TOTALBasketball

The Ultimate Basketball Encyclopedia

TOTALBasketball

The Ultimate Basketball Encyclopedia

www.sportclassicbooks.com

Published in the United States of America by Sport Media Publishing Inc.,
Wilmington, Delaware, and simultaneously in Canada.

For information about permission to reproduce selections from this book,
please write to:

Permissions
Sport Media Publishing, Inc.,
21 Carlaw Ave.,
Toronto, Ontario, Canada, M4M 2R6
www.sportclassicbooks.com

Cover design: Paul Hodgson / pHd
Front cover photo of Yao Ming and Kevin Garnett: AFP/CORBIS/Magmaphoto.com
Back cover photo of Bob Cousy: Ozzie Sweet

Back cover photos of (clockwise from top left): Hank Luisetti, Artis Gilmore,
Alex Groza, Goose Tatum: The SPORT Collection
Back flap photos of Carl Braun (left) and Joe Fulks: The SPORT Collection
Interior design and layout : Paul Hodgson / pHd, Greg Oliver and John Pasternak

ISBN: 1-894963-01-6

Library of Congress Control Number: 2003111745

Printed in United States of America

For Leonard Koppett (1923-2003), a giant among sports literary figures whose ground-breaking, analytical approach to basketball reporting influenced a generation of writers and unwittingly laid the foundation for Total Basketball.

Acknowledgements

A project of this magnitude could not have been contemplated, let alone completed, without the support of legions of writers, researchers, editors, statisticians, programmers, photographers, designers and proofreaders. In many cases, these contributions are acknowledged in the table of contents or on the contributors page at the back of this book. But there are many others whose efforts were equally important and deserving of recognition.

First among these is Greg Oliver, our jack of all trades, whose many and varied contributions defy a simple job description. He was the primary liaison with editor Ken Shouler and, at one time or another, acted as a copy editor, strategist, layout editor, proofreader, and page designer. Simply put, he kept the project moving on several fronts. Think of a basketball team that had in its backcourt a single player that could shoot like Michael Jordan, pass like John Stockton and defend like Bill Russell. That's Greg.

And if Greg controlled our backcourt, his equivalent on the frontcourt was Peter Grucza. Peter's primary task was to massage the database so that it could churn out the thousands of lines of data required for the player register and the other statistics and records sections of the book. He became our fact checker and our go-to guy whenever an issue of accuracy or clarity arose. And in is his spare time he leant his considerable expertise to photo selection and preparation.

Pete Palmer deserves thanks for the many hours he spent to help sort out various database issues, particularly with respect to trade data, game starts and disqualifications.

Credit for the design of the player register belongs to John Pasternak, while Paul Hodgson's talented hand is evident in the overall page design, as well as the wonderful work on the dust jacket. Joe O'Leary chipped in with photo scanning and data management, while Julie Leahey's office administration was indispensable.

Our sincere gratitude goes out to the Association for Professional Basketball Research (www.apbr.org), particularly its president, Robert Bradley, and member extraordinaire John Grasso. The following APBR members also provided invaluable assistance: Dean LaVergne, Keith Ellis, Dean Oliver, Al Hoffman, Michael Tamada, J Michael Kenyon, Mike Goodman and Charlie Board. Their basketball knowledge and passion for the game is reflected throughout this book.

We also must acknowledge the contribution of David Neft, whose ground-breaking book *The Sports Encyclopedia: Pro Basketball* (last published in 1992) provided the bedrock upon which many sections of the book were constructed. For general research, thanks go to Greg Spira, Vladislav Yushin, as well as ABL specialists John Hogrogian and Richard Hancock.

The photographs that grace the pages of this book come from various sources, but special thanks goes to Robin Deutsch of the Naismith Memorial Basketball Hall of Fame, as well as to the proprietors of The SPORT Collection (the archive of *SPORT* magazine), SPORT Media Enterprises, Inc.

For marketing and promotional advice, we are grateful for the wise counsel of Wes Seeley. Finally, we must acknowledge the contribution of John Thorn, who originated the "Total" reference-book concept in 1989 by publishing the first of seven editions of *Total Baseball*. He followed with two editions each of *Total Football* and *Total Hockey* and laid the groundwork for *Total Basketball* before passing the torch to us.

As we said at the outset, a work of this magnitude requires the dedication of a large team. However, given the scope of the project, we acknowledge that, inevitably, there will remain some errors in fact or omission. For these, the publisher accepts full responsibility. We have pooled a considerable amount of talent to make the first edition of *Total Basketball* as good as humanly possible, and now it's up to you, dear reader, to help make subsequent editions even better. We view this as a work in progress. Therefore, we welcome your comments and suggestions. So if you spot something that is wrong, or something that can be made better, visit us at totalbasketball.com and let us know what you think.

Table of Contents

Table of Contents

LeBron James, 2003 A $90 million man before lacing on Nikes in his first Pro Summer League game, here against the Washington Wizards, his is the face of the future.

Introduction

From Peach Baskets To World Acclaim: The Ultimate Game

By Sam Smith

Memo: To Dr. James Naismith.
From: Pro Basketball in the 21st Century.

Your game has come a long way, dude.
Bigger, better, faster, devoid of racism and xenophobia, a melting pot of athletic and economic accomplishment, hip guys with a lot of hop, basketball has come from that makeshift gymnasium in Springfield, Mass., where Canadian Dr. James Naismith was entrusted with coming up with an activity for the restless boys of winter. From that, basketball would become the second most popular sport on the planet, played by more than 400 million participants worldwide by the third millennium.

Only soccer, known as football in most parts of the world, holds a participant edge over basketball. No team sport world-wide has grown like basketball, whose international expansion has come back to the founding United States with a record 21 players among the 58 selected in the 2003 NBA draft and with almost 20 percent of the rosters of NBA teams in the 2002-03 season being comprised of players representing 34 different countries and territories outside the United States.

The global appeal of basketball, spawned in large part by the fabulous 1992 NBA Dream Team at the Barcelona Olympics, appears to be the next great step for the sport that has its roots and heritage in the U.S. About 20 percent of all NBA brand merchandise now is sold outside the U.S. and about 15 percent of the league's broadcast revenues come from outside the United States with almost 150 TV partners in more than 200 countries. It all is leading to, according to NBA commissioner David Stern, some form of NBA expansion or brand sale outside the U.S. Possibilities include NBA teams being set up in Europe, South America and Asia and playing teams from the U.S. once travel considerations are made possible, or NBA-established leagues in different countries. And the day is coming soon when the NBA champion will play a true world championship series against the best team outside the U.S. in what could become the greatest sporting event in the world.

All from those humble beginnings with a bunch of rambunctious school boys in 1891 who attempted to toss a ball into a peach basket for 30 minutes. In the end, one basket was scored. And so basketball was born, and it hasn't stopped growing.

The latest height was to the drafting and almost immediate crowning of a high school graduate, LeBron James of Akron, Ohio, to become the next great thing in basketball with his selection as the first overall pick in the 2003 NBA draft, that coming just weeks after the teenager had signed a $90-million endorsement contract with Nike. Just a decade earlier the notion of high school teenagers being able to come directly to the NBA was viewed as a dream and impractical. But with James' selection, and the selection of 18-year-old Darko Milicic of Serbia-Montenegro as the second overall pick in the 2003 draft, high schoolers were the rage of the NBA. Many of the league's greatest stars, like Kobe Bryant, Tracy McGrady and Kevin Garnett, went directly from high school to the NBA. And others were on the verge of stardom, like Eddy Curry and Tyson Chandler in Chicago. They're tattooed and ready to reverse slam dunk.

So James seemed at that point certain to become the next great American sports star following those who seemingly would never be topped, from George Mikan to Wilt Chamberlain to Kareem Abdul-Jabbar to Julius Erving to Magic Johnson, Larry Bird and Michael Jordan. After watching Jordan score 63 points in a playoff game against his great Boston Celtics team, Bird described Jordan as "God disguised as Michael Jordan." Top that, LeBron.

Basketball, in fact, has transcended sport.

Few figures in American, even world, society have become as popular and famous as NBA players. Jordan, of course, topped the list for most of the 1990s and into 2003, when he finished his playing career with the Washington Wizards. The longtime Chicago Bulls star wore the crown as the world's most eminent athlete, his Chicago Bulls team becoming legendary around the globe. Celebrities in the world of entertainment, even world leaders, flocked to watch, be near and meet NBA stars.

Young men like Shaquille O'Neal, Bryant, Bird, Johnson, Erving, Allen Iverson, Garnett, Vince Carter, Karl Malone and Grant Hill became American icons through their participation in the NBA. No sport featured its stars like the NBA, a clever marketing strategy devised by Stern in the early 1980s and popularized by Jordan and his image making machinery. It led to the NBA, if not becoming the most watched and favorite American sport, producing the biggest sports stars America had to offer. Sports clothing, from sneakers to jerseys, became fashion statements around the world that continue to grow. Wearing so called "retro" jerseys of former players, mostly from the NBA, became a major fashion trend among youth and Hollywood by early 2003.

The NBA agreed to admit a 30th team for the 2004-05 season in Charlotte, N.C.—the original Charlotte team moving to New Orleans, La., in 2002—for an entry fee of a record $300 million. Fully two thirds of the existing teams had new arenas built or major renovations done in the 1990s. And while TV ratings sagged at the beginning of the new millennium with the splintering effect of cable TV and hundreds of viewing choices, pro basketball was like America at the turn of

the 20th Century. The world was coming to share in this great wealth of talent and riches.

Such a journey was hard to imagine in the late 1890s, almost like flight and motor vehicle travel. Though there were few major innovations and little technological change in basketball. Even in that first game, the basket was 10 feet high. It happened to be the height of the above running track where the peach basket could be nailed. It never changed.

The recreation area where the game was played was about 35 feet by 55 feet. As the game developed, the dimensions of the court were different because of the availability of arenas and gyms. Today, the standard basketball court is 94 feet by 50 feet. But it's always been the same essential rectangle shape. That first game had nine per side, there being 18 boys in Naismith's class. The peach basket had a bottom, there were no half court designations or backboard for bank shots and a soccer ball was used. Naismith added the backboard in 1893 because kids sitting on the railing above the peach basket would knock the attempted shots away, though it was several decades before backboards were standard and many of the first leagues in the early 20th Century played games without the backboard. But many of the rules for that first game carried forward to the present, including rules against goaltending, traveling with the ball, five seconds for a throw-in from out of bounds, fouling out and halftime.

The game was first known as Basket Ball, but soon incorporated into one word and, in effect, one game. Before the turn of the century, professional games were played. But its finesse and balletic appeal would not appear for many years. NBA stars are widely considered the most talented athletes in the world, men almost seven feet tall and more than 250 pounds able to twist and contort their bodies like petite ballerinas, taking steps and performing moves one would only see in great dance. The power and grace of today's basketball stars in unequalled in any endeavor.

The early years of basketball more mirrored American football with brutal, physical play that so enlivened the spectators that steel, and later rope, cages were erected to protect the players from the often unruly fans. It led to the nickname "cagers" for basketball players, a moniker that stuck for many decades afterward. A center jump after baskets continued until 1936, after which the ball was given to the team that was scored upon. The game constantly evolved and merged to the point that in 2002, the NBA changed its defense rules to allow zones, which long were permitted in international play, thus helping merge the U.S. game with the game played around the world.

But it was in the United States where basketball grew and prospered.

Initially, basketball was an Eastern United States games from its roots in Massachusetts. The first reported professional game was played in New Jersey in 1896, and within two years several leagues were formed around Philadelphia, New Jersey, New York and the New England States. It was in one of those New England league games in Lowell, Mass. in 1902 when Harry Lew became the first black to play in a professional game. Blacks weren't officially welcomed into professional basketball and the NBA until 1950 when Earl Lloyd, Sweetwater Clifton, Chuck Cooper and Hank DeZonie, the latter after the season started, came to the NBA.

Baseball, actually, had been the purveyor of racism in American sport. The NFL had many black players through the 1920s until white players demanded the exclusion of blacks in 1933. That ban lasted until 1946 when the All-American Conference was integrated and challenged the NFL. Before Lloyd, Clifton and Cooper were allowed into the NBA in 1950, scores of black players competed in primarily white pro leagues throughout the first half of the 20th Century. Many blacks also participated in the then-acknowledged World Championship tournament which was staged in Chicago. The tournament's prime was from 1939 through 1948. The National Basketball League, which ran from 1935 through 1949 and saw several of its teams join the merger which created the NBA in 1946, had teams of mostly black players during the World War II years, some five years before Jackie Robinson played for the Brooklyn Dodgers, and in its final season admitted the New York Rens, the touring all-black team that became the first all-black team to play in the predominantly white league.

There certainly was deep segregation, mostly exclusion and hardships for blacks who played any sport, including basketball, in the then segregated and often racist America of the early 20th Century. But more blacks did get the chance to play in white leagues in basketball, in part because the leagues were so splintered then.

The game still was in its infancy and leagues were more curiosities. They'd pop up from year to year around the East, and players would play for a team in one league on one night and then in another league on the next. It wasn't until the 1920s, with the American Basketball League, that there was any stability. The league was the first to require backboards in all games and players were signed to exclusive contracts so they could not jump leagues between games. The ABL was the first national league of sorts with teams in the Midwest. But the stock market crash of 1929 and the ensuing Great Depression soon put it out of business.

Players were left again to barnstorm, which became the primary basketball mode of the first 35 years of the 20th Century. It also was the prime outlet for the black players, who were only permitted in the all-white leagues in limited numbers. Barnstorming, the playing of games while traveling the country, which also was popular in the winter with great baseball players like Babe Ruth, actually was easier in many respects than league play.

There weren't enough arenas back then for regularly scheduled seasons, and the arenas that could accommodate large crowds were booked for other events. In fact, it would be the need to fill arenas by hockey owners in the 1940s that led to the creation of the NBA.

It wasn't long after the game was founded that the first great barnstorming team started. It was the Buffalo Germans, a group of teenagers from the local YMCA. Their team played into the mid-1920s and, according to the Basketball Hall of Fame in Springfield, compiled a 792-86 record and once won 111 straight games.

The Germans are enshrined in the Hall of Fame along with the Original Celtics, the New York Renaissance Five and the Harlem Globetrotters, all barnstorming attractions, the latter

two all-black teams.

The other great barnstorming attraction of the era was the SPHA's, the South Philadelphia Hebrew Association team. While blacks were discriminated against, so were other immigrant groups, like Jews. It's why in the early 1900s many of the top professional boxers were Jewish. Groups discriminated against often found themselves seeking fame and fortune in the activities shunned by the upper classes, like boxing, and then also basketball.

The SPHA's, like the Original Celtics, who were from New York City, occasionally joined leagues. But they usually were so superior from years of playing together that they caused the destruction of the leagues or were run out for being too dominant. The Boston Celtics of the NBA named themselves after the Original Celtics, in part because of the Original Celtics' entertaining fast break style, which was carried on by Red Auerbach's teams of the 1950s and 1960s with Bob Cousy and Bill Russell. The Original Celtics were great innovators, playing zone defenses at times, though developing the style of the era that led to today's game.

One player was in the middle and he was relied on primarily to rebound and make the jump at the center of the court after every basket, thus becoming known as the center. The two players beside the center were relied on to score in those days, that being the offense popularized by Dick Motta with Chicago and Washington in the 1970s, those players forward of the others toward the basket. The other two players on the court were expected primarily to guard the opposition, thus becoming known as guards.

The first of the great black barnstorming teams was the Renaissance, who became known as the Rens. They were formed in 1923, named for the Renaissance Casino Ballroom in Harlem. The dance floor became their arena with chandelier and bandstand. They went on the road mostly fulltime in 1928. Accounts of all records from those eras aren't exact, but the Rens were said to be about 500-50 between 1932 and 1936 and in their history before folding in 1949 2,318-381 by one historical account. They were a fast breaking, athletic wonder of the era, once running off 88 consecutive wins before being beaten by the Original Celtics, the Celtics' one win in eight games that year against the Rens. The Rens won the world title in the Chicago tournament in 1939 over the NBL Oshkosh All Stars and in the final World Professional Basketball Tournament in Chicago in 1948, the Rens lost by just four points to the burgeoning power of the NBA, the Minneapolis Lakers.

The Lakers were the standard of the early NBA, and it was the Harlem Globetrotters who defeated them in serious games in Chicago in 1948 and 1949 even as the Globetrotters had begun to develop their popular comedy act that still tours.

The Globetrotters, formed by Chicago businessman Abe Saperstein, started play in Hinckley, Ill., outside Chicago in 1927. They originally were a Chicago ballroom team, like the Rens from New York, named the Savoy Big Five for the Savoy Ballroom in Chicago. They were so successful and won so easily against teams from around the Midwest, the Globetrotters slowly began adding comedic touches and ball handling routines to their play that eventually would become their staple.

This was basketball in America in the 1920s and 1930s with one relatively stable league, the NBL, while basketball also made its first appearance in the Olympics in 1936. The NBL was a compendium of teams representing cities and businesses, like tire and auto companies. It was little Oshkosh in Wisconsin that dominated the early years of the NBL along with the Zollner Pistons, owned by piston maker Fred Zollner, whose teams eventually became the Fort Wayne Pistons and Detroit Pistons. But even these teams wanted for arenas, often playing in high school gyms and ballrooms, and even into the 1950s, NBA players coming to Fort Wayne would hire local teenagers to drive them to the games from the train from the East Coast, which didn't stop in Fort Wayne. As late as 1955, when Fort Wayne was in the NBA Finals, the Fort Wayne Coliseum arena had been rented out for a bowling tournament. So the middle three games, Fort Wayne's so called "home" games, were played in Indianapolis with Syracuse eventually winning a seventh game back in New York for the title.

The essence of the game began to change in the latter stages of the NBL with the emergence of George Mikan from DePaul University in Chicago, the game's first giant. He developed the first so called sky hook and won championships in seven of his first eight seasons in professional basketball and five of six in the NBA. His dominance forced the first major rules change of the first NBA era, widening the three-second lane from six feet to 12 feet in 1951. The lane would be widened again, in 1964 from 12 to today's 16 feet, to try to offset the dominance of another giant, Wilt Chamberlain.

Because of the difficulty of finding arenas even after the NBA began, the New York Knicks often were forced to play in a National Guard armory because dates for Madison Square Garden were booked. Meanwhile, Mikan had an advantage in the Minneapolis Auditorium, which was somewhat smaller in width than most NBA arenas of the time.

Though it was coming time for the competing factions and forces to begin falling away and creating the merger than would produce the strength and power of basketball, the National Basketball Association.

Although it wasn't until 1949 that the name NBA represented the best basketball league in the world, it was 1946 when the men who would carve out this new league came together. They were, essentially, businessmen, arena owners looking to secure more dates for their arenas simply to make more money. It never was about creating a great basketball league. That merely was the vehicle to get them there.

The great American sports in the 1920s and 1930s were horse racing and boxing. Arenas and stadium were built to accommodate those events, and indoor arenas began to spring up for track meets, boxing and eventually ice shows after the success of U.S. ice skaters in the 1936 Olympics. With that, the arena owners began to import more hockey games as well. The basketball that was flourishing at the time was in college. The pro leagues were regional and not greatly respected. The barnstorming teams generally were regarded as the best. Meanwhile, the college game was growing more popular and in the so called basketball capital of the world, New York City, an annual postseason tournament known as the National Invitation

Tournament was started in 1938 and became a success. The collegiate governing body, the National Collegiate Athletic Association, started a national tournament the following year. It captured the nation's imagination quickly and soon was a premier event, naming a national collegiate basketball champion. New York capitalized on the phenomenon with college doubleheaders in Madison Square Garden, which became among the arena's most popular events.

So no one believed pro basketball would become particularly popular. But the arena owners hoped to sell some tickets.

On June 6, 1946, the owners of arenas in New York, Boston, Detroit, Toronto, Cleveland, Philadelphia, Chicago, Pittsburgh, Providence, Washington and St. Louis formed the Basketball Association of America. A 60-game schedule was established with 48-minute games, eight minutes longer than college games, supposedly to give fans more for their money.

Joe Fulks, generally credited with being the first great jump shooter, became the league's scoring star and a young coach named Arnold "Red" Auerbach led Washington to the regular season title. Zone defenses were allowed when the season began, but eventually eliminated. It didn't help as slowdown and roughhouse tactics kept scores low. Plus, teams frequently couldn't use their assigned arenas because they already were booked for more profitable ice shows. Though the big problem for the inaugural BAA was that the players who fans recognized as the best were in the rival NBL.

The biggest one, in many ways, was Mikan, who played for the Chicago American Gears in the 1946-47 season and led them to the title. But owner Maurice White then tried to start his own league with Mikan, the Professional Basketball League of America. These continuing struggles only served to weaken the credibility of professional basketball leagues while college basketball prospered.

White's PBLA didn't last long and Mikan was signed by the Minneapolis Lakers of the NBL and led them to the title in 1947-48. Meanwhile, the BAA was sinking. Four of the original 11 franchises folded and to cut costs the schedule was reduced to 48 games and rosters cut from 12 to 10 players. They went into the minor leagues to add a team from Baltimore and it won the championship.

It was then that BAA commissioner Maurice Podoloff saved the future NBA. He persuaded the top NBL teams, Fort Wayne, Rochester, Indianapolis and Minneapolis with Mikan to join the BAA. Again, Mikan's team won the championship. The NBL finished out that 1948-49 season with the Anderson Duffy Packers winning the championship. The BAA then absorbed the rest of the NBL for the 1949-50 season and changed its name to National Basketball Association.

Though it was hardly time to celebrate. There were now an unwieldy 17 teams. Teams played 62, 64 or 68 games. The playoffs were an incomprehensible round robin. Six teams went out of business in the off-season and Washington would fold during the season. The first three black players, Lloyd, Clifton and Cooper, were signed to contracts, effectively finally breaking the color line in the NBA, but again schedules weren't even and teams were losing money and in danger of folding.

But then came the big break for pro basketball that broke the college stranglehold on basketball.

In January 1951, a Manhattan College player, Junius Kellogg, told the Bronx District Attorney he was approached by gamblers to shave points. The ensuing investigation nearly destroyed college basketball. It was disclosed that almost 100 games were fixed in a four-year period. The big New York programs, like New York University and City College of New York, which led the doubleheaders that filled Madison Square Garden, were implicated. Two University of Kentucky players, now in the pros, Alex Groza and Ralph Beard, were banned from the NBA as a result. The NBA escaped without serious damage to its credibility and the nation began to look to it for reliable basketball. Plus, with the demand for doubleheaders over, the NBA teams could move into the major arenas for the choice dates.

At the same time, the Knicks went to the Finals and played an exciting seven game series with Rochester and then the following year with Mikan and Minneapolis. With New York the center of basketball, having the Knicks in the big games created more interest and the NBA began to become a national story.

Then it fixed its game and the march to international acclaim was on.

The NBA still was too slow and dull. Minneapolis, the perennial champion, liked to walk the ball up and drop it in to Mikan and watch him score. When teams got ahead, they'd often go into a stall. Fouling was brutal and frequent. Some games had more than 100 free throws shot and lasted longer than three hours (with no commercials for TV). In 1950, Fort Wayne beat Minneapolis 19-18 in a game. There were overtime games in which the team that got the tip would hold the ball the entire period for a last shot.

Syracuse owner Danny Biasone, who persuaded the league to install a time clock, supplied the answer. Biasone came up with the equation, figuring in a well-played game at the time each team attempted 60 shots. He took the 48-minute game—2,880 seconds—and divided. The result was 24 seconds per shot. It saved the NBA.

Points per game went up by more than 13 that first season with the shot clock, 1954-55, when the title, ironically, was won by Biasone's Syracuse Nationals. It also helped that Mikan retired to go into law so he could make a better living. No, the NBA wasn't bigtime yet with its greatest star leaving to earn more money.

Scoring continued to surge, and the league's evolution was under way. The move began to leave the small cities, like Syracuse, Fort Wayne and Rochester to become big-time. And then national. In 1960, the Lakers left Minneapolis for Los Angeles and two years later, Philadelphia moved to San Francisco, with Syracuse filling in as the new Philadelphia team. The NBA was becoming a truly national league of big cities. Now, it just needed some big stars, and they were on the way.

There had been Mikan and the Minneapolis Lakers, but they mostly labored in the obscurity of the NBA's dark ages, meaning before the introduction of the 24-second clock. That technological change represented the NBA's so called modern era, and as it dawned came the greatest dynasty in the history of pro sports, the Boston Celtics.

Red Auerbach was there and so was Bob Cousy, the flashy guard from Holy Cross in Massachusetts. They had talent, but not the power and rebounding to deal with the Lakers and Rochester Royals. And then the Celtics put together perhaps the most significant trade in NBA history. There have been many versions and explanations over the years of what truly happened. Rochester with the No. 1 overall pick in the draft supposedly couldn't afford the 1956 Olympic Games star center from the University of San Francisco, Bill Russell. They had Maurice Stokes, then one of the game's top rebounders. But Celtics owner Walter Brown, so the story goes, provided financially ailing Rochester a financial inducement to skip over Russell in the draft. Supposedly Brown steered the profitable ice capades to Rochester for two years as payment. St. Louis had the No. 2 overall pick, one ahead of Boston.

But St. Louis then was the southern most city in the NBA with southern attitudes toward blacks. Russell would become the highest paid player on the Hawks, and management supposedly felt there would be community and team resentment. Because of the Olympics being played in Australia, and thus in the fall, Russell wouldn't be available until after the season started. So St. Louis agreed to make a deal. They'd get St. Louis native Ed McCauley and University of Kentucky star Cliff Hagen, who was coming out of the military.

The deal was done and a dynasty started.

The Celtics won their first title in 1957 in a double overtime seventh game over the Hawks. Auerbach believed in a running, fast break style with a limited number of plays, said to be seven at the time. Auerbach didn't believe in high scoring, offensive stars to center a team around but an overall team concept that was built around Russell's defense, rebounding and outlet passing. St. Louis came back to win the title in 1958 after Russell hurt his ankle in Game 3 of the final series. It would be the last championship for the Hawks' franchise, which eventually would move to Atlanta, and the last NBA championship team to have all white players. The Celtics then went on to win the NBA championship the next eight consecutive seasons, a streak unparalleled in American teams sports. Overall, Russell would play for 11 championship teams with the Celtics, the last two when he became the first black coach in NBA history, Russell thus becoming the greatest winner in NBA history.

Though Russell would become the most prolific champion, he would be just one of the stars in arguably the greatest individual era in NBA history. Not by accident it coincided with NBA teams opening the door to the flood of black talent waiting to take the league to new heights. By 1960, a quarter of the players in the NBA would be black after just one or two on most teams in the late 1950s in sort of quota system that could not dam up the rushing waters of great talent available.

It started in 1958 with Elgin Baylor, who was the godfather of air, the first man who seemed to hang in the air when shooting. He began a line that went through Dr. J, Jordan and the current high flying stars of the NBA, like Bryant, McGrady and Carter.

And in 1959 came Wilt Chamberlain, most likely the most dominant player ever in the NBA. He wasn't the greatest winner, and by the 1990s, the Chicago Bulls' Michael Jordan was widely regarded as the game's greatest player. But no one dominated the game in his time like Chamberlain, whose offensive records remain the most unreachable in NBA annals. Chamberlain scored 100 points in a game and averaged more than 50 points in a season. An ironman who never fouled out of a game, he once averaged more than 48 minutes per game over an entire season. He came to Philadelphia under the then territorial draft rule. The NBA still struggled for recognition and revenues in the 1950s and 1960s, so teams were allowed exclusive rights to the best college player in their "territory" in the draft. Though Chamberlain went to the University of Kansas and played one season for the Globetrotters before coming to the NBA (players couldn't play in the NBA in those days before their college classes graduated), Philadelphia had made Chamberlain a territorial pick when Chamberlain was in high school in Philadelphia. Chamberlain became the league's first big gate attraction as well. He broke all sorts of records as a rookie averaging 37.6 points and 27 rebounds and being named MVP and rookie of the year. Though Russell's Celtics would be champions, a familiar pattern in their duels over the years. Chamberlain would win the statistics battle while Russell's team filled with future Hall of Famers, like Cousy, Bill Sharman, Tom Heinsohn, K.C. Jones and Sam Jones would win the games.

The year 1960 brought Jerry West, whose fundamentally solid style would become the future logo for the NBA. There was Oscar Robertson, who went on to become the only player in NBA history to average a triple double—double figures in points, rebounds and assists—in a single season. And there was Lenny Wilkens, who would go into the Hall of Fame as a player and coach and become the first coach to pass 1,000 wins after a great playing career.

Great stars continued to enter the game, like Jerry Lucas, Walt Bellamy, Nate Thurmond, Rick Barry and Earl Monroe. Monroe came from Winston Salem State, a black college, breaking down another racial door and exposing another vein of great talent. Monroe brought to the NBA the so-called street ball that is popular today with a series of twisting behind the back moves with the basketball that excited crowds, a sort of jazz music of basketball, an improvisational repertoire of movements that continues to be expanded upon today. The players in the current era are able to make the moves in the air, which wasn't common then by other than Baylor and Connie Hawkins, who was banned for a time for an alleged role in the college betting scandals, but was exonerated and finished his career in the NBA after playing in the American Basketball Association.

The ABA would be the NBA's only great rival since its inception, and while the ABA never was a commercial success and was folded into the NBA in 1976, it had a profound effect on the NBA. It is generally credited with introducing the three-point shot for a longer field goal, though that was first tried in the little known American Basketball League, a 1961-63 experiment by Globetrotters' owner Saperstein. Hawkins got his start there while being banned from the NBA, Bill Sharman was a player coach and Cleveland shipbuilder George Steinbrenner for his start in sports ownership there. But with the NBA struggling at the time, the nation wasn't ready for a rival pro basketball league and the ABL failed in less than two seasons.

The ABA, though, wasn't far behind. It was formed in 1967 and hired Mikan as commissioner. Its franchises moved and folded with regularity and games witnessed by a few hundred spectators were common in some cities as the NBA retained the credibility of the basketball public and the key arenas. But the ABA grew and developed some of the greatest stars in basketball history. It's where the careers of Erving, George Gervin, Artis Gilmore, Dan Issel and Moses Malone started. It attracted NBA stars like Barry and Billy Cunningham. In 1969, it began the revolution that has taken on greater impact today when the league persuaded collegiate star Spencer Haywood to leave college after his sophomore year to join the ABA. The courts agreed Haywood couldn't be denied his right to earn a living in pro basketball, and the gates swung open, changing the future of pro and college basketball.

Although college basketball would continue to prosper with great UCLA teams in the 1970s and stars like Jordan, Patrick Ewing, James Worthy, Magic Johnson and Larry Bird in championship games, the talent drain would begin. College had been a wonderful feeder system for the NBA, but that began to change as undergraduate players had more success in the NBA and with the development of Garnett, who skipped college to go directly to the NBA in 1995, the college game began to lose its greatest potential stars. By the early 2000s, NBA All-Stars like Bryant, McGrady, Garnett and Jermaine O'Neal never attended college and many other top NBA players, like Jason Kidd, Stephon Marbury, Elton Brand and Iverson attended college for just one or two years.

After Haywood came George McGinnis, Jim Chones and Erving, all leaving college early and Moses Malone, who skipped college. Although Malone had a Hall of Fame career, there were only a few, including Darryl Dawkins and Bill Willoughby, who went directly from high school to the NBA and it wasn't until Garnett's success that it became accepted that players could skip college and be successful in the NBA. In the 2001 draft, three of the top four selections, Kwame Brown, Tyson Chandler and Eddy Curry, were picked out of high school, and in the 2003 draft, the No. 1 overall pick and most anticipated pro since Kareem Abdul-Jabbar, then known as Lew Alcindor, was high schooler LeBron James.

The ABA would eventually falter after nine seasons as four teams, the Indiana Pacers, Denver Nuggets, San Antonio Spurs and New Jersey Nets paid for admittance to the NBA and the remainder of the league was disbanded. It wasn't until 1999 when a former ABA team, the Spurs, won an NBA title and in 2003, the Nets and Spurs played for the championship, the first Finals' pairing of former ABA teams.

While the NBA was fighting off the ABA, it also fought off its players and agreed in 1973 to the league's first collective bargaining agreement with the players' association.

The Celtics came back in the 1970s to win two more titles and Bill Walton, coming out of his UCLA success, had a brilliant, albeit brief, shining moment with one NBA championship in Portland. But the wars with the ABA took their toll and the NBA was staggering. Rumors of rampant drug use among players hurt the league's image. In many quarters, it was regarded as an outlaw league.

Until it was saved by two Midwestern kids, Earvin "Magic" Johnson and Larry Bird. Johnson's Michigan State team defeated Bird's Indiana State team in the 1979 NCAA championship game, and they took their rivalry—black against white, scorer against passer, city kid against country kid—to the NBA. The Lakers, who were among the top teams, were able to get Johnson as the No. 1 overall pick in the draft after winning a coin flip with the Chicago Bulls (top picks were decided that way until the draft lottery started in 1985) because the Lakers had received compensation, which was the old free agency rules, for the Jazz' signing of Gail Goodrich, then an All-Star. The compensation was the Jazz' No. 1 pick in 1979. And Auerbach had done it again for the Celtics, selecting Bird in the 1978 draft after his fourth year in college. But he had a year of eligibility left after transferring and wasn't graduating until 1979. Bird was the sixth overall pick in 1978.

One or the other was in the NBA Finals every year from 1980 through 1989 and they played one another three times. Philadelphia with Erving and Moses Malone made three Finals appearances in the decade as it became perhaps the era of the last great rivalries, between both teams and players. Magic and Bird rivaled the great duels of Chamberlain and Russell of the 1960s and began the boom for the NBA that carried into the 1990s.

Still, team finances weren't great in the early 1980s and the league's TV contract even had some Finals games on tape delay. The result was the pioneering financial vehicle that became a model for all sports. In 1983, the NBA and its players agreed to a so-called salary cap concept which limited the amount of money teams could spend on their players. It was not unique as leagues over the years, especially in the pre-NBA years, had mandated such so-called caps. But it was unheard of in the modern era of pro sports. Its inauguration along with the coming of Jordan and the special marketing associated with him and other individual players turned NBA players into international stars and the NBA into a dynamo.

Jordan was a successful player at the University of North Carolina, even hitting a game winning shot for a championship in 1982. But no one expected him to become the premier player of his era and most important financial and marketing figure in pro sports history. Jordan was the No. 3 pick in the 1984 draft, going behind Hakeem Olajuwon and Sam Bowie. Even the Chicago Bulls didn't know what they had at the time. General manager Rod Thorn said not to expect too much from a shooting guard as teams never have won before led by a shooting guard.

The Bulls wouldn't win a championship for seven years with Jordan. But during that time, Jordan built up an impressive array of endorsements that made him the richest team sport athlete ever with major contracts for everything from shoes to hamburgers. His electric smile and stunningly exciting game played well off the ground made him a fan favorite and eventually a national icon and treasure. Jordan's dunking became his trademark. Once rejected in the NBA, in part because of the fear of backboards breaking, which were costly, and deemed unsportsmanlike, dunking became the art form of the game after the 1976 ABA All Star game in which Erving dunked on a jump from the free throw line.

Erving's unique and spectacular athleticism was passed on to

Jordan and by the new millennium to Carter and Bryant with expectations of many that James will take the baton of creative brilliance into basketball's next decade.

Johnson's Lakers won five championships in the 1980s, but Jordan's Bulls became the next NBA dynasty with six championships in the 1990s, a run of three straight from 1991 through 1993, after which Jordan decided he'd accomplished all he could and retired. It came a year after he led the famous 1992 U.S. Olympic "Dream Team" to the gold medal in a show of American basketball might and celebrity that changed international basketball forever.

FIBA, the international basketball governing body, changed its rules in 1989 to allow professionals into the Olympics and international events. The result was the Dream Team of great U.S. stars, like Jordan, Johnson, Bird, Charles Barkley, Ewing, David Robinson and Karl Malone. It was a U.S. domination, but it would be an inspiration for world basketball as youngsters took up the game in greater numbers, producing the international stars in the NBA in the new millennium, like Dirk Nowitzki, Pega Stojakovic, Pau Gasol and Yao Ming.

As for Jordan, he played professional baseball in the minor leagues for a year, but then returned to the NBA in 1995 amidst the greatest anticipation in the history of the game. Even President Bill Clinton talked about it in his speeches. For Jordan's first full season back in 1995-96, the Bulls added the unpredictable Dennis Rodman, a longtime rebounding champion with the Detroit Pistons and San Antonio Spurs who was known for his bizarre antics. With coach Phil Jackson and Scottie Pippen, the Bulls were both basketball team and a traveling show to rival any of the touring rock bands. Fans followed them everywhere. They won a record 72 games in the 1995-96 season and championships in 1996, 1997 and 1998 before Jordan retired again, only to return for two seasons, though with less success, for the Washington Wizards from 2001 through 2003.

That 2002-03 season, Jordan's last as a player as he turned 40 years old, also saw the end of the league's newest dynasty, the O'Neal and Bryant Lakers under former Chicago Bulls coach Jackson, whose success as a coach carried him past Auerbach and Pat Riley among the winningest ever in playoffs. Those Lakers' teams won championships in 2000, 2001 and 2002 and after yielding to eventual champion San Antonio, it appeared the Lakers were on the way back with signings in the summer of 2003 of veteran stars Karl Malone and Gary Payton. However, the Lakers run for a championship hit an unexpected hurdle when Bryant was charged with a single count of felony sexual assault stemming from an alleged incident at a Colorado resort. Bryant denied the charges and was preparing for a court date as his teammates prepared for training camp.

In the beginning of the 2000s, the NBA had become the hip hop of sports, popular among the young rap singers and entertainers, who moved easily among NBA stars. NBA fashion has become the fashion of the streets and with the stars, from jerseys to sneakers. Tattoos became popular among players, with many players painting their bodies with more than a dozen pieces of the body art. In many ways, basketball merged with the youth oriented entertainment industry in the United States, the rhythmic movements of the game an inspiration for the music of the day. A ballet of sport and a symphony of movement. Yes, the game of basketball has come a long way.

Section **1**

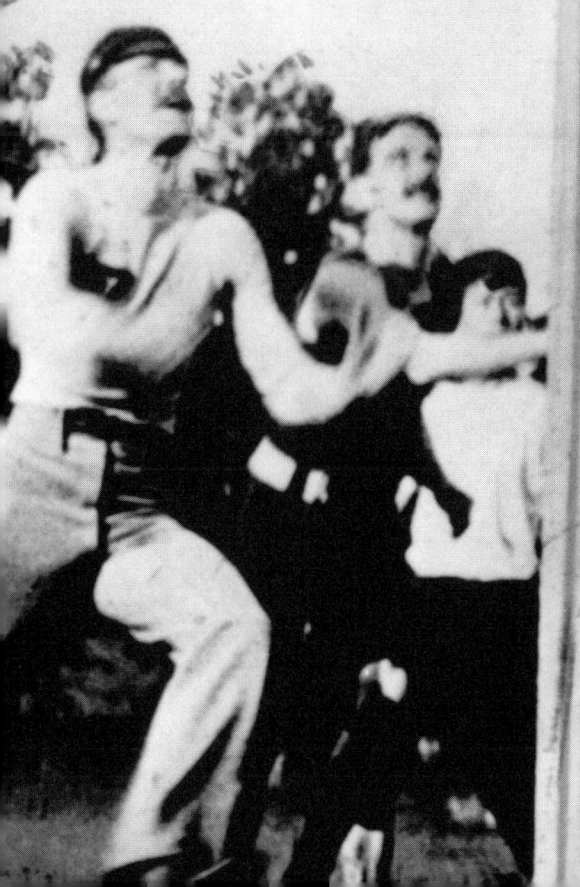

In the Beginning
1891-1945

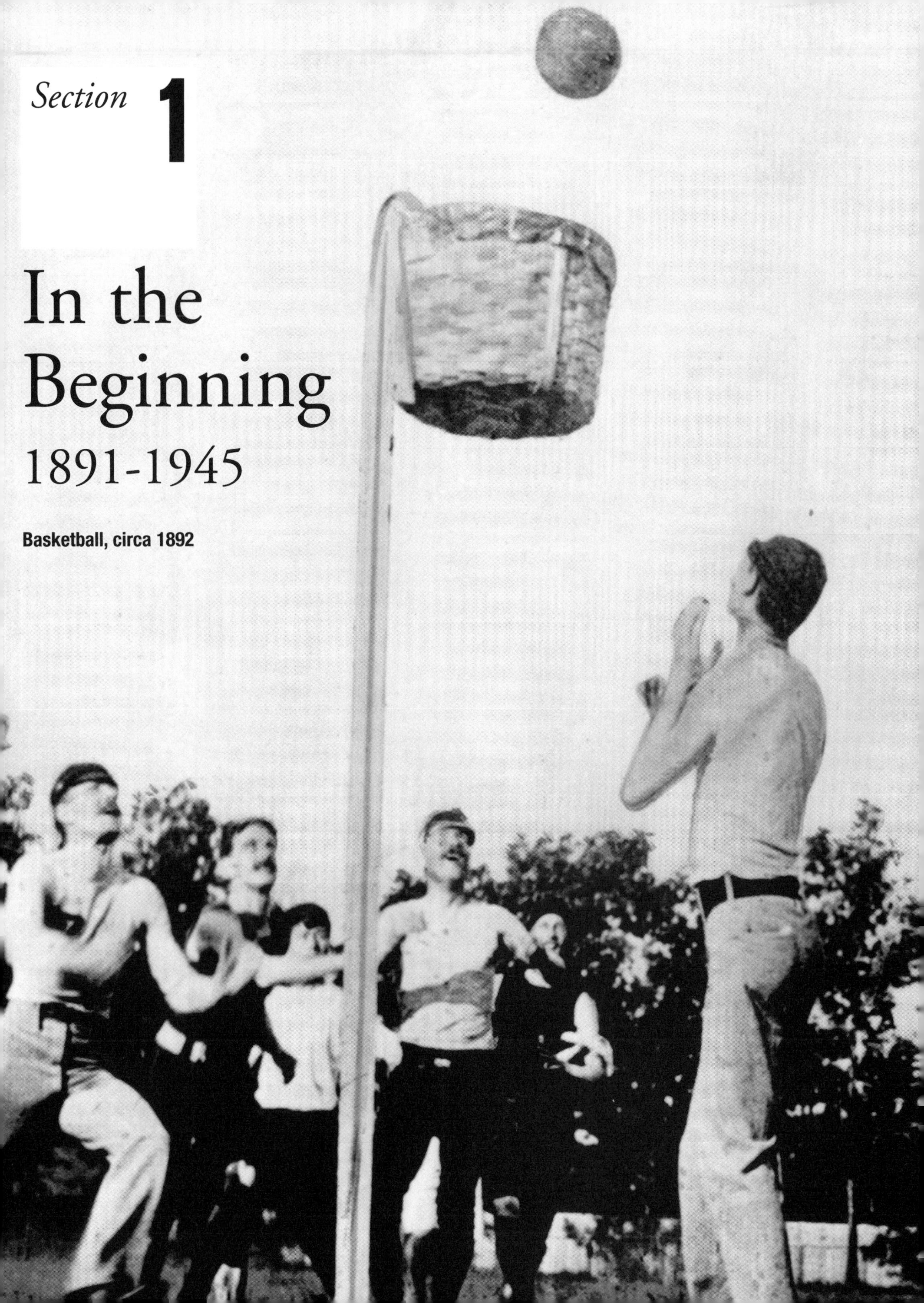

Basketball, circa 1892

Chapter 1

James Naismith: The Invention of the Game

By Robert Peterson

Unlike our other major sports, basketball did not evolve out of an older game. Sports historians agree that baseball grew out of the ancient English bat and ball game called rounders and a variant called town ball that was played in colonial America. Football developed from English rugby and soccer, and the progenitor of hockey was a kid's game in Canada during the 19th century.

Basketball's birth was different. It was invented in 1891 to meet a particular need at a particular time and place. The inventor was James Naismith, a 30-year-old Canadian who was a second-year student and an instructor at the International Training School of the Young Men's Christian Association in Springfield, Mass. The school had two types of students: those preparing for careers as YMCA physical directors, and those being trained as Y general secretaries. The 18 students in the secretaries' class were mature men—some as old as Naismith—and they did not take kindly to the gymnastics and calisthenics that were the staples of their required physical education classes.

In the fall and early spring they could go outside and play football or baseball, but Springfield's chilly autumns and cold winters kept them indoors. By mid-fall of 1891, the students had proven to be so rebellious over working with dumbbells and mats that two instructors had left the class.

James Naismith was happily teaching boxing, wrestling, swimming and canoeing to prospective physical directors. He was fulfilled. Naismith was an exemplar of what was called "muscular Christianity" and was fully in sympathy with the YMCA's growing emphasis on a sound mind in a sound body.

At faculty meetings Naismith had told his colleagues that a different approach was needed for the general secretaries' class. "The trouble is not with the men but with the system we are using," he said. "The kind of work for this particular class should be of a recreative nature, something that would appeal to their play instincts." Naismith had also told Dr. Luther H. Gulick, the phys-ed department chairman, that he thought he could invent a game that would be "interesting, easy to learn, and easy to play in the winter and by artificial light."

Gulick told Naismith to take over the secretaries' class and see what he could do with the recalcitrant students. Before long Naismith was calling them the "incorrigibles." He stopped the calisthenics and the work on parallel bars and other apparatus and tried to interest them in some simple boys' games such as Prisoner's Base. No sale. Next Naismith tried modifying rugby, soccer and lacrosse but the resulting games were either too tame or too rough. Recalling his dilemma many years later, he wrote that after two weeks of working with the class, he was thoroughly discouraged.

James Naismith, 1929
Born and raised in Almonte, Ontario, he was 30 when he invented basketball to appease a bored group of YMCA charges in 1891.

But he was no man to assent to failure without a fight, so, with only a day remaining before he was due to report to the faculty about his progress with the "incorrigibles," Naismith´ decided to make a systematic study of popular sports. He noted that all of them were played with a ball or puck, so his new game would have a ball. Should it be large or small? All sports using a small ball required intermediate equipment such as a bat or racquet. Naismith was striving for simplicity so the choice was easy. The ball would be large.

What should be done with it? Naismith thought that rugby, which was morphing into American football in the United States, was the most interesting game but it could not be played on the hardwood floor of a gymnasium because tackling was an essential feature. How could tackling be eliminated? By forbidding the player with the ball from running with it. What could he do with the ball? For one thing, he could pass it to a teammate. Naismith all but screamed, 'Eureka!' He later wrote, "I can still recall how I snapped my fingers and shouted, 'I've got it!'"

Up to this point, James Naismith had only invented the game today's boys call keepaway which was not likely to find favor with grown men. He needed a method of scoring. Such sports as hockey, football, soccer, and lacrosse have ground-level goals at which the players drive the ball with all their strength, making them undesirable for indoor play. Naismith's thoughts drifted back to his Canadian boyhood and a popular pastime called Duck on the Rock. In this game "It" places his "duck"— a stone about the size of a softball—on a boulder and the other players take turns trying to knock it off with their own ducks. A player who is tagged by "It" after a missed throw as he runs to retrieve his duck becomes the new "It." If "It's" duck is knocked off the boulder, he must put it back before giving chase. Boys soon learned that it was better to throw their duck in an arc so that it would not go far if they missed, thus giving "It" less chance to tag them. Naismith reasoned that if the goal for his new game were high and horizontal, finesse would be more desirable than force. That night, after mentally playing the first game of basketball in bed, Naismith slept the sleep of the untroubled for the first time in weeks.

In the morning he asked the school's janitor whether he had two boxes about 18 inches square. "No," the janitor replied, "I haven't any boxes, but I'll tell you what I do have. I have two old peach baskets down in the storeroom if they will do you any good." Thus did the new game miss being called boxball. Naismith asked the janitor to get the baskets and a ladder. Mounting the ladder, he nailed a basket to the lower rail of the gymnasium's balcony at both ends of the 65-by-45-foot gym. It happened that the balcony rail was 10 feet above the gym floor, establishing the basket's height for the ages (although there have been attempts to raise it). Naismith then wrote the rules for the new game on a scratch pad and asked the school stenographer to type them. The rules were:

- *The ball to be an ordinary Association football (soccer ball).*
- *The ball may be thrown in any direction with one or both hands.*
- *The ball may be batted in any direction with one or both hands (never with the fist).*
- *A player cannot run with the ball. The player must throw it from the spot on which he catches it, allowance to be made for a man who catches the ball when running at a good speed if he tries to stop.*
- *The ball must be held in or between the hands; the arms or body must not be used for holding it.*
- *No shouldering, holding, pushing, or striking, in any way, the person of an opponent shall be allowed; the first infringement of this rule by any person shall count as a foul, the second shall disqualify him until the next goal is made, or if*

there was evident intent to injure the person for the whole of the game, no substitute allowed.
- *A foul is striking at the ball with the fist, violation of Rules 3, 4, and such as described in Rule 5.*
- *If either side makes three consecutive fouls, it shall count a goal for the opponents. (Consecutive means without the opponents in the meantime making a foul.)*
- *A goal shall be made when the ball is thrown or batted from the grounds into the basket and stays there, providing those defending the goal do not touch or disturb the goal. If the ball rests on the edge and the opponent moves the basket, it shall count as a goal.*
- *When the ball goes out of bounds, it shall be thrown into the field and played by the person first touching it. In case of a dispute, the umpire shall throw it straight into the field. The thrower-in is allowed five seconds. If he holds it longer, it shall go to the opponent. If any side persists in delaying the game, the umpire shall call a foul on them.*
- *The umpire shall be the judge of the men and shall note the fouls and notify the referee when three consecutive fouls have been made. He shall have the power to disqualify men according to Rule 5.*
- *The referee shall be the judge of the ball and shall decide when the ball is in play, in bounds, to which side it belongs, and shall keep the time. He shall decide when a goal has been made, and keep account of the goals, with any other duties that are usually performed by a referee.*
- *The time shall be two 15-minute halves, with five minutes rest between.*
- *The side making the most goals in that time shall be declared the winners. In case of a draw, the game may, by agreement of the captains, be continued until another goal is made.*

It was almost class time when the steno finished typing the rules. Naismith tacked them up on the bulletin board and greeted arriving students. The first to appear was Frank Mahan, a tackle on the school football team and the ringleader of the "incorrigibles." He looked at the soccer ball in Naismith's hands and the peach baskets on the balcony rail and scoffed, "Huh! Another new game!" When all 18 secretaries were on hand, Naismith appointed two captains and had them choose sides. The nine men on each team were designated as three forwards, three centers, and three backs who were chiefly defensemen. The first game got under way when Naismith threw up the soccer ball between two opposing centers. "It was the start of the first basketball game and the finish of the trouble with that class," Naismith wrote in his book, *Basketball: Its Origin and Development*, published 50 years after the first game. "The game was a success from the time the first ball was tossed up," he added. "The players were interested and seemed to enjoy the game. Word soon got around that they were having fun in Naismith's gym class, and only a few days after the first game we began to have a gallery."

Neither Naismith nor the students ever gave a detailed description of the first game. In his book he wrote that "as was to be expected, they made a great many fouls at first; and as a foul was penalized by putting the offender on the side lines

until the next goal was made, sometimes half of a team would be in the penalty area. It was simply a case of no one knowing just what to do. There was no team work, but each man did his best…Any man on the field was close enough to the basket to throw for goal, and most of them were anxious to score."

That seems to imply that several goals were scored in the first game, but that's not what the players told interviewers many years later. All agreed that only one basket was made that morning. In most accounts, the goal was credited to William R. Chase of New Bedford, Mass.; others say the scorer was either William H. Davis or Lyman W. Archibald, one of seven Canadians in the secretaries' class.

The date of basketball's birth is as uncertain as the first scorer, but it must have been in mid-December. Within days the noontime basketball games were drawing spectators who crowded the balcony. Among them were women teachers from a nearby elementary school who stopped in on their way to lunch. After a couple of visits, they asked Naismith whether girls could play his new game. He replied that he saw no reason they could not, and they promptly formed the first of many early girls teams. (One of the girls' teams included Maude E. Sherman, the daughter of a widow at whose home Naismith and several other Training School faculty members had room and board. Miss Sherman later became Naismith's wife.)

By the time the Christmas holiday break arrived, the secretaries' class was hooked on the game, and some of the students introduced it in their hometown YMCAs. When they returned to school, Frank Mahan asked Naismith what he planned to call the new game and suggested that it might be called Naismith ball. "I laughed and told him that I thought that name would kill any game," Naismith wrote. Mahan said, "Why not call it basketball?"

The Training School's newspaper, *The Triangle*, which went to YMCAs around the country, published the first report about the game in January, 1892. It was titled "Basket Ball" and was written by Naismith and illustrated with a line drawing of players in action. Naismith did not say that he had invented the game, but he wrote that it "seems to have those elements in it which ought to make it popular among the associations." The article listed the rules and gave sketchy advice about the court. Teams might have from three to 40 players, depending on the size of the court. "The fewer players down to three, the more scientific it may be made, but the more players the more fun, and the more exercise for quick judgment," he wrote.

Perhaps because nine-men teams played the first game, Naismith recommended that number as best. Three would be defenders called a goalkeeper and two guards. Three were centers. And three were offensive men—two wings and a "home man," who stationed himself under his team's goal.

Naismith had wanted to keep roughness out of the new game, but it must have already appeared because he deplored it in the *Triangle* article. He wrote: "The very men who are rough in playing will be the very first ones to oppose the game on this account, for there is that in man's nature which will retaliate, and the rough player generally gets the worst of the roughness. If there is need for such a game, let it be played as any other game of science and skill, then men will value it. But there is neither science nor skill in taking a man unawares, and shoving

him, or catching his arm and pulling him away, when he is about to catch the ball. A dog could do as much as that."

Naismith had considered the idea of awarding free throws for fouls but dismissed it because "after a little practice, a good thrower could convert it into a goal almost every time, because of the limits of the ordinary gymnasium." But he urged the Y's physical directors to keep a firm hand on the game so that roughness would be minimized. "If men will not be gentlemanly in their play, it is our place to encourage games that may be played by gentlemen in a manly way, and show them that science is superior to brute force with a disregard for the feelings of others," Naismith wrote.

By late winter, Naismith had organized the first basketball team, with Frank Mahan as captain. The nine-man team played at the Training School and traveled in New England and upstate New York to demonstrate the new game. In May, 1892, *Physical Education*, the YMCA's monthly for physical directors, published the team's picture and reported that it had never lost a game. The peach baskets used in the earliest games had apparently been abandoned because the photo shows two wire-mesh baskets that look to be about 15 inches in diameter and 30 inches deep. That spring basketball was introduced in New York City as part of the opening of new YMCA athletic facilities. In reporting on the event, *The New York Times* called the game "a substitute for football without its rough features."

In Springfield there had been public games of basketball even earlier in 1892. On February 12 and March 15, the Armory Hill and Central branches of the YMCA there played match games, and on March 11, a team of faculty members, including Naismith, had demonstrated the game in a match with the students' team. The students won, five goals to one. The faculty's only goal was scored by Amos Alonzo Stagg, an All-American football player at Yale who was, like Naismith, an instructor in the physical education department, and who went on to become the dean of college football coaches. Stagg's football training hampered him as a basketball player and he was frequently charged with fouls for pushing opponents. Naismith groused afterward, "I wish Lonnie could have made that point without fouling everybody."

Naismith and Stagg were kindred spirits and became lifelong friends. Both were theological school graduates—Stagg from Yale Divinity School and Naismith from Montreal's Presbyterian College—and both were idealists who believed that clean sport inclined a person to a virtuous life, and both lived that creed. They were influenced by Dr. Luther H. Gulick, who was imbued with the idea of "working for young men, not simply for their bodies, minds, and souls, but for the salvation, development and training of the whole man complete as God made him." Gulick used that idea to pioneer modern physical training.

At Gulick's request, Stagg formed a football team for the Training School in 1890. Recruiting from the student body and faculty, he assembled a team that matched up well with Ivy League teams, even though some of his recruits had never played football before. The average weight of the team was under 160 pounds, and they were soon dubbed "Stagg's Stubby Christians." As the climax to the 1890 season, the team played mighty Yale in the first indoor football game at New York City's Madison Square Garden. Yale escaped with a 16-10 victory.

Naismith played every minute of every game in both the 1890 and 1891 football seasons as a tough center who gave up 20 pounds to his opponent. He had played English rugby at McGill University in Montreal and learned the American football game at Springfield. Once he asked Stagg, "Lonnie, why do you play me at center?" Presumably Stagg was kidding when he replied, "Jim, I play you at center because you can do the meanest things in the most gentlemanly manner."

Naismith was a wrestler and lacrosse player as well as a gridder, and he enjoyed these rough sports, but he was an exemplary sportsman. He bore a cauliflower ear as a badge of participation in rough sports and devised the first football helmet to protect the other ear. The headgear consisted of several layers of flannel tied over the ears and fastened under the chin; a later model was made of chamois skin. Neither saved his head from hard knocks but they did keep his ears from further damage.

Within a year of its birth, basketball was the rage in YMCA gyms around the country. Physical directors found the game to be the perfect end to an evening workout largely devoted to calisthenics and working with weights. The young business and professional men who frequented the gyms loved the game and came back for more. They were long on enthusiasm but short on skill. Marvin A. Riley, a veteran newspaperman, described the first game ever played in the Trenton YMCA gym in the fall of 1892 this way 30 years later:

There were about 80 young men on the floor of the YMCA gymnasium that opening night, and in order that no one would feel slighted it was decided that (physical director) William J. Davidson and I would choose sides. This we did, the result being that each of us had a fighting force of 40 good men and true. Dave mobilized his regiment in one end of the gym, and I got mine in the other, and he gave his battlers his ideas as to how the game was played; and I gave my bunch of huskies what I had gathered from witnessing games in Boston.

I do not know what Dave told his bunch, but I told mine that the sole object of the gentle pastime was to toss the ball in the basket of the other team, and stop them from tossing the ball in our basket—not to trip if it could be avoided—not to hold unless absolutely necessary, and not to slug excepting as a final resort in extreme emergency.

A referee was selected, who was told to blow a whistle to begin the contest and at any and all other times he might deem necessary or advisable for the safety of the players or the good name of the Association.

Both teams lined up at opposite ends of the hall, presenting the appearance of shock-absorbing regiments. The referee blew the whistle and we never saw nor heard of him again until an armistice finally was declared, with about one-fourth of those who went over the top still on their feet.

That first game was surely the cat's meow. Very few of the 80 who started in with nice new gym uniforms came out with their shirts on their backs, and most of us were artistically tattooed with fingernail scratches. Frequently there were 20 or more fairly good wrestling matches going on simultaneously and occasional scientific sparring exhibitions took place without in any slightest way interfering with the progress of the game.

I cannot recall the scoring of any goals because the defensive work was so remarkable that no one of the 80 players engaged secured an open shot for the bushel basket. If any player did get his hands on the ball it took several minutes to dig him out from under the mob that immediately hopped him.

That free-for-all in Trenton was not typical of games in basketball's pioneer days. For one thing, few early games had 80 contestants. Nine-man teams played most of them, as Naismith recommended. Most games probably were not quite as rough as the game in Trenton either. In an article titled "Basket Ball and Its Success" in November 1893, *The New York Times* wrote:

Basket ball is a modified kind of football with every element of roughness eliminated. It is particularly adapted for indoor practice, and may be played on any gymnasium floor or other suitable place. When it is known that the game is played in hundreds of gymnasiums from New York to San Francisco, has recently been introduced into Japan, is a popular sport with young athletes in Australia, and is played by scores of handsome athletic young ladies in Wellesley and Smith Colleges, it will be seen that it possesses more than ordinary elements of interest....

The game is simple, easily learned, and not incumbered with a list of difficult rules....Many of the football terms are retained, although the pastime lacks such incidental features of the genuine game as sprained ankles, dislocated shoulders, broken noses, and other casualties to which spectators of a contest between brawny college teams frequently witnesses.

The baskets are the goals and the aim of the teams is to throw the ball into the opponents' goal. At first thought this may appear as a comparatively simple thing to do, but five minutes' play by a novice would convince him of the adage that "appearances are deceptive," and he would begin to realize that a considerable amount of skill and practice are necessary to make a goal.

In 1893 the official YMCA rules suggested that teams should have five men if the court was small, nine if it was large. A year later the number was set at five if the court was less than 1,800 square feet, seven if it was up to 3,600 square feet, and nine if it was bigger than that. It was not until 1897 that teams were finally fixed at five.

Other rules were evolving, too. At first, field goals earned one point and there were no free throws; the penalty for fouls was temporary benching of the offender. Then free throws were introduced for fouling, including such infractions as running with the ball or kicking it, as well as for hacking, holding, or pushing an opponent. The free throw line was 20 feet from the basket until 1894 when it was cut to 15 feet. In 1893, the time for each half was lengthened from 15 to 20 minutes and the intermission from five to 10 minutes. The Y's rule-makers tinkered with scoring too, setting the value of a field goal at three points and penalizing fouls by adding a point to the opponents' score. Finally, for the 1895-96 season, they settled on two points for a field goal, one for a free throw.

To start each half, and after each score, the referee threw the ball up between opposing centers, who might tap it to a teammate or catch it themselves. The referee and umpire ranged

along the sidelines. The referee ruled on out-of-bounds plays, which team had the ball, when it was in play, and when goals were made. He also kept the time. The umpire called all fouls, including what are now called violations.

For a short time, the court was marked off into three segments, and forwards, centers and guards or backs were restricted to their sector, although any player could shoot so long as he stayed in his assigned sector. But even when all players could go anywhere on the court it was the usual practice for guards to spend nearly the whole game near the opponents' goal.

Naismith apparently did not foresee development of the dribble. His Rule Number 2 said that the ball "may be batted in any direction with one or both hands," but it seems likely that he had in mind an alternative to throwing the ball to a teammate, not running while bouncing the ball on the floor.

In any case, the pioneering players discovered that when they were being closely guarded in a corner and no teammate was open for a pass, they could escape by bouncing the ball a short distance away, then beating their opponent to it. The continuous dribble soon followed. The amateur rules forbade double dribbles and also prohibited a dribbler from trying for a field goal. He had to pass off when he neared the basket until the rule was changed in 1908. For a time before the turn of the 20th century the "air" dribble was permitted. A player would run down the court while batting the ball a few inches above his hand, a technique that was just short of traveling with the ball, so the rule was changed to require that it must be batted above the dribbler's head. That rule change ended the air dribble.

Until 1898 the YMCA rules allowed a dribbler to bounce the ball with both hands on it, but a new clause in the rules stated that during a dribble, a player could not touch the ball with two hands more than once. Commenting on the rule change ending the two-hand dribble, Luther H. Gulick wrote, "The object of the rule (change) is to largely do away with dribbling. To give a definite illustration: A man cannot dribble the ball down the floor even with one hand and then throw for goal. He must pass it. One man cannot make star plays in this style. The game must remain what it was originally intended to be—a passing game. Dribbling has introduced all of the objectionable features that are hurting the game. It gives the advantage to heavy men and to rough play."

The pioneering professionals went along with most YMCA rules, but not this one. Many pro leagues continued the two-hand dribble well into the 1930s, putting a premium on the strong, bulky player who could bull his way down court, double-dribbling with two hands and backing into opponents who got in the way.

Defense was entirely man-to-man in the early years, and defenders took pride in denying shots to their opponent. Often several minutes went by before either team had a shot at the basket. One-handed shots were rare except when a player was directly below the basket. Slam dunks were the stuff of fantasy.

Here is how one of the early experts described shooting methods and team play:

The two best methods of throwing for goal are the underhand toss, giving a reverse rotation to the ball, and the overhand shot from the chest, in which the ball is pushed or shot

upward and outward toward the goal.

A favorite method of scoring is for one attack (forward) to throw to the basket. Should the ball fail to enter, another attack quickly places himself under the basket, catches the ball as it descends and pushes it into the basket. The tallest attack should always play under the basket, as the shorter the space between his outstretched hand and the goal the better for him.

The center men are so placed as to assist the forwards or help the backs, and, as the strain comes on each of these divisions, they should be able to make a good shot for goal and be quick enough to stop a good play of an opponent. Their aim should be to keep feeding the ball forwards to their own men and keep them in a position to score goals.

The backs, to whom the defense is entrusted, should be the biggest and heaviest men on the team. They should not be so big nor so heavy, though, as to be clumsy and slow, for quickness of the foot and eye is indispensable in basketball, and no other qualities can make up for its lack. It is exceedingly difficult for an attack to make a goal if the defense sticks closely to him and plays him well, so that the first and foremost thought in the mind of a back should be to stick to his opponent like glue and he should follow these tactics without varying. In fact, if a back should prevent his opponent from throwing a goal, and yet during the whole game has not once touched the ball himself, he has a right to think he has played a good game.

The early advocates of basketball believed that low scores meant good basketball. As one alleged expert put it in 1893, "Six points is a good score in a well-played game, but poorer teams may roll up twenty or more."

A donnybrook often followed when the ball went out of bounds because the original rules stated that it belonged to the first player to touch it. In his reminiscences, Naismith wrote: "It was not uncommon to see a player who was anxious to secure the ball make a football dive for it, regardless of whether he went into the apparatus that was stored around the gym or into the spectators in the bleachers." He recalled an incident when the ball flew into the balcony and "immediately the players from one team scrambled for the narrow stairway, crowding it so that they could make little speed. Two of the players on the other team boosted one of their mates up until he could catch the lower part of the balcony, swing himself up, and regain the out-of-bounds ball."

In those early days, there was much talk of good basketball as "scientific" because it was obvious that cleverness and the ability to feint and fake out an opponent were huge assets. H.G. Reynolds, who was a member of the Central YMCA team in Chicago in 1893, reminisced about the team in the *Converse Basketball Year Book* of 1922:

George Eller, the Central physical director, was insisting on thorough preparation and scientific study in connection with the game. Our team was composed of gym class squad leaders, and before our class could play the game we had to go through the regular work, calisthenics, apparatus, and conditioning exercises. Class basketball followed....The team itself then took the floor for scrimmage or practice to develop its passing game,

ending with a conditioning mile run, which Ehler made us jog in less than six minutes. We had regular meetings to discuss the plays we had seen, or which had developed on the floor in action, analyzing each, diagramming in chalk-talks the mechanics of more scientific play, and contributing whatever any one had evolved to the general knowledge and theory of play. Out of this forerunner to the modern skull practice, we gradually worked up the fundamentals of team play. We early observed the almost unavoidable tendency of players to be drawn in toward the ball, and reasoning from that discovery we systematized our team work. Having received a cross pass, our players knew the next throw would be along the side, or a pass along the side would be followed by a cross throw. We developed a knowledge of where the play would be, saving the fraction of a second which, in the long run, meant the difference in score between winner and loser.

H.G. Reynolds, who went on to become a well-known coach and referee, said the Central YMCA's players opposed the reduction of players on a team from nine to seven in 1894 and again when it dropped to five in 1897. "We looked with suspicion at the new departure, fearing that it would slow up the game. It was a great surprise to us when it proved instead to speed up play," he wrote. "We all thought it was a big mistake. But it was the thing which made basketball. It eliminated the larger part of the bodily contact which marred the early game, clearing the floor and rendering scientific team play possible," Reynolds said. "Team play, in fact, became an absolute necessity, and the most dense observer could not help seeing that fact."

During basketball's first four or five years, all of the best teams were in YMCA branches, but colleges and high schools were taking up the game. In the fall of 1892, Stagg introduced the game at the University of Chicago. It also appeared at the University of Iowa and Geneva College in Beaver Falls, Pa. By 1895 basketball was an intramural sport at many colleges, including Yale, Stanford, Ohio State, Hamline, Wesleyan, and Smith College for women in Northampton, Mass. The game was first played at Smith in 1893 and male spectators were banned because the players wore bloomers. Three years later, men were welcomed at an inter-class game at Smith because the costumes had changed. In a lengthy story about a game pitting Smith's sophomores against the freshmen, *The New York Times* included this fashion note: "The usual gymnasium suit of dark blue, with short, divided skirts, blouse waists, and full sleeves, was the costume. This, relieved by the crimson '98 across the front, crimson belts, ties, and arm bands is, besides being extremely comfortable, remarkably becoming in all cases, and very picturesque. Thick, heavy knee pads are also essential."

Men's uniforms would not have excited such admiration. They varied from the trousers, tights, and short-sleeved shirts used in the typical gym to track suits and even football pants.

Intercollegiate competition began February 9, 1895, according to historian Zander Hollander, when the Minnesota State School of Agriculture whipped Hamline, 9-3, in a game of nine-man teams. (Earlier, teams representing colleges had faced YMCA teams; Vanderbilt defeated the Nashville YMCA as early as March 1893.) The first intercollegiate game with five-man teams is believed to have been a 15-12 victory by the University of Chicago over the University of Iowa on January 16, 1896. The Iowa team, however, was actually the Iowa City YMCA club, all of whose members attended the university. In eastern college circles, the first five-man game was between the University of Pennsylvania and Yale. It was played at New Haven on March 20, 1897, with Yale winning, 32-10.

In the early years it was not uncommon for a college varsity to play YMCA and high school teams. Often the high schoolers more than held their own. In his reminiscences, Naismith noted that in 1900 Holyoke, Mass. High School defeated Dartmouth, Holy Cross, and other strong college teams. He found it unsurprising, since many of the high school players had played basketball in YMCAs before they joined their school team and thus had developed a level of skill beyond that of players who took up the game in college.

Naismith was, of course, the authority on basketball for the first four years until he left Springfield in 1895 to become physical director of the YMCA in Denver and study medicine at Gross Medical College there. He earned his medical degree in April 1898, but he did not hang out a shingle; rather, he planned to use his medical training to enhance his work in physical education. Soon after he got the medical degree, his life took a new turn. Stagg recommended him for the position of chapel director at the University of Kansas. It happened that there were also openings for "manager of athletics" and head of the newly established Department of Physical Education at the university. It is hard to think of three positions better suited to Naismith's qualifications and interests. (The story goes that Stagg's telegram of recommendation read: "Recommend James Naismith, inventor of basket-ball, medical doctor, Presbyterian minister, tee-totaler, all-around athlete, non-smoker, and owner of vocabulary without cuss words.")

Naismith was hired for the three positions and took up his post in September 1898. His duties as chapel director were to preach and lead prayers and hymns every day. As manager of athletics, he was disappointed with the university's offerings; the only sport of consequence was football. Basketball had been introduced a year before he arrived as a sport for women students but it did not take root.

Naismith formed eight basketball teams made up of male students and faculty members for intramural play. Most of the players had never seen a basketball game before they played in one. But the game proved popular on campus, and soon the student newspaper was hailing the game as all the rage on campus. "At present it appears that basket ball would carry all before it," the newspaper editorialized.

In early February 1899 Naismith organized a varsity team made up of the best players on the intramural teams. The Jayhawk basketeers lost their first game to the Kansas City, Missouri YMCA team, 16-5. Later that season the Jayhawks evened the score with a 17-14 victory over the YMCA. Naismith was, in effect, the coach of the university team, although he did not take the job seriously. In fact, he didn't believe a basketball team needed a coach. When a friend told him that he was going to coach a college team, Naismith replied, "Basketball is just a game to play. You don't coach it." Nevertheless, he "taught" the varsity for several seasons,

compiling a won-lost record of 54-44. After he left the post, he attended the team's home games, but he seemed only mildly interested in the proceedings, according to other spectators.

When Naismith left Springfield for Kansas in 1895, his old mentor, Luther H. Gulick, took over as basketball's guide and arbiter of rules. He was well suited to the task. The History of the Y.M.C.A. in North America credits Gulick with developing the philosophy and methods that took the YMCA's programs from the days when its gym superintendents were retired boxers and circus acrobats into the age of professional physical directors who aimed to "Christianize" the gym. Gulick had been a gymnasium superintendent himself and had earned a medical degree from New York University before going to Springfield in 1897. He spent 13 years leading the Y's physical training program into the modern age.

Gulick faced plenty of problems after Naismith left, not so much with the rules of the game as with the love-hate relationship that YMCA general secretaries and physical directors had for basketball. On the one hand, basketball was attracting new members and was enhancing interest in the community in the wider work of the local Y. As an article in the YMCA's journal titled Physical Education noted in the summer of 1894, "One of the best solutions to the difficulty of maintaining the interest of the members has been the judicious introduction of the play element into the work; and in this line nothing has been so peculiarly and generally satisfactory as Basket Ball." The article also noted that basketball leagues stimulated community interest; thus inter-YMCA competition was valuable, even though it required charging a nominal entrance fee for games to pay traveling expenses of visiting teams and other costs.

On the other hand, some physical directors were asking, "Is Basket Ball a Danger?" That was the title of an article in another YMCA publication, Young Men's Era, that same summer in which five physical directors spoke their minds. The consensus was, "No, not necessarily,' although all five expressed concern that basketball might be permitted to push calisthenics and dumbbell drills out of gym activities and monopolize the floor for too much time.

In a typical reply, Thomas Cornelius of the Baltimore YMCA advised: "The new game of basket-ball, which is the most popular of all gymnasium games, and deservedly so, takes nearly an hour to play, and very little else can be done the same evening. It is an all-around game, decidedly more so than any other game I know….

"It is also recreative, which class work generally is not," Cornelius continued, "but it was never intended to take the place of regular systematic class work, and should be kept under control, never allowing it to crowd out the other."

Cornelius added, "It should be played at stated times: say, once a week for afternoon classes and once a week for night classes, and the ball religiously kept off the floor at all other times. Properly managed it is an aid to our work and a drawing card, improperly managed it will do harm."

Two years later, in 1896, a survey of leaders of 26 YMCAs around the country found that they believed basketball was beneficial to most Ys. By and large, attendance was up in their gyms, and the majority described inter-YMCA play and games

with colleges and National Guard teams as "helpful" to the aims of the YMCA. A minority of the leaders complained of too much roughness in the play, incompetent officials, and frequent bad feelings between teams, especially in games outside the local gym.

The Camden, N.J. YMCA barred basketball from its gymnasium in the fall of 1896 on grounds that the game was too brutal to be played in a Christian organization. In January 1897 Gulick spoke against roughness in the pages of the YMCA's Association Men. He wrote:

> *The game must be kept clean. It is a perfect outrage for an institution that stands for Christian work in the community to tolerate not merely discourteous and ungentlemanly treatment of guests, but slugging and that which violates the elementary principles of morals. It hurts the religious life of the Association; it hurts the influence of the Association in the community; it hurts the personal influence of the general secretary and physical director of the Association; it injures the character of the men who play. If the fact were generally known, it would influence the financial support of the Association. It would have a large measure of influence in determining the amount of credence that the young men should give to the claims of the Association that it aims to lead men into a high Christian life.*

Other YMCA executives echoed Gulick's views in the pages of *Association Men*. "Is basketball of such vital importance that it must be included in our instruction?" asked H.L. Chadwick of Philadelphia rhetorically. "Our apparatus has not grown rusty, neither do we see any loss in our attendance, or in the legitimate work of the gymnasium, since we refused to allow any game to usurp the whole of the gymnasium for hours at a time, and finally to usurp our time. The few who considered the game of paramount value deserted the gymnasium and hired outside places to play, but the business and professional men, the students, clerks and mechanics go on steadily with their exercises and are not crazed over games of basketball."

Chadwick's attack brought plenty of responses defending basketball, but by this time basketball had outgrown the YMCA's ability to control it. While the debate simmered in the pages of *Association Men* during the winter of 1896-97, the first professionals were on the court.

The first admitted play-for-pay team was one of those mentioned by H.L. Chadwick who had deserted YMCA gyms. It was a team in Trenton, N.J. which had represented the YMCA there from 1892 until it left at the beginning of the 1896-97 season, evidently after friction developed with the Y's leaders. Trenton's *Daily True American* reported in its October 31, 1896 issue that the players "are no longer sailing under the colors of the YMCA but have organized independently this year, through some difficulties." The newspaper did not explain what the difficulties were.

A 10-man roster was announced for the Trenton Basketball Team, headed by Fred Cooper, captain, and Al Bratton, the YMCA team's stars for three years. Fred Padderatz and W.S. Saunderson, two local sportsmen, were to handle the team's business affairs.

What was probably the first advertisement for a basketball

game appeared in the *True American* on November 4. It was a one-column, two-inch ad among the notices for public sales and church bazaars and announced the "Grand Opening of the Season of the National Champions" on Saturday, November 7, at Trenton's Masonic Hall. The Trenton team, which had claimed the mythical national championship in 1895-96 after beating YMCAs and college and high school teams in New Jersey, New York, and eastern Pennsylvania, would face the Brooklyn YMCA, described as "champions of New York."

The team's new home, the Masonic Temple, was a sprawling, three-story building in downtown Trenton, with stores on the first floor, the Masonic lodge rooms on the second, and a large social hall with a high ceiling on the third. Padderatz and Saunderson arranged to erect portable baskets in the third-floor hall. The hall may have had electric lights; most public buildings of the era were lit by gaslight, but Trenton's downtown was being wired for electricity around that time.

The hall was also fitted out with basketball's first cage enclosing the court. The cage was a 12-foot wire fence set on the court's boundaries, with doors at both ends to allow access. *The True American* said the purpose of the cage was "so that the ball will never go among the spectators." This is a reasonable explanation because the rule giving an out-of-bounds ball to the first player to touch it was still in effect, and it would have been bad for business to have players wrestling in the laps of paying customers for possession of the ball. With the cage the ball was never out of bounds.

Trenton basketball historian Marvin A. Riley had a different explanation for the cage. Writing a quarter century later, Riley said, "The Trentons conceived the idea that the cage would make the game faster by stopping all out-of-bounds delays." Even later, Fred Cooper, the team captain, had still a third twist on the cage's origin. Cooper said that a local sports editor had commented after a team practice, "They played like a lot of monkeys and should be put in a cage." Fred Padderatz, a carpenter by trade, promptly built a cage and put the team in it, Cooper said.

Other teams did not seize upon the idea for a cage. In fact, they derided the structure as "Trenton's monkey cage." Nevertheless, acceptance of the cage grew among eastern independent teams, and the first professional league, formed in 1898, made the cage mandatory. For three decades the cage was a fixture among pro teams in the East. Most players thought the purpose was to protect players from rabid fans. Cages were rare in the Midwest and were never used by college and high school teams, but they continued in vogue in the East long after the rules were changed to eliminate scrimmages on out-of-bounds balls by giving possession of the ball to the opponents of the team that caused it to go out.

The cage lived on in the nation's sports pages for two generations after its disappearance from the court because sports editors found "cagers" and "cage game" were fitted more easily into headlines than "basketball players" and "basketball."

The Trenton Basketball Team, smartly clad in red, sleeveless jerseys, black, padded knickers and wool stockings opened the 1896 season by whipping the Brooklyn YMCA, 16-1, a fairly typical score for that era. The game attracted 700 spectators. Padderatz and Saunderson had built risers in the hall so that

those who had seats well back from the court could see over those at courtside.

Each team had seven players—two forwards, two "defense," a center, and two "side centers." The first Trenton field goal was scored by side center Newt Bugbee after seven minutes of "fierce playing," the *True American* reported. Fred Cooper, a forward, led the scoring with six points on three field goals. Brooklyn's only point came on a free throw by a player named Simonson with three minutes left in the game. Trenton's starting seven played the whole game, and Brooklyn had only one sub.

Following the usual practice, the home team named the referee and the visitors the umpire. The Trentons selected Marvin A. Riley to referee, giving the future historian a close-up view of what is presumed to be the first professional, or at least semi-pro, game. The qualifier "presumed to be" is necessary because neither Riley nor any of the other participants ever pinpointed the first play-for-pay game, except to say that it happened that year, but it seems probable that when the players left the YMCA for the Masonic Hall, they did so with profit in mind.

Legend has it that the Trenton players earned $15 each for the game, with Cooper receiving an extra dollar as captain and, in effect, coach, although that title was not used. The amount seems improbably high, even if 700 people were crammed into the hall and the box office took in $150. Trenton would have had to pay the hall rental, traveling costs for the Brooklyn team, and fees for the officials before dividing what remained. Unless Padderatz, Saunderson, and the three Trenton players who did not get into the game received nothing, it seems unlikely that each man's share would have been more than $5.

The Trenton Basketball Team played 19 more games that year and finished with a 19-1 record. Their only loss was at Millville, a small town in southern New Jersey with a strong YMCA team whose court was a onetime roller skating rink. Millville blanked the Trentons, 8-0. Trenton avenged the loss by shutting out Millville, 14-0, back home in their cage. Presumably all of their other opponents were simon-pure amateurs. They included several other YMCA teams, Philadelphia's Central High School and Manual Training School, Temple College and the University of Pennsylvania. In their season finale, the Trentons whipped their amateur successors at the Trenton YMCA, 14-2. Earlier in the season, the YMCA's board of directors had forbidden the Y team to play a scheduled game against the professionals.

The success of the Trentons was due largely to the ability of Cooper and Bratton, both soccer players, in adapting soccer's passing patterns to basketball, Riley wrote. His descriptions are not very specific but they suggest that Cooper and Bratton were the first to make a series of short, snappy passes on the run toward the basket. "Time and again I have seen Cooper and Bratton in those early days, pass the ball back and forth between them—no one else touching it—and score against the efforts of an entire opposing team," wrote Riley. "I have seen them do this trick away from home and witnessed the spectators rise en masse and cheer the brilliant exhibition in spite of the fact that it was done by invading players."

Riley did not give similarly glowing descriptions of the basket-shooting techniques used by Cooper and Bratton, but the only approved methods at the time were the layup near the

basket and the two-hand set shot. The set shot might be launched underhand or from chest level.

Pro teams proliferated after the success of the Trentons. Other independent teams began playing for pay after the 1896-97 season, including some in other YMCAs. The YMCA's Athletic League, which was established in 1896 to govern all of the organization's sports programs, was soon reporting instances of local Y's paying membership fees for good basketball players and others forming leagues with "unregulated" teams. The League's monthly newsletters urged physical directors to uphold the principles of "clean sport." The league advised that "much of the outlaw basketball could be eliminated by an explanation of the aims and purposes of registering the men and the necessity of upholding pure amateurism."

In dealing with teams outside YMCAs, local Ys followed the rules of the Amateur Athletic Union, which had been established in 1888 to control amateur sports. By 1899, the AAU decided that a pro team could play amateurs so long as the pros were properly registered as professionals. The Y's Athletic League Letter advised that YMCA teams "desiring to play registered professional teams should, when arranging for games, get a written statement from the team to the effect that they are professionals." The idea was to prevent the pros from playing at one time as professionals and the next as amateurs. "A man that knowingly becomes a professional cannot be reinstated, so such action prevents him from entering amateur sports again," the Athletic League ruled.

As the turn of the 20th century neared, basketball was firmly established in YMCAs, some colleges and high schools, and among a handful of independent amateur teams. There were scores of professional teams in the New York–Philadelphia corridor, and in southern New England, the Hudson River Valley of New York State, and eastern and southwestern Pennsylvania. They were not pros in today's meaning—only in the sense that the players were paid. There were no contracts, and pay was by the game. Sometimes a visiting professional team was given a guarantee; at other times they played for a percentage of the gate receipts and divided the take.

The AAU held the first national basketball tournament in 1897 in New York City, although it was national in name only. Twelve amateur teams were entered, most of them from New York. The 23rd Street YMCA team won the title and the gold medals that went with it. The team promptly decided to turn professional to capitalize on its modest measure of fame and, honest to a fault, informed the AAU of its intention. The team was banned from the 23rd Street Y's gym, and the players were denied memberships.

With no home court, the 23rd Streets became a traveling team, the first of the barnstormers. A Philadelphia sportswriter dubbed them the "Wanderers" And the name stuck. Recalling the Wanderers' peregrinations many years later, John L. Wendelken, a forward on the team, wrote:

"With our reputation established, Bob Abadie, who was named Manager, had no difficulty in dating teams in New England, New Jersey, Pennsylvania, and Hudson (Valley) and Mohawk Valley clubs (in upstate New York). The remunerations for these games averaged $12 to $15 above expenses per player, depending on the number making the trip. We always kept it a minimum," he added dryly. Unlike later barnstorming teams which would hit the road for a week or more, the Wanderers scheduled midweek games in towns within easy railroad reach of New York so that they could return after the game for their regular jobs or studies. (Wendelken and another player were medical students.)

On weekends, the Wanderers would venture farther afield, and over the Thanksgiving, Christmas, New Year's, and Easter holidays they would be on the go for three or four days. Their most exhausting trip, over the New Year's holiday in 1901, found them playing four games within a 24-hour period in western Pennsylvania and East Liverpool, Ohio. On New Year's Eve, they whipped Pittsburgh South Side and then played morning, afternoon, and evening games on January 1.

The game was changing during this period. The most notable change was reduction in the number of players on a team to five for the 1897-98 season, which led to faster, more open play and a little less emphasis on brute strength. Because the typical basketball court was small, cutting the number of players from 14 to 10 put more value on speed, quickness, and effective passing and less on sheer strength.

Still, the professional game was no place for shrinking violets. Marvin A. Riley was a busy referee in the early professional era. He had this to say about what was allowed:

In those days you must know that when a guard met a forward, or any other player, head-on—no hipping or shouldering—just plain front-to-front—it was not called a foul. All that was necessary was to make the play on the ball, just as you make the play in football on the man who is carrying the ball—excepting, or course, you could not hold or use your hands—but you could play the ball and put all you wanted in back of your play. If the player who was dribbling happened to be right in back of the ball—that was his fault.

Despite the ample allowance for rough play, basketball—for both amateurs and professionals—was no longer just a massed battle for the ball. Many teams were copying the Trentons' short passing game, and the first designed plays were appearing. Originally, all plays were off the center jump. The center, or occasionally the team captain, would indicate by a slight movement of the hand or head the direction the center hoped to tap the ball. "Guards down" was the most common play off the jump; the center would tap the ball to one of his forwards and one of the guards would race past, take a pass from the forward, and dribble near the basket to the other guard coming from the opposite side of the floor for the shot. (The rules prohibited the dribbling guard from shooting.)

As the turn of the 20th century neared, basketball was growing in popularity, but it was still a minor sport. That would soon begin changing.

Chapter 2

Coming of Age: Basketball Through World War II

By Robert Peterson

Basketball made great strides on the road to its present popularity during the first two decades of the 20th century. The game still played second fiddle to baseball and football, but by the time the United States became embroiled in World War I in 1917, virtually all colleges and most high schools, especially those in cities, were represented by basketball teams.

There were good reasons for the game's growth. For one thing, basketball offered plenty of fast, continuous action, thrilling both players and spectators. For another, small rural high schools that would have had a hard time rounding up enough athletes to form a representative team in football or baseball could assemble the few needed for basketball. Equipment was cheaper, too. Just after the turn of the century, a basketball player could be outfitted with jersey, knee-length pants, long stockings, canvas shoes with rubber soles, and a warm-up sweater for as little as $4.35. A top-of-the-line outfit in the A.G. Spalding & Bros. catalogue went for $14.35.

Most colleges and high schools had gymnasiums, although some of them were far from ideal for basketball. Some gyms had low ceilings, making it impossible to shoot a long, arching shot, and a few were heated by pot-bellied stoves at courtside, making it hazardous to run along the sideline with an opponent in pursuit. But the gym could be converted into a basketball court inexpensively merely by marking out boundary lines, free throw lines, and a center circle, and screwing a pair of goals ($4 per pair) into the end walls or fastening them to standards. An official ball cost $4 or $5, depending on quality.

Basketball's rules were still in flux. As late as 1914, five sets of rules were in use—two by professional leagues, and one each by colleges, Amateur Athletic Union members, and women's teams. The National Collegiate Athletic Association was founded in 1906 and began bringing some order to the collegiate chaos. Its Collegiate Rules Committee struggled with varying ideas about rules for the dribble. Some purists pointed out that basketball began as a passing game and objected to the fact that some players sought to thrill the crowd by dribbling the length of the court. Proponents of the dribble noted that it could be an exciting play if it was performed well, which, by the way, was not as easy as it is today because the basketball was rarely a true sphere. For one thing, the bladder's inflation needle was tucked under a heavy thong lacing, making a slight bump on the ball's surface. For another, "Irregularities in the ball were commonplace," according to Thomas Allan Knudson, who studied early basketball equipment for his doctoral dissertation. "In shooting for the goal," he wrote, "the thrower was advised to hold the ball each time in a particular way so that the hands became

Senda Berenson and Students, 1893
These women refute the idea that basketball is only for boys, due to the "evil influence of such excitement upon the nervous feminine nature."

familiar with the many peculiarities in the shape of the ball" (Walter "Dutch" Wohlfarth, an early professional, achieved fame as the "Blind Dribbler" for his unusual ability to dribble without looking at the ball).

In 1915 the collegians and the Amateur Athletic Union agreed on a uniform rule for dribbling. One-handed dribbling would be allowed, and at the end of a dribble the dribbler could shoot. Heretofore, the AAU rules specified that the dribbler had to pass to a teammate and could not shoot.

In 1911 the Rules Committee had approved a proposal that the umpire, who was also timekeeper, would signal the end of each half by firing a revolver. The following winter, before that rule took effect, the committee reconsidered when it was pointed out that in New York State, a gun-toting umpire who did not have a gun license could be arrested for violating the state's Sullivan Law. Taking the advice of umpires, the committee changed from guns to whistles.

In 1913 the Collegiate Rules Committee put an end to the scrimmages that resulted from James Naismith's original rule calling for an out-of-bounds ball to go to the first player to touch it. The new rule gave an out-of-bounds ball to an opponent of the player who caused it to go out. No longer would opposing players wrestle each other for the right to throw it back into play. At the same time, the Rules Committee called for opposing centers to jump with one hand behind their backs on the center jumps that started each half and followed each field goal and successful free throw. Their thinking was that roughness would be reduced if centers couldn't use the free hand to push the opponent.

The two professional leagues in operation at this time went along with most college rules, but not all. The Eastern League, centered in the Philadelphia-Trenton, N.J. area, required that courts be 65 by 35 feet and enclosed in wire cages. The New York State League, in northeastern New York, did not require cages, and only the Troy Trojans had one; it was made of rope netting rather than wire mesh. No backboards were used in the New York State League. The baskets were hung from a rod coming down from the rafters, and all shots had to be made "clean." Both of the pro leagues permitted the discontinued (double) dribble with two hands.

But the pro leagues' rules differed in another respect besides the dribble and the use of backboards and cages. In the New York State League, a player who was fouled took the free throw himself while the Eastern League followed the intercollegiate practice of having a designated free-throw shooter take all of his team's free throws. Before the decade was over, the Eastern League ruled that each player would shoot his own free throws. The colleges did not adopt that rule until 1924.

When free-throw specialists were in their heyday, they invariably led their leagues in scoring. In the final season of the Central League in 1911-12, for example, Bill Kummer of the Connellsville, Pa. team was the top scorer with 1,404 points in 62 games. That gave him an average of nearly 23 points a game at a time when team totals were mostly in the 20s and 30s. Of that remarkable total, 938 points were free throws. Kummer had 233 field goals that season. So did Dutch Wohlfarth of the Johnstown, Pa. team. But Wohlfarth did not have a single free throw in 58 games, so he finished sixth in the scoring race behind Kummer and four other free-throw specialists.

Several women's colleges adopted basketball in the early 20th century, mostly for intramural play. The game enjoyed growing popularity among high school girls, too. Not everyone was pleased. The Victorian age perception of women as hothouse flowers still persisted, as Lucille Eaton Hill of Wellesley College for women demonstrated in 1903. She told the New England Association of Colleges and Preparatory Schools that girls under college age should never play basketball, and women

college students playing the game should be carefully supervised. *The New York Times* reported that Miss Hill said "the physical effects upon young girls at a critical period of their growth into womanhood, the chances of permanent injury to beauty and health, the evil influence of such excitement upon the nervous feminine nature, and the tendency to unsex a player—for she declared that the competitive game, with its traveling about, its exhibitions before mixed audiences, and its cultivation of the win-at-any-cost spirit, was not womanly, and made neither for character or refinement—were all urged against the game for young girls."

On the other hand, Senda Berenson, who had introduced basketball to Smith College's students in 1893, wrote that the game was very beneficial for young women if it was well supervised by a woman coach or instructor and if the women's rules were followed. "The rules for men are injurious to girls physically because they give too severe a test to her powers of endurance," Miss Berenson wrote. "They also contain elements of roughness that are bad for her social and moral character." Nevertheless, some girls' teams played men's rules and were coached by men.

Women's rules were designed to eliminate roughness and to reduce the amount of exertion required to play basketball. The court was divided into three equal parts, and each of a team's six players—two forwards, two centers, and two guards—was required to stay in her assigned sector. Players were not allowed to bat or snatch the ball from an opponent's hands or even to touch it. No bodily contact was permitted in guarding. Dribbling wasn't allowed either, and a player could hold the ball for only three seconds before passing or shooting.

Commenting on the rules, Berenson, who was Smith's director of physical training, wrote that the rule prohibiting a player from snatching the ball from an opponent "does away with personal contact and the evil passions that may thus be aroused in the heat and excitement of the game. The time limit of three seconds for holding the ball makes the game less of a mad whirl and relieves the too great strain on the heart." Also to ease such strains, the women's rules called for 15-minute halves rather than the 20-minute halves for men's games.

The first professional basketball league began play in 1898. It was grandly called the National Basketball League despite the fact that all six member teams were in the Philadelphia area and southern New Jersey. The league was formed under the leadership of newspaper sports editors. Horace Fogel of the Philadelphia *Public Ledger* was elected president. Franchises were granted to the Trenton Basketball Team; the former Millville, N.J. YMCA club; Camden, N.J., Germantown, Pa. and two Philadelphia teams, the Clover Wheelmen and the Hancock Athletic Association.

Formation of the league was not without disputes. Making a schedule was difficult because all teams wanted home games on Saturdays. Some teams were slow to build cages on their courts, which the league's rules mandated. Some of the courts may have been illuminated by gaslights because the rules required lighting satisfactory to the referee. Not more than eight players per team could appear in a game.

Apparently there was no league limit on salaries. Trenton basketball historian Marvin A. Riley said that Trenton's players

earned $2.50 each for a home game, $1.25 on the road. The league paid its four referees, including Marvin Riley, $3 per game. Even with such modest costs, three teams ran into financial trouble early in the season and dropped out. Trenton won the first championship with an 18-2-1 record; the runner-up was Millville with 14-6-2.

The National League continued to operate for five more seasons, though with several franchise changes. The New York Wanderers joined the league in 1899-00 and won the pennant in 1900-01. The league had to fight off challenges from other short-lived circuits in the New York, Philadelphia, and Wilmington, Del. areas, competing fiercely for fans and players. The National Basketball League finally succumbed on January 2, 1904, when leagues in New England lured away many of its star players, including John Wendelken of the Wanderers. He was offered $50 a game for two or three games a week, a princely wage at the time, by the team in Springfield, Mass.

Most of the good professional teams preferred the stability of league play to barnstorming, and in the Northeast they had plenty of opportunities to join a league, although without assurance that the league would survive very long. From 1900 until World War I there was at least one pro league in operation each season and often three or four. In addition, many cities and small towns had semipro teams on which a player could supplement his income from a regular job.

Nearly all of the pros and semipros on these teams came out of teams in YMCAs, high schools, athletic clubs and settlement houses. College players seldom turned pro after graduation until well after the Great War. One reason was that while a professional career could be lucrative (by the standards of the time) it was also precarious. Players were not given no-cut contracts (in most cases they had no contracts at all), and injured players had no paydays. Also, there was still a stigma attached to professional sports. Luther Gulick voiced the view of many amateur sportsmen in 1904. He wrote that professionalism "has ruined every branch of athletics to which it has come. When men commence to make money out of sport, it degenerates with most tremendous speed, so that those who love sport have come to set their faces like a flint against every tendency toward professionalism in athletics. It has in the past inevitably resulted in men of lower character going into the game, for, on the average, men of serious purpose in life do not care to go into that kind of thing."

This somewhat elitist view of professional sports was typical of a gentleman around the turn of the century, although it was beginning to change as college athletes like Christy Mathewson began coming into major league baseball. But the vast majority of pros in both baseball and basketball were athletically gifted young men from the working class, not well educated, but having no more character flaws than their fellow citizens.

The pioneering professional basketball leagues were confined to the Northeast because it was the prime seedbed for basketball and because population centers were close enough together to make league play practicable. The age of easy air travel, which brought the possibility of transcontinental leagues, was decades away. Most basketball teams got around by railroad and interurban trolley; a few clubs used the newfangled automobile for short trips.

All of the early "major leagues" were unstable, with only two surviving longer than six seasons. (They were "major" only in the sense that they attracted the best pro players, not in being nationally known). These were the earliest professional leagues:

National League: 1898-1904. Teams in southern New Jersey, southeastern Pennsylvania, New York, and Delaware.
New England League: 1902-05. Teams in Massachusetts and New Hampshire.
Central Massachusetts League: 1902-03. Teams in Massachusetts and Connecticut.
Philadelphia League: 1903-09.
Western Massachusetts League: 1903-04. Teams in Massachusetts and Connecticut.
Central League: 1906-12. Teams in western Pennsylvania and eastern Ohio.
Eastern League: 1909-23. Teams in southeastern Pennsylvania, New Jersey, and New York. (Cancelled season in 1918-19 because of World War I.)
Hudson River League: 1909-12. Teams in eastern New York and New Jersey.
New York State League: 1911-17, and 1919-23. Teams in eastern and central New York, Massachusetts, and New Jersey.
Pennsylvania State League: 1914-1918, and 1919-1921. Teams in the coal region of Pennsylvania and Paterson, N.J.
Interstate League: 1915-17 and 1919-20. Teams in New York, New Jersey, and Connecticut.
Connecticut State League: 1917-18 and 1920-21. Teams in Connecticut and New Jersey.

None of these leagues attracted widespread attention. Not until the mid-1920s did reports of professional basketball begin appearing with any regularity in major newspapers, and even then the stories tended to be sketchy at best, deprecatory at worst. All of the early leagues had frequent franchise shifts as fan support waned and players sought greener pastures. There were no inter-league agreements to prevent players and whole teams from jumping where they wished, and it was not uncommon for a team to cancel a league game if it had the prospect of a better payday for a game with a team outside their league.

By 1909 some professional players were wearing the colors of five or more teams each season. William Scheffer wrote in the *Reach Official Basket Ball Guide* that year that he had been told by a team manager in New Jersey that just twenty men represented the ten teams he had booked for home games the previous season.

Several of the early leagues had teams in Philadelphia, New York, and Pittsburgh, but most professional teams were in smaller cities; some were much smaller. The strongest team in the 1906-07 season, for example, represented East Liverpool, Ohio, a pottery manufacturing city of 17,000 on the Ohio River, 40 miles west of Pittsburgh. The team manager, William Hocking, scoured the eastern cities where pro basketball had been played for a decade and secured the services of Joe Fogarty, John "Snake" Deal, Ed Ferat, Bill Keenan, Winnie Kincaid, and John Pennino, all established stars of the cage game in the New York-Philadelphia corridor.

The East Liverpool Potters were entered in the new Central League, which included the South Side club of Pittsburgh and teams in four nearby small cities. The Potters' home games were played in a cage in a theater with movable seats. They drew from 500 to 1,000 rabid fans per game, some of whom displayed their enthusiasm with cowbells, tin whistles, and sleigh bells. The fans were prepared to back the Potters with hard cash, and sometimes up to $2,000 was bet on an important game.

By early December 1906, the basketball Potters were entrenched as local favorites. For a game in Pittsburgh against South Side, 400 East Liverpudlians rode a special train to the big city. East Liverpool's victory was celebrated the next day with the lead story on the front page of the *Evening Review*. The newspaper reported that when the rooters got home at two a.m., "they were joined by a hundred more at the station. Rockets were sent up, redfire was burned, and cowbells and horns awoke the town."

The Potters shared the league championship title with South Side when an agreement could not be reached on terms for a playoff. The next season they walked off with the pennant, posting a 53-19 record. The season after that, all the team's stars deserted for other clubs in the Central League, and the makeshift club that represented East Liverpool finished dead last with a mark of 4-67, 44-1/2 games behind the first-place Homestead Young Americans. That was the end of East Liverpool's day in the pale sun of professional basketball.

The Central League continued to operate through the 1911-12 season, although without a franchise in East Liverpool. The circuit vied with the Eastern League and Hudson River League for players and regional prestige. Central Leaguers earned salaries as high as $100 a month, so eastern stars continued to go west. The McKeesport Tubers won the Central League championship in 1910 and in 1911 with several eastern stars, including Andy Sears, the most noted designated free-throw shooter in the game. In the latter year, the Tubers challenged the DeNeri club of Philadelphia, Eastern League champion, to basketball's first "world series." If there was any doubt of the Central League's strength, it was dispelled when McKeesport routed DeNeri in four straight games in a best-of-seven series. The series was arranged by the team managers, not by the leagues, and McKeesport's claim to the world championship rang hollow because no series was played against the Troy Trojans, champions of the Hudson River League.

The McKeesport-DeNeri "world series" in 1911 was not the only inter-league test in the early years. In 1913 the only two circuits operating—the Eastern and New York State Leagues—sanctioned a series. Reading, Pa. of the Eastern League won three of five games from Troy of the New York State loop. The results were not very conclusive because the home team in each game decided what rules would be used, and the Eastern League rules mandated backboards while the New York State League did not. As a result, the team at home won every game. (On their home court, in a National Guard armory, the Troy Trojans demolished the Eastern League champions, 28-14 and 47-13.) Reading won the flip of a coin to decide the site of the deciding game and eked out a 31-29 victory at home.

Another "world" title was contested that season in Fond du

Lac, Wis., one of the seedbeds of professional basketball in the Midwest. Fond du Lac's Company E of the National Guard defeated the touring New York Nationals, 28-25 and 43-23, in what was billed as a series for the professional championship of the United States. Three years later, in 1916, the winners of the three leagues then in operation planned a series to decide supremacy, though without the sanction of the leagues. Greystroke of Philadelphia, the Eastern League champions, split two games with the Paterson Crescents of the Interstate League and claimed the third game by forfeit. The Penn State League titlists, the Wilkes-Barre Barons, also bested Paterson in two games, but by the time they finished that series it was too late in the season to have a playoff between Greystroke and Wilkes-Barre.

Possibly the best of the pioneering professional teams was the Troy Trojans. Their nucleus was four young men—Ed and Lew Wachter, Bill Hardman, and Jimmy Williamson—who had learned the game at the Troy, N.Y. YMCA in the last decade of the 19th century. From 1905 through the 1915-16 season they won the unofficial AAU title once and took four pennants in five years of play in professional leagues. Their leader was 6-foot-1 Edward A. Wachter, who is generally regarded as the best center of the 1900-20 era. His brother, Louis W. "Lew" Wachter, and Hardman and Williamson were not quite in his class, but when joined by sharp-shooting Jack Inglis and Charles "Chief" Muller they were a formidable team.

Ed Wachter was first paid to play with Ware in the Western Massachusetts League in 1903. Late in that season, his contract was sold for $100 to Haverhill, Massachusetts in the New England League, apparently the first sale of a basketball player's contract. For the 1904-05 season, he joined his brother Lew, Williamson, Hardman, and two friends, Ray Snow and Jim Kennedy, to represent Company E of the National Guard in Schenectady, N.Y. At the time, the line between amateurs and professionals was exceedingly fuzzy; despite Ed Wachter's pro experience the Company E team apparently qualified as amateur, because the team challenged the best AAU team in the Midwest, the Blue Diamonds of the Kansas City Athletic Club, to a series for the unofficial AAU championship (The AAU held no official national tournaments between 1905 and 1909).

Company E beat Kansas City in three straight games at Kansas City's Convention Hall to win the amateur "world championship." The first two games were donnybrooks, so rough that the second game had to be ended with four minutes left to play after a Kansas City player decked Hardman.

For the next two seasons, Ed Wachter and company wore the colors of Company G of Gloversville, New York. There was no league in their locale so they toured as independents throughout the Northeast. In 1909 the Wachter brothers, Williamson, and Hardman went home to Troy to play as the Troy Trojans of the new Hudson River League. The Trojans won the pennant by one game over the Paterson, N.J. Crescents (who were also representing Princeton, N.J. in the Eastern League). In the league's second and final full season, the Trojans again edged out the Crescents and the Kingston, N.Y. Colonials for the title.

All of the Hudson River League teams played in large National Guard armories, and crowds of several thousand were

not uncommon; Troy averaged 3,000 for home games. Despite the general prosperity, there was turmoil over the league's leadership, and before the 1911-12 season began Troy and three other teams dropped out. The Trojans joined the newly formed New York State League and won pennants in the first two seasons. Thus Troy became the only team in pro basketball's early years to win league championships in four consecutive years.

The New York State League broke up because of poor attendance midway through the 1914-15 season, so the Troy Trojans hit the road. They wandered through Wisconsin, Minnesota and into Montana, then east again through North Dakota, Minnesota, Wisconsin, and Illinois, playing 29 games in 49 days and winning them all. Back home in the East, the Trojans ended the season with nine straight victories over teams in Massachusetts and New York.

The Troy Trojans' secret of success was teamwork. Throughout the 10 years when the Trojans were probably the best professional team, the Wachter brothers, Hardman, and Williamson stayed together—loyal to one another if not necessarily to Schenectady, Gloversville, or Troy. Ed Wachter, who was in effect coach although he did not have the formal title, is sometimes credited with having invented the bounce pass and the fast break. It seems more likely that both had been used before Wachter became a star, but no doubt he popularized them by incorporating them into the Trojans' attack.

Ed Wachter took great pride in team play and crisp passing, both as a player and later as coach at Williams College and Harvard University. Writing many years after the fact, he recalled with pleasure that James Naismith had visited the dressing room after Wachter's Schenectady team had beaten the Kansas City Blue Diamonds in 1905. He wrote that Naismith, the game's inventor, told the team, "You boys play the game of basketball as it was intended to be played, by passing the ball from one player to another until a player reaches an advantageous position to make a try for the basket."

Styles of play varied not only among professional leagues but also among colleges and other amateur teams in different regions of the country. At the turn of the 20th century, most colleges with basketball teams were in the East, and the game was not a prominent part of student activities. Frank S. Archibald, manager of the Dartmouth College team, wrote in the *Spalding Basket Ball Guide* for 1900-01:

A college basket ball team has disadvantages to overcome that other sports—foot ball, base ball, and track athletics—do not have. The game is not recognized as a college sport in the true sense of the word. In many cases the gymnasium can be had for practice only at inconvenient times, if at all. Unless arrangements can be made for the use of the gym, only out-of-town games can be played, and only a few of these. Like every innovation, the game is looked at askance by some, and as it is not really recognized, many good men won't come out.

A few years later, basketball was accepted as an intercollegiate sport at most colleges in the East, and at many in other regions. In the 1905-06 *Spalding Guide*, Hugh E. Leach of the University of Minnesota team commented on the differences between the game in the East and West (by which he meant the Upper Midwest). He wrote:

Unfortunate though it may be, it is nevertheless true that the rules as formulated for basketball may be variously interpreted. When played under a strict interpretation of the rules, the style of the game is much different than when the play is conducted according to the more liberal ruling. In nearly all the Western universities the tendency has been toward the stricter interpretation. Under this more rigid ruling all technicalities are observed strictly, and while this makes a cleaner game, the continual calling of fouls, when there is a tendency to rough play, breaks up the team work, and this, from the spectators' standpoint, detracts from the interest of the game. Players that have been coached to observe the rules strictly are much handicapped when opposed by men that have been taught the rougher tactics....To compare the East with the West in this branch of athletics would be a very difficult proposition. The style of play in the two sections has always been radically different. The East has become accustomed to the rougher game, and Columbia, who, I believe claims the championship, with this style of play, would have defeated any western team. Played according to the more technical interpretations of the rules, both Chicago and Minnesota could, with justice, I believe, dispute this claim. Until the style of play becomes more uniform, no real satisfaction will be gained in comparing the East with the West. A too strict interpretation of the rules retards the progress of the play, and spoils fast team work, yet if the rougher game is encouraged, instead of being a test of skill and endurance, the game will develop into a test of physical strength. Doubtless, however the rougher style of play will prevail, as this is more interesting to the spectator, and within a few years the West will conform to the East. Without doubt, basket ball has come to play an important part in the field of athletics in the West as well as the East. It will not be very strange to see, within a few years, that the indoor game attracts as much interest during the winter months, as does foot ball in the fall or base ball in the spring.

Hugh Leach was right, at least in part. By the time the U.S. entered World War I in 1917, basketball had overtaken baseball in popularity on college campuses, although it still trailed football by a considerable margin. As was true for football, the Ivy League led the way in basketball. Yale formed a team in the spring of 1895, but basketball was not then recognized as a varsity sport. The team played YMCA teams in New York, but no college teams, in the 1895-96 season. By the turn of the century, most schools in the Ivy League had varsity teams. The Eastern Intercollegiate League began play in 1901-02, with Yale winning the championship with a 6-2 record. Columbia, Harvard, Princeton and Cornell trailed in that order. The University of Pennsylvania joined the league in 1903 to make it a six-team circuit and won the championship in 1905-06 and again in 1907-08.

Penn was challenged at the end of the 1907-08 season by the University of Chicago team, which was the acknowledged Western Intercollegiate champion. A three-game series was planned, but only two were played. Chicago beat the Quakers in Chicago, 18-15. Eighteen hundred spectators turned out,

indicating the game's growing popularity. Penn was beaten again, 16-15, back home in Philadelphia.

In the *Reach Official Basket Ball Guide* of 1908-09, the editor, William J. Scheffer, said that the eastern college teams were rougher than those in the West and suffered for it. Scheffer wrote: "There was no questioning that Pennsylvania had the best team in the East, in the college ranks, but when it came to the meeting with the West the latter showed that they were advanced a little farther. All this can be attributed to one case—clean play. Fouls are called in the West, not five or six to a team, but thirty and forty. Players know that they will be ruled off the floor and do not attempt foul means to win games." (At the time a player could be charged with an unlimited number of fouls; the rule disqualifying a player for five fouls was effective the following season).

A handful of colleges dropped basketball for a year or two after early trials. Among them was Harvard, whose president, Dr. Charles Eliot, blamed "rough play" when he discontinued the basketball team in 1909. Also dropping the game that year were the University of California, University of Connecticut, and Western Reserve University in Cleveland. Westminster College in Pennsylvania dropped out because its faculty decided that basketball "interfered with good scholarship." On the other hand, several colleges took up the game for the first time that season. Among them was Midland College in Nebraska, which started a men's team after having had a women's team for 10 years.

Sports reflected the larger society. A "gentlemen's agreement" among owners of big league baseball teams kept black players off major league rosters, and only a handful of blacks appeared on sports teams in colleges with mostly white student bodies. Arthur Ashe, detailing the careers of black athletes in his three-volume *Hard Road to Glory*, listed just eight who played basketball at "white" colleges from the turn of the century to the end of World War I. They were Samuel Ransom at Wisconsin's Beloit College (1904-08); Wilbur Wood at Nebraska (1907-10); Fenwich Watkins at Vermont (1907-09); Cumberland Posey at Penn State (1909) and Duquesne (1916); Sol Butler at Dubuque, Iowa (1916); William Kindle at Springfield, Mass. College (1911); Cleveland Abbott at South Dakota State (1913); and Paul Robeson at Rutgers (1915-18). Robeson was by far the best known. He was a football All-American and a star in baseball and track and field and went on to become a famed singer, actor, and civil rights activist.

Several historically black colleges had basketball teams in the early part of the 20th century, among them Howard University in Washington, D.C. and Lincoln University in Oxford, Pa. By law in the South and by custom in the North, they played only other all-black teams.

Fewer than a half-dozen black players were on integrated professional rosters before World War I. A black man named Bucky Lew played for Newbury and Haverhill in the New England League in 1904. Three years later Frank "Dido" Wilson integrated the minor Mohawk Valley League with Fort Plain, N.Y. The Eastern League may have had a black player on its rosters in 1911 and again in 1917. No other integrated professional teams are known after that time until the mid-1930s.

By necessity, most black athletes who wanted to play bas-ketball joined all-black teams. The seedbed was the YMCA, just as it was for whites. "Colored" Ys in the cities and in black colleges popularized the game in the first decade of the 20th century. Basketball was introduced to the segregated black high schools in Washington, D.C. in 1905 by Edwin B. Henderson, a black graduate of Harvard who became the first historian of African-American sports. Henderson was a key figure in organizing the District's Interscholastic Athletic Association, which promoted sports for high school students.

The first independent black team, outside the YMCA, was the Smart Set Club in Brooklyn, N.Y. The Smart Set had a track team as well as a basketball team. Soon Smart Set was joined by several other black athletic clubs in the New York area in forming the Olympia Athletic League. Similar athletic clubs and leagues appeared in other northern and border cities with significant African-American populations. In the South, few black athletes played basketball until after World War I. As Arthur Ashe noted, in southern states "warm weather the year round lessened the impetus for a winter game. There were no gymnasiums (for blacks), equipment was poor, coaching was out of an A.G. Spalding manual. The YMCAs had too few indoor facilities. Yet the YMCA's outdoor play areas offered the only hope for a time."

About 1910, the Incorporators, a semipro club, was formed in New York and was soon recognized as probably the strongest black team in the metropolitan region until after World War I. In Pittsburgh, the Monticello Delaney Rifles were started about the same time by Cumberland Posey, the former player at Penn State and Duquesne. Monticello and their Pittsburgh successors, the Loendi Big Five, also started by Cum Posey, regularly traveled east to play the strongest black teams in New York and New Jersey and more than held their own. The *New York Age*, a black newspaper, reported in 1912 that the "colored basketball world will be forced to recognize Monticello as one of the fastest colored quints….It has not met defeat in two years, playing all white teams" (presumably white teams in the Pittsburgh area).

The Loendi Big Five is generally regarded as the best black professional team until the Renaissance Big Five arrived on the basketball scene in the 1920s. So far as is known, Loendi was never invited to play any of the teams in the all-white professional leagues of its day.

While college and professional basketball teams were beginning to thrive in the first two decades of the 20th century, teams that belonged to the Amateur Athletic Union—chiefly YMCAs, athletic associations, and independent teams who were not pros—continued to do well. At the time it was thought that weight was important for a basketball player, and of course it was in the rough and tough professional game. But the AAU took the idea to the extreme of conducting its regional tournaments by weight classes. Often there were regional tourneys for teams whose players weighed 115 pounds or less. The next weight class might be 135 or 145, and teams whose players were over 145 pounds were placed in the unlimited, or heavyweight, division.

If players were to be divided by physique, why wasn't the deciding factor height, since tallness is such a distinct advantage in basketball? Curiously, in the early days little importance was

placed on height. In the first book on basketball skills and techniques, published in 1904 with the title *How to Play Basket Ball*, readers were advised: "Height is a more important consideration in choosing a center than in choosing a forward. Without height many good plays between center and forwards, when the ball is put in play, cannot be carried out. But along with height the center must be able to correctly determine the exact time at which to jump in order to get the ball at just the right height, not too low nor too high. The ability to thus judge the jump correctly, of course, improves with practice. However, let a quick man be the first choice, height being of secondary importance."

The AAU's national tournaments were for unlimited division teams. The first three titles—for 1897, 1899, and 1900—were won by YMCA teams from New York City. After that, the AAU's balance of power began shifting westward. The national winners beginning in 1901 up to World War I were from Chicago, Buffalo, Portage, Wis., San Francisco, and Utah. Not until 1920, when New York University beat Rutgers, 49-24, in the final did an eastern team again take the AAU title.

In 1906 the AAU tried to foster the adaptation of basketball to roller skating, which was gaining favor among athletes. *The New York Times* reported that several experimental games of basketball on skates had been played at Madison Square Garden, and that 50 teams had been organized. The rules forbidding traveling with the ball had to be modified for skaters, the newspaper noted. *The Times* added, "When skating it is practically impossible to follow the existing rules, as frequently the players are unable to preserve their equilibrium, and often bring one or more players down with them when they fall." Despite such drawbacks, James E. Sullivan, secretary-treasurer of the AAU, predicted that roller basketball would become a valuable addition to indoor sports. He was wrong; basketball on skates never got beyond the novelty stage.

World War I had significant effects on basketball, as it did on other aspects of American life. The military's draft took many young athletes into the services. The AAU cancelled its national tournament for 1918, the second year of America's involvement in the war. The professional New York State League had to suspend operations for the latter part of the 1916-17 season and all of 1917-18 because all of its teams played in National Guard armories, and the armories were closed when the Guardsmen were summoned to active service.

After the war ended in November 1918, with America and its Allies victorious over Germany, basketball got international exposure at tournaments played in France. Army Lt. Max (Marty) Friedman, who had been a professional star since 1910, organized a 600-team tournament among the soldiers in the American Expeditionary Force. Friedman's own team, representing a U.S. Army unit stationed in the French city of Tours, won the championship, ending an undefeated season with 19 wins. Two of his teammates were also veterans of the professional Eastern League.

After the AEF tournament, Friedman helped to organize Inter-Allied Games involving a U.S. Army team that he captained, and teams from the French and Italian military forces. The games were played in the open air at Pershing Stadium in Paris. Fifteen thousand spectators, a record for basketball, were

on hand for the first game, pitting the U.S. against Italy. Not surprisingly, the U.S. won easily, 53-11. The Yanks also had no trouble whipping France, 93-8. Despite the possible blows to Italian and French pride, Lt. Friedman said afterwards, "The game is the only one of the purely American sports which the Allies can easily grasp and adapt themselves to. And," he predicted, "there is no doubt in my mind of its successful adoption by all the countries of Europe."

Time would prove him right.

The Heyday of the Barnstormers

While the pioneering professional leagues were struggling for stability, several barnstorming teams crisscrossed the country trying to make a living by playing the college teams, National Guard clubs, and athletic association and town teams that were springing up like weeds. Television and radio were far in the future, and so such entertainments as outdoor band concerts, moving pictures, vaudeville shows, and barnstorming baseball and basketball teams were eagerly welcomed.

The most famous of the early barnstormers were the Buffalo Germans. The team began in 1895 when a group of youngsters, most of them 14 years old, was learning the game in the German department of the YMCA in Buffalo, N.Y. Their teacher was F.W. Burkhardt, an alumnus of the Y's International Training School where the game had been born four years earlier. In six years of play against amateur teams in the Buffalo area, the Germans won 87 games and lost six.

In 1901, Buffalo hosted the Pan-American Exposition, a summer-long festival celebrating international flora, fauna, crafts, and entertainment. One feature was the all-around championships of the Amateur Athletic Union, including a basketball tournament. The Buffalo Germans, now 18 and 19 years old, entered the AAU tourney, along with seven other teams, all from the Northeast. The others were St. Joseph's Literary Institute of Cambridge, Mass.; the Entre Nous Athletic Club of Paterson, N.J.; St. Joseph's, also of Paterson; the National Athletic Club of Brooklyn, N.Y. the 17th Separate Company (National Guard) of Flushing, N.Y.; the Institute Athletic Club of Newark, N.J.; and St. John's School of Manlius, N.Y.

The three-day round-robin tourney was played outdoors on grass, a common venue at the time. The youthful Germans won all seven of their games by scores ranging from 16-3 to 9-3. If the scores seem unusually low, even for that low-scoring time, it was because the games were only 20 minutes long, half the regulation time. On the last day of the tournament, the Germans were scheduled for two games. One had been booked for morning, but because several of the Germans had school examinations that day, their captain, Alfred (Allie) Heerdt, got the agreement of their opponent, St. John's School, to shift the game to 4:00 p.m. *The Buffalo Express* reported:

Capt. Heerdt evidently overlooked the fact that his team was scheduled to play St. Joseph's of Paterson at an earlier hour and the latter seeing a chance to help out Entre Nous, also of Paterson, declined to wait for the Buffalo players longer than the rules required. At the end of the stipulated 15 minutes, only three German Y.M.C.A. representatives were on hand—

(William) Rhode, (Hank) Faust and (Johnny) Maier—but rather than see the game go by default they determined to make a fight against the other team....They did nobly and their determination to play was cheered on all sides. For nearly five minutes of the first half they held their own against the great odds, playing all around their opponents, who undoubtedly felt very cheap about putting the only blur on the three-day sport. Each side had scored a goal from a foul when (Eddie) Miller was seen to enter the Stadium....A united shout brought him to a realization of the situation his team was placed in. Throwing off his outer garments as he ran, Miller was soon in the thickest of the mixup and the St. Joseph's chances dropped 50 percent. Miller had no sooner warmed up than Capt. Heerdt had arrived upon the grounds. Heerdt's face denoted that he was both surprised and indignant that his team had been caught in a trap, but without waiting for explanation, he followed Miller's plan....During the intermission Miller and Heerdt donned their uniforms and the way they sailed into St. Joseph's was delightful, running up a score of nine against a blank for the others.

That dramatic 10-1 victory laid the foundation for the Buffalo Germans' legend. Continuing to play as amateurs, the Germans enhanced their reputation by winning the vast majority of their games. They closed out the 1903-04 season with a cumulative record over eight years of 100 victories and only eight defeats. Captain Allie Heerdt decided to enter his team in the basketball tournament planned in conjunction with the 1904 Olympic Games in St. Louis. (Basketball did not become an Olympic sport until the 1936 Games in Berlin; in 1904 it was what is today called a demonstration sport.)

The tournament in St. Louis was the first truly national tourney for basketball. Entered besides the Buffalo Germans were the Central YMCA of Chicago, Turner's Tigers of Los Angeles, the Missouri Athletic Club and Central YMCA of St. Louis, and the Xavier Athletic Club of New York. The Germans won three of their first four games by lopsided scores and the fourth by eight points. All four games were played outdoors on clay. In the final they beat Chicago's Central YMCA, 39-28, in Washington University's gymnasium. The game had to be moved indoors because of a downpour.

On the strength of their victories at the Pan-American Exposition and the Olympic Games tournament, the Buffalo Germans began billing themselves as world champions. After their triumph in St. Louis, they were the toast of Buffalo. They led a parade through downtown streets in a coach drawn by four horses, and they were tendered a reception by local dignitaries.

The Buffalo Germans turned professional in the 1904-05 season and took to the road. Barnstorming from Portsmouth, N.H. to Kansas City, K.S., they won 69 games and lost 19. For the following 20 seasons they were primarily barnstormers, although they never took another extended trip. There was talk of a world tour in 1913, but it did not materialize, and for the most part they stuck fairly close to home. During their best years as professionals from 1904 through 1916, the Germans played most of their games in western New York and northwestern Pennsylvania. Eighty percent of their games were on

the road. All of the players had jobs in Buffalo so they rarely traveled far except when they took winter vacations and ventured into Ohio and northeastern New York. At least one pro league was in operation every season during the Germans' peak years, but the Germans never entered, primarily because Buffalo was hundreds of miles away and transportation problems would have been insurmountable.

Their most notable achievement was a 111-game winning streak that began in 1908 and ended in 1911. Two weeks before the streak started, the Germans had taken a drubbing from the Troy Trojans in a day-night doubleheader, 51-33 and 56-13, but when they started winning, they seemed invincible. The vast majority of their victims were YMCAs, college teams, semi-pros playing under National Guard colors, and town teams, some from hamlets of less than 1,000 souls. During the 111-game streak, the Germans did not meet a single team from the professional Central, Eastern, or Hudson River Leagues. The string was finally ended when they did meet a good pro team wearing the colors of the 31st Separate Company (National Guard) of Herkimer, N.Y. The Buffalo Germans are one of five full teams enshrined in Basketball's Hall of Fame. (The others are the first team in Springfield, the Original Celtics, the all-black Renaissance Big Five and the Harlem Globetrotters.)

The 31st Separate Company team that ended the Buffalo Germans' long string of victories was managed by Frank J. Basloe, the most colorful of professional basketball's pioneers. Basloe, who was born in Hungary in 1887, was a sometime basketball player, vaudeville comedian, and promoter of marathon runs, motorcycle races, and prize fights. He had a barnstorming basketball team on the road every year from 1903 to 1923, except for a one-year hiatus during World War I. Until 1913, his teams traveled mostly in New York State and New England. Beginning in 1914, Basloe barnstormed through Pennsylvania, Ohio, Indiana, and the Upper Midwest every year with teams called the Oswego, New York, Indians and Basloe's Globe Trotters. They played 100 to 130 games a season, appearing wherever they could get a guarantee of at least $100.

On occasion, Basloe negotiated for more money while a game was in progress. Once, for example, he had agreed to play a three-game series against Fond du Lac, Wis. for $300. When Basloe's team took the floor for the first game, they saw 3,500 people jammed into the armory, a lovely sight for a promoter. While the game was going on, Basloe went up into the stands, pretending to be a local fan. He shouted, "Those New Yorkers think we Fond du Lac people are a bunch of farmers. I wish I had an armful of garbage—I would let them have it for sure."

It happened that many fans *did* have garbage—the remains of their lunches—and they happily heaved it onto the floor. After the subsequent riot, the Fond du Lac manager found Basloe and asked, "Now what's the hold-up? How much is it going to cost me for the next two games?" Basloe demanded $1,200 more, and he got it. At the end of the series, he was also given a cowboy suit and the title of "Hold-Up Manager" by the fans and manager of Fond du Lac.

Over 19 seasons, Basloe's touring teams won 1,324 games, lost 127, and traveled 95,000 miles, mostly by train, at a time when most Americans rarely left their home county.

Frank Basloe's Globe Trotters and the Buffalo Germans were

not the only barnstormers before World War I. Often when a league disintegrated in mid-season, member teams would go on the road, as the Troy Trojans did in 1915. And in the 1906-07 season, the Crescent Five of Evanston, Ill. did not play a single game at home. They went on the road on Dec. 12 and did not see home again until April 6. The Crescents won 55 games and lost 18 against YMCAs, colleges, National Guard units, and athletic clubs on a tour that took them as far east as Rochester, N.Y., and Toronto, Canada, westward through Kansas City, Denver, and Salt Lake City to Los Angeles, north through San Francisco and Vancouver, British Columbia, and back home via Seattle, Spokane, St. Paul and Milwaukee.

Without doubt the best-known—and perhaps best—team in basketball's first 40 years was the Original Celtics of New York. Although the Celtics spent part or all of four seasons in professional leagues, they were primarily barnstormers. No team, not even Basloe's Globe Trotters, traveled as extensively as the Celtics did during the 1920s ands '30s. In most seasons, they were barnstorming from late September to April, playing upwards of 100 games in the East, Midwest, and sometimes the South. They were the dominant pro team of the Twenties, although they were not quite as dominant as later legend had it. It is sometimes claimed that the Celtics never lost a season series to any team. Not true. It is also said that they broke up every league they entered because they were too good. Also not true. Still, it must be said that their success rate was the best of their time.

The Celtics had their origins in 1914 as a team for teenagers in a settlement house in the Chelsea district of Manhattan. The first Celtics justified the team name with players named Morrisey, McArdle, and Barry. By the 1916-17 season they had moved into the semipro ranks as the New York Celtics. Playing home games at the Amsterdam Opera House on West 44th Street, the Celtics won 3l, lost 10, and tied one against metropolitan area semipros. In their one game against full-fledged professionals, the Celtics were beaten, 29-17, by the Newark Turners of the Interstate League.

In 1918 the Celtics were taken over by a promoter named James A. Furey. Their first manager, Frank "Tip" McCormack, declined to allow use of the name New York Celtics, so Furey changed it to Original Celtics and booked games with metropolitan area teams. For the season they won 65 and lost only four. Their home games in the Central Opera House attracted crowds of 4,000; one game, against the touring Edison Indians of New London, Wis., drew 6,500 fans.

For the next season, Furey signed three veteran professionals, and the Original Celtics began their march to fame. The newcomers were Johnny Beckman, a high-scoring, 5-foot-8 forward who had been starring for teams in the New York State, Eastern, and Penn State Leagues since 1913; Oscar (Swede) Grimstead, a pro since 1911, including one season with Basloe's Globe Trotters, and Henry G. (Dutch) Dehnert, a sturdy, 5-foot-11 guard who, at 22 years of age, already had four years of professional experience under his belt. Also on the team were veterans Mike Smolick and Ernie Reich. Of the *real* Originals, only Pete Barry and player-manager John J. Whitty remained.

The Celtics were challenged for dominance in the New York area by a new team organized by Tex Rickard, a boxing promoter who planned to bring pro basketball into Madison Square Garden. The team was called the New York Whirlwinds and opened the season by beating Camden, the Eastern League champions, before only 1,428 spectators in the Garden. Disappointed with the crowd, Rickard exiled the Whirlwinds to armories around the city.

The Whirlwinds were worthy of better quarters. Their scoring leader was 5-foot-4 Barney Sedran, who had played for City College of New York from 1908 to 1911 and was the first professional star to come from the college ranks. He had once scored the astonishing total of 17 field goals in a New York State League game. His running mate at forward was Nat Holman, another college man who had already made a name in the pro game as a floor general and set-shot artist. At center was Chris Leonard, a five-year professional. The guards were Max (Marty) Friedman, the former Army lieutenant who had run the AEFs basketball tournament in Paris after the Great War, and 5-foot-10 Harry Riconda, an experienced cager who later spent six years as a major league infielder.

In the spring of 1921 a three-game series was arranged between the Celtics and the Whirlwinds to decide the unofficial championship of the metropolitan region. The first game drew 11,000 fans to the 71st Regiment Armory to see the Whirlwinds bury the Celtics, 40-27, in a game played by amateur rules with plenty of whistle blowing and no double dribbling. Twenty-eight personal fouls were called against the Whirlwinds and twenty-five against the Celtics. One player was permitted to shoot all free throws (the amateurs did not change that rule until 1924) and so Nat Holman led the Whirlwind scorers with 22 points, all on free throws. For the Celtics, Johnny Beckman scored 25 points—all but two on free throws.

The second game was played under professional rules before a crowd of 6,000 at the 69th Regiment Armory. The Celtics won a seesaw battle, 26-24. The third game was not played. The following year's *Reach Basket Ball Guide* suggested that there may have been fears that players would be bribed. The *Guide* reported: "The series created so much interest that certain gamblers tried to connect in the fixing of one of the games. Thanks to two of the games' star players, a basket ball Black Sox scandal was averted" (The reference is to the fixing of the 1919 baseball World Series by Chicago White Sox players.)

Two weeks after the inconclusive test of strength between the Whirlwinds and Celtics, Jim Furey signed Whirlwind stars Nat Holman and Chris Leonard for his Celtics for the 1921-22 season. He also added George (Horse) Haggerty, a 6-foot-4, 220-pound bruiser to his roster. On the strength of these additions, Furey began billing his team as "national champions," even though they had never ventured out of the metropolitan area. The Celtics spent the next year in the struggling Eastern and Metropolitan Leagues. The Celts were leading the Metropolitan circuit in early 1922, having won all 12 of their games but finding very lean financial pickings, when they dropped out to become full-time barnstormers. Beginning in September and ending in late April, the Original Celtics played the astounding total of 205 games. They claimed 193 victories, 11 defeats, and one tie. It was estimated that a half-million spectators saw the Celtics in their tours through 13 states of the Northeast and Midwest. They even spent a couple of weeks as

the Atlantic City franchise in the Eastern League before that circuit died in January 1923.

The next season—their first as full-time barnstormers—the Original Celtics won 134, lost six, and played a 32-32 tie with a team in Mt. Vernon, N.Y. It is not known why that game was not decided by overtime, but there is a story that sometimes the Celtics would deliberately play to a tie at the end of regulation time and then demand more money to finish the game. In the 1926-27 season, the Celtics returned to league play, winning two straight championships in the American Basketball League—the first professional league with national aspirations.

By that time the Celtics had added 6-foot-5 Joe Lapchick, who was considered a giant in those days, and speedy Davey Banks to their roster and were clearly the best team of the period. Their game featured ball possession, short passes, and high-percentage shots. They played a tenacious man-to-man defense and may have originated switching on defense. On offense the Celtics favored constant movement with and without the ball. They are sometimes credited with having originated the pivot play and the give and go. In some accounts, Dutch Dehnert is said to have invented the pivot play to thwart the Chattanooga Rail-Lites' "standing guard," who stayed in the backcourt to foil easy baskets by the opposition. Dehnert suggested stationing himself in front of the standing guard with his back to the basket, receive passes from teammates, and then return the ball to them as they cut for the basket. If the guard tried to go around Dehnert to intercept the ball, Dutch would pivot the other way and go in for an easy layup.

No doubt the Celtics perfected the pivot play, but according to the recollections of John Wendelken, the New York Wanderers were using a very similar play around 1900. It also seems unlikely that the Celtics invented the give and go, in which a player passes the ball to a teammate and immediately cuts for the basket and takes a return pass for an easy score. The give and go is an almost instinctive move and surely would have been common before the Celtics were formed.

The Original Celtics went back to barnstorming during the 1930s, but they were no longer the best. The black Renaissance Big Five of New York had that distinction after beating the Celts in eight of 14 games in 1932-33. With the financial help of popular singer Kate Smith, the fading Celtics played on until the early 1940s.

The Rens and Celtics were not alone on the barnstorming trail during the Twenties and Thirties. In the Midwest, the Harlem Globetrotters were laying the foundation for the worldwide reputation they have today for mixing first-rate basketball skills and comedy in equal measure. Equally well-known during the Depression years were the barnstorming Olson's Terrible Swedes. Each year several other traveling clubs hit the road, some of them based on novelty. Often a group of players would grow beards and tour as the House of David, trading on the fame of a bearded barnstorming baseball team sponsored by the Israelite House of David, a religious sect based in Benton Harbor, Mich. Another traveling team used the same whiskery gimmick and called themselves the Bearded Beauties. For one season, the Hong Wah Q'ues, a team of Chinese players, wandered through the Midwest playing independent teams.

Olson's Terrible Swedes were organized in 1920 by C.M. (Ole) Olson of Coffeyville, Kansas, a player, manager, and promoter who filled his roster with AAU players from the Midwest and Southwest. During their first decade, the Swedes booked 80 to 90 games a season in the Midwest, South, and West. By 1929 they included the East in their annual itinerary.

Ole Olson was a player as well as manager and was noted for behind-the-back passes and one-hand shots from the corners. Despite such bits of flashiness, the Terrible Swedes played straight basketball. Naturally they were billed as "world champions." In 1935 Olson took the Swedes off the road. The following year he began touring with the All-American Red Heads, a women's team that for the next 40 years was surpassed only by the Harlem Globetrotters as a barnstorming attraction. Playing exclusively men's teams, mostly amateurs in small towns, the Red Heads typically covered 30 states and played 185 games during their six-month-long seasons. In some years their travels took them to Mexico, the Philippines, and Hawaii.

Olson recruited players from women's teams in high schools and AAU leagues. Among the stars was Hazel Walker, a seven-time AAU All-American for teams in Tulsa and Little Rock and one of the best female players of the 1930s and '40s. She held the women's free-throw shooting championship and regularly defeated male challengers in half-time contests at Red Heads' games.

The appeal of the Red Heads was based on equal parts of skillful basketball, the novelty in those pre-women's liberation days of watching accomplished female athletes working up a sweat, and the battle of the sexes. Over the years they built up a repertoire of trick plays and gags to amuse the fans—dribbling with the knees, a variety of trick shots, and the piggyback play in which a petite guard hopped on the back of 6-foot-4 Gene (Careless) Love and dropped the ball through the hoop. During their first decade, the Red Heads were said to have won 50 percent of their games. In later years they did better than that, winning about 85 percent, according to Orwell Moore, who began coaching them in 1948 and owned the team from 1955 to 1975. The organization was so successful that during the 1950s two or three Red Head teams were on the road at the same time.

With the coming of television and the demise of teams in small towns, barnstorming was increasingly a tough way to make a living by that time, and the Red Heads left the road in 1975. Only the Harlem Globetrotters, who carried their own opposing team with them, carried on the barnstorming tradition.

Chapter 3

African-Americans in Basketball: Breaking Down the Barriers

By Roland Lazenby and Mikhail Horowitz

Michael Jordan laughing at the laws of gravity, lifting off from the foul line and grazing the constellations as he sails above the rim. Bill Russell and Wilt Chamberlain jostling under the boards like mythical giants locking in mortal combat. Earvin "Magic" Johnson bounding like an antelope down the court, looking to his left and flipping a pinpoint pass to a streaking James Worthy on his right.

Now imagine the game without them.

It's hard to believe, as we enter the third millennium, that there was a time when black athletes were barred from competing against their white counterparts, much the same as black doctors were prohibited from practicing in white hospitals and black students were not accepted into white colleges. It's especially hard to believe that the NBA, a professional league in which three-quarters of the players are African-American, was an exclusively Caucasian playground for its first four seasons. But segregation—the policy and practice of excluding people from participating as equals in society because of the color of their skin—held sway in the United States for the greater portion of the 20th century. It took many years of struggle by determined athletes, coaches, and social reformers to pave the way for the Jordans, Chamberlains, and Johnsons to revolutionize the game with their extraordinary gifts.

Certainly, the sacrifice of so many African-Americans in the service of their country during World War II was a major factor in the acceleration of integration, first in sports and then in the courts, schools, and workplaces of the land. Jackie Robinson, who had been an all-Pacific Coast Conference basketball player with UCLA in 1940-41 as well as a second lieutenant in the army during the war, ended 60 years of segregation in major league baseball when he debuted with the Brooklyn Dodgers in 1947. Other stars of the Negro Leagues—Larry Doby, Sam Jethroe, the ageless Satchel Paige—began to trickle into the "show," although it would be more than a decade before each of the big league teams would be integrated.

Paralleling the postwar trend in major league baseball, the decade of the 1950s brought a growing integration of professional basketball, which soon followed suit in the college game. But that progress came largely on the small, frustrating gains made by blacks in the earlier decades of the 20th century.

Early Attempts at Integration

African-Americans took up basketball shortly after the game's invention, and by the early 1900s were beginning to gain limited prominence. By 1906, black athletic clubs in Brooklyn, New Jersey and New York had begun sponsoring teams.

One of black America's first major connections to basketball

Charles "Tarzan" Cooper, 1939
The ultimate center of his day, he led the New York Rens to more than 1,300 wins, and the 1939 world title.

was Edwin Henderson, a Washington, D.C. schoolteacher who learned the game in 1904 while attending Harvard. Henderson returned to Washington and introduced the game into black high schools in the District of Columbia. In 1909, he became an instructor at Howard University. Using the high school talent he had developed locally, Henderson quickly organized a fine team at Howard.

Soon college programs followed. By 1910, Lincoln University, Howard University, Hampton Institute, and Virginia Union University had entered into competition. Two years later, the Colored Intercollegiate Athletic Association was

created, and the next year Tuskegee, Fisk, Talladega. Clark, Alabama State, Morehouse, Florida A&M, Morris Brown, Knoxville College, and Jackson formed the Southeastern Conference. Soon black colleges across the country had adopted basketball, and before long their competition was organized into more than a half dozen athletic conferences. Even though these black teams quickly showed an affinity for the game, they found themselves ignored by white fans and the mainstream media.

The idea of a black school playing against a major white university seemed ludicrous in that age of segregation. Yet in the late 1920s, teams from both Howard and Hampton ventured north to compete against Ivy League schools. The experiment was brief, and soon the black schools were again competing only against themselves.

The 1920s brought limited integration of some college teams. At Columbia, sophomore George Gregory gained notoriety as the All-Eastern Conference center for 1928-29. Described in *Spalding's Guide* as "the tall colored boy who played center" and "the graceful Columbia center," Gregory ranked fourth in the conference in scoring and second in free throws made. Of his play, Penn athletic director Ralph Morgan wrote, "Gregory had height; he got the tap; he was fast and could shoot. The coaches were clearly right when they selected him [to the all-conference team]."

That same season Western Illinois State Teacher's College had two black players, one of which, a guard named Page, was selected all-conference. For 1928-29, teams representing Southern Cal, Brooklyn College of Pharmacy, and Columbia College of Pharmacy all had an African-American player. High school and junior high teams in Pennsylvania showed extensive integration in 1928-29. Elsewhere, there were incidents of integration from Yankton (South Dakota) High to Peoria, Illinois, and Warwick, New York, which, although isolated, helped break down the sturdy racial barriers in the college game. In the 1920s, '30s, and '40s, noted African-American players began to appear, including Paul Robeson (later to win fame as a pro football player, singer, and political activist) at Rutgers, Wilbur Woods at Nebraska, Wilmeth Sadat-Singh at Syracuse, Dolly King at Long Island University, and the first black All-American, UCLA's Don Barksdale in 1947. Unfortunately, segregation remained a way of life throughout America, and many southern colleges didn't begin to integrate their teams until 1970.

The Rens

Pro basketball, which by most accounts originated in 1896, offered blacks a limited opportunity in the variety of leagues that flowered over the first decades of the 20th century. There had been instances of integration in pro basketball as early as 1904, when Bucky Lew played with two New England League teams. Historian William F. Himmelman, known for his extensive research of the early game, has cited other instances:

- Frank "Dido" Wilson played in the Mohawk Valley League in 1907.
- In 1911 and 1917, the Eastern League appears to have included an African-American whose name has been lost to posterity.
- The 1935 roster of the Buffalo Bisons, a Midwest

Basketball Conference team, included the 6-foot-4 center Hank Williams.

Perhaps the best pro team of the 1930s was the Renaissance Big Five from Harlem. Known as the Rens, this club stacked up 2318 wins against 381 losses over 26 seasons. Like the Original Celtics, the Rens were barnstormers who relied on the passing game and a stifling defense. But there was one big difference between the clubs—the Rens were black.

There was no Negro pro basketball league during the era, so African-Americans had to travel a narrow path to success. They had to be good enough to draw crowds and smart enough to avoid the Jim Crow troubles that plagued the country. The Rens were able to do both. In 1932-33, they toured the deep South and pulled it off handily. Just about everywhere they traveled, even across the Northeast and Midwest, they encountered the meanness of segregation. But the Rens always got their money before they played, and they practiced a brand of clean, exciting basketball that opened many closed minds. Honey Russell once described the Rens as "one of the cleanest teams I ever played against. They just played basketball that was so good they didn't have to resort to any kind of rough stuff." And John Wooden, UCLA's great coach, who played against the Rens several times in the late 1930s as a member of the Indianapolis Kautsky Grocers, simply called them "the best I ever saw."

Robert Douglas, an immigrant from the West Indies who played ball in Harlem, founded the club in 1922. He wanted to call the team the Spartans, but he needed sponsorship. The Renaissance Casino in Harlem agreed to provide a home in its ballroom, so the club became the Renaissance Big Five. They gained notoriety in the mid-1920s during a series of games with the Original Celtics. Over three seasons, the Rens met the Celtics nine times and won four games. The Rens also beat every major American Basketball League team they faced. By the 1930s, they were playing 130 games a year and winning just about all of them. Their big men were Wee Willie Smith at 6-foot-5 and Charles "Tarzan" Cooper at 6-foot-3; two other stars, Clarence "Fat" Jenkins and Bill Yancey, also played baseball in the Negro Leagues. The 1932-33 team rolled up an 88-game winning streak on its way to a 120-8 record. They played the aging Celtics 14 times that season and won eight, but the Celtics ended their winning streak.

Even at the height of their success, the Rens had to endure the discomfort of segregation. Many hotels and restaurants refused them service, so they often ate cold cuts and arranged to stay in private homes. Many nights they had to drive extra miles to find a place to sleep. Their road secretary carried a pistol just in case of trouble, and sometimes there were tense moments. But Douglas paid them well and kept them together, which meant they just got better with time.

"We loved being the Renaissance," said Hall of Famer William "Pop" Gates to historian Robert Peterson, "because we thought we were the best, and we were happy and proud to represent the Negro people and give them something they could be proud of and adhere to."

In 1939, the Chicago *Herald-American* began sponsorship of a pro tourney that ran for the next decade. Played in Chicago

Stadium, the tournament drew 12 to 16 teams each year from the various league champions and top barnstorming teams. In some years the crowds reached 20,000, and the pro players considered it a "world series" event that settled their championship. The Rens, led by Gates, then a 21-year-old rookie, ran through the first tournament field, beating the Oshkosh All Stars, champions of the National Basketball League, 34-25, for the world championship.

World War II soon put the brakes on the nation's barnstorming acts, causing Douglas to shut down the Rens for a time. But Cooper, Smith and several other Rens played as the Washington Bears and again won the Chicago tournament in 1943. They regrouped after the war and played during 1948-49 as the Dayton Rens in the National Basketball League, which pioneered the eventual eradication of pro basketball's color line.

The Globetrotters

The Harlem Globetrotters got their start in Chicago in 1926, but in their first incarnation they were strictly a regional team. It would take more than a decade before they began to garner "global" attention.

The Trotters began existence as the Savoy Big Five, playing out of Chicago's Savoy Ballroom. In 1926, they encountered a portly 23-year-old promoter, Abe Saperstein, from Chicago's north side. He began booking the team and within months took over its management. In January 1927, he dubbed them Saperstein's New York and booked them for a game in nearby Hinckley, Illinois. None of the players were from New York, but the name sounded worldly to Saperstein. Later they would become just plain "New York" and still later "Saperstein's Harlem New York." Finally, after about eight years or so, they became the Harlem Globetrotters.

In later years, the Trotters would become world famous for their flamboyant humor, precisely orchestrated slapstick routines and slick ball-handling, often performed to the accompaniment of *Sweet Georgia Brown*. But in the early days, the Globetrotters played their basketball straight. They did, however, apparently have their warm-up "circle" in those days, which over the years evolved into the world's classiest ball-handling routine. The dazzling entertainment and infectious good humor were a means of deflecting the ugly racial moods the team sometimes encountered on the road. Plus, if the local teams had fun and the crowd laughed, people didn't mind losing, and the Globetrotters were often invited back.

During the Depression the Globetrotters played some of the country's great barnstorming teams, but they still hadn't traveled very far from Chicago. In fact, they hadn't even played in Harlem. Their breakthrough came with the 1939 season, when they rolled up a 148-13 record, good enough for an invitation to the Chicago tournament. The Globetrotters lost a close game to the Rens, but the closeness of the contest showed how good they were. In 1940, with a starting five of Bernie Price, Babe Pressley, Sonny Boswell, Hillery Brown, and Inman Jackson, the Globetrotters won the tournament, beating the NBL's Chicago Bruins (owned by George Halas), 31-29, in overtime. The victory soon led to a new team bus and what would become the team's signature red-white-and-blue uniforms, and the Globetrotters were on their way.

In the 1940s, Saperstein signed a pair of stars who would come to typify the Globetrotters' unique mix of amazing talent and hilarious antics. Reece "Goose" Tatum, a baseball player from Arkansas, had huge hands, long arms, and a wonderful wit. Marques Haynes, a virtuoso with a basketball in his hands, was enticed by Saperstein to join the club after his Langston University (Oklahoma) team beat the Trotters. Building on Tatum's creativity, the Globetrotters abandoned the straight game to offer fans their hugely entertaining brand of hoops, filled with gimmicks, gags, and razzle-dazzle dribbling and passing. But they paused in this conversion long enough to beat George Mikan and the Minneapolis Lakers in several exhibition games at Chicago Stadium after World War II (they would play exhibition games against the Lakers through the 1950s).

Meadow Lemon, a boy growing up in Wilmington, North Carolina, saw a newsreel featuring the Trotters in the late 1940s and described it this way: "I could hardly stay in my seat with that jumpin', jivin', whistlin', music blaring. It made you want to dance, and that's what these guys, these Harlem Globetrotters were doing. Smiling, singing, slapping each other on the back, tumbling from the locker room to a basketball court, a big one with thousands of fans in the stands." Lemon would later become Meadowlark Lemon, one of the Trotters' brightest stars.

The team toured Alaska in 1949, then headed for Western Europe and North Africa the next year. In 1951, they toured South and Central America, drawing a crowd of 50,000 in Rio de Janeiro. Later that summer, they achieved official "ambassador" status when the U.S. government asked the Trotters to tour Berlin to help improve relations with Germany after the war. In the same open-air stadium where Adolph Hitler had refused to recognize African-American Olympians 15 years earlier, a crowd of 75,000 showered the Globetrotters with applause. The highlight of the show was the surprise appearance of four-time Olympic gold medalist Jesse Owens, who had been one of those snubbed in 1936. When the Trotters returned home, they found they were an even bigger attraction in the States.

In 1952, the Harlem Globetrotters celebrated their 25th anniversary, and later performed their routines for Pope Pius XII. In 1958, they added center Wilt Chamberlain, who had left the University of Kansas a year early and was waiting to enter the NBA. Even after joining the NBA, Chamberlain spent his summer months touring with the Trotters in Europe. In the early 1960s, at the peak of the Cold War, the team toured the Soviet Union and met Nikita Khrushchev.

In 1961, Saperstein founded the American Basketball League to compete with the NBA, but the venture failed. (During the league's short life, John McLendon coached the Cleveland Pipers, becoming the first black coach in a pro league.) Saperstein died in 1966, and in 1967 a group of investors bought the Globetrotters for $3.7 million. By then the Trotters had grown to a network of several touring teams, each spreading the gospel of *Sweet Georgia Brown* across the globe. In 2001, they celebrated their 75th anniversary. Without question, they are the longest-running team in the history of the game.

The War and Integration

The bombing of Pearl Harbor on December 7, 1941 had an

immediate effect on the pro game. The country mobilized for war, and suddenly the supply of players dried up. To fill the roster of his team, the Toledo Jim White Chevrolets, promoter Sid Goldberg came up with a novel idea—integration. The league's other owners weren't thrilled with the idea, but Goldberg pulled together six whites and four blacks—Zano Wast, Al Price, Casey Jones, and Shannie Barnett—to make a team for the 1942-43 season. This integrated squad lost all four games it played and promptly folded in December.

Despite the team's failure, the NBL owners had learned something from the experiment: the integrated teams hadn't brought the public outcry they had expected. The Chicago Studebakers were also integrated that season, half the team consisting of Harlem Globetrotters and the other half of white college players. The popularity of the Trotters helped the predominantly white crowds accept the change. But the Studebakers broke up before the Chicago tournament when former Loyola of Chicago star Mike Novak had a spat with former Globetrotter Sonny Boswell. Some at first thought the disagreement was racial, but the team's players later told historian Robert Peterson that Novak was merely upset because Boswell was shooting too much and passing too little.

Breakthroughs in the College Game

John McLendon holds the distinction of having been the coach who integrated college basketball. His main battle in 1940s America was the notion that blacks were inferior athletes. McLendon, a young coach at little North Carolina College in 1941, once recalled that he and other black coaches "knew in our hearts" that their teams and their players were as good or better than those at the segregated white schools. But before they could convince whites of that they had to convince blacks.

"Even the black population didn't know it and didn't believe it," McLendon recalled in a 1991 interview. "They had succumbed to the one-sided propaganda." Racist caricatures and ideology spewed nonstop from 1940s American mainstream culture, spurred by the overwhelmingly popular radio show *Amos and Andy*, which based its humor on the idiocy of its two black characters. Those messages ran deep in the American mind and psyche. The only way that African-American athletes could battle the stereotype was to win, and winning became McLendon's specialty.

One of the first black students at the University of Kansas in the 1930s, McLendon was ignored when he tried out for the basketball team. On the Kansas faculty at that time was Dr. James Naismith, the game's inventor. Naismith took McLendon under his wing and helped land him a part-time job coaching a local black high school team.

McLendon learned the game under the guidance of its inventor, then went on to earn a master's degree at the University of Iowa and proceeded into the coaching ranks at North Carolina College, one of dozens of traditionally black colleges that offered African-Americans the opportunity that the predominantly white state universities would not.

Throughout his coaching career, McLendon made the most of that opportunity. He guided Tennessee State to three consecutive NAIA championships in 1957, 1958, and 1959. He also coached at Hampton Institute, Kentucky State College,

and Cleveland State College, where in 1966 he became the first black coach to be hired by a predominantly white school. "Coach McLendon was a man of many firsts," said Clarence "Big House" Gaines, himself a trailblazer as the long-time coach at Winston-Salem State. "He was a true pioneer of the game. He was the first college coach to win multiple national championships when he coached Tennessee State, the first black team to win a national white tournament. He helped integrate a lot of hotels and restaurants in the cities where he played and coached. He was the first black man to coach a professional team when they hired him to coach the Cleveland Pipers in the old American Basketball League [in 1959, seven years before Bill Russell became the NBA's first black coach]."

When he began in North Carolina, it was unthinkable that whites and blacks would share the same court. But McLendon, who compiled a lifetime record of 729-240 in 34 years of coaching college and pro basketball, soon gained a reputation with his winning ways. On one occasion a white coach at a nearby Atlantic Coast Conference school invited McLendon to sit on the bench with him during a game, the only stipulation being that the black coach would have to wear a white coat to suggest that he was a locker room attendant. McLendon quietly declined. "I was fortunate to avoid a situation where I'd lose my self-respect," he said. "I never went voluntarily into a segregated situation."

During World War II, a military team at Duke's medical school made up of top white college players gained widespread publicity for its prowess. McLendon had an undefeated team at North Carolina College that received no publicity, so his team manager phoned up the Duke coach and suggested they play a game. The Duke medical coach said he would only play a "secret game" on a Sunday morning, on the condition that no fans or media were allowed in the gym. McLendon agreed. By half-time, his aggressively-pressing team had doubled the score on its high-profile opponents, and the white players came over to his bench and suggested that the roster be evenly divided among blacks and whites for the second half.

Another chink in the armor of segregated college basketball came in 1949, when McLendon's North Carolina College team defeated a Marine squad from Camp LeJeune in one of the first public interracial games in the South.

"My goal was to keep a team ready if integration ever came," McLendon recalled. "In that sense we were always working toward a goal beyond the present competition. Our players were playing beyond what it took to beat other black teams. I wanted them to be ready. If the door ever opened we could show the world that we could play basketball."

In 1954 he assumed the coaching reins at Tennessee State in Nashville, where he put together a run of great teams led by Dick Barnett, who would go on to fame as a key member of the New York Knicks' 1970 NBA championship team. At that time McLendon and several other black coaches petitioned the NCAA Coaches Association at their annual convention in New York City to invite black colleges to the NCAA Tournament. The executive committee approved their petition unanimously, but the NCAA's governing body declared that no "apparatus" existed that would accommodate participation by Negro colleges. The NAIA national tournament in Kansas City, however,

was willing to allow McLendon's team to compete. After Tennessee State won three straight NAIA titles from 1957 through 1959—along with the NAIA's prestigious Christmas Invitational Tournament in 1954—the talents and the competitive drive of African-American basketball players could no longer be denied.

In addition to the blessing of the NAIA, McLendon also received support from Converse, the shoe manufacturer, which showed an exemplary willingness in the 1950s to feature African-Americans in its marketing campaigns. Through his work with Converse, McLendon would appear at a variety of predominantly white universities to put on clinics for the coaches there. "I'm talking about the top colleges in America," said Gaines. "They'd fly Mac in and shut up the gym, and he'd spend a few days in there teaching coaches and players. Then other guys would end up getting credit for many of the things he created. And Mac wouldn't get a nickel." One of McLendon's innovations was the "Four Corners" delay offense; in an unusual twist of irony, he watched a bright young coach named Dean Smith gain fame for using it.

McLendon's reward was his election to the Basketball Hall of Fame in the Contributors category and his revered status among modern basketball heroes who know some history. One of those is Indiana Pacers coach Isiah Thomas, who, upon joining the Toronto Raptors as an executive in 1995, promptly hired McLendon, whom he considered to be the "father of fastbreak basketball," as a consultant for the team. The indomitable coach and unwavering advocate for the advancement of his race died in 1999, having lived to see the integration of Naismith's game at all levels of competition.

The end of segregation

The year 1950 saw three milestones in the integration of the NBA: the drafting of Chuck Cooper by the Boston Celtics, the signing of Nat "Sweetwater" Clifton by the New York Knicks, and, on October 31, the participation in a game by Earl Lloyd of the Washington Capitols, who became the first black player to step onto the NBA hardwood when he took the court against the Rochester Royals. More players followed. Don Barksdale, who had been the first black All-American at UCLA, became the first member of his race to play in an NBA All-Star Game in 1952. (Barksdale had also been the first African-American to play for the U.S. Olympic basketball team, at the London games in 1948, giving him the unique distinction of having achieved a "triple crown" as a trailblazer.) Some other black stars of collegiate ball entering the league in that decade were Sihugo Green, Walter Dukes, Ray Felix, Maurice Stokes, Willie Naulls, Sam Jones, K. C. Jones, Bennie Swain, Wayne Embry, Elgin Baylor, and the two dominant players of the era, Bill Russell and Wilt Chamberlain.

The college game saw progress as well, but it was uneven, given the regional nature of basketball conferences and the incremental gains of Civil Rights legislation. For instance, although both Arizona and Arizona State had integrated teams as early as 1953-54, Auburn—in the SEC—did not have a black player until Henry Harris began his three-year varsity career in 1969-70. Segregation undoubtedly prevented the SEC

from becoming one of the country's dominant conferences in the 1960s and early '70s. Among the many gifted African-American players who would have certainly attended SEC universities had they been able to, but instead wound up starring for other schools, were Wes Unseld, Artis Gilmore, Howard Porter, Elvin Hayes, Willis Reed, Butch Beard, Walt Frazier, and Jim Barnes.

The event that finally forced Southern schools to acknowledge the competitive handicap of segregation was the championship game of the 1966 NCAA Tournament. For the first time in an NCAA Final, five black starters—representing Texas Western—opposed an all-white squad, Adolph Rupp's Kentucky Wildcats, the nation's top-ranked team. Coached by Don Haskins and led by David "Big Daddy" Lattin, the Miners, who exemplified the exciting, freewheeling style of black basketball, whupped Kentucky, 72-65, in one of the most memorable upsets in the annals of the college game. The victory inspired young black basketball players throughout the U.S. and greatly accelerated the capitulation of the old guard at Southern and Atlantic Coast colleges. As Frank Fitzpatrick noted in his book about the contest, *And the Walls Came Tumbling Down: Kentucky, Texas Western, and the Game That Changed American Sports*, "in the next four years, a 1972 study would note, the most substantial increase in integration in the history of college sports took place."

As the sight of black players on basketball courts in Alabama, Mississippi, Kentucky and Florida began to be commonplace, the next logical wall to be breached was the one that prohibited African-Americans from coaching at major colleges. (The pros were another story—the NBA had integrated its coaching ranks in 1966-67, when Bill Russell assumed the duties of player-coach for the Boston Celtics. Since then, the NBA has had the best record of any pro sports league when it comes to hiring blacks for top coaching positions.) As black coaches began to demonstrate that they could win as effectively as their white colleagues, however, the barriers gave way. Fred Snowden, at the helm of Arizona, became the first black coach to have his team finish in the top 20 of a national poll in 1974-75. Nolan Richardson became the first to integrate the coaching ranks of the old Southwest Conference when he took the reins at Arkansas in 1985-86; Bob Wade integrated the ACC at Maryland the next year, and Wade Houston all but erased what was left of the color line in the SEC when he took over at Tennessee in 1989-90.

As the game invented by James Naismith and reinvented by African-American athletes entered the third millennium, with its popularity ballooning into all corners of the globe, it could truly pride itself as a sport that provides opportunity to players and coaches in direct proportion to their talent and regardless of their race. That is not to say that some barriers do not remain for African-Americans who seek a career in basketball. More representation would certainly be welcome in the spheres of team administration and ownership, for example. But progress is happening: Terdema Ussery was commissioner of the CBA in the mid-'90s and Robert Johnson is the owner of the WNBA's Charlotte Sting and the Charlotte Bobcats, the $300-million entry into the NBA for the 2004-05 season.

Chapter 4

Basketball in Flux: How the NBA Rose From the Turmoil

By Leonard Koppett

For American Sports fans of 1939, major league professional basketball simply did not exist. "Major League" meant that teams that got daily nationwide coverage, not just in the cities or areas involved. Baseball had created that idea in 1876. College football, with its few major bowl games and name-recognition traditions, had it from 1920 on. Canada's National Hockey League reached that status in 1926, when it added four United States cities. The National Football League was still trying to break through the perception of its inferiority to the major college games.

Although no teams were based further west than St. Louis (because of the limitations of train travel), newspapers in California, Texas, Florida and Maine, and everywhere in between, commonly carried results, league standings and comment, far beyond the home areas of the participating teams.

And what wasn't in the papers got no attention from the general sports fan. Negro League Baseball, in particular, suffered from this kind of invisibility. And the pro basketball leagues of the 1920s, driven into bankruptcy by the Depression of the 1930s, hadn't lasted long enough to establish a widespread following.

Basketball, even though it could (and did) arouse intense interest locally on the college, high school and amateur levels, had neither nationwide impact nor generally accepted pro respectability.

But changes were in motion.

Ned Irish, then a young sportswriter, had started promoting college doubleheaders in New York's Madison Square Garden in 1934. These became a big hit in the next two years, as abolition of the center jump after every score made basketball a faster and far more attractive spectator game. And anything that happened at Madison Square Garden warranted national attention, since the three main wire services—-which papers everywhere depended upon and used—were based in New York. To fill out this program, Irish brought in teams from all regions, including the far west, and those teams could be booked for similar double-headers in Chicago, Boston, Buffalo, and Philadelphia on their way in and out.

College stars from such teams, therefore, acquired a market value after graduation they previously lacked. Their only chance to keep playing after school was to barnstorm with independent teams or go to work for a company sponsoring an industrial team, sanctified as "amateur" by the Amateur

Danny Biasone, 1993
He championed the adoption of the 24-second clock in 1954, which saved the game.

Athletic Union because of the player's status as an employee.

In 1937, to take advantage of the star-creation the colleges were providing, a National Basketball League was formed. In 1938, the Garden (at the instigation of the New York basketball writers) started a post-season National Invitation Tournament, magnifying the impact of the top college teams. In 1939, the NCAA copied it, created its own championship tournament, and soon moved its title game to the Garden. The time was ripe for cashing in on the new flood of outstanding collegians.

Three top industrial teams—the Goodyear and Firestone tire companies of Akron, Ohio and General Electric in Fort Wayne, Indiana—joined with 10 independent pro teams for a 13-team National League. The next two years, there were only eight, playing a 28-game schedule.

Then World War II began, disrupting normal life in every way. The National League went through 1940-41 and 1941-42 seasons with seven teams, then with only five, four, and six the next three years.

But college basketball, especially at the Garden, thrived in wartime. Some of the biggest stars were too tall to be drafted into military service; others were still too young; and many servicemen assigned to training on college campuses remained eligible to play. The two post-season tournaments flourished,

gaining disproportionate attention while the standard pro sports were in a curtailed mode.

Then, before the 1945-46 season opened, the war was over and the road was open to full exploitation of the college-generated talent and interest.

In many minds, in many places, the thought was insistent: if this game, in such a setting, could be so successful for colleges, why not for pros? Why should all these star reputations, nurtured by the new popularity of the college game, lose or waste their money-making potential after graduation? Why must the pros of that day—either in ill repute in the large cities, or playing in such inherently limited leagues as the National in the midwest or the American farther east—remain so limited? Why not put on, professionally, college-style and college-atmosphere games, with college-developed players—and why not cash in on the economic advantages of an alliance between an arena and a promoter, the way Irish and the Garden did to their mutual benefit?

These ideas were in the air—but in a few specific minds they were not just a thought: they were an intention.

In Boston, a man named Walter Brown, and in Cleveland, a man named Al Sutphin, were about to join forces to bring into being what would eventually become today's National Basketball Association.

In New York, a man named Max Kase hoped to operate a New York franchise in such a league.

And in New Haven, Connecticut, a remarkable little man named Maurice Podoloff was about to take on the task of making this league a reality, although he didn't know it and had never given basketball a thought.

The Beginning

Max Kase was the sports editor of *The Journal-American,* New York's largest afternoon paper, a part of the Hearst chain. He had been a baseball writer for a while, and had worked in Boston. There he had become friendly with Walter Brown, who was the president of the Boston Garden. This building was Boston's equivalent of Madison Square Garden and Brown's interests were, naturally, centered around the hockey Bruins that the Garden owned. But he was a man who involved himself in all the other activities that came through the arena, and was always receptive to new ideas.

In 1944, Kase had been involved in the promotion of a pro basketball game for war relief. It was played at Manhattan Center, a sort of assembly hall-auditorium with portable seats, on 34th Street in New York. It drew so large an overflow crowd that Kase became convinced pro basketball's future could be better than its present. He pressed the point informally, but persuasively, to Brown.

Nothing really happened, however, until the spring of 1946. With the war out of the way, Brown was eager to try a basketball experiment. By now, he and Kase—and many others—had discussed the subject thoroughly. Kase had already begun negotiating with Nat Holman, the most famous of the Original Celtics and then a distinguished and successful coach at City College of New York, to be coach of a New York team in whatever league was formed.

Brown had ready-made connections. Through the National Hockey League, he was already a sort of partner of the arena

owners in New York, Chicago, Detroit, and Toronto. The NHL had close ties with the American Hockey League, the top minor league, and this included Cleveland, Philadelphia, Pittsburgh, Providence, and St. Louis, where the hockey teams were prime tenants of arenas.

The operator of the Cleveland American Hockey League team was Al Sutphin.

By now, the arena operators had an even stronger tie. One of the biggest moneymakers of all their attractions was the ice show, a music-and-skating extravaganza made popular by Sonja Henie in the 1930s. The ice show would come into the arena for two weeks at a time, and move on to the next arena. Its tour combined the fiscal advantages of the circus with a tinge of sports interest (since Olympic stars would move on into this profession). And since the ice show could play only in arenas equipped with rinks—not in theaters, ballparks, or gymnasiums—the working relationship between the arenas and the ice show was particularly close. The big man in the ice show business was John Harris, of Pittsburgh.

As talk of pro basketball's possibilities swirled around at various meetings of the hockey leagues and the arena owners' associations, Brown and Sutphin became the leaders of a move to take action. They would start a league, and bring as many of their colleagues into it as possible.

Kase and Brown, naturally, were sensitive to each other's interests. Any major league would need a New York entry, as a matter of course. Kase was ready and eager to rent Madison Square Garden for a New York team, and had drawn up tentative plans for a league (with such matters as schedule, salary limits, etc., blocked out). The one difference in their viewpoints was that Kase was more oriented towards established pros, Brown towards the new crop of collegians.

To rent Madison Square Garden, Kase had to talk to Irish. For himself, Irish could not have been less interested in embarking upon a new, unproven project. This was the spring of 1946. In the basketball season just completed, more than half a million spectators had paid their way into the Garden to watch the game. The attendance table is worth looking at, to realize what Irish had going for him:

21 regular-season double-headers:	380,346
National Invitation Tournament:	73,894
NCAA Tournament:	55,302
East-West All-Star Game:	18,157
	527,699

The capacity of the Garden for basketball was 18,499. The average attendance for these 29 programs was 18,196, or 98 percent.

Nevertheless, Irish was aware of pro basketball's potential, for the very reasons that had others interested. While he had no desire to look for a new world to conquer, he could not, realistically, allow someone else to move into the Garden and produce an eventual success.

Fortunately, he had something to fall back on. The idea of an arena-owned pro league had been discussed before Kase came up with a specific proposal. The arena owners had made an agreement, Irish explained, that if any of them went into it, all would go. The whole idea, after all, was that the teams be arena-owned. So although Irish wouldn't care to start one, if there was going

to be such a league, the Garden would be in it, with its own team, just as it had the Rangers in the National Hockey League.

Therefore, when the first organizational meeting was finally held, Ned Irish, representing the Garden, had the New York franchise. Kase received, eventually, a cash settlement for his prior efforts—several thousand dollars—and the best evidence that it was a satisfactory settlement is that Kase continued as a sports editor for 20 years and never had any visible friction with Irish, whatever his private regrets.

Meanwhile, Brown and Sutphin were pushing their idea and rounding up support. First of all, they needed someone to take charge of organizational details: every organization must have a head. Since they intended to be club owners in the new league, neither could also be the central administrator. A president had to be found.

Brown suggested Podoloff.

Maurice Podoloff, about five feet tall, appropriately round, born in Russia, raised since infancy in New Haven, graduate of Yale, lawyer, banker, and real-estate entrepreneur, was at that time the president of the American Hockey League. He had come to that position because his family (father and brothers) had built the New Haven Arena before the Depression, and owned the New Haven franchise in the AHL.

Podoloff knew little about sports, including hockey, and never tried to hide the fact. But a league president doesn't have to play, coach, or referee a game: he must handle legal matters, settle disputes, and, above all, find ways to let (or make) the separate club owners live together. In a league, the franchise holders are in the unusual situation of being, simultaneously, bitter rivals and partners. Presiding over such a group takes special talent.

In his own way, Podoloff was a wizard at this sort of thing, and although his career turned out to be a stormy one, replete with criticism that sometimes bordered on insult, he proved to be an excellent choice. The league's success would not have been possible without his particular contributions, even though many of his specific actions were to be open to challenge. He was criticized for "minor-league thinking," but it was precisely this shrewdness that enabled the young league to survive.

On June 6, 1946, the first meeting was held at the Hotel Commodore in New York, adjacent to Grand Central Station.

The league would be called The Basketball Association of America. The charter members were:

The Boston Celtics, represented by Brown, who chose the name "Celtics" for its double associations to the most famous professional basketball team of the past, and to Boston's Irish population.

The Chicago Stags, represented by Arthur Morse, a lawyer who had connections with the Norris family which ran the Chicago Stadium and the Chicago Black Hawks hockey team (and which also had a hand in the Detroit Olympia and Madison Square Garden).

The Cleveland Rebels, represented by Sutphin of the Cleveland Arena.

The Detroit Falcons, owned by the Olympia. (The Detroit hockey team that James Norris, father of the clan, acquired in 1933 along with the Olympia, had been called the Falcons; Norris had changed that to Red Wings.)

The New York Knickerbockers, represented by Irish.

The Philadelphia Warriors, represented by Pete Tyrell, who ran the Philadelphia Arena and the Philadelphia Rockets of the AHL.

The Pittsburgh Ironmen, represented by John Harris, who along with his arena and general ice show interests was head of the AHL Pittsburgh Hornets.

The Providence Steamrollers, represented by Lou Pieri, who ran the Providence Reds of the AHL and the arena there, a close friend of Walter Brown.

The St. Louis Bombers, represented by Emory D. Jones of the St. Louis Arena and the AHL team based there.

The Toronto Huskies, put forth by the Maple Leaf Gardens (which owned the NHL Maple Leafs).

The Washington Capitols, represented by Mike Uline, who owned the Uline Arena, the biggest building of its type in the nation's capital.

All but Morse were members of the Arena Managers Association of America, the group that had made the "if any, all" agreement that shut out Kase.

Of the 11, five were Podoloff's associates in the AHL. Five others were part of major-league hockey operations, with extensive farm-club relationships to the AHL. Only Uline was not closely involved with hockey.

What was significant about this lineup was that it had no connection whatever with the existing professional basketball structure (with one partial exception that we'll come to in a moment).

This disassociation had several consequences. For one thing, it enabled the new league to deal with editors and reporters on a new basis. Whatever prejudices had grown up about pro basketball, the BAA people could not automatically be saddled with them. Since they already had well-established contacts with their local newspapers through their other activities, they received a respectful hearing in the burgeoning battle for space in the crowded sports pages. They were free of any stigma previous pro teams may have accumulated, and were given from the start a degree of acceptance that would not have been available to "outsiders."

For another, it forced many of the teams into a policy that reflected the best feature of their idea—college players, with college reputations and the "clean" aura, and a college style of play. If the BAA had been an outgrowth of the existing pros, not only would its psychology have been different, but many college players simply couldn't have held their own against older pros in the competition for jobs. This way, many experienced pros simply were not available: either they found the existing pro leagues profitable and satisfactory, or they weren't approached by a new league quite conscious of the supply of cheaper fresh talent. Thus the less-experienced mass of recent collegians had a chance to develop as a group, and to set the tone of the new league.

A third plus—and perhaps the most important—was that all the new owners had extensive experience in sports promotion and business methods. This had been lacking in all the other pro basketball organizations. The BAA owners took for granted that their players would be full-time employees, like baseball players; that the schedule, and the authority of the league, would be basically tamper-proof; that the side issues of efficient publicity, concessions income, and first-class travel were not really side issues at all, but fundamentals.

A fourth effect of the hockey experience was the concept,

from the start, of championship playoffs at the end of the regular schedule. Nothing outrages purists more than this elaborate post-season competition, which reduces the whole long regular season to a jockeying for position; but nothing, in practice, is more essential to sports that have necessarily limited incomes (because indoor arenas can't be as large as ballparks) and that must generate some worthwhile prize money to keep player incentives functioning during a long schedule—which must be long to produce enough gross income.

There were negative consequences, too. Accustomed to the hockey pattern that a good fistfight peps up a game and brings back customers, many BAA owners took much too lenient a view of rowdyism in the early days. Unfamiliar, for the most part, with the nature of basketball and with the tricks pro players quickly master, they never gave referees sufficient authority over abusive players and coaches, nor made sufficiently clear the type of game the referee was to call.

But their advantages greatly outweighed their disadvantages. They had the buildings. New players were plentiful. The audience was eager. Expenses, compared to other team sports, were moderate (because squads were small).

Then, one by one, these advantages were chipped away.

The BAA

On November 1 1946, the Basketball Association of America began play. In Toronto, the New York Knicks defeated the Huskies, 68-66, even though Ed Sadowski, Toronto's player-coach, was high scorer with 18 points.

Both teams were in the Eastern Division, along with Washington, Philadelphia, Boston, and Providence. The other five entries comprised the Western Division. Each division's standings were kept separately, but each team played all the other teams in both divisions the same number of times. The schedule called for 60 games.

Ironically, the Knicks were seldom able to use Madison Square Garden as their home court. The building that had started the whole chain of thought leading to the BAA simply had no room for them. The college double-headers now numbered 28, not counting tournaments. These programs not only used up all the desirable dates, but were almost guaranteed sell-outs. Irish wasn't anxious to make room in the Garden's profitable pattern for an unknown quantity. So the Knicks had only six dates in the "Mecca of Basketball." The other 24 home games were played at the 69th Regiment Armory, which the Garden leased and outfitted with new seats. Nothing could symbolize more clearly the comparative importance of college and pro basketball at that time; the poor-relation status of the pros with respect to the flourishing collegians.

The best, and most experienced, pro players were still largely active in the National League and the American League. The National had teams in Rochester, Fort Wayne, Syracuse, Toledo, Oshkosh, Indianapolis, Sheboygan, Anderson (Indiana), Youngstown, Moline (Illinois), Detroit—and Chicago, which was most important of all because it had George Mikan, the 6-foot-10 giant from DePaul University in Chicago. Mikan had been the most overwhelming, and the most publicized of the college stars.

The American League was an eastern circuit, a combination

of earlier circuits named the Eastern and Metropolitan Leagues. Its activity was concentrated on weekends. It had been dominated by the South Philadelphia Hebrew Association team (the Sphas) coached by Eddie Gottlieb, and also had teams in Baltimore, Wilmington, Trenton, Paterson, Elizabeth, Jersey City, Troy, Brooklyn, and New York.

While most of the National League players stayed with it when the BAA was formed, much of the cream of the American League went into the new circuit—including Gottlieb, who took over as coach of the Philadelphia Warriors for Tyrell. Gottlieb soon emerged as the most important single acquisition of the new league—the exception mentioned earlier—the one man who had lifelong professional basketball experience and background, with all the good and bad things that meant.

The fact that Mikan was coming out of college, in the spring of 1946, had been an appreciable stimulant to the formation of the BAA. The realization that there would be, eventually, other Mikans coming along, and that this Mikan might play for many years, certainly figured in the calculations of the arena men when they deliberated about their new business. That he did not choose to join them when they did organize was something of a disappointment, but by his mere existence he was helping them even while he played elsewhere. He created interest and excitement in the pro game, because he was playing it, and this helped spread seeds of interest embedded in a layer of respectability.

A split in policy developed almost immediately, and it was to permeate the league's formative years. To have the best teams, competitively, it was necessary to rely on experienced pro players and, to some extent, on their rugged techniques; to have the shiny new product envisioned for long-term prosperity, it was necessary to cultivate the new college stars. In another sense, the two viewpoints boiled down to rate of growth: how quickly did competitive excellence have to be established, for a quick return at the gate? Or, how long could money be spent (and lost) to build for a sounder future, even if the immediate gate lagged?

Some owners went in one direction, some in the other, and the way they selected their original coaches was revealing.

In New York, Irish hired Neil Cohalan, who had coached Manhattan College and was well-known locally. In Chicago, the Stags landed Harold Olsen, who had just led Ohio State to a Big Ten championship and national prominence—and Chicago, of course, was the heart of Big Ten country. In St. Louis, the Bombers took Ken Loeffler, a scholarly sort whose college coaching background included Yale. In Detroit, the Falcons came up with Glenn Curtis, whose Indiana State team had just gone to the finals of the small-college national championships.

Thus the three most powerful arenas (New York, Chicago, and Detroit, with interlocking ownership through the Norris family) and the large (15,000 seat) St. Louis Arena went wholeheartedly for college flavor.

In Boston, Walter Brown seemed to get the best of both worlds. Honey Russell had been a famous pro player about a decade before, but also had college-coaching exposure.

However, in Philadelphia, Gottlieb was in command. In Cleveland, the coach was Dutch Dehnert, a famous member of the Original Celtics (and credited with the invention of the pivot play). In Pittsburgh, Paul Birch was another former Celtic, who had coached extensively in earlier pro leagues (and

who had been a college star as a player at Duquesne). Toronto's Sadowski was an active prominent pro player.

These four, then, were building with hard-core pros.

The Providence coach was Robert Morris, who had been a prominent high school coach in Rhode Island for many years.

And the Washington Capitols, the organization that least fit the pattern of the others, had a 29-year-old local boy, who had never coached even a college team, fresh out of the Navy and known as pretty successful at the high school level. His name was Arnold (Red) Auerbach, and he talked Uline into giving him the job by persuading him that he could recruit a good team from fellow servicemen who had been playing plenty of freelance pro basketball on weekends.

The rules of play, on the other hand, were agreed upon along college-style lines. With three exceptions, the college rules were taken over intact: the games were to last 48 minutes instead of 40 (to make it a long-enough show without double-headers); the zone defense, which tended to slow down action, was prohibited; and the limit on personal fouls was raised from five to six at the end of the season, in proportion to the increase in time played;

In the past, pro leagues had tried all sorts of different rules. There were two-handed dribbles, baskets without backboards, and, of course, the game inside a cage, where the ball could not go out of bounds so that action was continuous. Among other things, games played for money were understandably rougher than amateur games—and this roughness, in turn, promoted a sort of reciprocal consideration, a live-and-let-live policy by players who were often opponents one week and teammates the next. If one drove for the basket a little too aggressively, one was dumped a little too roughly—and the boys played nice after that. This sort of thing added to pro basketball's disrepute; but when the games were for blood the opposite became true. Experienced players could use little tugs, nudges, bumps and grabs that quickly took a game out of the referee's hands. Two of the goals implicit in "college style" ball, therefore, were the reproduction of enthusiasm of college players, and the physically cleaner and faster game.

It became pretty evident, right off the bat, that the pro approach was the correct one as far as winning was concerned. Coaches did not play, and did not even, in some cases, choose the players who made up the squads. But Gottlieb and Auerbach certainly had complete control of the personnel question, and they went heavily for men with previous pro experience.

What the coaches did do was reflect the approaches of their managements, and in the Western Division, Olsen and Loeffler, for all their college backgrounds, quickly committed themselves to established players. When, in the cases of Boston and Pittsburgh, the management didn't get as good material, it didn't make any difference that the coaches were pro-oriented.

So, almost as soon as the first season began, the Washington Capitols under the unknown Auerbach ran off and hid from the rest. A 17-game winning streak enabled the Caps to spread-eagle the Eastern division before the season was half over.

By the time the season was over, Washington had a 49-11 record (which was to remain unsurpassed for 20 years).

Fourteen games behind Washington, but with nothing to apologize for, were Gottlieb's Warriors. He had come up with

the individual prize, a 6-foot-5 Kentuckian named Joe Fulks, whose shot-making ability was so unbelievable that people simply refused to believe it until they saw him.

In those days, a basketball player was still considered sensational if he scored 20 points in a game. It was a standard of achievement not unlike, in the sports fan's mind, hitting two home runs in one baseball game. In recent years, fantastic scoring totals had been posted by Mikan and a few others, but it was understandable—if marvelous or ridiculous, according to one's viewpoint—that an oversized player could produce oversized statistics by using his height near the basket. But Fulks wasn't all that big, and he wasn't scoring from close to the basket. So when fans read that Fulks averaged 23.2 points per game over a 60-game season, and that he had scored 30 or more in 12 different games (going as high as 41), they just couldn't swallow it.

"There must be something funny about that pro game," said countless reading fans, who hadn't seen for themselves. They didn't know what was "funny," but something must be. Perhaps pro defense was being cooperative. The years of suspicion and unrespectability couldn't be sloughed off so easily.

Yet, what Fulks was really doing was pointing the way to the future. His fantastic scoring was the result of fantastic scoring skill, pure and simple. The jump shot, properly executed, cannot be stopped without fouling; a defender can force the jump shooter to take the shot prematurely, or from an undesirable angle, but he can't do anything about the shot itself. Fulks was the pioneer of the shot that was to become pro basketball's primary weapon.

The opposition, and the relatively small crowds that saw Fulks in action, had no trouble appreciating him. He was the only unanimous choice for the all-league team, and as scoring champion he averaged almost seven points per game more than the runner-up (Bob Feerick with 16.8). Not until 1962, when Wilt Chamberlain made all statistics meaningless (in a totally different style of game) did a scoring champion produce a bigger margin of superiority.

According to the playoff pattern settled upon, the first-place teams in each division met each other, the second-place teams played, and the third-place teams met. That was the first round. The division leaders had to play a best-of-seven set, which allowed the others, playing best of three, to play an extra round before producing a survivor to play for the championship.

The Western Division, during the regular season, had produced the closest possible race: a tie between Chicago and St. Louis. Chicago won the one-game playoff for first place (in overtime, no less)—and proceeded to knock off Washington, four games to two.

In beating Washington, the Stags reversed one of the first trends of basketball, the home-court advantage. During the regular season, the Caps had won 29 of their 30 home games, a lopsided proportion that was symptomatic of many of the difficulties that would follow. But in the playoffs, the Stags won the first two games played in Washington, by 16-point margins. They won the third at home, taking an insurmountable 3-0 lead, and ran out the series in six games.

Philadelphia, meanwhile, disposed of St. Louis by winning the third and deciding game on the other team's court.

Then Philadelphia polished off the Knicks in two straight,

and moved into the finals against Chicago. It turned out to be the Warriors, in no uncertain terms: two decisive victories at Philadelphia, a split of close games in Chicago, and an 83-80 victory at Philadelphia to wrap it up.

And so, on April 22, the first season of the BAA had ended. In the sense that it had been completed at all, and that outstanding players had proved themselves, it could be called a success. But its impact on the public, in its own cities, was still quite secondary, and on the general sports public nil. Financially, there was a great deal of wreckage.

The three trailing teams in the Western Division—Cleveland, Detroit, and Pittsburgh—closed up shop. They abandoned the original conception because they didn't have the resources, or the will, to keep spending money. Whatever the salaries had been the first year—few players got more than $6,000—it was obvious that these would rise. The travel, by rail, in a league that stretched from Toronto to Washington and Boston to St. Louis cost an appreciable sum. Pittsburgh had a rich college basketball tradition and was "a good basketball town," but its arena simply didn't generate the kind of year-round income Madison Square Garden could rely on. Cleveland and Detroit, by and large, were not "good basketball towns."

In the East, Toronto and Boston had tied for last. Walter Brown, of course, had no intention of quitting, since he was one of the chief advocates of the league in the first place. But Toronto, with neither a fertile field for basketball in its area (although Naismith was born in Ontario), nor a winning team, pulled out.

Those four defections left only seven teams, and a serious question of survival. In money, the BAA hadn't done as well as the National League. Freelance teams, especially the Harlem Globetrotters, were still the real money-makers, and while the sports world as a whole didn't pay too much attention, a world championship pro tournament held annually in Chicago was still a big event within the pro basketball sphere.

As the owners faced retrenchment and reorganization, what may be called political positions started to harden. Irish, who had gone into the enterprise with doubts that now seemed at least partially justified, was firmly committed to a sort of ruthless major-leagueism. He wanted things done with "class," he wanted a college-type game, and he was willing to go on losing money now to make it later—because the Garden had plenty of money. He had no patience with the struggles of less affluent promoters, or the traditional scrambling for a few extra bucks or a slight competitive advantage that characterized the older pros.

Some might call Irish's viewpoint admirable, and perhaps it was in theory. In practice, however, it simply antagonized most of his colleagues, who didn't have comparable resources behind them. Podoloff, as president, sided with the poorer members—out of political instinct, personal inclination, and business experience. Podoloff bent his efforts to juggling disasters as best he could—overlooking a debt here, bending a rule there, trying to make decisions that would assist existence rather than perfection.

This way, there arose two camps: the Podoloff camp, characterized by any expedient for survival, and the Irish camp, pressing for big-league standards and the devil take the hindmost. The reality of life made it inevitable that Podoloff's camp was always larger.

In retrospect, it is easy to see that both attitudes were useful, and that the league eventually succeeded out of their synthesis. Without Irish's insistence that the original grand concepts not be lost sight of, the BAA could easily have gone down the fruitless path of all the other pro basketball leagues. But without Podoloff's manipulations to let the weaker members stay in business, there would not have been any league at all to grow to maturity. But at the time, it often seemed that conflict polarized by Irish and Podoloff might rip the league apart.

The immediate problems, looking to the second season, were:
1. Finding enough teams to have a schedule.
2. Cutting back on expenses.
3. Bringing in a larger number of players whose college reputations would mean something to the fans in each city.

To answer the first, the seven survivors took in the Baltimore Bullets, who had been in the league that Gottlieb had abandoned. To balance the divisions, Baltimore and Washington were put in the "West" (with Chicago and St. Louis), while New York, Philadelphia, Boston, and Providence comprised the East.

This arrangement, for the East at least, certainly cut down on travel expense. A cutback to a 48-game schedule also served this purpose. The teams played eight times against every opponent in the same division, and six times against the teams in the other division.

For the third problem, the BAA relied on that great invention of professional sports promotion, the draft. By drafting the rights to graduating college players, the teams could avoid bidding against each other for the more desirable talent. By letting teams draft in reverse order of the previous year's standings, they could strengthen the weakest teams the most, and keep up the competitive balance on which close races depended.

To make maximum use of local interest, however, the BAA added a gimmick called "the territorial draft choice." In the first round, a team could pick a player from its own area regardless of which turn it was entitled to, so that if a college star had made his reputation in Philadelphia, the Warriors would be able to get him and to cash in on his fame whether or not they finished low in the standings.

As an immediate gate-booster to teams trying to build public support from the ground up, the territorial draft was a fine idea. Eventually, it became unnecessary and was abandoned.

The situation in New York, so crucial to the league's search for an image and for press attention, was considerably improved.

Irish had hired a new coach—Joe Lapchick, one of the most famous Original Celtics, the first widely-known "giant" because he was 6-foot-5 (which was gigantic in the early 1920s), and now at the peak of his success as coach of St. John's, one of the regular Garden teams. He was as big a name and as popular a person as basketball had to offer.

The Chicago Stags picked up two big local names, Andy Phillip and Gene Vance. Before the war, they had been the leaders of the famous Whiz Kids of Illinois, and although they failed to win another Western Conference title when they returned to school as veterans, they were important.

Still, the National League got at least as many prominent graduating collegians as the BAA, even though it was also going through wholesale reorganization. The Chicago team had folded, and Mikan had moved to the new Minneapolis franchise, where

John Kundla, of the University of Minnesota, was coaching.

Competitively, the 1947-48 season was a dazzling success: The Warriors, defending champions, met Baltimore, the only new team, for the title—and Baltimore took it, in six games.

One couldn't ask for a better season—if one were a fan. If one were an owner, the picture was quite different. The 48-game schedule proved to be disastrous: it cut down on income far more than it did on expenses. And the competition for talent was serious: college players were playing off one league against the other in negotiation, and the pros themselves had somewhere to go if they wanted to move.

Another such season, Podoloff felt, might be the last.

Irish, as usual, did not quite agree. His Knicks had made progress, and a longer schedule meant finding more dates on a crowded calendar. "Be patient and build," Irish advocated. "I've got to do something, and quick," Podoloff felt.

And Podoloff knew what that "something" must be. One way or another, the cream of the National League must be brought into the BAA.

He found a way.

The Merger

Originally, Podoloff's office had been up on Madison Avenue, where the American Hockey League office was, but soon the central office of the NBA was moved into the Empire State Building, on the 80th floor. This gave the league the highest office, and the shortest commissioner, in sports—an obvious sort of joke that was repeated frequently and that fairly represented the attitude of most of the sports world towards the two-year-old circuit. The older columnists knew, with the certainty of fossilized prejudices, that pro basketball "wouldn't work" and that basketball was a game either for sissies or "goons." The younger writers, exposed at high intensity to the exciting college scene, were predisposed in favor of the new venture—but repeatedly appalled at the bush-league aspects that were too glaring to overlook: the squabbling in public among owners, the abuse heaped upon referees by owners and coaches as well as players, the last-minute schedule changes, and the rapid turnover of franchises. Most of all, in New York, where so much opinion was formed, Irish's unconcealed lack of respect for Podoloff did little to enhance the league's dignity—and Podoloff's penchant for double talk in countless syllables didn't help either. The very technique of equivocation and filibustering, legitimately helpful in private when warring owners had to be reconciled for the sake of league business, was a damaging handicap when applied to press and public.

To handle the league's publicity, Podoloff had hired Walter Kennedy, who had come out of Notre Dame in the mid-1930s and had done social work, coaching, and publishing. Kennedy was knowledgeable and energetic, but kept pretty much in the background in a setup that had the league president himself and various owners so much in the limelight.

Neither Kennedy nor Podoloff had the slightest suspicion, at the that time, that Kennedy would eventually succeed Podoloff.

First-hand knowledge of Podoloff's maneuvers, however, was giving Kennedy invaluable background, because Podoloff was really maneuvering.

The 1947-48 season had been an artistic success but a financial flop for the BAA. For the National League, operating on a smaller scale, it had been more successful financially, but a little disturbing artistically, since the Minneapolis team built around Mikan and Pollard threatened to become too strong for healthy competition. But the National League people had more reason for optimism than the BAA people, despite—or perhaps because of—their less grandiose ideas.

During the summer of 1948, as both leagues prepared for necessary expansion, it was more and more obvious that a real battle for talent was around the corner. The returned G.I.s, now finishing interrupted college careers, were about to graduate in large numbers with bigger reputations than ever, older than most graduates, more prepared to be pros. The college tournaments had become so large, and so well-publicized (and attended), that nationally-known stars were being produced in unprecedented numbers—which made it all the more important for any particular team, or league, to get the top names.

The underlying conditions for a merger were plain, if not quite irresistible: the National League had the players, the BAA had the cities and the arenas.

But the real question was, merger on what terms, and into what? Podoloff probed, in informal conversations, all summer. The Minneapolis Lakers, under Max Winter, were not particularly interested, since they were on the verge of establishing a dynasty in their own league. The second-best team, year in and year out, was Rochester, loaded with hard-nosed pros and New York area products—but what would the BAA want with a city the size of Rochester?

Yet, there had to be an entering wedge somewhere—and Podoloff found it in two men: Paul Walk of Indianapolis and Carl Bennett of Fort Wayne.

Walk was the general manager of the Indianapolis Kautskys, owned by a florist. Bennett ran the Fort Wayne team for Fred Zollner, the piston man. Podoloff convinced both, one way or another, that their future lay in the more prestigious big arenas, playing as much on the social-climbing (in terms of sports) inclinations of their owners as on logic. But there was logic, too: if they were in basketball for the publicity, obviously they'd get more of it in a league with the biggest cities.

Indianapolis and Fort Wayne decided to jump to the BAA. "Betrayal!" screamed the other National League clubs—with plenty of justification. But screaming was a reaction, not a policy. If the National League was going to break ranks, the Lakers would go along with the times. Winter and Ben Berger, the principal owner, decided to accept the BAA invitation too.

But that left Rochester, in particular, out in the cold. Lester and Jack Harrison, who operated the Royals (with Lester as coach), simply weren't going to take that. They threatened, pleaded and argued—and the BAA decided to take them too, without allowing questions of damage to go too far.

It was a victory of staggering proportions. All of a sudden, almost on the eve of the 1948-49 season, the very players whose absence had become a reason to downgrade the BAA, were in it: Mikan, Pollard, Bob Davies and Arnie Risen of Rochester, a half-dozen lesser but visible lights.

In effect, the National League was dead, then and there, although it went on with nine teams: Syracuse, Anderson (Indiana), Hammond (Indiana), and Detroit in one division;

Oshkosh, Sheboygan, Tri-Cities (Moline and Rock Island, Illinois, and Davenport, Iowa), Waterloo (Iowa) and Denver in the other. It still had Harry Boykoff, and Al Cervi (one of the Rochester greats who had become playing-coach at Syracuse), Frank Brian, and 7-foot-0 Don Otten, out of Bowling Green—but the names of the cities were enough to brand it as inescapably minor league.

To the BAA, the bonanzas were Mikan and the near elimination of competition for next year's college stars. Wherever Mikan went, as a visiting player, he filled the house. In a league in which home teams kept all the receipts, that made him as popular as (and synonymous with) money.

To Irish, specifically, Mikan and the highly-regarded Rochester team meant something new to justify more Garden dates for his Knicks. He complained of the minor-league connotations of the names on the shirts—Minneapolis, Rochester, Fort Wayne, for heaven's sakes!—but he accepted the reality. In fact, a larger league than the eight-team circuit of 1947-48 seemed essential to one of his main precepts: in Madison Square Garden, he felt, the public had been conditioned to double-headers by the colleges, and double-headers it must have from the pros.

By double-header, of course, Irish meant two games involving four teams, and this created a scheduling nightmare. To have any double-headers at all, anywhere, meant abandoning any idea of a completely balanced home-and-away schedule. If all teams played the same number of double-headers, however, it would be possible to have an equal number of games at home and away and a set number of "neutral" games. But not all teams wanted double-headers, which were neither necessary nor desirable in smaller arenas that could be filled with one game, and not all wanted the same number. In order to provide a "first" game for a Garden double-header (or one in Boston or Philadelphia or Chicago), some other team would have to transfer one of its home games.

And this, in turn, meant that more games had to be scheduled in the first place, to provide extras for this "neutral pool."

This problem did not make its full impact immediately, but started to grow when the National League teams came in.

The 12-team BAA that played the 1948-49 season had a 60-game schedule, a return to the original number. Washington and Baltimore were now in the East, where they belonged, and the four newcomers were in the Western Division with Chicago and St. Louis. Washington, still coached by Auerbach and with substantially the same veteran club, won the Eastern race handily, by a six-game margin over New York with Baltimore, Philadelphia, Boston, and Providence trailing in that order.

But in the West there was a surprise: even though Minneapolis and Rochester dominated the league, as the better-informed experts had expected, it was Rochester that finished first, by a one-game margin.

The year before, Chicago's Max Zaslofsky had beaten out Fulks for the scoring championship, but now Mikan took over. Even though Fulks raised his own average to 26 points a game, Mikan posted 28.3. (Zaslofsky was third with 20.6). Then in 10 playoff games, big George, elbows swinging and eyeglasses glittering, poured in 303 points.

Meanwhile, the emasculated National League went through the motions. Anderson won in the East, Oshkosh (in a close

race) in the West, and both went through to the playoff finals, where Anderson won the title by taking three straight.

Irish was a still powerful but increasingly isolated voice. The four new teams had shifted the proportions of block voting—a shift that Podoloff could not avoid welcoming, since it strengthened his own position. There were now 12 teams and only half of them really stemmed from the original arena-owned, college-style concept. The immigrants from the National League, and Baltimore, had orthodox pro histories and viewpoints, and Washington had been a special case from the beginning. The problems and goals, as well as the ideas of how to operate, were quite different for owners in Minneapolis and Fort Wayne than for those in New York and Boston. The conflicts that arose in league meetings now, therefore, were no mere personality clashes—although Irish's characteristic aloof, imperious, and humorless manner added to his difficulties; there were, now, authentic conflicts of interest.

Meanwhile, a peculiar facet of a much larger problem touched the basketball league: the color line.

So far—in the spring of 1949—there were no Negro players in the BAA. Traditionally, in pro basketball, all-Negro teams had competed freely against all-white teams, and the Negro teams often won championships; but integration within a team was rare. By this time, however, Jackie Robinson was playing his third season with the Brooklyn Dodgers, and baseball's stubbornly-held color line had been broken. On the college level, in all sports including basketball, it was being shattered more thoroughly every day. The BAA owners were no more, and no less, enlightened on this question than other promoters of the time: they shared the same context of prejudice that pervaded American society, but as promoters they thought even more specifically and less idealistically. Whatever unconscious motivations may have been at work, on the surface they simply feared change. Would their predominantly white audiences "accept" Negro stars, and "identify" with them?

So the BAA drifted on the color question, while outstanding Negro players went on to Olympic competition and joined AAU teams, or freelanced as pros.

But there was one special circumstance that made the pro basketball situation different from baseball's or football's. The most successful, in money, pro basketball team ever assembled was an all-Negro institution, Abe Saperstein's Harlem Globetrotters.

On sheer playing ability, the Trotters had been good enough to win world pro titles in the freelance competitive pattern that preceded the BAA. Even now, passing into the 1950s, they were strong enough to battle the best league teams on even terms (as they were soon to prove). But they had become world famous, and had made millions of dollars for Saperstein, by clowning rather than by winning. They had developed comedy routines, incorporated into their games with the cooperation of their own "opposing" team (or without the cooperation of less skillful local teams). Even though they no longer concentrated on straight basketball—or maybe because of this—they were, without comparison, the biggest basketball attraction anywhere.

This meant that they could, and did, fill the biggest arenas, and that they were highly desirable tenants. This meant, in turn, that the Globetrotters developed close, friendly relations with the arena managers who had launched the BAA.

This meant that the Globies were available, a couple of times a year, to stir basketball interest in any town they visited, to make a good payday for the arena (even after the Globies got their cut), and to help bring in crowds to see a BAA game by playing their own game as a preliminary. A spring tour against college seniors became a highly publicized annual series.

And this meant, of course, that the BAA owners were not likely to raid the Globetrotters for experienced talent, even if they could afford to, which was doubtful.

And the Globetrotter management was not, understandably, bursting with impatience to see its stars offered a profitable alternative.

Finally, emphasizing how close these relationships were, there was the circumstance that the New York office of the Globetrotters (who were based in Chicago) was sublet from the BAA and located in the suite of rooms on the 80th floor of the Empire State Building.

Actually, the color bars were about to fall. By the fall of 1949, it was already clear that Negro players would be taken into the league for the next season. (The first one drafted turned out to be Chuck Cooper, of Duquesne, by the Boston Celtics, but he didn't actually play any sooner than Nat [Sweetwater] Clifton did for the Knicks, who set a precedent by purchasing his contract from the Globetrotters, or Earl Lloyd for the Caps). In a short time, Negro stars were to become more numerous than in any other major-league sport, but the beginnings were hesitant and humiliating.

The slowness of the BAA in accepting Negroes was underlined by what happened in the summer of 1949. The inevitable formal merger with the remnants of the National League took place, creating a 17-team league, comprising about 200 players and a host of teams needing help—and even in this expansion, no place was found for a single Negro.

By taking in the National League survivors (in August, 1949), the BAA not only formally eliminated competition, but conclusively altered its own nature. It finished the process, at the top, of changing into an old-fashioned pro league with only vestiges of the arena-owned blueprint. Paradoxically, at the bottom, it was building a body of college stars and public acceptance that would, eventually, evolve back towards the founders' concepts. But for the time being, the forces of traditional professionalism had proved dominant.

To begin with, the league adopted a new name: the National Basketball Association.

Then it gathered itself into three divisions. The real reason for this unwieldy setup was the insistence of the vintage BAA members—like Irish—that there be the least disruption of the patterns the enlarged BAA had developed in 1948-49.

Thus, the previous year's Eastern and Western Divisions were kept substantially intact, although the Western was now called the "Central." A new "Western" division comprised most of the remaining National Leaguers.

But that wasn't all. Other franchise changes had taken place. Providence finally gave up, and its owner, Lou Pieri, became a partner of Brown's in the Boston Celtics, who had also gone through three years of heavy losses. Their demise reduced the Eastern Division to five—New York, Boston, Washington, Baltimore, and Philadelphia.

The Indianapolis Jets also went out of business, although another Indianapolis entry was in the wings. This reduced the old Western Division to five.

Four National League teams were being brought in: Syracuse, Anderson, Tri-Cities, and Sheboygan.

Two other teams, Denver and Waterloo, had started the 1948-49 season in the National League but had not finished it. They were also admitted to the enlarged circuit.

The 17th team was unusual and important: it was the Kentucky team graduating en masse, going into business for itself as the Indianapolis Olympians.

The Olympians and five of the six National League newcomers comprised the Western Division of the National Basketball Association.

Syracuse was moved into the Eastern Division, filling the gap left by Providence. But, for scheduling purposes, Syracuse was to play the pattern set for the Western Division—a triumph of illogic that typified much of the lack of realism that permeated the whole merger.

In short, what the BAA had done was to invite the dying remnants of the National League to join in their own financial burial. It would have been more forthright (but perhaps sticky legally, on anti-trust grounds) to refuse to admit them. On the other hand, it is no one's right or duty to refuse to adult, competent businessmen a chance to lose money if they want to; that was the view of the BAA. That the end could only be further shaking down to stronger franchises, no one really doubted.

However, the merger did represent a historic accomplishment. For the first time, all players (or at least, all teams) with major-league pretensions were brought together under one organizational roof—except for Negroes, of course. Structurally, the consolidation that constituted an essential to growth had been effected, and if the character of the "only major league in basketball" was not quite what its formulators had foreseen, it did—at least and at last—exist. Its fourth season, and its first under its new name, was sure to be eventful.

The Shakeout

To keep up with what happened during the 1949-50 season, a basketball fan needed eyes in the back of his head, unlimited leisure and subscriptions to newspapers from more than a dozen cities. Few were that interested.

Those who cared, and settled for the limited view afforded from any particular city, could notice some distinct changes: hysteria was on the increase; home courts were becoming impregnable; more outstanding players were on hand than ever before; and the rough old-pro style was becoming more prevalent.

The schedule itself was a mishmash that violated all big-league traditions. The teams in the Eastern Division were supposed to play each other six times, the Central Division teams six times and the Western Division teams twice (to save on travel expenses, and so that the big cities wouldn't have to give up dates with the better-known old BAA teams for the sake of these newcomers). The Central Division followed the same pattern: six inside the division, six with the East and two with the West. The Western teams were to play each other seven times, and everyone else only twice.

Right off the bat, that made a ridiculous imbalance. Here, in

one league, were Eastern and Central teams scheduled to play 68 games, and Western Division teams scheduled for 62.

But the real joker was Syracuse. Its record would count in the Eastern Division standings—but its schedule would be that of the tacked-on Western group. So Syracuse would play only 10 games against the other teams in its own division, while all the others played 26.

Finally, just to keep things from coming out too even, Syracuse played two extra games with Indianapolis, and Tri-Cities played two extra games with Anderson, for no other reason than a little extra gate.

So here was a league where 10 teams played a 68-game schedule, four played 64 and three played 62. And after all that, 12 of the teams would begin playoffs.

Such a schedule satisfied nobody, and results conspired to emphasize its ludicrous aspects.

Syracuse, led by Cervi and Dolph Schayes, ran off with the Eastern title. Syracuse finished with a 51-13 record, 13 games ahead of the second-place Knicks, and swept through the Eastern playoffs by knocking off Philadelphia in two straight and the Knicks in two out of three.

In the Central Division, the powerful Minnesota and Rochester teams finished in a flat tie, at 51-17, and had to play off for first place before they could start the playoffs. The game was played at Rochester on March 21 and the Lakers came from behind to win it, 78-76, as Mikan poured in 35 points. There was also a tie for third, 11 games behind the leaders, and in that playoff Fort Wayne defeated Chicago at Fort Wayne. Then the Pistons knocked out the disappointed Rochester team in the "regular playoffs" in two straight, leaving the Lakers a clear path. The Lakers polished off Chicago, Fort Wayne and Anderson (the Western Division survivor) without losing a game, to reach the championship series against Syracuse. There the Nats put up more resistance, but the Lakers took the series, four games to two, and were established as a "dynasty" with two straight titles.

It was enough basketball—593 games decided, 94,952 points scored, 32,205 personal fouls committed—to make the most resolute fan bleary-eyed.

Long before the 1949-50 season was complete, it was evident that the death rate among franchises would be appalling. Sure enough, the summer brought the demise of six clubs and serious changes in a couple of others.

Sheboygan, Waterloo, and Anderson were simply too small, in population and resources, to even dream of keeping up with the big cities. They folded. Denver was simply too far away at a time when air travel was not yet universal, nor so time-saving. It folded. And, surprisingly, so did Chicago and St. Louis, two of the charter BAA clubs. In Chicago, the Stadium itself had never actually taken command of the team, letting friends and associates run it (Arthur Morse and Judge John Sbarbaro) without really integrating basketball into the building's operation. In St. Louis, business just wasn't that good.

Going into the 1950-51 season, therefore, the NBA was back to 11 teams, a wieldy number. New York, Boston, Syracuse, Philadelphia, Baltimore, and Washington formed a compact Eastern division, with few travel and schedule problems. Minneapolis, Rochester, Fort Wayne, Indianapolis and Tri-Cities composed the Western Division, with more travel

difficulties, smaller incomes, but excellent player strength and competitive balance.

The differences in playing facilities now emerged as a major question. New York, Boston, and Philadelphia, the only remaining representatives of the original hopes and concepts of the BAA, had large seating capacities, huge population areas to draw from, and a definite need for at least some double-headers.

Elsewhere it was another story. The Baltimore Coliseum, an old building, seated 4,000. The Fort Wayne Pistons played in North Side High School, with 3,800 seats. Rochester's Edgerton Park Sports Arena held 5,000. Syracuse played in the State Fair Coliseum, well out of town, where 7,500 could be accommodated. Washington's Uline Arena listed its capacity as 8,000, and the Lakers in Minneapolis claimed 10,000 at the Auditorium, although they had to use other local courts too. Tri-Cities played in the Wharton Fieldhouse, in Moline, where 6,000 could be handled.

Only Indianapolis, using the Butler Field House with 17,000 seats, could match New York and Boston in capacity, but this was not a commercial arena with the attendant advantages.

These others, then, had no need of double-headers. Nor could they hope to cash in on big attractions. Their only chance to make money was to play many games—a longer schedule, even if that involved diluting the quality and the excitement of any one particular game. Irish, whose interest it was to keep travel (and player fatigue) to a minimum while aiming at crowds of 18,000 for a hot event, was for a shorter schedule.

To no one's surprise, Irish lost again. The new schedule was set at 68 games, matching the maximum of the previous year.

Solidification and Scandal

For the 1950-51 season, Irish had managed to squeeze in 18 Madison Square Garden dates for his Knicks. Four of them involved double-headers. And it was really a squeeze: there were 28 regular-season college double-headers scheduled, and the "circuit" was going full blast: the Boston Garden had eight college programs, the Chicago Stadium nine, the Cleveland Arena 12, the Buffalo Memorial Auditorium 21, Philadelphia's Convention Hall 13, the San Francisco Cow Palace 18, and the University of Pennsylvania's Palestra (where Penn and Villanova teamed up as the host teams) 16. Counting the various tournaments, just as many college games were being offered in big-league commercial settings as major-league pro games.

Then the college bubble burst.

In January, a Manhattan College player, Junius Kellogg, reported to the Bronx District Attorney that he had turned down a bribe to "shave" points—that is, not lose the game, but win by less than the margin set as a handicap for the gamblers.

But investigation showed that a couple of his teammates had accepted such bribes, and had acted upon them.

Within a month, a parallel investigation by New York District Attorney Frank Hogan made the Manhattan College incident a minor aberration: the games had been crooked, Hogan discovered and the players confessed, on a vast scale.

City College's Cinderella Team of the previous year, the heroic double champions—all were implicated. So were the leading players from LIU, a perennial Garden power. Some NYU players were involved. St. John's players were accused but

not indicted. The shock that went through the sports world could only be compared to baseball's Black Sox Scandal of 1920, when it was revealed that the Chicago White Sox had conspired to throw the 1919 World Series to the Cincinnati Reds.

And all the revulsion focused on the Garden—and on Irish. He had made basketball big-time; he had created the large money stake that made schools recruit so uninhibitedly. It was Irish who had made the game so popular that gamblers moved in; it was Irish who controlled the "commercial arena programs" that college administrators—who had been profiting from them for years and building up their own careers—suddenly found so dangerous and immoral. It was Irish who, somehow, had failed to police his preserve.

Remaining games were canceled. Self-righteously, one conference after another declared the Garden "unsuitable" for college events. New York, as all right-thinking Americans knew, was the center of sin and corruption and Madison Square Garden was Sodom and Gomorrah, rolled into one.

And if the college boys were crooked, surely the pros must be too? That question blew like a cold wind through the NBA. At that moment, its comparative obscurity was a life-saving blessing. There was no hint, from the underground gambling circles that were now a prime source of information for journalists, that pros were involved. Carryover suspicion of the pros, and the primacy of the college action, had kept betting on the pros on a relatively small scale. Treading on eggs, but for the time being untarnished, the NBA finished its season in good order.

Well, not exactly in good order. The Washington franchise had collapsed on January 9, and the players had been redistributed (Freddy Scolari to Syracuse, Bones McKinney to Boston). But this was a bearable loss, since it balanced the two divisions at five teams apiece and eliminated another weak sister financially.

By the time the NBA playoffs were starting, in late March, the first shock was past. The college season had ended; the pros had not been implicated. The whole business, obviously, was a peculiarly New York evil.

In this touchy atmosphere, the NBA went through an eventful set of playoffs. The Knicks, who had finished third, were the hot club. Having finished third, the Knicks polished off Boston in two straight, while fourth-place Syracuse did the same to first-place Philadelphia. In a ferocious five-game semi-final, the Knicks had the odd game at home and won it by two points, 83-81. In the west, both Minneapolis and Rochester had to go three games to survive the first round, and then Rochester upset the Lakers, three games to one, as Mikan was partially hobbled by a bad ankle.

Now the Knicks and Rochester met for the championship, with all the New York games scheduled for the little Armory (capacity, 5,000) because the Garden had long since been occupied by its annual April tenant, the circus. For the first time, New York had a team in what was becoming basketball's equivalent of a World Series, but the big city was hardly aware of it, let alone interested, as the Yankees, Giants, and Dodgers were all coming north. Rochester, quite properly, was heavily favored, and won the first two games, at Rochester, by one-sided margins (92-65 and 99-84). In New York, the Royals took the third game, 78-71, and they were leading by six points with eight minutes to play in the fourth game.

However, that close to elimination, the Knicks rallied. They pulled out that game, 79-73, then startled everyone by winning the fifth in Rochester, 92-89. In New York, with Zaslofsky gaining momentum, the Knicks evened the series, 80-73.

On April 21, at Rochester, a hectic finals was won by Rochester, but only after the Knicks had fought back again to tie with one minute to play. In the records, Rochester had its championship, but the real appeal of the Knicks to New York—an appeal that was to have a great effect on the growth of the league in the next few crucial years—stemmed from the battle they put up in this series.

Meanwhile, back on March 2, another big step towards major-league status had been taken. Walter Brown, midway through the season, before there had been any hint of scandal to weaken the college structure, had come up with a marvelous idea: an all-star game. It was held in Boston, on March 2, with 10 top players from the Eastern Division (coached by Lapchick) playing 10 from the West (coached by Kundla). The East won, 111-94.

As both pro and college seasons receded into history, no sensational headway had been made by the NBA, now down to 10 clubs. It seemed obvious that the Knicks would be used to fill gaps in the Garden schedule created by the defection of the morally upright colleges from other sections of the country, and the badly-burned New York schools—but this was a New York problem, or condition, or story; it didn't touch the NBA as a whole too seriously.

Until the other shoe dropped.

In July, it was learned that the Bradley team had been crooked too.

Hogan's investigation had continued. Each interrogation of accused players turned up new leads. Toledo was in it, too.

And on October 19, on the eve of the 1951-52 NBA season, after a charity all-star game in Chicago, two more players were picked up: Groza and Beard.

The Kentucky boys, it seemed, had been the original fixers of the current cycle, going into "business" right after returning from the 1948 Olympics.

By the time Hogan's exposures were complete, the statistics were: Games had been fixed in 22 cities in 17 states.

There was firm evidence against 33 players from six colleges.

On the record, 90 games between 1947 and 1951 had been discussed for manipulation, and 49 were actually rigged.

And no one with any sense of realism could doubt that this was only the visible tip of a very large iceberg. (In years to come, new investigations and new scandals were to touch a dozen more schools. The fixers had focused on the big arenas because that's where the games were; when the games were moved back to college gyms, the fixers moved there just as easily.)

Scandals of such scope put everything in a different light—including the NBA.

It was no longer a matter of bad old Madison Square Garden, and a New York problem. Large-scale commercialized college basketball had been dealt a body blow everywhere; the very idea of it was suspect.

Which meant that pro basketball had a golden opportunity. By a sudden twist, it was the more respectable of the two.

College basketball's tragedy, then, proved to be the turning

point for the pros. All the preliminary steps that had been taken under their own power—the merger, the consolidation, the building up of resources, the creation of stars, and the establishment of a rudimentary tradition and following—could now pay off.

The same 10 teams that finished in 1951 were starting the new season, even though one of them had moved. Kerner took his Hawks from Tri-Cities to Milwaukee, where a brand new 11,000-seat arena had just been built in the middle of the city. This was certainly a step up in class, towards major leagueism, rather than a mark of failure. So for the first time, stability of ownership had been maintained over a summer.

In a positive sense, therefore, the 1951-52 season was uneventful—off the court. Syracuse, strengthened by the acquisition of Rocha and a brilliant rookie backcourt man in George King, finished first in the East, one game ahead of Boston, which now had a spectacular scoring trio in Macauley, Cousy, and Bill Sharman, but weak rebounding and defense. In the West, Rochester nosed out the Lakers by one game, making season-long consistency overcome the fact that the Lakers won seven out of nine from the Royals hand-to-hand.

Neither first-place finisher, however, reached the finals of the playoffs. The Knicks, who had finished third, again emerged as the hot club. They got by Boston by winning the third game in double overtime in Boston (on what Auerbach, to this day, insists was a "terrible call," which gave Vandeweghe two free throws at the buzzer), and disposed of Syracuse in what was to be a five-game set, four games to one. The Lakers polished off Indianapolis in two and Rochester in four.

Again, the final series went the full seven games, with the heavily-favored western team winning against unexpected resistance. This time the Knicks did not come quite as close, taking an 82-65 licking in the final game at Minneapolis.

A similar structural stability endured through the 1952-53 season. Again the same 10 teams started and finished the season. Again Minneapolis defeated New York in the final round of the playoffs, although the Lakers needed only five games to do it this time, winning four straight after losing the first. Since both the Knicks and Lakers had finished first in their divisions during the regular season (the Knicks by half a game over Syracuse and one and a half over Boston, the Lakers by four games over Rochester), this was the "truest" world-series type championship the league had had so far.

Over this apparent tranquility, however, hung clouds. The apprehension, and trials, of players and gamblers involved in the college scandals kept making the papers, and an atmosphere of unease continued. The Grand Jury that had started hearing the basketball cases in February, 1951, was not discharged until April 29, 1953—three weeks after that year's NBA playoffs had ended.

And at one point, the NBA had been touched directly. It came out, during the 1952-53 season, that one of the league's referees, Sol Levy, had received $3,000 in bribes to affect the outcome of three games in 1950. Fortunately for the NBA, everyone seemed to take Levy's immediate dismissal in stride, without projecting further suspicions. But it was a subject that could not be brushed aside.

Other troubles were building, too, behind closed doors. The deceptive serenity and solidification of 1951-53 was about to be shattered on three fronts—the game itself, financial problems,

and gambling, all coming to a head in the 1953-54 season that seemed to be starting so calmly and optimistically.

To see them in context, however, we'll have to stop for a moment to examine the type of basketball that had evolved in the early '50s, which can be called the Mikan Era.

The Mikan Era

Rough.

That's the word for the brand of basketball evolved in the NBA during its first eight years.

It was a combination of college philosophy and old pro technique. The BAA founders had insisted upon, and had succeeded in planting, the collegiate enthusiasm, the uncompromising standard of maximum effort at all times that so many previous pro leagues had lacked. But the individual principles of established pro play were clearly the most effective—especially when added to such heightened motivation.

The result was a bruising, body-contact type of game. With so many large men moving quickly in a confined space, there was enough legitimate reason for accidental collision. But there were three distinct causes of collision-on-purpose, as well.

The first, and foremost, was test of manhood: as soon as possible, pros "put the question" (as Lapchick liked to say) to all newcomers. How much guts did the newcomer have? Establishing respect, therefore, was necessity number one for every new player. And the only way to establish respect was to hit back, promptly and effectively.

The second basic invitation to rough stuff was strategic. Obviously, the referees couldn't see everything, and couldn't call everything they did see. If they did, the whole game would quickly become a parade to the foul line, nullifying the very thing the owners were trying to sell—high-speed, college-style basketball.

For this condition, the owners were responsible. By being afraid to insist that the referees call a tight game because "it would slow up the action," they were encouraging their players and coaches to do more and more of the body contact that made slowing up the game inevitable. After all, if you gained an advantage by getting away with six belts out of 10, you gained still more by getting away with 12 out of 20, or 18 out of 30.

The third factor was embedded in the rules, and was as much of a problem in college and amateur basketball as in the pros: as a close game came nearer and nearer to the final buzzer, there were substantial tactical advantages to fouling. The fact that a basket was worth two points and a free throw only one made it worthwhile to try to trade a foul—which could cost one point—for a chance to score two points.

Among pros, then, such tactics took on greater value. On a pro team, almost every player was expected to be able to make his free throws under pressure—so if the defense decided to "give a foul," it might as well be a healthy enough whack to leave the victim a trifle shaken as he stepped to the free throw line. A few such "tactical" exchanges quickly led to emotional ones: tempers rose, retaliations became progressively rougher, and the referee's task became impossible.

For that matter, the referee's task was impossible to begin with. As the smaller towns came in, with single-minded fan support, the sense of being physically threatened by a mob was hard to shake. Coaches and home-team players systematically

incited the crowd. And the one person who could ease the situation—the owner—as often as not sat on the bench and added his screams to the rest.

If an owner, who is actually paying your salary and freely complaining about you to the press and in the privacy of league meetings, is actually on the bench during a game, jumping up and shouting insults, waving his fist in the air, stomping out into the court itself—if an owner acts this way, the message is hard to miss. He wants you to "let things go" (for his side only, of course) and he is, when all is said and done, the man who is paying the freight. So if you want to keep your career as a referee thriving, you give the man what he wants—not "favorable" calls, which would be dishonest, but a minimum of whistles, which is fair, honorable, and even conceptually defensible.

This ruggedness has to be stressed for two reasons—because it had such great effect on the reforms that were to follow in a few years, and because the charge of "sissiness" or "a game for goons" rankled so much. For plain physical punishment, the pro basketball player did not have to apologize to the football or hockey player.

Men who are merely tall, therefore, have no place in so athletic a game—and they didn't in the NBA, from the beginning. Those who were exceptionally tall were also tough, determined, muscular, well-coordinated, and blessed with endurance. Without these qualities, they couldn't last out a season.

And this was the factor that finally determined the style of play NBA teams produced: an abundance of big men who were not merely big, but talented athletes.

At the beginning, in the BAA days, the "big man" was only the center. Every team had someone in the 6-foot-8 to 6-foot-10 size range, but men between 6-foot-5 and 6-foot-8 could operate effectively at that position. (Gallatin was 6-foot-6, Groza 6-foot-7, Miasek 6-foot-7.)

When Mikan came along, he was the biggest of the centers, in bulk as well as in height, but he represented a difference only in degree. He was still the only really outsized man on his team.

The forwards, in those days, ranged from 6-foot-2 to 6-foot-6 and were still fundamentally what their name implied, the front line of offense. The idea was still to get as close to the basket as possible for a lay-up or an easy shot, so forwards did a lot of driving and helped with the rebounding.

The guards included many men well under six feet tall. A 6-foot-2 guard was considered tall, 6-foot-4 a freak.

The guards also still had classical functions: shoot from outside, deliver the ball to the forwards, drive in when possible.

The centers scored almost entirely from the pivot, by hooking or wheeling in, or on tap-ins and other rebounds. The good shooters among the guards still used the two-handed set shot as a primary weapon, but even one-hand shooters "set" themselves as often as they fired on the run. The new breed, the jump shooters a la Fulks, were almost always the corner men.

In this era, then, teams developed distinct personalities.

The Rochester Royals were, in a sense, the most perfect team. Davies and Wanzer could hit from far out, and drive. Risen could pivot, hand off, move, and rebound at center. Arne Johnson could hit the boards, and Jack Coleman could do that and score too. Holzman, like Davies and Wanzer, had the full complement of backcourt skills. All were reliable from the free throw line. But their biggest assets were balance, ball handling, and court sense. Their scoring was evenly distributed, they really looked for one another, and they were alert to all openings. In the six seasons between 1949 and 1954, the Royals won 266 regular season games while the Lakers won only 267, and the Royals actually finished ahead of them twice.

What made this so remarkable was the one Rochester deficiency: size. The Lakers, especially when they added Mikkelsen to Mikan and Pollard, simply overpowered the Royals in a show-down. Over those years, the Lakers defeated Rochester 38 times (including playoffs) and lost only 28 times—and that was enough to make it the Mikan Era instead of the Royals' Era. Against other teams, not so overmatched physically, Rochester won even more often than the Lakers did.

The Minneapolis game was simple, and, to many ardent fans, unattractive. Mikan, Mikkelsen, or Pollard would clear the defensive board when the opposition missed. The Lakers would bring the ball up slowly, waiting for the lumbering Mikan to get into position in the pivot. Then they would concentrate on getting the ball in to Big George, whose huge left elbow would open a swath as he turned in towards the basket. Since the opposition was concerned almost entirely with trying to stop Mikan somehow, or to keep the ball from going in to him, plenty of opportunities arose for Pollard, Mikkelsen, Martin, or any one else, to operate individually. And what anyone missed, one of the front three was likely to tap in.

It was simple—and it was effective. Mikan was simply too big in bulk to be blocked out. He couldn't jump very high, but didn't have to. He couldn't run, but didn't have to. But he had tremendous competitive fire and pride to go along with his size, and excellent timing, and knowledge of his assets. Determination was one of his most important characteristics.

Everything revolved around him. He scored more than anyone ever had, but not so much more as to distort statistics (as Wilt Chamberlain would later), because the slow-moving offense made the Lakers a relatively low-scoring team.

What Mikan was really proving, as the championships piled up, was the inescapable importance of possession of the ball. The well-schooled basketball people had always known that, of course; but now, even the casual fan couldn't miss it. The only answer to a team with Mikan on it was to get enough bigger players to attain an even break in rebounding—somehow, somewhere. People Mikan's size weren't easy to find, and some who were—Don Otten, Charlie Share, Larry Foust—never matched Mikan's abilities. More plentiful were players of comparable height who were considerably thinner, but perhaps more agile; and players in the 6-foot5 to 6-foot-8 range who could really leap.

So Mikan's presence intensified the search for "big men." A big center was no longer enough. Now you needed at least one rugged 6-foot-7 forward—to handle Mikkelsen, for instance. And a bigger backcourt man became useful too, since one of the ways to combat the big forwards was to maneuver them away from the basket to let the little men operate. Once the little men got inside, the 6-foot-2 man had the same advantage over the 5-foot-11 man that the 6-foot-8 had over the 6-foot-5: he could take him into the pivot.

By the end of the Mikan era, then, at least two men who would have been centers at the beginning of it were standard

equipment for every team, and backcourt men in the 6-foot-3 range were becoming common. For all teams, roughness and fouling were the central problems, precisely because getting possession through a rebound was so important, and so difficult when there was a discrepancy in size.

The owners recognized the problem. There was much talk about devising ways "to counteract the big man"—but what was really involved was counteracting the deliberate fouling used against the game the big men created, since it was perfectly plain that the stars of the future would be bigger and bigger—and better.

The closer the game, the worse the problem. Just when excitement should be reaching its peak, a tight battle deteriorated into foul trading. The team that was ahead by a few points, confident of its ability to handle the ball, (since these were pros), did not try to score; it sat back and tried to run out the clock. If the trailing team fouled, to try to trade one point for two, the leading team fouled right back. Yet, the trailing team had to keep fouling and hope for a miss, since there was no other way to try to win.

For the 1950-51 season—the first "shakedown" season after the merger, when the league was down to 11 teams—a new rule was tried. In the last three minutes of the game, there would be a jump ball after every successful free throw (but not, naturally, after the first try of a two-shot foul). This meant a team couldn't be sure of getting possession even after the free throw, so that "trading one for two" took on an added element of risk.

It helped a little—but only a little. All it really did was push up the foul-trading segment to before the three-minute mark. And it didn't really deter. For instance, in the third game of the final round of the playoffs, at the 69th Regiment Armory in New York, the Royals had a six-point lead over the Knicks with four and a half minutes to play. The Knicks rallied, and cut this margin to 62-61 just as the three-minutes-to-play point was reached.

In the next 70 seconds, the Royals shot—and made—seven consecutive one-shot fouls. They won the game 78-71.

For the next season, 1951-52, the jump-ball rule was applied to the last two minutes, instead of three. But a more important change was made, this one aimed directly at the big centers and specifically at Mikan. The free-throw lane, the area in which an offensive player is not allowed to be for more than three seconds, was widened from six to 12 feet.

This meant that Mikan (or anyone else) had to take up his pivot position further from the basket—six feet away instead of three feet away. It meant an extra step in wheeling in, and a changed trajectory on hook shots—and a much better shot at the rebound for the defensive team. It also meant that the alley for driving was opened up. In every respect, this was a progressive change, which proved permanent, although it failed partially in its primary objective: Mr. Mikan adjusted quite well. His scoring average did drop from 28.4 to 23.8, and the scoring championship did go to Arizin (with 25.4), but Mikan and the Lakers did win the playoffs, which they had not done the previous year. They won the next two championships, too, although Mikan's scoring totals continued to drop—as much in response to better balance among the Lakers and the acceptance of the percentages, as from any "impossibility" created for the big man.

By now, the tireless and fertile imaginations of the pros had found a new flaw in the jump-ball rule. The jump was between the man who was fouled and the man who committed the foul. All you had to do, then, was to have your big man foul their little man, and the chances were you'd get the ball after the jump. So, for the 1952-53 season, the rule was changed: now the jump would be between the man who was fouled and "the player whom the fouled player was playing immediately before"—in other words, the normal match-up.

None of this was having much effect, and game after game was ending in shambles. The players and coaches complained, the referees suffered, the owners squabbled about which team was getting an advantage in which game—and the customers showed their disapproval in the most convincing fashion, by walking out and not coming back. Early in the 1950-51 season, two particular games focused attention on the inherent weaknesses in the rules.

On November 22, 1950, at Minneapolis, the Fort Wayne Pistons defeated the Lakers—19-18. Among their other advantages, the Lakers had a home court that was shorter and narrower than normal, which made their bulk all the more effective and their lack of speed less significant. The Pistons, who were a pretty rugged bunch themselves, simply held the ball out.

Less than two weeks later, in Rochester, the Royals played a five-overtime game with Indianapolis, the longest ever played in the league. What could be more exciting? Lots of things. In this one, during each of the overtime periods, the team that got the tap merely held the ball for one last shot. Even the rabid Rochester fans, with their team on its way to a championship, first booed and then walked out in droves while the game was still on. Finally, the Olympians won, 75-73.

Bad as things were during the regular schedule, they were much worse in playoffs, because the stakes were greater. The tighter the game, the more fouls; the more fouls, the more bickering about the ones that weren't called; the more bickering, the more frustration for all concerned—no dignity in winning, a feeling of being cheated in losing.

At this point, the referees were living under siege, permanent villains no matter what they did. From time to time they would need police protection in leaving an arena. The rough play led to frequent fistfights among players, which in turn incited the courtside fans and added to the hysterical atmosphere.

For the 1953-54 season, the most gimmicky rule tried yet was adopted. In an attempt to reduce fouling, each player was limited to two personals committed in any one period; if he committed a third, he had to sit out the rest of the quarter—although his game limit was still six.

Nothing helped. In one of the 1953 playoff games, Boston and Syracuse battled through four overtimes, before Boston won, 111-105. In that game, Bob Cousy scored 50 points—with only 10 baskets and 30 free throws. For all the playoff games that year, the average was 80 free throw attempts per game (40 for each team).

In such circumstances, the stronger teams were virtually unbeatable on their own courts.

What was happening, then, was all too clear. For all the improved financial stability, the shaking out of weaker franchises, the opportunity for attention afforded by college basketball's burst bubble, the influx of new stars, and the traditions

already established, the NBA was starting to fail in its one crucial aspect—the product. The game itself was going the way so many pro leagues had taken it in the past, towards oblivion.

But the owners, now more involved in acting like rabid fans than like businessmen, weren't ready to face up to the facts. The 1953-54 season would force them to.

The Brink of Disaster

The NBA owners, who called themselves the Board of Governors, had every reason to feel optimistic as they looked ahead to the 1953-54 season—as long as they were willing (and stubbornly eager) to ignore the deterioration of their game on the floor.

During the previous season, the Dumont Television Network had televised 14 Saturday afternoon games. Now NBC was ready to step in with a larger program, and this was Podoloff's pet. He might still not know too much about the technicalities of basketball, but as a businessman he certainly grasped the importance of nationwide television exposure. Pretty soon, the bustling little figure of Podoloff, moving up and down the sidelines during televised games and being interviewed polysyllabically whenever possible, was to be a familiar sight on home screens.

And what would the expanded audience see? A compact nine-team circuit in which all the teams had at least four years of continuous identity behind them. Indianapolis had finally dropped out, but that was a small loss, since Groza and Beard had been caught. Syracuse, Fort Wayne, and Milwaukee had bright new arenas, municipally built, to play in. The league structure was certainly in the best shape it had ever been in.

The players were a dream. So many exciting ones were coming out of the college ranks that the effects of the scandals were all but forgotten. Clyde Lovellette, of Kansas, the giant of the college season of 1952, had decided to join Minneapolis as Mikan's heir apparent after spending a year in the AAU ranks. Another star abandoning the AAU was George Yardley, joining Fort Wayne.

Coming out of college was Walter Dukes, a seven-footer who had led Seton Hall through an undefeated season. From Columbia, there was 6-foot-7 Jack Molinas, who had performed a similar feat for the Lions in 1951 as a sophomore. There was also Ray Felix, a skinny 6-foot-11 LIU product who had not been touched by the scandals because, as a sophomore, he had been simply left out of the deals.

However, there was a booby trap in each of these promising elements.

The television program languished. The individual owners couldn't look beyond selfish interests: who was to get more money by having his team make more TV appearances? Who wanted to schedule a Saturday afternoon game when a Saturday night game would draw more at the gate? Instead of pulling together and making the televised games as attractive as possible, they bogged down in bickering for small advantages. Here, again, the basic conflict of interest showed itself. Irish, with the Knicks now the most important feature of Garden basketball, had little interest in the small fees television could bring. He wanted the big live crowds. For the shoestring operators in smaller cities, on the other hand, no fee looked small and every

little bit of exposure was welcome. Podoloff, siding as usual with the have-nots, never succeeded in arranging a TV schedule that gave the uncommitted audience the best available games instead of the games particular owners wanted most to sell.

On the matter of franchise stability, a cruel trick had been played on one member, through no fault of his own or of the league. When Kerner moved from Tri-Cities to Milwaukee, it was a major step up in class, even though Milwaukee could hardly be considered a hotbed of basketball interest. Still, he had brought a major-league sport to a city that didn't have any such representation, and that resented being in Chicago's shadow. With a new, 11,000-seat arena to play in, he had all the building blocks of a success, and during the first year there had done well.

Then, without warning, in March of 1953, the Boston Braves moved to Milwaukee. Suddenly, Milwaukee was a major league baseball town, wild about its new status, commercially committed to giving baseball every support. Suddenly, Kerner and the NBA were forgotten and ignored.

Since the Baltimore franchise was also struggling, and Philadelphia was having lean years, one-third of the league wasn't as solid as it had seemed a few months before.

And a snag developed on the player front, too.

The Knicks, having finished first in the East, with a record second only to Minneapolis', did not rate a high draft choice—but they were confronted with an embarrassment of riches. Under the territorial draft rule, they could pick Dukes, Molinas, or Felix, generally regarded as the three most desirable properties.

Irish chose—characteristically—the one with the biggest reputation, Dukes. Baltimore, picking first in the regular draft, grabbed Felix. The next pick was Milwaukee's, and Kerner took Bob Houbregs. Then Fort Wayne took Molinas.

It soon appeared that Irish had guessed wrong all around. Again characteristically, he refused to meet the $17,000 bonus that the Globetrotters gave Dukes, and wound up with nothing. Felix, who would have been grateful to join the Knicks on any terms, went on to become the rookie of the year and the number five scorer in the league—ranking between Schayes and Mikan—under Bee's tutelage.

And Molinas, in the first half of the season, proved himself a real find, all doubt about his talents dispelled. He had the shots, the mobility and the size to be a major-league.

But he also had something else: a desire to gamble.

In late December, the news broke. Through Ike Gellis, sports editor of the *New York Post*, Podoloff had been informed that there were rumors about Molinas. An investigation led to direct questioning of Molinas by Podoloff and Zollner. Molinas would admit only that he had bet small sums, occasionally, and only on his own team to win. Even this, however, was enough for Podoloff to act upon. The player contract specifically prohibited betting of any sort on any game played by an NBA club.

Podoloff acted promptly, and was backed up unanimously for once. Molinas was barred, period. Further investigations were conducted and nothing was turned up to indicate that any other player had been involved. ("A personal psychiatric aberration," Podoloff called it, and years later no one could deny that Molinas had his own strange attitudes about the subject. After becoming a lawyer, and striving repeatedly for reinstatement, Molinas was found in the fixer's role in a new wave of college

scandals, and actually went to prison.)

There was no mistaking the shudder that went through the NBA at this point.

For the first time, the scandal had touched the pros directly. Was it just Molinas? Had the cancer really been caught in time and cut out?

As things turned out, however, the Molinas case was a turning point. Because there was no terrible aftermath, because no further incidents cropped up, and because this one had been faced frankly and investigated instead of glossed over, faith in the league's integrity took firmer root than it might have otherwise.

Meanwhile, an immediate improvement of image was needed, something to counteract the ugly thoughts. Fortunately, it was at hand.

The 1954 All-Star Game had been scheduled for January 21 at Madison Square Garden. After the first two All-Star games in Boston, which were Walter Brown's personal productions, the third had been played in Fort Wayne (and won by the West, 79-75, with Mikan the outstanding player).

Now this extravaganza was to be put on, for the first time, in the most appropriate setting, that Mecca of basketball that still had such glamorous connotations for all players and most of the public. And the boys really put on a show.

Ray Felix, the skinny, awkward rookie whose reflexes were never first-rate, played Mikan—and played him even most of the game. Pollard, meanwhile, made six baskets in the first half en route to a 23-point total, high for the game. Davies and Wanzer on one side, Cousy and McGuire with Sharman on the other, set off backcourt fireworks that had the crowd of 16,478 ecstatic.

With seven minutes to play in the game, the West was ahead, 73-69. But the East roared back, led 76-73, was caught, and went into the final minute with an 82-80 lead.

Lapchick sent in Cousy, to kill the remaining 50 seconds by dribbling—but Davies stole the ball, drove and tied it up with 33 seconds left. Cousy, biding his time for a final shot, sent up a long one-hander with only three seconds to go, and made it, for an 84-82 lead. But the West was able to call time out, then get the ball in to Mikan, who wheeled on Felix—and was fouled.

With the clock showing one second to play, George calmly stepped to the line and sank the two free throws, sending the game into overtime.

In the extra period, Cousy went wild. He hit from outside, he drove in for a three-pointer, and then sank five more free throws as the game ran out, a 98-93 victory for the East, all the while dribbling to kill time and passing perfectly.

This spectacular game gave the basketball world something to talk about for weeks, when something positive and exhila-rating was most needed.

For the rest of the season, close pennant races maintained interest. The Knicks finished first in the East again, but didn't clinch first until the next to last day of the season, as Syracuse and Boston tied for second, two games behind. In the West, the Lakers beat out Rochester by a two-game margin also. Neil Johnston won the scoring title again, with a 24.4 average, but no other player in the league succeeded in averaging 20 points or more. In fact, the team average of 79.5 points per game was the lowest since 1947-48, the league's second year. This decrease in scoring was a symptom of the increased roughness and orientation toward fouling.

Then came the playoffs. Shambles.

One of the worst ideas ever to come out of the councils of the Board of Governors was the playoff pattern for 1954. When the Indianapolis team had folded, leaving the Western Division with four teams, it was no longer possible to have four teams qualify for the playoffs. To accommodate three teams in the first round, a round robin was devised. Having just completed a 72-game schedule, the top three teams in each division would now play a six-game round robin, each pair playing once at home and once away—to eliminate one of the three. The two survivors would then have a two-out-of-three semi-final, and the usual best-of-seven final would follow.

Although this was as silly a procedure as one could find, it wasn't, in itself, the cause of the shambles. Fouling was.

Once again, one game symbolized things out of proportion. The Knicks, having finished first, were crushed by the Celtics in the first game of the round robin at home, then beaten at Syracuse. In between, Syracuse nipped Boston in overtime.

That meant that the Knicks had to win at Boston to stay alive, since Syracuse already had two victories. This could be Boston's second, and it would leave the Knicks with only a meaningless game to play against Syracuse if they lost.

It happened to fall on Saturday afternoon, March 20—on national television. The game encompassed all the repulsive fea-tures of the grab-and-hold philosophy. It lasted three hours, and the final seconds of a one-point game were finally abandoned by the network. The arguments with the referees were interminable and degrading. What had been happening, as a matter of course, in dozens of games for the last couple of years, was shown to a nationwide audience in unadulterated impurity.

Boston won, 79-78. The round robin was completed, with Syracuse beating the Knicks and Boston again—and then Syracuse beat Boston two more times in the next round. In the West, the Royals and Lakers followed the same cumbersome pro-cedure to get rid of Fort Wayne, which had finished third any-how, and then the Lakers took two out of three from the Royals.

In the final round, Syracuse managed to push the Lakers through a full seven-game series before yielding. The Nats had no physical means of coping with Mikan, Lovellette, and Mikkelsen, even though George was slowing down. He was now 30 years old and thinking of retirement. But it was all anti-climax now. A Syracuse-Minneapolis final—"minor-league cities"—was not calculated to absorb the American public in early April, with the baseball season starting.

The identity of the cities involved in the finals, the foul-filled style of play, the touch of scandal—all these things represented the final triumph of the "old pro" context represented by the old National League over the "college-style" idea with which the BAA started. Two-thirds of the nine-team league now had noth-ing whatever to do with arena control, even indirectly. Of the original three, the Knicks had prospered but had been touched most closely by the college scandals and had not succeeded in bringing home the big prize, a playoff title; the Celtics, too, had never become quite good enough and had cost Brown hundreds of thousands of dollars; and the Warriors had passed entirely into Gottlieb's hands, making him an owner-coach like Bee and Harrison. And although few people put it in such terms, it was

a fact that no league in which three of the nine teams have owner-coaches can have big-league aura or reality.

The original dream, it seemed, was gone, and not only that—the whole league might go. As the 1954 season ended, the ostriches on the Board of Governors could no longer escape confrontation with their weaknesses. They were being vilified on all sides as "bush league," and whatever merit there was to such a charge, the attitudes that invited it could not be separated from the unsatisfactory quality of the games themselves.

Something had to be done. Promptly. Something was.

The New Rule

On April 22, 1954, the NBA owners met. The playoff fiasco had come to an end only 10 days before. The Molinas case still sent shivers of apprehension through many minds. The financial problems in Milwaukee and Baltimore were acute. The television ratings—and income—had been unsatisfactory. And from all sides, criticism of the league's games and "bush league qualities" was reaching new intensity.

One radical idea was in the air, but less often discussed than most others: a time limit on one team's possession of the ball without attempting a shot. At last, a radical solution found fertile soil. At last, the owners were ready to admit their difficulties weren't trivial. They decided to put petty pursuits of minor advantages aside and to really seek something better.

Danny Biasone, of Syracuse, got behind the time limit idea. He proposed a 24-second rule: each team would have to take a shot at the basket within 24 seconds of getting full possession of the ball. That Biasone would suggest it was significant. This short, somewhat dour, rather unpolished man had come in through the National League merger. He wasn't given to making long speeches, but when he did speak, he said exactly what he meant, his Italian origins a trifle audible in his vowels—and then lived up to what he said.

He represented no major financial power. His city was not essential to the league. He was not one of the arena operator originals, with prior associations with Irish, Brown, Podoloff, or Winter. He was not an independent millionaire like Zollner. In the acrimonious rivalries that marked those years, he had insisted on his right to sit on his team's bench, to root, and to bait referees. When the Nats and Knicks had some of their bitter battles, he had been singled out by Irish—to the press—as the sort of "small town" owner that the league didn't need.

Underneath, however, those who came to know Biasone better found a man with intense loyalties and great common sense. In this crisis, his common sense and sincerity proved priceless.

Biasone had arrived at 24 seconds as the time limit by the simple method of dividing the number of shots taken in typical games into time played. Twenty-four seconds meant 120 shots a game—60 per team. In the season just completed, each team had averaged 75-80 shots per game. Obviously, the new rule would not be too restrictive. And 24 seconds was a long time. A team had to get the ball past the centerline within 10 seconds anyhow; usually this took only two or three. And the average basketball play, with a couple of cuts off the pivot and other maneuvers, seldom took as long as 10 seconds to execute. Without a limit, the NBA had averaged about one shot every 18 seconds. The new rule would be reasonable.

It was adopted.

But it wasn't enough by itself, they could see that.

A time limit, by itself, might encourage more fouling. If the offense had to shoot within 24 seconds, it might be a good idea to foul it first, and give up one point instead of two. Some way had to be found to nullify the strategic advantage of fouling.

The answer was: a limit on team fouls. Up to now, the only limitation in basketball had been applied to the individual player: six personals, and he was out of the game. Now the fouls would be charged against the team as well as against the man—and only six team fouls per quarter were to be permitted. After that, every additional foul committed would cost an extra free throw: if on an ordinary one-shot foul, an extra free throw for an extra point; if on what would be a two-shot foul (in the act of shooting, for instance), three chances to make two points.

In this way, an extra foul would be too great a price to pay deliberately. Once the quota of six was used up, a foul would mean a near certainty of two points (among the good pro foul shooters). Since one didn't have to foul to get possession—the 24-second rule took care of that—it was better to try to force a missed field goal than to give up two free throws.

This combination, the time limit on shooting and the team limit on fouls, saved the NBA.

Literally.

The game that resulted was so superior that, in retrospect, all concerned were soon willing to admit that without this change the league would have died. That the basic idea was sound was soon confirmed by the fact that international amateur rules (including the Olympics and eventually college rules) were changed accordingly.

Two important refinements went along with the new rules. Since the whole purpose was to reduce or eliminate strategic fouling, offensive fouls could be punished differently. The team that already had the ball had nothing to gain from committing a foul; offensive fouls were always overzealous attempts to score. Therefore, the penalty was changed as follows: the individual player was still charged with a personal, towards his own limit of six, but the team was not; and the victimized team did not get a free throw, but only possession of the ball out of bounds. An offensive foul, made in an attempt to score, was thus more properly punished by the deprivation of a chance to score—and the long walks to the foul line at the other end of the floor, which used to be the annoying aftermath of offensive fouls, were eliminated.

The other refinement was the backcourt foul, meaning anything beyond the center line. This automatically called for two shots now—so there was no sense fouling a man before he got into scoring range, to save seconds in the closing moments.

In that one meeting, the NBA owners accomplished more than they had in eight years, although the magnitude of their achievement was not seen at the time, even by them.

Over the summer, as special 24-second clocks were designed, built and tested, they looked ahead to the 1954-55 season with trepidation as deep as the unjustified optimism they had experienced the year before.

(Excerpted from 24 Seconds to Shoot: The Birth and Improbable Rise of the NBA, *by Leonard Koppett, with permission from Sport Media Publishing, Inc.)*

Original Celtics, 1923
The first great team, the Original Celtics, featuring (left to right), Johnny Beckman, Johnny Whittey, Nat Holman, Jack Barry and Chris Leonard.

Chapter 5

The Original Celtics

Basketball was their religion, and they spread their gospel all over, wherever you could put up a couple of baskets and attract a crowd.

By Tom Meany
SPORT Magazine, February 1949

It was balmy that Winter in Miami, perhaps the balmiest Winter Florida's great resort city ever was to know, both as to weather and real estate prices. The great hurricane of 1926 was still many months away. In fact, it wasn't until the following September that it came swooshing out of the Caribbean to send buildings and prices tumbling.

The great storm was still in the future, and January and February were months of enjoyment. Every night was New Year's Eve; every afternoon was the Fourth of July. Jack Dempsey, still the heavyweight king, was building a hotel—as who wasn't in Miami in those days?—and looking for an "added attraction." William Jennings Bryan, the Great Commoner, was lending his silver tongue to the sale of lots in Coral Gables, so Dempsey cast about for an antidote. He chose, of all people, the Original Celtics, the greatest basketball team the world had ever seen.

It was a lucrative lark for the Celtics, as were all their basketball junkets in those days. They went Julius Caesar one better, for they came, they saw, they conquered—and they had a rollicking good time. Along with Bryan, with Al Schacht and Nick Altrock, the baseball comedy team, the Celtics, too, made their contribution to the sound and fury of Miami in that hectic season.

Soon it was time for the Celtics to go to work again. Jim Furey, their energetic and industrious manager, had booked them for a game in Chattanooga, Tennessee. There were complications, too, as there so often were in those pioneering days of professional basketball. Nat Holman, one of the most valued operatives on the Celtics roster, had to return to New York for business reasons.

Losing a player, even a star like Holman, never bothered the Celtics. One of their members happened to find Benny Borgmann, a star scorer from Paterson, New Jersey, at a dog track one night. So Benny was brought along, like many others before and since, to wear the shamrock jersey and be a member of the Original Celtics, even if only for a one-night stand.

It was characteristic of the Celtics that they neither knew nor cared how many miles it was from Miami to Chattanooga. Furey merely booked a game for them and they went and played it. The next stop was always just around the corner as far as the Celtics were concerned. That Chattanooga was almost as far from Miami as Chicago is from New York came as a distinct surprise to the Celts, the most traveled of all basketball teams but also the most disinterested as to the details of their journeys.

"We were dog-dirty and tired when we got off the train at Chattanooga," recalls Dutch Dehnert. "There were a bunch of guys on the platform, a committee or something, to greet the great Celtics. And there we were, five of us—Johnny Beckman, Pete Barry, Joe Lapchick, Borgmann, and me. And crummy-looking too, after being on the train about 20 hours.

"Naturally, these guys want to know where the rest of the squad is. So Beckie says, 'This is all there is, there isn't any more.' Then he tells them they can cut out the sightseeing tour they had planned for us, just get us to the hotel, let us get a hot bath, a shave, and an hour's nap. 'We'll be in the dressing room at eight,' he tells them although it is then nearly five.

"Well, I don't know about the others, but they had a tough time waking me up at seven thirty. Beckman is going around whacking us on the soles of our feet with a shoe to get us out of bed.

"We were playing in some auditorium, and they had a good crowd with lots of standees. The club we were playing was the Chattanooga Railites, a local industrial outfit and rated pretty good. They were already out on the court when we come on, about a dozen of them in nice new uniforms, zipping the ball around and putting on a great show.

"They stopped to watch us when we came out, and I'll never forget how surprised they looked. The crowd started to give us a hand and then stopped almost before it started. There had been no time to get our uniforms laundered, and we looked like five guys who'd just wandered in off the street.

"There was silence when we started to warm up, because we just stood back and took lazy pop shots and lobbed the ball to one another. The crowd didn't know what to make of it. They probably figured they'd been jobbed, and the promoter had rung in a lot of stumble-bums. Finally, we broke a sweat and practiced a little faster and then the game got under way.

"Lapchick was a dandy at getting the tap. We had set plays from the tap, which no other club had ever heard of in those days. Beckie went in and took the first tap from Joe, passed over his head to me, and I went under and laid one up, coming up from guard position. Then Lapchick batted the next tap back to Barry, the other guard, and Pete dribbled in to score. We must have scored eight goals in two minutes, and we're in front 30 to 1 before there's a time out.

"The Railites were using a standing guard, something which

has long since gone out of basketball. This fellow stood right on his own foul line and never went up-court, even when his own club had the ball.

"In the time out, Beckman said, 'We'll have to move that guard out of there. He's breaking up our passes when we cut.' Then I volunteered to stand in front of him, explaining that instead of him breaking up our passes, they could pass to me and I could give it back.

"When play was resumed, I moved up in front of this fellow. Beckman passed to me and I passed to Borgmann, who was coming in from the other side. Then Barry passed to me, kept coming, and I passed right back to him. All of a sudden a great light dawned, and I took time out.

"We all went into a huddle and discussed the possibilities of this maneuver we had accidentally hit on. Beckman was enthusiastic, and we knew if Beckie liked it we had something, because Johnny was the smartest man who ever played basketball.

"This was the pivot play, but we didn't even know it at the time. A couple of minutes later, however, the standing guard, in an effort to bat the ball out of my hands, moved around to my right side. All I had to do was pivot to my left, take one step, and lay the ball up for a basket."

⊛ ⊛ ⊛

This, then, is the story, among other things, of the birth of the pivot play, one of the many great contributions the Celtics made to basketball. The manner in which it was developed was characteristic of the Shamrock five. Looking for something new, they stumbled on this efficacious play by accident. If the birth of the pivot play was accidental that night in Chattanooga, however, its subsequent development through the years was deliberate. The Celts knew a good thing when they saw it. They were to basketball what the Baltimore Orioles were to baseball just before the turn of the century. You'll recall that it was the Orioles of John McGraw and Hughey Jennings, of Uncle Wilbert Robinson and Kid Gleason, who brought most of the current strategic refinements into baseball—the hit-and-run, the delayed steal, the double steal, the drag bunt, and many more.

The beginnings of the Celtics, who did much the same for the cage game, are lost in what passes for antiquity in basketball. The late Garry Schmeelk, one of the greatest shots professional basketball ever knew, told me back in 1941 that he didn't think one basketball fan in a thousand could name the Original Celtics. Schmeelk, long since retired from the courts by this time, operated a package store on New York's West Side. In the window he had a group picture of the "original" Original Celtics, if you'll overlook the redundancy.

Schmeelk offered any of his customers, a case of liquor of their own choosing if they could identify the players. He never had to give up so much as a dram. The players in the photograph were Hart, McCormick, Goggin, Mally, Calhoun, Witte, Barry, and F. McCormick, the latter, judging from the picture, a brother of uninitiated McCormick. Witte and Barry went on with the more famous Celtics but this squad, captioned "New York Celtics, 1914-17" undoubtedly was the original squad. The others dropped out before the Celtics became nationally known.

It was some five years later before the Celtics began their march to glory. In the Winter of 1922-23, Jim Furey, a far-seeing promoter, took the first step that was to bring order out of chaos in basketball. There were hundreds of basketball teams at that time. They were teams in the sense that they were uniformed and had a court on which to play, but not teams in the sense that they played together as such. Their composition was not static. Players were with one team one night and with another, quite possibly their opponents of the night before, on the next. Informal, what?

It was here that the genius of Furey asserted itself. He hired the Seventy-first Regiment Armory in Manhattan for Sunday nights and organized the Original Celtics to play for him and solely for him. There was to be no more wildcat barnstorming, no more playing at so much a night. The Celtics signed contracts with him and were guaranteed straight salaries, instead of having to depend on varying pay scales on a per game basis. These were the first individual contracts in the history of basketball, although previously promoters had reached the point of signing team contracts when scheduling games.

The members of this first Celtic team were Pete Barry, who appeared in the 1914-17 group picture, Dutch Dehnert, Horse Haggerty, Johnny Beckman, Joe Trippe, and Ernie Reich. The latter, who died while still at the height of his playing career, was a brother of the heavyweight prizefighter, Al Reich, who later was to achieve a modicum of fame as the bodyguard for Dr. John F. (Jafsie) Condon in the Lindbergh kidnapping case. The team was coached by another veteran of the 1914 group, Johnny Witte.

These were the Original Celtics as the public came to know them—a squad of six men, you'll note, although Coach Witte could play in a pinch. Later there were important additions—Nat Holman and Chris Leonard from the New York Whirlwinds, Joe Lapchick from the Brooklyn Visitations, Davey Banks, Carl Husta, and Nat Hickey.

⊛ ⊛ ⊛

If the Celtics had a great tradition, they also had a bizarre one. Organized as a neighborhood team in 1914, remnants of this great team were playing as late as 1942. There was a Winter or two when the squad put its shamrock insignia under the banner of Kate Smith, the radio songstress. Through her business manager, Ted Collins, himself an old basketball player, now the owner of the Boston football Yankees, Miss Smith took the Celtic deficits and tried to keep the club afloat at the old Hippodrome. The Hipp is gone now and so are the Celtics—except in the memories of those who saw them when they were an almost legendary team on the court.

What the Celtics had, over and above all else, was pride in their organization, the same fierce pride which made the Orioles the terrors of baseball in the 1890's. Whether it was a league contest or an exhibition game, they wanted to win. And they did, too, most of the time.

Witte was called out of retirement to handle the revived Celtics back in the early 30's. Lapchick, Dehnert, and Barry decided to go barnstorming. They picked up two additional players from their rivals, (the Visitations), in the person of Willie Scrill, as aggressive a player as ever wore rubber soles and John (Red) Conaty who could go and grab a tap with any

player who over lived.

"It was then we found out we weren't the Celtics any longer," related Lapchick years later to Leonard Lewin, N. Y. *Daily Mirror* basketball writer. "We were beaten badly in Philadelphia. Then we played a few more games, looking worse each time. Witte called us together and said:

"'Let's call it off, fellas. Let's not drag the reputation of the Celtics in the mud. It took too long to build it up.'

"And Johnny meant it. He was taking himself right out of a job, but he didn't care. He felt that the genuine, deep pride he had—and all of us had—in the great name of the Celtics was worth more than trying to squeeze a last few extra dollars out of that name."

What had happened to the Celtics was what happens to all great sports organizations. As Dehnert bluntly put it, "We got old on ourselves."

Not only did the Celtics get old on themselves, but so did the entire game of professional basketball in the East. It virtually died out until it was reborn in the Basketball Association of America, with the New York Knickerbockers, now coached by Lapchick, playing in Madison Square Garden and the 69th Regiment Armory, and the pro game then spreading out among other BAA teams around the country.

As the Celtics and their contemporaries aged, the game of professional basketball underwent a change, subtle at first and then at a pace which might be called "to hell in a bucket." And not the bucket play Dutch Dehnert set up that night in Chattanooga, either.

In an effort to compensate for their lost speed, the Celtics, and others, slowed down the game. Basketball began to resemble wrestling, and to enjoy about the same popularity as the mat game did around the big city, which was nil at that time. The Shamrocks once played Fort Wayne, Indiana, for a championship and won by the unbelievable low score of 16 to 15. This was under the old center-tap rules, of course, but under any rules it hardly was a score for a championship game.

College teams began to copy the Celtics' style, to the detriment of the game itself. One of the most successful teams between 1929 and 1931 was St. John's, of Brooklyn, called the "Wonder Five." With Max Posnack employed in the pivot, St. John's, then coached by Buck Freeman who was later succeeded by Lapchick, controlled the ball for most of the game. Back court, their superb passing enabled them to maintain possession almost at will. When Posnack went into the bucket, St. John's could maintain possession interminably. It was slick—and very uninteresting—basketball. St. John's once kept a fine City College team scoreless from the floor for 38 consecutive minutes. In another game, the Wonder Five held Manhattan College scoreless from the field for the entire contest—if "contest" is the right word for this particular affair.

While the Middle West was employing fast-break basketball and filling the field houses of the Big Ten, the East was stressing possession and sneering at the Midwestern game as being "fire-horse basketball." While the purists of the East remained aloof, basketball boomed in the West. Nearly all the top-flight pros went into Fort Wayne, Chicago, Detroit, and Oshkosh for jobs. A pro basketball player in Sheboygan, Wisconsin, could make more than one in New York.

When the intercollegiate rules restricted the number of seconds a player could stand in the bucket position, eliminated the center tap, and forced the team with the ball to bring it past mid-court and into the attack zone within 10 seconds, basketball became a different, and better, game. The East had to go along or wither on the vine.

Before the Celtics passed out entirely, they had one brief fling of sunset glory. Playing now with a six-man squad and comparatively for peanuts, the Celts booked two games on a Sunday. One was in the afternoon at Hoboken, New Jersey where they were made to look bad against a team which wouldn't have belonged on the same court with them in older days. The other game was booked at night for the Renaissance Casino in Harlem against the popular "Rens," one of the greatest of all Negro teams.

After the Hoboken debacle in the afternoon, Ray Kennedy, the sixth man on the Celts, announced he was through. That left Manager Witte with five men to face the Rens. But Dutch Dehnert suddenly got word that his mother was dying. He hastened to her bedside and the Celtics had four players left—and two hours in which to dig up a fifth.

Witte thought of Johnny Beckman. He took a handful of nickels and disappeared into a phone booth. He finally located Beckman in a tavern he was operating in Elizabeth, New Jersey and told him about the Celtics' plight.

"I'm retired, Johnny," Beckie argued. "I haven't had a uniform on or a basketball in my hand for a couple of years."

"Look, Beckie," said Witte, "the Celtics need you."

That did it. "I'll see you at the hall," responded Beckman. "Get me some things."

Among the "things" Witte collected for Beckman that night were a pair of basketball shoes owned by Cappy Ricks, the great Negro ball handler—shoes which were two sizes too large for Beckman. The shoes were what Lapchick called "two-step shoes," meaning that Beckman had to take two steps before he was able to move one.

When the game was over, Beckman, 39 years old and for some seasons retired from basketball, had led the Celtics to a surprising victory. It was not only a victory, but a most decisive one. He was top scorer in the game with 13 points—good going in those days. And the soles of his feet were like two slices of raw beef, the result of the blisters he raised while racing up and down the floor in Cappy's "two-step shoes."

Nevertheless, it was a happy Beckman who accepted the congratulatory thumps of his sweaty teammates.

"Thanks for having me back, fellas," said he. "It was great to do it just once more."

"And now, Beckie," said Witte, "here's your share of the guarantee."

"I don't want any money," declared Beckman. "I enjoyed myself too much to be paid."

The stubborn Witte insisted Beckman take his rightful cut of the gate. Equally as stubbornly, Beckie refused. Finally he thought of a compromise.

"Tell you what we'll do," grinned Beckie. "Gimme the money and we'll go out and drink it up."

All agreed this was an eminently fair proposition.

⊛ ⊛ ⊛

To get a proper perspective on the Celtics, the reader must condition himself to the realization that the Shamrock players were pioneers. They lived as pioneers did—from day to day, from game to game. No team of today would go out and drink up the receipts as the Celtics did after Beckman's return to glory. It wasn't habitual with the Celts, either, but in this particular case, they realized that they had reached the end of an era. They had seen the last performance of a player they believed the best who had ever played the game.

Like the professional baseball players of the period preceding the first World War, the Celtics were rough, earthy guys— "red necks," as the old-timers fondly refer to the diamond heroes of the second decade of this century.

⊛ ⊛ ⊛

Most of the Celtics came from a rough, brawling neighborhood on New York's West Side, a neighborhood which produced racketeers and statesmen, hoodlums and prelates. It also produced basketball players. In an area which ran North from 23rd St. to 29th St. and West from Eighth Avenue to Tenth Avenue, there sprang up at the same time some of the greatest basketball players the game has ever seen—Pete Barry, Johnny Witte, Ernie Reich, Johnny Beckman, Dutch Dehnert, and Nat Hickey.

Of this group, Barry, Witte, Reich, Dehnert, and Beckman were with the "original" Original Celtics—the first group organized by Jim Furey to play together as a unit. All, except Reich, who died while still an active player, went on to distinguish themselves as coaches in the game, Witte with his old teammates, Barry with Kate Smith's Celtics, Dehnert with teams in Detroit and Sheboygan, as well as an ex-GI team which won the Hearst Professional Basketball Tournament in Chicago, and Beckman with Baltimore in the American League. All this talent from one section of the city—an area which a pedestrian could completely cover at a leisurely pace within a half-hour's time.

The beginnings of the Celtics were rough. The leagues in which they played were rough.

Once, their backer was a mysterious gentleman named Donovan. He had been unearthed somewhere by Witte to bankroll the club. Donovan met the players once and once only. He explained that the pressure of his "outside business" would prevent him from spending much time with them, that he knew little about basketball, but that he had confidence in Witte. Most of the Celtics thought Mr. Donovan an engaging little chap, even though he didn't bother to explain what his "outside business" was.

They were soon to find out. Crossing Tenth Avenue one night, a sedan whizzed by Mr. Donovan, and there was a lot of popping which didn't come from the exhaust. Mr. Donovan was picked up full of lead and very dead. It seems he brewed and sold beer, a profession both profitable and precarious in those Volstead days. The gentlemen in the sedan were business rivals. And Witte went scurrying around to find a new backer, preferably one whose bankroll had been acquired in a more conservative business.

High jinks was the order of the day with the Celts. Their road trips were not only business ventures but gay excursions as well. There was that night in Hudson, New York, when

Beckman, on his way back to the hotel after the game, passed a delicatessen where several cases of milk were piled up in the doorway, with a huge cake of ice on top. Beckie picked up the cake of ice, which must have weighed 50 pounds, and lugged it into the hotel with him.

"Check this," said Beckman to the night clerk, as he slithered the block of ice along the counter of the desk. Instead of checking in the ice, the clerk checked out the Celtics.

⊛ ⊛ ⊛

None of the sanitation connected with modern basketball was found among the Shamrocks. They wore their uniforms for weeks on end without laundering them, simply because they never had time to have them laundered. Each man carried his own equipment in a small hand grip. The soiled, sweaty uniforms were stuffed in after each game, never to see daylight or feel fresh air until the following night when they were pulled out of the bag for the next game on the schedule. Eventually somebody would think of ordering a new set, and the old ones would be discarded.

Like the baseball Orioles, the Celtics thought physicians were only for the rich. They had their own home remedies for everything, most of them devised by Beckman, who must have had a touch of faith-healer, or witchdoctor in him.

Lapchick recalls being clawed up pretty thoroughly in one of the rougher games the Celtics played. A day later the scratches developed an infection. Beckman diagnosed, prescribed, and treated. He soaked a Turkish towel in steaming hot water and wrapped it tightly around Lapchick's arm. Then he proceeded to rub the scabs from Joe's arm with the towel. The final step was to pour a bottle of bootleg brandy over the open wounds.

"You'll be okay for tomorrow night, kid," said Beckman lightly. After all it wasn't his arm. The odd part of it was that Lapchick was able to play in the next game, although he didn't get much sleep after Beckie's ministrations.

But these were the Celtics, men among men. Basketball was their religion, and they set up altars in strange and faraway places. They spread the gospel through the Middlewest and the South, playing professional, amateur or college teams and, when time permitted, holding clinics after the game. So widespread was their fame that high school coaches sent their squads as far as 150 miles to see the Celts play when the team was in their region.

Because they were so far ahead of most of the contemporaries whom they met on these barnstorming tours, the Celtics had plenty of time in which to experiment. When they enjoyed a comfortable lead, they gave brilliant passing exhibitions without attempting to score. And after games they stayed up far into the night, talking basketball, arguing, discussing the game, working out new tactics.

Most teams of that era used a man-to-man defense. There was no time for team work in a sport in which players were constantly changing sides, and the men against whom you played tonight might be on your side tomorrow.

⊛ ⊛ ⊛

It was the Celtics who brought the "switch" into basketball, a play which is now standard equipment even with scholastic teams, just as the pivot play is. Before the advent of the switch, a player, asked how had he fared in the game, was likely to reply,

"I got three goals and my man only got one." It was strictly individual, with each player being responsible for the player who lined up opposite him at the tap-off.

Not the Celtics, however. They played the game as a team, not as individuals. When the other side had the ball, the Celtic player always guarded the man nearest, whether he was the personal opponent of that particular player or not. Lapchick found this all a little bewildering when he had served his apprenticeship with lesser clubs and was tapped for the Shamrocks.

"The rules for a center in those days," recalls Joe, "were for the center to get the tap and then get the hell out of the way, so he wouldn't get hurt. The tap, of course, was important then, since the ball was centered for a jump after each score, instead of merely at the beginning of each half or after a technical foul as is done now.

"I found out it was all different with the Celtics. A center had to work along with the rest of the team. And your defensive duties entailed more than merely guarding the fellow who jumped against you. They were constantly switching on the defense and I couldn't figure out how they did it, except by instinct. Certainly they never practiced it.

"As a result, I was always getting in somebody's way. My teammates were getting picked off right and left. There was a time when the Celtics considered dropping me because of my inability to switch.

"It was Johnny Witte who saved me. I consider Witte one of the greatest psychologists I've ever met, although Johnny would laugh in my face and tell me I was crazy if I told him he was a psychologist.

"All the others on the team were giving me tongue lashings and telling me what a dope I was not to be able to understand a simple thing like switching. And then Witte would take me aside and tell me what a great basketball player I was going to be, with my physical equipment and my speed, as soon as I mastered the technique.

"'It isn't how many goals you get, Joe,' Witte used to say, 'or how often you get the tap. We know what you can do *with* the ball. It's how good you are *without* the ball that determines how good a basketball player you are.'

"And there, I think Witte summed up the creed of the Celtics. It's how good you are *without* the ball that makes you a basketball player."

Basketball, as the Celtics played it, was a science. But their way of preparing for it was hardly scientific. Their Summers were lazed away with no attempt to stay in condition. Some of the fellows followed the ponies. One, indeed, made himself a bundle as a bookmaker. He used a couple of his teammates as runners. That was in the days of what was euphemistically known as "oral betting" at the New York tracks. The duties of a runner were to find out what odds rival bookies were quoting and, when necessary, to bet off some of the wagers their bookies had accepted. It was exciting, but hardly a good way to keep in condition. When the time came to start another season, the Celtics reported hog fat. They played themselves into shape during their first half-dozen games. Dutch Dehnert, for instance, usually reported at 210 but weighed only about 180 pounds when the season ended.

⊕ ⊕ ⊕

The basketball of the Celtic era, of course, was not as physically grueling as the basketball of today. The halves were 20 minutes; there was a center jump after each score; and there was no compulsion to bring the ball to the forecourt within 10 seconds. A team which was physically spent could stall in the backcourt with the ball. The courts averaged 60 feet by 40. They were bandboxes compared to the 90 by 50 courts prevalent now. In a game today, there are frequently more field goals than there were points in the days of the Celtics.

Despite the handicap of not being in shape, plus the blithe disregard many of their members had for training, the Celts averaged better than five victories out of six starts, even when they started going downhill. What made them so truly great was that the Celtics literally won as they pleased most of the time. They rarely poured it on—first, because rolling up the score was bad business and had a deleterious effect upon the gate for a return game and second, because it was exhausting. Some of the few defeats the Celtics sustained in a season—usually 15 or 20 losses against 100 victories—occurred because a team with which the Shamrocks were toying suddenly got hot in the closing minutes and poured through enough points to erase the Irish margin.

Never, all the Celtic survivors are careful, nay, insistent to point out, was a game lost because the Celts wanted to lose it. Nor was the score ever kept close merely to accomplish a betting coup. There is only one recorded instance of the Celtics betting on a basketball game—and then they bet on themselves to thwart a bookmaker they had reason to believe had double-crossed them. More about that later.

Replacements gradually came to the first Celtic team Furey had organized, but the replacements were carefully screened before acceptance. Horse Haggerty, a giant of a man who had originally come from mining districts around Scranton, Pennsylvania, but who reached the Celtics from Springfield, Massachusetts, was beginning to wear out. First Joe Trippi and later Lapchick were hired as replacements.

Haggerty could be a story in himself, for he was the Paul Bunyan of the courts, a man of surprising speed for one of his height and weight. There were times when Haggerty and the hefty Dehnert were called upon to double-team some obstreperous individual on the opposing team. When they did, he was no longer obstreperous and scarcely an individual.

⊕ ⊕ ⊕

One of the most gifted of all the Celtic additions was Nat Holman, who came out of New York's teeming East Side to win himself an education and fame through the medium of professional basketball. Smart and glib, the suave Holman also was one of the truly great passers in basketball history. He could thread a needle with his passes, throwing the ball with no spin, making it easy to handle. It was Holman who fed Dehnert in the pivot most of the time, and it was Nat who taught the Dutchman the trick of coming forward to take the pass. When Dehnert stepped forward to take the ball, he was able to return the pass without hindrance from the defensive player.

While much of the magic of Holman's passing went unappreciated, his superb faking did not. Nat could feint basketball players into knots as easily as the wily Benny Leonard could tie up opponents in the ring. And when the Celts were in a tight

game, where one point meant a great deal, Holman was a master at drawing a foul. Dribbling up the floor, or cutting to take a pass, Nat would recoil from an opposing player like a man who had just been hit by a truck, although actually there may have been no bodily contact at all. Or, if there was, it was Holman who established it.

One night at Madison Square Garden, the Celtics faced the Brooklyn Visitations. Willie Scrill of the visitors was so angry at being made to look foolish by Holman's feints that he blew his top and lit into Nat with the evident intention of taking him apart. The length of the court they went, Willie throwing punches with both hands as fast as he could, Holman back-pedaling like Gene Tunney against Jack Dempsey the night of the long count in Chicago. Nat feinted, bobbed and weaved so dexterously that not one of the dozens of punches Scrill threw at him landed. Holman never tried to punch back. When Scrill finally stopped from exhaustion, Nat calmly shot the foul which was awarded him.

Holman, who came to the Celtics from the New York Whirlwinds, was eager to get ahead in the world. He studied at Savage Institute, received a degree as a physical instructor, and, while still playing pro ball, became basketball coach at the College of the City of New York, more familiarly known as CCNY. Here he achieved the dignified rating of an assistant professor. He is recognized as an authority on the game, precisely as Lapchick at St. John's University and later among the pros.

Holman took up college coaching early. Lapchick did not do so until 1936 when his playing days were behind him. And, although the rivalry between City and St. John's is among the most intense in the metropolitan area, the two men always have remained firm friends. As a matter of fact, when Nat, a bachelor until he was 49, found the charms of Miss Ruth Jackson irresistible, it was Lapchick, his old Celtic teammate, who officiated as best man at Nat's marriage on November 2, 1945.

There was a certain shy aloofness about Holman when he first joined the Celtics. He couldn't quite see their way of playing after the game, but he certainly could appreciate their way of playing during the game. And he added much to it, with his skillful passing and feinting—to say nothing of his accurate shooting.

Later, long after Lapchick had joined Holman with the Celtics, there was another addition to the Shamrocks worth mentioning. That was Davie Banks, a chunky little fellow built like a Shetland pony, who could run all night. Banks, with a barnstorming team featuring Bob McDermott, one of the best of the latter-day professionals to come from New York, and Polly Birch, the great Duquesne center, kept the name of the Celtics going well into the 1940's touring the country and meeting all comers. Not, however, with the same success as the old Celtics.

There were two phases of Celtic greatness before the team petered out. The first was with Haggerty, Barry, Beckman, Dehnert, Holman, and Witte. The second was when Lapchick, Banks, Leonard, and Hickey teamed up with Barry, Beckman, Dehnert, and Holman. One team merged into the other, overlapping, as it were. They kept the Celtics booming until the American League split up the team in the late 20's. And even

after that, the barnstorming performances by Holman, Dehnert, Barry, Lapchick, and Banks as a unit kept green the memory of the great Shamrock clubs.

⊕ ⊕ ⊕

Something new was added to basketball in the mid-20's when George Preston Marshall, the Washington laundry tycoon, decided to take the professionals out of the dance halls and make the sport big-league in every sense of the term. Marshall, current owner of the Washington Redskins of the National Football League, is an unpredictable genius who resembles Larry MacPhail more than any other individual in the field of sports promotion.

Marshall was simply ahead of his time with the American Basketball League. The idea was good and the promotion sound, but there was no way to cope with the Original Celtics, who continued to play exhibition games, beating the tar out of league teams and making more money than any of the players on the league teams. The late Joseph Carr, who was to become president of the National Football League, finally solved the problem by blacklisting the Celtics. No league team was allowed to play exhibitions against the Celts, who thus found their revenue sharply curtailed.

The cold war worked, and the Celtics went into the league in its second season, taking over the defunct Brooklyn franchise—and, with it, the poor record Brooklyn had compiled. The Celtics won the second half of the schedule and might have won the first half, too, had not Cleveland been too far in front when the Celtics assumed the Brooklyn burden.

Cleveland, whose representatives played under the trade name of Rosenblums, succumbed before the Celtics in the play-offs in three straight games. The next year, the Celtics won both halves of the pennant race. Since they couldn't very well play themselves, the league arranged for them to meet Fort Wayne, the American League's top Western team. The Celtics won that series, too. By now, the league was fresh out of ideas.

So superior were the Celtics to the rest of the league that they were threatening to bring about its dissolution. In Washington, Marshall's Palace Club, named after the laundry he operated there, had cost him $65,000 in an ever-changing stream of high salaried personnel. And still he wasn't able to beat the Celtics. "We'll break you yet, George," Dehnert used to yell at Marshall on the sidelines as the Celts rolled to another victory.

⊕ ⊕ ⊕

With attendance falling off in the cities where the clubs trailed the Celtics, which was in all the cities in the league, a drastic move was made. The Celtics were broken up and their members allocated to other cities in the league so that some semblance of balance might be achieved. This action, I believe, is unparalleled in professional sport.

The great Beckman left to become player-coach of Baltimore. Banks, who had replaced him, and Holman were sent to the New York Hakoahs. Dutch Dehnert and Pete Barry went to Rochester. Lapchick was slated for Cleveland and Chris Leonard retired. Johnny Witte, the manager, was out of a job and out of a team.

One threat of separation was enough for the Celtics. Barry, Dehnert, and Lapchick jumped the league, signed up Scrill and

Conaty, looked up Witte, and put him back on the job as manager. After a few games, however, Witte called the whole deal off, as has been related earlier in this story. Johnny didn't want to make money if it meant making a monkey out of the Celtics' name and tradition.

Although this was before the invention of radio's popular package deal, Lapchick, Barry, and Dehnert sold themselves to Cleveland as a package. The Rosenblums, who had lost their first two games, won the next eight with the combination of the three Celts, Nat Hickey, and Carlie Husta. Once again the race had been blown wide open. The league was confronted with the same old Celtic problem—this time under the name of the Rosenblums. So the league amputated Hickey and awarded him to George Halas' team in Chicago.

The Rosenblums won one-half of the race in each of the next two seasons, and grabbed the playoff, each time. It was too much for the league.

The losing teams moved their home dates to the courts of the opposing teams in an effort to escape the flow of red ink which was inundating their box offices. That meant that in the cities where basketball had been drawing, there was a falling off because fans were getting double doses of the poorer teams. The crowds of 7,000 in Cleveland, for instance, dwindled to 1,500. Cleveland dropped out of the league and its players were transferred to Toledo in 1929, as the American League made one more stab at keeping afloat.

The players were cut $500 a month at Toledo, which meant a reduction of 50 percent in many cases. And the management piled barnstorming games on top of the 44-game league schedule in an effort to get its investment back. Barry, Dehnert, and Lapchick had to drive 200 miles to play an exhibition in Dayton, Ohio, then drive right back to play a league game that same night in Toledo. It wasn't much fun and it showed in the play of the Celtic survivors, who finished last as the league folded with a resounding crash.

Thus it was that the Celtics, broken up lest they break up the league, finally broke it up anyway. Although it was financially disastrous, it was in many ways quite the greatest compliment any team in organized sport ever received. The teams the Celtics were beating were not teams representing whistle-stops on a barnstorming junket but the best professional basketball players in the country. The best of the rest simply wasn't good enough for the Celtics.

Some years ago, in baseball's American League, there was a great cry of "Break up the Yankees!" It arose because the Yanks, under Miller Huggins, won six pennants out of a possible eight and later, under Joe McCarthy, won seven out of a possible eight. Yet these were Yankee teams of constantly changing personnel, teams which were getting the cream of the crop in replacements from their farm system.

It was different with the Celtics. These were the same fellows, tearing the league apart year after year. It was a team which was literally forced to go barnstorming because in league play all semblance of competition had been removed. When the American Basketball League folded, the Celtics were like Alexander. They had to hit the road, seeking new worlds to conquer.

⊕ ⊕ ⊕

And hit the road was precisely what the Celtics did. Barry, Dehnert, Lapchick, Banks, Hickey, and Husta returned to the old grind of barnstorming. They found it wasn't quite the same, though, because in the early 30's there was something abroad in this land of ours called a Depression. The Celtics used to play road games for a set guarantee of $400, with the privilege of taking a percentage. Invariably, their share of the gross amounted to more than the guarantee. Now, however, the Celtics were playing for $250 per appearance. And they weren't traveling first class any more. It wasn't Pullmans now, but an old jalopy which cost a couple of hundred bucks and had room for seven passengers—provided the passengers were relatives of Singer's Midgets. It made for crowded going. Lapchick not only had to jump center, but also keep the bus moving.

For six years, these remnants of the once great Celtics traveled in this gypsy fashion. It is to their credit that they managed to keep the Shamrock reputation alive, and to win as high a percentage of their games as the old originals had. From 1930 until 1936, when Lapchick quit to become head coach at St. John's, the Celtics kept on the go—and kept the opposition on the go, too.

There was still magic in the Celtic name. Lou O'Neill, sports editor of the Long Island Star-Journal and one of the metropolitan district's finest horse handicappers, discovered that magic when he took a fling at basketball promoting in the early 30's at a time when, as he himself expresses it, "a buck was scarce."

O'Neill thought he would go Jim Furey one better in promoting. He lined up a basketball squad, and made it his object to keep the players busy every night in the week and twice on Sundays. But not under the same team name. They represented Long Island City one night, other spots on Long Island other nights, but always as the "home" team. Lou paid them less per game than they had been in the habit of receiving, but kept them so busy that they actually received more per week.

⊕ ⊕ ⊕

One of the spots represented by O'Neill's club was West Sayville, Long Island. They played there as the West Sayville Volunteer Firemen and played their games in the spacious firehouse, using the half not being used as a garage for the fire apparatus. The chief was on the level about it, too. He had them all sworn in as volunteer firemen, although all the players lived 50 or 100 miles from the town of West Sayville and any conflagration there could have burned out the town before these "volunteers" reached it.

When the team, on successive weeks, defeated Rody Cooney's Brooklyn Visitations and Eddie Wilde's Jewels, (the team which had been the St. John's "Wonder Five" before graduation), the chief was tremendously enthused. "Get us the Celtics," he demanded.

The Celtics demanded $300 as a guarantee. To meet this, it was decided to tilt the admission price from 75 cents to a dollar and a half, a stiff price in those depression days of the early 30's.

"The night the Celtics were scheduled to play us in West Sayville," recalled O'Neill, "was one of the coldest that section of Long Island had ever experienced. It was one above zero. Yet the Celtics were such a drawing card that we had to close the

doors a half hour before game time. One of the local cops decided that the crowd represented a fire hazard. Can you imagine that, when there were two fire engines in the other half of the hall?"

And what about the game?

"They beat us," admitted Lou. "But I learned one of the Celtic tricks that night. As soon as the first foul was called against them, all five of them charged the referee, demanded to know if they were getting a jobbing, where he got off to call such a foul, and so on. I realized later that this was standard operating procedure with them. They played in so many strange courts, and with even stranger officiating, that they had to protect themselves right from the start by jumping the referee. After that first blast, the whistle-blower usually thought twice before he called a foul."

Elmer Ripley, a great set shot who has coached at Columbia, Yale, and Georgetown, served his time with the Celtics. He remembers distinctly their troubles with officials, particularly in the pre-Lapchick days when Horse Haggerty was the center. The Horse was six feet, four inches tall and weighed 240 pounds when he was in shape, which was all the time. Haggerty, who could palm a basketball in one of his ham-like hands, was such an attraction that the personal foul rule was usually waived so the spectators could get a full-time view of the Horse in action.

"One night we were playing in Lancaster, Ohio," recollected Ripley with a chuckle, "and the opposition wouldn't waive the rule. That made Horse mad.

"On the opening tap, he deliberately fouled the center jumping against him. Three times more they jumped and each time Horse fouled the fellow. He was out of the game before a minute of playing time had elapsed.

"Then the promoter pleaded with Haggerty to stay in the game. 'Not me,' said the Horse, a stickler for playing the code when it suited him. 'Rules are rules.' "

It wasn't usual, but neither was it rare for the Celtics to find themselves playing six men on some of their barnstorming spots—the referee lining himself up with the hometown team. Dutch Dehnert one night noticed the referee huddled with the opposition during a time out and dropped by to overhear the conversation. "Take it easy," Dutch overheard the official say. "I'll call so many fouls on the Celtics you'll win without any trouble."

Dehnert reported this intelligence to his mates. There was a jump ball at center. Johnny Beckman hit the referee high and the Dutchman hit him low. He went out like a light. This was the spot for Haggerty. He dashed to the sidelines, grabbed the water bucket, and emptied its contents on the unconscious (and unscrupulous) official.

"Where am I?" gasped the half-drowned whistle tooter.

"You're practically in the ashcan right now, chum," growled Haggerty. "Call them right from here on or we'll really go to work on you."

⊕ ⊕ ⊕

One of the great basketball officials of those rough and ready days was Herman Baetzel, who had his share of troubles with the Horse. He called a foul on Haggerty which Haggerty didn't like, it being one of his quaint delusions that he never committed any fouls.

"If you call one more like that, I'll kill you," threatened Haggerty, looking as though he meant it.

A few seconds later Baetzel's whistle tooted again and play halted.

"This may be the last act of an honest career," declared the official, bravely, "but, Haggerty, I'm calling a foul on you."

Far from assaulting the referee, Haggerty laughed out loud. The Horse appreciated courage and personal integrity when he saw it.

There was a time when Haggerty did assault Baetzel but it wasn't in anger—not really. The massive Haggerty just couldn't resist the chance to put over what he considered a practical joke. He thought he had been picked off and Baetzel thought otherwise.

"I tell you, Herman," screamed Haggerty, "he picked me off. Like this . . ." And then the Horse demonstrated with his hands just how he had been blocked out, a move which delighted the spectators, who booed Haggerty with abandon, much to the latter's annoyance.

Baetzel, conscious of the crowd's reaction and trying to prove that even the great Haggerty couldn't intimidate him, closed his eyes and shook his head emphatically from side to side. "No," he bellowed, still with his eyes shut tight. "No, no!" That was just too much for Haggerty. He hauled off and "let him have it," as they say. When Baetzel regained consciousness, he pointed a trembling finger at Haggerty. "You're out of the game," he stated.

"Why?" asked Haggerty with disarming guile.

"You punched me," declared Baetzel.

"How do you know it was me?" Haggerty wanted to know. "Maybe it was somebody else. After all, you didn't see it happen. You had your eyes closed."

P.S.: Baetzel, eyes closed or not, had the last word. And, in this case, the last word was "Out."

Before Haggerty and Nat Holman played together on the Celtics, they played against each other. Holman's slick faking caused an official to call a foul against Haggerty, who, for a wonder, was wholly innocent of a foul this time. Horse was outraged. "You won't fake me again like that," he declared. But Nat did. A few seconds later, Holman was missing, out cold on one end of the floor, where Haggerty had left him.

"As long as I'm going to be charged with fouls I don't commit," explained the Horse, "I may as well get my money's worth."

Despite that stormy beginning, Haggerty and Holman became fast friends in their six years on the Celtics. "Horse was my personal bodyguard," recalled Nat. "Any time I was hit, and I was hit a lot in those early days, Haggerty would go over to the fellow who fouled me, give him a robust nudge in the ribs, and say, 'now we're even.' They always knew what he meant, too."

After leaving the Celtics, Haggerty took one fling with George Marshall's Washington team. With seconds left to play, the Marshall-men led the Celtics by a point and it looked as though George was about to realize his great ambition of finally beating the Celtics. Washington had the ball out of bounds and Haggerty took it to pass it in. All he had to do was throw

it to a teammate and the game was over. Holman sized up the situation and although it was Washington's ball, Nat cut for the basket. "Horse!" he called. Six years of playing together had left their mark. Instinctively, Haggerty passed to the flying Holman, who laid up the ball for what were the winning points.

Lapchick, who succeeded Haggerty as the Celtics' center, played against him. He still remembers the beatings he used to absorb. "Horse would beat a tattoo on your ribs and it would be a couple of days before you could breathe properly," recalled Joe with a shudder.

"And strong? I remember one time a fan kept riding Haggerty all through the game. After we dressed and left the arena, Horse spotted the guy outside on the sidewalk and grabbed him.

"The fellow held Haggerty by the coat lapel, pleading with Horse not to hit him. When the Horse let him have it, the fellow shot 20 feet into the gutter—with Haggerty's lapel still in his hand!"

Although the Celtics traveled the country, all that I talked to about this story agreed unanimously that the roughest court they ever played on was Prospect Hall in Brooklyn. It was known, and not with affection, to visiting basketball players and officials as "The Bucket of Blood."

"Even the kids among the rooters were tough," relates Dick Meehan, another of the truly great officials of basketball's early days. "I remember reporting there to work as a referee one night. As I'm walking into the hall with my handgrip, a kid comes up to me and asks, 'Let me carry your bag so I can get in to see the game, mister.'

"I told him he could carry my bag. Then he asked me if I was playing with the Visitations, the home team. I told him I wasn't and then he looked a little hesitant. 'Playing with the visitors?' he asked.

"I told him I wasn't and a great light dawned in the kid's eyes. He put the bag down on the ground and edged away from me. 'You must be the referee, then,' he said. 'Before you even start, I'll bet two to one you're lousy.' That's the way the kid fans were at Prospect Hall. You can imagine what the grown-up rooters were like!"

Prospect Hall was, and still is, a dance hall in South Brooklyn. It has housed some great players in its day—Rody Cooney, Joe Brennan, Swede Grimstead, Harry Knoblock, Red Conaty, Willie Scrill, and many others. It was always packed when the Celtics played there. There was dancing before and after the game and between the halves.

"I used to wonder how they could get so many people into the place," remarked Dutch Dehnert. "It seemed as though they were hanging from the rafters. And the guys in the rafters thought nothing of shying a bottle at you when you were trying to shoot a foul. That was bad enough, but the fellows sitting on the sidelines would trip you up when you were going down the court. Once a fellow stuck a lighted cigarette into the back of my leg as I was trying to pass a ball in from out of bounds. They were holy terrors."

Under such conditions, it isn't remarkable that tempers often ran short. And when a fight broke out, whether among the players or the spectators, the management had one set solution. That was for the orchestra leader, Professor John J. Nolan, to break out with a lively dance number.

"I think the number was 'Dardenella'," mused Lapchick. "Believe me, Professor Nolan got a lot of practice playing that one."

⊕ ⊕ ⊕

It was not at Prospect Hall but over in Perth Amboy, New Jersey, that the mighty Haggerty met his comeuppance. Arthur Daley, talented sports columnist of *The New York Times* and an authority on the escapades of the Horse, tells the story this way:

"The Horse gave it out, but he could also take it. At Perth Amboy one night, Haggerty was indiscreet enough to put the slug on a local official, to the great indignation of the assembled populace. The game was played in a garage with a sink in the corner serving as a shower room. Last to trudge down toward the waiting automobile was Haggerty. He never made it. Some 30 wild-eyed fans mobbed him. The other Celtics didn't miss him until he showed up a half hour later, his clothes torn and his face bloody. There wasn't a whisper out of him. He dismissed it with a shrug of his broad shoulders."

One of the idiosyncrasies of the Celtics was that they played a tie game on occasion. A tie game in basketball today is unheard of, unless both teams happen to drop from exhaustion after playing umpty-nine extra periods. Lapchick explained the tie games in the Celtics' record to Dick Young, sportswriter of the New York *Daily News*.

"Tie games weren't uncommon in our barnstorming days," said Joe. "If the game was deadlocked at the end of the regulation time, our manager would enter into hasty negotiations with the local promoter on the sidelines. If the promoter agreed to pay us extra for the overtime, we'd resume. If he refused, the game ended right there with no decision. We had originally contracted only for 40 minutes—and, besides, a tie was good business. It left the fans talking and brought them out in droves when we returned there later that season or the following year."

It was the aftermath of a tie game which led to the only recorded instance of the Celtics betting on a game. During the season of 1921-22, the Shamrock five played a tie with the Coffee Club in Pittsburgh. The tie wasn't played off and there was great excitement the next winter when the Celts returned to play the Coffee Club again.

The day before the game, Johnny Beckman received a wire from a friend of his in Pittsburgh saying that he could get big odds betting that the Celtics would win by 20 points.

"If we can't beat them by 20 points," commented Holman, "we ought to hang up."

Dutch Dehnert nodded in agreement. So did all the others, all except Joe Lapchick, then in his first year with the Celts and getting $50 a game. He liked the idea of getting $300 but he couldn't see risking his week's pay against a team which had held the Celtics even the year before.

"We took it easy on them last year, kid. They just happened to get hot," assured Chris Leonard. "It won't happen again."

The decision was made to bet the bundle to win by 20 points and the game wasn't very old before Lapchick realized his fears had been groundless. At half-time, the Celtics were in front by more than 20 points and in a position to win as they pleased.

There was a rude awakening before the second half started.

Beckman's friend burst into the dressing room with the startling news that the bookie hadn't been able to place all of the $2,000 he had been given to bet-only $250 of it. The Celtics realized immediately that they had been caught in a swindle. Their first reaction was to loaf through the second half and win by fewer than 20 points, but they were hooked there, too, for $250 of their own money was at stake. What happened, of course, was that the gambler had placed the bulk of the money for himself. If the Celtics failed to win by 20 points, he was sunk but so was their $250. It would have cost each of the Celtics about $35 apiece to teach him a lesson.

It was Beckman who finally solved the puzzle. The plan was to take the Coffee Club in stride and protect the $250 and then hang the gambler out to dry the next night, as the Celtics were remaining over in Pittsburgh to play the Loendi Club. Becky told his friend to tip off the gambler that the Celts wouldn't beat Loendi by more than 11 points. On the basis of this supposedly inside information, the welcher would be a cinch to bet all his previous night's winnings. And the Celtics planned to cover these bets through a middle man. They did, and they walloped Loendi by more than 30 points.

⊕ ⊕ ⊕

That lesson, learned the hard way, taught the Celtics that betting on basketball games was more uncertain than playing in them. Actually, the Shamrocks did nothing wrong in betting since they bet on their own skill and didn't retard the scoring. As a matter of fact, there was little betting on basketball games in the 20's. The first price lines and "point-spreads" on basketball bobbed up during the season of 1930-31 around New York City and then the betting was confined to college games, there being very little of it in professional games.

Hackneyed, even corny as it may sound, with the Celtics the game was the thing. In the matter of salaries, they were born too soon. But they averaged around $7,500 a season with the minimum being about $5,000 and with some of the better players getting as much as $10,000. They looked on this as ample, which it was in those low cost days, and they didn't mind the rigors of travel in the least.

Like all great athletic groups, the Celtics had to come to the end of the trail some time. After Johnny Witte had abandoned the barnstorming tour with the plain statement that the receipts didn't justify dragging the great name of the Celtics into the dust, they made one more stab, in the mid-30's. They were to play a team of former collegians, kids in their first year of pro ball, at New York's Seventy-first Regiment Armory, the scene of the Celtics' first organized success.

⊕ ⊕ ⊕

Now, college kids were meat and drink to the Celtics. When Vic Hanson, the Syracuse star, first came into the American League, the Celts made him look silly, although before the sea-

son was over, Hanson developed into one of the league's best players. And then there was the case of Homer Stonebreaker, the gangling long shot of Fort Wayne, who had an uncanny eye. Homer made six goals against Chris Leonard the first time he played against the Celtics but the next night Chris blanked Stonebreaker and scored five or six times himself. He had analyzed Homer and discovered that he brought both hands almost to the ground before starting a shot. Leonard played the Fort Wayne ace close and he never got a shot off.

It was always like that with the Celtics. They spotted a weakness in an individual and exploited it to the hilt. Like the time Lapchick scored 17 goals in two successive games against Al Kellett, a player who later became a center of rare ability. Al was new to the game at the time. While guarding Lapchick he couldn't resist turning his head every so often to see what Dehnert was doing with the ball in the pivot. Every time Al turned his head, Joe cut for the basket. He scored eight times the first night and nine times the next. After that Kellett stopped turning his head and kept his eyes on Joe.

Coming up to the game with the ex-collegians, however, Dehnert was a little dubious. He and Lapchick talked over a plan of action. Dutch regarded Ralph Kaplowitz, a former Long Island University player, as a positive menace because of his speed and shooting skill.

"Joe," said the Dutchman to Lapchick, "these kids have too much speed and stamina for us. They'll run us bow-legged before the night is over. Here is what I think we should do. Let's break fast on them and jump into an early lead before they get warmed up and then I'll go into the pivot and hold the ball out on them. That'll save our legs and force them to play our game."

Lapchick listened and thought it sounded all right to him. Once the Celtics got in front, the college boys would be under pressure and would be bound to make mistakes.

"What happened," related Dehnert years later, "was just the reverse. The kids jumped into the early lead instead of us and they went into the pivot, with a big lad from NYU, Irwin (King Kong) Klein in the bucket. We couldn't get the ball away from them. They made us look silly. We wanted them to play our game and they were playing it, all right, better than we could ourselves at that time!"

It was the last stand of the Celtics. They had not only builded well, but too well. They were beaten with weapons they had forged themselves. Once that happened, there was nothing to do but quit. They were left only with memories—but what memories! Memories of the greatest days the professional court game has ever known—the era of the Celtics.

(Reprinted with permission, Sport Media Enterprises, Inc., 2003)

Chapter 6

Hank Luisetti, Basketball Revolutionary

It hardly seems possible today, but basketball was once a slow-moving, low-scoring game. A college kid with a "crazy" shot changed it forever.

By Jack Orr
SPORT Magazine, March 1962

Once upon a time—and you young guys aren't going to believe this—the total score of a basketball game was frequently 25 points or less. In 1926, for instance, City College of New York beat Villanova, 11-9, and lost a tough one to Carnegie Tech, 13-12. City also beat Dickinson, 15-7, and in a high-scoring game, defeated Temple, 15-14.

Then, one day 26 years ago, a young kid named Angelo Enrico (Hank) Luisetti came out of the West and did for basketball what Babe Ruth did for baseball and what Red Grange did for football. That is, he revolutionized the game. Playing for Stanford University, he made the one-handed shot famous—and basketball hasn't been the same since.

There are those who say Luisetti was the best player ever. "I can't remember anybody who could do more things," Clair Bee, one of the best of the basketball coaches, said not long ago. "He was an amazing marksman, a spectacular dribbler and an awfully clever passer," said Nat Holman, one of the Original Celtics. "The thing I remember about him," said Joe Lapchick, another old Celtic, "was his uncanny ability to control the ball while going at top speed."

"He was as far ahead of his time as Bob Cousy is ahead of the others today," said Pic Picariello, a Long Island University coach who goes back 35 years or so. In a poll of sportswriters taken a few years ago to determine the best basketball player of the half-century, only George Mikan drew more votes than Luisetti.

The game that made Luisetti took place December 29, 1936. Stanford came into Madison Square Garden that night to play Long Island University. New York was the capital of basketball in those days. The country's best college teams were the New York schools and the best of them all in 1936 was LIU, which had won an unprecedented 43 games in a row. LIU was a slick ball-handling team. Its players could shoot from the outside to open up an opponent's defenses, and when they had succeeded in doing that, they could pass them dizzy under the basket. Furthermore, the LIU team—coached by Bee—was fiery and tenacious on defense.

Stanford, coached by John Bunn, had done well on the West Coast. Luisetti's scoring had amazed Californians and newspaper reports raving about his shooting had preceded him East. But New York fans were skeptical. Sure he's good, they said, but we've seen wonder teams before. They come into the Garden

Hank Luisetti, 1939
His one-handed shot revolutionized the game.

and they fold. So what if he does average 22 points a game? (An unbelievable figure in those days when there was a time-consuming center jump after every basket.) We'll contain him.

At the beginning of the game, it looked as if the New York fans were right, LIU scored first, Stanford missed its first shot and then LIU sunk a foul. Ho hum, said the Garden customers. Another West Coast flop. They settled back to watch big Art

Hillhouse and his LIU teammates take apart Stanford.

But suddenly things began to happen. It was unbelievable the way the Stanfords shot. Remember, no Easterner had seen this kind of basketball. Luisetti, began popping them one handed. Now everybody knew that the *only* way to shoot from outside was with two hands gripping the ball firmly. By half-time Stanford was in front by eight points, as substantial possibly as a 30-point lead today.

"I'll never forget the look on Art Hillhouse's face when I took that first shot," Luisetti, who is now 45, was saying not long ago. "He was about 6-foot-8 and he never expected a shot like that to be thrown. Guess he'd never seen one.

"When it hit I could just see him saying, 'Boy, is this guy lucky.' But that was the way we shot. That was what made it for us. Nobody but us believed we would win that night."

But win they did—and convincingly. In the second half Stanford pulled away to an implausible 45-31 victory. The long reign of LIU was over, but, more significantly, so was Eastern style basketball. The offense based around Luisetti was electrifying. His strong, slim body moving gracefully, his handsome head held high, he was all over the court. He rebounded, getting up so high it was hard to believe he was only 6-foot-3. He dribbled. He passed. And he shot. Oh, how he shot. On the run he pushed the ball gently toward the basket—one handed. To everybody's amazement, the ball usually went in.

"It seemed Luisetti could do nothing wrong," wrote an awed gentleman from *The New York Times*. "Some of his shots would have been deemed foolhardy if attempted by anybody else, but with Luisetti shooting, these were accepted by the enchanted crowd." Wrote another reporter: "LIU was run practically out into the middle of Eighth Avenue." As the man who once sold the *Brooklyn Eagle* on Flatbush Avenue said upon hearing that the Dodgers were moving to the West Coast: "It is the end of an area." Clair Bee said Luisetti was the best player he ever laid eyes on.

There were skeptics, too. "I'll quit coaching," said Holman, "if I have to teach one-handed shots to win. Nobody can convince me that a shot predicated on a prayer is smart basketball." But it wasn't long thereafter that kids in New York City playgrounds, and those elsewhere, too, could be seen trying to emulate the sharpshooter from the West. His one-handed shots started the scoring era which produced scores such as the 173-139 game between the Boston Celtics and the Minneapolis Lakers a couple of years ago.

"I guess we didn't really know what we were starting that night," Luisetti said recently. "We actually had no idea that we would bring on a revolution. You know, I've thought about that night many times over the years. I had no notion what that one game would mean to me. Getting all that publicity in New York changed my life, my whole life. It made me a national figure with stories about me in the *Saturday Evening Post* and *Collier's* and all that. I had just been a local kid up till then."

Now that he looks back at it all, he understands the significance. He is proud of it.

"I wasn't too bad a ballplayer," he told a reporter recently. "I had the whole game. I had flash, but I had more. I was all around. I could shoot long, shoot short, drive, tip rebounds, play defense and in tough games I was a clutch player.

"That's when I rose. I laughed a lot, we all did, but inside I guess I had the killer instinct. Inside I was serious as hell. I would do well today. I'd do well any day. Maybe I wouldn't get as many tips, with somebody like Wilt Chamberlain around because I wouldn't get in close—but I'd get my points."

One of the things they used to say about Luisetti was that he was a reluctant shooter.

"I guess so," he said. "I got as much kick out of passing off as I did from scoring. But sometimes those other guys would bug me and make me shoot."

There was the time Stanford was playing a fine Duquesne club. Though Hank was averaging 22 points a game, he began passing off. His teammates decided to teach him a lesson. The Indians came roaring down the floor on a quick break. Luisetti spun a pass to Art Stoefen, Stanford's big blond center. Stoefen dribbled once and threw the ball back to Luisetti underneath the basket. Luisetti again refused to shoot and whipped the ball back to Stoefen. Stoefen threw it right back. Luisetti scored. Then Howie Turner took a Luisetti feed—and threw it right back to him. By then, Hank realized that the other guys were in on a plot.

"Aw, come on, fellers," he said. "Cut it out."

But it was too late. They had Luisetti on the hip. Every time the Indians got the ball, they fed Luisetti. Every time he passed to a teammate, the man would return it immediately. By the end of the night, Luisetti had set a record of 50 points.

Luisetti may have been the most versatile man ever to play the college game. When he and Stanford played City College in Madison Square Garden, he only had six points at half-time, though he had set up dozens of plays for his teammates. Then City caught fire and soon was breathing down the Stanford neck. Luisetti took charge. "In a breathtaking exhibition of exquisite artistry," wrote a goggle-eyed reporter, "Luisetti scored 13 consecutive points and blew the game wide open."

Another time, in the first of a two-game series with Oregon, he scored 20 points mainly by tap-ins under the basket. Next night Oregon massed its defenses to keep him on the outside. He stood back and threw in 26 points.

He was a tremendous dribbler as well. One basketball expert says that he was incomparable. "Well," he adds "possibly Lou Boudreau was close. And there is always Cousy. But they are the three top ones in 30 years."

Luisetti, son of a restaurant chef, was born in the Telegraph Hill waterfront section of San Francisco that produced Joe DiMaggio, Tony Lazzeri and Frank Crosetti. He was an only child and began shooting baskets when he was six. At Galileo High School in San Francisco he began developing his feathery one-hand shot.

"I don't know how I came to think of it," he said. "It just seemed to be a natural way to get the ball in the air."

"I let him do it," said his high school coach, Tommy Denike, "because the ball seemed to drop in the basket more often than not. Boy, wouldn't I have felt funny if I had tried to change his style."

By the time Luisetti was a freshman at Stanford, his one-hander was the talk of the campus. By then he was able to work it with either hand, an art particularly appreciated by his freshman coach, Johnny Bunn, who was to handle Hank through

his varsity years as well.

"When I was a freshman I asked John Bunn if I could stay with the one-hander, even though most coaches in those days would die if you tried it," Luisetti said. "I was standing near the corner in practice and I popped one in. Bunn said, 'Stay with it, boy.'"

As a freshman, Luisetti led his club to an undefeated season. He scored 305 points in 18 games. Over one weekend series, in two games, he made 70 points.

He made All-America in his sophomore year with 416 points. He made All-America again as a junior and a senior. Against the Trojans of Southern California when he was still a soph, Stanford trailed by what seemed an insurmountable 15 points (at least for those days). There were only ten minutes remaining. Luisetti scored 24 points from there on in, including the last 14 in succession, and Stanford won, 51-47.

Prior to Luisetti, Stanford had won just a single Pacific Coast Conference basketball title—in 1920. In Hank's three varsity years, Stanford won three titles and was voted college team of the year in 1937. Luisetti was named college player of the year twice.

"Let me tell you what Luisetti was like in those days," Stanford publicity man Don Liebendorfer once said. "I've been around college basketball 37 years and there never was a finer man. When he was a freshman, he was talking to me in my office and I said, 'You shoot pretty well, but remember to keep that hat band the same size.' And from that day on, every Monday morning he would show up at my office and say, 'How's the hat band size look to you?' "

Coach Bunn, who later became dean of men at Stanford before moving on to Springfield (Massachusetts) College, admired Hank's personality, too. "He was not only the greatest player I ever had," Bunn said, "but he also is one of the finest men I've ever known.

"Those were great clubs to coach. Every regular was a crack player who could score, pass and run. The only way they could have stopped Luisetti and our center Stoefen, would have been to put a lid on the top of the basket. No mere commonplace defense ever could keep them from scoring.

"Luisetti was a dream player. Once I remember he missed six foul shots in a row. He came rushing over to the bench. 'Take me out, coach,' he said. 'I'm terrible!'

"So I took him out and gave him a rest for a few minutes. Then he went back in. Oh, yes, he managed to pop in ten before the game ended. And that was on a bad day.

"They used to ask me how I felt about coaching the best basketball player of the age. Well, my answer was always the same: I always said that Hank Luisetti is the young man who made a coach out of John Bunn. He could have made a coach out of anybody."

Many people think Luisetti would have been a great coach himself. Jack Calderwood, who was Hank's teammate and college roommate, said he learned as much about basketball from Hank in one year as he did all the rest of his life.

"He was completely unselfish and, I think, a natural-born leader," Calderwood said. "It may sound corny for these times, but at Stanford we were extremely rah-rah boys. Before a game our five starters—Dinty Moore, Turner, Stoefen, Hank and I—

would go into a huddle, clasp hands and chant, 'One for all, all for one, all for Stanford.' Then Hank would show the crowd and the opposing club what the game was all about.

"He was an easy guy to room with. He heaved hash at Deke house to help get himself through college. (Despite Hank's fame and popularity, he had to work to support himself. Basketball was not yet popular enough as a big-time sport to bring him fringe benefits with his scholarship. That has changed, of course, due in large part to him, but the change came later.)

"Hank would come home at night pretty tired after a day of classes, basketball practice and hash-slinging," Calderwood said, "but he was always a considerate man to have around and he was always free and loose and ready to go.

"He was enormously proud of his family and he wrote home practically every day. They were proud of him, too, and I remember that his mother had a velvet pillow on which she pinned his various medals and it was prominently displayed in the living room. I used to go home with him some weekends.

"At college, he and I often practiced ricocheting basketballs on the floor of our room—until the guys underneath complained. On the court we could duplicate the bounce passes and the give-and-go's we practiced up in the room.

"We used to love to play. Once, I remember, we were in against UCLA and were ahead by two points with about a minute left to play. Moore, the captain that year, said, 'How about letting them score to tie it up? I want to play some more.' We all laughed and Hank said, 'Sure, let's do it.' Well, we went into overtime and Luisetti scored something like 12 points in the overtime period. Coach Bunn saw what was going on and almost flipped his lid."

After Stanford beat LIU in that historic 1936 game, the Indians traveled to Philadelphia to play Temple.

Stanford was such a great draw that the crowd was 9,000, and several hundred more had to be turned away. It was a night of great confusion and a third of the people who had tickets couldn't get through the milling crowd. Finally, three riot calls were put out.

As the game was about to start a Stanford substitute player came over to the press bench, situated under one of the baskets. "A word of warning to you fellows," the sub said. "When we drive in, we come fast. So we'd appreciate it a lot if you would put your hands up to protect our boys from banging into the seats."

"How do you like that?" said a reporter. "It isn't bad enough we have to pluck wrestlers out of our laps. Now we got to keep our guard up against basketball players."

The Stanfords were bouncing off typewriters and telegraph keys all night long—and they made mincemeat out of the Temples and laughed all the while. If a fancy play worked, a Stanfordite would chuckle and slap his opponent on the back: "How'd you like that one?" If it didn't work, it didn't seem to matter. There was the same display of good nature: "Nearly had you that time."

Perhaps the biggest night, statistically speaking, for Hank and Stanford came on March 4, 1938. First place in the Pacific Coast Conference's southern division was at stake that night, and a lot more besides. Always bitter rivals, Stanford, with

a 9-2 conference record, and California, 8-3, were playing in the Berkeley Pavilion in the final southern division game of the season. The winner would go on to play for the league championship. Hank, a senior, was within reach of the national college career scoring record and the conference single-season scoring record.

With people packed in every seat and standing-room space, waves of wild noise rolled down onto the court as the game began. Six minutes went by and Hank didn't have a point. He was fouled then by Bill Garetson, a California guard. Hank scored his foul shot, then, two minutes later, he scored a set shot from 25 feet out. Seconds later, he let loose a one-hander from the corner. The ball went in. Time after time, Hank shot—and scored. With the first half about to end, he hit the mid-court line with his left foot, swept his right arm up and, still on the run, threw up a one-hander. The ball went cleanly through the basket-a 50-foot field goal. California had 20 points. Stanford had 36, 17 by Hank.

With nine minutes remaining in the second half, the ball bounced loose near midcourt. Luisetti dove for it. So did Garetson. So did California's Ed Dougery.

In the pileup Dougery's elbow crashed into Hank's chin. Hank stood up, took two steps and fell full-length on his face. He was out cold.

They worked over Hank for two minutes, then carried him, still unconscious, to the dressing room. Stanford and California rooters rose united to applaud him. The game began again and Stanford held its lead. Then, with three minutes to play, Luisetti, pale and shaken, returned to the game. He scored five more points, a total 22, and Stanford won, 63-42.

As the teams trooped to the dressing room, reporters began writing historic news. Hank Luisetti had become the leading college scorer of all time. His 22 points had given him a career record of 1,550 and a conference record of 232 points in 12 games.

After college some of Hank's teammates wanted to go on a basketball barnstorming trip, but he had other projects. He was invited to Hollywood to make a movie with Betty Grable and he wanted to marry Jane Rossiter, a girl he had met at Stanford. He did both. The movie, *Campus Confessions*, was a flop, but it did make history. It was the first time basketball had been a movie subject.

The film turned out to be a financial trouble-maker allround for Hank. The Amateur Athletic Union suspended him for a year because, they said, he had directly capitalized on his sports for profit. He was ineligible to play in the big amateur basketball tournament that traditionally was the sport's premier attraction outside the college game. A year later, though, in 1940, Hank played in the AAU tournament, set a tournament scoring record and was voted the outstanding player. Moreover he proved he was still the No. 1 gate attraction in the game.

"Luisetti's presence," an AAU spokesman said, "added at least $5,000 to the gate."

Hank played amateur ball in 1941 for the Phillips Oilers and though hobbled most of the season by aftermaths of a torn knee ligament, he still averaged 11.1 points a game. Then, as World War II began, he enlisted in the Navy and was assigned to St. Mary's Pre-Flight Base, where he played more basketball

and, according to many people, reached his peak. Luisetti was continually double guarded and still he managed to score 30 or more points often enough to keep people gaping.

In Luisetti's two seasons at St. Mary's, 1942 and 1943, the team won 20 straight games. In 1944, he was transferred to Norfolk, Virginia, for assignment to the aircraft carrier, *Bonhomme Richard*. A few days before he shoved off for sea duty, Hank grew ill.

"All at once," he said later, "I was running a high fever and then I passed out. They rushed me to the hospital and found I had spinal meningitis."

For two months he fought the killer virus. For a week he was in a coma, kept alive by drug injections. Not much publicity leaked out. The public didn't know Hank was on the brink of death.

His wife, Jane, flew to his hospital bed. Hank's weight plunged to 158 pounds, and then, the tide turned. "It was an overtime affair," Hank said, "but I licked it. They began to stuff me with vitamins and tonics and I came out okay."

Not all okay. When the war ended and pro basketball began to grow, the teams—and the industrial league teams, too—bid for Luisetti. He wasn't yet 30, he had built himself into good physical shape again and he still scored well when he occasionally fooled around on the court. But his formal basketball career was over. "What would you do," Hank said, "if the doctors warned you that a comeback might mean losing your health? I mean, permanently?"

When word was out that Luisetti definitely would play no more basketball, coaching offers were made to him. He turned them down. "I just don't have the temperament to be a coach," he said.

Instead Hank went into the business world. These days he works for the E. F. MacDonald travel agency in San Francisco. He is up by seven a.m., then drives 22 miles from Burlingame, where he lives in a seven-room house, to San Francisco. His work involves calling on executives and outlining travel plans for them. His name is still a hallowed one in the Bay area and he is highly successful. Then he drives home where, Jane Luisetti says, he changes into blue denims and big boots. "The boots," says Jane, "as often as not, are stuck up on my coffee table as he watches a ball game on television and smokes a cigar.

"Hank is still very much dedicated to basketball. He puts on a clinic for the *San Francisco Examiner* every winter and he loves to work with youngsters. He certainly has helped our son, Mike. (The Luisettis have a 20-year-old daughter, Nancy, too.) Mike was captain and high scorer of the Mills High School team last year. He has quite a cross to bear, being the son of the famous Hank Luisetti and being expected to perform miracles."

Recently, Hank was asked what he thought about the changes in basketball. "Imagine what it has become," he said. "We thought we used to do well when our team scored 50 a game."

Did he realize what he had contributed to those changes?

"I think I do," said Hank Luisetti, "Maybe we didn't realize it at the time, but I think we did bring in the fast break and though those guys back East didn't think we could do it, we showed that you can shoot with one hand."

(Reprinted with permission, Sport Media Enterprises, Inc., 2003)

Chapter 7

The Globetrotters: Basketball's Greatest Road-Show

Harlem Globetrotters On The Road, 1955 Abe Saperstein, center, launched the Trotters in 1927.

Slapstick comedy and pure athletic genius made the Harlem Globetrotters smash box office from California to Casablanca

By Al Stump
SPORT Magazine, January 1951

Sweet Willie Oliver, while falling out of a second-story barn door one night, uttered a cry that sums up the history of basketball's greatest road-show—the Harlem Globetrotters. Willie had just scored a Trotter goal by banking the ball off his opponent's head into the hoop when a 200-pound farmer peevishly clipped him with a meaty hip. Oliver crashed through the thinly-boarded hayloft door, yelling as he went: "This ain't in the act . . . !"

Maybe it wasn't, but the Globetrotters have never been a team to stick to their own daffy script. Players and spectators rushed from the loft, expecting to find Oliver broken into several pieces. Instead, he was virtually buried from sight in a fertilizer heap. After a quick sluicing down at a nearby horse trough, he was ready to resume action. Thereafter he became "Sweet Willie" to Globetrotter addicts—which is to say

2,000,000 fans from Casablanca to California.

Oliver's switch from the scenario is topped in Globetrotter legend only by the Walter (Toots) Wright affair, which took place during another Midwest exhibition. This time the scene was a drafty dance hall, warmed by two pot-bellied stoves at either end of the court. There was a furious scrimmage under the basket followed by a horrible howl from Wright. Toots had come down a-straddle one of the heaters. Fanning his pants, he streaked for the showers in a cloud of smoke. Later, Wright accosted owner Abe Saperstein to complain, "Listen, boss, there's nothing in my contract says I have to catch fire."

"True, Toots," replied Saperstein. "But you're undoubtedly the hottest player I've had since the team started barnstorming. Here's a $50 bonus."

The Original Harlem Globetrotters (from Chicago, not Harlem), who have played to more customers for more money on more continents than any professional basketball club in history, no longer must book themselves into cow barns and rural ballrooms. Once impoverished, they are the game's richest property today. Their gross receipts in a 215-game tour of the U.S., Canada, Europe, and North Africa last season reached a phenomenal $3,250,000. But the Trotters are always happy to throw in an ad lib with every dribble. This is one reason why such experts as Chuck Taylor, Dutch Dehnert, Phog Allen, and Eddie Gottlieb call them the greatest, most hilarious act on court record. Dehnert, it's worth noting, starred with the fabulous Original Celtics and Gottlieb helped pioneer the almost-as-famed Philadelphia Sphas.

Another reason for Trotter raves is their unbelievable win record. In 23 years of touring from Madison Square Garden to Moose Jaw, Saskatchewan, performing nightly on strange courts and with hometown referees, the Negro wizards have played 3,667 games. They've won 3,421 of 'em, losing only 245 and tieing one—a .933 victory percentage!

Mostly against soft, small-town competition, you say? Ten years ago the Harlem outfit clowned to the world professional title over the Chicago Bruins, 31-29. In 1948, their casual tomfoolery chastened George Mikan and the Minneapolis Lakers, basketball's best white team, 61-59. The next year, they trick-passed and stunt-shot the Lakers to another defeat, 49-45, before 22,000 fans at Chicago Stadium—the largest indoor cage crowd ever assembled. Last season, the Trotters staged an 18-game, coast-to-coast tour with one of the most powerful college squads yet put together. The All-Stars included Paul Arizin of Villanova, Bob Cousy of Holy Cross, Kevin O'Shea of Notre Dame, Don Rehfeldt of Wisconsin, and Gerry Calabrese of St. John's and had more All-Americans on the bench. The collegians played with a grim intensity born of pride irt their reputations. The Trotters, as always, played for laughs. They shot sitting down, riding piggy-back, and on their heads. They scored baskets by bouncing the ball in off the floor. At times, three of the five regulars were in the stands, autographing programs, while two Trotters went on a spectacular passing spree that kept the ball from the vainly grabbing All-Stars.

The college heroes looked and felt foolish. In the Boston Garden game, the sleight-of-hand of the pros had Cousy, O'Shea, and Irv Dambrot, the CCNY flash, bumping their heads together. It was impossible to follow the Trotter fakes,

backward passes, and hocus pocus ball-handling. Once, huge Nat (Sweetwater) Clifton passed between O'Shea's legs to the gorilla-armed Trotter captain, Babe Pressley, Before O'Shea could turn, Pressley shot the ball back the same way. The Babe then laid the ball on the floor and strolled away. Two All-Stars dived for it. But Pressley, wheeling sharply, place-kicked it to grinning Reece (Goose) Tatum under the basket for two easy points as the Stars sprawled on their faces. The score was a runaway 72-59. And the Trotters threw away another 20 points with their gagging.

It was slapstick, but also basketball raised to the highest scientific level. In some cities, after running up a substantial lead, the Trotters would purchase newspapers from a passing vendor and turn the ball over to one man—Marques Haynes, billed as the world's greatest dribbler. Haynes then proved it. While his mates sprawled on the floor, scanning the news, Haynes kept the ball away from America's finest college talent. Sometimes he ran them in circles for two minutes. The All-Stars never did catch up with the light-brown magician who can dribble equally well standing, seated, or flat on his back.

Before the tour ended, the nutsy nomads had to reach for still crazier comedy effects to avoid an All-Star whitewashing. Nobody doubted that the five of 18 games won by the Stars came with the sly aid of the Globetrotters.

Basketball's most imposing player, the six-foot 10-inch George Mikan, learned about the Trotters the same painful way. Around Chicago Stadium, fans declared that the Trotter voodoo stuff wouldn't make a monkey out of him. Early in the game, Mikan found himself guarding Roscoe (Duke) Cumberland, one of the gaudiest gents in Saperstein spangles for 13 years.

"Now you sees it, now you don't," chanted Cumberland, palming and "cuffing" the ball in a lightning series of motions. Suddenly, Mikan didn't see it. The crowd's delighted roar told him that he, like the greenest rube, had been slickered by the oldest of all Trotter tricks. Cumberland, before walking away, had gently placed the ball on top of the dazed Mikan's head. Before the furious hoop king could snatch it off his locks, another Trotter sneaked up from behind and recaptured the ball.

Some substantial critics believe that, year in and out, the Globetrotters form the greatest basketball aggregation of all time. Not even the Celtics could afford to make with the funny stuff for 12 to 15 minutes out of every 40-minute game. Only the Trotters are physically freakish and skilled enough to get away with it against all comers. "They're a combination of the old shell game, the Marx Brothers, and a pompom gun," says Johnny Wooden, the UCLA coach and all-time All American at Purdue. "A two-hour workout with the Trotters is worth a full season of ordinary basketball training. You can't explain what makes them so unbeatable. You just marvel at them."

Many of their goofy takeoffs defy not only rules and reason, but all laws governing flying objects. Sometimes the Trotters, late in the game and after victory has been salted away, go into football T-formation. At Port Angeles, Washington, one evening, Sonny Boswell, playing "quarterback," drop-kicked the full length of an 80-foot court for a perfect basket. Accident? Bernie Price did the same at Makoto, Minnesota. Last season, Clarence Wilson, who came from Tennessee State's

national Negro champs to the Trotters, booted two incredible goals on successive nights at Anderson, Indiana, and Cleveland. Boomerang-artist Babe Pressley can put so much backspin on the ball that he bounce-passes to an enemy player across the court. and makes the ball return to him as if on a string. The specialty of Goose Tatum, the highest-paid man in basketball at $25,000 a year, is to dribble around his guard, using only his elbows to bounce the ball, and sink a surefire basket without once glancing at the hoop. The Trotters never had a finer crowd-panicker than Inman Jackson, who could stand at mid-court before a game and sink a dozen to 20 straight 40-foot field goals.

Occasionally, the Trotter reputation for uncanny shooting exceeds even their ability. At Wembley Stadium, London, last Summer, 10,000 Britishers uttered appropriate gasps as the razzle-dazzle unfolded. To top it off, Saperstein ordered the side-splitting "sleeper" play. In this one, Tatum, a Stepin Fetchit type, sneaks away during a scramble under the Trotter net and yells for the ball. He's all alone under the opponent's basket as Babe Pressley uncorks a towering, court-length pass. Tatum catches. Then he recalls that his shoelace needs knotting. He sits down to struggle with a balky lace while all five opponents rush upon him. When he's sufficiently surrounded, Tatum uncoils, shimmies, shakes, twitches, spins until all hands are faked dizzy—and sinks a languid basket.

But in London the act misfired. Pressley, falling out of bounds at the far end, threw off balance. The pass was too high for Tatum. It was just high enough, however, to smack the basket dead-center and go through. The miracle—probably the longest competitive field goal ever scored—didn't get a tumble from the English. By this time they were convinced that anything was possible. So they just murmured politely to themselves.

"The first time it happened in 23 years!" cries Saperstein, a volatile little (five feet, three inches) butterball. "And they thought we did it on purpose!"

Now and then somebody makes the error of accusing the Trotters of overdoing the comedy. The charge is that they make a travesty of the game because it's the only sure way they can win. This gets an automatic answer. Irked by a Canadian all-star team's wisecracks one night, the dusky dervishes cut out the nonsense and played it straight—for a final score of 122-20. Another time, in Iowa, they turned loose Al (Runt) Pullins for 34 baskets and seven free throws. Nobody else bothered to score. Pullins' 75 points alone accounted for an easy victory.

Opponents often resent the ribbing. The only tie game in Trotter experience came in 1935 when the New York Celtics pulled up to a 32-32 score with two minutes to play. The Celtics called time out, collected their gear, and walked off the floor, never to return. "Found—a way to keep from losing to the Trotters!" sardonically reported a writer the next morning.

Saperstein Sports Enterprises is today strictly a major-league operation. Wealthy Abe, with headquarters in Chicago and an office suite in Manhattan's Empire State Building, spends $75,000 a year on publicity alone. He covers the country with scouts who will spend a small fortune uncovering one star of Trotter stature. But in the beginning, you could have bought Abe's rights for a plank steak. That was in 1927. Saperstein, an immigrant boy out of Whitechapel, London, was coaching the Savoy Big Five, a Chicago Negro quintet sponsored by a dance hall. Times grew tough. The sponsor threw them out in favor of a roller-skating troupe. Inventing the name "Harlem Globetrotters," a phony alias, Abe hit the Illinois back-country with his athletes just before the depression struck.

"We earned just enough to get from town to town—but never enough to get us home. So we just kept going until we hit the Pacific Ocean," recalls Abe. "We played anywhere—in livestock barns, warehouses, old op'ry houses, cowsheds and, once, in a drained swimming pool. Plenty times we staggered through three games in two days on one meal consisting of hamburgers. Poor? Why, five men had to play virtually a complete game each day. We had one sub—me, the owner. One time, to keep from starving, we bucked dirt roads for 250 miles to play in a Minnesota jerkwater gym. It was freezing weather, with no heat in the joint. Even our eyelashes froze. Our end of the gate was $5. There were nights when we slept in the town jail just to have a roof over our heads."

Travel was by rattletrap fiivver. Outside Miles City, Montana, they hit a blinding blizzard. The flivver wheezed into a snowdrift, dumping Saperstein & Co. out an their heads. "I sat there in the snow wondering what the hell would become of us," reports Abe. "Then we saw the lights of a sheepherder's shack—we were saved!"

After a miserable 48 hours cooped up in one room with the herder and some sheep, the troupe shoved on to Shelby, Montana, rip-roaring site of the Dempsey-Gibbons fight. Here they were instructed by gun-toting local fans either to throw the game to the home club or be shipped out of town in boxes.

"We were mulling that over," shudders Abe, "when along combs another delegation with guns to say that they were backing us heavy to win—or else. We were scared stiff. But I figured the second gang had more members and bigger six-shooters. So we dunked in our first 11 shots, walloped 'em good, and lammed for the city limits."

The Trotters somehow won 101 out of 107 that first year. And more important, they perfected their show. They learned to bounce balls into the bucket off their heads, to throw blind passes that never missed, to dropkick baskets and spin balls off their index fingers. Fans roared for more. In a few years, Saperstein had more dates than he could fill. He no longer needed to buckle the short pants around his pudgy belly as the team's only substitute.

Great Trotters of the past form a "Who's Who" of colored basketball in the U.S.—Rock Anderson, Fats Long, Zack Clayton, Ted Strong, Razor Frazier, Sam Sharpe, Sonny Boswell, Bill Ford, Andy Washington . . . They have never won less than 135 games or lost more than 18 in a season since their first year's 101-6 record. Few hamlets in America have missed them. The 152-2 record of the 1934 squad and 154-3 mark of his 1947 edition are all-time best winning performances. Abe's personal all-time Trotter all-star team includes Babe Pressley, Goose Tatum, and Ermer Robinson of his present squad, Sonny Boswell, Inman Jackson, inventor of much Trotter dipsy-do, Runt Pullins, Harry Rusan, and the amazing 220-pound Ted Strong. Strong, with the hugest hands in the game palming the ball like a grape, was so brilliant for 15 years that many

coaches rate him the greatest cager of them all.

Coping with these engaging buffoons has cut years off his life, Saperstein admits. He pays Trotter rookies—carefully screened by a national spy network—$400 a month and expenses. Stars in the Tatum and Marques Haynes class drive limousines and earn $2,000 a month. And a Trotter schedule runs 10 months a year. But the gala life is a better attraction. Saperstein is never sure how many Globetrotters will come trucking out of the dressing room on a given night. Last season in Casablanca, Tatum, the team's No. 1 box-office draw, vanished for the fourth time in six months. Abe and his aides were combing the streets at 4 a.m. when along clattered a horse-drawn native lack, loaded to the axles with whoopee-making Moroccans.

"Climb aboard, boss—if you can get a handhold!" cried a familiar tenor. It was the Goose, grinning down from behind the reins.

Tatum potted 24 points that night, sparking a Trotter win over a picked team of American white pros that included Leo Barnhorst of Notre Dame and Tony Lavelli of Yale. What could Saperstein say? Especially when the Goose convulsed an audience that included the Sultan of Morocco by dangling one-handed from the basket rim and emitting chimpanzee howls after tip-ins.

"I've fined him a dozen times, suspended him, farmed him out, and even assigned him a bodyguard, but it's no use," says Saperstem. "Tatum is the Babe Ruth of basketball—he makes his own rules."

A hotel bed-check on Tatum usually starts at 3 a.m., but with little hope that he'll be in the sack. At Pullman, Washington, he disappeared and wasn't seen for a week as the Trotters headed West. Taking the court at Seattle, Abe spotted his missing link in the crowd, hauled him forth, and into a suit. Cincinnati fans once almost ripped out the seats because Tatum failed to appear as advertised. Again, en route from Chicago to play Creighton University at Omaha, Saperstein took his eyes off Tatum for perhaps a minute. The Goose jumped off the train during a stop for water and didn't appear until Bismarck, North Dakota, 20-odd games later.

But this zaniest of Globetrotters with the seven-foot wing-spread once scored 27 field goals for the Chicago Stadium one-game record. You can't enforce rules on a producer like that.

Others among these carefree characters have sheriff trouble, wife trouble, and bottle trouble. Abe patiently bails them out, patches up romances, and explains that not even a Harlem Globetrotter can exist exclusively on a liquid diet. "Trouble with that is that one of Abe's biggest stars was the most prolific boozer ever seen in sports," confides a team attache. "Playing in a haze, he was still an All-Pro selection in his forties!"

Any team that wins .933 of its games is likely to produce strutting prima donnas. This is the one thing Saperstein won't tolerate. "We don't even keep a scorebook," Abe tells you, "because we don't care who makes the points. What counts is who helps make them." His only real fathead trouble came in 1939, just before the world championship tourney semi-finals with the Renaissance Big Five. Four of his first stringers revolted, demanding more control of Trotter affairs. Saperstein

fired them, cancelled two weeks of bookings, brought in a quartet of untested rookies from Detroit, and lost to the Rens by two points.

Nobody doubts now that the smallest guy in basketball is supreme commander of its most celebrated show. Among the Trotters, Saperstein is known as "Little Caesar."

Abe's wonderfully wacky talent comes from everywhere. Boyd Buie, a onearmed wonder who averaged over 20 points a game, captained Tennessee State's Negro kingpins. Sweetwater Clifton was a fugitive from the Cleveland Indians baseball farm system. Haynes was the idol of Langston, Oklahoma U. Ermer Robinson, set shot dead-eye from San Diego, joined the Trotters after setting a National AAU scoring record at Denver. Goose Tatum was playing an indifferent outfield for the Birmingham Black Barons when Saperstein spotted his 84-inch arms—the longest lunch-hooks in bigtime sport. When Abe tried to convert the awkward Tatum to basketball, veteran Trotters accused him of insanity. Now Tatum, who plays one side of the double-post favored by the Trotters, is good for 20 to 30 points a game when bearing down. Where Saperstein recently sold Sweetwater Clifton to the New York Knicker-bockers for $25,000, he wouldn't part with Tatum for $50,000.

And you couldn't buy the Globetrotters for $1,000,000. They are an international panic, with sell-out houses behind them in 34 countries. At the *Palais du Sport* in Paris last June, they drew 60,000 in five nights. At Oporto, Portugal, a police cordon had to be thrown around their hotel to restrain fanatical admirers. A dozen police riot cars were needed when 3,000 angry patrons broke loose at the Los Angeles Pan-Pacific last January after the "sold-out" sign went up. Basketball never saw the like of Saperstein spurning a $100,000 offer from Jack Solomons, the British promoter, and cleaning up twice that sum with a 73-game tour through 14 European countries. A $6 ticket top for the team that one wintry Minnesota night settled for a total payoff of $5 is now nothing unusual for the Globetrotters. This season more than 2,500,000 will see them all the way from Lima, Peru, to Israel—the grandest tour Saperstein has yet arranged.

"They told me that Negro basketball couldn't succeed on a national scale," says Saperstein. "There was a big amateur wheel who called me into his office, got on the phone, and killed every game I had booked in two states. Rivals infringed on the team's name and I had to go to court to stop."

The little man with the belly like a basketball pauses, wheezing lightly. "Take a look at this," he adds in a voice full of pride.

This is a fat contract for a full-scale A-class production of "The Harlem Globetrotter Story" by Columbia Studios, due to hit the country's movie screens this month. Along with it is a letter from a certain governmental agency.

"The Globetrotters have proven themselves ambassadors extraordinary of good will wherever they have gone," it says. "On any future tours, please call on the State Department of the United States of America for any help we can give."

Abe's five hungry clowns in their beat-up fever have come a long, long way to become the greatest road-show in the history of basketball, if not in all sport.

(Reprinted with permission, Sport Media Enterprises, Inc., 2003)

Early Days
1946–1970

Carl Braun, 1949
The Knicks may have been owned by Madison Square Garden, but they rarely got to play there until the mid '50s, instead toiling before maximum crowds of 5,000 in the old 69th Regiment Armory on Lexington Avenue.

Chapter 8

The First 25 Years

At the end of World War II, professional basketball was very much secondary to the college game. The National Basketball League for the most part played before small crowds in small towns, and had little appeal outside its local communities.

But that began to change in 1946 with the creation of the Basketball Association of America. The pro game moved into large cities like New York, Boston and Philadelphia. Eventually, the NBL and BAA would merge to form the NBA. There would be many challenges along the way, and many franchises would come and go, but what emerged over the next 25 years was a unified league that stretched from coast to coast.

The post-war years were a remarkable time for pro basketball. Not everyone agreed that basketball would ever become a truly big-time sport regarded on the same level as the National Football League, Major League Baseball or even the National Hockey League. But gradually the pieces came together. The pro game developed and marketed its first star players, George Mikan, Bob Pettit and Bob Cousy. It opened its doors—albeit slowly—to African Americans, starting with Nat 'Sweetwater' Clifton, Earl Lloyd and Chuck Cooper. The rule makers adopted the 24-second clock, a game-saving innovation that cut down on fouls and sped up the game. It weeded out small-market teams like Sheboygan, Tri-Cities and Fort Wayne (to name just three) and focused all its efforts on the big cities. The young league responded quickly and decisively when confronted with a betting scandal. And it wasted no time in getting a foothold when a new medium called television arrived on the scene with talk of revolutionizing the way Americans watched sports.

All of those developments were important, but perhaps the primary impetus for the success of the pro game was the advent of a host of outstanding players through the latter part of the 1950s and early 1960s. These men changed the game. They took it above the rim. They made it more athletic. Size and strength mattered more, but not at the expense of agility and speed. The gap that once existed between the plodding, pure ball-control game of the early pros and the fast-paced acrobatics of the barnstormers like the Harlem Globetrotters was narrowed. And the fans responded.

It's impossible to overemphasize the contributions of players like Wilt Chamberlain, Bill Russell, Elgin Baylor, Jerry West, Oscar Robertson and a host of others who gave the NBA the gift of credibility. These men filled arenas, made newspaper headlines and attracted TV moguls. That's not to say the NBA was without problems during these years, but the problems—and there were many—never seemed quite so worrisome as long as Russell was anchoring another Celtics dynasty or Chamberlain was rewriting the record book.

By the mid-'60s pro basketball was firmly enough ensconced

Bob Pettit, 1961
The elegant forward replaced George Mikan as the game's biggest star, but would soon be supplanted by Russell and Chamberlain.

to encourage a group of entrepreneurs to launch a rival league to the NBA. The American Basketball Association began in 1967 and, although it had many troubles, it would popularize the three-point basket and give the game such stars as Julius Erving, George Gervin and Artis Gilmore. As the 1960s ended, the NBA remained the dominant league but merger talks with the ABA had already begun. Professional basketball had come a long way in 25 years.

But it was only the beginning.

1946-47

Another new season, another new league– or was this different?

By Phil Berger

It wasn't love of the game that prompted the owners of this nation's major arenas to forge a new pro basketball league in 1946. With the Axis powers vanquished, America was ready to leave behind the material deprivations of World War II and enjoy its hard-earned leisure. For the men who ran facilities like, say, Madison Square Garden, Uline Arena, Olympia Stadium, and St. Louis Arena, pro basketball seemed a product that could keep their calendars filled, and their profits flowing through winters previously given over to hockey, ice shows, rodeos and college basketball.

The Basketball Association of America (BAA)—a pro league with eleven franchises east of the Mississippi River—was founded on June 16, 1946, in New York by a group comprised largely of members of the Arena Managers Association of America.

Although no one knew it at the time, the BAA would go through multiple franchise shakeouts over the next few years and end up re-named the National Basketball Association, the most successful pro league in the long history of Dr. James Naismith's game.

But back then basketball as a pro spectacle was only a few steps removed from the game played decades before in ballrooms on whose slippery floors patrons danced afterward. In 1946, pro hoops had nothing like the hold of major-league baseball and football on the popular imagination. What's more, past attempts to go pro had soured the public because of unstable leagues whose players might jump teams from month to month and whose ballclubs often folded before a season ran its course.

Those unfortunate precedents did not deter the men behind the BAA. They launched with a regular-season schedule of sixty games to be followed by championship playoffs. In contrast to the 40-minute college game, BAA contests were 48 minutes, on the overly optimistic notion that the public would feel it was getting more for its money.

The eleven franchises were divided into two divisions: the New York Knickerbockers, Philadelphia Warriors, Boston Celtics, Toronto Huskies, Providence Steamrollers, and Washington Capitols in the East; the Cleveland Rebels, Pittsburgh Ironmen, Chicago Stags, Detroit Falcons and St. Louis Bombers in the West.

Each team was obliged to ante up a $10,000 franchise fee to help defray operating expenses and cover the salary of the league's president, Maurice Podoloff (who doubled as president of the American Hockey League).

The game itself was nothing like the game we know today. Players did not routinely double pump or slam dunk. The fact of the matter was that BAA players did not, and could not,

Jumpin' Joe Fulks
The running, gunning 6-foot-5 ex-Marine from Kentucky emerges as the new league's first star, "The Babe Ruth of Basketball."

jump to the ozone. Nor was there a 24-second clock to acclerate the action. Teams had unlimited time to get off a shot. A radical notion for that era was the jump shot, and those who took it defied the conventional wisdom of some coaches that nothing but trouble occurs when a fellow leaves his feet for a shot.

From the ball itself, which BAA players insist was larger, to the trouble they had shooting it—only one BAA player, Washington's Bob Feerick, hit better than 40% of his field goals in 1946-47—the game was markedly different.

⊕ ⊕ ⊕

In the BAA's first season not a single black man was on any of the eleven rosters. The league was lily-white, and many of the players had just returned from military service. For them, the notion of earning a living wage for playing a boy's game—albeit for a modest salary, typically between $3,500 and $6,500—was simply wondrous. Besides, that was decent money for the time, though not enough to keep most BAA players from needing off-season jobs.

BAA teams in the league's first season were assembled by various means. Geography figured in the rosters of franchises like the Providence Steamrollers, who relied heavily on former Rhode Island State College players, and the Pittsburgh Ironmen, who chose players from within a 100 mile radius of the city. The Knicks' roster was top-heavy with players from New York-area colleges.

Then there was 29-year-old Arnold [Red] Auerbach, coach of the Washington Capitols. During the war, Auerbach had coached the Norfolk Naval Training Station team, which exposed him to a number of talented G.I.s. He recruited players who had impressed him during intra-military competitions. It didn't trouble him that these men lived all over the country.

As the teams fleshed out their rosters over the summer, salaries were negotiated and contracts finalized. In a new operation like the BAA, one player, Tom King of the Detroit Falcons, saw an opportunity to expand his role. King, who would average 5.2 points per game in 58 contests in the first season, recalled: "When I reported to the Falcons training camp, it was obvious to me they had a coach, a gym and that the uniforms were ordered. What they didn't have was a publicity director or business manager. I had a B.S. in business administration from the University of Michigan. I knew how to write and type—in high school I'd been a stringer for the Lansing, Mich. *State Journal*—and I knew how to keep the books. So I asked for the jobs of publicity director and business manager of the Falcons and was hired by Arthur Wirtz and James Norris (who owned not only the Falcons' Olympia Stadium but also Chicago Stadium and St. Louis Arena, home courts of the Stags and Bombers). They'd paid me an $8,000 salary as a player and a $500 bonus to sign. I said I could do this other, additional work for $8,000 more."

King, who later became president of the Merchandise Mart and Apparel Center in Chicago—at the time the largest whole-sale-buying complex of its kind in the world—earned $16,500 during 1946-47, more than any player in the league.

Typical of those times was the reception that a pair of Celtics—one 6-foot-7, the other 6-foot-8—got the day they reported to the Boston Garden: a secretary, assuming they were circus freaks, directed them to the hotel where the bigtop's personnel were staying. Eventually, the misdirected lads made it to the Celtics training camp, a dormitory facility they shared with a minor-league hockey team. It proved an incompatible setup, leading to fist fights between the teams that on one occasion at least brought the local gendarmes out.

⊕ ⊕ ⊕

The BAA's first season commenced Nov. 1, 1946 in Toronto—Knicks versus the Huskies.

Back then a ticket could be had for as little as a dollar. The game that the paying customer saw was largely earthbound, its perfect expression the now-defunct two-hand set shot. A shooter planted his feet and, gripping the ball along the seams with both hands, routinely fired it 25 to 35 feet from the basket—easily beyond today's three-point distance.

Players back then didn't operate as comfortably off the dribble. A two-hand set-shot artist required more time and room than the jump-shooter of today's game. To free him up, teams ran a weave that kept players in constant motion and the ball hopping among the five starters. When executed properly, the weave would free a man for that distant two-hander or, with a cunning cut, result in an easy layup. The distinctions common to today's game of power and small forward, of point and off guard, did not apply then. In an offense built around the weave, all but the pivot man were interchangeable.

That man in the pivot sustained the flow, acting as a feeder to teammates crisscrossing off him. Those times he chose to ignore his cutters, he might shoot a sweeping hook shot—a standard shot in a big man's arsenal as he played at close quarters in the six foot lane then in use.

BAA teams were hard-pressed to find an audience that first season. Auerbach's Capitols, the best team in regular-season play with a 49-11 record, averaged only 3,000 fans in Uline Arena, whose capacity was 5,500. In other cities the turnout was even more negligible. There was a night in Pittsburgh, whose 15-45 record was the worst in the league, when only 819 paying customers materialized. It was no surprise when the Ironmen were disbanded at the end of the season. (Cleveland and Toronto also folded their operations.)

Over the course of the season, only Philadelphia and New York drew better than 100,000 paid admissions for their '46-47 home dates. In all, the net receipts for the first season totaled $1,089,949.

While crowds tended to be sparse, those fans that made it to the arena became part of the rowdy atmosphere of that inaugural season. Bearing the brunt of this was the referee, who was accorded the sort of treatment given a no-talent act on an amateur night billing.

"The game," said former referee Sid Borgia, "had what you'd call an uncouth manner. You had no control then, as refs do now. Now coaches can't open their mouths about refs to the press. They can't come on to the court. But back then . . . there was no limit on what was said. All the power you had then was calling a technical foul. And in those days if you called a technical foul, it gave the fans the right to come out and almost put you on a cross—right on the middle of the floor. That's what a technical meant—just like persecution."

The art of self-defense was practically a prerequisite for referees, particularly against fans. "In Philadelphia," said Borgia, "the fans would wait for you as you came by at the end of the game. You had no cops to take you on and off the floor. It was nothing for the fans to spit and kick at you."

⊕ ⊕ ⊕

The BAA tried mightily to interest the public in their game. One idea that was tried was a longer game. In Chicago—whose owners were pushing the concept—the Stags experimented with a few 60-minute games (four 15-minute quarters). The hope, unfounded as it turned out, was that the paying customer

would feel he was getting more bang-for-his-buck.

To publicize its existence, the BAA relied on newspapers and radio. Only Washington televised its contests. "When the Falcons would go on the road," said Detroit's player-publicist-business manager Tom King, "I would carry my old portable Remington typewriter with me and write advances for the papers back in Detroit, and sometimes game accounts for the wire services, who paid by-the-word." The press often managed to report the day-to-day foulups that crimped the BAA's operations—floors that were laid over hockey rinks that then turned slippery from condensation; the failure to provide a doctor to tend to injured players; scorekeepers' errors; "dead" spots on courts that would not give a ball a true bounce.

In its first season, BAA rosters included some men who were not wholeheartedly in the basketball business. Cleveland's Frank Baumholz, among the top scorers in the league with a 14-point average, would cut short his season in February 1947 to report to the Cincinnati Reds' spring training camp. He would play ten seasons with the Reds, Cubs and Phillies as a lifetime .290 hitter. Baumholtz would be joined by at least five others—Detroit's Stan Miasek, St. Louis' Aubrey Davis, and Boston's Al Brightman, John Simmons and Chuck Connors—who would leave the BAA for major league baseball.

The game itself was subject to the same sort of unrest. By January, the league had outlawed the zone defense, a rule change that did not entirely deter teams from playing disguised forms of the zone, which in those days meant frequent cries of "switch." The rule change grew from the league's concern that zone defences made the game less crowd-pleasing. Another problem was, although the forward-thinking Auerbach enjoyed success by having his team fast break at every opportunity, other old-guard coaches viewed any deviation from the slower, patterned game as heresy.

As 1946-47 unfolded, a few players were shooting an innovative shot that saw them leap first into the air and then let fly the ball. That shot, the jump shot, would change basketball completely. But like Stanford's Hank Luisetti, who popularized the running one-hand shot in the 1930s, the jump shooter was often regarded as a basketball eccentric. Some coaches prohibited their players for taking jump shots.

One man who did not resist the future that the jump shot pointed to was Philadelphia coach Eddie Gottlieb, who was known as The Mogul. Gottlieb was an all-round sports promoter whose "main forte," in the words of an associate of his, was basketball. In the Warriors' Joe Fulks, Gottlieb saw a player who could get his shot off—that airborne jumper—at will. And that, thought The Mogul, offered box-office possibilities.

Fulks—called the Babe Ruth of Basketball by *Time* magazine that year—did top BAA scorers in '46-47. His 23.2 ppg scoring average may not seem like much to today, but to his peers Fulks was a revolutionary figure. In that first season, he took a league-high 1,557 field-goal tries (an average of nearly 26 shots a game) at a time when there was no 24-second clock. His 23.2 ppg led the league by more than six points a game.

Remarkable though Fulks' scoring totals were, it should be noted that he played in a game not dominated, as it would be later, by big men. The two players listed as seven-footers, Elmore Mergenthaler (Providence: 14 games, 1.4 ppg) and

Ralph Siewert (St. Louis: 21 games, 1.0 ppg) had little impact. In fact, the BAA's all-league center that year, Stan Miasek of Detroit, was only 6-foot-6, 210 pounds, and had no high school or college basketball experience.

⊕ ⊕ ⊕

For players of any size, the BAA road life took getting used to. Constant rail travel was hard on players accustomed to the weekend schedules of the American League or the shorter season of the collegians.

But after the horrors of World War II to which many of them had been exposed, basketball life on the run was taken in stride. Much of the traveling was by rail. Many pros killed time during long train rides at card tables. On railway coaches occupied by Pittsburgh Ironmen, that meant setting down newspapers on the floor so that tobacco-chewing card sharps like Press Maravich and Stan Noszka could spit without soiling railroad property. In hotel rooms, they set their newspapers by the side of the bed.

For Maravich, whose son Pete later starred in the NBA, the card games were not what they'd been the year before, when he had played for the Youngstown Bears in the National League and allied himself with Bear teammate, Frank Baumholtz, against the team's card-playing coach, Paul Birch. It was Press' habit to fold his hand, then casually look over Birch's cards, revealing their contents to Baumholtz by singing in Serbian. "Un ima kral"—he has a king. Afterward he and Baumholtz would divvy up Birch's losses and laugh about their conniving.

For non-stop antics, nobody topped the Celtics' Chuck Connors, who went on to become TV's *Rifleman*. Connors was a lovable and garish character, who was forever "on." In the stands during preliminary games, or in a railway station, without prompting Connors would spout Shakespearean excerpts and poetry like *Face on the Barroom Floor* or *Casey at the Bat*. In Boston's first season, he was a publicity man's dream, ever ready to spread the then-dubious name of the Celtics to service clubs or radio audiences—any place where a hambone would do.

Teammate John Simmons: "I saw him once in a train station go up to this short guy—total, total stranger—4-foot-10 maybe. Walk up to him and lift up the guy and say, 'Dad, where have you been? I haven't seen you in a while.' Chuck was 6-foot-7 . . . and had this big booming voice. And everybody would be laughing at this little guy that's his 'father.'

Connors, like the Celtics, often stumbled during the first season, but he and his mates got through the year with elan. Take the road trip that saw the Celtics stop in St. Louis for a game. Boston led by five points with half a minute to play. It was then that Celtic coach Honey Russell called a timeout. In his huddle, the coach said the only way the team could lose was to get sloppy with the basketball, and he cited the hypothetical example of Connors doing X, Y and Z—a prophetic flash, it turned out, of what happened. Through Connors' miscues, St. Louis tied the game in regulation and won it in overtime.

When the team assembled at the St. Louis train station, Boston's trainer had the tickets that Honey usually gave out. As the tickets were being dispersed, Connors was paged. Reporting to the station master's office, he found this message: "You're the only person in the world smart enough to blow a five-point lead with 30 seconds. If you're that smart, figure out a way to get

back to Boston without a ticket."

Over the regular-season schedule, one team—the Washington Capitols—proved far and away the best in the league, winning games by an average of nearly ten points a contest. By contrast, the best team in the Western Division, Chicago, had an average margin of victory of fewer than four points a game.

No small part of the Washington team's success owed to its young, aggressive coach, Auerbach. Though short on credentials when he landed in Washington—he'd coached at St. Alban's Prep school and Roosevelt High—Auerbach did not let that undercut his legitimacy. He made it plain who was in charge, and if the task was complicated by his being as young as his players, he never allowed that to interfere.

"I told 'em," said Auerbach, "'If I'm going to lose my job, I'm going to lose it because I can't coach.' Not because those guys are forming opinions and attitudes. Like I'd take a guy out of a ballgame. He'd say, 'Hey, what are you taking me out for?' And I would say, 'Hey, I hired you. I'll fire you. You just play, I'll coach. I won't listen to any crap.'"

Auerbach, who would coach three seasons in Washington, then one season at Tri-Cities before landing in Boston in 1950-51 was, like some of the veteran coaches, dictatorial in his approach, but with Red there was a subtlety to his methods that raised him above the crowd. He had a psychological force on his players—little tricks to get them up.

He was not averse to using disparaging remarks that he swore other coaches had made to stir his players, or to "innocently" question whether, say, 6-foot-3 John Norlander was tall enough—read, "good enough"—to guard a stalwart of the opposition's. He kept his players off balance, his mood changes unnerving some of them.

"It was the way he acted," said Fred Scolari, a starting guard at Washington. "Sometimes he'd come in and be in a good mood, and just charm you. Other times, he'd just say things that made you mad. I think it was his way to psych us. I know

he had a way of making me mad, making me feel as if I'd never won a job."

As a game coach, Auerbach used wit and a white-heat anger to succeed. At a time when a coach could substitute on a jump ball for any man on the floor, he is credited with being the first to rush in the tallest man on his bench when a smaller player was scheduled to jump. He did not tread softly through the first season. He pushed his team, using his reserves sparingly, and running up the score when he could. He worked the referees too, baiting them and rallying Uline Arena crowds to the team's cause.

"Yelling and screaming," said Howie McHugh, the longtime Celtic publicity man. "All the time. Stomping on the floor. Spitting. Doing everything. Oh Jesus. Spitting: p-toooo, p-tooo. It was awful the show he put on. Get the fans screaming mad. They'd think they were being cheated."

Auerbach's Capitols won the Eastern Division by 14 games. But in a first season that resisted logic, the sudden demise of Washington—eliminated from the playoffs in the opening round—fit the cockeyed spirit of the BAA's inaugural campaign. Fulks' Warriors ended up as the league's first champions, and the teetotaling Gottlieb celebrated by consuming the five martinis he'd vowed to drink in one sitting if his Warriors triumphed. Knocked them down with no apparent effect.

For a league that eventually would prosper beyond a pro basketball pioneer's wildest imagination, the BAA of 1946-47 came off looking like a monetary and artistic failure. That's how the league's own president, Mr. Podoloff, regarded it at the time.

But 1946-47 provided a beginning, even if it was a bumpy one. Then again, beginnings are often like that. And for those who were part of that first season, the spirit of it is really all that matters. It was, as Chuck Connors puts it, ". . . a night in the flower of a guy's youth and enthusiasm. Where could he have had it better than to be among a bunch of ballplayers and playing ball? With people yelling and screaming for him."

1946-47 BAA SEASON HIGHLIGHTS

STANDINGS

Eastern Division

	W	L	Pct.	GB
Washington	49	11	.817	—
Philadelphia	35	25	.583	14
New York	33	27	.550	16
Providence	28	32	.467	21
Toronto	22	38	.367	27
Boston	22	38	.367	27

Western Division

	W	L	Pct.	GB
Chicago	39	22	.639	—
St. Louis	38	23	.623	1
Cleveland	30	30	.500	8.5
Detroit	20	40	.333	18.5
Pittsburgh	15	45	.250	23.5

ALL-STAR TEAMS

FIRST TEAM		SECOND TEAM	
Joe Fulks	Philadelphia	Ernie Calverley	Providence
Bob Feerick	Washington	Frank Baumholtz	Cleveland
Stan Miasek	Detroit	John Logan	St. Louis
Bones McKinney	Washington	Chuck Halbert	Chicago
Max Zaslofsky	Chicago	Fred Scolari	Washington

PLAYOFFS

FINALS

Philadelphia 4, Chicago 1
Apr. 16: Chicago 71 at Philadelphia 84
Apr. 17: Chicago 74 at Philadelphia 85
Apr. 19: Philadelphia 75 at Chicago 72
Apr. 20: Philadelphia 73 at Chicago 74
Apr. 22: Chicago 80 at Philadelphia 83

EASTERN DIVISION
SEMI-FINALS

Chicago 4, Washington 2
Apr. 2: Chicago 81 at Washington 65
Apr. 3: Chicago 69 at Washington 53
Apr. 8: Washington 55 at Chicago 67
Apr. 10: Chicago 69 at Washington 76
Apr. 12: Washington 67 at Chicago 55
Apr. 13: Washington 61 at Chicago 66

QUARTER-FINALS

Philadelphia 2, St. Louis 1
Apr. 2: St. Louis 68 at Philadelphia 73
Apr. 5: Philadelphia 51 at St. Louis 73
Apr. 6: Philadelphia 75 at St. Louis 59

WESTERN DIVISION
SEMI-FINALS

Philadelphia 2, New York 0
Apr. 12: New York 70 at Philadelphia 82
Apr. 14: Philadelphia 72 at New York 53

QUARTER-FINALS

New York 2, Cleveland 1
Apr. 2: New York 51 at Cleveland 77
Apr. 5: Cleveland 74 at New York 86
Apr. 9: Cleveland 71 at New York 93

BAA LEADERS

SCORING

	GP	FGM	FTM	PTS	PPG
Joe Fulks, PHW	60	475	439	1389	23.2
Bob Feerick, WSC	55	364	198	926	16.8
Stan Miasek, DTF	60	331	233	895	14.9
Ed Sadowski, TRH/CLR	53	329	219	877	16.5
Max Zaslofsky, CHS	61	336	205	877	14.4
Ernie Calverley, PRO	59	323	199	845	14.3
Chick Halbert, CHS	61	280	213	773	12.7
John Logan, SLB	61	290	190	770	12.6
Leo Mogus, CLR/TRH	58	259	235	753	13.0
Colby Gunther, PIT	52	254	226	734	14.1

FIELD GOALS

	FGM	FGA	FG%
Bob Feerick, WSC	364	908	.401
Ed Sadowski, TRH/CLR	329	891	.369
Earl Shannon, PRO	245	722	.339
Colby Gunther, PIT	254	756	.336
Max Zaslofsky, CHS	336	1020	.329
Don Carlson, CHS	272	845	.322
Connie Simmons, BOS	246	768	.320
Johnny Norlander, WSC	223	698	.319
Kenny Sailors, CLR	229	741	.309
Mel Riebe, CLR	276	898	.307

FREE THROWS

	FTM	FTA	FT%
Fred Scolari, WSC	146	180	.811
Tony Kappen, BOS/PIT	128	161	.795
Stan Stutz, NYK	133	170	.782
Bob Feerick, WSC	198	260	.762
John Logan, SLB	190	254	.748
Max Zaslofsky, CHS	205	278	.737
Joe Fulks, PHW	439	601	.730
Leo Mogus, CLR/TRH	235	325	.723
George Mearns, PRO	126	175	.720
Tony Jaros, CHS	128	181	.707

ASSISTS

	GP	AST	APG
Ernie Calverley, PRO	59	202	3.4
Kenny Sailors, CLR	58	134	2.3
Ossie Schectman, NYK	54	109	2.0
Howie Dallmar, PHW	60	104	1.7
Mickey Rottner, CHS	56	93	1.7
Stan Miasek, DTF	60	93	1.6
Leo Mogus, CLR/TRH	58	84	1.4
Earl Shannon, PRO	57	84	1.5
John Logan, SLB	61	78	1.3
Bob Feerick, WSC	55	69	1.3

THE YEAR IN BASKETBALL

November 1, 1946 The Basketball Association of America, later to become the National Basketball Association, begins play as the New York Knickerbockers defeat the Toronto Huskies, 68-66, at Maple Leaf Gardens in Toronto. Ozzie Schectman scores the first basket in new league's history before a crowd of 7,090. Ed Sadowski, the Huskies' player/coach, leads all scorers with 18 points. The league grants free admittance to any fans taller than Huskies' center, 6-foot-8, George Nostrand.

November 5, 1946 The Boston Celtics make their home debut, playing at Boston Arena. The game is delayed because Boston's Chuck Connors, later to become television's "Rifleman," shatters the glass backboard in pre-game warm-ups.

November 7, 1946 In the Philadelphia Warriors' first-ever game, five Pittsburgh players foul out, leaving the Ironmen with only four eligible players. When Paul Birch, Pittsburgh's coach, refuses the Warriors' offer to allow one of the disqualified players to continue playing, the teams finish the game in a four-on-four contest. Philly wins, 81-75. Joe Fulks leads the Warriors with 25 points.

December 11, 1946 In an experiment, the Chicago Stags and the Cleveland Rebels play a game that features 15-minute quarters instead of the usual 12-minute quarters. The Stags win, 88-70.

January 9, 1947 Less than three months into the inaugural season, Don Martin of Providence sets a BAA record for most points in a game when he scores 40 vs. Cleveland.

January 11, 1947 After using zone defenses for over two months, the BAA outlaws them.

January 14, 1947 Five days after Don Martin sets the league record for most points in a game, Joe Fulks breaks the record by a point, when he scores 41 against Toronto.

March 24, 1947 Utah upsets Kentucky, 49-45, to win the tenth annual NIT. Arnie Ferrin and Vern Gardner lead the Utes with 15 points each. Alex Groza and Jim Line (12 points apiece) lead Kentucky, which was 34-2, entering the game.

March 25, 1947 Holy Cross wins the NCAA tournament with a 58-47 defeat of Oklahoma. George Kaftan is the Crusaders' hero, scoring 30 points against powerful CCNY in the semifinals and 18 in the title tilt. In that finale, Kaftan and two teammates score 48 of Holy Cross's 58 points. Freshman Bob Cousy is a reserve player for the Crusaders.

April 11, 1947 The Indianapolis Kautskys win the 9th annual World Professional Tournament, defeating the Toledo Jeeps, 62-47. Kautskys' forwards Leo Klier, Gus Doerner, and Bill Closs lead the way, combining for 33 points.

April 16, 1947 Joe Fulks of Philadelphia scores a record 29 points in a half in a playoff game against Chicago. Twenty-one of Fulks' points come in a single quarter.

April 22, 1947 The Philadelphia Warriors beat the Chicago Stags, 83-80, in Game 5 of the championship series to win the inaugural BAA title. Joe Fulks, Philadelphia's All-Star forward, leads his club with 34 points while forward Tony Jaros tops Chicago with 21, in a game played at Philadelphia Arena.

1947-48

Four teams disappear, but lone newcomer #1 with a bullet

The BAA came out of its first season on shaky legs. Attendance and press coverage of league games fell far short of expectations, and the franchises in Cleveland, Detroit, Pittsburgh, and Toronto folded over the summer. With three-fifths of the Western Division gone and league enrollment down to seven clubs, league president Maurice Podoloff acted to get the circuit back into working order. He talked the Baltimore Bullets into jumping over from the American Basketball League, the old East Coast circuit which was living out its last few seasons in minor-league fashion. With only eight teams instead of eleven, Podoloff pared down the schedule from 60 to 48 games, and put Washington and Baltimore in the Western Division with Chicago and St. Louis.

But even with the shaky condition of the league, the BAA clubs generally strengthened themselves with a tonic of fresh talent. Players from the disbanded clubs helped some of the teams; Boston got veterans Ed Sadowski and Mel Reibe, Baltimore signed ex-NBL players Kleggie Hermsen and Dick Schulz, Providence wound up with guard Kenny Sailors after he made quick stops in Chicago and Philadelphia, and Chicago picked up Stan Miasek, last season's all-league center. After getting Miasek, the Stags then dealt their center, Chick Halbert, to the Philadelphia Warriors, who needed a big man.

Several rookies also brightened the BAA scene. The New York Knicks signed guard Sid Tannenbaum, a popular player from NYU and forward Carl Braun from Colgate. Chicago added Andy Phillip and Gene Vance, two of the Illinois Whiz Kids who led their school to Big Ten championships during the War. St. Louis signed center Red Rocha from Oregon State, and Baltimore inked forward Paul Hoffman of Purdue. Although none of these rookies were as famous as George Mikan, they nevertheless had reputations which added to the big-league image of the BAA. Another key addition to the league was New York coach Joe Lapchick, a representative of the best of old-time pro ball, and more recently the popular coach at St. John's.

The best news for the league's survival was a torrid first-place battle in both divisions. All four Western teams fought down to the wire in a pack, with St. Louis finishing at 29-19 and Baltimore, Chicago, and Washington all at 28-20. The Bombers now had a top center in rookie Rocha to go along with backcourt aces Johnny Logan and Belus Smawley. The Stags got important help from newcomers Miasek, Phillip, and Vance, but holdover guard Max Zaslofsky led the team in scoring with a 21.0 average. The Washington Caps, transplanted to the Western Division, fielded essentially the same team as last year's first-place entry, headed by guard Bob Feerick. Baltimore, the new club on the block, had a veteran squad which played methodical, ball-control basketball. Player coach Buddy Jeannette brought in NBL veterans Kleggie Hermsen, Dick

Joe Lapchick
Old pro arrives from St. John's University with instant credibility in tow.

Schulz, and Chick Reiser, traded for centers Connie Simmons and Grady Lewis during the season, and had a poised rookie in Paul Hoffman.

The Eastern Division race came down to a struggle between Philadelphia and New York. The Warriors, last year's playoff champs, added a strong center in Chick Halbert to complement forwards Joe Fulks and Howie Dallmar; Fulks led the BAA with a 22.1 scoring average although he trailed Max Zaslofsky in total points scored. The Knicks finished one game back with a quartet of talented young players: Carl Braun, Bud Palmer, Dick Holub, and Sid Tannenbaum. The 20-year-old

Braun used his deadly one-handed shot to score 47 points against Providence on December 6, and he soon added to his arsenal a jump shot which he learned from Palmer, a handsome forward from Princeton. Tannenbaum, from NYU and Holub, from LIU, both had lots of past exposure in Madison Square Garden.

The two New England clubs fared the worst in the league. The Boston Celtics had the all-league center in Ed Sadowski but little else, while the Providence Steamrollers had a stable of fine guards with no one of note up front. The Celtics captured the final playoff spot with a 20-28 record, while Providence was the league punching bag at 6-42.

The regular season eliminated only Providence from the playoffs, since three Western clubs were in a deadlock for the final two playoff spots. A round robin was set up, with Chicago beating Washington and Baltimore beating Chicago. The Caps were thus shut out of the playoffs despite a record only one game below the best in the league.

The playoff procedure was the same as last year, with first, second, and third place finishers meeting each other in the opening round. The first-place Bombers and Warriors split the first six games of their series before the ailing St. Louis squad went down to a crushing 85-46 defeat in the final game at Philadelphia. In the second place matchup, New York and Baltimore split their first two games and met in the rubber

game in Baltimore; the Knicks held a three-point lead with less than two minutes to play, but the Bullets fired back to surge out to an 84-77 victory. The third place series also went the full route of three games, with the Chicago Stags eliminating Boston.

Baltimore and Chicago met to decide an opponent for Philadelphia in the finals, and the old-pro Bullets proved a match for the fast-breaking Stags. With Connie Simmons continuing to show the hot hand he showed late in the regular season after coming over from Boston, the Bullets took 73-67 and 89-72 victories to head into the championship round.

The defending champion Warriors confirmed their status as favorites by whipping the Bullets 71-60 in the opening game before 7,201 fans in Philadelphia. The Warriors evidently began relishing their victory too soon when they led 41-20 at half-time in the second game; the Bullets came on in the last half to win a 66-63 decision to even the series. The Bullets then ran off 72-70 and 78-75 victories in Baltimore to take full charge of the series. The Warriors took the next game in Philadelphia by a score of 91-82, but the Bullets ended it with an 88-73 win on their own home floor. With the Bullets, a dull club to watch and one without any big-name players, as reigning champs, the BAA couldn't honestly hold up its champion as the best pro basketball had to offer. But better things were on the way starting next year.

1947-48 BAA SEASON HIGHLIGHTS

STANDINGS

Eastern Division

	W	L	Pct.	GB
Philadelphia	27	21	.563	—
New York	26	22	.542	1
Boston	20	28	.417	7
Providence	6	42	.125	21

Western Division

	W	L	Pct.	GB
St. Louis	29	19	.604	—
Washington	28	20	.583	1
Chicago	28	20	.583	1
Baltimore	28	20	.583	1

ALL-STAR TEAMS

FIRST TEAM		**SECOND TEAM**	
Joe Fulks	Philadelphia	John Logan	St. Louis
Max Zaslofsky	Chicago	Carl Braun	New York
Ed Sadowski	Boston	Stan Miasek	Chicago
Howie Dallmar	Philadelphia	Fred Scolari	Washington
Bob Feerick	Washington	Buddy Jeannette	Baltimore

PLAYOFFS
FINALS
Baltimore 4, Philadelphia 2
  Apr. 10: Baltimore 60 at Philadelphia 71
  Apr. 13: Baltimore 66 at Philadelphia 63
  Apr. 15: Philadelphia 70 at Baltimore 72
  Apr. 17: Philadelphia 75 at Baltimore 78
  Apr. 20: Baltimore 82 at Philadelphia 91
  Apr. 21: Philadelphia 73 at Baltimore 88

EASTERN DIVISION
SEMI-FINALS
Philadelphia 4, St. Louis 3
  Mar. 23: Philadelphia 58 at St. Louis 60
  Mar. 25: Philadelphia 65 at St. Louis 64
  Mar. 27: St. Louis 56 at Philadelphia 84
  Mar. 30: St. Louis 56 at Philadelphia 51
  Apr. 1: Philadelphia 62 at St. Louis 69
  Apr. 3: St. Louis 61 at Philadelphia 84
  Apr. 6: Philadelphia 85 at St. Louis 46
QUARTER-FINALS
Baltimore 2, New York 1
  Mar. 27: New York 81 at Baltimore 85
  Mar. 28: Baltimore 69 at New York 79
  Apr. 1: New York 77 at Baltimore 84

WESTERN DIVISION
SEMI-FINALS
Baltimore 2, Chicago 0
  Apr. 7: Baltimore 73 at Chicago 67
  Apr. 8: Chicago 72 at Baltimore 89
QUARTER-FINALS
Chicago 2, Boston 1
  Mar. 28: Chicago 79 at Boston 72
  Mar. 31: Chicago 77 at Boston 81
  Apr. 2: Chicago 81 at Boston 74
WESTERN DIVISION TIEBREAKERS
  Mar. 23: Washington 70 at Chicago 74
  Mar. 25: Baltimore 75 at Chicago 72

BAA LEADERS

SCORING

	GP	FGM	FTM	PTS	PPG
Max Zaslofsky, CHS	48	373	261	1007	21.0
Joe Fulks, PHW	43	326	297	949	22.1
Ed Sadowski, BOS	47	308	294	910	19.4
Bob Feerick, WSC	48	293	189	775	16.1
Stan Miasek, CHS	48	263	190	716	14.9
Carl Braun, NYK	47	276	119	671	14.3
John Logan, SLB	48	221	202	644	13.4
Bud Palmer, NYK	48	224	174	622	13.0
Red Rocha, SLB	48	232	147	611	12.7
Fred Scolari, WSC	47	229	131	589	12.5

FIELD GOALS

	FGM	FGA	FG%
Bob Feerick, WSC	293	861	.340
Ed Sadowski, BOS	308	953	.323
Carl Braun, NYK	276	854	.323
Max Zaslofsky, CHS	373	1156	.323
Chick Reiser, BLB	202	628	.322
Bud Palmer, NYK	224	710	.315
Red Rocha, SLB	232	740	.314
Mel Riebe, BOS	202	653	.309
Belus Smawley, SLB	212	688	.308
Stan Miasek, CHS	263	867	.303

FREE THROWS

	FTM	FTA	FT%
Bob Feerick, WSC	189	240	.787
Max Zaslofsky, CHS	261	333	.784
Joe Fulks, PHW	297	390	.762
Buddy Jeannette, BLB	191	252	.758
Howie Dallmar, PHW	157	211	.744
Bud Palmer, NYK	174	234	.744
John Logan, SLB	202	272	.743
Johnny Norlander, WSC	135	182	.742
Chick Reiser, BLB	137	185	.741
Fred Scolari, WSC	131	179	.732

ASSISTS

	GP	AST	APG
Howie Dallmar, PHW	48	120	2.5
Ernie Calverley, PRO	47	119	2.5
Jim Seminoff, CHS	48	89	1.9
Chuck Gilmur, CHS	48	77	1.6
Andy Phillip, CHS	32	74	2.3
Ed Sadowski, BOS	47	74	1.6
Buddy Jeannette, BLB	46	70	1.5
John Logan, SLB	48	62	1.3
Carl Braun, NYK	47	61	1.3
Saul Mariaschin, BOS	43	60	1.4

THE YEAR IN BASKETBALL

January 10, 1948 Washington scores a record 20 points in overtime as they beat Philadelphia.

January 18, 1948 George Mikan of the Minneapolis Lakers scores an all-time NBL high of 41 points in a game against Rochester.

February 24, 1948 In an exhibition game, the Harlem Globetrotters defeat the Minneapolis Lakers on an Ermer Robinson shot at the buzzer.

March 17, 1948 St. Louis, led by Ed Macauley's 24 points, wins the NIT by knocking off NYU, 65-52.

March 23, 1948 Behind All-Americans Alex Groza and Ralph Beard, who combine for 26 points, Adolph Rupp's Kentucky wins the NCAA tournament with a 58-42 defeat of Baylor.

April 11, 1948 George Mikan pours in 40 points to lead the Minneapolis Lakers to a 75-71 victory over the New York Rens in the title game of the World Professional Tournament in Chicago. Nat (Sweetwater) Clifton paces the Rens with 24. The game is the final one played in the acknowledged world tournament, which began in 1939 and ran consecutively for 10 years.

April 13, 1948 Trailing 41-20 at halftime, the Baltimore Bullets rally to beat the Philadelphia Warriors, 66-63, in Game 2 of the BAA finals.

April 21, 1948

The Baltimore Bullets defeat the Philadelphia Warriors, 88-73, to win the BAA championship in six games. The Bullets feature a balanced scoring attack. Guard Chick Reiser (16 points) leads five Bullets in double figures. Joe Fulks leads Philadelphia with 28 points.

August 1948 The United States pummels France, 65-21, to clinch the gold medal at the Summer Olympics in London. The victory concludes an 8-0 march through the international tournament. (Note: The 1940 Olympic Games were originally scheduled to be held in Tokyo, but several countries planned to boycott the Games there because Japan was waging an aggressive war in Asia and then Japan itself decided the Games would be a distraction to their military goals. The Games were rescheduled to be held in Helsinki, Finland, but the start of World War II in 1939 caused the Games to be cancelled. The 1944 Olympic Games were also not held because of World War II.)

1948-49

Rest of BAA no match for league-jumping Mikan and Lakers

It was an ingenious move. It didn't insure survival, but it gave the BAA a strong upper hand in the war between the leagues. BAA president Maurice Podoloff convinced the Minneapolis Lakers, Rochester Royals, Fort Wayne Zollner Pistons, and Indianapolis Kautskys to leave the NBL and cast their lots with the newer league. Podoloff had the big arenas and big cities to offer these clubs, and they had the first-rate players that the BAA needed to draw customers into those arenas. With George Mikan and Bob Davies and their team-mates now in the circuit, the BAA was certainly the best professional league in the country.

All eight BAA clubs from last season returned for this campaign, giving Podoloff a lineup of twelve teams. Baltimore and Washington joined New York, Philadelphia, Boston, and Providence in the Eastern Division, while the four new members combined with Chicago and St. Louis to form the Western Division. Fort Wayne and Indianapolis caused a mild surprise by finishing at the bottom of standings in the West. The Pistons had been a winning club in the tough NBL last season, but age was cutting into the squad. The Indianapolis team, renamed the Jets, also was declining into ineptitude. The other two newcomers, however, went right to the head of the class.

The Lakers and Royals had met in last year's NBL championship series, and their rivalry resumed in the regular campaign in the BAA. The Lakers had George Mikan, the man the entire league was talking about. A famous college player at DePaul and a fabulously successful pro in two seasons in the NBL, Mikan had the biggest name in the world of basketball. In the realm of college ball, only Alex Groza and Ralph Beard of the University of Kentucky could rival Mikan's reputation. Now Mikan was coming into cities like New York, Philadelphia, and Boston as a pro, and crowds were filling the arenas there to see him play. Indeed, the Madison Square Garden marquee advertised an upcoming event as "Tonite: George Mikan vs. Knicks." Big George rarely disappointed the customers, averaging 28.3 and hitting over 45 points six times.

But the Lakers had more than just the high-scoring Mikan. Jim Pollard at forward relied on grace as much as Mikan did on strength. A tremendous leaper with a soft shooting touch, Pollard would score when opponents double-teamed and triple-teamed Mikan. Just as easily, he could shoot passes into Mikan when the big man was free to score. Herm Schaefer and Swede Carlson were the guards who fed the ball to Mikan and Pollard, and the other forward was Arnie Ferrin, who had led Utah to the NCAA championship in 1944 and the NIT title in 1947.

The Rochester Royals, however, conceded nothing to the Lakers and actually finished one game ahead of them in the West. The Royals had in Arnie Risen a center who was not as strong as Mikan but who was much more mobile. Risen ranked fourth in league scoring with a 16.6 average and he led the

George Mikan
The game's first truly dominant center, he uses his six-foot-10, 245-pound frame to fearsome effect in and around the basket.

league in field goal percentage. The Royals lacked the Lakers' strength up front, but they clearly outclassed them in the backcourt. Even without Al Cervi, who left the team to join the NBL Syracuse Nats, the Royals had Bob Davies, Red Holzman, and Bobby Wanzer. Davies was the BAA's top driving guard and a master at triggering the fast break.

Behind these two titans and ahead of Fort Wayne and Indianapolis came the Chicago Stags and St. Louis Bombers, old-line BAA clubs. The Stags had two top guards in set-shooter Max Zaslofsky and playmaker Andy Phillip and a very

competent center in rookie Ed Mikan, George's baby brother, but they put together an ordinary 31-20 record until coach Ole Olsen was canned. Under Phil Brownstein, the Stags streaked to a 7-2 mark down the stretch. The Bombers fell under .500 despite continued good play from guards Johnny Logan and Belus Smawley.

The Eastern Division had only old-line BAA clubs. The Washington Capitols took first place with a 38-22 record, the same mark that earned Chicago third place in the West. Coach Red Auerbach still had Freddie Scolari, Bob Feerick and Bones McKinney in his starting lineup, but he got Kleggie Hermsen from Baltimore to take over the center job. Six games back in second place came the New York Knicks. Forwards Carl Braun and Bud Palmer did most of the scoring in the early going, with rookie Ray Lumpp helping out after coming over from Indianapolis in a mid-season deal. Rookie Harry Gallatin joined the team after the first eight games of the season, and played in every single contest until he retired in 1958, a career of 746 consecutive games.

The other Eastern teams all finished below the .500 mark. The defending champion Bullets were getting old and had to work some new blood into the lineup. Philadelphia got good scoring from Joe Fulks and Ed Sadowski, but an injury to Howie Dallmar severely hurt the team. The Boston Celtics had a new coach in Doggie Julian, a blue-chip rookie in George

Kaftan, and lots of new faces via trades; the result, unfortunately, was a 25-35 record and no playoff berth. The Providence Steamrollers had the worst record in the league despite the fine play of guards Kenny Sailors and Ernie Calverley.

Eight teams made it to the playoffs, with an entirely new playoff schedule. The first two rounds would decide divisional representatives for the finals, so that the two first-place clubs theoretically could meet in the championship series. The opening round saw Washington down Philadelphia and New York eliminate defending champion Baltimore in the East. In the West, Rochester knocked off St. Louis, and Minneapolis beat Chicago. Washington then bested New York two games to one while the basketball universe paid most of its attention to the Rochester-Minneapolis showdown. The Lakers took an 80-79 decision in Rochester, then beat the Royals 67-55 in St. Paul after trailing 52-49 after three periods. The finals, then, came down to Minneapolis versus Washington.

The Lakers ran off three quick victories in the best-of-seven set, with Mikan scoring 42, 10 and 35 points. In the fourth game, Mikan netted 27, but the Caps broke his wrist and won the game 83-71. George sported a cast for the fifth game and scored 22 points while the Caps won 74-66. Ahead by only a 3-2 margin, the Lakers wrapped up the BAA title with a 77-56 victory in St. Paul.

1948-49 BAA SEASON HIGHLIGHTS

STANDINGS

Eastern Division

	W	L	Pct.	GB
Washington	38	22	.633	—
New York	32	28	.533	6
Baltimore	29	31	.483	9
Philadelphia	28	32	.467	10
Boston	25	35	.417	13
Providence	12	48	.200	26

Western Division

	W	L	Pct.	GB
Rochester	45	15	.750	—
Minneapolis	44	16	.733	1
Chicago	38	22	.633	7
St. Louis	29	31	.483	16
Fort Wayne	22	38	.367	23
Indianapolis	18	42	.300	27

ALL-STAR TEAMS

FIRST TEAM		SECOND TEAM	
George Mikan	Minneapolis	Arnie Risen	Rochester
Joe Fulks	Philadelphia	Bob Feerick	Washington
Bob Davies	Rochester	Bones McKinney	Washington
Max Zaslofsky	Chicago	Ken Sailors	Providence
Jim Pollard	Minneapolis	John Logan	St. Louis

PLAYOFFS

FINALS

Minneapolis 4, Washington 2
Apr. 4: Washington 84 at Minneapolis 88
Apr. 6: Washington 62 at Minneapolis 76
Apr. 8: Minneapolis 94 at Washington 74
Apr. 9: Minneapolis 71 at Washington 83
Apr. 11: Minneapolis 66 at Washington 74
Apr. 13: Washington 56, Minneapolis (at St. Paul) 77

EASTERN DIVISION

SEMI-FINALS

Washington 2, New York 1
Mar. 29: New York 71 at Washington 77
Mar. 31: Washington 84 at New York 86, OT
Apr. 2: New York 76 at Washington 84

QUARTER-FINALS

Washington 2, Philadelphia 0
Mar. 23: Washington 92 at Philadelphia 70
Mar. 24: Philadelphia 78 at Washington 80

New York 2, Baltimore 1
Mar. 23: New York 81 at Baltimore 82
Mar. 24: Baltimore 82 at New York 84
Mar. 26: Baltimore 99 at New York 103, OT

WESTERN DIVISION

SEMI-FINALS

Minneapolis 2, Rochester 0
Mar. 27: Minneapolis 80 at Rochester 79
Mar. 29: Rochester 55, Minneapolis (at St. Paul) 67

QUARTER-FINALS

Rochester 2, St. Louis 0
Mar. 22: St. Louis 64 at Rochester 93
Mar. 23: Rochester 66 at St. Louis 64

Minneapolis 2, Chicago 0
Mar. 23: Chicago 77 at Minneapolis 84
Mar. 24: Minneapolis 101 at Chicago 85

BAA LEADERS

SCORING

	GP	FGM	FTM	PTS	PPG
George Mikan, MPL	60	583	532	1698	28.3
Joe Fulks, PHW	60	529	502	1560	26.0
Max Zaslofsky, CHS	58	425	347	1197	20.6
Arnie Risen, ROC	60	345	305	995	16.6
Ed Sadowski, PHW	60	340	240	920	15.3
Belus Smawley, SLB	59	352	210	914	15.5
Bob Davies, ROC	60	317	270	904	15.1
Kenny Sailors, PRO	57	309	281	899	15.8
Carl Braun, NYK	57	299	212	810	14.2
John Logan, SLB	57	282	239	803	14.1

FIELD GOALS

	FGM	FGA	FG%
Arnie Risen, ROC	345	816	.423
George Mikan, MPL	583	1403	.416
Ed Sadowski, PHW	340	839	.405
Jim Pollard, MPL	314	792	.396
Red Rocha, SLB	223	574	.389
Bobby Wanzer, ROC	202	533	.379
Connie Simmons, BLB	299	794	.377
Herm Schaefer, MPL	214	572	.374
Belus Smawley, SLB	352	946	.372
Howie Shannon, PRO	292	802	.364

FREE THROWS

	FTM	FTA	FT%
Bob Feerick, WSC	256	298	.859
Max Zaslofsky, CHS	347	413	.840
Bobby Wanzer, ROC	209	254	.823
Herm Schaefer, MPL	174	213	.817
Howie Shannon, PRO	152	189	.804
Hal Tidrick, INJ/BLB	164	205	.800
John Logan, SLB	239	302	.791
Jake Pelkington, FTW/BLB	211	267	.790
Walt Budko, BLB	244	309	.790
Joe Fulks, PHW	502	638	.787

ASSISTS

	GP	AST	APG
Bob Davies, ROC	60	321	5.4
Andy Phillip, CHS	60	319	5.3
John Logan, SLB	57	276	4.8
Ernie Calverley, PRO	59	251	4.3
George Senesky, PHW	60	233	3.9
Jim Seminoff, BOS	58	229	3.9
George Mikan, MPL	60	218	3.6
Kenny Sailors, PRO	57	209	3.7
Bob Feerick, WSC	58	188	3.2
Bobby Wanzer, ROC	60	186	3.1

THE YEAR IN BASKETBALL

November 25, 1948 Howie Dallmar of the Philadelphia Warriors goes 0-for-15 from the field to tie the BAA record he set a year earlier. Dallmar's goose eggs would be matched seven times in coming years and exceeded only 43 years later, in the '91-92 season, when Tim Hardaway goes 0-17.

December 4, 1948 The Washington Capitols defeat the Baltimore Bullets, 83-82, running their record to 15-0, the best start in BAA history. The Houston Rockets will tie the Capitols' record in 1983.

December 18, 1948 The Knicks' Carl Braun sets a single-game high by scoring 47 points in a game versus Providence.

January 18, 1949 The Associated Press publishes its first weekly national basketball poll. The rankings have Saint Louis first, followed by Kentucky, Western Kentucky, Minnesota, Oklahoma A&M, San Francisco, Illinois, Hamline, Villanova, and Utah.

February 10, 1949 Joe Fulks of Philadelphia scores an NBA record 63 points in a game against Indianapolis. Fulks goes 27 of 56 (.482) from the floor and scores 33 in the second-half.

February 22, 1949 George Mikan of the Minneapolis Lakers scores 48 points in a game against the New York Knicks.

March 21, 1949 The New York Rens, playing in the NBL as the Denver Rens, plays its final game, vs. the Denver Nuggets, in Rockford, Ill. Through three decades the Rens record was 2,588-529 (.830).

March 26, 1949 Kentucky, defeated in the opening round of this year's NIT, wins its second consecutive NCAA tournament, defeating Oklahoma A&M, 46-36. Alex Groza, the Wildcats' sterling center, tosses in 25 to lead the victory. The game matches two Hall of Fame coaches and their differing styles, Kentucky's Adolph Rupp preferred fast breaks and A&M's Hank Iba liked the slow-down game. Later, Kentucky is implicated in point-shaving in its NIT loss to Loyola-Chicago. In 1952, Groza, Ralph Beard, and Dale Barnstable will admit to the offense and are banned from the NBA.

March 26, 1949 Jack Toomey of the Baltimore Bullets commits a record 8 fouls in an overtime game vs. New York. As a team, Baltimore commits a record 53 fouls. Eleven players foul out, including 6 Bullets.

April 13, 1949 The Minneapolis Lakers win their first BAA title, whipping the Washington Capitols, 77-56, to take the series, four games to two. George Mikan, the Lakers' big center, dominates inside with 29 points. Lakers' guard Herm Schaefer adds 17.

1949-50

NBL comes aboard, but Capt. Mikan, Lakers keep cruising

Three years of financial warfare ended with the merger of the BAA and the NBL, giving birth to a far-flung hodgepodge called the National Basketball Association. From last year's BAA came New York, Boston, Philadelphia, Washington, Baltimore, Rochester, Minneapolis, Chicago, St. Louis, and Fort Wayne. From the NBL came Syracuse, Anderson, Tri-Cities, Waterloo, Sheboygan, and Denver. Debuting in the pro ranks were the Indianapolis Olympians, composed mostly of graduated University of Kentucky stars. The seventeen clubs stretched from Boston to Denver as the merger weeded out only five teams. The BAA clubs of Providence and Indianapolis and the NBL entries of Hammond, Oshkosh, and Dayton fell by the wayside.

League commissioner Maurice Podoloff faced tremendous scheduling problems. He put the new Indianapolis club and five NBL teams into the Western Division, kept the BAA's western wing together as the Central Division, and put Syracuse, the strongest of the NBL clubs, in with the BAA's eastern clubs. The demands of travel, especially in an era before flying was common, led to an unbalanced schedule: Eastern and Central teams played 68 games, Syracuse, Anderson and Tri-Cities played 64 games, and Denver, Waterloo and Sheboygan played 62 games.

But as chaotic as it seemed, this league admittedly had the nation's top pro teams (with the possible exception of the Globetrotters). The two best teams battled it out at the top of the Central Division. The Minneapolis Lakers had George Mikan at center, and he was at the peak of his game; he led the circuit with a 27.4 scoring average, hit for a high game of 51 points in one contest, and was brutally effective as a rebounder and defender. Forward Jim Pollard headed up the supporting cast, that included three top rookies: 6-foot-7 rebounder Vern Mikkelsen, 5-foot-10 playmaker Slater Martin, and 6-foot-3 reserve forward Bud Grant, a future great football coach. As strong as the Lakers were, the Rochester Royals tied them for first place with a late-season winning streak of 15 games. Relying on mobility and ball-handling, the Royal attack centered on veteran guards Bob Davies and Bobby Wanzer and on center Arnie Risen. Both the Lakers and Royals finished at 51-17.

Alex Groza
Joining the Indianapolis Olympians with Kentucky teammate Ralph Beard in tow, rookie blossoms immediately into one of the league's best.

Tied for third were the Fort Wayne Zollner Pistons, with a hot rookie in forward Fred Schaus, and the Chicago Stags, with guards Max Zaslofsky and Andy Phillip still the heart of the team. The St. Louis Bombers signed rookie Ed Macauley, a weak-rebounding but high-scoring center from St. Louis University, but the Bombers nevertheless finished last.

In the West, only Indianapolis and Anderson finished above .500. The Olympians had two of the best-known college players of the postwar years: center Alex Groza and guard Ralph Beard. Both reacted splendidly to their new pro surroundings.

Groza finished second to Mikan with a 23.4 scoring average, three times going over 40 points in one game. The Anderson Packers had won the final NBL championship, and led by guard Frankie Brian, they made their only season in the NBA a winning one. The Tri-Cities Blackhawks came in third despite owner Ben Kerner hiring Red Auerbach as coach after he was fired by Washington. Sheboygan won the fourth playoff spot with a 22-40 record, while Waterloo and Denver finished out of sight in the depths of the West.

Playing a heavy schedule against the weaker Western teams, the Syracuse Nats put together the best record in the league, a sparkling 51-13 mark. The schedule didn't explain how the Nats won nine of ten games against Eastern teams and seven of ten from Central teams; their talent did that. Old pro Al Cervi was the backcourt leader and coach, and Dolph Schayes, now a rugged star who could score both with long set shots and with inside muscle, was the ace scorer. Other key men on this scrappy squad included strong center George Ratkovicz, forward Alex Hannum, and guards Billy Gabor and Paul Seymour.

The New York Knicks finished a strong second in the East, with coach Joe Lapchick putting together a deep squad which excelled at running and team basketball. Bud Palmer had quit to concentrate on a broadcasting career, but shooter Carl Braun and rebounder Harry Gallatin returned from last year's team. Center Connie Simmons came over from Baltimore, and rookies Vince Boryla, Dick McGuire, and Ernie Vandeweghe added their college reputations and solid talent. The stocky Boryla had just finished setting scoring records at the University of Denver with his hook shot, McGuire came from St. John's with a poor

shot but great playmaking ability, and Colgate's Vandeweghe added forward strength whenever he could get away from his medical studies. The Washington Capitols, without coach Auerbach but with lots of veteran players, finished third. Philadelphia barely managed to take the fourth playoff spot ahead of Baltimore and Boston as Joe Finks had a poor season.

After Minneapolis beat Rochester and Fort Wayne beat Chicago in one-game tie-breakers in the Central Division, the opening round of the playoffs began. Six clubs bit the dust in that round, and the second round left Syracuse, Minneapolis, and Anderson as the divisional champs. The Lakers then polished off the Packers in two straight games and readied themselves for the Nats in the title series.

The Lakers took the first game in Syracuse 68-66 on a last-second heave by Bob Harrison. The Nats won the second game 91-85, but the Lakers were happy to come away with a split on enemy territory. Back in Minnesota, the Lakers drilled out 91-77 and 77-69 victories, using their superior strength to beat down the well-coordinated Nats. The scene for the sixth game shifted to Syracuse, and the Nats used new tactics to combat the Lakers. Coach Cervi put tough Paul Seymour on Jim Pollard as a watchdog, and he sent his big men into the game in relays to physically work George Mikan over. The strategy worked, as the Nats held a 21-point lead with only six minutes left and coasted to an 83-76 triumph. But once the teams got back to Minneapolis, the Lakers took the upper hand, with Mikan muscling his way to 40 points, and with several fights enlivening the proceedings, the Lakers pounded out a 110-95 victory that brought them the first NBA championship.

1949-50 SEASON HIGHLIGHTS

STANDINGS

Central Division

	W	L	Pct.	GB
Minneapolis	51	17	.750	—
Rochester	51	17	.750	—
Fort Wayne	40	28	.588	11
Chicago	40	28	.588	11
St. Louis	26	42	.382	25

Eastern Division

	W	L	Pct.	GB
Syracuse	51	13	.797	—
New York	40	28	.588	13
Washington	32	36	.471	21
Philadelphia	26	42	.382	27
Baltimore	25	43	.368	28
Boston	22	46	.324	31

Western Division

	W	L	Pct.	GB
Indianapolis	39	25	.609	—
Anderson	37	27	.578	2
Tri-Cities	29	35	.453	10
Sheboygan	22	40	.355	16
Waterloo	19	43	.306	19
Denver	11	51	.177	27

ALL-STAR TEAMS

FIRST TEAM		SECOND TEAM	
George Mikan	Minneapolis	Frank Brian	Anderson
Jim Pollard	Minneapolis	Fred Schaus	Fort Wayne
Alex Groza	Indianapolis	Dolph Schayes	Syracuse
Bob Davies	Rochester	Al Cervi	Syracuse
Max Zaslofsky	Chicago	Ralph Beard	Indianapolis

PLAYOFFS
FINALS
Minneapolis 4, Syracuse 2
Apr. 8: Minneapolis 68 at Syracuse 66
Apr. 9: Minneapolis 85 at Syracuse 91
Apr. 14: Syracuse 77, Minneapolis (at St. Paul) 91
Apr. 16: Syracuse 69, Minneapolis (at St. Paul) 77
Apr. 20: Minneapolis 76 at Syracuse 83
Apr. 23: Syracuse 95 at Minneapolis 110
SEMI-FINALS
Minneapolis 2, Anderson 0
Apr. 5: Anderson 50 at Minneapolis 75
Apr. 6: Minneapolis 90 at Anderson 71

EASTERN DIVISION FINALS
Syracuse 2, New York 1
Mar. 26: New York 83 at Syracuse 91, OT
Mar. 30: Syracuse 76 at New York 80
Apr. 2: New York 80 at Syracuse 91
CENTRAL DIVISION FINALS
Minneapolis 2, Fort Wayne 0
Mar. 27: Fort Wayne 79 at Minneapolis 93
Mar. 28: Minneapolis 89 at Fort Wayne 82
WESTERN DIVISION FINALS
Anderson 2, Indianapolis 1
Mar. 28: Anderson 74 at Indianapolis 77
Mar. 30: Indianapolis 67 at Anderson 84
Apr. 1: Anderson 67 at Indianapolis 65
EASTERN DIVISION SEMI-FINALS
Syracuse 2, Philadelphia 0
Mar. 22: Philadelphia 76 at Syracuse 93
Mar. 23: Syracuse 59 at Philadelphia 53
New York 2, Washington 0
Mar. 21: New York 90 at Washington 87
Mar. 22: Washington 83 at New York 103

CENTRAL DIVISION SEMI-FINALS
Fort Wayne 2, Rochester 0
Mar. 23: Fort Wayne 90 at Rochester 84
Mar. 25: Rochester 78 at Fort Wayne 79, OT
Minneapolis 2, Chicago 0
Mar. 22: Chicago 75 at Minneapolis 85
Mar. 25: Minneapolis 75 at Chicago 67
WESTERN DIVISION SEMI-FINALS
Anderson 2, Tri-Cities 1
Mar. 21: Tri-Cities 77 at Anderson 89
Mar. 23: Anderson 75 at Tri-Cities 76
Mar. 26: Tri-Cities 71 at Anderson 94
Indianapolis 2, Sheboygan 1
Mar. 21: Sheboygan 85 at Indianapolis 86
Mar. 23: Indianapolis 85 at Sheboygan 96
Mar. 25: Sheboygan 84 at Indianapolis 91
TIEBREAKERS
Mar. 20: Chicago 69 at Fort Wayne 86
Mar. 21: Minneapolis 78 at Rochester 76

NBA LEADERS

SCORING

	GP	FGM	FTM	PTS	PPG
George Mikan, MPL	68	649	567	1865	27.4
Alex Groza, INO	64	521	454	1496	23.4
Frankie Brian, AND	64	368	402	1138	17.8
Max Zaslofsky, CHS	68	397	321	1115	16.4
Ed Macauley, SLB	67	351	379	1081	16.1
Dolph Schayes, SYR	64	348	376	1072	16.8
Carl Braun, NYK	67	373	285	1031	15.4
Kenny Sailors, DNN	57	329	329	987	17.3
Jim Pollard, MPL	66	394	185	973	14.7
Fred Schaus, FTW	68	351	270	972	14.3

FIELD GOALS

	FGM	FGA	FG%
Alex Groza, INO	521	1090	.478
Dick Mehen, WAT	347	826	.420
Bobby Wanzer, ROC	254	614	.414
Harry Boykoff, WAT	288	698	.413
George Mikan, MPL	649	1595	.407
John Hargis, AND	223	550	.405
Red Rocha, SLB	275	679	.405
Vern Mikkelsen, MPL	288	722	.399
Ed Macauley, SLB	351	882	.398
Jack Toomay, DNN	204	514	.397

FREE THROWS

	FTM	FTA	FT%
Max Zaslofsky, CHS	321	381	.843
Chick Reiser, WSC	212	254	.835
Al Cervi, SYR	287	346	.829
Belus Smawley, SLB	260	314	.828
Fran Curran, ROC	199	241	.826
Frankie Brian, AND	402	488	.824
Fred Scolari, WSC	236	287	.822
Fred Schaus, FTW	270	330	.818
Leo Kubiak, WAT	192	236	.814
Bobby Wanzer, ROC	283	351	.806

ASSISTS

	GP	AST	APG
Dick McGuire, NYK	68	386	5.7
Andy Phillip, CHS	65	377	5.8
Bob Davies, ROC	64	294	4.6
Al Cervi, SYR	56	264	4.7
George Senesky, PHW	68	264	3.9
Dolph Schayes, SYR	64	259	4.0
Jim Pollard, MPL	66	252	3.8
Jim Seminoff, BOS	65	249	3.8
Carl Braun, NYK	67	247	3.7
John Logan, SLB	62	240	3.9

THE YEAR IN BASKETBALL

August 3, 1949 The National Basketball Association comes into being when the Basketball Association of America grants admittance to six surviving teams of the National Basketball League. Maurice Podoloff, the BAA's first president, continues as president of the resulting 17-team league.

November 20, 1949 The Knicks' Paul Noel fouls out of a game versus Philadelphia in 9 minutes. At the time, it is the quickest disqualification in NBA history.

November 24, 1949 Don Otten of the Tri-Cities Hawks commits a record 8 personal fouls in a game at Sheboygan.

November 27, 1949 Syracuse beats Anderson, 125-123, in 5 overtimes. Anderson commits a record 66 personal fouls and the Nats attempt a record 86 free throws, making 59.

March 10, 1950 The Sheboygan Redskins tally 61 field goals and 51 assists, both records, in a game vs. Denver.

March 18, 1950 CCNY defeats Bradley, 69-61, to win the NIT.

March 29, 1950 CCNY becomes the only team in history to win both the NIT and NCAA post-season tournaments when they edge Bradley for the second time in nine days, 71-68, to win the NCAA crown. The Beavers' Irwin Dambrot, who tallies 15 points in the clinching game, is named Most Outstanding Player.

April 23, 1950 Led by George Mikan's 40 points, the Minneapolis Lakers defeat the Syracuse Nationals, 110-95, to win the first NBA championship in six games. Dolph Schayes leads the losers with 23 in Game 6.

April 25, 1950 Chuck Cooper becomes the first African-American to be drafted by an NBA team when the Celtics tab him on the second round of the draft. Later, in the ninth round, Washington selects another black player, Earl Lloyd.

April 27, 1950 The Boston Celtics, coming off four consecutive losing seasons, hire Arnold (Red) Auerbach as head coach. Boston will go 39-30 in 1950-51. In 16 seasons, Auerbach will lead Boston to nine NBA titles.

The color of the basket is changed to bright orange after studies show the color improves shooting accuracy.

May 24, 1950 Nat "Sweetwater" Clifton of the Harlem Globetrotters becomes the first black player to sign with an NBA team when he inks a pact with the Knicks.

1950-51

Cooper, Lloyd, Clifton break color barrier, Royals shock Lakers

The shock waves rippled throughout college basketball: Manhattan College star Junius Kellogg reported in January that he had been offered a bribe from gamblers to shave points in a game in Madison Square Garden. District Attorney Frank Hogan followed up with an investigation that shocked the basketball world. College games at the Garden, it turned out, had often been fixed, and several New York powerhouses were directly implicated. Practically the entire City College of New York (CCNY) squad, winners of both the National Invitation Tournament (NIT) and National Collegiate Athletic (NCAA) crowns last spring, confessed to point shaving; players from Long Island University (LIU) and New York University (NYU) were also involved, and the St. John's squad was mentioned but never indicted. With the college basketball world recoiling in horror, pro ball now had its first opportunity to capture some of the hoop spotlight in New York, the media capital of the nation.

The NBA, which offered an alternative to college ball, had consolidated into ten teams by early 1951; Chicago, St. Louis, Anderson, Sheboygan, Waterloo, and Denver had all dropped out after last season, and the Washington Capitols folded on January 9 after compiling a 10-25 record in relative privacy. The ten remaining clubs snapped up the top players from these defunct teams, making the league a much tougher circuit. Black players were admitted into the league this year, with Boston's Chuck Cooper, Syracuse's Earl Lloyd and New York's Sweetwater Clifton the trailblazers at the start of the season. There was now even an All-Star game, a March affair in Boston won by the East, 111-94.

But although the West lost the exhibition, the two strongest clubs were still in that division. The Minneapolis Lakers had the All-Star front line of George Mikan, Jim Pollard, and Vern Mikkelsen, plus a backcourt ace in Slater Martin. The Rochester Royals had a smart, veteran club featuring Bob Davies, Bobby Wanzer, and Arnie Risen. As usual, these two clubs finished first and second in their division, with the Lakers this season taking first place by three games.

The next two playoff spots went to the Fort Wayne Zollner Pistons, who were helped by 6-foot-9 rookie center Larry Foust, and the Indianapolis Olympians, with Alex Groza and Ralph Beard among the top ten scorers in the league. Tri-Cities, a surprise survivor of the league consolidation, got backcourt star Frankie Brian out of the wreckage of the folded teams in a very complicated fashion. After Anderson left, the Chicago Stags picked up Brian's contract; the Stags then sent Brian to Tri-Cities for an unproven rookie named Bob Cousy.

A star at Holy Cross, Cousy found himself passed around like a bad check before he had even played a game. After the Boston Celtics had passed over the local star, Tri-Cities signed him and sent him to Chicago; then Chicago folded, leaving

Bob Cousy
An ignominious start belies the incredible career that lay ahead.

Cousy without a team. Three guards from the Chicago roster went into a pot, with New York, Philadelphia, and Boston drawing their names out of a hat. The Knicks took Max Zaslofsky, a top shooter and the prize of the bunch. The Warriors picked next and came up with Andy Phillip, a great playmaker. The Celtics were stuck with Cousy, a popular New England player but one that new coach Red Auerbach figured as an unlikely pro.

The 6-foot-1 Cousy proved Auerbach wrong and made a winning coach out of him in the process. Cousy immediately set the league on its ear with his fancy-Dan passes, rocketing

the ball from behind his back to open teammates, shoveling it blind to waiting Celtics. His dribbling also delighted spectators, as he could put the ball behind his back or between his legs without losing a step. That he could score was evident in his 15.6 average.

Easy Ed Macauley came to the Celtics in a special draft of the players from the disbanded St. Louis team. This draft was held after commissioner Podoloff refused to allow the Knicks to buy the Bombers franchise to obtain Macauley. With these two new aces and with Auerbach's fast break philosophy, the Celtics broke the .500 barrier for the first time and finished a strong second behind the Philadelphia Warriors. The Warriors also came back from a poor campaign last season. A return to form by Joe Fulks, the playmaking of newcomer Andy Phillip, and the scoring of star rookie Paul Arizin, a jump shooter with a line drive shot and the ability to hang at the top of his jump, made the Warriors practically a new club.

The Knicks finished third in the East despite the loss of Carl Braun to the Army. Coach Joe Lapchick replaced Braun with Max Zaslofsky and added rebounding help by purchasing Sweetwater Clifton from the Harlem Globetrotters. Clifton was short for a center at 6-foot-6, but he was very strong and had years of experience with the Globetrotters and New York Rens. Glueing the Knicks together was the playmaking of guard Dick McGuire. Syracuse slumped to fourth place; Dolph Schayes was now an established star at forward, but Al Cervi was playing less at guard. The weak Baltimore Bullets finished fifth, and the Washington club didn't finish at all.

The playoffs began with Minneapolis and Rochester winning their opening matches in the West as expected, and with New York and Syracuse upsetting Philadelphia and Boston in the East. The Lakers began the Western finals with a 76-73 victory at home, but the Royals then outmaneuvered the larger Lakers for three straight victories and a trip to the finals. In the East, the Syracuse-New York series came down to a decisive fifth game; the Nats led by a 70-58 count with 10 minutes left, but the Knicks then caught fire and took an 83-81 victory to put themselves into the title round.

With the Knicks in their first championship series, New York City fans were excited about their professional team. That enthusiasm took a severe beating when the Royals captured the first three games, but the Knicks at least saved a little face by winning Game 4, 79-73, with a late rally in front of the home-town fans. Back in Rochester, Connie Simmons' 26 points led the Knicks to a 92-89 win and brought the series back to New York. Game six went to the Knicks, 80-73, and the series was suddenly tied at three games all. The championship now came down to a seventh-game showdown. The two teams battled on an even basis all game, with the score knotted at 75-75 with 40 seconds left. Bob Davies then got two foul shots on a blocking foul against McGuire, and he canned both to put the Royals ahead 77-75. The rules called for a jump ball after successful free throws in the final three minutes of a game, and the Royals grabbed the jump, held on to the ball, and scored at the buzzer for a 79-75 triumph over the gallant New York squad.

1950-51 SEASON HIGHLIGHTS

STANDINGS

Eastern Division

	W	L	Pct.	GB
Philadelphia	40	26	.606	—
Boston	39	30	.565	2.5
New York	36	30	.545	4
Syracuse	32	34	.485	8
Baltimore	24	42	.364	16
*Washington	10	25	.286	—

*Washington dropped out January 9, 1951.

Western Division

	W	L	Pct.	GB
Minneapolis	44	24	.647	—
Rochester	41	27	.603	3
Fort Wayne	32	36	.471	12
Indianapolis	31	37	.456	13
Tri-Cities	25	43	.368	19

ALL-STAR GAME
Boston Garden, Boston
Friday, March 2, 1951
East 111, West 94
MVP: Ed Macauley

ALL-STAR TEAMS

FIRST TEAM		SECOND TEAM	
George Mikan	Minneapolis	Dolph Schayes	Syracuse
Alex Groza	Indianapolis	Frank Brian	Tri-Cities
Ed Macauley	Boston	Vern Mikkelsen	Minneapolis
Bob Davies	Rochester	Joe Fulks	Philadelphia
Ralph Beard	Indianapolis	Dick McGuire	New York

PLAYOFFS
FINALS
Rochester 4, New York 3
Apr. 7: New York 65, at Rochester 92
Apr. 8: New York 84, at Rochester 99
Apr. 11: Rochester 78, at New York 71
Apr. 13: Rochester 73, at New York 79
Apr. 15: New York 92, at Rochester 89
Apr. 18: Rochester 73, at New York 80
Apr. 21: New York 75, at Rochester 79

EASTERN DIVISION
DIVISION FINALS
New York 3, Syracuse 2
Mar. 28: Syracuse 92, at New York 103
Mar. 29: New York 80, at Syracuse 102
Mar. 31: Syracuse 75, at New York 97
Apr. 1: New York 83, at Syracuse 90
Apr. 4: Syracuse 81, at New York 83
DIVISION SEMI-FINALS
New York 2, Boston 0
Mar. 20: New York 83, at Boston 69
Mar. 22: Boston 78, at New York 92
Syracuse 2, Philadelphia 0
Mar. 20: Syracuse 91, at Philadelphia 89, OT
Mar. 22: Philadelphia 78, at Syracuse 90

WESTERN DIVISION
DIVISION FINALS
Rochester 3, Minneapolis 1
Mar. 29: Rochester 73, at Minneapolis 76
Mar. 31: Rochester 70, at Minneapolis 66
Apr. 1: Minneapolis 70, at Rochester 83
Apr. 3: Minneapolis 75, at Rochester 80
DIVISION SEMI-FINALS
Rochester 2, Fort Wayne 1
Mar. 20: Fort Wayne 81, at Rochester 110
Mar. 22: Rochester 78, at Fort Wayne 83
Mar. 24: Fort Wayne 78, at Rochester 97
Minneapolis 2, Indianapolis 1
Mar. 21: Indianapolis 81, at Minneapolis 95
Mar. 23: Minneapolis 88, at Indianapolis 108
Mar. 25: Indianapolis 80, at Minneapolis 85

NBA LEADERS

SCORING

	GP	FGM	FTM	PTS	PPG
George Mikan, MPL	68	678	576	1932	28.4
Alex Groza, INO	66	492	445	1429	21.7
Ed Macauley, BOS	68	459	466	1384	20.4
Joe Fulks, PHW	66	429	378	1236	18.7
Frankie Brian, TRI	68	363	418	1144	16.8
Paul Arizin, PHW	65	352	417	1121	17.2
Dolph Schayes, SYR	66	332	457	1121	17.0
Ralph Beard, INO	66	409	293	1111	16.8
Bob Cousy, BOS	69	401	276	1078	15.6
Arnie Risen, ROC	66	377	323	1077	16.3

FIELD GOALS

	FGM	FGA	FG%
Alex Groza, INO	492	1046	.470
Ed Macauley, BOS	459	985	.466
George Mikan, MPL	678	1584	.428
Jack Coleman, ROC	315	749	.421
Harry Gallatin, NYK	293	705	.416
George Ratkovicz, SYR	264	636	.415
Paul Arizin, PHW	352	864	.407
Vince Boryla, NYK	352	867	.406
Vern Mikkelsen, MPL	359	893	.402
Bobby Wanzer, ROC	252	628	.401

FREE THROWS

	FTM	FTA	FT%
Joe Fulks, PHW	378	442	.855
Belus Smawley, BLB/SYR	227	267	.850
Bobby Wanzer, ROC	232	273	.850
Fred Scolari, SYR/WSC	279	331	.843
Vince Boryla, NYK	278	332	.837
Fred Schaus, FTW	404	484	.835
Sonny Hertzberg, BOS	223	270	.826
Frankie Brian, TRI	418	508	.823
Al Cervi, SYR	194	237	.819
Red Rocha, BLB	242	299	.809

ASSISTS

	GP	AST	APG
Andy Phillip, PHW	66	414	6.3
Dick McGuire, NYK	64	400	6.2
George Senesky, PHW	65	342	5.3
Bob Cousy, BOS	69	341	4.9
Ralph Beard, INO	66	318	4.8
Bob Davies, ROC	63	287	4.6
Frankie Brian, TRI	68	266	3.9
Fred Scolari, SYR/WSC	66	255	3.9
Ed Macauley, BOS	68	252	3.7
Dolph Schayes, SYR	66	251	3.8

REBOUNDS

	GP	TRB	RPG
Dolph Schayes, SYR	66	1080	16.4
George Mikan, MPL	68	958	14.1
Harry Gallatin, NYK	66	800	12.1
Arnie Risen, ROC	66	795	12.0
Alex Groza, INO	66	709	10.7
Larry Foust, FTW	68	681	10.0
Vern Mikkelsen, MPL	64	655	10.2
Paul Arizin, PHW	65	640	9.8
Ed Macauley, BOS	68	616	9.1
Jack Coleman, ROC	67	584	8.7

THE YEAR IN BASKETBALL

1950-51 Clair Bee, whose LIU teams compiled a 412-87 (.826) record in 21 years, steps down as LIU shelves basketball because of a point-fixing scandal. The scandal is part of a wide investigation that implicates 32 players at seven colleges in plots to fix 86 games.

October 5, 1950 When the Chicago Stags fold, the Celtics draw lots for three members of the defunct franchise. The lottery yields Bob Cousy for whom Boston pays $8,500.

October 22, 1950 The first men's World Championships are played in Buenos Aires, Argentina, under FIBA's direction. Argentina wins the championship, beating the United States, 64-50, in the final game.

October 31, 1950 Earl Lloyd becomes the first African-American to appear in an NBA game, when his Washington Capitols open the season in Rochester against the Royals. The next day, Chuck Cooper becomes the second black player when the Boston Celtics play their first game.

November 4, 1950 Future Hall of Famer Paul Arizin makes his pro debut for the Philadelphia Warriors, in a 77-68 victory over the Celtics.

November 22, 1950 The Fort Wayne Pistons beat the Minneapolis Lakers, 19-18, in the lowest-scoring game in NBA history.

December 28, 1950 Dolph Schayes of Syracuse snatches 35 rebounds, then an NBA record, in a game against the Warriors in Philadelphia. Schayes' feat comes in the first season in which rebounds are a recorded statistic.

January 6, 1951 In the longest game in NBA history, the Indianapolis Olympians and the Rochester Royals both play stall ball in a six-overtime game, in which the Olympians prevail, 75-73. The score is tied 65-65 after regulation, but both team's slowdown tactics yield a mere 18 total points throughout all overtimes. Arnie Risen of Rochester leads all scorers with 26. Ralph Beard and Alex Groza top Indianapolis with 17 apiece.

January 9, 1951 The NBA's Washington Capitols disband. The Caps had gotten off slowly, winning just 10 of its first 35 games. Its players were distributed to other clubs

January 21, 1951 Boston ties the record for most points in an overtime period by netting 20 in a win vs. the Fort Wayne Pistons.

February 2, 1951 Bob Cousy tallies a record 12 points in overtime, in a game between his Celtics and Syracuse.

February 18, 1951 Seven players from the champion City College of New York team are arrested for bribery and charged by the Manhattan District Attorney with conspiring to fix games. While collegians from five other schools also are rounded up for similar allegations, the spotlight is on the CCNY group, which the previous season captured New York City's heart by becoming the only team ever to win both the NCAA and NIT titles. CCNY cancels basketball for the rest of the season.

March 2, 1951 The East defeats the West, 111-94, in the first NBA All-Star game, at Boston Garden.

March 27, 1951 Kentucky, led by center Bill Spivey and featuring future NBA stars Cliff Hagan and Frank Ramsey, wins the NCAA basketball championship by defeating Kansas State, 68-58.

April 21, 1951 In Game 7 of the NBA finals, the Rochester Royals edge the New York Knicks, 79-75, to win the championship.

1951-52

Groza, Beard history but NBA a beneficiary of college scandals

The stink of scandal now hung heavy over all of big-time college basketball. New York's Madison Square Garden had been disgraced by last year's disclosures of widespread fixing of games between large local schools, but the stain had spread far beyond New York when new revelations were made over the summer. Players on prominent teams all over the country had been shaving points while on the take from professional gamblers. The two most spectacular discoveries were that Bradley and Kentucky had been doing business with the gamblers. Coach Adolph Rupp of Kentucky had said that gamblers, "couldn't touch my boys with a ten-foot pole," but stars Alex Groza and Ralph Beard were found to have been rigging games after returning from their triumphs in the 1948 Olympics. A series of hearings and trials brought the sordid details out into the open, and basketball fans, betting or otherwise, thought twice when faced with a college match.

With new audiences now available, the NBA offered a tight ten-team circuit which had stepped up in class with the transfer of the Tri-Cities Blackhawks to Milwaukee. The still glamorous Madison Square Garden hosted most New York home games, and most of the top college players of recent seasons displayed their polished skills in this professional setting. Addressing the collegiate scandals, Groza and Beard were banned because of their college improprieties.

So with more eyes watching than ever before, both divisions staged blistering battles for first place. The Rochester Royals and Minneapolis Lakers as usual slugged it out for the top spot in the West. Bob Davies, Bobby Wanzer, and Arnie Risen led the Royals to a 41-25 record, tops in the league and one game better than the Lakers. Minneapolis still had the all-star front line of George Mikan, Jim Pollard, and Vern Mikkelsen. To negate Mikan's brute strength, the league would widen the foul lane from six feet to twelve feet for the 1952-53 season; in 1951-52, Big George kept wheeling in, however, and averaged 23.8 points per game, with a high-water mark of 61 against the Royals on January 20. Although the Lakers finished second, both clubs expected to meet again in a showdown in the playoffs.

The rest of the Western teams trailed the Royals and Lakers by a big margin. Indianapolis had lost their top players and gate attractions with the disgrace of Groza and Beard, but the club pulled itself together and actually improved on last season's record. The Fort Wayne Pistons picked up star guard Frankie Brian from Milwaukee in a deal, but the good play of Brian, Larry Foust and Fred Schaus could not lift the Pistons up to the .500 level. The Milwaukee Hawks came in a dismal fifth just as they did last year in Tri-Cities, but the club got a warm reception from the Wisconsin fans who had supported strong clubs in Sheboygan and Oshkosh for years.

The Eastern Division produced a dogfight just as fierce as the Royals-Lakers battle. Syracuse and Boston finished one

Paul Arizin
One of the game's first jump shooters, his accuracy nets 25.4 points per game, halting George Mikan's scoring title run at three.

game apart in the standings after five months of regular season play. Just like the Royals and Lakers, the Nats and Celtics played two different styles of ball. Syracuse coach Al Cervi schooled his men in a tough, scrappy brand of defense and a ball-control offense which worked the ball around until someone got open for a shot. Forward Dolph Schayes led the Nats in scoring and rebounding, and he typified the battling spirit of the team. Center Red Rocha came over from Baltimore to help Schayes in the forecourt, while rookie George King joined Paul Seymour in a top-flight defensive backcourt.

While the Nats played a tight team-oriented game, the Celtics relied on three stars for most of the scoring. Bob Cousy, now in his second season, upped his scoring average to 21.7 while continuing to dazzle opponents and audiences with his passing and dribbling. Ed Macauley scored at a 19.2 pace at center, while guard Bill Sharman, a superb outside shooter, signed with Boston after spending part of last season with the defunct Washington team. Coach Red Auerbach had all his theories of fast-break basketball in good order, but the Celtics lacked the good rebounder to make it work at peak efficiency.

Finishing a close third were the New York Knicks; with essentially the same squad as last season, the New Yorkers hoped to win a return trip to the playoff finals. The Philadelphia Warriors fell off from their 1950-51 form but still captured a playoff spot behind Paul Arizin's league-leading 25.4 scoring and Andy Phillip's league-leading 539 assists. The Baltimore Bullets limped home a weak fifth.

When the top eight teams started the season all over again in the playoffs, there was only one minor surprise in the opening round; the Knicks upset the Celtics, taking the deciding match of the three-game series with an 88-87 double overtime win. The Lakers, Royals, and Nats all marched to expected victories. The Royals had whipped the Lakers in last year's play-offs, but the Lakers turned the tables this year, taking three straight games after losing the first game. The Syracuse-New York series excited fans in both cities. The Knicks took the first game 87-85 in Syracuse, with Max Zaslofsky and Connie Simmons leading the way back from a 16-point half-time deficit. The Nats won Game 2 by a 102-92 margin, but the Knicks then captured hard-fought 99-92 and 100-93 decisions in New York to move into the finals against the Lakers.

In the opening game, the Knicks lost two points in the early going when the referees called a foul on the Lakers but did not see Al McGuire's shot go in; McGuire missed both foul shots, and the Knicks went on to lose, 83-79, in overtime. The Knicks surprisingly took Game 2 in St. Paul 80-72, and headed back to New York with a split. With the Garden tied up with the circus, the Knicks played in the 69th Regiment Armory and lost Game 3, 82-73, but fought back to even the series with a 90-89 win in overtime. The Lakers took Game 5 in St. Paul, 102-89, with Mikan and Pollard both notching 32 points, but the Knicks took Game 6 in New York, 76-68. With all the marbles riding on one game, the Lakers hosted the Knicks on April 25; their hospitality was hardly warm, as the Minneapolis team rolled to an 82-65 victory and their second NBA title in three seasons.

1951-52 SEASON HIGHLIGHTS

STANDINGS

Eastern Division

	W	L	Pct.	GB
Syracuse	40	26	.606	—
Boston	39	27	.591	1
New York	37	29	.561	3
Philadelphia	33	33	.500	7
Baltimore	20	46	.303	20

Western Division

	W	L	Pct.	GB
Rochester	41	25	.621	—
Minneapolis	40	26	.606	1
Indianapolis	34	32	.515	7
Fort Wayne	29	37	.439	12
Milwaukee	17	49	.258	24

ALL-STAR GAME

Boston Garden, Boston
Monday, February 11, 1952
East 108, West 91
MVP: Paul Arizin

ALL-STAR TEAMS

FIRST TEAM

George Mikan	Minneapolis
Ed Macauley	Boston
Paul Arizin	Philadelphia
Bob Cousy	Boston
Bob Davies	Rochester
Dolph Schayes	Syracuse

SECOND TEAM

Larry Foust	Fort Wayne
Vern Mikkelsen	Minneapolis
Jim Pollard	Minneapolis
Bob Wanzer	Rochester
Andy Phillip	Philadelphia

PLAYOFFS

FINALS

Minneapolis 4, New York 3
Apr. 12: New York 79, Minneapolis (at St. Paul) 83, OT
Apr. 13: New York 80, Minneapolis (at St. Paul) 72
Apr. 16: Minneapolis 82 at New York 77
Apr. 18: Minneapolis 89 at New York 90, OT
Apr. 20: New York 89, Minneapolis (at St. Paul)102
Apr. 23: Minneapolis 68 at New York 76
Apr. 25: New York 65 at Minneapolis 82

EASTERN DIVISION
DIVISION FINALS

New York 3, Syracuse 1
Apr. 2: New York 87 at Syracuse 85
Apr. 3: New York 92 at Syracuse 102
Apr. 4: Syracuse 92 at New York 99
Apr. 8: Syracuse 93 at New York 100

DIVISION SEMI-FINALS

Syracuse 2, Philadelphia 1
Mar. 20: Philadelphia 83 at Syracuse 102
Mar. 22: Syracuse 95 at Philadelphia 100
Mar. 23: Philadelphia 73 at Syracuse 84

New York 2, Boston 1
Mar. 19: New York 94 at Boston 105
Mar. 23: Boston 97 at New York 101
Mar. 26: New York 88 at Boston 87, 2OT

WESTERN DIVISION
DIVISION FINALS

Minneapolis 3, Rochester 1
Mar. 29: Minneapolis 78 at Rochester 88
Mar. 30: Minneapolis 83 at Rochester 78
Apr. 5: Rochester 67 at Minneapolis 77
Apr. 6: Rochester 80 at Minneapolis 82

DIVISION SEMI-FINALS

Minneapolis 2, Indianapolis 0
Mar. 23: Indianapolis 70 at Minneapolis 78
Mar. 25: Minneapolis 94 at Indianapolis 87

Rochester 2, Fort Wayne 0
Mar. 18: Fort Wayne 78 at Rochester 95
Mar. 20: Rochester 92 at Fort Wayne 86

NBA LEADERS

SCORING

	GP	FGM	FTM	PTS	PPG
Paul Arizin, PHW	66	548	578	1674	25.4
George Mikan, MPL	64	545	433	1523	23.8
Bob Cousy, BOS	66	512	409	1433	21.7
Ed Macauley, BOS	66	384	496	1264	19.2
Bob Davies, ROC	65	379	294	1052	16.2
Frankie Brian, FTW	66	342	367	1051	15.9
Larry Foust, FTW	66	390	267	1047	15.9
Bobby Wanzer, ROC	66	328	377	1033	15.7
Arnie Risen, ROC	66	365	302	1032	15.6
Vern Mikkelsen, MPL	66	363	283	1009	15.3

FIELD GOALS

	FGM	FGA	FG%
Paul Arizin, PHW	548	1222	.448
Harry Gallatin, NYK	233	527	.442
Ed Macauley, BOS	384	888	.432
Bobby Wanzer, ROC	328	772	.425
Vern Mikkelsen, MPL	363	866	.419
Jack Coleman, ROC	308	742	.415
George King, SYR	235	579	.406
Paul Walther, INO	220	549	.401
Red Rocha, SYR	300	749	.401
Bob Lavoy, INO	240	604	.397

FREE THROWS

	FTM	FTA	FT%
Bobby Wanzer, ROC	377	417	.904
Al Cervi, SYR	219	248	.883
Bill Sharman, BOS	183	213	.859
Frankie Brian, FTW	367	433	.848
Fred Scolari, BLB	353	423	.835
Fred Schaus, FTW	310	372	.833
Joe Fulks, PHW	250	303	.825
Bill Tosheff, INO	182	221	.824
Paul Arizin, PHW	578	707	.818
Bob Cousy, BOS	409	506	.808

ASSISTS

	GP	AST	APG
Andy Phillip, PHW	66	539	8.2
Bob Cousy, BOS	66	441	6.7
Bob Davies, ROC	65	390	6.0
Dick McGuire, NYK	64	388	6.1
Fred Scolari, BLB	64	303	4.7
George Senesky, PHW	57	280	4.9
Bobby Wanzer, ROC	66	262	4.0
Leo Barnhorst, INO	66	255	3.9
Dugie Martin, MPL	66	249	3.8
Fred Schaus, FTW	62	247	4.0

REBOUNDS

	GP	TRB	RPG
Larry Foust, FTW	66	880	13.3
Mel Hutchins, MLH	66	880	13.3
George Mikan, MPL	64	866	13.5
Arnie Risen, ROC	66	841	12.7
Dolph Schayes, SYR	63	773	12.3
Paul Arizin, PHW	66	745	11.3
Nathaniel Clifton, NYK	62	731	11.8
Jack Coleman, ROC	66	692	10.5
Vern Mikkelsen, MPL	66	681	10.3
Harry Gallatin, NYK	66	661	10.0

THE YEAR IN BASKETBALL

The NBA adopts a rule to widen the foul lane from 6 feet to 12 feet.

October 20, 1951 Ralph Beard and Alex Groza are banned from the NBA after admitting to point-shaving while at Kentucky.

January 17, 1952 Dolph Schayes cans 23 of 27 free throws in a wild triple-overtime game between Syracuse and Minneapolis. Schayes' total free throws made and attempted are both new records.

January 20, 1952 George Mikan sets a Lakers' record when he pours in 61 points in a game versus Rochester.

January 28, 1952 Norma Schoulte, a high school player in Monona, Louisiana, scores 111 points in a single game.

February 21, 1952 In a marketing ploy, the Boston Celtics host the Fort Wayne Pistons in a game that starts at midnight. Billed as the Milkman's Special (at a time when milkmen rose early to deliver milk to customers' homes), Bob Cousy leads Boston with 24 points and the Celtics win, 88-67, before a crowd of 2,368.

March 19, 1952 Led by freshman sensation Tom Gola, LaSalle defeats Dayton, 75-64, to win the NIT championship.

March 22, 1952 Clyde Lovellette, the nation's leading scorer, tallies 44 points in Kansas' 74-55 pounding of Saint Louis in the West regional final of the NCAA tournament.

March 26, 1952 Lovellette hits for 33 points as Kansas wins the national title with an 80-63 drubbing of St. John's in the NCAA tourney final.

March 29, 1952 George Mikan of the Minneapolis Lakers scores 47 points in a playoff game vs. Rochester. Mikan's effort sets a playoff standard for most points scored in a game. The record is broken less than a year later when Bob Cousy nets 50 against Syracuse.

April 25, 1952 The Minneapolis Lakers win their second NBA crown, with a convincing 82-65 victory over New York in Game 7 of the NBA finals. Before 8,612 fans at the Minneapolis Auditorium, the Lakers win with a balanced attack led by George Mikan's 20 points. Frank Saul and Bob Harrison each contribute 14, while Vern Mikkelsen scores 13.

August 1952 The United States downs the Soviet Union, 36-25, to capture the gold medal at the Summer Olympics in Helsinki, Finland. The Soviets' tactics of stalling in the final contest fails to perturb the Americans, who are led by Bob Kurland and Clyde Lovellette.

1952-53

Lakers dynasty intact, but too many fouls, stodgy play a worry

The NBA was slowly carving a permanent place in America's winter sports menu. The league had ten stable franchises, all returning from last season, and while smaller cities like Fort Wayne, Rochester, Syracuse, and Indianapolis were still on the circuit, the large outposts of New York, Boston, and Philadelphia created a "big-league" aura in the public's eyes. And although television was still in its infancy, it was bringing NBA games to many fans who had never seen a pro basketball game before. Most important, however, the NBA had escaped the scandals which had seriously discredited college ball; word did come out that an official had taken bribes to affect games in 1950, but immediate dismissal of the official nipped the affair in the bud. Star players gave almost every team gate appeal, with Laker center George Mikan and Celtic guard Bob Cousy the premier attractions in the league.

But offsetting these assets in large measure was the unattractive style of play in the NBA. The widening of the foul lane from six feet to twelve feet opened the game up a bit, but roughhouse tactics were still the order of the day close to the basket. Action ground to a virtual halt toward the end of many games, when tension should have been at its highest. Strategic fouling and seemingly endless trips to the foul line gummed up the final minutes of games, and freezing the ball frequently ended the day's scoring with quite a bit of time left on the clock. Reforms were needed in the playing rules, but these were not to come for several seasons.

Regardless of the problems in playing style, the NBA could still boast of five top-flight teams with distinct images. The Minneapolis Lakers relied on their frontcourt muscle, with George Mikan, Vern Mikkelsen, and Jim Pollard combining bulk with talent. Little Slater Martin, a mere 5-foot-10 tall, handled the ball in the backcourt and did most of the running for the Western Division champion Lakers. Short on size but long on guile, the smart Rochester Royals finished a close second in the West. Key veterans Bob Davies, Bobby Wanzer, and Arnie Risen had been together since the days of the NBL, and the savvy of the squad showed up in reserves Jack McMahon, Alex Hannum, and Red Holzman, all future NBA coaches.

The Eastern Division counted three superior clubs in its ranks. The New York Knicks blended a horde of talented players together into a tight unit. Coach Joe Lapchick got shooter Carl Braun back from the Army, and the ex-Colgate star moved right into a starting post at guard. Harry Gallatin, Sweetwater Clifton, Connie Simmons, Ernie Vandeweghe, Max Zaslofsky, Dick McGuire, Vince Boryla, and Al McGuire formed the rest of the Knick chassis. After a blazing start, the team cooled off toward the end of the season after Zaslofsky broke his arm in January and various other, less serious, injuries

Neil Johnston
By refining the game's first great hook shot, he averages 22.3 points for the Warriors to win the first of three consecutive scoring titles.

dogged other players.

Another club relying on teamwork, good passing, and tough defense was the Syracuse Nats. Dolph Schayes and Paul Seymour epitomized the Syracuse team, both being able scorers and rough characters in their floor play. The Boston Celtics finished practically even with New York and Syracuse despite channeling most of the scoring to three men. Bob Cousy, Bill Sharman, and Ed Macauley all placed in the top six scorers in the league, thus offsetting the Boston weaknesses in defense and rebounding.

The league's five lesser franchises offered less to the general fan. The Fort Wayne Pistons captured third place in the West with a transfusion of healthy new blood. Rookie Monk Meineke of Dayton added muscle to the frontcourt while newcomers Freddie Scolari, Andy Phillip, and Dick Groat bolstered the guard positions. Trades brought Scolari from Baltimore and Phillip from Philadelphia, and these two combined with Frankie Brian in furnishing experience in the backcourt. Groat, a high-scoring All-American from Duke, played well in the first half of the season before going into the service; after his discharge, he gave up basketball for a career as shortstop for the Pittsburgh Pirates. With center Larry Foust leading the scoring, the Pistons took a playoff spot with a 36-33 record. The final Western playoff position went to the Indianapolis Olympians, struggling along without the scandal-disgraced Alex Groza and Ralph Beard. One game back in fifth place came the Milwaukee Hawks, whose defense was nearly invisible.

The Eastern Division fielded the two weakest entries in the league—the Baltimore Bullets and Philadelphia Warriors—with the Bullets winning a playoff berth practically by default. Clair Bee, longtime coach at LIU, took over the management of the Bullets but could do little with this mediocre squad. The Philadelphia team won only 12 of 69 contests, a mighty fall from the first-place finish of 1951. Scoring champion Paul Arizin marched off into the service, but coach Eddie Gottlieb came up with another scoring champion in second-year center Neil Johnston. With his teammates feeding him the ball

steadily, the hook-shooting Johnston put together a 22.3 scoring average, tops in the circuit. Joe Fulks, meanwhile, had slowed down to 11.9 in his final season as a regular.

At the start of the playoffs, the Knicks and Lakers swept to easy victories over the Bullets and Olympians. Fort Wayne, meanwhile, upset Rochester by taking the deciding third game by a score of 67-65 on the enemy's court. In the remaining first-round series, Boston downed Syracuse with straight wins, the second one a drawn-out 111-105 victory in four overtimes. The Celtics couldn't survive the next round, however, bowing to the Knicks in four games. The Pistons extended the Lakers to their fullest but came up short in the deciding fifth game, dropping a 74-58 decision to Mikan and Co.

The championship series then shaped up as a rematch of last year's New York-Minneapolis tilt. The series opened in Minneapolis with a surprising 96-88 Knick victory, as Connie Simmons and Sweetwater Clifton did a good job controlling Mikan. The Lakers took Game 2 73-71, with fouling slowing the game practically to a walk for the final eight minutes. With a split on the road, the Knicks hoped to make hay at home; instead, the Lakers plowed them under. The three contests in New York all were hard fought, close games, but the Lakers came out on top in all three of them. For the third straight season, the Knicks had lost in the finals. And for the third time in four NBA seasons, George Mikan and the Lakers had won the crown.

1952-53 SEASON HIGHLIGHTS

STANDINGS

Eastern Division

	W	L	Pct.	GB
New York	47	23	.671	—
Syracuse	47	24	.662	.5
Boston	46	25	.648	1.5
Baltimore	16	54	.229	31
Philadelphia	12	57	.174	34.5

Western Division

	W	L	Pct.	GB
Minneapolis	48	22	.686	—
Rochester	44	26	.629	4
Fort Wayne	36	33	.522	11.5
Indianapolis	28	43	.394	20.5
Milwaukee	27	44	.380	21.5

AWARDS

Top Rookie
Don Meineke, Fort Wayne

ALL-STAR TEAMS

FIRST TEAM

George Mikan	Minneapolis
Bob Cousy	Boston
Neil Johnston	Philadelphia
Ed Macauley	Boston
Dolph Schayes	Syracuse

ALL-STAR GAME

Memorial Coliseum, Fort Wayne,
Tuesday, January 13, 1953
West 79, East 75
MVP: George Mikan

SECOND TEAM

Bill Sharman	Boston
Vern Mikkelsen	Minneapolis
Bob Wanzer	Rochester
Bob Davies	Rochester
Andy Phillip	Philadelphia

PLAYOFFS

FINALS
Minneapolis 4, New York 1
Apr. 4: New York 96 at Minneapolis 88
Apr. 5: New York 71 at Minneapolis 73
Apr. 7: Minneapolis 90 at New York 75
Apr. 8: Minneapolis 71 at New York 69
Apr. 10: Minneapolis 91 at New York 84

EASTERN DIVISION
DIVISION FINALS
New York 3, Boston 1
Mar. 25: Boston 91 at New York 95
Mar. 26: New York 70 at Boston 86
Mar. 28: Boston 82 at New York 101
Mar. 29: New York 82 at Boston 75

DIVISION SEMI-FINALS
New York 2, Baltimore 0
Mar. 17: Baltimore 62 at New York 80
Mar. 20: New York 90 at Baltimore 81
Boston 2, Syracuse 0
Mar. 19: Boston 87 at Syracuse 81
Mar. 21: Syracuse 105 at Boston 111, 4OT
WESTERN DIVISION
DIVISION FINALS
Minneapolis 3, Fort Wayne 2
Mar. 26: Fort Wayne 73 at Minneapolis 83
Mar. 28: Fort Wayne 75 at Minneapolis 82
Mar. 30: Minneapolis 95 at Fort Wayne 98
Apr. 1: Minneapolis 82 at Fort Wayne 85
Apr. 2: Fort Wayne 58 at Minneapolis 74

DIVISION SEMI-FINALS
Fort Wayne 2, Rochester 1
Mar. 20: Fort Wayne 84 at Rochester 77
Mar. 22: Rochester 83 at Fort Wayne 71
Mar. 24: Fort Wayne 67 at Rochester 65
Minneapolis 2, Indianapolis 0
Mar. 22: Indianapolis 69 at Minneapolis 85
Mar. 23: Minneapolis 81 at Indianapolis 79

NBA LEADERS

SCORING

	GP	FGM	FTM	PTS	PPG
Neil Johnston, PHW	70	504	556	1564	22.3
George Mikan, MPL	70	500	442	1442	20.6
Bob Cousy, BOS	71	464	479	1407	19.8
Ed Macauley, BOS	69	451	500	1402	20.3
Dolph Schayes, SYR	71	375	512	1262	17.8
Bill Sharman, BOS	71	403	341	1147	16.2
Jack Nichols, MLH	69	425	240	1090	15.8
Vern Mikkelsen, MPL	70	378	291	1047	15.0
Bob Davies, ROC	66	339	351	1029	15.6
Bobby Wanzer, ROC	70	318	384	1020	14.6

FIELD GOALS

	FGM	FGA	FG%
Neil Johnston, PHW	504	1114	.452
Ed Macauley, BOS	451	997	.452
Harry Gallatin, NYK	282	635	.444
Bill Sharman, BOS	403	925	.436
Vern Mikkelsen, MPL	378	868	.435
Ernie Vandeweghe, NYK	272	625	.435
Jack Coleman, ROC	314	748	.420
Dugie Martin, MPL	260	634	.410
Bob Lavoy, INO	225	560	.402
George King, SYR	255	635	.402

FREE THROWS

	FTM	FTA	FT%
Bill Sharman, BOS	341	401	.850
Fred Scolari, FTW/BLB	276	327	.844
Dolph Schayes, SYR	512	619	.827
Carl Braun, NYK	331	401	.825
Fred Schaus, FTW	243	296	.821
Odie Spears, ROC	199	243	.819
Paul Seymour, SYR	340	416	.817
Bob Cousy, BOS	479	587	.816
Bobby Wanzer, ROC	384	473	.812
Bill Tosheff, INO	253	314	.806

ASSISTS

	GP	AST	APG
Bob Cousy, BOS	71	547	7.7
Andy Phillip, FTW/PHW	70	397	5.7
George King, SYR	71	364	5.1
Dick McGuire, NYK	61	296	4.9
Paul Seymour, SYR	67	294	4.4
Bob Davies, ROC	66	280	4.2
Ed Macauley, BOS	69	280	4.1
Leo Barnhorst, INO	71	277	3.9
George Senesky, PHW	69	264	3.8
Bobby Wanzer, ROC	70	252	3.6

REBOUNDS

	GP	TRB	RPG
George Mikan, MPL	70	1007	14.4
Neil Johnston, PHW	70	976	13.9
Dolph Schayes, SYR	71	920	13.0
Harry Gallatin, NYK	70	916	13.1
Mel Hutchins, MLH	71	793	11.2
Jack Coleman, ROC	70	774	11.1
Larry Foust, FTW	67	769	11.5
Nathaniel Clifton, NYK	70	761	10.9
Arnie Risen, ROC	68	745	11.0
Joe Graboski, INO	69	687	10.0

THE YEAR IN BASKETBALL

November 12, 1952 The Milwaukee Hawks commit 55 fouls in game against Baltimore, the most fouls committed by a team in a non-overtime game. (In November 1949, Sheboygan committed 66 in a tilt that lasted 4 overtimes.)

November 15, 1952 Three days after Milwaukee commits 55 fouls in a game, Syracuse is whistled for 60 in an overtime contest versus Baltimore. A record eight Nats and five Bullets foul out in a game that Baltimore wins, 97-91.

January 2, 1953 The Bullets begin a 32-game road losing streak.

January 10, 1953 Clarence (Bevo) Francis of Rio Grande (Pa.) College scores 116 points in a game versus Ashland Junior College. Francis makes 47 field goals and 22 of 29 free throws. Rio Grande wins the game, 150-85.

January 11, 1953 The Celtics set the record for most assists in a half, with 24, in a game versus Baltimore.

January 13, 1953 Don Barksdale, a Celtics' forward, becomes the first African-American to make an NBA All-Star team.

February 6, 1953 Dick Bogenrife of Sedalia High School in Midway, Ohio scores 120 points in a game.

February 14, 1953 Bill Chambers of William & Mary grabs 51 rebounds in a 105-84 victory over Virginia.

March 12, 1953 Seton Hall (31-2) tops St. John's, 58-46, to win the NIT. Only two weeks earlier the then-undefeated Pirates suffered successive losses to Dayton and Louisville, before returning to form for the NIT.

March 6, 1953 Ed Macauley of Boston scores a career-high 46 points versus George Mikan and the Minneapolis Lakers.

March 7, 1953 The first women's World Championships, as organized by FIBA, are played in Santiago, Chile

March 17, 1953 Bob Leonard of Indiana hits a free throw with 27 seconds left in the game, giving the Hoosiers a 69-68 victory and the national title over defending champ Kansas. Center Don Schlundt scores 30 points to lead the Hoosiers.

March 21, 1953 Bob Cousy fires in 50 points, including a record 30 of 32 free throws, in a four-overtime playoff game in Syracuse, as the Celtics outlast the Nationals, 111-105. The Eastern Division semifinal contest sees each team score over 50 points from the line. Syracuse commits a record 55 fouls. Six Nats and three Celtics foul out.

April 10, 1953 For the second consecutive year, the Minneapolis Lakers defeat the New York Knicks in the NBA finals. This year, the Lakers do it in five games (compared with seven the prior season). In the finale, played in New York's 69th Street Regiment Armory, six Lakers score in double figures, led by Jim Pollard's 17, as Minneapolis wins 91-84.

1953-54

Fifth title in six years
Mikan's parting gift
to Minneapolis Lakers

Things looked brighter for the NBA at the start of this season than at any other time in its short history. The National Broadcasting Company thought enough of the product to start a modest program of national telecasts. With the weak Indianapolis franchise dropped from the league, there were now nine teams to show to the country. Veteran pro players stocked these nine clubs with deep benches, and a slew of new talent came into the league from several sources. Rookies Ray Felix of LIU, Jack Molinas of Columbia, Bob Houbregs of Washington, and Ernie Beck of Pennsylvania turned pro after prominent college careers. In addition, former All-Americans Clyde Lovellette, George Yardley, Ernie Barrett, Don Sunderlage, and Walt Davis came into the league after playing AAU ball. With plenty of talent compressed into nine teams, and with a television program to spark interest, how could this help but be the NBA's most profitable campaign?

Simply stated, the season was a flop because the game itself was degenerating into a pushing and shoving match reminiscent of the notorious days of pro ball before the growth of stable leagues. The area under the basket was no-man's-land, with guards rarely daring to drive in close to the hoop. Hot-handed shooters were often cooled off with heavy-handed policing. Officials tried to keep order by calling fouls, but a steady succession of charity throws reduced action to a yawn. Indeed, coaches found it best to have their players repeatedly foul the enemy in the final minutes of a contest, giving up a probable one point in return for a chance at two. Add an occasional policy of sitting on a lead in the fourth quarter, and the NBA's product was wasted in a boring match of technicalities.

Another problem which sent a shudder through the circuit involved rookie Jack Molinas of Fort Wayne. A talented forward, Molinas enjoyed gambling, and a story broke in December about his betting on games. Molinas admitted that he had bet small sums on the Pistons to win in several games, and although there was no question of his throwing a game, Commissioner Podoloff banned him from the NBA. Several years later Molinas was convicted of being a "fixer" in a new round of college basketball scandals, and was sent to prison.

But even with all the problems that turned many fans off, the NBA played through its fifth season. With the Western Division down to four teams, the league governors allotted only three playoff spots to each division this year. Minneapolis, Rochester, and Ft. Wayne took those berths in the West, leaving Milwaukee far behind in the dust. Bothered by bad knees, George Mikan fell to an 18.1 scoring average, fourth best in the league; he still ranked second in the league in rebounding, however, and his strength made driving on the Lakers a risky proposition. The Rochester Royals, too, were starting to creak with age but they still finished a strong second behind their longtime rivals from Minnesota. With Bobby

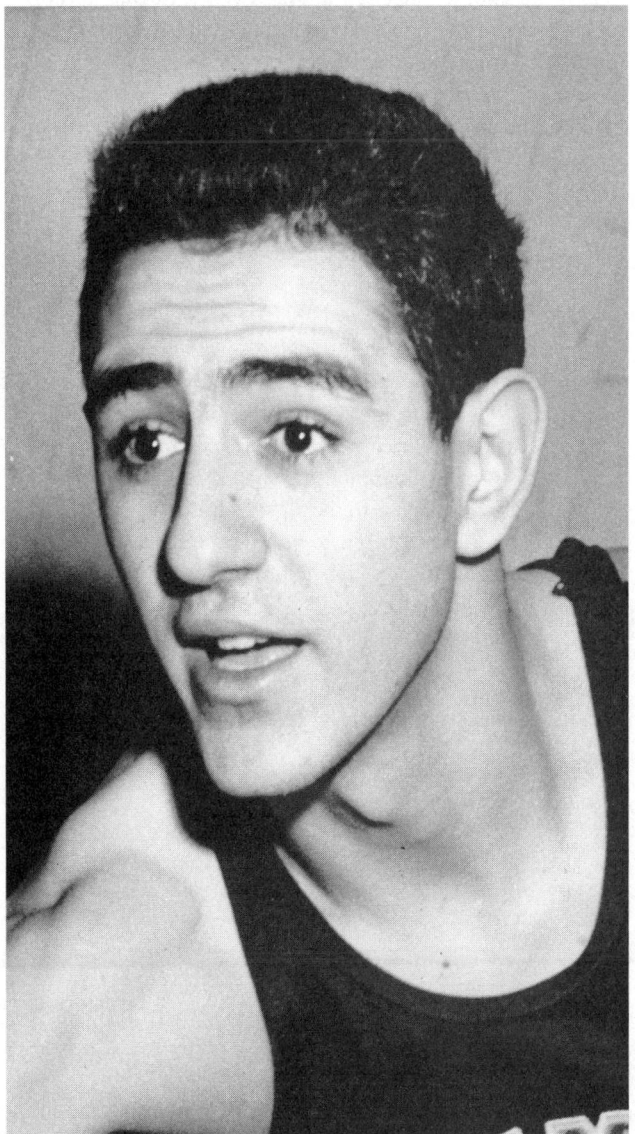

Jake Molinas
Banned for betting on—but not against—his own Fort Wayne Pistons, he'd go on to become notorious as basketball's great "fixer."

Wanzer, Bob Davies, and Arnie Risen all starting to slow down, the Royals were to slip into mediocrity after this season.

Fort Wayne, on the other hand, looked like a team on the way up. Despite losing an outstanding young talent in Molinas, the Pistons added George Yardley, an explosive jump-shooter, to the holdover forward corps of Mel Hutchins and Monk Meineke. Larry Foust gave the team a high-scoring center, and veteran guards Max Zaslofsky and Leo Barnhorst came over in mid-season to help old hands Andy Phillip, Freddie Scolari, and Frankie Brian in the backcourt. Although only third-place

finishers this year, the Pistons were good bets to pass the Royals next season. The last-place Hawks were a team easily forgotten, with Red Holzman's coaching debut the squad's only claim to fame.

New York, Boston, and Syracuse captured the Eastern play-off spots with little trouble from Baltimore and Philadelphia. After three straight flops in the playoff finals, the Knicks were itching for another shot at the title. Even with Max Zaslofsky traded away and Ernie Vandeweghe rarely able to get away from his medical studies, the Knicks captured first place with a blend of different talents, ranging from Carl Braun's hot shooting to Harry Gallatin's league-leading rebounding. The Celtics and Nats tied for second place on the strength of hot offenses. Boston fans were now accustomed to the fine shooting of Bob Cousy, Bill Sharman, and Ed Macauley, and to the lack of defense and rebounding muscle on the squad. The Nats had one of pro ball's best offensive weapons in forward Dolph Schayes, and they had a tough defense led by guard Paul Seymour. The problem with the Nats was that they didn't have a legitimate starting center. The also-ran Bullets and Warriors each had a high-scoring center; Baltimore rookie Ray Felix scored at a 17.6 clip, while Warrior veteran Neil Johnston retained his scoring championship with a 24.4 average.

With only three teams in the playoffs from each division, the league set up a round robin to whittle the field down to two clubs in each sector. After this confusing first round was over,

the Knicks and Pistons had been eliminated. That left Syracuse and Boston in the East, with the Nats then winning a place in the championship series with two straight victories. The Lakers and Royals squared off in what was to be the last of their classic battles in the West. The Lakers took Game 1, 89-76, the Royals won Game 2, 74-73, and the Lakers captured the deciding game by an 82-72 score.

The championship series between Syracuse and Minneapolis involved so-called "minor league" cities but definitely major league teams. The Lakers used their size in a 79-68 first game triumph, but the Nats came back to take Game 2, 62-60, on a bucket by Paul Seymour with seven seconds left. Mikan's 30 points led the Lakers to an 81-67 win in Game 3, with the Nats coming back with an 80-69 triumph in the fourth game. When the Lakers took Game 5, 84-73, in Syracuse and headed back to Minneapolis for the final two contests with a one-game edge, the series was all but over. The scrappy Nats then battled the Lakers to a standstill in the sixth game and won, 65-63, on a Jim Neal basket with four seconds left in the game. But the Lakers' superior size came out in the rubber game, with an 87-80 triumph bringing Minneapolis its third straight NBA championship. It was a fitting way for George Mikan to go out, as the big man would announce his retirement before the next season. And it was the end of an era in another way, as the 24-second rule was about to change the entire complexion of the game.

1953-54 SEASON HIGHLIGHTS

STANDINGS

Eastern Division

	W	L	Pct.	GB
New York	44	28	.611	—
Boston	42	30	.583	2
Syracuse	42	30	.583	2
Philadelphia	29	43	.403	15
Baltimore	16	56	.222	28

Western Division

	W	L	Pct.	GB
Minneapolis	46	26	.639	—
Rochester	44	28	.611	2
Fort Wayne	40	32	.556	6
Milwaukee	21	51	.292	25

AWARDS

Top Rookie
Ray Felix, Baltimore

ALL-STAR TEAMS

FIRST TEAM

Bob Cousy	Boston
Neil Johnston	Philadelphia
George Mikan	Minneapolis
Dolph Schayes	Syracuse
Harry Gallatin	New York

SECOND TEAM

Ed Macauley	Boston
Jim Pollard	Minneapolis
Carl Braun	New York
Bob Wanzer	Rochester
Paul Seymour	Syracuse

ALL-STAR GAME

Madison Square Garden, New York
Thursday, January 21, 1954
East 98, West 93, OT
MVP: Bob Cousy

PLAYOFFS

FINALS
Minneapolis 4, Syracuse 3
Mar. 31: Syracuse 68 at Minneapolis 79
Apr. 3: Syracuse 62 at Minneapolis 60
Apr. 4: Minneapolis 81 at Syracuse 67
Apr. 8: Minneapolis 69 at Syracuse 80
Apr. 10: Minneapolis 84 at Syracuse 73
Apr. 11: Syracuse 65 at Minneapolis 63
Apr. 12: Syracuse 80 at Minneapolis 87

EASTERN DIVISION
DIVISION FINALS
Syracuse 2, Boston 0
Mar. 25: Boston 94 at Syracuse 109
Mar. 27: Syracuse 83 at Boston 76
ROUND ROBIN
Mar. 16: Boston 93 at New York 71
Mar. 17: Syracuse 96 at Boston 95, OT
Mar. 18: New York 68 at Syracuse 75
Mar. 20: New York 78 at Boston 79
Mar. 21: Syracuse 103 at New York 99
Mar. 22: Boston 85 at Syracuse 98

WESTERN DIVISION
DIVISION FINALS
Minneapolis 2, Rochester 1
Mar. 24: Rochester 76 at Minneapolis 89
Mar. 27: Minneapolis 73 at Rochester 74
Mar. 28: Rochester 72 at Minneapolis 82
ROUND ROBIN
Mar. 16: Fort Wayne 75 at Rochester 82
Mar. 17: Rochester 88 at Minneapolis 109
Mar. 18: Minneapolis 90 at Fort Wayne 85
Mar. 20: Fort Wayne 73 at Minneapolis 78
Mar. 21: Rochester 89 at Fort Wayne 71
Mar. 23: Minneapolis at Rochester (canceled)

NBA LEADERS

SCORING

	GP	FGM	FTM	PTS	PPG
Neil Johnston, PHW	72	591	577	1759	24.4
Bob Cousy, BOS	72	486	411	1383	19.2
Ed Macauley, BOS	71	462	420	1344	18.9
George Mikan, MPL	72	441	424	1306	18.1
Ray Felix, BLB	72	410	449	1269	17.6
Dolph Schayes, SYR	72	370	488	1228	17.1
Bill Sharman, BOS	72	412	331	1155	16.0
Larry Foust, FTW	72	376	338	1090	15.1
Carl Braun, NYK	72	354	354	1062	14.8
Bobby Wanzer, ROC	72	322	314	958	13.3

FIELD GOALS

	FGM	FGA	FG%
Ed Macauley, BOS	462	950	.486
Bill Sharman, BOS	412	915	.450
Neil Johnston, PHW	591	1317	.449
Clyde Lovellette, MPL	237	560	.423
Ray Felix, BLB	410	983	.417
Larry Foust, FTW	376	919	.409
Eddie Miller, BLB	244	600	.407
Jack Coleman, ROC	289	714	.405
Harry Gallatin, NYK	258	639	.404
Mel Hutchins, FTW	295	736	.401

FREE THROWS

	FTM	FTA	FT%
Bill Sharman, BOS	331	392	.844
Dolph Schayes, SYR	488	590	.827
Carl Braun, NYK	354	429	.825
Paul Seymour, SYR	299	368	.813
Zeke Zawoluk, PHW	186	230	.809
Bob Cousy, BOS	411	522	.787
Harry Gallatin, NYK	433	552	.784
George Mikan, MPL	424	546	.777
Odie Spears, ROC	183	238	.769
Ed Macauley, BOS	420	554	.758

ASSISTS

	GP	AST	APG
Bob Cousy, BOS	72	518	7.2
Andy Phillip, FTW	71	449	6.3
Paul Seymour, SYR	71	364	5.1
Dick McGuire, NYK	68	354	5.2
Bob Davies, ROC	72	323	4.5
Jack George, PHW	71	312	4.4
Paul Hoffman, BLB	72	285	4.0
George King, SYR	72	272	3.8
Ed Macauley, BOS	71	271	3.8
Danny Finn, PHW	68	265	3.9

REBOUNDS

	GP	TRB	RPG
Harry Gallatin, NYK	72	1098	15.3
George Mikan, MPL	72	1028	14.3
Larry Foust, FTW	72	967	13.4
Ray Felix, BLB	72	958	13.3
Dolph Schayes, SYR	72	870	12.1
Neil Johnston, PHW	72	797	11.1
Arnie Risen, ROC	72	728	10.1
Mel Hutchins, FTW	72	695	9.7
Lew Hitch, MLH	72	691	9.6
Joe Graboski, PHW	71	670	9.4

THE YEAR IN BASKETBALL

January 21, 1954 In the first overtime game in All-Star history, Bob Cousy hits for 10 points in the extra period, giving the East a 98-93 victory. Cousy wins the game's MVP honors.

February 2, 1954 Clarence (Bevo) Francis scores 113 points in an intercollegiate game, as his Rio Grande squad trounces Hillsdale College, 134-91. Francis pours in 38 field goals and hits 37 of 42 free throws.

February 13, 1954 Frank Selvy of Furman scores 100 points in a 149-95 victory over Newberry. In front of his mother, who is watching Selvy play for the first time, Selvy makes his final two points on a shot from near half-court in the closing seconds. Selvy, who will lead the nation in scoring with a 41.7 per-game average, goes 41 for 66 from the field and 18 of 22 from the line.

March 7, 1954 In an experiment, the Minneapolis Lakers and Milwaukee Hawks play a regular season game with 12-foot baskets. The result is a low-scoring affair, in which the Hawks "outshoot" the Lakers from the floor, 31.7% to 28.6%. From the line, Minneapolis makes 21 of 31 (.677) foul shots while the Hawks manage 11 of 25 (.440). Bill Calhoun, a Hawks forward, leads all scorers with 22.

March 8, 1954 The Milwaukee Hawks and Baltimore Bullets play a doubleheader—the only time in NBA history that two teams have played each other twice on the same day. The twinbill produces nearly identical results. In the opener Milwaukee wins, 64-54. In the finale, the Hawks prevail 65-54. Bob Harrison of Milwaukee scores 14 points in each game to earn high-scoring honors for the day.

March 14, 1954 The Baltimore Bullets end a 32-game road losing streak.

March 17, 1954 Bob Cousy tallies 12 points in overtime in a game between the Celtics and Syracuse.

March 13, 1954 Holy Cross beats Duquesne, 71-62, to win the NIT. The Crusaders' Maurice Stokes is named the tournament's top player.

March 20, 1954 LaSalle wins the NCAA tournament championship by defeating Bradley, 92-75, in the title game in Kansas City.

April 12, 1954 The Minneapolis Lakers win their third successive NBA title, an unprecedented feat at the time. The Lakers win the crown with an 87-80 victory in Game 7 over Syracuse. Forward Jim Pollard leads the Lakers with 21 points. The title is the Lakers' fifth in six years.

April 23 1954 NBA officials vote to allow the 24-second clock into the game and to limit each team to six personal fouls per quarter, after which each foul results in an opposition free throw. The 24-second clock is the idea of Danny Biasone, the Syracuse Nationals' owner.

1954-55

Saved by the clock, NBA sees scoring jump by 14 ppg

Two changes in the rules this season streamlined the NBA's play and turned the standings practically upside down. The new 24-second clock kept teams from stalling by forcing them to shoot within 24 seconds of gaining possession of the ball. The league also cut down on intentional fouling by limiting each team to five infractions in each period; when a team notched its sixth foul of the period, the opponent would receive a penalty shot on all free throw situations. Thus, NBA games crammed a lot more action into their 48 minutes than ever before.

This change in playing style brought on a shift in power in the league. The Minneapolis Lakers, champions for the last three years, suffered from the 24-second rule as well as from the retirement of George Mikan. Moving upstairs as general manager, Mikan left a large gap at center into which Clyde Lovellette was thrown; the young center scored frequently enough, but could not approach Mikan's value as a rebounder or defender. Vern Mikkelsen and Slater Martin kept pace with the quicker play demanded by the new rules, but Jim Pollard endured a sub-par season before retiring. The Lakers adapted well enough to finish eight games over .500 and only three games out of first place in the West, but the defending champs no longer were the intimidating powerhouse of old. The Rochester Royals fell a lot farther and a lot more quickly. Although age had been slowly catching up with key men Arnie Risen, Bob Davies, and Bobby Wanzer, the 24-second clock made the Royals' lack of speed a painful liability. The Royals thudded to a 29-43 mark and barely grabbed off the third Western playoff spot ahead of the Milwaukee Hawks.

With Minneapolis and Rochester coming down from the twin peaks they had held for years, Syracuse and Fort Wayne became the new NBA powers. New York and Boston remained close contenders, and Philadelphia, Milwaukee, and Baltimore continued in the also-ran category. Baltimore had a blue-chip rookie in Furman's Frank Selvy, the collegiate scoring champion who had poured in 100 points in a single undergraduate contest. The Bullets, however, drew few paying customers and were in full financial retreat until the club finally called it quits on November 27 with a 3-11 record. A draft parcelled the players to the other clubs, with Selvy going to Milwaukee. The Hawks had another rookie forward who would become one of the NBA's superstars Bob Pettit, a slim 6-foot-9 graduate of Louisiana State, went uncompromisingly to the boards on rebounds and used a fine-tuned jump shot to accumulate points at a rapid rate; the Hawks were still a cellar team, but Pettit was the cornerstone around which owner Ben Kerner would build a champion. The Philadelphia Warriors got jump-shooter Paul Arizin back from the military and paired him with center Neil Johnston in a potent one-two scoring punch. The Warriors had too many holes to make the playoffs this year, but

Dolph Schayes
The big forward, shown here fighting through Philadelphia's Woody Sauldsberry (14) and Jack George, leads Syracuse to its lone title.

like the Hawks, they were very close to a championship season.

The Knicks and Celtics, meanwhile, made the playoffs despite some pressing problems. The Knicks were rebuilding; Connie Simmons and Al McGuire were traded, while Vince Boryla, Freddie Schaus, and Ernie Vandeweghe retired. Coach Joe Lapchick still got scoring from Carl Braun and rebounding from Hang Gallatin, and he brought in new help in the persons of center Ray Felix from Baltimore and guard Gene Shue from Philadelphia. Up in Boston, Celtic coach Red Auerbach had the guns to run a fast-break attack in Bob Cousy, Bill Sharman,

and Ed Macauley, but a persistent weakness on the boards and on defense kept the Celts a .500 club. Auerbach did uncover one fine rookie in swingman Frank Ramsey, the first of the high-scoring "sixth men" that are standard equipment in the NBA today.

The two clubs that rose to the top in the new setup were the Syracuse Nationals and the Fort Wayne Pistons. The Nats had finished second in the East last season and had made it to the finals in the playoffs before losing to the Lakers. This year, they finished first in the East by five games over New York. Dolph Schayes supplied the big offensive spark from his forward position, and guard Paul Seymour spearheaded the NBA's most hard-nosed defense. Coach Al Cervi counted his riches when he came up with two competent centers; veteran Red Rocha returned after a season in retirement, and rookie Johnny Kerr brought mobility and fine passing skill to the pivot position.

The Fort Wayne club matched Syracuse by taking first place in the West. Owner Fred Zollner hired referee Charlie Eckman to run the Pistons. Lacking any coaching experience, Eckman kept his men loose with fast-flowing stories and good-humored profanity, leaving most of the basketball strategy up to the good sense of his veteran squad. Larry Foust, George Yardley, Mel Hutchins, Max Zaslofsky, Andy Phillip, and Frankie Brian had all demonstrated All-Star skills in the past, and the weakening of the Lakers and Royals gave them a chance to bring Fort Wayne to the top for the first time in the Western Division.

The playoffs produced exciting, attractive basketball games, testaments to the good sense of the new rules changes. The Celtics edged the Knicks two-to-one in a series of high-scoring contests in the Eastern semifinal, while the Lakers also had to go the limit to eliminate old rival Rochester in the West. Then the first-place clubs stepped into the picture, with the Nats beating Boston and the Pistons beating Minneapolis in four games each. The two division winners, then, got ready for the final.

The Pistons were saddled with a heavy disadvantage when their home court was unavailable, forcing them into a smaller gym in Indianapolis for their home games. The first two games were played in Syracuse, with both going to the Nats in close finishes. Back in Indiana, the veteran Pistons relaxed and copped three straight games, putting themselves in the driver's seat. Back in Syracuse for the sixth game, Dolph Schayes' 28 points led the Nats to a 109-104 victory. The final game came down to the wire, tied up at 91-all; with 12 seconds left, George King sank a free throw to put Syracuse up 92-91. The Nats promptly stole the ball back and had their first (and only) NBA championship in their hip pocket.

1954-55 SEASON HIGHLIGHTS

STANDINGS

Eastern Division

	W	L	Pct.	GB
Syracuse	43	29	.597	—
New York	38	34	.528	5
Boston	36	36	.500	7
Philadelphia	33	39	.458	10
Baltimore *	3	11	.214	—

* Baltimore folded November 27, 1954

Western Division

	W	L	Pct.	GB
Fort Wayne	43	29	.597	—
Minneapolis	40	32	.556	3
Rochester	29	43	.403	14
Milwaukee	26	46	.361	17

AWARDS

Top Rookie
Bob Pettit, Milwaukee

ALL-STAR TEAMS

FIRST TEAM		SECOND TEAM	
Neil Johnston	Philadelphia	Vern Mikkelsen	Minneapolis
Bob Cousy	Boston	Harry Gallatin	New York
Dolph Schayes	Syracuse	Paul Seymour	Syracuse
Bob Pettit	Milwaukee	Slater Martin	Minneapolis
Larry Foust	Fort Wayne	Bill Sharman	Boston

ALL-STAR GAME

Madison Square Garden, New York
Tuesday, January 18, 1955
East 100, West 91
MVP: Bill Sharman

PLAYOFFS

FINALS
Syracuse 4, Fort Wayne 3
Mar. 31: Fort Wayne 82 at Syracuse 86
Apr. 2: Fort Wayne 84 at Syracuse 87
Apr. 3: Syracuse 89, Fort Wayne (at Indianapolis) 96
Apr. 5: Syracuse 102, Fort Wayne (at Indianapolis) 109
Apr. 7: Syracuse 71, Fort Wayne (at Indianapolis) 74
Apr. 9: Fort Wayne 104 at Syracuse 109
Apr. 10: Fort Wayne 91 at Syracuse 92

EASTERN DIVISION
DIVISION FINALS
Syracuse 3, Boston 1
Mar. 22: Boston 100 at Syracuse 110
Mar. 24: Boston 110 at Syracuse 116
Mar. 26: Syracuse 97 at Boston 100, OT
Mar. 27: Syracuse 110 at Boston 94
DIVISION SEMI-FINALS
Boston 2, New York 1
Mar. 15: New York 101 at Boston 122
Mar. 16: Boston 95 at New York 102
Mar. 19: Boston 116 at New York 109

WESTERN DIVISION
DIVISION FINALS
Fort Wayne 3, Minneapolis 1
Mar. 20: Minneapolis 79, Fort Wayne (at Elkhart, Ind.) 96
Mar. 22: Minneapolis 97, Fort Wayne (at Indianapolis) 98, OT
Mar. 23: Fort Wayne 91 at Minneapolis 99, OT
Mar. 27: Fort Wayne 105 at Minneapolis 96
DIVISION SEMI-FINALS
Minneapolis 2, Rochester 1
Mar. 16: Rochester 78, Minneapolis (at St. Paul) 82
Mar. 18: Minneapolis 92 at Rochester 94
Mar. 19: Rochester 110, Minneapolis (at St. Paul) 119

NBA LEADERS

SCORING

	GP	FGM	FTM	PTS	PPG
Neil Johnston, PHW	72	521	589	1631	22.7
Paul Arizin, PHW	72	529	454	1512	21.0
Bob Cousy, BOS	71	522	460	1504	21.2
Bob Pettit, MLH	72	520	426	1466	20.4
Frank Selvy, MLH/BLB	71	452	444	1348	19.0
Dolph Schayes, SYR	72	422	489	1333	18.5
Vern Mikkelsen, MPL	71	440	447	1327	18.7
Clyde Lovellette, MPL	70	519	273	1311	18.7
Bill Sharman, BOS	68	453	347	1253	18.4
Ed Macauley, BOS	71	403	442	1248	17.6

FIELD GOALS

	FGM	FGA	FG%
Larry Foust, FTW	398	818	.487
Jack Coleman, ROC	400	866	.462
Tom Marshall, ROC	223	505	.442
Neil Johnston, PHW	521	1184	.440
Ray Felix, NYK	364	832	.438
Clyde Lovellette, MPL	519	1192	.435
Bill Sharman, BOS	453	1062	.427
Ed Macauley, BOS	403	951	.424
Vern Mikkelsen, MPL	440	1043	.422
Red Kerr, SYR	301	718	.419

FREE THROWS

	FTM	FTA	FT%
Bill Sharman, BOS	347	387	.897
Frankie Brian, FTW	217	255	.851
Dolph Schayes, SYR	489	587	.833
Dick Schnittker, MPL	298	362	.823
Jim Baechtold, NYK	279	339	.823
Harry Gallatin, NYK	393	483	.814
Odie Spears, ROC	220	271	.812
Paul Seymour, SYR	300	370	.811
Bob Cousy, BOS	460	570	.807
Carl Braun, NYK	274	342	.801

ASSISTS

	GP	AST	APG
Bob Cousy, BOS	71	557	7.9
Dick McGuire, NYK	71	542	7.6
Andy Phillip, FTW	64	491	7.7
Paul Seymour, SYR	72	483	6.7
Dugie Martin, MPL	72	427	5.9
Jack George, PHW	68	359	5.3
Bob Davies, ROC	72	355	4.9
George King, SYR	67	331	4.9
Bill Sharman, BOS	68	280	4.1
Ed Macauley, BOS	71	275	3.9

REBOUNDS

	GP	TRB	RPG
Neil Johnston, PHW	72	1085	15.1
Harry Gallatin, NYK	72	995	13.8
Bob Pettit, MLH	72	994	13.8
Dolph Schayes, SYR	72	887	12.3
Ray Felix, NYK	72	818	11.4
Clyde Lovellette, MPL	70	802	11.5
Jack Coleman, ROC	72	729	10.1
Vern Mikkelsen, MPL	71	722	10.2
Arnie Risen, ROC	69	703	10.2
Larry Foust, FTW	70	700	10.0

THE YEAR IN BASKETBALL

August 1954 Danny Biasone, owner of the Nationals, invites NBA officials to Syracuse to witness the 24-second clock in action. In a practice game with Dolph Schayes and other locals, NBA owners such as Boston's Walter Brown and New York's Ned Irish witness a faster-paced game. Later, Maurice Podoloff, the NBA commissioner, pronounces, "The adoption of the shot clock was the most important event in NBA history and Danny Biasone is the most important man in the NBA."

1954-55 The NBA adopts a rule introducing the 24-second clock. At the same time, it also mandates the awarding of a penalty foul shot after a team's fifth personal foul in a period. The combined rules change the game significantly by speeding up the previously ponderous pace of play, increasing scoring, and reducing the number of fouls that teams commit.

October 30, 1954 The 24-second clock is used in an NBA game for the first time as the Cincinnati Royals best the Boston Celtics, 98-95.

December 30, 1954 The Fort Wayne Pistons hold their opponent under 100 points for the 28th consecutive game. The streak sets a record that will stand for 46 years, until the New York Knicks break it in the 2000-01 season with 33 consecutive games.

December 31, 1954: Fort Wayne and Minneapolis combine to attempt 127 free throws, the most ever in an NBA game. Minneapolis wins the foul-marred contest, 103-91.

January 8, 1955 Kentucky's 129-game home winning streak ends when the Wildcats lose, 59-58, to Georgia Tech.

January 22, 1955 Bob Davies of Rochester passes for a record 20 assists in a game versus Boston.

February 25, 1955 In the lowest-scoring game since the inception of the 24-second clock, Boston beats Milwaukee, 62-57. A slippery court in the Providence Auditorium hampers play, but Charley Share, the Hawks' center, manages 19 points anyway as the game's high scorer.

March 19, 1955 Duquesne, which lost the title game of the NIT in 1954, goes all the way this season, defeating Dayton, 70-58, for the championship. Sihugo Green leads the way for the Dukes, with 33 points. Maurice Stokes of fourth-place St. Francis (Pa.) is named tournament MVP, averaging 31 ppg in four contests.

March 19, 1955 San Francisco, with Bill Russell, wins the NCAA basketball championship with a 77-63 victory over LaSalle and Tom Gola. Russell scores 23 points and grabs 25 boards in the title contest, while teammate K.C. Jones holds Gola, a three-time All-American, to 16 points and scores 24 himself.

March 19, 1955 Dick Ricketts and Sihugo Green combine for 56 points to lead 22-4 Duquesne to a 70-58 triumph over Dayton in the NIT championship tilt.

April 10, 1955 The Syracuse Nationals defeat the Fort Wayne Pistons, 92-91, in Game 7 to win the NBA championship. George King is the Nationals' hero; he hits two decisive free throws with 12 seconds left, and then steals the ensuing inbounds pass to seal the win.

1955-56

Pettit leads league in scoring, rebounding, adds inaugural MVP

With a minimum of personnel changes, the Philadelphia Warriors soared from last place to the top of the Eastern Division this season. The first champions of the BAA back in 1947, the Warriors had recently fallen on hard times and finished at the bottom of the East last year with a 33-39 mark. Owner-coach Eddie Gottlieb began the rebuilding process by turning over the coaching reins to George Senesky, a long-time player under Gottlieb with the old Sphas and with the Warriors. A second step in building the Warriors back up to a position of strength was the signing of rookie Tom Gola. Acclaimed as one of the best all-around players in collegiate history, Gola led LaSalle to the NIT championship in 1952 and to the NCAA finals in 1955 before losing to San Francisco and Bill Russell. Reserve forward Ernie Beck also returned to the club from the military, but no other key personnel changes were made.

The Warriors had a lot of talented players who suddenly started pulling together under Senesky's direction. Paul Arizin and Neil Johnston finished two-three in the league scoring tables, giving the Warriors an unmatched outside-inside scoring tandem. Arizin popped in enough jump shots from his forward slot to average 24.2 despite an asthma condition which often set him coughing and wheezing while running up and down court. Johnston, a tough 6-foot-8 center, used a hook shot to average over 20 points per game for the fourth straight season. These two scorers were the established stars on the club. The supporting cast, however, surprised the league with its solid play. Veteran forward Joe Graboski furnished muscle to the forecourt, and guard Jack George blossomed into a first-rate playmaker in his third pro season. Gola helped the Warriors immensely as the other starting guard; a 6-foot-6 forward in college, he smoothly converted to the backcourt, giving the Warriors the NBA's biggest guard and giving the league's other clubs a sizeable problem on defense. With the bench making occasional contributions, with the offense as potent as ever, and with the defense tightened up considerably, the Warriors leapfrogged all the way to first place with a 45-27 record, the best in the league.

The Boston Celtics trailed the Warriors by six games, still missing the rebounding muscle and defense to make its fast-break offense pay top dividends. Bob Cousy, Bill Sharman, and Ed Macauley all finished in the top ten in scoring, but the Celtics had to wait for a first-class center before they could reach championship status. Nevertheless, coach Red Auerbach continued adding serviceable bodies to his squad by signing rookie forward Jim Loscutoff, a rugged rebounder who soon became known around the league as a "hatchet man."

Falling under the .500 level were the New York Knicks, who were in the midst of a rebuilding program that would show scant results until the late 1960's. Rookie forward Kenny Sears,

Tom Gola
Rookie from LaSalle emerges to support the scoring exploits of vets Paul Arizin and Neil Johnston and deliver the Warriors' second crown.

a pencil-thin shooter, and center Walter Dukes, a refugee from the Harlem Globetrotters, were this year's key additions to the aging squad. The biggest loss to the New York squad was coach Joe Lapchick, a very popular figure with the press and the public; having lost the confidence of team president Ned Irish, Lapchick resigned in February, and Vince Boryla took over as the new coach. The Knicks finished in a tie for third with the Syracuse Nats who slumped badly from last season's championship form. With the final playoff spot at stake, the Nats beat the Knicks in a one-game showdown at the end of the regular

season, thus shutting the New Yorkers out of the playoffs for the first time ever.

While the Eastern Division was thoroughly shaking up its standings, the Western clubs finished in practically the same order as last season. The Fort Wayne Pistons won six less games than they did last season, but they still captured first place with a 37-35 record. Forward George Yardley and center Larry Foust continued to pace the team's scoring, but coach Charlie Eckman rebuilt his backcourt by releasing Max Zaslofsky, benching Frankie Brian, and replacing these two veterans with rookies Chuck Noble and Corky Devlin.

Finishing four games back in a tie for the remaining playoff berths were the Minneapolis Lakers and the St. Louis Hawks. The Lakers slipped under .500 for the first time despite fine scoring from center Clyde Lovellette and fine playmaking from guard Slater Martin. Jim Pollard had retired, but when the Lakers began to panic in mid-season, they prevailed upon George Mikan to come out of retirement to play center. Mikan was overweight and rusty at first, but he played himself back into shape by the time the playoffs began; he could not, however, again be the dominant force he had been, since his age and the 24-second clock worked against him.

Tying the Lakers for second place were the Hawks, transplanted to St. Louis by owner Ben Kerner in a move which paid off at the box office. The improving Hawks got help from former Royals Jack Coleman and Jack McMahon, but the major force on the club was the vastly improving Bob Pettit. A glowing competitor and hard worker, Pettit led the NBA both in scoring and rebounding, and he led the Hawks into the playoffs for the first time since 1950, when the club was still in Tri-Cities.

The Royals tumbled into last place and out of the playoffs for the first time in the club's history. Veteran guard Bob Davies quit, and center Arnie Risen was dispatched to Boston; coach Les Harrison installed three rookies in his starting lineup: forwards Maurice Stokes and Jack Twyman and guard Ed Fleming. A product of tiny St. Francis (Pa.), Stokes gave the Royals a top-notch strong forward, while Twyman brought polished shooting skills from his career at the University of Cincinnati. But the fans were showing up in smaller numbers at Royal games, and Harrison was already thinking of greener pastures elsewhere.

The early matches in the playoffs all went the limit. Syracuse beat Boston and St. Louis beat Minneapolis in three-game series, and Philadelphia beat Syracuse and Fort Wayne beat St. Louis in five-game series. With the 24-second clock now filling all the games with basketball action, the NBA expected an exciting seven-game championship series between the Warriors and Pistons. It didn't happen, however, as the Warriors upended the Pistons in five games to easily take their first NBA title. Starting next year, though, a new champion would take the crown and prove very difficult to dislodge from the throne.

1955-56 SEASON HIGHLIGHTS

STANDINGS

Eastern Division

	W	L	Pct.	GB
Philadelphia	45	27	.625	—
Boston	39	33	.542	6
Syracuse	35	37	.486	10
New York	35	37	.486	10

Western Division

	W	L	Pct.	GB
Fort Wayne	37	35	.514	—
Minneapolis	33	39	.458	4
St. Louis	33	39	.458	4
Rochester	31	41	.431	6

AWARDS

MVP
Bob Pettit, St. Louis
Top Rookie
Maurice Stokes, Rochester

ALL-STAR TEAMS

FIRST TEAM

Bob Pettit	St. Louis
Paul Arizin	Philadelphia
Neil Johnston	Philadelphia
Bob Cousy	Boston
Bill Sharman	Boston

SECOND TEAM

Dolph Schayes	Syracuse
Maurice Stokes	Rochester
Clyde Lovellette	Minneapolis
Slater Martin	Minneapolis
Jack George	Philadelphia

ALL-STAR GAME

War Memorial Auditorium, Rochester
Tuesday, January 24, 1956
West 108, East 94
MVP: Bob Pettit

PLAYOFFS

FINALS
Philadelphia 4, Fort Wayne 1
Mar. 31: Fort Wayne 94 at Philadelphia 98
Apr. 1: Philadelphia 83 at Fort Wayne 84
Apr. 3: Fort Wayne 96 at Philadelphia 100
Apr. 5: Philadelphia 107 at Fort Wayne 105
Apr. 7: Fort Wayne 88 at Philadelphia 99
EASTERN DIVISION
DIVISION FINALS
Philadelphia 3, Syracuse 2
Mar. 23: Syracuse 87 at Philadelphia 109
Mar. 25: Philadelphia 118 at Syracuse 122
Mar. 27: Syracuse 96 at Philadelphia 119
Mar. 28: Philadelphia 104 at Syracuse 108
Mar. 29: Syracuse 104 at Philadelphia 109

DIVISION SEMI-FINALS
Syracuse 2, Boston 1
Mar. 17: Syracuse 93 at Boston 110
Mar. 19: Boston 98 at Syracuse 101
Mar. 21: Syracuse 102 at Boston 97
Second-Place Game
Mar. 16: Minneapolis 103 at St. Louis 97
Third-Place Game
Mar. 15: New York 77 at Syracuse 82

WESTERN DIVISION
DIVISION FINALS
Fort Wayne 3, St. Louis 2
Mar. 22: St. Louis 86 at Fort Wayne 85
Mar. 24: Fort Wayne 74 at St. Louis 84
Mar. 25: St. Louis 84 at Fort Wayne 107
Mar. 27: Fort Wayne 93 at St. Louis 84
Mar. 29: St. Louis 97 at Fort Wayne 102
DIVISION SEMI-FINALS
St. Louis 2, Minneapolis 1
Mar. 17: Minneapolis 115 at St. Louis 116
Mar. 19: St. Louis 75 at Minneapolis 133
Mar. 21: St. Louis 116 at Minneapolis 115

NBA LEADERS

SCORING

	GP	FGM	FTM	PTS	PPG
Bob Pettit, STL	72	646	557	1849	25.7
Paul Arizin, PHW	72	617	507	1741	24.2
Neil Johnston, PHW	70	499	549	1547	22.1
Clyde Lovellette, MPL	71	594	338	1526	21.5
Dolph Schayes, SYR	72	465	542	1472	20.4
Bill Sharman, BOS	72	538	358	1434	19.9
Bob Cousy, BOS	72	440	476	1356	18.8
Ed Macauley, BOS	71	420	400	1240	17.5
George Yardley, FTW	71	434	365	1233	17.4
Larry Foust, FTW	72	367	432	1166	16.2

FIELD GOALS

	FGM	FGA	FG%
Neil Johnston, PHW	499	1092	.457
Paul Arizin, PHW	617	1378	.448
Larry Foust, FTW	367	821	.447
Kenny Sears, NYK	319	728	.438
Bill Sharman, BOS	538	1229	.438
Clyde Lovellette, MPL	594	1370	.434
Chuck Share, STL	315	733	.430
Bob Houbregs, FTW	247	575	.430
Bob Pettit, STL	646	1507	.429
Mel Hutchins, FTW	325	764	.425

FREE THROWS

	FTM	FTA	FT%
Bill Sharman, BOS	358	413	.867
Dolph Schayes, SYR	542	632	.858
Dick Schnittker, MPL	304	355	.856
Bob Cousy, BOS	476	564	.844
Carl Braun, NYK	320	382	.838
Dugie Martin, MPL	329	395	.833
Paul Arizin, PHW	507	626	.810
Vern Mikkelsen, MPL	328	408	.804
Neil Johnston, PHW	549	685	.801
Jim Baechtold, NYK	233	291	.801

ASSISTS

	GP	AST	APG
Bob Cousy, BOS	72	642	8.9
Jack George, PHW	72	457	6.4
Dugie Martin, MPL	72	445	6.2
Andy Phillip, FTW	70	410	5.9
George King, SYR	72	410	5.7
Tom Gola, PHW	68	404	5.9
Dick McGuire, NYK	62	362	5.8
Bill Sharman, BOS	72	339	4.7
Maurice Stokes, ROC	67	328	4.9
Carl Braun, NYK	72	298	4.1

REBOUNDS

	GP	TRB	RPG
Bob Pettit, STL	72	1164	16.2
Maurice Stokes, ROC	67	1094	16.3
Clyde Lovellette, MPL	71	992	14.0
Dolph Schayes, SYR	72	891	12.4
Neil Johnston, PHW	70	872	12.5
Chuck Share, STL	72	774	10.8
Harry Gallatin, NYK	72	740	10.3
Jack Coleman, ROC/STL	75	688	9.2
George Yardley, FTW	71	686	9.7
Larry Foust, FTW	72	648	9.0

THE YEAR IN BASKETBALL

December 15, 1955 Minneapolis and Syracuse set a league record by combining to score 268 points in a game. The Nationals prevail, 135-133, in triple overtime. Seven players score 20 points or more in the contest.

December 27, 1956 Bill Sharman's consecutive free throw streak ends at 55. Sharman's record will last 19 years until Calvin Murphy breaks it in 1980.

January 6, 1956 Jeanette Hays of Henry, Tenn. scores 100 points in a high school game.

January 24, 1956 With 20 points and 24 rebounds, Bob Pettit of St. Louis wins the first of his NBA-record four All-Star MVP awards, leading the West to a 108-94 victory over the East in Rochester.

March 12, 1956 Dick Farley of Syracuse fouls out after playing just five minutes, at the time the fastest disqualification in NBA history, in a game against St. Louis.

March 19, 1956 The Minneapolis Lakers throttle the St. Louis Hawks, 133-75, in Game 2 of the Western Conference semifinals, the largest margin of victory (58 points) in NBA playoff history.

March 23, 1956 Louisville beats Dayton, 93-80, to win the NIT. The Cardinals' Charlie Tyra takes the MVP award.

March 23, 1956 Bill Russell leads undefeated San Francisco to an 83-71 win over Iowa to win the NCAA basketball championship. The victory makes the Dons the first tournament champion to go undefeated through an entire season and runs their two-year winning streak to 55.

March 27, 1956 Syracuse attempts a record-tying 56 foul shots in a playoff contest against Philadelphia. The two teams combine to grab a record-setting 159 rebounds, of which the Warriors get 89.

April 7, 1956 The Philadelphia Warriors win the NBA championship, defeating the Fort Wayne Pistons in four games to two. In the final game, Warriors forward Joe Graboski and Paul Arizin score 29 and 26 points, respectively, to lead Philadelphia to a 99-88 victory.

April 29, 1956 The St. Louis Hawks trade the draft rights to Bill Russell to the Boston Celtics in exchange for Ed Macauley and Cliff Hagan.

April 30, 1956 Bill Russell of the University of San Francisco is selected third overall in the NBA draft by the St. Louis Hawks. Later, the Hawks trade Russell to Boston.

1956-57

Celtic dynasty launched by Game 7, 2OT win over Hawks

The Boston Celtics had long owned a full stable of hot shooters, but lacked a strong rebounder to get the ball for the gunners. This season, coach Red Auerbach found his man in 6-foot-9 Bill Russell, a lean center who had just led the University of San Francisco to 55 straight wins and two NCAA championships. A master at gaining position for rebounds and a magician at blocking shots, Russell seemed so much an answer to Auerbach's dreams that the Boston coach sent veteran center Ed Macauley and rookie forward Cliff Hagan to St. Louis for the Hawks' number two pick in the first round of the draft. After the Royals passed him by, the Celtics picked Russell and outbid the Harlem Globetrotters to sign him to a lucrative contract. The only problem was that Russell planned to play in the Olympic Games in Melbourne, which would keep him out of the pro ranks until mid-December.

Thus Auerbach had to wait for his rookie star; he had other new help to tide the team over until then. Veteran guard Andy Phillip came from Ft. Wayne to provide wisdom for the bench, and rookie Tom Heinsohn won a starting forward position. Called "Ack-Ack" because of his love of shooting the ball, the 6-foot-7 Heinsohn excited Boston fans with his offense the way Russell would with his defense. With the incomparable Bob Cousy quarterbacking the club, Bill Sharman throwing in long-range jumpers with automatic accuracy, and Jim Loscutoff muscling his way to rebounds, the Celtics caught fire in the early going and ran off a 10-game winning streak with Heinsohn in the pivot. The Celtics cooled off to a 16-8 mark by December 22, the day that Bill Russell joined the team.

After getting settled with the Celtics, Russell went on to revolutionize pro basketball with his rebounding, defense, and shot-blocking. He made the foul lane posted territory for opposing drivers, and his rebounds on the defensive boards usually triggered the fabled Celtic fast-break, led by Cousy. The starting five of Russell, Heinsohn, Loscutoff, Cousy, and Sharman was the class unit of pro ball, and swingman Frank Ramsey added zip to the shock troops after his discharge from the service in January. An eight-game win streak in January put the Celtics out of reach in the East.

The Syracuse Nats came on strong near the end of the season to finish second behind Boston. A slow start had driven coach Al Cervi to resign, but veteran guard Paul Seymour sta-

Bill Russell
A revolutionizing force, here powering over Syracuse's Bob Hopkins as Tom Heinsohn (15) and Joe Holup look on, is unleashed on the pro game.

bilized the club after taking over as the new mentor. On the floor, Syracuse's biggest asset still was Dolph Schayes, third in the NBA in both scoring and rebounding. The Philadelphia Warriors slumped to 37-35 this season and barely squeaked into the playoffs; Paul Arizin and Neil Johnston still scored at prolific rates, but the loss of Tom Gola to the military hurt the backcourt. The Knicks finished last and out of the money despite a respectable 36-36 record; two key additions to the roster were guard Richie Guerin, a rookie from Iona by route of the military service, and forward Willie Naulls, a rookie from

UCLA picked up from the St. Louis Hawks in a trade for Slater Martin.

Over in the Western Division, all four clubs finished below the .500 level that had earned New York last place in the East. Three clubs deadlocked for first place with mediocre 34-38 marks. The Fort Wayne Pistons managed to hold on to a share of first place despite a continued slide in the win column. George Yardley was the only consistent scoring threat, and coach Charlie Eckman continued to revise his backcourt by sending Andy Phillip to Boston and picking up Gene Shue from New York. The Minneapolis Lakers also grabbed a portion of first place while unloading veteran players. George Mikan retired for good, and guard Slater Martin had been traded to New York before the season started for center Walt Dukes. Clyde Lovellette and Dick Garmaker led the Laker offense by placing in the NBA's top ten scoring leaders.

The third co-leader, the St. Louis Hawks, added lots of new talent, but got off to a very disappointing start. The Russell trade with Boston brought Ed Macauley, a popular figure from his college days at the University of St. Louis, and Cliff Hagan, a muscular 6-foot-4 forward just discharged from the Army. Slater Martin came over in mid-season after a short stint in New York, and he immediately filled the bill of feeding Bob Pettit and the other Hawk frontcourt men. Pettit finished second in the NBA scoring race to Paul Arizin, an imposing fact when one considers that a broken wrist forced Pettit to wear a cast on his hand after mid-February. The Hawks went through three coaches this season, beginning under Red Holzman, playing eight games under Slater Martin before he decided to

concentrate on playing, and finishing the campaign under the direction of reserve forward Alex Hannum, who had been picked up on waivers earlier in the year. Under Hannum, the Hawks jelled late in the season and entered the playoffs in fine condition. The last-place Rochester Royals enjoyed good seasons by Jack Twyman and Maurice Stokes, but the club was on shaky legs both on the court and at the box office.

Unlike last season, the playoffs produced lopsided early matches, with the Celtics and Hawks finally emerging as the contestants in the championship round. Neither club had won an NBA crown before, and the Celtics were heavily favored to break the ice. Large crowds filled the houses in both Boston and St. Louis and gave this series a large jolt of electricity. The Hawks surprised the Celtics with a 125-123, double overtime win in Boston in Game 1, with the Celtics evening the series the next night. In St. Louis, the Hawks took Game 3 only to drop the next two contests to the Celtics. The sixth game went to the Hawks when Bob Cousy missed a free throw with 12 seconds left; the Hawks came downcourt, Bob Pettit missed a shot, and Cliff Hagan tapped it in at the buzzer for a 96-94 triumph. The final game of the series was a seesaw affair, with two Pettit foul shots tying the game at 103-all at the end of regulation time. Jack Coleman's shot with nine seconds left tied the score again at 113, and sent the game into a second over-time period. Tension mounted as the clubs battled into this extra period. With the Celtics up 125-123 with two seconds left the Hawks heaved the ball inbounds at the backboard, and Pettit soared up to tap it in; it rolled around the rim and dropped out. The Celtics were champs for the first time.

1956-57 SEASON HIGHLIGHTS

STANDINGS

Eastern Division

	W	L	Pct.	GB
Boston	44	28	.611	—
Syracuse	38	34	.528	6
Philadelphia	37	35	.514	7
New York	36	36	.500	8

Western Division

	W	L	Pct.	GB
St. Louis	34	38	.472	—
Minneapolis	34	38	.472	—
Fort Wayne	34	38	.472	—
Rochester	31	41	.431	3

AWARDS
MVP
Bob Cousy, Boston
Top Rookie
Tom Heinsohn, Boston

ALL-STAR TEAMS
FIRST TEAM

Paul Arizin	Philadelphia
Dolph Schayes	Syracuse
Bob Pettit	St. Louis
Bob Cousy	Boston
Bill Sharman	Boston

SECOND TEAM

George Yardley	Fort Wayne
Maurice Stokes	Rochester
Neil Johnston	Philadelphia
Dick Garmaker	Minneapolis
Slater Martin	St. Louis

ALL-STAR GAME
Boston Garden, Boston
Tuesday, January 15, 1957
East 109, West 97
MVP: Bob Cousy

PLAYOFFS
FINALS
Boston 4, St. Louis 3
Mar. 30: St. Louis 125 at Boston 123, 2OT
Mar. 31: St. Louis 99 at Boston 119
Apr. 6: Boston 98 at St. Louis 100
Apr. 7: Boston 123 at St. Louis 118
Apr. 9: St. Louis 109 at Boston 124
Apr. 11: Boston 94 at St. Louis 96
Apr. 13: St. Louis 123 at Boston 125, 2OT

EASTERN DIVISION
DIVISION FINALS
Boston 3, Syracuse 0
Mar. 21: Syracuse 90 at Boston 108
Mar. 23: Boston 120 at Syracuse 105
Mar. 24: Syracuse 80 at Boston 83
DIVISION SEMI-FINALS
Syracuse 2, Philadelphia 0
Mar. 16: Syracuse 103 at Philadelphia 96
Mar. 18: Philadelphia 80 at Syracuse 91

WESTERN DIVISION
DIVISION FINALS
St. Louis 3, Minneapolis 0
Mar. 21: Minneapolis 109 at St. Louis 118
Mar. 24: Minneapolis 104 at St. Louis 106
Mar. 25: St. Louis 143 at Minneapolis 135, 2OT
DIVISION SEMI-FINALS
Minneapolis 2, Fort Wayne 0
Mar. 17: Fort Wayne 127 at Minneapolis 131
Mar. 19: Minneapolis 110 at Fort Wayne 108
TIEBREAKERS
Mar. 14: Fort Wayne 103 at St. Louis 115
Mar. 16: Minneapolis 111 at St. Louis 114

NBA LEADERS

SCORING

	GP	FGM	FTM	PTS	PPG
Paul Arizin, PHW	71	613	591	1817	25.6
Bob Pettit, STL	71	613	529	1755	24.7
Dolph Schayes, SYR	72	496	625	1617	22.5
Neil Johnston, PHW	69	520	535	1575	22.8
George Yardley, FTW	72	522	503	1547	21.5
Clyde Lovellette, MPL	69	574	286	1434	20.8
Bill Sharman, BOS	67	516	381	1413	21.1
Bob Cousy, BOS	64	478	363	1319	20.6
Ed Macauley, STL	72	414	359	1187	16.5
Dick Garmaker, MPL	72	406	365	1177	16.3

FIELD GOALS

	FGM	FGA	FG%
Neil Johnston, PHW	520	1163	.447
Chuck Share, STL	235	535	.439
Jack Twyman, ROC	449	1023	.439
Bob Houbregs, FTW	253	585	.432
Bill Russell, BOS	277	649	.427
Clyde Lovellette, MPL	574	1348	.426
Paul Arizin, PHW	613	1451	.422
Ed Macauley, STL	414	987	.419
Kenny Sears, NYK	343	821	.418
Ray Felix, NYK	295	709	.416

FREE THROWS

	FTM	FTA	FT%
Bill Sharman, BOS	381	421	.905
Dolph Schayes, SYR	625	691	.904
Dick Garmaker, MPL	365	435	.839
Paul Arizin, PHW	591	713	.829
Neil Johnston, PHW	535	648	.826
Bob Cousy, BOS	363	442	.821
Carl Braun, NYK	245	303	.809
Vern Mikkelsen, MPL	342	424	.807
Joe Holup, SYR	204	253	.806
Harry Gallatin, NYK	415	519	.800

ASSISTS

	GP	AST	APG
Bob Cousy, BOS	64	478	7.5
Jack McMahon, STL	72	367	5.1
Maurice Stokes, ROC	72	331	4.6
Jack George, PHW	67	307	4.6
Dugie Martin, NYK/STL	66	269	4.1
Carl Braun, NYK	72	256	3.6
Gene Shue, FTW	72	238	3.3
Larry Costello, PHW	72	236	3.3
Bill Sharman, BOS	67	236	3.5
Dolph Schayes, SYR	72	229	3.2

REBOUNDS

	GP	TRB	RPG
Maurice Stokes, ROC	72	1256	17.4
Bob Pettit, STL	71	1037	14.6
Dolph Schayes, SYR	72	1008	14.0
Bill Russell, BOS	48	943	19.6
Clyde Lovellette, MPL	69	932	13.5
Neil Johnston, PHW	69	855	12.4
Red Kerr, SYR	72	807	11.2
Walter Dukes, MPL	71	794	11.2
George Yardley, FTW	72	755	10.5
Jim Loscutoff, BOS	70	730	10.4

THE YEAR IN BASKETBALL

December 1, 1956 The United States men's basketball team wins its fourth straight Olympic gold medal in Melbourne. In the medal-clinching game, U.S. defeats Russia, 89-55, led by Bill Russell and K.C. Jones.

December 3, 1956 In his college debut, Wilt Chamberlain scores 52 points in a Kansas victory.

December 24, 1956 Corky Devlin of Fort Wayne ties an NBA record by going 0-for-15 from the field against the Minneapolis Lakers.

December 27, 1956 Bill Sharman's record NBA free-throw streak ends at 55 games.

March 17, 1957 The Minneapolis Lakers beat the Fort Wayne Pistons, 131-127—at that time the most points scored by two teams in a playoff game.

March 23, 1957 Bradley nips Memphis St., 84-83, on a three-point play by Shellie McMillon with 30 second left in the game to claim the NIT Tournament. Memphis State's Win Wilfong, who tallies 30 points in the final, is named tournament MVP.

March 23, 1957 In a thriller, North Carolina edges Kansas, 54-53, in triple overtime to win NCAA championship. The undefeated Tar Heels also topped Michigan State in triple overtime in the semifinals by a 74-70 score. In the final, Kansas' Wilt Chamberlain managed a game-high 23 despite being double- and triple-teamed all game.

March 25, 1957 In a wild contest, the St. Louis Hawks best the Minneapolis Lakers, 143-135, in a double-overtime playoff game that sets records for most points scored by two teams. The Hawks shoot 52 of 126 (.413) from the floor and the Lakers make 46 of 117 (.393) field-goal attempts.

April 9, 1957 Bob Cousy dishes out a record 19 assists in Boston's playoff contest versus St. Louis. As a team, the Celtics garner 33 assists, also a playoff record.

April 13, 1957 In one of the most exciting Game 7's in NBA finals history, the Boston Celtics defeat the St. Louis Hawks, 125-123, in double overtime to win the NBA title. The game ends when Bob Pettit misses a layup in the final seconds after catching Alex Hannum's full-court pass. Pettit, the Hawks center, scores 39 points and grabs 19 rebounds. Boston's Tommy Heinsohn scores 37 points and gets 23 boards. Bill Russell scores 19 with 32 rebounds.

1957-58

Hawks rebound to upset Celtics behind Pettit's 50-point finale

Like a caterpillar changing into a butterfly, the NBA was slowly shedding its small-time image and changing into a big-league operation. Fort Wayne and Rochester, two traditional basketball towns that had come into the NBA from the old NBL, were replaced on the circuit by Detroit and Cincinnati, a pair of larger cities that had long held big-league status through the exploits of their baseball teams. Owner Fred Zollner moved his Pistons to Detroit and Les Harrison took the Royals to Cincinnati, both men hoping to expand their profits with a larger population base. Another old-line franchise, the Minneapolis Lakers, was sold to Bob Short, who felt no obligation to stay in Minnesota if attendance did not pick up. So the compact, eight-team NBA was moving into the big cities, with Minneapolis and Syracuse the smallest outposts still in operation.

This growing big-league image was further nourished by the glamour of the Boston Celtics, the defending champions. Coach Red Auerbach had fine tuned his club to excellence, with a firehouse fast break offense and a tenacious, pressing defense. Bob Cousy fueled his national reputation by making outrageously spectacular passes and drives as the middle man in the fast break, while Bill Sharman and Tom Heinsohn kept the attack in high gear with their long-range shooting. Center Bill Russell started the fast break moving with his rebounds and quick outlet passes to Cousy, and his unmatched shot-blocking ability freed the Celtic guards to press on defense, confident that anyone who got through the middle would be stopped by Russell. The key subs were veteran players, but rookie guard Sam Jones, a superb shooter from North Carolina College, caught on as the tenth man and as a diamond in the rough for the future. With Russell around for the entire season, the Celtics improved to a 49-23 record, the best in the league.

The rest of the Eastern teams entertained little hope of catching the Celtics during the regular season. Syracuse came closest, finishing eight games back in second place. Dolph Schayes was still the heart and soul of the Nats, but he got strong supporting performances from Johnny Kerr, Ed Conlin,

Maurice Stokes
A third straight all-star season, then, inexplicably, the day after the above game where he guarded Detroit's league-leading scorer, George Yardley, tragedy struck.

and Larry Costello, a set-shooter picked up from the Philadelphia Warriors. The Warriors still had two hot scorers in Paul Arizin and Neil Johnston, and they got Tom Gola back from the military in mid-season, but they barely edged out New York for the third playoff spot. The Knicks sent veterans Harry Gallatin, Sweetwater Clifton, and Dick McGuire to Detroit in a general housecleaning which saw the team finish out of the playoffs for the third straight year.

Out on the banks of the Mississippi, the St. Louis Hawks made the playoffs with a talented, experienced club. After coming of age in the playoff finals against Boston last spring, the Hawks soared to a 41-31 record and an easy first-place finish in the Western Division. Coach Alex Hannum had the deepest frontcourt in the NBA Bob Pettit led the Hawks by example, ranking second in the NBA in rebounding and third in scoring with a 24.6 clip. Cliff Hagan took over the other

forward spot and scored at a 19.9 pace. Ed Macauley added offensive skills to the front line while Chuck Share concentrated on defense and rebounding. Guards Slater Martin and Jack McMahon limited themselves to feeding the ball inside to the big men and playing tough defense on enemy guards. In contrast to the Celtics, the Hawks played a pattern, control offense which relied on the inside scoring of the forwards.

Behind the Hawks, the transplanted Pistons and Royals tied for the remaining playoff spots. The Pistons made lots of changes but still wound up at 33-39: coach Charlie Eckman was canned in favor of Red Rocha; Mel Hutchins was sent to New York for Harry Gallatin, Sweetwater Clifton, and Dick McGuire; and Larry Foust and Corky Devlin were traded to Minneapolis for Walt Dukes. The high note of the campaign was George Yardley's winning the NBA scoring crown with a 27.8 average and setting a league record with 2001 points.

The Royals, too, were of little note on the court. Clyde Lovellette came from Minneapolis to join Maurice Stokes and Jack Twyman in a first-rate frontcourt, but the Royals still needed to build themselves back up from their collapse in the last few seasons in Rochester. The Lakers, meanwhile, hit bottom, tumbling into the basement with a chaotic 19-53 season. Owner Short made George Mikan coach of the Lakers, but the club fell apart under the great center's tutelage. John Kundla came out of the front offfice to resume the coaching duties in the second half of the campaign, but the talent-poor club could not make a comeback. The team's leading scorer was forward Vern Mikkelsen, the last remaining veteran of the championship squads of the early 1950's.

With the Lakers out of the playoffs for the first time in NBA history, the Celtics and Hawks started out as favorites to meet again in the championship series. The semi-final rounds had to be played first, with the Warriors upsetting the Nats in the East and the Pistons downing the Royals in the West. The Royals lost more than the series, however; they lost star forward Maurice Stokes. Although he struck his head on the floor during the last game of the regular season, Stokes was able to play in the first game of the playoffs. However, he went into a coma the next day. At first the diagnosis was encephalitis, but later it was found that his coma and subsequent paralysis were caused by his head injury. Stokes never recovered, and the Royals would search in vain for a replacement in the years to come.

In the divisional finals, the Celtics and Hawks both swept into the finals by soundly beating the contending Warriors and Pistons.

The rematch between the Celtics and Hawks sparked a heated interest in the championship series. The Hawks edged out a 104-102 victory in Game 1, while the Celtics easily took Game 2, 136-112. In Game 3, disaster hit the Celtics as Bill Russell injured his ankle, opening the way for a 111-108 Hawk win. Using subs Arnie Risen and Jack Nichols, the Celtics pulled even with a 109-98 fourth game victory, but the Hawks again pulled ahead with a 102-100 squeaker in Game 5. With their backs to the wall, the Celtics called on Russell for 20 minutes of action in Game 6; his ankle, however, stripped him of all mobility and forced coach Auerbach to lift him from the lineup. Pettit, meanwhile, scored a playoff record 50 points and led his mates to the title with a 110-109 victory. The Celtics had been dethroned after only one year on top, but they would be back.

1957-58 SEASON HIGHLIGHTS

STANDINGS

Eastern Division	W	L	Pct.	GB		Western Division	W	L	Pct.	GB
Boston	49	23	.681	—		St. Louis	41	31	.569	—
Syracuse	41	31	.569	8		Detroit	33	39	.458	8
Philadelphia	37	35	.514	12		Cincinnati	33	39	.458	8
New York	35	37	.486	14		Minneapolis	19	53	.264	22

AWARDS

MVP
Bill Russell, Boston

Top Rookie
Woody Sauldsberry, Philadelphia

ALL-STAR TEAMS

FIRST TEAM

Dolph Schayes	Syracuse
George Yardley	Detroit
Bob Pettit	St. Louis
Bob Cousy	Boston
Bill Sharman	Boston

SECOND TEAM

Cliff Hagan	St. Louis
Maurice Stokes	Cincinnati
Bill Russell	Boston
Tom Gola	Philadelphia
Slater Martin	St. Louis

ALL-STAR GAME

St. Louis Arena, St. Louis
Tuesday, January 21, 1958
East 130, West 118
MVP: Bob Pettit

PLAYOFFS

FINALS
St. Louis 4, Boston 2
Mar. 29: St. Louis 104 at Boston 102
Mar. 30: St. Louis 112 at Boston 136
Apr. 2: Boston 108 at St. Louis 111
Apr. 5: Boston 109 at St. Louis 98
Apr. 9: St. Louis 102 at Boston 100
Apr. 12: Boston 109 at St. Louis 110

EASTERN DIVISION
DIVISION FINALS
Boston 4, Philadelphia 1
Mar. 19: Philadelphia 98 at Boston 107
Mar. 22: Boston 109 at Philadelphia 87
Mar. 23: Philadelphia 92 at Boston 106
Mar. 26: Boston 97 at Philadelphia 111
Mar. 27: Philadelphia 88 at Boston 93
DIVISION SEMI-FINALS
Philadelphia 2, Syracuse 1
Mar. 15: Philadelphia 82 at Syracuse 86
Mar. 16: Syracuse 93 at Philadelphia 95
Mar. 18: Philadelphia 101 at Syracuse 88

WESTERN DIVISION
DIVISION FINALS
St. Louis 4, Detroit 1
Mar. 19: Detroit 111 at St. Louis 114
Mar. 22: St. Louis 99 at Detroit 96
Mar. 23: Detroit 109 at St. Louis 89
Mar. 25: St. Louis 145 at Detroit 101
Mar. 27: Detroit 96 at St. Louis 120
DIVISION SEMI-FINALS
Detroit 2, Cincinnati 0
Mar. 15: Cincinnati 93 at Detroit 100
Mar. 16: Detroit 124 at Cincinnati 104

NBA LEADERS

SCORING

	GP	FGM	FTM	PTS	PPG
George Yardley, DET	72	673	655	2001	27.8
Dolph Schayes, SYR	72	581	629	1791	24.9
Bob Pettit, STL	70	581	557	1719	24.6
Clyde Lovellette, CIN	71	679	301	1659	23.4
Paul Arizin, PHW	68	483	440	1406	20.7
Bill Sharman, BOS	63	550	302	1402	22.3
Cliff Hagan, STL	70	503	385	1391	19.9
Neil Johnston, PHW	71	473	442	1388	19.5
Kenny Sears, NYK	72	445	452	1342	18.6
Vern Mikkelsen, MPL	72	439	370	1248	17.3

FIELD GOALS

	FGM	FGA	FG%
Jack Twyman, CIN	465	1028	.452
Cliff Hagan, STL	503	1135	.443
Ray Felix, NYK	304	688	.442
Bill Russell, BOS	456	1032	.442
Clyde Lovellette, CIN	679	1540	.441
Kenny Sears, NYK	445	1014	.439
Neil Johnston, PHW	473	1102	.429
Ed Macauley, STL	376	879	.428
Larry Costello, SYR	378	888	.426
Bill Sharman, BOS	550	1297	.424

FREE THROWS

	FTM	FTA	FT%
Dolph Schayes, SYR	629	696	.904
Bill Sharman, BOS	302	338	.893
Bob Cousy, BOS	277	326	.850
Carl Braun, NYK	321	378	.849
Dick Schnittker, MPL	201	237	.848
Larry Costello, SYR	320	378	.847
Gene Shue, DET	276	327	.844
Willie Naulls, NYK	284	344	.826
Kenny Sears, NYK	452	550	.822
Ron Sobie, NYK	196	239	.820

ASSISTS

	GP	AST	APG
Bob Cousy, BOS	65	463	7.1
Dick McGuire, DET	69	454	6.6
Maurice Stokes, CIN	63	403	6.4
Carl Braun, NYK	71	393	5.5
George King, CIN	63	337	5.3
Jack McMahon, STL	72	333	4.6
Tom Gola, PHW	59	327	5.5
Richie Guerin, NYK	63	317	5.0
Larry Costello, SYR	72	317	4.4
Jack George, PHW	72	234	3.2

REBOUNDS

	GP	TRB	RPG
Bill Russell, BOS	69	1564	22.7
Bob Pettit, STL	70	1216	17.4
Maurice Stokes, CIN	63	1142	18.1
Dolph Schayes, SYR	72	1022	14.2
Red Kerr, SYR	72	963	13.4
Walter Dukes, DET	72	954	13.2
Larry Foust, MPL	72	876	12.2
Clyde Lovellette, CIN	71	862	12.1
Vern Mikkelsen, MPL	72	805	11.2
Willie Naulls, NYK	68	799	11.8

THE YEAR IN BASKETBALL

November 16, 1957 Bill Russell grabs a record 49 rebounds in a game between Boston and Philadelphia. Thirty-two of Russell's boards come in one half. Still, Russell's rebounds are less than half of his team's total as the Celtics establish a new record for rebounds by a team in one game—103.

December 21, 1957 The St. Louis Hawks set a new record for points in a game, by romping over Syracuse, 146-136. In the process, the Hawks set new standards for free throws made and attempted in a quarter by hitting 24 of 29 (.828).

January 11, 1958 The Detroit Pistons amass 83 points in the second half en route to a 129-102 win over the Minneapolis Lakers.

January 12, 1958 Dolph Schayes becomes the NBA's all-time leading scorer, succeeding the retired George Mikan, who scored 11,764 career points. In passing Mikan, Schayes nets 23 markers in Syracuse's 135-108 win over Detroit.

January 22, 1958 The Knicks set records for most field goals attempted in a half (77) and in a quarter (41) vs. Detroit.

February 4, 1958 Cliff Hagan scores 26 points in a quarter in a game between his St. Louis Hawks and the New York Knicks. Hagan makes 10 of 15 field goals, plus six free throws, en route to his spectacular performance.

March 15, 1958 Cincinnati Royals' star Maurice Stokes collapses during a playoff game. He will be diagnosed as having encephalitis and become permanently disabled.

March 19, 1958 The Celtics grab a playoff record 91 rebounds versus Philadelphia.

March 22, 1958 Xavier wins its first NIT title, defeating Dayton, 78-74, in overtime. The game marks Dayton's third loss in four years in the title game and fifth overall.

March 22, 1958 Vern Hatton and Johnny Cox combine for 54 points to lead Kentucky to an 84-72 victory over Seattle in the NCAA championship game. The Wildcats overcome 25 points by Seattle's Elgin Baylor, who shoots 9 for 32 from the field.

March 23, 1958 Bill Russell grabs a record 40 rebounds for the Celtics in a playoff game versus Philadelphia.

March 30, 1958 The Celtics record 85 rebounds in Game 2 of the NBA Finals, en route to a 136-112 victory over the St. Louis Hawks.

April 12, 1958 Bob Pettit performs one of the greatest playoff feats in history when he scores 50 points in Game 6 of the NBA Finals to propel St. Louis over Boston, 110-109, giving the Hawks the NBA championship. The victory becomes the Hawks' franchise's only NBA title ever. Meanwhile, it is one of only two NBA titles the Celtics do not win in a 13-year span that will end in 1969. The Hawks also become the last all-white team to win an NBA title.

1958 Bill Russell of Boston wins the NBA's Most Valuable Player award, becoming the first African-American to do so.

1958-59

Celts survive Nat scare, display mastery over Baylor-led Lakers

Elgin Baylor arrived on the pro basketball scene with a spark that lit a new fire of interest in the sporting public. A strong 6-foot-5 forward out of the University of Seattle, Baylor stepped into the Minneapolis Lakers' lineup and displayed a set of moves unknown to most basketball fans. A tough rebounder and sound ball handler, Baylor shone most brightly when putting the ball in the hoop. He tapped in rebounds, he sank long jumpers, and he seemed to soar and float in his ad lib drives to the basket. The rookie scored at a 24.9 clip, fourth best in the NBA, and drew curious crowds in all the league cities. In fact, the NBA enjoyed its highest attendance yet as it played its tenth season.

One of the clubs enjoying the attendance boom was the New York Knicks, who drew a record 18,496 fans to one of their games in Madison Square Garden. With Fuzzy Levane the new coach, the Knicks spurred fan interest by winning 10 of their first 11 games to take an early lead in the Eastern Division. But the rebuilt Knick squad, headed by guard Richie Guerin and forwards Kenny Sears and Willie Naulls, could not hold off the Boston Celtics for long. With Bill Russell, Bob Cousy, and Bill Sharman all first-team All-Stars, and with Jim Loscutoff back after an illness and K.C. Jones joining the club as a rookie guard after an Army stint, the Celtics had more assets in hand than ever. The Boston club caught up with the slumping Knicks in mid-season and ran away to a 12-game lead by the end of the regular season.

The third-place Syracuse Nationals added rookie Hal Greer to the backcourt and strengthened the forecourt by trading Ed Conlin to Detroit for George Yardley, last season's scoring champ. This deal made the Nats a club to contend with in the playoffs. Philadelphia finished last, hurt most by the loss of center Neil Johnston for most of the schedule because of a knee injury. For assets, the Warriors counted the continued high scoring of Paul Arizin, the poised play of rookie guard Guy Rodgers, and the future draft rights to Wilt Chamberlain, who quit the University of Kansas this season to tour with the Harlem Globetrotters. But the Warriors played this season without a big-league center.

The St. Louis Hawks captured a playoff spot and first place in the West despite a case of rotating coaches. Owner Ben Kerner found coach Alex Hannum too strong-willed for his liking, so he fired him despite last season's championship banner. Kerner hired Andy Phillip as the new coach but tired of him 10 games into the season. Ed Macauley then got the job; the easygoing Macauley was a popular local favorite who was at the end of his playing career. The chaotic coaching situation did not spoil the talent on the floor. Bob Pettit and Cliff Hagan handled the bulk of the scoring and rebounding from the forward positions, with Pettit scoring a record 2105 points. Clyde Lovellette was obtained from Cincinnati to split the

Elgin Baylor
Grappling here with the Pistons' Walter Dukes (23) and Dick McGuire, he brings an all-new aspect of artistry and showmanship to the game.

center duties with Chuck Share. Guards Slater Martin and Jack McMahon confined most of their attention to feeding the forwards and playing defense. This blend of talents ran away with the Western crown.

The Lakers improved to 33-39 and a second-place finish, strengthened tremendously by the rookie Baylor. The Pistons took the third playoff spot practically by default, with Detroit's 28-44 record outdone in futility by Cincinnati's 19-53 log. The Royals suffered tremendously from the loss of star forward Maurice Stokes, who was still paralyzed.

A local group purchased the Royals from Les Harrison, and the new owners canned coach Bobby Wanzer early in the campaign and replaced him with Tom Marshall, a young player in his fifth pro season. The only true bright spot in the Royals' season was Jack Twyman, the sharp-shooting forward who blossomed into one of the NBA's hottest scorers; only Bob Pettit finished ahead of Twyman in the NBA scoring race.

Pettit and his Hawks enjoyed a bye in the opening round of the playoffs while the Lakers and Pistons squared off in the Western semifinal. The Pistons had no one to match young Baylor, and the Lakers eliminated the Pistons two games to one. The rejuvenated Lakers then took on the first-place Hawks in what many fans mistakenly wrote off as a mismatch. The unheralded Lakers had two solid veterans in center Larry Foust and forward Vern Mikkelsen, whose career bridged the Mikan and Baylor eras. Minneapolis guards Dick Garmaker and Hot Rod Hundley also scored more than their St. Louis counterparts. The Hawks nevertheless were favored to reach the finals for a third straight season. The Hawks seemed in control when they captured two out of the first three games, but then the Lakers came storming back. With Baylor's hot hand leading the way, the Lakers took three straight victories to send the defending champion Hawks home and to head on into the champi-

onship round against the Celtics.

While all this activity had been going on in the West, the Eastern rounds played off in routine fashion. Syracuse appeared stronger for the playoffs than they had been during the season, and they confirmed this appraisal by knocking off the Knicks in two quick decisions. The Nats stood second in talent only behind the Celtics. Dolph Schayes, George Yardley, Hal Greer, and Larry Costello all could score from the outside, and Schayes and Johnny Kerr hit the boards effectively. Most important, the Nats played a selfless brand of team ball, flowing on offense and tenacious on defense. The Nats pressed the Celtics to their limit in the Eastern finals, but the Celtics emerged from Game 7 with a 130-125 victory that sent them into the championship round.

The Lakers had made it to this series by upsetting the Hawks, but the deep Boston team was too much for the rebuilt Lakers to handle. The Celtics had beaten the Lakers 18 straight times heading into the playoffs, and the pattern held true as the Celtics took four consecutive victories and swept into the throne room. After a year as bridesmaid, the Celtics again held the center spotlight and would not give it up until they had built one of the greatest dynasties of sports history.

1958-59 SEASON HIGHLIGHTS

STANDINGS

Eastern Division

	W	L	Pct.	GB
Boston	52	20	.722	—
New York	40	32	.556	12
Syracuse	35	37	.486	17
Philadelphia	32	40	.444	20

Western Division

	W	L	Pct.	GB
St. Louis	49	23	.681	—
Minneapolis	33	39	.458	16
Detroit	28	44	.389	21
Cincinnati	19	53	.264	30

AWARDS
MVP
Bob Pettit, St. Louis
Top Rookie
Elgin Baylor, Minnesota

ALL-STAR TEAMS
FIRST TEAM
Bob Pettit	St. Louis
Elgin Baylor	Minneapolis
Bill Russell	Boston
Bob Cousy	Boston
Bill Sharman	Boston

ALL-STAR GAME
The Olympia, Detroit
Friday, January 23, 1959
West 124, East 108
MVPs: Elgin Baylor and Bob Pettit

SECOND TEAM
Paul Arizin	Philadelphia
Cliff Hagan	St. Louis
Dolph Schayes	Syracuse
Slater Martin	St. Louis
Richie Guerin	New York

PLAYOFFS
FINALS
Boston 4, Minneapolis 0
Apr. 4: Minneapolis 115 at Boston 118
Apr. 5: Minneapolis 108 at Boston 128
Apr. 7: Boston 123, Minneapolis (at St. Paul) 110
Apr. 9: Boston 118 at Minneapolis 113

EASTERN DIVISION
DIVISION FINALS
Boston 4, Syracuse 3
Mar. 18: Syracuse 109 at Boston 131
Mar. 21: Boston 118 at Syracuse 120
Mar. 22: Syracuse 111 at Boston 133
Mar. 25: Boston 107 at Syracuse 119
Mar. 28: Syracuse 108 at Boston 129
Mar. 29: Boston 121 at Syracuse 133
Apr. 1: Syracuse 125 at Boston 130
DIVISION SEMI-FINALS
Syracuse 2, New York 0
Mar. 13: Syracuse 129 at New York 123
Mar. 15: New York 115 at Syracuse 131

WESTERN DIVISION
DIVISION FINALS
Minneapolis 4, St. Louis 2
Mar. 21: Minneapolis 90 at St. Louis 124
Mar. 22: St. Louis 98 at Minneapolis 106
Mar. 24: Minneapolis 97 at St. Louis 127
Mar. 26: St. Louis 98 at Minneapolis 108
Mar. 28: Minneapolis 98 at St. Louis 97, OT
Mar. 29: St. Louis 104 at Minneapolis 106
DIVISION SEMI-FINALS
Minneapolis 2, Detroit 1
Mar. 14: Detroit 89 at Minneapolis 92
Mar. 15: Minneapolis 103 at Detroit 117
Mar. 18: Detroit 102 at Minneapolis 129

NBA LEADERS

SCORING

	GP	FGM	FTM	PTS	PPG
Bob Pettit, STL	72	719	667	2105	29.2
Jack Twyman, CIN	72	710	437	1857	25.8
Paul Arizin, PHW	70	632	587	1851	26.4
Elgin Baylor, MPL	70	605	532	1742	24.9
Cliff Hagan, STL	72	646	415	1707	23.7
Dolph Schayes, SYR	72	504	526	1534	21.3
Kenny Sears, NYK	71	491	506	1488	21.0
Bill Sharman, BOS	72	562	342	1466	20.4
Bob Cousy, BOS	65	484	329	1297	20.0
Richie Guerin, NYK	71	443	405	1291	18.2

FIELD GOALS

	FGM	FGA	FG%
Kenny Sears, NYK	491	1002	.490
Bill Russell, BOS	456	997	.457
Cliff Hagan, STL	646	1417	.456
Clyde Lovellette, STL	402	885	.454
Hal Greer, SYR	308	679	.454
Red Kerr, SYR	502	1139	.441
Bob Pettit, STL	719	1640	.438
Larry Costello, SYR	414	948	.437
Sam Jones, BOS	305	703	.434
Paul Arizin, PHW	632	1466	.431

FREE THROWS

	FTM	FTA	FT%
Bill Sharman, BOS	342	367	.932
Dolph Schayes, SYR	526	609	.864
Kenny Sears, NYK	506	588	.861
Bob Cousy, BOS	329	385	.855
Willie Naulls, NYK	258	311	.830
Clyde Lovellette, STL	205	250	.820
Paul Arizin, PHW	587	722	.813
Vern Mikkelsen, MPL	286	355	.806
Gene Shue, DET	338	421	.803
Larry Costello, SYR	280	349	.802

ASSISTS

	GP	AST	APG
Bob Cousy, BOS	65	557	8.6
Dick McGuire, DET	71	443	6.2
Larry Costello, SYR	70	379	5.4
Richie Guerin, NYK	71	364	5.1
Carl Braun, NYK	72	349	4.9
Dugie Martin, STL	71	336	4.7
Jack McMahon, STL	72	298	4.1
Elgin Baylor, MPL	70	287	4.1
Tom Gola, PHW	64	269	4.2
Guy Rodgers, PHW	45	261	5.8

REBOUNDS

	GP	TRB	RPG
Bill Russell, BOS	70	1612	23.0
Bob Pettit, STL	72	1182	16.4
Elgin Baylor, MPL	70	1050	15.0
Red Kerr, SYR	72	1008	14.0
Dolph Schayes, SYR	72	962	13.4
Walter Dukes, DET	72	958	13.3
Woody Sauldsberry, PHW	72	826	11.5
Cliff Hagan, STL	72	783	10.9
Joe Graboski, PHW	72	751	10.4
Willie Naulls, NYK	68	723	10.6

THE YEAR IN BASKETBALL

October 1959 Nine seasons after the first African-American plays in an NBA game, the St. Louis Hawks become the last NBA team to integrate when they sign Sihugo Green.

February 25, 1959 Elgin Baylor scores 55 points against Cincinnati.

February 27, 1959 The Celtics score a record 173 points en route to a 173-139 demolishing of Minneapolis. Bob Cousy sets an NBA record for assists with 28 and also scores 31 points to supplement Tommy Heinsohn's 43, Bill Sharman's 29, and Frank Ramsey's 20. Boston piles up 90 points in the second half. Each team grabs over 80 rebounds.

February 28, 1959 Forward Jack Twyman of Cincinnati scores 50 points against the St. Louis Hawks.

March 21, 1959 St. John's wins its third NIT championship, edging Bradley, 76-71, in overtime. The Johnnies' Tony Jackson, tourney MVP, led the way with 21 points and 27 rebounds.

March 21, 1959 California edges Jerry West and West Virginia,

71-70, to win the NCAA title. Darrell Imhoff, California's center, tips in the winning bucket with 17 seconds left. West scores 28 points and is named the tournament's MOP.

April 7, 1959 Bob Cousy passes for 19 assists to tie a playoff record, as the Celtics defeat Minneapolis, 123-110, in Game 3 of the NBA finals.

April 9, 1959 Boston wins the NBA championship—its first in a string of eight consecutive titles—with a 118-113 win over Minneapolis. The victory concludes a four-game sweep of the once-dominant Lakers and begins a string of many prominent wins by the Celtics over the Lakers. In the game, Bill Sharman leads Boston with 29. Elgin Baylor paces Minneapolis with 30.

March 31, 1959 Wilt Chamberlain, formerly of the University of Kansas and the Harlem Globetrotters, is drafted as a territorial pick by the Philadelphia Warriors.

1959-60

Russell, Celtics best Pettit, Hawks in seven-game classic

Pro basketball fans had never seen anyone like Wilt Chamberlain, the rookie center of the Philadelphia Warriors. Standing 7-foot-1 with awesome strength, Wilt had signed with the Warriors for a reported $65,000, a sum previously unheard-of in the sport. Warrior owner Eddie Gottlieb spent his money wisely, for Chamberlain not only would be a massive asset on the court, but he also would draw crowds eager to see the giant they had heard so much about. A native of Philadelphia, Chamberlain had played two well-publicized seasons at the University of Kansas, then had passed up his senior year to travel with the Harlem Globetrotters. Now that he was bringing his reputation into the league, the NBA owners were gleefully anticipating greater attendance.

On the playing floor, Chamberlain provided just the show that the curiosity seekers were looking for. Very quick in addition to very big, Wilt averaged a record 37.6 points per game. He tapped in offensive rebounds in bunches, he sank fall-away jumpers with surprising accuracy, and he made the dunk shot famous, soaring above the basket and slamming the ball down through the hoop with backboard-rattling force. He went over 50 points in six games, and also led the NBA in rebounding. He played almost every minute of every game and never fouled out, intimidating enemy drivers without having to foul them. Wilt did have some clashes with coach Neil Johnston, whose job as center had been usurped by the rookie, but his effectiveness on the floor for the Warriors was obvious to anyone. With Wilt the hub of the team, and with a solid supporting cast of Paul Arizin, Tom Gola, Guy Rodgers, and Woody Sauldsberry, the Warriors jumped to an impressive 49-26 mark.

But the Boston Celtics, with Bill Russell, put together an even more impressive 59-16 record to take first place in the East for the fourth straight year. Russell starred on defense as spectacularly as Wilt did on offense; he blocked shots and rebounded with an enthusiastic flair. The scoring for Boston was left mostly to long range-gunners like Tom Heinsohn, Bob Cousy, Bill Sharman, and Frank Ramsey. The Celtic bench shuttled fresh help into the breach whenever needed, with young guards Sam Jones and K.C. Jones and forward Gene Conley (a major league baseball pitcher in the summer) the important shock troops. At one point during the season, the Celtics ran off a 17-game winning streak, and their ten-game final margin over Philadelphia underlined the team's class.

Finishing just behind the Warriors in third place in the East were the Syracuse Nationals, whose 45-30 record was only one game worse than the first-place record in the West. Rookie guard Dick Barnett, a fine shooter, strengthened the Syracuse bench, while veteran Dolph Schayes led the club in scoring as usual and sank his 15,000th career point during the campaign. Finishing far out of the playoffs were the New York Knicks, whose disappointing play after a promising showing last season

Wilt Chamberlain
Scoring and rebounding titles, plus rookie-of-the-year and MVP honors, in the most dominant rookie season ever in any major sport.

cost coach Fuzzy Levane his job. Veteran player Carl Braun took over as coach in mid-season but he could not put the disjointed Knicks back together again.

While the Knicks were rebuilding at the bottom of the East, the St. Louis Hawks were doing some minor refurbishing at the top of the West. The Hawks had been knocked off by the Lakers in the Western finals of last season's playoffs, and owner Ben Kerner and coach Ed Macauley acted to prevent further decay from setting in. The starting front line of Bob Pettit, Cliff Hagan, and Clyde Lovellette needed no alteration, but backup

help was obtained in the persons of veterans Larry Foust and Dave Piontek. Slater Martin continued to quarterback the Hawks, but the other guard spot was filled by younger men, Johnny McCarthy and Si Green. Although the Hawks seemed no stronger than three of the Eastern clubs, they easily captured first place in the West with a 16-game margin over Detroit. The Pistons hadn't had a winning season since moving to Detroit, and coach Red Rocha paid with his job, replaced in mid-season by veteran guard Dick McGuire; nevertheless, the team's 30-45 record was good enough for second place in the weak Western Division. Guard Gene Shue led the Pistons in scoring and won a place on the first team All-League squad. The Lakers captured third place despite a relapse into the chaotic situation of two years ago. Elgin Baylor upped his scoring average to 29.6, but the rest of the squad fell apart under the coaching reins of John Castellani, who had coached Baylor at the University of Seattle. Old favorite Jim Pollard replaced Castellani mid-way through the schedule, but a combination of trades and rookie help could not stop a skid to a 25-50 record and a continued lethargy at the ticket window. The punchless Cincinnati Royals finished far back in last place despite Jack Twyman's 31.2 scoring average, second only to Chamberlain in the NBA

The Western Division semi-final playoff series between Detroit and Minneapolis was a battle of losers, with the Lakers getting past the Pistons in two straight games largely on the back of Elgin Baylor. The Eastern semi-final pitted Philadelphia and Syracuse against each other, with the Warriors triumphing in three games. The divisional finals then matched the Boston Celtics against the Warriors and Wilt Chamberlain, while the St. Louis Hawks took on the Lakers and Elgin Baylor. The Celtics could not keep Chamberlain from scoring, but they did play a better team game than the Warriors; the defending champs thus eliminated the Warriors four games to two. The Hawks had more trouble with the upstart Lakers; playing their final series as a representative of Minneapolis, the Lakers took a three-to-two edge in games before the veteran Hawks came back to take the final two games.

In the championship round, the Celtics clearly seemed to be the better team, but the Hawks pushed the series to a decisive seventh game in Boston. A second period Boston blitz, outscoring the Hawks 41-23, broke the game wide open and made the second half a futile basket-trading affair. Now it was three titles in four years for the Celtics, and the league's first repeat at the top since the Lakers of George Mikan.

1959-60 SEASON HIGHLIGHTS

STANDINGS

Eastern Division

	W	L	Pct.	GB
Boston	59	16	.787	—
Philadelphia	49	26	.653	10
Syracuse	45	30	.600	14
New York	27	48	.360	32

Western Division

	W	L	Pct.	GB
St. Louis	46	29	.613	—
Detroit	30	45	.400	16
Minneapolis	25	50	.333	21
Cincinnati	19	56	.253	27

AWARDS
MVP
Wilt Chamberlain, Philadelphia
Top Rookie
Wilt Chamberlain, Philadelphia

ALL-STAR TEAMS
FIRST TEAM

Bob Pettit	St. Louis
Elgin Baylor	Minneapolis
Wilt Chamberlain	Philadelphia
Bob Cousy	Boston
Gene Shue	Detroit

SECOND TEAM

Jack Twyman	Cincinnati
Dolph Schayes	Syracuse
Bill Russell	Boston
Richie Guerin	New York
Bill Sharman	Boston

ALL-STAR GAME
Convention Hall, Philadelphia
Friday, January 22, 1960
East 125, West 115
MVP: Wilt Chamberlain

PLAYOFFS
FINALS
Boston 4, St. Louis 3
Mar. 27: St. Louis 122 at Boston 140
Mar. 29: St. Louis 113 at Boston 103
Apr. 2: Boston 102 at St. Louis 86
Apr. 3: Boston 96 at St. Louis 106
Apr. 5: St. Louis 102 at Boston 127
Apr. 7: Boston 102 at St. Louis 105
Apr. 9: St. Louis 103 at Boston 122

EASTERN DIVISION
DIVISION FINALS
Boston 4, Philadelphia 2
Mar. 16: Philadelphia 105 at Boston 111
Mar. 18: Boston 110 at Philadelphia 115
Mar. 19: Philadelphia 90 at Boston 120
Mar. 20: Boston 112 at Philadelphia 104
Mar. 22: Philadelphia 128 at Boston 107
Mar. 24: Boston 119 at Philadelphia 117
DIVISION SEMI-FINALS
Philadelphia 2, Syracuse 1
Mar. 11: Syracuse 92 at Philadelphia 115
Mar. 13: Philadelphia 119 at Syracuse 125
Mar. 14: Syracuse 112 at Philadelphia 132

WESTERN DIVISION
DIVISION FINALS
St. Louis 4, Minneapolis 3
Mar. 16: Minneapolis 99 at St. Louis 112
Mar. 17: Minneapolis 120 at St. Louis 113
Mar. 19: St. Louis 93 at Minneapolis 89
Mar. 20: St. Louis 101 at Minneapolis 103
Mar. 22: Minneapolis 117 at St. Louis 110, OT
Mar. 24: St. Louis 117 at Minneapolis 96
Mar. 26: Minneapolis 86 at St. Louis 97
DIVISION SEMI-FINALS
Minneapolis 2, Detroit 0
Mar. 12: Minneapolis 113 at Detroit 112
Mar. 13: Detroit 99 at Minneapolis 114

NBA LEADERS

SCORING

	GP	FGM	FTM	PTS	PPG
Wilt Chamberlain, PHW	72	1065	577	2707	37.6
Jack Twyman, CIN	75	870	598	2338	31.2
Elgin Baylor, MPL	70	755	564	2074	29.6
Bob Pettit, STL	72	669	544	1882	26.1
Cliff Hagan, STL	75	719	421	1859	24.8
Gene Shue, DET	75	620	472	1712	22.8
Dolph Schayes, SYR	75	578	533	1689	22.5
Tom Heinsohn, BOS	75	673	283	1629	21.7
Richie Guerin, NYK	74	579	457	1615	21.8
Paul Arizin, PHW	72	593	420	1606	22.3

FIELD GOALS

	FGM	FGA	FG%
Kenny Sears, NYK	412	863	.477
Hal Greer, SYR	388	815	.476
Clyde Lovellette, STL	550	1174	.468
Bill Russell, BOS	555	1189	.467
Cliff Hagan, STL	719	1549	.464
Wilt Chamberlain, PHW	1065	2311	.461
Bill Sharman, BOS	559	1225	.456
Bailey Howell, DET	510	1119	.456
Sam Jones, BOS	355	782	.454
George Yardley, SYR	546	1205	.453

FREE THROWS

	FTM	FTA	FT%
Dolph Schayes, SYR	533	597	.893
Gene Shue, DET	472	541	.872
Kenny Sears, NYK	363	418	.868
Bill Sharman, BOS	252	291	.866
Larry Costello, SYR	249	289	.862
Willie Naulls, NYK	286	342	.836
Clyde Lovellette, STL	316	385	.821
George Yardley, SYR	381	467	.816
Cliff Hagan, STL	421	524	.803
Paul Arizin, PHW	420	526	.798

ASSISTS

	GP	AST	APG
Bob Cousy, BOS	75	715	9.5
Guy Rodgers, PHW	68	482	7.1
Richie Guerin, NYK	74	468	6.3
Larry Costello, SYR	71	449	6.3
Tom Gola, PHW	75	409	5.5
Dick McGuire, DET	68	358	5.3
Hot Rod Hundley, MPL	73	338	4.6
Dugie Martin, STL	64	330	5.2
Johnny McCarthy, STL	75	328	4.4
Cliff Hagan, STL	75	299	4.0

REBOUNDS

	GP	TRB	RPG
Wilt Chamberlain, PHW	72	1941	27.0
Bill Russell, BOS	74	1778	24.0
Bob Pettit, STL	72	1221	17.0
Elgin Baylor, MPL	70	1150	16.4
Dolph Schayes, SYR	75	959	12.8
Willie Naulls, NYK	65	921	14.2
Red Kerr, SYR	75	913	12.2
Walter Dukes, DET	66	883	13.4
Kenny Sears, NYK	64	876	13.7
Cliff Hagan, STL	75	803	10.7

THE YEAR IN BASKETBALL

October 18, 1959 Elgin Baylor of Minneapolis scores 52 points in the season's opening game, against Detroit.

October 24, 1959 In his first NBA game, Wilt Chamberlain of Philadelphia scores 43 points—the most ever by a rookie on opening night—versus New York at Madison Square Garden. Chamberlain's performance signals the dawn of a great career. It also is the first of 1,045 straight games in which he will not foul out.

November 8, 1959 Elgin Baylor scores an NBA-record 64 points in Minneapolis' 136-115 win over Boston. Baylor's performance breaks Joe Fulks' record of 63 points, which stood for 11 years.

January 13, 1960 Dolph Schayes becomes the first player to score 15,000 for a career when he tallies 34 points in Syracuse's 127-120 win over Boston. Schayes will hold the career scoring mark until 1963-64 when Bob Pettit overtakes him.

January 22, 1960 Pete Cimino of Bristol, Pa. scores 114 points in a high school game.

January 25, 1960 Rookie Wilt Chamberlain scores 58 points as his Philadelphia Warriors beat Detroit, 127-117. The point total sets a rookie record, which Chamberlain ties less than a month later.

January 26, 1960 Danny Heater of Burnsville High School (W.V.)

scores 135 points in his team's 173-43 victory over Widen High. Heater's mark comes in a game played on a small court.

February 5, 1960 Bill Russell breaks his own rebounding record of 49 by pulling down 51 as Boston tops Syracuse, 124-100.

February 6, 1960 All-American Oscar Robertson of Cincinnati becomes the NCAA all-time leading scorer with 2,589 points, as he scores 29 in the Bearcats' win over Houston.

March 19, 1960 Ohio State shoots 84% from the field in the first half and goes on to win the NCAA title with a 75-55 rout over California. Jerry Lucas, a consensus All-American, paces the Buckeyes with 16 points. Guard Mel Nowell adds 15, future great John Havlicek scores 12.

March 19, 1960 Bradley takes the NIT, winning the championship game, 88-72 against Providence. Mack Herndon leads Bradley with 26 points. Lenny Wilkens scores 25 for the Friars

March 29, 1960 Bill Russell sets an NBA finals' record by grabbing 40 rebounds in a losing effort in Game 2. St. Louis wins the game, 113-103.

April 9, 1960 The Celtics beat the St. Louis Hawks, 122-103, in Game 7 to win the NBA championship. Bill Russell leads Boston with 22 points and 35 rebounds.

1960-61

Lakers head west, the Big O checks in, Celtics roll to 4th title

For the first time, the NBA stretched from coast to coast, joining major league baseball and pro football in California. Just as baseball had moved two tradition-steeped clubs, the Brooklyn Dodgers and New York Giants, to the virgin territory, the NBA sent the Minneapolis Lakers to open up the West Coast for pro basketball. The Lakers had been going nowhere on the floor and downhill at the ticket window since George Mikan retired, and owner Bob Short decided to take his club to Los Angeles, where the baseball Dodgers and football Rams had struck it rich. The Lakers, too, would prosper here, and the entire NBA reaped the benefits of high attendance and publicity in one of the nation's most glamorous cities.

But Los Angeles was not the only new asset in the NBA this season; two new superstars turned pro after superb college careers. The Cincinnati Royals made Oscar Robertson the number one pick in the college draft, taking the product of the University of Cincinnati both for his local gate appeal and his playing ability. A 6-foot-5 guard, the Big O combined more skills than any other player ever in the public eye. His outside shot rang up points in a steady flow, his passes threaded the tightest of openings between defenders, his ball-handling created opportunities both for himself and his teammates, and he could rebound as well as many forwards. As a rookie, Oscar scored at a 30.5 clip, third best in the league, and he made the first-team All-League squad. As an overall player, only Elgin Baylor of the Lakers approached Robertson.

Baylor was the Lakers' biggest asset, scoring a record 71 points in one game against New York. But he had a worthy partner this season in Jerry West, a rookie guard out of the University of West Virginia. West was not as big as Robertson, but his shooting, ball-handling, and competitive drive were just as keen. West got off to a slow start, acclimating himself to the rigors of play and travel in the NBA, but by the end of the regular season, he and Baylor gave the Lakers an unmatched inside-outside scoring punch, a duo that would carry the Lakers for years.

But while one new city and two new stars changed the NBA scene, the same clubs remained dominant in each division, the Boston Celtics in the East and the St. Louis Hawks in the West. The Celtics took first place by nine games over the Warriors, compiling the league's best record with a 57-22 mark. The Celtics by now were a public institution, known even by non-fans as the paragon of basketball excellence. Some fans celebrated guard Bob Cousy as the key element in the dynasty, pointing to his passing and ball-handling on the fast break as the indispensable ingredient. Other fans pointed out that the Celtics had never won a title until center Bill Russell arrived; with his rebounding and defensive prowess in the pivot, the Celtics had never finished out of first place.

Tom Heinsohn
Twisting for two here against the Nats' Larry Costello, his 19.7 ppg leads a balanced Celts' attack in which five average 16-plus points.

The remaining Celtics held less of the limelight but nevertheless had definite identities in the eyes of pro basketball fans. Tom Heinsohn and Bill Sharman were the scorers, the shooters the Celtics went to in a pinch. Frank Ramsey hustled and shot from the other forward spot. With Sharman's playing time cut down by injuries, Sam Jones and K.C. Jones got more playing time this season. Sam was a pure shooter, with a classic jump shot; K.C. rarely shot, but played some of the tightest defense in the league. Veterans Jim Loscutoff and Gene Conley furnished reserve muscle to the forward wall, and rookie forward

Satch Sanders began earning his reputation as a tough defender and rebounder. Orchestrating all this talent was coach Red Auerbach, considered by some fans to be the biggest star of all. His frequent storming at referees riled fans up all over the circuit, and his victory cigar, lit when the Celtics had the game in hand, became a symbol of Celtic supremacy.

The St. Louis Hawks had no coach as distinctive as Auerbach; in fact, owner Ben Kerner fired his coaches quite frequently. Paul Seymour was this year's new coach, put in charge of a talented squad which repeated as Western champion. The front line of Bob Pettit, Cliff Hagan, and Clyde Lovellette averaged 72 points per game, and veteran guards Si Green and Johnny McCarthy were joined by rookie Lenny Wilkens, a top-flight ball-handler from Providence College. The Hawk reserves were veteran performers who rarely captured the public's attention. The spotlight on the Hawks fell on Pettit, third in the NBA in rebounding and fourth in scoring. The Hawks finished first in the Western Division race, and first in the NBA in attendance. They even seemed capable of upending the Celtics in the playoffs.

The other NBA clubs took a backseat to the Celtics and Hawks both on the court and in the newspapers. The Philadelphia Warriors were the only other club to finish over .500, capturing second place in the East with a 46-33 record; Wilt Chamberlain upped his scoring average to 38.4 in taking

his second scoring crown in two pro seasons. Syracuse had a new coach in Alex Hannum, got a good season out of old standby Dolph Schayes, lost George Yardley to retirement, and took the last Eastern playoff berth with a 38-41 record. The New York Knicks finished a distant last again as their first draft choice, center Darrall Imhoff, was a sore disappointment.

In the Western Division, the Lakers took second place with a 36-43 mark, unveiling the combination of Baylor and West to their new Los Angeles fans. The Detroit Pistons, led by veterans Gene Shue and Bailey Howell, edged out the Cincinnati Royals, led by young Robertson, for the final playoff berth.

The first round of the playoffs produced one upset and one near upset. Syracuse minimized the damage Wilt Chamberlain could do by closely pressing the rest of the Philadelphia players, and the Nats took three straight games to win the series. The Pistons took the Lakers to a decisive fifth game before bowing out in the West. In the divisional finals, the Celtics and Hawks won, the Celtics handily and the Hawks barely.

Fans watched to see if the Hawks could knock the Celtics off in the title round, but 129-95 and 116-108 Boston victories in the first two games served notice that the crown was staying in Boston for another year. The Hawks won Game 3, but the Celtics stood for no more nonsense as Red Auerbach enjoyed a good smoke toward the end of the fourth and fifth games and counted his fourth championship in the last five years.

1960-61 SEASON HIGHLIGHTS

STANDINGS

Eastern Division

	W	L	Pct.	GB
Boston	57	22	.722	—
Philadelphia	46	33	.582	11
Syracuse	38	41	.481	19
New York	21	58	.266	36

Western Division

	W	L	Pct.	GB
St. Louis	51	28	.646	—
Los Angeles	36	43	.456	15
Detroit	34	45	.430	17
Cincinnati	33	46	.418	18

AWARDS
MVP
Bill Russell, Boston
Top Rookie
Oscar Robertson, Cincinatt

ALL-STAR TEAMS
FIRST TEAM

Elgin Baylor	Los Angeles
Bob Pettit	St. Louis
Wilt Chamberlain	Philadelphia
Bob Cousy	Boston
Oscar Robertson	Cincinnati

SECOND TEAM

Dolph Schayes	Syracuse
Tom Heinsohn	Boston
Bill Russell	Boston
Larry Costello	Syracuse
Gene Shue	Detroit

ALL-STAR GAME
Onondaga County War Memorial Auditorium, Syracuse
Tuesday, January 17, 1961
West 153, East 131
MVP: Oscar Robertson

PLAYOFFS
FINALS
Boston 4, St. Louis 1
Apr. 2: St. Louis 95 at Boston 129
Apr. 5: St. Louis 108 at Boston 116
Apr. 8: Boston 120 at St. Louis 124
Apr. 9: Boston 119 at St. Louis 104
Apr. 11: St. Louis 112 at Boston 121

EASTERN DIVISION
DIVISION FINALS
Boston 4, Syracuse 1
Mar. 19: Syracuse 115 at Boston 128
Mar. 21: Boston 98 at Syracuse 115
Mar. 23: Syracuse 110 at Boston 133
Mar. 25: Boston 120 at Syracuse 107
Mar. 26: Syracuse 101 at Boston 123
DIVISION SEMI-FINALS
Syracuse 3, Philadelphia 0
Mar. 14: Syracuse 115 at Philadelphia 107
Mar. 16: Philadelphia 114 at Syracuse 115
Mar. 18: Syracuse 106 at Philadelphia 103

WESTERN DIVISION
DIVISION FINALS
St. Louis 4, Los Angeles 3
Mar. 21: Los Angeles 122 at St. Louis 118
Mar. 22: Los Angeles 106 at St. Louis 121
Mar. 24: St. Louis 112 at Los Angeles 118
Mar. 25: St. Louis 118 at Los Angeles 117
Mar. 27: Los Angeles 121 at St. Louis 112
Mar. 29: St. Louis 114 at Los Angeles 113, OT
Apr. 1: Los Angeles 103 at St. Louis 105
DIVISION SEMI-FINALS
Los Angeles 3, Detroit 2
Mar. 14: Detroit 102 at Los Angeles 120
Mar. 15: Detroit 118 at Los Angeles 120
Mar. 17: Los Angeles 113 at Detroit 124
Mar. 18: Los Angeles 114 at Detroit 123
Mar. 19: Detroit 120 at Los Angeles 137

NBA LEADERS

SCORING

	GP	FGM	FTM	PTS	PPG
Wilt Chamberlain, PHW	79	1251	531	3033	38.4
Elgin Baylor, LAL	73	931	676	2538	34.8
Oscar Robertson, CIN	71	756	653	2165	30.5
Bob Pettit, STL	76	769	582	2120	27.9
Jack Twyman, CIN	79	796	405	1997	25.3
Dolph Schayes, SYR	79	594	680	1868	23.6
Willie Naulls, NYK	79	737	372	1846	23.4
Paul Arizin, PHW	79	650	532	1832	23.2
Bailey Howell, DET	77	607	601	1815	23.6
Gene Shue, DET	78	650	465	1765	22.6

FIELD GOALS

	FGM	FGA	FG%
Wilt Chamberlain, PHW	1251	2457	.509
Jack Twyman, CIN	796	1632	.488
Larry Costello, SYR	407	844	.482
Oscar Robertson, CIN	756	1600	.472
Bailey Howell, DET	607	1293	.469
Barney Cable, SYR	266	574	.463
Clyde Lovellette, STL	599	1321	.453
Dick Barnett, SYR	540	1194	.452
Wayne Embry, CIN	458	1015	.451
Hal Greer, SYR	623	1381	.451

FREE THROWS

	FTM	FTA	FT%
Bill Sharman, BOS	210	228	.921
Dolph Schayes, SYR	680	783	.868
Gene Shue, DET	465	543	.856
Frank Ramsey, BOS	295	354	.833
Paul Arizin, PHW	532	639	.833
Clyde Lovellette, STL	273	329	.830
Dave Gambee, SYR	291	352	.827
Kenny Sears, NYK	268	325	.825
Oscar Robertson, CIN	653	794	.822
Cliff Hagan, STL	383	467	.820

ASSISTS

	GP	AST	APG
Oscar Robertson, CIN	71	690	9.7
Guy Rodgers, PHW	78	677	8.7
Bob Cousy, BOS	76	587	7.7
Gene Shue, DET	78	530	6.8
Richie Guerin, NYK	79	503	6.4
Johnny McCarthy, STL	79	430	5.4
Larry Costello, SYR	75	413	5.5
Cliff Hagan, STL	77	381	4.9
Elgin Baylor, LAL	73	371	5.1
Hot Rod Hundley, LAL	79	350	4.4

REBOUNDS

	GP	TRB	RPG
Wilt Chamberlain, PHW	79	2149	27.2
Bill Russell, BOS	78	1868	23.9
Bob Pettit, STL	76	1540	20.3
Elgin Baylor, LAL	73	1447	19.8
Bailey Howell, DET	77	1111	14.4
Willie Naulls, NYK	79	1055	13.4
Walter Dukes, DET	73	1028	14.1
Dolph Schayes, SYR	79	960	12.2
Red Kerr, SYR	79	951	12.0
Wayne Embry, CIN	79	864	10.9

THE YEAR IN BASKETBALL

October 19, 1960 In their first game as the Los Angeles Lakers, the former Minneapolis franchise loses in Cincinnati, 140-123. Before moving to L.A., the franchise had called Minneapolis home for 13 years and had won five championships.

November 4, 1960 Wilt Chamberlain scores 44 points but goes 0-10 from the line to set an NBA record, in a game against Detroit.

November 15, 1960 In a dominating performance, Elgin Baylor breaks his own single-game record when he scores 71 points in the L.A. Lakers' 123-108 defeat of the Knicks.

November 24, 1960 Wilt Chamberlain of Philadelphia snatches a record 55 rebounds in a 132-129 loss to Bill Russell and Boston.

December 24, 1960 The Boston Celtics grab a record 109 rebounds in a 150-106 victory over the Detroit Pistons.

December 25, 1960 The Syracuse Nationals rout the New York Knicks, 162-100, setting a record for margin of victory (62 points).

January 16, 1961 The NBA admits the Chicago Packers and a Pittsburgh franchise into the association. The Packers become the league's first new franchise since the merger of the BAA and NBL in 1949. The team's owners, led by David Tregar and Max Winter, pay $200,000 to gain admittance. The following season the team changes its name to the Chicago Zephyrs. A year after that, the franchise moves to Baltimore and is known as the Bullets.

January 17, 1961 One day after gaining admittance into the NBA, John Harris, the owner of the new Pittsburgh franchise, pulls his club out. After announcing that Celtics' star Bill Sharman will be his team's first head coach, Harris is roundly criticized by Celtics' owner Walter Brown. Harris acknowledges a misunderstanding between he and Brown and withdraws, saying, "I have been aware of my lack of knowledge about basketball, but now I'm firmly convinced that I know nothing about it."

January 17, 1961 Cincinnati's Oscar Robertson, 22, becomes the youngest player to take home the All-Star Game MVP award, after he scores 23 points with 14 assists in the West's 153-131 win in Syracuse.

February 18, 1961 Bob Pettit of the St. Louis Hawks scores a career-high 57 points in a 141-138 overtime victory over Detroit.

February 22, 1961 Johnny Morris of Norcom High in Portsmouth, Va. scores 127 points in a single game.

March 5, 1961 Bill Russell scores a career-high 37 points as Boston defeats Philadelphia, 146-127.

March 25, 1961 Providence edges St. Louis, 62-59, to win its first NIT. The Friars' Vin Ernst is named tournament MVP.

March 25, 1961 The year after Oscar Robertson leaves the University of Cincinnati, the Bearcats win the NCAA title, with a 70-65 overtime victory over previously undefeated Ohio State. The Buckeyes' Jerry Lucas who is named Most Outstanding Player.

April 11, 1961 Boston wins its third consecutive NBA championship, defeating St. Louis in Game 5 at Boston Garden, 121-112. Bill Russell scores 30 points to lead the Celtics.

June 5, 1961 The American Basketball League, a new entity that will begin play in 1961-62, announces that it will award three points for any shot made behind a line that is placed 22 feet from the basket.

1961-62

Missed Selvy shot gives Celtics 2nd life, 5th title soon theirs

It was a year of expansion, new competition, a scoring explosion, military activation, a fading power, a rising power, and a continuing power. The expansion brought the Chicago Packers into the league, the first new franchise in the NBA's history. Star rookie Walt Bellamy and a bunch of castoff veterans stocked the Packers, who finished a distant last in the Western Division. The poor showing disappointed the Packers' fans, and the league itself found the low attendance figures most disappointing. Chicago had never warmed up to the Stags, who competed in the NBA until 1950, and pro basketball again seemed to be failing in the nation's second largest city.

But the Packers were not the only new team on the pro basketball scene this season. Abe Saperstein, the owner of the Harlem Globetrotters, organized and presided over the new American Basketball League. Los Angeles, Chicago, Hawaii, Kansas City, Pittsburgh, Washington, Cleveland, and San Francisco fielded teams for the ABL's inaugural season and scrounged for players to put on the floor. Only a handful of NBA players jumped over to the ABL, the most prominent of which were Dick Barnett and Ken Sears; Bill Sharman ended his career with the Boston Celtics to coach the Los Angeles franchise.

Most of the ABL players were NBA rejects, older players past their peak, and several players whom the NBA had barred because of some connection with the college betting scandals of 1960. In fact, the ABL's leading scorer and most exciting player was Connie Hawkins of Pittsburgh, who had been barred by the NBA and the University of Iowa for not reporting a bribe offer. The Western Division champs turned out to be the Kansas City Steers, who featured rookies Bill Bridges and Gene Tormohlen and veteran Larry Staverman, while the Eastern crown plus the playoff championship went to the Cleveland Pipers, who had Dick Barnett, Lang Siegfried, Connie Dierking, Ben Warley, and John Barnhill.

The ABL broke ice on two fronts. It employed a black coach, John McLendon of Cleveland. It also made all baskets from more than 25 feet out worth three points. But the players in the ABL were in no way comparable to those in the NBA, and by the end of the season, Los Angeles had folded, Washington had moved to New York, and the entire ABL was treading water in a sea of red ink.

While the ABL was going through its faceless season, the NBA was raking in publicity over the unprecedented scoring feats of Wilt Chamberlain. Frank McGuire, the new coach of the Philadelphia Warriors, wanted big Wilt to go to the basket as much as possible, and the Big Dipper responded by averaging 50.4 points a game. No one could stop Wilt near the basket, and the giant center

Wilt Chamberlain
On March 2, 1962, before 4,124 fans in Hershey, Pa., a game for the ages— his dunk with 46 seconds to play caps a 100-point night.

demonstrated his full offensive might against the New York Knicks on March 2 at Hershey, Pennsylvania. With the Knicks helpless to stop him, Wilt hit for 36 field goals and 28 of 32 free throws to score 100 points in a 169-147 Warrior triumph. Newspapers devoted much space to the event, and basketball fans throughout the country had either good or bad things to say about Wilt; very few ignored him. Some fans believed that his overwhelming size was ruining the game, but it was a fact that even stars of a smaller size were scoring at paces unheard of years ago. Elgin Baylor, Walt Bellamy, Bob Pettit, Oscar Robertson, and Jerry West all topped the 30 points per game mark, a plateau broken for the first time only two seasons ago.

Baylor compiled a 38.3 average, second in the league, while playing only on weekends after mid-season. The activation of military reserve units for the Berlin crisis had called Baylor away into uniform and only on weekend passes could he get back into his basketball outfit. The NBA, however, made out better than either baseball or football in the call-up; aside from Baylor, the only other star player to be activated was guard Lenny Wilkins of St. Louis.

The loss of Wilkins triggered the collapse of the Hawks, who had finished first in the West for the past five years. The back-court had no other first-rate playmaker besides Wilkins, and the frontcourt suffered after Clyde Lovellette went out in mid-season with a heel injury. To add to the chaos, owner Ben Kerner kept the coaching situation in disarray; he canned Paul Seymour early in the campaign, replaced him with Fuzzy Levane, and then replaced Levane with six games to go by putting Bob Pettit in charge on an interim basis. Pettit and Cliff Hagan still performed at All-Star levels at the forward positions, but the Hawks finished out of the playoffs with a 29-51 mark.

The Los Angeles Lakers filled the power vacuum left by the fall of the Hawks. Elgin Baylor and Jerry West spearheaded the Laker offense, and the Laker club had enough supporting strength to keep on winning even when Baylor was away. Rudy LaRusso, Frank Selvy, and Jim Krebs filled the other Los Angeles starting slots, while Tom Hawkins, Hot Rod Hundley, and Ray Felix came off the bench to provide a lift when needed. Enjoying life at the top, the Lakers would be at or near the head of the West for years to come. For this season, the Cincinnati Royals and Detroit Pistons joined them in the playoffs, while the Hawks and the newborn Packers finished out of the money.

In the East, the Boston Celtics kept right on rolling along. Despite the defection of Bill Sharman to the ABL, the Celtics finished in first place for the sixth straight year. Bill Russell, Bob Cousy, and Tom Heinsohn were at the peak of their games, and Sam Jones, K.C. Jones and Satch Sanders were distinguishing themselves with more playing time. The Celtics' 60-20 record was the best in the NBA and topped the Philadelphia Warriors by 11 games in the East. The Syracuse Nats, with Dolph Schayes slowing down, took the third playoff spot, ahead of the New York Knicks.

The two most interesting playoff series involved the Celtics. In the Eastern finals, the Warriors and Celtics battled into a decisive seventh game, which the Celtics won 109-107 when the Warriors failed in a last-second play to Chamberlain. In the championship series, the Lakers and Celtics also went into a seventh game. In a match of sizzling competition, the clubs battled to a 100-all deadlock after regulation time, with LA's Selvy missing a short jumper at the buzzer. That was the closest the Lakers came to dethroning the Celtics; the defending champs outscored the challengers 10-7 in the overtime period to take the title game 110-107. When Selvy's last-second shot skipped off the rim, the Celtics still wore the crown for the fourth straight year.

1961-62 SEASON HIGHLIGHTS

STANDINGS

Eastern Division

	W	L	Pct.	GB
Boston	60	20	.750	—
Philadelphia	49	31	.613	11
Syracuse	41	39	.513	19
New York	29	51	.363	31

Western Division

	W	L	Pct.	GB
Los Angeles	54	26	.675	—
Cincinnati	43	37	.538	11
Detroit	37	43	.463	17
St. Louis	29	51	.363	25
Chicago	18	62	.225	36

AWARDS

MVP
Bill Russell, Boston

Top Rookie
Walt Bellamy, Chicago

ALL-STAR TEAMS

FIRST TEAM		SECOND TEAM	
Bob Pettit	St. Louis	Tom Heinsohn	Boston
Elgin Baylor	Los Angeles	Jack Twyman	Cincinnati
Wilt Chamberlain	Philadelphia	Bill Russell	Boston
Jerry West	Los Angeles	Richie Guerin	New York
Oscar Robertson	Cincinnati	Bob Cousy	Boston

ALL-STAR GAME

St. Louis Arena, St. Louis
Tuesday, January 16, 1962
West 150, East 130
MVP: Bob Pettit

PLAYOFFS
FINALS
Boston 4, Los Angeles 3
Apr. 7: Los Angeles 108 at Boston 122
Apr. 8: Los Angeles 129 at Boston 122
Apr. 10: Boston 115 at Los Angeles 117
Apr. 11: Boston 115 at Los Angeles 103
Apr. 14: Los Angeles 126 at Boston 121
Apr. 16: Boston 119 at Los Angeles 105
Apr. 18: Los Angeles 107 at Boston 110, OT

EASTERN DIVISION
DIVISION FINALS
Boston 4, Philadelphia 3
Mar. 24: Philadelphia 89 at Boston 117
Mar. 27: Boston 106 at Philadelphia 113
Mar. 28: Philadelphia 114 at Boston 129
Mar. 31: Boston 106 at Philadelphia 110
Apr. 1: Philadelphia 104 at Boston 119
Apr. 3: Boston 99 at Philadelphia 109
Apr. 5: Philadelphia 107 at Boston 109
DIVISION SEMI-FINALS
Philadelphia 3, Syracuse 2
Mar. 16: Syracuse 103 at Philadelphia 110
Mar. 18: Philadelphia 97 at Syracuse 82
Mar. 19: Syracuse 101 at Philadelphia 100
Mar. 20: Philadelphia 99 at Syracuse 106
Mar. 22: Syracuse 104 at Philadelphia 121

WESTERN DIVISION
DIVISION FINALS
Los Angeles 4, Detroit 2
Mar. 24: Detroit 108 at Los Angeles 132
Mar. 25: Detroit 112 at Los Angeles 127
Mar. 27: Los Angeles 111 at Detroit 106
Mar. 29: Los Angeles 117 at Detroit 118
Mar. 31: Detroit 132 at Los Angeles 125
Apr. 3: Los Angeles 123 at Detroit 117
DIVISION SEMI-FINALS
Detroit 3, Cincinnati 1
Mar. 16: Cincinnati 122 at Detroit 123
Mar. 17: Detroit 107 at Cincinnati 129
Mar. 18: Cincinnati 107 at Detroit 118
Mar. 20: Detroit 112 at Cincinnati 111

NBA LEADERS

SCORING

	GP	FGM	FTM	PTS	PPG
Wilt Chamberlain, PHW	80	1597	835	4029	50.4
Walt Bellamy, CHP	79	973	549	2495	31.6
Oscar Robertson, CIN	79	866	700	2432	30.8
Bob Pettit, STL	78	867	695	2429	31.1
Jerry West, LAL	75	799	712	2310	30.8
Richie Guerin, NYK	78	839	625	2303	29.5
Willie Naulls, NYK	75	747	383	1877	25.0
Elgin Baylor, LAL	48	680	476	1836	38.3
Jack Twyman, CIN	80	739	353	1831	22.9
Cliff Hagan, STL	77	701	362	1764	22.9

FIELD GOALS

	FGM	FGA	FG%
Walt Bellamy, CHP	973	1875	.519
Wilt Chamberlain, PHW	1597	3159	.506
Jack Twyman, CIN	739	1542	.479
Oscar Robertson, CIN	866	1810	.478
Al Attles, PHW	343	724	.474
Larry Foust, STL	204	433	.471
Clyde Lovellette, STL	341	724	.471
Cliff Hagan, STL	701	1490	.470
Wayne Embry, CIN	564	1210	.466
Rudy LaRusso, LAL	516	1108	.466

FREE THROWS

	FTM	FTA	FT%
Dolph Schayes, SYR	286	319	.897
Willie Naulls, NYK	383	455	.842
Larry Costello, SYR	247	295	.837
Frank Ramsey, BOS	334	405	.825
Cliff Hagan, STL	362	439	.825
Tom Meschery, PHW	216	262	.824
Richie Guerin, NYK	625	762	.820
Hal Greer, SYR	331	404	.819
Tom Heinsohn, BOS	358	437	.819
Sam Jones, BOS	243	297	.818

ASSISTS

	GP	AST	APG
Oscar Robertson, CIN	79	899	11.4
Guy Rodgers, PHW	80	643	8.0
Bob Cousy, BOS	75	584	7.8
Richie Guerin, NYK	78	539	6.9
Gene Shue, DET	80	465	5.8
Jerry West, LAL	75	402	5.4
Frank Selvy, LAL	79	381	4.8
Slick Leonard, CHP	70	378	5.4
Cliff Hagan, STL	77	370	4.8
Bucky Bockhorn, CIN	80	366	4.6

REBOUNDS

	GP	TRB	RPG
Wilt Chamberlain, PHW	80	2052	25.7
Bill Russell, BOS	76	1790	23.6
Walt Bellamy, CHP	79	1500	19.0
Bob Pettit, STL	78	1459	18.7
Red Kerr, SYR	80	1176	14.7
Johnny Green, NYK	80	1066	13.3
Bailey Howell, DET	79	996	12.6
Oscar Robertson, CIN	79	985	12.5
Wayne Embry, CIN	75	977	13.0
Elgin Baylor, LAL	48	892	18.6

THE YEAR IN BASKETBALL

October 27, 1961 The American Basketball League, founded by Globetrotter owner Abe Saperstein, begins play.

October 1961 Boston's Bill Russell is roundly criticized after he refuses to play in an exhibition game in Lexington, Ky. because he and his black teammates were refused service in a restaurant.

November 25, 1961 Bob Cousy, scores his 15,000th career point. At the time, only Dolph Schayes had scored more.

December 8, 1961 In a thrilling game for the ages, Wilt Chamberlain scores a record-breaking 78 points in Philadelphia's 151-147 triple-overtime victory over Los Angeles. Elgin Baylor, whose record Chamberlain breaks, scores 63 for the Lakers.

December 16, 1961 Chamberlain begins a record streak of seven consecutive games in which he scores 50 or more points.

January 13, 1962 Chamberlain scores 73 points as he leads the Warriors to a 135-117 victory over Chicago.

February 17, 1962 Chamberlain drops in 67 points versus St Louis. In the process he makes first of what will become an NBA record 35 consecutive field goals without a miss.

February 25, 1962 Chamberlain scores 67 points, but Philadelphia loses to the Knicks, 149-135, and Richie Guerin, who pours in 50.

March 2, 1962 Chamberlain scores an NBA single-game record of 100 points against the New York Knicks, in a game at Hershey (Pa.) Arena. Despite the Knicks' stalling tactics in the final minutes, Chamberlain's dunk with 46 seconds left gives him his 99th and 100th points. In all, Chamberlain makes 36 of 63 field goal attempts and 28 of 32 foul shots. The Warriors win the game, 169-147, setting another record—most points scored by two teams in a game.

March 4, 1962 Chamberlain records his fifth straight game of 50 or more points, when he pours in 58 against the Knicks.

March 10, 1962 Oscar Robertson ends a season in which he averages a triple-double, long before the term was invented. Robertson's feat consists of per-game marks of 30.8 points, 12.5 rebounds, and a league-leading 11.4 assists. It is the only time an NBA player averages double figures in three categories for an entire season.

March 24, 1962 Dayton finally wins the NIT. A runner-up five times in the title game in the previous 11 years, the Flyers come out on top, dropping St. John's, 73-67. Bill Chmielewski is named tourney MVP.

March 24, 1962 Cincinnati, an upset NCAA champion in 1961, does it again. Behind Paul Hogue's 22 points and Tom Thacker's 21, the Bearcats topple Ohio State, 71-59, in the title game for the second consecutive year. Hogue, who outplays an injured Jerry Lucas in the final, is named the tournament's Most Outstanding Player.

April 14, 1962 Elgin Baylor sets an NBA Finals record by scoring 61 points in the Lakers' 126-121 victory over Boston in Game 5.

April 18, 1962 Boston wins its fourth straight NBA title and its fifth in six years, with a thrilling 110-107 overtime victory over the Lakers in Game 7. The Lakers nearly win in regulation but Frank Selvy's last-second shot rims the basket.

May 23, 1962 The NBA announces that the Philadelphia Warriors will move to San Francisco.

1962-63

Cousy hangs 'em up, Celtics celebrate with fitting send-off

Pro basketball had flourished in Philadelphia long before the NBA was born. Strong leagues had operated in the area before World War I, and the Philadelphia Sphas had won respect as one of the strongest pro teams in the years between the World Wars. The Philadelphia Warriors joined the BAA at its start in 1946, and had competed in the NBA ever since its creation in 1949. The Warriors had produced Joe Fulks, Paul Arizin, and Wilt Chamberlain and two championships—one in 1947 and another in 1956. But now the Warriors were leaving, and Philadelphia no longer had a professional basketball team. Owner Eddie Gottlieb, who had ran the Sphas before starting the Warriors, sold his club to a San Francisco group who moved it to that city. So now pro basketball had joined baseball and pro football in posting bases in both Los Angeles and San Francisco. The Warriors now lined up in the Western Division, with Cincinnati shifting over to take their place in the East.

While the Warriors headed West, the rival league, the ABL, headed toward oblivion. After stumbling through a debt-ridden first year, the ABL began its new season with only six clubs; many of the better players had left to sign with NBA teams. The only bright spot for the ABL was the signing of All-American forward Jerry Lucas of Ohio State by the Cleveland Pipers, but even that turned to dust as the Pipers were financially unable to get a team on the floor. Lucas sat out the entire basketball season, and the rest of the ABL joined him on the sidelines on New Year's Eve, when the league gave up the fight and collapsed, a failure at challenging the NBA for a portion of the pro basketball dollar. Although some of the players caught on with NBA clubs, most of them returned to minor league ball or civilian pursuits.

Dick Barnett, who had played in the ABL last year, helped keep the Los Angeles Lakers atop the Western Division. Barnett's keen jump shot complemented the offensive power of Elgin Baylor and Jerry West, and became even more important when West missed time with injuries. The Lakers were strong everywhere but at center, where veteran Jim Krebs and rookies Leroy Ellis and Gene Wiley acted as stopgaps. But even without the sort of imposing center who could rival Bill Russell and Wilt Chamberlain, the Lakers repeated as the first-place finisher in the West.

The St. Louis Hawks regrouped from last year's disastrous campaign and finished second to the Lakers, five games back. New coach Harry Gallatin retained only Bob Pettit and Cliff Hagan from the squad that finished the 1961-62 campaign. Rookie Zelmo Beaty and veteran Phil Jordon, picked up from New York, filled the center spot left vacant with Clyde Lovellette's sale to Boston. Lenny Wilkins returned from military service to quarterback the club from the backcourt, and ABL ex-patriot John Barnhill and rookie Chico Vaughn filled

Dave DeBusschere
Fresh from his rookie season as a Chicago White Sox pitcher, the wide-eyed rookie averages 20 points as a Piston.

the other guard spot. Gallatin brought in three new forwards in veteran Woody Sauldsberry, who came over from the Chicago club in a mid-season trade, and Mike Farmer and Bill Bridges, both of whom came from the ABL Another ABL product, center Gene Tormohlen, joined the Hawks near the end of the season. But with all the personnel changes, Pettit was still the ace, the leading scorer and rebounder.

After the Hawks, the other three Western clubs finished under .500. The Detroit Pistons captured third place with a big team. Bailey Howell, Bob Ferry, and Ray Scott gave the Pistons

a lot of beef up front and forced rookie Dave DeBusschere, a natural forward, to spend some of his court time playing guard alongside Don Ohl. A local favorite from the University of Detroit, DeBusschere also drew a salary as a pitcher with the Chicago White Sox.

Behind the Pistons, in fourth place, were the disappointing Warriors. Although Wilt Chamberlain again led the NBA with a 44.8 average, opposing teams found success in stopping Wilt's teammates. Paul Arizin had retired rather than go to San Francisco, and Tom Gola was traded to New York early in the season for Willie Naulls and Ken Sears. But trades could not shore up the Warriors, and they fell out of the playoffs with a 31-49 record, an inauspicious start on the West Coast. The Chicago Zephyrs, with a new nickname but few new fans, had two high scorers in Walt Bellamy and rookie Terry Dischinger, but again finished in last place.

Although the Warriors suffered through a bad season, the Boston Celtics had viewed their move to the West as the removal of their strongest rival. But regardless of the Warriors the Celtics were stronger than ever, stocking perhaps their best squad in history. Boston's one dim note was Bob Cousy. Cousy, the NBA's most popular player through the years, announced that this would be his last season. Although he played less than usual, Cousy's floor play stood up to the highest standards of his career and when the aging star was not playing, shooter Sam Jones and ball-hawk K.C. Jones kept the Boston backcourt in fine shape. Bill Russell was still the unsurpassed master at defense and clutch rebounding at center, and he had backup help from veteran Clyde Lovellette, who had been picked up from St. Louis. At forward, Tom Heinsohn was the offensive ace, Satch Sanders the defensive star, and Jim Loscutoff furnished muscle when needed from the bench. For swingmen, the Celtics had the game's best in veteran Frank Ramsey and rookie John Havlicek. Both played guard and forward, and both could shoot and run.

Behind the Celtics came the Syracuse Nats, a club which on appearances had no right to finish at 48-32. Veteran star Dolph Schayes, at 34, was on his last legs as a player and the team lacked size. But the Nats hustled their way into the playoffs, followed in the third spot by the Cincinnati Royals. The New York Knicks, as usual, finished fourth and out of the playoffs.

In the playoffs, the Celtics and Lakers went through a seven-game divisional series, with the Celtics downing Cincinnati and the Lakers beating back the Hawks. The Lakers had come within one shot of dethroning the Celtics last season, but this year's title was never in doubt. The Celtics defeated the Lakers in six games to win their fifth straight championship, the sixth in the last seven years.

1962-63 SEASON HIGHLIGHTS

STANDINGS

Eastern Division

	W	L	Pct.	GB
Boston	58	22	.725	—
Syracuse	48	32	.600	10
Cincinnati	42	38	.525	16
New York	21	59	.263	37

Western Division

	W	L	Pct.	GB
Los Angeles	53	27	.663	—
St. Louis	48	32	.600	5
Detroit	34	46	.425	19
San Francisco	31	49	.388	22
Chicago	25	55	.313	28

AWARDS

MVP
Bill Russell, Boston
Top Rookie
Terry Dischinger, Chicago
Coach of Year
Harry Gallatin, St. Louis

ALL-STAR TEAMS

FIRST TEAM

Elgin Baylor	Los Angeles
Bob Pettit	St. Louis
Bill Russell	Boston
Oscar Robertson	Cincinnati
Jerry West	Los Angeles

SECOND TEAM

Tom Heinsohn	Boston
Bailey Howell	Detroit
Wilt Chamberlain	San Francisco
Bob Cousy	Boston
Hal Greer	Syracuse

ALL-STAR GAME

Los Angeles Sports Arena, L.A.
Wednesday, January 16, 1963
East 115, West 108
MVP: Bill Russell

PLAYOFFS
FINALS
Boston 4, Los Angeles 2
Apr. 14: Los Angeles 114 at Boston 117
Apr. 16: Los Angeles 106 at Boston 113
Apr. 17: Boston 99 at Los Angeles 119
Apr. 19: Boston 108 at Los Angeles 105
Apr. 21: Los Angeles 126 at Boston 119
Apr. 24: Boston 112 at Los Angeles 109

EASTERN DIVISION
DIVISION FINALS
Boston 4, Cincinnati 3
Mar. 28: Cincinnati 135 at Boston 132
Mar. 29: Boston 125 at Cincinnati 102
Mar. 31: Cincinnati 121 at Boston 116
Apr. 3: Boston 128 at Cincinnati 110
Apr. 6: Cincinnati 120 at Boston 125
Apr. 7: Boston 99 at Cincinnati 109
Apr. 10: Cincinnati 131 at Boston 142
DIVISION SEMI-FINALS
Cincinnati 3, Syracuse 2
Mar. 19: Cincinnati 120 at Syracuse 123
Mar. 21: Syracuse 115 at Cincinnati 133
Mar. 23: Cincinnati 117 at Syracuse 121
Mar. 24: Syracuse 118 at Cincinnati 125
Mar. 26: Cincinnati 131 at Syracuse 127, OT

WESTERN DIVISION
DIVISION FINALS
Los Angeles 4, St. Louis 3
Mar. 31: St. Louis 104 at Los Angeles 112
Apr. 2: St. Louis 99 at Los Angeles 101
Apr. 4: Los Angeles 112 at St. Louis 125
Apr. 6: Los Angeles 114 at St. Louis 124
Apr. 7: St. Louis 100 at Los Angeles 123
Apr. 9: Los Angeles 113 at St. Louis 121
Apr. 11: St. Louis 100 at Los Angeles 115
DIVISION SEMI-FINALS
St. Louis 3, Detroit 1
Mar. 20: Detroit 99 at St. Louis 118
Mar. 22: Detroit 108 at St. Louis 122
Mar. 24: St. Louis 103 at Detroit 107
Mar. 26: St. Louis 104 at Detroit 100

NBA LEADERS

SCORING

	GP	FGM	FTM	PTS	PPG
Wilt Chamberlain, SFW	80	1463	660	3586	44.8
Elgin Baylor, LAL	80	1029	661	2719	34.0
Oscar Robertson, CIN	80	825	614	2264	28.3
Bob Pettit, STL	79	778	685	2241	28.4
Walt Bellamy, CHZ	80	840	553	2233	27.9
Bailey Howell, DET	79	637	519	1793	22.7
Richie Guerin, NYK	79	596	509	1701	21.5
Jack Twyman, CIN	80	641	304	1586	19.8
Hal Greer, SYR	80	600	362	1562	19.5
Don Ohl, DET	80	636	275	1547	19.3

FIELD GOALS

	FGM	FGA	FG%
Wilt Chamberlain, SFW	1463	2770	.528
Walt Bellamy, CHZ	840	1595	.527
Oscar Robertson, CIN	825	1593	.518
Bailey Howell, DET	637	1235	.516
Terry Dischinger, CHZ	525	1026	.512
Dave Budd, NYK	294	596	.493
Jack Twyman, CIN	641	1335	.480
Al Attles, SFW	301	630	.478
Sam Jones, BOS	621	1305	.476
Red Kerr, SYR	507	1069	.474

FREE THROWS

	FTM	FTA	FT%
Larry Costello, SYR	288	327	.881
Richie Guerin, NYK	509	600	.848
Elgin Baylor, LAL	661	790	.837
Tom Heinsohn, BOS	340	407	.835
Hal Greer, SYR	362	434	.834
Frank Ramsey, BOS	271	332	.816
Dick Barnett, LAL	343	421	.815
Adrian Smith, CIN	223	275	.811
Jack Twyman, CIN	304	375	.811
Oscar Robertson, CIN	614	758	.810

ASSISTS

	GP	AST	APG
Guy Rodgers, SFW	79	825	10.4
Oscar Robertson, CIN	80	758	9.5
Bob Cousy, BOS	76	515	6.8
Si Green, CHZ	73	422	5.8
Elgin Baylor, LAL	80	386	4.8
Lenny Wilkens, STL	75	381	5.1
Richie Guerin, NYK	79	348	4.4
Bill Russell, BOS	78	348	4.5
Larry Costello, SYR	78	334	4.3
Don Ohl, DET	80	325	4.1

REBOUNDS

	GP	TRB	RPG
Wilt Chamberlain, SFW	80	1946	24.3
Bill Russell, BOS	78	1843	23.6
Walt Bellamy, CHZ	80	1309	16.4
Bob Pettit, STL	79	1191	15.1
Elgin Baylor, LAL	80	1146	14.3
Red Kerr, SYR	80	1039	13.0
Johnny Green, NYK	80	964	12.1
Wayne Embry, CIN	76	936	12.3
Bailey Howell, DET	79	910	11.5
Bob Boozer, CIN	79	878	11.1

THE YEAR IN BASKETBALL

October 23, 1962 Coming off a 1961-62 season, in which he averaged over 50 points, Wilt Chamberlain opens the '62-63 campaign with 56 points against Detroit. It is the most points ever scored by a player on the season's opening night.

November 3, 1962 Chamberlain erupts for 72 points against the Lakers.

November 16, 1962 Chamberlain scores 73 points, including 45 in the first half, to lead San Francisco to a 127-111 victory over the New York.

December 31, 1962 Abe Saperstein's high hopes end when the American Basketball League, which he founded, suspends operations. The league was in its second season.

January 11, 1963 Chamberlain pours in 65 points against the Lakers.

January 11, 1963 Walter Garrett of Birmingham West End High in Birmingham, Ala. scores all of his team's points in West End's 97-54 victory.

January 17, 1963 Chamberlain scores 67 points in a game against the Lakers.

March 10, 1963 Chamberlain pours in 70 points versus Syracuse.

March 14, 1963 Guy Rodgers of San Francisco matches Bob Cousy's NBA record of 28 assists in a 114-109 loss to St. Louis.

March 17, 1963 Bob Cousy makes a tearful farewell speech on Bob Cousy Day at Boston Garden. A Celtic for 13 years, Cousy will retire after the playoffs.

March 23, 1963 Providence takes its second NIT championship in three years, turning back Canisius, 81-66. The Friars' Ray Flynn is named tournament MVP.

March 23, 1963 Loyola of Chicago stops Cincinnati's bid for a third straight NCAA title, when the Ramblers win a 60-58 overtime contest over the Bearcats in the tournament title game. Forward Vic Rouse hits a follow-up with two seconds left for the victory. The Bearcats' starting five plays the entire game. Cincinnati plays six men.

April 24, 1963 The Boston Celtics again defeat the Los Angeles Lakers, 112-109, to win their fifth consecutive NBA championship. The Celtics' six-game victory is their third defeat of the Lakers in the past five championship series. Bob Cousy scores 18 points in what was intended to be his final game. Seven years later, as coach of the Cincinnati Royals, Cousy suits up and plays seven games.

1963-64

Russell out-duels Wilt as Celtics lay claim to sixth straight title

Three familiar institutions were gone from the NBA picture this season: Commissioner Maurice Podoloff, the Syracuse Nationals, and Bob Cousy. Podoloff had reached age 73 and retired as the NBA's chief executive. He had been president of the BAA at its founding in 1946, and had presided over the NBA since its creation in 1949. Through the lean years of the 1940's and 1950's, the colorful Podoloff had kept the league going through compromise and improvisation, and was now leaving behind a solid circuit which had just set a new attendance record.

The man the owners chose for a new commissioner was Walter Kennedy, the BAA's original publicity director and since then the mayor of Stamford, Connecticut—a background which helped him overcome a threatened strike at the All-Star game when the players demanded that a pension plan be instituted. Kennedy talked the players into going through with the game, and then he arranged a modest pension plan after the season. Attendance kept climbing under Kennedy's reign, passing the 2,500,000 mark this season.

Another departure this season was the move of the Syracuse Nationals to Philadelphia, where they became known as the 76ers. The Nats had come into the NBA from the NBL in the 1949 merger, and they had won the league crown in 1955. Never a physically big club, the Nats had one star in Dolph Schayes and had always shown as inexhaustible supply of hustle. But Schayes was at the end of the line as a player, and the small base of Syracuse was off the main travel routes and the area was too small to compete with the large cities on the circuit. So owner Danny Biasone sold the club to a Philadelphia group, who moved the club in as a replacement for the departed Warriors. Dolph Schayes went along as player coach.

The missing face most talked about by fans however, was that of Bob Cousy. As the dynasty of the Boston Celtics extended, even non-basketball fans knew about Cousy. His fancy dribbling and razor-sharp passes brought fans to their feet and his leading of the firehouse Boston fast break made him the most noticeable element in the Celtic machine. Some fans figured that the Celtic string of championships had to end now that Cousy was gone, but others claimed that the dynasty would go on, because the key element was not Cousy but the defensive-minded Bill Russell.

The Celtics again came in first place and thus partially answered the question. The Celtic fast break kept rolling without Cousy and the pressing defense even improved. Sam Jones and K.C. Jones started in the backcourt, the perfect blend of an offensive and a defensive star. Tom Heinsohn and Satch Sanders were the same combination of offense and defense at forward, and Russell held all the pieces together with his rebounding, his shotblocking, and his unnoticed 15 points per game scoring. The leading scorer on the club didn't even start;

Jerry Lucas
His brilliant rebounding and overall play combines with the superb skills of Oscar Robertson to lift Cincinnati.

John Havlicek came off the bench, played both forward and guard, never shied away from a shot, and ran up and down the court without a sign of exhaustion. His performance won him the title of the NBA's best sixth man, an honor taken away from teammate Frank Ramsey, who was still a dangerous man in stretches. Willie Naulls came from the San Francisco Warriors to provide backup strength at forward, and Clyde Lovellette and Jim Loscutoff were still available for spot duty.

But even with all of coach Red Auerbach's talented squad, the Celtics got a chase from the Cincinnati Royals, who fin-

ished only four games back with a 55-25 mark. Oscar Robertson shot, passed, dribbled, and rebounded as well or better than any other guard in the NBA In the frontcourt, Jerry Lucas signed with the Royals after sitting out a season. He ranked third in the NBA in rebounding, behind only Chamberlain and Russell. In addition to his rebounding talent, Lucas had a fine outside shot and averaged 17.7 points per game in his pro debut. With bulky Wayne Embry setting picks and boxing out at center, with Jack Twyman and Tom Hawkins playing forward opposite Lucas, and with Adrian Smith and Arlen Bockhorn in the backcourt with Oscar, the Royals stayed hot on the Celtics' heels all season.

The Philadelphia 76ers, hurt by a foot injury to Larry Costello, a knee injury to Lee Shaffer, and Dave Gambee's broken foot, fell to a 34-46 mark in their first season in Philadelphia, yet still beat out the New York Knicks for the final playoff spot. The Knicks added Len Chappell, Bob Boozer, Johnny Egan. and Bill McGill in trades and had the first-picked rookie in Art Heyman, but they still finished with the worst record in the league 22-58.

Over in the Western Division, the San Francisco Warriors joined the Lakers and Hawks as the major powers in the division. The Warriors came in first under new coach Alex Hannum, who installed a deliberate style into the team's offense and affirmed a new concentration on defense. Hannum convinced Wilt Chamberlain to concentrate on blocking shots, a la Bill Russell, and passing the ball off more often; Wilt's scoring average thus "fell" to 36.9, still the best in the league, while his value as a defender and playmaker from the pivot increased. The Warriors controlled the boards against most teams, with 6-foot-11 rookie Nate Thurmond joining veterans Tom Meschery and Wayne Hightower in the forward corps which grabbed off any loose rebounds Chamberlain didn't get. Guy Rodgers, Al Attles, and Gary Phillips handled the backcourt chores.

Two games back of the Warriors came the St. Louis Hawks, who added ex-Knick Richie Guerin to the backcourt and used rebounder Bill Bridges more extensively at forward. Bob Pettit still paced the club in scoring and rebounding, with Cliff Hagan, Lenny Wilkens, and Zelmo Beaty key contributors. The Lakers finished a strong third, with a weakness at center partially offsetting the scoring feats of Elgin Baylor and Jerry West. Finishing fourth were the Baltimore Bullets, who had moved from Chicago, and fifth were the Detroit Pistons, who lost Dave DeBusschere to the military.

The playoffs further answered the question as to whether Cousy or Russell was the key factor in the Celtic dynasty. Both Boston and San Francisco made it to the title scenes, with Russell and Chamberlain facing each other for the crown. Chamberlain outscored Russell; but Russell's defense and rebounding combined with the other talent on the Boston roster to blow the Warriors out in five games.

1963-64 SEASON HIGHLIGHTS

STANDINGS

Eastern Division

	W	L	Pct.	GB
Boston	59	21	.738	—
Cincinnati	55	25	.688	4
Philadelphia	34	46	.425	25
New York	22	58	.275	37

Western Division

	W	L	Pct.	GB
San Francisco	48	32	.600	—
St. Louis	46	34	.575	2
Los Angeles	42	38	.525	6
Baltimore	31	49	.388	17
Detroit	23	57	.288	25

AWARDS

MVP
Oscar Robertson, Cincinatti
Top Rookie
Jerry Lucas, Cincinatti
Coach of Year
Alex Hannum, San Francisco

ALL-STAR TEAMS

FIRST TEAM

Bob Pettit	St. Louis
Elgin Baylor	Los Angeles
Wilt Chamberlain	San Francisco
Oscar Robertson	Cincinnati
Jerry West	Los Angeles

SECOND TEAM

Tom Heinsohn	Boston
Jerry Lucas	Cincinnati
Bill Russell	Boston
John Havlicek	Boston
Hal Greer	Philadelphia

ALL-STAR GAME

Boston Garden, Boston
Tuesday, January 14, 1964
East 111, West 107
MVP: Oscar Robertson

PLAYOFFS
FINALS
Boston 4, San Francisco 1
Apr. 18: San Francisco 96 at Boston 108
Apr. 20: San Francisco 101 at Boston 124
Apr. 22: Boston 91 at San Francisco 115
Apr. 24: Boston 98 at San Francisco 95
Apr. 26: San Francisco 99 at Boston 105

EASTERN DIVISION
DIVISION FINALS
Boston 4, Cincinnati 1
Mar. 31: Cincinnati 87 at Boston 103
Apr. 2: Cincinnati 90 at Boston 101
Apr. 5: Boston 102 at Cincinnati 92
Apr. 7: Boston 93 at Cincinnati 102
Apr. 9: Cincinnati 95 at Boston 109
DIVISION SEMI-FINALS
Cincinnati 3, Philadelphia 2
Mar. 22: Philadelphia 102 at Cincinnati 127
Mar. 24: Cincinnati 114 at Philadelphia 122
Mar. 25: Philadelphia 89 at Cincinnati 101
Mar. 28: Cincinnati 120 at Philadelphia 129
Mar. 29: Philadelphia 124 at Cincinnati 130

WESTERN DIVISION
DIVISION FINALS
San Francisco 4, St. Louis 3
Apr. 1: St. Louis 116 at San Francisco 111
Apr. 3: St. Louis 85 at San Francisco 120
Apr. 5: San Francisco 109 at St. Louis 113
Apr. 8: San Francisco 111 at St. Louis 109
Apr. 10: St. Louis 97 at San Francisco 121
Apr. 12: San Francisco 95 at St. Louis 123
Apr. 16: St. Louis 95 at San Francisco 105
DIVISION SEMI-FINALS
St. Louis 3, Los Angeles 2
Mar. 21: Los Angeles 104 at St. Louis 115
Mar. 22: Los Angeles 90 at St. Louis 106
Mar. 25: St. Louis 105 at Los Angeles 107
Mar. 28: St. Louis 88 at Los Angeles 97
Mar. 30: Los Angeles 108 at St. Louis 121

NBA LEADERS

SCORING

	GP	FGM	FTM	PTS	PPG
Wilt Chamberlain, SFW	80	1204	540	2948	36.9
Oscar Robertson, CIN	79	840	800	2480	31.4
Bob Pettit, STL	80	791	608	2190	27.4
Walt Bellamy, BAL	80	811	537	2159	27.0
Jerry West, LAL	72	740	584	2064	28.7
Elgin Baylor, LAL	78	756	471	1983	25.4
Hal Greer, PHI	80	715	435	1865	23.3
Bailey Howell, DET	77	598	470	1666	21.6
Terry Dischinger, BAL	80	604	454	1662	20.8
John Havlicek, BOS	80	640	315	1595	19.9

FIELD GOALS

	FGM	FGA	FG%
Jerry Lucas, CIN	545	1035	.527
Wilt Chamberlain, SFW	1204	2298	.524
Walt Bellamy, BAL	811	1582	.513
Terry Dischinger, BAL	604	1217	.496
Bill McGill, BAL/NYK	456	937	.487
Jerry West, LAL	740	1529	.484
Oscar Robertson, CIN	840	1740	.483
Bailey Howell, DET	598	1267	.472
Johnny Green, NYK	482	1026	.470
Bob Pettit, STL	791	1708	.463

FREE THROWS

	FTM	FTA	FT%
Oscar Robertson, CIN	800	938	.853
Jerry West, LAL	584	702	.832
Hal Greer, PHI	435	525	.829
Tom Heinsohn, BOS	283	342	.827
Richie Guerin, NYK/STL	347	424	.818
Cliff Hagan, STL	269	331	.813
Bailey Howell, DET	470	581	.809
Elgin Baylor, LAL	471	586	.804
Wayne Hightower, SFW	260	329	.790
Paul Neumann, PHI	210	266	.789

ASSISTS

	GP	AST	APG
Oscar Robertson, CIN	79	868	11.0
Guy Rodgers, SFW	79	556	7.0
K.C. Jones, BOS	80	407	5.1
Jerry West, LAL	72	403	5.6
Wilt Chamberlain, SFW	80	403	5.0
Richie Guerin, NYK/STL	80	375	4.7
Hal Greer, PHI	80	374	4.7
Bill Russell, BOS	78	370	4.7
Lenny Wilkens, STL	78	359	4.6
Johnny Egan, DET/NYK	66	358	5.4

REBOUNDS

	GP	TRB	RPG
Bill Russell, BOS	78	1930	24.7
Wilt Chamberlain, SFW	80	1787	22.3
Jerry Lucas, CIN	79	1375	17.4
Walt Bellamy, BAL	80	1361	17.0
Bob Pettit, STL	80	1224	15.3
Ray Scott, DET	80	1078	13.5
Gus Johnson, BAL	78	1064	13.6
Red Kerr, PHI	80	1017	12.7
Elgin Baylor, LAL	78	936	12.0
Wayne Embry, CIN	80	925	11.6

THE YEAR IN BASKETBALL

September 1, 1963 Walter Kennedy succeeds Maurice Podoloff as NBA president. Podoloff had held the post since 1946. Four years after Kennedy's appointment, his title is changed to commissioner.

December 28, 1963 Johnny (Red) Kerr of the Philadelphia Warriors plays in his 707th straight game to break the NBA record held by Dolph Schayes. Kerr would ultimately play in 844 straight before the streak ends because of injury on November 5, 1965

February 3, 1964 Coach Adolph Rupp of Kentucky gets his 700th career win as the Wildcats pummel Georgia, 108-83.

February 8, 1964 Bob Pettit surpasses Dolph Schayes as the NBA's all-time leading scorer, with an 18-point performance in St. Louis' 103-97 loss to San Francisco. Pettit will hold the record for only two seasons before Wilt Chamberlain passes him.

March 21, 1964 Despite finishing third in the Missouri Valley Conference during the regular season, Bradley wins its third NIT title in eight years, throttling New Mexico, 86-54. Lavern Tart is named the tournament's top player.

March 21, 1964 In the start of a dynasty, UCLA (30-0) completes an unbeaten season by downing Duke, 98-83, to win the NCAA championship. Gail Goodrich leads the John Wooden-led Bruins with 27 points. Kenny Washington, a five-points-per-game scorer during the season, adds 26.

April 26, 1964 The Boston Celtics win their sixth straight NBA championship, beating the San Francisco Warriors, 105-99, in Game 5 of the NBA finals. The Celtics place six players in double figures to offset Wilt Chamberlain's 30 points in the contest.

June 9, 1964 The Baltimore Bullets and Detroit Pistons pull off the largest trade in NBA history (at the time). The deal sends forward Bailey Howell and Bob Ferry, guard Don Ohl, and the rights to rookies Wally Jones and Les Hunter to Baltimore for forwards Terry Dischinger and Don Kojis and guard Rod Thorn.

1964-65

Shocker: Wilt dealt, with new Philly mates almost stops Celts

The East beat the West 124-123 in the annual All-Star game on January 13, but newspapers the next morning gave headline coverage to another basketball story; Wilt Chamberlain had been traded. The greatest scorer in basketball history, Wilt was averaging 38.9 points per game for the San Francisco Warriors. The Warriors, however, decided that they could do better by unloading Wilt and holding on to Nate Thurmond in the pivot. After winning the Western Division last season, the team dropped 16 of its first 21 games of this season to drop far back in the standings.

The Warriors couldn't put their winning formula back together after that, and they had practically fallen out of the running for a playoff berth by the All-Star break. Nate Thurmond, a potentially great center, was playing out of position at forward for the Warriors and would cover the team's needs at center. And finally, the Warriors had drawn only moderate crowds on the West Coast so far, with fans failing to warm up to Chamberlain; if Wilt's high salary were dropped and he were sold for a lot of money, perhaps the Warriors would have sufficient capital to build an attractive squad.

Within hours after the All-Star game, the Warriors traded Wilt to the Philadelphia 76ers. The Warriors got a lot of money plus three players, guard Paul Neumann, center Connie Dierking, and forward Lee Shaffer. (Shaffer was a holdout with the 76ers, he did not sign with the Warriors, and he never played again in the NBA.) Wilt went back to his hometown, with the team that had been known as the Syracuse Nats until two years ago. He again had an admiring public, and was playing on a team that had always emphasized teamwork and defense but had lacked a big man at center. Hal Greer, Larry Costello, Chet Walker, Dave Gambee, Al Bianchi, and Johnny Kerr all came out of the Syracuse tradition, as did head coach Dolph Schayes, and now Chamberlain and rookie Luke Jackson would give the club the rebounding strength it had never had. The rest of the regular season would be taken up by working Wilt into the 76er system, but the club posed a new threat to the Boston Celtics in the playoffs.

The Celtics had sewn up their ninth straight Eastern Division first-place finish by winning their first 11 games and slowing up very little after that. It was a season of transition for the Celtics, as team owner and founder Walter Brown died and veteran players Frank Ramsey, Jim Loscutoff, and Clyde Lovellette retired. Tom Heinsohn missed 13 games because of

Jerry West
Driving here against the Big O, he finishes second to Wilt in the scoring race, though his record 46.3 ppg in the final can't lift Los Angeles past Boston.

injuries, and Larry Siegfried started to see considerable action as a backup guard. But the core of the Celtics remained the same, with Bill Russell, Satch Sanders, and K.C. Jones the defensive stars and Sam Jones, John Havlicek, and Heinsohn the offensive aces. Coach Red Auerbach lit his victory cigar 62 times during the season, going without his smoke only 18 times.

The Cincinnati Royals finished a distant second at 48-32; playmaker-scorer Oscar Robertson and rebounder-scorer Jerry Lucas made the Royals a dangerous club, but they were unable

to press the Celtics as closely as they did last season. The 76ers finished third at 40-40, biding their time until the playoffs. The Knicks finished fourth again, but found hope for the future in rookies Willis Reed, Jim Barnes, Howie Komives, and Emmette Bryant.

While the Celtics wrapped up their division early, the Los Angeles Lakers did the same in the West by winning 15 of their first 21 games. With Elgin Baylor and Jerry West good for 58.1 points per game, the Lakers built up a 49-31 record for the regular season. The St. Louis Hawks got off to a slow start, due largely to a knee injury to Bob Pettit and a leg injury to Richie Guerin. With the team's record at 17-16, owner Ben Kerner fired coach Harry Gallatin and made Guerin a player coach; the Hawks played better the rest of the way and made an unsuccessful run on first place late in the season.

The surprise winner of the third playoff spot was the Baltimore Bullets, only two years removed from their Chicago origins. Coached by Buddy Jeannette, who had taken an earlier version of the Bullets to the BAA championship in 1948, the Baltimore club made a key trade by sending Terry Dischinger and Rod Thorn to the Detroit Pistons in exchange for Bailey Howell, Don Ohl, and Bob Ferry. Howell and Ohl fit into a high-scoring starting lineup which included holdovers Walt Bellamy, Gus Johnson, and Kevin Loughery. With Johnson developing into one of the NBA's best forwards, and with the veteran firepower picked up from Detroit, the Bullets immediately became a club to contend with. The trade worked out less well for the Pistons, who finished six games behind the Bullets in fourth place. Dischinger helped the club with his shooting, but the key addition was Dave DeBusschere, who returned after missing most of last season because of military service. The trade with Baltimore opened up room for him in the frontcourt, where his rebounding skill blossomed, and his leadership qualities were called upon when owner Fred Zollner fired coach Charlie Wolf and made DeBusschere, a mere 24 years old, the player coach of the team. With his added basketball duties, DeBusschere decided to end his burgeoning career as a pitcher with the Chicago White Sox. Finishing far back in last place were the Warriors. For the Pistons and Warriors, there were no playoffs this season.

Again this year, the most publicized playoff series involved the Celtics. In the Eastern finals, the 76ers had every hope of ending the Celtic domination. The Celtics took the first game at Boston, 108-98, with the 76ers taking the second at Philly, 109-103. The pattern repeated in the next two games, with each club winning on its home court. The fifth and sixth games also went to the home teams, bringing the clubs together for a seventh game in Boston.

The Celtics streaked out to a 30-12 lead in the first period, but the 76ers slowly came back. With five seconds left in the game, Boston led 110-109 and had the ball out of bounds. In trying to throw the ball into play, Bill Russell hit a wire supporting the backboard, and the 76ers got the ball. The 76ers now had a final shot at a victory, but the inbounds pass from Hal Greer was deflected by John Havlicek. With the 76ers disposed of, the rest was easy for the Celtics. Their opponent in the championship series was the Lakers, who had lost Elgin Baylor to a knee injury. Although Jerry West played heroically, averaging 40 points per game, the Lakers went down in five games, victims of the Celtics' seventh straight title.

1964-65 SEASON HIGHLIGHTS

STANDINGS

Eastern Division

	W	L	Pct.	GB
Boston	62	18	.775	—
Cincinnati	48	32	.600	14
Philadelphia	40	40	.500	22
New York	31	49	.388	31

Western Division

	W	L	Pct.	GB
Los Angeles	49	31	.613	—
St. Louis	45	35	.563	4
Baltimore	37	43	.463	12
Detroit	31	49	.388	18
San Francisco	17	63	.213	32

AWARDS

MVP
Bill Russell, Boston

Top Rookie
Willis Reed, New York

Coach of Year
Red Auerbach, Boston

ALL-STAR TEAMS

FIRST TEAM

Elgin Baylor	Los Angeles
Jerry Lucas	Cincinnati
Bill Russell	Boston
Oscar Robertson	Cincinnati
Jerry West	Los Angeles

SECOND TEAM

Bob Pettit	St. Louis Louis
Gus Johnson	Baltimore
Wilt Chamberlain	San Francisco-Philadelphia
Sam Jones	Boston
Hal Greer	Philadelphia

ALL-STAR GAME

St. Louis Arena, St. Louis
Wednesday, January 13, 1965
East 124, West 123
MVP: Jerry Lucas

PLAYOFFS

FINALS
Boston 4, Los Angeles 1
Apr. 18: Los Angeles 110 at Boston 142
Apr. 19: Los Angeles 123 at Boston 129
Apr. 21: Boston 105 at Los Angeles 126
Apr. 23: Boston 112 at Los Angeles 99
Apr. 25: Los Angeles 96 at Boston 129

EASTERN DIVISION
DIVISION FINALS
Boston 4, Philadelphia 3
Apr. 4: Philadelphia 98 at Boston 108
Apr. 6: Boston 103 at Philadelphia 109
Apr. 8: Philadelphia 94 at Boston 112
Apr. 9: Boston 131 at Philadelphia 134, OT
Apr. 11: Philadelphia 108 at Boston 114
Apr. 13: Boston 106 at Philadelphia 112
Apr. 15: Philadelphia 109 at Boston 110
DIVISION SEMI-FINALS
Philadelphia 3, Cincinnati 1
Mar. 24: Philadelphia 119 at Cincinnati 117
Mar. 26: Cincinnati 121 at Philadelphia 120
Mar. 28: Philadelphia 108 at Cincinnati 94
Mar. 31: Cincinnati 112 at Philadelphia 119

WESTERN DIVISION
DIVISION FINALS
Los Angeles 4, Baltimore 2
Apr. 3: Baltimore 115 at Los Angeles 121
Apr. 5: Baltimore 115 at Los Angeles 118
Apr. 7: Los Angeles 115 at Baltimore 122
Apr. 9: Los Angeles 112 at Baltimore 114
Apr. 11: Baltimore 112 at Los Angeles 120
Apr. 13: Los Angeles 117 at Baltimore 115
DIVISION SEMI-FINALS
Baltimore 3, St. Louis 1
Mar. 24: Baltimore 108 at St. Louis 105
Mar. 26: Baltimore 105 at St. Louis 129
Mar. 27: St. Louis 99 at Baltimore 131
Mar. 30: St. Louis 103 at Baltimore 109

NBA LEADERS

SCORING

	GP	FGM	FTM	PTS	PPG
Wilt Chamberlain, SFW/PHI	73	1063	408	2534	34.7
Jerry West, LAL	74	822	648	2292	31.0
Oscar Robertson, CIN	75	807	665	2279	30.4
Sam Jones, BOS	80	821	428	2070	25.9
Elgin Baylor, LAL	74	763	483	2009	27.1
Walt Bellamy, BAL	80	733	515	1981	24.8
Willis Reed, NYK	80	629	302	1560	19.5
Bailey Howell, BAL	80	515	504	1534	19.2
Terry Dischinger, DET	80	568	320	1456	18.2
Don Ohl, BAL	77	568	284	1420	18.4

FIELD GOALS

	FGM	FGA	FG%
Wilt Chamberlain, SFW/PHI	1063	2083	.510
Walt Bellamy, BAL	733	1441	.509
Jerry Lucas, CIN	558	1121	.498
Jerry West, LAL	822	1655	.497
Bailey Howell, BAL	515	1040	.495
Terry Dischinger, DET	568	1153	.493
Johnny Egan, NYK	258	529	.488
Zelmo Beaty, STL	505	1047	.482
Oscar Robertson, CIN	807	1681	.480
Paul Neumann, PHI/SFW	365	772	.473

FREE THROWS

	FTM	FTA	FT%
Larry Costello, PHI	243	277	.877
Oscar Robertson, CIN	665	793	.839
Howard Komives, NYK	212	254	.835
Adrian Smith, CIN	284	342	.830
Jerry West, LAL	648	789	.821
Sam Jones, BOS	428	522	.820
Bob Pettit, STL	332	405	.820
Jerry Lucas, CIN	298	366	.814
Dave Gambee, PHI	299	368	.812
Hal Greer, PHI	335	413	.811

ASSISTS

	GP	AST	APG
Oscar Robertson, CIN	75	861	11.5
Guy Rodgers, SFW	79	565	7.2
K.C. Jones, BOS	78	437	5.6
Lenny Wilkens, STL	78	431	5.5
Bill Russell, BOS	78	410	5.3
Jerry West, LAL	74	364	4.9
Hal Greer, PHI	70	313	4.5
Kevin Loughery, BAL	80	296	3.7
Elgin Baylor, LAL	74	280	3.8
Larry Costello, PHI	64	275	4.3

REBOUNDS

	GP	TRB	RPG
Bill Russell, BOS	78	1878	24.1
Wilt Chamberlain, SFW/PHI	73	1673	22.9
Nate Thurmond, SFW	77	1395	18.1
Jerry Lucas, CIN	66	1321	20.0
Willis Reed, NYK	80	1175	14.7
Walt Bellamy, BAL	80	1166	14.6
Gus Johnson, BAL	76	988	13.0
Luke Jackson, PHI	76	980	12.9
Zelmo Beaty, STL	80	966	12.1
Elgin Baylor, LAL	74	950	12.8

THE YEAR IN BASKETBALL

October 23, 1964 Walt Hazzard and Bill Bradley power an undefeated United States Olympic team to a sixth consecutive gold medal at the Summer Games in Tokyo. In the medal-winning game, the U.S. downs Russia, 73-59.

November 10, 1964 Twenty-four-year-old Dave DeBusschere, the Pistons' player/coach and the youngest head coach in NBA history, records his first coaching victory, 119-117, against Baltimore.

November 13, 1964 Bob Pettit becomes the first NBA player to score 20,000 career points when he tallies 29 in St. Louis' 123-106 loss to the Cincinnati Royals at Cincinnati Gardens.

November 13, 1964 Gus Johnson (41 points) and Walt Bellamy (40) become the first teammates to score 40 points or more in the same game as their Baltimore Bullets beat the Lakers, 127-115.

November 23, 1964 The Baltimore Bullets are sold to a group of Washington, D.C. businessmen, including Abe Pollin, the franchise's current owner.

December 18, 1964 Oscar Robertson scores 56 points, including 18 in the fourth quarter, as he leads Cincinnati to a 111-107 triumph over the Lakers.

January 15, 1965 The San Francisco Warriors trade Wilt Chamberlain to the Philadelphia 76ers for center Connie Dierking, guard Paul Neumann, forward Lee Shaffer and cash.

March 11, 1965 Bill Russell grabs 49 rebounds, the third-highest total in NBA history, in a 112-100 win over Detroit at Providence.

March 14, 1965 Boston wins its 61st game of the regular season to set a new NBA record.

March 18, 1965 Amos Alonzo Stagg, the great college football coach who played a significant role in the early development of basketball, dies at 102.

March 19, 1965 In a match-up of two dazzling All-Americans, Cazzie Russell of Michigan scores 28 points—one less than Princeton's Bill Bradley—as the Wolverines top the Tigers, 93-76 in an NCAA semi-final tilt.

March 20, 1965. St. John's wins its fourth NIT, besting Villanova, 55-51, in the title game at Madison Square Garden. The Redmen's Ken McIntyre wins the tournament MVP award.

March 20, 1965 UCLA makes it two NCAA titles in a row, with a 91-80 victory over Michigan. Gail Goodrich leads the Bruins with 42 points.

April 15, 1965 The Celtics advance to the NBA finals by defeating the 76ers, 110-109, in Game 7 of the Eastern Conference finals. The game is remembered for Celtics' announcer Johnny Most's call of "Havlicek stole the ball!" on Hal Greer last-second inbounds pass. Sam Jones of Boston leads all scorers with 37 points.

April 25, 1965 The Celtics score 42 points in the fourth quarter of Game 5 to win their seventh straight NBA championship, routing the Los Angeles Lakers, 129-96. Bull Russell leads Boston with 22 points and 30 rebounds. Jerry West scores 33 to lead L.A., which plays without injured All-Star Elgin Baylor.

1965-66

Eighth staight title, ninth overall for Celts, as Auerbach departs

The Philadelphia 76ers had come within one shot of beating the Boston Celtics in last spring's playoffs, and they started this season with high hopes of ending the Celtics' long string of NBA championships. Wilt Chamberlain had a half season of experience in the 76er system, and he eagerly anticipated answering those critics who said that he lacked the competitive zeal of rival center Bill Russell of the long-successful Celtics. Around Wilt's scoring, rebounding, and defense in the pivot, coach Dolph Schayes had offensive aces in Hal Greer, Chet Walker, rookie Billy Cunningham, and newcomer Wally Jones, obtained from Baltimore. He had a strong rebounder in Luke Jackson, and two experienced reserves in Syracuse veterans Al Bianchi and Dave Gambee. Chamberlain began to change his style, going to the basket less frequently, passing off more often to his sharp-shooting teammates, and concentrating on defense and blocking shots. He still managed to lead the league in scoring as well as rebounding and field goal percentage, and finished seventh in the NBA in assists.

Bill Russell was still the shot-blocker without equal, but he and the Celtics started to feel the inevitable creep of time. Tom Heinsohn retired, and coach Red Auerbach replaced him at forward by starting veteran Willie Naulls and using super-sub John Havlicek more often at that position. Further forward help came from Don Nelson, who blossomed into a key reserve after Auerbach picked him up from Los Angeles on waivers. The other starters were familiar figures, with Russell, Sam Jones, K.C. Jones, and Satch Sanders identified in the public's mind with the excellence of the Celtic dynasty. Various injuries kept several of these veterans out of the lineup for stretches of time and made the Celtics' task of repeating that much harder.

But they did look like they were on the way to another first place finish in the East when they held a four-game lead over the 76ers on New Year's Day. On February 12, the Celtics met their rivals from Philly head-on in Syracuse and beat them 85-

Oscar Robertson
Swinging by Baltimore's Kevin Loughery toward a fifth straight top three finish in MVP voting, and sixth straight first team all-star berth.

83; this victory put the Celtics five up in the win column and three up in the loss column. But then the tide turned, as the Celtics dropped three straight games while the 76ers won three straight. Now Boston's record stood at 42-22 and Philadelphia's at 40-22. On March 5 and 6, the two rivals squared off in a home-and-away series which swung the balance of power; the 76ers won 102-85 at home and 113-110 in Boston. The 76ers then swept their last eight games, and not even a sweep of their last six games could save the Celtics from finishing one game behind the 76ers. For the first time since 1956, the Celtics were

in second place.

The Cincinnati Royals, led as usual by Oscar Robertson and Jerry Lucas, took the third Eastern playoff berth with a 45-35 record, which would have been good enough for first place in the West. The fourth place team, as always, was the New York Knicks, who slowly but surely were building back into respectability. First draft pick Bill Bradley, the All-American forward from Princeton, turned down pro ball to accept a Rhodes scholarship to Oxford, but the Knicks did come up with a pair of solid rookie forwards in Dick Van Arsdale and Dave Stallworth. In addition, trades brought in new offensive power in center Walt Bellamy and guard Dick Barnett, although the acquisition of Bellamy forced talented second-year man Willis Reed to play an unfamiliar forward spot.

There was nothing unfamiliar about the Los Angeles Lakers taking first place in the West for the fourth time in five years. Bad knees kept Elgin Baylor out of the lineup for a long stretch and cut his effectiveness far below normal when he did play. But Jerry West kept scoring at a 31.3 level, and the supporting cast of Rudy LaRusso, Walt Hazzard, Leroy Ellis, and Bob Boozer picked up some of the slack left by Baylor's injuries.

The four other Western teams all finished under the .500 mark. The Baltimore Bullets came in second with a 38-42 record, Gus Johnson's bad knees kept him on the shelf for half the season and forced the team to trade center Walt Bellamy to New York for forward Jim Barnes, who turned out to be less helpful than expected. Veteran Johnny Kerr took over at center, and he finally missed a game early in the campaign after playing 917 consecutive regular season and playoff games. Behind Baltimore came the St. Louis Hawks, who dearly felt the absence of retired star Bob Pettit. The San Francisco Warriors just missed the playoffs in fourth place, but unveiled a new scoring star in rookie forward Rick Barry, a thin 6-foot-7

shooting ace from the University of Miami. The Detroit Pistons had picked center Bill Buntin as their first draft choice, and his poor season helped the team reserve another high draft place by finishing last with a 22-58 record.

But with the end of the regular season, attention focused on the playoff situation in the East. The Celtics, humbled by their second place finish, had to compete in the opening round for the first time in ten years. Paired with the Royals, the defending champions dropped two of the first three games before winning the fourth and fifth games to take the series. Now the stage was set for the rematch of Russell and Chamberlain, of Boston and Philadelphia. The 76ers had enjoyed the first-round bye given to the divisional champion, and the two weeks of inactivity seemed to dull the sharp edge developed in their closing spurt of 18 out of 21 games and the last 11 in a row. The Celtics, however, got their house in order in the Cincinnati series and came roaring into the confrontation. The defending champs knocked the 76ers off 114-93 in the opening game in Philly, and then took a commanding edge with a 114-93 win in Boston. The 76ers then won Game 3 at home, but a 114-110 overtime win for the Celtics in Game 4 foretold the final outcome. Game five at Philly went to the Celtics, and the 76ers went home for the summer with the taste of victory still unrealized. The Celtics, meanwhile, headed into the championship series for the tenth straight year, and captured their eighth straight title with a seven-game triumph over the Lakers.

During the series, Red Auerbach announced that he was stepping down as coach next season, to concentrate on his duties as general manager, with Bill Russell succeeding him as player coach. After running off an incredible string of nine titles in ten years, Auerbach's victory cigar would no longer glow from the Boston bench.

1965-66 SEASON HIGHLIGHTS

STANDINGS

Eastern Division

	W	L	Pct.	GB
Philadelphia	55	25	.688	—
Boston	54	26	.675	1
Cincinnati	45	35	.563	10
New York	30	50	.375	25

Western Division

	W	L	Pct.	GB
Los Angeles	45	35	.563	—
Baltimore	38	42	.475	7
St. Louis	36	44	.450	9
San Francisco	35	45	.438	10
Detroit	22	58	.275	23

AWARDS
MVP
Wilt Chamberlain, Philadelphia
Top Rookie
Rick Barry, San Francisco
Coach of Year
Dolph Schayes, Philadelphia

ALL-STAR TEAMS
FIRST TEAM		SECOND TEAM	
Rick Barry	San Francisco	John Havlicek	Boston
Jerry Lucas	Cincinnati	Gus Johnson	Baltimore
Wilt Chamberlain	Philadelphia	Bill Russell	Boston
Oscar Robertson	Cincinnati	Sam Jones	Boston
Jerry West	Los Angeles	Hal Greer	Philadelphia

ALL-STAR GAME
Cincinnati Gardens, Cincinnati
Tuesday, January 11, 1966
East 137, West 94
MVP: Adrian Smith

PLAYOFFS
FINALS
Boston 4, Los Angeles 3
Apr. 17: Los Angeles 133 at Boston 129, OT
Apr. 19: Los Angeles 109 at Boston 129
Apr. 20: Boston 120 at Los Angeles 106
Apr. 22: Boston 122 at Los Angeles 117
Apr. 24: Los Angeles 121 at Boston 117
Apr. 26: Boston 115 at Los Angeles 123
Apr. 28: Los Angeles 93 at Boston 95

EASTERN DIVISION
DIVISION FINALS
Boston 4, Philadelphia 1
Apr. 3: Boston 115 at Philadelphia 96
Apr. 6: Philadelphia 93 at Boston 114
Apr. 7: Boston 105 at Philadelphia 111
Apr. 10: Philadelphia 108 at Boston 114, OT
Apr. 12: Boston 120 at Philadelphia 112
DIVISION SEMI-FINALS
Boston 3, Cincinnati 2
Mar. 23: Cincinnati 107 at Boston 103
Mar. 26: Boston 132 at Cincinnati 125
Mar. 27: Cincinnati 113 at Boston 107
Mar. 30: Boston 120 at Cincinnati 103
Apr. 1: Cincinnati 103 at Boston 112

WESTERN DIVISION
DIVISION FINALS
Los Angeles 4, St. Louis 3
Apr. 1: St. Louis 106 at Los Angeles 129
Apr. 3: St. Louis 116 at Los Angeles 125
Apr. 6: Los Angeles 113 at St. Louis 120
Apr. 9: Los Angeles 107 at St. Louis 95
Apr. 10: St. Louis 112 at Los Angeles 100
Apr. 13: Los Angeles 127 at St. Louis 131
Apr. 15: St. Louis 121 at Los Angeles 130
DIVISION SEMI-FINALS
St. Louis 3, Baltimore 0
Mar. 24: St. Louis 113 at Baltimore 111
Mar. 27: St. Louis 105 at Baltimore 100
Mar. 30: Baltimore 112 at St. Louis 121

NBA LEADERS

SCORING

	GP	FGM	FTM	PTS	PPG
Wilt Chamberlain, PHI	79	1074	501	2649	33.5
Jerry West, LAL	79	818	840	2476	31.3
Oscar Robertson, CIN	76	818	742	2378	31.3
Rick Barry, SFW	80	745	569	2059	25.7
Walt Bellamy, BAL/NYK	80	695	430	1820	22.8
Hal Greer, PHI	80	703	413	1819	22.7
Dick Barnett, NYK	75	631	467	1729	23.1
Jerry Lucas, CIN	79	690	317	1697	21.5
Zelmo Beaty, STL	80	616	424	1656	20.7
Sam Jones, BOS	67	626	325	1577	23.5

FIELD GOALS

	FGM	FGA	FG%
Wilt Chamberlain, PHI	1074	1990	.540
Johnny Green, NYK/BAL	358	668	.536
Walt Bellamy, BAL/NYK	695	1373	.506
Al Attles, SFW	364	724	.503
Happy Hairston, CIN	398	814	.489
Bailey Howell, BAL	481	986	.488
Bob Boozer, LAL	365	754	.484
Oscar Robertson, CIN	818	1723	.475
Zelmo Beaty, STL	616	1301	.473
Jerry West, LAL	818	1731	.473

FREE THROWS

	FTM	FTA	FT%
Larry Siegfried, BOS	274	311	.881
Rick Barry, SFW	569	660	.862
Howard Komives, NYK	241	280	.861
Jerry West, LAL	840	977	.860
Adrian Smith, CIN	408	480	.850
Oscar Robertson, CIN	742	881	.842
Paul Neumann, SFW	265	317	.836
Kevin Loughery, BAL	297	358	.830
Richie Guerin, STL	362	446	.812
Hal Greer, PHI	413	514	.804

ASSISTS

	GP	AST	APG
Oscar Robertson, CIN	76	847	11.1
Guy Rodgers, SFW	79	846	10.7
K.C. Jones, BOS	80	503	6.3
Jerry West, LAL	79	480	6.1
Lenny Wilkens, STL	69	429	6.2
Howard Komives, NYK	80	425	5.3
Wilt Chamberlain, PHI	79	414	5.2
Mahdi Abdul-Rahman, LAL	80	393	4.9
Richie Guerin, STL	80	388	4.8
Hal Greer, PHI	80	384	4.8

REBOUNDS

	GP	TRB	RPG
Wilt Chamberlain, PHI	79	1943	24.6
Bill Russell, BOS	78	1779	22.8
Jerry Lucas, CIN	79	1668	21.1
Nate Thurmond, SFW	73	1312	18.0
Walt Bellamy, BAL/NYK	80	1254	15.7
Zelmo Beaty, STL	80	1086	13.6
Bill Bridges, STL	78	951	12.2
Dave DeBusschere, DET	79	916	11.6
Willis Reed, NYK	76	883	11.6
Rick Barry, SFW	80	850	10.6

THE YEAR IN BASKETBALL

October 16, 1965 Bill Russell of Boston grabs 36 rebounds versus Cincinnati—the most ever by a player in his team's season opener.

November 4, 1965 Johnny Kerr plays in the last of 844 consecutive games, a record that spanned 12 seasons, as his Baltimore Bullets lost, 108-107, at New York. Randy Smith, who goes on to play in 906 consecutive games, will break Kerr's streak in the 1981-82 season.

November 21, 1965 Two days after missing a flight to broadcast a Lakers' game, Chick Hearn works a Lakers-76ers game, beginning a streak of broadcasting more than 3,200 consecutive Lakers' regular season and playoff games.

December 14, 1965 Rookie Rick Barry of San Francisco scores 57 points in the Warriors' 141-137 loss to New York at Madison Square Garden. Barry's total is the second-highest by a rookie in an NBA game and his 21 free throws in 22 attempts ties Frank Selvy's rookie mark for most free throws made in a game.

January 12, 1966 Red Auerbach becomes the first NBA coach to record 1,000 coaching victories (regular season and playoffs) as his Celtics defeat the Lakers, 114-102, at Boston Garden.

January 14, 1966 Led by Wilt Chamberlain, the Philadelphia 76ers defeat Boston, 112-110, to win the first of what was then an NBA record 36 consecutive home games.

January 27, 1966 The Chicago Bulls are granted admission to the NBA as an expansion franchise. The Bulls follow the defunct Chicago Stags and the Chicago Packers as the NBA's third franchise in the Windy City. The Bulls' entry grows the league to 10 teams and begins an era of expansion for the league; seven additional clubs will gain admittance in the following four years.

February 7, 1966 Wilt Chamberlain scores 65 points in a game against the Lakers

February 14, 1966 Wilt Chamberlain passes Bob Pettit as the NBA's all-time leading scorer when he nets 41 points in a 149-123 victory over Detroit. Chamberlain will hold the career mark for the next 18 years, until Kareem Abdul-Jabbar succeeds him. Pettit's record was 20,880 points.

March 15, 1966 Abe Saperstein, founder of the Harlem Globetrotters and the short-lived American Basketball Association, dies at age 62.

March 19, 1966 Texas Western, featuring an all-black starting lineup, beats all-white Kentucky, 72-65, to win the NCAA championship. Because of Texas Western's disciplined style of play, the game is thought to dispel the idea that blacks couldn't play patterned basketball.

March 19, 1966 Brigham Young defeats NYU, 97-84, to win the NIT.

April 28, 1966 The Boston Celtics win their eighth successive NBA title—the longest streak in NBA history—by edging the Lakers, 95-93, in Game 7 at Boston Garden. Once again, Bill Russell paces Boston in the deciding game with 25 points and 32 rebounds. Following the season, Red Auerbach, the Celtics' long-time coach, retires. Russell replaces him, becoming a player/coach and the first black to coach an NBA team. It is fifth time in the eight-year streak that Boston has defeated the Lakers in the finals.

1966-67

A long time coming, Wilt sips champagne as 76ers new champs

After two unsuccessful attempts to put the nation's second largest city on the NBA circuit, the league once again took a chance at securing a foothold in the Windy City. The first failure for the NBA came in 1950 when the Chicago Stags went out of business. The second attempt came when the Packers, who changed their name to the Zephyrs in 1962, picked up and moved to Baltimore for the start of the 1963-64 season.

In order to accommodate this third attempt, the NBA expanded its ranks to ten members, the newest one named the Chicago Bulls. With Johnny Kerr as head coach, the Bulls got off to a fast start and wound up winning a playoff berth in the Western Division, in addition to winning a paying clientele among Chicago sports fans. The addition of this tenth member forced some changes in the league, namely, the shift of Baltimore from the West to the East, and the revision of the playoff system to include the first four finishers in each division.

So while the NBA was taking another shot at Chicago, the Philadelphia 76ers were ready to take another shot at the Boston Celtics. The 76ers had taken first place in the East away from the Celtics last season, only to collapse in the playoffs. Coach Dolph Schayes was fired as a result of that disappointment, with Alex Hannum taking over as the new coach. Hannum had taken the San Francisco Warriors to the playoff finals several years before, with Wilt Chamberlain playing a large role in passing the ball and on defense. Hannum again had Wilt pass the ball off more often than shoot, with Chamberlain dipping to a 24.1 scoring average, the lowest in his career and the first not to win him the NBA scoring crown. But Wilt ranked first in shooting percentage, first in rebounds, and third in assists, and his accumulation of blocked shots rivaled that of Boston's Bill Russell. The forward corps had two offensive aces in Chet Walker and Billy Cunningham, plus a tough rebounder in Luke Jackson. Hal Greer spearheaded the backcourt with his playmaking and precision jump-shooting. The other guard was Wally Jones, and the reserves were rookies Matt Guokas and Billy Melchionni, and veteran Larry Costello, who came out of retirement only to injure his knee midway through the campaign. Coach Hannum welded this crew into a tight unit, but the 76ers still had to deal with the champion Celtics.

Although Boston had lost first place last year, they had still won the championship in the playoffs, and the addition of veterans Bailey Howell and Wayne Embry more than offset the retirement of Willie Naulls and the trade of Mel Counts. The big question mark for the Celtics was Bill Russell, not as a player but as the coach. Red Auerbach had retired to the sanctuary of the general manager's office, and the public wondered if the Celtics would continue as champions under Russell, the first

Rick Barry
Pushing past Cincinnati defenders en route to two of his 2,775 points, enough to end Wilt Chamberlain's run of seven straight scoring titles.

black coach in major league sports.

The Celtics actually improved under Russell, moving up to a 60-21 record, but they couldn't come close to keeping the amazing pace set by the 76ers. With Wilt clogging up the middle on defense, clearing the boards, and passing the ball to Greer, Walker, and Cunningham, the 76ers flattened all the regular season competition, winning 45 of their first 49 and cruising to a 68-13 season's tally. The 76ers were the most powerful team in pro basketball, and the Celtics would have to muster all their guile to upset them again in the playoffs.

The Cincinnati Royals, still paced by Oscar Robertson and Jerry Lucas, and the New York Knicks, in the playoffs for the first time since 1959, also qualified for the post-season tournament, but had no hope of upsetting either Philadelphia or Boston. Baltimore, the second-place finisher in the West last season, fell apart and finished last in the East this season.

The first-place finisher in the West last season, the Los Angeles Lakers, also slipped, falling under the .500 level and finishing a distant third. Although Elgin Baylor had recovered from his knee troubles to rejoin Jerry West in a superb one-two offensive punch, the Lakers suffered at center, where the trade of Leroy Ellis left the position in Darrall Imhoff's hands, and at forward, where Rudy LaRusso retired after being traded to Detroit in mid-season.

Replacing the Lakers at the top of the heap were the San Francisco Warriors, coached by ex-Celtic Bill Sharman. Nate Thurmond gave the Warriors strength at center to fight Russell and Chamberlain, and forward Rick Barry shot often and straight enough to win the scoring championship, the first man to unseat Chamberlain since Wilt came into the league. A supporting cast of tried veterans and untested youngsters meshed into a solid outfit behind the two stars.

The St. Louis Hawks finished second, with rookie shooter Lou Hudson replacing the retired Cliff Hagan. The fledgling Bulls took the fourth playoff spot with a scrappy club led by veterans Guy Rodgers and Bob Boozer and by second-year pro Jerry Sloan, rescued from the Baltimore bench in the expansion draft. The Pistons had a fine rookie guard in Dave Bing and a

fine veteran forward in Dave DeBusschere, who turned over the coaching reins to assistant Donnie Butcher late in the season to concentrate on playing, but the club nevertheless missed the playoffs for the fourth straight year.

The Western playoffs took the expected shape, with the Warriors emerging as the divisional representative in the championship series. In the East, all eyes focused on the Philadelphia-Boston series; the physically overwhelming 76ers versus the poised Celtics. The first game in Philly opened some eyes, as Chamberlain outscored Russell 32-15 and the 76ers swamped the Celtics 127-113. The Celtics took an early lead in Game 2 at Boston, but the 76ers wore the champions down and won, 107-102. With their backs to the wall, the Celtics started super-subs John Havlicek and Larry Siegfried and sprinted out to a 24-15 lead in the first nine minutes of Game 3. But Chamberlain's rebounding and clutch shooting by Greer and Wally Jones brought the 76ers all the way back to a 115-104 win. The handwriting was on the wall for the Celtics, their string of eight championships was about to end. The outgoing champs won Game 4 121-117 in Boston, but the 76ers simply overpowered the Celtics in Game 5; the final buzzer ended the 140-116 76er victory and also the Celtic reign. It seemed strange not to have the Celtics in the title round, but Chamberlain and his 76ers had decisively proven the better team. And they continued proving it to the end by dispensing with the Warriors in six games. Now, after seven years of scoring titles, Wilt Chamberlain was able to enjoy his first NBA championship.

1966-67 SEASON HIGHLIGHTS

STANDINGS

Eastern Division

	W	L	Pct.	GB
Philadelphia	68	13	.840	—
Boston	60	21	.741	8
Cincinnati	39	42	.481	29
New York	36	45	.444	32
Baltimore	20	61	.247	48

Western Division

	W	L	Pct.	GB
San Francisco	44	37	.543	—
St. Louis	39	42	.481	5
Los Angeles	36	45	.444	8
Chicago	33	48	.407	11
Detroit	30	51	.370	14

AWARDS

MVP
Wilt Chamberlain, Philadelphia
Top Rookie
Dave Bing, Detroit
Coach of Year
Johnny Kerr, Chicago

ALL-STAR TEAMS

FIRST TEAM	
Rick Barry	San Francisco
Elgin Baylor	Los Angeles
Wilt Chamberlain	Philadelphia
Jerry West	Los Angeles
Oscar Robertson	Cincinnati

SECOND TEAM	
Willis Reed	New York
Jerry Lucas	Cincinnati
Bill Russell	Boston
Hal Greer	Philadelphia
Sam Jones	Boston

ALL-STAR GAME

Cow Palace, San Francisco
Tuesday, January 10, 1967
West 135, East 120
MVP: Rick Barry

PLAYOFFS

FINALS
Philadelphia 4, San Francisco 2
Apr. 14: San Francisco 135 at Philadelphia 141, OT
Apr. 16: San Francisco 95 at Philadelphia 126
Apr. 18: Philadelphia 124 at San Francisco 130
Apr. 20: Philadelphia 122 at San Francisco 108
Apr. 23: San Francisco 117 at Philadelphia 109
Apr. 24: Philadelphia 125 at San Francisco 122

EASTERN DIVISION
DIVISION FINALS
Philadelphia 4, Boston 1
Mar. 31: Boston 113 at Philadelphia 127
Apr. 2: Philadelphia 107 at Boston 102
Apr. 5: Boston 104 at Philadelphia 115
Apr. 9: Philadelphia 117 at Boston 121
Apr. 11: Boston 116 at Philadelphia 140
DIVISION SEMI-FINALS
Boston 3, New York 1
Mar. 21: New York 110 at Boston 140
Mar. 25: Boston 115 at New York 108
Mar. 26: New York 123 at Boston 112
Mar. 28: Boston 118 at New York 109
Philadelphia 3, Cincinnati 1
Mar. 21: Cincinnati 120 at Philadelphia 116
Mar. 22: Philadelphia 123 at Cincinnati 102
Mar. 24: Cincinnati 106 at Philadelphia 121
Mar. 25: Philadelphia 112 at Cincinnati 94

WESTERN DIVISION
DIVISION FINALS
San Francisco 4, St. Louis 2
Mar. 30: St. Louis 115 at San Francisco 117
Apr. 1: St. Louis 136 at San Francisco 143
Apr. 5: San Francisco 109 at St. Louis 115
Apr. 8: San Francisco 104 at St. Louis 109
Apr. 10: St. Louis 102 at San Francisco 123
Apr. 12: San Francisco 112 at St. Louis 107
DIVISION SEMI-FINALS
St. Louis 3, Chicago 0
Mar. 21: Chicago 100 at St. Louis 114
Mar. 23: St. Louis 113 at Chicago 107
Mar. 25: Chicago 106 at St. Louis 119
San Francisco 3, Los Angeles 0
Mar. 21: Los Angeles 108 at San Francisco 124
Mar. 23: San Francisco 113 at Los Angeles 102
Mar. 26: Los Angeles 115 at San Francisco 122

NBA LEADERS

SCORING

	GP	FGM	FTM	PTS	PPG
Rick Barry, SFW	78	1011	753	2775	35.6
Oscar Robertson, CIN	79	838	736	2412	30.5
Wilt Chamberlain, PHI	81	785	386	1956	24.1
Jerry West, LAL	66	645	602	1892	28.7
Elgin Baylor, LAL	70	711	440	1862	26.6
Hal Greer, PHI	80	699	367	1765	22.1
John Havlicek, BOS	81	684	365	1733	21.4
Willis Reed, NYK	78	635	358	1628	20.9
Bailey Howell, BOS	81	636	349	1621	20.0
Dave Bing, DET	80	664	273	1601	20.0

FIELD GOALS

	FGM	FGA	FG%
Wilt Chamberlain, PHI	785	1150	.683
Walt Bellamy, NYK	565	1084	.521
Bailey Howell, BOS	636	1242	.512
Oscar Robertson, CIN	838	1699	.493
Willis Reed, NYK	635	1298	.489
Chet Walker, PHI	561	1150	.488
Bob Boozer, CHI	538	1104	.487
Tom Hawkins, LAL	275	572	.481
Happy Hairston, CIN	461	962	.479
Dick Barnett, NYK	454	949	.478

FREE THROWS

	FTM	FTA	FT%
Adrian Smith, CIN	343	380	.903
Rick Barry, SFW	753	852	.884
Jerry West, LAL	602	686	.878
Oscar Robertson, CIN	736	843	.873
Sam Jones, BOS	318	371	.857
Larry Siegfried, BOS	294	347	.847
Wali Jones, PHI	223	266	.838
John Havlicek, BOS	365	441	.828
Kevin Loughery, BAL	340	412	.825
Elgin Baylor, LAL	440	541	.813

ASSISTS

	GP	AST	APG
Guy Rodgers, CHI	81	908	11.2
Oscar Robertson, CIN	79	845	10.7
Wilt Chamberlain, PHI	81	630	7.8
Bill Russell, BOS	81	472	5.8
Jerry West, LAL	66	447	6.8
Lenny Wilkens, STL	78	442	5.7
Howard Komives, NYK	65	401	6.2
K.C. Jones, BOS	78	389	5.0
Richie Guerin, STL	79	345	4.4
Paul Neumann, SFW	78	342	4.4

REBOUNDS

	GP	TRB	RPG
Wilt Chamberlain, PHI	81	1957	24.2
Bill Russell, BOS	81	1700	21.0
Jerry Lucas, CIN	81	1547	19.1
Nate Thurmond, SFW	65	1382	21.3
Bill Bridges, STL	79	1190	15.1
Willis Reed, NYK	78	1136	14.6
Darrall Imhoff, LAL	81	1080	13.3
Walt Bellamy, NYK	79	1064	13.5
Leroy Ellis, BAL	81	970	12.0
Dave DeBusschere, DET	78	924	11.8

THE YEAR IN BASKETBALL

October 15, 1966 Bill Russell debuts as the NBA's first African-American head coach, leading the Celtics to a 121-113 win over San Francisco at the Boston Garden.

December 3, 1966 Lew Alcindor, later known as Kareem Abdul-Jabbar, is a smash hit in his college debut with UCLA. He scores 56 points as the Bruins defeat USC.

December 20, 1966 Representatives from San Diego and Seattle are granted NBA franchises. The San Diego club will adopt the name Rockets. After four losing years in San Diego, the team moves to Houston. Seattle will name itself the SuperSonics.

January 18, 1967 Goose Tatum, for many years the clown prince of the Harlem Globetrotters, dies at age 45.

February 2, 1967 The American Basketball Association is formed at a press conference at the Carlyle Hotel in New York. The 11-team league will begin play in October 1967, seeking to rival the success of the NBA. Former NBA great George Mikan is named the league's first commissioner.

February 16, 1967 Rick Barry of San Francisco scores 52 points against Chicago for his second consecutive 50-point game.

February 24, 1967 Wilt Chamberlain goes 18 for 18 from the field in a 149-118 victory over Baltimore. Chamberlain's performance sets an NBA record for most field goals in a game without a miss.

March 18, 1967 Junior guard Walt Frazier impresses the Madison Square Garden crowd for the first time, leading Southern Illinois to the NIT championship, 71-56, over Marquette. Frazier, who will go on to greatness with the New York Knicks, tallies 21 points and is named the tourney's top player.

March 25, 1967 UCLA, led by Lew Alcindor's 20 points, caps a 30-0 season by beating Dayton, 79-64, for the NCAA title.

April 11, 1967 Philadelphia ousts Boston from the playoffs with a 140-116 win in Game 5 of the Eastern Conference finals. The loss snaps Boston's run of eight straight NBA championships.

April 24, 1967 Philadelphia beats San Francisco, 125-122, to win the NBA championship in six games. Wilt Chamberlain paces Philadelphia with 24 points and 23 rebounds. Rick Barry's 44 points for the Warriors are not enough. It is the first time in nine years that the Celtics are not crowned champions.

May 25, 1967 UCLA, coached by John Wooden, wins the first of seven consecutive NCAA national championships, beating Dayton, 79-64.

1967-68

ABA hits the floor, Celtics up to old tricks, dump Lakers in final

The NBA added two new teams this season, with the addition of the Seattle SuperSonics and San Diego Rockets, two expansion teams created mostly from castoffs from other clubs. The NBA also had two new arenas to play in; the Forum in Los Angeles and the new Madison Square Garden in New York opened their doors in mid-season. And the NBA had new competition, as the American Basketball Association began play with eleven new clubs.

The ABA made no dent in the NBA's attendance figures, but the new league did spirit away Rick Barry, the established league's scoring champion. Barry jumped from the San Francisco Warriors to sign a lucrative contract with the new Oakland Oaks (coached by Bruce Hale, Barry's father-in-law), but the Warriors took Barry to court to force him to play under the reserve clause of his San Francisco contract. The court ruled that Barry could sit out the season and join the Oaks next year, and Barry spent the campaign broadcasting the Oaks' games. But no other major players jumped to the ABA, leaving the balance of power relatively undisturbed.

Wielding the most power in the NBA were the Philadelphia 76ers, the defending champions. With Wilt Chamberlain leading the league in rebounds, assists, and field goal percentage, and with Hal Greer, Chet Walker, Billy Cunningham, Wally Jones, and Luke Jackson working tightly around Wilt, the 76ers still were the class of the league. They couldn't keep the torrid pace of last season, but 24 wins in their last 29 games made the 76ers easy winners of the Eastern Division.

The 76ers were simply too strong for the aging Boston Celtics over an 82-game schedule. K.C. Jones had retired to become a college coach, and Bill Russell and Sam Jones were feeling the pains of injury and age. But even if they were no longer the invincible champions, the Celtics still had plenty of talent and cohesion, and they finished second with a 54-28 record.

The New York Knicks captured third place on the strength of their first .500 season since 1958-59. The addition of rookies Walt Frazier and Phil Jackson, plus the signing of Princeton great Bill Bradley, after two years in England as a Rhodes scholar, plus a short Air Force hitch, gave the Knicks a very deep squad which somehow got off to a poor start under coach Dick McGuire. Red Holzman took over as coach on December 27, and his constant stress on defense and team-oriented offense paid immediate dividends. Under Holzman, the Knicks compiled a 28-17 record.

The Detroit Pistons, shifted to the Eastern Division to make room for Seattle and San Diego, also improved markedly, as their 40-42 record was their best since 1955-56. Rookie guard Jimmy Walker and veteran Terry Dischinger, back from two years of military service, joined scoring champ Dave Bing and Dave DeBusschere as key men on this fourth-place club.

Dave Bing
Dipsy-doodling to a 27.1 ppg average and his only scoring title.

Finishing out of the playoffs were the Cincinnati Royals, who missed Oscar Robertson when he sat out with a thigh injury, and the Baltimore Bullets, who lost forward Gus Johnson to injuries. The Royals lost first draft pick Mel Daniels to the ABA, but the Bullets had an ace rookie in flashy guard Earl (The Pearl) Monroe.

The St. Louis Hawks almost lost Lou Hudson to the ABA, but the high scorer changed his mind about jumping shortly after announcing that he would change leagues. As it turned out, Hudson played only a part of the season before getting called into the Army. The Hawks didn't let Hudson's status

upset the team, as they used a tough pressing defense to lead the West with a 56-26 record. Coach Richie Guerin had retired as a player, leaving the backcourt chores to Lenny Wilkens, Don Ohl, and Dick Snyder. Zelmo Beaty, Bill Bridges, and Paul Silas hit the boards with a lot of muscle for the Hawks. The Los Angeles Lakers couldn't match the Hawks for strength up front, but the combination of Elgin Baylor and Jerry West spurred them home in second place; young guard Archie Clark developed into an offensive threat while West missed 31 games with an injury.

Without Rick Barry, the Warriors finished a distant third, helped not at all by an injury which sidelined center Nate Thurmond for the second half of the season. The Chicago Bulls captured the last playoff spot with a 29-53 mark, while the expansion teams in Seattle and San Diego, as expected, lost plenty of games; San Diego, in fact, had the worst record of any team since 1950.

The playoffs this year had two clear favorites in the 76ers and the Hawks, with the Celtics and Lakers outside shots. The Celtics came back from a 2-1 deficit to beat the Pistons in six games in their Eastern semifinals, while the 76ers ran into trouble with the upstart Knicks. The two clubs split the first four games, with Billy Cunningham going out with a fractured arm and Walt Frazier with an injured leg. The 76ers won games five and six, but the loss of Cunningham robbed the club of any punch its bench had. The Western semifinals saw a major upset

when the Warriors bumped off the Hawks in six games, while the Lakers, as expected, easily eliminated the Bulls. The Lakers then beat the Warriors to head into the title series against the Eastern representative, Philadelphia or Boston.

The Eastern showdown between the 76ers and Celtics had the air of a rematch for the heavyweight championship of the world; the Celtics had beat the 76ers two years ago; the 76ers had won last year. The opening game, one day after the assassination of Dr. Martin Luther King, saw the Celtics use long-range shooting to take a 127-118 victory. But then the 76ers settled down to their power game and took three straight from the Celtics. With their backs to the wall, the Celtics staved off elimination with a 122-104 win in Philly. Then, back in Boston, they evened the series at three games all with a 114-106 win. With the series riding now on a seventh game, it came down to the 76er muscle vs. the Celtic savvy. Chamberlain concentrated on feeding his teammates, who had a collective off-night in the shooting department. The Celtics stayed right with the stronger 76ers and led 97-95 with 34 seconds left on the clock. Russell then sank a foul shot, blocked a shot by Chet Walker, grabbed a rebound of Hal Greer's shot, and got the ball out to Sam Jones, who sunk a final basket for a 100-96 victory. The Celtic dynasty was back in business, and Russell and company were not about to let a championship slip away; they knocked off the Lakers in six games and savored their return to the top of the hill.

1967-68 SEASON HIGHLIGHTS

STANDINGS

Eastern Division	W	L	Pct.	GB		Western Division	W	L	Pct.	GB
Philadelphia	62	20	.756	—		St. Louis	56	26	.683	—
Boston	54	28	.659	8		Los Angeles	52	30	.634	4
New York	43	39	.524	19		San Francisco	43	39	.524	13
Detroit	40	42	.488	22		Chicago	29	53	.354	27
Cincinnati	39	43	.476	23		Seattle	23	59	.280	33
Baltimore	36	46	.439	26		San Diego	15	67	.183	41

AWARDS

MVP
Wilt Chamberlain, Philadelphia
Top Rookie
Earl Monroe, Baltimore
Coach of Year
Richie Guerin, St. Louis

ALL-STAR TEAMS

FIRST TEAM		SECOND TEAM	
Elgin Baylor	Los Angeles	Willis Reed	New York
Jerry Lucas	Cincinnati	John Havlicek	Boston
Wilt Chamberlain	Philadelphia	Bill Russell	Boston
Dave Bing	Detroit	Hal Greer	Philadelphia
Oscar Robertson	Cincinnati	Jerry West	Los Angeles

ALL-STAR GAME

Madison Square Garden, New York
Tuesday, January 23, 1968
East 144, West 124
MVP: Hal Greer

PLAYOFFS

FINALS
Boston 4, Los Angeles 2
Apr. 21: Los Angeles 101 at Boston 107
Apr. 24: Los Angeles 123 at Boston 113
Apr. 26: Boston 127 at Los Angeles 119
Apr. 28: Boston 105 at Los Angeles 119
Apr. 30: Los Angeles 117 at Boston 120, OT
May 2: Boston 124 at Los Angeles 109
EASTERN DIVISION
DIVISION FINALS
Boston 4, Philadelphia 3
Apr. 5: Boston 127 at Philadelphia 118
Apr. 10: Philadelphia 115 at Boston 106
Apr. 11: Boston 114 at Philadelphia 122
Apr. 14: Philadelphia 110 at Boston 105
Apr. 15: Boston 122 at Philadelphia 104
Apr. 17: Philadelphia 106 at Boston 114
Apr. 19: Boston 100 at Philadelphia 96

DIVISION SEMI-FINALS
Philadelphia 4, New York 2
Mar. 22: New York 110 at Philadelphia 118
Mar. 23: Philadelphia 117 at New York 128
Mar. 27: New York 132 at Philadelphia 138, 2OT
Mar. 30: Philadelphia 98 at New York 107
Mar. 31: New York 107 at Philadelphia 123
Apr. 1: Philadelphia 113 at New York 97
Boston 4, Detroit 2
Mar. 24: Detroit 116 at Boston 123
Mar. 25: Boston 116 at Detroit 126
Mar. 27: Detroit 109 at Boston 98
Mar. 28: Boston 135 at Detroit 110
Mar. 31: Detroit 96 at Boston 110
Apr. 1: Boston 111 at Detroit 103

WESTERN DIVISION
DIVISION FINALS
Los Angeles 4, San Francisco 0
Apr. 5: San Francisco 105 at Los Angeles 133
Apr. 10: San Francisco 112 at Los Angeles 115
Apr. 11: Los Angeles 128 at San Francisco 124
Apr. 13: Los Angeles 106 at San Francisco 100
DIVISION SEMI-FINALS
San Francisco 4, St. Louis 2
Mar. 22: San Francisco 111 at St. Louis 106
Mar. 23: San Francisco 103 at St. Louis 111
Mar. 26: St. Louis 109 at San Francisco 124
Mar. 29: St. Louis 107 at San Francisco 108
Mar. 31: San Francisco 103 at St. Louis 129
Apr. 2: St. Louis 106 at San Francisco 111
Los Angeles 4, Chicago 1
Mar. 24: Chicago 101 at Los Angeles 109
Mar. 25: Chicago 106 at Los Angeles 111
Mar. 27: Los Angeles 98 at Chicago 104
Mar. 29: Los Angeles 93 at Chicago 87
Mar. 31: Chicago 99 at Los Angeles 122

NBA LEADERS

SCORING

	GP	FGM	FTM	PTS	PPG
Dave Bing, DET	79	835	472	2142	27.1
Elgin Baylor, LAL	77	757	488	2002	26.0
Wilt Chamberlain, PHI	82	819	354	1992	24.3
Earl Monroe, BAL	82	742	507	1991	24.3
Hal Greer, PHI	82	777	422	1976	24.1
Oscar Robertson, CIN	65	660	576	1896	29.2
Mahdi Abdul-Rahman, SEA	79	733	428	1894	24.0
Jerry Lucas, CIN	82	707	346	1760	21.5
Zelmo Beaty, STL	82	639	455	1733	21.1
Rudy LaRusso, SFW	79	602	522	1726	21.8

FIELD GOALS

	FGM	FGA	FG%
Wilt Chamberlain, PHI	819	1377	.595
Walt Bellamy, NYK	511	944	.541
Jerry Lucas, CIN	707	1361	.519
Jerry West, LAL	476	926	.514
Len Chappell, CIN/DET	235	458	.513
Oscar Robertson, CIN	660	1321	.500
Tom Hawkins, LAL	389	779	.499
Terry Dischinger, DET	394	797	.494
Don Nelson, BOS	312	632	.494
Hank Finkel, SDR	242	492	.492

FREE THROWS

	FTM	FTA	FT%
Oscar Robertson, CIN	576	660	.873
Larry Siegfried, BOS	236	272	.868
Dave Gambee, SDR	321	379	.847
Fred Hetzel, SFW	395	474	.833
Adrian Smith, CIN	320	386	.829
Sam Jones, BOS	311	376	.827
Flynn Robinson, CIN/CHI	288	351	.821
John Havlicek, BOS	368	453	.812
Jerry West, LAL	391	482	.811
Cazzie Russell, NYK	282	349	.808

ASSISTS

	GP	AST	APG
Wilt Chamberlain, PHI	82	702	8.6
Lenny Wilkens, STL	82	679	8.3
Oscar Robertson, CIN	65	633	9.7
Dave Bing, DET	79	509	6.4
Mahdi Abdul-Rahman, SEA	79	493	6.2
Art Williams, SDR	79	391	4.9
Al Attles, SFW	67	390	5.8
John Havlicek, BOS	82	384	4.7
Guy Rodgers, CHI/CIN	79	380	4.8
Hal Greer, PHI	82	372	4.5

REBOUNDS

	GP	TRB	RPG
Wilt Chamberlain, PHI	82	1952	23.8
Jerry Lucas, CIN	82	1560	19.0
Bill Russell, BOS	78	1451	18.6
Clyde Lee, SFW	82	1141	13.9
Nate Thurmond, SFW	51	1121	22.0
Ray Scott, BAL	81	1111	13.7
Bill Bridges, STL	82	1102	13.4
Dave DeBusschere, DET	80	1081	13.5
Willis Reed, NYK	81	1073	13.2
Walt Bellamy, NYK	82	961	11.7

THE YEAR IN BASKETBALL

October 10, 1967 Long-time University of Rhode Island coach Frank Keaney dies.

October 13, 1967 The ABA opens its inaugural season as the Oakland Oaks edge the Anaheim Amigos, 134-129, before 4,828 at Oakland Coliseum.

December 16, 1967 Wilt Chamberlain scores 68 points to lead Philadelphia to a 143-123 win over the Chicago Bulls.

January 20, 1968 In an historic game played before 52,693 at the new Houston Astrodome, Elvin Hayes scores 29 points in the first half and outplays Lew Alcindor as the Houston Cougars snap UCLA's 47-game win streak in a 71-69 victory. The game is broadcast in prime time on a Friday night to a rapt national audience.

January 22, 1968 Milwaukee and Phoenix basketball fans celebrate as franchises from their cities each gain admission into the NBA. The expansion brings to 14 the number of teams in the league.

January 23, 1968 Denise Long, a legendary high school player from Union Whitten, Iowa, scores 111 points in a single game. It is one of three times in Long's career that she exceeds the century mark.

January 29, 1968 Adolph Rupp of Kentucky becomes the winningest coach in collegiate history with 772 victories, as the Wildcats beat Mississippi.

February 17, 1968 The Naismith Basketball Hall of Fame opens on the campus of Springfield College in Springfield, Mass. The museum costs $650,000 to build and is named after the inventor of the game and former instructor at the Springfield Training School.

March 23, 1968 Dayton, led by All-American Don May, wins the NIT for the second time, by toppling Kansas, 61-48.

March 22, 1968 Avenging their defeat at the Astrodome in January, UCLA and Lew Alcindor thrash the undefeated Houston Cougars, with Elvin Hayes, 101-69, in the NCAA tournament's semi-finals. Alcindor outscores Hayes, 19-10.

March 22, 1968 UCLA, behind Lew Alcindor's 34 points, win their second consecutive NCAA title with a 78-55 rout of North Carolina.

May 2, 1968 The Celtics beat the Lakers, 124-109, to win the NBA championship in 6 games. John Havlicek scores 40 points for Boston in the deciding game, which is played at L.A.'s Forum.

May 4, 1968 The Pittsburgh Pipers defeat the New Orleans Buccaneers, 122-113, to win the inaugural ABA championship in seven games. Star forward Connie Hawkins, ostracized by the NBA, scores 20 points for the Pipers in the deciding game, which draws over 11,000 fans to the Pittsburgh Civic Center. The ABA ends its inaugural season with a $2.5 million operating loss.

1968-69

West magnificent, but Celtics hang on to beat Lakers in seven

The Boston Celtics came into this season as the defending champions, but one deal during the summer had established the Los Angeles Lakers as the odds-on favorite to take the NBA title this year; they traded for Wilt Chamberlain. After the Philadelphia 76ers had lost to Boston in the playoffs last spring, coach Alex Hannum jumped to the Oakland Oaks of the ABA and general manager Jack Ramsay took over as coach. He wanted to turn the 76ers into a running club, and his first move was to send Chamberlain to Los Angeles for guard Archie Clark, center Darrall Imhoff, and forward Jerry Chambers, plus cash. With Chamberlain, Elgin Baylor, and Jerry West on the same club, the league and the fans immediately classified the Lakers as the new superteam of the NBA. After all, Baylor and West had regularly led the Lakers into the playoff finals without winning the title, so the addition of the most powerful center in basketball filled the only weak spot on the team.

The NBA not only had a new glamour team, but it had two new franchises and a transplanted old team. The Milwaukee Bucks and Phoenix Suns came into the league as expansion clubs, and the St. Louis Hawks moved to Atlanta, as owner Ben Kerner sold the club after helping found it in 1946 and then moving it from Buffalo to Tri-Cities to Milwaukee to St. Louis. The rival ABA also moved a few franchises, but the new league failed to make much of a dent on the NBA in terms of playing personnel. Coaches Alex Hannum of Philadelphia and Bill Sharman of San Francisco moved over to the ABA, but centers Elvin Hayes and Wes Unseld, the cream of the rookie class, signed with NBA teams after enjoying a bidding war which drove pro basketball contracts to new heights.

Chamberlain, too, used the new league to boost his bargaining power, signing a four-year contract worth one million dollars. As the season progressed, Wilt's rebounding and defense made the Lakers a very tough club, but they were not the powerhouse that fans had expected. It took time for the other Lakers to get used to Wilt, Jerry West lost some time to injuries, and coach Butch Van Breda Kolff and Wilt had cool personal relations right from the start. The Lakers nevertheless logged a 55-27 record and easily copped the Western Division title.

The transplanted Hawks finished second in the West, seven games behind the Lakers. The return of Lou Hudson from military service bolstered the Hawks, but a salary dispute forced the trade of Lenny Wilkens to Seattle for Walt Hazzard, a deal which hurt the Hawks in the leadership department. The San Francisco Warriors came in a distant third, and the surprising San Diego Rockets took the final playoff spot with a respectable 37-45 record, thanks mostly to the league-leading 28.4 scoring of rookie Elvin Hayes.

The Chicago Bulls came in fifth and out of the playoffs, but started putting together the elements of a contending club;

Wes Unseld
Muscling by Jerry Lucas during an improbable MVP season in which his rebounding and passing helped lift the Bullets from worst to first.

Dick Motta was the new coach, Tom Boerwinkle was the rookie center, and subs Bob Love and Bob Weiss came from Milwaukee in a minor deal. Seattle finished sixth despite Wilkens, and the new Phoenix club finished last despite solid seasons from Gale Goodrich and Dick Van Arsdale.

Last season's cellar club in the East, the Baltimore Bullets, shocked the league by shooting to the top of the division with a 57-25 record, the best in the NBA The Bullets already had shooters in Earl (The Pearl) Monroe, Kevin Loughery, and Jack Marin, and Wes Unseld's rebounding and quick outlet passes

instantly turned the Bullets into a dangerous fast-breaking team. Unseld won both the MVP and Rookie of the Year awards, and the Bullets became the first major league pro team to rocket from last to first place in one season.

The Philadelphia 76ers finished a close second, getting along fine without Chamberlain in their new wide open format. Billy Cunningham and Hal Greer handled the burden of the scoring, and not even a leg injury to Luke Jackson, who had succeeded Chamberlain at center, seriously disrupted the new pattern. Close behind in third place were the New York Knicks, who enjoyed a great second half of the season after getting Dave DeBusschere in December from the Detroit Pistons for Walt Bellamy and Howie Komives. The trade gave the Knicks one of the game's best all-around forwards, enabled Willis Reed to move back to his normal center position, and made room for Walt Frazier in the starting lineup. After the trade, the Knicks went 36-11 despite injuries which sidelined Cazzie Russell and Phil Jackson and reduced the bench to a skeleton crew.

Back in fourth place came the Boston Celtics, one year older and apparently no longer a power to be contended with; Bill Russell suffered from a bad knee, Sam Jones sat out a few games with a pulled groin muscle, and only the insertion of John Havlicek into the starting lineup late in the season pumped some semblance of the old spark back into the Celtics. The Cincinnati Royals and Detroit Pistons both had severe weaknesses up front and finished out of the playoffs along with the fledgling Milwaukee Bucks.

The playoffs went according to schedule in the West, with the Lakers emerging as divisional representatives in the championship series. The East, however, produced plenty of surprises, starting with the Baltimore-New York series. With

starters Willis Reed, Dave DeBusschere, Bill Bradley, Walt Frazier, and Dick Barnett forced to play most of the game because of injuries to Russell and Jackson, the Knicks blitzed the Bullets with a pressing defense and sharp passing attack and eliminated the startled Baltimore squad with four straight wins. The Celtics, meanwhile, exercised some of their old-time playoff magic by kayoing Philadelphia in five games. The Eastern final matched the rising powers from New York against the experienced but aging powers from Boston. It went against logic, but somehow seemed normal, when the Celtics forced the Knicks into making errors, won the first two games to take command of the series, and closed it out in six.

For the second straight season, the Celtics finished out of first place in the East, yet made it to the championship final. So now the Celtics and Russell faced another crucial showdown with Wilt Chamberlain, this time in a Los Angeles uniform. The Lakers captured the first two games to move comfortably out in front, but the old pros from Boston took Game 3 to stay in contention. The fourth game came down to two seconds left, with the Lakers leading 88-87; but at the buzzer, Sam Jones hit on an off-balance jumper to give the Celtics an 89-88 win.

The two clubs split the next two games, and the showdown seventh game shaped up as perhaps the final hurrah of the Boston dynasty. The Celtic old men ran from the opening whistle on, and while the Lakers made a move to catch up in the fourth period. Wilt hurt his leg and left the game with five minutes left. Without the big man in the game, the Laker drive fell short, and the Celtics came away with a 108-106 win. This was it for the Celtic dynasty, the final championship for the dominant team of the sixties; Bill Russell and Sam Jones retired at this point, going out as unparalleled winners.

1968-69 SEASON HIGHLIGHTS

STANDINGS

Eastern Division

	W	L	Pct.	GB
Baltimore	57	25	.695	—
Philadelphia	55	27	.671	2
New York	54	28	.659	3
Boston	48	34	.585	9
Cincinnati	41	41	.500	16
Detroit	32	50	.390	25
Milwaukee	27	55	.329	30

Western Division

	W	L	Pct.	GB
Los Angeles	55	27	.671	—
Atlanta	48	34	.585	7
San Francisco	41	41	.500	14
San Diego	37	45	.451	18
Chicago	33	49	.402	22
Seattle	30	52	.366	25
Phoenix	16	66	.195	39

AWARDS

MVP
Wes Unseld, Baltimore

Top Rookie
Wes Unseld, Baltimore

Coach of Year
Gene Shue, Baltimore

ALL-STAR TEAMS

FIRST TEAM

Billy Cunningham	Philadelphia
Elgin Baylor	Los Angeles
Wes Unseld	Baltimore
Earl Monroe	Baltimore
Oscar Robertson	Cincinnati

SECOND TEAM

John Havlicek	Boston
Dave DeBusschere	Detroit-NY
Willis Reed	New York
Hal Greer	Philadelphia
Jerry West	Los Angeles

ALL-STAR GAME

Baltimore Civic Center, Baltimore
Tuesday, January 14, 1969
East 123, West 112
MVP: Oscar Robertson

PLAYOFFS

FINALS
Boston 4, Los Angeles 3
Apr. 23: Boston 118 at Los Angeles 120
Apr. 25: Boston 112 at Los Angeles 118
Apr. 27: Los Angeles 105 at Boston 111
Apr. 29: Los Angeles 88 at Boston 89
May 1: Boston 104 at Los Angeles 117
May 3: Los Angeles 90 at Boston 99
May 5: Boston 108 at Los Angeles 106

EASTERN DIVISION
DIVISION FINALS
Boston 4, New York 2
Apr. 6: Boston 108 at New York 100
Apr. 9: New York 97 at Boston 112
Apr. 10: Boston 91 at New York 101
Apr. 13: New York 96 at Boston 97
Apr. 14: Boston 104 at New York 112
Apr. 18: New York 105 at Boston 106

DIVISION SEMI-FINALS
New York 4, Baltimore 0
Mar. 27: New York 113 at Baltimore 101
Mar. 29: Baltimore 91 at New York 107
Mar. 30: New York 119 at Baltimore 116
Apr. 2: Baltimore 108 at New York 115

Boston 4, Philadelphia 1
Mar. 26: Boston 114 at Philadelphia 100
Mar. 28: Philadelphia 103 at Boston 134
Mar. 30: Boston 125 at Philadelphia 118
Apr. 1: Philadelphia 119 at Boston 116
Apr. 4: Boston 93 at Philadelphia 90

WESTERN DIVISION
DIVISION FINALS
Los Angeles 4, Atlanta 1
Apr. 11: Atlanta 93 at Los Angeles 95
Apr. 13: Atlanta 102 at Los Angeles 104
Apr. 15: Los Angeles 80 at Atlanta 99
Apr. 17: Los Angeles 100 at Atlanta 85
Apr. 20: Atlanta 96 at Los Angeles 104

DIVISION SEMI-FINALS
Los Angeles 4, San Francisco 2
Mar. 26: San Francisco 99 at Los Angeles 94
Mar. 28: San Francisco 107 at Los Angeles 101
Mar. 31: Los Angeles 115 at San Francisco 98
Apr. 2: Los Angeles 103 at San Francisco 88
Apr. 4: San Francisco 98 at Los Angeles 103
Apr. 5: Los Angeles 118 at San Francisco 78

Atlanta 4, San Diego 2
Mar. 27: San Diego 98 at Atlanta 107
Mar. 29: San Diego 114 at Atlanta 116
Apr. 1: Atlanta 97 at San Diego 104
Apr. 4: Atlanta 112 at San Diego 114
Apr. 6: San Diego 101 at Atlanta 112
Apr. 7: Atlanta 108 at San Diego 106

NBA LEADERS

SCORING

	GP	FGM	FTM	PTS	PPG
Elvin Hayes, SDR	82	930	467	2327	28.4
Earl Monroe, BAL	80	809	447	2065	25.8
Billy Cunningham, PHI	82	739	556	2034	24.8
Bob Rule, SEA	82	776	413	1965	24.0
Oscar Robertson, CIN	79	656	643	1955	24.7
Gail Goodrich, PHO	81	718	495	1931	23.8
Hal Greer, PHI	82	732	432	1896	23.1
Elgin Baylor, LAL	76	730	421	1881	24.8
Lenny Wilkens, SEA	82	644	547	1835	22.4
Don Kojis, SDR	81	687	446	1820	22.5

FIELD GOALS

	FGM	FGA	FG%
Wilt Chamberlain, LAL	641	1099	.583
Jerry Lucas, CIN	555	1007	.551
Willis Reed, NYK	704	1351	.521
Terry Dischinger, DET	264	513	.515
Walt Bellamy, NYK/DET	563	1103	.510
Joe Caldwell, ATL	561	1106	.507
Walt Frazier, NYK	531	1052	.505
Tom Hawkins, LAL	230	461	.499
Lou Hudson, ATL	716	1455	.492
Jon McGlocklin, MIL	662	1358	.487

FREE THROWS

	FTM	FTA	FT%
Larry Siegfried, BOS	336	389	.864
Jeff Mullins, SFW	381	452	.843
Jon McGlocklin, MIL	246	292	.842
Flynn Robinson, CHI/MIL	412	491	.839
Oscar Robertson, CIN	643	767	.838
Fred Hetzel, MIL/CIN	299	357	.838
Jack Marin, BAL	292	352	.830
Jerry West, LAL	490	597	.821
Bob Boozer, CHI	394	489	.806
Chet Walker, PHI	369	459	.804

ASSISTS

	GP	AST	APG
Oscar Robertson, CIN	79	772	9.8
Lenny Wilkens, SEA	82	674	8.2
Walt Frazier, NYK	80	635	7.9
Guy Rodgers, MIL	81	561	6.9
Dave Bing, DET	77	546	7.1
Art Williams, SDR	79	524	6.6
Gail Goodrich, PHO	81	518	6.4
Mahdi Abdul-Rahman, ATL	80	474	5.9
John Havlicek, BOS	82	441	5.4
Jerry West, LAL	61	423	6.9

REBOUNDS

	GP	TRB	RPG
Wilt Chamberlain, LAL	81	1712	21.1
Wes Unseld, BAL	82	1491	18.2
Bill Russell, BOS	77	1484	19.3
Elvin Hayes, SDR	82	1406	17.1
Nate Thurmond, SFW	71	1402	19.7
Jerry Lucas, CIN	74	1360	18.4
Willis Reed, NYK	82	1191	14.5
Bill Bridges, ATL	80	1132	14.2
Walt Bellamy, NYK/DET	88	1101	12.5
Billy Cunningham, PHI	82	1050	12.8

THE YEAR IN BASKETBALL

October 16, 1968 The Milwaukee Bucks make their NBA debut, losing, 89-84, to the Chicago Bulls before 8,467 fans at Milwaukee Arena.

November 28, 1968 Penny Ann Early becomes the first woman to "play" in a men's professional league. In a publicity stunt, the Kentucky Colonels sign Early and have her inbound the ball in a game against the Los Angeles Stars. Early wears a miniskirt for the occasion. After she tosses the ball to a teammate, the Colonels call timeout. As she leaves the court, fans give her a standing ovation.

December 19, 1968 The Knicks acquire forward Dave DeBusschere from Detroit in exchange for center Walt Bellamy and guard Howard Komives. The acquisition of DeBusschere becomes an important building block to the Knicks' championship in the '69-70 season.

February 10, 1969 LSU's Pete Maravich scores 66 points, but the Tigers lose to Tulane 101-94.

March 22, 1969 Behind tournament MVP Terry Driscoll, Temple beats Boston College, 89-76, to win the NIT.

March 19, 1969 The Milwaukee Bucks win a coin toss, giving them first pick in the 1969 NBA draft. The Bucks will select and eventually sign Lew Alcindor. Phoenix, which loses the toss, will pick Neal Walk.

March 22, 1969 UCLA becomes the first collegiate team to capture three consecutive NCAA championships by defeating Purdue, 92-72.

Lew Alcindor, with 37 points in the deciding game, wins his third consecutive tournament MVP award. Under coach John Wooden, and with Alcindor in the middle, UCLA went 90-2 (.978) in the three seasons.

April 2, 1969 The ABA's Houston Mavericks, a notoriously poor draw, play their final home game. The announced crowd for the contest against the New York Nets is 89.

April 23, 1969 Jerry West scores 53 points, leading the Lakers to a 120-118 triumph over the Celtics in the opening game of the NBA finals.

May 5, 1969 With player/coach Bill Russell leading the way, the Celtics win their 11th NBA title in 13 years, with a 108-106 victory over rival Los Angeles in Game 7 of the finals. Boston is helped in the final minutes when Don Nelson's jumper bounces high off the back of the rim and drops through the net. Jerry West, who tallies 42 points, 13 rebounds, and 12 assists in the final game, is the series' MVP. Russell and guard Sam Jones both retire after the season and the Celtics' remarkable string of championships ends.

May 7, 1969 The Oakland Oaks win the second-ever ABA championship, when they defeat the Indiana Pacers, 135-131, in overtime in Game 5 of the finals. Warren Jabali scores 39 points in the final game to lead Oakland.

1969-70

Knicks' turn to deny West, Chamberlain in seven-game final

The Celtics had won the playoffs as aged underdogs the last two seasons and now the Boston dynasty crashed to the end with the retirement of Bill Russell and Sam Jones. Russell had played on 11 championship squads in his 13 seasons, and Jones had played on 10 of them. The Celtics could in no way make up for their defense, rebounding, shooting, experience, and class. Tommy Heinsohn took over as coach, but with Henry Finkel at center, the Celtics collapsed to a 34-48 record, a fall to sixth place in the East.

But a new club embodied the fine precision of the Celtic machine in its heyday. The New York Knicks, with a deep squad built around center Willis Reed, forward Dave DeBusschere, and guard Walt Frazier, came roaring out of the gate to take an early lead which held up all season. The New Yorkers won their first game, then dropped one to San Francisco, and then proceeded to run off a record 18 straight victories. The Knick calling card was a pressing defense which stayed well-oiled with frequent substitutions, and the team's offensive slogan was, "Hit the open man," a capsule summary of the selfless passing game which kept the ball constantly moving.

And if the Knicks were acting like a new version of the Celtics, the league had a new Bill Russell in Lew Alcindor (later Kareem Abdul-Jabbar), the 7-foot-2 center out of UCLA. Combining the defensive awareness of Russell with the offensive power of Wilt Chamberlain, Alcindor signed a five year, $1.2 million contract with the Milwaukee Bucks, who had won a coin toss with the Phoenix Suns for the first draft pick and rights to Alcindor. Big Lew immediately proved that he was worth every penny, changing the Bucks from a cellar dwellers into title contenders. With some help from fellow rookie Bob Dandridge, Alcindor sparked the Bucks to a 56-26 season, finishing only four games behind New York. Baltimore and Philadelphia took the third and fourth playoff spots in the East.

Fifth place in the East went to the Cincinnati Royals, coached by Russell's old teammate, Bob Cousy. The former star guard actually played in a few games, but his main concern was to change the Royals into a running team in the image of the old Celtics. Rookie guards Norm Van Lier and Herm Gilliam fit right into this new style, but veterans Jerry Lucas and Oscar Robertson, long-time Cincinnati stars, felt more at home in the old pattern offense. Cousy dealt Lucas off early in the season to San Francisco for the surprisingly cheap price of Jim King and Bill Turner. He then tried to send Robertson to Baltimore for Gus Johnson, only to have the Big O exercise a contractual right to veto the deal. Finishing behind the Royals were the Celtics, out of the playoffs for the first time since 1950, and the perennially-weak Detroit Pistons.

In Los Angeles, Wilt Chamberlain spent a restless season on the sidelines. In the Lakers' ninth game of the year, he hurt his knee and underwent surgery. Elgin Baylor also had problems

Willis Reed
Injured here in Game 5 of the Final, his inspirational return for Game 7 against the Lakers capped MVP season and the Knicks' first title.

with his knees, so the Lakers were often down to one superstar, Jerry West. Winning his first scoring title with a 31.2 average, West often carried the team single-handedly, and the Lakers finished second in the Western Division with a 46-36 record.

The Atlanta Hawks finished in first place despite some personnel problems. Center Zelmo Beaty signed with the ABA and sat out his option season, leaving sub Jim Davis to hold down the pivot position until Walt Bellamy came down from Detroit in a late-season trade. Another trade hurt the Hawks, as the Phoenix Suns took rebounder Paul Silas off their hands for

the less-talented Gary Gregor.

The Chicago Bulls and Phoenix Suns took the third and fourth playoff spots with identical 39-43 records. Coach Dick Motta had his Bulls playing a physical, ball-control style of play, and a major portion of the team's offensive power came from the new forward combination of Chet Walker and Bob Love. Walker came to Chicago from Philadelphia in a swap for Jim Washington, and Love was promoted to a starting role after three years of bench sitting for the Royals, Bucks, and Bulls; the pair scored an average of 42.5 points per game.

The Suns got off to a slow start, which cost coach Johnny Kerr his job, but they came on strong late in the season with their completely revamped front wall. First draft pick Neal Walls shared the center job with veteran Jim Fox, Paul Silas held down one forward spot, and the famous Connie Hawkins filled the other forward spot. The NBA admitted Hawkins into the league as part of an out-of-court settlement to his damage suits, eight years after he was barred for not reporting a bribe offer while a freshman at the University of Iowa. Long celebrated as the best of the one-on-one players, "the Hawk" broke into the NBA with a 24.6 scoring average and a first-team All-Star berth, proving himself a star in this league as he had in the ABA for the past two seasons. Seattle, San Francisco, and San Diego all had new coaches either at the start of the season or during the campaign, and all of them finished out of the playoffs.

The first round of the playoffs went as expected, with the Knicks, Bucks, Hawks, and Lakers emerging victorious. The young Bucks relied entirely on Alcindor, but the Knicks used a well-balanced team performance to kayo them in five games in the Eastern final. In the West, the Lakers had Chamberlain and Baylor back in working order for the playoffs and disposed of the Hawks in four straight games. The title series would be between the team-oriented Knicks and the star-oriented Lakers.

The Knicks ran away with a 124-112 win in the opening game in a packed Madison Square Garden, as Wills Reed hit for 37 points against Chamberlain. Jerry West's 34 points three days later helped the Lakers even the series with a 105-103 win. The third game, in California, was knotted at 100-all until Dave DeBusschere put New York ahead with a bucket with three seconds left. Chamberlain then threw the ball in to West, and the star guard heaved it from deep in the backcourt, 55 feet away, into the basket to tie the score at the buzzer. Undaunted, the Knicks took a 111-108 win in overtime. The fourth game also went into overtime, with little-used sub John Tresvant sparking the Lakers in the extra period to a 121-115 win.

Game five in New York started well for the Knicks, but then Wills Reed collapsed with a torn thigh muscle; down by 13 points at the half, coach Red Holzman used a no-center lineup in the second half, with DeBusschere and Dave Stallworth covering Chamberlain. It worked, as a pressing defense and pin-point shooting led the Knicks back to a rousing 107-100 win. Reed sat out Game 6, and Chamberlain jammed home 45 points against the helpless Knicks in a 135-113 Laker victory. Back in New York for the seventh game, the Knicks took the floor without Reed, but he limped onto the floor to a huge ovation. Reed couldn't move, but he leaned on Chamberlain and kept him away from the basket; he also hit the first basket of the day, a jumper from the head of the key. The rest of the Knicks, inspired by Reed and cheered on by their fans, clicked with their pressing defense and outside shooting. They pulled away from the Lakers and never stopped running on the way to a 113-99 victory which brought New York its first NBA title.

1969-70 SEASON HIGHLIGHTS

STANDINGS

Eastern Division

	W	L	Pct.	GB
New York	60	22	.732	—
Milwaukee	56	26	.683	4
Baltimore	50	32	.610	10
Philadelphia	42	40	.512	18
Cincinnati	36	46	.439	24
Boston	34	48	.415	26
Detroit	31	51	.378	29

Western Division

	W	L	Pct.	GB
Atlanta	48	34	.585	—
Los Angeles	46	36	.561	2
Phoenix	39	43	.476	9
Chicago	39	43	.476	9
Seattle	36	46	.439	12
San Francisco	30	52	.366	18
San Diego	27	55	.329	21

AWARDS

MVP
Willis Reed, New York
Top Rookie
Lew Alcindor, Milwaukee
Coach of Year
Red Holzman, New York

ALL-STAR TEAMS

FIRST TEAM

Billy Cunningham	Philadelphia
Connie Hawkins	Phoenix
Willis Reed	New York
Jerry West	Los Angeles
Walt Frazier	New York

SECOND TEAM

John Havlicek	Boston
Gus Johnson	Baltimore
Lew Alcindor	Milwaukee
Lou Hudson	Atlanta
Oscar Robertson	Cincinnati

ALL-STAR GAME

The Spectrum, Philadelphia
Tuesday, January 20, 1970
East 142, West 135
MVP: Willis Reed

PLAYOFFS
FINALS

New York 4, Los Angeles 3
Apr. 24: Los Angeles 112 at New York 124
Apr. 27: Los Angeles 105 at New York 103
Apr. 29: New York 111 at Los Angeles 108, OT
May 1: New York 115 at Los Angeles 121, OT
May 4: Los Angeles 100 at New York 107
May 6: New York 113 at Los Angeles 135
May 8: Los Angeles 99 at New York 113

EASTERN DIVISION
DIVISION FINALS
New York 4, Milwaukee 1
Apr. 11: Milwaukee 102 at New York 110
Apr. 13: Milwaukee 111 at New York 112
Apr. 17: New York 96 at Milwaukee 101
Apr. 19: New York 117 at Milwaukee 105
Apr. 20: Milwaukee 96 at New York 132

DIVISION SEMI-FINALS
Milwaukee 4, Philadelphia 1
Mar. 25: Philadelphia 118 at Milwaukee 125
Mar. 27: Philadelphia 112 at Milwaukee 105
Mar. 30: Milwaukee 156 at Philadelphia 120
Apr. 1: Milwaukee 118 at Philadelphia 111
Apr. 3: Philadelphia 106 at Milwaukee 115

New York 4, Baltimore 3
Mar. 26: Baltimore 117 at New York 120, 2OT
Mar. 27: New York 106 at Baltimore 99
Mar. 29: Baltimore 127 at New York 113
Mar. 31: New York 92 at Baltimore 102
Apr. 2: Baltimore 80 at New York 101
Apr. 5: New York 87 at Baltimore 96
Apr. 6: Baltimore 114 at New York 127

WESTERN DIVISION
DIVISION FINALS
Los Angeles 4, Atlanta 0
Apr. 12: Los Angeles 119 at Atlanta 115

Apr. 14: Los Angeles 105 at Atlanta 94
Apr. 16: Atlanta 114 at Los Angeles 115, OT
Apr. 19: Atlanta 114 at Los Angeles 133

DIVISION SEMI-FINALS
Atlanta 4, Chicago 1
Mar. 25: Chicago 111 at Atlanta 129
Mar. 28: Chicago 104 at Atlanta 124
Mar. 31: Atlanta 106 at Chicago 101
Apr. 3: Atlanta 120 at Chicago 131
Apr. 5: Chicago 107 at Atlanta 113

Los Angeles 4, Phoenix 3
Mar. 25: Phoenix 112 at Los Angeles 128
Mar. 29: Phoenix 114 at Los Angeles 101
Apr. 2: Los Angeles 98 at Phoenix 112
Apr. 4: Los Angeles 102 at Phoenix 112
Apr. 5: Phoenix 121 at Los Angeles 138
Apr. 7: Los Angeles 104 at Phoenix 93
Apr. 9: Phoenix 94 at Los Angeles 129

NBA LEADERS

SCORING

	GP	FGM	FTM	PTS	PPG
Jerry West, LAL	74	831	647	2309	31.2
Lew Alcindor, MIL	82	938	485	2361	28.8
Elvin Hayes, SDR	82	914	428	2256	27.5
Billy Cunningham, PHI	81	802	510	2114	26.1
Lou Hudson, ATL	80	830	371	2031	25.4
Connie Hawkins, PHO	81	709	577	1995	24.6
Bob Rule, SEA	80	789	387	1965	24.6
John Havlicek, BOS	81	736	488	1960	24.2
Earl Monroe, BAL	82	695	532	1922	23.4
Dave Bing, DET	70	575	454	1604	22.9

FIELD GOALS

	FGM	FGA	FG%
Johnny Green, CIN	481	860	.559
Darrall Imhoff, PHI	430	796	.540
Lou Hudson, ATL	830	1564	.531
Jon McGlocklin, MIL	639	1206	.530
Dick Snyder, PHO/SEA	456	863	.528
Jim Fox, PHO	413	788	.524
Lew Alcindor, MIL	938	1810	.518
Wes Unseld, BAL	526	1015	.518
Walt Frazier, NYK	600	1158	.518
Dick Van Arsdale, PHO	592	1166	.508

FREE THROWS

	FTM	FTA	FT%
Flynn Robinson, MIL	439	489	.898
Chet Walker, CHI	483	568	.850
Jeff Mullins, SFW	320	378	.847
John Havlicek, BOS	488	578	.844
Bob Love, CHI	442	525	.842
Earl Monroe, BAL	532	641	.830
Lou Hudson, ATL	371	450	.824
Jerry West, LAL	647	785	.824
Hal Greer, PHI	352	432	.815
Gail Goodrich, PHO	488	604	.808

ASSISTS

	GP	AST	APG
Lenny Wilkens, SEA	75	683	9.1
Walt Frazier, NYK	77	629	8.2
Clem Haskins, CHI	82	624	7.6
Jerry West, LAL	74	554	7.5
Gail Goodrich, PHO	81	605	7.5
Mahdi Abdul-Rahman, ATL	82	561	6.8
John Havlicek, BOS	81	550	6.8
Art Williams, SDR	80	503	6.3
Norm Van Lier, CIN	81	500	6.2
Dave Bing, DET	70	418	6.0

REBOUNDS

	GP	TRB	RPG
Elvin Hayes, SDR	82	1386	16.9
Wes Unseld, BAL	82	1370	16.7
Lew Alcindor, MIL	82	1190	14.5
Bill Bridges, ATL	82	1181	14.4
Gus Johnson, BAL	78	1086	13.9
Willis Reed, NYK	81	1126	13.9
Billy Cunningham, PHI	81	1101	13.6
Tom Boerwinkle, CHI	81	1016	12.5
Paul Silas, PHO	78	916	11.7
Clyde Lee, SFW	82	929	11.3

THE YEAR IN BASKETBALL

October 18, 1969 Lew Alcindor (later known as Kareem Abdul-Jabbar) makes his professional debut by scoring 29 points, grabbing 12 rebounds, and handing out six assists as his Milwaukee Bucks post a 119-110 win.

November 15, 1969 Off to the best start in NBA history, the Knicks best the Celtics, 113-98, to bring their record to 17-1.

November 28, 1969 The Knicks break an NBA record with their 18th consecutive win. The victory comes when New York rallies late in the final quarter. Bob Cousy, the Royals' coach, inserts himself into the game in the final minutes but cannot thwart the Knicks' victory.

December 22, 1969 Pete Maravich makes 30 of 31 foul shots to set an NCAA record and scores 46 points to lead LSU over Georgia, 98-89.

February 6, 1970 The NBA adds three more franchises—Buffalo, Cleveland, and Portland—to the league, swelling the number of teams to 17, nearly twice what it was a decade earlier.

February 21, 1970 Kentucky overcomes Pete Maravich's 64 points as Dan Issel scores 51, to lead the Wildcats to a 121-105 win over LSU.

March 4, 1970 Jacksonville becomes the first major college basketball team to average over 100 points a game, as they close their regular season with a 101-97 win over Miami (Fla.).

March 7, 1970 Austin Carr of Notre Dame scores a record 61 points as the Irish beat Ohio State, 112-82, in a first-round NCAA tourney game.

March 19, 1970 Pete Maravich is "held" to 20 points as his LSU Tigers lose to Marquette, 101-79, in the NIT semifinals in Maravich's last college game. For the third successive year Maravich sets an all-time college basketball single-season scoring record. In this, his senior year, he scores 1,381 points, to average 44.5 points per game. In three years at LSU, "Pistol Pete" averaged 44.2 points per game, scoring a record 3,667 points. Marquette goes on to win the NIT title, beating St. John's in the final, 65-53. Dean Meminger is named the tournament's MVP.

March 21, 1970 UCLA beats Jacksonville, 80-69, for its fourth consecutive NCAA championship. Curtis Rowe scores 19 points and Sidney Wicks adds 17 points and grabs 18 rebounds as the Bruins' defense forces Artis Gilmore into a 9-for-29 shooting performance.

April 12, 1970 The Indiana Pacers set an ABA team-scoring record in a 177-135 romp over Pittsburgh. Eight Pacers score in double-figures, led by John Barnhill's 31 points, as Indiana racks up a record 43 assists.

April 21, 1970 Bob Cousy and Bob Pettit are inducted into the Basketball Hall of Fame.

April 29, 1970 The Knicks defeat the Lakers, 111-108, in overtime in Game 3 of the NBA finals. New York overcomes Jerry West's sensational shot from beyond half court that sends the game into overtime. The win gives New York a two-games-to-one lead in the series.

May 8, 1970 The New York Knicks win their first NBA title by beating the Lakers, 113-99, in Game 7 of the NBA finals. Willis Reed, the Knicks' injured captain, limps dramatically on to the court during pre-game warm-ups to inspire both his teammates and the Madison Square Garden crowd. Then Reed hits his first two shots and the Knicks go on to victory. Walt Frazier leads New York with 36 points and has 19 assists in the win.

May 25, 1970 Led by Roger Brown's 45 points, the Indiana Pacers defeat the Los Angeles Stars, 111-107, to win the ABA championship.

Chapter 9

The NBA's First African-Americans

By Kenneth Shouler

When Earl Lloyd walked onto the court of Edgerton Park Sports Arena in Rochester, New York, on October 31, 1950, he became the first African-American player ever to appear in an NBA game. He was playing for the Washington Capitols in their season opener against the Royals. "I stepped onto the court and the world kept spinning," Lloyd said, recalling the moment in a matter-of-fact tone. "No one said a word—fans, players, anybody. Nothing was ever said about me being the first black. They acted as if I was a player, period. I don't recall any mention in the newspapers about me being the first black to play in an NBA game." He grabbed a game-high 10 rebounds, the Caps lost 78-70, and the world kept right on spinning.

"It's amazing, but it was fairly uneventful," continued Lloyd, the only living member of the pioneering African-American trio that integrated the NBA in the fall of 1950. "Rochester was a place where the school system was already integrated." He recalled that the Capitols offered him a salary of $5,000 after they drafted him the previous spring. "I signed immediately—$5,000 for a rookie! That was for six months work, so you were making more than a whole bunch of people."

While Lloyd was the first black player to actually play on an NBA court, he was not the first to sign. That distinction belonged to Nat Clifton. On May 25, 1950, five months before Lloyd's historic appearance, a one-column headline in *The New York Times* sports pages read:

CLIFTON, NEGRO ACE, GOES
TO KNICKERBOCKER FIVE

The inconspicuous three-paragraph article, in the back of the sports pages, was lost between vacation ads for "Golf at the Concord in Kiamesha Lake, New York" and "Grossinger's Country Club." The very sparseness of the article was perfectly in tune with the perceived insignificance of this event.

"It wasn't that momentous," confirmed Leonard Lewin, who began covering the basketball beat for the *New York Post* in 1946. "It was relatively insignificant."

Clifton joined the Knicks after playing with the New York Renaissance (or "Rens") and the Harlem Globetrotters, both all-black teams. The Knicks had purchased his contract from the Globetrotters for $10,000. Of that, Clifton saw $2,500.

Earl Lloyd, 1958
Lloyd, background, joins teammate Bob Hopkins (9) in doing what a lot of folks did when Bill Russell was about—hope for a bounce and a rare rebound.

"For me, that was a lot of money," he said later. In fact, only five players in the NBA were making five-digit salaries at the time, with the highest salary being the $17,500 paid to George Mikan, the star center of the Minneapolis Lakers. The following fall, on November 4, Clifton would become only the third black player to set foot on an NBA court.

The second black player to suit up, and first ever drafted, was Charles Cooper. A graduate of Duquesne, where he had been named All-American several times, Cooper was drafted by

the Boston Celtics on April 25, 1950, and made his first appearance in an NBA game against Fort Wayne on November 1, 1950, one day after Lloyd played his first contest. Because the Capitols played their season opener a day before both the Celtics and Knicks did, Lloyd was the first to play. "I don't think a scheduling quirk should detract from Cooper," the modest Lloyd told the *Detroit Free Press* in 1992.

Despite the threesome's pioneering achievements, Lloyd was right: their entry into the league barely raised the dust.

Why was the NBA's integration so downright uneventful? One reason was that in the early 1950s, basketball, especially professional basketball, trailed far behind baseball in popularity. "In 1950, basketball was almost a nonentity," Lloyd remembered.

Jackie Robinson and the integration of Major League Baseball had come and gone. Lloyd, Cooper, and Clifton were blazing a trail, but Robinson had already cleared away the brush. It wasn't until April 15, 1947 that Jackie Robinson played his first game for the Brooklyn Dodgers. Nothing put that unconscionably late date in perspective so much as the action of a black protester who attended a game at Yankee Stadium in New York in 1946. "If we can stop bullets, why not balls?" read the man's banner. So even though the NBA was not integrated until three years and six months after baseball, the overdue integration of the National Pastime had deflected all the attention from basketball.

Baseball had drawn all the slings and arrows, receiving criticism from management, writers, players, and fans who opposed segregation. Then, too, the pinnacle of baseball achievement and its most popular forum was the Major Leagues; in 1950, basketball's most celebrated stage was not NBA hardwood.

Casual fans and aficionados of the hoops game had choices. They could watch any number of powerful college teams or follow the best barnstorming teams in the world, the New York Rens and the Harlem Globetrotters. The Rens were so good that during the 1930s and 1940s they barnstormed across America and compiled a 2,588-529 won-lost record. In 1948 they barely lost to the Minneapolis Lakers in the Chicago World Tournament, the highest-level competition of the time. Clifton scored 24 points for the Rens, but Mikan poured in 40 as Minneapolis won, 75-71.

The Trotters could also play the game at an exquisite level. In February 1950 they beat the Lakers in a hard-fought 61-59 game. The result showed that they could play the game straight, without their patented tricks and clowning. They were at their zenith in talent, with outstanding players like Marques Haynes and Goose Tatum. While not the Trotters' best player, Clifton was talented, amiable, and fit in well with the team's showy routines. And in Abe Saperstein the Trotters had a savvy owner who knew how to make the turnstiles click by playing to the crowd.

Meanwhile, NBA basketball—and the Basketball Association of America (BAA) and National Basketball League (NBL) before it—had not captured the public's fancy. Attendance at games was sparse. Before Lloyd, Clifton and Cooper began their careers, many league officials thought that bringing black players in might cause a further decline in white patronage. In hindsight, that hypothesis looks remarkably

wrongheaded these days. Today more than 85 percent of NBA players are black, while league attendance is at its peak. But luring patrons was different a half century ago, and owners, perhaps with justification, thought that a team with black players would fail to draw.

Pro basketball in general was tottering on a precipice. Between 1947 and 1951 NBA franchises in Cleveland, Detroit, Pittsburgh, Toronto, Providence, Chicago, and St. Louis folded. Washington also went bust on January 9, 1951, 34 games after Lloyd made his historic debut. The team had compiled a 10-25 record and was struggling at the gate. After spending part of the 1951 campaign and all of the following season in the Army, Lloyd was picked up by Syracuse for the 1952-53 season. Not all of his former Washington teammates were as fortunate: Chuck Gilmur, Ed Bartels, and several other Capitols never played again after the team folded.

To assist attendance, NBA arenas often staged doubleheaders with one pro game and one Trotters game. Ticket sales soared. "In the first five years of the NBA, the Globetrotters helped carry the league," said Dolph Schayes, a Hall of Famer and Lloyd's teammate when he played with Syracuse. "They drew fans that weren't into basketball. They came for the entertainment and then maybe stayed around to watch the NBA game after the Globetrotters. I played in games where the arena was packed for the Globetrotters in the opener, then we took the court for the NBA game and half the fans left. And it is very true that Abe Saperstein did a lot for black players when no one else would give them the time of day. But when the NBA started to sign blacks, Abe was so upset that he stopped playing doubleheaders with some of the franchises."

Harvey Pollack, then the PR man for the Philadelphia Warriors, confirms Schayes's point. "I was at doubleheaders in places such as Fargo, North Dakota, where the NBA game was the preliminary game, then the Globetrotters played the nightcap. Saperstein cut the NBA teams in on the gate almost from the goodness of his heart, and we'd make more from the game than we would from one of our own home games."

So NBA owners had to consider if signing black players was worth the risk of losing the Globetrotter revenues. Why bite Saperstein's hand when it was the only one feeding them?

At an owners' meeting in Chicago on April 25, 1950, Celtics owner Walter Brown selected Cooper in the second round of the college draft. One of the other owners said, "Walter, don't you know he's a Negro?" Brown responded, "I don't give a damn if he's striped, plaid, or polka-dot! Boston takes Chuck Cooper of Duquesne!" Informed of Brown's selection, Saperstein threatened to boycott the Boston Garden. Brown's response to the threat was swift. "[Saperstein] is out of the Boston Garden now, as far as I'm concerned!" he said. "It would be different if we were signing an established Globetrotter." For his part, Cooper sent Brown a telegram that read: "Thank you for having the courage to offer me a chance in pro basketball. I hope I'll never give you cause to regret it."

Although Brown was the first owner to draft a black player, Knicks owner Ned Irish was the first to actually sign one—Nat Clifton, nicknamed "Sweetwater" for his insatiable love of soda pop. "My friends couldn't get over how much of that stuff I drank, so they started calling me Sweetwater," he told the *New*

York Post. Like Jackie Robinson, who had played in the Negro National League for several years before breaking into the white pros, Clifton had played pro ball with the Globetrotters and was 28 by the time he played his first NBA game.

At 6-foot-7 and 225 pounds, Clifton was already a star. Often shown palming a ball in each hand in publicity photos, he played with razzle-dazzle—a Globetrotter prerequisite—and was a great leaper. Cal Ramsey, a former pro and currently the New York Knicks' director of special projects, remembered that "Clifton was a great post player. He had honed his skills with the Trotters." He also recalled Clifton excelling on fast breaks, and how his large hands allowed him to play tricks with the ball.

"Clifton was more the modern black player," said Nelson George, author of Elevating the Game. "He was a precursor of players with flash and real vertical games."

His basketball experience was richer than either Cooper's or Lloyd's. After graduating Xavier in Louisiana, Clifton served in Europe with the Army's all-black 369th Battalion from 1944 to 1947. "All we were allowed to do was deliver supplies," Clifton said of his role in the Army, which anticipated what he felt was his limited role in the NBA. He then joined the Dayton Metropolitans, an integrated team of three blacks and nine whites. He moved from Dayton to the Harlem Rens for about six months before settling in Chicago with the Trotters in late 1947.

Clifton became a key member of the Knicks teams that made five consecutive playoff appearances and three straight trips to the NBA Finals in the early 1950s. He led the Knicks in rebounding for the 1951-52 season, with 11.8 boards per game, good enough for seventh in the NBA. "That was game, my strength, getting inside," he told the *New York Post.* "A rugged rebounder—that's how they wrote about me mostly."

The comment suggests some displeasure with his role on the court. Clifton once told reporters that NBA fans never saw his best game. He said he could have scored more and been a more colorful player, but he felt that the NBA wanted him to stick to fundamental basketball. "When I first came to the Knicks I found I had to change over, you know," he said. "They didn't want me to do anything fancy... What I was supposed to do is rebound and play defense. I wanted to play ball like they do now," he said in 1990. "Guess I was born 30 years too soon."

Clifton's remarks were echoed by Dolph Schayes, who had teamed with Earl Lloyd at Syracuse. "Earl got the short end of the stick as far as playing was concerned; he was always doing the dirty work," Schayes told the *Detroit Free Press* in 1992. "He helped me a great deal, because with him in there, I was free to rebound and get a lot of glory, since his game was to guard the other team's offensive ace."

Cooper, too, felt that he had to compromise his game. "The major things I had to adjust to upon entering the pros," he told the *Amsterdam News* in 1978, "was the stationary pivot. In college, with my size and agility, I liked to go down low and utilize that space, but in the pros a big man in the pivot would clog that area." Cooper also complained that his career was marred by coaching decisions that limited his offensive role.

Cooper played for six years in the NBA. He was a contributor in his first season. The 6-foot-5, 215-pounder scored 9.3 points per game, placing him fourth on the team behind Ed Macauley (20.4), Bob Cousy (15.6), and Sidney Hertzberg (9.8). His 8.5 rebounding average was second only to Macauley's. The Celtics improved by 17 games and finished second in the division with a 39-30 mark. Cooper never exceeded the promise of those rookie averages. But his pioneering contributions to the game were noted: at age 24 he was listed in *Who's Who in Colored America.*

Lloyd enjoyed a longer career than either Clifton or Cooper. Despite a two-year stint with the Army, he played six seasons with Syracuse, including the championship campaign in 1955. "The Big Cat," as Lloyd was called for his quick, aggressive defense and rebounding, enjoyed his best year in 1955, contributing 10.2 points and 7.7 rebounds a game during the Nats' title season. He played his last two years with the Detroit Pistons. At 32, he thought it was time to get out, since Wilt Chamberlain had entered the league for the 1959-60 season, Lloyd's last.

While Clifton, Cooper and Lloyd had varying roles on the court, all three claimed fair treatment from their teammates. Said Lloyd, "I never had problems with other NBA players. I never got called a name by a player. The guy who was the hero to all of the black basketball players was Jackie Robinson. He blazed the trail. With Jackie, they dropped black cats, spiked him, insulted him. Joe Louis came around when black folks couldn't do anything but he became a hero beating up white folks. Basketball players were college people. If they did harbor any racial prejudice, they were smart enough to keep it to themselves."

Bob Cousy remembers Cooper. "Red [Auerbach, the Boston coach] treated Chuck Cooper like he would any new player and we treated him the same way. He showed us that he could help on the court and he was a great guy to be around. He wasn't singled out—he got a fair chance and then he proved himself." Cooper, for his part, remembered Cousy with the same kindness. "Cousy is about as free of the affliction of racism as any white person I've ever known," he once said. Red Auerbach recalls, "Our players didn't give a damn what color Cooper was. Cousy roomed with him and so did Bones McKinney. He had no problem with anyone on our team."

But while teammates were receptive to their black comrades, many NBA cities were not. The NBA's early black players had no easy time of it. They were separated from their white teammates and routinely shuttled to black hotels in Baltimore and Washington. In Indianapolis black players were permitted to stay in the same hotel as the white players, but could not eat in the hotel's restaurants. When their teams played exhibition games in southern cities, black players usually stayed at home. Snubbed by many eateries on the road, Lloyd recalls eating more than his share of room-service meals in hotel rooms. Among his dining partners was Horace "Bones" McKinney, who was a player-coach for Washington during Lloyd's first season, before finishing the year with Boston. "He knew and I knew we weren't going to change things immediately, and it was important to know he was in my corner."

Even a decade later, in the fall of 1959, Cal Ramsey encountered prejudice. A graduate of New York University, Ramsey was then playing for the St. Louis Hawks. One night he went

to the Sheraton Jefferson Hotel in St. Louis. "I went to get a steak and a baked potato," he recalled, but was not allowed to eat it on the premises. "They ordered me to 'take it out.' Another time I went with Sihugo Green, my idol, to another St. Louis hotel for a pregame meal. We had to eat our meal in a back room, partitioned off from the main dining room." Ramsey also remembered that two of his star teammates, Cliff Hagan and Bob Pettit—southerners who were reputed to be prejudiced—would often invite him out to dinner with them.

Each of the three players enjoyed a full life after their careers. After retiring from the NBA, Cooper joined Marques Haynes's Harlem Magicians for a few years. An auto accident in the late '50s led to his retirement. In the years between the end of his career and his death at the age of 57 in February 1984, Cooper made a comfortable life for himself as a Pittsburgh businessman. At age 35, Clifton played his eighth and last year with Detroit, one season before reuniting with Haynes and Tatum for four years with the Harlem Magicians. His NBA career averages were impressive for the time—10 points and 8.2 rebounds per game, while playing nearly 30 minutes a night. Ironically, he ended his career back with the Trotters. Clifton played for Abe Saperstein until 1965, when, at 42, his career was ended by a knee injury. Then he drove a cab in his hometown of Chicago, where he lived with his mother, son, and daughter. On August 31, 1990, while driving his cab, he suffered a fatal heart attack; he died that day in a hospital emergency room at age 67.

Just before Clifton died, Cal Ramsey remembered being with him. "He said, 'Cal, people think that I'm destitute because I drive a cab. But I own several cabs and live in a big house in Chicago.'" "He was a prince," said Lloyd. "Anybody who didn't like Sweets had a problem. He didn't bother nobody and nobody would bother him." Dick McGuire, Clifton's

teammate on the Knicks, laughs recalling Sweetwater. "He was a great guy, a card player. He never got out of a pot, what you call a chaser. If you had four aces, he'd stay in. He had big hands, palmed the ball, shot the ball with no rotation, very strong. People liked him. He had a very, very nice way about him."

Lloyd became an assistant coach with the Pistons in the early 1970s before going on to work for the Detroit Board of Education. "I was the administrator of skills training programs for public school kids from low income families," he recalls. "With the training they had to sell themselves." Many of his closest friends didn't know of his earlier accomplishment as a basketball player until the 1980s, when his name appeared as an answer on the television show Jeopardy.

Even Pistons' great Isiah Thomas, a true student of the game, didn't know who Lloyd was. "I never heard of him," Thomas told the *Free Press*. "But tell him I said thanks for the opportunity."

After retiring from that job in 1993, Lloyd's been coordinating community relations for the Bing Group, four companies owned by Hall of Fame Detroit guard Dave Bing, who in 1996 was named by the NBA as one of the best 50 players of all time.

While neither Lloyd, Clifton nor Cooper were Hall of Fame players, they all paved the way for the growth of the NBA. The first great black players—Bill Russell, Elgin Baylor, Wilt Chamberlain and Oscar Robertson—got their starts between 1956 and 1960. But Cooper, Clifton and Lloyd remind us of the game's humble origins and of how difficult things were for black players in the fledgling years of NBA basketball.

In September 2003, Lloyd's long journey was recognized by his induction into the Naismith Memorial Basketball Hall of Fame as a contributor.

THE NBA'S FIRST AFRICAN-AMERICANS

1st year – 1950-51
Nat "Sweetwater" Clifton, New York Knickerbockers*
Chuck Cooper, Boston Celtics*
Hank DeZonie, Tri-Cities Blackhawks*
Earl Lloyd, Washington Capitols*

1951-52
Don Barksdale, Baltimore Bullets*
Davage Minor, Baltimore Bullets
Bob Wilson, Milwaukee Hawks

1952-53
Blaine Denning, Baltimore Bullets

1953-54
Ray Felix, Baltimore Bullets
Rollen Hans, Baltimore Bullets
Isaac "Rabbit" Walthour, Milwaukee Hawks

1954-55
Bobby Knight, New York Knickerbockers
Ken McBride, Milwaukee Hawks
Jackie Moore, Philadelphia Warriors*
Jim Tucker, Syracuse Nationals*

1955-56
Jesse Arnelle, Fort Wayne Pistons*
Walter Dukes, New York Knickerbockers
Ed Fleming, Rochester Royals*
Dick Ricketts, Rochester Royals
Maurice Stokes, Rochester Royals
Bob Williams, Minneapolis Lakers*

1956-57
John Barber, St. Louis Hawks
Sihugo Green, Rochester Royals
Bob Hopkins, Syracuse Nationals
Hal Lear, Philadelphia Warriors
Willie Naulls, New York Knickerbockers
Bill Russell, Boston Celtics

1957-58
George R. Brown, Minneapolis Lakers
McCoy Ingram, Minneapolis Lakers
Sam Jones, Boston Celtics
Worthy Patterson, St. Louis Hawks
Woody Sauldsberry, Philadelphia Warriors

1958-59
Elgin Baylor, Minneapolis Lakers
Alex "Boo" Ellis, Minneapolis Lakers
Wayne Embry, Cincinnati Royals
Hal Greer, Syracuse Nationals
Andy Johnson, Philadelphia Warriors
K.C. Jones, Boston Celtics
Shellie McMillon, Detroit Pistons
Guy Rodgers, Philadelphia Warriors
Ben Swain, Boston Celtics

1959-60
Dick Barnett, Syracuse Nationals
Wilt Chamberlain, Philadelphia Warriors
Johnny Green, New York Knickerbockers
Tom Hawkins, Minneapolis Lakers
Maurice King, Boston Celtics
Cal Ramsey, New York Knickerbockers

* first African-American player with franchise

Chapter 10

The Great Wave of Talent: The '50s and '60s

By Sam Smith

Red Auerbach saw them all. He was there when it all began for the National Basketball Association in the 1940s, then as coach with the old Washington Capitols and the Tri-City Blackhawks, and for the rest of the century a coach, general manager, president and advisor for the Boston Celtics.

So one day just after the turn of the century, early in the year 2000, Auerbach was asked about what is generally regarded as the greatest basketball team ever assembled, the 1992 U.S. Olympic "Dream Team" with Michael Jordan, Magic Johnson, Larry Bird, Karl Malone, Charles Barkley, John Stockton and David Robinson. It was an awesome array of talent at what was perhaps the peak of the golden era of pro basketball in the U.S.

Auerbach merely sniffed.

"They may have been a little more spectacular," the great sage of the Celtics remarked, "but nobody is going to tell me that any team would beat a team with Bill Russell, Wilt Chamberlain, Elgin Baylor, Bob Pettit, Oscar Robertson, and Jerry West."

And nobody probably would, because even at the very adolescence of the NBA, there was an explosion of talent that effectively saved and established pro basketball in the U.S. and started it on the road to the major sports status and glamour game it would become. It was not unlike the wave of immigration throughout the 19th Century and into the 20th Century that helped turn the United States from a modest agrarian nation to a world superpower. Its borders were opened, and great talent fused with established natural resources to produce a nation to be admired and envied.

It was much the same with the NBA when the walls of racism and ignorance began to collapse and black players were welcomed in the NBA along with white players. It was, in effect, the beginning of basketball as we know it now, a graceful game of great beauty and unusual individuality, like a jazz band. Pro basketball had long been a much choreographed game with players executing precision movements in a team structure. It could be effective, but was not necessarily entertaining.

But then came Russell, and Chamberlain and Baylor—then Robertson, Willis Reed, Gus Johnson, Walt Bellamy and Earl Monroe. With West and Rick Barry, John Havlicek, Jerry Lucas and Pettit, basketball never would be the same. It was a collection of talent so astounding that it changed the way the game would be played, and no group since then could claim that.

Rules were changed because Chamberlain so dominated the offensive game and strategies were reconsidered because Russell so dominated the defensive game. No one had ever seen a

Earl Monroe, 1968
Powering past Knicks' Walt Frazier during Baltimore's remarkable Cinderella season of 1968-69, in which they went from last to first.

player glide in the air and seem to be suspended like Baylor, and no one had ever seen a guard so powerful and complete as Robertson. The NBA even took the visage of West and made it the logo symbol of the league. Gus Johnson became the model for the athletic power forwards for the next 40 years. And Monroe would follow Bob Cousy by effectively popularizing the school yard, street-type game that enchanted audiences. These players were magicians with the basketball, though also fundamentally sound and intelligent. They were strong and

athletic, blessed with individual skills and team abilities.

It truly was the beginning of the NBA's golden age.

Although there were great white players at the time—and would continue to be players like West, Havlicek, Pettit and Barry—it was the influence of the black players that made basketball whole, as racial unity does for society in general. Not that it was much expected in those times.

Major league baseball was integrated in 1947 by Jackie Robinson and the Brooklyn Dodgers. But it wouldn't be until the 1950-51 season that the NBA welcomed its first black players. Chuck Cooper of Duquesne was the first black player to be drafted, and went to the Boston Celtics and Nat "Sweetwater" Clifton became the first black to sign an NBA contract when he went from the Harlem Globetrotters to the New York Knicks. And Earl Lloyd from West Virginia State was the first black to play in an NBA game when his Washington Capitols' team opened the season first.

None, though, had a major impact as the NBA, still without a shot clock, was a league dominated by players shooting two-handed and one-hand set shots in slow, patterned games. There also was a feeling among blacks, if not an outright rule, that there was a limitation on black players. Even into the 1960s, many black players felt there was a three-player limit of black players for many teams, and the fact that St. Louis was considered a southern city back then probably changed the course of history of pro sports. In fact, Russell was one of the few public critics of what he maintained was the NBA's covert racial discrimination policy of the 1950s. Bill Russell said the NBA's practice was to "put two black athletes in the game at home, put three on the road, and put five in when you get behind."

The St. Louis Hawks in 1956 had the chance to get Russell, who was the first black superstar, undoubtedly the game's greatest winner, and probably the player who marked the change in the way the game was played. Russell represented the first wave in a great ocean of talent rolling up on the NBA shores of the late 1950s.

Russell was a collegiate star at the University of San Francisco. With future teammate K.C. Jones, he led the Dons to two straight NCAA titles and 55 straight victories. He was a shot-blocking marvel. No one had seen anything like him before. He was skinny, and about 6-foot-10, but unusually quick with incredible timing. Blocked shots were uncommon in basketball at the time, and when shots were blocked they were simply swatted away. What Russell specialized in was changing the shot, and blocking a part of the ball. He could block the bottom of the ball so that the ball would go up in the air and to himself. He could then pitch out for a fast break. And as a result of the way Russell played for the Boston Celtics, their style became the blueprint for success in the NBA. Challenging an offensive player then was not a crucial part of the NBA game. Now it is the essence of the game and it is because of the way Russell played.

St. Louis had the second pick in that 1956 draft and it was becoming clear that Russell was the best player in college. But St. Louis was regarded as a southern city. Russell was uncertain about playing there and talked about playing for the Harlem Globetrotters, which was the principal stopping place for talented black basketball players of the era.

In fact, Abe Saperstein, who founded the Globetrotters in Illinois, wasn't exactly a booster of NBA integration. He did work a deal with the Knicks for Clifton in 1950. But Saperstein did have something of a monopoly on the great black talent of the era and didn't want to see it end, according to Auerbach.

Wayne Embry, who played for the Cincinnati Royals with Robertson in the late 1950s and later became one of the NBA's most respected executives and a member of the Basketball Hall of Fame, said it always was his dream to play for the Globetrotters. "Our aspirations were not to play in the NBA," recalled Embry. "You didn't see African-Americans in the NBA. What you wanted to do was play for the Globetrotters. There were no blacks in the NBA. You didn't know much about the NBA." Embry was drafted by St. Louis, but traded to Cincinnati before he could play a game there, but recalls on trips to St. Louis as a player in the late 1950s not being able to eat with the team at the team hotel. "We had to go across the tracks," Embry recalled.

In 1956 the Hawks didn't have a black player and there was talk Russell wanted a big contract, about $25,000 per season, which was unheard of at the time. St. Louis long had financial problems and would eventually move to Atlanta. So ownership was not anxious to meet Russell's financial demands and uncertain about the impact of a black man being the highest paid on a team in the South. Also, the decision became somewhat easier for St. Louis with word that Russell wouldn't be able to play the first part of the season because of his Olympic commitment. And there was a deal to be made. The Celtics' Ed Macauley was a St. Louis native and was eager to finish his career back home. He was one of the league's top scorers, averaging more than 20 points per game in two seasons. Plus, the Celtics had the rights to Kentucky star Cliff Hagan, who was coming out of the U.S. Army. It was a farsighted tactic of Auerbach's that would pay dividends in the future. (It was in 1978 that Auerbach drafted Larry Bird even though Bird said he would stay in college one more season and the Celtics had to sign him before the 1979 draft to keep him. So five teams passed on Bird, and the Celtics got him with the sixth pick and Bird went on to lead Boston to three more titles and become one of the great players in NBA history.)

As for Hagan, he would be used as one of the biggest chips in any NBA poker game. Not sure about taking Russell, the Hawks agreed to the deal for their No. 2 draft pick. The Celtics owned the No. 3 pick in that draft, but under rules extant at the time, they would surrender that pick for the "territorial" rights to Holy Cross star Tom Heinsohn. Attendance was weak in the NBA in that era and one way to boost attendance was to steer local talent to local teams through the so-called territorial draft.

But there still was Rochester with the No. 1 pick. They had Maurice Stokes, then one of the great rebounders in the game, and he would lead the NBA in rebounding in Russell's rookie season before eventually being forced out of the game early by disease after just three seasons in the NBA, all of which he was an All Star and never lower than second in the league in rebounding. The notion was Rochester needed scoring, so they selected Sihugo Green of Duquesne, a first team all-American and high scoring guard who didn't have a successful NBA

career. There also have been rumors for many years that the Celtics provided Rochester, which was soon to move to Cincinnati, a financial inducement for the struggling franchise. It was said that Celtics owner Walter Brown steered the profitable Ice Capades to Rochester for two years as an inducement for the Royals to pass on Russell.

Russell first went to the U.S. Olympic team in the games in Melbourne, Australia that fall and didn't join the Celtics until December. In 21 minutes in his first game he grabbed 16 rebounds and blocked three of Bob Pettit's shots. St. Louis quickly got a taste of that deal, though they would get a title by the next season and, for at least two years, it appeared as if they got a good deal. Players like high-scoring Neil Johnston, who used a hook shot to win three consecutive scoring titles in the early 1950s, found the staple of their offensive game riddled by Russell's laser quick reflexes and jumping. The Celtics, in a stunning seventh game of the NBA finals decided in double overtime, beat St. Louis for the NBA title in Russell's rookie season. Boston then lost to St. Louis in the finals the next season when Russell was injured and missed two games, and then set a standard that still exists in American professional sports with eight consecutive NBA titles.

And who would interrupt them, if only briefly? Wilt Chamberlain of course, then playing for the Philadelphia 76ers. Chamberlain once lamented he'd get to the championship and always lose to the Celtics, and in 1962 and 1965 Chamberlain with Philadelphia did lose seventh games of the Eastern Conference finals to Russell and the Celtics by two points and one point, respectively.

But if Russell changed the game with his defense, it was Chamberlain coming into the NBA in 1959 who changed the game with his offense.

Pro sports had never seen anything quite like Chamberlain. He was Babe Ruth. He brought the offense to the game of basketball that truly popularized the game, and possessed gargantuan appetites for records, women and fun that rivaled the great Bambino's. Certainly George Mikan was as dominant a center as basketball had ever seen. And, as with Chamberlain, the keepers of the game began to tinker with the rules to try to control him since no players could.

The league widened the foul lane from six to 12 feet to try to get Mikan farther from the basket. A similar tactic greeted Chamberlain when he came on the scene, as the lane was widened from 12 feet to its current 16 feet. One time the NBA even experimented with a 12-foot high basket (instead of the normal 10 feet) in a regular season game late in the 1953-54 season. But it didn't have much effect since Mikan still was the closest to the basket and still dominated.

Mikan came out of DePaul University in Chicago in 1946 to join the then rival to the NBA, the National Basketball League. The forerunner to the NBA was the Basketball Association of America, but Mikan rejected the Chicago Stags of that league and went with the older, more established NBL. But Mikan fought his new team over contracts and when Mikan's Chicago Gears team was pulled out of the NBL, he signed with the Minneapolis Lakers of the BAA. Minneapolis would go on to five championships in six seasons with Mikan, the first great dynasty of the NBA, before Mikan retired after

the 1953-54 season at age 30. Basketball wasn't a lucrative profession in those days, and with a law degree Mikan figured to make much more money not playing basketball.

Russell, of course, was a great center, but not the kind of scorer that Mikan was. Mikan won the scoring title in 1949, 1950 and 1951 and was runner up in 1952 and 1953.

When Chamberlain came along he obliterated scoring records like Ruth obliterated the home run records of his day, hitting two and three times as many as the runner-up. Before Chamberlain came into the NBA, no player had ever averaged more than 30 points per game in a season. Chamberlain averaged 37.6 points per game as a rookie, raised that to 38.4 in his second season and then an astounding 50.4 points per game in his third season in the NBA. And in each of those seasons Chamberlain also set records for rebounding, averaging at least 27 rebounds per game his first two seasons in the NBA and then 25.7 per game in his third season. It also was during that season that Chamberlain established what figures to be one of the unbreakable records, like Joe DiMaggio's hit streak or Wayne Gretzky's scoring. Chamberlain scored 100 points against the Knicks on March 2, 1962 in a 169-147 win.

If Chamberlain's scoring feats seemed superhuman, so did he. He was tireless and relentless. In addition to dominating the scoring and rebounding, he never left the games. In the 1961-62 season, he averaged more than 48 minutes per game for the season by playing through all the overtimes. He actually sat out fewer than 10 minutes total for the entire season. And this was a time when travel was difficult, with no charter jets or elegant hotels. Teams often played three or four nights in a row and in barnstorming type games in smaller cities to help increase attendance. In fact, Chamberlain's 100-point game was played in Hershey, Pa., and after the game Chamberlain hitched a car ride to New York City with some of the players from the Knicks to be there for the next game.

And it was in that 1961-62 season that the talent explosion ignited a passion for the NBA game. Oscar Robertson, now in his second year out of the University of Cincinnati, averaged a triple double, another statistical marvel that hasn't since been approached. It is easy to forget about Robertson because TV had yet to catch up to pro basketball, but what Robertson was doing would never be approached by the great guards of the next era, like Magic Johnson and Michael Jordan. Robertson averaged 30.8 points, 12.5 rebounds and 11.4 assists per game for the entire season.

Even more overlooked that season was the top rookie, Walt Bellamy, from Indiana University. Another future Hall of Famer, Bellamy averaged 31.6 points and 19 rebounds per game as a rookie. It would have been one of the great seasons of all-time in the NBA if Bellamy hadn't finished in second place, more than 18 points per game behind league-leader Chamberlain. Bellamy's third-place slot in the rebounding race was almost seven per game behind Chamberlain and almost five per game behind Russell.

It was easy to be overlooked then with the giant Chamberlain casting a shadow of talent over the entire NBA. But there were bright spots all about and perhaps none brighter than the 1960 U.S. Olympic team, which was truly the first "Dream Team." That team was led by Robertson and included

Bellamy. But it also featured Jerry West, the high-scoring guard from the University of West Virginia. By his second season in the NBA, West averaged more than 30 points per game and was fifth in the league in scoring. Ten of the 12 members of that 1960 Olympic team would go on to play in the NBA, many as stars including Terry Dischinger, Jerry Lucas, Adrian Smith and Bob Boozer. That team rolled to eight easy wins, averaging more that 100 points per game and winning by an average margin of more than 40 points per game. It was an astounding performance and caught the eye of Americans not yet enamored by professional basketball.

With these players joining the likes of Chamberlain, Russell and Baylor in the NBA, professional basketball now had stars, rivalries and, in the Boston Celtics, a dynasty. All the pieces were starting to fall into place for a trip into the outer reaches of professional sports. Forget Sputnik and Mercury, the NBA was blasting off into its own unchartered territories.

But the players who made this possible, players like Chamberlain and Russell and Baylor and Robertson, never imagined growing up that they'd be the thrust to drive pro basketball's engine. Heck, they never even imagined being able to get on board.

And if they did, it would be in the back.

With African-Americans not permitted to play in major professional sports, teams of all black players, like the baseball Negro Leagues, emerged. In basketball, it was the New York Renaissance Five, better known as the Rens. And they became perhaps the elite professional basketball team in the nation. It would be almost 30 years before blacks would be welcomed into the NBA in great numbers, allowing for the blossoming of talent on the NBA's tree. But until then, the Rens, and later the Harlem Globetrotters, served as the inspiration.

Organized leagues from the 1920's through 1940s had difficulty surviving with failing ownerships, so the better teams barnstormed the country, though mostly in the East. They accepted challenges and played in tournaments. The Original Celtics, descended from the New York Celtics of the early 1910's, were the premier team of the 1920's, but by the 1930s they were eclipsed by the Rens. In 1933 it was the Celtics who ended an 88-game Rens' winning streak, but it was just one of eight games between the teams that season the Celtics won. The Rens were quick and ran a fast break much copied by the later Boston Celtics, who under Auerbach had the first all black starting five in the NBA with Russell, Sam Jones, K.C. Jones, Satch Saunders and Willie Naulls.

The Rens were a remarkable 112-7 in 1939 and won the tournament in Chicago of the best professional teams in the U.S., including the teams from the fledgling NBL, which eventually would be absorbed into the BAA for the merger in 1949 that created the NBA. The Rens finally disbanded after World War II with a record of 2,588 wins and 529 losses. In that 1939 tournament, the Rens also defeated the Globetrotters, who next year returned to win the tournament as it was growing clear that the all-black teams had remarkable talent that probably surpassed the all-white teams of the era. But Abe Saperstein, who founded and ran the Globetrotters, had other ideas for his team, which he turned into a world barnstorming troupe geared both for basketball and entertainment. Denied a chance

to play in the organized professional leagues like the NBL and BAA, stars like Goose Tatum and Marques Haynes joined the Globetrotters and sold out arenas around the world.

The Rens actually came out of Harlem in the borough of Manhattan in New York City and the Globetrotters would not play their first game in Harlem until 1968. Chicago had an all-black team in the 1920's called the Savoy Big Five, which was named for playing its games in the Savoy Ballroom on Sundays. Saperstein actually became involved as the black man who ran the Savoy Big Five found it hard to book his team on the road in what remained a most segregated country. So in 1927, Saperstein booked his team into Hinckley, Ill. for the first game of the new Harlem Globetrotters. It was a serious team then and went 361-32 its first three seasons. With black players barred or largely absent from the top pro leagues, the Globetrotters provided excellent basketball and entertainment, though not the measure of clowning they became famous for. NBA teams often were the first game with the Globetrotters the main event in double headers. The Globetrotters usually outplayed college all-star teams in exhibitions and even the NBA champion Minneapolis Lakers on one occasion. Sweetwater Clifton, a former Globetrotter, was the first black so-called "impact" player in the NBA and many of the prized additions to the pro game that are popular today, like the fast break, slam dunk, weave, behind-the-back pass and between-the-legs dribble, are credited to Globetrotters' teams over the years.

Even though the NBA began to sign a trickle of black players in the 1950s, playing for the Globetrotters still remained a prime option, and it's where Chamberlain went after his junior year at Kansas. College players were unable to join the NBA before their eligibility expired. So Chamberlain played one season for the Globetrotters before his much anticipated arrival with the Philadelphia Warriors.

Chamberlain was never the winner that Russell was, though the Celtics surrounded Russell with a virtual Hall of Fame of players. Chamberlain led the NBA in scoring his first seven years in the NBA and in rebounding in eight of his first 10. And to prove he could do just about anything, he would later lead the league in total assists. Chamberlain played on two championship teams, but they would go down as two of the greatest, most dominant teams in NBA history. His 1966-67 76ers were 68-13 and his 1971-72 Lakers were 69-13 with a record 33 straight victories.

When Chamberlain scored his 100 points in a game in 1962, it broke the league scoring record of 71 points that was held by another player who recently came into the fast integrating NBA, Elgin Baylor.

Baylor came out of Seattle University in 1958 and immediately began producing impressive scoring and rebounding totals, averaging 24.9 points and 15 rebounds, both in the top five in the league, in his rookie season. Baylor would have a 55-point game as a rookie, which already would be the third best scoring game in league history. By his third season, Baylor averaged 34.8 points and 19.8 rebounds and went to 38.3 per game the following season.

But it wasn't just the impressive statistics for this new group of players. They were redefining every position on the court and the way the game would be played. Russell, of course, became

the model for defensive play and Chamberlain was the offensive force non pareil. But they were centers, men who needed to either get the ball from someone else or knock it back at someone else to be effective.

Baylor took that a step farther. The 6-foot-5 forward effectively invented hang time. It was, of course, popularized by Connie Hawkins, Julius Erving and Michael Jordan. But it was Baylor who introduced the seemingly gravity-defying game to the NBA. It was Baylor who could take the ball to the basket, go up and over or around defenders. He was remarkably agile and strong, being able to both muscle players for rebounds and spring over them with a soft touch around the basket.

The game was getting a bounce, not only in popularity, but on the basketball court from players with great reflexes, speed, jumping ability and brilliant hand-eye coordination that enabled them to be strong and accurate.

Although the greatest impact was being delivered by the new era of African-American players who were getting a legitimate chance to play in the NBA, it wasn't only the influence of the black players that changed the game at the time. Jerry West was one of those new stars. He was often compared with Robertson since both graduated college the same year. He came into the NBA playing behind fellow West Virginian Hot Rod Hundley. But by his second season West averaged more than 30 points per game and became the so-called "two guard," the scoring guard that became the model for players in the NBA until Michael Jordan came along. Auerbach liked to say West was unstoppable. "Play him loose, close, keep him away from the ball. He still finds a way to get his 25 to 30 points," remarked Auerbach. It was how opponents would later describe the great Jordan. West wasn't the acrobat on the court that Jordan was, but he played as hard, was quick with a great shooting touch and an unyielding competitive spirit like that which defined Jordan.

Was West the perfect player? Someone at the NBA apparently thought so as when the league went looking for a logo figure to best express itself it drew up a player in mid-drive that most agreed precisely resembled West.

The turnover was now beginning, the changes underway. Before the 1962-63 season, Bob Cousy, the ball-handling wizard, said he would retire after the season, but the rookies who would be great kept coming. There was John Havlicek, Zelmo Beaty and Dave DeBusschere and Jerry Lucas in 1962, Nate Thurmond in 1963 and Willis Reed in 1964.

Reed lasted until the second round of the draft, which was just 10 picks then with just nine teams in the league. But it still was significant because another barrier was being removed that blocked the flow of talent into the NBA. It was the small, exclusively black colleges in the south. As the major southern universities began to open their doors to blacks in the late 1950s and early 1960s, the teams began to recruit some of the top black players. The thinking was that the smaller colleges, like Grambling, Winston Salem, Prairie View, Pan American and Tennessee A&I simply couldn't attract the talent that could succeed at an NBA level.

It also should be remembered that in that era there was little or no collegiate scouting in the NBA, something that had become a virtual science by the 1980s. Pro teams didn't even

have assistant coaches then, so few could afford to send scouts to watch collegiate talent, and those that would send observers didn't bother with the smaller schools. Teams relied on collegiate magazines and word of mouth from coaches about players. As remarkable as it seems now, teams purchased pre-season college preview magazines and often used it for their scouting. So a player like Reed could slip through the cracks, even though he would go on to be one of the top centers of his era and an inspiration for basketball players everywhere with his much replayed and related attempt to play the seventh game of the 1970 finals for the New York Knicks against the Lakers, an effort which inspired his team to go on to the championship.

But the mark players leave sometimes is not in their statistics or their legacy of championships. Often it is their impact on the game and how it changed because of them, like with Russell on defense, Chamberlain on offense, Baylor in the air, inventing the modern game, as some have suggested. Another pioneer was Earl Monroe.

Monroe would be selected as one of the best 50 players in the history of the NBA. He was on one NBA championship team, had a career average of 18.8 points per game, and wasn't a great rebounder or passer. But Monroe influenced a generation of players. He was the embodiment of the Harlem Globetrotters and the Rucker League in the NBA. He played for NAIA Winston Salem State in the mid-1960s after growing up in Philadelphia. Monroe legitimized playground basketball. Even as the game rolled into the 1960s with a vast improvement in the talent level, the game still resembled the structured play of the previous decade. It was quicker and more airborne, but hardly stylish, other than with a few exceptions, like Baylor. But Baylor did his human levitation act as a way to simply avoid the defense and score.

Monroe wasn't a great jumper or exceptionally fast, so he needed to employ misdirection to succeed. But Monroe also delighted in his tricks and stylish play, the first true jazz performer in the game that most resembles a great jazz band when it is at its best, making sweet music out of brilliant individual expression. Monroe's hallmarks were the hesitation dribble, the spin dribble, pump fakes, head fakes, shots from below the waist, from various angles, spinning the ball on his hand, dropping it up and down like it was a yoyo, but with no string.

There was a growing separation at the time of Monroe's arrival in the NBA in 1967. Those tricks and gimmicks were for the Globetrotters, the actors. The NBA was for the serious player, the intelligent player who studied plays and followed a pattern. Monroe's play obliterated all that. He was rookie of the year in 1968, averaging 24.3 points, 5.7 rebounds and 4.3 assists. He hit his career high of 25.8 per game the next season. He was a joy to watch and behold. He was a rare basketball player who brought the elements of showmanship and greatness to pro basketball: You couldn't turn away because you didn't know what you might miss. It would be much the same in later years with Dr. J., Julius Erving, and his astonishing slam dunking and graceful flights all the way through Michael Jordan's air time and hang time. Monroe didn't dunk and he didn't hang in the air. But he was no less thrilling and entertaining to watch.

A few years earlier, a skinny kid from the University of

Miami named Rick Barry came into the NBA, and he probably is the most underrated superstar in the history of the league. Some of that is due to his penchant for changing leagues from the NBA to the ABA and back to the NBA, for missing a season as a result, for being in court, for being out of order when he was on the court, basketball, that is. Barry was a demanding person who one might say suffered no fools. Those included his teammates. But he has to rank with Larry Bird, Bob Pettit and Elgin Baylor as one the best forwards ever to play the game.

Barry is most remembered as a great scorer, and he did lead the NBA in scoring in his second season, averaging 35.6 per game. This was after a rookie season in which Barry averaged 25.7 points and more than 10 rebounds per game. And Barry was regarded as perhaps the second best passing forward ever behind Larry Bird. He was one of the best shooters in the history of the game, shooting 90 percent for his career from the free throw line, and he had great range. He played before the three-point shot was accepted in the NBA, and would have averaged several points per game more given the range he routinely shot from. He even led the NBA in steals one season, the calling card for the great defenders. And Barry was a big-game player, increasing his scoring average from the regular season to the playoffs in his NBA and ABA years, winning an MVP and a championship in the ABA as well as an NBA championship. That second NBA season when he led the league in scoring, Barry was a marvel in the NBA Finals against the team, the Philadelphia 76ers, that some regard as the greatest ever after its 68-13 regular season record. The Sixers went on to win the NBA championship, but Barry almost overshadowed it by averaging 41 per game in the series and 44 in a losing effort in the final game. Barry won his NBA championship in 1975 in leading a seemingly hopelessly undermanned and underdog Golden State team to a four-game sweep of the more powerful Washington Bullets by averaging 29.5 per game. That gave Barry an all-time record average of 36 points per game in NBA Finals' games.

So go ahead and make your list of the greatest players in the history of the NBA. Sure, Michael Jordan will be on that list and so will Magic Johnson, Larry Bird and Kareem Abdul-Jabbar. But there's a good chance the rest of the top 10 would come from that period in the late 1950s and early 1960s when the integration finally overran the game. There was a greater pool of talent to choose from, and undoubtedly the increasing level of competition improved the game for all the players.

Fill out the remainder of that top-10 list. Wilt Chamberlain and Bill Russell have to be there, and they have to remain the top two centers in the history of the NBA. Abdul-Jabbar scored more points, but no one, even 40 years later, has had the impact and effect on the game that Russell and Chamberlain did. No one has ever been a better defensive player than Russell and no one has ever been a better offensive player than Chamberlain.

Has there ever been a better guard than Robertson? It is generally agreed it has to be Jordan, who overwhelmed the game with his unique individual ability and Russell's competitiveness. But no one, not even Jordan, has been as multi-faceted as Robertson. He scored, rebounded and created assists in double digits per game like no one ever has. And few have scored like West, other than Jordan. He was a machine, a brilliant competitor like Russell and Jordan and so influential as to be the model for what an NBA guard should be. Jordan and Johnson now are regarded as the two top guards in NBA history. But going against a backcourt of Robertson and West would make for a heck of a match.

Many now say Bird is the best of the forwards, an all-around performer and winner. But who comes next? Probably Baylor, maybe Pettit, or Barry. That's three of the top four coming in by the mid-1960s, and Julius Erving shortly thereafter. And there were more, like Walt Bellamy, Jerry Lucas, John Havlicek, Dave DeBusschere. Nate Thurmond, Gus Johnson, Billy Cunningham, Jerry Sloan and Dave Bing, all coming into the NBA by the mid-1960s, effectively setting the period from Russell's emergence to Monroe's as the greatest decade in NBA history. It has been much said that the 1980s, which recreated the great Boston Celtics-Los Angeles Lakers rivalry and brought Jordan and the Chicago Bulls to the American consciousness, was the golden era of the NBA. But, truly, there's been nothing to rival the great wave of talent from the mid-1950s to mid-1960s. It changed the game of professional basketball forever. It was a Renaissance of artists, painters and sculptors and musicians of their sport who were creating not only masterpieces, but establishing the rules and methods for those to follow for years to come. It was a time that will be looked back on by scholars of the sport for its influences for ages.

Like the 15th and 16th centuries of the cultural Renaissance, this time was a transition from a medieval to a modern form of the sport. Gone would be the gothic style of basketball of two-handed set shots, bruising, physical play and low-scoring, dull affairs. Scoring never would be higher. Remarkable feats would occur that never would be matched. Names would become legend, and need only a mention to stir images of greatness. It would be merely Michelangelo or Machiavelli or Erasmus, and there would be Russ, Wilt, the Big O and West. And many more. It was the best of times.

George Mikan, 1954 The end of the NBA's first era was marked by the 24-second rule and the retirement, to his law practice, of its greatest player.

Chapter 11

Mr. Basketball, George Mikan

They broke his bones, bloodied his nose and knocked out his teeth but
The Big Fellow kept on smashing every scoring record in the books.

By Norman Katkov
SPORT Magazine, March 1959

How good was George Mikan? No other sport casts aside old stars and embraces new ones quite so swiftly as professional basketball, so how does Mikan, officially proclaimed as the greatest basketball player of the first half of the 20th Century—and unofficially as the greatest since Dr. Naismith invented the game—stack up today, five seasons after his retirement? You have to ignore those few months in 1956 when an over-age, creaky Mikan gave up his lawyer's office for another brief fling at the game that made him famous. He was only a 6-foot-10 shadow of himself by then.

The answer, in case you had any doubt, is that Mikan still stands as the very best. He was the finest scorer and rebounder ever to play the game of basketball; he was the heart and soul of the Minneapolis Lakers, five times world champions; he was the gate attraction that procured major-league status for professional basketball. He was so good that when every other possible defense against him, fair or foul, had been tried and found wanting, the league had to widen the lanes under the baskets from six feet to 12. All that succeeded in doing was to cut big George's scoring average from 28 to 24 points a game.

Joe Lapchick, a pioneer professional with the original New York Celtics and later coach of the New York Knickerbockers, still is awed by the memory of the bespectacled giant who wore the distinctive number 99. "Big George reminds me of Babe Ruth," he once said. "Everyone forgot Ruth was once an exceptional pitcher and that he was a fine outfielder. Everyone also forgets that Mikan was the best feeder out of the pivot that the game ever had. Cover him normally and he'd kill you with his scoring. Cover him abnormally and he murdered you with his passes. Why, if he'd been playing when I was with the Celtics, he'd have scored a million points. I take that back. Make it two million."

As it was, George Mikan scored 11,764 points, the second highest total of all time. At one time he practically monopolized the record books in scoring and rebound statistics. He scored 44 points or more in nine different games, his greatest effort being 61 points against Rochester in 1952—after the anti-Mikan 12-foot rule was put in effect. He holds the all-time seasonal scoring average of 28.4 points; he held the total season scoring record of 1,932 points until George Yardley broke it by becoming the game's first 2,000-point man in 1958; and he still holds the career marks for scoring average, with 22.6, and field

goals, with 4,091. In the seven categories of scoring in which the NBA keeps official records, Mikan has two firsts, two thirds, a fourth, a tenth and an eleventh. He also ranks 13th in rebounds and—just to keep the records straight—fourth in personal fouls.

In his six big seasons with Minneapolis, from 1948 to 1954, Mikan led the league in scoring three times, was second twice, and fourth in his last and worst year. He made the league all-star first team each of the six years.

George's records were not come by cheaply. High scorers in basketball are fair game for organized mayhem, the penalty for which is a couple of free-throws—always considered a cheap payment for crippling or intimidating a high-point man. The fact that Mikan packed a solid 245 pounds on his huge frame earned him no immunity. If anything, his size made him more of a target.

Each of George's legs was broken once. His right foot, the arch of his left foot, his right wrist, his nose and his thumb also suffered broken bones. Three of his fingers were broken. His nose was ripped open twice. He has had a total of 166 stitches, ranging from three to 16 at a sitting.

No sissy himself, Mikan could give out as much punishment as he took when the occasion warranted. His usual method was simply to hurl his massive body at a particularly annoying guard, either going in for a shot or up for a rebound. Nobody ever could out-muscle him under the basket.

Once, after a rough game in New York, a reporter walked into the Lakers' dressing room and told Mikan, who sat exhausted in front of his locker, his blue uniform so soaked with perspiration that the famous number 99 was hardly visible, that the Knicks had accused him of illegally elbowing them all evening. Without a word, George peeled off his jersey and showed the surprised reporter a torso literally criss-crossed with black-and-blue welts.

"Ask them what they think these are," Mikan said. "Birthmarks?"

In the dog-eat-dog competition of professional basketball, Mikan and Minneapolis were one—just like Babe Ruth and Yankees. And just as the Babe made the home-run hitter baseball's greatest gate attraction, so Mikan made the high-scoring big man into the salvation of basketball.

Just as there were home-run hitters before Ruth, there were outsized basketball players before Mikan. But none of them combined great height with great skill. Most coaches, in fact, were suspicious of unusually tall players, feeling they couldn't

possibly be real athletes. Big George changed all that.

If there was any doubt among players and fans that the big man was destined to take over basketball, it ceased in a remarkable 30-day period at the end of Mikan's first NBA season in 1949. It started, oddly, only 12 days after Philadelphia's Joe Fulks had set the still-standing league record of 63 points in a single game. On February 22, Mikan celebrated Washington's Birthday by scoring 48 points against New York. Four days later, against Baltimore, he hit for 53. Fifteen days later, against New York again, it was 51, and six days after that it was 46 against Rochester. Mikan had crammed four of his seven most prolific scoring nights into a single month of his career and the dazzled observers added a new nickname to go with the Big Fellow, the Tall Pine, Specs and Engine 99. It was simply Mr. Basketball, a title they have never taken away from him.

George Mikan is from Joliet, Ill., home of 52,460 free souls and several thousand behind bars in the Illinois State Penitentiary, His father was Joseph G. Mikan, a Croatian; his mother was Minnie Mikan, a Lithuanian. Both were of average height.

There were three sons: George, Joe, Jr., who is now a farmer, and Ed, who was a pretty good basketball player himself. All of the sons worked in the Mikan's restaurant and bar, and all the Mikans lived above the "business."

George Mikan as a boy didn't know anything else but going to school, working in the restaurant and, after an ordinary working day of 12 or 14 hours, joining the rest of the family upstairs. Nor did he know, because Joseph and Minnie Mikan wouldn't allow it, that there were other grades to get in school besides the best grades. In immigrant families the best grades are important, and anything less than the first ten in the class is somehow relegated to abysmal failure.

George wasn't that interested in basketball as a boy. He played a pretty good game in the neighborhood backyard competition, but being a gentle soul he preferred his piano lessons or even shooting marbles. George was so good at shooting marbles that he was the champion of Will County at ten, and was rewarded with a day as honorary mayor of Joliet and a meeting with the great Babe Ruth in Chicago.

So George Mikan was too busy to play basketball until he had only one year left at Joliet Catholic High School. He wasn't going to play then, either, but his younger brother, Ed, was on the team and talked him into it.

That summer George, Ed and several other players from Joliet rode all the way across Cook County to Waukegan for a scrub game, just for kicks.

"Somebody borrowed a truck," George Mikan remembers. "It was a pretty hot day. We got into Waukegan just a few minutes before the game. They were a strong bunch of kids. Big kids. I was just another player."

When the game started that afternoon in Waukegan, George Mikan jumped center. He was 5-foot-11, shorter than his adversary, but he tipped the ball to his brother Ed and ran for the basket. Ed turned, feinted, feinted once more, and moved to his left, dribbling and looking for brother George.

Brother George was there, floundering around in front of the basket like a beached trout. In those days perpetual motion was his best tactic against the opposing center's defense. Since he never stopped moving, he was always a difficult target for a feeding pass. This occasion proved no exception. When Ed finally threw the ball, George had to pivot sharply to catch the pass. He turned on his right foot and reached far out for the ball. The opposing center came across the right leg hard, unable to check his advance.

George Mikan went down and couldn't get up. The leg was cleanly broken. It was the first in what was to become a staggering list of serious injuries.

"Ed got some splints on the leg," George remembers, "and they got me out to the truck. They laid me out in the back of the truck while the game continued. After the game was over, we went home."

If you remember that the distance between Waukegan and Joliet is close to 100 miles; if you can imagine how it is to ride in the flat bed of a truck with all your bones intact; if you remember the last scorching hot day you were subjected to without shade, it is hardly a mystery that George spent the next 18 months flat on his back in his bed above the restaurant in Joliet.

Quite apart from the pain, those 18 months above the family restaurant produced a remarkable change in him—a metamorphosis that was to petrify the sports world in years to come.

George was put into traction one night when he was 5-foot-11. He took his first hesitant steps 18 months later, stooping to get through the door to the kitchen, because he was 6-foot-7. What was now present on the basketball horizon in the untutored, unsophisticated 79 inches of George Mikan, testing his healed leg on the bedroom floor, was the new era of the big man in basketball.

A basketball team in those days was composed of five players, and the fellow closest to six feet in height was the center. He stationed himself on offense almost always in the free throw circle—crouched, bent forward, and waiting for the pass from his guards. When he got the pass, he fed it to one or the other of his forwards, or, if the guarding was close, back out to one of his guards, so the maneuvering could begin again. A team that scored more than 35 points had gone wild, and a quintet that scored more than 50 had obviously run amok.

Then George Mikan broke his leg, began to grow and forgot to stop, and that kind of basketball was finished forever.

George was finished at Joliet Catholic High as well. When he was mobile once more, he was hopelessly behind his old classmates. So he registered at Quigley Prep in Chicago. He had a notion about studying for the priesthood and had set his mind on attending the University of Notre Dame. Meantime he played basketball, studied hard and worked in the family restaurant with that single goal in mind.

"I'd be on the bus for Chicago by six o'clock every morning," he said. "I'd study on the bus going into Chicago and at night coming out. I always tried to get a six o'clock bus coming out. There was school, there was practice and there was work to do in the restaurant."

They were busy years for growing George Mikan. Not only was he playing a lot of basketball, but he also showed promise as a baseball pitcher. His windup looked like a hopeless tangle of arms and legs, but when the complicated maneuver reached

its climax, the ball rocketed toward the plate with surprising speed and accuracy. No less than four major-league teams—the Cubs, White Sox, Yankees and Pirates—were interested enough to offer minor-league contracts. But Mikan, already torn between the priesthood and the idea of playing basketball, turned down the baseball offers.

Eventually it was Greek which swung the scales toward basketball. George needed to pass Greek in order to study for the priesthood and he failed miserably at it. Try as he might, he couldn't muster a satisfactory grade in the language of Homer and Aristotle, and finally he gave up the idea of devoting his life to the Church.

Years later, Joe Lapchick heard about Mikan's early ambition and commented sadly, "I'm certain George would have donned the cloth had he visualized the sorrow he would bring to us poor coaches."

George played four years for Quigley Prep, and when he applied for admission to Notre Dame, his grades were fine. Scholastically, he was above and beyond the minimum for Notre Dame, but a college education is expensive and he had worked four years for an athletic scholarship—and he didn't get it.

Notre Dame coach George Keogan took one look at Mikan during a brief demonstration in the gymnasium and shook his head. "He's too awkward," he said to his assistant, Ray Meyer, "and he wears glasses!"

"I guess they just didn't think I had it," George recalls now. "They just about broke my heart, I'll tell you that. There were a couple of days when I didn't know what I was going to do." It was 1942 and George Mikan, now 6-foot-8, wore glasses a quarter of an inch thick. While he was finishing his last term at Quigley Prep, unable to think beyond the flat refusal at South Bend, Paul Mettei, who was athletic director at De Paul University in Chicago, sent for him.

"He'd never even seen me play," Mikan says. "He just said, 'Do you want to go to school?' He knew the answer to that one. Then he said, 'They tell me you play basketball.' I said, yes, I played basketball. He said, 'Ray Meyer is our coach. Have you heard of him?' Well, naturally I'd heard of Ray Meyer. So it was all settled. I came home and told the family, 'I'm going to De Paul.' They thought it was wonderful. I'd be able to live home and I could still help downstairs.

"Ray Meyer taught me basketball," he says flatly. "He taught me everything I know. I didn't know anything when he got hold of me that first year."

Meyer hadn't forgotten the big, awkward kid with the glasses who had tried out at South Bend. When he was named basketball coach at De Paul for the 1942-43 season, he told Mettei about the big boy from Joliet and both agreed he might be worth a gamble. De Paul usually got only the leftovers from the Chicago area anyhow, after Notre Dame, Northwestern, Illinois and even Loyola of Chicago had bid higher for the best talent. What did they have to lose?

Meyer put Mikan through a complete schedule of exercises designed to give the towering, 240-pound freshman the agility and coordination he lacked. Before Mikan ever touched a basketball in the De Paul gym, he spent dozens of hours jumping rope, shadow boxing and doing road work. Then,

before he was allowed to take part in a scrimmage, he spent more hours shooting at the basket. He shot hundreds of times, using every conceivable kind of shot. Slowly, under the sharp eyes of Ray Meyer, he familiarized himself with the weapons that were to enable him to outclass all opposition.

"At De Paul," the Big Fellow said flatly, "that first year, I was a freak. I was like the Fat Lady in the circus, or the Tattooed Man. I was big and I was alive, I could get the ball on the jump, but what other use could I be? I would stand under the basket and just reach out for the ball if it came off the backboard in my direction. But I was really regarded by the fans like that midget Bill Veeck used when he had the St. Louis Browns. So I worked on the hook shot. The hook shot was what started them—the opposition—thinking."

⊕ ⊕ ⊕

There was one other factor that started the opposition thinking. It was a personality factor; a characteristic of the Big Fellow and as much a part of the man as his height and his myopia—his courage. Certainly George could connect with the hook shot. But he knew, it became painfully apparent within a few weeks after unveiling the new weapon, that practically every time he shot, he was going down; he was going to hit the deck with at least two, and usually more, defending players on top of him.

Knowing it, he just kept shooting and became an All-America three years running. Knowing that any time he pivoted toward the basket and came up with that long arm, he might be pushed, tripped, wrestled or thrown to the floor, he went into the finals for the National Collegiate Athletic Association title at Madison Square Garden. He went up against high-scoring Rhode Island State College on an early spring evening in 1945 when every bone in his body ached from almost a week of tournament play.

They triple-teamed George Mikan that night. The instant the big fellow came within 20 feet of the basket, three Rhode Island players would surround him, like Secret Service men guarding a distinguished personage. George suffered from torn ligaments even before the game began; he had spent most of the day in bed in a vain attempt to rest pulled muscles and weary bones. Then, within 60 seconds of the jump at center, the ball came into him, off to one side of the free throw circle, and three men came at him as he made his turn. The three men rose with him as he started up with the long arm moving toward the basket, the three men fouled him as he arched the ball, and the three men came down on top of him as he fell heavily to the floor.

Mikan made that basket, and he dropped in the free throw after crossing himself before the attempt, and then he scored 50 more points before the game was over, for a total of 53. It was a new Madison Square Garden record.

But you have to remember that these were amateurs, mere neophytes at the art of roughing up a high scorer. In his very first game as a pro, with the Chicago Gears, in 1946, George traveled to Oshkosh, Wis., where an opponent with the sturdy name of Cowboy Edwards was put on the Big Fellow and promptly knocked out four of his teeth.

"They really wanted me out of that game," George recalled more than a decade later. It seemed absurd to ask if the abrupt

absence of four teeth had accomplished what no amount of physical injury before or since has been able to accomplish. In his first six years with the Minneapolis Lakers, beginning November 20, 1947, Mikan missed exactly two games, both absences brought on by prolonged respiratory infections, and the Lakers lost both games.

It may seem odd to state flatly that after a college career that included such triumphs as three straight years of being chosen All-America, George Mikan's star was just beginning to rise, but that was precisely the case. His collegiate records may be likened to the years—the highly successful years—that a baseball player spends in the minor leagues. But they only pay off in the major leagues, and George Mikan's college career was nearly forgotten as he rose in professional basketball ranks to heights never reached by any player, before or since.

George had signed a five-year contract with the Chicago Gears of the old National Basketball League, but he was unhappy with his new team and his performance suffered. Fortunately for Mikan, the team folded soon after its owner decided to change leagues at the beginning of the 1947-48 season, and its players were split up among the other teams in the National League. Mikan was assigned to the brand-new Minneapolis entry which had been created by a franchise shift from Detroit. In Detroit the team had won exactly four out of 44 games. But with Mikan and new surroundings, they became the darlings of basketball.

Mikan began his spectacular association with the Lakers five games after they had secured their franchise. His coach was Johnny Kundla, who had played for the University of Minnesota. His teammates were Jim Pollard, Jack Dwan, Herm Schaefer, Tony Jaros and Swede Carlson. Their arena was the beautiful Minneapolis Auditorium. Minneapolis won the National League title as Mikan scored 1,195 points in 56 games. He got every one of the 240 possible votes as the league's most valuable player. The rival Basketball Association of America—now the National Basketball Association—had no chance to get Mikan, so they did the next best thing. They talked Minneapolis owner Ben Berger into shifting his team into their league. The Lakers proceeded to tear the league apart.

They won five BAA-NBA titles in six years. After they won the title in 1954, for the fifth time, Maurice Podoloff, head of the NBA, said, "I will say it was the greatest team in the history of basketball and deserves a place not earned by any team in any other type of athletics. The Lakers have been the greatest contributing factor to the success of the NBA. The record of the Lakers will remain unchallenged for years to come."

Of Mikan, a writer remarked, "He's six feet ten, and couldn't be any greater even if he was ten feet six."

Of himself, Mikan said in 1952, after compiling the second highest score in NBA history, "There was a lot of fuss about my 61 points the other night; 99 per cent of it about me. That's the penalty for being a team player. Jim Pollard, Dugie Martin and the rest of the boys hardly got a mention. Yet if it hadn't been for them I couldn't have gotten 21 points. Jim threw me seven beautiful passes. Dugie gave me six. There's 13 baskets, 26 points. I got four more from Vern Mikkelsen. That's eight more points, 34 points all told. So you see how easy it is to get 34

points. All you have to do on this club is stand around and wait for somebody to throw you the ball.

"Then, after the game, somebody asked, 'Why do they always throw the ball to you in the clutch? They know you're going to be heavily guarded.' Well, that's the reason right there. Usually the defensive team gangs up on me in a spot like that. Where better can you pick up a foul? If I manage to get the ball, I can try a shot and maybe it'll go in. But whether the ball goes in or not, I'm certain to be fouled in all that congestion. And free throws win games, the same as field goals. So trying to get the ball in to the pivot man actually has a two-to-one better chance for points than a long shot from the floor."

The Big Fellow's modesty was characteristic. The fouls he was talking about were as easy to come by as a Purple Heart at Anzio. There was the night in Minneapolis when an opposing player went at him with fingers spread like an eagle's talons. When Mikan got up on his hands and knees, his nose was torn into bloody strips.

Kundla insisted that Mikan go home for the night, but George just sat down heavily on the bench while the team physician went to work. It was a tribute as much to the doctor's facility with the sutures as to George Mikan's hardiness that the Big Fellow took his own two free throws for that particular foul. It should also be noted that he made them both.

⊕ ⊕ ⊕

But that was nothing compared to the 1949 playoff game in Washington when he went down and came up with a broken wrist. It was broken, and he knew it, but since the playoff money was worth between $1,000 and $1,500 per winning player, the Big Fellow didn't even ask for time.

George Mikan finished the game with the broken right wrist, and then spent most of the night in a hospital emergency room, waiting for an intern to set the break. When at last it was in plaster, the sun was rising beyond the Potomac and he had just enough time to catch the plane which was taking the Lakers home for the next game in the series. He had time only to change clothes in his suburban home, and almost convince his skeptical wife, Patricia, that the wrist was only sprained. He even had the newspapermen convinced, but the opposing Capitols were a bit more curious. They began, almost from the opening of the game, to test the rumors about the Big Fellow's wrist.

Even though his right arm hung almost uselessly at his side, and George played the entire game shooting only with his left hand, he didn't try a single shot when at least two defensive players weren't chopping at his right arm. Mikan averaged 30.3 points per game as the Lakers won their first championship.

But Old Specs, as he was beginning to be called, wasn't bitter about the tactics. He even condoned them by saying, "There's a way in professional basketball, as well as in any other sport, to separate the men from the boys. Pressure is the big factor. The playoffs put more pressure on the individual players than anything else. You can have all the talent in the world, but if you're not interested in making the full use of that talent, victory is unlikely."

It was simply a way of life for Mikan, this will to win despite hardships. He had, all through the early years of his professional career, gone back to Chicago every summer to

study in the law school at De Paul University. He was, as determined to be a good lawyer as he was to be a great basketball player. He flunked his bar examination.

He flunked it three times running before passing it in Minnesota, but while he was studying—and flunking—he was creating a legend on the basketball floor.

In nine seasons as a professional he scored 11,764 points, all but 413 of them for the Minneapolis Lakers. He was unanimous choice as *SPORT*'s top cage performer four straight years. In 1953-1954, to take one year at random, he scored 1,306 points in 2,362 minutes of play, or a point every 1.8 minutes. And remember, please, that this was in professional play, where there were four other men on his team accomplished at getting the ball through the basket, and five more on the opposing team with a yen for shooting themselves.

In desperation, the league passed the only rule ever aimed at curbing a single player. By making the foul lanes double their usual six feet, and making it an automatic violation to be in the expanded lane more than three seconds, they hoped to reduce the deadly threat of Mikan, who liked to do his devastating work just outside the lane. All the rule did was force the Big Fellow to become even greater. Strangely, Mikan himself likes the rule and claims it makes for a better game.

It was at the height of his career, just after reaching his 30th birthday, that Mikan quietly walked into the office of the Minneapolis Lakers' general manager on the morning of September 25, 1954, and quit basketball. He said he wanted to quit when he was still good; he said he had passed the bar and wanted to begin his new career; he said he was a stranger to his kids and wanted to get to know his growing family.

"This should even up the league," was the glum comment of Johnny Kundla, faced with fielding a team that would, for only the third time in seven years, be minus the services of Old Specs.

From New York came a wire service comment: "They turned the most colorful page of basketball history today. George Mikan, who is Mr. Basketball of the Half Century and more, put the game behind him forever in a surprise retirement announcement."

For almost a year and a half that valedictory was substantiated. George devoted himself to his family, his Minneapolis law practice, the construction of a suburban home, and a front-office position with the Lakers. The 1954-1955 season came and went, and the early part of the 1955-56 season as well. Then, in January, with the season well under way. No. 99 was suddenly back in the team lineup.

There were many reasons given for the brief comeback. Today George Mikan says he wanted only to play basketball again. But all through Minneapolis that winter there ran stories of Mikan's financial involvement with the Lakers, and of his return as a move to protect his investment, estimated as a one-third ownership of the team.

The Lakers were going to Boston when it was announced George Mikan would be back in the lineup. The Celtics had drawn a top attendance of 7,800 spectators for the season to that date, but when the Big Fellow came bounding out on the floor in that inimitable lope of his, there were 12,235 people on their feet cheering him. He got two points—two points for the entire game, that is.

But the next day, against the New York Knickerbockers in the 69th Regiment Armory, he hit for 20 points. And the night following his Manhattan appearance, he started in Fort Wayne, doubled their existing attendance record for the season, and beat them, even though he played half the game with a broken finger. In 37 games, every one of them an agony of aching muscles, he finished off his career with a creditable 390 points and helped the Lakers into the playoffs.

The Mikan story should really end there with his last fling as a player. Certainly his brief career as the Lakers' coach, during the first half of the 1957-1958 season, was an abject failure. The team started out with seven straight defeats, and by the time Johnny Kundla was restored as coach, it had a dismal 9-30 record.

Today, George Mikan, a little heavier and a little grayer than the feared pivot man of a decade ago, is a successful lawyer and civic leader in Minneapolis. He and his wife Pat almost have a basketball team of their own in their strapping sons Larry, Terry, Pat and Mike. The Big Fellow has been bitten by the political bug and has already run for Congress once. He'll probably try it again. And if he doesn't make it then, he'll try again.

George always has been that kind of a competitor. There comes a time when even the most restrained chronicler discovers, usually to his chagrin, that he can no longer proceed with the prescribed dignity. The subject demands more. Your hero's accomplishments demand superlatives—line after line of superlatives.

There is a glowing example in the career of George Mikan, a career which began in the gymnasium of Joliet Catholic High School and ended, finally and irrevocably, with the finish of the 1955-56 basketball season. It is an example of tenacity, of strength of will, of courage so completely an extension of a man's personality that it is indistinguishable from the man.

What it accomplished was probably summed up in the mute but magnificent tribute that always greeted the Mikan-led Lakers when they came to New York. There on the marquee of Madison Square Garden, the mecca of American indoor sports, it was stated in its simplest possible terms:

TONITE

GEORGE MIKAN

VS.

KNICKS

(Reprinted with permission, Sport Media Enterprises, Inc., 2003)

Bob Pettit, 1961 The NBA's first MVP—in 1955-56—he would repeat three years later, the first of what would eventually number 10 multiple winners.

Chapter 12

Bob Pettit: The Polished Pro

The Hawks' slick captain played with poise and grace. He appeared to be a true natural but, actually, he had a tough time while battling to the top of his sport.

By Al Stump
SPORT Magazine, February 1965

It had been a week, as the Bayou folk of Bob Pettit's home country put it, to raise alligator bumps on a man's hide. It opened in Los Angeles early last November as Pettit found himself on the foul line after the game's final buzzer. The buzzer had burped with the Lakers leading, 115-114, but at the buzzer, Leroy Ellis had knocked Pettit sprawling.

In stunned rage, some 10,000 fans roared, "Miss it!" as Pettit stood, groggily, on the foul line for a pair of free throws. Under the thick wave of sound Pettit scored both shots and the St. Louis Hawks won, 116-115.

The following morning Pettit opened his mouth to say something and part of a tooth fell out. "Brother, I must be getting old," said Bob.

Now it was November 3 and the Hawks had moved into San Francisco to play the Warriors. Pettit had slept until 11 a.m. and he was moodily eyeing his "breakfast"-a whole-size order of pot roast, whipped potatoes, salad, rolls and a pitcher of milk. At 6-foot-9 and 235 pounds, Pettit is rawboned, but lean, and no matter how he stuffs down rich food, he is always fighting to keep from losing weight. He averages four hefty meals per day, featuring 20-ounce steaks and chocolate shakes.

"And think what today is," he said glumly in his low drawl. "It's the day we elect a United States President. You'd believe I'd be able to vote, wouldn't you? But I can't lift a finger."

On Election Day, although Bob is a large-scale taxpayer in Louisiana, a longtime registered voter and a thoughtful student of politics, he could not vote. Louisiana makes no provision for the casting of absentee ballots.

One night later the 32-year-old with the thickly tufted shoulders and chest, chiseled, handsome face and receding hairline went out against the Warriors to demonstrate why he is the greatest scorer in professional basketball history. He was feeling loose and in the mood for a 30- or 40-point night. But everything went wrong. His favorite shot, the jumper, was so cold he missed it five straight times. Nate Thurmond, 6-foot-11, was guarding the 6-foot-9 Pettit, crowding him, jabbing elbows into him, stepping on his feet. Pettit was unable to score until five minutes had passed.

Then the week of alligator bumps was over. Though not scoring, Pettit outjumped Thurmond on rebounds and set up the Hawks' fast break. He fed Len Wilkens and Zelmo Beaty. He kept the Hawks fired up. When Referee Don Murphy called

a fourth foul on the Hawks' Bill Bridges, after Wilt Chamberlain and Bridges had collided, Pettit said, "Why don't you bring out a chair and put it on the foul line for Chamberlain? He's been camped there all night!"

In the fourth quarter Pettit began to score. With the game tied 96-96 and two minutes left he maneuvered Thurmond into a foul and scored. Pettit was drenched in sweat, obviously feeling his 11 seasons of pro play; but he forced the pace and with San Francisco leading, 100-99 and time almost out, he slammed in from the right corner, grabbed a pass between Chamberlain and Thurmond, spun high and steered in a jump shot from the keyhole.

The Hawks won and Pettit, their captain had again proven his versatility, a versatility on display through more than 800 NBA games and more than 32,000 minutes of NBA play. The hard work has often left him with a set of aching size-15 feet and a trick stomach.

"If it wasn't for aids like Alka Seltzer and Rolaids," Pettit says, "I might not make it through the season. After a game I'm starved and eat a very big meal. My stomach kicks up and before I can even think about sleep I have to go to the seltzers, bicarbs and anti-alkaline pills."

Curiously, Bob is laconic, easygoing, a non-worrier and downright doctrinal in following every training dogma stressing the clean life laid down since the time of Amos Alonzo Stagg. He can relax under pressure. Yet, he has a trick stomach.

"What it is with me, I guess," Pettit says, "is that as you go along in life and work hard, you reach new plateaus of accomplishment. With each plateau you reach, the demands upon you become greater. And your pride increases to meet the demands. You drive your self harder than before. You can't afford negative thinking, so you always believe you'll win. You build an image of yourself that has nothing to do with ego-but it has to be satisfied.

"When I fall below what I know I can do, my belly growls and growls. Anytime I'm not playing up to my very best I can count on a jolt of indigestion."

Pettit can count on other jolts in pro basketball, too, physical jolts. He has learned to give back the jolts, though at the beginning the rough and tumble of pro basketball overwhelmed him. When he began his career with the Hawks, then based in Milwaukee, he was a 205-pounder who had been an All-America at Louisiana State University. Against the Minneapolis Lakers he was bounced into the seats and shoved around easily by 260-pound Vern Mikkelsen. Clyde Lovellette,

who was even bigger, contemptuously slapped Pettit across the face when Pettit challenged for the ball. Pettit swung back finally, aiming at little Slater Martin. Martin ducked and the punch caught Mikkelsen alongside the jaw.

The Lakers charged and the Hawks' coach, Red Holzman, pulled Pettit off the floor. "You're getting racked up like an eight ball," Holzman said. "I'll tell you right now. You'll never make the pros if you don't start getting rough with the big guys."

But even smaller opponents gave Pettit trouble. Once, Holzman pulled him out of a game and screamed, "Even the midgets make you look lousy!"

With such a beginning, Pettit could have become a self-fighter, a brooder or he could have lost confidence. But his rookie year wasn't many weeks old when he began to learn the knack of rudely blocking players before leaving his feet on a rebound, which is the proper way to make the play. And he developed a series of feints that bigger but slower men of the league found difficult to stop. Shifted from center (his college position) to forward he taught himself to shoot from the outside and perfected what some call the "Pettit angle."

This refers to the body slant at which he plays his man on offensive rebounds. "Basketball is mostly jockeying the guy checking you into a position where you have the best control," says Bob. "You've got to find ways not to let your man get behind you or to get caught back to back with some bruiser the size of Darrall Imhoff, Tom Hoover or Walt Bellamy. They'll lay the back and hips into you and you're all off balance. I play them with my body at a slant to theirs, where the angle enables me to get an arm over their shoulder when we're fighting for a rebound and then roll free with the ball."

Pettit studied and practiced-("I've averaged three hours a day of practice almost every day since I was a sophomore in high school")-until he became technically the most perfect of players. "Outside of one-man-on-one situations, I don't compare to him," admits Elgin Baylor of the Lakers. "The game is mostly one of working with others, taking and giving help, and that's where Pettit's the greatest." Says Bill Sharman: "Bob's a forward, but right now, even at his age he's so great he could play the pivot against Russell or Chamberlain and hold his own. He's the best I ever saw at both ends of the court-Mr. Consistency. The last year I played with the Celtics was my best year, in regard to field-goal percentage and about everything else, because I'd learned how to break from slumps and knew the habits of every man I went against. Pettit is the same way. Right now he's the master of such things as going up for a shot and using one arm to fend off a guard while he pops one in. He's the best at knowing the exact time to shoot. Nobody ever went after the second or third rebound with his know-how and fight. As a fast-break starter, he's one of the hardest drivers among big men. And on top of all this he scores very high. Pettit gets you 20 to 30 or more almost every game. He's also got a helluva sense of comedy and knows how to clown just enough to keep a team relaxed. He's a student of people who never stops trying to understand how he can help them be better-the perfect leader of any team."

A rookie announcer this year, Sharman asked Pettit to be his first interview subject. Bob spoke smoothly about a trip he made to Europe last summer with a State Department All-Star team, then, when finished with the interview, Pettit began to make horrible faces at Sharman-who was still talking into the mike-and Bob also messed up the sheets of Sharman's script until poor Bill couldn't find the next line. Sharman survived the ordeal without breaking into laughter or tears, but barely. "After this," Pettit told him, "the job will seem easy to you."

Some jobs have come easy to Pettit but mostly he has worked hard and with intelligence to master them. Since he was very young, Bob has known how and where he wanted to channel his life and he seldom has deviated from any set goal, a direct-line approach which is evident in many ways. When he's driving a car in a strange town, for example, he memorizes street names and studies maps until he knows the short-cuts. Six years ago he began to like golf, and to Pettit the only answer was to buy a home adjoining the Webb Memorial Golf Course in Baton Rouge. Now, by simply walking a few yards, he can practice shots in early morning and the twilight when the course is empty. He was only briefly a 100-shooter, quickly moving into the 80s. He's a collector of modern art who long ago determined not to make bad buys. In New York and Europe he consulted veteran collectors, read expertise on the subject, spent hours in museums, even bought his own canvas and paints. Today he owns ivory figurines he found in Egypt, Romanian wood carvings, some fine Paul Jenkins paintings and is learning the craft of restoring antique furniture from his Hawk roommate and old friend, Cliff Hagan, who has a basement workshop in St. Louis designed for such craftsmanship.

Pettit is enthusiastic when he describes a particular piece of furniture in his home: "At my Baton Rouge place, which sits on a great big 120-by-420-foot lot, with big old trees all around," he says, "I have a couch facing a picture window, overlooking the golf course. The couch is done in a jungle print of black, olive and orange. It was custom-built by Vallee of New York and it's over 12 feet long-which makes it plenty long enough for me to stretch out on for a nap. Also, it's handsome. My living room chairs are large and heavy and done in an avocado color. There's an orange rug on the floor and the walls have big, black Oriental pieces on them. It's very colorful and contemporary and I'm glad to say I had a lot to do with the decorating."

He also has decorated the all-time National Basketball Association record tables. In 16 seasons Dolph Schayes, now retired, amassed a lifetime league record of 19,249 points. On February 8, 1964, Pettit passed that figure and last November 13, against the Cincinnati Royals, he reached the 20,000-point plateau. He did it in only a fraction over ten seasons at an average of better than 26 points per game. Huge thrill? "Yes, because I began aiming for it a couple of years ago when Schayes was nearing retirement and it looked like I had a chance," Pettit says soberly. "It's nice to be the first man to accomplish anything. If I can make it 25,000 points, I will. But even if I should get hurt and have to quit sometime soon, the 20,000 will stand up for a while." Wilt Chamberlain presently is short of 17,000.

Cliff Hagan proudly points to the fact that Bob is only ninth on the all-time list in number of games played, yet has outscored everyone in pro history-besides which he owns the all-time NBA record for most field goals made, and is crowding Bill Russell for first place in all-time rebounds captured. In All-

Star Game play Pettit has appeared every year since 1956, has scored more points - 211-than any other player, and three times has been named the game's Most Valuable Player. In playoff competition, Pettit is the leader with 2194 points in 84 appearances, a 26.1 average.

"Most all-time season points, most All-Star points, most playoff points! How can anyone wonder who the top player in the history of the world is?" asks Hagan. "And did you know that Bob has more stitches in his face than many prizefighters?"

Pettit has had 125 stitches, some of which are memorable. Against the Boston Celtics one evening, for example, just before half-time, Tommy Heinsohn slashed Bob across the left brow and left him cold on the floor. Bleeding heavily, Bob was taken to the locker room, where Dr. Stan London inspected the wound. "It's deep and it'll take a lot of repair work," said the doctor. "I think we'd better call for an ambulance."

"Doc," said Pettit, "let's just delay the hospital thing until after the second half. Can't you sort of patch me up for another 25 minutes?"

London made 14 stitches and, insisting on starting the third period of the game, Pettit scored 18 points in the second half to beat Boston.

Another time, 17 stitches were taken in Pettit's mouth and jaw and he didn't miss more than a few minutes of play.

In February of his third NBA season, 1957, Pettit led a fast break, went in for a layup and flipped over Jim Loscutoff of the Celtics. He landed on his arm and snapped the metacarpal bone. "PETTIT OUT FOR SEASON," advised one newspaper. The good chance the Hawks had for the divisional title was given up by those closest to the picture.

"I told Ben Kerner, our owner, that there had to be some sort of cast that could be invented to enable me to shoot, even with a broken wrist," says Bob. "The doctors got busy and built one." The cast forced Pettit to walk around with his hand turned at a peculiar angle, but when he lifted it, the hand was fixed in a shooting position. He missed just one game and in an amazing display went on to pile up 1,755 points-close behind the league leader, Paul Arizin, at 1,817.

"And with guys hacking and chopping at that bad hand," Ben Kerner says, "Bob picked up a squad that had only one other man who averaged as much as 16 points on the season and led us to a three-way tie with the Lakers and Fort Wayne on the final day of play. He showed the way while we won the playoff. Against Boston, for the world title, he was fantastic. We carried the Celtics down to the seventh game before losing by two points. With an arm and a half, Bob scored 298 points in ten playoff games-almost 30 per game. Russell, Cousy, Schayes, none of those guys were even close to him."

Kerner's ballclub, then recently shifted to St. Louis from Milwaukee, had cost him a lot; he was desperately floating loans and in danger of collapse at this point.

The great '57 showing of the Hawks saved Kerner's financial life. "I'd taken a better than $100,000 bath," Kerner says, "and didn't know where to turn. Bobby Pettit changed my world. After our first division title that year, Kiel Auditorium fans loved us and began to pack the place." The Hawks went on, behind Pettit, to become a ranking power; and the upward of $50,000-a-year Pettit now is paid by Kerner is only one token

of the owner's appreciation.

"Ben is one of the closest men in the world to me," says Pettit. "Maybe it's partly because we're both unmarried and think a lot alike, or it may be something else; but I feel as if he's a member of my own family."

During the 1958 Christmas holidays, Pettit again broke a bone this one just below the thumb, and on his shooting hand. Another cast was built. Pettit entered the All-Star game wearing the cast, and he was pitted often under the boards against Bill Russell.

"Don't take any chances," Kerner instructed Bob. "We've got a chance to go all the way this season, so for God's sake play it safe."

But Pettit's pride, which compels him to fly against practicality, was stung when, early in the game, Russell twice knocked away his jump shot. Driving in, Bob grabbed both rebounds. On his third try he twisted and faked, swept clear for a split second and scored.

That night he scored 28 points, an All-Star record, took 26 rebounds, another record, and was named the game's Most Valuable Player. Bothered by the broken bone for weeks, he gunned the Hawks to the Division championship, then into another playoff final with the Celtics.

Bill Sharman paced the Celtics in scoring in the six-game series that followed, one of the wildest in history. "Let me tell you about the final game," Sharman says. "The Hawks led us three games to two and we had to win. But Pettit was a madman. He was going up in the keyhole so high that 6-10 Arnie Risen couldn't stay with him. In every huddle we asked each other: 'How can we stop Pettit?' We tried sagging on him and then two-manning him when he made his move. We tried to stop the Hawks from passing to him. We even tried using Tommy Heinsohn to guard him face-to-face when he didn't have the ball. We might as well have tried to bribe the guy to take it easy."

Of the Hawks' final 20 points that night, Pettit scored 19 and his 50 points for the night beat the Celtics, 110 to 109. This was his finest hour.

"After it was over, all I could do was sit on the locker bench with my head in my hands, gasping," remembers Pettit. "I have only a hazy memory of the last few minutes. I don't have any idea of how I got to the dressing room, I was so exhausted."

The Hawks remained powerful for some years, with Pettit starring, then slumped. Under coach Harry Gallatin they came back.

"Bob's help was a big factor in the comeback of the Hawks," Gallatin says. "Zelmo Beaty, for example, had all the moves, but was afraid to use them. Bob worked with Zelmo and gave him the confidence to become the great young player he is."

Several times, while Ben Kerner was roasting coaches in the St. Louis oven and rarely finding them able to stand the heat, Bob Pettit has taken over as temporary head coach. "I've said it 1000 times: NEVER would I take a coaching job in the NBA or anywhere," Pettit says. "I'm in love with another kind of life, you see. When I'm finished playing, you'll find me right where I have planned to be for years and years."

This future also is very much Bob's present-and it concerns what may be the most remarkable side of one of the most

remarkable of the New Breed of business-minded money-making athletes. Today, Pettit probably is the richest basketball player in the country. "Hell, he's independently wealthy right now," says one Hawk official. "He could buy his own NBA franchise any day."

In impressive order, Pettit is:

● Assistant vice-president of the American Bank & Trust of Baton Rouge, the largest banking emporium in that city.

● A partner in Goodwin-Pettit-Shores Insurance Agency, of the same city and doing business throughout the South.

● Partner with Herbert Brown, prominent real estate developer, in Brown-Pettit Projects, which wheels and deals in big land purchases and construction. This company owns a 92-unit apartment building in Lafayette, Louisiana, worth more than $2 million, a 76-unit in Gulfport, Mississippi, a 64-unit in Mobile, Alabama, and a 48-unit in Biloxi, Mississippi. "These are garden-type apartments with swim pools and steam rooms," says Bob. "Very plush living. We also own a shopping center in Baton Rouge and sections of land as far away as Las Vegas."

In one deal, Pettit and Brown spotted some raw land near Baton Rouge, liked it, bought it for $52,000 and sold it for $82,000 a year later, without a penny of other expenditure. In another, they acquired 90 acres in Las Vegas, which they are holding for a profit. As an LSU student, Pettit majored in business administration, with a B average. "I'm in three businesses at once," he says. "In the off-season, I get up at 6:45 a.m. and I'm at my desk at the American Bank & Trust by 8 o'clock. I'm there until 5 p.m., working with customers, servicing new accounts and handling relations with other banks. This job takes me on the road to many states. Some years back, I studied insurance courses at Hartford, Connecticut, and then formed my own company, Pettit Insurance Co., in 1955, which I've since combined with two partners. Fire and casualty coverage are my particular specialties. I work on the insurance business during weekends. And I cram in land development work whenever I can. To me there's no thrill like finding a piece of land with an old house on it, conceiving how it can become a shopping center, financing it and building it."

The black Lincoln convertible with the burgundy interior which Bob drives, his custom-made shirts, the country club estate he lives in at home are just some of the rewards of his commercial acumen, and his contacts.

If you're looking for a powerful indication of where Pettit's perfectionist drive, coupled with his cool ability to handle tough situations, derives from, gaze upon his father, Robert E. Lee Pettit, Sr., of Baton Rouge-six feet, four inches of accomplishment, and a fast-draw adventurer most of his life. "Few men, I believe," says Bob, "have lived a more exciting life than my father."

Pettit's father, who grew up in Colorado, played baseball and basketball prior to World War I at Westminster College. He went into the Army in 1917 and after 18 months with the artillery—including much combat action in France and Belgium—he returned to sign on as a Colorado State Ranger. Some 10,000 striking Colorado miners were at war with the constabulary at the time. Nobody with proper survival instinct wanted any part of the Rangers and the first question asked Pettit's father by the recruiting sergeant was: "Where do you

want your body buried?" Surviving bullets and scoring an impressive record as a Ranger, the father of Bob finished a tour of duty and headed for Baton Rouge, seeking more redblooded action.

He found it. Successively, he served 16 years as a chief criminal deputy in the sheriff's office and then a term, 1932-1936, as County Sheriff. "Huey Long ran Louisiana with a grip of iron," reports a Baton Rouge source close to the scene, "and Bob's father was on the opposite political side from Long. He was one of the very few who stood up to Huey-and survived. If he wasn't so tough and fast with a gun he'd have been dead a dozen times."

Young Bob was born the year his dad became sheriff and had the inspiration of later seeing him-despite the violent anti-Long position-win the appointment of Baton Rouge postmaster and still later become State Director of Institutions. "We've been described as a rich family," says Bob, Jr. "But very well-to-do would be closer to it. We had a big house and when I entered college in 1950, the folks gave me a new Plymouth convertible. My mother was the daughter of a Mississippi doctor and grew up on a plantation.

"Get it straight: I was never allowed to loaf as a boy," says Pettit. "As a nine-year-old I had to work for 15 cents an hour at Lobdell Hardware, a store owned by my grandfather and his sons. Later on, my mother ran Pettit Realty Company in Baton Rouge and when I reached college age she put me to work learning the real estate business. I listed houses and later learned to show them to prospects. Gosh, what a thrill it was when I made my first sale. I unloaded a house for $15,000 and made myself a $400 commission."

Whatever this family has touched has succeeded, yet through his early adolescence, Bob was a study in silent misery. More than anything he ever yearned for, he wanted to win a high-school letter sweater. But he was an athletic joke. He had no coordination and little height or strength. "I weighed 118 when I entered Baton Rouge High and I was only 5-9. At 14, I had more of a figure than a build and on the jayvee basketball team I went the whole season without scoring a point. I spent most of my time sitting on my tail on the floor when the going got rough. In baseball I was the first kid cut from the squad. In football I got into one game for one play-as a defensive left tackle. The Catholic High School guys took one look, ran at me and the ballcarrier went 65 yards for a touchdown. In my sophomore year the basketball coach ran out of uniforms before he got to me and I could only stand around and watch."

At home, Bob's folks watched him suffer.

"If it means so much, let's get some lumber and nails," said Bob's father. Together, they erected a basket in the family backyard and by the light of a couple of lamps positioned in a window, Bob shot a few million times at the hoop, with his folks joining in, and then his dad encouraged him to add rope-skipping and table tennis as coordination-builders. The herky-jerky push shot Bob had been using began to smooth out, but his legs still continued to cross themselves and he just didn't have enough bulk to stand the punishment of any contact game. He grew taller-and skinnier.

Entering a Church League composed of unskilled kids, Bob managed to get in the first real playing time of his basketball

experience. Plus this he made some important friends. Bob Pettit is the sort who makes a friend and keeps that friend the rest of his life.

"I would go home after games and take some old sash-weights from windows and practice lifting them in front of a mirror," says Pettit. "I was now about 5-11 tall and the way you could count my ribs I looked like a walking xylophone."

Still, he developed a workable hook shot, dribbling ability and the one-handed turnaround shot.

In his junior high school year, Bob's growth center went wild and he elevated five inches, and then two inches more, in succeeding months, to stand 6-foot-6. Every item of clothing he owned had to be discarded. He made the school first team, averaging 14 points per game. No one thought him at all remarkable until his final prep year, when he exploded for 33 points in one game. A siege of mumps knocked him out of nine games and Baton Rouge High lost all nine. He was now 6-foot-7 and full of newborn confidence and, upon his return to the lineup, his team won 18 games in a row and the city championship; then went into the State Tournament finals at Hammon, Louisiana. Coach Kenner Day, of Baton Rouge High, asked about his lanky star, predicted, "He developed late and he hasn't begun to understand the game, but I'll bet anyone this: Before he's through, this boy will break down basketball into all its components and he'll be just as great at all of them as constant work and natural smartness ever made anyone." In the state finals, Pettit's team won, with Bob scoring 32 points in one game. He was put on parade before college scouts in the All-American High School North-South Game at Murray, Kentucky.

Always highly conscious of his shortcomings, Bob objected to his folks' attendance at the season's games. But they were on hand every time he faced off on a center jump. "Please stay away, you make me nervous," Bob begged.

"We pay our money like everyone else," his father said, "so don't tell us we can't be there." A little family pressure on him at this point to fire up and become an important star was needed, and the parents didn't miss any cues.

At the Murray tournament, against the top talent in the country, Bob hit the climax of his amazing improvement-he was picked to the first-string tournament team and 14 college and university coaches began to woo him with offers ranging from the illegal to the orthodox room-board-tuition and $15 a month. "The smartest move I ever made was to stay right at home, where the business opportunity would be later, and play under Harry Ravenhorst at LSU," Pettit says. "At LSU I could live at home, close to my folks, which was also important. We're a family short of heirs. As the only child, the last of the Pettits, I wanted to stick close and enjoy those years all I could."

To this day, Pettit takes many of his meals at his mother's table. He hails her cooking as the quintessence of all that is fine in the southern culinary art, particularly her Trout Margarite, her bouillabaisse and her Pompano Supreme. And no loving mother ever had a son with a more flattering appetite. "I can put away most of one of her big pot roasts and a platter of mashed potatoes and feel no pain whatever," he says. His team-mates kid Bob that no one woman he might someday take in matrimony could ever cook often and large enough to satisfy his endless food need.

At Louisiana State, he set records that still stand: 50 points vs. Georgia, 45 vs. Georgia Tech, 60 vs. Louisiana College and many seasonal and career marks. "Maybe I was an All-America, but I learned humbleness at LSU," he says. "I got sick with pneumonia and while I was out four games, LSU won every one of them."

Pettit's unruffled poise, his lack of temper, irritate opponents. In the pros, he stays out of fights and rarely flares up. The exception came last season when, while on the foul line, he was needled by Guy Rodgers of San Francisco, who kept telling him: "You'll never make it, you big bum." Suddenly exploding, Pettit heaved the ball into Rodgers' stomach. "Now shut up!" he roared.

Maybe the story that best typifies Pettit's concentration on the practical, his ability to think on his feet at all times, concerns his European trip last year with the State Department All-Stars, coached by Boston's Red Auerbach. "Bob Cousy and I were walking down the street in Krakow, Poland," he tells it, "when we saw a man being thrown into the air by a crowd of college students. They were celebrating the 600th anniversary of Krakow University. When we got close, we saw it was Auerbach. The kids were tossing him up and catching him, just to let Red know they liked Americans.

"Well, Red saw us and hollered: 'Get those guys; they're Americans, too!'

"Cousy, the big coward, ran away, but the crowd grabbed me and began tossing me high into the air. Up I went and down I came. It was a kind of frightening thing, you know."

Pettit grins with some satisfaction, as he finishes the story.

"But all the time it was happening, I remembered to do two things-to keep one hand tight on my passport and the other on my wallet. I took quite a kidding about that from the All-Stars, but what's a guy to do when he's flying through the air in Krakow?"

If anyone would know what to do, it would be Bob Pettit, the polished pro.

(Reprinted with permission, Sport Media Enterprises, Inc., 2003)

Chapter 13

The Winning Ways Of Red Auerbach

The winningest coach in NBA history had a simple credo: "A ballclub is a dictatorship and I'm the dictator." Not everyone loved him, but Auerbach was respected by all.

By Irv Goodman
SPORT Magazine, March 1965

*Show me a good loser, and
I'll show you a loser.
— Arnold Auerbach*

The Boston Celtics had won 11 in a row and now they had lost one. Ahead by 24 points in the third quarter, they let the game get away from them. They lost their poise. They made mistakes. They forced shots. When the final buzzer sounded, they were down by one point and Madison Square Garden gave out the loudest roar of the night. A winner had lost.

In the passageway along the Fiftieth Street side of the Garden, Red Auerbach stepped out of the Celtics' dressing room. For the three or four minutes he had been in there, he was a quiet, consoling coach. "They feel rotten enough," he said. "I'm tough with them when we win, not when we lose."

People were waiting in the passageway for Auerbach. A couple of businessmen wanted to talk business—Auerbach is in the polyethelene-bag business. "Did you see what they did to us tonight?" Auerbach said. "They took the game away from us." He was talking about the referees.

A priest was there with a college boy, a good basketball player meeting the right people. "Father," Auerbach said, "How can you give away 24 points all by yourself in one quarter? You can't. They got to take

Red Auerbach, 1964
It was hard to tell what annoyed his rivals most—his Celtic teams winning so often, or his habit of blowing cigar smoke on all and sundry.

some of those points from you." He was still talking about the referees.

Auerbach turned to me. I had been traveling with him for a while and would do so for a few days more. "Let's walk," he said. "I'm not ready to go any place."

We walked the back end of the tunnel, away from the crowds, and around to the Forty-Ninth Street side. The teams

were still warming up for the second game of the double-header and the basketball people were congregated along the steps that lead down from center court.

Sid Borgia, the league's supervisor of referees, said hello. There was a time when these two didn't talk to each other. "How you, Red?" said Borgia.

"You got to do something about those referees, Sid," said

Auerbach.

"Be seeing you, Red," said Borgia.

Walter Kennedy, the commissioner of the league, was standing around. Before the start of the 1963-64 season, in what was practically his first official act in office, Kennedy fined Auerbach $500, an NBA record, for pulling his team off the court for two minutes during an exhibition game in Oceanside, Long Island. The most Auerbach had been fined before, as he remembers it, was $300, for a fist fight in a league game.

Auerbach took Kennedy by the arm and walked him into a corner. "Walt, they're at it again. If we're 24 points up and they're pressing, how can we get into trouble? But we get hit with five fouls and they get only one ..." Their voices trailed off and what Kennedy said to Auerbach couldn't be heard. But neither man was smiling.

Auerbach kept at it. With Eddie Gottlieb, who used to own the Warriors when they were in Philadelphia and is still a power in the NBA. And with Haskell Cohen, the league's publicity man, who didn't talk to Auerbach for about two years and does now because Joe Reichler, the Associated Press sportswriter, got them together. And with Joe Lapchick, who used to coach in the NBA and is, at 65, in his last year at St. John's University.

Then the buzzer sounded for the start of the second game and the basketball people walked back up the steps to the arena. Red Auerbach buttoned his overcoat and said, "Let's get going."

Red Auerbach is always going. On this night, into the cold of a New York night, out to the airport, onto the shuttle and back to Boston where he lives alone in a corner room of the Hotel Lenox. On other nights, to Detroit, and St. Louis, and Los Angeles, and San Francisco, and Baltimore, and Cincinnati, and Providence, and Minneapolis, and any place else the NBA chooses to play a basketball game. And on a few nights, when there is no game and no flight and no scouting, to Washington, D.C., where his wife and two daughters wait for him in a big and beautiful old house that is home.

What makes Red run? Why is he still at it? Why when he is already the most successful coach in the history of major spectator sports—eight division titles in a row, seven of them ending in championships? Why when the next oldest coach in term of service has, when you add up his hirings and firings, maybe five years in the league? Why when Auerbach now has from the Celtics what people figured he always wanted—the general manager's job in title as well as in fact? Why when in the opinion of many of his friends—and he has more friends than he permits himself to acknowledge—he has nothing left to prove in professional basketball?

No one knows why. No one can. Sure, he is proud of his personal record of accomplishment and he might want to keep building on it. Sure, he is proud of his teams that won with Bob Cousy and is proud of his team that won last year without Bob Cousy and maybe is waiting around to be proud of his team that wins without Bill Russell.

But pride alone isn't the answer. Nor is success. Nor money. Red Auerbach likes to win, and even that isn't the answer. Many men love victory. But Auerbach loves it and respects it and, toughest of all, understands it. He comprehends better than most men that winning is its own reward. The cheers, the silver cup, the gold coins, the bowed head and upraised hand-these come after the fact. The fact itself, the only fact, is winning.

Take the matter of the Coach of the Year award. Alex Hannum of San Francisco won it last season. Jack McMahon of Cincinnati was second. Auerbach was tied with Charley Wolf (Charley Wolf?) of Detroit for third. Boston beat San Francisco by 11 games during the season, and beat Cincinnati by four. Nobody even bothered to count Detroit. Did it bother Auerbach? Oh, a little bit, sure. For the record, at least, he complained. "It's the biggest joke I ever saw," he said. "It's ridiculous." But when I asked him, he said, "Get out of here. I'm like my team. We get nobody among the top scorers. We don't get many named to the All-Star teams. We just win."

Or take that plane trip back from New York. Auerbach lit up a cigar, his first since before the ballgame. When the Celtics win, he lights up immediately. When they lose, it takes a while. Now, two hours after the loss, that first puff tasted good.

A stewardess came by and said, "You'll have to put out that cigar."

Auerbach was smiling but he wasn't about to put out his cigar. "Honey," he said, "that sign doesn't say no smoking cigars."

"Sorry, but for the comfort of all passengers, we don't permit cigar smoking."

"So then why don't you ask the passengers if my cigar smoke bothers them."

"I'm sorry sir but I'll have to insist."

"Don't be afraid, honey, and don't insist."

The shuttle run between New York and Boston is not a choice assignment and may even be dealt out to those stewardesses in a slump. The young lady clearly not at the top of her game and no match for Auerbach. Nothing in her training manual covered a not-so-red-headed coach who had lost a ballgame that night didn't mean to lose this, too. She gave a non-stewardess grumble and strutted on down the cabin. Auerbach took a long pull on his cigar. When we got off plane, he smiled at the stewardess. She smiled at Tom Heinsohn.

Or consider the game the next night against the Los Angeles Lakers. Although Auerbach didn't get to bed the night before until one a.m.—we had to stop for Chinese food, his favorite meal, on the way in from the airport—he was up early in the morning. He had a nine a.m. business appointment with a bag customer. Then meetings at the Boston Garden. Then an interview with a radio station that wanted to put him on they air three times a week with a 15-minute opinion-and-comment program. Then a meeting with two retailers who wanted to sell Celtic tickets at their stores. Then a get-together with his trainer, Buddy LeRoux, who reported on the physical condition of the players. It wasn't until seven in the evening that Auerbach was able to sit back in his office—redone since he became general manager—and relax. He hadn't thought once about the Lakers. But the Lakers had been thinking about him. Particularly their coach, Fred Schaus.

Schaus doesn't talk to Auerbach. "I respect him as a coach," Schaus says, "but that doesn't mean I must like him as a person." Schaus's irritation may have begun earlier but didn't fester until the final 1962 playoffs. Pro teams are supposed to win at home and the Lakers came home to Los Angeles leading Boston, three games to two. But the Lakers blew the sixth game

and then, back in Boston, blew the seventh game, too.

In 1963, it was the same. Before the playoffs even began, Schaus accused Auerbach of accusing referee-in-chief Borgia of wanting to see the Celtics lose. "Auerbach isn't fooling anyone," Schaus said at the time. "He's looking to back Borgia into a psychological corner."

"Bah," Auerbach said, or something to that effect.

"Lots of luck," Bill Russell said as he took personal charge of the playoffs and the Celtics won in six games.

Last year Los Angeles lost not to Boston, but to St. Louis in the opening-playoff round. St. Louis lost to San Francisco, and it was San Francisco that lost to Boston in the finals.

This year Schaus's frustration is eyeball-high. "I guess I want to beat Auerbach more than I want to beat anyone else," he said early in the season. "Everyone does. He's had the champs for a long time. But there's more to it than that."

Then Schaus proceeded to tick off complaints: "Auerbach intimidates the officials. He's got that baiting of his down to a science. He knows just how far to go." Schaus admits that he is as guilty; he's just not as successful. "You find out," he said, "that if you don't start beefing on every call, you're going to get the worst of it. I've got to protect my team against bad calls." Then why resent Auerbach? "Auerbach isn't sincere. His actions are calculated, not the result of momentary frustration. And he gets away with twice as much as anyone else." Color that green.

Some of his other complaints: Auerbach has all his players foul deliberately at once. The referees can only call one. Meanwhile, the Celtics have taken something out of the other team. Auerbach gets the schedule he wants and plays the weaker teams earlier in the season. Auerbach arouses his players emotionally.

Sitting there in Auerbach's office, the telephone no longer ringing, the ballplayers gone after picking up extra tickets for friends, I recited these complaints to the Boston coach.

He smiled, that great little needler, and said, "Schaus is a very fine coach. He has a very fine team. I don't know why they haven't done better."

We went downstairs to the floor of the arena. Auerbach likes to stand around the court while his players gather in the dressing room. He gets a feel of the court this way, he says, a sense of the mood that will be there soon, a taste for the competition to come.

As he walked around the Garden, shaking hands with a guard, accepting a cigar from a fan, needling a newspaperman, I couldn't help but think how remarkable this man's work really is. His critics used to say he couldn't win without Bob Cousy. They used to say Cousy ran the team. They used to say Frank Ramsey, who retired after last season, really coached the team. The truth is, of course, that Auerbach runs *his* team more than any other coach, runs *his* team. Even Schaus concedes this. "Auerbach is a great, great coach," Schaus said. "A tough coach. His technical knowledge of the game is second to none. He is the only coach in the league that I worry more what he's going to do than what I'm going to do. His substitutions, his matchups, his moves are so good that you're always looking around to see what he's up to so you can figure out how to meet it." Then comes the demurrer again; nobody delivers unencumbered testimonials to the winner. "I can respect him as a

coach," Schaus continued, "without respecting him as a person."

On the jump ball at the start of the game, Russell tapped to Heinsohn, who tapped to Tom Sanders, who was breaking toward the basket. Sanders went up with the ball and was hacked. The whistle blew. "Two shots." Auerbach, on the bench, yelled out to the referee, "What took you so long blowing that damn whistle?" The coach who is supposed to have baiting down to a science was at work in his laboratory.

Sanders made the two shots and the Lakers brought the ball downcourt. A Laker palmed the ball and Auerbach was off the bench in an instant, calling the violation before the referee called it. But the referee did call it. Part of the man's science must be to watch everything.

A little later a Laker double-dribbled and the referee didn't see it. He was, at that moment, looking at Auerbach, and he knew he had missed the call. Now he was glaring—that's the only word for it—and Auerbach was yelling. "Watch the game, willya. Watch it. How we gonna live if you miss them."

A little later, as he came by the Boston bench, the official grumbled at Auerbach. "Accuse me, that's all you do is accuse me. Why you always on me?"

Toward the end of the quarter, Russell walked as he went in for a hanging dump shot. The referee missed this one, too, and Schaus sprang from his bench screaming. The referee called a technical foul. He had taken all he was going to from those coaches. Schaus pulled at his hair. Auerbach sat silently on his bench. He had nothing more to say to the officials.

With 50 seconds remaining in the half, K.C. Jones ran by and yelled to Auerbach: "Now?"

"No, next time," Auerbach answered.

Boston shot and scored. Now there were 28 seconds left. "Okay," Auerbach called to Jones and, as the Lakers brought the ball across the center line, Jones fouled Dick Barnett. Barnett made his one shot. Boston held the ball out and, with three seconds left, passed into Russell for a jumper and two more points. The way Auerbach works the game of basketball, this was giving away one point and getting four. Although they weren't playing good ball, the Celtics went off the court leading, 59-52.

The second half was different. The Celtics still weren't playing up to their game, and Heinsohn jammed his finger going in for a driving layup and had to sit down, and Elgin Baylor got hot, and the Lakers won by two points when, with 12 seconds left, the Celtics set up for one last shot by Sam Jones and Jones never got the shot off.

Now it was two losses in a row, and Boston doesn't often drop two at a time. Their tiny dressing room under the end arena was very quiet. Players scolded themselves for bad moves. One or two praised Baylor's bold play in the second half. Heinsohn soaked his finger and said softly to Auerbach when the coach came by: "A tough one, Red." Auerbach nodded and walked out of the steamy room. He had a late supper date with friends who had come up from New York for the game. "I'd like to go to bed," he said before he left, "but what can you do? They're friends." The Celtics had to be in Philadelphia the next day, Saturday, for a game with the 76ers, and the coach had to go off somewhere and be pleasant with people. He wasn't

hungry and he had had only one meal all day.

Saturday morning in Boston was clear and cold. Auerbach met me in the coffee shop at the Hotel Lenox at 8:15 for breakfast. "No breakfast for me," he said. "I can't eat this early." We got into a small convertible sports car he had purchased for his older daughter and would be driving from Philadelphia to Washington after the ballgame that night. At ten we stopped for gas. I had coffee, he had a Coke and cookies. Then we drove and talked.

About his beginnings: "I'm from the Williamsburgh section of Brooklyn and I learned my basketball at a gym built outdoors, on the roof of Public School 122. Unless it snowed or rained, we played. In high school, I made the all-Brooklyn second team, and my players kid me about it now. What they don't know is that we had more good basketball players in Brooklyn in those days than there were in all the rest of the United States.

"At George Washington, I had a tough time making the club. There were six backcourt men trying out for varsity and only one job open. I had four fistfights in the first two weeks of practice, but I got the job.

"The point is, I guess, I was always a bit brash. I was 29 and right out of the Navy when I walked in on Mike Uline and told him I was the guy to coach his Washington team that was being organized for the new Basketball Association of America. I don't know why, but Mike bought my brag. I recruited my team in a phone booth, calling all over the country to players I had known in the Navy. Bob Feerick and John Norlander and Irv Torgoff and Fred Scolari and Bones McKinney. We won the division title our first year. In fact, do you know that in each of the 18 years I've been in pro ball we made the playoffs?"

About continuing to coach: "I've been given all the honors a coach could want. I've met the President. I've been around the world. I'm still at it because of one man, Walter Brown. He was like a father to me. We never even had a contract. Just a handshake every year. Like last year, just a couple of minutes before he died. We were coming back from lunch and Brown stopped right in North Station. 'There'll be people back in the office,' he said. 'We'd better talk here. What are you going to do?'

"'I'll be back,' I said.

"'Okay, what do you want?'

"I told him.

"'Okay,' he said, and we went back to the office. That's the way we got along. If he wanted out, I'd leave. If I wanted out, he'd let me leave."

About last year: Some people think it was Auerbach's toughest season and his greatest accomplishment. First, his team had to learn to play without Bob Cousy. Secondly, Frank Ramsey signed a magazine piece about dirty play in the NBA. Then Russell spoke out in a magazine piece rapping the color line in the game. Then Heinsohn, as player rep, was called "the biggest heel in sports" by Walter Brown and for a while there was talk that Heinsohn would quit. Such a string of headlines can ruin a team. People began looking for a blowup among the Celtics, and when it didn't happen, either they were surprised or they gave more credit to Auerbach. "The whole thing couldn't mean less to me," Auerbach said but not too convincingly. "My only concern is that when my players get out on the court they give me everything they've got."

About next year: "Sometimes I think I'd kind of like to make it an even 20 years in pro ball. But, truthfully, I don't know. I might retire at the end of this year. I might do it next year. We have been shopping around for a replacement, though. It's not easy to find the kind of coach we want." He meant it isn't easy to find another Auerbach. One of the men they've been thinking about, though, is an Auerbach product—Frank Ramsey.

About wives: "I never get involved in the personal lives of my players. I never meet them socially. I don't mix with their wives. Wives have no room on my club, not unless they can score."

About his hobbies: "I got two. I collect letter openers. Don't ask me how come, I don't know. I just started and now I've got 500 of them cluttering up the house.

"My other hobby is getting kids into colleges. Kids who deserve to go. I've come to know a lot of college people and I find it gratifying to steer kids to schools where they'll fit.

"I had this kid once, his father wanted him to get into Harvard. The kid had good marks but that was all. Kids with marks are a dime a dozen, I told his father. You want me to try to help the kid, you got to listen to me. First thing, he's got to learn how to shake hands. None of this shaking with the tips of the fingers. He's got to shake. When he's interviewed, the Harvard people will notice. Then we got to get him into athletics. He can't play ball, so we'll get the high-school coach to name him manager of the baseball team. I worked with that kid his whole last year in high school and we got him into Harvard. He's still a shnook but now he's a shnook with a Harvard diploma."

Auerbach didn't talk about the game lost the night before or the game to be played this night. He was too concerned to talk. He wanted to win.

It was almost three o'clock when we pulled up to the Penn-Sheraton Hotel in Philadelphia. Auerbach parked the car in a no-parking zone and we went to eat. I had dinner and he had a grilled salami sandwich and a Coke. (This didn't shock me. Once, years before, when we went out for breakfast, we ate at a candy store because Auerbach wanted an egg cream and chocolate cake.) Then Auerbach went up to sleep for a while. I promised to wake him at six.

The team had arrived that morning, coming down on an early flight, as Auerbach had ordered. He wanted them resting in Philly, not running in Boston. The lobby was quiet. The players were sleeping or eating or watching television.

When I knocked at his door at six, Auerbach was up and dressed. He had soaked in a bathtub for a while, read the Philadelphia papers, napped for perhaps half an hour, and now was thirsty. We had Cokes again downstairs. Then he called his wife. She said she would meet him at a Toddle Shoppe in Washington at about 2:30 in the morning. He was pleased about this.

We drove the three blocks to Convention Hall. There was no ticket on his car. (There never is. Auerbach has a great talent for talking his way out of trouble with motorcycle cops, too.) The players were all there when Auerbach entered the dressing room on the second floor of the cavernous hall. Tom Sanders was in a corner reading a paperback novel. Willie Naulls, down to his shorts, was lying on a bench, his eyes shut.

The room was quiet, too quiet.

Auerbach didn't want this mood. Too easy to think about the night before. ("In my dressing room you think about winning," he preaches.) But he waited and watched. Then he decided. This was no night for a growl, no night for hard basketball talk.

He started with Sam Jones. "Let's see the three coins, Sam." Jones placed coins on the knuckles of the first three fingers of his right hand, flipped them up in the air and caught them, one at a time, in his right hand.

"How's the place doing?" he asked Russell. Russell had recently purchased a night club in Boston.

"Great, Red," he said. "I never knew a place could do so good. I got two juke boxes going there and I'm ashamed to tell you how much money they make. They pay the rent."

Russell, who usually vomits before a game to help relax himself, was belching. This wasn't going to be an easy night for him. His stomach was tight. But he knew what his coach was working at and he joined in. "Hey, Sam, what's this about a new life insurance I hear about? You can collect before you die."

Sam Jones sells insurance during the off-season. "I'll take all the insurance you want to buy, Russ," he said. "Any provisions you want. Just include those slaves you got down in Africa." (Russell also owns a couple of plantations in Liberia.)

Now Heinsohn picked it up. His finger was swollen to double its size and he would not play tonight. But he would work. "Red, remember that fight you had, you wanted me to appear as a witness?"

Auerbach grinned.

"Red comes to me," Heinsohn continued, "and says, 'Heiny, I'll need you in court to testify.' 'But, Red,' I say, 'I didn't even see the fight. I was in the locker room by then.' 'Yeah,' Red says, 'I know. But you'll testify.'"

Russell: "Remember the time Red got hit with the egg? That yolk running down his face. He thought he was dead."

The younger players were listening now. "I had a bodyguard there for a while," Auerbach said, "an ex-FBI man. They thought I needed him because I'd had a few fights in places like Syracuse and St. Louis. This bodyguard, I guess, knew his business, and he's standing behind me, protecting me from stuff that might come out of the seats. So this guy comes right out on the court and walked up practically next to me and lets fly. Hits me right in the middle of the forehead. I thought I'd been shot. No kidding. I didn't know what hit me. And when I feel that egg yolk running down, I figure it's blood."

The banter was easy now, one story topping another. Five minutes before they were due to go out on the court, Auerbach looked up. That meant everybody out. It is a firm Auerbach rule. Only his trainer can remain when Auerbach talks to his men. Since I was the only other person in the room, I left.

Five minutes later, Auerbach and his men came out on the court. "What did you say to them?" I asked. "What did I have to say?" Auerbach answered. "I told them to play ball. That's all. This is no night for pepping them up."

It isn't always so with the Celtics. Some nights Auerbach will work on them for ten minutes or more. He calls it "psyching" and it works. Once, before a game, Auerbach had a pain in his back and sat in the whirlpool bath instead of getting his players up. Just before the start of the game, Russell came over to the bench. "Red, baby, you didn't get me up for this one," he said.

"Listen, baby," Auerbach answered, "you owe me a few. You psyche me up tonight." It worked better than a pep talk would have that evening. Russell laughed and was ready to play.

There was a small and noisy Saturday night crowd in Convention Hall. "Hey, Red," a man yelled at Auerbach. "I didn't think you'd show up tonight." Auerbach smiled. Another man hollered, "How many you giving away, Auerbach?" He walked over to where they were sitting, just to the side of the Boston bench. When he's holding short, Auerbach will give the crowd a shot at him. His skin doesn't blister.

The Celtics were introduced. Each player was cheered. When it was Auerbach's turn, up came a boo. Auerbach waved. He claims these boos are mostly friendly. "I know the difference between a boo from a friend and a boo from an enemy." He says. "I should."

The game started sloppily, but not a word from Auerbach to the officials, not yet, at least. Dolph Schayes, the 76er coach, was up early complaining about the calls, and Auerbach was letting him have the floor. At the six-minute mark, Schayes was clipped with a technical foul for his stomping and shouting. Kindly Red Auerbach slouched back, his hands folded across his chest.

Late in the quarter Sam Jones stole a 76er pass and looped the ball to Russell coming down on the fast break. The ball went off Russell's hands and out of bounds. On the way back downcourt, Russell turned to Jones and mouthed: "Good pass, Sam." This is as good a sign as any of the closeness of the Celtics. The club has no cliques, and Russell, who could easily form one around himself, doesn't. A proud, intelligent man who is willing to say what he thinks, Russell is like Auerbach in that he cares about winning. He knows that comes first.

Russell has had bad knees since his college days—they may even be arthritic—and he needs to have them rubbed every night before he plays. "The pain," he says, "is like a toothache in the knee." But he plays 48 minutes a game, sitting down only on the few occasions when Auerbach feels the game is under control.

"This is a very smart man," Auerbach tells you. "I always tell my players I got to worry about eleven of them. The eleven of them only have to worry about one of me. Russell takes the time to study me, to know when I'm feeling good and when I'm feeling grumpy. He knows when to come to ask me for something. Like in the locker room before tonight's game. He came over quietly to ask if he could leave Philadelphia after the game instead of traveling back with the team at ten tomorrow morning. The way he starts it, he says, 'Can I see you a minute?' I figure I know what he wants but I say, 'Whatever it is, the answer is no.' He starts to walk away, slowly, because he knows I'll call him back. 'Yeah, you can go,' I say. I figured I owe him one. Last week he asked if he could go from Philadelphia to New York and then on to Chicago. I said yes because I knew he expected me to say no. He was figuring I'd say no this time and I'd owe him a yes next time. It's a game we play. And he's good at it." So, by the way, is Auerbach.

Moving the ball into the corner, Sam Jones was shoved. No words were exchanged with the officials but as he came back,

Jones told Auerbach. The Celtics know that Auerbach does the yelling for them.

At a time out Auerbach said to John Havlicek: "Knock off the fancy dribbling." Nothing else had to be said. Auerbach doesn't yell in a huddle, whatever the situation. "They're keyed up enough," he says. "It's my job to ease the tension."

Philadelphia was having trouble with its passes in the first half. K.C. Jones stole two in a row. This was no happenstance. The Celtics still play the best defense in the league. It is an Auerbach mark. Defense, he explains over and over again, is concentration. That's why Celtics are required to yell out, "That's my man. That's my man." It reminds them they're playing the other half of the game.

If you are bored with the racehorse offense of pro ball, watch the Celtics on defense once. It should perk you up. The way the Celtics play, the man with the ball has got to get past three men on his way to the basket. Then, if he makes it, he has to face the large hands and brilliant timing of Bill Russell. The Celtics close up the middle. They force the ball to the weaker or newer offensive opponent. They squeeze on a man from several directions if he is driving in. And they've always got their hands up.

Credit for this must go to the coach. Everyone likes to shoot but no pro fit for the name likes to play defense. Auerbach makes them play it. He drills it during preseason training and repeats it in practice sessions held every day at home when the club is not scheduled to play that night. "I'll let a man rest on offense," he explains, "but not on defense. If I see him loafing, out he comes. With Russell on the club, we're a step ahead of the rest of the league on defense, and I mean to keep us there." Auerbach won't comment on the point but other coaches contend that the Celtic defense is worth ten points a game or better.

This sturdy defense is just one innovation—if innovation doesn't strike you as too shocking a word to use to describe the simple act of guarding another man on the court—Auerbach has brought to pro ball. He was the first to use precisely detailed out-of-bounds plays, for example. In the first half against the 76ers, the Celtics had three out-of-bounds chances. They lined up for each in a different formation, peeled off as if by the numbers, and scored each time. The 76ers had two out-of-bounds under their basket and gave up the ball each time without scoring.

Near the end of the first half, Auerbach began to work on the senior of the two referees. The Celtics were only ahead by five at the time. "Hey, Earl, that's a foul," he said not too loudly. This was a soft workout, remember. "Hey, Earl, watch his feet." "Earl, stop him from pushing." "Foul, Earl." Once as the referee went by, he shouted to Auerbach: "Go ahead, say it again. Watch the foul, Earl." The Boston bench, without a signal, responded in loud, unison: "Okay, watch the foul, Earl." The referee smothered his smile. And Auerbach was content. The score at half-time was 61-50.

Before the start of the second half, Russell became ill. His stomach hurt. He began to belch and pop Tums into his mouth. "Red," he said. "I'm gonna be sick."

"Later," Auerbach said. "Now play."

It wasn't a joke. Auerbach wanted this ballgame. With Heinsohn out, he was worried enough. With Russell out, too,

he would be upset. Heinsohn began cheerleading from the bench. "Big defense, men, big defense." That was one way to hold what you had, and Heinsohn, co-captain of the Celtics with Russell, knew it. "I hate to lose," Auerbach had told me earlier in the day, "but him, he really hates to lose."

The funny thing is that when Heinsohn first joined the club as a territorial choice, Auerbach said he was too cocky a kid to make the pros. "He loafs too much," Auerbach said then. Heinsohn was upset but he did something about it. He showed Auerbach he was tough.

"Right away, he was a pro's pro," the coach said. "He wears this knee brace because a lateral ligament is gone. Now that's supposed to be bad. But he plays on it without a comment. He just hates to miss a game. Watch him tonight. He'll die on that bench."

I watched. And Heinsohn worked and wiggled and wore himself out urging on his teammates. On almost every play, he was up from the bench, his hands pumping as if, somehow, he were helping move the ball to the basket.

After four minutes of play and two failures to follow up a shot under the boards, Russell began to move. His stomach muscles loosened, his belches became audible as he ran down the court, and he began to do his job under the defensive board. This is where he is a genius. "There have been four or five men who have revolutionized the game," Auerbach said earlier. "Hank Luisetti with his one-handed shot. George Mikan, who made the pivot an offensive weapon. Cousy, who showed what playmaking and the fast break could do. And Russell. He changed the entire game. He developed defense as a weapon. He made the blocked shot a popular play. Before him, men used to jump with the shooter.

Russell showed them that you have to wait a second and jump just after the shot. Then you can block the shot. Today kids practice it in the playground. Blocking a shot is now a factor in winning or losing."

It was this night. Russell's work was needed in the second half. The Celtics' offense remained sub-par. The team seemed sluggish with the ball. Sam Jones wasn't hitting. And Tom Sanders was having a rare off-night.

Sanders has the toughest game assignment on the team. He must play a full-time defense against the opponent's highest scoring cornerman. That means people like Elgin Baylor and Jerry Lucas and Bob Pettit. And on most nights he does the job. He has long arms and strong legs, and can run, and isn't afraid to mix it, and understands the game. Does he like to play defense? "How do I know?" Auerbach answered when I once asked him this. "I didn't ask him. I told him. I tell everybody. A ballclub is a dictatorship, and I'm the dictator. You start asking ballplayers what they like and you're done."

Sanders was available as a No. 1 draft choice for the Celtics, who always pick last, because the New York Knicks decided to skip him. "When he came to camp," Auerbach said, "I was shocked. He didn't look like any basketball player. He wore elbow pads and knee pads halfway up his legs and glasses. He must have been carrying 20 pounds of equipment around on him. First thing I did, I told him to get contact lenses, that we'd pay for them. Then I told Frank Ramsey to steal his knee guards. He came over to me the next day and said, 'I can't find

my knee guards.'

"'Knee guards?' I said. 'Who the hell wears knee guards?'

"'I do,' he said, 'always.'

"'Why?' I asked him. 'You got bad knees?'

"'No, sir!' he said, 'I got good knees.'

"'Then why the knee guards? Forget 'em. They're just extra weight. I don't want you wearing one ounce of extra weight.'" Sanders never wore knee guards again.

Toward the end of the third quarter, Willie Naulls came in for Sanders and began hitting with a few one-handers from the corner. Naulls is another of the NBA veterans Auerbach keeps picking up and rejuvenating.

When Naulls joined the Celtics last season, he reported to camp at 248 pounds. In the first day of training, he collapsed from sheer exhaustion. "Every other club I was on," Naulls said, "we took it easy until the season started. Here I was down to 218 by the opening game."

Some coaches believe a team should play its way into shape. Not Auerbach. "This isn't professional wrestling. While they're playing into shape, my team is winning the first 14 out of 15 games."

How does he do it? With concentrated drills and very little rest. "A man is in shape only after he is really tired. Then the conditioning means something. We work for two days, twice a day, without the ball. After that, we drill only with the ball. I don't believe in road work. It doesn't apply to basketball. I have them running sideways and backwards, with their hands up, with short stops and starts. For two weeks we do this. Then we spend a week playing exhibitions. Then another week of conditioning. When the season starts, we're ready.

"I have a standing order. Don't come into camp out of shape and don't ever get out of shape."

The Celtics kept running and holding a five-point lead against the 76ers. Their shooting wasn't good enough to widen the lead but their defense was tough enough to avoid narrowing it. At one point, John Havlicek—the team's high scorer last season and today a strong, hardnosed, confident competitor—committed an obvious foul. He raised his hand to signal that he was the guilty party even before the referee announced the call. Swiftly, Auerbach jumped off the bench. "Johnny," he yelled. "Don't raise your hand. You don't tell them."

Midway in the fourth quarter, Philadelphia trimmed the Celtics' lead to one point with the two quick baskets. Auerbach dropped his head between his knees. But K.C. Jones stole another pass and the Celtics had momentum again. "What a kid," Auerbach said. Earlier in the day, he had given K.C. the kind of praise a man reserves for his first-born son. "This is one

of the finest boys I have ever coached. Never complains. Never blows. Loyal. Unselfish. You've got to keep bugging him or else he won't tell you when he's hurting. Whoever gets that kid to work for him, after he retires, will get the very best.

"After I drafted him, people said he couldn't shoot. Trade him, they said. But I wanted to take a look. I like kids who've been with winners. I broke him in with the club and got nothing but 100 percent hustle from him. I found that I never lost ground when I put him in. He was fast and quick and durable and smart. He knew how to play defense. True, he had to learn to shoot. So he went to work at it. Now he's getting confidence in his shooting. And I won't say a word. If he misses a hundred, I won't say a word. I've never bawled that kid out, he's that great. He's always been overshadowed, at San Francisco U. and here."

With 2:30 minutes remaining in the game, Sam Jones sank a foul and the Celtics were ahead by seven. Auerbach turned to me (I was sitting next to him) and said, "We got this one." Then he allowed a smile. "Up the guzzuppy," he said, "we got it." He had wanted that win.

A few minutes later I was hearing my first noisy Celtic locker room. "Good win," Auerbach was saying. "Not a good game but a good win. We needed that one."

Russell's stomach still hurt him. (In fact, the next day he had to check into a Boston hospital for observation, but was out in time for the next game the following Wednesday.) K.C. Jones had a bruise on his leg. But the Celtics were happy and they were going to celebrate. And Auerbach was saying that's a good idea. He doesn't bother much with curfews and bed checks and gumshoeing. "Who am I kidding?" he said.

"It takes me two hours to unwind, and I don't play. I can't tell them to go to bed. These are grown men. They know how to take care of themselves. And they know that I'll know when things are getting out of hand. If they play for me, they're ready to play or they're gone. I don't bawl a man out in public. I don't give him a serious fine. If he's that kind of trouble, I got to get rid of him anyway."

Auerbach asked Heinsohn about his finger. It looked as if it would be ready for Wednesday. He spoke to Sanders. "Your game was off but your try was good." Sanders, who won't say the wrong thing if he lives to be 100, smiled. "Don't kid me, Red. I was off."

Then Auerbach put on his hat and coat and said, "I got to go. I'll see you Wednesday." He had a date for 2:30 in the morning at a Toddle Shoppe in Washington and he wanted to be on time.

(Reprinted with permission, Sport Media Enterprises, Inc., 2003)

The Modern Game

1970-2003

Willis Reed, over Jerry West and teammate Jerry Lucas, 1973
A career cut short by injuries, but Reed's courage in playing the final game of the 1970 final despite a torn thigh muscle lifted his sport to a new level.

Section **3**

Chapter 14

The Magic, Larry and Michael Show

As the 1970s began, basketball remained No. 4 behind baseball, football and hockey among North American professional leagues. But by the time the millennium was finished, basketball was challenging football for the top spot in North America and had ascended to the No. 2 ranking behind soccer as the most popular team sport on the planet.

The reasons for the ascendancy are many. In 1975, four ABA franchises joined the NBA and the others disbanded, leaving one nation-wide major pro league that happily accepted such ABA stars as Julius Erving, George Gervin, Artis Gilmore, Dan Issel and Moses Malone. They joined a league that had been welcoming its own fresh crop of stars, including Lew Alcindor, Bill Walton and Earl Monroe. Still, the 1970s were difficult years because of an image problem created in part by persistent rumors of rampant drug use among players.

The turnaround began in the 1979-80 season with the coming of Magic Johnson in Los Angeles and Larry Bird in Boston. The arrival of these two budding stars, coupled with a league crackdown on the drug problem and a collective-bargaining agreement between the owners and the players that established a salary cap, resulted in NBA fortunes taking a dramatic upturn. From 1980 to 1989, every NBA final featured either Bird or Johnson, including three times when both appeared. They conjured memories of the great Bill Russell-Wilt Chamberlain battles of the 1960s and ignited interest among waves of new fans, corporate sponsors and television executives.

The growth fueled by Bird and Johnson was only a harbinger of what was to come. By the end of the 1980s, Michael Jordan had emerged as the game's dominant player and, before retiring in 2003, would be largely recognized as the greatest player ever. More than unparalleled ability, he brought the NBA a marquee figure whose worldwide celebrity would translate into unprecedented international growth of the game— and new-found riches for the NBA that were reaped from marketers eager to climb aboard the Jordan bandwagon.

With Jordan as its centerpiece, the NBA formed the Dream Team to compete in the 1992 Summer Olympics. The U.S. easily won the gold medal but, more significantly, demonstrated the power of celebrity. The worldwide popularity of basketball exploded after 1992. Today almost 20 percent of all players in the NBA were born outside of the United States, there is a team in Canada and the league has begun thinking about the possibility of operating in Europe, South America and Asia.

In the U.S., pro basketball is at an all-time high in popularity. The NBA's clever marketing has made household names of players such as Shaquille O'Neal, Kevin Garnett and Jason Kidd. Its popularity has continued despite run-ins with the law by some of its biggest names. Kobe Bryant, who might have been the most marketable NBA player in the post-Jordan era,

Dan Issel and Julius Erving, 1974
A league existing perpetually on the precipice of disaster, but the ABA's legacy on the game of basketball has been great.

entered the 2003-04 season proclaiming his innocence to a charge of felony sexual assault. Still, the league will add its 30th team in 2004, ticket sales are strong and TV revenues high.

And the talent pool has never been deeper, driven in no small part by several players who are graduating to the NBA directly from high school. The latest among the teenage sensations is LeBron James, who would debut with the Cleveland Cavaliers in 2003-04 after signing approximately $100-million in endorsement contracts before taking his first shot in the NBA.

1970-71

Bullets upset Knicks, but no one can match dominant Bucks

Undaunted by a stagnant national economy and motivated to shut the rival ABA out of as many markets as possible, the NBA indulged in another round of expansion which brought the Buffalo Braves, Cleveland Cavaliers, and Portland Trail Blazers into the circuit. The new clubs were typically forgettable on the floor, with the Cavaliers starting their maiden campaign with 15 straight losses and ending it with a total of 15 wins in 82 contests. But their presence forced the NBA into a major structural change, the creation of two divisions within both the Eastern and Western Conferences; two clubs from each of the four divisions would compete in the playoffs.

The Midwest Division was the strongest sector and had the league's strongest team, the Milwaukee Bucks. Last season center Lew Alcindor had turned the Bucks from an expansion team into a contender; this season guard Oscar Robertson turned them from a contender into a championship team. The Big O was unhappy under Bob Cousy in Cincinnati and was a sure bet to be traded as last season ended; the Bucks were able to pick up the all-time great guard for the relatively low price of Flynn Robinson and Charlie Paulk. Oscar furnished the ball-handing, outside shooting, and back-court leadership that could complement and increase Alcindor's dominance in the front-court. With Bob Dandridge, John McGlocklin, and Greg Smith filling out the starting lineup, the Bucks won recognition as the NBA's latest superteam. The Bucks obviously were not team-oriented in the usual sense, relying most heavily on Alcindor and Robertson. Twice the Bucks strung together long winning binges, taking 16 in a row at one point and later winning a record 20 straight. The only fly in the ointment for the Bucks was their inability to beat the defending champion New York Knicks, dropping four of five contests to the New Yorkers. The Bucks easily took first place in the most competitive division in the NBA, with the Bucks, Chicago Bulls, Phoenix Suns, and Detroit Pistons all finishing way over the .500 level.

The Bulls blossomed into a devastatingly physical club in Dick Motta's third year as coach and they had the third best record in the league at 51-31. Phoenix enjoyed its first winning season in its three-year history, and the Pistons had their first winning season since moving to Detroit, thanks largely to veteran guard Dave Bing, a nine-game winning streak to open

Lew Alcindor
Wreaking havoc with his sky hook, he nails the first of his MVP six-pack.

the season, and strong contributions from big rookie center Bob Lanier.

The Los Angeles Lakers had no rookie center in winning the Pacific Division title; they simply had Wilt Chamberlain back after missing most of last season with a knee injury. Chamberlain and Jerry West were a front-back combination to match Alcindor and Robertson in Milwaukee, but the Lakers lost their third superstar when forward Elgin Baylor had to sit out the season with bad knees. The Lakers did pick up some valuable new help by getting veteran guards Gail Goodrich and Pat Riley in deals and by signing rookie forward Jim McMillian.

The big but slow San Francisco Warriors edged out the San Diego Rockets, who relied on high-scoring Elvin Hayes, for the second playoff berth. The Rockets had one of the league's most colorful rookies in 5-foot-9 Calvin Murphy, the slick shooter and ball-handler out of Niagara College. The fourth-place Seattle Supersonics had the most controversial rookie in forward Spencer Haywood. The star of the 1968 Olympics, Haywood had left school after his sophomore season to sign with the ABA Denver Rockets last season. Midway through this season, however, he declared his contract with Denver void and signed with the Supersonics. The other league members stormed Commissioner Walter Kennedy with protests that Haywood had not gone through the college draft, and thus the Sonics had no right to sign him. The threats of penalties and lawsuits filled the air, but the Seattle team kept Haywood and thus won themselves an All-Star forward. The expansion Portland club had a fine rookie in guard Geoff Petrie but had very little else.

The New York Knicks got little help from any rookies, but they had enough returning talent to easily win the Atlantic Division with a 52-30 mark. Walt Frazier had developed into the NBA's best defensive guard and playmaker, and center Willis Reed's fine performance belied the fact that a bad knee and a bad shoulder were severely bothering him. The Philadelphia 76ers had a gaping hole at center but held on to the second playoff berth ahead of the vastly improved Boston Celtics. Given a hard dose of reality during last season's tumble into the ranks of losers, the Celtics had unloaded Larry Siegfried, Bailey Howell, and Em Bryant. They built a new starting lineup out of veteran forwards John Havlicek and Don Nelson, young guards Jo Jo White and Don Chaney, and hustling rookie center Dave

Cowens. This new Celtic outfit possessed the potential to run and press as well as the departed champs. The new Buffalo team was competitive but a distant last.

None of the teams in the Central Division created much excitement, with a 42-40 record earning the Baltimore Bullets first place. The Atlanta Hawks fell under the .500 level to 36-46, hurt by Joe Caldwell's jump to the ABA and by having to adjust to the fancy dribbling and passing of rookie guard Pete Maravich, the NCAA scoring champ for three seasons at Louisiana State. Minus Jerry Lucas and Oscar Robertson, the Cincinnati Royals dropped to 33-49 despite 6-foot Nate Archibald's emergence as a first-rate offensive threat. The new Cleveland team needed a telescope even to see a playoff berth.

As the playoffs began, fans anticipated a Milwaukee-New York final, with the star-heavy Bucks facing the smart, balanced Knicks. But while the Bucks easily handled the Warriors and Lakers in the West, Willis Reed's physical ills put the Knicks in deep trouble. They disposed of the Hawks in five games but met their match in the fast-breaking Bullets.

The New Yorkers looked safe after winning the first two games, but then Wes Unseld and Gus Johnson took control of the boards away from the Knicks. The Bullets won games three, four, and six to force a seventh game, and they walked off the court 93-91 victors as Bill Bradley missed a jump shot at the buzzer. For the Bullets, the victory over New York was the finest of the campaign, but the taste of triumph was short-lived. Unseld could not contain Alcindor, and the well-rested Bucks walked over the tired Bullets in four straight games, winning the NBA championship only three seasons after joining as a weak expansion outpost.

1970-71 SEASON HIGHLIGHTS

STANDINGS

Eastern Conference
Atlantic Division

	W	L	Pct.	GB
New York	52	30	.634	—
Philadelphia	47	35	.573	5
Boston	44	38	.537	8
Buffalo	22	60	.268	30

Central Division

	W	L	Pct.	GB
Baltimore	42	40	.512	—
Atlanta	36	46	.439	6
Cincinnati	33	49	.402	9
Cleveland	15	67	.183	27

Western Conference
Midwest Division

	W	L	Pct.	GB
Milwaukee	66	16	.805	—
Chicago	51	31	.622	15
Phoenix	48	34	.585	18
Detroit	45	37	.549	21

Pacific Division

	W	L	Pct.	GB
Los Angeles	48	34	.585	—
San Francisco	41	41	.500	7
San Diego	40	42	.488	8
Seattle	38	44	.463	10
Portland	29	53	.354	19

AWARDS
MVP
Lew Alcindor, Milwaukee
Top Rookie (tie)
Geoff Petrie, Portland
Dave Cowens, Boston
Coach of Year
Dick Motta, Chicago
ALL-STAR TEAMS
FIRST TEAM

John Havlicek	Boston
Billy Cunningham	Philadelphia
Lew Alcindor	Milwaukee
Jerry West	Los Angeles
Dave Bing	Detroit

ALL-STAR GAME
International Sports Arena, San Diego
Tuesday, January 12, 1971
West 108, East 107
MVP: Lenny Wilkens

SECOND TEAM

Gus Johnson	Baltimore
Bob Love	Chicago
Willis Reed	New York
Walt Frazier	New York
Oscar Robertson	Milwaukee

PLAYOFFS
FINALS
Milwaukee 4, Baltimore 0
Apr. 21: Baltimore 88 at Milwaukee 98
Apr. 25: Milwaukee 102 at Baltimore 83
Apr. 28: Baltimore 99 at Milwaukee 107
Apr. 30: Milwaukee 118 at Baltimore 106
EASTERN CONFERENCE
CONFERENCE FINALS
Baltimore 4, New York 3
Apr. 6: Baltimore 111 at New York 112
Apr. 9: Baltimore 88 at New York 107
Apr. 11: New York 88 at Baltimore 114
Apr. 14: New York 80 at Baltimore 101
Apr. 16: Baltimore 84 at New York 89
Apr. 18: New York 96 at Baltimore 113
Apr. 19: Baltimore 93 at New York 91
CONFERENCE SEMI-FINALS
New York 4, Atlanta 1
Mar. 25: Atlanta 101 at New York 112
Mar. 27: Atlanta 113 at New York 104

Mar. 28: New York 110 at Atlanta 95
Mar. 30: New York 113 at Atlanta 107
Apr. 1: Atlanta 107 at New York 111
Baltimore 4, Philadelphia 3
Mar. 24: Philadelphia 126 at Baltimore 112
Mar. 26: Baltimore 119 at Philadelphia 107
Mar. 28: Philadelphia 103 at Baltimore 111
Mar. 30: Baltimore 120 at Philadelphia 105
Apr. 1: Philadelphia 104 at Baltimore 103
Apr. 3: Baltimore 94 at Philadelphia 98
Apr. 4: Philadelphia 120 at Baltimore 128
WESTERN CONFERENCE
CONFERENCE FINALS
Milwaukee 4, Los Angeles 1
Apr. 9: Los Angeles 85 at Milwaukee 106
Apr. 11: Los Angeles 73 at Milwaukee 91
Apr. 14: Milwaukee 107 at Los Angeles 118
Apr. 16: Milwaukee 117 at Los Angeles 94
Apr. 18: Los Angeles 98 at Milwaukee 116

CONFERENCE SEMI-FINALS
Milwaukee 4, San Francisco 1
Mar. 27: Milwaukee 107 at San Francisco 96
Mar. 29: San Francisco 90, Milwaukee (at Madison, WI) 104
Mar. 30: San Francisco 102, Milwaukee (at Madison, Wis.) 114
Apr. 1: Milwaukee 104 at San Francisco 106
Apr. 4: San Francisco 86, Milwaukee (at Madison, WI) 136
Los Angeles 4, Chicago 3
Mar. 24: Chicago 99 at Los Angeles 100
Mar. 26: Chicago 95 at Los Angeles 105
Mar. 28: Los Angeles 98 at Chicago 106
Mar. 30: Los Angeles 102 at Chicago 112
Apr. 1: Chicago 86 at Los Angeles 115
Apr. 4: Los Angeles 99 at Chicago 113
Apr. 6: Chicago 98 at Los Angeles 109

NBA LEADERS

SCORING

	GP	FGM	FTM	PTS	PPG
Lew Alcindor, MIL	82	1063	470	2596	31.7
John Havlicek, BOS	81	892	554	2338	28.9
Elvin Hayes, SDR	82	948	454	2350	28.7
Dave Bing, DET	82	799	615	2213	27.0
Lou Hudson, ATL	76	829	381	2039	26.8
Bob Love, CHI	81	765	513	2043	25.2
Geoff Petrie, POR	82	784	463	2031	24.8
Pete Maravich, ATL	81	738	404	1880	23.2
Billy Cunningham, PHI	81	702	455	1859	23.0
Tom Van Arsdale, CIN	82	749	377	1875	22.9

FIELD GOALS

	FGM	FGA	FG%
Johnny Green, CIN	502	855	.587
Lew Alcindor, MIL	1063	1843	.577
Wilt Chamberlain, LAL	668	1226	.545
Jon McGlocklin, MIL	574	1073	.535
Dick Snyder, SEA	645	1215	.531
Greg Smith, MIL	409	799	.512
Bob Dandridge, MIL	594	1167	.509
Wes Unseld, BAL	424	846	.501
Jerry Lucas, SFW	623	1250	.498
Archie Clark, PHI	662	1334	.496
Oscar Robertson, MIL	592	1193	.496

FREE THROWS

	FTM	FTA	FT%
Chet Walker, CHI	480	559	.859
Oscar Robertson, MIL	385	453	.850
Ron Williams, SFW	331	392	.844
Jeff Mullins, SFW	302	358	.844
Dick Snyder, SEA	302	361	.837
Stan McKenzie, POR	331	396	.836
Jerry West, LAL	525	631	.832
Jimmy Walker, DET	344	414	.831
Bob Love, CHI	513	619	.829
Calvin Murphy, SDR	356	434	.820

ASSISTS

	GP	AST	APG
Norm Van Lier, CIN	82	832	10.1
Lenny Wilkens, SEA	71	654	9.2
Oscar Robertson, MIL	81	668	8.2
John Havlicek, BOS	81	607	7.5
Walt Frazier, NYK	80	536	6.7
Mahdi Abdul-Rahman, ATL	82	514	6.3
Ron Williams, SFW	82	480	5.9
Nate Archibald, CIN	82	450	5.5
Archie Clark, PHI	82	440	5.4
Dave Bing, DET	82	408	5.0

REBOUNDS

	GP	TRB	RPG
Wilt Chamberlain, LAL	82	1493	18.2
Wes Unseld, BAL	74	1253	16.9
Elvin Hayes, SDR	82	1362	16.6
Lew Alcindor, MIL	82	1311	16.0
Jerry Lucas, SFW	80	1265	15.8
Bill Bridges, ATL	82	1233	15.0
Dave Cowens, BOS	81	1216	15.0
Tom Boerwinkle, CHI	82	1133	13.8
Nate Thurmond, SFW	82	1128	13.8
Willis Reed, NYK	73	1003	13.7

THE YEAR IN BASKETBALL

October 14, 1970 Nate (Tiny) Archibald debuts for the Cincinnati Royals, in a home game versus New York. Playing for the same franchise two seasons later, he will become the only player to ever lead the league in scoring and assists in the same year, averaging 34.0 points and 11.4 assists per game for the Kansas City-Omaha Kings.

October 17, 1970
Pistol Pete Maravich, the college game's most prolific scorer, makes his NBA debut for the Atlanta Hawks at home against Milwaukee. The Bucks win, 107-86.

November 12, 1970 After starting life 0-15, the expansion Cleveland Cavaliers win their first game, beating the expansion Portland Trail Blazers, 105-103, in Portland.

November 13, 1970 John Brisker of the ABA's Pittsburgh Condors scores 50 points versus Texas, one night after scoring 53 against Indiana.

January 5, 1971 The Harlem Globetrotters lose to the New Jersey Reds, 100-99, breaking a 2,495-game winning streak.

January 11, 1971 The NBA names its 25th Anniversary team, comprised of Paul Arizin, Bob Cousy, Bob Davies, Joe Fulks, Sam Jones, George Mikan, Bob Pettit, Bill Russell, Dolph Schayes, and Bill Sharman.

January 23, 1971 Robert Douglas, the owner and coach of the great New York Rens for over 25 years, is the first black elected to the Basketball Hall of Fame.

January 29, 1971 Hal Greer of the 76ers becomes the sixth player in NBA history to score 20,000 points in a 142-118 loss to Milwaukee.

January 30, 1971 UCLA begins an 88-game winning streak with a 74-61 win over Cal-Santa Barbara.

March 27, 1971 North Carolina wins its first and only NIT title, thumping Georgia Tech, 84-66. The Tar Heels' Bill Chamberlain is named tournament MVP.

March 30, 1971 UCLA becomes the first team ever to win five consecutive NCAA basketball titles when they defeat Villanova, 68-62.

March 30, 1971 A Los Angeles county judge rules that the NBA cannot prevent collegiate underclassman Spencer Haywood from playing for the Seattle Supersonics. The ruling effectively ends the NBA's dictate against underclassmen from joining the league.

April 19, 1971 In a fiercely played series, the Baltimore Bullets nip the Knicks, 93-91, in Game 7 of the Eastern Conference finals. In the finale, Earl Monroe paces Baltimore with 26. Dick Barnett and Willis Reed lead New York with 26 and 24 points, respectively.

April 30, 1971 The Milwaukee Bucks win the NBA championship in a four-game sweep of the Baltimore Bullets. Lew Alcindor scores 27 points to give the Bucks the title in only their third season in the league.

May 18, 1971 The Utah Stars, led by Zelmo Beaty's 36 points, beat the Kentucky Colonels, 131-121, to win the ABA championship. The Stars overcome Dan Issel's 41 points for the Colonels.

May 1971 Wayne Embry becomes the first black general manager in NBA history when the Milwaukee Bucks elevate him to that post.

1971-72

Lakers finally champs on ninth trip to final in post-Mikan era

As a weapon against the rival ABA's signing of undergraduate stars before their senior year, the NBA now permitted the drafting of undergrads if they could be classified as hardship cases; this ruling retroactively covered the signing of Spencer Haywood by Seattle last season, and it allowed Baltimore to sign guard Phil Chenier after his junior year at California. But with the ABA seriously bidding for the services of the top college talent, this year's rookies were no longer hardship cases after signing their pro contracts. Sidney Wicks, Austin Carr, Elmore Smith, Curtis Rowe, and Howard Porter all accepted lucrative pacts from NBA teams, and while top collegians Artis Gilmore, George McGinnis, and Julius Erving signed with the ABA, the older league struck back by hiring two young ABA stars, Charlie Scott and Jim McDaniels. They were signed late in the season after they had found escape clauses in their contracts.

In addition to the rich new faces around the league, the NBA also had a new city, as the San Diego Rockets abandoned the West Coast to set up shop in Houston, where an ABA team had failed earlier. The San Francisco Warriors changed their name to the Golden State Warriors, and Milwaukee center Lew Alcindor changed his name to Kareem Abdul-Jabbar because of his Islamic religious beliefs.

And the mantle of super-team also changed hands this season, passing from the Milwaukee Bucks to the Los Angeles Lakers. Elgin Baylor's knees had forced his retirement early in the campaign, but new Laker coach Bill Sharman, back in the NBA after three years in the ABA, nevertheless welded together a balanced, talented outfit that put together the best record in NBA history. Wilt Chamberlain's scoring average was down to 14.8, but, even in his thirteenth season, his strength under the boards was still unmatched by any other player. Jerry West directed the team from the backcourt and scored at a 25.8 clip, while fellow guard Gail Goodrich blossomed into the Lakers' top scorer with a 25.9 average. At the forwards, Happy Hairston concentrated on rebounding and defense, while Jim McMillian inherited Baylor's spot and oiled the offense with his quick driving and shooting. Experienced subs Flynn Robinson, Leroy Ellis, and Pat Riley fit right into the Laker pattern when called upon.

The Lakers played almost mistake-free basketball from the start of the season, and a 110-106 victory over Baltimore on November 5 started the club on the longest winning streak in NBA annals. The Lakers played excellent team basketball, with different men starring on different nights, and the team kept winning right through November and December. For two months, the Lakers won every game they played, with the streak reaching 33 games on January 7. Two nights later, the Milwaukee Bucks ended the string with a 120-104 decision, but the Lakers had long passed the old standard of 20 consec-

Gail Goodrich
With Elgin Baylor injured, Goodrich picks up the slack (even edging Jerry West for the team scoring lead) as Lakers win 69 games.

utive wins set by the Bucks last year. By the season's end, the Lakers had a record total of 69 wins, one better than the 1966-67 Philadelphia 76ers.

The Golden State Warriors, Los Angeles' competition in the Pacific Division, were left far behind, but still played interesting basketball. They added speed in Cazzie Russell and Jim Barnett, and finished a much-improved second. Player coach Lenny Wilkins also had his Seattle Supersonics playing good ball, but they finished out of the playoffs despite a 47-35 record. The Rockets slumped in their new Houston home, and

Portland again had a horrendous record despite the addition of rookie Sidney Wicks.

In the Midwest Division, last year's super-team, the Milwaukee Bucks, were still outstanding. Illness sidelined Oscar Robertson part of the time, but Lucius Allen developed into a competent backcourt leader. Of course, the newly-named Abdul-Jabbar exhibited all of his old prowess by leading the NBA in scoring with a 34.8 average. The Chicago Bulls again muscled their way into second place, with Bob Love, Chet Walker, Jerry Sloan, Tom Boerwinkle, and Bob Weiss joined this season by rookie center Cliff Ray and third-year guard Norm Van Lier, who was picked up in a trade with Cincinnati. The strong Phoenix Suns compiled a 49-33 record despite the lack of any bench strength, and the Detroit Pistons relapsed into their old losing ways after losing guard Dave Bing for the first two months of the season with a detached retina.

The Eastern Conference made a worse showing than the West, with only two of the eight clubs posting a winning record for the season. The Boston Celtics regained the excellence characteristic of the days of Bill Russell, compiling a 56-26 record to take first place in the Atlantic Division. John Havlicek and Don Nelson were the veterans on the team, and Dave Cowens, Jo Jo White, and Don Chaney were the young starters who were improving with each season.

The New York Knicks underwent some mid-season readjustments, yet finished with a strong 48-34 record in second place behind Boston. A bad knee knocked center Willis Reed out of action for most of the campaign, so the Knicks had to use 6-foot-8 Jerry Lucas, obtained from the Warriors in a trade for Cazzie Russell, in the middle. Lucas was not the rebounder or shot-blocker that Reed was, but his outside shooting drew larger opposition centers outside and opened up the middle for the Knicks to drive. The Knicks also sent Mike Riordan and Dave Stallworth to Baltimore for guard Earl (The Pearl) Monroe, who had trouble fitting his flashy offensive skills into the New York pattern after coming over in November.

Finishing out of the playoffs in the Atlantic Division were the Philadelphia 76ers, despite an All-Star performance by Billy Cunningham, and the Buffalo Braves, despite good play from rookies Elmore Smith and Randy Smith. All the Central Division clubs finished with losing records, with Baltimore and Atlanta qualifying for playoff berths.

The Celtics, Knicks, Bucks, and Lakers emerged from the first round of the playoffs as expected, but the next matchups were harder to predict. It was the up-and-coming young Celtics against the experienced Knicks, and the New Yorkers sent the Bostonians back for more seasoning by winning their series in five games. Meanwhile, the Western finals pitted the phenomenal Lakers against the defending-champion Bucks, and a titanic matchup between Wilt Chamberlain and Kareem Abdul-Jabbar. Even with Oscar Robertson slowed by muscle pulls, the Bucks managed a split of the first four games, but the Lakers then won two straight to move on to the championship series heavily favored over New York.

The Knicks won the first game, 114-92, with superb outside shooting, but the lack of a New York center strong enough to cope with Chamberlain could not be denied any longer. The Lakers then won four straight games and made Jerry West a member of a championship team for the first time in his 12-year pro career.

1971-72 SEASON HIGHLIGHTS

STANDINGS

Eastern Conference
Atlantic Division

	W	L	Pct.	GB
Boston	56	26	.683	—
New York	48	34	.585	8
Philadelphia	30	52	.366	26
Buffalo	22	60	.268	34

Central Division

	W	L	Pct.	GB
Baltimore	38	44	.463	—
Atlanta	36	46	.439	2
Cincinnati	30	52	.366	8
Cleveland	23	59	.280	15

Western Conference
Midwest Division

	W	L	Pct.	GB
Milwaukee	63	19	.768	—
Chicago	57	25	.695	6
Phoenix	49	33	.598	14
Detroit	26	56	.317	37

Pacific Division

	W	L	Pct.	GB
Los Angeles	69	13	.841	—
Golden State	51	31	.622	18
Seattle	47	35	.573	22
Houston	34	48	.415	35
Portland	18	64	.220	51

AWARDS
MVP
Kareem Abdul-Jabbar, Milwaukee
Top Rookie
Sidney Wicks, Portland
Coach of Year
Bill Sharman, LA Lakers

ALL-STAR TEAMS

FIRST TEAM

John Havlicek	Boston
Spencer Haywood	Seattle
Kareem Abdul-Jabbar	Milwaukee
Jerry West	Los Angeles
Walt Frazier	New York

ALL-STAR GAME
The Forum, Inglewood
Tuesday, January 18, 1972
West 112, East 110
MVP: Jerry West

SECOND TEAM

Bob Love	Chicago
Billy Cunningham	Philadelphia
Wilt Chamberlain	Los Angeles
Nate Archibald	Cincinnati
Archie Clark	Philadelphia-Baltimore

FINALS
Los Angeles 4, New York 1
Apr. 26: New York 114 at Los Angeles 92
Apr. 30: New York 92 at Los Angeles 106
May 3: Los Angeles 107 at New York 96
May 5: Los Angeles 116 at New York 111, OT
May 7: New York 100 at Los Angeles 114

EASTERN CONFERENCE
CONFERENCE FINALS
New York 4, Boston 1
Apr. 13: New York 116 at Boston 94
Apr. 16: Boston 105 at New York 106
Apr. 19: New York 109 at Boston 115
Apr. 21: Boston 98 at New York 116
Apr. 23: New York 111 at Boston 103

CONFERENCE SEMI-FINALS
Boston 4, Atlanta 2
Mar. 29: Atlanta 108 at Boston 126
Mar. 31: Boston 104 at Atlanta 113
Apr. 2: Atlanta 113 at Boston 136
Apr. 4: Boston 112 at Atlanta 112
Apr. 7: Atlanta 114 at Boston 124
Apr. 9: Boston 127 at Atlanta 118

New York 4, Baltimore 2
Mar. 31: New York 105 at Baltimore 108, OT
Apr. 2: Baltimore 88 at New York 110
Apr. 4: New York 103 at Baltimore 104
Apr. 6: Baltimore 98 at New York 104
Apr. 9: New York 106 at Baltimore 82
Apr. 11: Baltimore 101 at New York 107

WESTERN CONFERENCE
CONFERENCE FINALS
Los Angeles 4, Milwaukee 2
Apr. 9: Milwaukee 93 at Los Angeles 72
Apr. 12: Milwaukee 134 at Los Angeles 135
Apr. 14: Los Angeles 108 at Milwaukee 105
Apr. 16: Los Angeles 88 at Milwaukee 114
Apr. 18: Milwaukee 90 at Los Angeles 115
Apr. 22: Los Angeles 104 at Milwaukee 100

CONFERENCE SEMI-FINALS
Milwaukee 4, Golden State 1
Mar. 28: Golden State 117 at Milwaukee 106
Mar. 30: Golden State 93 at Milwaukee 118
Apr. 1: Milwaukee 122 at Golden State 94
Apr. 4: Milwaukee 106 at Golden State 98
Apr. 6: Golden State 100 at Milwaukee 108

Los Angeles 4, Chicago 0
Mar. 28: Chicago 80 at Los Angeles 95
Mar. 30: Chicago 124 at Los Angeles 131
Apr. 2: Los Angeles 108 at Chicago 101
Apr. 4: Los Angeles 108 at Chicago 97

NBA LEADERS

SCORING

	GP	FGM	FTM	PTS	PPG
Kareem Abdul-Jabbar, MIL	81	1159	504	2822	34.8
Nate Archibald, CIN	76	734	677	2145	28.2
John Havlicek, BOS	82	897	458	2252	27.5
Spencer Haywood, SEA	73	717	480	1914	26.2
Gail Goodrich, LAL	82	826	475	2127	25.9
Bob Love, CHI	79	819	399	2037	25.8
Jerry West, LAL	77	735	515	1985	25.8
Bob Lanier, DET	80	834	388	2056	25.7
Archie Clark, PHI/BAL	77	712	514	1938	25.2
Elvin Hayes, HOU	82	832	399	2063	25.2

FIELD GOALS

	FGM	FGA	FG%
Wilt Chamberlain, LAL	496	764	.649
Kareem Abdul-Jabbar, MIL	1159	2019	.574
Walt Bellamy, ATL	593	1089	.545
Dick Snyder, SEA	496	937	.529
Jerry Lucas, NYK	543	1060	.512
Walt Frazier, NYK	669	1307	.512
Jon McGlocklin, MIL	374	733	.510
Chet Walker, CHI	619	1225	.505
Lucius Allen, MIL	441	874	.505
Lou Hudson, ATL	775	1540	.503

FREE THROWS

	FTM	FTA	FT%
Jack Marin, BAL	356	398	.894
Calvin Murphy, HOU	349	392	.890
Gail Goodrich, LAL	475	559	.850
Chet Walker, CHI	481	568	.847
Dick Van Arsdale, PHO	529	626	.845
Stu Lantz, HOU	387	462	.838
John Havlicek, BOS	458	549	.834
Cazzie Russell, GST	315	378	.833
Stan McKenzie, POR	315	379	.831
Jimmy Walker, DET	397	480	.827

ASSISTS

	GP	AST	APG
Jerry West, LAL	77	747	9.7
Lenny Wilkens, SEA	80	766	9.6
Nate Archibald, CIN	76	701	9.2
Archie Clark, PHI/BAL	77	613	8.0
John Havlicek, BOS	82	614	7.5
Norm Van Lier, CIN/CHI	79	542	6.9
Billy Cunningham, PHI	75	443	5.9
Jeff Mullins, GST	80	471	5.9
Walt Frazier, NYK	77	446	5.8
Mahdi Abdul-Rahman, BUF	72	406	5.6

REBOUNDS

	GP	TRB	RPG
Wilt Chamberlain, LAL	82	1572	19.2
Wes Unseld, BAL	76	1336	17.6
Kareem Abdul-Jabbar, MIL	81	1346	16.6
Nate Thurmond, GST	78	1252	16.1
Dave Cowens, BOS	79	1203	15.2
Elmore Smith, BUF	78	1184	15.2
Elvin Hayes, HOU	82	1197	14.6
Clyde Lee, GST	78	1132	14.5
Bob Lanier, DET	80	1132	14.2
Bill Bridges, ATL/PHI	78	1051	13.5

THE YEAR IN BASKETBALL

Women's rules are changed, reducing the number of players on a side from six to five. A 30-second shot clock debuts in women's college games.

September 21, 1971 In the first interleague game between the NBA and rival ABA, the Milwaukee Bucks edge the ABA's Dallas Chaparrals, 106-103, in a preseason contest. The two leagues will play 155 exhibitions from 1971-1975, with the ABA winning the series, 79-76.

October 5, 1971 The previous season's NBA and ABA champions meet in a preseason game. The result: The NBA's Bucks beat counterpart Utah, 122-114, in Salt Lake City.

November 4, 1971 Elgin Baylor retires because of knee problems.

November 4, 1971 The Pittsburgh Condors of the ABA encounter "John Brisker Intimidation Night" in a game in Salt Lake City versus the Utah Stars. The promotion is named after the ferocious Brisker, the Condors' star forward/guard.

November 5, 1971 In a seemingly innocuous victory, the Los Angeles Lakers replace the retired Elgin Baylor in the starting lineup with forward Jim McMillian. The new starter scores 22 points and grabs 13 rebounds, as the Lakers beat the Baltimore Bullets, 110-106. The win is the first of 33 in a row for Los Angeles.

December 22, 1971 The Lakers break the record for the longest winning streak in pro team sports, with their 27th straight NBA win, 127-120 over Baltimore. Baseball's 1916 New York Giants won 26 in a row.

January 9, 1972 The Lakers' winning streak ends at 33 games, when the Milwaukee Bucks prevail.

January 18, 1972 Jerry West sinks a last-second, 20-foot jumper giving the West a 112-110 All-Star game victory. West is named MVP.

January 28, 1972 Dianne Campbell, a high school player in Claude, Tex. Scores 100 points in a game.

January 25, 1972 In a brawl that haunts Bill Musselman for the rest of his coaching career, players from his University of Minnesota team badly injure Ohio State's seven-foot center Luke Witte during a melee.

February 16, 1972 Wilt Chamberlain reaches 30,000 career points.

March 14, 1972 The Cincinnati Royals announce they are moving to Kansas City at the end of the season.

March 18, 1972 Memphis' Larry Miller sets ABA record by scoring 67 points in a game.

March 19, 1972 In the first Association for Intercollegiate Athletics for Women (AIAW) collegiate championship, Immaculata College downs West Chester State, 52-48.

March 19, 1972 The Lakers beat Golden State, 162-99, to attain the largest margin of victory (63 points) in NBA history.

March 1972 Maryland takes the NIT championship.

March 25, 1972 Bill Walton scores 24 points to lead undefeated UCLA to an 81-76 victory over Florida State in the NCAA title game.

March 27, 1972 Adolph Rupp of Kentucky retires after 42 years.

May 7, 1972 Capping a record season, the Lakers beat the Knicks in five games to win the NBA championship. The Lakers clinch the title with a 114-100 victory, in which four players—Wilt Chamberlain, Gail Goodrich, Jerry West, and Jim McMillian—each score 20 points or more.

May 20, 1972 Indiana defeats New York to capture the ABA title.

1972-73

Knicks toast of NY after upsetting Celtics, then Lakers

The executioner's axe stayed sharp this season as coaches went to the chopping block with some degree of regularity. At Phoenix, Butch van Breda Kolff, hired to replace Cotton Fitzsimmons, lasted just eight games before general manager Jerry Colangelo decided that he had made a mistake in hiring coaches and took over the job himself. Colangelo and star forward Connie Hawkins found each other's company quite distasteful, with the result that Hawkins' scoring average fell to 16.1 and the Suns fell to a 38-44 record. At Detroit, Earl Lloyd was on shaky ground as the season started, and a 2-5 record out of the gate did him in, with former Piston player Ray Scott assuming the task of trying to get the Pistons to work together as a team.

In Seattle, new coach Tom Nissalke started out with two strikes against him. Lenny Wilkens had decided to concentrate on playing and to give up the coaching reins, which went to Nissalke. To avoid a potentially sticky situation, the Sonics dealt the popular Wilkens to Cleveland which both alienated the fans and removed the team's backcourt leader. With Jim McDaniels and John Brisker, two expensive ABA defectors, joining Spencer Haywood in the lineup, Nissalke (himself a former ABA coach) was expected to win immediately. But without Wilkens, the Sonics lacked a dependable playmaker, and they stumbled to a horrible start amidst rumors that the players would not put out their best for Nissalke. With the team record standing at 13-32, Nissalke was canned and Bucky Buckwalter appointed head coach. At the season's end, the Sonics had fallen from the preseason favorite's role in the Pacific Division to a poor 26-56 record. Tex Winter's problem in Houston was that he couldn't get the Rockets to play defense, and he was fired late in the campaign in favor of Johnny Egan, who directed the club to a 16-19 mark down the stretch.

But the most abominable situation belonged to Roy Rubin, the freshman coach of the Philadelphia 76ers. Making his pro debut after many years at Long Island University, Rubin took charge of a team that had been the class of the NBA six years ago but had now fallen on hard times. One bad draft after another had minimized the young talent coming to the club, and a series of bad deals had sent away the stars of the 1966-67 championship squad without bringing much in return. The courts this year ruled that star forward Billy Cunningham had signed a legal contract with the Carolina Cougars of the ABA and was obligated to play there. This was the straw that broke the camel's back in Philly. Rubin fielded a miserable outfit, lacking in speed and board strength and making a multitude of mental errors. With veteran Hal Greer relegated to the bench, rookie Freddie Boyd was given the playmaker's job, a task he handled in very unsure fashion. The 76ers had expected this to be a rebuilding year, but the team lost so regularly and by such big margins that Rubin was ousted with the 76ers beaten down

Dave Cowens
The big man, working here against the Knicks' Jerry Lucas, posts an MVP season as the fast-breaking Celtics dominate the regular season.

to a 4-47 level. Guard Kevin Loughery took over as coach and could coax only a slight improvement out of the squad, with the 76ers setting a new record for futility with a 9-73 record, much like the early New York Mets without the charm of being an expansion team.

Fifty-nine games ahead of the 76ers in the Atlantic Division were the Boston Celtics, whose sparkling 68-14 record was the class of the league. These new Celtics relied on the fast break just as earlier editions of the team had, and they often won games simply by running the opposition down. John Havlicek

had won All-Star notices for several years, but the critics this year acclaimed center Dave Cowens as the league MVP. The biggest addition to the Celtics this year was rebounding forward Paul Silas, who came from Phoenix as compensation for the Suns' signing of Charlie Scott, who had been a Boston draft choice. The New York Knicks finished a strong second, with Willis Reed rounding into shape as the season progressed and with Earl (The Pearl) Monroe fitting smoothly into the New York style of play. Buffalo finished a weak third, but got a strong season out of rookie forward Bob McAdoo.

Although the Baltimore Bullets did get help from rookie guard Kevin Porter, a new pair of forwards sparked the club's improvement to a 52-30 record and first place in the Central Division. Elvin Hayes came from Houston in a trade for Jack Marin and teamed with center Wes Unseld to give the Bullets two first-rate big men, while 6-foot-4 Mike Riordan blossomed into stardom as a small forward. Phil Chenier and Porter held down the backcourt positions while Archie Clark sat out the first half of the season in a salary dispute. The Hawks improved to 46-36 under new coach Cotton Fitzsimmons and took the second playoff berth in the Central Division.

The two playoff berths in the Midwest Division went as expected to the Milwaukee Bucks, with Kareem Abdul-Jabbar, and the Chicago Bulls, who lost center Tom Boerwinkle to a knee injury but got solid work out of subs Clifford Ray and Dennis Awtrey. Detroit improved in the later stages of the season to finish third, and the Kansas City-Omaha Kings, who were the transplanted Cincinnati Royals, finished last despite an outstanding performance by 6-foot Nate Archibald, who became the first player ever to lead the circuit in scoring and

assists. With mostly mediocre talent in the lineup with him, Archibald combined speed, moves, and fine shooting to notch a league-leading 34.0 points per game and to make himself an instant gate attraction.

In the Pacific Division, the Lakers didn't put together any 33-game winning streaks this year but still managed to win first place with a 60-22 record. Behind Los Angeles in second place were the Golden State Warriors, who rejoiced over the return of star forward Rick Barry from the ABA. Phoenix, Seattle, and Portland brought up the rear in the division.

The West Coast produced the only upset of the first round of the playoffs, as the Warriors, behind Nate Thurmond's rugged interior defense on Kareem Abdul-Jabbar, stunned the Bucks by eliminating them in six games. Boston and New York won handily, while the Lakers had to take a 95-92 decision in Game 7 to get past the Bulls. The Eastern final was a copy of last year's, as the second-place Knicks upended the first-place Celtics, with New York taking a 94-78 seventh game victory (the first time a team had ever beaten Boston on their home floor in a seventh game) in which John Havlicek was disabled with a bad shoulder.

The Lakers disposed of the Warriors in the West and were favored to repeat as champions over the Knicks as they had last year. One factor was different this season, however, New York center Willis Reed was healthy and able to battle Chamberlain under the boards. The Lakers won the first game, 115-112, but then the Knicks pressed the Lakers and held them under 100 points for the next four games, all of which were victories for the New Yorkers, who had their second NBA championship in four years.

1972-73 SEASON HIGHLIGHTS

STANDINGS

Eastern Conference
Atlantic Division

	W	L	Pct.	GB
Boston	68	14	.829	—
New York	57	25	.695	11
Buffalo	21	61	.256	47
Philadelphia	9	73	.110	59

Central Division

	W	L	Pct.	GB
Baltimore	52	30	.634	—
Atlanta	46	36	.561	6
Houston	33	49	.402	19
Cleveland	32	50	.390	20

Western Conference
Midwest Division

	W	L	Pct.	GB
Milwaukee	60	22	.732	—
Chicago	51	31	.622	9
Detroit	40	42	.488	20
KC-Omaha	36	46	.439	24

Pacific Division

	W	L	Pct.	GB
Los Angeles	60	22	.732	—
Golden State	47	35	.573	13
Phoenix	38	44	.463	22
Seattle	26	56	.317	34
Portland	21	61	.256	39

AWARDS
MVP
Dave Cowens, Boston
Top Rookie
Bob McAdoo, Buffalo
Coach of Year
Tom Heinsohn, Boston

ALL-STAR TEAMS
FIRST TEAM

John Havlicek	Boston
Spencer Haywood	Seattle
Kareem Abdul-Jabbar	Milwaukee
Nate Archibald	KC-Omaha
Jerry West	Los Angeles

SECOND TEAM

Elvin Hayes	Baltimore
Rick Barry	Golden State
Dave Cowens	Boston
Walt Frazier	New York

ALL-STAR GAME
Chicago Stadium, Chicago
Tuesday, January 23, 1973
East 104, West 84
MVP: Dave Cowens

PLAYOFFS
FINALS
New York 4, Los Angeles 1
May 1: New York 112 at Los Angeles 115
May 3: New York 99 at Los Angeles 95
May 6: Los Angeles 83 at New York 87
May 8: Los Angeles 98 at New York 103
May 10: New York 102 at Los Angeles 93
EASTERN CONFERENCE
CONFERENCE FINALS
New York 4, Boston 3
Apr. 15: New York 108 at Boston 134
Apr. 18: Boston 96 at New York 129
Apr. 20: New York 98 at Boston 91
Apr. 22: Boston 110 at New York 117, 2OT
Apr. 25: New York 97 at Boston 98
Apr. 27: Boston 110 at New York 100
Apr. 29: New York 94 at Boston 78

CONFERENCE SEMI-FINALS
Boston 4, Atlanta 2
Apr. 1: Atlanta 109 at Boston 134
Apr. 4: Boston 126 at Atlanta 113
Apr. 6: Atlanta 118 at Boston 105
Apr. 8: Boston 94 at Atlanta 97
Apr. 11: Atlanta 101 at Boston 108
Apr. 13: Boston 121 at Atlanta 103
New York 4, Baltimore 1
Mar. 30: Baltimore 83 at New York 95
Apr. 1: Baltimore 103 at New York 123
Apr. 4: New York 103 at Baltimore 96
Apr. 6: New York 89 at Baltimore 97
Apr. 8: Baltimore 99 at New York 109
WESTERN CONFERENCE
CONFERENCE FINALS
Los Angeles 4, Golden State 1
Apr. 17: Golden State 99 at Los Angeles 101
Apr. 19: Golden State 93 at Los Angeles 104
Apr. 21: Los Angeles 126 at Golden State 70

Apr. 23: Los Angeles 109 at Golden State 117
Apr. 25: Golden State 118 at Los Angeles 128
Apr. 22: Milwaukee 115 at Chicago 99
CONFERENCE SEMI-FINALS
Golden State 4, Milwaukee 2
Mar. 30: Golden State 90 at Milwaukee 110
Apr. 1: Golden State 95 at Milwaukee 92
Apr. 5: Milwaukee 113 at Golden State 93
Apr. 7: Milwaukee 97 at Golden State 102
Apr. 10: Golden State 100 at Milwaukee 97
Apr. 13: Milwaukee 86 at Golden State 100
Los Angeles 4, Chicago 3
Mar. 30: Chicago 104 at Los Angeles 107, OT
Apr. 1: Chicago 93 at Los Angeles 108
Apr. 6: Los Angeles 86 at Chicago 96
Apr. 8: Los Angeles 94 at Chicago 98
Apr. 10: Chicago 102 at Los Angeles 123
Apr. 13: Los Angeles 93 at Chicago 101
Apr. 15: Chicago 92 at Los Angeles 95

NBA LEADERS

SCORING

	GP	FGM	FTM	PTS	PPG
Nate Archibald, KCO	80	1028	663	2719	34.0
Kareem Abdul-Jabbar, MIL	76	982	328	2292	30.2
Spencer Haywood, SEA	77	889	473	2251	29.2
Lou Hudson, ATL	75	816	397	2029	27.1
Pete Maravich, ATL	79	789	485	2063	26.1
Charlie Scott, PHO	81	806	436	2048	25.3
Geoff Petrie, POR	79	836	298	1970	24.9
Gail Goodrich, LAL	76	750	314	1814	23.9
Sidney Wicks, POR	80	761	384	1906	23.8
Bob Lanier, DET	81	810	307	1927	23.8

FIELD GOALS

	FGM	FGA	FG%
Wilt Chamberlain, LAL	426	586	.727
Matt Guokas, KCO	322	565	.570
Kareem Abdul-Jabbar, MIL	982	1772	.554
Curtis Rowe, DET	547	1053	.519
Jim Fox, SEA	316	613	.515
Jerry Lucas, NYK	312	608	.513
Mike Riordan, BAL	652	1278	.510
Archie Clark, BAL	302	596	.507
Bob Kauffman, BUF	535	1059	.505
Walt Bellamy, ATL	455	901	.505

FREE THROWS

	FTM	FTA	FT%
Rick Barry, GST	358	397	.902
Calvin Murphy, HOU	239	269	.888
Mike Newlin, HOU	327	369	.886
Jimmy Walker, HOU	244	276	.884
Bill Bradley, NYK	169	194	.871
Cazzie Russell, GST	172	199	.864
Dick Snyder, SEA	186	216	.861
Dick Van Arsdale, PHO	426	496	.859
John Havlicek, BOS	370	431	.858
Jack Marin, HOU	248	292	.849

ASSISTS

	GP	AST	APG
Nate Archibald, KCO	80	910	11.4
Lenny Wilkens, CLE	75	628	8.4
Dave Bing, DET	82	637	7.8
Oscar Robertson, MIL	73	551	7.6
Norm Van Lier, CHI	80	567	7.1
Pete Maravich, ATL	79	546	6.9
John Havlicek, BOS	80	529	6.6
Herm Gilliam, ATL	76	482	6.3
Charlie Scott, PHO	81	495	6.1
Jo Jo White, BOS	82	498	6.1

REBOUNDS

	GP	TRB	RPG
Wilt Chamberlain, LAL	82	1526	18.6
Nate Thurmond, GST	79	1349	17.1
Dave Cowens, BOS	82	1329	16.2
Kareem Abdul-Jabbar, MIL	76	1224	16.1
Wes Unseld, BAL	79	1260	15.9
Bob Lanier, DET	81	1205	14.9
Elvin Hayes, BAL	81	1177	14.5
Walt Bellamy, ATL	74	964	13.0
Paul Silas, BOS	80	1039	13.0
Spencer Haywood, SEA	77	995	12.9

THE YEAR IN BASKETBALL

June 23, 1972 Title IX becomes law as part of the Higher Education Amendments Act of 1972. The legislation bars sexual bias in athletics and other activities at colleges receiving federal assistance. It will lead the way in the growth of many women's collegiate sports, including basketball.

September 10, 1972 At the Olympic Games in Munich, the U.S. basketball team suffers their first-ever defeat in Olympic competition, losing the gold-medal game, 51-50, to the USSR in a disputed finish. With three seconds left, Doug Collins of the U.S. sinks two free throws to give the Americans a 50-49 lead. Time expires but the officials put three seconds back on the clock when the Soviet coach argues that he called a timeout after Collins' second free throw. The Soviets throw a court-length pass to center Alexander Belov, who sinks the winning layup at the buzzer. The U.S. protests and refuses the silver medal. The loss breaks America's 62-game Olympic basketball winning streak.

October 20, 1972 The Buffalo Braves amass an NBA record 58 points in the fourth quarter yet lose by eight, 126-118, to the Celtics at the Boston Garden.

October 21, 1972 In an amazing reversal, the day after setting an NBA record by scoring 58 points in a quarter, Buffalo scores an NBA record-low four points in the third quarter of a 91-63 loss to the Milwaukee Bucks in Buffalo.

November 18, 1972 Down by 18 points with just over five minutes to play in the fourth quarter, the Knicks score the game's final 19 points to edge the Bucks, 87-86, at Madison Square Garden.

January 27, 1973 UCLA defeats Notre Dame, 82-63, to break the University of San Francisco's all-time college basketball record of 60 consecutive wins, set in 1956.

March 24, 1973 Immaculata wins the second AIAW basketball title, beating Queens College, 59-52.

March 24, 1973 Nate (Tiny) Archibald of Kansas City-Omaha becomes the first player in NBA history to lead the league in both scoring (34.0 ppg) and assists (11.4 apg) in the same season.

March 25, 1973 Bobby Stevens hits a 20-footer at the buzzer to give Virginia Tech the NIT championship, in a 92-91 win over Notre Dame. The Fighting Irish's John Shumate is named the tournament's Most Valuable Player.

March 26, 1973 Bill Walton puts on one of the greatest individual performances in collegiate history, scoring 44 points by making 21 of 22 field goal attempts, leading UCLA to its seventh straight NCAA title, 87-66, over Memphis State. The victory was UCLA's 60th in a row.

April 1, 1973 John Havlicek scores 54 points to lead the Celtics over Atlanta, 134-109, in Game 1 of the Eastern Conference Semifinals.

May 10, 1973 New York beats Los Angeles, 102-93, in Game 5 to win their second NBA championship in four years. Willis Reed is named the Finals MVP for the second time.

May 12, 1973 Indiana defeats Kentucky, 88-81, in Game 7 of the ABA finals. George McGinnis' 27 points leads the Pacers to the championship.

1973-74

Cowens out-duels Kareem as Celtics re-ascend to throne

Wilt Chamberlain, the all-time NBA scoring and rebounding leader, made his exit from the league this season by signing as a player-coach with the San Diego Conquistadors of the ABA. A court order, however, forbade him from playing with the ABA club since he had not played out his option with the Los Angeles Lakers, so he spent the year as a bench coach in San Diego. His departure from the NBA closed the books on one of the league's most colorful personalities and left Kareem Abdul-Jabbar of Milwaukee as the undisputed king of the big men on the circuit.

Chamberlain's old rival, Bill Russell, crossed Chamberlain in the other direction, quitting his post as television commentator to go to Seattle as coach of the Supersonics. Other old Celtics who had played with Russell on the great Boston clubs of the 1950's and 1960's were also on the move. Satch Sanders finally retired as an active player, leaving the Celtics to become head coach at Harvard. Bob Cousy resigned as coach of the Kansas City-Omaha Kings, tired of losing and unsuccessful in building the franchise after four and a half years. And K.C. Jones came back to the NBA as coach of the Capital Bullets, who had moved from Baltimore to an arena near Washington, D.C.

The present-day Celtics did quite well for themselves, finishing comfortably in first place in the Atlantic Division for the third straight season. Veteran John Havlicek was the thread connecting this club to its illustrious ancestors, and center Dave Cowens was the key to the present, battling larger giants with mobility and hustle. The New York Knicks relied on their defense and took second place despite losing Earl Monroe with a leg injury in the early going and losing Willis Reed for most of the campaign with knee trouble.

The big news in the Atlantic Division, however, was the sudden emergence of the Buffalo Braves as a coming power. General manager Eddie Donovan and coach Jack Ramsay cleaned a lot of deadwood away and replaced it with fine young talent. They signed rookie guard Ernie DiGregorio from Providence College, a superb playmaker who led the NBA in assists in his rookie year. They obtained a power forward in Gar Heard through a minor trade with Chicago. And they took a big chance by trading young center Elmore Smith, a potential star, to the Los Angeles Lakers for Jim McMillian, one of the NBA's top small forwards. The gamble paid off when McMillian had a good season, and second-year man Bob McAdoo blossomed into an immediate star when shifted to the center spot. A rangy 6-foot-10, McAdoo used a sharp shooting eye to lead the NBA in scoring with a 30.6 average. These men, along with improving holdover Randy Smith, formed a powerful starting unit, and Donovan and Ramsay built up the bench with a late-season deal that brought Jack Marin and Matt Guokas from Houston. The Braves still had to learn to play top notch defense, but their offensive power took them into the

Bob McAdoo
Shift to center for 6-foot-10 sharpshooter results in first of three straight scoring titles, and sudden respectability for Buffalo Braves.

playoffs this year under a new rule, since their record was better than the second-place team in the central division.

Behind them this season, in fourth place, were the Philadelphia 76ers. Despite losing first draft choice Doug Collins for most of the season with a leg injury, new coach Gene Shue at least made the 76ers competitive, finding an unexpected treasure in Steve Mix, who had been playing semi-pro ball in the Midwest after flopping with the Detroit Pistons.

The Central Division was dominated by the Bullets, who built a 47-35 record despite losing Archie Clark and Wes

Unseld for long stretches with injuries. Atlanta fell to a 35-47 level and failed to win a playoff spot despite edging Houston for second place. Cleveland had the rookie disappointment of the year in Jim Brewer, and as usual was not a factor in the race for the playoffs.

The hottest fight for playoff position was in the Midwest Division, where the Chicago Bulls and Detroit Pistons slugged it out for second place behind the Milwaukee Bucks. Both teams relied on muscle and ball-control offenses, with the Bulls having the edge at forward with Bob Love and Chet Walker, the Pistons having an advantage at center with Bob Lanier, and with Dave Bing, Chris Ford, Jerry Sloan, and Norm Van Lier making the backcourts an even match. Coach Ray Scott had the Pistons playing the best ball in the team's history in Detroit, and the club record of 52-30 was better than anything in the Pacific Division, thus clinching a playoff berth despite losing second place to the Bulls. In Kansas City-Omaha, Nate Archibald suffered an Achilles tendon injury and this instantly ruined the entire King offense.

The Los Angeles Lakers lost veteran star Jerry West to an injury and had to struggle for the playoffs in the Pacific Division. Chamberlain was gone, and his leaving prompted the trade of Jim McMillian to Buffalo for Elmore Smith. A mid-season trade for Connie Hawkins produced poor results, but Gail Goodrich emerged in the transitional surroundings as the team's scoring ace with a 25.3 average. The Golden State Warriors finished only three games behind Los Angeles despite

losing big men Nate Thurmond and Clyde Lee on injuries, but their 44-38 final record wasn't good enough to earn them a playoff spot over the Pistons. Bill Russell's coaching couldn't turn Seattle into a winning club, and Phoenix and Portland did even worse.

The new playoff rule created a stronger field for the first round. The Celtics took the measure of the young Braves in six games, while the Knicks had to win a seventh game from the Bullets. In the West, the Bucks downed the weakened Lakers in five games, while the Bulls and Pistons beat on each other for seven games, with the Bulls winning a 96-94 decision in the deciding contest. After knocking heads with the tough Pistons for seven games, the Bulls simply could not stand up to the Bucks and lost four straight games to Abdul-Jabbar and Co. In the Eastern finals, Willis Reed and Dave DeBusschere were hobbled with injuries, and the Knicks bowed to the Celtics after upsetting them for the past two years.

In the championship series, the Bucks were hurting in the backcourt, with Lucius Allen out with a knee injury and with Oscar Robertson slowed down from his peak. The Celtics won the first game. The clubs then took turns winning the next five games, with the Bucks taking a 102-101 double-overtime victory in Game 6 with their backs up against the wall. Dave Cowens hit for 28 points in the seventh game, outscoring Abdul-Jabbar by two, and the Celtics outscored the Bucks 102-87 to reclaim the title after an absence of five years.

1973-74 SEASON HIGHLIGHTS

STANDINGS

Eastern Conference
Atlantic Division

	W	L	Pct.	GB
Boston	56	26	.683	—
New York	49	33	.598	7
Buffalo	42	40	.512	14
Philadelphia	25	57	.305	31

Central Division

	W	L	Pct.	GB
Capital	47	35	.573	—
Atlanta	35	47	.427	12
Houston	32	50	.390	15
Cleveland	29	53	.354	18

Western Conference
Midwest Division

	W	L	Pct.	GB
Milwaukee	59	23	.720	—
Chicago	54	28	.659	5
Detroit	52	30	.634	7
KC-Omaha	33	49	.402	26

Pacific Division

	W	L	Pct.	GB
Los Angeles	47	35	.573	—
Golden State	44	38	.537	3
Seattle	36	46	.439	11
Phoenix	30	52	.366	17
Portland	27	55	.329	20

AWARDS

MVP
Kareem Abdul-Jabbar, Milwaukee
Top Rookie
Ernie DiGregorio, Buffalo
Coach of Year
Ray Scott, Detroit

ALL-STAR TEAMS

FIRST TEAM		SECOND TEAM	
John Havlicek	Boston	Elvin Hayes	Capital
Rick Barry	Golden State	Spencer Haywood	Seattle
Kareem Abdul-Jabbar	Milwaukee	Bob McAdoo	Buffalo
Walt Frazier	New York	Dave Bing	Detroit
Gail Goodrich	Los Angeles	Norm Van Lier	Chicago

ALL-STAR GAME

Seattle Center Coliseum, Seattle
Tuesday, January 15, 1974
West 134, East 123
MVP: Bob Lanier

PLAYOFFS
FINALS
Boston 4, Milwaukee 3
Apr. 28: Boston 98 at Milwaukee 83
Apr. 30: Boston 96 at Milwaukee 105, OT
May 3: Milwaukee 83 at Boston 95
May 5: Milwaukee 97 at Boston 89
May 7: Boston 96 at Milwaukee 87
May 10: Milwaukee 102 at Boston 101, 2OT
May 12: Boston 102 at Milwaukee 87

EASTERN CONFERENCE
CONFERENCE FINALS
Boston 4, New York 1
Apr. 14: New York 88 at Boston 113
Apr. 16: Boston 111 at New York 99
Apr. 19: New York 103 at Boston 100
Apr. 21: Boston 98 at New York 91
Apr. 24: New York 94 at Boston 105

CONFERENCE SEMI-FINALS
Boston 4, Buffalo 2
Mar. 30: Buffalo 97 at Boston 107
Apr. 2: Boston 105 at Buffalo 115
Apr. 3: Buffalo 107 at Boston 120
Apr. 6: Boston 102 at Buffalo 104
Apr. 9: Buffalo 97 at Boston 100
Apr. 12: Boston 106 at Buffalo 104
New York 4, Capital 3
Mar. 29: Capital 91 at New York 102
Mar. 31: New York 87 at Capital 99
Apr. 2: Capital 88 at New York 79
Apr. 5: New York 101 at Capital 93, OT
Apr. 7: Capital 105 at New York 106
Apr. 10: New York 92 at Capital 109
Apr. 12: Capital 81 at New York 91

WESTERN CONFERENCE
CONFERENCE FINALS
Milwaukee 4, Chicago 0
Apr. 16: Chicago 85 at Milwaukee 101
Apr. 18: Milwaukee 113 at Chicago 111
Apr. 20: Chicago 90 at Milwaukee 113
Apr. 22: Milwaukee 115 at Chicago 99
CONFERENCE SEMI-FINALS
Milwaukee 4, Los Angeles 1
Mar. 29: Los Angeles 95 at Milwaukee 99
Mar. 31: Los Angeles 90 at Milwaukee 109
Apr. 2: Milwaukee 96 at Los Angeles 98
Apr. 4: Milwaukee 112 at Los Angeles 90
Apr. 7: Los Angeles 92 at Milwaukee 114
Chicago 4, Detroit 3
Mar. 30: Detroit 97 at Chicago 88
Apr. 1: Chicago 108 at Detroit 103
Apr. 5: Detroit 83 at Chicago 84
Apr. 7: Chicago 87 at Detroit 102
Apr. 9: Detroit 94 at Chicago 98
Apr. 11: Chicago 88 at Detroit 92
Apr. 13: Detroit 94 at Chicago 96

NBA LEADERS

SCORING

	GP	FGM	FTM	PTS	PPG
Bob McAdoo, BUF	74	901	459	2261	30.6
Pete Maravich, ATL	76	819	469	2107	27.7
Kareem Abdul-Jabbar, MIL	81	948	295	2191	27.0
Gail Goodrich, LAL	82	784	508	2076	25.3
Rick Barry, GST	80	796	417	2009	25.1
Rudy Tomjanovich, HOU	80	788	385	1961	24.5
Geoff Petrie, POR	73	740	291	1771	24.3
Spencer Haywood, SEA	75	694	373	1761	23.5
John Havlicek, BOS	76	685	346	1716	22.6
Bob Lanier, DET	81	748	326	1822	22.5

FIELD GOALS

	FGM	FGA	FG%
Bob McAdoo, BUF	901	1647	.547
Kareem Abdul-Jabbar, MIL	948	1759	.539
Rudy Tomjanovich, HOU	788	1470	.536
Calvin Murphy, HOU	671	1285	.522
Butch Beard, GST	316	617	.512
Clifford Ray, CHI	313	612	.511
Don Nelson, BOS	364	717	.508
Happy Hairston, LAL	385	759	.507
Bob Lanier, DET	748	1483	.504
Bob Dandridge, MIL	583	1158	.503

FREE THROWS

	FTM	FTA	FT%
Ernie DiGregorio, BUF	174	193	.902
Rick Barry, GST	417	464	.899
Jeff Mullins, GST	168	192	.875
Chet Walker, CHI	439	502	.875
Bill Bradley, NYK	146	167	.874
Calvin Murphy, HOU	310	357	.868
Dick Snyder, SEA	194	224	.866
Gail Goodrich, LAL	508	588	.864
Fred Brown, SEA	195	226	.863
Jim McMillian, BUF	325	379	.858

ASSISTS

	GP	AST	APG
Ernie DiGregorio, BUF	81	663	8.2
Calvin Murphy, HOU	81	603	7.4
Lenny Wilkens, CLE	74	522	7.1
Walt Frazier, NYK	80	551	6.9
Dave Bing, DET	81	555	6.9
Norm Van Lier, CHI	80	548	6.9
Oscar Robertson, MIL	70	446	6.4
Rick Barry, GST	80	484	6.0
John Havlicek, BOS	76	447	5.9
Kevin Porter, CAP	81	469	5.8

REBOUNDS

	GP	ORB	DRB	TRB	RPG
Elvin Hayes, CAP	81	354	1109	1463	18.1
Dave Cowens, BOS	80	264	993	1257	15.7
Bob McAdoo, BUF	74	281	836	1117	15.1
Kareem Abdul-Jabbar, MIL	81	287	891	1178	14.5
Happy Hairston, LAL	77	335	705	1040	13.5
Spencer Haywood, SEA	75	318	689	1007	13.4
Sam Lacey, KCO	79	293	762	1055	13.4
Bob Lanier, DET	81	269	805	1074	13.3
Clifford Ray, CHI	80	285	692	977	12.2
Gar Heard, BUF	81	270	677	947	11.7

STEALS

	GP	STL	SPG
Larry Steele, POR	81	217	2.68
Steve Mix, PHI	82	212	2.59
Randy Smith, BUF	82	203	2.48
Jerry Sloan, CHI	77	183	2.38
Rick Barry, GST	80	169	2.11
Phil Chenier, CAP	76	155	2.04
Norm Van Lier, CHI	80	162	2.02
Walt Frazier, NYK	80	161	2.01
Calvin Murphy, HOU	81	157	1.94
Jim Price, LAL	82	157	1.91

BLOCKS

	GP	BLK	BPG
Elmore Smith, LAL	81	393	4.85
Kareem Abdul-Jabbar, MIL	81	283	3.49
Bob McAdoo, BUF	74	246	3.32
Bob Lanier, DET	81	247	3.05
Elvin Hayes, CAP	81	240	2.96
Gar Heard, BUF	81	230	2.84
Sam Lacey, KCO	79	184	2.33
Clifford Ray, CHI	80	173	2.16
Spencer Haywood, SEA	75	106	1.41
Zaid Abdul-Aziz, HOU	79	104	1.32

THE YEAR IN BASKETBALL

September 23, 1973 Julius Erving plays the first of two preseason games for the Atlanta Hawks. Dr. J. scores 28 points and has 18 rebounds in a 112-99 victory over the ABA's Kentucky Colonels. The NBA responds by fining the Hawks $25,000 because the Milwaukee Bucks own Erving's rights. In his second and final game with the Hawks a week later, Erving cans 32 points in a 120-106 win over the ABA's Carolina Cougars.

October 28, 1973 Less than a month after the NBA begins recording blocked shots, Elmore Smith of the Lakers blocks a record 17 in a 111-98 win over Portland. The record still stands. In the same game, Smith's teammate, guard Gail Goodrich, scores 49 points

December 15, 1973 Tennessee beats Temple, 11-6—the fewest amount of points scored in an NCAA game since 1938. Playing stall-ball, Temple does not attempt a field goal in the final 11:44 of the first half—yet only trails by two, 7-5, at halftime. In the second half, Tennessee does not attempt a field goal, but makes four foul shots to win.

January 1, 1974 Flashy passer Ernie DiGregorio of the Buffalo Braves dishes out 25 assists in a 120-119 win over the Portland Trail Blazers. Ernie D's total establishes a single-game record for a rookie. DiGregorio will go on to win Rookie-of-the-Year.

January 19, 1974 Notre Dame ends UCLA's 88-game winning streak with a 71-70 victory in South Bend.

January 20, 1974 Essex County (N.J.) Community College wipes out Englewood Cliffs, 210-67, to set a small-college scoring record.

March 7, 1974 The city of New Orleans is granted an NBA franchise, becoming the league's 18th team. The price tag is $6.15 million.

March 24, 1974 Purdue captures its first NIT championship, whipping Utah, 97-81. Utah's Mike Sojourner is named tournament MVP.

March 23, 1974 North Carolina State ends UCLA's seven-year reign as NCAA basketball champions, with a scintillating 80-77 double-overtime victory in the tournament semifinals.

March 25, 1974 North Carolina State wins the NCAA championship, downing Marquette, 76-64. David Thompson, the tournament's Most Outstanding Player, leads the Wolfpack with 21 points.

April 17, 1974 Moses Malone is drafted by the Utah Stars in the first round of the ABA draft. He will become the first modern basketball player to jump from high school directly to the professional ranks.

May 10, 1974 En route to an NBA title, the Bucks defeat the Celtics, 102-101, in double overtime in Game 6 of the NBA finals. John Havlicek plays all 58 minutes and leads Boston with 36 points. Kareem Abdul-Jabbar also plays the entire game, finishing with 34.

May 10, 1974 Julius Erving's New York Nets beat the Utah Stars, 111-100, in Game 5 to win the ABA championship.

May 12, 1974 The Boston Celtics win the NBA championship for the 12th time in 18 years by defeating Milwaukee, 102-87, in Game 7 of the Finals. Center Dave Cowens leads Boston with 28 points in the clincher.

May 1974 Ray Scott of the Detroit Pistons becomes the first African-American to be named coach of the year in any major American team sport. Scott's honor comes after he guides Detroit to a 52-30 record in the '73-74 season.

1974-75

Awesome Bullets shocked in four by Barry and kids

A full squad of perennial All-Stars hung up their sneakers this season while their clubs swan-dived into the lower levels of the NBA after years at or near the top. The retirement of Jerry West triggered the collapse of the Los Angeles Lakers into the cellar in the Pacific Division with a 30-52 record, better only than the New Orleans Jazz, this year's expansion club. The defection of Wilt Chamberlain to the ABA and the trade of Jim McMillian to the Buffalo Braves had broken up the championship unit of 1971-72, and West's retirement plus Cazzie Russell's knee injury finished the Lakers as contenders.

The Milwaukee Bucks also finished last, trailing the field in the Central Division after playing in last year's championship series. Oscar Robertson's retirement in a salary dispute left the Bucks without a backcourt leader, and when Kareem Abdul-Jabbar broke his hand against a backboard in a fit of anger in a pre-season game, the Bucks were condemned to a slow start. The club compiled a 3-13 mark without Jabbar, but when the 7-foot-2 center returned to the lineup, the Bucks continued their lukewarm play and ended with a 38-44 record. To add to coach Larry Costello's distress, Jabbar made a mid-season request to be traded to either Los Angeles or New York, where the cultural life was more to his taste than in Milwaukee. In New York, the Knicks lost all their forecourt muscle with the retirement of Willis Reed, Dave DeBusschere, and Jerry Lucas. Guards Walt Frazier and Earl Monroe carried more than their share of the load, but opponents regularly killed the Knicks on the boards. Only a last-day victory coupled with Cleveland's 95-94 loss to Kansas City-Omaha enabled the Knicks to sneak into the playoffs as the Eastern wildcard team in the new playoff set-up, and the New Yorkers quickly were ousted by Houston.

While the Lakers. Bucks, and Knicks were driven back to the drawing board to rebuild, the Portland Trail Blazers, Detroit Pistons, and Chicago Bulls failed to fully live up to their preseason expectations. The Blazers signed center Bill Walton, a three-time All-American at UCLA, to a $2.5 million contract and immediately were branded title contenders in the Pacific Division. But Walton missed most of the season with a bone spur in his foot, and the Blazers finished at 38-44, an improvement over last season but not a championship showing. The Detroit Pistons also had hopes of moving into the front

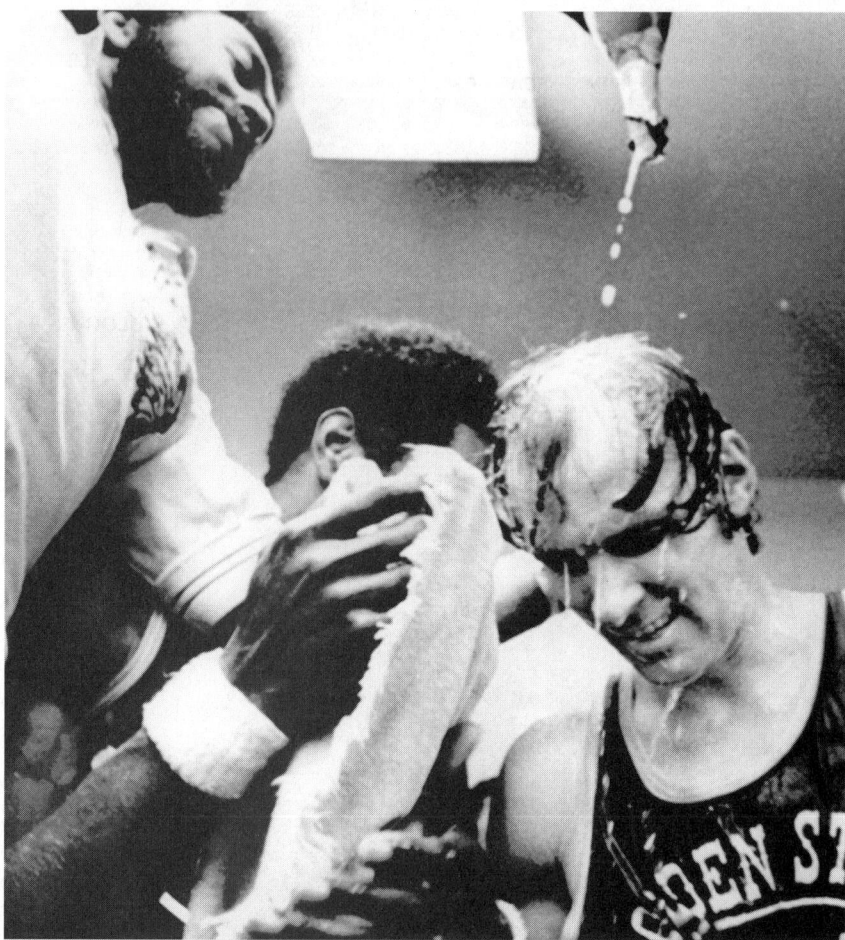

Rick Barry
In his finest all-round season, finishes second in league scoring and is the Finals MVP.

ranks of the NBA after last season's strong record, but after an early spurt fueled by the star duo of Bob Lanier and Dave Bing, the mid-season release of forward Don Adams shot the club through with dissension and sent the team into a tailspin which lasted through a first-round playoff elimination. The Chicago Bulls captured first place in the Midwest Division, but their 47-35 record didn't measure up to the super expectations fanned by the acquisition of center Nate Thurmond from Golden State. The Bulls boasted of an All-Star starting five of Bob Love, Chet Walker, Thurmond, Norm Van Lier, and Jerry Sloan, but holdouts by Love, and Van Lier, plus a drop-off in scoring by Thurmond made the Bulls less super than expected.

So while several clubs were falling or failing to make progress, the Boston Celtics, Buffalo Braves, Washington Bullets, and Golden State Warriors rose to the top of the league this season. Team cohesion kept the Celtics together through the early going when center Dave Cowens was sidelined with a broken foot. Unlike the Bucks, the Celtics managed to stay

around the .500 level without their star center, and with Cowens back in the lineup, the Celtics moved into high gear to easily capture first place in the Atlantic Division. The Buffalo Braves dropped back into second place once the Celtics started moving, but the Braves blossomed into an offensive power mainly on the strength of Bob McAdoo's phenomenal scoring. With the outside shooting touch of a forward and enough jumping ability to play center, the 6-foot-10 McAdoo scored at a 34.5 clip to win his second straight NBA scoring title and led the Braves into second place despite costly injuries to Gar Heard, Jim McMillian, and Ernie DiGregorio.

Over in the Central Division, the Washington Bullets had first place to themselves all season long. Known two years ago as the Baltimore Bullets and last year as the Capital Bullets, they tied the Celtics for the league's best record with a 60-22 season. Elvin Hayes and Phil Chenier did the heavy-duty scoring, Mike Riordan and Kevin Porter kept the floor play fluid, and Wes Unseld recovered from last year's sore knees to again dominate the boards in his accustomed manner. The deep bench featured sophomore forward Nick Weatherspoon, ex-ABA All-Star guard Jimmy Jones, and rookie muscleman Len (Truck) Robinson. The Houston Rockets won a playoff berth in the division although they finished 19 games behind the Bullets.

The Midwest Division had a much tighter spread, with Chicago taking first place and Kansas City-Omaha and Detroit qualifying for the playoffs. The Golden State Warriors opened up a big gap in the Pacific Division, but their mid-season slump coupled with a late-season Seattle spurt made the final standings relatively close. The Warriors apparently were heading into

a rebuilding season when they traded Nate Thurmond to Chicago, lost Clyde Lee to Atlanta in the completion of a past deal, and saw Cazzie Russell play out his option and sign with the Lakers. But with Rick Barry playing the best all-around ball of his career at the head of a young supporting cast, the Warriors streaked out to an early divisional lead and held on to beat out the Bill Russell coached, rookie-laden Seattle Supersonics.

The Warriors survived some rocky play in the Western finals to beat the Chicago Bulls in their seventh game to move into the championship series. The Eastern series was a confrontation between the Celtics and Bullets, the clubs with the best records in the league. The Bullets came from behind to take the first game in Boston and went on to defeat the proud Celtics in six games. But branded as overwhelming favorites in the championship series, the Bullets suddenly fell apart. Jones was out with a knee injury, Hayes and Weatherspoon lost the shooting touches that killed Boston, and the club seemed confused on the floor. The younger Warriors, with Rick Barry leading the way, pulled a major upset by taking the NBA crown with four straight victories.

As the NBA ended the season with a new champion in the Warriors, the league statistics also had taken on a new look. With defense emphasized more than in the past, the average team score per game dropped to 102.6, the lowest since the 99.6 average of 1956-57. Another changing aspect of the NBA was at the top, where commissioner Walter Kennedy was resigning at the end of the season to be replaced by political figure Larry O'Brien.

1974-75 SEASON HIGHLIGHTS

STANDINGS

Eastern Conference
Atlantic Division

	W	L	Pct.	GB
Boston	60	22	.732	—
Buffalo	49	33	.598	11
New York	40	42	.488	20
Philadelphia	34	48	.415	26

Central Division

	W	L	Pct.	GB
Washington	60	22	.732	—
Houston	41	41	.500	19
Cleveland	40	42	.488	20
Atlanta	31	51	.378	29
New Orleans	23	59	.280	37

Western Conference
Midwest Division

	W	L	Pct.	GB
Chicago	47	35	.573	—
KC-Omaha	44	38	.537	3
Detroit	40	42	.488	7
Milwaukee	38	44	.463	9

Pacific Division

	W	L	Pct.	GB
Golden State	48	34	.585	—
Seattle	43	39	.524	5
Portland	38	44	.463	10
Phoenix	32	50	.390	16
Los Angeles	30	52	.366	18

AWARDS
MVP
Bob McAdoo, Buffalo
Top Rookie
Keith Wilkes, Golden State
Coach of Year
Phil Johnson, KC-Omaha

ALL-STAR TEAMS
FIRST TEAM

Rick Barry	Golden State
Elvin Hayes	Washington
Bob McAdoo	Buffalo
Nate Archibald	KC-Omaha
Walt Frazier	New York

SECOND TEAM

John Havlicek	Boston
Spencer Haywood	Seattle
Dave Cowens	Boston
Phil Chenier	Washington
Jo Jo White	Boston

Citizenship Award
Wes Unseld, Washington

ALL-STAR GAME
Veterans Memorial Coliseum, Phoenix
Tuesday, January 14, 1975
East 108, West 102
MVP: Walt Frazier

PLAYOFFS
FINALS
Golden State 4, Washington 0
  May 18: Golden State 101 at Washington 95
  May 20: Washington 91 at Golden State 92
  May 23: Washington 101 at Golden State 109
  May 25: Golden State 96 at Washington 95
EASTERN CONFERENCE
CONFERENCE FINALS
Washington 4, Boston 2
  Apr. 27: Washington 100 at Boston 95
  Apr. 30: Boston 92 at Washington 117
  May 3: Washington 90 at Boston 101
  May 7: Boston 108 at Washington 119
  May 9: Washington 99 at Boston 103
  May 11: Boston 92 at Washington 98
CONFERENCE SEMI-FINALS
Boston 4, Houston 1
  Apr. 14: Houston 106 at Boston 123
  Apr. 16: Houston 100 at Boston 112
  Apr. 19: Boston 102 at Houston 117
  Apr. 22: Boston 122 at Houston 117
  Apr. 24: Houston 115 at Boston 128

Washington 4, Buffalo 3
  Apr. 10: Buffalo 113 at Washington 102
  Apr. 12: Washington 120 at Buffalo 106
  Apr. 16: Buffalo 96 at Washington 111
  Apr. 18: Washington 102 at Buffalo 108
  Apr. 20: Buffalo 93 at Washington 97
  Apr. 23: Washington 96 at Buffalo 102
  Apr. 25: Buffalo 96 at Washington 115
FIRST ROUND
Houston 2, New York 1
  Apr. 8: New York 84 at Houston 99
  Apr. 10: Houston 96 at New York 106
  Apr. 12: New York 86 at Houston 118
WESTERN CONFERENCE
CONFERENCE FINALS
Golden State 4, Chicago 3
  Apr. 27: Chicago 89 at Golden State 107
  Apr. 30: Golden State 89 at Chicago 90
  May 4: Golden State 101 at Chicago 108
  May 6: Chicago 106 at Golden State 111
  May 8: Chicago 89 at Golden State 79
  May 11: Golden State 86 at Chicago 72
  May 14: Chicago 79 at Golden State 83

CONFERENCE SEMI-FINALS
Golden State 4, Seattle 2
  Apr. 14: Seattle 96 at Golden State 123
  Apr. 16: Seattle 100 at Golden State 99
  Apr. 17: Golden State 105 at Seattle 96
  Apr. 19: Golden State 94 at Seattle 111
  Apr. 22: Seattle 100 at Golden State 124
  Apr. 24: Golden State 105 at Seattle 96
Chicago 4, Kansas City-Omaha 2
  Apr. 9: KC-Omaha 89 at Chicago 95
  Apr. 13: Chicago 95 at KC-Omaha 102
  Apr. 16: KC-Omaha 90 at Chicago 93
  Apr. 18: Chicago 100 at KC-Omaha 104, OT
  Apr. 20: KC-Omaha 77 at Chicago 104
  Apr. 23: Chicago 101 at KC-Omaha 89
FIRST ROUND
Seattle 2, Detroit 1
  Apr. 8: Detroit 77 at Seattle 90
  Apr. 10: Seattle 106 at Detroit 122
  Apr. 12: Detroit 93 at Seattle 100

NBA LEADERS

SCORING

	GP	FGM	FTM	PTS	PPG
Bob McAdoo, BUF	82	1095	641	2831	34.5
Rick Barry, GST	80	1028	394	2450	30.6
Kareem Abdul-Jabbar, MIL	65	812	325	1949	30.0
Nate Archibald, KCO	82	759	652	2170	26.5
Charlie Scott, PHO	69	703	274	1680	24.3
Bob Lanier, DET	76	731	361	1823	24.0
Elvin Hayes, WSB	82	739	409	1887	23.0
Gail Goodrich, LAL	72	656	318	1630	22.6
Spencer Haywood, SEA	68	608	309	1525	22.4
Fred Carter, PHI	77	715	256	1686	21.9

FIELD GOALS

	FGM	FGA	FG%
Don Nelson, BOS	423	785	.539
Butch Beard, GST	408	773	.528
Rudy Tomjanovich, HOU	694	1323	.525
Kareem Abdul-Jabbar, MIL	812	1584	.513
Bob McAdoo, BUF	1095	2138	.512
Kevin Kunnert, HOU	346	676	.512
Paul Westphal, BOS	342	670	.510
Bob Lanier, DET	731	1433	.510
Dick Snyder, CLE	498	988	.504
Jim McMillian, BUF	347	695	.499

FREE THROWS

	FTM	FTA	FT%
Rick Barry, GST	394	436	.904
Calvin Murphy, HOU	341	386	.883
Bill Bradley, NYK	144	165	.873
Nate Archibald, KCO	652	748	.872
Jim Price, LAL/MIL	169	194	.871
John Havlicek, BOS	289	332	.870
Jack Marin, BUF	193	222	.869
Mike Newlin, HOU	265	305	.869
Chet Walker, CHI	413	480	.860
Jimmy Walker, KCO	247	289	.855

ASSISTS

	GP	AST	APG
Kevin Porter, WSB	81	650	8.0
Dave Bing, DET	79	610	7.7
Nate Archibald, KCO	82	557	6.8
Randy Smith, BUF	82	534	6.5
Pete Maravich, NOJ	79	488	6.2
Rick Barry, GST	80	492	6.2
Slick Watts, SEA	82	499	6.1
Walt Frazier, NYK	78	474	6.1
Gail Goodrich, LAL	72	420	5.8
Norm Van Lier, CHI	70	403	5.8

REBOUNDS

	GP	ORB	DRB	TRB	RPG
Wes Unseld, WSB	73	318	759	1077	14.8
Dave Cowens, BOS	65	229	729	958	14.7
Sam Lacey, KCO	81	228	921	1149	14.2
Bob McAdoo, BUF	82	307	848	1155	14.1
Kareem Abdul-Jabbar, MIL	65	194	718	912	14.0
Happy Hairston, LAL	74	304	642	946	12.8
Paul Silas, BOS	82	348	677	1025	12.5
Elvin Hayes, WSB	82	221	783	1004	12.2
Bob Lanier, DET	76	225	689	914	12.0
Curtis Perry, PHO	79	347	593	940	11.9

STEALS

	GP	STL	SPG
Rick Barry, GST	80	228	2.85
Walt Frazier, NYK	78	190	2.44
Larry Steele, POR	76	183	2.41
Slick Watts, SEA	82	190	2.32
Fred Brown, SEA	81	187	2.31
Phil Chenier, WSB	77	176	2.29
Jerry Sloan, CHI	78	171	2.19
Lucius Allen, MIL/LAL	66	136	2.06
Norm Van Lier, CHI	70	139	1.99
Elvin Hayes, WSB	82	158	1.93

BLOCKS

	GP	BLK	BPG
Kareem Abdul-Jabbar, MIL	65	212	3.26
Elmore Smith, LAL	74	216	2.92
Nate Thurmond, CHI	80	195	2.44
Elvin Hayes, WSB	82	187	2.28
Bob Lanier, DET	76	172	2.26
Bob McAdoo, BUF	82	174	2.12
Sam Lacey, KCO	81	168	2.07
Tom Burleson, SEA	82	153	1.87
Gar Heard, BUF	67	120	1.79
Jim Chones, CLE	72	120	1.67

THE YEAR IN BASKETBALL

September 16, 1974 Forrest (Phog) Allen, one of the game's earliest dominant coaches, dies at age 88.

September 28, 1974 The Indiana Pacers of the ABA play their first game in Market Square Arena, in a preseason tilt versus the NBA's Milwaukee Bucks. Led by George McGinnis' 24 points, the Pacers defeat the Bucks, 118-115, despite 46 points from Milwaukee forward Bobby Dandridge and 26 from Kareem Abdul-Jabbar.

October 3, 1974 "Mr. Clutch" calls it quits. Jerry West, selected to the All-NBA first team ten times in his 14-year career, retires.

October 18, 1974 Chicago center Nate Thurmond records the NBA's first quadruple-double, with 22 points, 14 rebounds, 13 assists, and 12 blocks in the Bulls' 120-115 overtime win against Atlanta in Chicago.

February 7, 1975 The New Orleans Jazz', playing in their first NBA season, end a 28-game road losing streak.

February 9, 1975 Bill Russell becomes the first African-American player elected into the Hall of Fame.

February 14, 1975 In the highest scoring game in ABA history, the San Diego Conquistadors defeat the New York Nets, 176-166 in four overtimes. Julius Erving of New York scores a career-high 63 points and grabs 23 rebounds. Guard Bo Lamar leads San Diego with 45 points.

February 23, 1975 Nearly 12,000 fans attend a women's game between Immaculata and Queens College in the opener of a double-header at Madison Square Garden. Immaculata, a three-time national champion, wins 65-61. Two men's teams, Fairfield and Massachusetts, play the nightcap but the *New York Times* reports that the crowd "dwin-dled to about 4,000 by halftime of the men's game."

March 22, 1975 Delta State wins the AIAW basketball title with a 90-81 victory over three-time champ, Immaculata.

March 31, 1975 UCLA wins its 10th championship in 12 years, beating Kentucky, 92-85. Two days earlier · coach John Wooden had announced his retirement.

April 6, 1975 Washington's Wes Unseld grabs 30 rebounds against New Orleans to win the rebounding title over Dave Cowens, 14.8 rpg to 14.7.

April 30, 1975 Larry O'Brien is named the third commissioner in NBA history, succeeding Walter Kennedy (who succeeded Maurice Podoloff).

April 30, 1975 A record 17,421 fans attend Game 6 of the ABA's Western Conference finals between home-standing Indiana and Denver. The Pacers, however, disappoint the throng, losing 104-99. Three nights later in Game 7, Indiana regroups and wins to advance to the ABA finals.

May 22, 1975 Kentucky defeats Indiana, 110-105, in Game 5 to win the ABA title. Artis Gilmore scores 28 points for the Colonels.

May 18, 1975 Golden State wins, 96-95, to sweep Washington in four games to win the NBA title. Butch Beard's foul shot with nine seconds left gives the Warriors the title. Rick Barry leads the winners with 20 points in the finale.

June 16, 1975 The Bucks trade Kareem Abdul-Jabbar, along with Walt Wesley, to Los Angeles for center Elmore Smith, guards Brian Winters and Junior Bridgeman, and forward Dave Meyers.

June 24, 1975 Wendell Ladner, a popular forward for the Nets, is killed in a plane crash at age 27.

1975-76

Celtics re-claim crown with Havlicek, White— and Glenn McDonald?

The best player in the NBA asked to be traded and got his wish. Kareem Abdul-Jabbar had played six seasons in Milwaukee. He had won three MVP awards, taken the Bucks to one championship, and made them perennial contenders. He decided, however, that he wanted to live either in New York, where he grew up, or in Los Angeles, where he attended college. The Bucks accommodated him in June of 1975 with a trade to the Lakers. The Bucks received center Elmore Smith, guard Brian Winters, and two rookies taken in the first round of the draft, forward David Meyers of UCLA and swingman Junior Bridgeman of Louisville. The four newcomers helped the Bucks rebound from last place to first in the Midwest Division.

Meanwhile, things did not go smoothly in Los Angeles or New York. With Kareem at center, the Lakers were expected to rise from last place to first in the Pacific Division. Kareem did post big numbers in scoring and rebounding and did win another MVP award. The Lakers, however, slumped in midseason and were eliminated from the playoffs in the last week of the regular season.

The Knicks didn't even get that close to the playoffs. Walt Frazier and Earl Monroe still starred in the backcourt, but the Knicks were weak up front. Over the summer, they had signed star ABA forward George McGinnis to a lucrative contract. NBA Commissioner Larry O'Brien, who succeeded Walter Kennedy in that position last spring, voided the contract because the Philadelphia 76ers held the draft rights to McGinnis. The Knicks did acquire forward Spencer Haywood from Seattle in October for a bundle of money, a move which bolstered the front line but did not prevent a last place finish in the Atlantic Division.

The best basketball was played up the coast from Los Angeles and New York, in mellower sites to the north. In Boston, the Celtics opened up a lead in the Atlantic Division after New Year's Day. Don Chaney had jumped to the ABA, but the Celtics reinforced the backcourt by trading Paul Westphal to Phoenix for Charlie Scott. Although the bench was thin, veterans John Havlicek, Dave Cowens, Jo Jo White, and Paul Silas kept the Celtic tradition alive for a fourteenth divisional title. The Buffalo Braves took second place on the strength of Bob McAdoo's third straight scoring title and Randy Smith's excellence at guard. Ernie DiGregorio lost playing time as the Braves adjusted poorly to his return from a knee injury. The 76ers tied Buffalo and also made the playoffs. They lost Billy Cunningham to a knee injury in December, but Doug Collins and newcomer McGinnis emerged as offensive weapons on a winning team.

A new champion reigned in the Central Division, as the Cleveland Cavaliers passed the Washington Bullets with a strong final month. Cleveland coach Bill Fitch blended a col-

Kareem Abdul-Jabbar
After three MVP awards in six seasons with Milwaukee, a yen to go urban results in trade to L.A.—and, eventually, three more MVPs.

lection of role players into an effective half-court team with balanced scoring. The Bullets lost their divisional crown by losing eight of their final twelve games. The Bullets had added Dave Bing from Detroit to complement veteran stars Wes Unseld, Elvin Hayes, and Phil Chenier. Houston finished out of the playoffs despite a deep stock of scorers, as did New Orleans despite Pistol Pete Maravich's talents. The Atlanta Hawks failed to sign their two first-round draft picks and collapsed from March onwards.

None of the Midwest Division teams had a winning record.

The Bucks squeezed past the Pistons by winning six of their final eight games. That hot stretch, however, raised Milwaukee's record only to 38-44. Bob Dandridge and Brian Winters took up the scoring slack left behind by Abdul-Jabbar. The Pistons were crippled by guard Kevin Porter's season-ending knee injury a month into the season. Without their newly-acquired playmaker, the Pistons could not use Bob Lanier and Curtis Rowe to best advantage. The Kansas City Kings dropped Omaha as a part-time home and disappointed high pre-season expectations despite Tiny Archibald's continued brilliance. The Chicago Bulls fell into a losing habit after Chet Walker retired and Jerry Sloan injured a knee.

In the Pacific Division, the Lakers did not blossom into instant champions with the arrival of Abdul-Jabbar. The Golden State Warriors defended last year's championship by winning the most games in the regular season. Rick Barry led the team in both scoring and assists, with Jamaal Wilkes complementing him at forward. The guard corps featured much-improved Phil Smith and rookie Gus Williams. Seattle and Phoenix finished far behind the Warriors but still earned play-off berths. Guards Slick Watts and Fred Brown were the heart of the Sonics. Phoenix improved as the season progressed, blending ex-Celtic guard Paul Westphal and rookie center Alvan Adams into a solid veteran cast. Last in the division were the Portland Trail Blazers cursed by a recurring series of injuries to Bill Walton.

In the playoffs, the Celtics beat Buffalo and Cleveland to advance to the championship series. In the west, Phoenix upset the Warriors in Oakland in Game 7, 94-86, to earn a shot at the Celtics and the title.

The championships series began on the parquet floor of the Boston Garden. In Game 1, the Suns suffered from a collective spell of bad shooting, as the Celtics won, 98-87. Game two was more of the same, as the veteran Celtics beat the upstart Suns 105-90. Back in Arizona, however, the Suns beat the Celtics, 105-98, in Game 3 and 109-107 in Game 4.

The usual sell-out crowd of 15,320 filled the Boston Garden for the pivotal fifth game. They saw a marathon of endurance and luck. Down by five points with 55 seconds remaining, the Suns tied the game with Westphal's jumper, steal, basket, and foul shot. The Celtics and Suns played a five-minute overtime without breaking the tie. With five seconds left in the second overtime, Curtis Perry hit a long jump shot to put Phoenix ahead, 110-109. The Celtics went to their clutch shooter, John Havlicek, who scored with two seconds left to put Boston ahead, 111-110. When Phoenix took an illegal time-out, the Celtics converted a free throw to go ahead, 112-110. The Suns then threw the ball in to Garfield Heard, who miraculously sunk a long prayer to send the game into a third overtime. Boston reserve Glenn McDonald scored six points in this final period to lead the Celtics to an exhausting 128-126 victory. When the teams reconvened in Phoenix, the Celtics ground out an 87-80 victory to reclaim their accustomed perch atop the NBA.

1975-76 SEASON HIGHLIGHTS

STANDINGS

Eastern Conference
Atlantic Division

	W	L	Pct.	GB
Boston	54	28	.659	—
Buffalo	46	36	.561	8
Philadelphia	46	36	.561	8
New York	38	44	.463	16

Central Division

	W	L	Pct.	GB
Cleveland	49	33	.598	—
Washington	48	34	.585	1
Houston	40	42	.488	9
New Orleans	38	44	.463	11
Atlanta	29	53	.354	20

Western Conference
Midwest Division

	W	L	Pct.	GB
Milwaukee	38	44	.463	—
Detroit	36	46	.439	2
Kansas City	31	51	.378	7
Chicago	24	58	.293	14

Pacific Division

	W	L	Pct.	GB
Golden State	59	23	.720	—
Seattle	43	39	.524	16
Phoenix	42	40	.512	17
Los Angeles	40	42	.488	19
Portland	37	45	.451	22

AWARDS

MVP
Kareem Abdul-Jabbar, LA Lakers
Top Rookie
Alvan Adams, Phoenix
Coach of Year
Bill Fitch, Cleveland

ALL-STAR TEAMS

FIRST TEAM

Rick Barry	Golden State
George McGinnis	Philadelphia
Kareem Abdul-Jabbar	Los Angeles
Nate Archibald	Kansas City
Pete Maravich	New Orleans

Citizenship Award
Slick Watts, Seattle

ALL-STAR GAME
The Spectrum, Philadelphia
Tuesday, February 3, 1976
East 123, West 109
MVP: Dave Bing

SECOND TEAM

Elvin Hayes	Washington
John Havlicek	Boston
Dave Cowens	Boston
Randy Smith	Buffalo
Phil Smith	Golden State

PLAYOFFS
FINALS
Boston 4, Phoenix 2
May 23: Phoenix 87 at Boston 98
May 27: Phoenix 90 at Boston 105
May 30: Boston 98 at Phoenix 105
June 2: Boston 107 at Phoenix 109
June 4: Phoenix 126 at Boston 128, 3OT
June 6: Boston 87 at Phoenix 80
EASTERN CONFERENCE
CONFERENCE FINALS
Boston 4, Cleveland 2
May 6: Cleveland 99 at Boston 111
May 9: Cleveland 89 at Boston 94
May 11: Boston 78 at Cleveland 83
May 14: Boston 87 at Cleveland 106
May 16: Cleveland 94 at Boston 99
May 18: Boston 94 at Cleveland 87
CONFERENCE SEMI-FINALS
Boston 4, Buffalo 2
Apr. 21: Buffalo 98 at Boston 107
Apr. 23: Buffalo 96 at Boston 101
Apr. 25: Boston 93 at Buffalo 98
Apr. 28: Boston 122 at Buffalo 124
Apr. 30: Buffalo 88 at Boston 99
May 2: Boston 104 at Buffalo 100

Cleveland 4, Washington 3
Apr. 13: Washington 100 at Cleveland 95
Apr. 15: Cleveland 80 at Washington 79
Apr. 17: Washington 76 at Cleveland 88
Apr. 21: Cleveland 98 at Washington 109
Apr. 22: Washington 91 at Cleveland 92
Apr. 26: Cleveland 98 at Washington 102, OT
Apr. 29: Washington 85 at Cleveland 87
FIRST ROUND
Buffalo 2, Philadelphia 1
Apr. 15: Buffalo 95 at Philadelphia 89
Apr. 16: Philadelphia 131 at Buffalo 106
Apr. 18: Buffalo 124 at Philadelphia 123, OT
WESTERN CONFERENCE
CONFERENCE FINALS
Phoenix 4, Golden State 3
May 2: Phoenix 103 at Golden State 128
May 5: Phoenix 108 at Golden State 101
May 7: Golden State 99 at Phoenix 91
May 9: Golden State 129 at Phoenix 133, 2OT
May 12: Phoenix 95 at Golden State 111
May 14: Golden State 104 at Phoenix 105
May 16: Phoenix 94 at Golden State 86

CONFERENCE SEMI-FINALS
Golden State 4, Detroit 2
Apr. 20: Detroit 103 at Golden State 127
Apr. 22: Detroit 123 at Golden State 111
Apr. 24: Golden State 113 at Detroit 96
Apr. 26: Golden State 102 at Detroit 106
Apr. 28: Detroit 109 at Golden State 128
Apr. 30: Golden State 118 at Detroit 116, OT
Phoenix 4, Seattle 2
Apr. 13: Phoenix 99 at Seattle 102
Apr. 15: Phoenix 116 at Seattle 111
Apr. 18: Seattle 91 at Phoenix 103
Apr. 20: Seattle 114 at Phoenix 130
Apr. 25: Phoenix 108 at Seattle 114
Apr. 27: Seattle 112 at Phoenix 123
FIRST ROUND
Detroit 2, Milwaukee 1
Apr. 13: Detroit 107 at Milwaukee 110
Apr. 15: Milwaukee 123 at Detroit 126
Apr. 18: Detroit 107 at Milwaukee 104

NBA LEADERS

SCORING

	GP	FGM	FTM	PTS	PPG
Bob McAdoo, BUF	78	934	559	2427	31.1
Kareem Abdul-Jabbar, LAL	82	914	447	2275	27.7
Pete Maravich, NOJ	62	604	396	1604	25.9
Nate Archibald, KCK	78	717	501	1935	24.8
Fred Brown, SEA	76	742	273	1757	23.1
George McGinnis, PHI	77	647	475	1769	23.0
Randy Smith, BUF	82	702	383	1787	21.8
John Drew, ATL	77	586	488	1660	21.6
Bob Dandridge, MIL	73	650	271	1571	21.5
Calvin Murphy, HOU	82	675	372	1722	21.0
Rick Barry, GST	81	707	287	1701	21.0

FIELD GOALS

	FGM	FGA	FG%
Wes Unseld, WSB	318	567	.56085
John Shumate, PHO/BUF	332	592	.56081
Jim McMillian, BUF	492	918	.536
Bob Lanier, DET	541	1017	.532
Kareem Abdul-Jabbar, LAL	914	1728	.529
Elmore Smith, MIL	498	962	.518
Rudy Tomjanovich, HOU	622	1202	.517
Doug Collins, PHI	614	1196	.513
Ollie Johnson, KCK	348	678	.513
Mike Newlin, HOU	569	1123	.507

FREE THROWS

	FTM	FTA	FT%
Rick Barry, GST	287	311	.923
Calvin Murphy, HOU	372	410	.907
Cazzie Russell, LAL	132	148	.892
Bill Bradley, NYK	130	148	.878
Fred Brown, SEA	273	314	.869
Mike Newlin, HOU	385	445	.865
Jimmy Walker, KCK	231	267	.865
Jim McMillian, BUF	188	219	.858
Jack Marin, BUF/CHI	161	188	.856
Keith Erickson, PHO	134	157	.854

ASSISTS

	GP	AST	APG
Slick Watts, SEA	82	661	8.1
Nate Archibald, KCK	78	615	7.9
Calvin Murphy, HOU	82	596	7.3
Norm Van Lier, CHI	76	500	6.6
Rick Barry, GST	81	496	6.1
Dave Bing, WSB	82	492	6.0
Randy Smith, BUF	82	484	5.9
Alvan Adams, PHO	80	450	5.6
Gail Goodrich, LAL	75	421	5.6
Mike Newlin, HOU	82	457	5.6

REBOUNDS

	GP	ORB	DRB	TRB	RPG
Kareem Abdul-Jabbar, LAL	82	272	1111	1383	16.9
Dave Cowens, BOS	78	335	911	1246	16.0
Wes Unseld, WSB	78	271	765	1036	13.3
Paul Silas, BOS	81	365	660	1025	12.7
Sam Lacey, KCK	81	218	806	1024	12.6
George McGinnis, PHI	77	260	707	967	12.6
Bob McAdoo, BUF	78	241	724	965	12.4
Elmore Smith, MIL	78	201	692	893	11.4
Spencer Haywood, NYK	78	234	644	878	11.3
Elvin Hayes, WSB	80	210	668	878	11.0

STEALS

	GP	STL	SPG
Slick Watts, SEA	82	261	3.18
George McGinnis, PHI	77	198	2.57
Paul Westphal, PHO	82	210	2.56
Rick Barry, GST	81	202	2.49
Chris Ford, DET	82	178	2.17
Larry Steele, POR	81	170	2.10
Phil Chenier, WSB	80	158	1.98
Norm Van Lier, CHI	76	150	1.97
Steve Mix, PHI	81	158	1.95
Fred Brown, SEA	76	143	1.88

BLOCKS

	GP	BLK	BPG
Kareem Abdul-Jabbar, LAL	82	338	4.12
Elmore Smith, MIL	78	238	3.05
Elvin Hayes, WSB	80	202	2.53
Harvey Catchings, PHI	75	164	2.19
George Johnson, GST	82	174	2.12
Bob McAdoo, BUF	78	160	2.05
Tom Burleson, SEA	82	150	1.83
Otto Moore, NOJ	81	136	1.68
Sam Lacey, KCK	81	134	1.65
Lloyd Neal, POR	68	107	1.57

THE YEAR IN BASKETBALL

October 8, 1975 The Denver Nuggets of the ABA play the first basketball game at new McNichols Arena, and defeat the NBA's Seattle Supersonics, 115-110, in a preseason tilt.

October 8, 1975 The ABA's San Antonio Spurs defeat the NBA's Atlanta Hawks, 109-107, in the first basketball ever game played in the Louisiana Superdome.

October 23, 1975 Moving from high school directly to the pros, Bill Willoughby debuts for the Atlanta Hawks. Willoughby, who played at Dwight Morrow High in Englewood, N.J., becomes the youngest player in league history at 18 years, five months and three days.

November 9, 1975 Mendy Rudolph retires after 23 years as an NBA referee. The colorful Rudolph officiated a record 2,113 games, more than any ref in league history at the time. Earl Strom eventually breaks Rudolph's record by officiating over 2,400 games in his 30-year career.

December 14, 1975 Kareem Abdul-Jabbar grabs a record 29 defensive rebounds in a 110-100 victory over Detroit.

March 21, 1976 Kentucky wins its first NIT in 30 years, defeating North Carolina-Charlotte, 71-67. UNC's Cedric Maxwell is voted the tourney's top player—the fourth straight year a member of the second-place team gets that honor.

March 27, 1976 Delta State beats Immaculata, 69-64, for its second straight AIAW title.

March 29, 1976 Indiana and Bobby Knight go undefeated at 32-0, beating Michigan, 86-68, in the NCAA tourney final. Scott May scores 26 points and Kent Benson 25 in the clinching victory.

May 1, 1976 With Julius Erving and the Nets in town, the Denver Nuggets draw 19,034 fans for an ABA championship game. Erving scores 45 points and hits the game-winning shot at the buzzer.

May 13, 1976 In the final ABA championship series, the New York Nets rally from 22 points down in the third quarter to beat the Denver Nuggets, 112-106, and win the crown in six games. The Nets' Julius Erving scores 31 points and John Williamson scores 28. Five weeks later, the ABA merges with the established NBA.

June 4, 1976 In one of the NBA's greatest games, the Boston Celtics defeat the Phoenix Suns, 128-126, in triple overtime in Game 5 of the NBA finals. Phoenix's Garfield Heard extends the game with a long turn-around jumper as time expires in the second overtime. But Boston battles back. Jo Jo White scores 33 points in 60 minutes of action for Boston. Two days later, the Celtics clinch their 13th title.

June 6, 1976 Boston wins its 13th NBA championship, defeating Phoenix in Game 6, 87-80.

June 17, 1976 The ABA merges with the NBA, increasing the number of NBA teams by four to 22. The Denver Nuggets, Indiana Pacers, New York Nets, and San Antonio Spurs are the ABA teams admitted into the established league.

July 23, 1976 The Soviet Union women's team thwarts the U.S. squad, 112-77, at the Olympics in Montreal. Led by their great center Uljana Semenova, who scores 32 points in 23 minutes, the Soviets go undefeated at the Games and win the gold medal. With Semjonova, the Soviet women's team was undefeated for 18 years in international play.

1976-77

Four ABA teams join, Walton, Trail Blazers cut wide swath to title

The four surviving ABA teams each paid over $3 million to enter the NBA promised land. They also had to pool another $3 million to pay off John Y. Brown, the owner of the Kentucky Colonels, who were left out of the merger. Brown promptly purchased a half-interest in the Buffalo Braves. In addition, the New York Nets had to pay about $4 million to the New York Knicks to share the New York territory. Despite the high financial toll on the ABA teams, ABA players figured prominently in all four divisional races.

The New York Nets had won the final ABA title and had high hopes in the Atlantic Division. Over the summer, they bolstered their backcourt by sending players and draft choices to Kansas City for Tiny Archibald. Star forward Julius Erving aggravated the team's financial woes, however, by demanding renegotiation of his contract and sitting out the team's pre-season schedule. Just before the season began, the Nets sold Erving's contract to the Philadelphia 76ers for approximately $3 million. While the deal eased the Nets' financial pressures, it ruined the team on the floor. When Archibald suffered a broken foot in January, the Nets' season became a fiasco.

The 76ers, meanwhile, became an elite team with the addition of Dr. J. George McGinnis and Doug Collins were also potent offensive weapons, supported by a deep cast of role players. The 76ers opened up a lead in the Atlantic Division after New Year's Day. The Celtics finished only six games back despite a series of misfortunes. Paul Silas was traded to Denver in a salary dispute, Dave Cowens left the team in November for two months for personal reasons, Charlie Scott suffered a broken arm in January and missed almost two months, and newly-acquired forwards Sidney Wicks and Curtis Rowe fit with difficulty into the Celtic system. The Knicks finished out of the playoffs despite acquiring Bob McAdoo and Jim McMillian from Buffalo. The Braves and Nets expectedly brought up the rear after dropping their star players.

In the Central Division, ABA survivor Moses Malone made a difference. After spending the pre-season with Portland, Malone was traded to Buffalo. After a week with the Braves, he was then sent to the Houston Rockets. Malone developed during the season into a superb rebounder at both forward and center. Rudy Tomjanovich was Houston's offensive leader. The Rockets closed strongly, with new coach Tom Nissalke, himself an ABA ex-patriot, taking them to the divisional title. Washington, San Antonio, and Cleveland all made the playoffs. New Orleans missed the playoffs despite Pete Maravich's scoring title, which featured 13 games of 40 points or more. Atlanta finished last again, with Ted Turner purchasing a controlling interest in the Hawks in January.

In the Midwest Division, an ABA team finished first. The Denver Nuggets had stars in David Thompson, Dan Issel, and Bobby Jones, veteran strength in ex-Celtic forward Paul Silas,

Pete Maravich
Firing here against the Nets' Jan Van Breda Kolff and Nate Archibald, Pistol Pete pops 40 or more points 13 times on way to scoring title.

an exciting fast break offense, and the best attendance in the league. Chicago and Detroit also made the playoffs from the Midwest. The Bulls lost 14 of their first 17 games, then came back and won 20 of their last 24 games. Star center Artis Gilmore came to Chicago from the defunct Kentucky Colonels. The Pistons enjoyed Bob Lanier's usual excellence and were disappointed by ex-ABA forward Marvin Barnes, whose season was overshadowed by a gun-related parole violation. Kansas City and Indiana were respectable also-rans while Milwaukee fell from first place to last.

In the Pacific Division, new coach Jerry West led the Los Angeles Lakers to the best record in the league. Kareem Abdul-Jabbar's dominance at center earned him another MVP award and lifted an otherwise ordinary team to a new level. Challenging the Lakers all season were the Portland Trail Blazers, beneficiaries of Bill Walton's relatively good health. New coach, Jack Ramsay traded away Sidney Wicks and Geoff Petrie, their leading scorers in recent years, and installed a running offense and tenacious defense. Maurice Lucas came from the ABA to help Walton with his strong inside game. Rick Barry, Phil Smith, and Jamaal Wilkes excelled in the Warriors' unsuccessful bid to repeat as Pacific champions. Seattle hovered around the .500 mark all season in Bill Russell's finale as coach. After their cinderella trip to last year's playoff finals, the Phoenix Suns finished in last place in the division. Paul Westphal continued his hot shooting, but injuries crippled the Suns at forward and sent them to 17 losses in their last 22 games.

In the playoffs, the four mini-series set up four interesting quarter-final series. In the west, Portland won the opener at Denver and then held home-court advantage to win six games. With Abdul-Jabbar scoring 40 points or better four times, the Lakers eliminated the Warriors in seven games. In the east, the young Houston Rockets beat the veteran Washington Bullets in six games.

In the other Eastern quarterfinal, the defending champion Celtics won the opener in Philadelphia 113-111 on a Jo Jo White jumper at the buzzer. The Sixers won Game 2 and recaptured the home-court advantage by winning Game 3 109-100 in Boston. The Celtics evened the series by taking Game 4 124-119 behind Cowens' 37 points. The Sixers won Game 5 in Philadelphia, and the Celtics captured Game 6 in Boston. In the finale in the Spectrum, the Sixers went ahead with a 10-2 spurt in the third period and won the deciding game by an 83-77 score.

In the semi-finals, the Sixers rolled on, overwhelming Houston in six games. In the West, Kareem Abdul-Jabbar and Bill Walton both played center at a superb level. The Blazers, however, simply had better personnel around Walton. They swept the Lakers in four straight games.

In the championship series, Philadelphia's individual stars matched up against Portland's team orientation. The Sixers won the first two games at home, as the Blazers were plagued with turnovers and cold shooting. With Bill Walton excelling in scoring, rebounding, and passing, the Blazers revived and handily captured the third and fourth games in Portland. Back in Philadelphia, the Blazers staged a 26-8 spurt in the third period and won the key fifth game, 110-104. The Sixers rallied in Game 6 but could not stem the Portland tide. The Trail Blazers won Game 6, 109-107, to take the NBA championship.

1976-77 SEASON HIGHLIGHTS

STANDINGS

Eastern Conference
Atlantic Division

	W	L	Pct.	GB
Philadelphia	50	32	.610	—
Boston	44	38	.537	6
New York	40	42	.488	10
Buffalo	30	52	.366	20
New York	22	60	.268	28

Central Division

	W	L	Pct.	GB
Houston	49	33	.598	—
Washington	48	34	.585	1
San Antonio	44	38	.537	5
Cleveland	43	39	.524	6
New Orleans	35	47	.427	14
Atlanta	31	51	.378	18

Western Conference
Midwest Division

	W	L	Pct.	GB
Denver	50	32	.610	—
Chicago	44	38	.537	6
Detroit	44	38	.537	6
Kansas City	40	42	.488	10
Indiana	36	46	.439	14
Milwaukee	30	52	.366	20

Pacific Division

	W	L	Pct.	GB
Los Angeles	53	29	.646	—
Portland	49	33	.598	4
Golden State	46	36	.561	7
Seattle	40	42	.488	13
Phoenix	34	48	.415	19

AWARDS

MVP
Kareem Abdul-Jabbar, LA Lakers
Top Rookie
Adrian Dantley, Buffalo
Coach of Year
Tom Nissalke, Houston
Citizenship Award
Dave Bing, Washington

ALL-STAR TEAMS

FIRST TEAM

Elvin Hayes	Washington
David Thompson	Denver
Kareem Abdul-Jabbar	Los Angeles
Pete Maravich	New Orleans
Paul Westphal	Phoenix

SECOND TEAM

Julius Erving	Philadelphia
George McGinnis	Philadelphia
Bill Walton	Portland
George Gervin	San Antonio
Jo Jo White	Boston

ALL-STAR GAME

Milwaukee Arena, Milwaukee
Sunday, February 13, 1977
West 125, East 124
MVP: Julius Erving

PLAYOFFS

FINALS
Portland 4, Philadelphia 2
  May 22: Portland 101 at Philadelphia 107
  May 26: Portland 89 at Philadelphia 107
  May 29: Philadelphia 107 at Portland 129
  May 31: Philadelphia 98 at Portland 130
  June 3: Portland 110 at Philadelphia 104
  June 5: Philadelphia 107 at Portland 109

EASTERN CONFERENCE
CONFERENCE FINALS
Philadelphia 4, Houston 2
  May 5: Houston 117 at Philadelphia 128
  May 8: Houston 97 at Philadelphia 106
  May 11: Philadelphia 94 at Houston 118
  May 13: Philadelphia 107 at Houston 95
  May 15: Houston 118 at Philadelphia 115
  May 17: Philadelphia 112 at Houston 109

CONFERENCE SEMI-FINALS
Philadelphia 4, Boston 3
  Apr. 17: Boston 113 at Philadelphia 111
  Apr. 20: Boston 101 at Philadelphia 113
  Apr. 22: Philadelphia 109 at Boston 100
  Apr. 24: Philadelphia 119 at Boston 124
  Apr. 27: Boston 91 at Philadelphia 110
  Apr. 29: Philadelphia 108 at Boston 113
  May 1: Boston 77 at Philadelphia 83

Houston 4, Washington 2
  Apr. 19: Washington 111 at Houston 101
  Apr. 21: Washington 118 at Houston 124, OT
  Apr. 24: Houston 90 at Washington 93
  Apr. 26: Houston 107 at Washington 103
  Apr. 29: Washington 115 at Houston 123
  May 1: Houston 108 at Washington 103

FIRST ROUND
Boston 2, San Antonio 0
  Apr. 12: San Antonio 94 at Boston 104
  Apr. 15: Boston 113 at San Antonio 109

Washington 2, Cleveland 1
  Apr. 13: Cleveland 100 at Washington 109
  Apr. 15: Washington 83 at Cleveland 91
  Apr. 17: Cleveland 98 at Washington 104

WESTERN CONFERENCE
CONFERENCE FINALS
Portland 4, Los Angeles 0
  May 6: Portland 121 at Los Angeles 109
  May 8: Portland 99 at Los Angeles 97
  May 10: Los Angeles 97 at Portland 102
  May 13: Los Angeles 101 at Portland 105

CONFERENCE SEMI-FINALS
Los Angeles 4, Golden State 3
  Apr. 20: Golden State 106 at Los Angeles 115
  Apr. 22: Golden State 86 at Los Angeles 95
  Apr. 24: Los Angeles 105 at Golden State 109
  Apr. 26: Los Angeles 103 at Golden State 114
  Apr. 29: Golden State 105 at Los Angeles 112
  May 1: Los Angeles 106 at Golden State 115
  May 4: Golden State 84 at Los Angeles 97

Portland 4, Denver 2
  Apr. 20: Portland 101 at Denver 100
  Apr. 22: Portland 110 at Denver 121
  Apr. 24: Denver 106 at Portland 110
  Apr. 26: Denver 96 at Portland 105
  May 1: Portland 105 at Denver 114, OT
  May 2: Denver 92 at Portland 108

FIRST ROUND
Golden State 2, Detroit 1
  Apr. 12: Detroit 95 at Golden State 90
  Apr. 14: Golden State 138 at Detroit 108
  Apr. 17: Detroit 101 at Golden State 109

Portland 2, Chicago 1
  Apr. 12: Chicago 83 at Portland 96
  Apr. 15: Portland 104 at Chicago 107
  Apr. 17: Chicago 98 at Portland 106

NBA LEADERS

SCORING

	GP	FGM	FTM	PTS	PPG
Pete Maravich, NOJ	73	886	501	2273	31.1
Billy Knight, IND	78	831	413	2075	26.6
Kareem Abdul-Jabbar, LAL	82	888	376	2152	26.2
David Thompson, DEN	82	824	477	2125	25.9
Bob McAdoo, BUF/NYK	72	740	381	1861	25.8
Bob Lanier, DET	64	678	260	1616	25.3
John Drew, ATL	74	689	412	1790	24.2
Elvin Hayes, WSB	82	760	422	1942	23.7
George Gervin, SAS	82	726	443	1895	23.1
Dan Issel, DEN	79	660	445	1765	22.3

FIELD GOALS

	FGM	FGA	FG%
Kareem Abdul-Jabbar, LAL	888	1533	.579
Mitch Kupchak, WSB	341	596	.572
Bobby Jones, DEN	501	879	.570
George Gervin, SAS	726	1335	.544
Bob Lanier, DET	678	1269	.534
Bob Gross, POR	376	711	.529
Swen Nater, MIL	383	725	.528
Bill Walton, POR	491	930	.528
Joe Meriweather, ATL	319	607	.526
Artis Gilmore, CHI	570	1091	.522

FREE THROWS

	FTM	FTA	FT%
Ernie DiGregorio, BUF	138	146	.945
Rick Barry, GST	359	392	.916
Calvin Murphy, HOU	272	307	.886
Mike Newlin, HOU	269	304	.885
Fred Brown, SEA	168	190	.884
Dick Van Arsdale, PHO	145	166	.873
Jo Jo White, BOS	333	383	.869
Junior Bridgeman, MIL	197	228	.864
Cazzie Russell, LAL	188	219	.858
Jan Van Breda Kolff, NYN	195	228	.855

ASSISTS

	GP	AST	APG
Don Buse, IND	81	685	8.5
Slick Watts, SEA	79	630	8.0
Norm Van Lier, CHI	82	636	7.8
Kevin Porter, DET	81	592	7.3
Tom Henderson, ATL/WSB	87	598	6.9
Rick Barry, GST	79	475	6.0
Jo Jo White, BOS	82	492	6.0
Mike Gale, SAS	82	473	5.8
Paul Westphal, PHO	81	459	5.7
John Lucas, HOU	82	463	5.6

REBOUNDS

	GP	ORB	DRB	TRB	RPG
Bill Walton, POR	65	211	723	934	14.4
Kareem Abdul-Jabbar, LAL	82	266	824	1090	13.3
Moses Malone, BUF/HOU	82	437	635	1072	13.1
Artis Gilmore, CHI	82	313	757	1070	13.0
Bob McAdoo, BUF/NYK	72	199	727	926	12.9
Elvin Hayes, WSB	82	289	740	1029	12.5
Swen Nater, MIL	72	266	599	865	12.0
George McGinnis, PHI	79	324	587	911	11.5
Maurice Lucas, POR	79	271	628	899	11.4
Larry Kenon, SAS	78	282	597	879	11.3

STEALS

	GP	STL	SPG
Don Buse, IND	81	281	3.47
Brian Taylor, KCK	72	199	2.76
Slick Watts, SEA	79	214	2.71
Quinn Buckner, MIL	79	192	2.43
Mike Gale, SAS	82	191	2.33
Bobby Jones, DEN	82	186	2.27
Lionel Hollins, POR	76	166	2.18
Chris Ford, DET	82	179	2.18
Rick Barry, GST	79	172	2.18
Randy Smith, BUF	82	176	2.15

BLOCKS

	GP	BLK	BPG
Bill Walton, POR	65	211	3.25
Kareem Abdul-Jabbar, LAL	82	261	3.18
Elvin Hayes, WSB	82	220	2.68
Artis Gilmore, CHI	82	203	2.48
Caldwell Jones, PHI	82	200	2.44
George Johnson, GST/BUF	78	177	2.27
Moses Malone, BUF/HOU	82	181	2.21
Dan Roundfield, IND	61	131	2.15
Billy Paultz, SAS	82	173	2.11
Elmore Smith, MIL/CLE	70	144	2.06

THE YEAR IN BASKETBALL

October 20, 1976 The New York Nets trade Julius Erving to the Philadelphia 76ers for cash.

October 22, 1976 Twin brothers Tom and Dick Van Arsdale play together in a game for the Phoenix Suns. They are the only brothers ever to compete for the same NBA franchise.

December 26, 1976 Larry Kenon of San Antonio sets an NBA record with 11 steals against the Kansas City Kings.

February 13, 1977 Julius Erving, in his first NBA All-Star Game, is voted MVP after he scores 30 points and gets 12 rebounds.

February 25, 1977 Pete Maravich scores 67 points—at the time the most ever by a guard in an NBA game—as New Orleans defeats New York, 124-107.

March 1, 1977 Carol Blazejowski, a 5-foot-10 forward, scores 52 points for Montclair (N.J.) State to beat Queens (N.Y.) College 102-91 on March 1, 1977. The point total is the highest by any man or woman since the new Madison Square Garden was built in 1968.

March 9, 1977 Anthony Roberts of Oral Roberts sets an NIT record by scoring 65 points in a 90-89 first round loss to Oregon. The tournament is eventually won by St. Bonaventure, which sparked by tourney MVP Greg Sanders, beats Houston for the title, 94-91.

March 26, 1977 Delta State wins the AIAW title for the third straight year, with a 68-55 victory over LSU.

March 28, 1977 In his final game as coach, Al McGuire leads his Marquette Warriors past North Carolina, 67-59, to capture the NCAA title. Butch Lee paces Marquette with 19.

May 22, 1977 The Portland Trail Blazers defeat the Philadelphia 76ers to win the NBA championship, becoming the first team to rally after losing the first two games of the series. In the clincher, Blazers' center Bill Walton scores 20 points, grabs 23 rebounds, and has 7 assists.

June 10, 1977 In the NBA draft, Milwaukee tabs Marques Johnson of UCLA with the first overall pick. In a later round, New Orleans chooses the first woman ever drafted by an NBA team—Lusia Harris, the three-time All-American from Delta State.

June 26, 1977 Former NBA commissioner Walter Kennedy dies.

1977-78

Powered by Unseld, Bullets finally claim first championship

With one post-merger season under its belt and a potentially great team poised to defend its championship, the NBA had reason to expect great things in 1977-78. Instead the season was marked by injuries, bickering and one near-tragedy.

The league revealed its still-shaky economic status when it reduced rosters to 11 men, an obvious cost-cutting measure that didn't set well with the player's association. Then a turf war erupted in New York between the Knicks and the Nets. The ABA expatriates expected to move to New Jersey, eventually taking up residence at a new arena in the Meadowlands complex. But the Knicks protested that the move violated the terms of the Nets' entry into the NBA In the end, the financially strapped Nets were allowed to move to a temporary home at Rutgers after forking over an additional $4 million penalty.

Early in the season, the Lakers' Kareem Abdul-Jabbar broke his hand when he punched Milwaukee rookie Kent Benson, earning himself a $5,000 fine in the process. Then, on Dec 9, another altercation nearly resulted in the NBA's first on-court death. In a game with Houston, L.A.'s Kermit Washington got into a scuffle with Kevin Kunnert of the Rockets. As the fight quickly escalated, Houston's Rudy Tomjanovich ran downcourt to act as a peace-maker. Washington, seeing an enemy jersey rushing at him from behind, turned and delivered a terrifying blow that smashed Tomjanovich's face and nearly killed him. Washington was fined $10,000 and suspended for 60 days (then shipped to Boston for Charlie Scott), but the near-tragedy left a cloud over the rest of the season.

Dismal luck plagued even defending champion Portland. The Trail Blazers looked like the NBA's next dynasty in rolling to a 50-10 record. But at that point Bill Walton, the league's MVP, went down with what seemed like a minor foot injury. In time it was diagnosed as a stress fracture, and the Blazers struggled to an 8-14 finish. Walton hobbled through only two games in the playoffs as the league's best team fell to upstart Seattle.

In New Orleans, Pete Maravich seemed on his way to

Rudy Tomjanovich
Nearly killed by this punch from Laker Kermit Washington, Houston's Tomjanovich played three more years.

another scoring title when he hurt his knee after 50 games and was lost for the season, costing the Jazz a chance at the rare distinction of having the league's top scorer and rebounder. The latter honor went to Truck Robinson, signed away from Atlanta as a free agent. But with Maravich out of the way, the race for the scoring crown came to a stirring conclusion. On the season's final afternoon, David Thompson of Denver scored 73 points against Detroit—the highest single-game total by anyone other than Wilt Chamberlain—to give him the lead over San Antonio's George Gervin. Needing 61 points that night for the title, the Iceman tallied 63 against New Orleans to edge Thompson by the slimmest of margins.

Having failed in their quest for the 1976-77 title, the Philadelphia 76ers had a promise for their fans: "We owe you one." A 2-4 start brought coach Gene Shue's dismissal, but the 76ers righted themselves under Billy Cunningham, as Julius Erving, George McGinnis and Doug Collins led the way to 55 wins and another Atlantic Division title. The Knicks sent Walt Frazier to Cleveland for Jim Cleamons, but wound up treading water despite the efforts of Bob McAdoo and new coach Willis Reed. Boston collapsed to 32-50 in John Havlicek's final sea-

son, as Satch Sanders replaced Tom Heinsohn as coach in mid-season. Dave Cowens led the team in points, rebounds and assists, but he didn't have much help. Buffalo had a new coach, Cotton Fitzsimmons, and two new stars, Billy Knight (acquired from Indiana for Adrian Dantley) and Nate Archibald. But Archibald tore an Achilles tendon in training camp, and Knight and Randy Smith couldn't make up for the loss. And in New Jersey, the Nets had rookie Bernard King and not much else.

With Gervin, Larry Kenon and Billy Paultz leading the way, San Antonio took the Central Division title, finishing comfortably ahead of Washington. The Bullets signed free agent Bob Dandridge but lost Phil Chenier to a back injury in mid-season. The team struggled for a while, but as Kevin Grevey got comfortable in Chenier's spot and Dandridge learned to complement Elvin Hayes and Wes Unseld, the Bullets began to look formidable. Injuries hampered Frazier in Cleveland, where the Cavaliers struggled to repeat last year's 43-39 record. Coach of the year Hubie Brown brought Atlanta in at 41-41, a 10-game improvement. The Hawks featured a tough defense and Charlie Criss, a 5-foot-8 rookie who had played for years in what is now the CBA. But Houston fell from first to last place in the wake of the Tomjanovich incident, despite a great year from the equally undersized Calvin Murphy.

David Thompson and Dan Issel led Denver to another Midwest title, ahead of Milwaukee, which improved with the addition of rookie Marques Johnson, who replaced the depart-ed Dandridge. Chicago and Detroit were also-rans despite the presence of two great centers in Artis Gilmore and Bob Lanier, respectively. Indiana traded off Dantley and John Williamson, its two top scorers, and Kansas City fired coach Phil Johnson in mid-season en route to identical 31-51 records.

Rookie of the Year, Walter Davis, joined Paul Westphal and Alvan Adams in Phoenix, and the result was 49 wins and second place in the Pacific Division. In Seattle, new coach Bob Hopkins had lots of talent in new faces Marvin Webster, Paul Silas, Gus Williams, Jack Sikma and John Johnson, but the result was a 5-17 start. Then Lenny Wilkens took over as coach, and the Sonics went 42-18 to finish third, two games ahead of the Lakers. Rookie Norm Nixon was a bright spot for L.A., but free agent Jamaal Wilkes was slowed by injuries. Meanwhile, Rick Barry and Phil Smith led Golden State to a 43-39 record but a last-place finish in the league's toughest division.

In the Eastern playoffs, Washington stunned division champs San Antonio and Philadelphia in matching six-game series. In the West, Seattle did the same to Portland (minus Walton and Bob Gross, out with a broken ankle) and Denver, setting up a championship meeting between two teams that no one had ever expected to be there. The result was an exciting seesaw battle, with Washington rallying from a 3-2 deficit behind playoff MVP Wes Unseld and winning the decisive seventh game on Seattle's court. After being swept twice in the Finals in the 1970s, the Bullets finally made the Fat Lady sing.

1977-78 SEASON HIGHLIGHTS

STANDINGS

Eastern Conference
Atlantic Division

	W	L	Pct.	GB
Philadelphia	55	27	.671	—
New York	43	39	.524	12
Boston	32	50	.390	23
Buffalo	27	55	.329	28
New Jersey	24	58	.293	31

Central Division

	W	L	Pct.	GB
San Antonio	52	30	.634	—
Washington	44	38	.537	8
Cleveland	43	39	.524	9
Atlanta	41	41	.500	11
New Orleans	39	43	.476	13
Houston	28	54	.341	24

Western Conference
Midwest Division

	W	L	Pct.	GB
Denver	48	34	.585	—
Milwaukee	44	38	.537	4
Chicago	40	42	.488	8
Detroit	38	44	.463	10
Indiana	31	51	.378	17
Kansas City	31	51	.378	17

Pacific Division

	W	L	Pct.	GB
Portland	58	24	.707	—
Phoenix	49	33	.598	9
Seattle	47	35	.573	11
Los Angeles	45	37	.549	13
Golden State	43	39	.524	15

AWARDS

MVP
Bill Walton, Portland
Top Rookie
Walter Davis, Phoenix
Coach of Year
Hubie Brown, Atlanta
Citizenship Award
Bob Lanier, Detroit

ALL-STAR TEAMS

FIRST TEAM		SECOND TEAM	
Leonard Robinson	New Orleans	Walter Davis	Phoenix
Julius Erving	Philadelphia	Maurice Lucas	Portland
Bill Walton	Portland	Kareem Abdul-Jabbar	Los Angeles
George Gervin	San Antonio	Paul Westphal	Phoenix
David Thompson	Denver	Pete Maravich	New Orleans

ALL-STAR GAME

The Omni, Atlanta
Sunday, February 5, 1978
East 133, West 125
MVP: Randy Smith

PLAYOFFS

FINALS
Washington 4, Seattle 3
May 21: Washington 102 at Seattle 106
May 25: Seattle 98 at Washington 106
May 28: Seattle 93 at Washington 92
May 30: Washington 120 at Seattle 116, OT
June 2: Washington 94 at Seattle 98
June 4: Seattle 82 at Washington 117
June 7: Washington 105 at Seattle 99
EASTERN CONFERENCE
CONFERENCE FINALS
Washington 4, Philadelphia 2
Apr. 30: Washington 122 at Philadelphia 117
May 3: Washington 104 at Philadelphia 110
May 5: Philadelphia 108 at Washington 123
May 7: Philadelphia 105 at Washington 121
May 10: Washington 94 at Philadelphia 107
May 12: Philadelphia 99 at Washington 101
CONFERENCE SEMI-FINALS
Philadelphia 4, New York 0
Apr. 16: New York 90 at Philadelphia 130
Apr. 18: New York 100 at Philadelphia 119
Apr. 20: Philadelphia 137 at New York 126
Apr. 23: Philadelphia 112 at New York 107

Washington 4, San Antonio 2
Apr. 16: Washington 103 at San Antonio 114
Apr. 18: Washington 121 at San Antonio 117
Apr. 21: San Antonio 105 at Washington 118
Apr. 23: San Antonio 95 at Washington 98
Apr. 25: Washington 105 at San Antonio 116
Apr. 28: San Antonio 100 at Washington 103
FIRST ROUND
New York 2, Cleveland 0
Apr. 12: New York 132 at Cleveland 114
Apr. 14: Cleveland 107 at New York 109
Washington 2, Atlanta 0
Apr. 12: Atlanta 94 at Washington 103
Apr. 14: Washington 107 at Atlanta 103, OT
WESTERN CONFERENCE
CONFERENCE FINALS
Seattle 4, Denver 2
May 5: Seattle 107 at Denver 116
May 7: Seattle 121 at Denver 111
May 10: Denver 91 at Seattle 105
May 12: Denver 94 at Seattle 100
May 14: Seattle 114 at Denver 123
May 17: Denver 108 at Seattle 123

CONFERENCE SEMI-FINALS
Seattle 4, Portland 2
Apr. 18: Seattle 104 at Portland 95
Apr. 21: Seattle 93 at Portland 96
Apr. 23: Portland 84 at Seattle 99
Apr. 26: Portland 98 at Seattle 100
Apr. 30: Seattle 89 at Portland 113
May 1: Portland 94 at Seattle 105
Denver 4, Milwaukee 3
Apr. 18: Milwaukee 103 at Denver 119
Apr. 21: Milwaukee 111 at Denver 127
Apr. 23: Denver 112 at Milwaukee 143
Apr. 25: Denver 118 at Milwaukee 104
Apr. 28: Milwaukee 117 at Denver 112
Apr. 30: Denver 91 at Milwaukee 119
May 3: Milwaukee 110 at Denver 116
FIRST ROUND
Milwaukee 2, Phoenix 0
Apr. 11: Milwaukee 111 at Phoenix 103
Apr. 14: Phoenix 90 at Milwaukee 94
Seattle 2, Los Angeles 1
Apr. 12: Seattle 90 at Los Angeles 102
Apr. 14: Seattle 99 at Los Angeles 105
Apr. 16: Los Angeles 102 at Seattle 111

NBA LEADERS

SCORING

	GP	FGM	FTM	PTS	PPG
George Gervin, SAS	82	864	504	2232	27.2
David Thompson, DEN	80	826	520	2172	27.2
Bob McAdoo, NYK	79	814	469	2097	26.5
Kareem Abdul-Jabbar, LAL	62	663	274	1600	25.8
Calvin Murphy, HOU	76	852	245	1949	25.6
Paul Westphal, PHO	80	809	396	2014	25.2
Randy Smith, BUF	82	789	443	2021	24.6
Bob Lanier, DET	63	622	298	1542	24.5
Walter Davis, PHO	81	786	387	1959	24.2
Bernard King, NJN	79	798	313	1909	24.2

FIELD GOALS

	FGM	FGA	FG%
Bobby Jones, DEN	440	761	.578
Darryl Dawkins, PHI	332	577	.575
Artis Gilmore, CHI	704	1260	.559
Kareem Abdul-Jabbar, LAL	663	1205	.550
Alex English, MIL	343	633	.542
Bob Lanier, DET	622	1159	.537
George Gervin, SAS	864	1611	.536
Bob Gross, POR	381	720	.529
Billy Paultz, SAS	518	979	.529
Walter Davis, PHO	786	1494	.526

FREE THROWS

	FTM	FTA	FT%
Rick Barry, GST	378	409	.924
Calvin Murphy, HOU	245	267	.918
Fred Brown, SEA	176	196	.898
Mike Newlin, HOU	152	174	.874
Scott Wedman, KCK	221	254	.870
Pete Maravich, NOJ	240	276	.870
John Havlicek, BOS	230	269	.855
Larry Kenon, SAS	276	323	.854
Ron Boone, KCK	322	377	.854
Walt Frazier, CLE	153	180	.850

ASSISTS

	GP	AST	APG
Kevin Porter, DET/NJN	82	837	10.2
John Lucas, HOU	82	768	9.4
Ricky Sobers, IND	79	584	7.4
Norm Nixon, LAL	81	553	6.8
Norm Van Lier, CHI	78	531	6.8
Henry Bibby, PHI	82	464	5.7
Foots Walker, CLE	81	453	5.6
Randy Smith, BUF	82	458	5.6
Quinn Buckner, MIL	82	456	5.6
Paul Westphal, PHO	80	437	5.5

REBOUNDS

	GP	ORB	DRB	TRB	RPG
Truck Robinson, NOJ	82	298	990	1288	15.7
Moses Malone, HOU	59	380	506	886	15.0
Dave Cowens, BOS	77	248	830	1078	14.0
Elvin Hayes, WSB	81	335	740	1075	13.3
Swen Nater, BUF	78	278	751	1029	13.2
Artis Gilmore, CHI	82	318	753	1071	13.1
Kareem Abdul-Jabbar, LAL	62	186	615	801	12.9
Bob McAdoo, NYK	79	236	774	1010	12.8
Marvin Webster, SEA	82	361	674	1035	12.6
Wes Unseld, WSB	80	286	669	955	11.9

STEALS

	GP	STL	SPG
Ron Lee, PHO	82	225	2.74
Gus Williams, SEA	79	185	2.34
Quinn Buckner, MIL	82	188	2.29
Mike Gale, SAS	70	159	2.27
Don Buse, PHO	82	185	2.26
Foots Walker, CLE	81	176	2.17
Ricky Sobers, IND	79	170	2.15
Randy Smith, BUF	82	172	2.10
Chris Ford, DET	82	166	2.02
Wilbur Holland, CHI	82	164	2.00

BLOCKS

	GP	BLK	BPG
George Johnson, NJN	81	274	3.38
Kareem Abdul-Jabbar, LAL	62	185	2.98
Tree Rollins, ATL	80	218	2.73
Bill Walton, POR	58	146	2.52
Billy Paultz, SAS	80	194	2.42
Artis Gilmore, CHI	82	181	2.21
Joe Meriweather, NOJ	54	118	2.19
Elmore Smith, CLE	81	176	2.17
Marvin Webster, SEA	82	162	1.98
Elvin Hayes, WSB	81	159	1.96

TURNOVERS

	GP	TO	TPG
Pete Maravich, NOJ	50	250	5.0
Ricky Sobers, IND	79	356	4.5
Artis Gilmore, CHI	82	369	4.5
Bob McAdoo, NYK	79	348	4.4
Kevin Porter, DET/NJN	82	360	4.4
Eric Money, DET	76	319	4.2
George McGinnis, PHI	78	312	4.0
Bernard King, NJN	79	308	3.9
Ron Boone, KCK	82	303	3.7
George Gervin, SAS	82	303	3.7

THE YEAR IN BASKETBALL

October 11, 1977 The Women's Basketball League, the first pro league of its kind, is incorporated in Ohio by founder Bill Byrne. The league will feature future Hall of Famers Nancy Lieberman, Carol Blazejowski, and Ann Myers, though it lasts only three seasons.

October 20, 1977 Kareem Abdul-Jabbar is fined a league record $5,000 for punching Milwaukee's Kent Benson the day before. It's double trouble for Abdul-Jabbar, who also broke his hand with the punch.

December 9, 1977 In one of the ugliest incidents in NBA history, Kermit Washington of the Lakers decks Houston's Rudy Tomjanovich with one punch. Tomjanovich suffers a broken nose, double fracture to his jaw, and a concussion when his head slams onto the court as he falls. Tomjanovich eventually recovers. Washington is suspended for 60 days and fined, and the incident follows him for the remainder of his career.

December 10, 1977 Adolph Rupp, head coach at the University of Kentucky, dies in Lexington, Kentucky at the age of 76.

December 24, 1977 Kevin Porter of New Jersey dishes out 29 assists in a 126-112 win over Houston. Porter's total sets an NBA record that will last 12 years.

March 1978 Texas defeats North Carolina State, 101-93, to win the NIT. Texas' point total is the highest in a championship game in the 41-year history of the tournament.

March 27, 1978 Jack Givens pours in 41 points to lead Kentucky to a 94-88 victory over Duke for the NCAA title.

April 9, 1978 In separate, outstanding performances that decide the NBA's scoring title on the last day of the regular season, David Thompson of Denver scores 73 points in an afternoon game against Detroit to temporarily pull ahead of George Gervin in the scoring race. That night, the Spurs' Gervin retaliates with 63 points against New Orleans to win the crown.

June 4, 1978 The Washington Bullets rout the Seattle Supersonics, 117-82, in Game 6 of the NBA finals. The margin of victory is the biggest in NBA Finals history.

June 7, 1978 The Bullets win the NBA title, taking Game 7 on the road against Seattle, with a 105-99 victory. The previous Baltimore pro team to win a title was the Baltimore Bullets of the BAA in 1948.

June 20, 1978 The Women's Professional Basketball League is formed and six franchises are awarded to representatives of Chicago, Dayton, Iowa, Milwaukee, Minnesota, and New Jersey.

July 7, 1978 The owners of the Buffalo Braves and Boston Celtics trade NBA franchises. In an unprecedented deal, the league approves a swap in which Braves' owner John Y. Brown and Harry Mangurian acquire the Celtics, while Boston owner Ira Levin gets the Braves.

1978-79

Back to old ways, Bullets misfire in yet another final

The off-season was enlivened by controversial news involving two of the league's biggest stars and its most celebrated franchise. Bill Walton's broken foot proved much more serious that anyone had imagined; it was to sideline him for all of 1978-79. Blaming Portland officials for pressuring him to play with the injury, Walton announced that he wouldn't return to the team when his contract was up. Meanwhile, free agent Rick Barry left Golden State to sign with Houston. But the league gave the Warriors John Lucas as compensation, somewhat negating the impact of Barry's arrival.

The most unusual development came when Buffalo owner John V. Brown and Boston owner Irv Levin swapped franchises. Levin moved his new team to San Diego and renamed them the Clippers. In the process, he picked up Kermit Washington. Kevin Kunnert and rookie Freeman Williams from the Celtics for Nate Archibald, Billy Knight and Marvin Barnes. The result was another dismal season in Boston, despite the emergence of Cedric Maxwell as a top-notch player in his second year. Even player-coach Dave Cowens, who replaced Satch Sanders as head man in mid-season, seemed to have lost his fire. But the Clippers lost the biggest prize of all when Red Auerbach refused to let them have Boston's top draft pick, a junior eligible named Larry Bird who had already announced that he planned to stay for his senior year at obscure Indiana State.

While Boston was falling to the Atlantic Division basement, new arrival Washington, shifted from the Central Division, took over the top spot. Led by one of the best front lines ever, with Elvin Hayes, Wes Unseld and Bob Dandridge backed up by Mitch Kupchak and Greg Ballard, the defending champs compiled the league's best record. Philadelphia disposed of Lloyd Free (to San Diego) and George McGinnis (to Denver for Bobby Jones), but slipped to second place when Doug Collins went down with a foot injury and even Julius Erving couldn't make up for the loss. Meanwhile, New Jersey jumped to 37 wins behind the high-scoring duo of Bernard King and John Williamson. In New York, the Knicks had high hopes after signing free agent Marvin Webster. But Webster was disappointing, Earl Monroe was hurt, and Red Holtzman, who replaced Willis Reed as coach early in the season, couldn't bring the team around. The Knicks dumped high-salaried Bob McAdoo and Spencer Haywood during a season brightened only by the play of second-year men Ray Williams and Toby Knight.

San Antonio again finished atop the Central Division, as James Silas returned from two injury-plagued seasons to complement George Gervin and Larry Kenon. Second place went to surprising Houston. Though the Barry-Lucas deal proved a toss-up, the Rockets got a fine year from Rudy Tomjanovich, back in form after his terrible injury a year earlier. Calvin Murphy was still at the top of his game, and Moses Malone

Dennis Johnson
Being named finals MVP was sweet redemption after going 0-for-14 from the floor in Seattle's Game 7 loss to the Bullets a year earlier.

pulled down 17 rebounds a game en route to his first MVP award. Atlanta added free agent Dan Roundfield to John Drew and improving sophomore Eddie Johnson, and the result was a third-place finish, just two games out of first. But Cleveland dropped to 31 wins despite a fine season from Campy Russell. Detroit, transplanted from the Midwest Division, lost Bob Lanier for 39 games and John Shumate for all 82. Though Kevin Porter shattered the season record for assists, the Pistons fell to 30-52 under new coach Dick Vitale. But that still left them four games ahead of New Orleans. Pete Maravich failed

to bounce back from his knee injury, the Jazz shipped its other star, Truck Robinson, to Phoenix, and Haywood, picked up from the Knicks, couldn't take up the slack.

In Kansas City, Coach of the Year Cotton Fitzsimmons and Rookie of the Year, Phil Ford, led the Kings to the Midwest title. Meanwhile, Denver struggled as McGinnis fouled out of 16 games and Dan Issel appeared to be getting old. Led by David Thompson, the Nuggets rallied after Donnie Walsh replaced Larry Brown as coach, but still fell a game short of K.C. Indiana picked up Johnny Davis (from Portland) and free agent Alex English (from Milwaukee) and improved to 38 wins. Milwaukee fell to the same total when a great year from Marques Johnson wasn't enough to overcome the loss of David Meyers to a back injury. Scotty Robinson replaced Chicago coach Larry Costello in mid-season as the Bulls dropped to the cellar despite good years from old pro Artis Gilmore and sophomore Reggie Theus.

In Seattle, the loss of Webster was only a minor irritant. The Sonics still had the NBA's best backcourt in Gus Williams and Dennis Johnson, and the league awarded them Lonnie Shelton as compensation for Webster. When Tommy LaGarde, the new center, went down with a knee injury, Jack Sikma moved to the pivot and the team didn't miss a beat en route to 52 wins and the Pacific title. Phoenix finished two games back, adding Truck Robinson to its nucleus of Paul Westphal, Walter Davis and

Alvan Adams. Kareem Abdul-Jabbar, the rejuvenated Jamaal Wilkes and second-year man Norm Nixon led Los Angeles to a strong third-place finish. In Portland, Tom Owens played very well at center. Maurice Lucas was still a star and the Blazers added rookies Mychal Thompson and Ron Brewer. But the loss of Walton proved debilitating, and it didn't help that Bob Gross and Lionel Hollins were slowed by knee and ankle injuries, respectively. New coach Gene Shue got fine seasons from Lloyd Free and Randy Smith as the new arrivals in San Diego finished just short of the final playoff spot. But Phil Smith was hampered by injuries and Golden State fell to last place despite good years from John Lucas and Robert Parish.

Phoenix forced Seattle to the limit in the Western playoff finals, building a 3-2 lead before the Sonics rallied to win in seven. In the East, the Bullets had an even tougher time. After outlasting Atlanta in seven games, they fell behind San Antonio 3-1 (the Spurs having survived their own seven-game showdown with Philadelphia), then staged an amazing comeback that culminated in a 107-105 win in the deciding game.

With Kupchak sidelined by a back injury, the Bullets looked tired in their championship rematch with the Sonics. After barely holding off a Seattle comeback in the series opener, they lost the next four, fading in the second half of each game. Dennis Johnson was named playoff MVP as the Sonics rolled to their first NBA title.

1978-79 SEASON HIGHLIGHTS

STANDINGS

Eastern Conference
Atlantic Division

	W	L	Pct.	GB
Washington	54	28	.659	—
Philadelphia	47	35	.573	7
New Jersey	37	45	.451	17
New York	31	51	.378	23
Boston	29	53	.354	25

Central Division

	W	L	Pct.	GB
San Antonio	48	34	.585	—
Houston	47	35	.573	1
Atlanta	46	36	.561	2
Cleveland	30	52	.366	18
Detroit	30	52	.366	18
New Orleans	26	56	.317	22

Western Conference
Midwest Division

	W	L	Pct.	GB
Kansas City	48	34	.585	—
Denver	47	35	.573	1
Indiana	38	44	.463	10
Milwaukee	38	44	.463	10
Chicago	31	51	.378	17

Pacific Division

	W	L	Pct.	GB
Seattle	52	30	.634	—
Phoenix	50	32	.610	2
Los Angeles	47	35	.573	5
Portland	45	37	.549	7
San Diego	43	39	.524	9
Golden State	38	44	.463	14

AWARDS

MVP
Moses Malone, Houston
Top Rookie
Phil Ford, Kansas City
Coach of Year
Cotton Fitzsimmons, Kansas City
Citizenship Award
Calvin Murphy, Houston

ALL-STAR TEAMS

FIRST TEAM

Marques Johnson	Milwaukee
Elvin Hayes	Washington
Moses Malone	Houston
George Gervin	San Antonio
Paul Westphal	Phoenix

SECOND TEAM

Walter Davis	Phoenix
Bobby Dandridge	Washington
Kareem Abdul-Jabbar	Los Angeles
Lloyd Free	San Diego
Phil Ford	Kansas City

ALL-STAR GAME

Silverdome, Pontiac
Sunday, February 4, 1979
West 134, East 129
MVP: David Thompson

PLAYOFFS

FINALS
Seattle 4, Washington 1
May 20: Seattle 97 at Washington 99
May 24: Seattle 92 at Washington 82
May 27: Washington 95 at Seattle 105
May 29: Washington 112 at Seattle 114, OT
June 1: Seattle 97 at Washington 93

EASTERN CONFERENCE
CONFERENCE FINALS
Washington 4, San Antonio 3
May 4: San Antonio 118 at Washington 97
May 6: San Antonio 95 at Washington 115
May 9: Washington 114 at San Antonio 116
May 11: Washington 102 at San Antonio 118
May 13: San Antonio 103 at Washington 107
May 16: Washington 108 at San Antonio 100
May 18: San Antonio 105 at Washington 107

CONFERENCE SEMI-FINALS
Washington 4, Atlanta 3
Apr. 15: Atlanta 89 at Washington 103
Apr. 17: Atlanta 107 at Washington 99
Apr. 20: Washington 89 at Atlanta 77
Apr. 22: Washington 120 at Atlanta 118, OT
Apr. 24: Atlanta 107 at Washington 103
Apr. 26: Washington 86 at Atlanta 104
Apr. 29: Atlanta 94 at Washington 100

San Antonio 4, Philadelphia 3
Apr. 15: Philadelphia 106 at San Antonio 119
Apr. 17: Philadelphia 120 at San Antonio 121
Apr. 20: San Antonio 115 at Philadelphia 123
Apr. 22: San Antonio 115 at Philadelphia 112
Apr. 26: Philadelphia 120 at San Antonio 97
Apr. 29: San Antonio 90 at Philadelphia 92
May 2: Philadelphia 108 at San Antonio 111

FIRST ROUND
Philadelphia 2, New Jersey 0
Apr. 11: New Jersey 114 at Philadelphia 122
Apr. 13: Philadelphia 111 at New Jersey 101

Atlanta 2, Houston 0
Apr. 11: Atlanta 109 at Houston 106
Apr. 13: Houston 91 at Atlanta 100

WESTERN CONFERENCE
CONFERENCE FINALS
Seattle 4, Phoenix 3
May 1: Phoenix 93 at Seattle 108
May 4: Phoenix 97 at Seattle 103
May 6: Seattle 103 at Phoenix 113
May 8: Seattle 91 at Phoenix 100
May 11: Phoenix 99 at Seattle 93
May 13: Seattle 106 at Phoenix 105
May 17: Phoenix 110 at Seattle 114

CONFERENCE SEMI-FINALS
Seattle 4, Los Angeles 1
Apr. 17: Los Angeles 101 at Seattle 112
Apr. 18: Los Angeles 103 at Seattle 108, OT
Apr. 20: Seattle 112 at Los Angeles 118, OT
Apr. 22: Seattle 117 at Los Angeles 115
Apr. 25: Los Angeles 100 at Seattle 106

Phoenix 4, Kansas City 1
Apr. 17: Kansas City 99 at Phoenix 102
Apr. 20: Phoenix 91 at Kansas City 111
Apr. 22: Kansas City 93 at Phoenix 108
Apr. 25: Phoenix 108 at Kansas City 94
Apr. 27: Kansas City 99 at Phoenix 120

FIRST ROUND
Phoenix 2, Portland 1
Apr. 10: Portland 103 at Phoenix 107
Apr. 13: Phoenix 92 at Portland 96
Apr. 15: Portland 91 at Phoenix 101

Los Angeles 2, Denver 1
Apr. 10: Los Angeles 105 at Denver 110
Apr. 13: Denver 109 at Los Angeles 121
Apr. 15: Los Angeles 112 at Denver 111

NBA LEADERS

SCORING

	GP	FGM	FTM	PTS	PPG
George Gervin, SAS	80	947	471	2365	29.6
World B. Free, SCS	78	795	654	2244	28.8
Marques Johnson, MIL	77	820	332	1972	25.6
Bob McAdoo, NYK/BOS	60	596	295	1487	24.8
Moses Malone, HOU	82	716	599	2031	24.8
David Thompson, DEN	76	693	439	1825	24.0
Paul Westphal, PHO	81	801	339	1941	24.0
Kareem Abdul-Jabbar, LAL	80	777	349	1903	23.8
Artis Gilmore, CHI	82	753	434	1940	23.7
Walter Davis, PHO	79	764	340	1868	23.6

FIELD GOALS

	FGM	FGA	FG%
Cedric Maxwell, BOS	472	808	.584
Kareem Abdul-Jabbar, LAL	777	1347	.577
Wes Unseld, WSB	346	600	.577
Artis Gilmore, CHI	753	1310	.575
Swen Nater, SCS	357	627	.569
Kermit Washington, SCS	350	623	.562
Walter Davis, PHO	764	1362	.561
Marques Johnson, MIL	820	1491	.550
Bill Robinzine, KCK	459	837	.548
Tom Owens, POR	600	1095	.548

FREE THROWS

	FTM	FTA	FT%
Rick Barry, HOU	160	169	.947
Calvin Murphy, HOU	246	265	.928
Fred Brown, SEA	183	206	.888
Robert Smith, DEN	159	180	.883
Ricky Sobers, IND	298	338	.882
Jo Jo White, BOS/GST	139	158	.880
Dave Twardzik, POR	261	299	.873
Mike Newlin, HOU	212	243	.872
Mike Dunleavy, HOU	159	184	.864
Brian Winters, MIL	237	277	.856

ASSISTS

	GP	AST	APG
Kevin Porter, DET	82	1099	13.4
John Lucas, GST	82	762	9.3
Norm Nixon, LAL	82	737	9.0
Phil Ford, KCK	79	681	8.6
Paul Westphal, PHO	81	529	6.5
Rick Barry, HOU	80	502	6.3
Ray Williams, NYK	81	504	6.2
Tom Henderson, WSB	70	419	6.0
Armond Hill, ATL	82	480	5.9
Quinn Buckner, MIL	81	468	5.8

REBOUNDS

	GP	ORB	DRB	TRB	RPG
Moses Malone, HOU	82	587	857	1444	17.6
Rich Kelley, NOJ	80	303	723	1026	12.8
Kareem Abdul-Jabbar, LAL	80	207	818	1025	12.8
Artis Gilmore, CHI	82	293	750	1043	12.7
Jack Sikma, SEA	82	232	781	1013	12.4
Elvin Hayes, WSB	82	312	682	994	12.1
Robert Parish, GST	76	265	651	916	12.1
Truck Robinson, NOJ/PHO	69	195	607	802	11.6
George McGinnis, DEN	76	256	608	864	11.4
Dan Roundfield, ATL	80	326	539	865	10.8

STEALS

	GP	STL	SPG
M.L. Carr, DET	80	197	2.46
Eddie Jordan, NJN	82	201	2.45
Norm Nixon, LAL	82	201	2.45
Foots Walker, CLE	55	130	2.36
Phil Ford, KCK	79	174	2.20
Randy Smith, SCS	82	177	2.16
Maurice Cheeks, PHI	82	174	2.12
Gus Williams, SEA	76	158	2.08
Kevin Porter, DET	82	158	1.93
Quinn Buckner, MIL	81	156	1.93

BLOCKS

	GP	BLK	BPG
Kareem Abdul-Jabbar, LAL	80	316	3.95
George Johnson, NJN	78	253	3.24
Tree Rollins, ATL	81	254	3.14
Robert Parish, GST	76	217	2.86
Terry Tyler, DET	82	201	2.45
Elvin Hayes, WSB	82	190	2.32
Dan Roundfield, ATL	80	176	2.20
Rich Kelley, NOJ	80	166	2.08
Caldwell Jones, PHI	78	157	2.01
Artis Gilmore, CHI	82	156	1.90

TURNOVERS

	GP	TO	TPG
George McGinnis, DEN	76	350	4.6
Pete Maravich, NOJ	49	201	4.1
Phil Ford, KCK	79	324	4.1
Kevin Porter, DET	82	336	4.1
Julius Erving, PHI	78	312	4.0
Moses Malone, HOU	82	328	4.0
Bernard King, NYK	82	320	3.9
Artis Gilmore, CHI	82	312	3.8
Mickey Johnson, CHI	82	312	3.8
Ricky Sobers, IND	81	308	3.8

THE YEAR IN BASKETBALL

November 8, 1978 One of the most peculiar games in NBA history begins—but won't end for four and a half months. In a contest between New Jersey and Philadelphia, a referee violates a rule by assessing three technical fouls against Nets' coach Kevin Loughery and star forward Bernard King. Upholding an appeal, the league rules the official was wrong and orders the game to be replayed on Mar. 23, 1979 from the point of the violation. But before the game is replayed, the Nets and Sixers complete a trade that sends Ralph Simpson to New Jersey and Eric Money and Harvey Catchings to Philly. All three players play for their new teams in the completed portion of the contest, thus officially appearing in the game for both teams. The Sixers win, 110-98.

December 9, 1978 The first game of the Women's Professional Basketball League draws over 7,000 fans to the Milwaukee Arena The Chicago Hustle beats the Milwaukee Does, 92-87. Debra Waddy-Rossow leads Chicago with 30 points.

March 1, 1979 ESPN gains exclusive rights to televise college basketball.

March 11, 1979 In the second round of the East regional in Raleigh, N.C., St. John's, the 10th and last seed, beats No. 2 seeded Duke, 80-78, and 9th seeded Penn upsets top-seeded North Carolina, 72-71.

March 23, 1979 The Sixers and Nets finish a game that began on Nov. 8, 1978. After the league upholds a protest by New Jersey, the game resumes from the point of the infraction. Three players—Eric Money, Harvey Catchings, and Ralph Simpson—play for both teams in the game because they are traded by Philadelphia and New Jersey before the resumption of the contest. Only Money plays a significant role, scoring 23 points for New Jersey in the first part of the game and 4 for Philly in the conclusion. The Sixers win, 110-98.

March 21, 1979 Sparked by tournament co-MVPs Butch Carter and Ray Tolbert, Indiana slips past Purdue, 53-52, to win the NIT.

March 26, 1979 Magic Johnson and Larry Bird begin their storied rivalry when Johnson's Michigan State defeats Bird's previously undefeated Indiana State, 75-64, to win the NCAA championship. Johnson scores 24 points, has seven rebounds, and four assists while Bird goes 7-for-21 from the field and scores 19 points, along with 13 rebounds.

April 19, 1979 The Los Angeles Lakers win a coin toss, giving them the right to select Magic Johnson in the first round of the 1979 draft. The Chicago Bulls lose the toss and will select David Greenwood of UCLA.

May 1, 1979 The Houston Angels defeat the Iowa Cornets, 111-104, in the deciding fifth game to win the inaugural Women's Basketball League championship, before 5,978 fans in Houston.

June 1, 1979 Seattle defeats Washington in five games to avenge their defeat in 1978 and capture the NBA championship. In the concluding contest, Seattle's backcourt of Gus Williams and Dennis Johnson combine for 44 points as the Sonics win, 87-83. Dennis Johnson wins the Finals MVP.

June 25, 1979 Earvin (Magic) Johnson of Michigan State is selected first overall in the NBA draft.

1979-80

Curtain goes up on Larry & Magic Show; first act ends magically

Plagued by declining TV ratings and a lack of charismatic teams, the NBA got a tremendous boost from the return to power of the league's proudest franchises, Boston and Los Angeles, behind the two most heralded rookies since Bill Walton.

The Celtics' improvement was more dramatic, coming on the heels of consecutive 32- and 29-win seasons. The catalyst was Rookie of the Year Larry Bird, who amassed all-pro statistics and made his teammates better as well. Nate Archibald bounced back from three injury-plagued years, Dave Cowens and Cedric Maxwell continued their strong play, and the result was 61 wins and a Coach of the Year award for Bill Fitch, who came over from Cleveland. Despite Red Auerbach's opposition to the rule, Boston also benefited from the newly instituted 3-point shot, with Bird and Chris Ford among the top long-range marksmen.

The Lakers, under flamboyant new owner Jerry Buss, shipped Adrian Dantley to Utah for Spencer Haywood and picked up Jim Chones from Cleveland. New coach Jack McKinney suffered a near-fatal bicycle accident after 14 games and was replaced temporarily by assistant Paul Westhead, but the Lakers kept rolling and finished with 60 wins. Leading the charge was Kareem Abdul-Jabbar, who won his sixth MVP award, but he had plenty of help from versatile rookie Magic Johnson, plus old standbys Jamaal Wilkes and Norm Nixon. By mid-season McKinney had recovered, but Buss chose to stay the course with Westhead, who was ultimately rewarded with a multi-year contract.

The league's other power was in Philadelphia, where Julius Erving, Maurice Cheeks and Bobby Jones again led the 76ers, along with Caldwell Jones and the improving Darryl Dawkins. Oft-injured Doug Collins failed to return to top form, but Lionel Hollins, from Portland, helped fill that gap, and the 76ers improved to 59-23, second in the Atlantic Division.

The previous Atlantic titlist, Washington, signed free agent playmaker Kevin Porter, but lost Thomas Henderson to Houston, and when Porter struggled, the team lacked direction. Bob Dandridge and Mitch Kupchak played in only 85 games between them, negating another great season from Elvin Hayes and the improvement of Greg Ballard, as the Bullets sank to 39-43. That tied them with the rising New York Knicks, who added rookie star Bill Cartwright to an exciting young backcourt of Ray Williams and Michael Ray Richardson. New Jersey's top rookie, Calvin Natt, went to Portland in mid-season for Maurice Lucas. Lucas and Mike Newlin, picked up from Houston, played well, but offered little hope for the future.

In the Central Division, John Drew, Dan Roundfield and Eddie Johnson led Atlanta to 50 wins, while Houston and San Antonio each slipped to 41-41. Under new coach Del Harris,

Larry Bird
His name to be forever linked with Magic Johnson's, he draws first professional blood by winning the rookie of the year award.

the Rockets again relied on Moses Malone and Calvin Murphy, but Rudy Tomjanovich and Rick Barry had sub-par seasons. For Barry, it would be his last. Meanwhile, the Spurs' failure to repeat as division champs despite good years from George Gervin, Larry Kenon and James Silas cost coach Doug Moe his job. Indiana, transplanted from the Midwest Division, lost Ricky Sobers through free agency, but got Mickey Johnson as compensation and didn't lose any ground. What did cost the Pacers in the long run was the mid-season trade of Alex English to Denver for fading George McGinnis. Cleveland improved

under new coach Stan Albeck as sophomore Mike Mitchell became a star, but Campy Russell missed half the season with injuries. Detroit gave up M.L. Carr and a No. 1 draft pick to get Bob McAdoo from Boston, rookie Greg Kelser was disappointing, and in a final gesture of futility, the Pistons traded Bob Lanier to Milwaukee for Kent Benson before finishing 16-66.

Marques Johnson, Junior Bridgeman and Brian Winters led the way as Milwaukee rebounded from a poor 1978-79 to win the Midwest Division. Besides picking up Lanier, the Bucks also got David Meyers back from a year's absence with a back injury. Kansas City finished two games back, led again by Otis Birdsong, Scott Wedman and Phil Ford. Denver collapsed to 30-52, with the loss of David Thompson for 43 games negating a big year from Dan Issel, but the McGinnis-for-English trade would pay dividends for the next decade. Chicago had a new coach, Jerry Sloan, a top rookie, David Greenwood, and a much-improved second-year man, Reggie Theus, but injuries plagued Artis Gilmore and kept the Bulls from going anywhere. The New Orleans Jazz went all the way to Salt Lake City, whereas the Utah Jazz finished last again, though in a different division. Pete Maravich was released in January, replaced by Dantley as the team's scoring star. The Jazz also sent Rich Kelley to New Jersey for Bernard King, but King, plagued by problems with alcohol, played only 19 games.

In the Pacific Division the Lakers faced strong challenges from Seattle and Phoenix. The Sonics had Gus Williams and Dennis Johnson in the backcourt, plus Jack Sikma and the league's top 3-point shooter in Fred Brown, while the Suns were led again by Paul Westphal, Walter Davis, Truck Robinson and Alvan Adams. Portland lost Mychal Thompson for the season with a broken leg, and four members of the 1977 champs—Lucas, Hollins, Dave Twardzik and Larry Steele—played their last in Portland. Free agent Bill Walton signed with San Diego, but the league's awarding of Kermit Washington, Randy Smith and Kevin Kunnert to Portland as compensation decimated the Clippers, and Walton re-injured his foot and played only 14 games. Lloyd Free averaged 30 points and Swen Nater, Walton's backup at UCLA, led the league in rebounding, but it was a long season in San Diego. It was even longer in Golden State, where injuries hampered Phil Smith and the Warriors dropped to 24 wins.

The best playoff series matched Seattle and Milwaukee in the Western semifinals, with the Sonics squeaking by in seven games before falling to the Lakers in five. Meanwhile, Philadelphia spoiled the possibility of a Magic vs. Bird matchup in the finals by blowing out Boston in five games. In the championship series, Abdul-Jabbar led the Lakers to a 3-2 lead but severely sprained an ankle while scoring 40 points in the fifth game. In his absence L.A. went to a small lineup featuring Johnson at center, and the rookie responded with 42 points and 15 rebounds as the Lakers won the sixth game and their first title since 1972. That performance earned Johnson the playoff MVP award in a close vote over Abdul-Jabbar.

1979-80 SEASON HIGHLIGHTS

STANDINGS

Eastern Conference
Atlantic Division

	W	L	Pct.	GB
Boston	61	21	.744	—
Philadelphia	59	23	.720	2
Washington	39	43	.476	22
New York	39	43	.476	22
New Jersey	34	48	.415	27

Central Division

	W	L	Pct.	GB
Atlanta	50	32	.610	—
Houston	41	41	.500	9
San Antonio	41	41	.500	9
Cleveland	37	45	.451	13
Indiana	37	45	.451	13
Detroit	16	66	.195	34

Western Conference
Midwest Division

	W	L	Pct.	GB
Milwaukee	49	33	.598	—
Kansas City	47	35	.573	2
Denver	30	52	.366	19
Chicago	30	52	.366	19
Utah	24	58	.293	25

Pacific Division

	W	L	Pct.	GB
Los Angeles	60	22	.732	—
Seattle	56	26	.683	4
Phoenix	55	27	.671	5
Portland	38	44	.463	22
San Diego	35	47	.427	25
Golden State	24	58	.293	36

AWARDS
MVP
Kareem Abdul-Jabbar, LA Lakers
Top Rookie
Larry Bird, Boston
Coach of Year
Bill Fitch, Boston
Citizenship Award
Austin Carr, Cleveland

ALL-STAR TEAMS
FIRST TEAM		SECOND TEAM	
Julius Erving	Philadelphia	Dan Roundfield	Atlanta
Larry Bird	Boston	Marques Johnson	Milwaukee
Kareem Abdul-Jabbar	Los Angeles	Moses Malone	Houston
George Gervin	San Antonio	Dennis Johnson	Seattle
Paul Westphal	Phoenix	Gus Williams	Seattle

ALL-STAR GAME
Capital Centre, Landover
Sunday, February 3, 1980
East 144, West 136, OT
MVP: George Gervin

PLAYOFFS
FINALS
Los Angeles 4, Philadelphia 2
May 4: Philadelphia 102 at Los Angeles 109
May 7: Philadelphia 107 at Los Angeles 104
May 10: Los Angeles 111 at Philadelphia 101
May 11: Los Angeles 102 at Philadelphia 105
May 14: Philadelphia 103 at Los Angeles 108
May 16: Los Angeles 123 at Philadelphia 107

EASTERN CONFERENCE
CONFERENCE FINALS
Philadelphia 4, Boston 1
Apr. 18: Philadelphia 96 at Boston 93
Apr. 20: Philadelphia 90 at Boston 96
Apr. 23: Boston 97 at Philadelphia 99
Apr. 24: Boston 90 at Philadelphia 102
Apr. 27: Philadelphia 105 at Boston 94

CONFERENCE SEMI-FINALS
Boston 4, Houston 0
Apr. 9: Houston 101 at Boston 119
Apr. 11: Houston 75 at Boston 95
Apr. 13: Boston 100 at Houston 81
Apr. 14: Boston 138 at Houston 121

Philadelphia 4, Atlanta 1
Apr. 6: Atlanta 104 at Philadelphia 107
Apr. 9: Atlanta 92 at Philadelphia 99
Apr. 10: Philadelphia 93 at Atlanta 105
Apr. 13: Philadelphia 107 at Atlanta 83
Apr. 15: Atlanta 100 at Philadelphia 105

FIRST ROUND
Philadelphia 2, Washington 0
Apr. 2: Washington 96 at Philadelphia 111
Apr. 4: Philadelphia 112 at Washington 104

Houston 2, San Antonio 1
Apr. 2: San Antonio 85 at Houston 95
Apr. 4: Houston 101 at San Antonio 106
Apr. 6: San Antonio 120 at Houston 141

WESTERN CONFERENCE
CONFERENCE FINALS
Los Angeles 4, Seattle 1
Apr. 22: Seattle 108 at Los Angeles 107
Apr. 23: Seattle 99 at Los Angeles 108
Apr. 25: Los Angeles 104 at Seattle 100
Apr. 27: Los Angeles 98 at Seattle 93
Apr. 30: Seattle 105 at Los Angeles 111

CONFERENCE SEMI-FINALS
Los Angeles 4, Phoenix 1
Apr. 8: Phoenix 110 at Los Angeles 119, OT
Apr. 9: Phoenix 128 at Los Angeles 131, OT
Apr. 11: Los Angeles 108 at Phoenix 105
Apr. 13: Los Angeles 101 at Phoenix 127
Apr. 15: Phoenix 101 at Los Angeles 126

Seattle 4, Milwaukee 3
Apr. 8: Milwaukee 113 at Seattle 114, OT
Apr. 9: Milwaukee 114 at Seattle 112, OT
Apr. 11: Seattle 91 at Milwaukee 95
Apr. 13: Seattle 112 at Milwaukee 107
Apr. 15: Milwaukee 108 at Seattle 97
Apr. 18: Seattle 86 at Milwaukee 85
Apr. 20: Milwaukee 94 at Seattle 98

FIRST ROUND
Phoenix 2, Kansas City 1
Apr. 2: Kansas City 93 at Phoenix 96
Apr. 4: Phoenix 96 at Kansas City 106
Apr. 6: Kansas City 99 at Phoenix 114

Seattle 2, Portland 1
Apr. 2: Portland 110 at Seattle 120
Apr. 4: Seattle 95 at Portland 105, OT
Apr. 6: Portland 86 at Seattle 103

NBA LEADERS

SCORING

	GP	FGM	FTM	PTS	PPG
George Gervin, SAS	78	1024	505	2585	33.1
World B. Free, SCS	68	737	572	2055	30.2
Adrian Dantley, UTJ	68	730	443	1903	28.0
Julius Erving, PHI	78	838	420	2100	26.9
Moses Malone, HOU	82	778	563	2119	25.8
Kareem Abdul-Jabbar, LAL	82	835	364	2034	24.8
Dan Issel, DEN	82	715	517	1951	23.8
Elvin Hayes, WSB	81	761	334	1859	23.0
Otis Birdsong, KCK	82	781	286	1858	22.7
Mike Mitchell, CLE	82	775	270	1820	22.2

FIELD GOALS

	FGM	FGA	FG%
Cedric Maxwell, BOS	457	750	.609
Kareem Abdul-Jabbar, LAL	835	1383	.604
Artis Gilmore, CHI	305	513	.595
Adrian Dantley, UTJ	730	1267	.576
Tom Boswell, DEN/UTJ	346	613	.564
Walter Davis, PHO	657	1166	.563
Swen Nater, SCS	443	799	.554
Kermit Washington, POR	421	761	.553
Bill Cartwright, NYK	665	1215	.547
Marques Johnson, MIL	689	1267	.544

THREE POINT FIELD GOALS

	3PM	3PA	3P%
Fred Brown, SEA	39	88	.443
Chris Ford, BOS	70	164	.427
Larry Bird, BOS	58	143	.406
John Roche, DEN	49	129	.380
Brian Taylor, SCS	90	239	.377
Brian Winters, MIL	38	102	.373
Kevin Grevey, WSB	34	92	.370
Joe Hassett, IND	69	198	.348
Rick Barry, HOU	73	221	.330
Freeman Williams, SCS	42	128	.328

FREE THROWS

	FTM	FTA	FT%
Rick Barry, HOU	143	153	.935
Calvin Murphy, HOU	271	302	.897
Ron Boone, LAL/UTJ	175	196	.893
James Silas, SAS	339	382	.887
Mike Newlin, NJN	367	415	.884
Terry Furlow, ATL/UTJ	171	196	.872
Roger Phegley, WSB/NJN	177	203	.872
Mike Bratz, PHO	141	162	.870
Kevin Grevey, WSB	216	249	.867
John Roche, DEN	175	202	.866

ASSISTS

	GP	AST	APG
Micheal Ray Richardson, NYK	82	832	10.2
Nate Archibald, BOS	80	671	8.4
Foots Walker, CLE	76	607	8.0
Norm Nixon, LAL	82	642	7.8
John Lucas, GST	80	602	7.5
Phil Ford, KCK	82	610	7.4
Magic Johnson, LAL	77	563	7.3
Maurice Cheeks, PHI	79	556	7.0
Eddie Jordan, NJN	82	557	6.8
Kevin Porter, WSB	70	457	6.5

REBOUNDS

	GP	ORB	DRB	TRB	RPG
Swen Nater, SCS	81	352	864	1216	15.0
Moses Malone, HOU	82	573	617	1190	14.5
Wes Unseld, WSB	82	334	760	1094	13.3
Caldwell Jones, PHI	80	219	731	950	11.9
Jack Sikma, SEA	82	198	710	908	11.1
Elvin Hayes, WSB	81	269	627	896	11.1
Robert Parish, GST	72	247	536	783	10.9
Kareem Abdul-Jabbar, LAL	82	190	696	886	10.8
Kermit Washington, POR	80	325	517	842	10.5
Larry Bird, BOS	82	216	636	852	10.4

STEALS

	GP	STL	SPG
Michael Ray Richardson, NYK	82	265	3.23
Eddie Jordan, NJN	82	223	2.72
Dudley Bradley, IND	82	211	2.57
Gus Williams, SEA	82	200	2.44
Magic Johnson, LAL	77	187	2.43
Maurice Cheeks, PHI	79	183	2.32
Julius Erving, PHI	78	170	2.18
Sonny Parker, GST	82	173	2.11
Foots Walker, CLE	76	155	2.04
Ray Williams, NYK	82	167	2.04

BLOCKS

	GP	BLK	BPG
Kareem Abdul-Jabbar, LAL	82	280	3.41
George Johnson, NJN	81	258	3.19
Tree Rollins, ATL	82	244	2.98
Terry Tyler, DET	82	220	2.68
Elvin Hayes, WSB	81	189	2.33
Harvey Catchings, MIL	72	162	2.25
Caldwell Jones, PHI	80	162	2.02
Ben Poquette, UTJ	82	162	1.98
Joe Meriweather, NYK	65	120	1.85
Julius Erving, PHI	78	140	1.79

TURNOVERS

	GP	TO	TPG
Michael Ray Richardson, NYK	82	361	4.4
Reggie Theus, CHI	82	344	4.2
Bob McAdoo, DET	58	238	4.1
Magic Johnson, LAL	77	308	4.0
George McGinnis, DEN/IND	73	281	3.8
Moses Malone, HOU	82	303	3.7
Campy Russell, CLE	41	148	3.6
Julius Erving, PHI	78	281	3.6
Kareem Abdul-Jabbar, LAL	82	295	3.6
Mickey Johnson, IND	82	287	3.5

THE YEAR IN BASKETBALL

The NBA adopts the three-point field goal for the first time. At the same time, the league eliminates a third referee on the court, which ends an experiment conducted during the 1978-79 season.

October 12, 1979 Chris Ford of the Celtics scores the first official three-point field goal in NBA history in the season opener between Boston and Houston. The Celtics win the game, 114-106, at Boston Garden.

December 9, 1979 Larry Bird and Magic Johnson meet for the first time as pros. Johnson's Lakers win, 123-105, behind Magic's 23 points, eight rebounds, and six assists. Bird gets 16 points, three boards, and three assists.

February 1980 Former Milwaukee Bucks coach Larry Costello resigns as head of the Milwaukee. Does of the Women's Pro Basketball League when the team is unable to pay his salary.

March 19, 1980 Virginia, led by center Ralph Sampson, topple Minnesota, 58-55, to claim the school's first NIT championship.

March 26, 1980 Behind Darrell Griffith, alias Dr. Dunkenstein, who scores 23 points, Louisville beats UCLA, 59-54, to win the NCAA title.

April 9, 1980 The New York Gems beat the Iowa Cornets, 125-114, in Game 4 of a best-of-five series to win the second Women's Basketball League title. Reserve guard Pearl Moore leads New York with 27 points.

May 1, 1980 Dallas gets an NBA franchise, bringing the number of teams to 23.

May 16, 1980 Rookie point guard Magic Johnson replaces the injured Kareem Abdul-Jabbar at center and scores 42 points, grabs 15 boards, and passes for 7 assists as the Lakers win Game 6 and the NBA championship with a 123-107 win over Philadelphia. The game is broadcast nationally on tape delay because of television networks' concern over viewer interest.

May 29, 1980 Kareem Abdul-Jabbar wins his sixth MVP award, surpassing Bill Russell's record of five.

June 9, 1980 The Celtics acquire Robert Parish and the third pick in the 1980 draft from Golden State in exchange for the first and 13th picks. With their pick, Boston's GM Red Auerbach selects Kevin McHale and two cornerstones of a soon-to-be-great team are in place.

1980-81

Anti-climactic final after Celtics edge 76ers in classic semi

The NBA expanded for the first time in six years, adding a third Texas team, this one in Dallas. The Mavericks hired Dick Motta as coach, but got little help from the other clubs in the expansion draft. Still, Jim Spanarkel (from Philadelphia) and Tom LaGarde (from Seattle) played well, as did Bill Robinzine, acquired from Cleveland early in the season. In December the Mavs picked up well-traveled (and often-released) Brad Davis from the CBA He alone from this 15-67 team would still be around when Dallas became an NBA power.

Among current NBA powers, the champs in Los Angeles had a tough year, losing Magic Johnson to an early-season knee injury and finishing behind Phoenix in the Pacific Division, despite fine seasons from Kareem Abdul-Jabbar, Jamaal Wilkes and Norm Nixon. Worse yet, when Johnson returned some of the Lakers thought he didn't fit in. That assessment looked prophetic when Magic played poorly in the mini-series against Houston and L.A. went down in a major upset. Still, owner Jerry Buss made it clear where his sympathies lay when he signed Magic to a 25-year, $25 million contract in June.

An eventful year in Boston began on draft day, when the Celtics sent the No.1 pick (acquired from Detroit for Bob McAdoo) to Golden State so the Warriors could take Joe Barry Carroll. In exchange Boston got Robert Parish and Kevin McHale, the No. 3 pick. The addition of two stellar big men proved crucial after Dave Cowens retired in training camp. The shaken Celtics started slowly, but Larry Bird led them in a season-long pursuit of Philadelphia that ended with a win over the 76ers on the final day. Both teams finished 62-20, but a better conference record gave Boston the Atlantic Division title.

Despite the disappointing finish, it was a good year in Philadelphia. Julius Erving won the MVP award, and rookie Andrew Toney stepped in for Doug Collins, who played only 12 games before giving up his comeback attempt. New York improved to 50 wins as Bill Cartwright, Ray Williams and Micheal Ray Richardson gave coach Red Holtzman his last winning season. But in Washington, new coach Gene Shue found that even Elvin Hayes was showing his age. Mitch Kupchak recovered from a back injury and played well, but Bob Dandridge played even less than a year ago, and Wes

Cedric Maxwell
Accepts *SPORT* magazine award as finals MVP, having stepped impressively into the breech while Houston's Robert Reid was shutting down Larry Bird.

Unseld ended his final season on the sidelines. New Jersey coach Kevin Loughery didn't survive the season, but the Nets had hopes for rookies Mike Gminski, Mike O'Koren and Darwin Cook, plus second-year man Cliff Robinson.

The addition of Dallas brought realignment in the Midwest and Central divisions, with Milwaukee and Chicago swapping places with San Antonio and Houston—and all four had successful seasons. Milwaukee lost David Meyers, who quit because of religious beliefs, but Marques Johnson, Junior Bridgeman, Bob Lanier and second-year man Sidney Moncrief led the Bucks to 60 wins and the Central title. A healthy Artis Gilmore and new arrival Larry Kenon joined Reggie Theus and David Greenwood as the Bulls improved to 45-37. That put them a game ahead of Indiana, where Billy Knight, Mike Bantom, Johnny Davis and James Edwards helped earn Jack McKinney the Coach of the Year award with his new team. Atlanta coach Hubie Brown wasn't so lucky, losing his job as his team plummeted to 31 wins. New Cleveland coach Bill Musselman was also fired, despite a fine year from Mike Mitchell and a promising rookie in Bill Laimbeer. Detroit's new coach, Scotty Robertson, did finish the season, but his team won just 21 games.

New San Antonio coach Stan Albeck made an effective center tandem of Dave Corzine (from Washington) and George Johnson (from New Jersey). With George Gervin and James Silas still going strong in the backcourt, the Spurs won the Midwest title easily. In Houston, Calvin Murphy was fading and Rudy Tomjanovich looked finished, but Moses Malone was better than ever, and he kept the Rockets at 40-42, tied with Kansas City. A 26-25 finish awakened hopes for the future in Denver, where Alex English, Dan Issel and a healthy David Thompson gave the Nuggets a trio of 20-point-per-game scorers. Two key moves came in December, when the Nuggets acquired Dallas's top draft pick, Kiki Vandeweghe, who had been a holdout, and Doug Moe replaced Donnie Walsh as coach. In Utah, Adrian Dantley and Darrell Griffith were all that kept the Jazz ahead of Dallas.

Phoenix replaced the Lakers at the top of the Pacific Division after a big trade that brought Dennis Johnson from Seattle for Paul Westphal. Johnson had been in Lenny Wilkens' doghouse, but he fit right in with Truck Robinson, Walter Davis and Alvan Adams. Meanwhile, in Seattle, Westphal broke his foot, Lonnie Shelton hurt his wrist, Gus Williams sat out the season in a contract dispute, and the Sonics fell to last place. Only a fine year from Jack Sikma kept them competitive. Portland got Mychal Thompson back, and he combined with rookie Kelvin Ransey and sophomore Jim Paxson to lead the Blazers to 45 wins. Rookie Joe Barry Carroll and new arrival Bernard King, recovered from his alcohol problem, helped Golden State, as did World Free, acquired from San Diego for Phil Smith. But the Clippers fell to last place under new coach Phil Silas after Bill Walton went down in the preseason.

The Western playoffs were up for grabs after Houston's shocking elimination of the Lakers, and the result was two seven-game struggles in the semi-finals. Injury-plagued Kansas City built a 3-1 lead and held on to upset Phoenix while Houston was outlasting favored San Antonio. Then the Rockets disposed of the Kings in five games to earn an unexpected trip to the championship series.

In the East, Milwaukee took Philadelphia to seven games before the 76ers eked out a 99-98 win in the finale. Then, in a rematch with Boston, the 76ers jumped out to a 3-1 lead and held a commanding advantage in the final minutes of the fifth game. But the Celtics beat the odds and rallied for a 111-109 win. Another two-point win evened the series, and Bird's last-minute jumper decided the seventh game, a 91-90 thriller.

The championship series was somewhat anticlimactic, but Houston put up a good fight before losing in six games. With Bird slowed for much of the series by the defense of Robert Reid, Boston's Cedric Maxwell was voted playoff MVP as the Celtics won their 14th NBA title.

1980-81 SEASON HIGHLIGHTS

STANDINGS

Eastern Conference
Atlantic Division

	W	L	Pct.	GB
Boston	62	20	.756	—
Philadelphia	62	20	.756	—
New York	50	32	.610	12
Washington	39	43	.476	23
New Jersey	24	58	.293	38

Central Division

	W	L	Pct.	GB
Milwaukee	60	22	.732	—
Chicago	45	37	.549	15
Indiana	44	38	.537	16
Atlanta	31	51	.378	29
Cleveland	28	54	.341	32
Detroit	21	61	.256	39

Western Conference
Midwest Division

	W	L	Pct.	GB
San Antonio	52	30	.634	—
Kansas City	40	42	.488	12
Houston	40	42	.488	12
Denver	37	45	.451	15
Utah	28	54	.341	24
Dallas	15	67	.183	37

Pacific Division

	W	L	Pct.	GB
Phoenix	57	25	.695	—
Los Angeles	54	28	.659	3
Portland	45	37	.549	12
Golden State	39	43	.476	18
San Diego	36	46	.439	21
Seattle	34	48	.415	23

AWARDS
MVP
Julius Erving, Philadelphia
Top Rookie
Darrell Griffith, Utah
Coach of Year
Jack McKinney, Indiana
Citizenship Award
Mike Glenn, New York

ALL-STAR TEAMS
FIRST TEAM
Julius Erving — Philadelphia
Larry Bird — Boston
Kareem Abdul-Jabbar — Los Angeles
George Gervin — San Antonio
Dennis Johnson — Phoenix

SECOND TEAM
Marques Johnson — Milwaukee
Adrian Dantley — Utah
Moses Malone — Houston
Otis Birdsong — Kansas City
Nate Archibald — Boston

ALL-STAR GAME
The Coliseum, Richfield, Ohio
Sunday, February 1, 1981
East 123, West 120
MVP: Nate Archibald

PLAYOFFS
FINALS
Boston 4, Houston 2
May 5: Houston 95 at Boston 98
May 7: Houston 92 at Boston 90
May 9: Boston 94 at Houston 71
May 10: Boston 86 at Houston 91
May 12: Houston 80 at Boston 109
May 14: Houston 102 at Boston 91
EASTERN CONFERENCE
CONFERENCE FINALS
Boston 4, Philadelphia 3
Apr. 21: Philadelphia 105 at Boston 104
Apr. 22: Philadelphia 99 at Boston 118
Apr. 24: Boston 100 at Philadelphia 110
Apr. 26: Boston 105 at Philadelphia 107
Apr. 29: Philadelphia 109 at Boston 111
May 1: Boston 100 at Philadelphia 98
May 3: Philadelphia 90 at Boston 91
CONFERENCE SEMI-FINALS
Philadelphia 4, Milwaukee 3
Apr. 5: Milwaukee 122 at Philadelphia 125
Apr. 7: Milwaukee 109 at Philadelphia 99
Apr. 10: Philadelphia 108 at Milwaukee 103
Apr. 12: Philadelphia 98 at Milwaukee 109
Apr. 15: Milwaukee 99 at Philadelphia 116
Apr. 17: Philadelphia 86 at Milwaukee 109
Apr. 19: Milwaukee 98 at Philadelphia 99
Boston 4, Chicago 0
Apr. 5: Chicago 109 at Boston 121
Apr. 7: Chicago 97 at Boston 106
Apr. 10: Boston 113 at Chicago 107
Apr. 12: Boston 109 at Chicago 103
FIRST ROUND
Chicago 2, New York 0
Mar. 31: Chicago 90 at New York 80
Apr. 3: New York 114 at Chicago 115, OT
Philadelphia 2, Indiana 0
Mar. 31: Indiana 108 at Philadelphia 124
Apr. 2: Philadelphia 96 at Indiana 85
WESTERN CONFERENCE
CONFERENCE FINALS
Houston 4, Kansas City 1
Apr. 21: Houston 97 at Kansas City 78
Apr. 22: Houston 79 at Kansas City 88
Apr. 24: Kansas City 88 at Houston 92
Apr. 26: Kansas City 89 at Houston 100
Apr. 29: Houston 97 at Kansas City 88
CONFERENCE SEMI-FINALS
Kansas City 4, Phoenix 3
Apr. 7: Kansas City 80 at Phoenix 102
Apr. 8: Kansas City 88 at Phoenix 83
Apr. 10: Phoenix 92 at Kansas City 93
Apr. 12: Phoenix 95 at Kansas City 102
Apr. 15: Kansas City 89 at Phoenix 101
Apr. 17: Phoenix 81 at Kansas City 76
Apr. 19: Kansas City 95 at Phoenix 88
Houston 4, San Antonio 3
Apr. 7: Houston 107 at San Antonio 98
Apr. 8: Houston 113 at San Antonio 125
Apr. 10: San Antonio 99 at Houston 112
Apr. 12: San Antonio 114 at Houston 112
Apr. 14: Houston 123 at San Antonio 117
Apr. 15: San Antonio 101 at Houston 96
Apr. 17: Houston 105 at San Antonio 100
FIRST ROUND
Houston 2, Los Angeles 1
Apr. 1: Houston 111 at Los Angeles 107
Apr. 3: Los Angeles 111 at Houston 106
Apr. 5: Houston 89 at Los Angeles 86
Kansas City 2, Portland 1
Apr. 1: Kansas City 98 at Portland 97, OT
Apr. 3: Portland 124 at Kansas City 119, OT
Apr. 5: Kansas City 104 at Portland 95

NBA LEADERS

SCORING

	GP	FGM	FTM	PTS	PPG
Adrian Dantley, UTJ	80	909	632	2452	30.7
Moses Malone, HOU	80	806	609	2222	27.8
George Gervin, SAS	82	850	512	2221	27.1
Kareem Abdul-Jabbar, LAL	80	836	423	2095	26.2
David Thompson, DEN	77	734	489	1967	25.5
Otis Birdsong, KCK	71	710	317	1747	24.6
Julius Erving, PHI	82	794	422	2014	24.6
Mike Mitchell, CLE	82	853	302	2012	24.5
World B. Free, GST	65	516	528	1565	24.1
Alex English, DEN	81	768	390	1929	23.8

FIELD GOALS

	FGM	FGA	FG%
Artis Gilmore, CHI	547	816	.670
Darryl Dawkins, PHI	423	697	.607
Cedric Maxwell, BOS	441	750	.588
Bernard King, GST	731	1244	.588
Kareem Abdul-Jabbar, LAL	836	1457	.574
Kermit Washington, POR	325	571	.569
Adrian Dantley, UTJ	909	1627	.559
Bill Cartwright, NYK	619	1118	.554
Swen Nater, SCS	517	935	.553
Marques Johnson, MIL	636	1153	.552

THREE POINT FIELD GOALS

	3PM	3PA	3P%
Brian Taylor, SCS	44	115	.383
Freeman Williams, SCS	48	141	.340
Joe Hassett, DAL/GST	53	156	.340
Mike Bratz, CLE	57	169	.337
Henry Bibby, SCS	32	95	.337
Kevin Grevey, WSB	45	136	.331
Chris Ford, BOS	36	109	.330
Scott Wedman, KCK	25	77	.325

FREE THROWS

	FTM	FTA	FT%
Calvin Murphy, HOU	206	215	.958
Ricky Sobers, CHI	231	247	.935
Mike Newlin, NJN	414	466	.888
Jim Spanarkel, DAL	375	423	.887
Junior Bridgeman, MIL	213	241	.884
John Long, DET	160	184	.870
Charlie Criss, ATL	185	214	.864
Larry Bird, BOS	283	328	.863
Billy McKinney, UTJ/DEN	162	188	.862
Billy Ray Bates, POR	170	199	.854

ASSISTS

	GP	AST	APG
Kevin Porter, WSB	81	734	9.1
Norm Nixon, LAL	79	696	8.8
Phil Ford, KCK	66	580	8.8
Micheal Ray Richardson, NYK	79	627	7.9
Nate Archibald, BOS	80	618	7.7
John Lucas, GST	66	464	7.0
Kelvin Ransey, POR	80	555	6.9
Maurice Cheeks, PHI	81	560	6.9
Johnny Davis, IND	76	480	6.3
Kenny Higgs, DEN	72	408	5.7

REBOUNDS

	GP	ORB	DRB	TRB	RPG
Moses Malone, HOU	80	474	706	1180	14.8
Swen Nater, SCS	82	295	722	1017	12.4
Larry Smith, GST	82	433	561	994	12.1
Larry Bird, BOS	82	191	704	895	10.9
Jack Sikma, SEA	82	184	668	852	10.4
Kenny Carr, CLE	81	260	575	835	10.3
Kareem Abdul-Jabbar, LAL	80	197	624	821	10.3
Artis Gilmore, CHI	82	220	608	828	10.1
Caldwell Jones, PHI	81	200	613	813	10.0
Elvin Hayes, WSB	81	235	554	789	9.7

STEALS

	GP	STL	SPG
Magic Johnson, LAL	37	127	3.43
Micheal Ray Richardson, NYK	79	232	2.94
Quinn Buckner, MIL	82	197	2.40
Maurice Cheeks, PHI	81	193	2.38
Ray Williams, NYK	79	185	2.34
Dudley Bradley, IND	82	186	2.27
Julius Erving, PHI	82	173	2.11
Ron Lee, DET	82	166	2.02
Robert Reid, HOU	82	163	1.99
Larry Bird, BOS	82	161	1.96

BLOCKS

	GP	BLK	BPG
George Johnson, SAS	82	278	3.39
Tree Rollins, ATL	40	117	2.93
Kareem Abdul-Jabbar, LAL	80	228	2.85
Robert Parish, BOS	82	214	2.61
Artis Gilmore, CHI	82	198	2.41
Harvey Catchings, MIL	77	184	2.39
Terry Tyler, DET	82	180	2.20
Mychal Thompson, POR	79	170	2.15
Ben Poquette, UTJ	82	174	2.12
Elvin Hayes, WSB	81	171	2.11

TURNOVERS

	GP	TO	TPG
Moses Malone, HOU	80	312	3.9
Magic Johnson, LAL	37	144	3.9
Micheal Ray Richardson, NYK	79	300	3.8
Phil Ford, KCK	66	244	3.7
Norm Nixon, LAL	79	284	3.6
Larry Bird, BOS	82	287	3.5
Adrian Dantley, UTJ	80	280	3.5
Wes Matthews, WSB/ATL	79	261	3.3
Nate Archibald, BOS	80	264	3.3
Bernard King, GST	81	267	3.3

THE YEAR IN BASKETBALL

October 30, 1980 In connection with its 35th anniversary, the NBA cites Bill Russell as the greatest player of all-time, Red Auerbach as the greatest coach, and the 1966-67 Philadelphia 76ers the greatest team. The 35th anniversary team consists of Kareem Abdul-Jabbar, Elgin Baylor, Wilt Chamberlain, Bob Cousy, Bob Pettit, Oscar Robertson, Julius Erving, John Havlicek, George Mikan, Jerry West, and Russell.

November 11, 1980 Billy Knight of Indiana scores a team-record 52 points to lead the Pacers over San Antonio, 119-113. Twelve years later, Reggie Miller will break Knight's record when he scores 57 points.

November 12, 1980: Dan Issel of Denver scores the 20,000th point of his career, with a fourth quarter lay-up in a 118-111 loss at New Jersey. Issel is the 12th player in pro basketball history to achieve the milestone.

December 21, 1980 Kareem Abdul-Jabbar becomes the fifth player in NBA history to score 25,000 career points as he gets a season-high 42 points in the L.A. Lakers' 135-102 defeat of San Antonio.

December 22, 1980 Ryan Roberts of Downs Tri-Valley (Ill.) High School, grabs 55 rebounds against Urbana University High, tying the national high school record for most rebounds in a game.

December 27, 1980 Calvin Murphy starts a record-breaking streak of making 78 consecutive free throws when he goes 16 for 16 from the line against Washington.

January 23, 1981 Annette Kennedy, a 5-foot-6 guard from SUNY Purchase (N.Y.), scores 70 points in a 116-21 win over Pratt. Kennedy's performance snaps the women's collegiate single-game mark of 60 set by Pearl Moore of Francis Marion in 1978.

February 28, 1981 Calvin Murphy of Houston sets an NBA record by sinking his 78th consecutive free throw.

March 25, 1981 Tulsa nips Syracuse, 86-84, in overtime to take the NIT championship. The winners' Greg Stewart is named tournament MVP.

March 29, 1981 Louisiana Tech demolishes Tennessee, 79-59, to win the AIAW title.

March 30, 1981 Sophomore Isiah Thomas scores 23 points to lead Indiana to a 63-50 victory over North Carolina for the NCAA championship.

April 20, 1981 The Nebraska Wranglers beat the Dallas Diamonds, 99-90, in the deciding fifth game to win the third and final Women's Professional Basketball League title. Rosie Walker scores 39 points in the final game.

May 14, 1981 Behind Larry Bird's 27 points, the Boston Celtics beat the Houston Rockets to take the NBA crown in six games.

1981-82

In a season that featured the deepest rookie crop in the league's history, Dallas and Detroit were the biggest beneficiaries. The Mavericks picked up forwards Jay Vincent and Mark Aquirre, plus guard Rolando Blackman, en route to a 28-54 record that represented a 13-game improvement over their inaugural season. The Pistons, coming off a dismal 21-61 season, got forward Kelly Tripucka and guard Isiah Thomas in the draft, then added second-year center Bill Laimbeer in a mid-season trade with Cleveland, and wound up with 39 wins. But despite these gains, both teams failed to make the playoffs.

In New Jersey, the Nets had a new coach, Larry Brown; a new high-scoring guard, Ray Williams, lured away from the Knicks as a free agent; and two productive rookies, Albert King and Rookie of the Year Buck Williams. They parlayed these changes into a 44-win season and a berth in the playoffs. There they fell to the Washington Bullets, who relied heavily on rookies Jeff Ruland and Frank Johnson and second-year man Rick Mahorn in a rebuilding season that earned Gene Shue his second Coach of the Year award.

The league's other top rookie, forward Tom Chambers, wasn't enough to keep San Diego from slipping into the Pacific Division cellar. And Indiana fell apart despite a good year from promising freshman Herb Williams. The arrival of Orlando Woolridge wasn't enough to keep the Chicago Bulls from losing 48 games, or coach Jerry Sloan from losing his job. Likewise, future all-star Larry Nance couldn't contribute enough as a rookie with Phoenix to offset the loss of Walter Davis for 37 games with a broken arm. As a result, the Suns slipped from first to third in the Pacific Division, though still posting 46 wins.

Of all the year's notable freshman, probably the least impressive was Boston's Danny Ainge, who was persuaded to give up his foundering baseball career for a shot at basketball. But the Celtics didn't appear to need him very much anyway. For the third consecutive year since the arrival of Larry Bird they posted the league's best record, highlighted by an 18-game winning streak. Even so, they were hard pressed to beat out Philadelphia, whose 58 wins were more than any other team in the league. Julius Erving again led the 76ers, but he had help from high-scoring guard Andrew Toney, emerging as a star in his second year. Meanwhile, the Knicks plunged to the bottom of the Atlantic Division in Red Holzman's final year as coach.

In the Central Division, Milwaukee suffered a lengthy hold-out by Marques Johnson and injuries to Brian Winters and Junior Bridgeman, but coach Don Nelson and versatile guard Sidney Moncrief led the Bucks to 55 wins and another title. Atlanta used a league-leading defense to gain the final playoff berth in the east. Cleveland went through four coaches, ending up with Bill Musselman (the first of their three coaches in 1980-81), but the net result was the league's worst record.

Riley, McAdoo final pieces of puzzle as Lakers win again

Magic Johnson
Leads revolt resulting in removal of Lakers coach Paul Westhead, then points the way with stellar playoff performance and finals MVP award.

San Antonio added high-scoring forward Mike Mitchell to scoring leader George Gervin and squeaked by Denver for the Mideast Division title. The Nuggets' frontcourt of Alex English, Dan Issel and Kiki Vandeweghe each averaged more than 20 points per game as the team set NBA records for points scored and points allowed. Houston, the surprise team of last year's playoffs, matched Denver with 46 wins. The Rockets got a good year from newly acquired Elvin Hayes, but their main man was still Moses Malone, who averaged 31.1 points, led the league in rebounding and won the MVP award. Among the

also-rans, Kansas City couldn't overcome the loss of Otis Birdsong and Scott Wedman, while Utah wasted another outstanding season from Adrian Dantley.

In Los Angeles, a near-rebellion led by Magic Johnson resulted in the ousting of Coach Paul Westhead after 11 games. Free-agent forward Mitch Kupchak went down shortly thereafter with a severe knee injury, but the Lakers regrouped under new coach Pat Riley and drove to the title in the strong Pacific Division. Seattle, with Gus Williams back after his year-long holdout, jumped from last place to second. Though failing to make the playoffs, Golden State won 45 games behind high scorers Bernard King and World Free. And Portland had an emerging star in second-year center Mychal Thompson.

The playoffs promised a matchup of Magic vs. Bird for the championship, but Boston ran into trouble against Philadelphia. Down 3-1, the Celtics rallied to force a seventh game, as they had a year earlier; but this time the 76ers refused to fold, winning in Boston Garden to earn the right to face Los Angeles. But balanced scoring and the all-around brilliance of playoff MVP Magic Johnson proved decisive for the Lakers, who emerged with a 4-2 series victory and their second title in three years.

1981-82 SEASON HIGHLIGHTS

STANDINGS

Eastern Conference
Atlantic Division

	W	L	Pct.	GB
Boston	63	19	.768	—
Philadelphia	58	24	.707	5
New Jersey	44	38	.537	19
Washington	43	39	.524	20
New York	33	49	.402	30

Central Division

	W	L	Pct.	GB
Milwaukee	55	27	.671	—
Atlanta	42	40	.512	13
Detroit	39	43	.476	16
Indiana	35	47	.427	20
Chicago	34	48	.415	21
Cleveland	15	67	.183	40

Western Conference
Midwest Division

	W	L	Pct.	GB
San Antonio	48	34	.585	—
Denver	46	36	.561	2
Houston	46	36	.561	2
Kansas City	30	52	.366	18
Dallas	28	54	.341	20
Utah	25	57	.305	23

Pacific Division

	W	L	Pct.	GB
Los Angeles	57	25	.695	—
Seattle	52	30	.634	5
Phoenix	46	36	.561	11
Golden State	45	37	.549	12
Portland	42	40	.512	15
San Diego	17	65	.207	40

AWARDS

MVP
Moses Malone, Houston
Top Rookie
Buck Williams, New Jersey
Coach of the Year
Gene Shue, Washington
Citizenship Award
Kent Benson, Detroit

ALL-STAR TEAMS

FIRST TEAM		SECOND TEAM	
Larry Bird	Boston	Alex English	Denver
Julius Erving	Philadelphia	Bernard King	Golden State
Moses Malone	Houston	Robert Parish	Boston
George Gervin	San Antonio	Magic Johnson	Los Angeles
Gus Williams	Seattle	Sidney Moncrief	Milwaukee

ALL-STAR GAME

Meadowlands Arena, East Rutherford
Sunday, January 31, 1982
East 120, West 118
MVP: Larry Bird

PLAYOFFS
FINALS
Los Angeles 4, Philadelphia 2
May 27: Los Angeles 124 at Philadelphia 117
May 30: Los Angeles 94 at Philadelphia 110
June 1: Philadelphia 108 at Los Angeles 129
June 3: Philadelphia 101 at Los Angeles 111
June 6: Los Angeles 102 at Philadelphia 135
June 8: Philadelphia 104 at Los Angeles 114
EASTERN CONFERENCE
CONFERENCE FINALS
Philadelphia 4, Boston 3
May 9: Philadelphia 81 at Boston 121
May 12: Philadelphia 121 at Boston 113
May 15: Boston 97 at Philadelphia 99
May 16: Boston 94 at Philadelphia 119
May 19: Philadelphia 85 at Boston 114
May 21: Boston 88 at Philadelphia 75
May 23: Philadelphia 120 at Boston 106
CONFERENCE SEMI-FINALS
Boston 4, Washington 1
Apr. 25: Washington 91 at Boston 109
Apr. 28: Washington 103 at Boston 102
May 1: Boston 92 at Washington 83
May 2: Boston 103 at Washington 99, OT
May 5: Washington 126 at Boston 131, 2OT

Philadelphia 4, Milwaukee 2
Apr. 25: Milwaukee 122 at Philadelphia 125
Apr. 28: Milwaukee 108 at Philadelphia 120
May 1: Philadelphia 91 at Milwaukee 92
May 2: Philadelphia 100 at Milwaukee 93
May 5: Milwaukee 110 at Philadelphia 98
May 7: Philadelphia 102 at Milwaukee 90
FIRST ROUND
Philadelphia 2, Atlanta 0
Apr. 21: Atlanta 76 at Philadelphia 111
Apr. 23: Philadelphia 98 at Atlanta 95, OT
Washington 2, New Jersey 0
Apr. 20: Washington 96 at New Jersey 83
Apr. 23: New Jersey 92 at Washington 103
WESTERN CONFERENCE
CONFERENCE FINALS
Los Angeles 4, San Antonio 0
May 9: San Antonio 117 at Los Angeles 128
May 11: San Antonio 101 at Los Angeles 110
May 14: Los Angeles 118 at San Antonio 108
May 15: Los Angeles 128 at San Antonio 123

CONFERENCE SEMI-FINALS
Los Angeles 4, Phoenix 0
Apr. 27: Phoenix 96 at Los Angeles 115
Apr. 28: Phoenix 98 at Los Angeles 117
Apr. 30: Los Angeles 114 at Phoenix 106
May 2: Los Angeles 112 at Phoenix 107
San Antonio 4, Seattle 1
Apr. 27: San Antonio 95 at Seattle 93
Apr. 28: San Antonio 99 at Seattle 114
Apr. 30: Seattle 97 at San Antonio 99
May 2: Seattle 113 at San Antonio 115
May 5: San Antonio 109 at Seattle 103
FIRST ROUND
Seattle 2, Houston 1
Apr. 21: Houston 87 at Seattle 102
Apr. 23: Seattle 70 at Houston 91
Apr. 25: Houston 83 at Seattle 104
Phoenix 2, Denver 1
Apr. 20: Phoenix 113 at Denver 129
Apr. 23: Denver 110 at Phoenix 126
Apr. 24: Phoenix 124 at Denver 119

NBA LEADERS

SCORING

	GP	FGM	FTM	PTS	PPG
George Gervin, SAS	79	993	555	2551	32.3
Moses Malone, HOU	81	945	630	2520	31.1
Adrian Dantley, UTJ	81	904	648	2457	30.3
Alex English, DEN	82	855	372	2082	25.4
Julius Erving, PHI	81	780	411	1974	24.4
Kareem Abdul-Jabbar, LAL	76	753	312	1818	23.9
Gus Williams, SEA	80	773	320	1875	23.4
Bernard King, GST	79	740	352	1833	23.2
World B. Free, GST	78	650	479	1789	22.9
Larry Bird, BOS	77	711	328	1761	22.9
Dan Issel, DEN	81	651	546	1852	22.9

FIELD GOALS

	FGM	FGA	FG%
Artis Gilmore, CHI	546	837	.652
Steve Johnson, KCK	395	644	.613
Buck Williams, NJN	513	881	.582
Kareem Abdul-Jabbar, LAL	753	1301	.579
Calvin Natt, POR	515	894	.576
Adrian Dantley, UTJ	904	1586	.570
Bernard King, GST	740	1307	.566
Bobby Jones, PHI	416	737	.564
Bill Cartwright, NYK	390	694	.562
Jeff Ruland, WSB	420	749	.561

THREE POINT FIELD GOALS

	3PM	3PA	3P%
Campy Russell, NYK	25	57	.439
Andrew Toney, PHI	25	59	.424
Kyle Macy, PHO	39	100	.390
Brian Winters, MIL	36	93	.387
Don Buse, IND	73	189	.386
Mike Dunleavy, HOU	33	86	.384
Mark Aguirre, DAL	25	71	.352
Kevin Grevey, WSB	28	82	.341
Mike Bratz, SAS	46	138	.333
Joe Hassett, GST	71	214	.332

FREE THROWS

	FTM	FTA	FT%
Kyle Macy, PHO	152	169	.899
Charlie Criss, ATL/SCS	141	159	.887
John Long, DET	238	275	.865
George Gervin, SAS	555	642	.864
Larry Bird, BOS	328	380	.863
James Silas, CLE	246	286	.860
Mike Newlin, NYK	126	147	.857
Kiki Vandeweghe, DEN	347	405	.857
Kevin Grevey, WSB	165	193	.855
Jack Sikma, SEA	447	523	.855

ASSISTS

	GP	AST	APG
Johnny Moore, SAS	79	762	9.6
Magic Johnson, LAL	78	743	9.5
Maurice Cheeks, PHI	79	667	8.4
Nate Archibald, BOS	68	541	8.0
Norm Nixon, LAL	82	652	8.0
Isiah Thomas, DET	72	565	7.8
Rickey Green, UTJ	81	630	7.8
Geoff Huston, CLE	78	590	7.6
Kelvin Ransey, POR	78	555	7.1
Micheal Ray Richardson, NYK	82	572	7.0

REBOUNDS

	GP	ORB	DRB	TRB	RPG
Moses Malone, HOU	81	558	630	1188	14.7
Jack Sikma, SEA	82	223	815	1038	12.7
Buck Williams, NJN	82	347	658	1005	12.3
Mychal Thompson, POR	79	258	663	921	11.7
Maurice Lucas, NYK	80	274	629	903	11.3
Larry Smith, GST	74	279	534	813	11.0
Larry Bird, BOS	77	200	637	837	10.9
Robert Parish, BOS	80	288	578	866	10.8
Artis Gilmore, CHI	82	224	611	835	10.2
Truck Robinson, PHO	74	202	519	721	9.7

STEALS

	GP	STL	SPG
Magic Johnson, LAL	78	208	2.67
Maurice Cheeks, PHI	79	209	2.65
Micheal Ray Richardson, NYK	82	213	2.60
Quinn Buckner, MIL	70	174	2.49
Ray Williams, NJN	82	199	2.43
Rickey Green, UTJ	81	185	2.28
Gus Williams, SEA	80	172	2.15
Isiah Thomas, DET	72	150	2.08
Johnny Moore, SAS	79	163	2.06
Don Buse, IND	82	164	2.00

BLOCKS

	GP	BLK	BPG
George Johnson, SAS	75	234	3.12
Tree Rollins, ATL	79	224	2.84
Kareem Abdul-Jabbar, LAL	76	207	2.72
Artis Gilmore, CHI	82	221	2.70
Robert Parish, BOS	80	192	2.40
Kevin McHale, BOS	82	185	2.26
Herb Williams, IND	82	178	2.17
Terry Tyler, DET	82	160	1.95
Caldwell Jones, PHI	81	146	1.80
Julius Erving, PHI	81	141	1.74

TURNOVERS

	GP	TO	TPG
Isiah Thomas, DET	72	302	4.2
Magic Johnson, LAL	78	289	3.7
Adrian Dantley, UTJ	81	300	3.7
Moses Malone, HOU	81	292	3.6
Micheal Ray Richardson, NYK	82	287	3.5
Ray Williams, NJN	82	287	3.5
Bernard King, GST	79	269	3.4
Reggie Theus, CHI	82	279	3.4
Kelly Tripucka, DET	82	279	3.4
Larry Bird, BOS	77	254	3.3

THE YEAR IN BASKETBALL

December 1, 1981 Kareem Abdul-Jabbar moves into second place on the NBA's career scoring list, when he passes Oscar Robertson in a Lakers' victory over Utah. In the game Abdul-Jabbar's total reaches 26,712 points, second only to Wilt Chamberlain's 31,419.

December 21, 1981 Doug Schloerner's 15-foot jumper with one second left in the seventh overtime gives Cincinnati a 75-73 victory over Bradley. The seven overtimes set an NCAA record.

January 9, 1982 John Roche of Denver sets an NBA record by hitting seven three-pointers in one half vs. Seattle.

January 22, 1982 With a 94-53 victory over Oral Roberts, Louisiana Tech sets a new women's collegiate record with its 52nd consecutive win.

January 26, 1982 Cheryl Miller, who will go on to fame at USC, scores 105 points for Riverside Poly High (Cal.) against Riverside North High. It is the most points scored by a female high schooler in a game of 5 on 5. (For much of the 1900's, women's basketball was played 6 on 6.)

January 29, 1982 Old Dominion defeats Louisiana Tech, ending the Lady Techsters' 54-game winning streak.

February 2, 1982 Moses Malone of Houston scores 53 points and hauls in 22 rebounds in a game versus San Diego.

February 19, 1982 Atlanta outlasts Seattle, 127-122, in four overtimes in the second-longest game in the NBA since the advent of the 24-second clock in 1954.

March 6, 1982 The Spurs defeat the Bucks, 171-166, in triple OT in San Antonio in what was then the highest scoring game in NBA history.

March 24, 1982 Bradley upends Purdue, 67-58, to win the NIT.

March 28, 1982 In the first NCAA women's tournament, Louisiana Tech beats Cheney State, 76-62, to win the championship. The tournament replaces the AIAW championship, which had been held since 1972.

March 29, 1982 Michael Jordan's jumper with 16 seconds left gives North Carolina a 63-62 win over Georgetown for the NCAA championship

June 8, 1982 The Lakers beat the 76ers in six games to win the NBA title. It is the second time in three years that Los Angeles tops Philadelphia in six games. Magic Johnson is Finals Most Valuable Player.

1982-83

Moses leads Erving, loyal band of 76ers to the promised land

The league signed a new cable television deal in 1982, with weekly game on ESPN supplementing the usual coverage on CBS (USA was added to the cable team a year later). Fittingly enough, the season that followed was about as predictable as a made-for-TV movie.

The script was written in the off-season when Philadelphia signed Houston's Moses Malone as a free agent. The addition of the two-time MVP to a cast including Julius Erving, Andrew Toney, Maurice Cheeks and Bobby Jones made the 76ers prohibitive favorites for the championship, and coach Billy Cunningham's crew lived up to that assessment during the regular season, rolling to a 65-17 record and finishing nine games ahead of Boston in the Atlantic Division. Though Larry Bird and Robert Parish again turned in outstanding seasons, an unsettled backcourt and dissatisfaction with coach Bill Fitch plagued the Celtics. Buck Williams led New Jersey to 49 wins, but coach Larry Brown was ousted just before the season's end after applying for a college post. The demoralized Nets staggered into the playoffs and lost in the first round to the Knicks, who had improved to 44-38 behind free agent acquisition Bernard King. Though out of the playoff picture, Washington posted the best record ever for a last-place team, winning 42 games with a rugged frontcourt of Jeff Ruland, Greg Ballard and Rick Mahorn.

Not much was new in the Central Division, where Sidney Moncrief and Marques Johnson led Milwaukee to another title, earning Don Nelson the Coach of the Year award. Second-place Atlanta improved by only a game despite the presence of veteran Dan Roundfield and rookie Dominique Wilkens. In Detroit, the Pistons slipped to 37-45, failing to put together an adequate supporting cast for Isiah Thomas, Bill Laimbeer and Kelly Tripucka. Chicago sent Artis Gilmore to San Antonio for Dave Corzine and Mark Olberding, but fell to 28 wins and wasted a fine season from Reggie Theus. Cleveland picked up World Free from Golden State and "improved" to 23-59, while Indiana fell to the basement despite the arrival of the league's second-best rookie in Clark Kellogg.

The addition of Gilmore, plus solid performances from George Gervin and Mike Mitchell, brought 53 wins and another Midwest Division title to San Antonio. Alex English and Kiki Vandeweghe, the league's two top scorers, led Denver to a second-place tie with surprising Kansas City. The Kings improved by 15 games, with Larry Drew emerging as a star under coach Cotton Fitzsimmons. Though missing the playoffs, Dallas gained 10 games in the standings through the development of its young players—particularly Mark Aquirre, who averaged 24 points a game as a sophomore. In Utah, the financially troubled Jazz were unable to sign Dominique Wilkins, their No. 1 draft choice, and shipped him off to Atlanta for John Drew and Freeman Williams. Drew, however,

Moses Malone
Twice league MVP with the Rockets, he signs with the 76ers as a free agent and wastes no time adding MVP #3—and another in the finals.

spent two months in drug rehabilitation and Williams was released in December. On top of that, Adrian Dantley missed 60 games with an injured wrist, and a fine season from Darrell Griffith couldn't compensate for the loss. Still, the Jazz finished comfortably ahead of 14-68 Houston.

In the Pacific Division, Kareem Abdul-Jabbar, Magic Johnson, Jamaal Wilkes and Norm Nixon led Los Angeles to another title, while rookie James Worthy showed star potential. Phoenix won 53 games with a balanced team featuring Walter Davis, Dennis Johnson, new acquisition Maurice Lucas and

much-improved sophomore Larry Nance. Gus Williams and Jack Sikma led Seattle to third place, two games ahead of Portland, where Jim Paxson and Calvin Natt were the scoring stars. Golden State lost its top scorers when Bernard King signed with New York and Free was traded to Cleveland, and slipped to 30 wins despite the emergence of two new 20-point men in Joe Barry Carroll and Purvis Short. The Return of Bill Walton was big news in San Diego, but Walton played only 33 games, and the Clippers finished last again despite adding Rookie of the Year Terry Cummings to second-year man Tom Chambers.

The big surprise of the playoffs was Milwaukee's four-game sweep of Boston in the Eastern semifinals. But in the Finals the Bucks were no match for the 76ers, who won in five games to advance to the championship series. Meanwhile, the Lakers rolled over Portland and San Antonio to win the West despite the absence of James Worthy, who missed the playoffs with a broken leg. With Worthy out, and Bob McAdoo and Nixon slowed by injuries, Los Angeles was no match for the 76ers, who swept to the title in four games, completing a 12-1 post-season. Malone averaged 26 points and 18 rebounds for the series, winning the playoff MVP trophy to go along with his second straight regular-season MVP award.

1982-83 SEASON HIGHLIGHTS

STANDINGS

Eastern Conference
Atlantic Division

	W	L	Pct.	GB
Philadelphia	65	17	.793	—
Boston	56	26	.683	9
New Jersey	49	33	.598	16
New York	44	38	.537	21
Washington	42	40	.512	23

Central Division

	W	L	Pct.	GB
Milwaukee	51	31	.622	—
Atlanta	43	39	.524	8
Detroit	37	45	.451	14
Chicago	28	54	.341	23
Cleveland	23	59	.280	28
Indiana	20	62	.244	31

Western Conference
Midwest Division

	W	L	Pct.	GB
San Antonio	53	29	.646	—
Kansas City	45	37	.549	8
Denver	45	37	.549	8
Dallas	38	44	.463	15
Utah	30	52	.366	23
Houston	14	68	.171	39

Pacific Division

	W	L	Pct.	GB
Los Angeles	58	24	.707	—
Phoenix	53	29	.646	5
Seattle	48	34	.585	10
Portland	46	36	.561	12
Golden State	30	52	.366	28
San Diego	25	57	.305	33

AWARDS

MVP
Moses Malone, Philadelphia
Top Rookie
Terry Cummings, San Diego
Coach of Year
Don Nelson, Milwaukee
Defensive Player of Year
Sidney Moncrief, Milwaukee

ALL-STAR TEAMS

FIRST TEAM

Larry Bird	Boston
Julius Erving	Philadelphia
Moses Malone	Philadelphia
Magic Johnson	Los Angeles
Sidney Moncrief	Milwaukee

Sixth Man Award
Bobby Jones, Philadelphia
Citizenship Award
Julius Erving, Philadelphia

ALL-STAR GAME

The Forum, Los Angeles
Sunday, February 13, 1983
East 132, West 123
MVP: Julius Erving

SECOND TEAM

Alex English	Denver
Buck Williams	New Jersey
Kareem Abdul-Jabbar	LA Lakers
George Gervin	San Antonio
Isiah Thomas	Detroit

PLAYOFFS
FINALS
Philadelphia 4, Los Angeles 0
May 22: Los Angeles 107 at Philadelphia 113
May 26: Los Angeles 93 at Philadelphia 103
May 29: Philadelphia 111 at Los Angeles 94
May 31: Philadelphia 115 at Los Angeles 108

EASTERN CONFERENCE
CONFERENCE FINALS
Philadelphia 4, Milwaukee 1
May 8: Milwaukee 109 at Philadelphia 111, OT
May 11: Milwaukee 81 at Philadelphia 87
May 14: Philadelphia 104 at Milwaukee 96
May 15: Philadelphia 94 at Milwaukee 100
May 18: Milwaukee 103 at Philadelphia 115

CONFERENCE SEMI-FINALS
Philadelphia 4, New York 0
Apr. 24: New York 102 at Philadelphia 112
Apr. 27: New York 91 at Philadelphia 98
Apr. 30: Philadelphia 107 at New York 105
May 1: Philadelphia 105 at New York 102

Milwaukee 4, Boston 0
Apr. 27: Milwaukee 116 at Boston 95
Apr. 29: Milwaukee 95 at Boston 91
May 1: Boston 99 at Milwaukee 107
May 2: Boston 93 at Milwaukee 107

FIRST ROUND
New York 2, New Jersey 0
Apr. 20: New York 118 at New Jersey 107
Apr. 21: New Jersey 99 at New York 105

Boston 2, Atlanta 1
Apr. 19: Atlanta 95 at Boston 103
Apr. 22: Boston 93 at Atlanta 95
Apr. 24: Atlanta 79 at Boston 98

WESTERN CONFERENCE
CONFERENCE FINALS
Los Angeles 4, San Antonio 2
May 8: San Antonio 107 at Los Angeles 119
May 10: San Antonio 122 at Los Angeles 113
May 13: Los Angeles 113 at San Antonio 100
May 15: Los Angeles 129 at San Antonio 121
May 18: San Antonio 117 at Los Angeles 112
May 20: Los Angeles 101 at San Antonio 100

CONFERENCE SEMI-FINALS
Los Angeles 4, Portland 1
Apr. 24: Portland 97 at Los Angeles 118
Apr. 26: Portland 106 at Los Angeles 112
Apr. 29: Los Angeles 115 at Portland 109, OT
May 1: Los Angeles 95 at Portland 108
May 3: Portland 108 at Los Angeles 116

San Antonio 4, Denver 1
Apr. 26: Denver 133 at San Antonio 152
Apr. 27: Denver 109 at San Antonio 126
Apr. 29: San Antonio 127 at Denver 126, OT
May 2: San Antonio 114 at Denver 124
May 4: Denver 105 at San Antonio 145

FIRST ROUND
Portland 2, Seattle 0
Apr. 20: Portland 108 at Seattle 97
Apr. 22: Seattle 96 at Portland 105

Denver 2, Phoenix 1
Apr. 19: Denver 108 at Phoenix 121
Apr. 21: Phoenix 99 at Denver 113
Apr. 24: Denver 117 at Phoenix 112, OT

NBA LEADERS

SCORING

	GP	FGM	FTM	PTS	PPG
Alex English, DEN	82	959	406	2326	28.4
Kiki Vandeweghe, DEN	82	841	489	2186	26.7
Kelly Tripucka, DET	58	565	392	1536	26.5
George Gervin, SAS	78	757	517	2043	26.2
Moses Malone, PHI	78	654	600	1908	24.5
Mark Aguirre, DAL	81	767	429	1979	24.4
Joe Barry Carroll, GST	79	785	337	1907	24.1
World B. Free, GST/CLE	73	649	430	1743	23.9
Reggie Theus, CHI	82	749	434	1953	23.8
Terry Cummings, SCS	70	684	292	1660	23.7

FIELD GOALS

	FGM	FGA	FG%
Artis Gilmore, SAS	556	888	.626
Steve Johnson, KCK	371	595	.624
Darryl Dawkins, NJN	401	669	.599
Kareem Abdul-Jabbar, LAL	722	1228	.588
Buck Williams, NJN	536	912	.588
Orlando Woolridge, CHI	361	622	.580
James Worthy, LAL	447	772	.579
Brad Davis, DAL	359	628	.572
Bill Cartwright, NYK	455	804	.566
Jeff Ruland, WSB	580	1051	.552

THREE POINT FIELD GOALS

	3PM	3PA	3P%
Mike Dunleavy, SAS	67	194	.345
Isiah Thomas, DET	36	125	.288
Darrell Griffith, UTJ	38	132	.288
Allen Leavell, HOU	42	175	.240

FREE THROWS

	FTM	FTA	FT%
Calvin Murphy, HOU	138	150	.920
Kiki Vandeweghe, DEN	489	559	.875
Kyle Macy, PHO	129	148	.872
George Gervin, SAS	517	606	.853
Adrian Dantley, UTJ	210	248	.847
Brad Davis, DAL	186	220	.845
Kelly Tripucka, DET	392	464	.845
Billy Knight, IND	343	408	.841
Larry Bird, BOS	351	418	.840
Jack Sikma, SEA	400	478	.837

ASSISTS

	GP	AST	APG
Magic Johnson, LAL	79	829	10.5
Johnny Moore, SAS	77	753	9.8
Rickey Green, UTJ	78	697	8.9
Larry Drew, KCK	75	610	8.1
Frank Johnson, WSB	68	549	8.1
Gus Williams, SEA	80	643	8.0
Ray Williams, KCK	72	569	7.9
Isiah Thomas, DET	81	634	7.8
Norm Nixon, LAL	79	566	7.2
Brad Davis, DAL	79	565	7.2

REBOUNDS

	GP	ORB	DRB	TRB	RPG
Moses Malone, PHI	78	445	749	1194	15.3
Buck Williams, NJN	82	365	662	1027	12.5
Bill Laimbeer, DET	82	282	711	993	12.1
Artis Gilmore, SAS	82	299	685	984	12.0
Jack Sikma, SEA	75	213	645	858	11.4
Dan Roundfield, ATL	77	259	621	880	11.4
Cliff Robinson, CLE	77	190	666	856	11.1
Jeff Ruland, WSB	79	293	578	871	11.0
Larry Bird, BOS	79	193	677	870	11.0
Terry Cummings, SCS	70	303	441	744	10.6

STEALS

	GP	STL	SPG
Micheal Ray Richardson, GST/NJN	64	182	2.84
Rickey Green, UTJ	78	220	2.82
Johnny Moore, SAS	77	194	2.52
Isiah Thomas, DET	81	199	2.46
Darwin Cook, NJN	82	194	2.37
Maurice Cheeks, PHI	79	184	2.33
Gus Williams, SEA	80	182	2.27
Magic Johnson, LAL	79	176	2.23
Allen Leavell, HOU	79	165	2.09
Fat Lever, POR	81	153	1.89

BLOCKS

	GP	BLK	BPG
Tree Rollins, ATL	80	343	4.29
Bill Walton, SCS	33	119	3.61
Mark Eaton, UTJ	81	275	3.40
Larry Nance, PHO	82	217	2.65
Artis Gilmore, SAS	82	192	2.34
Kevin McHale, BOS	82	192	2.34
Alton Lister, MIL	80	177	2.21
Herb Williams, IND	78	171	2.19
Kareem Abdul-Jabbar, LAL	79	170	2.15
Moses Malone, PHI	78	157	2.01

TURNOVERS

	GP	TO	TPG
Ray Williams, KCK	72	338	4.7
Isiah Thomas, DET	81	324	4.0
Reggie Theus, CHI	82	320	3.9
Micheal Ray Richardson, GST/NJN	64	248	3.9
Magic Johnson, LAL	79	300	3.8
Jeff Ruland, WSB	79	300	3.8
Adrian Dantley, UTJ	22	81	3.7
Ricky Sobers, WSB	41	148	3.6
Larry Drew, KCK	75	270	3.6
Joe Barry Carroll, GST	79	284	3.6

THE YEAR IN BASKETBALL

October 29, 1982 Dominique Wilkins makes his NBA debut for the Atlanta Hawks in a 94-86 loss at Detroit.

December 7, 1982 The Utah Jazz set an NBA record by making all of 39 attempts from the free throw line. They lose, however, to Portland, 137-121.

December 20, 1982 In the first-ever sanctioned intercollegiate game played north of the Arctic Circle, the University of Alaska defeats Northeast Missouri State, 74-72, in Kotzebue, Alaska.

December 24, 1982 Tiny Chaminade University upsets No. 1-ranked Virginia and Ralph Sampson, 77-72, in the Honolulu holiday basketball tournament.

January 22, 1983 The Houston Rockets fail to score in overtime, the only NBA team to ever do so, in a 113-96 loss to Portland.

March 13, 1983 Randy Smith's record consecutive-game streak ends at 906.

March 1983 Fresno State wins its first NIT by turning back DePaul, 69-60, behind the stellar play of forward Ron Anderson, who garners tournament MVP. Note to Editor: No exact date for this game.

April 3, 1983 USC beats Louisiana Tech, 69-67, to win the second NCAA women's championship.

April 4, 1983 Lorenzo Charles dunks at the buzzer after Derek Whittenburg's 35-foot desperation shot falls short to give Jim Valvano's North Carolina State a stunning 54-52 triumph over Houston in the NCAA basketball championship.

May 20, 1983 Clair Bee, noted basketball coach and author, dies in Cleveland.

May 31, 1983 Capping a four-game sweep, the 76ers defeat the Lakers, 115-108, to win the NBA title. Magic Johnson plays all 48 minutes, scoring 27 points and passing for 13 assists, in the concluding game. Moses Malone is voted the Finals MVP.

1983-84

Let off hook by Lakers in early games, Celtics win in seven

Two legends of the NBA passed important milestones and a potential legend began his pro career. In the end, however, the 1983-84 season belonged to another legend-in-the making in Boston.

Elvin Hayes, winding up his 16-year career in Houston as Ralph Sampson's backup, passed John Havlicek as the all-time leader in games played. He finished as the third-leading scorer and rebounder in NBA history. Meanwhile, under the tutelage of Hayes and new coach Bill Fitch, the 7-foot-4 Sampson captured the Rookie of the Year award. The Rockets improved by 15 games, but couldn't escape the Midwest Division cellar.

In Los Angeles, Kareem Abdul-Jabbar was still going strong in his 15th season. On April 5 he passed Wilt Chamberlain's career scoring mark of 31,419 points; in addition he replaced Moses Malone as center on the all-pro team while leading the Lakers to their third straight Pacific Division title.

Though he led the league's rebounders for the fourth time in a row, Malone had a disappointing season in Philadelphia. Picked by most to repeat as champs, the 76ers fell to 52 wins, then suffered a shocking first-round playoff loss to New Jersey. Replacing them atop the Atlantic Division were the revitalized Celtics. New coach K.C. Jones eliminated the dissension that had developed under Fitch; Dennis Johnson, acquired from Phoenix, added stability in the backcourt; Robert Parish and Kevin McHale provided power up front; and when all else failed, Boston called on Larry Bird, who was named MVP after finishing second in the balloting three times in a row.

Many thought the award should have gone to New York's Bernard King, who led the Knicks to a 47-35 record. In fact, King edged Bird by two votes for Player of the Year in a Sporting News poll of the league's players. New Jersey had no MVP candidates, but Buck Williams and Otis Birdsong led the Nets to 45 wins under new coach Stan Albeck, Washington's Jeff Ruland emerged as a major force at center, but the Bullets fell to 35-47. Still, they qualified for the last playoff spot under the league's new expanded format.

In the Central Division, Sidney Moncrief and Marques Johnson led Milwaukee to its fourth straight title, a game ahead of Detroit. The Pistons, under new coach Chuck Daly, won 49 games, relying usually on their "class of 1981-82"—Isiah Thomas, Kelly Tripucka and Bill Laimbeer. Atlanta also slipped into the playoffs, but Cleveland, Chicago and Indiana managed only 81 wins among them.

Scoring champion Adrian Dantley and Coach of the year Frank Layden led Utah, the league's surprise team, to the Midwest Division title. The Jazz backed up Dantley with scorers Darrell Griffith and John Drew and shot-blocker Mark Eaton. Dallas, two games back, continued to improve with the nucleus they picked up in the 1981 draft—Mark Aquirre and Rolando Blackman in particular. Despite the scoring of Kiki

Elvin Hayes
Ends his career having played more NBA games (1,303) than anyone to date and ranking third all-time in scoring and rebounding.

Vandeweghe and Alex English, Denver fell to 38-44. A 186-184 triple-overtime loss to Detroit, the highest-scoring game in league history, epitomized their frustrating season. Kansas City and San Antonio also fell off, with the Kings edging out the Spurs for the final playoff berth in the West.

All that earned them the right to be demolished in three games by the Lakers, who lost their usual first-round bye with the playoff field increased from 12 to 16 teams. Rookie Byron Scott, obtained from San Diego for Norm Nixon, was erratic, and a stomach infection hampered Jamaal Wilkes late in the

season, but the Lakers moved in Michael Cooper and James Worthy as starters and scarcely missed a beat. Portland finished second with a balanced offense orchestrated by coach Jack Ramsey; Seattle and Phoenix made the playoffs though falling to 42 and 41 wins, respectively. Golden State missed out by a game despite the scoring of Purvis Short and Joe Barry Carroll, and San Diego again brought up the rear despite the presence of Nixon, Terry Cummings and Bill Walton.

Phoenix upset Portland and Utah in the playoffs before falling to Los Angeles in the Western finals. In the east, Boston survived a seven-game series with New York, then disposed of

Milwaukee in five games. Then the Lakers and Celtics squared off for the first time since the days of Bill Russell. In addition, it was the first confrontation between Magic Johnson and Larry Bird since the 1979 NCAA championship game. The Lakers won the first and third games easily, but lost the second and fourth, both in overtime. Boston took the next one, but the Lakers came back to force a seventh game. The largest TV audience in NBA history watched as the Celtics scratched out a 111-102 win. Bird, the playoff MVP, led everyone with 27 points and 11 rebounds per game, providing a taste of what was to come in the next few years.

1983-84 SEASON HIGHLIGHTS

STANDINGS

Eastern Conference
Atlantic Division

	W	L	Pct.	GB
Boston	62	20	.756	—
Philadelphia	52	30	.634	10
New York	47	35	.573	15
New Jersey	45	37	.549	17
Washington	35	47	.427	27

Central Division

	W	L	Pct.	GB
Milwaukee	50	32	.610	—
Detroit	49	33	.598	1
Atlanta	40	42	.488	10
Cleveland	28	54	.341	22
Chicago	27	55	.329	23
Indiana	26	56	.317	24

Western Conference
Midwest Division

	W	L	Pct.	GB
Utah	45	37	.549	—
Dallas	43	39	.524	2
Denver	38	44	.463	7
Kansas City	38	44	.463	7
San Antonio	37	45	.451	8
Houston	29	53	.354	16

Pacific Division

	W	L	Pct.	GB
Los Angeles	54	28	.659	—
Portland	48	34	.585	6
Seattle	42	40	.512	12
Phoenix	41	41	.500	13
Golden State	37	45	.451	17
San Diego	30	52	.366	24

AWARDS

MVP
Larry Bird, Boston
Top Rookie
Ralph Sampson, Houston
Coach of Year
Frank Layden, Utah
Defensive Player of Year
Sidney Moncrief, Milwaukee

ALL-STAR TEAMS

FIRST TEAM

Larry Bird	Boston
Bernard King	New York
Kareem Abdul-Jabbar	Los Angeles
Magic Johnson	Los Angeles
Isiah Thomas	Detroit

Sixth Man Award
Kevin McHale, Boston
Citizenship Award
Frank Layden, Utah

ALL-STAR GAME

McNichols Sports Arena, Denver
Sunday, January 29, 1984
East 154, West 145, OT
MVP: Isiah Thomas

SECOND TEAM

Julius Erving	Philadelphia
Adrian Dantley	Utah
Moses Malone	Philadelphia
Sidney Moncrief	Milwaukee
Jim Paxson	Portland

PLAYOFFS
FINALS
Boston 4, Los Angeles 3
May 27: Los Angeles 115 at Boston 109
May 31: Los Angeles 121 at Boston 124, OT
June 3: Boston 104 at Los Angeles 137
June 6: Boston 129 at Los Angeles 125, OT
June 8: Los Angeles 103 at Boston 121
June 10: Boston 108 at Los Angeles 119
June 12: Los Angeles 102 at Boston 111
EASTERN CONFERENCE
CONFERENCE FINALS
Boston 4, Milwaukee 1
May 15: Milwaukee 96 at Boston 119
May 17: Milwaukee 110 at Boston 125
May 19: Boston 109 at Milwaukee 100
May 21: Boston 113 at Milwaukee 122
May 23: Milwaukee 108 at Boston 115
CONFERENCE SEMI-FINALS
Boston 4, New York 3
Apr. 29: New York 92 at Boston 110
May 2: New York 102 at Boston 116
May 4: Boston 92 at New York 100
May 6: Boston 113 at New York 118
May 9: New York 99 at Boston 121
May 11: Boston 104 at New York 106
May 13: New York 104 at Boston 121
Milwaukee 4, New Jersey 2
Apr. 29: New Jersey 106 at Milwaukee 100
May 1: New Jersey 94 at Milwaukee 98
May 3: Milwaukee 100 at New Jersey 93
May 5: Milwaukee 99 at New Jersey 106
May 8: New Jersey 82 at Milwaukee 94
May 10: Milwaukee 98 at New Jersey 97

FIRST ROUND
Boston 3, Washington 1
Apr. 17: Washington 83 at Boston 91
Apr. 19: Washington 85 at Boston 88
Apr. 21: Boston 108 at Washington 111, OT
Apr. 24: Boston 99 at Washington 96
Milwaukee 3, Atlanta 2
Apr. 17: Atlanta 89 at Milwaukee 105
Apr. 19: Atlanta 87 at Milwaukee 101
Apr. 21: Milwaukee 94 at Atlanta 103
Apr. 24: Milwaukee 97 at Atlanta 100
Apr. 26: Atlanta 89 at Milwaukee 118
New York 3, Detroit 2
Apr. 17: New York 94 at Detroit 93
Apr. 19: New York 105 at Detroit 113
Apr. 22: Detroit 113 at New York 120
Apr. 25: Detroit 119 at New York 112
Apr. 27: New York 127 at Detroit 123, OT
New Jersey 3, Philadelphia 2
Apr. 18: New Jersey 116 at Philadelphia 101
Apr. 20: New Jersey 116 at Philadelphia 102
Apr. 22: Philadelphia 108 at New Jersey 100
Apr. 24: Philadelphia 110 at New Jersey 102
Apr. 26: New Jersey 101 at Philadelphia 98
WESTERN CONFERENCE
CONFERENCE FINALS
Los Angeles 4, Phoenix 2
May 12: Phoenix 94 at Los Angeles 110
May 15: Phoenix 102 at Los Angeles 118
May 18: Los Angeles 127 at Phoenix 135, OT
May 20: Los Angeles 126 at Phoenix 115
May 23: Phoenix 126 at Los Angeles 121
May 25: Los Angeles 99 at Phoenix 97

CONFERENCE SEMI-FINALS
Los Angeles 4, Dallas 1
Apr. 28: Dallas 91 at Los Angeles 134
May 1: Dallas 101 at Los Angeles 117
May 4: Los Angeles 115 at Dallas 125
May 6: Los Angeles 122 at Dallas 115, OT
May 8: Dallas 99 at Los Angeles 115
Phoenix 4, Utah 2
Apr. 29: Phoenix 95 at Utah 105
May 2: Phoenix 102 at Utah 97
May 4: Utah 94 at Phoenix 106
May 6: Utah 110 at Phoenix 111, OT
May 8: Phoenix 106 at Utah 118
May 10: Utah 82 at Phoenix 102
FIRST ROUND
Utah 3, Denver 2
Apr. 17: Denver 121 at Utah 123
Apr. 19: Denver 132 at Utah 116
Apr. 22: Utah 117 at Denver 121
Apr. 24: Utah 129 at Denver 124
Apr. 26: Denver 111 at Utah 127
Dallas 3, Seattle 2
Apr. 17: Seattle 86 at Dallas 88
Apr. 19: Seattle 95 at Dallas 92
Apr. 21: Dallas 94 at Seattle 104
Apr. 24: Dallas 107 at Seattle 96
Apr. 26: Seattle 104 at Dallas 105, OT
Phoenix 3, Portland 2
Apr. 18: Phoenix 113 at Portland 106
Apr. 20: Phoenix 116 at Portland 122
Apr. 22: Portland 103 at Phoenix 106
Apr. 24: Portland 113 at Phoenix 110
Apr. 26: Phoenix 117 at Portland 105
Los Angeles 3, Kansas City 0
Apr. 18: Kansas City 105 at Los Angeles 116
Apr. 20: Kansas City 102 at Los Angeles 109
Apr. 22: Los Angeles 108 at Kansas City 102

NBA LEADERS

SCORING

	GP	FGM	FTM	PTS	PPG
Adrian Dantley, UTJ	79	802	813	2418	30.6
Mark Aguirre, DAL	79	925	465	2330	29.5
Kiki Vandeweghe, DEN	78	895	494	2295	29.4
Alex English, DEN	82	907	352	2167	26.4
Bernard King, NYK	77	795	437	2027	26.3
George Gervin, SAS	76	765	427	1967	25.9
Larry Bird, BOS	79	758	374	1908	24.2
Mike Mitchell, SAS	79	779	275	1839	23.3
Terry Cummings, SCS	81	737	380	1854	22.9
Purvis Short, GST	79	714	353	1803	22.8

FIELD GOALS

	FGM	FGA	FG%
Artis Gilmore, SAS	351	556	.631
James Donaldson, SCS	360	604	.596
Mike McGee, LAL	347	584	.594
Darryl Dawkins, NJN	507	855	.593
Calvin Natt, POR	500	857	.583
Jeff Ruland, WSB	599	1035	.579
Kareem Abdul-Jabbar, LAL	716	1238	.578
Larry Nance, PHO	601	1044	.576
Bob Lanier, MIL	392	685	.572
Bernard King, NYK	795	1391	.572

THREE POINT FIELD GOALS

	3PM	3PA	3P%
Darrell Griffith, UTJ	91	252	.361
Mike Evans, DEN	32	89	.360
Johnny Moore, SAS	28	87	.322
Michael Cooper, LAL	38	121	.314
Ray Williams, NYK	25	81	.309

FREE THROWS

	FTM	FTA	FT%
Larry Bird, BOS	374	421	.888
John Long, DET	243	275	.884
Bill Laimbeer, DET	316	365	.866
Walter Davis, PHO	233	270	.863
Ricky Pierce, SCS	149	173	.861
Adrian Dantley, UTJ	813	946	.859
Billy Knight, KCK	243	283	.859
Jack Sikma, SEA	411	480	.856
Kiki Vandeweghe, DEN	494	580	.852
Dennis Johnson, BOS	281	330	.852

ASSISTS

	GP	AST	APG
Magic Johnson, LAL	67	875	13.1
Norm Nixon, SCS	82	914	11.1
Isiah Thomas, DET	82	914	11.1
John Lucas, SAS	63	673	10.7
Johnny Moore, SAS	59	566	9.6
Rickey Green, UTJ	81	748	9.2
Gus Williams, SEA	80	675	8.4
Ennis Whatley, CHI	80	662	8.3
Larry Drew, KCK	73	558	7.6
Brad Davis, DAL	81	561	6.9

REBOUNDS

	GP	ORB	DRB	TRB	RPG
Moses Malone, PHI	71	352	598	950	13.4
Buck Williams, NJN	81	355	645	1000	12.3
Jeff Ruland, WSB	75	265	657	922	12.3
Bill Laimbeer, DET	82	329	674	1003	12.2
Ralph Sampson, HOU	82	293	620	913	11.1
Jack Sikma, SEA	82	225	686	911	11.1
Robert Parish, BOS	80	243	614	857	10.7
Cliff Robinson, CLE	73	156	597	753	10.3
Dave Greenwood, CHI	78	214	572	786	10.1
Larry Bird, BOS	79	181	615	796	10.1

STEALS

	GP	STL	SPG
Rickey Green, UTJ	81	215	2.65
Isiah Thomas, DET	82	204	2.49
Gus Williams, SEA	80	189	2.36
Maurice Cheeks, PHI	75	171	2.28
Magic Johnson, LAL	67	150	2.24
T.R. Dunn, DEN	80	173	2.16
Ray Williams, NYK	76	162	2.13
Darwin Cook, NJN	82	164	2.00
Lester Conner, GST	82	162	1.98
Julius Erving, PHI	77	141	1.83

BLOCKS

	GP	BLK	BPG
Mark Eaton, UTJ	82	351	4.28
Tree Rollins, ATL	77	277	3.60
Ralph Sampson, HOU	82	197	2.40
Larry Nance, PHO	82	174	2.12
Artis Gilmore, SAS	64	132	2.06
Roy Hinson, CLE	80	145	1.81
LaSalle Thompson, KCK	80	145	1.81
Julius Erving, PHI	77	139	1.81
Kareem Abdul-Jabbar, LAL	80	143	1.79
Joe Barry Carroll, GST	80	142	1.77

TURNOVERS

	GP	TO	TPG
Jeff Ruland, WSB	75	345	4.6
Magic Johnson, LAL	67	308	4.6
Andrew Toney, PHI	78	296	3.8
Isiah Thomas, DET	82	303	3.7
Ralph Sampson, HOU	82	295	3.6
Mark Aguirre, DAL	79	284	3.6
Moses Malone, PHI	71	249	3.5
Joe Barry Carroll, GST	80	272	3.4
Ennis Whatley, CHI	80	272	3.4
Adrian Dantley, UTJ	79	261	3.3

THE YEAR IN BASKETBALL

September 28, 1983 The NBA announces that any player convicted of taking illegal drugs, or admitting to having taken them, will be banned from the league for life.

December 13, 1983 In the highest scoring game in NBA history, the Detroit Pistons defeat the Denver Nuggets, 186-184, in triple overtime at Denver's McNichols Arena. Kiki Vandeweghe of Denver leads all scorers with 51 points and teammate Alex English pours in 47. Isiah Thomas leads the Pistons with 47, while backcourt mate John Long scores 41. Four players—Kent Benson and David Thirdkill of Detroit and Howard Carter and Ken Dennard of Denver—go scoreless.

January 5, 1984 Adrian Dantley of Utah ties Wilt Chamberlain's 22-year-old record when he makes 28 free throws in a game.

January 8, 1984 The NCAA announces that it will expand its Division I tournament field to 64 teams, beginning in 1985.

January 21, 1984 Annette Kennedy of the State University of New York sets a modern-day women's collegiate record when she scores 70 points in a game.

February 1, 1984 David Stern succeeds Larry O'Brien to become the fourth commissioner in NBA history.

March 1984 Michigan takes home the NIT trophy after an 83-63 thumping of Notre Dame in the title contest. Wolverines' center Tim McCormick is named MVP.

April 2, 1984 John Thompson's Georgetown wins the NCAA title beating Houston, 84-75 in the clinching game.

April 5, 1984 Kareem Abdul-Jabbar becomes the leading scorer in NBA history when he overtakes Wilt Chamberlain's career total of 31,419 points. Abdul-Jabber's record-breaking points come against Utah when he hits his patented sky hook from the right baseline.

April 1984 Darryl Dawkins ends the regular season with a record 386 fouls. Despite infinite promise, the high schooler turned professional was known more for breaking backboards with monstrous dunks and getting himself in foul trouble than he was for his productivity.

June 12, 1984 In Game 7 of the NBA finals, the Celtics beat the Lakers, 111-102, to win the championship. Cedric Maxwell, the Finals MVP from three years before, scored 24 points and Dennis Johnson adds 22 to lead Boston, overcoming a 29-point performance by Kareem Abdul-Jabbar. Larry Bird grabbed series MVP honors.

June 19, 1984 In an NBA draft that will yield several all-time greats, the Houston Rockets select Akeem Olajuwon of the University of Houston as the first pick overall. Chicago selects Michael Jordan of North Carolina (third), Philadelphia selects Charles Barkley of Auburn (fifth), and Utah picks John Stockton of Gonzaga (16th).

A standard women's basketball, 28.5 inches in circumference, or one inch less than the standard balls used by men, is adopted.

1984-85

Air Jordan takes off, Lakers gain revenge in final win over Celtics

The exceptional rookies grabbed headlines, but another important newcomer was Ted Turner's WTBS, which replaced ESPN and USA as the cable portion of the league's TV package. The expanded coverage on the "superstation" contributed to the NBA's unprecedented growth for the rest of the decade. So did Rookie of the Year Michael Jordan, who joined the Chicago Bulls and immediately evoked comparisons to Julius Erving with his electrifying style of play. The other top rookie, Akeem Olajuwon, teamed with Ralph Sampson in Houston to give the Rockets the most dominating pair of big men in NBA history.

Still, the new favorites had to take a back seat to two NBA standbys, the Boston Celtics and the Los Angeles Lakers, who staged a season-long battle for the league's best record, with Boston finishing on top, 63 wins to 62. The Celtics sent Gerald Henderson to Seattle and installed Danny Ainge as a starter, but their most improved player may have been Larry Bird, who averaged nearly 29 points and became the most feared 3-point shooter in the league en route to his second straight MVP award. Jamaal Wilkes had reached the end of the line in Los Angeles, but the development of James Worthy and Byron Scott, plus the continued excellence of Kareem Abdul-Jabbar and Magic Johnson, made the Lakers better than ever.

The league's other top teams were both in the East. Milwaukee got Terry Cummings in a blockbuster deal with San Diego, and he teamed with Sidney Moncrief to lead the Bucks to 59 wins and help Don Nelson win another Coach of the Year award. Meanwhile, with powerful rookie Charles Barkley joining veterans Moses Malone, Julius Erving and Andrew Toney in Philadelphia, the 76ers regained some of the ground they'd lost a year earlier, and finished with 58 wins.

After Boston and Philadelphia, the big story in the Atlantic Division was injuries. New Jersey lost three of its starters for long stretches and relied on Micheal Ray Richardson and Buck Williams in a 42-40 season. Washington lost center Jeff Ruland for half the season and finished 40-42 despite good play from a backcourt of Gus Williams, acquired from Seattle, and second-year man Jeff Malone. Hardest-hit were the Knicks, who lost their whole frontcourt and fell to 24 wins. The worst blow was a career-threatening knee injury to league scoring champion Bernard King.

In Detroit, the Pistons hoped to move up with the addition of Dan Roundfield from Atlanta, but he was hampered all year by injuries. Jordan and Orlando Woolridge gave Chicago more than 50 points per game, but the Bulls had little else. Cleveland squeezed into the playoffs for the first time in seven years as new coach George Karl got good seasons from Roy Hinson and Phil Hubbard up front to go with the outside scoring of World Free. With Roundfield gone, Dominique Wilkens averaged 27 points for Atlanta, and Doc Rivers made strides as a point

Kareem Abdul-Jabbar
Not quite the dominant force of old, but plays like a young Buck in the playoffs, averaging 26 points and gaining nod as MVP of the finals.

guard, but the Hawks still sank to 34 wins. Likewise, promising youngsters Clark Kellogg, Herb Williams, Vern Fleming and Steve Stipanovich couldn't lift Indiana out of last place.

The revitalized Denver Nuggets took the Mideast Division crown, winning 52 games. Alex English had another fine season, and he had help from Calvin Natt and Lafayette Lever, both acquired from Portland for Kiki Vandeweghe. Meanwhile, Houston's "Twin Towers", Sampson and Olajuwon, led the Rockets to 48 wins. Dallas added rookie Sam Perkins but dropped a notch to third, behind Houston. Adrian Dantley's

holdout and John Drew's suspension hurt Utah, but the Jazz won 41 games, but new coach Cotton Fitzsimmons could take comfort in the fact that he finished 10 games ahead of his old team, Kansas City.

In Portland, Vandeweghe had trouble adjusting to Jack Ramsay's patterned offense; still other than the Lakers, the Trail Blazers were the only Pacific Division team over .500. Injuries to Walter Davis crippled Phoenix, while Seattle collapsed in the wake of the Gus Williams trade. The Clippers moved to Los Angeles in search of big crowds but found that losing teams don't draw anywhere. And Golden State lost Joe Barry Carroll to Italy and dropped to last place despite the play of Purvis Short and Sleepy Floyd.

As expected, Boston and Los Angeles met again in the championship series after easy victories in the conference playoffs. The Celtics looked unbeatable in a 148-114 opening-game win, but the Lakers asserted themselves thereafter and won the series in six games, clinching the title in Boston Garden. Elbow and finger injuries hampered Bird's shooting in the series, but the deciding factor was the play of Abdul-Jabbar, who averaged 26 points and won the playoff MVP award.

1984-85 SEASON HIGHLIGHTS

STANDINGS

Eastern Conference
Atlantic Division

	W	L	Pct.	GB
Boston	63	19	.768	—
Philadelphia	58	24	.707	5
New Jersey	42	40	.512	21
Washington	40	42	.488	23
New York	24	58	.293	39

Central Division

	W	L	Pct.	GB
Milwaukee	59	23	.720	—
Detroit	46	36	.561	13
Chicago	38	44	.463	21
Cleveland	36	46	.439	23
Atlanta	34	48	.415	25
Indiana	22	60	.268	37

Western Conference
Midwest Division

	W	L	Pct.	GB
Denver	52	30	.634	—
Houston	48	34	.585	4
Dallas	44	38	.537	8
San Antonio	41	41	.500	11
Utah	41	41	.500	11
Kansas City	31	51	.378	21

Pacific Division

	W	L	Pct.	GB
LA Lakers	62	20	.756	—
Portland	42	40	.512	20
Phoenix	36	46	.439	26
LA Clippers	31	51	.378	31
Seattle	31	51	.378	31
Golden State	22	60	.268	40

AWARDS

MVP
Larry Bird, Boston
Top Rookie
Michael Jordan, Chicago
Coach of Year
Don Nelson, Milwaukee
Defensive Player of Year
Mark Eaton, Utah

ALL-STAR TEAMS
FIRST TEAM

Larry Bird	Boston
Bernard King	New York
Moses Malone	Philadelphia
Magic Johnson	LA Lakers
Isiah Thomas	Detroit

Sixth Man Award
Kevin McHale, Boston
Citizenship Award
Dan Issel, Denver

ALL-STAR GAME
Hoosier Dome, Indianapolis
Sunday, February 10, 1985
West 140, East 129
MVP: Ralph Sampson

SECOND TEAM

Terry Cummings	Milwaukee
Ralph Sampson	Houston
Kareem Abdul-Jabbar	LA Lakers
Michael Jordan	Chicago
Sidney Moncrief	Milwaukee

PLAYOFFS
FINALS
L.A. Lakers 4, Boston 2
May 27: L.A. Lakers 114 at Boston 148
May 30: L.A. Lakers 109 at Boston 102
June 2: Boston 111 at L.A. Lakers 136
June 5: Boston 107 at L.A. Lakers 105
June 7: Boston 111 at L.A. Lakers 120
June 9: L.A. Lakers 111 at Boston 100

EASTERN CONFERENCE
CONFERENCE FINALS
Boston 4, Philadelphia 1
May 12: Philadelphia 93 at Boston 108
May 14: Philadelphia 98 at Boston 106
May 18: Boston 105 at Philadelphia 94
May 19: Boston 104 at Philadelphia 115
May 22: Philadelphia 100 at Boston 102

CONFERENCE SEMI-FINALS
Boston 4, Detroit 2
Apr. 28: Detroit 99 at Boston 133
Apr. 30: Detroit 114 at Boston 121
May 2: Boston 117 at Detroit 125
May 5: Boston 99 at Detroit 102
May 8: Detroit 123 at Boston 130
May 10: Boston 123 at Detroit 113

Philadelphia 4, Milwaukee 0
Apr. 28: Philadelphia 127 at Milwaukee 105
Apr. 30: Philadelphia 112 at Milwaukee 108
May 3: Milwaukee 104 at Philadelphia 109
May 5: Milwaukee 112 at Philadelphia 121

FIRST ROUND
Boston 3, Cleveland 1
Apr. 18: Cleveland 123 at Boston 126
Apr. 20: Cleveland 106 at Boston 108
Apr. 23: Boston 98 at Cleveland 105
Apr. 25: Boston 117 at Cleveland 115

Milwaukee 3, Chicago 1
Apr. 19: Chicago 100 at Milwaukee 109
Apr. 21: Chicago 115 at Milwaukee 122
Apr. 24: Milwaukee 107 at Chicago 109
Apr. 26: Milwaukee 105 at Chicago 97

Philadelphia 3, Washington 1
Apr. 17: Washington 97 at Philadelphia 104
Apr. 21: Washington 94 at Philadelphia 113
Apr. 24: Philadelphia 100 at Washington 118
Apr. 26: Philadelphia 106 at Washington 98

Detroit 3, New Jersey 0
Apr. 18: New Jersey 105 at Detroit 125
Apr. 21: New Jersey 111 at Detroit 121
Apr. 24: Detroit 116 at New Jersey 115

WESTERN CONFERENCE
CONFERENCE FINALS
L.A. Lakers 4, Denver 1
May 11: Denver 122 at L.A. Lakers 139
May 14: Denver 136 at L.A. Lakers 114
May 17: L.A. Lakers 136 at Denver 118
May 19: L.A. Lakers 120 at Denver 116
May 22: Denver 109 at L.A. Lakers 153

CONFERENCE SEMI-FINALS
L.A. Lakers 4, Portland 1
Apr. 27: Portland 101 at L.A. Lakers 125
Apr. 30: Portland 118 at L.A. Lakers 134
May 3: L.A. Lakers 130 at Portland 126
May 5: L.A. Lakers 107 at Portland 115
May 7: Portland 120 at L.A. Lakers 139

Denver 4, Utah 1
Apr. 30: Utah 113 at Denver 130
May 2: Utah 123 at Denver 131, OT
May 4: Denver 123 at Utah 131
May 5: Denver 125 at Utah 118
May 7: Utah 104 at Denver 116

FIRST ROUND
L.A. Lakers 3, Phoenix 0
Apr. 18: Phoenix 114 at L.A. Lakers 142
Apr. 20: Phoenix 130 at L.A. Lakers 147
Apr. 23: L.A. Lakers 119 at Phoenix 103

Denver 3, San Antonio 2
Apr. 18: San Antonio 111 at Denver 141
Apr. 20: San Antonio 113 at Denver 111
Apr. 23: Denver 115 at San Antonio 112
Apr. 26: Denver 111 at San Antonio 116
Apr. 28: San Antonio 99 at Denver 126

Utah 3, Houston 2
Apr. 19: Utah 115 at Houston 101
Apr. 21: Utah 96 at Houston 122
Apr. 24: Houston 104 at Utah 112
Apr. 26: Houston 96 at Utah 94
Apr. 28: Utah 104 at Houston 97

Portland 3, Dallas 1
Apr. 18: Portland 131 at Dallas 139, 2OT
Apr. 20: Portland 124 at Dallas 121, OT
Apr. 23: Dallas 109 at Portland 122
Apr. 25: Dallas 113 at Portland 115

NBA LEADERS

SCORING

	GP	FGM	FTM	PTS	PPG
Bernard King, NYK	55	691	426	1809	32.9
Larry Bird, BOS	80	918	403	2295	28.7
Michael Jordan, CHI	82	837	630	2313	28.2
Purvis Short, GST	78	819	501	2186	28.0
Alex English, DEN	81	939	383	2262	27.9
Dominique Wilkins, ATL	81	853	486	2217	27.4
Adrian Dantley, UTJ	55	512	438	1462	26.6
Mark Aguirre, DAL	80	794	440	2055	25.7
Moses Malone, PHI	79	602	737	1941	24.6
Terry Cummings, MIL	79	759	343	1861	23.6

FIELD GOALS

	FGM	FGA	FG%
James Donaldson, LAC	351	551	.637
Artis Gilmore, SAS	532	854	.623
Otis Thorpe, KCK	411	685	.600
Kareem Abdul-Jabbar, LAL	723	1207	.599
Larry Nance, PHO	515	877	.587
James Worthy, LAL	610	1066	.572
Kevin McHale, BOS	605	1062	.570
Maurice Cheeks, PHI	422	741	.570
Magic Johnson, LAL	504	899	.561
Orlando Woolridge, CHI	679	1225	.554

THREE POINT FIELD GOALS

	3PM	3PA	3P%
Byron Scott, LAL	26	60	.433
Larry Bird, BOS	56	131	.427
Brad Davis, DAL	47	115	.409
Trent Tucker, NYK	29	72	.403
Dale Ellis, DAL	42	109	.385
Andrew Toney, PHI	39	105	.371
World B. Free, CLE	71	193	.368
Mike Evans, DEN	57	157	.363
Darrell Griffith, UTJ	92	257	.358
Don Buse, KCK	31	87	.356

FREE THROWS

	FTM	FTA	FT%
Kyle Macy, PHO	127	140	.907
Kiki Vandeweghe, POR	369	412	.896
Brad Davis, DAL	158	178	.888
Kelly Tripucka, DET	255	288	.885
Alvan Adams, PHO	250	283	.883
Larry Bird, BOS	403	457	.882
Maurice Cheeks, PHI	175	199	.879
Junior Bridgeman, LAC	181	206	.879
Eddie Johnson, KCK	325	373	.871
Rickey Green, UTJ	232	267	.869

ASSISTS

	GP	AST	APG
Isiah Thomas, DET	81	1123	13.9
Magic Johnson, LAL	77	968	12.6
Johnny Moore, SAS	82	816	10.0
Norm Nixon, LAC	81	711	8.8
John Bagley, CLE	81	697	8.6
Micheal Ray Richardson, NJN	82	669	8.2
Reggie Theus, KCK	82	656	8.0
Rickey Green, UTJ	77	597	7.8
Eddie Johnson, ATL	73	566	7.8
Gus Williams, WSB	79	608	7.7

REBOUNDS

	GP	ORB	DRB	TRB	RPG
Moses Malone, PHI	79	385	646	1031	13.1
Bill Laimbeer, DET	82	295	718	1013	12.4
Buck Williams, NJN	82	323	682	1005	12.3
Hakeem Olajuwon, HOU	82	440	534	974	11.9
Mark Eaton, UTJ	82	207	720	927	11.3
Larry Smith, GST	80	405	464	869	10.9
Robert Parish, BOS	79	263	577	840	10.6
Larry Bird, BOS	80	164	678	842	10.5
Artis Gilmore, SAS	81	231	615	846	10.4
LaSalle Thompson, KCK	82	274	580	854	10.4

STEALS

	GP	STL	SPG
Micheal Ray Richardson, NJN	82	243	2.96
Johnny Moore, SAS	82	229	2.79
Fat Lever, DEN	82	202	2.46
Michael Jordan, CHI	82	196	2.39
Doc Rivers, ATL	69	163	2.36
Isiah Thomas, DET	81	187	2.31
Gus Williams, WSB	79	178	2.25
Clyde Drexler, POR	80	177	2.21
Maurice Cheeks, PHI	78	169	2.17
Lester Conner, GST	79	161	2.04

BLOCKS

	GP	BLK	BPG
Mark Eaton, UTJ	82	456	5.56
Hakeem Olajuwon, HOU	82	220	2.68
Sam Bowie, POR	76	203	2.67
Wayne Cooper, DEN	80	197	2.46
Tree Rollins, ATL	70	167	2.39
Roy Hinson, CLE	76	173	2.28
Artis Gilmore, SAS	81	173	2.14
Bill Walton, LAC	67	140	2.09
Alton Lister, MIL	81	167	2.06
Kareem Abdul-Jabbar, LAL	79	162	2.05

TURNOVERS

	GP	TO	TPG
Jeff Ruland, WSB	37	178	4.8
Magic Johnson, LAL	77	308	4.0
Ralph Sampson, HOU	82	328	4.0
Bernard King, NYK	55	204	3.7
Isiah Thomas, DET	81	300	3.7
Reggie Theus, KCK	82	303	3.7
Moses Malone, PHI	79	284	3.6
Herb Williams, IND	75	263	3.5
Michael Jordan, CHI	82	287	3.5
Norm Nixon, LAC	81	275	3.4

THE YEAR IN BASKETBALL

December 6, 1984 The Bucks retire Bob Lanier's uniform number 16. Lanier was an eight-time NBA All-Star. Ten years later, the Pistons will retire the same number, which Lanier wore for Detroit for eight years.

December 12, 1984 Georgeann Wells becomes the first woman to dunk in a game as her Virginia team slams Charleston, 110-82.

January 4, 1985 The Boston Celtics honor team president and former head coach Red Auerbach by retiring uniform No. 2.

January 10, 1985 Lenny Wilkens becomes the first person to play and coach in 1,000 games, when he coaches Seattle to a 106-105 win over Cleveland. The next season, he will become the Cavaliers coach.

February 23, 1985 Bobby Knight is ejected five minutes into Indiana's 72-63 loss to Purdue when he throws a chair across the court.

March 1, 1985 Herb Kohl, a Milwaukee businessman who will become a United States Senator, purchases the Milwaukee Bucks.

March 29, 1985 Behind sharpshooter Reggie Miller, UCLA wins the NIT at Madison Square Garden, beating Indiana, 65-62.

March 31, 1985 Old Dominion beats Georgia, 70-65, to win the women's NCAA championship.

March 31, 1985 Boston's Scott Wedman hits an NBA-record 11th straight three-pointers without a miss.

April 1, 1985 Villanova upsets No. 1-ranked Georgetown, 66-64, to win the NCAA championship.

April 2, 1985 The NCAA Rules Committee adopts the 45-second shot clock for men's basketball.

May 12, 1985 The first NBA draft lottery takes place.

May 16, 1985 Michael Jordan is named the NBA's Rookie of the Year after placing third in the league in scoring with a 28.2 average.

May 27, 1985 In a game known as the Memorial Day Massacre, the Lakers, brimming with title hopes, are crushed by the Celtics, 148-114, at Boston Garden in Game 1 of the Finals. Three days later, again in the Garden, they beat the Celts by seven, and go on to win the title.

June 18, 1985 Patrick Ewing is selected first overall by the New York Knicks in a modified NBA draft, in which the number of rounds is reduced from 10 to 7. Utah picks Karl Malone 13th in the first round.

June 30, 1985 The relocated Naismith Basketball Hall of Fame opens its doors for the first time in downtown Springfield, Mass.

1985-86

Third strike for Richardson, Celtics reel off 82 wins

In a season of highs and lows, no one stood higher than 7-foot-6 Manute Bol, drafted by Washington, and no one was "lower" than 5-foot-7 Spud Webb, who joined Atlanta. Despite criticism that the NBA was becoming a freak show, both proved they belonged: Bol led the league in shot-blocking, and Webb's speed fueled a running game that turned the Hawks around.

Also in the "high" category were New Jersey's Micheal Ray Richardson, kicked out of the league after failing his third drug test; John Lucas, released by Houston after a similar failure; and Walter Davis of Phoenix, who missed a month getting treatment for his drug problem.

The "lows" included 11 major players who missed more than half the season with injuries. Once again New York had the worst of it; Rookie of the Year Patrick Ewing, who missed 32 games, was the healthiest member of the Knicks projected front line. In Philadelphia, a stress fracture sidelined Andrew Toney. The emergence of Charles Barkley as a major star, however, kept the 76ers in the running for the title under new coach Matt Guokas until Moses Malone went out with an eye injury just before the playoffs. Chicago lost only one player, but it was Michael Jordan, who broke a bone in his foot and missed 64 games. The Bullets' Jeff Ruland missed 52, and Bol and Jeff Malone weren't enough to save coach Gene Shue's job. Likewise, Indiana added Wayman Tisdale to its promising young front line, but a knee injury to Clark Kellogg negated the gain.

It was the same story in the West. San Antonio got off to a good start, then collapsed after losing Johnny Moore to meningitis. The 44-game absence of Sam Bowie and a 12-game losing streak in mid-season dropped Portland under .500. Utah picked up a gem in rookie Karl Malone, but Darrell Griffith was out all year with a stress fracture. And the Clippers' leading scorer, Derek Smith, missed 71 games for knee surgery.

Even Boston's Larry Bid was dragged down by a back injury that reduced him to a mere All-Star for the first half of the season. But treatment by a chiropractor finally corrected the problem, and Bird soared back to his accustomed heights, winning his third straight MVP award. Another change in Boston was the presence of former MVP Bill Walton, acquired from San Diego. Though a series of foot injuries had made it impossible for Walton to play full-time, he proved as effective as ever when limited to 20 minutes a game. And with Walton, veteran Scott Wedman and new acquisition Jerry Sichting coming off the bench, the Celtics climbed to a 67-15 record. Meanwhile, the Lakers picked up Walton's former teammate Maurice Lucas from Phoenix. Though he led them in rebounding, Lucas had trouble fitting in with the Lakers' high-speed offense. Still, Los Angeles rolled to 62 wins and another Pacific Division title.

In Milwaukee, the blue-collar Bucks topped 50 wins and

Larry Bird
Overcomes ailing back to collect third consecutive Most Valuable Player award, then adds second finals MVP in three years.

topped the Central Division for the sixth straight time. Right behind them was the season's surprise team, the Atlanta Hawks. Coach of the Year Mike Fratello's young team improved by 16 games, led by Dominique Wilkins, "The Human Highlight Film". Houston also reached the 50-win level as Akeem Olajuwon and Ralph Sampson improved with experience. Two other rising teams, Detroit and Dallas, made key additions to their talented nucleus: Detroit, with rookie guard Joe Dumars, and Dallas, with center James Donaldson, acquired from the Clippers.

It was the season of disappointment in Cleveland, where the Cavaliers' high hopes dissolved and coach George Karl was dismissed during a 29-win season. Golden State was only a game better despite the return of Joe Barry Carroll and the addition of rookie Chris Mullin. Seattle had a new coach, Bernie Bickerstaff, and rookie star Xavier McDaniel, but couldn't improve on last year's 31-51 record. Also disappointing were the Nets, who collapsed after a strong start despite fine seasons from big men Buck Williams and Mike Gminski. But the Kings found a way to make mediocrity pay; they moved to Sacramento and sold out every home game while going 37-45. The Celtics' toughest playoff challenge may have come in

the opening round against Chicago. The high-flying Jordan had returned just in time to lead the Bulls into the playoffs, and he scored 49 and 63 points in the first two games. But the Celtics' overall superiority was just too much, and the Bulls fell in three games. Meanwhile, the Lakers' season ended with a shocking 4-1 loss to Houston in the Western finals. The championship series featured a fifth-game-free-for-all started by Sampson, but in the end Boston had too much talent, too much depth, and too much Larry Bird. The Celtics' 4-2 victory gave them 82 playoff and regular-season wins, the highest total in NBA history, and Bird added another playoff MVP trophy to his collection.

1985-86 SEASON HIGHLIGHTS

STANDINGS

Eastern Conference
Atlantic Division

	W	L	Pct.	GB
Boston	67	15	.817	—
Philadelphia	54	28	.659	13
New Jersey	39	43	.476	28
Washington	39	43	.476	28
New York	23	59	.280	44

Central Division

	W	L	Pct.	GB
Milwaukee	57	25	.695	—
Atlanta	50	32	.610	7
Detroit	46	36	.561	11
Chicago	30	52	.366	27
Cleveland	29	53	.354	28
Indiana	26	56	.317	31

Western Conference
Midwest Division

	W	L	Pct.	GB
Houston	51	31	.622	—
Denver	47	35	.573	4
Dallas	44	38	.537	7
Utah	42	40	.512	9
Sacramento	37	45	.451	14
San Antonio	35	47	.427	16

Pacific Division

	W	L	Pct.	GB
LA Lakers	62	20	.756	—
Portland	40	42	.488	22
LA Clippers	32	50	.390	30
Phoenix	32	50	.390	30
Seattle	31	51	.378	31
Golden State	30	52	.366	32

AWARDS
MVP
Larry Bird, Boston
Top Rookie
Patrick Ewing, New York
Coach of Year
Mike Fratello, Atlanta
Defensive Player of Year
Alvin Robertson, San Antonio
Sixth Man Award
Bill Walton, Boston
Most Improved Player
Alvin Robertson, San Antonio
ALL-STAR TEAMS
FIRST TEAM

Larry Bird	Boston
Dominique Wilkins	Atlanta
Kareem Abdul-Jabbar	LA Lakers
Magic Johnson	LA Lakers
Isiah Thomas	Detroit

SECOND TEAM

Charles Barkley	Philadelphia
Alex English	Denver
Hakeem Olajuwon	Houston
Sidney Moncrief	Milwaukee
Alvin Robertson	San Antonio

Citizenship Awards
Michael Cooper, LA Lakers
Rory Sparrow, New York

ALL-STAR GAME
Reunion Arena, Dallas
Sunday, February 9, 1986
East 129, West 132
MVP: Isiah Thomas

PLAYOFFS
FINALS
Boston 4, Houston 2
May 26: Houston 100 at Boston 112
May 29: Houston 95 at Boston 117
June 1: Boston 104 at Houston 106
June 3: Boston 106 at Houston 103
June 5: Boston 96 at Houston 111
June 8: Houston 97 at Boston 114
EASTERN CONFERENCE
CONFERENCE FINALS
Boston 4, Milwaukee 0
May 13: Milwaukee 96 at Boston 128
May 15: Milwaukee 111 at Boston 122
May 17: Boston 111 at Milwaukee 107
May 18: Boston 111 at Milwaukee 98
CONFERENCE SEMI-FINALS
Boston 4, Atlanta 1
Apr. 27: Atlanta 91 at Boston 103
Apr. 29: Atlanta 108 at Boston 119
May 2: Boston 111 at Atlanta 107
May 4: Boston 94 at Atlanta 106
May 6: Atlanta 99 at Boston 132
Milwaukee 4, Philadelphia 3
Apr. 29: Philadelphia 118 at Milwaukee 112
May 1: Philadelphia 107 at Milwaukee 119
May 3: Milwaukee 103 at Philadelphia 107
May 5: Milwaukee 109 at Philadelphia 104
May 7: Philadelphia 108 at Milwaukee 113
May 9: Milwaukee 108 at Philadelphia 126
May 11: Philadelphia 112 at Milwaukee 113

FIRST ROUND
Boston 3, Chicago 0
Apr. 17: Chicago 104 at Boston 123
Apr. 20: Chicago 131 at Boston 135, 2OT
Apr. 22: Boston 122 at Chicago 104
Milwaukee 3, New Jersey 0
Apr. 18: New Jersey 107 at Milwaukee 119
Apr. 20: New Jersey 97 at Milwaukee 111
Apr. 22: Milwaukee 118 at New Jersey 113
Philadelphia 3, Washington 2
Apr. 18: Washington 95 at Philadelphia 94
Apr. 20: Washington 97 at Philadelphia 102
Apr. 22: Philadelphia 91 at Washington 86
Apr. 24: Philadelphia 111 at Washington 116
Apr. 27: Washington 109 at Philadelphia 134
Atlanta 3, Detroit 1
Apr. 17: Detroit 122 at Atlanta 140
Apr. 19: Detroit 125 at Atlanta 137
Apr. 22: Atlanta 97 at Detroit 106
Apr. 25: Atlanta 114 at Detroit 113, 2OT
WESTERN CONFERENCE
CONFERENCE FINALS
Houston 4, L.A. Lakers 1
May 10: Houston 107 at L.A. Lakers 119
May 13: Houston 112 at L.A. Lakers 102
May 16: L.A. Lakers 109 at Houston 117
May 18: L.A. Lakers 95 at Houston 105
May 21: Houston 114 at L.A. Lakers 112
CONFERENCE SEMI-FINALS
L.A. Lakers 4, Dallas 2
Apr. 27: Dallas 116 at L.A. Lakers 130
Apr. 30: Dallas 113 at L.A. Lakers 117
May 2: L.A. Lakers 108 at Dallas 110
May 4: L.A. Lakers 118 at Dallas 120
May 6: Dallas 113 at L.A. Lakers 116
May 8: L.A. Lakers 120 at Dallas 107

Houston 4, Denver 2
Apr. 26: Denver 119 at Houston 126
Apr. 29: Denver 101 at Houston 119
May 2: Houston 115 at Denver 116
May 4: Houston 111 at Denver 114, OT
May 6: Denver 103 at Houston 131
May 8: Houston 126 at Denver 122, 2OT
FIRST ROUND
L.A. Lakers 3, San Antonio 0
Apr. 17: San Antonio 88 at L.A. Lakers 135
Apr. 19: San Antonio 94 at L.A. Lakers 122
Apr. 23: L.A. Lakers 114 at San Antonio 94
Houston 3, Sacramento 0
Apr. 17: Sacramento 87 at Houston 107
Apr. 19: Sacramento 103 at Houston 111
Apr. 22: Houston 113 at Sacramento 98
Denver 3, Portland 1
Apr. 18: Portland 126 at Denver 133
Apr. 20: Portland 108 at Denver 106
Apr. 22: Denver 115 at Portland 104
Apr. 24: Denver 116 at Portland 112
Dallas 3, Utah 1
Apr. 18: Utah 93 at Dallas 101
Apr. 20: Utah 106 at Dallas 113
Apr. 23: Dallas 98 at Utah 100
Apr. 25: Dallas 117 at Utah 113

NBA LEADERS

SCORING

	GP	FGM	FTM	PTS	PPG
Dominique Wilkins, ATL	78	888	577	2366	30.3
Adrian Dantley, UTJ	76	818	630	2267	29.8
Alex English, DEN	81	951	511	2414	29.8
Larry Bird, BOS	82	796	441	2115	25.8
Purvis Short, GST	64	633	351	1632	25.5
Kiki Vandeweghe, POR	79	719	523	1962	24.8
Moses Malone, PHI	74	571	617	1759	23.8
Hakeem Olajuwon, HOU	68	625	347	1597	23.5
Mike Mitchell, SAS	82	802	317	1921	23.4
World B. Free, CLE	75	652	379	1754	23.4
Kareem Abdul-Jabbar, LAL	79	755	336	1846	23.4

FIELD GOALS

	FGM	FGA	FG%
Steve Johnson, SAS	362	573	.632
Artis Gilmore, SAS	423	684	.618
Larry Nance, PHO	582	1001	.581
James Worthy, LAL	629	1086	.579
Kevin McHale, BOS	561	978	.574
Charles Barkley, PHI	595	1041	.572
Kareem Abdul-Jabbar, LAL	755	1338	.564
Adrian Dantley, UTJ	818	1453	.563
Alton Lister, MIL	318	577	.551
Robert Parish, BOS	530	966	.549

THREE POINT FIELD GOALS

	3PM	3PA	3P%
Craig Hodges, MIL	73	162	.451
Trent Tucker, NYK	41	91	.451
Ernie Grunfeld, NYK	26	61	.426
Larry Bird, BOS	82	194	.423
World B. Free, CLE	71	169	.420
Kyle Macy, CHI	58	141	.411
Michael Cooper, LAL	63	163	.387
Dale Ellis, DAL	63	173	.364
Kevin McKenna, WSB	27	75	.360
Mike McGee, LAL	41	114	.360

FREE THROWS

	FTM	FTA	FT%
Larry Bird, BOS	441	492	.896
Chris Mullin, GST	189	211	.896
Mike Gminski, NJN	351	393	.893
Jim Paxson, POR	217	244	.889
George Gervin, CHI	283	322	.879
Franklin Edwards, LAC	132	151	.874
Magic Johnson, LAL	378	434	.871
Kiki Vandeweghe, POR	523	602	.869
Brad Davis, DAL	198	228	.868
Jeff Malone, WSB	322	371	.868

ASSISTS

	GP	AST	APG
Magic Johnson, LAL	72	907	12.6
Isiah Thomas, DET	77	830	10.8
Reggie Theus, SAC	82	788	9.6
John Bagley, CLE	78	735	9.4
Maurice Cheeks, PHI	82	753	9.2
Sleepy Floyd, GST	82	746	9.1
John Lucas, HOU	65	571	8.8
Norm Nixon, LAC	67	576	8.6
Doc Rivers, ATL	53	443	8.4
Clyde Drexler, POR	75	600	8.0

REBOUNDS

	GP	ORB	DRB	TRB	RPG
Bill Laimbeer, DET	82	305	770	1075	13.1
Charles Barkley, PHI	80	354	672	1026	12.8
Buck Williams, NJN	82	329	657	986	12.0
Moses Malone, PHI	74	339	533	872	11.8
Ralph Sampson, HOU	79	258	621	879	11.1
Larry Smith, GST	77	384	472	856	11.1
Larry Bird, BOS	82	190	615	805	9.8
LaSalle Thompson, SAC	80	252	518	770	9.6
James Donaldson, LAC/DAL	83	171	624	795	9.6
Robert Parish, BOS	81	246	524	770	9.5

STEALS

	GP	STL	SPG
Alvin Robertson, SAS	82	301	3.67
Micheal Ray Richardson, NJN	47	125	2.66
Clyde Drexler, POR	75	197	2.63
Maurice Cheeks, PHI	82	207	2.52
Fat Lever, DEN	78	178	2.28
Isiah Thomas, DET	77	171	2.22
Charles Barkley, PHI	80	173	2.16
Paul Pressey, MIL	80	168	2.10
Larry Bird, BOS	82	166	2.02
Darwin Cook, NJN	79	156	1.97

BLOCKS

	GP	BLK	BPG
Manute Bol, WSB	80	397	4.96
Mark Eaton, UTJ	80	369	4.61
Hakeem Olajuwon, HOU	68	231	3.40
Wayne Cooper, DEN	78	227	2.91
Benoit Benjamin, LAC	79	206	2.61
Jawann Oldham, CHI	52	134	2.58
Herb Williams, IND	78	184	2.36
Tree Rollins, ATL	74	167	2.26
Patrick Ewing, NYK	50	103	2.06
Kevin McHale, BOS	68	134	1.97

TURNOVERS

	GP	TO	TPG
Charles Barkley, PHI	80	352	4.4
Jeff Ruland, WSB	30	120	4.0
Reggie Theus, SAC	82	328	4.0
Magic Johnson, LAL	72	274	3.8
Isiah Thomas, DET	77	293	3.8
Clyde Drexler, POR	75	285	3.8
Ralph Sampson, HOU	79	284	3.6
Joe Barry Carroll, GST	79	277	3.5
Sleepy Floyd, GST	82	287	3.5
Moses Malone, PHI	74	259	3.5

THE YEAR IN BASKETBALL

November 13, 1985 Lynette Woodard, a former University of Kansas All-American, makes her debut with the Harlem Globetrotters in Spokane, Wash. Woodard's appearance makes her the first female Globetrotter.

December 14, 1985 The Utah Jazz retire Pete Maravich's number seven uniform.

January 4, 1986 David Robinson, Navy's All-American center, blocks a Division I record 14 shots in a game versus UNC-Wilmington. Roy Rogers of Alabama in 1996 and Loren Woods of Arizona in 2000 will tie Robinson's record.

February 23, 1986 Kareem Abdul-Jabbar passes Elvin Hayes as the NBA's leader in career games played with 1,304.

March 26, 1986 Ohio State defeats Wyoming, 73-63, to win the NIT.

March 30, 1986 Texas wins the women's NCAA basketball title with a 97-81 victory over USC.

March 31, 1986 Louisville beats Duke, 72-69, to win the NCAA title championship as Pervis Ellison hits two free throws with 27 seconds left.

April 2, 1986 The NCAA adopts the three-point field goal, which will be instituted in the 1986-87 season.

April 13, 1986 The Boston Celtics end the regular season at Boston Garden with a 135-107 victory over the New Jersey Nets. The win gives the Celtics a 40-1 (.976) home mark. In the process, Boston sets records for most home wins and highest home winning percentage in a season.

April 20, 1986 Michael Jordan of Chicago scores an NBA playoff record 63 points in a 135-131 double-OT loss in Boston.

May 21, 1986 Ralph Sampson hits an off-balance jumper as time expires as Houston eliminates the defending champion Lakers, four games to one, with a 114-112 victory.

June 8, 1986 The Boston Celtics win their 16th NBA title, beating the Houston Rockets, 114-97, to take the series in six games.

June 10, 1986 Nancy Lieberman becomes the first woman to play in a regular season men's pro basketball game when she takes the floor for the Springfield (Mass.) Fame in a United States Basketball League game.

June 19, 1986 Len Bias, the Maryland star who was taken second overall by Boston in the NBA draft, is found dead of a cocaine overdose.

1986-87

Scoring title Jordan's, but Magic takes two MVPs as Lakers romp

Draft-day deals resulted in the creation of a potential new dynasty and the death of an old one. The big winners were the Cleveland Cavaliers. General manager Wayne Embry sent Roy Hinson to Philadelphia for the No. 1 pick and took center Brad Daugherty, who made the all-rookie team, where he joined fellow Cavs Ron Harper and John (Hot Rod) Williams. It wasn't enough to lift Cleveland out of the Central Division cellar, but new coach Lenny Wilkens had a contender in the making.

Not so successful were the 76ers, who also sent Moses Malone to Washington for Jeff Ruland. A knee injury limited Ruland to five games and forced his premature retirement. Andrew Toney's comeback got mixed reviews, and Hinson proved disappointing. Only the inspired play of Charles Barkley kept them above .500. It was fitting that Julius Erving, whose arrival in 1976 had begun a new era in Philadelphia, ended his 16-year pro career at the end of the season.

The Celtics looked like winners in the draft, using the second pick (acquired from Seattle for Gerald Henderson) to grab forward Len Bias. But Bias's death two days later of cocaine intoxication was a serious blow. With Bill Walton and Scott Wedman sidelined most of the season, the Celtics were forced to rely almost exclusively on their starters, who were showing the effects of overwork by playoff time.

The Lakers had also appeared to be slowing down in their playoff loss to Houston last spring. So they let Maurice Lucas go in favor of the younger and faster A.C. Green at power forward. Coach Pat Riley also moved the focus of the offense away from Kareem Abdul-Jabbar and relied more on Magic Johnson, who averaged 24 points and ended Larry Bird's three-year reign as MVP.

As for Bird, he again led the Celtics to the best record in the East, with help from Kevin McHale, having the best season of his career. Boston was chased to the wire by the Hawks, who won 57 games en route to the Central Division title. Many thought Atlanta would dethrone the Celtics in the playoffs, but Detroit stopped the Hawks cold in five games. The Pistons, still in need of inside scoring, sent Kelly Tripucka to Utah for Adrian Dantley, and jumped to 52 wins. Milwaukee won its usual 50 games, but coach Don Nelson resigned after the season, citing differences with owner Herb Kohl.

Jack Ramsey left Portland to coach Indiana and moved the Pacers to the .500 mark, with help from Rookie of the Year Chuck Person. New Chicago coach Doug Collins gave Michael Jordan free reign, and Jordan led the league with 37 points a game as the Bulls improved to 40 wins. But in Washington the acquisition of Moses Malone lifted the Bullets to only 42 wins.

There was trouble in Phoenix, where five players were implicated in a drug scandal and coach John Macleod was fired as the Suns fell short of the playoffs again. Still, they won three

Len Bias
Dies of cocaine intoxication two days after being picked No. 2 by Celtics.

times as many games as the L.A. Clippers, who lost Marques Johnson and Norm Nixon to injuries and challenged the NBA record for futility before finishing at 12-70.

Things were better in Portland, where Mike Schuler replaced Ramsey and became Coach of the Year as the Trail Blazers improved to 49 wins behind Kiki Vandeweghe and Clyde Drexler. In Dallas, the talented Mavericks finally put it all together, winning 55 games, while second-year man Karl Malone made Utah fans forget the departed Dantley. But in Houston, drugs brought the expulsion of guards Mitchell Wiggins and Lewis Lloyd, and Ralph Sampson missed 39

games with injuries—problems that even the play of Akeem Olajuwon couldn't overcome. Golden State, under new coach George Karl, made the playoffs for the first time in 10 years; and Seattle improved to 39 wins as three players—Dale Ellis (acquired from Dallas), Tom Chambers and Xavier McDaniel—averaged 23 points or better.

The Sonics took off in the playoffs, upsetting Dallas and Houston before falling to the Lakers in the Western finals. In the East, the Celtics looked tired in a seven-game victory over Milwaukee, then looked beaten in the next series when Detroit had a one-point lead and the ball with five seconds left in the pivotal fifth game. But Bird stole Isiah Thomas's pass and passed to Dennis Johnson for the winning basket; then, after Detroit won the sixth game, Boston prevailed, 117-114, setting up another meeting with Los Angeles.

McHale was playing on a broken foot, Robert Parish on a sprained ankle, and the Celtics looked sad as the Lakers won the first two games easily. Boston rallied at home, winning two of the three—but the fourth game proved decisive. Bird's 3-pointer put the Celtics up by two with seconds remaining; but after a free throw by Abdul-Jabbar, Johnson sank a "junior sky hook" to sink Boston. The Lakers went on to win in six games, and Johnson was an easy choice as playoff MVP.

1986-87 SEASON HIGHLIGHTS

STANDINGS

Eastern Conference
Atlantic Division

	W	L	Pct.	GB
Boston	59	23	.720	—
Philadelphia	45	37	.549	14
Washington	42	40	.512	17
New Jersey	24	58	.293	35
New York	24	58	.293	35

Central Division

	W	L	Pct.	GB
Atlanta	57	25	.695	—
Detroit	52	30	.634	5
Milwaukee	50	32	.610	7
Indiana	41	41	.500	16
Chicago	40	42	.488	17
Cleveland	31	51	.378	26

Western Conference
Midwest Division

	W	L	Pct.	GB
Dallas	55	27	.671	—
Utah	44	38	.537	11
Houston	42	40	.512	13
Denver	37	45	.451	18
Sacramento	29	53	.354	26
San Antonio	28	54	.341	27

Pacific Division

	W	L	Pct.	GB
LA Lakers	65	17	.793	—
Portland	49	33	.598	16
Golden State	42	40	.512	23
Seattle	39	43	.476	26
Phoenix	36	46	.439	29
LA Clippers	12	70	.146	53

AWARDS

MVP
Magic Johnson, LA Lakers
Top Rookie
Chuck Person, Indiana
Coach of Year
Mike Schuler, Portland
Defensive Player of Year
Michael Cooper, LA Lakers
Sixth Man Award
Ricky Pierce, Milwaukee
Most Improved Player
Dale Ellis, Seattle

ALL-STAR TEAMS

FIRST TEAM

Larry Bird	Boston
Kevin McHale	Boston
Hakeem Olajuwon	Houston
Magic Johnson	LA Lakers
Michael Jordan	Chicago

Citizenship Award
Isiah Thomas, Detroit

ALL-STAR GAME

Kingdome, Seattle
Sunday, February 8, 1987
West 154, East 149, OT
MVP: Tom Chambers

SECOND TEAM

Dominique Wilkins	Atlanta
Charles Barkley	Philadelphia
Moses Malone	Washington
Isiah Thomas	Detroit
Lafayette Lever	Denver

PLAYOFFS

FINALS
L.A. Lakers 4, Boston 2
June 2: Boston 113 at L.A. Lakers 126
June 4: Boston 122 at L.A. Lakers 141
June 7: L.A. Lakers 103 at Boston 109
June 9: L.A. Lakers 107 at Boston 106
June 11: L.A. Lakers 108 at Boston 123
June 14: Boston 93 at L.A. Lakers 106

EASTERN CONFERENCE
CONFERENCE FINALS
Boston 4, Detroit 3
May 19: Detroit 91 at Boston 104
May 21: Detroit 101 at Boston 110
May 23: Boston 104 at Detroit 122
May 24: Boston 119 at Detroit 145
May 26: Detroit 107 at Boston 108
May 28: Boston 105 at Detroit 113
May 30: Detroit 114 at Boston 117

CONFERENCE SEMI-FINALS
Detroit 4, Atlanta 1
May 3: Detroit 112 at Atlanta 111
May 5: Detroit 102 at Atlanta 115
May 8: Atlanta 99 at Detroit 108
May 10: Atlanta 88 at Detroit 89
May 13: Detroit 104 at Atlanta 96

Boston 4, Milwaukee 3
May 5: Milwaukee 98 at Boston 111
May 6: Milwaukee 124 at Boston 126
May 8: Boston 121 at Milwaukee 126, OT
May 10: Boston 138 at Milwaukee 137, 2OT
May 13: Milwaukee 129 at Boston 124
May 15: Boston 111 at Milwaukee 121
May 17: Milwaukee 113 at Boston 119

FIRST ROUND
Boston 3, Chicago 0
Apr. 23: Chicago 104 at Boston 108
Apr. 26: Chicago 96 at Boston 105
Apr. 28: Boston 105 at Chicago 94

Milwaukee 3, Philadelphia 2
Apr. 24: Philadelphia 104 at Milwaukee 107
Apr. 26: Philadelphia 125 at Milwaukee 122, OT
Apr. 29: Milwaukee 121 at Philadelphia 120
May 1: Milwaukee 118 at Philadelphia 124
May 3: Philadelphia 89 at Milwaukee 102

Detroit 3, Washington 0
Apr. 24: Washington 92 at Detroit 106
Apr. 26: Washington 85 at Detroit 128
Apr. 29: Detroit 97 at Washington 96

Atlanta 3, Indiana 1
Apr. 24: Indiana 94 at Atlanta 110
Apr. 26: Indiana 93 at Atlanta 94
Apr. 29: Atlanta 87 at Indiana 96
May 1: Atlanta 101 at Indiana 97

WESTERN CONFERENCE
CONFERENCE FINALS
L.A. Lakers 4, Seattle 0
May 16: Seattle 87 at L.A. Lakers 92
May 19: Seattle 104 at L.A. Lakers 112
May 23: L.A. Lakers 122 at Seattle 121
May 25: L.A. Lakers 133 at Seattle 102

CONFERENCE SEMI-FINALS
Seattle 4, Houston 2
May 2: Seattle 111 at Houston 106, OT
May 5: Seattle 99 at Houston 97
May 7: Houston 102 at Seattle 84
May 9: Houston 102 at Seattle 117
May 12: Seattle 107 at Houston 112
May 14: Houston 125 at Seattle 128, 2OT

L.A. Lakers 4, Golden State 1
May 5: Golden State 116 at L.A. Lakers 125
May 7: Golden State 101 at L.A. Lakers 116
May 9: L.A. Lakers 133 at Golden State 108
May 10: L.A. Lakers 121 at Golden State 129
May 12: Golden State 106 at L.A. Lakers 118

FIRST ROUND
L.A. Lakers 3, Denver 0
Apr. 23: Denver 95 at L.A. Lakers 128
Apr. 25: Denver 127 at L.A. Lakers 139
Apr. 29: L.A. Lakers 140 at Denver 103

Golden State 3, Utah 2
Apr. 23: Golden State 85 at Utah 99
Apr. 25: Golden State 100 at Utah 103
Apr. 29: Utah 95 at Golden State 110
May 1: Utah 94 at Golden State 98
May 3: Golden State 118 at Utah 113

Houston 3, Portland 1
Apr. 24: Houston 125 at Portland 115
Apr. 26: Houston 98 at Portland 111
Apr. 28: Portland 108 at Houston 117
Apr. 30: Portland 101 at Houston 113

Seattle 3, Dallas 1
Apr. 23: Seattle 129 at Dallas 151
Apr. 25: Seattle 112 at Dallas 110
Apr. 28: Dallas 107 at Seattle 117
Apr. 30: Dallas 98 at Seattle 124

NBA LEADERS

SCORING

	GP	FGM	FTM	PTS	PPG
Michael Jordan, CHI	82	1098	833	3041	37.1
Dominique Wilkins, ATL	79	828	607	2294	29.0
Alex English, DEN	82	965	411	2345	28.6
Larry Bird, BOS	74	786	414	2076	28.1
Kiki Vandeweghe, POR	79	808	467	2122	26.9
Kevin McHale, BOS	77	790	428	2008	26.1
Mark Aguirre, DAL	80	787	429	2056	25.7
Dale Ellis, SEA	82	785	385	2041	24.9
Moses Malone, WSB	73	595	570	1760	24.1
Magic Johnson, LAL	80	683	535	1909	23.9

FIELD GOALS

	FGM	FGA	FG%
Kevin McHale, BOS	790	1307	.604
Artis Gilmore, SAS	346	580	.597
Charles Barkley, PHI	557	937	.594
James Donaldson, DAL	311	531	.586
Kareem Abdul-Jabbar, LAL	560	993	.564
Buck Williams, NJN	521	936	.557
Robert Parish, BOS	588	1057	.556
Steve Johnson, POR	494	889	.556
Rodney McCray, HOU	432	783	.552
Larry Nance, PHO	585	1062	.551

THREE POINT FIELD GOALS

	3PM	3PA	3P%
Kiki Vandeweghe, POR	39	81	.481
Detlef Schrempf, DAL	33	69	.478
Danny Ainge, BOS	85	192	.443
Byron Scott, LAL	65	149	.436
Trent Tucker, NYK	68	161	.422
Kevin McKenna, NJN	52	124	.419
Larry Bird, BOS	90	225	.400
Michael Cooper, LAL	89	231	.385
Sleepy Floyd, GST	73	190	.384
Mike McGee, ATL	86	229	.376

FREE THROWS

	FTM	FTA	FT%
Larry Bird, BOS	414	455	.910
Danny Ainge, BOS	148	165	.897
Bill Laimbeer, DET	245	274	.894
Byron Scott, LAL	224	251	.892
Craig Hodges, MIL	131	147	.891
John Long, IND	219	246	.890
Kiki Vandeweghe, POR	467	527	.886
Jeff Malone, WSB	376	425	.885
Rolando Blackman, DAL	419	474	.884
Ricky Pierce, MIL	387	440	.880

ASSISTS

	GP	AST	APG
Magic Johnson, LAL	80	977	12.2
Sleepy Floyd, GST	82	848	10.3
Doc Rivers, ATL	82	823	10.0
Isiah Thomas, DET	81	813	10.0
Terry Porter, POR	80	715	8.9
Reggie Theus, SAC	79	692	8.8
Nate McMillan, SEA	71	583	8.2
John Stockton, UTJ	82	670	8.2
Fat Lever, DEN	82	654	8.0
Maurice Cheeks, PHI	68	538	7.9

REBOUNDS

	GP	ORB	DRB	TRB	RPG
Charles Barkley, PHI	68	390	604	994	14.6
Charles Oakley, CHI	82	299	775	1074	13.1
Buck Williams, NJN	82	322	701	1023	12.5
James Donaldson, DAL	82	295	678	973	11.9
Bill Laimbeer, DET	82	243	712	955	11.6
Michael Cage, LAC	80	354	568	922	11.5
Larry Smith, GST	80	366	551	917	11.5
Hakeem Olajuwon, HOU	75	315	543	858	11.4
Moses Malone, WSB	73	340	484	824	11.3
Robert Parish, BOS	80	254	597	851	10.6

STEALS

	GP	STL	SPG
Alvin Robertson, SAS	81	260	3.21
Michael Jordan, CHI	82	236	2.88
Maurice Cheeks, PHI	68	180	2.65
Ron Harper, CLE	82	209	2.55
Clyde Drexler, POR	82	204	2.49
Fat Lever, DEN	82	201	2.45
Derek Harper, DAL	77	167	2.17
John Stockton, UTJ	82	177	2.16
Doc Rivers, ATL	82	171	2.09
Terry Porter, POR	80	159	1.99

BLOCKS

	GP	BLK	BPG
Mark Eaton, UTJ	79	321	4.06
Manute Bol, WSB	82	302	3.68
Hakeem Olajuwon, HOU	75	254	3.39
Benoit Benjamin, LAC	72	187	2.60
Alton Lister, SEA	75	180	2.40
Patrick Ewing, NYK	63	147	2.33
Kevin McHale, BOS	77	172	2.23
Larry Nance, PHO	69	148	2.14
Roy Hinson, PHI	76	161	2.12
Charles Jones, WSB	79	165	2.09

TURNOVERS

	GP	TO	TPG
Charles Barkley, PHI	68	320	4.7
Isiah Thomas, DET	81	340	4.2
Ron Harper, CLE	82	344	4.2
Magic Johnson, LAL	80	304	3.8
Reggie Theus, SAC	79	292	3.7
Patrick Ewing, NYK	63	227	3.6
Charles Oakley, CHI	82	295	3.6
Steve Johnson, POR	79	277	3.5
Sleepy Floyd, GST	82	279	3.4
Buck Williams, NJN	82	279	3.4

THE YEAR IN BASKETBALL

November 26, 1986 Don Nelson gets his 500th career coaching win, as his Bucks beat the Bullets, 122-103. Nelson achieved 500 wins faster than any coach in history. (Pat Riley has bettered Nelson's mark.)

December 2, 1986 The Celtics lose, 117-109, to Washington, ending a string of 38 consecutive home wins. The game is played at the Hartford Civic Center, where the Celtics occasionally play home games.

January 2, 1987 Coach Jack Ramsey gets his 800th NBA victory as Indiana defeats the L.A. Clippers, 116-106.

February 11, 1987 Dean Smith gets his 600th career coaching win.

February 14, 1987 Dick Baldwin gets his 876th collegiate coaching win—one more than Adolph Rupp of Kentucky. Baldwin coaches at Broome County Community College in upstate New York.

February 23, 1987 Seattle's Nate McMillan sets an NBA rookie record with 25 assists in a 124-112 victory over the Los Angeles Clippers.

February 24, 1987 Kareem Abdul-Jabbar, the NBA's all-time leading scorer, makes the first and only three-point field goal of his career.

March 26, 1987 Southern Mississippi defeats LaSalle, 84-80, to win the 50th National Invitation Tournament.

March 29, 1987 Tennessee routs Louisiana Tech, 67-44, to win the NCAA women's championship.

March 30, 1987 Keith Smart hits a 16-foot baseline jumper with four seconds as Indiana beats Syracuse, 74-73, for the NCAA championship.

April 16, 1987 Michael Jordan pours in 61 points but the Bulls lose to Atlanta, 117-114. Jordan becomes only the second player in history, after Wilt Chamberlain, to eclipse 3,000 points in a season.

April 22, 1987 For the first time in seven years, the NBA expands, admitting franchises from Charlotte, Miami, Minnesota, and Orlando.

April 24, 1987 Michael Jordan wins his first of seven consecutive scoring titles, and a record ten in all.

May 26, 1987 Larry Bird steals Isiah Thomas' inbounds pass and hits Dennis Johnson for the winning basket, as Boston snatches a victory from Detroit, 108-107, in Game 5 of the Eastern Conference finals.

June 14, 1987 The L.A. Lakers beat Boston , 106-93, to win the NBA crown. The victory gives L.A. their fourth championship in eight seasons.

1987-88

Flirting with disaster, Lakers escape with three 7th-game wins

Just as many were wondering when the NBA would produce a team capable of challenging the Lakers and Celtics, the league produced four legitimate contenders, with another on the horizon. But somebody forgot to tell the Lakers.

For most of the season the spotlight was on the Central Division. In Detroit, Dennis Rodman, John Salley and the rest of the league's strongest bench backed up an already powerful first team, a combination that added up to 54 wins and a first-place finish and becoming the first team to draw more than a million fans. Atlanta won 50 for the third straight time as Dominique Wilkins continued to shine despite poor seasons from Kevin Willis and Randy Wittman. And Michael Jordan led Chicago to the 50-win level while earning his second scoring title and first MVP award. The emergence of Mark Price as a star brought visions of a title in Cleveland's future, and the Cavs reacted by sending No. 1 draft pick Kevin Johnson to Phoenix for all-star Larry Nance. For once, "Wait till next year" was a legitimate slogan in Cleveland. Meanwhile, the aging Milwaukee Bucks slipped to 42 wins under new coach Del Harris, and the young Indiana Pacers collapsed in mid-season to finish 38-44.

The Celtics, with Larry Bird still in near-MVP form, had no competition in the Atlantic Division, where no one else could manage a winning record but everyone had a new coach: Wes Unseld in Washington, Rick Pitino in New York, Jim Lyman in Philadelphia and Willis Reed in New Jersey. The Bullets' Moses and Jeff Malone, the Knicks' Patrick Ewing and Rookie of the Year Mark Jackson, the 76ers' Charles Barkley and the Nets' Buck Williams were stars for the also-rans. Also noteworthy was Washington rookie Tyrone 'Muggsy' Bogues, the smallest player in NBA history at 5-foot-3.

Meanwhile, Denver reclaimed the Midwest Division title and earned Doug Moe the Coach of the Year award with strong seasons from Alex English and pesky guards Lafayette Lever and Michael Adams. Dallas finished a game back with John Macleod replacing Dick Motta as coach and Roy Tarpley blossoming as an outstanding sixth man. John Stockton emerged as a star in Utah, setting a record for assists and blending with Karl Malone to give the Jazz their strongest team yet. Houston took a big gamble, sending Ralph Sampson to Golden State for Joe Barry Carroll and Sleepy Floyd. Floyd, however, failed to solve the Rockets' problems at guard. Still Akeem Olajuwon led them to 46 wins. Meanwhile, San Antonio was waiting for No. 1 draft pick David Robinson to get out of the Navy (target date: 1989), and Sacramento was waiting for a miracle in the form of a winning season. The smart money was on San Antonio.

Out West the smart money was on the Lakers, as a 38-4 streak beginning in December made coach Pat Riley's

James Worthy
Awesome Game 7 performance—36 points and 16 rebounds—earns him Finals MVP, and Lakers their fifth title in nine years.

guarantee of a repeat championship look almost reasonable. Kareem Abdul-Jabbar, who turned 41 in April, was fading, but Mychal Thompson was a solid backup, A.C. Green was improving, and Byron Scott was emerging as a star. A late-season injury to Magic Johnson slowed the Lakers a bit, but they still finished with 62 wins, comfortably ahead of Portland. Clyde Drexler led the Trail Blazers to 53 wins with help from Jerome Kersey and Terry Porter, and Seattle improved by five games as Dale Ellis, Xavier McDaniel and Tom Chambers all repeated as 20-point-per-game scorers. Phoenix cleaned house

during a 28-win season; Golden State sank to 20-62 with Sampson injured and Chris Mullin missing time for alcohol rehabilitation; and the Clippers played like—well, like the Clippers.

The playoffs brought severe tests for the Lakers and the Celtics, and only the Lakers passed. Atlanta extended Boston to seven games, losing only when Bird exploded for 20 points in the fourth quarter of the finale; then Detroit wore down the Celtics' overworked starters in an extremely physical six-game series to earn a shot at the title. Meanwhile, the Lakers ran up against a stout Utah defense built around Mark Eaton. With sixth man Thurl Bailey complementing Stockton and Malone on offense, the Jazz scared Los Angeles before falling in seven

games. Next came Dallas, and again the Lakers were forced to the brink of elimination; but again the champs came through, earning a return to the finals with another seven-game win.

Detroit split two games in Los Angeles, then took two of three at home, and returned to L.A. with a 3-2 lead. The Lakers won the sixth game despite 43 points from Isiah Thomas, playing on a badly sprained ankle, then hung on for a 108-105 win in the climactic game behind 36 points and 16 rebounds from James Worthy—a performance that earned him the playoff MVP award. No team had ever won three straight seven-game series, and no team had repeated since 1969—but then, Riley had guaranteed it.

1987-88 SEASON HIGHLIGHTS

STANDINGS

Eastern Conference
Atlantic Division

	W	L	Pct.	GB
Boston	57	25	.695	—
Washington	38	44	.463	19
New York	38	44	.463	19
Philadelphia	36	46	.439	21
New Jersey	19	63	.232	38

Central Division

	W	L	Pct.	GB
Detroit	54	28	.659	—
Atlanta	50	32	.610	4
Chicago	50	32	.610	4
Milwaukee	42	40	.512	12
Cleveland	42	40	.512	12
Indiana	38	44	.463	16

Western Conference
Midwest Division

	W	L	Pct.	GB
Denver	54	28	.659	—
Dallas	53	29	.646	1
Utah	47	35	.573	7
Houston	46	36	.561	8
San Antonio	31	51	.378	23
Sacramento	24	58	.293	30

Pacific Division

	W	L	Pct.	GB
LA Lakers	62	20	.756	—
Portland	53	29	.646	9
Seattle	44	38	.537	18
Phoenix	28	54	.341	34
Golden State	20	62	.244	42
LA Clippers	17	65	.207	45

AWARDS
MVP
Michael Jordan, Chicago
Top Rookie
Mark Jackson, New York
Coach of Year
Doug Moe, Denver
Defensive Player of Year
Michael Jordan, Chicago
Sixth Man Award
Roy Tarpley, Dallas
Most Improved Player
Kevin Duckworth, Portland

ALL-STAR TEAMS
FIRST TEAM

Larry Bird	Boston
Charles Barkley	Philadelphia
Hakeem Olajuwon	Houston
Michael Jordan	Chicago
Magic Johnson	LA Lakers

SECOND TEAM

Karl Malone	Utah
Dominique Wilkins	Atlanta
Patrick Ewing	New York
Clyde Drexler	Portland
John Stockton	Utah

Citizenship Award
Alex English, Denver

ALL-STAR GAME
Chicago Stadium, Chicago
Sunday, February 7, 1988
East 138, West 133
MVP: Michael Jordan

PLAYOFFS
FINALS
L.A. Lakers 4, Detroit 3
June 7: Detroit 105 at L.A. Lakers 93
June 9: Detroit 96 at L.A. Lakers 108
June 12: L.A. Lakers 99 at Detroit 86
June 14: L.A. Lakers 86 at Detroit 111
June 16: L.A. Lakers 94 at Detroit 104
June 19: Detroit 102 at L.A. Lakers 103
June 21: Detroit 105 at L.A. Lakers 108
EASTERN CONFERENCE
CONFERENCE FINALS
Detroit 4, Boston 2
May 25: Detroit 104 at Boston 96
May 26: Detroit 115 at Boston 119, 2OT
May 28: Boston 94 at Detroit 98
May 30: Boston 79 at Detroit 78
June 1: Detroit 102 at Boston 96, OT
June 3: Boston 90 at Detroit 95
CONFERENCE SEMI-FINALS
Boston 4, Atlanta 3
May 11: Atlanta 101 at Boston 110
May 13: Atlanta 97 at Boston 108
May 15: Boston 92 at Atlanta 110
May 16: Boston 109 at Atlanta 118
May 18: Atlanta 112 at Boston 104
May 20: Boston 102 at Atlanta 100
May 22: Atlanta 116 at Boston 118
Detroit 4, Chicago 1
May 10: Chicago 82 at Detroit 93
May 12: Chicago 105 at Detroit 95
May 14: Detroit 101 at Chicago 79
May 15: Detroit 96 at Chicago 77
May 18: Chicago 95 at Detroit 102

FIRST ROUND
Boston 3, New York 1
Apr. 29: New York 92 at Boston 112
May 1: New York 102 at Boston 128
May 4: Boston 100 at New York 109
May 6: Boston 102 at New York 94
Detroit 3, Washington 2
Apr. 28: Washington 87 at Detroit 96
Apr. 30: Washington 101 at Detroit 102
May 2: Detroit 106 at Washington 114, OT
May 4: Detroit 103 at Washington 106
May 8: Washington 78 at Detroit 99
Chicago 3, Cleveland 2
Apr. 28: Cleveland 93 at Chicago 104
May 1: Cleveland 101 at Chicago 106
May 3: Chicago 102 at Cleveland 110
May 5: Chicago 91 at Cleveland 97
May 8: Cleveland 101 at Chicago 107
Atlanta 3, Milwaukee 2
Apr. 29: Milwaukee 107 at Atlanta 110
May 1: Milwaukee 97 at Atlanta 119
May 4: Atlanta 115 at Milwaukee 123
May 6: Atlanta 99 at Milwaukee 105
May 8: Milwaukee 111 at Atlanta 121
WESTERN CONFERENCE
CONFERENCE FINALS
L.A. Lakers 4, Dallas 3
May 23: Dallas 98 at L.A. Lakers 113
May 25: Dallas 101 at L.A. Lakers 123
May 27: L.A. Lakers 94 at Dallas 106
May 29: L.A. Lakers 104 at Dallas 118
May 31: Dallas 102 at L.A. Lakers 119
June 2: L.A. Lakers 103 at Dallas 105
June 4: Dallas 102 at L.A. Lakers 117

CONFERENCE SEMI-FINALS
L.A. Lakers 4, Utah 3
May 8: Utah 91 at L.A. Lakers 110
May 10: Utah 101 at L.A. Lakers 97
May 13: L.A. Lakers 89 at Utah 96
May 15: L.A. Lakers 113 at Utah 100
May 17: Utah 109 at L.A. Lakers 111
May 19: L.A. Lakers 80 at Utah 108
May 21: Utah 98 at L.A. Lakers 109
Dallas 4, Denver 2
May 10: Dallas 115 at Denver 126
May 12: Dallas 112 at Denver 108
May 14: Denver 107 at Dallas 105
May 15: Denver 103 at Dallas 124
May 17: Dallas 110 at Denver 106
May 19: Denver 95 at Dallas 108
FIRST ROUND
L.A. Lakers 3, San Antonio 0
Apr. 29: San Antonio 110 at L.A. Lakers 122
May 1: San Antonio 112 at L.A. Lakers 130
May 3: L.A. Lakers 109 at San Antonio 107
Denver 3, Seattle 2
Apr. 29: Seattle 123 at Denver 126
May 1: Seattle 111 at Denver 91
May 3: Denver 125 at Seattle 114
May 5: Denver 117 at Seattle 127
May 7: Seattle 96 at Denver 115
Dallas 3, Houston 1
Apr. 28: Houston 110 at Dallas 120
Apr. 30: Houston 119 at Dallas 108
May 3: Dallas 93 at Houston 92
May 5: Dallas 107 at Houston 97
Utah 3, Portland 1
Apr. 28: Utah 96 at Portland 108
Apr. 30: Utah 114 at Portland 105
May 4: Portland 108 at Utah 113
May 6: Portland 96 at Utah 111

NBA LEADERS

SCORING

	GP	FGM	FTM	PTS	PPG
Michael Jordan, CHI	82	1069	723	2868	35.0
Dominique Wilkins, ATL	78	909	541	2397	30.7
Larry Bird, BOS	76	881	415	2275	29.9
Charles Barkley, PHI	80	753	714	2264	28.3
Karl Malone, UTJ	82	858	552	2268	27.7
Clyde Drexler, POR	81	849	476	2185	27.0
Dale Ellis, SEA	75	764	303	1938	25.8
Mark Aguirre, DAL	77	746	388	1932	25.1
Alex English, DEN	80	843	314	2000	25.0
Hakeem Olajuwon, HOU	79	712	381	1805	22.8

FIELD GOALS

	FGM	FGA	FG%
Kevin McHale, BOS	550	911	.604
Robert Parish, BOS	442	750	.589
Charles Barkley, PHI	753	1283	.587
John Stockton, UTJ	454	791	.574
Walter Berry, SAS	540	960	.563
Dennis Rodman, DET	398	709	.561
Buck Williams, NJN	466	832	.560
Cliff Levingston, ATL	314	564	.557
Patrick Ewing, NYK	656	1183	.555
Mark West, CLE/PHO	316	573	.551

THREE POINT FIELD GOALS

	3PM	3PA	3P%
Craig Hodges, MIL/PHO	86	175	.491
Mark Price, CLE	72	148	.486
John Long, IND	34	77	.442
Gerald Henderson, NYK/PHI	69	163	.423
Kelly Tripucka, UTJ	31	74	.419
Danny Ainge, BOS	148	357	.415
Larry Bird, BOS	98	237	.414
Trent Tucker, NYK	69	167	.413
Dale Ellis, SEA	107	259	.413
Leon Wood, SAS/ATL	52	127	.409

FREE THROWS

	FTM	FTA	FT%
Jack Sikma, MIL	321	348	.922
Larry Bird, BOS	415	453	.916
John Long, IND	166	183	.907
Mike Gminski, NJN/PHI	355	392	.906
Johnny Dawkins, SAS	198	221	.896
Walter Davis, PHO	205	231	.887
Chris Mullin, GST	239	270	.885
Jeff Malone, WSB	335	380	.882
Winston Garland, GST	138	157	.879
Kiki Vandeweghe, POR	159	181	.878

ASSISTS

	GP	AST	APG
John Stockton, UTJ	82	1128	13.8
Magic Johnson, LAL	72	858	11.9
Mark Jackson, NYK	82	868	10.6
Terry Porter, POR	82	831	10.1
Doc Rivers, ATL	80	747	9.3
Nate McMillan, SEA	82	702	8.6
Isiah Thomas, DET	81	678	8.4
Maurice Cheeks, PHI	79	635	8.0
Fat Lever, DEN	82	639	7.8
Dennis Johnson, BOS	77	598	7.8

REBOUNDS

	GP	ORB	DRB	TRB	RPG
Michael Cage, LAC	72	371	567	938	13.03
Charles Oakley, CHI	82	326	740	1066	13.00
Hakeem Olajuwon, HOU	79	302	657	959	12.1
Karl Malone, UTJ	82	277	709	986	12.0
Buck Williams, NJN	70	298	536	834	11.9
Charles Barkley, PHI	80	385	566	951	11.9
Roy Tarpley, DAL	81	360	599	959	11.8
Moses Malone, WSB	79	372	512	884	11.2
Otis Thorpe, SAC	82	279	558	837	10.2
Bill Laimbeer, DET	82	165	667	832	10.1

STEALS

	GP	STL	SPG
Michael Jordan, CHI	82	259	3.16
Alvin Robertson, SAS	82	243	2.96
John Stockton, UTJ	82	242	2.95
Fat Lever, DEN	82	223	2.72
Clyde Drexler, POR	81	203	2.51
Mark Jackson, NYK	82	205	2.50
Maurice Cheeks, PHI	79	167	2.11
Nate McMillan, SEA	82	169	2.06
Hakeem Olajuwon, HOU	79	162	2.05
Michael Adams, DEN	82	168	2.05

BLOCKS

	GP	BLK	BPG
Mark Eaton, UTJ	82	304	3.71
Benoit Benjamin, LAC	66	225	3.41
Patrick Ewing, NYK	82	245	2.99
Hakeem Olajuwon, HOU	79	214	2.71
Manute Bol, WSB	77	208	2.70
Larry Nance, PHO/CLE	67	159	2.37
Jawann Oldham, SAC	54	110	2.04
Herb Williams, IND	75	146	1.95
Hot Rod Williams, CLE	77	145	1.88
Roy Hinson, PHI/NJN	77	140	1.82

TURNOVERS

	GP	TO	TPG
Karl Malone, UTJ	82	328	4.0
Charles Barkley, PHI	80	304	3.8
Magic Johnson, LAL	72	266	3.7
Ralph Sampson, HOU/GST	48	173	3.6
Patrick Ewing, NYK	82	287	3.5
Brad Daugherty, CLE	79	269	3.4
Isiah Thomas, DET	81	275	3.4
Benoit Benjamin, LAC	66	224	3.4
Reggie Theus, SAC	73	234	3.2
Moses Malone, WSB	79	253	3.2

THE YEAR IN BASKETBALL

October 23-25, 1987 The first international tournament to be sanctioned by FIBA involving NBA teams is played in Milwaukee. Called the McDonald's championship, the Bucks compete against the Italian League champ, Tracer Milan, and the Soviet Union national team. The Bucks win the two-day tourney.

November 21, 1987 Bobby Knight is ejected from an exhibition game against the touring Soviet National team. With 15:05 remaining in the game and Indiana trailing, 66-43, Knight takes the Hoosiers off the court, ending the game.

January 5, 1988 Pete Maravich dies suddenly of a heart attack at age 40 while playing a pickup game in Pasadena, Ca.

January 25, 1988 Rickey Green, a Utah Jazz point guard, scores the NBA's 5,000,000th point as the Jazz beat Cleveland, 119-96.

March 30, 1988 Connecticut wins the NIT by besting Ohio State, 72-67, behind tourney MVP Phil Gamble.

April 3, 1988 Louisiana Tech wins the NCAA women's championship with a 56-54 come-from-behind victory over Auburn.

April 4, 1988 Danny Manning scores 31 points to lead Kansas to its second NCAA national title, an 83-79 upset victory over Oklahoma.

April 26, 1988 The NBA votes to permanently add a third referee.

May 25, 1988 In a fourth-quarter shootout between Larry Bird and Dominique Wilkins, the Boston Celtics eliminate the Atlanta Hawks and advance to the Eastern Conference finals. Wilkins scores 16 points in the final stanza and finishes with 47. Bird scores 20 in the fourth and totals 34.

June 8, 1988 In perhaps the "tallest" trade ever, the Bullets deal 7-foot-6 Manute Bol to the Warriors for 7-foot-0 David Feitl.

June 19, 1988 On a sprained ankle, Isiah Thomas scores 25 points in the third quarter of Game 6 of the NBA Fnals. But the Lakers beat Thomas' Pistons, 103-102, to even the series at three games apiece.

June 21, 1988 The Los Angeles Lakers beat the Detroit Pistons, 108-105, in Game 7 to become the first NBA team in 19 years to repeat as NBA champions. James Worthy is the Finals MVP.

July 25, 1988 Becoming the first NBA team to play in the Soviet Union, the Atlanta Hawks beat the Soviet Georgia All-Stars, 85-84.

1988-89

42-year drought ends as Pistons beat Lakers, ruin Kareem's farewell

In a season of transition, the NBA welcomed two new teams and said goodbye to a legend. The standings also indicated a league in flux, with 12 teams moving up or down by nine games or more. It was only fitting that the championship went to a franchise that had never won a title in its long history.

The legend, of course, was Kareem Abdul-Jabbar, who became only a part-time player for the Lakers while making a grand farewell tour of the league in his twentieth season. The pomp and circumstance didn't seem to distract his teammates, though, as they won 57 games and their eighth straight Pacific Division title, led by MVP Magic Johnson, plus James Worthy, Byron Scott and A.C. Green.

The two expansion teams took different approaches in stocking their rosters. The Charlotte Hornets blended veterans Kelly Tripucka, Robert Reid and Kurt Rambis with rookie Rex Chapman, but the Miami Heat went almost entirely for youth, with top draft pick Rony Seikaly the most recognizable name. Charlotte got better results, winning 20 to Miami's 15, but both finished last in their respective divisions, as expected.

Among the teams in transition, the biggest gains came in Phoenix and Golden State, where veteran coaches Cotton Fitzsimmons and Don Nelson returned and worked miracles. Fitzsimmons won Coach of the Year honors by leading the Suns to 55 wins, a 27-game improvement, behind free agent acquisition Tom Chambers, second-year man Kevin Johnson and Eddie Johnson. With Ralph Sampson slowed all year by injuries, Nelson started a lineup of four guards and a forward, and installed a motion offense, as the Warriors improved by 23 games, led by Chris Mullin, back from a bout with alcoholism, and Rookie of the Year Mitch Richmond.

Another success story was written in Cleveland, where the Cavaliers got off to a 30-8 start behind Larry Nance and young stars Brad Daugherty, Ron Harper, Mark Price and John (Hot Rod) Williams. Unfortunately for the Cavs, they were in the same division with Detroit. The Pistons started slowly, but took off after sending moody Adrian Dantley to Dallas for Mark Aquirre. Aided by a Cleveland slump, they overtook the Cavs and finished with 63 wins.

Atlanta picked up Moses Malone and Reggie Theus, but failed to move up when Kevin Willis missed the whole season. Milwaukee improved to 49 wins as Larry Krystowiak showed signs of becoming a star (before a serious knee injury in the playoffs) and Terry Cummings remained one. Second-year men Scottie Pippen and Horace Grant made progress in Chicago, but again the main man was Michael Jordan, who shifted to point guard but still won another scoring title. Though losing the MVP award to Johnson by an eyelash, Jordan won the player's vote in *The Sporting News* by a lopsided 84-37 margin.

In the Atlantic Division, New York coach Rick Pitino saw

Joe Dumars
Rejected here by Knicks' Kenny Walker, but not often while averaging 27 points per game in the finals.

his young team win the title behind Patrick Ewing, Mark Jackson and Charles Oakley, picked up from Chicago for Bill Cartwright. Meanwhile, Philadelphia added Ron Anderson (from Indiana) and rookie Hersey Hawkins to Charles Barkley and Mike Gminski, and the result was 46 wins and second place. That put them ahead of Boston, one of the year's big losers. The Celtics' season went up in smoke when bone spurs finished Larry Bird after only six games. Just behind the Celtics came the Washington Bullets, minus Moses Malone. Coach Wes Unseld went without a center for most of the season, but

a new motion offense brought out the best in Jeff Malone, John Williams and Bernard King. In New Jersey even Buck Williams was beginning to slip as the Nets finished ahead of Charlotte.

The Midwest Division saw three of the year's biggest declines in Dallas, Denver and San Antonio. The Mavericks lost Roy Tarpley to knee surgery and drug rehabilitation and went downhill from there. Alex English scored 2,000 points for a record eighth season in Denver, and Lafayette Lever was better than ever, but sub-par play from the big men brought the Nuggets down.

The Midwest title went to the Utah Jazz, who won 51 games despite the mid-season resignation of coach Frank Layden, who moved to the front office and handed the reins to Jerry Sloan. Karl Malone and John Stockton again led the offense, and Mark Eaton anchored an outstanding defense. But the Jazz fell apart in the playoffs, losing three straight to Golden State. In Houston, another great season from Akeem Olajuwon and the acquisition of Otis Thorpe didn't boost the Rockets to the top.

In the Pacific Division, coach Mike Schuler lost his job as Portland fell to 39 wins despite the presence of Clyde Drexler,

Kevin Duckworth, Terry Porter and Jerome Kersey, and new coach Rick Adelman couldn't stop the slide. Seattle moved up again as Michael Cage replaced Chambers, sophomore Derrick McKey made great strides. Sacramento, transplanted from the Midwest Division, added Danny Ainge and Wayman Tisdale to improving sophomore Kenny Smith, but it had little immediate effect. And the Clippers fired coach Gene Shue after No. 1 draft pick Danny Manning went out with a knee injury.

With Jordan playing brilliantly, the Bulls were the surprise team of the playoffs, upsetting Cleveland and New York and throwing a scare into Detroit before falling to the Pistons in six games. Meanwhile, the Lakers romped through the Western playoffs, winning 11 straight games and setting up a rematch with the Pistons for the championship. Many fans had visions of Abdul-Jabbar bowing out with a third consecutive title, but when hamstring injuries sidelined Byron Scott and Magic Johnson, the Lakers were unable to handle Detroit's backcourt. With playoff MVP Joe Dumars averaging 27 points, the Pistons won four straight to complete their long climb to the top.

1988-89 SEASON HIGHLIGHTS

STANDINGS

Eastern Conference
Atlantic Division

	W	L	Pct.	GB
New York	52	30	.634	—
Philadelphia	46	36	.561	6
Boston	42	40	.512	10
Washington	40	42	.488	12
New Jersey	26	56	.317	26
Charlotte	20	62	.244	32

Central Division

	W	L	Pct.	GB
Detroit	63	19	.768	—
Cleveland	57	25	.695	6
Atlanta	52	30	.634	11
Milwaukee	49	33	.598	14
Chicago	47	35	.573	16
Indiana	28	54	.341	35

Western Conference
Midwest Division

	W	L	Pct.	GB
Utah	51	31	.622	—
Houston	45	37	.549	6
Denver	44	38	.537	7
Dallas	38	44	.463	13
San Antonio	21	61	.256	30
Miami Heat	15	67	.183	36

Pacific Division

	W	L	Pct.	GB
LA Lakers	57	25	.695	—
Phoenix	55	27	.671	2
Seattle	47	35	.573	10
Golden State	43	39	.524	14
Portland	39	43	.476	18
Sacramento	27	55	.329	30
LA Clippers	21	61	.256	36

AWARDS

MVP
Magic Johnson, LA Lakers
Top Rookie
Mitch Richmond, GS
Coach of Year
Cotton Fitzsimmons, Phoenix
Defensive Player of Year
Mark Eaton, Utah
Sixth Man Award
Eddie Johnson, Phoenix
Most Improved Player
Kevin Johnson, Phoenix
Citizenship Award
Thurl Bailey, Utah

ALL-STAR GAME
Astrodome, Houston
Sunday, February 12, 1989
West 143, East 134
MVP: Karl Malone

ALL-STAR TEAMS

FIRST TEAM

Karl Malone	Utah
Charles Barkley	Philadelphia
Hakeem Olajuwon	Houston
Magic Johnson	LA Lakers
Michael Jordan	Chicago

SECOND TEAM

Tom Chambers	Phoenix
Chris Mullin	Golden State
Patrick Ewing	New York
John Stockton	Utah
Kevin Johnson	Phoenix

THIRD TEAM

Dominique Wilkins	Atlanta
Terry Cummings	Milwaukee
Robert Parish	Boston
Dale Ellis	Seattle
Mark Price	Cleveland

PLAYOFFS

FINALS
Detroit 4, L.A. Lakers 0
June 6: L.A. Lakers 97 at Detroit 109
June 8: L.A. Lakers 105 at Detroit 108
June 11: Detroit 114 at L.A. Lakers 110
June 13: Detroit 105 at L.A. Lakers 97

EASTERN CONFERENCE
CONFERENCE FINALS
Detroit 4, Chicago 2
May 21: Chicago 94 at Detroit 88
May 23: Chicago 91 at Detroit 100
May 27: Detroit 97 at Chicago 99
May 29: Detroit 86 at Chicago 80
May 31: Chicago 85 at Detroit 94
June 2: Detroit 103 at Chicago 94

CONFERENCE SEMI-FINALS
Chicago 4, New York 2
May 9: Chicago 120 at New York 109, OT
May 11: Chicago 97 at New York 114
May 13: New York 88 at Chicago 111
May 14: New York 93 at Chicago 106
May 16: Chicago 114 at New York 121
May 19: New York 111 at Chicago 113

Detroit 4, Milwaukee 0
May 10: Milwaukee 80 at Detroit 85
May 12: Milwaukee 92 at Detroit 112
May 14: Detroit 110 at Milwaukee 90
May 15: Detroit 96 at Milwaukee 94

FIRST ROUND
New York 3, Philadelphia 0
Apr. 27: Philadelphia 96 at New York 102
Apr. 29: Philadelphia 106 at New York 107
May 2: New York 116 at Philadelphia 115, OT

Detroit 3, Boston 0
Apr. 28: Boston 91 at Detroit 101
Apr. 30: Boston 95 at Detroit 102
May 2: Detroit 100 at Boston 85

Chicago 3, Cleveland 2
Apr. 28: Chicago 95 at Cleveland 88
Apr. 30: Chicago 88 at Cleveland 96
May 3: Cleveland 94 at Chicago 101
May 5: Cleveland 108 at Chicago 105, OT
May 7: Chicago 101 at Cleveland 100

Milwaukee 3, Atlanta 2
Apr. 27: Milwaukee 92 at Atlanta 100
Apr. 29: Milwaukee 108 at Atlanta 98
May 2: Atlanta 113 at Milwaukee 117, OT
May 5: Atlanta 113 at Milwaukee 106, OT
May 7: Milwaukee 96 at Atlanta 92

WESTERN CONFERENCE
CONFERENCE FINALS
L.A. Lakers 4, Phoenix 0
May 20: Phoenix 119 at L.A. Lakers 127
May 23: Phoenix 95 at L.A. Lakers 101
May 26: L.A. Lakers 110 at Phoenix 107
May 28: L.A. Lakers 122 at Phoenix 117

CONFERENCE SEMI-FINALS
Phoenix 4, Golden State 1
May 6: Golden State 103 at Phoenix 130
May 9: Golden State 127 at Phoenix 122
May 11: Phoenix 113 at Golden State 104
May 13: Phoenix 135 at Golden State 99
May 16: Golden State 104 at Phoenix 116

L.A. Lakers 4, Seattle 0
May 7: Seattle 102 at L.A. Lakers 113
May 10: Seattle 108 at L.A. Lakers 130
May 12: L.A. Lakers 91 at Seattle 86
May 14: L.A. Lakers 97 at Seattle 95

FIRST ROUND
L.A. Lakers 3, Portland 0
Apr. 27: Portland 108 at L.A. Lakers 128
Apr. 30: Portland 105 at L.A. Lakers 113
May 3: L.A. Lakers 116 at Portland 108

Golden State 3, Utah 0
Apr. 27: Golden State 123 at Utah 119
Apr. 29: Golden State 99 at Utah 91
May 2: Utah 106 at Golden State 120

Phoenix 3, Denver 0
Apr. 28: Denver 103 at Phoenix 104
Apr. 30: Denver 114 at Phoenix 132
May 2: Phoenix 130 at Denver 121

Seattle 3, Houston 1
Apr. 28: Houston 107 at Seattle 111
Apr. 30: Houston 97 at Seattle 109
May 3: Seattle 107 at Houston 126
May 5: Seattle 98 at Houston 96

NBA LEADERS

SCORING

	GP	FGM	FTM	PTS	PPG
Michael Jordan, CHI	81	966	674	2633	32.5
Karl Malone, UTJ	80	809	703	2326	29.1
Dale Ellis, SEA	82	857	377	2253	27.5
Clyde Drexler, POR	78	829	438	2123	27.2
Chris Mullin, GST	82	830	493	2176	26.5
Alex English, DEN	82	924	325	2175	26.5
Dominique Wilkins, ATL	80	814	442	2099	26.2
Charles Barkley, PHI	79	700	602	2037	25.8
Tom Chambers, PHO	81	774	509	2085	25.7
Hakeem Olajuwon, HOU	82	790	454	2034	24.8

FIELD GOALS

	FGM	FGA	FG%
Dennis Rodman, DET	316	531	.595
Charles Barkley, PHI	700	1208	.579
Robert Parish, BOS	596	1045	.570
Patrick Ewing, NYK	727	1282	.567
James Worthy, LAL	702	1282	.548
Kevin McHale, BOS	661	1211	.546
Otis Thorpe, HOU	521	961	.542
Benoit Benjamin, LAC	491	907	.541
Larry Nance, CLE	496	920	.539
John Stockton, UTJ	497	923	.538

THREE POINT FIELD GOALS

	3PM	3PA	3P%
Jon Sundvold, MIA	48	92	.522
Dale Ellis, SEA	162	339	.478
Mark Price, CLE	93	211	.441
Hersey Hawkins, PHI	71	166	.428
Craig Hodges, PHO/CHI	75	180	.417
Eddie Johnson, PHO	71	172	.413
Ricky Berry, SAC	65	160	.406
Harold Pressley, SAC	119	295	.403
Reggie Miller, IND	98	244	.402
Byron Scott, LAL	77	193	.399

FREE THROWS

	FTM	FTA	FT%
Magic Johnson, LAL	513	563	.911
Jack Sikma, MIL	266	294	.905
Scott Skiles, IND	130	144	.903
Mark Price, CLE	263	292	.901
Chris Mullin, GST	493	553	.892
Kevin Johnson, PHO	508	576	.882
Joe Kleine, SAC/BOS	134	152	.882
Walter Davis, DEN	175	199	.879
Mike Gminski, PHI	297	341	.871
Jeff Malone, WSB	296	340	.871

ASSISTS

	GP	AST	APG
John Stockton, UTJ	82	1118	13.6
Magic Johnson, LAL	77	988	12.8
Kevin Johnson, PHO	81	991	12.2
Terry Porter, POR	81	770	9.5
Nate McMillan, SEA	75	696	9.3
Sleepy Floyd, HOU	82	709	8.6
Mark Jackson, NYK	72	619	8.6
Mark Price, CLE	75	631	8.4
Isiah Thomas, DET	80	663	8.3
Michael Jordan, CHI	81	650	8.0

REBOUNDS

	GP	ORB	DRB	TRB	RPG
Hakeem Olajuwon, HOU	82	338	767	1105	13.5
Charles Barkley, PHI	79	403	583	986	12.5
Robert Parish, BOS	80	342	654	996	12.5
Moses Malone, ATL	81	386	570	956	11.8
Karl Malone, UTJ	80	259	594	853	10.7
Charles Oakley, NYK	82	343	518	861	10.5
Mark Eaton, UTJ	82	227	616	843	10.3
Otis Thorpe, HOU	82	272	515	787	9.6
Bill Laimbeer, DET	81	138	638	776	9.6
Michael Cage, SEA	80	276	489	765	9.6

STEALS

	GP	STL	SPG
John Stockton, UTJ	82	263	3.21
Alvin Robertson, SAS	65	197	3.03
Michael Jordan, CHI	81	234	2.89
Fat Lever, DEN	71	195	2.75
Clyde Drexler, POR	78	213	2.73
Hakeem Olajuwon, HOU	82	213	2.60
Doc Rivers, ATL	76	181	2.38
Ron Harper, CLE	82	185	2.26
Winston Garland, GST	79	175	2.22
Lester Conner, NJN	82	181	2.21

BLOCKS

	GP	BLK	BPG
Manute Bol, GST	80	345	4.31
Mark Eaton, UTJ	82	315	3.84
Patrick Ewing, NYK	80	281	3.51
Hakeem Olajuwon, HOU	82	282	3.44
Larry Nance, CLE	73	206	2.82
Benoit Benjamin, LAC	79	221	2.80
Wayne Cooper, DEN	79	211	2.67
Mark West, PHO	82	187	2.28
Alton Lister, SEA	82	180	2.20
Rik Smits, IND	82	151	1.84

TURNOVERS

	GP	TO	TPG
Magic Johnson, LAL	77	316	4.1
Kevin Johnson, PHO	81	324	4.0
Chuck Person, DET	80	312	3.9
John Stockton, UTJ	82	312	3.8
Isiah Thomas, DET	80	296	3.7
Danny Manning, LAC	26	94	3.6
Gary Grant, LAC	71	256	3.6
Michael Jordan, CHI	81	292	3.6
Karl Malone, UTJ	80	288	3.6
Alvin Robertson, SAS	65	234	3.6

THE YEAR IN BASKETBALL

January 21, 1989 Michael Adams of Denver ties an NBA record held by John Roche when he hits seven three-point field goals in one half of a game vs. Milwaukee.

January 28, 1989 Before the largest regular-season crowd in collegiate history, LSU upsets Georgetown, 82-80. The turnstile count in the Superdome is 54,321, though a total of 65,913 tickets are sold.

January 31, 1989 Loyola Marymount defeats U.S. International, 181-150, setting several NCAA records, including most total points (331) by two teams and the most points by a losing team.

February 12, 1989 A crowd of 44,735, the largest in All-Star Game history, nearly fills the Houston Astrodome to watch the West beat the East, 143-134. Utah's Karl Malone wins MVP honors with 28 points.

March 29, 1989 St. John's, propelled by the play of tournament MVP Jayson Williams, wins a record 5th NIT, 73-65, over Saint Louis.

April 2, 1989 Tennessee beats Auburn, 76-60, to win the NCAA woman's championship.

April 3, 1989 Rumeal Robinson hits two free throws with three seconds left in overtime to give Michigan an 80-79 win over Seton Hall in the NCAA championship game.

April 8, 1989 FIBA votes to eliminate the distinction between amateurs and professionals, thereby allowing NBA players to participate in international events, such as the Olympics and the World Championships. The decision opens the way for the future U.S. Dream Team to compete in Barcelona at the 1992 Olympics.

April 23, 1989 Kareem Abdul-Jabbar of the L.A. Lakers retires as the leading scorer in NBA history, with 38,387 points in 1,560 games.

May 7, 1989 Michael Jordan hits a do-or-die jumper from the key as time expires, giving the Bulls a 101-100 victory over Cleveland in Game 5 of the best-of-five series. The Bulls will reach the Eastern Conference finals before losing to Detroit.

June 13, 1989 In a four-game sweep, the Pistons reverse the results of the previous year by beating the Lakers, 105-97, to win the NBA championship. Joe Dumars, who won Finals MVP honors, scores 23 points to lead Detroit. James Worthy gets 40 to lead the Lakers, who play without the injured Magic Johnson. The game marks the end of Kareem Abdul-Jabbar's career.

1989-90

Attendance soars as Minny, Orlando rev up, Pistons keep chugging

Brian Shaw and Danny Ferry (Cleveland's number one draft choice) opted to play in Italy, but the NBA picked up five foreigners from Europe and most did quite well: Vlade Divac (Yugoslavia), L.A. Lakers; Sarunas Marciulionis (USSR), Golden State; Zarko Paspalj (Yugoslavia), San Antonio; Drazen Petrovic (Yugoslavia), Portland; Alexander Volkov (USSR), Atlanta. More than 70 ex-NBA or CBA players were on rosters in the Italian League with another thirty on rosters in the Spanish League.

For the second year in a row expansion became a part of the NBA. The addition of the Minnesota Timberwolves and the Orlando Magic brought the NBA up to 27 teams. The Timberwolves outdid the Magic with 22 wins to 18 wins.

Record-setting attendance was attained by the NBA, with 17,368,659 fans going through the turnstiles. The top club was Minnesota with over a million and an average of 26,160. Last year's expansion team, Charlotte, was second, averaging 23,901.

On the court the biggest gain was by the San Antonio Spurs, who enjoyed a 35-game improvement in the win column, the best turn-around in NBA history. The big additions to the Spurs were starting rookies David Robinson and Sean Elliott. Also new were Terry Cummings, Caldwell Jones, David Wingate and the return of Johnny Moore.

In the Atlantic Division, Charles Barkley led the Philadelphia 76ers to the crown, edging the Celtics by one game. The addition of Rick Mahorn and Hersey Hawkins helped offset the loss of guard Maurice Cheeks.

Boston, with a healthy Larry Bird, felt the loss of Brian Shaw. Reggie Lewis and the arrival of John Bagley took up the slack. Kevin McHale had an excellent year as the sixth man, but at times the Celtics showed their age.

The Knicks had a new young coach in Stu Jackson and a great year from Patrick Ewing, who broke the team scoring record. Injuries shelved Kiki Vandeweghe again and took their toll on Charles Oakley. The Knicks were on top or second in the division until March, when they lost 12 of 16. The late addition of Cheeks, from the Spurs, helped pull the team together.

Washington, Miami and New Jersey were also-rans in the Atlantic Division. The Bullets missed the playoffs for only the fourth time in 21 seasons. The Heat, in their second year, overtook the Nets, who had the worst record in the NBA. The Nets used 19 players during the season and had an eleven-game losing streak in March.

There was no question of who would lead the Central Division, as the Pistons ran off a 13-game winning streak in the middle of the season. The loss of Mahorn was eased with the play of James Edwards and Dennis Rodman. The Pistons were on the verge of a dynasty with strong play at every position with a still fairly young team.

The Bulls tried to make it a close race but couldn't stay with

Isiah Thomas
Calmly quarterbacked Detroit's "Bad Boys" to second-straight NBA Championship, and his first Finals MVP.

the Pistons. For the fourth successive year Michael Jordan led the league in scoring average—his fourth year in-a-row with over a 30 ppg average. On March 28th Jordan scored 69 points and had a career high 18 rebounds against the Cavaliers.

The rest of the Central Division, except for Orlando, was challenging for third place with the Bucks, the Cavs and the Pacers all making the playoffs and the Hawks just missing. The Bucks were led by the best sixth man in the league, Ricky Pierce, but were hurt by a bad knee injury to starting forward Larry Krystkowiak. The Bucks again activated assistant coach

Mike Dunleavy, who after the season was named head coach of the L.A. Lakers. Jack Sikma surpassed 10,000 rebounds.

The much improved Spurs won the Midwest Division by one game over the Jazz. David Robinson was Rookie of the Year. Utah was again led by Karl Malone, second to Jordan with a 31.0 ppg average and John Stockton who set an all-time NBA record with 1,134 assists. Stockton became the first NBA player to record three successive 1,000 assist seasons.

Hakeem Olajuwon led the league in rebounds and blocked shots, and averaged 24.3 points per game. Olajuwon became only the third player in NBA history to record a quadruple double, against the Bucks on March 29.

If the Lakers missed Kareem Abdul-Jabbar it certainly didn't show in the standings as they had the NBA's best record and won their ninth straight division crown to qualify for the play-offs for the 14th consecutive year.

Portland increased 20 games in the win column. The big acquisition was Buck Williams who came in an off-season trade for Sam Bowie. Phoenix, coached by Cotton Fitzsimmons, was led by Tom Chambers, who set a club record with 60 points in a win over Seattle. The Suns broke a league record on April 9 versus the Jazz when they made 61 of 80 free throws.

When the playoffs began, a Lakers-Pistons Final was predicted. But the Lakers lost in the second round to Phoenix.

The Conference Finals pitted Detroit against Chicago and Portland against Phoenix. The Pistons won a low-scoring series in seven to gain their third consecutive trip to the Finals. The home team won each game with Jordan scoring 47 and 42 points respectively in Games 3 and 4. The Portland-Phoenix series went six games with the home team winning the first five games but Portland won Game 6 in Phoenix 112-109.

Detroit beat Portland to become the sixth team to repeat as champion. The Series lasted just five games, with Detroit only losing a Game 2 overtime contest.

After the season, a judge ordered Brian Shaw to honor a contract with the Celtics. But Shaw, who was refused permission to play in Italy, stated he would not play in Boston. NBA players were declared eligible for play in the 1992 Olympics.

1989-90 SEASON HIGHLIGHTS

STANDINGS

Eastern Conference
Atlantic Division

	W	L	Pct.	GB
Philadelphia	53	29	.646	—
Boston	52	30	.634	1
New York	45	37	.549	8
Washington	31	51	.378	22
Miami Heat	18	64	.220	35
New Jersey	17	65	.207	36

Central Division

	W	L	Pct.	GB
Detroit	59	23	.720	—
Chicago	55	27	.671	4
Milwaukee	44	38	.537	15
Cleveland	42	40	.512	17
Indiana	42	40	.512	17
Atlanta	41	41	.500	18
Orlando	18	64	.220	41

Western Conference
Midwest Division

	W	L	Pct.	GB
San Antonio	56	26	.683	—
Utah	55	27	.671	1
Dallas	47	35	.573	9
Denver	43	39	.524	13
Houston	41	41	.500	15
Minnesota	22	60	.268	34
Charlotte	19	63	.232	37

Pacific Division

	W	L	Pct.	GB
LA Lakers	63	19	.768	—
Portland	59	23	.720	4
Phoenix	54	28	.659	9
Seattle	41	41	.500	22
Golden State	37	45	.451	26
LA Clippers	30	52	.366	33
Sacramento	23	59	.280	40

AWARDS

MVP
Magic Johnson, LA Lakers
Top Rookie
David Robinson, San Antonio
Coach of Year
Pat Riley, LA Lakers
Defensive Player of Year
Dennis Rodman, Detroit
Sixth Man Award
Ricky Pierce, Milwaukee
Most Improved Player
Rony Seikaly, Miami
Citizenship Award
Glenn Rivers, Atlanta

ALL-STAR GAME
Miami Arena, Miami
Sunday, February 11, 1990
East 130, West 113
MVP: Magic Johnson

ALL-STAR TEAMS

FIRST TEAM

Karl Malone	Utah
Charles Barkley	Philadelphia
Patrick Ewing	New York
Magic Johnson	LA Lakers
Michael Jordan	Chicago

SECOND TEAM

Larry Bird	Boston
Tom Chambers	Phoenix
Hakeem Olajuwon	Houston
John Stockton	Utah
Kevin Johnson	Phoenix

THIRD TEAM

James Worthy	LA Lakers
Chris Mullin	Golden State
David Robinson	San Antonio
Clyde Drexler	Portland
Joe Dumars	Detroit

PLAYOFFS
FINALS
Detroit 4, Portland 1
June 5: Portland 99 at Detroit 105
June 7: Portland 106 at Detroit 105, OT
June 10: Detroit 121 at Portland 106
June 12: Detroit 112 at Portland 109
June 14: Detroit 92 at Portland 90
EASTERN CONFERENCE
CONFERENCE FINALS
Detroit 4, Chicago 3
May 20: Chicago 77 at Detroit 86
May 22: Chicago 93 at Detroit 102
May 26: Detroit 102 at Chicago 107
May 28: Detroit 101 at Chicago 108
May 30: Chicago 83 at Detroit 97
June 1: Detroit 91 at Chicago 109
June 3: Chicago 74 at Detroit 93
CONFERENCE SEMI-FINALS
Chicago 4, Philadelphia 1
May 7: Philadelphia 85 at Chicago 96
May 9: Philadelphia 96 at Chicago 101
May 11: Chicago 112 at Philadelphia 118
May 13: Chicago 111 at Philadelphia 101
May 16: Philadelphia 99 at Chicago 117
Detroit 4, New York 1
May 8: New York 77 at Detroit 112
May 10: New York 97 at Detroit 104
May 12: Detroit 103 at New York 111
May 13: Detroit 102 at New York 90
May 15: New York 84 at Detroit 95

FIRST ROUND
New York 3, Boston 2
Apr. 26: New York 105 at Boston 116
Apr. 28: New York 128 at Boston 157
May 2: Boston 99 at New York 102
May 4: Boston 108 at New York 135
May 6: New York 121 at Boston 114
Detroit 3, Indiana 0
Apr. 26: Indiana 92 at Detroit 104
Apr. 28: Indiana 87 at Detroit 100
May 1: Detroit 108 at Indiana 96
Philadelphia 3, Cleveland 2
Apr. 26: Cleveland 106 at Philadelphia 111
Apr. 29: Cleveland 101 at Philadelphia 107
May 1: Philadelphia 95 at Cleveland 122
May 3: Philadelphia 96 at Cleveland 108
May 5: Cleveland 97 at Philadelphia 113
Chicago 3, Milwaukee 1
Apr. 27: Milwaukee 97 at Chicago 111
Apr. 29: Milwaukee 102 at Chicago 109
May 1: Chicago 112 at Milwaukee 119
May 3: Chicago 110 at Milwaukee 86
WESTERN CONFERENCE
Portland 4, Phoenix 2
May 21: Phoenix 98 at Portland 100
May 23: Phoenix 107 at Portland 108
May 25: Portland 89 at Phoenix 123
May 27: Portland 107 at Phoenix 119
May 29: Phoenix 114 at Portland 120
May 31: Portland 109 at Phoenix 109
CONFERENCE SEMI-FINALS
Portland 4, San Antonio 3
May 5: San Antonio 94 at Portland 107

May 8: San Antonio 112 at Portland 122
May 10: Portland 98 at San Antonio 121
May 12: Portland 105 at San Antonio 115
May 15: San Antonio 132 at Portland 138, 2OT
May 17: Portland 97 at San Antonio 112
May 19: San Antonio 105 at Portland 108, OT
Phoenix 4, L.A. Lakers 1
May 8: Phoenix 104 at L.A. Lakers 102
May 10: Phoenix 100 at L.A. Lakers 124
May 12: L.A. Lakers 103 at Phoenix 117
May 13: L.A. Lakers 101 at Phoenix 114
May 15: Phoenix 106 at L.A. Lakers 103
FIRST ROUND
L.A. Lakers 3, Houston 1
Apr. 27: Houston 89 at L.A. Lakers 101
Apr. 29: Houston 100 at L.A. Lakers 104
May 1: L.A. Lakers 108 at Houston 114
May 3: L.A. Lakers 109 at Houston 88
Phoenix 3, Utah 2
Apr. 27: Phoenix 96 at Utah 113
Apr. 29: Phoenix 105 at Utah 87
May 2: Utah 105 at Phoenix 120
May 4: Utah 105 at Phoenix 94
May 6: Phoenix 104 at Utah 102
San Antonio 3, Denver 0
Apr. 26: Denver 103 at San Antonio 119
Apr. 28: Denver 120 at San Antonio 129
May 1: San Antonio 131 at Denver 120
Portland 3, Dallas 0
Apr. 26: Dallas 102 at Portland 109
Apr. 2: Dallas 107 at Portland 114
May 1: Portland 106 at Dallas 92

NBA LEADERS

SCORING

	GP	FGM	FTM	PTS	PPG
Michael Jordan, CHI	82	1034	593	2753	33.6
Karl Malone, UTJ	82	914	696	2540	31.0
Patrick Ewing, NYK	82	922	502	2347	28.6
Tom Chambers, PHO	81	810	557	2201	27.2
Dominique Wilkins, ATL	80	810	459	2138	26.7
Charles Barkley, PHI	79	706	557	1989	25.2
Chris Mullin, GST	78	682	505	1956	25.1
Reggie Miller, IND	82	661	544	2016	24.6
Hakeem Olajuwon, HOU	82	806	382	1995	24.3
David Robinson, SAS	82	690	613	1993	24.3
Larry Bird, BOS	75	718	319	1820	24.3
Jeff Malone, WSB	75	781	257	1820	24.3

FIELD GOALS

	FGM	FGA	FG%
Mark West, PHO	331	530	.625
Charles Barkley, PHI	706	1177	.600
Robert Parish, BOS	505	871	.580
Karl Malone, UTJ	914	1627	.562
Orlando Woolridge, LAL	306	550	.556
Patrick Ewing, NYK	922	1673	.551
Kevin McHale, BOS	648	1181	.549
Otis Thorpe, HOU	547	998	.548
James Worthy, LAL	711	1298	.548
Buck Williams, POR	413	754	.548

THREE POINT FIELD GOALS

	3PM	3PA	3P%
Steve Kerr, CLE	73	144	.507
Craig Hodges, CHI	87	181	.481
Drazen Petrovic, POR	34	74	.459
Jon Sundvold, MIA	44	100	.440
Byron Scott, LAL	93	220	.423
Hersey Hawkins, PHI	84	200	.420
Craig Ehlo, CLE	104	248	.419
John Stockton, UTJ	47	113	.416
Reggie Miller, IND	150	362	.414
Fat Lever, DEN	36	87	.414

FREE THROWS

	FTM	FTA	FT%
Larry Bird, BOS	319	343	.930
Eddie Johnson, PHO	188	205	.917
Walter Davis, DEN	207	227	.912
Joe Dumars, DET	297	330	.900
Kevin McHale, BOS	393	440	.893
Terry Porter, POR	421	472	.892
Magic Johnson, LAL	567	637	.890
Chris Mullin, GST	505	568	.889
Hersey Hawkins, PHI	387	436	.888
Mark Price, CLE	300	338	.888

ASSISTS

	GP	AST	APG
John Stockton, UTJ	78	1134	14.5
Magic Johnson, LAL	79	907	11.5
Kevin Johnson, PHO	74	846	11.4
Muggsy Bogues, CHA	81	867	10.7
Gary Grant, LAC	44	442	10.0
Isiah Thomas, DET	81	765	9.4
Mark Price, CLE	73	666	9.1
Terry Porter, POR	80	726	9.1
Tim Hardaway, GST	79	689	8.7
Darrell Walker, WSB	81	652	8.0

REBOUNDS

	GP	ORB	DRB	TRB	RPG
Hakeem Olajuwon, HOU	82	299	850	1149	14.0
David Robinson, SAS	82	303	680	983	12.0
Charles Barkley, PHI	79	361	548	909	11.5
Karl Malone, UTJ	82	232	679	911	11.1
Patrick Ewing, NYK	82	235	658	893	10.9
Rony Seikaly, MIA	74	253	513	766	10.4
Robert Parish, BOS	79	259	537	796	10.1
Moses Malone, ATL	81	364	448	812	10.0
Michael Cage, SEA	82	306	515	821	10.0
Buck Williams, POR	82	250	550	800	9.8

STEALS

	GP	STL	SPG
Michael Jordan, CHI	82	227	2.77
John Stockton, UTJ	78	207	2.65
Scottie Pippen, CHI	82	211	2.57
Alvin Robertson, MIL	81	207	2.56
Derek Harper, DAL	82	187	2.28
Tyrone Corbin, MIN	82	175	2.13
Fat Lever, DEN	79	168	2.13
Hakeem Olajuwon, HOU	82	174	2.12
Lester Conner, NJN	82	172	2.10
Tim Hardaway, GST	79	165	2.09

BLOCKS

	GP	BLK	BPG
Hakeem Olajuwon, HOU	82	376	4.59
Patrick Ewing, NYK	82	327	3.99
David Robinson, SAS	82	319	3.89
Manute Bol, GST	75	238	3.17
Benoit Benjamin, LAC	71	187	2.63
Mark Eaton, UTJ	82	201	2.45
Charles Jones, WSB	81	197	2.43
Mark West, PHO	82	184	2.24
Rik Smits, IND	82	169	2.06
Hot Rod Williams, CLE	82	167	2.04

TURNOVERS

	GP	TO	TPG
Gary Grant, LAC	44	207	4.7
Isiah Thomas, DET	81	324	4.0
Hakeem Olajuwon, HOU	82	320	3.9
Magic Johnson, LAL	79	292	3.7
Karl Malone, UTJ	82	303	3.7
Kevin Johnson, PHO	74	266	3.6
John Stockton, UTJ	78	273	3.5
Patrick Ewing, NYK	82	279	3.4
Scottie Pippen, CHI	82	279	3.4
Tim Hardaway, GST	79	261	3.3

THE YEAR IN BASKETBALL

October 21, 1989 Betram Lee and Peter Bynoe become the first black owners of a major sports team when they buy the Nuggets for $65M.

November 9, 1989 Seattle's Dale Ellis sets a record by playing 69 out of 73 minutes in a five-OT game won by Milwaukee, 155-154.

November 18, 1989 Two players from the Soviet Union—the Hawks' Alexander Volkov and Warriors' Sarunas Marciulionis—compete against each other in a NBA game for the first time in history.

January 15, 1990 Trent Tucker of the Knicks catches, spins, and fires a three-point shot all with one-tenth of a second on the clock to beat Chicago, 109-106. The Bulls argue that no one can catch and release a shot within that time, but the basket counts. The controversy leads to a rule that states a player needs at least three-tenths of a second to make a shot.

February 17, 1990 Lisa Leslie of Morningside High School in Inglewood, Cal., scores 101 points *in the first half* against South Torrance High. Trailing 102-24 at half-time and upset over Morningside's tactic of purposely feeding Leslie, the South Torrance coach refuses to bring his team out for the second half, ending the game.

March 4, 1990 Hank Gathers, Loyola Marymount's star forward and the nation's leading scorer and rebounder, collapses and dies during a West Coast Conference tournament game against Portland. He was 23.

March 28, 1990 Michael Jordan scores 69 points, his career best, as Chicago beats Cleveland, 117-113, in OT and clinches a playoff spot.

March 28, 1990 Vanderbilt win the NIT by edging Saint Louis, 74-72.

April 1, 1990 Stanford beats Auburn, 88-81, to win the NCAA women's championship.

April 2, 1990 UNLV crushes Duke, 103-73 to give coach Jerry Tarkanian his first NCAA championship.

April 28, 1990 The Celtics set playoff records for most points in a game and highest field goal percentage, when they rout the Knicks, 157-128, in Game 2 of the Eastern Conference finals in Boston.

June 14, 1990 Vinnie Johnson hits a 15-footer with 0.7 seconds left, propelling Detroit to its second straight NBA title, over Portland, 92-90.

1990-91

Changing of the guard as Jordan leads Bulls' run

With the NBA starting its first season in the new decade, it was apparent that some things hadn't changed. In the first week of the new season Golden State defeated Denver, 162-158, setting an NBA record for most points scored by two teams in a regulation game. A week later Denver played toreador defense again, letting Phoenix ring up 173 points, including a record 107 in the first half. Even without Alex English, who had led the previous decade in scoring and had gone to Dallas as a free agent, the Nuggets had no trouble panning for points. They led the league with 120 a game. But they also gave up 131 a game. The result was a 20-62 mark under coach Paul Westhead, the worst record in the league.

Playing his second season in Atlanta and third decade overall, Moses Malone was still up to his old ways, getting to the free throw line. In the new season's first week he broke Oscar Robertson's career free throws record (7,694).

One of the biggest steps was taken by Orlando in their second season. They improved from 18 wins to 31. Chicago's leap from 55 to 61 wins wasn't nearly as dramatic, though they made up an impressive 15 games in the standings, finishing 11 games ahead of Detroit to take the Central title, instead of four behind them as in 1989-90.

Michael Jordan was in his familiar spot on the leader boards. He clinched his fifth consecutive scoring title (31.5), comfortably ahead of Karl Malone (29). Jordan was also third in the league in steals (2.72), joining teammate Scottie Pippen (2.35) for top ten in the theft department Third in scoring was Washington's Bernard King (28.4), fully recovered from the anterior cruciate ligament tear he suffered with New York more than five years before. Fulfilling his goal, King made the All-Star team. Charles Barkley enjoyed another all-around season. He finished fourth in scoring (27.6) and field goal percentage (.570), though Philadelphia won nine less games than the year before. Patrick Ewing (26.6) enjoyed his best scoring season to date and joined teammate Charles Oakley among the top ten finishers in caroms.

Detroit still brandished its physical, defensive swagger, led by Bill Laimbeer, Joe Dumars, Dennis Rodman, James Edwards, and John Salley off the bench. They allowed just 97 points per game, three ahead of anyone else. Los Angeles, Utah, and Chicago were just behind them in defense and Chicago was also sixth in the league in scoring (110), giving them a nine-point margin of victory, the circuit's largest differential.

It was a season for other milestones. Moses Malone and Alex English both reached 25,000 points and Larry Bird reached 20,000. Michael Jordan reached 15,000 points in just his 460th career game (32.6). The only player to reach it faster was Wilt Chamberlain (358 games, 41.9).

Malone wasn't the only player to set an all-time record.

Michael Jordan
In tears, hugging the Larry O'Brien Championship Trophy after leading Chicago to its first-ever NBA title over the Lakers in five games.

Orlando's 6-foot-1 Scott Skiles got 30 assists in a December 30, 1990 game against—you guessed it—Denver. Kevin Porter had held the mark of 29, set more than a decade before. John Stockton broke his own single season assist record, finishing with 1,164, breaking his previous high of 1,134 set the year before. On April 15, Magic Johnson logged 19 assists to pass Oscar Robertson and move into first place on the all-time list. Vernon Maxwell also found his way into the record books when he became only the fifth player to score 30 points in a quarter, joining Wilt Chamberlain, David Thompson, George Gervin and Michael Jordan in that distinction. Maxwell's 30 came in the fourth quarter of a 103-97 win over Cleveland.

The most remarkable part of All-Star weekend in the Charlotte Coliseum didn't involve the game itself. Chicago's Craig Hodges hit an astounding 19 consecutive three-pointers in the three-point competition. Sloppy play ruled the East-West game. Despite 51 turnovers, the game had a dramatic finish. With the West trailing 116-114, Kevin Johnson hoisted a three-pointer that looked on the mark. But Utah's Karl Malone inexplicably grabbed the ball to redirect the shot and was called

for offensive goal-tending with 2.9 seconds left. On the strength of 22 rebounds, the most since Wilt Chamberlain plucked that many in 1967, Barkley was awarded the game MVP.

As the post-season began, it looked as if the Finals would bring together Portland and Chicago, the teams with the best records. Chicago, winners of 61, began a determined march through the Eastern Conference with a three-zip elimination of New York. Meanwhile, Portland, winners of a league-best 63, had to go the limit in a mini-series with Seattle, before routing Utah in five. For the fourth straight season, Chicago would have to face Detroit, who had used a physical style of play to defeat them the last three years in a row. Chicago won the first two games and then a third in Detroit. In Game 4 Chicago won easily 115-94, with several Pistons walking off the court before the game ended. This was payback for Jordan's remark that the Pistons were not true champs because of their rough play.

An anticipated Final between Portland and Chicago did not occur, as Los Angeles topped Portland in six games. It was Los Angeles vs. Chicago, the old guard and winner of five titles, Magic Johnson, versus the league's best player still in search of a championship, Michael Jordan. After a Jordan jumper, the Bulls led Game 1, 91-89, with 23 seconds left. L.A. coach Mike Dunleavy diagrammed a three-pointer for Sam Perkins, who connected with 9 seconds left. Chicago called Jordan's number but his shot went in and out at the buzzer. In Game 2, the Bulls won easily, 107-86. The change occurred at half-time, when Chicago had Pippen guard Magic, since Jordan was picking up fouls. In Game 3, the Lakers took a 13-point lead. But the Bulls came back to tie the game at 74 with 8 minutes left in the third quarter. Pippen fouled out on a Vlade Divac three-pointer, but Jordan, with seconds remaining, hit a jumper over Byron Scott and Divac to send the game into overtime, where Chicago won 104-96. Chicago won 97-82 in Game 4. A late six-point run by L.A. put them up briefly in Game 5 but Chicago prevailed, 108-101. Jordan hit 56 percent of his shots, and averaged 31 points, 11 assists and 6 rebounds to win the Finals MVP. In Michael Jordan's seventh season he finally got the championship he coveted.

1990-91 SEASON HIGHLIGHTS

STANDINGS

Eastern Conference
Atlantic Division

	W	L	Pct.	GB
Boston	56	26	.683	—
Philadelphia	44	38	.537	12
New York	39	43	.476	17
Washington	30	52	.366	26
New Jersey	26	56	.317	30
Miami Heat	24	58	.293	32

Central Division

	W	L	Pct.	GB
Chicago	61	21	.744	—
Detroit	50	32	.610	11
Milwaukee	48	34	.585	13
Atlanta	43	39	.524	18
Indiana	41	41	.500	20
Cleveland	33	49	.402	28
Charlotte	26	56	.317	35

Western Conference
Midwest Division

	W	L	Pct.	GB
San Antonio	55	27	.671	—
Utah	54	28	.659	1
Houston	52	30	.634	3
Orlando	31	51	.378	24
Minnesota	29	53	.354	26
Dallas	28	54	.341	27
Denver	20	62	.244	35

Pacific Division

	W	L	Pct.	GB
Portland	63	19	.768	—
LA Lakers	58	24	.707	5
Phoenix	55	27	.671	8
Golden State	44	38	.537	19
Seattle	41	41	.500	22
LA Clippers	31	51	.378	32
Sacramento	25	57	.305	38

AWARDS

MVP
Magic Johnson, LA Lakers
Top Rookie
Mitch Richmond, GS
Coach of Year
Cotton Fitzsimmons, Phoenix
Defensive Player of Year
Mark Eaton, Utah
Sixth Man Award
Eddie Johnson, Phoenix
Most Improved Player
Kevin Johnson, Phoenix
Citizenship Award
Thurl Bailey, Utah

ALL-STAR GAME
Astrodome, Houston
Sunday, February 12, 1989
West 143, East 134
MVP: Karl Malone

ALL-STAR TEAMS

FIRST TEAM

Karl Malone	Utah
Charles Barkley	Philadelphia
David Robinson	San Antonio
Michael Jordan	Chicago
Magic Johnson	LA Lakers

SECOND TEAM

Dominique Wilkins	Atlanta
Chris Mullin	Golden State
Patrick Ewing	New York
Kevin Johnson	Phoenix
Clyde Drexler	Portland

THIRD TEAM

James Worthy	LA Lakers
Bernard King	Washington
Hakeem Olajuwon	Houston
John Stockton	Utah
Joe Dumars	Detroit

PLAYOFFS

FINALS
Chicago 4, L.A. Lakers 1
June 2: L.A. Lakers 93 at Chicago 91
June 5: L.A. Lakers 86 at Chicago 107
June 7: Chicago 104 at L.A. Lakers 96, OT
June 9: Chicago 97 at L.A. Lakers 82
June 12: Chicago 108 at L.A. Lakers 101

EASTERN CONFERENCE
CONFERENCE FINALS
Chicago 4, Detroit 0
May 19: Detroit 83 at Chicago 94
May 21: Detroit 97 at Chicago 105
May 25: Chicago 113 at Detroit 107
May 27: Chicago 115 at Detroit 94

CONFERENCE SEMI-FINALS
Chicago 4, Philadelphia 1
May 4: Philadelphia 92 at Chicago 105
May 6: Philadelphia 100 at Chicago 112
May 10: Chicago 97 at Philadelphia 99
May 12: Chicago 101 at Philadelphia 85
May 14: Philadelphia 95 at Chicago 100

Detroit 4, Boston 2
May 7: Detroit 86 at Boston 75
May 9: Detroit 103 at Boston 109
May 11: Boston 115 at Detroit 83
May 13: Boston 97 at Detroit 104
May 15: Detroit 116 at Boston 111
May 17: Boston 113 at Detroit 117, OT

FIRST ROUND
Chicago 3, New York 0
Apr. 25: New York 85 at Chicago 126

Apr. 28: New York 79 at Chicago 89
Apr. 30: Chicago 103 at New York 94

Boston 3, Indiana 2
Apr. 26: Indiana 120 at Boston 127
Apr. 28: Indiana 130 at Boston 118
May 1: Boston 112 at Indiana 105
May 3: Boston 113 at Indiana 116
May 5: Indiana 121 at Boston 124

Detroit 3, Atlanta 2
Apr. 26: Atlanta 103 at Detroit 98
Apr. 28: Atlanta 88 at Detroit 101
Apr. 30: Detroit 103 at Atlanta 91
May 2: Detroit 111 at Atlanta 123
May 5: Atlanta 81 at Detroit 113

Philadelphia 3, Milwaukee 0
Apr. 25: Philadelphia 99 at Milwaukee 90
Apr. 27: Philadelphia 116 at Milwaukee 112, OT
Apr. 30: Milwaukee 100 at Philadelphia 121

WESTERN CONFERENCE
CONFERENCE FINALS
L.A. Lakers 4, Portland 2
May 18: L.A. Lakers 111 at Portland 106
May 21: L.A. Lakers 98 at Portland 109
May 24: Portland 92 at L.A. Lakers 106
May 26: Portland 95 at L.A. Lakers 116
May 28: L.A. Lakers 84 at Portland 95
May 30: Portland 90 at L.A. Lakers 91

CONFERENCE SEMI-FINALS
L.A. Lakers 4, Golden State 1
May 5: Golden State 116 at L.A. Lakers 126
May 8: Golden State 125 at L.A. Lakers 124
May 10: L.A. Lakers 115 at Golden State 112

May 12: L.A. Lakers 123 at Golden State 107
May 14: Golden State 119 at L.A. Lakers 124, OT

Portland 4, Utah 1
May 7: Utah 97 at Portland 117
May 9: Utah 116 at Portland 118
May 11: Portland 101 at Utah 107
May 12: Portland 104 at Utah 101
May 14: Utah 96 at Portland 103

FIRST ROUND
Portland 3, Seattle 2
Apr. 26: Seattle 102 at Portland 110
Apr. 28: Seattle 106 at Portland 115
Apr. 30: Portland 99 at Seattle 102
May 2: Portland 89 at Seattle 101
May 4: Seattle 107 at Portland 119

Golden State 3, San Antonio 1
Apr. 25: Golden State 121 at San Antonio 130
Apr. 27: Golden State 111 at San Antonio 98
May 1: San Antonio 106 at Golden State 109
May 3: San Antonio 97 at Golden State 110

L.A. Lakers 3, Houston 0
Apr. 26: Houston 92 at L.A. Lakers 94
Apr. 27: Houston 98 at L.A. Lakers 109
Apr. 30: L.A. Lakers 94 at Houston 90

Utah 3, Phoenix 1
Apr. 25: Utah 129 at Phoenix 90
Apr. 27: Utah 92 at Phoenix 102
Apr. 30: Phoenix 98 at Utah 107
May 2: Phoenix 93 at Utah 101

NBA LEADERS

SCORING

	GP	FGM	FTM	PTS	PPG
Michael Jordan, CHI	82	990	571	2580	31.5
Karl Malone, UTJ	82	847	684	2382	29.0
Bernard King, WSB	64	713	383	1817	28.4
Charles Barkley, PHI	67	665	475	1849	27.6
Patrick Ewing, NYK	81	845	464	2154	26.6
Michael Adams, DEN	66	560	465	1752	26.5
Dominique Wilkins, ATL	81	770	476	2101	25.9
Chris Mullin, GST	82	777	513	2107	25.7
David Robinson, SAS	82	754	592	2101	25.6
Mitch Richmond, GST	77	703	394	1840	23.9

FIELD GOALS

	FGM	FGA	FG%
Buck Williams, POR	358	595	.602
Robert Parish, BOS	485	811	.598
Kevin Gamble, BOS	548	933	.587
Charles Barkley, PHI	665	1167	.570
Vlade Divac, LAL	360	637	.565
Olden Polynice, SEA/LAC	316	564	.560
Otis Thorpe, HOU	549	988	.556
Kevin McHale, BOS	504	912	.553
David Robinson, SAS	754	1366	.552
John Paxson, CHI	317	578	.548

THREE POINT FIELD GOALS

	3PM	3PA	3P%
Jim Les, SAC	71	154	.461
Trent Tucker, NYK	64	153	.418
Jeff Hornacek, PHO	61	146	.418
Terry Porter, POR	130	313	.415
Scott Skiles, ORL	93	228	.408
Danny Ainge, POR	102	251	.406
Hersey Hawkins, PHI	108	270	.400
Larry Bird, BOS	77	198	.389
Glen Rice, MIA	71	184	.386
Tim Hardaway, GST	97	252	.385

FREE THROWS

	FTM	FTA	FT%
Reggie Miller, IND	551	600	.918
Jeff Malone, UTJ	231	252	.917
Ricky Pierce, MIL/SEA	430	471	.913
Kelly Tripucka, CHA	152	167	.910
Magic Johnson, LAL	519	573	.906
Scott Skiles, ORL	340	377	.902
Kiki Vandeweghe, NYK	259	288	.899
Jeff Hornacek, PHO	201	224	.897
Eddie Johnson, PHO/SEA	229	257	.891
Larry Bird, BOS	163	183	.891

ASSISTS

	GP	AST	APG
John Stockton, UTJ	82	1164	14.2
Magic Johnson, LAL	79	989	12.5
Michael Adams, DEN	66	693	10.5
Kevin Johnson, PHO	77	781	10.1
Tim Hardaway, GST	82	793	9.7
Isiah Thomas, DET	48	446	9.3
Pooh Richardson, MIN	82	734	9.0
Gary Grant, LAC	68	587	8.6
Sherman Douglas, MIA	73	624	8.5
Scott Skiles, ORL	79	660	8.4

REBOUNDS

	GP	ORB	DRB	TRB	RPG
David Robinson, SAS	82	335	728	1063	13.0
Dennis Rodman, DET	82	361	665	1026	12.5
Charles Oakley, NYK	76	305	615	920	12.1
Karl Malone, UTJ	82	236	731	967	11.8
Patrick Ewing, NYK	81	194	711	905	11.2
Brad Daugherty, CLE	76	177	653	830	10.9
Robert Parish, BOS	81	271	585	856	10.6
Benoit Benjamin, LAC/SEA	70	157	566	723	10.3
Otis Thorpe, HOU	82	287	559	846	10.3
Derrick Coleman, NJN	74	269	490	759	10.3

STEALS

	GP	STL	SPG
Alvin Robertson, MIL	81	246	3.04
John Stockton, UTJ	82	234	2.85
Michael Jordan, CHI	82	223	2.72
Tim Hardaway, GST	82	214	2.61
Scottie Pippen, CHI	82	193	2.35
Mookie Blaylock, NJN	72	169	2.35
Michael Adams, DEN	66	147	2.23
Hersey Hawkins, PHI	80	178	2.23
Kevin Johnson, PHO	77	163	2.12
Chris Mullin, GST	82	173	2.11

BLOCKS

	GP	BLK	BPG
Hakeem Olajuwon, HOU	56	221	3.95
David Robinson, SAS	82	320	3.90
Patrick Ewing, NYK	81	258	3.19
Manute Bol, PHI	82	247	3.01
Chris Dudley, NJN	61	153	2.51
Larry Nance, CLE	80	200	2.50
Mark Eaton, UTJ	80	188	2.35
Kevin McHale, BOS	68	146	2.15
Benoit Benjamin, LAC/SEA	70	145	2.07
Pervis Ellison, WSB	76	157	2.07

TURNOVERS

	GP	TO	TPG
Magic Johnson, LAL	79	316	4.0
Bernard King, WSB	64	256	4.0
Isiah Thomas, DET	48	187	3.9
Sherman Douglas, MIA	73	270	3.7
Michael Adams, DEN	66	238	3.6
Patrick Ewing, NYK	81	292	3.6
John Stockton, UTJ	82	295	3.6
Kevin Johnson, PHO	77	270	3.5
Benoit Benjamin, LAC/SEA	70	233	3.3
Ron Harper, LAC	39	129	3.3

THE YEAR IN BASKETBALL

November 2, 1990 In the first regular season NBA game played outside North America by any major pro sports league, the Phoenix Suns beat the Utah Jazz, 119-96, in Tokyo. The next night Utah wins, 102-101.

November 2, 1990 Golden State beats Denver, 162-158, in Denver, setting an NBA record of most points scored in a OT game.

November 3, 1990 Moses Malone of Atlanta passes Oscar Robertson for most career free throws made when he makes seven of nine foul shots in a 121-120 win over Indiana at the Omni in Atlanta.

November 10, 1990 Phoenix scores an NBA-record 107 points in the first half against a defenseless Nuggets' squad, in a 173-143 victory.

December 3, 1990 The Boston Celtics honor announcer Johnny Most by unveiling a banner bearing a microphone.

December 23, 1990 In a game that took 26 days to decide, the Celtics beat the Hawks, 132-104, at Boston Garden. The game began on November 28, but a wet playing surface, caused by condensation from the ice underneath the parquet floor, forced postponement of the game 90 seconds into the second quarter with the Celtics ahead, 37-22.

December 30, 1990 Scott Skiles of Orlando gets an NBA-record 30 assists in a 155-116 defeat of Denver.

February 2, 1991 New Hampshire snaps its record 32-game home losing streak with a 72-56 win over Holy Cross.

March 27, 1991 Stanford, behind star forward Adam Keefe, wins its first NIT, stopping Oklahoma, 78-72.

March 31, 1991 Tennessee captures its third NCAA women's title with a 70-67 overtime victory over Virginia.

April 1, 1991 Duke defeats Kansas, 72-65, in the NCAA title game.

April 15, 1991 The Sacramento Kings set an NBA record by losing their 35th consecutive road game.

April 15, 1991 Magic Johnson of the Lakers hands out 19 assists in a 112-106 win over Dallas. The total propels Johnson past Oscar Robertson into first place on the career assist list.

April 18, 1991 John Stockton breaks his own single-season assist record as Utah routs Seattle, 130-103. Stockton's 11 assists give him 1,136 for the season, two more than the record he set in 1989-90.

June 12, 1991 The Chicago Bulls win their first NBA title, defeating the Lakers, 108-101, in Game 5.

1991-92

Magic a magic all-star, but Jordan's MVPs prove torch has passed

The new season hadn't begun when Roy Tarpley, a center of great promise for the Dallas Mavericks, was banned from the NBA for life after violating the league's anti-drug agreement. (In actuality, he would play 55 more games the following season before bowing out permanently.) The season had barely begun when Magic Johnson addressed a phalanx of reporters, telling them he would retire because he contracted HIV, the virus that causes AIDS.

It would fall to the Sacramento Kings to bring some levity to the league, winning their first road game after a league record 43 consecutive losses. Their win in Orlando came a year and three days after their last road win in Washington. Miami could also laugh, though not right away. In December they lost to Cleveland, 148-80, the 68-point difference representing the largest margin of victory in league history. The Heat trailed by "only" 20 at the half, before Cleveland iced them with a 75-27 second half.

Magic Johnson
His November 1991 press conference announcing he had tested positive for the HIV virus didn't end his on-court career. He returned for the All-Star Game, the Olympics and later, briefly, to the Lakers.

Given the big picture, Miami had cause for celebration. Led by Glen Rice and Rony Seikaly, they jumped from 24 wins to 38, good enough to make the playoffs in their fourth season. New York also did an about-face under their new coach Pat Riley. After a year spent broadcasting, Riley signed a five-year deal with New York and lifted them from their previous 39 wins to 51 for a tie with Boston atop the Atlantic Division. In the west, Golden State took a leap forward. Behind Chris Mullin, Tim Hardaway and Sarunas Marciulionis, they scored a league-best 119 points a game.

With Magic Johnson's name on the All-Star Game ballot, fans voted him into the starting lineup for the West. Johnson was outstanding, putting up 25 points and nine assists, and winning the MVP award in the only game he played in the entire season.

The game itself was a 153-113 blowout for the West, but emotions ran high. After the pre-game introductions, the entire East team walked to the other side of the court and embraced Johnson. The game concluded with Johnson, in a pair of good-natured one-on-one duels in the final minute. First, with the ball in Isiah Thomas' hands, Johnson signaled his friend to try and drive on him. Thomas dribbled between his legs and behind his back, then moved toward the basket and tried a jumper with Johnson contesting him. The shot missed. A few seconds later, Johnson went one-on-one with Michael Jordan, who gave Johnson a head fake before sinking a jump shot. Johnson owned the final highlight, though, hoisting an off-balance three-pointer to cap a memorable event.

Chicago stormed out of the gates, beginning with a 14-3 record. They won 67 games, earning homecourt advantage throughout the playoffs.

In the post-season, they first faced Miami, who must have wondered about the value of reaching their first post-season. The Bulls took both games in Chicago, 113-94 and 120-90. Jordan scored 56 in Game 3 three for a 119-114 finish. Next came New York, who shocked the Bulls in Game 1, beating them, 94-89, in Chicago. Defense was on the menu in Games 2 and 3 as Chicago won, 86-78 and again, 94-86, to regain homecourt advantage. With Xavier McDaniel and Charles Oakley getting as physical and intimidating as the rules would allow, New York won two of the next three and got a seventh game. But Chicago won a blowout in Game 7, 110-81. Cleveland was next. The Cavaliers stomped Chicago 107-81 in Game 2 and knotted the series at two games each in Cleveland. But Chicago won easily in Game 5, 112-89, and then at Cleveland 99-94.

In the Western Conference, Portland throttled L.A. in four games, avenging the loss the year before. Phoenix and Utah were the next victims and now came a showdown between the teams with the best records in each conference and the two players now considered to be the league best—Jordan and Clyde Drexler.

Jordan was awarded his third MVP before the 1992 Finals. Despite Portland hitting their first seven field goal attempts, Chicago breezed to a 122-89 win as Michael Jordan hit six consecutive three-pointers. In the second game Chicago led by ten points in the fourth quarter. But Danny Ainge and Terry Porter sparked a comeback. Tied at 97, the Bulls had the ball with 13.2 seconds left. Jordan missed at the buzzer to send it into overtime, where Ainge and Porter dominated, as Portland won 115-104.

Accomplishing what would become their trademark, Chicago took back homecourt advantage in Game 3, 94-84. Portland evened the series at home but dropped Game 5, 119-106. Facing elimination, the Blazers used the running game to take a 73-58 lead with 2:32 remaining in the third period of Game 6. They led 79-64 after three quarters. With Jordan on the bench, a Chicago reserve, Bobby Hansen, hit a three. Then a flagrant foul against Portland gave Chicago free throws and possession. Portland unraveled. After a 14-2 run, Chicago had the lead down to three. Jordan then returned and Chicago won, 97-94, with Jordan pacing the Bulls with 33 points. He was awarded his second consecutive Finals MVP.

1991-92 SEASON HIGHLIGHTS

STANDINGS

Eastern Conference
Atlantic Division

	W	L	Pct.	GB
Boston	51	31	.622	—
New York	51	31	.622	—
New Jersey	40	42	.488	11
Miami Heat	38	44	.463	13
Philadelphia	35	47	.427	16
Washington	25	57	.305	26
Orlando	21	61	.256	30

Central Division

	W	L	Pct.	GB
Chicago	67	15	.817	—
Cleveland	57	25	.695	10
Detroit	48	34	.585	19
Indiana	40	42	.488	27
Atlanta	38	44	.463	29
Charlotte	31	51	.378	36
Milwaukee	31	51	.378	36

Western Conference
Midwest Division

	W	L	Pct.	GB
Utah	55	27	.671	—
San Antonio	47	35	.573	8
Houston	42	40	.512	13
Denver	24	58	.293	31
Dallas	22	60	.268	33
Minnesota	15	67	.183	40

Pacific Division

	W	L	Pct.	GB
Portland	57	25	.695	—
Golden State	55	27	.671	2
Phoenix	53	29	.646	4
Seattle	47	35	.573	10
LA Clippers	45	37	.549	12
LA Lakers	43	39	.524	14
Sacramento	29	53	.354	28

AWARDS
MVP
Michael Jordan, Chicago
Top Rookie
Larry Johnson, Charlotte
Coach of Year
Don Nelson, Golden State
Defensive Player of Year
David Robinson, San Antonio
Sixth Man Award
Detlef Schrempf, Indiana
Most Improved Player
Pervis Ellison, Washington
Citizenship Award
Magic Johnson, LA Lakers

ALL-STAR GAME
Orlando Arena, Orlando, Florida
Sunday, February 9, 1992
West 153, East 113
MVP: Earvin "Magic" Johnson

ALL-STAR TEAMS
FIRST TEAM

Karl Malone	Utah
Chris Mullin	Golden State
David Robinson	San Antonio
Michael Jordan	Chicago
Clyde Drexler	Portland

SECOND TEAM

Scottie Pippen	Chicago
Charles Barkley	Philadelphia
Patrick Ewing	New York
Tim Hardaway	Golden State
John Stockton	Utah

THIRD TEAM

Dennis Rodman	Detroit
Kevin Willis	Atlanta
Brad Daugherty	Cleveland
Mark Price	Cleveland
Kevin Johnson	Phoenix

PLAYOFFS
FINALS
Chicago 4, Portland 2
June 3: Portland 89 at Chicago 122
June 5: Portland 115 at Chicago 104, OT
June 7: Chicago 94 at Portland 84
June 10: Chicago 88 at Portland 93
June 12: Chicago 119 at Portland 106
June 14: Portland 93 at Chicago 97

EASTERN CONFERENCE
CONFERENCE FINALS
Chicago 4, Cleveland 2
May 19: Cleveland 89 at Chicago 103
May 21: Cleveland 107 at Chicago 81
May 23: Chicago 105 at Cleveland 96
May 25: Chicago 85 at Cleveland 99
May 27: Cleveland 89 at Chicago 112
May 29: Chicago 99 at Cleveland 94

CONFERENCE SEMI-FINALS
Cleveland 4, Boston 3
May 2: Boston 76 at Cleveland 101
May 4: Boston 104 at Cleveland 98
May 8: Cleveland 107 at Boston 110
May 10: Cleveland 114 at Boston 112, OT
May 13: Boston 98 at Cleveland 114
May 15: Cleveland 91 at Boston 122
May 17: Boston 104 at Cleveland 122

Chicago 4, New York 3
May 5: New York 94 at Chicago 89
May 7: New York 78 at Chicago 86
May 9: Chicago 94 at New York 86
May 10: Chicago 86 at New York 93
May 12: New York 88 at Chicago 96
May 14: Chicago 86 at New York 100
May 17: New York 81 at Chicago 110

FIRST ROUND
Chicago 3, Miami 0
Apr. 24: Miami 94 at Chicago 113
Apr. 26: Miami 90 at Chicago 120
Apr. 29: Chicago 119 at Miami 114

Boston 3, Indiana 0
Apr. 23: Indiana 113 at Boston 124
Apr. 25: Indiana 112 at Boston 119, OT
Apr. 27: Boston 102 at Indiana 98

Cleveland 3, New Jersey 1
Apr. 23: New Jersey 113 at Cleveland 120
Apr. 25: New Jersey 96 at Cleveland 118
Apr. 28: Cleveland 104 at New Jersey 109
Apr. 30: Cleveland 98 at New Jersey 89

New York 3, Detroit 2
Apr. 24: Detroit 75 at New York 109
Apr. 26: Detroit 89 at New York 88
Apr. 28: New York 90 at Detroit 87, OT
May 1: New York 82 at Detroit 86
May 3: Detroit 87 at New York 94

WESTERN CONFERENCE
CONFERENCE FINALS
Portland 4, Utah 2
May 16: Utah 88 at Portland 113
May 19: Utah 102 at Portland 119
May 22: Portland 89 at Utah 97
May 24: Portland 112 at Utah 121
May 26: Utah 121 at Portland 127, OT
May 28: Portland 105 at Utah 97

CONFERENCE SEMI-FINALS
Portland 4, Phoenix 1
May 5: Phoenix 111 at Portland 113
May 7: Phoenix 119 at Portland 126
May 9: Portland 117 at Phoenix 124
May 11: Portland 153 at Phoenix 151, 2OT
May 14: Phoenix 106 at Portland 118

Utah 4, Seattle 1
May 6: Seattle 100 at Utah 108
May 8: Seattle 97 at Utah 103
May 10: Utah 98 at Seattle 104
May 12: Utah 89 at Seattle 83
May 14: Seattle 100 at Utah 111

FIRST ROUND
Portland 3, L.A. Lakers 1
Apr. 23: L.A. Lakers 102 at Portland 115
Apr. 25: L.A. Lakers 79 at Portland 101
Apr. 29: Portland 119 at L.A. Lakers 121, OT
May 3: Portland 102, L.A. Lakers (at Las Vegas) 76

Utah 3, L.A. Clippers 2
Apr. 24: L.A. Clippers 97 at Utah 115
Apr. 26: L.A. Clippers 92 at Utah 103
Apr. 28: Utah 88 at L.A. Clippers 98
May 3: Utah 107, L.A. Clippers (at Anaheim.) 115
May 4: L.A. Clippers 89 at Utah 98

Seattle 3, Golden State 1
Apr. 23: Seattle 117 at Golden State 109
Apr. 25: Seattle 101 at Golden State 115
Apr. 28: Golden State 128 at Seattle 129
Apr. 30: Golden State 116 at Seattle 119

Phoenix 3, San Antonio 0
Apr. 24: San Antonio 111 at Phoenix 117
Apr. 26: San Antonio 107 at Phoenix 119
Apr. 29: Phoenix 101 at San Antonio 92

NBA LEADERS

SCORING

	GP	FGM	FTM	PTS	PPG
Michael Jordan, CHI	80	943	491	2404	30.1
Karl Malone, UTJ	81	798	673	2272	28.0
Chris Mullin, GST	81	830	350	2074	25.6
Clyde Drexler, POR	76	694	401	1903	25.0
Patrick Ewing, NYK	82	796	377	1970	24.0
Tim Hardaway, GST	81	734	298	1893	23.4
David Robinson, SAS	68	592	393	1578	23.2
Charles Barkley, PHI	75	622	454	1730	23.1
Mitch Richmond, SAC	80	685	330	1803	22.5
Glen Rice, MIA	79	672	266	1765	22.3

FIELD GOALS

	FGM	FGA	FG%
Buck Williams, POR	340	563	.604
Otis Thorpe, HOU	558	943	.592
Horace Grant, CHI	457	790	.578
Brad Daugherty, CLE	576	1010	.570
Michael Cage, SEA	307	542	.566
Charles Barkley, PHI	622	1126	.552
David Robinson, SAS	592	1074	.551
Danny Manning, LAC	650	1199	.542
Pervis Ellison, WSB	547	1014	.539
Larry Nance, CLE	556	1032	.539

THREE POINT FIELD GOALS

	3PM	3PA	3P%
Dana Barros, SEA	83	186	.446
Drazen Petrovic, NJN	123	277	.444
Jeff Hornacek, PHO	83	189	.439
Mike Iuzzolino, DAL	59	136	.434
Dale Ellis, MIL	138	329	.419
Craig Ehlo, CLE	69	167	.413
John Stockton, UTJ	83	204	.407
Larry Bird, BOS	52	128	.406
Dell Curry, CHA	74	183	.404
Hersey Hawkins, PHI	91	229	.397

FREE THROWS

	FTM	FTA	FT%
Mark Price, CLE	270	285	.947
Larry Bird, BOS	150	162	.926
Ricky Pierce, SEA	417	455	.916
Rolando Blackman, DAL	239	266	.898
Jeff Malone, UTJ	256	285	.898
Scott Skiles, ORL	248	277	.895
Jeff Hornacek, PHO	279	315	.886
Kevin Gamble, BOS	139	157	.885
Johnny Dawkins, PHI	164	186	.882
Ron Anderson, PHI	143	163	.877

ASSISTS

	GP	AST	APG
John Stockton, UTJ	82	1126	13.7
Kevin Johnson, PHO	78	836	10.7
Tim Hardaway, GST	81	807	10.0
Muggsy Bogues, CHA	82	743	9.1
Rod Strickland, SAS	57	491	8.6
Mark Jackson, NYK	81	694	8.6
Pooh Richardson, MIN	82	685	8.4
Micheal Williams, IND	79	647	8.2
Michael Adams, WSB	78	594	7.6
Mark Price, CLE	72	535	7.4

REBOUNDS

	GP	ORB	DRB	TRB	RPG
Dennis Rodman, DET	82	523	1007	1530	18.7
Kevin Willis, ATL	81	418	840	1258	15.5
Dikembe Mutombo, DEN	71	316	554	870	12.3
David Robinson, SAS	68	261	568	829	12.2
Hakeem Olajuwon, HOU	70	246	599	845	12.1
Rony Seikaly, MIA	79	307	627	934	11.8
Greg Anderson, DEN	82	337	604	941	11.5
Patrick Ewing, NYK	82	228	693	921	11.2
Karl Malone, UTJ	81	225	684	909	11.2
Charles Barkley, PHI	75	271	559	830	11.1

STEALS

	GP	STL	SPG
John Stockton, UTJ	82	244	2.98
Micheal Williams, IND	79	233	2.95
Alvin Robertson, MIL	82	210	2.56
Mookie Blaylock, NJN	72	170	2.36
David Robinson, SAS	68	158	2.32
Michael Jordan, CHI	80	182	2.27
Chris Mullin, GST	81	173	2.14
Muggsy Bogues, CHA	82	170	2.07
Sedale Threatt, LAL	82	168	2.05
Mark Macon, DEN	76	154	2.03

BLOCKS

	GP	BLK	BPG
David Robinson, SAS	68	305	4.49
Hakeem Olajuwon, HOU	70	304	4.34
Larry Nance, CLE	81	243	3.00
Patrick Ewing, NYK	82	245	2.99
Dikembe Mutombo, DEN	71	210	2.96
Manute Bol, PHI	71	205	2.89
Duane Causwell, SAC	80	215	2.69
Pervis Ellison, WSB	66	177	2.68
Mark Eaton, UTJ	81	205	2.53
Andrew Lang, PHO	81	201	2.48

TURNOVERS

	GP	TO	TPG
Derrick Coleman, NJN	65	247	3.8
Dikembe Mutombo, DEN	71	249	3.5
Kevin Johnson, PHO	78	273	3.5
John Stockton, UTJ	82	287	3.5
Tim Hardaway, GST	81	267	3.3
Isiah Thomas, DET	78	250	3.2
Clyde Drexler, POR	76	243	3.2
Charles Barkley, PHI	75	233	3.1
Scott Skiles, ORL	75	233	3.1
Mitch Richmond, SAC	80	248	3.1

THE YEAR IN BASKETBALL

October 16, 1991 Roy Tarpley of the Dallas Mavericks is banned from the NBA for life after violating the league's anti-drug agreement.

November 7, 1991 Magic Johnson announces his retirement because he has contracted HIV, the virus that causes AIDS.

November 23, 1991 The Sacramento Kings finally win a road game. After losing an NBA-record 43 consecutive away games, the Kings eke out a 95-93 win against the Orlando Magic.

December 17, 1991 In the biggest margin of victory in NBA history, Cleveland defeats Miami, 148-80, to win by 68 points.

January 13, 1992 In a wild game, Troy State defeats DeVry Institute, 258-141, in a game that breaks numerous NCAA records, including most points by one team, most points by both teams and most points in a half (Troy St., 135). It is also the first time in NCAA history that one team scores over 200 points.

February 27, 1992 Winless Prairie View sets an NCAA Division I record for most losses in a season, when they drop their 28th of the year in a 112-79 loss to Mississippi Valley State.

April 1, 1992 Virginia takes the NIT, beating Notre Dame 81-76 in OT.

April 5, 1992 Stanford, led by junior guard Molly Goodenbour, wins its second women's championship, beating Western Kentucky, 78-62.

April 6, 1992 Duke becomes the first team since UCLA in 1972 and 1973 to repeat as NCAA champs when they beat Michigan 71-51.

May 11, 1992 In the highest-scoring playoff game in NBA history, Portland edges Phoenix, 153-151, in double OT in Game 4 of the Western Conference semis. The Blazers' three guards—Clyde Drexler, Terry Porter, and Danny Ainge—combine for 89 points.

May 25, 1992 Danny Biasone, inventor of the 24-second rule and one-time owner of the Syracuse Nationals, dies at 83.

June 3, 1992 Michael Jordan scores a record 35 points, including six 3-pointers, in the first half as the Bulls beat Portland 122-89 in Game 1 of the NBA Finals. Jordan finishes with 39 points as Chicago wins, 122-89.

June 14, 1992 The Bulls win their second consecutive NBA championship, beating Portland, 97-93, in Game 6 of the finals at Chicago Stadium. Michael Jordan's 33 points pace the Bulls.

June 17, 1992 Philadelphia trades Charles Barkley to Phoenix for Jeff Hornacek, Tim Perry, and Andrew Lang.

1992-93

Sir Charles lifts Suns, but no one eclipses Jordan-led Bulls

Following the 1992 season, several teams made improvements in order to catch Chicago. Phoenix traded Jeff Hornacek, Tim Perry and Andrew Lang to Philadelphia for Charles Barkley. The Suns had won more than 50 games four years in a row. The Western Conference title seemed within their grasp if they could just land a superstar to go with scorer and assist man Kevin Johnson and distance bomber Dan Majerle. Now, with Barkley, Phoenix led the league in scoring with 113 points a game and won a league best 62 games.

While the Suns were getting stronger, it could be debated whether the Knicks were. New York picked up Doc Rivers, who brought his smart, measured approach to the guard position. New York won 60 games for the best record in the conference. But they had traded Xavier McDaniel, a forward with attitude who had excelled in the playoffs the previous year.

Boston had won 51 games last year and would win 48 in 1992-93. But an era was over. Dealing with chronic back pain, Larry Bird retired at the age of 35, following his summer with the "Dream Team" at the 1992 Barcelona Olympics. Reggie Lewis was the Celtics leading scorer for the second straight year.

In the Atlantic Division, Orlando jumped from 21 to 41 wins with the arrival of number one overall draft pick Shaquille O'Neal, who finished in the top ten in scoring, field goal percentage, rebounding, and blocks and was Rookie of the Year. Charlotte, another expansion team, made strides, too, winning 44 games, primarily due to the play of Alonzo Mourning.

Though still the team to beat, Chicago won ten less games than the year before.

The Delta Center in Utah played host to the All-Star Game. Patrick Ewing of the Knicks forced overtime by connecting on a 15-foot hook with eight seconds left. The West then pulled the game out, 135-132. Utah teammates John Stockton and Karl Malone were voted co-MVPs before the Salt Lake City faithful. Stockton had 15 assists and Malone scored 28 points in addition to pulling down 10 rebounds.

Michael Jordan (32.6) tied Wilt Chamberlain's record of seven consecutive scoring titles. But Chicago had larger goals—they were attempting to do what no NBA team had done since 1966: win three titles in a row. George Mikan and the Lakers had won three straight, and the Bill Russell-led Celtics won eight in a row. But there were fewer teams and fewer playoff series then; now teams had to win 15 post-season games.

Chicago tore through Atlanta and Cleveland without a loss, but looked vulnerable after losing the first two games of the Conference Finals in New York. The press then reported that Jordan was gambling in Atlantic City with his father James early in the morning after the second loss.

Jordan claimed he had left the casino earlier and angrily shut himself off from the press. The Bulls circled the wagons, rallying around their teammate. Chicago won the next two games,

Dominique Wilkins
"The Human Highlight Film" scored over 2,000 points for eighth time in career, but couldn't lead Hawks past first round of the playoffs.

including a 54-point performance by Jordan in Game 4. In Game 5 a three-pointer by B.J. Armstrong put the Bulls up by one. Ewing drove, fumbled the ball, got it to Charles Smith, who attempted four shots. The first was blocked by Grant, the second stripped by Jordan and the next two by Pippin. Chicago won, 97-94, and then won at home, 96-88.

Phoenix had been tested in the early rounds, losing the first two to Los Angeles before winning three straight. It then took them six games to dispose of San Antonio and they went the full seven to eliminate a Seattle team that won 55 games.

Chicago looked forward to a more wide open style of play in the Finals. In six games against New York they had reached 100 points just twice, both times on their home court. But they topped 100 four times against Phoenix, including their first two on the road. In Game 1 they had built a 20-point lead and won 100-92. In Game 2 Phoenix ran out early, but the Bulls charged back. Chicago led 104-98 with 1:48 left. Danny Ainge nailed a three-pointer but Scottie Pippen blocked his next three attempts and Chicago held on for a 111-108 victory.

In Game 3 Dan Majerle rained threes on Chicago early. It was 103-103 at the end of regulation. With each team missing opportunities to end the game, Majerle sealed the third overtime and Phoenix had a victory. In Game 4, Barkley continued to score on Horace Grant inside. But Jordan drove every time he got his hands on the ball. With under a minute left, he drove and was fouled. His three-point conversion made it 109-104.

He scored 55 points and the Bulls won 111-105. Facing elimination in Chicago, Phoenix won 108-98.

In Game 6, the Bulls clicked on all cylinders early on. But by the fourth quarter they unraveled, not able to get shots up before the 24-second clock. The Suns led 98-94, with the ball, and 45 second left. But Frank Johnson missed a wide open 15-footer and Jordan went coast to coast to cut the lead to two. Now Majerle, with a wide-open baseline jumper from 15 feet, shot an air ball. The Bulls had the ball, with 14 seconds left, trailing by 2. Phoenix' defense broke down when Barkley went for a steal against Pippen, who drove, dished to Grant under the basket, who kicked it back to John Paxson at the three-point line. Paxson drained it with 3 seconds left, Chicago's first points in the quarter not scored by Jordan. In the final seconds, Grant blocked a short jumper by Kevin Johnson and the Bulls had won their third straight title.

1992-93 SEASON HIGHLIGHTS

STANDINGS

Eastern Conference
Atlantic Division

	W	L	Pct.	GB
New York	60	22	.732	—
Boston	48	34	.585	12
New Jersey	43	39	.524	17
Orlando	41	41	.500	19
Miami Heat	36	46	.439	24
Philadelphia	26	56	.317	34
Washington	22	60	.268	38

Central Division

	W	L	Pct.	GB
Chicago	57	25	.695	—
Cleveland	54	28	.659	3
Charlotte	44	38	.537	13
Atlanta	43	39	.524	14
Indiana	41	41	.500	16
Detroit	40	42	.488	17
Milwaukee	28	54	.341	29

Western Conference
Midwest Division

	W	L	Pct.	GB
Houston	55	27	.671	—
San Antonio	49	33	.598	6
Utah	47	35	.573	8
Denver	36	46	.439	19
Minnesota	19	63	.232	36
Dallas	11	71	.134	44

Pacific Division

	W	L	Pct.	GB
Phoenix	62	20	.756	—
Seattle	55	27	.671	7
Portland	51	31	.622	11
LA Clippers	41	41	.500	21
LA Lakers	39	43	.476	23
Golden State	34	48	.415	28
Sacramento	25	57	.305	37

AWARDS
MVP
Charles Barkley, Phoenix
Top Rookie
Shaquille O'Neal, Orlando
Coach of Year
Pat Riley, New York
Defensive Player of Year
Hakeem Olajuwon, Houston
Sixth Man Award
Cliff Robinson, Portland
Most Improved Player
Chris Jackson, Denver
Citizenship Award
Terry Porter, Portland

ALL-STAR GAME
Delta Center, Salt Lake City, Utah
Sunday, February 21, 1993
West 135, East 132, OT
MVPs: Karl Malone and John Stockton

ALL-STAR TEAMS
FIRST TEAM

Charles Barkley	Phoenix
Karl Malone	Utah
Hakeem Olajuwon	Houston
Michael Jordan	Chicago
Mark Price	Cleveland

SECOND TEAM

Dominique Wilkins	Atlanta
Larry Johnson	Charlotte
Patrick Ewing	New York
John Stockton	Utah
Joe Dumars	Detroit

THIRD TEAM

Scottie Pippen	Chicago
Derrick Coleman	New Jersey
David Robinson	San Antonio
Tim Hardaway	Golden State
Drazen Petrovic	New Jersey

PLAYOFFS
FINALS
Chicago 4, Phoenix 2
June 9: Chicago 100 at Phoenix 92
June 11: Chicago 111 at Phoenix 108
June 13: Phoenix 129 at Chicago 121, 3OT
June 16: Phoenix 105 at Chicago 111
June 18: Phoenix 108 at Chicago 98
June 20: Chicago 99 at Phoenix 98
EASTERN CONFERENCE
CONFERENCE FINALS
Chicago 4, New York 2
May 23: Chicago 90 at New York 98
May 25: Chicago 91 at New York 96
May 29: New York 83 at Chicago 103
May 31: New York 95 at Chicago 105
June 2: Chicago 97 at New York 94
June 4: New York 88 at Chicago 96
CONFERENCE SEMI-FINALS
New York 4, Charlotte 1
May 9: Charlotte 95 at New York 111
May 12: Charlotte 101 at New York 105, OT
May 14: New York 106 at Charlotte 110, 2OT
May 16: New York 94 at Charlotte 92
May 18: Charlotte 101 at New York 105
Chicago 4, Cleveland 0
May 11: Cleveland 84 at Chicago 91
May 13: Cleveland 85 at Chicago 104
May 15: Chicago 96 at Cleveland 90
May 17: Chicago 103 at Cleveland 101
FIRST ROUND
New York 3, Indiana 1
Apr. 30: Indiana 104 at New York 107
May 2: Indiana 91 at New York 101
May 4: New York 93 at Indiana 116
May 6: New York 109 at Indiana 100, OT

Chicago 3, Atlanta 0
Apr. 30: Atlanta 90 at Chicago 114
May 2: Atlanta 102 at Chicago 117
May 4: Chicago 98 at Atlanta 88
Cleveland 3, New Jersey 2
Apr. 29: New Jersey 98 at Cleveland 114
May 1: New Jersey 101 at Cleveland 99
May 5: Cleveland 93 at New Jersey 84
May 7: Cleveland 79 at New Jersey 96
May 9: New Jersey 89 at Cleveland 99
Charlotte 3, Boston 1
Apr. 29: Charlotte 101 at Boston 112
May 1: Charlotte 99 at Boston 98, 2OT
May 3: Boston 89 at Charlotte 119
May 5: Boston 103 at Charlotte 104
WESTERN CONFERENCE
CONFERENCE FINALS
Phoenix 4, Seattle 3
May 24: Seattle 91 at Phoenix 105
May 26: Seattle 103 at Phoenix 99
May 28: Phoenix 104 at Seattle 97
May 30: Phoenix 101 at Seattle 120
June 1: Seattle 114 at Phoenix 120
June 3: Phoenix 102 at Seattle 118
June 5: Seattle 110 at Phoenix 123
CONFERENCE SEMI-FINALS
Phoenix 4, San Antonio 2
May 11: San Antonio 89 at Phoenix 98
May 13: San Antonio 103 at Phoenix 109
May 15: Phoenix 96 at San Antonio 111
May 16: Phoenix 103 at San Antonio 117
May 18: San Antonio 97 at Phoenix 109
May 20: Phoenix 102 at San Antonio 100

Seattle 4, Houston 3
May 10: Houston 90 at Seattle 99
May 12: Houston 100 at Seattle 111
May 15: Seattle 79 at Houston 97
May 16: Seattle 92 at Houston 103
May 18: Houston 95 at Seattle 120
May 20: Seattle 90 at Houston 103
May 22: Houston 100 at Seattle 103, OT
FIRST ROUND
Phoenix 3, L.A. Lakers 2
Apr. 30: L.A. Lakers 107 at Phoenix 103
May 2: L.A. Lakers 86 at Phoenix 81
May 4: Phoenix 107 at L.A. Lakers 102
May 6: Phoenix 101 at L.A. Lakers 86
May 9: L.A. Lakers 104 at Phoenix 112, OT
Houston 3, L.A. Clippers 2
Apr. 29: L.A. Clippers 94 at Houston 117
May 1: L.A. Clippers 95 at Houston 83
May 3: Houston 111 at L.A. Clippers 99
May 5: Houston 90 at L.A. Clippers 93
May 8: L.A. Clippers 80 at Houston 84
Seattle 3, Utah 2
Apr. 30: Utah 85 at Seattle 99
May 2: Utah 89 at Seattle 85
May 4: Seattle 80 at Utah 90
May 6: Seattle 93 at Utah 80
May 8: Utah 92 at Seattle 100
San Antonio 3, Portland 1
Apr. 29: San Antonio 87 at Portland 86
May 1: San Antonio 96 at Portland 105
May 5: Portland 101 at San Antonio 107
May 7: Portland 97 at San Antonio 100, OT

NBA LEADERS

SCORING

	GP	FGM	FTM	PTS	PPG
Michael Jordan, CHI	78	992	476	2541	32.6
Dominique Wilkins, ATL	71	741	519	2121	29.9
Karl Malone, UTJ	82	797	619	2217	27.0
Hakeem Olajuwon, HOU	82	848	444	2140	26.1
Charles Barkley, PHO	76	716	445	1944	25.6
Patrick Ewing, NYK	81	779	400	1959	24.2
Joe Dumars, DET	77	677	343	1809	23.5
Shaquille O'Neal, ORL	81	733	427	1893	23.4
David Robinson, SAS	82	676	561	1916	23.4
Danny Manning, LAC	79	702	388	1800	22.8

FIELD GOALS

	FGM	FGA	FG%
Cedric Ceballos, PHO	381	662	.576
Brad Daugherty, CLE	520	911	.571
Dale Davis, IND	304	535	.568
Shaquille O'Neal, ORL	733	1304	.562
Otis Thorpe, HOU	385	690	.558
Karl Malone, UTJ	797	1443	.552
Larry Nance, CLE	533	971	.549
Frank Brickowski, MIL	456	836	.545
Larry Stewart, WSB	306	564	.543
Antoine Carr, SAS	379	705	.538

THREE POINT FIELD GOALS

	3PM	3PA	3P%
B.J. Armstrong, CHI	63	139	.453
Chris Mullin, GST	60	133	.451
Drazen Petrovic, NJN	75	167	.449
Kenny Smith, HOU	96	219	.438
Jim Les, SAC	66	154	.429
Mark Price, CLE	122	293	.416
Terry Porter, POR	143	345	.414
Trent Tucker, CHI	53	131	.405
Danny Ainge, PHO	150	372	.403
Dennis Scott, ORL	108	268	.403

FREE THROWS

	FTM	FTA	FT%
Mark Price, CLE	289	305	.948
Mahmoud Abdul-Rauf, DEN	217	232	.935
Eddie Johnson, SEA	234	257	.911
Micheal Williams, MIN	419	462	.907
Scott Skiles, ORL	289	324	.892
Ricky Pierce, SEA	313	352	.889
Reggie Miller, IND	427	485	.880
Kenny Smith, HOU	195	222	.878
Drazen Petrovic, NJN	315	362	.870
Reggie Lewis, BOS	326	376	.867

ASSISTS

	GP	AST	APG
John Stockton, UTJ	82	987	12.0
Tim Hardaway, GST	66	699	10.6
Scott Skiles, ORL	78	735	9.4
Mark Jackson, LAC	82	724	8.8
Muggsy Bogues, CHA	81	711	8.8
Micheal Williams, MIN	76	661	8.7
Isiah Thomas, DET	79	671	8.5
Mookie Blaylock, ATL	80	671	8.4
Kenny Anderson, NJN	55	449	8.2
Mark Price, CLE	75	597	8.0

REBOUNDS

	GP	ORB	DRB	TRB	RPG
Dennis Rodman, DET	62	367	765	1132	18.3
Shaquille O'Neal, ORL	81	342	780	1122	13.9
Dikembe Mutombo, DEN	82	344	726	1070	13.0
Hakeem Olajuwon, HOU	82	283	785	1068	13.0
Kevin Willis, ATL	80	335	693	1028	12.8
Charles Barkley, PHO	76	237	691	928	12.2
Patrick Ewing, NYK	81	191	789	980	12.1
Rony Seikaly, MIA	72	259	587	846	11.8
David Robinson, SAS	82	229	727	956	11.7
Derrick Coleman, NJN	76	247	605	852	11.2
Karl Malone, UTJ	82	227	692	919	11.2

STEALS

	GP	STL	SPG
Michael Jordan, CHI	78	221	2.83
Mookie Blaylock, ATL	80	203	2.54
John Stockton, UTJ	82	199	2.43
Nate McMillan, SEA	73	173	2.37
Alvin Robertson, MIL/DET	69	154	2.23
Ron Harper, LAC	80	177	2.21
Eric Murdock, MIL	79	174	2.20
Micheal Williams, MIN	76	165	2.17
Gary Payton, SEA	82	177	2.16
Scottie Pippen, CHI	81	173	2.14

BLOCKS

	GP	BLK	BPG
Hakeem Olajuwon, HOU	82	342	4.17
Shaquille O'Neal, ORL	81	286	3.53
Dikembe Mutombo, DEN	82	287	3.50
Alonzo Mourning, CHA	78	271	3.47
David Robinson, SAS	82	264	3.22
Larry Nance, CLE	77	198	2.57
Pervis Ellison, WSB	49	108	2.20
Manute Bol, PHI	58	119	2.05
Patrick Ewing, NYK	81	161	1.99
Clifford Robinson, POR	82	161	1.96

TURNOVERS

	GP	TO	TPG
Jim Jackson, DAL	28	115	4.1
Shaquille O'Neal, ORL	81	308	3.8
Isiah Thomas, DET	79	284	3.6
Scott Skiles, ORL	78	265	3.4
Christian Laettner, MIN	81	275	3.4
Tim Hardaway, GST	66	218	3.3
Patrick Ewing, NYK	81	267	3.3
Derrick Coleman, NJN	76	243	3.2
Hakeem Olajuwon, HOU	82	262	3.2
John Stockton, UTJ	82	262	3.2

THE YEAR IN BASKETBALL

October 27, 1992 In the first NBA game ever in Latin America, the Rockets defeat the Mavericks, 104-102, in preseason at the Mexico City Sports Palace. Over 19,500 fans attend.

November 8, 1992 The Kings defeat the Lakers at the Great Western Forum, 124-111, to snap a 43-game regular season losing streak on the Lakers' home court. The Kings' previous road win against L.A. had occurred Oct. 20, 1974.

January 8, 1993 Michael Jordan reaches the 20,000-point mark in his 620th game, faster than anyone except Wilt Chamberlain (499 games).

January 15, 1993 Hank Iba, longtime Oklahoma A&M coach and Hall of Famer dies at age 88.

February 25, 1993 Vermont beats Northeastern, 50-40, for its 50th straight win, breaking the women's Division I record for consecutive wins.

April 2, 1993 Cleveland's Mark Price misses a foul shot, stopping his consecutive free throw streak end at 77. The miss leaves Price one short of Calvin Murphy's NBA record of 78 straight free throws.

April 4, 1993 Sheryl Swoopes shatters the women's title game record by scoring 47 points to lead Texas Tech to an 84-82 win over Ohio State.

April 5, 1993 North Carolina downs Michigan, 77-71, in the NCAA title game, featuring Chris Webber's famed illegal timeout in the final minute.

April 8, 1993 Brian Shaw sets an NBA record by hitting 10 three-pointers in Miami's 117-92 win over Milwaukee.

April 25, 1993 Michael Williams breaks Calvin Murphy's streak of making 78 consecutive free throws, when he goes 10-for-10 in Minnesota's victory over Utah.

April 28, 1993 Jim Valvano dies of cancer at age 47.

May 9, 1993 Phoenix beats the Lakers, 112-104, in overtime in Game 5 of their opening round playoff series. The win makes the Suns the first NBA team to lose two playoff games at home and comeback to win three straight in a best-of-five series.

June 7, 1993 Drazen Petrovic is killed in an auto accident in Germany. He was 28.

June 20, 1993 The Bulls become the first franchise in 28 years to win three consecutive NBA championships, as they defeat Phoenix, 99-98.

July 27, 1993 Reggie Lewis, the Celtics' star forward, dies of a heart ailment while shooting baskets at Brandeis University. Lewis was 27.

1993-94

With Jordan retiring, Hakeem and Rockets grab centre stage

With few exceptions, the same NBA powers that sat atop the standings last year were there again at the close of the 1993-94 regular season. Seattle, without a player in the top ten in scoring, rebounding, or assists, led the circuit with 63 wins. Rudy Tomjanovich coached his Rockets to 58 wins and another Midwest Division title. Atlanta was a genuine surprise, winning 57 games behind new coach Lenny Wilkens to finish ahead of the Bulls in the Central. New York again set the standard for stinginess, leading the league in defense and winning its second straight Atlantic Division crown. Boston fell from 48 wins last year to 32. Their star player, Reggie Lewis, died of a heart attack while practicing before the season.

Orlando was climbing the ranks because of the most dominant young center to enter the league since Lew Alcindor was drafted by Milwaukee in 1969. Shaquille O'Neal finished second in scoring (29.3) and rebounding (13.2). His field goal percentage (.599) was tops in the league by far and he finished sixth in blocked shots.

But the biggest change in the balance of power was due to the absence of one player. On October 6, prior to the start of the season, Michael Jordan announced that he was retiring from basketball. He had grown weary of the game even before Chicago had won its third straight title last June. The press was dissecting his life to an unbearable degree and not allowing him the freedom to move. His father, James, said as much after the son's trip to Atlantic City made headline news the previous spring. Two months later, authorities found the body of James, who had been missing for weeks. Analysis proved that he had been murdered. While the motive for the murder was robbery—he had pulled over to the side of a road to sleep and was robbed and shot—some members of the press speculated that his death was payback for the son's unpaid gambling debts. At the Chicago press conference, Jordan chastised the press for their lack of sensitivity and claimed he had "nothing more to prove" playing basketball. He had won seven scoring titles and led his team to three consecutive championships. The consensus was that Jordan—even at the tender age of 30 and having played just nine years—was the greatest ever to play the game.

A less noticed run came to an end early in the season. Michael Williams of Minnesota finally missed a free throw, ending his record of 97 consecutive charity tosses made dating back to the previous season.

As the months wore on, however, the suspense of the season centered on how the Bulls would fare without Jordan. By the All-Star break the Bulls were making the doubters look foolish with a record of 34-14 (.723). In February, at about the time Jordan signed a contract to play baseball in the Chicago White Sox organization, the All-Star Game took place at the Target Center in Minneapolis. The West employed triple-teams on

Hakeem Olajuwon
Truly a Dream Season: League MVP, Finals MVP, Defensive Player of the Year, First-Team All-Star and NBA champion for the first time.

Shaquille O'Neal, intent on not allowing him any of the spotlight. The strategy backfired and helped the East to a 127-118 win. The mob scene around O'Neal left the perimeter wide open and Pippen hit nine of his 15 field goal attempts, with five of his connections coming from beyond the three-point line. Armstrong and Cleveland's Mark Price also found the mark and the East set an All-Star record with 10 three-pointers. In addition to his game-high 29 points, Pippen had 11 rebounds and was a unanimous choice as the game's MVP.

Not long after, David Robinson recorded a quadruple-

double with 34 points, 10 rebounds, 10 assists and 10 blocks in the Spurs' 115-96 win over visiting Detroit. Then, with his teammates feeding him for 41 field goal attempts in the season's final game, Robinson scored 71 points to edge out O'Neal and win the NBA scoring title.

In an astounding playoff series, eighth seeded Denver eliminated top-seeded Seattle, 98-94, in overtime in Game 5. It was the first time an eight-seed defeated a one-seed. Several days later Isiah Thomas retired after 13 years and two titles with Detroit.

Phoenix got off to a loud start in the post-season. Charles Barkley scored 56 points, including a playoff record 38 in the first half, to lead Phoenix to a 140-133 victory to eliminate Golden State in the opening round. A week later, the Suns, down 20 points with 10 minutes left, rallied for a 124-117 overtime victory to go up two games over Houston in the Western Conference semifinals. Houston then blitzed Phoenix three straight and, after a Suns' victory, won Game 7 on their homecourt, 104-94.

New York got by Chicago in Game 5, when a questionable foul call on Pippen put Hubert Davis on the line for two shots. New York won in seven and then did the same against Indiana. The Rockets got past Utah in five to meet New York in the Finals.

In a series in which neither team scored 100 points, the Rockets, after trailing 3-2 in games, beat New York 90-84 in Game 7 of the finals. Olajuwon tallied 25 points, 10 rebounds, seven assists and three blocks and earned the Finals MVP. He was previously named MVP and Defensive Player of the Year.

1993-94 SEASON HIGHLIGHTS

STANDINGS

Eastern Conference
Atlantic Division

	W	L	Pct.	GB
New York	57	25	.695	—
Orlando	50	32	.610	7
New Jersey	45	37	.549	12
Miami Heat	42	40	.512	15
Boston	32	50	.390	25
Philadelphia	25	57	.305	32
Washington	24	58	.293	33

Central Division

	W	L	Pct.	GB
Atlanta	57	25	.695	—
Chicago	55	27	.671	2
Cleveland	47	35	.573	10
Indiana	47	35	.573	10
Charlotte	41	41	.500	16
Detroit	20	62	.244	37
Milwaukee	20	62	.244	37

Western Conference
Midwest Division

	W	L	Pct.	GB
Houston	58	24	.707	—
San Antonio	55	27	.671	3
Utah	53	29	.646	5
Denver	42	40	.512	16
Minnesota	20	62	.244	38
Dallas	13	69	.159	45

Pacific Division

	W	L	Pct.	GB
Seattle	63	19	.768	—
Phoenix	56	26	.683	7
Golden State	50	32	.610	13
Portland	47	35	.573	16
LA Lakers	33	49	.402	30
Sacramento	28	54	.341	35
LA Clippers	27	55	.329	36

AWARDS

MVP
Hakeem Olajuwon, Houston
Top Rookie
Chris Webber, Golden State
Coach of Year
Lenny Wilkens, Atlanta
Defensive Player of Year
Hakeem Olajuwon, Houston
Sixth Man Award
Dell Curry, Charlotte
Most Improved Player
Don MacLean, Washington
Citizenship Award
Joe Dumars, Detroit

ALL-STAR GAME

Target Center, Minneapolis, Minnesota
Sunday, February 13, 1994
East 127, West 119
MVP: Scottie Pippen

ALL-STAR TEAMS

FIRST TEAM

Scottie Pippen	Chicago
Karl Malone	Utah
Hakeem Olajuwon	Houston
John Stockton	Utah
Latrell Sprewell	Golden State

SECOND TEAM

Shawn Kemp	Seattle
Charles Barkley	Phoenix
David Robinson	San Antonio
Mitch Richmond	Sacramento
Kevin Johnson	Phoenix

THIRD TEAM

Derrick Coleman	New Jersey
Dominique Wilkins	Atlanta-L.A.
Clippers	
Shaquille O'Neal	Orlando
Mark Price	Cleveland
Gary Payton	Seattle

PLAYOFFS

FINALS
Houston 4, New York 3
June 8: New York 78 at Houston 85
June 10: New York 91 at Houston 83
June 12: Houston 93 at New York 89
June 15: Houston 82 at New York 91
June 17: Houston 84 at New York 91
June 19: New York 84 at Houston 86
June 22: New York 84 at Houston 90

EASTERN CONFERENCE
CONFERENCE FINALS
New York 4, Indiana 3
May 24: Indiana 89 at New York 100
May 26: Indiana 78 at New York 89
May 28: New York 68 at Indiana 88
May 30: New York 77 at Indiana 83
June 1: Indiana 93 at New York 86
June 3: New York 98 at Indiana 91
June 5: Indiana 90 at New York 94

CONFERENCE SEMI-FINALS
New York 4, Chicago 3
May 8: Chicago 86 at New York 90
May 11: Chicago 91 at New York 96
May 13: New York 102 at Chicago 104
May 15: New York 83 at Chicago 95
May 18: Chicago 86 at New York 87
May 20: New York 79 at Chicago 93
May 22: Chicago 77 at New York 87

Indiana 4, Atlanta 2
May 10: Indiana 96 at Atlanta 85
May 12: Indiana 69 at Atlanta 92
May 14: Atlanta 81 at Indiana 101
May 15: Atlanta 86 at Indiana 102
May 17: Indiana 76 at Atlanta 88
May 19: Atlanta 79 at Indiana 98

FIRST ROUND
Atlanta 3, Miami 2
Apr. 28: Miami 93 at Atlanta 88
Apr. 30: Miami 86 at Atlanta 104
May 3: Atlanta 86 at Miami 90
May 5: Atlanta 103 at Miami 89
May 8: Miami 91 at Atlanta 102

New York 3, New Jersey 1
Apr. 29: New Jersey 80 at New York 91
May 1: New Jersey 81 at New York 90
May 4: New York 92 at New Jersey 93, OT
May 6: New York 102 at New Jersey 92

Chicago 3, Cleveland 0
Apr. 29: Cleveland 96 at Chicago 104
May 1: Cleveland 96 at Chicago 105
May 3: Chicago 95 at Cleveland 92, OT

Indiana 3, Orlando 0
Apr. 28: Indiana 89 at Orlando 88
Apr. 30: Indiana 103 at Orlando 101
May 2: Orlando 86 at Indiana 99

WESTERN CONFERENCE
CONFERENCE FINALS
Houston 4, Utah 1
May 23: Utah 88 at Houston 100
May 25: Utah 99 at Houston 104
May 27: Houston 86 at Utah 95
May 29: Houston 80 at Utah 78
May 31: Utah 83 at Houston 94

CONFERENCE SEMI-FINALS
Houston 4, Phoenix 3
May 8: Phoenix 91 at Houston 87
May 11: Phoenix 124 at Houston 117, OT
May 13: Houston 118 at Phoenix 102
May 15: Houston 107 at Phoenix 96
May 17: Phoenix 86 at Houston 109
May 19: Houston 89 at Phoenix 103
May 21: Phoenix 94 at Houston 104

Utah 4, Denver 3
May 10: Denver 91 at Utah 100
May 12: Denver 94 at Utah 104
May 14: Utah 111 at Denver 109, OT
May 15: Utah 82 at Denver 83
May 17: Denver 109 at Utah 101, 2OT
May 19: Utah 91 at Denver 94
May 21: Denver 81 at Utah 91

FIRST ROUND
Denver 3, Seattle 2
Apr. 28: Denver 82 at Seattle 106
Apr. 30: Denver 87 at Seattle 97
May 2: Seattle 93 at Denver 110
May 5: Seattle 85 at Denver 94, OT
May 7: Denver 98 at Seattle 94 , OT

Houston 3, Portland 1
Apr. 29: Portland 104 at Houston 114
May 1: Portland 104 at Houston 115
May 3: Houston 115 at Portland 118
May 6: Houston 92 at Portland 89

Phoenix 3, Golden State 0
Apr. 29: Golden State 104 at Phoenix 111
May 1: Golden State 111 at Phoenix 117
May 4: Phoenix 140 at Golden State 133

Utah 3, San Antonio 1
Apr. 28: Utah 89 at San Antonio 106
Apr. 30: Utah 96 at San Antonio 84
May 3: San Antonio 72 at Utah 105
May 5: San Antonio 90 at Utah 95

NBA LEADERS

SCORING

	GP	FGM	FTM	PTS	PPG
David Robinson, SAS	80	840	693	2383	29.8
Shaquille O'Neal, ORL	81	953	471	2377	29.3
Hakeem Olajuwon, HOU	80	894	388	2184	27.3
Dominique Wilkins, ATL/LAC	74	698	442	1923	26.0
Karl Malone, UTJ	82	772	511	2063	25.2
Patrick Ewing, NYK	79	745	445	1939	24.5
Mitch Richmond, SAC	78	635	426	1823	23.4
Scottie Pippen, CHI	72	627	270	1587	22.0
Charles Barkley, PHO	65	518	318	1402	21.6
Glen Rice, MIA	81	663	250	1708	21.1

FIELD GOALS

	FGM	FGA	FG%
Shaquille O'Neal, ORL	953	1591	.599
Dikembe Mutombo, DEN	365	642	.569
Otis Thorpe, HOU	449	801	.561
Chris Webber, GST	572	1037	.552
Shawn Kemp, SEA	533	990	.538
Loy Vaught, LAC	373	695	.537
Cedric Ceballos, PHO	425	795	.535
Rik Smits, IND	493	923	.534
Dale Davis, IND	308	582	.529
Hakeem Olajuwon, HOU	894	1694	.528
John Stockton, UTJ	458	868	.528

THREE POINT FIELD GOALS

	3PM	3PA	3P%
Tracy Murray, POR	50	109	.459
B.J. Armstrong, CHI	60	135	.444
Reggie Miller, IND	123	292	.421
Steve Kerr, CHI	52	124	.419
Scott Skiles, ORL	68	165	.412
Eric Murdock, MIL	69	168	.411
Mitch Richmond, SAC	127	312	.407
Kenny Smith, HOU	89	220	.405
Dell Curry, CHA	152	378	.402
Hubert Davis, NYK	53	132	.402

FREE THROWS

	FTM	FTA	FT%
Mahmoud Abdul-Rauf, DEN	219	229	.956
Reggie Miller, IND	403	444	.908
Ricky Pierce, SEA	189	211	.896
Sedale Threatt, LAL	138	155	.890
Mark Price, CLE	238	268	.888
Glen Rice, MIA	250	284	.880
Jeff Hornacek, PHI/UTJ	260	296	.878
Scott Skiles, ORL	195	222	.878
Terry Porter, POR	204	234	.872
Kenny Smith, HOU	135	155	.871

ASSISTS

	GP	AST	APG
John Stockton, UTJ	82	1031	12.6
Muggsy Bogues, CHA	77	780	10.1
Mookie Blaylock, ATL	81	789	9.7
Kenny Anderson, NJN	82	784	9.6
Kevin Johnson, PHO	67	637	9.5
Rod Strickland, POR	82	740	9.0
Sherman Douglas, BOS	78	683	8.8
Mark Jackson, LAC	79	678	8.6
Mark Price, CLE	76	589	7.8
Micheal Williams, MIN	71	512	7.2

REBOUNDS

	GP	ORB	DRB	TRB	RPG
Dennis Rodman, SAS	79	453	914	1367	17.3
Shaquille O'Neal, ORL	81	384	688	1072	13.2
Kevin Willis, ATL	80	335	628	963	12.0
Hakeem Olajuwon, HOU	80	229	726	955	11.9
Olden Polynice, DET/SAC	68	299	510	809	11.9
Dikembe Mutombo, DEN	82	286	685	971	11.8
Charles Oakley, NYK	82	349	616	965	11.8
Karl Malone, UTJ	82	235	705	940	11.5
Derrick Coleman, NJN	77	262	608	870	11.3
Patrick Ewing, NYK	79	219	666	885	11.2

STEALS

	GP	STL	SPG
Nate McMillan, SEA	73	216	2.96
Scottie Pippen, CHI	72	211	2.93
Mookie Blaylock, ATL	81	212	2.62
John Stockton, UTJ	82	199	2.43
Eric Murdock, MIL	82	197	2.40
Penny Hardaway, ORL	82	190	2.32
Gary Payton, SEA	82	188	2.29
Tom Gugliotta, WSB	78	172	2.21
Latrell Sprewell, GST	82	180	2.20
Dee Brown, BOS	77	156	2.03

BLOCKS

	GP	BLK	BPG
Dikembe Mutombo, DEN	82	336	4.10
Hakeem Olajuwon, HOU	80	297	3.71
David Robinson, SAS	80	265	3.31
Alonzo Mourning, CHA	60	188	3.13
Shawn Bradley, PHI	49	147	3.00
Shaquille O'Neal, ORL	81	231	2.85
Patrick Ewing, NYK	79	217	2.75
Oliver Miller, PHO	69	156	2.26
Chris Webber, GST	76	164	2.16
Shawn Kemp, SEA	79	166	2.10

TURNOVERS

	GP	TO	TPG
Jim Jackson, DAL	82	336	4.1
Christian Laettner, MIN	70	259	3.7
Penny Hardaway, ORL	82	295	3.6
Kevin Johnson, PHO	67	235	3.5
Isiah Thomas, DET	58	203	3.5
Danny Manning, LAC/ATL	68	233	3.4
Hakeem Olajuwon, HOU	80	272	3.4
Patrick Ewing, NYK	79	261	3.3
Shawn Kemp, SEA	79	261	3.3
Alonzo Mourning, CHA	60	198	3.3

THE YEAR IN BASKETBALL

October 6, 1993 Michael Jordan announces his retirement, saying he has nothing left to accomplish.

November 4, 1993 The NBA goes Canadian, when the league's Board of Governors votes to place a franchise in Toronto.

November 9, 1993 Michael Williams of Minnesota misses a free throw, ending a record streak of 97 consecutive free throws made.

February 7, 1994 Michael Jordan signs a contract to play baseball with the Chicago White Sox.

February 12, 1994 Connecticut's men's and women's teams are both ranked first in the AP and USA Today/Coaches polls

March 24, 1994 Askia Jones of Kansas State scores 62 points in 28 minutes in a 115-77 victory over Fresno State in the NIT quarter-finals. Villanova eventually wins the championship, 80-73, over Vanderbilt.

March 27, 1994 Magic Johnson returns to the Lakers as head coach and the Lakers win, 110-101, over Milwaukee. Johnson will coach the remaining 15 games of the season, but does not return the next season.

April 3, 1994 Charlotte Smith's three-pointer at the buzzer gives North Carolina a 60-59 win over Louisiana Tech in the NCAA women's title game.

April 4, 1994 Arkansas wins its first national championship with a 76-72 victory over Duke.

April 24, 1994 The Spurs' David Robinson scores 71 points on the final day of the season to edge out Shaquille O'Neal for the NBA scoring title. With his teammates feeding him constantly, Robinson dominates the L.A. Clippers in the 112-87 win by making 26 of 41 field goal attempts and hitting 18 of 25 foul shots.

April 27, 1994 Vancouver joins the NBA.

May 7, 1994 In a major upset, eighth-seeded Denver eliminates top-seeded Seattle, 98-94, in overtime in Game 5 of their best-of-five first-round series. It is the first time an eight-seed defeats a one-seed.

May 11, 1994 Isiah Thomas retires after 13 years and two NBA titles.

May 11, 1994 The Suns, down 20 with 10 minutes left, rally for a 124-117 OT win over Houston in Game 2 of the Western Conference semis.

June 22, 1994 The Houston Rockets, led by Hakeem Olajuwon, win their first NBA title, beating New York 90-84 in Game 7 of the finals.

1994-95

Shaq attack, Jordan back, but it's still Hakeem's show

That this would be no ordinary year—from beginning to end—was apparent from the get go. In the first week of the new season, Glenn Robinson, a 6-foot-7 scoring machine from Purdue University, signed the most lucrative rookie contract in NBA history—a 10-year, $68 million deal with the Milwaukee Bucks. Not two weeks later, Golden State, one day after signing Chris Webber, traded him to Washington for Tom Gugliotta and first-round draft picks in 1996, 1998, and 2000. Milwaukee would jump to 34 wins, up from 20 last year. It would take several years before Webber would improve the Bullets.

When the dust had finally cleared on money matters and deals, the play on the hardwood proved worth the wait. The 1994-95 campaign proved that there were several uppity new kids on the block. Let the record show that the league could barely contain the talent of 22 year-old *wunderkind* Shaquille O'Neal. He could be found where no other NBA center could be: in the top ten in scoring, rebounding, blocks, and field goal percentage. Orlando reaped the windfall, winning the Atlantic Division with 57 wins. O'Neal was getting major help from 6-foot-7 second-year guard Penny Hardaway, a 20-point scorer who led the team in assists and steals. Unrestricted free agent Horace Grant had signed with Orlando, bringing rebounding help and 57 percent accuracy from the floor. Orlando ranked first in league scoring and owned the best home record at 39-2.

Indiana and Charlotte were also making moves. The Pacers combined a second-tier offense with a first-tier defense (95.5), fourth in the league behind Cleveland, New York and Atlanta. Getting major contributions from Alonzo Mourning and Larry Johnson, Charlotte won 50 games.

On January 6, Atlanta coach Lenny Wilkens became the NBA's all-time winning coach, moving past Red Auerbach when he notched his 939th victory, beating Washington, 112-90. Several weeks later, John Stockton broke Magic Johnson's all-time career assists record of 9,921, in the Jazz' 129-88 rout of Denver. In the All-Star Game, held in Phoenix, Shaquille O'Neal led the East squad with 22 points, but Sacramento's Mitch Richmond hit 10 of 13 from the field for 23 points, and was voted MVP. Two days after the game, Clyde Drexler was traded to Houston, where he was reunited with college teammate Hakeem Olajuwon.

All these occurrences, however, were upstaged by Michael Jordan's return to the Bulls on March 17 after a 21-month layoff. Ten days later, he scored 55 points against New York at Madison Square Garden.

Phoenix continued their excellent play, getting double-digit scoring from seven players to finish 59-23 and win the Pacific Division. San Antonio won the Midwest with a league-best 62 wins, two games ahead of Utah. Defending champ Houston was a distant third, 15 games out.

David Robinson
After being named league MVP, "The Admiral" couldn't lead San Antonio past Houston in the Western Conference Finals.

Last year Houston played in three games where a loss would end their season. Their triumph earned them the tag, "Clutch City," which showed up on t-shirts around the city.

Now, in the conference semi-finals, Phoenix won three of the first four, including Game 4 in Houston. With 17.9 seconds left and Phoenix leading by two in Game 5, Barkley missed two free throws. Houston took advantage and won, 103-97. Houston won Game 6, 116-103. In Game 7 at Phoenix, Mario Elle hit a three-pointer with seconds left and Houston held on to win, 115-114. Houston had faced two

elimination games in the first round versus Utah and now faced three more. Olajuwon outplayed league MVP David Robinson in the Conference Finals and Houston won in six.

Jordan found the playoffs rough going. In his first playoff game he scored 48 as the Bulls topped the Hornets, 108-100. But after taking the Hornets in four games, the Bulls lost to Orlando in six, as Jordan looked out of sync with his mates in key spots.

Against New York, Reggie Miller scored eight points on two three-pointers and two free throws in the final 16.4 seconds to win Game 1. That stolen game was the difference, as the Pacers won 97-95 over host New York in Game 7 of the conference semis. In the Conference Finals against Orlando, Indiana got to a seventh game but found O'Neal too much to deal with, losing 105-81.

In the Finals, Houston was down by 20 in the second quarter of Game 1 and Olajuwon sitting with his third foul. With ten seconds left, Nick Anderson missed four straight free throws that would have clinched the game. With the game in overtime, an Olajuwon tip-in gave Houston a stunning victory. Houston swept the next three, giving Clutch City a double clutch with back-to-back titles.

1994-95 SEASON HIGHLIGHTS

STANDINGS

Eastern Conference
Atlantic Division

	W	L	Pct.	GB
Orlando	57	25	.695	—
New York	55	27	.671	2
Boston	35	47	.427	22
Miami Heat	32	50	.390	25
New Jersey	30	52	.366	27
Philadelphia	24	58	.293	33
Washington	21	61	.256	36

Central Division

	W	L	Pct.	GB
Indiana	52	30	.634	—
Charlotte	50	32	.610	2
Chicago	47	35	.573	5
Cleveland	43	39	.524	9
Atlanta	42	40	.512	10
Milwaukee	34	48	.415	18
Detroit	28	54	.341	24

Western Conference
Midwest Division

	W	L	Pct.	GB
San Antonio	62	20	.756	—
Utah	60	22	.732	2
Houston	47	35	.573	15
Denver	41	41	.500	21
Dallas	36	46	.439	26
Minnesota	21	61	.256	41

Pacific Division

	W	L	Pct.	GB
Phoenix	59	23	.720	—
Seattle	57	25	.695	2
LA Lakers	48	34	.585	11
Portland	44	38	.537	15
Sacramento	39	43	.476	20
Golden State	26	56	.317	33
LA Clippers	17	65	.207	42

AWARDS

MVP
David Robinson, San Antonio
Top Rookie (tie)
Jason Kidd, Dallas
Grant Hill, Detroit
Coach of Year
Del Harris, LA Lakers
Defensive Player of Year
Dikembe Mutombo, Denver
Sixth Man Award
Anthony Mason, New York
Most Improved Player
Dana Barros, Philadelphia
Citizenship Award
Joe O'Toole, Atlanta

ALL-STAR GAME

America West Arena, Phoenix, Arizona
Sunday, February 12, 1995
West 139, East 112
MVP: Mitch Richmond

ALL-STAR TEAMS

FIRST TEAM

Karl Malone	Utah
Scottie Pippen	Chicago
David Robinson	San Antonio
John Stockton	Utah
Anfernee Hardaway	Orlando

SECOND TEAM

Charles Barkley	Phoenix
Shawn Kemp	Seattle
Shaquille O'Neal	Orlando
Gary Payton	Seattle
Mitch Richmond	Sacramento

THIRD TEAM

Detlef Schrempf	Seattle
Dennis Rodman	San Antonio
Hakeem Olajuwon	Houston
Reggie Miller	Indiana
Clyde Drexler	Houston

PLAYOFFS
FINALS
Houston 4, Orlando 0
June 7: Houston 120 at Orlando 118, OT
June 9: Houston 117 at Orlando 106
June 11: Orlando 103 at Houston 106
June 14: Orlando 101 at Houston 113

EASTERN CONFERENCE
CONFERENCE FINALS
Orlando 4, Indiana 3
May 23: Indiana 101 at Orlando 105
May 25: Indiana 114 at Orlando 119
May 27: Orlando 100 at Indiana 105
May 29: Orlando 93 at Indiana 94
May 31: Indiana 106 at Orlando 108
June 2: Orlando 96 at Indiana 123
June 4: Indiana 81 at Orlando 105

CONFERENCE SEMI-FINALS
Indiana 4, New York 3
May 7: Indiana 107 at New York 105
May 9: Indiana 77 at New York 96
May 11: New York 95 at Indiana 97, OT
May 13: New York 84 at Indiana 98
May 17: Indiana 95 at New York 96
May 19: New York 92 at Indiana 82
May 21: Indiana 97 at New York 95

Orlando 4, Chicago 2
May 7: Chicago 91 at Orlando 94
May 10: Chicago 104 at Orlando 94
May 12: Orlando 110 at Chicago 101
May 14: Orlando 95 at Chicago 106
May 16: Chicago 95 at Orlando 103
May 18: Orlando 108 at Chicago 102

FIRST ROUND
Orlando 3, Boston 1
Apr. 28: Boston 77 at Orlando 124
Apr. 30: Boston 99 at Orlando 92
May 3: Orlando 82 at Boston 77
May 5: Orlando 95 at Boston 92

Indiana 3, Atlanta 0
Apr. 27: Atlanta 82 at Indiana 90
Apr. 29: Atlanta 97 at Indiana 105
May 2: Indiana 105 at Atlanta 89

New York 3, Cleveland 1
Apr. 27: Cleveland 79 at New York 103
Apr. 29: Cleveland 90 at New York 84
May 1: New York 83 at Cleveland 81
May 4: New York 93 at Cleveland 80

Chicago 3, Charlotte 1
Apr. 28: Chicago 108 at Charlotte 100, OT
Apr. 30: Chicago 89 at Charlotte 106
May 2: Charlotte 80 at Chicago 85
May 4: Charlotte 84 at Chicago 85

WESTERN CONFERENCE
CONFERENCE FINALS
Houston 4, San Antonio 2
May 22: Houston 94 at San Antonio 93
May 24: Houston 106 at San Antonio 96
May 26: San Antonio 107 at Houston 102
May 28: San Antonio 103 at Houston 81
May 30: Houston 111 at San Antonio 90
June 1: San Antonio 95 at Houston 100

CONFERENCE SEMI-FINALS
San Antonio 4, L.A. Lakers 2
May 6: L.A. Lakers 94 at San Antonio 110
May 8: L.A. Lakers 90 at San Antonio 97, OT
May 12: San Antonio 85 at L.A. Lakers 92
May 14: San Antonio 80 at L.A. Lakers 71
May 16: L.A. Lakers 98 at San Antonio 96, OT
May 18: San Antonio 100 at L.A. Lakers 88

Houston 4, Phoenix 3
May 9: Houston 108 at Phoenix 130
May 11: Houston 94 at Phoenix 118
May 13: Phoenix 85 at Houston 118
May 14: Phoenix 114 at Houston 110
May 16: Houston 103 at Phoenix 97, OT
May 18: Phoenix 103 at Houston 116
May 20: Houston 115 at Phoenix 114

FIRST ROUND
San Antonio 3, Denver 0
Apr. 28: Denver 88 at San Antonio 104
Apr. 30: Denver 96 at San Antonio 122
May 2: San Antonio 99 at Denver 95

Phoenix 3, Portland 0
Apr. 28: Portland 102 at Phoenix 129
Apr. 30: Portland 94 at Phoenix 103
May 2: Phoenix 117 at Portland 109

Houston 3, Utah 2
Apr. 27: Houston 100 at Utah 102
Apr. 29: Houston 140 at Utah 126
May 3: Utah 95 at Houston 82
May 5: Utah 106 at Houston 123
May 7: Houston 95 at Utah 91

L.A. Lakers 3, Seattle 1
Apr. 27: L.A. Lakers 71 at Seattle 96
Apr. 29: L.A. Lakers 84 at Seattle 82
May 1: Seattle 101 at L.A. Lakers 105
May 4: Seattle 110 at L.A. Lakers 114

NBA LEADERS

SCORING

	GP	FGM	FTM	PTS	PPG
Shaquille O'Neal, ORL	79	930	455	2315	29.3
Hakeem Olajuwon, HOU	72	798	406	2005	27.8
David Robinson, SAS	81	788	656	2238	27.6
Karl Malone, UTJ	82	830	516	2187	26.7
Jamal Mashburn, DAL	80	683	447	1926	24.1
Patrick Ewing, NYK	79	730	420	1886	23.9
Charles Barkley, PHO	68	554	379	1561	23.0
Mitch Richmond, SAC	82	668	375	1867	22.8
Glen Rice, MIA	82	667	312	1831	22.3
Glenn Robinson, MIL	80	636	397	1755	21.9

FIELD GOALS

	FGM	FGA	FG%
Chris Gatling, GST	324	512	.633
Shaquille O'Neal, ORL	930	1594	.583
Horace Grant, ORL	401	707	.567
Otis Thorpe, HOU/POR	385	681	.565
Dale Davis, IND	324	576	.562
Gheorghe Muresan, WSB	303	541	.560
Dikembe Mutombo, DEN	349	628	.556
Shawn Kemp, SEA	545	997	.547
Danny Manning, PHO	340	622	.547
Olden Polynice, SAC	376	691	.544

THREE POINT FIELD GOALS

	3PM	3PA	3P%
Steve Kerr, CHI	89	170	.524
Detlef Schrempf, SEA	93	181	.514
Dana Barros, PHI	197	425	.464
Hubert Davis, NYK	131	288	.455
John Stockton, UTJ	102	227	.449
Hersey Hawkins, CHA	131	298	.440
Wesley Person, PHO	116	266	.436
Kenny Smith, HOU	142	331	.429
B.J. Armstrong, CHI	108	253	.427
Dell Curry, CHA	154	361	.427

FREE THROWS

	FTM	FTA	FT%
Spud Webb, SAC	226	242	.934
Mark Price, CLE	148	162	.914
Dana Barros, PHI	347	386	.899
Reggie Miller, IND	383	427	.897
Muggsy Bogues, CHA	160	180	.889
Scott Skiles, WSB	179	202	.886
Mahmoud Abdul-Rauf, DEN	138	156	.885
B.J. Armstrong, CHI	206	233	.884
Jeff Hornacek, UTJ	284	322	.882
Keith Jennings, GST	134	153	.876

ASSISTS

	GP	AST	APG
John Stockton, UTJ	82	1011	12.3
Kenny Anderson, NJN	72	680	9.4
Tim Hardaway, GST	62	578	9.3
Rod Strickland, POR	64	562	8.8
Muggsy Bogues, CHA	78	675	8.7
Nick Van Exel, LAL	80	660	8.2
Avery Johnson, SAS	82	670	8.2
Pooh Richardson, LAC	80	632	7.9
Mookie Blaylock, ATL	80	616	7.7
Jason Kidd, DAL	79	607	7.7

REBOUNDS

	GP	ORB	DRB	TRB	RPG
Dennis Rodman, SAS	49	274	549	823	16.8
Dikembe Mutombo, DEN	82	319	710	1029	12.5
Shaquille O'Neal, ORL	79	328	573	901	11.4
Patrick Ewing, NYK	79	157	710	867	11.0
Tyrone Hill, CLE	70	269	496	765	10.9
Shawn Kemp, SEA	82	318	575	893	10.9
David Robinson, SAS	81	234	643	877	10.8
Hakeem Olajuwon, HOU	72	172	603	775	10.8
Karl Malone, UTJ	82	156	715	871	10.6
Popeye Jones, DAL	80	329	515	844	10.6

STEALS

	GP	STL	SPG
Scottie Pippen, CHI	79	232	2.94
Mookie Blaylock, ATL	80	200	2.50
Gary Payton, SEA	82	204	2.49
John Stockton, UTJ	82	194	2.37
Nate McMillan, SEA	80	165	2.06
Eddie Jones, LAL	64	131	2.05
Jason Kidd, DAL	79	151	1.91
Elliot Perry, PHO	82	156	1.90
Hakeem Olajuwon, HOU	72	133	1.85
Dana Barros, PHI	82	149	1.82

BLOCKS

	GP	BLK	BPG
Dikembe Mutombo, DEN	82	321	3.91
Hakeem Olajuwon, HOU	72	242	3.36
Shawn Bradley, PHI	82	274	3.34
David Robinson, SAS	81	262	3.23
Alonzo Mourning, CHA	77	225	2.92
Shaquille O'Neal, ORL	79	192	2.43
Vlade Divac, LAL	80	174	2.17
Patrick Ewing, NYK	79	159	2.01
Bo Outlaw, LAC	81	151	1.86
Oliver Miller, DET	64	116	1.81

TURNOVERS

	GP	TO	TPG
Glenn Robinson, MIL	80	312	3.9
Chris Mullin, GST	25	93	3.7
Tim Hardaway, GST	62	217	3.5
Scottie Pippen, CHI	79	269	3.4
Penny Hardaway, ORL	77	262	3.4
Hakeem Olajuwon, HOU	72	238	3.3
John Stockton, UTJ	82	271	3.3
Latrell Sprewell, GST	69	228	3.3
Joe Dumars, DET	67	221	3.3
Rod Strickland, POR	64	211	3.3

THE YEAR IN BASKETBALL

November 3, 1994 Glenn Robinson of Purdue signs the most lucrative rookie contract in NBA history—a 10-year, $68 million contract with the Milwaukee Bucks.

November 16, 1994 One day after signing Chris Webber, Golden State trades him to Washington for Tom Gugliotta and first-round draft picks in 1996, 1998, and 2000.

January 6, 1995 Lenny Wilkens becomes the NBA's winningest head coach when he notches his 939th victory, as his Atlanta Hawks topple Washington, 112-90. Wilkens' win total moves him past Red Auerbach. Following the game, Wilkens lights a cigar—Auerbach's trademark—in honor of the man whose record he surpassed.

February 1, 1995 Utah Jazz guard John Stockton breaks Magic Johnson's all-time NBA career assists record of 9,921, in the Jazz' 129-88 rout of Denver.

February 14, 1995 Clyde Drexler is traded to the Houston Rockets, where he is reunited with college teammate Hakeem Olajuwon.

March 17, 1995 Michael Jordan announces that he is ending his 17-month retirement and will rejoin the Chicago Bulls immediately. Ten days later, he scores 55 points in a Bulls' victory over the New York Knicks at Madison Square Garden.

March 29, 1995 Virginia Tech captures its second NIT title, nipping Marquette, 65-64, in overtime. The Hokies' Shawn Smith is MVP.

April 2, 1995 Connecticut completes a 35-0 season by defeating Tennessee, 70-64, for the NCAA women's championship.

April 3, 1995 UCLA wins its first national championship in 20 years and 11th overall, defeating Arkansas, 89-78. Ed O'Bannon is MVP.

April 28, 1995 In his first playoff game since returning, Michael Jordan scores 48 points as the Bulls beat the Hornets, 108-100.

June 14, 1995 The Houston Rockets win their second consecutive NBA title, defeating the Orlando Magic, 113-101, to complete a four-game sweep. Rockets' center Hakeem Olajuwon scores 35 points in outplaying Shaquille O'Neal, who tallies 25.

June 1995 High schooler Kevin Garnett is selected fifth overall by the Minnesota Timberwolves in the NBA draft. Garnett, who played at Chicago's Farragut Academy, is the first player to jump directly from high school to the NBA in 20 years.

1995-96

Raptors, Grizzlies join, but Rodman pushes Bulls back to top

The 1995-1996 season had something new, followed by something familiar. Before the season began Minnesota had selected high school phenom Kevin Garnett fifth overall in the draft. A standout as Chicago's Farragut Academy, Garnett became the first player to jump directly from high school to the NBA in 20 years. Also new were the Toronto Raptors and Vancouver Grizzlies, Canada's two NBA entries that brought the number of teams to 29. Amazingly, each newcomer won its opener. Before 33,000 fans at SkyDome, the Raptors defeated New Jersey, 94-79. (In the months to follow, Toronto's distinctions were historically dubious: in January they went 0-for-3 from the foul line to set an NBA record for fewest free throws made in a game). Meanwhile in Portland, the Grizzlies overran the Blazers, 92-80.

A month before the season began the Bulls sought to strengthen their front line and acquired Dennis Rodman from San Antonio. The king of eccentricity had won four consecutive rebounding titles but had worn out his welcome in San Antonio with oddball behavior, like removing his sneakers in a playoff huddle. Thus Rodman was available for the bargain price of backup center Will Perdue. In Miami, Pat Riley wooed Alonzo Mourning and got him, with Pete Myers and big man LeRon Ellis, in exchange for forward Glen Rice (who had scored 56 points last April), point guard Khalid Reeves, center Matt Geiger, and a 1996 first round draft pick.

With no one in the NBA requiring proof of his greatness, Hakeem Olajuwon became the eleventh player in history to score 20,000 points and grab 10,000 rebounds. Other landmarks involved an official and a coach: referee Jake O'Donnell retired after officiating more than 2,100 NBA regular-season games, 279 playoff games, and 39 NBA Finals games in 28 seasons. Dallas coach Dick Motta became just the third coach to win 900 games, when his Mavericks defeated Vancouver, 103-101, in a double-overtime contest.

Magic Johnson came out of retirement to help a rejuvenated Laker team and logged 19 points, eight rebounds and 10 assists in his first game in five years, sparking the Lakers to a 128-118 victory over Golden State. He retired for good at the end of the season. In April, Robert Parish of Charlotte played in his 1,561st game, breaking Kareem Abdul-Jabbar's career record. Orlando's Dennis Scott made a record 11 three-pointers in a victory over Atlanta.

But all events this year were lesser sideshows compared to what was going on in Chicago. Denver was the unlikely team to defeat Chicago in February and snap the Bulls' franchise-record 18-game winning streak—the fourth-longest in NBA history. By the All-Star break Chicago was an ungodly 42-5. Jordan scored 20 points in 22 minutes and was named MVP as the East beat the West, 129-118. Shaquille O'Neal led all scorers with a game-high 25 points.

Dennis Rodman
"The Worm" tutored as a Bad Boy in Detroit, but grew into a higher-profile trouble maker during his championship stints with the Bulls.

On March 26, Orlando's NBA record 40-game home winning streak ended with a 113-91 loss to the Lakers. A week later, the Bulls wiped out the mark with a 44th straight home win. The Bulls had balance: Jordan had scored 40 points ten times and 50 once, leading the circuit in scoring; Scottie Pippen contributed 19 points and hellacious defense (Rodman, Pippen and Jordan were First Team all-defensive players); Toni Kukoc earned Sixth Man of the Year; Steve Kerr made threes at a .515 clip, and the team coupled a league best offense (105.2) with the third best defense. When they won in Milwaukee on

April 16th their record was 70-9, the first team to win 70 in a season.

The coming showdown was Chicago and Orlando, who won 60, leaving New York in the dust, 13 games behind them in the Atlantic Division. Orlando was hot, chopping down Detroit and Atlanta in the playoffs with a 7-1 record. Chicago also enjoyed a 7-1 mark versus Cleveland and New York. Chicago served ominous notice to Orlando with a 121-83 win in Game 1 of the Conference Finals. Jordan accepted his MVP Award before Game 2, but the Bulls were down by 20 points before their stifling defense turned the deficit into a 93-88 victory. They won the next two easily.

Seattle presented a problem. They won a Western-best 64 games and had swept two-time defending champs Houston in the second round. They beat Utah on their homecourt in

seven games. Chicago-Seattle was the match-up of the two best records in Finals history. The Bulls won Game 1, 107-90. Rodman set an NBA Finals record with 11 offensive rebounds in Game 2. Chicago led 76-65 and led by three with 8 seconds left, and Pippen missed two. Rodman got the rebound and forced a jump ball and the Bulls held on 92-88. In Seattle for Game 3, Jordan scored 36 and the Bulls won in a blowout, 108-86. Seattle woke up, prevailing 107-86 in Game 4. In Game 5, the score was tied at 51 midway through the third quarter, but Seattle's defense—and Shawn Kemp, Hersey Hawkins, and Defensive Player of the Year, Gary Payton, each scoring 20—turned up the heat for a 89-78 win. Rodman again snatched 11 offensive rebounds to clean up Chicago's poor shooting in Game 6 and the Bulls prevailed 87-75 for their fourth title in six years.

1995-96 SEASON HIGHLIGHTS

STANDINGS

Eastern Conference
Atlantic Division

	W	L	Pct.	GB
Orlando	60	22	.732	—
New York	47	35	.573	13
Miami Heat	42	40	.512	18
Washington	39	43	.476	21
Boston	33	49	.402	27
New Jersey	30	52	.366	30
Philadelphia	18	64	.22	42

Central Division

	W	L	Pct.	GB
Chicago	72	10	.878	—
Indiana	52	30	.634	20
Cleveland	47	35	.573	25
Atlanta	46	36	.561	26
Detroit	46	36	.561	26
Charlotte	41	41	.500	31
Milwaukee	25	57	.305	47
Toronto	21	61	.256	51

Western Conference
Midwest Division

	W	L	Pct.	GB
San Antonio	59	23	.720	—
Utah	55	27	.671	4
Houston	48	34	.585	11
Denver	35	47	.427	24
Dallas	26	56	.317	33
Minnesota	26	56	.317	33
Vancouver	15	67	.183	44

Pacific Division

	W	L	Pct.	GB
Seattle	64	18	.780	—
LA Lakers	53	29	.646	11
Portland	44	38	.537	20
Phoenix	41	41	.500	23
Sacramento	39	43	.476	25
Golden State	36	46	.439	28
LA Clippers	29	53	.354	35

AWARDS
MVP
Michael Jordan, Chicago
Top Rookie
Damon Stoudamire, Toronto
Coach of Year
Phil Jackson, Chicago
Defensive Player of Year
Gary Payton, Seattle
Sixth Man Award
Tony Kukoc, Chicago
Most Improved Player
Gheorghe Muresan, Washington
Citizenship Award
Chris Dudley, Portland

ALL-STAR GAME
Alamodome, San Antonio, Texas
Sunday, February 11, 1996
East 129, West 118
MVP: Michael Jordan

ALL-STAR TEAMS
FIRST TEAM

Scottie Pippen	Chicago
Karl Malone	Utah
David Robinson	San Antonio
Michael Jordan	Chicago
Anfernee Hardaway	Orlando

SECOND TEAM

Shawn Kemp	Seattle
Grant Hill	Detroit
Hakeem Olajuwon	Houston
Gary Payton	Seattle
John Stockton	Utah

THIRD TEAM

Charles Barkley	Phoenix
Juwan Howard	Washington
Shaquille O'Neal	Orlando
Mitch Richmond	Sacramento
Reggie Miller	Indiana

PLAYOFFS

FINALS
Chicago 4, Seattle 2
June 5: Seattle 90 at Chicago 107
June 7: Seattle 88 at Chicago 92
June 9: Chicago 108 at Seattle 86
June 12: Chicago 86 at Seattle 107
June 14: Chicago 78 at Seattle 89
June 16: Seattle 75 at Chicago 87

EASTERN CONFERENCE
CONFERENCE FINALS
Chicago 4, Orlando 0
May 19: Orlando 83 at Chicago 121
May 21: Orlando 88 at Chicago 93
May 25: Chicago 86 at Orlando 67
May 27: Chicago 106 at Orlando 101

CONFERENCE SEMI-FINALS
Chicago 4, New York 1
May 5: New York 84 at Chicago 91
May 7: New York 80 at Chicago 91
May 11: Chicago 99 at New York 102, OT
May 12: Chicago 94 at New York 91
May 14: New York 81 at Chicago 94

Orlando 4, Atlanta 1
May 8: Atlanta 105 at Orlando 117
May 10: Atlanta 94 at Orlando 120
May 12: Orlando 102 at Atlanta 96
May 13: Orlando 99 at Atlanta 104
May 15: Atlanta 88 at Orlando 96

FIRST ROUND
Chicago 3, Miami 0
Apr. 26: Miami 85 at Chicago 102
Apr. 28: Miami 75 at Chicago 106
May 1: Chicago 112 at Miami 91

Orlando 3, Detroit 0
Apr. 26: Detroit 92 at Orlando 112
Apr. 28: Detroit 77 at Orlando 92
Apr. 30: Orlando 101 at Detroit 98

Atlanta 3, Indiana 2
Apr. 25: Atlanta 92 at Indiana 80
Apr. 27: Atlanta 94 at Indiana 102, OT
Apr. 29: Indiana 83 at Atlanta 90
May 2: Indiana 83 at Atlanta 75
May 5: Atlanta 89 at Indiana 87

New York 3, Cleveland 0
Apr. 25: New York 106 at Cleveland 83
Apr. 27: New York 84 at Cleveland 80
May 1: Cleveland 76 at New York 81

WESTERN CONFERENCE
CONFERENCE FINALS
Seattle 4, Utah 3
May 18: Utah 72 at Seattle 102
May 20: Utah 87 at Seattle 91
May 24: Seattle 76 at Utah 96
May 26: Seattle 88 at Utah 86
May 28: Utah 98 at Seattle 95, OT
May 30: Seattle 83 at Utah 118
June 2: Utah 86 at Seattle 90

CONFERENCE SEMI-FINALS
Seattle 4, Houston 0
May 4: Houston 75 at Seattle 108
May 6: Houston 101 at Seattle 105
May 10: Seattle 115 at Houston 112
May 12: Seattle 114 at Houston 107, OT

Utah 4, San Antonio 2
May 7: Utah 95 at San Antonio 75
May 9: Utah 77 at San Antonio 88
May 11: San Antonio 75 at Utah 105
May 12: San Antonio 86 at Utah 101
May 14: Utah 87 at San Antonio 98
May 16: San Antonio 81 at Utah 108

FIRST ROUND
Seattle 3, Sacramento 1
Apr. 26: Sacramento 85 at Seattle 97
Apr. 28: Sacramento 90 at Seattle 81
Apr. 30: Seattle 96 at Sacramento 89
May 2: Seattle 101 at Sacramento 87

San Antonio 3, Phoenix 1
Apr. 26: Phoenix 98 at San Antonio 120
Apr. 28: Phoenix 105 at San Antonio 110
May 1: San Antonio 93 at Phoenix 94
May 3: San Antonio 116 at Phoenix 98

Utah 3, Portland 2
Apr. 25: Portland 102 at Utah 110
Apr. 27: Portland 90 at Utah 105
Apr. 29: Utah 91 at Portland 94, OT
May 1: Utah 90 at Portland 98
May 5: Portland 64 at Utah 102

Houston 3, L.A. Lakers 1
Apr. 25: Houston 87 at L.A. Lakers 83
Apr. 27: Houston 94 at L.A. Lakers 104
Apr. 30: L.A. Lakers 98 at Houston 104
May 2: L.A. Lakers 94 at Houston 102

NBA LEADERS

SCORING

	GP	FGM	FTM	PTS	PPG
Michael Jordan, CHI	82	916	548	2491	30.4
Hakeem Olajuwon, HOU	72	768	397	1936	26.9
Shaquille O'Neal, ORL	54	592	249	1434	26.6
Karl Malone, UTJ	82	789	512	2106	25.7
David Robinson, SAS	82	711	626	2051	25.0
Charles Barkley, PHO	71	580	440	1649	23.2
Alonzo Mourning, MIA	70	563	488	1623	23.2
Mitch Richmond, SAC	81	611	425	1872	23.1
Patrick Ewing, NYK	76	678	351	1711	22.5
Juwan Howard, WSB	81	733	319	1789	22.1

FIELD GOALS

	FGM	FGA	FG%
Gheorghe Muresan, WSB	466	798	.584
Chris Gatling, GST/MIA	326	567	.575
Shaquille O'Neal, ORL	592	1033	.573
Anthony Mason, NYK	449	798	.563
Shawn Kemp, SEA	526	937	.561
Dale Davis, IND	334	599	.558
Arvydas Sabonis, POR	394	723	.545
Bison Dele, LAC	416	766	.543
Chucky Brown, HOU	300	555	.541
John Stockton, UTJ	440	818	.538

THREE POINT FIELD GOALS

	3PM	3PA	3P%
Tim Legler, WSB	128	245	.522
Steve Kerr, CHI	122	237	.515
Hubert Davis, NYK	127	267	.476
B.J. Armstrong, GST	98	207	.473
Jeff Hornacek, UTJ	104	223	.466
Brent Price, WSB	139	301	.462
Bobby Phills, CLE	93	211	.441
Terry Dehere, LAC	139	316	.440
Mitch Richmond, SAC	225	515	.437
Allan Houston, DET	191	447	.427

FREE THROWS

	FTM	FTA	FT%
Mahmoud Abdul-Rauf, DEN	146	157	.930
Jeff Hornacek, UTJ	259	290	.893
Terrell Brandon, CLE	338	381	.887
Dana Barros, BOS	130	147	.884
Brent Price, WSB	167	191	.874
Hersey Hawkins, SEA	247	283	.873
Mitch Richmond, SAC	425	491	.866
Reggie Miller, IND	430	498	.863
Tim Legler, WSB	132	153	.863
Spud Webb, ATL/MIN	125	145	.862

ASSISTS

	GP	AST	APG
John Stockton, UTJ	82	916	11.2
Jason Kidd, DAL	81	783	9.7
Avery Johnson, SAS	82	789	9.6
Rod Strickland, POR	67	640	9.6
Damon Stoudamire, TOR	70	653	9.3
Kevin Johnson, PHO	56	517	9.2
Kenny Anderson, NJN/CHA	69	575	8.3
Tim Hardaway, GST/MIA	80	640	8.0
Mark Jackson, IND	81	635	7.8
Gary Payton, SEA	81	608	7.5

REBOUNDS

	GP	ORB	DRB	TRB	RPG
Dennis Rodman, CHI	64	356	596	952	14.9
David Robinson, SAS	82	319	681	1000	12.2
Dikembe Mutombo, DEN	74	249	622	871	11.8
Charles Barkley, PHO	71	243	578	821	11.6
Shawn Kemp, SEA	79	276	628	904	11.4
Hakeem Olajuwon, HOU	72	176	608	784	10.9
Patrick Ewing, NYK	76	157	649	806	10.6
Alonzo Mourning, MIA	70	218	509	727	10.4
Loy Vaught, LAC	80	204	604	808	10.1
Jayson Williams, NJN	80	342	461	803	10.0

STEALS

	GP	STL	SPG
Gary Payton, SEA	81	231	2.85
Mookie Blaylock, ATL	81	212	2.62
Michael Jordan, CHI	82	180	2.20
Jason Kidd, DAL	81	175	2.16
Alvin Robertson, TOR	77	166	2.16
Penny Hardaway, ORL	82	166	2.02
Eric Murdock, MIL/VAN	73	135	1.85
Eddie Jones, LAL	70	129	1.84
Hersey Hawkins, SEA	82	149	1.82
Tom Gugliotta, MIN	78	139	1.78

BLOCKS

	GP	BLK	BPG
Dikembe Mutombo, DEN	74	332	4.49
Shawn Bradley, PHI/NJN	79	288	3.65
David Robinson, SAS	82	271	3.30
Hakeem Olajuwon, HOU	72	207	2.88
Alonzo Mourning, MIA	70	189	2.70
Elden Campbell, LAL	82	212	2.59
Patrick Ewing, NYK	76	184	2.42
Gheorghe Muresan, WSB	76	172	2.26
Shaquille O'Neal, ORL	54	115	2.13
Jim McIlvaine, WSB	80	166	2.08

TURNOVERS

	GP	TO	TPG
Shawn Kemp, SEA	79	316	4.0
Jason Kidd, DAL	81	324	4.0
Rod Strickland, POR	67	255	3.8
Damon Stoudamire, TOR	70	266	3.8
Robert Pack, DEN	31	115	3.7
Juwan Howard, WSB	81	300	3.7
Alonzo Mourning, MIA	70	259	3.7
Jerry Stackhouse, PHI	72	252	3.5
Hakeem Olajuwon, HOU	72	245	3.4
Glenn Robinson, MIL	82	279	3.4

THE YEAR IN BASKETBALL

September 13, 1995 The Harlem Globetrotters lose their first game in 24 years, 91-85, in Vienna, Austria, to a team led by ex-Lakers' star Kareem Abdul-Jabbar. The Trotters had won 8,829 straight games.

January 12, 1996 New York holds Boston's Dana Barros without a three-pointer in a 105-92 Knicks' victory, ending Barros' NBA record streak of 89 consecutive games with at least one three-point basket.

January 30, 1996 Magic Johnson comes out of retirement to get 19 points, eight rebounds and 10 assists, sparking the Lakers to a 128-118 victory over Golden State at the Great Western Forum.

February 20, 1996 John Stockton breaks Maurice Cheeks' all-time record for steals in a career, with 2,311, as Utah defeats Boston, 112-98.

March 12, 1996 Denver's Mahmoud Abdul-Rauf, who has refused to stand during the national anthem because of his Islamic beliefs, is suspended without pay. Two days later, Abdul-Rauf and the league agree on a compromise: The guard will stand and say a silent prayer during the anthem.

March 18, 1996 Dennis Rodman of the Chicago Bulls is fined $20,000 and suspended for six games for assaulting a referee.

March 26, 1996 Orlando's 40-game home winning streak ends.

March 31, 1996 Freshman Chamique Holdsclaw scores 16 points and grabs 14 rebounds to lead Tennessee to its fourth NCAA women's title, in an 83-65 victory over Georgia.

April 1, 1996 Kentucky wins its first national title in 18 years with a 76-67 victory over Syracuse.

April 6, 1996 Robert Parish of Charlotte plays in his 1,561st game, breaking Kareem Abdul-Jabbar's career record.

April 16, 1996 The Bulls win their 70th game, breaking the 1971-72 Lakers' record of 69 wins in a season.

April 21, 1996 The Bulls beat Washington to finish with a 72-10 (.878) regular season record, giving them the most wins in NBA history.

April 24, 1996 The NBA's board of governors approves the formation of a women's basketball league, to be called the WNBA.

May 14, 1996 Magic Johnson retires for the second time.

June 16, 1996 Led by Michael Jordan's 22 points, the Bulls win their fourth NBA title in six years, by beating Seattle, 87-75, in Game 6.

July 18, 1996 Shaquille O'Neal joins the Los Angeles Lakers in a record seven-year deal worth $121 million.

1996-97

Shaq goes Hollywood, but real power base still in Windy City

Chicago opened the season with a torrid 17-1 mark, bringing their record over the last 100 regular season games to 89-11 (.890). It seemed possible, even probable, that they would win 70 games again.

As the Bulls appeared ascendant, the Magic began to decline. On July 18 Shaquille O'Neal, a free agent, signed a seven-year deal with Los Angeles worth $121 million. Following three-consecutive 50-win seasons, Orlando had to face the future without their 24-year old behemoth in the middle. In December they lost a game to Cleveland, 84-57, matching the NBA record for fewest points in a game since the 24-second clock debuted in 1954. O'Neal missed 31 games with a knee injury but still led Los Angeles in points, rebounds, field goal percentage and blocks. O'Neal would be joined by Kobe Bryant, who, straight from high school, made his debut on November 3 at 18 years and four months—becoming the youngest player in NBA history. In December Jermaine O'Neal of Portland, who had turned 18 on Oct. 13, became the youngest player ever in an NBA game, eclipsing the record of Bryant a month before.

Another major transaction sent Charles Barkley to Houston. Barkley lent muscle and scoring to the duet of Hakeem Olajuwon and Clyde Drexler. Irrepressible as ever on the boards, Barkley gathered 33 caroms in one game and 27 in another—the highest totals of the season. Houston jumped from 48 to 57 wins and hoped to return to championship form.

Behind second-year coach Jeff Van Gundy, New York won 57 games. But they gazed upward in the standings to find their old coach, Pat Riley, and the Miami Heat, winners of 61 games and the Atlantic Division title. In just over a year Riley had molded the team into a force in the Eastern Conference. He had a scorer-playmaker in Tim Hardaway, a prolific three-point man in Voshon Lenard, and a 20-point scorer, rebounder, fierce defender and shot-blocker in Alonzo Mourning. The defensive influence Riley exerted in New York was visited on the Heat, as his troops allowed a stingy 89 points per game. Chicago and Utah tied for the league lead in defense.

The All-Star Game in Cleveland brought together 47 of the greatest 50 players of all-time for a half-time ceremony. Battling back from a 23-point deficit, the East took charge by scoring 40 points in the third quarter, 20 of them by Charlotte's Glen Rice, who finished with 26 and took MVP honors.

In April, a Philadelphia rookie gave the league a glimpse of years to come. Guarded by Michael Jordan, Allen Iverson scored 44 points against the Bulls, the most by a rookie in four years. He later became the only rookie ever to score 40 or more points in five consecutive NBA games.

The changes in the league could not slow Chicago. Deprived of winning 70 games by consecutive losses to Miami and New York to end the season, the Bulls still won a best-ever

Karl Malone
A First-Team All-Star and league MVP, "The Mailman" couldn't deliver the NBA Championship to Utah, falling to the Bulls in six games.

141 games in consecutive seasons. They were 42-6 at the All-Star break and would likely have surpassed 70 wins if Dennis Rodman didn't kick a sideline cameraman in the groin, drawing an 11-game suspension from the league.

New York eliminated themselves from the conference semifinals against Miami. After they took a 3-1 lead, a brawl in Game 5 led to the suspension of three New York players, including Patrick Ewing. Miami won the last three games, sealing the deal when Tim Hardaway scored 18 of his 38 points in the third quarter of Game 7, as Miami won 101-90. For their

troubles Miami got run over by Chicago in five games.

In the Western Conference, Houston got by Seattle, last year's finalist, in seven games. But John Stockton took over the fourth quarter of Game 6 against Houston, culminating in his three-pointer at the buzzer to send Utah to its first-ever NBA Finals in a dramatic 103-100 win.

From the start, the Utah-Chicago tilt was tightly played. In Game 1 a three-pointer by Scottie Pippen made it 81-79, but a Stockton three with 52 seconds left tied the score at 82. A Stockton miss and Karl Malone rebound put Malone on the line, where the MVP missed both free throws. Chicago set up a play for Jordan with 7.5 seconds left. Bryon Russell lunged for a steal, but Jordan side-stepped him and hit a jumper to win it, 84-82. In Game 2 the Bulls won 97-85. Malone's 37 points in Game 3 helped Utah to a 104-93 win. The Bulls led 71-66 with 2:27 left in Game 4. Then, following a time out, Stockton hit

a three, stole the ball from Jordan and threw a perfect outlet to a driving Malone. Utah won 78-73.

Jordan played Game Five in Utah with the flu. The Jazz led by 16 in the second quarter. Jordan brought Chicago back but they still trailed 53-49 at the half. A Stockton three-pointer gave Utah a lead, but a Jordan three with 26 seconds left gave Chicago a two-point 90-88 victory. In Game 6 Chicago was down 10 in the second quarter but Jordan led them back. Chicago took a late lead behind threes by Judd Buechler and Steve Kerr. A three by Russell tied the game with 28 seconds left. With seconds left, Stockton double-teamed Jordan. Jordan found Kerr open in the lane and he hit a 15-footer with 5 seconds left. Pippen then stole the inbounds pass and the Bulls, after a Toni Kukoc basket, won 90-86. The Bulls had won five of the last seven titles and Jordan had his fifth Finals MVP.

1996-97 SEASON HIGHLIGHTS

STANDINGS

Eastern Conference
Atlantic Division

	W	L	Pct.	GB
Miami Heat	61	21	.744	—
New York	57	25	.695	4
Orlando	45	37	.549	16
Washington	44	38	.537	17
New Jersey	26	56	.317	35
Philadelphia	22	60	.268	39
Boston	15	67	.183	46

Central Division

	W	L	Pct.	GB
Chicago	69	13	.841	—
Atlanta	56	26	.683	13
Charlotte	54	28	.659	15
Detroit	54	28	.659	15
Cleveland	42	40	.512	27
Indiana	39	43	.476	30
Milwaukee	33	49	.402	36
Toronto	30	52	.366	39

Western Conference
Midwest Division

	W	L	Pct.	GB
Utah	64	18	.780	—
Houston	57	25	.695	7
Minnesota	40	42	.488	24
Dallas	24	58	.293	40
Denver	21	61	.256	43
San Antonio	20	62	.244	44
Vancouver	14	68	.171	50

Pacific Division

	W	L	Pct.	GB
Seattle	57	25	.695	—
LA Lakers	56	26	.683	1
Portland	49	33	.598	8
Phoenix	40	42	.488	17
LA Clippers	36	46	.439	21
Sacramento	34	48	.415	23
Golden State	30	52	.366	27

AWARDS

MVP
Karl Malone, Utah
Top Rookie
Allen Iverson, Philadelphia
Coach of Year
Pat Riley, Miami
Defensive Player of Year
Dikembe Mutombo, Denver
Sixth Man Award
John Starks, New York
Most Improved Player
Isaac Austin, Miami
Citizenship Award
P.J. Brown, Miami

ALL-STAR GAME
Gund Arena, Cleveland, Ohio
Sunday, February 9, 1997
East 132, West 120
MVP: Glen Rice

ALL-STAR TEAMS

FIRST TEAM

Karl Malone	Utah
Grant Hill	Detroit
Hakeem Olajuwon	Houston
Michael Jordan	Chicago
Tim Hardaway	Miami

SECOND TEAM

Scottie Pippen	Chicago
Glen Rice	Charlotte
Patrick Ewing	New York
Gary Payton	Seattle
Mitch Richmond	Sacramento

THIRD TEAM

Anthony Mason	Charlotte
Vin Baker	Milwaukee
Shaquille O'Neal	Los Angeles
John Stockton	Utah
Anfernee Hardaway	Orlando

PLAYOFFS

FINALS
Chicago 4, Utah 2
June 1: Utah 82 at Chicago 84
June 4: Utah 85 at Chicago 97
June 6: Chicago 93 at Utah 104
June 8: Chicago 73 at Utah 78
June 11: Chicago 90 at Utah 88
June 13: Utah 86 at Chicago 90

EASTERN CONFERENCE
CONFERENCE FINALS
Chicago 4, Miami 1
May 20: Miami 77 at Chicago 84
May 22: Miami 68 at Chicago 75
May 24: Chicago 98 at Miami 74
May 26: Chicago 80 at Miami 87
May 28: Miami 87 at Chicago 100

CONFERENCE SEMI-FINALS
Chicago 4, Atlanta 1
May 6: Atlanta 97 at Chicago 100
May 8: Atlanta 103 at Chicago 95
May 10: Chicago 100 at Atlanta 80
May 11: Chicago 89 at Atlanta 80
May 13: Atlanta 92 at Chicago 107

Miami 4, New York 3
May 7: New York 88 at Miami 79
May 9: New York 84 at Miami 88
May 11: Miami 73 at New York 77
May 12: Miami 76 at New York 89
May 14: New York 81 at Miami 96
May 16: Miami 95 at New York 90
May 18: New York 90 at Miami 101

FIRST ROUND
Chicago 3, Washington 0
Apr. 25: Washington 86 at Chicago 98
Apr. 27: Washington 104 at Chicago 109
Apr. 30: Chicago 96 at Washington 95
Miami 3, Orlando 2
Apr. 24: Orlando 64 at Miami 99
Apr. 27: Orlando 87 at Miami 104
Apr. 29: Miami 75 at Orlando 88
May 1: Miami 91 at Orlando 99
May 4: Orlando 83 at Miami 91
New York 3, Charlotte 0
Apr. 24: Charlotte 99 at New York 109
Apr. 26: Charlotte 93 at New York 100
Apr. 28: New York 104 at Charlotte 95
Atlanta 3, Detroit 2
Apr. 25: Detroit 75 at Atlanta 89
Apr. 27: Detroit 93 at Atlanta 80
Apr. 29: Atlanta 91 at Detroit 99
May 2: Atlanta 94 at Detroit 82
May 4: Detroit 79 at Atlanta 84

WESTERN CONFERENCE
CONFERENCE FINALS
Utah 4, Houston 2
May 19: Houston 86 at Utah 101
May 21: Houston 92 at Utah 104
May 23: Utah 100 at Houston 118
May 25: Utah 92 at Houston 96
May 27: Houston 91 at Utah 96
May 29: Utah 103 at Houston 100
CONFERENCE SEMI-FINALS
Utah 4, L.A. Lakers 1
May 4: L.A. Lakers 77 at Utah 93
May 6: L.A. Lakers 101 at Utah 103
May 8: Utah 84 at L.A. Lakers 104
May 10: Utah 110 at L.A. Lakers 95
May 12: L.A. Lakers 93 at Utah 98, OT

Houston 4, Seattle 3
May 5: Seattle 102 at Houston 112
May 7: Seattle 106 at Houston 101
May 9: Houston 97 at Seattle 93
May 11: Houston 110 at Seattle 106, OT
May 13: Seattle 100 at Houston 94
May 15: Houston 96 at Seattle 99
May 17: Seattle 91 at Houston 96
FIRST ROUND
Utah 3, L.A. Clippers 0
Apr. 24: L.A. Clippers 86 at Utah 106
Apr. 26: L.A. Clippers 99 at Utah 105
Apr. 28: Utah 104 at L.A. Clippers 92
L.A. Lakers 3, Portland 1
Apr. 25: Portland 77 at L.A. Lakers 95
Apr. 27: Portland 93 at L.A. Lakers 107
Apr. 30: L.A. Lakers 90 at Portland 98
May 2: L.A. Lakers 95 at Portland 91
Houston 3, Minnesota 0
Apr. 24: Minnesota 95 at Houston 112
Apr. 26: Minnesota 84 at Houston 96
Apr. 29: Houston 125 at Minnesota 120
Seattle 3, Phoenix 2
Apr. 25: Phoenix 106 at Seattle 101
Apr. 27: Phoenix 78 at Seattle 122
Apr. 29: Seattle 103 at Phoenix 110
May 1: Seattle 122 at Phoenix 115, OT
May 3: Phoenix 92 at Seattle 116

NBA LEADERS

SCORING

	GP	FGM	FTM	PTS	PPG
Michael Jordan, CHI	82	920	480	2431	29.6
Karl Malone, UTJ	82	864	521	2249	27.4
Glen Rice, CHA	79	722	464	2115	26.8
Mitch Richmond, SAC	81	717	457	2095	25.9
Latrell Sprewell, GST	80	649	493	1938	24.2
Allen Iverson, PHI	76	625	382	1787	23.5
Hakeem Olajuwon, HOU	78	727	351	1810	23.2
Patrick Ewing, NYK	78	655	439	1751	22.4
Kendall Gill, NJN	82	644	427	1789	21.8
Gary Payton, SEA	82	706	254	1785	21.8

FIELD GOALS

	FGM	FGA	FG%
Gheorghe Muresan, WSB	327	541	.604
Tyrone Hill, CLE	357	595	.600
Rasheed Wallace, POR	380	681	.558
Shaquille O'Neal, LAL	552	991	.557
Chris Mullin, GST	438	792	.553
Karl Malone, UTJ	864	1571	.550
John Stockton, UTJ	416	759	.548
Dale Davis, IND	370	688	.538
Danny Manning, PHO	426	795	.536
Gary Trent, POR	361	674	.536

THREE POINT FIELD GOALS

	3PM	3PA	3P%
Glen Rice, CHA	207	440	.470
Steve Kerr, CHI	110	237	.464
Kevin Johnson, PHO	89	202	.441
Joe Dumars, DET	166	384	.432
Mitch Richmond, SAC	204	477	.428
Reggie Miller, IND	229	536	.427
Dell Curry, CHA	126	296	.426
Terry Mills, DET	175	415	.422
Mario Elie, HOU	120	286	.420
Voshon Lenard, MIA	183	442	.414

FREE THROWS

	FTM	FTA	FT%
Mark Price, GST	155	171	.906
Terrell Brandon, CLE	268	297	.902
Jeff Hornacek, UTJ	293	326	.899
Ricky Pierce, DEN/CHA	139	155	.897
Mario Elie, HOU	207	231	.896
Reggie Miller, IND	418	475	.880
Malik Sealy, LAC	254	290	.876
Hersey Hawkins, SEA	258	295	.875
Darrick Martin, LAC	218	250	.872
Glen Rice, CHA	464	535	.867

ASSISTS

	GP	AST	APG
Mark Jackson, DEN/IND	82	935	11.4
John Stockton, UTJ	82	860	10.5
Kevin Johnson, PHO	70	653	9.3
Jason Kidd, DAL/PHO	55	496	9.0
Rod Strickland, WSB	82	727	8.9
Damon Stoudamire, TOR	81	709	8.8
Tim Hardaway, MIA	81	695	8.6
Nick Van Exel, LAL	79	672	8.5
Robert Pack, NJN/DAL	54	452	8.4
Stephon Marbury, MIN	67	522	7.8

REBOUNDS

	GP	ORB	DRB	TRB	RPG
Dennis Rodman, CHI	55	320	563	883	16.1
Dikembe Mutombo, ATL	80	268	661	929	11.6
Anthony Mason, CHA	73	186	643	829	11.4
Ervin Johnson, DEN	82	231	682	913	11.1
Patrick Ewing, NYK	78	175	659	834	10.7
Chris Webber, WSB	72	238	505	743	10.3
Vin Baker, MIL	78	267	537	804	10.3
Shawn Kemp, SEA	81	275	532	807	10.0
Loy Vaught, LAC	82	222	595	817	10.0
Tyrone Hill, CLE	74	259	477	736	9.9
Karl Malone, UTJ	82	193	616	809	9.9

STEALS

	GP	STL	SPG
Mookie Blaylock, ATL	78	212	2.72
Doug Christie, TOR	81	201	2.48
Gary Payton, SEA	82	197	2.40
Eddie Jones, LAL	80	189	2.36
Rick Fox, BOS	76	167	2.20
David Wesley, BOS	74	162	2.19
Allen Iverson, PHI	76	157	2.07
John Stockton, UTJ	82	166	2.02
Greg Anthony, VAN	65	129	1.98
Kenny Anderson, POR	82	162	1.98

BLOCKS

	GP	BLK	BPG
Shawn Bradley, NJN/DAL	73	248	3.40
Dikembe Mutombo, ATL	80	264	3.30
Shaquille O'Neal, LAL	51	147	2.88
Alonzo Mourning, MIA	66	189	2.86
Ervin Johnson, DEN	82	227	2.77
Patrick Ewing, NYK	78	189	2.42
Vlade Divac, CHA	81	180	2.22
Hakeem Olajuwon, HOU	78	173	2.22
Kevin Garnett, MIN	77	163	2.12
Marcus Camby, TOR	63	130	2.06

TURNOVERS

	GP	TO	TPG
Allen Iverson, PHI	76	334	4.4
Robert Pack, NJN/DAL	54	218	4.0
Latrell Sprewell, GST	80	320	4.0
Jerry Stackhouse, PHI	81	316	3.9
Tom Gugliotta, MIN	81	292	3.6
Damon Stoudamire, TOR	81	292	3.6
Hakeem Olajuwon, HOU	78	281	3.6
Shawn Kemp, SEA	81	284	3.5
Glenn Robinson, MIL	80	272	3.4
Patrick Ewing, NYK	78	265	3.4

THE YEAR IN BASKETBALL

November 3, 1996 Kobe Bryant makes his debut at 18 years and four months—becoming the youngest player in NBA history—when he goes scoreless in six minutes in a Lakers' victory.

December 5, 1996 Jermaine O'Neal of Portland, who turned 18 on Oct. 13, becomes the youngest player ever in an NBA game, eclipsing the standard set by Kobe Bryant a month before.

January 15, 1997 Dennis Rodman of Chicago kicks a sideline cameraman in the groin. He is suspended for 11 games and fined $25,000.

February 12, 1997 NBA refs Henry Armstrong and George Toliver are indicted on tax-evasion charges for allegedly downgrading first-class airline tickets, pocketing the price difference, and not reporting it as income.

March 15, 1997 North Carolina head coach Dean Smith gets his 877th career win, becoming the winningest coach in NCAA history.

March 30, 1997 Tennessee beats Old Dominion, 68-59 to win its second consecutive women's basketball championship.

March 31, 1997 Arizona defeats Kentucky, 84-79, in overtime to win the NCAA championship.

April 12, 1997 Allen Iverson scores a career-high 50 points and becomes the only rookie to score 40 or more points in four straight games.

May 6, 1997 Kentucky head coach Rick Pitino announces that he is leaving to coach the Boston Celtics.

May 12, 1997 Larry Bird is named the Pacers' new head coach.

May 19, 1997 Long-time Knicks' and NBC announcer Marv Albert is indicted for allegedly biting a woman and forcing her to perform oral sex in an Arlington, Va. hotel room. Albert will deny the charges, then plead guilty to an assault and battery misdemeanor.

May 29, 1997 John Stockton hits a three-pointer at the buzzer to send Utah to its first-ever NBA finals in a dramatic 103-100 win over Houston in Game 6 of the Western Conference finals.

June 13, 1997 The Chicago Bulls defeat the Utah Jazz, four games to two, to win their fifth NBA championship in seven years. Michael Jordan, who scores 39 points in the deciding game, is voted MVP.

June 21, 1997 The New York Liberty and Los Angeles Sparks play the first game in WNBA history, at L.A.'s Great Western Forum.

August 30, 1997 The Houston Comets defeat the New York Liberty, 65-51, in Houston, to win the inaugural WNBA championship.

1997-98

Bulls look mortal, but Malone and Stockton can't quite get it done

The Chicago Bulls seemed vulnerable from the very start of the season. Scottie Pippen began the year injured and played only 44 games. After 15 games, the Bulls were 8-7. Their offense fell to ninth in the league—an anemic 96 points a game. Their strength was defense, which ranked third in a league, allowing just 89 points a game. Still, they won 62 games, giving them the best three-year total of all-time at 203-43. Their 62 wins tied Utah for league best, with the Lakers and Seattle finishing with 61 each.

Reminders of changes in the NBA abounded. Kevin Garnett averaged a modest 17 points and 9 rebounds last season. Just two years out of high school, Garnett signed a six-year, $123-million contract with the Minnesota Timberwolves, giving the 21-year-old the richest deal in sports history. Weeks later the NBA hired two female referees, Dee Kantner and Violet Palmer. Both officiated a full slate of games over the season.

Within months, several records were set. In November, A.C. Green played his 907th consecutive game to break Randy Smith's NBA record. The next month Bubba Wells, unbelievably, fouled out of a game in 3 minutes, the quickest disqualification in league history. Another mark of fabulous futility was set by the Denver Nuggets, who lost 93-77, their 23rd consecutive defeat to set an NBA record. A day later they beat the Clippers to end the streak.

In the All-Star Game in New York, Michael Jordan scored 23 points in a 135-114 win and won MVP honors for the third time. A month later a crowd of 62,046 packed Atlanta's football stadium, the Georgia Dome, to watch Jordan and the Bulls defeat the Hawks, 89-74.

San Antonio finished its season at 56-26 to set an NBA record for the largest single-season improvement—36 games. Rookie All-Star Tim Duncan, who averaged 21 points and nearly 12 rebounds a game, had much to do with the turn-around, but so did the return of David Robinson, who missed 76 games last year with a back injury.

Larry Bird, who helped Indiana to 58 wins, 19 more than last year, became only the fourth rookie head coach to win the Coach of the Year. Bird saw his defensive-oriented team through highs and lows. In a game against Portland in February the Pacers won 124-59, becoming the first NBA team ever to score twice as many points as an opponent. Not a month later Indiana set the record for fewest points in a game in the modern era when they lost to San Antonio, 74-55.

Jordan won his tenth scoring title and was voted MVP. Dennis Rodman won his seventh consecutive rebounding title. Jordan and Pippen were both voted by NBA coaches to the All-Defensive team, Jordan's ninth selection and Pippen's seventh. Karl Malone was voted to the All-Defensive team for the first time.

Michael Jordan
With this shot, "His Airness" finished the Jazz and claimed his sixth NBA Championship, sixth NBA Finals MVP and subsequently retired.

Utah, last year's finalist, faced elimination in the first round. Eighth-seeded Houston won two of three. But Utah's defense shut down the Rockets, holding them to 71 and then 70 points in the last two games. They sailed past San Antonio in five games and then swept the Lakers in the Conference Finals.

Chicago had uneventful sprints past New Jersey and Charlotte but Indiana stretched them to the limit. The Bulls won the first two games, but the next two were decided by two-points each—both Indiana victories. In Game 4 Pippen missed a pair of free throws and a Reggie Miller three-pointer with two

seconds left won it, 96-94. Back in Chicago, the Bulls won by 19, 106-87. In Indiana, the Pacers won Game 6, 92-89. In Game 7, Jordan promised victory. But the Pacers led by five with minutes left and had a jump ball. Jordan stole the tip from Rick Smits and Kerr hit a three to tie the game. The Bulls won 88-83. It was the Bulls first seven-game test since 1992, when New York took them to the limit in the conference semi-finals.

Utah ran their playoff win streak to seven with a Game 1 victory in overtime, 88-85. Game 2 saw Chicago break the home-court advantage with a 93-86 win. In Game 3 Chicago held Utah to an NBA-record low for points in a game, in a 96-54 victory. The 42-point margin of victory was a Finals' record. Game 4 was a squeaker, with Chicago prevailing 86-82. The Bulls looked to close it out in Game 5. But Karl Malone

had perhaps his best playoff game ever, scoring 39 points to lead Utah to an 83-81 victory. The series went back to Utah. In Game 6, Jordan scored 23 in the first half, but Pippen had wrenched his back on a dunk early in the game and Jordan had to carry the load. At the half the Jazz led 49-45. John Stockton hit a three-pointer with less than a minute left to give Utah a three-point lead with 41 seconds left, 86-83. But Jordan drove for a score and in the next possession he blindsided Malone and stole the ball. With 5 seconds left he drove right on Bryon Russell, and pulled up for a foul-line jumper to make it 87-86. A last second fling by Stockton was short and the Bulls, for the second time in the decade, had won their third consecutive title. Finishing with 45 points, Jordan was awarded the Finals MVP, his sixth.

1997-98 SEASON HIGHLIGHTS

STANDINGS

Eastern Conference
Atlantic Division

	W	L	Pct.	GB
Miami Heat	55	27	.671	—
New Jersey	43	39	.524	12
New York	43	39	.524	12
Washington	42	40	.512	13
Orlando	41	41	.500	14
Boston	36	46	.439	19
Philadelphia	31	51	.378	24

Central Division

	W	L	Pct.	GB
Chicago	62	20	.756	—
Indiana	58	24	.707	4
Charlotte	51	31	.622	11
Atlanta	50	32	.610	12
Cleveland	47	35	.573	15
Detroit	37	45	.451	25
Milwaukee	36	46	.439	26
Toronto	16	66	.195	46

Western Conference
Midwest Division

	W	L	Pct.	GB
Utah	62	20	.756	—
San Antonio	56	26	.683	6
Minnesota	45	37	.549	17
Houston	41	41	.500	21
Dallas	20	62	.244	42
Vancouver	19	63	.232	43
Denver	11	71	.134	51

Pacific Division

	W	L	Pct.	GB
LA Lakers	61	21	.744	—
Seattle	61	21	.744	—
Phoenix	56	26	.683	5
Portland	46	36	.561	15
Sacramento	27	55	.329	34
Golden State	19	63	.232	42
LA Clippers	17	65	.207	44

AWARDS

MVP
Michael Jordan, Chicago
Top Rookie
Tim Duncan, San Antonio
Coach of Year
Larry Bird, Indiana
Defensive Player of Year
Dikembe Mutombo, Atlanta
Sixth Man Award
Danny Manning, Phoenix
Most Improved Player
Alan Henderson, Atlanta
Citizenship Award
Steve Smith, Atlanta

ALL-STAR GAME
Madison Square Garden, New York
Sunday, February 8, 1998
East 135, West 114
MVP: Michael Jordan

ALL-STAR TEAMS

FIRST TEAM
Karl Malone	Utah
Tim Duncan	San Antonio
Shaquille O'Neal	LA Lakers
Michael Jordan	Chicago
Gary Payton	Seattle

SECOND TEAM
Grant Hill	Detroit
Vin Baker	Seattle
David Robinson	San Antonio
Tim Hardaway	Miami
Rod Strickland	Washington

THIRD TEAM
Scottie Pippen	Chicago
Glen Rice	Charlotte
Dikembe Mutombo	Atlanta
Mitch Richmond	Sacramento
Reggie Miller	Indiana

PLAYOFFS
FINALS
Chicago 4, Utah 2
June 3: Chicago 85 at Utah 88, OT
June 5: Chicago 93 at Utah 88
June 7: Utah 54 at Chicago 96
June 10: Utah 82 at Chicago 86
June 12: Utah 83 at Chicago 81
June 14: Chicago 87 at Utah 86
EASTERN CONFERENCE
CONFERENCE FINALS
Chicago 4, Indiana 3
May 17: Indiana 79 at Chicago 85
May 19: Indiana 90 at Chicago 104
May 23: Chicago 105 at Indiana 107
May 25: Chicago 94 at Indiana 96
May 27: Indiana 87 at Chicago 106
May 29: Chicago 89 at Indiana 92
May 31: Indiana 83 at Chicago 88
CONFERENCE SEMI-FINALS
Chicago 4, Charlotte 1
May 3: Charlotte 70 at Chicago 83
May 6: Charlotte 78 at Chicago 76
May 8: Chicago 103 at Charlotte 89
May 10: Chicago 94 at Charlotte 80
May 13: Charlotte 84 at Chicago 93
Indiana 4, New York 1
May 5: New York 83 at Indiana 93
May 7: New York 77 at Indiana 85
May 9: Indiana 76 at New York 83
May 10: Indiana 118 at New York 107, OT
May 13: New York 88 at Indiana 99

FIRST ROUND
Chicago 3, New Jersey 0
Apr. 24: New Jersey 93 at Chicago 96, OT
Apr. 26: New Jersey 91 at Chicago 96
Apr. 29: Chicago 116 at New Jersey 101
Charlotte 3, Atlanta 1
Apr. 23: Atlanta 87 at Charlotte 97
Apr. 25: Atlanta 85 at Charlotte 92
Apr. 28: Charlotte 64 at Atlanta 96
May 1: Charlotte 91 at Atlanta 82
Indiana 3, Cleveland 1
Apr. 23: Cleveland 77 at Indiana 106
Apr. 25: Cleveland 86 at Indiana 92
Apr. 27: Indiana 77 at Cleveland 86
Apr. 30: Indiana 80 at Cleveland 74
New York 3, Miami 2
Apr. 24: New York 79 at Miami 94
Apr. 26: New York 96 at Miami 86
Apr. 28: Miami 91 at New York 85
Apr. 30: Miami 85 at New York 90
May 3: New York 98 at Miami 81
WESTERN CONFERENCE
CONFERENCE FINALS
Utah 4, LA Lakers 0
May 16: LA Lakers 77 at Utah 112
May 18: LA Lakers 95 at Utah 99
May 22: Utah 109 at LA Lakers 98
May 24: Utah 96 at LA Lakers 92
CONFERENCE SEMI-FINALS
LA Lakers 4, Seattle 1
May 4: L.A. Lakers 92 at Seattle 106
May 6: L.A. Lakers 92 at Seattle 68
May 8: Seattle 103 at L.A. Lakers 119
May 10: Seattle 100 at L.A. Lakers 112
May 12: L.A. Lakers 110 at Seattle 95

Utah 4, San Antonio 1
May 5: San Antonio 82 at Utah 83
May 7: San Antonio 106 at Utah 109, OT
May 9: Utah 64 at San Antonio 86
May 10: Utah 82 at San Antonio 73
May 12: San Antonio 77 at Utah 87
FIRST ROUND
Utah 3, Houston 2
Apr. 23: Houston 103 at Utah 90
Apr. 25: Houston 90 at Utah 105
Apr. 29: Utah 85 at Houston 89
May 1: Utah 93 at Houston 71
May 3: Houston 70 at Utah 84
San Antonio 3, Phoenix 1
Apr. 23: San Antonio 102 at Phoenix 96
Apr. 25: San Antonio 101 at Phoenix 108
Apr. 27: Phoenix 88 at San Antonio 100
Apr. 29: Phoenix 80 at San Antonio 99
L.A. Lakers 3, Portland 1
Apr. 24: Portland 102 at L.A. Lakers 104
Apr. 26: Portland 99 at L.A. Lakers 108
Apr. 28: L.A. Lakers 94 at Portland 99
Apr. 30: L.A. Lakers 110 at Portland 99
Seattle 3, Minnesota 2
Apr. 24: Minnesota 83 at Seattle 108
Apr. 26: Minnesota 98 at Seattle 93
Apr. 28: Seattle 90 at Minnesota 98
Apr. 30: Seattle 92 at Minnesota 88
May 2: Minnesota 84 at Seattle 97

NBA LEADERS

SCORING

	GP	FGM	FTM	PTS	PPG
Michael Jordan, CHI	82	881	565	2357	28.7
Shaquille O'Neal, LAL	60	670	359	1699	28.3
Karl Malone, UTJ	81	780	628	2190	27.0
Mitch Richmond, SAC	70	543	407	1623	23.2
Antoine Walker, BOS	82	722	305	1840	22.4
Shareef Abdur-Rahim, VAN	82	653	502	1829	22.3
Glen Rice, CHA	82	634	428	1826	22.3
Allen Iverson, PHI	80	649	390	1758	22.0
Chris Webber, WAS	71	647	196	1555	21.9
David Robinson, SAS	73	544	485	1574	21.6

FIELD GOALS

	FGM	FGA	FG%
Shaquille O'Neal, LAL	670	1147	.584
Bo Outlaw, ORL	301	543	.554
Alonzo Mourning, MIA	403	732	.551
Tim Duncan, SAS	706	1287	.549
Vin Baker, SEA	631	1164	.542
Dikembe Mutombo, ATL	399	743	.537
Antonio McDyess, PHO	497	927	.536
Rasheed Wallace, POR	466	875	.533
Karl Malone, UTJ	780	1472	.530
Bryant Reeves, VAN	492	941	.523

THREE POINT FIELD GOALS

	3PM	3PA	3P%
Dale Ellis, SEA	127	274	.464
Jeff Hornacek, UTJ	56	127	.441
Chris Mullin, IND	107	243	.440
Hubert Davis, DAL	101	230	.439
Steve Kerr, CHI	57	130	.438
Glen Rice, CHA	130	300	.433
Wesley Person, CLE	192	447	.430
Reggie Miller, IND	164	382	.429
Dell Curry, CHA	61	145	.421
Eldridge Recasner, ATL	62	148	.419

FREE THROWS

	FTM	FTA	FT%
Chris Mullin, IND	154	164	.939
Jeff Hornacek, UTJ	285	322	.885
Ray Allen, MIL	342	391	.875
Derek Anderson, CLE	275	315	.873
Kevin Johnson, PHO	162	186	.871
Tracy Murray, WAS	182	209	.871
Reggie Miller, IND	382	440	.868
Hersey Hawkins, SEA	177	204	.868
Christian Laettner, ATL	306	354	.864
Mitch Richmond, SAC	407	471	.864

ASSISTS

	GP	AST	APG
Rod Strickland, WAS	76	801	10.5
Jason Kidd, PHO	82	745	9.1
Mark Jackson, IND	82	713	8.7
Stephon Marbury, MIN	82	704	8.6
John Stockton, UTJ	64	543	8.5
Tim Hardaway, MIA	81	672	8.3
Gary Payton, SEA	82	679	8.3
Brevin Knight, CLE	80	656	8.2
Damon Stoudamire, TOR/POR	71	580	8.2
Sam Cassell, NJN	75	603	8.0

REBOUNDS

	GP	ORB	DRB	TRB	RPG
Dennis Rodman, CHI	80	421	780	1201	15.0
Jayson Williams, NJN	65	443	440	883	13.6
Tim Duncan, SAS	82	274	703	977	11.9
Dikembe Mutombo, ATL	82	276	656	932	11.4
David Robinson, SAS	73	239	536	775	10.6
Karl Malone, UTJ	81	189	645	834	10.3
Anthony Mason, CHA	81	177	649	826	10.2
Antoine Walker, BOS	82	270	566	836	10.2
Arvydas Sabonis, POR	73	149	580	729	10.0
Kevin Garnett, MIN	82	222	564	786	9.6

STEALS

	GP	STL	SPG
Mookie Blaylock, ATL	70	183	2.61
Brevin Knight, CLE	80	196	2.45
Doug Christie, TOR	78	190	2.44
Gary Payton, SEA	82	185	2.26
Allen Iverson, PHI	80	176	2.20
Eddie Jones, LAL	80	160	2.00
Jason Kidd, PHO	82	162	1.98
Kendall Gill, NJN	81	156	1.93
Hersey Hawkins, SEA	82	148	1.80
Clyde Drexler, HOU	70	126	1.80

BLOCKS

	GP	BLK	BPG
Marcus Camby, TOR	63	230	3.65
Dikembe Mutombo, ATL	82	277	3.38
Shawn Bradley, DAL	64	214	3.34
Theo Ratliff, DET/PHI	82	258	3.15
David Robinson, SAS	73	192	2.63
Tim Duncan, SAS	82	206	2.51
Michael Stewart, SAC	81	195	2.41
Shaquille O'Neal, LAL	60	144	2.40
Alonzo Mourning, MIA	58	130	2.24
Bo Outlaw, ORL	82	181	2.21

TURNOVERS

	GP	TO	TPG
Glenn Robinson, MIL	56	202	3.6
Sam Cassell, NJN	75	270	3.6
Antoine Walker, BOS	82	295	3.6
Grant Hill, DET	81	284	3.5
Rod Strickland, WAS	76	266	3.5
Tim Duncan, SAS	82	279	3.4
Shawn Kemp, CLE	80	272	3.4
Jim Jackson, PHI/GST	79	262	3.3
Ray Allen, MIL	82	262	3.2
Jason Kidd, PHO	82	262	3.2

THE YEAR IN BASKETBALL

October 1, 1997 Kevin Garnett, two years out of high school, signs a six-year, $123 million contract with the Minnesota Timberwolves. The 21-year-old's pact is the richest in sports history.

October 9, 1997 Dean Smith retires as North Carolina's basketball coach after 36 years and more victories than anyone else.

October 28, 1997 The NBA hires two female referees, Dee Kantner and Violet Palmer. Both officiate a full slate of games in the season.

November 20, 1997 Ironman A.C. Green plays his 907th consecutive game to break Randy Smith's NBA record.

December 1, 1997 Golden State guard Latrell Sprewell assaults head coach P.J. Carlesimo. Sprewell is suspended for 10 games.

December 29, 1997 Dallas' Bubba Wells fouls out of a game in 3 minutes of play, the quickest disqualification in league history.

January 23, 1998 The Denver Nuggets lose their 23rd consecutive game to set an NBA single-game record, with a 93-77 defeat to Phoenix. A day later, Denver wins one, 99-81, over the Clippers.

March 26, 1998 Minnesota topples Penn State, 79-72, to win its second NIT championship in six years.

March 29, 1998 The Tennessee Lady Volunteers win their third straight women's college basketball title, defeating Louisiana Tech, 93-75.

March 30, 1998 The Kentucky Wildcats rally to defeat the Utah Utes, 78-69, to win their second national title in three seasons.

April 19, 1998 San Antonio ends its season with a win over Denver, 96-82, to finish 56-26 and set an NBA record for the largest single-season improvement—36 games.

May 12, 1998 Larry Bird becomes only the fourth rookie head coach to win the Coach of the Year as he guides his Pacers to a 58-24 record, a 19-game improvement from the previous season.

June 6, 1998 In Game 3 of the NBA finals, Chicago holds Utah to an NBA-record low for points in a game, in a 96-54 thrashing. The 42-point margin is a Finals' record.

June 14, 1998 Michael Jordan hits a game-winning jumper at the buzzer to give his Bulls the championship in Game 6 of the NBA finals.

June 29, 1998 With negotiations on a new labor agreement with the players' union deadlocked, the NBA announces that a lockout will be imposed, beginning midnight on June 30.

1998-99

With Jordan gone again, Spurs make most of short season

By June 29, 1998 negotiations on a new labor agreement with the players' union reached an impasse. Thus the NBA announced that a lockout would be imposed, beginning midnight on June 30. In October, the NBA cancelled the first two weeks of the 1998-99 season because of the lockout. In sum, the dispute cancelled the first three months of the regular season. For the NBA it was unprecedented: the league had gone 48 seasons and over 30,000 games without a single game being cancelled due to labor problems.

Before a settlement, more of the league's past had passed on. On November 13, Red Holzman, a former player who coached the New York Knicks to the franchise's only two championship titles and was inducted into the Hall of Fame in 1991, died in New York.

By January 6, an agreement between the NBA owners and the player's association ended a six-month player lockout. A reduced schedule called for each team to begin in February and play 50 regular season games. It was the fewest games played since 1947-48. That year the BAA schedule called for a reduction from 60 to 48 games to accommodate the smaller number of teams: of the 11 teams that played in the 1946-47 season, three had folded.

With nearly 40 percent of the season lopped off, the NBA title was there for the taking. Michael Jordan had retired. Scottie Pippen went to Houston in a trade and Dennis Rodman had been picked up on waivers by Los Angeles. What remained of the Bulls' dynasty were Toni Kukoc, Ron Harper, Dickey Simpkins, Randy Brown, and Bill Wennington and they finished last in the Central Division with a 13-37 mark. On April 10, Chicago's ineptitude set new standards: they lost 82-49 to Miami, the lowest point total since the introduction of the shot clock in 1954. Chicago's offense, at 81.9 per games, was by far the worst in the league. The league seemed to forget how to score: just one team—Sacramento—averaged 100 points a game

Charles Barkley, Hakeem Olajuwon, and Scottie Pippen made for a curious triumvirate in Houston, and the Rockets took off to 31-19. But the top records in the league belonged to San Antonio and Utah: they posted 37-13 marks in the mini-season. Portland won the Pacific Division, while Miami, Orlando and Indiana tied for the best marks in the east at 33-17.

Miami and New York met in the post-season for the third consecutive year and, predictably, it played out as a paradigm of bump and grind defensive basketball. New York had finished fourth in the Atlantic Division, but they now had four players capable of making a basket: Patrick Ewing, Latrell Spreewell, Allan Houston, and Larry Johnson. The margin of victory in the first four games was between 10 and 20 points, but the final game came down to a last second shot by Houston that rattled

Tim Duncan
In just his sophomore year in the NBA, he led the Spurs to the title over the Knicks—the first former ABA team to claim the big prize.

around and fell in. New York then swept Atlanta and—with the size and agility of Marcus Camby and a four-point shot by Larry Johnson—bested Indiana in six games.

San Antonio had a smoother path, getting by Minnesota in four games before sweeping Los Angeles and Portland for an 11-1 record. At times, they seemed fated to win. Down by 18 points in the third quarter of Game 2 against Portland, they came back but still trailed 85-83 with 12 seconds left. Then Sean Elliot made a three-pointer as he was falling out of bounds and San Antonio won, 86-85. They won Games 3 and 4 by a

combined 36 points.

San Antonio had never won a basketball title, not in the NBA or ABA, dating back to their entry in the league in 1973. In more than a quarter of a century they had not even been to an ABA or NBA Final. Teammates George Gervin and Artis Gilmore had not been able to bring them a title and neither could David Robinson, the first pick of the 1987 draft.

For the 1998-99 season they had added capable scorers Steve Kerr, Jerome Kersey, and Mario Elie. They started out 6-8 and then exploded to 31-5 to close out the year. In Tim Duncan and David Robinson they owned the best Twin Tower effect ever, with both finishing in the top ten in rebounds, blocks, and field goal percentage. Duncan was also sixth in scoring and was voted to the All-Defensive Team.

Against New York they took Game 1, 89-77. In the second game defense kept New York close, but San Antonio prevailed 80-67, as their big men dominated inside against a Knick defense that battled gamely without an injured Patrick Ewing. New York won Game 3 at home, 89-81. San Antonio would score above 90 for the only time in Game 4, winning 96-89. The Knicks led by 8 early in Game 5 and held a 75-72 lead with three minutes left. A three-pointer by Elie tied it. The Knicks led by a point but a short baseline jumper by Avery Johnson with 2 seconds left gave San Antonio a 78-77 lead with 2.1 seconds left. A last second fall-away by Sprewell was well short and San Antonio won its first championship. Tim Duncan was awarded Finals MVP. San Antonio became the first of the old ABA teams to win an NBA championship.

1998-99 SEASON HIGHLIGHTS

STANDINGS

Eastern Conference
Atlantic Division

	W	L	Pct.	GB
Miami	33	17	.660	—
Orlando	33	17	.660	—
Philadelphia	28	22	.560	5
New York	27	23	.540	6
Boston	19	31	.380	14
Washington	18	32	.360	15
New Jersey	16	34	.320	17

Central Division

	W	L	Pct.	GB
Indiana	33	17	.660	—
Atlanta	31	19	.620	2
Detroit	29	21	.580	4
Milwaukee	28	22	.560	5
Charlotte	26	24	.520	7
Toronto	23	27	.460	10
Cleveland	22	28	.440	11
Chicago	13	37	.260	20

Western Conference
Midwest Division

	W	L	Pct.	GB
San Antonio	37	13	.740	—
Utah	37	13	.740	—
Houston	31	19	.620	6
Minnesota	25	25	.500	12
Dallas	19	31	.380	18
Denver	14	36	.280	23
Vancouver	8	42	.160	29

Pacific Division

	W	L	Pct.	GB
Portland	35	15	.700	—
LA Lakers	31	19	.620	4
Phoenix	27	23	.540	8
Sacramento	27	23	.540	8
Seattle	25	25	.500	10
Golden State	21	29	.420	14
LA Clippers	9	41	.180	26

AWARDS

MVP
Karl Malone, Utah
Top Rookie
Vince Carter, Toronto
Coach of Year
Mike Dunleavy, Portland
Defensive Player of Year
Alonzo Mourning, Miami
Sixth Man Award
Darrell Armstrong, Orlando
Most Improved Player
Darrell Armstrong, Orlando
Citizenship Award
Brian Grant, Portland

ALL-STAR GAME

Scheduled for Sun., Feb. 14, 1999 at the First Union Center, Philadelphia, Game not played because of the lockout by the owners of the players.

ALL-STAR TEAMS

FIRST TEAM

Karl Malone	Utah
Tim Duncan	San Antonio
Alonzo Mourning	Miami
Allen Iverson	Philadelphia
Jason Kidd	Phoenix

SECOND TEAM

Chris Webber	Sacramento
Grant Hill	Detroit
Shaquille O'Neal	Los Angeles
Gary Payton	Seattle
Tim Hardaway	Miami

THIRD TEAM

Kevin Garnett	Minnesota
Antonio McDyess	Denver
Hakeem Olajuwon	Houston
Kobe Bryant	Los Angeles
John Stockton	Utah

PLAYOFFS

FINALS
San Antonio 4, New York 1
June 16: at San Antonio 89, New York 77
June 18: at San Antonio 80, New York 67
June 21: at New York 89, San Antonio 81
June 23: San Antonio 96, at New York 89
June 25: San Antonio 78, at New York 77

EASTERN CONFERENCE
CONFERENCE FINALS
New York 4, Indiana 2
May 30: New York 93, at Indiana 90
June 1: at Indiana 88, New York 86
June 5: at New York 92, Indiana 91
June 7: Indiana 90, at New York 78
June 9: New York 101, at Indiana 94
June 11: at New York 90, Indiana 82

CONFERENCE SEMI-FINALS
Indiana 4, Philadelphia 0
May 17: at Indiana 94, Philadelphia 90
May 19: at Indiana 85, Philadelphia 82
May 21: Indiana 97, at Philadelphia 86
May 23: Indiana 89, at Philadelphia 86

New York 4, Atlanta 0
May 18: New York 100, at Atlanta 92
May 20: New York 77, at Atlanta 70
May 23: at New York 90, Atlanta 78
May 24: at New York 79, Atlanta 66

FIRST ROUND
New York 3, Miami 2
May 8: New York 95, at Miami 75
May 10: at Miami 83, New York 73
May 12: at New York 97, Miami 73
May 14: Miami 87, at New York 72
May 16: New York 78, at Miami 77

Atlanta 3, Detroit 2
May 8: at Atlanta 90, Detroit 70
May 10: at Atlanta 89, Detroit 69
May 12: at Detroit 79, Atlanta 63
May 14: at Detroit 103, Atlanta 82
May 16: at Atlanta 87, Detroit 75

Philadelphia 3, Orlando 1
May 9: Philadelphia 104, at Orlando 90
May 11: at Orlando 79, Philadelphia 68
May 13: at Philadelphia 97, Orlando 85
May 15: at Philadelphia 101, Orlando 91

Indiana 3, Milwaukee 0
May 9: at Indiana 110, Milwaukee 88
May 11: at Indiana 108, Milwaukee 107, OT
May 13: Indiana 99, at Milwaukee 91

WESTERN CONFERENCE
San Antonio 4, Portland 0
May 29: at San Antonio 80, Portland 76
May 31: at San Antonio 86, Portland 85
June 4: San Antonio 85, at Portland 63
June 6: San Antonio 94, at Portland 80

CONFERENCE SEMI-FINALS
San Antonio 4, L.A. Lakers 0
May 17: at San Antonio 87, L.A. Lakers 81
May 19: at San Antonio 79, L.A. Lakers 76
May 22: San Antonio 103, at L.A. Lakers 91
May 23: San Antonio 118, at L.A. Lakers 107

Portland 4, Utah 2
May 18: at Utah 93, Portland 83
May 20: Portland 84, at Utah 81
May 22: at Portland 97, Utah 87
May 23: at Portland 81, Utah 75
May 25: at Utah 88, Portland 71
May 27: at Portland 92, Utah 80

FIRST ROUND
San Antonio 3, Minnesota 1
May 9: at San Antonio 99, Minnesota 86
May 11: Minnesota 80, at San Antonio 71
May 13: San Antonio 85, at Minnesota 71
May 15: San Antonio 92, at Minnesota 85

L.A. Lakers 3, Houston 1
May 9: at L.A. Lakers 101, Houston 100
May 11: at L.A. Lakers 110, Houston 98
May 13: at Houston 100, L.A. Lakers 88
May 15: L.A. Lakers 98, at Houston 88

Utah 3, Sacramento 2
May 8: at Utah 117, Sacramento 87
May 10: Sacramento 101, at Utah 90
May 12: at Sacramento 84, Utah 81, OT
May 14: Utah 90, at Sacramento 89
May 16: Utah 99, Sacramento 92, OT

Portland 3, Phoenix 0
May 8: at Portland 95, Phoenix 85
May 10: at Portland 110, Phoenix 99
May 12: Portland 103, at Phoenix 93

NBA LEADERS

SCORING

	GP	FGM	FTM	PTS	PPG
Allen Iverson, PHI	48	435	356	1284	26.8
Shaquille O'Neal, LAL	49	510	269	1289	26.3
Karl Malone, UTJ	49	393	378	1164	23.8
Shareef Abdur-Rahim, VAN	50	386	369	1152	23.0
Keith Van Horn, NJN	42	322	256	916	21.8
Tim Duncan, SAS	50	418	247	1084	21.7
Gary Payton, SEA	50	401	199	1084	21.7
Stephon Marbury, MIN/NJN	49	378	222	1044	21.3
Antonio McDyess, DEN	50	415	230	1061	21.2
Grant Hill, DET	50	384	285	1053	21.1

FIELD GOALS

	FGM	FGA	FG%
Shaquille O'Neal, LAL	510	885	.576
Otis Thorpe, WAS	240	440	.545
Hakeem Olajuwon, HOU	373	725	.514
Alonzo Mourning, MIA	324	634	.511
David Robinson, SAS	268	527	.509
Rasheed Wallace, POR	242	476	.508
Bison Dele, DET	216	431	.501
Vitaly Potapenko, CLE/BOS	204	412	.495
Danny Fortson, DEN	191	386	.495
Tim Duncan, SAS	418	845	.495

THREE POINT FIELD GOALS

	3PM	3PA	3P%
Dell Curry, MIL	69	145	.476
Chris Mullin, IND	73	157	.465
Hubert Davis, DAL	65	144	.451
Walt Williams, POR	63	144	.438
Dale Ellis, SEA	94	217	.433
Michael Dickerson, HOU	71	164	.433
Jeff Hornacek, UTJ	34	81	.420
Clifford Robinson, PHO	58	139	.417
George McCloud, PHO	69	166	.416
Jud Buechler, DET	61	148	.412

FREE THROWS

	FTM	FTA	FT%
Reggie Miller, IND	226	247	.915
Chauncey Billups, DEN	157	172	.913
Darrell Armstrong, ORL	161	178	.904
Ray Allen, MIL	176	195	.903
Hersey Hawkins, SEA	119	132	.902
Jeff Hornacek, UTJ	125	140	.893
Chris Mullin, IND	80	92	.870
Glenn Robinson, MIL	140	161	.870
Mario Elie, SAS	103	119	.866
Eric Piatkowski, LAC	88	102	.863

ASSISTS

	GP	AST	APG
Jason Kidd, PHO	50	539	10.8
Rod Strickland, WAS	44	434	9.9
Stephon Marbury, MIN/NJN	49	437	8.9
Gary Payton, SEA	50	436	8.7
Terrell Brandon, MIL/MIN	36	309	8.6
Mark Jackson, IND	49	386	7.9
Brevin Knight, CLE	39	302	7.7
John Stockton, UTJ	50	374	7.5
Avery Johnson, SAS	50	369	7.4
Nick Van Exel, DEN	50	368	7.4

REBOUNDS

	GP	ORB	DRB	TRB	RPG
Chris Webber, SAC	42	149	396	545	13.0
Charles Barkley, HOU	42	167	349	516	12.3
Dikembe Mutombo, ATL	50	192	418	610	12.2
Danny Fortson, DEN	50	210	371	581	11.6
Tim Duncan, SAS	50	159	412	571	11.4
Alonzo Mourning, MIA	46	166	341	507	11.0
Antonio McDyess, DEN	50	168	369	537	10.7
Shaquille O'Neal, LAL	49	187	338	525	10.7
Kevin Garnett, MIN	47	166	323	489	10.4
David Robinson, SAS	49	148	344	492	10.0

STEALS

	GP	STL	SPG
Kendall Gill, NJN	50	134	2.68
Eddie Jones, LAL/CHA	50	125	2.50
Allen Iverson, PHI	48	110	2.29
Jason Kidd, PHO	50	114	2.28
Doug Christie, TOR	50	113	2.26
Penny Hardaway, ORL	50	111	2.22
Gary Payton, SEA	50	109	2.18
Darrell Armstrong, ORL	50	108	2.16
Eric Snow, PHI	48	100	2.08
Mookie Blaylock, ATL	48	99	2.06

BLOCKS

	GP	BLK	BPG
Alonzo Mourning, MIA	46	180	3.91
Shawn Bradley, DAL	49	159	3.24
Theo Ratliff, PHI	50	149	2.98
Dikembe Mutombo, ATL	50	147	2.94
Greg Ostertag, UTJ	48	131	2.73
Patrick Ewing, NYK	38	100	2.63
Tim Duncan, SAS	50	126	2.52
Hakeem Olajuwon, HOU	50	123	2.46
David Robinson, SAS	49	119	2.43
Antonio McDyess, DEN	50	115	2.30

TURNOVERS

	GP	TO	TPG
Shareef Abdur-Rahim, VAN	50	186	3.7
Grant Hill, DET	50	184	3.7
Chris Webber, SAC	42	148	3.5
Allen Iverson, PHI	48	167	3.5
Stephon Marbury, MIN/NJN	49	164	3.3
Karl Malone, UTJ	49	162	3.3
Rod Strickland, WAS	44	142	3.2
Scottie Pippen, HOU	50	159	3.2
Keith Van Horn, NJN	42	133	3.2
Darrell Armstrong, ORL	50	158	3.2

THE YEAR IN BASKETBALL

October 13, 1998 The NBA cancels the first two weeks of the 1998-99 season because of the lockout. Ultimately, the dispute will cancel the first three months of the regular season after 51 NBA seasons and over 35,000 games without a cancellation due to labor problems. Finally, an agreement will be reached and the 82-game season will be reduced to 50 games for each team.

November 13, 1998 Red Holzman, who coached the New York Knicks to the franchise's only two championship titles and was inducted into the Hall of Fame in 1991, dies in New York.

December 22, 1998 Officials from the American Basketball League (ABL), a pro league for women that rivals the better-known WNBA, announce that they are closing down operations and filing for bankruptcy.

January 6, 1999 An agreement between NBA owners and the player's association ends a six-month player lockout. The labor dispute had threatened something unprecedented—to erase the entire 1998-99 season. When the season gets underway, teams will play an abbreviated 50-game regular season schedule.

January 8, 1999 John Thompson, Georgetown's basketball coach for 27 years, resigns in mid-season for personal reasons.

February 9, 1999 In a game between two undefeated teams, Penn blows a 27-point lead to Princeton in the final 15 minutes, losing, 50-49, at the Palestra in Philadelphia.

February 12, 1999 Four-time all-star guard Mark Price retires.

March 6, 1999 UConn upsets top-ranked Duke, 77-74, to win the school's first men's national championship. Richard Hamilton leads third-ranked Connecticut (34-2) with 27 points.

March 25, 1999 California gets past Clemson, 61-60, to win the NIT. The Bears' Sean Lampley is named tournament MVP.

April 10, 1999 The Chicago Bulls fail to break 50 points in an 82-49 loss to Miami. The Bulls' total is the lowest since the introduction of the shot clock in 1954.

June 25, 1999 San Antonio becomes the first of the old ABA teams to win the NBA Finals, outlasting New York, 78-77, in Game 5 of the finals. Tim Duncan, who scores 31 points, is named finals' MVP.

August 19, 1999 Kim Perrot, point guard for the WNBA champion Houston Comets, dies of cancer.

1999-2000

Shaq, Kobe thrive in Jackson's Zen world, usher in new dynasty

In the seven seasons from 1993-99 with Orlando and Los Angeles, Shaquille O'Neal had been part of winning teams every year. In two of those seasons (1996 and 1998) his teams won 60 games and five times they won 50 or more. But when the light shone brightest, O'Neal's teams had been swept from the post-season six out of seven times. Coach Phil Jackson was brought in for the 1999-2000 season.

As he once corrected Michael Jordan, telling him he must trust his teammates more, so Jackson now told O'Neal that he should improve his rebounding and disinterested defense. O'Neal won his second scoring title and finished first (as usual) in field goal percentage, second in rebounding, and third in blocks. With O'Neal and Kobe Bryant combining for 51 points a game, the Lakers ran out to a 37-11 record by the All-Star Game. Tim Duncan (24 points) and O'Neal (22) shared MVP honors as the West won the All-Star Game, 137-126.

As those two centers reached their peaks, another great pivot man had passed on. On October 12, Wilt Chamberlain was found dead in his Los Angeles home at the age of 63. The cause of death was congestive heart failure. The owner of dozens of records, Chamberlain was a titan for his time and all-times: he won seven scoring consecutive titles (1960-66), was the only player to average 50 points in a season (no one else ever averaged 40), and scored 100 points in a game. Chamberlain was just the second of the NBA's 50 greatest players to pass away. Pete Maravich died of a heart attack in 1988.

A month into the season Houston's Charles Barkley tore a tendon in his knee, effectively ending his career. He would rehabilitate the knee and play one last game—the last contest of the '99-00 season—before retiring for good. In January, Bobby Phills, a guard for the Hornets, died at age 30 in a car accident outside the Hornets' training facility. In May, Malik Sealy, a guard and forward for Minnesota, was killed in a head-on auto accident. The driver of the other car survived and was later found to have been drunk. Sealy was 30.

Did the season offer any surprises in the standings? No and yes. No, Pat Riley got the absolute maximum effort from his troops—nothing new there—and Miami snatched the Atlantic Division title for the fourth consecutive time. No, Utah copping the Midwest title was no headline grabber; their uncannily consistent run of regular-season excellence was routine, extending back to the mid-eighties. But yes, the Indiana Pacers, perhaps getting inspiration from last year's former-ABA champion San Antonio, hadn't been to a NBA Final in the 23 years since the merger. No less surprising was defending champ San Antonio's first-round exit against Phoenix. Tim Duncan was injured and missed the first round.

But this Pacer team was different. It wasn't, as with recent Pacer teams, modeled on the scoring of one hyperkinetic player, Reggie Miller, with the rest filling subordinate roles.

Vince Carter
Soared to NBA Slam Dunk title at the All-Star Weekend, and cued the league's marketing gurus to push another North Carolina alumnus.

Jalen Rose led Indiana in scoring and Rose, Austin Croshere, Travis Best, and Mark Jackson shared heaving duties from three-point land. Dale Davis was still a rock of granite inside and Rik Smits provided some scoring in the pivot. In his third and last year of coaching, Larry Bird had directed his team to the Finals, as he promised he would.

Weeks before the playoffs began, Shaquille O'Neal served notice of what was in store. He posted 61 points and 23 boards in a game versus the Clippers. The Lakers got a scare in the best-of-five series against Sacramento before prevailing in the

fifth game, 113-86. Phoenix proved easier competition in the conference semis but Los Angeles needed to dig deep to get past Portland. Scottie Pippen had been traded to the Blazers before the season and gave them needed playoff experience. It was working. They won 59 games, their best total in nine years and second-best in their 30-year history. They got through Minnesota and Utah with a 7-2 record before they fell behind Los Angeles three games to one. They then won consecutive games and in Game 7 led by 15 points entering the fourth quarter, just 12 minutes away from the Finals. But in the fourth quarter none of their players could make a big shot and slow the tide of the Laker comeback led by Kobe Bryant and O'Neal.

In the Finals, O'Neal set the tone with 43 points and 19 rebounds in Game 1. In Game 2 Rose, Miller and Croshere combined for 75 points, but O'Neal had 40 points and 24 rebounds and Los Angeles got a combined 42 from Glen Rice and Ron Harper. Back in Indianapolis, Indiana owned Game 3, with Miller netting 33 and Rose adding 21. But to make a series of it, Indiana needed Game 4 at home. It turned out to be the most thrilling game of the series. Bryant's status was questionable, since he rolled an ankle in Game 2. With the score tied at 104 at the end of regulation, Travis Best missed a jumper that would have won it for Indiana. In overtime O'Neal fouled out with 2:33 left and Bryant took over the game, scoring eight of L.A.'s 16 points in a 120-118 win. Bryant and O'Neal had combined for 64 points, offsetting 35 from Miller and 24 from Smits. With a 3-1 lead, the Lakers could even shake off their 120-87 blowout loss in Game 5 and return home for Game 6. The Pacers led 84-79 after three quarters, but L.A. rallied behind O'Neal's 41 points and won their first title in 12 years. Averaging 38 points and 17 rebounds, O'Neal was awarded Finals MVP.

1999-2000 SEASON HIGHLIGHTS

STANDINGS

Eastern Conference
Atlantic Division

	W	L	Pct.	GB
Miami	52	30	.634	—
New York	50	32	.610	2
Philadelphia	49	33	.598	3
Orlando	41	41	.500	11
Boston	35	47	.427	17
New Jersey	31	51	.378	21
Washington	29	53	.354	23

Central Division

	W	L	Pct.	GB
Indiana	56	26	.683	—
Charlotte	49	33	.598	7
Toronto	45	37	.549	11
Detroit	42	40	.512	14
Milwaukee	42	40	.512	14
Cleveland	32	50	.390	24
Atlanta	28	54	.341	28
Chicago	17	65	.207	39

Western Conference
Midwest Division

	W	L	Pct.	GB
Utah	55	27	.671	—
San Antonio	53	29	.646	2
Minnesota	50	32	.610	5
Dallas	40	42	.488	15
Denver	35	47	.427	20
Houston	34	48	.415	21
Vancouver	22	60	.268	33

Pacific Division

	W	L	Pct.	GB
LA Lakers	67	15	.817	—
Portland	59	23	.720	8
Phoenix	53	29	.646	14
Seattle	45	37	.549	22
Sacramento	44	38	.537	23
Golden State	19	63	.232	48
LA Clippers	15	67	.183	52

AWARDS

MVP
Shaquille O'Neal, LA Lakers
Top Rookie (tie)
Elton Brand, Chicago
Steve Francis, Houston
Coach of Year
Doc Rivers, Orlando
Defensive Player of Year
Alonzo Mourning, Miami
Sixth Man Award
Rodney Rogers, Phoenix
Most Improved Player
Jalen Rose, Indiana
Citizenship Award
Vlade Divac, Sacramento

ALL-STAR GAME

The Arena, Oakland, California
Sunday, February 13, 2000
West 137, East 126
MVPs: Shaquille O'Neal & Tim Duncan

ALL-STAR TEAMS

FIRST TEAM

Tim Duncan	San Antonio
Kevin Garnett	Minnesota
Shaquille O'Neal	LA Lakers
Jason Kidd	Phoenix
Gary Payton	Seattle

SECOND TEAM

Karl Malone	Utah
Grant Hill	Detroit
Alonzo Mourning	Miami
Allen Iverson	Philadelphia
Kobe Bryant	LA Lakers

THIRD TEAM

Chris Webber	Sacramento
Vince Carter	Toronto
David Robinson	San Antonio
Eddie Jones	Charlotte
Stephon Marbury	New Jersey

PLAYOFFS

FINALS

L.A. Lakers 4, Indiana 2
June 7: Indiana 87 at L.A. Lakers 104
June 9: Indiana 104 at L.A. Lakers 111
June 11: L.A. Lakers 91 at Indiana 100
June 14: L.A. Lakers 120 at Indiana 118, OT
June 16: L.A. Lakers 87 at Indiana 120
June 19: Indiana 111 at L.A. Lakers 116

EASTERN CONFERENCE
CONFERENCE FINALS

Indiana 4, New York 2
May 23: New York 88 at Indiana 102
May 25: New York 84 at Indiana 88
May 27: Indiana 95 at New York 98
May 29: Indiana 89 at New York 91
May 31: New York 79 at Indiana 88
June 2: Indiana 93 at New York 80

CONFERENCE SEMI-FINALS

Indiana 4, Philadelphia 2
May 6: Philadelphia 91 at Indiana 108
May 8: Philadelphia 97 at Indiana 103
May 10: Indiana 97 at Philadelphia 89
May 13: Indiana 90 at Philadelphia 92
May 15: Philadelphia 107 at Indiana 86
May 19: Indiana 106 at Philadelphia 90

New York 4, Miami 3
May 7: New York 83 at Miami 87
May 9: New York 82 at Miami 76
May 12: Miami 77 at New York 76, OT
May 14: Miami 83 at New York 91
May 17: New York 81 at Miami 87
May 19: Miami 70 at New York 72
May 21: New York 83 at Miami 82

FIRST ROUND

Indiana 3, Milwaukee 2
Apr. 23: Milwaukee 85 at Indiana 88
Apr. 27: Milwaukee 104 at Indiana 91
Apr. 29: Indiana 109 at Milwaukee 96
May 1: Indiana 87 at Milwaukee 100
May 4: Milwaukee 95 at Indiana 96

Philadelphia 3, Charlotte 1
Apr. 22: Philadelphia 92, Charlotte 82
Apr. 24: Philadelphia 98 at Charlotte 108, OT
Apr. 28: Charlotte 76 at Philadelphia 81
May 1: Charlotte 99 at Philadelphia 105

New York 3, Toronto 0
Apr. 23: Toronto 88 at New York 92
Apr. 26: Toronto 83 at New York 84
Apr. 30: New York 87 at Toronto 80

Miami 3, Detroit 0
Apr. 22: Detroit 85 at Miami 95
Apr. 25: Detroit 82 at Miami 84
Apr. 29: Miami 91 at Detroit 72

WESTERN CONFERENCE
CONFERENCE FINALS

L.A. Lakers 4, Portland 3
May 20: Portland 94 at L.A. Lakers 109
May 22: Portland 106, L.A. Lakers 77
May 26: L.A. Lakers 93, Portland 91
May 28: L.A. Lakers 103 at Portland 91
May 30: Portland 96 at L.A. Lakers 88
June 2: L.A. Lakers 93 at Portland 103
June 4: Portland 84, L.A. Lakers 89

CONFERENCE SEMI-FINALS

L.A. Lakers 4, Phoenix 1
May 7: Phoenix 77 at L.A. Lakers 105
May 10: Phoenix 96 at L.A. Lakers 97
May 12: L.A. Lakers 105 at Phoenix 99

May 14: L.A. Lakers at Phoenix 117
May 16: Phoenix 65 at L.A. Lakers 87

Portland 4, Utah 1
May 7: Utah 75 at Portland 94
May 9: Utah 85 at Portland 103
May 11: Portland 103 at Utah 84
May 14: Portland 85 at Utah 88
May 16: Utah 79 at Portland 81

FIRST ROUND

L.A. Lakers 3, Sacramento 2
Apr. 23: Sacramento 107 at L.A. Lakers 117
Apr. 27: Sacramento 89 at L.A. Lakers 113
Apr. 30: L.A. Lakers 91 at Sacramento 99
May 2: L.A. Lakers 88 at Sacramento 101
May 5: Sacramento 86 at L.A. Lakers 113

Phoenix 3, San Antonio 1
Apr. 22: Phoenix 72 at San Antonio 70
Apr. 25: Phoenix 70 at San Antonio 85
Apr. 29: San Antonio 94 at Phoenix 101
May 2: San Antonio 78 at Phoenix 89

Portland 3, Minnesota 1
Apr. 23: Minnesota 88 at Portland 91
Apr. 26: Minnesota 82 at Portland 86
Apr. 30: Portland 87 at Minnesota 94
May 2: Portland 85 at Minnesota 77

Utah 3, Seattle 2
Apr. 22: Seattle 93 at Utah 104
Apr. 24: Seattle 87 at Utah 101
Apr. 29: Utah 78 at Seattle 89
May 3: Utah 93 at Seattle 104
May 5: Seattle 93 at Utah 96

NBA LEADERS

SCORING

	GP	FGM	FTM	PTS	PPG
Shaquille O'Neal, LAL	79	956	432	2344	29.7
Allen Iverson, PHI	70	729	442	1989	28.4
Grant Hill, DET	74	696	480	1906	25.8
Vince Carter, TOR	82	788	436	2107	25.7
Karl Malone, UTJ	82	752	589	2095	25.5
Chris Webber, SAC	75	748	311	1834	24.5
Gary Payton, SEA	82	747	311	1982	24.2
Jerry Stackhouse, DET	82	619	618	1939	23.6
Tim Duncan, SAS	74	628	459	1716	23.2
Kevin Garnett, MIN	81	759	309	1857	22.9

FIELD GOALS

	FGM	FGA	FG%
Shaquille O'Neal, LAL	956	1665	.574
Dikembe Mutombo, ATL	322	573	.562
Alonzo Mourning, MIA	652	1184	.551
Ruben Patterson, SEA	354	661	.536
Rasheed Wallace, POR	542	1045	.519
David Robinson, SAS	528	1031	.512
Wally Szczerbiak, MIN	342	669	.511
Karl Malone, UTJ	752	1476	.509
Antonio McDyess, DEN	614	1211	.507
Othella Harrington, VAN	420	830	.506

THREE POINT FIELD GOALS

	3PM	3PA	3P%
Hubert Davis, DAL	82	167	.491
Jeff Hornacek, UTJ	66	138	.478
Matt Bullard, HOU	79	177	.446
Rodney Rogers, PHO	115	262	.439
Allan Houston, NYK	106	243	.436
Terry Porter, SAS	90	207	.435
Lindsey Hunter, DET	168	389	.432
Tracy Murray, WAS	113	263	.430
Jon Barry, SAC	66	154	.429
Wesley Person, CLE	106	250	.424

FREE THROWS

	FTM	FTA	FT%
Jeff Hornacek, UTJ	171	180	.950
Reggie Miller, IND	373	406	.919
Darrell Armstrong, ORL	225	247	.911
Terrell Brandon, MIN	187	208	.899
Ray Allen, MIL	353	398	.887
Predrag Stojakovic, SAC	135	153	.882
Jim Jackson, ATL	186	212	.877
Derek Anderson, LAC	271	309	.877
Mitch Richmond, WAS	298	340	.876
Sam Cassell, MIL	390	445	.876

ASSISTS

	GP	AST	APG
Jason Kidd, PHO	67	678	10.1
Nick Van Exel, DEN	79	714	9.0
Sam Cassell, MIL	81	729	9.0
Gary Payton, SEA	82	732	8.9
Terrell Brandon, MIN	71	629	8.9
John Stockton, UTJ	82	703	8.6
Stephon Marbury, NJN	74	622	8.4
Mike Bibby, VAN	82	665	8.1
Mark Jackson, IND	81	650	8.0
Eric Snow, PHI	82	624	7.6

REBOUNDS

	GP	ORB	DRB	TRB	RPG
Dikembe Mutombo, ATL	82	304	853	1157	14.1
Shaquille O'Neal, LAL	79	336	742	1078	13.6
Tim Duncan, SAS	74	262	656	918	12.4
Kevin Garnett, MIN	81	223	733	956	11.8
Chris Webber, SAC	75	190	598	788	10.5
Shareef Abdur-Rahim, VAN	82	218	607	825	10.1
Elton Brand, CHI	81	348	462	810	10.0
Dale Davis, IND	74	256	473	729	9.9
David Robinson, SAS	80	193	577	770	9.6
Jerome Williams, DET	82	277	512	789	9.6

STEALS

	GP	STL	SPG
Eddie Jones, CHA	72	192	2.67
Paul Pierce, BOS	73	152	2.08
Darrell Armstrong, ORL	82	169	2.06
Allen Iverson, PHI	70	144	2.06
Mookie Blaylock, GST	73	146	2.00
Jason Kidd, PHO	67	134	2.00
Terrell Brandon, MIN	71	134	1.89
Gary Payton, SEA	82	153	1.87
Kendall Gill, NJN	76	139	1.83
John Stockton, UTJ	82	143	1.74

BLOCKS

	GP	BLK	BPG
Alonzo Mourning, MIA	79	294	3.72
Dikembe Mutombo, ATL	82	269	3.28
Shaquille O'Neal, LAL	79	239	3.03
Theo Ratliff, PHI	57	171	3.00
Shawn Bradley, DAL	77	190	2.47
David Robinson, SAS	80	183	2.29
Tim Duncan, SAS	74	165	2.23
Raef LaFrentz, DEN	81	180	2.22
Greg Ostertag, UTJ	81	172	2.12
Marcus Camby, NYK	59	116	1.97

TURNOVERS

	GP	TO	TPG
Steve Francis, HOU	77	306	4.0
Jerry Stackhouse, DET	82	311	3.8
Jason Williams, SAC	81	296	3.7
Stephon Marbury, NJN	74	270	3.6
Shawn Kemp, CLE	82	291	3.5
Lamar Odom, LAC	76	258	3.4
Jason Kidd, PHO	67	226	3.4
Kevin Garnett, MIN	81	268	3.3
Sam Cassell, MIL	81	267	3.3
Allen Iverson, PHI	70	230	3.3

THE YEAR IN BASKETBALL

August 27, 1999 In an 11-player transaction, Houston deals Michael Dickerson, Othella Harrington, Brent Price, Antoine Carr, and a future first-round pick to Vancouver as part of a three-way deal. The trade gives Houston the draft rights to Steve Francis, along with Tony Massenburg from Vancouver, and Don MacLean and a future first-round pick from Orlando. The Magic receive Michael Smith, Rodrick Rhodes, Lee Mayberry, and Makhtar N'diaye from Vancouver.

October 12, 1999 Wilt Chamberlain is found dead in his Los Angeles home at the age of 63.

November 24, 1999 The NBA expels journeyman center Stanley Roberts because he tested positive for an amphetamine-based drug.

December 2, 1999 William (Pop) Gates, one of the best players of basketball's barnstorming era in 1930s and 1940s, dies.

December 8, 1999 Charles Barkley of Houston tears a tendon in his knee in a game in Philadelphia, effectively ending his career. Barkley will rehabilitate his knee and play one final game, the last one of the 1999-00 season, before retiring for good.

January 12, 2000 Bobby Phills, a Charlotte Hornets' guard, dies at age 30 in a single-car accident outside the Hornets' training facility.

January 19, 2000 Michael Jordan joins the Washington Wizards as part owner and president of basketball operations.

March 6, 2000 Shaquille O'Neal of the Lakers nets 61 points to go with 23 boards in a game versus the Clippers.

March 30, 2000 Wake Forest defeats Notre Dame, 71-61, to win the NIT title. The Demon Deacons' Robert O'Kelley get the tournament MVP award.

April 3, 2000 Behind the gutsy play of point guard Mateen Cleaves, Michigan State wins its second national championship with an 89-76 victory over Florida.

May 20, 2000 Malik Sealy, a guard/forward for the Timberwolves is killed in a head-on auto accident. The driver of the other car survives and is later found to have been drunk. Sealy was 30.

June 19, 2000 The Lakers, behind Shaquille O'Neal (41 points) and Kobe Bryant (26), win the NBA championship, beating Indiana, 116-111, in Game 6 of the Finals. The game marks coach Phil Jackson's seventh title and Larry Bird's final game as Pacers' coach.

2000-01

Saving best for last, Lakers lose once–in OT–in playoff romp

Los Angeles won 56 games, 11 fewer than the previous year. But then the Lakers faced elimination games against Sacramento and Portland in post-season play. In 2001, they romped through the post-season with a 15-1 mark, their lone blemish coming in a Finals loss to Philadelphia.

For the Philadelphia 76ers, it had been a long time between drinks. The 1983 Sixers, riding Moses Malone's bullish inside game and MVP season, won 65 games and finished 12-1 in the post-season. They had four 50-win seasons since, with the Malone, Julius Erving and Charles Barkley teams to follow. But they never reached an NBA Final from 1984 through 2000. Since the draft of Allan Iverson in the first round in 1996 it had been a slow climb. Larry Brown nurtured Iverson's all-world talent and frequent disregard for rules and regulations. In 1999-2000, they won 49 games and then 56 in 2001.

Iverson's 31.1 average won him a second scoring title and he led the circuit in steals. He was All-NBA First Team for the second time and he won the MVP. He also led the league in heart, routinely risking life and limb in the paint by leading with his 6-foot, 160-pound frame. Iverson had major help from Dikembe Mutombo, also from Georgetown by way of Zaire. Mutombo led the league in rebounds a second consecutive year. He was also fifth in blocks and won Defensive Player of the Year Honors. He also won the All-Star MVP when he scored 15 of his 25 points in the fourth period to help the East erase a 21-point fourth quarter deficit and win, 111-110.

The season began with Pat Riley becoming the second coach in NBA history to win 1,000 games when the Heat defeated the Magic in Miami, 105-79. Later in November, John Stockton played his 1,271st career game for Utah—the most an NBA player has played with the same team. Stockton broke the mark previously held by Boston forward John Havlicek.

Scoring marks were set early and often. Golden State forward Antawn Jamison scored 51 points versus Seattle in early December and then posted 51 in the very next game. Kobe Bryant scored 51 in the same game, but the Warriors defeated the Lakers 125-122 in overtime. It was the first NBA game in which opposing players scored 50 or more points since December 14, 1962, when Wilt Chamberlain tallied 63 for the Philadelphia Warriors and Elgin Baylor notched 50 for the Lakers. The night before Jamison's back-to-back fifties, Karl Malone passed Wilt Chamberlain's 31,419 points to move into second place on the all-time scoring list. Detroit's Jerry Stackhouse capped the scoring records in April, scoring an NBA season-high 57 points in a win over Chicago.

A defensive streak stopped when New York's record of 33 consecutive games holding teams below 100 points ended in a 105-91 loss to Milwaukee. The last time they allowed 100 points was in Boston on November 10, 2000. During the streak the Knicks went 21-12, allowing opponents a stingy

Allen Iverson
"The Answer" had the answer to Philadelphia's desires: MVP of the league, the All-Star Game and a trip to the NBA Finals.

average of 82.8 points a game.

That record for smothering defense didn't help New York in the playoffs, when they lost to Toronto in Game 5 of the first round at home. Philadelphia then fell behind spunky Toronto in the semi-final series, but advanced by the slightest of margins, winning Game 7 by one point at home. The 76ers also went the full seven before beating Milwaukee.

The Lakers had no comparable tests of their mettle. They breezed through Portland and Sacramento with a 7-0 record. Now they had to face San Antonio, who won a league-best

58 games and, unlike the last post-season, had a healthy Tim Duncan. But the anticipated competition was never joined. The Lakers won four straight, even winning the last two by margins of 39 and 29 points.

Now the Lakers had to wait ten days for Philadelphia to finish off Milwaukee and for the Finals to begin. If they were rusty, Allan Iverson was quick to exploit it. Iverson scored 48 points, enough to offset 44 points and 20 rebounds by Shaquille O'Neal. In Game 2 Bryant scored 31, redeeming himself for a lackluster 7-for-22 effort in Game 1. O'Neal added 28 points, 20 rebounds, and eight blocks and Los Angeles won, 98-89.

When O'Neal fouled out of Game 3 with over two minutes left, it was Robert Horry who saved the day. The forward with the knack for hitting three-pointers scored seven points in 47 seconds, including a three-point clincher for a 96-91 win. The Laker margin of victory in Game 4 was 14 points, as O'Neal had 34 points and 14 rebounds. In Game 5, the Lakers led by 15 after three quarters and were never challenged. Iverson scored 37 (and averaged 35.6 for the series) but Los Angeles prevailed 108-96. O'Neal hit 57 percent of his shots and averaged 33 points, 16 rebounds, five assists, and three blocks and was awarded his second consecutive Finals MVP.

2000-01 SEASON HIGHLIGHTS

STANDINGS

Eastern Conference
Atlantic Division

	W	L	Pct.	GB
Philadelphia	56	26	.683	—
Miami	50	32	.610	6
New York	48	34	.585	8
Orlando	43	39	.524	13
Boston	36	46	.439	20
New Jersey	26	56	.317	30
Washington	19	63	.232	37

Central Division

	W	L	Pct.	GB
Milwaukee	52	30	.634	—
Toronto	47	35	.573	5
Charlotte	46	36	.561	6
Indiana	41	41	.500	11
Detroit	32	50	.390	20
Cleveland	30	52	.366	22
Atlanta	25	57	.305	27
Chicago	15	67	.183	37

Western Conference
Midwest Division

	W	L	Pct.	GB
San Antonio	58	24	.707	—
Dallas	53	29	.646	5
Utah	53	29	.646	5
Minnesota	47	35	.573	11
Houston	45	37	.549	13
Denver	40	42	.488	18
Vancouver	23	59	.280	35

Pacific Division

	W	L	Pct.	GB
LA Lakers	56	26	.683	—
Sacramento	55	27	.671	1
Phoenix	51	31	.622	5
Portland	50	32	.610	6
Seattle	44	38	.537	12
LA Clippers	31	51	.378	25
Golden State	17	65	.207	39

AWARDS

MVP
Allen Iverson, Philadelphia
Top Rookie
Mike Miller, Orlando
Coach of Year
Larry Brown, Philadelphia
Defensive Player of Year
Dikembe Mutombo, Philadelphia-Atlanta
Sixth Man Award
Aaron McKie, Philadelphia
Most Improved Player
Tracy McGrady, Orlando
Citizenship Award
Dikembe Mutombo, Philadelphia

ALL-STAR GAME

MCI Center, Washington, D.C.
Sunday, February 11, 2001
West 137, East 126
MVP: Allen Iverson

ALL-STAR TEAMS

FIRST TEAM

Tim Duncan	San Antonio
Chris Webber	Sacramento
Shaquille O'Neal	Los Angeles
Allen Iverson	Philadelphia
Jason Kidd	Phoenix

SECOND TEAM

Kevin Garnett	Minnesota
Vince Carter	Toronto
Dikembe Mutombo	Atlanta-Phil
Kobe Bryant	Los Angeles
Tracy McGrady	Orlando

THIRD TEAM

Karl Malone	Utah
Dirk Nowitzki	Dallas
David Robinson	San Antonio
Gary Payton	Seattle
Ray Allen	Milwaukee

PLAYOFFS

FINALS

L.A. Lakers 4, Philadelphia 1
June 6: Philadelphia 107 at L.A. Lakers 101, OT
June 8: Philadelphia 89 at L.A. Lakers 98
June 10: L.A. Lakers 96 at Philadelphia 91
June 13: L.A. Lakers 100 at Philadelphia 86
June 15: L.A. Lakers 108 at Philadelphia 96

EASTERN CONFERENCE
CONFERENCE FINALS

Philadelphia 4, Milwaukee 3
May 22: Milwaukee 85 at Philadelphia 93
May 24: Milwaukee 92 at Philadelphia 78
May 26: Philadelphia 74 at Milwaukee 80
May 28: Philadelphia 89 at Milwaukee 83
May 30: Milwaukee 88 at Philadelphia 89
June 1: Philadelphia 100 at Milwaukee 110
June 3: Milwaukee 91 at Philadelphia 108

CONFERENCE SEMI-FINALS

Philadelphia 4, Toronto 3
May 6: Toronto 96 at Philadelphia 93
May 9: Toronto 92 at Philadelphia 97
May 11: Philadelphia 78 at Toronto 102
May 13: Philadelphia 84 at Toronto 79
May 16: Toronto 88 at Philadelphia 121
May 18: Philadelphia 89 at Toronto 101
May 20: Toronto 87 at Philadelphia 88

Milwaukee 4, Charlotte 3
May 6: Charlotte 92 at Milwaukee 104
May 8: Charlotte 90 at Milwaukee 91
May 10: Milwaukee 92 at Charlotte 102
May 13: Milwaukee 78 at Charlotte 85
May 15: Charlotte 94 at Milwaukee 86
May 17: Milwaukee 104 at Charlotte 97
May 20: Charlotte 95 at Milwaukee 104

FIRST ROUND

Philadelphia 3, Indiana 1
Apr. 21: Indiana 79 at Philadelphia 78
Apr. 24: Indiana 98 at Philadelphia 116
Apr. 28: Philadelphia 92 at Indiana 87
May 2: Philadelphia 88 at Indiana 85

Toronto 3, New York 2
Apr. 22: Toronto 85 at New York 92
Apr. 26: Toronto 94 at New York 74
Apr. 29: New York 97 at Toronto 89
May 2: New York 93 at Toronto 100
May 4: Toronto 93 at New York 89

Charlotte 3, Miami 0
Apr. 21: Charlotte 106 at Miami 80
Apr. 23: Charlotte 102 at Miami 76
Apr. 27: Miami 79 at Charlotte 94

Milwaukee 3, Orlando 1
Apr. 22: Orlando 90 at Milwaukee 103
Apr. 25: Orlando 96 at Milwaukee 103
Apr. 28: Milwaukee 116 at Orlando 121, OT
May 1: Milwaukee 112 at Orlando 104

WESTERN CONFERENCE
CONFERENCE FINALS

L.A. Lakers 4, San Antonio 0
May 19: L.A. Lakers 104 at San Antonio 90
May 21: L.A. Lakers 88 at San Antonio 81
May 25: San Antonio 72 at L.A. Lakers 111
May 27: San Antonio 82 at L.A. Lakers 111

CONFERENCE SEMI-FINALS

San Antonio 4, Dallas 1
May 5: Dallas 78 at San Antonio 94
May 7: Dallas 86 at San Antonio 100
May 9: San Antonio 104 at Dallas 90
May 12: San Antonio 108 at Dallas 112
May 14: Dallas 87 at San Antonio 105

L.A. Lakers 4, Sacramento 0
May 6: Sacramento 105 at L.A. Lakers 108
May 8: Sacramento 90 at L.A. Lakers 96
May 11: L.A. Lakers 103 at Sacramento 81
May 13: L.A. Lakers 119 at Sacramento 113

FIRST ROUND

San Antonio 3, Minnesota 1
Apr. 21: Minnesota 82 at San Antonio 87
Apr. 23: Minnesota 69 at San Antonio 86
Apr. 28: San Antonio 84 at Minnesota 93
Apr. 30: San Antonio 97 at Minnesota 84

Dallas 3, Utah 2
Apr. 21: Dallas 86 at Utah 88
Apr. 24: Dallas 98 at Utah 109
Apr. 28: Utah 91 at Dallas 94
May 1: Utah 77 at Dallas 107
May 3: Dallas 84 at Utah 83

Sacramento 3, Phoenix 1
Apr. 22: Phoenix 86 at Sacramento 83
Apr. 25: Phoenix 90 at Sacramento 116
Apr. 29: Sacramento 104 at Phoenix 96
May 2: Sacramento 80 at Phoenix 78

L.A. Lakers 3, Portland 0
Apr. 22: Portland 93 at L.A. Lakers 106
Apr. 26: Portland 88 at L.A. Lakers 106
Apr. 29: L.A. Lakers 99 at Portland 86

NBA LEADERS

SCORING

	GP	FGM	FTM	PTS	PPG
Allen Iverson, PHI	71	762	585	2207	31.1
Jerry Stackhouse, DET	80	774	666	2380	29.8
Shaquille O'Neal, LAL	74	813	499	2125	28.7
Kobe Bryant, LAL	68	701	475	1938	28.5
Vince Carter, TOR	75	762	384	2070	27.6
Chris Webber, SAC	70	786	324	1898	27.1
Tracy McGrady, ORL	77	788	430	2065	26.8
Paul Pierce, BOS	82	687	550	2071	25.3
Antawn Jamison, GST	82	800	382	2044	24.9
Stephon Marbury, NJN	67	563	362	1598	23.9

FIELD GOALS

	FGM	FGA	FG%
Shaquille O'Neal, LAL	813	1422	.572
Bonzi Wells, POR	387	726	.533
Marcus Camby, NYK	304	580	.524
Kurt Thomas, NYK	314	614	.511
Wally Szczerbiak, MIN	469	920	.510
Darius Miles, LAC	318	630	.505
John Stockton, UTJ	328	651	.504
Donyell Marshall, UTJ	427	849	.503
Corliss Williamson, TOR/DET	325	647	.502
Clarence Weatherspoon, CLE	347	692	.501

THREE POINT FIELD GOALS

	3PM	3PA	3P%
Brent Barry, SEA	109	229	.476
John Stockton, UTJ	61	132	.462
Shammond Williams, SEA	61	133	.459
Hubert Davis, DAL/WAS	78	171	.456
Danny Ferry, SAS	70	156	.449
Toni Kukoc, PHI/ATL	70	157	.446
Patrick Garrity, ORL	97	224	.433
Ray Allen, MIL	202	467	.433
Rashard Lewis, SEA	123	285	.432
Dell Curry, TOR	62	145	.428

FREE THROWS

	FTM	FTA	FT%
Reggie Miller, IND	323	348	.928
Allan Houston, NYK	279	307	.909
Doug Christie, SAC	280	312	.897
Steve Nash, DAL	231	258	.895
Mitch Richmond, WAS	143	160	.894
Steve Smith, POR	309	347	.890
Ray Allen, MIL	348	392	.888
Darrell Armstrong, ORL	220	249	.884
Eric Piatkowski, LAC	158	181	.873
Terrell Brandon, MIN	195	224	.871

ASSISTS

	GP	AST	APG
Jason Kidd, PHO	77	753	9.8
John Stockton, UTJ	82	713	8.7
Nick Van Exel, DEN	71	600	8.5
Mike Bibby, VAN	82	685	8.4
Gary Payton, SEA	79	642	8.1
Andre Miller, CLE	82	657	8.0
Mark Jackson, TOR/NYK	83	661	8.0
Sam Cassell, MIL	76	580	7.6
Stephon Marbury, NJN	67	506	7.6
Terrell Brandon, MIN	78	583	7.5

REBOUNDS

	GP	ORB	DRB	TRB	RPG
Dikembe Mutombo, ATL/PHI	75	307	708	1015	13.5
Ben Wallace, DET	80	303	749	1052	13.2
Shaquille O'Neal, LAL	74	291	649	940	12.7
Tim Duncan, SAS	82	259	738	997	12.2
Antonio McDyess, DEN	70	240	605	845	12.1
Kevin Garnett, MIN	81	219	702	921	11.4
Chris Webber, SAC	70	179	598	777	11.1
Shawn Marion, PHO	79	220	628	848	10.7
Antonio Davis, TOR	78	274	513	787	10.1
Elton Brand, CHI	74	285	461	746	10.1

STEALS

	GP	STL	SPG
Allen Iverson, PHI	71	178	2.51
Mookie Blaylock, GST	69	163	2.36
Doug Christie, SAC	81	183	2.26
Jason Kidd, PHO	77	166	2.16
Baron Davis, CHA	82	170	2.07
Terrell Brandon, MIN	78	161	2.06
Ron Artest, CHI	76	152	2.00
Darrell Armstrong, ORL	75	135	1.80
Steve Francis, HOU	80	141	1.76
Antoine Walker, BOS	81	138	1.70

BLOCKS

	GP	BLK	BPG
Theo Ratliff, PHI	50	187	3.74
Jermaine O'Neal, IND	81	228	2.81
Shawn Bradley, DAL	82	228	2.78
Shaquille O'Neal, LAL	74	204	2.76
Dikembe Mutombo, ATL/PHI	75	203	2.71
Adonal Foyle, GST	58	156	2.69
Raef LaFrentz, DEN	78	206	2.64
David Robinson, SAS	80	197	2.46
Tim Duncan, SAS	82	192	2.34
Ben Wallace, DET	80	186	2.33

TURNOVERS

	GP	TO	TPG
Jerry Stackhouse, DET	80	326	4.1
Antoine Walker, BOS	81	301	3.7
Jason Kidd, PHO	77	286	3.7
Lamar Odom, LAC	76	264	3.5
Allen Iverson, PHI	71	237	3.3
Steve Francis, HOU	80	265	3.3
Kobe Bryant, LAL	68	220	3.2
Andre Miller, CLE	82	265	3.2
Paul Pierce, BOS	82	262	3.2
Larry Hughes, GST	50	152	3.0

THE YEAR IN BASKETBALL

September 20, 2000 In the largest trade in NBA history, New York deals Patrick Ewing to Seattle as part of a four-team swap. New York receives Glen Rice, Travis Knight and a future first-round draft pick from the Lakers, Luc Longley from Phoenix, Vernon Maxwell, Vladimir Stepania, Lazaro Borrell, a future first-round pick and two future second-round picks from Seattle. The Lakers receive Horace Grant, Chuck Person, Greg Foster, and Emanuel Davis from Seattle. Phoenix receives Chris Dudley and a future first-round pick from New York.

October 25, 2000 The NBA punishes the Minnesota Timberwolves for entering into a secret contractual agreement with forward Joe Smith and his agent Eric Fleischer that violated the league salary cap rules. The league fines the Timberwolves $3.5 million and orders the forfeiture of the team's first-round picks in the 2001, 2002, 2003, 2004, and 2005 drafts.

November 26, 2000 John Stockton plays his 1,271st career game for Utah—the most an NBA player has played with the same team—in the Jazz' 94-79 victory over Detroit.

December 5, 2000 Karl Malone enters into second place on the NBA's career scoring list in a Jazz win over Toronto.

January 13, 2001 Atlanta retires Dominique Wilkins' #21 jersey.

January 23, 2001 The Knicks' record streak of 33 straight games holding teams below 100 points ends in a 105-91 loss to Milwaukee. The last time they allowed 100 points was in Boston on November 10, 2000 when they beat the Celtics in overtime, 103-101.

January 26, 2001 Hall of Fame coach Al McGuire dies at 72.

February 8, 2001 The Continental Basketball Association, in its 55th season, suspends operations.

March 29, 2001 Tulsa whips Alabama, 79-60, to win the NIT title.

April 1, 2001 Ruth Riley makes two foul shots with 5.8 seconds to give the Notre Dame women's team its first national championship, 68-66, over Purdue. Riley is named the Most Outstanding Player of the tourney.

April 2, 2001 Duke wins the men's national collegiate title beating Arizona, 82-72. The victory is the school's third championship.

June 15, 2001 The Lakers claim their second consecutive NBA title, beating the 76ers in Game 5, 108-96.

July 3, 2001 The NBA approves the relocation of Vancouver to Memphis, effective for the 2001-02 season.

2001-02

Nets stand in for 76ers, rest of Lakers script remains same

The rise of old ABA teams was apparently contagious. For the third time in four seasons, one of the four ABA merger teams from 1976 reached the NBA Finals. San Antonio started the ABA revival show in 1999, winning their first crown—the first ever by a former ABA squad. Then Indiana, the most dominant ABA team ever with three championships and five Finals appearances—but dormant for a quarter of a century in the NBA—reached the 2000 Finals. Now the New Jersey Nets—once the New York Nets, playing at drafty Commack Arena and later the Nassau Coliseum—had their first trip to the Finals since 1976. In the waning days of the nine-year ABA it was Julius Erving who levitated nightly and carried the Nets past Denver—the remaining merger team. Erving had taken the title ride two years before and by the time of the merger the two-time MVP was rightly recognized as the greatest talent the ABA ever produced. But the Nets could not afford Erving's price and he went to Philadelphia, getting to four NBA Finals and winning a title in the next seven years. Meanwhile, the story of the plummeting Nets might be described as "the curse of Julius Erving."

Stephon Marbury had averaged 23 points and eight assists in two seasons in New Jersey, but he had not galvanized his youthful mates and the team wallowed near the basement of the Atlantic Division, with 31 wins in 2000 and 26 the following season. Thus the trade of Marbury for Jason Kidd—a point guard who couldn't score with Marbury but had an irrepressible, fast breaking, shove-it-down-your throat mindset—was an educated gamble. Kidd had won three consecutive assist titles. Despite shooting 39 percent from the floor in 2001, Kidd doubled the Nets performance with 52 wins and finished runner-up in the MVP voting to Tim Duncan.

In an Eastern Conference that hadn't claimed a title since Chicago won in 1998, the path to the Finals was wide open. The league's top four teams were all west of St. Louis: Sacramento (61 wins), San Antonio and Los Angeles (58 each) and Dallas (57). Detroit took the Central Division crown but their best player, Ben Wallace, a rebounder and shot blocker *par excellence*, didn't score and the team's attack lacked the voltage to go far. Only Boston, with the scoring duo of Paul Pierce (26 ppg) and Antoine Walker (22 ppg), had the juice to do damage.

Before the season, the Vancouver Grizzlies were approved to relocate to Memphis. In Washington former Wizard executive Michael Jordan, now 38, vowed to make a second comeback. With Jordan, the horrible Wizards improved by 18 wins, falling short of the post-season at 37-45. Jordan led the team in scoring (22.9 ppg) and the team, predictably, led the league in attendance.

January was a time for appreciating the present and recalling the past. Kobe Bryant went off for 56 points, a league-high

Jason Kidd
Established himself as the league's best back court player after trade to New Jersey, leading the Nets to the Finals for the first time.

mark, in a Lakers rout of Memphis. One day later, Allen Iverson—on his way to his third scoring title in six years—did Bryant a bucket better, hitting for 58 in a win against Houston.

On January 18, Alex Hannum died at age 78. Hannum was the only coach to win titles in both the ABA and NBA. In fact, Hannum coached the St. Louis Hawks in 1958 (when Bob Pettit scored 50 points in Game 6 to beat Boston) and the 68-13 Philadelphia 76ers in 1967—two title teams sandwiching Boston's run of eight titles and keeping them from winning 13 straight. After he led Philadelphia to a 62-20 mark

in 1968, he coached the Oakland Oaks to a 60-18 mark in the ABA, and the Oaks turned back the Pacers in five games in the ABA Finals.

In the All-Star Game in Philadelphia, Kobe Bryant scored 31 points and was named game MVP, as the West defeated the East, 135-120.

In the Eastern Conference, it took the Nets until the overtime of Game 5 to dispose of Indiana, 120-109. The next test came in the Conference Finals. New Jersey hadn't been in the playoffs since 1998; Boston, not since 1995. The teams split the first two games and New Jersey had a 20-point lead in the fourth quarter of Game 3. But a two-barrel comeback led by Paul Pierce and Antoine Walker gave Boston a stunning victory. After that demoralizing collapse, the Nets dug out a tight Game 4 and then won the next two.

The Lakers rolled over Portland in three games and San Antonio, while playing tighter contests than last year, still lost in five. Sacramento then backed L.A. to the wall. Owners of a league-best 61 wins and a Pacific Division title, Sacramento got help from seven double-digit scorers and owned the league's second best offense. Riding standouts Chris Webber and scorer-playmaker Mike Bibby, they held a 2-1 lead in games and a 20-point fourth quarter lead in Game 4. But they collapsed and were done in when Robert Horry hit a three-pointer to win it. The Kings won Game 5 but lost the last two, including Game 7 in overtime at home.

Even a stellar Final series by Jason Kidd, with his per-game marks of 21 points, 10 assists and 7 rebounds, could not avert a Laker sweep. Kobe Bryant and Shaquille O'Neal combined for 63 points a game. O'Neal's portion was 36 points (with .595 accuracy), 12 rebounds, 4 assists and 3 blocks. Proving an unstoppable force for a third straight year, he won his third Finals MVP.

2001-02 SEASON HIGHLIGHTS

STANDINGS

Eastern Conference
Atlantic Division

	W	L	Pct.	GB
New Jersey	52	30	.610	—
Boston	49	33	.598	3
Orlando	44	38	.537	8
Philadelphia	43	39	.524	9
Washington	37	45	.451	15
Miami	36	46	.439	16
New York	30	52	.366	22

Central Division

	W	L	Pct.	GB
Detroit	50	32	.610	—
Charlotte	44	38	.537	6
Toronto	42	40	.512	8
Indiana	42	40	.512	8
Milwaukee	41	41	.500	9
Atlanta	33	49	.402	17
Cleveland	29	53	.354	21
Chicago	21	61	.256	29

Western Conference
Midwest Division

	W	L	Pct.	GB
San Antonio	58	24	.707	—
Dallas	57	25	.695	1
Minnesota	50	32	.610	8
Utah	44	38	.537	14
Houston	28	54	.341	30
Denver	27	55	.329	31
Memphis	23	59	.280	35

Pacific Division

	W	L	Pct.	GB
Sacramento	61	21	.744	—
LA Lakers	58	24	.707	3
Portland	49	33	.598	12
Seattle	45	37	.549	16
Los Angeles	39	43	.476	22
Phoenix	36	46	.439	25
LA Clippers	21	61	.256	40

AWARDS

MVP
Tim Duncan, San Antonio
Top Rookie
Pau Gasol, Memphis
Coach of Year
Rick Carlisle, Detroit
Defensive Player of Year
Ben Wallace, Detroit
Sixth Man Award
Corliss Williamson, Detroit
Most Improved Player
Jermaine O'Neal, Indiana
Citizenship Award
Alonzo Mourning, Miami

ALL-STAR GAME
First Union Center, Philadelphia
Sunday, February 10, 2002
West 135, East 120
MVP: Kobe Bryant

ALL-STAR TEAMS

FIRST TEAM

Tim Duncan	San Antonio
Tracy McGrady	Orlando
Shaquille O'Neal	LA Lakers
Jason Kidd	New Jersey
Kobe Bryant	LA Lakers

SECOND TEAM

Kevin Garnett	Minnesota
Chris Webber	Sacramento
Dirk Nowitzki	Dallas
Gary Payton	Seattle
Allen Iverson	Philadelphia

THIRD TEAM

Ben Wallace	Detroit
Jermaine O'Neal	Indiana
Dikembe Mutombo	Philadelphia
Paul Pierce	Boston
Steve Nash	Dallas

PLAYOFFS

NBA FINALS
L.A. Lakers 4, New Jersey 0
June 5: New Jersey 94 at L.A. Lakers 99
June 7: New Jersey 83 at L.A. Lakers 106
June 9: L.A. Lakers 106 at New Jersey 103
June 12: L.A. Lakers 113 at New Jersey 107

EASTERN CONFERENCE
CONFERENCE FINALS
New Jersey 4, Boston 2
May 19: Boston 97 at New Jersey 104
May 21: Boston 93 at New Jersey 86
May 25: New Jersey 90 at Boston 94
May 27: New Jersey 94 at Boston 92
May 29: Boston 92 at New Jersey 103
May 31: New Jersey 96 at Boston 88

CONFERENCE SEMI-FINALS
New Jersey 4, Charlotte 1
May 5: Charlotte 93 at New Jersey 99
May 7: Charlotte 88 at New Jersey 102
May 9: New Jersey 97 at Charlotte 115
May 12: New Jersey 89 at Charlotte 79
May 15: Charlotte 95 at New Jersey 103

Boston 4, Detroit 1
May 5: Boston 84 at Detroit 96
May 8: Boston 85 at Detroit 77
May 10: Detroit 64 at Boston 66
May 12: Detroit 79 at Boston 90
May 14: Boston 90 at Detroit 81

FIRST ROUND
New Jersey 3, Indiana 2
Apr. 20: Indiana 89 at New Jersey 83
Apr. 22: Indiana 79 at New Jersey 95
Apr. 26: New Jersey 85 at Indiana 84
Apr. 30: New Jersey 74 at Indiana 97
May 2: Indiana 120 at New Jersey 109, 2OT

Detroit 3, Toronto 2
Apr. 21: Toronto 63 at Detroit 85
Apr. 24: Toronto 91 at Detroit 96
Apr. 27: Detroit 84 at Toronto 94
Apr. 29: Detroit 83 at Toronto 89
May 2: Toronto 82 at Detroit 85

Boston 3, Philadelphia 2
Apr. 21: Philadelphia 82 at Boston 92
Apr. 25: Philadelphia 85 at Boston 93
Apr. 28: Boston 103 at Philadelphia 108
May 1: Boston 81 at Philadelphia 83
May 3: Philadelphia 87 at Boston 120

Charlotte 3, Orlando 1
Apr. 20: Orlando 79 at Charlotte 80
Apr. 23: Orlando 111 at Charlotte 103, OT
Apr. 27: Charlotte 110 at Orlando 100, OT
Apr. 30: Charlotte 102 at Orlando 85

WESTERN CONFERENCE
CONFERENCE FINALS
L.A. Lakers 4, Sacramento 3
May 18: L.A. Lakers 106 at Sacramento 99
May 20: L.A. Lakers 90 at Sacramento 96
May 24: Sacramento 103 at L.A. Lakers 90
May 26: Sacramento 99 at L.A. Lakers 100
May 28: L.A. Lakers 91 at Sacramento 92
May 31: Sacramento 102 at L.A. Lakers 106
June 2: L.A. Lakers 112 at Sacramento 106, OT

CONFERENCE SEMI-FINALS
Sacramento 4, Dallas 1
May 4: Dallas 91 at Sacramento 108
May 6: Dallas 110 at Sacramento 102
May 9: Sacramento 125 at Dallas 119
May 11: Sacramento 115 at Dallas 113
May 13: Dallas 101 at Sacramento 114

L.A. Lakers 4, San Antonio 1
May 5: San Antonio 80 at L.A. Lakers 86
May 7: San Antonio 88 at L.A. Lakers 85
May 10: L.A. Lakers 99 at San Antonio 89
May 12: L.A. Lakers 87 at San Antonio 85
May 14: San Antonio 87 at L.A. Lakers 93

FIRST ROUND
Sacramento 3, Utah 1
Apr. 20: Utah 86 at Sacramento 89
Apr. 23: Utah 93 at Sacramento 86
Apr. 27: Sacramento 90 at Utah 87
Apr. 29: Sacramento 91 at Utah 86

L.A. Lakers 3, Portland 0
Apr. 21: Portland 87 at L.A. Lakers 95
Apr. 25: Portland 96 at L.A. Lakers 103
Apr. 28: L.A. Lakers 92, Portland 91

Dallas 3, Minnesota 0
Apr. 21: Minnesota 94 at Dallas 101
Apr. 24: Minnesota 110 at Dallas 122
Apr. 28: Dallas 115 at Minnesota 102

San Antonio 3, Seattle 2
Apr. 20: Seattle 89 at San Antonio 110
Apr. 22: Seattle 98 at San Antonio 90
Apr. 27: San Antonio 102 at Seattle 75
May 1: San Antonio 79 at Seattle 91
May 3: Seattle 78 at San Antonio 101

NBA LEADERS

SCORING

	GP	FGM	FTM	PTS	PPG
Allen Iverson, PHI	60	665	475	1883	31.4
Shaquille O'Neal, LAL	67	712	398	1822	27.2
Paul Pierce, BOS	82	707	520	2144	26.1
Tracy McGrady, ORL	76	715	415	1948	25.6
Tim Duncan, SAS	82	764	560	2089	25.5
Kobe Bryant, LAL	80	749	488	2019	25.2
Vince Carter, TOR	60	559	245	1484	24.7
Dirk Nowitzki, DAL	76	600	440	1779	23.4
Karl Malone, UTJ	80	635	509	1788	22.4
Antoine Walker, BOS	81	666	240	1794	22.1
Gary Payton, SEA	82	737	267	1815	22.1

FIELD GOALS

	FGM	FGA	FG%
Shaquille O'Neal, LAL	712	1229	.579
Elton Brand, LAC	532	1010	.527
Donyell Marshall, UTJ	343	661	.519
Pau Gasol, MEM	551	1064	.518
John Stockton, UTJ	401	775	.517
Alonzo Mourning, MIA	447	866	.516
Ruben Patterson, POR	319	619	.515
Corliss Williamson, DET	411	806	.510
Tim Duncan, SAS	764	1504	.508
Brent Barry, SEA	401	790	.508

THREE POINT FIELD GOALS

	3PM	3PA	3P%
Steve Smith, SAS	116	246	.472
Jon Barry, DET	121	258	.469
Eric Piatkowski, LAC	111	238	.466
Wally Szczerbiak, MIN	87	191	.455
Steve Nash, DAL	156	343	.455
Hubert Davis, WAS	57	126	.452
Tyronn Lue, WAS	63	141	.447
Michael Redd, MIL	88	198	.444
Wesley Person, CLE	143	322	.444
Ray Allen, MIL	229	528	.434

FREE THROWS

	FTM	FTA	FT%
Reggie Miller, IND	296	325	.911
Richard Hamilton, WAS	300	337	.890
Darrell Armstrong, ORL	182	205	.888
Damon Stoudamire, POR	174	196	.888
Steve Nash, DAL	260	293	.887
Chauncey Billups, MIN	207	234	.885
Chris Whitney, WAS	154	175	.880
Steve Smith, SAS	159	181	.878
Predrag Stojakovic, SAC	283	323	.876
Troy Hudson, ORL	176	201	.876

ASSISTS

	GP	AST	APG
Andre Miller, CLE	81	882	10.9
Jason Kidd, NJN	82	808	9.9
Gary Payton, SEA	82	737	9.0
Baron Davis, CHA	82	698	8.5
John Stockton, UTJ	82	674	8.2
Stephon Marbury, PHO	82	666	8.1
Jamaal Tinsley, IND	80	647	8.1
Jason Williams, MEM	65	519	8.0
Steve Nash, DAL	82	634	7.7
Mark Jackson, NYK	82	605	7.4

REBOUNDS

	GP	ORB	DRB	TRB	RPG
Ben Wallace, DET	80	318	721	1039	13.0
Tim Duncan, SAS	82	268	774	1042	12.7
Kevin Garnett, MIN	81	243	738	981	12.1
Danny Fortson, GST	77	290	609	899	11.7
Elton Brand, LAC	80	396	529	925	11.6
Dikembe Mutombo, PHI	80	254	609	863	10.8
Jermaine O'Neal, IND	72	188	569	757	10.5
Dirk Nowitzki, DAL	76	120	635	755	9.9
Shawn Marion, PHO	81	211	592	803	9.9
P.J. Brown, CHA	80	273	513	786	9.8

STEALS

	GP	STL	SPG
Allen Iverson, PHI	60	168	2.80
Ron Artest, CHI/IND	55	141	2.56
Jason Kidd, NJN	82	175	2.13
Baron Davis, CHA	82	172	2.10
Doug Christie, SAC	81	160	1.98
Darrell Armstrong, ORL	82	157	1.91
Karl Malone, UTJ	80	152	1.90
Paul Pierce, BOS	82	154	1.88
Kenny Anderson, BOS	76	141	1.86
John Stockton, UTJ	82	152	1.85

BLOCKS

	GP	BLK	BPG
Ben Wallace, DET	80	278	3.48
Raef LaFrentz, DEN/DAL	78	213	2.73
Alonzo Mourning, MIA	75	186	2.48
Tim Duncan, SAS	82	203	2.48
Dikembe Mutombo, PHI	80	190	2.38
Jermaine O'Neal, IND	72	166	2.31
Erick Dampier, GST	73	.167	2.29
Adonal Foyle, GST	79	168	2.13
Pau Gasol, MEM	82	169	2.06
Shaquille O'Neal, LAL	67	137	2.04

TURNOVERS

	GP	TO	TPG
Allen Iverson, PHI	60	237	4.0
Steve Francis, HOU	57	221	3.9
Jerry Stackhouse, DET	76	266	3.5
Jason Kidd, NJN	82	286	3.5
Stephon Marbury, PHO	82	284	3.5
Jamaal Tinsley, IND	80	270	3.4
Lamar Odom, LAC	29	97	3.3
Jason Williams, MEM	65	214	3.3
Karl Malone, UTJ	80	263	3.3
Shareef Abdur-Rahim, ATL	77	250	3.2

THE YEAR IN BASKETBALL

October 30, 2001 After three years in retirement, 38-year-old Michael Jordan returns to the NBA with the Washington Wizards and scores 19 points in a 93-91 loss to the Knicks.

December 24, 2001 With his team's record at 4-21, Tim Floyd resigns as head coach of the Chicago Bulls.

January 18, 2002 Alex Hannum, the only coach to win championships in both the ABA and NBA, dies at age 78.

February 1, 2002 Phil Jackson gets the 700th win of his NBA coaching career, as the Lakers beat Memphis, 100-85. Jackson is the fastest coach to win 700, doing it in 946 games.

February 20, 2002 Michael Redd of Milwaukee hits 8 three-pointers and scores 26 points in the fourth quarter of the Bucks' 115-76 win over Houston. The three-pointers set an NBA mark for most in a quarter.

March 28, 2002 Memphis wins the NIT, beating South Carolina, 72-62. Freshman Dajuan Wagner is the tournament's top player.

March 31, 2002 Connecticut's women's team completes a perfect 39-0 season by defeating Oklahoma, 82-70, for the school's third cham-pionship. The Connecticut team sets an NCAA season record by winning their games by an average of 35.4 ppg.

April 2, 2002 Maryland beats Indiana, 64-52, to win the school's first men's collegiate national championship. Guard Juan Dixon scores 18 point in the clincher and is named the tournament's MOP.

May 5, 2002 Panathinaikos defeats Kinder Bologna, 89-83, to win the European championship, in Bologna, Italy. Dejan Bodiroga of Panathinaikos scores 21 points and is named the game's MVP.

May 31, 2002 The New Jersey Nets, long an NBA doormat, qualify for the NBA finals for the first time, by beating the Celtics in six games.

June 12, 2002 The Lakers sweep the Nets in four games to win their third consecutive NBA title. Phil Jackson ties Red Auerbach by winning his ninth title as head coach.

June 26, 2002 The Houston Rockets select China's Yao Ming, a 7-foot-6 center, with the first pick in the NBA draft.

August 5, 2002 Chick Hearn, the Lakers' Hall of Fame play-by-play announcer for 42 years, dies at age 85.

2002-03

Duncan sweeps MVPs, leads Spurs to title in Robinson's swan song

It was a year for Hall of Famers moving on and new blood infusing the NBA.

Hakeem Olajuwon retired after playing the 2001-02 season with Toronto. In his 18-year career "The Dream" twice led Houston to NBA titles (1994, '95), winning the Finals MVP in both seasons. He was league MVP (1994), twice Defensive Player of Year (1993, '94), and six times All-First Team (1987, '88, '89, '93, '94, '97). His number 34 was retired by the Rockets. Shortly after in June, Houston made China's Yao Ming, a 7-foot-6 center, their first pick in the NBA draft.

In 2000-03 there were just two teams that won 60 games— San Antonio and Dallas. Close behind were the Sacramento Kings (59 wins) and four other fifty-win teams—Minnesota (51) and Detroit, Portland, and Los Angeles, all tied with 50. Those numbers foretold the fortunes of the Western teams. For the Lakers, 50 wins was their lowest total in a full season since 1994-95, two seasons before Shaquille O'Neal arrived.

Michael Jordan started his last All-Star Game when Toronto's Vince Carter graciously gave up his starting spot. Jordan came through in the final seconds of the first overtime, hitting a baseline jumper over Shawn Marion to put the East ahead, 138-136. But a pair of free throws by Kobe Bryant sent the game into a second overtime where Kevin Garnett took over, scoring nine of his game-high 37 points, giving the West a 10-point win and brining Garnett the game MVP.

The Lakers eliminated a vastly improved Minnesota team in six games in the first round, overcoming a huge performance from Kevin Garnett (27 points, 16 rebounds, and five assists per game). The Lakers rode their potent twosome of Kobe Bryant (32 ppg) and O'Neal (29 ppg). But they could ride that twosome no further.

The Lakers were out of step early on. A summer foot operation hobbled O'Neal and he missed 15 games. Kobe Bryant finished runner-up in scoring to Tracy McGrady, but he couldn't compensate for the decreased production from the Lakers' bench. The supporting cast was vital to the Lakers' run of three straight championships, but their contribution declined. Rick Fox missed eight playoff games. Bryan Shaw had no impact and Robert Horry, who repeatedly hit clutch shots in the past, was invisible. In the Conference Semi-Finals the Lakers faced San Antonio and consecutive-MVP forward Tim Duncan. The Spurs had beaten Los Angeles four straight during the season and a combined 57 points from Bryant and O'Neal couldn't offset Tim Duncan's 28 points per game and the team effort from San Antonio in the post-season. In Game 6 in Los Angeles, San Antonio won by 28 points to eliminate the Lakers and end their run of three titles and 13 consecutive post-season series won.

Sacramento put together another excellent season but their chances of advancing were dealt a severe blow when Chris Webber (averaging 27.5 points) sustained a knee injury in

Tracy McGrady
Once buried in his cousin Vince Carter's shadow in Toronto, flew to new heights in Orlando and established himself as a bonafide All-Star.

Game 2 of the conference semis against Dallas and missed the last five games. Dallas won in seven, getting support from their big three, Dirk Nowitzski (21 ppg, 14 rebounds), Steve Nash (19 ppg, seven apg), and Michael Finley (19 ppg). Dallas also got a surprising boost came from Nick Van Exxel (25.3 ppg) and prevailed in seven games.

That matched Dallas against San Antonio. Again, Duncan dominated, posting 28 points and 17 rebounds a game. But in Game 6, after the Spurs trailed by 13 with 11 minutes to play, it was Stephen Jackson and Manu Ginobili who supplied the fire

power. The Spurs outscored the Mavs 34-9 in the final 12 minutes to win 90-78. The comeback reversed the equally wild outcome of Game 5, when the Spurs had a 19-point lead, but were dusted 29-10 in the fourth quarter for a 103-91 Dallas victory.

New Jersey had little problem repeating as Eastern Conference champions. After going six games with Milwaukee, they swept Detroit and Boston, giving them a 10-game winning streak. But the Jason Kidd-led fast break that averaged 101 points against Boston didn't get a foothold in the Finals. San Antonio held the Nets to 82 points a game. In Game 6, a 19-0 Spurs run finished the Nets, 88-77. Finals MVP Tim Duncan played a balanced series, averaging 24 points, 17 rebounds, five assists and five blocks.

Following the season, John Stockton, one of the great small guards of all-time and the NBA's all-time assists and steals leader,

announced his retirement after 19 years with the Utah Jazz. At 41, Stockton closed his career with 15,806 assists—over 5,500 more than anyone else in NBA history. Several weeks later Hall of Famer Dave DeBusschere died after suffering a heart attack while walking in New York City. He was 62. It was the acquisition of DeBusschere from Detroit in 1968 that changed the fortunes of the Knicks and they won NBA titles in 1970 and 1973. DeBusschere was voted to the All-Defensive First Team six consecutive years, from 1969 through 1974.

Even the sadness of a great player passing was balanced by a new era dawning. LeBron James, the most heralded high school player ever, was drafted No. 1 overall by the Cleveland Cavaliers. The 6-foot-8, 240-pound James was a consensus high school All-American in his sophomore, junior, and senior seasons.

2002-03 SEASON HIGHLIGHTS

STANDINGS

Eastern Conference
Atlantic Division

	W	L	Pct.	GB
New Jersey	49	33	.598	—
Philadelphia	48	34	.585	1
Boston	44	38	.537	5
Orlando	42	40	.512	7
Washington	37	45	.451	12
New York	37	45	.451	12
Miami	25	57	.305	24

Central Division

	W	L	Pct.	GB
Detroit	50	32	.610	—
Indiana	48	34	.585	2
New Orleans	47	35	.573	3
Milwaukee	42	40	.512	8
Atlanta	35	47	.427	15
Chicago	30	52	.366	20
Toronto	24	58	.293	26
Cleveland	17	65	.207	33

Western Conference
Midwest Division

	W	L	Pct.	GB
San Antonio	60	22	.732	—
Dallas	60	22	.732	0
Minnesota	51	31	.622	9
Utah	47	35	.573	13
Houston	43	39	.524	17
Memphis	28	54	.341	32
Denver	17	65	.207	43

Pacific Division

	W	L	Pct.	GB
Sacramento	59	23	.720	—
LA Lakers	50	32	.610	9
Portland	50	32	.610	9
Phoenix	44	38	.537	15
Seattle	40	42	.488	19
Golden State	38	44	.463	21
LA Clippers	27	55	.329	32

AWARDS
MVP
Tim Duncan, San Antonio
Top Rookie
Amare Stoudemire, Phoenix
Coach of Year
Gregg Popovich, San Antonio
Defensive Player of Year
Ben Wallace, Detroit
Sixth Man Award
Bobby Jackson, Sacramento
Most Improved Player
Gilbert Arenas, Golden State
Citizenship Award
David Robinson, San Antonio

ALL-STAR GAME
Philips Arena, Atlanta
Sunday, February 9, 2003
West 155, East 145, 2OT
MVP: Kevin Garnett

ALL-STAR TEAMS
FIRST TEAM

Tim Duncan	San Antonio
Kevin Garnett	Minnesota
Shaquille O'Neal	LA Lakers
Tracy McGrady	Orlando
Kobe Bryant	LA Lakers

SECOND TEAM

Dirk Nowitzki	Dallas
Chris Webber	Sacramento
Ben Wallace	Detroit
Jason Kidd	New Jersey
Allen Iverson	Philadelphia

THIRD TEAM

Paul Pierce	Boston
Jamal Mashburn	New Orleans
Jermaine O'Neal	Indiana
Stephon Marbury	Phoenix
Steve Nash	Dallas

PLAYOFFS
FINALS
San Antonio 4, New Jersey 2
June 4: New Jersey 89 at San Antonio 101
June 6: New Jersey 87 at San Antonio 85
June 8: San Antonio 84 at New Jersey 79
June 11: San Antonio 76 at New Jersey 77
June 13: San Antonio 93 at New Jersey 83
June 15: New Jersey 77 at San Antonio 88

EASTERN CONFERENCE
CONFERENCE FINALS
New Jersey 4, Detroit 0
May 18: Boston 76 at Detroit 74
May 20: Boston 88 at Detroit 86
May 22: Detroit 85 at New Jersey 97
May 24: Detroit 82 at New Jersey 102

CONFERENCE SEMI-FINALS
Detroit 4, Philadelphia 2
May 6: Philadelphia 87 at Detroit 98
May 8: Philadelphia 97 at Detroit 104
May 10: Detroit 83 at Philadelphia 93
May 11: Detroit 82 at Philadelphia 95
May 14: Philadelphia 77 at Detroit 78
May 16: Detroit 93 at Philadelphia 89, OT

New Jersey 4, Boston 0
May 5: Boston 93 at New Jersey 97
May 7: Boston 95 at New Jersey 104
May 9: New Jersey 94 at Boston 76
May 12: New Jersey 110 at Boston 101

FIRST ROUND
Detroit 4, Orlando 3
Apr. 20: Orlando 99 at Detroit 94
Apr. 23: Orlando 77 at Detroit 89
Apr. 25: Detroit 80 at Orlando 89
Apr. 27: Detroit 92 at Orlando 100
Apr. 30: Orlando 67 at Detroit 98
May 2: Detroit 103 at Orlando 88
May 4: Orlando 93 at Detroit 108

New Jersey 4, Milwaukee 2
Apr. 19: Milwaukee 96 at New Jersey 109
Apr. 22: Milwaukee 88 at New Jersey 85
Apr. 24: New Jersey 103 at Milwaukee 101
Apr. 26: New Jersey 114 at Milwaukee 119
May 29: Milwaukee 82 at New Jersey 89
May 1: New Jersey 113 at Milwaukee 101

Boston 4, Indiana 2
Apr. 19: Boston 103 at Indiana 100
Apr. 21: Boston 77 at Indiana 89
Apr. 24: Indiana 83 at Boston 101
Apr. 27: Indiana 92 at Boston 102
Apr. 29: Boston 88 at Indiana 93
May 1: Indiana 90 at Boston 110

Philadelphia 4, New Orleans 2
Apr. 20: New Orleans 90 at Philadelphia 98
Apr. 23: New Orleans 85 at Philadelphia 90
Apr. 26: Philadelphia 85 at New Orleans 99
Apr. 28: Philadelphia 96 at New Orleans 87
Apr. 30: New Orleans 93 at Philadelphia 91
May 2: Philadelphia 107 at New Orleans 103

WESTERN CONFERENCE
CONFERENCE FINALS
San Antonio 4, Dallas 2
May 19: Dallas 113 at San Antonio 110
May 21: Dallas 106 at San Antonio 119
May 23: San Antonio 96 at Dallas 83
May 25: San Antonio 102 at Dallas 95
May 27: Dallas 103 at San Antonio 91
May 29: San Antonio 90 at Dallas 78

CONFERENCE SEMI-FINALS
San Antonio 4, L.A. Lakers 2
May 5: L.A. Lakers 82 at San Antonio 87
May 7: L.A. Lakers 95 at San Antonio 114
May 9: San Antonio 95 at L.A. Lakers 110
May 11: San Antonio 95 at L.A. Lakers 99
May 13: L.A. Lakers 94 at San Antonio 96
May 15: San Antonio 110 at L.A. Lakers 82

Dallas 4, Sacramento 3
May 6: Sacramento 124 at Dallas 113
May 8: Sacramento 132 at Dallas 110
May 10: Dallas 141 at Sacramento 137
May 11: Dallas 83 at Sacramento 99
May 13: Sacramento 93 at Dallas 112
May 15: Dallas 105 at Sacramento 115
May 17: Sacramento 99 at Dallas 112

FIRST ROUND
San Antonio 4, Phoenix 2
Apr. 19: Phoenix 96 at San Antonio 95, OT
Apr. 21: Phoenix 76 at San Antonio 84
Apr. 25: San Antonio 99 at Phoenix 86
Apr. 27: San Antonio 84 at Phoenix 86
Apr. 29: Phoenix 94 at San Antonio 82
May 1: San Antonio 87 at Phoenix 85

Sacramento 4, Utah 1
Apr. 19: Utah 90 at Sacramento 96
Apr. 21: Utah 95 at Sacramento 108
Apr. 26: Sacramento 104 at Utah 107
Apr. 28: Sacramento 79 at Utah 91
Apr. 30: Utah 78 at Sacramento 101

Dallas 4, Portland 3
Apr. 19: Portland 86 at Dallas 96
Apr. 23: Portland 99 at Dallas 103
Apr. 25: Dallas 115 at Portland 103
Apr. 27: Dallas 79 at Portland 98
Apr. 30: Portland 103 at Dallas 99
May 2: Dallas 103 at Portland 125
May 4: Portland 95 at Dallas 107

L.A. Lakers 4, Minnesota 2
Apr. 20: L.A. Lakers 117 at Minnesota 98
Apr. 22: L.A. Lakers 91 at Minnesota 119
Apr. 24: Minnesota 114 at L.A. Lakers 113
Apr. 27: Minnesota 97 at L.A. Lakers 102
Apr. 29: L.A. Lakers 120 at Minnesota 90
May 1: Minnesota 85 at L.A. Lakers 101

NBA LEADERS

SCORING

	GP	FGM	FTM	PTS	PPG
Tracy McGrady, ORL	75	829	576	2407	32.1
Kobe Bryant, LAL	82	868	601	2461	30.0
Allen Iverson, PHI	82	804	570	2262	27.6
Shaquille O'Neal, LAL	67	695	451	1841	27.5
Paul Pierce, BOS	79	663	604	2048	25.9
Dirk Nowitzki, DAL	80	690	483	2011	25.1
Tim Duncan, SAS	81	714	450	1884	23.3
Chris Webber, SAC	67	661	215	1542	23.0
Kevin Garnett, MIN	82	743	377	1883	23.0
Ray Allen, MIL/SEA	76	598	316	1713	22.5
Allan Houston, NYK	82	652	363	1845	22.5

FIELD GOALS

	FGM	FGA	FG%
Eddy Curry, CHI	335	573	.585
Shaquille O'Neal, LAL	695	1211	.574
Carlos Boozer, CLE	331	618	.536
P.J. Brown, NOH	319	601	.531
Rados Nesterovic, MIN	400	762	.525
Nene Hilario, DEN	321	619	.519
Tim Duncan, SAS	714	1392	.513
Matthew Harpring, UTJ	521	1020	.511
Pau Gasol, MEM	569	1116	.510
Brian Grant, MIA	344	676	.509

THREE POINT FIELD GOALS

	3PM	3PA	3P%
Bruce Bowen, SAS	101	229	.441
Michael Redd, MIL	182	416	.438
Wesley Person, MEM	100	231	.433
David Wesley, NOH	134	316	.424
Wally Szczerbiak, MIN	61	145	.421
Steve Nash, DAL	111	269	.413
Matthew Harpring, UTJ	66	160	.412
Anthony Peeler, MIN	87	212	.410
Mike Bibby, SAC	56	137	.409
Eddie Jones, MIA	98	241	.407

FREE THROWS

	FTM	FTA	FT%
Allan Houston, NYK	363	395	.919
Ray Allen, MIL/SEA	316	345	.916
Steve Nash, DAL	308	339	.909
Troy Hudson, MIN	208	231	.900
Reggie Miller, IND	207	230	.900
Jason Terry, ATL	259	292	.887
Dirk Nowitzki, DAL	483	548	.881
Chauncey Billups, DET	318	362	.878
Jerry Stackhouse, WAS	455	518	.878
Darrell Armstrong, ORL	165	188	.878

ASSISTS

	GP	AST	APG
Jason Kidd, NJN	80	711	8.9
Jason Williams, MEM	76	631	8.3
Gary Payton, SEA/MIL	80	663	8.3
Stephon Marbury, PHO	81	654	8.1
John Stockton, UTJ	82	629	7.7
Jamaal Tinsley, IND	73	548	7.5
Jason Terry, ATL	81	600	7.4
Steve Nash, DAL	82	598	7.3
Andre Miller, LAC	80	537	6.7
Eric Snow, PHI	82	544	6.6

REBOUNDS

	GP	ORB	DRB	TRB	RPG
Ben Wallace, DET	73	293	833	1126	15.4
Kevin Garnett, MIN	82	244	858	1102	13.4
Tim Duncan, SAS	81	259	784	1043	12.9
Jermaine O'Neal, IND	77	202	594	796	10.3
Brian Grant, MIA	82	241	596	837	10.2
Troy Murphy, GST	79	228	578	806	10.2
Dirk Nowitzki, DAL	80	81	710	791	9.9
Shawn Marion, PHO	81	199	574	773	9.5
Jerome Williams, TOR	71	231	419	650	9.2
P.J. Brown, NOH	78	243	458	701	9.0

STEALS

	GP	STL	SPG
Allen Iverson, PHI	82	225	2.74
Ron Artest, IND	69	159	2.30
Shawn Marion, PHO	81	185	2.28
Doug Christie, SAC	80	180	2.25
Jason Kidd, NJN	80	179	2.24
Kobe Bryant, LAL	82	181	2.21
Paul Pierce, BOS	79	139	1.76
Caron Butler, MIA	78	137	1.76
Steve Francis, HOU	81	141	1.74
Jamaal Tinsley, IND	73	125	1.71

BLOCKS

	GP	BLK	BPG
Theo Ratliff, ATL	81	262	3.23
Ben Wallace, DET	73	230	3.15
Tim Duncan, SAS	81	237	2.93
Elton Brand, LAC	62	158	2.55
Adonal Foyle, GST	82	205	2.50
Shaquille O'Neal, LAL	67	159	2.37
Jermaine O'Neal, IND	77	178	2.31
Andrei Kirilenko, UTJ	80	175	2.19
Shawn Bradley, DAL	81	170	2.10
Erick Dampier, GST	82	154	1.88

TURNOVERS

	GP	TO	TPG
Jason Kidd, NJN	80	296	3.7
Steve Francis, HOU	81	299	3.7
Paul Pierce, BOS	79	288	3.6
Glenn Robinson, ATL	69	248	3.6
Gilbert Arenas, GST	82	290	3.5
Kobe Bryant, LAL	82	288	3.5
Ricky Davis, CLE	79	277	3.5
Allen Iverson, PHI	82	286	3.5
Jalen Rose, CHI	82	285	3.5
Antoine Walker, BOS	78	260	3.3

THE YEAR IN BASKETBALL

September 7, 2002 Spain defeats the United States, 81-75, at the World Championships in Indianapolis. The loss is the third in nine games for the U.S., which fields a roster filled with NBA all-star caliber players. The loss places the Americans sixth in the final standings.

September 25, 2002 The U.S. women's team edges Russia, 79-74, to go 9-0 and win the World Championships in Nanjing, China.

Dec. 17, 2002 Hank Luisetti, a three-time All-American forward who revolutionized basketball in the 1930s with a running one-handed shot, dies at age 86.

January 10, 2003 Robert Johnson, founder and CEO of the Black Entertainment Television network, becomes the first African-American majority owner of a major American sports team when the league's board of governors approves the awarding of a franchise to Charlotte.

April 3, 2003 St. John's wins its sixth NIT championship, besting Big East rival Georgetown, 70-67, at Madison Square Garden.

April 6, 2003 Connecticut wins its second consecutive women's national championship, 73-68, over Tennessee.

April 7, 2003 Syracuse, led by freshman sensation Carmelo Anthony, wins the NCAA tournament, by defeating Kansas, 81-78. The victory is the first national championship for the Orangemen.

May 2, 2003 John Stockton, the NBA's all-time assists and steals leader, announces his retirement after 19 years with the Utah Jazz. Stockton, 41, ends his career with 15,806 assists—over 5,500 more than anyone else in NBA history.

May 11, 2003 FC Barcelona wins the European league title, 76-65, at home over Benetton Treviso. Dejan Bodiroga, who scores 20 points for the victors, is named game MVP for the second year in row.

May 15, 2003 Hall of Famer Dave DeBusschere dies after suffering a heart attack while walking in New York City. He was 62.

June 15, 2003 The San Antonio Spurs erupt with a 19-0 fourth-quarter run to defeat the New Jersey Nets, 88-77, to win the NBA title.

June 26, 2003 LeBron James, the most heralded high school player ever, is drafted No. 1 overall by the Cleveland Cavaliers in the NBA Draft. The 6'8", 240-pound James was a consensus high school All-American.

Chapter 15

Goodbye Schlitz, Hello Smog: Kareem Goes West Again

The oversized Muslim convert from Harlem never felt at home in Milwaukee, so Abdul-Jabbar was happy to leave for a fresh start with the L.A. Lakers.

By Barry Farrell
SPORT Magazine, February 1976

The P.A. system at Los Angeles' "Fabulous" Forum sounds mighty like the voice of creation when it declares that the tall fellow in the goggles is "The World's Greatest Basketball Player"— but this is Hollywood, sweetheart, and that's what we call faint praise. When you've got a myth in motion making hoop history right here in Tinseltown, you can't get by on simple bragging any more than you can with newspaper ads for home games saying,

KAREEM!

LAKERS!

in that order, or program notes alleging that Number 33 on our side is "THE FORCE in pro basketball." When the standard hype fails to exaggerate the powers of a loved one—especially a loved one returning from a cold northern exile to the comforts of a five-year contract worth between 2.5 and 4 million dollars—the local idea of grandeur requires the boosters' chorus to come up with a new song and dance. That's what I imagined I was hearing last summer, when L.A. began to buzz with a story worthy of daytime TV: Six Milwaukee winters had worked wonders on the Lakers' new dynasty-maker, so that now, besides being the game's greatest player, Kareem Abdul-Jabbar was also the world's nicest guy.

No news could have been more welcome in Los Angeles, where feelings of unrequited fandom were a plague upon the two great houses of basketball. Wilt Chamberlain had stalked off the Lakers to sack the ABA franchise in San Diego, and was now pursuing a bizarre obsession with volleyball. Jerry West had retired sooner than expected to become a gentleman golfer and unconvincing television shill. Gail Goodrich and the Lakers were then said to be more than $100,000 apart in contract talks. But cheers rang particularly thin in memory for the heroes of Westwood, Lew

Kareem Abdul-Jabbar, 1975
Finding sunshine anew in Southern California.

Alcindor and Bill Walton, whose teams in six championship seasons had won 174 games out of 180 for coach John Wooden and UCLA. The enigmatic Alcindor had left town in what many took to be a huff, only to become the sulky Abdul-Jabbar; the embarrassing Walton, meanwhile, had emerged as a left-

wing Mortimer Snerd, a Dresden-doll rookie whose more-organic-than-thou approach to life had him leading the NBA only in sick calls.

Kareem's accomplishments were not to be disputed—he was twice the collegiate Player of the Year, three times the NBA's Most Valuable Player, four times a first-team All-Pro, and the league leader in career scoring average, with 30.4 a game. But the impression lingered that Southern California had failed to charm him, that life in Los Angeles had left him feeling, as he once remarked, like a man "on a raft in the middle of the ocean." So while no one doubted that the Lakers had done well to invest in his talents, the town was in need of consolations not to be found on the court alone, and the press was primed to quiz him on his loyalty to Lotusland when it assembled at the Forum for the grand unveiling.

The lights fell dramatically as the master of ceremonies intoned the Arabic words for "Noble and Powerful Servant of Allah," a name that for all its Islamic piety could hardly be better for basketball—"Kareem!" (the sound of a rebound) "Abdul!" (an elbow in the eye) "Jabbar!" (slam-dunk). A pin spotlight clawed its way up the crack in the curtain until it found the smiling, bearded face. Then, to the scribes' loud applause, the prodigal returned, shambling up to the dais like a stretched-out Jimmy Stewart. Kareem made many assurances that he was pleased to be back in L.A., and his calm and cosmopolitan manner was all it took to convince the grateful city that he was just what the Lakers were claiming—"a new super center with a new super attitude."

Sensing that the demands of folklore had somehow got the best of the principles of psychology, I made arrangements to meet Kareem one afternoon after a Lakers practice. The team had looked ragged winning at the Forum the night before, and coach Bill Sharman was running the players through what seemed to be an intense and spirited scrimmage. Kareem worked hard in the thick of it, wrestling down rebounds, passing smartly, paying special attention to the rookies, laughing and hustling like a man with a new super attitude. The few times he took a shot himself, his teammates whooped it up for him, glad to be a part of Sky Hook Enterprises. Kareem scrimmaged for ten or 15 minutes, then went over to a hoop at the side of the court to practice shooting free throws. He made 42 out of 49 and I was waiting for number 50 when he left the gym, beckoning me to follow.

I had to skip to keep up with his antelope stride as we made our way out into bright sunshine. We were on the Loyola Marymount University campus in southwest Los Angeles, a place of palm trees and succulents and hard green lawns, flat and interchangeable. Kareem walked to his car and leaned on the right front fender of the Mercedes. We had hardly exchanged a word, but now I saw that his eyes were flashing an ON THE AIR sign.

"Everybody's been saying what a changed man you are," I began. Watching the scrimmage had cast some doubt on my assumption that the story was a hype, and I could hear new uncertainty entering in my voice. "Can this be true? Are you going to have to come up with a bright and sunny disposition to live up to all your clippings?"

"No, not really," Kareem said after a moment's silence. "I'm

just going to be myself, and in doing that, I think they might realize that the other ideas they've had about me were pretty far off. There's no way you can add me up to some of the things that have been printed."

"So your attitude isn't one hundred and eighty degrees different from what it was this time last year."

"No, no, there's no way. This is the first time I've been in Southern California when I've been able to speak freely to the press. Also, when I was in L.A. before, I was an adolescent. Now I'm a man. That makes a whole new way of relating."

"So you do expect to relate to L.A. better than you could to Milwaukee?" I asked.

"Definitely. The Southern California life-style is completely different from what you find in the Midwest. I mean look...." His arm swept across the semitropical tableau, a scene more like Marrakesh than Milwaukee. "See, I'm from Harlem. That means I'm from the cultural capital of Afro-America. Truly. People like W.E.B. DuBois, Dizzy Gillespie, Charlie Parker, Nikki Giovanni, LeRoi Jones, they all derive from Harlem. In Milwaukee, there was just very little for me to relate to. This is not to put Milwaukee down, by no means, but it can be a pretty lonely life if you've got nothing to relate to."

The conversation proceeded along these lines, guarded, perhaps, but pleasant and cordial. We discussed matters of mutual interest in a friendly manner. We enjoyed a frank exchange of views. Overhearing us, you might have guessed that he was the Saudi ambassador and I the protocol man from the State Department. I had gleaned a list of adjectives used to describe Jabbar in newspaper articles over the years and, with his indulgence, I tried them out on him one by one.

"How about 'reclusive'?"

"No, not at all. I'm not hiding from anybody. Definitely not. I spend time alone, but reclusive I'm not. I've got a lot of friends. I spend time with people I like and who I'm pretty sure like me."

"'Aloof'?"

"I can be aloof. But I think that has to do with meeting people who come at me as if I'm an object. Forgive this example, but I guess I might have a lot in common with a beautiful woman. A beautiful woman has to meet people who don't care anything about her, who just want to see her up close. And for me, I meet a lot of people who want to ask me how tall I am. Actually. That's their first and only remark to me. After a while, you see them coming, and you become what they call aloof."

"How about 'skeptical' and 'suspicious'?"

"I'm not ... no, maybe I am a little suspicious. That might be true. It is true. I think it comes from growing up in this world. It's a tough world. A little suspicion can put you on a good survival track."

"'Quiet'?"

"Initially, I am kind of quiet. I lay back at first and watch. That's a New Yorker's way. You do a lot of people-watching in New York, and I think I do that still."

"What about 'mentally hyperactive'?"

Kareem raised his eyebrows and looked far away. "I'm very curious about a lot of things. You talk about something new and I'll be all ears. But 'mentally hyperactive' sounds like a psychiatrist's term. I know I don't have to make any effort to

clear my mind to play, not after doing it so long. It's my living, it's my blood. I suppose if my mind were hyperactive that might be a problem. Last year, when my hand was broken and I wasn't playing, that was the first time since I was in the fourth grade that my basketball season didn't start in the late summer. I had a chance to think about a lot of things. I might have been a little hyperactive then, I guess." He shook his head in a kind of baffled amusement.

"Would you say you're 'short-tempered'?" I asked, choosing another description from the list.

"No. Definitely not."

"Didn't you break your hand by getting so mad you smashed it against the backboard?"

"Against the backboard standard, yes. I punched it. The guy who drove me to the hospital told me that one time he was working in his basement shop and he put a drill-bit through his thumb. It made him so mad that he kicked the wall and broke his foot. People do these things. It happens. That was my only consolation."

He stood up and jingled his car keys, agreeing to meet at the Forum before the game the following night. Before I could gather my belongings, he was gone. It occurred to me that even though our meeting had been perfectly pleasant, Kareem would have had a hard time picking me out of a police lineup if I had snatched those keys and made off with his Mercedes.

⊕ ⊕ ⊕

The sportswriters of Milwaukee—authors of most of the words on my list—did not seem to be mourning Kareem's departure.

"Kareem was inaccessible a lot of the time," Rel Bochat, the basketball writer for the *Milwaukee Sentinel*, told me when I called. "We had confidential home numbers for all the players except him. That's just an example. Then a lot of times if you asked what he thought was a dumb question, he'd just give you the 'look.' Or else he'd say 'Excuse me,' and barge right past, leaving you standing there with your pencil. On the road he was better. We'd go into New York, and those guys could ask all the dumb questions they wanted. They'd ask him about his Islamic faith and all that, and he'd sit there talking to them.

"The press here didn't ride him or anything like that. Once about three years back he made an obscene gesture on the floor, raised his finger, and the *Journal* ran a picture the next afternoon. He got pretty corked off about that. And then once I did a piece in which I mentioned that Lew Alcindor had set some record, and Kareem didn't like that one little bit. I tried to explain that I didn't mean to offend him, that Lew Alcindor was his name at the time he set the record. But he gave me a big lecture about it anyhow. When he left, the town was divided, but as far as I'm concerned he won't be missed. The team's making money, we're getting some full houses, and we're going to win some games. Give my regards to Lew Alcindor."

Kareem patted the chair beside him when he saw me enter the Lakers' locker room. He was trying to work some comfort into a new basketball shoe, and he didn't speak or look up while I settled down beside him. I had been forewarned that he didn't enjoy talking about basketball much, feeling that his idea of the game is adequately expressed on the court, but still I began our second talk by asking him if he had any further personal objectives as a player.

"No, no," Kareem said, not lifting his eyes from the shoe. "I've accomplished everything anybody could hope to accomplish as a basketball player. I just want to continue to play like I've been playing, and that's enough. It's put me at the top of the profession."

He continued to knead the shoe, calm and deliberate in motion as well as word. His matter-of-fact answer left no room for elaboration. I asked him about his attempt to break the NBA gag rule last season, when he said after a game that referee Jerry Loeber "sets a standard for ineptitude that is unequaled," adding that he would, if necessary, ask the American Civil Liberties Union to defend his right to speak his mind.

"Oh, that ended up pretty well defused," he said. "They fined me. I refused to pay. My team paid for me. And that was it. I think it might have shook a few people up, but I didn't expect any immediate change to come out of it. The pro basketball official has the roughest job of any sports official. We couldn't play the game if it wasn't for them. There'd be fights out there, one after another.

"It's just that the officiating has to be more consistent. If they're going to allow some roughness, they should make it the same for all players all over the court. They allow a lot more roughness under the basket than anywhere else. To the point of bloodshed, literally. The bigger you are, the taller you are, the more they allow people to do to you. They all blow calls, they're human, but the good officials will at least blow the whistle. It's the officials who don't blow the whistle at all, who just watch the game, that make it hard on you. The game just gets out of hand."

Kareem's teammates were assembling in the locker room, a roomful of well-paid athletes whose quiet manner produced an atmosphere more like the haughty downtown athletic club than the grab-ass locker rooms common to basketball. Kareem had a nod or a greeting for all of them, but, as in a decorous gentlemen's club, no one came over to intrude on his conversation. Kareem had shown immediate enthusiasm for the team, missing no practices and making no complaints, "as dedicated as a rookie," coach Sharman said. Kareem was glad to be free of the pattern-bound game of Larry Costello, whose Bucks playbook is said to be as thick as the Manhattan Yellow Pages. The Lakers' style is more like a city game, a pickup game, and that's the way Kareem likes to play.

As he dressed for the game, Kareem was recalling an important summer in his life, the summer before he graduated from high school. He was putting out a newspaper for a community project in Harlem, and his work took him often to the Schomburg Center for Research in Black Culture, on 135th Street in Manhattan. At Power Memorial Academy, where his teams won 71 games in a row, he was not only a superstar but also a seven-foot black at a midtown Catholic school; Jack Donohue, his high-school coach, had said to him, "Lewie, let's face it, you're a minority of one." But at the library, Kareem discovered a larger context for his sense of being a person apart, and that led him to open his eyes to what was going on in Harlem. That summer, he became aware of black nationalist groups, of the Black Muslims, of various Yoruba groups, and of

Malcolm X.

"My father always knew about our family history," he said, "back to the man who brought us over. We knew that we were Yoruba, that we'd gone from the Yoruba country straight to Trinidad. I really have to credit my father with giving me some knowledge of my roots. All of us are supposed to have roots, but the Afro-American's roots have been just ... crushed out, you know. I wasn't in that position. I knew things about my family history which gave me some pride, and that was a good thing, because I was going to a school with a lot of Irish kids, and they could be sort of unkind. Then that summer came along, and I became aware of many new things."

Three months after Malcolm X was assassinated in Harlem on February 21, 1965, Ferdinand Lewis Alcindor appeared at a press conference to announce his decision to attend UCLA; the summer he arrived in Los Angeles was the summer Watts burned. His freshman team beat the UCLA varsity in his first appearance at Westwood, and Lew Alcindor was at once the toast of the town. But Kareem's reaction to Los Angeles was colored by dismay at the bland vanilla grins that greeted him on campus, the idle chatter that went no further than "How ya dune?" He turned inward, kept company with foreign students, read *The Autobiography of Malcolm X* and Frantz Fanon's *The Wretched of the Earth* and *Black Skin, White Masks*.

"Malcolm X had a big influence on me," Kareem said, now in his uniform and ready to play. "The contrast he made between Islam and Christianity was very concrete to me. Then I read the Fanon books. There were some Algerians at school, and they were telling me things, and one of them was teaching me a little about Islam. So in that atmosphere I absorbed it very deeply. Frantz Fanon—what struck me most about his thinking was the way he put down any kind of racism. We're dealing with human beings, so humanism is the only answer ...."

Sharman moved around behind Kareem and made eyes at the clock, signaling me to scoot. When Kareem saw me looking past him to the coach, he stopped talking at once. "Come on back after the game if you feel like it," he said as I departed.

⊕ ⊕ ⊕

The Lakers looked slewfooted beating the Atlanta Hawks that night. The freelance game was out of whack, and with only one starter back from last year's squad, the team was forced into a patterned offense which no one played with any assurance. Although Kareem has an outlet pass as quick and strong as any in the league except, perhaps, Wes Unseld's, the Lakers weren't giving him much of a chance to use it, with the guards breaking too fast or not at all and the forwards chugging downcourt late on offense.

But Kareem's play was superb, marked by what the hometown fans took to be a new exuberance. He dribbled the ball, loped downcourt for lay-ins, raised a power fist after satisfying baskets, and behaved as though he was having a wonderful time. His ideas on how to play the game of basketball were all there to be seen in the way he planted himself and looked toward the action, waving for the ball, passing into thickets of movement for many sharp assists. And when he went up for his patented sky hook, his arm described an arc of supremacy that was his alone, the dimension of his game that makes his presence on the court the most dominant in basketball. His

performance seemed part game, part recital, and when it was announced that he had scored 39 points, taken 23 rebounds and blocked ten shots, the crowd reacted with a giant whew!, as though unaware of how much Jabbar had been doing.

Outside the locker room, Sharman was like a movie-star's manager, a smiling man with a luxurious problem. "Fellas, like I say, I hate to keep picking him out all the time, but what can I tell you?" he told the crowd of reporters. "He just did it all. He made us win a game we might not have deserved. It's going to take some time for the team to come together, two or three months, maybe longer. The thing about Kareem is that he can help us win some of these subpar games."

Sharman had said that he was "a little apprehensive about the guy" before Kareem arrived, but that as soon as practice started his worries vanished. "Some stars, you know, they're a little bit special, but not Kareem. He's not that way. He wanted to play, and that's a great big inspiration for the others, that someone as great as he is will practice with such dedication. And he's a very unselfish player. He's got great vision, he looks to pass before he shoots. He's great for a team with rookies, because he's going to give you the ball if you get open, and he's got such great hands that he can catch a bad pass and make you look good. I just can't say enough about him. He's a serious man, a reader, a good conversationalist, good company, a pleasure to be around. He's just a super player with a super attitude."

The first Laker road trips had produced some anecdotes about Kareem—small stories that made his teammates feel attached to him. He'd said something funny on the bus, told a good story in the locker room, got mad playing against Seattle's Tom Burleson (the only man in the NBA taller than he is) and declared a 12-minute jihad, scoring 15 points in the first quarter. Ted Green, who covers the Lakers for the *L.A. Times*, said that once you comprehend the ordeal of passing through public places at Kareem's altitude, his reputation as distant and aloof comes into a new focus. "I couldn't believe what happened just going through the L.A. airport," Green said. "I was walking with him, and I counted, and between the ticket counter and the boarding ramp he was stopped seventeen times by people who actually said, 'How's the weather up there?' and 'How tall are you?' And Kareem just kept walking as though he didn't hear. It's sad. He has to run away from the world so much of the time."

⊕ ⊕ ⊕

Kareem patted the chair next to him and picked up where we'd left off, talking about *The Wretched of the Earth*. It was only ten minutes after the game, but he didn't seem the least bit flushed or fatigued. He maintained a dignified reserve, even in the course of applying a generous amount of powder to his peninsula-sized feet. Talking about Fanon led him back to the practice of Islam.

Kareem's sense of privacy, his reticence about his home life, his caution, derive in large part from the dangers that attach to speaking out as an orthodox Muslim in America. Threats have come his way, and three years ago seven members of the Hanafi, a division of his Sunnite faith, were murdered by intruders in a house he owned in Washington, D.C. The four persons convicted of the killings were all Black Muslims. There was,

Kareem said, "the same mentality" about the killings as in the assassination of Malcolm X—people trying to quiet down those who expose the lies.

"What the so-called Black Muslims believe is not Islam. Heaven and Hell are not on Earth. Any Muslim knows this. So that means these people are lying, or what they believe in is a lie, even if they accept it sincerely. They want to quiet that fact down. I don't see them as a danger, just something to test my faith. I have to live it. There have always been obstacles to test Muslims. There've been other false prophets. These people just aren't Muslims. They use Islamic trappings, but that's all."

"How about Muhammad Ali?"

"Cassius Clay is not a Muslim. He's just sowing confusion. If you asked the average American in Waukegan about the Muslims, he'd probably think first and foremost of Cassius Clay."

"You don't call him by his adopted name?"

"He's not a Muslim, so I can't call him by a Muslim name. If he should choose to become a Muslim, I'll call him by whatever name he wishes to use."

Kareem, who has studied Arabic at Harvard, said, "I want to become completely bilingual by the time I'm through playing, because there's a great deal of anticipation and speculation as to our dealings with the Arab world and after I'm finished playing I definitely would like to respond to that."

The locker room was just about empty, Kareem was dressed, and his car keys were beginning to jingle. He said he still enjoyed the basketball life, didn't mind the road trips, tried not to let his interests be thwarted by the impossibility of being anonymous in public.

"I've been this height since I was fourteen or fifteen, you know, so I've learned how to deal with it. I've learned a whole lot about stealth, about how to sneak in and out, to walk fast, to watch people and know when their attention is going to be misdirected so I can go right on by. It can be hard to deal with, but I've always had positive identities about my height. When I've thought about what I am, I've identified with the Empire State Building and redwood trees. Seriously. That's exactly the truth. If you're going to be different, make yourself really different. Make it a mark of excellence."

(Reprinted with permission, Sport Media Enterprises, Inc., 2003)

Chapter 16

The Hick From French Lick Puts Magic in His Act

Bostonians were unsure what to expect when Larry Bird arrived from Terre Haute, Indiana. They soon realized, however, they'd landed a superstar.

Larry Bird, 1980 A private man, beginning to show a little of his own Magic.

By Bob Ryan
SPORT Magazine, May 1981

Larry Bird had just completed doing to the Los Angeles Lakers what Magic Johnson had done to the Philadelphia 76ers nine months earlier—what the car-insurance people call a "total"—and now it was time for postmortems in the Boston Celtics' lockerroom.

Standing in front of a locker was the Most Famous Laker of Them All, Jerry West. And, yes, the former Laker player and coach had been impressed.

"The 36 points weren't what impressed me," said West. "What impressed me was that every little thing Bird did was

important. He was a thought ahead of everyone else on every offensive play."

What West and 17,504 other observers in the L.A. Forum had seen on that February night in 1981 was a personal basketball clinic, conducted at the Lakers' expense. Bird had scored 36 points, collected 21 rebounds, passed for 6 assists, leaped for 3 blocks and stripped the ball from five Lakers. After a slow first quarter he connected on 15 of 17 shots. In short, he had played the most complete game of his professional basketball career, a game that matched, or perhaps even exceeded, the 42-point, 15-rebound, 7-assist gem that Magic Johnson had thrown at Philadelphia in the final game of the 1979-80 NBA championship series.

Bird had played magnificent games for the Celtics in his rookie season of 1979-80, but there had been times when he was, well, a first-year player, albeit a talented one. The game Bird played in the Forum clearly signaled his on-court coming of age. Not until that night had he shaped an entire game to his own image. That could not have happened during his rookie season, if only because, unlike the more ebullient Magic Man, his personality would not have permitted it.

"The things that make you a veteran in this league," says Celtic Coach Bill Fitch, "are knowing the cities, the fans, the travel, the teams and the way they'll come at you like hired guns. That's what having experience in the NBA is all about.

"Larry went through last year as a very sound fundamental basketball player who was still learning these things. Last year fans would say, 'He's an excellent player,' but in a sense he was still a babe in the woods. This year you'd swear he's a 10-year veteran because he's learned so much."

The on-court Bird is easy to define. He is the consummate team player. Though he likes to play golf and tennis, he relates best to team play. It would be difficult to envision Bird competing in an individual sport for a living. As much as any contemporary basketball player—perhaps as much as any basketball player ever—he perceives the essence of this game; namely, that there are five people with five sets of feelings and only one basketball. It never occurs to him to demand exclusive control of the basketball, for which his teammates and his coach and the city of Boston are grateful. And he wants desperately to win. "Larry would kill to win a game of jacks," Fitch says.

But the off-court Bird remains a private figure to outsiders. "In college I didn't do interviews," Bird says. "I don't like to put myself in somebody's hands." As a Celtic he continues to guard his private life closely. What is known is that he lives in Newton, Mass., a suburb of Boston, with a girl named Dinah Mattingly. (His ex-wife, from a short-lived teenage marriage, and his daughter live in Terre Haute, Ind.) He is called the "Hick From French Lick," referring to the town in Indiana where he grew up, and that self-deprecating image was the one this shy 24-year-old generally held up to the outside world.

But this year the Hick began to show other facets of himself. By season's end he had refined his postgame interviews with reporters into a smooth, though cliche-ridden, oration. The oration is delivered as he stares over the heads of the media people who are crowded around him in the lockerroom. It is spoken in an impersonal tone and with the obvious hope that it will pacify the inquisitors and send them on quickly to somebody else. It usually does.

A sample: "We wuz just not playin' our game tonight. We let 'em git too many easy shots, and I thought we wuz goin' one-on-one too much. We might have been a little tarred [i.e., tired] from our trip, but that's no excuse. I wuz havin' a little trouble gettin' my rhythm early so I wuz concentratin' on reboundin' and defense until I could get something good goin' offensively. They've got a good basketball team, and you can't afford to take them lightly."

Even the cliches do not come easily. "I'm a very private person," he says. "At Indiana State I knew everyone. Of course, coming to the Celtics, I had to meet new people. I've been more open this year than last year, and I hope to be more open next year. But I want my time for myself and for my friends. I'd like to keep my friends and to enjoy myself with them."

Bird has no difficulty relating to his teammates, but then he never has. There is a sameness to the interrelationships within every male athletic aggregation known to man, from Little League to the major leagues, and Bird relishes this army-barracks camaraderie. One of his favorite postgame diversions is to go out and drink beer with his teammates. He may not be the next Don Rickles or even the next Bill (One-Liner) Fitch but he is handy with the ego-puncturing needle. He spares no one in his comments. ("New shirt?" he'll ask a player who has worn the same shirt three straight days.) It is his voice that loosens up the bus en route to the airport at 8 a.m. There is not even a hint of aloofness in this man whose estimated $650,000-a-year salary sets him apart from the everyday factory worker and even from the everyday pro athlete.

When M.L. Carr was idled with a bone fracture in his left foot this season, Bird inquired of Red Auerbach in the Celtics' lockerroom, "Hey, is M.L. still on the payroll?" That was before he gently reminded Carr that the team, at that point, was 4-3 with him and 29-5 without him.

After he finished his postgame shower, Bird invited Rick Robey to use Bird's now vacated shower stall. Just as Robey stepped in, Bird turned the water to ice cold.

"In a restaurant," says Carr, "he'll want to give the tip to the cook instead of to the waitress because he says the cook is the one who did all the work."

Says Robey, "The first time he ever was in New York we had a steak dinner. It cost $52 for both of us to eat. 'In French Lick you can eat on that for a week,' Larry said. I told him, 'Larry, we've got to leave a tip.' Larry wasn't too happy. He said, 'For that kind of money we should get the dishes and the tableware.'"

After playing one-on-one with the venerable Auerbach, who at age 63 still occasionally takes to the court following Celtic practices, Bird said of his boss, "He's the only guy who goes one-on-one with an oxygen tank on his back."

Bird enjoys a close relationship with Walter Randall, the septuagenarian equipment manager, masseur and confidant of the Celtics ("I can talk to him like a son," Randall says proudly), and he is generally as respectful of the feelings of the team's lowest members as he is of his own. Though he clearly has a closer relationship with subs Rick Robey and Kevin McHale than with any other teammate, he gets along well with everyone, black teammates as well as white.

Consider the viewpoint of Eric Fernsten, a journeyman backup center-forward. "I mentioned to some of the guys that I didn't have a contract with an equipment company. 'Who did you sign with?' Larry asked me. 'Nobody,' I told him. So he asked his agent, Bob Woolf, to talk to Converse. I got the contract.

"Let's face it. Some superstars are arrogant. There would be a lot of teams in this league who would be better off if the stars treated their teammates a bit better. Bird treats everyone well-on and off the court. When you sit next to the coach night after night and you hear him yell at Bird, 'Shoot it! Shoot it!' that's got to register with you. That kind of unselfishness is rare, very

rare, and it's very nice."

Opponents, however, see a different Bird. "He's one of the meanest sons of a bitch in the league. I don't worry about anyone intimidating him," says Fitch. "He's as tough and as rugged as you could ask. He has no fear threshold. He may be a hick from French Lick but he's street-wise. If you bully Larry Bird, you picked the wrong guy."

Allan Bristow of Utah discovered the same thing one night this season.

The two forwards had been going at it for most of the game, whacking each other around as if there were nobody else on the court. Bird and the Celtics believed that Bristow was trying to provoke him into a fight, perhaps even to get him ejected. Since his first day in rookie camp, Bird had come across people who wanted to test him. Though both Bristow and Utah Coach Tom Nissalke vehemently denied they had intended any such thing, the Celtics felt Bristow had been sent in as a hatchet man.

The eruption came late in the third period. Following a Boston basket, the two players became entangled in the backcourt. Bristow landed on the floor, with Bird standing over him. Bird didn't move. When Bristow's request for him to move was repeated and rejected, the Utah forward reached out and tackled Bird. When Bird got up he landed a solid left, at which point the combatants began the usual athletic waltz.

Both men were ejected, and the Jazz—leading by 10 at the time—went on to an upset win over the Celtics. Bird had already scored 25 points and pulled down 12 rebounds and was the only Celtic player who was performing well.

"You talk about great players like Jerry West, John Havlicek and Clyde Frazier," says M.L. Carr, "but you never see a concentration level like Bird's when the game is on the line. It's not a selfish thing. He wants to win so bad, but it's in the role of a team player, setting up teammates for easy baskets, rebounding and playing defense. Larry can very easily go out and score 30-35 points a game but he's constantly aware of his teammates and what it takes to win the ballgame."

During a two-game stretch this season, Celtic forward Cedric (Cornbread) Maxwell went through one of his periodic scoring droughts. "Max isn't getting the ball," Bird said after the second game, his anger toward himself showing. "And it's my fault because he isn't getting the ball often enough. I know how to get him the ball but I'm not doing it."

Fitch has to yell, "Shoot!" fewer times than he did last year, however. "There might be a time when I do say, 'Shoot!'" says the Celtic coach, "but then he does something that I didn't see coming."

"I want people to think of me as someone who plays as hard as he can and is a team player," says Bird. "I've grown up on the team aspect of the game."

Bird recalls that during his senior year at Spring Valley High School in French Lick, Coach Jim Jones threatened to make him remove his uniform at half-time if he didn't start shooting the ball more. Bird had spent most of his junior year feeding a star player named Danny King but as a senior he was trying to reward players who had less talent than either he or King.

"He doesn't want people to think of him as a gunner," Fitch said this season. "His shot selection is typical of most of the

decisions he makes as a basketball player—it's pretty damn good."

⊕ ⊕ ⊕

The scene: the Celtics are gathered at Boston's Logan Airport awaiting a late-season flight and the start of another road trip. They feel as if they have done nothing but fly in airplanes and inhabit coffee shops for the past month. They are about to close out a period of 14 road games in 18 playing dates.

Bird is dressed in blue jeans and a pullover top and is talking with some of his teammates. He sees a well-dressed man standing 20 feet away, focusing a camera on him.

"Hey," Bird shouts at the man. "Why don't you ask me first if it's all right to take my picture?"

The man is embarrassed. "Is it okay'" he says sheepishly to Bird.

"Yeah.

A little girl comes up and requests an autograph. Bird complies with a smile.

There is a difference between the way Bird deals with children and the way he deals with adults. "When a kid comes up speaking for himself," he says, "and says, 'Thank you,' it's a helluva lot more important to me than when a guy comes up and says, 'Can I have an autograph for my kids?' You can see it in the kids' eyes. that it means so much more to them."

Rather than sign autographs, Bird prefers to have a conversation, even with a complete stranger. "I'd prefer that somebody shake my hand and have a conversation than ask for an autograph. When people ask to talk to you, they want to know about you. That's the kind of people you give your time to."

At the end of that day's flight, after the team arrives at the airport in Dallas, Bird runs into that type of admirer. As he sits on a baggage rack waiting for his luggage, a middle-aged couple comes up to him.

"Don't go too hard on our Mavs," the man says. Bird laughs. He and the couple engage in an animated conversation for the next 10 minutes; Bird does about as much listening as talking. When the strangers leave, Bird is smiling.

Still, life on the road is more difficult for Bird than for the other Celtics. Most of the players receive about as much recognition as a team from Italy would. "He's got a tougher life," says Robey, who despite his 6-foot-10 height can dine in relative anonymity in hotel coffee shops. "He can't go anywhere. We get harassed sometimes. He gets it all the time. We can come down and have breakfast without being bothered; he can't."

Sometimes Bird resents being bothered. "Every person wants to preserve a part of his privacy," says Carr, "and Bird's is very limited. Somebody may come up to him and say, 'Hi,' and it may turn him off because they don't know how he feels that day. It all depends on the situation—whether he's played 48 minutes the night before, or it he's banged up physically."

In one very important sense Bird is *always* subpar physically. He is not the 58-percent shooter he was in college for one simple reason—he has a badly mangled right index finger. It is without question the most underpublicized aspect of a person about whom people want to know everything.

Bird broke the finger in the spring of his senior year at Indiana State. Playing in a softball game, he tried to catch a

liner off the bat of his brother Mike. The result was a finger that was smashed rather than simply fractured. Two operations later Bird is left with a misshapened finger on his shooting hand.

After that big night in Los Angeles Bird admitted that his shooting touch in that game had been the best since "I hurt my finger." He seldom discusses the injury and never complains about it, but it is obviously on his mind. "It is frustrating," he has admitted. "But there isn't anything I can do about it."

Because of the injury, Bird does not have complete physical confidence. He began his professional career worried that he would reinjure the finger. He played the 1979 exhibition season and the first 10 regular season games with the finger taped to the one alongside it, to protect it from being jammed. But he tore the tape off at half-time of a game, explaining that "I've got to stop babying myself."

Nobody can baby himself in the NBA. "The grind definitely gets me down," Bird admits. "Last year I was going to new cities, seeing new things. It's very tough this year because everything is the same. But when the games start, everything changes—I have a whole different attitude. I am ready to play." If Bird should get hurt, however, his willingness to play might change. "If, say, five or six years from now I am playing injured, I don't know if I want to be in this league. If I feel I'm playing for the money, that I can't perform, that I get no excitement out of the game, I'll get out of it."

There is no doubt that Bird has adjusted far better to the playing style of the NBA than to the lifestyle. His reservations about the length of his career are sincere, but his love of the game is equally sincere. The chances are that Bird will let go of his pro basketball career with the greatest reluctance. He is fully aware of the dimensions of his talents.

Regardless of how long he plays, Bird expects to remain the same person. "The money I earn and being a celebrity haven't changed my style," he says. "But maybe the people around me have changed. If I like them I'll tell them so, and if I don't like them I'll tell them so. I try to be as honest as I can."

During Bird's senior year at Indiana State, Dave Cowens, who was then the Celtic coach, flew to Terre Haute to watch Bird play. He brought along Robey and another Celtic, Jeff Judkins, who is now with Utah. After the game they took Bird on a tour of Terre Haute bars. When Cowens returned to Boston, he talked about Bird. "He is a good guy, a guy with a sense of humor," Cowens said. "He's not that sullen, unstable hick we've been reading about in the papers. He's someone who has to be understood."

Bird may have changed in some ways and remained the same in others, but no Celtic would amend what Cowens said about him that day.

(Reprinted with permission, Sport Media Enterprises, Inc., 2003)

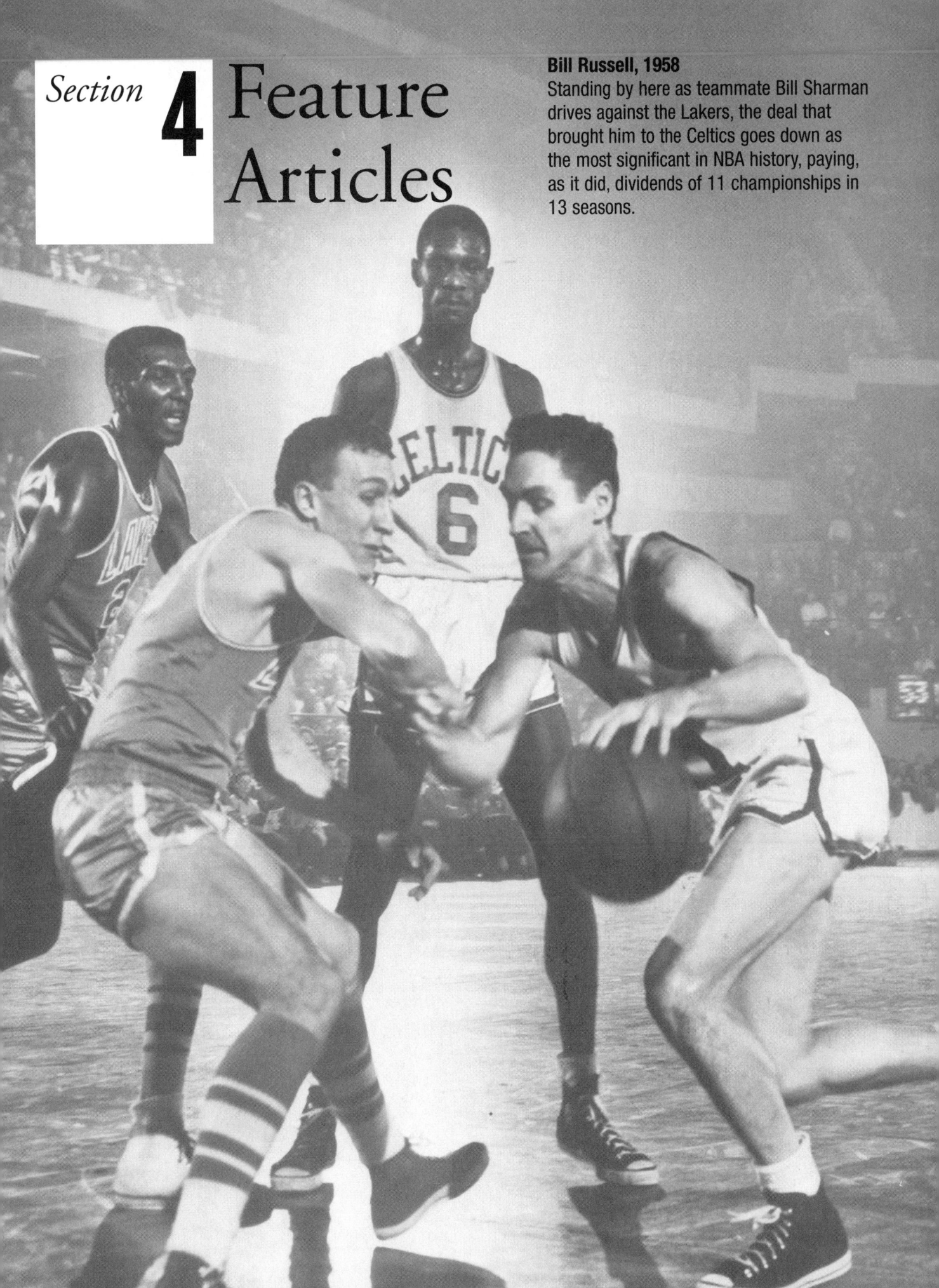

Section **4** Feature Articles

Bill Russell, 1958
Standing by here as teammate Bill Sharman drives against the Lakers, the deal that brought him to the Celtics goes down as the most significant in NBA history, paying, as it did, dividends of 11 championships in 13 seasons.

Chapter 17

The Top 50 Magical Moments in Basketball

By Alex Sachere

Writer, editor and former NBA executive Alex Sachere ranks 50 events that shaped the game.

1. Humble Beginnings

Luther Gulick had a problem. The winter of 1891 was fast approaching, and the head of physical education at the YMCA Training School in Springfield, Mass., needed an indoor activity that would enable his students to stay in shape and burn off excess energy, to say nothing of calories, while it was cold and snowy outside. Gulick turned to James Naismith, a young, Canadian-born instructor, and asked him to devise an indoor game that would challenge the young men physically and also hold their interest.

Naismith thought about the most popular outdoor games of the time—rugby, soccer and lacrosse. While he liked the physical exercise they provided, he rejected the idea of moving them indoors because he felt they were too physical for such a confined space. He recalled an activity he had devised as a student at McGill University in Montreal, where he had helped the school's rugby players stay in shape during the winter by having them run in the gymnasium and toss a ball into a box on the floor. He also remembered a game he had played as a child, called Duck on a Rock, where the object was to knock a stone off the top of a larger boulder by tossing smaller stones, or "ducks," at it. By combining the two, he had his answer.

Naismith asked the school's custodian, Pop Stebbins, to find a couple of boxes and nail them from the overhead running track that encircled the school gym, providing targets for the game's players. The idea of elevating the goals was important to Naismith, as it would promote hand-eye coordination and reduce the physical pounding that he considered inevitable if the target was on the ground. Stebbins couldn't find any boxes but returned with a pair of peach baskets, so the game became "basket ball" (eventually shortened to one word) instead of "box ball." Balls were no problem—the school had plenty of soccer balls around.

To fit the time frame of a physical education class period, the first basketball game was 30 minutes long, divided into two 15-minute halves. There were 18 students in Naismith's class, so each team consisted of nine players. Naismith's original 13 rules included no running with the ball, which could only be advanced by passing it from one player to another, and no striking an opponent. Since the gym at the Springfield YMCA was just 50 feet long and 35 feet wide, those became the dimensions of the first basketball court (less than half the area of today's standard NBA or college court, which measures 94 x 50).

Naismith later wrote that there were many fouls in that first

Frank Selvy, 1954
He played a role in Numbers 10 and 16 on our Top 50 list.

game, as players were unaccustomed to the rules. He also noted that there was little teamwork, because the playing area was so small that players could reach the goals from anywhere on the court, and so they were constantly shooting instead of passing. Apparently only one player was successful, however, since while Naismith's own account of that first game did not provide a final score, other reports pegged it at 1-0. Even who scored the sport's first basket is in doubt—some reports have William R. Chase scoring on a 25-foot toss, while others credit the game's only score to Lyman W. Archibald or W.H. Davis.

From that humble beginning, basketball quickly flourished.

Hundreds lined up to watch the daily noontime games, and students spread word of the game when they returned home from school. Within months it was being played in gyms throughout much of the United States and Canada. College teams began playing the game the following year, and the first women's game was played in 1893. By 1896 there is even record of a professional game, as players in Trenton, N.J., unable to use the local YMCA, booked a Masonic Hall, charged admission and split the proceeds, earning $15 apiece after expenses. There was an extra dollar left over, which was awarded to Fred Cooper, the game's principal organizer.

2. Rens Rule

For basketball's first half-century, the professional ranks were dominated by barnstorming teams. Although leagues existed in the East and Midwest, teams found they could do better financially by remaining independent, traveling the country and playing any opponent that was willing to put up a good fee. Some of the best early pro teams did both, playing in leagues and also playing other opponents whenever they could. One of these was the Original Celtics, a New York-based club that dominated the sport in the 1920s with stars like Joe Lapchick, Johnny Beckman, Dutch Dehnert and Nat Holman. Other tops clubs of the '20s and '30s included the SPHAs run by Eddie Gottlieb of Philadelphia, the Cleveland Rosenblums, and the Harlem Globetrotters, who discovered in the mid-'30s that they could increase their bookings around the country if they mixed a little razzle-dazzle and clowning in with their basketball.

Another great team from the barnstorming era was the New York Renaissance Big Five, founded by Bob Douglas and named after the Renaissance Casino ballroom in Harlem. The Rens were organized in 1922, some five years before the Globetrotters, and were the first team comprised solely of African Americans to gain prominence on the pro circuit. As such, the players on the Rens faced obstacles unknown to the white teams of the era—verbal and even physical abuse from fans, meals that had to be eaten on the team bus because no restaurant would serve them, and long drives out of their way to find hotels that would put them up for the night.

The Rens won 88 games in a row in the first three months of 1933 and finished that winter with a record of 120-8; they compiled a remarkable 473-49 mark from 1932 through 1936 because Douglas brought together some of the best players of that era and kept them together. The team was led by speedy 5-foot-7 playmaker Clarence "Fat" Jenkins and two outstanding big men, 6-foot-5 "Wee" Willie Smith and 6-foot-4 Charles "Tarzan" Cooper, who was described by Lapchick as the greatest center he had ever seen. The 1932-33 Rens team is one of only four clubs inducted into the Basketball Hall of Fame.

The Rens enjoyed a remarkable run, taking on all comers and beating most of them, winning anywhere from 100 to 150 games a year through the 1930s. Their finest moment came in 1939 when they compiled a 112-7 record and capped the year by winning the first-ever World Professional Tournament in Chicago. The event, which lasted for 10 years and was sponsored by the *Chicago Herald-American,* was conceived as the first true "world series" of basketball, bringing together 12 to 16 of the top teams in the games, both league champions and the

best of the barnstormers. The Rens, now led by future Hall of Famer William "Pop" Gates as well as Cooper, Smith, Eyre Saitch, Zack Clayton and Johnny Isaacs and coached by Jenkins, swept all four of their games, beating the National Basketball League champion Oshkosh All-Stars 34-25 in the final to validate their status as the best in basketball.

Travel restrictions in World War II cut into their operations and the Rens finally disbanded in 1949, by which time they were known as the Dayton Rens. One source lists their record over 26 seasons as 2,318 won and 381 lost, another as 2,588 won 529 lost—either way, a remarkable run.

3. The Birth of the NBA

On June 6, 1946, the owners and managers of arenas in major cities in the Eastern half of the United States as well as Toronto gathered in New York. Many owned hockey teams that played in those arenas, and now, anticipating boom times following the end of World War II, they were looking for another sport that would fill their buildings on dates they would otherwise be dark. They turned to basketball.

There already was a professional circuit, the National Basketball League, but it was national in name only. It operated in the Midwest, with franchises in towns like Sheboygan and Oshkosh as well as cities like Chicago and Detroit. Formed in 1935 as the Midwest Basketball Conference and renamed two years later, the NBL did have the biggest star in the game, 6-foot-10 George Mikan, a three-time All-American who would develop into the game's first truly dominant giant. The arena owners who met in New York figured they could coexist with the NBL; there even was talk of a potential world series between the champions of the two leagues, along baseball's lines.

Thirteen franchises were granted at that meeting at the old Commodore Hotel alongside Grand Central Terminal, but Buffalo and Indianapolis dropped out over the summer. Maurice Podoloff, operator of the New Haven (Conn.) Arena and president of the American Hockey League, chaired the meeting and reminded those in attendance that "the newly organized Association was a major league in every possible meaning of the term," a declaration that helped get him elected president of the new venture.

The 11 charter members of the Basketball Association of America, as the league called itself, were Boston, New York, Philadelphia, Providence, Toronto and Washington in the Eastern Division and Chicago, Cleveland, Detroit, Pittsburgh and St. Louis in the Western Division. That roster of large cities provided a stark contrast to the NBL's smaller towns and in time would seal the older league's fate, even though at the outset most of the veteran pros chose to remain in the NBL rather than jump to the new league.

The BAA adopted the prevailing college rules, which meant that there was once a time when zone defenses were legal in the pro game; it wasn't until two months into the inaugural campaign that the league banned them in a move to speed up play. Another little-known fact is that the league operated under a salary cap in its first season, with each team allowed to spend up to $55,000 to fill out its 12-man roster. One major difference from the college game was that the BAA decided to play games of four 12-minute quarters instead of two 20-minute

halves, the reasoning being that the paying fans would thus be getting more for their money.

The league's first game was played at Maple Leaf Gardens in Toronto, an appropriate site since the sport was invented by the Canadian-born James Naismith. The visiting team was the New York Knickerbockers, and the first basket in league history was scored by Oscar "Ozzie" Schechtman of the Knicks on a lay-up. Despite a game-high 18 points by Toronto player-coach Ed Sadowski, the Knicks won that first game 68-66.

Tickets for that first game were priced from 75 cents to a high of $2.50, but even then the league had a penchant for promotions: Any person taller than 6-foot-8 Toronto center George Nostrand was admitted free of charge.

4. Mikan, Lakers Establish Dominance

The 1948-49 season was a landmark in the growth of professional basketball. The Basketball Association of America, despite having large arenas in major cities, was struggling after two seasons. It had yet to carve its niche in the consciousness of most sports fans. That "major league" status, however, was achieved in one bold move.

Just before the start of the season, the four strongest teams from the rival National Basketball League agreed to join the BAA. Suddenly, the NBL, the Midwest-based loop that had been around for more than a decade and boasted nearly all of the top players of that era, found itself without its prize teams: the champion Minneapolis Lakers, the runner-up Rochester Royals, the Fort Wayne Pistons and the Indianapolis Jets. The NBL was doomed. It would struggle on for one more year before packing it in, with five more teams joining the BAA, which took advantage of its place as the only major league by changing its name to the National Basketball Association. The rest of the NBL faded into memory.

As much as the first wave of defections weakened the NBL, it solidified the BAA. All of a sudden the young league, which had dipped to eight teams the previous season, was a solid, 12-team circuit with a strong presence in the Midwest as well as along the Eastern seaboard. What's more, the move meant that many of the best players in the game could now showcase their talents in the major arenas that were the BAA's strength.

Biggest of all, literally and figuratively, was George Mikan. Sure he stood 6-foot-10, but Mikan worn thick-lense glasses and was considered too awkward as a teenager to be offered a scholarship to Notre Dame, where coach George Keogan told him to go back to Chicago because he'd make a better scholar than a ballplayer. So Mikan enrolled at DePaul and blossomed into a three-time All-American under the tutelage of Ray Meyer.

When he graduated in 1946, Mikan was pursued by several teams in the fledgling BAA but chose instead to sign with his hometown Chicago American Gears of the NBL, who offered him a multi-year contract for $60,000, a huge amount in those days. The Gears won the 1947 title and Mikan led the league in scoring, but then owner Maurice White decided to pull out of the NBL and form his own 24-team league, with the Gears as the showpiece. Woefully under-financed, the venture was doomed from the start and lasted only a matter of weeks. When it folded, all its players became free agents and Mikan returned to the NBL, signing a one-year contract for $15,000 with the

Minneapolis Lakers. As he had a year earlier, Mikan led the league in scoring and carried his team to the championship, so it was with open arms that he was welcomed into the BAA for the 1948-49 season. How much did Mikan mean to the BAA? The marquee outside New York's Madison Square Garden one night read: "Tonite: Geo. Mikan vs. Knicks." He took a lot of ribbing from his teammates because of that, but it underscored the basic truth that he was the game's premier attraction.

Despite Mikan and other top players including Jim Pollard, a forward who was among the best all-around players in the game, the Lakers finished the 1948-49 BAA regular season one game behind the Rochester Royals, who were led by the outstanding backcourt trio of Bob Davies, Bobby Wanzer and Red Holzman. But the Lakers swept both Chicago and Rochester by 2-0 counts to advance to the finals against the Washington Capitols, coached by a 31-year-old named Red Auerbach who would later achieve success with the Boston Celtics.

The Lakers won the first two games of the Finals at home, then took Game 3 at Washington's Uline Arena 94-74 and seemed headed for a sweep. But Mikan suffered a broken wrist in Game 4 after a collision with Washington's Kleggy Hermsen, and the Capitols stayed alive with an 83-71 win. Mikan showed up for Game 5 with a big cast on his broken wrist and scored 22 points, but Washington won again 74-66. Game 6 was in Minnesota, however, and even with a cast, there was no stopping Mikan and the Lakers this time as they posted a 77-56 victory, adding the BAA crown to the one they had captured in the NBL the year before.

Mikan, who averaged 30.3 points per game in the playoffs after leading the league during the regular season at 28.3 ppg, would go on to lead his team to four more championships in the next five years, establishing the Minneapolis Lakers as the NBA's first dynasty.

5. CCNY's Unique Double

What City College of New York accomplished in 1950 had never been done before in basketball history, hasn't been done in the half-century since, and is very unlikely ever to be done in the future. CCNY, an urban, commuter school that was known as the "working man's Harvard" for offering a quality, free (since changed to moderately priced) education to all residents of the city, won the championships of both the National Invitation Tournament and the National Collegiate Athletic Association Tournament in the 1949-50 season, beating Midwest power Bradley in the finals of both events.

CCNY was coached by Nat Holman, who played for the Original Celtics during basketball's barnstorming era, and had a starting unit that consisted of one senior, 6-foot-4 Irwin Dambrot, and a quartet of sophomores—Floyd Layne, Ed Warner, Al "Fats" Roth and 6-foot-6 Ed Roman.

In that era the NIT was a major event, the lure of New York's Madison Square Garden drawing the nation's top teams. It was played two weeks before the NCAA held its own tournament, so teams could compete in both if they were invited. Today the tournaments are staged concurrently and the NIT has become a second-tier event.

Since 1939, when the NCAA tournament was inaugurated, four teams had entered both events and three of them had won

one tournament but been beaten in the other; none had been able to survive the pressure of every game being winner-take-all and win both.

CCNY went into the 1950 NIT with momentum following late regular-season wins over intra-city rivals NYU and St. John's, and added to it by soundly defeating defending champion San Francisco 65-46 in its opener and then routing two-time NCAA titlist Kentucky 89-50 in the quarter-finals. Next was Duquesne, and the Beavers' 62-52 victory not only moved them into the NIT final but also earned them a berth in the NCAA Tournament that was to follow.

But first came the NIT Final against Bradley, the top-ranked team in the nation with a 29-3 record. CCNY fell behind by 11 points in the early going, trimmed the gap to 30-27 by half-time and pulled away after intermission to win 69-61 behind Dambrot's 23 points. Holman, who coached despite a 103 degree fever, knew his team was on a roll and saw the chance to achieve the unprecedented double.

CCNY got a break in that the NCAA Eastern Regional was in New York, so the Beavers could play before their home fans and Holman could spend as much time as possible recuperating. After edging Ohio State 56-55, the Beavers beat North Carolina State 78-73 to advance to the NCAA Finals and a rematch against Bradley, which had taken the Western Regional with wins over UCLA and Baylor.

CCNY stretched a 39-32 half-time lead to 58-47 with 10 minutes left before Bradley went to a full-court, man-to-man press. The Beavers were nursing a 69-63 lead with 57 seconds remaining, but a free throw by Joe Stowell and a lay-up, a steal and another lay-up by Gene Melchiorre brought Bradley to within one. Then Melchiorre made another steal and drove to the basket, but his shot attempt was blocked by CCNY's Dambrot, who recovered the loose ball and spotted Norman Mager at the other end of the floor. Mager caught Dambrot's court-length pass and scored the clinching basket with less than 10 seconds to play. CCNY had a 71-68 victory and its historic double championship.

6. Breaking the NBA's Color Barrier

Who was the NBA's Jackie Robinson? There's no simple answer, although the distinction of being the first African American to compete in a league game goes to Earl Lloyd.

African Americans have played a prominent role in the history of professional basketball, as much if not more so than in the other major sports. There were no major national professional leagues for basketball's first half-century, so the fact that the leagues that existed were all-white wasn't of great consequence. The fact is some of the best teams made their mark not by competing in leagues but by barnstorming—traveling from town to town, taking on all comers. The all-black New York Renaissance Big Five were one of the premier teams of this barnstorming era, from the 1920s through the 1940s. So were the Harlem Globetrotters, who were in the top echelon of competitive clubs back then and remain on the scene today with crowd-pleasing comedy routines featured in their repertoire.

The most significant professional league of the late 1930s and 1940s was the Midwest-based National Basketball League, and several blacks were on team rosters during World War II.

In 1946-47 (the same year the NBA was born in the form of its predecessor, the Basketball Association of America), Dolly King played for the Rochester Royals and Pop Gates for the Tri-Cities Blackhawks of the NBL.

The NBA did not stay all-white for very long. In 1950, prior to the league's fifth season, the Boston Celtics selected Chuck Cooper of Duquesne (not to be confused with Charles "Tarzan" Cooper, a star with the barnstorming Rens in earlier years) in the second round of the draft. As the story goes, at an owners' meeting in Chicago on April 25, 1950, Celtics owner Walter Brown selected Cooper in the second round of the college draft. One of the other owners said, "Walter, don't you know he's a Negro?" Brown responded, "I don't give a damn if he's striped, plaid, or polka-dot! Boston takes Chuck Cooper of Duquesne!" Later, on the eighth round of the same draft, the Washington Capitols selected Earl Lloyd of West Virginia State.

Neither, however, was the first African American player to sign a contract with an NBA team. Shortly after the draft the New York Knicks signed Nat "Sweetwater" Clifton away from the Harlem Globetrotters for a reported $25,000.

The distinction of becoming the first African American player to appear in an NBA game fell to Lloyd, as the only game scheduled for opening night had the Washington Capitols playing at the Rochester Royals on October 31, 1950. Rochester won that game 78-70 and went on to capture the league championship, while the Washington team was disbanded in mid-season. Lloyd, a 6-foot-6 center who was nicknamed "Big Cat," played in only seven games that season before being drafted into military service, but he went on to have a productive nine-year career in which he averaged 8.4 points and 6.4 rebounds per game. He was the starting center on the Syracuse Nationals team that won the 1955 NBA championship.

Clifton had the best career of the trio, playing eight NBA seasons, seven of them with the Knicks, and averaging 10.0 points and 8.2 rebounds per game. He later played with the Harlem Magicians, a barnstorming team that worked comedy routines into their basketball games much like the Globetrotters. Clifton, a 6-foot-7-1/2 center, played in the 1957 NBA All-Star Game, scoring eight points and grabbing 11 rebounds to help the East beat the West 109-97. He wasn't the first African American to make the All-Star Game—that honor belongs to Ray Felix, a 6-foot-11 center who represented Baltimore in his rookie season of 1954.

Cooper, a 6-foot-5 center, played six seasons in the league, four of them with the Celtics, and averaged 6.7 points and 5.9 rebounds per game for his career.

7. The Birth of the Shot Clock

One of the most important games in NBA history was also one of the most boring.

It took place on November 22, 1950 in Minneapolis. Matched up against the defending champion Minneapolis Lakers, who boasted stars like George Mikan, Jim Pollard, Vern Mikkelsen and Slater Martin, the visiting Fort Wayne Pistons knew they were unlikely to win if they tried to play a running game. So coach Murray Mendanhall ordered his team to do just the opposite.

Knowing the Lakers couldn't score if it didn't have the ball,

the Pistons conducted their offense with all deliberate speed. They held the ball, and then they held it some more. As the 7,021 in attendance voiced their displeasure with the lack of action, the Pistons patiently stood around and watched the seconds tick away while Minneapolis, not wanting to be caught off guard, refused to press them. Fort Wayne led 8-7 at the quarter, trailed 13-11 at half-time, and 17-16 after three quarters, then outscored the Lakers 3-1 in the final 12 minutes to win by a score of 19-18—the lowest scoring game in NBA history.

The two teams combined for a total of eight baskets in 48 minutes of action, or inaction. George Mikan, basketball's biggest star, scored 15 points for the Lakers; nobody else had more than five. For a league that was struggling to find its place on the American sports scene, this game was a black eye. And it was only one of many, though clearly the most glaring.

"The game was stagnant," said Bob Cousy, the Boston Celtic Hall of Famer who was a rookie in 1950-51. "Teams literally started sitting on the ball in the third quarter. That was the way the game was played: Get a lead and put the ball in the icebox, while the paying customers started reading the program."

By 1954, it became clear to one and all that something drastic had to be done. The pace of the game had slowed dramatically; when teams weren't standing around holding the ball, they were fouling each other in an effort to gain possession, resulting in repeated parades from foul line to foul line. "Things were going from bad to worse," said Maurice Podoloff, the league's president. "The games were interminable. Attendance was suffering. We were in a desperate situation."

Danny Biasone, owner of the Syracuse Nationals, saw a possible solution. "Basketball needed a time limit," he said. "In baseball you get three outs and in football you have to gain 10 yards in four plays or give up the ball. But in basketball, if you had the lead and a good ball-handler, you could play around all night."

So Biasone and his general manager, Leo Ferris, devised a formula to set a time limit within which a team must attempt a shot. They looked at statistics for the previous couple of seasons and determined that in a game without stalling, each team should average about 60 shots with no trouble, or a total of 120. They then divided this into the length of a game, which is 48 minutes or 2,880 seconds, and the result came to 24. Thus was born the 24-second shot clock. "But the number of seconds really wasn't that important," Biasone emphasized. "No matter what, the game needed a time element."

Biasone organized a pickup game in Syracuse over the summer to try out his idea. The other owners thought it might work and decided to give it a try, also adopting a rule that limited the number of fouls a team could commit in any one quarter to six (later reduced to five and then four) without incurring penalty shots. The two innovations complemented each other—the shot clock preventing stalling, the foul limit preventing excessive fouling.

The results were immediate and dramatic. Average team scores went from 79.5 points in 1953-54 to 93.1 points in 1954-55, an 18 percent increase. The Boston Celtics, at 101.4 points per game, became the first team to crack the century mark over a full season. Three teams scored 100 points or more in the 1954 playoffs, while 18 did it in 1955. And with the shot clock preventing Fort Wayne from stalling, Biasone's Syracuse Nationals rallied from a 17-point deficit to beat the Pistons 92-91 in Game 7 of the Finals to win the NBA championship.

"Everyone kidded me that I thought of the clock just to win the championship, but that wasn't so," said Biasone. "I just wanted to see a whole game."

Biasone's idea for a shot clock worked so well that it not only has been maintained by the NBA to this day, but it has been adopted, albeit with varying time limits, by the governing bodies of college basketball and the international game as well. The addition of the shot clock was deemed so essential that Biasone ended up in the Basketball Hall of Fame.

8. The Globetrotters Captivate Berlin

It was a stunning sight as more than 75,000 spectators filled the Olympic Stadium in Berlin on August 22, 1951, to watch the Harlem Globetrotters. What made it so special was that this was the same arena where Adolf Hitler had snubbed American track star Jesse Owens 15 years earlier, walking out on the medal ceremony rather than watch the gold be awarded to a black man.

The Globetrotters had experienced many snubs in their distinguished history, which dates back to 1926. A Chicago promoter named Abe Saperstein was coaching a team of African-Americans called the Savoy Big Five at the time, but when the Savoy Ballroom on Chicago's South Side decided it no longer wanted to sponsor the team, he renamed his team the Harlem Globetrotters—Harlem to identify the players as African-Americans, Globetrotters to give them a worldly image.

The Trotters didn't have to trot much of the globe for their first game, however. Their first trip covered about 50 miles, from Chicago to Hinckley, Ill., where they beat a local team on January 7, 1927, for their first win under their new name.

In pro basketball's barnstorming era, when leagues quickly came and went and teams survived by traveling the country and taking on all comers, the Globetrotters ranked alongside the Rens, the Harlem Renaissance Ballroom Big Five, as the top African-American teams of the 1920s and '30s. The Globetrotters compiled a record of 101-16 in 1927 even though they played every game on the road and often were denied access to convenient hotels and restaurants because of the color of their skin.

Saperstein, seeking to ensure his team's survival, realized that riding into town, beating the local team in its own gym and then moving on down the road was a dangerous formula. After a few years, when the host team had been beaten in front of its fans each time, Saperstein feared it would stop inviting the Globetrotters back. Losing on purpose was out of the question, as the Globetrotters rightfully prided themselves on being one of the best teams in the country. So Saperstein hit on the idea of working comedy in with the basketball for a different kind of entertainment package. Make the fans laugh, he thought, and they won't mind it as much if their home team gets beaten and they'll want the Globetrotters to come back.

So the Globetrotters began working trick shots, slick ball-handling and fancy passing into their basketball repertoire, and the formula was a big hit. The Globetrotters remained one of the most highly competitive teams in the country, yet they were

uniquely entertaining as well, and as a result they managed to survive long after other barnstorming clubs folded.

Following World War II, with the birth of the NBA and its growth by absorbing the best teams from the NBL, the Globetrotters, with gifted crowd-pleasing players like Goose Tatum and Marcus Haynes, carved their niche as the game's premier barnstorming team. They became true globetrotters, traveling all over the world and winning millions of new fans for the sport of basketball with their unique performances. The U.S. State Department dubbed them "Ambassadors of Good Will," and in 1951 asked the Globetrotters to include a visit to Berlin in their tour of Europe. It was only six years following the end of World War II, and the American government saw this as an opportunity to mend fences with Germany.

That is why, on August 22, 1951, the Globetrotters found themselves in the middle of the Olympic Stadium in Berlin, playing a German team and delighting more than 75,000 spectators with their special routines. This was one game where the result was unimportant; the very fact that it could be played, between a team of African-Americans and a team of Germans, was what was so important. This was underscored at half-time, when a helicopter landed on the field near the basketball floor, and out stepped a black man in a running suit—Jesse Owens. Mayor Ludwig Shreiber of West Berlin greeted Owens by saying, "Fifteen years ago on this field, Hitler refused to offer you his hand. Now I give you both of mine." Owens then stepped onto the running track and ran a lap around the stadium as the fans roared their tribute.

The Harlem Globetrotters, basketball's Ambassadors of Good Will, had helped make a remarkable moment possible.

9. The First NBA All-Star Game

The NBA was still seeking its place in the sports consciousness of Americans in 1950-51, its fifth season. The league, which had begun with 11 teams, had shrunk to eight, then ballooned to 17 following the demise of the NBL before settling back to 11 in the summer of 1950. In addition to this instability, the game itself was suffering from too much stalling and physical play, factors which were alienating many fans.

Maurice Podoloff, the league's president (the position has since been renamed commissioner), called a brainstorming session in his office with Walter Brown, the founder of the Boston Celtics, and Haskell Cohen, the NBA's publicity man. The agenda was simple—come up with an idea that would spark interest and attract fans to the game.

It was Cohen who suggested that the NBA borrow a page from major league baseball's book and stage a mid-season All-Star Game, bringing the league's best players from all teams together for a one-game exhibition. Brown immediately embraced the idea.

"It was at the time of the college (point-shaving) scandals and basketball had a black eye," Brown said. "Things were going so badly that even my wife wanted me to get out of the business. But I thought the All-Star Game would be a good thing. I told the league I would take care of all the expenses, and all the losses if there were any."

So Podoloff gave the go-ahead for the inaugural All-Star Game to be played at Boston Garden on March 2, 1951. The 10 players chosen from each division were given train fare to Boston and, as "Easy" Ed Macauley of the Celtics recalled, a $25 U.S. Savings Bond.

"There wasn't even a luncheon," said Macauley, relating how the players arrived during the day as if for any other game, played the game at night and then took the train back to rejoin their teams. "A lot of the owners did not want to have the game. They were afraid only 5,000 people would show up. The New York press, at the time, was the only one that mattered, and the owners were afraid they would ridicule the game. But Walter Brown believed in it."

The fans of Boston proved him right. A crowd of 10,094 turned out for the game and went home happy as Macauley scored 20 points to lead the East team to a 111-94 victory. Macauley also harassed the better-known George Mikan of the Minneapolis Lakers, the center for the West team, into a 4-for-17 shooting performance and limited him to 12 points. "They ganged up on me pretty good," said Mikan. "They had a game plan on defense and it worked."

Joe Fulks of Philadelphia added 19 points for the East, which jumped out to a 31-22 first-quarter lead and was never caught. Dolph Schayes of Syracuse had 15 points and a game-high 14 rebounds for the East, Paul Arizin of Philadelphia scored 15 points and Bob Cousy of Boston and Andy Phillip of Philadelphia each had eight assists. For the West, Alex Groza of Indianapolis led the way with 17 points and 13 rebounds.

Today's record book lists Macauley as the game's most valuable player, but he did not receive the award at the time. "They first picked an MVP in the third game (in 1953)," said Macauley. "Then they decided they had better go back and pick one for the first two."

From that humble beginning, the NBA All-Star Game has grown into a gala weekend celebration of the sport of that attracts fans and media members from all around the world and is televised in over 200 countries.

10. Francis, Selvy Top Century Mark

Two of the most remarkable scoring feats in college basketball history took place just nine days apart.

On February 4, 1954, Clarence "Bevo" Francis of Rio Grande College in Ohio set an all-time collegiate scoring record of 113 points against Hillsdale. Just nine days later, Frank Selvy of Furman netted an even 100 points against Newberry on February 13, 1954. Selvy is listed as the holder of the NCAA Division I, or major college, scoring record, while Francis stands atop the Division II list.

The 6-foot-9 Francis, who got the nickname because his father was fond of Beve Beer, a root beer-like soft drink, had played high school ball in Wellsville, Ohio under coach Newt Oliver and went with him to Rio Grande, a tiny school in the southeastern part of the state. Rio Grande went 39-0 in 1952-53 and Francis averaged 50.1 points per game for the season, scoring 116 points in a game against Ashland Junior College. But the NCAA wouldn't recognize Francis's achievements as records because of the level of the opposition, and Rio Grande failed to gain national recognition for its unbeaten season because most of its opponents were small schools or junior colleges. So the next season, Oliver tried to upgrade his opponents

and took his team on the road, playing in the major arenas.

Having the NCAA reject his 116-point game burned at Francis. "I never cared much about points before," he said, "but I really did want to break 100 sometime this year." Oliver agreed, saying, "I became more determined than ever that Bevo would again go over the 100-point mark in scoring."

They found their chance in a late-season game against Hillsdale, a weak team that had lost to Rio Grande 82-45 earlier in the season. Francis had 43 points at half-time, at which point Oliver declared, "This was the game that was to be heard round the world." Francis came out and scored 31 of his team's 33 points in the third quarter (games were played in four 10-minute quarters then, rather than two 20-minute halves), and 39 of his team's 43 in the fourth quarter to finish with 113 points as Rio Grande won 134-91.

"I didn't know I had gotten 113 points until I was coming out of the shower after the game and a couple of players told me," said Francis, who left school after two years and played with a team that competed against the Harlem Globetrotters. "I knew I'd been shooting well, but getting 113 points! I had no idea. I still can't believe it."

Nine days later, Selvy, a jump-shooting guard, hit the century mark against Newberry. It was the first Furman game to be televised state-wide, and also the first time Selvy's mother saw him play college ball in person. She was among several hundred fans who traveled from Corbin, S.C. to Greenville for the game.

Early on, it was apparent this was to be Selvy's night. Bobby Bailey, the Newberry player assigned to guard him, fouled out after just 2:43 of the first quarter. Selvy poured in 24 points in the first quarter and 13 more in the second for a school-record 37 at half-time, but that was just the beginning. Coach Lyles Alley, recognizing the opportunity, ordered every play in the second half run for Selvy and urged his other players to pass up shots in order to get Selvy more scoring opportunities.

Selvy scored 26 of his team's 32 points in the third quarter and 37 of 40 in the fourth, finishing with 100 as Furman beat Newberry 149-95. He reached the plateau in dramatic fashion, scoring six points in the game's final 30 seconds and connecting on a 70-foot heave as the final buzzer sounded.

"It was my night," said Selvy, who would go on to a productive, nine-year career in the NBA, "because that ball went right through the basket and hit nothing but net. It was one of those shots where more luck than skill was involved. But when a player scores 100 points, there has to be plenty of both."

11. The Real-Life "Hoosiers"

The movie *Hoosiers*, released in 1986, told an inspirational story about a basketball team from a small high school in rural Indiana. Spurred by a coach who preached the values of teamwork and sacrifice and self-discipline, that team beat bigger and stronger opponents to win the state championship.

It seemed like a typical Hollywood Cinderella story, and it was. It also was true.

The real-life Hoosiers came from Milan High School, and despite an enrollment of just 161 students, they won the Indiana state championship in 1954, beating far-bigger Muncie Central 32-30 on a last-second basket, just like in the movie.

To appreciate the achievement, one must understand how big high school basketball is in Indiana. From the larger cities to the most far-flung rural towns, people passionately follow the fortunes of their local high school and kids dream of suiting up and playing for the varsity. It all culminates in "Hoosier Hysteria," the nickname given to the statewide high school basketball tournament that culminates in a showdown in the state capital of Indianapolis. In most states, schools are grouped into different classifications based on enrollment and compete against other schools of roughly the same size. But until 1996-97, Indiana held just one statewide tournament for all schools, big or small, so Milan's victory over Muncie Central was truly a triumph of David over Goliath.

Milan, which had reached the tournament semi-finals the year before, defeated Crispus Attucks of Indianapolis, a team featuring a sophomore named Oscar Robertson, to advance to the 1954 final four, then beat Terre Haute Gerstmeyer 60-48 to move into the title game against Muncie Central. But Bob Engel, one of Milan's biggest and best players, was out with a back injury, and coach Marvin Wood knew his team would have to slow down the pace against Muncie Central, a school that has won eight state titles. Muncie's frontcourt players stood 6-foot-5, 6-foot-4 and 6-foot-2; Milan's tallest player, Ron Truitt, was 6-foot-2, and its starting center, Gene White, was just 5-foot-11.

Milan, spreading the floor and working deliberately for its shots, led 25-17 at the half, but Muncie gradually wore down its smaller opponent and moved in front 28-26 by holding Milan without a basket in the third quarter. Wood wasn't about to panic; he decided to take the air out of the ball, even though his team was down by two. Bobby Plump held the ball for 4 minutes, 14 seconds, to the amazement of the crowd at Butler Fieldhouse.

"Everybody was going crazy wondering what the hell was going on out there," said Plump. "We're behind in the tournament and yet we're holding the ball. I looked over at Coach Wood, and he's just sitting there nonchalantly."

Explained Wood, "I felt, hey, we have to do everything we can to conserve what energy we have to give us a chance at the end of the game. So we slowed it down earlier than we ever had."

Wood called a timeout with a little over 3-1/2 minutes left and brought his team out of the stall. Plump missed a jumper, but Muncie turned the ball over against the press and Ray Craft tied the game with a jumper, then Milan went ahead 30-28 on two free throws by Plump with 1:42 to play. After Muncie's Gene Flowers responded with a basket to tie the score, Plump held the ball until there were 18 seconds left and called another timeout.

Wood called a clear-out play for Plump to drive and then either shoot or pass to an open teammate. Plump crossed midcourt and with five seconds left started his move against Jimmy Barnes, who at 5-foot-10 was about the same size as Plump. He faked left, drove right and pulled up to launch a shot from about 15 feet that sailed through at the buzzer, giving tiny Milan the state championship.

"Yes, I knew," Plump said of his game-winning buzzer-beater. "When you shoot, you usually know when it's good."

"Now that I look back on it, I'm not so sure it wasn't destiny," said Wood.

12. Tar Heels Slay Goliath

"Nobody roots for Goliath," Wilt Chamberlain often said.

North Carolina coach Frank McGuire played on that theme by sending 5-foot-11 Tommy Kearns out for the opening center jump against the 7-foot-1 Chamberlain when the Tar Heels took on the Kansas Jayhawks in the 1957 NCAA championship game.

"I told him (Kearns) if he jumped high enough, he might reach Wilt's stomach," McGuire said. "Wilt looked freakish standing there, so far above our man. Wilt looked 10 feet tall towering over Tommy, but they made such a ridiculous picture together that Chamberlain must have felt no bigger than his thumb—at least, that was the state of mind we wanted him to get into."

McGuire figured his unbeaten Tar Heels were better than Kansas at every position other than center. So he focused everything, physically and psychologically, on containing Chamberlain, the Jayhawks' sophomore star who could take over a game all by himself. "I said he was so good, maybe we had better not show up," McGuire recalled of his pre-game talk to his team. "I said he might stuff some of them through the basket with the ball. I said we didn't have a chance unless our entire team defensed him at all times, and he'd still probably beat us so bad it would be embarrassing to go home. Of course, I was kidding them and they knew it, but it was psyching them up and loosening them up at the same time."

Kearns was not concerned that the Tar Heels, who had beaten Michigan State 74-70 in three overtimes in the national semi-finals, would be intimidated. "We're a chilly club—I mean, we just keep cool," he said. "We play it chilly all the time. Chamberlain won't give us the jitters like he did to all those clubs."

Just to make sure, McGuire sent Kearns out for the opening tap. "I think Wilt was taken aback, as I think the whole team was," said Kearns. "It set a tone for the game, and we jumped off to a very big lead as a result. I think it was a daring move by Coach McGuire, and it had an awful lot to do with us winning the game."

North Carolina jumped out to a 9-2 lead and Chamberlain went five minutes before getting his first basket. The Tar Heels led 19-7 after 10 minutes and 29-22 at half-time, but after being cautioned at half-time by first-year coach Dick Harp not to panic, the Jayhawks bounced right back and pulled even early in the second half. North Carolina star Lennie Rosenbluth fouled out with 1:45 remaining and Kansas in front 46-43 on Gene Elstun's three-point play, off a feed from Chamberlain.

A basket by Joe Quigg cut the margin to one, and after Ron Loneski turned the ball over on the inbounds pass, Kearns sank a free throw with 20 seconds left to send the game into overtime tied 46-46. Both teams played slowdown after that; each scored one basket in the first overtime, none in the second.

Kearns' layup and two free throws gave North Carolina a 52-48 lead in the third OT, but Chamberlain's three-point play and a free throw by Maurice King tied the score. North Carolina tried to play for a final shot, but Kansas' John Parker stole the ball from Quigg and fed Elstun, who was fouled by Kearns and made one of two free throws. Kansas led 53-52 with 31 seconds left.

On the ensuing play, Kearns' driving shot attempt was rejected by Chamberlain. The loose ball bounced to Quigg at the top of the key and when he tried to drive to the basket, his shot also was swatted away by Chamberlain. But King, helping out on the play, fouled Quigg with six seconds left. Quigg made both foul shots, and a pass intended for Chamberlain was tipped away by Quigg and recovered by Kearns, who dribbled once and shot the ball. Time expired before it came down, and North Carolina had its second straight triple overtime victory—and a national championship, 54-53.

13. The Celtics Start A Dynasty

In 1956-57, the Boston Celtics figured they finally had the ingredients for a championship team. They had added a pair of brilliant rookies, center Bill Russell and forward Tom Heinsohn, to complement their brilliant backcourt of Bob Cousy and Bill Sharman. When the title was on the line, in Game 7 of the NBA Finals, it was the rookies who would make up for woeful 5-for-40 shooting from the guards, combining for 56 points and 55 rebounds to bring Boston its first NBA crown.

The Celtics met the St. Louis Hawks in an evenly matched NBA Finals that saw two games go to double overtime. Four of the seven games were decided by a margin of two points apiece including Game 6, which the Hawks won 96-94 on a tip-in by rookie Cliff Hagan. Game 7 was nationally televised (a rarity in those days) and turned out to be a thriller.

Although Cousy shot 2-for-20 and Sharman 3-for-20, Heinsohn and Russell made up for their lack of production, Heinsohn getting 37 points and 23 rebounds and Russell 19 points and 32 rebounds, plus five blocks. St. Louis led by four with under two minutes to go before Boston scored six in a row, only to have the Hawks send it to overtime on a pair of free throws by Bob Pettit, their brilliant forward who had 39 points and 19 points in Game 7 and averaged 29.8 points and 16.8 rebounds per game for the series.

Jack Coleman of St. Louis, who had hit the game-winning shot in the series opener, sank another clutch jumper to force a second overtime period. That went down to the wire as Boston took a 125-123 lead on a pair of free throws by Jim Loscutoff with two seconds remaining, then survived a remarkable last-second play designed by Hawks player-coach Alex Hannum.

Hannum decided to take the ball out of bounds himself and try to fire a court-length baseball pass over everyone's heads and off the backboard at the opposite end of the floor, hoping that a teammate like Pettit could grab the carom and attempt the shot. As Hannum outlined the plan in the huddle during the timeout, the St. Louis players were skeptical. "There were nine guys around Hannum and we all were nodding like we knew what he was talking about," said Macauley. "But I was like everyone else. I was thinking that Alex had a hard time hitting the backboard from 15 feet, so how was he going to do it from 94 feet?" Echoed Pettit, "I kept thinking I'd never heard anything like it before. And Alex was so sure of himself. He looked right at me and said, 'Pettit, you'll get the rebound and tip it in.'"

It very nearly worked. Hannum fired the ball the length of the court, hitting the opposite backboard 94 feet away, and the ball caromed toward Pettit, who grabbed the loose ball but hurried his shot to make sure he got it off in time. "I caught the

ball in midair and shot it before I came down," said Pettit. "The ball rolled around the rim and came out. Really, as crazy as it sounds, I should have made the shot. Alex's pass was perfect."

The Celtics had survived. Cousy called that championship the most satisfying of his career, and Russell chooses to wear the ring he received after that season from among the 11 he earned. It was the start of the greatest dynasty in American professional sports history—11 NBA titles in 13 years for the Boston Celtics.

14. Pettit's Revenge

Bob Pettit, the St. Louis Hawks' brilliant forward who played in the All-Star Game in each of his 11 seasons in the NBA, didn't have to wait long to make up for missing the last shot of the 1957 NBA Finals against the Boston Celtics. The teams met again for the title the following year, and this time Pettit was not to be denied.

Boston was favored, but St. Louis stunned the Celtics by winning the opening game of the series at Boston Garden 104-102. Boston evened the series with a 136-112 rout in Game 2, but the third game would turn out to be calamitous for the defending champions.

Center Bill Russell suffered a sprained ankle in the third minute of play, an injury that would sideline him for the next two games and limit him to 20 minutes at half-speed in Game 6. Without the shot-blocking Russell lurking in the lane, or with him at less than 100 percent, the Hawks felt free to attack the hoop.

St. Louis won Game 3 111-108, but Boston rallied in Russell's absence and took Game 4 109-98. With the series tied at 2-2, the Hawks went into Boston Garden and came away with a 102-100 win in Game 5, giving them a chance to wrap up the title on their home floor. And Pettit was never better than in Game 6.

He scored 31 points in the first three quarters, then tallied 19 of his team's final 21 points for a total of 50 for the game. His last two points came on a jumper with 15 seconds remaining and gave the Hawks a 110-107 lead, enough to withstand one last Celtic basket. St. Louis' 110-109 victory produced the franchise's only NBA championship.

"In his day, Bob Pettit was the best power forward there was," said Red Auerbach, the coach of the Celtics. "Pettit was Mr. Clean, Mr. All America. He was like John Havlicek, a clean liver, just a super guy, but very, very competitive. He would play all out, whether he was 50 points ahead or 50 behind. It didn't matter. That's the only way he knew how to play—all out."

"Bob made 'second effort' a part of the sport's vocabulary," said Russell. "He kept coming at you more than any man in the game. He was always battling for position, fighting you off the boards."

Pettit's 50 points matched the record for an NBA Playoff game set by Bob Cousy of Boston against Syracuse in 1953. Cousy, however, had the benefit of a four-overtime game, and one that was so marked by fouls that 30 of his points came from the free throw line (as opposed to 12 by Pettit). Pettit had 19 field goals (in 34 attempts), to just 10 field goals by Cousy.

"We won that title because Bobby Pettit would not let us lose," said teammate Charlie Share.

15. Wilt Scores 100

Wilt Chamberlain was the most dominating offensive force the game of basketball has ever seen, and never more so than on March 2, 1962. That's when he scored 100 points against the New York Knicks in leading his Philadelphia Warriors to a 163-147 victory before 4,124 in Hershey, Pa., where the Warriors played a few of their home games in the early '60s in an effort to draw extra fans.

"It is a mythic game because Wilt scored exactly 100, no more, no less," said Harvey Pollack, who was in charge of publicity and statistics for Philadelphia and who filed stories about the game for the Associated Press, United Press International and the *Philadelphia Inquirer*, none of whom sent their own reporters.

The 7-foot-1, 275-pound Chamberlain often spoke of how the game is shrouded in mystery, since it was not televised and no videotape exists. "People have been able to embellish it without facts getting in the way," he observed. "Over the years the memories get better. It's like your first girlfriend—the picture you have in your head is always better than how she looked in real life."

Chamberlain was unstoppable that night. The Knicks' starting center, Phil Jordan, was suffering from the flu and did not play, and his replacements, Darrall Imhoff and Cleveland Buckner, were helpless in trying to contain Chamberlain. He scored 23 points in the first quarter and had 41 by half-time, then added 28 in the third quarter.

As the fans began to chant, "Give It To Wilt! Give It To Wilt!" the Warriors did just that, feeding Chamberlain every time they could in the fourth quarter. The Knicks tried fouling other Philadelphia players to keep the ball away from Chamberlain, but to little avail. "When we got the ball, they were fouling everyone except Wilt so he wouldn't get 100," recalled Philadelphia forward Tom Meschery. "So we would take the ball out of bounds and throw high lobs directly to Wilt near the basket. When Wilt wanted the ball, he was big enough and strong enough to go get it. Guys were hanging on his back and he was still catching the pass and scoring."

Chamberlain reached the century mark with 46 seconds left to play, taking a pass from Joe Ruklick, who had collected an offensive rebound, and laying it in. Fans poured onto the court, stopping the game, and Chamberlain went to the locker room where PR man Pollack wrote "100" on a sheet of paper and had Chamberlain hold it up for photographers.

Chamberlain shot 36-for-63 from the field and 28-for-32 from the foul line for his 100 points, which erased his own NBA single-game scoring record of 78 points set earlier that season. He went on to average an NBA-record 50.4 points per game and become the only player to surpass 4,000 points in one season, finishing with 4,029. He also led the league in rebounding at 25.7 rpg, was second in field goal percentage at .506 and set an NBA record by averaging 48.5 minutes per game—an amazing feat when you remember that a regulation NBA game lasts only 48 minutes. Seven of Philadelphia's games went into overtime that season and Chamberlain played 3,882 of a possible 3,890 minutes, going the distance in 79 of the team's 80 games.

But the record that captured fans' imagination was the

100-point game. Even Chamberlain, who downplayed the feat as "inevitable" when it first happened, came to embrace it before he died in 1999. "As time goes by," he said, "I feel more and more a part of that 100-point game. It has become my handle, and I've come to realize just what I did."

16. One That Got Away

Frank Selvy set an NCAA Division I record by scoring 100 points for Furman against Newberry, and tallied more than 6,000 points in a nine-year NBA career. In 1961-62, starting alongside Jerry West in the backcourt for the Los Angeles Lakers, he averaged 14.7 points, 5.2 rebounds and 4.8 assists per game. But the shot that would always haunt him, and the one long-time Lakers fans can't forget, is one he missed against the Boston Celtics at the end of Game 7 of the 1962 NBA Finals.

"I would trade all my points for that last basket," said Selvy. But it was not to be.

The Celtics had won three NBA titles in a row, but the Lakers were a team on the rise in their second season on the west coast after having moved from Minneapolis. They had won the Western Division by 11 games behind stars like West, who averaged 30.8 points per game, and Elgin Baylor, who was second in the league behind Wilt Chamberlain at 38.3 ppg even though Army reserve duty limited him to 48 games.

The Celtics and Lakers split the first four games of the NBA Finals before Baylor put on an amazing one-man show in Game 5, scorching Boston Garden for a Finals-record 61 points and grabbing 22 rebounds as Los Angeles won 126-121. But the Lakers blew a chance to end the series at home, bowing to Boston 119-105 in Game 6 to set up a winner-take-all Game 7 showdown.

The teams battled to a 75-75 tie through three quarters. Boston moved in front 100-96 and seemed in command when the Lakers' Rudy LaRusso was called for an offensive foul with one minute to play. But Selvy grabbed a rebound and drove the length of the floor to cut the lead in half, then West stole a Bob Cousy pass and fed it to Selvy, who this time missed his shot but grabbed his own rebound and scored to tie it at 100-100 with 18 seconds to go.

On the ensuing play, Boston's Frank Ramsey tried a running hook shot but missed and LaRusso grabbed the rebound and called a timeout with five seconds on the clock. Lakers coach Fred Schaus went to a three-guard lineup and put the ball in Hundley's hands, with Baylor the first option and West the second. When play resumed, however, both of them were well covered and Hundley spotted Selvy open along the left baseline, since Cousy had left his man to double-team West. Hundley fired the inbounds pass to Selvy as Cousy scrambled to recover.

"It was a fairly tough shot," recalled Selvy. "I was almost on the baseline."

His eight-footer bounced off the rim, and the rebound was grabbed by Russell as time expired. Boston went on to win 110-107 in overtime, starting a frustrating eight-year period in which the Lakers would lose to the Celtics six times in the NBA Finals. The Celtics had their fourth consecutive championship, and Selvy and his teammates had the memory of a chance that got away.

17. Rouse Tames the Bearcats

The Cincinnati Bearcats had won two NCAA championships and boasted the best defense in the country, allowing a mere 52.9 points per game. The Loyola of Chicago Ramblers had never appeared in an NCAA tournament, but they were the highest scoring team in the nation at nearly 92 points per game.

The 1963 NCAA championship game was a classic showdown of offense vs. defense, the unstoppable force against the immovable object. The conventional wisdom going in was that whoever controlled the tempo of the game would win. A high-scoring, run-and-gun affair favored Loyola; a low-scoring struggle gave the edge to Cincinnati.

Sometimes, you can throw conventional wisdom out the window. Cincinnati controlled the tempo and kept the score low—and still lost.

"Our game plan worked for us 99 out of 100 times," said Cincinnati guard Tony Yates. "On this night, it didn't."

Loyola shot a woeful .274 from the field, 23-for-84. But the Ramblers took care of the ball, committing only three turnovers in the overtime contest to 16 by Cincinnati. And despite falling behind early and trailing by as many as 15 points in the second half, when the opportunity to win presented itself, Loyola didn't let it slip away.

Cincinnati led 29-21 at half-time and seemed comfortably in control with a 45-30 advantage six minutes into the second half. But Loyola went to a desperate full-court press and the Bearcats began to unravel. They started turning the ball over and missing their shots, and Yates, star forward Tom Thacker and center George Wilson each picked up their fourth personal fouls.

This was the opportunity Loyola was seeking. The Ramblers went on a 15-3 run, capped by a steal and basket by Jerry Harkness, to close the gap to 48-45 with 4:26 to play. Les Hunter finally cut the deficit to one at 53-52 by tipping in a shot by Harkness, who quickly fouled Cincinnati's Larry Shingleton to stop the clock with 12 seconds remaining.

Shingleton made the first free throw but missed the second and Harkness's basket with four seconds left tied it at 54-54, forcing overtime.

After the teams exchanged baskets until it was 58-58, Loyola tried to hold the ball for a last shot. Harkness went up for a jumper but Cincinnati's Ron Bonham got a hand on the ball, so Harkness passed to Les Hunter to the left of the lane instead. Hunter's shot hit the rim and bounced long, but Vic Rouse, alone on the right side of the basket, collected the rebound and laid it back in at the buzzer for a 60-58 victory.

"I felt suspended in air—you could almost say it was an out-of-body experience—and totally focused," Rouse said. "I didn't tip it, I grabbed it tight, jumped up and laid it in. I'd missed a couple like that before and I wanted to be so sure. Oh, my, it felt good! It was like a blessing."

18. Houdini's Last Act

Even though he had been a college star at nearby Holy Cross, Bob Cousy was not the player Red Auerbach wanted for the Boston Celtics in 1950. When he bypassed the 6-foot-1 Cousy in favor of drafting 6-foot-11 Charlie Share, Auerbach curtly explained, "Little men are a dime a dozen. I'm supposed

to win, not go after local yokels."

Cousy was drafted by the Chicago Stags, but that team folded before the start of the 1950-51 season. Three players' names went into a hat for dispersal—veterans Max Zaslofsky and Andy Phillip and the rookie Cousy. Zaslofsky was picked by the Knicks, Phillip was selected by Philadelphia and Boston got the player who was left, the "local yokel."

Cousy would make Auerbach eat his words. A deft ball-handler and passer who earned the nickname "Houdini of the Hardwood," Cousy became a Celtics mainstay and an NBA All-Star for 13 consecutive seasons. He made the All-NBA First Team 10 years in a row beginning in 1952, his second season with the club, and was the league's Most Valuable Player in 1957. The Celtics' career leader with 6,945 assists, he was the league's top playmaker for seven consecutive seasons beginning in 1953.

With Cousy in place as their floor general and running the fast break that would become their trademark, the Celtics won their first NBA championship in 1957 after adding a pair of key rookies, forward Tom Heinsohn and center Bill Russell. Cousy also was the quarterback of five more title teams, from 1959 through 1963, as the Celtics established the greatest dynasty in American professional sports, winning eight championships in a row and 11 in 13 seasons.

"Cooz was the absolute offensive master, the best play-making guard that ever played the game," said Heinsohn. "Once that ball reached his hands, the rest of us just took off, never bothering to look back. We didn't have to. He'd find us. When you got into position to score, the ball would be there."

Cousy played the game with a flair that was unknown to the sport in the 1950s, when dunking was considered a sign of poor sportsmanship. From look-away passes to behind-the-back dribbling, Cousy brought a taste of playground ball to the NBA and paved the way for players like Pete Maravich and Earl Monroe, Walt Frazier and Tiny Archibald and so many more by combining style with substance.

"The rest of us have to think about the things we do. He does them instinctively," said K.C. Jones, who succeeded Cousy as the Celtics' point guard.

Cousy's last game as a Celtic came on April 24, 1963, as Boston was trying to wrap up its fifth consecutive championship. The Celtics led the Lakers 3-2, with Game 6 of the Finals in Los Angeles. Boston led by nine points early in the fourth quarter before Cousy suffered a sprained left ankle and had to leave the game. While he was on the bench, the Lakers closed the gap to one.

Cousy reentered the game with five minutes to go, and the Lakers' comeback stalled. A steal and basket by Heinsohn put the Celtics up by four with two minutes to go, after which Cousy's ball-handling baffled the Lakers, who were forced to foul in order to stop the clock. As the Celtics hit their free throws to stay in front, Cousy dribbled out the final seconds of his career and tossed the ball high in the air as the buzzer sounded ending the Celtics' 112-109 victory.

19. Bradley, Russell Duel At the Garden

In the 1960s, holiday college basketball tournaments were still a novelty, and the most glamorous event on the calendar

was the ECAC Holiday Festival in New York's Madison Square Garden. These were the days before so many games were nationally televised, when a trip to New York to compete at the "mecca of basketball" was considered a recruiting coup, so the tournament had no trouble attracting the best teams and most exciting players in the land.

In 1964, those players were Cazzie Russell of Michigan and Bill Bradley of Princeton, two 6-foot-5 forwards who would earn All-America status and lead their schools to national prominence. Both were great all-around players, Bradley perhaps a slightly better long-range shooter and Russell a bit quicker and more explosive driving to the basket. Both were outstanding offensive players who scored despite being double-teamed or running up against zones designed to keep them in check.

The teams took on their stars' personalities. Princeton played a patient, ball-control offense that worked the ball for a good shot and tried to control the tempo of the game, while Michigan liked to run at every opportunity and rely on its talent to outscore opponents.

Coincidentally, each of the stars scored 36 points in the first round of the Holiday Festival, as Princeton beat Syracuse 77-67 and Michigan defeated Manhattan 90-77. That whetted fans' appetites for the showdown, which attracted more than 18,000 to the old Madison Square Garden on Eighth Avenue.

Bradley was brilliant, foiling Michigan's plan to play him straight up, man-to-man. He scored from inside and out, posting up, shooting jumpers and driving to the hoop. He outscored Russell 23-8 in the first half, but Michigan's stronger supporting cast, which included future pros Bill Buntin and Oliver Darden, picked up most of the slack and the Wolverines trailed only 39-37 at half-time.

Michigan changed tactics for the second half, going to a full-court press to try to keep the ball out of Bradley's hands. The Princeton star responded by scoring 18 points in 15 minutes as the Tigers extended their lead to 76-63. But Bradley was called for his fifth personal foul with 4:37 remaining and had to leave the game with 41 points, and the Wolverines sensed an opportunity.

Suddenly, Michigan's press rattled the Tigers, who didn't have their star to bail them out. Russell, meanwhile, stepped into the spotlight, scoring six points in a quick 10-0 Michigan run that wiped out most of the deficit. With a minute to go Russell scored on a three-point play and the game was tied 78-78, as Bradley watched helplessly from the bench.

Following a Princeton miss, the Wolverines decided to hold for the last shot. The Tigers assumed Russell would take it, but they could do nothing to stop him. Russell got the ball, shook free and put up a 15-foot jumper that went in with three seconds left, giving Michigan an 80-78 victory.

The Wolverines had outscored Princeton 17-4 after Bradley had been disqualified, Russell scoring 11 of his 27 points in that stretch run.

Bradley had won the battle, outscoring Russell 41-27, but Russell had survived to help Michigan win the war. The two teams met again in the NCAA Final Four, with similar if less dramatic results; Bradley scored 29 points before fouling out with six minutes to play, while Russell scored 28 to lead Michigan to a 93-76 victory.

20. DeMatha Beats Power, Kareem

Kareem Abdul-Jabbar (then known as Lew Alcindor) was perhaps the most renowned high school basketball player ever. He was 6-foot-8 when he entered New York's Power Memorial and quickly grew past 7 feet during his freshman year. After being embarrassed by a more experienced Erasmus Hall High School team in a scrimmage prior to his first season, Abdul-Jabbar vowed it would never happen again and worked tirelessly on his game, learning to use both his height and his athletic skills to best advantage. His team lost six games during his freshman year, but by the time he began his sophomore season he was well on his way to greatness.

Abdul-Jabbar led Power Memorial to 71 consecutive victories in one stretch, a streak that was broken in his senior year by DeMatha Catholic High School, a perennial powerhouse from the Washington suburb of Hyattsville, Md. It was Abdul-Jabbar's only loss in his last three years of high school, and one the man who would go on to lead UCLA to three NCAA crowns and become the NBA's all-time leading scorer has never forgotten. "They were a good, well-trained team with a winning tradition—and the serious desire to beat our behinds," Abdul-Jabbar said of DeMatha.

The man behind DeMatha was Morgan Wooten, who has amassed more than 1,000 victories and won over 85 percent of his games since becoming the school's basketball coach in 1956. "It was the high school game of the year in the nation, maybe of all time," said Wooten, whose team took a 29-game winning streak of its own into the showdown against Power. "They beat us the year before in the last minute by three points and Kareem scored 38 points. Our strategy in the 1964 game was to let Kareem score whatever he could while we stopped everybody else. For the '65 rematch, I reversed our strategy: We would try to stop Kareem. The other Power players would have to pick up the slack, if they could. If they couldn't, we would win."

To get his players accustomed to facing an agile, athletic 7-footer, Wooten put a tennis racket in the hands of his best player, 6-foot-8 Sid Catlett, and had him impersonate Abdul-Jabbar on defense during practice sessions. "Sid had firm orders from me to block every shot he could," said Wooten. "With his height and that tennis racket added to it, he looked like the Washington Monument in a DeMatha uniform. With his jumping ability added to everything else, our shooters had to put enough arch on their shots to bring rain."

Offensively, the DeMatha players patiently worked the ball around until they could get off a good shot, and they made sure they could get it over Abdul-Jabbar. Defensively, their big men ganged up on Abdul-Jabbar and held him in check, and the other Power players couldn't pick up the slack. The result was a taut defensive struggle in which Abdul-Jabbar's dominating presence was negated.

"DeMatha came prepared," recalled Abdul-Jabbar. "They had two 6-foot-8 big men, Bob Whitmore and Sid Catlett, who both went on to play at Notre Dame, and they sandwiched me, tried to deny me the ball. They slowed the game down, walked the ball up the court when they had it, and double- and triple-teamed me on our end. The game was close, but they played well, made the crucial shot at the end, and won it 46-43."

"We did it by stopping Abdul-Jabbar and taking away Power's inside game, holding him to 16 points, 14 below his average," said Wooten. And by being able to score over him, thanks to some preparation with a tennis racket.

21. "Havlicek Stole the Ball!"

Even though he scored more than 30,000 points in his brilliant career with the Boston Celtics, John Havlicek is perhaps best remembered for a basket he prevented with a steal in the 1965 playoffs. The play was immortalized by the late Johnny Most, the long-time radio play-by-man of the Boston Celtics whose gravely voice brought the Celtics to millions of listeners throughout New England.

Boston had won six consecutive championships, but in 1965 it was threatened in the Eastern Divison Finals by a Philadelphia team that had added Wilt Chamberlain to a roster that already included Hal Greer, Chet Walker and Luke Jackson. Boston, as division champion, had a bye through the first round of the playoffs while Philadelphia defeated Cincinnati. In the division finals, the home team won each of the first six games, with the deciding Game 7 at Boston Garden going down to the closing seconds.

Boston was trying to stave off a Philadelphia rally that had cut the Celtics' lead to five points, then three, then one at 110-109 with five seconds to play. And when Boston center Bill Russell tried to inbound the ball from under his own basket, it hit one of the guide wires that ran down from the ceiling of Boston Garden and helped support the backboards. Referee Earl Strom called the violation and awarded possession to Philadelphia.

During the ensuing timeout, Philadelphia coach Dolph Schayes was worried that if his team got the ball to Chamberlain, the Celtics would foul him since he was a notoriously poor free throw shooter. "Wilt's problems at the foul line weighed on my mind, so I set up a play where Hal Greer would pass the ball to Chet Walker, and Johnny Kerr would set a pick to free Walker for a shot," said Schayes.

Greer took the ball out under the basket. He looked toward the 7-foot-1 Chamberlain in the low post, but Russell stepped in between them. Meanwhile, Celtics guard K.C. Jones was leaping along the baseline and frantically waving his arms to distract Greer, who turned his attention to Walker out beyond the key. Havlicek had taken a position several feet off the direct line of sight between Greer and Walker, making it look like Walker was open when really he wasn't.

"I knew they had five seconds to put the ball in play," said Havlicek. "My thought was, as the official handed Greer the ball, to start counting, 'one thousand one, one thousand two, one thousand three.' When I got to 'one thousand four' and the ball still hadn't been passed in, I took a peek over my shoulder and saw that Greer was about to lob a pass to Walker. I knew that it wasn't a good pass and that I would have a good chance of deflecting or intercepting it. I made a controlled deflection to Sam Jones, who was right near me. He went down the sideline dribbling out the clock and the game was over. As soon as the buzzer went off, the crowd went bananas. It was hysteria and euphoria.

"The incident would have ended right there," added Havlicek, "except that our announcer, Johnny Most, went

almost completely haywire at the end of the game. He had established a reputation as an excitable broadcaster long before that night, but something about the drama of this particular ending really hit him and he launched into one of the most famous spiels in Boston sports broadcasting history."

"*Greer is putting the ball into play. He gets it out deep,*" Most slowly intoned. Then, suddenly, his voice rose in a frenzy. "*Havlicek steals it. Over to Sam Jones. Havlicek stole the ball! It's all over! Johnny Havlicek stole the ball!*"

"I didn't realize it was that outstanding a play until I heard Johnny Most," Havlicek said. "The next day, radio station WHDH, which did our games in those days, kept repeating the tape of the game ending, including Johnny Most's semi-hysterical ending. All over Greater Boston, the phrase, 'Havlicek stole the ball' meant a great deal. The play has gotten bigger as time goes on."

The Celtics had the win, and would go on to capture their seventh consecutive championship, beating the Los Angeles Lakers in five games.

22. Texas Western Beats Kentucky

Some games have an impact that extends far beyond the boundaries of the court, long after the final buzzer has sounded. Such was the case with the 1966 NCAA championship game between Kentucky and Texas Western (now the University of Texas-El Paso).

Kentucky was a traditional basketball power going for its fifth national title, coached by the legendary Adolph Rupp. The team was nicknamed "Rupp's Runts" since no starter was taller than 6-foot-5, but the lineup included players like Pat Riley, Louie Dampier and Larry Conley.

Texas Western was the outsider. Although it had compiled a 23-1 record during the regular season, it had not beaten a single Top 10 team. Its players came from the inner city playgrounds of cities like New York and Detroit, Houston and Gary, Ind., and none of them attracted national attention.

Then there was the inescapable racial sub-plot to the game, which was played at a time when race relations had become a major national issue. All five Texas Western starters were African Americans. Kentucky was an all-white team from a Southern state that had never even recruited a black player.

If ever a team was to shatter a stereotype, it was Texas Western. Even though the Miners' players came from the inner cities, the team played anything but a schoolyard game. Hall of Fame coach Don Haskins, a disciple of the legendary Henry Iba, preached discipline and defense, and those became the team's trademarks, honed in countless hours of grueling practice sessions. "Every day after practice I wanted to shoot him," guard Bobby Joe Hill said of Haskins—but in the end all the hard work paid off.

To take on Rupp's Runts, Haskins decided to go with a shorter, quicker lineup. He benched 6-foot-8 center Nevil Shed and went with a three-guard system featuring the 5-foot-10 Hill, 6-foot-1 Orsten Artis and 5-foot-6 Willie Worsley. Their quickness made all the difference.

Hill scored 20 points, Artis added 15 and Worsley led an aggressive defense that pestered the Wildcats into turnovers and held Kentucky to under 39 percent shooting from the field. On consecutive first-half plays that typified the game, Hill converted steals into lay-ups for the Miners, putting them ahead to stay. Texas Western led 34-31 at half-time, and its ball-handlers forced Kentucky to foul during the second half. The Miners cashed in at the foul line, sinking 28 of 34 attempts to maintain its lead, finally winning by a 72-65 margin.

Years later, Haskins tried to downplay the racial aspect of the game. "I never thought a thing about it," he said, "but after we won the title with five black guys, everybody made a big deal out of it. You play your five best guys."

Nevertheless, the game would prove to be a positive landmark as soon afterward major Southern universities, Kentucky included, began recruiting African American players. A barrier had been lifted, thanks in large measure to a group of unheralded players from a little-known school that won an NCAA championship.

23. Showdown in the Astrodome

If one game can be said to have placed college basketball squarely in the spotlight, making it a major part of the American sports scene, it was the showdown between UCLA and Houston in the Astrodome on January 20, 1968.

It had everything: Two unbeaten teams, No. 1 UCLA vs. No. 2 Houston; defending national champions vs. hometown heroes; a clash of consensus All-Americans and future Hall of Famers in Kareem Abdul-Jabbar of UCLA vs. Elvin Hayes of Houston. Most of all, it was a spectacle.

The game attracted a crowd of 52,693, the largest ever to see a basketball game to that point. Interestingly, none was seated within 100 feet of the court, which had been set up where second base normally would have been, at the center of the nearly circular building. Only the Astrodome's permanent seats were used, other than tables and chairs for scorers, officials and media, meaning the players looked tiny from even the best seat in the house—yet no one seemed to mind.

The build-up for this game had been tremendous. UCLA had won 47 consecutive games, including the 1967 NCAA championship, and had never lost with the 7-foot-2 Abdul-Jabbar, a junior, in the lineup. Houston also was undefeated, having won 17 straight games since bowing to the Bruins 73-58 in the previous Final Four, and was led by the 6-foot-9 Hayes, a senior.

Abdul-Jabbar had suffered a scratched left cornea eight days earlier in a game against California, missing two games and wearing an eyepatch for most of the week leading up to the showdown, when he was unable to practice with the team. "I overestimated myself, and so did Coach (John) Wooden. The game wasn't five minutes old before I was exhausted, and I had no second wind," said Abdul-Jabbar.

Houston, calling Hayes' number at every opportunity, jumped in front by as many as 15 points before taking a 46-43 lead into intermission, at which point the Big E already had 29 points. The pace of the second half was more deliberate, and with 3:02 to play the score was tied 65-65. Hayes scored on a baseline jumper and teammate Don Chaney added a 15-footer to make it 69-65, but UCLA guard Lucius Allen hit a bucket and two free throws to make it 69-69 with 44 seconds left.

Houston worked the ball to Hayes down low, and as he

moved toward the left corner for a turnaround jumper he was fouled by Jim Nielsen with 28 seconds left. Though just a 60 percent free throw shooter, Hayes sank both shots for a 71-69 lead. After UCLA's inbounds pass went out of bounds off one of the Bruins, Houston managed to run out the clock for the win. Hayes finished with 39 points, 15 rebounds and 8 blocked shots, while Abdul-Jabbar had 15 points and 12 rebounds and shot just 4-for-18 from the field.

UCLA's streak was over, but the Bruins were able to exact revenge in the NCAA tournament, when the teams again met in the Final Four. This time Houston was No. 1 and UCLA was No. 2, but not for long. With Lynn Shackelford shadowing Hayes in a diamond-and-one defense, the Houston star managed just 10 points and the Cougars were no match for the deeper Bruins. UCLA coasted to a 101-69 victory as all five starters scored in double figures. The Bruins went on to beat North Carolina 78-55 in a championship game that Abdul-Jabbar described as "an after-thought" following the emotion-charged revenge rout of Houston.

24. A Leprechaun Helps Russell Go Out A Winner

During the late 1950s and 1960s, rivals often suggested there were leprechauns loose in Boston Garden, helping the Celtics to their string of eight consecutive championships and 11 in 13 seasons. Sometimes they appeared when opposing players were headed upcourt on a fast break and guided the ball to the famed dead spots in the parquet floor, inevitably resulting in turnovers. Other times they seemed to perch atop the backboards, guiding in errant Celtics' shots. And other times they seemed to travel with the team.

One such creature surely was with the Celtics, May 5, 1969, when the Celtics won the last title in their glorious run. There's no other way to explain the basket by Boston's Don Nelson in the final minute that clinched the Game 7 victory over the arch-rival Los Angeles Lakers in Bill Russell's final game with the Celtics.

Russell had added the coaching duties to his playing responsibilities before the 1966-67 season, succeeding Red Auerbach on the bench. The Celtics were beaten by the Philadelphia 76ers in five games in the Eastern Division Finals that year, but exacted revenge over the 76ers en route to the championship the following season. In 1968-69, they did it again. Though they finished just fourth in the East with a 48-34 record, when it came playoff time they were ready, beating Philadelphia in five games and New York in six for another date against the Lakers in the Finals.

Los Angeles had the home-court advantage, and that loomed large after each of the first six games of the series went to the home team. Before Game 7, Lakers owner Jack Kent Cooke had thousands of balloons blown up and floated to the rafters in the Forum, to be released as the Southern Cal marching band played *Happy Days Are Here Again* after the anticipated Los Angeles victory. That's the way it read in the script Auerbach—now the Boston team's president—got his hands on.

"Red mentioned that before the game," said Nelson, a forward with the Celtics who would later achieve coaching prominence himself. "You could see the balloons by the thousands. It was definitely a mistake on their part to do that, and he let his feelings be known."

The Celtics responded by hitting eight of their first 10 shots and racing to a 24-12 lead. The Lakers closed the spread to 59-56 at half-time, but early in the fourth quarter Boston had stretched it out to 17 points. The Lakers closed to 103-94 with just under six minutes to play, but at that point Lakers center Wilt Chamberlain went to the bench with a bruised shin. Despite the loss of their big center, who had 27 rebounds at that point, the Lakers continued to eat into the Celtics' lead. With three minutes to go, a jumper by reserve 7-footer Mel Counts brought the Lakers within one. Chamberlain seemed ready to come back in, but Lakers coach Butch van Breda Kolff opted to keep him on the bench and go with the players who had brought the team back—a move that would later haunt him and the Lakers.

The game remained tight, and with under a minute left and Boston in possession in its offensive end, Lakers guard Jerry West knocked the ball free. Nelson scooped up the loose ball as the shot clock was running down and hoisted up a shot from around the foul line. That's where the leprechaun came in. Nelson's line-drive shot hit the back rim and bounced straight up into the air, to the top of the backboard, where it magically plummeted straight through the net, as if guided by unseen hands.

"That was the luckiest shot I ever made in my life," said Nelson. "Havlicek made a move, somebody from behind hit the ball and it came right to me. I was cutting across the paint. I just grabbed it and shot it very poorly, and it made that crazy bounce and went in. I shot it too hard. I shot it very quickly and it hit the back of the rim and went up real high and came back through.

"There was no time to chuckle—it was like I planned it that way."

Nelson's basket took the starch out of the Lakers' comeback, and Boston held on to win 108-106. Russell, in his final game as player-coach, played all 48 minutes and hauled down 21 rebounds. Afterwards he announced his retirement, leaving with this remarkable record: In his NBA Playoff career he played in 11 seventh games or deciding fifth games, and his team won all 11.

25. Reed Limps Onto the Court

The New York Knicks were in trouble. They were matched up against a Los Angeles Lakers team that boasted three of the greatest players of all time: Wilt Chamberlain, Elgin Baylor and Jerry West. And it looked like they would have to play Game 7 of the 1970 NBA Finals without their captain, Willis Reed, their only true big man.

After the teams split the first two games of the series, the Knicks won Game 3 111-108 in overtime, surviving a 60-foot buzzer-beater by West that had tied the score at the end of regulation—it was only worth two points instead of three, since the NBA did not adopt the three-point field goal rule till the end of the decade. The Lakers bounced right back to tie the series by taking Game 4 121-115.

Early in Game 5, Reed tripped and suffered a torn muscle in his right thigh. The Knicks' 6-foot-10 warrior, whose move from forward to center a season earlier had turned the team

from a good one to a championship contender, hobbled off the court. His replacement, journeyman backup Nate Bowman, was no match for Chamberlain in terms of size or skills, and by half-time the Lakers led by 13. So Red Holzman, the canny Knicks coach who had been around pro basketball since before the NBA was founded, pulled the 6-foot-10 Bowman and threw a tag team of forwards, 6-foot-7 Dave Stallworth and 6-foot-6 Dave DeBusschere, at the massive, 7-foot-1 Chamberlain. The strategy worked as the Lakers focused so intently on trying to take advantage of the Chamberlain mismatch, they stopped playing their normal game. The Knicks rallied and stole a 107-100 victory.

But they needed one more win for the championship, and with time to prepare for the Reed-less Knicks, the Lakers easily captured Game 6 in Los Angeles 135-113. Chamberlain was unstoppable, scoring 45 points and hauling down 27 rebounds.

Game 7 was in New York, and as the fans filled Madison Square Garden, the question was whether or not Reed would play. It appeared to be answered when the two teams emerged from the locker rooms for their warmups: Reed was not among the Knicks on the court. Instead he was deep in the bowels of the building, taking a last-minute injection of cortisone in his injured leg in hopes it would ease the pain just enough.

"I wanted to play," Reed recalled three decades later. "That was for the championship, the one great moment you play for all your life. I didn't want to have to look at myself in the mirror 20 years later and say I wished I had tried to play."

Moments before tipoff, Reed limped through the tunnel beneath the stands and onto the court, greeted by a deafening roar that grew and grew. It didn't matter that he could barely hobble, much less run—his presence elevated the Knicks and seemed to stun the Lakers. He scored the first two baskets of the game, then let his teammates carry him the rest of the way. With Walt Frazier playing one of the great games in NBA Finals history, swishing 36 points and dishing 19 assists, the Knicks raced to a 61-37 half-time lead and coasted to a 113-99 win and the first NBA championship in franchise history.

"I had no idea that it would become such a great moment in sports history," Reed said. "It was a big moment for us because it was a chance for the Knicks to win a championship for the first time. I'm happy to know that so many people remember it. It was a great moment in my life."

26. The Olympic Game That Ended Three Times

When isn't the final buzzer final? In the gold medal game of the 1972 Olympics in Munich, Germany, the closing seconds were replayed not once but twice after the "final" buzzer sounded. As a result, what appeared to be a 50-49 victory for the United States turned into a 51-50 triumph for the Soviet Union, the United States' first "loss" ever in Olympic competition.

The Soviet Union led for most of the game, but with three seconds left Doug Collins drove to the basket and was knocked to the floor by Zurab Sakandelidze. A dazed Collins got up, stepped to the line and sank both free throws to give the United States a 50-49 lead. The Soviets inbounded the ball, but play was stopped with one second left when some fans ran onto the court. When play resumed, the Soviets threw the ball off the backboard, the Americans recovered as the buzzer sounded and

headed off to celebrate their victory.

Some five minutes later, an official of the International Basketball Federation went to the locker-room and told the team to get back onto the floor. The Soviet coach apparently had requested a timeout after Collins' free throws, and so three seconds were put back on the clock. The Soviets inbounded the ball once again, a shot was missed and the buzzer sounded, and again the Americans began to celebrate.

But again it was premature. The timer had mistakenly set the game clock to 0:50 instead of 0:03 before play resumed, and officials ordered the ending replayed once again. This time, Ivan Edeshko threw a court-length pass toward Aleksander Belov near the opposite free throw line. Belov and Kevin Joyce of the United States collided while going for the ball, but no foul was called. Belov caught the pass, turned and shot, the ball going through at the buzzer. This time—their third attempt to score a basket—it was the Soviets who were celebrating, and this time the 51-50 victory stood.

The Americans protested the way the end of the game was conducted, but to no avail. They voted not to accept their silver medals, believing to this day they deserved the gold.

Collins, who later starred for the Philadelphia 76ers, coached the Chicago Bulls and Detroit Pistons and did commentary for NBC and TNT, remembers that game as if it was played yesterday.

"It was a very bittersweet experience for me, to be a member of the first U.S. men's basketball team to lose in the Olympics, but I still don't believe that we lost. It was something that was out of our hands," he said.

"We were down by one with about 10 seconds to go, but I was able to steal a pass and was heading for a lay-up when I was fouled with three seconds left. I slid under the basket and hit my head on the basket support. I was unconscious for a few seconds, and when I went to the foul line I still felt groggy. But I think that helped me, because I didn't feel the pressure. I made two shots, and we were ahead by one.

"That's when all the confusion began. The Russians got two (extra) chances to win it and they finally put one in and won 51-50. After being so happy about the two free throws I had made, I was the most dejected person in the world.

"I think the one thing I regret more than anything else is not having that feeling you get standing on the platform, getting the gold medal around your neck, and listening to the national anthem. I feel we were robbed of that."

27. Notre Dame Stops UCLA's Winning Streak at 88

No team has dominated a sport the way UCLA dominated college basketball in the 1960s and early '70s. Starting in 1963-64, when legendary coach John Wooden led the Bruins to a perfect 30-0 mark and their first NCAA crown, UCLA lost a total of just 22 games in 12 seasons, and eight of them came in 1965-66 when Kareem Abdul-Jabbar was a freshman and ineligible to compete for the Bruins varsity. Eliminate that season and you have 14 losses in 11 years—barely more than one per season!

UCLA had four 30-0 seasons in that stretch and won 10 NCAA championships, including seven in a row from 1966-67 through 1972-73. And from January 30, 1971 through January

17, 1974, the Bruins set an NCAA record by winning 88 consecutive games.

That streak might have been much longer, but Notre Dame had defeated UCLA 89-82 on January 26, 1971, ending a 47-game Bruin winning streak. That left UCLA short of the record of 60 consecutive wins set by the University of San Francisco team that featured Bill Russell and K.C. Jones.

UCLA immediately began another winning streak, and this time it got the record—and Notre Dame was its victim in the record-breaking win. On January 28, 1973, the Bruins made sure of the record by pulling away to a 61-39 lead midway through the second half and coasting to an 82-63 victory behind center Bill Walton's triple-double of 16 points, 15 rebounds and 10 blocks.

Nearly one year later, the winning streak was up to 88 games when UCLA faced Notre Dame once again on January 19, 1974. The Bruins were ranked No. 1, but Walton had suffered a back injury and had not played in 12 days before the matchup with the No. 2-ranked Irish, who were led by future pros Adrian Dantley, John Shumate and Gary Brokaw.

Showing no effects of the layoff, Walton sank 12 of his first 13 shots and dominated the paint, leading UCLA to a 70-59 lead with 3-1/2 minutes remaining. That's when Wooden ordered his team into a delay game in an attempt to kill the clock, but it killed UCLA's momentum instead.

Notre Dame went to a full-court press that rattled the Bruins, who suddenly began turning the ball over. Two baskets by Shumate and one apiece by Dantley and Brokaw cut the lead to three, and after another turnover, Brokaw scored again to make it 70-69 with 1:11 left.

UCLA's woes continued as forward Jamaal Wilkes was called for a charging foul, the fifth consecutive possession on which the Bruins had turned the ball over. With all eyes focused on Notre Dame's three stars, it was a member of the supporting cast who stepped into the hero's role.

"We wanted Shumate and Brokaw to set up a two-on-one situation on one side, because they had been so effective," said Dwight Clay, who played the guard position alongside Brokaw. "Curtis Rowe began to cheat and help Wilkes stop their action. That left me alone in the corner and I waved my hands. Brokaw read it and got me the ball."

Clay caught the pass in the right corner and went right up with his jumper. It sailed through the net with 29 seconds left on the clock. "I knew it was good as soon as it left my hands," said Clay, whose basket gave Notre Dame a 71-70 victory. The Irish had scored the last 12 points of the game to end the longest winning streak in college basketball history.

28. Wooden Goes Out A Winner

The man behind the greatest dynasty in college basketball history, the UCLA juggernaut that won 10 championships in 12 years, including seven in a row from 1966-67 through 1972-73, was coach John Wooden.

So remarkable were Wooden's coaching accomplishments that only those steeped in basketball history know that he was a great player as well. Long before he became the "Wizard of Westwood," he was known as the "Indiana Rubber Man" because he used to bounce his body onto the floor and into the

stands chasing down loose balls. But he was more than a hustler—he was a three-time All-State player who led Martinsville to the Indiana state championship, and a three-time Helms Foundation All-American who led Purdue to the NCAA title. He played pro ball in the 1930s, leading his league in scoring once and finishing second twice, and supplemented his income by teaching and coaching high school ball, compiling a record of 218-42 in 11 seasons. After World War II he served as coach and athletic director at Indiana State for two seasons, then followed Horace Greeley's advice and headed west.

In 1964, Wooden coached a UCLA team led by guards Gail Goodrich and Walt Hazzard to the NCAA championship. The Bruins won again the following season, then failed to qualify for the tournament in 1965-66, when Kareem Abdul-Jabbar was a freshman and ineligible to compete for the varsity. After that the Bruins, led first by Abdul-Jabbar and later by Bill Walton, reeled off seven titles in a row before surrendering the crown to North Carolina State in 1974.

Wooden's 1975 team lacked a dominating center, but he made up for it by using the agile 6-foot-9 Richard Washington in between forwards Marques Johnson and Dave Meyers. The Bruins went 23-3 in the regular season and then beat Michigan (in overtime), Montana and Arizona State to advance to the Final Four. In the national semi-finals against Louisville, UCLA erased a four-point deficit in the closing minute of regulation play to send the game into overtime, then pulled out a 75-74 victory when Louisville guard Terry Howard, who had not missed a free throw all season in 28 attempts to that point, failed to convert on the front end of a one-and-one.

In the title game against a Kentucky team led by Kevin Grevey, UCLA led 43-40 at the half and 66-56 with eight minutes left, but the Wildcats whittled it down to one, 76-75. On the next play Meyers was called for a charge after colliding with Grevey, then nailed with a technical for arguing the call. That gave Kentucky a chance for five points: the one-and-one, the technical and possession of the ball. Instead, the Wildcats came up empty as Grevey missed the front end of the one-and-one and the technical, then Kentucky turned the ball over on the ensuing possession. It was all UCLA needed as the Bruins slowly edged away to a 92-85 victory.

So how did Wooden feel at the end of his 29-year coaching career? "I suppose anyone would like to go out with a victory," he replied. "The fact that the victory was for the national championship doesn't lessen the pleasure."

29. The Shot Heard Round the World

Many call the Boston Celtics' 128-126 triple overtime victory over the Phoenix Suns in the 1976 NBA Playoffs the greatest game ever played. It's hard to argue, because it was a game that had everything—buzzer-beating shots, high stakes, surprise heroes, innovative strategy, controversial calls and pandemonium in the arena.

The veteran Celtics, whose roster included John Havlicek, Dave Cowens and Jo Jo White, were favored over the Suns, an eight-year-old expansion franchise that was making its first Finals appearance. Boston easily won the first two games at home, but Phoenix came back and won two close contests on its home floor to set up the pivotal Game 5 at Boston Garden.

The Celtics jumped out to a 32-12 lead and appeared headed for their third easy home-court win. But Phoenix closed the gap to 15 points at half-time and then stunned the Garden crowd by holding the Celtics to 34 points in the second half. The game went into overtime tied at 95-95 after Curtis Perry of Phoenix and Havlicek of Boston each missed two late free throws.

Each team scored six points in overtime, which ended amidst controversy when Boston's Paul Silas signaled for a time-out in the closing seconds. The Celtics already had used all their timeouts and would have been charged a technical foul had the request been granted, but referee Richie Powers either didn't see Silas or ignored him, and let the final seconds tick off the clock. Phoenix was furious at the non-call, but the game went into a second overtime.

Boston jumped in front and held a three-point lead with 19 seconds left when Dick Van Arsdale scored for the Suns. Paul Westphal then came up with a steal and Curtis Perry put in his own rebound to put Phoenix in front 110-109 with four seconds left.

Havlicek took Don Nelson's inbounds pass near midcourt, drove toward the lane and banked in a 12-footer. "There was this tremendous roar and I looked at the clock and I think there may have been one second showing, but then there were none. I assumed the game was over," said Havlicek.

He was wrong. Though hundreds of fans had poured over the courtside press tables and onto the parquet floor, referees Powers and Don Murphy had one second put back on the clock, then set about clearing the court and getting the players back out to the benches from the locker rooms, where many had gone during the commotion.

During that time, Westphal suggested to Suns coach John MacLeod that Phoenix call a timeout and purposely draw a technical foul. While Boston would get a free throw attempt that might stretch the lead to two points, the Suns would get to inbound the ball from mid-court instead of from under their own basket and thus have a better chance at a possible game-tying basket.

MacLeod okayed the idea and White made the free throw, making Boston's lead 112-110. Perry inbounded the ball to Gar Heard, standing to the right of the top of the key. The Phoenix forward caught it and arched a rainbow jumper that sailed right in, tying the game and stunning everyone in the building.

Just when it appeared that Phoenix's young legs might overcome Boston's experience, seldom-used reserve forward Glenn McDonald stepped to the fore for the Celtics. With Cowens, Charlie Scott and Paul Silas all having fouled out, McDonald put the Celtics ahead to stay with a basket with 1:39 remaining in the third overtime. He also hit a corner jumper and two free throws for six points in the five-minute period. Two free throws by backup center Jim Ard stretched Boston's lead to six points, enough to offset a pair of baskets by Westphal, and the Celtics had a 128-126 victory.

The Celtics went to Phoenix and closed out the series with an 87-80 victory in Game 6 for their 13th NBA championship, but Game 5 is the one everyone remembers.

"People immediately began calling it the most exciting or best-played game they had ever seen," said Havlicek, "and I'd have to say it was the most exciting I've ever been in. There were so many highs and lows, so many times when we went from winning to losing and back to what we thought was winning again."

30. Putting the Women's Game on the Map

Women have been playing basketball almost as long as men, but it took the better part of a century for the women's game to achieve a place of prominence on the American sports scene.

The first college basketball game on record between two women's teams took place on April 4, 1896, barely five years after the sport was invented. Stanford beat California 2-1 in a game which no men were permitted to attend. When one basket fell and had to be fixed by male attendants, it was reported that "the Berkeley team screamed and hid in a corner" until the men left the gym.

Much has changed since those early days. Now the screaming comes from the sellout crowds at the women's NCAA Final Four, the WNBA Playoffs or the women's basketball competition in the Olympic Games.

For many years, women's basketball was played with six per side and the court divided in half, with players not permitted to cross the midcourt line—this was considered more genteel than the way men ran up and down the court. In the 1960s, things began changing in a hurry. First two of the players were designated as rovers and allowed to cross midcourt, then in 1969 teams began experimenting using five players per side with no restrictions. In 1971 this became the standard for women's play, although "six-girl basketball" remained popular in some parts of the country for another two decades.

Women's basketball was controlled by the Amateur Athletic Union until 1969, when the first intercollegiate tournament was held. Two years later the Association of Intercollegiate Athletics for Women was formed, and this group coordinated the growth of the women's game before giving way to the NCAA in 1982. The passage by Congress of Title IX of the Educational Amendments of 1972, which sought to promote gender equity by mandating that schools receiving federal financial aid must devote comparable resources to women's programs (including athletics) as to men's, gave a big boost to the women's college game.

In 1987, a crowd of 24,563 saw Texas beat Tennessee 97-78 in a women's college game, and the NCAA Women's Final Four soon became an annual sellout. Major colleges like Tennessee, Stanford, North Carolina and Connecticut became the powers of the sport, replacing pioneers like Louisiana Tech, Old Dominion, Delta State and Immaculata, which had dominated in the 1970s. A much-ballyhooed USA Basketball Women's National Team was formed in 1995, practiced together for a year and then won the gold medal at the 1996 Olympics in Atlanta. Two professional leagues were formed after that, and while the ABL soon folded, the WNBA—with the backing of the men's NBA—has not only survived but thrived.

Women stars have begun to receive widespread recognition. The days of a Nera White, who played for Nashville Business College and was a 10-time MVP of the AAU tournament yet remained unknown to the general sports fan, are long gone. Players like Lusia Harris, Carol Blazejowski, Ann Meyers, Ann

Donovan and Cheryl Miller achieved acclaim for their skill and the way they played the game, paving the way for today's stars like Cynthia Cooper, Sheryl Swoopes, Rebecca Lobo, Lisa Leslie, Teresa Weatherspoon, Ruthie Bolton-Holifield and Chamique Holdsclaw to achieve widespread acclaim.

One of the landmark days in the growth of women's basketball came on March 6, 1977, when a college doubleheader at New York's Madison Square Garden drew 12,336 fans and national media attention. No. 1-ranked Delta State beat second-ranked Immaculata 79-62 in the nightcap, but what the fans went home talking about took place in the opener.

Carol Blazejowski, a 5-foot-10 forward who could drive to the basket or hit jump shots from anywhere on the court, scored 52 points as Montclair (N.J.) State beat Queens (N.Y.) College 102-91. At the time it was the most points scored, by a man or a woman, since the new Garden was built in 1968.

"The crowd, the excitement, it was all very stimulating. Not just for me but for the team. I couldn't believe it," said Blazejowksi, who went on to play for the 1979 World University and Pan Am Games U.S. teams, was a member of the 1980 Olympic team that boycotted the Games in Moscow and is now president of the WNBA's New York Liberty.

Blazejowski scored 38 of her points in the second half, when she made 17-of-21 shots from the field. When she left the game with 47 seconds remaining, she received a standing ovation and photographers rushed to catch her reaction. "It had to be the greatest thrill of my life," she said.

That performance, in the media mecca of New York, opened doors for the women's game that had been closed for many years, and boosted it on its way to its current prominence.

31. Bird, Magic Begin A Rivalry for the Ages

Earvin "Magic" Johnson and Larry Bird formed one of basketball's great rivalries, changing the face of professional basketball in the 1980s with their unselfish, team-first attitude and dedication to winning.

"Basketball is a game where no one player is more important than the team," said Johnson, who sparked the Los Angeles Lakers' "Showtime" offense that produced five NBA titles in the 1980s. "Both of us want to bring out the best in our teammates. We think the same way about the game," said Bird, who led the revival of the storied Boston Celtics franchise with three titles in the '80s.

Johnson and Bird met in one of the landmark games in college basketball history, the 1979 NCAA championship game in Salt Lake City that attracted major media attention because of the two superstars and raised the sport's public profile. "The buildup for the game was crazy," recalled Bird. "The idea of the two of us playing for the NCAA title had captured everyone's imagination."

Bird, who had elected to postpone signing with Boston so he could complete his final year of eligibility at Indiana State, had led the little-known Sycamores to an unbeaten record going into the title game. Michigan State, with Johnson in his sophomore year playing along with future NBA frontcourtmen Greg Kelser and Jay Vincent, had lost six games but had gotten better as the season wore on.

The game did not live up to its buildup, as a sore thumb and Michigan State's 2-3 zone defense caged Bird. After scoring 35 points and shooting 16-for-19 in the national semi-finals against DePaul, Bird could only manage 19 points and 7-for-21 shooting against the Spartans' front line of Johnson, Kelser and Vincent, all of whom would be first-round NBA draft choices. "I never saw him so far off," said Vincent. "He shot two over the basket."

Bird didn't use his injured thumb as an excuse, crediting Michigan State's defense. "We thought we had proved that we could beat every kind of defense, but we had never seen anything like that zone of theirs," he said. "I couldn't do anything at all against it. They did a really good job on me."

The Spartans jumped out to a 37-28 lead and extended it to 50-34 early in the second half. Indiana State pulled within six midway through the period, but could come no closer. Johnson scored seven of his game-high 24 points in the next five minutes and Michigan State pulled away to a 75-64 victory and the NCAA crown.

"What impressed me most about Larry came near the end, when we were celebrating," said Johnson. "He had his head in a towel, crying. Losing really hurt him, and that's the sign of a true competitor."

"I have always admired the way Magic handles himself," Bird would say many years later, after both had made their marks in the pros. "I feel he's the greatest all-around team player in basketball. I have always looked up to him because he knows how to win. Magic plays basketball the way I think you should play the game."

Johnson and Bird formed one of basketball's great rivalries, and helped spur the growth of basketball not just in the United States but worldwide.

32. Dr. J's Greatest House Call

Much of Julius Erving's pro career was a highlight film. After playing college ball at a time when dunking was illegal, Erving was unshackled when he turned pro and emerged as one of the game's high-flying innovators, carrying the torch from Elgin Baylor to Michael Jordan in the evolution of the game's aerial artistry. "I would never have had the visions I had if I hasn't seen Dr. J in his prime," said Jordan.

Erving won two titles with the ABA's New York Nets, where his spectacular presence went a long way toward keeping the struggling league alive long enough to finally effect a merger with the NBA. Upon joining the more established league, he turned the Philadelphia 76ers into championship contenders, finally teaming with Moses Malone to win the title in 1983.

Yet for all his success within the team framework, it was his individual play that created the legend of Dr. J. One of the most talked-about moments in basketball history came at the 1976 ABA All-Star Game, when Erving won a dunking contest by racing from one end of the floor, taking off from just inside the foul line and soaring to the hoop before slamming it down.

That was a dunking contest, however. What was his greatest play during a game? Picking a highlight of highlights is difficult, but many would point to a driving basket he made during the fourth quarter of Game 4 of the 1980 NBA Finals against the Los Angeles Lakers at the Spectrum in Philadelphia.

Erving had the ball on the right side, where he was guarded

by Mark Landsberger, a burly forward who had a size advantage but couldn't match Erving's quickness or leaping ability. Erving drove past him toward the baseline and then elevated toward the hoop.

Kareem Abdul-Jabbar, the Lakers' 7-foot-2 center, came over in the lane to try to block the shot. Erving, already airborne, brought the ball down and shifted his body behind the backboard to elude Abdul-Jabbar's outstretched arms. Then he somehow seemed to float just enough to his left, back toward the court, so he could hook his right arm toward the basket on the reverse side and lay it in.

As the crowd erupted in cheers, the players, Sixers and Lakers alike, could only admire what they'd seen. "Here I was trying to win a championship, and my mouth just dropped open," said Lakers guard Magic Johnson. "'He actually did that?' I thought, 'What should we do? Should we take the ball out, or should we ask him to do it again?' It's still the greatest move I've ever seen in basketball, the all-time greatest."

The "Baseline Move," as the play became known, helped the Sixers win 105-102 and even the series at two games apiece, although the Lakers went on to take the title in six.

33. Magic Fills In for the Big Fella

The Los Angeles Lakers held a 3-2 lead over the Philadelphia 76ers in the 1980 NBA Finals, but they were in trouble. Kareem Abdul-Jabbar had suffered a sprained ankle late in the third quarter of Game 5, and when doctors took a look at it after the game, they told him to forget about flying to Philadelphia for Game 6. Even recovery in time for a possible Game 7 was questionable, they said.

Abdul-Jabbar was the league's MVP and the Lakers' mainstay, their leading scorer (24.8 ppg) and rebounder (10.8 rpg) and the top shot-blocker (3.41 bpg) in the league. He had not missed a game all season, and Coach Paul Westhead was understandably worried about what effect Abdul-Jabbar's absence would have on his team—physically and psychologically.

The Lakers had gone through the regular season with Jim Chones, their starting power forward, doubling as Abdul-Jabbar's backup at center. But since the Lakers' best bench player was a guard, Michael Cooper, Westhead decided to try the unorthodox. He turned to his point guard, 6-foot-9 Earvin "Magic" Johnson, and told the 20-year-old rookie he was needed to play center.

Johnson had last played center three years earlier, when he was a senior in high school, but he embraced the challenge of filling in for Abdul-Jabbar, both physically and psychologically. When the Lakers gathered for the flight to Philadelphia for Game 6 and word spread that their team captain would not be joining them, Johnson took matters into his own hands. He planted himself into Abdul-Jabbar's customary front-row aisle seat, stretched out and pulled a blanket over his head, just the way Abdul-Jabbar normally did. Then he winked at Westhead, turned to his teammates scattered about the first-class cabin and announced: "Never fear, E.J. is here!"

Johnson's brashness immediately lifted his teammates' spirits. Then he backed it up with one of the greatest clutch performances in NBA Playoff history.

The ever-confident Johnson was grinning when he stepped into the center circle for the opening tip against hulking Darryl Dawkins, and the Sixers were taken aback. The Lakers scored the first seven points of the game and went up 11-4 before Philadelphia seemed to come out of shock. With Steve Mix coming off the bench and slicing unimpeded toward the basket, Philadelphia rallied to take a 52-44 lead in the second quarter before going into half-time tied at 60-60.

Reinvigorated after intermission, Los Angeles scored the first 14 points of the third quarter, but again Philadelphia fought back and closed the gap to 103-101 with five minutes to play. But Johnson rose to the challenge, scoring nine points down the stretch as L.A. outscored Philadelphia 20-6 to win 123-107 and wrap up the first of five NBA championships of the 1980s.

Johnson's stat line reflected his all-around dominance: 42 points, 15 rebounds, 7 assists, 3 steals and 1 block. It could not reflect the emotional impact he had in lifting the Lakers from uncertainty to the ecstasy of a championship.

After the game, Johnson looked into the TV cameras and sent a message to Abdul-Jabbar back in his home in Bel-Air: "We know you're hurtin', Big Fella, but we want you to get up and do a little dancin' tonight. This one's for you!"

34. Boston's Comeback Specials

For many years, the Boston Celtics and Philadelphia 76ers owned one of pro basketball's most spirited rivalries. After Bill Russell led the Celtics to eight consecutive championships, it was Wilt Chamberlain and the 76ers who broke the string in 1967. And for eight seasons, from 1980 through 1987, either Boston or Philadelphia represented the Eastern Conference in the NBA Finals.

Never was the Boston-Philly rivalry more intense than in 1981, when the Celtics, led by Larry Bird, staged one of the most remarkable repeated comebacks in basketball history against the 76ers and Julius Erving. Trailing 3-1 in the best-of-7 Eastern Conference Finals, the Celtics erased second-half deficits in three consecutive games to win the series, taking Game 7 by one point after winning the two previous games by two points each.

The teams had matched 62-20 records during the regular season, but Philadelphia had sent the Celtics to the brink of elimination by gaining a split of the first two games in Boston, then winning twice at home. Celtics GM Red Auerbach, for one, wasn't ready to throw in the towel. M.L. Carr of the Celtics recalled the way Auerbach addressed the team before Game 5:

"Red told us, 'Until they beat you one more time, they can't win a championship. They've got to beat you. And if you don't let 'em beat you one more time, you win it.' So we never thought of it that way—'Gee, we're down 3-1.' We thought, 'Red said they got to beat you one more time. Don't let 'em do it tonight.' You do that three times, you win it."

Nonetheless, when Boston fell behind 59-49 at half-time of Game 5 on its home floor, the situation looked bleak. Philadelphia led by six with 1:51 to play, but a block by Cedric Maxwell set up a three-point play by Tiny Archibald, then a steal and basket by Bird drew Boston within one. Another steal, this time by Carr, led to a pair of free throws, then another free throw by Carr closed out the scoring. Boston had scored the

last eight points to win 111-109 and stay alive.

Though stunned, the 76ers went home buoyed by the knowledge that they had beaten Boston the last 11 times the teams had met in Philadelphia. And when they opened a 12-point half-time lead, it appeared that Game 6 would make it 12 in a row. But once again Boston fought back, Maxwell leading the charge and finally hitting two key free throws as the Celtics won 100-98.

When the teams headed back up to Boston for Game 7, the spirits of the 76ers had to be sagging. But somehow they regrouped and broke in front, taking a 31-26 lead after one quarter and a 53-48 advantage at half-time. For the third game in a row, the Celtics were 24 minutes from elimination.

Philadelphia kept up the pressure and led 89-83 with 4:34 remaining. But from that point on, boosted by the fans at Boston Garden, the Celtics stopped the Sixers cold. Philadelphia got the ball 10 times, but came away from those 10 possessions with just a solitary free throw.

While Boston's defense was stifling the Sixers, its offense managed to produce eight points—the final two when Bird brought the ball up the left side, stopped at the foul line extended and took a page from Hall of Famer Sam Jones' book by going glass for an 18-footer and the game-winning basket with 1:03 to play. Philadelphia's Maurice Cheeks was fouled with 29 seconds left but made just one of two free throw attempts and Boston held on to win 91-90.

Never has a team put together three such comebacks against a quality opponent in consecutive, pressure-packed situations, as did the Celtics, who won Games 5, 6 and 7 by a total of just five points.

35. Jordan, Worthy Give Dean Smith His First Title

It was a tough spot for a freshman, but this was no ordinary freshman. So despite the presence of veterans like forward James Worthy and center Sam Perkins in his North Carolina lineup, it was a slender 6-foot-6 first-year named Michael Jordan whom Dean Smith turned to in the closing seconds of the 1982 NCAA championship game between North Carolina and Georgetown.

The game, which began with goaltending calls against Georgetown's 7-foot freshman center, Patrick Ewing, on North Carolina's first four baskets, was close throughout. The Hoyas led 32-31 at half-time, and neither team led by more than four points throughout the second half. A jumper in the lane by Eric "Sleepy" Floyd gave Georgetown a 62-61 lead with 57 seconds left, then North Carolina ran 25 seconds off the clock before calling a timeout.

Worthy, an All-American who had scored 28 points on 13-for-17 from the field, seemed the most likely candidate for the final attempt because if he didn't hit his shot, he might be apt to draw a foul. But Smith decided to use Worthy as a decoy and ran a play for Jordan instead.

Jimmy Black, North Carolina's point guard, faked a pass into the pivot, and when Floyd stepped back for a double-team, he swung the ball to a wide-open Jordan on the left side. "I was all kinds of nervous," Jordan said. "But I didn't have time to think about doubts."

Without hesitating, Jordan put up a 16-foot jumper that

went in with 15 seconds left, giving North Carolina a 63-62 lead. "I didn't look at the ball at all," said Jordan. "I just prayed. I had a feeling it was going in, but I didn't see it go in. That shot put me on the basketball map."

The Hoyas still had 15 seconds left to make something happen. Sophomore point guard Fred Brown brought the ball upcourt and looked to the left baseline for Floyd, a consensus All-American, but the North Carolina defense was keying on him and had shut down the passing lane. Brown next turned to pivot, hoping to get the ball into the low post to Ewing or the Hoyas' other big man, Ed Spriggs. But there was a cluster of bodies in the lane and Brown didn't want to risk an entry pass. With those options denied, Brown figured senior Eric Smith might be open on the right wing.

"I thought I saw Smitty out of the right corner of my eye," Brown said. "My peripheral vision is pretty good, but this time it failed me. It was only a split second, but that's all it takes to lose a game."

The player Brown thought was Smith turned out to be Worthy, and Brown's pass went straight to the North Carolina forward. Nobody in the crowd of 61,612 at the Louisiana Superdome, or among those watching on television, was more surprised than Worthy. "I thought he'd try to lob it over me or throw it away from me. I was surprised that it was right in my chest," said Worthy, who actually wasn't where he was supposed to be on the play.

"James had gone for a steal on a fake moments earlier and was out of position," said Smith. "He shouldn't have been where he was on the court, and it fooled Brown, and James went for the steal."

"I knew it was bad as soon as I let it go," Brown said. "I wanted to reach out and grab it back. If I'd had a rubber band, I would have yanked it back."

Worthy's steal enabled the Tar Heels to kill three seconds off the clock, and although Worthy then missed two free throws, Georgetown only had enough time left for a desperation heave that wasn't close. North Carolina had a one-point victory and Smith had his first NCAA title.

"This is one we'll always remember," said Worthy, who was chosen the Most Outstanding Player of the Final Four. "It was the one that made us and Dean Smith champions."

And it's one Brown will never forget, although he was able to put his miscue in proper perspective. "This is part of growing up," he said. "It was a great game. I loved playing it. I just wish the score was reversed at the end."

36. Charles Dunks Phi Slamma Jamma

They were the men of Phi Slamma Jamma, the fraternity of dunk, and they liked nothing better than to throw the ball down. "The team with the most dunks wins the game. That's our slogan," declared University of Houston coach Guy Lewis.

So how did the high-flying Cougars lose the 1983 NCCA championship game?

On a last-second dunk, of course.

North Carolina State, 25-10, was trying to become the first team to win an NCAA championship with a double-digit loss total. In their way was top-ranked Houston, 31-2, with a line-up better suited for the NBA than the NCAA featuring

Hakeem Olajuwon and Clyde Drexler.

"I've never seen anything like that in 16 years of coaching college basketball," N.C. State coach Jim Valvano said after watching Houston dunk Louisville 94-81 in the national semi-finals. "We'll try to handle their team by playing, shall I say, a slower tempo. If we get the opening tip [in the Monday night game], we may not take a shot until Tuesday morning."

Thurl Bailey of N.C. State scored the opening basket of the game on a dunk, then the Wolfpack concentrated on its deliberate offense while using a zone defense that sagged around the basket to try to short-circuit Houston's running game. The strategy limited Houston to just one dunk in the first half; settling mostly for jump shots, the Cougars shot just .313 and trailed 33-25 at the half.

Even with Drexler on the bench in foul trouble, Houston got untracked in the second half and outscored N.C. State 17-2 to move in front 42-35. Then Lewis took Olajuwon out for a rest and ordered his team into its slowdown, "locomotion" offense, which gave N.C. State the opening it needed. The change in tempo allowed the Wolfpack to regroup and took Houston out of its rhythm—the Cougars would get just four baskets the rest of the way. Valvano ordered his players to foul at every opportunity, taking advantage of Houston's weak free throw shooting, and the Wolfpack gradually came back and finally tied the score at 52-52 on a long shot by Dereck Whittenberg with 1:59 left.

After Houston freshman Alvin Franklin missed the front end of a one-and-one, N.C. State held the ball for a final shot. Whittenberg had the hot hand, but Bailey's pass to him was tipped away by Drexler. Whittenberg scrambled to recover the ball and heaved up a desperation, off-balance shot from 30 feet away that was off target, short of the rim.

That's when Lorenzo Charles, a 6-foot-7 sophomore who had spent much of the night trying to keep Olajuwon out of position, made the play of his life.

"I knew when Whit let the shot go that it was short," Charles said. "I didn't know where Hakeem was, just that he was behind me. I knew I was the closest one to the basketball."

Charles followed the arc of Whittenberg's shot, caught it in mid-air just in front of the basket and dunked it home with one second remaining. N.C. State had an improbable 54-52 victory and the championship.

"We figure the team with the most dunks will win," Oljauwon had said, echoing his coach's philosophy. And that's exactly what happened—Charles' shot gave North Carolina State the edge in dunks, 2-1, and Houston was beaten with its own favorite weapon.

37. Villanova's Perfect Game Beats Georgetown
Georgetown-Villanova for the 1985 NCAA championship looked like a classic mismatch. The Hoyas, featuring dominating center Patrick Ewing, were the defending champs, ranked No. 1 after losing only two games by a total of three points. Villanova, on the other hand, had lost 10 games during the regular season, with two of the losses coming to Georgetown.

"I'd have to put [the Hoyas] with the great San Francisco teams of Bill Russell and the great Kentucky teams, Alex Groza and that club," said Hall of Fame coach Lou Carnesecca, whose

St. John's team played both Finals clubs in Big East action and lost to Georgetown in the national semi-finals . "I'd also have to put them with the great UCLA clubs and the Indiana team (1976) that had five (future) pros. We tried everything, but when a club like Georgetown is performing at that level of proficiency, there's nothing you can do."

Nothing, that is, except play 40 minutes of near-perfect basketball, which is what Villanova did on April 1, 1985. The Wildcats set an NCAA Tournament record by shooting .786 from the field, 22-for-28. They took 10 shots in the second half and made all but one of them. To cap things off they sank 11 free throws in the final 2:11, icing the 66-64 upset victory. When it was over, Georgetown coach John Thompson had his players applaud the victors in the post-game ceremony.

"Any time you shoot that percentage," said Thompson, "you deserve the praise. You couldn't get much better."

Before the game, it had been Villanova coach Rollie Massimino who was lobbing the plaudits at the Hoyas and Ewing.

"Georgetown is as good a team as has ever been assembled, and that's because of Patrick," said Massimino. "He's the best to ever play college basketball. When it comes time to make the decision to win or lose in the last four minutes, he's involved in every single defensive play."

But Villanova was no stranger to good defense—its two regular season losses to Georgetown had come by scores of 57-50 and 52-50, the latter in overtime. And it had advanced to the championship game by beating Memphis State 52-45, the fourth time in five games it held an opponent under 50 points. So Massimino made sure his players weren't awed by the Hoyas' reputation. "I told all the kids to go to their rooms, sit for 15 minutes and tell themselves, 'You're not going to play to lose. You're going to play to win,'" said Massimino. "I told them, 'You can't play tentative; you can't play scared; you can't play not to lose. You're as good as the team you're playing tonight.'"

Or better.

The Wildcats shot 13-for-18 in the first half and went into intermission with a 29-28 lead, having kept the tempo at the slow pace they preferred. But if their first half was good, their second half was even better. Offensively, they shot 9-for-10. Defensively they limited Ewing to six points, for a game total of just 14, and blanked Reggie Williams, who had scored 10 in the first half. And with the game on the line, they made the foul shots they needed to win.

Harold Jensen's jumper from the right side with 2:36 to play gave Villanova a 55-54 lead and was the Wildcats' last field goal. They went into a delay game and forced Georgetown to foul, made 11 free throws and stayed in front till the finish.

The Hoyas had shot 55 percent from the field, yet were outshot by more than 20 percentage points. "It was frustrating," said Georgetown guard Harold Broadnax. "We were right in their faces (on defense) and they kept hitting and hitting."

Even the Villanova players seemed stunned. "They're definitely the better team. If we played 10 times, they'd probably win a majority of them," said Villanova's Ed Pinckney.

But they only played once when the title was on the line, and Villanova's near-perfect game resulted in a championship.

38. "God Disguised As Michael Jordan"

The legend of Michael Jordan was just beginning to be written when the Chicago Bulls faced the Boston Celtics in the 1986 NBA Playoffs. Jordan was so young back then, he was still Hair Jordan: photos from the game show him with neatly cropped hair.

To be sure, he's already provided glimpses of what was to come. He'd hit the game-winning jumper as a freshman to give North Carolina the NCAA championship over Georgetown, he'd won the Naismith and Wooden awards as the top college player in the nation two years later, he'd starred in the 1984 Los Angeles Olympics, and he'd captured the NBA Rookie of the Year award in 1985. Nike had even named a sneaker after him.

But he had suffered a broken foot early in 1985-86, an injury that shelved him for most of his second pro season. He wouldn't have come back at all that year if Bulls management had its way, but Jordan insisted on returning to action and helping his team secure the final playoff berth in the East despite a modest 30-52 record.

Boston, which had won a league-high 67 games during the season, easily won the opener at Boston Garden 123-104 despite Jordan's 49 points. It was a remarkable scoring effort in a losing cause, but it was nothing compared with what was next.

Chicago got off to a fast start in Game 2, which was also at the Garden, and then Jordan seemed to score every time Boston tried to come back. The Bulls led by as many as 10 points in the third period, but by the end of the quarter the Celtics had closed the gap to one at 84-83, despite 36 points by Jordan. Jordan scored 18 more points in the fourth quarter, and Chicago needed them all. Boston had edged in front by two points before Jordan was fouled attempting a three-pointer with 17 seconds to play. Jordan made both free throws—the league had not yet changed the rule giving a player fouled on an attempted three-pointer three foul shots instead of two—tying the score at 116-116 and sending the game into overtime.

"Michael was doing so much and so well, I found myself just wanting to stop and watch him—and I was playing!" said Bulls guard John Paxson.

Jordan tallied seven points in the five-minute overtime, giving him 61 and tying Elgin Baylor's NBA Playoff record set in 1962, and his trey put Chicago up 125-121 with 1:39 left. But buckets by Jerry Sichting and Danny Ainge tied the score for Boston, and Jordan, with the clock ticking down, missed a left side jumper that would have won it. Was he mortal after all?

Late in the second overtime, Jordan drove past Celtics center Robert Parish for a slam that gave him a Playoff-record 63 points, and kept the game tied. But Sichting broke the tie with a basket with 57 seconds left, and Boston won 135-131. Two nights later, the Celtics completed the series sweep, and seven weeks later they would be crowned NBA champions for the 16th time in franchise history.

But for one afternoon, Jordan had turned Boston Garden into his personal playground, making a lasting impression on none less than Larry Bird.

"I didn't think anyone was capable of doing what Michael has done to us," said the Celtic legend. "He is the most exciting, awesome player in the game today. I think it's just God disguised as Michael Jordan."

39. Bird Picks Pistons' Pockets

Put two players with the basketball skills and instincts of Larry Bird and Dennis Johnson on the floor at the same time and anything can happen. The Detroit Pistons found that out the hard way in the 1987 NBA Playoffs.

Bill Fitch, Bird's first coach with the Boston Celtics, perhaps described Bird's basketball instincts best when he said, "Larry's mind takes an instant picture of the whole court. He sees the creative possibilities." He also brings out the best in his teammates, including the versatile Johnson, whom Bird called the smartest player he ever played with.

The Celtics were the defending champions in 1987, but they were aging and weakened by injuries. The rising power in the Eastern Conference was the Detroit Pistons, with a strong guard trio of Isiah Thomas, Joe Dumars and Vinnie Johnson and a deep frontcourt. The Pistons were still a year or two away from achieving "Bad Boys" notoriety, but they were hungry and eager to knock the Celtics from their perch.

The teams split the first four games of their best-of-7 Eastern Conference Finals, but while Boston's wins were struggles, Detroit's came more easily, including a 26-point rout in Game 4. Riding that momentum, the Pistons matched the Celtics stride for stride in the pivotal Game 5 in Boston Garden and took a 107-106 lead into the final minute.

A driving shot attempt by Bird was blocked by Dennis Rodman, then a young, un-tattooed Pistons reserve, but went out of bounds off a Boston player. All the Pistons had to do was run the final five seconds off the clock and they'd be heading home with a chance to close out the series, so coach Chuck Daly tried to call a timeout to make sure his team had all its ducks in a row. But the ball was at the far end of the court and none of the Pistons heard him amidst the bedlam of the Garden, so play continued.

Thomas was handed the ball and looked to throw it in. While guarding his man, Bird managed to sneak a peek at Thomas just as the Detroit captain looked at teammate Bill Laimbeer. Anticipating the toss into the post, Bird raced into the passing lane and got there before the ball could reach Laimbeer's outstretched hands.

"I saw Laimbeer open down low and I automatically headed toward him," Bird said. "At the last instant, I reached in and just barely tipped it. I was trying to get control of the ball while practically falling out of bounds on the left baseline and I was just getting ready to throw it up when I saw a blur, a white jersey streaking down the lane."

The blur was Dennis Johnson, who had been guarding his man out above the foul line but instinctively cut to the basket when he saw Bird go for the steal. "If D.J. hadn't made the cut down the lane, we would have been dead ducks," said Bird. "I couldn't get my feet positioned right. I didn't really want to have to shoot it, but there wasn't much time left, so I needed to have D.J. react perfectly. A lot of players would still be standing there."

Instead of being forced to attempt a hurried, off-balance shot, Bird fired a pass to Johnson who laid it in with one second to play for a 108-107 win. Although Detroit took Game 6, Boston came back home and won Game 7 to maintain its domination in the Eastern Conference for another season.

40. Keith Smart Lifts Indiana Over Syracuse

Steve Alford was "Mr. Basketball" in Indiana, one of the most honored and revered high school players in the history of that hoops-crazy state. When he decided to attend Indiana University, visions of NCAA championships danced in many a Hoosier head.

But it took an unheralded junior college transfer named Keith Smart, who wasn't even recruited out of high school in Louisiana, to make those dreams come true for Bob Knight's team and its legions of followers in 1986.

Knight had only begun accepting juco transfers two years earlier, when he recruited Smart and Dean Garrett. Garrett, a 6-foot-10 center, gave the Hoosiers a shot-blocking presence and went on to a lengthy pro career in Europe and the NBA. Smart's quickness and ability to penetrate and break down a defense complemented Alford's brilliant spot-up shooting.

Smart was a late bloomer. He was only 5-foot-3 as a junior in Baton Rouge, La., and while he grew to 5-foot-9 as a senior, a broken wrist kept him from attracting college recruiters. "I had the spirit," Smart said. "I just didn't have the body."

So after high school he spent a year working at McDonald's, playing pickup ball around the city and growing to 6 feet tall. The coach at Garden City Community College in Kansas agreed to give him a tryout and liked what he saw, and after two years there Smart's quickness attracted Knight's interest and he transferred to Indiana.

The Hoosiers' road to the 1986 title game wasn't an easy one. They trailed Auburn by 14 points before rallying to win an early-round game, then fell behind LSU by 12 points in the second half before coming back to win the Midwest Regional final 77-76 on a late basket by Rick Calloway. The national semifinal against UNLV was a track meet, the Hoosiers barely outrunning the Runnin' Rebels 97-93 to move into the championship game against Syracuse.

Syracuse's aim was to stop Alford, a two-time All-American and Indiana's career scoring leader. The Orangemen employed a variety of defenses, including a box-and-one with 6-foot-5 Howard Triche guarding the 6-foot-2 Alford, but the Indiana star still managed to shake free and nail four three-pointers in five attempts for a 34-33 half-time lead.

Alford, who scored a game-high 23 points, hit three more treys in the second half before the defensive harassment wore him down and held him scoreless for the final four minutes. But when a defense concentrates that hard on one player, it's taking risks elsewhere, and the man who made Syracuse pay was Smart, who was playing the title game in his home state at the Superdome in New Orleans.

He repeatedly drove to the basket for layups or short jumpers, scoring 12 of his team's last 15 points to finish with 21 for the game. After a free throw by Triche gave Syracuse a 73-70 lead with 38 seconds left, Smart raced the ball upcourt and scored on a short jumper. On the ensuing inbounds pass, Smart immediately fouled Derrick Coleman, stopping the clock with 28 seconds to play. Coleman, a future All-American and NBA star, was just a freshman, and he missed the front end of the one-and-one.

Indiana got the rebound and Smart brought the ball over the midcourt line. He first looked for Alford but found him covered, so he sent it into the post to Daryl Thomas. As Coleman and Triche collapsed on him, Thomas passed it back to Smart who was cutting toward the left baseline. He put up a 16-footer that went through with five seconds on the clock, beating Syracuse 74-73 and giving Knight his third NCAA title.

41. Magic's "Junior, Junior Sky-hook" Beats Boston

Magic Johnson delved into the repertoire of Los Angeles Lakers teammate Kareem Abdul-Jabbar for the shot that beat the Boston Celtics in the key game of the 1987 NBA Finals, the rubber series between those two arch-rivals who defined pro basketball for the better part of the decade.

The sky-hook was Abdul-Jabbar's trademark, the cornerstone of his game from his schoolboy days at Power Memorial in New York through three NCAA crowns at UCLA and on to the NBA, where he would become the league's all-time leading scorer. Johnson, whose playmaking ability added years onto Abdul-Jabbar's career and made the latter stages far more productive, took pride in adding something to his game each year. He improved his free throw shooting, extended his jump shot to three-point range and developed an array of post-up moves—including a hook shot borrowed from the master, which he used to drive a stake through the Celtics' collective heart.

The Lakers and Celtics of the 1980s formed one of sports' greatest rivalries boasting two of its most appealing stars, Johnson of the Lakers and Larry Bird of the Celtics, two team-oriented players with burning passions to excel and to win. Because they played in opposite conferences they only met twice during the regular season, but each was a nationally televised event that attracted media coverage from around the world. They did meet three times with the NBA championship at stake, the Celtics winning the 1984 Finals in seven games, the Lakers taking the title in six games in 1985. The 1987 NBA Finals was the rubber match, the third and final time these two great teams, and individuals, would contest a crown.

The Lakers took a 2-1 lead in the series, the home team winning every game. That made Game 4 at Boston Garden a vital one for the Celtics, or else they faced the daunting prospect of being down 3-1 with two of the potential remaining three games in Los Angeles. Boston responded by building a 16-point half-time lead, and still had a seemingly comfortable eight-point margin with three minutes to play.

But the Lakers rallied and closed the gap to 103-102 with 30 seconds to play, then took the lead as Johnson fed Abdul-Jabbar on a pick-and-roll. Bird responded by coolly canning a three-pointer to put the Celtics back on top 106-104 with 12 seconds left. Abdul-Jabbar was fouled on the next possession and made the first free throw but missed the second, which would have tied the score. But the rebound bounced out of bounds off Boston, giving the Lakers one more chance.

Following a timeout called by Lakers coach Pat Riley, Johnson took the inbounds pass near the left sideline. He thought about shooting a jumper, but 6-foot-11 Kevin McHale stood in his way. So he dribbled to his right, with McHale in pursuit and Bird and Robert Parish moving over to help out. Before they could converge on him beneath the foul line, however, Johnson launched a running hook shot that sailed through and gave L.A. the lead with two seconds left to play. After a

timeout, Bird somehow managed to shake loose for a jumper but it was off target as the horn sounded, and the Lakers had a pulsating 107-106 victory. The Celtics survived for one more game, but the Lakers wrapped up the championship by winning Game 6 in Los Angeles 106-93.

"That was my junior, junior sky-hook," said Johnson, when he was asked in the Lakers locker room to describe the winning shot. Down the hall, in the Boston room, Bird just shook his head. "You expect to lose to the Lakers on a sky-hook," he said. "You don't expect it to be from Magic."

42. Shootout on Causeway Street

When Larry Bird and Dominique Wilkins squared off in Game 7 of the 1988 Eastern Conference semi-finals between the Boston Celtics and the Atlanta Hawks, it was like a scene from a Western movie. "It was like two gunfighters waiting to blink," said Kevin McHale, a teammate of Bird on that Celtics squad. "There was one stretch that was as pure a form of basketball as you're ever going to see."

The old Boston Garden on Causeway Street served as the O.K. Corral for this Game 7 shootout, and the stakes were high. The Celtics were an aging team that had been to the NBA Finals four years in a row, winning twice, and were hopeful of one more shot at a ring. The Hawks were a team that had made the playoffs nine times in 11 years but had never gotten out of the first round, and they knew their window of opportunity wouldn't remain open much longer, either.

The shootout featured two of the premier scorers in NBA history. Bird's shooting ability and fundamental excellence made him the idol of purists, while Wilkins was the high-flying Human Highlight Film whose aerial acrobatics excited a new generation of fans. Bird, 6-foot-9, had a one-inch height advantage over Wilkins, but 'Nique was by far the better jumper. Although both played the small forward position, they did not always match up against each other. Wilkins usually guarded Bird, but when Atlanta had the ball, the lanky 6-foot-11 McHale had the assignment of trying to contain Wilkins.

The shootout, simmering all game, heated up with the score tied 86-86 and 10:26 to play in the fourth quarter, when the season was on the line for both teams. "They each put their team on their back and said, 'Let's go,'" said Hawks coach Mike Fratello. Bird's jumper with 10:03 to play touched off a barrage of nine points in less than two minutes. But the Hawks wouldn't let the Celtics pull away and Wilkins' basket tied the score again at 99-99 with 5:57 remaining.

Bird scored 11 points after that, including a go-ahead basket with 3:34 left and a stunning three-pointer over Wilkins at the 1:43 mark. Wilkins responded by scoring 11 points of his own following Bird's go-ahead basket, including seven in the game's final 1:31, to keep his team in the chase.

"He hit that three-pointer with my hands dead in his face—what can you do?" Wilkins said later. "I thought I did everything I possibly could on the offensive end, and defensively I was all over him. He hit the big shots, I hit the big shots."

In the end, Wilkins was put in a position where he had to miss. Boston led 118-115 with one second left and Wilkins at the foul line for two free throws. After he made the first, he knew Atlanta's only hope was if he intentionally missed the

second and one of his teammates could get the rebound for a put-back to tie the score. Wilkins carefully took aim and did exactly what he wanted, banging the free throw off the rim, but Boston center Robert Parish tipped the rebound to teammate Dennis Johnson and time expired. Boston had the win and the series, and while the Celtics would be eliminated by Detroit in the Conference Finals, the Hawks would not make it past the second round of the playoffs for the rest of the century.

Wilkins finished the game with 47 points, including 16 in the fourth quarter, having shot a stunning 19-for-23 from the field. "That's as hard as I've ever worked to guard a guy who wound up with 47," said McHale.

Bird, meanwhile, wound up with 34 points on 15-for-24 shooting, getting 20 of his points in the final 10:03. "He wanted it," said Hawks assistant coach Don Chaney, who had been a teammate of Bird's late in his own playing career. "He wanted the ball and he came through. That's what superstars are made of."

43. Jordan Hits "The Shot"

It is best-known as "The Shot," and it changed the courses of two NBA franchises, the Chicago Bulls and Cleveland Cavaliers, one for better and one for worse.

When the teams met in the first round of the 1989 NBA Playoffs, both had high hopes. The Bulls had been building for several years around Michael Jordan, and with Scottie Pippen and Horace Grant on board, were beginning to have title aspirations. The Cleveland Cavaliers, meanwhile, had assembled one of the NBA's finest young teams with a nucleus of Brad Daugherty, Larry Nance, Mark Price and Ron Harper and felt this might be their year since they had won 57 games during the regular season, 10 more than Chicago.

It was a rematch of their series from 1988, when Chicago won the deciding Game 5 107-101. This time, however, Cleveland had the home-court advantage and had beaten the Bulls six straight times during the regular season. Nonetheless, before the playoffs Jordan brashly predicted that Chicago would win the series.

Chicago stole that home-court advantage by winning the opening game of the best-of-5 series in Cleveland 95-88. But after each team won a home game, the Bulls turned the advantage back over to Cleveland by failing to close out the Cavs in Game 4, dropping a 108-105 overtime decision.

Momentum seemed to be on Cleveland's side at it headed back to the Coliseum in Richfield, Ohio, where the Cavs had compiled a 37-4 record during the regular season including 22 wins in a row. It seemed unlikely that Cleveland would lose twice on its home floor in a span of 10 days.

The game was tight from start to finish, coming down to a spectacular final play. With three seconds left on the clock, Cleveland held a 100-99 lead but Chicago had the ball following a timeout.

The Bulls set up to inbound the ball from midcourt on the right sideline. The Cavs knew Chicago would try to get the ball into Jordan's hands right away, so they set up a double-team with Nance joining Craig Ehlo, their best defensive guard, to try to deny him the ball. Jordan came out from the lane, running directly at Nance, then cut to his left and beat Ehlo to the

inbounds pass near the right sideline, above the top of the circle.

He took one dribble to his left, then another, moving into the key just above the foul line. Nance was behind him and out of the play, while Ehlo was struggling to keep pace. What happened next is perhaps the ultimate example of hang time. Jordan went up for his jump shot while gliding slightly to his left, and Ehlo cut in front of him from right to left and made a running leap to attempt a block, his hand in Jordan's face. Jordan seemed to hang suspended in mid-air, his right hand under the ball in shooting position, his left hand on its side to guide it, as Ehlo reached the apex of his leap and then sailed past him on the way down. It was only once Ehlo had hit the floor that Jordan, on his way down but still at least a foot off the court, released his shot. The 16-footer went through at the buzzer. When he landed Jordan pumped his fist in celebration and leaped into the air once again, a reaction that was caught by the national TV cameras and replayed again and again.

"I put my credibility on the line by predicting we would win. I had to make the shot," said Jordan. "There's nothing like it in the world, that feeling of having the ball in the final seconds as the clock slowly ticks off, going up and hanging in the air and then hitting the shot. Man, that is total control. There's just no other feeling like it. None."

Following the 101-100 victory, Chicago beat New York in six games to advance to the Eastern Conference Finals, where they were ousted by the Detroit Pistons in six. Beating the Cavaliers for the second year in a row, and this time by taking the decisive game on the road, was an important step in the team's growth into a champion. Two years later the Bulls would win the first of their six championships in the 1990s.

Cleveland, meanwhile, has never been the same after losing Game 5 to the Bulls for the second straight year. The Cavs dipped to 42-40 in 1989-90, a drop of 15 games, and once again were unable to get out of the first round of the playoffs, this time bowing to the 76ers in five games. Cleveland failed to make the playoffs in 1990-91, has a 14-26 record in its postseason appearances since then and never reached the NBA Finals.

44. Hill to Laettner Beats Kentucky

Duke's bid to repeat as national champion seemed doomed after Sean Woods drove past Bobby Hurley and scored on a 12-foot bank shot to give Kentucky a 103-102 lead with 2.1 seconds left in overtime of the 1992 East Regional final.

It had been a remarkable game between two of the nation's most successful programs and high-profile coaches, Rick Pitino of Kentucky and Mike Krzyzewski of Duke. The Blue Devils missed a chance to win in regulation when Hurley's driving jumper with two seconds left rimmed out, then the two teams slugged it out in OT like a pair of heavyweights exchanging haymakers in a 15-round title bout.

John Pelphrey hit a three-pointer for Kentucky at 3:58 of overtime, Hurley answered at 2:40. Pelphrey sank two free throws at 2:17, Christian Laettner matched them at 1:53. Laettner's running eight-footer edged Duke in front 100-98 with 31.5 seconds left, Jamal Mashburn one-upped him for Kentucky by converting a three-point play after being fouled on a driving layup, giving the Wildcats a one-point lead with 19.6 seconds left. But Mashburn fouled out on the next play

and Laettner converted both free throws at 14.1 seconds to put Duke back in front 102-101. Kentucky called a timeout with 7.2 seconds left to set up Woods' basket, after which Duke called a timeout of its own for one final play.

Duke's championship reign seemed about to end, but Coach K would have none of it. "No matter what situation we were in, he was confident," said Duke forward Grant Hill. "We all came to the huddle still burned by the shot that put Kentucky up, and Coach K had a plan already mapped out on the board. He said, 'Okay, here's how we win the game: Grant, you throw to Christian here and he'll take the shot to win.' And that's exactly how it happened."

When the teams took the floor, Laettner braced himself at the foul line, his back to the basket. Once Hill was handed the ball under the basket at the far end of the court, the 6-foot-11 Laettner—three inches taller than any Kentucky player on the floor—spread his arms to give his teammate a large target.

Hill fired a baseball pass some 75 feet, his aim perfect. Pelphrey, one of two Wildcats covering Laettner, thought about trying for an interception but backed off, not wanting to foul. Laettner caught it with his back to the hoop, and the clock on the scoreboard—and the one in his head—started ticking. He quickly faked to his right, then took one dribble and made a spin move to his left. Pelphrey was off balance and Deron Feldhaus, the other Kentucky defender, was left anchored on the floor as Laettner rose up and shot a 16-foot, right-handed jumper that sailed through the net as time ran out.

"Totally incredible—I didn't even see it go in," said Laettner, who was engulfed by a swarm of Duke players and fans at the climax of what had been a perfect shooting night: 10-for-10 from the field, 10-for-10 from the foul line.

Krzyzewski saw it, or didn't see it, the same way. "As soon as he let it go, I knew it was going in," he said, "but I didn't see it because everyone jumped in front of me."

Then he spoke about the competitive zeal of Laettner, who went on to become the first collegian to start in four Final Fours and set an NCAA Tournament career scoring record with 407 points. "Christian has this hunger for competition that I've never seen in anybody else," said Krzyzewski. "He's never afraid to make the play, be it a shot, rebound, pass, block, whatever. He wants to be there when the game is decided.

"You've heard of guys who burn to win? This guy's got a forest fire inside him."

45. The Dream Team's Dream Game

The best basketball team of all time? Few would argue against the original Dream Team, which represented the United States at the 1992 Olympics in Barcelona.

Start with Michael Jordan, arguably the greatest player of all time. Add Magic Johnson and Larry Bird, past their primes perhaps, but still two of the greatest team players in history. At center were two great 7-footers, David Robinson and Patrick Ewing. At power forward, two more perennial all-pros, Karl Malone and Charles Barkley. The NBA's all-time leader in assists and steals, John Stockton, shared time with Magic at point guard. Two-way standout Scottie Pippen and offensive stars Chris Mullin and Clyde Drexler could play either small forward or big guard, while the lone collegian on the squad, Christian

Laettner, was available as an emergency center or big forward.

"Dream Team is a lot of name to live up to," said Chuck Daly, the Hall of Famer who led the Detroit Pistons to a pair of NBA championships and was head coach of the Olympic team. "But if anything, the 1992 U.S. Olympic men's basketball team exceeded all hopes and expectations. I think we truly gave the world a glimpse—only a glimpse, since we were never seriously challenged—of what basketball can be like at its highest level."

Indeed, the Dream Team won its Olympic opener against Angola 116-48 and its eight games by an average of nearly 44 points. In the gold medal game it fell behind a team from Croatia led by future NBA players Toni Kukoc, Dino Radja and Drazen Petrovic 25-23 midway through the first half but regrouped to lead by 14 at half-time en route to a 117-85 win.

The Dream Team's most intense competition came a week before the start of the Olympics, during a closed, intra-squad scrimmage witnessed only by a few officials from USA Basketball. The 20-minute practice, played with referees, a scoreboard and a clock to simulate game conditions, may well have been the greatest basketball game you've never seen.

Jordan and his Chicago Bulls teammate, Pippen, were on one team with Robinson, Malone and Laettner. Johnson and Bird, longtime rivals, headed the other team along with Ewing, Barkley and Mullin. Stockton and Drexler were nursing injuries and did not play.

Johnson recalls the game vividly, if not happily, because he made the mistake of tugging on Superman's cape—or in basketball terms, engaging in a little trash-talking with Jordan. "We were leading 14-2 and I let Michael know about it," said Johnson. "I told him he'd better get into the show or it's all over. I don't know why I said that. All of a sudden he said, 'I'm bringing us back,' and he did. Single-handedly."

Jordan scored one basket, then another, then another. He called his own number, waving away teammates so he could go one-on-one against Johnson, then fed an open teammate if they tried to double-team him. It wasn't long before Jordan's team caught up, and eventually edged in front for a 40-36 win.

Johnson could only admire what he had witnessed. "I pushed him to his level, the highest that he can go," he said. "I didn't like it at the time, but at the same time, I did enjoy it. It was really something. Your mind says you want to stop him, but the other side of it says you have no chance. He just starts jumping over you. Every time I looked up, he had his shoes on my No. 15. It was as good a demonstration of basketball as I've ever seen in my life, everything a basketball player could want."

Jordan summed it up this way: "I'm not sure people will ever see the true greatness of this team because we may never be pressed to that level, but a little of it came out today and it was really a beautiful thing."

46. Sheryl Swoopes to the Hoop

Sheryl Swoopes was the 1991 National Junior College Player of the Year at South Plains (Texas) J.C., but when she tried out for the 1992 U.S. Olympic team and had to compete against older players with experience in international competition, she was cut.

"I was just a baby at it," she said. "I was very young, and honestly, I had never really played against so many great, talented players."

Instead of getting discouraged, she went about improving her game. "There's always something every day you can get better at, things you can work on," she said. "Of course, you get tired, and it's really hard to get out there and keep going all the time. But you have to remember, in the back of my mind, all I'm thinking of is '96, gold medal . . . I just made myself come out every day and pushed myself."

Swoopes transferred to Texas Tech and led the Lady Raiders to a 58-8 record over two seasons, winning the Southwest Conference title both years. A 6-foot forward, she averaged 21.6 ppg and 8.9 rpg in 1991-92, then revved it up a notch to 28.1 ppg (second in the nation) and 9.2 rpg in 1992-93. She capped her college career by setting 11 NCAA Tournament, Final Four or Championship records in a brilliant postseason as she led Texas Tech to the 1993 NCAA championship.

Swoopes carried her team to the Final Four in Atlanta, scoring 33 points against Southern Cal, 30 against Washington and 36 against Colorado. Before the national semi-finals, Swoopes was named the Division I Player of the Year and the Naismith Award winner as the top player in the nation. But if those honors represented any extra pressure, she shrugged it off and scored 31 as Texas Tech upset top-ranked Vanderbilt 60-46.

Those performances only hinted at what was to come. On April 4, Swoopes set an NCAA championship game record by scoring 47 points as Texas Tech won its first title 84-82 over Ohio State. The Buckeyes led 55-54 before Swoopes scored 16 of her points in the final 10-1/2 minutes as Texas Tech took control. She scored a pair of baskets and a three-point play to put Texas Tech in front 80-73 with 58 seconds left, and four free throws down the stretch nailed down the victory.

She'd proven herself a champion, but one goal remained unfulfilled: the Olympics. She turned down an offer to play in the men's USBL and went to Italy, where she averaged 23 ppg for Bari, then returned to play for the U.S. in the 1994 World Championships and the 1994 Goodwill Games.

Her Olympic dream was about to come true. Swoopes was selected for the USA Basketball Women's National Team that practiced together and compiled a 52-0 record in the year leading up to the 1996 Olympics. That earned her a spot on the Olympic team, and she averaged 13.0 points, 3.5 rebounds and 3.9 assists and shot .606 from the field in leading the United States to the gold medal in Atlanta.

She went on to star in the WNBA as one of the league's early marquee signings, but only after the birth of her son Jordan (named after Michael Jordan). She missed most of the league's inaugural season while pregnant, but joined the Houston Comets two weeks after Jordan was born and played a supporting role as Cynthia Cooper led the Comets to the league's first championship.

She then teamed with Cooper to lead the Comets to two more titles, earning All-WNBA honors in 1998 as she averaged 15.6 points, 5.1 rebounds and 2.48 steals per game and in 1999 as she averaged 18.3 points, 6.3 rebounds, 4.0 assists and 2.38 steals per game. On July 27, 1999, Swoopes became the first woman in WNBA history to post a triple-double when she had 14 points, 15 rebounds and 10 assists in the Comets' 85-46 rout of the Detroit Shock.

47. Paxson's Three Gives Chicago the Three-Peat

John Paxson of the Chicago Bulls was a role-player who played his role to perfection at the end of Game 6 of the 1993 NBA Finals. Then again, he'd had plenty of practice.

"I just caught the ball and shot it, as I have my whole life," said Paxson, who grew up with a basketball in his hand, since his father and brother played in the NBA.

"I've been playing basketball since I was 8 years old, and I've shot like that in my driveway hundreds of thousands of times. It was just reaction."

He wasn't in his driveway this time, however, but at America West Arena in Phoenix. The Bulls, seeking their third consecutive NBA crown, led the Phoenix Suns three games to two, but they had watched an eight-point fourth quarter lead in Game 6 slip away and were trailing 98-94 with 2:23 left, facing the prospect of having to play a Game 7 on Phoenix's home court against a team that was riding momentum.

But the Suns could not close it out. In fact, neither team could score until Michael Jordan grabbed a rebound for the Bulls and went coast to coast to cut the lead in half with 38 seconds left. Phoenix ran as much time as it could off the clock but could manage only a Dan Majerle airball, so the Bulls regained possession and called a timeout with 14.1 seconds to play.

The obvious strategy was to get the ball to Jordan and let the greatest player in the game work his magic. But Chicago coach Phil Jackson was keeping his options open. He put three guards on the floor, Paxson and B.J. Armstrong joining Jordan, plus forwards Pippen and Horace Grant—all good shooters who could handle the ball.

What unfolded was the kind of play coaches dream about, all five players touching the ball and staying one step ahead of the defense, ending with an open jumper by one of the game's best pure shooters. Jordan inbounded to Armstrong, took a return pass and brought the ball upcourt, then surprised the Suns by feeding to Pippen, who found Grant near the baseline. But Grant was mired in a shooting slump and didn't want to risk even a short jumper in traffic, so as the defense converged on him he kicked it back out to Paxson, spotted up behind the three-point arc.

"Once Paxson got the ball," said Jordan, "I knew it was over."

It was catch and shoot, just what Paxson does best.

"I got a clean look at it," he said. "There was no one around me and it felt good when it left. I just caught the ball and shot it—as I have my whole life."

Paxson's three-pointer sailed through the net with 3.9 seconds remaining and gave the Bulls a 99-98 victory and the three-peat.

"It was like a dream come true," said Paxson. "You're a kid out in your driveway, shooting shots to win championships. When you get down to it, it's still just a shot in a basketball game. But I think a lot of people could relate to that experience."

Phoenix Suns coach Paul Westphal was among those who could. A fine shooter and prolific scorer as an NBA player, Westphal could appreciate what the moment felt like for Paxson.

"I just had to smile to myself," he said, despite the disappointment of losing. "It's a shot every kid dreams about. John Paxson got to live that dream out."

48. Another No. 23 Wins A Title for North Carolina

David Thompson was one of the great leapers in basketball history. A 6-foot-4 guard/forward who was nicknamed "Skywalker," Thompson led North Carolina State to the 1974 NCAA title and then averaged 22.1 points per game in a pro career cut short after nine seasons by drug abuse and injuries.

In 1994, he was sitting with his niece, Charlotte Smith, who played for the North Carolina basketball team, prior to the 1994 women's Final Four at the Richmond (Va.) Coliseum.

"Maybe two decades later, it will be your niece who wins a national title," Smith suggested to her uncle.

Sure enough, she did.

The 6-foot Smith grabbed 23 rebounds, an NCAA Women's Final Four record, and scored the game-winning basket as North Carolina edged Louisiana Tech 60-59 for the title in what ranks as the most exciting women's championship game in NCAA history. The 23 boards matched her uniform number, a number she chose not in honor of that other noted Tar Heel, Michael Jordan, but for her mother, Etta, who wore No. 23 when she played high school ball.

Louisiana Tech had taken a 59-57 lead with 14 seconds to play on a 16-foot jumper by Pam Thomas. North Carolina's Tonya Sampson attempted a driving layup, but she missed the shot and the scramble for the rebound resulted in a jump ball. North Carolina retained possession with four seconds to play thanks to the alternating possession arrow.

Sylvia Hatchell, the North Carolina coach, called a timeout to sketch out a final play, then took another timeout. But when the Tar Heels put the ball in play, it was knocked away by Louisiana Tech and went out of bounds with just seven-tenths of a second left on the clock. It was just enough time for a tip-in or a catch-and-shoot, but nothing else.

As Stephanie Lawrence took the ball to throw it in, the Louisiana Tech defenders clogged the middle to prevent Smith or 6-foot-5 center Sylvia Crawley from getting a shot around the basket. Sampson and point guard Marion Jones tried to shake free on the perimeter, but they also were covered.

So Smith moved out from the lane to the right side and found an open area just beyond the three-point line. The Lady Techsters didn't follow her outside, since Smith was known for her inside game and not her long-distance shooting. When Lawrence saw Smith find some open space, she knew this likely would be the best opportunity the Tar Heels would get.

Lawrence's pass found Smith, who caught it and went up for the shot without hesitation, knowing there wasn't enough time to make any kind of move toward the basket. Her jumper came from just beyond the three-point arc, the buzzer sounding soon after the ball left her right hand and before it nestled through the net, giving North Carolina the victory and its first-ever NCAA women's basketball title.

"I just prayed and shot. Then the mob hit me," said Smith, who was quickly swallowed by her teammates in a wild on-court celebration.

And so, 12 years after another No. 23—Jordan—had hit a game-winning shot to give North Carolina's men an NCAA title, and 20 years after her uncle, David Thompson, had led N.C. State to the championship, Smith had beaten the clock to give North Carolina the women's crown.

49. Jordan Goes Out In Style

Leave it to Michael Jordan to finish in a blaze of glory.

Arguably the greatest player in basketball history, Jordan ended the second phase of his NBA career with a flourish, faking Utah's Bryon Russell out of position and then sinking the jumper that gave the Chicago Bulls the 1998 NBA title.

The shot was reminiscent of how Jordan had burst upon the national scene with a similar basket 16 years earlier, when as a freshman he hit the jumper that gave North Carolina the 1982 NCAA crown over Georgetown.

Jordan's final basket came in a game he would rather not have played.

The Bulls had taken a 3-1 series lead over Utah, but had muffed a chance to end it at home when the Jazz posted an 83-81 victory in Game 5. "I would have loved to have won it here at home," Jordan said after that game. "That would have been a great scenario."

"We blew our opportunity," added Jordan, "but this has happened to us before. It's a duplicate situation as in 1993." Five years earlier, Chicago had missed a similar chance to close out the Phoenix Suns in Game 5 at home, then had barely managed to eke out a one-point win in Game 6 in Phoenix on a late three-pointer by John Paxson.

Now they headed for Salt Lake City and a Game 6 that also would go down to the last shot.

Utah gave Chicago all it could handle in the game and moved in front 86-83 when John Stockton nailed a three-pointer with 41.9 seconds left. The prospect of a Game 7, with momentum on Utah's side, suddenly was very real, just as it had been in Phoenix five years earlier. But Jordan wouldn't let it happen.

He took the ensuing inbounds pass and drove the lane, scoring easily to cut the deficit to one as just 4.8 seconds ticked off the clock. That meant Utah could not run out the clock and Chicago didn't have to foul to get the ball back. Utah tried to get it to Karl Malone in the low post, but Jordan sneaked in on a double-team and made the steal. Instead of calling a timeout to set up a final play, Chicago pushed the ball upcourt, preferring not to give Utah a chance to set its defense.

Jordan moved the ball into the frontcourt with Steve Kerr on the left wing. He knew Stockton wouldn't leave the Chicago marksman unguarded, which meant he'd be able to go one-on-one against Russell until someone else could come over from the weak side to double-team. Without hesitating, Jordan made sure the help would not arrive in time.

He stutter-stepped as Russell reached for the ball, then drove past him toward the middle of the court. Russell was off balance, and Jordan made him more so by using his left arm to brush him away and create enough open to go up for his jumper from 18 feet out. It sailed through with 5.2 seconds remaining, giving Chicago an 87-86 win and its sixth title in eight years.

"When Russell reached, I took advantage of the moment," said Jordan, who finished with 45 points and won the NBA Finals MVP award for a record sixth time. "I never doubted myself. I never doubted the whole game."

"That was the best performance I've seen in a critical situation and critical game in a series," said Bulls coach Phil Jackson. "Michael is one of the great sharks. When the game is on the line, he wants to win."

50. UConn Upsets Mighty Duke

Duke appeared to be in a class of its own as the 1999 NCAA tourney began. The Blue Devils not only had Elton Brand, the college Player of the Year who was destined to go No. 1 in the NBA Draft, but three other players who would join Brand in the first half of the first round, something no other school had ever achieved. Duke had lost just once during the season and was eager to capture its third NCAA title of the 1990s, and stamp itself as college basketball's team of the decade.

Connecticut, meanwhile, was rated by most experts as the second-best team in the nation, a notch below the Blue Devils. Coach Jim Calhoun's team, however, had several things going for it. It had the support of an entire state, which had rallied around the UConn women's team during its unbeaten 1995 season. It was looking to settle an old score, having lost to Duke in the 1990 East Regional on a Christian Laettner buzzer-beater. And it was out to show it could do better than three previous Elite Eight appearances in the '90s.

Duke intimidated most opponents, but not the Huskies. Calhoun was not afraid to have his team run with the Blue Devils; rather than worry about matching up with Duke's players, he wanted Duke to worry about containing UConn's most athletic players, forward Richard Hamilton and guards Khalid El-Amin and Ricky Moore. Meanwhile, Connecticut forward Kevin Freeman helped center Jake Voskuhl double-team Brand and kept him from dominating the game, limiting him to a quiet 15 points and 13 rebounds. "I never knew where the double-team was coming from," Brand would say later.

UConn kept its poise even though Duke jumped in front early, and were only down 39-37 at the half. It was going to be close to the end, and with 4:07 left the score was tied at 68-68. During a timeout, El-Amin later related, "Me and Richard (Hamilton) looked at each other and said, 'It's winning time.'"

Hamilton, who finished with a game-high 27 points, sank two free throws and a three-pointer to give UConn a five-point lead, but a free throw by Chris Carrawell and a three-pointer by Trajan Langdon closed it to one. El-Amin hit a floater over Brand, William Avery offset that with two free throws, and after a missed shot by El-Amin, Duke had the ball with 20 seconds left. That's when the tenacious Moore made the defensive stop of his life. "I heard Coach K (Duke coach Mike Krzyzewski) yelling to Trajan, 'Go get the ball and take him,'" said Moore. "I loved that. Him against me. All I had to do was get one stop. I started smiling because I knew he wasn't going to score. I knew it was him against me, and I knew my will to win would prevail."

Langdon faked, trying to find a path to the basket or room for a jumper, but Moore stayed with him and finally forced Langdon into a traveling violation with 5.4 seconds left. Duke quickly fouled El-Amin, and his two free throws gave the Huskies a 77-74 advantage with 5.2 seconds left. Rather than call a timeout to set up a final three-point try, Langdon took the inbounds pass and raced upcourt, trying to get free for a shot. But before he could do so he lost his balance and the ball skittered away, and the Blue Devils' hopes went with it.

Connecticut finally had won the big prize, and it had done it by beating the top-ranked team in the country. "The kids wanted Duke," said Calhoun. "They wanted to play the best and beat the best—and they did."

Chapter 18

Basketball Arenas

Celtic Pride
The Boston Garden's famous parquet floor, built out of oak scraps for $10,000 in 1946, came to stand as a symbol of the Celtics' dominance.

By Charles Salzberg

Dr. James Naismith did not have spectators in mind when he invented basketball. It was supposed to be a strictly private affair, a recreational activity between the football and baseball seasons for 40 student teachers.

However, basketball quickly gained in popularity and spread well beyond the confines of small gymnasiums, moving into other venues, including armories, meeting halls, social clubs, stadiums, and eventually into large arenas. Many of these arenas have traditionally housed other events, like circuses, ice hockey, boxing, rodeo, concerts, and, today, even football.

The Early Days: Gymnasiums

In the first game ever played at the Springfield, Massachusetts YMCA in December 1891, 18 players were jammed together on the floor of the basement gym, cluttered with all kinds of athletic equipment. The playing surface was about 35 feet wide and 50 feet long. At opposite ends of the gym peach baskets were suspended from the balcony, courtesy of janitor "Pop" Stebbins, whose job it was to retrieve any successful shots from the basket.

Years later Dr. Naismith recalled the venue where his brain-child was played: "I remembered the dim lights that were set in the ceiling, the great mass of apparatus that was shoved into the corners, the walls lined with clubs, dumbbells and wands, and the gallery that ran completely the length of the floor."

At first, any number of players could be on a team, and this sometimes created crowd control problems on the court, as Naismith revealed in his book, *Basketball: Its Origin and Development*, written almost 50 years after his inaugural game. "Ed Hitchcock Jr., the physical director at Cornell, had a class of about one hundred students. Following our idea, he divided this class into two teams and threw up the ball for a game. The result was that when the ball went to one end of the gym, all of the players would rush after it. Someone would get his hands on the ball and would return it to the other end of the gym, and back across the floor would dash those one hundred students. On the second day, Hitchcock decided that this plan would not do, as there was grave danger of serious damage to the building. He decided that fifty men on a side were two many for basketball."

Eventually, Naismith and others came to a more reasonable compromise that took into consideration the size of the building in which they were playing. "Five men were suggested for small gymnasiums, and nine men for the larger ones. In 1894, the

rules set the number of men on a team at five when the playing space was less than eighteen hundred square feet, at seven when it was between eighteen hundred and thirty-six hundred square feet, and at nine when the floor was larger. In 1895, the number was fixed at five, unless otherwise mutually agreed upon. It was definitely settled in 1897 that a basketball team should consist of five men." Naismith well may have added "women," for they, too were getting into the act, with the first woman's game played in a gymnasium at Smith College, in Northampton, Massachusetts, in 1893.

Basketball spread from the northeast, the south, and then westward, but the venues remained much the same, as did the inherent drawbacks of playing in such small spaces. Ron Newlin, the former director of the Indiana Basketball Hall of Fame, described a typical game played in a gymnasium between two local Indiana teams, one from the Crawfordsville YMCA and the other from the Lafayette YMCA:

"The playing floor took up the entire room. There was a running track above the floor where you would have watched the game. There was a potbelly stove in one corner, so you probably would want to avoid chasing a ball into that corner. Just as so frequently the spectators would be in the balconies behind the basket watching the game, the hometown fans would help out a little bit by reaching through the railing and swatting away the other team's shots or guiding the home team's shots into the basket. In later years backboards were not created so much to give players something to bank the ball off of as it was to prevent spectators from goaltending."

Due to the relatively loose rules of basketball, the gymnasium itself became an unplanned participant in the game, sometimes even acting as a sixth defender. Often, shots couldn't be taken from the corners because of the overhanging oval track. Players were allowed to bounce the ball off the walls and the ceilings, and in some gyms, where the backboard was attached to the wall as opposed to being suspended from the ceiling or balcony, a player might use the wall as a springboard, jump against it, then launch himself upward, toward the hoop, to shoot the ball or, if he were skillful enough, dunk it.

Since these gymnasiums were built for other purposes, many of the buildings had roof supports in the middle of the floor—the YMCA in Trenton, New Jersey, had two steel pillars smack in the center of the floor—gym equipment pushed up against the walls, and there might even be a potbelly stove in a corner, used to heat the room. In one Pennsylvania gym, hot steam pipes lined the walls and players risked being seriously burned if they happened too close. One former player, Fred Cooper, recalled that Temple College's court in Philadelphia was long and narrow and that there was a large boiler at one end of the court. "If the ball did not drop," he said, "we knew we had scored." A smart coach might (and would) create plays that used these obstructions, having players bounce the ball off them, as if there was another player on the court.

Courts came in different shapes and sizes. Naismith wrote, "In 1894, the rules specified that there must be a well-defined line around the playing area at least three feet from the wall or fence. The boundary line naturally followed the contour of the gymnasium walls, which in many cases had projections to accommodate stairways or offices. Many courts were of irregular shape, frequently being wider at one end than the other. The team that played on the narrow end was therefore handicapped. In 1903, a clause was inserted in the rules stating that the boundary lines must be straight. Later the rules specifically stated that the court must be a rectangle.

"As the game was originally designed to be played on any court, there was no regulation size, the only stipulation being that the larger the court, the greater the number of players. In 1896, when a basketball team was definitely cut to five men, the rules contained a provision that the court should not exceed thirty-five hundred square feet of playing space. This size court was official until 1908, when the maximum court was set as 90 feet long and 55 feet wide. The width of the court was reduced to 50 feet in 1915."

It wasn't until the 1916-17 season that end walls were ruled out of bounds, which effectively shortened the career of those players who regularly used those walls as a launching pad to score.

Moving On: National Guard Armories and Social Halls

Eventually, due to exceedingly rough play, basketball was banned from most YMCAs. As a result, the game was forced to move to other available venues, which included National Guard armories and social halls, many of which were gas-lit. Since these auditoriums, some capable of holding as many as 1,500 or more, were rented, spectators had to be charged entrance fees. Thus, being forced to leave YMCA gyms resulted in opening up basketball to a larger audience, which in turn meant the larger arenas were in greater demand.

The quality of these venues differed widely. Some were quite good, offering plenty of room for the game and for spectators, while others offered only the bare minimum standards. Some of the baskets varied in width by as much as two inches, while backboards, either made of wood, glass or wire, were sometimes set as far away from the hoop as a foot, making it almost impossible to bank a shot in.

Playing conditions, whether in an armory or a social hall, were often far from perfect from the point of view of the players. Chuck Chuckovits, who played for the Toledo Jim White Chevrolets, complained about the terrazzo floor in the Civic Auditorium in Toledo, saying, "It was slipperier than hell. [We] would get shin splints from running on that floor."

Playing in armories, which were the preferred venue because they could hold so many spectators, sometimes produced unexpected and potentially comical complications. For instance, J. Emmett " Flip" Dowling, who played for Cohoes in the New York State League, recalled "we actually had to join the National Guard to play in the armory. We never went to drills or anything like that, and when the season was over they gave us a discharge."

The first documented professional game was most likely the one held in Trenton, New Jersey, on November 7, 1896. The Trenton Basketball team, formerly the Trenton YMCA team, played the Brooklyn YMCA's team at Trenton's Masonic Temple Hall, a three-story building in downtown Trenton. On the street level there were several stores; the second floor held several Masonic lodge rooms, and on the third floor there was a large social hall with a ceiling high enough to accommodate

the two basketball goals. As Robert E. Peterson points out in *Cages to Jumpshots*, it's very possible that the hall was illuminated by electric lights (as opposed to gaslights), as the city was in the process of being wired for electricity.

For the game, portable baskets were moved into the hall. In addition, an 8-to-12-foot chicken-wire mesh fence with two doors at either end was built around the court by Fred Padderatz, a carpenter and Trenton part-time manager. Legend has it he came up with the idea after a local sportswriter wrote of an exhibition game, ". . . these fellows play like monkeys and should be put in a cage." As famed referee of the time, Marvin A. Riley, wrote, "The Trenton's conceived the idea that the cage would make the game faster by stopping all out-of-bounds delays." And, after the game was completed, Riley reported that the cage "did make the game faster and more enjoyable for the spectators."

There was good reason for a cage in those days, because the rules allowed the team that first touched the ball after it went out of bounds to retain possession. If a wild pass or a missed shot went down a stairwell, or onto a balcony, players from both teams could and would race after it, running through anyone who might be in their path. As Naismith pointed out, "It was not uncommon to see a player who was anxious to secure the ball make a football dive for it, regardless of whether he went into the apparatus that was stored around the gym or into the spectators in the bleachers. Lloyd Ware, one of the boys who played on an early team of mine, takes great pleasure when in a jovial mood, in exhibiting a scar that he got when he dived for the ball and came into contact with the sharp corner of a radiator.

"One other incident that I remember distinctly was a game played in a gymnasium with a balcony. Early in the first half, the ball went into the gallery, and immediately the players from one team scrambled for the narrow stairway, crowding it so that they could make little speed. Two of the players on the other team boosted one of their mates up until he could catch the lower part of the balcony, swing himself up, and regain the out-of-bounds ball."

Others argued that the real reason for "cages" (hence the term "cagers" to describe basketball players) was to protect the players from the fans. The latter could get pretty rowdy, sometimes even going so far as to burn opposing players' legs with cigarette butts.

For whatever reason, Padderatz's concept caught on. Courts across the country were enclosed with wire meshing, or rope, or nylon. As William Scheffer reported in the *Reach Guide*, "Basketball is seen at its best when played in a wire cage of regulation size and the fans of New York [where they weren't using wire-mesh cages yet] have not witnessed basketball at its best."

By the late 1920s, cages had been outlawed, although occasionally you could still find games being played under these conditions in smaller towns well into the 1930s.

Barnstorming

As basketball grew in popularity professional teams began barnstorming the country. If they were lucky, they managed to book games in a spacious armory or a large social hall. But this wasn't always the case and many times they found themselves playing in rather odd venues.

The Oswego Indians, also known as Basloe's Globe Trotters, which traveled the northeast during the 1912-13 season, experienced the ups and downs of playing in all manner of small town social halls and armories, some of which were simply large community rooms lit by kerosene lamps. One of the finest armories they played in was in Fond du Lac, one of the few in that area where the court was enclosed in a cage—in this case, a three-foot wooden fence covered with advertising posters, a la modern day baseball stadiums. What a comedown it must have been then, when they later found themselves playing a game in a schoolroom, to a packed audience of 40 spectators!

Some teams were forced to play their games in unusual, not to mention highly unlikely, places. Moe Spahn, for instance, who played for a variety of semipro teams after he graduated from CCNY, even recalled playing in a fire station after the firemen pulled their engines out and set up an improvised court.

Buddy Jeannette, who played for the White Horses-Colonels, recalled another odd occurrence: "One day we were supposed to play a New York-Penn League game in Hazleton, Pennsylvania. In those days, to find the gym you drive into town and you look for the biggest building. We drove up to this bar and I got out of the car and ran inside and said to the bartender, 'Hey, we're supposed to play a basketball game in this town today. Can you tell me where it is?' He said, 'This is the place.' I look around and there are tables all over the room.

"So we went in and got dressed, and when we came out to play they had shoved all the tables back. They had a basket on one wall, and on the other side they let down a basket that had been drawn up to the ceiling. The floor was maybe 70 or 80 feet long. The referee went out to the middle of the court and drew a big round circle, and at each end he marked off 15 feet for the foul lines. Then they let a net down on the side where the people sat at the tables. And when the game began, the damnedest fight you ever saw started. That was a real education."

New Century, New Rules

As basketball rolled into the 20th century, professional leagues began to proliferate and the rules of the game and under what conditions it should be played became more codified. In the *Reach Official Book of Basketball Rules of 1903-04*, as played by the National League of Professional Basket Ball Teams of the United States, arenas had to certain stipulations, including the installation of actual cages built around the court, the innovation introduced by Fred Padderatz in Trenton almost a decade earlier.

Rule I

The Floor

All National League championship games must be played in a hall sufficiently large (and clear of posts or other obstructions) to allow of the placing of a cage of the regulation size. Slippery floors must be rosined on demand of either team's captain.

Rule II

The Cage

The cage must be sixty-five feet long and thirty-five feet wide. The wire screen must be no less than eleven feet from the floor and be kept in good repair. The corners of the cage must be round (under no circumstances can a floor be more than five

feet short in either length or width, and then only by two-thirds vote of Managers). Should any Manager find it compulsory to complain to President that any cage is in poor condition he (the President) should order Secretary to write to said Manager to repair said cage before the next League game, which order must be obeyed or said Manager fined for negligence.

Rule III

Light

The playing space must be illuminated to the satisfaction of the referee, and should any of the floors be poorly illuminated and complaint made by visiting Manager, the President should order the negligent Manager to better light up said floor or be fined at least twenty-five dollars ($25.00) for neglecting to do so when ordered by the President.

In addition, backboards were to be 4 by 4 foot wire screens, and the rim of the basket was to extend twelve inches from the backboard.

Extra-Added Attractions

It didn't take long for clever promoters to realize that they could piggyback events, thereby drawing more people and maximizing the space, not to mention swelling the coffers. As a result, basketball games were hooked up with dances; most times the game was first, then the dance. As player Flip Dowling recalled, "A group of fellows who called themselves the Elm Club used to run dances in the Catholic Union Hall, which had been an armory . . . and every Friday night they'd have a basketball game and a dance."

In Philadelphia, games were scheduled at the Musical Fund Hall, the Auditorium, and at the Broadwood Hotel, as well as other dance halls in the area. The game became part of the dance hall's promotion, either as the main attraction or the preliminary to the dance. Sometimes there would be dancing both before and after the game, with management treating the floor with resin when necessary. Again, the conditions were often less than ideal, as described by New York Celtics' guard Johnny Beckman: "The smoke was so bad, it was impossible to see."

The Philadelphia Sphas (South Philadelphia Hebrew Association,) forerunner of the Philadelphia Warriors, were owned and coached by Eddie Gottlieb. The team played many of its games in the marbled ballroom of the Broadwood, sometimes in front of as many as 3,000 fans who lounged in comfortable upholstered seats. Gottlieb, a brilliant promoter and entrepreneur, promised "a fight in every game, guaranteed." And so players like Moe Goldman and Chick Passion made it a point to pick fights with opposing players, just to fulfill Gottlieb's guarantee. One Spha, Gil Fitch, was also a bandleader, and after the game he would quickly change out of his uniform and into his tuxedo and take his place at the head of the band.

In the 1930s basketball also made its debut on legitimate theater stages. The Kate Smith Celtics (yes, that Kate Smith—the singer) played in the huge Hippodrome theater, in New York City, and the Brooklyn Jewels took to the court on the 80 by 40 foot stage of the Brooklyn Paramount Theater, where Jewels manager, Eddie Wilde, took credit for boosting attendance from 1,500 on a normal movie night to 5,000 when his team played there. And in Albany, Sammy Kaplan, who played

for the Kate Smith Celtics, recalled running up and down on a stage court between a scheduled movie and a vaudeville bill headlined by Red Skelton.

In Whiting, Indiana, during the 1930s, Rex Williams, owner of the Hoosier Theater, often booked basketball games as warm-up entertainment before a Hollywood film. A typical ad of the period, run in the *Whiting Times*, read, "See the 'Ball Tossers,' featuring the Oklahoma Oilers world champion professional exhibition of fast and furious playing that will put you on the edge of your seat breathless with excitement. Their entire bag of trick plays, lightning speed and dazzling brilliance is shown in a style that emphasizes the stellar caliber of this champion team. Whether you are a dyed-in-the-wool basketball enthusiast or not, you will get a slant on this popular sport that will surprise you."

Basketball player Robert Dietz, who played for the Indianapolis Kautskys (named for owner Frank Kautsky, a grocery store owner by trade), recalled one of the first games he played in. "The gym in Sheboygan had a stage on one end. People sat on the stage and jumped up and down. Well, the supports for the goal were on the stage, so when they jumped, the goal swayed. So you not only had to play against your opponents. You had to play against the crowd, as well."

Black Basketball: The Rens and The Globetrotters

The Renaissance Casino in Harlem was owned and operated by William Roche. One day in 1922 he was approached by Bobby Douglas, a native of St. Kitts, Jamaica, who coached and played for the Spartans, a team of all black players. The Spartans played at the Rockland Casino at 155th Street or the 369th Regiment Armory; Douglas wasn't happy with either of those sites and wanted a place that his team could call its home court. "They had just built the building," Douglas explained later, "and it wasn't going so good. And I told him if you take me there you'll get some good, good business." Roche was interested, but only if Douglas would agree to rename his team the Renaissance, which he believed would help promote his dance hall. "Now who in the hell wanted to name a team Renaissance?" Douglas thought, but he agreed to the terms and the Spartans became the Renaissance and began playing at the Casino, giving Roche 40 percent of the admissions. Tables were moved out and portable goals were wheeled onto the dance floor of the high-ceiling ballroom, making a small court somewhere in the neighborhood of 60 feet by 35 feet. The musicians' bandstand was on one side and on the other there was a wooden barrier surrounding the dance floor. "It was," recalled William "Pop" Gates, one of the Rens' star players, "a very slippery floor. They had baskets that they put up before every ball game and markers they put down for the foul lines and so forth. The spectators were seated at tables in loges on the second tier and in boxes on the third tier. That was supposed to be an elite area . . . The ballroom had a high ceiling, so you didn't have to worry about your shots. All you had to worry about was running into that hard wooden barrier around the floor because it had sharp edges. Sometimes when the game got rough, the guys would be flying over that barrier into people's laps."

John J. O'Brien Jr., who played for the Brooklyn Visitations,

described the unusual crowd. "The fans were the wealthiest black people in Harlem, dressed, believe it or not, in tuxedos. A good-looking crowd—handsome women, good-looking guys—and they loved the basketball game, but they loved to get the game over for dancing afterward."

Games were played before, between, and around the breaks of some of the most famous bands of the period—including Duke Ellington, Cab Calloway, Count Basie, Jimmy Lunceford, and Benny Goodman.

On Thanksgiving the Renaissance, now known as the Rens, would play their arch-rival, the Sphas and the lines would start forming by five o'clock in the evening. "If you didn't get there 'round about seven," said Douglas, "you had a tough time getting in." With as many as 2,000 spectators crammed into the Casino, Douglas put on a preliminary game at 7:30 between two teams of local kids, followed by a band performance, or perhaps a boxing exhibition. Then, at 9:30, with the crowd chomping at the bit, the Rens would face the Sphas.

Meanwhile, in 1926, on Chicago's South Side, the Savoy Ballroom—a carbon copy of the legendary Savoy in Harlem, which had been the inspiration for Benny Goodman's "Stompin' at the Savoy"—opened to disappointing crowds. The business manager of the black basketball team that represented the Giles Post of the American Legion had an idea that he thought might boost business for the struggling nightspot. "You're right in the middle of a sports-minded area," he told the owner. "You oughta cash in on that." The owner took the bait and the next thing he knew he had an all-Negro team led by ex-football star Dick Hudson and known as the Savoy Big Five, who played their games to a crowd anticipating the upcoming performances by such musical greats as Cab Calloway and Peg Leg Bates.

Unfortunately, Hudson was having trouble booking games throughout the Midwest, as promoters balked at scheduling games against an all-Negro team. In an attempt to raise the sagging fortunes of the team, Hudson got together with his friend, Walter Ball, a former all-star hurler with the Negro National League's Chicago American Giants, and they decided that if they hired a white promoter and manager they might be able to book more games and bring in more money. They settled on a short, squat, Jewish, English-born, cigar-smoking businessman/promoter named Abe Saperstein, offering him a fee of $100 plus 10 percent of all the bookings. Saperstein renamed the team Saperstein's Harlem Globetrotters, then enlisted his tailor father to create new uniforms for his team, swathing them in red, white and blue.

Unfortunately, despite the new name and new uniforms, fans did not flock to the Savoy to see the Globetrotters. And so, while the Savoy booked another hoped-for crowd-pleaser— roller skating—Saperstein hit upon another idea for his team— barnstorming.

In the ensuing years, the Globetrotters played all over the country, often appearing before overflowing crowds in venues like Chicago's Soldier Stadium, New York's Madison Square Garden, Pasadena's Rose Bowl, San Francisco's Cow Palace, and the Palais des Sports in Paris, France. In Los Angeles, the Globetrotters played before a crowd of 36,256, and in an after-

noon/evening double-header, they drew a total of 35,548 fans in Madison Square Garden. But Saperstein's team was not choosy. They also played at far less vaunted arenas, some of them decidedly makeshift, ranging from high school gymnasiums to armories, to social halls and even a swimming pool—drained, of course.

Over the years, of course, the Globetrotters have expanded their playing field to the rest of the world, and although they no longer play all comers—rather settling on regular patsies like the old Washington Generals—they are still capable of playing the odd venue every now and then. For instance, this reminiscence from a recent look at the Globetrotter Memories page on the Web: "During a promotion with a local grocery chain, our Advanced Ambassador, James 'Jumbo' Bacon took over the store! With *Sweet Georgia Brown* theme music pumping from the PA system in-between the color commentary from Jumbo, the store and its customers were taken into the world of the Harlem Globetrotters. In-between announcements, Jumbo made small work of the store: dribbling down the aisles, shooting jump shots into the shopper's grocery carts, committing a turnover near the poultry freezer. The promotion ended with Jumbo slam-dunking the ball into the bread baskets! Shopping will never be the same for those lucky people who experienced a moment in the Harlem Globetrotter world!"

A Giant Step: From Armories To Arenas

As professional leagues proliferated and fan popularity rose, games began to be played in actual arenas built especially for spectacles like the circus or rodeo, or other sporting events like hockey. In New York City, there was the Madison Square Garden. Tex Rickard, primarily a boxing promoter, was the principal operator of Madison Square Garden, which at the time was a rundown building located at 25th Street in Manhattan, in an area called Madison Square. Unfortunately, the conditions for playing basketball there were less than perfect. Teams complained about the fishnet enclosure around the court (the management promised to switch over to the more accepted wire cage, but evidently never did) as well as the slippery floor, on which players, especially visiting teams who weren't used to the surface, had a hard time standing upright. Another problem with the Garden was that often, too often, games were arbitrarily cancelled, usually because another event, like the circus or a bike race, had been booked. Naturally, the home teams, like the Whirlwinds, would then have to scamper about looking for an alternative site, usually places like the 69th Regiment Armory, or Brooklyn's Prospect Hall, which didn't particularly please opponents or fans.

Spotting the rising popularity of basketball and other sporting events, Rickard pushed to have a new Madison Square Garden erected. In 1925, the first of two reincarnations of Madison Garden was opened on Eighth Avenue between 49th and 50th streets. Capable of seating more than 18,000, it became a primary home for boxing, featuring heavyweights like Jack Dempsey. In addition to boxing, the Garden was also home for track meets and special events, like wrestling, dog shows, rodeos, conventions, six-day bike races and horse shows, as well as ice hockey, and now and then a handful of professional basketball games.

It wasn't until the late 1930s, however, that Ned Irish, a sportswriter for the *New York World-Telegram* and part-time publicist for the New York football Giants, having realized that college basketball had become too big for the gym, approached the Garden management about renting it out to present a slate of games between college teams. Garden management was obviously impressed enough by Irish's idea that they allowed him to book their arena without putting up a cent. Instead, they cut themselves in for a larger than usual percentage of the gross.

The Beginning of the Modern Era: The Birth of the NBA

By the 1940s, professional basketball leagues as we now know them were proliferating. Many of the teams were located in smaller cities and the arenas were often smaller than those available in big cities like New York and Chicago. In the 1941-42 season the Fort Wayne Zollner Pistons (named after Fred Zollner and his piston making business) played their first game at the Fort Wayne North Side High School gymnasium. As recalled by Carlisle Towery, a former All-American at Western Kentucky, "The floor at the North Side gym was small, and I think the arena only held about 4,000 people. And it was full just about every ball game—exhibitions, as well as league games."

On June 6, 1946, 11 northeastern arena owners, 10 of whom had ice hockey franchises either in the National or American Hockey Leagues, met in New York City with the aim of forming a professional basketball league encompassing 11 cities: New York, Boston, Detroit, Toronto, Philadelphia, Providence, Cleveland, Pittsburgh, Washington, St. Louis, and Chicago. This move was purely economically motivated, since their idea was to use their arenas on nights that were empty of other events, thereby optimizing their investments. Among those meeting were Walter Brown of Boston and Al Sutphin of Cleveland. At this time, along with hockey, the Ice Show was the major attraction for their arenas. They were well aware that Madison Square Garden was packing fans in to watch college double-headers promoted by Ned Irish; smart business men all, they wanted a piece of the roundball action. They chose attorney Maurice Podoloff, who at the time was president of the American Hockey League, as their new league's president.

Thus was born the Basketball Association of America. It already had a competitor in the National Basketball League, which included much smaller cities like Fort Wayne, Sheboygan, and Rochester. In fact, two NBL teams, the Rochester Royals and the Fort Wayne Pistons, had played the first exhibition of professional basketball in Toronto in front of 12,000 Canadians jammed into Maple Leaf Gardens. They could hardly be called fans, because most of them had never actually seen a professional basketball game before; according to Pistons general manager Carl Bennett, the fans were eerily quiet, most likely because they didn't know exactly what they were watching.

Most of the teams in the NBL played in relatively small arenas. The Baltimore Coliseum seated 4,000; Rochester's Edgerton Park Sports Arena held 5,000; Syracuse played in the State Fair Coliseum, a good distance from the city, where 7,500 could be accommodated; Washington's Uline Arena listed its capacity as 8,000; Tri-Cities played in the Wharton Fieldhouse, in Moline, with a capacity of 6,000; and the Minneapolis Lakers could accommodate 10,000 at the Auditorium, although they had to use other local courts, too. Only the Indianapolis team, which used the Butler Field House with 17,000 seats, could match New York or Boston in seating capacity.

The Anderson Packers played at the Wigwam, where, as former player Howie Shultz recalled, "we drew well. The Wigwam might have held about 3,500 people, but there were probably about 4,000 people that would come out to our games. And those fans were so close to the floor. It was an intimate environment, and a tough place for opposing teams to come in and do well. The fans were very vocal." Former Packer Ed Stanczak also recalled the Wigwam fondly: "I think our fast-break offense created a real spirited atmosphere in there. We'd hit those 100-point games, and the fans would just love it. There was a real enthusiasm for it. The fans were so close that members of other teams would be taking the ball out of bounds, and the fans would get right up in their ears and yell 'Boo!' loudly. Make no mistake about it. Those fans loved their Packers."

In 1948, five players from the University of Kentucky, including Ralph Beard, Alex Groza and Wah Wah Jones, won the gold medal in the London Olympics. When they returned to the States, they borrowed $30,000 from the NBA and the city of Indianapolis and formed their own team, renting the Butler Fieldhouse for $800 a night. "That," said Beard, "was considered the greatest floor in the league at that time. And the fans really embraced us. Whenever we'd play Minneapolis, or Anderson, or Fort Wayne, we'd pack that Butler Fieldhouse— 15,000 fans. Boy, we were really in the tall cotton then. We were rolling. By the end of our first year in the league, we had paid off our $30,000 debt to the city; we'd paid ourselves the generous salary of $5,000 each for five months, we'd given ourselves a $5,000 bonus each, and had $28,000 in the bank to boot." Unfortunately, this euphoria was not to last long, since Beard and others on the team were accused of fixing games when they were at Kentucky and subsequently were banned from the league.

On September 28, 1952, the Fort Wayne Pistons, who had been playing in a high school gym, opened the spacious Allen County War Memorial Coliseum, which held just under 10,000 fans. However, when the Coliseum was booked for the Fort Wayne Komets hockey team, various musical performances including folks like Gene Autry, Holiday on Ice exhibitions, or the American Bowling Congress National tour, the Pistons found themselves once again having to find alternate arenas. One of these was the local Armory, which guard Slater Martin found less than ideal. "The floor was built on concrete and so it was just as hard as playing on concrete, except there's a floor there," he recalled. "That wasn't easy when you fell, because it didn't give."

Martin also recalled playing in the North Side gym, which presented other problems, especially for superstar George Mikan, who dominated the league. "They used to get on George wherever he went. Like in Fort Wayne, they found out Mikan didn't like smoke, so everybody came to the game in this

little North Side gym and filled the place with smoke. They closed all the windows and you couldn't even see. They were puffing smoke in there all afternoon."

Martin also commented on the hazards of playing in small gyms or armories when it came to fan behavior. "I had them pull the hair on my legs. But there's always a cure for things like that. We'd take the ball out, see, and since there wasn't much room between you and the fans, they could reach out and pull the hair on your legs. But the next time down the court, you'd just have a guy stand in front of him and then he'd move away real quickly and you'd hit the guy with the ball right in the face and that was over with."

Sometimes the fans became an integral part of the game—and its outcome—because of the way the arenas were set up. Johnny Kerr, who played for the Syracuse Nationals and for a long time held the "Iron Man" title, recalled one particular incident. "I can remember playing in Madison Square Garden and I'm getting ready to shoot a free throw and all of a sudden the basket starts shaking like hell, it's moving, going around in circles. The ref says, 'Shoot the ball. You got ten seconds.' I say, 'The basket's moving.' They look up and sure enough some guy in the balcony is wiggling that thing, the guide wire, and the basket's moving like hell."

Many teams found themselves homeless when the large arenas they played in were booked for other events. The Knicks, for instance, when the circus or the rodeo or the dog show was in town, had to move from Madison Square Garden on 49th and Eighth to much smaller quarters in the 69th Regiment Armory. Sweetwater Clifton, the ex-Globetrotter who helped to break the color line in the NBA, had an interesting theory as to why the Knicks didn't dominate the way he thought they should have. "The reason why I think we never did win a championship was because when I was there every time we'd get ready to play in the playoffs they would switch us from the Garden to the Armory. It was because the circus or the rodeo came to town. I think they had some kind of contract with the Garden. I think we'd have won the championship a lot of times, maybe three, if they'd kept us in the Garden, because that was our floor and there we were fast and we were good."

And the sharp-eyed shooting Celtic Hall of Famer Bill Sharman offered this theory as to why shooting percentages suffered in those days. "In Baltimore, we used to play in a roller skating rink. In Syracuse, we played in an old building at the fairgrounds that had a leaky roof, a warped floor, and very little heat. They had very few basketball arenas as they do today and most of them had poor lighting, all kinds of different, inadequate floors, bad temperatures, etc. Many were used for hockey and we would play right over the ice with no insulation except for the basketball floor itself. Suffice to say, with cold, stiff hands and fingers, it certainly didn't help the shooting touch and percentages."

Legendary Arenas
Boston Garden

Over the years, there have been many arenas that have become major parts of basketball folklore. One that tops the list is certainly Boston Garden, home of the Celtics. Tex Rickard, the New York promoter, planned to mass-produce Madison Square Garden, building carbon copies in six major cities. He began in Boston, erecting the Boston Garden on top of North Station, the hub of the Boston and Maine Railroad. (Larry Bird once commented, "I thought it was pretty neat that the railroad station was below and the gym was up above.") It took less than a year to build the Garden, and it was christened on November 17, 1928, with a boxing match between Honeyboy Finnegan and Andre Routis. (Over the years, some of the other boxers who appeared at the Garden included Joe Louis, Sugar Ray Robinson, Jake LaMotta, Gene Tunney, Rocky Marciano, and Muhammad Ali.) The Bruins hockey team moved in not long afterwards. Eventually, after Rickard's death, the building passed on to Boston millionaire Henry Lapham and George V. Brown. The *Boston Evening American* held a rename-the-building contest and a woman named Ruth Fassano came up with the clever idea of calling it "Boston Garden."

In 1929, the Ringling Brothers & Barnum & Bailey Circus played the Garden, and into the 1930s the arena was host to a variety of events, including a six-day bicycle race, a hunting and fishing show, a Notre Dame football game, a winter ski exhibition, midget auto races, the Sonja Henie Ice Revue, and the rodeo. In the 1940s Brown widened his scope, booking women's softball, the Shriners Ball, book shows, and big bands. Calvin Coolidge spoke at the Garden, and in 1940, a rally for presidential candidate Franklin Delano Roosevelt was held there. Bob Hope entertained there during an Army-Navy relief show and, during World War II, the Garden was home to War Bond shows featuring Judy Garland, Gene Kelly, and Greer Garson. In the 1950s, Bishop John J. Writer celebrated a Mass for 11,000 of the faithful; Liberace played and signed autographs until 4 a.m. In 1960, JFK held his final presidential campaign rally in the Garden, and the Beatles played there in 1964. In 1972, the same night that Boston Mayor Kevin White bailed them out of a Rhode Island jail, the Rolling Stones performed a midnight rambler show.

The Boston Garden was primarily built as a showcase for boxing; hence, all the seating had a pronounced vertical slant, and the incline was particularly steep upstairs. (The second version of Madison Square Garden, on 49th and Eighth, was no different; from the upstairs seating, it felt as if you could topple over. As kids, relegated to the cheap seats, we used to call it the "nosebleed" section.) The Garden was also infamous for its obstructed-view seats. Since the arena was built for boxing, not basketball, less than one-quarter of the seating capacity of 14,890 was on the desirable sideline.

The checkerboard patterned parquet floor was, of course, the focal point for anyone who either attended a game at the Boston Garden or played there. In 1946, the floor was built at a cost of $10,000. Due to the shortage of hardwood during World War II, the Brookline, Massachusetts fellow named DiNatale who was responsible for building it had to take oak scraps cut from a Tennessee forest. The boards were an inch-and-a-half thick and particularly strong because they were cut against the grain. The five-by-five foot panels were arranged in an alternating pattern that formed the parquet effect. The floor lasted until the Garden was abandoned in 1995, but it was brought over to the new Fleet Center and laid there. Finally, it was replaced.

While examining the floor in 1987, Cleveland guard Ron Harper remarked, "Man, my driveway is better than this." And Magic Johnson once observed, "Some courts are fast and some are slow. This one here is a little softer. Here you have to dribble that much harder just to make the ball come up." Former Celtic Danny Ainge put his finger on one of the problems encountered by players who weren't used to the floor: "A lot of times you're dribbling the ball upcourt, the ball won't come back to you. So the guys who do a lot of fancy dribbling, they never know. They go behind their back and they come up empty." And the final word goes to Tom Meschery, who obviously didn't think there was anything quaint about that legendary surface: "The floor looked great on television, but that checkerboard was a disgrace because of loose screws, dead spots and everything else. Nonetheless, that floor became a symbol for winning."

Incredibly, there was no air-conditioning in the Garden, and sometimes the players suffered badly for it. For instance, during Boston's pivotal Game 5 victory against the Lakers in the 1984 Finals, the temperature in the arena was close to 100 degrees, causing Kareem Abdul-Jabbar to suck oxygen from a mask late in the game.

The locker rooms were also a disgrace, and not only for the visiting team. Tom Heinsohn blew *that* myth apart. "I have heard players that played in Boston Garden say the visiting locker room was overheated and all kinds of other stuff. In fact, we were treated as poorly as the visitors by Boston Garden management in my early days with the Celtics. Our locker room, in the heyday when we were winning all those championships, consisted of two nails for everybody. I was stationed between Bill Russell and Bob Cousy, practically in the corner. We had one shower that would overflow and flood the locker room so everybody would rush to get out fast so their shoes wouldn't get wet. In Philadelphia, you'd go play at Convention Hall and you didn't even get a hook. We used to lay our clothes out on a table in some dingy conference room. So facilities weren't the best. Nowadays players go first class, everybody has their own room. Never happened in my day."

John Havlicek agreed. "The dressing rooms were some wooden benches located under the bleachers. That meant the taller guys had to dress in the front of the room where the ceiling was higher. As you went deeper into the room, the ceiling sloped down and that was where the smaller guys were. To call it a locker room is a misnomer, because there were no lockers. Just a strip on the wall with nails pounded into it. You hung your clothes on the nails and hooks. There was a six-foot area that had four showers and there was only one toilet, so guys would line up before the game."

Syracuse War Memorial

The Syracuse War Memorial was another unique arena, both for its physical attributes and for the fans that frequented the games. As Dolph Schayes once remarked, the Syracuse arena held only "6,400 seats and the fans were right on top of you."

The War Memorial had thick iron piping that formed the base of the basket supports, and there was a crossbar about five inches above the floor. During one game, Knick Harry Gallatin

drove toward the basket, tripped and went sprawling on the ground and got his head wedged under the pipe. To some fans watching, it appeared as if he'd been guillotined. It looked as if he might be permanently stuck there, but eventually he managed to work himself free and, amazingly, he stayed in the game.

But far worse than any structural hazards were the Syracuse fans and the havoc they wrought. Rumor had it that when it was time to come to Syracuse, many opposing players suddenly came down with a case of what was dubbed the "Syracuse flu," making them suddenly unable to make the trip. "The Syracuse fans were out of control," recalled the Celtics' Frank Ramsey. "They'd throw cups full of Coke, programs, even batteries at you. That place was a hockey arena with sideboards." One night, when there was a fight between Dolph Schayes and "Jungle" Jim Loscutoff, "the fans knocked over those hockey boards to get on the court and some of the fans were hurt when they ended up under the boards. It was like a stampede."

Hershey, Pennsylvania

A historic moment took place at an off-the-beaten-track arena when Philadelphia Warriors center Wilt Chamberlain scored 100 points in a game. The Warriors were facing the Knicks, and instead of playing in Philadelphia, the owner, Eddie Gottlieb, chose to play the game in Hershey, Pennsylvania, where the team sometimes held practices in the off-season.

Tom Meschery recalled the arena, which at capacity held only 4,124 spectators: "Hershey had one of those dreary, old, dungeon-like arenas with overlapping rafters. Because the Hershey Company was there, the whole town smelled like fresh chocolate. We had trained in Hershey, so we were acquainted with the gym."

It was March 2, 1962. There were five games left in the season and the Warriors, having clinched a playoff spot, were playing out the string against the last-place Knicks. Harvey Pollack, the Warriors' PR director, remembered the game: "There was no television, only a few reporters and about 4,000 fans. I know because I wrote stories for two wire services and a Philadelphia newspaper that night. One of the few photographs that exist shows Wilt holding a piece of paper with 100 written on it. That's my handwriting. But if you talk to people today, 50,000 of them will tell you they were there the night Chamberlain scored 100 points in a single game."

"In the Hershey arena lobby," Pollack added, "they had a pinball machine and one of those target practice machines, and Wilt said he set records on both of those."

"I do recall him sitting in that little locker room," said Frank McGuire. " It was nothing more than a high school dressing room with one long wooden bench in the middle where everyone sat."

The ABA: A Step Back In Time

With the introduction of the American Basketball Association in1967-68, arenas took a step backward in time. With most of the big venues already booked, some of the teams in the new league had to make do with whatever they could

find. The Floridians, for instance, played some of their games "at a place in Coconut Grove where there were so many cockroaches in the dressing rooms that the visiting teams just changed at the hotel," said public relations man Rudy Martzke.

And, recalled ABA guard Gene Littles, the real arena, which was nothing more than an old auditorium on Miami Beach, wasn't much better. "They had the kind of baskets you just roll out there, they'd throw down the floor and then you'd play— before 200."

"One time I came to Miami with Kentucky," said Dan Issel, "and the Ice Capades was going in the other part of the building. I got my ankles taped and, in uniform, I walked over to watch the show. They had about 8,000 for the ice show and about 1,500 for our game."

"The walls in the dressing rooms were so thin and the two teams' rooms were next to each other, so everybody could hear everything," recalled former player Steve Jones. "I was in there with New Orleans and we were up by about 20 points at half. [New Orleans coach] Babe McCarthy said, 'Shush up, fellas. I want ya'll to lissen to what's going on next door.' [Miami coach] Hal Blitman was going nuts, screaming and cussing everyone out. Babe was biting his lip to keep from laughing and we were doing the same thing—we didn't want them to hear us. As we walked out on the floor, all Babe said was, 'That's what I'm gonna sound like after the game if we blow this one.' Florida was the only place in the league where you could hear the other teams' half-time talk."

In the meantime, the New Orleans Buccaneers, who had 42 home games, had to play 11 of them on the road in such places as Jackson, Tennessee; Greenville, Mississippi; and Jackson, Mississippi, because their own arena was booked for those dates. One game had an announced crowd of 465 spectators, or maybe it would be more precise to call them witnesses.

But perhaps the top spot in the Hall of Shame of arenas belongs to the New Jersey Nets, then called the Americans, who played their first season in the 4,800-seat Teaneck Armory. The team had fewer than 50 ticket holders and a crowd anywhere in the vicinity of 500 was considered cause for celebration. The height of absurdity came that first year when New Jersey was awarded the home court advantage for a one-game playoff with Kentucky. Unfortunately, the Teaneck Armory was booked, and the only substitute Americans' owner Arthur Brown could come up with was the Commack Arena on Long Island. Louie Dampier, who played for Kentucky, remembered the incident well.

"We ended up in a tie with New Jersey, and we had to have a one game play-off," he recalled. "Their arena was occupied, so we went to this place to play, I think it was set up for ice skating, basically. They only seated about two thousand, I think. They couldn't move their floor over there for some reason. They got a temporary floor from somebody else and they hauled it in. We arrived for the game and they were still putting the floor together. And we thought, 'There's going to be a delay.' And it was freezing in that building, too. We walked out curious, even though it was much warmer in the dressing room. As we watched them we saw these guys with hammers out there. They were actually repairing holes in the floor, some of them bigger than a basketball. They were just bringing pieces

of wood out there and trying to nail them together. And the basketball supports were made of metal or iron pipe, and they were close to the end of the floor. They weren't professional goals. They had jagged edges of metal on them, and they were rusty so they tried to cover that up with pieces of tape. I don't even know if the baskets even had nets on them or not. It was just a real bad situation."

It was so bad that ABA Commissioner George Mikan stepped in and forfeited the game to the Colonels, putting the Americans out of the playoffs.

But the Nets' story gets even more absurd because the following season Brown moved the Americans to the Commack Arena. They got a new floor and changed their name to the Nets, which was meant to endear them to New York fans, who already had the Jets and the Mets.

"There are so many stories about guys freezing their butts off at Commack," said sportswriter Jeff Denberg. "Brown even installed several large heaters to blow hot air around, but that didn't have much impact. One game, Bob Verga was sitting on the bench wearing his overcoat. Brown sent a note to the bench, 'Tell Verga to take off his coat.' Verga refused. Brown sent down another note, and Verga still wouldn't take his coat off. Finally, Brown sent a note to coach Max Zaslofsky: 'Put Verga in the game.' Verga went into the game and yes, he did take off his coat."

"Guys would sit on the bench at Commack wearing coats and gloves trying to stay warm," said player Steve Jones. "Nobody wanted to play for the Nets and have that icebox as your home court."

Eventually, the team moved to the Island Garden, which wasn't much better. "I never played at Commack," said Dan Issel, "but when the Nets moved to the Island Garden, that wasn't any better. It was still cold. Guys on the bench still wore coats over their warm-ups. The dressing rooms were brutal. They should have called the place the Long Island Toilet."

"The Island Garden was like an airline hangar," explained player's agent Ron Grinker. "It gave you that kind of airy, vacant feeling."

"Without a doubt, the Island Garden was the least professional, lowest-class facility in pro basketball," said sportswriter Bob Ryan. "No one would dare dress in the locker room. Everyone dressed at the hotel first. On one side of the arena were about five rows of stands, reminiscent of a high school gym. The other side had about 15 rows. I couldn't believe how rinky-dink the place was."

And Roy Boe, former owner of the Nets, concurred. "The Island Garden was terrible. We got all the complaints about the toilets not working and there being no hot water in the showers. If the circus had just left, the parking lot would be littered with elephant excrement."

Top of the Line: Today's Arenas

Today every professional team, the WNBA included, plays in a modern arena—many of them, like the Phillips Arena (Atlanta Hawks), and the ARCO Arena (Sacramento Kings), named after corporate sponsors. Some bemoan the loss of uniqueness or the history and color of, say, the second-generation Madison Square Garden (which made way for the

present Garden, which opened for the 1963-64 season and stands directly above the Pennsylvania Railroad Station at 33rd Street and Seventh Avenue) or the old Boston Garden. Take, for instance, this early description of the San Antonio Spurs' Alamodome:

"The Alamodome is what is known as a 'third generation' facility. It features the very latest in dome architecture and engineering technology, with column-free spans for unobstructed viewing and a curtain wall system for configuration flexibility. So whatever your event, chances are the Alamodome can accommodate you.

"In fact, it has been designed to meet the specific needs of 24 different events—including tradeshows, small and large assemblies, football, basketball and hockey, and assemblies-in-the-round. It has 160,000 gross square feet of contiguous exhibit floor space with room for up to 885 10' x 10' booths with aisles, and an additional 30,000 square feet of conference room space. The Alamodome also has state-of-the-art lighting, sound and A/V systems, including video transport via fiber optics, television broadcast support and video production capabilities.

"And it's all under a ceiling that's just 125 feet high to its lowest truss. So you get all the advantages of a dome-sized facility, but still keep an intimate, human-scale feeling."

It may have all that, but in 2002 the Spurs got a newer home—the SBC Center. The new arena, on the city's eastside, is named after a local communications firm. Its function is to serve as home for the Spurs and the San Antonio Livestock Association.

How would the ghosts of those players who toiled in the first half of the 20th century feel as they stare upward at sold-out arenas, plastered with advertisements for beer and running shoes and telephone companies and fast food franchises, and then outward at the enormous, for the most part well-behaved, star-studded crowd, some of them paying astronomical amounts for courtside seats?

They might have been in a state of disbelief but also a little proud.

TODAY'S NBA ARENAS

Team	Name of Arena	Capacity	Year Built	Team	Name of Arena	Capacity	Year Built
Atlanta	Phillips Arena	20,000	1999	Minnesota	Target Center	19,006	1990
Boston	FleetCenter	18,624	1995	New Jersey	Continental Airlines Arena	20,049	1981
Chicago	United Center	21,711	1994	New Orleans,	New Orleans Arena	17,200	2002
Cleveland	Gund Arena	20,562	1994	New York	Madison Square Garden	19,763	1968
Dallas	American Airline Center	18,042	2001	Orlando	TD Waterhouse Centre	17,248	1989
Denver	Pepsi Center	19,309	1999	Philadelphia	Wachovia Center	20,444	1996
Detroit	Palace of Auburn Hills	22,076	1988	Phoenix	America West Arena	19,023	1992
Golden State	Arena in Oakland	19,596	1966/97	Portland	Rose Garden	19,980	1995
Houston	Toyota Center	18,300	2003	Sacramento	ARCO Arena	17,317	1988
Indiana	Conseco Fieldhouse	18,500	1999	San Antonio	SBC Center	18,500	2002
L.A. Clippers	Staples Center	19,282	1999	Seattle	Key Arena	17,072	1995
L.A. Lakers	Staples Center	19,282	1999	Toronto	Air Canada Centre	19,800	1999
Memphis Grizzlies	FedExForum	18,400	2003	Utah	Delta Center	19,911	1991
Miami	American Airlines Arena	19,600	2000	Washington	MCI Center	20,674	1997
Milwaukee	Bradley Center	18,717	1988				

Chapter 19

NBA Attendance

By Ted Brock

In his book *Cages to Jumpshots: Pro Basketball's Early Years*, sports historian Robert W. Peterson notes that the Basketball Association of America, formed in the summer of 1946, "was born because arena managers wanted to fill seats."

Indeed, all 11 of the BAA's original franchises were owned by the arenas in which the teams played.

"There is a certain irony," Peterson writes, "in the fact that basketball, the uniquely American sport, would play second fiddle to (hockey) and be used to provide an attraction for arenas when the hockey teams were out of town." A crowd of 17,205 watched the New York Knicks' first game at Madison Square Garden. The Knicks lost to the Chicago Stags that night and would play only five more of their 30 home games at the Garden, hosting the other 24 at the 69th Regiment Armory.

Peterson's attendance chart for the BAA's maiden season reveals that only three of the teams—Philadelphia, New York and St. Louis—averaged paid attendance of more than 3,000 per game. Overall interest in the BAA product got a nudge, though, from the 239,311 complimentary admissions that filled arenas, adding to the 800,757 who paid from 70 cents to $2.50 to watch the 11 teams. Four squads—Cleveland, Detroit, Pittsburgh and Toronto—barely made it through the inaugural season and dropped out.

Peterson notes the BAA's second season saw a subtle increase in average attendance. Crowds averaging more than 4,000 showed up to watch the two attendance leaders, Philadelphia and New York, and overall the league averaged 3,000 a game—helped once again by substantial complimentary admissions.

In the BAA's early years, professional basketball's style of play still bore many of the characteristics it had carried through the first half of the century. Speed and ball movement were paramount. The two-handed set shot was considered the ultimate outside weapon. The jump shot was a novelty, used by few and mastered mainly by the Philadelphia Warriors' Joe Fulks. The idea of shooting one-handed at all had been on the national scene slightly more than a decade—introduced by Stanford's Hank Luisetti in the mid-1930s and refined by Toledo's Chuck Chuckovits.

The BAA labored in the shadow of the more popular college game, as did the rival National Basketball League, whose Chicago American Gears featured 6-foot-10 center George Mikan. Player popularity had been the calling card of the NBL, which drew on such talents as Chuckovits, Oshkosh's 6-foot-4 center Leroy (Cowboy) Edwards and Fort Wayne's sharp-shooting Bob McDermott.

The NBL had begun in 1937-38, struggled through the

Rooting For the Home Team, 1974

period of World War II, maintained a healthy and respectful relationship with the BAA with regard to drafting and signing players—and then folded in 1949.

The newly formed National Basketball Association absorbed the NBL's healthiest franchises—Indianapolis, Fort Wayne, Rochester and Minneapolis—and several off the beaten path, such as Sheboygan, Wisconsin, and Waterloo, Iowa. By its second season, the league had pared its three-division, 17-team luggage to two divisions and 11 teams. Minneapolis, with Mikan at center, entered the 1950-51 season as the champion of the league's maiden year.

The game's drawing power was limited, and some small towns survived the first cut. Fort Wayne's ball-freezing 19-18 victory over Mikan and the Lakers on November 11, 1950—the lowest-scoring game in NBA history—served as the perfect emblem: a game whose low excitement level was cutting into its appeal.

"To give you an idea of where the league was, attendance-wise, you have to remember Fort Wayne still was playing its games in a high school gym," says Zelda Spoelstra, alluding to the town's 3,800-seat North Side High School facility.

Spoelstra came by this information first-hand. She was one of six employees in the original NBA office, and today still serves the league as its manager of special projects.

She recalls that one of the few crowd-building devices the league could muster in the early '50s was the occasional doubleheader at New York's Madison Square Garden.

"You'd see the Knicks and three other teams," she says, "and they counted on the Knicks to draw the crowd."

Attendance-wise, times were lean during the NBA's first two years. The figures for 1950-51 included 3,267 paying spectators per game. Syracuse and Minneapolis averaged 5,185 and 4,728 respectively, and New York and Philadelphia were the only others among the league's eight teams to average above 4,000.

Former broadcaster Hank Greenwald covered the NBA in both Syracuse and Rochester before doing play-by-play with the Golden State Warriors in the 1960s and '70s. Greenwald recalls one inexpensive move by Danny Biasone, owner of the Syracuse Nats from the late 1940s until the early '60s.

"Biasone took advantage of the deathly cold Syracuse winter," Greenwald says. "He'd leave the doors of the arena wide open, hoping to lure anyone in from the street."

Biasone, a member of the Basketball Hall of Fame, didn't stop there. His creative mind also contributed what Spoelstra and a consensus of NBA historians regard as the single most important turning point in league history: the 24-second shot clock.

Introduced in the 1954-55 season, the shot clock had the twin effect of speeding up the game and increasing scoring. The average point production per team per game went from 79.5 in 1953-54 to 93.1 in 1954-55.

Eventually, the rules makers would add a new scoring dimension by drawing an arc 22 feet from the basket. Shots made from beyond the arc would be worth three points. The 3-pointer had its impact, but its effect on fan interest was nothing like the shot clock's.

The game's faster pace paralleled the introduction of more African-American players to the league. Earl Lloyd of the Washington Capitols, Chuck Cooper of the Boston Celtics and Nat "Sweetwater" Clifton of the Knicks had become the NBA's first black players in 1950-51. In 1954-55, Lloyd and Jim Tucker, playing for Biasone's Nats, became the first black players on an NBA championship team.

The middle of the decade brought an even stronger African-American presence, as Bill Russell, K.C. Jones and Sam Jones formed the nucleus of the Boston Celtics teams that would win the league title 1956-57 and eight straight championships between 1958-59 and 1965-66.

It also should be noted that between 1957-58—when Russell became the first black man to be named the league's most valuable player—and 1983-84, when Boston's Larry Bird won the first of his three consecutive MVP awards, only three other white players received the award. Bob Pettit of St. Louis won it in 1958-59, Boston's Dave Cowens in 1972-73 and Portland's Bill Walton in 1977-78.

While the game might have been growing more fan-friendly, Spoelstra points out, "There were no NBA games on television until 1954. Mr. Podoloff (Maurice Podoloff, whose presidency of the BAA had continued with the formation of the NBA) negotiated with (the independent DuMont Network) for 13 games that year at $3,000 a game. Even then there was no sharing the receipts. The home team kept the money." Although NBC came into the picture the following year for a contract worth more than $100,000, TV's interest in the league remained lukewarm for most of the next two decades.

A remark by Syracuse Nats star Dolph Schayes in Terry Pluto's *Tall Tales*, an anecdotal history of the NBA's early years, points to one of the league's first successful attendance strategies:

"In the first five years of the NBA, the (Harlem) Globetrotters helped carry the league. They drew fans who weren't into basketball, they came for the entertainment and then maybe they stayed around to watch the NBA game . . . I played in games where the arena was packed for the Trotters in the opener, then we took the court for the NBA game and half the fans left."

The arrival of Wilt Chamberlain, who joined the Philadelphia Warriors in 1959-60 after a year with the Globetrotters, drew attention to the prolific scoring and rebounding of the 7-foot-1, 275-pound Kansas All-American. It also meant a bigger gate for the Russell-Chamberlain match-ups.

Still, filling arenas around the league was an inexact science. On March 2, 1962, when Chamberlain scored 100 points to set the still-standing NBA single-game scoring record, only 4,124 were on hand to see it. The game took place in Hershey, Pennsylvania, home of the Warriors' training camp. Philadelphia owner Eddie Gottlieb scheduled a handful of games there as a reward for the town's support. Chamberlain's feat only highlighted the disparity between product and promotion.

Harvey Pollack, the venerated Philadelphia 76ers public relations man (he began in the days of the Warriors) and the NBA's resident statistical guru, remembers how barren the league's promotional landscape really was, during its first two decades.

"The league didn't have marketing departments," Pollack says. "They didn't have promotional gimmicks. They didn't have the resources."

What they had instead was resourcefulness. It occasionally surfaced in the mid-1950s, when owner Ben Kerner, $94,000 in debt, moved the Milwaukee Hawks to St. Louis.

In *Tall Tales*, Pluto quotes Kerner's flamboyant publicity man Marty Blake:

"When we moved to St. Louis (in 1955), they promised us that we'd have a base of 1,000 season ticket holders. We had 55. So we scrambled for money. We played a million exhibition

games. We promoted before promotion was fashionable. I mean, we had acts such as Count Basie, Guy Lombardo, the Four Freshmen, Tommy Dorsey—all big names and they all played after our games. We gave away prizes."

Media relations was another concept the league was slow to grasp. Pollack says it's worth noting the NBA didn't require its teams to publish media guides until 1969. (Pluto quotes Pollack as remembering that when Warriors owner Eddie Gottlieb hired him, initially as an assistant public relations director, Gottlieb dictated that Pollack keep his $26-a-week job on the sports staff of the *Philadelphia Inquirer*; that way the team would have a contact at the paper. Make that two contacts: Warriors' P.R. director Herb Goode worked at the *Inquirer*, too.)

Professional basketball owners, since 1946, had sought to take advantage of the college game's popularity. One device, the territorial draft, gave a franchise the right to select a player from its surrounding area (determined by the league) by giving up its first-round pick for that season.

Veteran sportswriter Leonard Koppett told Pluto the story of Wilt Chamberlain and the territorial draft, the year Chamberlain graduated from Philadelphia's Overbrook High School:

". . . There were about 130 colleges after Wilt, which was absolutely unheard of in those days. Word was that Red Auerbach was angling to get Wilt to attend a college in the Boston area (Chamberlain told Pluto it was Harvard), so the Celtics would have him in their territory. But Eddie Gottlieb was not about to let that happen."

Harvey Pollack: "Eddie went to the league and said, 'Our territorial pick is Wilt Chamberlain.'

"The NBA said, 'Hey, you can't take him. He's still in high school.'

"Eddie said, 'Why not? Listen, I guarantee that Wilt will be our first-round pick after his senior year in college and I'm taking him now. If he breaks a leg, if he can't play—I still get him. I'm taking a gamble on the guy.' "

Koppett: ". . . Gottlieb was a power in the league, one of the founding fathers. So they gave him the rights to Wilt."

Auerbach: "The league felt sorry for Eddie, so they made a special provision for him. We didn't like it in Boston, but back then deals were made all the time."

The territorial draft was abandoned in 1965.

Throughout the 1960s, professional basketball's signature showed signs of flamboyance and abundant talent, stoked by the presence of African-American stars such as Oscar Robertson, Elgin Baylor, Dave Bing and Walt Frazier. Meanwhile, the talents of Julius Erving and George Gervin helped make the rival American Basketball Association an attraction. By the time the ABA merged with the NBA in the mid-1970s, tough guys had joined the mix, among them Kareem Abdul-Jabbar, Bob Lanier, Robert Parrish and Willis Reed.

Marquee players with speed, quickness and leaping ability were becoming the thing, and in the 1980s one man became the catalyst who converted flash to cash.

David Stern took over for Larry O'Brien as NBA commissioner in 1984. Stern's marketing of name value—with stars such as Magic Johnson and Larry Bird—filled arenas. His leadership led to improved relations between the league office and the players' association. He cultivated lucrative sponsorships and gave the league a true presence on network and cable television. A flood of licensed products spread worldwide.

Stern's promotional model took off, literally, on the success of Michael Jordan. Thanks to Stern's steering public attention toward high-profile performers, the game's best player ever had a marketing motor waiting for him as his career began to blossom in the late 1980s.

One NBA market took extra time to get it. In 1990-91, the season before the New Jersey Nets hired Jon Spoelstra, Zelda Spoelstra's nephew, as their president, every NBA team except one sold out its arena when Jordan came to town.

"New Jersey couldn't even come out for the greatest player ever," Jon Spoelstra says.

Spoelstra came to the Nets from the Portland Trail Blazers, where he'd served as vice president-general manager for 11 years. During that time, he had built a reputation as a sports marketing expert. He wrote the book many consider the bible of the art—*How to Sell the Last Seat in the House*—as well as its sequel, *Ice to the Eskimos*.

Spoelstra explains how he enticed the Jordan no-shows:

"When we packaged and bundled the (ticket) program we sold out five games," he says, "including the two Chicago games."

The other three games in the package offered two appearances by Larry Bird and the Boston Celtics and one by Magic and the Los Angeles Lakers.

"That's my rocket science," Spoelstra says.

"What it really is, is getting them to come back. All we did was say, 'How do we increase their frequency?'"

Over the NBA's 52-year history, teams and cities have built larger and more attractive venues, for obvious reasons. Arenas seating 15,000 to 20,000 became the norm in the 1990s. Occasionally, a franchise has moved from a mega-house to a more intimate building with better sight lines and more seats closer to the court. On March 27, 1998, at the Georgia Dome in Atlanta, the Chicago Bulls defeated the Hawks 89-74 before a crowd of 62,046—the largest ever to watch an NBA game.

In the 1987-88 season, the Pistons became the first team to go over 1,000,000 in regular-season attendance. That was the year they lost to Los Angeles in the NBA Finals. The next year, they beat the Lakers in the NBA Finals, and drew "only" 879,614. Of course they'd moved from the massive Pontiac Silverdome to the Palace at Auburn Hills, where they sold out from 1988-89 to 1992-93.

The only other team to break a million, Minnesota, did so in its first year. The Timberwolves' 1,027,572 in 1989-90, however, couldn't top the Pistons' record 1,066,505.

Into the 21st century began, professional basketball historians noted the following:

● Regular-season attendance around the NBA increased in 1999-2000, despite a drop-off in television ratings.

● Post-season attendance in 1999-2000 averaged more than 19,000 for the third time in NBA history.

● League-wide, regular-season attendance holds steady, above 85 percent of capacity.

Certain attendance figures from the NBA's early and middle years have a way of reflecting social values. In 1956-57, Bill Russell was rookie year in Boston, the Celtics averaged 10,517 in the regular season, a jump more than 25 percent above the 8,063 average the previous season.

Yet during the championship-rich Russell era, the team's average home attendance hung in the 7,000s-8,000s, dipping to 6,852 in 1961-62.

Then, in 1966-67, the Celtics went from a 7,942 average house to 10,409—despite going uncrowned for only the second time in Russell's career.

Why the spike? More important, why the drop-off and doldrums while the great Red Auerbach teams were writing basketball history? Pluto and others have documented acts of racial hatred against Russell during his time in Boston. It might not be air-tight scholarship to suggest a correlation between attendance lag and community bias against the Celtics' commitment to African-American players. By the same token, it would be foolish to count that out.

That issue and numerous others form a body of folklore embedded in the figures that follow. Most of the crowd numbers from the professional basketball's early days have been retrieved and archived alongside the league's official statistics from 1969-70 onward. Here they are for your inspection and speculation. Choose a point in NBA history, and count the house.

NBA FRANCHISE ATTENDANCE HISTORY

Atlanta Hawks

Year	Total	Avg
2002-03	528,655	12,894
2001-02	506,110	12,344
2000-01	560,330	13,667
1999-00	601,138	14,662
1998-99	331,831	13,273
1997-98	715,452	17,450
1996-97	585,802	14,288
1995-96	496,679	12,114
1994-95	504,807	12,312
1993-94	546,749	13,335
1992-93	491,229	11,981
1991-92	511,903	12,485
1990-91	529,171	12,907
1989-90	573,731	13,993
1988-89	644,291	15,714
1987-88	583,073	14,221
1986-87	549,652	13,406
1985-86	377,678	9,212
1984-85	299,794	7,312
1983-84	292,059	7,123
1982-83	292,690	7,139
1981-82	308,889	7,534
1980-81	362,702	8,846
1979-80	449,843	10,972
1978-79	329,064	8,026
1977-78	304,050	7,416
1976-77	214,775	5,238
1975-76	227,815	5,556
1974-75	205,341	5,008
1973-74	312,128	7,613
1972-73	304,802	7,434
1971-72	230,784	5,629
1970-71	245,910	5,998
1969-70	197,990	5,210
1968-69	178,979	4,474

Baltimore Bullets

Year	Total	Avg
1972-73	263,660	6,431
1971-72	272,339	6,642
1970-71	251,130	6,125
1969-70	225,569	6,096
1968-69	290,147	7,635
1967-68	171,146	4,754
1966-67	129,799	4,056
1965-66	174,880	4,602
1964-65	187,124	4,564
1963-64	195,783	5,020

Boston Celtics

Year	Total	Avg
2002-03	709,049	17,293
2001-02	659,751	16,091
2000-01	629,201	15,346
1999-00	683,608	16,673
1998-99	440,602	17,624
1997-98	743,422	18,132
1996-97	664,022	16,196
1995-96	732,841	17,874
1994-95	606,870	14,802
1993-94	604,867	14,753
1992-93	608,495	14,841
1991-92	610,976	14,902
1990-91	611,537	14,916
1989-90	611,537	14,916
1988-89	611,537	14,916
1987-88	611,222	14,908
1986-87	611,222	14,908
1985-86	610,581	14,892
1984-85	610,727	14,896
1983-84	606,857	14,801
1982-83	621,829	15,167
1980-81	595,444	14,523
1979-80	596,349	14,545
1978-79	417,926	10,193
1976-77	517,391	12,619
1975-76	539,589	13,161
1974-75	486,270	11,860
1973-74	355,261	11,102
1972-73	423,234	10,852
1971-72	346,701	8,456
1970-71	313,768	8,045
1969-70	277,632	7,504
1968-69	322,130	8,948
1967-68	320,788	8,670
1966-67	322,690	10,409
1965-66	246,189	7,942
1964-65	246,529	8,218
1963-64	223,347	7,445
1962-63	262,581	8,753
1961-62	191,855	6,852
1960-61	201,569	7,199
1959-60	209,374	7,755
1958-59	244,642	8,155
1957-58	240,943	8,308
1956-57	262,918	10,517
1955-56	209,645	8,063
1954-55	175,675	7,027
1953-54	156,912	7,472
1952-53	161,808	6,742
1951-52	160,167	5,523
1950-51	197,888	6,184
1949-50	110,552	4,252
1948-49	144,275	4,975
1947-48	90,264	3,761
1946-47	108,240	3,608

Buffalo Braves

Year	Total	Avg
1977-78	252,457	6,157
1976-77	319,398	7,790
1975-76	418,696	10,212
1974-75	467,267	11,397
1973-74	427,270	10,421
1972-73	321,710	7,847
1971-72	350,852	8,557
1970-71	204,053	4,977

Capital Bullets

Year	Total	Avg
1973-74	414,202	10,102

Charlotte Hornets

Year	Total	Avg
2001-02	462,738	11,286
2000-01	615,424	15,010
1999-00	732,827	17,874
1998-99	480,807	19,232
1997-98	959,634	23,406
1996-97	985,722	24,042
1995-96	985,722	24,042
1994-95	971,618	23,698
1993-94	971,618	23,698
1992-93	971,618	23,698
1991-92	971,618	23,698
1990-91	980,141	23,906
1989-90	979,941	23,901
1988-89	950,064	23,172

Chicago Bulls

Year	Total	Avg
2002-03	804,309	19,617
2001-02	776,311	18,934
2000-01	888,654	21,674
1999-00	907,064	22,124
1998-99	560,012	22,400
1997-98	983,517	23,988
1996-97	978,453	23,865
1995-96	969,149	23,638
1994-95	926,278	22,592
1993-94	759,816	18,532
1992-93	759,656	18,528
1991-92	759,969	18,536
1990-91	757,745	18,482
1989-90	754,564	18,404
1988-89	736,964	17,975
1987-88	740,482	18,061
1986-87	650,718	15,871
1985-86	469,226	11,445
1984-85	487,370	11,887
1983-84	260,950	6,365
1982-83	301,050	7,343
1981-82	369,611	9,015
1980-81	389,718	9,505
1979-80	363,605	8,868

Cincinnati Royals

Year	Total	Avg
1978-79	368,968	8,999
1977-78	548,844	13,386
1976-77	476,636	11,625
1975-76	258,406	6,303
1974-75	438,860	10,704
1973-74	334,183	8,151
1972-73	424,944	10,364
1971-72	435,282	10,617
1970-71	414,857	10,118
1969-70	331,668	10,051
1968-69	151,608	3,790
1967-68	131,165	3,975
1966-67	171,793	4,772

Cincinnati Royals

Year	Total	Avg
1971-72	151,186	3,687
1970-71	131,734	3,992
1969-70	155,818	4,869
1968-69	113,822	4,065
1967-68	124,668	4,156
1966-67	156,931	4,755
1965-66	208,865	6,329
1964-65	169,570	5,299
1963-64	228,012	6,909
1962-63	137,739	4,174
1961-62	146,468	4,725
1960-61	194,017	6,259
1959-60	58,244	1,879
1958-59	68,470	2,445
1957-58	105,590	3,641

Cleveland Cavaliers

Year	Total	Avg
2002-03	471,374	11,496
2001-02	596,115	14,539
2000-01	650,775	15,873
1999-00	603,702	14,724
1998-99	352,992	14,120
1997-98	694,629	16,942
1996-97	692,684	16,895
1995-96	730,095	17,807
1994-95	833,850	20,338
1993-94	753,686	18,383
1992-93	751,469	18,329
1991-92	677,408	16,522
1990-91	623,906	15,217
1989-90	695,710	16,969
1988-89	730,925	17,827
1987-88	504,847	12,313
1986-87	447,125	10,905
1985-86	390,842	9,533
1984-85	323,984	7,902
1983-84	208,095	5,075
1982-83	160,537	3,916
1981-82	236,523	5,769
1980-81	224,489	5,475
1979-80	322,788	7,873
1978-79	325,616	7,942
1977-78	454,961	11,097

Year	Total	Avg
1976-77	570,445	13,913
1975-76	519,010	12,659
1974-75	334,582	8,161
1973-74	164,520	4,013
1972-73	186,477	4,548
1971-72	214,119	5,222
1970-71	144,252	3,518

Dallas Mavericks

Year	Total	Avg
2002-03	816,429	19,912
2001-02	802,703	19,578
2000-01	680,138	16,589
1999-00	666,177	16,248
1998-99	362,837	14,513
1997-98	541,545	13,208
1996-97	619,178	15,102
1995-96	684,138	16,686
1994-95	678,433	16,547
1993-94	526,414	12,839
1992-93	554,724	13,530
1991-92	649,741	15,847
1990-91	683,927	16,681
1989-90	691,570	16,868
1988-89	695,056	16,953
1987-88	695,592	16,966
1986-87	696,333	16,984
1985-86	693,052	16,904
1984-85	684,466	16,694
1983-84	583,134	14,223
1982-83	487,158	11,882
1981-82	390,292	9,519
1980-81	319,347	7,789

Denver Nuggets

Year	Total	Avg
2002-03	607,813	14,824
2001-02	633,846	15,460
2000-01	619,300	15,105
1999-00	637,698	15,554
1998-99	296,965	11,879
1997-98	483,791	11,800
1996-97	461,408	11,254
1995-96	675,426	16,474
1994-95	704,011	17,171
1993-94	673,738	16,433
1992-93	603,459	14,719
1991-92	534,323	13,032
1990-91	438,103	10,685
1989-90	519,404	12,668
1988-89	555,498	13,549
1987-88	520,913	12,705
1986-87	494,943	12,072
1985-86	531,814	12,971
1984-85	448,464	10,938
1983-84	462,397	11,278
1982-83	496,307	12,105
1981-82	475,688	11,602
1980-81	423,287	10,324
1979-80	527,208	12,859
1978-79	603,356	14,716
1977-78	657,673	16,041
1976-77	703,133	17,150

Detroit Pistons

Year	Total	Avg
2002-03	839,278	20,470
2001-02	760,807	18,556
2000-01	607,323	14,813
1999-00	678,470	16,548
1998-99	444,585	17,783
1997-98	794,567	19,380
1996-97	820,585	20,014
1995-96	730,573	17,819
1994-95	719,090	17,539
1993-94	785,187	19,151
1992-93	879,614	21,454
1991-92	879,614	21,454
1990-91	879,614	21,454
1989-90	879,614	21,454
1988-89	879,614	21,454
1987-88	1,066,505	26,012
1986-87	908,240	22,152

Year	Total	Avg
1985-86	695,239	16,957
1984-85	691,540	16,867
1983-84	652,865	15,924
1982-83	522,063	12,733
1981-82	406,317	9,910
1980-81	228,349	5,569
1979-80	333,233	8,128
1978-79	389,936	9,511
1977-78	223,382	5,448
1976-77	303,792	7,410
1975-76	251,352	6,131
1974-75	307,180	7,492
1973-74	300,565	7,331
1972-73	212,094	5,173
1971-72	188,763	4,604
1970-71	283,913	6,925
1969-70	167,648	4,412
1968-69	201,433	5,301
1967-68	224,164	7,005
1966-67	193,782	6,459
1965-66	120,013	4,000
1964-65	121,239	4,041
1963-64	100,386	3,346
1962-63	144,150	4,805
1961-62	143,081	4,769
1960-61	164,230	5,298
1959-60	178,007	5,742
1958-59	119,351	3,978
1957-58	134,411	4,800

Fort Wayne Pistons

Year	Total	Avg
1948-49	N/A	
1949-50	N/A	
1950-51	107,019	3,148
1951-52	N/A	
1952-53	N/A	
1953-54	N/A	
1954-55	N/A	
1955-56	128,102	4,745
1956-57	108,054	3,859

Golden State Warriors

Year	Total	Avg
2002-03	634,935	15,486
2001-02	593,182	14,468
2000-01	591,981	14,439
1999-00	509,172	12,419
1998-99	335,837	13,433
1997-98	500,260	12,201
1996-97	621,844	15,167
1995-96	616,025	15,025
1994-95	616,025	15,025
1993-94	616,025	15,025
1992-93	616,025	15,025
1991-92	616,025	15,025
1990-91	616,025	15,025
1989-90	616,025	15,025
1988-89	587,820	14,337
1987-88	465,348	11,350
1986-87	423,997	10,341
1985-86	401,279	9,787
1984-85	300,580	7,331
1983-84	337,817	8,239
1982-83	341,243	8,323
1981-82	401,646	9,796
1980-81	413,480	10,085
1979-80	344,483	8,402
1978-79	427,252	10,421
1977-78	474,715	11,578
1976-77	479,328	11,691
1975-76	490,846	11,972
1974-75	360,740	8,799
1973-74	265,095	6,466
1972-73	244,504	5,964
1971-72	200,917	5,740

Houston Rockets

Year	Total	Avg
2002-03	565,166	13,784
2001-02	481,227	11,737
2000-01	518,555	12,648
1999-00	624,594	15,234

Year	Total	Avg
1998-99	407,125	16,285
1997-98	667,685	16,285
1996-97	667,685	16,285
1995-96	667,685	16,285
1994-95	653,389	15,936
1993-94	615,224	15,005
1992-93	554,210	13,517
1991-92	592,790	14,458
1990-91	613,230	14,957
1989-90	649,697	15,846
1988-89	680,728	16,603
1987-88	681,051	16,611
1986-87	660,175	16,102
1985-86	604,644	14,747
1984-85	569,018	13,878
1983-84	435,852	10,631
1982-83	307,131	7,491
1981-82	480,128	11,710
1980-81	385,354	9,399
1979-80	413,572	10,087
1978-79	434,400	10,595
1977-78	384,905	9,388
1976-77	347,920	8,486
1975-76	261,518	6,378
1974-75	187,457	4,572
1973-74	158,059	3,855
1972-73	189,773	4,629
1971-72	203,599	4,966

Indiana Pacers

Year	Total	Avg
2002-03	670,461	16,352
2001-02	686,537	16,745
2000-01	733,444	17,889
1999-00	752,145	18,345
1998-99	404,536	16,181
1997-98	645,302	15,739
1996-97	636,735	15,530
1995-96	673,967	16,438
1994-95	655,028	15,976
1993-94	543,815	13,264
1992-93	530,891	12,949
1991-92	517,352	12,618
1990-91	475,291	11,592
1989-90	528,275	12,885
1988-89	468,912	11,437
1987-88	502,319	12,252
1986-87	520,007	12,683
1985-86	460,969	11,243
1984-85	437,677	10,675
1983-84	421,202	10,273
1982-83	197,364	4,814
1981-82	318,062	7,758
1980-81	409,839	9,996
1979-80	433,402	10,571
1978-79	367,160	8,955
1977-78	501,759	12,238
1976-77	432,726	10,554

Kansas City Kings

Year	Total	Avg
1984-85	262,812	6,410
1983-84	370,270	9,031
1982-83	340,359	8,301
1981-82	280,564	6,843
1980-81	336,585	8,209
1979-80	375,387	9,156
1978-79	442,354	10,789
1977-78	315,722	7,701
1976-77	330,526	8,062
1975-76	272,675	6,651
1974-75	308,906	7,534
1973-74	232,692	5,675
1972-73	261,860	6,387

Los Angeles Clippers

Year	Total	Avg
2002-03	706,471	17,231
2001-02	740,185	18,053
2000-01	601,587	14,673
1999-00	559,714	13,652
1998-99	256,568	10,263
1997-98	408,693	9,968

Year	Total	Avg
1996-97	400,637	9,772
1995-96	414,560	10,111
1994-95	438,254	10,689
1993-94	471,034	11,489
1992-93	532,632	12,991
1991-92	500,200	12,200
1990-91	522,104	12,734
1989-90	486,621	11,869
1988-89	450,623	10,991
1987-88	359,674	8,773
1986-87	316,140	7,711
1985-86	341,614	8,332

Los Angeles Lakers

Year	Total	Avg
2002-03	777,888	18,972
2001-02	778,777	18,995
2000-01	776,336	18,935
1999-00	771,420	18,815
1998-99	430,007	17,200
1997-98	691,994	16,878
1996-97	697,132	17,003
1995-96	649,634	15,845
1994-95	591,125	14,418
1993-94	545,915	13,315
1992-93	633,655	15,455
1991-92	699,240	17,055
1990-91	697,185	17,005
1989-90	712,498	17,378
1988-89	717,349	17,496
1987-88	714,477	17,426
1986-87	681,707	16,627
1985-86	689,905	16,827
1984-85	613,826	14,971
1983-84	622,398	15,180
1982-83	648,244	15,811
1981-82	605,367	14,765
1980-81	538,537	13,135
1979-80	582,882	14,217
1978-79	482,611	11,771
1977-78	534,017	13,025
1976-77	501,434	12,230
1975-76	524,976	12,804
1974-75	474,287	11,568
1973-74	603,145	14,711
1972-73	664,872	16,216
1971-72	668,340	16,301
1970-71	566,108	13,808
1969-70	536,513	13,086
1968-69	483,262	11,787
1967-68	421,326	10,276
1966-67	435,008	11,154
1965-66	426,467	10,935
1964-65	392,004	10,316
1963-64	322,331	8,954
1962-63	285,462	8,396
1961-62	190,321	6,139
1960-61	151,344	5,045

Memphis Grizzlies

Year	Total	Avg
2002-03	611,322	14,910
2001-02	591,030	14,415

Miami Heat

Year	Total	Avg
2002-03	628,242	15,322
2001-02	655,549	15,989
2000-01	678,186	16,541
1999-00	707,325	17,252
1998-99	378,813	15,153
1997-98	614,864	14,997
1996-97	615,160	15,004
1995-96	606,091	14,783
1994-95	598,761	14,604
1993-94	617,242	15,055
1992-93	614,923	14,998
1991-92	613,583	14,965
1990-91	615,328	15,008
1989-90	615,238	15,006
1988-89	612,754	14,945

Milwaukee Bucks

Year	Total	Avg
2002-03	665,966	16,243
2001-02	745,305	18,178
2000-01	683,125	16,662
1999-00	628,605	15,332
1998-99	381,948	15,278
1997-98	638,034	15,562
1996-97	636,083	15,514
1995-96	647,088	15,783
1994-95	670,720	16,359
1993-94	634,107	15,466
1992-93	661,269	16,129
1991-92	635,515	15,500
1990-91	676,687	16,505
1989-90	659,602	16,088
1988-89	700,984	17,097
1987-88	452,057	11,026
1986-87	450,987	11,000
1985-86	443,064	10,806
1984-85	422,924	10,315
1983-84	414,250	10,104
1982-83	425,572	10,380
1981-82	443,288	10,812
1980-81	448,366	10,936
1979-80	446,972	10,902
1978-79	443,926	10,827
1977-78	435,057	10,611
1976-77	396,947	9,682
1975-76	426,784	10,409
1974-75	425,173	10,370
1973-74	373,135	9,819
1972-73	372,951	9,815
1971-72	372,439	10,346
1970-71	378,106	10,503
1969-70	360,650	9,491
1968-69	212,362	6,246

Minneapolis Lakers

Year	Total	Avg
1948-49	N/A	
1949-50	N/A	
1950-51	172,410	5,388
1951-52	N/A	
1952-53	N/A	
1953-54	N/A	
1954-55	N/A	
1955-56	112,360	4,494
1956-57	82,211	2,652
1957-58	107,874	3,596
1958-59	164,197	7,464
1959-60	106,859	4,110

Minnesota Timberwolves

Year	Total	Avg
2002-03	643,684	15,699
2001-02	731,673	17,846
2000-01	717,371	17,497
1999-00	665,999	16,244
1998-99	427,974	17,119
1997-98	738,572	18,014
1996-97	597,727	14,579
1995-96	585,669	14,285
1994-95	603,518	14,720
1993-94	733,419	17,888
1992-93	754,593	18,405
1991-92	769,035	18,757
1990-91	779,470	19,011
1989-90	1,027,572	25,063

New Jersey Nets

Year	Total	Avg
2002-03	622,574	15,184
2001-02	564,194	13,761
2000-01	556,573	13,575
1999-00	643,623	15,698
1998-99	415,353	16,614
1997-98	718,523	17,525
1996-97	670,628	16,357
1995-96	638,144	15,564

1994-95	684,102	16,685
1993-94	658,304	16,056
1992-93	620,416	15,132
1991-92	517,356	12,618
1990-91	489,915	11,949
1989-90	497,838	12,142
1988-89	519,601	12,673
1987-88	476,054	11,611
1986-87	452,686	11,041
1985-86	483,554	11,794
1984-85	501,963	12,243
1983-84	512,441	12,499
1982-83	530,808	12,947
1981-82	568,861	13,875
1980-81	302,061	7,367
1979-80	257,418	6,278
1978-79	198,990	4,853
1977-78	199,090	4,856

New Orleans Hornets

Year	Total	Avg
2002-03	641,683	15,650

New Orleans Jazz

Year	Total	Avg
1978-79	364,205	8,883
1977-78	527,351	12,862
1976-77	444,138	10,833
1975-76	513,282	12,519
1974-75	203,141	4,955

New York Knicks

Year	Total	Avg
2002-03	779,479	19,011
2001-02	810,283	19,763
2000-01	810,283	19,763
1999-00	810,283	19,763
1998-99	494,075	19,763
1997-98	810,283	19,763
1996-97	810,283	19,763
1995-96	810,283	19,763
1994-95	810,283	19,763
1993-94	810,283	19,763
1992-93	804,840	19,630
1991-92	731,371	17,838
1990-91	654,962	15,975
1989-90	730,432	17,815
1988-89	746,851	18,216
1987-88	586,752	14,311
1986-87	538,058	13,123
1985-86	592,486	14,451
1984-85	457,317	11,154
1983-84	495,944	12,096
1982-83	438,823	10,703
1981-82	444,189	10,834
1980-81	546,441	13,328
1979-80	508,597	12,405
1978-79	545,715	13,310
1977-78	626,815	15,288
1976-77	644,811	15,727
1975-76	672,745	16,408
1974-75	760,786	18,556
1973-74	784,433	19,133
1972-73	790,031	19,269
1971-72	785,298	19,154
1970-71	763,487	18,622
1969-70	761,226	18,566
1968-69	569,153	15,383
1967-68	534,568	14,448
1966-67	410,057	11,716
1965-66	369,812	10,566
1964-65	322,870	9,225
1963-64	293,704	8,392
1962-63	302,775	8,905
1961-62	265,153	8,035
1960-61	326,895	10,215

New York Nets

Year	Total	Avg
1976-77	284,259	6,933

Orlando Magic

Year	Total	Avg
2002-03	605,901	14,778
2001-02	621,121	15,149
2000-01	605,031	14,757
1999-00	576,409	14,059
1998-99	411,091	16,444
1997-98	701,647	17,113
1996-97	687,958	16,779
1995-96	707,168	17,248
1994-95	656,410	16,010
1993-94	626,931	15,291
1992-93	621,191	15,151
1991-92	621,191	15,151
1990-91	617,668	15,065
1989-90	617,468	15,060

Philadelphia 76ers

Year	Total	Avg
2002-03	807,097	19,685
2001-02	842,976	20,560
2000-01	805,692	19,651
1999-00	756,929	18,462
1998-99	436,444	17,458
1997-98	655,417	15,986
1996-97	626,478	15,280
1995-96	489,327	11,935
1994-95	507,809	12,386
1993-94	509,444	12,425
1992-93	515,284	12,568
1991-92	574,128	14,003
1990-91	634,210	15,469
1989-90	574,710	14,017
1988-89	558,292	13,617
1987-88	513,113	12,515
1986-87	587,748	14,335
1985-86	513,459	12,523
1984-85	572,569	13,965
1983-84	588,139	14,345
1982-83	646,788	15,775
1981-82	506,847	12,362
1980-81	469,355	11,448
1979-80	479,727	11,701
1978-79	506,485	12,353
1977-78	644,456	15,718
1976-77	632,949	15,438
1975-76	509,699	12,432
1974-75	296,721	7,237
1973-74	171,159	4,626
1972-73	182,921	5,901
1971-72	326,493	8,824
1970-71	336,815	8,636
1969-70	311,976	8,210
1968-69	361,161	10,622
1967-68	304,631	8,704
1966-67	246,275	8,209
1965-66	145,372	5,815
1964-65	108,729	4,349
1963-64	108,271	3,609

Philadelphia Warriors

Year	Total	Avg
1961-62	161,795	5,579
1960-61	196,223	6,766
1959-60	226,412	8,086
1958-59	153,566	5,906
1957-58	156,988	5,607
1956-57	158,004	5,097
1955-56	164,929	5,890
1946-47	129,142	4,305

Phoenix Suns

Year	Total	Avg
2002-03	666,559	16,257
2001-02	668,939	16,316
2000-01	737,586	17,990
1999-00	773,115	18,856
1998-99	472,283	18,891
1997-98	779,943	19,023
1996-97	779,943	19,023
1995-96	779,943	19,023

1994-95	779,943	19,023
1993-94	779,943	19,023
1992-93	779,943	19,023
1991-92	594,336	14,496
1990-91	589,591	14,380
1989-90	578,661	14,114
1988-89	511,076	12,465
1987-88	461,293	11,251
1986-87	471,172	11,492
1985-86	455,969	11,121
1984-85	493,446	12,035
1983-84	445,703	10,871
1982-83	465,603	11,356
1981-82	487,215	11,883
1980-81	482,693	11,773
1979-80	480,659	11,723
1978-79	465,010	11,342
1977-78	470,009	11,464
1976-77	411,294	10,032
1975-76	295,293	7,202
1974-75	253,103	6,173
1973-74	284,324	6,935
1972-73	342,117	8,344
1971-72	342,922	8,364
1970-71	332,945	8,121
1969-70	281,821	7,617
1968-69	160,565	4,340

Portland Trailblazers

Year	Total	Avg
2002-03	796,258	19,420
2001-02	797,821	19,459
2000-01	831,376	20,277
1999-00	835,078	20,368
1998-99	486,556	19,462
1997-98	843,647	20,577
1996-97	852,799	20,800
1995-96	850,338	20,740
1994-95	529,759	12,921
1993-94	528,408	12,888
1992-93	528,408	12,888
1991-92	528,408	12,888
1990-91	528,244	12,884
1989-90	528,244	12,884
1988-89	527,008	12,854
1987-88	519,306	12,666
1986-87	519,306	12,666
1985-86	519,306	12,666
1984-85	519,306	12,666
1983-84	519,306	12,666
1982-83	519,306	12,666
1981-82	519,306	12,666
1980-81	519,306	12,666
1979-80	519,306	12,666
1978-79	519,306	12,666
1977-78	519,306	12,666
1976-77	499,302	12,178
1975-76	413,992	10,097
1974-75	441,506	10,768
1973-74	327,495	7,988
1972-73	333,480	8,134
1971-72	279,506	6,988
1970-71	245,383	6,135

Rochester Royals

Year	Total	Avg
1952-53	79,285	2,478
1948-49	121,499	4,190

Sacramento Kings

Year	Total	Avg
2002-03	709,997	17,317
2001-02	709,997	17,317
2000-01	709,997	17,317
1999-00	687,410	16,766
1998-99	418,751	16,750
1997-98	605,434	14,767
1996-97	709,997	17,317
1995-96	709,997	17,317
1994-95	709,997	17,317
1993-94	709,997	17,317
1992-93	709,997	17,317
1991-92	697,574	17,014
1990-91	697,574	17,014
1989-90	697,574	17,014
1988-89	677,197	16,517
1987-88	423,653	10,333
1986-87	423,653	10,333
1985-86	423,653	10,333

San Antonio Spurs

Year	Total	Avg
2002-03	735,970	17,950
2001-02	906,390	22,107
2000-01	913,176	22,273
1999-00	889,444	21,694
1998-99	537,357	21,494
1997-98	783,455	19,109
1996-97	706,641	17,235
1995-96	811,422	19,791
1994-95	920,413	22,449
1993-94	904,167	22,053
1992-93	658,337	16,057
1991-92	658,337	16,057
1990-91	651,965	15,902
1989-90	603,660	14,723
1988-89	459,514	11,208
1987-88	346,960	8,462
1986-87	328,368	8,009
1985-86	336,407	8,205
1984-85	364,398	8,888
1983-84	375,900	9,168
1982-83	397,489	9,695
1981-82	434,243	10,591
1980-81	440,553	10,745
1979-80	468,657	11,431
1978-79	489,207	11,932
1977-78	373,707	9,115
1976-77	376,136	9,174

San Diego Clippers

Year	Total	Avg
1983-84	228,710	5,578
1982-83	158,887	3,875
1981-82	178,103	4,344
1980-81	257,597	6,283
1979-80	325,012	7,927
1978-79	311,789	7,605

San Diego Rockets

Year	Total	Avg
1970-71	264,206	6,775
1969-70	232,684	6,123
1968-69	248,217	6,054
1967-68	188,865	4,606

San Francisco Warriors

Year	Total	Avg
1970-71	195,935	5,156
1969-70	189,642	5,268
1968-69	194,683	4,748
1967-68	185,322	4,520
1966-67	216,352	7,727
1965-66	124,160	4,775
1964-65	76,963	2,138
1963-64	132,678	3,402
1962-63	101,218	3,067

Seattle Supersonics

Year	Total	Avg
2002-03	637,194	15,541
2001-02	633,516	15,452
2000-01	640,847	15,630
1999-00	615,730	15,018
1998-99	426,800	17,072
1997-98	699,952	17,072
1996-97	699,952	17,072
1995-96	697,301	17,007
1994-95	633,748	15,457
1993-94	601,969	14,682
1992-93	632,205	15,420
1991-92	586,929	14,315
1990-91	510,166	12,443
1989-90	502,014	12,244
1988-89	529,733	12,920
1987-88	492,312	12,008
1986-87	356,362	8,692
1985-86	329,296	8,032
1984-85	303,342	7,399
1983-84	446,970	10,902
1982-83	574,986	14,024
1981-82	750,059	18,294
1980-81	675,097	16,466
1979-80	890,713	21,725
1978-79	747,243	18,225
1977-78	504,668	12,309
1976-77	532,196	12,980
1975-76	557,304	13,593
1974-75	524,692	12,797
1973-74	491,856	11,996
1972-73	387,382	9,448
1971-72	444,302	11,108
1970-71	372,612	9,315
1969-70	278,444	7,735
1968-69	210,232	5,840
1967-68	202,263	6,525

St. Louis Hawks

Year	Total	Avg
1967-68	201,215	6,288
1966-67	198,039	6,829
1965-66	267,008	8,344
1964-65	265,645	6,641
1963-64	290,840	7,457
1962-63	284,849	7,699
1961-62	256,747	7,336
1960-61	291,084	8,561
1959-60	277,502	8,409
1958-59	265,000	8,548
1957-58	224,512	7,242
1956-57	217,300	7,010
1955-56	156,009	6,000

Syracuse Nationals

Year	Total	Avg
1949-50	N/A	
1950-51	174,094	5,276
1951-52	N/A	
1952-53	N/A	
1953-54	N/A	
1954-55	N/A	
1955-56	140,714	4,539
1956-57	118,883	3,835
1957-58	112,386	3,625
1958-59	107,455	3,466
1959-60	110,000	3,667
1960-61	112,394	4,014
1961-62	112,486	4,017
1962-63	161,593	5,771

Toronto Raptors

Year	Total	Avg
2002-03	777,507	18,963
2001-02	810,160	19,760
2000-01	793,256	19,348
1999-00	756,496	18,451
1998-99	439,190	17,568
1997-98	675,255	16,470
1996-97	748,927	18,267
1995-96	950,330	23,179

Utah Jazz

Year	Total	Avg
2002-03	786,034	19,171
2001-02	766,108	18,686
2000-01	792,196	19,322
1999-00	801,268	19,543
1998-99	493,120	19,725
1997-98	815,889	19,900
1996-97	813,073	19,831
1995-96	813,073	19,831
1994-95	811,159	19,784
1993-94	814,502	19,866
1992-93	815,892	19,900
1991-92	806,653	19,674
1990-91	514,751	12,555
1989-90	517,256	12,616
1988-89	509,501	12,427
1987-88	503,969	12,292
1986-87	491,382	11,985
1985-86	477,842	11,655
1984-85	373,808	9,117
1983-84	407,818	9,947
1982-83	355,819	8,679
1981-82	313,864	7,655
1980-81	307,825	7,508
1979-80	320,649	7,821

Vancouver Grizzlies

Year	Total	Avg
2000-01	563,218	13,737
1999-00	569,864	13,899
1998-99	417,966	16,719
1997-98	660,457	16,109
1996-97	679,422	16,571
1995-96	704,489	17,183

Washington Wizards

Year	Total	Avg
2002-03	827,093	20,173
2001-02	839,567	20,477
2000-01	638,653	15,577
1999-00	616,593	15,039
1998-99	402,481	16,099
1997-98	801,240	19,542
1996-97	700,646	17,089
1995-96	688,354	16,789
1994-95	701,084	17,100
1993-94	619,756	15,116
1992-93	559,265	13,641
1991-92	505,988	12,341
1990-91	487,097	11,880
1989-90	474,166	11,565
1988-89	402,377	9,814
1987-88	433,376	10,570
1986-87	485,352	11,838
1985-86	373,802	9,117
1984-85	383,188	9,346
1983-84	324,701	7,920
1982-83	368,601	8,990
1981-82	369,807	9,020
1980-81	375,360	9,155
1979-80	466,823	11,386
1978-79	524,356	12,789
1977-78	446,539	10,891
1976-77	467,745	11,408
1975-76	440,837	10,752
1974-75	383,775	9,360

Chapter 20

Family Matters: Tracing Basketball's Deep Bloodlines

By David Hereen

The Pittsburgh Pirates, at the peak of Willie Stargell's Hall of Fame career, adopted a rallying cry: We Are Family. But as a literal slogan it was actually a better fit for the New York Knicks' backcourt two decades earlier.

During the early 1950s, when the Knicks reached the NBA championship series three straight times, the team's guards included brothers Dick and Al McGuire, and Ernie Vandeweghe. Vandeweghe married the sister of an NBA player and they had a son, Kiki, who would play for the Knicks 40 years later while Dick McGuire still was employed by the team.

Besides being called Tricky Dick before a man named Nixon, Dick McGuire became known for handling jobs in all three critical areas of professional basketball—playing, coaching, and player evaluation. Brother Al also proved capable in the same three areas.

The McGuires were the first brothers elected to the Basketball Hall of Fame. They are the only related players in the Hall, although that may change in a few years when Reggie Miller becomes eligible to join his sister Cheryl.

Including recent additions to research done by John Grasso and Robert Bradley, 160 men have played in major professional basketball leagues and have had at least one relative playing in one of these leagues (see below).

The most prolific basketball families were the Bruce Hale-Rick Barry family and the Jones brothers of McGehee, Ark.

Al, mom and Dick McGuire, 1953
Al salutes big brother Dick, who would follow him to form the Naismith Memorial Basketball Hall of Fame's first and only brother combination.

Counting Hale, Barry and their offspring, this family had seven members who became professional basketball players, including five NBA players. The Jones family sent four brothers to the NBA, headed by Caldwell Jones, who played three seasons in the ABA before going to the NBA for 14 more.

These two families illustrate the point that, in families where more than one member played professional basketball, there was often a great disparity of talent. Barry, for example, was a Hall of Famer, one of the greatest small forwards ever to put on a basketball uniform. Hale, his father-in-law, was also a standout player. But the other five members of the family were either secondary NBA players or players who were not quite good enough to make it in the NBA. Caldwell Jones was an exceptional player, but his three brothers were career reserves in the NBA.

The imbalance in talent did not apply, however, to the McGuires. Any way you look at it, Dick and Al McGuire were among the pioneers in this aspect of basketball tradition. The

McGuire brothers were born during the mid-1920s in New York City. Both attended Catholic high schools in the city and both went to St. John's University. Dick was 31 months older than Al. At 6-foot-2, Al was two inches taller than Dick.

The two young men had in common a love for basketball and an intense desire to win. This was evident in weekend pickup games at Rockaway Beach on Long Island, on a basketball court near the ocean.

Sometimes Dick and Al would be matched up against each other. They played with intensity. "I would let him shoot from the outside anytime he wanted to, that's for sure," Dick said jokingly. Al was a notoriously poor shooter.

By the time the McGuire brothers reached the NBA, Dick was known as one of the better playmakers in the game. Of his contemporary point guards, only Bob Cousy and Bob Davies were considered better. He played 11 seasons in the NBA with New York and Detroit and seven times was chosen to play in the league's All-Star Game.

Midway through his final season as a player, 1959-60, he took over as Detroit's head coach when Red Rocha was fired. After his playing career ended, he coached three more seasons for Detroit and three for New York. He then became a scout for the Knicks and helped them assemble their two-time champion team led by Walt Frazier, Willis Reed, and Dave DeBusschere. Currently the Knicks' director of scouting services, he has been employed by the team for 47 years.

Al McGuire was a scrappy player, not as skilled as Dick. He lasted only three seasons in the NBA before becoming a college coach for 22 years.

His best job was head coach of the Marquette University team. Through wise recruiting, masterful motivating, and shrewd coaching, he was able to lead Marquette to an NIT title in 1970, a 28-1 record in 1970-71 and an NCAA championship in 1977. One of his recruits was his son, Allie, who went on to play one season for the Knicks after graduating from Marquette. Al's 13-season coaching record at Marquette was 295-80.

Marquette's title in 1977, achieved by a 67-59 victory over North Carolina in McGuire's final game as a coach, is still considered one of the great upsets in NCAA history.

Al then became a television commentator and even that sensitive job did not soften his brazen nature. In 1989, while commenting on a college game, he bluntly declared: "Tim Hardaway is the best college basketball player in America and should be the No. 1 draft choice." None of the NBA scouts rated Hardaway anywhere close to that high. He was considered a mid-first round draft choice and was selected at No. 14. In retrospect, however, it is clear that McGuire was right.

Hardaway was the best player in that draft.

McGuire Contemporaries

The players who had the most to do with defeating the McGuire-led Knick teams in the championship series were Bob Davies (with Rochester in 1950) and George Mikan (with Minneapolis in 1951 and 1952). Both of these men became Hall of Famers. Both had basketball-playing brothers. George Mikan was the best player of his era. He played in all three top

professional leagues of that time. After graduating from DePaul he played in the National Basketball League (NBL) and the Basketball Association of America (BAA), which evolved into the NBA. He led the Minneapolis Lakers to a BAA title in 1949 and to NBA titles in 1950, 1952, 1953, and 1954.

At 6-foot-10, Mikan seemed to tower over other players. He weighed 245 pounds and was notorious for swinging his elbows. At the peak of his career his per-game averages were about 28 points, 14 rebounds, and five blows to the ribs. He led the NBA at least once in nearly every statistical category, including personal fouls. He was voted the greatest player of the first half-century of basketball.

Mikan had a brother and a son in the NBA. His brother Ed was a journeyman who played for six teams in six seasons, never averaging double-figure scoring.

His son, Larry, played one season for the Cleveland Cavaliers. In 1970-71, Larry played 536 minutes for the Cavaliers, scoring 158 points (3.0 per game).

Davies was a clever guard who did most of the flashy things Bob Cousy was credited with inventing before Cousy did them. He mastered the between-the-legs dribble and the behind-the-back and over-the-shoulder passes. He even was nicknamed Houdini before Cousy.

As a senior at Seton Hall University in 1942, Davies was chosen MVP of the College All-Star Game. After a three-year stint in the U.S. Navy, he played for teams in the NBL, the BAA, and the NBA. He was named a first team all-star in all three leagues.

In the 1951 NBA championship series, Davies outplayed Dick McGuire in a head-to-head match-up. He sank two tie-breaking free throws with 17 seconds remaining in the seventh game and the Royals went on to win 79-75. Davies was honored as the championship series MVP.

After the death of his father, Bob Davies helped raise a brother, Dick, 16 years younger than himself. An LSU graduate, Dick Davies played summer basketball for a team coached by Red Auerbach. Auerbach named him captain of the team, which had several pro players on the roster, and invited him to try out for the Boston Celtics in 1961. Davies likely could have made the Celtics' roster at the peak of their dynasty.

"But when I found out I would be earning $7,500 with the Celtics when I could be making $8,800 as a starting salary with Goodyear [Tire and Rubber Company], I decided to go with Goodyear," Davies said. He went on to become Goodyear's vice president of manufacturing.

In 1964, Dick Davies was among a group of AAU players who formed a team to compete with seven NCAA teams at the U.S. Olympic Basketball Tryouts at St. John's University. The AAU team shocked the NCAA players, defeating an NCAA team led by Bill Bradley in the final game of the tryouts. Five AAU players, including Davies, were named to the U.S. Olympic Team, which swept through the Olympics without being challenged and defeated a Soviet Union team for the gold medal.

Dick Davies' enshrinement in the Olympic Hall of Fame as a basketball player made himself and Bob Davies the only brother combination to hold membership in basketball's two most prestigious halls of fame. They are also the only brothers

where one possesses an NBA championship ring and the other an Olympic gold medal.

Ernie Vandeweghe was not a member of any major basketball Hall of Fame. In fact, he was only a part-time professional basketball player. Vandeweghe was a backcourt teammate of Dick McGuire on the Knicks from 1949-50 through 1955-56. (He sat out the 1954-55 season.) He was one of the most efficient shooters in the NBA at that time, always hitting more than 40 percent of his shots during an era when few players shot that well.

But Vandeweghe's name appeared among the shooting percentage leaders only once, in 1952-53. He was listed in a tie for fifth place with his .435 percentage that season and averaged 12.0 points per game.

Vandeweghe was a full-time medical student. During his six seasons with the Knicks he missed 185 games, many of them because of the demands of his studies. While in the NBA he met and married the sister of Mel Hutchins, an NBA all-star.

After earning his doctorate in pediatrics, Vandeweghe retired from basketball, moved to California and raised a son, Kiki. Ernie later became a sports physician.

Kiki Vandeweghe's main athletic interest as a child was swimming. But when he settled into basketball, he outdid his father. At his peak with the Denver Nuggets, in 1983-84, he averaged 29.4 points per game. For his 13-season career, he averaged 19.7 points. He led all scorers with 51 points in the most prolific scoring game in NBA history—a 186-184 triple-overtime victory for Detroit over Denver on Dec. 13, 1983.

Kiki Vandeweghe was one of the NBA's all-time great shooters. Often shooting from long range, his career field-goal percentage was .525. He averaged .368 from three-point range and .872 on free throws.

The Hale-Barry Connection

Bruce Hale was a contemporary of Bob Davies. Hale was an All-American basketball player at Santa Clara University. He graduated from Santa Clara in 1941 and joined the Air Force, hoping to become a pilot. But an eye problem kept him grounded, so he went through Officers Training School and helped train recruits during World War II.

During most of his service tenure he was stationed in Florida. He played for the Five by Five basketball team consisting of five former collegiate All-Americans. The team toured Florida, playing exhibition games before large crowds on military bases.

Hale also organized a military service league and coached a team in the Miami area during the war. The service teams played a very high quality of basketball because most of the good young players were in one branch of the military or another at that time.

Hale had no idea then that he and a child who was two years old when he was discharged from service in 1946 would become known a half-century later as the patriarchs of basketball.

The two-year-old was Rick Barry.

From 1946 through 1951, Hale played for teams in the NBL, the BAA, and the NBA. He then coached briefly in the NBA before becoming the head men's basketball coach at the University of Miami. Hale's daughter, Pam, 10, was the Hurricanes' ball girl during Hale's first season at UM, 1954-55.

Seven years later, Hale tried to recruit Barry, who was starring at Roselle Park High School in New Jersey. Hale visited Barry and showed him a postcard of Miami Beach, where the Hurricanes played home games. Barry signed with the Hurricanes without visiting the campus in Coral Gables, about 20 miles from Hale's idyllic postcard scene. In three varsity seasons at UM, Barry averaged 29.8 points and 16.5 rebounds per game. He led the nation in scoring during his senior season with an average of 37.4 points.

He also met and married Pam Hale.

During Barry's tenure at Miami, Bruce Hale was fond of saying: "Rick may miss his first 10 shots, but he'll make the next 10." Hale helped Barry work on his complete game, and Rick responded by becoming a versatile player.

Hale was an innovator. He experimented with the three-point field goal. He fastened tape to the court in the shape of an arc beyond the free-throw circle and talked an opposing coach into using the shot in an intercollegiate game. That is believed to have been the first time a three-point shot was used at the collegiate or professional level.

Barry became Miami's best long-range shooter and his great shooting range would be an important element of his game as a professional. Using a variety of acrobatic offensive moves, with effective range up to 25 feet, Barry averaged 30.5 points in four ABA seasons and 23.2 points in 10 NBA seasons. He led the NBA at least once in scoring, field goals attempted, field goals made, free throws made, free throw percentage and steals.

A great passer, Barry accumulated the second highest assists-per-game average (5.1) of any forward in NBA history. The only frontcourt player to complete an NBA career with a higher average was Larry Bird. Barry was MVP of the 1975 NBA championship series, leading the Golden State Warriors to the title. He was elected to the Basketball Hall of Fame. On most all-time lists he is ranked among the top three or four small forwards.

Rick and Pam Barry raised four sons, three of whom have been active NBA players in recent seasons—Brent, Jon and Drew. The fourth, Scooter, was a member of an NCAA champion team at Kansas in 1988. Scooter played professionally for many years in Europe after trying out for the Boston Celtics and narrowly failing to make the team. "Both Kevin McHale and Larry Bird told me Scooter should have made [the Celtics], but they weren't going to cut a first-round draft choice to keep him," Rick Barry said.

Bruce Hale also has a son, Alan, who played three seasons for a professional team in Europe.

And Rick Barry's brother, Dennis, at one time was considered as good a player as Rick. At Roselle Park High School, the Barrys patterned their game after Elgin Baylor. Both put up huge scoring and rebounding numbers. But Dennis Barry's career was terminated by a severe knee injury. He never played a game of collegiate or professional basketball.

Even though Scooter Barry and Alan Hale fell just short of having prominent careers and Dennis Barry sustained the disappointing injury, the Hale-Barry family placed a record five

players in the NBA and a record seven players in professional basketball.

Other Brothers

Even the prolific Hale-Barry family could not claim credit for placing the largest set of brothers in the NBA. This distinction went to the Jones boys of McGehee, Ark.

The oldest of the four Jones brothers, and the shortest at 6-foot-8, was Wil. Like the three brothers who would follow him to the NBA, he played collegiate basketball at Albany State (Ga.). He then played seven solid seasons in the ABA and two as a reserve in the NBA. In his best season, he averaged 14.9 points and 10.4 rebounds for Memphis in the ABA.

Caldwell was the tallest (6-foot-11) and best of the Jones brothers. He excelled for three seasons in the ABA, averaging 15.8 points, 13.1 rebounds, and 3.4 blocked shots. Though he never came close to matching those numbers in the NBA, he played 14 NBA seasons for a career total of 17.

Major Jones (6-foot-9) played six NBA seasons for Houston and Detroit. Almost exclusively in a reserve role, he averaged 4.4 points and 3.5 rebounds.

The last of the Jones brothers, Charles (6-foot-9), also was primarily a reserve. He averaged only 2.5 points and 4.5 rebounds. But he hung on for 15 years in the NBA before retiring after the 1997-98 season. Counting all four brothers, the Jones family posted 10 seasons in the ABA and 37 in the NBA.

The Russell brothers—Frank, Campy and Walker—grew up in Michigan during the same era as the Joneses in Arkansas. Frank, the oldest, was born two years after Wil Jones. After graduating from Detroit University, he played one season for the Chicago Bulls. Campy Russell, three years younger than Frank, attended the University of Michigan and then averaged 15.8 points per game over a nine-season NBA career. The youngest Russell brother, Walker, went to Western Michigan University and played six seasons as a reserve in the NBA.

When Bernard and Albert King were high school players, Albert received acclaim as one of the top young players in the United States. But by the time they were finished with their NBA careers, Bernard was by far the better known brother.

Albert played nine NBA seasons, averaging 12.1 points per game. Despite a horrendous knee injury at the peak of his career, Bernard averaged 22.5 points for 14 seasons. He was having arguably the best season of anybody in the NBA in 1984-85, leading the league by a wide margin with 32.9 points per game, when he was injured in the 55th game. He came back from the injury two years later and had several more good seasons. But he wasn't as good as he had been before the injury.

Bernard King is a Hall of Fame candidate in spite of his severe injury. Mark Price would have been one except for his. Price was at the peak of an outstanding career when he wrecked a knee during his ninth season in a freak accident. He was knocked into a sign hanging from a press table beside the court. He never came close to regaining his previous form.

At the peak of his game, Price had seasons in which he averaged 19.6 points and 10.4 assists. One of the best pure shooters in NBA history, he shot nearly 50 percent from two-point range, over 40 percent from three-point range, and over 90 percent from the free-throw line. He holds the NBA record with a career free-throw percentage of .907. Price's younger brother, Brent, played most of the decade of the 1990s as an NBA reserve.

There was one other brother tandem named Price in pro basketball. Guards Jim and Mike Price played professionally during the 1970s. Jim averaged 10 points in seven NBA seasons. Mike garnered little playing time as a reserve in three NBA seasons and one in the ABA.

Two prolific scorers who had brothers in the NBA were Hall of Famer George Gervin and Hall candidate Dominique Wilkins. The rail-thin Gervin averaged 21.9 points in four ABA seasons, then posted a 26.2 average in 10 NBA seasons, winning four scoring titles. The prototypical player who never saw a shot he didn't like, Gervin played 35,597 minutes of professional basketball and took 27,405 shots. But Gervin's shooting-gallery attitude paid off. For his full career his field goal percentage was .506 and his free throw percentage was .841. He is usually ranked among the top five shooting guards of all time. His brother, Derrick, played two NBA seasons.

Another prolific shooter and scorer, Dominique Wilkins averaged 24.8 points and 6.7 rebounds during a 15-season NBA career. He totaled 26,668 points and won a scoring title. He holds the St. Louis-Atlanta Hawks franchise records for points and steals. A spectacular athlete, nicknamed the "Human Highlight Reel," he twice won the slam-dunk contest during the NBA's All-Star Game Weekend. He is a certain Hall of Famer. His brother, Gerald, averaged 13.0 points in 13 seasons. The Wilkins brothers wound up their careers as teammates for the Orlando Magic during the 1998-99 season.

A brother tandem that was much more equal in ability was Gus and Ray Williams. Both were standout guards. Gus played 11 seasons, averaging 17.1 points and 5.6 assists. A great clutch player, he averaged 19.5 points in playoff games and played a starring role for Seattle's NBA champion team in 1979. Ray averaged 15.5 points and 5.8 assists for six teams in 10 NBA seasons.

Even harder to separate in ability were the Van Arsdale brothers. Both were 6-foot-5 and they were identical twins. Dick Van Arsdale averaged 16.4 points in 12 NBA seasons for New York and Phoenix. Tom Van Arsdale had a less stable career, playing for six NBA teams. But he also played 12 seasons. His scoring average was 15.3.

Another prominent set of basketball-playing twins is Horace and Harvey Grant. But they are easier to tell apart. The 6-foot-9 Harvey averaged 9.9 points and 4.4 rebounds for 11 NBA seasons. The 6-foot-10 Horace has averaged about 12 points and eight rebounds and is still active. Horace's rebounding and post defense were crucial to the Chicago Bulls in their championship seasons of 1991, 1992, and 1993.

Fathers and Sons

Pete Maravich may have been the only player in basketball history who was actually asked to downgrade his game. Under the tutelage of his father, Press, Pete became so good at Louisiana State University that his teammates could not keep up with him. The situation did not improve during his professional career with the Atlanta Hawks and New Orleans Jazz,

two of the NBA's weaker teams.

Characterized by floppy socks and moppy hair, Pistol Pete averaged 44.2 points, 6.4 rebounds and 5.1 assists in three varsity seasons at LSU. He set several NCAA scoring records that may never be challenged. He averaged 16.7 field goals per game, and it is a near certainty that close to six per game were from beyond the distance that today is worth three points. This means that, with today's rules, Maravich would have averaged about 50 points per game.

In the NBA, his career averages were 24.2 points, 5.4 assists, and 4.2 rebounds. In his best season, 1976-77, he led the NBA in field goals attempted, free throws made, points and scoring average (31.1).

Maravich had such great shooting range that defenders would have to get in his face as soon as he crossed half-court. He was almost always double-teamed. The NBA's three-point distance was easy for Pete. In his final NBA season, 1979-80, the league introduced a 23-foot, 9-inch three-point shot. Even at that age, with creaky knees, in limited playing time, he sank 10 of 15 threes. If the NBA had had three-point shots his entire 10-season career, Maravich probably would have averaged over 28 points per game instead of his actual 24.2.

The parts of Maravich's game that were a problem for teammates were his ball-handling and passing. Some of his teammates were slow to react, and the ball would bounce off a shoulder or an ear when Maravich made his snappy deliveries. Much of Pete's practice on his slick moves was spent under the watchful eyes of his father at all hours of the day and night.

Press Maravich played professionally before becoming a coach. He played one season for the Youngstown Bears in the NBL (1945-46) and one for the Pittsburgh Ironmen of the BAA (1946-47). He averaged 4.6 points while shooting .272 from the field and .517 from the free-throw line.

Another noteworthy father-son combination was Dolph and Dan Schayes. Dolph became a Hall of Famer after averaging over 20 points a game for six straight seasons and over 12 rebounds per game for 11 straight seasons for the Syracuse Nationals. He played 16 professional seasons. Dan was not the player his father was, but he did surpass his dad with 18 seasons in the NBA.

Joe "Jelly Bean" Bryant played eight respectable seasons in the NBA, but his son, Kobe, has made more of a name for himself. Signed by the Los Angeles Lakers right out of high school, Kobe is regarded as the best shooting guard in the league. Barring injuries, he is a near certain future Hall of Famer.

Danny Manning is a player whose potential Hall of Fame career was impaired by an injury. Manning won of the Naismith and Wooden awards as the college Player of the Year in 1988 after leading Kansas to the NCAA title. He was named the NCAA Tournament's Most Outstanding Player. However, he blew out a knee during his rookie season with the Los Angeles Clippers. He has played well during a 15-season NBA career, but has not regained the durability or athleticism he possessed before the injury. His father, Ed, played four seasons in the NBA and five in the ABA.

Father-son combinations worthy of special mention are brothers Jim and Jon Paxson, whose father Jim also played in the NBA; star guard Jimmy Walker, whose son Jalen Rose has developed into a fine forward/guard with the Indiana Pacers, and the phenomenal shooting tandem of Walt and Wally Szczerbiak.

Copycat Cousins

One of the major stories of recent NBA seasons was the outlandish effort the league made to promote Vince Carter as the next Michael Jordan. A secondary story to the Carter hype concerned efforts by the Toronto Raptors to convince Tracy McGrady not to try to emulate his teammate before McGrady signed with Orlando. While attempting to take the ball to the basket for spectacular dunks like Carter's, McGrady was prone to turn the ball over. Not any more: McGrady won a scoring title in 2002-03, his sixth NBA season. The thread tying the two stories together is this: Carter and McGrady are distant cousins. So it isn't strange that McGrady, the younger of the two at age 24, should want to imitate the venerable Carter, 26.

With his explosive drives and thunderous jams, the 6-foot-5 Carter is certainly a showcase player. His scoring average rose in each of his first three seasons in the NBA, before injuries came and his offense declined. It's doubtful of course if he or anyone else will match Jordan's 10 scoring titles.

McGrady has emerged from Carter's shadow. Signed right out of high school, he has improved in each of his six NBA seasons. An athletic 6-foot-8 backcourt man, McGrady already has broken one of Jordan's records. During the 1999-2000 season he blocked 151 shots, 20 more than Jordan's record number for a guard.

Newly inducted into the Basketball Hall of Fame, Robert Parish played a record 21 seasons in the NBA, winning three league championship rings with the Boston Celtics. Before retiring in 1997, he scored 23,334 points, collected 10,117 rebounds and blocked 2,361 shots. A second cousin of Parish's, Larry Robinson, played four NBA seasons.

Exceptionally fast for a 6-foot-6 player, "The Greyhound" Walter Davis scored 19,521 points in 15 NBA seasons and is the all-time scoring leader of the Phoenix Suns. He was a member of the U.S. Gold Medal winning Olympic Team in 1976 and won the NBA's Rookie of the Year award in 1978. He is the uncle of guard Hubert Davis, still active after 11 NBA seasons.

Grant Long and Terry Mills have much in common. Both are nephews of John Long. The two Longs and Mills all were born and raised in Michigan and played college basketball for Michigan schools. All three played at least 10 seasons in the NBA, and each of the three played at least one season for the Detroit Pistons.

Glenn (Doc) Rivers enjoyed a prosperous 13-season career in the NBA, and since retiring as a player he has coached the Atlanta Hawks and the Orlando Magic. Two of Rivers' relatives—cousin Byron Irvin and uncle Jim Brewer—also played in the NBA.

Three other sets of professional-basketball playing cousins were Evers Burns-Len Elmore, Danny Vranes-Jeff Judkins and Lamond and Tracy Murray.

Only twice in professional basketball history were there grandfather-grandson combinations. One was Bruce Hale with grandsons Brent, Jon and Drew Barry. The other was grandpa

Johnny Townsend and grandson Eric Montross.

Although he never had a relative in professional basketball, Miami Heat coach Pat Riley is noteworthy because of unique family ties. Riley has spent 28 seasons in the NBA as player and coach and has won five championship rings. He is the son of Leon Riley, who played major league baseball in 1944. He is the brother of Lee Riley, who played six seasons in the National Football League.

With members in three major professional sports the Rileys are probably unique but, hey, it's all in the family.

RELATIVES IN THE NBL, BAA, NBA & ABA

FATHERS & SONS

BARRY - Rick and Brent, Jon & Drew
BIBBY - Henry and Mike
BRYANT - Joe and Kobe
CHAPMAN - Wayne and Rex
DUMAS - Rich and Richard
DUNLEAVY - Mike and Mike, Jr.
ELLIS - Leroy and Leron
FERRY - Bob and Danny
GUOKAS - Matt and Matt, Jr.
HIGGINS - Earle and Sean
HOSKET - Bill and Bill
JONES - Wali and Askia
MANNING - Ed and Danny
MARAVICH - Press and Pete
McGUIRE - Al and Allie
MIKAN - George and Larry
MOUNT - Pete and Rick
PAXSON - Jim, Sr. and Jim, Jr. & John
PIATKOWSKI - Walt and Eric
SALVADORI - Al and Kevin
SCHAYES - Dolph and Danny
SZCZERBIAK - Walt and Wally
VAN BREDA KOLFF - Bill and Jan
VANDEWEGHE - Ernie and Kiki
VAUGHN - David and David III
WAGNER - Milt and Dajuan
WALKER - Jimmy and Jalen Rose

BROTHERS

ANDERSON - Willie and Shandon
BARRY - Brent, Jon and Drew
BRADLEY - Charles and Dudley
COLLINS - Jarron and Jason (twins)
CORLEY - Ken and Ray
DAVIS - Brad and Mickey
DOUGLAS - John and Leon
FISHER - Derek and WASHINGTON - Duane
FITZGERALD - Bob and Dick
GERVIN - George and Derrick
GONDREZICK - Glen and Grant
GRANT - Harvey and Horace (twins)
GUOKAS - Al and Matt, Sr.
JOHNSON - Eric and Vinnie
JONES - Caldwell, Charles, Major and Wil
JONES - Nick and Steve
KING - Albert and Bernard
LEE - Ron and Russell
McCRAY - Rodney and Scooter
McGUIRE - Al and Dick
MELCHIONNI - Bill and Gary
MIKAN - Ed and George
NATT - Calvin and Kenny
NORRIS - Audie and Sylvester
O'BANNON - Ed and Charles
OGDEN - Bud and Ralph
OTTEN - Don and Mac
PAXSON - Jim Jr. and John
PEARCY - George and Henry
PERSON - Chuck and Wesley
PRICE - Brent and Mark
PRICE - Jim and Mike
ROGERS - Harry and Marshall
ROLLINS - Kenny and Phil
RUSSELL - Campy, Frank and Walker
SASSER - Jason and Jeryl
SCHEFFLER - Steve and Tom
SHORT - Eugene and Purvis
SIMMONS - Connie and Johnny
SOJOURNER - Mike and Willie
STITH - Sam and Tom
THOMAS - Carl and Charles (twins)
TRAPP - George and John Q.
VAN ARSDALE - Dick and Tom (twins)
VINCENT - Jay and Sam
WILEY - Michael and Morton
WILKINS - Dominique and Gerald
WILLIAMS - Gus and Ray

COUSINS

Evers Burns and Len Elmore
Vince Carter and Tracy McGrady
Jevon Crudup and Robert Parish
Byron Irvin and Doc Rivers
Stephon Marbury and Jamal Thomas
Lamond and Tracy Murray
Willis Reed and Orlando Woolridge
Danny Vranes and Jeff Judkins

SECOND COUSINS

Jonathan Bender and Morris Peterson
Robert Parish and Larry Robinson

UNCLES AND NEPHEWS

Jim Brewer and Doc Rivers
Walter Davis and Hubert Davis
Al Guokas and Matt Guokas, Jr.
Mel Hutchins and Kiki Vandeweghe
John Long and Grant Long
John Long and Terry Mills
Dick McGuire and Allie McGuire
Ed Mikan and Larry Mikan

GRANDFATHER AND GRANDSON

Johnny Townsend and Eric Montross
Bruce Hale and Brent, Jon & Drew Barry

—Compiled by John Grasso and Robert Bradley

Chapter 21

Multi-Sport Stars:
Men For Two
(or Three) Seasons

Gene Conley
Pride of the Celtics.

Gene Conley
Pride of the Red Sox.

By Ted Brock

I t's a shame Michael Jordan never made it to the major leagues. He could have joined the elite group of athletes who have played at the top levels of basketball and one other sport.

The names of these versatile athletes comprise a roster that spans six decades—from Otto Graham in the 1940s and '50s to Danny Ainge in the 1970s, '80s and '90s. The paths of some of these athletes crossed on the playing field, and there are parallels in some of their stories. But if you're looking for the magic hinge that binds them all, forget it. No overarching theme runs across their careers, other than a love of playing games, countless hours of practice, and occasional good fortune.

Jordan would have fit right in with these multi-achievers. Too bad for him the curveball looked more like a golf ball than a basketball. Otherwise, Michael could have been to the White

Sox and the South Side of Chicago what Frank Baumholtz was to the Cubs and the North Side.

Granted, you won't find a pair of Air Baumholtz sneakers at auction on the Internet. But the 5-foot-10 guard from Midvale, Ohio, did lace up canvas high-tops for the Youngstown Bears of the National Basketball League in 1945-46. The following season he helped get the NBA off the ground, averaging 14 points in 45 games with the Cleveland Rebels, who finished the new league's first season with a 30-30 record, good for third place in the Western Division.

Baumholtz's pro basketball career ended when he broke in as an outfielder with the Cincinnati Reds in April 1947, beginning an 11-year major league career that took him to the Cubs in 1949 and the Philadelphia Phillies in 1956. In taverns along Chicago's Rush Street, the answer to the trivia question, "Who had the Cubs' highest overall batting average in the 1950s?" ought to be worth a beer or two. The answer's not Ernie Banks,

not Ralph Kiner, but Frank Baumholtz, with .300.

"Frank Baumholtz was a pain in the rear end," said Gene Conley, whose careers in the NBA and the major leagues became the envy of his contemporaries. "He drove you nuts. What a good contact hitter, a slap hitter." Conley, a lean, hard-throwing 6-foot-8, 225-pound righthander, came out of Richland, Washington, and debuted with the Boston Braves in the spring of 1952 after minor league stops in Hartford, Milwaukee, and Toledo.

Conley had attended Washington State University, where he'd played basketball and made an impression on University of Southern California guard Bill Sharman. In Sharman's second year with the Boston Celtics, 1952, he recommended the team give Conley a look. (Sharman, incidentally, was another two-sport star; a Dodgers prospect, he was in the Brooklyn dugout when Bobby Thomson hit his fabled homer in 1951.)

"So I get this call from the East Coast from a guy who said his name was Red Auerbach," Conley recalled. "I thought, 'Who in the Sam Hill is Red Auerbach?'

"He said, 'How would you like to play basketball?'

"I said, 'Is there any money involved?'

"He said, 'Never mind about the money.'

"I worked out for him, and he said, 'We'll keep you anyway.'"

Conley asked for $5,000, signed for $4,500, and played in 39 games that year, averaging 2.3 points and 4.4 rebounds a game as a backup center and forward.

"The only reason I decided to play was that I was in the minor leagues making $700-800 a week," he said. "When spring training began, I didn't have to play basketball. Auerbach didn't mind because I wasn't helping him."

How far out of his depth did Conley feel? "I played against [Minneapolis Lakers stars and future Hall of Famers] George Mikan and Jim Pollard when I was 22. They said Mikan would push me in and I should just jump straight up. They forgot to tell me he hooked you with his arm. He'd have liked to put me in the third row."

Conley's 0-3 record and 7.82 ERA with the Braves in the spring of 1952 quickly punched his ticket back to the minors. He came up for good in 1954, after the club had moved to Milwaukee. Conley joined a starting rotation that included Warren Spahn and Lew Burdette. He went 14-9 with a 2.96 ERA.

He made that year's National League All-Star team, faced one batter in the eighth inning and was the game's losing pitcher. The next year, in the middle of an 11-7 season, he made the All-Star team again and struck out the side in the top of the 12th inning to get the victory. At the time, only Dizzy Dean and Lefty Gomez had previously figured in back-to-back All-Star Game decisions. (Several pitchers have done it since.)

In 1958 the Braves won the World Series, which put an extra $5,000 in Conley's pocket. That wasn't enough, however, to offset the financial strain that came with the new house he was having built in Milwaukee, so he did what any sensible professional athlete would do: he called Red Auerbach and asked if he could play for the Celtics again.

"[Red] said he'd pay my way there, but if I didn't make it I'd have to pay my own way back," Conley recalled. "I packed a big footlocker full of clothes, and when I got there [Celtics owner] Walter Brown said, 'Red I don't know if this guy can play but he's got a lot of clothes here, so he must think he can play.' I was ready. I had a lot of confidence."

After a five-year hiatus, during which the only basketball he'd played was "at the YMCA or shooting around in the off-season," Conley spent the next three seasons with the Celtics, picking up three championship rings.

"Red kept me around," Conley said. "I could shoot, I played hard-nosed defense, and I fouled too much."

He was proud and humbled to be part of the Celtics dynasty and mystique. "We'd go into a city and nobody liked us because we were the champions. We were the big bullies. If we were down at half-time, nobody worried because we knew we were going to take their lunch in the third quarter."

Conley, whose natural position was center, often played alongside Bill Russell. On offense, Auerbach used Conley as a forward in the corner ("If I got six or eight points, I earned them"). On defense, he marked the opposing center.

"I played a lot against Wilt Chamberlain," he said. "I loved it. I'm not telling you it was a picnic, because Red had me play in front of him and, if they lobbed it over me, [Tom] Heinsohn would crash into him. Wilt was a nice guy. He could've picked you up and thrown you in the bleachers if he'd wanted to."

Auerbach's coaching genius left its mark on Conley one night in Cincinnati during the 1959-60 season. "Red said, 'Gene, I want you to take [Royals center] Wayne Embry. He's strong, he's big, he'll crash the backboard. Keep him off the board is all I ask, then let Russ take [Jerry] Lucas.'

"Wayne about beat me up, but Russ got 51 rebounds. Russ was like a windshield wiper. I told Red afterward, 'That was a good idea, but it's kind of rough on me.'"

In 1961, the Celtics traded Conley to New York, but the Knicks left him unprotected in the expansion draft. After a year with the Washington/New York Tapers of the American Basketball League, he caught on with the Knicks and played two seasons. On his first visit back to Boston, he recalled, "I was jumping center and I said to Russell, 'Russ, you're not going to do it to me in front of all these people, are you?'

"He said, 'I got to do it,' and sure enough the first two times down he blocked me. When we came down the third time I stayed outside and threw one up from 35 feet. Nothing but net. As we were running back down the court, he was laughing that laugh. He said, 'Are you shittin' me?' I said, 'Russ, I got to do it.' It was then I realized, though, how great the Celtics were. By then they had [John] Havlicek, and I thought they had six guys on the court."

Conley retired from basketball in 1964 with NBA career averages of nearly 16.5 minutes, 5.9 points and 6.3 rebounds in 351 games over six seasons.

The 1963 baseball season turned out to be Conley's last in the major leagues. He'd made the National League All-Star team in 1959, the year the Braves traded him to the Phillies. The Phillies dealt him to the Boston Red Sox in 1961, and despite a 15-win season in 1962, his hard throwing caught up with him in 1963.

Cleveland Indians general manager Gabe Paul offered Conley the chance to pick up the pieces with the Indians'

Kinston franchise in the Class A Carolina League.

"I went down and pitched in a couple of games," Conley said. "Guys were knocking me around and my arm hurt. I went into church on a Sunday before I came home to Boston. I was sitting there in the back row thinking, 'I haven't got a job, I've got no college education, I've got kids . . . All of a sudden I started bawling. The old pastor came up to me and said, 'What's the matter son, did you lose your mother?' I said, 'No, I lost my fastball.'"

Conley finished his major league career with 91 wins, 96 losses, and a 3.82 earned run average. "I had a poor move to first," he says, "and I always wished I had a good double-play ball, that hard sinker or change."

Good double-play ball or no good double-play ball, thousands of kids all over America longed for a taste of what Gene Conley represented. Even his contemporary, longtime major league shortstop Dick Groat, tried to use the big righthander's example as a bargaining chip in 1952.

Groat, who says, "Basketball was my first love," first caught the country's eye when he was college basketball's leading scorer in his junior and senior years as a guard at Duke University.

Groat played 95 games with the Pittsburgh Pirates in the summer of 1952, and followed that with 26 games in the 1952-53 season for the NBA's Fort Wayne Pistons. In 14 major league seasons with Pittsburgh, St. Louis, Philadelphia, and San Francisco, Groat had a .286 career batting average and played on five All-Star teams. In 1960, the Pirates' world championship season, he led the National League with a .325 average and was voted the league's Most Valuable Player. But baseball wasn't his first love.

"Two sports was something I had set in my mind when I was nine years old," Groat said. "I was five when my brother put up a 10-foot hoop. I lived and died basketball. Even when I was playing American Legion baseball in high school, I'd play basketball all afternoon. It was the sport I played the best without a doubt. Baseball was work. Basketball was fun. [I decided that] I was going to the major leagues without playing in the minor leagues and I would play pro basketball."

Groat reached both goals, thanks to a little ingenuity on the Pistons' part.

In Groat's sophomore year at Duke, the Blue Devils' coaching staff included Red Auerbach. "Auerbach made me a complete player," Groat said. "When I won the scoring titles [under head coach Harold Bradley], I always guarded the easy guy. I was proud of the fact the Pistons had me guard Bobby Wanzer or Bob Davies when we played the Royals, and Bob Cousy when we played the Celtics. It came from my days with Red. His philosophy then was 'work on defense and rest on offense.'"

With his college eligibility spent, Groat joined the Pittsburgh Pirates for the summer of '52 and returned to the Durham, North Carolina campus in the fall to complete the 10 course credits he needed for graduation. He played semi-pro basketball in the early fall, and signed a contract with the Pistons in November. But because his academic career at Duke was tied to a military obligation, Groat was able to play with Fort Wayne only on weekends. Tougher yet, his Monday political science class convened at 8:10 a.m., and three

cuts meant failure.

"Fort Wayne, Indiana, was not the easiest place to fly from," Groat recalled. "I'd take a charter from there to Detroit; then Capitol Airlines from Detroit to Norfolk, Virginia; then Piedmont Airlines, arriving in Durham at 7:45."

Six games into his NBA career, Groat found himself grounded in Detroit the third time he took that route. He phoned the Pistons and said, "You people have been great to me but I just can't keep playing."

A week later the Pistons called him back and said they'd take care of everything. "They rented a plane out of Durham and flew me to wherever they'd be playing on Saturday," Groat said. "Sundays we'd play in Fort Wayne, and the rented plane would get me back in time for class. That was more fun than I'd ever had in my life."

The fun was just a memory when Groat returned to the Pirates after being discharged from the service in 1955. Three years earlier, before signing with Pittsburgh, he'd tried to convince general manager Branch Rickey that he could handle two sports year-round.

"Even the fact that I used Gene Conley [as an example] didn't work," he recalled. "Mr. Rickey said it wasn't a fair comparison. 'Gene Conley is a backup center and a starting pitcher who goes out every fourth day,' he said. 'You're a shortstop who's going to be playing 150 games a year. The human body cannot take that kind of beating.' Looking back, of course, he was right."

Groat won his World Series championship ring in 1960, thanks to one of the most dramatic home runs in baseball history: Bill Mazeroski's blast in the bottom of the ninth inning of Game 7. Fourteen years later, another two-sport star would figure in another memorable homer. For the record, when Hank Aaron hit his 715th career home run at Atlanta on April 8, 1974, the winning pitcher was the Braves' Ron Reed, who, like Conley and Groat, also had played in the NBA.

Coincidentally, Reed played with the Pistons of the mid-1960s, who by then had moved to Detroit. Not coincidentally, Reed's boyhood hero had been Gene Conley, and now he was pitching for the franchise that brought Conley into the majors.

Growing up in La Porte, Indiana, Reed was a high school basketball and baseball star. He still holds the University of Notre Dame record for rebounds in a game, 17, set in his junior year, 1964.

The Milwaukee Braves signed Reed to a minor league contract in 1965, the same year the Pistons drafted him in the fourth round. He spent two years pitching in the minors before making it up for a full season in Atlanta in 1968, the Braves' third year there. Reed went 11-10 with a 3.35 ERA and was named to his only All-Star team, pitching the first two-thirds of the ninth inning in the National League's 1-0 win at the Astrodome.

Reed was a Brave until 1975, when he was traded to St. Louis, which dealt him to Philadelphia the next year. He spent eight seasons with the Phillies before finishing with the Chicago White Sox in 1984. His odyssey landed him on a World Series champion, the 1980 Phillies.

The big winners in all this are Reed's grandchildren. They only have to say the word, and Reed will be happy to tell them

about racing to home plate as soon as Aaron's No. 715 cleared the left field fence.

"That home run put me ahead," Reed said with a laugh. "They put the box score from that game in the Hall of Fame. That's the only way I was going to get to Cooperstown."

After that bedtime tale, though, it will take every bit of Reed's considerable gift for storytelling to convince them of what happened one night in 1963 at Detroit's Cobo Arena. Reed and the Pistons faced Wilt Chamberlain and the Philadelphia 76ers.

"There was a fast break, and I was one of the lagging guys," Reed said. "We got the rebound, and the pass came back out to me at about half-court. I turned, and there was one guy between me and the basket."

It was Wilt Chamberlain.

Reed didn't hesitate. He went straight at Chamberlain, leaped and dunked over the Big Dipper.

"We were coming back up court, and he looked at me and said, 'Little white boy, don't you ever do that again.'"

A few years later Reed and his Atlanta Braves teammates had just boarded a bus parked outside their New York hotel for the ride to Shea Stadium to face the Mets, when one of the players spotted Chamberlain walking up the street.

"Henry Aaron knew Wilt," Reed said, "so he got off the bus, invited Wilt aboard and said, 'Come back here, I've got to ask you a question.' Henry walked Wilt back to where I was sitting and said, 'This guy says he dunked on you. Is that true?' When Wilt said it was true, I said, 'Thank you, sir.'"

Not long before Chamberlain's death in 1999, the two men met by chance at an Atlanta sports memorabilia show.

"We spent an hour together, and with that amazing memory of his he recalled the dunk incident," Reed said. "He asked, 'You still telling those lies?' and I said, 'I sure am.'"

Reed finished his rookie year in the NBA, 1965-66, with averages of 17-plus minutes, 7-plus points and 5-plus rebounds in 57 games as the Pistons finished at 22-58, the worst record in the nine-team NBA.

When it was over, he drove to LaPorte, dropped off his winter gear, packed for summer and headed to Waycross, Georgia, where the Braves' minor leaguers trained. "Those guys were running eight or 12 sprints from the foul line to center field and huffing and puffing," said Reed, who arrived with a fitness level well beyond his new teammates' wildest dreams. "I thought that was funniest thing I'd seen in my whole life."

His second year in the NBA, the Pistons went 30-51. They'd picked up a sensational rookie named Dave Bing, yet still finished second-worst in a 10-team league. Reed's stats went up a little; the stories got better, too.

Reed's old Pistons teammate Dave DeBusschere, who died in 2003, also belonged to the double-duty sport stars club, although DeBusschere's career took the opposite direction from Reed's. Upon leaving Detroit University, DeBusschere saw limited action in the first of his two seasons with the Chicago White Sox, appearing in 12 games and giving up 23 bases on balls in 18 innings of the 1962 campaign. That autumn, he began an NBA career that stretched to 1974 and climaxed with the New York Knicks' 1973 NBA championship.

In Reed's second year with the Pistons, DeBusschere was player-coach. The two men seldom spent time together off the court, but the former backup forward remembers one night that they did, after a particularly horrendous performance in Philadelphia. Debusschere, as Reed recalled it, "took me to a bar where they played a lot of Frank Sinatra records, and after 10 or 12 beers I lost count. He did what he set out to do."

DeBusschere often assigned Reed to the opposition's surest scorer. "I'd always draw Havlicek," Reed says. "The man didn't breathe. I'd guard Gus Johnson, Elgin Baylor, and once in a while Rick Barry."

On one occasion, the NBA scheduled a regular season game with San Francisco in Miami, and it was billed as "Welcome Home Rick Barry Night." "DeBusschere comes up right before the game and says to me, 'I'm down with the flu.' I think I held Barry to 44," Reed said.

DeBusschere's brief major league career took an upturn in 1963. His two-year line included three wins and four losses in 102-1/3 innings pitched, with 61 strikeouts, 57 walks and a 2.90 ERA.

And one base hit. "I got it off Camilo Pascual," DeBusschere would later recall. "He threw me his curveball, and he was known as the best curveball pitcher around at the time."

DeBusschere's abiding memory of the Knicks teams of the early 1970s is expressed by one word: unselfishness. The team, he said, had "the willingness to sacrifice for each other without anything in return. We were probably the best passing team in history. [Coach Red] Holzman was a genius, a wonderful man who understood the psyche of each person. He knew just where he had to stroke Walt Frazier, and he knew what to say to each of the others."

Another coach, Bud Grant of the Minnesota Vikings, was winning football games at a remarkable rate during the same period that Reed and DeBusschere were successfully competing at both hardball and hoops. Grant took over the Vikings in 1967 and coached them to 11 NFC Central Division titles and four Super Bowls. He was inducted into the Pro Football Hall of Fame in 1994—yet another former NBA player who reached the top tier of another sport.

Grant joined the Minneapolis Lakers in 1949-50, and shared in the team's second straight NBA championship, seeing limited duty on a team that included George Mikan and Jim Pollard. Grant, who made $3,500 that year (Mikan made $33,000), appeared in 35 games that season, averaging 2.6 points. The following year, his last in the NBA, he played 61 games, with the same scoring average, as the Lakers lost to eventual NBA champion Rochester in the Western Division play-offs.

Grant was the Lakers' seventh man. "As the second man off the bench," he says, "My job was more defense than offense. I'd go in and bang other guys around. Most of the time I played against bigger people. I could get up and down the floor on the break, and whatever scoring I did was in transition . . .

"One thing I could do that Mikan liked: I could get him the ball, whereas the other guys would want to drive, shoot and score. I was good at positioning myself on the floor, moving the defensive man around. In those days we had the narrow lane, so Mikan could maneuver. It wasn't long before I realized I wasn't going to be a star in that setup."

At 6-foot-3 and 200 pounds, Grant was hailed as the greatest all-around schoolboy athlete in Wisconsin state history at Central High School in Superior. He spent a year in the U.S. Navy at the Great Lakes Training Center, where he played football under future Hall of Fame coaches Paul Brown and Weeb Ewbank. After his discharge in 1946, he enrolled at the University of Minnesota, where he won nine letters as an end in football, a forward in basketball, and a pitcher and outfielder in baseball before graduating in 1949.

The Philadelphia Eagles drafted Grant in 1950, and after a year of playing every position on the defensive line, he beat out receivers Bobby Walston and Pete Pihos and finished second in the NFL with 56 receptions in 1952, earning a trip to the Pro Bowl.

Grant made history that year—off the field. "My contract had an option," said Grant, whose football salary in 1950 was $7,000. "The Eagles wouldn't give me a raise, so I played out my option in 1951. Bert Bell said, 'You're setting a dangerous precedent.'"

Having unwittingly struck a theme for athletes' migratory patterns in the second half of the 20th century, Grant left Philadelphia for greener pastures north of the border, signing an $11,000 contract with the Winnipeg Blue Bombers of the Canadian Football League. He played four years there as an end and cornerback, leading the CFL in receptions three times and making a record five interceptions in one game. At age 29, he replaced Allie Sherman as the Blue Bombers' coach and compiled a 102-56-2 record in 10 seasons, with six Western Conference titles and four Grey Cup championships, before accepting the Vikings job in 1967.

Grant's taking over as coach of the Blue Bombers also meant giving up the sport that brought him more money than basketball or football. From the time he was in high school, he'd barnstormed the states of Minnesota and Wisconsin from May to September as a "hired gun" on semi-pro baseball teams.

"After the war there was no entertainment," Grant said.

"People were still on a high from money and jobs generated by the war effort. Baseball was everything in small towns. Towns put up lights. I must have played in 100 light dedication games.

"I could pitch three days a week and I could hit, so I played all summer long and made $50 to $100 a game. I made more than that, actually, because I'd bet my money on the team I'd be playing for."

In his coaching days with the Vikings, Grant often drew on his full athletic background. He was good at delegating responsibility among his assistants, but never relinquished control over the kicking game. There, he averred, the parallels with basketball were strong, and he loved arranging football players using the "space" principles common to both games.

"When it would rain," Grant said, "I used to take our football players into the gym and watch them play basketball. I could tell which ones would work hard on defense, positioning, getting up and down the floor. When the ball turned over, where did they go? I could tell the good players."

So perhaps there is a common thread running through multi-sport stars, after all. Maybe it's an appreciation for the shared detail in all sport, and for the way different games mirror each other in technique, strategy, and spirit.

It's the sort of detail that informs Ron Reed. In one moment, Reed acknowledges his pride in having picked up the save for Steve Carlton as the Phillies took a 2-0 lead en route to their World Series championship in 1980. In the next moment, he reminds you he's most proud of sharing the modern-day record for fewest home runs allowed in at least 250 innings—a mark he tied in 1975, when he allowed five homers in 251 innings.

Then again, maybe the common thread we're looking for isn't measurable at all. Maybe we can get it from Reed's response to Wilt Chamberlain after he'd dunked on Wilt and the big man told him "don't you ever do that again."

Reed looked Chamberlain in the eye and said, "I don't have to."

MULTI-SPORT BASKETBALL PLAYERS

Two Careers at the Top

Neal Adams
NBL, 1942-43: Oshkosh
AAFC, 1946-47: Brooklyn
Danny Ainge
MLB, 1979-1981: Toronto
NBA, 1981-1995: Boston, Sacramento, Portland, Phoenix
Ernie Andres
NBL, 1939-48: Indianapolis
MLB, 1946: Boston (AL)
Lou Barle
NBL, 1939-1943: Oshkosh
NFL, 1938-39: Detroit, Cleveland
Connie Mack Barry
NBL, 1939-1948: Oshkosh, Chicago
NFL, 1939-1946: Detroit, Cleveland, Chicago
Frank Baumholtz
NBL, 1945-46: Youngstown
BAA, 1946-47: Cleveland
MLB, 1947-1957: Cincinnati, Chicago (NL), Philadelphia
Hank Biasatti
BAA, 1946-47: Toronto
MLB, 1949: Philadelphia
Lou Boudreau
NBL, 1938-39: Hammond
MLB, 1938-1952: Cleveland, Boston
Frank Carswell
NBL, 1947-48: Flint
MLB, 1953: Detroit
Gene Conley
NBA, 1952-53, 1958-61, 1962-64: Boston, New York
ABL, 1961-62: Washington/New York
MLB, 1952-1963: Boston (NL), Milwaukee, Philadelphia, Boston (AL)
Chuck Connors
BAA, 1946-48: Boston
MLB, 1949, 1951: Brooklyn, Chicago (NL)
Ted Cook
NBL, 1947-49: Minneapolis, Sheboygan, Hammond
NFL, 1947-50: Detroit, Green Bay
Hal Crisler
BAA, 1946-47: Boston
NFL, 1946-1950: Washington, Baltimore
George Crowe
NBL, 1948-49: Dayton
MLB, 1952-1961: Boston (NL), Milwaukee, Cincinnati, St. Louis
Cookie Cunningham
NBL, 1938-39: Columbus
NFL, 1927-1931: Cleveland, Chicago Bears, Staten Island
Armand Cure
BAA, 1946-47: Providence
AAFC, 1947: Baltimore
Dave DeBusschere
NBA, 1962-1974: Detroit, New York
MLB, 1962-63: Chicago (AL)
Jack Dugger
NBL, 1946-47: Syracuse
AAFC, 1946: Buffalo
NFL, 1947-49: Detroit, Chicago Bears
Don Eliason
BAA, 1946-47: Boston
NFL, 1942, 1947: Brooklyn, Boston
Dick Evans
NBL, 1941-43: Sheboygan, Hammond, Chicago
NFL, 1940-43: Green Bay, Chicago Cardinals
Len Ford
NBL, 1948-49: Dayton
AAFC, 1948-49: Los Angeles
NFL, 1950-58: Cleveland, Green Bay
Johnny Gee
NBL, 1946-47: Syracuse
MLB 1939-1946: Pittsburgh, New York (NL)
Gorham Getchell
BAA, 1946-47: Pittsburgh
AAFC, 1947: Baltimore

Otto Graham
NBL, 1945-46: Rochester
AAFC, 1946-49: Cleveland
NFL, 1950-55: Cleveland
Bud Grant
NBA, 1949-1951: Minneapolis
NFL, 1951-52: Philadelphia
CFL, 1953-56: Winnipeg
Don Grate
MLB, 1945-46: Philadelphia (NL)
NBL, 1947-50: Indianapolis, Sheboygan
Dick Groat
NBA, 1952-53: Fort Wayne
MLB, 1952-1967: Pittsburgh, St. Louis, Philadelphia, San Francisco
Steve Hamilton
NBA, 1958-1960: Minneapolis
MLB, 1961-1972: Cleveland, Washington, New York (AL), Chicago (AL), San Francisco, Chicago (NL)
Vern Huffman
NFL, 1937-38: Detroit
NBL, 1938-39: Indianapolis
Bob MacLeod
NFL, 1939: Chicago Bears
NBL, 1939-1940: Chicago
Joel Mason
NFL, 1939-1945: Chicago Cardinals, Green Bay
NBL, 1942-43: Sheboygan
Bill McCahan
MLB, 1946-49: Philadelphia (AL)
NBL, 1948-49: Syracuse
Max Morris
NBL, 1946-1950: Chicago, Sheboygan
AAFC, 1946-48: Chicago, Brooklyn
Cotton Nash
NBA, 1964-65: Los Angeles, San Francisco
ABA, 1967-68: Kentucky
MLB, 1967, 1969-1970: Chicago (AL), Minnesota
Irv Noren
NBL, 1946-47: Chicago
MLB, 1950-1960: Washington, New York, Kansas City, St. Louis (NL), Chicago (NL), Los Angeles (NL)
Ray Ramsey
NBL, 1947-48: Tri Cities
BAA, 1947-49: Baltimore
AAFC, 1947-49: Chicago, Brooklyn
NFL, 1951-53: Chicago Cardinals
Ron Reed
NBA, 1965-67: Detroit
MLB, 1966-1984: Atlanta, St. Louis, Philadelphia, Chicago (AL)
Del Rice
NBL, 1945-46: Richmond
MLB, 1945-1961: St. Louis (NL), Milwaukee, Chicago (NL), Baltimore, Los Angeles (AL)
Dick Ricketts
NBA, 1955-58: St. Louis, Richmond, Cincinnati
MLB, 1959: St. Louis
Frank Sachse
NBL, 1943-45: Oshkosh
NFL, 1943-45: Brooklyn, Boston
Jim Spruill
NBL, 1948-49: Indianapolis
AAFC, 1948-49: Baltimore
George Svendsen
NFL, 1935-1941: Green Bay
NBL, 1939-40: Sheboygan
Rusty Saunders
MLB, 1927: Philadelphia (AL)
NBL, 1940-46: Detroit, Indianapolis
Howie Schultz
MLB, 1943-48: Brooklyn, Philadelphia (NL), Cincinnati
NBL, 1946-49: Anderson Packers
NBA, 1949-1953: Anderson Packers, Minneapolis Lakers, Fort Wayne Pistons
Otto Schnellbacher
BAA, 1948-49: Providence, St. Louis
AAFC, 1948-49: New York Yankees
NFL, 1950-51: New York Giants 1948-51

Bill Schroeder
NBL, 1946-47: Sheboygan
AAFC, 1946-47: Chicago
Bob Shaw
NBL, 1945-47: Cleveland, Youngstown, Toledo
NFL, 1945-46, 1949-50: Cleveland, Los Angeles, Chicago Cardinals
John Simmons
BAA, 1946-47: Boston
MLB, 1949: Washington
Clint Wager
NFL, 1942-45: Chicago Bears, Chicago Cardinals, Card-Pitt
NBL, 1943-49: Oshkosh, Hammond
NBA, 1949-50: Fort Wayne
George Wilson
NFL, 1937-1946: Chicago Bears
NBL, 1939-40: Chicago
Lonnie Wright
AFL, 1966-67: Denver
ABA, 1967-1972: Denver

Careers with Asterisks

Jud Buechler
NBA, Pro Beach Volleyball
Wilt Chamberlain
NBA, Pro Beach Volleyball
Harry Gallatin
NBA, Minor League Baseball
Jack Haley
NBA, Competitive Surfing
Michael Jordan
NBA, Minor League Baseball
Greg Lee
ABA, NBA, Pro Beach Volleyball
John Lucas
NBA, World Team Tennis
Mark McNamara
NBA, Pro Beach Volleyball
Randy Smith
NBA, North American Soccer League

Drafted by Both the NBA and Another Pro League

Scott Burrell
NBA (Charlotte 1993), MLB (Seattle 1989)
Dell Curry
NBA (Utah), MLB (Baltimore)
Tony Gwynn
NBA (San Diego Clippers 1981), MLB (San Diego 1981)
John Havlicek
NBA (Boston 1962), NFL (Cleveland 1962)
Kevin Johnson
NBA (Cleveland 1987), MLB (Oakland 1986)
K.C. Jones
NBA (Boston 1956), NFL (Los Angeles 1955)
Dave Logan
NBA (Kansas City Kings 1976), NFL (Cleveland Browns 1976), MLB (Cincinnati 1976)
Pat Riley
NBA (San Diego Rockets 1967), NFL (Dallas 1967)
Brett Roberts
NBA (Sacramento 1992), MLB (Cincinnati 1988, Minnesota 1991)
Corey Williams
NBA (Chicago 1992), NFL (Kansas City 1992)
Dave Winfield
MLB (San Diego 1973), NBA (Atlanta 1973), ABA (Utah 1973), NFL (Minnesota 1973)

Chapter 22

Moving On: Free Agency and the 20 Top Deals

By Bob Bellotti

Free agency was an alien concept in the NBA when the players first considered forming a union. The NBA declined even to recognize the players' association started by president Bob Cousy in 1954. Key issues for the players at the time—in a league that was losing money—were the $2 a day meal money and teams playing more than 20 exhibition games per season to increase revenues.

By 1957, the NBA had merely entered into discussions about such player issues as pensions, minimum wage, health benefits, and per diems. There was no discussion about players becoming free agents and having the right to move to the team of their choice. The NBA operated, much like Major League Baseball, under the assumption that there was a so-called "reserve" clause that reserved a player's rights for his team in perpetuity.

It wasn't until 1964 that the NBA recognized a players' union, two years after Larry Fleisher was hired as the association's general counsel. That resulted after the famous near boycott of the 1964 All Star game, which was the first to be nationally televised. The players gathered under the basket just before the game and agreed not to play unless the league agreed to a pension plan. The game would start 10 minutes late and the league agreed to a pension plan as well as an increase in per diem—to a whopping $8 per day on the road. But the players' union then operated more like a traditional labor union, concerned exclusively with issues of employee benefits.

In effect, free agency for the NBA began in 1968. That was the year Rick Barry was permitted to play for the Oakland Oaks of the American Basketball Association. Barry was an All Star for the Golden State Warriors when he signed a contract with the Oaks of the rival league before the 1967-68 season. The standard NBA contract at the time had an option clause which was renewable by the team and could be renewed any number of times.

Barry and the ABA went to court and the court ruled that the team had merely a one-year option on a player's rights. So Barry sat out one year and was then permitted to leave Golden State and play for Oakland in the ABA. With that, in 1970 a

Cliff Hagan, 1958
Hagan was on the wrong end of one of the most lopsided deals in NBA history.

group of NBA players, led by union president Oscar Robertson, filed a class action suit challenging the league's rules restricting player movement and its attempt to merge with the rival ABA.

Oddly, the turning point for basketball came when a baseball arbitrator ruled that pitchers Dave McNally and Andy Messersmith could be free agents. A year later, in 1976, the NBA and the players' association entered into a collective bargaining agreement to settle the Robertson case. It was the first official recognition of free agency in the NBA. There was

an official one-year option, a reduction in the number of rounds of the draft so not as many players would be tied to teams, and then—if a player elected to become a free agent after his contract ended and he wanted to go to another team—the commissioner could award compensation to the team that was losing a player with the wording "making that team whole" as the key in the agreement. The 1976 deal also paved the way for the ABA to cease operations and four teams to be absorbed into the NBA.

Some of the major compensation cases involved Bill Walton, Spencer Haywood, and Gail Goodrich. Walton, angered by what he felt was inadequate medical care for his foot problems in Portland and an eventual lawsuit, signed September 18, 1979 with the San Diego Clippers near his home. The Trail Blazers were awarded as compensation Kevin Kunnert, Kermit Washington, a 1980 first-round draft pick, and cash. Since Walton was injured again and would play little for the Clippers, such awards discouraged free agent signings. Haywood was the first college underclassman to come into the ABA when he challenged the status quo and signed with the ABA in 1969. Goodrich's signing by the New Orleans Jazz in 1976 may have been the most costly in NBA history. The Lakers received two first round draft picks and a second as compensation. They used one of those picks to select Magic Johnson, who went on to lead L.A. to five NBA championships and be considered one of the top 10 NBA players of all-time.

Compensation was written in for a five-year period, and then in 1981 teams had a right of first refusal in free agency. That meant a team had the right to match an offer made for its player and thereby retain that player. Often a team would match the offer, but really didn't want the player. So then the two teams would make a trade involving the "free agent" player and another player, so the team losing the player would get something and the player would not have to go back to the team he wanted to leave.

In 1983 the players and the NBA agreed for the first time in American professional sports to establish a salary cap on teams limiting how much they could spend on salaries. Players were guaranteed 53 percent of the revenues of the league, and there was the "Larry Bird exception," allowing teams to exceed the salary cap to resign its own players.

The 1976 agreement outlining the elements of free agency expired in 1987 and the players filed another antitrust suit led by association president Junior Bridgeman. This resulted, in 1988, in a new collective bargaining agreement, in which free agency was modified and the right of first refusal only applied to a player's first contract. Thus was established the first unrestricted free agency.

A no lockout/no strike agreement was put in place for the 1994-1995 season with the collective bargaining agreement expiring in 1994. The new agreement in 1995 eliminated all restricted free agency, which previously applied to that first contract. The NBA got the right to re-open that contract issue if revenues to the players increased beyond a certain level, and the league did, leading to the lockout to begin the 1998-1999 season. That lasted into January 1999, when a new collective bargaining agreement was signed. It re-instituted the concept of restricted free agency, but just for rookie

contracts after the third year, while veterans remained free to sign with any team once their contract expired with no compensation unless agreed upon between the teams in a so-called sign-and-trade deal.

Thus free agency and trading were locked hand-in-hand through commissioner's compensation, right of first refusal and eventual sign-and-trade deals. Here's *Total Basketball*'s ranking of the 20 most significant trades and signings in NBA history.

1. April 1956: Ed Macauley and Cliff Hagan (Boston) for Bill Russell (University of San Francisco)

Red Auerbach saw what few others did in 1956—that Bill Russell would be a revolutionary figure in the game. The Celtics had the No. 3 pick in the 1956 draft, and intended to use it for territorial choice Tom Heinsohn. So Auerbach checked with Macauley, who was a star for the Celtics and would one day have his number retired. Macauley was a St. Louis native and said he wouldn't mind returning. Also, St. Louis was the most southern city in the NBA at the time and owners were concerned about the reaction to a top pick being a black player. So Auerbach traded Macauley and the rights to Cliff Hagan, who was coming out of the Army, for the No. 2 pick in the draft. Then, as the story goes, Celtics' owner Walter Brown agreed to steer the high grossing Ice Capades to Rochester for two years if the Royals would pass on Russell with the No. 1 pick. Rochester, which already had one of the game's top rebounders in Maurice Stokes, selected Sihugo Green with the top pick and the Celtics got both Russell and Heinsohn and went on to create the greatest dynasty in American team sports history with 11 titles over the next 13 years.

2. June 1975: Elmore Smith, Brian Winters, Dave Meyers, and Junior Bridgeman (Los Angeles) for Walt Wesley and Kareem Abdul-Jabbar (Milwaukee)

The Bucks won a coin flip for the right to make the No. 1 pick in the 1968-1969 draft and selected Lew Alcindor, who in his second year led the NBA in scoring and led the Bucks to their only NBA championship. The title quest was aided by the Bucks' acquisition of Hall of Fame guard Oscar Roberston before that championship 1970-71 season for Flynn Robinson and Charlie Paulk. Robertson was at the end of his career and would play three more seasons with Milwaukee and then retire.

After six seasons in Milwaukee, Abdul-Jabbar, who was from New York City and played in college at UCLA in Los Angeles, told Bucks management the city of Milwaukee was too small and confining for him for both cultural and religious reasons. Abdul-Jabbar requested to be traded to New York or Los Angeles and the Lakers were able to put together the best package. Teamed with Magic Johnson, Abdul-Jabbar went on to play on five more championship teams in the 1980s. Though fielding competitive teams, the Bucks never made it back to the NBA Finals.

3. July 1976: Two first-round picks and a second-round pick from the New Orleans Jazz to the Los Angeles Lakers as compensation for the signing of Gail Goodrich

In the early era of NBA free agency, the commissioner

was permitted to compensate the team that lost a player as a free agent with the mission of "making the team whole" again. The Lakers used the 1977 first-round pick for Kenny Carr and the 1979 first-round pick, which was No. 1 number in the 1979 draft, for Earvin "Magic" Johnson from Michigan State. Johnson went on to become one of the greatest guards in NBA history, revolutionized guard play in the NBA, and orchestrated of five championship teams with the Lakers.

4. June 1980: Draft picks Joe Barry Carroll (No. 1) and Rickey Brown (No. 13) for Robert Parish (Golden State) and Kevin McHale (No. 3 draft pick)

When Boston was routed four games to one in the Eastern Conference finals by the Philadelphia 76ers in 1980, it set in motion a trade that eventually produced perhaps the greatest forward line in NBA history and three NBA championships. The Celtics were overwhelmed by the bigger 76ers, and had the No. 1 choice in the upcoming draft thanks to the Detroit Pistons' signing of M.L. Carr. To work out the compensation in the deal, the Pistons took former scoring champion Bob McAdoo and gave the Celtics two No. 1 draft picks, one of which became the top pick in the 1980 draft. Joe Barry Carroll of Purdue University was regarded as the nation's top collegian. But Celtics' coach Bill Fitch had always pined for Robert Parish, a center for the Warriors who was regarded as lazy. The Celtics also had interest in lanky University of Minnesota center Kevin McHale.

So a deal was made. The Celtics traded the No. 1 and No. 13 picks in the first round of the 1980 draft for Parish and the No. 3 pick, which they used for McHale. Golden State selected Carroll, who had a troubled, up and down career and used the No. 13 pick for Rickey Brown, a forward who played for parts of five seasons for the Warriors and Atlanta Hawks. The Utah Jazz selected Darrel Griffith from Louisville with the No. 2 pick in the draft. By adding McHale and Parish to a front line with Larry Bird, the Celtics put together a group of three future Hall of Famers to challenge the Los Angeles Lakers through the 1980s and produce, arguably, the great rivalry in NBA history.

5. July 1996: Shaquille O'Neal (Orlando) to the Los Angeles Lakers as a free agent

Shaquille O'Neal played out his contract with the Orlando Magic and, with no rules requiring compensation or the ability to match an offer, O'Neal went to the Lakers with the Orlando Magic receiving nothing in return. The trade paid dividends four seasons later, as O'Neal, the league MVP, led the Lakers past Indiana in six games in the 2000 Finals. O'Neal, averaging 38 points and 17 rebounds, was the Finals MVP. Indomitably strong in the pivot, O'Neal won two more Finals' MVP awards and the Lakers won three straight championships before being defeated in the 2003 playoffs by the San Antonio Spurs.

6. December 1968: Walt Bellamy and Howard Komives (New York) for Dave BeBusschere (Detroit)

DeBusschere was a hometown hero in Detroit and the youngest coach in team sports history when he was named player-coach at 24 in 1964. The 6-foot-6 forward was a professional baseball player with the Chicago White Sox. Bellamy, a future Hall of Famer, averaged more than 31 points and 19 rebounds as a rookie in 1961-62 for the old Chicago Packers, who moved to Baltimore and became the Bullets. He was traded to the Knicks in 1965. Now his trade to Detroit freed up the pivot, allowing the Knicks to move young Willis Reed to center and install DeBusschere as an athletic, tough power forward and set the stage for two NBA championships. Bellamy, who would finish his career with more than 20,000 points and 10,000 rebounds, was traded from the Pistons after one season.

7. January 1965: Paul Neumann, Connie Dierking, Lee Shaffer (Philadelphia) and $150,000 for Wilt Chamberlain (San Francisco)

Chamberlain had been in the hospital the summer before the 1964-1965 season. He originally was diagnosed as having had a heart attack, and always had irregular EKG readings. Eventually, his doctor determined he had pancreatitis. Chamberlain still was the league's scoring leader, but his average dropped below 40 points per game the previous season as the Warriors used their first round pick on center Nate Thurmond. Chamberlain returned for the 1964-1965 season, but the team started poorly and fears remained that Chamberlain really had had a heart attack and would have future problems. The Warriors were 10-34 going into the All Star game. Shortly after the game concluded, the trade of Chamberlain to the Philadelphia 76ers was announced. Two seasons later, with Chamberlain averaging 24 points and 24 rebounds and finishing third in the NBA in assists, the 76ers put together what many consider the greatest team ever in winning 68 games and the championship.

8. July 1968: Jerry Chambers, Archie Clark and Darrall Imhoff (Los Angeles) for Wilt Chamberlain (Philadelphia)

As was often the case, Chamberlain became the scapegoat when the 76ers were beaten in the 1968 Eastern Conference finals by the Celtics. After all, he was so big and strong and could do everything, it was said. Relations with surviving owner Irv Kosloff soured after the death of co-owner Ike Richman. Why? What did the death have to do with it? Jack Ramsey was hired as general manager and believed the team needed changes. Chamberlain was considering trying to jump to the ABA, but wanted to live in Los Angeles. So the deal was worked out with owner Jack Kent Cooke and the Lakers won the NBA championship in 1972 with Chamberlain being named Finals MVP.

9. September 1982: Caldwell Jones (Philadelphia) and 1983 first-round pick for Moses Malone (Houston)

In 1982, Moses Malone was the reigning MVP, the second time he'd won the award, when he became a free agent. Under the rules at the time, the Rockets could match any offer for him, which they did. But Malone wanted to go to the 76ers, who had made the Finals three times since acquiring Julius

Erving in 1976 from the ABA, but had never won a title. Malone was named league MVP again in 1983 and the 76ers established a playoff record with 12 wins in 13 games for the title.

10. 1950-51: Charlie Share (Boston) for Bill Sharman (Washington)

Bill Sharman played a season with Washington in 1950-1951 and when the team disbanded, he was selected by Ft. Wayne. When Sharman did not report to Fort Wayne, he was traded to Boston. Share ended up in Fort Wayne. Sharman went on to play 10 seasons with the Celtics, competing on four championship teams (1957, 1959-61) in the beginning of the Celtics' dynasty. He also was a professional baseball player in the minor leagues and a great shooter in an era of poor shooting in the NBA.

11. November 1971: Dave Stallworth, Mike Riordan and cash (New York) for Earl Monroe (Baltimore)

Monroe, one of the first to bring the schoolyard style of basketball to the NBA, had been in classic battles for the Bullets against Walt Frazier and the Knicks in the late 1960s and early 1970s. So it was a shock that Monroe went to the Knicks to be paired in the backcourt with Frazier. Dave Stallworth had been with New York since 1965 and Mike Riordan since 1968. Both had been invaluable players off the bench, especially during the Knicks championship season of 1969-70. Despite the clamor of observers who said that "one ball wasn't enough" for Frazier and Monroe, "The Pearl" reigned in his free-form game and helped the Knicks to the NBA title in 1973.

12. July 2001: Jason Kidd and Chris Dudley (Phoenix) for Stephon Marbury, Johnny Newman and Soumaila Samake (New Jersey).

It was the trade that made the Nets. New Jersey went to the NBA Finals two straight seasons in 2002 and 2003 behind Jason Kidd, who seemed to bring the fast break back to a league with more than its fill of controlled offenses. It was the franchise's first finals appearances in a quarter-century. They had last made the trip as the New York Nets in the ABA. That was in 1976, when Julius Erving averaged 34.7 in the post-season and led them past Denver in the Finals.

The Suns fell out of the playoffs as Marbury played hurt and had surgery after the 2001-02 season.

13. February 1989: Adrian Dantley (Detroit) and a No. 1 draft pick for Mark Aguirre (Dallas)

The Pistons had been on the verge of getting to the NBA Finals, but lost to the Boston Celtics in the conference finals in 1986 and 1987. The Pistons felt they needed a scorer who moved the ball better than Dantley, who was a 6-foot-5 post-up player. They acquired Aguirre, who was close friends with Pistons' star guard Isiah Thomas, and the Pistons finally made it to the Finals and won championships in 1989 and 1990.

14. June 1972: Jack Marin (Baltimore) for Elvin Hayes (Houston)

Hayes, the University of Houston star, started with the San Diego Rockets, but after one season in Houston when the team moved there, he was dealt to Baltimore. He was traded for Jack Marin, a small forward. The Bullets, after moving to Washington, went to the Finals in three of Hayes' first five seasons there and won a championship in 1978 before Hayes was traded back to Houston in 1981 to finish his career.

15. February 1980: George McGinnis (Denver) for a first-round draft pick and Alex English (Indiana)

Desperate to improve attendance after their move to the NBA following the breakup of the ABA, the Pacers went for the rapidly aging George McGinnis, an Indianapolis native and star at Indiana University. They gave up the lanky Alex English, who didn't get much chance to play in Milwaukee and was just developing with the Pacers. English went on to average at least 23 points per season for Denver for nine straight seasons and become the franchise's all-time leader in scoring and assists. In the 1980s he scored more points than anyone in the league.

16. September 1982: John Drew, Freeman Williams (both of Atlanta) and cash for Utah's draft rights to Dominique Wilkins

Wilkins was the third pick in the 1982 draft from the University of Georgia. He went on to become the Hawks' all-time leading scorer, lead the league in scoring in 1986, and become one of the most spectacular players in league history for his dunking.

17. June 1992: Jeff Hornacek, Tim Perry, and Andrew Lang (Phoenix) for Charles Barkley (Philadelphia)

Charles Barkley had become one of the elite players in the NBA in eight seasons in Philadelphia, but was controversial and unpredictable. With the team missing the playoffs in 1991-92, Barkley began demanding to be traded and Philadelphia obliged. Remaining as serious as he could be, Barkley won his only MVP award in 1993 and the Suns, with the league's best record, lost in the sixth game of the NBA Finals to the Chicago Bulls on John Paxson's three-pointer with three seconds remaining. After three more seasons in Phoenix, Barkley again forced a trade, this time to Houston, where he declared his retirement after a knee injury during the 1999-2000 season.

18. February 1997: Shawn Bradley, Robert Pack, Khalid Reeves and Ed O'Bannon (New Jersey) for Jim Jackson, Chris Gatling, Sam Cassell, George McCloud, and Eric Montross (Houston)

The trade between Dallas and New Jersey had little impact on either team, but involved the most players in NBA history between two teams. It surpassed an eight-player trade between Detroit and Baltimore in 1964 that involved Bailey Howell, Don Ohl, Bob Ferry, Les Hunter, Terry Dischinger, Rod Thorn, and Don Kojis. Before the 1999-2000 season, Vancouver, Houston, and Orlando were involved in a deal in which 11 players changed teams, the key being Steve Francis going to Houston and Michael Dickerson and Othella Harrington going to Vancouver.

19. June 1998: Bucks trade the draft rights to Dirk Nowitzki and Pat Garrity to Dallas Mavericks for draft rights to Robert "Tractor" Traylor

The deal built the Mavericks as Dirk Nowitzki emerged as an MVP candidate and the Mavs used the Garrity pick as part of the deal that got them Steve Nash from Phoenix. Traylor was a bust in Milwaukee and eventually moved onto the Hornets to be a backup.

20. August 2000: Grant Hill (Detroit) for Ben Wallace and Chucky Atkins (Orlando)

Hill was a free agent and could have signed outright with Orlando. But under the collective bargaining agreement rules, a players' own team can pay a player more. To get Hill the maximum contract, the Pistons and Magic agreed on a so-called sign and trade deal. Hill signed with the Pistons and was traded for reserves Ben Wallace and Chucky Atkins. Wallace went on to become Defensive Player of the Year and the Pistons had back-to-back 50-win seasons in 2001-02 and 2002-03 after the deal. Hill played little because of foot and ankle problems that led to four surgeries through the summer of 2003.

Chapter 23

NBA Short Players Have Stood Tall

By William Heller

When Dr. James Naismith invented the game of basketball in December 1891, could he have possibly imagined his creation was so well-conceived that more than a century later, 5-foot-11 Speedy Claxton and 7-foot-1 David Robinson would not only compete on the same court, but be integral members of the same championship team?

Or, in a sport where increased height brings one closer to a 10-foot high basket, that a 1945 vote of coaches in the National Basketball League, one of the NBA's ancestors, would tab 5-foot-11 Bobby McDermott as the greatest player ever?

Or that 55 years after that, 5-foot-3 Muggsy Bogues, who was ridiculed in his high school for being so short, would be completing his 13th season in the NBA—a league whose average height was 6-foot-7?

Of course, players have grown in professional basketball. The average height of the NBA's first champion, the 1949-50 Minneapolis Lakers, was 6-foot-3.1 inches. A decade later, the average height of the champion Boston Celtics was 6-foot-4.8. The 1969-70 champion Knicks came in at 6-foot-5.8, while the 1979-80 champs, the Los Angeles Lakers, were at 6-foot-6.3. The 1989-90 champion Detroit Pistons averaged 6-foot-6.6, and the 1999-2000 Lakers were 6-foot-7.1. By opening day, 2003, the league average had grown more skyward: 6-foot-7.4 inches.

In 1947-48, the eight teams in the NBA, then known as the Basketball Association of America, had 18 players under six feet tall. In 1973, with twice as many NBA teams, there was just one sub-six-footer: future Hall of Famer Calvin Murphy with the Houston Rockets.

But thirty years later, during the 2002-2003 season, eight NBA teams had a player under six feet contributing, continuing a legacy of talented players who have not only overcome their lack of height, but also the perceptions of others.

Being shorter than other players may be an impediment. It has never been and likely never will be an impenetrable barrier at any level of basketball.

In the eighth grade, Monty Towe, who would grow to be 5-foot-7 and lead North Carolina State to a national championship, was matched in a junior high tournament championship game against a team led by John Garrett, who would grow to be 6-foot-11 and became an All-American at Purdue. Towe scored 20 and his team won 45-31. "I don't have a Napoleon complex, but if you're a short person, you have to make people notice you," Towe said.

Spud Webb, standing 5-foot-7, did precisely that when he won the 1986 NBA Slam Dunk Contest. Ditto Barney Sedran,

Spud Webb, 1993
He was the NBA's Slam Dunk champ, a giant on the court at 5-foot-7.

at 5-foot-4, 74 years earlier. It was 1912, and Sedran, known as the "Mighty Mite of Basketball," turned to pro ball with the Newburgh (New York) Club in the Hudson River League after three outstanding seasons at the City College of New York.

Nearly 90 years later, there are still outstanding players under six feet tall making careers in professional basketball.

"It's a disadvantage, but you can overcome it if you have exceptional skills," said 6-foot-1 Hall of Fame guard Bob Cousy. "It's still a game where speed and quickness separate the men from the boys."

But even after basketball bounces into the 21st century, some people cling tenaciously to old notions. They see an undersized player, at any level of basketball, and trigger the word "can't" in a knee-jerk reaction. The biggest obstacles in the careers of short players are frequently not their heights, but the perceptions of others. And they can begin at an early age.

Ralph "Buckshot" O'Brien, a prolific scorer at Butler University who played in the NBA in the early '50s, got his nickname at the age of four when the neighborhood grocer determined that O'Brien would grow up to be "no bigger than a buckshot." In the eighth grade, O'Brien was 4-foot-8 and weighed 84 pounds. He was actually asked to work out on a stretching machine and also to repeat the eighth grade to give him more time to grow. He declined both. "I said, 'Hey look, whatever He's given me, He's given me,'" O'Brien said. "When it was time for me to grow, I did. I went from 4-8 to 5-5 in two years."

He grew to be 5-foot-9, but he never outgrew some people's misconceptions. In 1951, O'Brien, playing with the Indianapolis Olympians, was psyched to play his first professional game at Madison Square Garden against the New York Knicks—maybe too psyched. "I'd lost my player's pass," O'Brien said. "The security guard wouldn't let me in. He said he'd been on that gate 25 years and he wanted to know whose bag I was carrying." Fortunately for O'Brien, his coach, Herm Schaefer, was nearby. After he stopped laughing, Schaefer told the guard that O'Brien, indeed, was an NBA player. After scoring 18 that night, O'Brien paid a visit to the guard and asked him, "Did you see the game?" The guard nodded.

Long after he retired from pro basketball to become an insurance man at the age of 26, O'Brien received the honor of a lifetime in 1975. He was named one of five former athletes chosen to receive the NCAA Silver Anniversary Award, which recognizes student athletes who have distinguished themselves after completing their collegiate athletic careers 25 years earlier. Also honored at that luncheon attended by 1,400 in Washington, D.C., January 7, 1975, was President Gerald Ford, who had been named winner of the NCAA's Theodore Roosevelt Award. "I couldn't believe I was sitting at the head table with the president of the United States," O'Brien said. O'Brien's height, or lack of it, never came up.

Like his 5-foot-9 contemporary O'Brien, Murray Wier made it to the NBA in its early days. Wier, a star for the University of Iowa who led the nation in scoring (21.0) in 1947-48, played the 1949-50 NBA season with the Tri-Cities Blackhawks, whose coach for part of that season was Red Auerbach. Auerbach replaced Roger Potter after a 1-6 start and went 28-29, his only losing season in 17 years of coaching in the NBA. "He was a hell of a coach, a bright guy with a brilliant basketball mind," said Wier, who went on to an outstanding high school coaching career. "I got along with him okay, but I don't think Red ever liked the Midwest or the people of the Midwest. People out here, to him I think, were hillbillies and farmers."

The Blackhawks relocated to Milwaukee as the Hawks in 1951, then migrated to St. Louis in 1955, and finally to Atlanta in 1968. Wier, 5-foot-8 Charlie Criss, and 5-foot-7 Spud Webb, three of only 13 players under 5-foot-10 to play in the

NBA's first 50 years, all played for the same franchise decades apart. In all, there were only 82 players less than six feet tall in the first 50 years of the NBA.

"On the road, we got $5 for meal money," Wier recalled. "But you could get a great meal for a buck-seventy-five. We traveled by train quite a bit. Sometimes we drove in three or four cars. We went all over the damn country. We played a lot of exhibition games. Most of the places we played in were the pits. You wouldn't put a dog in them. If today's players had to play just one week the way we did, they'd quit. But the NBA was just getting started. Nobody thought a whole lot about it. You just accepted that was it."

There were few NBA impact players shorter than six feet before the 1960s. Al Cervi and Buddy Jeannette, outstanding players in the late 1940s and early '50s, were 5-foot-11. Slater "Dugie" Martin, who helped the Minneapolis Lakers win five NBA titles in six years in the late '50s, was 5-foot-10. All three are in the Hall of Fame.

Hershey Carl, 5-foot-9-1/2, thought he'd never get to play college ball, let alone in the NBA. He graduated Van Steuben High School as the leading scorer in the city of Chicago, averaging 34 points a game his senior season in 1955-56. All of four college teams recruited him: Kansas (which had Wilt Chamberlain at the time), the University of Illinois, Bradley University, and DePaul in Chicago. Wanting to experience life away from home, Carl visited Kansas and Bradley, though neither team had bothered to scout him in person. Carl did not make a sizable impression at either school. "The coaches didn't say I was too short, but I saw the way they looked at me up and down," he said. "I could see that they were surprised, because I was the leading scorer in the city. They never said anything. I left and they never contacted me. You can't add inches. If they'd seen me play, then maybe it would have been different. Maybe."

Neither school offered a scholarship, so Carl accepted a partial one to the University of Illinois. Freshmen were ineligible for varsity then, and Carl was the last player on the 1956-57 Illinois freshman basketball team. He was told not to bother to dress for the annual freshman/varsity scrimmage.

At the tender age of 18, Carl had reached a common destination for undersized players. He was forced to ask himself whether he was right in believing in himself and in his ability, or whether a system denying him an opportunity to play would dictate his life.

He transferred to DePaul, where legendary coach Ray Meyer was happy to provide Carl a chance to play. "We were glad to take him," Meyer said. "He was a little guy who was an extremely fine shooter. If he had played with the three-point shot, he probably would have led the country in scoring."

Even so, Carl took down 6-foot-10 Hall of Famer George Mikan's single-game scoring record of 37 points in DePaul's Alumni Hall. In an 81-78 overtime win against Marquette on December 23, 1960, Carl scored 43. He led DePaul in scoring and free-throw percentage for all three seasons he played and was named to the Little All-American Team for players under six feet. Meyer told Carl that he had been considered for the 1960 Olympic Team, but had been passed over for a couple of guys named Oscar Robertson and Jerry West. Still, Carl made

it to the NBA, playing one season with the Chicago Packers, appearing in 31 games and averaging 5.5 points. He had more than proven himself, but he just as easily could have given up during that frustrating first year at the University of Illinois.

Sometimes, people's perceptions of short players' limitations border on the comical. Philadelphia 76ers coach Larry Brown, who is 5-foot-9 and played in the American Basketball Association for five years, remembered when he was drafted by the Baltimore Bullets of the NBA. "Their general manager came to see me," Brown said. "He said, 'Golly, you're smaller than we thought. How are you going to guard Oscar Roberston or Jerry West or Havlicek?' My response was that nobody was guarding them. They were averaging 30 to 35 points a game. I don't know if he appreciated that. They didn't invite me to camp." A second team ABA All-Star in 1968 and MVP of the 1968 ABA All-Star Game, Brown set the ABA record for most assists in a game (23) before turning to a coaching career, where's he's enjoyed success in the ABA and NBA, as well as collegiately at UCLA and Kansas. At 5-foot-7, Jerry Dover was the only other ABA player under 5-foot-10.

Another 5-foot-9 guard, Hall of Famer Calvin Murphy, never understood other people's misconceptions about height. "It didn't dawn on me," he said. "I thought the best players played: midgets, giants, whatever. I never looked at myself as a little guy. I played basketball. I was always the underdog in the minds of other people, not in mine. All of that is the figment of the imagination: that because of my size, I was an underdog. If you allow yourself to think that way, you're going to lose because that's negative thinking. My being successful isn't about me being small. I succeeded because I was talented. I get a lot of mail from the average-sized player asking me how they can make it. I tell them, if you think about it that way, you'll never succeed. I heard people say to me, 'Murph, what if you were 6-4? You would have been bitchin'.' I say, 'At 6-4, I couldn't do anything more. I made the Hall of Fame.'"

His high school coach in Norwalk, Connecticut, Jack Cronin, testified that Murphy, indeed, never thought twice about his height: "He didn't care about his size. And he didn't care if you were 6-5. He'd run right through you."

Murphy set a single season record for free throw percentage in the NBA—.958 in 1980-81—and averaged 17.9 points in his outstanding 13-year career with the Rockets, the only pro team he ever played for.

In 1969, the Basketball Hall of Fame established the Frances Pomeroy Naismith Award. Named for basketball founder James Naismith's daughter-in-law, it honors the best senior player in the country six feet or under. At the time, Murphy at Niagara University, "Pistol Pete" Maravich at LSU and Rick Mount at Purdue, all members of the class of 1970, were waging the greatest battle for three consecutive collegiate scoring titles ever seen in the history of college basketball. Murphy scored 68 in a game against Syracuse, December 7, 1968, but the 6-foot-5 Maravich topped that with 70 against Alabama, February 7, 1970. Exactly three weeks later, the 6-foot-4 Mount scored a career high 61 vs. Iowa. Maravich, Murphy, and Mount posted career scoring averages of 44.2, 33.1, and 32.3 respectively. Lord knows what their numbers would have been with the three-point shot, which was added to collegiate basketball in

1986, seven years after the NBA approved it.

Monte Towe had little of Murphy's scoring firepower, yet carved a niche for himself anyway at the height of 5-foot-7. David Thompson will never forget the first time he saw his future teammate—not only in college at North Carolina State, but also with the Denver Nuggets in their final season in the American Basketball Association and their first season in the NBA. "We were checking in at Sullivan Dorm at North Carolina State, and some of the other guys were there," Thompson said. "A guy named Joe Cafferky had this little guy with him. I thought he was his brother. He had cut off jeans and a tank top. I thought he was 14 years old. I didn't know who he was. When they told me who he was, I said, 'Man, we're going to be in trouble.' Later that evening we played in some pick-up games and his team always won. Right then, I found out Monte was a winner."

Together, they perfected the alley-oop pass. Thompson, a scoring machine who was one of the greatest leapers to ever grace a basketball court, would streak to the basket and Towe would catch him in perfect stride for a lay-in—the NCAA had outlawed the dunk from 1967 to 1977. "We practiced it, but after a while, it was eye contact," Thompson said. "We played so much together, he knew when I'd go back door. He'd throw it up and I'd go get it. He was a great passer, the best passer I ever played with. He had a flair for the game."

In one of the greatest collegiate games ever played, Towe made the play that changed the game. UCLA was at its zenith, having crafted ungodly winning streaks of 47, 41, and 88 games on the way to nine national championships in 10 years heading into the 1973-74 season. In a mid-season showdown of unbeaten teams, UCLA—led by 6-foot-11 center Bill Walton, one of the greatest college players ever and certainly the best passing center the game has ever seen—crushed North Carolina State, 84-66, on a neutral court in St. Louis. "Our motivation the rest of the year was to get into the NCAA Tournament to get another shot at them," Towe said.

The Wolfpack did, barely. The Tournament was then only 25 teams, and NC State had to win the Atlantic Coast Conference Championship to qualify. In the championship game, NC State led a deeply talented University of Maryland team 101-100 when Towe was fouled with six seconds left. It was one-and-one, not two foul shots. Towe made both, and the Wolf Pack won, 103-100.

NC State beat Providence in the first round of the Tournament, and then crushed Pittsburgh by 28 points despite losing Thompson, who went down in a frightening mid-air collision. He made it back for the national semi-finals and a rematch with UCLA and scored 28 points in one of the most exciting games in Final Four history.

The Wolfpack looked hopelessly beaten in double overtime when UCLA got possession of the ball with 2:07 remaining with a seven-point lead. "Monte kept us fired up," Thompson said. "He wouldn't let us quit." On the in-bounds pass, Towe jumped in front of Walton, 16 inches taller, and drew a charge. Towe got a one-and-one, made both foul shots, and NC State went on to win, 80-77. Two nights later, NC State won the national championship, 76-64 over Marquette, with Towe scoring 16.

After two years of playing professionally in the ABA and NBA for coach Larry Brown with Denver, averaging 2.1 and 2.5 points, respectively, Towe was an assistant at NC State, then a head coach in the Global Basketball Association, and an assistant to current Minnesota Timberwolves head coach Flip Saunders with Sioux Falls in the Continental Basketball Association. Towe later became the head coach at Chipola Junior College in Marianna, Florida, then at Santa Fe Community College in Gainesville, Florida, and is now is head coach for the University of New Orleans Privateers.

When asked if Towe the coach would have recruited Towe the player, he said, "I probably wouldn't. I didn't fit the ideal prototype."

Neither did Charlie Criss, who heard the negative comments longer than any other professional player until he became the oldest NBA rookie ever at the ancient basketball age of 28 in 1977. All he did with the opportunity was stick in the NBA for eight seasons, averaging double figures in points for two of them—quite an accomplishment for a man who was cut from the roster of a team in the weekends-only Eastern League, the ancestor of the CBA.

"I always believed I would play in the NBA," Criss said. "Other people told me I wouldn't make it, but that kept me going. It motivated me to show them they were wrong, and they sure were."

His "they" included his coaches at New Mexico State. After he arrived in the NBA, Criss got a letter from his former assistant coach there, Eddie Murphy. "He had said I'd never make it to the NBA, that I was too small," Criss said. "He sent me a letter 10 years later apologizing. He thought they weren't going to take small guys. At that time, they weren't."

Lou Henson, Criss' head coach at New Mexico State, shared Murphy's opinion. After watching the 5-foot-8 Criss fail to reach the NBA for years, he offered him this advice in 1975: face reality. "I told him, 'You've been trying for years. You're not going to make it in the NBA. You need to do something else and get on with your life,'" Henson said. "But Charlie had that burning desire. He showed me that he could make it."

He showed everyone, to the delight of the people who gave him that opportunity with the Atlanta Hawks. "Everybody loved him," said Frank Layden, then an assistant coach under Hubie Brown. Layden was Calvin Murphy's coach at Niagara University. "Charlie is one of the most wonderful persons I've ever known," Layden said. "He came up the hard way. He was tough as nails, an over-achiever. He knew how to pass; he knew how to shoot. A tough guy. He had to be."

Hubie Brown was on the same page with Layden. "Charlie was extremely likable, very coachable, and a very, very hard worker," Brown said. "The only two players who I ever coached in the pros in 14 years that I thought really enjoyed playing were Eddie Johnson and Charlie Criss. They played one-on-one a half-hour before practice; practiced for two hours, and played one-on-one half an hour after practice. They were always working on their game. You can't be Charlie's size and excel at the NBA level without having a great heart. Because not only does it take incredible physical discipline, but also mental discipline. The game is so demanding when you are that size."

There is another prerequisite: earmuffs, so you will not hear the endless stream of negatives. "I didn't listen to it," 5-foot-7 Spud Webb said. "If I listened to it, I would have been a season ticket holder somewhere."

Instead, Webb built an NBA career that included a spectacular moment in the spotlight during his rookie season with the Atlanta Hawks, when he rearranged a lot of perceptions about shorter players. It was the NBA's Slam Dunk Contest, February 3, 1986, in his native Dallas. With an entire arena chanting, "Spud! Spud! Spud," he took one last look at the rim, and then tossed a ball high in the air in front of him. He accelerated towards the basket, timed his jump perfectly, intercepted the ball, cradled it in his hands for a moment and slammed it through the net. The arena, including the NBA players watching him, exploded. "I think it changed the way people looked at little guys," he said.

Heck, it changed the way his Atlanta Hawks teammates looked at him. "He'd never dunked like that in a game or in practice," said Doc Rivers, who later became the coach of the Orlando Magic. "We didn't know he could do it."

It's a phrase Muggsy Bogues has heard most of his young life. The 5-foot-3 eighth wonder of the world enjoyed a 14-year NBA career.

"People always say we'll never see another Larry Bird," said Alan Bristow, who coached Bogues with the Charlotte Hornets. "But I've always felt we have a better chance of seeing another Larry Bird than we do another Muggsy Bogues. Nobody has done what Muggsy is doing."

Bogues led the NBA in assist-to-turnover ratio for six years. All he ever wanted was an opportunity, which has often eluded players who concede inches. From 1963 to 1970, there was not a single NBA player shorter than 5-foot-10.

Bogues, though, never paid attention to numbers. "Believe it or not, I never doubted myself," he said. "It may be arrogant, but I always believed. It comes from my mom. It comes from my upbringing. I was a hard-nosed guy who wouldn't take 'no' for an answer. I felt it's very hard for others to believe in you if you don't believe in yourself. I always thought I could play."

The ones who believed he couldn't usually paid a price. In his junior and senior years at famed Dunbar High in Baltimore, he led the Poets to successive seasons of 28-0 and 31-0. But Bogues received little respect when Dunbar traveled to Camden High School in New Jersey in his junior season to face the nation's No. 1 ranked team, which featured future college stars Billy Thompson, Milt Wagner, and point guard Kevin Walls, a trio that led the University of Louisville to the 1986 NCAA National Championship. When the line-ups were introduced that night in New Jersey, Bogues heard snickering. "I could see the players and the fans laughing and joking," Bogues said. "Kevin Walls came out, and when he came near me he laughed and pointed at me, and then at himself, as if he was telling the crowd, 'Hey, I got the little one.' He thought I was a joke. When he pointed at me, the entire crowd laughed at me."

Not after the game. Bogues stole the ball from Walls seven times, including three in a row, and held him to nine points as Dunbar crushed Camden, 84-59.

Walls would be the first of many opposing guards to discover just how big a nuisance Bogues could be. "He's crazy on defense," Tim Hardaway said. "He's just a pain in the butt."

Sherman Douglas once said, "He's so annoying you want to slap him."

Milwaukee Bucks coach George Karl found Bogues more enjoyable. "Muggsy was probably my favorite player," Karl said. "He just played with such a passion. It's what I call the right way to play. He just enjoyed it. He had a good attitude. He had a relationship with his teammates all the time. I think, because of that, he was a real good floor leader."

Bogues' odds of making it to the NBA at 5-foot-3 were astronomical, but still not as large as Greg Grant's 11 years later. Grant, at 5-foot-7, was not only vertically challenged, but also hampered by the fact that he had played college basketball in Division III. From 1974, when small colleges were split into Division II with scholarships and Division III without them, only four Division III players before Grant had ever played a single game in the NBA, and none of them—Clint Wheeler, Derrick Rowland, Michael Harper, and Sam "The Bam" Pellom—were 5-foot-7.

Yet Grant always knew he would make the NBA. "I came up through a lot of negatives," he said. "I came up a little harder because of my size. I always had that negative hanging over my head. I was too short to make it. I was too skinny to make it. It sounds like a cliché, but it you really want to do something, you can do it. I always knew I was going to be a professional basketball player. I put that in my high school yearbook under 'What You Want to Become.' That was what I was going to do."

But he might have spent a lifetime working in a fish market had Rutgers University coach Kevin Bannon, then the coach at Trenton State, not been persistent enough to recruit Grant a second time after failing the first. "My cholesterol level went down 20 percent recruiting Greg," Bannon laughed.

Bannon had recruited Grant out of Trenton High School, but Grant elected to play at Morris Brown College in Atlanta, Georgia. He stayed briefly before returning to Trenton. His fiancee, Aretha, was pregnant with the first of their two children. Grant took a job in the shipping department of an air conditioning factory, but got laid off after six months. So he did construction work with his dad. "I really didn't want to do that," Grant said. "It was too hard."

He found a new job at the Crab Shack, where he sold and cleaned fish. But he also kept playing ball and was averaging 42 points a game in the summer when Bannon decided to recruit him again. "He was just tearing up the summer leagues," Bannon said. "He was enormously talented. I just loved the way he played. I wouldn't want to play against him—that tough, that quick, that fast, and he just never got tired."

Bannon offered Grant another chance at college, and Grant happily accepted. He wanted an education and another chance at basketball. As a sophomore at Trenton State, he averaged 28.5 points, 4.0 rebounds, 3.0 steals and 2.8 assists, while setting a school record by scoring 51 points in a game at Montclair State. As a junior, he scored 52 in a game at Wilmington College; finished second in the nation in scoring (30.6); set an NCAA Division III Tournament record by scoring 85 points in two games; was named an All-American, and was the only non-Division I player named to the UPI Small All-American Team. In his senior year, he led Trenton State to a 30-2 record, the best of any college in any division that

season; led the country in scoring (32.6); was named the Division III Player of the Year, and became the top single season scoring leader in New Jersey history by scoring 1,044 points—108 more than the former record set by Bill Bradley.

After college, Grant paved a professional basketball career the hard way: playing for six different NBA teams. To do so, he twice had to resurrect his NBA career in the CBA. Each time, he again had to prove himself.

"There are certain ways you can face obstacles in your life," Bannon said. "Greg's way was to meet obstacles head on. He was never an excuse guy. He was a guy who always wanted to find a way. Find a way to do it. As a coach, I wish I could bottle that."

You cannot. Nor can you always measure talent and skills by inches.

"If the game was played at one size, it just wouldn't be exciting," said Memphis Grizzlies guard Brevin Knight, who began his NBA career with the Cleveland Cavaliers. "If everyone was 6-6 or 7-feet, it wouldn't be a challenge. Instead, it's a smaller, quicker guy against a taller guy. That's the nature of the game."

Knight, who is 5-foot-10, thinks the game of basketball will have room for smaller players forever. "Always," he said. "We're the ones they put the ball in the hands of. We're the ones that run the team."

During the 2002-2003 season, Knight was one of several NBA guards under six-feet. Listed at 5-foot-11 were: Chucky Adkins of Detroit; Miami's Travis Best; Speedy Claxton of San Antonio, and Dallas' Avery Johnson, who led the Mavs' Texas rival Spurs to their first NBA title in 1998-99. Knight was one of three NBA players at 5-foot-10, joined by Portland's Damon Stoudamire and Mike Wilkes of Minnesota. And Earl Boykins, the 5-foot-5 guard of the Golden State Warriors, conceded inches to all his under six-foot contemporaries. Yet he outdid them all, averaging 8.8 points and 3.3 assists while shooting .377 on 3's and .865 at the foul line.

Best averaged 8.4 points and 3.5 assists for the Heat, while Adkins averaged 7.1 points and 2.7 assists. Stoudamire checked in at 6.9 points and 3.5 assists, starting in 59 games for the Trail Blazers and averaging 22.3 minutes, and Claxton, who missed the entire 2000-2001 season with a torn ACL, contributed 5.8 points and 2.5 assists for the Spurs in 30 games.

Terrell Brandon, a two-time NBA All-Star despite his 5-foot-11 height, averaged 13.8 points, 6.1 assists and 1.58 steals in his 12-year career.

"People think the only way you can play is if you're tall," Knight said. "You have to be tall to be able to dunk. But all shapes and sizes play basketball. I really heard it when it came time to go to college: people said I was too small to play. After college, people said I was too small to play in the NBA. It motivated me. I worked that much harder on my game."

His game at Stanford was pretty phenomenal, and Knight figured he'd be the first point guard taken in the 1997 NBA draft. He figured wrong. Though he was taken in the first round as the 16th pick by the Cavs, he was the third point guard chosen after Chauncey Billups, Boston's No. 3 pick, and Antonio Daniels, Vancouver's No. 4 pick. "To me, I felt I was the best point guard and I still got chosen third," he said. "Still,

people were telling me I was too small and couldn't do it."

But he did. In his rookie season, Knight finished second in the NBA in steals (2.45) and eighth in the league in assists (8.2) while averaging 9.0 points, as he was named to the First Team All Rookie Team. In the strike-shortened 1998-99 season, he averaged 9.6 points, 7.7 assists (eighth in the NBA) and 1.8 steals before breaking a bone in his hand late in the season, missing seven games.

His response to the injury? He stayed in Cleveland the whole summer to practice. "After breaking my hand last season, I knew I had to come back better," Knight said. "To get better, I had to commit to working. I stayed the whole summer and worked on my shooting."

Knight's work ethic had already been noted by his teammates, who had elected him a tri-captain before the 1998-99 season, a rare honor for an NBA sophomore who was the youngest member of the team. None of his teammates used a tape measure before voting.

"I don't care what height you are," Cavs coach Randy Whitman said. "If you have the talent, you can play. Brevin has the talent to play in this league, and he's proved that, of course. Most little guys who come into the league are very strong willed. They've heard, 'You're too small to make it' all their lives. They deal with it."

During the 1999-2000 season, in a game matching the Cavs and the Toronto Raptors, Knight found himself with a rare height advantage matched up against Muggsy Bogues. "It was a little weird," Knight said. "You're used to playing against bigger guys all the time, and now he's shorter than me. He has been an inspiration to me, him, Calvin Murphy, Nate Archibald (6-foot-1) and Spud Webb. Those guys came in and did a great job in the NBA."

So did 5-foot-7 Keith "Mister" Jennings, who didn't let ACL knee surgery eight games into his 1992-93 NBA rookie season prevent him from returning to the Golden State Warriors for two full seasons. The 1991 Naismith Award winner from East Tennessee State averaged 7.4 points and 4.7 assists for the Warriors in 1994-95.

Eleven other players at 5-foot-10 made it to the NBA: Ralph Beard (Indiana), Jimmy Darrow (St. Louis), Sonny Herzberg (Boston), future Knicks coach Red Holzman (Rochester/Milwaukee), "Fast Eddie" Hughes (Utah/Denver), Paul "Bucky" McConnell (Milwaukee), Bob Royer (Denver), Jerry Rullo (Philadelphia), Kenny Sailors (Denver/Boston/Baltimore), Zeke Sinicola (Fort Wayne) and Willie Somerset (Baltimore). They showed again that while you can measure a player's height, you can't measure his heart.

When Knight and guard Cedric Henderson were injured midway through the 1999-2000 season, the Cavs signed 5-foot-5 Boykins from Eastern Michigan, who followed Knight as the 1998 winner of the Naismith Award. On February 17, 2000, Boykins came off the Cavs' bench for 22 points and 10 assists, both career highs, in a 119-101 win over Denver, earning a rare standing ovation at Cleveland's Gund Arena. Yet another short player had stood tall in the NBA.

Chapter 24

Basketball and The Law

By Gary D. Hailey

Most of the events with which this book is concerned took place on the court—the basketball court. This chapter is about the significant events in basketball history that took place in a courtroom, where the players were not tall young men wearing sneakers and shorts, but usually middle-aged men of average size wearing dark suits or black robes.

By using a computerized legal database, you can find thousands of published court decisions involving the sport of basketball. The legal questions addressed in those decisions run the gamut, reflecting of the wide variety of disputes that find their way into our court system for resolution. For example, in *Lambert v. West Virginia State Board of Education*, 447 S.E.2d 901 (1994), a West Virginia court held that it was unconstitutional gender-based discrimination for that state to schedule girls' high-school basketball games in the fall rather than the winter. In *Continental Basketball Association v. Ellerstein Enterprises*, 669 N.E.2d 134 (1996), the owner of the CBA's Evansville team argued that the league's attempt to take away his franchise was legally invalid because the league had not complied with federal and state regulations that protected franchisees' rights. In *NBA v. Sokolofsky*, 496 N.E.2d 222 (1986), an NBA referee who had declared himself permanently disabled after suffering a heart attack in 1977 failed to persuade a New York court that the NBA's refusal to reinstate him five years later was illegal discrimination on the basis of his physical condition. And in *ABA v. AMF Voit, Inc.*, 358 F. Supp. 981 (1973), the issue was whether the ABA's red, white, and blue basketball was entitled to protection under federal trademark law. (The court held that it was not.)

This chapter, however, has a narrower focus—namely, the contract and antitrust disputes between NBA players and the league (or, in some cases, a maverick team owner and the league), including cases that involved basketball legends like Oscar Robertson, Julius Erving, Rick Barry, and Spencer Haywood.

⊕ ⊕ ⊕

Lawsuits cost money, and early-day professional basketball teams couldn't afford to spend a lot of money on lawyers. One of the few consistently profitable basketball-related enterprises was the Harlem Globetrotters, who were founded in 1926 by Abe Saperstein. The Globetrotters spawned a number of imitators, including an Iowa-based group of "colored" barnstormers who called themselves the "Famous Globetrotters" ("Des Moines Globetrotters" just doesn't have the right ring, does it?). After World War II, the Famous Globetrotters (who also used the term "Original" in their advertising) began to

Lou Hudson, 1969
Hudson employed the "unclean hands" defense to stay in St. Louis.

book themselves into arenas far away from Des Moines, and sportswriters and basketball fans alike began to confuse the two organizations.

Saperstein filed suit in federal court in Iowa in 1949—the year the NBA began play—alleging that these Johnny-come-latelies were infringing his trademark. The Harlem Globetrotters had never registered their name as a trademark; in fact, the judge who heard the case held that "Globetrotters" was too generic a term to be registered under the trademark laws (*Saperstein v. Grund*, 85 F. Supp 647 [1949]). But the

team's name had acquired what lawyers called "secondary meaning," meaning that it had become sufficiently well known that its use by a competitor would confuse or deceive the public. And while there was no law preventing the Iowa barnstormers from using black basketball players, or combining basketball with comedy to entertain its fans, it had to come up with a name that clearly distinguished it from Saperstein's Globetrotters.

By 1961, however, the NBA was successful enough to attract a rival professional league—the American Basketball League, which was the brainchild of Harlem Globetrotters' owner Abe Saperstein.

⊕ ⊕ ⊕

Players and attorneys usually prosper when an upstart challenges an established pro sports league, and the brief NBA-ABL rivalry was no exception to that rule. New leagues need to attract star players to achieve major-league status in the eyes of sports fans, but you don't find many star players hanging around the local playgrounds or YMCAs—most of them are already the property of established pro teams. The ABL was able to sign Connie Hawkins without a fight because the NBA had banned him due to his alleged involvement in a point-shaving scandal at the University of Iowa, but just about every other top-caliber player had to be pried away from a NBA team.

One young NBA star who found the ABL's siren song irresistible was Dick Barnett, a guard who had been the first draft choice of the Syracuse Nationals in 1959. Barnett may not have been in Oscar Robertson's class, but he was a very good young player, averaging 16.9 points per game in the 1960-61 season, which ranked 19th among all NBA players.

Barnett had signed the standard NBA one-year contract in March 1960—he was paid $8,500 for the 1960-61 season—and the Nats' general manager Danny Biasone offered him a $3,000 raise to play the next season for Syracuse. Biasone (who later testified that Barnett had orally accepted his offer) then mailed Barnett a new contract in May 1961. He began to wonder what was going on when Barnett didn't return the contract and then didn't return telephone calls. What was going on was that Barnett had decided to sign a $13,000 contract with the Cleveland Pipers of the ABL, whose primary owner was none other than George Steinbrenner.

The standard NBA contract contained a provision that was similar to the so-called "reserve clause" that had been a part of major-league baseball agreements for decades. Paragraph 22(A) of that contract provided that if a club and one of its players did not agree on a new deal by November 1, the club could unilaterally renew the player's old contract for an additional season on the same terms—except that it could cut the player's salary by up to 25%. So even if a player did not sign a new contract, he would not become a free agent immediately upon expiration of the old one.

When he didn't hear back from Barnett, Biasone sent him a letter explaining that the club believed it had a valid contract with him for the upcoming season because Barnett had agreed to Biasone's $11,500 salary offer on the telephone, and had later asked for an advance against that salary, which the team sent him (although he never cashed the check). To protect himself legally, Biasone went on to say that he was renewing Barnett's contract pursuant to the terms of Paragraph 22(A). Rather than cutting Barnett's pay, however, the Nats' GM stood by his previous $11,500 offer.

Entertainers and athletes have been known to sign a deal to perform for one employer, and then decide to accept a better offer from someone else. Traditionally, courts are reluctant to order an entertainer or athlete who has signed a personal services contract to perform for a particular employer. But they are not so reluctant to punish that entertainer or athlete for his breach of contract by ordering him not to perform for anyone else.

When it later found out that Barnett had signed with the ABL, Syracuse filed suit in a Cleveland court, winning an injunction against Barnett and the Pipers that prevented Barnett from playing in the ABL (*Central New York Basketball, Inc. v. Barnett*, 181 N.E. 2d 506 [1961]). An injunction is usually issued only when the plaintiff will otherwise suffer an injury for which monetary compensation is inadequate. If Syracuse could have replaced Barnett with an equally talented basketball player, his signing with Cleveland would not have caused Syracuse such an injury. But Syracuse argued that Barnett was a uniquely talented player whose extraordinary skill and ability made it virtually impossible to replace him. "He has all the talent of a great basketball player," Biasone testified. "He is terrific all the way around."

The ABL club and Barnett were forced to argue the opposite. The Pipers' coach testified that Barnett was only "pretty good," while Barnett himself modestly told the court that he did not have exceptional and unique skill and ability as a basketball player. But the judge noted the obvious inconsistency between Cleveland's eagerness to add Barnett to its roster—evidenced by its offer to pay him more than Syracuse—and its testimony that he was nothing special as a player.

The ABL and Barnett next argued that the reserve clause in the standard NBA contract was legally invalid as a "perpetual service" contract because it bound a player to the NBA team that drafted him forever. But according to the NBA, if a player did not sign a new contract before the beginning of a new season, his team could renew his old one for only one additional year. So a player like Barnett who did not sign a contract would be bound to his team for an additional season (and might even have to play for up to 25% less pay), but would then become a free agent. By the time that would have happened in this case, the short-lived ABL had folded its tent and the NBA was, once again, the only game in town when it came to professional basketball.

Taking the position that Paragraph 22(A) of the standard NBA player contract allowed clubs to renew an expired contract only one time was a wise legal strategy. The league could have asserted (as had major league baseball) that the provision was self-perpetuating—that renewing an expired contract for another season automatically gave a team a new option to renew for an additional season, and then another, for as long as the team wanted to retain rights to a player. But the court might have then viewed the contract provision as too one-sided and refused to enforce it at all. The NBA also may have thought that no star player would sit out for a full season

in order to become a free agent. And even if one did do something so radical, NBA owners might have thought their fellow owners could be counted on not to sign another team's player.

But the NBA didn't anticipate the formation of another rival league, the American Basketball Association, nor did it anticipate someone like Rick Barry coming along. Barry led the San Francisco Warriors in scoring as a rookie, averaging 25.7 points per game in 1965-66, then topped himself the next year, leading the NBA with a 35.6 average. The Warriors had paid Barry $75,000 in 1966-67, but the Oakland Oaks of the fledgling ABA were willing not only to match that salary but also promise Barry a piece of the team and a percentage of the gate. When Barry announced prior to the beginning of the 1967-68 season that he had signed a three-year deal with the Oaks, the Warriors immediately went to court and won an injunction that ordered Barry not to play for any other team until September 30, 1968—the last day of the one-year renewal period provided for in Barry's contract for the 1966-67 season.

Barry refused to knuckle under to the Warriors, and instead sat out the entire 1967-68 season while collecting $75,000 from the Oaks. Relying on a California law that said a personal services contract could not bind an employee for more than seven years, the Warriors argued that Barry should be enjoined from playing for the Oaks for seven seasons, not just one season. But a California court held that Barry's contract was valid for at most two seasons—the original one-year contract term plus the option year (*Lemat Corp. v. Barry*, 80 Cal. Rptr. 240 [1969]). Even though Barry had breached the contract by refusing to play for the Warriors during his option year, that breach did not entitle the Warriors to an injunction that lasted longer than the original term of the contract. The star was free to play for the Oaks in 1968-69.

Unfortunately, even with Barry—who led the ABA in scoring that season until he was injured—the Oaks' average home attendance in 1968-69 was only about 1,800. That summer, the Oaks were sold to a Washington, D.C., investor and renamed the Washington Capitols. But Barry apparently had something against the East Coast, so he did an about-face and re-signed with the Warriors (who gave him a five-year deal that more than doubled his Oakland salary) just after the sale of the Oaks was announced. Not surprisingly, the Oaks/Capitols went to court to enforce the terms of their contract with Barry.

Barry's lawyers offered several defenses. First, they argued that the assignment of Barry's contract by the Oaks to the new Washington team was invalid. But Barry's contract, like nearly all professional sports contracts, expressly provided that the Oaks had the right to trade Barry or otherwise assign his contract to any other ABA team without his permission.

Barry also argued that the Capitols were not entitled to an injunction because the team had "unclean hands." This legal term originated hundreds of years ago, when there were two completely separate court systems in England—courts of law (which punished wrongdoing by awarding monetary damages to successful litigants), and courts of equity (which issued injunctions in cases where money damages were insufficient to right a wrong). Today, American courts usually have both legal

and equitable authority, but the legal rules sometimes differ depending on whether a plaintiff is seeking money or an injunction.

It is an ancient principle of Anglo-American equity jurisprudence that "he who comes into equity must come with clean hands." In other words, even if the defendant is plainly guilty of breaking the law, a court of equity will not lift a finger against him if the plaintiff's conduct also has been improper. Barry argued that the Oaks were guilty of improperly inducing him to breach his original contract with the Warriors, and that the Oaks' "unclean hands" tainted their legal successor, the Capitols, as well.

The court must have been tempted to comment on Barry's *chutzpah* in raising an "unclean hands" defense, but did not. Instead, it simply pointed out that the alleged misconduct by the Oaks did not taint the Capitols just because the Capitols had bought the Oaks' ABA franchise (*Washington Capitols Basketball Club, Inc. v. Barry*, 304 F. Supp. 1193 [1969]). The Oaks may have misbehaved, but the Washington team's ownership had done nothing wrong.

The "unclean hands" defense was successfully raised in another NBA-ABA lawsuit. Lou Hudson, who was voted NBA Rookie of the Year after leading the St. Louis Hawks in scoring in 1966-67, started negotiating with the new ABA Minnesota Muskies while the Hawks were still in the playoffs. Soon after St. Louis was eliminated, Hudson inked a lucrative three-year deal with the Muskies on May 3, 1967. The signing was announced at a press conference in Minneapolis later that month.

Exactly one week later, the Hawks filed suit to enforce the reserve clause in their 1966-67 contract with Hudson and enjoin him from playing in the ABA in the upcoming season. Hudson's teammate and close friend Bill Bridges called him and questioned the wisdom of his decision to jump to the ABA, and Hudson changed his mind and inked a new five-year deal with the Hawks on June 5. Without Hudson, the Muskies lost over half a million dollars in the team's inaugural 1967-68 season, and the team was sold and became the Miami Floridians in the summer of 1968—just weeks after the Hawks moved to Atlanta.

A federal court refused to enjoin Hudson from playing for the Hawks because the Muskies "soiled its hands" when the team approached him during the 1967 NBA playoffs, and offered him a contract even though it knew that the reserve clause in his St. Louis contract gave the Hawks the rights to his services for the 1967-68 season (*Minnesota Muskies, Inc. v. Hudson*, 294 F. Supp. 979 [1969]). "This is not to say that Hudson was an innocent bystander," said the court. "On the contrary, viewed strictly from the standpoint of business morality, his position in this litigation, like that of the Muskies, is not an enviable one."

It mattered not that the Hawks also had been guilty of unlawful conduct when they signed Hudson to a second contract with full knowledge that he had signed an agreement to play for the Muskies. "It is irrelevant that the conduct of St. Louis may have been more reprehensible than that of the Muskies," the court held. "The doors of a court of equity are closed to one tainted" by misconduct such as that committed

by the Muskies.

It is difficult to reconcile the decisions in the Barry and Hudson cases. Given the holding in the Barry case that the Capitols should not be penalized just because the Oaks had unclean hands, one might wonder why the court in the Hudson case punished the Floridians for the sins of the Muskies. The judge who presided over the Hudson lawsuit did not discuss this issue in detail, but stated simply that the Miami club "acquired no greater rights to the services of Hudson than those acquired by the Muskies."

Judges rarely let their personal feelings about the parties to a lawsuit show in their written opinions. But judges occasionally do let it all hang out. "This case presents another chapter in the history of contract jumping by famous American athletes," is how the opinion in *Erving v. Virginia Squires Basketball Club*, 468 F.2d 1064 (1972), begins. "As usual the amounts paid by the competing teams are fantastic." After reading only those two sentences, Julius Erving's lawyer must have known his client was in trouble.

The famous "Dr. J" signed a four-year contract with the ABA Squires after his junior year of college. But after only one season with the Squires, Erving accepted a more lucrative offer from the Atlanta Hawks. When the Squires objected, Erving sued, arguing that his contract with the ABA team should be set aside because of fraud. The Squires countersued, seeking an injunction preventing Erving from playing for the Hawks. The team arguing that a clause in its contract with Erving that provided that any disputes between the player and team be submitted to binding arbitration should be enforced.

The federal appeals court that ruled on Erving's appeal of his defeat in a lower court observed that "the charge of fraud [against the Squires] in inducing this innocent collegian to leave college and play for four years for the inadequate sum of $500,000 is repeated *ad nauseam* by Erving's counsel in various colorful phrases." The Squires insisted that "this is just a plain, ordinary case of contract jumping to get more money, that the claim of fraud did not originate until two months or more after Dr. J. had signed his contract with the Hawks, and that the whole sorry business is nothing more nor less than the usual maneuvering by a greedy young athlete to sell out to the highest bidder." Upholding the arbitration clause in the contract, the court chose not to pass upon the parties' conflicting claims "as they are the very issues to be determined by the arbitration of the dispute."—but you don't have to be a legal genius to figure out which side the judge thought deserved to prevail in the arbitration.

⊛ ⊛ ⊛

The NBA-ABA rivalry spawned not only contract-jumping lawsuits, but also antitrust litigation. The plaintiffs in the two most significant antitrust cases of the era were veteran guard Oscar Robertson and *wunderkind* forward Spencer Haywood.

With only a year of junior college experience under his belt, Haywood led the 1968 U.S. Olympic basketball team to a gold medal. He enrolled at the University of Detroit that fall, but left after just one season to play for the ABA's Denver Rockets. As a 20-year-old rookie, Haywood led the ABA in scoring and rebounding, and was named MVP of the league.

In the spring of 1970—before he had reached his 21st birth-day—Haywood renegotiated his contract with the Rockets, eventually signing a six-year deal valued at $1.9 million. On closer examination, however, the contract signed on Haywood's account by his legal guardian was riddled with loopholes that allowed much of his compensation to be deferred for years, or made certain payments subject to various contingencies. The young superstar could be sure of receiving only about a fifth of the nominal value of the contract, while the remainder of the promised compensation was "illusory and indefinite," in the words of the judge who heard Haywood's antitrust suit. After consulting an attorney, Haywood notified the Rockets that their contract was legally invalid because they had fraudulently misrepresented its value, and then signed a six-year contract to play with the Seattle SuperSonics of the NBA.

But there was a fly in the Haywood-Seattle ointment: sections 2.05 and 6.03 of the NBA's by-laws. Those provisions—sometimes termed "the four-year rule"—stated that a player who had started college but dropped out could not be drafted or play in the NBA until his college class had graduated. Haywood had first enrolled in junior college in 1967, and would have been a member of the University of Detroit class of 1971 if he had not dropped out to sign with Denver. So he was not eligible to play in the NBA until the beginning of the 1971-72 season.

The NBA commissioner, Walter Kennedy, had refused to approve Haywood's contract with the SuperSonics, and the NBA Board of Governors quickly passed a resolution directing the commissioner to consider bringing charges against Seattle and to advise the board of "the most drastic penalties lawfully at its command" if the charges were sustained, ranging from fines to loss of draft choices to the expulsion of the franchise from the league. In addition, Seattle's opponents began to file protests of each game in which Haywood appeared in a Sonics uniform. Haywood went to court, claiming that NBA by-law sections 2.05 and 6.03 violated Section 1 of the Sherman Antitrust Act, which declares illegal "[e]very contract, combination . . . or conspiracy, in restraint of trade or commerce."

Soon after the Sherman Act became law in 1890, the Supreme Court ruled that this language should not be read too literally, but that only unreasonable contracts, combinations, or conspiracies that unduly restrained trade were illegal. In 1954, the NBA suspended Jack Molinas of the Fort Wayne Pistons indefinitely after he admitted that he had bet on several Pistons games. In 1961, after he graduated from Brooklyn Law School, Molinas filed an antitrust suit against the NBA. But the court held that the league's suspension of Molinas and its subsequent refusal to reinstate him was not an unreasonable restraint of trade in violation of the antitrust laws.

"[E]very disciplinary rule which a league may invoke, although by its nature it may involve some sort of a restraint, does not run afoul of the antitrust laws," the court reasoned. "And a disciplinary rule invoked against gambling seems about as reasonable a rule as could be imagined" (*Molinas v. NBA*, 190 F. Supp. 241 [1961]). Molinas argued to no avail that he had only bet on his team to win. But the judge noted that, at the time Molinas had been suspended, public confidence in basketball had been shattered due to a series of gambling incidents, which justified the NBA's strict anti-wagering rules.

(Molinas was not the only loser in this litigation. The publicity engendered by the lawsuit brought to light his relationship with New York City playground legend Connie Hawkins, who was subsequently kicked out of the University of Iowa before he played a single varsity game. The NBA banned Hawkins as well, who bounced from the ABL to the Harlem Globetrotters to the ABA. In 1969, he sued the NBA, which eventually agreed to pay him a million dollars to settle the case and allowed him to sign with the Phoenix Suns.)

Determining whether an agreement among competitors is an unreasonable restraint of trade can require a court to engage in complex economic analysis, but a full-blown "rule of reason" analysis is not required in all Section 1 cases. The Court has identified certain types of practices that generally have such a pernicious effect on competition and lack "any redeeming virtue" that they can be conclusively presumed to be unreasonable. For example, an agreement among competitors on the minimum price to be charged for something is *per se* illegal, and the competitors are not allowed to argue that the price they have agreed to charge is a fair one.

Another practice that is often presumed to be illegal is the group boycott, which has been defined as a "concerted refusal by traders to deal with other traders." Here, according to Haywood's suit, the NBA clubs were a group of traders who were refusing to deal with potential pro basketball players whose college classes had not yet graduated from college. But the NBA argued that there was precedent for allowing "rule of reason" justifications in certain group boycott cases. Here, the NBA's stated justification was its altruistic desire to encourage basketball players to finish college and prepare for a career outside of basketball. Haywood had a more cynical view of the league's reasons for imposing the four-year rule. College basketball was an efficient and almost costless means of developing young talent for the NBA; unlike major league baseball, the NBA did not have to subsidize minor-league teams to give younger players a place to hone their skills.

The federal judge who heard Haywood's application for a preliminary injunction against enforcement of the four-year rule gave the NBA's rule-of-reason argument short shrift. If the NBA by-laws had been more flexible, allowing for exceptions to the four-year rule in appropriate cases and providing for appeals or other procedural safeguards for individual players, those by-laws might have survived antitrust attack. But sections 2.05 and 6.03 were "absolute" and "overly broad." So the court ordered the NBA not to take any action that prevented or interfered with Haywood playing for the SuperSonics (*Denver Rockets v. All-Pro Management, Inc.*, 325 F. Supp. 1049 [1971]).

A general policy that encourages aspiring professional athletes to attend college for four full years before turning pro may, in fact, do more good than harm. But the facts in the Haywood case cried out for an exception to the usual NBA rule. In the first place, Haywood had already played a full season in the ABA before signing with Seattle, which made him ineligible to play college basketball ever again. And given his "hardship" status—Haywood was one of 10 children in a single-parent household—it is naive to argue that it was in Haywood's best interest to require him to go back to college (without a basketball scholarship, how was he to pay for

college?) before he was allowed to earn a living playing basketball. The judge might have been more sympathetic to the NBA's arguments if Haywood was fresh out of high school rather than an established professional star, but by choosing not to make an exception for Haywood, the NBA shot itself in the foot.

Would it have been wiser for the NBA to bend its four-year rule for Haywood but require him to go through the regular college draft, or some sort of special draft? Perhaps, but such a course might have taken the league from the frying pan and dumped it into the fire. The judge was able to dispose of Haywood's complaint without ruling on his allegation that the NBA college draft was also an antitrust violation, but strongly hinted that he would have found against the NBA on this issue if it had been necessary for him to rule on it. A decision that the college draft was illegal would have had much more serious consequences for the league than the judge's overturning of the four-year rule as it had been applied to Haywood.

From a college athlete's point of view, a professional league's amateur draft may look like a blatantly anticompetitive practice—in essence, it's an agreement among teams that they will not compete for the top young talent, which keeps salaries artificially low and leaves the player with no say as to which team he plays for. After all, they might argue, do high-tech companies draft the graduates of top science and engineering schools? Of course not—a number of firms may make job offers to a new graduate, who chooses an employer based on how much money he or she will make, the city in which the firm is located, and numerous other factors.

But sports teams are different from high-tech companies (or law firms, or automobile makers) in one crucial respect. Sports teams are members of a league, and the league is more important than any individual team. Where would the Michael Jordan-era Chicago Bulls have been without the Jazz, the Knicks, the Lakers and the rest of the NBA? Without the NBA regular season and playoff structure, culminating in a winner-take-all championship series, the Bulls could have been little more than modern-day barnstormers, traveling from city to city putting on exhibitions.

Unlike other businesses, sports league members are completely interdependent on one another. They are what lawyers call "joint venturers." A company like GM doesn't need Ford or Toyota to exist in order to be able to make money by selling cars. But the Chicago Bulls need the Indiana Pacers and the Miami Heat and other NBA teams to be successful in the basketball business. While GM doesn't lose any sleep if its rivals lose money or even go bankrupt, the Bulls have no interest in running the Pistons or the Nets out of business. In fact, they have some interest in seeing their on-the-court rivals succeed. That's because sports leagues thrive when teams are competitively balanced, not when certain teams are so dominant (or so hapless) that the outcome of games is a foregone conclusion.

Perhaps the best analogy for a professional sports league and its member teams in the non-sports world is a network of franchised restaurants under local ownership. The relationship between the members of a restaurant chain is characterized more by cooperation than competition. Local restaurant owners usually contribute to a national advertising fund that

promotes all chain members equally. Each location is required to meet certain quality standards, which are intended to protect the reputation of all the franchisees. (If a family has a bad experience at one McDonald's or Wendy's, it lowers the chance that they will patronize other members of the chain in the future, and vice versa.)

So while each restaurant owner is a separate legal entity, the relevant entity for antitrust purposes will generally be the chain as a whole, not each individual location. A single corporation acting alone can violate Section 2 of the Sherman Act, which prohibits monopolization, but it takes two independent firms, working in concert, to violate Section 1. So whether the individual members of a restaurant chain are viewed as a single economic entity or a group of competing firms can be very significant to the outcome of antitrust litigation.

The owner of a local McDonald's may compete to some degree with other McDonald's—although such intra-brand competition is usually limited by territorial restrictions on how close a new restaurant can be to an existing chain member—but his or her real competition is the Burger King or the Wendy's down the street. And while the Nets and the Knicks (or the Lakers and the Clippers) may compete to some degree for season-ticket buyers, NBA teams do not really compete economically with one another. They compete with the NHL, college basketball, and other spectator sports—not to mention movie theaters, amusement parks, even bowling alleys.

In litigation among team owners involving disagreements over team relocation or broadcast rights, as we shall see later, the courts have been more sympathetic to a "joint venture" (or "single entity") analysis that does not automatically condemn all league rules and regulations as antitrust violations. In antitrust suits between owners and players, however, courts have tended to view mechanisms like the college draft and the salary cap—which do help level the playing field among rival sports teams and promote competitive balance and the health of the league as a whole—more as anticompetitive restrictions that hurt players than as a procompetitive regulation that enables a league to compete more successfully against other forms of entertainment.

The most significant player-versus-owner lawsuit in NBA history was clearly *Robertson v. NBA.* The plaintiffs in that suit—which challenged not only the college draft and the reserve clause in the standard NBA player contract, but also a proposed NBA-ABA merger that was announced in May 1970—were all 14 elected player representatives, including not only Oscar Robertson, but also Bill Bradley, John Havlicek, and Wes Unseld.

The players' first priority was to prevent the rival leagues from merging, which would have brought an end to the sky-rocketing salaries that had resulted from the frenzied inter-league competition for players. Shortly after their complaint in the case was filed in federal court, a judge enjoined the planned merger. (The court did allow the leagues to negotiate a proposed agreement for the sole purpose of seeking a special antitrust exemption from Congress, but the exemption legislation never got out of committee.) Later, the judge modified his original order by allowing the leagues to negotiate a merger agreement if and only if they could come to terms with the players' union on the college player draft and the reserve clause.

The next important development in the case came almost five years after the case was filed—on Valentine's Day, 1975—by which time three of the original 14 plaintiffs (including Robertson) were no longer pro basketball players. Not to put too fine a point on it, the court handed the NBA its head in what might be viewed as a latter-day Valentine's Day Massacre for the owners.

The owners had moved for summary judgment on the players' allegations. Summary judgment, which is a way for a judge to decide a case without an actual trial, is appropriate only when there is no real dispute over what the relevant facts are, just a disagreement over the legal consequences of those facts. For example, the parties to a contract may not dispute that each of them signed a particular document, but may disagree over the legal implications of certain language in that contract. In such a case, there is no need to call witnesses.

After considering the owners' summary judgment motion, the court not only rejected most of the owners' arguments, but came close to ruling in favor of the players right on the spot (389 F. Supp. 867 [1975]). It held that "practically all" of the intra- and inter-league restraints challenged by the players appeared to be *per se* violations of the antitrust laws. For example, according to the judge, the player draft was an illegal group boycott and analogous to price-fixing, which is also *per se* illegal.

The reserve clause, which allowed a team to unilaterally renew the player's contract with the team for an additional season, barely avoided immediate condemnation. The players argued that the reserve clause granted each club a perpetual right of renewal, and the judge agreed that a reserve clause that had perpetual effect would certainly have been struck down. But the NBA countered by asserting, as it had in the earlier contract-jumping cases, that a player could become a free agent no later than one year after his contract expired, assuming that his team had exercised its option to renew. (The league also pointed out as proof of its reasonableness that it no longer allowed a team that renewed a player's contract to cut his previous year's salary by up to 25%.)

The problem with the NBA's position was that the league had adopted a variant of the NFL's "Rozelle Rule," which required any team that signed a free agent to compensate the player's former team for its loss. The new team might have to forfeit future draft choices, or surrender one or more of its players if the NBA Commissioner felt the former team deserved such recompense. Not surprisingly, few NBA teams chose to sign free agents. But because there was some disagreement over the exact details of the compensation system—they weren't written down anywhere—it would have been premature for the judge to rule on the legality of the compensation system without first holding a trial.

The judge's sympathy for the players' position was obvious, and his opinion made it clear that a trial in the case might be little more than a formality. "I must confess that it is difficult for me to conceive of any theory or set of circumstances pursuant to which the college draft [and other practices attacked by the players] could be saved from Sherman Act condemnation," the judge wrote. "The life of these restrictions,

therefore, appears to be all but over, although their formal interment must await further developments in this case." The owners saw the legal handwriting on the wall and negotiated a settlement with the players in 1976. As part of that settlement, the owners signed a new collective bargaining agreement that made significant concessions to the players and provided for continued oversight of the NBA by the court for the next decade.

But the collective bargaining agreement did allow the NBA-ABA merger to be consummated at long last, although by this time the ABA was but a shadow of its former self. (In 1970, when the leagues originally agreed to merge, 10 ABA teams planned to join the NBA. By 1976, only six ABA franchises were still around, and only four were involved in the merger.) And it blessed the college draft and a modified version of the NBA's "Rozelle Rule."

That's right—the NBA players' union agreed in the course of negotiations over a collective bargaining agreement to allow the NBA to engage in some of the very same practices which it had attacked as anticompetitive in the *Robertson* litigation. But a funny thing happens when practices by an employer that might otherwise be condemned under the antitrust laws are incorporated in a collective bargaining agreement between that employer and an employees' union—those practices are no longer subject to antitrust attack.

The so-called "labor exemption" to the antitrust laws—which says that provisions of collective bargaining agreements between employers and unions are generally exempt from the antitrust laws—represents an attempt by the courts to reconcile federal antitrust laws with federal labor laws. Without this exemption, collective bargaining efforts by trade unions to obtain higher wages and other benefits for its members—efforts that are protected and even encouraged by the labor laws—could be attacked as anticompetitive behavior that violated the antitrust laws. So when the NBA players' union agreed in exchange for concessions on other issues to enter into a collective bargaining agreement with the NBA that provided for a college draft, for compensation to teams that lost free agents, and for other arguably anticompetitive restrictions, those restrictions could not be challenged in an antitrust suit.

Just how far the labor exemption extends is apparent from the decision in Leon Wood's 1984 lawsuit against both the NBA and the players' association. Wood, the Philadelphia 76ers' first-round draft choice in 1984, was offered a one-year contract for only $75,000 under the league's new salary cap rules.

In 1983, the league had narrowly averted its first strike when the players agreed to a limitation on player salaries—a salary cap—that the NBA had insisted was necessary to save the league from a fiscal Armageddon. The cap was simple in concept, but maddeningly complex and loophole-ridden in practice. One thing that was clear was that any rookie who was unlucky enough to be drafted by a team that was at or above the maximum team salary found himself at a real disadvantage. First-round choices of teams that were over the cap could be paid a maximum of $75,000 and could not be signed to multi-year contracts. In other words, these rookies became free agents after only one season, which was terrific if they had great rook-

ie seasons, but not so great if they played little or got hurt.

Wood argued that his value in the open market was far greater than $75,000, which was undoubtedly true, but the court held that the salary cap provisions of the collective bargaining agreement were immune to antitrust attack (*Wood v. NBA*, 602 F. Supp. 525 [1984]). The salary paid to employees is a mandatory subject of collective bargaining when said employees are represented by a union; that is, the employer cannot change salaries without negotiating with the union first. It was clear that the salary cap provisions in the 1983 collective bargaining agreement had been agreed to only after intensive arms-length negotiations between the NBA and the players' association. "As such these provisions come under the protective shield of our national labor policy and are exempt from the reach of the Sherman Act," said the court.

Union members who don't like the deal their union cuts with their employer just have to grin and bear it; the majority rules. Wood argued that the agreement could not bind him because he was not even a union member when it was negotiated. But collective bargaining agreements apply not only to those who are employees when an agreement is signed, but also to those who become employees after an agreement is signed. Wood and his fellow collegians were stuck with the teams that drafted them because the veterans in the players' union had agreed that the NBA could divvy up college players through the draft and put a cap on rookie salaries, even though none of those union members would ever be subject to the draft or the rookie cap. Under the law, the veterans were perfectly free to bargain away the rookies' freedom in exchange for a few additional pieces of silver.

In 1987, a group of NBA players went to court to challenge the league's salary cap provisions as invalid because the old collective bargaining agreement that contained them had expired. But the court held that even though the old collective bargaining agreement was no longer in effect, the labor exemption still shielded the cap from antitrust challenge until it became clear that the next collective bargaining agreement would not contain such provisions. The NBA and players' union then came to terms on a new seven-year collective bargaining agreement in 1988. That agreement contained a new salary cap exception that became known as the "Larry Bird Rule," which allowed a team to re-sign its own veteran free agents without violating the cap.

In 1996, in *Brown v. Pro Football*, 518 U.S. 231, the Supreme Court went even further, holding that the labor exemption applied to the provisions in an expired collective bargaining agreement—and to new provisions implemented unilaterally by a league after it reached a bargaining impasse with its players' union (which is legal under the labor laws)—as long as the parties still had a collective bargaining "relationship." Once players form a union and bargain collectively with a league, they can take advantage of the protections afforded to unions under the labor laws, but must forfeit their rights under the antitrust laws. As Justice Breyer, the author of the *Brown* opinion, observed while the case was being argued, "I was brought up at my mother's knee to believe that antitrust and labor law do not mix." In other words, a union can't have its cake and eat it, too. (If this seems somehow unfair to unions,

it's not; after all, the labor exemption was created to prevent employers from using the antitrust laws against unions. The labor exemption protects both employers and unions from antitrust attacks.)

If players really want to bring an antitrust suit against a group of owners, they can—they just have to dissolve their union. Frustrated by its inability to win a satisfactory collective bargaining agreement with the National Football League, the NFL Players' Association did just that in 1989 and converted itself from an honest-to-God labor union into a mere "association"—an action that was somewhat reminiscent of the famous Vietnam-era line about having to destroy a village in order to save it—so that it could pursue an antitrust challenge against the NFL. (After winning their suit, the players quickly re-formed their union. A future court may not look so kindly on the NFL players if they try that tactic again.)

When the 1988 NBA collective bargaining agreement expired in 1995 and the league locked out the players in an attempt to strengthen its bargaining hand, some NBA players (led by Michael Jordan and Patrick Ewing) also tried to force the NBA players' union to relinquish its status as the players' exclusive bargaining agent and dissolve itself. The dissidents preferred to bring an antitrust suit against the league rather than accept the terms of a tentative new agreement negotiated by the union's executive director. Eventually, the players voted not to decertify their union, and a modified collective bargaining agreement was signed in 1996.

The peace between the NBA owners and players was short-lived, however. Salaries continued to spiral upward, and when Kevin Garnett—the 1990s' version of Spencer Haywood—signed a $126 million contract in 1997, you could almost hear the league's owners repeating Popeye's classic mantra, "That's all I can stands, I can't stands no more." The owners exercised their option to reopen the collective bargaining agreement in 1998, and imposed another lockout that summer when the players refused to agree to certain changes to that agreement. For the first time in NBA history, regular-season games—and the NBA All-Star Game—had to be cancelled because of labor strife.

After more than a third of the regular season had been lost and it appeared that the entire season might be cancelled, the two sides settled their differences in January 1999. For once, the poor got richer, and the very, very rich got a little bit poorer. Individual salaries were capped at $14 million for 10-year veterans, $11 million for players with seven to nine years in the NBA, and $9 million for less experienced players. Minimum salaries were increased across the board, reducing to some degree the huge disparity between the salaries for superstars and those for journeymen.

⊕ ⊕ ⊕

While the most significant legal clashes in basketball history have involved owner-player or league-union confrontations, occasionally a maverick owner will rebel against his fellow owners and challenge a league's rules in court.

The most notorious such litigation involved Oakland Raiders owner Al Davis's decision to move the Raiders to Los Angeles. Perhaps not surprisingly, a Los Angeles jury agreed with Davis that the NFL's refusal to grant him permission to move his team was an unlawful conspiracy among team owners in violation of the antitrust laws. What was surprising was that a federal appeals court upheld that verdict. To add to the confusion, that same court issued a subsequent decision that undercut much of the effect its initial ruling. When the legal dust finally cleared, the Raiders had been allowed to move to Los Angeles, but the jury's award of damages to the team was reversed because the franchise had wrongfully expropriated for itself an asset belonging to the league as a whole—that asset being the value of a second NFL franchise in the Los Angeles market (which the league could have exploited through the sale of an expansion franchise if the Raiders hadn't moved there first).

After the decision in the first appeal in the Raiders case, the NBA's San Diego Clippers also decided the grass was greener in Los Angeles. The NBA approved the team's move, but asked a court to rule that its policy of requiring league approval prior to the relocation of a franchise was legal. After the second appeal in the NFL litigation was decided, the same federal appeals court held that such a restriction was legal unless it was applied unreasonably—usually, a question left to the tender mercies of a jury (*NBA v. SDC Basketball Club*, 815 F.2d 562 [1987]).

One prominent antitrust expert has written that the Raiders and Clippers decisions were "so confusing, devoid of substantive antitrust analysis, and internally inconsistent that their precedential value should have been nil" (Roberts, "Antitrust Issues in Professional Sports," in G. Uberstine, *The Law of Amateur and Professional Sports* 19-16 [1998 ed.]). Subsequent litigation over team relocations has generally recognized that there are many legitimate reasons for a sports league to place limits on the ability of its franchises to pull up stakes and move to new cities whenever the urge for a new taxpayer-financed stadium strikes. But the NFL in particular remains a bit gun-shy when it comes to saying "no" to owners who want to relocate. Since the Raiders litigation, the team has been permitted to move back to Oakland, the Cardinals have left St. Louis only to be replaced by the Rams, the Colts and Browns have played musical chairs in Baltimore, and the Oilers have moved to Nashville (after taking a detour through Memphis).

Of course, most of the money earned by professional sports leagues comes from television, so it is not surprising that there has been considerable litigation over broadcast rights to league games. In fact, the first significant antitrust decision that went against a sports league resulted from a 1953 Justice Department challenge of the NFL's restrictions on the sale of broadcast rights by NFL teams. (In those days, individual pro football teams retained the rights to televise their games; the league had the rights to only the NFL All-Star and Championship games.)

The judge in that case held that any restrictions on telecasts of NFL games in an NFL city were legal when that city's team was playing at home—presumably, broadcasts of either that game or any other NFL game might hurt home-game ticket sales—but not legal when the team was playing on the road. After the upstart AFL negotiated a favorable television deal with ABC, the NFL wanted to sign a deal with CBS providing that each NFL team's road games would be televised in its home territory, but that all of its home games would be blacked out. When the judge who had issued the 1953 ruling against the

NFL held that the NFL-CBS contract violated that ruling, the league went hat in hand to Congress.

Congress responded to the NFL's plea for help by passing the Sports Broadcasting Act of 1961, 15 U.S.C. 1291 *et seq.*, which exempted certain league television contracts from the antitrust laws. Generally speaking, that law allowed leagues to prohibit game broadcasts in a team's home territory when the team was playing a home game, but did not exempt other restrictions on televised games from antitrust scrutiny.

In 1991, the NBA argued that the 1961 statute exempted its restrictions on the sale of television rights to "superstations" by individual NBA teams. The NBA had sold the rights to televise a limited number of its games to NBC and TNT, but individual teams were given considerable freedom to sell the TV rights to their other games. There was one significant string attached, however: the teams could not allow superstations like WGN and WTBS (local broadcast stations that now were carried by hundreds of local cable TV systems throughout the United States) to broadcast more than a certain number of their games. When the league voted to reduce the maximum number of superstation game broadcasts from 25 to 20 games per season, the Chicago Bulls and Chicago superstation WGN sued.

The court that heard the case ruled that the Sports Broadcasting Act's antitrust exemption applied only to provisions in league contracts with a television network, not a league's restrictions on the sale of broadcast rights by individual teams (*Chicago Professional Sports v. NBA*, 754 F. Supp. 1336 (1991); *affirmed*, 961 F.2d 667 [1992] ["WGN I"]). It then held that the new NBA policy violated the "rule of reason" because it reduced output—here, the number of Bulls games that could be broadcast on WGN or any other superstation—in the same way that an agreement among the big oil companies to shut down their refineries on weekends would reduce the output of gasoline (and, presumably, cause the price of gasoline to go up). Ironically, while the new 20-game superstation limit was found to be illegal, the old 25-game rule was not overturned.

The NBA tried to restructure its deals with NBC and TNT to qualify for the Sports Broadcasting Act's antitrust exemption. After the first attempt to do so was rebuffed in court, 808 F. Supp. 646 (1992) ("WGN II"), the NBA amended its by-laws so that the copyrights to all game telecasts were the property of the league rather than individual teams. The NBA then assigned those copyrights to NBC, which agreed to televise only a few regular-season games itself, and to assign the rights to other games to TNT. The rights to the remaining games reverted to the NBA, which then authorized individual teams to sell rights to their games to local broadcasters, but not to superstations. Anticipating a new legal challenge, the NBA had a back-up plan: if the ban on superstation telecasts was found illegal, a team that sold broadcast rights to a superstation had to pay the league a special fee.

To no one's surprise, the Bulls and WGN took the league to court for a third time. The district court ruled in favor of the plaintiffs (874 F. Supp. 844 [1995]). But the appeals court was more sympathetic to the NBA's arguments. In particular, it held that the league and its member teams might be considered a "single entity" for antitrust purposes rather than each NBA team being viewed as an independent economic actor—which would mean that its superstation rule could not be challenged under Section 1 of the Sherman Act because there can be no illegal "combination" or "conspiracy" unless there are two or more entities to combine or conspire. Consequently, the appeals court sent the case back to the lower court for a new trial (95 F.3d 593 [1996] ["WGN III"]).

As the WGN decision indicates, the courts are showing more sympathy to arguments that a sports league like the NBA is really a single economic unit rather than a group of independent competitors. Many newly formed professional sports leagues have organized themselves in such a way to make a "single entity" defense even more likely to succeed. For example, for the first several years of its existence, WNBA teams were not independent legal entities like NBA teams. Individual NBA teams did not own individual WNBA teams— the members of the NBA owned the WNBA collectively. In other words, the Lakers didn't own the Sparks and the Knicks didn't own the Liberty; the Lakers and the Knicks owned a share of every team in the WNBA, but were allocated a bigger share of the WNBA's revenues because they operated and administered the teams that played in their arenas. (Last fall, the NBA restructured the women's league, offering its owners the chance to buy their WNBA "little sisters." Several NBA owners declined, which resulted in the league's contraction and a couple of franchise relocations. The Orlando Magic moved to Connecticut and became the first WNBA team to play in a non-NBA city under non-NBA ownership—namely, the Mohegan Sun casino, which does not permit sports betting.)

Being structured as a single legal entity (as well as being a single economic entity, at least arguably) might not have made much difference when it came to disputes between the WNBA and its players because the labor laws are more important than the antitrust laws in that context. But it could have largely eliminated antitrust challenges by dissident owners over broadcast rights, licensing and sponsorship deals, and other issues.

Chapter 25

From Naismith To Jordan: Basketball Pioneers

By Steve Popper

There are some who would believe that the game began when Michael Jordan first wagged his tongue as he soared almost sideways over defenders. Understandable, since it is difficult to see a line from basketball's humble beginnings to the current incarnation, the set shot replaced by 360-degree jams, the chest pass nearly gone, displaced by killer crossover dribbles, and the peach basket a distant memory in a world of luxury box-filled arenas. The timeline bristles with action, from the start to the present—the line leaps airborne at times, thunders with power at others, and slips almost unseen through deft hands.

But there is a timeline to Jordan and beyond, one that begins perhaps with Elgin Baylor and proceeds through Connie Hawkins, then David Thompson and Julius Erving, all players who floated above the fray, eschewing the fundamentals for the fantastic. And there is a timeline that slithers through the history of the game, providing the necessary ingredients for the game to reach the worldwide status that it occupies today. David Stern would not be possible without Maurice Podoloff, who would not have been heard from without Dr. Naismith. The beginnings, then the innovations, and the struggles all were necessary to find the game that some would believe Jordan built. Here, then, is *Total Basketball*'s tribute to 10 (okay, 11) pioneers who have done the most to shape the game:

DR. JAMES NAISMITH

It would be nice if the story went something like this: December 1891, Dr. Naismith tacks a peach basket to the wall at a YMCA gymnasium in Springfield, Mass., and in a matter of moments, the gathered players were whipping passes behind their backs, tossing up long, arching jump shots behind a hastily drawn 3-point line, all with Naismith conducting the action in a fit of inspiration.

But Naismith's place in history is not that simple to detail. True, his inspiration led to the hanging of peach baskets, and a month later he published a set of rules, 13 precepts that are mostly long forgotten by now. But that is the point of contention with Naismith; his contributions are all but forgotten now, with his biggest legacy being the moment those baskets were nailed to the wall.

Naismith created the sport, a variation on games played on other continents long before—like the game "duck on a rock" from his youth—as an activity for his charges at the Y, and after that had little to do with the product that developed. He did not seek to further the competition and nine years after he tacked up the basket, he took his first coaching job. He was a failure at coaching, leaving a legacy that names him as the only

Phog Allen, 1951
A student of James Naismith, but an innovator in his own right.

coach in the storied history of Kansas basketball with a losing record, 55-60.

But just as the nailing of the baskets spawned the game, Naismith's tenure at Kansas also gave birth to a cradle of coaches that have dominated the game since its beginnings. When he stepped down at Kansas, Forrest "Phog" Allen took over, beginning a career of coaching that not only set a standard for the profession, but also continued the lineage through history with his own students, Adolph Rupp and Dean Smith, coaches who occupy the top two spots on college basketball's

all-time victory list.

The influence that Dr. Naismith had upon the game has been debated and will likely continue to be argued, but there is no question that he provided the roots that the game has sprouted from. But he never enjoyed the competitive nature, instead reveling in its use as a game of leisure.

"I am sure that no man can derive more pleasure from money or power than I do from seeing a pair of basketball goals in some out of the way place," he once said. "Deep in the Wisconsin woods an old barrel hoop nailed to a tree, or a weather-beaten shed on the Mexican border with a rusty iron hoop nailed to one end."

FORREST "PHOG" ALLEN

There is a story that goes like this: Forrest Allen was playing basketball at the University of Kansas in 1906 and he approached his coach, Dr. James Naismith, and inquired about the possibility of becoming a basketball coach. "You don't coach basketball, Forrest, you play it."

For a while, it might have seemed that Naismith offered him sound advice, as Allen took over the program from Naismith in 1907, and was gone by the next season. But he showed his inclination to make it a career, searching out jobs at Baker University and the Haskell Institute that he handled in the same season, juggling all three jobs, before stepping out of the profession for four years. He then returned to coaching in 1912, handling the duties for all sports at Central Missouri State University, where he posted a 102-7 record in seven seasons.

Kansas came calling again and he became the school's athletic director and coach of basketball and football. He spent 39 seasons as the Jayhawks' basketball coach, compiling a record of 590-219, making him the winningest coach in Kansas history. All told, he won 746 games, a record that stood until it was broken by one of his students, Adolph Rupp.

Even after Rupp broke the record, he said of Allen, "He'll go down in history as the greatest basketball coach ever."

If he was the most dominant coach, Allen did it with wit and class that would influence his students. Told that Wilt Chamberlain had enrolled at Kansas, he dryly noted, "Fine, fine, I certainly hope he comes out for the basketball team."

Allen's competitive spirit would do more to further the game than his mentor and the inventor of the game, Dr. Naismith, would ever do. He was one of the founders of the National Basketball Coaches Association and served as its first president. He was an instrumental force behind the inclusion of basketball in the Olympics and also in the implementation of the NCAA Tournament. He guided his teams to 24 conference championships, but just one NCAA title, in 1952.

HANK LUISETTI

Many people remember the day that Angelo 'Hank' Luisetti and Stanford came to Madison Square Garden in 1936 as a game that changed the face of basketball forever. They might recall the odd sight of Luisetti's running one-handed shot or the huge crowd crammed into every corner of the arena to see Stanford put an end to Long Island University's 43-game winning streak. On that day, Luisetti became the first star of the sport, having already established his reputation on the west coast and now on the game's grandest stage, taking on the best team in the nation and winning with a novel new approach.

Luisetti grew up in California, learning how to play at a Boys Club where he watched a young Joe DiMaggio play baseball. He never played in the National Basketball Association, after developing spinal meningitis during his time in the Navy. He briefly coached an AAU team from California, winning a national championship in 1951 before giving it up, then worked for Standard Oil, then sold life insurance and finally worked in the automobile business before retiring.

He watched the game regularly up until his death in December 2002, and was surprised at the lasting memory that his team made during their brief stay on the east coast after a six-day rail journey to play in the game.

"It helped us a lot that we got the publicity for this game," Luisetti said. "Basketball wasn't that big. But to be in New York and beat that LIU team put west coast basketball on the map."

Not long before his death, the 87-year-old Luisetti spoke by phone with Leo Merson, the player who had been assigned to guard him that night. Merson told of how he had played with a flu and how he just was not himself. Perhaps if the story had come out in 1936, rather than the rave reviews for Luisetti's 15-point performance in Stanford's 45-31 win, Merson might have earned some of the notoriety that follows Luisetti to this day.

"I never realized how important that game was until now," said Merson.

Luisetti replied: "Well, neither did we until this time. Everybody thought we would lose because LIU had won so many games. If we hadn't won in New York I never would have gotten the recognition I got for the one-handed shooting. We had a good ballclub."

The stage proved as good for basketball as it was for Luisetti, lifting the college game to another level and putting his shooting style on display for generations to emulate and take to another level.

GEORGE MIKAN

To put the performance of George Mikan in perspective, imagine Michael Jordan taking off for the first time along the baseline, soaring skyward and slamming in a dunk over awed defenders. Then imagine the league's officials eyeing this scene, grabbing their pencils and protractors, and cranking the basket from 10 feet to 12 feet, and inserting a rule in the books that a player may not remain airborne for more than one second. Satisfied, they would have prevented Jordan from discouraging the rest of the players with his uncommon skills.

It happened to George Mikan less than a decade into the National Basketball Association's history. He was the first of the dominating big men, a 6-foot-10 giant blessed with skills beyond the scope of most smaller players, able to drop in uncannily accurate hook shots with either hand and deliver a consistent set shot, too. And on defense, he stood in the lane, guarding the basket while his teammates spread out in a zone and swatted away shots above the rim. A brute a full 25 years before Shaquille O'Neal was born, Mikan led the league in personal fouls in three different seasons. And even Jordan never

inspired a marquee like the one at Madison Square Garden on December 13, 1949, when it read, "Geo. Mikan vs. Knicks." (Mikan was surprised to find his teammates still in civilian clothes as the game neared. He asked for an explanation and one said, "Oh, we thought you were going to play the Knicks by yourself.")

In the first year of the NBA, in a game that provided only one other scorer who could top 20 points per game, Mikan averaged 27.4 points. And in the postseason, he led the Minneapolis Lakers to the league's first championship by averaging 31.3 points per game. The following season, the league began to chart rebounding figures and Mikan grabbed 14.1 per game—second only to Dolph Schayes of the Syracuse Nationals—and scored a career-best 28.4 points per game.

The one-man show had to end and the league put a stop to it the only way it could. The key was expanded from a slender six feet wide to 12 feet, pushing him away from the basket. Mikan could no longer plant himself under the basket where the smaller players would helplessly try to stop him.

He still led the Lakers to their third consecutive championship in the 1953-54 season, averaging 18.1 points and 14.3 rebounds. But the following year, with the 24-second shot clock taking effect, he opted to walk away from the game. He was elected to the initial class of the Hall of Fame and was named as the greatest basketball player of the first half-century, finishing with 139 of the 380 votes cast in an Associated Press poll in 1950. Hank Luisetti finished a close second with 123 votes. Had the poll been taken several years later, after the Minneapolis titles, the vote would not have been nearly so close. With white kneepads and spectacles, Mikan was hardly the image projected by the likes of Chamberlain and O'Neal, but he was the first of the big men to set a course that they would someday follow.

DANNY BIASONE

While Naismith gave the game its roots and coaches like Allen and Rupp provided the structure that is still adhered to today, it was Danny Biasone who gave the game the prod it needed to reach the heights it has today.

Ask most NBA fans who Danny Biasone is and you get a puzzled look, although perhaps a little less so since he was inducted into the Basketball Hall of Fame in 2000. It was too late for Biasone to issue any, 'told you sos' (the induction coming six years after his death) but it recognized the contributions of a man who provided the league's saving innovation: the 24-second shot clock.

Biasone, who was the owner of the Syracuse Nationals in the infancy of professional basketball, had accomplished enough to merit a place in the sports annals even before he calculated the math to create the shot clock. He had created one of the sport's early success stories, guiding the Nats through the NBL and then into the NBA, where the team made the league's first Finals.

Mikan's dominance was an example of a troublesome aspect of the game. It led to a boring style of play in which teams funneled the ball into the post and went into a ball-control offense once they established a lead. This style was taken to its apex in 1950, when the Fort Wayne Pistons, determined to counteract

Mikan and the Lakers, held the ball, stalling the game into a 19-18 decision (Mikan scored 15 of the 18), the lowest-scoring game in league history.

Biasone was part of a group searching for a way to avoid the path the game seemed stuck on. Biasone figured the game could be prodded forward by limiting the time that a team could possess the ball. He derived his formula by calculating that teams had hoisted a combined average of 120 total shots in a game, and he divided that into the 48-minute game time and came up with 24 seconds.

The clock was tested in a scrimmage with the league's owners gathered to watch and there was no question that the game was seeing a renaissance in this near-empty gymnasium. The 24-second clock had an immediate impact as scoring went up dramatically, with the league scoring average jumping 14 points per game from 79.5 to 93.1. And Mikan, who had beaten Biasone in that first league Finals, saw rules that conspired against him and opted for retirement.

WILT CHAMBERLAIN

When Wilt Chamberlain was still a student at Overbrook High School in Philadelphia, he would spend his summers in the Catskill Mountains of New York, waiting tables at Kutsher's Country Club. And when he would take off the work clothes, he would step into the small gymnasium at the Country Club and find himself cast into games with members of the NBA ranks—players who were already mean, experienced and tough. And just as he would when he joined them in the pros, Chamberlain already had their numbers.

"Red Auerbach was the coach," he recalled three years before his death when he sat down for an interview in the NBA offices. "He had me go against some of his Boston Celtics boys, and I used to try to beat them to death."

Wilt would follow a statement like that with a huge, bellowing laugh, slapping his massive hands on his knees that stretched out in long paths from his chair. But everything he did was big, outsized, and off the scale of the average person. He once said it was not easy being Goliath, but he seemed to relish it more than any other big man to find his way onto the court.

"I think that my legacy should be that I gave credence that you could be big, bigger than most, and still have athletic ability," Chamberlain said. "Even though George Mikan had done a great deal before me, I think I embodied what a big man was able to do. I think they had no way to compare what I was doing. It was so far out of the realm of believability. People came to a game and they said, 'He's capable of scoring 100 points,' and every night they were looking for 100 points. It had to be very, very special for them to say, 'Wow, Wilt did this or did that.' So 50 points was shrugged off, like, 'Well, he can do that anytime he wants.'"

In retrospect though, it is those staggering numbers that Chamberlain is remembered for. He was 7-foot-1, 275 pounds, and athletic, able to outrun guards and with a vertical leap that would rival Jordan's. He led the NBA in scoring seven straight seasons, amassing 31,419 points. He is the only player to score 100 points in a game, a number that he landed on exactly against the Knicks in 1962. He is the only player to total 4,000

points in a season. In the 1961-62 season, he averaged 50.4 points per game, a number that makes a player a star today if he reaches it in one game.

As a rookie, he averaged 37.6 points and 27 rebounds, being named the league's Rookie of the Year, Most Valuable Player, and MVP of the All-Star Game. In perhaps his best season, he averaged 24 points and 24 rebounds for the Lakers in 1966-67 and finished third in the league in assists. The following year, the player who once shot 63 times in a game actually led the league in assists.

BILL RUSSELL

He was the antithesis to everything that Wilt Chamberlain was. Chamberlain was huge, larger than life. Russell was 6-foot-11, but just 220 pounds. Russell would say his piece in a few carefully chosen words, sometimes ironic, sometimes caustic, but always painfully accurate.

Chamberlain's place in basketball lore is set by his outsized numbers. Russell's lasting impression is championship trophies. And just as Chamberlain set statistical marks that may never be approached, Russell's knack for leadership and courage set a standard for winning that no one has come near.

Russell won back-to-back NCAA titles at the University of San Francisco, then an Olympic gold medal, before joining the Celtics in a draft-day trade in 1956 and setting a standard for excellence that is still staggering today. In 13 seasons with the Celtics, Russell's squads won 11 league titles. He faced 11 decisive games in that time, 10 seventh games and one Game 5 of a best-of-five series, and he never lost one of them. He simply would not allow it.

"His will to win made the difference," his teammate Bob Cousy once told reporters. "He did not have the all-around skills of guys like Wilt or Kareem [Abdul-Jabbar]. But with his intensity, he raised himself to a level above both of them."

And it was the players and coaches who faced Russell who most appreciated that intensity and the skills he possessed. Think of Wilt and you think 100 points in one game or 50.4 points per game in one season. Think of Russell and it is hard to think of anything other than the championships. But Russell was much more than just a leader. He is one of only a few players in college basketball history to average 20 points and 20 rebounds for his career. And in the NBA, he came up with big numbers, usually at the biggest times. Enough to secure a place in history among his basketball contemporaries, being voted as the greatest player in the history of the NBA in a poll of writers for the 35th anniversary of the league.

He had 22 points and 35 rebounds in Game 7 of the 1960 Finals. He scored 30 points in Game 7 of the 1962 Finals. In the 1964 Finals, it was an astounding 30 points and 40 rebounds in an overtime Game 7 against the Lakers. In those 11 decisive games, he averaged 29.5 rebounds. Blocked shots, the trademark of his game, were not tabulated by the league during his career, and it was the impact of the plays, not their numbers, that made him so frightening to opposition. He was everywhere, with no player on the court safe from his wingspan.

"He's the one player I would pick to be at my side in the seventh game of the NBA championship finals," said former Celtic Bill Sharman.

"It's his focus, his tenacity," Julius Erving said at a tribute to Russell. "Never when I saw him play did I look at him as the most talented player on the court. But he would be the best player because of what he could bring to the table and how he could make everyone better and how he was in the clutch and how he was always a step ahead."

It was that way from the 55 consecutive victories his San Francisco squad compiled, through the 11 NBA titles, to his final game, a 48-minute effort in Game 7 of the 1969 Finals against Chamberlain and the Lakers. On that day, Russell grabbed 21 rebounds and the Celtics won one last time. That is a legacy that will remain when the individual numbers are forgotten.

DAVID STERN

In a league of giants and spectacular athletes, the short and rotund lawyer has towered over almost all of them, guiding the National Basketball Association since 1984 to undreamed of heights, both in the United States and worldwide.

As the fourth commissioner of the NBA, Stern has overseen the most dramatic growth spurt the league has ever witnessed. The league, which appeared to be limping towards the millennium, has flourished under his charge, enjoying a five-fold increase in revenues, adding six new franchises. As the NBA has grown, he has conquered new fronts, launching the WNBA, the reigning women's professional basketball league, in affiliation with the established NBA.

Before he took charge, he served as outside counsel and then the league's general counsel, having a hand in the 1976 settlement between the league and the players that led to free agency. He also helped shape the collective bargaining agreement that introduced the salary cap and revenue sharing; pro sports' first anti-drug agreement; and the development of NBA Properties as the league's marketing arm, as well as the creation of NBA Entertainment.

Stern has always been ahead of the curve, utilizing television and now the internet to send his message to the masses. He may be the Svengali behind the curtain and the players merely the puppets, but he happily pushes them forward as ready-for-prime-time stars, and the world has been only too happy to gobble them up.

LARRY BIRD AND EARVIN "MAGIC" JOHNSON

Rivalries have fueled sports for decades. In basketball, it was no different, whether it be feuding coaches or the meetings of Wilt Chamberlain and Bill Russell that sparked the game's growth. But the game was believed to be dying a slow death from an assortment of maladies in the late 1970s. The integration of the sport nearly 30 years earlier, in October 1950, had done little to slow the racist leanings of fans who saw the league as a harbor for a playground style of basketball played by drug-fueled malcontents. The perception may have been no more harbored in truth than any other racist notion, but the perception was there, nonetheless.

And it took a white man from tiny French Lick, Indiana, population 2,059, and a black man—the Lansing, Michigan, child of a school custodian and a General Motors assembly-line

worker—to change all that. Small town and inner city, white and black, the two combined to close all the barriers with humble attitudes and engaging smiles, not to mention perhaps the greatest assemblage of skill and savvy to ever to grace the courts of the NBA.

They came to the stage together, from very different paths. Bird moved unsteadily from French Lick to Indiana University, before finding his way through junior college to Indiana State University. He single-handedly turned that small-time program into the unbeaten and number one team in the nation in 1979, as they came upon the NCAA Tournament's championship game.

Awaiting was powerhouse Michigan State and its magnificent freshman point guard, Earvin Johnson. Bird was the player of the year that season, but it was Johnson who led his team to the title, sparking off the first salvo in a magnificent rivalry, one that remains staked in friendship more than hatred or envy.

The numbers alone would place each in their rightful place among the greatest players the sport has ever seen. Bird was a 12-time all-star, and only the third player and first non-center to ever win three consecutive Most Valuable Player Awards. Magic was a revolution to the game, measuring the same 6-foot-9 as Bird, but becoming the tallest point guard in league history at the time. He, too, won Most Valuable Player honors three times, and also captured the Finals MVP award three times. He surpassed Oscar Robertson's career assists record, a mark that would later be overtaken by John Stockton.

But it was not the numbers that made these two. It was the style they played with, a pure and fundamentally sound game that was a throwback to perhaps a time that never really existed, only taking place in failed memories and Hollywood movies. They passed the ball, making their teammates better, and they did the passing with a flair and purpose that thrilled both coaches and fans.

And in crafting their own magical performances, they somehow managed to always intersect. Bird was drafted by the Celtics after his junior year, but he opted to go back and play his final year of college ball. Without his services, the Celtics went 29-53 that year, and when he arrived the following year, they improved to 61-21 as he earned rookie of the year honors and led Boston in scoring (21.3), rebounding (10.4), steals (1.7) and three-pointers (58 total).

Johnson joined the league that year, too, bypassing his final two seasons of college eligibility. While Bird got the rookie honors, Johnson began to carve his own niche, becoming the first rookie since Elvin Hayes 11 years earlier to start in the All-Star Game and finished the year with an amazing performance to win his first NBA title. With Kareem Abdul-Jabbar sidelined with a badly sprained ankle, the 20-year-old rookie jumped center and manned the middle, sky-hooking his way to a 42-point, 15-rebound, seven-assist effort in becoming the first rookie to win the Finals MVP.

While they had their moments apart, it was when they were on the floor together that they truly were magic, alternating as champions usually at the other's expense. When it was over, Bird said of his rival, "Magic is head and shoulders above every-

body else. I've never seen [anybody] as good as him." Of Bird, David Stern said: "Larry Bird helped define the way a generation of basketball fans has come to view and appreciate the NBA."

They came and went, attached like Siamese twins, from college to the pros, and turned the game back into something even better than the good old days.

MICHAEL JORDAN

For Babe Ruth, it was not stretching the truth when Yankee Stadium was called, "The House That Ruth Built." He was there at its inception, providing some of its greatest memories. For Jordan, it isn't as clear-cut.

The league that Jordan built was already there, struggling through the hard times and rising from the ashes, all before he first went airborne for the Chicago Bulls in 1984. If the league (the house) was built already, Jordan reworked it, reconfigured it, the way that Ray Kroc turned the hamburger into something akin to a religion.

Jordan may not have built the house, but he took the bricks and stones that were laid by all of those before him and made himself the keystone. Jordan was not the first basketball player to flout the conventions of gravity, so perhaps he was stepping on stones that we could not see, stones that were Elgin Baylor, Julius Erving, and every other skywalker before him. Michael Jordan is arguably the greatest player the game has ever seen, and he may not have been the first to do too many things, or even the best at any of them. But he was the most complete package of skills the game has ever seen.

The all-around game, the defensive intensity, the ability to rebound when it was needed, was Oscar Robertson. The showmanship was built on ground paved by Bob Cousy, by Pete Maravich and even Meadowlark Lemon. And Jordan even took the best of Willis Reed when he wobbily made his way through Game 5 of the 1997 Finals, scoring 38 points and the decisive three-point play with a flu that was thought bad enough to sideline him. Maybe he didn't have as many titles as Russell or average a triple-double for a season as Robertson did (though he didn't play point guard, which helps greatly in registering a triple-double) but he combined the attributes of each of the greats.

He could dunk like Erving and Dominique Wilkins, drop in cold-blooded jumpers like Larry Bird, and will his team to victory like Russell or Magic. Even when his Air Time flights came closer to earth, he still dominated, mostly with a deadly fall-away jumper. Perhaps what he did better than any of those before him was sell himself. He was the most celebrated athlete in the world and the most marketable, with his endorsements dwarfing the advertising world in the same way his name found its way throughout the National Basketball Association record book. He made us "Just Do It" and he was "Air." He wore sneakers and it was not just kids, but even other professional athletes who wanted to wear them. We wanted to be like Mike.

That is the way it was with Jordan. He was a little of all before him, but none of them—like none of us—can really be like Mike.

Chapter 26

The History of NBA Expansion

By Bob Bellotti

'We want to win now," proclaimed Pat Williams, the Orlando Magic president, before the franchise had played its first game.

"When the winning starts, it will be a great feeling," Rolando Blackman, Dallas's young guard, said as the team entered its second season. "But it will take a few years."

"I feel like we have the capability of being a contender," Lenny Wilkens, Seattle's head coach, said before the club's third season.

"Within five years, we hope to have a shot at that last playoff spot," said Stu Inman, the Miami Heat's player personnel director in Miami's first year.

"We are like flower children." said Dick Motta, upon coaching the struggling Chicago Bulls in 1968, their third season. "We run around the country spreading joy and happiness wherever we go."

And there you have it. NBA expansion teams produce a range of emotions for the people involved with them: optimism, anxiety, exuberance, caution, laughter, frustration. Management, coaches, players, and fans of expansion teams have reason to expect almost anything, including short-term coaching assignments, a coin flip that decides whether a franchise will contend for the NBA title, a $200,000 admission fee, a 23-game losing streak, terrific rookies, division realignment that forces an East Coast team to play one-third of its games against West Coast teams, and 17 straight losses to start life. All of these things occurred to expansion organizations before their second season.

"It was one of the happiest times of my life," said Jerry Sloan, picked by Chicago in the 1966 player dispersal draft.

⊕ ⊕ ⊕

Let us define our central topic: an NBA expansion team is a team created from scratch that has never before played as an entity in any league under any name in any form.

With that definition, we rule out the many teams that played in the 1940s in the Basketball Association of America and those in the National Basketball League that merged with the BAA in 1949 when the league became known as the National Basketball Association. We also disengage the Denver

The Bobcats Are Coming, 2003
NBA commissioner David Stern, left, owner Robert Johnson and Charlotte mayor Pat McCrory launch the league's newest franchise.

Nuggets, Indiana Pacers, New Jersey Nets, and San Antonio Spurs, who entered the NBA in 1976 after several years of full-fledged membership in the ABA. Finally, we disregard franchises that moved to start life anew in a different city—unless, of course, like the Utah (nee New Orleans) Jazz they were an expansion team to begin with.

We are left with 17 franchises—nearly 60 percent of the teams that comprise today's NBA:

Buffalo Braves	Charlotte Hornets	Cleveland Cavaliers
Chicago Bulls	Chicago Packers	Dallas Mavericks
Miami Heat	Milwaukee Bucks	Minnesota Timberwolves
New Orleans Jazz	Orlando Magic	Phoenix Suns
Portland Trail Blazers	San Diego Rockets	Seattle SuperSonics
Toronto Raptors	Vancouver Grizzlies	

Most of these organizations were burdened for years with the expressive signature of expansion squads: prolonged losing. For the New Orleans/Utah Jazz, a .500 season was a distant goal that took the team 10 years to attain. The San Diego/Houston Rockets, created 22 years earlier, took eight seasons to reach that break-even point. The Minnesota Timberwolves, the only team to call Minneapolis home since the legendary Lakers left the city in 1960, played below .500 for nine years before rising above the fold. The Portland Trail Blazers were a sub-.500 squad that never made the playoffs until Bill Walton showed them how in 1976-77—the year the

Blazers won the NBA title. And then there's the most losing expansion team of them all—the futile Vancouver/Memphis Grizzlies, for whom even a mediocre season remains a dream.

Not all expansion teams, however, have suffered so badly for so long. Some, like the Dallas Mavericks, became winners by following a master plan that rooted out marginal players and replaced them with wisely chosen, talented draft picks. Others, such as the Seattle SuperSonics, rose slowly and surely, improving in small increments season after season. One blessed franchise, the Milwaukee Bucks, endured the frustration of cellar-dwelling for only a year.

NBA expansion has always been an uncertain business. New teams entering the league have dealt with front-office instability, rising debt, the lack of a suitable playing arena, and the wooing of fickle fans, not to mention the biggest obstacle to success, the dearth of talented players. But all 17 expansion teams have survived. As of 2003, all are still in existence today and only six of them (the Packers, Rockets, Braves, Jazz, Grizzlies and Hornets) changed cities along the way.

On the court, some vital statistics give a perspective on the plight of a new club. The 17 teams have yielded 12 championships (six by the Bulls) in 482 team years from 1961-62 through 2002-03. The average expansion team makes its initial playoff appearance in its fifth year and achieves its first .500 season in its sixth season. After seven seasons, the Grizzlies are the only team that hasn't made the grade in either category. The average new club wins 25% of its games in its first year and 35% its second. In years three through five, the average win rates are 37%, 46% and 49%, respectively.

Stability? You won't find it among head coaches of expansion teams. "The expansion coach is usually a sacrificial lamb," said Motta, who coached Dallas for its first seven years, an unusually long tenure. Ten of the 17 coaches hired to shepherd new franchises were gone inside of two years. One, Scotty Robertson of New Orleans, lasted 15 games. The average tenure of a team's first skipper is 2.8 years, and it is only that high because three head men had long tenures by any standards. In addition to Motta, Bill Fitch coached the Cavs for nine seasons and Larry Costello headed Milwaukee for eight years. Ron Rothstein, Miami's first head coach, who lasted three seasons, chuckled before his team had played a game, "I have a great lawyer who negotiated my contract—it says I can't be fired until the team has three wins."

On Jan. 10, 2003, the NBA Board of Governors unanimously approved the granting of an expansion team to Charlotte, North Carolina, to be owned by Robert Johnson. The fee? A mere $300 million, but that included the Charlotte Sting of the WNBA. The team adopted the nickname Bobcats, and begins play in the 2004-05 season.

Expansion marks the growth of any strong modern league and, if the NBA continues to flourish in the first decade of the new century, as it has done for most of the past 30 years, future growth will be a natural outcome. Perhaps the league's next franchise will be in St. Louis, or Nashville, or Kansas City, or Tampa; or maybe in Lexington, Kentucky or Baltimore or Pittsburgh or Honolulu or San Juan. It's also a possibility that the league will expand into a third country and place a team in, say, Mexico City.

But whichever city is chosen, the NBA should consider this: the quality of play of expansion teams since the expansion boom of the late 1960s and early '70s is suffering. The most recent crop of new squads was the least successful. The gap between the best teams and the worst is widening. Modern-day expansion clubs, such as Vancouver and Minnesota, have fared more poorly than did teams that grew out of the '60s and '70s increase. Consider that the first 11 expansion teams that joined the league from 1961 (Chicago Packers) through 1980 (Dallas) had a cumulative winning percentage of .418 after five seasons in the league. The six latest teams that joined, from 1988 (Miami and Charlotte) through 1995 (Toronto and Vancouver), have a .313 winning percentage over the same period. The latter group has won about eight fewer games per team per year.

The year-by-year figures show the trend:

	Season					
	1st Avg. W-L	2nd Avg. W-L	3rd Avg. W-L	4th Avg. W-L	5th Avg. W-L	5-Year Pct.
10 teams from 1961 – 1980	21-60	31-50	35-47	41-41	42-40	.418
7 teams from 1980 – 1995	18-64	24-59	20-62	27-45	36-46	.313
Decline by latter group	-3.5	-8	-15	-14	-6	-.105

Ironically, the reason for the decline by present-day clubs is probably expansion itself. A league with more teams employs more players. More players usually means less talented players enter the league. Through the dispersal draft, expansion teams are stocked with second-rung talent, players that other teams consider expendable. The typical team's first-year roster is packed with reserves and low-grade free agents. If the front office is good, the team will select a star with its allotted high first-round draft pick. That helps mitigate the talent gap, but not by much—the best record of any of the past six expansion squads within their first three years is 31-51.

⊕ ⊕ ⊕

Milwaukee captured a championship earlier than any expansion team, winning the trophy in its third season. Only five other expansion franchises have reached the summit: the Trail Blazers (in their seventh year); the SuperSonics (12th); the Packers/Zephyrs/Bullets/Wizards (17th); the Bulls (25th, 26th 27th, 30th, 31st, 32nd), and the Rockets (27th and 28th). Three others—the Suns, Jazz, and Magic—have reached the NBA Finals and lost. The remaining eight clubs have never gotten that far.

The makings of the Bucks' title began on March 19, 1969 when the team won a coin toss over the Phoenix Suns. The Suns picked "heads," the coin came up "tails." The Bucks, who finished 27-55 in their inaugural season, won the right to select first in the 1969 NBA draft. The decision of whom to pick was easy. Lew Alcindor, soon to be Kareem Abdul-Jabbar, was perhaps the best collegian ever at that time. A three-time All-American, he had led UCLA to a 79-2 record and three consecutive NCAA titles.

But signing the big man was another matter. The American Basketball Association had recently finished its second season of play. That it was still intact was a major achievement. Plagued by financial difficulties, erratic attendance, and franchise instability, the ABA entered a bidding war with the NBA for

Alcindor. The New York Nets of the newer league were awarded the rights to the big man because of the hometown draw; Alcindor was a New Yorker, who had starred at Power Memorial High.

At the time, the ABA's future was thought to be riding on whether it could ink Alcindor. The Bucks' future was riding on him as well. Alcindor gave the new league a fair shot at him. He effectively set the terms of negotiation by asking each league to submit one sealed contract bid.

The ABA's strategy was fiendishly clever, a viable threat to the Bucks. Each of the ABA's teams would pay a share in Alcindor's contract, thus enabling the league to submit a huge offer. But the ABA men in charge of the deal, Commissioner George Mikan (ironically the NBA's first great pivotman) and Nets owner Art Brown, inexplicably submitted a bid lower than what the team representatives had agreed to. When Alcindor announced the NBA's bid was higher, surprised ABA officials rushed in with a $1 million counter-offer. But Alcindor stuck to his word and signed with the Bucks. While the ABA lasted another seven seasons before merging four teams into the NBA, its inability to sign Alcindor changed the future of both leagues.

In Milwaukee, Big Lew was an immediate hit. In his first year, he finished second in the league in scoring (28.8 points per game), and third in rebounds (14.5 per game). Supported by guards Flynn Robinson (21.8 points) and Jon McGlocklin (17.6 points), the Bucks improved by 29 games to finish four games behind the Knicks in the Eastern Division.

The next season, the Bucks won the championship. A key move in winning the title occurred just after the 1969-70 season ended. On April 21, 1970, the Bucks acquired the great Oscar Robertson from the Cincinnati Royals in exchange for Robinson and reserve forward Charlie Paulk. With the Royals, Robertson had been first-team All-NBA for nine consecutive seasons, but had never been on a championship team. With Alcindor and "The Big O," Milwaukee raced to a 66-16 record, the league's best—14 games better than the second-best team. They amassed winning streaks of 16 and 20 games. Alcindor led the league in scoring (31.7 points per game), finished second in field goal percentage (.577), and fourth in rebounding (16 per game). Robertson, at 32, made an outstanding supporting player (19.4 points, 8.2 assists, and 5.7 rebounds). Bobby Dandridge, a second-year pro who could run the floor as well as any forward in the league, added punch (18.4 points and 8 rebounds). The Bucks won by a remarkable average of 12.2 points per game.

The playoffs brought the anticipation of a Bucks-Knicks match-up. The Knicks were the defending champions, had the league's second-best record, and had beaten the Bucks in four of five regular-season contests. But in the second round, the Knicks lost to the Baltimore Bullets by two points in Game 7 when Bill Bradley missed a shot at the buzzer.

Meanwhile, in the West, Milwaukee buzzed through one opponent after another. In the first round, they stomped Nate Thurmond, Jerry Lucas and the San Francisco Warriors, four games to one. After losing Game 4, the Bucks' won the final game by 50 points. The Bucks met the vaunted Lakers in round two. But Wilt Chamberlain could not match Alcindor's dominance and Milwaukee took the series in five games. In the Finals, the Bucks thrashed Wes Unseld, Earl Monroe and the Bullets in four straight.

The Bucks, recently so pleased just to be a part of the league, won the crown in their third season by going 12-2 in the playoffs and outscoring their opponents by an average of 14.5 points per game.

The Chicago Packers, the NBA's first expansion team, had humbler beginnings. The franchise gained approval to enter the association at a league meeting in Syracuse on January 16, 1961. The Packers' owners, led by David Tregar and Max Winter, paid $200,000 for the team. (By comparison, the most recent expansion teams, Toronto and Vancouver, which both entered in 1995, paid $125 million each.) Tregar named the team after his packing company. The nickname was appropriate because the team's arena, the Chicago Amphitheater, was near the city's meat-packing stockyards. (In its second season, the team changed its nickname to the Zephyrs—a reference to the wind that roars through the lake city.)

A Pittsburgh club, headed by ice-show businessman John Harris, was also awarded a franchise on the same day that the Packers gained entry. It was to start play the next year, same as the Packers. That night Harris announced that Boston Celtics star Bill Sharman would be Pittsburgh's first head coach. Celtics owner Walter Brown, a friend of Harris, admitted ignorance of the announcement, saying he was "absolutely flabbergasted."

"That's what I get for trying to help a friend," Brown said, "I hope Pittsburgh drops out of the league tomorrow." Unexpectedly, Pittsburgh did. The next day, Sharman said he knew nothing about the offer. Harris said he must have misunderstood something Brown had told him. "I have been aware of my lack of knowledge about basketball, but now I'm firmly convinced that I know nothing about it," Harris said, as his one-day-old franchise folded.

Pittsburgh's withdrawal pleased the Packers because it gave them dibs on all of the players who were available in the league expansion draft, which took place in April and May 1961. Chicago began play in the '61-62 season. The team came armed with a new star, 22-year-old center Walt Bellamy, whom Chicago had selected with the first pick in the 1962 collegiate draft. Knowing the Packers would take Bellamy, the league awarded Chicago the first pick because of the appeal the Indiana University player brought to the nearby big city. (The league also awarded the Packers the first five picks in the second round.)

Bellamy delivered one of the greatest rookie seasons in NBA history (31.6 points and 19 rebounds per game). But many fans hardly noticed Bellamy's achievements because they occurred in the same season that Wilt Chamberlain was demolishing opponents by averaging 50.4 points and 25.7 rebounds a game for Philadelphia. Although Bellamy finished second in the league in scoring, the margin between Chamberlain and himself was a whopping 18.8 points per game.

Despite Bellamy's terrific season, Chicago fans never embraced the ballclub, partly because it had competition. That same year, Abe Saperstein, the Harlem Globetrotters' owner, established a new league, the American Basketball League. The ABL placed a franchise in Chicago, called the Majors, which was coached by former NBA star Andy Phillip. In that initial

season Packers attendance lagged, and the Packers did likewise. They finished at 18-62, the worst record in the league.

In the early days of expansion, obtaining the right to play in a suitable arena was sometimes challenging. The Amphitheater sat 11,000 people and was considered a temporary home court until the team could move into the larger Chicago Stadium. But negotiations for moving there didn't succeed. So, with attendance still low after a 25-55 second season, Tregar and Winter sold the franchise to a group of Washington, D.C. businessmen for $1.1 million—a hefty profit on their original $200,000 investment. The new owners, one of whom was present-day Wizards owner Abe Pollin, placed the team in Baltimore, which had just built a new midtown arena. The team took the Bullets as its moniker. The relocation gave the franchise two distinctions: the shortest time in which an expansion team has moved from its city of origin, and the only NBA team to have three nicknames in its first three seasons.

The Zephyrs' move to Baltimore was the second time an NBA franchise had failed in Chicago. In 1950, the Stags went out of business after four winning seasons. But the NBA was undaunted. A third Chicago franchise, the Bulls, began play in 1966-67. Where did they play their home games? In the same Amphitheater abandoned by the Packers/Zephyrs. Under the leadership of former NBA star Johnny "Red" Kerr, the team succeeded immediately, winning its first three games and making the playoffs in its first year. The team had a terrific backcourt of veteran Guy Rodgers, who led the league in assists, and young Jerry Sloan, a rare find in the dispersal-draft. Kerr was named Coach of the Year. That St. Louis swept the Bulls in three straight in the first playoff round seemed to matter little. But in the stands, attendance problems remained. The team averaged only 4,772 fans per game that first year, a figure that declined in the two succeeding seasons.

Atypical for an expansion team, the Bulls qualified for postseason play in eight of their first nine years. Under Dick Motta, who replaced Kerr as head coach for the franchise's third season, Chicago soon established one the top starting fives in the league. With Sloan, forwards Bob Love and Chet Walker, and center Tom Boerwinkle, the Bulls won 51 games in 1970-71. Point guard Norm Van Lier joined the following year and Chicago went 57-25, 51-31, 54-28, and 47-35, respectively, from 1971-72 through '74-75. Unfortunately, the Bucks were an elite team during those years, and the Bulls were in the same division as Milwaukee. Consequently, those Chicago teams never made it to the NBA Finals.

By 1967-68, the NBA had become a staple American professional sport, behind major-league baseball and the NFL. The Boston Celtics and Los Angeles Lakers dominated the tableau, with highly appealing battles between Bill Russell and Wilt Chamberlain getting the most attention. The league also had a bundle of other terrific players—Robertson in Cincinnati, Jerry West and Elgin Baylor in L.A., Sam Jones and John Havlicek in Boston, Hal Greer of Philadelphia and youngsters such as Willis Reed of New York and Rick Barry of San Francisco.

So it was not unexpected that, in 1967, the NBA continued broadening its appeal, creating the first of two great waves of expansion that the league has experienced. Building on its 10-team base, the NBA admitted seven new teams in the four years

from 1967 through 1970. With a strong following in the East and Midwest already established, the league focused on improving its visibility in Western cities, while also adding franchises in key Eastern and Midwestern markets. In 1967, the San Diego Rockets and Seattle SuperSonics joined the league. The following season the Phoenix Suns were admitted, along with the Milwaukee Bucks. In 1971, three franchises received berths: the Portland Trail Blazers, Cleveland Cavaliers, and Buffalo Braves.

The 17-team league was restructured into four divisions, two in each conference, for the 1970-71 season. By '71-72, with the San Diego franchise having moved to Houston, the setup looked like this:

Eastern Conference

Atlantic Division	Central Division
Boston Celtics	Atlanta Hawks
Buffalo Braves	Baltimore Bullets
New York Knicks	Cincinnati Royals
Philadelphia 76ers	Cleveland Cavaliers

Western Conference

Midwest Division	Pacific Division
Chicago Bulls	Golden State Warriors
Detroit Pistons	Houston Rockets
Milwaukee Bucks	Los Angeles Lakers
Phoenix Suns	Portland Trail Blazers
	Seattle Supersonics

As expected, most of the new franchises did poorly. San Diego and Phoenix managed to squeeze into the playoffs in their second seasons of play, but the success was short-lived.

The Rockets' plight was typical of the ups and downs a new team faces when entering the league. In their first season, 1967-68, they went 15-67, eight games behind Seattle, also in its first year.

A rare win in that season stands out in head coach Jack McMahon's mind. On February 18, 1968, the world champion Philadelphia 76ers came to town. The 76ers had demolished the Rockets five times already that season by an average of 17.8 points per game. San Diego entered the contest on a 17-game losing streak. Philly featured all-stars Chamberlain, Greer, and Billy Cunningham. San Diego featured Art "Hambone" Williams, who averaged 8.1 points per game. "I sent in Williams, a local guy we picked up from the playground," McMahon said in an interview published in 1988. "I mean, he went on a streak. From being seven points down, we won the game [111-106]."

The lift didn't last long—the win was the final one for the Rockets that year. They lost their remaining 15 games, including a 134-103 drubbing at the Sixers' hands the next time the teams met.

In its second season, San Diego made major strides, winning 37 games, largely because the team drafted Elvin Hayes. Hayes led the league in scoring (28.4 points per game) and finished fifth in rebounding (1,406 boards, in the final season in which league leaders were determined by total rebounds instead of per-game average).

In year three, Hayes finished third in the league in scoring (27.5 points) and first in rebounding (16.9). But support was weak and the team declined to 27 wins. In '70-71—the final season in San Diego—the team neared the .500 mark, improving by 13 games to 40-42.

That summer, the franchise was sold to a group of Houston businessmen. The new owners moved the team to Houston, where Elvin Hayes played college ball. The team played its home games the first season in multiple places—the Astrodome, Hofheinz Pavilion, and Astrohall, all in Houston, and three other Texas cities, El Paso, San Antonio, and Waco. While Rockets fans were happy to see their returning star, the franchise didn't reach respectability until the late 1970s, about a decade after the club's birth.

The Seattle SuperSonics began life on December 20, 1966, when the NBA announced it was awarding a team to the Pacific port city. In the expansion draft, Seattle went the veteran route, choosing experienced players who mostly were in the middle of their careers. Its first selection was Tom Meschery, a forward for the San Francisco Warriors, who promptly announced he would retire rather than play for Seattle. (He later changed his mind.)

Seattle's won-lost record was average as expansion teams go. The club won 23 games in its first year and 30 in its sophomore season. Atypically, however, the Sonics suffered no ups and downs in their record. Through year five, Seattle had improved its wins each season, a feat of which only two other expansion teams (Chicago Packers and Dallas) can boast. In the fifth season, 1971-72, the team finished 47-35, an improvement of nine games from the year before. Unfortunately, the Sonics missed the playoffs by four games in an era when only four teams per conference qualified for the postseason.

The Phoenix Suns nearly became a dominant team in just their second season, a year in which they won only 39 games. If only they had won the coin flip for the rights to draft the future Hall of Famer now known as Kareem Abdul-Jabbar. But they lost the toss, and were left to pick second in the 1969 draft. Phoenix chose Neal Walk, a center from Florida. (Perhaps to lighten the disappointment of not getting Alcindor, Phoenix also selected Bob Beamon, the great Olympic long jumper, in the 15th round. Beamon did not make the team.) Walk's play in no way mitigated losing the coin toss. Although he was the team's center for five years, and averaged over 20 points a game in one campaign, Walk played only eight years and on balance had a mediocre career that ended in 1976-77.

The Buffalo Braves began life in peculiar fashion—they were sold before they played their first game in 1970. The team's original owners transferred ownership of the ballclub to Paul Snyder on October 13, 1970. The exchange must have suited the team—the next day, the Braves won their opener against Cleveland, another expansion team.

The Braves' early years were characterized by poor teams. The team won 22 games in each of its first two seasons, and 21 in its third year. In the first two seasons, center/forward Bob Kauffman led the team in scoring (20.4 and 18.9 points per game, respectively). The next year, future great Bob McAdoo arrived, fresh out of the University of North Carolina. McAdoo played four seasons and parts of a fifth with the Braves. He led the league in scoring in three of those years.

After eight years in Buffalo, the Braves moved to the West Cost, becoming the San Diego Clippers. Precipitating the move was a franchise swap by two owners. Boston's Ira Levin traded the Celtics to John Y. Brown in exchange for the controlling interest in the Braves. Levin's West Coast business interests led him to move the team to San Diego.

Portland began play in 1970 with a squad that featured rookie Geoff Petrie, a Princeton grad (in an era when Ivy League teams produced a fair share of solid pros). Petrie was a 22-year-old sharpshooter, who was Portland's first draft pick. He had an excellent first season, leading the team in scoring (24.8 points) and assists (4.8), and was named co-Rookie of the Year, with Dave Cowens of Boston. Under rookie coach Rolland Todd, the Blazers beat the previous year's NBA finalists a total of three times (champion Milwaukee once and Baltimore twice). The team finished 29-53, the best record of the three clubs that began play that year. But 16 of the Blazers' 29 wins were against the other two teams (Buffalo and Cleveland), creating a false sense of optimism.

In its second season of play, the team declined by 11 games and finished at 18-64. Todd was canned after 56 games. Stu Inman, Portland's director of player personnel, succeeded him. Petrie gave way to Sidney Wicks as the first option on offense. Wicks became Portland's second consecutive Rookie of the Year, but he and Petrie were unable to keep the team afloat by themselves. The supporting players were mostly career second-stringers, such as Stan McKenzie, Dale Schlueter, and Gary Gregor, who were cast into roles more prominent than their talents suggested. The Blazers went another three seasons before improving on the 29 wins they achieved in year one.

The Cleveland Cavaliers started life as the laughingstock of the league, thanks partly to inept play and partly to their humorous head coach, Bill Fitch. To begin with, in 1970-71 the franchise lost the first 15 games it played. After finally posting its first win ever, a 105-103 squeaker against the expansion Trail Blazers, the Cavs dropped another 12 straight. Their second win was another two-point victory, over Buffalo. Then they lost seven more. Thus, the Cavs started life with a depressing 2-33 (.057) record. How bad was it? One night guard Johnny Warren went the wrong way for a layup, sinking the bucket in opposing Portland's basket. (Leroy Ellis, the Blazers center, tried to block the shot.) As Fitch was known to quip, things generally dropped off from there.

By season's end, Cleveland was firmly mired in the cellar, seven games worse than any other team in the league. The second season was only slightly better, as the Cavaliers won 23 games. Fitch's mood, however, seemed unshaken. He graced reporters with one-liner after one-liner about his team's plight. Two examples among many: "Just remember, the name is Fitch, not Houdini." "I phoned Dial-a-Prayer, but when they found out who it was, they hung up."

At 0-15, Cleveland was on the verge of breaking the record for most consecutive losses to start a season, set by the old Denver Nuggets in 1949-50. Before the 16th game, Fitch bought a cast-iron skull in an antique store and used it as a motivational device in his pregame talk. "This," he told his players, "is all that remains of the Nuggets' coach." (The voodoo worked; Cleveland won its first game.)

Fitch's jokes did not gain him a guest appearance as a comedian on *The Ed Sullivan Show*, but they did allay some of the criticism hurled toward his players. His reign with the Cavaliers lasted nine years, during which Cleveland made three playoff

appearances. The high point came in year six when the team edged Washington in the first round, four games to three, and then took Boston, the NBA's eventual champion, to six games in the Eastern Conference Finals. But in Fitch's last season, the team fell to 30-52, and the Cavs seemed stuck again with the expansion-team reputation it firmly held at the start of the Fitch years.

⊕ ⊕ ⊕

Following the rapid growth in the late 1960s and early '70s, NBA expansion cooled. Only two teams entered the league over the next 17 years, the New Orleans Jazz in 1974 and the Dallas Mavericks in 1980.

The Jazz's early years were the signature of one man—Pete Maravich, the flashy, high-scoring guard who was a Louisiana legend. For four years at Louisiana State, Maravich shattered NCAA scoring records, averaging 44.2 points per game. In the NBA Maravich was a potent scorer, though he didn't reach the heights he had in college. For New Orleans, he was that quintessential drawing card: a fabulous star with homegrown roots. He played with the team for five-plus years, capturing the league's scoring title in 1976-77 (31.1 points per game).

But Maravich's scoring did not translate into many wins. The Jazz lost 14 of their first 15 games under head coach Scotty Robertson before he was abruptly canned. After Elgin Baylor, the club's assistant coach, coached one game, Butch van Breda Kolff stepped in and finished the season. New Orleans wound up winning only 23 games that season and no more than 39 in any season during the Maravich years. In fact, their first playoff appearance came in their ninth year (1983-84) when, as the Utah Jazz, they had a 45-37 ledger.

For the blueprint on how to build a successful team from scratch, the Mavericks' front office was widely regarded as senior engineers. Dallas built through the draft, trading players for future draft picks. Kiki Vandeweghe, for example, the team's first draft pick, found himself traded to Denver after his contract negotiations lasted past the start of the season. Dallas's price was two first-round picks, one in 1981, the other in 1985. The Mavericks also were fortunate to have dealt with the Cleveland Cavaliers of that era. Under the misguided ownership of Ted Stepien, the Cavs decimated their club through trades. The Cavs "gave" four first-round picks to the Mavericks for players whose sum value was borderline to average. Partly as a result of those deals, the NBA later banned Cleveland from making trades without the league's consent.

Within six years the Mavericks had built an ideal draft history: Vandeweghe (1980), Mark Aguirre, Rolando Blackman, and Jay Vincent (1981), Dale Ellis and Ron Harper (1983), Sam Perkins (1984), Detlef Schrempf (1985), and Roy Tarpley and Mark Price (1986). While not all stayed with Dallas—Price, for example, was traded to Cleveland (ironically) for a second-round pick—the group's composite accomplishments went on to include 17 All-Star Game appearances.

President Norm Sonju, director of player personnel Rick Sund, and head coach Dick Motta worked the Mavericks' master plan. Strangely, part of the plan was based on the hope that Dallas would be one of the league's two worst teams after its third year, 1982-83. Ralph Sampson, the giant center from Virginia, was the target. Dallas was counting on winning the

coin flip between the two teams with the poorest records and picking Sampson in the '83 draft. The Mavs, however, weren't close to being that bad; eight teams had poorer records in the '82-83 season. "This is where I didn't want to be," Motta said. "I was afraid to death of this." Dallas picked Dale Ellis ninth.

Sampson's absence notwithstanding, Dallas maintained slow, sure success. Small forward Aguirre, playmaker Derek Harper and off-guard Blackman, along with power forward Perkins, formed the team's backbone from 1983-84 through '88-89. Center Roy Tarpley, plagued by substance addiction, was terrific when healthy. Contributing players included guard Brad Davis, forwards Ellis and Vincent, and center James Donaldson. The team won only 15 games in its first season, but improved or maintained its number of wins annually for the first seven years of existence. In the eighth year, 1987-88, with a 53-29 record, the Mavericks reached the Western Conference finals before losing to the Lakers, four games to three.

⊕ ⊕ ⊕

The second substantial wave of expansion involved fewer franchises than the spate of teams that were added between 1967 and 1970. With the NBA glorying in the battles between Magic Johnson's Lakers and Larry Bird's Celtics, with Michael Jordan displaying unrivaled performances, and with record-breaking attendance and television revenue, the league added four teams, two in 1988-89 and two in 1989-90.

Charlotte and Miami were the first group, followed the next season by Minnesota and the Orlando Magic. Then, in 1995, two Canadian clubs, Toronto and Vancouver, were admitted.

The Hornets took hold in a state known for its rabid college basketball fans. Playing in the new 23,698-seat Charlotte Coliseum, the Hornets led the league in attendance in seven of their first eight years. Still, the team's on-court fortunes bore little relation to interest in the team. General manager Carl Scheer said the talent available to Charlotte in the 1988 dispersal draft was worse than he had imagined. "Sobering," he called it. Right he was. In the draft, Charlotte did manage to select shooting guard Dell Curry and point man Muggsy Bogues, both of whom went on to long, productive NBA careers. But other selections included point guard Michael Holton and center Dave Hoppen, two borderline NBAers, who wound up in Charlotte's regular rotation the first year.

Though the Hornets did not win very often, it was exciting when they did. In year one, they won five of their 20 games on a shot made in the final five seconds (details below). No other team had as many last-second wins that year.

Date	Player	Secs. Left	Type of Shot	Opp.	Score
11/19/88	Tripucka, Kelly	2.0	2 free throws	@ S.A.	107-105
12/1/88	Tripucka, Kelly	4.0	Layup	Phi.	109-107
12/23/88	Rambis, Kurt	0.0	Layup	Chi.	103-101
1/26/89	Rambis, Kurt	0.0	Layup	@ Uta.	89-88
2/3/89	Kempton, Tim	2.0	Layup	Sea.	108-106

The Heat set a dispersal-draft standard with their first pick, selecting from Dallas a player named Arvid Kramer, a war-horse of eight NBA games, who had last played in the league nine years earlier. The Heat's reasoning for the seemingly screwy selection became apparent after the draft. The Mavericks had three prospects—Steve Alford, Uwe Blab, and Bill Wennington—that they could not protect without breaking

their core rotation. So they negotiated a deal with Miami. The Heat agreed to select Kramer—and not to select any of the three—in return for Dallas's first-round pick in that year's collegiate draft. Kramer never played a game for Miami.

It was smart move by Miami. With the draft pick, they selected DePaul's Kevin Edwards, who played five seasons with the team. Some teams, after seeing Miami's strategy, set up similar deals in future drafts, in effect paying a team that was picking ahead of them for not selecting a certain player. Unusual? Yes. That same characteristic also arose when the NBA placed Miami in the Midwest Division for its first season. Playing mostly Western Conference teams, including six on the West Coast, Miami's travel schedule was brutal.

The Heat's overall strategy was to build through the draft, and their first two drafts picks, Rony Seikaly and Kevin Edwards, both wound up having distinguished careers with the team. Nonetheless, the strategy did not have a noticeable impact on the team's record. Miami's first season was marked by a streak of 17 consecutive losses at the start of the season. No NBA team, expansion or otherwise, had ever begun a season so badly. The Heat won 15 games that season and suffered through two more relatively miserable campaigns, winning 18 and 24 games in their second and third years, respectively. Bright spots emerged, however. Glen Rice, the Heat's first-round pick in the 1989 draft, gave Miami more long-range shooting. Grant Long, a hustling 6-foot-8 power forward, made an impact on the boards.

None of the four teams that started play in 1988 and 1989 were as bad for as long as Minnesota. Like other expansion franchises, the Wolves intended to build through youth. But they selected a plethora of veterans in the expansion draft, including Rick Mahorn, Steve Johnson, Tyrone Corbin, and Brad Lohaus. Mahorn, coming off a championship season with the Pistons, refused to join the Timberwolves, and it was downhill from there. Billy McKinney, the team's player personnel director, and head coach Bill Musselman disagreed on personnel moves. After posting 22-60 and 29-53 records in the first two seasons, the team fired Musselman.

Jimmy Rodgers, a season removed from being fired as the Celtics' skipper, replaced Musselman for 1991-92. Rodgers was burdened by two unproductive centers, Felton Spencer and Luc Longley, both lottery picks, who combined to average less than 11 points a game. In year three, Minnesota went 15-67. The following season, Rodgers was fired after 29 games; Sidney Lowe replaced him, and the Wolves won 19 games, eight fewer than any expansion team in its fourth year (until Vancouver came along).

At the gate, however, the Timberwolves, like the other expansion teams of their era, were a big hit. The team drew 35,000 people for its first exhibition game, against the Lakers. The Timberwolves played their home games in the Metrodome, a baseball and football stadium, where they drew 1,027,572 fans (25,063 per game)—an NBA single-season record. The following season, playing in the new, smaller Target Center, the Wolves drew an average of 19,011 for home games, the league's third-best figure.

Like Minnesota, Orlando started play in 1989-90 and did well at the box office. The team won its first game, a preseason tilt over the world champion Pistons. "The impact of our first exhibition game," said Pat Williams, the Magic's president, "was so enormous it really set the tone for the whole year." The Magic sold out most of their games that first season in the Orlando Arena. The raucous atmosphere of the "O-rena," as it came to be known, intensified when the Magic won four home games in the first month and went 7-7 in their first 14 games of the year.

That optimism, however, faded under the rigor of an 82-game schedule. The Magic wound up 18-64. Terry Catledge, a journeyman forward selected in the expansion draft, led the team in scoring (19.4 points per game). In year two, Orlando improved by 13 games to 31-51. Playmaker Scott Skiles had a solid season (17.2 points, 8.4 assists). Rookie Dennis Scott scored 15.7 points per game, and second-year man Nick Anderson scored at a 14.1 clip. But large-scale success was nearby.

The rise of the Magic drew comparisons with that of the expansion Milwaukee Bucks, who won the NBA championship in their third year. Both franchises were fortunate. The Bucks acquired the rights to Kareem Abdul-Jabbar by winning a coin flip. The Magic acquired the rights to Shaquille O'Neal by winning the NBA draft lottery. Both teams were built around their dominating centers. Both teams reached the NBA Finals, with Milwaukee winning and Orlando losing (4-0, to Houston). Both centers had a huge impact on their team's record. In Abdul-Jabbar's first year, Milwaukee improved by 29 games. In O'Neal's, the Magic improved by 20.

The difference was that even with a 20-game jump, Orlando finished with a modest 40-40 record. O'Neal certainly had a terrific rookie campaign (23.4 points, 13.9 rebounds) and surpassed those numbers in his second season. But he did not catapult his team to a title in two years.

The admission of Toronto and Vancouver in 1995 was contingent on a unique legal clause that nearly killed the deal. The NBA insisted the teams could only enter if their respective home provinces of Ontario and British Columbia banned government-sponsored betting on NBA games. In British Columbia, a furor erupted over whether a sports league could dictate govermental policy. The year before, British Columbians bet $1.56 million on NBA games. The government's profits went primarily to support B.C.'s health-care services.

After a long dispute, Michael Harcourt, premier of British Columbia, forged a resolution with Grizzlies owner Arthur Griffiths. Griffiths agreed to ante $500,000 a year for five years. Half of the money would go to the health-care system, the other half to a hospice for needy children. In exchange, the government banned betting on NBA games, and agreed to the argument that the Grizzlies would generate a projected $10 million in taxes per year to B.C. and the Canadian federal government.

The Raptors were beset by management turmoil in the club's early years. By the time the team entered its third season, it was doing so with its third ownership group and second head coach. On the court, Toronto slogged to a first-year record of 21-61, but managed wins against Chicago and Seattle, the NBA's finalists the previous season. In its second season, under

fiery coach Darrell Walker, the Raptors played hard and rose to a surprising 30 wins. Behind star point guard Damon Stoudamire, the team looked optimistically toward the 1997-98 season. The Raptors signed Doug Christie, Stoudamire's backcourt partner, to an expensive seven-year contract. "Making the playoffs is our goal this season," Christie said. "Nothing less."

The Raptors settled for a lot less. Midway through the season, Stoudamire and forwards Walt Williams and Carlos Rogers were traded to Portland for Kenny Anderson, forward Gary Trent, guard Alvin Williams, and two first-round draft choices. Team president Isiah Thomas also left the club that season. The Raptors fell hard, ending their third year at 16-66.

At the box office, though, the Raptors were terrific. An average of 23,179 fans descended on the SkyDome in 1995-96, placing Toronto third in NBA attendance.

Following Vancouver's expansion draft, on June 24, 1995, head coach Brian Winters said, "I think we picked a pretty good team." Yeah, sure. The initial squad lost 23 in a row at one point, the league's longest single-season skein of futility, and finished 15-67.

The Grizzlies undoubtedly have been the league's worst expansion team. Through five seasons, Vancouver had won about one game in every five. The Grizzlies lost 100 games more quickly than any other team in NBA history. They were the first team to lose by an average of 10 points or more in two consecutive seasons (-10.0 ppg in 1995-96, -10.2 in '96-97). The Grizzlies had fewer wins in their first, second, and fourth seasons (15, 14, and 8, respectively—the latter figure in a lock-out-shortened 50-game season) than any other expansion team at the same point.

The Grizzlies' plan was to obtain cornerstone players in the rookie draft, use veterans to help the rookies learn, and sign prominent free agents by the time the team entered its third year. Unfortunately, the franchise failed to reach its first and third goals. After five seasons, the team had only one cornerstone player, forward Shareef Abdur-Rahim, and had not signed any prominent free agents. Steve Francis, a budding star selected second in the 1999 draft, refused to play for the Grizzlies and forced a trade to Houston (in which Vancouver received two promising youngsters, Othella Harrington and Michael Dickerson).

Now located in Memphis, the Grizzlies can look back on a very dubious record: After five seasons, Vancouver's record was 78-300 (.206), the poorest record for any expansion team after five years. Perhaps the Grizzlies would agree with Bill Fitch. "War is hell," Fitch said, "But expansion is worse."

HISTORY OF NBA EXPANSION

NBA Expansion Teams' Five-Year Records

Team	First Season	1st W-L	2nd W-L	3rd W-L	4th W-L	5th W-L	5-Year Average
Chicago Packers	1961-62	18-62	25-55 *	31-49 **	37-43	38-42	30-50 (.375)
Chicago Bulls	1966-67	33-48	29-53	33-49	39-43	51-31	37-45 (.451)
San Diego Rockets	1967-68	15-67	37-45	27-55	40-42	34-48 ***	31-51 (.378)
Seattle SuperSonics	1967-68	23-59	30-52	36-46	38-44	47-35	35-47 (.427)
Milwaukee Bucks	1968-69	27-55	56-26	66-16	63-19	60-22	54-28 (.659)
Phoenix Suns	1968-69	16-66	39-43	48-34	49-33	38-44	38-44 (.463)
Buffalo Braves ****	1970-71	22-60	22-60	21-61	42-40	49-33	31-51 (.378)
Cleveland Cavaliers	1970-71	15-67	23-59	32-50	29-53	40-42	28-54 (.341)
Portland Trail Blazers	1970-71	29-53	18-64	21-61	27-55	38-44	27-55 (.329)
New Orleans Jazz	1974-75	23-59	38-44	35-47	39-43	26-56	32-50 (.390)
Dallas Mavericks	1980-81	15-67	28-54	38-44	43-39	44-38	34-48 (.415)
Charlotte Hornets	1988-89	20-62	19-63	26-56	31-51	44-38	28-54 (.341)
Miami Heat	1988-89	15-67	18-64	24-58	38-44	36-46	26-56 (.317)
Minnesota T'wolves	1989-90	22-60	29-53	15-67	19-63	20-62	21-61 (.256)
Orlando Magic	1989-90	18-64	31-51	21-61	41-41	50-32	32-50 (.390)
Toronto Raptors	1995-96	21-61	30-52	16-66	23-27	45-37	27-49 (.357)
Vancouver Grizzlies	1995-96	15-67	14-68	19-63	8-42	22-60	16-60 (.206)
Avg W-L		**20-61**	**29-53**	**30-52**	**36-43**	**40-42**	**527-853**
Avg. Pct.		**.247**	**.354**	**.366**	**.456**	**.488**	**.380**

* Known as Chicago Zephyrs   ** Moved to Baltimore becoming the Bullets   *** Moved to Houston   **** Known today as the Los Angeles Clippers

First Games of Expansion Teams

Team	Date	Opponent	W/L	Score
Chicago Packers	Oct. 19, 1961	New York	L	103-120
Chicago Bulls	Oct. 15, 1966	St. Louis	W	104-97
San Diego	Oct. 14, 1967	St. Louis	L	98-99
Seattle	Oct. 13, 1967	San Francisco	L	116-144
Milwaukee	Oct. 16, 1968	Chicago	L	84-89
Phoenix	Oct. 18, 1968	Seattle	W	116-107
Buffalo	Oct. 14, 1970	Cleveland	W	107-92
Cleveland	Oct. 14, 1970	Buffalo	L	92-107
Portland	Oct. 16, 1970	Cleveland	W	115-112

Team	Date	Opponent	W/L	Score
New Orleans	Oct. 17, 1974	New York	L	74-89
Dallas	Oct. 11, 1980	San Antonio	W	103-92
Charlotte	Nov. 4, 1988	Cleveland	L	93-133
Miami	Nov. 5, 1988	L.A. Clippers	L	91-111
Minnesota	Nov. 3, 1989	Seattle	L	94-106
Orlando	Nov. 4, 1989	New Jersey	L	106-111
Toronto	Nov. 3, 1995	New Jersey	W	94-79
Vancouver	Nov. 3, 1995	Portland	W	92-80

First-round Collegiate Draft Picks of Expansion Teams

Team	Year	First-round pick	College
Chicago Packers	1961	Walt Bellamy	Indiana
Chicago Bulls	1966	Dave Schellhase	Purdue
San Diego	1967	Pat Riley	Kentucky
Seattle	1967	Al Tucker	Okla. Baptist
Milwaukee	1968	Charlie Paulk	N.E. Oklahoma
Phoenix	1968	Gary Gregor	So. Carolina
Buffalo	1970	John Hummer	Princeton
Cleveland	1970	John Johnson	Iowa
Portland	1970	Geoff Petrie	Princeton
New Orleans	1974	None	—
Dallas	1980	Kiki Vandeweghe	UCLA
Charlotte	1988	Rex Chapman	Kentucky
Miami	1988	Rony Seikaly	Syracuse
Minnesota	1989	Pooh Richardson	UCLA
Orlando	1989	Nick Anderson	Illinois
Toronto	1995	Damon Stoudamire	Arizona
Vancouver	1995	Bryant Reeves	Okla. St.

Expansion Drafts

1961 Expansion Draft (April/May 1961)

Chicago Packers

Player	From	Player	From
Dave Budd	New York	Andy Johnson	Philadelphia
Barney Cable	Syracuse	Bob Leonard	L.A. Lakers
Gene Conley	Boston	Dave Pointek	St. Louis
Ralph Davis	Cincinnati	Larry Staverman	Cincinnati
Archie Dees	Detroit		

Note: The league conducted an expansion draft in the spring of 1961 to stock the Chicago Packers. The new team was allowed to select one player from each other NBA team for $50,000 per player. While this writer's research could not locate an official list of players selected, an examination of the Packers' all-time player list, using a franchise media guide, yielded the set of players (above) whom the Packers are believed to have selected. Robert Bradley, founder of the Association for Professional Basketball Research, provided the list.

1966 Expansion Draft (April 30-May 1, 1966)

Chicago Bulls

Player	From	Player	From
John Barnhill	Detroit	Jim King	Los Angeles
Al Bianchi	Philadelphia	Don Kojis	Detroit
Ron Bonham	Boston	McCoy McLemore	San Francisco
Bob Boozer	Los Angeles	Jeff Mullins	St. Louis
Nate Bowman	Cincinnati	Jerry Sloan	Baltimore
Len Chappell	New York	Tom Thacker	Cincinnati
Barry Clemens	New York	John Thompson	Boston
Keith Erickson	San Francisco	Gerry Ward	Philadelphia
John Kerr	Baltimore	Jim Washington	St. Louis

1967 Expansion Draft (May 1, 1967)

San Diego Rockets

Player	From	Player	From
Jim Barnett	Boston	Johnny Green	Baltimore
John Barnhill	Baltimore	Toby Kimball	Boston
John Block	Los Angeles	Don Kojis	Chicago
Henry Finkel	Los Angeles	Jon McGlocklin	Cincinnati
Dave Gambee	Philadelphia	Jim Ware	Cincinnati

Seattle Supersonics

Player	From	Player	From
Henry Akin	New York	Bud Olsen	San Francisco
Nate Bowman	Philadelphia	Ron Reed	Detroit
Dave Deutsch	New York	Rod Thorn	St. Louis
Richie Guerin	St. Louis	Ben Warley	Baltimore
Walt Hazzard	Los Angeles	Ron Watts	Boston
Tom Kron	St. Louis	Bob Weiss	Philadelphia
Tom Meschery	San Francisco	George Wilson	Chicago
Dorie Murrey	Detroit		

1968 Expansion Draft (May 6, 1968)

Milwaukee Bucks

Player	From	Player	From
Len Chappell	Detroit	Jon McGlocklin	San Diego
Larry Costello	Philadelphia	Jay Miller	St. Louis
Johnny Egan	Baltimore	Bud Olsen	Seattle
Wayne Embry	Boston	George Patterson	Detroit
Dave Gambee	San Diego	Jim Reid	Philadelphia
Gary Gray	Cincinnati	Guy Rodgers	Cincinnati
Fred Hetzel	San Francisco	Tom Thacker	Boston
Johnny Jones	Boston	Bob Warlick	San Francisco
Bob Love	Cincinnati	Bob Weiss	Seattle

Phoenix Suns

Player	From	Player	From
John Barnhill	San Diego	Bill Melchionni	Philadelphia
Emmette Bryant	New York	Dave Schellhase	Chicago
Gail Goodrich	Los Angeles	Dick Snyder	Atlanta
Dennis Hamilton	Los Angeles	Craig Spitzer	Chicago
Neil Johnson	New York	Gene Tormohlen	Atlanta
David Lattin	San Francisco	Dick Van Arsdale	New York
Paul Long	Detroit	Roland West	Baltimore
Stan McKenzie	Baltimore	John Wetzel	Los Angeles
McCoy McLemore	Chicago	George Wilson	Seattle

1970 Expansion Draft (May 11, 1970)

Buffalo Braves

Player	From	Player	From
Emmette Bryant	Boston	Paul Long	Detroit
Fred Crawford	Milwaukee	Mike Lynn	Los Angeles
Dick Garrett	Los Angeles	Don May	New York
Herm Gilliam	Cincinnati	Ray Scott	Baltimore
Bill Hosket	New York	George Wilson	Philadelphia
Bailey Howell	Boston		

Cleveland Cavaliers

Player	From	Player	From
Butch Beard	Atlanta	Loy Petersen	Chicago
Len Chappell	Milwaukee	Luther Rackley	Cincinnati
Johnny Egan	Los Angeles	Bobby "Bingo" Smith	San Diego
Bobby Lewis	San Francisco	John Warren	New York
McCoy McLemore	Detroit	Walt Wesley	Chicago
Don Ohl	Atlanta		

Portland Trail Blazers

Player	From	Player	From
Rick Adelman	San Diego	Stan McKenzie	Phoenix
Jerry Chambers	Phoenix	Dorie Murray	Seattle
Leroy Ellis	Baltimore	Pat Riley	San Diego
Fred Hetzel	Philadelphia	Dale Schlueter	San Francisco
Joe Kennedy	Seattle	Larry Siegfried	Boston
Ed Manning	Chicago		

1974 Expansion Draft (May 20, 1974)

New Orleans Jazz

Player	From	Player	From
Dennis Awtrey	Chicago	Bob Kauffman	Buffalo
Jim Barnett	Golden State	Toby Kimball	Philadelphia
Walt Bellamy	Atlanta	Steve Kuberski	Boston
John Block	K.C.-Omaha	Stu Lantz	Detroit
Barry Clemens	Cleveland	Dean Meminger	New York
E.C. Coleman	Houston	Louie Nelson	Washington
Lamar Green	Phoenix	Curtis Perry	Milwaukee
Nate Hawthorne	Los Angeles	Bud Stallworth	Seattle
Ollie Johnson	Portland		

1980 Expansion Draft (May 28, 1980)

Dallas Mavericks

Player	From	Player	From
Del Beshore	Chicago	Abdul Jeelani	Portland
Winford Boynes	New Jersey	Jeff Judkins	Boston
Alonzo Bradley	Houston	Arvid Kramer	Denver
Mike Bratz	Phoenix	Tom LaGarde	Seattle
Marty Byrnes	Los Angeles	Billy McKinney	Kansas City
Austin Carr	Cleveland	Wiley Peck	San Antonio
Jim Cleamons	Washington	Bingo Smith	San Diego
Terry Duerod	Detroit	Jim Spanarkel	Philadelphia
Jack Givens	Atlanta	Raymond Townsend	Golden State
Joe Hassett	Indiana	Richard Washington	Milwaukee
Geoff Huston	New York	Jerome Whitehead	Utah

1988 Expansion Draft (June 23, 1988)

Miami Heat

Player	From	Player	From
Hansi Gnad	Philadelphia	Jon Sundvold	San Antonio
Scott Hastings	Atlanta	Billy Thompson	L.A. Lakers
Conner Henry	Sacramento	Andre Turner	Houston
Arvid Kramer	Dallas	Darnell Valentine	L.A. Clippers
Fred Roberts	Boston	Dwayne Washington	New Jersey
John Stroeder	Milwaukee	Kevin Williams	Seattle

Charlotte Hornets

Player	From	Player	From
Tyrone Bogues	Washington	Dave Hoppen	Golden State
Michael Brooks	Denver	Ralph Lewis	Detroit
Mike Brown	Chicago	Bernard Thompson	Phoenix
Dell Curry	Cleveland	Sedric Toney	New York
Rickey Green	Utah	Clinton Wheeler	Indiana
Michael Holton	Portland		

1989 Expansion Draft (June 15, 1989)

Orlando Magic

Player	From	Player	From
Mark Acres	Boston	Jerry Reynolds	Seattle
Terry Catledge	Washington	Scott Skiles	Indiana
Jim Farmer	Utah	Otis Smith	Golden State
Sidney Green	New York	Reggie Theus	Atlanta
Frank Johnson	Washington	Sam Vincent	Chicago
Keith Lee	New Jersey	Marlon Wiley	Dallas

Minnesota Timberwolves

Player	From	Player	From
Gunther Behnke	Cleveland	Rick Mahorn	Detroit
Tyrone Corbin	Phoenix	Maurice Martin	Denver
Mark Davis	Milwaukee	David Rivers	L.A. Lakers
Steve Johnson	Portland	Scott Roth	San Antonio
Shelton Jones	Philadelphia	Eric White	L.A. Clippers
Brad Lohaus	Sacramento		

1995 Expansion Draft (June 24, 1995)

Vancouver Grizzlies

Player	From	Player	From
Greg Anthony	New York	Derrick Phelps	Sacramento
Benoit Benjamin	New Jersey	Trevor Ruffin	Phoenix
Rodney Dent	Orlando	Byron Scott	Indiana
Blue Edwards	Utah	Reggie Slater	Denver
Doug Edwards	Atlanta	Larry Stewart	Washington
Kenny Gattison	Charlotte	Gerald Wilkins	Cleveland
Antonio Harvey	L.A. Lakers		

Toronto Raptors

Player	From	Player	From
Willie Anderson	San Antonio	Oliver Miller	Detroit
B.J. Armstrong	Chicago	Ed Pinckney	Milwaukee
Acie Earl	Boston	John Salley	Miami
Andres Guibert	Minnesota	Doug Smith	Dallas
Keith Jennings	Golden State	Zan Tabak	Houston
Jerome Kersey	Portland	B.J. Tyler	Philadelphia
Tony Massenburg	L.A. Clippers	Dontonio Wingfield	Seattle

Players selected in three expansion drafts

Player	Teams
John Barnhill	Chi. '66, S.D. '67, Phoe. '68
Len Chappell	Chi. '66, Milw. '68, Cleve. '70
McCoy McLemore	Chi. '66, Phoe. '68, Cleve. '70
George Wilson	Sea. '67, Phoe. '68, Buff. '70

Players selected in two expansion drafts

Player	Teams
Jim Barnett	S.D. '67, N.O. '74
John Block	S.D. '67, N.O. '74
Nate Bowman	Chi. '66, Sea. '67
Emmette Bryant	Phoe. '68, Buff. '70
Barry Clemens	Chi. '66, N.O. '74
Johnny Egan	Milw. '68, Cleve. '70
Dave Gambee	S.D. '67, Milw. '68
Fred Hetzel	Milw. '68, Port. '70
Toby Kimball	S.D. '67, N.O. '74
Don Kojis	Chi. '66, S.D. '67
Arvid Kramer	Dal. '80, Mia. '88
Paul Long	Phoe. '68, Buff. '70
Jon McGlocklin	S.D. '67, Milw. '68
Stan McKenzie	Phoe. '68, Port. '70
Dorie Murrey	Sea. '67, Port. '70
Bud Olsen	Sea. '67, Milw. '68
Bingo Smith	Cleve. '70, Dal. '80
Tom Thacker	Chi. '66, Milw. '68
Bob Weiss	Sea. '67, Milw. '68

Chapter 27

The Evolution of Equipment

The Armory Cage, Paterson, New Jersey, 1929
Home to the Whirlwinds and Crescents of the American Basketball League (1925-31), the armory's basketball setup included the mesh cage common in the east through the early '30s.

By Robert Peterson

The Ball

The first basketball was, in fact, a soccer ball, and it was chosen almost by happenstance. James Naismith, the game's inventor, had worked out most of the details for his new game in December 1891. He knew he wanted the ball to be large and not easily hidden, but he did not decide on the type until just before he was to meet his phys-ed class.

As he entered his office that morning, Naismith recalled in *Basketball: Its Origin and Development*, "Side by side on the floor lay two balls, one a football and the other a soccer ball. I noticed the lines of the football and realized that it was shaped so that it might be carried in the arms." There was to be no running with the ball in the new game, so the choice was easy; it would be the soccer ball.

The soccer ball (then called "Association football") was used for basketball in the game's first two years. In 1894, the YMCA's rules committee, which consisted of Naismith and Dr. Luther H. Gulick, chairman of Springfield's phys-ed department, decided that an official basketball should be between 30 and 32 inches in circumference, about four inches bigger than a soccer ball. They left no record telling why they chose that size, but we may speculate that Naismith and Gulick believed the larger ball would be more easily handled than a soccer ball. The official ball's circumference did not appear in the YMCA's

rules until 1895.

The Overman Wheel Company, a bicycle manufacturer, made the first official YMCA basketballs in Chicopee Falls, Massachusetts, according to Naismith. Overman's western sales agent was A.G. Spalding & Bros. of Chicago, which made sporting goods, and that company advertised its own "official" basketball in the 1894 edition of the *Spalding Official Basket Ball Guide*. It is possible that Spalding collaborated with Overman in designing the first basketball.

That ball, and all others that followed it for the next four decades, was handcrafted by skilled workers. First they cut four or eight oddly shaped panels from tanned cowhide and cemented a lining of heavy canvas on the hide's inside surface. The panels were then machine-stitched together with the wrong side out so that the thick seams would be inside the ball when it was turned right side out. A rubber bladder with a nipple opening for inflating it was then inserted and the panel ends hand-stitched together. After the ball was inflated, the nipple (later a valve) was tucked under the rawhide laces that closed the opening.

"Disadvantages were obvious," wrote H.V. Porter, who studied the process on behalf of the Naismith Memorial Basketball Hall of Fame. "Only a small percentage would finish out with a shape near enough a perfect sphere to be top grade balls . . . The thick inside seams affected bouncing and reaction at backboard and ring, depending on whether contact was over a seam or between seams. During a game the leather under pressure at the seam edges wore thin and stretched to develop flat panels or the shape of a pumpkin, balloon or oblong."

Even a top-grade ball could be hard to handle, according to Thomas Allan Knudson in his 1972 doctoral dissertation on amateur basketball rules. He wrote, "Irregularities in the ball were commonplace for any ball . . . and in shooting for the goal, the thrower was advised to hold the ball each time in a particular way so that eventually 'the hands becoming familiar with any peculiarities in the shape of the ball, they adapt themselves to it and the ball is thrown with better judgment and with more chance of success.'"

In 1896 the YMCA's rule-makers, led by Gulick (Naismith had left Springfield to study medicine in Denver, Colorado), tried to eliminate seriously lopsided balls. The committee decreed that a top-grade ball could not vary by more than a quarter-inch in three diameters and should weigh between 18 and 20 ounces. The Amateur Athletic Union, including the YMCA, and college rule-makers had slightly different weight specifications for basketballs until 1915, when they agreed that the ball should weigh between 20 and 23 ounces. The increase in weight limits came about because manufacturers wanted to use heavier leather to ensure a more durable shape for basketballs.

The Great Depression of the 1930s had many effects on American life, and at least one on the sport of basketball. Because ball manufacture was labor-intensive, balls were always quite expensive. In the early days, a top-grade ball cost $6—a couple of days' wages for a laborer. When the Depression struck, a good basketball was priced at $16 and up, and a typical high school team could afford only one or two balls. The National Federation of State High School Associations assigned

H.V. Porter of the Illinois Association to "devise a more efficient type of construction to eliminate the waste in number of rejects and the short life of a well-shaped ball."

The job of developing such a ball was given to Henry T. Winterbauer and John T. Clark, both manufacturers. After a year of trial and error, they succeeded in making the first molded ball. Porter explained the method: "Two hemispheres of fabric were formed in a hot steel mold similar to those used in making a bowler hat. These half spheres were pressed together around a rubber bladder which was then inflated and wound with cord as in a baseball and impregnated with a mixture of raw latex and leather fibre and cured under heat in a steel mold which was also used to cure and shape the elastic with which the leather cover was attached to the carcass. Later a partially cured bladder was used."

Soon after the first molded ball was introduced, Milton Reach patented the "Last-Bilt" ball, which was molded around a hollow sphere, or last, of wax. The molded balls, Porter wrote, "are exact in size, in shape and in reaction regardless of which part makes contact with the floor, backboard, ring or hand. They retain these qualities through many days or weeks of use." The molded balls did not, however, gain instant favor with players and coaches. Especially in the colleges, diehards insisted on using the old sewn ball. They complained that the molded ball "didn't feel right" or "it acted different" or "bounced funny." It was not until 1950 that colleges accepted the molded ball as official. By that time, the specifications called for a circumference between 29-1/2 and 30 inches and weight between 20 to 22 ounces. In 1956 rubber- and composition-covered balls were approved for high schools and YMCA teams, but not for colleges and AAU teams.

The National Basketball Association also had some diehards who favored the sewn ball. When Wilson Sporting Goods Company, which supplied the NBA's balls, introduced the Last-Bilt molded ball in 1952, some team owners objected. In a letter to Commissioner Maurice Podoloff, Boston Celtics president Walter A. Brown made an impassioned plea for the new molded ball, at least in part because he had financial support from one of Wilson's executives. "Are we opposed to all progress?" he asked rhetorically. "If two thousand colleges find this type of ball acceptable . . . why shouldn't we?" Brown's view prevailed and the NBA adopted the molded ball.

Basketballs in the early days were brown or a deep tan in color. Beginning in the 1930s, experiments began with balls of different colors—white, black, orange, and other colors—according to Knudson. "Serious studies and experimentation with ball color accompanied the development of molded type basketballs with an artificial cover and the acceptance of the color orange as the best for visibility," he wrote. The orange ball became official in 1960, although the old natural tan ball remained official, too, until manufacturers' stocks ran out.

Today's best-grade basketballs for college men's teams and the NBA are leather-covered, 29 to 30 inches in circumference, and are priced at about $80 retail. Basketballs for women, which are an inch less in circumference, also cost about $80. Lesser-grade balls and rubber or composition balls are available for as little as $11.50.

Today's balls retain their shape well for long periods, are rel-

atively inexpensive, and are very durable. Boys play with official basketballs at a young age, either in the school gym or on the playground. "The results are obvious," Knudson noted. "Today's players shoot better, dribble and pass with more finesse, use a greater variety of shots and passes, use either hand for dribbling, shooting and passing and in general have a feel for handling the ball unknown in earlier days."

The Basket

Basketball's first goals were the now legendary peach baskets that James Naismith nailed to the lower rail of the balcony in the Springfield College gymnasium in December 1891. The rail was 10 feet above the floor, and that has remained the official height of the baskets to this day. The flimsy peach baskets did not last long. A photo of the first organized team at Springfield College in the spring of 1892 shows two wire-mesh baskets alongside the players. The hoops appear to be about 15 inches in diameter and 30 inches deep.

Lew Allen of Hartford, Connecticut got the idea in 1892 of making 15-inch cylindrical baskets of heavy woven wire, and it may be that the ones shown in the Springfield team's photo were his. A year later the Narragansett Machine Company of Providence, Rhode Island manufactured baskets with iron rims and cord nets. Because Naismith's original rules said a thrown ball must stay in the basket to count as a goal, the nets were closed. To get the ball out after a score, it was punched out with a long pole, or a player got a ladder to reach it.

By the 1894-95 season, the Narragansett company was making a basket with an 18-inch diameter rim to accommodate the new official basketball. It had a long cord hanging down, which, when pulled, lifted the net, causing the ball to roll out. It was not until 1912 that the bottom was cut out of the net so that the ball would drop through.

Backboards were not part of Naismith's original plan for the goals. They were authorized in the 1895-96 season, not to aid shooters but to inhibit spectators. Basketball games were already attracting partisan fans, and when games were played in gymnasiums with galleries for spectators, it was easy for a fervid fan to reach over the rail and guide the shots of his favorites into the basket or deflect those of opponents. So in 1895 the rules called for a four-by-six-foot wire or wooden screen behind the basket to keep fans from interfering with shots. The wire screens were soon dented by repeated rebounds, giving the home team an advantage because the players knew the peculiarities of their own backboards, and so gradually wood replaced the wire mesh boards. Glass backboards first appeared in 1909, and fan-shaped boards were authorized in 1940 (the latter were subsequently disapproved for college games). Today's goals in the National Basketball Association are clear glass or fiberglass six feet wide by three feet deep. To give shooters a target for banked shots, there is a 24-by-18-inch white rectangle on the board directly behind the rim. To keep slam dunkers from breaking the backboard, the rim has a pressure-release device so that it will bend but not break when a 250-pound behemoth hangs on it after a dunk.

In the early days the goals and backboards were not standard in every gymnasium. On some courts, the baskets would be set out 12 inches from the board instead of six inches as the amateur rules required. On others, there might be no board at all; the basket was attached to a rod coming down from the ceiling. Occasionally, especially on some National Guard armory courts in northern New York State, the basket's diameter was 16 inches instead of the regulation 18 inches.

Over the decades, particularly during the 1940s when tall men began coming into the college and professional game in droves, there have been calls to raise the height of the basket. Even earlier, in the 1930s, Forrest C. "Phog" Allen of the University of Kansas had proposed baskets 12 feet high as a counter to the move to eliminate the center jump after every score, according to Knudson. (The center jump after successful foul shots was ended in 1936 and after field goals in 1937. The scored-upon team took the ball under its own basket.) Knudson wrote: "Dr. Allen felt the higher basket would equalize the alleged advantage of the tall player over the short one."

However, Knudson also wrote, "The effect that no one had anticipated, and that practically ruled out the rise of the basket, was the effect it had on the big man . . . It was found that the big man was even more effective than before and the change hurt the little man most in the game." Worst of all, raising the goals changed the whole complexion of the game, because when the rim was raised the little man no longer drove for the basket but was content to hang back and shoot from 20 feet.

The Court

The first basketball game—at Springfield College in 1891—was played on a court about 50 feet long and 35 feet wide. Boundary lines were imaginary since the court was not marked out; gym equipment like Indian clubs, dumbbells, parallel bars and other apparatus were shoved out on the way, and Naismith, the referee that day, evidently ruled on out-of-bounds balls by guesstimate. The court was less than 40 percent as big as today's official court, and with nine-man teams that day, there must have been a lot of bumping and shoving.

Naismith's original rules made no mention of a mandated size for a basketball court. As the rules for the game evolved during the first few years, the number of players determined the size of the court. Nine-man teams used the biggest space and seven- and five-man teams had smaller courts. In 1896, when teams were set at five men, the rules said the court should not exceed 3,500 square feet—twice the expanse of the first court at Springfield. In 1908 the maximum size was established at 90 feet long by 55 feet wide; seven years later the width was reduced to 50 feet. (Today's playing space for colleges and the NBA is 94 by 50 feet. High school courts may be as small as 74 by 50 feet.)

Fewer than 200 YMCAs around the country had gymnasiums when basketball was born, and gyms weren't ubiquitous in colleges and high schools, either. Even the gyms that did exist were not ideal for basketball. Most were illuminated by gaslight or carbon lights that sometimes flared up and then dimmed. By 1894 the rules specified that there should be sidelines at least three feet from the walls or fences, and often the courts had irregular projections to accommodate stairways or offices. Some courts were wider at one end than the other, handicapping the team whose goal was at the narrow end. It was not until 1903 that sidelines and end lines had to be straight, and even later

before it was specified that the court must be a rectangle.

Some gymnasiums had structural deficiencies. The YMCA gym at Trenton, New Jersey, had two steel posts in the center of the court to support the roof. The first professional team, which started in the Trenton Y, thus developed the first "post" plays. In many other YMCA gyms, shots from the corners of the court were impossible because an oval gallery with a running track overhung the court.

The court at Philadelphia's Temple College (now University) was long and narrow with a big boiler at one end. Players would shoot over that boiler, and if they did not hear the ball drop, they knew they had scored because the ball stayed in the basket. At Nanticoke, Pennsylvania, hot steam pipes lined the walls at courtside, inflicting severe burns on hapless players who were pushed against them. A similar hot time was in store for visitors to the gym at Wilmington, Delaware, because it was heated by a potbelly stove near the sideline.

By 1920 most college teams were playing on adequate courts, but there were exceptions. One was New York University, which had no gym and played its home games wherever the Violets were welcomed. The team even played a game or two on a barge anchored in the Hudson River on Manhattan's west side. NYU had a storied rivalry with the City College of New York, and for their meeting in March 1920 they were booked into the 168th Street Regimental Armory. Nearly 10,000 basketball fans were on hand to see NYU beat CCNY, 39-21—the largest crowd ever to see a college game up to that time and a harbinger of the throngs that jammed Madison Square Garden for basketball doubleheaders during the 1930s.

Many teams, especially independents and professionals in northern New York and New England, played in National Guard armories during the first half of the 20th century. The armories were barnlike halls capable of seating 1,500 spectators or more around a spacious court. Some teams represented National Guard units, and players were required to sign on as Guardsmen, although they didn't have to drill and received honorable discharges after the season.

Barnstorming teams often found unusual venues on the road. Frank Basloe, who led barnstorming teams from 1904 to 1923, had games in halls that were studded with posts so that the players could play hide-and-seek, scores of National Guard armories, and in Masonic halls, Elmwood Music Hall in Buffalo, and Grange halls lit by kerosene lamps. In the hamlet of Pine River, Minnesota, Basloe's GlobeTrotters played the town team in a schoolroom before a packed house of 40 spectators. The Harlem Globetrotters, who were born six years after Basloe left the barnstorming trail, once played a game in a drained swimming pool, surely the most unusual court in basketball history.

One feature of courts for the professional game, especially in the East, was the cage, a wire-mesh or rope-net enclosure. The theory was that the game became faster because the ball was never out of bounds. Players bounced the ball and each other off the cage, making the pro game even rougher than it was without the cage. They also learned to tie up an opponent by grabbing the cage on either side of him.

Cages were used in the East until about 1930. In the New York-Philadelphia area and western Pennsylvania, wire-mesh was favored. In the Hudson River Valley and New England, rope nets were usually the choice. A handful of courts in the Midwest had cages, too, usually of net. Cages were almost never used by college teams and never by high schools.

Many old pros who played in cages were partial to them. Albert Cooper Jr., son of one of the first professional stars and a pro himself during the 1920s, said, "I played in cages up to 1929 when they stopped using them in Trenton. When they eliminated the cages, I never cared for basketball after that. All of the basketball players in those days enjoyed playing in a cage because there was less chance of injury than there is today. You learned to protect yourself. If you got jammed against the cage, it didn't bother you."

There were dissenters to that view. One of them was Joel S. "Shikey" Gotthoffer, a star for the Philadelphia Sphas, one of the best professional teams of the 1930s. When the Sphas had no game scheduled, the owner gave him permission to go to Nanticoke and earn some extra dollars. "I got $150 a ball game," Gotthoffer remembered, more than twice his per-game wage with the Sphas. "The owner of the ball club also owned a gin mill and money didn't mean anything to him.

"I played the first few games at Nanticoke in a cage, and I came home with the cage's markings on me," Gotthoffer recalled. "You could play tic-tac-toe on everybody after a game because the cage marked you up; sometimes you were bleeding and sometimes not. You were like a gladiator, and if you didn't get rid of the ball you could get killed."

Joe Schwarzer, who had earned All-American honors in both football and basketball at Syracuse University, recalled that when he came home after his first game in the New York State League, he took off his shirt and exposed rope burns all over his back. "Oh, my God," his wife exclaimed, "you've been in a fight!"

Courtside spectators were close enough to the cage that they could reach out and touch it. From their vantage point, the players must have looked like a zoo full of hyperactive gorillas. The memories of pros of the period are replete with tales of having been stabbed with hatpins and knitting needles and being burned by lighted cigarettes thrust through the cage. In towns in the Pennsylvania coal region, fans were noted for heating nails with miner's lamps and tossing them over the net at opposing foul shooters.

One of the last cages was on an unusual court in Hazleton, Pennsylvania in the late 1930s, long after they had disappeared elsewhere. In the 1938-39 season, Harry E. "Buddy" Jeannette, who is enshrined in basketball's Hall of Fame, was playing on a team that represented Cleveland in the National Basketball League and doubled as the Elmira, New York team in the New York-Pennsylvania League. Jeannette remembered:

> One day we were supposed to play a New York-Penn League game in Hazleton. In those days, to find the gym you drive into town and look for the biggest building. We drove up to this bar and I got out of the car and ran inside and said to the bartender, "Hey, we're supposed to play a basketball game in this town today. Can you tell me where it is?" He said, "This is the place." I look around and there are tables all over the room.

So we went in and got dressed, and when we came out to play they had shoved all the tables back. They had a basket on one wall, and on the other side they let down a basket that had been drawn up to the ceiling. The floor was maybe 70 or 80 feet long. The referee went to the middle of the court and drew a big round circle, and at each end he marked off 15 feet for the foul lines. Then they let a net down on the side where people sat at the tables. And when the game began, the damnedest fight you ever saw started. That was a real education.

For three decades beginning about 1910, many dance halls in large cities included basketball games as added attractions. In New York City's Harlem, the Manhattan Casino often scheduled two games between outstanding black teams followed by dancing. On December 30, 1910, the Casino advertised a doubleheader pitting the Jersey City Athletic Club against the St. Cyprian Heavyweight team and Howard University opposing the New York All Stars. The games did not start until 8:45 p.m., so no doubt they were shorter than regulation time because they were followed by dancing. General admission was 50 cents, and you could buy a box—seating eight—for $2.

The Renaissance Big Five, or New York Rens, called the Renaissance Casino in Harlem their home, although they were there only over holidays. When they were home over Thanksgiving and Christmas, the Rens attracted full houses of people in evening clothes who were eager for the game and the dancing that followed. The court was small—perhaps 60 by 35 feet—with the musicians' bandstand on one side and a wooden barrier surrounding the dance floor/basketball court. "It was a very slippery floor," remembered William "Pop" Gates, a Hall of Famer. "They had baskets that they put up before every ball game and markers that they put down for the foul lines and so forth. The spectators were seated at loges on the second tier and box seats on the third tier. That was supposed to be an elite area.

"The ballroom had a high ceiling, so you didn't have to worry about your shots," Gates continued. "All you had to worry about was running into that hard wooden barrier around the floor because it had sharp edges. Sometimes when the game got rough, guys would be flying over that barrier into people's laps."

The Philadelphia Sphas also shared billing with dancing. Their home court during the 1930s was the ballroom of the Broadwood Hotel. The Sphas were a predominantly Jewish team, and their games were highlights on the social calendar of Jewish singles, in part because they liked basketball and in part because of the dancing that followed. When ex-Temple star Gil Fitch, a musician, was on the Sphas' roster, he would change quickly into a tuxedo after the game and lead his band for the dance.

Professional basketball had a brief vogue on theater stages during the 1930s. The New York Celtics, who were getting financial help from popular singer Kate Smith, played some home games in the Hippodrome Theater in Manhattan. Across the East River, the Brooklyn Jewels were an attraction on the 80-by-40-foot stage of the Brooklyn Paramount Theater. Jewels

manager Eddie Wilde reported enthusiastically in the 1936 *Converse Basketball Year Book* that the introduction of basketball had boosted theater attendance on some nights from 1,500 to 5,000. Sammy Kaplan, who starred on the Kate Smith Celtics and American Basketball League teams in the '30s, remembered playing on a stage in Albany, New York. The basketball game complemented a movie and a vaudeville bill headlined by top banana Red Skelton. There was talk of a theater basketball league for deluxe theaters with big stages, but nothing came of it.

The Uniforms

Basketball uniforms have varied over the decades. In the beginning, players wore ordinary gymnasium attire, including long trousers, tights, and short-sleeved shirts; some had football pants and tracksuits. The first team at Springfield dressed in long trousers, sweaters, and soft leather shoes with leather soles. The first professionals in Trenton, New Jersey, wore red, sleeveless jerseys, black padded knickers, and wool stockings. In 1901 A.G. Spalding & Bros. introduced the first uniform specifically designed for basketball. Spalding offered a choice of knee-length jersey tights, knee-length padded pants, and short padded pants, and shirts both with and without sleeves.

Five years later, in the 1906-07 edition of its *Official Basket Ball Guide*, Spalding explained what the well-dressed player should wear. Top-of-the-line shoes cost $8 a pair and had soles of pure gum rubber, which would "enable a player to keep his footing on the most slippery floor," Spalding promised. For those with less money to spend, Spalding offered a pair for $4.50. "The wearer cannot slip with these shoes because of the unique construction of the sole, which is made of rubber with holes in it, so as to form a suction when in contact with the floor, and yet not enough to interfere with the freest action of the player," the company claimed.

Shorts made of sateen, a glossy cotton fabric, or of heavy twilled cotton, cost from 50 cents to $1.25, depending on quality; stripes down the sides added 50 cents per pair. There were also shorts made of canvas or flannel and padded at the hips. Sleeveless worsted wool shirts with a four-inch stripe around the chest cost $1.50, while cotton shirts were only 75 cents.

Spalding advertised warm-up sweaters for $4 to $6. The most expensive sweater was of lamb's wool and "is the official sweater worn by all the leading university and college teams," the company claimed. Most teams wore colorful above-the-knee stockings; Spalding's best had horizontal stripes and cost $3.25 a pair.

The East Liverpool, Ohio Potters—Central League champions in 1906-07—would not look out of place today, just slightly quaint. They had sleeveless jerseys with "EL" on the front, and the knee-length droopy drawers that have been de rigueur in the National Basketball Association since Michael Jordan began setting the style.

In the 1920s, shorts became briefer. There were no two-piece warm-up suits. Instead, players donned heavy wool sweaters when they were not in the game. By the 1940s, basketball uniforms looked a lot like those of today, except that the shorts were much shorter. Uniforms were primarily made of

nylon and such natural fabrics as wool and cotton rather than the polyesters and nylon mini-meshes of today. Two-piece warm-up suits were in vogue by the '40s.

The most important part of a player's uniform, his shoes, evolved too. The pioneers wore the high-topped leather shoe with a soft leather sole that was standard in the gymnasium. In the late 1890s, many teams adopted the tennis sneaker, and by 1900 the first shoe designed for basketball—canvas high-top with a rubber sole pitted with holes for better traction—was in use.

By 1940 basketball shoes were much more comfortable and serviceable than they were in the early days. Shoes had canvas uppers, sponge insoles with cushioned arches, and soles designed for good traction. More expensive models had leather tops in basic white or black.

Basketball shoes began going high-tech and making fashion statements with the arrival of Jordan in the NBA in the mid-1980s. His multimillion-dollar endorsement contracts for Nike shoes led to signing bonuses for other stars with Reebok, Adidas, and other companies, and fueled a sneaker boom that lasted into the mid '90s.

Technically, today's basketball shoes are far beyond those of a generation ago. Some have cells combining unpressurized air and a high-performance rubber polymer that provide cushioning and stability for the foot. Some shoes imitate the shape and biomechanics of a player's foot. Others provide better ankle support. All of the major shoe manufacturers have extensive laboratories where designers, biomechanics engineers, material specialists, molding technicians, and computer scientists work together to enhance performance of basketball shoes. The results are excellent shoes costing from $35 to $150 and up.

Other Leagues

David Thompson, 1976
The NBA's No. 1 draft pick signed instead with the ABA's Denver Nuggets, but a year later he—plus the rest of the Nuggets and three other franchises—would become part of the established league.

Chapter 28

The Early Pro Leagues

By Robert Bradley and John Grasso

Before Michael, Dr. J., Kareem, Wilt and Big George there was Harry, Barney, Benny, Dutch, The Kid, and a host of other pro basketball stars—virtually none of whom are remembered today.

More than 100 years ago basketball was played professionally in organized leagues with regular schedules, playoffs and league championships—and even a "World Series". Individual game statistics were kept and published.

Although some of these leagues were short-lived and players moved around somewhat there was more continuity then is generally thought. One of these leagues—the Eastern Basket Ball League, a six-team league centered around Philadelphia, played eight consecutive seasons with no franchise changes until the first World War caused the league to suspend play. This league stability was not matched by any professional basketball league (including the NBA) in the twentieth century!

Records also were set that have been forgotten. In the 1908-09 Central Basket Ball League Bill Keenan scored 76 points in one game on 38 field goals—a record not surpassed in pro basketball until 1961 when Wilt Chamberlain scored 78 in a triple-overtime game.

Thanks largely to the efforts of William J. Scheffer much of their story can be told today. Scheffer was a sports writer for the *Philadelphia Press* and editor of the *Reach Official Basket Ball Guide* in addition to his duties as the President-Secretary-Treasurer of the Philadelphia Basket Ball League. These annual guides, published by the A.J. Reach Company, Base Ball and Sporting Goods Manufacturers of Philadelphia, PA were issued primarily to promote the sales of sporting goods but to an historian they have proved invaluable. Although nearly half of the guide (priced at 10 cents) was devoted to advertising the company's products (including the company's Official Basket Ball priced at $6.00), the remainder of the guide contained photos of the leading professional, college and high school teams and team and individual statistics of the various leagues. Also included in the guides were the "National Rules—For the government and protection of the game of Basket Ball."

The guides were published annually for 26 years beginning with the 1901-02 issue and provide the source for much of the material contained in this section. Reach's rival, A.G. Spalding & Bros., also published a basket ball annual but their emphasis was on NCAA, YMCA and AAU basketball and contained little of interest to the pro basket ball fan. (Interesting sidelight is that both companies were founded by ex-pro baseball players—Alfred James Reach and Albert Goodwill Spalding—both of whom played in the National Association from 1871-75.)

Local newspapers such as the *Philadelphia Inquirer, Trenton*

Ed Wachter, 1911
A passing maven, he is thought to be the first player sold—in 1903 from a team in Ware, Mass., to one in nearby Haverhill, for $100.

State-Gazette, Utica Daily Observer and *Paterson Evening News* provided detailed accounts of virtually every league game played by their hometown teams. As was the custom during the early twentieth century references to players were often only by their last names. This has presented a challenge to the researcher but for the most part the challenge was met successfully.

Thanks to Mr. Scheffer's diligence—and the invention of microfilm—the information contained in the following section was developed.

Robert Peterson's eloquent essay in Chapter 2 of this volume provides an excellent description of professional basketball during this era. This chapter provides some of the statistics.

NATIONAL BASKETBALL LEAGUE
[1898-99 TO 1903-04]

LEAGUE MEMBERS

Bristol Pile Drivers	Bristol, PA	1899-00 to 1902-03
Burlington Shoe Pegs	Burlington, NJ	1900-01, 1902-03
Camden Electrics	Camden, NJ	1898-99 to 1899-00,
		1902-03 to 1903-04
Camden Skeeters	Camden, NJ	1900-01 to 1901-02
Chester	Chester, PA	1899-00
Clover Wheelmen [Bikers]	Philadelphia, PA	1898-99
Conshohocken [Conshos]	Conshohocken, PA	1902-03 to 1903-04
Germantown A.A. [Nationals]	Philadelphia, PA	1898-99
Hancock Athletic Association	Philadelphia, PA	1898-99
Millville Glass Blowers	Millville, NJ	1899-00 to 1901-02, 1903-04
New York Wanderers	Road team	1899-00 to 1902-03
Pennsylvania Bicycle Club	Philadelphia, PA	1899-00 to 1900-01
Philadelphia Clover		
Wheelmen [Bikers]	Philadelphia, PA	1898-99
Philadelphia Phillies	Philadelphia, PA	1901-02 to 1902-03
St. Bridgets [Biddies]	Philadelphia, PA	1903-04
Trenton [Trentons]	Trenton, NJ	1899-00 to 1900-01
Trenton Nationals	Trenton, NJ	1898-99, 1901-02
Trenton Potters	Trenton, NJ	1902-03 to 1903-04
Wilmington	Wilmington, DE	1902-03
Wilmington Peaches	Wilmington, DE	1902-03

1898-99 NBL

Organized on July 30, 1898 at a meeting at the Hotel Vendig in Philadelphia. At the meeting were William E. Morgenweck of Camden, James McMurray of Millville, H.W. Junghurth of the Germantown "Big Five" and Philadelphia sports editor Peter E. Wurfflein who represented Frank Smith of Trenton. Horace S. Fogel of Philadelphia was elected league president. Theodore E. Nichols, later to become prominent in real estate, entered the league shortly afterwards with a team representing the Hancock A.A. of Philadelphia. Trenton was the only club which used a cage at the time and insisted on its use in league play. Thus, it became the league standard. League rules did not permit overtime to break ties; tie games were to be replayed at a future date. First tie game was a 16-16 tie between Clover and Millville on December 10, 1898 at Millville. The game was replayed on December 28, 1898 and won by Millville 21-8.

Germantown and Hancock encountered financial difficulties during the season, dropping out shortly after its start at which time the "Big Five of Clover Wheelmen were renamed "the Big Five of Philadelphia".

On March 11, 1899 Millville annihilated Philadelphia 64-3, leading 30-3 at the half with Frank Bomhoff's 21 points leading the Glassblowers.

The season's final game played was on April 8, 1899 when Trenton defeated Millville 24-13. The last scheduled league game on April 12, 1899 was forfeited to Camden when the Millville team did not show up. Trenton was officially declared season champions on the basis of their season record without need of a playoff and won the 35' long pennant designed by the A.G. Spalding company.

	W	L	T	PCT.
Trenton Nationals	18	2	1	.900
Millville Glassblowers	14	6	2	.700
Camden Electrics	7	13	1	.350
Clover Wheelmen/				
Philadelphia Clover Wheelmen***	5	14	1	.263
Germantown A.A.*	1	4	0	.200
Hancock Athletic Association**	0	6	1	.000

*Germantown played their last game on December 29, 1898 and dropped out of the league shortly afterwards as Town Hall in Germantown was considered to be not suitable for the game.
**Hancock failed to show for a game in Camden on December 31, 1898. Shortly afterwards a letter dated December 28, 1898 was received by the League from Hancock team manager Theodore E. Nichols which read in part "In view of the poor showing made by the Hancock team resulting from the loss of the services of four of its best players I deem it advisable to withdraw from the league." In so doing, Nichols avoided a heavy fine and forfeit of his bond. On January 7, 1899 a league meeting was held in which the Hancock franchise was officially annulled, Nichols was fined $50 and his bond was returned.
***Since the loss of the Hancock franchise left the city of Philadelphia with just one team, the "Big Five of the Clover Wheelmen" were ordered to rename their team "the Big Five of Philadelphia" for the balance of the season.

1899-00 NBL

The NBL faced its first competition as Peter Wurfflein, who had left the NBL after a disagreement over franchise rights, organized the Interstate League. The IL provided direct competition as it fielded franchises in Conshohocken, Philadelphia (Penn, Hancock, Germantown, Tannhaeuser) and Millville (which had defected from the NBL after the Mercer County Wheelmen had applied for a franchise). Albert Austermuhl, who had played for Camden in the league's first year, replaced Wurfflein as the league's secretary-treasurer and league president Horace Fogel was re-elected.

Mercer County withdrew their application for membership and on September 16, 1899, Bristol (PA), Chester (PA), New York (who would play all of their games on

the road) and Pennsylvania joined the returning Trenton and Camden clubs to bring the league's membership back up to six teams. Chester dropped out during the first half of the season after failing to post a victory but Millville returned from the IL for the second half of the season to take their place.

Trenton again won the league championship, successfully defending it by finishing the first half of the season with an 8-0 record, and stretching their winning streak to 15 league games but stumbled and were caught by Millville in the second half, with both clubs finishing with identical 14-4-1 records. Trenton then bested Millville for the second half title by winning two of three games in a post-season matchup, with the second game forfeited to Trenton when Millville had an ineligible player, Hilly Wallace, in their lineup.

	FIRST HALF				SECOND HALF				SEASON TOTALS			
	W	L	T	PCT.	W	L	T	PCT.	W	L	T	PCT.
Millville Glassblowers**	..	..	..	.....	14	4	1	.778	14	4	1	.778
Trenton	8	0	0	1.000	14	4	1	.778	22	4	1	.746
New York Wanderers	3	2	0	.600	13	7	0	.650	16	9	1	.640
Camden Electrics	4	4	0	.500	11	9	0	.550	15	13	0	.536
Bristol Pile Drivers	3	6	0	.333	6	14	1	.300	9	20	1	.310
Pennsylvania Bicycle Club	4	4	0	.500	0	20	0	.000	4	24	0	.143
Chester*	0	6	0	.000	..	..	..	.....	0	6	0	.000

*Chester dropped out during the first half.
**Millville joined the league on January 3, 1900.

SECOND HALF NBL PLAYOFF

Apr. 28, 1900 at Bristol - Millville 18, Trenton 13
(Game protested by Trenton since Millville used Hilly Wallace, who was ineligible to play for them; League President Fogel ruled that game was to be replayed.)
May 5, 1900 at Camden - Trenton 4, Millville 0 forfeit (Millville refused to play game since they wanted to use Wallace)
May 8, 1900 at Camden - Trenton 22, Millville 19

NBL CHAMPIONSHIP

Trenton wins NBL championship by winning both halves of the season

1900-01 NBL

The 1900 off-season proved to be the NBL's most stable. All six franchises returned for another season in addition to a new member in Burlington.

Unlike the previous year, the season was not divided into halves, but at the midway point of the season Camden was leading the league with a 10-4 record followed by Trenton at 10-5, with New York at the bottom with a 6-7 record. The "Wanderers" then put on a spurt winning 16 of 18 games to capture the league championship. The new Burlington team struggled to an 0-12 record before dropping out during the first half. The regular season concluded on April 11 as New York defeated Trenton 35-28. There were no playoffs as New York won the league championship outright.

After the season on April 13 in Philadelphia a special "National League Tournament" was held in which all six teams were invited to participate but Trenton and Millville didn't appear. The remaining teams played games of 15-minute halves with the following results: New York 20, Bristol 10; Camden 19, Penn BC 7 and in the tournament championship final: New York 17, Camden 5.

A "goal-throwing" contest also was held in which Heite of the Penn BC (who had been scoreless in the regular season in only two games) won a gold-mounted pair of pearl opera glasses with his 9 of 13 shooting.

	W	L	PCT.
New York Wanderers	23	9	.719
Trenton	20	12	.625
Millville Glassblowers	18	14	.563
Bristol Pile Drivers	17	15	.531
Camden Skeeters	16	16	.500
Pennsylvania Bicycle Club	8	24	.250
Burlington*	0	12	.000

*Burlington dropped out during the season.

LEAGUE LEADERS
Regular Season

	G	FG	FT	TP	PPG
Albert Cooper, Trenton	27	63	164	290	10.7
Charlie Klein, Bristol	28	121	17	259	9.3
John Deal, Penn BC	21	61	134	256	12.2
John Wendelken, New York	31	116	13	245	7.9
Bill Everingham, Bristol	27	31	169	231	8.6
Harry Hough, Bristol	32	92	29	213	6.7
Bill Reid, New York	31	64	81	209	6.7
Ed Ferat, Camden	31	44	108	196	6.3
Walter "Red" Barber, Millville	28	49	89	187	6.7
Hilly Wallace, Millville	27	58	61	177	6.6

1901-02 NBL

Philadelphia joined the league in 1901 taking the place of the Pennsylvania club. And for the second time in three years a rival league was organized, with the American League placing teams in Burlington (NJ), Camden (NJ), Chester (PA), Norristown (PA), Trenton, Wilmington and Philadelphia (Penn and St. James) providing direct competition for the NBL.

Bristol outdistanced Camden in the regular season to win the league title, and then proved the superiority of the NBL as they defeated American League champions Wilmington and New England League champion Manchester in a post-season tournament.

	W	L	PCT.
Bristol Pile Drivers	28	12	.700
Camden Skeeters	25	15	.625
Trenton Nationals	23	17	.575
Millville Glassblowers	21	19	.525
New York Wanderers	18	21	.461
Philadelphia Phillies	4	35	.103

LEAGUE LEADERS

Regular Season	G	FG	FT	TP	PPG
John Deal, Camden	42	112	381	605	14.4
Charlie Klein, Bristol	39	145	73	363	9.3
Walter "Red" Barber, Millville	35	83	189	355	10.1
Harry Stout, Trenton	39	99	135	333	8.5
Bill Everingham, Bristol	29	35	254	324	11.2
Harry Hough, Bristol	39	137	31	305	7.8
Kid Eberlein, New York	36	90	88	268	7.4
Albert Cooper, Trenton	30	54	136	244	8.1
Jack Hitchens, Millville	37	65	104	234	6.3
John Wendelken, New York	36	108	0	216	6.0

1902-03 NBL

Ernest C. Crowhurst of Philadelphia was elected League President as the season began play in mid-October 1902. Shortly afterwards the Philadelphia League was organized and played its first game on January 5 providing some competition for the NBL. The NBL again had membership changes as Millville dropped out and Burlington, Conshohocken and Wilmington were brought in to bring the league's membership up to eight clubs.

Camden and New York dominated the first part of the schedule, with Camden leading the league with a 15-2 record. To restore interest in the pennant race the decision was made in mid-season to split the league into two halves awarding the first half championship to Camden. In the second half, which began on January 1, Camden continued its dominance and easily outdistanced Burlington capturing the league title.

	FIRST HALF			SECOND HALF			SEASON TOTALS		
	W	L	PCT.	W	L	PCT.	W	L	PCT.
Camden Electrics	15	2	.882	21	7	.750	36	9	.800
Bristol Pile Drivers**	12	5	.706	..	..	.....	12	5	.706
New York Wanderers	11	2	.846	11	14	.440	22	16	.579
Philadelphia Phillies*	10	7	.588	..	..	.....	10	7	.588
Trenton Potters	6	9	.400	14	15	.483	20	24	.455
Burlington Shoe Pegs**	2	12	.143	16	11	.593	18	23	.439
Wilmington/									
Wilmington Peaches*	2	14	.125	14	12	.538	16	26	.381
Conshohocken	4	11	.267	4	21	.160	8	32	.200

*Dec. 21, 1902 Philadelphia resigns from league after first half. Phillies manager Frank Morgenweck purchases the Wilmington franchise from Charles Kraus.

**Dec. 30, 1902 Burlington resigns from league after first half. Burlington Manager Reber purchases the Bristol franchise and has the former Bristol team represent Burlington.

NBL CHAMPIONSHIP

As Camden won both halves of the season, they were awarded the NBL pennant and cup without the necessity of any playoff games.

LEAGUE LEADERS

Regular Season	G	FG	FT	TP	PPG
John Deal, Camden	47	144	452	740	15.7
Harry Hough, Bristol/Burlington	45	206	236	648	14.4
Al Cooper, Trenton	34	75	346	496	14.6
Steve White, Phil/Wilmington	39	83	267	433	11.1
Jack Reynolds, Wilm/Consho	47	74	280	428	9.1
Hilly Wallace, Wilmington	45	170	6	346	7.7
Charles Bossert, Camden	46	138	42	318	6.9
Kid Eberlein, New York	36	126	59	311	8.6
Ed Ferat, Camden	47	126	41	293	6.2
Harry Stout, Trenton	44	82	83	247	5.6

Note: Free throws were listed as "Goals from Offenses".

1903-04 NBL

At a league meeting on October 19th it was decided to disband the National Basketball League as Burlington, New York and Wilmington had dropped out. Shortly afterwards a new five-team American Basketball League was organized. The NBL owners decided to make another attempt and reorganized a five-team league with Millville and St. Bridget's joining Trenton, Camden and Conshohocken.

With many of the league's better players signing with rival leagues which were offering higher salaries, fan interest in the NBL began to decline. Financial problems ensued for the league's five clubs and the league disbanded in December with Camden in first place. The highlight of the brief season was on December 10th when Willie Keenan, center for Camden, scored 21 field goals to set a new league record in the 67-16 victory over St. Bridgets: a team also referred to as the Hillclimbers from the Falls of Schuykill.

The last league game was played on January 2, 1904 as Millville defeated St. Bridget's 52-21.

At a meeting in Camden on January 3, the league officially declared the 1st half closed and Camden the winner of the 1st half. Secretary-Treasurer William Scheffer resigned. Plans were made for Trenton to be included in the 2nd half to begin play on January 16, 1904 but they never materialized. When the Conshohocken team was accepted into the PBL on January 18 all plans for a resumption of the NBL ended.

	W	L	PCT.
Camden Electrics**	10	4	.714
Conshohocken	8	4	.667
Trenton Potters*	8	5	.615
Millville Glass Blowers	6	9	.400
St. Bridget's Biddies	2	12	.143

*Trenton resigned from league on Dec. 26, 1903.
**Camden resigned from league on Dec. 31, 1903.

NATIONAL BASKETBALL LEAGUE: 1898-1904

Teams	1898-99	1899-00	1900-01	1901-02	1902-03	1903-04	Totals
Bristol	x	9-20	17-15	28-12	12-5	x	66-52
Burlington	x	x	0-12	x	18-23	x	18-35
Camden	7-13	15-13	16-16	25-15	36-9	10-4	109-70
Chester	x	0-6	x	x	x	x	0-6
Clover	5-14	x	x	x	x	x	5-14
Conshohocken	x	x	x	x	8-32	8-4	16-36
Germantown	1-4	x	x	x	x	x	1-4
Hancock	0-6	x	x	x	x	x	0-6
Millville	14-6	14-4	18-14	21-19	x	6-9	73-52
New York	x	16-9	23-9	18-21	22-16	x	79-55
Penn Bicycle Club	x	4-24	8-24	x	x	x	12-48
Philadelphia	x	x	x	4-35	10-7	x	14-42
St. Bridgets	x	x	x	x	x	2-12	2-12
Trenton	18-2	22-4	20-12	23-17	20-24	8-5	111-64
Wilmington	x	x	x	x	16-26	x	16-26
Total games played	45	80	102	119	142	34	522

Note: tie games not shown above.

Team Records

League–Most Championships: 2, Camden, Trenton
League–Most Games Played: 179, Camden
League–Most Games Won: 111, Trenton
League–Most Games Lost: 70, Camden
League–Highest Won-Lost Percentage: .634, 111-64, Trenton
League–Lowest Won-Lost Percentage: .000, 0-6, Chester
.000, 0-6, Hancock

Season–Most Games Played: 45, 1902-03, Camden
Season–Most Games Won: 36, 1902-03, Camden
Season–Most Games Lost: 35, 1901-02, Philadelphia
Season–Highest Won-Lost percentage: .900, 18-2 1898-99, Trenton
Season–Lowest Won-Lost percentage: .000, 0-12 1900-01, Burlington
.000, 0-6 1898-99, Hancock
.000, 0-6 1899-00, Chester

Individual Records (records based on available data)

League–Most Games Played: 119, Ed Ferat
League–Most Field Goals: 435, Harry Hough
League–Most Free Throws: 967, John Deal
League–Most Total Points: 1,601, John Deal
League–Highest PPG average: 14.6, John Deal

Season–Most Games Played: 47, 1902-03, several
Season–Most Field Goals: 206, 1902-03, Harry Hough
Season–Most Free Throws: 452, 1902-03, John Deal
Season–Most Total Points: 740, 1902-03, John Deal
Season–Highest PPG average: 15.7, 1902-03, John Deal

Individual Summary: 3 or more Seasons

Player	Seasons	Yrs.	Teams	G	FG	FT	TP	PPG
Bob Abadie	1899-03	4•••	NYK	63	29	0	58	0.9
Kid Abadie	1899-02	3••	NYK	28	49	0	98	3.5
Walter Barber	1898-04	6•••	MIL/PHI/WIL	73	159	369	687	9.4
Charles Bennett	1899-04	5•••	BRI/BUR/CON	72	87	0	174	2.4
Frank Bomhoff	1898-04	6•••	MIL/BUR	73	159	3	321	4.4
Charles Bossert	1899-03	4•••	CHE/CAM	94	265	77	607	6.5
Al Bratton	1898-01	3•	TRE	1	0	0	0	0.0
Charlie Carr	1899-02	3••	CAM/PHI	29	40	0	80	2.8
George Cartledge	1898/02	3•	TRE/PHI	14	9	0	18	1.3
Al Cooper	1898-04	6•••	TRE	91	192	646	1030	11.3
Fred Cooper	1898-01	3•	TRE	1	2	0	4	4.0
Red Cramer	1898-02	4••	CAM/PHI	48	74	89	237	4.9
John Deal	1898-03	5•••	CLO/CAM/ CHE/PHI	110	317	967	1601	14.6
Mother Dietrich	1899-03	4•••	NYK	69	35	1	71	1.0
Bob Dippy	1899-02	3••	CAM	61	28	0	56	0.9
Bill Donlon	1898-02	4••	GER/PHI	21	36	29	101	4.8
Kid Eberlein	1898-03	5•••	NYK	74	219	147	585	7.9
Gus Endebrock	1898-03	5•••	TRE	49	90	0	180	3.7
Bill Everingham	1899-04	5•••	BRI/TRE/BUR	64	76	444	596	9.3
Ed Ferat	1898-03	5•••	CAM	119	258	154	670	5.6
Al Geddes	1898-02	4••	CLO/CHE/PHI	10	4	0	8	0.8
Frank Geddes	1898-01	4•••	CLO/CHE	13	8	0	16	1.2
Walter Grief	1899-03	4•••	NYK	58	96	128	320	5.5
Jud Hancock	1900-04	4•••	CAM/PHI/WIL	51	46	3	95	1.9
Bill Harrison	1899-04	4•••	TRE	67	33	0	66	1.0
Jack Hitchens	1898-04	6•••	MIL/BUR	65	93	148	334	5.2
Harry Hough	1900-03	3•••	BRI	116	435	296	1166	10.0
E.A. Keen	1899/03	3••	PHI/WIL	27	37	4	78	2.9
Bill Keenan	1901-04	3••	PHI/CAM	57	152	6	310	5.4
Charlie Klein	1899-03	4•••	BRI/BUR	84	367	170	904	10.8
Walter Lewis	1899-03	4•••	TRE	18	12	2	26	1.4
Billy Lindsay	1898-03	5•••	TRE	38	64	70	198	5.2
Billy Markwardt	1901-04	3••	PHI/CAM	49	43	0	86	1.8
Al Mellick	1898-03	5•••	TRE/BRI/ CAM/BUR	23	10	0	20	0.9
Budge Middleton	1898-04	6•••	CAM	80	58	1	117	1.5
Fred Mulliner	1900-03	3•••	BRI/BUR	46	51	20	122	2.7
Bart Newman	1901-04	3••	PHI/CAM	40	80	30	190	4.8
John Plant	1899-03	4•••	BRI/BUR	85	40	6	86	1.0
Firman Reeves	1898-04	6•••	MIL/BUR	57	67	24	158	2.8
Dan Reick	1898-02	4••	MIL	38	10	0	20	0.5
Billy Reid	1899-03	4•••	NYK	72	133	102	368	5.1
Pete Riley	1899-04	5•••	TRE	72	163	1	327	4.5
Sandy Shields	1899/03	3••	NYK/BRI	35	131	92	354	10.0
Percy Smith	1898-01	3•	CLO/BUR/BRI	7	3	0	6	0.9
Ray Snow	1899-02	3••	BRI/TRE/PHI	9	6	0	12	1.3
Chris Stinger	1898-03	5•••	TRE	84	51	0	102	1.2
Harry Stout	1898-04	6•••	TRE	112	237	275	749	6.7
Bill Thomas	1899-02	3••	PHI/CAM	20	15	5	35	1.8
Walter Thompson	1898-02	4••	CLO/CAM/ CHE/PHI/NYK	12	3	0	6	0.5
Hilly Wallace	1898-04	6•••	MIL/CAM/ PHI/WIL	110	320	79	719	6.5
John Wallace	1898/04	5•••	MIL	48	35	0	70	1.5
John Wendelken	1899-03	4•••	NYK	80	323	13	659	8.2
Steve White	1901-04	3••	PHI/WIL/CAM	44	95	303	493	11.2

* data only available for 1 year
*+ data only available for 1-1/2 years
** data only available for 2 years
**+ data only available for 2-1/2 years
*** data only available for 3 years

FIRST GAME DETAILS

This is the *Philadelphia Inquirer* article from Friday, December 2, 1898 describing the first professional basketball league game.

BASKET BALL IS ON
THE OPENING OF THE REGULAR
NATIONAL LEAGUE SEASON IN THIS CITY
Trenton Beats Hancock
In an Exceedingly Close and Interesting
Game the Jerseymen Win by the
Score of 21 to 19

The Trenton and Hancock athletic association teams met last evening at Textile Hall in the opening game of the National Basket Ball League, and after forty minutes of hard and fast playing Trenton was the victor by the score of 21 to 19. This was the first appearance of the Trenton team in Philadelphia and everybody present were prepared to see some of the passing of which they are famous for. The audience couldn't have been disappointed, as the applause that greeted this kind of play was deafening. About 900 people were present, and cheers and hisses were mingled with good and bad playing. No less than forty-one fouls were called during the game, and the people who were present unjustly hissed the referee who only enforced the new National League rules, which makes all rough playing and three men in a scrimmage fouls. The play had only started when Harrison ran with the ball and Ruckhardt scored the first point on a free throw, the first score in the National League. The half ended by the score of 11 to 8 in favor of the Hancock, and victory looked perched on Hancock's banner. The second half saw the fastest playing that has been witnessed in this city. Trenton showed great judgment in changing the attacks for the half, and it undoubtedly won the game for Trenton. Although Hancock led during this half until ten minutes was left of time, when Trenton by fast playing, won out, to the disappointment of the large crowd. Both teams played a good game, but Hancock was undoubtedly the better in individual play, while Trenton excelled in team work. Of the 41 fouls called, 22 were called on Hancock and the rest on Trenton. Trenton scored 11 of their 23 points on foul throws and Hancock 9. The line-up:

Trenton	Positions	Hancock
Cooper, Lindsey	Attack	West
Stout, Bratton	Attack	Reichhardt
Hamilton, Enderbock	Center	King
Cartledge	Defense	Kendig
Harrison	Defense	Hackett

Goals from field: Hackett 3; Cooper, 2; Bratton, 2; Harrison, West, Reickhardt
Goals from foul: Lindsey, 7; Reickhardt, 9; Stout, 1; Cooper, 3
Fouls: Kendig, 6; West, 6; King, 6; Reickhardt, 2; Hackett, 2; Stout, 2; Harrison, 4; Cartledge, 2; Hamilton, 3; Enderbock, 2; Lindsey, 1
Referee: E.C. Rutsckman
Time: 20 minute halves
Editor's Notes: Spelling and grammar is as it was in the article. Name of first player to score appeared variously as "Ruckhardt", "Reickhardt", "Reichhardt".

PHILADELPHIA BASKET BALL LEAGUE
[1902-03 TO 1908-09]

LEAGUE MEMBERS

Baldwin [Locomotives]	Philadelphia, PA	1905-06
Beacon [Churchmen]	Philadelphia, PA	1905-06
Bridesburg	Philadelphia, PA	1905-06
Columbia Field Club	Philadelphia, PA	1902-03 to 1903-04
Conshohocken Giants	Conshohocken, PA	1903-04 to 1904-05
Conshohocken Iron Men	Conshohocken, PA	1906-07 to 1907-08
Covenant Guild Nationals	Philadelphia, PA	1902-03
DeNeri	Philadelphia, PA	1904-05 to 1908-09
East Falls [Cliff Climbers, Hessians]	Philadelphia, PA	1902-03 to 1907-08
Germantown	Philadelphia, PA	1907-08 to 1908-09
Gray's Ferry	Road team	1904-05
Greystock	Philadelphia, PA	1902-03
Jasper Athletic Club [A.C.s]	Philadelphia, PA	1902-03 to 1905-06
Manayunk [Yunkers]	Philadelphia, PA	1904-05 to 1907-08
National A.C.	Philadelphia, PA	1903-04
North Philadelphia Phillies	Philadelphia, PA	1903-04 to 1908-09
North Wales	North Wales, PA	1907-08 to 1908-09
Philadelphia Strattons	Philadelphia, PA	1907-08 to 1908-09
St. John	Philadelphia, PA	1902-03 to 1903-04
St. Luke	Philadelphia, PA	1907-08
St. Simeon [Saints]	Philadelphia, PA	1902-03 to 1908-09
South Philadelphia	Philadelphia, PA	1903-04
Trenton E.L. Kerns	Trenton, NJ	1905-06
Xavier	Philadelphia, PA	1902-03 to 1903-04
West Philadelphia	Philadelphia, PA	1903-04
West Philadelphia	Philadelphia, PA	1904-05

Note: Columbia FC withdrew in Jan. 1905 and players finished the season as "Gray's Ferry."

1902-03 PBL

With basket ball gaining in popularity, a professional league was organized in Philadelphia in 1902 with William J. Scheffer as league president. The initial eight clubs were: the Columbia Field Club, Jasper Athletic Club, East Falls, St. John's, St. Simeon's, Xavier, Covenant Guild and Tioga. The latter failed to appear at the final pre-season league organization meeting and had their franchise vacated. Greystock AC was invited to replace them. Doubleheaders were scheduled by the league featuring the clubs' second or junior teams playing the preliminary game. "Clean Sport" was the league's motto and it was written that "any player found slugging would be disqualified and suspended for one game for the first infraction, two games for the second infraction and expelled for the season for the third."

The opening league game was on January 5, 1903 at Columbia Hall in Philadelphia where the Jasper AC defeated the Covenant Guild 32-10. Although the league did not initially have the same level of star players as the National League it was nonetheless competitive and popular with the fans.

	W	L	PCT.
Columbia Field Club	22	5	.815
East Falls	20	8	.714
Jasper Athletic Club	14	14	.500
St. John	12	14	.462
Greystock	12	15	.444
St. Simeon	12	16	.429
Xavier	10	17	.370
Covenant Guild Nationals	6	19	.240

LEAGUE LEADERS

Regular Season	G	FG	FT	TP	PPG
Harry Bates, Columbia	27	86	237	409	15.1
Flynn, St. Simeon	23	80	178	338	14.7
Neill, Greystock	28	49	211	309	11.0
Bill Clayton, East Falls	24	65	158	288	12.0
Schwer, Jasper	26	45	184	274	10.5
John McGowan, Xavier	25	72	71	215	8.6
Neiler, Covenant	23	48	108	204	8.9
Schaeffer, St. John	26	24	137	185	7.1
John Donohue, Xavier	28	81	1	163	5.8
Cole, East Falls	25	61	39	161	6.4

1903-04 PBL

In its second season the league continued its successful ways with six of eight teams returning. President Scheffer showed that his penchant for clean play would be upheld. He suspended John McGraw of the Jasper AC and Arthur Atwood of East Falls for the season after their roughhousing during a game was continued in a street altercation afterwards.

John McGowan of the last place Xavier club won a special league "Goal Throwing" contest by making 11 of 13 shots. Dan Haggerty finished last of the eight contestants with a 1 for 13 score.

The season was scheduled to end on Saturday, March 12 but was extended one week in order to play off tied and postponed games even though none had a bearing on the final league championship.

	W	L	PCT.
Jasper Athletic Club	24	4	.857
Columbia Field Club	18	8	.692
St. John	18	10	.643
East Falls	14	14	.500
West Philadelphia/North Philadelphia Phillies*	12	16	.429
South Philadelphia/National Athletic Club/ Conshohocken Giants**	10	17	.370
St. Simeon	9	18	.333
Xavier	5	23	.179

*West Philadelphia moved to North Philadelphia during the season.
**South Philadelphia dropped out in Dec. 1903 and were replaced by National who were dropped from the league Jan. 17, 1904 and replaced by Conshohocken.

LEAGUE LEADERS

Regular Season	G	FG	FT	TP	PPG
Schwer, Jasper	25	59	214	332	13.3
Harry Bates, Columbia	24	52	213	317	13.2
Cole, East Falls/St. Simeon	24	82	104	268	11.2
Flynn, St. Simeon	17	48	149	245	14.4
Scherer, St. John	25	63	107	233	9.3
Al Bloom, St. John	18	34	135	203	11.3
Whitey Mallon, Jasper	24	96	1	193	8.0
Schaeffer, North Philadelphia	20	16	143	175	8.8
Bill Clayton, East Falls	24	45	84	174	7.3
Al McWilliams, Columbia	24	83	7	173	7.2

1904-05 PBL

The third season of the PBL opened on October 29, 1904, with eight teams each scheduled for 40 games. Manayunk and DeNeri were added to replace Xavier and St. John. The Columbia F.C., the most successful league member in the first two seasons, was forced to withdraw in January 1905 due to the loss of its hall. The Columbia players finished the season on the road as the "Gray's Ferry" club and only managed to play 33 games. The Conshohocken Giants outscored their opponents by an average of more than 10 points per game and won the league championship. The previous season's winners, the Jasper A.C. lost their top scorer, Schwer, after only 13 games and finished in third place. Jack Reynolds of North Philadelphia set a league scoring record with 616 points—460 on free throws. Bill Keenan was the only league player to score a field goal in every game and finished the season with a league-leading 157 field goals. After the close of the season on March 29, the victorious Conshohocken team went on a tour of Western Pennsylvania and won six of eight games against independent teams losing only to Indiana, Pa. and the powerful Southside A.C. of Pittsburgh.

	W	L	PCT.
Conshohocken Giants	31	8	.795
West Philadelphia/North Philadelphia Phillies	28	13	.683
Jasper Athletic Club	26	15	.634
DeNeri	22	17	.564
East Falls	18	22	.450
St. Simeon	13	26	.333
Manayunk	11	29	.275
Columbia Field Club/Gray's Ferry*	7	26	.212

Note: there were two tie games—DeNeri-East Falls and DeNeri-Manayunk
*Columbia dropped out in January 1905. Columbia players played as "Gray's Ferry."

LEAGUE LEADERS

Regular Season	G	FG	FT	TP	PPG
Jack Reynolds, North Philadelphia	39	78	460	616	15.8
Sam White, Conshohocken	37	137	304	578	15.6
John McGraw, Jasper	39	88	238	414	10.6
Al Bloom, Manayunk	31	54	262	370	11.9
Mink, DeNeri	33	33	302	368	11.2
Bill Keenan, Conshohocken	37	157	1	315	8.5
Cole, St. Simeon	31	104	99	307	9.9
Walter Brady, DeNeri	40	112	41	265	6.6
Charlie Bossert, Conshohocken	38	112	40	264	7.0
Bill Clayton, East Falls	29	70	111	251	8.7

1905-06 PBL

As was to be expected the last place Columbia/Gray's Ferry group did not rejoin the league for its fourth season. Surprisingly though, the league champion Conshohocken Giants also left to play as an independent team. Beacon and Bridesburg were selected as replacements. Bridesburg quit on December 20 and was replaced by a Trenton team which lasted only one month and which was in turn replaced by Baldwin on January 26, 1906. The 28-game season ended in turn on March 16 in a tie between DeNeri and Manayunk. As per league rules, a best-of-three playoff was scheduled. Before "the largest crowd to ever see a basketball game in Philadelphia" DeNeri defeated Manayunk 24-18 at the National AC hall on March 30. The following night at Manayunk's hall DeNeri became league champions by a 52-24 score as Charlie Bossert's 23 points and Joe Fogarty's 9 field goals led the team.

	W	L	PCT.
DeNeri	22	6	.786
Manayunk	22	6	.786
St. Simeon	18	10	.643
East Falls	17	11	.607
North Philadelphia Phillies	15	13	.536
Jasper Athletic Club	9	19	.321
Beacon	5	23	.179
Bridesburg/Trenton E.L. Kerns/Baldwin	4	24	.143

Notes: Regular season ended in a tie.
Bridesburg dropped out on Dec. 20. 1905 and were replaced by Trenton on Dec. 21, who dropped out of league on Jan. 19 and were replaced by Baldwin on Jan. 26.

PBL PLAYOFF SERIES
Mar. 30, 1906 at National AC - DeNeri 24, Manayunk 18
Mar. 31, 1906 at Manayunk Hall - DeNeri 52, Manayunk 24

LEAGUE LEADERS

Regular Season	G	FG	FT	TP	PPG
William "Kid" Dark, St. Simeon	29	51	256	358	12.3
Charlie Bossert, DeNeri	28	88	164	340	12.1
Scherer, Manayunk	26	62	203	327	12.6
John Donohue, Beacon	26	49	188	286	11.0
Bill Clayton, East Falls	26	59	149	267	10.3
John McGraw, Jasper	25	65	131	261	10.4
Howard Thomas, North Philadelphia	23	37	164	238	10.3
Ed Toner, St. Simeon	28	96	28	220	7.9
Joe Fogarty, DeNeri	10	63	80	206	20.6
Al McWilliams, Manayunk	28	98	1	197	7.0

1906-07 PBL

For its fifth season the league's membership was reduced from eight to six teams, primarily due to difficulties in obtaining suitable places to play. The Jasper A.C., a charter member of the league, dropped out as did the two bottom-place teams of the previous year—Beacon and Baldwin.

Replacing them was the league champion of the 1904-05 season, Conshohocken, who again captured the league title. For the first time in league history, each team played a balanced schedule of 30 games, meeting each other six times. The league's overall balance was also apparent as each team defeated every other team at least once.

The establishment of the Central Basket Ball League with teams in Western Pennsylvania and Ohio hurt the Philadelphia League, since several stars of previous years preferred to play in the new league. Kid Dark, the 1905-06 scoring leader was among them. The DeNeri team, 1905-06 champions, was especially hard hit, losing Joe Fogarty and several other of their best players. Consequently, they could finish no better than fifth in the six team league. Other former Philadelphia League stars who switched leagues included John Featherstone, Bill Keenan, Ed Ferat and Winnie Kincaide.

The 1906-07 Philadelphia League unofficial all-star team as selected by the ubiquitous William J. Scheffer (League President-Secretary-Treasurer, editor of the Reach Official Basket Ball Guide and sports writer for the Philadelphia Press) featured four Conshohocken players: league-leading scorer Sam White, Bill Lukens, Al McWilliams, Bill Herron and Charles Bossert of the DeNeri club.

	W	L	PCT.
Conshohocken Iron Men	22	8	.733
Manayunk	19	11	.633
East Falls	15	15	.500
St. Simeon	14	16	.467
DeNeri	11	19	.367
North Philadelphia Phillies	9	21	.300

LEAGUE LEADERS

Regular Season	G	FG	FT	TP	PPG
Sam White, Conshohocken	29	103	206	412	14.2
Jack Reynolds, Manayunk	26	30	258	318	12.2
Charlie Bossert, DeNeri	27	73	146	292	10.8
John McGraw, St. Simeon	28	66	129	261	9.3
Bill Lukens, Conshohocken	29	98	29	225	7.8
Murphy, East Falls	25	54	111	219	8.8
John Donohue, St. Simeon	28	57	73	187	6.7
Bill Clayton, East Falls	22	53	74	180	8.2
Howard Thomas, DeNeri	13	32	104	168	12.9
Al Glassey, Conshohocken	31	81	0	162	5.2

1907-08 PBL

Season six of the PBL featured the addition of two teams, Stratton and Germantown, restoring the league to its original eight team status. A former power in the Philadelphia amateur leagues, Germantown dominated the season winning three-quarters of its games including an 85-20 defeat of the second place St. Simeon club in the pennant-clinching game. They featured a balanced attack with six of their seven players finishing among the top 30 league scorers. Conshohocken, the previous year's champion, again dropped out of the league and were replaced by North Wales. East Falls, the only remaining team from the league's inaugural 1902-03 season also dropped out in mid-season. For the second straight year several star players were lost to the Central Basketball League in Western Pennsylvania.

	W	L	PCT.
Germantown	21	7	.750
St. Simeon	17	11	.607
DeNeri	15	10	.600
Conshohocken Iron Men/North Wales*	16	11	.593
Manayunk	13	11	.542
Philadelphia Strattons	13	13	.500
North Philadelphia Phillies	6	18	.250
St. Luke**	3	23	.115
East Falls**	8	8	.500

*Conshohocken dropped out and was replaced by North Wales.
**East Falls dropped out and was replaced by St. Luke.

LEAGUE LEADERS

Regular Season	G	FG	FT	TP	PPG
Howard Thomas, DeNeri	20	50	238	338	16.9
William Reilly, Germantown	25	81	148	310	12.4
John Donohue, St. Simeon	26	89	70	248	9.5
John McGraw, St. Simeon	28	70	97	237	8.5
Al Glassey, Germantown	26	46	134	226	8.7
Al McWilliams, North Wales/Manayunk	28	92	23	207	7.4
George Bell, North Wales	22	36	133	205	9.3
Army Fitzgerald, Stratton	22	58	87	203	9.2
Bill Lukens, North Wales	23	90	9	189	8.2
Jack Reynolds, North Wales	17	26	123	175	10.3

1908-09 PBL

The seventh season of the Philadelphia League was its last as the Central League continued to attract players. William Scheffer claimed that the league's demise was not caused by lack of fan interest but, rather, due to rowdyism among the players and a lack of support of the referees on the part of the team managers.

In the 1909-10 Reach guide he wrote: "Managers must learn to know that there are strict rules to govern the game, and that officials are put there to see that the rules are strictly enforced. If the officials are not backed up, the games become regular indoor foot ball contests, players being injured and spectators becoming disgusted. The latter are the ones to look after, as without public support, no sport will last."

Tragedy struck the league on January 2 as Charles Ritter of the North Wales team died during the game against Stratton.

There were four weeks left in the first half of the season on January 6 when North Philadelphia, North Wales and St. Simeon dropped out. North Wales left for financial reasons while North Philadelphia was upset over the season suspension of Joe Cavanaugh for fighting with referee Schoenhut and St. Simeon disputed a fine for non-appearance in a game at Germantown. Three days later Germantown dropped out of the league to compete as an independent leaving only the Stratton and DeNeri teams remaining. Germantown was considered by Scheffer to be league champion as their 11-2 record easily surpassed that of the second place North Philadelphia team. John Featherstone, seventh in total points, scored all 82 via field goals although he was shut out twice. In one game he made 10 field goals—a feat matched only by Germantown teammate Ivan Loos.

	W	L	PCT.
Germantown**	11	2	.846
North Philadelphia Phillies*	7	5	.583
St. Simeon*	7	6	.538
Philadelphia Strattons	5	6	.454
DeNeri	4	8	.333
North Wales*	2	9	.182

*North Philadelphia, North Wales and St. Simeon dropped out on Jan. 6, 1909.
**Germantown dropped out on Jan. 9, 1909.

LEAGUE LEADERS

Regular Season	G	FG	FT	TP	PPG
John Donohue, St. Simeon	12	28	94	150	12.5
Jack Reynolds, North Wales	11	13	112	138	12.6
William Reilly, Germantown	8	24	61	109	13.6
Harry Bates, North Philadelphia	8	10	81	101	12.6
Al Glassey, Germantown	12	38	15	91	7.6
Ford, De Neri	11	28	33	89	8.1
John Featherstone, Germantown	11	41	0	82	7.5
Jimmy Rumsey, North Philadelphia	11	14	45	73	6.6
Charles Klein, DeNeri	12	27	14	68	5.7
Preusch, North Philadelphia	12	21	23	65	5.4

Team Records

League–Most Championships: 2, Conshohocken, Germantown
League–Most Games Played: 193, St. Simeon
League–Most Games Won: 90, St Simeon
League–Most Games Lost: 103, St Simeon
League–Highest Won-Lost Percentage: .781, 32-9, Germantown
League–Lowest Won-Lost Percentage: .115, 3-23, St. Luke

Season–Most Games Played: 41, 1904-05, Jasper, North Philadelphia
Season–Most Games Won: 31, 1904-05, Conshohocken
Season–Most Games Lost: 29, 1904-05, Manayunk
Season–Highest Won-Lost %: 846, 11-2, 1908-09, Germantown
Season–Lowest Won-Lost %: 115, 3-23, 1907-08, St. Luke

Individual Records - (records for 1902-04 are incomplete)

League–Most Games Played: 150, Cole
League–Most Field Goals: 388, A.M. McWilliams
League–Most Free Throws: 1,077, Jack Reynolds
League–Most Total Points: 1,401, Jack Reynolds
League–Highest PPG average: 14.0, Sam White

Season–Most Games Played: 40, 1904-05, Walter Brady; 40, 1904-05, Ford
  40, 1904-05, Dippy Obermier; 40, 1904-05, Dan Haggerty
Season–Most Field Goals: 157, 1904-05, Bill Keenan
Season–Most Free Throws: 460, 1904-05, Jack Reynolds
Season–Most Total Points: 616, 1904-05, Jack Reynolds
Season–Highest PPG average: 16.9, 1907-08, Howard Thomas

Individual Summary: 3 or more Seasons

Player	Seasons	Yrs.	Teams	G	FG	FT	TP	PPG
Herman Baetzel	1902-06	4**	JAS	18	35	0	70	3.9
Harry Bates	1902-09	7	COL/BEA/ DEN/STR/NPH	133	265	709	1239	9.3
Charles Bennett	1903/07	3*	CON	23	26	0	52	2.3
Al Bloom	1903/08	4	STJ/MAN/DEN	70	114	479	707	10.1
Charles Bossert	1904-09	5	CON/DEN/STR	121	314	412	1040	8.6
Jack Boyd	1903-07	4*	STS/DEN	73	33	2	68	0.9
Andy Cameron	1902-09	7**	JAS/STS	102	45	0	90	0.9
Archie Cavanaugh	1906-09	3	MAN/NPH	45	96	1	193	4.3
Joe Cavanaugh	1906-09	3	MAN/NPH	57	124	30	278	4.9
W. Cavanaugh	1906-09	3	MAN/NPH	50	24	1	49	1.0
Bill Clayton	1902-09	7	EFL/STS	140	313	630	1256	9.0
Cole	1902-09	7	EFL/STS/ STR/NWL	150	386	328	1100	7.3
Connor	1902/08	5**	XAV/STS/ CON/NWL	20	22	39	83	4.2
Craig	1902/06	3**	COL/BEA	12	2	0	4	0.3
C. Devine	1903/09	4*	EFL/STR	61	105	14	224	3.7
Devlin	1902-06	4**	XAV/STS	37	18	19	55	1.5
John Donohue	1902/09	6	XAV/COL/ BEA/STS	135	321	428	1070	7.9
Clarence Enos	1903/09	4*	STJ/EFL/ STR/NWL	25	45	33	123	4.9
John Featherstone	1903/09	4*	JAS/GER	64	139	1	279	4.4
Flynn	1902-05	3	STS/EFL/JAS	63	182	416	780	12.4
Ford	1903-09	6*	WPH/DEN	115	364	34	762	6.6
Al Glassey	1903-09	6*	CON/MAN/GER	118	294	154	742	6.3
Elwood Gowdy	1902-09	7**	COV/NAT/ NPH/STR/	100	273	9	555	5.6
Dan Haggerty	1903-07	4*	NAT/NPH	95	205	0	410	4.3
L. Haggerty	1903/07	3*	NAT/NPH	30	30	0	60	2.0
Harveson	1904-09	5	JAS/BEA/STS	56	118	7	243	4.3
Haug	1902/09	4*	COV/BEA/ NPH/NWL	32	25	10	60	1.9
Bill Herron	1904/08	3	CON/NWL	85	87	16	190	2.2
Kerswell	1903-07	4*	NAT/NPH	40	17	0	34	0.9
King	1903-08	5*	EFL	81	96	0	192	2.4
Gus Krueger	1902-08	6**	STJ/MAN/DEN	94	116	8	240	2.6
Ivan Loos	1904-09	5	MAN/GER	75	162	0	324	4.3
William Loos	1904-09	5	MAN/GER	87	92	7	191	2.2
Bill Lukens	1904/08	3	CON/NWL	53	188	38	414	7.8
Charles Mallon	1903/08	4	JAS/EFL/STS	64	158	1	317	5.0
Billy Markwardt	1903-08	5*	XAV/DEN/NPH	73	105	0	210	2.9
McBurney	1904/08	3	DEN	20	9	0	18	0.9
Walter McCallion	1902-05	3*	GRE/COL	17	34	0	68	4.0
Jack McCullough	1904/09	3*	STJ/MAN/NPH	37	9	0	18	0.5
John McGowan	1902-06	3	XAV/BAL	33	80	90	250	7.6
John McGraw	1902-09	7**	JAS/STS	132	312	598	1222	9.3
McIlvaine	1906-09	3	NPH	7	4	0	8	1.1
Al McWilliams	1902-08	6*	GRE/COL/ MAN/CON/NWL	126	388	41	817	6.5
Murphy	1904/08	3	EFL	77	105	288	498	6.5
Myers	1902-05	3**	EFL/CON/STS	24	21	87	129	5.4
Dippy Obermier	1902-09	7**	JAS/NPH/NWL	116	158	36	352	3.0
George Patterson	1902/06	3**	JAS/WPH/BRI	5	7	13	27	5.4
Jack Reynolds	1903-09	6*	CON/NPH/ MAN/NWL	106	162	1077	1401	13.2
Schaeffer	1902-07	5	STJ/NPH/NAT	130	70	409	549	4.2
Scherer	1902-07	5*	STJ/MAN	92	185	495	865	9.4
Schwer	1902-08	5	JAS/EFL	89	153	566	872	9.8
Shock	1903/08	4*	EFL	42	25	0	50	1.2
Howard Thomas	1904-09	5	STS/NPH/ DEN/GER	67	145	551	841	12.6
Ed Toner	1905/09	3	STS	50	168	112	448	9.0
Sam White	1904-08	4	CON/BAL/STL	79	267	575	1109	14.0
Wick	1903-08	5	STS/EFL	47	86	2	174	3.7
Mike Wilson	1902-07	5**	STS/COL/EFL	60	138	119	395	6.6
Lew Winch	1902-09	7**	JAS/STS	129	154	1	309	2.4

*data unavailable for 1 year
**data unavailable for 2 years

CENTRAL BASKET BALL LEAGUE
[1906-07 TO 1911-12]

LEAGUE MEMBERS

Alliance	Alliance, OH	1908-09
Butler	Butler, PA	1906-07
Canton	Canton, OH	1906-07
Charleroi [Cherubs]	Charleroi, PA	1911-12
Connellsville [Cokers]	Connellsville, PA	1910-11 to 1911-12
East Liverpool Potters	East Liverpool, OH	1906-07 to 1908-09
Greensburg	Greensburg, PA	1906-07 to 1908-09
Greensburg Billikens	Greensburg, PA	1909-10
Homestead Young Americans	Homestead, PA	1906-07 to 1909-10
Homestead Steeltowners	Homestead, PA	1910-11
Johnstown Johnnies	Johnstown, PA	1908-09 to 1911-12
McKeesport Tubers	McKeesport, PA	1906-07 to 1910-11
Pittsburgh South Side	Pittsburgh, PA	1906-07 to 1911-12
Uniontown [Berets, Braves]	Uniontown, PA	1908-09 to 1911-12
Washington Georges	Washington, PA	1911-12

1906-07 CBL

The Central Basket Ball League was organized in the fall of 1906 in Pittsburgh, PA. Charles B. Powers, sports editor of the *Pittsburgh Dispatch*, was elected league president and Joseph Leithead, a former player for the Pittsburgh South Side AC, was named secretary-treasurer. The league began its first season with four teams (South Side, Homestead, Butler and McKeesport) using local players and two teams, East Liverpool led by Joe Fogarty and Greensburg led by Kid Dark, signing top pro players from throughout the region. During the season South Side added Harry Hough and Jimmy Kane. East Liverpool finished the first half of the season with a 22-8 record, easily outdistancing South Side by five games. After the conclusion of the 30-game schedule, a 20-game post-season began. McKeesport signed the players from the Tamaqua club, and Homestead, which dropped out of the league, was replaced by Canton. South Side, led by Harry Hough's 15.3 scoring average, finished the post-season with a 16-3 record, but league plans to match East Liverpool and South Side in a championship series never materialized as the two clubs failed to agree on referees to officiate the series.

REGULAR SEASON	W	L	PCT.	POST-SEASON SERIES	W	L	PCT.
East Liverpool Potters	22	8	.733	Pittsburgh South Side	16	3	.842
Greensburg	17	13	.567	East Liverpool Potters	12	7	.632
Pittsburgh South Side	17	13	.567	McKeesport Tubers	11	7	.611
Homestead Americans	15	14	.517	Young Butler	9	11	.450
Butler	11	19	.367	Greensburg	8	12	.400
McKeesport Tubers	7	22	.241	Canton*	1	17	.056

*Canton replaced Homestead for the post-season series.

CBL CHAMPIONSHIP

East Liverpool refused to play Pittsburgh, since they could not agree on officials.

LEAGUE LEADERS

Regular Season	G	FG	FT	TP	PPG
Jackie Adams, Homestead	28	100	205	405	14.5
Joe Fogarty, East Liverpool	29	131	99	361	12.4
Harry "Bushel" Beggs, Butler	24	91	108	290	13.8
William "Kid" Dark, Greensburg	30	57	141	255	8.5
Bill Keenan, East Liverpool	28	124	4	252	9.0
Harry Liebau, Pittsburgh	21	49	144	242	11.5
Harry Hough, Pittsburgh	16	69	82	220	13.8
Roy Steele, Homestead	29	109	2	220	7.6
Ed Toner, Greensburg	24	83	10	176	7.3
John "Snake" Deal, East Liverpool	21	69	34	172	8.2

Post-Season	G	FG	FT	TP	PPG
Harry Hough, Pittsburgh	17	62	136	260	15.3
Joe Fogarty, East Liverpool	18	69	95	233	12.9
Alois Getzsinger, McKeesport	17	61	78	200	11.8
Steve White, Greensburg	16	40	96	176	11.0
Anderson, East Liverpool/Butler	17	80	0	160	9.4
Fred Mulliner, McKeesport	17	69	18	156	9.2
Jackie Adams, Butler	14	43	67	153	10.9
Harry "Bushel" Beggs, Butler	11	36	75	147	13.4
Jimmy Kane, Pittsburgh	17	67	1	135	7.9
Roy Steele, Butler	19	62	7	131	6.9

1907-08 CBL

Although Butler withdrew from the league prior to the 1907-08 season, the CBL still managed to play an ambitious schedule of 176 games. The South Side AC of Pittsburgh was hampered by injuries to key players and the loss of Jimmy Kane in mid-season to the Pittsburgh Pirates baseball team. As a result, East Liverpool was easily able to win the league title. The league established its superiority over the Philadelphia Basketball League in a series of post-season exhibition games between the PBL champion Germantown team and several CBL teams. Depressed economic conditions in Western Pennsylvania hurt the league financially.

	W	L	PCT.
East Liverpool Potters	53	19	.736
Pittsburgh South Side	42	28	.600
Homestead Young Americans	32	38	.457
Greensburg	28	42	.400
McKeesport Tubers	21	49	.300

LEAGUE LEADERS

Regular Season	G	FG	FT	TP	PPG
Steve White, Greensburg	65	152	668	972	15.0
Harry Hough, Pittsburgh	51	234	482	950	18.6
Andy Sears, McKeesport	69	136	640	912	13.2
Jack Adams, Homestead	67	146	605	897	13.4
Joe Fogarty, East Liverpool	60	251	373	875	14.6
Ed Ferat, East Liverpool	65	247	42	536	8.3
Jimmy Kane, Pittsburgh	49	222	11	455	9.3
Roy Steele, Homestead	67	226	3	455	6.8
John Deal, East Liverpool	41	160	92	412	10.1
Bill Keenan, East Liverpool	55	188	0	376	6.9

1908-09 CBL

By adding Johnstown and Uniontown to the league, the CBL expanded to seven teams for its third season. Five of the stars of the previous year's East Liverpool championship team were acquired by the two new teams. The East Liverpool franchise was acquired by new interests led by J. and L. Rhinehard. Ex-New York star Alexander "Sandy" Shields was hired as team captain. They failed miserably in their efforts to recruit a winning team and Shields quit mid-season to become a referee. To conclude the disastrous season, the owners released their players and hired an amateur team from Alliance, OH for the last ten games of the season. The situation reached ridiculous depths on March 16 when Johnstown defeated Alliance 110-9 on 55 field goals—38 of them by Bill Keenan in 35 minutes of play. Keenan's professional record of 76 points in a game was not surpassed until 1961 when Wilt Chamberlain scored 78 in a triple-overtime game. The other six teams engaged in a spirited battle for the league championship with Homestead edging McKeesport and Pittsburgh South Side AC.

	W	L	PCT.
Homestead Young Americans	49	23	.681
McKeesport Tubers	46	26	.639
Pittsburgh South Side	43	28	.606
Greensburg	41	31	.569
Johnstown Johnnies*	38	33	.535
Uniontown	30	43	.411
Alliance	0	10	.000
East Liverpool Potters**	4	57	.066

*Johnstown was added to the league after they acquired several players who were to play for Uniontown.
**East Liverpool (4-57) was replaced by Alliance (0-10).

LEAGUE LEADERS

Regular Season	G	FG	FT	TP	PPG
Steve White, Greensburg	70	162	750	1074	15.3
Andy Sears, McKeesport	67	159	658	976	14.6
Joe Fogarty, Johnstown	67	222	377	821	12.3
Harry Hough, Pittsburgh	49	121	399	641	13.1
Jackie Adams, Uniontown	49	166	267	599	12.2
Bill Herron, Homestead	65	63	441	567	8.7
Fred Mulliner, Uniontown	67	125	273	523	7.8
Roy Steele, Homestead	65	205	2	412	6.3
Chief Muller, Pittsburgh	56	193	19	405	7.2
John Deal, Johnstown	55	151	82	384	7.0
Bill Keenan, Johnstown	54	188	2	378	7.0

1909-10 CBL

Although league President Powers resigned in December and was replaced by Joseph Leithead, the fourth season of the CBL was the smoothest-run in the league's brief existence. As was to be expected, the troubled East Liverpool franchise was dropped from the league and the remaining six teams played a balanced schedule, meeting each other 14 times. The race was very close and at the start of the last month of play—only two games separated the top four teams. McKeesport, known for its defensive prowess, won the title by three games.

	W	L	PCT.
McKeesport Tubers	49	21	.700
Johnstown Johnnies	46	24	.657
Greensburg Billikens	41	29	.586
Homestead Young Americans	37	33	.529
Pittsburgh South Side	24	46	.343
Uniontown	13	57	.186

LEAGUE LEADERS

Regular Season	G	FG	FT	TP	PPG
Andy Sears, McKeesport	70	160	925	1245	17.8
Joe Fogarty, Johnstown	63	192	736	1120	17.8
Walter Brady, Pittsburgh	70	133	731	997	14.2
Bill Kummer, Greensburg	62	168	570	906	14.6
Steve White, Uniontown	60	118	547	783	13.1
Fred Mulliner, Uniontown	64	118	273	509	8.0
Bill Herron, Homestead	66	81	321	483	7.3
Jack Adams, Homestead	44	132	196	460	10.5
Bill Keenan, Johnstown	63	224	0	448	7.1
Doc Newman, Johnstown	66	176	67	419	6.4

1910-11 CBL

The Greensburg team moved to Connellsville to start the league's fifth season. McKeesport, using only six players, repeated as league champions, clinching the title on the last day of the season, even though Pittsburgh South Side's Harry Hough had been offered a bonus for winning the pennant. Financially, the Pittsburgh team lost significantly since they had spent heavily in their quest for the crown. With 10 games remaining in the season, the Homestead team forfeited their franchise. League records were established by Andy Sears, McKeesport's designated foul shooter, when he netted 26 of 29 in a game, including 16 consecutively. At the conclusion of the season a World Series was played between McKeesport and the Eastern Basketball League champion DeNeri team which McKeesport won in four straight games.

	W	L	PCT.
McKeesport Tubers	49	21	.700
Pittsburgh South Side	48	22	.686
Johnstown Johnnies	40	30	.571
Connellsville	31	39	.443
Homestead Steeltowners*	22	48	.314
Uniontown	20	50	.286

*Homestead dropped out, forfeiting their final 10 games

WORLD SERIES OF BASKETBALL

[DeNeri - EL, McKeesport - CBL]
Apr. 1, 1911 at Philadelphia - McKeesport 33, DeNeri 22
Apr. 8, 1911 at Philadelphia - McKeesport 35, DeNeri 21
Apr. 12, 1911 at Pittsburgh - McKeesport 42, DeNeri 22
Apr. 15, 1911 at Pittsburgh - McKeesport 57, DeNeri 20

LEAGUE LEADERS

Regular Season	G	FG	FT	TP	PPG
Harry Hough, Pittsburgh	64	157	963	1277	20.0
Andy Sears, McKeesport	67	169	924	1262	18.8
Joe Fogarty, Johnstown	63	207	799	1213	19.3
Jackie Adams, Homestead	60	164	762	1090	18.2
Bill Kummer, Connellsville	56	170	678	1018	18.2
James Brown, Uniontown	40	99	245	443	11.1
Kid Dark, Connellsville	67	138	81	357	5.3
Jimmy Kane, Pittsburgh	51	166	15	347	6.8
Dutch Wohlfarth, Homestead	54	158	0	316	5.9
Bill Keenan, Johnstown	48	157	0	314	6.5

1911-12 CBL

The sixth and final season began minus the league champion McKeesport team whose players were acquired by Uniontown. Charleroi, PA and Washington, PA were added to keep the league at six teams. Washington, who received a franchise just one week before the season began, was completely outclassed and, after losing the first 30 games, was dropped by the league. For a brief time Washington was represented by the Hudson River League's Trenton team who played simultaneously in both leagues. Pittsburgh South Side lost several stars to the Eastern league and dropped out of the league in February, leaving the remaining four teams to conclude the season. Johnstown, with four players among the top ten individual scoring leaders, won the league championship. Bill Kummer of Connellsville set a league record with 20 free throws in 20 attempts to better his previous record of 18-18.

	W	L	PCT.
Johnstown Johnnies	48	18	.727
Uniontown	45	21	.682
Connellsville	35	31	.530
Charleroi	26	40	.394
Pittsburgh South Side*	20	34	.370
Washington Georges**	0	30	.000

*Pittsburgh dropped out.
**Washington dropped out.

LEAGUE LEADERS
Regular Season

	G	FG	FT	TP	PPG
Bill Kummer, Connellsville	62	233	938	1404	22.7
Jack Adams, Charleroi	63	206	895	1307	20.8
Joe Fogarty, Johnstown	65	203	856	1262	19.4
Andy Sears, Uniontown	65	175	905	1255	19.3
Walter Brady, Pittsburgh	45	111	537	759	16.9
Dutch Wohlfarth, Johnstown	58	233	0	466	8.0
James Brown, Charleroi	63	200	9	409	6.5
Doc Newman, Johnstown	62	198	0	396	6.4
Bill Keenan, Johnstown	64	194	0	388	6.1
Roy Steele, Pittsburgh	46	160	6	326	7.1

1912-13 CBL

Although the 1911-12 season ended with just four teams, the Pittsburgh South Side returned for the 1912-13 season. Charleroi relocated in Homestead and the league began its exhibition season with Connellsville, Homestead, Johnstown, Pittsburgh South Side and Uniontown. After playing just a few exhibitions the league was disbanded on November 12, 1912.

CENTRAL BASKETBALL LEAGUE - 1906-12

Teams	1906-07	1907-08	1908-09	1909-10	1910-11	1911-12	Totals
Butler	20-30	x	x	x	x	x	20-30
Canton	1-17	x	x	x	x	x	1-17
Charleroi	x	x	x	x	x	26-40	26-40
Connellsville	x	x	x	x	31-39	35-31	66-70
East Liverpool	34-15	53-19	4-67	x	x	x	91-101
Greensburg	25-25	28-42	41-31	41-29	x	x	135-127
Homestead	15-14	32-38	49-23	37-33	22-48	x	155-156
Johnstown	x	x	38-33	46-24	40-30	48-18	172-105
McKeesport	18-29	21-49	46-26	49-21	49-21	x	183-146
Pittsburgh South Side	33-16	42-28	43-28	24-46	48-22	20-34	210-174
Uniontown	x	x	30-43	13-57	20-50	45-21	108-171
Washington	x	x	x	x	x	0-30	0-30
Total games played	146	176	251	210	210	174	1167

Team Records
League–Most Championships: 2, McKeesport
League–Most Games Played: 384, Pittsburgh South Side
League–Most Games Won: 210, Pittsburgh South Side
League–Most Games Lost: 174, Pittsburgh South Side
League–Highest Won-Lost Percentage: .621, 172-105, Johnstown
League–Lowest Won-Lost Percentage: .000, 0-30, Washington

Season–Most Games Played: 73, 1908-09, Uniontown
Season–Most Games Won: 53, 1907-08, East Liverpool
Season–Most Games Lost: 67, 1908-09, East Liverpool
Season–Highest Won-Lost Percentage: .736, 53-19, 1907-08, East Liverpool
Season–Lowest Won-Lost Percentage: .000, 0-30, 1911-12, Washington

Individual Records
League–Most Games Played: 365, Joe Fogarty
League–Most Field Goals: 1,275, Joe Fogarty
League–Most Free Throws: 4,052, Andy Sears
League–Most Total Points: 5,885, Joe Fogarty
League–Highest PPG average: 17.0, Harry Hough

Season–Most Games Played: 71, 1907-08 Winnie Kincaide
71, 1908-09 Winnie Kincaide
72, 1908-09 George Henschel
73, 1908-09 Bobby Mayham
Season–Most Field Goals: 251, 1907-08 Joe Fogarty
Season–Most Free Throws: 963, 1910-11 Harry Hough
Season–Most Total Points: 1,404, 1911-12 Bill Kummer
Season–Highest PPG average: 22.7, 1911-12 Bill Kummer

Game–Most Field Goals: 38, 1908-09, Bill Keenan
Game–Most Free Throws: 26, 1910-11, Andy Sears
Game–Most Total Points: 76, 1908-09, Bill Keenan
Game–Most consecutive free throws made: 20, 1911-12, Bill Kummer

Individual Summary - 3 or more Seasons

Player	Seasons Yrs	Teams	G	FG	FT	TP	PPG
Jack Adams	1906-12 6	HOM/BUT/UNT/CHR	325	957	2997	4911	15.1
Bushel Beggs	1906-12 4	BUT/GRN/CON	203	504	311	1319	6.5
Mio Boggio	1908-12 4	MCK/UNT	234	473	11	957	4.1
Walter Brady	1906-12 6	PIT	301	589	1381	2559	8.5
Allie Brown	1906-12 6	HOM/BUT/PIT/UNT/CHR	294	501	0	1002	3.4
Jimmy Brown	1909-12 3	UNT	118	332	259	923	7.8
Kid Dark	1906-12 6	GRN/CON	306	609	368	1586	5.2
John Deal	1906-09 3	ELP/JOH	117	380	208	968	8.3
Doherty	1908-12 4	GRN/CON	224	443	0	886	4.0
Doyle	1908-11 3	MCK/GRN/CON	78	155	5	315	4.0
Leon Egolf	1909-12 3	GRN/CON	83	111	0	222	2.7
Ed Ferat	1906/12 5	ELP/UNT/WAS	225	655	74	1384	6.2
Joe Fogarty	1906-12 6	ELP/JOH	365	1275	3335	5885	16.1
Alois Getzinger	1906-11 5	MCK	297	612	164	1388	4.7
Flo Haggerty	1908-11 3	JOH	159	289	8	586	3.7
Jimmy Hahn	1906-09 3	MCK/ELP	121	302	77	681	5.6
Johnny Halsall	1908-11 3	UNT/JOH	114	103	0	206	1.8
George Henschel	1906/12 4	MCK/PIT	182	204	3	411	2.3
Bill Herron	1908-12 4	HOM/CHR	209	223	864	1310	6.3
Harry Hough	1906/11 4	PIT	197	643	2062	3348	17.0
Jimmy Kane	1906-11 5	PIT	201	802	93	1697	8.4
Bill Keenan	1906-12 6	ELP/JOH	319	1104	6	2214	6.9
Winnie Kincaide	1906/12 6	ELP/UNT/JOH	321	331	183	845	2.6
Bill Kummer	1906-12 6	BUT/GRN/CON	282	870	2213	3953	14.0
Kunkle	1909-12 3	PIT/WAS	49	107	12	226	4.6
Harry Liebau	1906-09 3	PIT/ELP	86	202	429	833	9.7
Bobby Mayham	1907/12 4	PIT/JOH	185	218	0	436	2.4
Allie McLaughlin	1906-11 5	GRN/MCK/JOH	299	216	26	458	1.5
George Morris	1909-12 3	MCK/UNT	160	161	0	322	2.0
Chief Muller	1906/10 3	PIT	158	468	38	974	6.2
Fred Mulliner	1906-10 4	MCK/PIT/UNT	215	464	577	1505	7.0
George Newman	1906-12 3	JOH	186	503	119	1125	6.1
Henry Nickel	1906-11 3	PIT/HOM	158	236	4	476	3.0
Chas. O'Donnell	1906/12 5	MCK/UNT	247	472	2	946	3.8
John Pennino	1906/12 5	ELP/UNT/PIT	271	331	40	702	2.6
Bill Powell	1906-12 6	GRN/HOM/PIT/UNT	290	631	32	1294	4.5
Andy Sears	1907-12 5	MCK/UNT	338	799	4052	5650	16.7
Roy Steele	1906-12 6	HOM/BUT/PIT	342	1105	20	2230	6.5
Walter Swenson	1908-12 4	MCK/UNT	97	175	0	350	3.6
Steve White	1906-11 5	GRN/UNT/CON	249	541	2283	3365	13.5
Dutch Wohlfarth	1907-12 5	HOM/JOH	261	811	37	1659	6.4

EASTERN LEAGUE
[1909-10 TO 1917-18, 1919-20 TO 1922-23]

LEAGUE MEMBERS

Atlantic City Celtics	Atlantic City, NJ	1922-23
Atlantic City Sandpipers	Atlantic City, NJ	1922-23
Bridgeport Blue Ribbons	Bridgeport, CT	1919-20
Camden	Camden, NJ	1917-18
Camden Alphas	Camden, NJ	1910-11 to 1916-17
Camden Crusaders	Camden, NJ	1917-18, 1919-20 to 1920-21
Camden Skeeters	Camden, NJ	1921-22 to 1922-23
Coatesville Coats [Highwaymen]	Coatesville, PA	1920-21 to 1922-23
DeNeri	DeNeri, PA	1909-10 to 1912-13, 1914-15 to 1917-18, 1919-20
DeNeri Dudes	DeNeri, PA	1913-14
Elizabeth [Lizzies]	Elizabeth, NJ	1909-10
Germantown	Philadelphia, PA	1909-10
Germantown G's [Germs]	Philadelphia, PA	1919-20 to 1920-21
Greystock Greys	Philadelphia, PA	1910-11 to 1917-18
Harrisburg [Hillers]	Harrisburg, PA	1921-22
New York Giants [Brickey's Giants]	New York, NY	1921-22
New York Celtics	New York, NY	1921-22
Newark	Newark, NJ	1920-21
North Philadelphia Phillies	Philadelphia, PA	1919-20
Philadelphia	Philadelphia, PA	1920-21 to 1921-22
Philadelphia Jasper Jewels	Philadelphia, PA	1909-10 to 1917-18, 1922-23
Philadelphia Jaspers	Philadelphia, PA	1922-23
Princeton Tigers	Princeton, NJ	1909-10
Reading Bears [Pretzels, Rubies]	Reading, PA	1909-10 to 1915-16, 1917-18, 1919-20 to 1922-23
Reading Coal Barons	Reading, PA	1916-17
Scranton Miners	Scranton, PA	1921-22
Sixth Regiment	Philadelphia, PA	1909-10
Trenton Potters	Trenton, NJ	1909-10 to 1917-18, 1919-20
Trenton Royal Bengals	Trenton, NJ	1921-22
Trenton Tigers	Trenton, NJ	1920-21, 1922-23
Wilkes-Barre [Coal Barons]	Wilkes-Barre, PA	1921-22

1909-10 EBL

Although William J. Scheffer's Philadelphia Basketball League folded during the 1908-09 season, he picked up the pieces and was back in business the following year. Using two ex-PBL clubs as a nucleus—DeNeri of South Philadelphia and Jasper AC of the Kensington section of Philadelphia—he added the Sixth Regiment from Philadelphia, the Reading Bears, a strong independent team, and two teams from New Jersey—Trenton and Elizabeth. During the season the Sixth Regiment relocated to the Germantown suburb of Philadelphia and the Elizabeth team was replaced by a team from Princeton, NJ. After struggling unsuccessfully throughout half the season, the Princeton team hired many of the Paterson Crescents who then competed simultaneously in both the Hudson River League and the Eastern Basketball League.

The season was a successful one, with all six franchises completing the 30-game schedule. The championship race ended in a tie and Trenton won three straight games in the best-of-three playoff for the league championship.

	W	L	PCT.
Trenton Potters	20	10	.667
Reading Bears	20	10	.667
Jasper Jewels	18	12	.600
DeNeri	15	15	.500
Sixth Regiment/Germantown**	11	19	.367
Princeton Tigers*	6	17	.261
Elizabeth	0	7	.000

*Elizabeth was replaced by Princeton Dec. 18, 1909.
**Sixth Regiment moved to Germantown Jan. 4, 1910.

EBL PLAYOFF
Mar. 22, 1910 at Trenton - Trenton 34, Reading 18
Mar. 24 at Reading - Trenton 29, Reading 24
Mar. 25 at Trenton - Trenton 33, Reading 24

LEAGUE LEADERS

Regular Season	GP	FGM	FTM	PNTS	PPG
Harry Hough, Trenton	30	92	336	520	17.3
Michael Wilson, DeNeri	30	80	302	462	15.4
John Donohue, Jasper	29	120	195	435	15.0
Howard Thomas, Germantown	28	57	186	300	10.7
Ed Ferat, Reading	30	79	137	295	9.8
Hodge Roland, Reading	30	79	106	264	8.8
Al Glassey, Germantown	30	88	12	188	6.3
Charles Klein, Trenton	25	90	0	180	7.2
John McNabb, Princeton	13	38	84	160	12.3
John Featherstone, Jasper	29	74	0	148	5.1

1910-11 EBL

Shortly before the league's second season, two of their six teams, Germantown and Princeton, dropped out. Fortunately for all concerned, two top independent clubs, Camden and Greystock, were available and were added to the league. This six-team circuit consisting of DeNeri, Jasper and Greystock in Philadelphia, Reading, PA and Camden and Trenton in New Jersey would then compete intact without franchise changes, relocations, league expansions or contractions for the next eight years. Until the First World War caused the league to suspend play in December, 1917, each one of these six teams played complete 40-game schedules every season from 1910-11 through 1916-17. Such league stability was unprecedented in professional basketball, and was not matched by any professional basketball league (including the NBA) in the twentieth century!

Four of the six teams were in contention throughout most of the 1910-11 season. But when Jasper lost their star Fred Eckhardt they slumped, and DeNeri won the league title by a five-game margin. Trenton, the previous year's champion, lost their leader Harry Hough to the CBL and finished last.

The league introduced the concept of recording assists for the first time. Camden led with 195 assists in scoring 359 field goals for the season.

At the conclusion of the season DeNeri met the CBL champion McKeesport team in an unofficial World Series of Basketball, arranged by the players and not the leagues. It turned out to be no contest as McKeesport won handily in four straight games as DeNeri managed only 17 field goals in the series and were outscored by Mio Boggio of McKeesport who had 18 field goals.

William Scheffer's unofficial all-star selections:
Forward - Elwood Gowdy, John Featherstone
Center - John Donohue
Guard - Al McWilliams, Gus Krueger

	W	L	PCT.
DeNeri	28	12	.700
Jasper Jewels	23	17	.575
Greystock Greys	22	18	.550
Reading Bears	21	19	.525
Camden Alphas	14	26	.350
Trenton Potters	12	28	.300

WORLD SERIES OF BASKETBALL
[DeNeri - EL, McKeesport - CBL]
Apr. 1, 1911 at DeNeri (Philadelphia) - McKeesport 33, DeNeri 22
Apr. 8 at DeNeri (Philadelphia) - McKeesport 35, DeNeri 21
Apr. 12 at Pittsburgh - McKeesport 42, DeNeri 22
Apr. 15 at Pittsburgh - McKeesport 57, DeNeri 20

LEAGUE LEADERS

Regular Season	G	FG	FT	TP	PPG
John Donohue, Jasper	39	94	350	538	13.8
Jack Boyd, Greystock	35	58	321	437	12.5
Michael Wilson, DeNeri	36	76	258	410	11.4
Hodge Roland, Reading	36	75	200	350	9.7
Army Fitzgerald, Camden	36	98	141	337	9.4
Howard Thomas, Camden	24	43	235	321	13.4
Fichthorn, Reading	36	54	143	251	7.0
William Reilly, DeNeri	40	69	103	241	6.0
Fred Mulliner, Trenton	21	35	161	231	11.0
John McGraw, Jasper	39	84	37	205	5.3

1911-12 EBL

By reacquiring the great Harry Hough from the CBL, the Trenton Potters went from last to a tie for first—the second time in three years that the regular season ended in a tie. As they did two years previously, Trenton won the playoff for the league championship, this time in a best-of-three series.

	W	L	PCT.
Trenton Potters	29	11	.725
Jasper Jewels	29	11	.725
Greystock Greys	20	20	.500
DeNeri	18	22	.450
Camden Alphas	13	27	.325
Reading Bears	11	29	.275

EBL CHAMPIONSHIP
Apr. 6, 1912 at Trenton - Trenton 30, Jasper 13
Apr. 11, 1912 at Jasper (Philadelphia) - Jasper 28, Trenton 22
Apr. 19, 1912 at Cooper Battalion Hall (Philadelphia) - Trenton 19, Jasper 15

LEAGUE LEADERS

Regular Season	G	FG	FT	TP	PPG
Harry Hough, Trenton	37	90	447	627	16.9
William Hardman, Reading	34	55	328	438	12.9
William Reilly, Jasper	40	69	284	422	10.6
Howard Thomas, Camden	36	35	314	384	10.7
John Donohue, Jasper	39	93	187	373	9.6
Army Fitzgerald, Camden	38	83	116	282	7.4
Jack Boyd, Greystock	30	23	225	271	9.0
Al Glassey, DeNeri	38	54	132	240	6.3
Michael Wilson, DeNeri	27	60	89	209	7.7
Al McWilliams, Greystock	38	61	74	196	5.2

1912-13 EBL

With the CBL's demise, the EBL gained more of pro basketball's best players. Jackie Adams, Jimmy Brown, Ed Dolin and Bill Herron of the previous year's CBL Charleroi team were hired to represent the Camden EBL team. But while Adams led the league in scoring, his team failed to improve upon their fifth-place status of the two prior years. The Reading Bears nipped DeNeri by one game for the league title.

After the season the Bears challenged the Troy Trojans of the NYSL in a best-of-five series billed for "the Eastern Championship." Since each league had its own set of rules, each of the first four games was played by the home team's rules and won easily by the home team. The fifth and deciding game at Reading (the site determined by a coin flip) was played with the first half under NYSL rules and the second half under EBL rules. Significant rules differences included no backboards and few fouls called and the player fouled had to shoot the foul in the NYSL.

Troy led at the end of the first half by 12-5. In William Scheffer's words "There was a vast difference in Reading's play when the second half opened under Eastern rules. The Eastern champions were like a squad of military police coming back from a month's outing in the bushes to city streets again. They tore into the final period with confidence smacking of victory, and in as thrilling a twenty minutes ever waged inside a cage they caught Troy's lead, then went ahead to a margin, although but slight, which swept them into the championship."

	W	L	PCT.
Reading Bears	30	10	.750
DeNeri	29	11	.725
Trenton Potters	21	19	.525
Jasper Jewels	20	20	.500
Camden Alphas	11	29	.275
Greystock Greys	9	31	.225

PLAYOFF SERIES FOR EASTERN TITLE

[Reading - EBL vs. Troy - NYSL]
Apr. 1, 1913 at Reading - Reading 38, Troy 24
Apr. 2 at Reading - Reading 33, Troy 16
Apr. 8 at Troy - Troy 28, Reading 14
Apr. 9 at Troy - Troy 47, Reading 13
Apr. 19 at Reading - Reading 31, Troy 29

LEAGUE LEADERS

Regular Season	G	FG	FT	TP	PPG
Jackie Adams, Camden	34	91	467	649	19.1
Andy Sears, Reading	34	70	468	608	17.9
Joe Fogarty, DeNeri	37	106	364	576	15.6
Harry Hough, Trenton	39	76	301	453	11.6
Billy Kummer, Jasper	29	49	349	447	15.4
T. Thomas, Greystock	21	15	219	249	11.9
Al Cooper, Trenton	35	48	152	248	7.1
Doc Newman, DeNeri	38	97	20	214	5.6
John Donahue, Jasper	40	72	54	198	5.0
Bill Keenan, DeNeri	37	91	0	182	4.9

1913-14 EBL

One of the greatest pennant races in the entire history of pro sports occurred in the EBL during the 1913-14 season. Jasper, Camden and Trenton finished in a three-way tie for first place, only one game ahead of fourth place Reading and three games ahead of fifth place DeNeri. The tie was broken in a round-robin series in which each team met each other twice in a home and home set. This playoff series nearly ended in a tie and was only decided in the sixth and final game when Jasper edged Trenton in Philadelphia. Had this score been reversed it would have set up a sudden death elimination championship series. The third game of the six-game playoff was noteworthy, since Jasper's defense held Camden without a field goal.

	W	L	PCT.
Jasper Jewels	23	17	.575
Camden Alphas	23	17	.575
Trenton Potters	23	17	.575
Reading Bears	22	18	.550
DeNeri Dudes	20	20	.500
Greystock Greys	9	31	.225

EBL PLAYOFF SERIES

Mar. 23, 1914 at Trenton - Trenton 30, Camden 24
Mar. 25 at Camden - Camden 34, Trenton 22
Mar. 26 at Jasper - Jasper 42, Camden 18
Mar. 27 at Trenton - Jasper 24, Trenton 20
Mar. 28 at Camden - Camden 33, Jasper 24
Mar. 30 at Jasper - Jasper 29, Trenton 20

LEAGUE LEADERS

Regular Season	G	FG	FT	TP	PPG
Billy Kummer, Jasper	39	110	477	697	17.9
Jackie Adams, Camden	39	76	507	659	16.9
Andy Sears, Reading	37	76	476	628	17.0
Joe Fogarty, DeNeri	35	69	403	541	15.5
Michael Wilson, Greystock	40	72	397	541	13.5
Harry Hough, Trenton	38	50	412	512	13.5
Jimmy Kane, Trenton	38	109	9	227	6.0
James Brown, Camden	38	98	14	210	5.5
Bushel Beggs, Reading	38	75	20	170	4.5
Dutch Wohlfarth, Jasper	40	82	0	164	4.1

1914-15 EBL

Unbelievable as it may seem, for the fourth time in its six-year history the Eastern league's regular season ended in a tie. This time, however, after splitting the first two playoff games the two teams could not agree on the terms for the deciding game and the series was abandoned.

After the season several rules were changed and future ties were to be settled by a one game playoff at a neutral site.

An innovation in measuring player effectiveness was added for this season. Since teams used designated foul shooters, the scoring champion was usually from among those players. To recognize the contributions of field goal shooters and play-makers, an EBL effectiveness rating was devised which added field goals and assists and divided by games played. Under this system George Steele finished first. Foul shooting effectiveness was also measured this year and Andy Sears led with a 70.2 percentage.

	W	L	PCT.
Camden Alphas	25	15	.625
Reading Bears	25	15	.625
Trenton Potters	20	20	.500
Greystock Greys	18	22	.450
DeNeri	17	23	.425
Jasper Jewels	15	25	.375

EBL PLAYOFF SERIES

Mar. 23, 1915 at Camden - Camden 45, Reading 35
Mar. 24 at Reading - Reading 52, Camden 29
[third game not played, as teams couldn't agree on site]

LEAGUE LEADERS

Regular Season	G	FG	FT	TP	PPG
Andy Sears, Reading	36	71	474	616	17.1
Jackie Adams, Camden	37	66	482	614	16.6
Joe Fogarty, DeNeri	38	95	417	607	16.0
Mike Wilson, Greystock	37	78	421	577	15.6
Harry Hough, Trenton	39	62	452	576	14.8
Billy Kummer, Jasper	22	59	243	361	16.4
Jimmy Kane, Trenton	39	133	0	266	6.8
James Brown, Camden	34	117	30	264	7.8
Roy Steele, Camden	40	114	0	228	5.7
Eddie Dolin, Camden	40	108	1	217	5.4

1915-16 EBL

A tri-cornered "World Series" was attempted between Interstate League champion Paterson, Pennsylvania State League champion Wilkes-Barre, and the Eastern league champion Greystock team. Greystock and Paterson split two games with the third scheduled for Philadelphia. Paterson declined to play and Greystock claimed a forfeit win. Wilkes-Barre then defeated Paterson in two straight games but didn't meet Greystock as "it was too late in the season."

	W	L	PCT.
Greystock Greys	27	13	.675
Reading Bears	23	17	.575
Camden Alphas	21	19	.525
DeNeri	20	20	.500
Jasper Jewels	17	23	.425
Trenton Potters	12	28	.300

WORLD SERIES CHAMPIONSHIPS

[Greystock - EBL, Paterson - IBL, Wilkes-Barre - PSL]
Apr. 7, 1916 at Greystock - Greystock 38, Paterson 16
Apr. 8 at Paterson - Paterson 30, Greystock 17
Third game scheduled at Greystock but Paterson declined to play and Greystock claimed forfeit victory
Apr. 12 at Wilkes-Barre - Wilkes-Barre 31, Paterson 22
Apr. 15 at Paterson - Wilkes-Barre 22, Paterson 17

LEAGUE LEADERS

Regular Season	G	FG	FT	TP	PPG
Jackie Adams, Camden	40	71	527	669	16.7
Andy Sears, Reading	40	70	519	659	16.5
Barney Sedran, Jasper	39	55	404	514	13.2
Michael Wilson, Greystock	35	60	381	501	14.3
Kid Dark, DeNeri	39	86	283	455	11.7
Joe Fogarty, Greystock	32	38	332	408	12.8
James Brown, Camden	39	132	2	266	6.8
Johnny Beckman, DeNeri	34	88	74	250	7.4
Doc Newman, DeNeri	40	95	17	207	5.2
Eddie Dolin, Camden	40	94	0	188	4.7

1916-17 EBL

For the first time the Eastern League went to a split-season format. Five of the six teams won at least 50 percent of their games in each half as last place DeNeri could win but 7 of 40 for the year. The first half winner Jasper lost Harry Hough to a shoulder dislocation in mid-season and were not nearly as effective in the second half. Hough returned for the league championship playoffs but could only manage one field goal in the three games.

Jasper's team featured several of the greatest of the early pro players: Barney

Sedran, Harry Hough, Marty Friedman, Davey Kerr and Jack Fox. Although Hough and Sedran each played professionally for more than 20 years, this season marked the only season in which they were teammates in league play.

	FIRST HALF			SECOND HALF			SEASON TOTALS		
	W	L	PCT.	W	L	PCT.	W	L	PCT.
Greystock Greys	12	8	.600	14	6	.700	26	14	.650
Jasper Jewels	14	6	.700	10	10	.500	24	16	.600
Reading Coal Barons	12	8	.600	10	10	.500	22	18	.550
Camden Alphas	11	9	.550	10	10	.500	21	19	.525
Trenton Potters	10	10	.500	10	10	.500	20	20	.500
DeNeri	1	19	.050	6	14	.300	7	33	.175

EBL CHAMPIONSHIP
Mar. 21, 1917 at Camden - Jasper 30, Greystock 26
Mar. 26, 1917 at Camden - Greystock 35, Jasper 17
Mar. 30, 1917 at Camden - Greystock 23, Jasper 21

LEAGUE LEADERS
Regular Season	G	FG	FT	TP	PPG
Joe Fogarty, Greystock	40	89	576	754	18.9
Jackie Adams, Camden	39	55	547	657	16.8
Sam Curlett, Trenton	40	39	533	611	15.3
Kid Dark, DeNeri/Jasper	39	51	445	547	14.0
Andy Sears, Reading	32	43	424	510	15.9
Barney Sedran, Jasper	38	91	219	401	10.6
James Brown, Camden	40	125	13	263	6.6
Harry Hough, Jasper	17	16	221	253	14.9
Johnny Beckman, Reading	38	92	54	238	6.3
Ray Cross, Greystock	39	106	0	212	5.4

1917-18 EBL
This was a year of turmoil as the United States entered World War I. The NYSL and the IBL both suspended play, but the Eastern league began play in mid-November. On December 3 the league disbanded abruptly as both Jasper and Greystock withdrew without warning. An unsuccessful attempt was made to reorganize with a four-team league and the league remained inactive until 1919-20.

Jasper had the highest percentage in the abbreviated season and was considered league champion even though second place DeNeri had played two more games and won one more game.

A significant rules change provided that the player was who fouled was required to shoot the free throw.

One of Camden's players during this abridged season was future Olympic rowing star, Jack Kelly. He later would become the father of Grace Kelly, movie star and Princess of Monaco.

After the abrupt season ending, Trenton and Camden agreed to play a best-of-seven series for the "Championship of New Jersey," with EBL President William J. Scheffer as referee. The first game was won by Camden 28-27 at Trenton on Dec. 10. Two days later a second game was played at Camden and Trenton was the victor, 47-19, but attendance was very poor. On Dec. 14, the Camden owner, Dr. Helm, called off the series due to the lack of fan interest.

	W	L	PCT.
Jasper Jewels	4	2	.667
DeNeri	5	3	.625
Trenton Potters	4	3	.571
Greystock Greys	4	3	.571
Camden	2	4	.333
Reading Bears	2	6	.250

The league suspended play on Dec. 3, 1917.

LEAGUE LEADERS
Regular Season	G	FG	FT	TP	PPG
Johnny Beckman, DeNeri	8	20	34	74	9.3
Chief Muller, DeNeri	8	20	20	60	7.5
Harry Franckle, Trenton	7	14	21	49	7.0
Doc Newman, Trenton	7	10	26	46	6.6
Mick Posey, Reading	7	14	17	45	6.4
Jack Lawrence, Greystock	7	12	20	44	6.3
James Brown, Camden	5	16	11	43	8.6
Tom Hargraves, Trenton	7	15	13	43	6.1
Maurice Tome, Trenton	7	12	18	42	6.0
George Norman, Jasper	6	12	17	41	6.8

1918-19 EBL
Among the EBLers in military service this season were players Marty Friedman, Chris Leonard, Frank Bruggy, Eddie White and Garry Schmeelk and referee Ward Brennan.

1919-20 EBL
Both Jasper and Greystock remained out of the league when it resumed activity, but they were replaced by teams from North Philadelphia and Germantown. The North Philadelphia team did not make it to the second half and were replaced by a team from Bridgeport, CT—the first Connecticut team to play in the EBL.

Camden won both halves of the season eliminating the need for a league championship series.

	FIRST HALF			SECOND HALF			SEASON TOTALS		
	W	L	PCT.	W	L	PCT.	W	L	PCT.
Camden Crusaders	15	5	.750	15	4	.789	30	9	.769
Germantown G's	11	9	.550	10	10	.500	21	19	.525
Trenton Potters	9	10	.474	11	9	.550	20	19	.513
Reading Bears	8	12	.400	10	8	.556	18	20	.474
DeNeri	10	10	.500	7	11	.389	17	21	.447
North Philadelphia Phillies*	6	13	.316	..	..	....	6	13	.316
Bridgeport Blue Ribbons	..	..	....	4	15	.211	4	15	.211

*North Philadelphia dropped out during the first half.

LEAGUE LEADERS
Regular Season	G	FG	FT	TP	PPG
James Campbell, Camden	37	91	93	275	7.4
Tom Barlow, Trenton	39	75	105	255	6.5
Eddie Dolin, Camden	37	78	66	222	6.0
Liz Powell, Germantown	40	65	90	220	5.5
James Brown, DeNeri	22	81	53	215	9.8
Ernie Reich, Reading	31	70	73	213	6.9
Roy Steele, Camden	37	79	52	210	5.7
Eddie White, Trenton	30	77	53	207	6.9
Nat Holman, Germantown	28	55	89	199	7.1
Dave Kerr, Camden	37	74	50	198	5.4

1920-21 EBL
Camden had the unusual distinction of having the best overall season record (29-11) and not being invited to the league championship series. This was because they failed to win either half of the season, finishing second by one game each time. Newark and Philadelphia were added to the league to replace DeNeri and Bridgeport but, after losing their first five games, Newark dropped out and was replaced by Coatesville. Although the first half ended in a tie, the first place playoff game did not take place until the end of the second half. The ruling was made that whichever of the two teams (Reading and Trenton) finished higher in the standings in the second half would be named first half champions. The two teams ended the second half deadlocked as well and thus the first half playoff occurred after the second half ended. Second half winner Germantown then defeated first half winner Reading in two straight games for the league championship.

	FIRST HALF			SECOND HALF			SEASON TOTALS		
	W	L	PCT.	W	L	PCT.	W	L	PCT.
Camden Crusaders	14	6	.700	15	5	.750	29	11	.725
Reading Bears	15	5	.750	11	9	.550	26	14	.650
Trenton Tigers	15	5	.750	11	9	.550	26	14	.650
Germantown	5	15	.250	16	4	.800	21	19	.525
Philadelphia	7	13	.350	4	16	.200	11	29	.275
Newark/Coatesville Coats*	4	16	.200	3	17	.150	7	33	.175

*Newark was dropped from the league on Nov. 20, 1920 with a record of 0-5 and was replaced by Coatesville who assumed their record.

EBL FIRST HALF PLAYOFF
Mar. 23, 1921 at Musical Hall (Philadelphia) - Reading 27, Trenton 19
EBL CHAMPIONSHIP
Mar. 24, 1921 at Germantown - Germantown 30, Reading 14
Mar. 26, 1921 at Reading - Germantown 30, Reading 25

LEAGUE LEADERS
Regular Season	G	FG	FT	TP	PPG
Nat Holman, Germantown	34	79	127	285	8.4
Frank Boyle, Reading	37	86	105	277	7.5
Eddie Dolin, Camden	38	99	73	271	7.1
Roy Steele, Camden	39	77	71	225	5.8
George Norman, Trenton	36	69	70	208	5.8
Dave Kerr, Camden	38	75	54	204	5.4
James Brown, Coatesville	34	77	49	203	6.0
Eddie White, Trenton	36	77	49	203	5.6
James Campbell, Camden	26	57	63	177	6.8
Chick Passon, Philadelphia	30	40	83	163	5.4
Neil Deighan, Camden	35	59	45	163	4.7

1921-22 EBL
As the Pennsylvania State League became defunct, two of their better teams, Wilkes-Barre and Scranton, were invited to join the Eastern league for the 1921-22 season. Harrisburg replaced Germantown and an eight-team league began play in the fall of 1921. The Harrisburg team played but three home games before selling their franchise to a New York group. One month later the Original Celtics acquired the franchise and played league basketball for the first time. With the season again split in halves, the Celtics won the second half by one game over Camden and

Trenton and then defeated the first half leader, Trenton in a best-of-three series for the league championship—holding Trenton to only one field goal in the final game. A sad occurrence during the season was the death of Celtic Ervine "Ernie" Reich of pneumonia on February 23.

	FIRST HALF			SECOND HALF			SEASON TOTALS		
	W	L	PCT.	W	L	PCT.	W	L	PCT.
Trenton Tigers	24	3	.889	15	5	.750	39	8	.830
New York Celtics***	..	..	....	16	4	.800	16	4	.800
Camden Skeeters	20	7	.741	15	5	.750	35	12	.745
Scranton Miners*	11	11	.500	..	..	....	11	11	.500
Wilkes-Barre	10	13	.435	3	13	.188	13	26	.333
Coatesville Coats	8	14	.364	5	14	.263	13	28	.317
Reading Bears	10	14	.417	2	15	.118	12	29	.293
Philadelphia**	5	15	.250	..	..	....	5	15	.250
Harrisburg/New York Giants***	5	16	.238	..	..	....	5	16	.238

*Scranton dropped out.
**Philadelphia dropped out.
***Harrisburg transferred to the New York Giants Nov. 16, 1921 who were dropped by the league on Dec. 21, 1922 and replaced by the New York Celtics during the first half.

EBL CHAMPIONSHIP
Mar. 31, 1922 at Trenton - New York 24, Trenton 20
Apr. 1 at New York - Trenton 22, New York 17
Apr. 5 at Camden - New York 27, Trenton 22

LEAGUE LEADERS

Regular Season	G	FG	FT	TP	PPG
James Campbell, Camden	45	136	136	408	9.1
Tom Barlow, Trenton	45	127	106	360	8.0
Joe Berger, Coatesville/Wilkes-Barre	38	70	170	310	8.2
Eddie Dolin, Camden	47	101	94	296	6.3
Bernie Dunn, Trenton	45	102	81	285	6.3
Stretch Meehan, Trenton	45	67	136	270	6.0
Dave Kerr, Camden	44	96	68	260	5.9
Gil Schwab, Reading	40	64	125	253	6.3
Frank Bruggy, Scranton/Wilkes-Barre	34	71	93	235	6.9
Roy Steele, Camden	46	89	56	234	5.1

1922-23 EBL

A six-team league began play as Atlantic City replaced the league champion Celtics and Philadelphia replaced Wilkes-Barre. After six games the Atlantic City owners acquired the Celtic team to play for them in Atlantic City but at the end of the first half the franchise dropped out of the league along with the Reading franchise. The remaining four teams attempted to continue the league but after playing only six games the EBL club owners on January 18 decided to suspend the season and attempt to reorganize the following year. The suspension was due to "one-sided races, high salaries and unusual overhead expenses." Before suspending play, every salary claim against Coatesville and Philadelphia was satisfied by the league and the Coatesville franchise was declared forfeited.

After being in existence longer than any professional league of the era, the Eastern Basketball League went out of existence.

	FIRST HALF			SECOND HALF			SEASON TOTALS		
	W	L	PCT.	W	L	PCT.	W	L	PCT.
Trenton Tigers	16	3	.842	2	1	.667	18	4	.818
Camden Skeeters	16	4	.800	2	1	.667	18	5	.783
Coatesville Coats	9	11	.450	2	2	.500	11	13	.458
Atlantic City Sandpipers/Celtics*	7	10	.412	..	..	....	7	10	.412
Philadelphia Jasper Jewels/Jaspers***	5	13	.278	0	2	.000	5	15	.250
Reading Bears**	3	15	.167	..	..	....	..	..	....

The league disbanded on Jan. 18, 1923 during the second half of the season.
*The Atlantic City Sandpipers were replaced by the Atlantic City Celtics who dropped out during the first half.
**Reading dropped out during the first half of the season.
***Philadelphia Jasper Jewels disbanded following the first half of the season and were replaced by the Philadelphia Jaspers.

LEAGUE LEADERS

Regular Season	G	FG	FT	TP	PPG
James Campbell, Camden	23	59	79	197	8.6
Thomas Barlow, Trenton	22	57	51	165	7.5
Bernie Dunn, Trenton	22	63	26	152	6.9
Stretch Meehan, Trenton	22	33	86	152	6.9
Roy Steele, Camden	22	57	31	145	6.6
George Glasco, Coatesville	24	45	54	144	6.0
Elmer Ripley, Coatesville	23	40	63	143	6.2
Dave Kerr, Camden	23	55	30	140	6.1
Louis Sugarman, Coatesville	24	38	44	120	5.0
Eddie Dolin, Camden	21	40	31	111	5.3

1923-24, 1924-25 EBL

The EBL did not reorganize for these seasons. A revived Philadelphia Basketball League featured the Philadelphia SPHAs, but it would be considered only semi-pro caliber.

EASTERN BASKETBALL LEAGUE - 1909-23

Teams	09-10	10-11	11-12	12-13	13-14	14-15	15-16	16-17
Atlantic City	x	x	x	x	x	x	x	x
Bridgeport	x	x	x	x	x	x	x	x
Camden	x	14-26	13-27	11-29	23-17	25-15	21-19	21-19
Coatesville	x	x	x	x	x	x	x	x
DeNeri	15-15	28-12	18-22	29-11	20-20	17-23	20-20	7-33
Elizabeth	0-7	x	x	x	x	x	x	x
Germantown	11-19	x	x	x	x	x	x	x
Greystock	x	22-18	20-20	9-31	9-31	18-22	27-13	26-14
Jasper	18-12	23-17	29-11	20-20	23-17	15-25	17-23	24-16
New York	x	x	x	x	x	x	x	x
N. Phila.	x	x	x	x	x	x	x	x
Philadelphia	x	x	x	x	x	x	x	x
Princeton	6-17	x	x	x	x	x	x	x
Reading	20-10	21-19	11-29	30-10	22-18	25-15	23-17	22-18
Scranton	x	x	x	x	x	x	x	x
Trenton	20-10	12-28	29-11	21-19	23-17	20-20	12-28	20-20
Wilkes-Barre	x	x	x	x	x	x	x	x
Total games	90	120	120	120	120	120	120	120

Teams	17-18	18-19	19-20	20-21	21-22	22-23	Totals
Atlantic City	x	N	x	x	x	7-10	7-10
Bridgeport	x	O	4-15	x	x	x	4-15
Camden	2-4		30-9	29-11	35-12	18-5	242-193
Coatesville	x	L	x	7-33	13-28	11-13	31-74
DeNeri	5-3	E	17-21	x	x	x	176-180
Elizabeth	x	A	x	x	x	x	0-7
Germantown	x	G	21-19	21-19	x	x	53-57
Greystock	4-3	U	x	x	x	x	135-152
Jasper	4-2	E	x	x	x	5-15	178-158
New York	x		x	x	21-20	x	21-20
N. Phila.	x		6-13	x	x	x	6-13
Philadelphia	x		x	11-29	5-15	x	16-44
Princeton	x		x	x	x	x	6-17
Reading	2-6		18-20	26-14	12-29	3-15	235-220
Scranton	x		x	x	11-11	x	11-11
Trenton	4-3		20-19	26-14	39-8	18-4	264-201
Wilkes-Barre	x		x	x	13-26	x	13-26
Total games	21		116	120	149	62	1398

Team Records
League–Most Championships: 3, Trenton
League–Most Games Played: 465, Trenton
League–Most Games Won: 264, Trenton
League–Most Games Lost: 220, Reading
League–Highest Won-Lost %: .568, 264-201, Trenton
League–Lowest Won-Lost %: .000, 0-7, Elizabeth
Season–Most Games Played: 47, 1921-22 Trenton, Reading, Camden
Season–Most Games Won: 39, 1921-22, Trenton
Season–Most Games Lost: 33, 1916-17, DeNeri
　　　　　　　　 33, 1920-21 Coatesville
Season–Highest Won-Lost %: .830, 39-8 1921-22, Trenton
Season–Lowest Won-Lost %: .000, 0-7 1909-10, Elizabeth

Individual Records
League–Most Games Played: 339, George Morris
League–Most Field Goals: 778, Jimmy Brown
League–Most Free Throws: 2,530, Jack Adams
League–Most Total Points: 3,248, Jack Adams
League–Highest PPG average: 17.2, Jack Adams
Season–Most Games Played: 47, 1921-22, Eddie Dolin
Season–Most Field Goals: 136, 1916-17, James "Soup" Campbell
Season–Most Free Throws: 576, 1916-17, Joe Fogarty
Season–Most Total Points: 754, 1916-17, Joe Fogarty
Season–Highest PPG average: 19.1, 1912-13, Jackie Adams

Individual Summary - 3 or more Seasons

Player	Seasons	Yrs	Teams	G	FG	FT	TP	PPG
Jack Adams	1912-17	5	CAM	189	359	2530	3248	17.2
Yummy Armpriester	1920-23	3	RDG	35	46	59	151	4.3
Armstrong	1916/21	3	DEN/GER/COA	10	5	4	14	1.4
Tom Barlow	1915-23	7	TRE/DEN	164	355	312	1022	6.2
Pete Barry	1919/23	3	BRI/NYK/ATC	19	24	21	69	3.6
John Beckman	1915/23	7	DEN/RDG/TRE/NYK/ATC	134	358	378	1094	8.2
Bushel Beggs	1912/20	6	RDG	135	233	80	546	4.0
Eggie Bilson	1912/21	7	GRE/DEN/GER	75	69	11	149	2.0
Blessing	1909-14	5	RDG/GRE	79	98	1	197	2.5
Kidder Bourquin	1910-13	3	CAM	71	95	3	193	2.7
Jack Boyd	1910-13	3	GRE	84	95	696	886	10.5
Frank Boyle	1919-22	3	RDG	97	181	238	600	6.2
Walter Brady	1912-15	3	DEN/JAS	70	91	118	300	4.3
Eddie Bredbenner	1911/20	4	RDG/DEN	56	76	11	163	2.9
Joe Brennan	1920-23	3	TRE/W-B/PHI	14	16	24	56	4.0
Catty Bressler	1910-13	3	RDG	74	160	18	338	4.6
W. Brooks	1909-14	5	GER/DEN/CAM/GRE	111	165	1	331	3.0
Jimmy Brown	1912/23	10	CAM/DEN/COA/PHI	265	778	220	1776	6.7
Frank Bruggy	1909/23	6	ELZ/DEN/GER/SC/WB/AC	69	151	170	472	6.8
Min Calhoun	1920-23	3	COA/PHI	17	22	40	84	4.9
Soup Campbell	1917/23	5	GRE/CAM	136	352	377	1081	7.9
Rube Cashman	1911/20	7	JAS/CAM/SC/WB/AC	152	166	63	395	2.6
Jimmy Clinton	1913/21	4	TRE/BRI/NEW	27	38	4	80	3.0
Cole	1909-12	3	PRI/TRE/RDG	9	23	0	46	5.1
Fred Cooper	1910/15	4	TRE	68	87	295	469	6.9
Ray Cross	1912/23	9	GRE/DEN/PHI/COA/ATC	285	477	158	1112	3.9
Kid Dark	1913-21	7	DEN/JAS/NPH/COA	189	308	888	1504	8.0
Dutch Dehnert	1919-22	3	BRI/DEN/PHI/NYK	39	54	52	160	4.1
Neil Deighan	1919-23	4	CAM	135	171	179	521	3.9
Rich Deighan	1919-23	4	CAM/COA	102	117	150	384	3.8
Eddie Dolin	1912/23	9	CAM	336	725	266	1716	5.1
John Donohue	1909-15	6	JAS	198	439	786	1664	8.4
Joe Dreyfus	1916/23	6	DEN/RDG/PHI	111	165	164	494	4.4
Tom Dunleavy	1915/23	5	GRE/TRE/PHI/COA	84	133	103	369	4.4
Bernie Dunn	1920-23	3	TRE	86	193	125	511	5.9
Fred Eckhardt	1909-15	6	JAS	187	136	0	272	1.5
John Featherstone	1909-13	4	JAS/CAM	85	163	0	326	3.8
Ed Ferat	1909/16	4	RDG/CAM	48	94	154	342	7.1
Fichthorn	1909-13	4	RDG	117	161	168	490	4.2
Army Fitzgerald	1909/20	8	GER/CAM/JAS	186	345	374	1064	5.7
Joe Fogarty	1912/20	7	DEN/GRE	187	405	2096	2906	15.5
Harry Franckle	1914/23	8	TRE/GER/HAR/PHI	202	318	188	824	4.1
Max Friedman	1915/23	5	JAS/NYK/PHI	89	142	29	313	3.5
Lenny Frost	1910/14	4	TRE	99	124	0	248	2.5
Jake Fuller	1915/20	3	JAS/BRI	34	32	5	69	2.0
Alois Getzinger	1911/21	7	TRE/DEN/GER	234	269	46	584	2.5
Fred Gieg	1913-17	4	TRE	112	123	0	246	2.2
George Glasco	1920-23	3	GER/COA	84	144	187	475	5.7
Elwood Gowdy	1909/21	6	DEN/GER	135	269	1	539	4.0
Bob Griebe	1920-23	3	COA	52	49	108	206	4.0
Swede Grimstead	1915/23	5	DEN/NPH/TRE/SC/CM/PH	99	160	59	379	3.8
George Haggerty	1913/23	9	RDG/NYK/ATC	234	240	50	530	2.3
Tom Hargraves	1915/22	6	TRE/DEN/COA	28	37	82	156	5.6
Bill Herron	1912-16	4	CAM	99	61	0	122	1.2
Leslie Hoffman	1915-22	3	TRE/COA/SCR	23	21	33	75	3.3
Nat Holman	1919-23	4	GER/NYK/ATC	93	191	315	697	7.5
Harry Hough	1909/22	10	TRE/JAS/GER/COA	251	441	2287	3169	12.6
Jimmy Kane	1912-15	4	CAM/TRE	105	322	9	653	6.2
Teddy Kearns	1920-23	3	TRE	102	170	78	418	4.1
Bill Keenan	1909/17	7	DEN/CAM/TRE/GRE	124	223	1	447	3.6
Dave Kerr	1915/23	6	RDG/JAS/CAM	185	363	211	937	5.1
Winnie Kincaide	1909/22	8	RDG/DEN/GRE/GER/COA	220	176	14	366	1.7
Turk Kirkpatrick	1909/15	5	GER/RDG/GRE/JAS	102	96	0	192	1.9
Babe Klotz	1919-22	3	DEN/PHI/RDG	58	25	89	139	2.4
Gus Krueger	1909-13	4	DEN/CAM	100	65	1	131	1.3
Bill Kummer	1912-15	3	JAS	90	218	1069	1505	16.7
Jack Lawrence	1913/23	9	GRE/GER/W-B/ATC/PHI	173	247	134	628	3.6
Chris Leonard	1916/23	6	JAS/BRI/COA/NYK/ATC	71	88	134	310	4.4
Billy Lloyd	1914/20	5	TRE/DEN	12	13	11	37	3.1
Bill Lukens	1909-12	3	DEN/CAM	57	88	30	206	3.6
Charles MacGregor	1910-17	7	GRE/DEN/JAS	169	262	43	567	3.4
Leo Malone	1919-22	3	DEN/RDG	49	49	142	240	4.9
Banty Marshall	1919/22	3	PRI/TRE	28	70	68	208	7.4
Bobby Mayham	1909/13	3	TRE	57	51	0	102	1.8
Walter McCallion	1909/13	4	CAM/GRE	116	178	105	461	4.0
Willis McCarter	1911/22	5	GRE/DEN/PHI	50	60	47	167	3.3
John McGraw	1909-14	5	JAS	162	271	48	590	3.6
Ally McWilliams	1910/23	11	GRE/DEN/PHI/ATC	221	276	57	609	2.8
Stretch Meehan	1919-23	4	GER/TRE	100	134	316	584	5.8
George Morris	1912/23	10	RDG	339	369	134	872	2.6
Chief Muller	1917/23	3	DEN/TRE/W-B	35	90	61	241	6.9
George Newman	1912/23	9	DEN/TRE/W-B/ATC	274	585	188	1358	5.0
George Norman	1915/22	6	RDG/DEN/JAS/TRE/W-B	108	191	298	680	6.3
Charlie O'Donnell	1912-18	6	RDG	163	286	1	573	3.5
Chick Passon	1917/23	5	DEN/PHI/ATC	55	63	134	260	4.7
Liz Powell	1916/21	4	DEN/GER/COA	83	108	169	385	4.6
Inky Regan	1919/23	3	GER/PHI	29	26	42	94	3.2
Ernie Reich	1916/22	4	DEN/RDG/NYK	79	159	128	446	5.6
William Reilly	1909-13	4	GER/DEN/JAS	82	143	309	595	7.3
Pete Riley	1909-13	4	TRE	86	192	12	396	4.6
Hodge Roland	1909-12	4	RDG	69	159	310	628	9.1
Garry Schmeelk	1915/23	5	JAS/GER/COA/NYK/RDG	46	121	120	362	7.9
Gil Schwab	1919-23	4	BRI/RDG	65	106	186	398	6.1
Andy Sears	1912-18	6	RDG	181	331	2367	3029	16.7
Barney Sedran	1915/23	4	JAS/NYK/PHI	90	167	546	880	9.8
Cy Simendinger	1915/22	3	TRE/GER/HAR	32	13	16	42	1.3
Roy Steele	1912/23	10	CAM	278	600	219	1419	5.1
Billy Steen	1920-23	3	COA	16	15	14	44	1.4
Lou Sugarman	1914/23	8	GRE/RDG/DEN/CM/PH/CO	213	380	180	940	4.4
Howard Thomas	1909-12	3	GER/CAM	88	135	735	1005	11.4
Kirk Thomas	1909-13	4	GER/CAM	106	143	0	286	2.7
Thompson	1909/17	6	DEN/GRE/CAM	121	170	8	348	2.9
Maury Tome	1916/23	6	TRE	185	259	177	695	3.8
Zip Trautwein	1919/23	3	NPH/W-B/PHI	26	22	39	83	3.2
Weaver	1909-13	4	DEN/CAM	52	18	3	39	0.8
White	1911/18	3	DEN/CAM/GRE/RDG/JAS	30	38	170	246	8.2
Eddie White	1919-23	4	TRE/W-B/ATC	101	227	182	636	6.3
Mike Wilson	1909-17	8	DEN/GRE	221	434	1850	2718	12.3
Lew Winch	1909-12	3	JAS	63	65	0	130	2.1
Skeets Wright	1919-22	3	BRI/PHI	65	82	175	339	5.2
Zahn	1915-18	3	TRE/DEN/GRE	15	14	28	56	3.7

HUDSON RIVER LEAGUE [1909-10 TO 1911-12]

LEAGUE MEMBERS

Catskill Beare-Cats	Catskill, NY	1910-11
Catskill Mystics	Catskill, NY	1909-10
Hudson Mixers	Hudson, NY	1909-10 to 1910-11
Kingston Colonials	Kingston, NY	1910-11
Kingston Company M	Kingston, NY	1911-12
Kingston Wild Cats	Kingston, NY	1909-10
Newburgh Bizzy Izzies	Newburgh, NY	1911-12
Newburgh Company E	Newburgh, NY	1910-11
Newburgh Rose Buds	Newburgh, NY	1909-10
Paterson Crescents	Paterson, NJ	1909-10 to 1911-12
Poughkeepsie Bridge Jumpers	Poughkeepsie, NY	1909-10 to 1910-11
Schenectady Indians	Schenectady, NY	1910-11
Trenton	Trenton, NJ	1911-12
Troy Trojans	Troy, NY	1909-10 to 1910-11
White Plains Lambs	White Plains, NY	1911-12
Yonkers Fourth Separates	Yonkers, NY	1909-10 to 1911-12

1909-10 HRL

John H. Poggi was the driving force behind the organization of the Hudson River Basket Ball League, which occurred on September 18 in Newburgh, N.Y. He served as league vice-president and secretary as well as unofficial public relations man and statistician. Major Albert Saulpaugh, Jr. of Catskill was elected League President. Lew Wachter of Troy and J.A. McQuillan of Yonkers also contributed to the league's organization.

The league's first season was successful both financially and competitively. Teams played in armories having relatively large seating capacities and often drew crowds of 4,000 for several games. Troy defeated Paterson 23-20 on March 9 in Paterson's last league game in Paterson. The Trojans then won their remaining four games to win the league championship by a one game margin over Paterson.

A planned three league World Series among the three league champions fell through when Eastern League champion Trenton could not get their court in mid-April. Troy then challenged the Central League champion McKeesport and defeated them.

	W	L	PCT.
Troy Trojans	24	4	.857
Paterson Crescents	23	5	.821
Kingston Wild Cats	14	13	.519
Catskill Mystics	14	14	.500
Yonkers Fourth Separates	13	14	.481
Hudson Mixers	12	14	.462
Poughkeepsie Bridge Jumpers	6	18	.250
Newburgh Rose Buds	2	26	.071

LEAGUE LEADERS

Regular Season	G	FG	FT	TP	PPG
Toby Matthews, Catskill	27	71	140	282	10.4
John McNabb, Paterson	27	51	118	220	8.1
Kid Eberlein, Yonkers	19	39	100	178	9.4
Bill Hardman, Troy	25	78	10	166	6.6
Jimmy Clinton, Poughkeepsie	18	41	80	162	9.0
Ed Wachter, Troy	17	35	89	159	9.4
Louis Sugarman, Hudson	17	28	84	140	8.2
Frank Hill, Paterson	24	69	0	138	5.8
Matt Love, Paterson	26	52	26	130	5.0
Harry Wallum, Paterson	26	58	4	120	4.6

Unofficial All-Star Team as selected by John H. Poggi

Forwards - Bill Hardman, John McNabb, Jimmy Clinton
Centers - Ed Wachter, Frank Hill
Guards - Ed Roach, John Callahan, Harry Wallum

1910-11 HRL

Drawing an average of more than 3,000 fans per game, the Troy Trojans repeated as league champions in the second season of the Hudson River Basket Ball League.

The second place Crescent AC of Paterson lost only one more game than the Trojans but won three less as the withdrawal of the Schenectady team (who had replaced the Poughkeepsie team) led to an unbalanced schedule. As was typical of teams of the era, the Crescents played nearly as many non-league games as league games and finished with an overall record of 59-11, with all 11 losses coming in league play. Among their non-league victories was a 104-14 rout of the Trenton EBL team.

A new league rule required the man fouled to shoot the free throw.

An attempt was made to organize a national commission of the three major leagues—the HRL, EBL and CBL—but although Poggi and Scheffer were in favor of the plan, they could not gain the agreement of the CBL.

	W	L	PCT.
Troy Trojans	29	10	.744
Paterson Crescents	26	11	.703
Kingston Colonials	26	14	.650
Yonkers Fourth Separates	18	17	.514
Newburgh Company E	16	23	.410
Hudson Mixers	13	21	.382
Catskill Beare-Cats	12	26	.316
Schenectady Indians*	2	20	.091

*The Poughkeepsie Bridge Jumpers were replaced by the Schenectady Indians who assumed Poughkeepsie's 0-6 league record. Schenectady dropped out before the season ended.

LEAGUE LEADERS

Regular Season	G	FG	FT	TP	PPG
Chief Muller, Troy	38	95	48	238	6.3
Bill Hardman, Troy	31	88	34	210	6.8
Sam Curlett, Kingston	39	77	52	206	5.3
Harry Wallum, Paterson	36	95	7	197	5.5
Toby Matthews, Catskill	38	83	30	196	5.2
Frank Hill, Paterson	34	74	39	187	5.5
Jimmy Clinton, Yonkers	32	82	19	183	5.7
Harry Franckle, Kingston	32	68	44	180	5.6
Kid Eberlein, Yonkers	33	77	26	180	5.5
Matt Love, Paterson	36	71	18	160	4.4

Unofficial All-Star Team as selected by John H. Poggi

Forwards - Chief Muller, Jimmy Clinton, Bill Hardman
Center - Ed Wachter
Guards - Ed Roach, Harry Wallum, George Henschel

1911-12 HRL

Politics caused the death of the Hudson River Basket Ball League in only its third year. At a pre-season league meeting Troy, Catskill, Hudson and Schenectady withdrew from the league since the other four clubs did not want to retain league president Albert Saulpaugh. After they withdrew, John H. Poggi was named president in addition to his other duties. White Plains and Trenton were added and a six-team league with a 40-game schedule was planned. After playing but three games most of the Kingston team jumped to play as the Pittsburgh Southside AC in the CBL. Newburgh also lost several stars to the CBL. After eight games the Trenton team dropped out of the league altogether. Meanwhile, the Paterson Crescent AC was also playing simultaneously in the new New York State Basket Ball League representing the city of Cohoes. With all this confusion and distraction the league terminated midway through their season. The cost of high salaries (with some players earning as much as 50 cents per minute) was cited as the cause for the league's demise.

The season was officially ended on Jan. 20, 1912. There was talk of consolidation between the HRL and the New York State League but this wasn't accomplished. Plans were made for Newburgh, Kingston and Paterson to play a series to determine the league champions. The first game of that series was scheduled for Paterson on Jan. 27, but plans were changed and a game between Paterson and the HRL All-Stars was played instead with Paterson winning 46-29. The new Kingston team found a home in the New York State League and continued their season there while the others finished the season as independent clubs.

	W	L	PCT.
Kingston Company M	14	8	.636
Newburgh Bizzy Izzies	14	9	.609
Paterson Crescents	13	9	.591
White Plains Lambs*	8	8	.500
Trenton**	3	5	.375
Yonkers Fourth Separates***	3	16	.158

*White Plains dropped out.
**Trenton dropped out following their game on Dec. 2, 1911.
***Yonkers dropped out.

LEAGUE LEADERS

Regular Season	G	FG	FT	TP	PPG
Ira Streusand, Newburgh	20	37	179	253	12.7
Sam Curlett, Kingston	15	14	148	176	11.7
John McNabb, Paterson	17	19	86	124	7.3
Frank Hill, Paterson	21	36	50	122	5.8
Jimmy Clinton, Yonkers	13	23	74	120	9.2
Walter Lamb, White Plains	15	29	60	118	7.9
Barney Sedran, Newburgh	23	56	2	114	5.0
Walter Brady, Trenton	8	12	63	87	10.9
Jake Fuller, Yonkers/Newburgh	23	42	0	84	3.7
Harry Wallum, Paterson	18	36	0	72	4.0

HUDSON RIVER LEAGUE - 1909-12

Teams	1909-10	1910-11	1911-12	Totals
Catskill	14-14	12-26	x	26-40
Hudson	12-14	13-21	x	25-35
Kingston	14-13	26-14	14-8	54-35
Newburgh	2-26	16-23	14-9	32-58
Paterson	23-5	26-11	13-9	62-25
Poughkeepsie	6-18	x	x	6-18
Schenectady	x	2-20	x	2-20
Trenton	x	x	3-5	3-5
Troy	24-4	29-10	x	53-14
White Plains	x	x	8-8	8-8
Yonkers	13-14	18-17	3-16	34-47
Total games played	108	142	55	305

Team Records

League–Most Championships: 2, Troy
League–Most Games Played: 89, Kingston
League–Most Games Won: 62, Paterson
League–Most Games Lost: 58, Newburgh
League–Highest Won-Lost %: .791, 53-14, Troy
League–Lowest Won-Lost %: .091, 2-20, Schenectady

Season–Most Games Played: 40, 1910-11, Kingston
Season–Most Games Won: 29, 1910-11, Troy
Season–Most Games Lost: 26, 1909-10, Newburgh
                1910-11, Catskill
Season–Highest Won-Lost Percentage: .857, 24-4, 1909-10, Troy
Season–Lowest Won-Lost Percentage: .071, 2-26, 1909-10, Newburgh

Individual Records

League–Most Games Played: 82, Matt Love
League–Most Field Goals: 189, Harry Wallum
League–Most Free Throws: 248, John McNabb
League–Most Total Points: 488, John McNabb
League–Highest PPG average: 7.4, Jimmy Clinton

Season–Most Games Played: 39, 1910-11, Sam Curlett
Season–Most Field Goals: 95, 1910-11, Chief Muller
                95, 1910-11, Harry Wallum
Season–Most Free Throws: 179, 1911-12, Ira Streusand
Season–Most Total Points: 282, 1909-10, Toby Matthews
Season–Highest PPG average: 12.7, 1911-12 ,Ira Streusand

Individual Summary - 3 Seasons

Player	Seasons Yrs	Teams	G	FG	FT	TP	PPG
Charles Biggane	1909-12 3	PAT	57	80	10	170	3.0
Johnny Callahan	1909-12 3	KIN/NEW	57	89	75	253	4.4
Jimmy Clinton	1909-12 3	POU/YON	63	146	173	465	7.4
Cowan	1909-12 3	NEW/HUD	11	16	17	49	4.5
Kid Eberlein	1909-12 3	YON	53	119	146	384	7.2
Frank Ernst	1909-12 3	HUD/YON	66	116	22	254	3.8
Fiske	1909-12 3	POU/YON/WHP	21	34	3	71	3.4
Max Friedman	1909-12 3	NEW/HUD	56	85	13	183	3.3
Jake Fuller	1909-12 3	HUD/YON/NEW	65	90	22	202	3.1
Jud Galloway	1909-12 3	NEW	23	13	1	27	1.2
Harry Haring	1909-12 3	PAT	70	74	15	163	2.3
Frank Hill	1909-12 3	PAT	79	179	89	447	5.7
Matt Love	1909-12 3	PAT	82	155	45	355	4.3
Johnny McNabb	1909-12 3	PAT	77	120	248	488	6.3
Jack Nolls	1909-12 3	HUD/NEW	26	48	9	105	4.0
Morgan O'Brien	1909-12 3	YON/POU/ HUD/WHP	62	82	13	177	2.9
John Otkens	1909-12 3	KIN/NEW/YON	61	81	16	178	2.9
Ed Roach	1909-12 3	YON	73	73	81	227	3.1
Lou Sugarman	1909-12 3	HUD/KIN	51	104	110	318	6.2
Harry Wallum	1909-12 3	PAT	80	189	11	389	4.9
Skeets Wright	1909-12 3	KIN/NEW	41	54	65	173	4.2

NEW YORK STATE LEAGUE
[1911-12 TO 1916-17, 1919-20 TO 1922-23]

LEAGUE MEMBERS

Adams	Adams, MA	1919-20
Albany	Albany, NY	1912-13
Albany Senators	Albany, NY	1919-20 to 1922-23
Amsterdam	Amsterdam, NY	1919-20 to 1922-23
Brooklyn Triangles [Dodgers]	Brooklyn, NY	1913-14
Catskill	Catskill, NY	1911-12 to 1912-13, 1915-16
Cohoes	Cohoes, NY	1911-12 to 1914-15, 1916-17
Cohoes	Cohoes, NY	1919-20 to 1922-23
Fort Plain	Fort Plain, NY	1915-16
Glens Falls	Glen Falls, NY	1916-17
Glen Falls	Glen Falls, NY	1920-21 to 1921-22
Gloversville	Gloversville, NY	1912-13 to 1915-16
Gloversville	Gloversville, NY	1919-20 to 1921-22
Hudson	Hudson, NY	1911-12
Hudson	Hudson, NY	1916-17
Hudson	Hudson, NY	1919-20
Kingston Colonials	Kingston, NY	1911-12 to 1914-15
Kingston	Kingston, NY	1921-22 to 1922-23
Mohawk Indians	Mohawk, NY	1915-16 to 1916-17, 1919-20 to 1921-22
Newark	Newark, NJ	1913-14
Newburgh	Newburgh, NY	1913-14
Paterson Crescents	Paterson, NJ	1913-14 to 1914-15
Pittsfield	Pittsfield, MA	1919-20
Pittsfield	Pittsfield, MA	1919-20 to 1920-21
Poughkeepsie	Poughkeepsie, NY	1913-14
Saratoga	Saratoga, NY	1916-17
Schenectady	Schenectady, NY	1911-12, 1915-16
Schenecrady	Schenectady, NY	1915-16 to 1916-17, 1919-20 to 1922-23
Syracuse	Syracuse, NY	1913-14
Troy Trojans	Troy, NY	1911-12 to 1915-16
Troy	Troy, NY	1919-20, 1921-22 to 1922-23
Utica	Utica, NY	1911-12
Utica Indians	Utica, NY	1913-14
Utica Utes	Utica, NY	1914-15, 1920-21 to 1921-22
Utica-Herkimer	Utika, NY	1911-12

1911-12 NYSL

Organized on October 8, 1911, the New York State Basket Ball League included charter members Troy, Catskill, Cohoes, Hudson, Schenectady and Gloversville. Each team was allowed to reserve eight players. Games were to be played with two 20-minute halves with all teams playing in armories with cages but no backboards. Gloversville, one of the best independent teams in the country, withdrew from the NYSBBL before the start of the season, even though the league attempted to induce them to play by offering them players.

A meeting of representatives of six Western New York cities was scheduled for Oswego, NY on October 8 with the intention of organizing a Western New York basketball league. Basketball fans from Utica, Oswego, Syracuse, Ogdensburg, Alexandria Bay and Troy had their hopes for a league shattered when several teams failed to send representatives to the meeting.

With league play already underway, James Coughlin of Utica was granted a franchise in the NYSBBL with the team to be known as Utica-Herkimer and to play games in both locations as the only NYSBBL team to play without a cage.

The fledgling league was not without violence. Among other incidents, on November 18 Johnny Callahan of Schenectady punched referee Irving Leon during a game with Utica. Mike Roberts of Utica then knocked Callahan unconscious.

The league placed a ban on participation in non-league games with the Gloversville team on December 6. Any NYSBBL players who took part in games against Gloversville would be fined $25 and suspended. Jimmy Conway of Utica was fined and suspended although Bell of Troy, Callahan and Wright of Schenectady and Bradshaw of Utica also played but were not suspended. Referee Irving Leon also was dismissed for officiating a Gloversville game.

The Schenectady franchise was offered for sale to Kingston on January 12. Purchase of the franchise would have entitled the buyer to Schenectady's won-lost record. Manager Fitzgerald of Kingston refused to pay the price and Manager Williamson of Cohoes, seeing the opportunity to raise his team's record in the standings, purchased the Schenectady franchise. Thus, for a brief time, Cohoes was the owner of two league franchises. Then Williamson sold the original Cohoes franchise to Kingston with Cohoes taking Schenectady's place in the standings and the new Kingston team assuming the former Cohoes' team's record. On January 31, as a result of the recent franchise trading, which resulted in the league standings showing more games won than lost, league president Perry W. Decker ruled that in order to balance the standings the Kingston team would be given a record of 16 wins and 16 losses.

Following the conclusion of the season and Troy's league championship, a league all-star game was played at Troy before 2,250 fans on March 29. The teams selected by the Troy newspapers were "All-Americans": forwards Jimmy Davey, Bobby Vance; center, Ed Wachter; guards Andy Suils, Jack Inglis, George Henschel. "All-Leaguers": forwards Chief Muller, Toby Matthews; center, Dick Leary; guards

Lew Wachter, Jimmy Williamson, George Haggerty. The All-Americans won the game handily, 30-18.

1911-12 NYSL

	W	L	PCT.
Troy Trojans	36	12	.750
Hudson	28	25	.528
Kingston Colonials**	24	26	.480
Catskill	23	27	.460
Schenectady/Cohoes**	21	32	.396
Utica-Herkimer/Utica Utes*	14	29	.326

*Utica began the season as Utica-Herkimer but dropped Herkimer from the team name on Dec. 10, 1911.

**On Jan. 21, 1912 the Schenectady franchise was sold to Cohoes who then assumed Schenectady's record. The original Cohoes franchise was then sold to Kingston who were arbitrarily assigned a record of 16-16.

Note: The final standings show more games won than lost as a result of the Jan. 21, 1912 transactions.

LEAGUE LEADERS

Regular Season	G	FG	FT	TP	PPG
Chief Muller, Troy	48	198	39	435	9.1
Bobby Vance, Hudson	53	187	48	422	8.0

1912-13 NYSL

Gloversville was finally added to the league, replacing Hudson who had dropped out shortly after the conclusion of the league's inaugural season. The Catskill team dropped out on February 25 and were replaced by Albany who ran up a 1-5 record before they, too, quit the league on March 28. Ironically Albany's one win (against Cohoes) was thrown out of the final standings becaused they used Cohoes' player Toby Matthews in violation of league rules.

Troy, led by Ed Wachter, Chief Muller and Jack Inglis, won their fourth consecutive professional league championship. The first two titles came in the Hudson River League.

	W	L	PCT.
Troy Trojans	35	13	.729
Gloversville	28	22	.560
Kingston Colonials	27	23	.540
Catskill/Albany*	18	27	.400
Utica	19	30	.388
Cohoes	18	30	.375

*Catskill dropped out on Feb. 25, 1913 and was replaced by Albany, who quit the league on Mar. 28, 1913.

LEAGUE LEADERS

Regular Season	G	FG	FT	TP	PPG
Jack Inglis, Troy	48	180	43	403	8.4
Ed Wachter, Troy	39	141	70	352	9.0
Jimmy Clinton, Kingston	47	120	76	316	6.7
Chief Muller, Troy	39	135	38	308	7.9
Dick Leary, Gloversville	48	125	53	303	6.3
Toby Matthews, Catskill/Cohoes	48	116	67	299	6.2
Barney Sedran, Utica	48	125	41	291	6.1
Louis Sugarman, Gloversville/Cohoes	43	108	62	278	6.5
George Henschel, Kingston/Albany	43	88	71	247	5.7
Peter Lamb, Catskill/Kingston	39	92	53	237	6.1

1913-14 NYSL

Charles P. Stack, the league's secretary added the jobs of league president and treasurer to his duties.

With the addition of the Paterson Crescents and teams in Newburgh and Poughkeepsie, the league expanded to eight teams. Of the three, only Paterson was stable as Newburgh relocated to Syracuse before dropping out in mid-March and Poughkeepsie moved to Brooklyn and then to Newark.

Utica, led by Swede Grimstead, Jack Fox and the "Heavenly twins" Barney Sedran and Max "Marty" Friedman, won the league title by one game and ended the Trojans consecutive championship string at four.

	W	L	PCT.
Utica Indians	46	17	.730
Troy Trojans	45	18	.714
Cohoes	34	30	.531
Gloversville	30	30	.500
Paterson Crescents	29	37	.439
Kingston Colonials	23	41	.359
Newburgh/Syracuse*	18	36	.333
Poughkeepsie/Brooklyn Triangles/Newark**	11	27	.289

*Newburgh moved to Syracuse in Jan. 1914 before dropping out Mar. 18, 1914.

**Poughkeepsie moved in Nov. 1913 to Brooklyn then to Newark in Jan. 1914. Newark dropped out of the league on Jan. 30, 1914.

LEAGUE LEADERS

Regular Season	G	FG	FT	TP	PPG
Louis Sugarman, Cohoes	63	187	164	538	8.5
Chief Muller, Troy	60	184	113	481	8.0
Jack Inglis, Troy	61	185	101	471	7.7
Barney Sedran, Utica	60	177	90	444	7.4
Dick Leary, Gloversville	59	154	106	414	7.0
Bobby Vance, Syracuse	59	159	91	409	6.9
Joe Johnson, Kingston	60	145	107	397	6.6
Jack Nolls, Cohoes	61	145	96	386	6.3
Garry Schmeelk, Paterson	61	143	100	386	6.3
Ed Wachter, Troy	56	111	143	365	6.5

1914-15 NYSL

As the six strongest teams returned, the league seemed ready for another prosperous season. Many of the era'a greatest players were on league rosters, including Jack Inglis, Ed Wachter, Barney Sedran, Tubby Lamb, Jimmy Clinton, Swede Grimstead and Chief Muller. But on January 2, the league drew the curtain on its season. The official reason given were the "heavy financial reverses at Gloversville, Cohoes and Kingston." It was disclosed that Utica, Troy and Paterson would have continued in the league had they been able to convince Kingston to stay. The Kingston team, which had been run by the players themselves for the past two months, refused to continue unless the league would guarantee their salaries. Had they continued, Rome and Oswego would have been offered league franchises to maintain a six-team league. A season-long glovemakers strike in Gloversville was the cause of that team's failure. Plans were made to reorganize the league for the following season. Utica and Troy continued as independent teams playing exhibitions.

	W	L	PCT.
Troy Trojans	19	8	.704
Utica Utes	15	11	.577
Gloversville	12	13	.480
Cohoes	13	15	.464
Kingston Colonials	9	13	.409
Paterson Crescents	7	15	.318

LEAGUE LEADERS

Regular Season	G	FG	FT	TP	PPG
Jack Inglis, Troy	27	78	31	187	6.9
Jimmy Clinton, Cohoes	27	65	51	181	6.7
Dick Leary, Troy	27	55	57	167	6.2
Chief Muller, Gloversville	24	58	38	154	6.4
Ed Wachter, Troy	21	48	49	145	6.9
Joe Johnson, Kingston	23	44	55	143	6.2
Marty Friedman, Utica	26	45	49	139	5.4
Barney Sedran, Utica	24	49	40	138	5.8
Frank Bruggy, Gloversville	25	51	34	136	5.4
Johnny Beckman, Kingston	20	46	39	131	6.6

1915-16 NYSL

The league began play on November 16 in Gloversville. Returning were many of the top pros from previous years, such as Walter "Wabby" Hammond, Ed Wachter, Charles "Blubs" Alberding, Trim McKinstry, Jack Nolls and Garry Schmeelk. The Utica team was led by player-manager Ed Wachter, whose brother Joe was also on the roster. The Troy team featured Wachter's two other brothers, Vic and Charlie, while big brother Lew spent the year in the Pennsylvania State League as manager of the Carbondale team. The Troy-Utica game on December 11 was one of several that season to feature all four Wachter brothers.

On January 3, the Troy franchise was turned over to the league, which replaced them with Fort Plain. The Troy players became free agents and the entire team was signed by Gloversville manager Trumble. On February 2, Hudson withdrew from the league and was replaced by Catskill, who assumed Hudson's record. Three days later, Hudson's management reversed their decision and was allowed to return to the league. In those three days, however, Catskill had played a league game which was added to Hudson's total in the standings.

A Schenectady defeat of Fort Plain on April 8 caused the season to end in a tie between Utica and Schenectady. A best-of-three series was played to determine the league champion, which was won by Schenectady in two straight games.

	W	L	PCT.
Schenectady	26	12	.684
Utica	26	12	.684
Mohawk	23	18	.561
Hudson**	16	20	.444
Troy/Fort Plain*	12	24	.333
Gloversville	9	26	.257

*Troy dropped out on Jan. 3, 1916 and was replaced by Fort Plain; Troy players became free agents and were immediately signed by Gloversville.

**Hudson dropped out on Feb. 2 and was replaced by Catskill; Hudson was reinstated on Feb. 5, but in the interim Catskill had played a game which counted in the standings.

NYSL CHAMPIONSHIP

Apr. 14 at Schenectady - Schenectady 21, Utica 16
Apr. 15 at Utica - Schenectady 21, Utica 18

LEAGUE LEADERS

Regular Season	G	FG	FT	TP	PPG
Jack Nolls, Mohawk	39	90	117	297	7.6
Ed Wachter, Utica	36	64	121	249	6.9
Herman Butch, Schenectady	37	85	70	240	6.5
Trim McKinstry, Hudson	38	75	53	203	5.3
Dave Beaver, Troy/Gloversville/Utica	32	56	66	178	5.6
Joe Evers, Troy/Gloversville	28	76	24	176	6.3
Al Schuler, Utica	30	72	28	172	5.7
Blubs Alberding, Utica	34	68	35	171	5.0
Jim Murnane, Mohawk	40	57	30	144	3.6
Ben Butch, Schenectady	39	55	33	143	3.7
Hass Bradshaw, Schenectady	32	56	28	140	4.4
Jerk Waters, Fort Plain	36	41	56	138	3.8
H. Fritz, Schenectady	34	48	21	117	3.4
Van Vliet, Hudson	38	44	23	111	2.9
Johnson, Mohawk	26	45	21	111	4.3

Note: The above players were the only ones whose statistics were listed by the league

1916-17 NYSL

The league planned to open this season with Amsterdam and Cohoes replacing Fort Plain and Gloversville but on November 11 Amsterdam backed out and the league's opening was delayed a week while a replacement team was sought. The Saratoga-Ballston team was selected (known henceforth simply as "Saratoga") and the league began play on November 23. On December 11 the Saratoga franchise was given permission to transfer operations to Ballston Spa and would be known as the Ballston Spa team for the next eight days until they withdrew from the league and were replaced by Glens Falls.

On January 6 it was reported that Cohoes had planned to withdraw from the league following the next week's games. On January 22 they were allowed back into the league. But the world off the courts was affecting play.

On February 3, headlines in regional papers read, "U.S. severs diplomatic relations with Germany." February 17 produced more of the same: "Nation is Grimly Preparing." Thus, on February 17 league president Edward K. Miller officially suspended the playing schedule, since all teams played in armories which would now be needed for military operations.

The season ended with Schenectady in front of Mohawk by one-half game.

	W	L	PCT.
Schenectady	15	7	.682
Mohawk Indians	15	8	.652
Hudson	13	9	.591
Utica Utes	12	12	.500
Glens Falls	3	6	.333
Cohoes	5	13	.278
Saratoga*	0	8	.000

The league suspended operations during the season due to World War I.
*Saratoga moved to Glens Falls during the season.

LEAGUE LEADERS

Regular Season	G	FG	FT	TP	PPG
Al Schuler, Utica	23	61	47	169	7.3
Jack Nolls, Mohawk	23	48	58	154	6.7
Herman Butch, Schenectady	22	31	59	121	5.5
Ernest Houghton, Hudson	23	34	32	100	4.3
Johnny Callahan, Hudson	23	36	25	97	4.2
Trim McKinstry, Hudson	22	31	21	83	3.8
Pat Doyle, Mohawk	21	22	36	80	3.8
Allie Brown, Utica	23	18	42	78	3.4
Bill Dowd, Mohawk	22	27	13	67	3.0
Charles Biggane, Cohoes	16	21	20	62	3.9

1917-18 NYSL

The league did not operate due to World War I.

1918-19 NYSL

The league did not operate due to World War I.

1919-20 NYSL

After a two and a half year stoppage due to World War I, the NYSBBL was reorganized in October 1919 and came back bigger, though not better, than ever. William H. Hepinstall of Albany led the reorganization efforts that resulted in Martin J.B. McDonough of Troy being elected league president and Louis N. Stolz, league secretary. A ten-team league with two teams in the Berkshire mountain region of Western Massachusetts began play the week of November 10. The league was dubbed the "twin city" league, since each league city had a neighboring one also in the league. The five pairs were: Utica-Mohawk, Gloversville-Amsterdam, Schenectady-Albany, Troy-Cohoes, and Pittsfield-Adams. For the first time the league would play a split season, with the first half ending on New Year's Day. Five of the teams played in nets and four others planned to install them but Schenectady remained netless as "the Schenectady fans preferred the open out-of-bound game." Also, for the first time in league history the league was "Wachter-less" as Lew was manager of the Scranton PSL team, Big Ed was coaching Williams and the other three only occasionally played independent ball.

The league did not permit more than one EBL pro player per team, causing Albany to drop the talented Nat Holman from their team.

On January 15, manager Joe Martin of Pittsfield transferred his team to Hudson, who assumed their 0-5 second half record. Three days later the Cohoes franchise was sold to Pittsfield interests, and Pittsfield assumed the Cohoes record. Ten days later Hudson dropped out of the league because they could not get adequate playing dates in their local armory, since an independent team had a prior claim on the venue.

Forfeits were also the order of the day, with three games forfeited within a ten-day period at the beginning of February due to teams failing to appear. Yet, at a league meeting it was decided, upon threats of withdrawal from the league by several teams, to throw out the forfeited games. Since Hudson was already out of the league all their remaining games were considered to be forfeits. Thus they finished with an official record of 0-36 for the season.

On March 12 Pittsfield was expelled from the league because they refused to pay a $100 fine for their failure to appear for a game in Albany.

The season ended on March 31 and the best three-of-five league championship series between Albany and Troy was scheduled to begin in Albany on April 7. Sites were to be alternated, with a coin toss to determine the Game 5 site if needed. On April 3 Troy refused to play unless the entire receipts from the series were pooled and divided. This did not happen and neither did the championship series.

At the conclusion of the season, meetings were scheduled with representatives from the four major professional basketball leagues toward the creation of a National Professional Basketball Committee to oversee the sport.

	FIRST HALF			SECOND HALF			SEASON TOTALS		
	W	L	PCT.	W	L	PCT.	W	L	PCT.
Troy	14	3	.824	27	5	.844	41	8	.837
Albany Senators	17	1	.844	25	9	.735	42	10	.808
Mohawk Indians	13	5	.722	18	15	.545	31	20	.608
Schenectady	13	5	.722	13	14	.481	26	19	.578
Adams	9	7	.563	14	11	.560	23	18	.561
Utica Utes	5	10	.333	18	13	.581	23	23	.500
Gloversville	5	13	.278	14	17	.453	19	30	.388
Amsterdam	1	17	.056	16	17	.485	17	34	.333
Cohoes/Pittsfield*	3	13	.188	8	16	.333	11	29	.275
Pittsfield/Hudson**	6	12	.333	0	36	.000	6	48	.111

*Pittsfield transferred to Hudson on Jan. 15, 1920 and assumed Pittsfield's 0-5 second half record. On Jan. 18 the Cohoes franchise was sold to Pittsfield interests who assumed Cohoes' second half record.
**Hudson dropped out of league on Jan. 25 and all remaining games were forfeited to their opponents.
**Pittsfield was expelled from league on Mar. 12.

NYSL CHAMPIONSHIP
Albany and Troy named co-champions after they failed to agree on a playoff.

LEAGUE LEADERS

Regular Season	G	FG	FT	TP	PPG
Jack Nolls, Mohawk	47	121	147	389	8.1
Harry Riconda, Albany	46	98	117	313	6.4
Marty Barry, Troy	42	90	99	279	6.6
Marty Friedman, Albany	40	97	58	252	6.1
Wabby Hammond, Amsterdam	40	98	45	241	6.0
Mike Johnson, Adams	34	99	39	237	7.0
Chief Muller, Troy	24	105	26	236	9.2
Ed Kearney, Gloversville	46	91	25	207	4.5
Barney Sedran, Albany/Troy	36	73	58	204	5.7
Joe Evers, Troy	40	89	21	199	5.0

1920-21 NYSL

The league dropped to eight teams as Troy, Adams and Hudson didn't return although Cohoes rejoined. The season was split in halves but not cleanly. On January 28 Pittsfield, with a 2-1 second-half record, played its final first half game against Cohoes. Another oddity during the first half was a 21-21 tie game between Mohawk and Amsterdam on New Year's Day. League rules called for five minute overtime periods, but with the score tied 18-18 at the end of regulation time, 20-20 after the first overtime and 21-21 after the second overtime, the teams agreed to call it a tie so that they could play each other again in the second game of a double-header.

On January 31 Albany quit the league after an unsuccessful attempt to have the Amsterdam team expelled from the league. Albany manager William Hepinstall complained that attacks on his players, and on a referee in a game at Amsterdam, were a sufficient cause to expel them. But the league did not agree on an expulsion, giving the Albany franchise to a team from Glens Falls. By February 10 Albany reconsidered and was allowed back into the league. Glens Falls remained, and the league then had nine teams for a short while.

On February 17 Pittsfield resigned with a record of 6-4. Hepinstall wanted their games to be stricken from the standings, but the league compromised and declared all unplayed Pittsfield games as forfeits.

Sportsmanship was demonstrated in a March 26 game between Utica and Schenectady. After Schenectady lost Joe Lapchick and Herm Butch to injury and were forced to play with four players, Utica manager Fay Inman withdrew Brad Hall from his team and the two teams finished the game with four players per side. At the time Utica was in a close battle with Albany for the second half championship. The season ended on March 30 as Albany defeated Utica 34-22 to finish in a tie at 12-4 each. A one-game playoff for the second half title was held and again Albany defeated Utica 35-16. As Albany had also won the first half, they were crowned

league champions without the need for a league championship series.

After the season Albany played a best-of-five series with PSL champion Scranton, but lost three games to two as the home team won all five games.

	FIRST HALF			SECOND HALF			SEASON TOTALS		
	W	L	PCT.	W	L	PCT.	W	L	PCT.
Albany**	22	6	.786	12	4	.750	34	10	.773
Schenectady	15	12	.556	9	5	.643	24	17	.585
Gloversville	13	14	.481	11	5	.688	24	19	.558
Utica Utes	12	16	.429	12	4	.750	24	20	.545
Cohoes	15	13	.536	6	6	.500	21	19	.525
Pittsfield***	11	17	.393	6	10	.375	17	27	.386
Mohawk Indians*	12	15	.444	2	8	.200	14	23	.378
Amsterdam*	10	17	.370	3	9	.250	13	26	.333
Glens Falls**	..	..	.....	3	13	.188	3	13	.188

*Mohawk and Amsterdam played 21-21 tie game on Jan, 1, 1921. The game was called after the second overtime so that the teams could play second game of a doubleheader.
**Albany withdrew from league on Jan. 31 and was replaced by Glens Falls. Albany rejoined league by Feb. 10.
***Pittsfield dropped out during the second half on Feb. 18.

PLAYOFF FOR SECOND HALF CHAMPIONSHIP
Apr. 2 at Albany - Albany 35, Utica 16

LEAGUE LEADERS

Regular Season	G	FG	FT	TP	PPG
Barney Sedran, Albany	40	99	126	324	8.4
Dick Leary, Utica	42	78	176	332	7.4
Marty Barry, Cohoes	38	85	114	284	7.2
Marty Friedman, Albany	41	83	113	279	6.8
Harry Riconda, Albany	36	52	158	262	7.3
Peter Gilligan, Pittsfield	38	72	85	229	6.0
Jerry Sullivan, Gloversville	40	58	102	218	5.4
Mike Smolick, Schenectady	32	64	98	226	7.1
Jack Nolls, Mohawk	37	56	108	220	5.9
William Kampmeier, Cohoes	34	67	71	205	6.0

1921-22 NYSL

With the return of Kingston and Troy it appeared the league would have ten teams for the 1921-22 season. But manager Hepinstall of Albany, the defending champions, opposed a ten-team league and dropped out. The league started play with nine teams, but transportation expenses became a factor as many of the better players were New York City area residents whose travel expenses to and from home for each game were borne by their teams. Most teams lost money due to "unsound economic conditions in New York State," coupled with high salaries, ranging from $25 to $100 per game per player and the extensive travel expenses.

Although leading the league, Schenectady was forced to drop out near the end of the first half and Gloversville, with the second best record, was declared first half champions. The Gloversville team then began a decline and went winless in the second half. The league championship series between Cohoes, the second half champion, and Gloversville was not held. Gloversville manager Herbert Painter blamed a lack of fan support as his reason for defaulting.

	FIRST HALF			SECOND HALF			SEASON TOTALS		
	W	L	PCT.	W	L	PCT.	W	L	PCT.
Albany***	..	..	.....	11	2	.846	11	2	.846
Schenectady*	19	7	.731	..	..	.....	19	7	.731
Cohoes	17	13	.567	11	2	.846	28	15	.651
Gloversville	20	9	.690	0	9	.000	20	18	.526
Amsterdam	13	15	.464	9	5	.643	22	20	.524
Kingston Colonials	14	15	.483	4	6	.400	18	21	.462
Utica Utes	13	13	.500	2	8	.200	15	21	.417
Troy	4	8	.333	5	5	.500	9	13	.409
Mohawk Indians	7	18	.280	5	5	.500	12	23	.343
Glens Falls**	7	16	.304	..	..	.....	7	16	.304

*Schenectady dropped out during the first half.
**Glens Falls dropped out during the first half.
***Albany did not play during the first half.

NYSL CHAMPIONSHIP

Cohoes named champion after Gloversville refused to play them.

LEAGUE LEADERS

Regular Season	G	FG	FT	TP	PPG
Michael Johnson, Cohoes	42	108	81	297	7.1
Benny Borgmann, Kingston	27	84	124	292	10.8
Dick Leary, Utica	36	63	147	273	7.6
Harry Riconda, Amsterdam/Albany	25	36	163	235	9.4
Marty Barry, Cohoes	30	72	86	230	7.7
Martin Trippe, Cohoes	41	70	63	203	5.0
David Wassmer, Schenectady/Amsterdam	37	62	76	200	5.4
William Kampmeier, Cohoes	39	58	81	197	5.1
Michael Smoleck, Schenectady/Amsterdam	30	57	82	196	6.5
Al Schuler, Utica	34	68	51	187	5.5

1922-23 NYSL

The tenth and final season of competition in the NYSBBL opened without Utica, the only club to have competed in all nine previous seasons. Schenectady returned, while Mohawk and Gloversville dropped out, and a six-team league resulted. A somewhat disorganized schedule had Kingston playing—and winning—many more games than their opponents. They played 42 games while the other team's totals ranged from 31 to 37 games each.

Kingston captured the championship in both halves of the season, making a league championship series unnecessary. In fact, in the four years that the NYSBBL played split seasons there never was a league championship series between first and second half winners.

The NYSBBL completed its season (at the same time the Eastern League folded), but the fans simply did not turn out and the New York State League managers decided not to continue in operation for subsequent years.

	FIRST HALF			SECOND HALF			SEASON TOTALS		
	W	L	PCT.	W	L	PCT.	W	L	PCT.
Kingston Colonials	20	4	.833	13	5	.722	33	9	.786
Albany	11	9	.550	8	5	.615	19	14	.576
Troy	10	9	.526	3	9	.250	13	18	.419
Cohoes	9	12	.429	6	9	.400	15	21	.417
Amsterdam	6	16	.273	9	6	.600	15	22	.405
Schenectady	6	12	.333	4	9	.308	10	21	.323

LEAGUE LEADERS

Regular Season	G	FG	FT	TP	PPG
Benny Borgmann, Kingston	39	136	186	458	11.7
Harry Riconda, Albany	30	48	135	231	7.7
Charles Powers, Kingston	41	65	75	205	5.0
Frank Boyle, Troy/Cohoes	30	48	104	200	6.7
Michael Smoleck, Amsterdam	35	38	120	196	5.6
Barney Sedran, Albany	28	55	68	178	6.4
Ray Kennedy, Amsterdam	31	38	102	178	5.7
Jerry Sullivan, Troy/Amsterdam	31	43	90	176	5.7
Joe Brennan, Troy/Amsterdam/Albany	31	46	83	175	5.6
Joe Trippe, Cohoes	25	42	79	163	6.5

NEW YORK STATE BASKET BALL LEAGUE - 1911-23

Teams	11-12	12-13	13-14	14-15	15-16	16-17	17-18	18-19
Adams	x	x	x	x	x	x	N	N
Albany	x	18-27	x	x	x	x		
Amsterdam	x	x	x	x	x	x	O	O
Catskill	23-27	x	x	x	x	x		
Cohoes	21-32	18-30	34-30	13-15	x	5-13	L	L
Fort Plain	x	x	x	x	12-24	x	E	E
Glens Falls	x	x	x	x	x	3-6	A	A
Gloversville	x	28-22	30-30	12-13	9-26	x	G	G
Hudson	28-25	x	x	x	16-20	13-9	U	U
Kingston	24-26	27-23	23-41	9-13	x	x	E	E
Mohawk	x	x	x	x	23-18	15-8		
Newark	x	x	11-27	x	x	x		
Paterson	x	x	29-37	7-15	x	x		
Pittsfield	x	x	x	x	x	x		
Saratoga	x	x	x	x	x	0-8		
Schenectady	x	x	x	x	26-12	15-7		
Syracuse	x	x	18-36	x	x	x		
Troy	36-12	35-13	45-18	19-8	x	x		
Utica	14-29	19-30	46-17	15-11	26-12	12-12		
Total games	146	145	236	75	112	63		

Teams	19-20	20-21	21-22	22-23	Totals
Adams	23-18	x	x	x	23-18
Albany	42-10	34-10	8-4	19-14	121-65
Amsterdam	17-34	13-26	22-20	15-22	67-102
Catskill	x	x	x	x	23-27
Cohoes	3-13	21-19	28-15	15-21	158-188
Fort Plain	x	x	x	x	12-24
Glens Falls	x	3-13	7-16	x	13-35
Gloversville	19-30	24-19	20-18	x	142-158
Hudson	0-36	x	x	x	57-90
Kingston	x	x	18-21	33-9	134-133
Mohawk	31-20	14-23	12-23	x	95-92
Newark	x	x	x	x	11-27
Paterson	x	x	x	x	36-52
Pittsfield	14-28	17-27	x	x	31-55
Saratoga	x	x	x	x	0-8
Schenectady	26-19	24-17	19-7	10-21	120-83
Syracuse	x	x	x	x	18-36
Troy	41-8	x	9-13	13-18	198-90
Utica	23-23	24-20	15-21	x	194-175
Total games	239	174	158	105	1453-1458

Team Records

League–Most Championships: 3, Troy
League–Most Games Played: 371, Utica
League–Most Games Won: 198, Troy
League–Most Games Lost: 188, Cohoes
League–Highest Won-Lost Percentage: .688, 198-90, Troy
League–Lowest Won-Lost Percentage: .000, 0-8, Saratoga

Season–Most Games Played: 66, 1913-14, Paterson
Season–Most Games Won: 46, 1913-14, Utica
Season–Most Games Lost: 41, 1913-14, Kingston
Season–Highest Won-Lost %: .837 41-8, 1919-20, Troy
Season–Lowest Won-Lost %: .000, 0-36, 1919-20, Hudson

Individual Records

League–Most Games Played: 299, Jack Nolls
League–Most Field Goals: 703, Chief Muller
League–Most Free Throws: 646, Jack Nolls
League–Most Total Points: 1,906, Jack Nolls
League–Highest PPG average: 8.2, Chief Muller

Season–Most Games Played: 64, 1913-14 Maurice Tome, Trim McKinstry
Season–Most Field Goals: 198, 1911-12, Chief Muller
Season–Most Free Throws: 186, 1922-23, Benny Borgmann
Season–Most Total Points: 528, 1913-14, Lou Sugarman
Season–Highest PPG average: 11.7, 1922-23, Benny Borgmann

New York State Basketball League: 1911-23

Individual Summary - 3 Seasons

Player	Seasons	Yrs	Teams	G	FG	FT	TP	PPG\
Blubs Alberding	1911/21	7*	UTI/COH/HUD	95	136	79	351	3.7
Sid Barger	1911-16	5**	CAT/UTI/TRY/HUD	117	77	63	217	1.9
Marty Barry	1919-23	4	TRY/COH	118	258	320	836	7.1
Tom Barry	1920-23	3	PIT/AMS	16	12	21	45	2.8
John Beckman	1913/20	3	KIN/ADM	66	164	119	447	6.8
Herman Bergkamp	1919-23	4	UTI/SCH/COH	104	137	176	450	4.3
Charlie Biggane	1912/17	4	COH	130	148	126	422	3.2
Bowe	1916/22	3	GLF	40	35	76	146	3.7
Frank Boyle	1915/23	3*	HUD/COH/TRY	38	57	106	220	5.8
Howard Bradshaw	1911/21	5*	UTI/TRY/GLV/SCH/AMS	103	110	74	294	2.9
Ray Bradshaw	1912/23	7	UT/AB/KN/COH/TR/SC/AM	92	68	39	175	1.9
Frank Brucker	1915/21	3*	SCH/GLV/ALB	70	127	75	329	4.7
Matt Brucker	1920-23	3	SCH/MOH	43	76	100	252	5.9
Frank Bruggy	1913-16	3*	GLV/HUD	83	210	75	495	6.0
Ben Butch	1915/21	4	SCH/GFL	91	124	57	305	3.4
Herman Butch	1915/22	5	SCH	147	197	235	629	4.3
John Callahan	1911/17	4*	SCH/COH/GLV/HUD	124	215	104	534	4.3
Chamberlain	1911/17	3**	UTI/GLV/FTP/COH	2	1	0	2	1.0
Jimmy Clinton	1911/23	9**	K/CO/HD/PT/U/GV/SC/T	180	420	302	1142	6.3
Cole	1911/16	3**	CAT/ALB/HUD	20	22	8	52	2.6
Eddie Connolly	1919-22	3	ALB/GLV	106	97	107	301	2.8
Tom Cosgrove	1920-23	3	PIT/AMS	66	51	104	206	3.1
Sam Curlett	1911/22	5	KIN	134	240	226	706	5.3
John Dakin	1915/20	3*	HUD/PIT/ADM	11	7	6	20	1.8
Doherty	1911/16	4**	SCH/COH/FTP/HUD	44	68	57	193	4.4
Bill Dowd	1915/22	5*	MOH	104	133	113	379	3.6
Joe Dreyfus	1913/23	5	UTI/COH/PIT/SCH/AMS	68	103	68	274	4.0
Leo Duval	1913/23	6	COH/ALB/PIT/TRY/AMS	117	112	75	299	2.6
Kid Eberlein	1911-14	3*	CAT/KIN	43	100	34	234	5.4
Joe Evers	1913/23	7	TRY/GLV/HUD/COH/SCH	162	321	144	786	4.9
Jack Fox	1911/20	6**	UTI/FTP/AMS	152	210	158	578	3.8
Marty Friedman	1911/23	8*	HUD/UTI/ALB/MOH	197	384	347	1115	5.7
H. Fritz	1915/20	3	SCH	54	70	33	173	3.2
Jake Fuller	1911/15	3*	HUD/KIN	79	97	122	316	4.0
Frank Gill	1915/20	3*	GVL/FTP/SCH	10	11	4	26	2.6
Pete Gilligan	1919-23	4	PIT/HUD/GLF/MOH/COH	106	168	186	522	4.9
Oscar Grimstead	1911/23	6*	TRY/COH/UT/GV/SCH/ALB	123	210	113	533	4.3
H. Grobe	1911/22	5*	CAT/COH/TRY	24	27	18	72	3.0

Player	Seasons	Yrs	Teams	G	FG	FT	TP	PPG\
George Haggerty	1911/22	5*	HUD/GLV/COH/TRY	115	192	55	439	3.8
Brad Hall	1911/22	9**	UTI/MOH	147	118	81	317	2.2
Walter Hammond	1914/23	5*	GLV/FTP/AMS	89	194	86	474	5.3
George Henschel	1911/22	5*	KIN/ALB/NEW/COH	103	147	159	453	4.4
Wm. Hepinstall	1919-23	4	ALB	22	18	23	59	2.7
Harold Hiser	1919-23	4	ADM/PIT/UTI/GLF/TRY	74	129	73	331	4.5
Jack Inglis	1911-15	4*	TRY	136	443	175	1061	7.8
Fay Inman	1911/22	6**	UTI/GLV/COH	54	44	39	127	2.4
Joe Johnson	1913/22	4	KIN/AMS	124	232	264	728	5.9
Mike Johnson	1920-23	3	PIT/COH	88	182	137	501	5.7
Bill Kampmeier	1920-23	3	COH	94	148	199	495	5.3
Ed Kearney	1919-22	3	GLV/MOH	54	101	31	233	4.3
Hugh Kling	1915/21	4*	SCH/AMS	79	40	58	138	1.7
Ray Kennedy	1920-23	3	ALB/AMS	101	141	207	489	4.8
Harry Knoblauch	1920-23	3	SCH/KIN	48	39	44	122	2.5
Walter Lamb	1911/15	3*	CAT/TRY/PAT	69	164	88	416	6.0
Joe Lapchick	1920-23	3	SCH/TRY	61	27	164	218	3.6
Dick Leary	1911/22	7*	HUD/GLV/TRY/UTI	228	523	575	1621	7.1
Chris Leonard	1916/21	3	GLF/UTI/COH/TRY	23	19	55	93	4.0
Ed Long	1911/23	7*	COH/UTI/ALB/MOH/TRY	66	66	55	187	2.8
Al McIntyre	1920-23	3	AMS/TRY/MOH/SCH	49	69	75	213	'4.3
Charlie Mallory	1919-22	3	MOH	81	84	82	250	3.1
Leo Malone	1919-23	3	SCH/TRY	17	23	60	106	6.2
Eddie Mathews	1919-23	4	TRY/AMS/GLF/GLV	113	142	81	365	3.2
Toby Matthews	1911/17	5**	CAT/COH/SYR/HUD/SCH	103	196	107	499	4.8
Hank McDermott	1915/23	6*	SCH/COH/MOH/UTI	137	141	127	409	3.0
Trim McKinstry	1911/22	7*	SCH/COH/FHUD/GL	214	345	217	907	4.2
Ed Mitchell	1919-23	3	MOH/AMS/SCH	6	1	4	6	1.0
Frank Morgenweck	1911-15	4	KIN/COH	10	2	2	6	0.6
Frank Morton	1919-23	4	AMS	12	2	7	11	0.9
Moynihan	1915/21	3*	SCH/GLF	23	36	20	92	4.0
Chief Muller	1911/22	7*	TRY/GLV/HUD	205#	703	278	1684	8.2
Jim Murnane	1911/22	7*	UTI/SYR/MOH	139	169	93	431	3.1
Jack Murray	1911/22	3	GLF/MOH	39	48	57	153	3.9
Hod Nestor	1919-22	3	UTI/GLV/AMS	103	112	183	407	4.0
Fred Nolls	1915/21	3*	MOH	5	7	7	21	4.2
Jack Nolls	1911/22	9*	SC/TR/CO/MO/UT/GF/GV	299	630	646	1906	6.4
Jack Nugent	1912/22	7	T/AL/SY/U/H/CO/AM/PI	180	95	87	277	1.5
Morgan O'Brien	1911/20	6**	CAT/COH/GLV/ADM	84	86	71	243	2.9
Tom O'Neill	1915/23	5*	TRY/GLV/COH	148	115	157	387	2.6
Owl Patrick	1915/22	4*	GLV	26	9	6	24	0.9
Jim Pelcher	1919-23	4	GLV	123	41	111	193	1.6
John Pennino	1912/22	4	KIN	119	65	113	243	2.0
Frank Peris	1919-22	3	GLV/TRY	62	90	45	225	3.6
Babe Petrick	1911-14	3*	UTI/SYR	24	44	12	100	4.2
Al Phillips	1912/20	5*	CAT/TR/UT/FP/HD/CO/PT	45	50	36	136	3.0
Posson	1915/20	3*	SCH/SAR/COH/PIT	29	29	28	86	3.0
Charlie Powers	1920-23	3	GLV/KIN	80	119	161	399	5.0
Harry Riconda	1919/23	4	ALB/AMS	137	234	573	1041	7.6
Mike Roberts	1911/20	5**	UTI/SYR	28	30	27	87	3.1
Leland Schell	1915/20	3*	MOH/FTP/COH/AMS	13	12	10	34	2.6
Garry Schmeelk	1912/22	7*	UTI/PAT/SCH/GLV	109	261	175	697	6.4
Al Schuler	1915/22	5	UTI	159	344	220	908	5.7
Joe Schwarzer	1919-22	3	GLV/MOH	42	54	76	184	4.4
Barney Sedran	1912/23	7	UTI/ALB/MOH/COH/TRY	224	556	428	1540	6.9
Mike Smolick	1914/23	5	COH/ALB/SCH/AMS	116	205	326	736	6.3
Dick Smythe	1920-23	3	AMS/COH	25	29	27	85	3.4
Jack Spault	1913/22	3	KIN/UTI/ALB/GLV	14	8	5	21	1.5
Al Stewart	1920-23	3*	AMS	74	73	106	252	3.4
Lou Sugarman	1911/23	4*	KIN/GLV/COH	118	315	247	877	7.4
Andy Suils	1911/22	6*	HUD/TRY/ADM/UTI	145	89	86	264	1.8

Player	Seasons	Yrs	Teams	G	FG	FT	TP	PPG\
Dewey Sullivan	1915/20	3	MOH	23	26	22	74	3.2
Jerry Sullivan	1919-23	4	ALB/PIT/GLV/ KN/TR/AM	128	187	324	698	5.5
Walter Swenson	1912-15	3	COH/KIN/PAT	48	43	73	159	3.3
Maury Tome	1911/23	5*	KIN	144	223	165	611	4.2
Joe Trippe	1920-23	3	COH	88	140	170	450	5.1
Van Vliet	1915/22	3	HUD/PIT/ UTI/GLF	51	52	37	141	2.8
Bobby Vance	1911-15	4	HUD/COH/ ALB/SYR/GLV	169#	479	212	1170	6.9
Charlie Wachter	1912/16	3*	TRY/GLV	9	1	0	2	0.2
Ed Wachter	1911/23	9*	TRY/UTI/ HUD/ALB/COH	165	374	408	1156	7.0
Lew Wachter	1911-15	4*	TRY	11	7	5	19	1.7
Harry Wallum	1911-15	4*	COH/ALB/PAT	81	141	45	327	4.0
Dave Wassmer	1919-23	4	PIT/SCH/AMS	67	97	140	334	5.0
Jerk Waters	1915/23	6	GLV/FP/GLF/ COH/MO/AM	108	91	132	314	2.9

* = data unavailable for 1 year
** = data unavailable for 2 years
# = Muller and Vance games played unavailable for 1911-12.
Estimates of 48 for Muller and 53 for Vance used to calculate PPG.

PENNSYLVANIA STATE LEAGUE
[1914-15 TO 1917-18, 1919-20 TO 1920-21]

LEAGUE MEMBERS

Carbondale Pioneers	Carbondale, PA	1915-16 to 1917-18
Freeland	Freeland, PA	1914-15 to 1916-17
Hazleton [Mountaineers]	Hazleton, PA	1914-15 to 1917-18
Nanticoke Nans [Nannies]	Nanticoke, PA	1914-15 to 1917-18, 1919-20 to 1920-21
Paterson Crescents	Paterson, NJ	1920-21
Pittston	Pittston, PA	1914-15 to 1917-18, 1919-20 to 1920-21
Plymouth Shawnees	Plymouth, PA	1915-16 to 1917-18, 1919-20 to 1920-21
Providence	Scranton, PA	1917-18
Scranton Miners	Scranton, PA	1915-16 to 1917-18, 1919-20 to 1920-21
Tamaqua	Tamaqua, PA	1914-15
Trenton	Trenton, NJ	1920-21
Wilkes-Barre Coal Barons	Wilkes-Barre, PA	1920-21
Wilkes-Barre Barons	Wilkes-Barre, PA	1916-17 to 1917-18, 1919-20

1914-15 PSL

Newspapermen Byron J. Lewis of Pittston and Michael U. Coll of Hazleton were the prime organizers of this new league in the Wyoming Valley coal-mining region of Northeastern Pennsylvania. Six towns, all within 25 miles of each other, comprised the league. A balanced 20-game schedule was played with most teams using local players. Pittston, who had been the independent champions of Pennsylvania for the past three years, easily won the league title behind league scoring leader John Haston.

	W	L	PCT.
Pittston	18	2	.900
Freeland	11	9	.550
Nanticoke Nans	9	11	.450
Wilkes-Barre Barons	9	11	.750
Hazleton Mountaineers	8	12	.400
Tamaqua	5	15	.250

LEAGUE LEADERS

Regular Season	G	FG	FT	TP	PPG
John Haston, Pittston	19	63	186	312	16.4
Sager, Hazleton	19	38	212	288	15.2
Butch Schaub, Freeland	18	30	184	244	13.6
Al Williams, Nanticoke	16	18	186	222	13.9
Willie McCarter, Wilkes-Barre	15	32	134	198	13.2
Fulmer, Tamaqua	15	39	51	129	8.6
Merle Harris, Pittston	19	63	0	126	6.6
Welsh, Freeland	18	47	6	100	5.6
Sassaman, Tamaqua	16	36	25	97	6.1
John Deal, Tamaqua	7	5	84	94	13.4

1915-16 PSL

Changes for the PSL's second season included withdrawal of the Tamaqua team and expansion to Scranton, Carbondale and Plymouth (still continuing along present-day Interstate 81) and a more ambitious 42-game schedule. A close six-team race was won by Wilkes-Barre. Financially, the league prospered, even though a trolley strike during the season hindered travel. After the season an inter-league series was played with Wilkes-Barre defeating the Interstate League champion Paterson Crescents twice. A subsequent series with the Eastern League champion Greystock team was not played due to failure of the teams to agree on terms for the games.

	W	L	PCT.
Wilkes-Barre Barons	29	13	.690
Freeland	25	17	.595
Carbondale Pioneers	24	18	.571
Nanticoke Nans	24	18	.571
Scranton Miners	22	20	.524
Pittston	18	24	.429
Hazleton Mountaineers	17	25	.405
Plymouth Shawnees	9	33	.214

WORLD SERIES CHAMPIONSHIPS

[Greystock: EBL, Paterson: IBL, Wilkes-Barre: PSL]
Apr. 7, 1916 at Philadelphia - Greystock 38, Paterson 16
Apr. 8 at Paterson - Paterson 30, Greystock 17
Apr. 12 at Wilkes-Barre - Wilkes-Barre 31, Paterson 22
Apr. 15 at Paterson - Wilkes-Barre 22, Paterson 17

LEAGUE LEADERS

Regular Season	G	FG	FT	TP	PPG
Sam Curlett, Wilkes-Barre	42	74	608	756	18.0
Novak, Freeland	42	45	575	665	15.8
Jack Inglis, Carbondale	41	130	192	452	11.0
Bill Clarke, Pittston	42	30	351	411	9.8
Pat Doyle, Scranton/Hazleton	28	43	294	380	13.6
Gilpin, Scranton	27	26	306	358	13.3
Sager, Hazleton/Pittston	33	63	211	337	10.2
Bobby Vance, Hazleton	24	59	217	335	14.0
Dick Leary, Nanticoke	42	86	79	251	6.0
Jimmy Kane, Scranton	37	102	28	232	6.3

1916-17 PSL

All eight teams returned for the 40-game schedule but Freeland dropped out after playing only part of their season. No longer did the purely local atmosphere prevail, as teams recruited players from the EBL and NYSL. Several well-known professionals such as Jack Inglis, Chief Muller, Garry Schmeelk, Elmer Ripley and Swede Grimstead were among those playing in the PSL and other professional leagues this season. Carbondale easily won the league championship with a 33-7 mark.

	W	L	PCT.
Carbondale Pioneers	33	7	.825
Wilkes-Barre Barons	28	12	.700
Nanticoke Nans	26	14	.650
Pittston	24	17	.585
Hazleton Mountaineers	17	23	.425
Plymouth Shawnees	15	25	.375
Scranton Miners	9	32	.220
Freeland	4	26	.133

LEAGUE LEADERS

Regular Season	G	FG	FT	TP	PPG
Jack Inglis, Carbondale	39	129	133	391	10.0
Chief Muller, Nanticoke	39	109	103	321	8.2
Garry Schmeelk, Pittston	40	102	109	313	7.8
Merle Harris, Pittston	37	80	152	312	8.4
Al McIntyre, Carbondale	39	97	85	279	7.2
Dick Leary, Nanticoke	40	75	122	272	6.8
Elmer Ripley, Carbondale	39	75	110	260	6.7
Oscar Grimstead, Plymouth	39	83	92	258	6.6
Willie McCarter, Wilkes-Barre	40	40	155	235	5.9
Haire, Plymouth	40	77	75	229	5.7

1917-18 PSL

Due to the United States' involvement in World War I, the Eastern Basketball League suspended play in December 1917 and the New York State and Interstate Leagues did not even start their seasons. But the Pennsylvania State League managed to play a complete season. With no other major professional leagues competing for players, the PSL attracted many of the era's top pros including the legendary Barney Sedran and Harry Hough. For the first time the league divided the season in two halves with the winners, Pittston and Hazleton, meeting for the league title. Providence, which replaced Freeland, was not able to start the second half and Carbondale and Scranton dropped out during the second half.

	FIRST HALF			SECOND HALF			SEASON TOTALS		
	W	L	PCT.	W	L	PCT.	W	L	PCT.
Providence*	19	8	.704	..	..	....	19	8	.704
Pittston	22	6	.786	7	11	.389	29	17	.630
Plymouth Shawnees	18	10	.643	7	12	.368	25	22	.532
Nanticoke Nans	9	18	.333	14	6	.700	23	24	.489
Wilkes-Barre Barons	12	14	.462	10	9	.526	22	23	.489
Hazleton Mountaineers	7	21	.250	15	5	.750	22	26	.458
Scranton Miners**	11	15	.423	4	9	.308	15	24	.385
Carbondale**	11	17	.393	4	9	.308	15	26	.366

*Providence dropped out during the first half.
**Carbondale and Scranton dropped out during the second half.

PSL CHAMPIONSHIP
Pittston defeated Hazleton 3 games to 1

LEAGUE LEADERS

Regular Season	G	FG	FT	TP	PPG
Dick Leary, Plymouth/Hazleton	46	80	135	295	6.4
Merle Harris, Pittston	44	74	143	291	6.6
Joseph Berger, Plymouth	42	71	135	277	6.6
Jimmy Kane, Scranton/Wikes-Barre	35	77	122	276	7.9
Barney Sedran, Carbondale/Wilkes-Barre	45	87	84	258	5.7
Garry Schmeelk, Pittston	37	93	69	255	6.9
Frank Bruggy, Providence/Scranton	36	80	94	254	7.1
Frank Boyle, Providence/Plymouth	36	73	102	248	6.9
Willie McCarter, Nanticoke/Hazleton	44	52	141	245	5.6
Chief Muller, Wilkes-Barre	31	78	88	244	7.9

1918-19 PSL
The league suspended play due to World War I.

1919-20 PSL

Prior to the start of the season Thomas J. Brislin took over the league presidency with William B. Loftus as secretary. Scranton returned but Hazleton didn't and the league remained at five members. Carbondale applied for membership but was unable to find a suitable place to play. The split season format was used again with Scranton and Nanticoke finishing in the top two positions in both halves.

	FIRST HALF			SECOND HALF			SEASON TOTALS		
	W	L	PCT.	W	L	PCT.	W	L	PCT.
Nanticoke Nans	16	8	.667	16	7	.696	32	15	.681
Scranton Miners	18	6	.750	14	10	.583	32	16	.667
Pittston	13	11	.542	14	10	.583	27	21	.562
Wilkes-Barre Barons	7	17	.292	12	11	.522	19	28	.404
Plymouth Shawnees	6	18	.250	3	21	.125	9	39	.188

PSL CHAMPIONSHIP
Mar. 29, 1920 at Scranton - Scranton 30, Nanticoke 23
Mar. 30 at Nanticoke - Nanticoke 42, Scranton 30
April 5 at Scranton - Nanticoke 23, Scranton 18
April 6 at Nanticoke - Nanticoke 32, Scranton 31

LEAGUE LEADERS

Regular Season	G	FG	FT	TP	PPG
John Beckman, Nanticoke	38	101	144	346	9.1
Frank Bruggy, Scranton	44	103	117	323	7.3
Frank Boyle, Pittston/Nanticoke	39	77	119	273	7.0
Garry Schmeelk, Pittston	45	97	62	256	5.7
Dick Leary, Nanticoke	42	65	109	239	5.7
Elmer Ripley, Scranton	43	67	89	223	5.2
Chris Leonard, Pittston	41	41	125	207	5.0
Leo Malone, Wilkes-Barre	29	56	86	198	6.8
Merle Harris, Pittston	34	55	87	197	5.8
Stretch Meehan, Scranton	42	47	96	190	4.5

1920-21 PSL

The Paterson Crescents joined the league for the first half but dropped out before the half ended. Plymouth replaced them for the second half but they, too, couldn't complete the full schedule. Pittston, the first half winners, met second-half winner Scranton for the league championship.

	FIRST HALF			SECOND HALF			SEASON TOTALS		
	W	L	PCT.	W	L	PCT.	W	L	PCT.
Trenton**	..	..	....	3	0	1.000	3	0	1.000
Scranton Miners	13	11	.542	12	5	.706	25	16	.610
Wilkes-Barre Barons	14	10	.583	8	6	.571	22	16	.579
Pittston	14	10	.583	6	8	.429	20	18	.526
Nanticoke Nans	10	14	.417	11	6	.647	21	20	.512
Paterson Crescents*	3	9	.250	..	..	....	3	9	.250
Plymouth Shawnees	..	..	....	0	12	.000	0	12	.000

*Paterson was dropped by the league on Dec. 14, 1920 for refusing to pay a $100 fine assessed for non-appearance in Wilkes-Barre for a scheduled game on Dec. 8.
**Joey Manze former part owner of the Trenton EBL franchise was awarded a PSL franchise on March 6, 1920. His Trenton team played their first PSL game on March 10, defeating Pittston 26-24 in overtime at Trenton. They then played and won two more PSL games defeating Pittston again on March 11, 1920, 30-25, and defeating Wilkes-Barre 32-20 on March 17. They are not included in the "official" league standings but the games were billed as regular Pennsylvania State League games.

PSL FIRST HALF PLAYOFF
Scranton defeated Wilkes-Barre in a one-game playoff

PSL CHAMPIONSHIP
Scranton defeated Pittston 2 games to 0

LEAGUE LEADERS

Regular Season	G	FG	FT	TP	PPG
John Beckman, Nanticoke	40	84	193	361	9.0
Joseph Berger, Scranton/Plymouth	34	65	129	259	7.6
Elmer Ripley, Scranton	40	64	127	255	6.4
Leo Malone, Wilkes-Barre	36	49	137	235	6.5
Chris Leonard, Pittston	36	42	145	229	6.4
Garry Schmeelk, Pittston	30	76	66	218	7.3
Dutch Dehnert, Scranton	33	60	78	198	6.0
Merle Harris, Pittston	34	53	90	196	5.8
Doc Newman, Wilkes-Barre	30	68	55	191	6.4
Frank Bruggy, Scranton	30	56	61	173	5.8

1921-22 PSL

Prior to the start of this season the league disbanded with Scranton and Wilkes-Barre joining the Eastern League.

PENNSYLVANIA BASKETBALL LEAGUE: 1914-21

Teams	14-15	15-16	16-17	17-18	18-19	19-20	20-21	Totals
Carbondale	x	24-18	33-7	15-26	N	x	x	72-51
Freeland	11-9	25-17	4-26	x	O	x	x	40-52
Hazleton	8-12	17-25	17-23	22-26		x	x	64-86
Nanticoke	9-11	24-18	26-14	23-24	L	32-15	21-20	135-102
Paterson	x	x	x	x	E	x	3-9	3-9
Pittston	18-2	18-24	24-17	29-17	A	27-21	20-18	136-99
Plymouth	x	9-33	15-25	25-22	G	9-39	0-12	58-131
Providence	x	x	x	19-8	U	x	x	19-8
Scranton	x	22-20	9-32	15-24	E	32-16	25-16	103-108
Tamaqua	5-15	x	x	x		x	x	5-15
Wilkes-Barre	9-11	29-13	28-12	22-23		19-28	22-16	129-103
Total games played	60	168	156	170	0	119	91	764

Team Records

League–Most Championships: 2, Pittston
League–Most Games Played: 237, Nanticoke
League–Most Games Won: 136, Pittston
League–Most Games Lost: 131, Plymouth
League–Highest Won-Lost Percentage: .704, 19-8, Providence
League–Lowest Won-Lost Percentage: .250, 3-9, Paterson
                                   .250, 5-15, Tamaqua

Season–Most Games Played: 48, 1917-18, Hazleton
                          48, 1919-20, Scranton
                          48, 1919-20, Pittston
Season–Most Games Won, 33, 1916-17, Carbondale
Season–Most Games Lost, 39, 1919-20, Plymouth
Season–Highest Won-Lost Percentage .900, 18-2, 1914-15, Pittston
Season–Lowest Won-Lost Percentage, .000, 0-12, 1920-21, Plymouth

Individual Records

League–Most Games Played: 217, Butch Schaub
League–Most Field Goals: 373, Merle Harris
League–Most Free Throws: 549, Butch Schaub
League–Most Total Points: 1,218, Merle Harris
League–Highest PPG average: 13.3, John Haston

Season–Most Games Played: 47, 1917-18, Oscar Grimsteadt
Season–Most Field Goals: 130, 1915-16, Jack Inglis
Season–Most Free Throws: 608, 1915-16, Sam Curlett
Season–Most Total Points: 756, 1915-16, Sam Curlett
Season–Highest PPG average: 18.0, 1915-16, Sam Curlett

Individual Summary - 3 or more Seasons

Player	Seasons Yrs		Teams	G	FG	FT	TP	PPG
John Beckman	1917-21	3	NAN	98	242	448	932	9.5
Joe Berger	1914-21	6	W-B/PLY/SCR/PIT	176	272	437	981	5.6
Herman Bergkamp	1916-20	3	HAZ/PLY/PIT	113	93	127	313	2.8
Boczkowski	1914-17	3	FRE	57	51	2	104	1.8
Frank Boyle	1917-21	3	PRO/PIT/NAN	85	163	237	563	6.6
Brogan	1914-17	3	FRE	42	22	4	48	1.1
Frank Bruggy	1917-21	3	PRO/SCR	110	239	272	750	6.8
Bill Clarke	1914-17	3	PIT	66	50	390	490	7.4
Lou Coopey	1914-21	6	NAN/W-B	173	219	267	705	4.1
Davis	1916-20	3	PLY/PRO/SCR/NAN	27	34	59	127	4.7
Joe Dreyfus	1916-21	3	SCR/PIT/PLY	11	18	14	50	4.5
Tommy Dunleavy	1916-21	4	W-B	90	164	127	455	5.1
Bernie Dunn	1914-21	5	PIT/W-B	162	216	178	610	3.8
Clarence Foster	1914-21	5	W-B	157	158	191	507	3.2
Hobby Fyfe	1916-20	3	PIT	69	125	123	373	5.4
Oscar Grimstead	1916-21	4	PLY/PIT/NAN/SCR	132	210	194	614	4.7
Merle Harris	1914-21	6	PIT	204	373	472	1218	6.0
Stan Bucky Harris	1915-21	5	PIT	141	167	264	598	4.2
Nick Harvey	1917-21	3	PRO/SCR	118	133	85	351	3.0
John Haston	1914-20	3	PIT	25	69	194	332	13.3
Hughes	1915-20	3	PLY	33	28	16	72	2.2
Hughes	1914-20	3	HAZ/W-B	27	16	6	38	1.4
Johnson	1914-17	3	FRE	60	100	2	202	3.4
Jimmy Kane	1915-18	3	SCR/W-B	94	237	219	693	7.4
Dick Leary	1915-20	4	NAN/PLY/HAZ	170	306	445	1057	6.2
Chris Leonard	1916-21	3	HAZ/PIT	79	84	279	447	5.7
MacLachlan	1914-17	3	PIT/PLY	95	60	27	147	1.5
Jim Mahon	1915-20	3	CAR/SCR	88	157	65	379	4.3
Leo Malone	1916-21	4	SCR/W-B	114	157	375	689	6.0
Margie	1916-21	3	PIT	21	19	28	66	3.1
Willis McCarter	1914-20	5	W-B/NAN/HAZ/PIT	164	210	462	882	5.4
Al McIntyre	1915-18	3	CAR	61	128	120	376	6.2
Chief Muller	1916-21	3	NAN/W-B	73	195	197	587	8.0
John Nolan	1916-21	3	CAR/W-B	64	118	45	281	4.4
Jack Nolls	1915-18	3	SCR/HAZ/PIT	100	176	146	498	5.0
Pfaff	1915-21	5	HAZ/W-B/NAN	132	168	140	476	3.6
Elmer Ripley	1915-21	5	CAR/W-B/SCR	179	288	415	991	5.5
Russell	1915-18	3	HAZ	99	72	64	208	2.1
Butch Schaub	1914-21	6	FRE/HAZ/NAN	217	243	549	1035	4.8
Schimmel	1915-21	4	NAN	91	42	62	146	1.6
Garry Schmeelk	1916-21	4	PIT	152	368	306	1042	6.9
Simmers	1915-21	4	PLY/W-B/NAN	10	6	13	25	2.5
Dick Smythe	1916-21	4	HAZ/PLY/PIT/W-B	100	190	145	525	5.3
Lou Sugarman	1917-21	3	CAR/W-B/PLY	45	79	61	219	4.9
Andy Suils	1915-21	4	CAR/PLY/PIT	120	63	55	181	1.5
Welsh	1914-17	3	FRE	83	134	43	311	3.7

INTERSTATE BASKET BALL LEAGUE
[1915-16 TO 1916-17, 1919-20]

LEAGUE MEMBERS

Ansonia Wrightlets	Ansonia, CT	1919-20
Bridgeport Blue Ribbons	Bridgeport, CT	1916-17, 1919-20
Brooklyn Trolley Dodgers [Dodgers]	Brooklyn, NY	1915-16
Brooklyn Dodgers	Brooklyn, NY	1919-20
Danbury Hatters	Danbury, CT	1916-17
Elizabeth	Elizabeth, NJ	1915-16
Elizabeth Bessies	Elizabeth, NJ	1915-16
Hoboken G's	Hoboken, NJ	1916-17
Jersey City Saints	Jersey City, NJ	1915-16
Jersey City Skeeters [St. Aedans, Saints]	Jersey City, NJ	1916-17, 1919-20
Kingston Pathfinders	Kingston, NY	1915-16
National Turners	Newark, NJ	1916-17
New York Cathedral Separate Five	New York, NY	1916-17
New York Treat 'em Roughs	New York, NY	1919-20
Newark Nationals	Newark, NJ	1919-20
Newark Turners	Newark, NJ	1916-17
North Hudson	Elizabeth, NJ	1915-16
Passaic Athletic Association	Passaic, NJ	1919-20
Paterson Crescents	Paterson, NJ	1915-16 to 1916-17
Paterson Silk Sox	Paterson, NJ	1920-21
Stamford	Stamford, CT	1915-16 to 1916-17
Troys of North Hudson	Union City, NJ	1915-16

1915-16 IBL

Organized by John J. O'Brien in 1915, the Interstate Basket Ball League placed teams in Stamford, CT; Brooklyn and Kingston, NY; and Jersey City, Paterson and Elizabeth, NJ. League play commenced on October 28, 1915. Elizabeth struggled early in the season and was replaced by North Hudson. North Hudson, however, refused to accept the 2-11 record of Elizabeth and the season was then split.

Kingston defeated Brooklyn 26-24 on the final day of the first half of the season to finish a game ahead of Jersey City. Kingston promptly applied to relocate to Elizabeth for the second half, citing increased rail travel as their reason. The move was granted and the league was awarded a new replacement franchise to North Hudson. Elizabeth continued to struggle financially, and the team was bought out by the North Hudson club, as the team continued to play in North Hudson with the league placing a new club in Elizabeth (their third IBL club in the inaugural season).

Paterson finished 13-4 in the second half to set up a playoff with Kingston (which had finished the season in North Hudson), as Paterson won the best-of-five series three games to two to win the IBL championship, a first for Paterson in pro league play.

	FIRST HALF			SECOND HALF			SEASON TOTALS		
	W	L	PCT.	W	L	PCT.	W	L	PCT.
Jersey City Skeeters	13	6	.684	12	6	.667	25	12	.676
Paterson Crescents	10	10	.500	13	4	.765	23	14	.622
Kingston Pathfinders/									
Elizabeth/North Hudson*	14	5	.737	6	9	.400	20	14	.588
Stamford	11	7	.611	7	9	.438	18	16	.529
Elizabeth***	..	..	....	2	6	.250	2	6	.250
Brooklyn Trolley Dodgers	6	12	.333	5	11	.312	11	23	.323
Elizabeth/North Hudson**	2	16	.125	..	..	....	2	16	.125

*Kingston moved to the Elizabeth Bessies Jan. 5, 1916 for the second half, and then where bought out by North Hudson in Jan. 1916.
**Elizabeth dropped out of the league Dec. 16, 1915 during the first half to operate as an independent team and was replaced by North Hudson.
***The Elizabeth franchise was commissioned by the league to replace the Elizabeth franchise that was purchased by North Hudson.

IBL CHAMPIONSHIP
Mar. 18, 1916 at Paterson - Paterson 24, Kingston 23
Mar. 23 at Jersey City - Kingston 13, Paterson 10
Mar. 25 at Paterson - Paterson 27, Kingston 25
Mar. 30 at Jersey City - Kingston 16, Paterson 14
Apr. 6 at Jersey City - Paterson 23, Kingston 17

WORLD SERIES CHAMPIONSHIPS
[Greystock - EBL, Paterson - IBL, Wilkes-Barre - PSL]
Apr. 7, 1916 at Philadelphia - Greystock 38, Paterson 16
Apr. 8 at Paterson - Paterson 30, Greystock 17
Apr. 12 at Wilkes-Barre - Wilkes-Barre 31, Paterson 22
Apr. 15 at Paterson - Wilkes-Barre 22, Paterson 17

LEAGUE LEADERS

Regular Season	G	FG	FT	TP	PPG
Chief Muller, Jersey City	35	87	98	272	7.8
Garry Schmeelk, Brooklyn	29	104	62	270	9.3
Joe Johnson, Kingston/North Hudson	35	81	79	241	6.9
George Norman, Stamford	33	72	75	219	6.6
Frank Bruggy, Kingston/North Hudson	33	72	74	218	6.6
George Smith, Stamford	32	76	54	206	6.4
Ernie Reich, Jersey City	36	72	58	202	5.6
Maurice Tome, Kingston/North Hudson	35	73	56	202	5.8
George Henschel, Kingston/North Hudson	34	64	65	193	5.7
Walter Swenson, Paterson	33	60	63	183	5.5

1916-17 IBL

Bridgeport, Danbury and New York were added for the 1916-17 season, as North Hudson, Brooklyn, and Elizabeth dropped out. Bridgeport and Danbury battled down to the final game of the first half, with Bridgeport finishing on top by a game. Bridgeport, Danbury and Stamford, the top three clubs in the first half, all dropped out after the first half, citing the long trips for the Connecticut clubs. Three New Jersey clubs—Newark, Hoboken and the National Turners—were added to fill out the league.

The second half featured a close pennant race as Paterson topped Newark 29-24 on April 22 to claim first place by a game. Bridgeport then returned to top Paterson 26-17 and 26-24 to win the league title in the IBL championship series. The games were played at neutral sites as both teams had lost the use of their home courts due to war orders.

	FIRST HALF			SECOND HALF			SEASON TOTALS		
	W	L	PCT.	W	L	PCT.	W	L	PCT.
Bridgeport Blue Ribbons*	15	4	.789	..	..	....	15	4	.789
Danbury Hatters*	14	5	.737	..	..	....	14	5	.737
Newark Turners	..	..	....	15	6	.714	15	6	.714
Paterson Crescents	8	10	.444	16	5	.762	24	15	.615
Jersey City Skeeters	8	11	.421	13	7	.650	21	18	.538
Stamford*	8	8	.500	..	..	....	8	8	.500
Hoboken G's	..	..	....	7	12	.368	7	12	.368
National Turners	..	..	....	6	13	.316	6	13	.316
New York Cathedral Separate Five	1	16	.059	2	16	.111	3	32	.086

*Bridgeport, Danbury, Stamford dropped out after the first half, retaining their franchise rights.

IBL CHAMPIONSHIP
Apr. 26, 1917 at West Hoboken - Bridgeport 26, Paterson 17
Apr. 29 at Newark - Bridgeport 26, Paterson 24

LEAGUE LEADERS

Regular Season	G	FG	FT	TP	PPG
Walter Swenson, Bridgeport/Jersey City	39	66	145	277	7.1
Hobby Fyfe, Jersey City	39	89	87	265	6.7
Frank Bruggy, Paterson	34	93	77	263	7.7
George Norman, Danbury/Newark	39	62	109	233	6.0
Leo Malone, Jersey City/National	32	52	120	224	7.0
Joe Dreyfus, Stamford/Newark	34	79	65	223	6.6
Gilbert Schwab, Stamford/National	27	83	49	215	8.0
Jimmy Clinton, Bridgeport/Paterson	34	65	77	207	6.1
Chris Leonard, Danbury/Newark	36	44	119	207	5.8
Eddie White, Bridgeport/Hoboken	29	72	54	198	6.8

1919-20 IBL

League play was suspended in 1917-18 and 1918-19 due to the outbreak of World War I, but the league returned for play on November 4, 1919 with Ansonia, Bridgeport, Newark, New York, Passaic and Jersey City as members.

Paterson dropped out during the first week of the season after failing to lease the Paterson Armory, which was being used by the Paterson Silk Sox baseball club for indoor on Saturday nights. When New York dropped out of the league soon after, a replacement club was awarded to Frank Morgenweck and Jimmy Clinton who placed it in Paterson, playing on Wednesday nights until indoor baseball proved to be a failure and they could return to Saturdays.

The league was in haphazard condition, and included incidents such as the Ansonia team "borrowing" a player named Robinson from Paterson for a league game against Paterson. Players were shuttled back and forth, with nearly all IBL players also freelancing in the EBL or PSL. Hobby Fyfe may have set a record of sorts: he actually played for New York, Brooklyn, Jersey City and Passaic in the short season.

Jersey City manager Harry Wallum sold his franchise to Garry Schmeelk on December 21. Schmeelk then moved the team to Brooklyn. The team paced the league until losses to Paterson and Ansonia gave the first half title to the Silk Sox, with the league then disbanding at the season's midpoint.

The last league game was played on January 10, 1920.

After the aborted season an "Eastern Championship" series was played with the Eastern Basketball League first-half champion Camden Crusaders. The second game of the series was noteworthy in that it was the second half of a doubleheader played by Paterson. The first game was a non-league game against the Superiors from the Passaic league and four of the five Paterson players played both games.

	FIRST HALF			SECOND HALF			SEASON TOTALS		
	W	L	PCT.	W	L	PCT.	W	L	PCT.
New York Treat 'em **									
Roughs/Paterson Silk Sox	10	6	.625	..	..	....	10	6	.625
Jersey City Skeeters/									
Brooklyn Dodgers***	9	7	.562	..	..	....	9	7	.562
Bridgeport Blue Ribbons	8	8	.500	..	..	....	8	8	.500
Ansonia Wrightlets	7	8	.467	..	..	....	7	8	.467
Passaic Athletic Association	6	9	.400	..	..	....	6	9	.400
Newark Nationals*	0	2	.000	..	..	....	0	2	.000

The league disbanded during the season.

*Newark played its last game on Dec. 3, 1919 and was officially dropped by the

league on Dec. 16, although it planned to compete in the league's second half.
**New York dropped out Nov. 18, 1919 and was replaced by Paterson.
***Jersey City was replaced by Brooklyn on Dec. 28, 1919.

EASTERN CHAMPIONSHIP
Jan 17 at Paterson - Camden 41, Paterson 40
Jan 20 at Paterson - Paterson 38, Camden 23
Feb 20 at Paterson - Paterson 43, Camden 25

INTERSTATE BASKETBALL LEAGUE - 1915-20

Teams	15-16	16-17	17-18	18-19	19-20	Totals
Ansonia	x	x	N	N	7-8	7-8
Bridgeport	x	15-4	O	O	8-8	23-12
Brooklyn	11-23	x			9-7	20-30
Danbury	x	14-5	L	L	x	14-5
Elizabeth	2-6	x	E	E	x	2-6
Hoboken	x	7-12	A	A	x	7-12
Jersey City	25-12	21-18	G	G	x	46-30
Kingston	14-5	x	U	U	x	14-5
National	x	6-13	E	E	x	6-13
New York	x	3-32			x	3-32
Newark	x	15-6			0-2	15-8
North Hudson	8-25	x			x	8-25
Passaic	x	x			6-9	6-9
Paterson	23-14	24-15			10-6	57-35
Stamford	18-16	8-8			x	26-24
Total games played	101	113			40	254

Team Records
League–Most Championships: 2, Paterson
League–Most Games Played: 93, Paterson
League–Most Games Won: 57, Paterson
League–Most Games Lost: 35, Paterson
League–Highest Won-Lost %: .737, 14-5, Danbury
.737, 14-5, Kinsgton
League–Lowest Won-Lost %: .086, 3-32, New York

Season–Most Games Played: 39, 1916-17, Paterson
39, 1916-17, Jersey City
Season–Most Games Won: 25, 1915-16, Jersey City
Season–Most Games Lost: 32, 1916-17, New York
Season–Highest Won-Lost Percentage: .790, 15-4, 1916-17, Bridgeport
Season–Lowest Won-Lost Percentage: .000, 0-2, 1919-20, Newark

Individual Summary - 3 or more Seasons
(statistics only available for 1915-16 and 1916-17 seasons)

Player	Seasons Yrs	Teams	G	FG	FT	TP	PPG
John Beckman	1915/20	3	PAT/BRI/ NEW/NYK/JER	30	49	76	174	5.8
Frank Bruggy	1915/20	3	KIN/NHD/PAT	67	165	151	481	7.2
Jimmy Clinton	1915/20	3	PAT/BRI/NYK	67	120	130	370	5.5
Joe Dreyfus	1915/20	3	STM/NEW/JER	68	132	116	380	5.6
Jake Fuller	1915/20	3	ELZ/NHD/ JER/NEW/ANS	21	30	52	112	5.3
Hobby Fyfe	1915/20	3	BKN/JER/NYK	68	151	145	447	6.6
Nick Harvey	1915/20	3	PAT	52	59	59	177	3.4
Stretch Harvey	1915/20	3	JER/BRI/ANS	62	70	75	215	3.5
Chris Leonard	1915/20	3	PAT/DAN/ NEW/NYK/JER	71	87	196	370	5.2
Al McIntyre	1915/20	3	ELZ/HOB/NEW	26	40	42	122	4.7
Chief Muller	1915/20	3	JER/BKN/ NEW/ANS	36	89	102	280	7.8
George Norman	1915/20	3	STM/DAN/ NEW/ANS	72	134	184	452	6.3
Ernie Reich	1915/20	3	JER/BRI	69	114	123	351	5.1
Elmer Ripley	1915/20	3	BKN/HOB/PAT	35	46	63	155	4.4
Ed Roach	1915/20	3	JER/DAN/ NAT/ANS	68	43	97	183	2.7
Garry Schmeelk	1915/20	3	BKN/PAT/NYK	30	105	64	274	9.1
Mike Smolick	1915/20	3	STM/HOB/ANS	23	32	34	98	4.3
Lou Sugarman	1915/20	3	ELZ/NYK/BKN	5	11	11	33	6.6
Eddie White	1915/20	3	ELZ/BRI/HOB	30	76	55	207	6.9

METROPOLITAN BASKET BALL LEAGUE
[1921-22 TO 1927-28]

LEAGUE MEMBERS

Albany Senators	Albany, NY	1927-28
Brooklyn Dodgers	Brooklyn, NY	1921-22 to 1922-23
Greenpoint Knights of St. Anthony	Brooklyn, NY	1921-22 to 1926-27
Brooklyn Prospect Big Five [Pros]	Brooklyn, NY	1921-22 to 1922-23
Brooklyn Visitations [Visitation Triangles]	Brooklyn, NY	1921-22 to 1927-28
Catskill	Catskill, NY	1927-28
Elizabeth	Elizabeth, NJ	1922-23
Hudson	Hudson, NY	1927-28
Kingston Colonials	Kingston, NY	1923-24 to 1924-25
Kingston Colonials	Kingston, NY	1926-27 to 1927-28
New York Celtics	New York, NY	1922-23
New York MacDowell Lyceum [Macs]	New York, NY	1921-22 to 1922-23
New York Pros	New York, NY	1925-26
Newark Bears	Newark, NJ	1925-26
Passaic Panthers	Passaic, NJ	1924-25
Passaic Mets	Passaic, NJ	1925-26 to 1927-28
Paterson Crescents	Paterson, NJ	1926-27
Paterson Legionnaires	Paterson, NJ	1922-23 to 1925-26
Paterson Pats	Paterson, NJ	1927-28
Paterson Power Brothers Five	Paterson, NJ	1921-22
Perth Amboy Mets	Perth Amboy, NJ	1925-26
Trenton Royal Bengals	Trenton, NJ	1923-24 to 1924-25
Troy Trojans	Troy, NY	1927-28
Yonkers Indians	Yonkers, NY	1925-26 to 1926-27
Yonkers Chippewas [Leaguers]	Yonkers, NY	1922-23 to 1924-25
West Brooklyn Assumption Triangles	Brooklyn, NY	1926-27

1921-22 MBL
Organized in January 1922 by John J. O'Brien with William Colgan as president, the Met League allowed only three established professional players per club in an effort to keep salaries down. The league's membership included six clubs: The Brooklyn Dodgers, Brooklyn Pros, Brooklyn Visitations, Greenpoint Knights, New York Macs and Paterson Powers Brothers Five.
The Brooklyn Dodgers and New York finished the regular season deadlocked with 12-8 records, and when the New York players went on strike in hopes of improving their financial situation, the league awarded the league title to Brooklyn.

	W	L	PCT.
Brooklyn Dodgers	12	8	.600
New York MacDowell Lyceum	12	8	.600
Brooklyn Prospect Big Five	11	9	.550
Brooklyn Visitations	9	11	.450
Greenpoint Knights of St. Anthony	9	11	.450
Paterson Power Brothers Five	7	13	.350

LEAGUE LEADERS

Regular Season	G	FG	FT	TP	PPG
Benny Borgmann, Paterson	18	71	76	218	12.1
Joe Brennan, Brooklyn Dodgers	20	65	57	187	9.4
Eddie Burke, Brooklyn Visitations	18	53	64	170	9.4
Richard Smyth, New York	19	50	32	132	6.9
Harry Riconda, Brooklyn Prospect Big Five	16	28	73	129	8.1
Frank Bruggy, Brooklyn Prospect Big Five	18	43	41	127	7.1
Leo Malone, Brooklyn Prospect Big Five.	19	29	69	127	6.7
George Norman, Brooklyn Dodgers	20	31	60	122	6.1
Garry Schmeelk, New York	16	36	43	115	7.2
Willie Carey, Greenpoint	17	36	43	115	6.8

MBL CHAMPIONSHIP
Brooklyn awarded championship when New York players went on strike.

1922-23 MBL
Every club except Paterson returned for the second season of the MBL, and in June, Elizabeth, the Paterson Legionnaires and the legendary New York Celtics joined the league. In that meeting the league also elected new league officers as Edward Thorp assumed the position of MBL president.
The overall standing of the league improved with the collapse of the Eastern and New York State Leagues, as the MBL gained recognition as the top pro basketball circuit. Many of the top players from the rival leagues signed with the MBL, strengthening the league. The Celtics went on to win all twelve of their games before dropping out of the league in November with a week remaining in the first half. The Yonkers Chippewas were recruited to replace them for the second half.
As the second half of the season wound down, Paterson, the Brooklyn Pros and Yonkers battled for first place, with Paterson and Brooklyn finishing in a tie as Yonkers faded and fell into fourth.
To decide the second-half championship Thorp ordered a best-of-three series, which Paterson won two games to one. In the ensuing league championship series Paterson topped Elizabeth two games to one.

	FIRST HALF			SECOND HALF			SEASON TOTALS		
	W	L	PCT.	W	L	PCT.	W	L	PCT.
New York Celtics/									
Yonkers Chippewas*	12	0	1.000	15	13	.536	27	13	.675
Greenpoint Knights of									
St. Anthony	7	5	.583	16	12	.571	23	17	.575
Brooklyn Pros	4	7	.364	18	10	.643	22	17	.564
Paterson Legionnaires	4	8	.333	18	10	.643	22	18	.550
Brooklyn Visitations	8	6	.571	14	13	.519	22	19	.537
Elizabeth	9	3	.750	9	14	.391	18	17	.514
New York MacDowell Lyceum	5	10	.333	7	19	.269	12	29	.293
Brooklyn Dodgers	2	12	.143	10	16	.385	12	28	.300

*New York dropped out on Nov. 17, 1922 during the first half and was replaced by Yonkers for the second half of the season.

MBL SECOND HALF PLAYOFF
Mar. 31, 1924 at Paterson - Paterson 42, Brooklyn Pros 39
Apr. 1 at Brooklyn - Brooklyn Pros 37, Paterson 23
Apr. 4 at Paterson - Paterson 32, Brooklyn Pros 24

MBL CHAMPIONSHIP
Apr. 14 at Brooklyn - Paterson 45, Elizabeth 31
Apr. 15 at Paterson - Elizabeth 30, Paterson 22
Apr. 18 at Paterson - Paterson 51, Elizabeth 34

LEAGUE LEADERS

Regular Season	G	FG	FT	TP	PPG
Benny Borgmann, Paterson	39	134	191	459	11.8
George Norman, Brooklyn Pros	38	119	117	354	9.3
Eddie White, Brooklyn Visitations	39	96	76	268	6.9
Stretch Meehan, N.Y. MacDowell	38	44	175	263	6.9
Willie Carey, Greenpoint	40	90	74	254	6.4
Frank Boyle, Greenpoint	38	64	123	251	6.6
George Smith, Greenpoint	35	76	99	251	7.2
James Campbell, Yonkers	31	77	72	226	7.3
Frank Bruggy, Elizabeth	31	64	70	198	6.4
Joe Brennan, Brooklyn Dodgers	34	53	91	197	5.8

1923-24 MBL

After the Brooklyn Dodgers, Brooklyn Pros, Elizabeth and New York dropped out of the league, officials decided to limit league membership to six clubs as Kingston of the NYSL and Trenton of the EBL were recruited to round out the league.

When the teams took the floor for the season, Brooklyn quickly took control of first place and hung on to edge Kingston for the first-half title. Paterson, who had finished strong in the first half, provided the competition in the second half but a win by Brooklyn over Trenton on the final day of the regular season wrapped up the second half and league championship for the Visitations.

	FIRST HALF			SECOND HALF			SEASON TOTALS		
	W	L	PCT.	W	L	PCT.	W	L	PCT.
Brooklyn Visitations	13	7	.650	13	7	.650	26	14	.650
Paterson Legionnaires	10	10	.500	12	8	.600	22	18	.550
Kinston Colonials	12	8	.600	9	11	.450	21	19	.525
Trenton Royal Bengals	11	9	.550	10	10	.500	21	19	.525
Greenpoint Knights of									
St. Anthony	7	13	.350	9	11	.450	16	24	.400
Yonkers Chippewas	7	13	.350	7	13	.350	14	26	.350

LEAGUE LEADERS

Regular Season	G	FG	FT	TP	PPG
Benny Borgman, Paterson	38	108	191	407	10.7
Joe Brennan, Brooklyn	39	115	140	370	9.5
Davey Banks, Brooklyn	33	85	108	278	8.9
James Campbell, Kingston	18	48	42	138	7.7
Carl Husta, Kingston	40	76	148	300	7.5
Eddie White, Yonkers	19	44	53	141	7.4
Stretch Meehan, Trenton	28	36	116	188	6.7
Harry Riconda, Greenpoint	32	39	125	203	6.3
George Glasco, Trenton	37	75	77	227	6.1
George Smith, Greenpoint	35	62	90	214	6.1

1924-25 MBL

Kingston relocated to Passaic for the 1924-25 season, but returned to Kingston on November 23, with the franchise staying put for the remainder of the season. In the first half Kingston edged Greenpoint by a single game, with a 33-32 win in Greenpoint providing the difference.

Brooklyn jumped out to an early lead in the second half, holding off a challenge from Paterson to capture the second half title. In the championship series Kingston captured the first game, but Brooklyn bounced back to win the next two games to claim the title.

	FIRST HALF			SECOND HALF			SEASON TOTALS		
	W	L	PCT.	W	L	PCT.	W	L	PCT.
Brooklyn Visitations	10	10	.500	14	5	.737	24	15	.615
Passaic Panthers/									
Kingston Colonials*	13	7	.650	8	9	.471	21	16	.568
Greenpoint Knights of									
St. Anthony	12	8	.600	9	8	.529	21	16	.568
Patterson Legionnaires	7	12	.368	11	7	.611	18	19	.486
Yonkers Chippewas	8	10	.444	4	11	.267	12	21	.382
Trenton Royal Bengals	8	11	.421	5	11	.312	13	22	.371

*The Passaic Panthers moved to the Kingston Colonials on November 23 during the first half.

MBL CHAMPIONSHIP
Mar. 22, 1925 at Brooklyn - Kingston 25, Brooklyn 20
Mar. 24 at Greenpoint - Brooklyn 31, Kingston 14
Apr. 11 at Paterson - Brooklyn 33, Kingston 29

LEAGUE LEADERS

Regular Season	G	FG	FT	TP	PPG
Benny Borgmann, Paterson	33	92	206	390	11.8
Bill McElwain, Yonkers	18	39	16	154	8.6
Carl Husta, Kingston	37	93	149	315	8.5
Joe Brennan, Brooklyn	38	96	122	314	8.3
Davey Banks, Brooklyn	35	78	125	281	8.0
Cliff Anderson, Greenpoint	37	59	166	284	7.7
Rody Cooney, Brooklyn	17	31	61	123	7.2
Harry Riconda, Kingston	31	41	143	224	7.2
Willie Marrin, Yonkers	33	58	106	222	6.7
Stretch Meehan, Paterson	34	28	164	220	6.4

1925-26 MBL

With the formation of the American Basketball League, the MBL declined in stature, but the 1925-26 season proved to be highly successful on the court. Trenton dropped out of the league and Kingston moved to Perth Amboy during the off-season. New York and Newark were added to bring the league back up to eight clubs.

In the first half Yonkers edged Paterson by a game in a race that was determined on the final day before the mid-season break. The league was reduced to six clubs when New York dropped out during the first half and Perth Amboy moved to Passaic in January for the second half of the season.

In the second half Greenpoint and Brooklyn finished tied with 8-1 records with Greenpoint winning two games from the Visitations to take the second half title. In the MBL championship series Greenpoint topped Yonkers two games to one, winning the decisive third game on the road 28-26.

	FIRST HALF			SECOND HALF			SEASON TOTALS		
	W	L	PCT.	W	L	PCT.	W	L	PCT.
Yonkers Indians	15	6	.714	4	5	.444	19	11	.633
Greenpoint Knights of									
St. Anthony	11	10	.524	8	1	.889	19	11	.633
Paterson Legionnaires	14	7	.667	4	6	.400	18	13	.581
New York Pros*	5	4	.556	..	..	....	5	4	.556
Brooklyn Visitations	8	13	.381	8	1	.889	16	14	.533
Perth Amboy Mets/Passaic**	8	11	.421	0	5	.000	8	16	.333
Newark Bears	4	14	.222	1	7	.125	5	21	.192

*New York dropped out during the first half.
**Perth Amboy moved to Passaic on January 26.

SECOND HALF PLAYOFF
Greenpoint defeated Brooklyn 2 games to 0

MBL CHAMPIONSHIP
Mar. 27, 1926 at Yonkers, Yonkers 25, Greenpoint 23
Mar. 28 at Greenpoint, Greenpoint 28, Yonkers 23
Apr. 6 at Brooklyn, Greenpoint 28, Yonkers 26

LEAGUE LEADERS

Regular Season	G	FG	FT	TP	PPG
Willie Marrin, Yonkers	29	43	145	231	8.0
Cliff Anderson, Greenpoint	29	45	126	216	7.4
Bill McElwain, Yonkers	29	37	139	213	7.3
Chick Passon, Paterson	22	47	125	209	9.5
Harry Riconda, Perth Amboy	20	35	117	187	9.4
Joe Brennan, Brooklyn	25	53	83	189	7.6
George Artus, Paterson	31	56	77	189	6.1
Davey Banks, Brooklyn	24	54	80	188	7.8
George Norman, Newark	25	52	80	184	7.4
Dutch Eggerts, Greenpoint	28	43	95	181	6.5

1926-27 MBL

Newark, Passaic and the Paterson Legionnaires dropped out during the off-season and the Paterson Crescents, West Brooklyn and Kingston were recruited to bring the league back up to six clubs. The MBL began to encounter serious financial troubles, forcing Greenpoint to drop out during the first half of the season and West Brooklyn and Yonkers followed during the second half, reducing the

circuit to three teams.

Brooklyn paced the league with an 8-2 record in the first half and Paterson dominated the league with a 7-0 record in the second with Brooklyn finishing 3-3 and Kingston last with an 0-3 record. Brooklyn returned to its first half form in the championship series however, taking three straight games from the Crescents for the title.

	FIRST HALF			SECOND HALF			SEASON TOTALS		
	W	L	PCT.	W	L	PCT.	W	L	PCT.
Paterson Crescents	6	4	.600	7	0	1.000	13	4	.765
Brooklyn Visitations	8	2	.800	3	3	.500	11	5	.688
West Brooklyn**									
Assumption Triangles	7	3	.700	0	2	.000	7	5	.583
Yonkers Indians***	4	6	.400	0	2	.000	4	8	.333
Greenpoint Knights of St. Anthony*	2	5	.286	..	..	.....	2	5	.286
Kingston Colonials	0	7	.000	0	3	.000	0	10	.000

*Greenpoint dropped out during the first half.
**West Brooklyn dropped out during the second half.
***Yonkers dropped out during the second half.

MBL CHAMPIONSHIP
Mar. 13, 1927 at Brooklyn - Brooklyn 24, Paterson 23
Mar. 19 at Paterson - Brooklyn 36, Paterson 30
Mar. 20 at Brooklyn - Brooklyn 33, Paterson 29

1927-28 MBL
Although the Paterson Crescents dropped out, Albany, Catskill, Hudson, the Paterson Pats and Troy were added to bring the NBL up to seven members for the 1927-28 season. The campaign got off to a shaky start, however, as Paterson drubbed Kingston 33-14 to win their first game and then promptly dropped out of the league. Kingston bounced back to lead the league with a 13-4 record when the league folded in January 1928, during the first half of the season.

	FIRST HALF			SECOND HALF			SEASON TOTALS		
	W	L	PCT.	W	L	PCT.	W	L	PCT.
Kingston Colonials	13	4	.765	..	..	.....	13	4	.765
Catskill	11	5	.688	..	..	.....	11	5	.688
Brooklyn Visitations	9	6	.600	..	..	.....	9	6	.600
Hudson	7	9	.438	..	..	.....	7	9	.438
Albany Senators	3	8	.237	..	..	.....	3	8	.273
Troy Trojans	1	11	.083	..	..	.....	1	11	.083
Paterson Pats*	0	1	.000	..	..	.....	0	1	.000

*Paterson defeated Kingston 33-14 at Paterson on November 5. Manager Joe Murray withdrew his team from the league on November 8 because he thought his team was too good for the competition. "After watching my club in action with the Kingston club Saturday night I realized I would not be giving the loyal fans of this city a good break by remaining in the league." Paterson continued as an independent team meeting ABL teams in exhibition games. For reasons unknown the official league standings list Paterson's record as 0 wins and 1 loss. It is possible that the league decided to forfeit the Paterson game.

Metropolitan Basketball League - 1921-28

Teams	21-22	22-23	23-24	24-25	25-26	26-27	27-28	Totals
Albany	x	x	x	x	x	x	3-8	3-8
Brooklyn Dodgers	12-8	12-28	x	x	x	x	x	24-36
Brooklyn Prospect	11-9	22-17	x	x	x	x	x	33-26
Brooklyn Visitation	9-11	22-19	26-14	24-15	16-14	11-5	9-6	117-84
Catskill	x	x	x	x	x	x	11-5	11-5
Elizabeth	x	18-17	x	x	x	x	x	18-17
Greenpoint	9-11	23-17	16-24	21-16	19-11	2-5	x	90-84
Hudson	x	x	x	x	x	x	7-9	7-9
Kingston	x	x	21-19	21-16	x	0-10	13-4	55-49
McDowell	12-8	12-29	x	x	x	x	x	24-37
New York	x	12-0	x	x	5-4	x	x	17-4
Newark	x	x	x	x	5-21	x	x	5-21
Passaic	x	x	x	x	0-5	x	x	0-5
Paterson	7-13	22-18	22-18	18-19	18-13	13-4	0-1	100-86
Perth Amboy	x	x	x	x	8-11	x	x	8-11
Trenton	x	x	21-19	13-22	x	x	x	34-41
Troy	x	x	x	x	x	x	1-11	1-11
West Brooklyn	x	x	x	x	x	7-5	x	7-5
Yonkers	x	15-13	14-26	12-21	19-11	4-8	x	64-79
Total games played	60	158	120	109	90	37	44	620

Team Records
League–Most Championships: 3, Brooklyn Visitations
League–Most Games Played: 201, Brooklyn Visitations
League–Most Games Won: 117, Brooklyn Visitations
League–Most Games Lost: 86, Paterson
League–Highest Won-Lost Percentage: .810, 17-4, New York
League–Lowest Won-Lost Percentage: .000, 0-5, Passaic

Season–Most Games Played: 41, 1922-23, Visitations, McDowell
Season–Most Games Won: 26, 1923-24, Brooklyn Visitations

Season–Most Games Lost: 29, 1922-23, McDowell
Season–Highest Won-Lost Percentage: 1.000, 12-0, 1922-23, New York
Season–Lowest Won-Lost Percentage: .000, 0-10, 1926-27, Kingston

Individual Records
(statistics only available 1921-26)

League–Most Games Played: 162, Bob Griebe
League–Most Field Goals: 416, Benny Borgmann
League–Most Free Throws: 674, Benny Borgmann
League–Most Total Points: 1,506, Benny Borgmann
League–Highest PPG average: 11.6, Benny Borgmann

Season–Most Games Played: 40, several
Season–Most Field Goals: 134, 1922-23, Benny Borgmann
Season–Most Free Throws: 206, 1924-25, Benny Borgmann
Season–Most Total Points: 459, 1922-23, Benny Borgmann
Season–Highest PPG average: 12.1, 1921-22, Benny Borgmann

Metropolitan Basketball League - 1921-28

Individual Summary - 3 or more Seasons
(statistics only available 1921-26)

Player	Seasons Yrs		Teams	G	FG	FT	TP	PPG
Cliff Anderson	1923-26	3	KIN/GRN	78	117	316	550	7.1
George Artus	1921-26	5	VIS/KIN/PAT	122	144	295	588	4.8
Tom Barlow	1922-26	4	GRN/TRE	116	185	250	620	5.3
Benny Borgmann	1921-26	5	PAT	130	416	674	1506	11.6
Joe Brennan	1921-26	5	DOD/VIS	156	382	493	1257	8.1
Frank Bruggy	1921/25	3	BKN/ELZ/PAT	50	108	112	328	6.6
Eddie Burke	1921/25	3	VIS	64	134	220	398	6.2
Jimmy Campbell	1922-26	4	BKN/YON/KIN/TRE/PAM	90	197	176	570	6.3
Willie Carey	1921-26	5	GRN/YON	158	272	306	850	5.4
Red Conaty	1922-25	4	VIS	83	148	100	396	4.8
Rody Cooney	1921-25	4	VIS	107	145	227	517	4.8
Joe Dreyfus	1921-26	5	VIS/PAT/YON/NEW	110	143	203	489	4.4
Bernie Dunn	1922-25	4	MCD/TRE	48	68	68	204	4.3
Dutch Eggerts	1921-26	5	GRN	116	168	285	621	5.4
Walter Garland	1921-26	5	GRN/VIS/YON	139	139	302	578	4.2
George Glasco	1921-26	5	VIS/YON/TRE/GRN	104	178	224	477	4.6
Bob Griebe	1921-26	5	DOD/VIS	162	156	332	644	4.0
Oscar Grimstead	1921-25	4	DOD/ELZ/VIS	108	122	123	367	3.4
George Haggerty	1921-24	3	VIS/NYK/PAT	19	10	13	33	1.7
Nick Harvey	1921-25	4	VIS/ELZ/PAT/KIN	115	160	175	495	14.3
Mickey Husta	1923-26	3	KIN/PAM/PAS	82	54	136	244	3.0
Teddy Kearns	1922-26	4	MCD/TRE/KIN/PAM	112	175	157	507	4.5
Ray Kennedy	1921-26	5	MCD/VIS/YON/PAT	107	122	271	515	4.8
Harry Knoblauch	1922-25	3	MCD/PAT/CON	79	66	158	290	13.7
Leo Malone	1921-26	5	VIS/GRN/TRE/NEW	153	186	427	789	5.2
Willie Marrin	1922-26	4	MCD/YON	91	147	316	490	5.4
Stretch Meehan	1921-26	5	MCD/TRE/PAT	147	154	630	938	6.4
George Newman	1922-25	3	DOD/ELZ/KIN/VIS	27	42	42	126	4.7
George Norman	1921/26	4	DOD/VIS/YON/NEW	108	239	312	790	7.3
Chick Passon	1923-26	3	KIN/PAT	25	50	125	225	9.0
Artie Powers	1921-26	5	PAT	140	150	325	625	4.5
Charlie Powers	1921-25	4	PAT/MCD/KIN	104	162	245	569	5.5
Harry Riconda	1921-26	5	VIS/GRN/KIN/PAM/PAS	118	178	514	849	7.2
Elmer Ripley	1921-24	3	DOD/ELZ/PAT	62	81	141	303	4.9
Honey Russell	1921-24	3	VIS/YON	59	94	81	269	4.6
Garry Schmeelk	1921-24	3	MCD/ELZ/YON	34	99	83	181	5.3
Barney Sedran	1921-24	3	DOD/YON	34	49	41	139	14.1
George Smith	1921-25	4	VIS/GRN	93	169	233	571	6.2
Dick Smythe	1921-26	5	MCD/GRN/YON	81	126	91	343	4.2
Eddie Stuchbury	1921/25	3	GRN/YON	49	101	78	172	13.5
Maury Tome	1922/26	4	MCD/TRE/KIN/PAM/PAS	100	138	108	384	3.8
Joe Trippe	1921-25	4	GRN/PAT	92	120	161	401	4.4
Dave Wassmer	1921-25	4	MCD/YON	97	142	176	460	4.7
Eddie White	1921-26	5	VIS/YON/NEW	127	285	295	855	6.7

AMERICAN BASKETBALL LEAGUE
[1925-26 TO 1930-31]

LEAGUE MEMBERS

Baltimore Orioles	Baltimore, MD	1926-27
Boston Whirlwinds	Boston, MA	1925-26
Brooklyn Arcadians	Brooklyn, NY	1925-26
Brooklyn Rockets	Brooklyn, NY	1926-27
Brooklyn Celtics	Brooklyn, NY	1926-27
Brooklyn Visitations	Brooklyn, NY	1927-28 to 1930-31
Buffalo Bisons [Germans]	Buffalo, NY	1925-26
Chicago Bruins	Chicago, IL	1925-26 to 1930-31
Cleveland Rosenblums [Rosies]	Cleveland, OH	1925-26 to 1930-31
Detroit Cardinals [Olympians]	Detroit, MI	1927-28
Detroit Lions	Detroit, MI	1926-27
Detroit Pulaski Post Five	Detroit, MI	1925-26 to 1926-27
Fort Wayne Hoosiers [Guards]	Fort Wayne, IN	1926-27 to 1930-31
Fort Wayne Caseys	Fort Wayne, IN	1925-26
New York Celtics	New York, NY	1927-28, 1929-30
New York Hakoahs	New York, NY	1928-29
Paterson Crescents	Paterson, NJ	1929-30 to 1930-31
Paterson Whirlwinds	Paterson, NJ	1928-29
Philadelphia Phillies [Quakers]	Philadelphia, PA	1926-27
Philadelphia Warriors [Quakers]	Philadelphia, PA	1926-27 to 1927-28
Rochester Centrals	Rochester, NY	1925-26 to 1930-31
Syracuse All-Americans	Syracuse, NY	1929-30
Toledo Red Man Tobaccos [Redmen]	Toledo, OH	1930-31
Trenton [Royal] Bengals	Trenton, NJ	1928-29
Washington Palace Five [Laundrymen, Palacians]	Washington, DC	1925-26 to 1927-28

1925-26 ABL

Organized by NFL President Joe Carr, the ABL aspired to take pro basketball to a higher level. Clubs were placed in major cities such as Boston, Brooklyn, Buffalo, Chicago, Cleveland, Detroit, Fort Wayne, Rochester, Washington, and East Liverpool (which dropped out before the season). And although the Original Celtics turned down an offer to join the league, the league could lay claim as basketball's first true major league.

The ABL chose to use Amateur Athletic Union (AAU) rules, including the elimination of the two-handed dribble and the use of backboard. In addition, league players were signed to exclusive contracts, a first in pro basketball, and gambling on games was prohibited.

In the season's first half Brooklyn edged Washington and Cleveland. Boston was expelled after the first half after a dispute over player contracts, leaving eight teams. Cleveland finished two games ahead of Washington for the second-half title.

In a playoff between Brooklyn and Cleveland, the Rosenblums won the series in three straight games. Attendance for the first two games of the series averaged about 10,000 in Cleveland, giving the league owners cause for optimism. The Original Celtics then challenged the Rosenblums to a best-of-five series, but owner Max Rosenblum declined their offer.

	FIRST HALF			SECOND HALF			SEASON TOTALS		
	W	L	PCT.	W	L	PCT.	W	L	PCT.
Cleveland Rosenblums	10	6	.625	13	1	.919	23	7	.767
Washington Palace Five	11	5	.688	11	3	.786	22	8	.733
Brooklyn Arcadians	12	4	.750	7	7	.500	19	11	.633
Rochester Centrals	9	7	.562	9	5	.643	18	12	.600
Fort Wayne Caseys	7	9	.438	6	8	.429	13	17	.433
Boston Whirlwinds*	6	10	.375	..	..	.....	6	10	.375
Buffalo Bisons	5	11	.322	5	9	.357	10	20	.333
Chicago Bruins	6	10	.375	3	11	.214	9	21	.300
Detroit Pulaski Post Five	6	10	.375	2	12	.143	8	22	.267

*Boston was expelled after the first half.

ABL CHAMPIONSHIP
Apr. 7, 1926 at Cleveland - Cleveland 36, Brooklyn 33
Apr. 8 at Cleveland - Cleveland 37, Brooklyn 21
Apr. 9 at New York - Cleveland 23, Brooklyn 22

LEAGUE LEADERS
Regular Season	G	FG	FT	TP	PPG
Rusty Saunders, Brooklyn/Washington	34	73	92	238	7.0
Ray Kennedy, Washington	27	66	84	216	8.0
Honey Russell, Cleveland	30	68	80	216	7.2
Nat Hickey, Cleveland	30	68	62	198	6.6
Elmer Ripley, Brooklyn	30	59	96	214	7.1
George Glasco, Brooklyn/Washington	35	64	70	198	5.7
Marty Barry, Rochester	27	50	81	181	6.7
Carl Husta, Cleveland	30	50	68	168	5.6
Red Conaty, Washington/Brooklyn	25	63	36	162	6.5

1926-27 ABL

The ABL's second season began with nine clubs, as Buffalo and Detroit dropped out and Baltimore, Detroit and Philadelphia were added to bolster the lineup. The Brooklyn Arcadians moved their games from Arcadian Hall and were renamed the Rockets.

Early in the season the struggling Detroit and Brooklyn teams dropped out of the league, with the Original Celtics assuming Brooklyn's record and home court as the league struck Detroit's games from the league record. The Celtics, playing as the Brooklyn Celtics, won 13 of their 16 remaining first-half games to finish at 13-8, good enough for fourth.

Cleveland dominated the first half after adding rookie Cookie Cunningham to their championship club, finishing one game ahead of Washington. The Orioles finished a woeful 1-20 in the first half of the season, but pulled off a coup when it purchased John Beckman from the Celtics.

The addition improved Baltimore, but did nothing to slow the Celtics as they dominated the second half of the season, finishing 19-2. Cleveland slumped to 9-12 in the second half after selling Honey Russell to the Chicago due to friction with owner Max Rosenblum. In the post-season matchup of the two champions, the Celtics swept the Rosenblums for the league title.

	FIRST HALF			SECOND HALF			SEASON TOTALS		
	W	L	PCT.	W	L	PCT.	W	L	PCT.
Brooklyn Rockets/ Brooklyn Celtics**	13	8	.619	19	2	.905	32	10	.762
Washington Palace Five	16	5	.762	14	7	.667	30	12	.714
Cleveland Rosenblums	17	4	.810	9	12	.429	26	16	.619
Philadelphia Warriors	14	7	.667	10	11	.476	24	18	.571
Fort Wayne Hoosiers	8	13	.381	15	6	.714	23	19	.548
Rochester Centrals	8	13	.381	6	15	.286	14	28	.333
Chicago Bruins	7	14	.333	6	15	.286	13	29	.310
Baltimore Orioles	1	20	.048	5	16	.238	6	36	.143
Detroit Lions*	0	6	.000	..	..	.....	0	6	.000

*Detroit dropped out during the season.
**The Brooklyn Rockets (0-5) dropped out with the New York Celtics assuming their record and playing as the Brooklyn Celtics during the first half.

ABL CHAMPIONSHIP
Apr. 6, 1927 at Cleveland - Brooklyn 29, Cleveland 21
Apr. 7 at Cleveland - Brooklyn 28, Cleveland 20
Apr. 9 at Brooklyn - Brooklyn 35, Cleveland 32

LEAGUE LEADERS
Regular Season	G	FG	FT	TP	PPG
Rusty Saunders, Washington	42	119	161	399	9.5
Benny Borgmann, Fort Wayne	34	87	206	380	11.2
Chick Passon, Philadelphia	41	93	181	367	9.0
Nat Hickey, Cleveland	41	103	137	343	8.4
Carl Husta, Cleveland	41	84	162	330	8.0
Johnny Beckman, Brooklyn/Baltimore	37	91	141	323	8.7
Ray Kennedy, Washington	40	68	172	308	7.7
Nat Holman, Brooklyn	34	82	135	299	8.8
Honey Russell, Cleveland/Chicago	40	61	134	256	6.4
Harry Topel, Rochester	37	81	91	253	6.8

1927-28 ABL

Detroit was added to the league as Baltimore dropped out and Brooklyn took on a new name—the New York Celtics—as they moved some of their games into Madison Square Garden. The league changed the basic format of its playoffs, going from one division playing a season with two halves to a two-division alignment with an additional round of playoff games. The Eastern Division consisted of New York, Philadelphia, Rochester and Washington; the Western Division included Chicago, Cleveland, Detroit and Fort Wayne. In an effort to curtail rough play, the league adopted a rule disqualifying players after five personal fouls and fines of $10 to $25 for fighting or profanity.

On January 3, Detroit and Washington folded. Washington was replaced by the Metropolitan League's Brooklyn club. New York again dominated the regular season, winning the East by 11 games. Fort Wayne finished on top of the West by five games as the Rosenblums sunk to a 22-29 record.

The first round of the playoffs featured two sweeps as Fort Wayne topped Cleveland and New York defeated Philadelphia. The Celtics then had little trouble with the Hoosiers in the championship series, winning the series three games to one.

EASTERN DIVISION	W	L	PCT.	WESTERN DIVISION	W	L	PCT.
New York Celtics	40	9	.816	Fort Wayne Hoosiers	27	24	.529
Philadelphia Warriors	30	21	.588	Cleveland Rosenblums	22	29	.431
Washington/ Brooklyn Visitations*	25	26	.490	Chicago Bruins	13	36	.265
Rochester Centrals	24	28	.462	Detroit Cardinals**	5	13	.278

*Washington dropped out Jan. 3, 1928 and were replaced by Brooklyn.
**Detroit dropped out Jan. 3.

ABL PLAYOFFS
Mar. 14, 1928 at Cleveland - Fort Wayne 22, Cleveland 15
Mar. 16 at Fort Wayne - Fort Wayne 31, Cleveland 25

Mar. 13 at Philadelphia - New York 27, Philadelphia 21
Mar. 14 at Brooklyn - New York 32, Philadelphia 24

ABL CHAMPIONSHIP
Mar. 21 at Fort Wayne - New York 30, Fort Wayne 21
Mar. 22 at Fort Wayne - Fort Wayne 28, New York 21
Mar. 23 at Fort Wayne - New York 35, Fort Wayne 18
Mar. 25 at New York - New York 27, Fort Wayne 26

LEAGUE LEADERS

Regular Season	G	FG	FT	TP	PPG
Harry Topel, Rochester	52	171	96	438	8.4
Davey Banks, New York	49	170	72	412	8.4
Benny Borgmann, Fort Wayne	51	128	143	399	7.8
Nat Hickey, Cleveland	47	155	69	379	8.1
Honey Russell, Chicago	49	137	85	359	7.3
Al Kellett, Philadelphia	43	132	82	346	8.0
Tom Barlow, Philadelphia	48	142	51	335	7.0
Rusty Saunders, Wash./Brooklyn/Fort Wayne	50	127	76	330	6.6
Red Conaty Washington/Brooklyn	47	148	28	324	6.9
Carl Husta, Cleveland	41	115	89	319	7.8

1928-29 ABL

New York dropped out in the off-season, as their manager, James Furey, served time in Sing Sing for embezzlement. The remaining clubs quickly gobbled up the Celtic players. With Philadelphia also dropping out, the league recruited Trenton and Paterson to bring the league membership back up to one eight-team division.

Cleveland paced the league in the first half despite being forced by the league to sell Nat Hickey to Chicago. Fort Wayne followed in second as Brooklyn and Chicago finished tied for third.

In the closely contested second half of the season, Fort Wayne held off Brooklyn and Cleveland for first, with a crucial 30-29 over Brooklyn on March 18 proving to be the difference. In the ABL championship series Cleveland defeated Fort Wayne in four straight games.

	FIRST HALF			SECOND HALF			SEASON TOTALS		
	W	L	PCT.	W	L	PCT.	W	L	PCT.
Cleveland Rosenblums	19	9	.679	10	4	.714	29	13	.690
Fort Wayne Hoosiers	18	10	.643	11	3	.786	29	13	.690
Brooklyn Visitations	15	12	.556	10	4	.714	25	16	.610
Chicago Bruins	15	12	.556	4	10	.286	19	22	.463
Rochester Centrals	11	15	.423	7	7	.500	18	22	.450
New York Hakoahs	13	16	.448	5	9	.357	18	25	.419
Trenton Bengals	12	16	.429	4	8	.333	16	24	.400
Paterson Whirlwinds	6	19	.240	3	9	.250	9	28	.243

ABL CHAMPIONSHIP
Mar. 27, 1929 at Cleveland - Cleveland 24, Fort Wayne 17
Mar. 28 at Cleveland - Cleveland 28, Fort Wayne 23
Mar. 30 at Fort Wayne - Cleveland 19, Fort Wayne 18
Apr. 1 at Fort Wayne - Cleveland 30, Fort Wayne 22

LEAGUE LEADERS

Regular Season	G	FG	FT	TP	PPG
Benny Borgmann, Fort Wayne	42	100	125	325	7.7
Nat Hickey, Cleveland/Chicago	46	124	74	322	7.0
Carl Husta, Cleveland	42	101	83	285	6.8
Lou Rabin, Rochester	40	110	54	274	6.9
Tom Barlow, Trenton	38	120	34	274	7.2
Johnny Beckman, Rochester/Cleveland	38	101	67	269	7.1
Rusty Saunders, Fort Wayne	42	104	50	258	6.1
Red Conaty, Brooklyn	39	107	37	251	6.4
Davey Banks, New York	42	98	48	244	5.8
Al Kellett, Trenton/Chicago	38	79	79	237	6.2

1929-30 ABL

Syracuse joined the league, as did the Celtics, but the Celtics were a shadow of their former selves. They struggled to a 5-5 mark and dropped out after before owner Jim Furey had sold off Davey Banks, Joe Brennan and Nat Holman. Syracuse didn't fare any better, dropping out later in the first half of the season with a 4-20 record (including four forfeits).

Cleveland used a win over Brooklyn late in the first half to help claim the first-half title, despite two forfeitures padding Brooklyn's record. In the second half Rochester edged the Rosenblums by a game to set up the championship series between the two clubs. Rochester took the first game of the series, but Cleveland rebounded to sweep the next four to claim the league championship.

	FIRST HALF			SECOND HALF			SEASON TOTALS		
	W	L	PCT.	W	L	PCT.	W	L	PCT.
Cleveland Rosenblums	17	7	.738	18	12	.600	35	19	.648
Rochester Centrals	14	10	.583	19	11	.633	33	21	.611
Brooklyn Visitations	15	9	.625	15	15	.500	30	24	.556
Chicago Bruins	12	12	.500	17	13	.567	29	25	.537
New York Celtics*	5	5	.500	..	..	....	5	5	.500
Fort Wayne Hoosiers	12	12	.500	13	17	.433	25	29	.463
Paterson Crescents	10	14	.417	8	22	.267	18	36	.333
Syracuse All-Americans**	4	20	.167	..	..	....	4	20	.167

*New York dropped out Dec. 19, 1929 during the first half and their games were stricken from the standings.
**Syracuse dropped out on Jan. 6 during the first half and forfeited their final four games.

ABL CHAMPIONSHIP
Mar. 20, 1930 at Rochester - Rochester 20, Cleveland 16
Mar. 21 at Cleveland - Cleveland 18, Rochester 17
Mar. 22 at Rochester - Cleveland 18, Rochester 13
Mar. 23 at Cleveland - Cleveland 23, Rochester 16
Mar. 24 at Cleveland - Cleveland 21, Rochester 15

LEAGUE LEADERS

Regular Season	G	FG	FT	TP	PPG
Benny Borgmann, Fort Wayne/Paterson	50	149	118	416	8.3
Gaza Chizmadia, Rochester	55	113	117	343	6.2
Carl Husta, Cleveland	56	135	61	331	5.9
Nat Hickey, Chicago	53	133	51	317	6.0
Davey Banks, New York/Fort Wayne	50	122	63	307	6.1
Joe Brennan, Brooklyn	43	108	61	277	6.4
Red Conaty, Brooklyn	54	109	40	258	4.8
Pat Herlihy, Brooklyn	53	101	37	239	4.5
Lloyd Kintzing, Rochester	52	100	32	232	4.5
Nat Holman, New York/Syracuse/Chicago	47	88	51	227	4.8

1930-31 ABL

The Great Depression hit the league hard during the 1930-31 season. Toledo was added to bring membership back up to seven clubs, but a new league rule mandating that each club carry two rookies pushed out many familiar faces, including Tom Barlow, Gaza Chizmadia, Johnny Beckman and Nat Holman. Cleveland floundered early in the season and folded after a 6-6 start. Paterson followed soon after, leaving the league with five clubs.

Brooklyn captured the title in the season's first half, but slipped to the middle of the pack in the second half when Joe Brennan left the club. Fort Wayne and Chicago battled down to the wire in the second half, finishing deadlocked with 11-5 records, but Fort Wayne claimed the tie-breaker 20-16 to move on to the post-season. Brooklyn then returned to their first half form and defeated Fort Wayne four games to two for the final league championship.

Financial losses forced league president John O'Brien to suspend operations after the season, and after two seasons of inactivity, the league resumed play on a smaller scale. It would be another 15 years before another league with the ABL's major league aspirations would return.

	FIRST HALF			SECOND HALF			SEASON TOTALS		
	W	L	PCT.	W	L	PCT.	W	L	PCT.
Fort Wayne Hoosiers	13	9	.591	11	5	.688	24	14	.632
Brooklyn Visitations	14	7	.667	8	8	.500	22	15	.595
Paterson Crescents**	9	9	.500	..	..	....	9	9	.500
Cleveland Rosenblums*	6	6	.500	..	..	....	6	6	.500
Chicago Bruins	7	14	.333	11	5	.688	18	19	.486
Rochester Centrals	10	9	.526	5	10	.333	15	19	.441
Toledo Red Man Tobaccos	8	13	.381	4	11	.274	12	24	.333

*Cleveland dropped out Dec. 8, 1930 during the first half.
**Paterson dropped out Dec. 30 during the first half.

ABL SECOND HALF TIEBREAKER
Feb. 28, 1931 at Chicago - Fort Wayne 20, Chicago 16

ABL CHAMPIONSHIP
Mar. 5 at Brooklyn - Brooklyn 14, Fort Wayne 10
Mar. 8 at Brooklyn - Brooklyn 21, Fort Wayne 13
Mar. 10 at Fort Wayne - Fort Wayne 24, Brooklyn 20
Mar. 11 at Fort Wayne - Fort Wayne 30, Brooklyn 26 (2 overtimes)
Mar. 13 at Fort Wayne - Brooklyn 18, Fort Wayne 13
Mar. 15 at Brooklyn - Brooklyn 24, Fort Wayne 18

LEAGUE LEADERS

Regular Season	G	FG	FT	TP	PPG
Benny Borgmann, Paterson/Chicago	33	111	68	290	8.8
Davey Banks, Toledo	34	94	66	254	7.5
Manny Hirsch, Rochester	28	81	49	211	7.6
Willie Scrill, Brooklyn	37	87	29	203	5.5
Frank Shimek, Fort Wayne	37	78	47	203	5.5
Al Kellett, Brooklyn	36	59	55	173	4.8
Carl Husta, Cleveland/Fort Wayne	35	64	42	170	4.9
Rusty Saunders, Fort Wayne	38	66	34	166	4.4
Cookie Cunningham, Toledo	35	53	44	150	4.5
Lou Spindell, Cleveland/Toledo	35	58	28	144	4.1

AMERICAN BASKETBALL LEAGUE: 1925-31

Teams	25-26	26-27	27-28	28-29	29-30	30-31	Totals
Baltimore	x	6-36	x	x	x	x	6-36
Boston	6-10	x	x	x	x	x	6-10
Brooklyn	19-11	32-10	18-10	25-16	30-24	22-15	146-86
Buffalo	10-20	x	x	x	x	x	10-20
Chicago	9-21	13-29	13-36	19-22	29-25	18-19	101-152
Cleveland	23-7	26-16	22-29	29-13	35-19	6-6	141-90
Detroit	8-22	0-6	5-13	x	x	x	13-41
Fort Wayne	13-17	23-19	27-24	29-13	25-29	24-14	141-116
New York	x	x	40-9	18-25	x	x	58-34
Paterson	x	x	x	9-28	18-36	9-9	36-73
Philadelphia	x	24-18	30-21	x	x	x	54-39
Rochester	18-12	14-28	24-28	18-22	33-21	15-19	122-130
Syracuse	x	x	x	x	4-20	x	4-20
Toledo	x	x	x	x	x	12-24	12-24
Trenton	x	x	x	16-24	x	x	16-24
Washington	22-8	30-12	7-16	x	x	x	59-36
Total games played	123	171	181	163	174	106	918

METROPOLITAN BASKETBALL LEAGUE
[1932 to 1932-33]

LEAGUE MEMBERS

Bronx St. Martins [Braves]	Bronx, NY	1932-33
Brooklyn Americans	Brooklyn, NY	1932-33
Brooklyn Hill House	Brooklyn, NY	1932-33
Brooklyn Jewels	Brooklyn, NY	1932 to 1932-33
Brooklyn Jewish Center	Brooklyn, NY	1932
Brooklyn Visitations [Visitation Triangles]	Brooklyn, NY	1932 to 1932-33
Corbett's Jamaicans	Jamaica, NY	1932-33
Hoboken Lisas	Hoboken, NJ	1932 to 1932-33
Jamaica St. Monicas [St. Monica Lyceum]	Jamaica, NY	1932
Jersey City Palace Diamonds [Diamonds]	Jersey City, NJ	1932-33
Long Island Pros [Imps, Pro-Imps]	Queens, NY	1932 to 1932-33
Paterson Continentals	Paterson, NJ	1932-33
Union City Reds	Union City, NJ	1932 to 1932-33
Yonkers Knights [Caseys]	Yonkers, NY	1932-33

1932 MBL

Organized on February 10, 1932 with John J. O'Brien presiding as president, the Metropolitan Basketball League fielded teams in Brooklyn (and three more from the American Basketball League), Hoboken, Jamaica, Long Island and Union City.

In an abbreviated season, the Visitations with Red Conaty, Rody Cooney, Al Kellett, Pat Herlihy and Willie Scrill, and the Brooklyn Jewels with Davey Banks, Matty Begovich, Rip Gerson, Mac Kinsbronner, Allie Schuckman, finished tied for first place with 10-2 records. In a best-of-three playoff series the Visitations took the decisive third game to win the league title.

	W	L	PCT.
Brooklyn Visitations	10	2	.833
Brooklyn Jewels	10	2	.833
Union City Reds	8	4	.667
Hoboken Lisas	6	6	.500
Brooklyn Jewish Center	4	8	.333
Long Island Pros	3	9	.250
Jamaica St. Monicas	1	11	.083

MBL PLAYOFFS

Apr. 15, 1932 at Arcadia Hall, Brooklyn - Brooklyn Visitations 23, Brooklyn Jewels 16
Apr. 17 at Elks Ballroom, Brooklyn - Brooklyn Jewels 29, Brooklyn Visitations 19
Apr. 25 at Elks Club, Brooklyn - Brooklyn Visitations 28, Brooklyn Jewels 25

LEAGUE LEADERS

Regular Season	G	FG	FT	TP	PPG
Mac Kinsbronner, Brooklyn Jewels	12	42	16	100	8.3
Allie Schuckman, Brooklyn Jewels	12	35	26	96	8.0
Willie Scrill, Brooklyn Visitations	12	36	11	83	6.9
T. Neppell, Jamaica	12	36	9	81	6.8
Mike Michelotti, Long Island	11	35	10	80	7.3
Red Conaty, Brooklyn Visitations	12	32	12	76	6.8
Al Kellett, Brooklyn Visitations	12	28	19	75	6.2
Joe Brennan, Union City	11	29	15	73	6.6
Gruden, Hoboken	10	28	15	71	7.1
Pat Herlihy, Brooklyn Visitations	12	29	8	66	5.5

1932-33 MBL

After the Brooklyn Jewish Center and Jamaica St. Monicas both dropped out during the off-season, the Brooklyn Hillhouse, Corbett's Jamaicans, Paterson Continentals and Yonkers Knights were added to increase the Met League's membership to nine clubs.

Early in the first half, after a 2-2 start, Brooklyn Hillhouse dropped out and were replaced by the Brooklyn Americans. The Brooklyn Jewels finished 13-3 to top Hoboken by 1-1/2 games in the first half. Jersey City joined the league for the second half of the season, and after a 2-7 start Brooklyn was replaced by the Bronx St. Martins. Union City and Brooklyn tied for the second-half title with Union City winning a double-overtime tiebreaker to set up a league championship against the Jewels who won two games for the league title.

On October 21 the four remaining MBL clubs, the Brooklyn Visitations, Brooklyn Jewels, Bronx Americans and Hoboken Thourots, along with the Philadelphia Hebrews and Trenton Moose of the Eastern League, were reorganized as the American Basketball League.

	FIRST HALF			SECOND HALF			SEASON TOTALS		
	W	L	PCT.	W	L	PCT.	W	L	PCT.
Brooklyn Jewels	13	3	.812	16	6	.727	29	9	.763
Union City Reds	9	7	.562	16	6	.727	25	13	.658
Hoboken Lisas	11	4	.733	12	9	.571	23	13	.639
Brooklyn Visitations	9	6	.600	12	8	.600	21	14	.600
Long Island Pros*	8	7	.533	..	..	....	8	7	.533
Yonkers Knights	8	8	.500	4	16	.200	12	24	.333
Brooklyn H.H./Brooklyn A./ Bronx St. Martins**	3	12	.200	7	13	.350	10	25	.286
Paterson Continentals*	3	9	.250	..	..	....	3	9	.250
Corbett's Jamaicans*	3	11	.214	..	..	....	3	11	.214
Jersey City Palace Diamonds***	..	..	....	1	10	.091	1	10	.091

*Corbett's, Long Island and Paterson dropped out during the first half.
**Brooklyn Hill House was replaced by the Brooklyn Americans during the first half, Brooklyn Americans were replaced by Bronx St. Martins Feb. 7, 1933 during the second half.
***Jersey City awarded franchise Feb. during the second half.

MBL SECOND HALF PLAYOFF

Mar. 31, 1933 at Union City - Union City 32, Brooklyn Jewels 28 (2OT)

MBL PLAYOFFS

Apr. 12 at Arcadia Hall, Brooklyn - Brooklyn Jewels 31, Union City 23
Apr. 16 at Elks Hall, Brooklyn - Brooklyn Jewels 31, Union City 16

AMERICAN BASKETBALL LEAGUE
[1933-34 TO 1952-53]

LEAGUE MEMBERS

Allentown Aces	Allentown, PA	1950-51
Atlantic City Sand Snipers	Atlantic City, NJ	1936-37
Baltimore Bullets	Baltimore, MD	1944-45 to 1946-47
Baltimore Clippers	Baltimore, MD	1939-40 to 1940-41
Boston Trojans	Boston, MA	1934-35
Bridgeport Aer-A-Sols	Bridgeport, CT	1949-50 to 1950-51
Bridgeport Newfield Steelers	Bridgeport, CT	1948-49
Bridgeport Roesslers	Bridgeport, CT	1951-52
Bronx Americans [St. Martin's]	Bronx, NY	1933-34
Bronx Yankees	Bronx, NY	1937-38
Brooklyn Celtics	Brooklyn, NY	1940-41
Brooklyn Gothams	Brooklyn, NY	1946-47 to 1948-49
Brooklyn Indians	Brooklyn, NY	1942-43 to 1943-44
Brooklyn Jewels	Brooklyn, NY	1933-34
Brooklyn Jewels	Brooklyn, NY	1936-37
Brooklyn Visitations	Brooklyn, NY	1933-34 to 1935-36
Brooklyn Visitations	Brooklyn, NY	1936-37 to 1938-39
Camden Brewers [Athletics]	Camden, NJ	1933-34
Camden Indians	Camden, NJ	1942-43
Carbondale Aces [Big Chiefs]	Carbondale, PA	1950-51 to 1951-52
Elmira Colonels	Elmira, NY	1951-52 to 1952-53
Elizabeth Braves	Elizabeth, NJ	1946-47 to 1947-48
Harrisburg Senators	Harrisburg, PA	1942-43
Hartford Hurricanes	Hartford, CT	1947-48 to 1949-50
Hoboken Thourots	Union City, NJ	1933-34
Jersey Reds	North Bergen, NJ	1934-35 to 1939-40
Jersey City Atoms	Jersey City, NJ	1946-47 to 1947-48
Kingston Colonials	Kingston, NY	1935-36 to 1939-40
Lancaster Roses	Lancaster, PA	1947-48
Manchester British Americans [BA's]	Manchester, CT	1951-52 to 1952-53
Middletown Guards	Middletown, CT	1951-52 to 1952-53
New Britain Jackaways	New Britain, CT	1934-35
New Britain Mules	New Britain, CT	1934-35
New Britain Palaces	New Britain, CT	1933-34
New Haven Jewels	New Haven, CT	1937-38
New York Americans	New York, NY	1943-44
New York Gothams	New York, NY	1944-45 to 1945-46
New York Harlem Yankees	New York, NY	1949-50
New York Jewels	New York, NY	1934-35
New York Jewels	New York, NY	1940-41 to 1942-43
New York Original Celtics	New York, NY	1936-37 to 1937-38
New York Yankees	Bronx, NY	1937-38
Newark Joe Fays [Bears]	Newark, NJ	1933-34
Newark Bobcats	Newark, NJ	1946-47
Newark Mules	Newark, NJ	1934-35
Passaic Red Devils [Reds]	Passaic, NJ	1935-36
Paterson Crescents	Paterson, NJ	1944-45 to 1950-51
Paterson Panthers	Paterson, NJ	1935-36
Paterson Visitations	Paterson, NJ	1936-37
Pawtucket Slaters	Pawtucket, RI	1952-53
Philadelphia Hebrews [SPHAs]	Philadelphia, PA	1933-34 to 1936-37
Philadelphia SPHAs	Philadelphia, PA	1937-38 to 1948-49
Saratoga Harlem Yankees	Saratoga Springs, NY	1949-50 to 1951-52
Saratoga-Glens Falls-Hazleton Yankees	Saratoga Springs, NY	1952-53
Schenectady Packers	Schenectady, NY	1949-50
Schenectady Yankees	Schenectady, NY	1951-52
Scranton Miners	Scranton, PA	1947-48 to 1952-53
Trenton Bengals [Moose]	Trenton, NJ	1935-36
Trenton Moose	Trenton, NJ	1933-34
Trenton Tigers	Trenton, NJ	1941-42 to 1949-50
Troy Celtics	Troy, NY	1939-40 to 1940-41
Troy Celtics	Troy, NY	1946-47
Troy Haymakers	Troy, NY	1938-39 to 1939-40
Union City Reds	Union City, NJ	1933-34
Utica Pros	Utica, NY	1950-51
Washington Brewers	Washington, DC	1940-41 to 1941-42
Washington Capitols	Washington, DC	1944-45
Washington Capitols	Washington, DC	1951-52
Washington Heurichs	Washington, DC	1938-39
Washington Heurich Brewers	Washington, DC	1939-40
Westchester Indians	White Plains, NY	1944-45
Wilkes-Barre Barons	Wilkes-Barre, PA	1938-39 to 1939-40
Wilkes-Barre Barons	Wilkes-Barre, PA	1947-48 to 1952-53
Wilmington Bombers	Wilmington, DE	1944-45 to 1946-47
Wilmington Blue Bombers	Wilmington, DE	1941-42
Wilmington Blue Bombers	Wilmington, DE	1943-44
Yonkers Chiefs	Yonkers, NY	1946-47

1933-34 ABL

John J. O'Brien, a long-time basketball executive, revived the American Basketball League in 1933. The new version of the ABL didn't have the same national vision as its predecessor. The league's membership consisted of clubs from the Northeast, taking in teams from the Metropolitan Basketball League (Bronx, the Brooklyn Jewels and Brooklyn Visitations, Hoboken, and Union City) and the Eastern League (Philadelphia and Trenton) as well as Newark which featured scoring star Benny Borgmann.

The league changed its game format from two 20-minute halves to three 15-minute periods. Trenton and Brooklyn proved the class of the league in the first half, finishing deadlocked at 22-6, well ahead of Philadelphia. Trenton defeated Brooklyn in a first half playoff to lay claim to first place. Hoboken was less successful as they moved to Camden after four games, and then New Britain.

Philadelphia went undefeated in 14 contests to finish well ahead of the pack in the second half and went on to the league championship, topping Trenton four games to two.

	FIRST HALF			SECOND HALF			SEASON TOTALS		
	W	L	PCT.	W	L	PCT.	W	L	PCT.
Brooklyn Jewels	22	6	.786	4	4	.500	26	10	.722
Philadelphia SPHAs	15	12	.556	14	0	1.000	29	12	.707
Trenton Moose	22	6	.786	6	7	3462	28	13	.683
Hoboken/Camden/ New Britain*	5	19	.208	7	5	.583	12	24	.333
Brooklyn Visitations	12	12	.500	1	8	.111	13	20	.394
Bronx Americans	10	15	.400	2	6	.250	12	21	.364
Union City Reds	10	18	.357	4	7	.364	14	25	.359
Newark Bears	9	17	.346	4	5	.444	13	22	.371

*The Hoboken Thourots moved to the Camden Brewers on Nov. 23, and the New Britain Palaces took over the team on Jan. 10.

ABL PLAYOFFS: FIRST HALF CHAMPIONSHIP
Mar. 8, 1934 at Trenton - Trenton 44, Brooklyn 23
Mar. 9 at Brooklyn - Trenton 21, Brooklyn 14

ABL CHAMPIONSHIP
Apr. 6 at Trenton - Philadelphia 28, Trenton 21
Apr. 7 at Philadelphia - Trenton 35, Philadelphia 21
Apr. 13 at Trenton - Philadelphia 32, Trenton 20
Apr. 14 at Philadelphia - Trenton 32, Philadelphia 29
Apr. 15 at Brooklyn - Philadelphia 32, Trenton 22
Apr. 21 at Philadelphia - Philadelphia 40, Trenton 34

LEAGUE LEADERS

Regular Season	G	FG	FT	TP	PPG
Benny Borgmann, Newark	32	120	81	321	10.0
Moe Spahn, New Britain	38	92	149	333	8.8
Nat Frankel, Bronx	32	105	66	276	8.6
Cy Kaselman, Philadelphia	39	115	102	332	8.5
Lou Spindell, Trenton	40	114	98	326	8.2
Allie Schuckman, Brooklyn Jewels	34	91	89	271	8.0
Mac Kinsbronner, Brooklyn Jewels	32	101	44	246	7.7
Shikey Gothoffer, Philadelphia	41	105	102	312	7.6
Louis Bender, Union City	9	28	12	68	7.6
Paulie Adamo, Union City	37	93	87	273	7.4

1934-35 ABL

There were lineup changes in the league's follow-up season as Bronx and Trenton dropped out and Boston joined the league. Other teams underwent name changes as the Brooklyn Jewels became the New York Jewels, Newark became the Newark Mules, Union City was renamed the Jersey Reds in order to receive more widespread support, and New Britain was rechristened the New Britain Jackaways.

New Britain didn't last long however as they dropped out of the league after a 6-14 start. On the same day the Mules moved to New Britain and became the New Britain Mules for the second half of the season. The Jewels finished on top of the standings in the first half with a 16-6 record, giving them a 3-1/2 game cushion over the second place Philadelphia club.

Philadelphia and Brooklyn battled down to the season's last day in the second half, and after the two teams finished with identical 12-7 records, Brooklyn claimed first place by winning two of three games in a playoff. In the championship series Brooklyn then defeated New York, who had struggled in the second half, three games to two.

	FIRST HALF			SECOND HALF			SEASON TOTALS		
	W	L	PCT.	W	L	PCT.	W	L	PCT.
New York Jewels	16	6	.727	8	10	.444	24	16	.600
Philadelphia Hebrews	13	10	.565	12	7	.632	25	17	.595
Brooklyn Visitations	13	11	.542	12	7	.632	25	18	.581
Newark Mules*	12	11	.521	..	..	.....	12	11	.521
New Britain Mules*	..	..	.....	9	9	.500	9	9	.500
Jersey Reds	7	14	.333	9	9	.500	16	23	.410
Boston Trojans	10	11	.476	4	12	.250	14	23	.378
New Britain Jackaways*	6	14	.300	..	..	.....	6	14	.300

*New Britain and Newark merged for the second half on Jan. 18.

ABL SECOND HALF PLAYOFF
Apr. 5, 1935 at New York - Philadelphia 24, Brooklyn 15
Apr. 6 at Philadelphia - Brooklyn 39, Philadelphia 30
Apr. 11 at Philadelphia - Brooklyn 26, Philadelphia 25

ABL CHAMPIONSHIP
Apr. 12 at Brooklyn - Brooklyn 26, New York 16
Apr. 13 at Philadelphia - New York 26, Brooklyn 25
Apr. 14 at New York - Brooklyn 29, New York 19
Apr. 21 at Brooklyn - New York 26, Brooklyn 25
Apr. 28 at Brooklyn - Brooklyn 26, New York 10

LEAGUE LEADERS

Regular Season	G	TP	PPG
Carl Johnson, Brooklyn	43	310	7.2

1935-36 ABL

During the off-season Boston and New Britain dropped out of the league. The ABL found replacements in Kingston, and Paterson, although Paterson moved to Trenton during the season's first half and then moved to the Passaic at mid-season.

Philadelphia continued their fine play, finishing as first-half leaders with a 14-5 record. They slumped to 9-11 in the second half, however, as the Brooklyn Visitations grabbed the second half crown with a 12-8 record, finishing one game ahead of the Jersey Reds. Brooklyn was led by its long-range set shooter Bobby McDermott who led the league in scoring.

In the championship series Philadelphia was pitted against Brooklyn for the title. Philadelphia, who had lost a post-season series to Brooklyn the previous year, turned the tables, winning four games to three, as each squad won all of its home contests.

	FIRST HALF			SECOND HALF			SEASON TOTALS		
	W	L	PCT.	W	L	PCT.	W	L	PCT.
Philadelphia SPHAs	14	5	.737	9	11	.450	23	16	.590
New York Jewels	11	8	.579	10	10	.500	21	18	.538
Brooklyn Visitations	10	10	.500	12	8	.600	22	18	.550
Jersey Reds	9	9	.500	11	9	.550	20	18	.526
Kingston Colonials	7	12	.368	9	10	.474	16	22	.421
Paterson/Trenton/Passaic*	4	11	.267	8	11	.421	12	22	.353

*The Paterson Panthers moved to the Trenton Bengals on Dec. 13 during the first half, then to the Passaic Red Devils for the second half on Jan. 2

ABL CHAMPIONSHIP
Mar. 28, 1936 at Philadelphia - Philadelphia 30, Brooklyn 28
Mar. 29 at Brooklyn - Brooklyn 27, Philadelphia 24
Apr. 4 at Philadelphia - Philadelphia 30, Brooklyn 27
Apr. 5 at Brooklyn - Brooklyn 31, Philadelphia 24
Apr. 11 at Philadelphia - Philadelphia 26, Brooklyn 23
Apr. 12 at Brooklyn - Brooklyn 31, Philadelphia 30
Apr. 18 at Philadelphia - Philadelphia 47, Brooklyn 34

LEAGUE LEADERS

Regular Season	G	FG	FT	TP	PPG
Bobby McDermott, Brooklyn	40	157	68	382	9.6
Lou Rabin, Passaic	27	84	63	231	8.6
Carl Husta, Kingston	38	109	74	292	7.7
Mac Kinsbronner, New York	39	114	64	292	7.5
Moe Spahn, Jersey	36	74	102	250	6.9
Shikey Gothoffer, Philadelphia	37	96	55	247	6.7
Petey Berenson, Brooklyn	40	79	101	259	6.5
Carl Johnson, Brooklyn	39	85	78	248	6.4
Willie Scrill, Jersey	37	92	42	226	6.1
Allie Schuckman, New York	35	83	48	214	6.1

1936-37 ABL

The season brought more league-wide changes as New York star Barney Sedran left the league in the off-season. New York then struggled through the season, moving to Brooklyn for the second half as they dropped to the bottom of the standings. Passaic would be the only team to drop out of the league during the off-season, as Atlantic City would be welcomed in to balance the league schedule but they dropped out after starting the season 0-10. The Brooklyn Visitations moved, becoming the Paterson Visitations just prior to the season, but the Paterson club lasted only one game before returning to Brooklyn in November.

The league, which was now down to five clubs, admitted the New York Original Celtics for the second half of the season. The top club in the first half would be Jersey, as they finished with a 14-4 record to finish two games ahead of Philadelphia.

Philadelphia edged Jersey by two games in the second half, and the two teams met in a thrilling league championship series. Down three games to one and losing the fifth game with just 15 seconds remaining, Philadelphia staged a miracle rally and prevailed four games to three.

	FIRST HALF			SECOND HALF			SEASON TOTALS		
	W	L	PCT.	W	L	PCT.	W	L	PCT.
Jersey Reds	14	4	.778	12	8	.600	26	12	.684
Philadelphia SPHAs	12	6	.667	14	6	.700	26	12	.684
Kingston Colonials	11	6	.647	9	11	.450	20	17	.540
New York Original Celtics	..	..	....	10	10	.500	10	10	.500
Paterson Visitations/ Brooklyn Visitations**	4	11	.237	10	9	.526	14	20	.412
New York Jewels/ Brooklyn Jewels***	7	10	.712	4	15	.211	11	25	.306
Atlantic City Sand Snipers*	0	10	.000	..	..	....	0	10	.000

*Atlantic City dropped out during the first half on Dec. 21.
**Paterson moved to the Brooklyn Visitations during the first half on Nov. 23.
***New York was renamed the Brooklyn Jewels for the second half.

ABL CHAMPIONSHIP
Mar. 27, 1937 at Philadelphia - Jersey 36, Philadelphia 31
Mar. 28 at North Bergen, NJ - Philadelphia 39, Jersey 36
Apr. 3 at Philadelphia - Jersey 34, Philadelphia 28
Apr. 4 at North Bergen, NJ - Jersey 34, Philadelphia 30
Apr. 10 at Philadelphia - Philadelphia 34, Jersey 33
Apr. 14 at North Bergen, NJ - Philadelphia 45, Jersey 23
Apr. 17 at Philadelphia - Philadelphia 44, Jersey 43 (OT)

LEAGUE LEADERS
Regular Season	G	FG	FT	TP	PPG
Lou Rabin, Kingston	37	187	114	488	13.2
Mac Kinsbronner, N.Y. Jewels/Brooklyn Jewels	34	135	76	346	10.1
Carl Johnson, N.Y. Celtics	20	62	65	189	9.5
Moe Spahn, Jersey	36	99	128	326	9.1
Nat Frankel, Brooklyn Visitations	24	77	53	207	8.6
Red Rosan, Philadelphia	36	101	100	302	8.4
Carl Husta, Kingston	37	124	51	299	8.1
Petey Berenson, N.Y. Celtics	19	40	72	152	8.0
Shikey Gothoffer, Philadelphia	32	91	61	243	7.6
Paulie Adamo, Jersey	36	83	88	254	7.1

1937-38 ABL
Just prior to the season, Nathan Podoloff, the manager of New Haven Arena and brother of future NBA President Maurice Podoloff, purchased the Brooklyn Jewels and moved them to New Haven. The move was unsuccessful and the team returned to Brooklyn after six games. The Philadelphia Hebrews were renamed the SPHAs (South Philadelphia Hebrew Association) and the Bronx Yankees joined the league, renaming themselves the New York Yankees before dropping out 12 games into the season.

In the first half of the season, Jersey, led by Moe Spahn and Moe Frankel, outdistanced the Jewels, who boasted a fine frontcourt of Mac Kinsbronner, Allie Schuckman, Willie Rubenstein and George Slott. The New York Jewels topped the league in the second half finishing 1-1/2 games ahead of Jersey while Brooklyn tumbled to the bottom of the league.

Jersey and the New York Jewels agreed to play a best-of-five championship series but were overruled by the league. In a best-of-seven affair Jersey won four games to two.

	FIRST HALF			SECOND HALF			SEASON TOTALS		
	W	L	PCT.	W	L	PCT.	W	L	PCT.
Jersey Reds	16	6	.727	13	7	.650	29	13	.690
New Haven Jewels/ New York Jewels*	12	8	.600	14	5	.737	26	13	.667
Philadelphia SPHAs	12	10	.545	11	9	.550	23	19	.548
New York Original Celtics	11	10	.524	7	11	.389	18	21	.462
Brooklyn Visitations	13	10	.565	2	15	.118	15	25	.375
Kingston Colonials	5	15	.250	9	9	.500	14	24	.368
Bronx Yankees/ New York Yankees**	1	11	.083	..	..	....	1	11	.083

*New Haven moved to the New York Jewels during the first half on Nov. 30.
**The Bronx Yankees were renamed the New York Yankees and then dropped out during the first half on Jan. 11.

ABL CHAMPIONSHIP
Apr. 2, 1938 at North Bergen, NJ - Jersey 35, New York 34
Apr. 3 at Brooklyn - New York 33, Jersey 30
Apr. 9 at North Bergen, NJ - Jersey 30, New York 22
Apr. 10 at Brooklyn - Jersey 26, New York 24
Apr. 13 at North Bergen, NJ - New York 37, Jersey 33
Apr. 17 at Brooklyn - Jersey 30, New York 28

LEAGUE LEADERS
Regular Season	G	FG	FT	TP	PPG
Lou Rabin, Kingston	39	203	108	514	13.2
Moe Spahn, Jersey	40	118	127	363	9.1
Inky Lautman, Philadelphia	42	136	87	359	8.5
Petey Berenson, N.Y. Celtics	38	106	110	322	8.5
Nat Frankel, N.Y. Celtics	41	127	81	345	8.4
Mac Kinsbronner, N.Y. Jewels	40	124	81	329	8.2
Cy Kaselman, Philadelphia	42	117	93	327	7.8
Shikey Gothoffer, Philadelphia	40	95	93	283	7.1
Carl Johnson, N.Y. Celtics	38	93	80	266	7.0
Moe Frankel, Jersey	40	111	51	273	6.8

1938-39 ABL
The 1938-39 season was the year the split-season format was abandoned. The New York Original Celtics migrated to Troy as Washington and Wilkes-Barre also joined the league in the off-season.

Kingston finished the season in first place, edging Philadelphia. But Kingston lost in the playoffs to Jersey, as New York topped Philadelphia. New York then grabbed the league title, by avenging their 1938 loss to Jersey with a three-game sweep.

	W	L	PCT.
Kingston Colonials	28	7	.800
Philadelphia SPHAs	24	9	.727
Jersey Reds	19	14	.576
New York Jewels	19	15	.559
Wilkes-Barre Barons	14	22	.389
Troy Haymakers	12	21	.364
Brooklyn Visitations	7	20	.259
Washington Heurichs	7	22	.241

ABL PLAYOFFS
Jersey defeated Kingston 2 games to 1

Mar. 18, 1939 at Philadelphia - New York 46, Philadelphia 44
Mar. 19 at New York - New York 31, Philadelphia 24

ABL CHAMPIONSHIP
Mar. 31 at North Bergen, NJ - New York 34, Jersey 30
Apr. 29 at Brooklyn - New York 40, Jersey 36
Apr. 9 at Brooklyn - New York 37, Jersey 34 (OT)

LEAGUE LEADERS
Regular Season	G	FG	FT	TP	PPG
Lou Rabin, Jersey	33	116	109	341	10.3
Moe Dubilier, Wilkes-Barre	34	114	92	320	9.4
Moe Spahn, Jersey	32	98	85	281	8.8
Mickey Schoenfeld, Washington	29	103	48	254	8.8
Allie Esposito, Brooklyn	26	85	55	225	8.7
Art Zahn, Washington	29	79	72	230	7.9
Nat Frankel, Kingston	35	102	72	276	7.9
Mickey Kupperberg, New York	30	76	71	223	7.4
Joe Polcher, Troy	21	62	31	155	7.4
Inky Lautman, Philadelphia	32	87	58	232	7.2

1939-40 ABL
The Troy Celtics joined the league for the 1939-40 season and Brooklyn moved to Baltimore, giving the league eight members to start the season. The league membership was reduced by three during the season as Kingston merged with Troy, Jersey merged with New York, and Wilkes-Barre dropped out.

Philadelphia edged Washington by a game and Troy by 1-1/2 to win the league's regular season title. Then, in a round-robin playoff tournament, Philly captured the league championship. Washington represented the league in the World Tournament, defeating the Waterloo Wonders 35-23. They then lost to the Chicago Bruins in the semi-final round, 46-38, before defeating the Syracuse Reds 41-30 for third place. After Philadelphia defeated Washington in a one-game playoff for first place, all five remaining teams embarked on a round-robin series of games to determine the league champion, with Philadelphia finishing the tournament 7-0 to win the league title.

	W	L	PCT.
Kingston Colonials*	8	4	.667
Philadelphia SPHAs	19	13	.594
Washington Heurich Brewers	19	13	.594
Troy Haymakers	19	15	.559
New York Jewels	15	15	.500
Baltimore Clippers	15	16	.484
Jersey Reds**	7	14	.333
Wilkes-Barre Barons***	5	17	.227

*Kingston merged with Troy on Dec. 19.
**Jersey merged with New York on Jan. 26.
***Wilkes-Barre dropped out on Feb. 2.

ABL PLAYOFFS: FIRST PLACE
Mar. 9, 1940 at Philadelphia - Philadelphia 34, Washington 27

ABL CHAMPIONSHIP: ROUND ROBIN PLAYOFF

Philadelphia defeated Washington, Troy, New York and Baltimore in a round-robin playoff

Mar. 6 at Troy - Troy defeated Baltimore
Mar. 8 (location unknown) - Baltimore 43, Washington 37
Mar. 10 (location unknown) - Washington 33, Baltimore 32
Mar. 13 at Troy - Troy 44, Washington 32
Mar. 15 at Baltimore - New York 34, Baltimore 33
Mar. 16 at Philadelphia - Philadelphia 32, Troy 29
Mar. 17 at New York - Philadelphia 33, New York 27
Mar. 23 at Philadelphia - Philadelphia 43, Baltimore 36
Mar. 27 at Troy - Troy 37, Baltimore 27
Mar. 29 at Baltimore - Troy 37, Baltimore 24
Mar. 30 at Philadelphia - Philadelphia 37, New York 35
Mar. 31 at New York - New York vs Troy
Apr. 3 at Troy - Philadelphia 32, Troy 28
Apr. 7 at Philadelphia - Philadelphia 51, Washington 44
Apr. 10 at Coatesville, PA - Philadelphia 48, Washington 30

Round-Robin Standings

Philadelphia	7-0
Troy	6-2
New York	3-4
Washington	1-5
Baltimore	1-7

LEAGUE LEADERS

Regular Season	G	FG	FT	TP	PPG
Bobby McDermott, Baltimore	31	130	81	341	11.0
Phil Rabin, Washington	34	108	72	288	8.5
Moe Dubilier, Washington	37	110	64	284	7.7
Allie Esposito, Baltimore	29	79	51	209	7.2
Inky Lautman, Philadelphia	33	92	49	233	7.1
Sammy Kaplan, Troy	34	87	57	231	6.8
Chick Reiser, Troy	33	73	78	224	6.8
Petey Rosenberg, Philadelphia	30	90	22	202	6.7
Moe Goldman, Philadelphia	33	86	42	214	6.5
Willie Rubinstein, New York	27	55	63	173	6.4

1940-41 ABL

In the off-season the New York Jewels renamed themselves the Brooklyn Jewels, as all six clubs which finished the 1939-40 season returned intact. Philadelphia edged Washington by 1/2 game in the first half of the season as Troy relocated to Brooklyn before mid-season.

In the second half of the season Brooklyn finished in front of New York as Philadelphia fell back to fifth. Philadelphia then defeated Brooklyn three games to one in the championship series to take the championship crown. Prior to winning the series Philadelphia played in the World Tournament where they would defeat the Bismarck Phantoms, 48-30, before losing to the Oshkosh All-Stars, 38-31, in the quarter-final round.

	FIRST HALF			SECOND HALF			SEASON TOTALS		
	W	L	PCT.	W	L	PCT.	W	L	PCT.
Troy Haymakers/ Brooklyn Celtics*	6	6	.500	11	4	.733	17	10	.629
Philadelphia SPHAs	9	7	.562	7	9	.438	16	16	.500
Washington Brewers	8	7	.533	7	8	.467	15	15	.500
New York Jewels	6	6	.500	8	8	.500	14	14	.500
Baltimore Clippers	5	8	.385	6	10	.375	11	18	.379

*Troy moved to Brooklyn during the first half.

ABL CHAMPIONSHIP

Apr. 5, 1941 at Philadelphia - Philadelphia 48, Brooklyn 38
Apr. 6 at Saratoga Springs, NY - Brooklyn 40, Philadelphia 26
Apr. 12 at Philadelphia - Philadelphia 50, Brooklyn 43
Apr. 13 at Brooklyn - Philadelphia 30, Brooklyn 29

LEAGUE LEADERS

Regular Season	G	FG	FT	TP	PPG
Petey Rosenberg, Philadelphia	31	122	31	275	8.9
Mickey Kupperberg, Troy/Brooklyn	26	81	45	207	8.0
Inky Lautman, Philadelphia	31	91	56	238	7.7
Lou Rabin, Washington	29	83	53	219	7.6
Moe Spahn, New York	30	79	55	213	7.1
Willie Rubinstein, New York	29	73	58	204	7.0
Chick Reiser, Troy/Brooklyn	26	59	61	179	6.9
Ace Goldstein, New York	29	88	23	199	6.9
Irv Torgoff, Philadelphia	31	88	37	213	6.9
Moe Dubilier, Washington	29	71	45	187	6.4

1941-42 ABL

During the 1941 off-season Brooklyn and Baltimore left the league, but Trenton and Wilmington were added to keep the league membership at five clubs.

Wilmington, led by star Ed Sadowski, who had been signed away from the Indianapolis Kautskys of the National Basketball League, and Moe Spahn took the first half of the season by 2-1/2 games over Philadelphia and Irv Torgoff. Washington

finished third, with Trenton bringing up the rear. New York, which had started the season with only one win in seven games, dropped out in January, leaving the league with four teams, its fewest total ever.

Wilmington also paced the league in a hotly contested second-half race as their 8-4 record put them two games ahead of Trenton, and with only four clubs in the circuit no post-season games were held.

	FIRST HALF			SECOND HALF			SEASON TOTALS		
	W	L	PCT.	W	L	PCT.	W	L	PCT.
Wilmington Blue Bombers	10	3	.769	8	4	.667	18	7	.720
Philadelphia SPHAs	8	6	.571	5	7	.417	13	13	.500
Trenton Tigers	5	8	.385	6	6	.500	11	14	.440
Washington Brewers	5	6	.454	5	7	.417	10	13	.435
New York Jewels*	1	6	.143	..	..	.....	1	6	.143

*New York dropped out in January during the first half.

LEAGUE LEADERS

Regular Season	G	FG	FT	TP	PPG
Nat Frankel, Washington	20	59	70	188	9.4
Irv Torgoff, Philadelphia	22	67	34	168	7.6
Dutch Hoefer, Washington	25	75	32	182	7.3
Ace Goldstein, Trenton	19	57	17	131	6.9
Ed Sadowski, Wilmington	24	65	34	164	6.8
Red Paris, Trenton	25	56	57	169	6.8
Mike Bloom, Trenton	17	42	32	116	6.8
Moe Spahn, Wilmington	20	49	38	136	6.8
Herb Gershon, Trenton	25	72	20	164	6.6
Bernie Fleigel, Wilmington	25	57	36	150	6.0

1942-43 ABL

Washington dropped out following the 1941-42 season, but Harrisburg was added to keep the league at four teams. Wilmington was forced to move out of their homecourt armory when it was needed for wartime use, and the club landed in Camden. The league abandoned the split-season format and Trenton dominated the league winning 11 of 13 games, led by Mike Bloom and Ace Goldstein. Philadelphia finished 3-1/2 games behind in second, and Brooklyn, who had moved from Camden during the season, followed them in third place. Harrisburg, with league leading scorer Steve Juenger, finished in fourth, while New York, returning from a brief hiatus to win only one of their seven games, finished last.

Philadelphia and Trenton met in the championship series as the league returned to its post-season schedule. Philadelphia prevailed in the best-of-seven series four games to three. A highlight of the seventh game was a 70' basket by Irv Torgoff to end the second period, a heave which proved to be the margin of victory.

	W	L	PCT.
Trenton Tigers	11	2	.846
Philadelphia SPHAs	8	6	.571
Camden Indians/Brooklyn Indians*	3	5	.375
Harrisburg Senators	4	8	.250
New York Jewels	1	6	.143

*Camden moved to Brooklyn on Jan. 18.

ABL CHAMPIONSHIP

Mar. 6, 1943 at Philadelphia - Trenton 36, Philadelphia 27
Mar. 7 at Trenton - Philadelphia 42, Trenton 35
Mar. 13 at Philadelphia - Trenton 37, Philadelphia 30
Mar. 14 at Trenton - Philadelphia 42, Trenton 39

Owners Girard Naples of Trenton and Eddie Gottlieb of Philadelphia agreed to postpone the fifth game for one week to rest several injured players

Mar 27 at Philadelphia - Trenton 48, Philadelphia 38
Mar 28 at Trenton - Philadelphia 34, Trenton 33
Apr 3 at Philadelphia - Philadelphia 44, Trenton 42

LEAGUE LEADERS

Regular Season	G	FG	FT	TP	PPG
Steve Juenger, Hartford	10	38	40	116	11.6
Ed Sadowski, Brooklyn	8	32	27	91	11.4
Bobby Holm, New York	6	24	12	60	10.0
Mike Bloom, Trenton	12	37	31	105	8.8
Ace Goldstein, Trenton	13	48	15	111	8.5
Chick Reiser, Brooklyn	7	22	14	58	8.3
Irv Torgoff, Trenton	11	34	20	88	8.0
Hagan Anderson, New York	9	23	23	69	7.7
Bob Fitzgerald, Trenton	9	25	17	67	7.4
Lou Rabin, New York	4	10	8	28	7.0

1943-44 ABL

The New York Jewels renamed themselves the Americans and the Brooklyn club returned to Wilmington when its home court armory was made available. Harrisburg dropped out of the league during the off-season, but a new Brooklyn Indians franchise joined the league to replace them, bringing a young guard named Bob Davies into the league. The ABL returned to the split season format as Wilmington, behind center Ed Sadowski, finished atop the league in the first half, 2-1/2 games ahead of New York. Brooklyn dropped out of the league at mid-season leaving the league with

four teams. Philadelphia edged Trenton by a game in the second half, setting up a series with Wilmington for the league title, as Wilmington came back from a 3-1 deficit to win the best-of-seven series.

Although Wilmington used Jake Ahearn, an ineligible player in game one of the championships, their victory was allowed to stand but Ahearn was barred from the remaining playoff games.

	FIRST HALF			SECOND HALF			SEASON TOTALS		
	W	L	PCT.	W	L	PCT.	W	L	PCT.
Wilmington Blue Bombers	12	4	.750	5	5	.500	17	9	.654
Trenton Tigers	8	6	.571	7	5	.583	15	11	.577
Philadelphia SPHAs	4	9	.308	8	4	.667	12	13	.480
New York Americans	9	6	.600	2	8	.200	11	14	.440
Brooklyn Indians*	2	9	.182	..	..	.....	2	9	.182

*Brooklyn dropped out during the first half.

ABL CHAMPIONSHIP
Mar. 4, 1944 at Philadelphia - Wilmington 44, Philadelphia 31
Mar. 5 at Wilmington - Philadelphia 42, Wilmington 35
Mar. 12 at Wilmington - Philadelphia 50, Wilmington 44
Mar. 18 at Philadelphia - Philadelphia 56, Wilmington 51
Mar. 19 at Wilmington - Wilmington 45, Philadelphia 38
Mar. 25 at Philadelphia - Wilmington 57, Philadelphia 33
Mar. 26 at Wilmington - Wilmington 57, Philadelphia 36

LEAGUE LEADERS
Regular Season	G	FG	FT	TP	PPG
Mike Bloom, Trenton	26	94	85	273	10.5
Ossie Schectman, Philadelphia	19	89	21	199	10.5
Sonny Hertzberg, New York	17	67	23	157	9.2
Irv Torgoff, Philadelphia	21	82	25	189	9.0
Ed Sadowski, Wilmington	23	78	43	199	8.7
Matt Guokas, Trenton	26	77	45	199	7.7
Inky Lautman, Philadelphia	25	76	41	193	7.7
Bob Tough, Trenton	22	70	27	167	7.6
Angelo Musi, Wilmington	21	69	21	159	7.6
Butch Schwartz, Philadelphia	20	54	27	135	6.8

1944-45 ABL
In a busy off-season New York moved to Westchester and Baltimore and Washington joined the league, bringing its membership back up to six teams. Early in the season Washington relocated to Paterson, where they would finish the season in the league cellar, and Westchester moved to New York.

The league again abandoned the split-season format as Philadelphia and Trenton battled down to the end of the season with Philadelphia finishing on top by a game. Philadelphia was then matched against Baltimore in the league championship series, defeating them two games to one.

	W	L	PCT.
Philadelphia SPHAs	22	8	.733
Trenton Tigers	21	9	.700
Wilmington Bombers	14	14	.500
Baltimore Bullets	14	16	.467
Westchester Indians/New York Gothams*	11	15	.423
Washington Capitols/Paterson Crescents**	3	23	.115

*Westchester moved to New York on Jan. 20.
**Washington moved to Paterson on Jan. 1.

ABL PLAYOFFS
Mar. 15, 1945 at Baltimore - Baltimore 48, Trenton 38
Mar. 16 at Trenton - Trenton defeated Baltimore (Trenton played in a pro tournament in Cleveland Mar. 17-18 and then in the World Professional Tournament from Mar. 19 to Mar. 24.)
Apr. 2 at Baltimore - Baltimore defeated Trenton

Mar. 17 at Philadelphia - Philadelphia 49, Wilmington 44
Mar. 21 at Wilmington - Wilmington 48, Philadelphia 29
Apr. 15 at Philadelphia - Philadelphia 48, Wilmington 41

ABL CHAMPIONSHIPS
(originally scheduled for 3 of 5 but changed to 2 of 3)
Apr. 5 at Baltimore - Philadelphia 57, Baltimore 32
Apr. 7 at Philadelphia - Baltimore 47, Philadelphia 46
Apr. 14 at Philadelphia - Philadelphia 46, Baltimore 40

LEAGUE LEADERS
Regular Season	G	FG	FT	TP	PPG
Steve Juenger, Paterson	25	92	89	273	10.9
Mike Bloom, Trenton	30	118	85	321	10.7
Mike Wallace, New York	13	48	27	123	9.5
Sol Broder, Paterson	14	53	25	131	9.4
Cy Boardman, Wilmington	28	94	67	255	9.1
Bob Tough, Trenton	28	103	49	255	9.1
Inky Lautman, Philadelphia	29	99	52	250	8.6
Ace Abbott, Trenton	30	98	34	230	7.7
Hagan Anderson, New York	18	47	42	136	7.6
Art Hillhouse, Philadelphia	29	83	49	215	7.4

1945-46 ABL
In the off-season New York's Bob Davies signed with Rochester of the NBL, but the Gothams replaced him by signing William "Red" Holzman. For the first time in league history the season opened with the same membership that finished the prior season.

In the regular season, Baltimore and Philadelphia finished with identical 21-13 records and were matched against each other in the ABL championship series where Baltimore prevailed three games to one. After the conclusion of the playoffs, the Bullets went on to the World Tournament in Chicago, defeating the Dayton Mickeys 61-58 and Anderson Chiefs 67-65, before losing to the NBL's Fort Wayne Zollner Pistons 50-49 in the tournament's semi-final round.

	W	L	PCT.
Baltimore Bullets	21	13	.618
Philadelphia SPHAs	21	13	.618
New York Gothams	18	16	.529
Wilmington Bombers	15	19	.441
Trenton Tigers	14	20	.412
Paterson Crescents	13	21	.382

ABL PLAYOFFS
Mar. 15, 1946 - Wilmington defeated Philadelphia
Mar. 17 at Wilmington - Philadelphia 69, Wilmington 65
Mar. 23 at Philadelphia - Philadelphia 75, Wilmington 72

Baltimore defeated New York in best two of three games series

ABL CHAMPIONSHIPS
Mar. 30 at Philadelphia - Philadelphia 63, Baltimore 48
Mar. 31 at Baltimore - Baltimore 65, Philadelphia 48

Teams interrupted their championship series to play in a national professional invitation tournament in Schenectady.
Apr. 11, 1946 at Schenectady - Baltimore 61, Philadelphia 58 (OT) in consolation round of that tournament

Apr. 13 at Philadelphia - Baltimore 68, Philadelphia 45
Apr. 14 at Baltimore - Baltimore 54, Philadelphia 39

LEAGUE LEADERS
Regular Season	G	FG	FT	TP	PPG
Art Hillhouse, Philadelphia	34	139	145	423	12.4
Stan Modzelewski, Baltimore	31	126	126	378	12.2
Sonny Hertzberg, New York	33	156	79	391	11.8
Bobby Dorn, Paterson	32	134	105	373	11.7
Tony Kappen, New York	30	106	127	339	11.3
Cy Boardman, Paterson	32	126	108	360	11.2
Leo Gottlieb, New York	34	157	52	366	10.8
Inky Lautman, Philadelphia	34	147	68	362	10.6
Ralph Kaplowitz, Philadelphia	20	83	46	212	10.6
Mike Bloom, Baltimore	35	123	118	364	10.4

1946-47 ABL
With the formation of the Basketball Association of American and the Eastern Pennsylvania Basketball League, competition for players increased. Several of the top ABL players jumped to rival leagues, but Baltimore managed to bolster themselves as they signed Buddy Jeannette. In October the league became a member of the National Association of Pro Basketball Leagues, entering them into an agreement to honor other league's contracts in an effort to curtail further contract jumping.

When the season began New York had renamed themselves the Brooklyn Gothams, and Elizabeth, Jersey City, Newark and Troy all entered the league, which was now split into Southern and Northern divisions. Newark started poorly and moved to Yonkers in January before disbanding during the season.

In the Northern Division Brooklyn finished ahead of the pack. Baltimore was even more dominant in the Southern Division, finishing with a 31-3 record, the best in league history, before eliminating New York in first round of the playoffs. Philadelphia defeated Jersey City and Trenton defeated Elizabeth before meeting in the second round where Trenton prevailed.

While waiting for the winner of the Trenton-Philadelphia series, Baltimore elected to play in the World Tournament as the league then declared Trenton the ABL champions.

SOUTHERN DIVISION	W	L	PCT.
Baltimore Bullets	31	3	.912
Philadelphia SPHAs	19	14	.576
Trenton Tigers	17	17	.500
Elizabeth Braves	15	18	.455
Wilmington Bombers	15	20	.429
NORTHERN DIVISION	**W**	**L**	**PCT.**
Brooklyn Gothams	24	10	.706
Jersey City Atoms	14	22	.389
Troy Celtics	13	22	.371
Paterson Crescents	11	23	.324
Newark Bobcats/Yonkers Chiefs*	7	17	.292

*Newark moved to Yonkers before dropping out during the season.

ABL PLAYOFFS
FIRST ROUND
Mar. 13, 1947 at Baltimore - Brooklyn 80, Baltimore 66
Mar. 16 at Brooklyn - Baltimore 80, Brooklyn 53
Mar. 20 at Baltimore - Baltimore 70, Brooklyn 46

Philadelphia defeated Jersey City 2 games to 1

Mar. 16 at Trenton - Trenton 67, Elizabeth 39
Mar. 18 at Elizabeth - Trenton 54, Elizabeth 52
SECOND ROUND
Mar. 23 at Trenton - Trenton 81, Philadelphia 64
Apr. 7 at Philadelphia - Philadelphia 46, Trenton 42
Apr. 12 at Philadelphia - Trenton 48, Philadelphia 46

ABL CHAMPIONSHIP
The best two-of-three games final was scheduled between Baltimore and Trenton but Baltimore quit the playoffs to participate in World Basketball Tournament and Trenton was declared league champions by default.

LEAGUE LEADERS

Regular Season	G	FG	FT	TP	PPG
Ash Resnick, Troy	35	191	181	563	16.1
Mike Bloom, Baltimore	34	171	166	508	14.9
Jack Hewson, Wilmington	22	102	100	304	13.8
Stan Brown, Philadelphia	32	158	116	432	13.5
Bobby Dorn, Paterson	30	127	135	389	13.0
Cy Boardman, Paterson	32	139	134	412	12.9
Buddy Jeannette, Baltimore	29	113	118	344	11.9
John Ezersky, Brooklyn	34	147	100	394	11.6
Paul Chaddick, Wilmington	35	166	71	403	11.5
Fred Frey, Brooklyn	25	93	96	282	11.3

1947-48 ABL
The 1947 off-season was a tumultuous one for the league as defending champion Baltimore left to join the BAA, and Troy and Wilmington dropped out of the league. Lancaster and Wilkes-Barre were then brought into the league as replacements, but Lancaster managed to play only six contests before the league folded it, leaving the circuit with seven clubs. Player losses were also significant as Mike Bloom, Stan Brown, Jack Hewson and Johnny Ezersky were among those jumping to the BAA.

Changes continued during the season as Elizabeth dropped out with the league awarding its franchise to Hartford, and Jersey City relocated to Scranton. Wilkes-Barre proved to be the top team in the regular season, finishing on top by 7-1/2 games. In the first round of the post-season Wilkes-Barre defeated Trenton and Paterson topped Scranton, both in two-game sweeps. Wilkes-Barre then defeated Paterson two games to one to claim the league title.

	W	L	PCT.
Wilkes-Barre Barons	26	8	.765
Paterson Crescents	19	16	.543
Trenton Tigers	17	15	.531
Jersey City Atoms/Scranton Miners*	16	16	.500
Elizabeth Braves/Hartford Hurricanes**	11	12	.478
Philadelphia SPHAs	13	19	.406
Brooklyn Gothams	8	20	.286
Lancaster Roses***	1	5	.167

*Scranton franchise was terminated by the league on Dec. 4.
**Elizabeth moved to Hartford on Dec. 19.
***Jersey City moved to Lancaster on Jan. 28.

ABL PLAYOFFS
Mar. 24, 1948 at Wilkes-Barre - Wilkes-Barre 53, Trenton 52
Mar. 28 at Trenton - Wilkes-Barre 102, Trenton 84

Mar. 27 at Paterson - Paterson 82, Scranton 68
Mar. 28 at Scranton - Paterson 92, Scranton 66

ABL CHAMPIONSHIP
Mar. 31 at Wilkes-Barre - Wilkes-Barre 70, Paterson 63
Apr. 4 at Paterson - Paterson 65, Wilkes-Barre 57
Apr. 17 at Wilkes-Barre - Wilkes-Barre 51, Paterson 43

LEAGUE LEADERS

Regular Season	G	FG	FT	TP	PPG
Cas Ostrowski, Wilkes-Barre	31	214	133	561	18.1
Bill Chanecka, Wilkes-Barre	30	188	129	505	16.8
Elmore Morganthaler, Philadelphia	28	167	147	481	17.2
Martin Powers, Paterson	35	128	223	479	13.7
Aaron Tanitsky, Philadelphia	32	155	90	400	12.5
Ed Boyle, Trenton	32	112	154	378	11.8
Mike Wallace, Scranton	15	129	69	327	21.8
Jerry Rullo, Philadelphia	30	129	43	301	10.0
Ted Hanauer, Wilkes-Barre	33	111	70	292	8.8
Herschel Baltimore, Wilkes-Barre	34	119	50	288	8.5

1948-49 ABL
Bridgeport was added to bring the league back to an even eight clubs, and players were signed exclusive contacts to ensure that they would no longer play for other teams during the season. The league still lost one of its top players as Elmore Morganthaler signed with Philadelphia of the BAA. In response the league managed to sign a few BAA players, as Dick Holub of the New York Knicks signed with Paterson and Ralph Kaplowicz of Philadelphia signed with Hartford.

Defending champion Wilkes-Barre again was the top team in the regular season and defeated Trenton in the first round of the playoffs. Second place Scranton edged Paterson to advance to the championship series, where they managed to push Wilkes-Barre to five games before losing three games to two.

	W	L	PCT.
Wilkes-Barre Barons	29	12	.707
Scranton Miners	26	15	.634
Trenton Tigers	25	16	.610
Paterson Crescents	24	17	.585
Bridgeport Newfield Steelers	24	17	.585
Hartford Hurricanes	13	26	.333
Brooklyn Gothams	10	30	.250
Philadelphia SPHAs	8	26	.235

ABL FOURTH PLACE PLAYOFF
Mar. 26, 1949 - Paterson defeated Bridgeport 99-80 for fourth place

ABL PLAYOFFS
Mar. 30 at Wilkes-Barre - Wilkes-Barre 106, Trenton 71
Apr. 3 at Trenton - Wilkes-Barre 93, Trenton 80

Mar. 31 at Scranton - Scranton 68, Paterson 66
Apr. 2 at Paterson - Scranton 67, Paterson 65

ABL CHAMPIONSHIP
Apr. 7 at Wilkes-Barre - Wilkes-Barre 71, Scranton 60
Apr. 10 at Scranton - Scranton 75, Wilkes-Barre 70
Apr. 12 at Wilkes-Barre - Scranton 74, Wilkes-Barre 62
Apr. 20 at Scranton - Wilkes-Barre 72, Scranton 56
Apr. 22 at Wilkes-Barre - Wilkes-Barre 58, Scranton 47

LEAGUE LEADERS

Regular Season	G	FG	FT	TP	PPG
Dick Holub, Paterson	41	285	265	835	20.4
Cas Ostrowski, Wilkes-Barre	41	304	143	751	18.3
Bill Chanecka, Wilkes-Barre	40	269	180	718	18.0
Mickey Homa, Bridgeport	40	253	199	705	17.6
Jack Hewson, Trenton	36	240	204	684	19.0
Hank Baietti, Brooklyn	40	205	230	640	16.0
William Zirkel, Bridgeport	40	220	156	596	14.9
Ralph Kaplowitz, Hartford	41	216	138	570	13.9
Peter Pasko, Wilkes-Barre	29	216	94	526	18.1
Mike Wallace, Scranton	41	192	124	508	12.4

1949-50 ABL
Major changes were on the menu. An era ended as Philadelphia, a member since the inaugural 1933-34 season, dropped out of the league during the off-season, as did Brooklyn. New York and Schenectady were added as members, although Schenectady only managed to put a team on the court for four games before folding, and New York transferred to Saratoga during the season. Trenton also dropped out during the season, ending a nine-year association with the league. The season was concluded with six clubs with Scranton finishing 3-1/2 games ahead of Bridgeport to claim the regular season title. In the playoffs Scranton defeated Wilkes-Barre and Bridgeport defeated New York in the first round, with Scranton capturing the championship in a series that went the five game limit.

	W	L	PCT.
Scranton Miners	27	11	.711
Bridgeport Aer-A-Sols	22	13	.629
Wilkes-Barre Barons	21	17	.552
New York Harlem Yankees**	20	17	.541
Paterson Crescents	17	18	.486
Hartford Hurricanes	11	26	.297
Trenton Tigers***	4	16	.200
Schenectady Packers*	0	6	.000

*Schenectady dropped out Nov. 23.
**New York moved to Schenectady during the season.
***Trenton dropped out Feb. 1.

ABL PLAYOFFS
Mar. 19, 1950 at Scranton - Scranton 60, Wilkes-Barre 49
Mar. 22 at Wilkes-Barre - Wilkes-Barre 89, Scranton 83
Mar. 26 at Scranton - Scranton 103, Wilkes-Barre 99 (3 overtimes)

Mar. 26 at Bridgeport - Bridgeport 81, New York 74
Mar. 27 at Saratoga - New York 80, Bridgeport 78
Mar. 29 at Bridgeport - Bridgeport 75, New York 73

ABL CHAMPIONSHIP
Apr. 2, 1950 at Scranton - Scranton 88, Bridgeport 67
Apr. 9 at Bridgeport - Scranton 85, Bridgeport 73
Apr. 12 at Scranton - Bridgeport 68, Scranton 65
Apr. 14 at Bridgeport - Bridgeport 78, Scranton 73
Apr. 16 at Scranton - Scranton 85, Bridgeport 59

LEAGUE LEADERS

Regular Season	G	FG	FT	TP	PPG
Elmore Morganthaler, Scranton	37	267	194	728	19.7
Hank DeZonie, New York	37	286	78	650	17.6
Bill Chanecka, Wilkes-Barre	37	233	141	607	16.4
Cas Ostrowski, Wilkes-Barre	38	223	152	598	15.7
Ike Walthour, New York	35	207	119	533	15.2
George Kok, Bridgeport	35	201	123	525	15.0
Dick Holub, Paterson	34	145	213	503	14.8
Johnny Bach, Hartford	37	164	171	499	13.5
George Crowe, New York	35	190	96	476	13.6
Irv Rothenberg, Paterson	33	167	135	469	14.2

1950-51 ABL

Hartford dropped out of the league in the off-season, as Allentown and Utica were brought in to bring the league membership up to seven teams for the season. Allentown started poorly, winning only one of their first 13 games, and moved to Carbondale on December 28. Wilkes-Barre dropped out on February 22 after Scranton insisted that they put up a $1,500 bond to ensure that they would be paid. Scranton easily outdistanced Paterson by 7-1/2 games to defend their title as regular season champions.

In the planned four-team playoffs, Utica voted not to participate against Scranton, and the league then decided to abandon their post-season plans citing the availibility of the armories in which the teams played, naming Scranton as league champion.

	W	L	PCT.
Scranton Miners	28	8	.778
Wilkes-Barre Barons**	28	11	.718
Paterson Crescents	21	16	.568
Bridgeport Aer-A-Sols	18	15	.545
Utica Pros	17	22	.436
Saratoga Harlem Yankees	5	25	.167
Allentown Aces/Carbondale Ace*	4	24	.105

*Allentown moved to Carbondale on Dec. 28 after a 1-12 start.
**Wilkes-Barre dropped out on Feb. 22 after Scranton demanded a $1,500 bond before they would play.

LEAGUE LEADERS

Regular Season	G	FG	FT	TP	PPG
Ike Walthour, Saratoga	29	201	185	587	20.2
John Ezersky, Wilkes-Barre	39	242	234	718	18.4
Joe Colone, Wilkes-Barre/Carbondale	23	150	107	407	17.7
Hank DeZonie, Saratoga	24	158	49	365	15.2
Cas Ostrowski, Carbondale	15	90	48	228	15.2
Walter Sheil, Carbondale	15	82	54	218	14.5
Alex Athas, Utica	21	99	103	301	14.3
Irv Rothenberg, Paterson	34	158	145	461	13.6
Chink Crossin, Wilkes-Barre	31	165	81	411	13.3
Joel Kaufman, Paterson	35	171	97	439	12.5

1951-52 ABL

In the league's penultimate season, Paterson and Utica left the league and were replaced by Elmira, Washington and Wilkes-Barre, as Saratoga relocated to Schenectady. Manchester joined the league to bring the membership to seven and Carbondale moved to Middleton after the season began. In January, Washington dropped out and the Schenectady club returned to Saratoga with Middleton dropping out in February. Defending champion Scranton proved to be the top club in the ABL, topping Elmira by 2-1/2 games and Wilkes-Barre by three games during the season. In the post-season Wilkes-Barre finished as league championship defeating Scranton four games to two.

	W	L	PCT.
Scranton Miners	24	11	.686
Washington Capitols**	15	7	.682
Elmira Colonels	22	18	.550
Wilkes-Barre Barons	20	19	.513
Saratoga Harlem Yankees/Schenectady Yankees/			
Saratoga Harlem Yankees*	12	16	.429
Manchester British Americans***	8	11	.421
Carbondale Aces/Big Chiefs/Middletown Guards****	7	13	.350
Bridgeport Roesslers	9	22	.290

*Saratoga moved to Schenectady on Jan. 15, and back to Saratoga on Feb. 5.
**Washington dropped out Jan. 11.
***Manchester entered on Jan. 1.
****Carbondale disbanded on Jan. 20 and their record was assumed by Middletown who dropped out on Feb. 21.

ABL PLAYOFFS
Wilkes-Barre defeated Elmira 4 games to 3
Scranton defeated Saratoga 3 games to 1

ABL CHAMPIONSHIP
Wilkes-Barre defeated Scranton 4 games to 2

LEAGUE LEADERS

Regular Season	G	FG	FT	TP	PPG
Joe Colone, Wilkes-Barre	39	260	242	762	19.5
Leo Mogus, Elmira	38	211	208	630	16.6
Jerry Fowler, Elmira	38	183	157	523	13.8
Joel Kaufman, Bridgeport	31	186	148	520	15.7
Earl Hawkins, Wilkes-Barre	39	166	175	507	13.0
Chuck Mrazovich, Wilkes-Barre	38	176	153	505	13.3
Matty Forman, Bridgeport	29	182	123	487	16.8
John Azary, Scranton	33	168	140	476	14.4
Don Savage, Elmira	37	176	103	455	12.3
Danny Finn, Scranton	30	182	87	451	15.0

1952-53 ABL

By mid-October the Jersey City Titans, who had signed former Indianapolis Olympians Alex Groza and Ralph Beard to go with Sherman White—three players who had been banned by the NBA after a point-shaving scandal—applied for membership in the ABL. Elmira had signed former University of Kentucky center Bill Spivey, who had also been implicated. The signings quickly became an issue with the remaining clubs in the league, and on October 23, Elmira and New Jersey dropped out of the league in protest. In response, the rest of the teams voted to disband the league rather than damage the relation the clubs had with the NBA.

On November 13 a six-team league was reorganized, with its membership eventually increasing to seven, but shortly after the season began it was down to five as Middletown and Glens Falls-Saratoga dropped out. Manchester edged Wilkes-Barre by 1-1/2 games for the regular season title.

In the post-season, Wilkes-Barre and Manchester advanced to the Championship, which Manchester won. After the conclusion of the season, the league disbanded with little fanfare, ending the run of the oldest professional basketball league in operation.

	W	L	PCT.
Manchester British Americans	19	9	.679
Wilkes-Barre Barons	20	11	.645
Elmira Colonels	17	11	.607
Scranton Miners	12	11	.522
Middletown Guards*	2	5	.286
Pawtucket Slaters	6	19	.240
Saratoga-Glens Falls-Hazleton Harlem Yankees**	1	11	.083

*Middletown dropped out on Jan. 8.
**Glens Falls-Saratoga-Hazleton dropped out on Feb. 6.

ABL PLAYOFFS
Mar. 10, 1953 at Wilkes-Barre - Elmira 91, Wilkes-Barre 85
Mar. 12 at Elmira - Wilkes-Barre 63, Elmira 56
Mar. 14 at Elmira - Elmira 74, Wilkes-Barre 71
Mar. 15 at Wilkes-Barre - Wilkes-Barre 90, Elmira 82
Mar. 19 at Wilkes-Barre - Wilkes-Barre 89, Elmira 81
Mar. 21 at Elmira - Elmira 63, Wilkes-Barre 60
Mar. 22 at Wilkes-Barre - Wilkes-Barre 75, Elmira 70

Mar. (day unknown) at Manchester - Manchester defeated Scranton
Mar. 14 at Scranton - Scranton 100, Manchester 94

Note: Game two at Scranton was protested because Scranton used Perry Del Purgatorio, who was recently discharged from service but who hadn't played in any previous games that season. League President John O'Brien acknowledged that the "league had operated with many rule infractions this season" and tried to get Manchester to drop their protest. They didn't so he ruled in their favor. Scranton quit in a huff and Manchester advanced to the finals.

ABL CHAMPIONSHIP
Manchester defeated Wilkes-Barre

LEAGUE LEADERS

Regular Season	G	FG	FT	TP	PPG
Ray Felix, Manchester	28	208	200	616	22.0
Jerry Fowler, Elmira	28	*190	167	547	19.5
Gerry Calabrese, Wilkes-Barre	31	160	134	454	14.6
Chuck Mrazovich, Wilkes-Barre	31	149	91	389	12.5
Roger Layne, Wilkes-Barre	30	137	88	362	12.1
Ed Earle, Elmira	28	133	88	354	12.6
Bobby Knight, Manchester	27	136	80	352	13.0
Tom Smith, Wilkes-Barre	26	106	119	331	12.7
Joel Kaufman, Scranton/Pawtucket	23	112	77	301	13.1
Leroy Watkins, Mid/Sar/Pawtucket	19	113	64	290	15.3

National Basketball League
[1937-1949]

LEAGUE MEMBERS

Akron Firestone Non-Skids	Akron, OH	1937-38-1940-41
Akron Goodyear Wingfoots	Akron, OH	1937-48-1941-42
Anderson Duffey Packers	Anderson, IN	1946-47-1948-49
Buffalo Bisons	Buffalo, NY	1937-38
Buffalo Bisons	Buffalo, NY	1946-47
Chicago American Gears	Chicago, IL	1944-45-1946-47
Chicago Bruins	Chicago, IL	1939-40-1941-42
Chicago Studebaker Flyers	Chicago, IL	1942-43
Cincinnati Comellos	Cincinnati, OH	1937-38
Cleveland Allmen Transfers	Cleveland, OH	1944-45-1945-46
Cleveland Chase Brassmen	Cleveland, OH	1943-44
Cleveland White Horses	Cleveland, OH	1938-39
Columbus Athletic Supply	Columbus, OH	1937-38
Dayton Metropolitans	Dayton, OH	1937-38
Dayton Rens	Dayton, OH	1948-49
Denver Nuggets	Denver, CO	1948-49
Detroit Eagles	Detroit, MI	1939-40-1940-41
Detroit Gems	Detroit, MI	1946-47
Detroit Vagabond Kings	Detroit, MI	1948-49
Flint Dow A.C.'s	Flint, MI	1947-48
Fort Wayne General Electrics	Fort Wayne, IN	1937-38
Fort Wayne Zollner Pistons	Fort Wayne, IN	1941-42-1947-48
Hammond Calumet Buccaneers	Hammond, IN	1948-49
Hammond Ciesar All-Americans	Hammond, IN	1938-39-1940-41
Indianapolis Kautskys	Indianapolis, IN	1937-38-1939-40
Indianapolis Kautskys	Indianapolis, IN	1941-42
Indianapolis Kautskys	Indianapolis, IN	1945-46-1947-48
Kankakee Gallagher Trojans	Kankakee, MI	1937-38
Midland Dow A.C.'s	Midland, MI	1947-48
Minneapolis Lakers	Minneapolis, MN	1947-48
Oshkosh All-Stars	Oshkosh, WI	1937-38-1948-49
Pittsburgh Pirates	Pittsburgh, PA	1937-38-1938-39
Pittsburgh Raiders	Pittsburgh, PA	1944-45
Richmond King Clothiers	Richmond, IN	1937-38
Rochester Royals	Rochester, NY	1945-46-1947-48
Sheboygan Redskins	Sheboygan, WI	1938-39-1948-49
Syracuse Nationals	Syracuse, NY	1946-47-1948-49
Toledo Jeeps	Toledo, OH	1946-47-1947-48
Toledo Jim White Chevrolets	Toledo, OH	1941-42-1942-43
Tri-City Blackhawks	Moline, IL	1946-47-1948-49
Warren Penn Oilers	Warren, PA	1937-38-1938-39
Waterloo Hawks	Waterloo, IA	1948-49
Whiting Ciesar All-Americans	Whiting, IN	1937-38
Youngstown Bears	Youngstown, OH	1945-46-1946-47

The National Basketball League, one of the forerunners of today's NBA, was born when three large corporations decided to enter the field of pro basketball. Firestone and Goodyear, both of Akron, Ohio, and General Electric, of Ft. Wayne, Indiana, had fielded strong amateur entries in the Midwest Basketball Conference, and decided to run their teams against professional competition in the 1937-38 season. These three teams then joined forces with 10 independent professional teams in the Midwest to form the NBL.

The eastern-most franchises were the Buffalo Bisons, the Pittsburgh Pirates, and the Warren Penns. Ohio had four clubs: the Columbus Athletic Supply, the Akron Firestone Non-Skids, the Akron Goodyear Wingfoots, and the Dayton Metros. Indiana had the Whiting Ciesar All-Americans, the Ft. Wayne General Electrics, the Indianapolis Kautskys, and the Richmond King Clothiers. The western fringe of the league was made up of the Kankakee Gallagher Trojans from Illinois and the Oshkosh All-Stars from Wisconsin.

The league organization during this first season left much to be desired. Under the direction of commissioner Hubert Johnson of Detroit, the league never created a uniform schedule, but left it to each team to arrange games. As a result, teams played an unequal number of games, and several clubs played their full league schedules against only three or four opponents.

On the subject of playing rules, the league could not agree on a uniform policy concerning the center jump. College ball had taken the revolutionary step of abolishing the center jump after every basket, automatically giving the ball to the team scored against. League meetings heatedly discussed the issue without reaching a decision. As a compromise, the decision to use the center jump rule was left to the home team.

The teams themselves were made up primarily of veteran players from each club's local area.

None of the teams had much success in signing graduating college stars. Guard Ed Campion from DePaul, who was signed by Whiting, was the biggest name among the league's rookies. The Firestone, Goodyear, and General Electric teams recruited players from schools across the country by offering management positions within the corporation.

The old-line pro teams settled for local college and sandlot products, mostly men who had regular day jobs. Many players coached high school or college teams;

Johnny Wooden, for instance, was starting his illustrious coaching career with a high school team while playing with Whiting.

The set shot was still the most common way of scoring and the defense was still a rough, bruising struggle much like football.

1937-38 NBL
The new league play began in November 1937.

In the Eastern Division, the Firestone and Goodyear teams battled for first place. Firestone was led by 6-foot-1 guard Jack Ozburn and Soup Cable, a solid all-round forward from the University of Akron. Goodyear, the archrival of Firestone and the 1937 champion of the Midwest Conference, got most of its scoring from career employee Chuck Bloedom and sandlot product Charley Shipp.

The General Electric team surged to the front in the Western Division, followed by Oshkosh and Whiting. The General Electrics had balanced scoring from Scotty Armstrong, Bart Quinn, and Jim Hilgemann, but Oshkosh and Whiting each had one shining star. Leroy (Cowboy) Edwards, a 6-foot-4 center, almost single-handedly kept the All-Stars in contention with a league-leading 16.2 points per game. The Whiting Ciesar All-Americans found a star in guard Johnny Wooden.

As the season progressed, several also-ran teams forfeited games by not showing up.

The cash-strapped Richmond franchise moved to Cincinnati. A late-season slump by Goodyear gave first place to Firestone. In the Western Division, Oshkosh and Whiting edged Ft. Wayne out of a playoff spot.

In the playoffs, Goodyear upset Firestone in two straight games, 26-21 and 37-31. In the best-of-three Western playoff, Oshkosh took the first game from Whiting 40-33 in Hammond, Indiana, and wrapped up the series with a 41-38 second-game triumph in which Wooden's 16 points led both teams.

The best-of-three championship series opened in Oshkosh with a 29-28 Goodyear victory. The All-Stars, led by Edwards' 16 points, won in Akron. In the final game, Edwards was held to nine points as Goodyear won 35-27 to capture the first NBL crown.

Eastern Division	W	L	Pct.	HW	HL	RW	RL	GB
Akron Firestone Non-Skids*	14	4	.778	8	1	5	3	—
Akron Goodyear Wingfoots	13	5	.722	8	1	5	4	1
Pittsburgh Pirates	8	5	.615	5	1	3	4	3.5
Buffalo Bisons	3	6	.333	2	2	1	4	6.5
Warren Penns	3	9	.250	2	3	1	6	8
Columbus Athletic Supply*	1	12	.091	1	3	0	7	10.5

*Akron Firestone includes one forfeit win, Columbus includes two forfeit losses.

Western Division	W	L	Pct.	HW	HL	RW	RL	GB
Oshkosh All-Stars	12	2	.857	9	1	2	1	—
Whiting Ciesar All-Americans	12	3	.800	7	0	5	3	0.5
Fort Wayne General Electrics*	13	7	.650	9	1	2	6	2.0
Indianapolis Kautskys*	4	9	.308	4	2	0	6	7.5
Richmond King Clothiers/ Cincinnati Comellos*	3	7	.300	3	1	0	5	7
Kankakee Gallagher Trojans	3	11	.214	1	4	0	7	9
Dayton Metropolitans	2	11	.154	2	4	0	5	9.5

*Richmond moved to Cincinnati Jan. 5, 1938.
*Fort Wayne includes two forfeit wins, Indianapolis includes one forfeit loss.

EASTERN DIVISION PLAYOFF
Feb. 24, 1938 at Akron, OH - Akron Goodyear 26, Akron Firestone 21
Feb. 25 at Akron, OH - Akron Goodyear 31, Akron Firestone 31
WESTERN DIVISION PLAYOFF
Feb. 22 at Hammond, IN - Oshkosh 40, Whiting 33
Feb. 27 at Oshkosh, WI - Oshkosh 41, Whiting 38
CHAMPIONSHIP SERIES
Feb. 28 at Oshkosh, WI - Akron Goodyear 29, Oshkosh 28
Mar. 3 at Akron, OH - Oshkosh 39, Akron Goodyear 31
Mar. 4 at Oshkosh, WI - Akron Goodyear 37, Oshkosh 35

1938-39 NBL
The NBL tried, but failed, to sign Hank Luisetti, the famous one-hand shooting whiz from Stanford, and Mike Bloom, the star from N.I.T.-champion Temple, but several other good college players joined the league.

The league shrunk from 13 teams to eight, with the Buffalo, Columbus, Ft. Wayne, Cincinnati, Kankakee, and Dayton franchises dropped. The Whiting team shifted to nearby Hammond, and the Sheboygan Redskins, formerly a semi-pro outfit in Wisconsin, joined the league. All teams played 28 games and the center jump rule was abolished.

Firestone won their first 17 games to wrap up the Eastern Division title by mid-February. Goodyear fielded essentially the same team that won the 1938 championship, but the rest of the league had improved enough to demote them to also-ran status. The Warren team, short of cash, shifted to Cleveland late in the season.

In the Western Division, Oshkosh got hot in February to win the title, led again by a league-high 11.9 points per game from Leroy Edwards.

Akron Firestones and Oshkosh All-Stars met in the five-game championship playoff. They split the first two games in Akron. Firestone easily won the third game in Oshkosh, 40-29, but Leroy Edwards scored 25 points as Oshkosh won Game 4, 49-37. The Firestones held Edwards to nine points in the final game to win 37-30.

After the season, Sheboygan and Oshkosh participated in the first annual World Tournament, an invitational event staged in Chicago by the *Chicago Herald American*. Sheboygan lost the consolation game to the Harlem Globetrotters 36-33, and Oshkosh lost the championship game to the New York Rens 34-25.

Eastern Division	W	L	Pct.	HW	HL	RW	RL	GB
Akron Firestone Non-Skids	24	3	.889	11	2	13	1	—
Akron Goodyear Wingfoots	14	14	.500	7	7	7	7	10.5
Warren Penns/ Cleveland White Horses*	14	14	.500	9	5	4	9	10.5
Pittsburgh Pirates	13	14	.481	9	5	4	9	11

*Warren moved to Cleveland Feb. 10, 1939.
*Warren/Cleveland includes one forfeit win.

Western Division	W	L	Pct.	HW	HL	RW	RL	GB
Oshkosh All-Stars	17	11	.607	10	4	7	7	—
Indianapolis Kautskys	13	13	.500	9	4	4	9	3
Sheboygan Red Skins	11	17	.393	7	7	4	10	6
Hammond Ciesar All-Americans	4	24	.143	4	9	0	14	13

Hammond includes one forfeit loss.

CHAMPIONSHIP SERIES
Mar. 14, 1939 at Akron, OH - Akron Firestone 50, Oshkosh 38
Mar. 15 at Akron, OH - Oshkosh 38, Akron Firestone 36
Mar. 17 at Oshkosh, WI - Akron Firestone 40, Oshkosh 29
Mar. 18 at Oshkosh, WI - Oshkosh 49, Akron Firestone 37
Mar. 20 at Oshkosh, WI - Akron Firestone 37, Oshkosh 30

1939-40 NBL
The league added two new franchises. The Detroit Eagles took over the Cleveland franchise and the Chicago Bruins, owned by George Halas, replaced Pittsburgh. The new clubs joined several other teams in heavily recruiting talented college seniors.

The Akron Firestones edged out Detroit for first place in the Eastern Division. In the Western Division, Oshkosh and Sheboygan tied for first place, one game ahead of Chicago. Leroy Edwards led the league in scoring for the third year.

The playoffs were expanded to two rounds. The Firestones eliminated Detroit in the Eastern semi-final. In the West, Oshkosh needed three games to eliminate Sheboygan to set up a rematch of the 1939 final. Oshkosh easily won the first two games, 47-37 and 60-46. The Firestones then won twice at home, 35-32 and 41-40. The final game, played in the Kent State University gym, seesawed back and before the Firestones won 61-60 for their second straight NBL crown.

Oshkosh then joined Sheboygan and Chicago at the second annual World Tournament in Chicago. Oshkosh and Sheboygan were eliminated in the quarter-finals, while Chicago lost 31-29 to the Harlem Globetrotters in the final.

Eastern Division	W	L	Pct.	HW	HL	RW	RL	GB
Akron Firestone Non-Skids	18	9	.667	10	3	8	6	—
Detroit Eagles	17	10	.630	12	2	5	8	1
Akron Goodyear Wingfoots	14	14	.500	8	6	6	8	4.5
Indianapolis Kautskys	9	19	.321	6	8	3	11	9.5

Western Division	W	L	Pct.	HW	HL	RW	RL	GB
Oshkosh All-Stars	15	13	.536	12	2	3	11	—
Sheboygan Red Skins	15	13	.536	11	3	4	10	—
Chicago Bruins	14	14	.500	10	4	4	10	1
Hammond Ciesar All-Americans	9	19	.321	7	7	2	12	6

EASTERN DIVISION PLAYOFF
Mar. 1940 at Akron, OH - Akron Firestone 48, Detroit 35
Mar. 8 at Detroit, MI - Detroit 49, Akron Firestone 37
Mar. 9 at Akron, OH - Akron Firestone 46, Detroit 35

WESTERN DIVISION PLAYOFF
Mar. 7 at Oshkosh, WI - Oshkosh 41, Sheboygan 24
Mar. 8 at Sheboygan, WI - Sheboygan 43, Oshkosh 42
Mar. 9 at Sheboygan, WI - Oshkosh 31, Sheboygan 29

CHAMPIONSHIP SERIES
Mar. 11 at Oshkosh, WI - Oshkosh 47, Akron Firestone 37
Mar. 12 at Oshkosh, WI - Oshkosh 60, Akron Firestone 46
Mar. 14 at Akron, OH - Akron Firestone 35, Oshkosh 32
Mar. 15 at Akron, OH - Akron Firestone 41, Oshkosh 40
Mar. 16 at Akron, OH - Akron Firestone 61, Oshkosh 60

1940-41 NBL
The league was reduced to seven teams when the Indianapolis Kautskys withdrew. The league consolidated into one division, with four teams making the playoffs.

Oshkosh went 10-1 to open the season and easily finished first.

In the playoffs, Sheboygan lost its first game against Detroit but rebounded with two straight wins to advance to the final. In the other series, Oshkosh unveiled a new offensive scheme—employing Bob Carpenter and center Leroy Edwards in a double pivot offense—that resulted in a 30-28 first-game victory. The second game went into overtime, where Edwards hit three baskets to lead Oshkosh to a 47-41 victory, and a spot in the championship series against Sheboygan.

Oshkosh romped to the title with three straight wins, 53-38, 49-38, and 54-36, and then entered the annual World Tournament in Chicago. The final became an NBL showdown between Oshkosh and Detroit, which was won by Detroit, 39-37.

	W	L	Pct.	HW	HL	RW	RL	GB
Oshkosh All-Stars	18	6	.750	11	1	7	5.	—
Sheboygan Red Skins	13	11	.542	7	5	6	6	5
Akron Firestone Non-Skids	13	11	.542	7	5	6	6	5
Detroit Eagles	12	12	.500	8	4	4	8	6
Chicago Bruins	11	13	.458	8	4	3	9	7
Akron Goodyear Wingfoots	11	13	.458	6	6	5	7	7
Hammond Ciesar All-American	6	18	.250	2	6	8	0	12

SEMI-FINALS
Mar. 4, 1941 at Akron, OH - Oshkosh 30, Akron Firestone 28
Mar. 6 at Oshkosh, WI - Oshkosh 47, Akron Firestone 41 [OT]

Mar. 6 at Detroit, MI - Detroit 43, Sheboygan 32
Mar. 7 at Sheboygan, WI - Sheboygan 22, Detroit 19
Mar. 8 at Sheboygan, WI - Sheboygan 54, Detroit 40

CHAMPIONSHIP SERIES
Mar. 10 at Oshkosh, WI - Oshkosh 53, Sheboygan 38
Mar. 11 at Oshkosh, WI - Oshkosh 44, Sheboygan 38
Mar. 12 at Oshkosh, WI - Oshkosh 54, Sheboygan 36

1941-42 NBL
Two weeks after the NBL season began, the United States entered World War II. The next several years would see several athletes join the military, but the impact was minimal in the first year. Of the league's front-line players, only Bob Carpenter and Herm Witasek of Oshkosh, Bob Calihan of Ft. Wayne, Bill Hapac and Stan Szukala of Chicago, Ernie Andres and Bob Dietz of Indianapolis, and Jack Ozburn of Toledo missed all or most of the season.

The Firestone corporation elected to drop out of pro basketball, so the league lost its only two-time champion. The Hammond Ciesar All-Americans folded after two miserable seasons, and the Detroit Eagles bolted the NBL to become an independent club. Three new clubs, previously independents, entered into the league—the Indianapolis Kautskys (which had dropped out a year before), the Toledo Jim White Chevrolets and the Ft. Wayne Zollner Pistons.

The Oshkosh All-Stars finished first for the fifth straight year. Goodyear and Ft. Wayne tied for second, with Indianapolis earning the final playoff spot.

In the playoffs, Oshkosh easily eliminated Indianapolis with 40-33 and 64-48 victories, while the Pistons needed a 49-43 win in Game 3 to get past the Goodyears. Ft. Wayne won Game 1 of the final on home court, but when the series shifted to Oshkosh, the All-Stars took control. Leroy Edwards scored 35 points in Game 2 as Oshkosh won 68-60. Edwards scored just one point in the final game, but Oshkosh won anyway, 52-46, for their second straight title. Oshkosh then won the World Tournament in Chicago, beating the Detroit Eagles in the championship game.

	W	L	Pct.	HW	HL	RW	RL	GB
Oshkosh All-Stars	20	4	.833	13	1	7	3	—
Fort Wayne Zollner Pistons	15	9	.625	11	3	4	6	5
Akron Goodyear Wingfoots	15	9	.625	11	2	4	7	5
Indianapolis Kautskys	12	11	.522	10	1	2	10	7.5
Sheboygan Red Skins	10	14	.417	8	5	2	9	10
Chicago Bruins*	8	15	.348	4	8	3	8	11.5
Toledo Jim White Chevrolets*	3	21	.125	2	4	0	16	17

*Chicago includes one forfeit win and one forfeit loss, Toledo includes one forfeit win and one forfeit loss.

SEMI-FINALS
Mar. 1, 1942 at Indianapolis, IN - Oshkosh 40, Indianapolis 35
Mar. 2 at Oshkosh, WI - Oshkosh 64, Indianapolis 48

at Akron, OH - Akron Goodyear 46, Fort Wayne 30
at Fort Wayne, IN - Fort Wayne 51, Akron Goodyear 48
at Fort Wayne, IN - Fort Wayne 49, Akron Goodyear 43

CHAMPIONSHIP SERIES
Mar. 2 at Fort Wayne, IN - Fort Wayne 61, Oshkosh 43
Mar. 5 at Oshkosh, WI - Oshkosh 68, Fort Wayne 60
Mar. 6 at Oshkosh, WI - Oshkosh 52, Fort Wayne 46

1942-43 NBL
The war caused an attrition of players and franchises. The Indianapolis Kautskys suspended operations for the duration of the war and Goodyear replaced pro basketball with an amateur program.

George Halas, owner of the Chicago Bruins, folded his team, but the league still fielded a Chicago franchise thanks to the local Studebaker plant. The Studebaker factory converted to war-industry production and the workers there were exempt from the draft. When several players got jobs at the plant, the United Auto Workers union picked up the NBL Chicago franchise. Working in the plant were Mike Novak and Dick Evans of the Bruins, Paul Sokody of Sheboygan, and a host of Harlem Globetrotters led by stars Sonny Boswell, Duke Cumberland, and Bernie Price. Thus the NBL had its first racially-integrated club.

The season got off to a wobbly start when Toledo opened with four losses and left the league, leaving the NBL with four franchises. The Studebakers started strong but the team became divided along racial lines and their season fell apart. Amid this turmoil, Ft. Wayne and Sheboygan grabbed the top two spots.

But the four teams started on even footing in the playoffs. In the opening round, Ft. Wayne eliminated Chicago and Sheboygan beat Oshkosh. The championship opened in Ft. Wayne. Sheboygan won the first game, 55-50. Ft. Wayne took Game 2 in overtime, 50-45, but Sheboygan won Game 3, and the title, 30-29.

	W	L	Pct.	HW	HL	RW	RL	GB
Fort Wayne Zollner Pistons	17	6	.739	10	2	7	4	—
Sheboygan Red Skins	12	11	.522	9	4	3	7	5
Oshkosh All-Stars	11	12	.478	7	5	4	7	6
Chicago Studebaker Flyers	8	15	.349	5	6	3	9	9
Toledo Jim White Chevrolets*	0	4	.000	0	0	0	4	...

*Toledo disbanded Dec. 14, 1942.

SEMI-FINALS

at Fort Wayne, IN - Fort Wayne 49, Chicago 37
at Chicago, IL - Chicago 45, Fort Wayne 32
at Fort Wayne, IN - Fort Wayne 44, Chicago 32

Feb. 20, 1943 at Sheboygan, WI - Sheboygan 38, Oshkosh 26
Feb. 21 at Oshkosh, WI - Sheboygan 56, Oshkosh 47

CHAMPIONSHIP SERIES

Mar. 1 at Fort Wayne, IN - Sheboygan 55, Fort Wayne 50
Mar. 2 at Sheboygan, WI - Fort Wayne 50, Sheboygan 45 [OT]
Mar. 9 at Fort Wayne, IN - Sheboygan 30, Fort Wayne 29

1943-44 NBL

When the Chicago Studebaker franchise folded, the league persuaded the Chase Brass Company of Cleveland to sponsor the fourth NBL franchise.

Just as last year, the Sheboygan Redskins finished second behind the Ft. Wayne Pistons in the regular season. Oshkosh, a shadow of their great team of two years ago, placed third. The club got off to a bad start from which it never recovered, and morale fell when star center Leroy Edwards was suspended for three games in December because of an uncooperative attitude. Edwards wound up the season with a 7.8 scoring average, his lowest mark ever as a pro.

In the playoffs, Ft. Wayne kayoed the Chase Brass outfit in the opening round, while Sheboygan eliminated Oshkosh in three games. In the finals, the Pistons took the first game, 55-53, on a long bomb by Bobby McDermott with only seconds left in the game. In the second game, the Pistons won easily, 36-26. The Zollner crew then wrapped up the league title with a 48-38 victory at home. Thus, with five straight wins in the playoffs, four of them by comfortable margins, the Pistons won their first NBL crown after two years of disappointing playoff failures.

The Pistons went on to the World Tournament in Chicago—along with the other three NBL teams—and won the tournament with three straight victories.

	W	L	Pct.	HW	HL	RW	RL	GB
Fort Wayne Zollner Pistons	18	4	.818	9	2	9	2	—
Sheboygan Red Skins	14	8	.636	8	3	6	5	4
Oshkosh All-Stars	7	15	.318	6	5	1	10	11
Cleveland Chase Brassmen	3	15	.167	3	6	0	9	13

SEMI-FINALS

at Fort Wayne, IN - Fort Wayne 64, Cleveland 37
at Cleveland, OH - Fort Wayne 42, Cleveland 31

Mar. 3, 1944 at Sheboygan, WI - Sheboygan 32, Oshkosh 31
Mar. 4 at Oshkosh, WI - Oshkosh 34, Sheboygan 32
Mar. 7 at Sheboygan, WI - Sheboygan 40, Oshkosh 27

CHAMPIONSHIP SERIES

Mar. 9 at Sheboygan, WI - Fort Wayne 55, Sheboygan 53
Mar. 12 at Sheboygan, WI - Fort Wayne 36, Sheboygan 26
Mar. 14 at Fort Wayne, IN - Fort Wayne 48, Sheboygan 38

1944-45 NBL

As the end of the war drew near, the NBL began a return to full strength. With Chicago and Pittsburgh entering the league, bringing the league to six teams, the divisional play was reinstated for the first time since 1939-40.

Ft. Wayne, led by Bobby McDermott's 20.1 ppg, easily won first place in the Eastern Division. The Sheboygan Redskins had little trouble winning the Western Division, while the new Chicago team earned a playoff spot by finishing ahead of Oshkosh, which had lost 12 players to the military.

In the playoffs, Ft. Wayne easily got past Cleveland, while Sheboygan needed three games to eliminate Chicago. Sheboygan won the first two games of the final but, at home for the final three, Ft. Wayne regrouped to win all three and repeat as league champs. The Pistons then won their second straight World Tournament.

Eastern Division	W	L	Pct.	HW	HL	RW	RL	GB
Fort Wayne Zollner Pistons	25	5	.833	14	1	11	4	—
Cleveland Allmen Transfers	13	17	.433	8	7	5	10	12
Pittsburgh Raiders	7	23	.233	5	9	2	14	18
Western Division	W	L	Pct.	HW	HL	RW	RL	GB
Sheboygan Red Skins	19	11	.633	12	3	7	8	—
Chicago American Gears	14	16	.467	5	11	4	3	12
Oshkosh All-Stars	12	18	.400	10	6	2	12	7

EASTERN DIVISION PLAYOFF

Mar. 6, 1945 at Fort Wayne, IN - Fort Wayne 78, Cleveland 50
Mar. 8 at Cleveland, OH - Fort Wayne 58, Cleveland 51

WESTERN DIVISION PLAYOFF

Mar. 5 at Sheboygan, WI - Chicago 50, Sheboygan 49
Mar. 7 at Chicago, IL - Sheboygan 49, Chicago 36
Mar. 9 at Sheboygan, WI - Sheboygan 57, Chicago 27

CHAMPIONSHIP SERIES

Mar. 11 at Sheboygan, WI - Sheboygan 65, Fort Wayne 53
Mar. 12 at Sheboygan, WI - Sheboygan 50, Fort Wayne 47
Mar. 15 at Fort Wayne, IN - Fort Wayne 58, Sheboygan 47
Mar. 16 at Fort Wayne, IN - Fort Wayne 58, Sheboygan 41
Mar. 18 at Fort Wayne, IN - Fort Wayne 59, Sheboygan 49

1945-46 NBL

A record crowd of 23,912 saw the Ft. Wayne Pistons win the annual College All-Star game held in November in Chicago. The success of this exhibition underlined the new vigor of pro basketball. Looking to cash in on the postwar economic boom, the NBL hired famous Purdue coach Piggy Lambert as commissioner and welcomed the Rochester Royals and Indianapolis Kautskys as the seventh and eighth members.

The two-time defending champion Zollner Pistons, with two straight championships under their belt, repeated as Eastern Division champs ahead of the new Rochester team. In the West, Sheboygan Redskins outbattled Oshkosh for first place.

While Sheboygan eliminated Oshkosh in five games in the first round of the playoffs, most attention was focused on the Eastern Division showdown between Ft. Wayne and Rochester. The Pistons took the first game on their home court, 54-44, with Big Ed Sadowski throwing in a game-high 21 points. The Royals, however, then won, 58-52, at the Ft. Wayne gym. When the series moved to Rochester, the Royals won twice more—including a 70-54 series clinching win—to dethrone the champs.

In the finals, the Royals swept three straight games from the bigger, slower Sheboygan Redskins, using a sharp passing attack to take 60-50, 61-54, and 66-48 decisions.

Eastern Division	W	L	Pct.	HW	HL	RW	RL	GB
Fort Wayne Zollner Pistons	26	8	.765	14	3	12	5	—
Rochester Royals	24	10	.706	14	3	10	7	2
Youngstown Bears	13	20	.394	9	8	4	12	12.5
Cleveland Allmen Transfers	4	29	.121	4	11	0	18	21.5
Western Division	W	L	Pct.	HW	HL	RW	RL	GB
Sheboygan Red Skins	21	13	.618	12	6	9	7	—
Oshkosh All-Stars	19	15	.559	13	5	6	10	2
Chicago American Gears	17	17	.500	10	7	7	10	4
Indianapolis Kautskys	10	22	.313	4	11	6	11	10

EASTERN DIVISION PLAYOFF

Mar. 12, 1946 at Fort Wayne, IN - Fort Wayne 54, Rochester 44
Mar. 13 at Fort Wayne, IN - Rochester 58, Fort Wayne 52
Mar. 15 at Rochester, NY - Rochester 58, Fort Wayne 52
Mar. 16 at Rochester, NY - Rochester 70, Fort Wayne 54

WESTERN DIVISION PLAYOFF

Mar. 12 at Sheboygan, WI - Sheboygan 46, Oshkosh 45
Mar. 13 at Sheboygan, WI - Oshkosh 53, Sheboygan 41
Mar. 14 at Oshkosh, WI - Oshkosh 58, Sheboygan 52
Mar. 16 at Oshkosh, WI - Oshkosh 68, Sheboygan 42
Mar. 17 at Sheboygan, WI - Sheboygan 65, Oshkosh 46

CHAMPIONSHIP SERIES

Mar. 19 at Rochester, NY - Rochester 60, Sheboygan 50
Mar. 21 at Rochester, NY - Rochester 61, Sheboygan 54
Mar. 24 at Sheboygan, WI - Rochester 66, Sheboygan 48

1946-47 NBL

The NBL added five new teams this season, but the biggest addition was rookie center George Mikan, who joined the Chicago American Gears before the 1947 World Tournament. The most famous college player since Hank Luisetti, Mikan had starred at DePaul.

But before the season was a month old Mikan left the team, claiming the financially-troubled Gears had tried to cut his $12,000 salary. Mikan stayed at home for six weeks, and the Gears fell to fifth place in the Western Division. Mikan finally came back at the same time the Gears purchased veteran guard Bobby McDermott from Ft. Wayne. They helped Chicago win 17 of their last 23 to make the playoffs, along with Oshkosh, Indianapolis and Sheboygan.

In the Eastern Division, Rochester easily captured first place, ahead of Ft. Wayne, and the expansion teams, Syracuse Nationals and Toledo Jeeps.

In the Western playoffs, Chicago upset Indianapolis in five games and Oshkosh eliminated Sheboygan, while, in the East, Rochester and Ft. Wayne advanced over Syracuse and Toledo respectively. In the semi-finals, Chicago beat Oshkosh in two straight and Rochester needed three games to get past Ft. Wayne.

The final was a Mikan showcase. After he was held to 14 points in a Game 1 Rochester win, Mikan scored 27 and 23 points respectively in Chicago victories in Games 2 and 3. Rochester held Mikan to 14 in Game 4 but Chicago got 22 points from Bob Calihan to win the title.

Eastern Division	W	L	Pct.	HW	HL	RW	RL	GB
Rochester Royals	31*	13	.705	19	3	12	10	—
Fort Wayne Zollner Pistons	25	19	.568	17	5	8	14	6
Toledo Jeeps	21	23	.477	13	9	8	14	10
Syracuse Nationals	21	23	.477	14	8	7	15	10
Tri-City Blackhawks	19	25	.432	12	10	7	15	12
Youngstown Bears	12	32	.273	10	12	2	20	19
Western Division	W	L	Pct.	HW	HL	RW	RL	GB
Oshkosh All-Stars	28	16	.636	19	3	9	13	—
Indianapolis Kautskys	27	17	.614	19	3	8	14	1
Chicago American Gears	26	18	.591	15	7	11	11	2
Sheboygan Red Skins	26	18	.591	20	2	6	16	2
Anderson Duffey Packers	24	20	.545	16	6	8	14	4
Detroit Gems	4	40	.091	4	18	0	22	24

EASTERN DIVISION OPENING ROUND
Mar. 18, 1947 at Rochester, NY - Rochester 66, Syracuse 64
Mar. 19 at Syracuse, NY - Syracuse 64, Rochester 61
Mar. 21 at Rochester, NY - Rochester 54, Syracuse 48
Mar. 22 at Syracuse, NY - Rochester 62, Syracuse 57

Mar. 18 at Fort Wayne, IN - Fort Wayne 65, Toledo 38
Mar. 20 at Fort Wayne, IN - Fort Wayne 54, Toledo 31
Mar. 24 at Toledo, OH - Toledo 56, Fort Wayne 46
Mar. 25 at Toledo, OH - Toledo 58, Fort Wayne 53
Mar. 26 at Fort Wayne, IN - Fort Wayne 64, Toledo 46

WESTERN DIVISION OPENING ROUND
Mar. 18 at Oshkosh, WI - Sheboygan 54, Oshkosh 48
Mar. 19 at Oshkosh, WI - Sheboygan 40, Oshkosh 35
Mar. 20 at Sheboygan, WI - Oshkosh 53, Sheboygan 44
Mar. 21 at Sheboygan, WI - Oshkosh 53, Sheboygan 45
Mar. 22 at Sheboygan, WI - Oshkosh 49, Sheboygan 47

Mar. 18 at Indianapolis, IN - Chicago 74, Indianapolis 72
Mar. 20 at Indianapolis, IN - Chicago 69, Indianapolis 61
Mar. 23 at Chicago, IL - Indianapolis 68, Chicago 67
Mar. 25 at Chicago, IL - Indianapolis 55, Chicago 54
Mar. 26 at Chicago, IL - Chicago 76, Indianapolis 62

EASTERN DIVISION SEMI-FINALS
Mar. 27 at Chicago, IL - Chicago 60, Oshkosh 54
Mar. 29 at Oshkosh, WI - Chicago 61, Oshkosh 60

WESTERN DIVISION SEMI-FINALS
Mar. 29 at Rochester, NY - Rochester 58, Fort Wayne 49
Mar. 30 at Fort Wayne, IN - Fort Wayne 56, Rochester 49
Apr. 1 at Rochester, NY - Rochester 76, Fort Wayne 47

CHAMPIONSHIP SERIES
Apr. 3 at Rochester, NY - Rochester 71, Chicago 66
Apr. 5 at Rochester, NY - Chicago 67, Rochester 63
Apr. 7 at Chicago, IL - Chicago 78, Rochester 70
Apr. 9 at Chicago, IL - Chicago 79, Rochester 68

1947-48 NBL
The NBL appeared to lose its biggest star when the Chicago Gears jumped leagues to join the Professional Basketball League of America. The NBL also lost Youngstown and Detroit, but added Flint and Minneapolis.

But Mikan was back within a month. The PBLA collapsed two weeks into its season and, in a dispersal draft of its players, Mikan was taken by the Minneapolis Lakers.

With the addition of Mikan to a front line that already boasted Jim Pollard, the Lakers easily took first place in the Western Division. The Tri-Cities Blackhawks, Oshkosh All-Stars, and Indianapolis Kautskys captured the remaining playoff berths, with the aging Sheboygan Redskins left out in the cold.

In the Eastern Division, the Rochester Royals added 6-foot-9 center Arnie Risen in mid-season and finished first, ahead of the Anderson Duffey Packers. Ft. Wayne and Syracuse took the final playoff spots.

The best-of-five playoffs opened with Anderson downing Syracuse in three games and Rochester beating Ft. Wayne in four. In the West, both series went four games, with the Lakers eliminating Oshkosh and Tri-Cities beating Indianapolis.

The Lakers then got past Tri-Cites, while Rochester beat Syracuse in a series that saw Risen sidelined for the rest of the season with a broken jaw. Without Risen in the final round, Rochester had no defense for Mikan, who scored 21 and 25 points as the Lakers took a 2-0 series lead. Mikan added 32 points in Game 3, but Rochester won, 74-60. Game 4 was back to form, however, as Mikan scored 27 and the Lakers clinched the title.

The Lakers then won the World Tournament in Chicago, with Mikan scoring 40 points in the final game against the New York Rens.

Eastern Division	W	L	Pct.	HW	HL	RW	RL	NW	NL	GB
Rochester Royals	44	16	.733	26	4	17	11	1	1	—
Anderson Duffey Packers	42	18	.700	27	2	13	15	2	1	2
Fort Wayne Zollner Pistons	40	20	.667	24	3	14	16	2	1	4
Syracuse Nationals	24	36	.400	15	14	7	19	2	3	20
Toledo Jeeps	22	37	.373	15	13	6	22	1	2	21.5
Flint Dow A.C.'s/										
Midland Dow A.C.'s*	8	52	.133	7	22	1	26	0	4	36
Western Division	**W**	**L**	**Pct.**	**HW**	**HL**	**RW**	**RL**	**NW**	**NL**	**GB**
Minneapolis Lakers	43	17	.717	23	5	15	11	5	1	—
Tri-City Blackhawks	30	30	.500	17	9	11	19	2	2	13
Oshkosh All-Stars	29	31	.483	20	8	8	20	1	3	14
Indianapolis Kautskys	24	35	.407	17	10	5	25	2	0	17.5
Sheboygan Red Skins	23	37	.383	13	14	8	21	2	2	20

*Flint moved to Midland during the season.

EASTERN DIVISION OPENING ROUND
Mar. 23, 1948 at Fort Wayne, IN - Rochester 65, Fort Wayne 56
Mar. 24 at Fort Wayne, IN - Fort Wayne 68, Rochester 65
Mar. 25 at Rochester, NY - Rochester 64, Fort Wayne 47
Mar. 27 at Rochester, NY - Rochester 71, Fort Wayne 71

Mar. 23 at Anderson, IN - Anderson 73, Syracuse 56
Mar. 24 at Anderson, IN - Anderson 72, Syracuse 54
Mar. 27 at Syracuse, NY - Anderson 79, Syracuse 68

WESTERN DIVISION OPENING ROUND
Mar. 23 at Minneapolis, MN - Minneapolis 80, Oshkosh 68
Mar. 24 at Minneapolis, MN - Minneapolis 88, Oshkosh 65
Mar. 26 at Oshkosh, WI - Oshkosh 69, Minneapolis 51
Mar. 27 at Oshkosh, WI - Minneapolis 61, Oshkosh 66

Mar. 23 at Indianapolis, IN - Tri-City 77, Indianapolis 67
Mar. 24 at Indianapolis, IN - Indianapolis 89, Tri-City 70
Mar. 26 at Moline, IL - Tri-City 70, Indianapolis 59
Mar. 27 at Moline, IL - Tri-City 74, Indianapolis 61

EASTERN DIVISION SEMI-FINALS
Mar. 30 at Anderson, IN - Rochester 71, Anderson 66
Apr. 2 at Rochester, NY - Anderson 76, Rochester 69
Apr. 3 at Rochester, NY - Rochester 74, Anderson 48

WESTERN DIVISION SEMI-FINALS
Mar. 30 at Moline, IL - Minneapolis 98, Tri-City 79
Mar. 31 at Minneapolis, MN - Minneapolis 83, Tri-City 59

CHAMPIONSHIP SERIES
Apr. 13 at Minneapolis, MN - Minneapolis 80, Rochester 72
Apr. 14 at Minneapolis, MN - Minneapolis 82, Rochester 67
Apr. 15 at Rochester, NY - Rochester 74, Minneapolis 60
Apr. 18 at Rochester - Minneapolis 75, Rochester 65

1948-49 NBL
The heart was cut out of the NBL during the summer when the Minneapolis Lakers, Rochester Royals, Ft. Wayne Pistons, and Indianapolis Kautskys joined the rival BAA Lured away by the prospect of playing teams in larger cities, these clubs took with them such top players as George Mikan, Jim Pollard, Bob Davies, and Arnie Risen. To add to the NBL's troubles, the Toledo and Flint franchises folded, and Commissioner Piggy Lambert resigned because of ill health.

But the league regrouped under a new commissioner, Doxie Moore, and staged an interesting season. New franchises were awarded to Hammond, Detroit, Waterloo (Iowa), and Denver to go with the five returning franchises—Anderson, Syracuse, Tri-City, Sheboygan, and Oshkosh.

In the east, the Anderson Packers took advantage of the watered-down league to easily finish in first place with a 49-15 record, comfortably ahead of Syracuse. In the west, Oshkosh edged out Tri-City for first place.

In the playoffs, the first-place teams got a bye as the second and third-place teams squared off. Syracuse easily disposed of the weaker Hammond squad with two straight wins, while Tri-City surprisingly took two straight from Sheboygan. In the divisional finals the Anderson fast break overcame the steady Syracuse attack to take their series three games to one, and Oshkosh veteran Gene Englund and Bob Carpenter led the All-Stars past the Blackhawks in four games. The championship series came down to the fast Anderson Packers against the physical Oshkosh All-Stars. Speed won, as the Packers took three straight games.

After the season, the NBL scored a major triumph by getting the graduating starters of the NCAA champion University of Kentucky team and members of the 1948 Olympic squad, to turn pro as the Indianapolis Olympians. This master stroke was the final blow in the war between the BAA and the NBL. The BAA decided to immediately move for a merger.

Eastern Division	W	L	Pct.	HW	HL	RW	RL	NW	NL	GB
Anderson Duffey Packers	49	15	.766	32	2	17	13	0	0	—
Syracuse Nationals	40	23	.656	27	4	7	19	6	0	8.5
Hammond Calumet Buccaneers	21	41	.339	15	16	5	25	1	0	30.5
Detroit Vagabond Kings/ Dayton Rens*	16	43	.271	5	9	9	30	2	4	30.5
Western Division	**W**	**L**	**Pct.**	**HW**	**HL**	**RW**	**RL**	**NW**	**NL**	**GB**
Oshkosh All-Stars	37	27	.578	27	8	9	18	1	1	—
Tri-City Blackhawks	36	28	.563	25	10	10	17	1	1	1
Sheboygan Red Skins	35	29	.547	24	7	10	21	1	1	2
Waterloo Hawks	30	32	.484	23	6	7	22	0	4	6
Denver Nuggets	18	44	.290	15	15	3	28	0	1	18

*Detroit disbanded on Dec. 17, 1948 and were replace by Dayton.

OPENING ROUND
Apr. 1, 1949 at Hammond, IN - Syracuse 80, Hammond 69
Apr. 3 at Syracuse, NY - Syracuse 72, Hammond 66

Apr. 2 at Moline, IL - Tri-City 75, Sheboygan 60
Apr. 3 at Sheboygan, WI - Tri-City 59, Sheboygan 51

EASTERN DIVISION SEMI-FINALS
Apr. 8 at Syracuse, NY - Anderson 89, Syracuse 74
Apr. 10 at Syracuse, NY - Syracuse 80, Anderson 62
Apr. 11 at Anderson, IN - Anderson 76, Syracuse 59
Apr. 13 at Anderson, IN - Anderson 90, Syracuse 84

WESTERN DIVISION SEMI-FINALS
Apr. 6 at Oshkosh, WI - Oshkosh 68, Tri-City 66
Apr. 9 at Oshkosh, WI - Oshkosh 73, Tri-City 73
Apr. 10 at Moline, IL - Tri-City 70, Oshkosh 64
Apr. 12 at Moline, IL - Oshkosh 70, Tri-City 69

CHAMPIONSHIP SERIES
Apr. 16 at Oshkosh, WI - Anderson 74, Oshkosh 70
Apr. 17 at Oshkosh, WI - Anderson 72, Oshkosh 70
Apr. 19 at Anderson, IN - Anderson 88, Oshkosh 64

PROFESSIONAL BASKETBALL LEAGUE OF AMERICA [1947-48]

LEAGUE MEMBERS

Atlanta Crackers	Atlanta, GA	1947-48
Birmingham Skyhawks	Birmingham, AL	1947-48
Chattanooga Majors	Chattanooga, TN	1947-48
Chicago American Gears	Chicago, IL	1947-48
Grand Rapids Rangers	Grand Rapids, MI	1947-48
Houston Mavericks	Houston, TX	1947-48
Kansas City Blues	Kansas City, KS	1947-48
Louisville Colonels	Louisville, KY	1947-48
New Orleans Hurricanes	New Orleans, LA	1947-48
Oklahoma City Drillers	Oklahoma City, OK	1947-48
Omaha Tomahawks	Omaha, NE	1947-48
St. Joseph Outlaws	St. Joseph, MO	1947-48
St. Paul Saints	St. Paul, MN	1947-48
Springfield Squires	Springfield, MO	1947-48
Tulsa Rangers	Tulsa, OK	1947-48
Waterloo Pro-Hawks	Waterloo, IA	1947-48

1947-48 PBLA

Organized in 1947 by Maurice White, owner of the National Basketball League's Chicago American Gears, the PBLA was formed with the intent of capitalizing on the superstar status of Gears' center George Mikan. The league placed 16 clubs throughout the Midwest and Southeast and included a handful of the game's better known players, as Mikan and Bobby McDermott played for Chicago and Bruce Hale suited up for St. Paul.

The season tipped off on October 25 as Atlanta defeated Oklahoma 44-43. The league failed to make it past the first month of its schedule as financial losses of $600,000 mounted due to poor attendance. The league folded and the undefeated Gears filed for bankruptcy. Des Moines, Kansas City, Oklahoma City, St. Joseph, Springfield and Tulsa then met to discuss the formation of a new league, the All-American Basketball Conference, but the plans for the new league fell through.

NORTHERN DIVISION	W	L	PCT.
Chicago Gears	8	0	1.000
St. Paul Saints	6	3	.667
Grand Rapids Rangers	3	3	.500
Louisville Colonels	2	4	.333
Omaha Omahawks	2	4	.333
Kansas City Blues	1	5	.167
Waterloo Pro-Hawks	1	5	.167
St. Joseph Outlaws	1	6	.143

SOUTHERN DIVISION	W	L	PCT.
Houston Mavericks	2	0	1.000
Atlanta Crackers	7	1	.875
Birmingham Skyhawks	5	2	.714
Tulsa Ranchers	7	3	.700
Chattanooga Majors	3	3	.500
Oklahoma City Drillers	2	3	.400
New Orleans Hurricanes	3	5	.375
Springfield Squires	1	7	.125

The league disbanded during the season on Nov. 13, 1947.

LEAGUE LEADERS

Regular Season	G	FG	FT	TP	PPG
George Mikan, Chicago	8	79	35	193	24.1
Colby Gunther, Atlanta	8	49	61	159	19.9
Bruce Hale, St. Paul	9	57	31	145	16.1
Bobby McDermott, Chicago	8	65	10	140	17.5
Jack Dwan, St. Paul	9	57	14	128	14.2
Jim Gibbs, Tulsa	10	50	25	125	12.5
Paul Seymour, New Orleans	8	43	27	113	14.1
Elmore Morganthaler, Birmingham	7	35	32	102	14.6
Norm Rosen, New Orleans	8	49	3	101	12.6
Al Ingerman, New Orleans	8	34	25	93	11.6
Darrel Lorance, Springfield	8	31	25	87	10.9

Chapter 29

National Professional Basketball League 1950-1951

By Roger Meyer

It was the spring of 1950 and the National Basketball Association was completing its first season. The league began operations as the Basketball Association of America in October 1946, but this had been its first year since the merger with the National Basketball League. There were some teams that didn't make the NBA from that merger and therein lies the story of the short-lived National Professional Basketball League of 1950-51.

The NBA in 1949-50 was a far-flung league, consisting of 17 teams spread out from Boston to Denver. The schedule was too long with too many teams, thus making travel costs exorbitant. Winning records did not reflect box office success (Anderson, Ind. made it to the Western Division finals but dropped out when owner Ike Duffey sold his interest in the team due to poor health). The NBA made plans to rectify these problems by requiring all clubs to post a $50,000 bond by the April 24 league meeting in Chicago, or they would be dropped. This move was clearly designed to force out the weaker small-market teams, namely Denver, Sheboygan and Waterloo. And while that's exactly what happened, those teams were prepared for that eventuality—they announced the formation of a new league headquartered in Lafayette, Indiana, with Doxie Moore, former NBL boss as commissioner. A fourth franchise was granted to Lon Darling of Oshkosh, but it wasn't clear if their games would be played in Oshkosh or Milwaukee. Each of the four teams put up $4,000 for operating expenses and put Moore's salary in escrow for one year.

Other interested cities were St. Paul, Kansas City, Hammond (Ind.), Rockford (Ill.), Colorado Springs, Grand Rapids (Mich.), Terre Haute (Ind.) and Evansville (Ind.). The intent was to operate a 10-team league. While the NBA wanted this reduction to happen all along, the formation of a new league caught them by surprise, and a full-fledged player war was expected.

In June, the league named itself the National Professional Basketball League and awarded four more franchises to Anderson, Dayton, St. Paul, and Toledo. Later in the month, franchises in Grand Rapids and Omaha replaced Milwaukee and Toledo. By July, Dayton was unable to secure the Fieldhouse for games and its franchise was taken by Louisville. When Omaha could not fulfill its obligations, Kansas City secured the eighth and final berth.

By late September, teams entered training camp to prepare for league play beginning on November 1. On October 20, presidents Maurice Podoloff of the NBA and Magnus Brinkman of the NPBL met in Anderson; they agreed to end player raids and reached a cash settlement for past raids. They

Bob Brannum, 1947
The pride of Kentucky, and of the Sheboygan Redskins one winter.

even agreed to schedule exhibition games with each other. Once the NPBL season was ready to start, each team was slated to play a 60-game schedule, playing every other team four times plus two extra games with its nearest neighbor.

St. Paul beat Louisville, 60-48, on November 1 in the league's inaugural game. Hal Haskins and Stan Miasek paced the Lights with 11 points each while Ken Rollins took game honors with 12 points for the Aluminites. Sheboygan dropped Louisville to 0-2 the next night before 2,700 fans at Municipal Auditorium, 86-80. Bob Brannum of the Redskins, with

37 points, showed everyone he would be the league's biggest draw. He wound up as the season's leading scorer, averaging 19 points per game. A bruising 6-foot-6, 220-pounder, Brannum overpowered his opponents to score most of his points from close in. He would go on to become the Boston Celtics' first memorable sixth man for four more years through 1955-56.

Anderson knocked off St. Paul, 83-67, on November 4 before a great crowd of 3,600 at the local high school. Reported attendance (not always reliable) for the first two weeks was encouraging throughout the league as games regularly drew an average of 2,000 fans.

In an effort to showcase their talent and perhaps convince local businessmen to support a new franchise, the NPBL scheduled a game in Casper, Wyoming between Denver and Grand Rapids on November 14. The Hornets lost the bitterly contested game, 73-72. Three players were ejected along with player-coach and legendary Hall-of-Famer Bob McDermott. His subsequent temper tantrum no doubt convinced the city not to support any team. McDermott received a technical foul after strenuously objecting to a call and was subsequently tossed following numerous profane remarks. He then reportedly ripped doors off lockers in the dressing room in his continuing tirade. The game three nights later against St. Paul would prove to be the last of the veteran's 18-year career as Moore, who clashed with McDermott when they were both with Sheboygan in 1947-48, suspended him for the rest of the season. Moore was determined to prevent further black marks against the NPBL, but would have his work cut out for him.

St. Paul won seven of 10 games, including all five at home, to get off to a good start. Led by Wally Osterkorn's 135 points, the Lights' other four starters all averaged over eight points a game. But they couldn't match Denver, which streaked to a perfect 8-0 mark before dropping three straight on the road. The Refiners were paced by forward Ed Dahler's 143 points and four other starters all averaging over 10 points per game.

Problems at the gate began to surface in early December, particularly at Kansas City, where figures like 100 and 200 paying patrons were reported. The Hi-Spots (name derived from Canada Dry's popular mixer drink) were 2-10 through December 3, and coach Paul Cloyd resigned the following day, but remained as a player. Gene Kurash took over, but after one of the out-of-town owners departed, Commissioner Moore stepped in on December 17 and removed the remaining one and enticed Canada Dry to invest another $5,000 to keep the team afloat. The players did their part by agreeing to play the remainder of the season for $75 a week apiece, thus canceling the premature folding report. Also, the team sought to improve its home venue by moving games from icy Pla-Mor Arena to Rockhurst College Fieldhouse.

On December 20, despite a 12-8 record, St. Paul folded, with president Dick Headley announcing losses of $40,000. Grand Rapids was also in serious trouble, with Moore giving the franchise an ultimatum to find new backers, fold the team, or move to a new city. General manager George Glamack was unable to accomplish any of the three and the Hornets followed suit on December 29. They finished with a 6-13 mark, giving up 85.2 points per game. The Hornets' attendance problems could be traced to competing for playing dates with an estab-lished hockey team plus having to play Tuesdays and Fridays in conflict with high schools. Players from both teams were disbursed to other clubs, most notably St. Paul's Osterkorn to Sheboygan and Miasek to Louisville, and Grand Rapids' Ralph O'Brien and 7-foot Elmore Morganthaler both to Waterloo.

After two months, the league had already lost two teams and there were signs more would soon follow. The NPBL dealt with the folding teams' records by expunging them from the record book and adjusting the remaining team's won-lost records as though the defunct teams never existed. So if you were following team standings in the newspaper, you might have seen your team go from 12-10 to 9-8 and wonder if you had slipped back into a time warp. The league simply eliminated games won and lost against defunct teams. Since that is no way to record history, the team and individual records that follow reflect all games played.

On the court through December, Denver's 14-7 record was tops while Kansas City's 4-13 mark left them in the cellar. Anderson, Louisville, Sheboygan and Waterloo, the four remaining teams, were all hovering around .500. But the Redskins, fresh off a four-game winning streak at the end of December and bolstered by the addition of Osterkorn, appeared ready to overtake Denver. Brannum had just set a single-game scoring record with 45 points in Sheboygan's 132-86 thrashing of Kansas City on December 28 before a good home crowd of 2,500. The team point total was also a new league record.

Through mid-January, Sheboygan won five of six while Denver went one better in reverse by dropping six of seven, thus vaulting Waterloo into first place in the west and putting the Redskins up by two games over Louisville in the east. The battle for league supremacy between Sheboygan and Waterloo would carry the league right through to its final days.

Although Kansas City was given a second life, there was to be no third, and the team was forced to fold on January 24. The Hi-Spots dropped their last seven games and were reduced to grabbing bodies out of the stands to play out the schedule. Four players on their roster are known only by their last names, as nothing else about them has ever been documented. Kansas City's final game was an 85-69 drubbing on January 22 against Denver in Sidney, Nebraska, before a gathering of 750. They finished with just four wins in 23 games and were outscored by an average of a little over 16 points per game.

Although Denver won that game, its victory gave added meaning to the phrase, "I have some good news and some bad news." The good news was center Milt Schoon set a new professional basketball single game scoring record with 64 points in the Refiners' 99-72 drubbing of Kansas City. His 29 field goals were also a record. The bad news was that the next day only 900 witnessed the contest in City Auditorium as Bud Robineau, president of Frontier Refining Company, announced that the refinery had withdrawn sponsorship of the team, thus making it their last home game. Denver played its final three games on the road, losing them by a whopping 159 points, and then folded. One of those losses was to Sheboygan on January 27, a record breaking 157-72 thrashing as four Redskins scored over 20, much to the delight of 1,800 fans. The league was now down to just four teams and clearly in deep, imminent trouble.

Both Kansas City and Denver had hoped for moves to new cities, but that never materialized. Efforts to merge players from both teams and secure a franchise in Marion, Indiana, fell through when suitable gymnasium arrangements could not be made. Waterloo, the last remaining Western Division team, joined the three other eastern clubs under combined standings. By the end of January, Sheboygan was in first place with only two games separating the rest. It was going to be a fight to the finish in more ways than one.

Louisville won five of six through February 1, bringing its record to 18-14. But after the Alumnites lost three straight on the road, the Reynolds Metals Company also found it impossible to continue its support and announced the team was dropping out on February 10 with losses reported at $120,000. The league, however, was buoyed by the addition of the Evansville Agogans on the same day. Carl Draper, the owner, was also the money behind the efforts to secure the Marion franchise earlier. The Agogans sadly proved to be nothing more than sacrificial lambs, losing all six of their games by an average of 22 points. Ollie Shoaf was the lone bright spot, averaging 20 points per contest.

Anderson was plugging along on heart alone, relying on its five-year-old fan base in basketball-crazy Indiana. The team's demise had been reported as early as mid-December, but various forms of financial aid came to the rescue at different times. But fans and management eventually reached the breaking point. The Packers dropped seven of the last 11 games, yet won their final game at home on March 13, 83-67 over Waterloo, after not playing for eight days. They simply didn't play any more, never issuing any official written notification. Any season-ending suspense was now left up to Sheboygan and Waterloo.

Sheboygan closed with a 10-4 mark from February 1 on, including four of seven from Waterloo. The Hawks were also impressive, going 11-6, but it was not enough to catch the Redskins. Such was their rivalry that the league, still trying to generate fan support, scheduled a five-game exhibition series between the two clubs in the Dakotas and Iowa in mid-February. But the climax to this tumultuous season, hollow though it was, came down to a home-and-home series between the two clubs.

On March 8, the Redskins pounded the Hawks, 93-76, before 1,300 exuberant fans. Scoring leader Brannum (injured foot) and Max Morris (appendectomy) were out for Sheboygan, but reserve John Pilch stepped up with 20 points in his best game of the year. Three nights later at Waterloo, 2,201 fans braved a raging snow storm to watch the Redskins edge the Hawks in a thriller, 102-101. The win gave Sheboygan an eight to seven edge in their season series and removed any doubt as to who should be considered the league champion. The loss ended the Hawks' 18-game unbeaten streak at home. Jack Burmaster (26), Johnny Givens (23), and Osterkorn (19) paced the Redskins.

The Hawks pushed for a playoff series, claiming their 32 wins made them the champions. But Sheboygan was not interested and the league had no clout left to force anything. Both the Redskins and Hawks attempted to keep the league going in 1951-52 as the Western Professional League with Waterloo's "Pops" Harrison as the commissioner. But Sheboygan opted to play as an independent and that ended any possibility of a new league.

NPBL STATISTICS

FINAL STANDINGS
EASTERN DIVISION

TEAM	W	L	PCT.	GB
Sheboygan Redskins	29	16	.644	—
Louisville Aluminites	18	17	.514	6.5
Anderson Packers	22	22	.500	6.5
Grand Rapids Hornets	6	13	.316	10

WESTERN DIVISION

TEAM	W	L	PCT.	GB
Waterloo Hawks	32	24	.571	—
St. Paul Lights	12	8	.600	2
Denver Refiners	18	16	.529	3
Kansas City Hi-Spots	4	19	.174	11.5

LEADING SCORERS
(Based on average with a minimum 200 points)

PLAYER & TEAM	GA	FGS	FTS	PTS	AVG.
Bob Brannum, Sheboygan	37	242	220	704	19.0
Jim Owens, Anderson	42	229	176	634	15.1
Ralph O'Brien, Grand Rapids/Waterloo	48	300	96	696	14.5
Chuck Mrazovich, Anderson	16	82	67	231	14.4
Don Boven, Waterloo	56	269	245	783	14.0
Milo Komenich, Anderson	30	176	63	415	13.8
Wally Osterkorn, St. Paul/Sheboygan	39	166	175	507	13.0
Johnny Givens, Sheboygan	44	188	193	569	12.9
John Payak, Waterloo	56	234	251	719	12.8
Bobby Cook, Sheboygan	45	226	115	567	12.6
Stan Miasek, St. Paul/Louisville	32	142	118	402	12.6
Odie Spears, Louisville	35	159	121	439	12.5
Elmore Morganthaler, Grand Rapids/Waterloo	35	143	145	431	12.3
Bob Kinney, Anderson	23	101	80	282	12.3
Max Morris, Sheboygan	43	180	165	525	12.2

FREE THROW PCT. LEADERS
(Minimum 75 Attempts)

PLAYER & TEAM	FTA	FTM	PCT.
Kenny Rollins, Louisville	93	80	.860
Dick Niemiera, Anderson	155	125	.806
Joe Nelson, St. Paul/Waterloo	119	94	.790
Glen Selbo, Denver	84	65	.774
John Payak, Waterloo	326	251	.770

ALL-STAR TEAMS
FIRST TEAM

	POS
Don Boven, Waterloo, 6-foot-4, 210	F
Odie Spears, Louisville 6-foot-5, 205	F
Bob Brannum, Sheboygan 6-foot-6, 220	C
Ralph O'Brien, Grand Rapids/Waterloo 5-foot-9, 160	G
* Stan Miasek, St. Paul/Louisville 6-foot-5, 215	G
* Actually a F-C	

SECOND TEAM

Jim Owens, Anderson 6-foot-3, 185	F
Wally Osterkorn, St. Paul/Sheboygan 6-foot-5, 205	F
Ed Dahler, Denver/Waterloo 6-foot-5, 190	C
John Payak, Waterloo 6-foot-4, 170	G
Jack Burmaster, Sheboygan 6-foot-3, 190	G

Chapter 30

American Basketball League 1961-62, 1962-63

By Roger Meyer

Professional basketball was entering unchartered waters as the 1960s began. The major league, the National Basketball Association, was blessed with outstanding young talent in seven-foot Wilt Chamberlain, flashy Elgin Baylor, and rookie phenoms Oscar Robertson and Jerry West—all under the age of 25 with years of promise ahead of them. Yet the league was not an unqualified success, which gave hope to Abe Saperstein, founder and owner of the world-famous Harlem Globetrotters.

Saperstein had supported the NBA on many occasions by sharing billing with NBA teams in doubleheaders. Arenas were usually filled to capacity to see the Trotters play, not necessarily the NBA teams. Even the two-time defending champion Boston Celtics couldn't half-fill the Boston Garden on average during the 1960-61 season. As the 1950s drew to a close, Saperstein had become frustrated by the league's refusal to grant him a franchise, a request he felt he had earned. He had even proposed the NBA expand to the West Coast, but league officials continued to rebuff him. It wasn't as if Saperstein didn't understand the league—he was part owner of the Philadelphia Warriors.

When the Minneapolis Lakers moved to Los Angeles for the 1960-61 season, Saperstein finally took no for an answer. But as a promoter for more than 30 years, his take on the word no was, "Fine, I'll start my own league." Thus the American Basketball League was born.

During the spring of 1960, Saperstein contacted business and community leaders across the country to enlist their financial backing and support in organizing his new basketball league. Franchises were granted to Washington, Pittsburgh, Cleveland, and Chicago in the east, and Kansas City, Los Angeles, San Francisco, and Hawaii in the west. Saperstein felt the sport was ready to go global, something he had seen first hand with the Globetrotters. It was decided to wait a year and begin operating in 1961-62 to give all the teams, and any new franchise approvals, a chance to start on an even basis. The

Abe Saperstein, 1962
His short-lived league did not match the success of his Globetrotters, but the ABL nonetheless left its mark on the game.

organizers met again later that summer, and each member posted a $10,000 league fee.

The next step was to get some players. Initially, the ABL planned to assign college seniors to teams from a pool and not hold a draft. However, this subsequently proved impractical and the ABL held a draft on March 19, 1961. Each team was allowed two territorial choices. Notables taken who signed were Larry Siegfried (Cleveland), Frank Burgess (Hawaii), and Roger Kaiser (Washington). NBA players were also contacted about joining up with the new league. The American Football League had done this on a limited basis to the established National Football League the year before, and Saperstein was determined

to make his league a success. Numerous second-line players, with more money and the prospects of starting, jumped to the ABL without much resistance from the NBA. But stars and semi-stars like New York's Kenny Sears (signed by San Francisco), Syracuse's Dick Barnett (went to Cleveland) and Boston's Bill Sharman, who left to become Los Angeles' player-coach, drew the two leagues into court. All three performed in the ABL while their cases dragged through the legal system. Former stars George Yardley, 33, signed with Los Angeles, and Nat "Sweetwater" Clifton, 39—who had played with the Globetrotters and, when he signed with the Knicks in 1950, became the was the first black player ever to sign with an NBA team—went with Chicago.

Others were invited to try out as the league opened full-scale training camps in September 1961. Some of the invitees raised eyebrows among the purists of the sport. Bill Spivey, taken by Cleveland, was implicated in the early 1950s college basketball scandal while at Kentucky, and was banned for life by the NBA. The same ban applied to Tony Jackson of St. John's (drafted by Pittsburgh) and Connie Hawkins, who was a freshman at Iowa during the most recent scandal in 1961. Hawkins went to Pittsburgh's camp as the ABL clearly indicated it wanted the best players available.

The lasting legacy of Saperstein and the ABL was the introduction of the 3-point field goal. Three points would be awarded on shots made beyond a 25-foot arc. Where the NBA had become a league dominated by big men, the ABL was determined to open things up and make the game more exciting for the fans, something Saperstein certainly had experience in. In addition to the 3-point shot, the ABL also adopted a 30-second shot clock and increased the foul lane from 12 to 18 feet. One last unique innovation was that visiting teams would share in gate receipts, unlike the NBA where the home team kept it all.

Saperstein eventually took ownership of the Chicago entry (originally, he was going to run the San Francisco team) and agreed to be the league's first commissioner for two years, without salary. And while most wondered what effect the ABL would have on the NBA, its real impact was felt by the amateur National Industrial Basketball League. When the Cleveland Pipers and New York-Washington Tapers (they moved to New York from Washington during the 1961-62 season) left to join the ABL, the NIBL was forced to fold after 14 years.

The ABL achieved credibility by filling the coaching ranks with six former NBA players—Andy Phillip in Chicago, Red Rocha in Hawaii, Jack McMahon in Kansas City, Bill Sharman in Los Angeles, Neil Johnston in Pittsburgh, and Stan Stutz in Washington. Unknown to the pros, Cleveland's John McLendon had been an outstanding college coach for 20 years at Tennessee State and San Francisco's Phil Woolpert, with Bill Russell playing the pivot, coached the University of San Francisco to back-to-back NCAA titles in 1954-55 and 1955-56. Now the ABL needed player recognition and, more importantly, identification with the fans.

Opening night was October 27 at San Francisco's Civic Auditorium where the Saints won a thriller over the Los Angeles Jets, 99-96. The Saints' big front line, with center Jim Francis, and forwards Kenny Sears and Mike Farmer, paced their attack most nights, with Francis and Sears finishing seventh and ninth in the season's final scoring leaders. Sears, at 6-foot-9, surprisingly led the league in assists. On November 2, Washington edged Chicago, 65-64, in the Washington Coliseum in the lowest-scoring game of the year. The Tapers were never able to draw fans or spark interest and moved to Long Island on New Year's Eve with a 14-22 record. Moving to New York made sense since The Technical Tape Corporation of New Rochelle owned 50 percent of the team.

The early going did show some promising results. Every team had at least one win and one loss after just a week of action, so heated competition was expected. One unique aspect of the scheduling occurred when teams played in Hawaii. Due to the long flight, teams stayed for one week and played five games. Conversely, Hawaii was on the road for extended lengths, as evidenced by playing their first 10 games on the road before opening at home on November 24. That's how their year went—two weeks at home followed by two weeks of travel. It's not surprising they finished at 29-53. But Spivey, after coming over from Los Angeles, was a huge surprise after not playing at a major league level for 10 years. He finished second in scoring (1,773 points), and field goal percentage (.5165).

The Los Angeles Jets, in spite of a 24-15 first-half mark that put them, 3-1/2 games behind Kansas City, suffered too much at the gate, averaging just 2,119 for 16 games, and became the league's first casualty by folding on January 15. The team's fate may have been decided on November 16 when owner Len Corbosiero died of a massive heart attack. Players were disbursed to the league's other clubs, most notably Spivey to Hawaii and Dan Swartz to New York. Like the original ABL, this version placed emphasis on standings at the halfway point, to such an extent that a best two-out-of-three playoff was scheduled. Through January 10, Cleveland led Pittsburgh by one game in the east and Kansas City topped Los Angeles in the west. Although no money or tangible award was won, Kansas City took the Pipers two out of three, winning the deciding game, 120-104, at home on January 14.

The league's showcase of the first half was the dynamic play of the Rens' Hawkins. The 19-year-old with no major college experience dazzled everyone with his high-flying moves and acrobatic dunks. No one had ever seen a player quite like "The Hawk," who exceeded 35 points seven times and led the league's scorers at the break with a 26.7-point average.

The second half continued to produce some outstanding play on the court but more problems off. Coach McLendon of the Pipers had a disagreement with owner George Steinbrenner (yes, the future New York Yankees' owner) and resigned January 30. His post was taken by Sharman, who had been unemployed after Los Angeles folded two weeks earlier. The following day, Ralph Wilson, owner of the AFL's Buffalo Bills, purchased the Pipers for an estimated $175,000. San Francisco's Saints won nine straight to start the second half, the 13th win in 15 games for Al Brightman, who took over for Woolpert on December 26. One interesting aspect to their streak was the 9,978 fans that turned out for the Saints' game January 19 against New York that featured—you guessed it— the Globetrotters as part of a doubleheader.

Hawkins poured in a season-high 54 points in a 110-108

loss to the Pipers on January 15. Cleveland continued to surrender individual record-breaking scoring the next night, allowing Kansas City's Bill Bridges to score 48 points, including a record 21 field goals, but lost this time, 120-100. Bridges was another bright young star who edged out Hawkins for the rebounding title, 1,059 to 1,038.

As the season progressed, only Kansas City really stood out as the team to beat. Every team usually gave a good effort and wins and losses were hard fought, not blowouts. Attendance everywhere but New York averaged between 3,000-4,000, if results printed in box scores could be believed. The one sticking point here may be that these figures included all those in attendance (special promotions, kids free and other corporate deals) and not just paid patrons. Otherwise, everything compared favorably to NBA numbers.

After losing seven of their first nine second half games, Cleveland turned things around once Sharman took over, winning nine of their last 11 games, including two out of three from Pittsburgh in the last three days to tie Chicago for the second-half title. Every team made the playoffs; because Kansas City was the first half champ, they drew a bye into the finals while everyone else scrambled for the other slot in a round-robin shootout. Surprising New York beat Hawaii and Chicago while Cleveland knocked off San Francisco and then New York. So the championship would be decided between Kansas City and Cleveland.

Kansas City won the first two games handily at home, 126-101 and 118-82. The Steers shot 58 percent in the first game and the Pipers' high-scoring Barnett was held to a season-low four points in the second. A total of 7,347 fans saw the two games. With the support of 7,624 fans, their largest crowd of the year, the Pipers fought back with a narrow 116-114 win in game three on April 5. The Pipers continued their never-say-die recovery with another two-point win, 100-98, on Connie Dierking's foul line hook shot with one second left before 4,115 delighted fans on April 7. So the series came down to a fifth and deciding game on April 9 back in Kansas City. Before a surprisingly low turnout of just 3,000, the Pipers capped their amazing comeback with a stunning 106-102 win.

Hawkins was voted the league's MVP and selected to the all-star team along with Bridges, Barnett, New York's Dan Swartz, and Kansas City's Larry Staverman. On balance, the situation wasn't all that bad for a first-year league. Cleveland and Kansas City were two good teams with a strong rivalry and there were young stars that gave the ABL hopes for the future.

On March 25 the second draft was held, with Cleveland taking center stage by selecting Ohio State's three-time All-American Jerry Lucas as one of their two territorial choices (teammate John Havlicek was the other). But Lucas had publicly stated he would not turn pro. Undeterred, the Pipers signed him in May and the ABL's future was looking brighter. Then in July, Steinbrenner dimmed everything by announcing the Pipers were awarded an NBA franchise. Subsequent reviews revealed the Pipers lacked sufficient financial backing and the franchise was revoked. Steinbrenner was refused re-entry to the ABL and Lucas was left in limbo. Saperstein made a last-gasp effort to sign him with Chicago but failed. It came out later that the Pipers had lost $170,000 in spite of winning the cham-

pionship. This whole mess proved very damaging to the ABL's image and future. Saperstein even admitted that the league lost over $1 million in its first season.

Other second-year changes found the Tapers, still unsuccessful in New York, playing in Philadelphia. Hawaii's Art Kim had lost $100,000 so the team was now based in Long Beach, California in an effort to curb excessive travelling expenses for everyone. The Long Beach Chiefs would play in a new 3,500-seat arena. And while pretty successful on and off the court, San Francisco shifted briefly to Denver before settling in Oakland. The league was now operating with the bare minimum of six teams.

It didn't take long for that to change. On October 24, Pittsburgh's owner, Lenny Litman, announced he could no longer afford to operate the team and was going to disband it. Saperstein furiously searched for a new owner and, two weeks later, convinced Philadelphia's Bill Rosensohn to finance the team for the balance of the season. The league was clearly in trouble.

In an effort to attract more fans, Saperstein booked his Chicago Majors for just 10 games at Chicago Stadium. He scheduled 15 games at other locations as doubleheaders with the Globetrotters, still a major draw.

On the court, Kansas City opened the season with a pair of victories at Oakland but quickly dropped their next three at Long Beach, the second a 103-74 drubbing, their worst loss of the year. They split the next four games with Chicago to leave them at 4-5. But they would regroup to go 18-4 the rest of the season to clearly be the class of the league. That wasn't saying much.

What little image remained of the ABL was beginning to self-destruct. Dayton University's 6-foot-10 sophomore, Bill Chmielewski, had quit the team in early November and signed with the Tapers on the 29th. Kansas City officials threatened to quit the ABL if he played since the league had a rule against signing underclassmen before graduation, except in the case of hardship. And who ruled on the hardship? Why, Paul Cohen the Tapers' president and acting commissioner, while Saperstein was somewhere in Africa. Chmielewski remained and so did hard feelings.

The league tried a novel experiment by having Chicago's game at Philadelphia on November 15 split into a doubleheader. Saperstein felt that most games were decided in the last few minutes, so the fans would get two exciting finishes instead of just one. Two half games were played before just 1,262, fans. The Tapers won the first, 51-46, and Chicago took the nightcap in overtime, 65-63. The fans were polled and 70 percent favored the usual four 12-minute quarters, so no further "doubleheaders" were played.

Attendance was down at most games, often less than 1,000. Kansas City was the only one doing well, yet its 2,400-average was modest by NBA standards (one newspaper account put its average crowd at 1,700). Bridges was emerging as the new star as Hawkins missed two weeks in December with an eye injury; he finished as the leading scorer, averaging 29.2 points per game, and also led in rebounding with 15.1 boards per game. Bridges had a season-high 55 points December 9th against Oakland and hit for over 35 seven other times. Had there been

a vote, he would have been the league's MVP.

Oakland had a roller coaster season under former Globetrotter star Ermer Robinson, the league's second black head coach. They were 2-12 and losers of 10 straight when they returned home and won nine straight, all by six points or less. Kansas City topped that streak, winning 10 straight, nine of them by 11 points or more. They had to be that good to finally overtake Long Beach, which began the season its own 10-game winning streak. The Chiefs played a rough brand of ball (they had nine fights in their first 13 games) and were led by the 33-year-old Spivey, who finished the season by scoring 37, 28, 38, and 31 points in the Chiefs' final four games. Hawkins returned for Pittsburgh's last four games and scored 109 points to lead the Rens to three wins, good enough to edge out the Oaks for third place. Philadelphia and Chicago finished fifth and sixth respectively.

What had seemed inevitable finally became official on New Year's eve when Saperstein announced the ABL would suspend operations due to lack of attendance, with little prospects for a substantial increase. There were encouraging signs in Kansas City, and both Long Beach and Oakland, but not one team operated in the black. Losses were estimated at $1.6 million for the 1-1/2-year league and the prospects for the future were bleak. One surprise revealed that Cohen, Philadelphia's owner, was also the actual owner of the Pittsburgh franchise, not Rosensohn, as originally reported. That was a major controversy, something the ABL seemed to specialize in.

The following players hooked up with the NBA: Bridges, Gene Tormohlen, and Nick Mantis of Kansas City signed with St. Louis; Maurice King and Staverman (also from the Steers) signed with Chicago; Long Beach's Ben Warley (originally drafted by Syracuse) went to the Nats and Ron Horn was taken by Los Angeles, and Oakland's Fred Lacour went with San Francisco. Other players signed with the Eastern League, and Saperstein planned to take about 15 players on tour with the Globetrotters.

Hawkins signed with the Globetrotters because he was still banned by the NBA. He would remain with the Trotters until 1967-68 when another new league, the American Basketball Association, was formed and needed talented players. He was still a great player and eventually won a $1 million suit that finally allowed him to play in the NBA in 1969-70.

The NBA was no doubt impacted by the ABL. Following the Lakers move to Los Angeles in 1960-61, Chicago was added for 1961-62, Philadelphia moved to San Francisco the following year, and Chicago moved to Baltimore in 1963-64. However, the league remained entrenched in its traditional play and did not incorporate the 3-point shot until 1979-80—18 years after the innovative American Basketball League first introduced it to the sport.

Trying to summarize the failure of a sports league 40 years later with no specific supporting documentation is presumptuous at best. But one only need look at the fledgling AFL, which first opposed the powerful NFL one year earlier. They had four owners who were wealthy in their own right and could afford to wait out the tough times until success came. The teams were based in major cities but with mostly no direct NFL competition. The ABL had neither of those factors. Without sufficient available capital, its assets quickly diminished. Saperstein had estimated yearly operating expenses of $250,000 per team and the ABL owners were not solvent enough to cover that.

ABL STATISTICS

LEAGUE MEMBERS

Chicago Majors	1961-63	Charter franchise, active when ABL disbanded
Cleveland Pipers	1961-62	Charter franchise, disbanded after season
Hawaii Chiefs	1961-62	Charter franchise, became Long Beach Chiefs
Kansas City Steers	1961-62	Charter franchise, active when ABL disbanded
Los Angeles Jets	1961-62	Charter franchise, disbanded during 1961-62 season
Long Beach Chiefs	1962-63	Formerly Hawaii Chiefs, active when ABL disbanded
New York Tapers	1961-62	Formerly Washington Tapers, moved during 1961-62 season became Philadelphia Tapers
Oakland Oaks	1962-63	Formerly San Francisco Saints, active when ABL disbanded
Philadelphia Tapers	1962-63	Formerly New York Tapers, active when ABL disbanded
Pittsburgh Rens	1961-63	Charter franchise, active when ABL disbanded
San Francisco Saints	1961-62	Charter franchise, became Oakland Oaks
Washington Tapers	1961-62	Charter franchise, Became New York Tapers during 1961-62 season

1961-62

Eastern Division	FIRST HALF W	L	Pct.	GB	SECOND HALF W	L	Pct.	GB	TOTAL W	L	Pct.	GB
Cleveland Pipers	24	18	.571	—	21	18	.538	—	45	36	.556	—
Pittsburgh Rens	23	19	.548	1	18	21	.462	3	41	40	.506	4
Chicago Majors	18	26	.409	7	21	18	.538	—	39	44	.470	7
Wash/NY Tapers	14	28	.333	10	17	22	.436	4	31	50	.448	14

Western Division	W	L	Pct.	GB	W	L	Pct.	GB	W	L	Pct.	GB
Kansas City Steers	28	12	.700	—	26	13	.667	—	54	25	.684	—
San Francisco Saints	19	17	.528	7	19	21	.475	7.5	38	38	.500	14.5
Hawaii Chiefs	13	28	.317	15.5	16	25	.390	11	29	53	.354	26.5
Los Angeles Jets*	24	15	.615									

*Los Angeles disbanded Jan. 10, 1962.

ABL FIRST HALF PLAYOFFS
Jan. 12 at KC - Kansas City 106, Cleveland 93
Jan. 13 at Cleveland - Cleveland 98, Kansas City 87
Jan. 14 at KC - Kansas City 120, Cleveland 104

ABL SECOND HALF PLAYOFFS
ABL PRELIMINARY ROUND
(Single elimination- Chicago and Cleveland drew first round byes)
Mar. 29 at Pittsburgh - San Francisco 107, Pittsburgh 103 (OT)
Mar. 29 at Pittsburgh - New York 125, Hawaii 116 (OT)

ABL QUARTERFINALS
Mar. 30 at Cleveland - Cleveland 117, San Francisco 112
Mar. 30 at Cleveland - New York 115, Chicago 108

ABL SEMIFINALS
Mar. 31 at KC - Cleveland 107, New York 84

ABL FINALS
(Kansas City drew a bye to the ABL Finals)
Apr. 1 at KC - Kansas City 126, Cleveland 101
Apr. 3 at KC - Kansas City 118, Cleveland 82
Apr. 5 at Cleveland - Cleveland 130, Kansas City 114
Apr. 7 at Cleveland - Cleveland 100, Kansas City 98
Apr. 9 at KC - Cleveland 106, Kansas City 102

ABL STATISTICS

1961-62 SCORING LEADERS

Player, Team	GP	Pts	PPG
Connie Hawkins, Pitt	78	2145	27.5
Bill Spivey, Haw	78	1773	22.7
Dan Swartz, Wash/NY	70	1739	24.8
Bill Bridges, KC	79	1697	21.4
Roger Kaiser, Wash/NY	80	1556	19.4
John Cox, Clev	80	1482	18.5
Jim Francis, SF	73	1395	19.1
Larry Staverman, KC	79	1387	17.5
Kenny Sears, SF	75	1330	17.7
Dick Barnett, Clev	50	1314	26.2

1961-62 AWARDS

First Team All-Stars	Second Team All-Stars
Bill Bridges, KC	Herschell Turner, Chi
Larry Staverman, KC	John Cox, Clev
Connie Hawkins, Pitt	Bill Spivey, Haw
Dan Swartz, Wash/NY	Nick Mantis, KC
Dick Barnett, Clev	Ken Sears, SF
Tony Jackson, Chi	

Most Valuable Player: Connie Hawkins, Pitt

1962-63

	W	L	Pct.	GB
Kansas City Steers	22	9	.710	—
Long Beach Chiefs	16	8	.667	2.5
Pittsburgh Rens	12	10	.545	5.5
Oakland Oaks	11	14	.440	8
Philadelphia Tapers	10	18	.357	10.5
Chicago Majors	8	20	.286	12.5

The ABL disbanded Dec. 31, 1962 with Kansas City declared league champions.

1962-63 SCORING LEADERS

Player, Team	GP	Pts	PPG
Bill Bridges, KC	29	849	29.2
Larry Staverman, KC	31	649	20.9
Bill Spivey, LB	24	542	22.5
Sy Blye, Phil	28	496	17.7
Kelly Coleman, Chi	26	494	19
Fred LaCour, Oak	25	494	19.7
Roger Kaiser, Phil	27	467	17.2
Tony Jackson, Chi	27	464	17.1
Maury King, KC	31	456	14.7
Ron Horn, LB	24	450	18.7

ALL-TIME ABL LEADERS

SCORING

Player, Teams	GP	Pts	PPG
Connie Hawkins, Pitt	94	2592	27.6
Bill Bridges, KC	108	2546	23.6
Bill Spivey, Haw/LB	102	2315	22.7
Larry Staverman, KC	110	2036	18.5
Roger Kaiser, Wash/NY/Phil	107	2023	18.9
Sy Blye, Wash/NY/Phil	109	1797	16.6
Dan Swartz, Wash/NY	70	1739	24.8
Tony Jackson, Chi	99	1724	17.4
Roger Taylor, Wash/NY/Phil	107	1596	14.9
Kelly Coleman, Chi	103	1591	15.4
Bucky Bolyard, Pitt-Chi	103	1515	14.7
John Cox, Clev	80	1482	18.5
Hershell Turner, Chi	99	1439	14.5
Jim Francis, SF	73	1395	19.1
Gene Tormohlen, KC	106	1380	13
Phil Rollins, Pitt	97	1332	13.7
Ken Sears, SF	75	1330	17.7
Dick Barnett, Clev	50	1314	26.2
Frank Burgess, Haw	80	1229	15.3
Herb Lee, Haw	84	1193	14.2
Nick Mantis, KC	77	1129	14.6
Jack Adams, Wash/NY	82	1123	13.6
Walt Mangham, Pitt	103	1067	10.4
Maury King, KC	109	1066	9.8
Bruce Spraggins, Wash/NY/Phil	105	1023	9.7

REBOUNDS

Player, Team	GP	Reb	RPG
Bill Bridges, KC	108	1496	13.9
Connie Hawkins, Pitt	94	1243	13.2
Gene Tormohlen, KC	106	1210	11.9
Bill Spivey, Haw/LB	102	1092	10.7
Larry Staverman, KC	110	956	8.7
Ben Warley, Clev/LB	96	943	9.8
Sy Blye, Wash/NY/Phil	109	905	8.3
Leroy Wright, Wash/NY/Phil	106	763	7.1
Jim Francis, SF	73	760	10.4
Kelly Coleman, Chi	103	749	7.2

ASSISTS

Player, Team	GP	Ast	APG
Roger Taylor, Wash/NY/Phil	107	457	4.3
Maury King, KC	109	424	3.9
Phil Rollins, Pitt	97	381	3.9
Gene Brown, SF/Oak	94	360	3.8
Ken Sears, SF	75	347	4.6
Whitey Bell, SF	71	322	4.7
Win Wilfong, KC	97	312	3.2
Roger Kaiser, Wash/NY/Phil	107	307	2.9
Larry Staverman, KC	110	304	2.8
Bucky Bolyard, Pitt-Chi	103	286	2.8

ABL COACHES

	1961-62	1962-63
Chicago Majors	Andy Phillip	Ron Sobieszczyk
Cleveland Pipers	John McLendon / Bill Sharman	—
Hawaii / Long Beach Chiefs	Red Rocha	Al Brightman
Kansas City Steers	Jack McMahon	John Dee
Los Angeles Jets	Bill Sharman	—
Wash / NY / Philadelphia Tapers	Stan Stutz	Mario Perri
Pittsburgh Rens	Neil Johnston	Neil Johnston
San Francisco Saints / Oakland Oaks	Phil Woolpert / Kevin O'Shea / Al Brightman	Ermer Rob

Chapter 31

American Basketball Association 1967-1976

By Terry Pluto

To most people, the old American Basketball Association will always be the red, white and blue ball.

Or Julius Erving, the Doctor who earned his Ph.D in the very first Slam-Dunk Contest.

Or the bikini-clad cheerleaders in Miami.

Or Movin' Marvin Barnes, who had 13 telephones in his apartment.

The old ABA will be always be basketball on the high-wire, with more than a few crash landings. After all, this was the league of Lefty Thomas. O.K., not for very long. But Larry Brown, who has coached in the pro game for more than two decades, loves to talk about the early days of the ABA, and he loves to mention Lefty Thomas.

It was the fall of 1967. Brown was a guard with a team called the New Orleans Buccaneers. Don't even try to find the Bucs—they didn't even live as long as the red, white and blue ball. But they did outlast Lefty Thomas.

Thomas was a shooter. What other position can you assign a guy who played 62 games and had only 55 assists while on the floor for about 30 minutes a night? "This guy Lefty Thomas scored 20 points against us, and I swear, he shot it every time," said Brown. So? "The guy had a ring on every finger," insisted Brown. "I'm telling you, 10 fingers, 10 rings. He played like that, with the rings."

Yes, Brown has his share of Julius Erving and George Gervin stories. And Hubie Brown, Dan Issel, Artis Gilmore, Rick Barry, and even Bob Costas stories (yes, *that* Bob

Julius Erving vs. Marvin Barnes, 1975
The Doctor goes for two but Marvelous Marvin has other notions.

Costas, who started in the old ABA before achieving pundit-hood as a high-profile sports commentator). But if the odd, dimly remembered names like Lefty Thomas roll off his tongue as often as more familiar names, that's because the odd, dimly remembered players like Lefty Thomas are as much a symbol of the old ABA as Julius Erving. The league was like basketball's Open Night at the Improv, where all comers could strut and stuff, or at least try.

It was a league where Les Selvage played for the Anaheim Amigos. Like Lefty Thomas, Selvage had his moments. He

went from working as a shipping clerk at Douglas Aircraft during the day to shooting away shamelessly for the Amigos at night. Selvage once took 26—count 'em—26 shots from behind the three-point line in a single game (for the record, he made 10). In all, during the ABA's first season he gunned a staggering 461 shots from downtown—more than a bunch of other ABA *teams*.

"Selvage didn't shoot 25 footers, he shot 30 footers," claimed Bob Bass. "He acted liked he'd get killed if he stepped inside the 3-point line." Bass, a longtime NBA executive whose

most recent stop was San Antonio, was also the guy who signed Lefty Thomas off the roster of the Harlem Clowns. If you don't know who the Clowns were, don't worry—neither did Bass, who signed Thomas anyway. What the heck, Larry Brown came to the ABA from the Akron Goodyears, an Industrial League team of the mid '60s. And Connie Hawkins, banned from the NBA because of alleged associations with gamblers, came to the ABA from a team called the Porky Chedwicks of the Young Men's and Women's Hebrew Association in Pittsburgh. All you need to know about that league is that admission to the games was 50 cents.

They were all tossed in the same kettle of stew, great players such as Hawkins, good ones like Brown, and the special cases like Thomas and Selvage. These men took center court in field houses, armories, and other long-forgotten buildings that served as pony express stations for this league, which was constantly galloping at full speed, even if it wasn't sure where it was going.

Consider that the New Jersey Americans played in a place called the Teaneck Armory, where it sometimes was so cold that the players wore coats while sitting on the bench during games. The Americans also had a playoff game forfeited because boards were missing from the floor. Then again, a game in New Orleans was held up for a half-hour because an opossum got loose in the electrical system. A game in Pittsburgh was held up for 20 minutes when the uniforms were "lost at the cleaners." In Dallas, they had a 35-minute opening night concert performed by the immortal Peanuts Hucko and his quartet. Then the Chapparals introduced "Miss Tall Texan," a woman named Brendo Darney who claimed to be "6-foot-7, give or a take a few inches with my hairdo."

The history books tell us that the American Basketball Association existed from 1967 to 1976. Then, it merged with the National Basketball Association, or at least four of its teams did—New Jersey, Denver, Indiana, and San Antonio. It's also a matter of record that the ABA gave us the 3-point shot, the Slam-Dunk Contest, and coaches wearing sandals and overalls.

On the subject of sandals, Wilt Chamberlain wore them during the 1973-74 season when he coached an ABA team called the San Diego Conquistadors, known as the Q's for short. The Q's played in a place called Golden Hall, with only 3,200 seats. This led to a baffling advertising campaign that played on the image of "The Tallest Coach in the Smallest Arena."

Initially, Chamberlain was supposed to play center and coach the Q's, but he was embroiled in a lawsuit with his old team, the Los Angeles Lakers. The judge ruled that Chamberlain could coach, but not play. It turned out to be a raw deal for the Q's, as Wilt wasn't exactly the second coming of Red Auerbach. He did come to most practices, although he commuted from his L.A. home to San Diego by helicopter. And the league *did* become a bit concerned about Wilt coaching in sandals, so they made a rule barring such footwear. But Chamberlain was still allowed to have celebrities such as Andy Williams and Archie Moore watch his practices, which usually were coached by assistant Stan Albeck.

As for the overalls, Larry Brown was permitted to coach in his Oh-My-Gosh-Oshkosh brand topped by a floppy, Beatles-like haircut. For his part, Doug Moe coached in white and black saddle shoes, and the venerable Alex Hannum coached in an impeccable coat and tie with a Marine haircut that made him look more like the head of the Joint Chiefs of Staff than the coach of the Oakland Oaks. This was the same Alex Hannum who, as coach of the 1958 St. Louis Hawks and the 1967 Philadelphia 76ers, provided the lone bumps in what would have been the Boston Celtics' run of 13 consecutive NBA titles from 1957 to 1969.

The ABA was a mixture of big names and small reputations. It was a league in a constant state of motion, continually reinventing itself, a league where the future Hall-of-Famers George Gervin and Julius Erving once found themselves on the same floor when a fan came out of the stands and hit official Ed Rush with a rubber chicken. It was a league in which the Virginia Squires took the court for their last year with a sandwich logo on their uniforms. The team had been purchased by a group headed by Van Cunningham, who owned a company that produces those premade sandwiches sold at convenience stores.

"I was with the group that owned the original Indiana Pacers," said Dick Tinkham. "The ABA gets a lot of credit for being bright and innovative, and I guess we were. But if there is one message I'd like to get across about the ABA, it's that we had no plan. Sure, we wanted to merge with the NBA. That was our goal. But a plan? We had none. We flew by the seat of our pants and made it up as we went along."

That's because the ABA wasn't even supposed to be a basketball league.

"Our idea was football," said Dennis Murphy, the patron saint of the ABA who later helped found the World Football League, the World Hockey Association and World Team Tennis. The year was 1965, and Murphy saw that the National Football League and the old American Football League were preparing to merge. He wanted to bring a pro football team to his home in Anaheim. But after the leagues merged, the Los Angeles Rams opposed any team in Anaheim, which they considered close enough to L.A. to possibly hurt their fan base. Murphy and a friend named Jim Hardy had raised some money for football, and frankly, they wanted to do something with the cash. Another baseball league would never work, so that left basketball or hockey.

"My favorite sport was basketball," said Murphy. "I knew nothing about hockey. So I thought, why not start another basketball league? There were only 10 NBA teams, so it seemed like there should be room for more."

Ah, the innocence of dreamers. Today, there would be an endless round of market studies done before any businessman would attempt such a thing. Consultants would be hired. Fans would be polled. The economies of prospective cities would be pondered.

Instead, Murphy talked to his friend, former Celtics great Bill Sharman, who had coached in another maverick hoops circuit, the American Basketball League, which limped along from 1961-1962 and failed miserably. Another thing to consider was that the NBA of the late 1960s was struggling, with few games on national TV and even fewer sellouts. Even the great Boston Celtics, according to Sharman, usually had "plenty of good seats available" for most of their games.

It made no sense to start another pro basketball league, and any objective marketing research would have revealed as much. But Murphy and his new pals were full of irrational exuberance. So what if more pro basketball would make little sense (and even fewer dollars)? These guys wanted a league of their own. And the miracle is that this league—which never should have been born, and once born never should have survived for more than one silly season—not only survived, but turned out to be such an incredible transfusion of ideas and energy for the NBA at a time when the old league desperately needed exactly that.

The new league was dubbed the American Basketball Association by Sharman and Murphy. Sharman recalled how the old ABL had a 3-point shot, and he liked it. Murphy said it sounded good to him. After all, it would be something different from the NBA, with its boring brown ball and every field goal counting for two points, no matter if the shot was made from three inches or 30 feet.

Then came the red, white and blue ball.

That idea began with George Mikan, the former Lakers center who was voted pro basketball's greatest player of the first 50 years of the 20th century. In 1967, Mikan was an attorney who owned a travel agency in Minneapolis. Murphy and his friends approached him about being the first ABA commissioner. After some haggling, the deal was done.

"We had a red, white and blue ball because I said we would," Mikan recalled. "We wanted our own identity, and what was the name of our league? The American Basketball Association. What are America's colors? Red, white, and blue. So let's have a red, white and blue ball. I also admit that I had a beef with the brown ball. I'd be sitting up in the balcony of some NBA arena, and I just couldn't see the darn thing. The arenas were dark back then, and the ball blended into the background. And when you watched a game on TV, that dirty brown ball didn't show up very well."

Not everyone liked the idea.

"The new owners acted like I wanted to burn the flag when I said to forget the brown ball," said Mikan. "I had to prove that there was nothing sacred about the brown ball. I did some research that showed there were over 50 shades of brown used on balls over the years. There was nothing 'natural' about a brown ball, it was dyed brown. But red, white and blue, that was something you could see from the balcony, you could see it on TV. When you shot it, the ball left a red, white and blue streak—like a rainbow."

Dennis Murphy backed Mikan. Yes, he liked the colored ball, but he also knew that Mikan was in love with it. And if Mikan didn't get his way with the ball, he would quit. Murphy knew that the ABA needed Mikan far more than Mikan needed the ABA. And if the other owners didn't want to go along, they could take their $5,000 and go home.

That's right, $5,000. That's how small the investment was for some of the league's first club owners. Of course, they had to buy their own red, white, and blue balls, which proved to be a problem, since no one was manufacturing them. For the first exhibition game, the ABA took some brown balls and had them painted red, white and blue. They were "slicker than a greased pig," as one player said afterwards. Turnovers ruled the day. Even after a factory began producing the balls, they still were

slippery, according to the players.

"That's because they were all new," said Steve Jones, the NBC-TV analyst and longtime ABA player. "If you watch a game today, they don't use a brand new basketball. That's because it's slick. You need a ball that is worn a bit."

"I was the first to say that the ball looked like it belonged on the nose of a seal," said Alex Hannum. "I was coaching in the NBA at the time. But when I went to the ABA, I liked the ball. It was a great tool for teaching shooting because it was very easy to see the rotation of the ball in the air."

Former ABA star Roger Brown said that watching the tricolored ball spin was "mesmerizing." He said he developed a move where he spun the ball in his hands, knowing a defender's eyes would he drawn to the colors. Then, he'd drive around the guy, who was staring at the ball. Brown, incidentally, was one of the truly underrated players in the history of pro basketball, a guy who became a legend in Indiana thanks to the ABA.

The red, white and blue ball was a favorite with kids, and more than 30 million were sold during the nine-year history of the league. That alone should have made the ABA millions upon millions upon millions. Alas, the league didn't patent the color scheme, meaning that anyone could produce the ball and not have to pay royalties—which is exactly what happened.

"If David Stern really wanted to do something different, he'd bring the red, white and blue ball into the NBA," said Johnny Kerr, a veteran NBA broadcaster who coached in the ABA. "That is the one idea from the ABA that the NBA missed. Can you imagine how many red, white and blue balls they'd sell to kids if the league switched right now? Can you imagine all the money the league could make?"

So the nascent league had a big-name commissioner, a 3-point shot, and a funny-looking ball. It also had Morton Downey Jr., who would later become notorious as one of the pioneers of scorch-the-earth talk shows. In 1967, according to Larry Brown, Downey had a desk sign that read SALES MANAGER, AMERICAN CAN on one side and PRESIDENT OF NEW ORLEANS BUCS on the other. He'd turn the sign to the appropriate side, depending upon what business he was doing at the moment. Downey signed Larry Brown and Doug Moe to their first ABA contracts; although he himself didn't survive that first season, Brown and Moe were his legacy, and both went on to enjoy tremendous careers.

Then there was the Dallas Chaparrals, so named because the team's first ownership meeting was held in the Chaparral Room at the Dallas Sheraton. Somebody noticed the name on the door and decided that a chaparral, which was another name for a roadrunner, would make a good nickname for the new team. Drafting the team proved a bit more difficult than naming it. The general manager was Max Williams, a former star at SMU. He put together a list of prospects, in alphabetical order. To save a few bucks, Dallas owner Roland Speth decided not to take Williams with him to New York for the first draft. He figured he'd just work off the list, mistakenly assuming that Williams had ranked the players in terms of desirability. Hence, the first five picks for Dallas were Matt Aitch, Jim Burns, Gary Gray, Pat Riley, and Jim Thompson—all in alphabetical order.

The Denver franchise was initially known as the Rockets,

after Rocket Truck Lines, which owned the team. The Kentucky Colonels were owned by a fellow named Joe Gregory, and he put a picture of his dog, Ziggy, in the first team program. The dog was even in one of the official team pictures. Ziggy was a Brussels griffon, a rare breed, valued at $10,000. "He's worth more than most of our players," cracked Bob Bass, who was coaching the team at the time.

"I remember when the ABA was formed," said Steve Jones. "Most of us said, It will never last. Then we said, Where do we try out? I made the Oakland roster, signed for $10,000."

Oakland also signed Rick Barry, who was then a star with the San Francisco Warriors. Barry received a lot of bad press for being a money-grubbing mercenary in high-topped sneakers. That's because he was the first NBA player to jump to the rival league, setting off a series of lawsuits, not to mention all the gnashing of teeth from NBA owners and officials. But Barry's move looks good in retrospect.

Consider that Oakland hired Bruce Hale as its coach. Then consider that Hale coached Barry at Miami University. Then consider that Barry was married to Hale's daughter. Imagine the discussions around the family table when Oakland made its bid to lure Barry away from the NBA. Yes, the money was bigger, but this was also about keeping things in the family and maintaining domestic tranquility. It also was about show business, as Oakland was partly owned by Pat Boone, who liked to play pickup games at UCLA when he wasn't singing or making movies. Barry saw signing with Oakland as a chance to break into Hollywood with the help of Boone. But Barry had to sit out that first year, benched by all the court cases. Without his star son-in-law, Bruce Hale was stuck with a horrible team, losing the final 17 games to finish with a 22-56 record, the worst in the league. As a result, Hale was fired just as Barry was cleared to play. Barry's father-in-law did remain with the team, however, as general manager.

Given all this chaos, why did the ABA make it? There's one easy answer: the players.

This was the fall of 1967. The NBA had just expanded from 10 to 12 teams, meaning there were no more than 150 professional pro basketball players. Europe was not the financially viable option it is today.

Think about that, only 150 NBA players. That meant a lot of really good players were out of work, at least as full-time pros. Furthermore, some superb players had been banned from the NBA for their "alleged" contact with gamblers. Connie Hawkins was the most famous, but there were others, such as Doug Moe and Roger Brown. One of the first moves made by Mikan was to invite Brown, Moe, Hawkins, and just about anyone else who wanted to try out to bring their shorts and shoes and pick a team. The ABA had 11 of them, from New Jersey to New Orleans to Dallas to Denver to Oakland to Anaheim. And all of them needed players.

Hawkins was the league's first star. He had huge hands, hands that made the basketball look like a softball. He waved that red, white and blue ball around as if he were the only adult on the court, holding the ball above the heads of a bunch of little kids who had absolutely no hope of jumping up to touch it. He seemed to play in cruise control for much of his first season, a 6-foot-8 forward with the arms of an 8-footer

who averaged 26.8 points and 13.5 rebounds. He drew raves from his teammates for his unselfishness. Hawkins led Pittsburgh to a Game 7 victory in the first ABA Finals, 122-113, over New Orleans, notching 20 points, 16 rebounds, and 9 assists.

"A basketball man could watch Connie Hawkins and see the subtle things—the passing, the blocked shots, the rebounding, how he helped his team on defense," said Mel Daniels, the star ABA center and later an assistant coach with the NBA's Indiana Pacers. "I'm convinced that the Connie Hawkins who led Pittsburgh to the first title could have dominated in the NBA as Magic Johnson and Larry Bird did. The Connie Hawkins who eventually made it to the NBA was 30, his knees were killing him, and he just wasn't the same guy who played in Pittsburgh."

Doug Moe averaged 24.2 points that first season, second best in the league. Larry Brown led the ABA in assists, a lot of them going to Moe.

The league claimed to average 2,800 fans per game, although some of them must have attended disguised as empty seats, because no one believed those attendance figures. Four of the 11 teams moved after that first season, including the champions, who left Pittsburgh for Minneapolis, which needed a team to replace its Minnesota Muskies, who had moved to Miami. The New Jersey Americans moved to Long Island and became the New York Nets, and the Anaheim Amigos moved to Los Angeles. The league put out word that anyone with a certified check for $50,000 against a purchase price of $650,000 could own their own ABA team. Somehow, the league with the red, white and blue ball was back for a second year.

In Year II of the ABA, Rick Barry played. And his father-in-law, Oakland GM Bruce Hale, made one of the great trades in league history, sending Steve Jones to New Orleans for Brown and Moe. Supposedly, New Orleans couldn't pay both players, and that was part of the deal. Oakland also hired Alex Hannum, who brought an approach to coaching that the league hadn't seen before. As one of his former players, Tom Merschery, once said, "When I think of Alex's training camps, I think of guys throwing up."

It's true that Hannum had a drill-sergeant mentality, but he also had a heart. His players knew that he had won in the NBA. They knew he listened to them, cared about them, wanted what was best for them—even if sometimes he thought what was best was to drive them until they were ready to lose their lunch.

"The only time Alex ever lost his composure with us was when we were doing sprints and Jim Hadnot just fell to the floor," recalled Moe. As the story goes, Hadnot said, "I can't catch my breath." Hannum asked, "Why not?" Hadnot replied, "You won't believe this, but I'm breathing through my ears."

Hannum's presence brought an aura of legitimacy to the league. He had coached Chamberlain to his first title over Bill Russell; he had coached one overachieving NBA team after another. "For years, virtually every NBA team was running the double-low post offense, which Alex Hannum had invented, only they called it something else," said Wayne Embry, former Cincinnati Royals center and executive. "He was more than a disciplinarian; he was an innovator."

Barry, too, made the league look good. ABA backers could sing hosannas to Moe, Brown, Hawkins, Daniels, and their other stars, but NBA people could counter, "So what? They never had to play against Bill Russell or Wilt Chamberlain." Well, Rick Barry did, and he had led the NBA in scoring.

In 1969 Oakland finished with a 60-18 regular season record—all the more amazing, considering that Barry played only 34 games before blowing out his knee. Yet Hannum drove the Oaks to win after win, usually led by Brown and Moe. Then the team beat Indiana in five games for the ABA title.

"You can't tell me that there was no place in the NBA for Larry Brown," said Rick Barry. "But no one would give him a chance because he was only 5-foot-9. Doug Moe was a Dave DeBusschere type, only better, because he could score more. In their primes, I'd take Moe over DeBusschere. The best thing about the ABA in the early days was the players. Some of the other stuff was so Mickey Mouse. One of my most vivid memories was a playoff game in Oakland. We finally had a big crowd, maybe 7,000, and George Mikan stands up before the game and tells the fans, 'It's great to be here in Oklahoma!'"

With the Oaks winning, Pat Boone did a lot of laughing that season. He had a business deal whose terms supposedly stipulated that it wasn't supposed to cost him much of anything to be one of the Oaks owners, or so he thought.

"I remember getting our championship ring," said Boone. "It's a long story, but things happened, and the next thing I knew, I was having to pay $1.3 million. Then the debt was over $2 million. I was praying, worrying that I'd go under."

The answer to Boone's prayers was a guy named Earl Foreman, who wanted to buy the Oaks and move them to Washington, D.C. "After all the deals were done, it ended up still costing me about $1.5 million," said Boone. "I remembered looking at the championship ring, and then I realized something—it wasn't diamond, it was made of glass."

For the second consecutive year, the ABA champion moved. Of course, so did three other franchises—including Gabe Rubin's Minnesota team, which relocated to its original home, Pittsburgh. But that was the essence of the ABA—a remarkable ability to find new owners, fresh sources of cash, men willing to bet on a dream that one day the two pro leagues would be one, and that they'd own an NBA franchise.

Consider the Houston Mavericks, 1967-68 to 1968-69. Lore has it that the team once drew the ABA's smallest crowd, all of 89 attendees. In its two years, Houston had a 52-104 record, so it's not like the folks who stayed away were missing much. The league then moved the franchise to North Carolina, where it became "regional," playing some games in Charlotte, Greensboro, and Raleigh. In theory, that wasn't a bad idea, because it exposed the pro game to fans throughout the state, which had always been (and remains) absolutely crazed by college hoops. But in reality, that meant the team needed three ticket offices in three different cities. It meant fans got confused where some of the games were being played. As for the athletes, they had no sense of a home court. The Washington, D.C. team later moved to Virginia and tried the same doomed plan, as did Miami in Florida. It never really worked anywhere.

But the ABA had another brainstorm. Why wait until a player graduated from college before drafting and signing him?

Where was it written that a player had to complete his college eligibility before turning pro? It was just a whispered agreement between the NBA and the NCAA, good for both parties. Colleges knew they had their players through their senior seasons. The NBA used the colleges as a farm system, letting the young men develop their skills under college coaching. Meanwhile, the players weren't paid, at least not according to NCAA rules.

An agent named Steve Arnold told the ABA owners, "Suppose a kid goes to MIT and he's a genius. IBM wants him to work for them after his junior year. Does IBM say, 'No, we have to let him finish his senior year?' Of course not, they make him an offer to come to work."

Why couldn't the ABA do the same?

"Are the NCAA rules legal?" asked Arnold. "Will they hold up in a court of law? What we are talking about is equal opportunity. A kid plays basketball very well and wants to support himself and his family. That's illegal?"

The more they talked about it, the more the owners liked it. This was a way to ambush the NBA, to get to the young talent first. "Only go after a few players," Arnold advised. "Call it the Hardship Case, meaning the kid has to support his family and has every legal right to do so. I believe the courts will support us."

Enter Spencer Haywood. The hero of the 1968 U.S. Olympic team, who had just completed his sophomore year at the University of Detroit, was courted and signed by Denver. The NBA couldn't believe it, and lawsuits flew. Haywood played. The NBA and the NCAA argued that the Free World As They Knew It would collapse if college players turned pro too early. The ABA didn't care. Haywood was an immediate star, averaging 30 points and nearly 20 rebounds per game. While some "purists" moaned how the ABA was depriving these young men of a chance to complete their education, most pro basketball people were aware of the hypocrisy of the argument. They knew many players didn't graduate, had no interest in graduating, and were simply staying eligible so they could play their senior years and then move on to the pros. The Haywood case eventually made it through the legal system, which ruled in favor of athletes having the same right to make a living as anyone else, adding that the NCAA's "Four-Year Rule" had no basis in law.

Suddenly, the ABA wasn't just that little league with the silly ball anymore. These guys were "stealing" players like Barry, Billy Cunningham, Zelmo Beaty, and other NBA mainstays. They even convinced veteran NBA officials John Vanak, Norm Drucker, Earl Strom, Joe Geshue, and Jack Madden to jump to their upstart league. This hurt the NBA more than the old league would ever admit, because these were some of its best officials. But the NBA didn't even pay them enough to make it a full-time job. The refs worked a full schedule, but most of them needed to moonlight to pay the bills. In 1969, the NBA was paying most if its officials about $15,000—the ABA offered them $25,000, plus a $25,000 signing bonus and other perks. Vanak said he made $22,000 in his final year in the NBA, and about $200,000 in his first three years in the ABA. Geshue and Strom later jumped back to the senior league, even though they took a financial hit, because they felt that the

uncertainty of the ABA, with its ever-shifting franchises, did not bode well for job security. But the others stuck it out. Ten officials who called ABA games worked in the NBA after the merger.

"By the final years of our league, our officials were an incredible collection of talent—they were even a bigger secret than the players," said Hubie Brown, whose first head coaching job as a pro was with the Kentucky Colonels.

But it was the ABA's quest for young talent that left a dramatic impact on the game. The hiring practices the league initiated remain a point of debate today, as both pro and college coaches moan about players turning pro too early—increasingly, even high school players.

At the time, however, the ABA, which was fighting to survive, didn't care about the long-range ramifications. It wanted to wound the NBA, to kick the giant in its shins and say, "Hey, take a look at me!" One tactic was to try to force a bidding war by jacking up the price of signing players. The ABA didn't worry about its own competitive balance. It never lost sight of the fact that the real enemy was the NBA.

Denver did not acquire the rights to Haywood by winning a lottery. Rather, Denver owner Bill Ringsby had the most money available at the time to offer Haywood. It was announced as a three-year, $450,000 contract, which stunned and outraged the NBA, as only established superstars were supposed to make $100,000 a year. And they were giving more than that to a kid, a college sophomore? The entire economic wagon that had carried pro basketball for so long was about to be upended.

Had the NBA taken a close look at Haywood's contract, however, a very different picture would have presented itself. The ABA operated on a system of deferred payments. So although it sounded like Haywood had broken into the vault at Fort Knox when his contract was announced, the truth was that he would receive $50,000 annually for three years, after which he'd receive $15,000 a year for 20 years, beginning when he was 40 years old! It was a classic case of buy now, pay later. And since the ABA owners knew they wouldn't be around 20 years later—some of them wondered if they'd make it through the next 20 days—they had no hesitation in giving out those kinds of contracts. Of course, players such as Haywood soon wised up to the situation. Haywood had several different contracts and switched agents while he was in Denver. Eventually, he jumped to the NBA, signing a six-year contract with Seattle for $1.5 million—all cash, none deferred.

Jim Chones remembered signing with the New York Nets for $1.5 million, but it was $150,000 annually for 10 years. Artis Gilmore signed a 10-year deal worth $150,000 annually, and he was to receive another $40,000 a year for 20 years starting in 1981.

"The NBA didn't get it," said veteran agent Ron Grinker. "The ABA was paying in phony dollars, the money spread out for 20 to 30 years. The NBA countered by paying those same kinds of big contracts, only over five years. Real dollars. The ABA was driving up the price of doing business, and the NBA was all too willing to go along. Both leagues were bleeding each other to death."

The ABA just made up the rules as it went along. When the league wanted to sign Rick Mount, the University of Indiana supershooter, it gave his draft rights to the Indiana Pacers. The idea was to keep Mount away from the NBA. Ditto for Dan Issel, a star at the University of Kentucky, whose rights were assigned to the ABA's Kentucky Colonels.

Then, the game turned serious. Enter Julius Erving.

Erving was not a hot prospect in college. His school, the University of Massachusetts, was hardly a basketball power. Word filtered down to Al Bianchi, coach of the Virginia Squires, that there was this kid at UMass who could really jump—and not only that, he wanted to jump to the pros after his junior year.

"All we had of Julius was the grainy black and white film from a National Invitational Tournament game," said Johnny Kerr, the Squires' general manager. "It was against North Carolina, and he got into foul trouble and didn't show that much, other than he was a good athlete. I did check his stats [27 points, 19 rebounds], and they were sensational."

Erving played in the low-profile Yankee Conference, and, this being the era of the "no dunk rule" in the NCAA, it was hard to project what he would do in a league where the dunk had become an art form. His agent, Steve Arnold, was calling all over the ABA, trying to find a team interested in Erving. Virginia owner Earl Foreman did a little checking on his own. He read some nice things about Erving in *Street & Smith's* magazine. Then Foreman ran into former St. John's coach Lou Carnesecca at a party, and Carnesecca said he liked Erving. Finally, Foreman called his son's summer camp counselor, who also was an assistant coach at Bates College in Maine.

"The coach told me, 'Forget Bob Cousy, Julius Erving is the best player ever to come out of New England,'" said Foreman. "So that was our scouting system—something mentioned at a party, [an article in] a magazine, and an assistant football coach from Bates College."

Erving was 20 years old when he met with Foreman and Kerr. He had two agents with him, Bob Woolf and Arnold. Woolf wanted Erving to return to school for his senior year. He was a traditional agent whose clients were nearly all NBA players. Arnold had been brokering players to the ABA for years by the time of this 1971 meeting. As for Erving, he said he felt that he had accomplished all he could in college and was ready to turn pro.

"We talked with Julius in a hotel room at the Philadelphia airport," said Kerr. "I remember seeing him sitting on the bed, and looking at his hands. I'd never seen such long fingers. They were the fingers of a pianist or a surgeon."

The deal was typical ABA: Announced as $500,000 for four years, it really was $75,000 annually with $50,000 per year in deferred payments.

"At the press conference where we announced that we had signed Doc, we had no idea what we had," said Bianchi. "I told reporters that Julius had big hands and could rebound."

"You should have seen our first tryout camp in Richmond after Julius signed," said Kerr. "He was running up and down the court, dunking on people. There was a shot that hit the back of the rim and banged straight up. It was one of those rebounds where it seemed five guys were jumping for it at the same time. Out of the middle of the pack came Julius, up, up,

up. He cupped the rebound with one hand and slammed it through the rim all in one motion. The gym went silent. All the players just stopped and stared at him. We got him off the court right after that; the last thing we wanted to do was get him hurt."

"The stuff you saw Michael Jordan do—the hanging in the air, the dunking in traffic, the great athleticism—well, Doc did it first," said Bianchi.

Julius acquired his nickname—Doctor J, or just Doc or the Doctor—after a player named Willie Sojourner, marveling at one of Erving's high-wire dunks, said, "There's the doctor diggin' into his bag again."

Joe Mullaney remembers being awed at seeing Erving dunk over 7-foot-2 Artis Gilmore. Others were stunned to see him throw the ball off the backboard, grab it with one hand and slam it through the rim, a trick he often did in pregame warm-ups. "The first time he did it, I asked Doc where that came from," said George Irvine, who played with Erving in Virginia. "Doc said, 'I never even tried it until today. I just had a dream the other night where I saw myself do it.' I thought, 'Man, this guy even dreams about dunking.' No one wanted to go in the pregame layup line behind Julius because he'd do one of those indescribable dunks, then you'd do a wimpy jam and the fans would boo you."

What even made Erving more impressive was his mature, kind, patient nature. As a rookie, his favorite food was Spaghetti O's. He was nice to fans, to media, to teammates, and despite his thunderous dunks, he didn't show up opponents with trash talk or gestures drawing attention to himself. Virginia tried every conceivable promotion with Erving, giving away life-sized posters and having a "Doctor Night" where everyone with a medicine bag or a stethoscope was admitted for a dollar. He averaged 27 points and 16 rebounds as a rookie. He was the most exciting new talent in all of pro basketball, but few fans knew it. Not only was he in "The Other League," he wasn't even with one of the ABA's more popular franchises. Virginia played some of its games in Richmond, some in suburban Norfolk, some in places no one can even remember. Seeing Erving there was like finding a Picasso in the dark, damp corner of a long-forgotten cellar.

After his first season, Erving realized that his deal with the Squires left a little to be desired. He tried to sign a new contract; Virginia refused. He tried to jump to Atlanta of the NBA, which was a problem because the Milwaukee Bucks still held his draft rights. Atlanta was fined by the NBA for signing Erving without first compensating Milwaukee. As usual when a player tried to switch leagues, lawsuits were filed. (If nothing else, the nine-year period that the ABA battled the NBA was a great era for lawyers.) Ultimately, the courts refused to let Erving play for Atlanta, sending him back to Virginia. The Squires knew they couldn't afford to keep him, so they agreed to trade him to the New York Nets. The consensus was that it was better to keep him in the ABA than lose him to the NBA.

Erving's game was emblematic of the style of basketball played in the ABA. The NBA had the great centers, but it was a league that seemed as boring as its brown ball, at least compared to the flamboyant players in the upstart league. Comparatively few fans got to see Erving, Willie Wise, Roger

Brown, Ron Boone, James Silas, Larry Kenon, Mel Daniels and so many others, however. It's worth recalling that the era, 1967-76, was before the advent of cable TV. Three networks—ABC, NBC, and CBS—held sway, and there was usually one NBA game a week, period, unless you lived in an NBA city that had broadcasts of the local teams. If a rival league with the likes of Erving, Gervin, David Thompson, and other ABA stars of that caliber was around today, just imagine what ESPN, ESPN2 and other cable outlets would pay for the rights to the games. Imagine, too, the exposure those cable networks would give the league and its players. But just as the ABA seemed to be ahead of its time with such innovations as the 3-point shot, the Slam-Dunk Contest, and a more up-tempo, high-wired style of play, the league was too early to be televised in living rooms across the country.

"In an era where sports is overexposed and over-televised, the ABA is the last significant sports venture that has any mystery about it," said Bob Costas. "Virtually everything that is known about the league comes by word of mouth, as if it happened centuries ago. The ABA was like basketball's Wild West, with Erving, Gervin, Silas and all the other stars as gunfighters. They are men of legend known to millions, but whose actual deeds were seen by few."

Costas has more than one reason to wax poetic about the ABA—his own broadcasting career was born there. The same question he asked of its players can be asked of him, namely, "How many people actually heard Costas call a St. Louis Spirits game on KMOX?"

The Spirits were around for the final two years of the ABA, and pro basketball has never seen a team quite like them, before or since. When the ABA folded, the Spirits had a front line of Marvin Barnes, Caldwell Jones, and Moses Malone. They had vintage power forward Lonnie Shelton under contract, ready to play the following year. They had Don Chaney and league legend Freddie Lewis in the backcourt, with M.L. Carr and Ron Boone coming off the bench. One of their coaches was Rod Thorn, the battle-scarred NBA executive who is now president of the New Jersey Nets. The Spirits also had Rudy Martzke in their front office, who later made a name for himself as *USA Today*'s sports TV critic. And they had Bob (known as Bobby) Costas behind the microphone.

"I remember when I was hired at KMOX, and the legendary Jack Buck asked me how old I was," said Costas. "I said I was 22. He looked at me and said, 'Kid, I have ties older than you.' That was the end of that encouraging exchange with a man whom I used to listen to while sitting in my father's driveway in Long Island, wishing I could be on a 50,000-watt station doing games like Jack Buck."

Despite all their talent, the Spirits had a 67-101 record over their two years in the league. Their one moment of glory came in the 1975 playoffs, when they upset defending champion New York and Julius Erving in the first round.

If Erving was the ABA's role model, its Good Soldier, Marvin Barnes was its dark side, a problem child from professional cradle to grave.

"I'll say this for Marvin, he once offered me a job," said Costas. "I had some problems at the station and I was sure I was about to be fired. I had committed a mortal sin for a broad-

caster—I had been late for a game. Anyway, I was sitting around after the game, telling the players about it, how I was in big trouble. Gus Gerard said, 'What can they do to you? They'll fine you, you'll pay it, and everything will be over.' Jack Buck told me, 'Kid, I've been in this business for 22 years, and I've never been late for anything.' I told the guys you don't get fined in radio, you get fired. Then Marvin Barnes said, 'Hey, bro, don't worry about it. I've been looking for a little white dude to drive me around in my Rolls-Royce.' If nothing else, Marvin was giving me something to fall back on."

Barnes was a star at Providence College, a 6-foot-9 forward/center who could score with ease inside, or from 18 feet. When in the mood, he was a tenacious rebounder and defender. He was the second pick in the 1974 NBA Draft, and the Philadelphia 76ers assumed they'd have no trouble signing him. Barnes' draft rights also belonged to Denver of the ABA, but St. Louis general manager Harry Weltman thought he had a chance to sign Barnes, so Denver took itself out of the picture. Weltman swooped down and quickly signed Barnes to an announced seven-year, $2.1-million contract, although it was really a deferred salary of $150,000 a year for 14 years.

"In my mind, the symbol of the Spirits will always be Marvin Barnes tooling down the street in his Rolls," said Costas. "He'd spot some kids on the corner, pick them up, drive them to an ice cream stand, treat them, then drive them home. But he was nothing more than a big kid himself. He missed something like 100 personal appearances in his two years, everything from lunches to charity events to boys clubs. He was constantly giving away tennis shoes and t-shirts to kids on the corner, but he was constantly late for practices, team flights and games."

Which leads to the story of the time St. Louis was playing a game in Kentucky. St. Louis is in the Central Time Zone, Louisville in the Eastern Time Zone. On the itinerary, Barnes noticed the flight left Kentucky at 8 a.m., and arrived in St. Louis at 7:58 a.m. He stared at that, uncomprehendingly, then said, "Man, Marvin ain't gettin' into no time machine. This plane goin' back in time." The real joke was no one expected Barnes to ever make a flight as early as 8 a.m.

On another occasion, the Spirits played a game one night in New York, the next in Norfolk. Barnes missed the flight to Norfolk the following morning, and several other flights. So he chartered a private plane from New York to Norfolk and arrived about 20 minutes before the game began. According to Steve Jones, Barnes walked into the dressing room wearing a wide-brimmed, Superfly Hat and his $10,000 floor-length mink coat, carrying a bag of McDonald's hamburgers and fries. He smiled and told the team, "Game Time is on time!" According to Costas, Barnes didn't start that night, but came off the bench to score 43 points and grab 19 rebounds.

"Late in the first half, the pilot of that chartered plane showed up by the Spirits bench," Costas recalled. "He didn't trust Marvin to mail him a check for the flight. He demanded to be paid, right then, in the middle of the game. Marvin sent the trainer to the dressing room to get his checkbook. During the next time out, all the players were around the coach except Marvin, who was standing there, sweat pouring off him, looking at his checkbook and asking the pilot, 'Hey, man, who

should I make this out to?' And then he wrote the pilot a check."

Barnes may not have had 13 telephones in his apartment, but he had one in almost every room. He was constantly buying cars, and constantly being fined for tardiness. Most of the time, he played relatively well, averaging 24 points and 16 rebounds, but he drove his coaches crazy because he hated to pass. "I don't know if he couldn't pass, or just wasn't interested in passing," said Thorn.

"I'm a basketball player, not a monk," Barnes once said, presumably in his defense. "I play the women. I play the clothes. I play the cars. I play everything I can play. There's players and playees. The playees are the ones who get played on by the players. I'm a player."

On another occasion, he declared, "I'm 22 and a 22-year-old ain't no genius. I don't want to act like an old man of 30 when I'm 22. But they keep telling me, 'You can't make any more mistakes, Marvin. Don't miss any more planes. Be on time, Marvin. Drink your milk, Marvin. Eat your vegetables, Marvin.'"

Barnes was known to his teammates as "BB," because they said his head was the size of a BB pellet. "The morning after a game, we'd be on the bus ready to go to the airport, and when Marvin did show up, he'd come out with a woman on each arm," said Steve Jones. "He'd kiss them both, then get on the bus. He had every physical ingredient you'd want in a big man, plus the killer spirit to go with it. He didn't just want to beat you, he wanted to embarrass you. When he was in the mood, he could get a rebound, throw a great outlet pass to a guard, then catch a return pass for a dunk. He had a good jumper from medium range, and a power game inside. But so much of what Marvin did was counterproductive to his career. He stayed up all night. He disdained practice, but then he'd go out and play a great game. You could see that God's hand touched the man and made him a great player, only he had no idea."

Barnes played a grand total of six years of pro ball—two with the Spirits, and four more in the NBA, during which he played with four teams, averaging only 9.2 points per game. He later ran afoul of the law and served time in prison.

At the other end of the spectrum, it was Erving who proved to be the major driving force between the two leagues finally merging. Starring for the New York Nets, Erving won two ABA titles in the league's final three seasons. With the Nets playing on Long Island, word of Erving's exploits was reaching the New York media. The Nets would never be covered with the same obsessive devotion as the NBA's Knicks, but a number of writers did venture out to see Erving play. They were impressed—not just by his game, but by his graceful personality. In the ABA's last playoff series, Erving averaged 38 points and 14 rebounds and shot 60 percent from the field as his Nets beat Denver in six games. Although he still remained a secret to most casual sports fans, hardcore types knew that Erving was special. Moreover, several NBA executives wanted to see him in their league to help its sagging attendance and TV ratings.

Enter the first Slam-Dunk Contest. In 1975-76, Denver had a great team. Coached by Larry Brown, the Nuggets boasted a formidable front line with David Thompson, Dan Issel and Bobby Jones. That season would prove to be the ABA's last, and

the league was down to seven teams. Most of the rosters were loaded with talent. Since there were so few clubs, the ABA decided to have the Nuggets (formerly the Rockets) play a team composed of players from six other franchises for the 1976 All-Star Game in Denver.

The ABA was desperate to put on a good show. Back then, there was no "All-Star Weekend" in the NBA. No sideshows, just one game, one night. The ABA wanted to do something special for the classic, which was going to be broadcast in several TV markets. Singers Glen Campbell and Charlie Rich were booked to do a pregame concert, but officials also wanted something unique for half-time. An ABA public relations man named Jim Bukata said, "Let's have a slam-dunk contest."

No one knew quite how to go about it, since there had never been an event like that before. "Our pregame warm-ups were almost like slam-dunk contests," recalled Dan Issel. "The dunk was a much bigger play in the ABA than it was in the NBA at that time. It went right to the heart of the ABA; it was a statement of your manhood and your talent." Players would watch each other dunk in warm-ups, and sort of verbally grade each effort, much as the judges do in figure skating. "The Slam-Dunk Contest was the natural extension of that," said Issel.

To save money, the league chose to invite only players who were already participating in the All-Star Game to take part in the Slam-Dunk Contest. The five selected were Artis Gilmore, Larry Kenon, George Gervin, David Thompson, and Erving. Thompson and Erving were the favorites. The winner was to receive $1,000 and a new stereo system.

Thompson, "The Next Erving," was a rookie out of North Carolina State, where his 42-inch vertical leap led his team to an NCAA title. Erving was still "The Doctor," the man who seemed to have invented the dunk.

"When I heard about the idea of a slam-dunk contest, it concerned me," said Erving. "I always considered myself a good dunker, but I'd never been in a contest before. I wanted to win, but my best dunks were always done in the game. I didn't think about them, I just did them. The other thing is that the contest was held at half-time, meaning we'd already been playing and our legs were a little tired. Really, none of us did much preparing, we just sort of winged it."

Today, the Slam-Dunk Contest does not take place on the same day as the All-Star Game. It's lost a bit of its luster, and most "name" players refuse to take part, either because they don't want to risk an injury or take a chance that they'd lose. So the contest generally features rookies, and the winner's name is usually forgotten after the last dunk. But everyone knows that Doctor J. won the inaugural Slam-Dunk Contest, and many fans recall the Doctor's "Dunk To End All Dunks."

"Julius planned to run the length of the court, take off from the foul line, and dunk it," recalled George Irvine. "Doug Moe said Julius would never be able to do it, jumping 15 feet out from the basket. That wasn't a knock on Julius by Doug. I mean, Doug Moe loved Julius. He just didn't think it was possible for anyone, even Doctor J., to dunk the ball from 15 feet out."

Before the contest, players began making bets about Doc's chances. Moe stood at the foul line, to make sure Erving took off from the right spot. This came after the players had tried several other dunks. Gervin took a basketball in each hand and tried to windmill one dunk after another, but he lost control of one of the balls. Gilmore sort of tried to tear down the rim with his dunks. Yes, there was power, but it had about as much grace as a jackhammer. David Thompson's best dunk was a drive from the corner, a 360-degree, no-look jam from under the hoop. He also had an amazing reverse dunk from a standstill position under the basket. Players will tell you that dunking from a standing spot—not being able to develop any momentum by driving to the hoop—is one of the most difficult feats.

"As the contest began, I had a plan," said Erving. "I had to do a dunk from the left side, so I did my 'Iron Cross.' I'd jump by the basket, spread my arms as if I were flying, then dunk the ball without even looking at the rim. For my standstill dunk under the basket, I took a basketball in each hand, then slammed one after another. From the right side, I drove under the basket, grabbed the rim with my right hand, then slammed the ball with my left hand."

That last dunk—the grabbing of the rim and using it like a chin-up bar—was a real jaw-dropper because none of the players had ever imagined such a thing. "The fans were going crazy during the contest, realizing they were seeing something that had never been seen before," said Carl Scheer, then the general manager of the Nuggets. "The players were enthralled. They all sat on the court, watching." The finalists were Thompson and Erving. For his last dunk, Thompson attempted to throw the ball off the backboard, catch it with one hand, and slam it. But he failed to hang on to the ball.

Then came Erving's last dunk, the one from the foul line that he promised. It was something he'd heard about being done by a New York playground legend named Jumpin' Jackie Jensen, the same guy who supposedly jumped up and took a quarter off the top of the backboard.

"Julius went to the foul line, turned around and starting pacing away from the basket," said Scheer. "He cradled the ball in his huge right hand as if it were a baseball, it looked that small. As he paced off, the crowd started screaming. Then he got about to three-quarters court, turned and dramatically faced the basket. There was utter silence in the arena. Julius stared at the basket for a moment. Then he took off with his long, majestic strides. The arena was so quiet you could hear his every step as his shoes touched the court. I can still see those long, galloping strides as if he were an antelope, that's how graceful he was. Then he was off, in the air, and he brought the ball back from behind himself somewhere, as if he were a helicopter. He took off from near the foul line, rammed the ball through the rim, and only when the ball hit the court, did the fans react."

If you watch the tape of that dunk, you'll see Doug Moe pointing to the foul line, indicating Erving's foot was on the line. "I did step on the line," said Erving. "But I told Doug, 'Look, I'm not doing that again. No one else can dunk from anywhere near as far out as I did.'"

Moe just laughed. So did the other players. The fans continued to roar. There would never be another Slam-Dunk Contest like this one. It was the first, it had Erving, and so much of it was so spontaneous, so fresh, not scripted and contrived as the contests are today.

Then again, the dunk today is taken for granted, mainly because it is seen so often and has become attached to the in-your-face, trash-talkin' style of basketball. Rather than the statement of grace and athleticism as it was for Erving and many of the other early high-flyers, it's now more violent, more self-absorbed. It's a put-down play, too often followed by mean stares and finger pointing at the opponent, despite the NBA's efforts to crack down on such gestures.

The 3-point shot was also born and bred in the ABA, even though the league had no 3-point shootout as the NBA now features in its All-Star weekends. In the league's first year, the idea of a 3-point shot was so new that people were confused by it. For example, there was a game between Indiana and Dallas on November 13, 1967. Dallas had a 118-116 lead with two seconds left. Indiana had the ball out under its own basket. The Pacers threw the ball to Jerry Harkness, who heaved up a desperation 92-foot hook shot, of all things, which banged off the board and popped right through the rim.

"Everyone in the arena was stunned," said Terry Stembridge, the Dallas radio announcer for that game. "But we figured, OK, now it's overtime. We forgot about it being a 3-pointer until the officials signaled the game was over." Ironically, it was the only 3-pointer that Harkness would make all season.

While the Harkness story is a fluke, the 3-point shot was designed to make the little man with the sharp-shooting touch more valuable, and it did just that. Hubie Brown coached Louie Dampier in Kentucky, "and he was Mark Price before there was Mark Price, the kind of 6-foot guard who could beat you with the shot or the pass. He was a good player who used the 3-point shot to make himself great."

Dampier played all nine years of his ABA career with Kentucky, and the "Little Guard from Pee Wee, Kentucky" was so durable he missed only 13 games. He was the ABA's all-time assists leader, and averaged 19 points a game—yet another tremendous player who was all but ignored because he played in the Other League. Brown was so enamored of Dampier's shooting that he set up plays for the guard to take a 3-pointer off the fast break, or a 3-pointer on out-of-bounds plays. A rim-rattling dunk might bring the fans to their feet, but it wasn't worth as many points as one of Dampier's long, arching jumpers, that red, white and blue ball a whirling rainbow as it went through the rim from 25 feet away.

"When the leagues merged, the NBA moguls didn't want the 3-point shot," said Angelo Drossos, the former owner of the San Antonio Spurs. "Red Auerbach hated it, and said the Celtics would never go along with it. He had everybody up in arms against it. Then a few years later, he drafted Larry Bird, and suddenly he thought the shot was a great idea. And the 3-point shootout is probably the best attraction of the All-Star Weekend."

Immediately after the league's 1975-76 season, the Virginia franchise shut down. That was a break for all concerned, as the poor Squires went through not one, not two, but five coaches on their way to compiling a dismal 15-68 record. The San Diego franchise had died after 11 games, and Utah went under after its 16th game.

Prior to the start of the 1975-76 season, New York and Denver bolted the ABA and went to the NBA, saying, "Take us,

and forget the rest of the league. Without us, the ABA is finished." Officials of the senior league thought about it, because they were tired of the ABA driving up salaries, tired of the ABA stealing their players and officials, tired of the ABA nipping at their heels. The NBA also was tired of the never-ending lawsuits, but one of those legal actions prevented the NBA from taking up Denver and New York on their offer. Called the Oscar Robertson Antitrust Suit, it was filed by the Players Association, which was against the merger. Why? Because the two leagues meant more money and more jobs for the players. A merger would probably lead to more control of salaries by the owners, and certainly fewer places for the players to work.

But by the summer of 1976, everyone in pro basketball knew that the leagues had to merge. The lawsuits had to be settled; the bleeding had to stop. So the owners worked out a deal with the players in which they set up some rules for free agency and allowed more player movement from team to team. High school players were allowed to formally apply for the NBA draft, something that had been started by the ABA, which signed had Moses Malone out of Petersburg High in Virginia.

That settlement cleared the way for the ABA and the NBA to negotiate. After nine years, 28 different franchises, and an estimated $50 million in losses, the ABA was told that it could bring four franchises into the NBA. That was a problem, because six teams remained: St. Louis, San Antonio, Kentucky, Indiana, Denver, and New York. The NBA also made it clear it didn't want Kentucky and St. Louis, and it was up to the ABA to cut a deal with the owners of those teams so the merger could proceed. By this time, Dave DeBusschere had emerged as the ABA's commissioner; his NBA counterpart was Larry O'Brien. They worked out a settlement whereby each of the four teams would pay $3.2 million to be admitted to the NBA. Also established was a system for allowing the other ABA players not on the four teams to be signed by NBA teams.

But the ABA still had to deal with Kentucky and St. Louis. Kentucky was owned by John Y. Brown. He agreed to fold his team if the other ABA owners would pay him $3 million, which they did. Then Brown turned around and bought the NBA's Buffalo Braves franchise for $1.5 million.

The real deal was cut by St. Louis owners Ozzie Silna, Danny Silna, and Don Schupak, who took $2.2 million in cash and a cut of the TV rights for each of the four teams heading into the NBA—and the TV deal was in perpetuity, meaning it went on forever. That deal has been worth megamillions, as Indiana, San Antonio, Denver and New Jersey each sends one-seventh of its national TV revenue each year to the owners of the old St. Louis Spirits.

The New York Nets (now New Jersey) had to pay the Knicks $4.8 million for the right to play in the Knicks' "territory." This led to the Nets selling Julius Erving to Philadelphia for $3 million, and dumping some of the other players who had helped the team win the last ABA title. The remaining ABA players were distributed among NBA teams: Kentucky star center Artis Gilmore went to Chicago, Marvin Barnes went to Detroit, Moses Malone and Maurice Lucas to Portland. The four ABA teams were not allowed to take part in the 1976 college draft.

Suddenly, after years of trashing the ABA players, the NBA couldn't wait to get these guys into uniform. And for good

reason. The record shows that in 1976-77, the first year after the merger, the old ABA stars took up where they had left off. Of the NBA's top 10 scorers, four had played in the ABA—Indiana's Billy Knight, Denver's Dan Issel and David Thompson, and San Antonio's George Gervin. Indiana's Don Buse led the league in assists and steals; Moses Malone was third in rebounding, and Gilmore fourth. Ten of the 24 NBA All-Stars that year had played in the ABA; of the 10 starters in the 1977 NBA Finals between Portland and Philadelphia, five were former ABA players: Dave Twardzik, Maurice Lucas, Caldwell Jones, George McGinnis, and Erving. Overall, of the 84 players on ABA rosters at the time of the merger, 63 of them found homes with NBA teams. Denver won the Midwest Division with a 50-32 record, second best in the league. San Antonio was a respectable 44-38, Indiana 36-46, and only the Erving-less Nets were subpar, finishing at 22-60.

It took a while, but the NBA eventually incorporated the 3-point shot. It made the Slam-Dunk Contest a part of its All-Star Weekend. Even the bikini-clad cheerleaders of the long-dead Miami franchise eventually resurrected themselves all over the NBA as "dance teams." And Julius Erving was the marquee player that the NBA needed for a few years, until the arrival of Magic Johnson and Larry Bird.

"The ABA had a strange split personality," said Bob Costas. "On the one hand, the ABA people knew what a great thing they had, how talented their players were and how entertaining. It was like we didn't want to share our little secret with the rest of the world. Yet, there was such pride in a league that had to endure so much just to survive, and we wanted the world to know how great our players were. It was an obvious contradiction, but both feelings were understandable. We saw so many of our players do well after the merger, it was incredible for those of us in the ABA. We could say to the world, 'See, we told you so.'"

ABA LEAGUE MEMBERS [1967-68 to 1975-76]

Anaheim Amigos	Anaheim, CA	1967-68
Carolina Cougars	Charlotte, NC	1969-70 to 1973-74
	Greensboro, NC	
	Raleigh, NC	
	Winston-Salem, NC	
Dallas Chaparrals	Dallas, TX	1967-68 to 1969-70,
		1971-72 to 1972-73
	Fort Worth, TX	
Denver Nuggets	Denver, CO	1974-75 to 1975-76
Denver Rockets	Denver, CO	1967-68 to 1973-74
Floridians	Miami, FL	1970-71 to 1971-72
	Jacksonville, FL	
	Miami Beach, FL	
	Tampa, FL	
	West Palm Beach, FL	
Houston Mavericks	Houston, TX	1967-68 to 1968-69
Indiana Pacers	Indianapolis, IN	1967-68 to 1975-76
Kentucky Colonels	Louisville, KY	1967-68 to 1975-76
	Lexington, KY	
	Cincinnati, OF	
Los Angeles Stars	Los Angeles, CA	1968-69 to 1969-70
Memphis Pros	Memphis, TN	1970-71 to 1971-72
	Greenville, MS	
	Jackson, MS	
Memphis Sounds	Memphis, TN	1974-75
Memphis Tams	Memphis, TN	1972-73 to 1973-74
Miami Floridians	Miami, FL	1968-69 to 1969-70
	Jacksonville, FL	
	Miami Beach, FL	
	Talahassee, FL	
	West Palm Beach, FL	

Minnesota Muskies	Bloomington, MN	1967-68
Minnesota Pipers	Bloomington, MN	1968-69
	Duluth, MN	
New Jersey Americans	Teaneck, NJ	1967-68
New Orleans Buccaneers	New Orleans, LA	1967-68 to 1969-70
New York Nets	Long Island, NY	1968-69 to 1975-76
	West Hemstead, NY	
Oakland Oaks	Oakland, CA	1967-68 to 1968-69
Pittsburgh Condors	Pittsburgh, PA	1970-71 to 1971-72
Pittsburgh Pipers	Pittsburgh, PA	1967-68, 1969-70
Spirits of St. Louis	St. Louis, MO	1974-75 to 1975-76
San Antonio Spurs	San Antonio, TX	1973-74 to 1975-76
San Diego Conquistadors	San Diego, CA	1972-73 to 1974-75
San Diego Sails	San Diego, CA	1975-76
Texas Chaparrals	Dallas, TX	1970-71
	Fort Wayne, TX	
	Lubbock, TX	
Utah Stars	Salt Lake City, UT	1970-71 to 1975-76
Virginia Squires	Norfolk, VA	1970-71 to 1975-76
	Hampton Roads, VA	
	Roanoke, VA	
	Richmond, VA	
Washington Capitols	Washington, DC	1969-70

1967-68

Into a brave new world as Davidson, pals launch new league

The American Basketball Association began its life with a big-name commissioner and mostly lesser-name players. Organized by a group of California promoters led by Gary Davidson, the ABA entered battle with the established and hostile NBA with George Mikan as the league's chief executive. Although Mikan had been the dominant figure in the NBA during his playing days with the Minneapolis Lakers, the players he now presided over were by and large rejects from the older circuit. The Oakland Oaks did sign Rick Barry, the NBA's leading scorer, but a court order forced him to sit our the season to fulfill the reserve clause of his contract with the San Francisco Warriors. Rookies Mel Daniels and Randy Mahaffey had been picked on the first round of the NBA draft but chose instead to sign with ABA clubs, and guards Louie Dampier, Bob Verga, and Bob Lloyd all were fresh out of college with All-American credentials.

But aside from these blue-chip athletes, the ABA clubs came up with whatever players were available to stock their rosters for this maiden campaign. There were old-time NBA veterans like Cliff Hagan, and marginal NBA journeymen like Ben Warley and Wayne Hightower. Men who had had a cup of coffee in the NBA now had another shot a pro basketball; this class of players included Larry Jones, Freddie Lewis, and Les Hunter, among many others. Other candidates for jobs had starred in college several years ago but had not broken into the NBA; Donnie Freeman, Walt Simon, Ollie Darden, Jim Hadnot, Willie Somerset, and Levern Tart ranked among those seeking to recall the glories of their undergraduate careers. Some rookies without big reputations but sizable talent also made the new squads, with Bob Netolicky, Trooper Washington, Jimmy Jones, Stew Johnson, and Byron Beck foremost among these. Connie Hawkins, Doug Moe, Roger Brown, and Tony Jackson were signed despite their peripheral involvement with the 1961 scandals which led the NBA to ban them. A handful of players came from industrial AAU teams and some came from the minor pro leagues, including several men who had played in the ABL which folded in 1963.

With this hodge-podge of players, the ABA opened its inaugural season with clubs in Pittsburgh, Minnesota, New Jersey, Indiana, Kentucky, New Orleans, Houston, Dallas, Denver, Anaheim, and Oakland; the Minnesota team played in Minneapolis, Indiana in Indianapolis, Kentucky in Louisville, and New Jersey in Teaneck, a suburb of New York City. Some of the head coaches had reputations as star players in the NBA; others were relatively unknown out of the college ranks.

Three innovations made the ABA games look very different from NBA contests. Just as in the ABL of 1961-62, field goals from beyond 25 feet away counted three points, and a 30-second clock gave the league clubs six extra seconds to work the ball around. Perhaps the most distinctive feature of the game

Connie Hawkins
Out of the wilderness to become a pied Piper in Pittsburgh, and the new league's inaugural Most Valuable Player.

was the red, white, and blue ball the ABA used, a stark contrast to the traditional brown ball.

Play started without a television contract, and attendance was sparse in most league cities, but the eleven teams headed into a championship race which was almost impossible to handicap ahead of time. The Western Division had three strong clubs in the New Orleans Buccaneers, Dallas Chapparals, and Denver Rockets, and three weak teams in the Houston Mavericks, Anaheim Amigos, and Oakland Oaks. The New Orleans squad was coached by Babe McCarthy and featured a

hustling lineup of Doug Moe, Jackie Moreland, Red Robbins, 5-foot-9 Larry Brown, and Jimmy Jones, with Jesse Branson and George Govan among the better subs in the league. Cliff Hagan came out of a year's retirement to coach and play forward for the Dallas Chaps, and he teamed with youngsters Cincy Powell and John Beasley in a high-scoring front line; rookie Bob Verga gave the Chaps a high-scoring guard until the Army snatched him away in mid-season. The Denver Rockets had the ABA's best all-around guard in NBA-castoff Larry Jones, with veteran Wayne Hightower and young Willie Murrell the stars up front.

These three clubs battled for first place most of the season with the final 1-2-3 standings showing New Orleans, Dallas, and Denver. Houston took fourth place under the direction of old NBA star Slater Martin. Out of the playoffs were the Anaheim Amigos, whose Les Selvage led the league in three-point tries, and the Oakland Oaks, who were owned by singer Pat Boone and used Rick Barry up in the broadcasting booth.

First place in the East went to the Pittsburgh Pipers, whose Connie Hawkins was the star of the league. A gifted one-on-one player who had played in the old ABL and with the Globetrotters after being banned by the NBA for not reporting a bribe offer while at the University of Iowa, "Hawk" started the season at forward, moved to center in mid-season, and led the ABA with a 26.8 scoring average. His mates in the starting line-up included forwards Trooper Washington and Art Heyman and guards Chico Vaughn and Charlie Williams, both good long-range shots. The Minnesota Muskies finished a close second with a strong nucleus made up of center Mel Daniels, forward Les Hunter, and guard Donnie Freeman.

The Indiana Pacers faded after a good start but hung on to third place, while Kentucky and New Jersey tied for the fourth and final playoff spot. These two clubs were scheduled to break their tie with a one-game playoff at Teaneck, but the Armory there was unavailable. The game was then set up in an arena in Commack, Long Island, but when the players showed up for the game, they found floor boards missing and bolts protruding from the floor; the Kentucky squad won the playoff berth by forfeit.

This incident cast the playoffs in a somewhat bush-league light, and crowds like the 661 who attended one opening round game in Minneapolis gave the players an embarrassing sense of privacy. The first two rounds went according to expectations, with Pittsburgh and New Orleans the contestants in the first ABA championship series. The Buccaneers had the tighter team and the stronger bench, but the Pipers had Connie Hawkins. New Orleans took a 3-2 lead in the series, but the Hawk led his mates to 118-112 and 122-113 victories in Games 6 and 7 to bring the first ABA crown to Pittsburgh, a city not long destined to be in the ABA circuit.

1967-68 SEASON HIGHLIGHTS

STANDINGS

Eastern Division

	W	L	Pct.	GB
Pittsburgh	54	24	.692	—
Minnesota	50	28	.641	4
Indiana	38	40	.487	16
Kentucky	36	42	.462	18
New Jersey	36	42	.462	18

Western Division

	W	L	Pct.	GB
New Orleans	48	30	.615	—
Dallas	46	32	.590	2
Denver	45	33	.577	3
Houston	29	49	.372	19
Anaheim	25	53	.321	23
Oakland	22	56	.282	26

AWARDS
MVP
Connie Hawkins, Pittsburgh
Rookie of the Year
Mel Daniels, Minnesota
Coach of the Year
Vince Cazetta, Pittsburgh

ALL-STAR TEAMS

FIRST TEAM

Connie Hawkins	Pittsburgh
Doug Moe	New Orleans
Mel Daniels	Minnesota
Larry Jones	Denver
Charlie Williams	Pittsburgh

SECOND TEAM

Roger Brown	Indiana
Cincy Powell	Dallas
John Beasley	Dallas
Larry Brown	New Orleans
Louie Dampier	Kentucky

ALL-STAR GAME
Hinkle Fieldhouse, Indianapolis
Tuesday, January 9, 1968
East 126, West 120
MVP: Larry Brown

PLAYOFFS
FINALS
Pittsburgh 4, New Orleans 3
Apr. 18: Pittsburgh 120, New Orleans 112
Apr. 20: New Orleans 109, Pittsburgh 100
Apr. 24: New Orleans 109, Pittsburgh 101
Apr. 25: Pittsburgh 106, New Orleans 105, OT
Apr. 27: New Orleans 111, Pittsburgh 108
May 1: Pittsburgh 118, New Orleans 112
May 4: Pittsburgh 122, New Orleans 113

EASTERN DIVISION
DIVISION FINALS
Pittsburgh 4, Minnesota 1
Apr. 4: Pittsburgh 125, Minnesota 117
Apr. 6: Minnesota 137, Pittsburgh 123
Apr. 10: Pittsburgh 107, Minnesota 99
Apr. 13: Pittsburgh 117, Minnesota 108
Apr. 14: Pittsburgh 114, Minnesota 105

DIVISION SEMI-FINALS
Minnesota 3, Kentucky 2
Mar. 24: Minnesota 115, Kentucky 102
Mar. 26: Kentucky 100, Minnesota 95
Mar. 27: Minnesota 116, Kentucky 107
Mar. 29: Kentucky 94, Minnesota 86
Mar. 30: Minnesota 114, Kentucky 108
Pittsburgh 3, Indiana 0
Mar. 25: Pittsburgh 146, Indiana 127
Mar. 26: Pittsburgh 121, Indiana 108
Mar. 27: Pittsburgh 133, Indiana 114
PLAYOFF FOR FOURTH PLACE
Mar. 23: Kentucky 2, New Jersey 0 (forfiet win)

WESTERN DIVISION
DIVISION FINALS
New Orleans 4, Dallas 1
Apr. 8: New Orleans 104, Dallas 99
Apr. 9: Dallas 112, New Orleans 109
Apr. 10: New Orleans 110, Dallas 107
Apr. 11: New Orleans 119, Dallas 103
Apr. 13: New Orleans 108, Dallas 107
DIVISION SEMI-FINALS
New Orleans 3, Denver 2
Mar. 26: New Orleans 130, Denver 104
Mar. 27: New Orleans 105, Denver 93
Mar. 30: Denver 105, New Orleans 98
Mar. 31: Denver 108, New Orleans 100
Apr 3: New Orleans 102, Denver 97
Dallas 3, Houston 0
Mar. 23: Dallas 111, Houston 110
Mar. 25: Dallas 115, Houston 97
Mar. 26: Dallas 116, Houston 103

SCORING

		G	FG	FT	PTS	AVG
Hawkins	Pit	70	635	603	1875	26.8
Moe	NO	78	665	551	1884	24.2
Tart	Oak-NJ	73	633	451	1718	23.5
Carrier	KY	77	643	395	1765	22.9
Jones	Den	76	602	530	1742	22.9

REBOUNDS

		G	REB	AVG
Daniels	Min	78	1213	15.6
Hawkins	Pit	70	945	13.5
J. Beasley	Dal	77	982	12.8
Harge	Pit-Oak	82	1038	12.7
Robbins	NO	73	894	12.2
Hadnot	Oak	77	936	12.2

ASSISTS

		G	AST	AVG
Brown	NO	78	506	6.5
Chubin	Ana	77	364	4.7
Hawkins	Pit	70	320	4.6
Brown	Ind	76	327	4.3
Heyman	NJ-Pit	73	276	3.8

1968-69

Musical franchises, tiny attendances, but a sense of progress

Poor attendance last year sent the league's weaker links looking for new lands to settle. The Anaheim team packed its bags for the big city of Los Angeles, a very unlikely challenger for the Los Angeles Lakers. The Minnesota Muskies fled to the warmer climes of Miami, and the champion Pittsburgh Pipers left town to move into Minneapolis, oblivious to the debt-ridden season of the Muskies.

The New Jersey Americans were reborn as the New York Nets, playing in an arena in Commack, Long Island which had been ruled unfit for play in last season's tie-breaker for a playoff spot. Opening day, this season didn't so much better, as the hockey ice over which the floor was laid began to melt and seep up through the boards during the pre-game drills, treating the crowd of 1,848 to the spectacle of players skidding and sliding all over the court. The heat in the building was turned off, the ice stopped melting, and the game started an hour late, with Kentucky winning the match, 99-92. In this damp, cold arena with sparse crowds, the Nets reminded no one of the New York Knicks and Madison Square Garden.

The ABA's attendance wasn't much better this season, rising from last year's average of 2,804 for regular season games to only 2,981. The new Miami team could pay off its outstanding debts in Minnesota only by selling All-Star center Mel Daniels to the Indiana Pacers for cash plus two insignificant players. The Houston club went broke early in the season, and Commissioner George Mikan kept the team going with league funds. One reason for the lack of enthusiasm over the ABA was its failure to sign any prominent rookies, with Elvin Hayes of Houston and Wes Unseld of Louisville spurning large offers from hometown ABA clubs to sign with the established league. Bill Sharman and Alex Hannum, two of the NBA's more famous coaches, joined ABA teams this year, but their press value was small. The major publicity event for the ABA was the debut of Rick Barry, who wore the uniform of the Oakland Oaks after sitting out his option year. Barry and Connie Hawkins of Minnesota were the stars, but both of them went out in mid-season with knee injuries.

Before hurting his knee, however, Barry got the Oakland club off to a flying start. Under the direction of Alex Hannum, who had made the Philadelphia 76ers the scourge of the NBA, the Oaks won 15 of their first 17 games and later strung together a 16-game winning streak to quickly amass an insurmountable lead in the Western Division. Barry had lots of help from the supporting cast. Forward Doug Moe and guard Larry Brown came in a trade from New Orleans to considerably

Warren Armstrong
A 28.8-point playoff average by the rookie (later known as Warren Jabali), leading Oakland Oaks to the title despite the loss of Rick Barry.

strengthen the club, and rookies Warren Armstrong, Henry Logan, and Jim Eakins joined with holdovers Ira Harge and Gay Bradds in making the Oaks the class of the league. Even after Barry took his 34.0 scoring average with him to the infirmary, the Oaks kept winning.

The New Orleans Bucs held second place, relying more on Jimmy Jones and Red Robbins in the absence of Moe and Brown. The Denver Rockets stood fast in third place, and the Dallas Chaps captured fourth place, with Cliff Hagan playing less frequently and with rookies Ron Boone and Glen Combs

making strong contributions. Bill Sharman coached the new Los Angeles Stars, who fielded a rookie-laden squad and finished out of the playoffs in fifth place. The Houston Mavericks came in last, with players coming and going in chaotic fashion while the front office affairs of the club approached the same state.

By contrast, the Indiana Pacers were one of the ABA's showcase franchises. Attendance reached acceptable levels, and the team was much strengthened by the addition of center Mel Daniels from the Miami franchise. A slow start of 2-7 cost coach Larry Staverman his job, but Bob Leonard came in and got the Pacers moving to a 42-27 clip. One game behind the first-place Pacers came the Miami Floridians, who remained a strong outfit despite the forced sale of Daniels. Coach Jim Pollard strung together a close-knit unit whose star was guard Donnie Freeman.

The Kentucky Colonels captured third place with a strong 42-36 record, relying on guards Louie Dampier and Darrel Carrier for the bulk of the team's scoring. In the midst of a controversy over whether women should be hired as professional jockeys, the Colonels won some press coverage by signing woman jockey Penny Ann Early to a player's contract. Miss Early threw the ball into play on an out-of-bounds play in a game against the Los Angeles Stars; the Colonels immediately called time out and took her out of the lineup forever.

The champion Pipers weren't enjoying any jokes in their new home in Minnesota. In addition to losing Connie Hawkins in mid-campaign with a knee injury, the Pipers had a most incompatible new coach in Jim Harding, a strict disciplinarian who freely yelled at his players and officials. He was so hot tempered that during the All-Star break, he punched team owner Gabe Rubin. After this, Vern Mikkelsen and then Gus Young handled the coaching duties, bringing the Pipers home a weak fourth. In last place were the New York Nets, who used a revolving door more for the players than the fans.

For the playoffs, Connie Hawkins was back in action for Minnesota while Rick Barry was still out for Oakland. Notwithstanding Hawk's presence, the Pipers lost in the opening round, while the Oaks joined Indiana, Miami, and New Orleans in moving into the second round. Both divisional finals were one-sided, with Indiana beating Miami in five games and Oakland taking four straight from New Orleans. The Pacers had two hot hands in Roger Brown and Freddie Lewis, plus two good big men in Mel Daniels and Bob Netolicky; the Oaks seemed weaker on paper without Barry. But rookie Warren Armstrong picked up the scoring slack left by Barry, averaging 28.8 for the playoffs, and the Oaks had a surprisingly easy time downing the Pacers in five games including an exciting 134-126 overtime win in Game 3. But in the shadow of the Celtics dramatic championship in the NBA, the ABA crown went almost completely unnoticed.

1968-69 SEASON HIGHLIGHTS

STANDINGS

Eastern Division

	W	L	Pct.	GB
Indiana	44	34	.564	—
Miami	43	35	.551	1
Kentucky	42	36	.538	2
Minnesota	36	42	.462	8
New York	17	61	.218	27

Western Division

	W	L	Pct.	GB
Oakland	60	18	.769	—
New Orleans	46	32	.590	14
Denver	44	34	.564	16
Dallas	41	37	.526	19
Los Angeles	33	45	.423	27
Houston	23	55	.295	37

AWARDS

MVP
Mel Daniels, Indiana
Rookie of the Year
Warren Armstrong, Oakland
Coach of the Year
Alex Hannum, Oakland

ALL-STAR TEAMS

FIRST TEAM

Connie Hawkins	Minnesota
Rick Barry	Oakland
Mel Daniels	Indiana
Jimmy Jones	New Orleans
Larry Jones	Denver

SECOND TEAM

John Beasley	Dallas
Doug Moe	Oakland
Red Robbins	New Orleans
Donnie Freeman	Miami
Louie Dampier	Kentucky

ALL-STAR GAME

Convention Center, Louisville, KY
Tuesday, January 28, 1969
West 133, East 127
MVP: John Beasley

PLAYOFFS

FINALS
Oakland 4, Indiana 1
Apr. 30: Oakland 123, Indiana 114
May 2: Indiana 150, Oakland 122
May 3: Oakland 134, Indiana 126, OT
May 5: Oakland 144, Indiana 117
May 7: Oakland 135, Indiana 131, OT
EASTERN DIVISION
DIVISION FINALS
Indiana 4, Miami 1
Apr. 20: Indiana 126, Miami 110
Apr. 22: Indiana 131, Miami 116
Apr. 23: Indiana 119, Miami 105
Apr. 25: Miami 114, Indiana 105
Apr. 26: Indiana 127, Miami 105
DIVISION SEMI-FINALS
Miami 4, Minnesota 3
Apr. 7: Miami 119, Minnesota 110
Apr. 9: Minnesota 106, Miami 99

Apr. 10: Minnesota 109, Miami 93
Apr. 12: Miami 116, Minnesota 109
Apr. 13: Miami 122, Minnesota 107
Apr. 15: Minnesota 105, Miami 100
Apr. 19: Miami 137, Minnesota 128
Indiana 4, Kentucky 3
Apr. 8: Kentucky 128, Indiana 118
Apr. 9: Indiana 120, Kentucky 115
Apr. 10: Kentucky 130, Indiana 111
Apr. 13: Kentucky 105, Indiana 104, OT
Apr. 14: Indiana 116, Kentucky 97
Apr. 15: Indiana 107, Kentucky 89
Apr. 17: Indiana 120, Kentucky 111
WESTERN DIVISION
DIVISION FINALS
Oakland 4, New Orleans 0
Apr. 19: Oakland 128, New Orleans 118
Apr. 21: Oakland 135, New Orleans 124
Apr. 23: Oakland 113, New Orleans 107
Apr. 25: Oakland 128, New Orleans 114

DIVISION SEMI-FINALS
Oakland 4, Denver 3
Apr. 5: Oakland 129, Denver 99
Apr. 6: Denver 122, Oakland 119
Apr. 8: Oakland 121, Denver 99
Apr. 10: Denver 109, Oakland 108
Apr. 12: Oakland 128, Denver 118
Apr. 13: Denver 126, Oakland 115
Apr. 16: Oakland 115, Denver 102
New Orleans 4, Dallas 3
Apr. 5: New Orleans 129, Dallas 106
Apr. 7: New Orleans 122, Dallas 108
Apr. 10: Dallas 130, New Orleans 106
Apr. 12: New Orleans 114, Dallas 107
Apr. 14: Dallas 123, New Orleans 112
Apr. 15: Dallas 136, New Orleans 118
Apr. 17: New Orleans 101, Dallas 95

SCORING

		G	FG	FT	PTS	AVG
L.Jones	Den	75	759	591	2133	28.4
J.Jones	NO	77	764	521	2050	26.6
Dampier	KY	78	713	308	1933	24.8
Daniels	Ind	76	712	400	1824	24.0
Somerset	Hou-NY	74	619	484	1758	23.8

REBOUNDS

		G	REB	AVG
Daniels	Ind	76	1256	16.5
Robbins	NO	76	1024	13.5
Thoren	Mia	78	1046	13.4
Rhine	Hou	73	804	11.0
Beck	Den	71	779	11.0

ASSISTS

		G	AST	AVG
Brown	Oak	77	544	7.1
Freeman	Mia	78	501	6.4
Dampier	NY	78	456	5.8
J.Jones	NO	77	437	5.7
Brown	Ind	75	345	4.6
Chubin	LA-Min-Ind-NY	77	354	4.6

1969-70

Hawkins defects, Barry stays put; Pacers claim title

The ABA's third season turned out to be a mixed bag of comings and goings. At the very top, Commissioner George Mikan was ousted by the team owners, who wanted a more aggressive leader to handle the growing "war" with the NBA. Mikan resigned under pressure on July 14, and Jim Gardner, the owner of the new Carolina franchise, moved in as temporary commissioner until a suitable occupant for the position could be found. Gardner took a more aggressive stand toward the established circuit, and actually lured away four of its top referees. In October, Jack Dolph won appointment to the commissioner's chair. A former executive at the Columbia Broadcasting System, Dolph wielded enough clout to get the ABA All-Star Game on CBS in primetime.

The shuffling in the league office was matched by the shuffling of franchises. For the second straight year, the defending ABA champion pulled up roots and moved to a new city, with the Oakland Oaks becoming the Washington Capitols. The Minnesota Pipers, who had won the league title the first year in Pittsburgh, returned to that city. The Houston Mavericks shifted headquarters to the cities of Charlotte, Raleigh, and Greensboro and adopting the name of the Carolina Cougars.

In the personnel department, both of the ABA's superstars jumped to the NBA. Connie Hawkins jumped after the NBA, in order to settle Hawkins' suit against the league, voted to rescind the ban it had imposed on him for his involvement in the college betting scandals of 1961. While Hawkins joined the Phoenix NBA club, Rick Barry had no desire to accompany the Oakland club to its new home in Washington, and he decided to jump back to the San Francisco Warriors, whom he had left two years ago after leading the NBA in scoring. But Earl Foreman, the new owner of the franchise, went to court and got an order forcing Barry to play out his ABA contract.

But beyond these two, the flow of incoming NBA and college personnel was encouraging for the league's survival. Zelmo Beaty of the Atlanta Hawks signed a contract with the Los Angeles Stars and sat out this option season, while Billy Cunningham of the Philadelphia 76ers inked a lucrative pact with the Carolina Cougars which would take effect in three years, and the Detroit Pistons' Dave Bing signed a contract with the Washington Caps, for the next season. Yet as things turned out for Bing, the failure of the team to stay in Washington nullified the pact before he ever suited up in an ABA game. But these signings buoyed the spirits of the younger league, as did the agreement of Lou Carnesecca, respected coach at St. John's University, to take charge of the New York Nets starting next year. The league also signed two first-round NBA draft picks in Larry Cannon and Simmie Hill, neither of whom, unfortunately, lived up to his advance billings.

The real prize among freshman pros came from the hardship category, which was the ABA's rationale for signing college

Spencer Haywood
After just two years in college, the first 'hardship' case cops a pro MVP.

undergraduates before the NBA could pluck them off at graduation. Spencer Haywood had starred in the 1968 Olympics and had won All-American honors at the University of Detroit in his sole season of varsity play; his signing with the Denver Rockets after his sophomore year put the ABA back into the sports headlines.

Haywood was an immediate hit with his rebounding and scoring, but the Denver club nevertheless got off to a disorganized start under coach John McLendon. With the team record at 9-19, McLendon was canned and replaced by former referee Joe Belmont. Under the new coach's reins, the Rockets pulled

an immediate about-face and won 17 of their first 19 contests. Haywood paced the ABA in both scoring and rebounding, while Larry Jones headed up the Denver backcourt. With Haywood leading the way, the Rockets stormed back from their limp start to win first place in the West with a 51-33 record.

The steady Dallas Chaparalls came in second with a 45-39 record. Chap coach Cliff Hagan decided to confine himself to the bench after two seasons as a playing coach, but the management seemingly found him less of an asset as a bench coach and fired him with the team record standing at 22-21. The Washington Caps slumped to third place in the West; both Rick Barry and Warren Armstrong suffered knee injuries, which took the starch out of new coach Al Bianchi's club.

Bill Sharman's Los Angeles Stars took fourth place, bolstered by rookies Mack Calvin and Willie Wise and by mid-season acquisitions Craig Raymond and Trooper Washington. The New Orleans Buccaneers started the year with a rush, winning 12 of their first 13 matches, but a knee injury to Jimmy Jones in December started the club on a skid which carried it out of the playoffs despite a final 42-42 record.

A 42-42 mark was good enough for third place in the East, with the new Carolina Cougars achieving that level. The Cougars stocked their club mostly with local talent, relying on familiar faces from college ball to win a following among the fans. The Indiana Pacers, meanwhile, won a secure following among their fans with a deep squad that put together a 59-25 record, the best in the league. Center Mel Daniels, forwards Bob Netolicky and Roger Brown, and guard Freddie Lewis all were carry-overs from the ABA's first year of existence, and they still ranked among the best at their positions. Veteran John Barnhill filled the fifth spot on the floor early in the season, with popular rookie Bill Keller coming on strong towards the end of the regular campaign.

The Kentucky Colonels finished a distant second, relying as usual on guards Louie Dampier and Darrel Carrier to carry the team's offense. After the third-place Carolina team came the New York Nets, who had their third home in as many years in an arena in Hempstead, Long Island. On the floor, the biggest improvement came in the backcourt, where NBA veteran Bill Melchionni teamed with ABA traveler Levern Tart to put some punch into the attack. The Pittsburgh and Miami clubs, which had been strong franchises in the ABA's initial season, collapsed in a heap at the bottom of the East and of the league.

The playoffs matched the strong Pacers against the unheralded Los Angeles Stars in the championship series. The Pacers had run through their Eastern competitors as expected, but the Stars surprised even their fans by beating Dallas in the first round and then by decisively upsetting Denver in five games. The ABA's first Cinderella team couldn't make it to midnight, however, bowing to the Goliath-like Pacers in six games.

1969-70 SEASON HIGHLIGHTS

STANDINGS

Eastern Division

	W	L	Pct.	GB
Indiana	59	25	.702	—
Kentucky	45	39	.536	14
Carolina	42	42	.500	17
New York	39	45	.464	20
Pittsburgh	29	55	.345	30
Miami	23	61	.274	36

Western Division

	W	L	Pct.	GB
Denver	51	33	.607	—
Dallas	45	39	.536	6
Washington	44	40	.524	7
Los Angeles	43	41	.512	8
New Orleans	42	42	.500	9

AWARDS

MVP
Spencer Haywood, Denver
Rookie of the Year
Spencer Haywood, Denver
Coach of the Year (tie)
Bill Sharman, Los Angeles
Joe Belmont, Denver

ALL-STAR TEAMS

FIRST TEAM		SECOND TEAM	
Rick Barry	Washington	Roger Brown	Indiana
Spencer Haywood	Denver	Bob Netolicky	Indiana
Mel Daniels	Indiana	Red Robbins	New Orleans
Bob Verga	Carolina	Louie Dampier	Kentucky
Larry Jones	Denver	Donnie Freeman	Miami

ALL-STAR GAME

State Fair Coliseum, Indianapolis
Saturday, January 24, 1970
West 128, East 98
MVP: Spencer Haywood

PLAYOFFS
FINALS
Indiana 4, Los Angeles 2
May 15: Indiana 109, Los Angeles 93
May 17: Indiana 114, Los Angeles 111
May 18: Los Angeles 109, Indiana 106
May 19: Indiana 142, Los Angeles 120
May 23: Los Angeles 117, Indiana 113
May 25: Indiana 111, Los Angeles 107
EASTERN DIVISION
DIVISION FINALS
Indiana 4, Kentucky 1
May 1: Kentucky 114, Indiana 110
May 2: Indiana 121, Kentucky 110
May 3: Indiana 114, Kentucky 110
May 5: Indiana 111, Kentucky 103
May 6: Indiana 117, Kentucky 103

DIVISION SEMI-FINALS
Indiana 4, Carolina 0
Apr. 18: Indiana 123, Carolina 105
Apr. 19: Indiana 103, Carolina 98
Apr. 22: Indiana 115, Carolina 106
Apr. 24: Indiana 110, Carolina 106
Kentucky 4, New York 3
Apr. 17: New York 122, Kentucky 118, OT
Apr. 18: Kentucky 113, New York 111
Apr. 19: New York 107, Kentucky 99
Apr. 22: Kentucky 128, New York 101
Apr. 26: New York 127, Kentucky 112
Apr. 28: Kentucky 116, New York 113
Apr. 29: Kentucky 112, New York 101
WESTERN DIVISION
DIVISION FINALS
Los Angeles 4, Denver 1
Apr. 30: Denver 123, Los Angeles 113, OT
May 1: Los Angeles 114, Denver 105
May 4: Los Angeles 119, Denver 113

May 5: Los Angeles 114, Denver 110
May 9: Los Angeles 109, Denver 107
DIVISION SEMI-FINALS
Los Angeles 4, Dallas 2
Apr. 17: Los Angeles 115, Dallas 103
Apr. 18: Dallas 129, Los Angeles 121
Apr. 20: Dallas 116, Los Angeles 104
Apr. 22: Los Angeles 144, Dallas 138
Apr. 24: Los Angeles 146, Dallas 139
Apr. 26: Los Angeles 124, Dallas 123
Denver 4, Washington 3
Apr. 17: Denver 130, Washington 111
Apr. 18: Denver 143, Washington 133
Apr. 19: Washington 125, Denver 120
Apr. 22: Washington 131, Denver 114
Apr. 23: Denver 132, Washington 110
Apr. 25: Washington 116, Denver 111
Apr. 28: Denver 143, Washington 119

SCORING

		G	FG	FT	PTS	AVG
Haywood	Den	84	986	547	2519	30.0
Verga	Car	82	867	458	2258	27.5
Freeman	Mia	79	766	626	2163	27.4
Dampier	KY	82	743	447	2125	25.9
Jones	Den	75	625	579	1870	24.9

REBOUNDS

		G	REB	AVG
Haywood	Den	84	1637	19.5
Daniels	Ind	83	1462	17.6
Robbins	NO	82	1332	16.2
Govan	NO	84	1217	14.5
Harge	Was	84	1177	14.0

ASSISTS

		G	AST	AVG
Brown	Was	80	580	7.1
Melchionni	NY	80	457	5.7
Calvin	LA	84	478	5.7
Jones	Den	75	426	5.7
Dampier	KY	82	447	5.5

1970-71

More turmoil, but Barry in New York, rookies create sizzle

For the first time, the ABA signed a group of first-rate rookies, All-Americans with national reputations. Dan Issel, Charlie Scott, Rick Mount, Mike Maloy, and Jim Ard all chose the ABA despite overtures from the established NBA. Also joining this talented quintet was Ralph Simpson, a hardship case from Michigan State. However, last year's showcase rookie, Spencer Haywood, sat out the first half of the season with a broken finger, demanded renegotiation of his contract, and then signed with the NBA's Seattle Supersonics late in the season. The loss of Haywood hurt the league's appeal, but the famous newcomers offset the loss.

While the good rookie crop was novel for the ABA, the shifting of franchises wasn't. For once, the league champion didn't move to a new city, but the Indiana Pacers did shift from the Eastern Division to the Western. This move balanced the transfer of the Washington Capitols, who moved to Norfolk and several surrounding cities in Virginia and became known as the Virginia Squires. Other shifted clubs this season were the Utah Stars, transplanted from Los Angeles, and the Memphis Pros, who played last season as the New Orleans Buccaneers. The trend to regional teams began last season with the Carolina Cougars and continued this year with the Virginia and Utah clubs, plus the transformation of the Dallas Chaps into the Texas Chaps and the Miami Floridians into the just plain Floridians. Attendance around the ABA in general, however, was still low enough to keep the teams in the red.

But one franchise was showing marked progress. The New York Nets had gone through two unnoticed seasons out on Long Island while the NBA Knicks monopolized all the publicity, attention, and attendance. But respectability started to come to the new team in town with the arrival of Lou Carnesecca, the colorful coach of St. John's University who stepped up into the pros with the Nets. The biggest addition, however, was Rick Barry, the superstar needed to make the New York franchise a viable entry in the nation's media center. Barry had most reluctantly played in Washington last season after the franchise was shifted from Oakland, and he openly rebelled against the idea of playing in southern Virginia, the site of the franchise for this season. So Squire owner Earl Foreman, seeing no gate appeal in a superstar who roundly criticized the home area of the team, sent Barry and his expensive contract on to New York. Although an injured knee cost him some playing time for the third straight season, Barry put the Nets back in the game on the court and in the publicity department.

The Virginia Squires, meanwhile, got along just fine without their reluctant star. Coach Al Bianchi had a new star in rookie Charlie Scott, a 6-foot-5 guard with a wide variety of shots and moves. Around his young offensive star, coach Bianchi welded together a tight unit of centers Jim Eakins and Ray Scott, forwards George Carter, Doug Moe, and Neil

Zelmo Beatty
His addition, move from L.A. to Utah, the charm as Stars claim crown.

Johnson, and guards Mike Barrett and Fatty Taylor. Although short on flashy talent outside of Scott, the Squires captured first place in the East with a strong 55-29 record.

The second-place Kentucky Colonels finished 11 games back, but came up with the league scoring champ in rookie Dan Issel, a strong center with a fine shooting touch. Issel's 29.9 scoring average marked the first time that the Colonels had any first-rate scoring punch in their forecourt. The New York team finished third, helped immeasurably by the addition of Barry, veteran forward Manny Leaks, and rookie center Billy Paultz, who accompanied coach Carnesecca from St. John's.

The Floridians had been a hopeless wreck last season, but new coach Bob Bass built a respectable outfit around guards Larry Jones and Mack Calvin, picked up in off-season deals. Pittsburgh had two ace scorers in John Brisker and George Thompson, but just missed the final playoff berth by finishing one game behind the Floridians. The Carolina Cougars finished last, but began to move away from just local talent by signing Joe Caldwell from the NBA Atlanta Hawks.

Last season's Eastern Division champ, the Indiana Pacers, won this season's Western title with a 58-26 record, only one game off last year's pace. Built around a nucleus of ABA originals, the Pacers won the most games in the league for the second straight year. The starting five of Mel Daniels, Roger Brown, Freddie Lewis, Bob Netolicky, and Bill Keller had new reserve support this season: Warren Armstrong, who was obtained from Kentucky after personal difficulties led to his suspension in the preseason; rookie Rick Mount, a three-year star at Purdue; and veterans Don Sidle and Wayne Chapman, picked up in a late-season deal with Denver. But even with the Pacers' depth and consistent excellence, the Utah Stars chased them to the wire and finished a mere game short of first place. The transplanted Stars had Zelmo Beaty in uniform, and the veteran NBA star gave the team strength in the middle unmatched by most competitors. The forward positions were ably handled by second-year man Willie Wise and veteran Red Robbins a fortuitous pickup from the Memphis club. The backcourt positions went to Ron Boone and Glen Combs after their mid-season arrival in a trade with the Texas Chaps.

After the Pacers and Stars, the quality fell off in the West. The Memphis Pros debuted at 41-43, while Texas and Denver both finished at 30-54. Denver's fall was particularly swift, tumbling from first place last season. Spencer Haywood's defection, plus the trading of guards Larry Jones and Jeff Congdon, sent the Rockets into a downward spiral which insured an early end to the season for coach Joe Belmont, a hero only last year.

This year's playoffs went according to expectations in the opening round, with Virginia, Kentucky, Indiana, and Utah emerging victorious. But in the divisional finals, Kentucky and Utah upset their favored opponents. Thus, the two second-place finishers met for the championship, with Utah the heavy favorite to win the crown. The Colonels contested every game and forced a decisive seventh game in Salt Lake City. Before a capacity crowd of 13,260, the Stars won the championship with a 131-121 victory.

1970-71 SEASON HIGHLIGHTS

STANDINGS

Eastern Division

	W	L	Pct.	GB
Virginia	55	29	.655	—
Kentucky	44	40	.524	11
New York	40	44	.476	15
Floridians	37	47	.440	18
Pittsburgh	36	48	.429	19
Carolina	34	50	.405	21

Western Division

	W	L	Pct.	GB
Indiana	58	26	.690	—
Utah	57	27	.679	1
Memphis	41	43	.488	17
Texas	30	54	.357	28
Denver	30	54	.357	28

AWARDS

MVP
Mel Daniels, Indiana
Rookie of the Year (tie)
Charlie Scott, Virginia
Dan Issel, Kentucky
Coach of the Year
Al Bianchi, Virginia

ALL-STAR TEAMS

FIRST TEAM		SECOND TEAM	
Roger Brown	Indiana	John Brisker	Pittsburg
Rick Barry	New York	Joe Caldwell	Carolina
Mel Daniels	Indiana	Zelmo Beaty	Utah (tie)
Mack Calvin	Floridians	Dan Issel	Kentucky (tie)
Charlie Scott	Virginia	Donnie Freeman	Texas
		Larry Cannon	Denver

ALL-STAR GAME

Greensboro Coliseum, Greensboro
Saturday, January 23, 1971
East 126, West 122
MVP: Mel Daniels

NBA vs ABA ALL-STAR GAME

The Astrodome, Houston
Friday, May 28, 1971
NBA 125, ABA 120
MVP: Walt Frazier

PLAYOFFS

FINALS
Utah 4, Kentucky 3
May 3: Utah 136, Kentucky 117
May 5: Utah 138, Kentucky 125
May 7: Kentucky 116, Utah 110
May 8: Kentucky 129, Utah 125, OT
May 12: Utah 137, Kentucky 127
May 15: Kentucky 105, Utah 101
May 18: Utah 131, Kentucky 121

EASTERN DIVISION
DIVISION FINALS
Kentucky 4, Virginia 2
Apr. 15: Kentucky 136, Virginia 132
Apr. 17: Virginia 142, Kentucky 122
Apr. 19: Virginia 150, Kentucky 137
Apr. 21: Kentucky 128, Virginia 110
Apr. 23: Kentucky 115, Virginia 107
Apr. 24: Kentucky 129, Virginia 117

DIVISION SEMI-FINALS
Kentucky 4, Floridians 2
Apr. 2: Kentucky 116, Floridians 112
Apr. 4: Kentucky 120, Floridians 110
Apr. 6: Floridians 120, Kentucky 102
Apr. 8: Floridians 129, Kentucky 117
Apr. 10: Kentucky 118, Floridians 101
Apr. 12: Kentucky 112, Floridians 103

Virginia 4, New York 2
Apr. 2: Virginia 113, New York 105
Apr. 4: Virginia 114, New York 108
Apr. 6: New York 135, Virginia 131
Apr. 7: New York 130, Virginia 127
Apr. 9: Virginia 127, New York 124
Apr. 10: Virginia 118, New York 114

WESTERN DIVISION
DIVISION FINALS
Utah 4, Indiana 3
Apr. 12: Utah 120, Indiana 118
Apr. 14: Indiana 120, Utah 107
Apr. 17: Utah 121, Indiana 107
Apr. 20: Utah 126, Indiana 99
Apr. 22: Indiana 127, Utah 109
Apr. 24: Indiana 105, Utah 102
Apr. 28: Utah 108, Indiana 101

DIVISION SEMI-FINALS
Utah 4, Texas 0
Apr. 2: Utah 125, Texas 115
Apr. 3: Utah 137, Texas 107
Apr. 4: Utah 113, Texas 101
Apr. 6: Utah 128, Texas 107

Indiana 4, Memphis 0
Apr. 2: Indiana 114, Memphis 98
Apr. 3: Indiana 106, Memphis 104
Apr. 5: Indiana 91, Memphis 90
Apr. 7: Indiana 102, Memphis 101

PLAYOFF FOR FOURTH PLACE
Apr. 1: Texas 115, Denver 109

SCORING

		G	FG	FT	PTS	AVG
Issel	KY	83	938	604	2480	29.9
Brisker	Pit	79	898	430	2315	29.3
Calvin	Fla	81	744	696	2201	27.2
Scott	Va	84	902	456	2276	27.1
Cannon	Den	80	751	606	2126	26.6

REBOUNDS

		G	REB	AVG
Daniels	Ind	82	1475	18.0
Keye	Den	83	1454	17.5
Beaty	Utah	76	1190	15.7
Govan	Mem	84	1138	13.6
Harge	Car-Fla	82	1085	13.2

ASSISTS

		G	AST	AVG
Melchionni	NY	81	672	8.3
Calvin	Fla	81	619	7.6
J. Jones	Mem	80	468	5.9
Scott	Va	84	472	5.6
Lehmann	Car	83	464	5.6

1971-72

New credibility with arrival of Erving, Gilmore

Money problems still hounded the majority of ABA team owners, but for the first time in the young league's history, the same lineup of clubs from last year returned this season. Only a few minor adjustments disturbed the returning array of teams; the Texas Chaparrals turned back into the Dallas Chaparrals after a one-year experiment with the new name, the New York Nets moved into the spanking new Nassau Coliseum on Long Island, and the Memphis Pros were sold to Charles O. Finley, the colorful owner of the Oakland Athletics baseball team.

But if the structural changes in the circuit were minor, the impact of the rookie class was major in every respect. Artis Gilmore, Jim McDaniels, Daniell Hillman, and Johnny Roche signed with the ABA despite the ready availability of lucrative contracts with the established NBA. In addition to these graduating collegians, the ABA brought in three noteworthy hardship undergrads in George McGinnis, Julius Erving, and Johnny Neumann. The biggest college reputations belonged to Gilmore, the 7-foot-2 center from Jacksonville, and Neumann, the 6-foot-6 guard from Mississippi who led the nation in scoring as a sophomore before turning pro.

Instant stardom came to Gilmore, Erving, and McGinnis. Gilmore was in a league by himself in the ABA, with no other center rivaling him either in size or shot-blocking ability; his presence in the middle made the Kentucky Colonels immediate favorites for the championship. Erving, who went under the name of Dr. J, sent the entire league aglow with his dazzling array of moves and shots, putting on glittering shows reminiscent of Elgin Baylor at his peak; teamed with Charlie Scott, Erving made the Virginia Squire offense as unstoppable as an impending flood seeping through a leaky dike. McGinnis, meanwhile, started the season slowly but soon won a starting job at forward because of his overwhelming rebounding muscle. Erving, Gilmore, and McGinnis were quickly recognized as the foremost properties of the ABA.

Two other blue-chip young players, Charlie Scott and Jim McDaniels, made unexpected exits from the league by signing with NBA clubs late in the season. Scott, a second-year guard with undeniable offensive skills, led the Virginia team through the bulk of the season with a league-pacing 34.4 scoring average, only to jump the club in March, claim a violation of his contract, and sign with the Phoenix Suns of the NBA. Rookie McDaniels of the Carolina Cougars ranked among the league leaders with a 26.8 scoring mark, but he also jumped his team in the spring to sign with the Seattle Supersonics. The loss of these two young stars set the league back a few steps in its struggle for national recognition.

But the development of the Kentucky Colonels into a genuinely entertaining club took some of the sting away. The Colonels had a new coach in Joe Mullaney, the ex-mentor of

Artis Gilmore
Manhandling the ball, not to mention the rest of the league.

the Los Angeles Lakers, plus a new center in the towering Gilmore. Dan Issel, last year's rookie scoring sensation, moved over to a forward spot to make room for Gilmore and upped his scoring average to 30.6 points per game. To go with these two young frontcourt aces, Mullaney retained Cincy Powell at forward and Louie Dampier at guard, and replaced the injured Darel Carrier at guard with rookies Mike Gale and Jimmy O'Brien. With the bench containing a mixture of experience and youth, the Colonels ran away with first place in the East, accumulating a record 68-16 mark during the regular season.

Charlie Scott and Julius Erving, two dynamic one-on-one

scorers, brought the Squires home in second place, but Scott's defection put the team in a doubtful condition for the playoffs. The New York Nets finished third in an enjoyable season, with their new arena boosting attendance and with Rick Barry staying healthy for the entire season for the first time in four ABA campaigns. Fourth place went to the Floridians, who partially overcame a chaotic frontcourt situation with solid play by guards Mack Calvin, Larry Jones, and Warren Jabali, who changed his name from Armstrong this year. The Carolina Cougars finished fifth despite an abundance of trades, and the Pittsburgh Condors finished last.

Good players abounded on the rosters of the Utah Stars and Indiana Pacers, the cream of the Western Division. The Stars had a new coach in LaDell Anderson, who replaced Bill Sharman after his jump back to the NBA. Utah's starting line-up of Zelmo Beaty, Red Robbins, Willie Wise, Jimmy Jones, and Glen Combs stacked up with any in the ABA, and Ron Boone contributed heavily as the sixth man. Indiana coach Bob Leonard also had a full cupboard of top players to choose from. At center, he had Mel Daniels; at forward, he had veterans Bob Netolicky and Roger Brown plus rookies McGinnis and Hillman; at guard, he had veterans Freddie Lewis and Bill Keller, second-year-man Rick Mount, and Larry Cannon,

whose personal troubles made him a bargain-price acquisition from Memphis. Although deep in talent, the turnover in personnel necessitated a period of adjustment, and the Pacers finished a distant second to the Stars. The Dallas Chaps came in third, with new coach Tom Nissalke winning Coach of the Year. The Denver Rockets hired the respected Alex Hannum as coach, but he could urge his charges to only a 34-50 season, good enough for a playoff spot only because the Memphis Pros totally collapsed in the first year of Finley's ownership there.

The fireworks in this year's playoffs began in the opening round, as the New York Nets stunned Kentucky by winning the first two games in Louisville and going on to take the series in six games. The divisional finals produced sparks in both series, as the Nets' continued their almost unbelievable surge by defeating the Squires in seven games, taking a 94-88 decision in the final match in Norfolk. In the West, the Pacers and Stars met for the second straight year, with the Pacers reversing last season's result by eliminating the Stars with a 117-113 victory in the seventh game. The sudden rise of the Nets won the ABA some needed press coverage emanating from New York, but the magic couldn't continue. The talent-heavy Pacers put the Nets back in their place with a six-game series triumph which made the Pacers the first two-time champ in the ABA.

1971-72 SEASON HIGHLIGHTS

STANDINGS

Eastern Division

	W	L	Pct.	GB
Kentucky	68	16	.810	—
Virginia	45	39	.536	23
New York	44	40	.524	24
Floridians	36	48	.429	32
Carolina	35	49	.417	33
Pittsburgh	25	59	.298	43

Western Division

	W	L	Pct.	GB
Utah	60	24	.714	—
Indiana	47	37	.560	13
Dallas	42	42	.500	18
Denver	34	50	.405	26
Memphis	26	58	.310	34

AWARDS
MVP
Artis Gilmore, Kentucky
Rookie of the Year
Artis Gilmore, Kentucky
Coach of the Year
Tom Nissalke, Dallas

ALL-STAR TEAMS
FIRST TEAM

Dan Issel	Kentucky
Rick Barry	New York
Artis Gilmore	Kentucky
Donnie Freeman	Dallas
Bill Melchionni	New York

SECOND TEAM

Willie Wise	Utah
Julius Erving	Virginia
Zelmo Beaty	Utah
Ralph Simpson	Denver
Charlie Scott	Virginia

ALL-STAR GAME
Freedom Hall, Louisville, KY
Saturday, January 29, 1972
East 142, West 115
MVP: Dan Issel

NBA vs ABA ALL-STAR GAME
Nassau Coliseum, Uniondale, NY
Thursday, May 25, 1972
NBA 106, ABA 104
MVP: Bob Lanier

PLAYOFFS
FINALS
Indiana 4, New York 2
May 6: Indiana 124, New York 103
May 9: New York 117, Indiana 115
May 12: Indiana 114, New York 108
May 15: New York 110, Indiana 105
May 18: Indiana 100, New York 99
May 20: Indiana 108, New York 105
EASTERN DIVISION
DIVISION FINALS
New York 4, Virginia 3
Apr. 13: Virginia 138, New York 91
Apr. 15: Virginia 115, New York 106
Apr. 24: New York 119, Virginia 117
Apr. 26: New York 118, Virginia 107
Apr. 29: Virginia 116, New York 107
May 1: New York 146, Virginia 136
May 4: New York 94, Virginia 88

DIVISION SEMI-FINALS
Virginia 4, Floridians 0
Mar. 31: Virginia 114, Floridians 107, OT
Apr. 1: Virginia 125, Floridians 100
Apr. 4: Virginia 118, Floridians 113
Apr. 6: Virginia 115, Floridians 106
New York 4, Kentucky 2
Apr. 17: New York 122, Kentucky 108
Apr. 18: New York 105, Kentucky 90
Apr. 19: Kentucky 105, New York 99
Apr. 22: New York 100, Kentucky 92
Apr. 26: Kentucky 109, New York 103
Apr. 28: New York 101, Kentucky 96
WESTERN DIVISION
DIVISION FINALS
Indiana 4, Utah 3
Apr. 15: Utah 108, Indiana 100
Apr. 17: Utah 117, Indiana 109
Apr. 19: Indiana 116, Utah 111
Apr. 22: Indiana 118, Utah 108

Apr. 24: Utah 139, Indiana 130
Apr. 26: Indiana 105, Utah 99
May 1: Indiana 117, Utah 113
DIVISION SEMI-FINALS
Utah 4, Dallas 0
Apr. 1: Utah 106, Dallas 96
Apr. 3: Utah 113, Dallas 107
Apr. 5: Utah 96, Dallas 89
Apr. 7: Utah 103, Dallas 99
Indiana 4, Denver 3
Mar. 31: Indiana 102, Denver 95
Apr. 1: Denver 106, Indiana 105
Apr. 4: Indiana 122, Denver 120, OT
Apr. 6: Denver 112, Indiana 106
Apr. 8: Indiana 91, Denver 79
Apr. 9: Denver 106, Indiana 99
Apr. 13: Indiana 91, Denver 89

SCORING

		G	FG	FT	PTS	AVG
Scott	Va	73	985	525	2524	34.6
Barry	NY	80	902	641	2518	31.5
Issel	KY	83	972	591	2538	30.6
Simpson	Den	84	920	457	2300	27.4
Erving	Va	84	910	467	2290	27.3

REBOUNDS

		G	REB	AVG
Gilmore	KY	84	1491	17.8
Daniels	Ind	79	1297	16.4
Erving	Va	84	1319	15.7
Govan	Mem	83	1182	14.2
Beaty	Utah	84	1110	13.2

ASSISTS

		G	AST	AVG
Melchionni	NY	80	669	8.4
Brown	Den	76	549	7.2
Jones	Utah	78	485	6.2
Dampier	KY	83	515	6.2
Jabali	Fla	81	495	6.1

1972-73

Barry departs, Billy C. arrives, Pacers net No. 3

The ABA took care of an expensive headache by folding the Pittsburgh and Florida franchises, two organizations populated by poor teams, very few paying fans, press indifference, and frustrated front offices. This paring of dead wood was one of commissioner Jack Dolph's last acts before resigning to return to the world of television.

Bob Carlson became the ABA's third chief executive, and under his direction the San Diego Conquistadors were created as the first ABA expansion club. This new team brought the league back up to 10 clubs for the upcoming season, but a quick look at the cities involved showed the difficulties the ABA had in obtaining a national television contract and national recognition. Only New York and Dallas were "big league" major metropolises; San Diego, Denver, Indianapolis, Louisville, Memphis, Salt Lake City, Norfolk, and Greensboro seemed minor league to most sports fans, and the television markets in these cities lacked the size to excite the networks. To make matters worse, the Dallas and Memphis clubs were largely ignored in their hometowns.

The New York club suffered a jolt to its gate appeal when star forward Rick Barry was ordered by the courts to report back to the Golden State Warriors on the grounds that he had signed a valid contract for future services with the NBA club when he had been dissatisfied with the shifting of his Oakland team to Washington and then to Virginia. Barry expressed a desire to stay in New York, where he could foster his ambitions of a career as a television commentator, but the courts upheld his contract with the Warriors. The loss of Barry hurt the entire league's drawing power, but the arrival of Billy Cunningham in Carolina somewhat softened the blow. A star forward with the Philadelphia 76ers, Cunningham had signed with the Cougars three years ago, and although he too expressed a desire to stay right where he was, the legal decision was that he had to fulfill his Carolina contract. So in the sum total of star veteran forward jumpings, the two leagues came out even.

The ABA teams also made out well in terms of playing personnel, when the Pittsburgh and Florida players were dispersed to the other teams in a special draft. This draft helped the teams more than the college draft, which turned up little help this year. The two most prominent rookies were Jim Chones and Brian Taylor, both hardship cases signed by the New York Nets.

The Carolina Cougars didn't need any key rookies to suddenly rush up to the top of the league with a 57-27 record. The Cougars did have a new coach in Larry Brown, who retired from his active career to preach the gospel of the fast break in Carolina. Newcomers Cunningham and Mack Calvin, late of the Floridians, fit right in with this new style, and the rest of the team came alive with the new coach and stars leading the way. Brown shuffled guards Calvin, Steve Jones, Ted McClain, and Gene Littles in and out, constantly keeping a fresh pair in

Julius Erving
With a league-leading 31.9 ppg, the Doctor was definitely in.

the game. Forwards Cunningham and Joe Caldwell had starred in running games during their NBA days, and they kept their younger mates from making many errors. The Cougars figured to have a problem at center when Mike Lewis went out with an injury early in the campaign, but Tom Owens plugged the hole in stop-gap fashion and kept the fast break running.

But the Cougars couldn't run away from the Kentucky Colonels, who finished only one game off the pace. The addition of Rick Mount and Wendell Ladner strengthened the Colonels, but the heart of the team again was the twin towers of Artis Gilmore and Dan Issel. Third place in the East went to

the Virginia Squires; Charlie Scott was lost to the NBA, but the Squires still had Julius Erving, whose 31.9 scoring average topped the league. Way down the ladder in fourth place were the New York Nets, who were 30-54 without Rick Barry. The Memphis club had a new name, the Tams. They also had a new coach, Bob Bass; a new scorer, George Thompson; and an abysmal 24-60 record.

The Western Division also had two top contenders, a strong middle club, and two weaklings trailing the rear. Utah and Indiana waged their annual battle for first place, with the Stars emerging on top this year by four games. The Stars bolstered their forward corps by picking up veterans Cincy Powell and George Govan, both ABA originals from 1967, but veteran Utah stars Willie Wise, Jimmy Jones, Ron Boone, and Zelmo Beaty were the key factors in the club's 55-29 record. The Pacers dropped veterans Bob Netolicky and Rick Mount to give more playing time to youngsters like George McGinnis and rookie Don Buse; McGinnis responded by blossoming into the ABA's foremost power forward, ranking second in scoring and fourth in rebounding. Veteran guard Donnie Freeman also added to the Pacers' strength, and the familiar trio of Mel Daniels, Roger Brown, and Freddie Lewis carried on as ever.

The Denver Rockets finished in the middle of the pack with a much improved 47-37 record, due greatly to Warren Jabali's steady backcourt leadership after coming over in the dispersal draft from Florida. The dregs of the West were the San Diego

Conquistadors and the Dallas Chaparrals, with the San Diego bunch the surprise winners of the fourth playoff spot. K.C. Jones coached the talent-thin Conquistadors to a 30-54 mark, relying heavily on the long-range shooting of Stew Johnson and Chuck Williams to offset the myriad array of weaknesses on the team. The Chaps, meanwhile, fell apart with the departure of coach Tom Nissalke to the NBA. Babe McCarthy replaced Nissalke and could muster little scoring power beyond Rich Jones and Bob Netolicky, and Netolicky disappointed the Chaps with his all-around play at center.

The Carolina, Kentucky, Utah, and Indiana clubs all got past their first round competition to set up the divisional finals between the ABA's strongest clubs. The Pacers and Stars split their first four games, but then the Pacers won game five in Salt Lake City and then wrapped it up in Indianapolis. The Cougars and Colonels, meanwhile, came down to a decisive seventh game, with the Colonels' size stopping the Cougar fast break in a 107-96 victory at Charlotte.

The championship series between the Pacers and Colonels also came down to a final seventh game, and before 16,597 fans in Louisville, the Pacers won the crown with an 88-81 triumph. This was the third ABA crown for the Pacers, and the first repeat championship in the league's short history. Just as prominent, however, was the repeated failure of the Colonels, a talented club with a consistently excellent record, to win their first ABA championship.

1972-73 SEASON HIGHLIGHTS

STANDINGS

Eastern Division

	W	L	Pct.	GB
Carolina	57	27	.679	—
Kentucky	56	28	.667	1
Virginia	42	42	.500	15
New York	30	54	.357	27
Memphis	24	60	.286	33

Western Division

	W	L	Pct.	GB
Utah	55	29	.655	—
Indiana	51	33	.607	4
Denver	47	37	.560	8
San Diego	30	54	.357	25
Dallas	28	56	.333	27

AWARDS

MVP
Billy Cunningham, Carolina
Rookie of the Year
Brian Taylor, New York
Coach of the Year
Larry Brown, Carolina

ALL-STAR TEAMS

FIRST TEAM		SECOND TEAM	
Billy Cunningham	Carolina	George McGinnis	Indiana
Julius Erving	Virginia	Dan Issel	Kentucky
Artis Gilmore	Kentucky	Mel Daniels	Indiana
Jimmy Jones	Utah	Ralph Simpson	Denver
Warren Jabali	Denver	Mack Calvin	Carolina

ALL-STAR GAME

Salt Palace, Salt Lake City, Utah
Tuesday, February 6, 1973
West 123, East 111
MVP: Warren Jabali

PLAYOFFS

FINALS
Indiana 4, Kentucky 3
Apr. 28: Indiana 111, Kentucky 107
Apr. 30: Kentucky 114, Indiana 102
May 3: Kentucky 92, Indiana 88
May 5: Indiana 90, Kentucky 86
May 8: Indiana 89, Kentucky 86
May 10: Kentucky 109, Indiana 93
May 12: Indiana 88, Kentucky 81

EASTERN DIVISION
DIVISION FINALS
Kentucky 4, Carolina 3
Apr. 11: Kentucky 113, Carolina 103
Apr. 14: Carolina 125, Kentucky 105
Apr. 16: Kentucky 108, Carolina 94
Apr. 18: Carolina 102, Kentucky 91
Apr. 20: Carolina 112, Kentucky 107
Apr. 21: Kentucky 119, Carolina 100
Apr. 24: Kentucky 107, Carolina 96

DIVISION SEMI-FINALS
Kentucky 4, Virginia 1
Mar. 30: Kentucky 129, Virginia 101
Apr. 1: Virginia 109, Kentucky 94
Apr. 3: Kentucky 115, Virginia 113
Apr. 6: Kentucky 108, Virginia 90
Apr. 7: Kentucky 114, Virginia 93

Carolina 4, New York 1
Mar. 30: Carolina 104, New York 96
Mar. 31: New York 114, Carolina 111
Apr. 3: Carolina 101, New York 91
Apr. 5: Carolina 112, New York 108
Apr. 6: Carolina 136, New York 113

WESTERN DIVISION
DIVISION FINALS
Indiana 4, Utah 2
Apr. 12: Utah 124, Indiana 107
Apr. 14: Indiana 116, Utah 110
Apr. 16: Indiana 118, Utah 108
Apr. 18: Utah 104, Indiana 103

Apr. 19: Indiana 104, Utah 102
Apr. 21: Indiana 107, Utah 98

DIVISION SEMI-FINALS
Utah 4, San Diego 0
Apr. 2: Utah 107, San Diego 93
Apr. 4: Utah 102, San Diego 92
Apr. 7: Utah 97, San Diego 96
Apr. 8: Utah 120, San Diego 98

Indiana 4, Denver 1
Mar. 31: Indiana 114, Denver 91
Apr. 1: Indiana 106, Denver 93
Apr. 3: Denver 105, Indiana 94
Apr. 5: Indiana 97, Denver 95
Apr. 7: Indiana 121, Denver 107

SCORING

		G	FG	FT	PTS	AVG
Erving	Va	71	892	475	2268	31.9
McGinnis	Ind	82	868	517	2261	27.6
Issel	KY	84	902	485	2292	27.3
Cunningham	Car	84	771	472	2028	24.1
Simpson	Den	81	732	421	1890	23.3

REBOUNDS

		G	REB	AVG
Gilmore	KY	84	1476	17.6
Daniels	Ind	81	1247	15.4
Paultz	NY	81	1015	12.5
McGinnis	Ind	82	1022	12.4
Erving	Va	71	867	12.2

ASSISTS

		G	AST	AVG
Williams	SD	83	582	7.0
Jabali	Den	82	539	6.6
Dampier	KY	80	521	6.5
Cunningham	Car	84	530	6.3
Neumann	Mem	79	470	6.0

1973-74

Chamberlain benched, Dr. J. brilliant as New York nails crown

The ABA added its biggest star ever—Wilt Chamberlain, the leading scorer in the history of pro basketball. The San Diego Conquistadors gave Wilt a massive contract to join the team as player-coach, but the NBA's Los Angeles Lakers immediately cancelled half of that deal by getting a court order forcing Wilt to sit out the option year on his contract. So the ABA found itself in a similar position with Wilt as it had been in 1967-68 with Rick Barry; his name was counted on to boost the gates around the circuit, but neither man could draw people when clad in his civies. Wilt traveled with San Diego as bench coach, but few people came out to the game just to see a 7-foot-1 coach urging his players on.

But other additions to the league this season turned out to be more beneficial than Wilt. The city of San Antonio enthusiastically welcomed the Dallas Chaparrals and took the rechristened Spurs to heart, turning out in respectable numbers to see the club. A group of talented rookies also came into the league; Mike Green, Larry Kenon, Sven Nater, Bo Lamar, Kevin Joyce, and Bird Averitt added some All-American glamour, but primarily improved the quality of play on the floor.

An old hand around the ABA but one in a new slot was Mike Storen, the new commissioner. As general manager at Indiana and Kentucky, Storen had built those franchises into going enterprises, and as commissioner, his main concern was to shore up the growing number of sick franchises. Carolina, Virginia, Memphis, and San Diego were all decidedly on shaky footing, both financially and artistically.

But the transfer most beneficial to the ABA in general was the move of star forward Julius Erving from the Virginia Squires to the New York Nets. As basketball's foremost crowd-pleaser because of his dazzling array of moves, Dr. J. made contract demands which the Virginia club simply could not meet, so they sent him along to the Nets for a bundle of cash plus forward George Carter. In New York, the press made Dr. J. an instant hit, both on a local and a national basis, and the Nets flourished both on the floor and at the ticket window. Erving turned the Nets into the league's most colorful and strongest club. Although they got off to a slow start under new coach Kevin Loughery, the Nets got untracked and streaked to a 55-29 record and first place in the Eastern Division. Other players filled in the slots around Erving's all-around brilliance. Larry Kenon skipped his senior year at Memphis State to join the Nets, and showed a knack for rebounding. At center, Billy Paultz had grown into such a competent player that young Jim Chones was sold to Carolina. The backcourt had two fine young players in Brian Taylor and rookie John Williamson, plus a steady veteran in Bill Melchionni. A mid-season deal shored up the bench by bringing in Wendell Ladner and Mike Gale from Kentucky, the Nets' chief rival for first place.

The Colonels made a slew of deals to strengthen their squad,

Billy Paultz
Leading the Nets (when Dr. J. was covered) to the ABA title.

but Dan Issel, Artis Gilmore, and Louie Dampier continued to carry the bulk of the scoring, rebounding, playmaking, and leadership duties. With Babe McCarthy the new coach this season, the Colonels ended the season a slim two games behind the Nets. A respectable third came the Carolina Cougars, who understandably fell off from last year's peak when Billy Cunningham went out with severe kidney trouble. Mack Calvin continued to play up to All-Star standards for the Cougars, who were playing to more and more empty seats in Carolina.

Far down in the depths of incompetency were the Virginia Squires and Memphis Tams, with the Squires winning a playoff

berth practically by default. Virginia owner Earl Foreman had money problems and resorted to selling off his better players to get working capital. Erving had gone to New York during the summer, powerful rookie center Sven Nater went to San Antonio in November, and second-year forward George Gervin followed Nater to San Antonio in February. Coach Al Bianchi was forced to get along with cheaper, less talented players, and the team's fans practically washed their hands of the club until Foreman later sold the team to a local group. Down in Memphis, owner Charlie Finley continued to lose money, and the Tams continued losing games in regular fashion.

With this transfer of talent from Virginia to San Antonio, the Spurs grew into a strong enough club to battle with the Utah Stars and Indiana Pacers for first place in the West. The Spurs had two solid ex-Dallas players in Rich Jones and James Silas, plus an offensive-minded rookie guard in Bird Averitt. The addition of Nater, known as Bill Walton's backup during his college days at UCLA, gave the Spurs a center strong enough to battle the likes of Gilmore, Beaty and Daniels. The later addition of Gervin, who signed with the Squires late last season after being ruled ineligible at Eastern Michigan, provided first rate offensive firepower in the forward spot opposite Rich Jones. Tom Nissalke returned to the franchise as coach after a disastrous year with the NBA in Seattle, and he orchestrated this talent into a strong third place finish at 45-39.

Utah took first place for the third straight season, with

Willie Wise, Jimmy Jones, and Ron Boone all winning honors on the first or second All-League teams. Indiana finished second, seemingly saving its best effort for the playoffs. In fourth and fifth, respectively, came the Denver Rockets and San Diego. The Denver club was a distinct disappointment, with coach Alex Hannum resigning at the conclusion of the campaign. The Conquistadors had two fine rookies in guard Bo Lamar and center Caldwell Jones, but coach Wilt Chamberlain was missing his greatest asset, player Wilt Chamberlain.

At the start of the playoffs, the New York Nets were downgraded because of their lack of experience. But this youngest team in pro basketball had engineered the best record in the ABA during the regular campaign, and they didn't slow down a bit in the playoffs. They disposed of the Virginia Squires in the opening round, then blew the Kentucky Colonels out in four straight, which cost Kentucky coach Babe McCarthy his job.

Against Utah in the finals, the Nets took game one, 89-85, behind Dr. J.'s 47 points, then took an easy 118-94 second-game win. When the series resumed in Salt Lake City, New York's Brian Taylor heaved in a three-pointer at the buzzer to tie the count at 94-94, with the Nets coming on to take a 103-100 overtime decision. The Stars took a rather meaningless fourth game victory by the score of 97-89, but then the Nets finished the job at home, using a balanced attack to take a 111-100 victory before 15,934 excited fans at the Nassau Coliseum who now took the Nets to heart just as rabidly as the Knicks.

1973-74 SEASON HIGHLIGHTS

STANDINGS

Eastern Division

	W	L	Pct.	GB
New York	55	29	.655	—
Kentucky	53	31	.631	2
Carolina	47	37	.560	8
Virginia	28	56	.333	27
Memphis	21	63	.250	34

Western Division

	W	L	Pct.	GB
Utah	51	33	.607	—
Indiana	46	38	.548	5
San Antonio	45	39	.536	6
Denver	37	47	.440	14
San Diego	37	47	.440	14

AWARDS
MVP
Julius Erving, New York
Rookie of the Year
Swen Nater, San Antonio
Coach of the Year (tie)
Babe McCarthy, Kentucky
Joe Mullaney, Utah

ALL-STAR TEAMS

FIRST TEAM		SECOND TEAM	
Julius Erving	New York	Dan Issel	Kentucky
George McGinnis	Indiana	Willie Wise	Utah
Artis Gilmore	Kentucky	Swen Nater	San Antonio
Jimmy Jones	Utah	Ron Boone	Utah
Mack Calvin	Carolina	Louie Dampier	Kentucky

ALL-STAR GAME
Norfolk Scope, Norfolk, VA
Wednesday, January 30, 1974
East 128, West 112
MVP: Artis Gilmore

PLAYOFFS
FINALS
New York 4, Utah 1
Apr. 30: New York 89, Utah 85
May 4: New York 118, Utah 94
May 6: New York 103, Utah 100, OT
May 8: Utah 97, New York 89
May 10: New York 111, Utah 100
EASTERN DIVISION
DIVISION FINALS
New York 4, Kentucky 0
Apr. 13: New York 119, Kentucky 96
Apr. 15: New York 99, Kentucky 80
Apr. 17: New York 89, Kentucky 87
Apr. 20: New York 103, Kentucky 90
DIVISION SEMI-FINALS
New York 4, Virginia 1
Mar. 29: New York 108, Virginia 96

Apr. 1: New York 129, Virginia 110
Apr. 4: Virginia 116, New York 115
Apr. 7: New York 116, Virginia 88
Apr. 8: New York 108, Virginia 96
WESTERN DIVISION
Kentucky 4, Carolina 0
Apr. 1: Kentucky 118, Carolina 102
Apr. 5: Kentucky 99, Carolina 96
Apr. 6: Kentucky 120, Carolina 110
Apr. 8: Kentucky 128, Carolina 119
DIVISION FINALS
Utah 4, Indiana 3
Apr. 13: Utah 105, Indiana 96
Apr. 15: Utah 106, Indiana 102
Apr. 17: Utah 99, Indiana 96
Apr. 18: Indiana 118, Utah 107
Apr. 22: Indiana 110, Utah 101
Apr. 25: Indiana 91, Utah 89
Apr. 27: Utah 109, Indiana 87

DIVISION SEMI-FINALS
Utah 4, San Diego 2
Mar. 30: Utah 114, San Diego 99
Apr. 1: Utah 119, San Diego 105
Apr. 3: San Diego 97, Utah 96
Apr. 4: San Diego 100, Utah 98
Apr. 6: Utah 100, San Diego 93
Apr. 8: Utah 110, San Diego 99
Indiana 4, San Antonio 3
Mar. 30: San Antonio 113, Indiana 109
Apr. 1: Indiana 128, San Antonio 101
Apr. 3: San Antonio 115, Indiana 96
Apr. 4: Indiana 91, San Antonio 89
Apr. 6: Indiana 105, San Antonio 100
Apr. 10: San Antonio 102, Indiana 86
Apr. 12: Indiana 97, San Antonio 86
PLAYOFF FOR FOURTH PLACE
Mar. 29: San Diego 131, Denver 111

SCORING

		G	FG	FT	PTS	AVG
Erving	NY	84	914	454	2299	27.4
McGinnis	Ind	80	789	488	2071	25.9
Issel	KY	83	829	457	2118	25.5
Gervin	Va-SA	74	672	378	1730	23.4
Wise	Utah	82	714	396	1826	22.3

REBOUNDS

		G	REB	AVG
Gilmore	KY	84	1538	18.3
McGinnis	Ind	80	1197	15.0
Jones	SD	79	1095	13.9
Nater	Va-SA	79	998	12.6
Mel Daniels	Ind	76	885	11.6

ASSISTS

		G	AST	AVG
Smith	Den	76	619	8.2
Williams	SD-KY	90	557	6.2
Dampier	KY	84	473	5.6
Taylor	Va	80	416	5.2
Jones	Utah	83	429	5.2
Erving	KY	84	434	5.2

1974-75

Colonels toss gauntlet, but NBA champs refuse to pick it up

To see the ABA in action this fall was something of a surprise; summer rumors indicated the imminent collapse of the circuit. But problems were worked out, and the 1974-75 season was played. Several franchises seemed to be on the edge of folding at the end of last season, but these weak members were propped up so that the league again fielded 10 clubs. The Carolina Cougars were given up as a failure, and the franchise became the Spirits of St. Louis. Commissioner Mike Storen resigned his post to become president of the Memphis Sounds, who had suffered as the Tams under the ownership of Charles O. Finley of baseball fame. The Utah Stars and Virginia Squires got new owners, and the Denver Rockets became the Denver Nuggets. Tedd Munchak had owned the Carolina franchise, but he found new work by replacing Storen as commissioner. Such reorganization kept the league afloat, but did not solve all its problems; the San Diego and Indiana franchises had financial problems during the season, and the lack of a national television contract hurt the entire league.

All the rumors of impending doom made it more difficult to sign graduating college stars, but the ABA did gather a core of attractive rookies. Marvin Barnes of Providence signed with St. Louis for $2 million, and other star collegians joining the league were Maryland's Len Elmore, North Carolina's Bobby Jones, and Pittsburgh's Billy Knight. But the most publicized rookie was Moses Malone, a 6-foot-11 teen who signed a contract with Utah directly out of a Virginia high school.

But the addition of the teenage "phenom" could not help the Stars hold onto first place in the West. The club that went into the championship series last spring before losing to New York broke up with the defection of center Zelmo Beaty and guard Jimmy Jones to the NBA and with the holdout of forward Willie Wise until his trade to Virginia late in the season. With Utah too weak to stay on top, the Nuggets moved to the front in the Western Division. General manager Carl Scheer and coach Larry Brown both joined the club from the defunct Carolina franchise, and they brought along with them guard Mack Calvin, a running playmaker who could command an effective fast break. The Nuggets also added two tough rookie forwards in Bobby Jones and Jan Van Breda Kolff and a smart veteran guard in Fatty Taylor, but much of the club's improvement came from development by center Mike Green and guard Ralph Simpson. This combination of old and new faces compiled an overwhelming 40-2 record at home during the regular season and finished the year at 65-19.

The second-place San Antonio Spurs had a fine starting quintet in Swen Nater, Rich Jones, George Gervin, Donnie Freeman, and James Silas, but a thin bench kept the club from challenging the Nuggets. The Indiana Pacers sent veterans Freddie Lewis, Roger Brown, and Mel Daniels to Memphis

Moses Malone
Making the unprecedented jump from high school to the pros.

during the summer, and coach Bob Leonard brought his club in third with a crew of mostly younger players; the focal point on the club was forward George McGinnis, who led the league with a 29.8 scoring average. Utah made the playoffs by finishing fourth, but the club had a weak bench and ended the year with three centers starting in the forecourt. The San Diego Conquistadors trailed the field with an abundance of shooters and a famine of defensive players. Wilt Chamberlain retired both as a player and coach before the season, and general manager Alex Groza filled in as coach for the first part of the schedule until Beryl Shipley could be hired.

While the Western title was sewed up early by Denver, the Eastern race was a two-team battle between the New York Nets and the Kentucky Colonels. The Nets had a new general manager in retired NBA star Dave DeBusschere, the ABA's most exciting star in Julius Erving, an All-Star guard in Brian Taylor, and an invigorating streak of confidence left over from last year's title. But a seemingly safe hold on first place vanished in a four-game losing streak in late March, enabling the Colonels to tie them for first place. The Colonels finished in a rush, winning their last nine games of the season. To go along with fore-court titans Artis Gilmore and Dan Issel and veteran guard Louie Dampier, the Colonels this year added a new coach in Hubie Brown, two new veteran forwards in Wilbert Jones and Marv Roberts, and three new veteran guards in Bird Averitt, Ted McClain, and Gene Littles. The new St. Louis club finished third with a bunch of talented, free-wheeling, unpolished rookies led by Marvin Barnes, who played top-notch ball after having jumped the club for several games early in the season.

At the bottom of the East came the league's two disaster franchises, Memphis and Virginia. The Sounds made the play-offs practically by default. Storen and new coach Joe Mullaney tried to build the team with deals for established players, but most of the acquired men had little left to offer. The Squires struggled through the season with a variety of castoffs and undisciplined rookies. When the season was over, the Squires had a 15-69 mark, the worst team record in ABA history.

With only the Squires and Q's excluded, the playoffs began with an Eastern Division tie-breaker between New York and Kentucky. The Colonels kept up their late-season heat by beating the Nets 108-99, then downed Memphis in five games. The Nets drew St. Louis as their first-round opponents. Having beaten the Spirits 11 straight times during the regular season, the Nets expected little trouble, but after winning the first game, they couldn't contain the young and big Spirit forwards and lost four straight to the rookie-laden team. With the defending champs thus upset, the Colonels did away with the Spirits in five games to move into the finals. Meanwhile, the Western Division had come down to a battle between Denver and Indiana, with the Pacers unexpectedly winning the seventh game on the Denver home floor. In the championship series, it was no contest; the Pacers had a big gun in George McGinnis, but the Colonels had a better balanced, deeper team. Taking the first three games in succession, then Game 5, the Colonels captured their first ABA title after years of knocking on the door.

At the season's end, Dave DeBusschere, the Nets' general manager, was named commissioner in a move to improve the ABA's image. DeBusschere's first move was to challenge the NBA champion Golden State Warriors to a best-of-five championship series with Kentucky. As expected, the answer was, "no".

1974-75 SEASON HIGHLIGHTS

STANDINGS

Eastern Division

	W	L	Pct.	GB
Kentucky	58	26	.690	—
New York	58	26	.690	—
St. Louis	32	52	.381	26
Memphis	27	57	.321	31
Virginia	15	69	.179	43

Western Division

	W	L	Pct.	GB
Denver	65	19	.774	—
San Antonio	51	33	.607	14
Indiana	45	39	.536	20
Utah	38	46	.452	27
San Diego	31	53	.369	34

AWARDS
MVP
Julius Erving, New York
George McGinnis, Indiana
Rookie of the Year
Marvin Barnes, St. Louis
Coach of the Year
Larry Brown, Denver

ALL-STAR TEAMS
FIRST TEAM

Julius Erving	New York
George McGinnis	Indiana
Artis Gilmore	Kentucky
Mack Calvin	Denver
Ron Boone	Utah

ALL-STAR GAME
HemisFair Arena, San Antonio
Tuesday, January 28, 1975
East 151, West 124
MVP: Freddie Lewis

ALL-STAR TEAMS
SECOND TEAM

Marvin Barnes	St. Louis
George Gervin	San Antonio
Swen Nater	San Antonio
Brian Taylor	New York
James Silas	San Antonio

PLAYOFFS
FINALS
Kentucky 4, Indiana 1
May 13: Kentucky 120, Indiana 94
May 15: Kentucky 95, Indiana 93
May 17: Kentucky 109, Indiana 101
May 19: Indiana 94, Kentucky 86
May 22: Kentucky 110, Indiana 105
EASTERN DIVISION
DIVISION FINALS
Kentucky 4, St. Louis 1
Apr. 21: Kentucky 112, St. Louis 109
Apr. 23: Kentucky 108, St. Louis 103
Apr. 25: St. Louis 103, Kentucky 97
Apr. 27: Kentucky 117, St. Louis 98
Apr. 28: Kentucky 123, St. Louis 103
DIVISION SEMI-FINALS
Kentucky 4, Memphis 1
Apr. 6: Kentucky 98, Memphis 91

Apr. 8: Kentucky 119, Memphis 105
Apr. 10: Kentucky 101, Memphis 80
Apr. 11: Memphis 107, Kentucky 93
Apr. 13: Kentucky 111, Memphis 99
St. Louis 4, New York 1
Apr. 6: New York 111, St. Louis 105
Apr. 9: St. Louis 115, New York 97
Apr. 11: St. Louis 113, New York 108
Apr. 13: St. Louis 100, New York 89
Apr. 15: St. Louis 108, New York 107
PLAYOFF FOR FIRST PLACE
Apr. 4: Kentucky 108, New York 99
WESTERN DIVISION
DIVISION FINALS
Indiana 4, Denver 3
Apr. 20: Denver 131, Indiana 128
Apr. 22: Indiana 131, Denver 124
Apr. 24: Indiana 118, Denver 112
Apr. 25: Denver 126, Indiana 109

Apr. 27: Indiana 109, Denver 109
Apr. 30: Denver 104, Indiana 99
May 3: Indiana 104, Denver 96
DIVISION SEMI-FINALS
Denver 4, Utah 2
Apr. 6: Denver 122, Utah 107
Apr. 7: Denver 126, Utah 120
Apr. 9: Utah 122, Denver 108
Apr. 11: Utah 132, Denver 110
Apr. 12: Denver 130, Utah 119
Apr. 14: Denver 115, Utah 113
Indiana 4, San Antonio 2
Apr. 5: Indiana 122, San Antonio 119, OT
Apr. 7: Indiana 98, San Antonio 93
Apr. 10: Indiana 113, San Antonio 103
Apr. 12: San Antonio 110, Indiana 109
Apr. 14: San Antonio 123, Indiana 117
Apr. 16: Indiana 115, San Antonio 100

SCORING

		G	FG	FT	PTS	AVG
McGinnis	Ind	79	873	545	2353	29.8
Erving	NY	84	914	486	2343	27.9
Boone	Utah	84	872	363	2117	25.2
Grant	SD	53	576	182	1335	25.2
Barnes	StL	77	777	295	1849	24.0

REBOUNDS

		G	REB	AVG
Nater	SA	78	1279	16.4
Gilmore	KY	84	1361	16.2
Barnes	StL	77	1202	15.6
Malone	Utah	83	1209	14.6
McGinnis	Ind	79	1126	14.3

ASSISTS

		G	AST	AVG
Calvin	Den	74	570	7.7
Williams	Mem	81	576	7.1
McGinnis	Ind	79	495	6.3
Jabali	SD	62	358	5.8
Lamar	SD	77	427	5.5
O'Brien	SD	79	439	5.5
Erving	NY	84	462	5.5

1975-76

Dr. J, Nets prevail in what becomes final ABA game, series

Dave DeBusschere took charge of the ABA just as it began to unravel. After one year as general manager of the Nets, DeBusschere was the surprise choice to become commissioner of the league in the summer of 1975. The good news that summer came out of Denver. The Nuggets signed rookies David Thompson and Marvin Webster, the first and third players chosen in the NBA draft. Thompson was the renowned acrobatic forward from North Carolina State, a much needed crowd pleaser for the ABA. Webster, who would later be tagged "The Human Eraser," was a shot-blocking center from Morgan State. The Nuggets would showcase these famous rookies in the new Sports Arena in Denver.

Negative news came out of Indiana. After years as an ABA star, George McGinnis bought his way out of his Pacer contract and signed with the Philadelphia 76ers of the NBA. The absence of a major television contract for the ABA had condemned McGinnis to play in relative obscurity. DeBusschere failed to improve the ABA television situation.

Without a television contract, teams had little media revenue to offset their losses. The Memphis franchise was, for all practical purposes, dead during the summer. In late August, however, DeBusschere arranged for its transfer to Baltimore. The Baltimore Claws got some instant credibility by buying Dan Issel from the financially-troubled Kentucky Colonels. Ten teams thus prepared for the ABA's ninth season.

On September 24, the Denver Nuggets and the New York Nets unexpectedly applied for admission to the NBA. The senior league took the applications under advisement. The resulting publicity painted the ABA as being on its last legs.

On October 8, the Baltimore Claws ominously traded Dan Issel to Denver for practically nothing. On October 20, three days before the season was to start, the underfinanced Claws went out of business. On that same day, the seven other ABA teams joined the Nuggets and the Nets in applying for admission to the NBA.

Once the season started, attendance was low. The league's image was one of instability. On November 11, the San Diego Sails folded. The league continued as an eight-team circuit only until December 2, when the Utah Stars ceased operations.

Down to seven teams, the league scrapped its divisional format. Each successive team collapse had resulted in dispersal of that team's players to other teams. The dispersals, in turn, caused a series of trades and other personnel moves. The ABA waited for the next shoe to drop. The Virginia Squires had an atrocious team and little money in the bank. The Spirits of St. Louis had very poor attendance at their games. These weak members hung on, however, and the ABA made it through the season as a seven-team league.

On the court, the ABA still offered entertaining, wide-open basketball. Its three-point shot created offensive possibilities

David Thompson
Scores 42 points, but ends up on the losing end of the last ABA game.

not found in the NBA. The Denver Nuggets blended old and new players into a winning combination. David Thompson scored often and with flair. Marvin Webster missed most of the season with hepatitis, but Dan Issel handled the center position in style after arriving from the still-born Baltimore team. Bobby Jones and Ralph Simpson contributed their skills to the winning mix. Although the Nuggets had sent Mack Calvin, Mike Green, and Jan van Breda Kolff to Virginia for the draft rights to Thompson. the team easily absorbed the loss of three key veterans. The high-scoring Nuggets enjoyed good attendance at their games.

The New York Nets had modest attendance at their games despite a winning team. The Nets relied most heavily on Julius Erving, the astounding offensive machine known as Dr. J. Guards Brian Taylor and John Williamson provided sharp outside shooting. A swap of big men with San Antonio turned out poorly, as center Swen Nater recovered slowly from a knee injury. San Antonio got more service from the ex-Nets Billy Paultz and Larry Kenon. Guards George Gervin and James Silas, however, were the offensive leaders of the Spurs.

The defending champion Kentucky Colonels suffered from the loss of Dan Issel, who had been sold to ease financial problems. The Colonels were built around center Artis Gilmore, the league's top rebounder and fourth-best scorer. A mid-season trade brought Maurice Lucas to Kentucky. The Indiana Pacers stayed competitive despite the loss of George McGinnis. Billy Knight took up the scoring slack, while Don Buse excelled at guard.

St. Louis shuffled its lineup in front of almost-empty seats. Marvin Barnes was hounded by legal problems and played erratically. When Utah folded, the Spirits obtained Moses Malone and Ron Boone. A mid-season trade brought Caldwell Jones to St. Louis. Virginia had hopes of rising this season, but a flood of injuries decimated the team. The Squires kept changing head coaches and had a precarious grip on financial life.

In the playoffs, Kentucky beat Indiana in a three-game miniseries. The two semi-final series each went to seven games. The Nets and Spurs went the limit despite the broken ankle suffered by James Silas in the opening game. Before 15,934 fans in the Nassau Coliseum, the Nets won the seventh game 121-114. In the other semi-final series, the Nuggets and Colonels faced off in a seventh game-before 18,821 fans in the Sports Arena in Denver, an ABA attendance record. The Nuggets won 133-110.

The championship series began in Denver before 19,034 fans, a new record. Julius Erving scored 45 points and hit a jumper at the buzzer for a 120-118 New York victory. In Game 2, yet another record crowd of 19,107 saw the Nuggets even the score 127-121 despite Erving's 48 points. In Game 3 in New York, Erving scored eight straight points in the final ninety seconds for a 117-111 Nets victory. The Nets also took Game 4, prohibiting the Nuggets from retaking the home court advantage. The Nuggets, however, won the fifth game at home to earn another trip to New York. In Game 6, David Thompson scored 42 points. The Nets, however, outscored the Nuggets 34-14 in the fourth quarter and won the game 112-106 to capture the league championship.

That championship was the ABA's last. The nine-year run was over. In June, the NBA announced that Denver, New York, San Antonio, and Indiana were joining the established league. Each team would pay $3.2 million for the privilege, with the Nets paying approximately an additional $4 million to the Knicks for invading their territory. Kentucky, St. Louis, and Virginia went out of business, as did the ABA itself. Its red, white, and blue ball would henceforth bounce only in playgrounds.

1975-76 SEASON HIGHLIGHTS

STANDINGS

	W	L	Pct.	GB
Denver	60	24	.714	—
New York	55	29	.655	5
San Antonio	50	34	.595	10
Kentucky	46	38	.548	14
Indiana	39	45	.464	21
St. Louis	35	49	.417	25
Virginia	15	68	.181	44
San Diego *	3	8	.273	—
Utah **	4	12	.250	—

**San Diego disbanded Nov. 12, 1976.
**Utah disbanded Dec. 2, 1976.

AWARDS

MVP
Julius Erving, New York
Rookie of the Year
David Thompson, Denver
Coach of the Year
Larry Brown, Denver

ALL-STAR TEAMS

FIRST TEAM

Julius Erving	New York
Billy Knight	Indiana
Artis Gilmore	Kentucky
James Silas	San Antonio
Ralph Simpson	Denver

SECOND TEAM

David Thompson	Denver
Bobby Jones	Denver
Dan Issel	Denver
Don Buse	Indiana
George Gervin	San Antonio

ALL-STAR GAME

McNichols Sports Arena, Denver
Tuesday, January 27, 1976
Denver 144, All-Stars 138
MVP: David Thompson

PLAYOFFS

FINALS
New York 4, Denver 2
May 1: New York 120, Denver 118
May 4: Denver 127, New York 121
May 6: New York 117, Denver 111
May 8: New York 121, Denver 112
May 11: Denver 118, New York 110
May 13: New York 112, Denver 106

SEMI-FINALS
Denver 4, Kentucky 3
Apr. 15: Denver 110, Kentucky 107
Apr. 17: Kentucky 138, Denver 119
Apr. 19: Kentucky 126, Denver 114
Apr. 21: Denver 108, Kentucky 106
Apr. 22: Denver 127, Kentucky 117
Apr. 25: Kentucky 119, Denver 115, OT
Apr. 28: Denver 133, Kentucky 110

New York 4, San Antonio 3
Apr. 9: New York 116, San Antonio 101
Apr. 11: San Antonio 105, New York 79
Apr. 14: San Antonio 111, New York 103
Apr. 18: New York 110, San Antonio 108
Apr. 19: New York 110, San Antonio 108
Apr. 21: San Antonio 106, New York 105
Apr. 24: New York 121, San Antonio 114
FIRST ROUND MINISERIES
Kentucky 3, Indiana 0
Apr. 8: Kentucky 120, Indiana 109
Apr. 10: Indiana 109, Kentucky 95
Apr. 12: Kentucky 100, Indiana 99

SCORING

		G	FG	FT	PTS	AVG
Erving	NY	84	949	530	2462	29.3
Knight	Ind	70	774	415	1969	28.1
Thompson	Den	83	807	541	2158	26.0
Gilmore	Ky	84	773	521	2067	24.6
Barnes	StL	67	681	251	1616	24.1

REBOUNDS

		G	REB	AVG
Gilmore	Ky	84	1303	15.5
Lucas	StL-Ky	86	970	11.3
Jones	SD-Ky-StL	76	853	11.2
Kenon	SA	81	897	11.1
Erving	NY	84	925	11.0
Issel	Den	84	923	11.0

ASSISTS

		G	AST	AVG
Buse	Ind	84	689	8.2
Simpson	Den	84	597	7.1
Calvin	Va	45	271	6.0
Dampier	Ky	82	467	5.7
Silas	SA	84	452	5.4

1968

Hinkle Fieldhouse, Indianapolis, Indiana
Tuesday, January 9, 1968
East 126, West 120
Coaches: West–Babe McCarthy, New Orleans; East–Jim Pollard, Minnesota
Most Valuable Player: Larry Brown
Officials: Joe Belmont, Ron Feiereisel
Attendance: 10,872

	1	2	3	4	Total
West	29	30	32	29	120
East	30	31	31	34	126

Mel Daniels of the Minnesota Muskies had 15 rebounds and 22 points, and he put the East ahead to stay in the fourth quarter. However, he was edged out of a Malibu convertible—the prize for the game's MVP—by Larry Brown of the New Orleans Buccaneers. Brown, at 5-foot-9 the smallest player on the floor, came off the West bench to score 17 points. Combined with his five assists and fine defensive play, Brown won the MVP balloting by a 10-9 vote over Daniels. Brown was a late replacement in the game, having been added to the West squad after Bob Verga of the Dallas Chaparrals went into the Army the previous week.

1969

Convention Center, Louisville, Kentucky
Tuesday, January 28, 1969
West 133, East 127
Coaches: West–Alex Hannum, Oakland; East–Gene Rhodes, Kentucky
Most Valuable Player: John Beasley
Officials: Andy Hershock, Ron Rakel
Attendance: 5,470

	1	2	3	4	Total
West	38	26	37	32	133
East	33	27	30	37	127

The story of the second ABA All-Star Game was mainly one of who wasn't there. Connie Hawkins of the Minnesota Pipers—the league's MVP the year before (when the Pipers were in Pittsburgh)—missed the game because of floating cartilage in his knee. On top of that, Pipers coach Jim Harding, who was to be the East coach, was replaced after he got into a fight with one of the Pipers' part-owners in the early morning of the day of the game.

Rick Barry, the Oakland Oaks' sensation playing his first season in the ABA after having sat out the previous year, did play but saw limited duty. Barry had just returned from a month-long layoff because of stretched ligaments in his left knee. Barry scored 10 points in 14 minutes. His coach with the Oaks, Alex Hannum, directed the West to a 133-127 win, giving him All-Star wins in the NBA and ABA in successive years.

1970

State Fair Coliseum, Indianapolis, Indiana
Saturday, January 24, 1970
West 128, East 98
Coaches: West–Babe McCarthy, New Orleans; East–Bob Leonard, Indiana
Most Valuable Player: Spencer Haywood
Officials: Earl Strom, John Vanak
Attendance: 11,932

	1	2	3	4	Total
West	34	27	25	42	128
East	18	23	33	24	98

As was the case with the NBA All-Star Game six years earlier, the ABA players used the leverage associated with a national television audience and a large in-house crowd to threaten a strike. As had happened in 1964, the dispute was resolved less than an hour before the scheduled starting time, as Commissioner Jack Dolph agreed to recognize the ABA Players Association. That done, the All-Stars left the Stouffer Inn in Indianapolis and, with a police escort, got to the State Fair Coliseum, where a standing-room-only crowd awaited them. Larry Jones of the Denver Rockets, president of the Players Association, shook off the stress of the labor negotiations and scored 12 points in the first quarter, en route to a game-high 30 points. But it was Jones' Denver teammate, rookie Spencer Haywood, who pulled down 19 rebounds and blocked seven shots to win the MVP award as the West won, 128-98.

1971

Greensboro Coliseum, Greensboro, North Carolina
Saturday, January 23, 1971
East 126, West 122
Coaches: West–Bill Sharman, Utah; Al Bianchi, Virginia
Most Valuable Player: Mel Daniels
Officials: Norm Drucker, Joe Gushue
Attendance: 14,407

	1	2	3	4	Total
West	29	40	28	25	122
East	33	26	33	34	126

An East squad, loaded with shooters, came back from an 18-point deficit to win,

126-122. But the team's coach, Al Bianchi of the Virginia Squires, said it was "better defense" than won the game. Relatively quiet for most of the night, Rick Barry of the New York Nets scored four points in the final minute—two on free throws to put the East ahead, 123-122, and two more on a driving lay up to give his team a three-point cushion.

Although his team lost, Mel Daniels of the Indiana Pacers—with 29 points and 13 rebounds—was named MVP of the game, an award worth $875. The amount was determined by the First Citizens Bank and Trust of Greensboro, which promoted the award, by opening an account in Daniels' name, putting $1,000,000 in the account, and then letting Daniels keep the interest that accrued over one week.

1971–NBA vs. ABA
(see Section 6, NBA All-Star Game)

1972

Freedom Hall, Louisville, Kentucky
Saturday, January 29, 1972
East 142, West 115
Coaches: West–LaDell Anderson, Utah; East–Joe Mullaney, Kentucky
Most Valuable Player: Dan Issel
Officials: John Vanak, Bob Serafin
Attendance: 15,378

	1	2	3	4	Total
West	31	35	23	26	115
East	36	29	32	45	142

Virginia Squires teammates Charlie Scott and Julius Erving provided early highlights by combining on several fast breaks, with Erving displaying the mid-air moves that would become his trademark. But the big explosion came in the fourth quarter when the East went on a 12-2 run to open up a 118-104 lead. The charge was led by Dan Issel of the Kentucky Colonels (and a product of the University of Kentucky), playing before the home-state fans, and Jim McDaniels of the Carolina Cougars, a seven-foot center from Western Kentucky University.

McDaniels led all players with 24 points and had 11 rebounds, but Issel, with 21 points and nine rebounds, was named MVP, earning a refrigerator, television, and a four-foot mounted jeweled sword worth, according to the ABA, $2,000.

1972–NBA vs. ABA
(see Section 6, NBA All-Star Game)

1973

Salt Palace, Salt Lake City, Utah
Tuesday, February 6, 1973
West 123, East 111
Coaches: East–Larry Brown, Carolina; West–LaDell Anderson, Utah
Most Valuable Player: Warren Jabali
Officials: Norm Drucker, Ed Middleton
Attendance: 12,556

	1	2	3	4	Total
East	28	37	27	19	111
West	28	24	32	39	123

Down by 19 early in the third quarter, the West cut the margin to eight by the end of the period and then scored the first 13 points of the final quarter. Warren Jabali of the Denver Rockets, the game's MVP, capped the West comeback with a three-point basket to tie the game, 92-92. Willie Wise of the Utah Stars put the West ahead with a pair of free throws, then added nine more points to finish as the game's top scorer.

The West double-teamed Julius Erving, shutting him off under the basket and stifling his efforts to get the East back in the game.

1974

Norfolk Scope, Norfolk, Virginia
Wednesday, January 30, 1974
East 128, West 112
Coaches: West–Joe Mullaney, Utah; East–Babe McCarthy, Kentucky
Most Valuable Player: Artis Gilmore
Officials: John Vanak, Wally Rooney
Attendance: 10,264

	1	2	3	4	Total
West	25	30	28	29	112
East	35	27	37	29	128

Artis Gilmore, the Kentucky Colonels' towering center, helped the East take a 9-0 lead. West coach Joe Mullaney sent San Antonio Spurs rookie Swen Nater into the game to try and slow Gilmore down. Nater had a tremendous game—29 points to lead all scorers and 22 rebounds to set an All-Star Game record—but Gilmore remained dominant enough to win the game's MVP award.

Julius Erving scored 14 points in spectacular fashion with an array of dunks and twisting lay ups in addition to some backhanded blocks of shots on defense.

1975

HemisFair Arena, San Antonio, Texas
Tuesday, January 28, 1975
East 151, West 124
Coaches: East–Kevin Loughery, New York; West–Larry Brown, Denver
Most Valuable Player: Freddie Lewis
Officials: Jack Madden, Jess Kersey
Attendance: 10,449

	1	2	3	4	Total
East	32	38	39	42	151
West	32	28	30	34	124

Freddie Lewis of St. Louis had 26 points and 10 assists to lead the East to a 151-124 win. Lewis scored 14 points in the first half and set up several other baskets with his passing. One of the shortest players in the game, and the oldest, Lewis won the MVP award as his performance overshadowed fine games by several others, including East teammates Julius Erving and Artis Gilmore.

For the West, George Gervin and James Silas of the host San Antonio Spurs each scored more than 20 points. Denver's Mack Calvin kept his conference in contention by scoring nine points in the first quarter.

The East took the lead for good in the second quarter on a free throw by Kentucky's Dan Issel. Dave Twardzik of Virginia then stole the ball and drove for a layup to make the score 35-32. Near the end of the half, Louie Dampier connected on a three-pointer and Erving buried a jumper to up the East's lead to 10 points.

1976

McNichols Sports Arena, Denver, Colorado
Tuesday, January 27, 1976
Denver 144, All-Stars 138
Coaches: All-Stars–Kevin Loughery, New York; Denver–Larry Brown
Most Valuable Player: David Thompson
Officials: Norm Drucker, Ed Middleton
Attendance: 17,798

	1	2	3	4	Total
All-Stars	31	25	41	41	138
Denver	32	23	37	52	144

With the ABA down to just seven teams, the All-Star Game became a match of the league's first-place team, the Denver Nuggets, against the best players from the other teams. David Thompson, the Nuggets' outstanding rookie, scored 29 points and led a fourth-quarter comeback as Denver beat the All-Stars, 144-138.

The event may be better remembered for the half-time entertainment, however, than for the game itself. Julius Erving, David Thompson, George Gervin, Larry Kenon, and Artis Gilmore took part in a slam-dunk contest. Erving started his performance by stuffing two balls at once and ended up as the contest winner.

Because of the lengthy half-time show, along with a pre-game concert featuring Glen Campbell and Charlie Rich, the game extended into the early hours of the next morning. Many fans left early and did not see the 52-point barrage by the Nuggets in the fourth quarter.

ABA INDIVIDUAL RECORDS, CAREER

POINTS

Louie Dampier	13,726
Dan Issel	12,823
Ron Boone	12,153
Mel Daniels	11,739
Julius Erving	11,662
Freddie Lewis	11,660
Don Freeman	11,544
Mack Calvin	10,620
Stew Johnson	10,538
Roger Brown	10,498
Jimmy Jones	10,465
Steve Jones	10,258
Ralph Simpson	9,953
Bob Netolicky	9,876
Cincy Powell	9,746
Larry Jones	9,651
Artis Gilmore	9,362
Willie Wise	9,110
George Carter	8,680
Byron Beck	8,353

REBOUNDS

Mel Daniels	9,494
Artis Gilmore	7,169
Gerald Govan	7,119
Red Robbins	6,155
Bob Netolicky	5,518
Dan Issel	5,426
Billy Paultz	5,406
Byron Beck	5,165
Jim Eakins	5,142
Ira Harge	4,995
Julius Erving	4,924
Jim Ligon	4,720
Wil Jones	4,602
Julius Keye	4,602
Cincy Powell	4,582
Gene Moore	4,360
Willie Wise	4,322
Tom Washington	4,271
Stew Johnson	4,263
John Beasley	4,257

ASSISTS

Louie Dampier	4,044
Mack Calvin	3,067
Bill Melchionni	3,044
Freddie Lewis	2,883
Jimmy Jones	2,786
Ron Boone	2,569
Larry Brown	2,509
Chuck Williams	2,420
Warren Jabali	2,389
Roger Brown	2,315
Fatty Taylor	2,275
Gerald Govan	2,164
Don Freeman	2,121
Billy Keller	1,980
Julius Erving	1,952
Ralph Simpson	1,878
Al Smith	1,793
Larry Jones	1,760
Glen Combs	1,639
George Lehmann	1,557

3-POINTS

Louie Dampier	794
Billy Keller	506
Glen Combs .	503
George Lehmann	409
Darel Carrier	398
Warren Jabali	322
Roger Brown	312
Chico Vaughn	306
Freddie Lewis	275
Steve Jones	269

GAMES PLAYED

Louie Dampier	728
Byron Beck	694
Freddie Lewis	686
Gerald Govan	681
Ron Boone	662
Jim Eakins	652
Stew Johnson	647
Steve Jones	640
Mel Daniels	628
Bob Netolicky	618
Roger Brown	605
Cincy Powell	599
Red Robbins	586
Don Freeman	584
Wil Jones	566
Fatty Taylor	561
Billy Keller	556
Jimmy Jones	546

MINUTES PLAYED

Louie Dampier	27,770
Freddie Lewis	24,038
Gerald Govan	22,925
Mel Daniels	22,340
Ron Boone	21,586
Roger Brown	21,454
Jimmy Jones	20,873
Bob Netolicky	20,554
Steve Jones	20,209
Donnie Freeman	19,546
Dan Issel	19,442
Stew Johnson	19,201
Red Robbins	18,745
Byron Beck	18,717
Cincy Powell	18,636
Mack Calvin	18,267
Artis Gilmore	17,449
Willie Wise	17,025
Billy Paultz	16,762
Larry Jones	16,721

SCORING AVERAGE

(min. 250 games)

Julius Erving	28.7
Dan Issel	25.6
George McGinnis	24.8
Artis Gilmore	22.3
George Gervin	21.9
Larry Jones	21.2
Bob Verga	21.2
Ralph Simpson	20.4
George Thompson	20.1
Darel Carrier	20.0
Mack Calvin	19.9
Don Freeman	19.8
Levern Tart	19.4
Willie Wise	19.2
Jimmy Jones	19.2
Zelmo Beaty	19.1
Louie Dampier	18.9
Mel Daniels	18.7
Ron Boone	18.4
George Carter	18.2
James Silas	18.2

FIELD GOAL PERCENTAGE

Artis Gilmore	.557
Zelmo Beaty	.536
Swen Nater	.532
Tom Washington	.532
Tom Owens	.521
George Irvine	.517
Julian Hammond	.514
Billy Knight	.510
Jimmy Jones	.510
Jim Eakins	.507
Byron Beck	.507
Julius Erving	.504
James Silas	.504
Billy Paultz	.502
Marvin Barnes	.500
Brian Taylor	.499
Mike Lewis	.498
Mike Green	.493
Dan Issel	.492
Bob Netolicky	.492

FREE THROW PERCENTAGE

Rick Barry	.880
Billy Keller	.872
Mack Calvin	.866
James Silas	.857
Darel Carrier	.851
John Brisker	.837
Art Becker	.835
George Gervin	.831
John Beasley	.831
Ron Boone	.830
Louie Dampier	.826
Steve Jones	.822
Steve Chubin	.820
Freddie Lewis	.819
Bill Melchionni	.819
Red Robbins	.818
George Carter	.813
Larry Brown	.813

SCORING AVERAGE

Ray Scott	1971-72	34.58
Rick Barry	1968-69	34.00
Julius Erving	1972-73	31.94
Rick Barry	1971-72	31.47
Dan Issel	1971-72	30.58
Connie Hawkins	1968-69	30.21
Spencer Haywoord	1969-70	29.99
Dan Issel	1970-71	29.88
George McGinnis	1974-75	29.78
Rick Barry	1970-71	29.39
Julius Erving	1975-76	29.31
John Brisker	1970-71	29.30
John Brisker	1971-72	28.92
Larry Jones	1968-69	28.44
Bill Knight	1975-76	28.13
Julius Erving	1974-75	27.89
Rick Barry	1969-70	27.73
George McGinnis	1972-73	27.57
Bob Verga	1969-70	27.54
Ralph Simpson	1971-72	27.38
Donnie Freeman	1969-70	27.38
Julius Erving	1973-74	27.37
Dan Issel	1972-73	27.29
Julius Erving	1971-72	27.26
Mack Calvin	1970-71	27.17

REBOUNDING

		REB	AVG
Spencer Haywood	1969-70	1637	19.49
Artis Gilmore	1973-74	1538	18.31
Mel Daniels	1970-71	1475	17.99
Artis Gilmore	1971-72	1491	17.75
Mel Daniels	1969-70	1462	17.61
Artis Gilmore	1972-73	1476	17.57
Julius Keye	1970-71	1454	17.52
Mel Daniels	1968-69	1256	16.53
Mel Daniels	1971-72	1297	16.42
Swen Nater	1974-75	1279	16.4
Red Robbins	1969-70	1332	16.24
Artis Gilmore	1974-75	1361	16.2
Julius Erving	1971-72	1319	15.7
Zelmo Beaty	1970-71	1190	15.66
Marvin Barnes	1974-75	1202	15.61

2-PT FG%

		FGA	FGM	PCT
Bobby Jones	1974-75	875	529	.605
Artis Gilmore	1971-72	1348	806	.598
Bobby Jones	1975-76	878	510	.581
Artis Gilmore	1974-75	1349	783	.580
Moses Malone	1974-75	1034	591	.572

3-PT FG%

		3PA	3PM	PCT
Brian Taylor	1975-76	76	32	.421
Billy Shepherd	1974-75	143	60	.420
Glen Combs	1971-72	254	103	.406
George Lehman	1970-71	382	154	.403
Louie Dampier	1974-75	96	38	.396

FREE THROW PERCENTAGE

		FTA	FTM	PCT
Mack Calvin	1974-75	530	475	.89622
Bill Keller	1975-76	183	164	.89617
Darel Carrier	1969-70	509	454	.892
Rick Barry	1970-71	507	451	.890
Jim Eakins	1975-76	223	198	.888

ASSISTS

		AST	AVG
Bill Melchionni	1971-72	669	8.36
Bill Melchionni	1970-71	672	8.30
Don Buse	1975-76	689	8.20
Al Smith	1973-74	619	8.14
George Lehman	1971-72	411	7.75

BLOCKED SHOTS

		BLK	AVG
Caldwell Jones	1973-74	316	4.00
Artis Gilmore	1973-74	287	3.42
Caldwell Jones	1974-75	246	3.24
Artis Gilmore	1972-73	259	3.08
Artis Gilmore	1974-75	258	3.07

STEALS

		STL	AVG
Don Buse	1975-76	346	4.12
Ted McClain	1973-74	250	2.98
Brian Taylor	1974-75	221	2.80
Fatty Taylor	1975-76	206	2.71
Fatty Taylor	1972-73	210	2.69

TEAM WINNING PERCENTAGE

		W	L	PCT
Kentucky	1971-72	68	16	.810
Denver	1974-75	65	19	.774
Oakland	1968-69	60	18	.769
Denver	1975-76	60	24	.714
Utah	1971-72	60	24	.714

MOST WINS, ONE SEASON

68	Kentucky Colonels, 1971-72
65	Denver Nuggets, 1974-75

MOST WINS, ALL TIME

448	Kentucky Colonels
427	Indiana Pacers
413	Denver Nuggets/Rockets

HIGHEST WINNING PERCENTAGE, ALL-TIME

.641	Minnesota Muskies
.608	Utah Stars
.602	Kentucky Colonels

MOST LOSSES, ONE SEASON

69	Virginia Squires, 1974-75
68	Virginia Squires, 1975-76

MOST LOSSES, ALL TIME

331	Denver Nuggets/Rockets
328	New York Nets
315	Indiana Pacers

LOWEST WINNING PERCENTAGE, ALL TIME

.321	Anaheim Amigos
.331	Memphis Pros/Tams/Sounds
.333	Houston Mavericks

Chapter 32

Women's Basketball

By Roland Lazenby

Modern women's basketball proceeded with a determined march through the last two decades of the twentieth century and into the twenty-first, but the game's beginnings were of a different nature—it was born of a leisurely lunchtime stroll.

A group of female teachers from Springfield's Buckingham Grade School happened to be walking by the YMCA in 1892 when they heard a round of shouting from the basement gymnasium. They walked inside and from the balcony above the gym floor they watched the organized mayhem below. There was young Jim Naismith lording over the activity just weeks after its invention.

It was instantly amusing to the women, this business of the soccer ball and the peach baskets. So they stayed and watched and laughed. Better yet, they returned to the gym for more sessions and eventually summoned the courage to ask Naismith if they could play. Being a gentleman, he agreed and set up a practice for the ladies.

Naismith described the scene in his autobiography: "When the time arrived, the girls appeared at the gymnasium, some with tennis shoes, but the majority with street shoes. None of them changed from their street clothes, costumes which were not made for freedom of movement. I shall never forget the sight that they presented in their long trailing dress with leg-of-mutton sleeves, and in several cases with the hint of a bustle." As the ladies suspected, playing the game was even better than watching it; so the practices became a regular thing at the YMCA. (This may have had something to do with the fact that Naismith and one of the teachers, Maude Sherman, were attracted to each other. They became a steady couple and later married.) The women enjoyed basket ball so much that they formed two teams at the YMCA and began competition.

By the fall of 1892, a women's team had formed at Stanford University. That season Stanford played the first of three games against Miss Head's School, a private preparatory school. The *Berkeley Daily Advocate* said basketball "is football modified to suit feminine capabilities. It is played in the gymnasium, and instead of goals there are baskets hung at either end of the room. The players line up, nine on a side. The umpire tosses the ball between the two lines, then a general scramble begins to get it in the basket."

By March 1893, the collegiate game had crossed the country to the east. Now Smith College in Northhampton, Massachusetts, had taken up the game. Senda Berensen, the physical director there, had learned about the sport through a seminar at Yale. She communicated with Naismith about the game and later set up two teams: one for the sophomores (the

Nikki Teasley, 2003
The Los Angeles Sparks' star leading the West over the East in the WNBA 2003 All-Star Game.

class of 1895), the other for the freshmen, (the class of '96). An intramural game between the two teams apparently created a great deal of fun and class pride, sending the women's sport on its way.

The first college basketball game on record between two women's teams took place on April 4, 1896, barely five years after the sport was invented. Stanford beat California 2-1 in a game which no men were permitted to attend. The *Berkeleyan* noted afterward that "the conservative few cannot say that there

was anything displeasing to the supposedly retiring nature of womankind." When one basket fell and had to be fixed by male attendants, it was reported that "the Berkeley team screamed and hid in a corner" until the men left the gym. About two weeks later, the University of Washington, using a misshapen ball and playing by a mix of men's and women's rules, beat Ellensburg State Normal School, 6-3.

"It was taken up promptly in the normal schools of physical training and spread to the women's colleges," wrote Dr. Luther Gulick in the 1897-98 edition of *Spalding's*. Gulick, of course, had a role in the game's invention less than a decade before: he was the director of the Springfield YMCA who had told Dr. Naismith to invent a game that would occupy the Training School students indoors during the fall and winter. "The game is played at Bryn Mawr, Vassar, Smith, and most of the other colleges for women," Gulick observed proudly. This quick growth brought with it a misunderstanding of rules that would keep the women's game divided for three quarters of a century.

In 1895, Clara Bair, a physical education instructor at Newcomb College in New Orleans, wrote to Naismith for information about his new game. He sent her materials, including an early diagram of the playing area. Naismith made notations on the diagram suggesting strategic locations for players. Bair misread the diagram, thinking that the players were confined to one of three areas on the court. She devised a women's game, which she called "Basquette," based on her misconception. These rules were caught up in the quick spread of the game and widely used. Other women's teams played by standard rules. The discrepancy created quite a controversy. In his comments on the women's game in 1897, Gulick made clear his dislike of the altered rules. "We understand that at Bryn Mawr and Vassar the game is played by the official rules," he wrote. "Some of the women's colleges play by other rules, the chief difference of which is that the floor is divided into either three or nine spaces . . . The players placed in these spaces are required to remain in them during the whole play; and also that each person securing the ball has a free throw. The ball cannot be taken by one player from another."

These changes weren't necessary, he continued, because "they seriously handicapped the most skillful, interesting and valuable plays of the game." He pointed out that some parties felt the official rules were too rough for women, but that the "advocates of the officials rules maintain that experience has demonstrated that this claim is not true."

Despite such objections, a four-woman committee headed by Berensen met in 1899 to establish standard women's rules, including:

● The allowance of five to nine players per side
● Forbidding one player to steal the ball from another
● Forbidding a player to hold the ball longer than three seconds
● Forbidding players from crossing out of their assigned areas on the floor

These rules reflected the view of women at the time. "Basketball . . . should be admitted only tentatively, and under professional supervision to a place among the sports open to women of a new age," wrote Lucille Eaton Hill of Wellesley College in 1903. "The chances of permanent injury to beauty and health, the evil influence of such excitement upon the emotional and nervous feminine nature, and the tendency to unsex the player, is not womanly." There were other detractors.

In 1922, the rules were modified to allow six to nine players per side; then in 1937, the number was set at six, half playing offense exclusively, half defense. The next year, the court was reduced from three to two sections. Still, the debate raged on, with various states and regions playing under different rules. In one sense, the six-player rule freed up the floor at the offensive end for three-on-three play. The format also made for some high-scoring averages, since the offense was restricted to three players. In 1924, Marie Boyd of Lonacoming Central in Maryland scored a staggering 156 points in a 163-3 win over Ursuline Academy. Her total consisted of 77 buckets and just two free throws.

For decades, the state of Iowa maintained six players to a side in high school basketball, which was immensely popular across the state. As a result, the nation's top career high school scorers all come from Iowa. They include: Lynne Lorenzen of Ventura, with 6,736 career points, 1983-87; Denise Long of Union Whitten, with 6,250 points, 1965-69; Debbie Coasts of Mediapolis, with 5,103 points, 1971-75; Sandra Fiete of Garnavillo, with 4,875 points, 1950-55; and Harriet Taylor of New Sharon, with 4,798 points, 1953-57. During her 112-game career, Lorenzen averaged 60.1 points and shot better than 70 percent from the floor.

⊕ ⊕ ⊕

The Edmonton Commercial Grads, a unique team in the history of sport, was formed in 1915 and ground out one of the best records in women's basketball over the next 25 years. Over that span, the Grads played with dynastic force, winning 522 games and losing just 20. Those figures included a 7-2 record against men's teams. At one point, their victory streak stretched to 147 games, and they claimed 14 Canadian championships.

A barnstorming bunch with no gym of their own, they played their home games outdoors, making their success all the more impressive because many of their wins came on the road. They played across the globe, touring the U.S., Canada and Europe and made Olympic exhibition appearances in Paris, Amsterdam, and Berlin.

In their 25-year history, they used just 38 players, most of whom were graduates of a commercial high school in Edmonton. Their coach, John Percy Page, declared that once a player married she had to leave the team. He stressed the credo that each Grad had to be a "lady first, a ball player second." Most of the players were teachers or stenographers.

The 1930s brought another group of women barnstormers, The All-American Red Heads, a team put together by an Arkansas businessman. They dyed their hair red and wore star-spangled, red, white, and blue uniforms. Their traveling covered about 60,000 miles each year, targeting the best men's teams in every town.

Although the faces changed, the Red Heads kept playing for decades. In 1974, they rolled to a 188-13 record. Their modern star was 5-foot-5 Jolene Ammons, who scored more than

21,000 points over 11 years with the team, the record for women players. "We are the best women's basketball team ever," declared Red Head Karen Logan in 1975. Indeed, it is easy to see the Red Heads as the female counterparts to a great barnstorming men's team of the 1930s: the New York Rens.

Another early outlet for the female competitive spirit was AAU basketball, which began a national tournament in 1926. Mildred "Babe" Didrikson, who went on to a career in professional women's golf, was a three-time AAU All-American. In February, 1930, a Dallas businessman had seen her play and offered her a $75-per-week job so she could play for the company team, the Employers Casualty Company Golden Cyclones, winners of the 1931 AAU national title. It would be an understatement to say she was a key player: she often scored thirty or more points in an era when a score of 20 for entire teams was considered respectable. During their five-game tournament run, the 19-year-old "Babe" scored 106 points. Her 21.2 average was amazing in that era of underhand free throws and set shots.

Even as a teenager she knew her purpose: "My goal was to be the greatest athlete who ever lived," she said. A versatile athlete without peer, Babe won five events at the AAU national track and field competition in 1932. Then she went to the Olympics and won two gold medals and one silver. Didrickson later pitched an exhibition baseball game against the St. Louis Cardinals and bowled a 200 game. She nearly broke world records in swimming and was a champion diver.

The Associated Press voted her the "Greatest Female Athlete" of the first half of the 20th century. The wire service also voted her Female Athlete of the Year six times—once for her track dominance and five times for her golfing prowess. No less a sportswriter than Grantland Rice was moved to write of the 5-foot-5 Babe, "She is beyond all belief until you see her perform; then you finally understand that you are looking at the most flawless section of muscle harmony, of complete mental and physical coordination, the world of sport has ever seen." Six years before she died of cancer at age 42, Didrickson was asked if there was anything she hadn't played. "Yeah," she quipped. "Dolls."

Other women's AAU stars included: Alline Banks Sprouse, who earned AAU All-America honors 11 consecutive years; Corine Jax Smith, who was an AAU All American nine times between 1931 and 1945; Patsy Neal, a three-time AAU All American who led Wayland Baptist College in Plainview, Texas, to the 1959 AAU national title.

The Wayland Baptist Flying Queens were a powerhouse during the 1950s, '60s, and '70s. In the mid-1950s, the Flying Queens ran up a 131-game winning streak and claimed AAU titles in 1955, '56, and '57. Their winning streak was broken when Nashville Business College beat them by four points for the 1958 AAU title. The Flying Queens came back to win the 1959 championship. They drew their sponsorship from local businessman Claude Hutcherson, who owned an airport. Thus the name, "Flying Queens." The team flew to its games in four Beechcraft Bonanzas and played an ambitious schedule each year. In 1959-60, the Queens played a series of games in Mexico.

Between 1958, when they upset the Flying Queens, the Nashville Business College team captured 10 AAU national titles and the team's star, Nera White, was selected the tournament's Most Valuable Player an incredible 10 times. As well, White was named an AAU All-America 15 consecutive years and in 1957-58 led the U.S. to the World Basketball Championship in Rio de Janeiro, where she earned another MVP honor. White toured Russia, West Germany, France, Brazil, Venezuela and Great Britain with various all-star teams.

Perhaps the most astonishing feat during the developmental years of women's basketball was the high-school coaching record of Bertha Teague, who retired in 1969 as the game's winningest coach with 1,152 victories. She began her career in 1926 at Cairo High School in Oklahoma, then the next year moved to Byng High School for another 42 seasons. Of her 42 teams there, 18 won 30 or more games, while 38 of her teams won conference titles. They also claimed 27 district championships. She coached eight state championship teams and from 1936 to 1938, her teams won 98 straight games. When she retired in 1969, the governor declared Bertha Teague Day in Oklahoma. She was enshrined in the state sports hall of fame in 1971.

⊛ ⊛ ⊛

Change came slowly in the women's game over the years. In the 1950s, most women's rules began to allow a single dribble before a player took a shot. A decade later, the dribble rule was expanded to three bounces. Eventually, the modern game came into line with its male counterpart. Any amount of dribbling was allowed. The result was a loosening of rules that allowed female players to demonstrate a growing athleticism. Despite the attention given to the Los Angeles Sparks Lisa Leslie for her new millennium dunk, in was in 1984 that Georgeann Wells of West Virginia became the first woman to dunk in collegiate competition.

Other developments came as follows:

1926—Pasadena, California, hosted the first women's AAU tournament. Play was based on the official five-player men's rules. The host team won.

1953—Santiago, Chile was the site of the inaugural FIBA World Championships for women.

1955—The United States sent a women's team to the Pan American games.

1969—The first National Invitational Tournament was held in West Chester, Pennsylvania. West Chester State won the first championship. This tournament was held twice more (1970 and 1971) at different locations.

1971—The Association of Intercollegiate Athletics for Women is formed, and this group coordinated the growth of the women's game before giving way to the NCAA in 1982.

1971—The number of women players allowed on the floor per team was reduced from six to five.

1972—The Association for Intercollegiate Athletics for Women began a national collegiate championship. Immaculata (of Philadelphia) won the first three national titles.

1975—Cyndi Meserve, 19, became the first woman to play on a men's collegiate basketball team. The 5-foot-8 guard went scoreless in one game and recorded a pair of free throws in another.

1976—Olympic medal competition for women's basketball began, with the Soviet Union socking the U.S. for the gold medal.

1977—One of the landmark days in the growth of women's basketball came on March 6, 1977, when a college double-header at New York's Madison Square Garden drew 12,336 fans and national media attention. No. 1-ranked Delta State beat second-ranked Immaculata 79-62 in the nightcap, but what the fans went home talking about took place in the opener.

1978—Title IX, the law requiring schools to provide equal athletic funding for women's sports, went into effect.

1982—The NCAA took over women's basketball, and the AIAW held its last tournament.

1984-85—The NCAA approved a smaller basketball for women. At 29 inches, it is one inch smaller in circumference and weighs 18-20 ounces, 2-1/2 ounces lighter than the men's ball.

1987—A crowd of 24,563 saw Texas beat Tennessee 97-78 in a women's college game, and the NCAA Women's Final Four soon became an annual sellout. Major colleges like Tennessee, Stanford, North Carolina and Connecticut became the powers of the sport, replacing pioneers like Louisiana Tech, Old Dominion, Delta State and Immaculata, which had dominated in the 1970s.

1987-88—The three-point goal was approved for all women's NCAA competition and for girl's high school play. The distance for both levels of competition is 19 feet, 9 inches.

1995—The USA Basketball Women's National Team was formed and practiced together for a year and then won the gold medal at the 1996 Olympics in Atlanta. Two professional leagues were formed soon after, and while the ABL soon folded, the WNBA—with the backing of the men's NBA—has survived and just finished its seventh season.

⊕ ⊕ ⊕

The beginning of the AIAW national championship series in 1972 thrust women's basketball toward modernization. A year earlier, the rules had standardized the five-player game. On March 20, 1972, Immaculata of Philadelphia defeated West Chester State, 52-48 for the first national championship, setting in motion a dynastic run. "I never would have played girls' basketball in high school if they hadn't changed the rules and let us play like the boys play," said Immaculata's star, Teresa Shank. "I hated girls' basketball rules."

Immaculata won the title the next two years—at one point winning 31 in a row—then appeared in what was then the biggest game in women's history, beating Queens College of New York, 65-61, before 12,000 fans at Madison Square Garden.

That spring, Margaret Wade's Delta State team, from Cleveland, Mississippi, dealt Immaculata its first tournament defeat in four years, 90-81, in the AIAW finals at Madison College (now James Madison University) in Harrisonburg, Virginia. Wade's Lady Statesmen finished the season 28-0, remarkable considering the program had been revived only two seasons earlier in 1973. Wade had run up a 453-89 record over 19 years at Cleveland (Mississippi) High School. When she moved into the college ranks at Delta State, her first team went 16-2, then zoomed off from there. The Lady Statesmen posted

a 33-1 record in 1975-76 and won a second AIAW title. Led by 6-foot-3 Lusia Harris, who averaged 25.9 points between 1974 and '78, they took a third consecutive title in 1977 with a 32-3 record. That same year, the Wade Trophy, recognizing the nation's outstanding women's collegiate player, was named in honor of Delta State's coach.

During their reign, the Lady Statesmen piled up 51 consecutive wins, the NCAA's women's record. The string ended in a 1976 defeat to Immaculata. Wade retired in 1979 with a 633-117 career record. In 1985, she, Senda Berensen Abbot, and Bertha Teague became the first three women enshrined in the Naismith Memorial Basketball Hall of Fame. Harris was enshrined in the Hall of Fame in 1992, along with Nera White.

In the years since, an additional dozen women have been added to the hall, namely: seven-foot Soviet star Uljana Semenova and UCLA stars Ann Meyers (1993) and Denise Curry (1997), Montclair State super-shooter Carol Blazejowski (1994), Old Dominion stars Anne Donovan (1995) and Nancy Liebermann (1996), USC stalwart Cheryl Miller (1995), AAU heroine Joan Crawford (1997) and coaches Jody Conradt (1998), Billie Moore (1999), Pat Head Summitt (2000) and Kay Yow (2002).

Semenova's incredible career spanned 18 years, in which her teams did not lose a single game, including gold medal runs at the 1976 and 1980 Olympic Games and three world championships.

The story of Ann Meyers' life could be opened to virtually any page to find something wondrous. Playing at UCLA in the 1970s, she became the first four-time All-American in women's college basketball. She led the Bruins to the 1978 AIAW national championship with a 90-74 win over Maryland. In the championship game, she scored 20 points and had 10 rebounds, nine assists, and eight steals. She went on to become the first and only woman signed by an NBA team. Then she married Baseball Hall of Famer Don Drysdale and started a family.

At 5-foot-9, 135 pounds, she was a complete player, with a nose for defense that matched the intensity of her offensive vision. One of 11 children, Meyers was raised in San Diego. Her older brother and competitor, Dave Meyer, earned a full basketball scholarship to UCLA. Ann soon followed in his footsteps, becoming the first woman player to earn a full ride with the Bruins. She averaged about 17 points a game over her four years in Los Angeles, and her play helped convince skeptics that women could play the game.

Indiana Pacers owner Sam Nassi seemed to believe that in 1979, when, without consulting his head coach, he drafted Meyers and gave her a guaranteed $50,000 contract. She was only the third woman in history drafted by an NBA team, but the other two—Denise Long in 1969 and Lusia Harris in 1977—never signed contracts. Nassi was roundly criticized for his move, but he insisted that it wasn't made for publicity purposes. At the Pacers' camp, Meyers was overwhelmed by writers and reporters wanting interviews. "I can dribble and make plays as well as anyone in the league," she told whoever asked. "I don't want to embarrass anyone, including myself."

She didn't. Still, she simply wasn't strong enough to compete

with the NBA's giants. Said Pacers coach Bob "Slick" Leonard after he cut her: "From a fundamentals standpoint, Ann is excellent. Some of the guys had better thank God that she doesn't have about six more inches and forty more pounds." Jack McCloskey, then a Pacers' assistant coach, was touched by Meyers' efforts. "She gave me a little peck on the cheek and a hug," he said. "It meant a lot to me. I've never gotten a kiss from a player who got cut." Meyers went on to the New Jersey Gems of the Women's Basketball League 1979 and 1980. In the short life of that professional circuit, she was twice selected league MVP.

For her part, Curry helped Meyers lead UCLA to the 1978 AIAW title and went on to average a double-double (24.6 ppg, 10.1 rpg) and pace the Bruins in scoring each of her four varsity seasons. She set 14 school records and still holds the school's mark as the all-time leading scorer (3,198 points) and rebounder (1,310). A three time Western Collegiate Athletic Conference (now Pac-10) Most Valuable Player, Curry was the 1981 UCLA All-University Athlete of the Year and a 1994 inductee into the UCLA Athletic Hall of Fame, where Curry had her jersey number 12 retired along with Kareem Abdul-Jabbar, Bill Walton and Meyers at the 25th anniversary of Pauley Pavilion.

Blazejowski, a 5-foot-10 forward who could drive hard down the lane or hit jump shots from anywhere on the court, scored 52 points as Montclair (N.J.) State beat Queens (N.Y.) College 102-91 on March 1, 1977. At the time it was the most points scored, by a man or a woman, since the new Madison Square Garden was built in 1968. The game was part of the first-ever women's basketball doubleheader at MSG. Blazejowski scored 38 of her points in the second half, when she made 17-of-21 shots from the field. When she left the game with 47 seconds remaining, she received a standing ovation and photographers rushed to catch her reaction. "It had to be the greatest thrill of my life," she said. "The crowd, the excitement, it was all very stimulating. Not just for me but for the team. I couldn't believe it."

That performance, in the media mecca of New York, opened doors for the women's game that had been closed for many years, and boosted it on its way to its current prominence. In her college career she scored 3,199 points, second only to Pete Maravich in all-time scoring among male or female college players. She still holds the single season (38.6 ppg; 1,235 pts) and career (31.7 ppg) NCAA scoring marks.

"Blaze," as she came to be known, was a member of the gold medal-winning 1979 World University Team, silver medal-winning 1979 Pan American Team and 1980 Olympic Team that did not participate in the XXIInd Olympiad in Moscow. In 1980-81, Blazejowski played with the New Jersey Gems of the Women's Basketball League (WBL) and was the league's leading scorer. She is now president of the WNBA's New York Liberty.

Led by All Americans Anne Donovan and Nancy Lieberman, the Old Dominion Monarchs captured two national championships. Donovan, a 6-foot-8 center, averaged 20 points and 14.5 rebounds per game over her career from 1979-83. "Anne was one of the first really talented big players," said CBS analyst Mimi Griffin. "She wasn't only big, but fluid.

She could post up low and run the floor well." Lieberman, a tough 5-foot-10 guard, was a two-time winner of the Wade award as national player of the year. She averaged 18.1 points and 8.7 rebounds per game from 1976-80. "She was on the cutting edge of a new style of basketball," Griffin told USA Today. "She popularized street ball in the women's game."

Cheryl Miller was a Southern California high school star who had a talented older brother on scholarship at UCLA. (Like Dave Meyer, Reggie Miller went on to play in the NBA.) But Cheryl didn't follow her brother to UCLA. Instead, she went to Southern Cal and used her considerable set of skills to put USC at the top of the women's game. By the time she enrolled at USC, Miller already owned a piece of the national record books. In high school at Riverside Poly in California, she had 1,604 career rebounds. On January 26, 1982, she scored 105 points against cross-town rival Riverside North Vista. Thirteen other girls had scored better than 100 points in a high-school game, but only Miller accomplished that feat while playing five-on-five basketball.

The next year the 6-foot-3 Miller earned All-America honors in leading USC (the team included All-American sisters Pam and Paula McGee) to the national championship, 69-67, over defending champions Louisiana Tech. As a freshman, Miller was named the tournament's Most Outstanding Player. The Trojans again claimed the championship in '84 with a win over Tennessee, and Miller again was named Most Outstanding Player. Miller also was voted the Naismith award as the national player of the year. Later that year, she helped the U.S. women to their first ever gold medal in Olympic competition in Los Angeles.

Southern Cal again returned to the national championship game in 1986, Miller's senior year, but lost to Texas. During her college career, Miller averaged 12 rebounds and 23.6 points while shooting 56.3 percent from the floor. She was a four-time All-American and a three-time national-player-of-the-year winner. She is among a small group of women to score more than 3,000 points and record more than 1,500 rebounds over a college career. Lynette Woodard, who finished her career at Kansas in 1981 with 3,649 points and 1,734 rebounds, and Susie Snider Eppers, who finished at Baylor in 1977 with 3,137 points and 1,823 rebounds, are among that group. "Cheryl Miller revolutionized the game of women's basketball," said Leon Barmore, who succeeded Sonja Hogg as coach at Louisiana Tech. "Her charisma as well as her talent helped bring the entertainment value of women's basketball to the forefront. She opened up the eyes of people who wouldn't otherwise watch the game."

Led by Miller, the 1980s brought an explosion in the women's game. With better coaches, better players, and better teams, NCAA women's basketball found that it could sell tickets. From 1982 to 1987, season-wide attendance at women's games increased from 2.39 million to 3.12 million fans. In 1987, Texas defeated Tennessee in Knoxville before 24,563 fans, the largest crowd for a women's game in NCAA history.

Joan Crawford, a 5-foot-11 center from Nashville, was an Amateur Athletic Union (AAU) star in the late 1950s and throughout the 1960s. A tough offensive player who possessed

solid rebounding and passing skills, Crawford played 14 AAU seasons (1955-1969), two with Clarendon in Texas and 12 with Nashville Business College (NBC). Crawford was named to 13 consecutive AAU All-America teams and won 10 AAU championships with Nashville Business College. She was named Most Valuable Player in the 1963 and 1964 National AAU Tournament.

⊕ ⊕ ⊕

In addition to Billie Moore, Meyers' and Curry's coach at UCLA, three other female coaches—Texas' Jody Conradt, Tennessee's Pat Head Summitt and North Carolina State's Kay Yow—have been added to the Naismith Memorial Basketball Hall of Fame in the past five years, with a fourth mentor of a female college team—Louisiana Tech's Leon Barmore—making it in 2003.

The most illustrious of the group is surely Summitt, who, despite her team losing the NCAA Final in April 2003, 73-68 to the University of Connecticut, is the winningest female college coach of all time. She won her 800th game on January 14, 2003 when her University of Tennessee Lady Vols defeated DePaul 76-57. Her 13 trips to the NCAA Final Four passed legendary UCLA coach John Wooden (12) for best in history. Not so strangely, Summitt's program at Tennessee brings to mind the glory days of UCLA in the 1960s and '70s when Wooden strung together 10 championship teams in Westwood with a succession of talent, from Walt Hazzard and Gail Goodrich to Lew Alcindor to Sidney Wicks to Bill Walton to Marques Johnson. This time, though, the setting was Knoxville, and the faces on the posters included Bridgette Gordon, Daedra Charles, Dena Head, Lisa Harrison, Nikki McCray, Michelle Marciniak, and Chamique Holdsclaw, a parade of stars highlighting Tennessee's best clubs over the years.

"I think we've set a standard here in which it's hard to leave the court or end a season with a defeat and feel that we've really been victorious," Summitt has said of her program. Perhaps none of her successes tasted sweeter than the 39-0 record her team rang up on the way to title number five in 1998. The Lady Vols' 1998 season falls in the realm of Clair Bee and his LIU Blackbirds, or Bill Russell and his San Francisco Dons, or Bill Walton and the 1973 Bruins, the only difference being that none of those aforementioned male powerhouses managed to win 39 games in a season.

Holdsclaw, the heart of the late-'90s Tennessee clubs, anchored three straight national championship teams and earned All-America honors three times. Those successes come on top of the fact that Holdsclaw led her high school team to four straight New York State titles. In the 1997 NCAA championship game against Old Dominion she scored 24 points and earned the Final Four's Most Outstanding Player honor (after averaging 20.6 points and 9.4 rebounds a game during the regular season). Many considered Holdsclaw the greatest ever, based on her clutch performances in big games. "That's the distinguishing feature of any great player," LSU coach Sue Gunter said. "She may have only six points in a game, but it'll be the most crucial six points of the evening, and it'll be six points that break your back. She has that drive, the initiative and creativity to get it done."

By sporting four starters 6-foot-1 or taller the 1998 Vols drew comparisons to other great women's teams: the undefeated 1995 University of Connecticut team and Southern California's 1983 and 1984 national championship teams with Pam and Paula McGee. The 1998 season was one of first in other ways, too. Summitt appeared on the cover of *Sports Illustrated*, the first women's college coach to make an *SI* cover, and released her own book, *Reach for the Summit*. Holdsclaw was featured in Ebony, and the entire program was the subject of an HBO documentary *A Cinderella Season: Lady Vols Fight Back*. These were media distractions, prompting Holdsclaw to declare the Lady Vols were "like a rock group. Cool. We're taking women's basketball to a new level."

In many ways, Summitt's career has epitomized the growth of the women's game. She was a mere graduate assistant when she was named to replace Margaret Hutson in 1974 as women's basketball coach at the University of Tennessee. "I was 22 years old," Summitt said. "It was my first coaching job. I was really in over my head." Her pay was a stipend. "It was about 250 or 260 bucks a month," she recalled. "My second year, I went full-time teaching and coaching and my salary was $8,900. I ate a lot of those really cheap hamburgers back then."

As her teams pressed through one victorious season after another, Title IX laws took effect, as did court challenges about the inequities in the pay of men's and women's college coaches, which helped. Outside of the litigation, however, Summitt's continued success made the case for her market value. By 1998, a raise boosted her salary package to about $400,000 a year, a sign of the progress in the women's game, progress that can be traced directly to her influence. "I think Tennessee has been a leader in women's basketball," she said. "The support we have had comes from the very top."

Her Lady Vols had won better than 83 percent of their NCAA tournament games, numbers that even Wooden and Kentucky's famed Adolph Rupp would be stretched to match. Summitt played collegiately at nearby University of Tennessee-Martin, where she developed an excellent all-around game, good enough to earn her a spot on the 1973 World University Games team. Her senior season in 1974 was interrupted by a knee injury, but Summitt battled back to make the 1976 Olympic team with which she earned a silver medal. A mere eight years later, she coached the first USA women's team to bring home the Gold medal. She did all of this, of course, as the very young head coach at Tennessee.

What followed would be national championships for her Vols in 1987, 1989, 1991, 1996, 1997 and 1998.

She took great pride in the growth of the women's game and the role her program played in that growth. "I think we've arrived," she said in 1997. "The television exposure is just tremendous. The impact has been phenomenal, and not only in the last five years, but even in the last year." As far as championship formulas, her ideas were clear and emphatic. "You win with players," she said. "So you want the positions intact. You want a 'go-to' player in the paint. Obviously, if I'm looking at two positions, I'm looking down the middle. I want my go-to player in the paint and I want that point guard that can be the quarterback of our basketball team.

"I think," she added, "when you get to the women's game

now, versus say maybe five years ago, you really have to have versatile players. You have to have creators and you have to have shooters. I think you have to be able to really spread the floor, and the three-point shot is obviously an important part of the game. However, we won the championship (in 1997) and we were 12th out of 12 teams in our league in three-point shooting."

⊕ ⊕ ⊕

The growth in the college game helped boost the prospects for the start up of two professional leagues in 1997: the WNBA, owned and operated by the NBA, and the American Basketball League, which folded in 1999, after struggling for two seasons. "With the ABL and the WNBA, there's obviously some more opportunity for exposure and for us to establish ourselves," Pat Head Summitt said in 1998. "But we can't rest on that. We have to continue to promote our game."

The WNBA witnessed the rise of the Houston Comets and the magical play of Cynthia Cooper, who led her team to the first four WNBA titles and retired after the 2000 championship at age 37 with four consecutive Championship MVP awards. The 5-foot-10 guard became the poster child for the revival of professional women's basketball in the United States, a venture undertaken with the capital and marketing savvy of the NBA. After being retired for two seasons, she returned in 2003 before shoulder surgery ended her season.

Cooper had led USC to NCAA championships in 1983 and 1984. She left USC in 1986 with career totals of 1,559 points, 381 assists and 256 steals. Cooper played on two U.S. Olympic teams, winning a gold medal in 1988 in Seoul and a bronze in the 1992 Barcelona Games. After sharpening her game overseas for 11 seasons in Spain and Italy, she returned to the United States in 1997 with the founding of the WNBA and quickly emerged as the new league's new star—at age 34.

"Coop can shoot, rebound, pass, lead, and guard the other team's best players," Comets Coach Van Chancellor, who would go on to coach Houston to four titles, said at the time. "That's about all of it, isn't it? She's one of the hardest-working players I've ever been around. I'm in awe of Cynthia Cooper." She averaged 21 points before her retirement and capped her remarkable four-year run by scoring 25 points in her final game, including six in overtime, as the Comets defeated the New York Liberty in the final game of the 2000 championship series (New York's third loss in the title game in four seasons). "Right now, I am just savoring the moment," Cooper said afterward. "This is a great moment for women's basketball and women's players."

Upon her return in 2003, Cooper fired 22 points in back-to-back games and averaged 16.6 before being injured. The 22-point performances came more than a month after her 40th birthday. Cooper is expected to return in 2004, but, already, a bevy of new stars has stepped in to help fill her shoes. Lisa Leslie of Los Angeles, Chamique Holdsclaw of Washington, Lauren Jackson of Seattle (the WNBA's 2003 MVP), Tamika Catchings of Indiana, Ruth Riley of Detroit and Houston's Sheryl Swoopes are superb athletes whose competitive fires burn intensely. Swoopes is arguably the best all-round player in the game, with two MVPs and three Defensive Player of the Year awards in the past four WNBA seasons.

Swoopes was the 1991 National Junior College Player of the Year at South Plains (Texas) J.C., but when she tried out for the 1992 U.S. Olympic team and had to compete against older players with experience in international competition, she was cut.

"I was just a baby at it," she said. "I was very young, and honestly, I had never really played against so many great, talented players."

Instead of getting discouraged, she went about improving her game. "There's always something every day you can get better at, things you can work on," she said. "Of course, you get tired, and it's really hard to get out there and keep going all the time. But you have to remember, in the back of my mind, all I'm thinking of is '96, gold medal . . . I just made myself come out every day and pushed myself."

Swoopes transferred to Texas Tech and led the Lady Raiders to a 58-8 record over two seasons, winning the Southwest Conference title both years. A 6-foot forward, she averaged 21.6 ppg and 8.9 rpg in 1991-92, then revved it up a notch to 28.1 ppg (second in the nation) and 9.2 rpg in 1992-93. She capped her college career by setting 11 NCAA Tournament, Final Four or Championship records in a brilliant postseason as she led Texas Tech to the 1993 NCAA championship.

Carrying her team to the Final Four in Atlanta, Swoopes scored 33 points against Southern Cal, 30 against Washington and 36 against Colorado. Before the national semi-finals, Swoopes was named the Division I Player of the Year and the Naismith Award winner as the top player in the nation. But if those honors represented any extra pressure, she shrugged it off and scored 31 points as Texas Tech upset top-ranked Vanderbilt 60-46.

Those performances only hinted at what was to come. On April 4, Swoopes set an NCAA championship game record by scoring 47 points as Texas Tech won its first title 84-82 over Ohio State. The Buckeyes led 55-54 before Swoopes scored 16 of her points in the final 10-1/2 minutes as Texas Tech took control. She scored a pair of baskets and a three-point play to put Texas Tech in front 80-73 with 58 seconds left, and four free throws down the stretch nailed down the victory.

She'd proven herself a champion, but one goal remained unfulfilled: the Olympics. She turned down an offer to play in the men's U.S. Basketball League and went to Italy, where she averaged 23 points per game for Bari, then returned to play for the United States in the 1994 World Championships and the 1994 Goodwill Games.

Her Olympic dream was about to come true. Swoopes was selected for the USA Basketball Women's National Team that practiced together and compiled a 52-0 record in the year leading up to the 1996 Olympics. That earned her a spot on the Olympic team, and she averaged 13.0 points, 3.5 rebounds and 3.9 assists and shot .606 from the field in leading the United States to the gold medal in Atlanta.

She went on to star in the WNBA as one of the league's early marquee signings, but only after the birth of her son Jordan (named after Michael Jordan). She missed most of the league's inaugural season while pregnant, but joined the Houston Comets two weeks after Jordan was born and played a supporting role as Cooper led the Comets to the

league's first championship.

She then teamed with Cooper to lead the Comets to two more titles, earning All-WNBA honors in 1998 as she averaged 15.6 points, 5.1 rebounds and 2.48 steals per game and in 1999 as she averaged 18.3 points, 6.3 rebounds, 4.0 assists and 2.38 steals per game. On July 27, 1999, Swoopes became the first woman in WNBA history to post a triple-double when she had 14 points, 15 rebounds and 10 assists in the Comets' 85-46 rout of the Detroit Shock.

In a new millennium she continued to amass new distinctions. She was twice been the WNBA's regular season MVP (2000, 2002). In the same years she was Defensive Player of the Year, an award she also claimed in 2003. She also added another Olympic gold medal to her collection in 2000.

⊕ ⊕ ⊕

One thing Swoopes hasn't been able to add, however, is another WNBA crown, to go with the four she, Cooper and the rest of the Comets shared during the league's first four seasons. The Los Angeles Sparks, led by Lisa Leslie, took the title in both 2001 and 2002 and came oh-so-close to making it three in a row on September 16, 2003 before falling, 83-78, to the Detroit Shock in the third and decisive game of the final. It was a dramatic final game played before the largest crowd in WNBA history, 22,076 at the Palace in Auburn Hills. With the crowd in a frenzy and chanting, "Beat L.A.! Beat L.A.!", the Shock's Deanna Nolan nailed a three-pointer from the corner to give the Shock a 75-73 lead with 53 seconds left. Then

Cheryl Ford—daughter of NBA all-timer Karl Malone—hit two free throws, and it was a four-point game with 43 seconds left. But the Sparks came surging back with a basket, then Nolan hit two more free throws, then L.A. nailed a three-pointer, then . . . L.A. fouled Nolan again and she calmly sank both, and it was truly over.

Over on the Sparks' bench, the team's coach, who had brought so much respectability to the Shock franchise—the worst in the league the previous season—leapt madly in the air. The coach's name? Bill Laimbeer, the very same tough and downright nasty leader of the Detroit Pistons "Bad Boys" who terrorized the NBA and won two championships in the late '80s and early '90s. The next day, at a rally that drew 700 fans back to the Palace, Laimbeer held the championship trophy aloft and declared, "This is only the first one. We want a few more of these." Outside, workmen were already preparing to change the address of the Palace from "2 Championship Drive" (in honor of the Pistons' two titles) to "3 Championship Drive."

In 1897, YMCA official Luther Gullick had complained that if the women's game was to be played by different rules, it shouldn't be called basketball at all. A century and a bit later, Gullick's complaint was no longer valid. The women's game in the 21st century is very much basketball, a competition brimming with savvy, style and every bit as much intensity, excitement and vigor as the men's game.

WOMEN'S PROFESSIONAL BASKETBALL LEAGUE STATISTICS

The WPBL was the idea of Bill Byrne, who had previous experience in the American Football League. By the summer of 1978, eight franchises, each costing $50,000, were selected. In July 1978, the first draft was held in New York City. Ann Meyers and Rita Easterling were the first two draft picks.

During its three seasons, the league, commonly known as the WBL, fielded teams across the U.S., from New York to San Francisco, but only three teams—Chicago, Minnesota and New Jersey last for the three campaigns.

Stars of the WBL included 'Machine Gun' Molly Bolin, Carol 'The Blaze' Blazejowski and 'Lady Magic' Nancy Lieberman.

1978-79

Eastern Division	W	L	Pct.	GB
Houston Angels	26	8	.768	—
New York Stars	19	15	.559	7
Dayton Rockets	12	22	.353	14
New Jersey Gems	9	25	.265	17
Midwest Division	**W**	**L**	**Pct.**	**GB**
Chicago Hustle	21	13	.618	—
Iowa Cornets	21	13	.618	—
Minnesota Fillies	17	17	.500	4
Milwaukee Does	11	23	.324	10

WBL EASTERN DIVISION
Apr. 11: Houston 97, New York 91
Apr. 13: Houston 93, New York 84

WBL MIDWEST DIVISION
Apr. 10: Chicago 112, Iowa 107, OT
Apr. 12: Iowa 114, Chicago 101
Apr. 14: Iowa 118, Chicago 117

WBL FINALS
Apr. 17: Houston 89, Iowa 85
Apr. 20: Houston 112, Iowa 98
Apr. 23: Iowa 110, Houston 101
Apr. 26: Iowa 89, Houston 79
May 1: Houston 111, Iowa 104

MVP: Rita Easterling, Chicago Hustle

1979-80

Eastern Division	W	L	Pct.	GB
New York Stars	28	7	.800	—
New Orleans Pride	21	13	.618	6.5
New Jersey Gems	19	17	.528	9.5
St. Louis Streak	15	21	.417	13.5
Washington Metros*	3	7	.300	—
Philadelphia Fox*	2	8	.200	—
Midwestern Division	**W**	**L**	**Pct.**	**GB**
Iowa Cornets	24	12	.667	—
Minnesota Fillies	22	12	.647	1
Chicago Hustle	17	19	.472	7
Milwaukee Does	10	24	.294	13
Western Division	**W**	**L**	**Pct.**	**GB**
Houston Angels	19	14	.576	—
San Francisco Pioneers	18	18	.500	2.5
California Dreams	11	18	.393	6
Dallas Diamonds	7	28	.200	13

*Philadelphia and Washington disbanded during the season

WBL QUARTER-FINALS
Mar. 17: Houston 90, San Francisco 75
Mar. 20: San Francisco 93, Houston 82
Mar. 22: San Francisco 98, Houston 95
Mar. 18: New Orleans 96, Minnesota 92
Mar. 21: Minnesota 97, New Orleans 93
Mar. 23: Minnesota 97, New Orleans 91

WBL SEMI-FINALS
Mar. 26: Minnesota 108, Iowa 87
Mar. 29: Minnesota 111, Iowa 128
Mar. 31: Iowa 95, Minnesota 92
Mar. 28: New York 104, San Francisco 97
Apr. 1: New York 91, San Francisco 90

WBL FINALS
Apr. 3: New York 128, Iowa 96
Apr. 5: New York 119, Iowa 99
Apr. 7: Iowa 119, New York 112
Apr. 9: New York 125, Iowa 114

MVPs: Molly Bolin, Iowa Cornets; Ann Meyers, New Jersey Gems

1980-81

Coastal Division	W	L	Pct.	GB
Dallas Diamonds	27	9	.750	—
New Jersey Gems	23	13	.639	4
New Orleans Pride	18	19	.486	9.5
San Francisco Pioneers	14	22	.389	13
New England Gulls*	2	10	.167	—
Central Division	**W**	**L**	**Pct.**	**GB**
Nebraska Wranglers	27	9	.750	—
Chicago Hustle	18	18	.500	9
St. Louis Streak	14	21	.400	12.5
Minnesota Fillies	7	28	.200	19.5

*New England disbanded during the season

WBL COSTAL DIVISION PLAYOFFS
Apr. 3: New Jersey 91, Dallas 86
Apr. 4: Dallas 92, New Jersey 85
Apr. 6: Dallas 107, New Jersey 88

WBL CENTRAL DIVISION PLAYOFFS
Apr. 4: Nebraska 97, Chicago 75
Apr. 5: Nebraska 81, Chicago 61

WBL FINALS
Apr. 14: Nebraska 89, Dallas 72
Apr. 15: Dallas 106, Nebraska 93
Apr. 17: Dallas 96, Nebraska 88
Apr. 18: Nebraska 94, Dallas 93
Apr. 20: Nebraska 99, Dallas 90

MVP: Nancy Lieberman, Dallas Diamonds

WOMEN'S AMERICAN BASKETBALL ASSOCIATION STATISTICS

Bill Byrne tried again with a fall league, with hopes of cashing in on the USA Olympic team's success in 1984. While some talented players played in the league (including Nancy Lieberman, Molly Bolin, Pam McGee and Paula McGee) most of the teams folded during the season. Chicago and Dallas survived to meet for the league title, which was won by Dallas.

	W	L	Pct.	GB
Dallas Diamonds	19	2	.905	—
Columbus Minks	12	5	.706	5
Atlanta Comets	7	6	.538	8
Virginia Wave	5	9	.357	10.5
Chicago Spirit	6	14	.300	12.5
Houston Shamrocks	3	14	.176	14

AMERICAN BASKETBALL LEAGUE (WOMEN) STATISTICS

Like the WABA, the American Basketball League started following the success of the American women's Olympic team on home soil. The ABL tipped off in October 1996, just months after the U.S. took gold in Atlanta. The league folded three seasons later, on December 23, 1998, prior to its All-Star game, unable to compete financially with the newly-formed WNBA.

1996-97

Eastern Conference	W	L	Pct.	GB
Columbus Quest	31	9	.775	—
Richmond Rage	21	19	.525	10
Atlanta Glory	18	22	.450	13
New England Blizzard	16	24	.400	15
Western Conference	**W**	**L**	**Pct.**	**GB**
Colorado Xplosion	25	15	.625	—
San Jose Lasers	18	22	.450	7
Seattle Reign	17	23	.425	8
Portland Power	14	26	.350	11

SEMI-FINALS
Feb. 23: Richmond 80, Colorado 77
Feb. 25: Richmond 82, Colorado 68

Feb. 23: Columbus 94, San Jose 69
Feb. 25: Columbus 81, San Jose 69

FINALS
Mar. 2: Columbus 90, Richmond 89

Mar. 4: Richmond 75, Columbus 62
Mar. 8: Richmond 72, Columbus 67
Mar. 9: Columbus 95, Richmond 84
Mar. 11: Columbus 77, Richmond 64
MVP: Nikki McCray, Columbus

New Pro Award: Crystal Robinson, Colorado
Defensive Player: Debbie Black, Colorado
Coach of the Year: Brian Agler, Columbus

1997-98

Eastern Conference	W	L	Pct.	GB
Columbus Quest	36	8	.818	—
New England Blizzard	24	20	.545	12
Atlanta Glory	15	29	.341	21
Philadelphia Rage	13	31	.295	23
Western Conference	**W**	**L**	**Pct.**	**GB**
Portland Power	27	17	.614	—
Long Beach StingRays	26	18	.591	1
Colorado Xplosion	21	23	.477	6
San Jose Lasers	21	23	.477	6
Seattle Reign	15	29	.341	12

SEMI-FINALS
Feb. 27: Long Beach 72, Portland 62
Mar. 1: Long Beach 70, Portland 69

Feb. 28: Columbus 94, San Jose 88
Mar. 1: Columbus 74, San Jose 62

FINALS
Mar. 8: Long Beach 65, Columbus 62
Mar. 9: Long Beach 71, Columbus 61
Mar. 11: Columbus 70, Long Beach 61
Mar. 13: Columbus 68, Long Beach 53
Mar. 15: Columbus 86, Long Beach 81
MVP: Natalie Williams, Portland

Rookie of the Year: Shalonda Enis, Seattle
Defensive Player: Yolanda Griffith, Long Beach
Coach of the Year: Lin Dunn, Portland
Finals MVP: Valerie Still, Columbus

1998-99

Eastern Conference	W	L	Pct.	GB
Columbus Quest	11	3	.786	—
Philadelphia Rage	9	5	.643	2
Chicago Condors	4	8	.333	6
Nashville Noise	4	11	.267	7.5
New England Blizzard	3	10	.231	7.5
Western Conference	**W**	**L**	**Pct.**	**GB**
Portland Power	9	4	.692	—
San Jose Lasers	9	6	.600	1
Seattle Reign	8	7	.533	2
Colorado Xplosion	5	8	.385	4

League disbanded Dec. 22, 1998

WOMEN'S NATIONAL BASKETBALL ASSOCIATION STATISTICS

1997

Eastern Conference	W	L	Pct.	GB
Houston Comets	18	10	.643	—
New York Liberty	17	11	.607	1
Charlotte Sting	15	13	.536	3
Cleveland Rockers	15	13	.536	3

Western Conference	W	L	Pct.	GB
Phoenix Mercury	16	12	.571	—
Los Angeles Sparks	14	14	.500	2
Sacramento Monarchs	10	18	.357	6
Utah Starzz	7	21	.250	9

SEMI-FINALS
Aug. 28: Houston 70, Charlotte 54
Aug. 28: New York 59, Phoenix 41
CHAMPIONSHIP GAME
Aug. 30: Houston 65, New York 51
MVP: Cynthia Cooper, Houston
Coach of the Year: Van Chancellor, Houston
Defensive Player: Teresa Weatherspoon, NY
Sportsmanship: Haixia Zheng, Los Angeles
Finals MVP: Cynthia Cooper, Houston

SCORING	GP	PTS	AVG
Cynthia Cooper, HOU	28	621	22.2
Ruthie Bolton-Holifield, SAC	23	447	19.4
Lisa Leslie, LOS	28	445	15.9
Wendy Palmer, UTH	28	443	15.8
Jennifer Gillom, PHO	28	440	15.7

REBOUNDING	GP	REB	AVG
Lisa Leslie, LOS	28	266	9.5
Wendy Palmer, UTH	28	225	8.0
Janice Braxton, CLE	25	189	7.6
Elena Baranova, UTH	28	207	7.4
Rebecca Lobo, NYL	28	202	7.2

FIELD GOAL PCT	GP	FGM	FGA	PCT
Zheng Haixia, LOS	28	110	178	.618
Trena Trice, NYL	28	51	92	.554
Linda Burgess, LOS	28	73	135	.541
Rushia Brown, CLE	28	64	123	.520
Greta Koss, UTH	13	15	29	.517

FREE THROW PCT.	GP	FTM	FTA	PCT
Judy Mosley-McAfee, SAC	12	11	11	1.000
Nicole Levesque, CHA	27	14	15	.933
Bridget Pettis, PHO	28	97	108	.898
Janeth Arcain, HOU	28	76	85	.894
Cynthia Cooper, HOU	28	172	199	.864

3-PT FIELD GOAL PCT.	GP	3FG	3FA	PCT
Milica Vukadinovic, CHA	1	1	1	1.000
Greta Koss, UTH	13	2	3	.667
Janice Braxton, CLE	25	5	10	.500
Rhonda Mapp, CHA	28	4	8	.500
Adrienne Johnson, CLE	25	2	4	.500
Linda Burgess, LOS	28	1	2	.500

ASSISTS	GP	AST	AVG
Teresa Weatherspoon, NYL	28	164	5.9
Penny Toler, LOS	28	143	5.1
Michele Timms, PHO	27	135	5.0
Chantel Tremitiere, SAC	28	135	4.8
Cynthia Cooper, HOU	28	131	4.7

BLOCKS	GP	BLK	AVG
Elena Baranova, UTH	28	63	2.3
Lisa Leslie, LOS	28	59	2.1
Vicky Bullett, CHA	28	55	2.0
Rebecca Lobo, NYL	28	51	1.8
Janice Braxton, CLE	25	28	1.1

STEALS	GP	STL	AVG
Teresa Weatherspoon, NYL	28	83	3.0
Michele Timms, PHO	27	71	2.6
Kim Perrot, HOU	28	69	2.5
Umeki Webb, PHO	28	68	2.4
Ruthie Bolton-Holifield, SAC	23	54	2.4

1998

Eastern Conference	W	L	Pct.	GB
Cleveland Rockers	20	10	.667	—
Charlotte Sting	18	12	.600	2
New York Liberty	18	12	.600	2
Detroit Shock	17	13	.567	3
Washington Mystics	3	27	.100	17

Western Conference	W	L	Pct.	GB
Houston Comets	27	3	.900	—
Phoenix Mercury	19	11	.633	8
Los Angeles Sparks	12	18	.400	15
Sacramento Monarchs	8	22	.267	19
Utah Starzz	8	22	.267	19

SEMI-FINALS
Phoenix 2, Cleveland 1
Aug. 22: Phoenix 78, Cleveland 68
Aug. 24: Cleveland 67, Phoenix 66
Aug. 25: Phoenix 71, Cleveland 60
Houston 2, Charlotte 0
Aug. 22: Houston 83, Charlotte 71
Aug. 24: Houston 77, Charlotte 61
CHAMPIONSHIP SERIES
Houston 2, Phoenix 1
Aug. 27: Phoenix 54, Houston 51
Aug. 29: Houston 74, Phoenix 69 OT
Sep. 1: Houston 80, Phoenix 71

MVP: Cynthia Cooper, Houston
Coach of the Year: Van Chancellor, Houston
Rookie of the Year: Tracy Reid, Charlotte
Defensive Player: Teresa Weatherspoon, NY
Sportsmanship: Suzie McConnell Serio, Cleveland
Finals MVP: Cynthia Cooper, Houston

SCORING	GP	PTS	AVG
Cynthia Cooper, HOU	30	680	22.7
Jennifer Gillom, PHO	30	624	20.8
Lisa Leslie, LA	28	549	19.6
Nikki McCray, WAS	29	512	17.7
Tamecka Dixon, LA	22	357	16.2

REBOUNDING	GP	REB	AVG
Lisa Leslie, LA	28	285	10.2
Cindy Brown, DET	30	301	10.0
Malgorzata Dydek, UTA	30	227	7.6
Jennifer Gillom, PHO	30	219	7.3
Tina Thompson, HOU	27	192	7.1

FIELD GOAL PCT	GP	FGM	FGA	PCT
Isabelle Fijalkowski, CLE	28	146	267	.547
Razija Mujanovic, DET	30	106	204	.520
Michelle Griffiths, PHO	30	93	184	.505
Janice Braxton, CLE	30	108	218	.495
Tracy Reid, CHA	30	151	310	.487

FREE THROW PCT.	GP	FTM	FTA	PCT
Sonia Chase, CHA	23	6	6	1.000
Erin Alexander, UTH	20	4	4	1.000
Nadine Domond, SAC	9	4	4	1.000
Sandy Brondello, SAC	30	96	104	.923
Andrea Congreaves, CHA	24	19	21	.905

3-PT FIELD GOAL PCT.	GP	3FG	3FA	PCT
Alicia Thompson, NYL	19	1	1	1.000
Albena Branzova, UTH	11	2	4	.500
Angela Hamblin, DET	6	1	2	.500
Yolanda Moore, HOU	30	1	2	.500
Dena Head, UTH	30	13	27	.481

ASSISTS	GP	AST	AVG
Ticha Penicheiro, SAC	30	224	7.5
Suzie McConnell Serio, CLE	28	178	6.4
Teresa Weatherspoon, NY	30	191	6.4
Michele Timms, PHO	30	158	5.3
Penny Toler, LA	30	143	4.8

BLOCKS	GP	BLK	AVG
Malgorzata Dydek, UTA	30	114	3.80
Lisa Leslie, LA	28	60	2.14
Tangela Smith, SAC	28	46	1.64
Vicky Bullett, CHA	30	46	1.53
Elena Baranova, UTA	20	30	1.10

STEALS	GP	STL	AVG
Teresa Weatherspoon, NY	30	100	3.33
Kim Perrot, HOU	30	84	2.80
Sheryl Swoopes, HOU	29	72	2.48
Ticha Penicheiro, SAC	30	67	2.23
Vickey Bullett, CHA	30	66	2.20

1999

Eastern Conference	W	L	Pct.	GB
New York Liberty	18	14	.560	—
Charlotte Sting	15	17	.469	3
Detroit Shock	15	17	.469	3
Orlando Miracle	15	17	.469	3
Washington Mystics	12	20	.375	6
Cleveland Rockers	7	25	.219	11

Western Conference	W	L	Pct.	GB
Houston Comets	26	6	.813	—
Los Angeles Sparks	20	12	.625	6
Sacramento Monarchs	19	13	.594	7
Phoenix Mercury	15	17	.469	11
Minnesota Lynx	15	17	.469	11
Utah Starzz	15	17	.469	11

SEMI-FINALS
New York 2, Charlotte 1
Aug. 27: Charlotte 78, New York 67
Aug. 29: New York 74, Charlotte 70
Aug. 30: New York 69, Charlotte 54
Houston 2, Los Angeles 1
Aug. 26: Los Angeles 75, Houston 60
Aug. 29: Houston 83, Los Angeles 55
Aug. 30: Houston 72, Los Angeles 52
CHAMPIONSHIP SERIES
Houston 2, New York 1
Sep. 3: Houston 73, New York 60
Sep. 4: New York 68, Houston 67
Sep. 5: Houston 59, New York 47

MVP: Yolanda Griffith, Sacramento
Coach of the Year: Van Chancellor, Houston
Rookie of the Year: Chamique Holdsclaw, Washington
Defensive Player: Yolanda Griffith, Sacramento
Sportsmanship: Dawn Staley, Charlotte
Finals MVP: Cynthia Cooper, Houston

SCORING	GP	PTS	AVG
Cynthia Cooper, HOU	31	686	22.1
Yolanda Griffith, SAC	29	545	18.8
Sheryl Swoopes, HOU	32	585	18.3
Natalie Williams, UTA	28	504	18.0
Nikki McCray, WAS	32	561	17.5

REBOUNDING	GP	REB	AVG
Yolanda Griffith, SAC	29	329	11.3
Natalie Williams, UTA	28	257	9.2
Chamique Holdsclaw, WAS	31	246	7.9
Lisa Leslie, LA	32	248	7.8
Taj McWilliams, ORL	32	239	7.5

FIELD GOAL PCT	GP	FGM	FGA	PCT
Muriel Page, WAS	32	105	183	.574
Yolanda Griffith, SAC	29	200	370	.541
Alisa Burras, CLE	31	103	191	.539
Latasha Byears, SAC	32	130	242	.537
DeLisha Milton, LA	32	125	236	.530

FREE THROW PCT.	GP	FTM	FTA	PCT
Eva Nemcova, CLE	31	62	63	.984
Dawn Staley, CHA	32	85	91	.934
Cynthia Cooper, HOU	31	204	229	.891
Korie Hlede, UTA	32	72	82	.878
Penny Toler, LA	30	39	45	.867

3-PT FIELD GOAL PCT.	GP	FGM	FGA	PCT
Jennifer Azzi, DET	28	30	58	.517
Sandy Brondello, DET	32	37	76	.487
Taj McWilliams, ORL	32	20	45	.444
Crystal Robinson, NY	32	76	174	.437
Gordana Grubin, LA	32	40	93	.430

ASSISTS	GP	AST	AVG
Ticha Penicheiro, SAC	32	226	7.1
Teresa Weatherspoon, NY	32	205	6.4
Dawn Staley, CHA	32	177	5.5
Cynthia Cooper, HOU	31	162	5.2
Debbie Black, UTA	32	161	5.0
Michele Timms, PHO	30	151	5.0

BLOCKS	GP	BLK	AVG
Malgorzata Dydek, UTA	32	77	2.41
Maria Stepnova, PHO	32	62	1.94
Yolanda Griffith, SAC	29	54	1.86
Lisa Leslie, LA	32	49	1.53
Sheryl Swoopes, HOU	32	46	1.44

STEALS

STEALS	GP	STL	AVG
Yolanda Griffith, SAC	29	73	2.52
Teresa Weatherspoon, NY	32	78	2.44
Debbie Black, UTA	32	77	2.41
Sheryl Swoopes, HOU	32	76	2.38
Nykesha Sales, ORL	32	69	2.16

2000

Eastern Conference	W	L	Pct.	GB
New York Liberty	20	12	.625	—
Cleveland Rockers	17	15	.531	3
Orlando Miracle	16	16	.500	4
Washington Mystics	14	18	.438	6
Detroit Shock	14	18	.438	6
Miami Sol	13	19	.406	7
Indiana Fever	9	23	.281	11
Charlotte Sting	8	24	.250	12

Western Conference	W	L	Pct.	GB
Los Angeles Sparks	28	4	.875	—
Houston Comets	27	5	.844	1
Sacramento Monarchs	21	11	.656	7
Phoenix Mercury	20	12	.625	8
Utah Starzz	18	14	.563	10
Minnesota Lynx	15	17	.469	13
Portland Fire	10	22	.313	18
Seattle Storm	6	26	.188	22

EASTERN CONFERENCE
CONFERENCE SEMI-FINALS
New York 2, Washington 0
- Aug. 12: New York 72, Washington 63
- Aug. 14: New York 78, Washington 57

Cleveland 2, Orlando 1
- Aug. 11: Orlando 62, Cleveland 55
- Aug. 13: Cleveland 63, Orlando 54
- Aug. 15: Cleveland 72, Orlando 43

CONFERENCE FINAL
New York 2, Cleveland 1
- Aug. 17: Cleveland 56, New York 43
- Aug. 20: New York 51, Cleveland 45
- Aug. 21: New York 81, Cleveland 67

WESTERN CONFERENCE
CONFERENCE SEMI-FINALS
Los Angeles 2, Phoenix 0
- Aug. 11: Los Angeles 86, Phoenix 71
- Aug. 13: Los Angeles 101, Phoenix 76

Houston 2, Sacramento 0
- Aug. 12: Houston 72, Sacramento 64
- Aug. 14: Houston 75, Sacramento 70

CONFERENCE FINAL
Houston 2, Los Angeles 0
- Aug. 17: Houston 77, Los Angeles 56
- Aug. 20: Houston 74, Los Angeles 69

WNBA CHAMPIONSHIP SERIES
Houston 2, New York 0
- Aug. 24: Houston 59, New York 52
- Aug. 26: Houston 79, New York 73, OT

MVP: Sheryl Swoopes, Houston
Coach of the Year: Michael Cooper, Los Angeles
Rookie of the Year: Betty Lennox, Minnesota
Defensive Player: Sheryl Swoopes, Houston
Sportsmanship: Suzie McConnell Serio, Cleveland
Most Improved: Tari Phillips, New York
Finals MVP: Cynthia Cooper, Houston

SCORING	GP	PTS	AVG
Sheryl Swoopes, HOU	31	643	20.7
Katie Smith, MIN	32	646	20.2
Brandy Reed, PHO	32	608	19.0
Natalie Williams, UTA	29	543	18.7
Lisa Leslie, LA	32	570	17.8

REBOUNDING	GP	REB	AVG
Natalie Williams, UTA	29	336	11.6
Yolanda Griffith, SAC	32	331	10.3
Lisa Leslie, LA	32	306	9.6
Tari Phillips, NY	31	247	8.0
Tina Thompson, HOU	32	245	7.7

FIELD GOAL PCT	GP	FGM	FGA	PCT
Muriel Page, WAS	32	131	222	.590
Kara Wolters, IND	31	148	264	.561
Yolanda Griffith, SAC	32	193	361	.535
Taj McWilliams, ORL	32	173	330	.524
Alicia Thompson, IND	31	131	255	.514

FREE THROW PCT.	GP	FTM	FTA	PCT
Jennifer Azzi, UTA	15	40	43	.930
Elena Tornikidou, DET	32	85	93	.914
Brandy Reed, PHO	32	128	142	.901
Becky Hammon, NY	32	61	69	.884
Vickie Johnson, NY	31	67	76	.882

3-PT FIELD GOAL PCT.	GP	3FG	3FA	PCT
Korie Hlede, UTA	31	25	58	.431
Tina Thompson, HOU	32	55	132	.417
Eva Nemcova, CLE	14	29	71	.408
Monica Maxwell, IND	32	62	156	.397
Betty Lennox, MIN	32	55	139	.396

ASSISTS	GP	AST	AVG
Ticha Penicheiro, SAC	30	236	7.9
Teresa Weatherspoon, NY	32	205	6.4
Dawn Staley, CHA	32	190	5.9
Shannon Johnson, ORL	32	169	5.3
Andrea Nagy, WAS	23	118	5.1

BLOCKS	GP	BLK	AVG
Margo Dydek, UTA	32	96	3.00
Lisa Leslie, LA	32	74	2.31
Tangela Smith, SAC	32	64	2.00
Cintia Dos Santos, ORL	32	63	1.97
Yolanda Griffith, SAC	32	61	1.91

STEALS	GP	STL	AVG
Sheryl Swoopes, HOU	31	87	2.81
Yolanda Griffith, SAC	32	83	2.59
Rita Williams, IND	32	76	2.38
Ticha Penicheiro, SAC	30	70	2.33
Brandy Reed, PHO	32	66	2.06

2001

Eastern Conference	W	L	Pct.	GB
Cleveland Rockers	22	10	.688	—
New York Liberty	21	11	.656	1
Miami Sol	20	12	.625	2
Charlotte Sting	18	14	.563	4
Orlando Miracle	13	19	.406	9
Indiana Fever	10	22	.313	12
Detroit Shock	10	22	.313	12
Washington Mystics	10	22	.313	12

Western Conference	W	L	Pct.	GB
Los Angeles Sparks	28	4	.875	—
Sacramento Monarchs	20	12	.625	8
Utah Starzz	19	13	.594	9
Houston Comets	19	13	.594	9
Phoenix Mercury	13	19	.406	15
Minnesota Lynx	12	20	.375	16
Portland Fire	11	21	.344	17
Seattle Storm	10	22	.313	18

EASTERN CONFERENCE
CONFERENCE SEMI-FINALS
Charlotte 2, Cleveland 1
- Aug. 16: Charlotte 53, Cleveland 46
- Aug. 18: Cleveland 69, Charlotte 51
- Aug. 20: Charlotte 72, Cleveland 64

New York 2, Miami 1
- Aug. 17: New York 62, Miami 46
- Aug. 19: Miami 53, New York 50
- Aug. 21: New York 72, Miami 61

CONFERENCE FINAL
Charlotte 2, New York 1
- Aug. 24: New York 61, Charlotte 57
- Aug. 26: Charlotte 62, New York 53
- Aug. 27: Charlotte 48, New York 44

WESTERN CONFERENCE
CONFERENCE SEMI-FINALS
Los Angeles 2, Houston 0
- Aug. 18: Los Angeles 64, Houston 59
- Aug. 20: Los Angeles 70, Houston 58

Sacramento 2, Utah 0
- Aug. 17: Sacramento 89, Utah 65
- Aug. 19: Sacramento 71, Utah 66

CONFERENCE FINAL
Los Angeles 2, Sacramento 1
- Aug. 24: Los Angeles 74, Sacramento 73
- Aug. 26: Sacramento 80, Los Angeles 60
- Aug. 27: Los Angeles 93, Sacramento 62

WNBA CHAMPIONSHIP SERIES
Los Angeles 2, Charlotte 0
- Aug. 30: Los Angeles 75, Charlotte 66
- Sep. 1: Los Angeles 82, Charlotte 54

MVP: Lisa Leslie, Los Angeles
Coach of the Year: Dan Hughes, Cleveland
Rookie of the Year: Jackie Stiles, Portland
Defensive Player: Debbie Black, Miami
Sportsmanship: Sue Wicks, New York
Most Improved: Janeth Arcain, Houston
Finals MVP: Lisa Leslie, Los Angeles

SCORING	GP	PTS	AVG
Katie Smith, MIN	32	739	23.1
Lisa Leslie, LA	31	606	19.5
Tina Thompson, HOU	30	579	19.3
Janeth Arcain, HOU	32	591	18.5
Chamique Holdsclaw, WAS	29	486	16.8

REBOUNDING	GP	REB	AVG
Yolanda Griffith, SAC	32	357	11.2
Natalie Williams, UTA	31	308	9.9
Lisa Leslie, LA	31	298	9.6
Chamique Holdsclaw, WAS	29	256	8.8
Tari Phillips, NY	32	257	8.0

FIELD GOAL PCT	GP	FGM	FGA	PCT
Latasha Byears, LA	32	133	221	.602
Ann Wauters, CLE	24	87	153	.569
Yolanda Griffith, SAC	32	192	368	.522
Rushia Brown, CLE	30	101	195	.518
Tari Phillips, NY	32	208	410	.507
Maria Stepanova, PHO	32	143	282	.507

FREE THROW PCT.	GP	FTM	FTA	PCT
Elena Baranova, Miami	32	66	71	.930
Allison Feaster, CHA	32	58	63	.921
Jennifer Azzi, UTA	32	88	96	.917
Janeth Arcain, HOU	32	135	150	.900
Katie Smith, MIN	32	246	275	.895
Dawn Staley, CHA	32	51	57	.895

3-PT FIELD GOAL PCT.	GP	3FG	3FA	PCT
Jennifer Azzi, UTA	32	38	74	.514
Ukari Figgs, LA	32	54	117	.462
Edna Campbell, SAC	32	43	94	.457
Elena Tornikidou, DET	32	22	49	.449
Andrea Stinson, CHA	32	29	65	.446

ASSISTS	GP	AST	AVG
Ticha Penicheiro, SAC	23	172	7.5
Teresa Weatherspoon, NY	32	203	6.3
Dawn Staley, CHA	32	179	5.6
Jennifer Azzi, UTA	32	171	5.3
Kristen Veal, PHO	29	125	4.3

BLOCKS	GP	BLK	AVG
Margo Dydek, UTA	32	113	3.53
Lisa Leslie, LA	31	71	2.29
Lauren Jackson, SEA	29	64	2.21
Maria Stepanova, PHO	32	64	2.00
Vicky Bullett, WAS	32	58	1.81

STEALS	GP	STL	AVG
Debbie Black, Miami	32	82	2.56
Rita Williams, IND	32	72	2.25
Nykesha Sales, ORL	32	70	2.19
Coquese Washington, HOU	32	69	2.16
Yolanda Griffith, SAC	32	63	1.97

2002

Eastern Conference	W	L	Pct.	GB
New York Liberty	18	14	.563	—
Charlotte Sting	18	14	.563	—
Washington Mystics	17	15	.531	1
Indiana Fever	16	16	.500	2
Orlando Miracle	16	16	.500	2
Miami Sol	15	17	.469	3
Cleveland Rockers	10	22	.313	8
Detroit Shock	9	23	.281	9

Western Conference	W	L	Pct.	GB
Los Angeles Sparks	25	7	.781	—
Houston Comets	24	8	.750	1
Utah Starzz	20	12	.625	5
Seattle Storm	17	15	.531	8
Portland Fire	16	16	.500	9
Sacramento Monarchs	14	18	.438	11
Phoenix Mercury	11	21	.344	14
Minnesota Lynx	10	22	.313	15

EASTERN CONFERENCE
CONFERENCE SEMI-FINALS
New York 2, Indiana 1
- Aug. 16: Indiana 73, New York 55
- Aug. 18: New York 84, Indiana 65
- Aug. 20: New York 75, Indiana 60

Washington 2, Charlotte 0
Aug. 15: Washington 74, Charlotte 62
Aug. 17: Washington 62, Charlotte 59
CONFERENCE FINAL
New York 2, Mystics 1
Aug. 22: Washington 79, New York 74
Aug. 24: New York 96, Washington 79
Aug. 25: New York 64, Washington 57
WESTERN CONFERENCE
CONFERENCE SEMI-FINALS
Los Angeles 2, Storm 0
Aug. 15: Los Angeles 78, Seattle 61
Aug. 17: Los Angeles 69, Seattle 59
Utah 2, Houston 1
Aug. 17: Utah 66, Houston 59
Aug. 18: Houston 83, Utah 77
Aug. 20: Utah 75, Houston 72
CONFERENCE FINAL
Los Angeles 2, Utah 0
Aug. 22: Los Angeles 75, Utah 67
Aug. 24: Los Angeles 103, Utah 77
WNBA CHAMPIONSHIP SERIES
Los Angeles 2, New York 0
Aug. 29: Los Angeles 71, New York 63
Aug. 31: Los Angeles 69, New York 66

MVP: Sheryl Swoopes, Houston
Coach of the Year: Marianne Stanley, Washington
Rookie of the Year: Tamika Catchings, Indiana
Defensive Player: Sheryl Swoopes , Houston
Sportsmanship: Jennifer Gillom, Phoenix
Most Improved: Coco Miller, Washington
Finals MVP: Lisa Leslie, Los Angeles

SCORING	GP	PTS	AVG
Chamique Holdsclaw, WAS	20	397	19.9
Tamika Catchings, IND	32	594	18.6
Sheryl Swoopes, HOU	32	592	18.5
Lauren Jackson, SEA	28	482	17.2
Lisa Leslie, LA	31	523	16.9

REBOUNDING	GP	REB	AVG
Chamique Holdsclaw, WAS	20	232	11.6
Lisa Leslie, LA	31	322	10.4
Margo Dydek, UTA	30	262	8.7
Tamika Catchings, IND	32	276	8.6
Natalie Williams, UTA	31	255	8.2

FIELD GOAL PCT	GP	FGM	FGA	PCT
Alisa Burras, POR	32	117	186	.629
Tamika Williams, MIN	31	124	221	.561
Ann Wauters, CLE	28	120	217	.553
Tammy Sutton-Brown, CHA	32	129	243	.531
Yolanda Griffith, SAC	17	93	179	.520

FREE THROW PCT.	GP	FTM	FTA	PCT
Sue Bird, SEA	32	102	112	.911
Ukari Figgs, POR	31	59	65	.908
Janeth Arcain, HOU	32	98	111	.883
Katie Douglas, ORL	32	58	67	.866
Tamara Moore, MIN	31	54	63	.857

3-PT FIELD GOAL PCT.	GP	3FG	3FA	PCT
Kelly Miller, CHA	32	24	51	.471
Jennifer Azzi, UTA	32	41	92	.446
Coquese Washington, IND	32	22	52	.423
Vickie Johnson, NY	31	32	76	.421
DeLisha Milton, LA	32	21	50	.420

ASSISTS	GP	AST	AVG
Ticha Penicheiro, SAC	24	192	8.0
Sue Bird, SEA	32	191	6.0
Teresa Weatherspoon, NY	32	181	5.7
Shannon Johnson, ORL	31	163	5.3
Dawn Staley, CHA	32	164	5.1

BLOCKS	GP	BLK	AVG
Margo Dydek, UTA	30	107	3.57
Lisa Leslie, LA	31	90	2.90
Lauren Jackson, SEA	28	81	2.89
Ruth Riley, Miami	26	41	1.58
Tangela Smith, SAC	32	46	1.44

STEALS	GP	STL	AVG
Tamika Catchings, IND	32	94	2.94
Sheryl Swoopes, HOU	32	88	2.75
Ticha Penicheiro, SAC	24	64	2.67
Sheri Sam, Miami	32	69	2.16
Nykesha Sales, ORL	32	60	1.88

2003

Eastern Conference	W	L	Pct.	GB
Detroit Shock	25	9	.735	—
Charlotte Sting	18	16	.529	7
Connecticut Sun	18	16	.529	7
Cleveland Rockers	17	17	.500	8
Indiana Fever	16	18	.471	9
New York Liberty	16	18	.471	9
Washington Mystics	9	25	.265	16

Western Conference	W	L	Pct.	GB
Los Angeles Sparks	24	10	.706	—
Houston Comets	20	14	.588	4
Sacramento Monarchs	19	15	.559	5
Minnesota Lynx	18	16	.529	6
Seattle Storm	18	16	.529	6
San Antonio Silver Stars	12	22	.353	12
Phoenix Mercury	8	26	.235	16

EASTERN CONFERENCE
CONFERENCE SEMI-FINALS
Detroit 2, Cleveland 1
Aug. 29: Detroit 76, Cleveland 74
Aug. 31: Cleveland 66, Detroit 59
Sep. 2: Detroit 77, Cleveland 63
Connecticut 2, Charlotte 0
Aug. 28: Connecticut 68, Charlotte 66
Aug. 30: Connecticut 68, Charlotte 62
CONFERENCE FINAL
Detroit 2, Connecticut 0
Sep. 5: Detroit 73, Connecticut 63
Sep. 7: Detroit 79, Connecticut 73
WESTERN CONFERENCE
CONFERENCE SEMI-FINALS
Los Angeles 2, Minnesota 1
Aug. 28: Minnesota74, Los Angeles 72
Aug. 30: Los Angeles 80, Minnesota69
Sep. 1: Los Angeles 74, Minnesota64
Sacramento 2, Houston 1
Aug. 29: Sacramento 65, Houston 59
Aug. 31: Houston 69, Sacramento 48
Sep. 2: Sacramento 70, Houston 68
CONFERENCE FINAL
Los Angeles 2, Sacramento 1
Sep. 5: Sacramento 77, Los Angeles 69
Sep. 7: Los Angeles 79, Sacramento 54
Sep. 8: Los Angeles 66, Sacramento 63
WNBA CHAMPIONSHIP SERIES
Detroit 2, Los Angeles 1
Sep. 12: Los Angeles 75 Detroit 63
Sep. 14: Detroit 62, Los Angeles 61
Sep. 16: Detroit 83, Los Angeles 78

MVP: Lauren Jackson, Seattle
Coach of the Year: Bill Laimbeer, Detroit
Rookie of the Year: Cheryl Ford, Detroit
Defensive Player: Sheryl Swoopes, Houston
Sportsmanship: Edna Campbell, Sacramento
Most Improved: Michelle Snow, Houston
Assist Award: Ticha Penicheiro, Sacramento
Finals MVP: Ruth Riley, Detroit

SCORING	GP	PTS	AVG
Lauren Jackson, SEA	33	698	21.2
Chamique Holdsclaw, WAS	27	554	20.5
Tamika Catchings, IND	34	671	19.7
Lisa Leslie, LOS	23	421	18.3
Katie Smith, MIN	34	620	18.2

REBOUNDING	GP	REB	AVG
Chamique Holdsclaw, WAS	27	294	10.9
Cheryl Ford, DET	32	334	10.4
Lisa Leslie, LOS	23	232	10.1
Lauren Jackson, SEA	33	307	9.3
Tari Phillips, NYL	33	280	8.5

FIELD GOAL PCT	GP	FGM	FGA	PCT
Tamika Williams, MIN	34	129	193	.668
Michelle Snow, HOU	34	126	253	.498
Ruth Riley, DET	34	115	231	.498
Yolanda Griffith, SAC	34	161	332	.485
Natalie Williams, IND	34	176	363	.485

FREE THROW PCT.	GP	FTM	FTA	PCT
Stephanie White, IND	28	45	48	.938
Chamique Holdsclaw, WAS	27	140	155	.903
Tamecka Dixon, LOS	30	82	92	.891
Sheryl Swoopes, HOU	31	110	124	.887
Sue Bird, SEA	34	61	69	.884

3-PT FIELD GOAL PCT.	GP	3FG	3FA	PCT
Becky Hammon, NYL	11	23	49	.469
Sandy Brondello, SEA	34	21	48	.438
Nikki Teasley, LOS	34	70	165	.424
Kelly Miller, CHA	34	22	52	.423
Deanna Nolan, DET	32	48	114	.421

ASSISTS	GP	AST	AVG
Ticha Penicheiro, SAC	34	229	6.7
Sue Bird, SEA	34	221	6.5
Nikki Teasley, LOS	34	214	6.3
Shannon Johnson, CON	34	196	5.8
Dawn Staley, CHA	34	174	5.1

BLOCKS	GP	BLK	AVG
Margo Dydek, SAN	34	97	2.9
Lisa Leslie, LOS	23	63	2.7
Lauren Jackson, SEA	33	64	1.9
Michelle Snow, HOU	34	62	1.8
Ruth Riley, DET	34	58	1.7

STEALS	GP	STL	AVG
Sheryl Swoopes, HOU	31	77	2.5
Tamika Catchings, IND	34	72	2.1
Ticha Penicheiro, SAC	34	61	1.8
Marie Ferdinand, SAN	34	58	1.7
Tari Phillips, NYL	33	56	1.7
Yolanda Griffith, SAC	34	57	1.7
Adrian Williams, PHO	34	57	1.7

WNBA Draft

1997 WNBA Draft
Elite Draft - First Round
1. Utah: Dena Head
2. Cleveland: Isabelle Fijalkowski
3. Charlotte: Rhonda Mapp
4. New York: Kym Hampton
5. Houston: Wanda Guyton
6. Sacramento: Judy Mosley-McAfee
7. Phoenix: Bridget Pettis
8. Los Angeles: Daedra Charles
Elite Draft - Second Round
9. Utah: Wendy Palmer
10. Cleveland: Lynette Woodard
11. Charlotte: Michi Atkins
12. New York: Vickie Johnson
13. Houston: Janeth Arcain
14. Sacramento: Mikiko Hagiwara
15. Phoenix: Nancy Lieberman-Cline
16. Los Angeles: Haixia Zheng
First Round
1. Houston: Tina Thompson
2. Sacramento: Pamela McGee
3. Los Angeles: Jamila Wideman
4. Cleveland: Eva Nemcova
5. Utah: Tammi Reiss
6. New York: Sue Wicks
7. Charlotte: Tora Suber
8. Phoenix: Toni Foster
Second Round
9. Phoenix: Tia Jackson
10. Charlotte: Sharon Manning
11. New York: Sophia Witherspoon
12. Utah: Jessie Hicks
13. Cleveland: Merlakia Jones
14. Los Angeles: Tamecka Dixon
15. Sacramento: Denique Graves
16. Houston: Tammy Jackson
Third Round
17. Houston: Racquel Spurlock
18. Sacramento: Chantel Tremitiere
19. Los Angeles: Katrina Colleton
20. Cleveland: Tina Nicholson
21. Utah: Raegan Scott
22. New York: Trena Trice
23. Charlotte: Debra Williams
24. Phoenix: Umeki Webb
Fourth Round
25. Phoenix: Monique Ambers
26. Charlotte: Andrea Congreaves
27. New York: Kisha Ford
28. Utah: Kim Williams
29. Cleveland: Anita Maxwell
30. Los Angeles: Travesa Gant
31. Sacramento: Tajama Abraham
32. Houston: Catarina Pollini

1998 WNBA Draft
First Round
1. Utah: Margo Dydek
2. Sacramento: Ticha Penicheiro
3. Washington: Murriel Page
4. Detroit: Korie Hlede
5. Los Angeles: Allison Feaster
6. Cleveland: Cindy Blodgett
7. Charlotte: Tracy Reid
8. Phoenix: Maria Stepanova
9. New York: Alicia Thompson
10. Houston: Polina Tzekova
Second Round
11. Utah: Olympia Scott
12. Sacramento: Tangela Smith
13. Washington: Rita Williams
14. Detroit: Rachael Sporn
15. Los Angeles: Octavia Blue
16. Cleveland: Suzie McConnell Serio
17. Charlotte: Christy Smith
18. Phoenix: Andrea Kuklova
19. New York: Nadine Domond
20. Houston: Nyree Roberts
Third Round
21. Utah: LaTonya Johnson
22. Sacramento: Quacy Barnes
23. Washington: Angela Hamblin
24. Detroit: Gergana Branzova
25. Los Angeles: Rehema Stephens
26. Cleveland: Tanja Kostic
27. Charlotte: Pollyanna Johns
28. Phoenix: Brandy Reed
29. New York: Albena Branzova
30. Houston: Amaya Valdemoro
Fourth Round
31. Utah: Tricia Bader
32. Sacramento: Adia Barnes
33. Washington: Angela Jackson
34. Detroit: Sandy Brondello
35. Los Angeles: Erica Kienast
36. Cleveland: Tammye Jenkins
37. Charlotte: Sonia Chase
38. Phoenix: Karen Wilkins
39. New York: Vanessa Nygaard
40. Houston: Monica Lamb

1999 WNBA Draft
First Round
1. Washington: Chamique Holdsclaw
2. Sacramento: Yolanda Griffith
3. Utah: Natalie Williams
4. Los Angeles: DeLisha Milton
5. Detroit: Jennifer Azzi
6. New York: Crystal Robinson
7. Minnesota: Tonya Edwards
8. Orlando: Tari Phillips
9. Charlotte: Dawn Staley
10. Phoenix: Edna Campbell
11. Cleveland: Chasity Melvin
12. Houston: Natalia Zasulskaya
Second Round
13. Washington: Shalonda Enis
14. Sacramento: Kedra Holland-Corn
15. Utah: Debbie Black
16. Los Angeles: Clarisse Machanguana
17. Detroit: Val Whiting
18. New York: Michele VanGorp
19. Minnesota: Trisha Fallon
20. Orlando: Sheri Sam
21. Charlotte: Stephanie McCarty
22. Phoenix: Clarissa Davis-Wrightsil
23. Cleveland: Mery Andrade
24. Houston: Sonja Henning
Third Round
25. Washington: Andrea Nagy
26. Sacramento: Kate Starbird
27. Utah: Adrienne Goodson
28. Los Angeles: Ukari Figgs
29. Detroit: Dominique Canty
30. New York: Tamika Whitmore
31. Minnesota: Andrea Lloyd Curry
32. Orlando: Taj McWilliams
33. Charlotte: Charlotte Smith
34. Phoenix: Lisa Harrison
35. Cleveland: Tracy Henderson

36. Houston: Kara Wolters
Fourth Round
37. Washington: Jennifer Whittle
38. Sacramento: Amy Herrig
39. Utah: Dalma Ivanyi
40. Los Angeles: La'Keshia Frett
41. Detroit: Astou Ndiaye
42. New York: Carolyn Jones-Young
43. Minnesota: Sonja Tate
44. Orlando: Carla McGhee
45. Charlotte: Angie Braziel
46. Phoenix: Amanda Wilson
47. Cleveland: Kellie Jolly Harper
48. Houston: Jennifer Rizzotti
49. Minnesota: Angie Potthoff
50. Orlando: Elaine Powell

2000 WNBA Draft
First Round
1. Cleveland: Ann Wauters
2. Washington: Tausha Mills
3. Detroit: Edwina Brown
4. Orlando: Cintia dos Santos
5. Minnesota: Grace Daley
6. Minnesota: Betty Lennox
7. Portland: Lynn Pride
8. Detroit: Tamicha Jackson
9. Seattle: Kamila Vodichkova
10. Minnesota: Maylana Martin
11. Charlotte: Summer Erb
12. Utah: Naomi Mulitauaopele
13. New York: Olga Firsova
14. Sacramento: Katy Steding
15. Los Angeles: Nicole Kubik
16. Houston: Elen Chakirova
Second Round
17. Cleveland: Helen Darling
18. Washington: Tonya Washington
19. Miami: Jameka Jones
20. Orlando: Jannon Roland
21. Phoenix: Adrain Williams
22. Minnesota: Marla Brumfield
23. Portland: Stacey Thomas
24. Minnesota: Keitha Dickerson
25. Seattle: Charisse Sampson
26. Indiana: Jurgita Streimikyte
27. Charlotte: Tiffany Travis
28. Detroit: Madinah Slaise
29. New York: Desiree Francis
30. Sacramento: Stacy Clinesmith
31. Los Angeles: Paige Sauer
32. Houston: Andrea Garner
Third Round
33. Cleveland: Monique Morehouse
34. Charlotte: Jill Morton
35. Utah: Stacy Frese
36. Orlando: Shawnetta Stewart
37. Phoenix: Tauja Catchings
38. Minnesota: Phylesha Whaley
39. Portland: Maxann Reese
40. Miami: Milena Flores
41. Seattle: Kirra Jordan
42. Indiana: Usha Gilmore
43. Charlotte: Peppi Browne
44. Detroit: Chavonne Hammond
45. New York: Jessica Bibby
46. Sacramento: Rhonda Banchero
47. Los Angeles: Marte Alexander
48. Houston: Latavia Coleman*
Fourth Round
49. Cleveland: Sophie Von Saldern
50. Indiana: Latina Davis*
51. Utah: Kristen Rasmussen
52. Orlando: Romana Hamzova
53. Phoenix: Shantia Owens**
54. Minnesota: Jana Lichnerova
55. Portland: Rhonda LaCher Smith
56. Minnesota: Shanele Stires
57. Seattle: Katrina Hibbert
58. Indiana: Renee Robinson*
59. Charlotte: Shaka Massey
60. Detroit: Cal Bouchard
61. New York: Natalie Porter
62. Sacramento: Jessica Zinobile
63. Los Angeles: Nicky McCrimmon
64. Houston: Abbie Willenborg

* Houston traded Latavia Coleman to Indiana in exchange for Latina Davis and Renee Robinson.
** Phoenix traded Shantia Owens to Miami in exchange for a fourth-round pick in the 2001 WNBA Draft.

2001 WNBA Draft
First Round
1. Seattle: Lauren Jackson
2. Charlotte: Kelly Miller
3. Indiana: Tamika Catchings
4. Portland: Jackie Stiles
5. Miami: Ruth Riley
6. Detroit: Deanna Nolan
7. Minnesota: Svetlana Abrosimova
8. Utah: Marie Ferdinand
9. Washington: Coco Miller
10. Orlando: Katie Douglas
11. Cleveland: Penny Taylor
12. Portland: LaQuanda Barksdale
13. Phoenix: Kristen Veal
14. Indiana: Kelly Schumacher
15. Houston: Amanda Lassiter
16. Los Angeles: Camille Cooper
Second Round
17. Seattle: Semeka Randall
18. Charlotte: Tammy Sutton-Brown
19. Indiana: Niele Ivey
20. Portland: Jenny Mowe
21. Miami: Georgia Schweitzer*
22. Detroit: Jae Kingi
23. Minnesota: Erin Buescher
24. Utah: Michaela Pavlickova
25. Washington: Tamara Stocks
26. Orlando: Brooke Wyckoff
27. Cleveland: Jaynetta Saunders
28. Minnesota: Janell Burse
29. Phoenix: Ilona Korstine
30. Sacramento: Jackie Moore
31. Houston: Tynesha Lewis
32. Los Angeles: Nicole Levandusky
Third Round
33. Houston: ShaRae Mansfield
34. Charlotte: Jennifer Phillips
35. Indiana: Marlena Williams
36. Portland: Rasheeda Clark
37. Miami: Levys Torres
38. Detroit: Svetlana Volnaya
39. Minnesota: Tombi Bell
40. Utah: Shea Ralph
41. Washington: Jamie Lewis
42. Orlando: Jaclyn Johnson
43. Cleveland: Angelina Wolvert
44. Washington: Yelena Karpova
45. Phoenix: Tere Williams
46. Sacramento: Maren Walseth
47. Houston: Shala Crawford
48. Los Angeles: Kelley Siemon
Fourth Round
49. Seattle: Juana Brown
50. Charlotte: Reshea Bristol
51. Indiana: April Brown
52. Portland: Natasha Pointer
53. Phoenix: Carolyn Moos
54. Detroit: Kelly Santos
55. Minnesota: Megan Taylor
56. Utah: Cara Consuegra
57. New York: Taru Tuukkanen
58. Orlando: Anne Thorius
59. Cleveland: Erin Batth
60. New York: Tara Mitchem
61. Phoenix: Megan Franza
62. Sacramento: Katie Smrcka-Duffy
63. Houston: Kristen Clement
64. Los Angeles: Beth Record
* Miami traded 21st pick Georgia Schweitzer to Minnesota in exchange for Marla Brumfield.

2002 WNBA Draft
First round
1. Seattle: Sue Bird
2. Detroit: Swin Cash
3. Washington: Stacey Dales-Schuman
4. Washington: Asjha Jones
5. Portland: Nikki Teasley
6. Minnesota: Tamika Williams
7. Charlotte: Sheila Lambert
8. Cleveland: Deanna Jackson
9. Charlotte: Shaunzinski Gortman
10. Houston: Michelle Snow
11. Utah: Danielle Crockrom
12. Sacramento: Hamchétou Maïga
13. Indiana: Tawana McDonald
14. Utah: LaNeisha Caufield
15. Miami: Tamara Moore
16. Los Angeles: Rosalind Ross
Second round
17. Indiana: Zuzi Klimesova
18. Detroit: Lenae Williams
19. Seattle: Lucienne Berthieu
20. Detroit: Ayana Walker
21. Detroit: Jill Chapman
22. Detroit: Kathy Wambe
23. Orlando: Davalyn Cunningham
24. Cleveland: Brandi McCain
25. Phoenix: Tootie Shaw
26. New York: Linda Fröhlich
27. Utah: Andrea Gardner
28. Seattle: Felicia Ragland
29. Miami: Lindsey Yamasaki
30. Los Angeles: Gergana Slavtcheva
31. Cleveland: Angie Welle
32. Los Angeles: Jackie Higgins
Third round
33. Washington: LaNisha Cartwel
34. Indiana: Kelly Komara
35. Seattle Takeisha Lewis
36. Washington: Teresa Geter
37. Portland: Mandy Nightingale
38. Minnesota: Lindsey Meder
39. Orlando: Saundra Jackson
40. Phoenix: Kayte Christensen
41. Charlotte: Edniesha Curry
42. Houston: Shondra Johnson
43. Utah: Edmarie Lumbsley
44. Sacramento: Alayne Ingram
45. Miami: Jerica Watson
46. New York: Tracy Gahan
47. Detroit: Ericka Haney
48. Los Angeles: Rashana Barnes
Fourth round
49. Indiana: LaKeisha Taylor
50. Portland: Melody Johnson
51. Sacramento: Jermisha Dosty
52. Indiana: Jillian Danker
53. Portland: Monique Cardenas
54. Minnesota: Shárron Francis
55. Orlando: Tomeka Brown
56. Phoenix: Amba Kongolo
57. Charlotte: Jessie Stomski
58. Houston: Cori Enghusen
59. Utah: Jaclyn Winfield
60. Sacramento: Elizabeth Pickney
61. Miami: Jerkisha Dosty
62. New York: Deedee Warley
63. Cleveland: Marché Strickland
64. Los Angeles: Tiffany Thompson

Chapter 33

Continental Basketball Association

By Nate Trela

The Continental Basketball Association is remembered by many fans as the league where anything could happen.

It was the place where Billings forward Sam Clancy could attract the attention of the National Football League despite not having played football in college. Clancy had a mean streak on the basketball court, fracturing the face of another player with a punch in the spring of 1982. The punch resulted in a three-week suspension, but the NFL took notice and he signed with the Seattle Seahawks that fall.

It was the league where Jose Slaughter and Barry Mitchell could be traded for each other, along with future considerations, during half-time of a game. Those "future considerations" turned out to be a couple of sweatsuits.

It was also the league where Rapid City coach Eric Musselman called up Albany forward Frankie Sanders the morning of a 1985 playoff game and told him, "I've got friends that have killed people." Musselman ended up with a fine, a suspension, and a police escort off the court in Albany. He would eventually become the first head coach of the NBA's Minnesota Timberwolves.

But it was also the league that inspired John Chaney to hop two buses and drive three hours on the weekend just to play in.

The CBA saw the rise of several coaching careers and the final days of several playing careers. For 57 seasons, it has been the league where NBA hopefuls went to hone their craft and be noticed. It is still the oldest professional league in the country, surviving formal bankruptcy once and several close calls.

"None of the owners ever made any money," said Stan Novak, who coached more than 300 games in the league. "Nobody really made any money ... There were just some great teams and some great players."

THE FIRST STEPS

Ironically, neither the man largely responsible for the founding of the Continental Basketball Association nor the man who owned it during its final days stayed actively involved with the league for more than one season.

In the early 1940s, Eddie White's Wilkes-Barre Barons were widely regarded as the best basketball team in eastern Pennsylvania. The Barons regularly held their own with whatever competition the National Basketball League had to offer. In fact, White paid up to $7,500 a season—a salary that rivaled what some players expected to make in the NBL—but he was committed to running his team as a minor-league organization.

More than anything, White was irritated by the disparity in the number of games the Barons played compared to the other

teams in the state. He was willing to play anybody, anywhere, but grew tired of traveling to Allentown and Hazleton. It seemed like the Barons were always on the road, and the home teams kept the bulk of the proceeds from the games. In his mind, there had to be a change.

On April 23, 1946, White and the owners of five other teams met and formed the Eastern Pennsylvania Basketball League—the CBA's original identity. William Morgan, owner of the Hazleton Mountaineers, would be installed as the league's first president.

The schedule wasn't perfectly balanced, with teams playing between 26 and 30 games, but it was the first organized season they had played. To nobody's surprise, the Barons cruised to the inaugural EPBL championship.

White, however, saw more opportunity with another fledgling league—the American Basketball League—and took Wilkes-Barre out of the EPBL. In fact, only four of the original six teams returned for a second season. But instead of collapsing, the league branched out, changed its name to the Eastern Professional Basketball League, and drove on under Morgan's guidance.

THE EASTERN LEAGUE

With the name change, a series of events began that set the stage for the EPBL to become what was arguably the second best basketball league in the country. The National Basketball League and the Basketball Association of America worked toward a merger and formed the National Basketball Association in 1949. Several existing teams folded as a result, which left dozens of talented players eager to find a team. Many turned to the EPBL.

But the teams they found were ragtag bunches, with distrust for the owners running rampant. It was common practice for one player on each road team to be assigned the duty of finding out which front office official would receive the club's share of the game-day proceeds. Far too many times, the players found themselves shortchanged if they did not collect their pay immediately following the contests. Nonetheless, the EPBL was succeeding, and it entered a period of relative financial stability.

Success wasn't limited to the front office. In 1949 Stan Novak began the finest coaching career in the history of the league. His 245-89 record and six Coach of the Year awards are impressive enough, but he also mentored several future coaches and general managers, most notably John Chaney, Jack McCloskey, and Hall-of-Fame coach Jack Ramsay. The CBA's Coach of the Year award would eventually be named in honor of Novak.

On the court, the early days of the league belonged to Bill Zubic, Joe Cackovic, and McCloskey. They were fixtures on the

all-league first teams, with Zubic winning the MVP award in 1950 and McCloskey taking the honors in 1953 and 1954.

At the same time, the league created an environment in which its players could settle into their communities. With games mostly on the weekends, players could work "real jobs" through the week while living out their hoop dreams on Fridays, Saturdays and Sundays.

The league was also developing a relationship with the NBA, but the bond was weakened by the EPBL's willingness to sign players with questionable reputations. The most severe damage may have been done in 1953, when the league signed Jack Molinas and Sherman White. Molinas had been banned from the NBA for life because he bet on games as a member of the Fort Wayne Zollner Pistons, while White never made it that far after being jailed for his role in a college point-shaving scandal.

It was hard to argue with the on-court performances of the two players, though. White became a regular selection to the all-league first team and picked up MVP honors in 1955. Molinas, who came aboard after the season began, picked up MVP honors in 1956 and was a three-time, first-team all-league player. But his career came to an end when he was convicted as the mastermind of a 1961 plot to fix pro and college games.

More disgraced players would follow the trail to the EPBL, and that willingness to embrace the sport's outcasts crushed any hopes the league might have had for a working relationship with the NBA. More than 15 years would pass before a formal deal would be reached with the NBA to develop talent. During that time, the EPBL could easily have folded. In 17 of the league's first 21 years, at least one team ceased operations or relocated either during or after the season.

Still, the league was able to find quality players to draw fans to games and keep its name floating in the public eye. Perhaps the most underappreciated player in the history of the league was Julius McCoy, who scored 7,782 points in a 12-year career. McCoy was the EPBL Rookie of the Year in 1959, and picked up all-league first-team honors that year. After going unrecognized for the next three seasons, McCoy ran off five straight appearances on the all-league first team (including winning the MVP award in 1966), and capped it off with an appearance on the all-league second team in 1968. Despite his accomplishments, McCoy never earned a shot in the NBA. Hal Lear and Stacey Arceneaux were also marquee names in the EPBL in the late 1950s. Lear averaged 25.6 points in 222 games and won the league's MVP award in 1957. Arceneaux was an equally prolific scorer, averaging 24.6 points in 292 games and winning an MVP award in 1960.

In 1962, the EPBL scored a major coup when future Hall-of-Famer Paul Arizin came out of retirement and suited up for the Camden Bullets. Arizin had called it a career at the end of the 1961-62 season when the NBA's Philadelphia Warriors moved to San Francisco. He still loved the game, but was unwilling to relocate to the West Coast. The EPBL provided the opportunity to continue both his life in the game and his new career at IBM. Arizin repaid the Bullets by averaging 25.6 points and 7.3 rebounds per game in three seasons.

The league received another potentially crushing blow in 1967, when the American Basketball Association was formed. Players jumped to the ABA en masse, attracted by contracts the

EPBL couldn't hope to match. It was the biggest talent drain the league had ever faced.

Even so, some quality players soldiered on in the EPBL. Ken Wilburn won the MVP award in the 1967-68 season, then went on to spend two seasons in the NBA. Over 209 Eastern League games from 1966 to 1975, he averaged 21.3 points per game and won another MVP award in 1974. He would later be named to the CBA's 50th anniversary team.

In 1970, the league changed its name to the Eastern Basketball Association as it struggled to find a place in professional basketball. The nine-team league slowly eroded, as owners overpaid players in the hopes of making an all-or-nothing run at the title. At the start of the 1974-75 season, the EBA was down to four teams and seemed to be on its last legs.

Its resurrection came in 1976, when the four ABA teams joined the NBA and the remaining five folded. The market was flooded with talented players, hungry to be on the court. One year after the merger the EBA had 10 teams—including its first club west of the Mississippi River.

Players like Charlie Criss made their mark in the reborn CBA. The 5-foot-8, 165-pound guard led the league in scoring three times and won MVP awards in 1976 and 1977, before spending six seasons in the NBA, mostly with the Atlanta Hawks. He would come back to the league later and wrap up his career in 1984.

At the end of the 1977-78 season, optimism was running high. The EBA negotiated a merger with the Western Basketball Association and, in anticipation of further western expansion, changed its name to the Continental Basketball Association on June 1, 1978. Although the WBA's teams all folded before the merger was completed, the name change stuck.

AFFILIATION DREAMS

As the 1970s drew to a close, the CBA found itself on the move. The NBA struck a deal with the league to develop referees in 1978-79, and four CBA veterans played in the NBA that season. Before the 1980-81 season, the two leagues signed their first agreement for player development. The deal paved the way for 10-day contracts that eventually would pay almost as much as a full season in the CBA.

One of the first success stories of the CBA era was Rickey Green, Golden State's first-round draft pick in 1977. Green spent his first two seasons in the NBA, but couldn't find a home in the league. He played in the CBA until 1981, but the Utah Jazz eventually found a place for him at point guard. Green became the first CBA veteran to play in an NBA All-Star Game and he led the Jazz to the Midwest Division title in 1984. He wound up playing a dozen NBA seasons following his CBA years.

The first developmental agreement also created a system of "reverse affiliations." Through the 1992-93 season, every CBA team had at least one full and one partial affiliation with an NBA team, through which it held a player's CBA rights. For example, if a player was released by the Indiana Pacers in the 1991-92 or 1992-93 seasons and wanted to play in the CBA for the first time, he had to join the Fort Wayne Fury. If that player was called back up by another NBA team and later released,

he still would come back to his original CBA club.

The affiliations were designed to keep the playing field level in the CBA, ideally preventing teams from getting into bidding wars for free agents. But some CBA clubs developed strong relationships with their counterparts, and certain NBA teams would hand over the final five rounds of their drafts to their affiliates.

In some cases, the CBA teams would discover players before the draft who ended up sticking in the NBA. Mark Eaton, for example, was drafted to be the Anchorage Knights' center in 1979, but Utah Jazz coach Frank Layden saw enough potential in the 7-foot-4 giant to keep him. That same year, the Jazz cut loose their second-round pick, Tico Brown. He began his career with the Knights and bounced through a handful of CBA teams on his way to becoming the league's career scoring leader with 8,538 points. Many observers point to Brown as the best CBA player never to reach the NBA.

His stats could have been more impressive if he hadn't joined the league behind Ron Davis, who set many of the scoring records that Brown broke. The two were teammates in Anchorage in 1979, and Davis' average of 31.7 points per game still stands as the highest career mark in the CBA era.

With scoring on the rise, the CBA slowly gathered attention in the national landscape. In 1982, the CBA All-Star Game became the league's first nationally televised event. Two seasons later, the NBA signed the CBA to another contract—a three-year, $1-million deal—for player and referee development.

The relationship between the two leagues helped the CBA land a cable deal, with a game-of-the-week televised nationally. For two months in the 1983-84 season, CBA referees worked NBA games as the league and its officials battled through a labor dispute.

During this period the CBA was serving as the springboard for several notable coaching careers. Phil Jackson spent four-and-a-half seasons as coach of the Albany Patroons, and even back then his unique coaching methods were effective. Jackson guided the franchise to a playoff appearance in each of his four full seasons and won the 1984 CBA championship. He was seen as a players' coach, who was comfortable both in teaching the triangle offense and chatting with his charges while he drove the team van on road trips. He's proven to be a bit of a rarity, posting a higher winning percentage in the NBA than his .565 mark in the CBA.

One can only imagine the contrast of playing for Jackson and his successor Bill Musselman, who led the Patroons to the CBA title in 1988, his first season at the helm. Championships were nothing new to Musselman, who won three straight titles with the Tampa Bay/Rapid City Thrillers before coming to Albany. He was well known for his relentless desire to win, doing everything he could to gain an advantage. Eventually, he turned his six CBA seasons—not to mention prior experience with the Cleveland Cavaliers and two ABA franchises—into a career in the NBA.

Yet another future NBA coach, George Karl, succeeded Musselman in Albany. Karl led the Montana Golden Nuggets to three playoff berths before the Cavaliers brought him on board as director of player acquisition in May 1983. His first NBA head-coaching job came in 1984, but Karl turned in a pair of sub-.500 seasons with the Cavs. Golden State gave him a chance in 1987-88, but a 16-48 start to the season led him to resign. With the Patroons, however, Karl proved that he was still a winner. In 1990-91, he led Albany to a 50-6 record, the best single-season winning percentage (.893) in a professional basketball league.

While the coaches developed, the league underwent an incredible jump in value. In 1978, expansion franchises cost just $8,000. By 1984, they cost $500,000 each. In 1986, the CBA signed its sweetest developmental deal with the NBA to that point—$1.8 million over three years.

THE RISE BEFORE THE FALL

The 1991-92 season probably marked the CBA's pinnacle—the league was admitted for the first time as an active member of USA Basketball and tipped off with an all-time high of 17 franchises. Even when the Bakersfield Jammers folded after just 24 games, optimism ran rampant in the league. In hindsight, the Jammers' collapse should have been the warning that the league was growing too quickly to be stable.

On the surface, the CBA seemed healthier than ever. Even though the NBA shortened its draft—and would eliminate the reverse affiliation system in 1993—the CBA seemed to be loaded with talent. At that time, its 16 teams were already drafting 112 players a season. The two leagues signed a three-year, multimillion dollar developmental deal in 1992, expanding their relationship to include marketing, broadcasting, public relations, community relations, and coaching development.

Vincent Askew, a 6-foot-6 swingman, was making the biggest splash of any CBA veteran playing at the time. After appearing in 14 games with the Philadelphia 76ers in 1987, he landed with the Savannah Spirits. He spent the next three seasons with the Albany Patroons, becoming the only CBA player to win back-to-back MVP awards, in 1990 and 1991. Golden State called Askew up at the end of 1990-91 season, and he didn't see the CBA again until 1998. Askew was the only active player named to the CBA's 50th anniversary team during the 1995-96 season.

Askew was soon exceeded in notoriety by Chris Childs, the reserve point guard for the New York Knicks' 1999 Eastern Conference championship team. For CBA players, the rule of thumb says your window of NBA opportunity closes after your second season in the minors. Of the 96 CBA veterans to appear in the NBA in 1998-99, only six played more than one uninterrupted season in the CBA. But Childs was a rarity. He spent five seasons with six teams in the CBA, where he was considered to be too temperamental to make it to the NBA. He received only one chance to show he belonged, when the New Jersey Nets signed him after he had led the Quad City Thunder to the 1994 CBA championship. Childs moved into the Nets' rotation right away and displaced starting point guard Kenny Anderson during the 1995-96 season. From there, he signed a lucrative free agent contract with the Knicks, and as of 2003 was firmly entrenched in the NBA.

In the mid-'90s, Childs had plenty of CBA refugees near him in New York. John Starks, a mercurial shooting guard, became the first CBA veteran to win an NBA award when he was named to the All-Defensive second team in 1993. Starks

had been released by the Golden State Warriors after his rookie season (1988-89), and found nobody in the NBA willing to take him. He joined the Cedar Rapids Silver Bullets in 1989 for his only CBA season, averaging 21.7 points, 5.5 assists, and 5.3 rebounds per game. The Knicks picked him up the next season and put Starks right into the rotation. He went on to win the NBA's Sixth Man Award in 1996-97.

Joining Starks in the Knicks' lineup was Anthony Mason, whose route to the NBA also passed through the CBA. After spending a year in Turkey and a year on the bench with New Jersey, Mason joined the Tulsa Fast Breakers in 1990. Coming out of Tennessee State, the 6-foot-7 Mason was thought to be too small to play power forward in the NBA, but he showed in Tulsa that he belonged in the paint. Over 26 games, Mason averaged 29.9 points, 14.8 rebounds, and 3.9 assists, which merited a brief stint with the Denver Nuggets. The Knicks signed him before the 1991-92 season, where he became a force off the bench. Mason won the NBA's Sixth Man Award for 1994-95 and moved into the starting lineup the following season.

The mid-'90s also saw the departure of Mauro Panaggio, the coach widely considered the greatest of the CBA era. In three stints, he won two titles and a league-record 446 games. Panaggio's career stretched over three decades, and he led his teams into four championship series.

CRASHING BACK DOWN

The CBA began the 1994-95 season with 16 teams, its sixth straight season at or above that mark. While two franchises folded at mid-season and three more collapsed after the playoffs, the league kept pushing forward and continued to expand into major markets. When the San Diego Wildcards, which relocated from Mexico City before the 1995-96 season, folded after just 21 games on the West Coast, the CBA started to reexamine its expansion and relocation criteria.

Despite the instability, the league never stopped producing talent for the NBA. Before the 1996-97 campaign, the two leagues agreed on another three-year extension of the developmental agreement. It resulted in a then record 45 call-ups, and, for the first time, all 29 NBA teams had at least once CBA veteran appear on their rosters.

Among them was Darrell Armstrong, although crediting the CBA for his development could be a bit of a stretch. When Armstrong left Fayetteville State in 1991, he headed for the Global Basketball League. When the league folded part way through the 1992-93 season, he played two games for the CBA's Capital Region Pontiacs and spent the next two summers in the USBL. The NBA's Orlando Magic gave him limited opportunities in the 1994-95 and '95-96 seasons, but he started to emerge in the fall of 1996. He was named the NBA's Most Improved Player and won the Sixth Man Award in 1999.

After the 1996-97 season, however, there was finally indisputable proof that the league was in trouble. Three teams folded, dropping the CBA below the 10-franchise minimum spelled out in the developmental agreement with the NBA. The addition of the Idaho Stampede for 1997-98 left the league one team shy of the minimum, but at least six teams were drowning in red ink.

In hindsight, it seems like a miracle that the CBA even made it that far. Starting with Eddie White in Wilkes-Barre, owners had a tendency to pay salaries that were not in line with the revenue their teams produced. But while White knew what he was doing, the relatively low cost of franchises made it possible for people who did not understand the business of basketball to jump into the league.

In many cases, owning a team was more about stroking one's own ego than doing what was best for basketball. The landscape is littered with franchises that folded because their owners valued success more than stability. The most glaring example came in 1997, when the Oklahoma City Cavalry folded just months after winning the CBA title. Starting with the 1978-79 season, the CBA went through 80 teams in 71 markets over 20 years.

At the height of irresponsibility, annual salaries—supplemented by endorsement deals—resulted in players earning six figures. Damon Bailey, for example, reportedly earned more than $100,000 with the Fort Wayne Fury in 1995-96. In many cases, this made the CBA a viable career choice for some players. An NBA minimum salary, the best many players could hope for, would have been a significant raise, but wasn't outrageously more than what they could make in the minor leagues. Teams in Europe might pay a little more, but the CBA provided a chance for stardom in the U.S.

Some individuals, like longtime CBA coach Bill Klucas, blame the financial woes of the league on more than just outrageous salaries. When Klucas was the coach of the Anchorage Northern Knights during the late 1970s and early 1980s, his team was effectively isolated from the rest of the league. In 1979-80, the Knights had to take the longest known road trip in American pro sports history—16 games in 31 days, entirely by bus. It would not be repeated.

The team responded by trading out sponsorship credits for all of the club's airfare between Anchorage and the hub airport in Seattle. But several other owners responded by forcing the Knights to pick up the tab for their flights into Alaska. In Klucas's mind, the contradictory desires of individual owners killed off a piece of the league.

Marty Blake, the long-time director of scouting services for the NBA and an employee of the original Wilkes-Barre Barons, believes there simply are not enough people who can run a basketball front office. The transition from college coach to professional coach is relatively easy to make. Learning how to line up $750,000 in corporate sponsorships, on the other hand, is something that can't be learned outside of minor-league sports.

A LEAGUE OF HIS OWN

In the summer of 1998, the CBA thought it had a plan for recovery. For the first time in four years, no teams were planning to fold or relocate. More than 100 CBA veterans appeared in the NBA in 1997-98, including Starks, Childs, Mason, and 63 others on opening day. And even though the CBA was still below the minimum number of teams specified in its contract with the NBA, it had plans to add franchises in St. Charles, Missouri and Trenton, New Jersey, for the 1999-2000 season.

Midway through the 1998-99 season, however, the league was back at square one. Both expansion groups backed away from the CBA and pledged to join the International Basketball League, which planned to pay higher salaries when it tipped off

the next season. The CBA filed a lawsuit, but could not prevent the move. After the season, ownership groups in several cities threatened to relocate or fold their teams if changes didn't happen. The Connecticut Pride lost a reported $700,000, more than one-third of the league's losses for the season.

The CBA found new hope in February 1999, when Isiah Thomas sat down with league commissioner Gary Hunter for a cup of coffee. Hunter thought Thomas was interested in purchasing an expansion team, but the Hall-of-Fame point guard had his eye on the nine teams that already existed.

On October 7, 1999, Thomas completed a nearly $10-million purchase of the league and transformed it into a single entity. At least one report indicated that the league could have folded if he did not make the purchase, and the NBA had threatened to not renew its developmental agreement with the CBA while Thomas was negotiating the acquisition. The move wasn't welcomed by all of the owners, especially those who sank millions of dollars into their teams and would walk away with a fraction of their investments. It took several months of debating before Thomas's offer was unanimously accepted.

Thomas spoke openly of developing direct affiliations between NBA and CBA teams, but found out the task was easier said than done. It quickly became clear that such a system would take years to put in place, and he signed a one-year renewal of the previous developmental deal. He needed to find a new way for the league to develop talent.

By moving to a single-entity structure, the CBA had the right system in place to solve its biggest problems. Thomas instituted "salary discipline" that slashed payrolls to a fraction of what they once were. Salaries topped out at $2,000 a week, slightly above the average salary of the previous year. It was now impossible for teams to get into outrageous bidding wars. Under the new system, the league office was also in charge of approving or rejecting all player signings. The measures kept teams from loading their rosters with players who could dominate at the CBA level but would never get a shot at the NBA, thus enhancing the CBA's goal of developing talent for the next level.

There was some concern when former CBA all-stars flocked to the rival IBL. But joining the IBL meant a player could not be called up to the NBA that season, effectively making a player admit that he belonged in the minor leagues. From the CBA's perspective, the IBL could have the retreads. Thomas felt it was important to make the CBA a place for developing young— and cheap—talent.

The most important change brought about by the single-entity structure was the way the operations of teams were interwoven. The financial struggles incurred by one team affected the others, and Thomas, as chairman and CEO of the league, used all of his resources. Three of the general managers at the end of the 1999-2000 season had positions in more than one team's front office. Before the 2000-01 season, their titles were changed to regional vice presidents to reflect their expanded roles.

(ALMOST) THE FINAL CHAPTER

When Isiah Thomas set his eyes set on becoming an NBA head coach in the summer of 2000, he was left in an unenviable position. The NBA saw his ownership of the CBA as a conflict of interest, and said he would have to sell the league to

accept a coaching job. But Thomas thought he deserved a return on his investment and set a price that reflected it. He turned down an offer from the NBA that would have turned into a tidy profit. He rebuffed former CBA owners who asked to buy their teams back, ignoring their warnings that he might never find another buyer.

When training camp approached and it appeared a sale would not happen in time, the CBA was placed in a blind trust. Thomas could not have anything to do with the league's operations and could not comment on the league, which had to be sold within the next year.

The rumor mill churned out a handful of possible buyers, from the National Basketball Players Association to the IBL to a woman claiming to be the heir to a fortune. The CBA's 55th season began amidst talk that it would be sold to a group of young investors, but the transaction never happened.

Attendance plummeted and players started jumping to other leagues, but that was just the tip of the iceberg. Bills went unpaid, roster spots went unfilled, and travel plans were cut. When the CBA's All-Star break arrived in February 2001, some officials knew a sale had to happen or the league would collapse.

Last-ditch efforts were made to sell the teams to their former owners and the IBL, but an agreement was never reached. On February 8, 2001, the league put out a statement saying its 10 teams were being "returned" to local ownership groups. The names and assets of five teams were bought and moved to the IBL, which picked players off the rosters of their fallen competitor. The CBA was no more.

Supporters of Thomas say he made a good-faith effort to sell the league, but he was hampered by his agreement with the NBA. When attendance fell, which in turn lowered revenues, he was not allowed to prop up the league with money out of his own pocket. As the red ink grew, the CBA's value plummeted.

Some of the league's officials were less forgiving. The league office incurred expenses that seemed out of line with its revenues, and many believed the league could have been stable if it had allowed some franchises to fold before the 2000-01 season.

Rich Coffey, the general manager of the Fort Wayne Fury, compared Thomas to Pontius Pilate, saying he "washed his hands of the league." There was anger over Thomas's refusal to sell the league when he had the chance, and at the way its players and front office personnel were left dangling in the wind. "There's a lot of built-up frustration and animosity . . . because we felt we were wronged," Coffey said at the time. "But we also wanted closure, and we got it."

BACK AGAIN

Long-time coach Charley Rosen famously referred to the CBA as the "Cockroach Basketball Association," noting its ability to survive anything. And sure enough, the league started to bounce back just months after collapsing into bankruptcy.

Shortly after the CBA folded, two of its rivals—the International Basketball Association and the IBL—also began to crumble. A vacuum was emerging in the second tier of professional basketball in North America.

Quietly, former CBA franchise owners Greg Heineman and Bill Ilett began speaking to potential ownership groups to gauge interest in reviving the league. Heineman had already bought

back the Sioux Falls Skyforce and placed the team in the IBL at the end of the 2000-01 season, while Ilett was considering buying back the Idaho Stampede. An August 2001 meeting in Minneapolis sealed the decision to resurrect the CBA, with the season set to start just three months later.

Although more than a dozen groups attended that meeting, only eight franchises played in the CBA's first season back—four of the teams that had made the move to the IBL, three franchises from the IBA, and one expansion team. Also, the environment for the return was less than ideal. The league was operating with two structures—the old CBA teams played a longer schedule and had a higher payroll than the IBA and expansion teams. The NBA had also launched its own minor league, the National Basketball Development League, which competed with the CBA to sign many of the same players.

With the short start-up time, teams had difficulty attracting sponsors and selling tickets. Two folded after the end of the season, but they were replaced by new incarnations of the Yakima Sun Kings and the Idaho Stampede.

Gary Hunter, the commissioner of the CBA both before and after Thomas's ownership of the league, said there is still hope for the league to one day reestablish its formal relationship with the NBA. He spoke with NBA officials twice about merging the NBDL with the CBA, but could not agree on terms. Fortunately, he said, the league runs on an improved financial model that should enable it to survive even without financial assistance from the NBA.

That is because the CBA has made a point of learning from its mistakes. Start-ups will be slower in the future, with ownership groups being held to a higher standard to prove they will be able to survive in the long term. Teams are clustered together so that road trips can be accomplished with more bus travel and less time on planes.

"We're trying not to repeat those mistakes of the past," Hunter said. "We suffered from volatile ownership in communities where we were doomed to fail from the very beginning because they were either not good sports communities or there was inadequate and poor management. Hopefully, there won't be quite as much movement or failure as there has been in the last 20 years."

EPBL/EBA/CBA STATISTICS

EASTERN PENNSYLVANIA BASKETBALL LEAGUE

1946-47 EPBL

	W	L	Pct.	GB
Wilkes-Barre Barons	22	5	.815	—
Lancaster Red Roses	20	10	.667	3.5
Reading Keys	15	13	.536	7.5
Hazleton Mountaineers	11	17	.393	11.5
Allentown Rockets	8	18	.308	13.5
Binghamton/Pottsville Pros	7	20	.259	15

EPBL SEMI-FINALS
Wilkes-Barre 45, Reading 41   Lancaster 76, Hazleton 63
Wilkes-Barre 62, Reading 58   Lancaster 64, Hazleton 53
EPBL FINALS
Lancaster 59, Wilkes-Barre 54
Wilkes-Barre 65, Lancaster 37
Wilkes-Barre 70, Lancaster 54

1947-48 EPBL

	W	L	Pct.	GB
Pottsville Packers	19	9	.679	—
Reading Keys	19	9	.679	—
Hazleton Mountaineers	18	10	.643	1
Lancaster Red Roses	14	14	.500	5
Sunbury Mercuries	13	15	.464	6
Harrisburg Senators	11	16	.407	7.5
Williamsport Billies	9	18	.333	9.5
Philadelphia Lumberjacks	8	20	.286	11

EPBL FIRST PLACE PLAYOFF
Pottsville 60, Reading 57
EPBL SEMI-FINALS
Pottsville 53, Hazleton 50   Lancaster 83, Reading 73
Hazleton 62, Pottsville 58   Reading 64, Lancaster 57
Hazleton 50, Pottsville 48   Reading 71, Lancaster 65
EPBL FINALS
Hazleton 61, Reading 53
Reading 69, Hazleton 59
Reading 54, Hazleton 52

1948-49 EPBL

	W	L	Pct.	GB
Williamsport Billies	18	12	.600	—
Reading Keys	18	12	.600	—
Harrisburg Senators	18	12	.600	—
Pottsville Packers	16	14	.533	2
York Victory A.C.	15	15	.500	3
Lancaster Red Roses	11	19	.367	7
Sunbury Mercuries	9	21	.300	9

EPBL FIRST PLACE PLAYOFF
Reading 68, Harrisburg 66
Williamsport 100, Reading 77

EPBL SEMI-FINALS
Pottsville 82, Williamsport 68   Harrisburg 83, Reading 73
Williamsport 89, Pottsville 79   Reading 97, Harrisburg 74
Pottsville 79, Williamsport 77   Harrisburg 57, Reading 51
EPBL FINALS
Pottsville 73, Harrisburg 70
Harrisburg 82, Pottsville 53
Pottsville 88, Harrisburg 69

1948-49 EPBL

NORTHERN DIVISION	W	L	Pct.	GB
Williamsport Billies	20	8	.714	—
Pottsville Packers	16	11	.593	3.5
Sunbury Mercuries	13	14	.482	6.5
Berwick Carbuilders	8	17	.320	10.5

SOUTHERN DIVISION	W	L	Pct.	GB
Lancaster Rockets	18	10	.643	—
Harrisburg Senators	16	12	.571	2
York Victory A.C.	9	17	.346	8
Reading Rangers	7	18	.280	9.5

EPBL FIRST PLACE PLAYOFF
Williamsport 90, Lancaster 87
EPBL SEMI-FINALS
Lancaster 85, Harrisburg 65   Williamsport 87, Pottsville 77
Harrisburg 84, Lancaster 60   Pottsville 83, Williamsport 79
Harrisburg 71, Lancaster 67   Williamsport 102, Pottsville 75
EPBL FINALS
Williamsport 92, Harrisburg 74
Harrisburg 73, Williamsport 67
Williamsport 100, Harrisburg 94

1950-51 EPBL

NORTHERN DIVISION	W	L	Pct.	GB
Sunbury Mercuries	23	5	.822	—
Williamsport Billies	16	12	.571	7
Berwick Carbuilders	15	13	.536	8
Pottsville Packers	12	16	.429	11

SOUTHERN DIVISION	W	L	Pct.	GB
York Victory A.C.	15	11	.577	—
Lancaster Rockets	12	15	.445	3.5
Harrisburg Senators	9	18	.333	6.5
Reading Rangers	8	20	.400	8

EPBL REGULAR SEASON CHAMPIONSHIP
Sunbury 80, York 75
EPBL SEMI-FINALS   Sunbury 84, Williamsport 77
York 78, Lancaster 64   Sunbury 77, Williamsport 66
York 69, Lancaster 68   Sunbury 77, Williamsport 70
EPBL FINALS
Sunbury 74, York 54
Sunbury 77, York 69

1951-52 EPBL

	W	L	Pct.	GB
Pottsville Packers	21	9	.700	—
Sunbury Mercuries	20	10	.667	1
Williamsport Billies	17	12	.586	3.5
Lancaster Rockets	13	16	.448	7.5
Reading Merchants	11	17	.393	9
Hazleton Mountaineers	6	20	.200	15

EPBL SEMI-FINALS
Pottsville 76, Williamsport 66   Sunbury 91, Lancaster 78
Pottsville 81, Williamsport 73   Sunbury 82, Lancaster 66
EPBL FINALS
Pottsville 76, Sunbury 69
Sunbury 96, Pottsville 77
Pottsville 83, Sunbury 76

1952-53 EPBL

	W	L	Pct.	GB
Sunbury Mercuries	17	3	.850	—
Williamsport Billies	13	7	.650	4
Lancaster Rockets	9	10	.474	7.5
Berwick Carbuilders	8	12	.400	9
Harrisburgh Capitols	7	12	.369	9.5
Lebanon Seltzers	5	15	.333	12

EPBL SEMI-FINALS
Berwick 80, Sunbury 59   Williamsport 81, Lancaster 64
Sunbury 73, Berwick 70
Berwick 95, Sunbury 90, OT
EPBL FINALS
Berwick 76, Williamsport 74
Williamsport 77, Berwick 73
Williamsport 81, Berwick 64

1953-54 EPBL

	W	L	Pct.	GB
Sunbury Mercuries	22	8	.733	—
Williamsport Billies	20	10	.667	2
Hazleton Hawks	15	15	.500	7
Lancaster Red Roses	15	15	.500	7
Berwick Carbuilders	14	16	.467	8
Lebanon Seltzers	4	26	.133	18

EPBL SEMI-FINALS
Lancaster 81, Sunbury 72   Williamsport 78, Hazleton 67
Lancaster 69, Sunbury 68   Hazleton 97, Williamsport 79
                             Williamsport 84, Hazleton 69
EPBL FINALS
Williamsport 99, Lancaster 89
Lancaster 105, Williamsport 71
Williamsport 110, Lancaster 87

1954-55 EPBL

	W	L	Pct.	GB
Williamsport Billies	19	11	.633	—
Wilkes-Barre Barons	18	12	.600	1
Scranton Miners	15	15	.500	4
Hazleton Hawks	15	15	.500	4
Sunbury Mercuries	13	17	.433	6
Lancaster Red Roses	10	20	.333	9

EPBL SEMI-FINALS
Williamsport 72, Hazleton 71   Wilkes-Barre 81, Scranton 70
Hazleton 100, Williamsport 91   Scranton 78, Wilkes-Barre 62
Hazleton 70, Williamsport 65   Wilkes-Barre 82, Scranton 70
EBPL FINALS
Wilkes-Barre 103, Hazleton 88, OT
Hazleton 81, Wilkes-Barre 65
Wilkes-Barre 76, Hazleton 71, OT

1955-56 EPBL

	W	L	Pct.	GB
Williamsport Billies	18	9	.667	—
Wilkes-Barre Barons	18	12	.600	1.5
Scranton Miners	14	13	.519	4
Sunbury Mercuries	13	13	.500	4.5
Hazleton Hawks	11	15	.423	6.5
New York-Harlem Yankees	2	14	.125	10.5

EPBL SEMI-FINALS
Williamsport 89, Sunbury 83   Wilkes-Barre 85, Scranton 82
Williamsport 77, Sunbury 74   Scranton 126, Wilkes-Barre 117
                                 Wilkes-Barre 86, Scranton 82
EPBL FINALS
Williamsport 88, Wilkes-Barre 86, OT
Wilkes-Barre 90, Williamsport 85
Wilkes-Barre 92, Williamsport 83
Wilkes-Barre 90, Williamsport 87

1956-57 EPBL

	W	L	Pct.	GB
Scranton Miners	21	9	.700	—
Hazleton Hawks	20	10	.667	1
Sunbury Mercuries	14	16	.467	7
Williamsport Billies	13	17	.433	8
Wilkes-Barre Barons	11	18	.379	9.5
Easton Madisons	10	19	.345	10.5

EPBL SEMI-FINALS
Williamsport 93, Scranton 90   Hazleton 111, Sunbury 103
Scranton 95, Williamsport 88   Sunbury 112, Hazleton 96
Scranton 111, Williamsport 89   Hazleton 107, Sunbury 105
EPBL FINALS
Scranton 114, Hazleton 107
Hazleton 120, Scranton 113
Scranton 106, Hazleton 99

1957-58 EPBL

	W	L	Pct.	GB
Wilkes-Barre Barons	19	10	.655	—
Hazleton Hawks	19	11	.633	0.5
Easton Madisons	18	11	.621	1
Sunbury Mercuries	18	11	.621	1
Scranton Miners	18	12	.600	1.5
Williamsport Billies	17	12	.586	2
Wilmington Jets	6	22	.214	12.5
Reading Keys	1	27	.036	17.5

EPBL SEMI-FINALS
Wilkes-Barre 117, Sunbury 114, OT   Easton 112, Hazleton 90
Wilkes-Barre 114, Sunbury 114, OT   Hazleton 97, Easton 92
                                       Easton 121, Hazleton 118
EPBL FINALS
Wilkes-Barre 119, Easton 107
Easton 124, Wilkes-Barre 109
Wilkes-Barre 143, Easton 124

1958-59 EPBL

	W	L	Pct.	GB
Scranton Miners	21	7	.750	—
Wilkes-Barre Barons	19	9	.679	2
Easton Madisons	17	11	.607	4
Hazleton Hawks	16	12	.571	5
Sunbury Mercuries	12	16	.429	9
Baltimore Bullets	12	16	.429	9
Williamsport Billies	9	19	.321	12
Allentown Jets	6	22	.214	15

EPBL SEMI-FINALS
Scranton 121, Hazleton 98   Easton 109, Wilkes-Barre 102
Hazleton 94, Scranton 78   Wilkes-Barre 119, Easton 109
Scranton 111, Hazleton 93   Wilkes-Barre 93, Easton 85
EPBL FINALS
Wilkes-Barre 112, Scranton 104
Scranton 109, Wilkes-Barre 98
Wilkes-Barre 113, Scranton 106

1959-60 EPBL

	W	L	Pct.	GB
Easton Madisons	21	7	.750	—
Baltimore Bullets	20	8	.714	1
Allentown Jets	15	12	.556	5.5
Scranton Miners	15	13	.536	6
Williamsport Billies	12	16	.439	9
Wilkes-Barre Barons	10	18	.357	11
Hazleton Hawks	9	18	.333	11.5
Sunbury Mercuries	9	19	.321	12

EPBL SEMI-FINALS
Easton 139, Scranton 102   Baltimore 103, Allentown 89
EPBL FINALS
Baltimore 112, Easton 110
Easton 131, Baltimore 120
Easton 114, Baltimore 107

1960-61 EPBL

	W	L	Pct.	GB
Baltimore Bullets	19	9	.679	—
Allentown Jets	19	9	.679	—
Scranton Miners	15	13	.536	4
Sunbury Mercuries	13	15	.464	6
Wilkes-Barre Barons	13	15	.464	6
Easton Madisons	11	16	.407	7.5
Williamsport Billies	11	16	.407	7.5
Hazleton Hawks	10	18	.357	9

EPBL SEMI-FINALS
Baltimore 132, Scranton 107   Allentown 129, Sunbury 97
EPBL CHAMPIONSHIP
Baltimore 119, Allentown 104

1961-62 EPBL

	W	L	Pct.	GB
Allentown Jets	22	5	.815	—
Williamsport Billies	18	8	.692	3.5
Sunbury Mercuries	16	11	.593	6
Trenton Colonials	13	13	.500	8.5
Wilkes-Barre Barons	13	15	.464	9.5
Camden Bullets	10	15	.400	11
Scranton Miners	8	16	.333	12.5
Hazleton Hawks	4	21	.160	17

EPBL SEMI-FINALS
Allentown 136, Trenton 115 Sunbury 120, Williamsport 114
Allentown 129, Trenton 125 Williamsport 139, Sunbury 133
 Williamsport 132, Sunbury 112

EPBL FINALS
Allentown 132, Williamsport 121
Williamsport 133, Allentown 117
Allentown 127, Williamsport 107

1962-63 EPBL

	W	L	Pct.	GB
Allentown Jets	20	8	.714	—
Camden Bullets	20	8	.714	—
Wilkes-Barre Barons	15	13	.536	5
Williamsport Billies	12	16	.429	8
Scranton Miners	11	17	.393	9
Trenton Colonials	10	18	.357	10
Sunbury Mercuries	10	18	.357	10

EPBL DIVISION TITLE GAME
Allentown 132, Camden 125
EPBL SEMI-FINALS
Allentown 153, Williamsport 121 Wilkes-Barre 126, Camden 120
Williamsport 114, Allentown 102 Wilkes-Barre 126, Camden 118
Allentown 121, Williamsport 110
EPBL FINALS
Allentown 144, Wilkes-Barre 126
Wilkes-Barre 124, Allentown 120
Allentown 132, Wilkes-Barre 115

1963-64 EPBL

	W	L	Pct.	GB
Camden Bullets	21	7	.750	—
Allentown Jets	21	7	.750	—
Scranton Miners	19	9	.679	2
Trenton Colonials	16	12	.571	5
Wilkes-Barre Barons	10	18	.357	11
Sunbury Mercuries	9	17	.346	11
Williamsport Billies	7	19	.269	13
Wilmington Blue Bombers	7	21	.250	14

EPBL SEMI-FINALS
Allentown 142, Trenton 137 Camden 132, Scranton 120
Trenton 121, Allentown 116 Scranton 123, Camden 105
Trenton 124, Allentown 120 Camden 131, Scranton 125
EPBL FINALS
Camden 131, Trenton 125
Camden 145, Trenton 138

1964-65 EPBL

	W	L	Pct.	GB
Camden Bullets	18	10	.643	—
Sunbury Mercuries	17	11	.607	1
Scranton Miners	17	11	.607	1
Allentown Jets	16	12	.571	2
Wilmington Blue Bombers	12	16	.429	6
Wilkes-Barre Barons	11	17	.393	7
Trenton Colonials	7	21	.250	11

EPBL SEMI-FINALS
Camden 124, Allentown 121 Sunbury 124, Scranton 123
Allentown 139, Camden 130 Scranton 137, Sunbury 129
Allentown 130, Camden 126, OT Scranton 123, Sunbury 121
EPBL FINALS
Scranton 128, Allentown 126
Allentown 142, Scranton 133
Allentown 131, Scranton 111

1965-66 EPBL

EASTERN DIVISION	W	L	Pct.	GB
Wilmington Blue Bombers	20	8	.714	—
Trenton Colonials	20	8	.714	—
Allentown Jets	15	13	.536	5
Camden Bullets	14	14	.500	6
New Haven Elms	8	20	.286	12

WESTERN DIVISION	W	L	Pct.	GB
Wilkes-Barre Barons	19	9	.679	—
Sunbury Mercuries	18	10	.643	1
Scranton Miners	13	15	.464	6
Harrisburg Patriots	10	18	.357	9
Johnstown C.J.'s	3	25	.107	16

EPBL EASTERN DIVISION TITLE GAME
Wilmington 124, Trenton 107

EPBL EASTERN SEMI-FINALS   **EPBL WESTERN SEMI-FINALS**
Trenton 133, Allentown 114   Sunbury 136, Scranton 132
EPBL EASTERN FINALS   **EPBL WESTERN DIVSION FINALS**
Wilmington 113, Trenton 110   Wilkes-Barre 109, Sunbury 103
Trenton 145, Wilmington 124   Sunbury 112, Wilkes-Barre 108
Wilmington 122, Trenton 110   Wilkes-Barre 113, Sunbury 107
EPBL FINALS
Wilkes-Barre 113, Wilmington 101
Wilmington 133, Wilkes-Barre 114
Wilmington 114, Wilkes-Barre 104

1966-67 EPBL

EASTERN DIVISION	W	L	Pct.	GB
Wilmington Blue Bombers	21	7	.750	—
Hartford Capitols	13	15	.464	8
Trenton Colonials	13	15	.464	8
New Haven Elms	7	21	.250	14
Asbury Park Boardwalkers	2	26	.071	19

WESTERN DIVISION	W	L	Pct.	GB
Scranton Miners	21	7	.750	—
Allentown Jets	19	9	.679	2
Sunbury Mercuries	19	9	.679	2
Wilkes-Barre Barons	14	13	.519	6.5
Harrisburg Patriots	10	17	.370	10.5

EPBL EASTERN SEMI-FINALS
Wilmington 136, New Haven119   Hartford 176, Trenton 170, OT
Wilmington 153, New Haven 130   Trenton 146, Hartford 139, OT
 Hartford 133, Trenton 123

EPBL WESTERN SEMI-FINALS
Scranton 119, Wilkes-Barre 108   Allentown 130, Sunbury 122
Wilkes-Barre 160, Scranton 151   Sunbury 135, Allentown 133
Scranton 141, Wilkes-Barre 130   Allentown 128, Sunbury 114
EPBL EASTERN FINALS   **EPBL WESTERN FINALS**
Wilmington 155, Hartford 138   Scranton 124, Allentown 122
Wilmington 141, Hartford 117   Scranton 139, Allentown 132
EPBL FINALS
Wilmington 119, Scranton 116
Scranton 149, Wilmington 142
Wilmington 121, Scranton 103
Scranton 147, Wilmington 129
Wilmington 143, Scranton 110

1967-68 EPBL

	W	L	Pct.	GB
Allentown Jets	23	9	.719	—
Hartford Capitols	21	11	.656	2
Wilkes-Barre Barons	20	12	.625	3
Wilmington Blue Bombers	21	12	.625	3
Sunbury Mercuries	18	14	.563	5
Scranton Miners	16	16	.500	7
Binghamton Flyers	10	22	.313	13
Asbury Park Boardwalkers	9	23	.281	14
Trenton Colonials	7	25	.219	16

EPBL SEMI-FINALS
Allentown 111, Wilmington 109   Hartford 132, Wilkes-Barre 130
Wilmington 127, Allentown 125   Wilkes-Barre 158, Hartford 116
Allentown 132, Wilmington 111   Wilkes-Barre 138, Hartford 124
EPBL FINALS
Allentown 121, Wilkes-Barre 111
Allentown 117, Wilkes-Barre 115
Wilkes-Barre 128, Allentown 108
Wilkes-Barre 119, Allentown 109
Allentown 109, Wilkes-Barre 104

1968-69 EPBL

EASTERN DIVISION	W	L	Pct.	GB
Wilmington Blue Bombers	20	7	.741	—
Trenton Colonials	13	12	.520	6
Hartford Capitols	11	15	.423	8.5
New Haven Elms	10	16	.385	9.5
Springfield*	0	18	.000	—
WESTERN DIVISION	**W**	**L**	**Pct.**	**GB**
Wilkes-Barre Barons	26	2	.929	—
Scranton Miners	15	12	.556	10.5
Allentown Jets	15	13	.536	11
Sunbury Mercuries	10	16	.385	15
Binghamton Flyers	9	18	.333	16.5

*Springfield disbanded during the season

EPBL EASTERN SEMI-FINALS
Wilmington 145, New Haven 142   Hartford 138, Scranton 115
Wilmington 151, New Haven 139   Hartford 135, Scranton 110

EPBL WESTERN SEMI-FINALS
Wilkes-Barre 138, Sunbury 88   Scranton 131, Allentown 119
Wilkes-Barre 132, Sunbury 126   Scranton 124, Allentown 118

EPBL EASTERN FINALS   **EPBL WESTERN FINALS**
Hartford 123, Wilmington 114   Wilkes-Barre 126, Scranton 108
Wilmington 140, Hartford 108   Wilkes-Barre 137, Scranton 122
Wilmington 140, Hartford 126

EPBL FINALS
Wilkes- Barre 116, Wilmington 93
Wilmington 114, Wilkes-Barre 110
Wilkes-Barre 122, Wilmington 115
Wilmington 123, Wilkes-Barre113
Wilkes-Barre 130, Wilmington 115

1969-70 EPBL

	W	L	Pct.	GB
Allentown Jets	20	8	.714	—
Wilmington Blue Bombers	19	9	.679	1
Hamden Bics	18	10	.643	2
Hartford Capitols	15	12	.556	4.5
Wilkes-Barre Barons	13	14	.481	6.5
Sunbury Mercuries	10	18	.357	10
Scranton Miners	8	19	.296	11.5
Binghamton Flyers	7	20	.256	12.5

EPBL SEMI-FINALS
Allentown 138, Hamden 131   Wilmington 138, Hartford 127
Hamden 128, Allentown 124   Hartford 120, Wilmington 108
Allentown 150, Hambed 133   Wilmington 140, Hartford 116

EPBL FINALS
Allentown 131, Wilmington 126
Wilmington 135, Allentown 113
Allentown 138, Wilmington 134
Wilmington 144, Allentown 130
Allentown 142, Wilmington 137

EASTERN BASKETBALL ASSOCIATION

1970-71 EBA

NORTHERN DIVISION	W	L	Pct.	GB
Hamden Bics	19	9	.679	—
Hartford Capitols	15	13	.536	4
Camden Bullets	12	16	.429	7
Delaware Blue Bombers	11	17	.393	8
SOUTHERN DIVISION	**W**	**L**	**Pct.**	**GB**
Scranton Apollos	21	7	.750	—
Allentown Jets	15	13	.536	6
Sunbury Mercuries	14	14	.500	7
Wilkes-Barre Barons	13	15	.464	8
Trenton Pat Pavers	6	22	.214	15

EBA NORTHERN SEMI-FINALS   **EBA SOUTHERN SEMI-FINALS**
Hartford 155, Camden 103   Allentown 137, Sunbury 128
Hartford 120, Camden 117   Sunbury 138, Allentown 125
                                       Allentown 133, Sunbury 117

EBA NORTHERN FINALS   **EBA SOUTHERN FINALS**
Hamden 139, Hartford 135, OT   Scranton 119, Allentown 110
Hartford 136, Hamden 106   Allentown 108, Scranton 105
Hamden 128, Hartford 123   Scranton 115, Allentown 114

EBA FINALS
Scranton 135, Hamden 103
Hamden 141, Scranton 119
Scranton 127, Hamden 125, OT
Scranton 126, Hamden 121, OT

1971-72 EBA

	W	L	Pct.	GB
Allentown Jets	21	9	.700	—
Scranton Apollos	17	13	.567	4
Hartford Capitols	17	13	.567	4
Trenton Pat Pavers	13	17	.433	8
Hazleton Bits	11	19	.367	10
Wilke-Barre Barons	11	19	.367	10

EBA SEMI-FINALS
Allentown 139, Trenton 116   Scranton 117, Hartford 110
Allentown 125, Trenton 116   Hartford 118, Scranton 109
                                    Scranton 108, Hartford 107

EBA FINALS
Allentown 124, Scranton 114
Scranton 128, Allentown 110
Scranton 123, Allentown 120
Allentown 119, Scranton 110
Allentown 115, Scranton 111

1972-73 EBA

	W	L	Pct.	GB
Hartford Capitols	25	7	.781	—
Wilkes-Barre Barons	22	10	.688	3
Scranton Apollos	20	12	.625	5
Allentown Jets	15	17	.469	10
Garden State Colonials	13	19	.406	12
Hamilton Pat Pavers	11	19	.367	13
Hamburg/Hazleton Bullets	4	26	.133	20

EBA SEMI-FINALS
Hartford 122, Allentown 111   Wilkes-Barre 114, Scranton 106
Hartford 115, Allentown 108   Wilkes-Barre 125, Scranton 113

EBA FINALS
Hartford 115, Wilkes-Barre 110
Wilkes-Barre 119, Hartford 109
Wilkes-Barre 132, Hartford 128
Hartford 120, Wilkes-Barre 117 (3OT)
Wilkes-Barre 120, Hartford 112

1973-74 EBA

EASTERN DIVISION	W	L	Pct.	GB
Hartford Capitols	19	8	.703	—
Hamilton Pat Pavers	14	13	.519	5
East Orange Colonials	8	19	.296	11
Cherry Hill Rookies	5	22	.185	14
WESTERN DIVISION	**W**	**L**	**Pct.**	**GB**
Allentown Jets	20	8	.714	—
Scranton Apollos	17	11	.607	3
Hazleton Bullets	15	12	.556	4.5

EBA EASTERN SEMI-FINALS   **EBA WESTERN SEMI-FINALS**
Hamilton 128, East Orange 112   Scranton 110, Hazleton 104
Hamilton 138, East Orange 113   Scranton 94, Hazleton 92

EBA EASTERN FINALS   **EBA WESTERN FINALS**
Hamilton 111, Hartford 109   Allentown 133, Scranton 108
Hartford 110, Hamilton 96   Scranton 131, Allentown 118
Hartford 120, Hamilton 117   Allentown 121, Scranton 115

EBA FINALS
Allentown 130, Hartford 114
Hartford 128, Allentown 111
Hartford 118, Allentown 103
Allentown 131, Hartford 125
Hartford 108, Allentown 107, OT

1974-75 EBA

	W	L	Pct.	GB
Hazleton Bullets	18	11	.620	—
Allentown Jets	16	14	.533	2.5
Scranton Apollos	15	14	.517	3
Cherry Hill Rookies	9	17	.346	7.5

EBA SEMI-FINALS
Allentown 133, Scranton 105
Allentown 111, Scranton 103

EBA FINALS
Allentown 115, Hazleton 98
Hazleton 109, Allentown 105
Allentown 117, Hazleton 105

1975-76 EBA

	W	L	Pct.	GB
Allentown Jets	24	3	.889	—
Scranton Apollos	21	5	.808	2.5
Lancaster Red Roses	19	5	.792	3.5
Hazleton Bullets	14	9	.609	8
Long Island Sounds	8	15	.348	14
Trenton Capitols	6	16	.261	16
Wilkes-Barre Barons	6	18	.250	6.5
Gold Coast*	—	—	—	—

*Gold Coast disbanded during the season

EBA SEMI-FINALS

Hazleton 130, Allentown 128   Lancaster 115, Scranton 114
Allentown 123, Hazleton 117   Scranton 128, Lancaster 120
Allentown 134, Hazleton 121   Lancaster 121, Scranton 103
Hazleton 134, Allentown 116   Scranton 116, Lancaster 106
Allentown 114, Hazleton 108   Lancaster 119, Scranton 111

EBA FINALS

Allentown 123, Lancaster 112
Lancaster 126, Allentown 116
Lancaster 159, Allentown 158 (2OT)
Allentown 128, Lancaster 114
Allentown 126, Lancaster 114

1976-77 EBA

	W	L	Pct.	GB
Allentown Jets	21	5	.808	—
Scranton Apollos	20	6	.769	1
Lancaster Red Roses	12	10	.545	7
Wilkes-Barre Barons	8	10	.444	9
Hartford Downtowners	5	19	.208	15
Jersey Shore Bullets	3	18	.143	15.5
Syracuse Centennials*	8	9	.471	—

*Syracuse disbanded during the season

EBA FINALS

Allentown 124, Scranton 123
Scranton 139, Allentown 128
Scranton 127, Allentown 123
Scranton 102, Allentown 101

1977-78 EBA

EASTERN DIVISION	W	L	Pct.	GB
Jersey Shore Bullets	20	11	.645	—
Long Island Ducks	15	15	.500	4.5
Quincy Chiefs	12	19	.387	8
Providence Shooting Stars	9	19	.321	9.5
Brooklyn Dodgers	8	22	.267	11.5
WESTERN DIVISION	**W**	**L**	**Pct.**	**GB**
Anchorage Northern Knights	24	7	.774	—
Wilkes-Barre Barons	23	8	.742	1
Lancaster Red Roses	19	12	.613	5
Allentown Jets	17	14	.548	7
Washington Metros	5	26	.167	18.5

EBA QUARTER-FINALS

Wilkes-Barre 143, Quincy 124   Lancaster 166, Long Island 149
Wilkes-Barre 143, Quincy 125   Lancaster 166, Long Island 149

EBA SEMI-FINALS

Lancaster 106, Anchorage 102   Wilkes-Barre 135, Jersey Shore 123
Anchorage 141, Lancaster 111   Wilkes-Barre 124, Jersey Shore 114
Lancaster 113, Anchorage 110   Jersey Shore 143, Wilkes-Barre 120
Anchorage 116, Lancaster 115   Wilkes- Barre 110, Jersey Shore 105
Lancaster 115, Anchorage 113

EBA FINALS

Wilkes-Barre 123, Lancaster 120
Lancaster 139, Wilkes-Barre 132
Wilkes-Barre 126, Lancaster 111
Lancaster 125, Wilkes-Barre 120
Wilkes-Barre 131, Lancaster 124

CONTINENTAL BASKETBALL ASSOCIATION

QW: Quarters won. Teams receive 3 points for a win, 1 point for each quarter won and 1/2 point for each quarter tied

1978-79 CBA

NORTHERN DIVISION	W	L	Pct.	GB
Rochester Zeniths	36	12	.750	—
Anchorage Northern Knights	27	22	.551	9.5
Jersey Shore Bullets	22	26	.458	14
Maine Lumberjacks	17	30	.362	18.5
SOUTHERN DIVISION	**W**	**L**	**Pct.**	**GB**
Wilkes-Barre Barons	22	22	.500	—
Allentown Jets	20	21	.488	0.5
Lancaster Red Roses	14	26	.350	6
Mohawk Valley Thunderbirds*	16	15	.516	—

*Mohawk Valley disbanded during the season

CBA FIRST ROUND

Jersey Shore 145, Allentown 120
Allentown 124, Jersey Shore 115
Allentown 144, Jersey Shore 140

CBA SEMI-FINALS

Anchorage 159, Wilkes-Barre 143   Rochester 140, Allentown 131
Anchorage 166, Wilkes-Barre 146   Allentown 130, Rochester 119, OT
Wilkes-Barre 157, Anchorage 151   Rochester 121, Allentown 120
Anchorage 173, Wilkes-Barre 137   Rochester 142, Allentown 132

CBA FINALS

Rochester 159, Anchorage 138
Rochester 148, Anchorage 136
Rochester 140, Anchorage 128
Rochester 134, Anchorage 129

1979-80 CBA

NORTHERN DIVISION	W	L	Pct.	GB
Rochester Zeniths	31	15	.674	—
Anchorage Northern Knights	29	16	.644	1.5
Maine Lumberjacks	21	23	.477	9
Hawaii Volcanos	20	25	.444	10.5
SOUTHERN DIVISION	**W**	**L**	**Pct.**	**GB**
Lehigh Valley Jets	19	12	.613	—
Pennsylvania Barons	14	17	.452	5
Lancaster Red Roses	12	22	.353	8.5
Utica Olympics	15	31	.326	12

CBA SEMI-FINALS

Maine 128, Lehigh Valley 105
Maine 130, Lehigh Valley 127
Rochester 127, Pennsylvania 126
Rochester 130, Pennsylvania 124

CBA EASTERN FINALS	**CBA WESTERN FINALS**
Rochester 140, Maine 132	Anchorage 127, Hawaii 122
Rochester 133, Maine 125	Hawaii 147, Anchorage 139
CBA FINALS	Hawaii 118, Anchorage 114
Rochester 116, Anchorage 113	Anchorage 139, Hawaii 130
Anchorage 132, Rochester 124	Anchorage 132, Hawaii 129
Anchorage 113, Rochester 109	
Anchorage 120, Rochester 117	
Rochester 105, Anchorage 96	
Rochester 113, Anchorage 96	
Anchorage 109, Rochester 99	

CBA 1980-81

EASTERN DIVISION	W	L	Pct.	GB
Rochester Zeniths	34	6	.850	—
Atlantic City Hi Rollers	22	18	.550	12
Philadelphia Kings	17	23	.425	17
Lehigh Valley Jets	16	24	.400	18
Maine Lumberjacks	16	24	.400	18
Scranton Aces	13	27	.325	21
WESTERN DIVISION	**W**	**L**	**Pct.**	**GB**
Montana Golden Nuggets	27	15	.643	—
Anchorage Northern Knights	25	17	.595	2
Billings Volcanos	23	19	.548	4
Alberta Dusters	11	31	.262	16

CBA EASTERN SEMI-FINALS	**CBA WESTERN SEMI-FINALS**
Rochester 132, Lehigh Valley 116	Montana 95, Alberta 87
Rochester 148, Lehigh Valley 123	Montana 120, Alberta 107
Philadelphia 134, Atlantic City 129	Billngs 123, Anchorage 119
Atlantic City 137, Philadelphia 136	Anchorage 109, Billings 103
Philadelphia 129, Atlantic City 125	Billings 110, Anchorage 95
CBA EASTERN FINALS	**CBA WESTERN FINALS**
Rochester 124, Philadelphia 116	Montana 134, Billings 128
Philadelphia 138, Rochester 137	Montana 134, Billings 125
Rochester 127, Philadelphia 103	Billings 132, Montana 129
	Montana 106, Billings 105

CBA FINALS
Rochester 131, Montana 112
Rochester 131, Montana 109
Rochester 136, Montana 121
Rochester 130, Montana 121

1981-82 CBA

EASTERN DIVISION	W	L	QW	Pts
Lancaster Lightning	34	12	105.0	207.0
Rochester Zeniths	29	17	102.0	189.0
Maine Lumberjacks	18	28	81.5	135.5
Atlantic City Hi Rollers	15	31	84.0	129.0
WESTERN DIVISION	**W**	**L**	**QW**	**Pts**
Billings Volcanoes	32	14	106.0	202.0
Montana Golden Nuggets	30	16	104.0	194.0
Alberta Dusters	12	34	81.5	117.5
Anchorage Northern Knights	14	32	72.0	114.0

CBA EASTERN FINALS
Lancaster 118, Rochester 96
Rochester 107, Lancaster 105
Lancaster 104, Rochester 91
Lancaster 112, Rochester 108

CBA WESTERN FINALS
Billings 122, Montana 121
Billings 121, Montana 109
Montana 118, Billings 114
Montana 135, Billings 133
Billings 108, Montana 107

CBA FINALS
Lancaster 110, Billings 98
Lancaster 98, Billings 94
Billings 110, Lancaster 102
Lancaster 131, Billings 120
Lancaster 125, Billings 113

1982-83 CBA

EASTERN DIVISION	W	L	QW	Pts
Rochester Zeniths	29	15	106.5	193.5
Lancaster Lightning	30	14	95.5	185.5
Maine Lumberjacks	22	22	88.0	154.0
Albany Patroons	16	28	75.5	123.5
CENTRAL DIVISION	**W**	**L**	**QW**	**Pts**
Detroit Spirits	26	18	92.0	170.0
Ohio Mixers	17	27	81.5	132.5
Wisconsin Flyers	14	30	78.0	120.0
WESTERN DIVISION	**W**	**L**	**QW**	**Pts**
Montana Golden Nuggets	33	11	104.0	203.0
Wyoming Wildcatters	22	22	86.0	152.0
Billings Volcanos	20	24	86.0	146.0
Las Vegas/Albuquerque*	17	27	85.0	136.0
Reno Bighorns	18	26	78.0	132.0

*Las Vegas Silvers moved and became the Albuquerque Silvers during the season

CBA EASTERN FINALS
Rochester 150, Detroit 125
Rochester 100, Detroit 98
Detroit 124, Rochester 119 (2OT)
Detroit 118, Rochester 114
Detroit 128, Rochester 116

CBA WESTERN FINALS
Montana 134, Wyoming 132
Wyoming 134, Montana 125
Montana 123, Wyoming 118
Montana 117, Wyoming 111

CBA FINALS
Detroit 99, Montana 94
Montana 110, Detroit 88
Detroit 109, Montana 107
Montana 109, Detroit 107
Detroit 136, Montana 128 (2OT)
Montana 107, Detroit 104
Detroit 106, Montana 102

1983-84 CBA

EASTERN DIVISION	W	L	QW	Pts
Puerto Rico Coquis	28	16	98.0	182.0
Albany Patroons	25	19	89.5	164.5
Bay State Bombardiers	22	22	95.0	161.0
Lancaster Lightning	24	20	88.5	160.5
Sarasota Stingers	16	28	81.5	129.5
Toronto Tornados	16	28	74.0	122.0
WESTERN DIVISION	**W**	**L**	**QW**	**Pts**
Wisconsin Flyers	27	17	101.0	182.0
Detroit Spirits	26	18	89.0	167.0
Wyoming Wildcatters	23	21	93.5	162.5
Ohio Mixers	23	21	88.0	157.0
Louisville Catbirds	23	21	87.0	156.0
Albuquerque Silvers	11	33	71.0	104.0

CBA EASTERN SEMI-FINALS
Bay State 110, Albany 100
Bay State 100, Albany 99, OT
Albany 117, Bay State 114, OT
Albany 116, Bay State 111
Albany 118, Bay State 101

Lancaster 114, Puerto Rico 109
Lancaster 110, Puerto Rico 103

CBA WESTERN SEMI-FINALS
Wyoming 118, Detroit 116
Wyoming 133, Detroit 115
Detroit 113, Wyoming 112
Wyoming 135, Detroit 124

Wisconsin 118, Ohio 110
Ohio 117, Wisconsin 116

Puerto Rico 103, Lancaster 93
Puerto Rico 112, Lancaster 95
Puerto Rico 98, Lancaster 87

CBA EASTERN FINALS
Albany 106, Puerto Rico 105
Puerto Rico 129, Albany 122
Albany 105, Puerto Rico 102, OT
Albany 114, Puerto Rico 109

Wisconsin 102, Ohio 101
Ohio 134, Wisconsin 120
Wisconsin 112, Ohio 97

CBA WESTERN FINALS
Wyoming 122, Wisconsin 121, OT
Wisconsin 116, Wyoming 101
Wyoming 89, Wisconsin 84
Wyoming 101, Wisconsin 94

CBA FINALS
Albany 129, Wyoming 121
Wyoming 128, Albany 126
Albany 120, Wyoming 111
Wyoming 128, Albany 112
Albany 119, Wyoming 109

1984-85 CBA

EASTERN DIVISION	W	L	QW	Pts
Albany Patroons	34	14	118.5	220.5
Tampa Bay Thrillers	35	13	108.0	213.0
Lancaster Lightning	28	20	102.5	186.5
Toronto Tornados	26	22	101.5	179.5
Puerto Rico Coquis	27	21	98.5	179.5
Bay State Bombardiers	20	28	93.0	153.0
Sarasota Stingers	21	27	89.5	152.5
WESTERN DIVISION	**W**	**L**	**QW**	**Pts**
Wyoming Wildcatters	24	24	99.0	171.0
Evansville Thunder	23	25	95.5	164.5
Detroit Spirits	23	25	94.0	163.0
Wisconsin Flyers	21	27	91.0	154.0
Louisville Catbirds	19	29	92.5	149.5
Cincinnati Slammers	17	31	84.0	135.0
Albuquerque Silvers	18	30	76.5	130.5

CBA EASTERN SEMI-FINALS
Tampa Bay 114, Lancaster 95
Tampa Bay 105, Lancaster 101
Tampa Bay 107, Lancaster 104, OT

Albany 133, Toronto 109
Toronto 124, Albany 114
Toronto 117, Albany 105
Albany 123, Toronto 111
Albany 132, Toronto 123

CBA WESTERN SEMI-FINALS
Detroit 139, Evansville 136
Evansville 150, Detroit 145
Detroit 132, Evansville 129
Detroit 173, Evansville 145

Wyoming 109, Wisconsin 97
Wyoming 112, Wisconsin 101
Wisconsin 121, Wyoming 98
Wisconsin 118, Wyoming 107
Wisconsin 98, Wyoming 84

CBA EASTERN FINALS
Tampa Bay 144, Albany 129
Albany 113, Tampa Bay 100
Tampa Bay 93, Albany 90
Albany 118, Tampa Bay 113
Tampa Bay 93, Albany 89, OT

CBA WESTERN FINALS
Detroit 121, Wisconsin 113
Detroit 122, Wisconsin 107
Detroit 133, Wisconsin 126

CBA FINALS
Tampa Bay 123, Detroit 119
Detroit 146, Tampa Bay 139
Tampa Bay 127, Detroit 106
Tampa Bay 134, Detroit 132
Detroit 107, Tampa Bay 103
Detroit 122, Tampa Bay 111
Tampa Bay 109, Detroit 105

1985-86 CBA

EASTERN DIVISION	W	L	QW	Pts
Tampa Bay Thrillers	34	14	109.0	211.0
Bay State Bombardiers	30	18	105.0	195.0
Baltimore Lightning	26	22	101.0	179.0
Albany Patroons	24	24	99.5	171.5
Florida Stingers	21	27	99.0	162.0
Maine Windjammers	18	30	84.0	138.0
Toronto/Pensacola*	15	33	81.5	126.5
WESTERN DIVISION	**W**	**L**	**QW**	**Pts**
Cincinnati Slammers	33	15	102.5	201.5
Evansville Thunder	25	23	97.5	172.5
Detroit Spirits	24	24	100.0	172.0
La Crosse Catbirds	24	24	98.5	170.5
Kansas City Sizzlers	25	23	94.0	169.0
Wyoming Wildcatters	21	27	93.0	156.0
Wisconsin Flyers	16	32	79.5	127.5

*Toronto Tornados moved and became the Pensacola Tornados during the season

CBA WESTERN QUARTERFINAL
Cincinnati 140, Kansas City 113
Cincinnati 129, Kansas City 103
Cincinnati 136, Kansas City 133, OT
Cincinnati 124 Kansas City 114

CBA EASTERN SEMI-FINALS
Albany 127, Tampa Bay 118
Tampa Bay 119, Albany 104
Tampa Bay 104, Albany 101
Albany 103, Tampa Bay 100
Albany 124, Tampa Bay 118

CBA WESTERN SEMI-FINALS
Cincinnati 126, Evansville 117
Cincinnati 108, Evansville 105, OT
Evansville 114, Cincinnati 111
Evansville 131, Cincinnati 116
Cincinnati 115, Evansville 104

Tampa Bay 134, Albany 111
Tampa Bay 118, Albany 110

Baltimore 121, Bay State 115
Bay State 135, Baltimore 132
Bay State 130, Baltimore 115
Bay State 136, Baltimore 130
Baltimore 125, Bay State 122
Bay State 118, Baltimore 114

CBA EASTERN FINALS
Tampa Bay 118, Bay State 100
Tampa Bay 112, Bay State 93
Bay State 107, Tampa Bay 104, OT
Tampa Bay 98, Bay State 97
Tampa Bay 119, Bay State 117

CBA FINALS
Tampa Bay 123, La Crosse 94
Tampa Bay 114, La Crosse 93
Tampa Bay 109, La Crosse 106
La Crosse 109, Tampa Bay 106
Tampa Bay 110, La Crosse 108

Detroit 117, La Crosse 114
Detroit 121, La Crosse 118, OT
La Crosse 123, Detroit 110
La Crosse 115, Detroit 105
Detroit 117, La Crosse 105
La Crosse 131, Detroit 117
La Crosse 108, Detroit 107

CBA WESTERN FINALS
Cincinnati 107, La Crosse 95
La Crosse 120, Cincinnati 102
La Crosse 100, Cincinnati 86
La Crosse 99, Cincinnati 92
Cincinnati 101, La Crosse 86
La Crosse 101, Cincinnati 93

1986-87 CBA

EASTERN DIVISION	W	L	QW	Pts
Tampa Bay Thrillers*	34	14	119.0	221.0
Albany Patroons	26	22	96.5	174.5
Jacksonville/Mississippi**	26	22	93.0	171.0
Pensacola Tornados	20	28	97.0	157.0
Charleston Gunners	20	28	82.5	142.5
Savannah Spirits	20	28	80.5	140.5
WESTERN DIVISION	**W**	**L**	**QW**	**Pts**
La Crosse Catbirds	28	20	103.0	187.0
Cincinnati Slammers	25	23	108.5	183.5
Topeka Sizzlers	24	24	91.5	163.5
Rockford Lightning	22	26	95.5	161.5
Wyoming Wildcatters	21	27	97.5	160.5
Wisconsin Wildcatters	22	26	87.5	153.5

*Tampa Bay moved to Rapid City at the conclusion of the regular season
**Jacksonville Jets moved and became the Mississippi Jets during the season

CBA EASTERN SEMI-FINALS
Albany vs Mississippi
Albany 150, Mississippi 130
Albany 116, Mississippi 115
Albany 111, Mississippi 103

Rapid City 108, Pensacola 99
Rapid City 108, Pensacola 100
Pensacola 111, Rapid City 100
Rapid City 103, Pensacola 82
Rapid City 99, Pensacola 89

CBA EASTERN FINALS
Rapid City 117, Albany 107
Rapid City 125, Albany 112
Rapid City 91, Albany 88, OT
Rapid City 113, Albany 112

CBA FINALS
Rockford 123, Rapid City 120
Rapid City 113, Rockford 108
Rapid City 126, Rockford 118
Rapid City 162, Rockford 125
Rapid City 127, Rockford 120

CBA WESTERN SEMI-FINALS
Cincinnati 118, Topeka 114, OT
Cincinnati 138, Topeka 105
Cincinnati 98, Topeka 93
Topeka 101, Cincinnati 100
Topeka 106, Cincinnati 103, OT
Topeka 106, Cincinnati 103, OT

Rockford 107, La Crosse 103
La Crosse 108, Rockford 99
La Crosse 107, Rockford 104
Rockford 98, La Crosse 94
La Crosse 136, Rockford 108
Rockford 99, La Crosse 96

CBA WESTERN FINALS
Rockford 127, Cincinnati 121
Cincinnati 101, Rockford 96
Rockford 117, Cincinnati 111
Rockford 117, Cincinnati 103
Rockford 107, Cincinnati 101

1987-88 CBA

EASTERN DIVISION	W	L	QW	Pts
Albany Patroons	48	6	149.5	293.5
Pensacola Tornados	28	26	101.5	185.5
Mississippi Jets	25	29	107.5	182.5
Savannah Spirits	22	32	100.0	166.0
Topeka Sizzlers	21	33	100.5	163.5
Charleston Gunners	14	40	88.0	130.0
WESTERN DIVISION	**W**	**L**	**QW**	**Pts**
La Crosse Catbirds	40	14	122.0	242.0
Rockford Lightning	37	17	118.5	229.5
Quad City Thunder	30	24	118.5	208.5
Wyoming Wildcatters	23	31	104.5	173.5
Rochester Flyers	20	34	104.5	164.5
Rapid City Thrillers	16	38	81.0	129.0

CBA EASTERN SEMI-FINALS
Albany 124, Savannah 104
Albany 119, Savannah 105
Savannah 119, Albany 114
Albany 122, Savannah 104
Albany 135, Savannah 91

CBA WESTERN SEMI-FINALS
La Crosse 109, Wyoming 94
La Crosse 105, Wyoming 92
Wyoming 106, La Crosse 104
Wyoming 108, La Crosse 107
Wyoming 103, La Crosse 92
Wyoming 96, La Crosse 89

Pensacola 127, Mississippi 104
Pensacola 115, Mississippi 111
Mississippi 121, Pensacola 103
Pensacola 131, Mississippi 111
Pensacola 112, Mississippi 99

CBA EASTERN FINALS
Albany 105, Pensacola 100
Albany 94, Pensacola 89
Albany 101, Pensacola 96
Albany 105, Pensacola 100
Albany 94, Pensacola 89

CBA FINALS
Wyoming 116, Albany 113, OT
Albany 95, Wyoming 83
Wyoming 83, Albany 80
Albany 104, Wyoming 85
Wyoming 109, Albany 90
Albany 102, Wyoming 81
Albany 105, Wyoming 96

Quad City 109, Rockford 96
Rockford 120, Quad City 117, OT
Quad City 127, Rockford 118
Rockford 111, Quad City 110
Rockford 92, Quad City 91
Quad City 114, Rockford 98
Rockford 99, Quad City 88

CBA WESTERN FINALS
Rockford 90, Wyoming 80
Wyoming 114, Rockford 110
Wyoming 103, Rockford 90
Wyoming 98, Rockford 93
Rockford 119, Wyoming 113
Wyoming 137, Rockford 134 (4OT)

1988-89 CBA

EASTERN DIVISION	W	L	QW	Pts
Albany Patroons	36	18	125.5	233.5
Tulsa Fast Breakers	28	26	114.0	198.0
Pensacola Tornados	30	24	104.5	194.5
Wichita Falls Texans	23	31	104.5	173.5
Charleston Gunners	20	34	97.5	157.5
Topeka Sizzlers	14	40	83.0	125.0
WESTERN DIVISION	**W**	**L**	**QW**	**Pts**
Rapid City Thrillers	38	16	131.5	245.5
Quad City Thunder	36	18	122.5	230.5
Rockford Lightning	34	20	121.5	223.5
Cedar Rapids Silver Bullets	30	24	100.5	190.5
La Crosse Catbirds	19	35	103.0	160.0
Rochester Flyers	16	38	88.0	136.0

CBA EASTERN SEMI-FINALS
Albany 113, Wichita Falls 111
Wichita Falls 106, Albany 98
Albany 106, Wichita Falls 97
Wichita Falls 106, Albany 97
Wichita Falls 101, Albany 100
Wichita Falls 107, Albany 100

CBA WESTERN SEMI-FINALS
Rapid City 96, Cedar Rapids 81
Rapid City 95, Cedar Rapids 89
Cedar Rapids 101, Rapid City 98
Rapid City, 104, Cedar Rapids 84
Rapid City 118, Cedar Rapids 109

Tulsa 113, Pensacola 103
Tulsa 114, Pensacola 99
Tulsa 135, Pensacola 113
Pensacola 114, Tulsa 113
Tulsa 112, Pensacola 103

CBA EASTERN FINALS
Tulsa 125, Wichita Falls 116
Tulsa 126, Wichita Falls 110
Tulsa 140, Wichita Falls 100
Tulsa 114, Wichita Falls 104

CBA FINALS
Tulsa 109, Rockford 103
Tulsa 117, Rockford 104
Tulsa 124, Rockford 107
Tulsa 114, Rockford 111

Quad City 118, Rockford 117
Quad City 105, Rockford 101
Rockford 120, Quad City 111
Rockford 101, Quad City 90
Rockford 109, Quad City 95
Rockford 120, Quad City 111

CBA WESTERN FINALS
Rapid City 117, Rockford 116
Rockford 100, Rapid City 93
Rockford 116, Rapid City 109
Rapid City 118, Rockford 115
Rockford 106, Rapid City 92
Rockford 105, Rapid City 93

1989-90 CBA

AMERICAN CONFERENCE

EASTERN DIVISION	W	L	QW	Pts
Albany Patroons	41	15	136.5	259.5
Pensacola Tornados	32	24	116.5	212.5
Grand Rapids Hoops	26	30	110.5	188.5
Columbus Horizon	18	38	97.0	151.0
CENTRAL DIVISION	**W**	**L**	**QW**	**Pts**
La Crosse Catbirds	42	14	127.5	253.5
Quad City Thunder	34	22	130.5	232.5
Cedar Rapids Silver Bullets	25	31	110.0	185.0
Rockford Lightning	22	34	108.5	174.5

NATIONAL CONFERENCE

MIDWEST DIVISION	W	L	QW	Pts
Rapid City Thrillers	42	14	123.5	249.5
Omaha Racers	29	27	118.0	205.0
Sioux Falls Skyforce	20	36	101.0	161.0
Topeka Sizzlers	10	46	85.0	115.0
WESTERN DIVISION	**W**	**L**	**QW**	**Pts**
Santa Barbara Islanders	37	19	112.0	223.0
Tulsa Fast Breakers	31	25	117.0	210.0
San Jose Jammers	23	33	106.5	175.5
Wichita Falls Texans	16	40	92.0	140.0

CBA AMERICAN FIRST ROUND
Grand Rapids 114, Pensacola 98
Pensacola 117, Grand Rapids 103
Pensacola 121, Grand Rapids 109

CBA WESTERN FIRST ROUND
San Jose 140, Omaha 120
Omaha 141, San Jose 127
San Jose 128, Omaha 120

CBA AMERICAN SEMI-FINALS
La Crosse 124, Quad City 104
La Crosse 117, Quad City 103
La Crosse 136, Quad City 124

Pensacola 123, Albany 117
Pensacola 128, Albany 127 (2OT)
Albany 145, Pensacola 107
Albany 137, Pensacola 133, OT
Albany 134, Pensacola 86
CBA AMERICAN FINALS
La Crosse 108, Albany 93
Albany 116, La Crosse 105
Albany 112, La Crosse 103
La Crosse 120, Albany 92
La Crosse 102, Albany 100
Albany 113, La Crosse 99
La Crosse 104, Albany 99, OT
CBA FINALS
La Crosse 128, Rapid City 109
La Crosse 111, Rapid City 98
Rapid City 127, La Crosse 109
La Crosse 114, Rapid City 105
La Crosse 113, Rapid City 101

CBA NATIONAL SEMI-FINALS
Tulsa 115, Santa Barbara 103
Santa Barbara 137, Tulsa 133, OT
Santa Barbara 118, Tulsa 116, OT
Tulsa 109, Santa Barbara 105
Santa Barbara 121, Tulsa 116

Rapid City 126, San Jose 93
San Jose 131, Rapid City 119
Rapid City 98, San Jose 97
San Jose 121, Rapid City 113
Rapid City 143, San Jose 107
CBA NATIONAL FINALS
Santa Barbara 116, Rapid City 110
Rapid City 122, Santa Barbara 110
Santa Barbara 119, Rapid City 111
Rapid City 119, Santa Barbara 117
Rapid City 127, Santa Barbara 100
Rapid City 140, Santa Barbara 97

1990-91 CBA
AMERICAN CONFERENCE

CENTRAL DIVISION	W	L	QW	Pts
Quad City Thunder	32	24	120.5	216.5
La Crosse Catbirds	32	24	111.0	207.0
Rockford Lightning	23	33	114.0	183.0
Cedar Rapids Silver Bullets	24	32	106.0	178.0
MIDWEST DIVISION	**W**	**L**	**QW**	**Pts**
Omaha Racers	39	17	127.0	244.0
Rapid City Thrillers	27	29	115.5	196.5
Sioux Falls Skyforce	26	30	100.0	178.0
Yakima Sun Kings	15	41	90.5	135.5

NATIONAL CONFERENCE

WESTERN DIVISION	W	L	QW	Pts
Tulsa Fast Breakers	34	22	124.0	226.0
Wichita Falls Texans	32	24	125.5	221.5
San Jose Jammers	21	35	93.0	156.0
Oklahoma City Cavalry	18	38	95.5	149.5
EASTERN DIVISION	**W**	**L**	**QW**	**Pts**
Albany Patroons	50	6	139.0	289.0
Grand Rapids Hornets	25	31	116.5	191.5
Pensacola Tornados	27	29	108.0	189.0
Columbus Horizon	23	33	106.0	175.0

CBA AMERICAN FIRST ROUND
Rapid City 125, Omaha 109
Omaha 115, Rapid City 102
Omaha 145, Rapid City 136
Rapid City 113, Omaha 109
Omaha 123, Rapid City 100

Quad City 118, La Crosse 108
La Crosse 108, Quad City 102
Quad City 117, La Crosse 105
La Crosse 110, Quad City 108, OT
Quad City 123, La Crosse 104
CBA AMERICAN FINALS
Quad City 117, Omaha 107
Quad City 123, Omaha 107
Omaha 113, Quad City 111
Quad City 122, Omaha 113
Quad City 129, Omaha 120

CBA FINALS
Wichita Falls 103, Quad City 99
Wichita Falls 100, Quad City 94
Quad City 114, Wichita Falls 97
Wichita Falls 100, Quad City 97
Quad City 108, Wichita Falls 97
Quad City 100, Wichita Falls 98
Wichita Falls 102, Quad City 90

CBA NATIONAL FIRST ROUND
Albany 102, Grand Rapids 89
Grand Rapids 105, Albany 102
Albany 101, Grand Rapids 89
Grand Rapids 119, Albany 102
Albany 100, Grand Rapids 87

Wichita Falls 115, Tulsa 102
Tulsa 115, Wichita Falls 112
Wichita Falls 107, Tulsa 105
Wichita Falls 111, Tulsa 87
CBA NATIONAL FINALS
Wichita Falls 121, Albany 99
Wichita Falls 110, Albany 99
Albany 99, Wichita Falls 91
Wichita Falls 95, Albany 88
Albany 100, Wichita Falls 91
Wichita Falls 87, Albany 84

1991-92 CBA
AMERICAN CONFERENCE

EASTERN DIVISION	W	L	QW	Pts
Grand Rapids Hoops	28	28	110.5	194.5
Birmingham Bandits	25	31	114.5	189.5
Albany Patroons	24	32	109.0	181.0
Columbus Horizon	18	38	88.0	142.0
MIDWEST DIVISION	**W**	**L**	**QW**	**Pts**
Quad City Thunder	42	14	136.5	262.5
La Crosse Catbirds	40	16	140.0	260.0
Rockford Lightning	21	35	98.0	161.0
Fort Wayne Fury	21	35	87.0	150.0

NATIONAL CONFERENCE

NORTHERN DIVISION	W	L	QW	Pts
Rapid City Thrillers	37	19	130.0	241.0
Omaha Racers	37	19	127.0	238.0
Tri-City Chinook	29	27	112.0	199.0
Sioux Falls Skyforce	24	32	104.0	176.0
Yakima Sun Kings	13	43	82.5	121.5
SOUTHERN DIVISION	**W**	**L**	**QW**	**Pts**
Oklahoma City Cavalry	33	23	114.5	213.5
Wichita Falls Texans	28	28	126.5	210.5
Tulsa Zone	24	32	108.0	180.0
Bakersfield Jammers*	16	8	52.0	100.0

*Bakersfield disbanded during the season

CBA AMERICAN FIRST ROUND
Birmingham 131, Albany 122
CBA AMERICAN SECOND ROUND
La Crosse 108, Grand Rapids 99
La Crosse 119, Grand Rapids 92
Grand Rapids 121, La Crosse 110
La Crosse 99, Grand Rapids 94

Quad City 109, Birmingham 99
Quad City 125, Birmingham 102
Birmingham 102, Quad City 97
Quad City 116, Birmingham 109
CBA AMERICAN FINALS
La Crosse 89, Quad City 86
Quad City 119, La Crosse 105
Quad City 118, La Crosse 114
La Crosse 116, Quad City 107
La Crosse 101, Quad City 95
CBA FINALS
La Crosse 105, Rapid City 95
Rapid City 114, La Crosse 105
La Crosse 107, Rapid City 101
Rapid City 102, La Crosse 94
Rapid City 110, La Crosse 103
La Crosse 125, Rapid City 120
La Crosse 101, Rapid City 98

CBA NATIONAL FIRST ROUND
Wichita 102, Tri-City 90
CBA NATIONAL SECOND ROUND
Omaha 126, Oklahoma City 110
Omaha 130, Oklahoma City 114
Oklahoma City 103, Omaha 97
Oklahoma City 135, Omaha 115
Omaha 106, Oklahoma City 98

Wichita Falls 108, Rapid City 103
Rapid City 105, Wichita Falls 95
Rapid City 98, Wichita Falls 72
Rapid City 100, Wichita Falls 90
CBA NATIONAL FINALS
Omaha 113, Rapid City 103
Rapid City 100, Omaha 98
Rapid City 93, Omaha 90
Omaha 104, Rapid City 90
Rapid City 108, Omaha 92

1992-93 CBA
AMERICAN CONFERENCE

EASTERN DIVISION	W	L	QW	Pts
Grand Rapids Hoops	35	21	125.0	230.0
Capital Region Pontiacs	28	28	113.0	197.0
Columbus Horizon	21	35	96.0	159.0
Fort Wayne Fury	20	36	98.5	158.5
MIDEAST DIVISION	**W**	**L**	**QW**	**Pts**
Rockford Lightning	44	12	138.0	270.0
Quad City Thunder	38	18	130.5	244.5
La Crosse Catbirds	32	24	123.0	219.0
Rochester Renegade	6	50	77.0	95.0

NATIONAL CONFERENCE

Midwest DIVISION	W	L	QW	Pts
Rapid City Thrillers	44	12	134.0	266.0
Omaha Racers	28	28	109.0	193.0
Sioux Falls Skyforce	26	30	110.5	188.5
Fargo-Moorhead Fever	18	38	95.0	149.0
WESTERN DIVISION	**W**	**L**	**QW**	**Pts**
Wichita Falls Texans	34	22	115.0	217.0
Tri-City Chinook	27	29	112.0	193.0
Oklahoma City Cavalry	25	31	112.5	187.5
Yakima Sun Kings	22	34	103.0	169.0

CBA AMERICAN FIRST ROUND
La Crosse 117, Rockford 101
La Crosse 121, Rockford 90
Rockford 140, La Crosse 100
Rockford 115, La Crosse 97
Rockford 127, La Crosse 121 (2OT)

Quad City 120, Grand Rapids 89
Quad City 99, Grand Rapids 88
Grand Rapids 100, Quad City 86

CBA NATIONAL FIRST ROUND
Rapid City 105, Tri-City 104
Rapid City 116, Tri-City 107
Rapid City 119, Tri-City 115

Omaha 98, Wichita Falls 94
Omaha 112, Wichita Falls 98
Wichita Falls 95, Omaha 83
Wichita Falls 101, Omaha 98
Omaha 103, Wichita Falls 102

Grand Rapids 115, Quad City 114, OT
Grand Rapids 98, Quad City 96

CBA AMERICAN FINALS **CBA NATIONAL FINALS**
Rockford 103, Grand Rapids 98   Omaha 134, Rapid City 130
Rockford 98, Grand Rapids 89   Omaha 119, Rapid City 112
Grand Rapids 97, Rockford 94   Rapid City 118, Omaha 105
Grand Rapids 104, Rockford 102   Rapid City 116, Omaha 115, OT
Grand Rapids 115, Rockford 110   Omaha 111, Rapid City 103

CBA FINALS
Omaha 106, Grand Rapids 98
Grand Rapids 113, Omaha 109, OT
Omaha 112, Grand Rapids 96
Omaha 119, Grand Rapids 111
Grand Rapids 103, Omaha 100
Omaha 106, Grand Rapids 98

1993-94 CBA
AMERICAN CONFERENCE

EASTERN DIVISION	W	L	QW	Pts
Grand Rapids Hoops	37	19	119.0	230.0
Fort Wayne Fury	19	37	104.5	161.5
Hartford Hellcats	18	38	100.0	154.0
Columbus Horizon	18	38	99.5	153.5
MIDEAST DIVISION	**W**	**L**	**QW**	**Pts**
La Crosse Catbirds	35	21	118.0	223.0
Rockford Lightning	32	24	122.0	218.0
Quad City Thunder	34	22	114.5	216.5
Rochester Renegades	31	25	112.0	205.0

NATIONAL CONFERENCE

MIDWEST DIVISION	W	L	QW	Pts
Rapid City Thrillers	37	19	125.5	236.5
Omaha Racers	30	26	113.5	203.5
Quad City Thunder	34	22	114.5	216.5
Fargo-Moorhead Fever	25	31	104.0	179.0
WESTERN DIVISION	**W**	**L**	**QW**	**Pts**
Tri-City Chinook	34	22	116.5	218.5
Wichita Falls Texans	26	30	118.0	196.0
Yakima Sun Kings	24	32	112.0	184.0
Oklahoma City Cavalry	24	32	105.5	177.5

CBA DAKOTA CAPITAL CLASSIC AMERICAN PLAYOFF QUALIFIER
Rochester 121, Fort Wayne 91   Quad City 82, Rochester 77, OT
CBA DAKOTA CAPITAL CLASSIC NATIONAL QUALIFIER
Sioux Falls 127, Yakima 121   Wichita Falls 119, Sioux Falls 101

CBA AMERICAN FIRST ROUND **CBA NATIONAL FIRST ROUND**
Grand Rapids 107, Quad City 88   Wichita Falls 115, Rapid City 112 (2OT)
Quad City 86, Grand Rapids 83   Rapid City 97, Wichita Falls 93
Quad City 85, Grand Rapids 77   Rapid City 97, Wichita Falls 94
Quad City 97, Grand Rapids 83   Wichita Falls 102, Rapid City 99
      Rapid City 103, Wichita Falls 97
La Crosse 115, Rockford 113, OT   Tri-City 140, Omaha 133, OT
La Crosse 104, Rockford 103   Tri-City 119, Omaha 105
La Crosse 109, Rockford 106   Omaha 111, Tri-City 98
      Omaha 117, Tri-City 115
CBA AMERICAN FINALS   Omaha 117, Tri-City 110
Quad City 119, La Crosse 100   **CBA NATIONAL FINALS**
Quad City 113, La Crosse 106   Rapid City 114, Omaha 109
Quad City 109, La Crosse 88   Omaha 114, Rapid City 100
CBA FINALS   Rapid City 118, Omaha 108
Quad City 127, Omaha 120 (2OT)   Omaha 104, Rapid City 102
Omaha 135, Quad City 134 (3OT)   Omaha 105, Rapid City 103
Quad City 103, Omaha 89
Quad City 110, Omaha 103
Quad City 132, Omaha 27, OT

1994-95 CBA
AMERICAN CONFERENCE

EASTERN DIVISION	W	L	QW	Pts
Pittsburgh Piranhas	27	29	119.0	200.0
Fort Wayne Fury	24	32	99.5	171.5
Harrisburg Hammerheads*	15	18	63.0	108.0
Hartford Hellcats*	11	23	57.5	90.5
MIDWEST DIVISION	**W**	**L**	**QW**	**Pts**
Quad City Thunder	33	23	116.5	215.5
Rockford Lightning	29	27	121.0	208.0
Chicago Rockers	28	28	118.0	202.0
Grand Rapids Mackers	29	27	114.0	201.0

NATIONAL CONFERENCE

WESTERN DIVISION	W	L	QW	Pts
Yakima Sun Kings	36	20	130.5	238.5
Sioux Falls Skyforce	34	22	131.0	233.0
Tri-City Chinook	32	24	127.5	223.5
Rapid City Thrillers	31	25	119.5	212.5
SOUTHERN DIVISION	**W**	**L**	**QW**	**Pts**
Oklahoma City Cavalry	35	21	106.0	211.0
Omaha Racers	26	30	97.5	175.5
Mexico Aztecas	19	37	100.5	157.5
Shreveport Crawdads	17	39	82.0	133.0

*Harrisburg and Hartford disbanded during the season

CBA AMERICAN FIRST ROUND
Grand Rapids 110, Chicago 104
Chicago 87, Grand Rapids 76
Chicago 102, Grand Rapids 94

Rockford 118, Fort Wayne 104
Rockford 117, Fort Wayne 108
CBA AMERICAN SECOND ROUND
Chicago 90, Quad City 86
Chicago 100, Quad City 97
Quad City 109, Chicago 77
Quad City 94, Chicago 90
Chicago 103, Quad City 100

Pittsburgh 119, Rockford 112
Pittsburgh 101, Rockford 93
Rockford 131, Pittsburgh 130, OT
Rockford 125, Pittsburgh 115
Pittsburgh 120, Rockford 113
CBA AMERICAN FINALS
Pittsburgh 99, Chicago 95
Pittsburgh 112, Chicago 110 (2OT)
Pittsburgh 96, Chicago 87

CBA FINALS
Yakima 110, Pittsburgh 97
Yakima 116, Pittsburgh 113
Pittsburgh 105, Yakima 100
Pittsburgh 106, Yakima 94
Yakima 102, Pittsburgh 99
Yakima 94, Pittsburgh 92

CBA NATIONAL FIRST ROUND
Tri-City 113, Rapid City 101
Tri-City 120, Rapid City 110

Omaha 119, Sioux Falls 114
Sioux Falls 118, Omaha 109
Omaha 197, Sioux Falls 104
CBA NATIONAL SECOND ROUND
Yakima 109, Tri-City 103, OT
Tri-City 103, Yakima 89
Yakima 106, Tri-City 102, OT
Yakima 115, Tri-City 102

Oklahoma City 110, Omaha 98
Omaha 118, Oklahoma City 111
Oklahoma City 117, Omaha 112
Omaha 105, Oklahoma City 101
Oklahoma City 108, Omaha 106, OT
CBA NATIONAL FINALS
Yakima 131, Oklahoma City 114
Oklahoma City 115, Yakima 97
Yakima 104, Oklahoma City 96
Yakima 116, Oklahoma City 102

1995-96 CBA
AMERICAN CONFERENCE

EASTERN DIVISION	W	L	QW	Pts
Grand Rapids Mackers	33	23	110.5	209.5
Fort Wayne Fury	25	31	113.0	188.0
Connecticut Pride	17	39	96.0	147.0
MIDEAST DIVISION	**W**	**L**	**QW**	**Pts**
Rockford Lightning	35	21	122.0	227.0
Quad City Thunder	37	19	116.0	227.0
Chicago Rockers	26	30	109.0	187.0

NATIONAL CONFERENCE

NORTHERN DIVISION	W	L	QW	Pts
Sioux Falls Skyforce	34	24	127.0	223.0
Omaha Racers	28	28	106.5	190.5
Yakima Sun Kings	19	37	104.5	161.5
SOUTHERN DIVISION	**W**	**L**	**QW**	**Pts**
Florida Beach Dogs	41	15	131.5	254.5
Oklahoma City Cavalry	34	22	121.5	223.5
Shreveport Storm	17	39	99.0	150.0
San Diego Wildcards*	4	17	34.5	46.5

*San Diego disbanded during the season

CBA AMERICAN FIRST ROUND **CBA NATIONAL FIRST ROUND**
Fort Wayne 127, Rockford 116   Florida 105, Omaha 87
Rockford 111, Fort Wayne 99   Florida 105, Omaha 96
Fort Wayne 103, Rockford 83   Florida 113, Omaha 91
Fort Wayne 97, Rockford 96
      Sioux Falls 120, Oklahoma City 97
Quad City 107, Grand Rapids 89   Sioux Falls 96, Oklahoma City 95
Grand Rapids 100, Quad City 91   Oklahoma City 119, Sioux Falls 111
Quad City 102, Grand Rapids 90   Sioux Falls 130, Oklahoma City 113
Quad City 104, Grand Rapids 97
CBA AMERICAN FINALS   **CBA NATIONAL FINALS**
Quad City 115, Fort Wayne 110   Florida 100, Sioux Falls 98
Fort Wayne 103, Quad City 101   Sioux Falls 106, Florida 104
Fort Wayne 96, Quad City 89, OT   Sioux Falls 112, Florida 111
Quad City 104, Fort Wayne 99   Florida 105, Sioux Falls 95
Fort Wayne 119, Quad City 107   Sioux Falls 97, Florida 95
CBA FINALS
Sioux Falls 131, Fort Wayne 123
Fort Wayne 113, Sioux Falls 105
Sioux Falls 121, Fort Wayne 115
Sioux Falls 123, Fort Wayne 122 (2OT)
Sioux Falls 118, Fort Wayne 117

1996-97 CBA

AMERICAN CONFERENCE

	W	L	QW	Pts
Florida Beachdogs	38	18	137.5	251.5
Grand Rapids Hoops	32	24	124.5	220.5
Quad City Thunder	27	29	110.0	191.0
Rockford Lightning	28	28	105.0	189.0
Connecticut Pride	21	35	107.5	170.5
Fort Wayne Fury	20	36	93.0	153.0

NATIONAL CONFERENCE

	W	L	QW	Pts
Sioux Falls Skyforce	47	9	134.0	275.0
Oklahoma City Cavalry	29	27	120.0	207.0
Yakima Suns Kings	25	31	103.0	178.0
Omaha Racers	22	34	97.5	163.5
La Crosse Bobcats	19	37	100.0	157.0

CBA AMERICAN FIRST ROUND

Florida 92, Rockford 85
Florida 89, Rockford 88
Florida 108, Rockford 84

Grand Rapids 102, Quad City 97
Grand Rapids 100, Quad City 94
Quad City 107, Grand Rapids 103
Quad City 92, Grand Rapids 89
Grand Rapids 114, Quad City 100

CBA NATIONAL FIRST ROUND

Sioux Falls 97, Omaha 88
Omaha 109, Sioux Falls 97
Omaha 120, Sioux Falls 108
Sioux Falls 107, Omaha 100
Omaha 98, Sioux Falls 92

Oklahoma City 103, Yakima 94
Yakima 97, Oklahoma City 93
Oklahoma City 86, Yakima 69
Yakima 110, Oklahoma City 96
Oklahoma City 120, Yakima 103

CBA AMERICAN FINALS

Grand Rapids 95, Florida 89
Florida 99, Grand Rapids 82
Florida 95, Grand Rapids 92
Grand Rapids 88, Florida 86
Florida 98, Grand Rapids 82

CBA NATIONAL FINALS

Oklahoma City 103, Omaha 91
Oklahoma City 119, Omaha 105
Omaha 107, Oklahoma City 102
Oklahoma City 108, Omaha 107

CBA FINALS

Florida 95, Oklahoma City 79
Oklahoma City 99, Florida 97
Oklahoma City 104, Florida 96
Florida 103, Oklahoma City 96
Oklahoma City 104, Florida 92
Oklahoma City 92, Florida 82

1997-98 CBA

AMERICAN CONFERENCE

	W	L	QW	Pts
Fort Wayne Fury	31	25	117.0	210.0
Rockford Lightning	29	27	114.0	201.0
Connecticut Pride	26	30	113.0	191.0
Grand Rapids Hoops	21	35	101.5	164.5

NATIONAL CONFERENCE

	W	L	QW	Pts
Quad City Thunder	38	18	130.0	244.0
Sioux Falls Skyforce	31	25	114.5	207.5
Yakima Sun Kings	26	30	110.0	188.0
Idaho Stampede	25	31	110.0	185.0
La Crosse Bobcats	25	31	98.0	173.0

CBA FIRST ROUND

Fort Wayne 102, Idaho 82
Idaho 91, Fort Wayne 90
Fort Wayne 104, Idaho 91
Idaho 109, Fort Wayne 103
Fort Wayne 112, Idaho 93

Rockford 98, Connecticut 85
Rockford 112, Connecticut 104
Rockford 102, Connecticut 96, OT

Quad City 99, La Crosse 95
Quad City 98, La Crosse 86
Quad City 106, La Crosse 85

Sioux Falls 113, Yakima 98
Sioux Falls 107, Yakima 101, OT
Yakima 102, Sioux Falls 95
Yakima 96 Sioux Falls 78
Sioux Falls 107, Yakima 96

CBA SECOND ROUND

Quad City 90, Rockford 89
Quad City 85, Rockford 83
Rockford 99, Quad City 81
Rockford 94, Quad City 92
Quad City 86, Rockford 80

Sioux Falls 91, Fort Wayne 85
Sioux Falls 93, Fort Wayne 91
Sioux Falls 106, Fort Wayne 99

CBA FINALS

Sioux Falls 95, Quad City 92
Quad City 82, Sioux Falls 81
Sioux Falls 94, Quad City 93
Quad City 108, Sioux Falls 106
Sioux Falls 107, Quad City 95
Quad City 107 Sioux Falls 85
Quad City 92, Sioux Falls 88

1998-99 CBA

AMERICAN CONFERENCE

	W	L	QW	Pts
Connecticut Pride	37	19	124.5	235.5
Grand Rapids Hoops	27	29	121.0	202.0
Fort Wayne Fury	28	28	103.5	187.5
Rockford Lightning	23	33	103.5	172.5

NATIONAL CONFERENCE

	W	L	QW	Pts
Sioux Falls Skyforce	32	24	128.5	224.5
Yakima Sun Kings	30	26	122.5	212.5
Quad City Thunder	29	27	100.0	187.0
Idaho Stampede	25	31	104.0	179.0
La Crosse Bobcats	21	35	100.5	163.5

CBA FIRST ROUND

Connecticut 132, Rockford 108
Connecticut 104, Rockford 102
Connecticut 124, Rockford 114, OT

Grand Rapids 100, Fort Wayne 85
Fort Wayne 99, Grand Rapids 92
Fort Wayne 101, Grand Rapids 80
Grand Rapids 86, Fort Wayne 84
Grand Rapids 91, Fort Wayne 78

Sioux Falls 109, Idaho 88
Sioux Falls 105, Idaho 91
Idaho 114, Sioux Falls 106
Idaho 127, Sioux Falls 126
Sioux Falls 99, Idaho 92

Yakima 99, Quad City 88
Quad City 88, Yakima 86
Yakima 87, Quad City 80
Quad City 84, Yakima 76
Quad City 89, Yakima 79

CBA SECOND ROUND

Connecticut 119, Grand Rapids 107
Connecticut 103, Grand Rapids 100
Grand Rapids 114, Connecticut 96
Connecticut 89, Grand Rapids 88

Sioux Falls 116, Quad City 107
Quad City 98, Sioux Falls 87
Sioux Falls 100, Quad City 98
Quad City 83, Sioux Falls 75
Sioux Falls 99, Quad City 86

CBA FINALS

Connecticut 109, Sioux Falls 104
Connecticut 115, Sioux Falls 97
Connecticut 115, Sioux Falls 105
Sioux Falls 135, Connecticut 111
Connecticut 105, Sioux Falls 103

1999-2000 CBA

AMERICAN CONFERENCE

	W	L	Pct.	GB
Rockford Lightning	30	26	.536	—
Connecticut Pride	29	27	.519	1.0
Grand Rapids Hoops	29	27	.519	1.0
Fort Wayne Fury	26	30	.464	4.0

NATIONAL CONFERENCE

	W	L	Pct.	GB
Quad City Thunder	35	21	.625	—
Yakima Sun Kings	33	23	.589	2.0
Sioux Falls Skyforce	30	26	.536	5.0
La Crosse Bobcats	21	35	.375	14.0
Idaho Stampede	19	37	.339	16.0

CBA PLAY-IN GAME

La Crosse 107, Idaho 94

CBA FIRST ROUND

La Crosse 111, Quad City 101
Sioux Falls 109, Connecticut 90
Yakima 98, Grand Rapids 96
Rockford 104, Fort Wayne 94

CBA SEMI-FINALS

La Crosse 99, Sioux Falls 90
Yakima 124, Rockford 102

CBA CHAMPIONSHIP

Yakima 109, La Crosse 93

2000-01 CBA

AMERICAN CONFERENCE

	W	L	Pct.	QW	Pts
Connecticut Pride	16	9	.640	55.0	103.0
Grand Rapids Hoops	15	10	.600	55.0	100.0
Fort Wayne Fury	11	9	.550	41.0	74.0
Rockford Lightning	12	13	.480	49.0	85.0
Gary Steelheads	9	15	.375	37.5	64.5

NATIONAL CONFERENCE

	W	L	Pct.	QW	Pts
Idaho Stampede	17	7	.708	49.0	100.0
Yakima Sun Kings	12	12	.500	55.5	91.5
Quad City Thunder	8	13	.381	42.0	66.0
La Crosse Bobcats	9	14	.391	41.5	68.5
Sioux Falls Skyforce	8	15	.348	42.5	66.5

League disbanded Feb. 8, 2001

2001-02 CBA

AMERICAN CONFERENCE	W	L	QW	Pts
Rockford Lightning	31	25	120.5	213.5
Sioux Falls Skyforce	33	23	114.5	213.5
Grand Rapids Hoops	30	26	114.0	204.0
Gary Steelheads	22	34	100.0	166.0
NATIONAL CONFERENCE	W	L	QW	Pts
Dakota Wizards	26	14	95.0	173.0
Fargo Moorhead Beez	25	15	80.5	155.5
Flint Fuze	17	23	77.5	128.5
Saskatchewan Hawks	8	32	66.0	90.0

CBA AMERICAN CONFERENCE SEMI-FINALS
Sioux Falls 95, Rockford 87
Rockford 110, Sioux Falls 106
Rockford 92, Sioux Falls 89
Rockford 104, Sioux Falls 93
CBA NATIONAL CONFERENCE SEMI-FINALS
Dakota 99, Fargo-Moorhead 98
Dakota 108, Fargo-Moorhead 107
Dakota 113, Fargo-Moorhead 101
CBA FINAL
Dakota 116, Rockford 109

2002-03 CBA

AMERICAN CONFERENCE	W	L	QW	Pts
Rockford Lightning	32	16	112.5	208.5
Grand Rapids Hoops	23	25	100.5	169.5
Gary Steelheads	25	23	93.5	168.5
Great Lakes Storm	19	29	80.5	137.5
NATIONAL CONFERENCE	W	L	QW	Pts
Dakota Wizards	31	17	119.5	212.5
Yakima Sun Kings	28	20	104.5	188.5
Idaho Stampede	17	31	87.5	138.5
Sioux Falls Skyforce	17	31	69.5	120.5

CBA AMERICAN CONFERENCE SEMI-FINALS
Rockford 149, Grand Rapids 146 (2OT)
Grand Rapids 128, Rockford 120
Grand Rapids 116, Rockford 108
Grand Rapids 127, Rockford 124
CBA NATIONAL CONFERENCE SEMI-FINALS
Dakota 100, Yakima 98
Yakima 110, Dakota 102
Yakima 109, Dakota 102
Yakima 105, Dakota 100
CBA FINALS
Yakima 117, Grand Rapids 107

EPBL/EBA/CBA CHAMPIONS AND AWARD WINNERS

EPBL/EBA/CBA CHAMPIONS
1946-47 Wilkes-Barre Barrons
1947-48 Reading Keys
1948-49 Pottsville Packers
1949-50 Williamsport Billies
1950-51 Sunbury Mercuries
1951-52 Pottsville Packers
1952-53 Williamsport Billies
1953-54 Williamsport Billies
1954-55 Wilkes-Barre Barrons
1955-56 Wilkes-Barre Barrons
1956-57 Scranton Miners
1957-58 Wilkes-Barre Barrons
1958-59 Wilkes-Barre Barrons
1959-60 Easton Madison
1960-61 Baltimore Bullets
1961-62 Allentown Jets
1962-63 Allentown Jets
1963-64 Camden Bullets
1964-65 Allentown Jets
1965-66 Wilmington Blue Bombers
1966-67 Wilmington Blue Bombers
1967-68 Allentown Jets
1968-69 Wilkes-Barre Barrons
1969-70 Allentown Jets
1970-71 Scranton Apollos
1971-72 Allentown Jets
1972-73 Wilkes-Barre Barrons
1973-74 Hartford Capitols
1974-75 Allentown Jets
1975-76 Allentown Jets
1976-77 Scranton Apollos
1977-78 Wilkes-Barre Barrons
1978-79 Rochester Zeniths
1979-80 Anchorage Northern Knights
1980-81 Rochester Zeniths
1981-82 Lancaster Lightning
1982-83 Detroit Spirits
1983-84 Albany Patroons
1984-85 Tampa Bay Thrillers
1985-86 Tampa Bay Thrillers
1986-87 Rapid City Thrillers
1987-88 Albany Patroons
1988-89 Tulsa Fast Breakers
1989-90 La Crosse Catbirds
1990-91 Wichita Falls Texans
1991-92 La Crosse Catbirds
1992-93 Omaha Racers
1993-94 Quad City Thunder
1994-95 Yakima Sun Kings
1995-96 Sioux Falls Skyforce
1996-97 Oklahoma City Cavalry
1997-98 Quad City Thunder
1998-99 Connecticut Pride
1999-2000 Yakima Sun Kings
2001-02: Dakota Wizards
2002-03: Yakima Sun Kings

MOST VALUABLE PLAYER
1949-50 Bill Zubic, Lancaster
1950-51 Jerry Rullo, Sunbury
1951-52 Chink Crossin, Pottsville
1952-53 Jack McCloskey, Sunbury
1953-54 Jack McCloskey, Sunbury
1954-55 Sherman White, Hazleton
1955-56 Jack Molinas, Wilmington
1956-57 Hal Lear, Easton
1957-58 Larry Hennessey, Wilkes-Barre
1958-59 Bill Spivey, Wilkes-Barre
1959-60 Stacey Arceneaux, Scranton
1960-61 Boo Ellis, Wilkes-Barre
1961-62 Roman Turmon, Allentown
1962-63 Paul Arizin, Camden
1963-64 Andy Johnson, Allentown
1964-65 Walt Simon, Allentown
1965-66 Julius McCoy, Scranton
1966-67 Willie Murrell, Scranton
1967-68 Ken Wilburn, Trenton
1968-69 Stan Pawlak, Wilkes-Barre
1969-70 Waitye Bellamy, Wilmington
1970-71 Willie Somerset, Scranton
1971-72 Hawthorne Wingo, Allentown
1972-73 Ed Johnson, Hartford
1973-74 Ken Wilburn, Allentown
1974-75 Jerry Baskerville, Hazleton
1975-76 Charlie Criss, Scranton
1976-77 Charlie Criss, Scranton
1977-78 Paul McCracken, Wilkes-Barre
1978-79 Andre McCarter, Rochester
1979-80 Ron Davis, Anchorage
1980-81 Willie Smith, Montana
1981-82 Ron Valentine, Montana
1982-83 Robert Smith, Montana
1983-84 Geff Crompton, Puerto Rico
1984-85 Steve Hayes, Tampa Bay
1985-86 Michael Young, Detroit
1986-87 Joe Binion, Topeka
1987-88 Michael Brooks, Albany
1988-89 Anthony Bowie, Quad City
1989-90 Vincent Askew, Albany
1990-91 Vincent Askew, Albany
1991-92 Barry Mitchell, Quad City
1992-93 Derek Strong, Quad City
1993-94 Ronnie Grandison, Rochester
1994-95 Eldridge Recasner, Yakima
1995-96 Shelton Jones, Florida
1996-97 Dexter Boney, Florida
1997-98 Jimmy King, Quad City
1998-99 Adrian Griffin, Connecticut
1999-2000 Jeff McInnis, Quad City
2001-02: Miles Simon, Dakota
2002-03: Andy Panko, Dakota

ROOKIE OF THE YEAR
1957-58 Dick Gaines, Easton
1958-59 Julius McCoy, Wilmington
1959-60 Alonzo Lewis, Sunbury
1960-61 Dave Gunther, Wilmington
1961-62 Jim Huggard, Sunbury
1962-63 Emerson Baynard, Sunbury
1963-64 Ken Rohloff, Sunbury
1964-65 Swish McKinney, Wilmington
1965-66 Bob Love, Trenton
1966-67 Ken Wilburn, Trenton
1967-68 Don Carlos, Hartford
1968-69 Rich Cornwall, Binghamton
1969-70 Ed Mast, Allentown
1970-71 Charlie Wallace, Trenton
1971-72 Craig Mayberry, Hartford
1972-73 Wincent White, Garden State
1973-74 Dennis Bell, Allentown
1974-75 Aulcie Perry, Allentown
1975-76 Mo Rivers, Lancaster/Walter Luckett, Long I.
1976-77 Major Jones, Allentown
1977-78 Bill Terry, Jersey Shore
1978-79 Billy Ray Bates, Main
1979-80 Edgar Jones, Leigh Valley
1980-81 Lee Johnson, Rochester
1981-82 Larry Spriggs, Rochester
1982-83 Mike Sanders, Montana
1983-84 Greg Jones, Wisconsin
1984-85 Eric Turner, Detroit
1985-86 Michael Adams, Bay State
1986-87 Ron Rowan, Topeka
1987-88 Jamie Waller, Charleston
1988-89 Daren Queenan, Charleston
1989-90 Clifford Lett, Pensacola
1990-91 Stephen Thompson, Rapid City
1991-92 Marcus Kennedy, Grand Rapids
1992-93 Gerald Madkins, Grand Rapids
1993-94 Alfonso Ford, Tri City
1994-95 Kendrick Warren, Rockford
1995-96 Ray Jackson, Grand Rapids
1996-97 Bernard Hopkins, Yakima/
    Jason Sasser, Sioux Falls
1997-98 Alvin Sims, Quad City
1998-99 Bakari Hendrix, Quad City
1999-2000 Jamel Thomas, Quad City
2001-02: Kenny Inge, Rockford
2002-03: Immanuel Mc Elroy, Grand Rapids

PLAYOFF/FINALS MVP

1975-76 Willie Sojourner, Lancaster/
    Greg Jackson, Allentown
1976-77 Ron Haigler, Scranton
1977-78 Phil Brown, Wilkes-Barre
1978-79 Larry Fogle, Rochester/
    Larry McNeill, Rochester
1979-80 Steve Hayes, Anchorage
1980-81 Lee Johnson, Rochester
1981-82 Ed Sherod, Lancaster

1982-83 Tico Brown, Detroit
1983-84 Andre Gaddy, Albany
1984-85 Freeman Williams, Tampa Bay
1985-86 Rod Higigins, Tampa Bay
1986-87 Cinton Wheeler, Tampa Bay
1987-88 Tod Murphy, Albany
1988-89 Dexter Shouse, Tulsa
1989-90 Andre Turner, La Crosse
1990-91 Ennis Whatley, Wichita Falls
1991-92 David Rivers, La Crosse
1992-93 Jim Thomas. Omaha
1993-94 Chris Childs, Quad City
1994-95 Aaron Swinson, Yakima
1995-96 Henry James, Sioux Falls
1996-97 Elmer Bennett, Oklahoma City
1997-98 Byron Houston, Quad City
1998-99 Adrian Griffin, Connecticut
1999-2000 Silas Mills, Yakima
2001-02: Miles Simon, Dakota
2002-03: Darrick Martin, Yakima

COACH OF THE YEAR

1975-76 Larry Cannon, Lancaster
1976-77 Stan Novak, Scranton
1977-78 Pete Monska, Wilkes-Barre
1978-79 Mauro Panaggio, Rochester
1979-80 Bill Klucas, Anchorage
1980-81 George Karl, Montana
1981-82 Cazzie Russell, Lancaster
1982-83 George Karl, Montana
1983-84 Herb Brown, Puerto Rico
1984-85 Phil Jackson, Albany
1985-86 Mauro Panaggio, Bay State
1986-87 Bill Musselman, Rapid City
1987-88 Bill Musselman, Albany
1988-89 Flip Saunders, Rapid City
1989-90 Gerald Oliver, Albany
1990-91 George Karl, Albany
1991-92 Dan Panaggio, Quad City/
    Flip Saunders, La Crosse
1992-93 Mauro Panaggio, Rockford
1993-94 Calvin Duncan, Tri City
1994-95 Morris McHone Yakima
1995-96 Brendan Suhr, Grand Rapids
1996-97 Morris McHone, Sioux Falls
1997-98 Dan Panaggio, Quad City
1998-99 Tyler Jones, Connecticut
1999-2000 Dan Panaggio, Quad City
2001-02: Dave Joerger, Dakota
2002-03: Chris Daleo, Rockford

NEWCOMER OF THE YEAR

1977-78 Ron Davis, Anchorage
1978-79 Andre McCarter, Rochester
1979-80 Brad Davis, Anchorage/
    Bobby Wilson, Hawaii
1980-81 Cazzie Russell, Philadelphia
1981-82 Brad Branson, Anchorage
1982-83 Mike Davis, Albany
1983-84 Steve Lingdenfelter, Wisconsin
1984-85 Don Collins, Lancaster
1985-86 John Drew, Wyoming
1986-87 Eddie Johnson, Tampa Bay
1987-88 Tony Campbell, Albany
1988-89 Randy Allen, Cedar Rapids
1989-90 Duane Ferrell, Topeka
1990-91 Albert King, Albany
1991-92 Stanley Brundy, Rapid City
1992-93 Derek Strong, Quad City
1993-94 Rodney Monroe, Rochester
1994-95 Marques Bragg, Grand Rapids
1995-96 Gaylon Nickerson, Oklahoma City
1996-97 Anthony Tucker, Florida
1997-98 Jeff McInnis, Quad City
1998-99 Damon Jones, Idaho
1999-2000 Charles Smith, Rockford
2001-02: Miles Simon, Dakota
2002-03: Damien Cantrell, Yakima

ALL-STAR GAME MVP

1978-79 Andre McCarter, Rochester
1981-82 Brad Branson, Anchorage
1982-83 Larry Spriggs, Albany
1983-84 Anthony Roberts, Wyoming
1984-85 Rick Lamb, Wyoming
1985-86 Don Collins, Tampa Bay
1986-87 Eddie Johnson, Tampa Bay
1987-88 Michael Brooks, Albany
1988-89 Dwayne McClain, Rockford
1989-90 Conner Henry, Rapid City
1990-91 Vincent Askew, Albany
1991-92 Conner Henry, Yakima
1992-93 Pat Durham, Fargo-Moorhead
1993-94 Jeff Martin, Grand Rapids
1994-95 Tony Dawson, Rockford
1995-96 Shelton Jones, Florida
1996-97 Dexter Boney, Florida
1997-98 Did not play
1998-99 Did not play
1999-2000 Dontae' Jones, La Crosse

DEFENSIVE PLAYER OF THE YEAR

1990-91 Clinton Smith, Albany
1991-92 Barry Mitchell, Quad City
1992-93 Stephen Bardo, Wichita Falls
1993-94 Stephen Bardo, Wichita Falls
1994-95 Mike Bell, Rockford
1995-96 Emanual Davis, Rockford
1996-97 Corey Beck, Sioux Falls
1997-98 Michael McDonald, Grand Rapids
1998-99 James Martin, Connecticut
1999-2000 Maceo Baston, Quad City
2001-02: Willie Murdaugh, Saskatchewan

MAN OF THE YEAR

1999-2000 Ryan Hoover, Rockford

EXECUTIVE OF THE YEAR

1983-84 James Coyne, Albany
1984-85 Jeff Gordon, Wyoming
1985-86 John E. Ligums, Bay State
1986-87 Bernie Giannon, Topeka
1987-88 Ron Minegar, La Crosse
1988-89 Anne Potter DeLong, Quad City
1989-90 Ron Minegar, La Crosse
1990-91 Chip Land, Oklahoma City
1991-92 Brooks Ellison, Yakima
1992-93 Brooks Ellison, Yakima
1993-94 Rich Coffey, Hartford
1994-95 Greg Heineman, Sioux Falls
1995-96 Tommy Smith, Sioux Falls
1996-97 Bob Przybysz, Grand Rapids
1997-98 Tommy Smith, Sioux Falls
1998-99 Bob Przybysz, Grand Rapids/
    Tommy Smith, Sioux Falls

JOHN F. KENNEDY SPORTSMANSHIP

1964-65 Bob McNeil, Camden
1965-66 George Blaney, Camden
1966-67 Dennis Cuff, Asbury Park
1967-68 Mike Riordan, Allentown
1968-69 Tony Upson. Trenton

50TH ANNIVERSARY TEAM

EPBL/EBA ERA

Charlie Criss, G
Hal Lear, G Jack McCloskey, G
Stacey Arceneaux, F
Bill Chanecka, F
Tom Hemans, F
Julius McCoy, F
Roman Turmon, C
Ken Wilburn, C
Stan Novak, Coach

Others receiving consideration: Paul Arizin, Waite
Bellamy, Jim Boeheim, George Bruns, Joe
Caokovio, John Chaney, Wally Choice, Rich
Cornwall, Chick Craig, Mack Daughtry, Alex Ellis,
Dick Gaines, Art Heyman, Jim Huggard, Bob Keller,
George Lehmann, Brendan McCann, Bob McNeill,
Jack Ramsay, John Richter, Jerry Rullo, Chink
Scott, Bill Zubic

CBA ERA

Tico Brown, G
Glenn Hagan, G
Robert Smith, G
Clinton Wheeler, G
Vince Askew, F
Don Collins, F
Ron Davis, F
Derrick Rowland, F
Claude Gregory, C
Charles Jones, C
Mauro Panaggio, Coach

Others receiving consideration: Geoff Crompton,
Joe Dawson, Larry Fogle, Jacky Dorsey, Ronnie
Grandison, Mario Elie, Steve Hayes, Cedric Hunter,
Phil Jackson, Lee Johnson, George Karl, Tim
Legler, Sidney Lowe, Bill Musselman, Kenny Natt,
Ed Nealy, Mike Sanders, DeWayne Scales, Al
Smith, Larry Spriggs, Andre Turner, A.J. Wynder

Chapter 34

United States Basketball League

By Christian Anderson

Most press conferences—sports or otherwise—feature a few big names, lots of smiling faces, and plenty of optimistic talk. The December 19, 1984, news conference to announce the formation of the United States Basketball League was no exception.

The league's founder, a 33-year-old former teacher and venture capitalist named Daniel Meisenheimer III, confidently announced that at least eight teams would play a 50-game schedule in the USBL's first season in the summer of 1985. He outlined his long-term plans for the league, which included national expansion from Boston to San Diego and hopes for a "farm system" relationship with the NBA.

Joining Meisenheimer at the press conference were Walt Frazier and Dick Barnett, the starting backcourt for the NBA's New York Knicks during the team's 1969-70 championship campaign. Frazier and Barnett were introduced as USBL franchise owners in Atlanta and White Plains, New York, respectively. Another former Knick, was there as well—Earl Monroe, a self-described "avid supporter" of the new league who would be appointed as its acting commissioner just prior to the tip-off of its inaugural season.

Meisenheimer's optimism continued to radiate after the news conference. He spoke of plans for an eight-division, 50-team league. He envisioned USBL teams in Albuquerque, Anaheim, Baltimore, Boston, Charlotte, Dallas, Denver, Houston, Las Vegas, Los Angeles, Pittsburgh, San Diego, San Francisco, Tampa, and Washington, D.C. He talked about per-team start-up costs of $1 million (although he would later claim that most USBL franchises operated with budgets of around one-fourth of that) and predicted that clubs would average 1,000 season tickets. Player salaries would range from $300-$1,000 per week.

Although the inaugural campaign didn't include Barnett or Frazier as owners, it did accomplish at least one goal: it provided a competitive summer outlet for players looking to earn some money, hone their skills, and gain additional visibility before heading off to the NBA, CBA, or European leagues in the fall.

⊛ ⊛ ⊛

The league's inaugural draft was held at Loew's Summit Hotel in New York City on April 10, 1985. Present were representatives from seven franchises. Among the first players selected in the "open" portion of the draft were Richie Adams (UNLV), Matt Doherty (North Carolina), and Ralph Dalton (Georgetown). Yet between the time of the draft and the start of the season on May 25, one franchise—the New York Golden Apples—had moved (to Westchester) and one coach, Rhode Island's Ernie DeGregorio, had been replaced (by Kevin Stacom).

The USBL's first season featured seven East Coast teams located in Long Island (Hempstead), New York; New Haven, Connecticut; Newport, Rhode Island; Springfield, Massachusetts; Wayne, New Jersey; Westchester (White Plains), New York; and Wildwood, New Jersey. An eighth team, a franchise in Boca Raton, Florida—the Gold Coast Manatees—decided to sit out the 1985 season and begin play in 1986 (as the Gold Coast Stingrays).

Each franchise featured a core of entertaining players, including John "Hot Rod" Williams; 7-foot-7 phenom Manute Bol, who would finish as runner-up in NBA Defensive Player of the Year voting; and Bol's tiny teammate Spud Webb, who would win the NBA Slam Dunk Contest at the 1986 All-Star Game. There were also several fringe NBA players and high-level CBA vets such as Geoff Huston, Brian Martin, Delaney Rudd, Butch Graves, Pete Davis, Joe Dawson, Bruce Kuczenski, Clinton Wheeler, Lowes Moore, Eddie Lee Wilkins, Derrick Rowland, Steve Burtt, and Jim Bostic. A few NBA vets, like Eddie Jordan, who played in nearly 500 NBA games for New Jersey and Los Angeles from 1977-83, also turned up on USBL rosters.

As an indication of the level of talent the USBL managed to attract, more than 40 percent of its 70 players were invited to NBA training camps prior to the 1985-86 season. So many, in fact, that on July 18, the league announced it was canceling the season, a month before the scheduled August 19 season-ender. After the mass exodus, league officials initially planned to revise the playoff schedule, but ultimately decided to call off the post-season altogether.

Springfield, coached by Gerald Oliver, a former NBA assistant in Cleveland during the Ted Stepien-Bill Musselman regime, sat atop the USBL standings at 19-6 when officials pulled the plug, 15 games short of the planned conclusion of regular season play. The Fame's roster boasted several of the league's top players, including guards Michael Adams, Sam Worthen, and Tracy Jackson, forwards Oliver Lee and Larry Lawrence (who later enjoyed a fine pro career overseas), and 7-foot center Ron Crevier.

The 5-foot-11 Adams would go on to win CBA Rookie of the Year honors in 1986 and put together a solid NBA career. Worthen, a Brooklyn native, had played in 64 games for Chicago during the 1980-81 NBA season and would later serve as head coach of the USBL's Miami Tropics in 1987 and New York Whitecaps in 1990.

Lee, who like Worthen had attended Marquette, followed up his USBL season by averaging 23 points per game in the CBA during the 1985-86 season. Lawrence had averaged 19

points per game for the CBA's Rochester Zeniths during the league's 1983 postseason. Jackson, who had appeared in more than 100 NBA games with Boston, Chicago, and Indiana from 1981-84, earned USBL Player of the Year honors after averaging nearly 19 points, 7 rebounds, and 3 steals per game for Springfield. Jackson's teammates Lawrence, Adams, and 6-foot-10 rookie Andre Goode would also garner postseason honors.

⊕ ⊕ ⊕

Despite losing $1.2 million in its inaugural season, the USBL expanded into Florida for the 1986 campaign, adding franchises in Tampa Bay and West Palm Beach (Gold Coast). A third new franchise, this one in Staten Island, New York, helped to offset the loss of three charter teams: Rhode Island, Connecticut, and Long Island. The New Jersey franchise was sold and moved from Wayne to Jersey City, where the team played at St. Peter's College.

Springfield replaced 1985 USBL Coach of the Year Gerald Oliver with former NBA guard Henry Bibby for the 1986 season, after Oliver moved over to coach the Staten Island entry. Bibby fared well, guiding the Fame to a 23-10 mark and earning USBL Coach of the Year honors. But the most notable move was the team's addition of Nancy Lieberman, a member of the gold-medal-winning U.S. Olympic women's basketball team in 1976, to its roster. While Lieberman's impact on the floor was minimal, playing just three minutes in her debut and averaging less than 2 points per game in 21 appearances, her presence was a milestone that helped generate valuable publicity for the two-year-old league.

Despite the hype that Lieberman's arrival brought from the media, league-wide average attendance at USBL games fell from just over 1,000 to 825 per game in 1986. In fact, two weeks into the season, Lieberman's Springfield team moved its games from the 8,000-seat Springfield Civic Center to a 2,000-seat arena at Springfield College after averaging about 1,200 fans for its first six home games.

For the second consecutive season, a mass exodus of players to NBA training camps interfered with the USBL's postseason plans. The league had hoped to stage a title game between its top two teams, Tampa Bay and Springfield, but with arenas being unavailable and NBA teams inviting 35 USBL players for tryouts, officials opted to end the season on August 24.

First-place Tampa Bay, which finished the season at 22-8, featured a powerful roster led by 6-foot-6 Don Collins, the 18th overall pick in the 1980 NBA draft and the USBL's leading scorer with 31.8 points per game. Collins had played in nearly 300 NBA games and averaged nearly 32 points to lead the Tampa Bay Thrillers to the CBA's 1986 title a few months before joining the USBL's Tampa Bay Flash. Collins, who finished his career overseas, singed the rim for 63 points in a 1986 CBA game and is still regarded as one of the most talented scorers in CBA history.

Joining Collins for the Flash was 6-foot-7 forward Ron Valentine, who had averaged 32 points per game in the CBA during his 1982 MVP season; forward Sam Mitchell, who put up 21 points per game in CBA action in 1985-86 and would later enjoy a solid NBA career; Kenny Stancell, who had averaged nearly 10 rebounds per game in 1985-86 CBA contests; and 6-foot-9 rookie center Curtis Kitchen, who would go on to

average more than 10 rebounds per game and lead the CBA in blocks as a rookie in 1986-87 before closing out his career in France, Belgium, and Argentina. At the point position was another CBA veteran, 6-foot-1 guard Leroy Witherspoon, the USBL's assists leader with 15 per game in 1986. "Spoon" also had a USBL record 28 assists in a 1986 game against Gold Coast. Two other NBA vets, the 6-foot-4 Carlos Clark, who earned championship rings in the NBA, CBA, and WBL, and 6-foot-8 Ken Green, who was coming off a 24-point, 13-rebound CBA season, rounded out the Flash roster.

⊕ ⊕ ⊕

In October 1986, the USBL took steps to avoid future scheduling conflicts with NBA camps, voting to begin its season in mid- to late May with regular season play ending by July 19, a week or two prior to the start of rookie camps. The move would enable the league to stage a postseason for the first time in its short history.

That same month, Bill Richey, chairman of Marketing Corporation of America, announced that he had contracted with the USBL to sell its teams and divisions beyond the Northeast, including a six-team division made up of franchises representing Charlotte, Lexington, Louisville, and Memphis.

But the stand-alone division never developed and teams in Springfield and Westchester, two of the league's charter franchises, did not return. Moreover, the Wildwood franchise moved to Philadelphia and Gold Coast changed its name to West Palm Beach. Then, in December, the ownership group of the Tampa Bay franchise announced that it had terminated its agreement with the league, citing disappointing financial performance. In a press release, the group said it decided to pull out of the USBL when "it appeared that even a break-even situation would be unlikely in the foreseeable future."

Despite its instability, the USBL managed to add new teams in Long Island and Miami (Miami actually began the season as the Miami-Kendall Tropics, but dropped Kendall, a Miami suburb, from its name midway through the season). New ownership saved the Tampa team, and the Rhode Island franchise, which had folded after the league's inaugural season in 1985, returned after a one-year absence. The "new" Gulls, which played the 1987 season at the 2,000-seat Community College of Rhode Island Field House in Warwick, lasted just one season despite reaching the USBL finals.

Highlighting the USBL's third season were two 30-something guards with NBA credentials: World B. Free and Michael "Sugar" Ray Richardson. The 33-year-old Free, an all-star who averaged more than 21 points per game in 12 NBA seasons, signed a $10,000 contract with the Miami Tropics on May 13, 1987, just two weeks before the team's first game. In Miami, Free teamed with veterans Mario Elie and Clinton Wheeler; the 6-foot-11 Ozell Jones, who would go on to earn All-CBA honors in 1990; and Bobby Parks, a 6-foot-5 guard who averaged 18 points per game in the CBA during the 1985-86 season.

Led by Free and coached by former NBA guard Sam Worthen, the Tropics beat a powerful Tampa Bay team that featured Don Collins, Mitchell Wiggins, Kenny Stancell, Leroy Witherspoon, Randy Allen, Curtis Kitchen, Tony Karasek, and rookie Norris Coleman to reach the finals. In the title game against George Whittaker's Rhode Island team, Free's 30 points

helped offset a 29-point effort by former NBA guard Andre Turner as Miami clipped the Gulls, 103-99, in front of 2800 spectators.

A late-season decision by league officials made Miami's title run more interesting. Just prior to the start of the playoffs, near the end of July, the league voted, 6-0, for a postseason format that divided the league into two divisions—North and South—even though it had played the entire season as an eight-team, one-division league. The decision forced Miami to move its first-round game against West Palm Beach to Tampa instead of the teams meeting on Miami's home court. In the end, it made little difference, as the Tropics scorched the Stingrays in the first round, winning by 16 points. But it was one more example of the sometimes puzzling thought-process of league officials.

While Free was guiding his team to a USBL championship, Richardson, a four-time NBA all-star who was released by the New Jersey Nets and banned by the league after violating its drug policy, was released by his first USBL team, the Long Island Knights, in mid-June. After the team's season opener, in which he scored 28 points, Richardson told *The New York Times*, "I'll be damned if I'm going to make this my career. I'm gonna put in my 10 weeks, say thank you very much, and never see this again."

Richardson was picked up four days later by the Jersey Jammers and made an inauspicious debut with them, scoring 14 points on 4-for-18 shooting from the field. For the season, however, Richardson averaged 25.5 points, 7.3 assists, and 2.5 steals. He would help the Albany Patroons to a CBA title in 1988 before leaving for Europe, where he enjoyed a long post-NBA career.

Other notable players logging minutes during the 1987 USBL season included Dwight Anderson, Ken "The Animal" Bannister, Muggsy Bogues, Tommy Collier, Mark Davis, Billy Donovan, Willie Glass, Stewart Granger, Geoff Huston, Harold Jensen, Ron Kellogg, Jim Lampley, Ralph Lewis, Bob McCann, Dirk Minniefield, Andrew Moten, Martin Nessley, Richard Rellford, Rob Rose, Dan Ruland, Frankie Sanders, McKinley Singleton, Ron Valentine, Ronnie Williams, Eddie Lee Wilkins, Nikita Wilson, and A.J. Wynder.

⊕ ⊕ ⊕

Soon after the end of the 1987 season, there was talk of expanding the league to 14 teams for the next year's campaign. While new franchises were added in Jacksonville, Jersey Shore, and New Haven, four others—Jersey, Rhode Island, Staten Island, and Tampa Bay—dropped out. And, for the third time in as many seasons, the West Palm Beach entry, which would play some of its games at North Shore High School, changed its name, this time trimming it to Palm Beach.

Coached by Rex Morgan, a former player for the Boston Celtics, Jacksonville was the most impressive of the league's new entries, going 21-9 in the regular season. The team had a strong roster that featured guards Craig Neal and Dexter Shouse (15.5 points per game), forwards Norris Coleman (28.4 points, 9.1 rebounds), Cedric Henderson (22.9 points, 12.9 rebounds), and Mitchell Wiggins (22.8 points), and center Alton Lee Gipson (9.3 rebounds). But Jacksonville was derailed in the postseason tournament by Palm Beach, which had finished just two games over .500 despite a roster that included Avery

Johnson, Richard Rellford, Tommy Davis, Kelvin Upshaw, Jerome Henderson, Andrew Moten, and Oscar Taylor. In the finals, Palm Beach was without many of its top players and lost to New Haven, 134-126, in front of a crowd of 621 at the Southern Connecticut State University gym. Bobby Parks led the Skyhawks with 27 points in the title game. Former Villanova star Dwayne McClain chipped in 20, and Leroy Combs, a 1987 all-star who had reached the finals that season as a member of the Rhode Island Gulls, had 24.

Miami was not on hand to defend its title. The Tropics, with Andre Turner, Ricky Wilson, Kannard Johnson, Ron Rowan, Sylvester Gray, and Ozell Jones, struggled through the season with a 13-10 record before the franchise folded, forcing the team to forfeit its final six games. Even before the team had ceased operations, several players had quit, claiming they had not been paid in four weeks.

Philadelphia, perhaps the league's most talented team with a roster featuring Lewis Lloyd, Michael Brooks, Ralph Lewis, Alex Bradley, Mark Plansky, Michael Anderson, and Tim Legler, was knocked out of the playoffs by New Haven in the semi-finals. Coached by Lefty Ervin, the Aces had narrowly lost to the USBL All-Stars in the league's fourth annual All-Star Game, held June 25, 1988, in Philadelphia. Lloyd, the game's MVP, scored 46 points, but the All-Stars, led by Lloyd's former NBA teammate Mitchell Wiggins—who tallied 21 points, 9 rebounds, and 7 assists—overcame a 14-point first quarter deficit by scoring 44 fourth-quarter points before downing the host team in overtime, 134-132. Former San Diego Clippers forward Michael Brooks had a remarkable performance in a losing effort, scoring 29 points, grabbing 16 rebounds, handing out 7 assists, and blocking 2 shots in 45 minutes of action.

⊕ ⊕ ⊕

On May 14, 1989, after four seasons of in-and-out franchises, shaky ownership, and tiny crowds, the USBL announced it would cancel its 1989 summer season and spend the year reorganizing the league. At the time, USBL Commissioner Dan Meisenheimer told the Associated Press that he made the decision after the owner of the Jacksonville franchise "moved out of town."

Meisenheimer also needed time to "get the kinks out" of his fast-food franchiser concept. Under the plan, the USBL would charge a $300,000 franchise fee that included instructions for operating the team. With operating budgets of $250,000 and a $68,000 salary cap for players, the idea was for the USBL to be the "least expensive franchise to purchase, and the least expensive to operate."

Despite a year of working to shore up its operations, the USBL had a rickety 1990 season. At the league's April 17 draft at Jacksonville, in which Kansas State guard Steve Henson was the first selection, six teams were present: the Connecticut Skyhawks, Jacksonville Hooters, Miami Kings, New York (Rockville Centre) Empires, Palm Beach Stingrays, and Philadelphia Aces. However, when the season tipped off on June 9, only five teams competed, down from a high of eight in 1987. Further, two of the clubs—Philadelphia and New York—folded after just six games. While information from the league promoting the 1991 season claimed that the 1990 campaign "was 20 games in length," official standings indicate that no

team played more than 16 games.

The abridged season was a challenge for USBL schedule makers. For example, in its first five games of the season, all of which were home contests, New Haven faced New York three times and Philadelphia twice. For fans, getting excited about the games was equally challenging, and that was reflected in the attendance figures. According to official statistics, the Skyhawks drew crowds of 164, 77, 70, 82, and 287 for their first five games, despite opening the season at 5-0 with a roster that featured 7-foot-2 center Petur Gudmundsson, forwards Damari Riddick, Tony Judkins and Gary Massey, and guards Shaun McDaniel and Phil Gamble.

When the season ended, Jacksonville again sat atop the league standings, as five of its players—forwards Randy Henry and Norris Coleman, guards Danny Pearson and Jerry Johnson, and rookie center Jessie Spinner—earned postseason honors. The Hooters featured the league's top-scoring offense (120.9 points per fame). Jacksonville also led the league in scoring defense, "limiting" opponents to 109.1 points per game. Incidentally, the league's worst defensive team, Palm Beach, surrendered 127 points per game.

⊕ ⊕ ⊕

The USBL was considerably stronger when it tipped off its sixth season on June 5, 1991, sporting two divisions for the first time in its history. The 1991 season also marked the league's expansion into Atlanta, giving the league franchises in two southern states, Florida and Georgia. In addition, a team in Glen Falls, New York, made its debut, while Miami rejoined the league two years after folding with debts of more than $70,000 and Long Island fielded a team for the first time since the 1988 campaign. The Gulf Coast of Florida also returned to the USBL fold for the 1991 season, this time with a team in Clearwater; the league had last featured a team in the Tampa Bay area in 1986 and 1987. Commissioner Meisenheimer owned all or part of the franchises in Atlanta, Miami, and New Haven.

New York City playground legend Lloyd Daniels, who had played in the CBA in 1987-88 and again in 1989-90, made his first appearance in the USBL during the 1991 season, averaging 14.7 points in 21 games with Miami. Daniels, whose career was considered to be over when he was shot in May 1989, joined veterans Shelton Jones, Derek Strong, Eric Mudd, Mouse McFadden, Steve Bucknall, Chuck Nevitt, Sean Gay and Ron Matthias and rookie Lorenzo Williams on the Tropics roster. Miami went 13-7 during the 20-game regular season to win the Southern Division title.

The 6-foot-3 Matthias, who played at Palm Beach Community College during the 1985-86 season before being expelled after a series of alleged incidents ranging from sexual harassment to vandalism to theft, was a classic example of a talented player with one significant limitation: He couldn't shoot the jumpshot. Scoring was never a problem for Matthias, a Bronx native who once scored 58 in a college game and consistently posted impressive scoring averages in the USBL and GBA. But he was an ineffective outside shooter. In a game against Long Island, Matthias scored 45 points without taking a jumpshot. "Where I come from, you don't [take jumpshots]," said Matthias. "You take your man to the hoop."

In the title game, which matched the top team from each

division, Philadelphia, the league's top-scoring team (117.5 points per game), downed Miami, 110-108, as Snoopy Graham, the 1991 USBL All-Star MVP, scored 25 points to earn championship MVP honors. Daniels scored 27 for Miami, which had split the regular season series with the Spirit, 1-1. Philly guard Michael Anderson, a veteran with NBA and CBA experience, left the Denver Nuggets' training camp to fly in for the championship game, which was played in front of a crowd of 1,500 in Philadelphia. He poured in 23 points for the Spirit, then hopped on a plane the next day to rejoin the Nuggets. Anderson earned USBL Player of the Year honors after averaging 23.7 points, a league-leading 10.3 assists, and 3.1 steals, which was also the league's best.

In the coaching ranks, former Cleveland State coach Kevin Mackey, who lost his college job after he was arrested in July 1990 for drunken driving and cocaine possession, took over for Eric Dennis in Miami in early July after the Tropics got off to a 6-6 start. Miami went 8-2 under Mackey, who began the season as an assistant in Atlanta and within a few weeks was named head coach of the GBA's Fayetteville Flyers.

In Atlanta, former NBA guard Charlie Criss guided the Eagles to a .500 mark, going 8-2 at home but winning just two of 10 on the road. Their roster included NBA vets Wes Matthews, Lanard Copeland, and Stephen Bardo. Criss was replaced the following season by Al Outlaw, the director of the Atlanta Pro-Am Basketball League. In Glen Falls, veteran CBA coach Jim Sleeper and his assistant, Gary Mazza, who won a CBA championship in Detroit in 1983, left Empire State after the Stallions started the season 4-5. Like Mackey, Sleeper went on to coach in the GBA.

Notable players making appearances in USBL games during 1991 included Derrall Dumas, Livingston Chatman, Anthony Mason, Earl Cureton, Keith Gatlin, Tharon Mayes, Dallas Comegys, Tim Legler, Keith Lee, and Keith Jennings, a 5-foot-7 rookie who would go on to play in the NBA.

⊕ ⊕ ⊕

Nine teams—an all-time high—competed for the 1992 USBL championship. Miami, Philadelphia, Long Island, Tampa (which had relocated from Clearwater), New Haven, Jacksonville, and Atlanta returned from 1991. The (Lakewood) New Jersey Jammers came back after a three-year absence. Another former franchise, the Palm Beach Stingrays, which was inactive in 1991 after four turbulent USBL seasons, also rejoined the league, but not without a struggle. A few days before the first game, the owners of the franchise pulled their support. A local businessman bought the team, but the players had just one practice together before the season opener, a 124-86 loss.

Jacksonville had its share of problems as well. The team, averaging about 300 fans per contest while playing at a local church, attempted to move its games to Florida Community College after players complained about the tile floor. College officials, however, denied the request, saying they didn't like the "slang connotation" associated with the team's nickname, Hooters.

Near the end the season, after an argument about travel from Jacksonville to New Jersey for a game, two of Jacksonville's top scorers—Wes Matthews and Randy Henry—opted not to make the trip. When head coach Rex Morgan had

not shown up two hours before game time, three other players who had driven up the coast for the game got back in their car and drove back to Florida, leaving the team with just four players. So the 43-year-old Morgan, who played for the Celtics during the early 1970s, was forced to put on a uniform to avoid paying the $5,000 forfeit penalty. New Jersey won the game, 154-137. Morgan finished with 12 points and 6 rebounds as his team was outrebounded, 76-33.

Another Florida team, Tampa Bay, failed to meet payroll for two weeks, forcing the league to pay the players. By then, half the team's players and the head coach had left. Jeff Cave, the team's 23-year-old assistant general manager, assumed head coaching duties and relocated the Sunblasters to Atlanta, which already had a USBL club. Left without a home arena, the team played an all-away schedule, traveling to its games in a van. The players, many of whom had been recruited out of the Atlanta area after the franchise folded, played for $20 per day in meal money. After 14 games in 17 days, the Sunblasters finished 4-22, including a 13-game losing streak to end the season.

While three of the Florida-based teams were battling problems, the fourth Florida team, Miami, garnered national media attention. A social experiment by former NBA guard John Lucas helped the Miami franchise to a league title in 1992, its first since 1987. In August 1991, Lucas bought the franchise, determined to use it as a means to help players with drug problems get their lives in order.

For Lucas, a former No. 1 NBA draft pick who was a recovering cocaine addict, finding candidates to fill his team's roster wasn't a problem. Roy Tarpley, Richard Dumas, Duane Washington, Chris Washburn, and Grant Gondrezick—all former NBA players who had attended Lucas's drug center in Houston—helped the Tropics win 15 of their first 16 games. Tarpley dominated, averaging 32 points and 17 rebounds per game on his way to earning Player of the Year honors. Against New Haven on May 30, Tarpley grabbed a USBL-record 28 rebounds as Miami trounced the Skyhawks, 125-97. Two weeks later, in a win over Jacksonville, Tarpley exploded for 47 points.

But the presence of NBA-caliber talent didn't have much of an effect on attendance at Tropics home games. For example, only 300 folks turned out for Tarpley's USBL debut, in which he scored 21 points.

The USBL took a week-long mid-season break so that two of its teams could compete in international competition. Minus Tarpley and Richard Dumas, the Tropics left Miami to take part in the Latin Cup in Panama City, where they won the gold medal after beating a team of all-stars from Puerto Rico's Superior League and the Panamanian National Team. At the same time, a team of USBL all-stars that included Michael Anderson, Darrell Armstrong, Norris Coleman, Tony Costner, Jay Edwards, Nate Johnston, and Tim Legler, downed the Canadian, Spanish, and Puerto Rican Olympic teams at the Copa V Cenenario tournament in San Juan, Puerto Rico, to bring home the gold medal.

When Miami resumed its season on June 25, Tarpley wasn't with the team and the Tropics lost in overtime to Atlanta. But behind strong performances from Richard Dumas, Ken Bannister, Duane Washington, and former Georgetown standout Michael Graham, the Tropics amassed a 6-2 mark without

him and a 22-4 record for the season. A 116-114 win over Philadelphia in the USBL title game capped Miami's storybook season. The 1992 Miami team still ranks as one of the most talented in minor league basketball history.

Lucas sold the team in April 1995, but not before Miami repeated as USBL champions in 1993 with players such as Chris Childs, Luther Burks, Cliff Robinson, Ricky Calloway, Freeman Williams, and Ken Bannister, who earned Player of the Year honors.

⊛ ⊛ ⊛

Only two of the USBL's top 10 scorers and one of the league's top 10 rebounders and assists leaders in 1992 returned to open the 1993 season. A number of the league's top players, as well as several CBA veterans, had signed with teams in the National Basketball League (NBL), a short-lived Canadian league that rose from the ashes of the old World Basketball League. The league-jumpers included Reggie Cross, Dan Cyrulik, Emanuel Davis, Derral Dumas, Jay Edwards, Matt Fish, Sean Gay, Michael Graham, Leonard Harris, Randy Henry, Kermit Holmes, Nate Johnston, Ralph Lewis, Roy Marble, Brian Martin, Gary Massey, Ron Matthias, Bob McCann, Dwayne McClain, Willie McDuffie, Eric Mudd, Tony Smith, Nikita Wilson, Ricky Wilson, A.J. Wynder, and Perry Young.

This wasn't the first time former USBL players had defected to a competing league. Before it went belly-up in 1992, the WBL had lured a number of top USBL alums—Carlos Clark, Tommy Collier, Willie Glass, Jerry Johnson, Anthony Jones, Shawn McDaniel, Andrew Moten, Craig Neal, Eric Newsome, Bobby Parks, Danny Pearson, Daren Queenan, McKinley Singleton, Greg Sutton, Andre Turner, Joe Ward, and Clinton Wheeler—to its ranks, although many returned to the league when the WBL folded.

With fewer top-name players than in previous seasons, teams struggled at the gate. Connecticut, which had changed its name from New Haven before the season, averaged a league-high 463 attendees per game. Westchester (292), Miami (280), Long Island (274), Daytona (246), and Atlanta (224) all averaged less than 300 fans per outing. Palm Beach drew less than 100 spectators per game.

⊛ ⊛ ⊛

Things were brighter in 1994. The league added new franchises in White Plains (Westchester), Memphis, and Gulfport, Mississippi, which played in the 12,000-seat Mississippi Coast Coliseum, huge when compared to the home floors of most USBL teams. Palm Beach, for example, played its home games at the Palm Beach Community College gym, a facility with no air conditioning. Westchester's home court was a 1,000-seat community center. Memphis and Atlanta played at local high schools.

In its first and only season in the league, Mississippi Coast, led by Greg Dennis, Terry Catledge, and Darren Chancellor, finished 18-8, tied with two-time USBL champion Miami for the best regular season record. But it was a veteran-heavy Jacksonville team, which had won only half of its games during the regular season, that won the league title, downing Atlanta for its first championship since 1990. The Hooters' lineup included former NBA players Clinton Wheeler, Norris

Coleman, and Kannard Johnson, along with 30-year-old Willie McDuffie, who had led the GBA in rebounds two years earlier, and forward Fred Lewis, the 1992 USBL Rookie of the Year and a 1993 All-USBL pick.

⊕ ⊕ ⊕

Sarasota, home to a CBA team in the mid-1980s, was one of three new USBL cities when the league tipped off its 1995 season on May 12. Hoboken and Jackson, Tennessee, former home of the GBA's Jackson Jammers, also entered the league, giving the USBL nine teams for the second consecutive season.

Eric Musselman, son of coaching veteran Bill Musselman, patterned his Florida team after the clubs he'd assembled in the CBA, where his teams had gone 270-122 over seven seasons, making him one of the winningest coaches in that league's history. Jay Edwards, Charles Smith, Wes Matthews, Nate Johnston and Stanley Jackson, all former NBA players, joined rookies Kevin Salvadori, Jessie Salters and Chuck Graham and minor league veteran Sylvester Gray to help the Sharks go undefeated at home en route to a 24-2 for the season. Florida, which won its last 15 games to set a USBL record for consecutive wins, downed Atlanta, 109-104, for the title.

The Sharks would repeat as champions the following season, this time going 25-1, including a 13-game winning streak to open the season. In his two seasons in the USBL, the 33-year-old Musselman was a remarkable 53-3. He left the minors following the 1996-97 CBA season to join the Orlando Magic as an assistant coach.

The following three seasons, Kevin Mackey, who'd coached in the CBA, GBA, and USBL, led the Atlantic City Seagulls to league titles, relying on talented players such as Chris Jent, Brent Dabbs, Brent Scott, Mike Jones, Mike Lloyd, Adrian Griffin, Robert Boykins, and LaMarr Greer.

⊕ ⊕ ⊕

The USBL swelled to 11 teams in 1996 and expanded to 12 franchises for the 1997 season, adding teams along the East Coast and Florida, and in North Carolina. Keeping with the league's franchising tradition, some former USBL markets, such as Tampa, Philadelphia, and Westchester, again fielded teams. By 1999, the USBL had expanded to a whopping 13 teams with its first franchises beyond the Mississippi River into Salina and Dodge City, Kansas, and Enid, Oklahoma.

Bolstered by stronger ownership groups and more savvy marketing, USBL attendance began to increase. Attendance marks that had stood for 15 years were shattered during the league's 2000 season. Still, franchises had their problems. One of the league's top teams, Atlantic City, reportedly lost more than $100,000 during the 1999 campaign. The Washington (D.C.) Congressionals played in borrowed practice jerseys for a string of games during the same season after the team's former coach, who had purchased game uniforms the previous season, refused to turn them over to the owner unless he was reimbursed. In April, the head coach of the Oklahoma City Storm resigned just 24 hours before the team was to tip off its expansion season. He was replaced by Denny Price, 62, the team's assistant general manager and the father of NBA guards Mark and Brent Price.

Meisenheimer, who created and nurtured the USBL, serving as its only commissioner in 15 years, has succeeded where the founders of the WBL, GBA, NBL, and countless other regional leagues failed. In some ways, the USBL is a microcosm of minor league basketball. Since 1985, it has frequently struggled with unstable franchises and shaky ownership, poor facilities, weak attendance, strange scheduling, and frequent roster changes. During the 30-game USBL 2000 season, for example, the league's 11 clubs combined for more than 200 transactions involving nearly 450 players.

But the league has also served an important role, providing quality players—especially rookies—with an opportunity for exposure. Each fall, dozens of former USBL players land on the rosters of CBA, NBA, and overseas teams.

Unlike summer pro-am leagues that operate in major cities around the country with players who are often good, but seldom great, USBL competition is consistently high-quality. Granted, the play isn't always disciplined or crisp, but USBL rosters have traditionally featured players quite capable of playing professionally at some level somewhere.

⊕ ⊕ ⊕

The 2001 season was best known for former NBA pivot man Darryl Dawkins' coaching the Pennyslvania ValleyDawgs (18-12) taking the title over Dodge City (15-15) 100-91. But the following season, the league's 17th, will go down as one of the league's best ever. There were ten franchises and two divisions. Parity reigned, with any team capable of winning on a given night. The league welcomed back seven franchises from the 2002 season. New additions included: the Adirondack Wildcats, (located in Glens Falls, New York), the St. Joseph Express, and the St. Louis SkyHawks. The Lakeland franchise relocated to Brevard, Florida for the 2002 Season. The Eastern Division was made up of the Adirondack Wildcats, Brevard Blue Ducks, Brooklyn Kings, Florida Sea Dragons, and the Pennsylvania ValleyDawgs. The Mid West Division was comprised of the Dodge City Legend, Kansas Cagerz, Oklahoma Storm, St. Joseph Express, and the St. Louis SkyHawks.

The USBL also witnessed an influx of former NBA players trying their hand at coaching. Eight former NBA players patrolled the sidelines this season, including Rex Morgan, St. Joseph Express; Mike Sanders, Adirondack Wildcats; Kenny Charles, Brooklyn Kings; Lionel Hollins, St. Louis SkyHawks; Harvey Grant, Brevard Blue Ducks; Cliff Levingston, Dodge City Legend; Darryl Dawkins, Pennsylvania ValleyDawgs; Kareem Abdul-Jabbar, Oklahoma Storm.

Media coverage came not only from the addition of coach Kareem Abdul-Jabbar but from an even more unlikely source. On April 16th, the Adirondack Wildcats announced the signing of NFL All-Pro Wide Receiver Terrell Owens to a contract. Owens appeared in five games. The league also saw 29 former players land in the NBA during the 2001-02 season.

In the post-season, behind the leadership of their coach Kareem Abdul-Jabbar, Oklahoma defeated the Cagerz 122-109 to capture their first USBL title behind the efforts of post-season MVP Ira Clark.

⊕ ⊕ ⊕

The 18th season of USBL play began in Salina, Kansas on April 17th 2003 when the Dodge City Legend faced the hometown Cagerz. The Legend won 93-76 and never looked back. They posted a league-best 25-8 marker, the second most wins in league history. They also played 15-0 at home. Behind Coach of

the Year Cliff Levingston and USBL Post-Season Festival MVP Darrin Hancock, Dodge City navigated the path to victory.

Excellence didn't belong to the Legend alone. The Pennsylvania ValleyDawgs finished 23-7, good enough to capture the Eastern Division crown. The expansion Westchester Wildfire, finishing 19-11, were exciting to watch as they took on the driven mindset of their coach John Starks. The Oklahoma Storm featured athletic players like USBL Player of the Year, Albert Mouring.

The Brooklyn Kings received local and national attention with the signing of Kwame James. James was one of the people who helped subdue the "shoe bomber" on a flight from France in December 2001. James—appearing in *USA Today*, *Sports Illustrated*, and as a guest on *Angles* and *Good Morning America*—explained his plight as a Canadian citizen who could not get a visa to stay in the country despite his heroic actions.

In the 11th Annual Post-Season Festival Championship were played in Dodge City. Three games went into overtime and three others were decided in the last minute of play. When the smoke cleared, Dodge City become the third consecutive host team to win the USBL Championship with a 97-96 win over Pennsylvania in overtime.

USBL STATISTICS

1985

	W	L	Pct.
Springfield Fame	19	6	.760
New Jersey Jammers	18	7	.720
Connecticut Colonials	13	10	.565
Rhode Island Gulls	11	14	.440
Westchester Golden Apples	9	15	.375
Long Island Knights	9	15	.375
Wildwood Aces	6	18	.250

PLAYOFF RESULTS
None.

ALL-USBL TEAM
First Team

Manute Bol	Rhode Island
Kenny Orange	Long Island
John "Hot Rod" Williams	Rhode Island
Lowes Moore	Westchester
Tracy Jackson	Springfield

Second Team

Jim Bostic	Westchester
Larry Lawrence	Springfield
Joe Dawson	Connecticut
Michael Adams	Springfield
Derrick Rowland	New Jersey

Coach of the Year: Gerald Oliver (Springfield)

SCORING LEADERS

Player	Team	PPG
John Williams	Rhode Island	23.1
Gene Waldron	Long Island	23.0
Lowes Moore	Westchester	21.5
Jeff Adkins	Wildwood	20.3
Spud Webb	Rhode Island	19.9
Derrick Rowland	New Jersey	19.0
Martin Clark	Rhode Island	18.8
Larry Lawrence	Springfield	18.8
Tracy Jackson	Springfield	18.8
Eddie Lee Wilkins	Connecticut	18.3

1986

	W	L	Pct.
Tampa Bay Flash	22	8	.733
Springfield Fame	23	10	.697
Wildwood Aces	21	10	.677
Staten Island Stallions	15	17	.469
Jersey Jammers	14	19	.424
Gold Coast Stingrays	7	25	.219
Westchester Golden Apples	5	18	.217

PLAYOFF RESULTS
None.

ALL-USBL TEAM
First Team

Jim Lampley	Wildwood
Don Collins	Tampa Bay
John "Hot Rod" Williams	Staten Island
Stewart Granger	Wildwood
Billy Goodwin	Springfield

Second Team

Jerome Henderson	Springfield
Ron Valentine	Tampa Bay
Greg Wendt	Gold Coast
Alvin Frederick	Westchester
Michael Adams	Springfield

Coach of the Year: Henry Bibby (Springfield)

SCORING LEADERS

Player	Team	PPG
Don Collins	Tampa Bay	31.8
Stewart Granger	Wildwood	26.5
Billy Goodwin	Springfield	26.4
Michael Adams	Springfield	26.1
Ron Valentine	Tampa Bay	25.3
Greg Wendt	Gold Coast	24.1
Dan Ruland	Gold Coast	23.9
Dwayne Johnson	Springfield	21.1
Ralph Lewis	Wildwood	21.0
Oliver Lee	Springfield	21.0

1987

	W	L	Pct.
Tampa Bay Stars	25	5	.833
Miami Tropics	18	12	.600
Rhode Island Gulls	17	13	.567
Long Island Knights	14	16	.467
Jersey Jammers	13	17	.433
Philadelphia Aces	13	17	.433
West Palm Beach Stingrays	11	19	.367
Staten Island Stallions	9	21	.300

PLAYOFF RESULTS
First Round
Miami 138, West Palm Beach 122
Tampa Bay 129, Staten Island 126, OT
Long Island 126, Jersey 123
Rhode Island 102, Philadelphia 97
Second Round
Miami 116, Tampa Bay 109
Rhode Island 122, Long Island 119
Championship (at Miami)
Miami 103, Rhode Island 99

ALL-USBL TEAM
First Team

Eddie Lee Wilkins	Staten Island
Don Collins	Tampa Bay
Richard Rellford	West Palm Beach
Muggsy Bogues	Rhode Island
World B. Free	Miami

Second Team

Hank McDowell	Rhode Island
Michael Brooks	Philadelphia Aces
Norris Coleman	Tampa Bay
Clinton Wheeler	Miami
Geoff Huston	Long Island

Coach of the Year: Gordon Gibbons (Tampa Bay)

SCORING LEADERS

Player	Team	PPG
Don Collins	Tampa Bay	31.0
Richard Rellford	W. Palm Beach	28.5
Eddie Lee Wilkins	Staten Island	27.1
Michael Ray Richardson	LI, Jersey	25.5
Mitchell Wiggins	Tampa Bay	25.5

1988

	W	L	Pct.
Jacksonville Hooters	21	9	.700
Philadelphia Aces	19	11	.633
New Haven Skyhawks	18	12	.600
Palm Beach Stingrays	16	14	.533
Jersey Shore Bucs	15	15	.500
Miami Tropics	13	17	.433
Long Island Knights	3	27	.100

PLAYOFF RESULTS
First Round
Philadelphia 134, Long Island 117
New Haven def. Jersey Shore (forfeit)
Second Round
New Haven 122, Philadelphia 118
Palm Beach 120, Jacksonville 111
Championship (at New Haven, Conn.)
New Haven 134, Palm Beach 126

ALL-USBL TEAM
First Team

Michael Brooks	Philadelphia
Norris Coleman	Jacksonville
Mike Jones	Jersey Shore
Lewis Lloyd	Philadelphia
Andre Turner	Miami

Second Team

Darryl Middleton	Long Island
Richard Rellford	Palm Beach
Cedric Henderson	Jacksonville
Bobby Parks	New Haven
Mitchell Wiggins	Jacksonville

SCORING LEADERS

Player	Team	PPG
Richard Rellford	Palm Beach	31.4
Mike Jones	Jersey Shore	31.3
Darryl Middleton	Long Island	31.3
Lewis Lloyd	Philadelphia	30.8
Tommy Davis	Palm Beach	29.0
Norris Coleman	Jacksonville	28.4
Michael Brooks	Philadelphia	26.9
Tim McAlister	Jersey Shore	24.3
Bobby Parks	New Haven	23.1
Cedric Henderson	Jacksonville	22.9

1989

League inactive.

1990

	W	L	Pct.
Jacksonville Hooters	15	1	.938
New Haven Skyhawks	7	7	.500
Palm Beach Stingrays	3	9	.250
New York Whitecaps	1	5	.167
Philadelphia Aces	1	5	.167

PLAYOFF RESULTS
None.

ALL-USBL TEAM
First Team

Alex Roberts	New York
Lewis Lloyd	Philadelphia
Randy Henry	Jacksonville
Jerry Johnson	Jacksonville
Terrance Allen	Palm Beach

Second Team

Ken McClary	Palm Beach
John Bailey	Palm Beach
Damari Riddick	New Haven
Shaun McDaniels	New Haven
Danny Pearson	Jacksonville

Coach of the Year: Rex Morgan (Jacksonville)

SCORING LEADERS

Player	Team	PPG
Lewis Lloyd	Philadelphia	26.8
John Bailey	Palm Beach	25.1
Randy Henry	Jacksonville	22.9
Norris Coleman	Jacksonville	22.6
Alex Roberts	New York	21.7

1991

Northern Division	W	L	Pct.
Philadelphia Spirit	15	5	.750
New Haven Skyhawks	10	10	.500
Long Island Surf	7	13	.350
Empire State Stallions	7	13	.350
Southern Division			
Miami Tropics	13	7	.650
Jacksonville Hooters	12	8	.600
Atlanta Eagles	10	10	.500
Suncoast Sunblasters	6	14	.300

PLAYOFF RESULTS
Championship (at Philadelphia)
Philadelphia 110, Miami 108

ALL-USBL TEAM
First Team

Earl Cureton	Philadelphia
Norris Coleman	Jacksonville
Anthony Mason	Long Island
Michael Anderson	Philadelphia
Wes Matthews	Atlanta

Second Team

Tony Costner	Philadelphia
Dallas Comegys	Philadelphia
Nate Johnston	Suncoast
Paul Graham	Philadelphia
Tharon Mayes	New Haven

Coach of the Year: Bill Lange (Philadelphia)

SCORING LEADERS

Player	Team	PPG
Norris Coleman	Jacksonville	29.3
Tharon Mayes	New Haven	28.0
Anthony Mason	Long Island	27.8
Michael Anderson	Philadelphia	23.7
Nate Johnston	Suncoast	20.3
Tim Legler	Philadelphia	19.6
Danny Pearson	Jacksonville	19.0
Brian Howard	Empire State	18.7
Dallas Comegys	Philadelphia	18.6
Randy Henry	Jacksonville	18.2

1992

Northern Division	W	L	Pct.
Philadelphia Spirit	21	5	.808
Long Island Surf	13	13	.500
New Jersey Jammers	11	15	.423
New Haven Skyhawks	10	16	.385
Southern Division			
Miami Tropics	22	4	.846
Atlanta Eagles	16	10	.615
Palm Beach Stingrays	13	13	.500
Jacksonville Hooters	7	19	.269
Tampa Bay Sunblasters	4	22	.154

PLAYOFF RESULTS
Division Play-Ins
Atlanta 118, Palm Beach 112
Long Island 118, New Jersey 99
Division Finals
Miami 118, Atlanta 103
Philadelphia 117, Long Island 115
Championship (at Miami)
Miami 116, Philadelphia 114

ALL-USBL TEAM
First Team

Roy Tarpley	Miami
Reggie Cross	Palm Beach
Richard Dumas	Miami
Jay Edwards	New Haven
Duane Washington	Miami

Second Team

Derrall Dumas	Jacksonville
Ken Miller	New Jersey
Anthony Pullard	New Haven
Michael Anderson	Philadelphia
Darrell Armstrong	Atlanta
Lloyd Daniels	Long Island

Coach of the Year: Al Outlaw (Atlanta)

SCORING LEADERS

Player	Team	PPG
Roy Tarpley	Miami	32.2
Richard Dumas	Miami	29.7
Ron Matthias	Palm Beach	28.3
Jay Edwards	New Haven	27.5
Wes Matthews	Jacksonville	25.8
Randy Henry	Jacksonville	25.3
Reggie Cross	Palm Beach	24.1
Kenny Miller	New Jersey	24.0
Lloyd Daniels	Long Island	23.7
Anthony Pullard	New Haven	22.8

1993

	W	L	Pct.
Daytona Beach Hooters	16	8	.667
Miami Tropics	14	10	.583
Atlanta	14	10	.583
Long Island Surf	14	10	.583
Westchester Stallions	12	12	.500
Connecticut Skyhawks	8	16	.417
Palm Beach Stingrays	6	18	.250

PLAYOFF RESULTS (at Milford, Conn.)
First Round
Atlanta 123, Palm Beach 110
Miami 130, Connecticut, 113
Westchester 128, Long Island 120
Second Round
Miami 135, Atlanta 120
Westchester 131, Daytona Beach 117
Championship
Miami 139, Westchester 127

ALL-USBL TEAM
First Team

Darrell Armstrong	Atlanta
Mark Brisker	Daytona Beach
Khari Jaxon	Palm Beach
Ken Bannister	Miami
Fred Lewis	Daytona Beach

Second Team

Elmer Anderson	Westchester
Luther Burks	Miami
Cliff Robinson	Miami
Sebastian Neal	Westchester
Stan Rose	Atlanta

Coach of the Year: John Lucas (Miami)

SCORING LEADERS

Player	Team	PPG
Ken Bannister	Miami	30.2
Luther Burks	Miami	24.5
Stan Rose	Atlanta	23.7
Mark Brisker	Daytona Beach	23.1
Khari Jaxon	Palm Beach	22.7
Darrell Armstrong	Atlanta	22.6
Fred Lewis	Daytona Beach	22.3
Danny Pearson	Daytona Beach	21.8
Elmer Anderson	Westchester	21.6
Ron Matthias	Connecticut	20.9

1994

	W	L	Pct.
Mississippi Coast Gamblers	18	8	.692
Miami Tropics	18	8	.692
Atlanta Trojans	17	9	.654
Jacksonville Hooters	13	13	.500
Long Island Surf	13	13	.500
Connecticut Skyhawks	12	14	.462
Westchester Stallions	10	16	.385
Memphis Fire	9	17	.346
Palm Beach Stingrays	7	19	.269

PLAYOFF RESULTS (at Jacksonville, Fla.)
First Round
Atlanta 124, Connecticut 121
Jacksonville 116, Long Island 111
Second Round
Atlanta 146, Miami 133
Jacksonville 103, Mississippi Coast 100
Championship
Jacksonville 117, Atlanta 109

ALL-USBL TEAM
First Team

Darrell Armstrong	Atlanta
Mark Brisker	Jacksonville
Greg Dennis	Mississippi Coast
Stan Rose	Atlanta
Kannard Johnson	Jacksonville

Second Team

Jean Prioleau	Long Island
Anderson Hunt	Miami
Keith Lee	Memphis
Kermit Holmes	Westchester
Joe Harvell	Memphis

Coach of the Year: Al Outlaw (Atlanta)

SCORING LEADERS

Player	Team	PPG
Stan Rose	Atlanta	27.6
Mark Brisker	Jacksonville	26.9
Anderson Hunt	Miami	25.1
Kannard Johnson	Jacksonville	23.3
Darrell Armstrong	Atlanta	22.5
Joe Harvell	Memphis	22.4
Kermit Holmes	Westchester	21.7
Greg Dennis	Mississippi	20.1
Ike Williams	Palm Beach	19.9
Ron Huery	Memphis	19.1

1995

	W	L	Pct.
Florida Sharks	24	2	.923
Jersey Turnpikes	20	5	.800
Atlanta Trojans	15	8	.652
Long Island Surf	14	12	.538
Jackson Jackals	11	15	.423
Memphis Fire	10	16	.385
Miami Tropics	8	18	.308
Connecticut Skyhawks	6	20	.231
Jacksonville Shooters	5	21	.192

PLAYOFF RESULTS (at Palmetto, Fla.)
Semi-finals
Atlanta 116, Jersey 102
Championship
Florida 109, Atlanta 104

ALL-USBL TEAM
First Team

Charles Smith	Florida
Jerry Reynolds	Atlanta
Brent Scott	Miami
Travis Williams	Florida
Frazier Johnson	Long Island

Second Team

Derrick Canada	Connecticut
Steve Worthy	Jersey
Dan O'Sullivan	Jersey
Sylvester Gray	Florida
Herman Alston	Long Island

Coach of the Year: Mike Mashak (Jersey)

SCORING LEADERS

Player	Team	PPG
Jerry Reynolds	Atlanta	26.3
Roger Crawford	Memphis	24.0
Marshall Grier	Connecticut	23.8
Fred Vinson	Atlanta	23.4
Derek Canada	Connecticut	23.1
Brent Scott	Miami	22.8
Anderson Hunt	Miami	21.7
Herman Alston	Long Island	19.8
Steve Worthy	Jersey	19.5
Nate Higgs	Miami	19.1

1996

Northern Division	W	L	Pct.
Atlantic City Seagulls	20	6	.769
Portland Mountain Cats	16	9	.640
Long Island Surf	14	12	.538
Connecticut Skyhawks	8	17	.320
New Hampshire Thunder Loons	6	19	.240
Southern Division			
Florida Sharks	25	1	.962
Tampa Bay Windjammers	13	11	.541
Jacksonville Barracudas	11	13	.423
Carolina Cardinals	6	11	.353
Treasure Coast Tropics	8	18	.308
Atlanta Trojans	6	16	.273

PLAYOFF RESULTS (at Atlantic City, NJ)
Semi-finals
Florida 130, Portland 119
Atlantic City 115, Tampa Bay 113
Championship
Florida 118, Atlantic City 115

ALL-USBL TEAM
First Team

Charles Smith	Florida
Greg Grant	Atlantic City
Brent Scott	Portland
Tom Kleinschmidt	Florida
Corey Williams	Long Island

Second Team

Kevin Ollie	Connecticut
Sean Green	Portland
Mark Strickland	Atlantic City
Ron Anderson	Atlantic City
Mike Hackett	Jacksonville

Coach of the Year: Eric Musselman (Florida)

SCORING LEADERS

Player	Team	PPG
Brent Scott	Portland	29.8
Greg Grant	Atlantic City	24.7
Corey Williams	Long Island	24.4
Ron Anderson	Atlantic City	24.3
Lonnie Harrell	New Hamp.	23.0
Sean Green	Portland	22.1
Ron Mathias	Portland	22.0
Tom Kleinschmidt	Florida	21.6
Roscoe Patterson	New Hamp.	21.2
John White	Jacksonville	20.9

1997

Northern Division	W	L	Pct.
Atlantic City Seagulls	20	6	.769
Long Island Surf	18	7	.692
Portland Wave	12	14	.462
Connecticut Skyhawks	11	13	.458
New Hampshire Thunder Loons	10	15	.400
Westchester Kings	9	14	.391
Philadelphia Power	10	16	.385
Southern Division			
Atlanta Trojans	17	8	.680
Raleigh Cougars	14	12	.539
Jacksonville Barracudas	12	13	.480
Florida Sharks	9	16	.360
Tampa Bay Windjammers	9	17	.346

PLAYOFF RESULTS (at Atlantic City, NJ)
Semi-finals
Long Island 121, Atlanta 102
Atlantic City 135, Raleigh 123
Championship
Atlantic City 114, Long Island 112

ALL-USBL TEAM
First Team

Herman Alston	Westchester
Dennis Edwards	Florida
Brent Scott	Atlantic City
Tim Moore	Jacksonville
John Strickland	Long Island

Second Team

Jerry McCullough	New Hampshire
Mark Baker	Atlantic City
Kevin Ollie	Connecticut
Donzel Rush	Tampa Bay
Ochiel Swaby	Tampa Bay

Coach of the Year: Kevin Mackey (Atlantic City)

SCORING LEADERS

Player	Team	PPG
Dennis Edwards	Florida	32.8
Herman Alston	Westchester	27.8
John Strickland	Long Island	27.1
Tyrone Hopkins	Raleigh	26.9
Ochiel Swaby	Tampa Bay	25.3
Curt Smith	Jacksonville	24.0
Tim Moore	Jacksonville	23.6
Steve Burtt	Long Island	22.1
Brent Scott	Atlantic City	21.9
Dathon Brown	Atlanta	21.7

1998

Mid-Atlantic Division	W	L	Pct.
Atlantic City Seagulls	18	8	.692
Washington, D.C. Congressionals	17	9	.654
New Jersey Shorecats	14	12	.538
Camden Power	11	15	.423
Northern Division			
Long Island Surf	18	7	.720
Connecticut Skyhawks	17	9	.654
Columbus Cagerz	9	16	.360
New Hampshire Thunder Loons	5	21	.192
Southern Division			
Jacksonville Barracudas	17	8	.680
Raleigh Cougars	11	14	.440
Atlanta Trojans	9	17	.346
Tampa Bay Windjammers	8	18	.308

PLAYOFF RESULTS (at Asbury Park, NJ)
First Round
Columbus 119, Camden 114
Connecticut 99, New Hampshire 86
Raleigh 119, Atlanta 112, OT
New Jersey 114, Tampa Bay 90
Second Round
Long Island 124, Columbus 121
Connecticut 133, Washington, D.C .114
Atlantic City 118, Atlanta 107
Jacksonville 112, New Jersey 102
Final Four
Long Island 110, Connecticut 105
Atlantic City 122, Jacksonville 107
Championship
Atlantic City 100, Long Island 96

ALL-USBL TEAM

Player	Team
First Team	
Curt Smith	Washington, D.C.
Mike Lloyd	Atlantic City
John Strickland	Long Island
Adrian Griffin	Atlantic City
Tyrone Hopkins	Raleigh
Second Team	
Seth Marshall	Connecticut
Silas Mills	Long Island
Tunji Awojobi	New Jersey
Ochiel Swaby	Tampa Bay
Andre Perry	Atlanta

Coach of the Year: Ray Hodge (Connecticut)

1SCORING LEADERS

Player	Team	PPG
Ochiel Swaby	Tampa Bay	26.2
Tyrone Hopkins	Raleigh	25.5
Seldon Jefferson	Raleigh	23.9
Kerry Thompson	Tampa Bay	23.0
Derrick Dial	Camden	23.0
John Strickland	Long Island	22.8
Curt Smith	Wash., D.C.	21.7
Marshall Grier	Connecticut	21.6
Seth Marshall	Connecticut	21.5
Mike Lloyd	Atlantic City	21.5

1999

Mid-Atlantic Division	W	L	Pct.
Atlantic City Seagulls	20	6	.769
Pennsylvania Valleydawgs	17	8	.680
New Jersey Shorecats	16	8	.667
Raleigh Cougars*	5	8	.385
Washington, D.C. Congressionals	1	21	.045
Northern Division			
Connecticut Skyhawks	15	8	.652
Brooklyn Kings	9	13	.591
Long Island Surf	11	14	.440
New Hampshire Thunder Loons	7	18	.280
Southern Division			
Kansas Cagerz	17	8	.680
Atlanta Trojans	14	9	.609
Gulf Coast Sundogs	9	14	.391
Tampa Bay Windjammers	9	15	.375

*Franchise ceased operations on June 4, 1999.

PLAYOFF RESULTS (at Salina, Kan.)
Quarter-finals
Atlanta 110, Pennsylvania 99
Atlantic City 111, Tampa Bay 99
Long Island 103, Kansas 96
Connecticut 97, New Jersey 86

Semi-finals
Atlantic City 97, Pennsylvania 94
Connecticut 99, Long Island 92
Championship
Atlantic City 83, Connecticut 77

ALL-USBL TEAM
First Team

Mike Lloyd	Atlantic City
Junie Sanders	Brooklyn
Adrian Griffin	Atlantic City
Andre Perry	Atlanta
Jermaine Walker	Gulf Coast

Second Team

Rasaun Young	Connecticut
Curt Smith	Connecticut
Roy Hairston	Kansas
Ace Custis	Pennsylvania
George Banks	Tampa Bay

Coach of the Year: Darryl Dawkins (Pennsylvania)
and Kevin Mackey (Atlantic City)

SCORING LEADERS

Player	Team	PPG
Mike Lloyd	Atlantic City	27.3
Junie Sanders	Brooklyn	27.0
Jermaine Walker	Gulf Coast	26.6
Adrian Griffin	Atlantic City	26.5
Greg Jones	Wash., D.C.	23.1
Kwan Johnson	Pennsylvania	22.4
Rasaun Young	Connecticut	21.6
Troy Bower	Long Island	21.1
Andre Perry	Atlanta	20.5
George Banks	Tampa Bay	20.5

2000

Northern Division	W	L	Pct.
Pennsylvania Valley Dawgs	20	10	.667
New Jersey Shorecats	19	11	.633
Long Island Surf	15	15	.500
Atlantic City Seagulls	12	18	.400
Brooklyn Kings	11	19	.366
Washington Congressionals	10	20	.334
Southern Division			
Dodge City Legend	22	8	.733
Kansas Cagerz	18	12	.600
Florida Sea Dragons	16	14	.533
Oklahoma Storm	14	16	.466
Gulf Coast SunDogs	8	22	.266

PLAYOFF RESULTS
Quarter-finals
Dodge City 122, Kansas 95
Atlantic City 107, Florida 92
New Jersey 116, Oklahoma 109
Long Island 103, Pennsylvania 106
Semi-finals
Dodge City 105, Oklahoma 95
Kansas 90, New Jersey 88
Championship
Dodge City 89, Oklahoma 86

ALL-USBL TEAM
First Team

Sean Colson	Dodge City
Kwan Johnson	Pennsylvania
Mark Blount	New Jersey
Ace Custis	Pennsylvania
Darrin Hancock	Dodge City

Second Team

Artie Griffin	Dodge City
Bryant Basemore	Kansas
Andre Perry	Florida
Willie Burton	Oklahoma
Raphael Edwards	Atlantic City

Coach of the Year: Kent Davidson (Dodge City)

SCORING LEADERS

Player	Team	PPG
Sean Colson	Wash., D.C.	28.2
Mike Lloyd	Atlantic City	24.6
Kwan Johnson	Pennsylvania	24.2
Jermaine Walker	Gulf Coast	21.4
Raphael Edwards	Atlantic City	20.4

2001

Northern Division

	W	L	Pct.
Maryland Mustangs	19	11	.633
Pennsylvania Valley Dawgs	18	12	.600
Long Island Surf	13	16	.448
Brooklyn Kings	12	17	.413
Atlantic City Seagulls	0	28	.000

Southern Division

	W	L	Pct.
Oklahoma Storm	20	10	.667
Kansas Cagerz	18	12	.600
Florida Sea Dragons	18	12	.600
Lakeland Blue Ducks	15	15	.500
Dodge City Legend	15	15	.500

PLAYOFF RESULTS

Quarter-finals
Long Island 122, Oklahoma 114
Dodge City 109, Maryland 106
Lakeland 124, Kansas 119
Pennsylvania 106, Florida 93

Semi-finals
Dodge City 95, Lakeland 79
Pennsylvania 118, Long Island 99

Championship
Pennsylvania 100, Dodge City 91

ALL-USBL TEAM

First Team

Aubrey Reese	Oklahoma
Jermaine Jackson	Kansas
George Evans	Maryland
Andre Perry	Florida
Jermaine Walker	Lakeland

Second Team

Kareem Reid	Pennsylvania
Dominick Young	Kansas
Kelvin Price	Dodge City
Gregory Springfield	Brooklyn
Johnny Jackson	Kansas

Coach of the Year: Robert Parish (Maryland)

SCORING LEADERS

Player	Team	PPG
Jermaine Walker	Lakeland	27.5
Aubrey Reese	Oklahoma	26.2
Raphael Edwards	Long Island	23.8
Corey Williams	Brooklyn	22.1
Jermaine Jackson	Kansas	21.8

2002

Eastern Division

	W	L	Pct.
Brevard Blue Ducks	21	9	.700
Adirondack Wildcats	21	9	.700
Pennsylvania ValleyDawgs	14	16	.466
Florida Sea Dragons	10	20	.333
Brooklyn Kings	7	23	.233

Midwest Division

	W	L	Pct.
Kansas Cagerz	21	9	.700
Oklahoma Storm	17	13	.566
St. Joseph Express	16	14	.533
Dodge City Legend	12	18	.400
St. Louis SkyHawks	11	19	.366

PLAYOFF RESULTS

Quarter-finals
Kansas 105, Dodge City 95
Adirondack 102, Pennsylvania 101
Brevard 117, St. Louis 101
Oklahoma 108, St. Joseph 106

Semi-finals
Kansas 139, Adirondack 138, 2OT
Oklahoma 96, Brevard 95

Championship
Oklahoma 122, Kansas 109

ALL-USBL TEAM

First Team

Greg Jones	St. Joseph Express
Kwan Johnson	Brevard Blue Ducks
Johnny Jackson	Kansas Cagerz
Ira Clark	Oklahoma Storm
Kenny Gregory	Dodge City Legend

Second Team

Todd Myles	Brooklyn Kings
Cory Hightower	Pennsylvania ValleyDawgs
Fred House	Adirondack Wildcats
Gary Williams	Kansas Cagerz
Oliver Miller	Kansas Cagerz

Scoring Leaders

Player	Team	PPG
Kwan Johnson	* Brevard	25.9
Greg Jones	St. Joseph	3.8
Corey Hightower	Pennsylvania	2.1
Gary Williams	Kansas	20.9
Terrance Roberson	Pennsylvania	20.6

2003

Eastern Division

	W	L	Pct.
Pennsylvania	23	7	.766
Westchester	19	11	.633
Adirondack	16	14	.533
Brooklyn	12	18	.400
Brevard	6	24	.200

Midwest Division

	W	L	Pct.
Dodge City	25	5	.833
Oklahoma	17	13	.566
Kansas	15	15	.500
Texas	2	28	.066

PLAYOFF RESULTS

Quarter-finals
Pennsylvania 122, Brooklyn 116
Westchester 97, Kansas 94
Oklahoma 143, Adirondack 135, OT
Dodge City 127, Brevard 103

Semi-Finals
Pennsylvania 106, Westchester 104
Dodge City 106, Oklahoma 100, OT

Championships
Dodge City 97, Pennsylvania 96, OT

ALL-USBL TEAM

First Team

Kareem Reid	Pennsylvania
Albert Mouring	Oklahoma
Ace Custis	Oklahoma
Darrin Hancock	Dodge City
John Jackson	Kansas

Second Team

Lenny Cooke	Brooklyn
Olden Polynice	Pennsylvania
Kevin Freeman	Westchester
Lee Benson	Kansas
Antonio Smith	Dodge City

Coach of the Year: Cliff Levingston (Dodge City)

Scoring Leaders

Player	Team	PPG
Lenny Cooke	Brooklyn	28.8
Albert Mouring	Oklahoma	28.4
Ace Custis	Pennsylvania	22.1
Q. Woody	Pennsylvania	26.0
Kareem Reid	Pennsylvania	19.7

Chapter 35

Global Basketball Association

By Christian Anderson

In the spring of 1991 Mike Storen, founder of the ABA's Indiana Pacers and one-time commissioner of the renegade league, unveiled plans for the Global Basketball Association (GBA). It was to be a truly international basketball league, with teams not only in the United States and Canada, but Europe, Central and South America, and the Pacific Rim. Ultimately, Storen's plans called for there to be 48 GBA teams around the world, including 20 or more in the States.

At a New York City news conference on March 6, the new league announced four U.S. franchises—Greensboro, North Carolina; Greenville, South Carolina; Nashville, Tennessee; and Raleigh, North Carolina—and two European teams, including one from Italy and one from the former Soviet Union.

From the start, Storen promoted the GBA as a "major league"—one that wouldn't be used as a training ground for the NBA or its developmental league, the Continental Basketball Association (CBA). To help position it as such, the GBA would play a 64-game schedule—eight games more than the CBA. The new league also promised to pay its players nearly twice as much as CBA teams did. Storen and other league officials hoped that increased salaries would help the GBA attract the best players from the CBA and European leagues.

Unlike the World Basketball League, which struck a deal with SportsChannel early on, the GBA did not have a television contract in place when the league's formation was announced. However, GBA officials claimed they were in "discussions" with at least two European cable networks and were exploring agreements with local cable systems.

By June, five months before play was scheduled to begin, the league had grown to nine franchises, with two additional U.S. teams—Huntsville, Alabama, and New York City—and another European club, this one in Brussels, Belgium. But that summer, while the GBA was preparing for its inaugural season, another new league—this one headed by Ted Stepien, the former owner of the Cleveland Cavaliers and a two-time CBA franchise owner—was also readying for a November launch. Pro Basketball USA (PBUSA), which had quietly pulled together teams in Albany, Georgia; Buffalo, New York; Fayetteville, North Carolina; Louisville, Kentucky; Memphis, Tennessee; Saginaw, Michigan; and Wichita, Kansas, had a planned salary structure similar to that of the GBA. Its franchise fees were also similar—$44,000 for the PBUSA, $55,000 for the GBA.

Initially, Stepien said that PBUSA had no plans for a merger. But on August 9, 1991, Storen and Stepien agreed to combine their new leagues, citing "geographical advantages" and a desire to avoid a bidding war for players. As part of the agreement,

Storen would serve as the league's commissioner and Stepien as president. The "new" GBA staged its first draft two days after the merger in Atlanta, where the league would be headquartered.

But the merger wasn't without sacrifice. PBUSA teams, concerned about the expense and marketability of international clubs, refused to travel to play the GBA's foreign franchises. Later, it was decided that the international teams would play a limited league schedule. But ultimately, it was the political unrest in the former Soviet Union that forced GBA officials to shelve their plans for international play altogether, at least for a year. In addition, ownership groups in Buffalo and New York City voted not to participate in the league's first season, instead opting to wait until the 1992-93 season to begin play. A franchise in St. Louis would join the GBA in its second season.

By the time it tipped off its inaugural season on November 18, 1991, the league that had started out as a multicontinent basketball operation resembled more of a regional outfit, with nine of 11 franchises located in southern states. With four teams in the Carolinas, two in Tennessee, and one each in Georgia, Kentucky, and Alabama, only former PBUSA franchises in Saginaw and Wichita were located above the Mason-Dixon line.

Featuring two divisions, 10-player rosters, and all-white leather basketballs, the GBA opened its 1991-92 season with a number of faces familiar to basketball fans. The Fayetteville Flyers hired former Cleveland State University coach Kevin Mackey to take the helm. Mackey, who compiled four consecutive 20-win seasons at CSU during the 1980s, was fired after being arrested and charged with driving under the influence and consuming alcohol in a motor vehicle. He later admitted to using cocaine. Just prior to joining the Flyers, Mackey had coached the USBL's Miami Tropics to the league's championship game.

Another well-known and controversial college coach, Dana Kirk, took over in coaching reigns in Memphis, a franchise co-owned by Stepien and Mike Wilcox, owner of the Saginaw franchise. Kirk, who also served as Memphis's general manager, had coached at Memphis State before being fired in 1986. He would later serve four months in prison for understating his income.

In Albany, Georgia, long-time CBA coach Mauro Panaggio signed on to coach the Sharp Shooters. Huntsville, Louisville, Nashville, and Saginaw also landed former CBA coaches in Jim Sleeper, Johnny Neumann, George Whittaker, and Cazzie Russell, respectively. And in Raleigh, former North Carolina State standout Monte Towe was named coach.

For the most part, each GBA team landed a handful of minor league veterans, including some top players from the CBA, WBL, and USBL. Standouts included guards James Blackwell, Charles Smith, Cedric Toney, John Crotty, Mouse

McFadden, James Martin, Milt Wagner, Eddie Hughes, Sean Gay, Jay Taylor, Joey Wright, Kevin Williams, Darryl Johnson, Andrew Moten, and Reggie Fox; forwards Mike Ratliff, Ricky Wilson, J.J. Eubanks, Alfrederick Hughes (who scored a GBA-record 54 points in a game during the 1991-92 season), Reggie Hansen, Danny Pearson, Richard Hollis, Winston Crite, Lloyd Daniels, Ronnie Thompkins, Dave Colbert, Michael Curry, Andy Toolson, Shelton Jones, Lorenzo Charles, and Bobby Parks; and centers Willie Simmons, Tommy Collier, Doug Roth, Stuart Gray, Dan O'Sullivan, Willie McDuffie, Lorenzo Williams, Ron Cavenall, Rich Antee, Keith Lee, Maurice Brittian, David Harris, and Chuck Nevitt.

Although most top-rated college players who failed to make NBA teams opted to sign with CBA clubs for the 1991-92 season, the GBA "discovered" a number of players who would go on to have successful careers in the CBA, a few of them even reaching the NBA. For example, Darrell Armstrong, the NBA's Most Improved Player and winner of the NBA Sixth Man Award in 1998-99, began his career in the GBA, averaging just 2.5 points in six games during the 1991-92 season. After a summer in the USBL, Armstrong returned to the GBA for its second season, increasing his scoring output to nearly 19 points per game over 12 outings. The GBA also launched the pro careers of Ricky Calloway, Chris Corchiani, Michael Curry, Jerome Harmon, and Eldridge Recasner, who would go on to have a solid NBA career.

Despite landing some talented players, GBA teams for the most part lagged behind their CBA counterparts in terms of talent. This was evidenced by the number of players who started for GBA teams, only to wind up being cut by teams in the CBA. Other players, who put up big numbers in GBA games, saw their stats dip in the CBA. Clifford Martin, for example, averaged nearly 12 points and 7 rebounds per game in 39 GBA outings. Two seasons later, in six CBA games, Martin managed just 2.3 points per game while shooting 19.2 percent from the field.

Similarly, average CBA players who moved to the GBA put up big numbers. Take Mike Morrison, a 6-foot-4 forward from Loyola (Maryland) who averaged less than 10 points per game in 46 CBA games in 1990-91. The next year, in the GBA, Morrison's scoring average jumped to nearly 24 points over 45 games. Another example was 6-foot-6 Danny Pearson, a solid player who had averaged around 13 points per game over the course of 100 CBA games. When Pearson hit the GBA, however, his scoring average was inflated to nearly 26 points per game in 54 contests. When Pearson returned to the CBA after the GBA folded, his average slipped back to 12.6 points per game.

A month into the GBA's inaugural season, commissioner Storen claimed that league-wide attendance was hovering around the 3,000-per-game mark. The Mid-Michigan club quickly established itself as the GBA's model franchise, setting the standard for operations, promotions, and management. The club's work earned it the right to host the league's first All-Star Game on March 21, 1992. Hoops legend Lloyd Daniels earned MVP honors as the Kevin Mackey-coached East squad downed Cazzie Russell's West team, 106-96.

Nonetheless, it was clear that some teams, especially those lacking any coherent marketing strategy, were already struggling to generate interest in their local markets. In Memphis, the HotShots regularly played in front of tiny crowds—even on opening night, when fewer than 800 fans turned out. Abruptly, in mid-January 1992, team owner Stepien, claiming to have lost $200,000 on the franchise, moved it to Pensacola, Florida, where he had operated a CBA club years earlier. But with no staff in place to promote the team and many players refusing to make the move, the HotShots fared no better in Florida. As one Memphis columnist put it, "It was a bad idea, poorly executed."

Despite the problems, the GBA completed its first regular season of play on March 30, 1992, a little more than a week after its All-Star Game. Seven teams were scheduled to continue playing into the postseason, but two—Albany and Louisville—declined, citing a lack of funding necessary to cover travel expenses and salaries. Of those remaining, the favorites to meet for the first GBA title were Mid-Michigan, from the Western Division, and Fayetteville, representing the Eastern Division; the former had won 42 games and the latter 41. Fayetteville, with James Martin and Ernest Hall in the backcourt and Stuart Gray, Tony Brown, and Lorenzo Williams up front, had gone 23-9 at home and won four of its five overtime games. Mid-Michigan, led by all-GBA guard Reggie Fox and a powerful frontcourt rotation of Paris McCurdy, Curtis Kidd, Scott Bailey, and veteran Ron Cavenall, had posted the league's second-best home record at 25-7.

Both favorites, however, failed to reach the finals. Greenville, led by three all-league performers—John Crotty, the league's assists leader; Willie McDuffie, its top rebounder; and Danny Pearson, its top scorer—swept Fayetteville, four-zip, in the second round. And Mid-Michigan, after advancing by way of Louisville's forfeit, ran into a determined Nashville club that had dumped Huntsville, two games to one, in the first round. Nashville, known as the Music City Jammers, battled back from a 2-0 series deficit to bounce Mid-Michigan, 4-3, and advance to the finals.

The Jammers had tied Pensacola for the last playoff spot, but advanced because of a 4-2 regular season series advantage. The franchise, which over the course of 1991-92 had endured two seven-game losing streaks and lost five games by more than 30 points, had moved from Nashville to Jackson, Tennessee, after going 24-40, including 6-26 on the road, in the regular season. The team changed coaches at the end of February after George Whitaker quit and Tommy Smith, a former assistant at Middle Tennessee State, took over.

The club came together behind the leadership of veteran guards Ricky Wilson and Darryl Johnson, a former WBL All-Star with CBA experience. The 27-year-old Wilson, a 1988 All-CBA pick who'd played in the NBA and overseas, teamed with Dave Colbert, another well-traveled vet who'd averaged 18 points per game during the 1988-89 CBA season, and 3-point gunner Darren Henrie to give the Jammers a solid scoring punch. In the finals, the underdog Jammers, who had lost three of their four regular season games to Greenville, came back from a 2-1 series deficit, winning three in a row to down the Spinners, 4-2, for the first GBA crown. Colbert earned series MVP for Music City.

Although the GBA had survived its inaugural season, it was far from stable. At a league meeting in late April, rumors surfaced about canceling the second season. Even before the play-

offs began, Greensboro officials had voiced concerns over the viability of the league. In June, Storen, perhaps sensing the impending trouble, resigned as commissioner in order to pursue "other business opportunities." Stepien took over as the GBA's chief official, moving the league's headquarters from Atlanta to Cleveland, where he made his home. A week later Stepien, who also owned a GBA franchise, moved it for the second time in six months, this time from Pensacola to Biloxi, Mississippi. The new commissioner had had a previous relationship with the city; in 1986, when he owned the CBA's Jacksonville Jets, he had moved the club to Biloxi before selling it.

Talk of securing ownership groups for franchises in Niagara Falls, New York, and London, Ontario, never materialized, and charter GBA teams in Huntsville, Wichita, Raleigh, and Greensboro pulled out of the league before the start of the second season. The Albany team changed its name from the SharpShooters to the SouthGA Blues for the second season and hired former all-CBA guard Al Smith as coach.

The league did manage to add a new franchise in Cedar Rapids, Iowa, coached by NBA Hall of Famer Rick Barry, which gave it enough for two four-team divisions. But it was a short-lived sophomore season. On November 25, just three games into the campaign, the financially strapped Louisville

team, coached by former NBA player Derek Smith, folded after failing to finalize a deal with a new ownership group in Cincinnati. Less than a month later, on December 20, 1992, the league ceased operations after owners of five of the remaining seven clubs voted to disband. At the time the league collapsed, the general manager of one franchise told the Associated Press, "You cannot continue to produce a product that nobody is buying." Soon after the league went belly-up, rumors began circulating of a new league featuring several former GBA clubs, but it failed to develop.

Insiders pointed to a lack of funding as the primary reason for the league's demise. According to GBA deputy commissioner Gary Youmans, a longtime CBA coach and general manager, GBA owners weren't prepared for the expenses associated with pro basketball, leaving the teams grossly undercapitalized and woefully understaffed.

The GBA's ill-fated second season had some bright spots, however. Melvin Newbern, a high-scoring guard for Cedar Rapids, connected on a GBA-record 18 field goals in a game against Mid-Michigan. SouthGA's James Blackwell set a new record for assists, collecting 19 in an early December game against Mississippi, and former North Carolina State standout Rodney Monroe hit 20 free throws in a game at Jackson.

GBA STATISTICS

1991-92

Western Division	W	L	Pct.	Home	Away
Mid-Michigan Great Lakers	42	22	.656	25-7	17-15
Louisville (Ky.) Shooters	35	29	.546	26-6	9-23
Huntsville (Ala.) Lasers	33	31	.515	21-11	12-20
Music City (Nashville) Jammers*	24	40	.375	18-14	6-26
Pensacola (Fla.) HotShots#	24	40	.375	20-12	4-28
Wichita (Kan.) Outlaws	23	41	.359	17-15	6-26

Eastern Division	W	L	Pct.	Home	Away
Fayetteville (N.C.) Flyers	41	23	.640	23-9	18-14
Greenville (S.C.) Spinners	36	28	.562	23-9	13-19
Albany (Ga.) Sharpshooters	35	29	.546	22-10	13-19
Greensboro (N.C.) Gaters	30	33	.476	23-9	7-24
Raleigh (N.C.) Bullfrogs	28	35	.444	20-11	8-24

*Franchise relocated to Jackson, Tennessee, at the end of the regular season
#Franchise relocated from Memphis to Pensacola on January 17, 1992

PLAYOFF RESULTS
First Round

Fayetteville 112, Greensboro 107   Music City 112, Huntsville 110
Fayetteville 97, Greensboro 85   Huntsville 113, Music City 108
     Music City 123, Huntsville 121

Michigan def. Louisville, forfeit
Second Round

Greenville 117, Fayetteville 113   Mid-Michigan 101, Music City 87
Greenville 119, Fayetteville 92   Mid-Michigan 125, Music City 123
Greenville 95, Fayetteville 93   Music City 96, Mid-Michigan 93
Greenville 99, Fayetteville 93   Music City 108, Mid-Michigan 105
     Music City 94, Mid-Michigan 84

Finals   Mid-Michigan 112, Music City 102

Greenville 128, Music City 126   Music City 105, Mid-Michigan 95
Music City 100, Greenville 94
Greenville 114, Music City 103
Music City 103, Greenville 101
Music City 103, Greenville 100
Music City 106, Greenville 101

ALL-GBA TEAM

First Team		Second Team	
John Crotty	Greenville	Mike Ratliff	Huntsville
Reggie Fox	Mid-Michigan	Joey Wright	Pensacola
Willie McDuffie	Greenville	Alfrederick Hughes	Louisville
Danny Pearson	Greenville	Jerome Harmon	Louisville
Lloyd Daniels	Greensboro	David Harris	Huntsville

Coach of the Year: Kevin Mackey (Fayetteville)

SCORING LEADERS

Player	Team	PPG
Danny Pearson	Greenville	25.5
Lloyd Daniels	Greensboro	24.3
Jerome Harmon	Louisville	21.9
Jay Taylor	Pensacola	21.4
Ricky Calloway	Wichita	21.0
Mike Ratliff	Huntsville	20.5
John Crotty	Greenville	20.3
Alfrederick Hughes	Louisville	19.4
Reggie Fox	Mid-Mich.	18.7
Ricky Wilson	Music City	18.0

1992-93 *

Northern	W	L	Pct
Cedar Rapids Sharpshooters	12	4	.750
Mid-Michigan Great Lakers	6	9	.400
Jackson (Tenn.) Jammers	6	12	.333
Louisville Shooters #	0	3	.000

Southern	W	L	Pct
Greenville (S.C.) Spinners	9	5	.643
Fayetteville (N.C.) Flyers	10	7	.588
SouthGA (Albany, Ga.) Blues	8	8	.500
Mississippi (Biloxi) Sharks	6	9	.400

*League folded prior to end of season
#Franchise folded after three games

SCORING LEADERS*
*At time league disbanded.

Player	Team	PPG
Dave Colbert	Jackson	30.0
Melvin Newbern	Cedar Rapids	29.6
Bobby Parks	Jackson	26.9
Rodney Monroe	Fayetteville	26.7
Fred Herzog	Cedar Rapids	24.9
Danny Pearson	Greenville	24.0
Jerome Harmon	Mid-Mich.	23.6
Anthony Jones	Mid-Mich.	21.2
Randy Henry	Jackson	20.8
Everick Sullivan	Greenville	19.2

Chapter 36

World Basketball League

By Christian Anderson

The World Basketball League (WBL) was born from the International Basketball Association (IBA), a league co-founded by Los Angeles sports entrepreneur Dennis Murphy and Canadian businessmen Ben Hatskin and Rocky Kalish, who in 1985 devised the idea of an international summer basketball league for players 6-foot-4 and under. Murphy and Hatskin had successfully started the World Hockey Association (WHA) in the early 1970s, and Murphy was a co-founder of the American Basketball Association. But unlike the WHA and ABA, the IBA never got off the ground. What did, however, was the WBL.

The WBL would be active for four seasons, from 1988-91. Paying out salaries from $12,000-$20,000, the intrepid league provided players with a chance to supplement their incomes—while showcasing their talents during the summer months—before moving on to NBA and CBA training camps in the fall.

The idea for the league was hatched in 1986. Murphy and Hatskin enlisted Hall of Fame guard Bob Cousy as an IBA consultant and he spent the summer of 1987 traveling the country promoting the upcoming league, which would feature players 6-foot-5 and under and a blue basketball decorated with a world map. "Watching Spud Webb dunk is exciting," Cousy said, in a line that would give the league its calling card. "Watching a 7-footer isn't."

The IBA initially planned for 12 franchises—in Dallas; San Jose; Orange County; Los Angeles; New York; Chicago; Fresno; Washington, D.C.; Vancouver; Toronto; Calgary; and Syracuse—to begin play in May 1988. Also under consideration were franchises in Louisville, Houston, Tampa, Philadelphia, Anchorage, Pittsburgh, New Orleans, and Seattle.

By the end of the summer of 1987, the IBA had written a league constitution and assembled an all-star team that beat a South Korean club in an exhibition game in Seoul. By the end of the year, teams in Los Angeles, Orange County, Vancouver, Syracuse, and Fresno had selected nicknames—Jaguars, Crush, Nighthawks, Shooting Stars, and Flames, respectively. In December 1987, the league staged a free-agent draft in New York City in which 10 franchises participated, selecting some 300 players, including Michael Jordan's 5-foot-9 brother Larry and former Auburn running back Bo Jackson.

But the would-be league started to show cracks early in 1988. On January 22, the IBA named 36-year-old Milt O. Thompson, a lawyer for the Pan American Games, as its first commissioner. The next day, the league backtracked, deciding to hold off for a few weeks before making an official announcement. It never came. In February, the Toronto franchise owner announced he was moving his yet-to-be-named team to Buffalo. A month later,

owners postponed the league's start until 1989.

At that point, the league was dead, but out of its ashes a group of IBA owners created the World Basketball League. They hired Steven E. Erhart, a lawyer and former executive with the Memphis Showboats of the United States Football League, as its first commissioner, and announced plans for a 54-game schedule from May-August 1988 with six teams: Calgary, Vancouver, Chicago, Fresno, Las Vegas, and Youngstown, Ohio.

According to Erhart, the league hoped to promote "quality pro basketball competition worldwide" by delivering a "speed game which forces every player to perform all the pure basketball fundamentals rather than relying on height alone." The idea was that it was much more entertaining to watch smaller, quicker, more athletic players than lumbering 7-footers. The concept of summer basketball was attractive enough to earn the new league a three-year TV deal with SportsChannel America, which was looking for live sports progamming to fill its summer schedule. Summer ball also enabled the WBL to sign players from leagues such as the Continental Basketball Association (CBA), which plays a traditional November-March schedule.

To maintain its credibility, league officials hired renowned accounting firm of Coopers & Lybrand to "observe and document" the measuring of every player. Players were measured "in an erect position" with their heels, backs of knees, buttocks, shoulder blades, and heads against a wall. Each team's general manager and head coach certified each player's height. Teams faced $10,000 fines if a player was found to exceed the league height limit. By 1992, WBL height restrictions had increased to 6-foot-7, but by then teams had figured out ways to use their measuring sticks "creatively" as to not violate the rules.

The Memphis-based WBL hoped to establish a European division by 1990, then add divisions in the Far East and South America. In the meantime, to maintain the momentum for international play, height-restricted WBL teams played full-sized touring all-star teams from the Soviet Union, Holland, Italy, Belgium, Germany, Spain, Yugoslavia, Finland, Norway, and other foreign countries in games that counted in the league standings. Over four seasons, from 1988-1991, WBL teams won 180 of 204 games against foreign competition.

The height restrictions weren't the only thing that set the WBL apart. The league used 10-minute quarters, the international 3-point line, players couldn't foul out, and games ending in a tie were decided by a seven-point sudden death overtime. The league also permitted zone defenses, which according to league officials, required "more strategic offensive patterns."

1988

For their inaugural seasons, WBL teams stocked their rosters with CBA veterans and former college standouts. Las Vegas'

backcourt, for example, featured former UNLV guards Mark Wade and Freddie Banks, who combined for 192 steals that first season on the way to leading the SilverStreaks to the first WBL championship. Other top players included Jim Les, Kevin Gamble, Scott Brooks, Clinton Wheeler, Alfrederick Hughes, Carlos Clark, Jim Thomas, Kenny Natt, Sindey Lowe, Eddie Hughes, Cedric Hunter, and Kelvin Ransey, all of whom saw or would see NBA action at some point during their careers. Others making appearances included Mitchell Wiggins, who was banned from the NBA for drug use; Boot Bond, one of the CBA's all-time leading scorers; Del Beshore, who led the CBA in assists in 1984-85; and Billy Ray Bates, who averaged more than 28 points during the 1981 NBA playoffs.

The first WBL All-Star game was played at the Olympic Saddledome in Calgary on July 7, 1988. A crowd of 7,000 watched as Vancouver's Jose Slaughter scored 24 to lead the West team, coached by Ted Owens, to a 131-120 win over the East, coached by Mike Thibault.

1989

As might be expected with any minor league, much changed between the WBL's first and second seasons. The Vancouver and Fresno franchises folded and the Chicago team relocated to Springfield, Ill., for the 1989 season, hiring former ABA and NBA center Dave Robisch as head coach. He went 56-34 over two seasons before the team folded after the 1990 campaign.

Fresno's owner claimed to have lost about $1 million during the team's first season in which the team averaged about 1,500 fans per game and went 4-15 over the last two months of the season. A franchise in Worcester, Mass., led by former ABA coach John Clark, was added to give the WBL five teams for its second campaign, which ran from May 10-August 25. SportsChannel broadcast 27 games, including the WBL all-star game and the championship. Youngstown, whose roster featured 24 different players over the course of the 44-game season, rolled to the league's second title, winning eight straight to end the regular season before cruising through the playoffs and championship series undefeated at 4-0.

Other notable players seeing WBL action in 1989 included Dave Henderson, Andre Turner, Delray Brooks, Keith Smart, Andrew Moten, Keith Gatlin, Marty Simmons, Ricky Grace, Lowes Moore, Bryan Warrick, Doug Lee, and Winston Morgan.

More than 10,000 fans attended the WBL's 1989 all-star game in Las Vegas at the host team, the SilverStreaks, downed a team of WBL all-stars, 155-148.

1990

The WBL began its third season with six teams, the most since its inaugural season in 1988. The Worcester, Mass., franchise folded after one season, but was replaced by teams in Erie (Pa.); Memphis; and Saskatoon, Saskatchewan. Coaching moves highlighted the 1990 season. Former ABA coach of the year Tom Nissalke, who'd also coached in the CBA, was named head coach of the Memphis Rockers, guiding the club to a fourth place finish with a 27-19 record. In Erie, former NBA center Steve Hayes took the coaching reigns, but was fired after winning only four of his first 15 games with the Wave, which failed to win a road game in 19 tries. And in Las Vegas, head

coach Denny Hovanec was fired after going 7-7 and replaced by former SMU and Nevada-Reno coach Sonny Allen, who went on to earn coach of the year honors after guiding the SilverStreaks to a 32-14 mark and a playoff spot.

But the focus again was on Youngstown, where the Pride broke the Boston Celtics pro basketball record of 32 consecutive home court victories by winning their 33rd in a row on July 6. The Pride's streak ended at 44 with a loss in the postseason to Calgary, but Youngstown went on to win its second consecutive league title behind strong postseason performances from league MVP Barry Mitchell, Mario Elie, Keith Smart, Mark Wade, and Richard Hollis. Youngstown also hosted the third annual WBL all-star game in which the West squad, coached by Nissalke, downed the East team, 150-123, as Vince Askew and Daren Queenan combined for 48 points to lead the West.

Despite a disappointing 19-27 record, Saskatchewan averaged crowds of 4,200, a WBL record. Unfortunately, the league's two other new clubs—Erie and Memphis—drew poorly and would eventually fold—Memphis after the 1991 season and Erie 28 games into the 1992 campaign.

1991

After playing with five and six teams in a single division for the first three seasons of its existence, the WBL expanded to eight teams and two divisions for the 1991 season, adding franchises in Boca Raton, Fla., and Dayton, Ohio, and relocating the Las Vegas franchise to Nashville. The SilverStreaks, one of the WBL's inaugural franchises, had played at UNLV's Thomas & Mack Center for most of its three seasons in Las Vegas, but moved into a smaller arena at Caesar's Palace near the end of the 1990 campaign after attendance wilted.

In Dayton, the expansion Wings began the season with Don Donoher as head coach and general manager. However, the day before training camp, Donoher, who guided University of Dayton teams to 16 postseason appearances, relinquished his head coaching duties, instead hiring one of his former assistants, Pat Haley, to coach the team. With little time to prepare, Haley, retired from basketball for more than a decade, got off to a rough start, going 3-5 to start the season. But then the Wings, led by veterans Alfrederick Hughes, Perry McDonald, Sedric Toney, Brook Steppe, Jaren Jackson, Troy Lewis, Eddie Hughes, Joe Ward, Darryl Johnson, Duane Washington, and Albert Springs, won 23 of their next 26 games.

Hughes, a former Loyola of Chicago star, started every regular season game in the history of the WBL through the 1991 season, including All-Star games. During his WBL career, he earned a reputation as one of the league's most competitive players.

At season's end, Dayton had won 36 games, the second most in WBL history. From there, the team cruised through the postseason undefeated, crushing traditional WBL power Calgary three games to none, winning by an average margin of 24 points per game. In his only season as coach (he moved into the front office the next season) Haley earned coach of the year honors.

In Halifax, despite finishing nine games under .500 and out of the playoffs, the Windjammers' average attendance was better than 4,700 fans per game, establishing the market as one of the league's best.

1992

The WBL continued its rapid growth in 1992, expanding from eight to 10 teams for its fifth season. The first signs of instability manifested on June 15, when just 19 games into its schedule, the Boca Raton (Fla.) franchise folded. Next, the Erie (Pa.) Wave, which in a search for fan support moved a few of its games to Pittsburgh, collapsed on July 19. And the WBL's defending champs, the Dayton Wings, shut down near the end of July. A few days later, on August 1, the WBL officially suspended operations.

Most franchise owners were left with debts ranging from $150,000-$200,000. Players failed to receive paychecks. WBL referees had not been paid in eight weeks.

The underlying reason for the league's demise soon became evident. Mickey Monus, owner of the WBL's succuessful Youngstown (Ohio) franchise and president and chief executive of the Youngstown-based Phar-Mor chain of drugstores, owned two other WBL franchises.

On the day the WBL ceased operations, Phar-Mor fired Monus, alleging that he had stolen millions of dollars of corporate funds to sustain the league. In 1995, three years after the WBL folded, Monus was indicted on 129 counts of fraud and conspiracy and convicted of directing a $1.1 billion fraud and embezzlement scheme. He was sentenced to more than 19 years in prison.

Among the better-known players who began their pro careers in the WBL were James Blackwell, who would go on to earn All-CBA honors; Luther Burks, Tank Collins, and Winston Crite, all future CBA All-Stars; Darryl Johnson, who would later post a 17-assist CBA game; Reggie Jordan, who went to play in the NBA; and Darryl McDonald, a CBA All-Defensive pick in 1992.

WBL STATISTICS

1988

	W	L	Pct
Calgary 88's*	32	22	.593
Las Vegas Silver Streaks	32	22	.593
Youngstown Pride	28	26	.519
Chicago Express	27	27	.500
Fresno Flames	25	29	.463
Vancouver Nighthawks	18	36	.333

*Seeded first by tiebreaker.

PLAYOFF RESULTS (at Las Vegas)
Semi-finals
Chicago 109, Calgary 107
Las Vegas 105, Youngstown 103
Championship Game
Las Vegas 102, Chicago 95

ALL-WBL TEAM
Carlos Clark, Calgary; Bryan Pollard, Vancouver; Anthony Jones, Las Vegas;
Jim Les, Chicago; Jamie Waller, Las Vegas
Coach of the Year: Mike Thibault (Calgary)

SCORING LEADERS

Player	Team	PPG
Jamie Waller	Las Vegas	26.7
Anthony Jones	Las Vegas	24.9
Freddie Banks	Las Vegas	21.5
Kenny Natt	Fresno	19.6
Alfrederick Hughes	Chicago	18.1
Jose Slaughter	Youngstown	17.9
Bryan Pollard	Vancouver	17.2

1989

	W	L	Pct
Calgary 88's	31	13	.705
Youngstown Pride	30	14	.682
Illinois Express	29	15	.659
Las Vegas Silver Streaks	26	18	.591
Worcester Counts	18	26	.409
International Teams	1	49	.020

PLAYOFF RESULTS (at Youngstown, Ohio)
Semi-finals
Calgary def. Las Vegas, 2-1
Youngstown def. Illinois, 2-0
Championship Game
Youngstown def. Calgary, 2-0

ALL-WBL TEAM
Willie Bland, Youngstown; David Henderson, Calgary; Alfrederick Hughes, Illinois;
Andre Turner, Calgary; Jamie Waller, Las Vegas
Coach of the Year: Bob Patton (Youngstown)

SCORING LEADERS

Player	Team	PPG
Jamie Waller	Las Vegas	21.7
Willie Bland	Youngstown	21.5
David Henderson	Calgary	21.1
Alfrederick Hughes	Illinois	20.9
Darryl Kennedy	Las Vegas	20.3
Chip Engelland	Calgary	19.4
Andrew Moten	Illinois	17.5

1990

	W	L	Pct
Youngstown Pride	38	8	.826
Las Vegas Silver Streaks	32	14	.696
Calgary 88's	29	17	.630
Illinois Express	27	19	.587
Memphis Rockers	27	19	.587
Saskatchewan Storm	19	27	.413
Erie Wave	12	34	.261
International Teams	5	51	.089

PLAYOFF RESULTS
First Round
Calgary def. Erie, 2-0
Las Vegas def. Saskatchewan, 2-0
Memphis def. Illinois, 2-1
Semi-finals
Calgary def. Las Vegas, 2-1
Youngstown def. Memphis, 2-1
Championship
Youngstown def. Calgary, 3-2

ALL-WBL TEAM
Fred Cofield, Youngstown; Mario Elie, Youngstown; Chip Engelland, Calgary
Alfrederick Hughes, Illinois; Jamie Waller, Las Vegas
Coach of the Year: Sonny Allen (Las Vegas)

SCORING LEADERS

Player	Team	PPG
Jamie Waller	Las Vegas	26.5
Mario Elie	Youngstown	23.1
Daren Queenan	Las Vegas	22.9
Luther Burks	Erie	22.4
Chip Engelland	Calgary	22.3
Perry Young	Calgary	21.6
Alfrederick Hughes	Illinois	21.2

1991

Northern Division	W	L	Pct
Calgary 88's	37	14	.725
Youngstown Pride	26	25	.510
Saskatchewan Storm	25	26	.490
Halifax Windjammers	21	30	.412
Erie Wave	18	33	.353
Southern Division			
Dayton Wings	36	15	.706
Florida Jades	30	21	.588
Memphis Rockers	29	22	.568
Nashville Stars	23	28	.451
International Teams	7	38	.156

PLAYOFF RESULTS
First Round
Saskatchewan def. Youngstown, 2-0
Florida def. Memphis, 2-1
Division Finals
Calgary def. Saskatchewan, 2-0
Dayton def. Florida, 2-0
Championship
Dayton def. Calgary, 3-0

ALL-WBL TEAM
Joe Dawson, Memphis; Alfrederick Hughes, Dayton; Tracy Moore, Florida
Daren Queenan, Nashville; Milt Wagner, Memphis
Coach of the Year: Pat Haley (Dayton)

SCORING LEADERS

Player	Team	PPG
Jamie Waller	Erie	26.3
Tracy Moore	Florida	25.2
Milt Wagner	Memphis	25.0
Steve Burtt	Halifax	24.9
Daren Queenan	Nashville	22.9
Joe Dawson	Memphis	22.9
Don Petties	Saskatchewan	22.4

1992 *

Northern Division	W	L	Pct
Calgary 88's	22	12	.647
Halifax Windjammers	19	14	.576
Hamilton Skyhawks	17	17	.500
Winnipeg Thunder	15	22	.405
Saskatchewan Storm	12	21	.364
Southern Division			
Dayton Wings	26	7	.788
Youngstown Pride	22	13	.629
Florida Jades**	9	10	.474
Erie Wave***	12	16	.429
Jacksonville Stingrays**	5	14	.263

*League suspended operations on August 1, 1992.
**Team folded on June 15, 1992.
***Team folded on July 20, 1992.

SCORING LEADERS

*At time league disbanded.

Player	Team	PPG
Jamie Waller	Youngstown	23.8
Fred Cofield	Youngstown	23.0
Jerry Stroman	Calgary	22.6
J.J. Eubanks	Winnipeg	21.9
Alfrederick Hughes	Dayton	21.9
Larry Robinson	Hamilton	20.9
Kelby Stuckey	Calgary	20.3

Awards,
Honors
and
Records

Walt Bellamy, 1963
Kicking up his feet as a
Chicago Zephyr, the
season after being
awarded the Eddie
Gottlieb Trophy as the
NBA's rookie of the year.

Chapter 37

NBA Awards and Honors

By Alex Sachere

Basketball is a team game, a game in which five talents and five egos learn to share one ball for the common good, so that the whole of the team becomes greater that the sum of its individual parts. When those five play as one and think as one, the ball moves swiftly and seamlessly about the floor, from player to player, before the open man sends it on its flight to the rim and it nestles through the net.

Basketball is a team game, yet within that framework lies ample opportunity for individual brilliance to come to the fore. Whether it is beating an opponent off the dribble for a clear path to the basket or boxing out a rival for position to grab a rebound, individual battles are constantly taking place on the basketball court, shaping and molding the context of the larger conflict between the two teams.

Almost since its inception, the NBA has formally recognized players for their individual excellence in addition to crowning a team champion. The number and range of awards has grown considerably over the years, reflecting the growth of the league itself.

The NBA dates its existence to 1946 and the creation of the Basketball Association of America—although several of its franchises were members of the Midwest-based National Basketball League, which merged with the BAA in 1949 to form the National Basketball Association. The Detroit Pistons, for example, began life in the NBL in 1941 as the Fort Wayne Zollner Pistons.

Since its first season, the league has honored its best players by naming All-NBA First and Second Teams, which were known as All-Star Teams in the early years before the inception in 1951 of the mid-season All-Star Game. The league began honoring an All-Rookie Team in 1962-63 and All-Defensive First and Second Teams in 1968-69. In 1988-89, with expansion having swelled the league to 25 teams, an All-NBA Third Team and an All-Rookie Second Team were added.

The first official individual honor came in 1952-53, when Don Meineke of Fort Wayne was named the league's Rookie of the Year (although there were local and regional honors for outstanding player or top rookie before that—but nothing league-wide). The NBA did not name its first Most Valuable Player until 1955-56, when Bob Pettit of the St. Louis Hawks was so honored. Its first Coach of the Year also was a Hawk, Harry Gallatin, who was honored following the 1962-63 season.

The NBA's awards are based solely on regular season play and are usually announced during the ensuing playoffs. There are two exceptions: The league has been honoring an All-Star Game MVP since 1953 (although it retroactively named MVPs for the first two All-Star contests) and an NBA Finals MVP

Bill Walton, 1974
A career cut sadly short by injuries, but a title in '77 and MVP in '78.

since 1969.

In the 1980s, with the league looking to generate more positive publicity, several new awards were created. A Comeback Player of the Year was first named in 1980-81, but after five seasons the league replaced this with the Most Improved Player Award, at least in part because winners had been coming back from drug or alcohol abuse or absence due to contract disputes. A Defensive Player of the Year and a Sixth Man Award were instituted in 1982-83. The Schick Pivotal Player Award, honoring a player for overall contributions based on a computer-

ized weighting of statistics, was created in 1983-84. The latter evolved into the IBM Award, which used a computerized formula to evaluate players but also factored in their teams' performance. This award was dropped following the 2001-02 season following the expiration of IBM's sponsorship agreement with the league.

The league lists three other individual awards in its official honor roll: the Executive of the Year, which has been selected by NBA team executives in a poll conducted by the sports weekly *The Sporting News* since 1972-73; the J. Walter Kennedy Citizenship Award, chosen by members of the Pro Basketball Writers Association since 1974-75; and the NBA Sportsmanship Award, inaugurated by the league in 1995-96 and chosen from among four division winners the following year.

Most of the NBA's awards are voted upon by panels of sports writers and broadcasters who regularly cover the league—beat writers who follow individual teams, national writers who cover the league as a whole, individual team broadcasters, and national network broadcasters. These media panels are chosen by the league's sports communications office, with input from team public relations personnel. Exceptions, in addition to those mentioned above, are the All-Rookie and All-Defensive Teams, which are chosen by a vote of the league's head coaches. In addition, the MVP was selected by a vote among league players from 1955-56 through 1979-80 before the voting was turned over to the media.

Award ballots are distributed during the final month of the regular season and are due back in the league office by the day after the completion of the campaign. That way, postseason performance cannot impact on a voter's judgment. Ballots for All-Star MVP are distributed during the fourth quarter of that contest and collected shortly before the final buzzer, with a re-vote taken should the game go into overtime. Ballots for Finals MVP similarly are collected moments before the end of the series-clinching game, with re-votes should the series be prolonged.

Fans can participate in the voting for All-Star MVP and Finals MVP through NBA.com, the league's official website. Fans vote for their choices online, and the results of the fan voting count as one ballot in the panel, which usually includes 8-10 media members.

In the early years, award winners received mention in the league's annual media guide, and of course could use their status in contract negotiations. Plaques later were presented by the league office, and All-Star and Finals MVPs sometimes received cars from the award sponsors; Adrian Smith of the Cincinnati Royals, surprise MVP of the 1966 All-Star Game, so prized his honor that he kept his powder-blue convertible in near-mint condition for more than three decades. Today, award-winners receive trophies or plaques, three of which are named for NBA pioneers, and two of the awards also carry corporate sponsorship. The MVP receives the Maurice Podoloff Trophy, named for the league's first commissioner. The Coach of the Year receives the Red Auerbach Trophy, named for the man who guided the Celtics to 10 championships, including eight in a row from 1959 through 1966. And the NBA Rookie of the Year receives the Eddie Gottlieb Trophy, named for the coach of the league's first championship, the 1947 Philadelphia Warriors, who later was the team's owner and the league's schedule-maker

for many years.

Various NBA awards have carried an assortment of title sponsors over the years, and these have changed as sponsorship agreements came and went. At the conclusion of the 2002-03 season, the got milk? NBA Rookie of the Year and the got milk? NBA All-Rookie Team were the league's only sponsored awards.

NBA Most Valuable Player (Maurice Podoloff Trophy)

The Most Valuable Player is the league's most prestigious award, honoring the outstanding individual player during the regular season. Voters are not given any specific criteria by which to judge players, but are asked to list their top five choices in order. Points are awarded on a 10-7-5-3-1 basis, and the player with the most points is the league's MVP. Thus, it is possible for one player to have more first place votes than another but still lose out based on overall points. (Note: For the NBA's other individual awards, voters were asked to choose one winner only up until the 2002-03 season, when they were asked to select their top three and points were assigned on a 5-3-1 basis.)

The list of league MVPs reads like a who's who of professional basketball in the second half of the 20th century. Every player who has won the award and is eligible for induction into the Basketball Hall of Fame has indeed been inducted; only those who have not yet met the five-year waiting period following retirement haven't been enshrined.

The list also says a lot about the changing nature of the league itself, from one dominated by pivotmen to one in which smaller, quicker players play leading roles. Beginning with Wilt Chamberlain's rookie season of 1959-60, a center won league MVP honors in 22 of the next 23 years. Since Larry Bird broke that run in 1983-84, the award has gone to a center only three times in 20 seasons.

Seven players have accounted for 29 MVP awards, with the other 19 being divided among 16 players. Kareem Abdul-Jabbar heads the list with six MVP awards in his trophy case, three each with the Milwaukee Bucks and Los Angeles Lakers. Bill Russell of the Boston Celtics and Michael Jordan of the Chicago Bulls each won five times. Wilt Chamberlain won four, one with the Philadelphia Warriors before the franchise moved to the Bay Area and three with the 76ers after he was dealt back to Philadelphia. Arch rivals Larry Bird of the Boston Celtics and Magic Johnson of the Los Angeles Lakers won three apiece, as did Moses Malone, who won two with the Houston Rockets and one with the Philadelphia 76ers. Malone, with Houston in 1981-82 and Philly in 1982-83, is the only player to win MVP honors in back-to-back seasons while playing for different teams, while Malone, Chamberlain, and Abdul-Jabbar are the only ones to win it while playing for more than one franchise.

The first MVP was 6-foot-9 Bob Pettit of the St. Louis Hawks, who led the NBA in both scoring and rebounding in 1955-56 and gained the honor even though his team compiled a 33-39 record. The only other time the league's MVP came from a team with a losing record was in 1975-76, when Abdul-Jabbar was honored despite the L.A. Lakers' 40-42 mark.

Two players earned MVP honors while also winning Rookie of the Year, Chamberlain in 1960 and Wes Unseld of the Baltimore Bullets (now the Washington Wizards) in 1969. Two players have been named MVP and Defensive Player of the Year

in the same season, Jordan in 1988 and Hakeem Olajuwon with the Houston Rockets in 1994.

Nine players have been accorded MVP honors for the regular season and the NBA Finals in the same campaign:

Player	Team	Year
Willis Reed	New York	1969-70
Kareem Abdul-Jabbar	Milwaukee	1970-71
Moses Malone	Philadelphia	1982-83
Larry Bird	Boston	1983-84, 1985-86
Magic Johnson	L.A. Lakers	1986-87
Michael Jordan	Chicago	1990-91, 1991-92, 1995-96, 1997-98
Hakeem Olajuwon	Houston	1993-94
Shaquille O'Neal	L.A. Lakers	1999-2000
Tim Duncan	San Antonio	2002-03

Of the above list, three players made it a triple by also winning All-Star Game MVP honors that season: Reed in 1970, Jordan in 1996 and 1998, and O'Neal (sharing the All-Star award with Duncan) in 2000.

Since the league began issuing the Most Valuable Player award based on the results of media balloting in 1980-81, the most lopsided result came in 1999-2000 when O'Neal received 1,207 of a possible 1,210 points from the 121-member panel. (There has never been a unanimous winner; the only unanimous winner of any individual NBA award was Ralph Sampson, who garnered all 76 votes for Rookie of the Year in 1983-84.) Shaq received first-place votes from 120 voters, with the lone exception, Fred Hickman (then of CNN), placing him second behind Allen Iverson of Philadelphia. Afterward, Hickman explained that he felt Iverson meant more to the Sixers than O'Neal did to the Lakers, that Los Angeles without Shaq was still a decent team but Philadelphia without Iverson was not.

There have been several close races for MVP, most recently in 1996-97 when Karl Malone edged Michael Jordan by just 29 points, 986-957. Magic Johnson beat out Charles Barkley of Philadelphia for the honor in 1989-90 by just 22 points, 636-614, at a time when fewer people voted for the award. And in the first year of media voting, 1980-81, Julius Erving edged Larry Bird by 31 points, 454-423. When the players voted for MVP, the closest votes came in 1956-57, when Bob Cousy received 31 votes to 20 for runner-up Bob Pettit at a time when players were asked to vote for just one person, and in 1975-76, when Kareem Abdul-Jabbar (409 points) won a three-way race against Bob McAdoo (393) and Dave Cowens (378) when players made three selections and points were awarded on a 5-3-1 basis.

How often has the Most Valuable Player (awarded, remember, based on regular-season play only) gone to a member of a team that went on to win the championship? Twelve players have done it a total of 20 times:

Player	Team	Year
Bob Cousy	Boston	1956-57
Bill Russell	Boston	1960-61, 1961-62, 1962-63, 1964-65
Wilt Chamberlain	Philadelphia	1966-67
Willis Reed	New York	1969-70
Kareem Abdul-Jabbar	Milwaukee, L.A. Lakers	1970-71, 1979-80
Moses Malone	Philadelphia	1982-83
Larry Bird	Boston	1983-84, 1985-86
Magic Johnson	L.A. Lakers	1986-87
Michael Jordan	Chicago	1990-91, 1991-92, 1995-96, 1997-98
Hakeem Olajuwon	Houston	1993-94
Shaquille O'Neal	L.A. Lakers	1999-2000
Tim Duncan	San Antonio	2002-03

Though less than half, the proportion of Most Valuable Players who played for championship teams is significant enough to be noteworthy. This came to the fore in the early 1960s, when Chamberlain was putting up prodigious numbers for Philadelphia but Boston was winning championships. No player has ever had a more amazing statistical season than Chamberlain did in 1961-62, when he averaged 50.4 points per game, set the all-time single-game record by scoring 100 points against the New York Knicks, and also averaged 48.5 minutes per game. In addition, he led the league in rebounding at 25.7 per game and was second with a field goal percentage of .506. That also was the season that Oscar Robertson, playing for the Cincinnati Royals, became the only player to average a triple-double for an entire season with 30.8 points, 12.5 rebounds and 11.4 assists per game. Yet it was Russell, the league's No. 2 rebounder but otherwise nowhere to be found on the statistical charts, who was voted by his peers as the league's MVP for 1961-62, presumably because of his role in anchoring the champion Celtics.

Despite his prolific scoring, Jordan was not recognized as MVP until 1988 and then not again until 1991, the first season the Bulls won the league crown. Robertson, acknowledged as the best all-around player in the game but one who did not win a title until he joined Milwaukee late in his career, won only one MVP award, in 1964. Jerry West, Robertson's long-time backcourt rival whose Lakers team played second fiddle to the Celtics throughout the 1960s, never won the award, not even when he finally got his championship ring in 1972, his next-to-last season.

How important is scoring to winning MVP honors? In Chamberlain's case, not very. When he won seven consecutive scoring titles from 1959-60 through 1965-66, he was accorded MVP honors in just the first and last years of that run. Russell got it in four of the intervening years and Robertson in one. Jordan's prolific scoring early in his career also did not persuade the MVP voters. He won only one MVP (1988) during the time before the Bulls became a championship team, but gained the honor four additional times when Chicago was champion.

In other cases, scoring has played a more significant role. For example, it clearly was the determining factor in Bob McAdoo, in the middle of a three-year reign as league scoring champion with the Buffalo Braves, winning MVP honors in 1975.

Here are the seven players who have won MVP honors a total of 13 times in the same season in which they led the league in scoring:

Player	Team	Year
Bob Pettit	St. Louis	1958-59
Wilt Chamberlain	Philadelphia	1959-60, 1965-66
Kareem Abdul-Jabbar	Milwaukee	1970-71, 1971-72
Bob McAdoo	Buffalo	1974-75
Michael Jordan	Chicago	1987-88, 1990-91, 1991-92, 1995-96, 1997-98
Shaquille O'Neal	L.A. Lakers	1999-2000
Allen Iverson	Philadelphia	2000-01

Following is the complete list of winners of the NBA Most Valuable Player award, selected from 1955-56 through 1979-80 by a vote among the league's players and since 1980-81 by a panel of sports writers and broadcasters:

Season	Player	Team
1955-56	Bob Pettit	St. Louis
1956-57	Bob Cousy	Boston
1957-58	Bill Russell	Boston
1958-59	Bob Pettit	St. Louis
1959-60	Wilt Chamberlain	Philadelphia
1960-61	Bill Russell	Boston
1961-62	Bill Russell	Boston
1962-63	Bill Russell	Boston
1963-64	Oscar Robertson	Cincinnati
1964-65	Bill Russell	Boston
1965-66	Wilt Chamberlain	Philadelphia
1966-67	Wilt Chamberlain	Philadelphia
1967-68	Wilt Chamberlain	Philadelphia
1968-69	Wes Unseld	Baltimore
1969-70	Willis Reed	New York
1970-71	Kareem Abdul-Jabbar	Milwaukee
1971-72	Kareem Abdul-Jabbar	Milwaukee
1972-73	Dave Cowens	Boston
1973-74	Kareem Abdul-Jabbar	Milwaukee
1974-75	Bob McAdoo	Buffalo
1975-76	Kareem Abdul-Jabbar	LA Lakers
1976-77	Kareem Abdul-Jabbar	LA Lakers
1977-78	Bill Walton	Portland
1978-79	Moses Malone	Houston
1979-80	Kareem Abdul-Jabbar	LA Lakers
1980-81	Julius Erving	Philadelphia
1981-82	Moses Malone	Houston
1982-83	Moses Malone	Philadelphia
1983-84	Larry Bird	Boston
1984-85	Larry Bird	Boston
1985-86	Larry Bird	Boston
1986-87	Magic Johnson	LA Lakers
1987-88	Michael Jordan	Chicago
1988-89	Magic Johnson	LA Lakers
1989-90	Magic Johnson	LA Lakers
1990-91	Michael Jordan	Chicago
1991-92	Michael Jordan	Chicago
1992-93	Charles Barkley	Phoenix
1993-94	Hakeem Olajuwon	Houston
1994-95	David Robinson	San Antonio
1995-96	Michael Jordan	Chicago
1996-97	Karl Malone	Utah
1997-98	Michael Jordan	Chicago
1998-99	Karl Malone	Utah
1999-00	Shaquille O'Neal	LA Lakers
2000-01	Allen Iverson	Philadelphia
2001-02	Tim Duncan	San Antonio
2002-03	Tim Duncan	San Antonio

NBA Finals Most Valuable Player

Jerry West of the Los Angeles Lakers put on such a compelling performance in the 1969 NBA Finals, he was named the Most Valuable Player of the series even though his team lost to the Boston Celtics. West scored 20 points or more in each of the seven games and averaged 37.9 points per game, starting the series with 53 points in Game 1 and ending it with a triple-double of 42 points, 13 rebounds, and 12 assists in Game 7, when he played despite a pulled hamstring.

Since that inaugural year, however, the NBA Finals MVP has gone to a member of the winning team every year. And not just to a member of the winning team, but almost exclusively to that team's premier player. Look at the most recent Finals MVPs. Michael Jordan won it in all six of the Chicago Bulls' championship seasons, and Hakeem Olajuwon of the Houston Rockets took it in the two years in between the Bulls' three-peats. Tim Duncan of the San Antonio Spurs won it in 1999, Shaquille O'Neal took the honor in each of the three years the Los Angeles Lakers won the title, then Duncan reclaimed it when the Spurs recaptured the crown in 2003.

Unlike the All-Star Game MVP, which can go to a player who steals the show with one great performance, the Finals MVP is decided over the course of a best-of-seven series in which things tend to balance out and the cream usually rises to

the top. More than one-third of NBA Finals MVPs, 13 out of 35, also won MVP honors that same season.

Of the eligible winners, 11 of 15 NBA Finals MVPs have been inducted into the Basketball Hall of Fame. And the four exceptions were hardly unheralded: Jo Jo White was one of the top scorers on the 1976 Boston Celtics, Dennis Johnson starred at both ends of the court for the 1979 Seattle SuperSonics, Cedric Maxwell was one of the veteran leaders on the 1981 Boston Celtics, and James Worthy was one of the top guns on the 1988 Los Angeles Lakers.

The award has not been without surprises. Kareem Abdul-Jabbar was the dominant figure though most of the 1980 NBA Finals, but he got hurt in Game 5 and that allowed rookie Magic Johnson to fill in at center, have a big Game 6 and steal away the MVP award. And it was the all-around play of the quiet, classy Joe Dumars that won the honor in 1989 over bolder, brasher teammates like Isiah Thomas and Bill Laimbeer on the Detroit Pistons' Bad Boys.

Perhaps the most surprising NBA Finals MVP was Maxwell of the 1981 Celtics, a team that also had stars like Larry Bird, Robert Parish, Kevin McHale and Nate Archibald. Even though Bird had both the most spectacular play of the six-game win over the Houston Rockets, an off-balance follow of his own miss in Game 1, and the shot that iced the championship, a three-pointer late in Game 6, he was not accorded MVP honors because of a mid-series slump that saw him held to eight points apiece in Games 3 and 4. The MVP honor instead went to Maxwell, the veteran who kept McHale in the role of sixth man by averaging 15.2 ppg in the regular season and then stepped it up to a team-high 17.7 ppg in the Finals.

Following is the complete list of winners of the NBA Finals Most Valuable Player award, as selected by a panel of writers and broadcasters:

Season	Finals MVP	Team
1968-69	Jerry West	LA Lakers
1969-70	Willis Reed	New York
1970-71	Kareem Abdul-Jabbar	Milwaukee
1971-72	Wilt Chamberlain	LA Lakers
1972-73	Willis Reed	New York
1973-74	John Havlicek	Boston
1974-75	Rick Barry	Golden State
1975-76	JoJo White	Boston
1976-77	Bill Walton	Portland
1977-78	Wes Unseld	Washington
1978-79	Dennis Johnson	Seattle
1979-80	Magic Johnson	LA Lakers
1980-81	Cedric Maxwell	Boston
1981-82	Magic Johnson	LA Lakers
1982-83	Moses Malone	Philadelphia
1983-84	Larry Bird	Boston
1984-85	Kareem Abdul-Jabbar	LA Lakers
1985-86	Larry Bird	Boston
1986-87	Magic Johnson	LA Lakers
1987-88	James Worthy	LA Lakers
1988-89	Joe Dumars	Detroit
1989-90	Isiah Thomas	Detroit
1990-91	Michael Jordan	Chicago
1991-92	Michael Jordan	Chicago
1992-93	Michael Jordan	Chicago
1993-94	Hakeem Olajuwon	Houston
1994-95	Hakeem Olajuwon	Houston
1995-96	Michael Jordan	Chicago
1996-97	Michael Jordan	Chicago
1997-98	Michael Jordan	Chicago
1998-99	Tim Duncan	San Antonio
1999-00	Shaquille O'Neal	LA Lakers
2000-01	Shaquille O'Neal	LA Lakers
2001-02	Shaquille O'Neal	LA Lakers
2002-03	Tim Duncan	San Antonio

NBA All-Star Game Most Valuable Player

The NBA All-Star Game is the ultimate playground game, with the best players in the league gathering annually to strut their stuff and put their best moves on one another. Freed from the constraints imposed by the team goal of trying to win a league championship, the All-Star Game becomes "Show me what you've got" taken to the extreme. Thunderous dunks and no-look passes are commonplace in this game played above the rim at breakneck speed. Michael Jordan shot free throws with his eyes closed; Isiah Thomas threw passes to teammates off the backboard; Magic Johnson waved everyone away so he could isolate for some one-on-one-upsmanship.

"It's a time when you can play without the specific pressure of knowing that what you do or don't do will show up in the standings," observed Hall of Famer Julius Erving, a five-time ABA All-Star and 11-time NBA All-Star. "You can exhibit your skills, all your skills, the way you know the majority of basketball fans want to see them. It's the one day you can cater completely to the fans who have made the game what it is. You perform simply for the love of the game of basketball."

"The All-Star Game is the ultimate in Showtime," said Magic Johnson, who came out of retirement to win MVP honors in the 1992 All-Star Game. A 12-time All-Star, Johnson also was the MVP of the 1990 game and holds the all-time record for single-game (22 in 1984) and career (127) assists. "We are all entertainers. When I go out on the floor and play a basketball game I'm always looking to have fun, and play in such a way that the fans also have fun watching me play. I love being in the All-Star Game, you better believe it. So tell the fans to get ready. Tell them, 'Don't be going out too much for popcorn. Stack it up and watch, because if you leave to go stand in line, you might miss the greatest plays.' You know you're going to make something happen. That's when you're at your best That's when you get to be you, because you create the situation. It's Smiletime then!"

If ever there was a game for which more than one ball was needed, this is it. And if ever there was a game destined to be dominated by guards, this is it, since guards bring the ball upcourt and control where it will go. Big men long have accepted the reality that their roles will be diminished in All-Star Games, where even future Hall of Famers are reduced to getting rebounds and then getting out of the way so that the flashier guards and small forwards have room to operate. If they want to score, big men have to put up shots just about every time the ball comes in to them, because if they pass it back out, they likely will not see it again.

Fifty-two NBA All-Star Games have been played since the mid-season game was instituted in 1951 (no game was played in the lockout-shortened 1999-2000 season), and guards have taken home MVP honors in 26 of them and shared the honor in one more. Since 1975, guards have won the MVP award in 16 of 28 games and shared it in another. Add the five MVPs taken by small forwards since 1975—six, if you want to include the 2003 MVP, 6-foot-11 Kevin Garnett, who plays multiple positions but spends most of his time at "small" forward—and the role of the big man really is put into perspective.

The Western Conference, with a starting front line of 7-foot Tim Duncan, 7-foot-1 Shaquille O'Neal, and 6-foot-11 Kevin Garnett backed up by 7-foot-1 David Robinson, 6-foot-9 Karl Malone, 6-foot-10 Chris Webber and 6-foot-11 Rasheed Wallace, overpowered the smaller East team 137-126 in the 2000 All-Star Game in Oakland. Duncan and O'Neal shared MVP honors in that game. But largely the same group, except for 7-foot-1 Vlade Divac replacing an injured O'Neal, couldn't stop the smaller East from erasing a 21-point deficit and pulling out a 111-110 victory in the 2001 All-Star Game in Washington. The MVP was Allen Iverson, barely 6 feet and 165 pounds, who shredded the tall timber by scoring 15 of his 25 points in the final nine minutes.

"Everybody was saying we couldn't win because of our size. It's not about size. It's about the size of your heart," Iverson said.

It's also about having the ball in your hands, with the opportunity to make things happen. Nobody knows this better than Isiah Thomas, the multi-talented guard who led the Detroit Pistons to two NBA titles and was a 12-time All-Star, winning MVP honors in 1984 and 1986. Thomas described the All-Star Game as "sheer fun" and said, "It's heaven for a guard. Wherever you throw the ball, whatever you do with it, it's right."

Ed Macauley of the host Boston Celtics was the MVP of the first All-Star Game, in 1951, although he wasn't so recognized at the time. The award wasn't created until 1953, when George Mikan of the Minneapolis Lakers was honored by a panel of media voters for his 22 points and 16 rebounds in the West's 79-75 victory in the third All-Star Game. Some years later, league officials retroactively named Macauley the MVP of Game 1, because he scored 20 points and helped hold Mikan to 4-for-17 shooting. At the same time, Paul Arizin of the Philadelphia Warriors was selected as the MVP of Game 2, in which he scored 26 points.

Game 4 was the first All-Star Game to go into overtime, and the original ballots that had Jim Pollard of Minneapolis as MVP were discarded and a second vote taken. Bob Cousy of the Boston Celtics, who scored 10 of his 20 points in the extra period to lead the East to a 79-75 victory, got the nod.

The award has been shared three times, in 1959 by Elgin Baylor of the Minneapolis Lakers and Bob Pettit of the St. Louis Hawks, in 1993 by Utah Jazz teammates Karl Malone and John Stockton (the fact that the game was played in Salt Lake City may well have impacted voters' judgment) and in 2002 by Tim Duncan of the San Antonio Spurs and Shaquille O'Neal of the Los Angeles Lakers.

Pettit, the forward who was an All-Star in each of his 11 NBA seasons, won the MVP award four times, more than any other player. He won it outright in 1956, 1958, and 1962 and shared it with Baylor in 1959. Oscar Robertson of the Cincinnati Royals (1961, 1964, 1969) and Michael Jordan of the Chicago Bulls (1988, 1996, 1998) each won the MVP award three times. Bob Cousy, Julius Erving and Magic Johnson won it twice apiece, and Karl Malone won it outright once and shared it with John Stockton once.

The great centers? George Mikan, Wilt Chamberlain and Bill Russell each won MVP honors once. Kareem Abdul-Jabbar, the league's all-time leading scorer, never won the award in his 20-year career.

Following is the complete list of winners of the NBA All-

Star Game Most Valuable Player award, as selected by a panel of writers and broadcasters covering the game:

Year	Player	Team
1951	Ed Macauley	Boston
1952	Paul Arizin	Philadelphia
1953	George Mikan	Minnesota
1954	Bob Cousy	Boston
1955	Bill Sharman	Boston
1956	Bob Pettit	St. Louis
1957	Bob Cousy	Boston
1958	Bob Pettit	St. Louis
1959	Bob Pettit	St. Louis
	Elgin Baylor	Minnesota
1960	Wilt Chamberlain	Philadelphia
1961	Oscar Robertson	Cincinnati
1962	Bob Pettit	St. Louis
1963	Bill Russell	Boston
1964	Oscar Robertson	Cincinnati
1965	Jerry Lucas	Cincinnati
1966	Adrian Smith	Cincinnati
1967	Rick Barry	San Francisco
1968	Hal Greer	Philadelphia
1969	Oscar Robertson	Cincinnati
1970	Willis Reed	New York
1971	Lenny Wilkens	Seattle
1972	Jerry West	LA Lakers
1973	Dave Cowens	Boston
1974	Bob Lanier	Detroit
1975	Walt Frazier	New York
1976	Dave Bing	Wash
1977	Julius Erving	Philadelphia
1978	Randy Smith	Buffalo
1979	David Thompson	Denver
1980	George Gervin	San Antonio
1981	Nate Archibald	Boston
1982	Larry Bird	Boston
1983	Julius Erving	Philadelphia
1984	Isiah Thomas	Detroit
1985	Ralph Sampson	Houston
1986	Isiah Thomas	Detroit
1987	Tom Chambers	Seattle
1988	Michael Jordan	Chicago
1989	Karl Malone	Utah
1990	Magic Johnson	LA Lakers
1991	Charles Barkley	Philadelphia
1992	Magic Johnson	LA Lakers
1993	Karl Malone	Utah
	John Stockton	Utah
1994	Scottie Pippen	Chicago
1995	Mitch Richmond	Sacramento
1996	Michael Jordan	Chicago
1997	Glen Rice	Charlotte
1998	Michael Jordan	Chicago
1999	no game	
2000	Tim Duncan	San Antonio
	Shaq O'Neill	LA Lakers
2001	Allen Iverson	Philadelphia
2002	Kobe Bryant	LA Lakers
2003	Kevin Garnett	Minnesota

NBA Coach of the Year (Red Auerbach Trophy)

A persuasive argument could be made for simply giving the NBA Coach of the Year award to the coach of the league's championship-winning team each season. After all, isn't guiding his team to the league title the ultimate goal of every coach?

But like the rest of the NBA's individual awards, the Coach of the Year is based on regular season performance only. Votes are cast and ballots collected in the final days of the regular season, so playoff performance doesn't enter into the equation.

In fact, since the award was established in 1962-63, only five times has it gone to the coach whose team went on to win the championship that season: Red Auerbach of the Boston Celtics in 1964-65, Red Holzman of the New York Knicks in 1969-70, Bill Sharman of the Los Angeles Lakers in 1971-72, Phil Jackson of the Chicago Bulls in 1995-96 and Gregg Popovich of the San Antonio Spurs in 2002-03. That's just five title-winners in the award's 41-year existence.

You have a better chance if you coach your team to the most wins during the regular season. Each of the five listed above did it that year, as well as five other winners of the Coach of the Year award: Dolph Schayes of the Philadelphia 76ers in 1965-66, Gene Shue of the Baltimore Bullets in 1968-69, Tom Heinsohn of the Boston Celtics in 1972-73, Bill Fitch of the Boston Celtics in 1979-80, and Pat Riley of the Los Angeles Lakers in 1989-90.

But that's still only 10 of the 41 winners, so it's apparent that success alone is not what the voters are looking for. It's success relative to the material a coach has to work with. It's success relative to the team's performance the year before and in recent seasons. It's success in the face of adversity, such as injuries to key players. These carry weight with the voters.

When Johnny Kerr led the expansion Chicago Bulls to a respectable 33 wins and a playoff berth in their first season, he was voted the Coach of the Year for 1966-67. When Ray Scott guided the Detroit Pistons to a 52-30 record, the first 50-win season in franchise history, he was voted the Coach of the Year for 1973-74. When Frank Layden coached the Utah Jazz to 45 wins, a division title and their first-ever playoff berth, he was voted the Coach of the Year for 1983-84. And when Glenn "Doc" Rivers took an Orlando team that had lost four of its five starters from the previous season and guided it to a .500 record and a playoff spot, he was voted the Coach of the Year for 1999-2000.

Riley has won the award more than any other coach, three times, and he did it with three different teams: the Los Angeles Lakers in 1989-90, the New York Knicks in 1992-93 and the Miami Heat in 1996-97. Four coaches have won the award twice: Shue with the Baltimore Bullets in 1968-69 and the Washington Bullets in 1981-82; Fitch with the Cleveland Cavaliers in 1975-76 and the Boston Celtics in 1979-80; Cotton Fitzsimmons with the Kansas City Kings in 1978-79 and the Phoenix Suns in 1988-89; and Don Nelson with the Milwaukee Bucks in 1984-85 and the Golden State Warriors in 1991-92.

Following is the complete list of winners of the NBA Coach of the Year Award, as selected by a panel of writers and broadcasters:

Year	Winner	Team
1962-63	Harry Gallatin	St. Louis
1963-64	Alex Hannum	San Francisco
1964-65	Red Auerbach	Boston
1965-66	Dolph Schayes	Philadelphia
1966-67	Johnny Kerr	Chicago
1967-68	Richie Guerin	St. Louis
1968-69	Gene Shue	Baltimore
1969-70	Red Holzman	New York
1970-71	Dick Motta	Chicago
1971-72	Bill Sharman	LA Lakers
1972-73	Tom Heinsohn	Boston
1973-74	Ray Scott	Detroit
1974-75	Phil Johnson	Kansas City-Omaha
1975-76	Bill Fitch	Cleveland
1976-77	Tom Nissalke	Houston
1977-78	Hubie Brown	Atlanta
1978-79	Cotton Fitzsimmons	Kansas City
1979-80	Bill Fitch	Boston
1980-81	Jack McKinney	Indiana
1981-82	Gene Shue	Washington
1982-83	Don Nelson	Milwaukee
1983-84	Frank Layden	Utah
1984-85	Don Nelson	Milwaukee
1985-86	Mike Fratello	Atlanta
1986-87	Mike Schuler	Portland
1987-88	Doug Moe	Denver
1988-89	Cotton Fitzsimmons	Phoenix
1989-90	Pat Riley	LA Lakers

1990-91	Don Chaney	Houston
1991-92	Don Nelson	Golden State
1992-93	Pat Riley	New York
1993-94	Lenny Wilkens	Atlanta
1994-95	Del Harris	LA Lakers
1995-96	Phil Jackson	Chicago
1996-97	Pat Riley	Miami
1997-98	Larry Bird	Indiana
1998-99	Mike Dunleavy	Portland
1999-00	Doc Rivers	Orlando
2000-01	Larry Brown	Philadelphia
2001-02	Rick Carlisle	Detroit
2002-03	Gregg Popovich	San Antonio

NBA Rookie of the Year (Eddie Gottlieb Trophy)

What do Bill Russell, Jerry West, and Magic Johnson have in common? All failed to win the NBA Rookie of the Year Award, then went on to brilliant careers that landed them in the Hall of Fame.

Russell, who joined the Boston Celtics midway through the 1956-57 season because he competed in the 1956 Olympics in Melbourne, lost out to high-scoring teammate Tom Heinsohn. West came to a Los Angeles Lakers team that already had two solid veteran guards, Rod Hundley and Frank Selvy, and thus was overshadowed in 1960-61 by Oscar Robertson, whose Cincinnati Royals had won just 19 games the previous season and were desperate for help.

Johnson came into the NBA in 1979 along with Larry Bird; the two had met in a memorable NCAA championship game, with Johnson's Michigan State team defeating previously unbeaten Indiana State and Bird. They joined two of the league's most storied franchises on opposite coasts, Johnson going to the Los Angeles Lakers and Bird to the Boston Celtics. Both had immediate impact, Bird leading the Celtics to a league-best 61 victories and Johnson helping the Lakers win 60. But their race for Rookie of the Year turned out to be a non-race, largely because Bird's Celtics had won just 29 games the year before while the Lakers had won 47. Recognizing what was at the time the greatest single-season improvement in NBA history, the voters gave the award to Bird in a landslide as he outpolled Johnson 63-3.

Johnson had the last laugh, however, albeit after the awards were announced. After the Philadelphia 76ers eliminated Boston in the Eastern Conference Finals, Johnson teamed with Kareem Abdul-Jabbar to lead the Lakers to an NBA championship, giving him NCAA and NBA titles in consecutive seasons. Johnson earned NBA Finals MVP honors after one of the most remarkable games in playoff history, when he moved over from his guard position to fill in for an injured Abdul-Jabbar at center in Game 6 and came up with 42 points, 15 rebounds and seven assists in the series-ending 123-107 victory.

The Rookie of the Year is the oldest individual award in the NBA, predating even the MVP award by three seasons. The first player to win Rookie honors was Don Meineke of the Fort Wayne Pistons, a 6-foot-7 forward who averaged 10.7 points and 6.9 rebounds per game in 1952-53, the best season of his five-year NBA career.

Going back to 1957-58, when the NBA first began recording its drafts by rounds, the Rookie of the Year Award has gone to (or been shared by) either a first-round draft pick or a territorial pick in 43 of 46 seasons. The last non-first-rounder to win the honor was Willis Reed of the New York Knicks, who

was selected with the first pick in the second round (the 10th overall selection) in 1964. Terry Dischinger of Chicago, a second-round pick in 1962, and Woody Sauldsberry of Philadelphia, an eighth-round pick in 1957, are the other winners from other than the first round.

Up until 1965, a team could designate a player from their immediate geographic area as their territorial pick before the start of the draft, and forfeit their normal first-round selection. The rule was intended to allow teams to be capitalize on the regional popularity of college stars, but Philadelphia's Eddie Gottlieb (for whom the Rookie of the Year trophy is named) persuaded his fellow team owners to allow him to extend it to include Wilt Chamberlain, who played college ball at Kansas but starred at Philadelphia's Overbrook High School.

The Rookie of the Year Award has been won (or shared) by the first overall pick in the draft, or a territorial pick, 15 times. Following are the overall No. 1 picks, and territorial choices, who went on to win Rookie of the Year honors:

Year	Winner	Team
1958-59	Elgin Baylor	Minneapolis
1959-60	Wilt Chamberlain	Philadelphia (territorial)
1960-61	Oscar Robertson	Cincinnati
1961-62	Walt Bellamy	Chicago
1963-64	Jerry Lucas	Cincinnati (territorial)
1969-70	Kareem Abdul-Jabbar	Milwaukee
1983-84	Ralph Sampson	Houston
1985-86	Patrick Ewing	New York
1990-91	Derrick Coleman	New Jersey
1991-92	Larry Johnson	Charlotte
1992-93	Shaquille O'Neal	Orlando
1993-94	Chris Webber	Golden State
1996-97	Allen Iverson	Philadelphia
1997-98	Tim Duncan	San Antonio
1999-00	Elton Brand	Chicago (tied)

Brand tied with Steve Francis of the Houston Rockets, one of three times the award has been shared. The others came in 1970-71, when Dave Cowens of the Boston Celtics and Geoff Petrie of the Portland Trail Blazers tied, and in 1994-95, when Grant Hill of the Detroit Pistons and Jason Kidd of the Dallas Mavericks shared the award.

Following is the complete list of winners of the got milk? NBA Rookie of the Year Award, as selected by a panel of writers and broadcasters:

Year	Winner	Team
1952-53	Don Meineke	Fort Worth
1953-54	Ray Felix	Baltimore
1954-55	Bob Pettit	Milwaukee
1955-56	Maurice Stokes	Rochester
1956-57	Tom Heinsohn	Boston
1957-58	Woody Sauldsberry	Philadelphia
1958-59	Elgin Baylor	Minnesota
1959-60	Wilt Chamberlain	Philadelphia
1960-61	Oscar Robertson	Cincinatti
1961-62	Walt Bellamy	Chicago
1962-63	Terry Dischinger	Chicago
1963-64	Jerry Lucas	Cincinatti
1964-65	Willis Reed	New York
1965-66	Rick Barry	San Francisco
1966-67	Dave Bing	Detroit
1967-68	Earl Monroe	Baltimore
1968-69	Wes Unseld	Baltimore
1969-70	K. Abdul-Jabbar	Milwaukee
1970-71	Dave Cowens	Boston
	Geoff Petrie	Portland
1971-72	Sidney Wicks	Portland
1972-73	Bob McAdoo	Buffalo
1973-74	Ernie DiGregorio	Buffalo
1974-75	Keith Wilkes	Golden State
1975-76	Alvan Adams	Phoenix
1976-77	Adrian Dantley	Buffalo

1977-78	Walter Davis	Phoenix
1978-79	Phil Ford	Kansas City
1979-80	Larry Bird	Boston
1980-81	Darrell Griffith	Utah
1981-82	Buck Williams	New Jersey
1982-83	Terry Cummings	San Diego
1983-84	Ralph Sampson	Houston
1984-85	Michael Jordan	Chicago
1985-86	Patrick Ewing	New York
1986-87	Chuck Person	Indiana
1987-88	Mark Jackson	New York
1988-89	Mitch Richmond	Golden State
1989-90	David Robinson	San Antonio
1990-91	Derrick Coleman	New Jersey
1991-92	Larry Johnson	Charlotte
1992-93	Shaquille O'Neal	Orlando
1993-94	Chris Webber	Golden State
1994-95	Jason Kidd	Dallas
	Grant Hill	Detroit
1995-96	Damon Stoudamire	Toronto
1996-97	Allen Iverson	Philadelphia
1997-98	Tim Duncan	San Antonio
1998-99	Vince Carter	Toronto
1999-00	Elton Brand	Chicago
	Steve Francis	Houston
2000-01	Mike Miller	Orlando
2001-02	Pau Gasol	Memphis
2002-03	Amare Stoudemire	Phoenix

NBA Most Improved Player

In 1980, the NBA's championship series between the Philadelphia 76ers and Los Angeles Lakers was televised nationally, but seen live only in those markets. The rest of the country saw it on delayed tape, usually following the late-night local news. So the league, hoping to stir interest, began thinking of new ways to spotlight its players and created several new awards, the first of which was the Comeback Player of the Year, instituted for the 1980-81 season. The idea was to recognize a high caliber player who slumped for a year or more, then came back to regain his former glory.

The initial winner was Bernard King of the Golden State Warriors, followed by Gus Williams of the Seattle SuperSonics, Paul Westphal of the New York Knicks, Adrian Dantley of the Utah Jazz, and Micheal Ray Richardson of the New Jersey Nets. After five years, however, it was clear that the original intent of the award was being blurred. Instead of players who came back from injuries or slumps, it was being won by players coming back from personal problems including drug and/or alcohol abuse (King, Richardson) or contract disputes (Williams sat out the 1980-81 seasons because he could not reach a contract agreement with Seattle).

So in 1985 the league shelved its Comeback Player of the Year Award and replaced it with the NBA Most Improved Player award. To win, a player need not be coming back from anything, but rather has only to show significant improvement over the previous season or more.

The first winner, in 1985-86, was Alvin Robertson of the San Antonio Spurs, who nearly doubled his averages from 9.2 points, 3.4 rebounds, and 3.5 assists per game as a rookie to 17.0 points, 6.3 rebounds, and 5.5 assists per game in his second pro season. He also led the league in steals at 3.67 per game, the highest average in league history and well over double his rookie mark of 1.61 steals per game.

The following season, Dale Ellis captured the award after being traded from the Dallas Mavericks to the Seattle SuperSonics. As a reserve in Dallas in 1985-86, Ellis averaged 7.1 points per game and shot .411 from the field. As a starter

in Seattle in 1986-87, he averaged 24.9 points per game and shot .516 from the field. Similarly, Kevin Duckworth won the award in 1987-88 after going from a reserve in San Antonio to a starter in Portland and improving from 5.4 points and 3.4 rebounds per game to 15.8 points and 7.4 rebounds per game.

Following is the complete list of winners of the NBA Most Improved Player Award, as selected by a panel of writers and broadcasters:

Year	Winner	Team
1985-86	Alvin Robertson	San Antonio
1986-87	Dale Ellis	Seattle
1987-88	Kevin Duckworth	Portland
1988-89	Kevin Johnson	Phoenix
1989-90	Rony Seikaly	Miami
1990-91	Scott Skiles	Orlando
1991-92	Pervis Ellison	Washington
1992-93	Chris Jackson	Denver
1993-94	Don MacLean	Washington
1994-95	Dana Barros	Philadelphia
1995-96	Gheorghe Muresan	Washington
1996-97	Isaac Austin	Miami
1997-98	Alan Henderson	Atlanta
1998-99	Darrell Armstrong	Orlando
1999-00	Jalen Rose	Indiana
2000-01	Tracy McGrady	Orlando
2001-02	Jermaine O'Neal	Indiana
2002-03	Gilbert Arenas	Golden State

Following is the complete list of winners of the NBA Comeback Player of the Year Award:

Year	Winner	Team
1980-81	Bernard King	Golden State
1981-82	Gus Williams	Seattle
1982-83	Paul Westphal	New York
1983-84	Adrian Dantley	Utah
1984-85	Micheal Ray Richardson	New Jersey

NBA Defensive Player of the Year

In 1982 the NBA launched two more awards, including the NBA Defensive Player of the Year, designed to recognize players for their contributions at the defensive end of the floor.

Defense can be difficult to quantify. While there are two statistical categories that specifically measure defensive achievements, namely blocked shots and steals, these only tell part of the story. What about the tenacious defender who plays his man tightly and doesn't let him get off his customary number of shots? What about the heady defender who keeps his man from getting to his favorite spots on the floor, or keeps him from getting the ball when he does get there? What about the quick defender who flashes down to double-team and then recovers in time to keep his man from scoring, or the rugged defender who is not afraid to help his team by stepping into the lane and taking a charge?

All of these go into playing superior defense, and to honor those players—not just the shotblocking and steals leaders—the NBA created the Defensive Player of the Year Award.

A perfect example of the kind of player the award's creators had in mind was Sidney Moncrief, the 6-foot-4 guard of the Milwaukee Bucks who won the first Defensive Player of the Year Award and was a repeat winner in 1983-84. Moncrief's name was nowhere to be found among the league leaders in steals or blocks. Yet he was adept at shutting down his own man and also helping out on double-teams.

Other times the award has gone to dominating shotblockers like Mark Eaton, David Robinson, Hakeem Olajuwon, Dikembe Mutombo, Alonzo Mourning and Ben Wallace, or

steals artists like Alvin Robertson and Gary Payton. Among the outstanding all-around defenders who have won it are Michael Cooper, Michael Jordan and Dennis Rodman.

Following is the complete list of winners of the NBA Defensive Player of the Year Award, as selected by a panel of writers and broadcasters:

Year	Winner	Team
1982-83	Sidney Moncrief	Milwaukee
1983-84	Sidney Moncrief	Milwaukee
1984-85	Mark Eaton	Utah
1985-86	Alvin Robertson	San Antonio
1986-87	Michael Cooper	LA Lakers
1987-88	Michael Jordan	Chicago
1988-89	Mark Eaton	Utah
1989-90	Dennis Rodman	Detroit
1990-91	Dennis Rodman	Detroit
1991-92	David Robinson	San Antonio
1992-93	Hakeem Olajuwon	Houston
1993-94	Hakeem Olajuwon	Houston
1994-95	Dikembe Mutombo	Denver
1995-96	Gary Payton	Seattle
1996-97	Dikembe Mutombo	Denver
1997-98	Dikembe Mutombo	Atlanta
1998-99	Alonzo Mourning	Miami
1999-00	Alonzo Mourning	Miami
2000-01	Dikembe Mutombo	Philadelphia-Atlanta
2001-02	Ben Wallace	Detroit
2002-03	Ben Wallace	Detroit

NBA Sixth Man Award

The other award instituted for the 1982-83 season was the NBA Sixth Man Award, designed to recognize contributions by non-starters. In order to qualify for the award, a player must have started fewer than half his team's games that season.

Reserves have long been integral to NBA success. Red Auerbach was among the first to keep at least one of his better, high-energy players on the bench at the start of the game and then insert him after a quarter or so, when the opposing team's starters were wearing down. It's not who starts the game that matters as much as who finishes it, Auerbach reasoned, and he always tried to have his best players on the floor for the finish. Frank Ramsey, John Havlicek, and Kevin McHale are among those who were particularly adept at filling the sixth man role for the Celtics.

Ramsey and Havlicek had retired by the time the award was created, but McHale became a two-time winner of the NBA Sixth Man Award before he was moved into the Boston starting lineup alongside Larry Bird and Robert Parish on one of the best front lines ever. McHale won Sixth Man honors in 1983-84 and 1984-85 after Bobby Jones of the Philadelphia 76ers, a defensive stopper and fine fast-break finisher, won the inaugural Sixth Man Award in 1982-83.

Joining McHale as two-time winners of the Sixth Man Award are Ricky Pierce, who won it in 1986-87 and 1989-90 with the Milwaukee Bucks, and Detlef Schrempf, who won it in 1990-91 and 1991-92 with the Indiana Pacers.

Following is the complete list of winners of the NBA Sixth Man Award, as selected by a panel of writers and broadcasters:

Year	Winner	Team
1982-83	Bobby Jones	Philadelphia
1983-84	Kevin McHale	Boston
1984-85	Kevin McHale	Boston
1985-86	Bill Walton	Boston
1986-87	Ricky Pierce	Milwaukee
1987-88	Roy Tarpley	Dallas
1988-89	Eddie Johnson	Phoenix
1989-90	Ricky Pierce	Milwaukee
1990-91	Detlef Schrempf	Indiana
1991-92	Detlef Schrempf	Indiana
1992-93	Cliff Robinson	Portland
1993-94	Dell Curry	Charlotte
1994-95	Anthony Mason	New York
1995-96	Tony Kukoc	Chicago
1996-97	John Starks	New York
1997-98	Danny Manning	Phoenix
1998-99	Darrell Armstrong	Orlando
1999-00	Rodney Rogers	Phoenix
2000-01	Aaron McKie	Philadelphia
2001-02	Corliss Williamson	Detroit
2002-03	Bobby Jackson	Sacramento

NBA Executive of the Year

The Sporting News, a St. Louis-based publishing company, has been selecting an NBA Executive of the Year since 1972-73 according to its own poll of executives around the league.

The award has been won each year by the chief basketball decision-maker in a team's front office, whether that person carried the title of general manager, vice president of basketball operations, or whatever. In two instances that person also was the team's principal owner—Angelo Drossos with the San Antonio Spurs in 1977-78 and Jerry Colangelo with the Phoenix Suns in 1992-93.

Colangelo has won the award more than anyone else, four times, all with the Phoenix Suns—in 1975-76, 1980-81, and 1988-89 as well as 1992-93. Two-time winners include Bob Ferry with the Washington Bullets in 1978-79 and 1981-82, Stan Kasten with the Atlanta Hawks in 1985-86 and 1986-87, Jerry Krause with the Chicago Bulls in 1987-88 and 1995-96, Bob Bass with the San Antonio Spurs in 1989-90 and the Charlotte Hornets in 1996-97, and Wayne Embry with the Cleveland Cavaliers in 1991-92 and 1997-98.

Following is the complete list of winners of the NBA Executive of the Year Award, as selected in a poll of NBA executives by *The Sporting News*:

Year	Executive	Team
1972-73	Joe Axelson	Kansas City-Omaha
1973-74	Eddie Donovan	Buffalo
1974-75	Dick Vertlieb	Golden State
1975-76	Jerry Colangelo	Phoenix
1976-77	Ray Patterson	Houston
1977-78	Angelo Drossos	San Antonio
1978-79	Bob Ferry	Washington
1979-80	Red Auerbach	Boston
1980-81	Jerry Colangelo	Phoenix
1981-82	Bob Ferry	Washington
1982-83	Zollie Volchok	Seattle
1983-84	Frank Layden	Utah
1984-85	Vince Boryla	Denver
1985-86	Stan Kasten	Atlanta
1986-87	Stan Kasten	Atlanta
1987-88	Jerry Krause	Chicago
1988-89	Jerry Colangelo	Phoenix
1989-90	Bob Bass	San Antonio
1990-91	Bucky Buckwalter	Portland
1991-92	Wayne Embry	Cleveland
1992-93	Jerry Colangelo	Phoenix
1993-94	Bob Whitsitt	Seattle
1994-95	Jerry West	LA Lakers
1995-96	Jerry Krause	Chicago
1996-97	Bob Bass	Charlotte
1997-98	Wayne Embry	Cleveland
1998-99	Geoff Petrie	Sacramento
1999-00	John Gabriel	Orlando
2000-01	Geoff Petrie	Sacramento
2001-02	Rod Thorn	New Jersey
2002-03	Joe Dumars	Detroit

IBM Award

Who is the best all-around player in the NBA? That was the

idea behind the IBM Award, which began its existence in 1983-84 as the Schick Pivotal Player Award, was shortened to the Schick Award in 1988, became the IBM Award in 1993 following a sponsorship change and then disappeared from the NBA's radar screen when IBM's sponsorship agreement with the league ended after the 2001-02 season.

The IBM Award utilized a computer evaluation of key offensive and defensive statistics to determine a player's overall contributions to a team, factoring in the team's victories. Here is the formula that was used:

$$\frac{\text{Player PTS - FGA + REB + AST + STL + BL - PF - TO + (team wins x 10)}}{\text{Team PTS - FGA + REB + AST + STL + BL - PF - TO}}$$

That is, a player's points, minus field goal attempts, plus rebounds, plus assists, plus steals, plus blocks, minus personal fouls, minus turnovers, plus his team's wins, times 10, is multiplied by 250, and then divided by his team's points minus field goal attempts, plus rebounds, plus assists, plus steals, plus blocks, minus personal fouls, minus turnovers to produce a final figure. The result was generally around 100 for the winner.

Note that statistics other than team wins are not weighted, so a rebound counts as much as a steal and a personal foul takes away as much as an assist adds on. Also, the number of shots a player attempts is subtracted from the number of points he scores, in an attempt to factor in shooting efficiency. Finally, the number of team victories, multiplied by 10, is added into each individual player's numerator in the equation to offset the advantage a good player on a bad team would otherwise have over a good player on a good team, where the denominator would be higher.

For an example of how the formula works, let's look at the 1997-98 winner, Karl Malone of the Utah Jazz. Here is his equation:

$$\frac{2190 - 1472 + 834 + 316 + 96 + 70 - 237 - 247 + (62 \times 10)}{8279 - 6113 + 3367 + 2070 + 648 + 412 - 1961 - 1260} \times 250$$

That comes out to 542,500 divided by 5,442 for a final point total of 99.69. Tim Duncan of the San Antonio Spurs was second that year with a score of 98.70, and Spurs teammate David Robinson was third with 96.66.

This formula tended to favor big men, since among the league leaders, total rebounds tend to be slightly higher than assists and blocks slightly higher than steals. Centers won the award in nine of its last 13 years, with Tim Duncan, Karl Malone and Dennis Rodman also winning during that stretch. The lone smaller player to win since 1989-90 was Grant Hill of the Detroit Pistons in 1996-97.

This formula was used since IBM took over sponsorship of the award; in its early years, a different formula (that was never announced) was used. That formula did not skew the award toward big men; in fact, guards and forwards won it in each of its first six years.

Following is the complete list of winners of the IBM Award (including when it was known as the Schick Pivotal Player Award and the Schick Award), as determined by a computer formula:

Year	Player	Team
1983-84	Magic Johnson	LA Lakers
1984-85	Michael Jordan	Chicago
1985-86	Charles Barkley	Philadelphia
1986-87	Charles Barkley	Philadelphia
1987-88	Charles Barkley	Philadelphia
1988-89	Michael Jordan	Chicago
1989-90	David Robinson	San Antonio
1990-91	David Robinson	San Antonio
1991-92	Dennis Rodman	Detroit
1992-93	Hakeem Olajuwon	Houston
1993-94	David Robinson	San Antonio
1994-95	David Robinson	San Antonio
1995-96	David Robinson	San Antonio
1996-97	Grant Hill	Detroit
1997-98	Karl Malone	Utah
1998-99	Dikembe Mutumbo	Atlanta
1999-2000	Shaquille O'Neal	LA Lakers
2000-01	Shaquille O'Neal	LA Lakers
2001-02	Tim Duncan	San Antonio

J. Walter Kennedy Citizenship Award

The J. Walter Kennedy Citizenship Award, named in honor of the NBA's second commissioner who served from 1963 through 1975, has been awarded annually since 1974-75 by the Professional Basketball Writers Association to an NBA player, coach or trainer in recognition of outstanding community service and charitable work. Members of the PBWA vote to select the winner.

Most of the winners have been players, although coach Frank Layden of the Utah Jazz won in 1983-84 and trainer Joe O'Toole of the Atlanta Hawks won in 1994-95. Magic Johnson was named the winner in 1991-92, the year after his initial retirement, for his work in spreading awareness of HIV and AIDS.

Following is the complete list of winners of the J. Walter Kennedy Citizenship Award, presented by the Pro Basketball Writers Association after a vote of its membership:

Year	Winner	Team
1974-75	Wes Unseld	Washington
1975-76	Slick Watts	Seattle
1976-77	Dave Bing	Washington
1977-78	Bob Lanier	Detroit
1978-79	Calvin Murphy	Houston
1979-80	Austin Carr	Cleveland
1980-81	Mike Glenn	New York
1981-82	Kent Benson	Detroit
1982-83	Julius Erving	Philadelphia
1983-84	Frank Layden	Utah
1984-85	Dan Issel	Denver
1985-86	Michael Cooper	LA Lakers
	Rory Sparrow	New York
1986-87	Isiah Thomas	Detroit
1987-88	Alex English	Denver
1988-89	Thurl Bailey	Utah
1989-90	Glenn Rivers	Atlanta
1990-91	Kevin Johnson	Phoenix
1991-92	Magic Johnson	LA Lakers
1992-93	Terry Porter	Portland
1993-94	Joe Dumars	Detroit
1994-95	Joe O'Toole	Atlanta
1995-96	Chris Dudley	Portland
1996-97	P.J. Brown	Miami
1997-98	Steve Smith	Atlanta
1998-99	Brian Grant	Portland
1999-00	Vlade Divac	Sacramento
2000-01	Dikembe Mutumbo	Philadelphia
2001-02	Alonzo Mourning	Miami
2002-03	David Robinson	San Antonio

NBA Sportsmanship Award

The NBA Sportsmanship Award was created by the league in 1996 to honor a player who best represents the ideals of sportsmanship on the court.

It is part of a larger program called the NBA Sportsmanship Initiative, which focuses on fostering the ideals of sportsmanship—ethical behavior, fair play and integrity—in amateur and professional basketball players. The program also includes the NBA Student-Athlete Sportsmanship Program and a public service awareness campaign.

Joe Dumars of the Detroit Pistons was the inaugural winner in 1995-96. Since then, four divisional winners have been selected as well as one overall winner.

Following is the complete list of winners of the NBA Sportsmanship Award, as selected by a panel of writers and broadcasters:

Year	Winner	Team
1995-96	Joe Dumars	Detroit
1996-97	Terrell Brandon	Cleveland
1997-98	Avery Johnson	San Antonio
1998-99	Hersey Hawkins	Seattle
1999-00	Eric Snow	Philadelphia
2000-01	David Robinson	San Antonio
2001-02	Steve Smith	San Antonio
2002-03	Ray Allen	Seattle

All-NBA Teams

The only award that goes back to the league's very first season, the All-NBA Teams have been selected by writers and broadcasters since 1946-47. First and Second Teams were chosen until 1988-89, when a Third Team was added to reflect the larger size of the league. Voters are asked to make their selections based on position; points were awarded on a 2-1 basis when two teams were chosen and on a 5-3-1 basis when three teams were selected.

Being chosen to the All-NBA First Team is among the highest honors in the sport, perhaps second only to being chosen Most Valuable Player. Interestingly, there have been four occasions when the league's MVP was not selected to the All-NBA First Team, all involving centers. This occurred at a time when the MVP was chosen by a vote among the league players and the All-NBA Teams were chosen by writers and broadcasters. The difference may also reflect different ways the awards are interpreted, with the MVP going to a player who contributes the most to his team's success and the All-NBA Team going to the outstanding players.

Bill Russell of the Boston Celtics was voted MVP in 1957-58 but only made the All-NBA Second Team, with Bob Pettit of the St. Louis Hawks getting the nod at center on the All-NBA First Team. Russell also won MVP honors in 1960-61 and 1961-62 but was beaten out for the All-NBA First Team center spot by Wilt Chamberlain of the Philadelphia Warriors. Dave Cowens of the Boston Celtics was voted MVP in 1972-73, but Kareem Abdul-Jabbar of the Milwaukee Bucks was voted to the All-NBA First Team at center.

Despite winning MVP honors five times and leading the Celtics to 11 championships in his 13 seasons, Russell was named to the All-NBA First Team only three times. He was selected to the Second Team eight times, more than any other player in history, finishing behind Chamberlain seven times

and Pettit once. The debate about who was "better," Chamberlain or Russell, Mr. Offense or Mr. Defense, the unstoppable force or the immovable object, dominated basketball throughout the 1960s, with advocates of each player believing to this day that they were right. From the balloting results, it's apparent that media voters placed a greater emphasis on offensive statistics when choosing the All-NBA Teams, and players valued defense and contributions to team success more when selecting the MVP. Chamberlain holds a 7-3 edge over Russell in All-NBA First Team selections, but Russell holds a 5-4 edge over Chamberlain in MVPs.

Karl Malone of the Utah Jazz has been named to the All-NBA First Team more than any other player, 11 times. Six players have been named to the First Team 10 times each: Kareem Abdul-Jabbar, Elgin Baylor, Bob Cousy, Michael Jordan, Bob Pettit, and Jerry West. Three players have been named to the First Team nine times apiece: Larry Bird, Magic Johnson and Oscar Robertson.

Abdul-Jabbar also was named to the Second Team five times, for a total of 15 selections to one of the All-NBA Teams, the most of any player in history. Malone, who has made the Second Team twice and the Third Team once, is next with 14 while Cousy (10 First, 2 Second), West (10 First, 2 Second), Dolph Schayes (6 First, 6 Second) and Hakeem Olajuwon (6 First, 3 Second, 3 Third) have been named 12 times apiece.

Following is the complete list of All-NBA Teams, as selected by a panel of writers and broadcasters:

1946-47

FIRST TEAM		SECOND TEAM	
Joe Fulks	Philadelphia	Ernie Calverley	Providence
Bob Feerick	Washington	Frank Baumholtz	Cleveland
Stan Miasek	Detroit	John Logan	St. Louis
Bones McKinney	Washington	Chuck Halbert	Chicago
Max Zaslofsky	Chicago	Fred Scolari	Washington

1947-48

FIRST TEAM		SECOND TEAM	
Joe Fulks	Philadelphia	John Logan	St. Louis
Max Zaslofsky	Chicago	Carl Braun	New York
Ed Sadowski	Boston	Stan Miasek	Chicago
Howie Dallmar	Philadelphia	Fred Scolari	Washington
Bob Feerick	Washington	Buddy Jeannette	Baltimore

1948-49

FIRST TEAM		SECOND TEAM	
George Mikan	Minneapolis	Arnie Risen	Rochester
Joe Fulks	Philadelphia	Bob Feerick	Washington
Bob Davies	Rochester	Bones McKinney	Washington
Max Zaslofsky	Chicago	Ken Sailors	Providence
Jim Pollard	Minneapolis	John Logan	St. Louis

1949-50

FIRST TEAM		SECOND TEAM	
George Mikan	Minneapolis	Frank Brian	Anderson
Jim Pollard	Minneapolis	Fred Schaus	Fort Wayne
Alex Groza	Indianapolis	Dolph Schayes	Syracuse
Bob Davies	Rochester	Al Cervi	Syracuse
Max Zaslofsky	Chicago	Ralph Beard	Indianapolis

1950-51

FIRST TEAM		SECOND TEAM	
George Mikan	Minneapolis	Dolph Schayes	Syracuse
Alex Groza	Indianapolis	Frank Brian	Tri-Cities
Ed Macauley	Boston	Vern Mikkelsen	Minneapolis
Bob Davies	Rochester	Joe Fulks	Philadelphia
Ralph Beard	Indianapolis	Dick McGuire	New York

1951-52

FIRST TEAM		SECOND TEAM	
George Mikan	Minneapolis	Larry Foust	Fort Wayne
Ed Macauley	Boston	Vern Mikkelsen	Minneapolis
Paul Arizin	Philadelphia	Jim Pollard	Minneapolis
Bob Cousy	Boston	Bob Wanzer	Rochester
Bob Davies	Rochester	Andy Phillip	Philadelphia
Dolph Schayes	Syracuse		

1952-53

FIRST TEAM		SECOND TEAM	
George Mikan	Minneapolis	Bill Sharman	Boston
Bob Cousy	Boston	Vern Mikkelsen	Minneapolis
Neil Johnston	Philadelphia	Bob Wanzer	Rochester
Ed Macauley	Boston	Bob Davies	Rochester
Dolph Schayes	Syracuse	Andy Phillip	Philadelphia

1953-54

FIRST TEAM		SECOND TEAM	
Bob Cousy	Boston	Ed Macauley	Boston
Neil Johnston	Philadelphia	Jim Pollard	Minneapolis
George Mikan	Minneapolis	Carl Braun	New York
Dolph Schayes	Syracuse	Bob Wanzer	Rochester
Harry Gallatin	New York	Paul Seymour	Syracuse

1954-55

FIRST TEAM		SECOND TEAM	
Neil Johnston	Philadelphia	Vern Mikkelsen	Minneapolis
Bob Cousy	Boston	Harry Gallatin	New York
Dolph Schayes	Syracuse	Paul Seymour	Syracuse
Bob Pettit	Milwaukee	Slater Martin	Minneapolis
Larry Foust	Fort Wayne	Bill Sharman	Boston

1955-56

FIRST TEAM		SECOND TEAM	
Bob Pettit	St. Louis	Dolph Schayes	Syracuse
Paul Arizin	Philadelphia	Maurice Stokes	Rochester
Neil Johnston	Philadelphia	Clyde Lovellette	Minneapolis
Bob Cousy	Boston	Slater Martin	Minneapolis
Bill Sharman	Boston	Jack George	Philadelphia

1956-57

FIRST TEAM		SECOND TEAM	
Paul Arizin	Philadelphia	George Yardley	Fort Wayne
Dolph Schayes	Syracuse	Maurice Stokes	Rochester
Bob Pettit	St. Louis	Neil Johnston	Philadelphia
Bob Cousy	Boston	Dick Garmaker	Minneapolis
Bill Sharman	Boston	Slater Martin	St. Louis

1957-58

FIRST TEAM		SECOND TEAM	
Dolph Schayes	Syracuse	Cliff Hagan	St. Louis
George Yardley	Detroit	Maurice Stokes	Cincinnati
Bob Pettit	St. Louis	Bill Russell	Boston
Bob Cousy	Boston	Tom Gola	Philadelphia
Bill Sharman	Boston	Slater Martin	St. Louis

1958-59

FIRST TEAM		SECOND TEAM	
Bob Pettit	St. Louis	Paul Arizin	Philadelphia
Elgin Baylor	Minneapolis	Cliff Hagan	St. Louis
Bill Russell	Boston	Dolph Schayes	Syracuse
Bob Cousy	Boston	Slater Martin	St. Louis
Bill Sharman	Boston	Richie Guerin	New York

1959-60

FIRST TEAM		SECOND TEAM	
Bob Pettit	St. Louis	Jack Twyman	Cincinnati
Elgin Baylor	Minneapolis	Dolph Schayes	Syracuse
Wilt Chamberlain	Philadelphia	Bill Russell	Boston
Bob Cousy	Boston	Richie Guerin	New York
Gene Shue	Detroit	Bill Sharman	Boston

1960-61

FIRST TEAM		SECOND TEAM	
Elgin Baylor	LA Lakers	Dolph Schayes	Syracuse
Bob Pettit	St. Louis	Tom Heinsohn	Boston
Wilt Chamberlain	Philadelphia	Bill Russell	Boston
Bob Cousy	Boston	Larry Costello	Syracuse
Oscar Robertson	Cincinnati	Gene Shue	Detroit

1961-62

FIRST TEAM		SECOND TEAM	
Bob Pettit	St. Louis	Tom Heinsohn	Boston
Elgin Baylor	LA Lakers	Jack Twyman	Cincinnati
Wilt Chamberlain	Philadelphia	Bill Russell	Boston
Jerry West	LA Lakers	Richie Guerin	New York
Oscar Robertson	Cincinnati	Bob Cousy	Boston

1962-63

FIRST TEAM		SECOND TEAM	
Elgin Baylor	LA Lakers	Tom Heinsohn	Boston
Bob Pettit	St. Louis	Bailey Howell	Detroit
Bill Russell	Boston	Wilt Chamberlain	San Francisco
Oscar Robertson	Cincinnati	Bob Cousy	Boston
Jerry West	LA Lakers	Hal Greer	Syracuse

1963-64

FIRST TEAM		SECOND TEAM	
Bob Pettit	St. Louis	Tom Heinsohn	Boston
Elgin Baylor	LA Lakers	Jerry Lucas	Cincinnati
Wilt Chamberlain	San Francisco	Bill Russell	Boston
Oscar Robertson	Cincinnati	John Havlicek	Boston
Jerry West	LA Lakers	Hal Greer	Philadelphia

1964-65

FIRST TEAM		SECOND TEAM	
Elgin Baylor	LA Lakers	Bob Pettit	St.Louis
Jerry Lucas	Cincinnati	Gus Johnson	Baltimore
Bill Russell	Boston	Wilt Chamberlain	SF-Philadelphia
Oscar Robertson	Cincinnati	Sam Jones	Boston
Jerry West	LA Lakers	Hal Greer	Philadelphia

1965-66

FIRST TEAM		SECOND TEAM	
Rick Barry	San Francisco	John Havlicek	Boston
Jerry Lucas	Cincinnati	Gus Johnson	Baltimore
Wilt Chamberlain	Philadelphia	Bill Russell	Boston
Oscar Robertson	Cincinnati	Sam Jones	Boston
Jerry West	LA Lakers	Hal Greer	Philadelphia

1966-67

FIRST TEAM		SECOND TEAM	
Rick Barry	San Francisco	Willis Reed	New York
Elgin Baylor	LA Lakers	Jerry Lucas	Cincinnati
Wilt Chamberlain	Philadelphia	Bill Russell	Boston
Jerry West	LA Lakers	Hal Greer	Philadelphia
Oscar Robertson	Cincinnati	Sam Jones	Boston

1967-68

FIRST TEAM		SECOND TEAM	
Elgin Baylor	LA Lakers	Willis Reed	New York
Jerry Lucas	Cincinnati	John Havlicek	Boston
Wilt Chamberlain	Philadelphia	Bill Russell	Boston
Dave Bing	Detroit	Hal Greer	Philadelphia
Oscar Robertson	Cincinnati	Jerry West	LA Lakers

1968-69

FIRST TEAM		SECOND TEAM	
Billy Cunningham	Philadelphia	John Havlicek	Boston
Elgin Baylor	LA Lakers	Dave DeBusschere	Detroit-NY
Wes Unseld	Baltimore	Willis Reed	New York
Earl Monroe	Baltimore	Hal Greer	Philadelphia
Oscar Robertson	Cincinnati	Jerry West	LA Lakers

1969-70

FIRST TEAM		SECOND TEAM	
Billy Cunningham	Philadelphia	John Havlicek	Boston
Connie Hawkins	Phoenix	Gus Johnson	Baltimore
Willis Reed	New York	Kareem Abdul-Jabbar	Milwaukee
Jerry West	LA Lakers	Lou Hudson	Atlanta
Walt Frazier	New York	Oscar Robertson	Cincinnati

1970-71

FIRST TEAM		SECOND TEAM	
John Havlicek	Boston	Gus Johnson	Baltimore
Billy Cunningham	Philadelphia	Bob Love	Chicago
Kareem Abdul-Jabbar	Milwaukee	Willis Reed	New York
Jerry West	LA Lakers	Walt Frazier	New York
Dave Bing	Detroit	Oscar Robertson	Milwaukee

1971-72

FIRST TEAM		SECOND TEAM	
John Havlicek	Boston	Bob Love	Chicago
Spencer Haywood	Seattle	Billy Cunningham	Philadelphia
Kareem Abdul-Jabbar	Milwaukee	Wilt Chamberlain	LA Lakers
Jerry West	LA Lakers	Nate Archibald	Cincinnati
Walt Frazier	New York	Archie Clark	Phil.-Baltimore

1972-73

FIRST TEAM		SECOND TEAM	
John Havlicek	Boston	Elvin Hayes	Baltimore
Spencer Haywood	Seattle	Rick Barry	Golden State
Kareem Abdul-Jabbar	Milwaukee	Dave Cowens	Boston
Nate Archibald	Kansas City-Omaha	Walt Frazier	New York
Jerry West	LA Lakers	Pete Maravich	Atlanta

1973-74
FIRST TEAM

John Havlicek	Boston
Rick Barry	Golden State
Kareem Abdul-Jabbar	Milwaukee
Walt Frazier	New York
Gail Goodrich	LA Lakers

SECOND TEAM

Elvin Hayes	Capital
Spencer Haywood	Seattle
Bob McAdoo	Buffalo
Dave Bing	Detroit
Norm Van Lier	Chicago

1974-75
FIRST TEAM

Rick Barry	Golden State
Elvin Hayes	Washington
Bob McAdoo	Buffalo
Nate Archibald	Kansas City-Omaha
Walt Frazier	New York

SECOND TEAM

John Havlicek	Boston
Spencer Haywood	Seattle
Dave Cowens	Boston
Phil Chenier	Washington
Jo Jo White	Boston

1975-76
FIRST TEAM

Rick Barry	Golden State
George McGinnis	Philadelphia
Kareem Abdul-Jabbar	LA Lakers
Nate Archibald	Kansas City
Pete Maravich	New Orleans

SECOND TEAM

Elvin Hayes	Washington
John Havlicek	Boston
Dave Cowens	Boston
Randy Smith	Buffalo
Phil Smith	Golden State

1976-77
FIRST TEAM

Elvin Hayes	Washington
David Thompson	Denver
Kareem Abdul-Jabbar	LA Lakers
Pete Maravich	New Orleans
Paul Westphal	Phoenix

SECOND TEAM

Julius Erving	Philadelphia
George McGinnis	Philadelphia
Bill Walton	Portland
George Gervin	San Antonio
Jo Jo White	Boston

1977-78
FIRST TEAM

Leonard Robinson	New Orleans
Julius Erving	Philadelphia
Bill Walton	Portland
George Gervin	San Antonio
David Thompson	Denver

SECOND TEAM

Walter Davis	Phoenix
Maurice Lucas	Portland
Kareem Abdul-Jabbar	LA Lakers
Paul Westphal	Phoenix
Pete Maravich	New Orleans

1978-79
FIRST TEAM

Marques Johnson	Milwaukee
Elvin Hayes	Washington
Moses Malone	Houston
George Gervin	San Antonio
Paul Westphal	Phoenix

SECOND TEAM

Walter Davis	Phoenix
Bobby Dandridge	Washington
Kareem Abdul-Jabbar	LA Lakers
Lloyd Free	San Diego
Phil Ford	Kansas City

1979-80
FIRST TEAM

Julius Erving	Philadelphia
Larry Bird	Boston
Kareem Abdul-Jabbar	LA Lakers
George Gervin	San Antonio
Paul Westphal	Phoenix

SECOND TEAM

Dan Roundfield	Atlanta
Marques Johnson	Milwaukee
Moses Malone	Houston
Dennis Johnson	Seattle
Gus Williams	Seattle

1980-81
FIRST TEAM

Julius Erving	Philadelphia
Larry Bird	Boston
Kareem Abdul-Jabbar	LA Lakers
George Gervin	San Antonio
Dennis Johnson	Phoenix

SECOND TEAM

Marques Johnson	Milwaukee
Adrian Dantley	Utah
Moses Malone	Houston
Otis Birdsong	Kansas City
Nate Archibald	Boston

1981-82
FIRST TEAM

Larry Bird	Boston
Julius Erving	Philadelphia
Moses Malone	Houston
George Gervin	San Antonio
Gus Williams	Seattle

SECOND TEAM

Alex English	Denver
Bernard King	Golden State
Robert Parish	Boston
Magic Johnson	LA Lakers
Sidney Moncrief	Milwaukee

1982-83
FIRST TEAM

Larry Bird	Boston
Julius Erving	Philadelphia
Moses Malone	Philadelphia
Magic Johnson	LA Lakers
Sidney Moncrief	Milwaukee

SECOND TEAM

Alex English	Denver
Buck Williams	New Jersey
Kareem Abdul-Jabbar	LA Lakers
George Gervin	San Antonio
Isiah Thomas	Detroit

1983-84
FIRST TEAM

Larry Bird	Boston
Bernard King	New York
Kareem Abdul-Jabbar	LA Lakers
Magic Johnson	LA Lakers
Isiah Thomas	Detroit

SECOND TEAM

Julius Erving	Philadelphia
Adrian Dantley	Utah
Moses Malone	Philadelphia
Sidney Moncrief	Milwaukee
Jim Paxson	Portland

1984-85
FIRST TEAM

Larry Bird	Boston
Bernard King	New York
Moses Malone	Philadelphia
Magic Johnson	LA Lakers
Isiah Thomas	Detroit

SECOND TEAM

Terry Cummings	Milwaukee
Ralph Sampson	Houston
Kareem Abdul-Jabbar	LA Lakers
Michael Jordan	Chicago
Sidney Moncrief	Milwaukee

1985-86
FIRST TEAM

Larry Bird	Boston
Dominique Wilkins	Atlanta
Kareem Abdul-Jabbar	LA Lakers
Magic Johnson	LA Lakers
Isiah Thomas	Detroit

SECOND TEAM

Charles Barkley	Philadelphia
Alex English	Denver
Hakeem Olajuwon	Houston
Sidney Moncrief	Milwaukee
Alvin Robertson	San Antonio

1986-87
FIRST TEAM

Larry Bird	Boston
Kevin McHale	Boston
Hakeem Olajuwon	Houston
Magic Johnson	LA Lakers
Michael Jordan	Chicago

SECOND TEAM

Dominique Wilkins	Atlanta
Charles Barkley	Philadelphia
Moses Malone	Washington
Isiah Thomas	Detroit
Lafayette Lever	Denver

1987-88
FIRST TEAM

Larry Bird	Boston
Charles Barkley	Philadelphia
Hakeem Olajuwon	Houston
Michael Jordan	Chicago
Magic Johnson	LA Lakers

SECOND TEAM

Karl Malone	Utah
Dominique Wilkins	Atlanta
Patrick Ewing	New York
Clyde Drexler	Portland
John Stockton	Utah

1988-89
FIRST TEAM

Karl Malone	Utah
Charles Barkley	Philadelphia
Hakeem Olajuwon	Houston
Magic Johnson	LA Lakers
Michael Jordan	Chicago

THIRD TEAM

Dominique Wilkins	Atlanta
Terry Cummings	Milwaukee
Robert Parish	Boston
Dale Ellis	Seattle
Mark Price	Cleveland

SECOND TEAM

Tom Chambers	Phoenix
Chris Mullin	Golden State
Patrick Ewing	New York
John Stockton	Utah
Kevin Johnson	Phoenix

1989-90
FIRST TEAM

Karl Malone	Utah
Charles Barkley	Philadelphia
Patrick Ewing	New York
Magic Johnson	LA Lakers
Michael Jordan	Chicago

THIRD TEAM

James Worthy	LA Lakers
Chris Mullin	Golden State
David Robinson	San Antonio
Clyde Drexler	Portland
Joe Dumars	Detroit

SECOND TEAM

Larry Bird	Boston
Tom Chambers	Phoenix
Hakeem Olajuwon	Houston
John Stockton	Utah
Kevin Johnson	Phoenix

1990-91
FIRST TEAM

Karl Malone	Utah
Charles Barkley	Philadelphia
David Robinson	San Antonio
Michael Jordan	Chicago
Magic Johnson	LA Lakers

THIRD TEAM

James Worthy	LA Lakers
Bernard King	Washington
Hakeem Olajuwon	Houston
John Stockton	Utah
Joe Dumars	Detroit

SECOND TEAM

Dominique Wilkins	Atlanta
Chris Mullin	Golden State
Patrick Ewing	New York
Kevin Johnson	Phoenix
Clyde Drexler	Portland

1991-92
FIRST TEAM

Karl Malone	Utah
Chris Mullin	Golden State
David Robinson	San Antonio
Michael Jordan	Chicago
Clyde Drexler	Portland

THIRD TEAM

Dennis Rodman	Detroit
Kevin Willis	Atlanta
Brad Daugherty	Cleveland
Mark Price	Cleveland
Kevin Johnson	Phoenix

SECOND TEAM

Scottie Pippen	Chicago
Charles Barkley	Philadelphia
Patrick Ewing	New York
Tim Hardaway	Golden State
John Stockton	Utah

1992-93

FIRST TEAM

		SECOND TEAM	
Charles Barkley	Phoenix	Dominique Wilkins	Atlanta
Karl Malone	Utah	Larry Johnson	Charlotte
Hakeem Olajuwon	Houston	Patrick Ewing	New York
Michael Jordan	Chicago	John Stockton	Utah
Mark Price	Cleveland	Joe Dumars	Detroit

THIRD TEAM

Scottie Pippen	Chicago
Derrick Coleman	New Jersey
David Robinson	San Antonio
Tim Hardaway	Golden State
Drazen Petrovic	New Jersey

1993-94

FIRST TEAM

		SECOND TEAM	
Scottie Pippen	Chicago	Shawn Kemp	Seattle
Karl Malone	Utah	Charles Barkley	Phoenix
Hakeem Olajuwon	Houston	David Robinson	San Antonio
John Stockton	Utah	Mitch Richmond	Sacramento
Latrell Sprewell	Golden State	Kevin Johnson	Phoenix

THIRD TEAM

Derrick Coleman	New Jersey
Dominique Wilkins	Atlanta-L.A. Clippers
Shaquille O'Neal	Orlando
Mark Price	Cleveland
Gary Payton	Seattle

1994-95

FIRST TEAM

		SECOND TEAM	
Karl Malone	Utah	Charles Barkley	Phoenix
Scottie Pippen	Chicago	Shawn Kemp	Seattle
David Robinson	San Antonio	Shaquille O'Neal	Orlando
John Stockton	Utah	Gary Payton	Seattle
Anfernee Hardaway	Orlando	Mitch Richmond	Sacramento

THIRD TEAM

Detlef Schrempf	Seattle
Dennis Rodman	San Antonio
Hakeem Olajuwon	Houston
Reggie Miller	Indiana
Clyde Drexler	Houston

1995-96

FIRST TEAM

		SECOND TEAM	
Scottie Pippen	Chicago	Shawn Kemp	Seattle
Karl Malone	Utah	Grant Hill	Detroit
David Robinson	San Antonio	Hakeem Olajuwon	Houston
Michael Jordan	Chicago	Gary Payton	Seattle
Anfernee Hardaway	Orlando	John Stockton	Utah

THIRD TEAM

Charles Barkley	Phoenix
Juwan Howard	Washington
Shaquille O'Neal	Orlando
Mitch Richmond	Sacramento
Reggie Miller	Indiana

1996-97

FIRST TEAM

		SECOND TEAM	
Karl Malone	Utah	Scottie Pippen	Chicago
Grant Hill	Detroit	Glen Rice	Charlotte
Hakeem Olajuwon	Houston	Patrick Ewing	New York
Michael Jordan	Chicago	Gary Payton	Seattle
Tim Hardaway	Miami	Mitch Richmond	Sacramento

THIRD TEAM

Anthony Mason	Charlotte
Vin Baker	Milwaukee
Shaquille O'Neal	LA Lakers
John Stockton	Utah
Anfernee Hardaway	Orlando

1997-98

FIRST TEAM

		SECOND TEAM	
Karl Malone	Utah	Grant Hill	Detroit
Tim Duncan	San Antonio	Vin Baker	Seattle
Shaquille O'Neal	LA Lakers	David Robinson	San Antonio
Michael Jordan	Chicago	Tim Hardaway	Miami
Gary Payton	Seattle	Rod Strickland	Washington

THIRD TEAM

Scottie Pippen	Chicago
Glen Rice	Charlotte
Dikembe Mutombo	Atlanta
Mitch Richmond	Sacramento
Reggie Miller	Indiana

1998-99

FIRST TEAM

		SECOND TEAM	
Karl Malone	Utah	Chris Webber	Sacramento
Tim Duncan	San Antonio	Grant Hill	Detroit
Alonzo Mourning	Miami	Shaquille O'Neal	LA Lakers
Allen Iverson	Philadelphia	Gary Payton	Seattle
Jason Kidd	Phoenix	Tim Hardaway	Miami

THIRD TEAM

Kevin Garnett	Minnesota
Antonio McDyess	Denver
Hakeem Olajuwon	Houston
Kobe Bryant	LA Lakers
John Stockton	Utah

1999-2000

FIRST TEAM

		SECOND TEAM	
Tim Duncan	San Antonio	Karl Malone	Utah
Kevin Garnett	Minnesota	Grant Hill	Detroit
Shaquille O'Neal	LA Lakers	Alonzo Mourning	Miami
Jason Kidd	Phoenix	Allen Iverson	Philadelphia
Gary Payton	Seattle	Kobe Bryant	LA Lakers

THIRD TEAM

Chris Webber	Sacramento
Vince Carter	Toronto
David Robinson	San Antonio
Eddie Jones	Charlotte
Stephon Marbury	New Jersey

2000-01

FIRST TEAM

		SECOND TEAM	
Tim Duncan	San Antonio	Kevin Garnett	Minnesota
Chris Webber	Sacramento	Vince Carter	Toronto
Shaquille O'Neal	LA Lakers	Dikembe Mutombo	Atlanta-Phil.
Allen Iverson	Philadelphia	Kobe Bryant	LA Lakers
Jason Kidd	Phoenix	Tracy McGrady	Orlando

THIRD TEAM

Karl Malone	Utah
Dirk Nowitzki	Dallas
David Robinson	San Antonio
Gary Payton	Seattle
Ray Allen	Milwaukee

2001-02

FIRST TEAM

		SECOND TEAM	
Tim Duncan	San Antonio	Kevin Garnett	Minnesota
Tracy McGrady	Orlando	Chris Webber	Sacramento
Shaquille O'Neal	LA Lakers	Dirk Nowitzki	Dallas
Jason Kidd	New Jersey	Gary Payton	Seattle
Kobe Bryant	LA Lakers	Allen Iverson	Philadelphia

THIRD TEAM

Ben Wallace	Detroit
Jermaine O'Neal	Indiana
Dikembe Mutombo,	Philadelpia
Paul Pierce	Boston
Steve Nash	Dallas

2002-03

FIRST TEAM

		SECOND TEAM	
Tim Duncan	San Antonio	Dirk Nowitzki	Dallas
Kevin Garnett	Minnesota	Chris Webber	Sacramento
Shaquille O'Neal	LA Lakers	Ben Wallace	Detroit
Kobe Bryant	LA Lakers	Jason Kidd	New Jersey
Tracy McGrady	Orlando	Allen Iverson	Philadelphia

THIRD TEAM

Paul Pierce	Boston
Jamal Mashburn	New Orleans
Jermaine O'Neal	Indiana
Stephon Marbury	Phoenix
Steve Nash	Dallas

NBA All-Rookie Teams

While the got milk? NBA Rookie of the Year award dates back to 1952-53, the first NBA All-Rookie Team was chosen following the 1962-63 season in a poll of the league's head coaches, who were not allowed to name a player from their own team on their ballot. One five-man team was chosen, without regard to position, until 1988-89, when a second team was added.

Unlike the All-NBA First Team, which four times has not included the league's MVP, every Rookie of the Year has been

named to the All-Rookie First Team, although he was not necessarily the leading vote-getter. The fact that the rookie team is chosen without regard to position helps avoid conflicts by allowing voters to select two centers, for example.

In 1992-93, the All-Rookie First Team consisted of two centers, Shaquille O'Neal and Alonzo Mourning, and three forwards, Christian Laettner, Tom Gugliotta and LaPhonso Ellis. Smaller players have dominated the team in other years such as 1998-99, when 6-foot-7 Matt Harpring was the biggest player on an All-Rookie First Team that also included point guards Jason Williams and Mike Bibby and swingmen Paul Pierce and Vince Carter.

It's interesting to look back on All-Rookie teams and see the groups of players who entered the NBA in the same season. Arguably the strongest group was in 1970-71, when the All-Rookie five consisted of Geoff Petrie, Dave Cowens, Pete Maravich, Calvin Murphy and Bob Lanier. All are enshrined in the Hall of Fame with the exception of Petrie, who shared Rookie of the Year honors with Cowens and averaged 21.8 points per game in a six-year career cut short by injury.

The Cleveland Cavaliers had three players on the 1986-87 All-Rookie Team: Brad Daugherty, Ron Harper, and John "Hot Rod" Williams. The only other team to have three players on the All-Rookie Team was the 1964-65 New York Knicks, who placed Willis Reed, Jim "Bad News" Barnes, and Howard Komives on the six-member team.

Since a Second Team was added, the Cavaliers are the only team to place four rookies on the two units in one season. Brevin Knight and Zydrunas Ilgauskas made the First Team in 1997-98, and Cedric Henderson and Derek Anderson made the Second Team.

Following is the complete list of the NBA All-Rookie Teams, as selected by the league's head coaches:

1962-63

Terry Dischinger	Chicago
Chet Walker	Syracuse
Zelmo Beaty	St. Louis
John Havlicek	Boston
Dave DeBusschere	Detroit

1963-64

Jerry Lucas	Cincinnati
Gus Johnson	Baltimore
Nate Thurmond	San Francisco
Art Heyman	New York
Rod Thorn	Baltimore

1964-65

Willis Reed	New York
Jim Barnes	New York
Howard Komives	New York
Lucious Jackson	Philadelphia
Wally Jones	Baltimore
Joe Caldwell	Detroit

1965-66

Rick Barry	San Francisco
Billy Cunningham	Philadelphia
Tom Van Arsdale	Detroit
Dick Van Arsdale	New York
Fred Hetzel	San Francisco

1966-67

Lou Hudson	St. Louis
Jack Marin	Baltimore
Erwin Mueller	Chicago
Cazzie Russell	New York
Dave Bing	Detroit

1967-68

Earl Monroe	Baltimore
Bob Rule	Seattle
Walt Frazier	New York
Al Tucker	Seattle
Phil Jackson	New York

1968-69

Wes Unseld	Baltimore
Elvin Hayes	San Diego
Bill Hewitt	LA Lakers
Art Harris	Seattle
Gary Gregor	Phoenix

1969-70

Kareem Abdul-Jabbar	Milwaukee
Bob Dandridge	Milwaukee
Jo Jo White	Boston
Mike Davis	Baltimore
Dick Garrett	LA Lakers

1970-71

Geoff Petrie	Portland
Dave Cowens	Boston
Pete Maravich	Atlanta
Cavin Murphy	San Diego
Bob Lanier	Detroit

1971-72

Elmore Smith	Buffalo
Sidney Wicks	Portland
Austin Carr	Cleveland
Phil Chenier	Baltimore
Clifford Ray	Chicago

1972-73

Bob McAdoo	Buffalo
Lloyd Neal	Portland
Fred Boyd	Philadelphia
Dwight Davis	Cleveland
Jim Price	LA Lakers

1973-74

Ernie DiGregorio	Buffalo
Ron Behagen	KC-Omaha
Mike Bantom	Phoenix
John Brown	Atlanta
Nick Weatherspoon	Capital

1974-75

Keith Wilkes	Golden State
John Drew	Atlanta
Scott Wedman	KC-Omaha
Tom Burleson	Seattle
Brian Winters	LA Lakers

1975-76

Alvan Adams	Phoenix
Gus Williams	Golden State
Joe Meriweather	Houston
John Shumate	Phoenix-Buffalo
Lionel Hollins	Portland

1976-77

Adrian Dantley	Buffalo
Scott May	Chicago
Mitch Kupchak	Washington
John Lucas	Houston
Ron Lee	Phoenix

1977-78

Walter Davis	Phoenix
Marques Johnson	Milwaukee
Bernard King	New Jersey
Jack Sikma	Seattle
Norm Nixon	LA Lakers

1978-79

Phil Ford	Kansas City
Mychal Thompson	Portland
Ron Brewer	Portland
Reggie Theus	Chicago
Terry Tyler	Detroit

1979-80

Larry Bird	Boston
Magic Johnson	LA Lakers
Bill Cartwright	New York
Calvin Natt	Portland
David Greenwood	Chicago

1980-81

Joe Barry Carroll	Golden State
Darrell Griffith	Utah
Larry Smith	Golden State
Kevin McHale	Boston
Kelvin Ransey	Portland

1981-82

Kelly Tripucka	Detroit
Jay Vincent	Dallas
Isiah Thomas	Detroit
Buck Williams	New Jersey
Jeff Ruland	Washington

1982-83

Terry Cummings	San Diego
Clark Kellogg	Indiana
Dominique Wilkins	Atlanta
James Worthy	LA Lakers
Quintin Dailey	Chicago

1983-84

Ralph Sampson	Houston
Steve Stipanovich	Indiana
Byron Scott	LA Lakers
Jeff Malone	Washington
Thurl Bailey	Utah (tie)
Darrell Walker	New York (tie)

1984-85

Michael Jordan	Chicago
Hakeem Olajuwon	Houston
Sam Bowie	Portland
Charles Barkley	Philadelphia
Sam Perkins	Dallas

1985-86

Xavier McDaniel	Seattle
Patrick Ewing	New York
Karl Malone	Utah
Joe Dumars	Detroit
Charles Oakley	Chicago

1986-87

Brad Daugherty	Cleveland
Ron Harper	Cleveland
Chuck Person	Indiana
Roy Tarpley	Dallas
John Williams	Cleveland

1987-88

Mark Jackson	New York
Armon Gilliam	Phoenix
Kenny Smith	Sacramento
Greg Anderson	San Antonio
Derrick McKey	Seattle

1988-89

FIRST TEAM		SECOND TEAM	
Mitch Richmond	Golden State	Brian Shaw	Boston
Willie Anderson	San Antonio	Rex Chapman	Charlotte
Hersey Hawkins	Philadelphia	Chris Morris	New Jersey
Rik Smits	Indiana	Rod Strickland	New York
Charles Smith	LA Clippers	Kevin Edwards	Miami

1989-90

FIRST TEAM		SECOND TEAM	
David Robinson	San Antonio	J. R. Reid	Charlotte
Tim Hardaway	Golden State	Sean Elliott	San Antonio
Vlade Divac	LA Lakers	Stacey King	Chicago
Sherman Douglas	Miami	Blue Edwards	Utah
Pooh Richardson	Minnesota	Glen Rice	Miami

1990-91

FIRST TEAM		SECOND TEAM	
Kendall Gill	Charlotte	Chris Jackson	Denver
Dennis Scott	Orlando	Gary Payton	Seattle
Dee Brown	Boston	Felton Spencer	Minnesota
Lionel Simmons	Sacramento	Travis Mays	Sacramento
Derrick Coleman	New Jersey	Willie Burton	Miami

1991-92

FIRST TEAM		SECOND TEAM	
Larry Johnson	Charlotte	Rick Fox	Boston
Dikembe Mutombo	Denver	Terrell Brandon	Cleveland
Billy Owens	Golden State	Larry Stewart	Washington
Steve Smith	Miami	Stanley Roberts	Orlando
Stacey Augmon	Atlanta	Mark Macon	Denver

1992-93

FIRST TEAM		SECOND TEAM	
Shaquille O'Neal	Orlando	Walt Williams	Sacramento
Alonzo Mourning	Charlotte	Robert Horry	Houston
Christian Laettner	Minnesota	Latrell Sprewell	Golden State
Tom Gugliotta	Washington	Clarence	
		Weatherspoon	Philadelphia
LaPhonso Ellis	Denver	Richard Dumas	Phoenix

1993-94

FIRST TEAM		SECOND TEAM	
Chris Webber	Golden State	Dino Radja	Boston
Anfernee Hardaway	Orlando	Nick Van Exel	LA Lakers
Vin Baker	Milwaukee	Shawn Bradley	Philadelphia
Jamal Mashburn	Dallas	Toni Kukoc	Chicago
Isaiah Rider	Minnesota	Lindsey Hunter	Detroit

1994-95

FIRST TEAM		SECOND TEAM	
Jason Kidd	Dallas	Juwan Howard	Washington
Grant Hill	Detroit	Eric Montross	Boston
Glenn Robinson	Milwaukee	Wesley Person	Phoenix
Eddie Jones	LA Lakers	Jalen Rose	Denver
Brian Grant	Sacramento	Donyell Marshall	Golden State (tie)
		Sharone Wright	Philadelphia (tie)

1995-96

FIRST TEAM		SECOND TEAM	
Damon Stoudamire	Toronto	Kevin Garnett	Minnesota
Joe Smith	Golden State	Bryant Reeves	Vancouver
Jerry Stackhouse	Philadelphia	Brent Barry	L.A.Clippers
Antonio McDyess	Denver	Rasheed Wallace	Washington
Arvydas Sabonis	Portland (tie)	Tyus Edney	Sacramento
Michael Finley	Phoenix (tie)		

1996-97

FIRST TEAM		SECOND TEAM	
Shareef Abdur-Rahim	Vancouver	Kerry Kittles	New Jersey
Allen Iverson	Philadelphia	Ray Allen	Milwaukee
Stephon Marbury	Minnesota	Travis Knight	LA Lakers
Marcus Camby	Toronto	Kobe Bryant	LA Lakers
Antoine Walker	Boston	Matt Maloney	Houston

1997-98

FIRST TEAM		SECOND TEAM	
Tim Duncan	San Antonio	Tim Thomas	Philadelphia
Keith Van Horn	New Jersey	Cedric Henderson	Cleveland
Brevin Knight	Cleveland	Derek Anderson	Cleveland
Zydrunas Ilgauskas	Cleveland	Maurice Taylor	LA Clippers
Ron Mercer	Boston	Bobby Jackson	Denver

1998-99

FIRST TEAM		SECOND TEAM	
Vince Carter	Toronto	Michael Dickerson	Houston
Paul Pierce	Boston	Michael Doleac	Orlando
Jason Williams	Sacramento	Cuttino Mobley	Houston
Mike Bibby	Vancouver	Michael Olowokandi	LA Clippers
Matt Harpring	Orlando	Antawn Jamison	Golden State

1999-2000

FIRST TEAM		SECOND TEAM	
Elton Brand	Chicago	Shawn Marion	Phoenix
Steve Francis	Houston	Ron Artest	Chicago
Lamar Odom	LA Clippers	James Posey	Denver
Wally Szczerbiak	Minnesota	Jason Terry	Atlanta
Andre Miller	Cleveland	Chucky Atkins	Orlando

2000-01

FIRST TEAM		SECOND TEAM	
Mike Miller	Orlando	Hidayet Turkoglu	Sacramento
Kenyon Martin	New Jersey	Desmond Mason	Seattle
Marc Jackson	Golden State	Courtney Alexander	Washington
Morris Peterson	Toronto	Marcus Fizer	Chicago
Darius Miles	LA Clippers	Chris Mihm	Cleveland

2001-02

FIRST TEAM		SECOND TEAM	
Pau Gasol	Memphis	Jamaal Tinsley	Indiana
Shane Battier	Memphis	Richard Jefferson	New Jersey
Jason Richardson	Golden State	Eddie Griffin	Houston
Tony Parker	San Antonio	Zeljko Rebraca	Detroit
Andrei Kirilenko	Utah	Vladimir Radmanovic	Seattle (tie)
		Joe Johnson	Boston-
			Phoenix (tie)

2002-03

FIRST TEAM		SECOND TEAM	
Yao Ming	Houston	Emanuel Ginobili	San Antonio
Amare Stoudemire	Phoenix	Gordan Giricek	Orlando
Caron Butler	Miami	Carlos Boozer	Cleveland
Drew Gooden	Orlando	Jay Williams	Chicago
Nene Hilario	Denver	J.R. Bremer	Boston

All-Defensive Teams

The inaugural All-Defensive Teams were selected in 1968-69 and included some of the greatest defensive players in NBA history: Bill Russell, Nate Thurmond, Dave DeBusschere, Walt Frazier and Jerry Sloan on the First Team, and Rudy LaRusso, Tom "Satch" Sanders, John Havlicek, Jerry West and Bill Bridges on the Second Team. That was the final season of Russell's playing career, and thus the only All-Defensive award for the player who had perhaps a greater impact on defense in the NBA than any other.

Frazier made the All-Defensive First Team in each of the first seven seasons it was selected by the league's coaches, and DeBusschere made it in each of the first six seasons. But the honor of most All-Defensive First Team placings belongs to Michael Jordan and Gary Payton, who were named nine times apiece, Jordan while playing for the Chicago Bulls and Payton while playing for the Seattle SuperSonics.

Scottie Pippen of the Portland Trail Blazers, for many years a teammate of Jordan on the Bulls, has made the All-Defensive First Team eight times and Second Team twice. The only other player with eight First Team selections is Bobby Jones of the Philadelphia 76ers, who made it in each of his first eight seasons after coming over from the ABA in 1976. Jones, who also made the All-Defensive Second Team once, was an ABA All-Defensive First Team selection twice as well.

Following is the complete list of NBA All-Defensive Teams, as selected by the league's head coaches:

1968-69

FIRST TEAM		SECOND TEAM	
Dave DeBusschere	New York	Rudy LaRusso	San Francisco
Nate Thurmond	San Francisco	Tom Sanders	Boston
Bill Russell	Boston	John Havlicek	Boston
Walt Frazier	New York	Jerry West	LA Lakers
Jerry Sloan	Chicago	Bill Bridges	Atlanta

1969-70

FIRST TEAM		SECOND TEAM	
Dave DeBusschere	New York	John Havlicek	Boston
Gus Johnson	Baltimore	Bill Bridges	Atlanta
Willis Reed	New York	Kareem Abdul-Jabbar	Milwaukee
Walt Frazier	New York	Joe Caldwell	Atlanta
Jerry West	LA Lakers	Jerry Sloan	Chicago

1970-71

FIRST TEAM		SECOND TEAM	
Dave DeBusschere	New York	John Havlicek	Boston
Gus Johnson	Baltimore	Paul Silas	Phoenix
Nate Thurmond	San Francisco	Kareem Abdul-Jabbar	Milwaukee
Walt Frazier	New York	Jerry Sloan	Chicago
Jerry West	LA Lakers	Norm Van Lier	Cincinnati

1971-72

FIRST TEAM		SECOND TEAM	
Dave DeBusschere	New York	Paul Silas	Phoenix
John Havlicek	Boston	Bob Love	Chicago
Wilt Chamberlain	LA Lakers	Nate Thurmond	Golden State
Jerry West	LA Lakers	Norm Van Lier	Chicago
Walt Frazier	New York (tie)	Don Chaney	Boston
Jerry Sloan	Chicago (tie)		

1972-73

FIRST TEAM		SECOND TEAM	
Dave DeBusschere	New York	Paul Silas	Boston
John Havlicek	Boston	Mike Riordan	Baltimore
Wilt Chamberlain	LA Lakers	Nate Thurmond	Golden State
Jerry West	LA Lakers	Norm Van Lier	Chicago
Walt Frazier	New York	Don Chaney	Boston

1973-74

FIRST TEAM		SECOND TEAM	
Dave DeBusschere	New York	Elvin Hayes	Washington
John Havlicek	Boston	Bob Love	Chicago
Kareem Abdul-Jabbar	Milwaukee	Nate Thurmond	Golden State
Norm Van Lier	Chicago	Don Chaney	Boston
Walt Frazier	New York (tie)	Dick Van Arsdale	Phoenix (tie)
Jerry Sloan	Chicago (tie)	Jim Price	LA Lakers (tie)

1974-75

FIRST TEAM		SECOND TEAM	
John Havlicek	Boston	Elvin Hayes	Washington
Paul Silas	Boston	Bob Love	Chicago
Kareem Abdul-Jabbar	Milwaukee	Dave Cowens	Boston
Jerry Sloan	Chicago	Norm Van Lier	Chicago
Walt Frazier	New York	Don Chaney	Boston

1975-76

FIRST TEAM		SECOND TEAM	
Paul Silas	Boston	Jim Brewer	Cleveland
John Havlicek	Boston	Jamaal Wilkes	Golden State
Dave Cowens	Boston	Kareem Abdul-Jabbar	LA Lakers
Norm Van Lier	Chicago	Jim Cleamons	Cleveland
Don Watts	Seattle	Phil Smith	Golden State

1976-77

FIRST TEAM		SECOND TEAM	
Bobby Jones	Denver	Jim Brewer	Cleveland
E. C. Coleman	New Orleans	Jamaal Wilkes	Golden State
Bill Walton	Portland	Kareem Abdul-Jabbar	LA Lakers
Don Buse	Indiana	Brian Taylor	Kansas City
Norm Van Lier	Chicago	Don Chaney	LA Lakers

1977-78

FIRST TEAM		SECOND TEAM	
Bobby Jones	Denver	E. C. Coleman	Golden State
Maurice Lucas	Portland	Bob Gross	Portland
Bill Walton	Portland	Kareem Abdul-Jabbar	LA Lakers (tie)
Lionel Hollins	Portland	Artis Gilmore	Chicago (tie)
Don Buse	Phoenix	Norm Van Lier	Chicago
		Quinn Buckner	Milwaukee

1978-79

FIRST TEAM		SECOND TEAM	
Bobby Jones	Philadelphia	Maurice Lucas	Portland
Bobby Dandridge	Washington	M. L. Carr	Detroit
Kareem Abdul-Jabbar	LA Lakers	Moses Malone	Houston
Dennis Johnson	Seattle	Lionel Hollins	Portland
Don Buse	Phoenix	Eddie Johnson	Atlanta

1979-80

FIRST TEAM		SECOND TEAM	
Bobby Jones	Philadelphia	Scott Wedman	Kansas City
Dan Roundfield	Atlanta	Kermit Washington	Portland
Kareem Abdul-Jabbar	LA Lakers	Dave Cowens	Boston
Dennis Johnson	Seattle	Quinn Buckner	Milwaukee
Don Buse	Phoenix (tie)	Eddie Johnson	Atlanta
Micheal Ray Richardson	New York (tie)		

1980-81

FIRST TEAM		SECOND TEAM	
Bobby Jones	Philadelphia	Dan Roundfield	Atlanta
Caldwell Jones	Philadelphia	Kermit Washington	Portland
Kareem Abdul-Jabbar	LA Lakers	George Johnson	San Antonio
Dennis Johnson	Phoenix	Quinn Buckner	Milwaukee
Micheal Ray Richardson	New York	Dudley Bradley	Indiana (tie)
		Michael Cooper	LALakers (tie)

1981-82

FIRST TEAM		SECOND TEAM	
Bobby Jones	Philadelphia	Larry Bird	Boston
Dan Roundfield	Atlanta	Lonnie Shelton	Seattle
Caldwell Jones	Philadelphia	Jack Sikma	Seattle
Michael Cooper	LA Lakers	Quinn Buckner	Milwaukee
Dennis Johnson	Phoenix	Sidney Moncrief	Milwaukee

1982-83

FIRST TEAM		SECOND TEAM	
Bobby Jones	Philadelphia	Larry Bird	Boston
Dan Roundfield	Atlanta	Kevin McHale	Boston
Moses Malone	Philadelphia	Wayne Rollins	Atlanta
Sidney Moncrief	Milwaukee	Michael Cooper	LA Lakers
Dennis Johnson	Phoenix (tie)	T. R. Dunn	Denver
Maurice Cheeks	Philadelphia (tie)		

1983-84

FIRST TEAM		SECOND TEAM	
Bobby Jones	Philadelphia	Larry Bird	Boston
Michael Cooper	LA Lakers	Dan Roundfield	Atlanta
Wayne Rollins	Atlanta	Kareem Abdul-Jabbar	LA Lakers
Maurice Cheeks	Philadelphia	Dennis Johnson	Boston
Sidney Moncrief	Milwaukee	T. R. Dunn	Denver

1984-85

FIRST TEAM		SECOND TEAM	
Sidney Moncrief	Milwaukee	Bobby Jones	Philadelphia
Paul Pressey	Milwaukee	Danny Vranes	Seattle
Mark Eaton	Utah	Hakeem Olajuwon	Houston
Michael Cooper	LA Lakers	Dennis Johnson	Boston
Maurice Cheeks	Philadelphia	T. R. Dunn	Denver

1985-86

FIRST TEAM		SECOND TEAM	
Paul Pressey	Milwaukee	Michael Cooper	LA Lakers
Kevin McHale	Boston	Bill Hanzlik	Denver
Mark Eaton	Utah	Manute Bol	Washington
Sidney Moncrief	Milwaukee	Alvin Robertson	San Antonio
Maurice Cheeks	Philadelphia	Dennis Johnson	Boston

1986-87

FIRST TEAM		SECOND TEAM	
Kevin McHale	Boston	Paul Pressey	Milwaukee
Michael Cooper	LA Lakers	Rodney McCray	Houston
Hakeem Olajuwon	Houston	Mark Eaton	Utah
Alvin Robertson	San Antonio	Maurice Cheeks	Philadelphia
Dennis Johnson	Boston	Derek Harper	Dallas

1987-88

FIRST TEAM		SECOND TEAM	
Kevin McHale	Boston	Buck Williams	New Jersey
Rodney McCray	Houston	Karl Malone	Utah
Hakeem Olajuwon	Houston	Mark Eaton	Utah (tie)
Michael Cooper	LA Lakers	Patrick Ewing	New York (tie)
Michael Jordan	Chicago	Alvin Robertson	San Antonio
		Lafayette Lever	Denver

1988-89

FIRST TEAM		SECOND TEAM	
Dennis Rodman	Detroit	Kevin McHale	Boston
Larry Nance	Cleveland	A. C. Green	LA Lakers
Mark Eaton	Utah	Patrick Ewing	New York
Michael Jordan	Chicago	John Stockton	Utah
Joe Dumars	Detroit	Alvin Robertson	San Antonio

1989-90

FIRST TEAM		SECOND TEAM	
Dennis Rodman	Detroit	Kevin McHale	Boston
Buck Williams	Portland	Rick Mahorn	Philadelphia
Hakeem Olajuwon	Houston	David Robinson	San Antonio
Michael Jordan	Chicago	Derek Harper	Dallas
Joe Dumars	Detroit	Alvin Robertson	Milwaukee

1990-91

FIRST TEAM		SECOND TEAM	
Michael Jordan	Chicago	Joe Dumars	Detroit
Alvin Robertson	Milwaukee	John Stockton	Utah
David Robinson	San Antonio	Hakeem Olajuwon	Houston
Dennis Rodman	Detroit	Scottie Pippen	Chicago
Buck Williams	Portland	Dan Majerle	Phoenix

1991-92

FIRST TEAM		SECOND TEAM	
Dennis Rodman	Detroit	Larry Nance	Cleveland
Scottie Pippen	Chicago	Buck Williams	Portland
David Robinson	San Antonio	Patrick Ewing	New York
Michael Jordan	Chicago	John Stockton	Utah
Joe Dumars	Detroit	Micheal Williams	Indiana

1992-93

FIRST TEAM		SECOND TEAM	
Scottie Pippen	Chicago	Horace Grant	Chicago
Dennis Rodman	Detroit	Larry Nance	Cleveland
Hakeem Olajuwon	Houston	David Robinson	San Antonio
Michael Jordan	Chicago	Dan Majerle	Phoenix
Joe Dumars	Detroit	John Starks	New York

1993-94

FIRST TEAM		SECOND TEAM	
Scottie Pippen	Chicago	Dennis Rodman	San Antonio
Charles Oakley	New York	Horace Grant	Chicago
Hakeem Olajuwon	Houston	David Robinson	San Antonio
Gary Payton	Seattle	Nate McMillan	Seattle
Mookie Blaylock	Atlanta	Latrell Sprewell	Golden State

1994-95

FIRST TEAM		SECOND TEAM	
Scottie Pippen	Chicago	Horace Grant	Orlando
Dennis Rodman	San Antonio	Derrick McKey	Indiana
David Robinson	San Antonio	Dikembe Mutombo	Denver
Gary Payton	Seattle	John Stockton	Utah
Mookie Blaylock	Atlanta	Nate McMillan	Seattle

1995-96

FIRST TEAM		SECOND TEAM	
Scottie Pippen	Chicago	Horace Grant	Orlando
Dennis Rodman	Chicago	Derrick McKey	Indiana
David Robinson	San Antonio	Hakeem Olajuwon	Houston
Gary Payton	Seattle	Mookie Blaylock	Atlanta
Michael Jordan	Chicago	Bobby Phills	Cleveland

1996-97

FIRST TEAM		SECOND TEAM	
Scottie Pippen	Chicago	Anthony Mason	Charlotte
Karl Malone	Utah	P.J. Brown	Miami
Dikembe Mutombo	Atlanta	Hakeem Olajuwon	Houston
Michael Jordan	Chicago	Mookie Blaylock	Atlanta
Gary Payton	Seattle	John Stockton	Utah

1997-98

FIRST TEAM		SECOND TEAM	
Scottie Pippen	Chicago	Tim Duncan	San Antonio
Karl Malone	Utah	Charles Oakley	New York
Dikembe Mutombo	Atlanta	David Robinson	San Antonio
Gary Payton	Seattle	Mookie Blaylock	Atlanta
Michael Jordan	Chicago	Eddie Jones	LA Lakers

1998-99

FIRST TEAM		SECOND TEAM	
Tim Duncan	San Antonio	P.J. Brown	Miami
Karl Malone	Utah	Theo Ratliff	Philadelphia
Scottie Pippen	Chicago	Dikembe Mutombo	Atlanta
Alonzo Mourning	Miami	Mookie Blaylock	Atlanta
Gary Payton	Seattle	Eddie Jones	Charlotte
Jason Kidd	Phoenix		

1999-00

FIRST TEAM		SECOND TEAM	
Tim Duncan	San Antonio	Scottie Pippen	Portland
Kevin Garnett	Minnesota	Clifford Robinson	Phoenix
Alonzo Mourning	Miami	Shaquille O'Neal	LA Lakers
Gary Payton	Seattle	Eddie Jones	Charlotte
Kobe Bryant	LA Lakers	Jason Kidd	Phoenix

2000-01

FIRST TEAM		SECOND TEAM	
Tim Duncan	San Antonio	Bruce Bowen	Miami
Kevin Garnett	Minnesota	P.J. Brown	Charlotte
Dikembe Mutombo	Philadelphia-Atlanta	Shaquille O'Neal	LA Lakers
Gary Payton	Seattle	Kobe Bryant	LA Lakers
Jason Kidd	Phoenix	Doug Christie	Sacramento

2001-02

FIRST TEAM		SECOND TEAM	
Tim Duncan	San Antonio	Bruce Bowen	San Antonio
Kevin Garnett	Minnesota	Clifford Robinson	Detroit
Ben Wallace	Detroit	Dikembe Mutombo	Philadelphia
Gary Payton	Seattle	Kobe Bryant	LA Lakers
Jason Kidd	New Jersey	Doug Christie	Sacramento

2002-03

FIRST TEAM		SECOND TEAM	
Tim Duncan	San Antonio	Ron Artest	Indiana
Kevin Garnett	Minnesota	Bruce Bowen	San Antonio
Ben Wallace	Detroit	Shaquille O'Neal	LA Lakers
Doug Christie	Sacramento	Jason Kidd	New Jersey
Kobe Bryant	LA Lakers	Eric Snow	Philadelphia

Chapter 38

The All-Star Game

By Stew Thornley

The first one was almost called off because the league president feared it would be such a bust that it would embarrass the National Basketball Association. But the All-Star Game was a success. It continued, it expanded, and it became not just a game but a multi-day extravaganza.

The idea for the All-Star Game came in the fall of 1950. Haskell Cohen, the NBA's public relations director, responded to a request from Maurice Podoloff, the NBA president, and Walter Brown, president of the Boston Celtics, for something that would bring exposure to professional basketball. At that time professional basketball did not hold the same place in the hearts of the fans as the college game did. Brown liked Haskell's idea and donated his building, the Boston Garden. Podoloff also was in favor, although the league president got cold feet as game drew closer and asked Brown to cancel it. "A few days before the game, Maurice Podoloff called me on the phone and asked me to 'call it off,'" Brown recalled years later. "He said that everybody he talked to said it would be a flop, and the league would look bad." Brown stuck with the game. Although he had more faith than Podoloff, Brown still wondered if they could draw 10,000 fans, which he projected would be needed for the game to break even financially.

The first All-Star Game was a success in all regards. It also came at a good time for the NBA and for basketball in general. In January of 1951, news began emerging about scandals in college basketball. Incidents of point-shaving and fixing of games, which had taken place over the past few years, eventually resulted in the banishment of a number of players, some of whom were already in the NBA—including two who played in the first All-Star Game. The scandals tarnished the image of college basketball, thereby opening the door for greater prestige for the pros, a process that wasn't hurt by the beginning of a yearly game featuring the NBA's best players.

The players in the first All-Star Game reportedly got nothing more than train fare to Boston and a $25 United States savings bond. Over the years, the compensation grew into the

The NBA's Dave Bing (left), and the ABA's Zelmo Beatty, 1971
An all-star game for the ages on May 28, 1971, as the NBA's stars lead the ABA's by just one in the dying moments before prevailing, 125-120.

thousands of dollars, with larger shares for the members of the winning team.

Sportswriters and broadcasters from the cities with NBA franchises initially chose the 10-player squads for each team. It was left to the coaches—who were the coaches of the first-place teams in each division at a designated point of the season—to then select the starting lineup. In 1966, East coach Red Auerbach left the choice of his starting center, between Wilt Chamberlain and Bill Russell, to the flip of a coin

(Chamberlain won). Within a few years, the starting status went to the players who were first in the balloting at each position. In 1974-75, the NBA began allowing the fans to vote for the starting lineup. Bob McAdoo of the Buffalo Braves received the highest vote total, 98,325, in the balloting for the 1975 All-Star Game. Michael Jordan became the only player to top two million in votes, with 2,451,136 for the 1997 All-Star Game.

The Game also provided an annual opportunity for teams and players to get together. The NBA often held league meetings in conjunction with the game. The players used the chance to convene as a means of trying to organize a player's association, a process that took many years and at times jeopardized the All-Star Game, as players threatened not to play if certain issues and grievances were not addressed by the owners.

The first NBA All-Star Games were carried on radio. Later they were televised, but were not always as a top priority with the networks. In 1959, only the second half of the All-Star Game was televised, in place of the Friday night fights. In 1969, the telecast was interrupted by President Lyndon Johnson's State of the Union address. When Johnson was done speaking, the remainder of the game was carried live, with taped highlights of the missing portion squeezed in. For many years, the games were weeknight affairs. Even when the games were played on the West Coast, the starting time was set to accommodate local fans, not those three time zones ahead on the East Coast.

Finally, in 1977, the regular game day was switched to Sunday. Seven years later, it became a weekend event as features like slam dunk contests, rookie games, and old-timer's games were added to the agenda. (Some of these events had taken place before, as preliminary or half-time events in the NBA and ABA. In 1984, they started on the Saturday of All-Star weekend. In 1993, the Jam Session, an interactive experience for the fans, was added to the festivities.) By this time, the All-Star Game was a major event for television, and by 2000, the game was being televised to more than 200 countries in more than 40 different languages.

It wasn't just the National Basketball Association that had an annual All-Star Game. The American Basketball Association held a game in each of its nine seasons. Because of a dwindling number of teams, the final ABA All-Star game featured its first-place team against the top players from the other teams. And for two years, a collection of All-Stars from the NBA and ABA squared off against one another. Even though NBA and ABA teams began playing pre-season exhibition games against one another starting in the fall of 1971 (four months after the first of the two NBA-ABA All-Star Games), the All-Star Games between the two leagues were unsanctioned events, arranged by the players' associations without the approval of the owners. In fact, the NBA owners were firmly opposed to their players engaging in such games.

Sometimes the All-Star Games were competitive, with several going into overtime, but usually the focus was on individual performances. Often with a big emphasis on style and little on fundamentals and defense, the games were normally high-scoring contests featuring a lot of freelancing and one-on-one play.

More than anything, the All-Star Game has been, and continues to be, a showcase for the NBA's best.

ALL-STAR GAME RESULTS

1951

Boston Garden, Boston, Massachusetts
Friday, March 2, 1951
East 111, West 94
Coaches: West–John Kundla, Minneapolis; East–Joe Lapchick, New York
Most Valuable Player: Ed Macauley
Officials: Pat Kennedy, Charley Eckman
Attendance: 10,094

	1	2	3	4	Total
West	22	20	22	30	94
East	31	22	30	28	111

A crowd of 10,094—94 more than Boston owner Walter Brown thought would be needed to break even—came to the Boston Garden to watch the first NBA All-Star Game. Many more listened to Marty Glickman's play-by-play descriptions over the Mutual Broadcasting System as the top players in the Eastern Division beat the best players from the West, 111-94.

The NBA's most dominant player, George Mikan, was stifled by Boston's Ed Macauley. Mikan collected only three points in the first half—all scored in the first quarter as both coaches played their starting five for the entire first period and the other players for the entire second—and 12 for the game.

In addition to the tough defense, Macauley was the standout scorer for the East, which played as a well-coordinated unit. No Most Valuable Player (MVP) was chosen at the time, but two years later—when the selection of an MVP started becoming a regular part of the game—MVP's for the first two games were selected retroactively with the 1951 award going to Macauley.

Two of the West starters—the Indianapolis Olympians' Alex Groza and Ralph Beard, who had been stars at the University of Kentucky—were among the players who were caught in the web of emerging investigations of the college basketball scandals and were banned from the NBA at the end of the 1950-51 season.

1952

Boston Garden, Boston, Massachusetts
Monday, February 11, 1952
East 108, West 91
Coaches: West–John Kundla, Minneapolis; East–Al Cervi, Syracuse
Most Valuable Player: Paul Arizin
Officials: Sid Borgia, Stan Stutz
Attendance: 10,211

	1	2	3	4	Total
West	22	22	27	20	91
East	26	23	33	26	108

The second NBA All-Star game turned into a duel between the two players who were also battling for the league's scoring title that year, George Mikan and Paul Arizin. Each player scored 26 points, but Arizin had a better supporting cast as five other players on the East squad scored in double figures.

The East built a 13-point lead in the second quarter, but Mikan led a comeback that cut the gap to five points at the end of the half. The East opened up another sizable lead and then held off another West surge in the fourth quarter before going on a final push that led to a 17-point win.

As was the case with the 1951 game, the MVP was selected retroactively with Paul Arizin receiving the honor.

1953

Memorial Coliseum, Fort Wayne, Indiana
Tuesday, January 13, 1953
West 79, East 75
Coaches: East–Joe Lapchick, New York; West–John Kundla, Minneapolis
Most Valuable Player: George Mikan
Officials: Sid Borgia, Bud Lowell
Attendance: 10,322

	1	2	3	4	Total
East	20	14	21	20	75
West	20	15	22	22	79

George Mikan dominated, but Bob Davies of the Rochester Royals was the player who poured it on in the final minutes of the game, sinking three field goals and two free throws to pull the West from a one-point deficit into a seven-point lead.

Andy Phillip of the Fort Wayne Pistons provided some outstanding playmaking and finished second in the balloting for the game's MVP to Mikan, who had 22 points and 16 rebounds to lead the West to its first victory.

1954

Madison Square Garden, New York, New York
Thursday, January 21, 1954
East 98, West 93, Overtime
Coaches: West—John Kundla, Minneapolis; East—Joe Lapchick, New York
Most Valuable Player: Bob Cousy
Officials: Mendy Rudolph, Sid Borgia
Attendance: 16,487

	1	2	3	4	OT	Total
West	25	19	23	17	9	93
East	28	20	17	19	14	98

A flurry of action in the final minute of the fourth quarter sent the All-Star Game into overtime for the first time. The East—which had battled back from a 13-point deficit—held an 82-80 lead with less than a minute to play, and Boston's Bob Cousy had the ball. Cousy planned on dribbling away the remaining time, but Rochester's Bob Davies stole the ball and scored to tie the game. However, Cousy redeemed himself by sinking a set shot with five seconds left to put the East back out in front. After using a pair of timeouts to move the ball upcourt, the West inbounded and got the ball to George Mikan, who wheeled and shot, drawing a foul as the horn sounded to end the period. With no time showing on the clock, Mikan stepped to the line and—in between smiling and joking with the referee—sank both his free throws to put the game into overtime.

In the extra period, Cousy took charge, scoring 10 points to give the East a 98-93 win and earn the game's MVP award. Jim Pollard of the Minneapolis Lakers led all players with 23 points and had been named the game's Most Valuable Player in a vote taken in the final minutes of regulation time. But after Pollard's teammate, Mikan, forced the game into overtime, another vote was taken with Cousy coming out on top.

1955

Madison Square Garden, New York, New York
Tuesday, January 18, 1955
East 100, West 91
Coaches: West—Charley Eckman, Fort Wayne; East—Al Cervi, Syracuse
Most Valuable Player: Bill Sharman
Officials: Phil Fox, Joe Serafin
Attendance: 15,564

	1	2	3	4	Total
West	21	29	21	20	91
East	21	28	21	30	100

Bill Sharman of the Boston Celtics opened up what had been a tight contest with a scoring spree in the fourth quarter to lead the East to a 100-92 win. Sharman produced 10 points during an eight-minute run while his backcourt mate with the Celtics, Bob Cousy, had seven points during that stretch.

The coach for the Western All-Stars, Charley Eckman, made his second All-Star appearance but only his first on the bench. Eckman had been an official in the NBA's first All-Star game.

For the second straight year, military teams played a preliminary game. Former University of Kentucky stars Lou Tsioropoulos and Cliff Hagan led a team from Andrews Air Force Base past a group of Armed Forces All-Stars.

1956

War Memorial Auditorium, Rochester, New York
Tuesday, January 24, 1956
West 108, East 94
Coaches: East—George Senesky, Philadelphia; West—Charley Eckman, Fort Wayne
Most Valuable Player: Bob Pettit
Officials: Arnie Heft, Lou Eisenstein
Attendance: 8,517

	1	2	3	4	Total
East	24	16	24	30	94
West	17	26	41	24	108

Bob Pettit—left out of the starting lineup by Charley Eckman, who chose three of his own Fort Wayne Pistons as starters—came off the bench to score 20 points and grab 24 rebounds and lead the West to a 108-94 win. Pettit had been the only unanimous choice to the All-Star team in the voting among sportscasters and writers to determine the 20 players to be in the game.

Eckman inserted Pettit, along with Vern Mikkelsen and Clyde Lovellette of the Minneapolis Lakers, after the West fell behind by 14 points in the first quarter. Packing the lineup with big men turned the game around for the West, who came back to take a three-point lead at the half and then open up a commanding lead with 41 points in the third period, 11 by Pettit.

1957

Boston Garden, Boston, Massachusetts
Tuesday, January 15, 1957
East 109, West 97
Coaches: West—Bobby Wanzer, Rochester; East—Red Auerbach, Boston
Most Valuable Player: Bob Cousy
Officials: Mendy Rudolph, Sid Borgia
Attendance: 11,178

	1	2	3	4	Total
West	26	17	23	31	97
East	18	23	33	35	109

The All-Star Game was back where it started, in Boston, and a pair of Celtics were the stars of a 109-97 win. Once again, it was the backcourt duo of Bob Cousy and Bill Sharman that provided the highlights, none bigger than a long pass Sharman attempted for Cousy in the first quarter. With the East trailing, 18-14, Sharman unleashed a one-handed, full-court pass for his teammate. The pass was too high for Cousy to reach, but it didn't matter; the ball went through the hoop for a 70-foot basket for Sharman.

It was Cousy, however, who was voted MVP for the game, primarily for his playmaking. Cousy fed Neil Johnston for three baskets in the third quarter, helping Johnston to score 15 points in the period and put the East in front. Cousy also thrilled the hometown fans with some behind-the-back dribbling and his usual dazzling display of ambidextrous ballhandling.

The preliminary for this year's All-Star Game was to be a prelude for an event at later contests—an old-timers' game, featuring such former stars as Bob Davies, Bones McKinney, and Al Cervi.

1958

St. Louis Arena, St. Louis, Missouri
Tuesday, January 21, 1958
East 130, West 118
Coaches: East—Red Auerbach, Boston; West—Alex Hannum, St. Louis
Most Valuable Player: Bob Pettit
Officials: Jim Duffy, Arnie Heft
Attendance: 12,854

	1	2	3	4	Total
East	30	31	31	38	130
West	31	35	25	27	118

Bob Cousy had another strong All-Star performance, scoring 16 points in the second half to lead the East to a 130-118 victory. While Cousy led the comeback, it was Paul Arizin of the Philadelphia Warriors who kept the East in the game in the opening quarters, scoring 15 first-half points. Dolph Schayes of Syracuse scored 18 points for the East with many of his points on "rainmakers," long set shots of more than 30 feet.

However, it was the West's Bob Pettit who won the game's MVP award, becoming the first player from the losing team to receive the honor. Playing with a cast on his left wrist, Pettit set All-Star Game records by scoring 28 points and grabbing 26 rebounds. Bill Russell, the defensive standout from the Boston Celtics, had little success in stopping Pettit in the first half (the St. Louis star has 17 of his 28 points in the half) and had little opportunity to do so in the second half, sitting on the bench for a lengthy period after picking up his fifth foul late in the third quarter.

The East led by 107-106 in the fourth quarter when Slater Martin of the St. Louis Hawks suffered a pulled muscle in his thigh and had to leave the game (continuing a run of bad luck for Martin, who had had his car stolen from a hotel parking lot earlier in the day). Cousy then scored seven straight points for the East to open up the lead.

1959

The Olympia, Detroit, Michigan
Friday, January 23, 1959
West 124, East 108
Coaches: East—Red Auerbach, Boston; West—Ed Macauley, Boston
Most Valuable Players: Elgin Baylor and Bob Pettit
Officials: Jim Duffy, Mendy Rudolph
Attendance: 10,541

	1	2	3	4	Total
East	31	21	32	24	108
West	27	34	30	33	124

The West dominated the East throughout the game, establishing dominance outside, inside, and underneath the boards at both ends of the court as it won for the third time in nine All-Star Games. Bob Pettit won his third MVP award, although this time he had to share it with a player making his first All-Star appearance, rookie Elgin Baylor of the Minneapolis Lakers. Both of the frontcourt men were outstanding with Baylor producing 24 points and 11 rebounds and Pettit topping that with 25 points and 16 rebounds.

One defender who did relatively well against Pettit was John Kerr of the Syracuse Nationals. Kerr's defense helped the East pull to within 98-93 in the fourth quarter. However, Kerr came out for a rest and was replaced by Bill Russell. Pettit, who had little trouble scoring on Russell in the previous All-Star Game (as well as during the regular season, as he was averaging 32 points in games against Russell's Celtics), went to work and converted a pair of three-point plays within a 40-second span to open up an 11-point lead for the West.

1960

Convention Hall, Philadelphia, Pennsylvania
Friday, January 22, 1960
East 125, West 115
Coaches: West–Ed Macauley, St. Louis; East–Red Auerbach, Boston
Most Valuable Player: Wilt Chamberlain
Officials: Arnie Heft, Sid Borgia
Attendance: 10,421

	1	2	3	4	Total
West	26	25	30	34	115
East	25	33	33	34	125

In front of his home fans, rookie Wilt Chamberlain of the Philadelphia Warriors performed well on offense and even better on defense, leading the East to a 125-115 win. Chamberlain had 23 points and 25 rebounds and easily won the game's MVP award before a full house at Philadelphia's Convention Hall.

Bill Russell—burned the last two years by Bob Pettit—also turned in a strong defensive game. As for Pettit, the St. Louis sharpshooter connected on only 4 of 15 shots from the field and finished with just 11 points. Jack Twyman of the Cincinnati Royals led all scorers with 27 points.

1961

Onondaga County War Memorial Auditorium, Syracuse, New York
Tuesday, January 17, 1961
West 153, East 131
Coaches: West–Paul Seymour, St. Louis; East–Red Auerbach, Boston
Most Valuable Player: Oscar Robertson
Officials: Norm Drucker, Richie Powers
Attendance: 8,016

	1	2	3	4	Total
West	47	37	31	38	153
East	19	43	35	34	131

For the third year in a row, a rookie was one of the dominant players in the All-Star Game. This time it was Oscar Robertson of the Cincinnati Royals, who helped the West get off to a fast start and go onto a 153-131 win.

Elgin Baylor of the L.A. Lakers scored seven of the West's first 11 points. Then Robertson and Bob Pettit chipped in, and the West held a 47-19 lead after one quarter. The East came back during the second period but got no closer than 15 points. Robertson contributed on both ends, scoring points, dishing off, and leaping high to pull rebounds away from giants like Bill Russell and Wilt Chamberlain.

Robertson finished one rebound shy of a triple-double. In addition to his nine rebounds, he had 23 points and 14 assists, the latter an All-Star Game record, to win the MVP award.

1962

St. Louis Arena, St. Louis, Missouri
Tuesday, January 16, 1962
West 150, East 130
Coaches: East–Red Auerbach, Boston; West–Fred Schaus, Los Angeles
Most Valuable Player: Bob Pettit
Officials: Sid Borgia, Willie Smith
Attendance: 15,112

	1	2	3	4	Total
East	32	28	34	36	130
West	35	29	41	45	150

Held to only 12 points in the previous All-Star Game, Wilt Chamberlain exploded for 42 points, breaking the record of 29 set the year before by Bob Pettit. However, Pettit's West squad still came out on top, 150-130, and Pettit won the game's MVP award, the fourth time he either shared the honor or won it outright. Pettit had another great game on the boards, setting a record with 27 rebounds, and also scored 25 points. Elgin Baylor, on a short leave from military duty, led the West with 32 points. It was the West's fifth win in the last seven games.

1963

Los Angeles Sports Arena, Los Angeles, California
Wednesday, January 16, 1963
East 115, West 108
Coaches: East–Red Auerbach, Boston; West–Fred Schaus, Los Angeles
Most Valuable Player: Bill Russell
Officials: Sid Borgia, Earl Strom
Attendance: 14,838

	1	2	3	4	Total
East	32	24	24	35	115
West	25	25	23	35	108

Bill Russell had a great night on the boards, pulling down 24 rebounds in the game with 11 of them coming in the first period against a front line for the West that averaged nearly seven-feet tall. West coach Fred Schaus even moved Elgin Baylor to a guard position so that he would have Walt Bellamy, Bob Pettit, and Wilt Chamberlain (now in the Western Division since his team, the Warriors, had moved from Philadelphia to San Francisco) up front. However, Russell foiled the strategy as the East got off to a 32-25 lead in the quarter.

The contest remained even in the ensuing quarters, but the West was never able to overcome the lead the East established in the opening period. With Russell on the bench in the final period, the West scored nine points in 80 seconds to close the gap, bringing Russell back onto the floor to help guard the lead in the waning minutes.

1964

Boston Garden, Boston, Massachusetts
Tuesday, January 14, 1964
East 111, West 107
Coaches: West–Fred Schaus, Los Angeles; East–Red Auerbach, Boston
Most Valuable Player: Oscar Robertson
Officials: Sid Borgia, Mendy Rudolph
Attendance: 13,464

	1	2	3	4	Total
West	22	27	28	30	107
East	25	34	27	25	111

The All-Star Game was back in its original home, the Boston Garden. Pre-game ceremonies featured another old-timers' game as well as an appearance by the Original Celtics. And camera crews stood by, ready to broadcast the game to a national television audience.

Meanwhile, greater drama was taking place beneath the grandstands, where the All-Stars—tired of being put off in their attempts to establish a pension plan—aired their grievances with the owners and made an implicit threat to not play the game. Seven years before, a dispute over the pension plan had brought about a threatened strike of that game, also in Boston. Then, at the get-together of players and owners for the 1961 All-Star Game in Syracuse, preliminary details of a pension plan had been worked out between the players and owners. But three years later (and seven years after the original threat to strike), a pension plan was still not yet in place. As a result, the 20 All-Stars gathered in the East squad's dressing room and confronted Walter Kennedy, who had succeeded Maurice Podoloff as NBA president four months before. At 8:55 p.m., only five minutes before the teams were scheduled to be introduced, the players finally told Kennedy that they would play (never having actually said that they wouldn't, although implying such a threat with their actions).

The game itself was nearly as suspenseful as the dressing room negotiations, but only for the first 21 minutes. The East then went on an 11-2 run for a 59-49 lead at half-time. The East increased the margin to 18 in the third quarter, then held off a late run by the West to win, 111-107.

With 26 points, 14 rebounds, and eight assists, Oscar Robertson won his second All-Star Game MVP award. It was Robertson's fourth All-Star Game, and he was a member of the winning team in all of them, two for the East and two for the West (since his Cincinnati Royals were moved to the Eastern Division after the 1961-62 season).

1965

St. Louis Arena, St. Louis, Missouri
Wednesday, January 13, 1965
East 124, West 123
Coaches: East–Red Auerbach, Boston; West–Alex Hannum, San Francisco
Most Valuable Player: Jerry Lucas
Officials: Mendy Rudolph, Joe Gushue
Attendance: 16,713

	1	2	3	4	Total
East	36	39	32	17	124
West	27	34	30	32	123

Oscar Robertson played on a winning All-Star team for the fifth year in a row and led all players with 28 points. His Cincinnati Royals teammate, Jerry Lucas, had 25 points to go with 10 rebounds, enough to earn him the All-Star Game MVP award. The East, which held a 107-91 lead after three quarters, held off the West in the final period to win, 124-123.

But the biggest story came immediately after the game with the announcement that the San Francisco Warriors had traded Wilt Chamberlain had traded to the Philadelphia 76ers. Playing in his third game for the West (since the move of the Warriors from Philadelphia to San Francisco and the team's transfer from the Eastern to Western Division), Chamberlain led all players with 16 rebounds.

1966

Cincinnati Gardens, Cincinnati, Ohio
Tuesday, January 11, 1966
East 137, West 94
Coaches: West–Fred Schaus, Los Angeles; East–Red Auerbach, Boston
Most Valuable Player: Adrian Smith
Officials: Norm Drucker, John Vanak
Attendance: 13,653

	1	2	3	4	Total
West	18	18	32	26	94
East	33	30	38	36	137

The voting for the game's MVP was as lopsided as the game itself. But the recipient of the award was one of the least likely players on either squad to be the game's best player. Among a group of stars that included Rick Barry, Nate Thurmond, Wilt Chamberlain, and Oscar Robertson, it was Adrian Smith of the Cincinnati Royals who was the game's high scorer and the winner of the award, out-distancing runner-up Wilt Chamberlain by a vote of 37-1/3 to 3-1/3.

Smith entered the game with the East already ahead, 29-12. Shortly after, Jerry West went down with an eye injury—the victim of a Bill Russell elbow—leaving the

West squad with little chance of a comeback. East coach Red Auerbach then evened out the playing time among the 10 players on the team, allowing Smith a greater opportunity to shine. In addition to his 24 points, Smith had eight rebounds in 26 minutes as the East won, 137-94. For his performance, Smith received a Ford Galaxie convertible, to date the most expensive prize awarded for the MVP.

1967

Cow Palace, San Francisco, California
Tuesday, January 10, 1967
West 135, East 120
Coaches: East–Red Auerbach, Boston; West–Fred Schaus, Los Angeles
Most Valuable Player: Rick Barry
Officials: Willie Smith, Earl Strom
Attendance: 13,972

	1	2	3	4	Total
East	33	34	28	35	120
West	39	38	27	31	135

A pair of San Francisco Warriors—the host team for the All-Star Game—stood out as the West won for the first time since 1962, 135-120. Nate Thurmond had 18 rebounds to go with 16 points while Rick Barry scored 38 points. The duo combined for 23 points in the first quarter, helping the West to a six-point lead. Dave DeBusschere, the Detroit Pistons' player-coach, then took over in the second quarter. He hit on his first six attempts from the field and ended up with 22 in the game.

Wilt Chamberlain, slowed by an injury that left his starting status in doubt until just before game time, still had enough to have a big night on the boards, pulling down a game-high 22 rebounds.

1968

Madison Square Garden, New York, New York
Tuesday, January 23, 1968
East 144, West 124
Coaches: West–Bill Sharman, San Francisco; East–Alex Hannum, Philadelphia
Most Valuable Player: Hal Greer
Officials: Mendy Rudolph, Don Murphy
Attendance: 18,422

	1	2	3	4	Total
West	25	34	32	33	124
East	37	27	37	43	144

The Warriors who led the West to victory in 1967 were missing from this game. Nate Thurmond was recovering from knee surgery, and Rick Barry—the previous season's scoring champion and All-Star MVP—was lured away by the rival American Basketball Association (ABA). A court order required Barry to sit out a season before he could play in the new league, but it still meant he was absent from the NBA game.

Even without Thurmond, the West controlled the boards, with Clyde Lee of the San Francisco Warriors and Zelmo Beaty of the St. Louis Hawks leading the way with 11 and 10 rebounds, respectively. But the East was much more accurate in its shooting, hitting nearly 60 percent of its shots from the floor, and won, 144-124. Hal Greer of the Philadelphia 76ers scored 21 points in just 17 minutes and was named MVP.

The game, in New York, was to be played in the new Madison Square Garden, which should have been completed by this time. However, the new arena was still a month away from being ready, and the old Madison Square Garden was the site for the game, which drew a crowd in excess of 18,000, a record for the All-Star Game.

1969

Baltimore Civic Center, Baltimore, Maryland
Tuesday, January 14, 1969
East 123, West 112
Coaches: West–Richie Guerin, Atlanta; East–Gene Shue, Baltimore
Most Valuable Player: Oscar Robertson
Officials: Joe Gushue, Norm Drucker
Attendance: 12,348

	1	2	3	4	Total
West	19	34	30	29	112
East	35	25	26	37	123

Oscar Robertson, who scored 26 points to win his third All-Star MVP award, was at his best in the fourth quarter. His basket and free throw put the East ahead, 97-96, and he converted on another three-point play shortly after to give his squad a 101-96 margin. A few minutes later, he made a spectacular pass to Baltimore's Gus Johnson, who was fouled and made his free throws to give the East an 11-point cushion.

Johnson was one of three Baltimore Bullets to score in double figures before the home fans. Johnson finished with 13 points, while Earl Monroe had 21, and Wes Unseld 11 points to go with eight rebounds.

1970

The Spectrum, Philadelphia, Pennsylvania
Tuesday, January 20, 1970
East 142, West 135
Coaches: West–Richie Guerin, Atlanta; East–Red Holzman, New York
Most Valuable Player: Willis Reed
Officials: Richie Powers, Jack Madden
Attendance: 15,244

	1	2	3	4	Total
West	21	38	26	50	135
East	36	35	35	36	142

Willis Reed had 21 points and 11 rebounds to win the MVP award. The Knicks' center was most effective early, leading the East to a 24-13 lead before being relieved by rookie Lew Alcindor of the Milwaukee Bucks. With the West struggling to deal with Alcindor's size, the East went on an 11-0 run and held a 15-point lead at the end of the first quarter.

The West fought back late in the second quarter, however, with Elvin Hayes, Bill Bridges, and Elgin Baylor scoring the last eight baskets of the half. A 10-1 spurt to start the second half pulled the West to within five points. The West stayed close until later in the third quarter when John Havlicek of the Boston Celtics scored nine straight points, helping the East open up a lead so large that even a 50-point explosion by the West in the fourth quarter wasn't enough to overcome it.

1971

International Sports Arena, San Diego, California
Tuesday, January 12, 1971
West 108, East 107
Coaches: East–Red Holzman, New York; West–Larry Costello, Milwaukee
Most Valuable Player: Lenny Wilkens
Officials: Mendy Rudolph, Ed T. Rush
Attendance: 14,378

	1	2	3	4	Total
East	26	34	23	24	107
West	30	32	20	26	108

Playing for the West squad after a realignment of the league put his Milwaukee Bucks in the Western Division, Lew Alcindor took a pass from Jerry West and hit a fallway jumper to break a 105-105 tie with less than a minute remaining in the game. Alcindor was fouled on the play by Gus Johnson and converted the free throw to give the West a three-point lead with 48 seconds left to play. JoJo White scored on a putback with 26 seconds to play to pull the East within one, but the West ran down the shot clock before Elvin Hayes fired a jumper that bounced high off the rim, high enough that the game was over by the time it came down.

Lenny Wilkens, the player-coach for the Seattle SuperSonics, scored 12 points in the second quarter and finished with 21 points to win the MVP trophy.

1971–NBA vs. ABA

The Astrodome, Houston, Texas
Friday, May 28, 1971
NBA 125, ABA 120
Coaches: NBA–Bill Russell (former NBA player-coach);
ABA–Larry Brown (former ABA coach)
Most Valuable Player: Walt Frazier
Attendance: 16,364

	1	2	3	4	Total
NBA	33	33	25	34	125
ABA	33	31	25	31	120

Walt Frazier came off the bench and hit six-of-seven field goal attempts in the first half, helping to offset early shooting problems by his teammates, and Elvin Hayes hit a basket at the buzzer to give the NBA a two-point lead at half-time. The game stayed close through the second half, and the NBA held only a 121-120 lead until Oscar Robertson and then Frazier each hit a pair of free throws to put the game out of reach. Frazier scored 26 points in the game and was named MVP.

The game was played for the benefit of the Whitney Young Foundation and the players' pension funds. Lew Alcindor, who had just led his Milwaukee Bucks to the NBA title, missed the game after being married that morning. Alcindor had planned to fly in from Washington, where the wedding was held, but then changed his mind, citing his Islamic faith, which prohibited him from playing so soon after the wedding.

1972

The Forum, Inglewood, California
Tuesday, January 18, 1972
West 112, East 110
Coaches: East–Tom Heinsohn, Boston; West–Bill Sharman, Los Angeles
Most Valuable Player: Jerry West
Officials: Darell Garretson, Manny Sokol
Attendance: 17,214

	1	2	3	4	Total
East	33	31	20	26	110
West	27	27	33	25	112

Poor free-throw shooting by the West allowed the East to stay close in the fourth quarter, but Jerry West made up for his mates' woes at the foul line. He stole the ball or deflected passes five times in the final eight minutes, and he put the West up by nine points with a steal and layup with just under three minutes to play. But the East battled back and tied the score on a jumper by Dave Cowens with 11 seconds to play.

After the first inbounds pass was knocked away, the West inbounded again, getting the ball to West, who came upcourt with Walt Frazier shadowing him. When he reached the top of the key, West unleashed a 21-footer that was good to give the West a 112-110 lead with a second to go. The late heroics made West the game's MVP with Connie Hawkins of the Phoenix Suns a close second.

1972–NBA vs. ABA

Nassau Coliseum, Uniondale, New York
Thursday, May 25, 1972
NBA 106, ABA 104
Coaches: NBA–Elgin Baylor (former NBA player); ABA–Al Bianchi, Virginia Squires
Most Valuable Player: Bob Lanier
Officials: John Vanak, Joe Gushue
Attendance: 14,086

	1	2	3	4	Total
NBA	21	29	33	23	106
ABA	30	26	25	23	104

Threats of fines and suspensions kept some NBA players away, but many defied the owners and showed up to play the ABA All-Stars before a sizable crowd at the home of the New York Nets on Long Island. It was another exciting game between the two leagues. Rick Barry of the Nets sank a three-pointer (the second half of the game was played with the ABA's rule of awarding three points for a field goal of 25 feet or longer) to pull the ABA to within a point with 13 seconds left. The ABA then fouled Archie Clark of Baltimore, sending him to the line. Clark made the first and missed the second, setting off a scramble for the rebound. Barry came away with the ball, raced across the mid-court line, and unleashed a 40-footer as the buzzer sounded. His shot would have been worth three points and a victory, but it fell short and the NBA narrowly won for the second year in a row.

1973

Chicago Stadium, Chicago, Illinois
Tuesday, January 23, 1973
East 104, West 84
Coaches: East–Tom Heinsohn, Boston; West–Bill Sharman, Los Angeles
Most Valuable Player: Dave Cowens
Officials: Richie Powers, Jake O'Donnell
Attendance: 17,527

	1	2	3	4	Total
East	27	23	26	28	104
West	27	18	20	19	84

The biggest cheers at Chicago Stadium during the 1973 All-Star Game came in the third quarter when the crowd was told of President Nixon's announcement of a cease-fire in Vietnam. Even a good game may not have competed with that news, but this one was anything but good. Lackadaisical defense couldn't outdo poor shooting and sloppy passing in producing a low-scoring contest. The West's 84 points were the fewest scored in an All-Star Game since the shot clock was introduced, and the East's 104 points were the lowest total for a winning team since 1955, the first season of the shot clock.

Dave Cowens and Elvin Hayes did stand out, both producing double figures in scoring and rebounding for the East. Spencer Haywood did the same for the West. Cowens, who sparked a third-quarter rally that broke a 57-57 tie and put the East up by 12, was named the game's MVP.

1974

Seattle Center Coliseum, Seattle, Washington
Tuesday, January 15, 1974
West 134, East 123
Coaches: East–Tom Heinsohn, Boston; West–Larry Costello, Milwaukee
Most Valuable Player: Bob Lanier
Officials: Don Murphy, Bob Rakel
Attendance: 14,360

	1	2	3	4	Total
East	29	18	38	38	123
West	39	27	35	33	134

The West opened up a 25-point lead in the second quarter, but the East got back into the game with a 14-0 run to start the second half. The West regrouped and built the lead back to 16 at the end of the third quarter. Once again, the East cut into the lead, coming as close as three points with 3:20 left in the game.

It was at this point that Bob Lanier, with some clutch shooting, earned his MVP award for the game. Lanier was assisted in this final stretch by Kareem Abdul-Jabbar, who contributed a key rebound and basket with a minute to go.

Lanier had 24 points and 10 rebounds and edged out Spencer Haywood of the host-team Seattle SuperSonics, who had 23 points and 11 rebounds, in the MVP balloting.

1975

Veterans Memorial Coliseum, Phoenix, Arizona
Tuesday, January 14, 1975
East 108, West 102
Coaches: East–K. C. Jones, Boston; West–Al Attles, Golden State
Most Valuable Player: Walt Frazier
Officials: Mendy Rudolph, Jerry Loeber
Attendance: 12,885

	1	2	3	4	Total
East	29	22	32	25	108
West	29	17	27	29	102

Walt Frazier of the New York Knicks scored 18 of his game-high 30 points in the second half to win the MVP Award as the East defeated the West, 108-102. Frazier and John Havlicek helped the East carry a comfortable lead into the final period, after a West rally—led by Nate Archibald, Rick Barry, and Kareem Abdul-Jabbar—in the third quarter had cut an 11-point East lead down to five points.

1976

The Spectrum, Philadelphia, Pennsylvania
Tuesday, February 3, 1976
East 123, West 109
Coaches: West–Al Attles, Golden; East–Tom Heinsohn, Boston
Most Valuable Player: Dave Bing
Officials: Paul Mihalak, Darell Garretson
Attendance: 17,511

	1	2	3	4	Total
West	23	27	30	29	109
East	28	17	38	40	123

Dave Bing scored all of his 16 points in the second half as the East came back to defeat the West, 123-109. Thought by some to be unworthy as one of the representatives in the game, Bing—who made seven of 11 shots from the floor and both of his attempts from the free-throw line—was named MVP.

Kareem Abdul-Jabbar led the West with 22 points and 15 rebounds.

1977

Milwaukee Arena, Milwaukee, Wisconsin
Sunday, February 13, 1977
West 125, East 124
Coaches: West–Larry Brown, Denver; East–Gene Shue, Philadelphia
Most Valuable Player: Julius Erving
Officials: Earl Strom and Lee Jones
Attendance: 10,938

	1	2	3	4	Total
West	23	35	39	28	125
East	34	34	21	35	124

The first All-Star Game following the merger of the NBA and ABA, this contest was a showcase for one of the ABA's greatest stars, Julius Erving. Erving scored 30 points in 30 minutes—several on dunks—and scored 13 in the final quarter in leading an East comeback that just fell short. Erving's first dunk of the night was a jam over 7-foot-2 Kareem Abdul-Jabbar that followed a rush down the floor and thrilled the fans in Milwaukee Arena. In addition to his 30 points, Erving was the game's leading rebounder with 12.

Bob McAdoo of the Buffalo Braves also had 30 points to go with 10 rebounds, with 14 of his points in the final quarter. Trailing by a point, the East had a chance to win, but Paul Westphal of the Phoenix Suns stole the ball from Pete Maravich of the New Orleans Jazz with six seconds to play.

1978

The Omni, Atlanta
Sunday, February 5, 1978
East 133, West 125
Coaches: West–Jack Ramsay, Portland; East–Billy Cunningham, Philadelphia
Most Valuable Player: Randy Smith
Officials: Jake O'Donnell, Jim Capers
Attendance: 15,491

	1	2	3	4	Total
West	39	27	34	25	125
East	28	29	35	41	133

John Havlicek was a late replacement for the East team, added to the squad by NBA Commissioner Larry O'Brien and inserted in the starting lineup when Doug Collins—who had been picked to start by his coach with the Philadelphia 76ers, Billy Cunningham—asked Havlicek to start in his place. Havlicek justified the selection by scoring six of the East's first eight points. However, it was Randy Smith, a guard with the Buffalo Braves, who came off the bench and helped the East stay in the game in the first half. Smith connected on a pair of long shots at the close of the first and second quarters.

Still down by eight points after three quarters, the East exploded for 41 points in the final period with Smith leading the charge. He scored eight straight points in the quarter and finished with 27 points, earning him the MVP award. In addition to outshooting the West, 62 percent to 39 percent, in the fourth quarter, the East dominated the boards, outrebounding the West by 18-7 in the final period.

1979

Silverdome, Pontiac, Michigan
Sunday, February 4, 1979
West 134, East 129
Coaches: West–Lenny Wilkens, Seattle; East–Dick Motta, Washington
Most Valuable Player: David Thompson
Officials: John Vanak, Jack Madden, Hugh Evans
Attendance: 31,745

	1	2	3	4	Total
West	36	44	24	30	134
East	27	31	40	31	129

A matchup of former ABA stars—David Thompson and Julius Erving—was a highlight of the 1979 All-Star Game. Thompson won the battle, helping the East build an 80-58 half-time lead with 14 points in the first half, none more spectacular than a thundering dunk he made after stealing the ball from Erving late in the second quarter. Thompson finished the game with 25 points and outplayed Erving, who had 29 points and eight rebounds, in the MVP balloting. Two other stars from the ABA stood out. George McGinnis—Thompson's teammate with the Denver Nuggets—had 16 points and six rebounds and also challenged Thompson for the MVP award. George Gervin of the San Antonio Spurs, who combined with Erving to help the East get back into the game in the third quarter, finished with 26 points.

1980

Capital Centre, Landover, Maryland
Sunday, February 3, 1980
East 144, West 136, Overtime
Coaches: West–Lenny Wilkens, Seattle; East–Billy Cunningham, Philadelphia
Most Valuable Player: George Gervin
Officials: Joe Gushue, Ed T. Rush
Attendance: 19,035

	1	2	3	4	OT	Total
West	37	27	27	37	8	136
East	28	36	44	20	16	144

George Gervin—en route to his third straight NBA scoring title—scored 34 points to lead the East to a 144-136 overtime win in a game short on defense but long on street basketball at its best. Gervin, the game's MVP, did his finest work in the third quarter, when the East scored 44 points to turn a half-time tie into a 17-point lead. He scored 11 points in a seven-minute stretch that featured an acrobatic reverse layup, a bank shot, and a rebound and tip-in. The West came back in the fourth quarter, tying the game, falling behind again, and retying it when Paul Westphal took a pass from Magic Johnson and buried an 18-foot jumper with 26 seconds left in the period. Larry Bird failed to win it in regulation time for the East when he missed an open shot with five seconds left, but he led the way in the overtime period with five points. Bird broke a 134-134 tie with a 21-foot jump shot with two minutes to play and then hit a three-point shot to open up the lead.

1981

The Coliseum, Richfield, Ohio
Sunday, February 1, 1981
East 123, West 120
Coaches: West–John MacLeod, Phoenix; East–Billy Cunningham, Philadelphia
Most Valuable Player: Nate Archibald
Officials: Paul Mihalak, Darell Garretson
Attendance: 20,239

	1	2	3	4	Total
West	27	31	30	32	120
East	23	38	36	26	123

With Nate "Tiny" Archibald of the Boston Celtics directing the offense, the East designed plays rather than just relying on one-on-one freelancing, the normal sight in an All-Star Game, and defeated the West by a score of 123-120. For his playmaking, which included nine assists, Archibald beat out Boston teammate, Robert Parish, who had 16 points and 10 rebounds, for the MVP award.

Archibald was at his best in the final periods, helping the East to build a sizable lead in the third quarter and then helping to maintain a dwindling lead in the fourth quarter. Archibald's driving lay up through the lane gave the East a 121-116 lead with a little over two minutes to play. The West came back and had a chance to send it into overtime, but Jack Sikma's three-point attempt bounced off the rim as the final horn sounded.

1982

Meadowlands Arena, East Rutherford, New Jersey
Sunday, January 31, 1982
East 120, West 118
Coaches: West–Pat Riley, Los Angeles; East–Bill Fitch, Boston
Most Valuable Player: Larry Bird
Officials: Jake O'Donnell, Wally Rooney
Attendance: 20,149

	1	2	3	4	Total
West	39	22	28	29	118
East	34	29	27	30	120

Celtics and Lakers were prominent in this game. Boston coach Bill Fitch, who directed the East squad, diagrammed plays to be run by Nate Archibald for fellow Celtics Robert Parish and Larry Bird. West coach Pat Riley countered with his Los Angeles stars, Magic Johnson, Kareem Abdul-Jabbar, and Norm Nixon. In the end, it was the Boston connection that prevailed, in part because of a miserable shooting performance by Abdul-Jabbar. Playing without the goggles that protected his eyes (forgotten in his hotel room across the Hudson River in New York City), Abdul-Jabbar missed his first eight shots and made only one of 10 in the game.

Bird, on the other hand, had the range. Midway through the fourth quarter he tied the game at 111 with a jumper from the top of the key, and then buried another from the same spot a half-minute later to put the East ahead. Another basket from the same area with 2:37 left made the score 118-114 in favor of the East, and a pair of free throws made the score 120-116 with 1:37 to play. Nixon countered with a jumper to cut the gap to two as the quarter entered its final minute. The West had chances to tie or take the lead but Gus Williams of Seattle missed a three-point attempt with eight seconds left, and Johnson—who looked to pass to Abdul-Jabbar but found the big man covered—kept the ball and drove to the basket, only to miss with two seconds left.

Bird finished with 19 points and 12 rebounds and was the game's MVP.

1983

The Forum, Los Angeles, California
Sunday, February 13, 1983
East 132, West 123
Coaches: East–Billy Cunningham, Philadelphia; West–Pat Riley, Los Angeles
Most Valuable Player: Julius Erving
Officials: Hugh Evans, Jess Kersey
Attendance: 17,505

	1	2	3	4	Total
East	42	27	34	29	132
West	31	33	26	33	123

Julius Erving dazzled the fans throughout the game with the greatest show coming in the third quarter, when he scored 11 points in under eight minutes. He started with a pair of dunks (one turning into a three-point play when he was fouled by Artis Gilmore) and then hit a bank shot and a 14-foot jumper. He added two more points before sitting down with just over four minutes left in the quarter, helping the East turn a 69-64 half-time lead into a 19-point margin.

Isiah Thomas, who finished as runner-up to Erving in the MVP balloting, was the star of the first half, coming up with eight points in the first quarter and four more before half-time. Thomas finished with 19 points and seven assists. Sidney Moncrief of the Milwaukee Bucks added 20 points, using his head, literally, for two of them. After a loose ball bounced off Moncrief's noggin and into the basket, East coach Billy Cunningham referred to "Moncrief's impersonation of Pele" as "the play of the game."

1984

McNichols Sports Arena, Denver, Colorado
Sunday, January 29, 1984
East 154, West 145, Overtime
Coaches: East–K. C. Jones, Boston; West–Frank Layden, Utah
Most Valuable Player: Isiah Thomas
Officials: Earl Strom, John Vanak
Attendance: 17,500

	1	2	3	4	OT	Total
East	32	30	37	33	22	154
West	40	36	31	25	13	145

A number of offensive records fell as the East outlasted the West in the third overtime game in NBA All-Star history. The West's 154 points set a new record, as did the 299 points combined by both teams. Magic Johnson broke his own All-Star mark, set two year before, with 22 assists, 13 of them in the first half. Johnson's teammate from the Lakers, Kareem Abdul-Jabbar, also had a big game with 25 points and 15 rebounds.

But the real standouts were East stars Julius Erving and Isiah Thomas. Thomas—who finished with 21 points (all scored in the second half and overtime) and 15 assists—beat out Erving, who ended up with a game-high 34 points, in initial MVP balloting, which was taken with four minutes remaining in regulation time and the East ahead by nine. But the West came back and tied the game on a bank shot by Johnson with 20 seconds left to send it into overtime.

As the East outscored the West, 22-13, in overtime, a new MVP ballot was taken with Thomas again prevailing over Erving. Ten of Thomas's points came in the third quarter as he helped the East whittle away at a 14-point West half-time lead.

The event also marked the beginning of the NBA's All-Star Weekend as an old-timers' game and slam-dunk contest were held the day before the game. In the dunk contest, Larry Nance of the Phoenix Suns executed a windmill dunk with balls in each hand to defeat Julius Erving and Dominique Wilkins.

1985

Hoosier Dome, Indianapolis, Indiana
Sunday, February 10, 1985
West 140, East 129
Coaches: East–K. C. Jones, Boston; West–Pat Riley, Los Angeles Lakers
Most Valuable Player: Ralph Sampson
Officials: Mike Mathis, Ed T. Rush
Attendance: 43,146

	1	2	3	4	Total
West	40	28	29	43	140
East	35	33	24	37	129

The first All-Star Game in a domed stadium produced a record crowd of 43,146 in Indianapolis. In what he described as a "playground game," Ralph Sampson of the Houston Rockets scored 24 points and grabbed 10 rebounds to win the MVP award as he led the West to a 140-129 win. But it was the playground moves that brought the biggest cheers in the Hoosier Dome—Julius Erving with a cradle dunk, Magic Johnson with a pass that was spectacular even beyond his usual standards, and George Gervin with a basket on a 15-foot shot from the hip.

Johnson finished the game with 15 assists and 21 points and was runner-up to Sampson in the MVP balloting. Detroit's Isiah Thomas scored 17 points in the first half, including a three-point shot that tied the game at the half. However, Thomas also caught a knee in the thigh shortly before his game-tying three-pointer and played little in the second half, finishing the game with 22 points.

1986

Reunion Arena, Dallas, Texas
Sunday, February 9, 1986
East 129, West 132
Coaches: East–K. C. Jones, Boston; West–Pat Riley, Los Angeles Lakers
Most Valuable Player: Isiah Thomas
Officials: Joe Crawford, Jack Madden
Attendance: 16,573

	1	2	3	4	Total
East	34	35	31	39	139
West	36	30	36	30	132

With the East trailing, 126-121, midway through the fourth quarter, East coach K.C. Jones decided to go with a one-guard offense. The strategy paid off as he teamed Isiah Thomas with four big men—Buck Williams, Moses Malone, Larry Bird, and Moses Malone. It was a lethal combination at both ends of the court. The added height helped the East dominate the boards in the closing minutes and outscore the West by an 18-6 margin. Thomas put the East ahead to stay with two free throws. He finished with 30 points and 10 assists to win his second All-Star MVP award.

1987

Kingdome, Seattle, Washington
Sunday, February 8, 1987
West 154, East 149, Overtime
Coaches: East–K. C. Jones, Boston; West–Pat Riley, Los Angeles Lakers
Most Valuable Player: Tom Chambers
Officials: Jess Kersey, Hue Hollins
Attendance: 34,275

	1	2	3	4	OT	Total
East	33	32	42	33	9	149
West	29	41	30	40	14	154

Tom Chambers of the Seattle SuperSonics had the chance to perform before the home fans when he was added to the West roster after an injury to Houston's Ralph Sampson the week before the game. Chambers sparked a comeback for the West, scoring 14 of his game-high 34 points in the fourth quarter to help send the game into overtime. He added four more in the extra period and was named MVP.

Moses Malone of the Washington Bullets had 27 points and 18 rebounds, including a tip-in with three seconds left in regulation time to put the East in front, 140-138. However, Rolando Blackman of Dallas—who finished with 29 points and was runner-up to Chambers in the MVP balloting—sank a pair of free throws with no time on the clock to force overtime.

1988

Chicago Stadium, Chicago, Illinois
Sunday, February 7, 1988
East 138, West 133
Coaches: West–Pat Riley, Los Angeles Lakers; East–Mike Fratello, Atlanta
Most Valuable Player: Michael Jordan
Officials: Darell Garretson, Jake O'Donnell
Attendance: 18,403

	1	2	3	4	Total
West	32	22	35	44	133
East	27	33	39	39	138

With the game in Chicago, the East players did all they could to get the ball in the hands of the Bulls' sensational shooting guard, Michael Jordan. Jordan did his part, scoring 40 points to lead the East to a 138-133 win. Jordan, who had won the slam dunk contest the day before, had 24 points but was in foul trouble and on the bench when the fourth quarter began. As the West began cutting into the East lead, coach Mike Fratello responded to the chants of "We want Michael" and put Jordan back into the game. Jordan responded with 16 points to secure the East victory, hitting his 40th point with 25 seconds left in the game. He missed a chance to tie Wilt Chamberlain's All-Star record of 42 points when he ignored a pass from Larry Bird with five seconds left, laughing as he watched the ball sail out-of-bounds. (Jordan and Fratello later said they were unaware of what the record was.) Jordan had eight rebounds, four steals, four blocked shots, and three assists to go with his 40 points.

1989

Astrodome, Houston, Texas
Sunday, February 12, 1989
West 143, East 134
Coaches: East–Lenny Wilkens, Cleveland; West–Pat Riley, Los Angeles Lakers
Most Valuable Player: Karl Malone
Officials: Hugh Evans, Dick Bavetta, Bill Saar
Attendance: 44,735

	1	2	3	4	Total
East	31	28	37	38	134
West	47	40	24	32	143

Coming up with 87 points in the first half, the West opened up a huge lead and then held on in the final two quarters to win, 143-134, before an All-Star Game record crowd in the Astrodome in Houston. Karl Malone of the Utah Jazz scored 18 of his 28 points in the big first half. Malone's Utah teammate, John Stockton, had 17 assists, nine in the first quarter, as he carried the load at point guard with Magic Johnson missing because of a partially torn hamstring.

1990

Miami Arena, Miami, Florida
Sunday, February 11, 1990
East 130, West 113
Coaches: West–Pat Riley, Los Angeles Lakers; East–Chuck Daly, Detroit
Most Valuable Player: Magic Johnson
Officials: Earl Strom, Bill Oakes, Paul Mihalak
Attendance: 14,810

	1	2	3	4	Total
West	23	29	31	30	113
East	40	25	35	30	130

The East was good on offense and even better on defense, opening up a 17-point lead after holding the West to a shooting percentage of 38% in the first quarter, and cruising to a 130-113 win. The only offense the West could muster came from Magic Johnson, who had 22 points to go with six rebounds and four assists as he became only the third member of the losing team to win the MVP award in the NBA All-Star Game.

1991

Charlotte Coliseum, Charlotte, North Carolina
Sunday, February 10, 1991
East 116, West 114
Coaches: West–Rick Adelman, Portland; East–Chris Ford, Boston
Most Valuable Player: Charles Barkley
Officials: Ed T. Rush, Mike Mathis, Lee Jones
Attendance: 23,530

	1	2	3	4	Total
West	23	35	34	22	114
East	22	45	27	22	116

The 1991 All-Star Game was a sloppy contest—with the teams combining for 51 turnovers—and one that ended with a gaffe by Utah's Karl Malone in the closing seconds. With the East leading, 116-114, Kevin Johnson of the Phoenix Suns put up a three-point attempt that had a chance win the game for the West. The shot looked true to many observers, but not to Malone, who tried to help the ball along as it came down and was called for offensive goaltending with 2.9 seconds left, taking away the West's last chance at victory.

On the positive side, Michael Jordan had 26 points, and Charles Barkley grabbed 22 rebounds, the highest total in 24 years. Barkley was the game's MVP.

1992

Orlando Arena, Orlando, Florida
Sunday, February 9, 1992
West 153, East 113
Coaches: West–Don Nelson, Golden State; East–Phil Jackson, Chicago
Most Valuable Player: Earvin "Magic" Johnson
Officials: Darell Garretson, Joe Crawford, Tommy Nunez
Attendance: 14,272

	1	2	3	4	Total
West	44	35	36	38	153
East	31	24	28	30	113

Magic Johnson stunned the basketball world with his announcement that he was infected with H.I.V. in November 1991 and retiring from the game as a result. However, his name was already on the ballot for the All-Star Game, and fans voted him into the starting lineup for the West. Johnson not only played in the game, he sparkled. With 25 points and nine assists, Johnson won the MVP award in the only game he played in the 1991-92 season.

It was an emotional event, and, following the pre-game introductions, the entire East roster walked to the other side of the court and embraced Johnson. The warm feelings continued through the game and ended with Magic in a pair of good-natured one-on-one duels in the final minute. With the West in command and the ball in the hands of the East's Isiah Thomas, Johnson signaled his friend to try and drive on him. Thomas dribbled between his legs and behind his back, then moved toward the basket and tried a jumper with Johnson contesting him. The shot missed. A few seconds later, Johnson went one-on-one with Michael Jordan, who had better luck, giving Johnson a head fake and then sinking a jump shot. Johnson still had the final highlight, though, making an off-balance three-pointer to cap a memorable event.

1993

Delta Center, Salt Lake City, Utah
Sunday, February 21, 1993
West 135, East 132, Overtime
Coaches: East–Pat Riley, New York; West–Paul Westphal, Phoenix
Most Valuable Players: Karl Malone and John Stockton
Officials: Jack Madden, Hue Hollins, Bennett Salvatore
Attendance: 19,459

	1	2	3	4	OT	Total
West	27	30	29	33	16	135
East	26	26	32	35	13	132

Patrick Ewing forced overtime by first sinking a 15-foot hook shot to tie the game with eight seconds left in regulation and then harassing John Stockton into missing a shot that could have won it for the West. However, the West still prevailed in the extra period and won the game, 135-132.

Stockton and his Utah teammate, Karl Malone, were voted co-MVPs in front of their home fans in Salt Lake City. Stockton had 15 assists, nearly half of them to Malone, who scored 28 points in addition to pulling down 10 rebounds.

1994

Target Center, Minneapolis, Minnesota
Sunday, February 13, 1994
East 127, West 119
Coaches: East–Lenny Wilkens, Atlanta; West–George Karl, Seattle
Most Valuable Player: Scottie Pippen
Officials: Jake O'Donnell, Jess Kersey, Dan Crawford
Attendance: 17,096

	1	2	3	4	Total
East	33	39	29	26	127
West	28	36	26	28	118

The West seemed determined to not let second-year star Shaquille O'Neal have the spotlight. Although they were able to shut down the big man from the Orlando Magic, the overall strategy backfired and helped the East to a 127-118 win. With O'Neal drawing double- and sometimes triple-teams, he made only two of 12 shots from the field. But the crowd around O'Neal left others open on the perimeter, most notably Scottie Pippen of the Chicago Bulls, who sank nine of his 15 field goal attempts, with five of his baskets and nine of his attempts coming from beyond the three-point line.

Pippen's Chicago teammate, B. J. Armstrong, and Cleveland's Mark Price also found the range from outside as the East set an All-Star record with 10 three-pointers. In addition to his game-high 29 points, Pippen had 11 rebounds and was a unanimous choice as the game's MVP.

1995

America West Arena, Phoenix, Arizona
Sunday, February 12, 1995
West 139, East 112
Coaches: East–Brian Hill, Orlando; West–Paul Westphal, Phoenix
Most Valuable Player: Mitch Richmond
Officials: Dick Bavetta, Steve Javie, Jack Nies
Attendance: 18,755

	1	2	3	4	Total
East	28	28	25	31	112
West	31	41	32	35	139

Free of the over-attentive defense that plagued him the year before, Shaquille O'Neal unleashed a pair of thunderous dunks in the first quarter and went on to lead the East squad with 22 points. However, the rest of his mates were quieter and allowed the West to build up a sizable lead through the second and third quarters. With the outcome no longer in doubt in the final period, both teams relaxed, and O'Neal even provided comic relief with a three-point attempt—one that resembled a shot put more than a jump shot—that fell well short of the basket.

Mitch Richmond of the Sacramento Kings was terrific for the West, hitting 10 of 13 from the field, including three from three-point range. With his game-high 23 points, Richmond was voted MVP.

1996

Alamodome, San Antonio, Texas
Sunday, February 11, 1996
East 129, West 118
Coaches: East–Phil Jackson, Chicago; West–George Karl, Seattle
Most Valuable Player: Michael Jordan
Officials: Ed T. Rush, Ed Middleton, Ronnie Nunn
Attendance: 36,037

	1	2	3	4	Total
East	33	28	41	27	129
West	32	26	22	38	118

Shaquille O'Neal and Michael Jordan combined for 21 points in the third quarter—more than half of their squad's total—as the East opened up an insurmountable lead on its way to a 129-118 win. The West was able to bring the East lead down to eight points with four minutes to play, but Anfernee Hardaway of Orlando sank a pair of three-pointers to put the East back up by 14.

O'Neal and Jordan were outstanding throughout the game. O'Neal had 15 points and 10 rebounds, although he was edged out by Jordan, who had 20 points, in the MVP balloting.

1997

Gund Arena, Cleveland, Ohio
Sunday, February 9, 1997
East 132, West 120
Coaches: West–Rudy Tomjanovich, Houston; East–Doug Collins, Detroit
Most Valuable Player: Glen Rice
Officials: Hugh Evans, Ron Garretson, Bill Oakes
Attendance: 20,562

	1	2	3	4	Total
West	34	26	27	33	120
East	21	36	40	35	132

In the presence of greatness, the East defeated the West, 132-120, with Glen Rice of the Charlotte Hornets leading the charge, coming off the bench to score a game-high 26 points. The East battled back from 13 points down at the end of the first quarter and a deficit that reached 23 points midway through the second quarter. The East chipped away at the lead through the remainder of the half and then took charge by scoring 40 points in the third quarter, 20 of them by Rice.

Michael Jordan had a triple-double—the first in the history of the All-Star Game—with 14 points, 11 rebounds, and 11 assists. However, the game's MVP award went to Rice, who scored 24 of his 26 points in the second half.

The biggest highlight of the event, though, may have been at half-time with the introduction of the NBA's all-time team. Forty-seven of the league's 50 greatest players were present for the ceremonies. George Mikan, Oscar Robertson, and Wilt Chamberlain were among the legends from the past who were introduced with current stars on the all-time team, including several who were playing in the All-Star Game that day.

1998

Madison Square Garden, New York, New York
Sunday, February 8, 1998
East 135, West 114
Coaches: West–George Karl, Seattle; East–Larry Bird, Indiana
Most Valuable Player: Michael Jordan
Officials: Hue Hollins, Bernie Fryer, Bob Delaney
Attendance: 18,323

	1	2	3	4	Total
West	25	33	33	23	114
East	33	34	34	34	135

In his last All-Star appearance as a Bull, Michael Jordan again stood out. He scored 23 points in a 135-114 win and won the game's MVP award for the third time.

Challenging Jordan for the spotlight was the Los Angeles Lakers' 19-year-old Kobe Bryant, the youngest player ever to start in the All-Star Game. The two went head-to-head for much of the first three quarters with Bryant outscoring Jordan during that time, 18 to 17. However, the showdown ended when West coach George Karl kept Bryant on the bench the entire fourth quarter. Jordan then scored six points in the final period to finish with a game-high 23.

1999

Scheduled for Sunday, February 14, 1999 at the First Union Center, Philadelphia, Pennsylvania.
Game not played because of the lockout of the players by the owners.

2000

The Arena, Oakland, California
Sunday, February 13, 2000
West 137, East 126
Coaches: East–Jeff Van Gundy, New York; Phil Jackson, Los Angeles Lakers
Most Valuable Players: Shaquille O'Neal and Tim Duncan
Officials: Joe Crawford, Terry Durham, Joe Forte
Attendance: 18,325

	1	2	3	4	Total
East	26	33	38	29	126
West	33	31	35	38	137

The 2000 All-Star game got off to a roaring start with a pair of early dunks by Toronto's Vince Carter, who had won the slam-dunk contest the day before. The game then settled down a bit before reverting to a show-time atmosphere in the third quarter, when Shaquille O'Neal performed a 360-degree dunk and Jason Kidd threw an alley-oop pass that turned into a basket when it banked in off the glass.

Playing more conventionally, Tim Duncan and Kevin Garnett paced the West with 24 points apiece, and each reached double figures in rebounds to help lead the West to a 137-126 victory. O'Neal chipped in with 22 points, and Kidd had 14 assists for the West.

Allen Iverson of the Philadelphia 76ers led all players with 26 points and also had nine assists.

2001

MCI Center, Washington, D. C.
Sunday, February 11, 2001
West 137, East 126
Coaches: East–Rick Adelman, Sacramento; Larry Brown, Philadelphia
Most Valuable Player: Allen Iverson
Officials: Dan Crawford, Don Vaden, Eddie F. Rush
Attendance: 20,374

	1	2	3	4	Total
West	30	31	28	21	110
East	17	33	20	41	111

Through three quarters, the West dominated the 2001 All-Star Game and took a 19-point lead into the final period. But led by Allen Iverson, Dikembe Mutombo, and Stephon Marbury, the East roared back for a 111-110 win. Iverson scored 15 of his game-high 25 points in the game in the fourth quarter and earned MVP honors. It was the second year in a row that Iverson led all scorers in the All-Star Game.

Helped greatly by the rebounding of Mutombo, who had 22 rebounds in the game, the East went on a 26-5 run to tie the game at 100-100 with just over three minutes to play. Kevin Garnett quickly put the West back in front with a turnaround jumper from inside the lane. Iverson answered with a three-point basket to give the East its first lead of the game at 103-102. Chris Webber's jump shot put the West back in front by a point, but Iverson buried a pair of free throws, completing his scoring for the evening, to give the East a 105-104 lead. Kobe Bryant connected from the left side to put the West back in the lead and then hit another jumper for a three-point lead. But Marbury tied the game at 108 with a three-point basket with under a minute to play. The West went ahead, 110-108, as Bryant sank his third basket in a row. But Marbury took the inbounds pass, dribbled downcourt, penetrated the three-point line, then retreated to behind the line and launched a long shot over a leaping Jason Kidd. The shot was good, giving the East a 111-110 lead with 28.4 seconds left. The West tried to counter as time ran down, but Vince Carter got in Tim Duncan's face, forcing a bad shot as time ran out.

2002

First Union Center, Philadelphia
Sunday, February 10, 2002
West 135, East 120
Coaches: West–Don Nelson, Dallas; East–Byron Scott, New Jersey
Most Valuable Player: Kobe Bryant
Officials: Derrick Stafford, Bennett Salvatore, Jess Kersey
Attendance: 19,581

	1	2	3	4	Total
West	32	40	28	35	135
East	24	31	22	43	120

The 2002 All-Star Game was held in Philadelphia, and the fans were hoping for a big game from 76ers star Allen Iverson. Instead, it was Philly native Kobe Bryant, playing for the West squad, who earned the Most Valuable Player award. Bryant scored 31 points, hitting on 12 of 25 field goal attempts to go with a perfect night at the free-throw line in leading the West to a 135-120 win. Gary Payton led the long-range barrage, sinking four of the West's record 13 three-point baskets. Tim Duncan was the game's leading rebounder, pulling down 14 missed shots while contributing 14 points on the offensive end.

Meanwhile, Iverson never found his shooting touch, making just two of his nine attempts from the field and finishing with five points. In fact, none of the East starters hit double-digits in scoring, although Dikembe Mutombo did get 10 rebounds.

2003

Philips Arena, Atlanta
Sunday, February 9, 2003
West 155, East 145, Double Overtime
Coaches: West–Rick Adelman, Sacramento; East–Isiah Thomas, Indiana
Most Valuable Player: Kevin Garnett, Minnesota
Officials: Jim Clark, Luis Grillo, Ted Bernhardt
Attendance: 20,325

	1	2	3	4	OT	2OT	Total
West	18	37	31	34	18	17	155
East	23	29	41	27	18	7	145

Toronto Raptor Vince Carter gave up his starting spot for the East to allow Michael Jordan of the Washington Wizards to be in the starting lineup for Jordan's final All-Star Game. For the second straight year, Jordan couldn't connect on more than a third of his field-goal attempts. By putting up 27 shots, however, Jordan was able to combine his nine field goals with a pair of free throws for 20 points.

Jordan missed a 14-foot shot that could have won the game in regulation time, but he came through in the final seconds of the first overtime period, sinking a baseline jumper over Shawn Marion to put the East ahead, 138-136. Jason Kidd then deflected the West's inbound pass, chased down the ball and heaved a three-point shot from the right corner as Jermaine O'Neal crashed into him. Bryant's desperation shot missed, but O'Neal was called for a foul, sending Bryant to the line with a chance to win the game with only a second left in the period. Bryant made his first free throw but missed the second. He converted the third to tie the game and send it into a second overtime.

Kevin Garnett took control in the second overtime period, scoring nine of his game-high 37 points, giving the West a 10-point win and Garnett the award as the game's MVP.

Chapter 39

The Evolution of Basketball Records

By Bob Bellotti

The evolution of professional basketball's records reflects the changing of the game. For instance, rough play and overt fouling characterized the ponderous pace of games in the early 1950s. Playing without a shot clock, a team would build a lead and frequently then would stall, forcing the opposition to foul to get the ball back. So it was that Don Meineke of the Fort Wayne Pistons set a record in 1952-53 that still stands: he fouled out of 26 of the 68 games in which he appeared.

In 1954-55, the shot clock was introduced and fouling gave way to scoring. With the addition of scoring dynamos such as Bob Pettit, George Yardley, Paul Arizin, Elgin Baylor, Wilt Chamberlain, Oscar Robertson, and Jerry West, the NBA's scoring average zoomed in the 1950s and early 1960s. It rose by 49 percent, from 79.5 points per game in 1953-54 to a record 118.8 points per game in 1961-62.

Scoring leveled off throughout the '70s, but offenses became more efficient. Shooting accuracy increased to where the league average for field goal percentage was .485 in 1978-79, the season before the 3-point shot became law.

The new rule caused a predictable decline in field goal percentage; shots taken further from the basket meant less accuracy. As such, the 3-pointer was not embraced quickly. Teams used the long-range shot sparingly and only a few players, such as "Downtown" Freddie Brown of Seattle, took 3-pointers with any regularity. Brown led the league in 3-point percentage in 1979-80, and was the career 3-point percentage leader over the shot's first four seasons. By the mid 1980s, however, many coaches began employing the 3-pointer as a weapon. As more players took the shot more often, percentages began to climb.

At the same time, however, offenses became more cautious in other ways. Teams ran more set plays with multiple options and defenses adjusted correspondingly. Offensive plays took longer to unfold, running more seconds off the shot clock, and offensive execution became a paramount concern. The result was a scoring decline, and by 1989-90 the league average for points per game had plummeted to 95.6, the lowest mark since 1954-55, the first year of the shot clock. In 1998-99, a season shortened by the owners' lockout of the players, scoring dipped further, to 91.6 per game.

In fact, other than new records for 3-point shooting, no significant offensive single-season record has been broken in the past 13 years, since John Stockton accumulated 1,164 assists in 1990-91, breaking his own record set a season earlier.

Who is on the record-breaking horizon? Karl Malone. If the premier power forward, who signed with the Los Angeles

Vern Mikkelson, 1959
Working here against the Knicks' Whitey Bell, his DQ mark—the NBA's longest-standing record at 48 years—may never be broken.

Lakers for the 2003-04 season, plays another two or three years, he is likely to break the career standards for total games (Parish, 1,611) and minutes played (Abdul-Jabbar, 57,446), points scored (Abdul-Jabbar, 38,387), and field goals made (Abdul-Jabbar, 15,837) and attempted (Abdul-Jabbar, 28,307). Malone already holds the records for most free throws made and taken.

The Most Points in a Game

Over the years, NBA records have provided both astonishing singular moments—Wilt Chamberlain grabbing 55 rebounds in a game against Boston and Bill Russell—and remarkable feats of endurance—Robert Parish playing in a record 1,611 games, the equivalent of playing nearly 20 seasons without rest.

But perhaps the most charismatic achievement is that of single-game scoring. How many points can a player score in a single game?

In the very early days of basketball, Bill Keenon scored 76 points in a March 1909 game in the Central Basket Ball League, according to the Association for Professional Basketball Research. Whether that was a record at the time or whether it withstood any challenges in later years is difficult to determine. Basketball records were hard to find or nonexistent in many of the leagues that sprang up across the country in the first half of the 20th century.

We do know that Bobby McDermott, among the game's greatest players in the '40s, once scored 56 points in a pro game. Milt Schoon, who played for the Denver Refiners in the National Professional Basketball League, scored 64 points on January 21, 1951.

In the college ranks, gangly Bevo Francis of tiny Rio Grande College in southeastern Ohio became a folk hero after scoring 116 points in a game in 1952-53 against Ashland College and 113 in a game a year later. He averaged 50.1 points per game in 1952-53, but the NCAA invalidated the record because it included several games against teams that were not four-year schools.

The next year, in Division I competition, Frank Selvy of Furman hit the century mark in a game. He scored 100 points versus Newberry College on February 13, 1954, a feat that has never been matched at that level of competition.

In 1982, Hall of Famer Cheryl Miller poured in 105 points in a California high school game. But that was nothing compared to what Lisa Leslie did. Leslie, now of the WNBA's Los Angeles Sparks, once scored 101 points *in the first half* of a high school game. Leslie scored every one of her team's points as her teammates purposely and continually fed her in an attempt to break Miller's record. The opposing team stuffed that gambit by refusing to play the second half.

In the fledgling NBA, Joe Fulks, a determined, awkward forward for the Philadelphia Warriors, set the early standard. Fulks, who popularized the jump shot during his career, had single-game highs of 41 and 47 points in each of the league's first two seasons, respectively. Then on February 10, 1949, Fulks scored an amazing 63 points in a game against Indianapolis, during a season in which the league average for a team was only 80 points per contest.

Ten years passed before Fulks's 63-point outburst was broken. Elgin Baylor, then a second-year pro for the Minneapolis Lakers, was the man to top Fulks. In November 1959, Baylor broke loose for 64 points in a game against Boston. A year later, Baylor smashed his own record, pouring in 71 points against the Knicks.

In that high-scoring era, few games matched the one in Philadelphia between the Warriors and Los Angeles Lakers on December 8, 1961. In a triple-overtime thriller, Chamberlain poured in 78 points to set a new single-game record. In the same game, Baylor scored 63 for L.A. Chamberlain's mark still stands as the second-highest total in NBA history. After the game, Frank McGuire, the Warriors' coach, became a prophet, saying, "He'll get 100 points someday."

In those days, the Warriors played a few of their games each season in Hershey, Pennsylvania, a short jaunt into dairy country from Philadelphia. Chamberlain had excelled in Hershey before. On December 29, 1961, on his way to averaging 50.4 points per game for the season, Wilt rattled the rim with 60 points in a game against the Los Angeles Lakers.

The Hershey games did not always draw well. So it was that on March 2, 1962, only 4,124 paid to see the Warriors play the rival Knicks in Hershey Arena. In the football hotbed of Pennsylvania some attendees may have had more interest in the preliminary game, which pitted players from two nearby NFL teams, the Philadelphia Eagles and Baltimore Colts.

The Knicks' starting center, Phil Jordan, did not play because he had the flu. Rugged Darrell Imhoff, a 6-foot-10 brute, replaced Jordan at center. A second-year pro, Imhoff was no match for Chamberlain and got into foul trouble early on. In the first quarter, Chamberlain had what for most players would have been an excellent game; he tallied 23 points, making 7 of 14 field goal attempts and all nine of his foul shots. He also grabbed 10 rebounds.

In the second quarter, with 6-foot-9 rookie Cleveland Buckner guarding him most of the time, Chamberlain dropped 18 points on the Knicks, giving him 41 for the half. Remarkably, the notoriously poor foul shooter made 13 of 15 from the line in the first 24 minutes. In the process, the Warriors had built an 11-point lead, 79-68.

With a variety of dunks, fadeaways, and finger rolls, Chamberlain's assault accelerated in the third quarter. Imhoff, Buckner, and 6-foot-7 Willie Naulls were helpless as the giant unloaded for 28 points on 10 of 16 from the floor and 8 of 8 from the line. Through three periods, Chamberlain had 69 points and seemed certain of breaking his own single-game mark of 78. Early in the fourth quarter, Imhoff fouled out and Chamberlain broke his own mark with a little less than eight minutes remaining.

With the Warriors enjoying a large lead, the outcome of the game was not in doubt. Philadelphia's tactics turned toward getting Wilt as many points as possible. They purposely fed him the ball time after time. The Knicks caught on quickly and, on each possession, held the ball for nearly the entire 24-second possession.

Still, Chamberlain kept scoring. With five minutes left, he had 89 points. The Knicks countered by fouling other Warriors players before they could get the ball to Wilt. The Warriors retaliated by fouling the Knicks to get the ball back more quickly. Chamberlain went over two minutes without scoring. Then he broke through several times and scored his 97th and 98th points with 1:19 left in the game. With 46 seconds left, he took a pass and dunked, giving him 100 points. Fans mobbed the court. Both Warriors and Knicks players shook his hand.

In achieving the awesome feat, Chamberlain had made 36 of 63 shots (57.1%) from the field. From the line, the 51% career foul shooter had made 28 of 32 attempts, an 87.5% conversion

rate. In the second half he had scored 59 points, including 31 in the final stanza.

Everyone else on the court that night became a footnote in history. Al Attles, the Warriors' second leading scorer, managed 17 points. Paul Arizin, a future Hall of Famer, and Tom Meschery both added 16. Guy Rodgers had 20 of Philadelphia's 39 assists. For the Knicks, Richie Guerin, New York's star guard, connected for 39 points; forward Naulls added 31. Buckner, who played only two NBA seasons and finished with a 6.0 career scoring average, had perhaps his best night as a pro. Coming off the bench, he scored 33 points and grabbed 8 boards.

And, oh, yes, the Warriors won the game, 169-147. But the final score hardly seemed relevant—except that it, too, set a record for most points in a game by two teams.

Introduction to the Records

The records that follow show the way that NBA standards have evolved, but, as with the *Total Basketball* Player Register, date back to 1937-38, the first season of the National Basketball League that eventually (in 1949-50) merged with the Basketball Association of America to create the NBA. Also

included are the records for players who performed in the ABA. Each record lists the players who have held records in numerous categories for a career, season, and single game.

For career records, each record-holder's mark is listed for the years it was held. Single-season records show that same information as well as the team or teams the player was with that year. Single-game records have an added bit of information: the opponent against which the mark was set.

A note of clarification: With some statistics—like points per game, rebounds per games and other averages—a player will hold a record, then lose it to another player. Thus Joe Fulks briefly held the career record for 23.9 points per game from 1947 to 1949. Then Fulks' average declined and George Mikan held the record at 22.6 ppg from 1949-56. At times a player holds a record, loses it for a time, and then gets it back again. So Wilt Chamberlain owned the record for points per game from 1959-1970 at 30.1. Kareem Abdul-Jabbar then surpassed him at 30.4 and held the record from 1970-75. Jabbar then fell back and Chamberlain owned it again until Jordan surpassed him. Similar record changes occurred with rebounds per game and steals per game.

ALL-TIME CAREER PLAYER RECORDS

Notes:

❖The first season listed in each category is the first time when statistics for the category were recorded and published.

❖When a player has held a record for more than one season, the figure shown is the player's total or average in the last year he held the mark. For example, Scotty Armstrong held the record for most games played in 1938-39 and '39-40. The figure shown, 72 games, was his total through '39-40.

❖In cases where two active players held the same career record in different seasons, both players' records are shown.

Games

Most games played

	Years Held	Record
Chuck Bloedorn	1937-38	18
Bud Lindbergh	1937-38	18
Bart Quinn	1937-38	18
Scotty Armstrong	1938-40	72
Herm Witasek	1940-41	93
Leroy Edwards	1941-47	266
Charley Shipp	1947-52	399
Red Holzman	1952-53	445
Bob Davies	1953-55	569
Arnie Risen	1955-58	727
Dolph Schayes	1958-71	1,059
Hal Greer	1971-76	1,122
John Havlicek	1976-83	1,270
Elvin Hayes	1983-85	1,303
Kareem Abdul-Jabbar	1985-95	1,560
Robert Parish	1995-2003	1,611

Minutes

Most minutes played

Paul Arizin	1951-52	2,939
Bob Cousy	1952-54	8,483
Mel Hutchins	1954-55	11,303
Bob Cousy	1955-60	23,574
Dolph Schayes	1960-61	26,532
Bob Cousy	1961-65	30,230
Bill Russell	1965-70	40,726
Wilt Chamberlain	1970-82	47,859
Elvin Hayes	1982-85	50,000
Kareem Abdul-Jabbar	1985-2003	57,446

Points

Highest points per game

Leroy Edwards	1937-43	11.3
Bobby McDermott	1943-46	15.1
Mel Riebe	1946-47	15.4
Joe Fulks	1947-49	23.9
George Mikan	1949-56	22.6
Bob Pettit	1956-59	24.9
Wilt Chamberlain	1959-70	30.1
Kareem Abdul-Jabbar	1970-75	30.4
Wilt Chamberlain	1975-88	30.06
Michael Jordan	1988-2003	30.12

Most points

Leroy Edwards	1937-48	3,199
Joe Fulks	1948-49	3,898
George Mikan	1949-57	11,764
Dolph Schayes	1957-63	19,113
Bob Pettit	1963-65	20,880
Wilt Chamberlain	1965-84	31,419
Kareem Abdul-Jabbar	1984-2003	38,387

Field Goals

Most field goals made

Leroy Edwards	1937-46	827
Bobby McDermott	1946-49	1,465
George Mikan	1949-58	4,097
Dolph Schayes	1958-62	5,868
Bob Cousy	1962-63	6,167
Bob Pettit	1963-64	6,953
Wilt Chamberlain	1964-83	12,681
Kareem Abdul-Jabbar	1983-2003	15,837

Most field goals attempted

Joe Fulks	1946-57	9,338
Bob Cousy	1957-64	16,465
Bob Pettit	1964-65	16,872
Wilt Chamberlain	1965-77	23,497
John Havlicek	1977-83	23,900
Elvin Hayes	1983-85	24,272
Kareem Abdul-Jabbar	1985-2000	328,307

Highest field goal percentage

Bob Feerick	1946-49	.365
George Mikan	1949-52	.411
Ed Macauley	1952-54	.448
Neil Johnston	1954-59	.444
Ken Sears	1959-60	.454
Wilt Chamberlain	1960-63	.502
Walt Bellamy	1963-66	.514
Wilt Chamberlain	1966-70	.530
Kareem Abdul-Jabbar	1970-75	.549
Artis Gilmore	1975-86	.582
Steve Johnson	1986-87	.587
James Donaldson	1987-89	.587
Artis Gilmore	1989-93	.582
Mark West	1993-98	.584
Artis Gilmore	1998-2003	.582

Three-point Field Goals

Most 3-point field goals made

Les Selvage	1967-68	147
Chico Vaughn	1968-69	282
Louie Dampier	1969-92	794
Dale Ellis	1992-97	1,461
Reggie Miller	1997-2003	2,330

Most 3-point field goals attempted

Les Selvage	1967-68	461
Chico Vaughn	1968-69	933
Louie Dampier	1969-91	2,217
Michael Adams	1991-95	2,816
Dale Ellis	1995-97	3,675
Reggie Miller	1997-2003	5,854

Highest 3-point field goal percentage

Darel Carrier	1967-79	.377
Fred Brown	1979-83	.387
John Roche	1983-85	.389
Trent Tucker	1985-88	.423
Mark Price	1988-89	.438
Hersey Hawkins	1989-90	.423
Steve Kerr	1990-2003	.454

Free Throws

Most free throws made

Soup Cable	1937-38	45
Leroy Edwards	1938-48	1,123
Joe Fulks	1948-49	1,238
George Mikan	1949-56	3,570
Dolph Schayes	1956-71	6,979
Oscar Robertson	1971-90	7,694
Moses Malone	1990-2000	8,531
Karl Malone	2000-2003	9,619

Most free throws attempted

Leroy Edwards	1945-46	200
Joe Fulks	1946-49	1,548
George Mikan	1949-56	4,597
Dolph Schayes	1956-67	8,274
Wilt Chamberlain	1967-2001	11,862
Karl Malone	2001-2003	12,963

Highest free throw percentage

Herm Fuetsch	1945-46	.813
Angelo Musi	1946-47	.829
Stan Stutz	1947-48	.807
Bobby Wanzer	1948-49	.824
Fred Schaus	1949-51	.828
Bobby Wanzer	1951-53	.839
Bill Sharman	1953-74	.883
Rick Barry	1974-91	.893
Mark Price	1991-2003	.904

Rebounds

Highest rebounds per game

Dolph Schayes	1950-52	14.4
George Mikan	1952-57	13.4
Bob Pettit	1957-59	15.7
Wilt Chamberlain	1959-2003	22.9

Most rebounds

Dolph Schayes	1950-52	1,853
George Mikan	1952-54	3,859
Dolph Schayes	1954-62	10,771
Bill Russell	1962-71	21,721
Wilt Chamberlain	1971-2003	23,924

Most offensive rebounds

Mel Daniels	1967-80	2,870
Moses Malone	1980-2003	6,731

Most defensive rebounds

Mel Daniels	1967-81	6,624
Kareem Abdul-Jabbar	1981-89	9,394
Moses Malone	1989-2001	10,452
Karl Malone	2001-2003	11,100

Assists

Highest assists per game

Ernie Calverley	1946-48	3.0
Andy Phillip	1948-49	4.3
Bob Davies	1949-50	5.0
Andy Phillip	1950-53	5.9
Bob Cousy	1953-63	7.6
Guy Rodgers	1963-64	8.0
Oscar Robertson	1964-84	9.5
Magic Johnson	1984-93	11.4
John Stockton	1992*-98	11.3
Magic Johnson	1998-2003	11.2

* Stockton shared the record with Johnson in 1992-93 with 11.4 apg.

Most assists

Ernie Calverley	1946-49	572
Andy Phillip	1949-57	3,638
Bob Cousy	1957-68	6,949
Oscar Robertson	1968-90	9,887
Magic Johnson	1990-94	9,921
John Stockton	1994-2003	15,806

Steals

Most steals

Ted McClain	1973-74	250
Larry Steele	1974-75	400
Don Buse	1975-86	1,818
Julius Erving	1986-91	2,272
Maurice Cheeks	1991-95	2,310
John Stockton	1995-2003	3,265

Highest steals per game

Ted McClain	1973-74	2.98
Larry Steele	1974-75	2.55
Don Buse	1975-83	2.16
Micheal Ray Richardson	1983-89	2.63
Alvin Robertson	1989-2003	2.71

Blocked Shots

Most blocked shots

Elmore Smith	1973-76	847
Kareem Abdul-Jabbar	1976-87	3,012
Artis Gilmore	1987-88	3,178
Kareem Abdul-Jabbar	1988-95	3,189
Hakeem Olajuwon	1995-2003	3,830

Highest blocked shots per game

Elmore Smith	1973-76	3.64
Kareem Abdul-Jabbar	1976-83	3.50
Tree Rollins	1983-87	3.03
Mark Eaton	1987-92	3.50
Hakeem Olajuwon	1992-94	3.63
David Robinson	1994-96	3.60
Dikembe Mutombo	1996-2000	3.57
Mark Eaton	2000-2003	3.50

Turnovers

Most turnovers

Larry Brown	1967-72	903
Mel Daniels	1972-74	1,233
Ron Boone	1974-78	2,076
Artis Gilmore	1978-79	2,255
Julius Erving	1979-90	3,940
Moses Malone	1990-2002	4,253
Karl Malone	2002-2003	4,421

Personal Fouls

Most fouls committed

Stan Miasek	1946-48	400
Ed Sadowski	1948-50	893
Joe Fulks	1950-54	1,774
Arnie Risen	1954-56	2,091
Vern Mikkelsen	1956-59	2,812
Dolph Schayes	1959-71	3,667
Hal Greer	1971-82	3,885
Elvin Hayes	1982-86	4,193
Artis Gilmore	1986-88	4,529
Kareem Abdul-Jabbar	1988-2003	4,657

Most disqualifications

Don Christensen	1950-51	19
Alex Hannum	1951-55	70
Vern Mikkelsen	1955-2003	127

'Notes:

⊕In cases where the same year is shown multiple times, the record was broken more than once in the season.

⊕The first season listed in each category is the first time when statistics for the category were recorded. In some cases the record for a half or a quarter was not published in the season in which the category was first recorded. For example, the most 3-pointers in a game was first recorded in 1979-80 but the record for most 3-pointers in a half or quarter did not appear until 1981-82.

⊕An asterisk (*) denotes one (1) overtime period.

⊕Robert Bradley, John Grasso, and Roger Meyer each provided research assistance for the single-season record of most points in a game.

Points

Most points, game

Player	Team	Opponent	Year Set	Total
Leroy Edwards	Oshkosh	Kankakee	1937-38	30
Chuck Chuckovits	Toledo	Sheboygan	1941-42	33
Leroy Edwards	Oshkosh	unknown	'42-43 or '43-44#	35
Bobby McDermott	Fort Wayne	Cleveland	1944-45	36
Stan Patrick	Chicago	Pittsburgh	1944-45	38
Bob Carpenter	Oshkosh	Cleveland	1945-46	40
Don Martin	Providence	Cleveland	1946-47	40
Joe Fulks	Philadelphia	Toronto	1946-47	41
George Mikan	Minneapolis	Rochester	1947-48	41
Carl Braun	New York	Providence	1947-48	47
George Mikan	Minneapolis	Chicago	1948-49	47
Joe Fulks	Philadelphia	Providence	1948-49	47
George Mikan	Minneapolis	Washington	1948-49	48
Joe Fulks	Philadelphia	Indianapolis	1948-49	63
Elgin Baylor	Minneapolis	Boston	1959-60	64
Elgin Baylor	Los Angeles	New York	1960-61	71
Wilt Chamberlain	Philadelphia	Los Angeles	1961-62	78***
Wilt Chamberlain	Philadelphia	New York	1961-62	100

The exact year and the opponent in the game in which Edwards scored 35 points are unknown.

Most points, half

Carl Braun	New York	Providence	1947-48	31
Joe Fulks	Philadelphia	Indianapolis	1948-49	33
George Mikan	Minneapolis	Rochester	1951-52	36
George Mikan	Minneapolis	Philadelphia	1951-52	36
Hal Greer	Syracuse	Boston	1958-59	39
Wilt Chamberlain	Philadelphia	Detroit	1959-60	39
Wilt Chamberlain	Philadelphia	Syracuse	1960-61	39
Wilt Chamberlain	Philadelphia	New York	1961-62	59

Most points, quarter

Carl Braun	New York	Providence	1947-48	19
Bob Pettit	Milwaukee	Rochester	1954-55	23
Cliff Hagan	St. Louis	New York	1957-58	26
Wilt Chamberlain	Philadelphia	New York	1961-62	31
David Thompson	Denver	Detroit	1977-78	32
George Gervin	San Antonio	New Orleans	1977-78	33

Most points, overtime period

Bob Cousy	Boston	Syracuse	1950-51	12
Earl Monroe	Baltimore	Detroit	1969-70	13
Joe Caldwell	Atlanta	Cincinnati	1969-70	13
Butch Carter	Indiana	Boston	1983-84	14

Field Goals

An asterisk (*) denotes one (1) overtime period.

Most field goals made, game

Bobby McDermott	Ft. Wayne	Cleveland	1944-45	16
Don Martin	Providence	Cleveland	1946-47	17
Bob Feerick	Washington	Providence	1946-47	17
Carl Braun	New York	Providence	1947-48	18
Joe Fulks	Philadelphia	Indianapolis	1948-49	27
Elgin Baylor	Los Angeles	New York	1960-61	28
Wilt Chamberlain	Philadelphia	Los Angeles	1961-62	31***
Wilt Chamberlain	Philadelphia	New York	1961-62	36

Most field goals made, half

Joe Fulks	Philadelphia	Indianapolis	1948-49	14
Cliff Hagan	St. Louis	New York	1957-58	14
Hal Greer	Syracuse	Boston	1958-59	18
Wilt Chamberlain	Philadelphia	New York	1961-62	22

Most field goals made, quarter

George Mikan	Minneapolis	New York	1948-49	10
Dick Garmaker	Minneapolis	New York	1957-58	10
Cliff Hagan	St. Louis	New York	1957-58	12
Wilt Chamberlain	Philadelphia	New York	1961-62	12
Lou Hudson	Atlanta	Kansas City	1976-77	12
David Thompson	Denver	Detroit	1977-78	13

Most field goals attempted, game

Joe Fulks	Philadelphia	Boston	1947-48	52
Joe Fulks	Philadelphia	Indianapolis	1948-49	56
Wilt Chamberlain	Philadelphia	Los Angeles	1961-62	62***
Wilt Chamberlain	Philadelphia	New York	1961-62	63

Most field goals attempted, half

Joe Fulks	Philadelphia	Indianapolis	1948-49	29
Wilt Chamberlain	Philadelphia	Chicago	1961-62	32
Wilt Chamberlain	Philadelphia	New York	1961-62	37

Most field goals attempted, quarter

Joe Fulks	Philadelphia	Indianapolis	1948-49	15
Tom Heinsohn	Boston	St. Louis	1956-57	15
Cliff Hagan	St. Louis	New York	1957-58	15
Bob Cousy	Boston	New York	1958-59	17
Elgin Baylor	Los Angeles	New York	1960-61	18
Bob Pettit	St. Louis	Philadelphia	1961-62	19
Wilt Chamberlain	Philadelphia	Chicago	1961-62	20
Wilt Chamberlain	Philadelphia	New York	1961-62	21

Three-point Field Goals

An asterisk (*) denotes 1 overtime period.

Most 3-point field goals made, game

Les Selvage	Anaheim	Denver	1967-68	10
Brian Shaw	Miami	Milwaukee	1992-93	10
Joe Dumars	Detroit	Minnesota	1994-95	10
George McCloud	Dallas	Phoenix	1995-96	10
Dennis Scott	Orlando	Atlanta	1995-96	11
Kobe Bryant	L.A. Lakers	Seattle	2002-03	12

Most 3-point field goals made, half

John Roche	Denver	Seattle	1981-82	7
Michael Adams	Denver	Milwaukee	1988-89	7
John Starks	New York	Miami	1993-94	7
Allan Houston	Detroit	Chicago	1994-95	7
Joe Dumars	Detroit	Orlando	1994-95	7
George McCloud	Dallas	Phoenix	1995-96	7
George McCloud	Dallas	Philadelphia	1995-96	7
Dennis Scott	Orlando	Atlanta	1995-96	7
Steve Smith	Atlanta	Seattle	1996-97	7
Henry James	Atlanta	New Jersey	1996-97	7
Glen Rice	L.A. Lakers	Portland	1998-99	7
Tim Thomas	Milwaukee	Portland	2000-01	8
Michael Redd	Milwaukee	Houston	2001-02	8
Ray Allen	Milwaukee	Charlotte	2001-02	8

Note: The ABA did not track records for a half in this category.

Most 3-point field goals made, quarter

John Roche	Denver	Seattle	1981-82	7
Steve Smith	Atlanta	Seattle	1996-97	7
Henry James	Atlanta	New Jersey	1996-97	7
Michael Redd	Milwaukee	Houston	2001-02	8

Note: The ABA did not track records for a quarter in this category.

Most 3-point field goals attempted, game

Les Selvage	Anaheim	Denver	1967-68	26

Most 3-point field goals attempted, half

John Roche	Denver	Seattle	1981-82	11
Michael Adams	Denver	L.A. Clippers	1990-91	13

Note: The ABA did not track records for a half in this category.
Note: The ABA did not track 3-point field goals made and attempted for a half or a quarter.

Free Throws

An asterisk (*) denotes 1 overtime period.

Most free throws made, game

Ernie Calverley	Detroit	Providence	1946-47	16
George Glamack	Indianapolis	not available	1947-48	20
George Mikan	Minneapolis	Anderson	1949-50	20
George Mikan	Minneapolis	Chicago	1949-50	20
Dolph Schayes	Syracuse	Minneapolis	1951-52	23***
Frank Selvy	Milwaukee	Minneapolis	1954-55	24
Wilt Chamberlain	Philadelphia	New York	1961-62	28
Adrian Dantley	Utah	Houston	1983-84	28

Most free throws made, half

Ken Sears	New York	Boston	1956-57	16
Wilt Chamberlain	Philadelphia	New York	1961-62	18
Oscar Robertson	Cincinnati	Baltimore	1964-65	19
Michael Jordan	Chicago	New York	1989-90	20

Most free throws made, quarter

Ken Sears	New York	Boston	1956-57	13
Oscar Robertson	Cincinnati	Baltimore	1964-65	13
Rick Barry	San Francisco	New York	1966-67	14
Pete Maravich	Atlanta	Buffalo	1973-74	14
Adrian Dantley	Detroit	Sacramento	1986-87	14
Michael Jordan	Chicago	Utah	1989-90	14
Michael Jordan	Chicago	Miami	1992-93	14
Johnny Newman	Denver	Boston	1997-98	14

Most free throws attempted, game

George Glamack	Indianapolis	not available	1947-48	27
Dolph Schayes	Syracuse	Minneapolis	1951-52	27***
Wilt Chamberlain	Philadelphia	Syracuse	1960-61	27
Wilt Chamberlain	Philadelphia	St. Louis	1961-62	34

Most free throws attempted, half

Ken Sears	New York	Boston	1956-57	17
George Yardley	Detroit	Minneapolis	1957-58	17
Wilt Chamberlain	Philadelphia	Boston	1959-60	18
Wilt Chamberlain	Philadelphia	New York	1961-62	18
Oscar Robertson	Cincinnati	Baltimore	1964-65	22
Tony Campbell	Minnesota	L.A. Clippers	1989-90	22
Michael Jordan	Chicago	Miami	1992-93	23

Most free throws attempted, quarter

George Yardley	Detroit	Minneapolis	1957-58	15
Wilt Chamberlain	Philadelphia	Syracuse	1961-62	15
Oscar Robertson	Cincinnati	Baltimore	1964-65	16
Stan McKenzie	Phoenix	Philadelphia	1969-70	16
Pete Maravich	Atlanta	Chicago	1972-73	16
Michael Jordan	Chicago	Miami	1992-93	16
Willie Burton	Philadelphia	Miami	1994-95	16
Johnny Newman	Denver	Boston	1997-98	16

Rebounds

An asterisk (*) denotes one (1) overtime period.

Most rebounds, game

Dolph Schayes	Syracuse	Philadelphia	1950-51	35
George Mikan	Minneapolis	Rochester	1951-52	36**
George Mikan	Minneapolis	Philadelphia	1951-52	36
Neil Johnston	Philadelphia	Syracuse	1953-54	39
Bill Russell	Boston	Philadelphia	1957-58	49
Bill Russell	Boston	Syracuse	1959-60	51
Wilt Chamberlain	Philadelphia	Boston	1960-61	55

Most rebounds, half

Bill Russell	Boston	Philadelphia	1957-58	32

Most rebounds, quarter

Neil Johnston	Philadelphia	Syracuse	1954-55	12
Maurice Stokes	Rochester	New York	1955-56	12
Bill Russell	Boston	Philadelphia	1957-58	17
Bill Russell	Boston	Cincinnati	1958-59	17
Bill Russell	Boston	Syracuse	1959-60	17
Wilt Chamberlain	Philadelphia	Syracuse	1959-60	17
Nate Thurmond	San Francisco	Baltimore	1964-65	18

Most offensive rebounds, game

Tim Bassett	San Diego	Indiana	1973-74	18
Moses Malone	Houston	Seattle	1981-82	21

Most offensive rebounds, half

(minimum 12)

Moses Malone	Houston	San Antonio	1977-78	12
Larry Smith	Golden St.	Denver	1985-86	12
Charles Barkley	Philadelphia	New York	1986-87	13

Note: The ABA did not track records for a half in this category.

Most offensive rebounds, quarter

(minimum 10)

Moses Malone	Milwaukee	Sacramento	1981-82	10
Larry Smith	Golden St.	Denver	1985-86	11
Charles Barkley	Philadelphia	New York	1986-87	11

Note: The ABA did not track records for a quarter in this category.

Most defensive rebounds, game

Artis Gilmore	Kentucky	New York	1973-74	34

Most defensive rebounds, half

(minimum 17)

Marvin Webster	Seattle	Atlanta	1977-78	17
Swen Nater	San Diego	Denver	1979-80	18

Note: The ABA did not track records for a half in this category.

Most defensive rebounds, quarter

(minimum 13)

Happy Hairston	Los Angeles	Philadelphia	1974-75	13

Note: The ABA did not track records for a quarter in this category.
Note: The ABA did not track records for a half or quarter for offensive or defensive rebounds. The NBA began recording offensive and defensive rebounds in 1973-74 but did not publish the league records for a half and a quarter until 1993.

Assists

An asterisk (*) denotes one (1) overtime period.

Most assists, game

Ernie Calverley	Providence	Pittsburgh	1946-47	8
Johnny Logan	St. Louis	Providence	1948-49	8
Dick McGuire	New York	Minneapolis	1949-50	16
Dick McGuire	New York	Boston	1949-50	16*
Andy Phillip	Philadelphia	Boston	1950-51	17
Dick McGuire	New York	Milwaukee	1951-52	17
Bob Cousy	Boston	New York	1952-52	18
Andy Phillip	Ft. Wayne	Minneapolis	1954-55	19
Bob Davies	Rochester	Boston	1954-55	20
Richie Guerin	New York	St. Louis	1958-59	21
Bob Cousy	Boston	Minneapolis	1958-59	28
Guy Rodgers	San Francisco	St. Louis	1962-63	28
Kevin Porter	New Jersey	Houston	1977-78	29
Scott Skiles	Orlando	Denver	1990-91	30

Most assists, half

Bob Cousy	Boston	Rochester	1951-52	11
Bob Cousy	Boston	Ft. Wayne	1956-57	12
Bob Cousy	Boston	Minneapolis	1958-59	19

Most assists, quarter

Dick McGuire	Detroit	Philadelphia	1957-58	9
Bob Cousy	Boston	Minneapolis	1958-59	12
John Lucas	Houston	Milwaukee	1977-78	12
John Lucas	Golden St.	Chicago	1978-79	12
Magic Johnson	L.A. Lakers	Seattle	1983-84	12
John Lucas	San Antonio	Denver	1983-84	14

Steals

An asterisk (*) denotes one (1) overtime period.

Most steals, game

Ted McClain	Carolina	New York	1973-74	12

Most steals, half

(minimum 8)

Quinn Buckner	Milwaukee	N.Y. Nets	1976-77	8
Fred Brown	Seattle	Philadelphia	1976-77	8
Gus Williams	Seattle	Washington	1978-79	8
Eddie Jordan	New Jersey	Chicago	1979-80	8
Dudley Bradley	Indiana	Utah	1980-81	8
Rob Williams	Denver	New Jersey	1982-83	8
Fat Lever	Denver	Indiana	1984-85	8
Michael Jordan	Chicago	Boston	1988-89	8
Clyde Drexler	Houston	Sacramento	1996-97	8
Doug Christie	Toronto	Philadelphia	1996-97	8
Michael Finley	Dallas	Philadelphia	2000-01	8

Note: The ABA did not track records for a half in this category.

Most steals, quarter

(minimum 7)

Quinn Buckner	Milwaukee	N.Y. Nets	1976-77	7
Fat Lever	Denver	Indiana	1984-85	8

Note: The ABA did not track steals records for a half or quarter. The NBA began recording steals in 1973-74 but did not publish the league records for a half and a quarter until 1992.
Note: The ABA did not track records for a quarter in this category.

Blocked Shots

An asterisk (*) denotes one (1) overtime period.

Most blocked shots, game

Julius Keye	Denver	Virginia	1972-73	12
Caldwell Jones	San Diego	Carolina	1973-74	12
Elmore Smith	Los Angeles	Detroit	1973-74	14
Elmore Smith	Los Angeles	Portland	1973-74	17

Most blocked shots, half

(minimum 11)

Elmore Smith	Los Angeles	Portland	1973-74	11
George Johnson	San Antonio	Golden St.	1980-81	11
Manute Bol	Washington	Milwaukee	1985-86	11

Note: The ABA did not track records for a half in this category.

Most blocked shots, quarter

(minimum 8)

Manute Bol	Washington	Milwaukee	1985-86	8
Manute Bol	Washington	Indiana	1986-87	8
Dikembe Mutombo	Philadelphia	Chicago	2001-02	8
Erick Dampier	Golden St.	L.A. Clippers	2001-02	8

Note: The ABA did not track blocked shots records for a half or quarter. The NBA began recording blocks in 1973-74 but did not publish the league records for a half and a quarter until 1993.
Note: The ABA did not track records for a quarter in this category.

Turnovers

An asterisk (*) denotes one (1) overtime period.

Most turnovers, game

Steve Chubin	Anaheim	Denver	1967-68	14
John Drew	Atlanta	New Jersey	1977-78	14
Jason Kidd	Phoenix	New York	2000-01	14

Personal Fouls

Most personal fouls, game

Don Otten	Tri-Cities	Sheboygan	1949-50	8

Most personal fouls, half

Many players		through 2002-03	6

Most personal fouls, quarter

Joe Hutton	Minneapolis	Boston	1951-52	5
Guy Sparrow	New York	St. Louis	1957-58	5
Many players		through 2002-03	6

ALL-TIME SINGLE-SEASON PLAYER RECORDS

Games

Most games played

Player	Team	Season Set	Total
Chuck Bloedorn	Akron Goodyear	1937-38	18
Bud Lindbergh	Fort Wayne	1937-38	
Bart Quinn	Fort Wayne	1937-38	

From 1938-39 through '43-44, 18 players shared the record with 28.
In 1944-45, 15 players shared the record with 30.
In 1945-46, 13 players shared the record with 34.

Charles Halbert	Chicago	1946-47	61
John Logan	St. Louis	1946-47	
George Nostrand	Toronto-Cleveland	1946-47	
Red Wallace	Boston-Toronto	1946-47	
Ray Wertis	Toronto-Cleveland	1946-47	
Max Zaslofsky	Chicago	1946-47	
Frank Brian	Anderson	1947-48	69
Ed Sadowski	Philadelphia-Baltimore	1949-50	69

From 1950-51 through '52-53, 11 players shared the record with 71.

Jack Nichols	Milwaukee-Rochester	1953-54	75
Jack Coleman	Rochester-Syracuse	1955-56	
Dave Piontek	Cincinnati-St. Louis	1959-60	77

In 1960-61, 22 players shared the record with 79.
In 1961-62 and '62-63, 40 players shared the record with 80.
From 1963-64 through '66-67, 17 players shared the record with 81.

John Tresvant	Cincinnati-Detroit	1967-68	85
Walt Bellamy	New York-Detroit	1968-69	88
Chuck Williams	San Diego-Kentucky	1973-74	90

Minutes

Most minutes played

Paul Arizin	Philadelphia	1951-52	2,939
Neil Johnston	Philadelphia	1952-53	3,166
Neil Johnston	Philadelphia	1953-54	3,296
Wilt Chamberlain	Philadelphia	1959-60	3,338
Gene Shue	Detroit	1959-60	3,338
Wilt Chamberlain	Philadelphia	1960-61	3,773
Wilt Chamberlain	Philadelphia	1961-62	3,882

Highest minutes per game

Paul Arizin	Philadelphia	1951-52	44.5
Neil Johnston	Philadelphia	1952-53	45.2
Neil Johnston	Philadelphia	1953-54	45.8
Wilt Chamberlain	Philadelphia	1959-60	46.4
Wilt Chamberlain	Philadelphia	1960-61	47.8
Wilt Chamberlain	Philadelphia	1961-62	48.5

Points

Most points, season

Leroy Edwards	Oshkosh	1937-38	210
Leroy Edwards	Oshkosh	1938-39	334
Leroy Edwards	Oshkosh	1939-40	361
Chuck Chuckovits	Toledo	1941-42	406
Mel Riebe	Cleveland	1944-45	607
Joe Fulks	Philadelphia	1946-47	1,389
George Mikan	Minneapolis	1948-49	1,698
George Mikan	Minneapolis	1949-50	1,865
George Mikan	Minneapolis	1950-51	1,932
George Yardley	Detroit	1957-58	2,001
Bob Pettit	St. Louis	1958-59	2,105
Wilt Chamberlain	Philadelphia	1959-60	2,707
Wilt Chamberlain	Philadelphia	1960-61	3,033
Wilt Chamberlain	Philadelphia	1961-62	4,029

Highest points per game

Leroy Edwards	Oshkosh	1937-38	16.2
Chuck Chuckovits	Toledo	1941-42	18.5
Mel Riebe	Cleveland	1944-45	20.2
Joe Fulks	Philadelphia	1946-47	23.2
George Mikan	Minneapolis	1948-49	28.3
George Mikan	Minneapolis	1950-51	28.4
Bob Pettit	St. Louis	1958-59	29.2
Wilt Chamberlain	Philadelphia	1959-60	37.6
Wilt Chamberlain	Philadelphia	1960-61	38.4
Wilt Chamberlain	Philadelphia	1961-62	50.4

Field Goals

Highest field goal percentage

Bob Feerick	Washington	1946-47	.401
Arnie Risen	Rochester	1948-49	.423
Alex Groza	Indianapolis	1949-50	.478
Bob Donham	Boston	1950-51	.507
Wilt Chamberlain	Philadelphia	1960-61	.509
Walt Bellamy	Chicago	1961-62	.519
Kenny Sears	N.Y.-S.F.	1962-63	.530
Wilt Chamberlain	Philadelphia	1965-66	.540
Wilt Chamberlain	Philadelphia	1966-67	.683
Wilt Chamberlain	Los Angeles	1972-73	.727

Most field goals made

Leroy Edwards	Oshkosh	1937-38	83
Leroy Edwards	Oshkosh	1938-39	124
Ernie Andres	Indianapolis	1939-40	130
Chuck Chuckovits	Toledo	1941-42	143
Bobby McDermott	Fort Wayne	1944-45	258
Joe Fulks	Philadelphia	1946-47	475
George Mikan	Minneapolis	1948-49	583
George Mikan	Minneapolis	1949-50	649
George Mikan	Minneapolis	1950-51	678
Clyde Lovellette	Cincinnati	1957-58	679
Bob Pettit	St. Louis	1958-59	719
Wilt Chamberlain	Philadelphia	1959-60	1,065
Wilt Chamberlain	Philadelphia	1960-61	1.251
Wilt Chamberlain	Philadelphia	1961-62	1,597

Most field goals attempted

Joe Fulks	Philadelphia	1946-47	1,557
Joe Fulks	Philadelphia	1948-49	1,689
Jack Twyman	Cincinnati	1958-59	1,691
Wilt Chamberlain	Philadelphia	1959-60	2,311
Wilt Chamberlain	Philadelphia	1960-61	2,457
Wilt Chamberlain	Philadelphia	1961-62	3,159

Three-point Field Goals

Highest 3-point field goal percentage

Darel Carrier	Kentucky	1967-68	.357
Darel Carrier	Kentucky	1968-69	.379
George Lehmann	Carolina	1970-71	.403
Glen Combs	Utah	1971-72	.406
Billy Shepherd	Memphis	1974-75	.420
Fred Brown	Seattle	1979-80	.443
Craig Hodges	Milwaukee	1985-86	.451
Kiki Vandeweghe	Portland	1986-87	.481
Craig Hodges	Milw.-Phoe.	1987-88	.491
Jon Sundvold	Miami	1988-89	.522
Steve Kerr	Chicago	1994-95	.524

Most 3-point field goals made

Les Selvage	Anaheim	1967-68	147
Louie Dampier	Kentucky	1968-69	199
John Starks	New York	1994-95	217
Dennis Scott	Orlando	1995-96	267

Most 3-point field goals attempted

Les Selvage	Anaheim	1967-68	461
Louie Dampier	Kentucky	1968-69	552
Michael Adams	Denver	1990-91	564
John Starks	New York	1994-95	611
George McCloud	Dallas	1995-96	678

Free Throws

Highest free throw percentage

Herm Fuetsch	Cleveland	1945-46	.813
Angelo Musi	Philadelphia	1946-47	.829
Bob Feerick	Washington	1948-49	.859
Bobby Wanzer	Rochester	1951-52	.904
Bill Sharman	Boston	1956-57	.905
Bill Sharman	Boston	1958-59	.932
Ernie DiGregorio	Buffalo	1976-77	.945
Rick Barry	Houston	1978-79	.947
Calvin Murphy	Houston	1980-81	.958

Most free throws made

Soup Cable	Akron Firestone	1937-38	45
Leroy Edwards	Oshkosh	1938-39	86
Leroy Edwards	Oshkosh	1939-40	139
Mel Riebe	Cleveland	1944-45	161
Joe Fulks	Philadelphia	1946-47	439
George Mikan	Minneapolis	1948-49	532
George Mikan	Minneapolis	1949-50	567
George Mikan	Minneapolis	1950-51	576
Paul Arizin	Philadelphia	1951-52	578
Neil Johnston	Philadelphia	1954-55	589
Dolph Schayes	Syracuse	1956-57	625
George Yardley	Detroit	1957-58	655
Bob Pettit	St. Louis	1958-59	667
Dolph Schayes	Syracuse	1960-61	680
Wilt Chamberlain	Philadelphia	1961-62	835
Jerry West	Los Angeles	1965-66	840

Most free throws attempted, season

Leroy Edwards	Oshkosh	1945-46	200
Joe Fulks	Philadelphia	1946-47	601
George Mikan	Minneapolis	1948-49	689
George Mikan	Minneapolis	1949-50	728
Neil Johnston	Philadelphia	1952-53	794
George Yardley	Detroit	1957-58	808
Bob Pettit	St. Louis	1958-59	879
Wilt Chamberlain	Philadelphia	1959-60	991
Wilt Chamberlain	Philadelphia	1960-61	1,054
Wilt Chamberlain	Philadelphia	1961-62	1,363

Rebounds

Highest rebounds per game

Dolph Schayes	Syracuse	1950-51	16.4
Bill Russell	Boston	1956-57	19.6
Bill Russell	Boston	1957-58	22.7
Bill Russell	Boston	1958-59	23.0
Wilt Chamberlain	Philadelphia	1959-60	27.0
Wilt Chamberlain	Philadelphia	1960-61	27.2

Most rebounds, season

Dolph Schayes	Syracuse	1950-51	1,080
Harry Gallatin	New York	1953-54	1,098
Bob Pettit	St. Louis	1955-56	1,164
Maurice Stokes	Rochester	1956-57	1,256
Bill Russell	Boston	1957-58	1,564
Bill Russell	Boston	1958-59	1,612
Wilt Chamberlain	Philadelphia	1959-60	1,941
Wilt Chamberlain	Philadelphia	1960-61	2,149

Most offensive rebounds

Mel Daniels	Minnesota	1967-68	502
Spencer Haywood	Denver	1969-70	533
Moses Malone	Houston	1978-79	587

Most defensive rebounds

Mel Daniels	Minnesota	1967-68	711
Mel Daniels	Indiana	1968-69	873
Spencer Haywood	Denver	1969-70	1,104
Elvin Hayes	Capital	1973-74	1,109
Kareem Abdul-Jabbar	Los Angeles	1975-76	1,111

Assists

Highest assists per game

Ernie Calverley	Providence	1946-47	3.4
Bob Davies	Rochester	1948-49	5.4
Andy Phillip	Philadelphia	1949-50	5.8
Andy Phillip	Philadelphia	1950-51	6.3
Andy Phillip	Philadelphia	1951-52	8.2
Bob Cousy	Boston	1955-56	8.9
Bob Cousy	Boston	1959-60	9.5
Oscar Robertson	Cincinnati	1960-61	9.7
Oscar Robertson	Cincinnati	1961-62	11.4
Oscar Robertson	Cincinnati	1964-65	11.5
Kevin Porter	Detroit	1978-79	13.4
Isiah Thomas	Detroit	1984-85	13.9
John Stockton	Utah	1989-90	14.5

Most assists, season

Ernie Calverley	Providence	1946-47	202
Bob Davies	Rochester	1948-49	321
Dick McGuire	New York	1949-50	386
Andy Phillip	Philadelphia	1950-51	414
Andy Phillip	Philadelphia	1951-52	539
Bob Cousy	Boston	1952-53	547
Bob Cousy	Boston	1954-55	557
Bob Cousy	Boston	1955-56	642
Bob Cousy	Boston	1959-60	715
Oscar Robertson	Cincinnati	1961-62	899
Guy Rodgers	Chicago	1966-67	908
Nate Archibald	K.C.-Omaha	1972-73	910
Kevin Porter	Detroit	1978-79	1,099
Isiah Thomas	Detroit	1984-85	1,123
John Stockton	Utah	1987-88	1,128
John Stockton	Utah	1989-90	1,134
John Stockton	Utah	1990-91	1,164

Steals

Highest steals per game

Fatty Taylor	Virginia	1972-73	2.69
Ted McClain	Carolina	1973-74	2.98
Don Buse	Indiana	1975-76	4.12

Most steals

Billy Cunningham	Carolina	1972-73	216
Ted McClain	Carolina	1973-74	250
Don Buse	Indiana	1975-76	346

Blocked Shots

Highest blocked shots per game

Artis Gilmore	Kentucky	1972-73	3.08
Elmore Smith	Los Angeles	1973-74	4.85
Mark Eaton	Utah	1984-85	5.56

Most blocked shots

Artis Gilmore	Kentucky	1972-73	259
Elmore Smith	Los Angeles	1973-74	393
Mark Eaton	Utah	1984-85	456

Turnovers

Most turnovers

Larry Brown	New Orleans	1967-68	355
Ron Boone	Dallas	1968-69	355
George McGinnis	Indiana	1972-73	401
George McGinnis	Indiana	1974-75	422

Personal Fouls

Most personal fouls

Stan Miasek	Detroit	1946-47	208
Chuck Gilmur	Chicago	1947-48	231
Joe Camic	Hammond	1948-49	295
George Mikan	Minneapolis	1949-50	297
George Mikan	Minneapolis	1950-51	308
Don Meineke	Ft. Wayne	1952-53	334
Bailey Howell	Baltimore	1964-65	345
Bill Bridges	St. Louis	1967-68	366
Gene Moore	Kentucky	1969-70	382
Darryl Dawkins	New Jersey	1983-84	386

Most disqualifications

Don Christensen	Tri Cities	1950-51	16
Don Meineke	Ft. Wayne	1952-53	26

ALL-TIME SINGLE-SEASON TEAM RECORDS

Wins and losses

Highest winning percentage
(minimum 60 games)

Team	Season Set	Record
Washington Capitols	1946-47	.817 (49-11)
Los Angeles Lakers	1971-72	.841 (69-13)
Chicago Bulls	1995-96	.878 (72-10)

Highest home winning percentage
(minimum 30 games)

Washington Capitols	1946-47	.967 (29-1)
Rochester Royals	1949-50	.971 (33-1)
Boston Celtics	1985-86	.976 (40-1)

Highest road winning percentage
(minimum 30 games)

Washington Capitols	1946-47	.667 (20-10)
Rochester Royals	1949-50	.667 (20-10)
Boston Celtics	1959-60	.719 (23-9)
Philadelphia 76ers	1966-67	.732 (26-8)
Los Angeles Lakers	1971-72	.816 (31-7)

Lowest winning percentage
(minimum 60 games)

Pittsburgh Ironmen	1946-47	.250 (15-45)
Flint Dow A.C.'s	1947-48	.133 (8-52)
Philadelphia 76ers	1972-73	.110 (9-73)

Lowest home winning percentage
(minimum 30 games)

Pittsburgh Ironmen	1946-47	.367 (11-19)
Providence Steamrollers	1948-49	.233 (7-23)
San Diego Rockets	1967-68	.195 (8-33)
Philadelphia 76ers	1972-73	.161 (5-26)

Lowest road winning percentage
(minimum 30 games)

Pittsburgh Ironmen	1946-47	.133 (4-26)
Denver Nuggets	1948-49	.097 (3-28)
Tri-Cities Blackhawks	1950-51	.067 (2-28)
Cleveland Cavaliers	1970-71	.051 (2-37)
Virginia Squires	1975-76	.049 (2-39)
Sacramento Kings	1990-91	.024 (1-40)

Points

Most points per game

Oshkosh All-Stars	1937-38	49.1
Oshkosh All-Stars	1941-42	49.3
Ft. Wayne Zollner Pistons	1942-43	51.1
Ft. Wayne Zollner Pistons	1944-45	56.9
Ft. Wayne Zollner Pistons	1945-46	58.7
Chicago Stags	1946-47	77.0
Minneapolis Lakers	1948-49	84.0
Rochester Royals	1948-49	84.0
Anderson Packers	1949-50	87.3
Boston Celtics	1951-52	91.3
Boston Celtics	1954-55	101.4
Philadelphia Warriors	1955-56	106.0
New York	1957-58	112.1
Boston Celtics	1958-59	116.4
Boston Celtics	1959-60	124.5
Philadelphia Warriors	1961-62	125.4
Oakland Oaks	1968-69	126.5
Denver Nuggets	1981-82	126.5

Most points allowed per game

Kankakee Gallagher Trojans	1937-38	53.3
Pittsburgh Raiders	1944-45	55.5
Cleveland Allmen Transfers	1945-46	56.4
Providence Steamrollers	1946-47	74.2
Providence Steamrollers	1947-48	80.1
Providence Steamrollers	1948-49	87.1
Denver Nuggets	1949-50	89.1
Baltimore Bullets	1952-53	90.1
Boston Celtics	1954-55	101.5
Philadelphia Warriors	1955-56	105.3
Minneapolis Lakers	1957-58	111.5
Cincinnati Royals	1958-59	112.0
New York Knicks	1959-60	119.6
Cincinnati Royals	1960-61	121.3
Philadelphia Warriors	1961-62	122.7
Seattle Supersonics	1967-68	125.1
Pittsburgh Condors	1971-72	126.4
Denver Nuggets	1990-91	130.8

Fewest points per game*

Milwaukee Hawks	1954-55	87.4
Chicago Bulls	1998-99	81.9

* since inception of shot clock in '54-55

Fewest points allowed per game*

Syracuse Nationals	1954-55	89.7
Cleveland Cavaliers	1995-96	88.5
Cleveland Cavaliers	1996-97	85.6
Atlanta Hawks	1998-99	83.4

* since inception of shot clock in '54-55

Field Goals

Most field goals made

Fort Wayne General Electrics	1937-38	290
Akron Firestone Non-Skids	1938-39 – 43-44	490
Fort Wayne Zollner Pistons	1944-45	670
Fort Wayne Zollner Pistons	1945-46	765
Chicago Stags	1946-47	1,879
Chicago Stags	1948-49	1,905
Minneapolis Lakers	1949-50	2,139
Boston Celtics	1952-53	2,177
Boston Celtics	1953-54	2,232
Boston Celtics	1954-55	2,604
Boston Celtics	1955-56	2,745
Boston Celtics	1956-57	2,808
Boston Celtics	1957-58	3,006
Boston Celtics	1958-59	3,208
Boston Celtics	1959-60	3,744
Philadelphia Warriors	1960-61	3,768
Philadelphia Warriors	1961-62	3,917
Philadelphia 76ers	1967-68	3,965
Virginia Squires	1970-71	4,014
Denver Nuggets	1975-76	4,059

Most field goals attempted

Chicago Stags	1946-47	6,309
Boston Celtics	1954-55	6,533
Boston Celtics	1955-56	6,913
Boston Celtics	1956-57	7,326
Boston Celtics	1957-58	7,759
Boston Celtics	1958-59	8,116
Boston Celtics	1959-60	8,971
Boston Celtics	1960-61	9,295

Highest field goal percentage

Chicago Stags	1946-47	.298
Baltimore Bullets	1947-48	.301
Rochester Royals	1948-49	.372
Rochester Royals	1949-50	.373
New York Knicks	1950-51	.379
Rochester Royals	1951-52	.389
Boston Celtics	1952-53	.392
Boston Celtics	1953-54	.400
Philadelphia Warriors	1955-56	.410
St. Louis Hawks	1958-59	.410
New York Knicks	1959-60	.421

Philadelphia Warriors	1960-61	.424
Cincinnati Royals	1961-62	.452
Cincinnati Royals	1962-63	.459
Los Angeles Lakers	1967-68	.477
Milwaukee Bucks	1969-70	.488
Milwaukee Bucks	1970-71	.50903
Denver Nuggets	1974-75	.50914
Los Angeles Lakers	1978-79	.517
Los Angeles Lakers	1979-80	.529
Los Angeles Lakers	1983-84	.535
Los Angeles Lakers	1984-85	.545

Three-point Field Goals

Most 3-point field goals made

Pittsburgh Pipers	1967-68	243
Kentucky Colonels	1968-69	335
New York Knicks	1988-89	386
Phoenix Suns	1992-93	398
Houston Rockets	1993-94	429
Houston Rockets	1994-95	646
Miami Heat	1996-97	678
Boston Celtics	2001-02	699
Boston Celtics	2002-03	719

Most 3-point field goals attempted

Pittsburgh Pipers	1967-68	790
Minnesota Pipers	1968-69	1,006
Indiana Pacers	1970-71	1,024
New York Knicks	1988-89	1,147
Houston Rockets	1993-94	1,285
Houston Rockets	1994-95	1,757
Houston Rockets	1995-96	1,761
Miami Heat	1996-97	1,865
Boston Celtics	2001-02	1,946
Boston Celtics	2002-03	2,155

Highest 3-point field goal percentage

Pittsburgh Pipers	1967-68	.308
Kentucky Colonels	1968-69	.353
Kentucky Colonels	1969-70	.358
Boston Celtics	1979-80	.384
Boston Celtics	1987-88	.384
Cleveland Cavaliers	1989-90	.407
Washington Bullets	1995-96	.407
Charlotte Hornets	1996-97	.428

Free Throws

Most free throws made

Akron Firestone Non-Skids	1937-38	183
Oshkosh All-Stars	1938-39	258
Oshkosh All-Stars	1939-40	329
Cleveland Allmen Transfers	1944-45	398
Oshkosh All-Stars	1945-46	481
Philadelphia Warriors	1946-47	1,098
Baltimore Bullets	1948-49	1,545
New York Knicks	1949-50	1,710
Syracuse Nationals	1950-51	1,912
Syracuse Nationals	1951-52	1,933
Syracuse Nationals	1952-53	2,197
New York Knicks	1957-58	2,300
Los Angeles Lakers	1961-62	2,378
Oakland Oaks	1968-69	2,607

Most free throws attempted

Oshkosh All-Stars	1945-46	657
Providence Steamrollers	1946-47	1,666
Rochester Royals	1948-49	2,060
New York Knicks	1949-50	2,404
Syracuse Nationals	1950-51	2,634
Syracuse Nationals	1952-53	2,950
New York Knicks	1957-58	3,056
Detroit Pistons	1960-61	3,240
Detroit Pistons	1961-62	3,240
Philadelphia Warriors	1966-67	3,411
Oakland Oaks	1968-69	3,434

Highest free throw percentage

Fort Wayne Zollner Pistons	1945-46	.720
Baltimore Bullets	1948-49	.753
Philadelphia Warriors	1950-51	.763
Boston Celtics	1954-55	.776
Minneapolis Lakers	1955-56	.786
Syracuse Nationals	1956-57	.79411
Utah Stars	1972-73	.79383
Houston Rockets	1973-74	.812
Kansas City-Omaha Kings	1974-75	.8205
Milwaukee Bucks	1988-89	.8207
Boston Celtics	1989-90	.832

Rebounds

Most rebounds

Ft. Wayne Pistons	1950-51	3,725
Baltimore Bullets	1951-52	3,780
New York Knicks	1952-53	4,007
New York Knicks	1954-55	4,379
Boston Celtics	1955-56	4,583
Boston Celtics	1956-57	4,963
St. Louis Hawks	1957-58	5,445
Boston Celtics	1958-59	5,601
Boston Celtics	1959-60	6,014
Boston Celtics	1960-61	6,131

Assists

Most assists

Cleveland Rebels	1946-47	494
St. Louis Bombers	1948-48	1,269
Boston Celtics	1949-50	1,473
Syracuse Nationals	1949-50	1,473
Boston Celtics	1950-51	1,579
Boston Celtics	1951-52	1,606
Boston Celtics	1952-53	1,666
Boston Celtics	1954-55	1,905
St. Louis Hawks	1960-61	2,136
Cincinnati Royals	1961-62	2,154
Philadelphia 76ers	1967-68	2,197
Seattle Supersonics	1969-70	2,214
Milwaukee Bucks	1970-71	2,249
Boston Celtics	1972-73	2,320
Denver Nuggets	1974-75	2,450
Milwaukee Bucks	1978-79	2,562
Los Angeles Lakers	1984-85	2,575

Steals

Most steals

Carolina Cougars	1973-74	1,005
Phoenix Suns	1977-78	1,059

Highest steals per game average

Carolina Cougars	1973-74	12.0
Phoenix Suns	1977-78	12.9

Blocked Shots

Most blocked shots

San Antonio Spurs	1973-74	600
Philadelphia 76ers	1979-80	652
Atlanta Hawks	1982-83	665
Utah Jazz	1984-85	697
Washington Bullets	1985-86	716

Highest blocked shots per game average

San Antonio Spurs	1973-74	7.1
Philadelphia 76ers	1979-80	8.0
Atlanta Hawks	1982-83	8.1
Utah Jazz	1984-85	8.5
Washington Bullets	1985-86	8.7

Turnovers

Fewest turnovers

Houston Mavericks	1967-68	1,093
Minnesota Timberwolves	1990-91	1,062
Detroit Pistons	1996-97	1,043
Dallas Mavericks	2001-02	992
Dallas Mavericks	2002-03	949

Note:* The Minnesota Timberwolves had a league-low 641 turnovers in 1998-99 when a lockout shortened the NBA schedule to 50- games schedule in effect due to lockout.

Fewest turnovers per game

Houston Mavericks	1967-68	14.0
Denver Nuggets	1989-90	13.9
Minnesota Timberwolves	1990-91	13.0
Detroit Pistons	1996-97	12.7
Dallas Mavericks	2001-02	12.1
Dallas Mavericks	2002-03	11.6

Personal Fouls

Most fouls committed, season

Chicago Stags	1946-47	1,473
Chicago Stags	1947-48	1,731
Ft. Wayne Pistons	1949-50	2,065
Tri-Cities Blackhawks	1950-51	2,092
Rochester Royals	1952-53	2,210
Syracuse Nationals	1960-61	2,280
Seattle Supersonics	1967-68	2,372
New York Nets	1969-70	2,381
Carolina Cougars	1972-73	2,394
Atlanta Hawks	1977-78	2,470

Most disqualifications, season

Tri-Cities Blackhawks	1950-51	79
Ft. Wayne Pistons	1950-51	79
Rochester Royals	1952-53	107

Chapter 40

NBA Records

(Records for "fewest" and "lowest" begin when the 24-second clock was introduced in 1954.)

SEASONS

Most

21	Robert Parish, 1976-77 to 1996-97
20	Kareem Abdul-Jabbar, 1969-70 to 1988-89
19	Moses Malone, 1976-77 to 1994-95
	James Edwards, 1977-79 to 1995-96
	John Stockton, 1984-85 to 2002-03

GAMES

Most, career

1,611	Robert Parish, 1976-77 to 1996-97
1,560	Kareem Abdul-Jabbar, 1969-70 to 1988-89
1,504	John Stockton, 1984-85 to 2002-03
1,434	Karl Malone, 1985-86 to 2002-03
1,329	Moses Malone, 1976-77 to 1994-95

Most consecutive, career

1,192	A.C. Green, Nov. 19/86 to Apr. 18/01
906	Randy Smith, Feb.18/72 to Mar.13/83
844	John Kerr Oct. 31/54 to Nov. 4/65

Most, one season

88	Walt Bellamy, 1968-69
87	Tom Henderson, 1976-77
86	McCoy McLemore, 1970-71
	Garfield Heard, 1975-76

MINUTES

(since 1951-52)

Most seasons leading league

8	Wilt Chamberlain
4	Elvin Hayes
3	Michael Jordan
	Michael Finley

Most consecutive seasons leading league

5	Wilt Chamberlain, 1959-60 to 1963-64
3	Wilt Chamberlain, 1965-66 to 1967-68
	Michael Jordan, 1986-87 to 1988-89

Most, career

57,446	Kareem Abdul-Jabbar, 1969-70 to 1988-89
53,479	Karl Malone, 1985-86 to 2002-03
50,000	Elvin Hayes, 1968-69 to 1970-71
47,859	Wilt Chamberlain, 1959-60 to 1961-62
47,764	John Stockton, 1984-84 to 2002-03
46,471	John Havlicek, 1962-63 to 1977-78

Highest average per game, career
(minimum 400 games)

45.8	Wilt Chamberlain, 1959-60 to 1961-62
42.3	Bill Russell, 1956-57 to 1968-69
42.2	Oscar Robertson, 1960-61 to 1969-70

Most, one season

3,882	Wilt Chamberlain, 1961-62
3,836	Wilt Chamberlain, 1967-68
3,806	Wilt Chamberlain, 1962-63
3,773	Wilt Chamberlain, 1960-61
3,737	Wilt Chamberlain, 1965-66

Robert Parish, 1992
Twenty-one seasons, four teams and an incredible 1,611 games—1,804 if you count playoffs and All-Star games.

Highest average per game, one season

48.5	Wilt Chamberlain, 1961-62	
47.8	Wilt Chamberlain, 1960-61	
47.6	Wilt Chamberlain, 1962-63	
47.3	Wilt Chamberlain, 1965-66	
46.8	Wilt Chamberlain, 1967-68	

Most, one game

69	Dale Ellis, Nov. 9/89, 5 OT
68	Xavier McDaniel, Nov. 9/89, 5 OT
64	Norm Nixon, Jan. 29/80, 4 OT
	Sleepy Floyd, Feb. 1/87, 4 OT

COMPLETE GAMES

Most, one season

79	Wilt Chamberlain, 1961-62

Most consecutive, one season

47	Wilt Chamberlain, Jan. 5-Mar. 14/62

SCORING

Most seasons leading league

10	Michael Jordan
7	Wilt Chamberlain

Most consecutive seasons leading league

7	Wilt Chamberlain, 1959-60 to 1965-66
	Michael Jordan, 1986-87 to 1992-93
3	George Mikan, 1948-49 to 1950-51
	Neil Johnston, 1952-53 to 1954-55
	Bob McAdoo, 1973-74 to 1975-76
	George Gervin, 1977-78 to 1979-80
	Michael Jordan, 1995-96 to 1997-98

POINTS

Most, career

38,387	Kareem Abdul-Jabbar, 1969-70 to 1988-89
36,374	Karl Malone, 1985-86 to 2002-03
32,292	Michael Jordan, 1984-85 to 2002-03
31,419	Wilt Chamberlain, 1959-60 to 1972-73
27,409	Moses Malone, 1976-77 to 1994-95

Highest average per game, career
(minimum 400 games)

30.12	Michael Jordan, 1984-85 to 2002-03
30.06	Wilt Chamberlain, 1959-60 to 1972-73
27.6	Shaquille O'Neal, 1992-93 to 2002-03
27.4	Elgin Baylor, 1958-59 to 1971-72
27.0	Jerry West, 1960-61 to 1973-74

Most, one season

4,029	Wilt Chamberlain, 1961-62
3,586	Wilt Chamberlain, 1962-63
3,041	Michael Jordan, 1986-87
3,033	Wilt Chamberlain, 1960-61
2,948	Wilt Chamberlain, 1963-64

Highest average per game, one season
(minimum 70 games)

50.4	Wilt Chamberlain, 1961-62
44.8	Wilt Chamberlain, 1962-63
38.4	Wilt Chamberlain, 1960-61
37.6	Wilt Chamberlain, 1959-60
37.1	Michael Jordan, 1986-87

Most, one game

100	Wilt Chamberlain, Mar. 2/62
78	Wilt Chamberlain, Dec. 8/61, 3 OT
73	Wilt Chamberlain, Jan. 13/62
	Wilt Chamberlain, Nov. 16/62
	David Thompson, Apr. 9/78
72	Wilt Chamberlain, Nov. 3/62
71	Elgin Baylor, Nov. 15/60
	David Robinson, Apr. 24/94

Most games, 50 or more, career

118	Wilt Chamberlain
31	Michael Jordan
18	Elgin Baylor
14	Rick Barry

Most games, 50 or more, one season

45	Wilt Chamberlain, 1961-62
30	Wilt Chamberlain, 1962-63
9	Wilt Chamberlain, 1963-64
	Wilt Chamberlain, 1964-65

Most consecutive games, 50 or more

7	Wilt Chamberlain, Dec. 16-Dec. 29/61
6	Wilt Chamberlain, Jan. 11-Jan. 19/62
5	Wilt Chamberlain, Dec. 8-Dec. 13/61
	Wilt Chamberlain, Feb. 25-Mar. 4/62

FIELD GOALS

Highest percentage, career
(minimum 2,000 made)

.599	Artis Gilmore, 1976-77 to 1987-88
.580	Mark West, 1983-84 to 1999-2000
.577	Shaquille O'Neal, 1992-93 to 2002-03

Highest percentage, season

.727	Wilt Chamberlain, 1972-73
.683	Wilt Chamberlain, 1966-67
.670	Artis Gilmore, 1980-81
.652	Artis Gilmore, 1981-82
.649	Wilt Chamberlain, 1971-72

Highest percentage, one game
(minimum 15 FGM)

1.000	Wilt Chamberlain, 15-15, Jan. 20/67
	Wilt Chamberlain, 18-18, Feb. 24/67
	Wilt Chamberlain 16-16, Mar. 19/67
.947	Wilt Chamberlain, 18-19, Nov. 27/63
.944	George Gervin, 17-18, Feb. 18/78

Most, career

15,837	Kareem Abdul-Jabbar, 1969-70 to 1988-89
13,335	Karl Malone, Utah, 1985-86 to 2001-03
12,681	Wilt Chamberlain, 1959-60 to 1972-73

Most, season

1,597	Wilt Chamberlain, 1961-62
1,463	Wilt Chamberlain, 1962-63
1,251	Wilt Chamberlain, 1960-61

Most attempts, career

28,307	Kareem Abdul-Jabbar, 1969-70 to 1988-89
25,810	Karl Malone, 1985-86 to 2002-03
24,272	Elvin Hayes, 1968-69 to 1983-84

Most attempts, one season

3,159	Wilt Chamberlain, 1961-62
2,770	Wilt Chamberlain, 1962-63
2,457	Wilt Chamberlain, 1960-61

Most attempts, one game

63	Wilt Chamberlain, Mar. 2/62
62	Wilt Chamberlain, Dec. 8/61, 3 OT
60	Wilt Chamberlain, Oct. 28/62, OT

THREE-POINT FIELD GOAL PERCENTAGE

(since 1979-80)

Highest percentage, career
(minimum 250 made)

.454	Steve Kerr, 1988-89 to 2002-03
.441	Hubert Davis, 1992-93 to 2002-03
.437	Drazen Petrovic, 1989-90 to 1992-93

Highest percentage, season

.524	Steve Kerr, 1994-96
.522	Tim Legler, 1995-96
.521	Jon Sundvold, 1988-89

THREE-POINT FIELD GOALS

(since 1979-80)

Most, career

2,330	Reggie Miller, 1987 to 2002-03
1,719	Dale Ellis, 1983-84 to 1999-2000
1,542	Tim Hardaway, 1989-90 to 2002-03

Most, one season

267	Dennis Scott, Orlando, 1995-96
257	George McCloud, 1995-96
231	Mookie Blaylock, 1995-96

Most, one game

11	Dennis Scott, Apr. 18/96
10	Brian Shaw, Apr. 8/93
	Joe Dumars, Nov. 8/94
	George McCloud, Dec. 16/95
	Ray Allen, Apr. 14/02

THREE-POINT FIELD GOAL ATTEMPTS

(since 1979-80)

Most attempts, career

5,854	Reggie Miller, 1987-88 to 2002-03
4,266	Dale Ellis, 1983-84 to 2000
4,345	Tim Hardaway, 1989-90 to 2002-03

Most attempts, one season

678	George McCloud, 1995-96
645	Antoine Walker, 2001-02
628	Dennis Scott, 1995-96

Most attempts, one game

20	Michael Adams, Apr. 12/91
	George McCloud, Mar. 5/96
19	Dennis Scott, Apr. 13/93
18	Joe Dumars, Nov. 8/94
	Dee Brown, Apr. 28/99

FREE THROWS

Highest percentage, career
(minimum 1,200 made)

.904	Mark Price, 1986-87 to 1997-98
.900	Rick Barry, 1965-66 to 1979-80
.892	Calvin Murphy, 1970-71 to 1982-83

Most made, none missed, one game

23	Dominique Wilkins, Dec. 8/92
19	Bob Pettit, Nov. 22/61
	Bill Cartwright, Nov. 17/81
	Adrian Dantley, Dec. 15/87, OT

Most attempts, none made, one game

11	Shaquille O'Neal, Dec. 8/00
10	Wilt Chamberlain, Nov. 4/60
9	Wilt Chamberlain, Feb. 19/67

Most made, career

9,619	Karl Malone, 1985-86 to 2002-03
8,531	Moses Malone, 1976-77 to 1994-95
7,694	Oscar Robertson, 1960-61 to 1973-74

Most made, season

840	Jerry West, 1965-66
835	Wilt Chamberlain, 1961-62
833	Michael Jordan, 1986-87

Most consecutive made

97	Micheal Williams, Mar. 24-Nov. 9/93
81	Mahmoud Abdul-Rauf, Mar. 15-Nov. 16/93
78	Calvin Murphy, Dec. 27/80-Feb. 28/81

Most made, one game

28	Wilt Chamberlain, Mar. 2/62
	Adrian Dantley, Jan. 4/84
27	Adrian Dantley, Nov. 25/83
26	Adrian Dantley, Oct. 31/80
	Michael Jordan, Feb. 26/87

Most attempts, career

12,963	Karl Malone, 1985-86 to 2002-03
11,862	Wilt Chamberlain, 1959-60 to 1972-73
11,090	Moses Malone, 1976-77 to 1994-95

Most attempts, one season

1,363	Wilt Chamberlain, 1961-62
1,113	Wilt Chamberlain, 1962-63
1,054	Wilt Chamberlain, 1960-61

NBA REGULAR SEASON INDIVIDUAL RECORDS

Most attempts, one game
34	Wilt Chamberlain, Feb. 22/62
32	Wilt Chamberlain, Mar. 2/62
31	Wilt Chamberlain, Dec. 8/61, 3 OT
	Adrian Dantley, Nov. 25/83
	Shaquille O'Neal, Nov. 19/99

REBOUNDS

(since 1950-51)
Most, career
23,924	Wilt Chamberlain, 1959-60 to 1972-73
21,620	Bill Russell, 1956-57 to 1968-69
17,440	Kareem Abdul-Jabbar, 1969-70 to 1988-89
16,279	Elvin Hayes, 1968-69 to 1983-84
16,212	Moses Malone, 1976-77 to 1994-95

Highest average per game, career
22.9	Wilt Chamberlain, 1959-60 to 1972-73
22.5	Bill Russell, 1956-57 to 1968-69
16.2	Bob Pettit, 1954-55 to 1964-65
15.6	Jerry Lucas, 1963-64 to 1973-74
15.0	Nate Thurmond, 1963-64 to 1976-77

Most, one season
2,149	Wilt Chamberlain, 1960-61
2,052	Wilt Chamberlain, 1961-62
1,957	Wilt Chamberlain, 1966-67
1,952	Wilt Chamberlain, 1967-68
1,946	Wilt Chamberlain, 1962-63

Most seasons, 1,000 or more
13	Wilt Chamberlain
12	Bill Russell
9	Bob Pettit
	Walt Bellamy
	Elvin Hayes

Highest average per game, one season
27.2	Wilt Chamberlain, 1960-61
27.0	Wilt Chamberlain, 1959-60
25.7	Wilt Chamberlain, 1961-62
24.7	Bill Russell, 1963-64
24.6	Wilt Chamberlain, 1965-66

Most, one game
55	Wilt Chamberlain, Nov. 24/60
51	Bill Russell, Feb. 5/60
49	Bill Russell, Nov. 16/57
	Bill Russell, Mar. 11/65
45	Wilt Chamberlain, Feb. 6/60
	Wilt Chamberlain, Jan. 21/61

OFFENSIVE REBOUNDS

(since 1973-74)
Most, career
6,731	Moses Malone, 1976-77 to 1996-97
4,526	Buck Williams, 1981-82 to 1997-98

Highest average per game, career
(minimum 400 games)
5.1	Moses Malone, 1976-77 to 1996-97
4.8	Dennis Rodman, 1986-87 to 1999-2000
3.97	Shaquille O'Neal, 1992-93 to 2002-03

Most, season
587	Moses Malone, 1978-79
573	Moses Malone, 1979-80
558	Moses Malone, 1981-82

Most, one game
21	Moses Malone, Feb. 11/82
19	Moses Malone, Feb. 9/79
18	Charles Oakley, Mar. 15/86, OT
	Dennis Rodman, Mar. 4/92, OT

DEFENSIVE REBOUNDS

(since 1973-74)
Most, career
1,412	Karl Malone, 1985-86 to 2002-03
10,117	Robert Parish, 1976-77 to 1996-97
9,714	Hakeem Olajuwon, 1984-85 to 2001-02

Highest average per game, career
(minimum 400 games)
9.8	Dave Cowens, 1973-74 to 1982-83
8.4	Dikembe Mutombo, 1991-92 to 2002-03
8.4	Wes Unseld, 1973-74 to 1980-81

Most, one season
1,111	Kareem Abdul-Jabbar, 1975-76
1,109	Elvin Hayes, 1973-74
1,007	Dennis Rodman, 1991-92

Most, one game
29	Kareem Abdul-Jabbar, Dec. 14/75
28	Elvin Hayes, Nov. 17/73
26	Rony Seikaly, Mar. 3/93

ASSISTS

Most, career
15,806	John Stockton, 1984-85 to 2002-03
10,215	Mark Jackson, 1987-88 to 2002-03
10,141	Magic Johnson, 1979-80 to 1995-96
9,887	Oscar Robertson, 1960-61 to 1973-74
9,061	Isiah Thomas, 1981-82 to 1993-94

Highest average per game, career
(minimum 400 games)
11.2	Magic Johnson, 1979-80 to 1995-96
10.5	John Stockton, 1984-85 to 2002-03
9.5	Oscar Robertson, 1960-61 to 1973-74
9.4	Jason Kidd, 1994-95 to 2002-03
9.3	Isiah Thomas, 1981-82 to 1993-94

Most, one season
1,164	John Stockton, 1990-91
1,134	John Stockton, 1989-90
1,128	John Stockton, 1987-88

Highest average per game, one season
(minimum 70 games)
14.5	John Stockton, 1989-90
14.2	John Stockton, 1990-91
13.9	Isiah Thomas, 1984-85

Most, one game
30	Scott Skiles, Dec. 30/90
29	Kevin Porter, Feb. 24/78
28	Bob Cousy, Feb. 27/59
	Guy Rodgers, Mar. 14/63
	John Stockton, Jan. 15/91

PERSONAL FOULS

Most, career
4,657	Kareem Abdul-Jabbar, 1975-76 to 1988-89
4,443	Robert Parish, 1976-77 to 1996-97
4,383	Hakeem Olajuwon, 1984-85 to 2001-02

Most, one season
386	Darryl Dawkins, 1983-84
379	Darryl Dawkins, 1982-83
372	Steve Johnson, 1981-82

Most, one game
8	Don Otten, Nov. 24/49
7	Alex Hannum, Dec. 26/50
	Cal Bowdler, Nov. 13/99

DISQUALIFICATIONS

(since 1950-51)
Most, career
127	Vern Mikkelsen, 1950-51 to 1958-59
121	Walter Dukes, 1955-56 to 1962-63
115	Shawn Kemp, 1989-90 to 2002-03

Most, one season
26	Don Meineke, 1952-53
25	Steve Johnson, 1981-82
23	Darryl Dawkins, 1982-83

STEALS

(since 1973-74)
Most, career
3,265	John Stockton, 1984-85 to 2002-03
2,514	Michael Jordan, 1984-85 to 2002-03
2,310	Maurice Cheeks, 1978-79 to 1992-93

Highest average per game, career
(minimum 400 games)
2.71	Alvin Robertson, 1984-85 to 1995-96
2.63	Micheal Ray Richardson, 1978-79 to 1985-86
2.35	Michael Jordan, 1984-85 to 2002-03

Most, one season
301	Alvin Robertson, 1985-86
281	Don Buse, 1976-77
265	Micheal Ray Richardson, 1979-80

Highest average per game, one season
3.67	Alvin Robertson, 1985-86
3.47	Don Buse, 1976-77
3.43	Magic Johnson, 1980-81

Most, one game
11	Larry Kenon, Dec. 26/76
	Kendall Gill, Apr. 3/99

BLOCKED SHOTS

(since 1973-74)
Most, one game
17	Elmore Smith, Oct. 28/73
15	Manute Bol, Jan. 25/86
	Manute Bol, Feb. 26/87
	Shaquille O'Neal, Nov. 20/93

Most, career
3,830	Hakeem Olajuwon, 1984-85 to 2002-03
3,189	Kareem Abdul-Jabbar, 1973-74 to 1988-89
3,064	Mark Eaton, 1982-83 to 1992-93

Highest average per game, career
(minimum 400 games)
3.50	Mark Eaton, 1982-83 to 1992-93
3.34	Manute Bol, 1985-86 to 1994-95
3.32	Dikembe Mutombo, 1991-92 to 2002-03

Most, one season
456	Mark Eaton, 1984-85
397	Manute Bol, 1985-86
393	Elmore Smith, 1973-74

Highest average per game, one season
5.56	Mark Eaton, 1984-85
4.97	Manute Bol, 1985-86
4.85	Elmore Smith, 1973-74

TURNOVERS

(since 1977-78)
Most, career
4,234	John Stockton, 1984-85 to 2002-03
4,423	Karl Malone, 1985-86 to 2002-03
3,804	Moses Malone, 1977-78 to 1994-95

Mast, one season
366	Artis Gilmore, 1977-78
360	Kevin Porter, 1977-78
359	Micheal Ray Richardson, 1979-80

Most, one game
14	John Drew, Mar. 1/78
	Jason Kidd, Nov. 17/00
13	Chris Mullin, Mar. 31/88

POINTS

Most, one team, one game:
186—Detroit at Denver, Dec. 13/83

Fewest, one team, one game:
49—Chicago vs. Miami, Apr. 10/99

Most, both teams, one game:
370—Detroit (186) at Denver (184),
Dec. 13/83, 3 OT

Fewest, both teams, one game:
119—Milwaukee (57) vs. Boston (62), at
Providence, Feb. 27/55

Most per game, one season:
126.5—Denver (82 games) 1981-82

Fewest per game, one season:
(Min. 50 games)
81.9—Chicago 1998-99

Most allowed per game, one season:
130.8—Denver, 1990-91

Fewest allowed per game, one season:
83.4—Atlanta, 1998-99

Largest margin of victory:
68—Cleveland vs. Miami, Dec.17/91 (148-80)

FIELD GOALS

Most per game, one season:
49.9—Boston, 1959-60

Fewest per game, one season:
30.4—Milwaukee, 1954-55

Most, one team, one game:
74—Detroit at Denver, Dec. 13/83, 3 OT

Fewest, one team, one game:
18—Chicago vs. Miami, Apr. 10/99

Most, both teams, one game:
142—Detroit (74) at Denver (68), Dec. 13/83, 3 OT

Fewest, both teams, one game:
45—Minnesota (22) vs. Atlanta (23), Apr. 12/97

Highest percentage, one team, one game:
.707 (53/75)—San Antonio at Dallas, Apr. 16/83

Lowest percentage, one team, one game:
.229 (22/96)—Milwaukee vs. Minneapolis, at
Buffalo, Nov. 6/54

Highest percentage, both teams, one game:
.632 (108/171)—Boston (.650) vs. New Jersey
(.615) at Hartford, Dec. 11/84

Lowest percentage, both teams, one game:
.246 (48/195)—Milwaukee (.229) vs. Minneapolis
(.263) at Buffalo, Nov. 6/54

Most made, one team, one season:
4,059—Denver, 1975-76

Most attempted, one team, one season:
9,295—Boston, 1960-61

Highest percentage, one team, one season:
.545—LA Lakers, 1984-85

Lowest percentage, one team, one season:
.362—Milwaukee, 1954-55

THREE-POINT FIELD GOALS
(since 1979-80)
Most, one team, one game:
19—Atlanta at Dallas, Dec. 17/96

Most, both teams, one game:
29—Denver (16) at Seattle (13), Mar. 20/97

Most per game, one team, one season:
8.96—Dallas, 1995-96

Fewest per game, one team, one season:
0.12—Atlanta, 1980-81; LA Lakers, 1982-83

Most made, one team, one season:
719—Boston, 2002-03

Most attempted, one team, one season:
2,155—Boston, 2002-03

Highest percentage, one team, one season:
.428—Charlotte, 1996-97

Lowest percentage, one team, one season:
.104—LA Lakers, 1982-83

FREE THROWS

Most made, one team, one game:
61—Phoenix vs. Utah, Apr. 9/90, OT

Fewest made, one team, one game:
0—Toronto vs. Charlotte, Jan. 9/96

Most made, both teams, one game:
116—Syracuse (59) vs. Anderson (57),
Nov. 24/49, 5 OT

Fewest made, both teams, one game:
7—Milwaukee (3) vs. Baltimore (4), Jan.1/73

Highest percentage, both teams, one game:
1.000 (16/16)—Atlanta vs. Toronto, Dec. 22/00

Lowest percentage, both teams, one game:
.410 (25/61)—LA Lakers (.386) at Chicago (.471),
Dec. 7/68

Most consecutive made, one team, one game:
39—Utah at Portland, Dec. 7/82

Lowest percentage, one team, one game:
.000 (0/3)—Toronto vs. Charlotte, Jan. 9/96

Most attempts, one team, one game:
86—Syracuse vs. Anderson, Nov. 24/49, 5 OT

Fewest attempts, one team, one game:
2—Cleveland vs. Golden State, Nov. 26/94

Most attempts, both teams, one game:
160—Syracuse (86) vs. Anderson (74),
Nov. 24/49, 5 OT

Fewest attempts, both teams, one game:
12—LA Lakers (3) vs. San Diego (9), Mar. 28/80

Most made, one team, one season:
2,607—Oakland, 1968-69

Most attempted, one team, one season:
3,434– Oakland, 1968-69

Most made per game, one team, one season:
31.9—New York, 1957-58

**Fewest made per game, one team,
one season:**
14.9—Boston, 1998-99

Highest percentage, one team, one season:
.832—Boston, 1989-90

**Lowest percentage, one team, one season,
season:**
.635—Philadelphia, 1967-68

**Most attempts per game, one team,
one season:**
42.4—New York, 1957-58

**Fewest attempts per game, one team,
one season:**
19.9—Phoenix, 2001-02

REBOUNDS
(since 1950-51)
Most, one team, one game:
109—Boston vs. Detroit, Dec. 24/60

Fewest , one team, one game:
18—Detroit vs. Charlotte, Nov. 28/01

Most, both teams, one game:
188—Philadelphia (98) vs. LA Lakers (90),
Dec. 8/61, 3 OT

Fewest, both teams, one game:
48—New York (20) vs. Fort Wayne (28), at Miami,
Feb. 14/55

Most made, one team, one season:
6,131—Boston, 1960-61

Most per game, one team, one season:
71.5—Boston, 1959-60

Fewest per game, one team, one season:
35.6—Cleveland, 1995-96

OFFENSIVE REBOUNDS
(since 1973-74)
Most, one team, one game:
39—Boston at Capital, Oct. 20/73

Fewest, one team, one game:
0—San Antonio at Utah, Jan. 23/02

Most both teams, one game:
60—Golden State (33) vs. Vancouver (27),
Apr. 18/01

Fewest both teams, one game:
6—Indiana (1) vs. Detroit (5), Jan. 18/02

Most per game, one team, one season:
18.54—Denver, 1990-91

Fewest per game, one team, one season:
9.43—New York, 2000-01

DEFENSIVE REBOUNDS
(since 1973-74)
Most, one team, one game:
61—Boston vs. Capital, March 17/74

Fewest, one team, one game:
10—Utah at LA Lakers, Apr, 1/90

Most, both teams, one game:
106—Portland (56) vs. Cleveland (50),
Oct. 18/74, 4 OT

Fewest, both teams, one game:
31—Utah (10) at LA Lakers (21), Apr. 1/90

Most per game, one team, one season:
37.5—Boston, 1973-74

Fewest per game, one team, one season:
24.9—Boston, 1997-98

ASSISTS

Most, one team, one game:
53—Milwaukee vs. Detroit, Dec. 26/78

Fewest, one team, one game:
3—Four Teams: Boston vs. Minneapolis, at
Louisville, Nov, 28/56; Baltimore vs. Boston,
Oct. 16/63; Cincinnati vs. Chicago, at
Evansville, Dec. 5/67; New York at Boston,
Mar. 28/76

NBA REGULAR SEASON TEAM RECORDS

Most, both teams, one game:
93—Detroit (47) at Denver (46), Dec. 13/83, 3 OT

Fewest, both teams, one game:
10—Boston (3) vs. Minneapolis (7), at Louisville, Nov. 28/56

Most, one team, one season:
2,575—LA Lakers, 1984-85

Most per game, one team, one season:
31.4—LA Lakers, 1984-85

Fewest per game, one team, one season:
15.6—Atlanta, 1998-99

PERSONAL FOULS

Most, one team, one game:
66—Anderson at Syracuse, Nov. 24/49
(Post 1954-55: 46—New York at Phoenix, Dec. 3/87)

Fewest, one team, one game:
5—Dallas at San Antonio, Nov. 20/99

Most, both teams, one game:
122—Anderson (66) at Syracuse (56), Nov. 24/49, 5 OT
(Post 1954-55: 84—Indiana (44) vs. Kansas City (40), Oct. 22/77)

Fewest, both teams, one game:
21—Phoenix (9) at Portland (12), Dec. 1/01

Most, one team, one season:
2,470—Atlanta, 1977-78

Most per game, one team, one season:
32.1—Tri-Cities, 1949-50
(Post 1954-55: 30.1—Atlanta, 1977-78)

Fewest per game, one team, one season:
18.0—Houston, 2001-02

DISQUALIFICATIONS

(since 1950-51)
Most, one team, one game:
8—Syracuse at Baltimore, Nov. 15/52, OT

Most, both teams, one game:
13—Syracuse (8) at Baltimore (5), Nov. 15/52, OT

Most, one team, one season:
107—Rochester, 1952-53

Most per game, one team, one season:
1.53—Rochester, 1952-53
Post 1954-55: 0.98—Atlanta, 1977-78

Fewest per game, one team, one season:
0.02—LA Lakers, 1988-89

STEALS

(since 1973-74)
Most, one team, one game:
27—Seattle vs. Toronto, Jan. 15/97

Fewest, one team, one game:
0—18 Teams, most recent: Cleveland vs. LA Lakers, Feb. 2/02

Most, both teams, one game:
40—Three times: Golden State (24) vs. LA Lakers (16), Jan. 21/75; Philadelphia (24) vs. Detroit (16), Nov. 11/78; Golden State (25) vs. San Antonio (15), Feb. 15/89

Fewest, both teams, one game:
2—Two times: Detroit (1) at New York (1), Oct. 9/73; San Antonio (1) at Charlotte (1), Feb. 6/66

Most, one team, one season:
1,059—Phoenix, 1977-78

Most per game, one team, one season:
12.9—Phoenix, 1977-78

Fewest per game, one team, one season:
5.94—Detroit, 1990-91

BLOCKED SHOTS

(since 1973-74)
Most, one team, one game:
23—Toronto vs. Atlanta, Mar. 23/01

Fewest, one team, one game:
0—By several teams

Most, both teams, one game:
34—Detroit (19) vs. Washington (15), Nov. 19/81

Fewest, both teams, one game:
0—Three times: Seattle at Portland, Nov. 22/73; Atlanta at Phoenix. Dec. 3/74; Kansas City at New York, Oct. 30/75

Most, one team, one season:
716—1985-86

Most per game, one team, one season:
8.7—Washington, 1985-86

Fewest per game, one team, one season:
2.6—Dallas, 1980-81

TURNOVERS

(since 1970-71)
Most one team, one game:
45—San Francisco vs. Boston, Mar. 9/71

Fewest, one team, one game:
3—Four Teams: Portland vs. Phoenix, Feb. 22/91; Orlando vs. New York, Mar. 31/96; Toronto at Houston, Jan. 16/01; LA Lakers vs. Houston, Dec. 30/01

Most, both teams, one game:
73—Twice: Philadelphia (38) vs. San Antonio (35), Oct. 22/76; Denver (38) vs. Phoenix (35), Oct. 24/80

Fewest, both teams, one game:
12—Cleveland (6) at Boston (6), Mar. 7/93

Most per game, one team, one season:
24.5—Denver, 1976-77

Fewest, one team, one season:
949—Dallas, 2002-03

Fewest per game, one team, one season:
11.6—Dallas, 2002-03

Most by opponent, per game, one season:
24.1—Atlanta, 1977-78

Fewest by opponents, per game, one season:
12.0—Houston, 2001-02

POINTS ALLOWED

Fewest per game, one team, one season:
83.4—Atlanta, 1998-99

Most per game, one team, one season:
130.8—Denver, 1990-91

OVERTIME

Most points, one team, one period:
25—New Jersey at LA Clippers, Nov. 30/96

Fewest points, one team, one period:
0—Eight teams, most recent: Houston vs. Portland, Jan. 22/83

Most points, both teams, one period:
46—Dallas (23) at Houston (23), Apr. 11/95 (1st OT)

Most OT games, one team, one season:
14—Philadelphia, 1990-91

Most losses, one team, one season:
10—Baltimore, 1952-53

Most wins, one team, one season:
9—Sacramento, 2000-01

Most OT periods, one game:
6—Indianapolis (75) at Rochester (73), Jan. 6/51

WINS AND LOSSES

Highest winning percentage, one team, one season:
.878 (72-10)—Chicago, 1995-96

Lowest winning percentage, one team, one season:
.110 (9-73)—Philadelphia, 1972-73

Highest home winning percentage, one season:
.976 (40-1)—Boston, 1985-86

Lowest home winning percentage, one season:
(Min. 30 games)
.161 (5-26)—Philadelphia, 1972-73

Lowest home winning percentage, one season:
.125 (3-21)—Providence, 1947-48

Highest road winning percentage, one season:
.816 (31-7)—LA Lakers, 1971-72

Lowest road winning percentage, one season:
(Min. 30 games)
.024 (1-40)—Sacramento Kings, 1990-91

Lowest road winning percentage, one season:
.000 (0-20)—Baltimore, 1953-54

Most consecutive wins, one team:
33—LA Lakers, Nov. 5/71 to Jan. 7/72

Most consecutive wins, one team, one season:
33—LA Lakers, Nov. 5/71 to Jan. 7/72

Most consecutive losses, one team:
24—Cleveland, Mar. 19 to Nov. 5/82

Most consecutive losses, one team, one season:
23—Vancouver, Feb. 16 to Apr. 2/96

Most consecutive home wins:
44—Chicago, Mar. 30/85 to Apr. 4/86

Most consecutive home losses:
19—Dallas, Nov. 6/93 to Jan. 21/94

Most consecutive road wins:
16—LA Lakers, Nov. 6/71 to Jan. 7/72

Most consecutive road losses:
43—Sacramento, Nov. 21/90 to Nov. 22/91

MINUTES

Most, one game:
67—Two Players: Red Rocha, Syracuse at Boston,
Mar. 21/53, 4 OT; Paul Seymour, Syracuse at
Boston, Mar. 21/53, 4 OT

Highest average per game, one series:
49.33—Wilt Chamberlain, Philadelphia vs.
New York, 1968

SCORING

Highest average, one series:
46.3—Jerry West, LA Lakers vs. Baltimore, 1965

Most points, one game:
63—Michael Jordan, Chicago at Boston,
Apr. 20/86, 2 OT

Highest field goal percentage, one game:
(Min. 8 made)
1.000—11 Players: Last, Horace Grant, Chicago
vs. Cleveland, May 13/93

Most field goals, one game:
24—Wilt Chamberlain, Philadelphia vs. Syracuse,
Mar. 14/60

Most three-point field goals, one game:
9—Three Players: Rex Chapman, Phoenix at
Seattle, Apr. 25/97; Vince Carter, Toronto vs.
Philadelphia, May 11/01; Ray Allen, Milwaukee
vs. Philadelphia, June 1/01

FREE THROWS

Most made, one game:
30—Bob Cousy, Boston vs. Syracuse,
Mar. 21/53, 4 OT
Most attempts, one game:
39—Shaquille O'Neal, LA Lakers vs. Indiana,
June 9/00

Most made, no misses, one game:
18—Karl Malone, Utal at LA Lakers, May 10/97

REBOUNDS

Highest average per game, one series:
32.0—Wilt Chamberlain, Philadelphia vs. Boston,
1967

Most, one game:
41—Wilt Chamberlain, Philadelphia vs. Boston,
Apr. 5/67

Most offensive rebounds, one game:
15—Moses Malone, Houston vs. Washington,
Apr. 21/77, OT

Most defensive rebounds, one game:
20—Five Times: Dave Cowens, Boston at Houston,
Apr. 22/75; Dave Cowens, Boston at
Philadelphia, May 1/77; Bill Walton, Portland at
Philadelphia, June 3/77; Bill Walton, Portland
vs. Philadelphia, June 5/77; Tim Duncan, San
Antonio at LA Lakers, May 14/02

ASSISTS

Highest average per game, one series:
17.0—Magic Johnson, LA Lakers vs. Portland,
1985

Most assists, one game:
24—Twice: Magic Johnson, LA Lakers vs. Phoenix,
May 15/84; John Stockton, Utah at LA Lakers,
May 17/88

PERSONAL FOULS

Most, one game:
8—Jack Toomay, Baltimore at New York,
March 26/49, OT

STEALS

Most, one game:
10—Allen Iverson, Philadelphia vs. Orlando,
May 13/99

BLOCKED SHOTS

Most, one game:
10—Two players: Mark Eaton, Utah vs. Houston,
Apr. 26/85; Hakeem Olajuwon, Houston at
LA Lakers, Apr. 29/90

TURNOVERS

Most, one game:
11—John Williamson, New Jersey at Philadelphia,
Apr. 11/79

SCORING

Most points, one team, one game:
157—Boston vs. New York, Apr. 28/90

Fewest points, one team, one game:
54—Utah at Chicago, June 7/98

Most points, both teams, one game:
304—Portland (153) at Phoenix (151),
May 11/92, 2 OT

Fewest points, both teams, one game:
130—Detroit (64) at Boston (66), May 10/02

Largest margin of victory, one game:
58 (133-75)—Minneapolis vs. St. Louis,
March 19/56

FIELD GOALS

Most, one team, one game:
67—Three times: Milwaukee at Philadelphia,
Mar. 30/70; San Antonio vs. Denver,
May 4/83; LA Lakers vs. Denver, May 22/85

Fewest, one team, one game:
19—Portland vs. San Antonio, Jun. 4/99

Most, both teams, one game:
119—Milwaukee (67) at Philadelphia (52),
Mar. 30/70

Fewest, both teams, one game:
48—Four times: Fort Wayne (23) vs. Syracuse (25)
at Indianapolis, Apr. 7/55; Cleveland (21) vs.
New York (27), May 1/95; Chicago (23) vs.
Miami (25), May 22/97; Portland (19) vs. San
Antonio (29) June 4/99

Highest percentage, one team, one game:
.670—Boston vs. New York, Apr. 28/90

Lowest percentage, one team, one game:
.233—Golden State vs. LA Lakers, Apr. 21/73

Highest percentage, both teams, one game:
.591—L.A. Lakers (.640) vs. Denver (.543),
May 11/85

Lowest field, both teams, one game:
.277—Syracuse (.275) vs. Fort Wayne (.280) at
Indianapolis, Apr. 7/55

THREE-POINT FIELD GOALS

Most, one team, one game:
20—Seattle vs. Houston, May 6/96

Most, both teams, one game:
33—Seattle (20) vs. Houston (13), May 6/96

FREE THROWS

Highest percentage, one team, one game:
1.000—Ten times, most recent:
Philadelphia vs. Toronto, May 16/01 (16-16)

Lowest percentage, one team, one game:
.261—Philadelphia at Boston, March 19/60 (6-23)

Highest percentage, both teams, one game:
.957—Chicago (.964) at Boston (.947), Apr. 23/87

Most made, one team, one game:
57—Boston vs. Syracuse, March 21/53, 4 OT;
Phoenix vs. Seattle, June 5/93

Fewest made, one team, one game:
2—Milwaukee at Philadelphia, May 24/01

Most made, both teams, one game:
108—Boston (57) vs. Syracuse (51),
Mar. 21/53, 4 OT

Fewest made, both teams, one game:
12—Boston (6) at Buffalo (6), Apr. 6/74

REBOUNDS

Highest percentage, one team, one game:
.723—LA Lakers vs. San Antonio,
Apr. 17/86 (47-65)

Most, one team, one game:
97—Boston vs. Philadelphia, Mar. 19/60

Fewest, one team, one game:
18—San Antonio at LA Lakers, Apr. 17/86

Most, both teams, one game:
169—Boston (89) vs. Philadelphia (80), Mar. 22/60

**Highest offensive percentage, one team,
one game:**
.609—New York vs. Indiana, June 5/94 (28-46)

Most offensive, one team, one game:
30—Seattle vs. Portland, Apr. 23/78

Fewest offensive, one team, one game:
2—Twice: New York at Boston, Apr. 19/74;
Golden State at Chicago, Apr. 30/75

Most offensive, both teams, one game:
51—Twice: Houston (27) vs. Atlanta (24), Apr.
11/79; Utah (27) at Houston (24), Apr. 28/85

Fewest offensive, both teams, one game:
9—Twice: New York (4) at Indiana (5), May 7/98;
Indiana (4) at New York (5), May 27/00

**Highest defensive percentage, one team,
one game:**
.952—Chicago vs. Golden State,
Apr. 30/75 (40-42)

Most defensive, one team, one game:
56—San Antonio vs. Denver, May 4/83

Fewest defensive, one team, one game:
12—Golden State at Seattle, Apr. 28/92

Most defensive, both teams, one game:
92—Denver (49) vs. Portland (43), May 1/77, OT

Fewest defensive, both teams, one game:
3—New Jersey (14) vs. Chicago (16), Apr. 29/98

ASSISTS
Most, one team, one game:
51—San Antonio vs. Denver, May 4/83

Fewest, one team, one game:
5—Twice: Boston at St. Louis, Apr. 3/60;
    Detroit at Chicago, Apr. 5/74

Most, both teams, one game:
79—LA Lakers (44) vs. Boston (35), Jun. 4/87

Fewest, both teams, one game:
16—Chicago (6) vs. LA Lakers (10), Mar. 29/68

PERSONAL FOULS
Most, one team, one game:
55—Syracuse at Boston, Mar. 21/53, 4 OT

Fewest, one team, one game:
9—Cleveland vs. Boston, May 2/92

Most, both teams, one game:
106—Syracuse (55) at Boston (51)
        Mar. 21/53, 4 OT

Fewest, both teams, one game:
25—Cleveland (10) at New Jersey (15) May 7/93

DISQUALIFICATIONS
Most, one team, one game:
7—Syracuse at Boston, Mar. 21/53, 4 OT

Most, both teams, one game:
12—Syracuse (7) at Boston (5), Mar. 21/53, 4 OT

STEALS
Most, one team, one game:
22—Golden State vs. Seattle, Apr. 14/75

Fewest, one team, one game:
0—Four teams, most recent: Indiana vs.
Philadelphia, May 2/01

Most, both teams, one game:
35—Golden State (22) vs. Seattle (13), Apr. 14/75

Fewest, both teams, one game:
2—Phoenix (0) at Seattle (2), Apr. 15/76

BLOCKED SHOTS
Most, one team, one game:
20—Philadelphia vs. Milwaukee, Apr. 5/81

Fewest, one team, one game:
0—By several teams

Most, both teams, one game:
29—Philadelphia (20) vs. Milwaukee (9), Apr. 5/81

Fewest, both teams, one game:
1—Portland (0) vs. Dallas (1), Apr. 25/85

PERSONAL FOULS
Most, one team, one game:
55—Syracuse at Boston, Mar. 21/43, 4 OT

Fewest, one team, one game:
9—Cleveland vs. Boston, May 2/92

Most, both teams, one game:
106—Syracuse (55) at Boston (51),
        Mar. 21/53, 4 OT

Fewest, both teams, one game:
25—Cleveland (10) at New Jersey (15), May 7/93

TURNOVERS
Most, one team, one game:
36—Chicago at Portland, Apr. 17/77

Fewest, one team, one game:
4—Detroit at Boston, May 9/91

Most, both teams, one game:
60—Golden State (31) at Washington (29),
        May 25/75

Fewest, both teams, one game:
13—Detroit (4) at Boston (9), May 9/91

Chapter 41

The Naismith Memorial Basketball Hall of Fame

By Ken Shoulder

It finally happened. After nearly 30 years of fundraising efforts, the Naismith Memorial Basketball Hall of Fame opened in a red brick building on the corner of the Springfield College campus in 1968. Nearly 77 years had passed since December 1891, when students played the faculty in the first known game at a YMCA gymnasium in Springfield, Mass.

Long before the building was ready, the first elections for the Hall had occurred in 1959. The first class of entrants included some 15 players, coaches, "contributors," a referee, and even two teams—the "First Team," comprised of 18 students at the YMCA Training School in 1891, and the Original Celtics, a wildly successful touring team, known previously as the New York Celtics in 1914.

The Class of 2003
New Basketball Hall of Fame members, from left, James Worthy, Earl Lloyd, Robert Parish, Meadowlark Lemon and Dino Meneghin, pose at their induction ceremony.

By far the most deserving of that inaugural class of inductees was the game's gentle inventor, Dr. James Naismith himself. Once, after attending a doubleheader with 18,000 paying fans at Madison Square Garden in 1937, Naismith could barely contain himself, exclaiming, "Good heavens, all these people would come to watch a basketball game?" On orders from his boss and head of physical education, Dr. Luther Gulick, Naismith had been given two weeks to devise a game that was a means to a pedagogical end: the school needed an indoor pastime, captivating and nonviolent, to occupy a class of "incorrigible" physical education students. The students were hopelessly bored with the usual run of childish gymnastic activities, designed to pacify them until the New England weather grew warm again. Naismith had his eureka moment while recalling "duck on a rock," a pastime from his childhood in Canada, in which an accurate, arced toss was more important that brute strength.

Years later, it was Naismith who made the first donation toward the Hall of Fame. The National Association of Basketball Coaches had sponsored his trip to attend the first basketball Olympics in Berlin. He returned his unused expense money to the association, saying "Here, why don't you start a Hall of Fame?" While he made no specifications, one can almost hear him saying that a Hall of Fame should be a record of the game's history, in the United States and abroad, and a record of all those people who contributed something signifi-

cant, on or off the court.

If those were his wishes, they were surely followed. Let the record show that aside from the First Team and the Original Celtics, there were four players in that initial group of 15 inductees in 1959. Two were stars from the early years, John Schommer and Charles Hyatt. The two more prominent members were Angelo "Hank" Lusietti and George Mikan. The Associated Press voted Mikan the greatest player of the first half-century. Who was voted second best? The whiz from Stanford, Hank Luisetti, whose jump shot in the 1930s thrilled audiences, in part because it looked like a skill born of another planet.

Since that first induction in 1959, the Hall has honored college and pro players and coaches, men and women, American and foreign-born competitors, referees and contributors. The class of 2003 typifies the diversity of inductess across the years. They include: two of the stars of the 1980s, Boston center Robert Parish and Los Angeles forward James Worthy; famous Harlem Globetrotter, Meadowlark Lemon; the long-time voice of the Lakers, Chick Hearn; Women's electee Leon Barmore, a coach for more than 20 years at Louisiana Tech University; Veteran's electee Earl Lloyd, who, in 1950, became the first African American to play in an NBA game; and, International electee Dino Meneghin, who played in four Olympics (1972, 1976, 1980 and 1984) and is regarded as the greatest Italian player of all-time.

There have actually been three Halls of Fame in Springfield. The first was on the Springfield College campus. The second was a $11.5-million, three-level building located off highway I-91. In September 2002, a new 80,000-square-foot, $45-million, basketball-shaped Hall of Fame opened in Springfield, offering hoops fans a true state-of-of-the-art interactive experience with trivia and skill contests, along with basketball-themed stores and a restaurant.

Like other sports, the Hall of Fame is not without controversy. If fans can debate whether the late Brooklyn Dodger Duke Snider deserves to have his plaque in Cooperstown, so too can we wonder what is taking the Hall of Fame so long to elect the great Boston guard Dennis Johnson, who Larry Bird called "the smartest player I ever played with." Inducting international and veteran players is unobjectionable, but what about Artis Gilmore and Mel Daniels, the two greatest centers in ABA history? Is it because their best years were recorded in the ABA and not the NBA that they are shunned?

Daniels was a two-time MVP and still holds the Pacers record for career rebounds (7,643) and for yearly rebound average (18), a record set in 1971. Gilmore is one of a select group to record 20,000 points and 10,000 rebounds. He also owns the highest field goal percentage of all-time (.582). Daniels won three ABA championships with Indiana, and Gilmore played on one title team with Kentucky. It is difficult to understand how Forrest DeBernardi is in the Hall—he was a dominant college and AAU player in the 1920s—but Daniels, Gilmore, and Johnson aren't.

NAISMITH MEMORIAL BASKETBALL HALL OF FAME

NAME	INDUCTION YEAR	NOTE
The First Team	1959	Team
Original Celtics	1959	Team
Forrest "Phog" Clare Allen	1959	Coach
Henry Clifford Carlson	1959	Coach
Dr. Luther Gulick	1959	Contributor
Edward J. Hickox	1959	Contributor
Charles D. Hyatt	1959	Player
Matthew P. Kennedy	1959	Referee
Angelo Luisetti	1959	Player
Walter E. "Doc" Meanwell, M.D.	1959	Coach
George L. Mikan	1959	Player
Ralph Morgan	1959	Contributor
Dr. James Naismith	1959	Contributor
Harold G. Olsen	1959	Contributor
John J. Schommer	1959	Player
Amos Alonzo Stagg	1959	Contributor
Oswald Tower	1959	Contributor
Ernest A. "Prof" Blood	1960	Coach
Victor A. Hanson	1960	Player
George T. Hepbron	1960	Referee
Frank W. Keaney	1960	Coach
Ward L. "Piggy" Lambert	1960	Coach
Edward C. (Ed) Macauley	1960	Player
Branch McCracken	1960	Player
Charles C. "Stretch" Murphy	1960	Player
Henry V. Porter	1960	Contributor
John R. Wooden	1960	Player
Buffalo Germans	1961	Team
Bernard Borgmann	1961	Player
Forrest S. DeBernardi	1961	Player
George H. Hoyt	1961	Referee
George E. Keogan	1961	Coach
Robert A. Kurland	1961	Player
John J. (Jack) O'Brien	1961	Contributor
Andy Phillip	1961	Player
Ernest C. "Quig" Quigley	1961	Referee
John S. Roosma	1961	Player
Leonard D. Sachs	1961	Coach
Arthur A. Schabinger	1961	Contributor
Christian Steinmetz	1961	Player
David Tobey	1961	Referee
Arthur L. Trester	1961	Contributor
Edward A. Wachter	1961	Player
David H. Walsh	1961	Referee
Jack McCracken	1962	Player
Frank "Pop" Morgenweck	1962	Contributor
Harlan O. "Pat" Page	1962	Player
Barney Sedran	1962	Player
Lynn W. St. John	1962	Contributor
John A. "Cat" Thompson	1962	Player
New York Rens	1963	Team
Robert F. Gruenig	1963	Player
William A. Reid	1963	Contributor
John W. Bunn	1964	Contributor
Harold E. Foster	1964	Player
Nat Holman	1964	Player
Edward S. Irish	1964	Contributor
R. William Jones	1964	Contributor
Kenneth D. Loeffler	1964	Coach
John D. "Honey" Russell	1964	Player
Walter A. Brown	1965	Contributor
Paul D. Hinkle	1965	Contributor
Howard A. "Hobby" Hobson	1965	Coach
William G. Mokray	1965	Contributor
Everett S. Dean	1966	Coach
Joe Lapchick	1966	Player
Clair F. Bee	1968	Contributor
Howard G. Cann	1968	Coach
Amory T. "Slats" Gill	1968	Coach
Alvin F. "Doggie" Julian	1968	Coach
Arnold J. "Red" Auerbach	1969	Coach
Henry G. Dehnert	1969	Player
Henry P. (Hank) Iba	1969	Coach
Adolph F. Rupp	1969	Coach
Charles H. Taylor	1969	Contributor
Bernard L. Carnevale	1970	Coach
Robert E. Davies	1970	Player
Robert (Bob) J. Cousy	1971	Player
Robert (Bob) L. Pettit	1971	Player
Abraham (Abe) Saperstein	1971	Contributor
Edgar A. Diddle	1972	Coach
Robert L. Douglas	1972	Contributor
Paul Endacott	1972	Player
Max Friedman	1972	Player
Edward Gottlieb	1972	Contributor
W. R. Clifford Wells	1972	Contributor
John Beckman	1973	Player
Bruce Drake	1973	Coach
Arthur C. Lonborg	1973	Coach
Elmer H. Ripley	1973	Contributor
Adolph (Dolph) Schayes	1973	Player
John R. Wooden	1973	Coach
Harry A. Fisher	1974	Contributor
Maurice Podoloff	1974	Contributor
Ernest J. Schmidt	1974	Player
Joseph R. Brennan	1975	Player
Emil S. "Liz" Liston	1975	Contributor
William F. (Bill) Russell	1975	Player
Robert P. "Fuzzy" Vandivier	1975	Player
Thomas J. Gola	1976	Player
Edward W. Krause	1976	Player
Harry Litwack	1976	Coach
William W. (Bill) Sharman	1976	Player
Elgin Baylor	1977	Player
Charles T. "Tarzan" Cooper	1977	Player
Lauren Gale	1977	Player
William C. "Skinny" Johnson	1977	Player
Frank J. McGuire	1977	Coach
Paul J. Arizin	1978	Player
Joseph F. Fulks	1978	Player
Clifford O. Hagan	1978	Player
John P. Nucatola	1978	Referee
James C. Pollard	1978	Player
Justin M. (Sam) Barry	1979	Coach
Wilton N. (Wilt) Chamberlain	1979	Player
James E. Enright	1979	Referee
Edgar S. Hickey	1979	Coach
John B. McLendon, Jr.	1979	Coach
Raymond J. Meyer	1979	Coach
Peter F. Newell	1979	Coach
Lester Harrison	1980	Contributor
Jerry R. Lucas	1980	Player
Oscar P. Robertson	1980	Player
Everett F. Shelton	1980	Coach
J. Dallas Shirley	1980	Referee
Jerry A. West	1980	Player
Thomas B. "Babe" Barlow	1981	Player
Ferenc Hepp	1981	Contributor
J. Walter Kennedy	1981	Contributor
Arad A. McCutchan	1981	Coach
Everett N. Case	1982	Coach
Alva O. Duer	1982	Contributor
Clarence E. "Bighouse" Gaines	1982	Coach
Harold E. Greer	1982	Player
Slater N. Martin	1982	Player
Frank V. Ramsey, Jr.	1982	Player
Willis Reed, Jr.	1982	Player
William W. (Bill) Bradley	1983	Player
David A. DeBusschere	1983	Player
Lloyd R. Leith	1983	Referee
Dean E. Smith	1983	Coach
John (Jack) K. Twyman	1983	Player
Louis G. Wilke	1983	Contributor
Clifford B. Fagan	1984	Contributor
James H. (Jack) Gardner	1984	Coach
John Havlicek	1984	Player
Samuel (Sam) Jones	1984	Player
Edward S. Steitz	1984	Contributor

NAME	INDUCTION YEAR	NOTE
Senda Berenson Abbott	1985	Contributor
W. Harold (Andy) Anderson	1985	Coach
Alfred N. Cervi	1985	Player
Marv K. Harshman	1985	Coach
Bertha F. Teague	1985	Contributor
Nate Thurmond	1985	Player
L. Margaret Wade	1985	Coach
William J. Cunningham	1986	Player
Thomas W. Heinsohn	1986	Player
William "Red" Holzman	1986	Coach
Zigmund "Red" Mihalik	1986	Referee
Fred R. Taylor	1986	Coach
Stanley H. Watts	1986	Coach
Richard F. Barry	1987	Player
Walter Frazier	1987	Player
Robert J. Houbregs	1987	Player
Peter P. Maravich	1987	Player
Robert Wanzer	1987	Player
Clyde E. Lovellette	1988	Player
Robert McDermott	1988	Player
Ralph H. Miller	1988	Coach
Westley S. Unseld	1988	Player
William "Pop" Gates	1989	Player
K. C. Jones	1989	Player
Leonard (Lenny) Wilkens	1989	Player
David Bing	1990	Player
Elvin E. Hayes	1990	Player
Donald Neil Johnston	1990	Player
Vernon Earl Monroe	1990	Player
Nathaniel Archibald	1991	Player
David W. Cowens	1991	Player
Lawrence Fleisher	1991	Contributor
Harry J. Gallatin	1991	Player
Robert M. (Bob) Knight	1991	Coach
Lawrence F. O'Brien	1991	Contributor
Borislav Stankovic	1991	Contributor
Sergei Belov	1992	Player
Louis P. Carnesecca	1992	Coach
Cornelius (Connie) L. Hawkins	1992	Player
Robert J. (Bob) Lanier	1992	Player
Alfred J. McGuire	1992	Coach
John (Jack) T. Ramsay	1992	Coach
Lusia Harris-Stewart	1992	Player
Nera D. White	1992	Player
Phillip D. Woolpert	1992	Coach
Walter Bellamy	1993	Player
Julius W. "Dr. J" Erving	1993	Player
Daniel P. Issel	1993	Player
Ann E. Meyers	1993	Player
Richard (Dick) S. McGuire	1993	Player
Calvin J. Murphy	1993	Player
Uljana Semjonova	1993	Player
William (Bill) T. Walton	1993	Player
Carol "Blaze" Blazejowski	1994	Player
Denzil (Denny) E. Crum	1994	Coach
Charles J. (Chuck) Daly	1994	Coach
Harry (Buddy) Jeannette	1994	Player
Cesare Rubini	1994	Coach
Anne Donovan	1995	Player
Aleksandr Gomelsky	1995	Coach
Kareem Abdul-Jabbar	1995	Player
John Kundla	1995	Coach
Vern Mikkelsen	1995	Player
Cheryl Miller	1995	Player
Earl Strom	1995	Referee

NAME	INDUCTION YEAR	NOTE
Kresimir Cosic	1996	Player
George Gervin	1996	Player
Gail Goodrich	1996	Player
Nancy Lieberman-Cline	1996	Player
David Thompson	1996	Player
George Yardley	1996	Player
Pete Carril	1997	Coach
Joan Crawford	1997	Player
Denise Curry	1997	Player
Antonio Diaz-Miguel	1997	Coach
Alex English	1997	Player
Don Haskins	1997	Coach
Bailey Howell	1997	Player
Larry Bird	1998	Player
Jody Conradt	1998	Coach
Alexander (Alex) Hannum	1998	Coach
Marques Haynes	1998	Player
Aleksandar Nikolic	1998	Coach
Arnold (Arnie) Risen	1998	Player
Leonard (Lenny) Wilkens	1998	Coach
Wayne Embry	1999	Contributor
Kevin McHale	1999	Player
Billie Moore	1999	Coach
John Thompson	1999	Coach
Fred Zollner	1999	Contributor
Danny Biasone	2000	Contributor
Robert McAdoo	2000	Player
Charles Newton	2000	Contributor
Pat Head Summit	2000	Coach
Isiah Thomas	2000	Player
Morgan Wootten	2000	Coach
John Chaney	2001	Coach
Mike Krzyzewski	2001	Coach
Moses Malone	2001	Player
Earvin "Magic" Johnson	2002	Player
Drazen Petrovic	2002	Player
Larry Brown	2002	Coach
Lute Olson	2002	Coach
Kay Yow	2002	Coach
Harlem Globetrotters	2002	Team
Robert Parish	2003	Player
James Worthy	2003	Player
Dino Meneghin	2003	Player
Leon Barmore	2003	Coach
Earl Lloyd	2003	Contributor
Meadowlark Lemon	2003	Contributor
Francis "Chick" Hearn	2003	Contributor

Curt Gowdy Media Awards

The Basketball Hall of Fame's media award is named in honor of Curt Gowdy, who served as president of the Hall of Fame for seven consecutive one-year terms. It was established by the Board of Trustees to single out members of the electronic and print media for outstanding contributions to basketball.

Curt Gowdy, electronic   1990
Dick Herbert, print (*Raleigh News & Observer*)
Marty Glickman, electronic   1991
Dave Dorr, print (*St. Louis Post-Dispatch*)
Chick Hearn, electronic   1992
Sam Goldaper, print (*New York Times*)
Johnny Most, electronic   1993
Leonard Lewin, print (*New York Post*)
Cawood Ledford, electronic   1994
Leonard Koppett, print (*NY Times* and *NY Post*)
Dick Enberg, electronic   1995
Bob Hammel, print (*Bloomington Herald Times*)
Billy Packer, electronic   1996
Bob Hentzen, print (*Topeka Capital-Journal*)
Marv Albert, electronic   1997
Bob Ryan, print (*Boston Globe*)
Dick Vitale, electronic   1998
Larry Donald, print (*Basketball Times*)
Dick Weiss, print (*New York Daily News*)
Bob Costas, electronic   1999
Smith Barrier, print (*Greensboro Daily News & Record*)
Hubie Brown, electronic   2000

Dave Kindred, print (*The Sporting News*)
Dick Stockton, electronic   2001
Curry Kirkpatrick, print
Jim Nantz, electronic   2002
Jim O'Connell, print
Rod Hundley, electronic   2003
Sid Hartman, print

Clair Bee Award

The Clair Bee Coach of the Year Award honors the active Division I basketball coach who has made the most significant positive contributions to his sport during the preceding year. The winner should reflect the character and professional qualities of Clair Bee, a Hall of Fame coach who many consider to be the best technical basketball coach in history, and a man who cared deeply about his players' well-being. The Hilton and Bee Awards were created by Chip Hilton Sports and the NCAA Foundation in 1996 as a way to promote positive character in the sport of basketball, a game upon which the legendary Bee had a great impact as a coach, administrator, innovator and teacher.

Clem Haskins, Minnesota		1997
Jim Phelan, Mount St. Mary's		1998
Jim O'Brien, Ohio State		1999
Jim Boeheim, Syracuse		2000
Lute Olson, University of Arizona		2001
Bob Knight, Texas Tech		2002
Tom Crean, Marquette		2003

John Bunn Award

The John Bunn Award is named for the first chairman of the Basketball Hall of Fame Committee (1949-69). The award, instituted by the Basketball Hall's Board of Trustees, annually honors an international or national figure who has contributed greatly to the game of basketball. Outside of Enshrinement, the John Bunn Award is the most prestigious award presented by the Basketball Hall of Fame.

John Bunn	1973
John Wooden	1974
J. Walter Kennedy	1975
Henry P. Iba	1976
Clifford B. Fagan	1977
Curt Gowdy	1978
Eddie Gottlieb	1979
Arnold "Red" Auerbach	1980
Ray Meyer	1981
Daniel Biasone	1982
Robert J. Cousy	1983
Lawrence F. O'Brien	1984
Lee Williams	1985
Grady W. Lewis	1986
David R. Gavitt	1987
Haskell Hillyard	1988
George E. Killian	1989
Pat Head Summitt	1990
Morgan B. Wootten	1991
Will Robinson	1992
Joe Vancisin	1993
William Wall	1994
Pete Carlesimo	1995
Vic Bubas	1996
C.M. Newton	1997
Tex Winter	1998
The Harlem Globetrotters	1999
Meadowlark Lemon	2000
Tom Jernstedt	2001
Harvey Pollack	2002
Joseph M. O'Brien	2003

Chip Hilton Award

The Chip Hilton Player of the Year Award is presented to a player who has demonstrated personal character both on and off the court, similar to the fictional Chip Hilton character depicted by Hall of Fame coach Clair Bee in the classic Chip Hilton Sports Series.

Tim Duncan, Wake Forest	1997
Hassan Booker, Navy	1998
Tim Hill, Harvard	1999
Eduardo Najera, Oklahoma	2000
Shane Battier, Duke	2001
Juan Dixon, Maryland	2002
Brandon Miller, Butler	2003

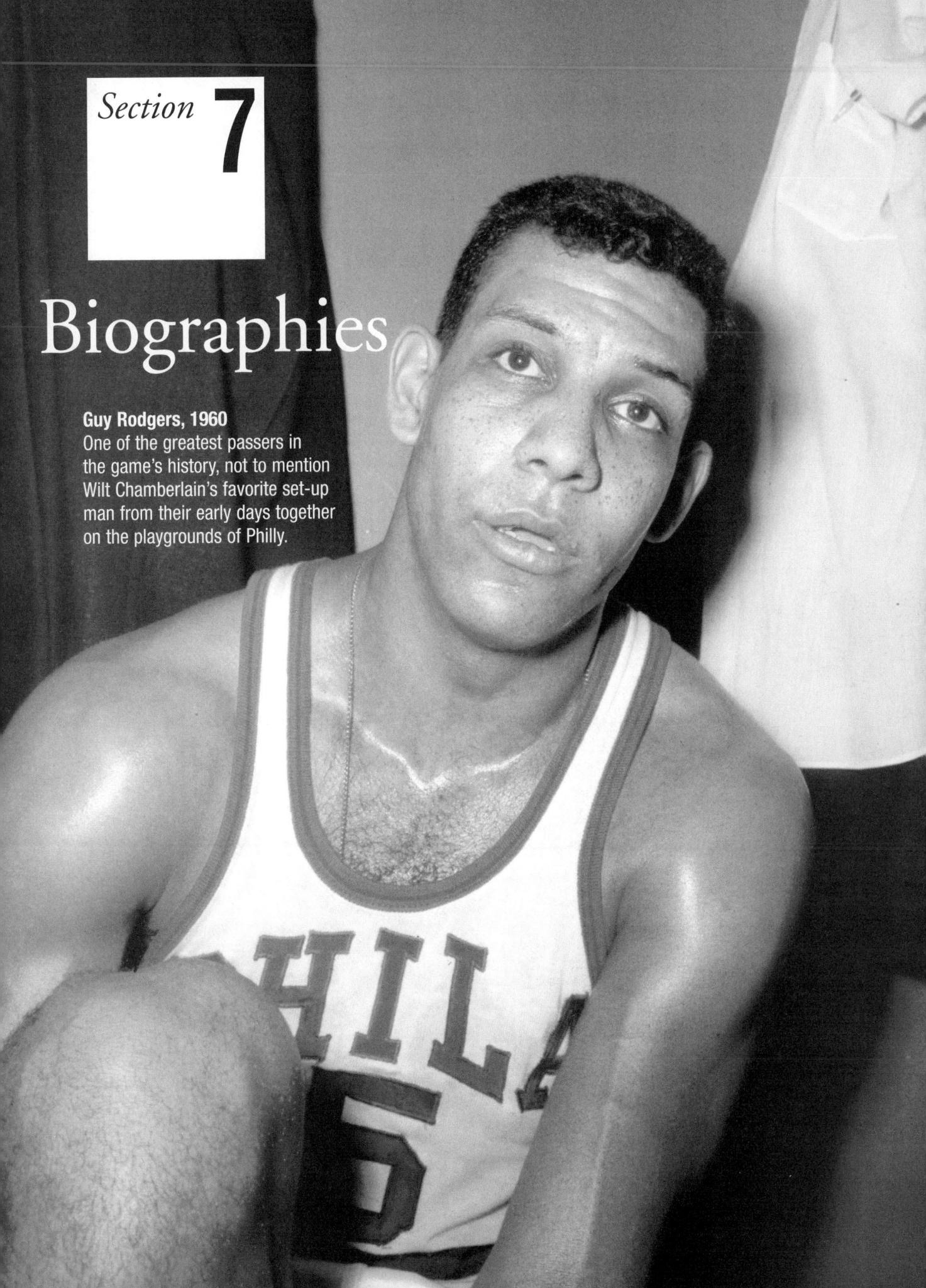

Section **7**

Biographies

Guy Rodgers, 1960
One of the greatest passers in the game's history, not to mention Wilt Chamberlain's favorite set-up man from their early days together on the playgrounds of Philly.

Chapter 42

The Incomparable Wilt Chamberlain

By Bob Ryan

I t does not quite equate to Voltaire's celebrated thesis concerning the Almighty. If Wilt Chamberlain had not existed, it would have been impossible to invent him.

Did an NBA player exist who averaged slightly in excess of 50 points per game for an entire season? Did an NBA player exist who scored 100 points in a regulation league game? Did an NBA player exist who pulled down 55 rebounds in a single contest? Did an NBA player exist who led the league in scoring in each of his first seven seasons, and then, almost as an act of defiance, lead the league in assists, the only man ever to do so from the center position?

Surely no one whose NBA experience pre-dates 1973 can believe that. Such a man must be the product of imaginations fueled by long nights spent nursing adult beverages, or mind-altering drugs.

But this man did exist. Not enough video exists as testimony to his spectacular prowess, but for those not privileged to live through the storied athletic times of the incomparable Wilton Norman Chamberlain, the record book bears witness to his NBA presence. As many, many people have observed, Wilt Chamberlain is not in the record book. He is the record book.

Wilt was, well, Wilt. Taller men have played in the NBA. Heavier men have played in the NBA. But his combination of size, intelligence, and sheer athleticism remains unique. A substantial case can be made that America has not produced a better pure athlete than Wilt Chamberlain. In fact, Wilt loved to make the case himself.

Take the subject of track and field, which most people would acknowledge is a reasonably fair test of all-around athleticism, and which Wilt always claimed to be his favorite athletic pursuit. In his 1973 autobiography, Wilt, he said the following:

"I high-jumped about 6-feet-6 and put the shot about 47 feet for my high school team, and ran the 440 in 48.6 and the 880 in 1:58.6 for the local AAU team. My senior year, after we won the city basketball championship, I was the only double winner in the public school championship track meet, taking firsts in the high jump and shot put."

There is very little doubt that Wilt could run. "Hell, I used to race all the quick little guards on the various pro teams I played for and—except for Al Attles, who ran a dead heat with me—I beat them all," he declared.

Wilt Chamberlain, 1958
A young Wilt, a year before he took the pro game and bent it to his will.

The man was a shade over 7-feet tall and in his playing prime he weighed anywhere from 275 to 320 pounds, depending on the time of the year.

Fortunately for posterity, there have been witnesses to Wilt's astonishing physical strength and dexterity, not to mention his innate competetiveness. One such observer was the great George Kiseda, who covered the NBA in Philadelphia for the *Philadelphia Bulletin* during Wilt's hometown NBA heyday and who became a good personal friend.

"Here are some of the things I've seen Wilt Chamberlain

do," Kiseda says. "I've seen Wilt Chamberlain palm a bowling ball (an ungrounded bowling ball with no holes, which means Wilt couldn't cheat); I've seen him do a flag, using a sapling on Long Island as his flagpole; I've seen him pick up a grown man by his pockets, holding him at arm's length in front of him while the guy spun his wheels.

"I've seen him throw 40 or 50-yard shovel passes with a football on the beach at Longport, N.J. (they weren't pop flies, either; they were projectiles); I've seen him break up a three-man fight at Convention Hall by grabbing one of the combatants with his right hand and shoving him out to arm's length to the right, grabbing another with his left hand and shoving him out to arm's length to the left, and, while keeping those two separated by the length of his wingspan, bumping the third guy out of the way with his chest."

Did Irving Berlin foresee Wilt Chamberlain when he wrote *Anything You Can Do, I Can Do Better?*

The Swiss Army Knife athletic versatility may have helped separate Chamberlain from the pack of generic great single-sport athletes, but, absent basketball, who would remember him? Wilt Chamberlain was Wilt Chamberlain because he was a truly amazing basketball player.

He was born in Philadelphia on August 21, 1936. One of nine children, he grew up in something less than affluent circumstances, but by the standards of the day (and perhaps this one, too) he was not poor. None of the Chamberlain children ever went to bed hungry. He always reasoned that his height came from his mother's side of the family, since his mother, at 5-foot-9-1/2, was slightly taller than his father.

The world first became aware of him at Overbrook High School. Even in those seemingly innocent days, there was fierce competition among not only colleges, but also high schools, for athletic talent, and so it was that before deciding upon entering Overbrook, the neighborhood school, he was recruited heavily by the city's premier Catholic schools.

He scored 32 in his first varsity game. Overbrook went 58-3 during his three varsity years, as Wilt broke Tom Gola's state scoring record with 2,252 points. It was the typical great player scenario, with coach Cecil Mosenson often pulling him from the game long before its conclusion. Wilt was particularly rough on Roxborough High, against whom he scored 71, 74, and 90.

Imagine the recruiting circus for a 7-footer who was being projected as perhaps the greatest center prospect ever. The interest far transcended college, since the NBA, and the Philadelphia Warriors in particular, had been watching him since 9th grade. The NBA had a so-called "territorial draft" that ceded the collegiate drafting rights to professional teams with geographic proximity. Even before Chamberlain shocked the known basketball world by passing up all the Eastern powers to attend Kansas, Warriors' owner Eddie Gottlieb pushed for an amendment to the territorial draft. Henceforth, the local professional team had the rights to local high-schoolers. Gottlieb was not about to allow Chamberlain out of his grasp.

Freshmen were not allowed to play varsity basketball in 1955. The Kansas freshmen did play the varsity before 14,000 people at Allen Field House and in that game Wilt Chamberlain announced himself to the next level of basketball

competition by scoring 42 points and grabbing 31 rebounds.

One year later he found himself playing for the national championship. It was No. 2 Kansas at 24-2 against No.1 North Carolina at 31-0, and it remains one of the most-discussed college basketball games ever played.

North Carolina was no different than any other opponent. Their primary goal was to neutralize Wilt Chamberlain.

It was essential for the Tar Heels to control the tempo, to limit, as they would say today, his "touches." In 55 minutes of basketball he would get off 13 shots, not counting the times he was fouled in the act of shooting. He finished with game-highs of 23 points and 14 rebounds, but North Carolina prevailed, 54-53.

There it began. Wilt was great, they said. But Wilt just wasn't a winner. The tag would follow him for the rest of his career.

What happened that night in Kansas City would be repeated many times, at least according to Wilt. "Never mind that I got 23 points—high for the game," he said in *Wilt*. "Never mind that I was named most valuable player in the tournament. Never mind that I had three or four men guarding me all night. Never mind that Ron Loneski threw a key pass away in the third overtime. Never mind that North Carolina—No. 1, undefeated, with a great coach (Frank McGuire) and great players—was actually favored going into the championship game. The people who were there (10,000 and no TV, of course) know what happened, but by the time I'd been a pro for a few years and lost to Boston a few times, everyone was pointing back to that North Carolina game as proof that I was a loser."

In later years Wilt would scoff at any notion that there was a legitimate comparison between himself and Bill Russell, citing, among other things, the fact that he was often guarded by two or three Celtics in any given sequence. In support of Wilt's thesis, many Celticologists concede that the Celtic who fouled Wilt the most over the years was not Russell, but 6-foot-1 guard K.C. Jones, who was forever double-teaming the Big Guy.

Wilt spent one more relatively unsatisfying season at Kansas before deciding that it was time to become a professional. College ball was fruitless. It was nothing but collapsing zone defenses and stall offenses and general aggravation. Besides, it was time to earn some money. Wilt was nothing if not entrepreneurial, and he had a great product to sell—himself.

But the times were different. He still had a year of college eligibility remaining, and was therefore ineligible to play in the NBA until his class had graduated. His only viable option for the 1958-59 season was to become a Harlem Globetrotter.

Globetrotter owner and founder Abe Saperstein came up with $65,000, and Wilt went on to spend a thoroughly happy year playing for the Globetrotters. All his life he would speak fondly of that season. Saperstein indulged him by allowing the big man to spend time in the backcourt. Off the court, Chamberlain reveled in the travel, especially the European tours. The relationship was mutually beneficial, because with Chamberlain in the lineup attendance for Globetrotter games was up significantly.

When the year was up, Chamberlain was the happy object

of a bidding war. In order to get him away from Saperstein, Gottlieb had to come up with the cash. Though announced at $35,000, when bonuses and side deals were tallied up his actual pay was closer to $100,000.

The Wilt Chamberlain of 1959 was not quite the same player as the Wilt Chamberlain who retired 14 years later. He was tall, and he was (relatively) skinny. Most of all, he was agile. That Wilt Chamberlain could handle the ball. He could drive baseline and execute fancy reverse lay-ups.

Skinny as he was, he was quite inherently strong. As the years progressed, he filled out and he became not just strong, but immensely powerful. The agility of his youth gave way to frightening physical might. A defender foolish enough to attempt blocking a Chamberlain dunk ran the risk of accompanying the basketball through the hoop.

Wilt was trouble for opposing centers because there was really nothing in the game he didn't like to do. He liked to rebound. He liked to block shots. He liked to run. He liked to pass, even as a young player. Most of all, he really, really, really liked to score. It was the source of his basketball identity.

All through his formative years, he scared people. He made them change the rules. Before he was through, they had outlawed offensive goaltending and they had widened the lane from 12 to 16 feet, all because of him. These things were a source of lifelong pride.

So he entered the NBA and took it apart. He averaged 37 points and 27 rebounds a game, each a record. With the zone defense prohibition in the NBA, he found it easier to score than at any time since his early days at Overbrook High. He maneuvered inside for dunks and little flips (later called "finger rolls" by legendary Laker announcer Chick Hearn). He fooled around with a banked turnaround jumper.

At that time the reigning big man in basketball was Boston's Bill Russell. It was only natural that people would choose to divorce their individual situation from the whole. The fact is that it was, and so remains, the greatest individual confrontation in NBA history. Over the next 10 years they would find themselves on rival teams 142 times, not counting exhibitions.

After the first one, in which the Celtics won by nine despite 30 points and 30 rebounds by Wilt (Russell had 22 and 35, respectively), Russell pondered the situation. "I said, 'Let's see. He's four or five inches taller. He's 40 or 50 pounds heavier. His vertical leap is at least as good as mine. He can get up and down the floor as well as I can. And he's smart. The real problem with all this is that I have to show up!'"

In the spring of 1960 the Celtics met the Philly Warriors in the Eastern Division Finals. Boston won, four games to two, the deciding sixth game being decided at the buzzer on a Tom Heinsohn tip-in. In the first Philadelphia victory Wilt had 29 points and 28 rebounds. In the second one he had—take a breath—50 points and 35 rebounds!

But, of course, in the eyes of his critics he was a loser.

The truth is that no one could touch the Boston Celtics. During Chamberlain's five and a half years as a member of the Philadelphia/San Francisco Warriors (the franchise re-located for the 1962-63 season) his great rival Russell played in the company of eight fellow Hall of Famers, only one of whom, Clyde Lovellette, was far past his prime. Chamberlain's best

Philadelphia teammate, and only Hall of Fame member, was Paul Arizin, who was 31 when Wilt joined the team. As a San Francisco Warrior he played alongside the young Nate Thurmond for 104 games. As a Philadelphia 76er he had two Hall of Fame teammates, Hal Greer and Billy Cunningham. As a Laker he had two, Jerry West, who had plenty left, and Elgin Baylor, who didn't.

But with Chamberlain as the focal point, the Philly Warriors lost a two-pointer in Game 7 to the Celtics in 1962 (Wilt: 37 points and 27 rebounds a game); the San Francisco Warriors went to the Finals in 1964 where they lost to the Celtics in five (Wilt: 29 points and 28 rebounds a game); the 1965 Philly 76ers (Wilt had been traded to Philly in January of 1965 when the Warriors couldn't afford his $200,000 salary) lost a seventh game one-pointer to the Celtics (Wilt: 26 points and 31 rebounds a game); and the 1966 76ers lost a five-game series to the Celtics (Wilt: 28 points and 30 rebounds a game). Can anyone look at those numbers and conjure up any reason other than Wilt's greatness to suggest how his teams even came close to beating the Boston Celtics?

On March 2, 1962 Wilt Chamberlain ensured his place in basketball history. That was the night he went 36-for-63 from the floor and a startling 28-for-32 from the line against the New York Knicks. The game was played in Hershey, Pa. and there were 4,124 in attendance. Contrary to that well-known entity, popular opinion, the Warriors won, 169-147.

Wilt was proud of the achievement, but only to a point. "I'm the world's worst foul shooter," he said in *Wilt*. "And I hit 28 of 32 that night. That shows anyone can get lucky . . . Besides, I always felt rebounding was more important than scoring. That's why I'm a lot prouder of my NBA record of 55 rebounds in one game than I am of the 100 points."

The fact is that the idea of Wilt scoring 100 in a game wasn't so weird. For 1961-62 was the season Wilt averaged 50.4 points per game. He says he did it because coach Frank McGuire, the same Frank McGuire who had coached the North Carolina team in 1957, asked him to. He averaged more than 48 minutes a game because he demanded to.

By the time the 1966-67 season rolled around, Wilt's general image was pretty well fixed. For every fan who applauded him for his phenomenal statistical achievements, there were at least two who derided him for not having a championship ring. There was only one way to shut them up, and that was to do what he and his teammates did that season.

Well, were the 1966-67 76ers the best team of all-time? The worst anyone can say is that they are in the dialogue. They won a then-record 68 games. At one point in the season they were 48-4. They averaged 125 points a game. They had superb scoring balance, with four men averaging over 18 and six over 12. They could beat you inside or out. Most of all, they had Wilt Chamberlain.

Discussion concerning the very best seasons any centers have ever had must begin with Wilt Chamberlain in 1966-67.

He averaged 24.1 points, 24.2 rebounds, and 7.8 assists a game. He was a monstrous defensive presence. It only took the 76ers five games to render the Celtics as ex-champions. Wilt averaged 20 points and 32 rebounds a game, saving his best for the convincing 140-116 clincher: 29 points, 36 rebounds, and

13 assists. (Attention Magic Johnson, Larry Bird, and Jason Kidd: Now that's a triple-double!)

The San Francisco Warriors were a little more stubborn, but the 76ers took them out in six. No longer could anyone say Wilt was not a winner, especially when he saved Game 6 with two crucial blocks in the waning seconds.

Wilt's career had three distinct phases. In Phase I which basically encompassed his first five years, he shot and shot and shot, always with the blessing, indeed, the urging, of his coach. Phase II was his well-balanced act, which crested in that magnificent 1966-67 season. In this phase he was capable of doing anything asked of him. He became more of a feeder, but if asked to get 45 or 50, he could still do it.

Later, there would be a third, curious phase. In this incarnation Wilt was almost obsessed with passing, and, even more to the point, not shooting. He was perfectly content to rebound, block shots, throw outlet passes and hit cutters. Scoring was an after-thought. Leading the league in field goal percentage was a major goal. That's the Wilt Los Angeles fans would come to know.

All this points to a very complex man. The fact is he did care what people thought of him. He was very conscious that many people would hold his size against him when evaluating him as a ballplayer. He was always interested in doing things that demonstrated his general athleticism and his intelligence.

Away from the action, he lived famously large. He was what we now call "high maintenance," making his own rules and living by them. When he played in Philadelphia, he lived in New York. Think he may have missed a practice or two? He bragged about his money, his sexual conquests, his non-athletic pursuits, his famous friends, and his ability to do whatever it was better than anybody else (He claimed to have driven cross-country, solo, in 36 hours). It may all have been true.

Doing it his way limited his productivity. He never developed a hook shot, for example, and he was in love with his fallaway jumper, a thoroughly counter-productive maneuver he kept in his repertoire as an ego stroke. In addition, he suffered from a classic case of Gentle Giant Syndrome. Wilt Chamberlain was, above all, a tremendously nice and courteous human being. Competitive? Yes. But ruthless? No. Cagey opponents, Bill Russell chief among them, knew how to take full advantage of Wilt's gentle nature.

If Wilt thought the brilliance of his 1966-67 contribution would represent permanent absolution in the Court of Public Opinion, he would be proven terribly wrong. For controversy returned only one year later when his 76ers lost a 3-1 series lead, and, eventually, the series itself to the hated Celtics. In the 100-96 Game 7 loss Wilt took but two shots from the floor, which became an immediate cause celebre.

In Wilt's mind, he had done nothing strange. The Celtics double and triple-teamed him, so he passed the ball. Again, from Wilt: "I kept passing the ball to them, and they kept missing. Hal (Greer) was 8-for-25. Wali (Jones) was 8-for-22. Matty (Guokas) was 2-for-10. Chet (Walker) was 8-for-22. Those four guys took most of our shots, and hit less than a third of them. But I got the blame."

He likewise got the blame in 1969 when his Lakers lost a

Game 7, and the championship, in their own building to, naturally, the Celtics. This time he had to come out of Game 7 when he hurt his knee. As soon as he felt ready to return, he told coach Butch van Breda Kolff, who refused to put him back in the game. The Celtics won by two, and when it was over Russell, whom he had considered to be a friend, made a crack to the effect that he would have had to have broken his leg in order to come out. A frustrated Wilt was left to sputter that the decision was the coach's, not his.

Unbelievably, Wilt found himself involved in more such controversy the following year, this time against the Knicks. The problems began in Game 5, when New York center Willis Reed went down with a first half hip injury. With Wilt being guarded by Lilliputians (i.e. no one over 6-foot-6), the Lakers blew a lead, and the ball game. Absent Reed, Wilt demolished the Knicks with 45 points and 27 rebounds in Game 6.

Game 7 was the historic affair when a hobbled Willis Reed hit the game's first two baskets—each mid-range jumpers—to ignite the Madison Square Garden crowd and the Knicks themselves. The real story of the game was Walt Frazier's 36 points and 19 assists, at the expense of Jerry West. But many decided the story was Wilt, as usual.

But Wilt's day as a Laker would come. Again the question must be asked: Were the 1971-72 Lakers the best team of all-time? And again the answer must be, well, they're certainly in the dialogue.

The Lakers hired a new coach for the 1971-72 season. Bill Sharman had proven to be a successful coach in both the ABA and NBA (Warriors). He was an advocate of fast break basketball, and he also had a policy of game-day practices, called "shootarounds," standard now but a radical idea in 1971. Wilt was a night owl, who seldom went to bed before dawn, home or away.

This was an ominous pairing of star player and strong-willed coach. Sharman convinced Wilt to try it, and Wilt had enough inherent respect for the man to go along with it. The Lakers won a record 33 straight games en route to a 69-13 season and then breezed through the playoffs, including a five-game pasting of New York in the Finals, avenging the defeat from two years before.

Wilt had a second ring at age 35.

That team had the most productive single-season backcourt of all-time in West and Gail Goodrich, who combined for 51 points a game. Happy Hairston was a brute power forward, the only man ever to grab 1,000 rebounds for himself while playing next to Wilt. Jim McMillian, who replaced Elgin Baylor in the lineup the day the 33-game streak began, was a clever scorer. And then there was Wilt, contenting himself with nine shots a game (the man who had once launched 63), rebounding (a league-leading 19 a game), outlet passing, defending, and finding cutters. In order to reach the Finals, the Lakers needed to defeat the defending champion Bucks, led by the great Kareem Abdul-Jabbar. Using every bit of his size, strength and considerable intellectual capacity, Wilt out-played the younger man.

The 1959 Wilt would not have recognized this guy. But the 1967 Wilt would have bought this one a beer. After all, the only other guy to anchor a team winning as many as 68 games in a

season had been himself.

With two rings now, Wilt was feeling pretty good about himself. He knew he would never win the Russell debate, so he contented himself with setting new records, this time shooting (or, should we say, dunking, tipping, and finger-rolling) his way to a .727 percentage, a figure that should stand for a millennia or two. His 1972-73 Lakers could not quite scale the mountain, losing the invaluable Hairston during the season to a knee injury and then coming up short against the Knicks in the Finals.

Wilt Chamberlain never really officially retired. He just stopped playing. He hemmed and hawed about continuing to play following the 1972-73 season, prompting an exasperated Laker management to trade for Buffalo center Elmore Smith. Wilt's response was to refer to Smith as "Elmo" in an interview. He then went back to his mountain-top home high above L.A. to get on with the rest of his fascinating life.

As it developed, that included signing as a player-coach with the San Diego Conquistadors of the American Basketball Association. When the Lakers went to court to prevent Chamberlain from playing, he coached the team instead—to a 37-47 record and a last place finish in the Western Division.

Wilt always played it coy on the subject of a comeback. He said he was contacted by upwards of nine teams about un-retiring, the last such overture coming in 1989. Do the math. Wilt was then 53 years old. The man who once declared that "my dogs could guard Marvin Webster" probably could have come back and rebounded in double figures, if nothing else. Wilt always stayed in great shape.

His post-career life was wonderfully diverse. He was always good with his money, and it safe to say he led a life of glorious conspicuous consumption. He sponsored a women's track team. He traveled widely. He practically turned his home into a social club. He was available for pontification on a variety of subjects, including politics (he was an outspoken Republican). In 1992, he was back in the news with his book, *A View from Above*, in which, among other things, he claimed to have had sexual relations with 20,000 women. Even for someone who always posted benumbing numbers—he registered 118 games of 50 or more points, with the runner-up, Michael Jordan, not reaching half that many—this was a stretch that he couldn't slip past wagging tongues. Still, he lived out most anyone's fantasies, and not just in the bedroom. He did what he wanted, when he wanted.

After years of estrangement, he made up with Bill Russell, who became a friend and confidant. As only Wilt would, he spent his own money in May 1999 to fly all night from the West Coast to participate in a Russell Tribute at the Fleet Center in Boston. He then allowed himself to be the butt of countless Russell and Celtics jokes, at both his and the team's expense. (It was widely noted that Russell would never have reversed roles.) It took a big man to do that, and Wilt was a very big man, in more ways than one.

Wilt Chamberlain died of heart failure at age 63 on October 12, 1999. All the old demons had been expunged years before. He was a man exceedingly comfortable in his own skin. Many people had many things to say on his behalf, but leave it to Wilt to have the best material ready to sum up his own incredible life.

In his last book, Wilt had posed the following philosophical question: "They say that good things come in small packages, but, all things being equal, wouldn't you rather have a 10-carat diamond than a one-carat diamond?"

Chapter 43

One Hundred To Remember

By Ken Shouler

Total Basketball's Editor Ken Shouler chooses the 100 greatest NBA players of all time, listed alphabetically.

Kareem Abdul-Jabbar
Center, Milwaukee, 1969-70 through 1974-75; LA Lakers, 1975-76 through 1988-89
Born: April 16, 1947 in New York 7-2, 267
High School: Power Memorial (New York)
College: UCLA

Ferdinand Lewis Alcindor, Jr. (who changed his name to Kareem Abdul-Jabbar when he converted to Islam in 1971) is lauded for having the most unstoppable shot in the history of basketball. Not only was his sky-hook rarely blocked, it was difficult for opposing centers to even disturb the rhythmic catch-dribble-extension of the shot. Alcindor first attempted the hook in junior high school. He developed it out of necessity, as a way of coping with kids who were beating on him. "It was the only shot I didn't get smashed back in my face," he explained. He missed the shot frequently at first, but his high-school coach Jack Donohue insisted he keep at it.

Power Memorial High School won 71 straight games and 78 of 79 games after Alcindor's freshman season. He was All-American three years and finished his high school career with 2,067 points and 2,002 rebounds, both New York City records.

At UCLA, the Bruins won the NCAA title each of the three years Alcindor played varsity. Then he won six NBA titles with Milwaukee and Los Angeles.

Abdul-Jabbar holds 10 NBA career regular season and playoff records, including most points, 38,387; six MVPs (1971, 1972, 1974, 1976, 1977, 1980); most minutes played, 57,446; most years in the post-season, 18; most games in post-season, 237. He was voted All-NBA first team 10 times and All-Defensive first team five times. Jabbar—while frequently being rated third behind Bill Russell and Wilt Chamberlain at center—may be the greatest ever for his combination of winning and individual achievements.

Born on April 16, 1947, he was 12 pounds, 11 ounces and 22 inches long at birth. His father, Ferdinand Lewis Alcindor,

Bob Lanier, 1974
Here bashing between Jerry Lucas and Bill Bradley, he was All-Star Game MVP in 1974 and third in league MVP voting the same year.

Sr. was 6-foot-2 and his mother, Cora, 5-foot-11, but young Lew probably got his height from his grandfather on his father's side, who was 6-foot-8. For three years the family lived on 111th Street and 7th Avenue in Harlem before moving to the Dyckman Housing Project in the Inwood section of Upper Manhattan, near the Cloisters.

His height was already a factor when he attended St. Jude's, a catholic grammar school. "But I am sitting," he replied from the back of the room to a nun who told him to sit down. His first introduction to racial prejudice came about when his

father, on a long bus ride to 125th Street, had to explain why they had to travel so far to find a barber who knew how to or would cut a black person's hair.

Since both his parents worked and no one could be watching Lew, he was sent to Holy Providence School in Cornwell Heights, Pennsylvania. There he was thrown in with black kids from Philadelphia, Washington, D.C. and Baltimore and got his education in physical schoolyard basketball.

In third grade he was 5-foot-4; in sixth grade he stood 6 feet. By the end of seventh grade he was 6-foot-6, 6-foot-8 in eighth grade (at age 13), and 6-foot-10 upon entering ninth grade. He had made honor roll ever year since the fifth grade at St. Jude's. Archbishop Molloy and Power Memorial High, the schools with the best basketball programs in New York, both wanted him. Even out-of-state schools—like the Hill School, a prep in Pottstown, Pennsylvania, that wanted him to become its first black athlete—considered Lew their quarry. He chose Power Memorial because of coach Jack Donohue, who had a winning reputation, and also because of proximity. Power was just 20 minutes by subway. Molloy was in Jamaica, Queens and would take two buses, a subway and 90 minutes of travel.

By the time his sophomore year rolled around, coach Donhue instituted his "no talk" ban. College coaches, scouts, newspapermen, photographers, and garden-variety curiosity seekers were showing up at Power in droves. The traffic flow had to be checked and no one—not even Donohue's friends—were permitted to talk to Alcindor without Donohue's permission. Alcindor granted no newspaper interviews and, by Donohue's urging, all letters sent to his home were forwarded, unopened, to Jack Donohue, care of Power Memorial High.

By now Alcindor was 7-foot-1 and 220 pounds. He could drop a hook shot with either hand and averaged 19 points and 16 rebounds in his first year. The team won 27 straight games his first year and took its first of three consecutive New York City Catholic high school championships

In his junior season he averaged 28 points, 18 rebounds, and Power ran its unbeaten streak to 52 wins, one short of the New York City record. The mirror image of Power in New York was DeMatha in Washington, D.C, a regional power that produced excellent teams and players. They too were unbeaten when the two met in the University of Maryland Fieldhouse in Hyattsville, Maryland before a crowd of 14,000. Power won 65-52 as Alcindor scored 35 and grabbed 21 rebounds.

The teams met again in Alcindor's senior season, with the Power winning streak at 71 straight. Using two 6-foot-8 players to play in front and in back of Alcindor, DeMatha shut down Power's inside game and forced them to shoot outside. The strategy worked and they won, 46-43.

In his last high school game on March 8, 1965, Power drubbed Rice High School 73-41 for the title. Alcindor entered the game needing 28 points to equal the all-time New York City scoring record. He netted 32, grabbed 22 rebounds, and blocked 8 shots. All told, Power Memorial High School won 78 of 79 games after Alcindor's freshman season.

Wild speculation surrounded Alcindor's next move. Alcindor visited UCLA, liked the quiet authority of coach John Wooden, didn't feel pressured, and knew that he would get an education. So he decided, against his parents' wishes for him to

go to a New York school, to travel 3,000 miles to play for the school that had just won an NCAA championship.

He entered UCLA in 1965. The UCLA freshman averaged 33.1 points and 21.5 rebounds per game, breaking the school's freshman record by more than 150 points. He also led the freshman team to 21 straight wins and an average of 113.2 points per game, exactly twice the opposition's 56.6.

On December 3, 1966, he scored 56 points in his varsity debut against USC at UCLA's Pauley Pavilion. He would top that total one other time, scoring 61 against Washington State.

It was routine for other teams to rough Alcindor up in the pivot, but Wooden didn't see the rough treatment as stopping him. "He always plays his best when it gets tough," Wooden said. Noticing the rough treatment allowed on road courts, Notre Dame's Johnny Dee said, "The only way to beat Alcindor is to hope for the three Fs—foreign court, friendly officials, and foul out Alcindor." None of it—not even freezing the ball—worked. "Lew-CLA," as the school was being called, went 30-0, including a defeat of Dayton in the 1967 NCAA Final, 79-64. Alcindor scored 20 points and grabbed 18 rebounds. He averaged 26.5 across five games and was MVP of the tournament.

Before he began his junior season, the NCAA Rules Committee made it a violation to dunk the ball. Facetiously known as the "Lew Alcindor Rule," the "no-dunk" ban seemed to incense Alcindor, who admitted that he hadn't played to the best of his ability as a sophomore and could still improve. After 47 straight wins, UCLA met Houston, ranked second. On January 20, 1968, a college record 52,693 fans in the Astrodome saw Houston upset UCLA, 71-69. Houston center Elvin Hayes outscored Alcindor, 39-15, and out-rebounded him 15-12. Guy Lewis, the Houston coach who saw UCLA eliminate his team from the NCAA semi-finals, 73-58, the year before, proclaimed "I wouldn't trade Hayes for two Alcindors."

He'd soon have occasion to reconsider that evaluation. UCLA met Houston for a third time in the NCAA semi-finals, on March 22, 1968. UCLA put on a team clinic and won 101-69. "That's the greatest exhibition I've ever seen," said coach Lewis. Elvin Hayes was held to ten points. In the Finals against North Carolina, UCLA breezed again, 78-55, with Alcindor netting 34 points (on 15 for 21 shooting) and pulling down 16 rebounds. "This is the best team of all time," said North Carolina coach Dean Smith, "and Alcindor is the greatest who ever played college basketball." With Alcindor, UCLA had won 59 of 60 games. He had won two NCAA championships and two tournament MVPs.

In 1967, Alcindor showed that his consciousness extended beyond the rectangular confines of the court. He headed to a Cleveland press conference—to join Jim Brown, Willie Davis, Bill Russell, and John Wooten—to support Muhammad Ali's refusal to be inducted in the United States Army.

While Alcindor had been involved in discussions of a possible boycott of the 1968 Summer Olympics with other black athletes, the protest never materialized. He had stated that a "boycott" was "one way to express yourself about racism in a racist society." When it came time to make his decision to stay or go to Mexico City, he said he did not want to sacrifice time at UCLA. He had a B-minus average, was on schedule to graduate in June of 1969, and didn't want to jeopardize his

standing. While the United States team swept through the foreign competition, Alcindor was home on the streets of Harlem, with friends Emmette Bryant and Freddie Crawford, working for Operation Sports Rescue, teaching ghetto kids to play basketball, and urging them to stay in school.

In the NCAA Finals during his senior year Alcindor shot 15 for 20, scored 37, and hauled in 20 rebounds as UCLA beat Purdue. Averaging 26 points and 16 rebounds over his college career, he led the Bruins to NCAA championships in 1967, 1968, and 1969. Each year he was voted the tournament's most outstanding player. In four seasons he compiled a stratospheric .639 field goal percentage.

As early as 1966 Alcindor had expressed a desire to play pro ball for New York. He knew the Knicks' general manager Eddie Donovan, and Jack Donohue was friendly with the Knicks. But in 1969 Alcindor's NBA rights belonged to the Milwaukee Bucks, the Eastern Division's last place club, who in a coin flip won the rights to the first pick over the West's last-place club, the Phoenix Suns. The Bucks had to contend with a $1 million offer from the ABA's New York Nets before signing Alcindor to a five-year contract for $1.4 million.

In his first game in 1969, the Bucks opposed Detroit and 6-foot-11 center Walt Bellamy. Alcindor had 19 points at the half, finished with 29, to go with 12 rebounds and 6 assists as Milwaukee won, 119-110. He also played the entire 48 minutes.

Before Alcindor arrived, the Bucks were 27-55 in 1969. In his first year they finished 56-26. He led the league in field goals and points and won the Rookie of the Year. In 1971, having changed his name to Kareem Abdul-Jabbar, he led the league in scoring (31.7), field goals, and points and led Milwaukee to a Finals sweep of the Baltimore Bullets. After just two seasons, Jabbar had an NBA title, an MVP and a Finals MVP. He upped his average again in 1972 (34.8), winning his second consecutive scoring title and an MVP award.

He won his third MVP and led the Bucks to the Finals again in 1974. He hit one of the momentous shots of all-time, a 15-foot baseline hook in overtime to win Game 6, but Boston won in seven games. With Jabbar missing six weeks with a hand injury, Milwaukee finished last the following season. His contract expired, and the Bucks offered to buy him a townhouse in New York City and let him commute to the games if he would re-sign. "I wanted to go to New York, but the Knicks didn't have the money," Jabbar said. But he was pursued by the owner of the Lakers, Jack Kent Cooke, and signed with Los Angeles.

In 1976 and 1977, his first two seasons with the pre-Showtime Lakers, he led the league in total rebounds and won his fourth and fifth MVPs (in eight years), tying Bill Russell. He played the full 164 games in his first two L.A. years, averaging 40 minutes a night.

He won his sixth MVP in 1980 (breaking Bill Russell's record of 5), when Earvin Johnson joined Los Angeles. The Lakers beat Philadelphia in six games. It was the first of five Lakers titles in the 1980s. They topped the 76ers in six games again in 1982. In 1984, his 15th season, Jabbar surpassed Chamberlain's 31,419 points to become the NBA's all-time scoring leader. Los Angeles beat Boston (the first team ever to eliminate them in the Finals on their home court) in 1985, with a 38 year-old Jabbar winning the Finals MVP.

After the Lakers were eliminated by the Rockets in 1986, Jabbar sought a strength training program that would make himself more immovable in the pivot. Lakers trainer Gary Vitti gave him a training manual to strengthen his upper and lower body. He went from 250 to 270 pounds and, after an early season game, Robert Parish announced, "He's tougher to knock off balance." In the 1987 Finals, Jabbar, then 40, outplayed the younger Parish, averaging 25 points in the Finals. In the 1988 Finals the Pistons led in Game 6 and were just seconds from a championship when Bill Laimbeer fouled Jabbar on a baseline hook shot. He went to the line and hit both free throws to give the Lakers a victory. They then won Game 7 to win the championship, the last of the Jabbar-Johnson era.

While the great Laker squads are often referred to as "Magic's Lakers," Pat Riley made no secret about the team's go-to man. "We called Kareem's number so often it was an act of arrogance," Riley said. Jabbar's teams had made it to the post-season in 18 of his 20 years. Only Robert Parish, with 21, played more seasons. Jabbar attributed his longevity to a training regimen, including stretching exercises, begun in the early '70s.

He was voted to the NBA's 35th anniversary team in 1980 and the 50th Anniversary All-Time team in 1996.

Since he retired Jabbar has written several books. *Black Profiles in Courage: A Legacy of African-American Achievement* is his examination of the lives of heroic African Americans, including Frederick Douglass, Harriet Tubman, Crispus Attucks, and others. *A Season on the Reservation: My Sojourn with the White Mountain Apache,* recounts his year (1998-99) coaching the high school team on the White Mountain Apache Reservation in Arizona. In 2000, Jabbar was an assistant coach with the Los Angeles Clippers. He is currently a commentator for basketball broadcasts.

Mark Aguirre

Guard, Dallas, 1981-82 to February 1989; Detroit, 1989 through 1992-93; LA Clippers, 1993-94
Born: December 10, 1959 in Chicago 6-6, 232 High School: Austin (Chicago), then Westinghouse Vocational (Chicago) College: DePaul

Mark Aguirre was a scoring machine in his three seasons at DePaul and continued through his first seven seasons in the pros. At his best he used a punishing low-post game in combination with a perimeter game that extended beyond the 3-point line. He was selected for the 1980 Olympics to be played in Moscow, but the United States did not play.

Dallas made Aguirre the number one pick (Isiah Thomas was number two) in the 1981 draft. Aguirre was a two-time all-American at De Paul, averaging 25 points and shooting 55 percent through his junior year.

Aguirre had his best scoring season in his third pro year, when he averaged 29.5 points per game. It was his first of three all-star selections. Dallas, with Rolando Blackman and Derek Harper, got out of the first round of playoffs and met Los Angeles in the conference semi-finals. Los Angeles blew them out in five games.

In six of seven full seasons with Dallas Aguirre averaged between 22 and 29 points (his only sub-20-point season was his rookie year, when he averaged 18.7 per game). Midway through

his eighth year, in February 1999, he was traded to Detroit for two-time scoring champion Adrian Dantley and a 1991 first-round draft choice (who turned out to be Doug Smith from Missouri).

Aguirre scored less in Detroit, but he gave them both post and mid-range scoring options. His interior play helped the Pistons to NBA titles in 1989 and 1990. Following Chicago's four-game sweep of Detroit in 1991, the Pistons unraveled and Aguirre unraveled with them. Aguirre, 32, averaged 11 points on .431 shooting in 1991-92—both numbers the lowest of his 11-year career. Disputes with management over his contract continued for the 1992-93 season—a year in which Aguirre became the 31st player in history to score 18,000 points—and the Pistons waived him before the 1993-94 season. The Clippers signed him for that season, Aguirre's last.

Nate "Tiny" Archibald

Guard, Cincinnati, 1970-71 through 1971-72; KC/Omaha, 1972-73 through 1974-75; Kansas City, 1975-76; New York, 1976-77; Buffalo, 1977-78; Boston, 1978-79 through 1982-83; Milwaukee, 1983-84
Born: September 2, 1948 in New York 6-1, 160 High School: DeWitt Clinton (Bronx, N.Y.) Junior College: Arizona Western College: Texas–El Paso

Selected by the Cincinnati Royals in the second round, and 19th overall in the 1970 draft, Nate "Tiny" Archibald made many NBA teams rue the choice to pass him by. Pro scouts were worried about his size and whether he would be durable. Archibald was a 6-foot-1, 160-pound guard with Allen Iverson-like speed. The greatest penetrator of his time, he drove by defenders at will, and could hit the perimeter shot. He first raised eyebrows in the NBA in his second season, when he finished second (behind Jabbar) in scoring by averaging 28 points and third in assists (behind West and Wilkens) with 9 per game.

Tiny still owns the large distinction that he achieved the following season. Playing for the Kansas City-Omaha Kings, who had moved from Cincinnati the year before, Archibald averaged 34 points and 11 assists, the first and last player to lead the NBA in both categories in the same season. Overall, he led the league in nine statistical categories.

One of seven children, Archibald came out of the Paterson Housing Project on Morris Avenue in the South Bronx. He played in boys' clubs and schoolyards, and a man named Floyd Layne convinced him that basketball might be the ticket out the neighborhood. He attended DeWitt Clinton High and went on to Arizona Western College and Texas-El Paso beginning his sophomore season.

His first two years with Cincinnati saw him score 16 and 28 points and become a standout point guard. But the third season was off the charts. Aside from the scoring and assist titles, he became just the fourth guard in 27 years of NBA history to lead the league in scoring, the previous three being Max Zaslofsky, Dave Bing, and Jerry West. He was the first guard ever to make 1,000 field goals (1,028) in a season. He did that while shooting a meaty 49 percent from the field and 78 percent from the free throw line.

Over the five seasons following his pace-setting 1973

campaign, Archibald missed almost half his games due to injury. He played only 35 games in 1973-74; 34 in 1976-77, his first and last season with the New York Nets; and a torn Achilles tendon forced him to miss the entire 1977-78 season.

After being traded to the Celtics for the 1978-79 season, Archibald never averaged 15 points in any of his five Boston seasons or his last year with Milwaukee. That's because for Boston he was less of a lethal scorer and more of a quarterback and was named to the All-Star team in three of his five seasons there, winning the All-Star MVP in 1981.

The Boston years followed a conversation with Bob Cousy when he still played with the Kings. Cousy knew the phenomenal scoring would pass. Said Archibald, "We talked about what the team needed in order to win, and basically it wasn't a guard who scored a lot of points. It was leadership. He actually predicted the future, because he said the time would come I'd be on a team where there'd be no more scoring 50 points a night and losing."

That time would come with the Celtics. In his first year with Boston the team won 29 and dropped 53. But Larry Bird joined the Celtics for the 1979-80 campaign and their record shot up to 61-21. Bird lead the team in scoring and rebounding and Archibald led in assists. That team lost in the Conference Finals to Philadelphia, but would hit its stride the following season. Boston won 62 and got revenge against Philadelphia, falling behind three-games-to-one but taking the next three of the Conference Finals by a total of five points. They then polished off Houston in six games in the Finals.

The five-time All Star retired from Milwaukee after the 1984 season. He was elected to the Hall of Fame in 1991 and voted to the NBA's All-Time Team in 1996.

Paul Arizin

Forward, Philadelphia, 1950-51 through 1961-62
Born: April 9, 1928 in Philadelphia 6-4, 200 High School: La Salle (Philadelphia) College: Villanova

At a time when the game was predominantly two-handed set shots and drives, Paul Arizin, a 6-foot-4 forward, was one of the few practitioners of the jump shot. He described his shot as coming about by "accident." "I was playing in the Catholic Club League in Philadelphia and our games were on a slick dance floor. When I tried to hook, my feet would go out from under me. So I jumped; the ceiling was low and I had to throw line drives. I just never changed."

The man known as "Pitchin' Paul" was a 20-point per game scorer at Villanova, the College Player of the Year in 1950, when he led all Division I players with 25.3 points per game. The Philadelphia Warriors chose him in the first round of the 1950 draft, with owner and coach Eddie Gottlieb offering him a $9000 contract. "That was a lot more than what most college graduates were getting in those days," Arizin said. He posted a rookie average of 17 points, and then led the league in the 1951-52 season with a 25.4 average, breaking George Mikan's three-year chokehold on the scoring title. Many NBA players before Arizin were making about 33 percent of their shots. In 1952 he led the league, connecting on 45 percent of his attempts. He also won the All-Star Game MVP that year.

After winning the scoring title Arizin served two years in the

Marines, but returned to average 21 points per game. In fact, he averaged between 21 and 26 points over his nine remaining NBA seasons. He was named to the All-Star team 10 times.

In 1956 he was All-NBA first team for the second of three times, averaged 24.2 points, and helped the Warriors to a league-best 45-27. Arizin and teammate Neil Johnston were second and third in the league in scoring, trailing only St. Louis' Bob Pettit. The Warriors topped Syracuse, the defending champions, in the Eastern Division Finals and had an easier time with Fort Wayne in five games. In the post-season, Arizin lead the Warriors with averages of 29 points and 8 rebounds. For Arizin, it was his greatest career moment. "Only one thing ever came close," he says. "That was being named to the NBA's 25th Anniversary All-Time, All-League Team in 1971."

He won another scoring title in 1957 with a 25.6 average. Twice he finished second in the league in scoring and finished in the top 10 nine times. Aside from his consistent scoring exploits, Arizin, whose nickname might well have been "Wheezing Paul," was known throughout his career for his panting and coughing up and down the court. While it appeared to be asthma, Arizin said it was from a persistent sinus condition he'd had since his youth.

Of all the players who began playing between 1945 and 1960, only three—Wilt Chamberlain (30.1), Elgin Baylor (27.4) and Bob Pettit (26.4)—had higher career averages than Arizin (22.8). In eight years of playoffs he raised that average to 24.2.

After the 1962 season Gottlieb took the Warriors to San Francisco. Arizin did not make the trip west, electing to retire. Instead he joined the Camden Bullets of the Eastern League, where he played from 1963 through 1965. He averaged 25 points with the Bullets and won league MVP honors in 1963. He was 37 when he played his last game in 1965.

He later worked as a marketing representative for IBM. Besides the NBA championship and two scoring titles, his career honors included being elected to the Hall of Fame in 1978. He was voted to the NBA's 50th Anniversary All-Time Team in 1996.

Charles Barkley

Forward, Philadelphia, 1984-85 through 1991-92; Phoenix, 1992-93 through 1995-96; Houston, 1996-97 through 1999-2000
Born: February 20, 1963 in Leeds, Ala. 6-5, 252 High School: Leeds College: Auburn

A veritable quote machine and villain wherever he played, Charles Barkley was never dull. He went by many labels—the "Round Mound of Rebound," "Sir Charles," or lately, "Mouth." Whatever the label, Charles Barkley is legendary for playing the power forward position in a way that made him seem much taller than his listed 6-foot-6. He shot 54 percent for his career and was at times was an unstoppable offensive player. In five seasons he averaged more than 25 points per game. He also showed a knack for playing inside and out. Perhaps the most rugged small rebounder in the game's history, Barkley was an All-Star 11 times, averaging 20 points and 10 rebounds for 11 consecutive seasons. In the history of basketball, only Wilt Chamberlain (12 consecutive years) and Kareem

Abdul-Jabbar (12), Bob Pettit (11), and Moses Malone (11) matched that run of excellence.

Barkley came to the pros by way of Leeds, Alabama and Auburn University. Philadelphia selected him fifth overall in the 1984 NBA draft and he made the All-Rookie team. Barkley played with Moses Malone, Julius Erving, Andrew Toney, Maurice Cheeks, and Bobby Jones that year, and Philly won 58 games but lost to Boston in five games in the 1985 Conference Finals. In 1986 the 76ers won 54 but lost to Milwaukee in the conference semis. With Malone and Toney gone and Erving playing his last season in 1987, Barkley led the circuit with 14.6 rebounds and scored 23 points on 59 percent shooting. He set two NBA records in one game, grabbing 11 offensive rebounds in one quarter and 13 in a half in a game against New York. Barkley could play like a power forward and a guard. It was typical to see him grab a rebound, charge the length of the floor, going behind-the-back as he needed, and finishing off with a monster slam at the other end.

In 1988 he had a career-best 28.3 average and began a string of four consecutive All-NBA first team selections. He won his third straight IBM Award, a statistical honor based on points, rebounds, and assists and measuring a player's overall contribution to his team. An All-Star in six of his eight Philadelphia seasons, Barkley won the league's MVP in 1991, scoring 17 points and grabbing 22 rebounds. "Can't no one on the planet Earth guard me," Barkley said to a *New York Times* writer. "No one. I mean that." Asked how he could rebound despite his size he answered, "If I were seven feet tall I'd be illegal in three states."

After eight seasons in Philadelphia, however, the team was getting further and further from an NBA title. After the 1992 season Philadelphia traded Barkley to Phoenix, getting in return a guard, a forward and a center—Jeff Hornacek, Tim Perry, and Andrew Lang.

Barkley played on the historic 1992 "Dream Team" in Barcelona and led the United States team in scoring, with 18 points per game, and field goal percentage (.711). Before a game against Angola Barkley was asked if he knew about his opponent. "I don't know anything about Angola but I know they're in trouble," he snapped.

Barkley's 1992-93 season, his first with Phoenix, may have been his best. The Suns won 62 and lost 20. Barkley averaged 26 points, 12 rebounds and a career-best 5 assists. He received the Most Valuable Player award and was named All-NBA first team for the fifth time.

In the Finals against the Bulls, Phoenix dug a hole by dropping consecutive home games, before prevailing in triple-over-time in Chicago, 129-121, as Barkley, who the previous game had 42 points and 13 rebounds, played 53 minutes and posted 24 points and 19 rebounds. Despite Barkley's 32 points and 12 rebounds, the Suns lost Game 4 when Jordan scored 55. But Phoenix again got a must-win with a 108-98 victory in Game 5, even as Chicago city officials boarded windows in anticipation of a post-game celebration. Back at home for Game 6, Phoenix rallied from a 9-point fourth quarter deficit and seemed to have the game in hand, leading by four points—with the ball!—with 49 seconds left. Then Frank Johnson missed a jumper and Jordan drove the length of the court, making it 98-96. Dan Majerle then shot a baseline air ball from 15 feet

away. After a Bulls' timeout, John Paxson buried a 3-pointer with three seconds left for a 99-98 Chicago victory.

Barkley was involved in his second blockbuster trade after the 1996 season, going to Houston to play with Hakeem Olajuwon and Clyde Drexler. Before the season began he played on his second Olympic team, helping America to its second consecutive gold medal. Houston won 57 games, with Barkley averaging 19 points and 13 rebounds, breaking his string of 11 straight 20-point, 10-rebound seasons. Utah defeated Houston in six games in the Conference Finals.

Late in his career, it was hard for Barkley to stay healthy. His last roar was the 1999 playoffs, when he averaged 24 points and 14 rebounds while Houston lost to Los Angeles in four games. Barkley contemplated retiring again.

After a devastating early-season knee injury, Barkley, 36, announced his retirement in the midst of his 16th season. But he returned for one last game after rehabilitating his leg. He finished with a 54 percent field goal percentage, the highest among all active forwards and third behind Bobby Jones and Kevin McHale among all forwards who ever played. He retired as the 18th highest scorer and 14th highest rebounder in (NBA-ABA) history. He was the 10th player ever to record 20,000 points and 10,000 rebounds. Barkley was voted to the NBA's 50th Anniversary All-Time Team in 1996.

Rick Barry

Forward, San Francisco, 1965-66 through 1966-67; 1967-68, did not play; Oakland (ABA), 1968-69; Washington Capitols (ABA), 1969-70; New York Nets (ABA), 1970-71 through 1971-72; Golden State Warriors, 1972-73 through 1977-78; Houston, 1978-79 through 1979-80
Born: March 28, 1944, in Elizabeth, N.J. 6-7, 220 High School: Roselle Park, N.J. College: Miami (Fla.)

When Rick Barry retired after the 1980 season, he was fifth all-time with 25,279 points. A scorer from any distance, Barry still holds the career record for points per game in the Finals. He averaged 36 points in the 10 NBA Finals games he played in 1967 and 1975. Barry is the only player to win scoring titles in the ABA (1968-69) and in the NBA (1966-67). Always known as a scorer and a brilliant passer off the dribble, Barry played his best offensive game on March 26, 1974 against Portland, when he scored 64 points, making 30 field goals. It was only the fourth time that a player made 30 field goals; Wilt Chamberlain did it on the other three occasions.

Barry was also notable for his underhanded free throw style. The shot allowed him to put the ball up softly, with backspin. At one point Barry worked with Chamberlain, who adopted the underhand approach, improved his percentage, but gave it up shortly after. Barry hit exactly 90 percent of his career free throw attempts. Mark Price shot slightly higher at 90.4 percent, but Price attempted only 2,362 while Barry attempted nearly twice that many, 4,243.

In his senior year at Miami Barry was the country's leading scorer with 37.4 points per game. The San Francisco Warriors made him their second pick (they chose Davidson's Fred Hetzel first) in the 1965 draft. When Barry came to the NBA, he needed no period of adjustment to the pro game. The 6-foot-7 forward played 35 minutes a night, averaged 26 points and won

Rookie of the Year. Wilt Chamberlain had run off seven consecutive scoring titles from 1960 through 1966. Then Rick Barry ended the Dipper's reign by ripping off 35.6 points in his second season.

"Next to Bird, Barry is the greatest passing forward ever to play," says Mike Gminski. "If he realized the jump shot was not going, he would drive to the basket," adds Guokas. "Although he was not as good a ball handler as Bird, he was more explosive going to the basket." In fact, in Barry's first nine pro seasons (five NBA and four ABA) he fell below 25 points per game on only one occasion and posted averages of 25.7, 35.6, 34.0, 27.7, 29.4, 31.5, 22.3, 25.1, and 30.6.

No one expected that Barry, not two months after the 1967 NBA Finals, would sign a three-year deal with the Oakland Oaks. The Warriors contested the deal, claiming that his contract with them was exclusive. A judge ruled he was bound to San Francisco for one year, but if he sat out for a season, he could play for the ABA franchise, if Oakland paid damages to the Warriors for loss of his services. During the year off he was a broadcaster for Oaks games and made endorsement appearances. Playing just 35 games the following year, he led the ABA in scoring but then tore up his knee. The Oaks won the 1968-69 ABA championship without him. He averaged better than 29 points per game over the next three seasons with the Washington Capitols (who had moved from Oakland for the 1969-70 season and to Virginia the following season), and for the New York Nets.

Barry played two years for Nets before returning to the Golden State Warriors for the 1972-73 season. By then a book about his nomadic life—*Confessions of A Basketball Gypsy*—had been published. His career average in the ABA was 30.5 points per game, the best in league history.

Barry made his second trip to the NBA Finals in 1975 against the Washington Bullets. He hit a jumper with the 24-second clock running down and 38 seconds left to win Game 1. In Game 2, Phil Chenier's 30 points weren't enough to offset Barry's 36. He hit two free throws with 23 seconds left to give the Warriors a 92-91 victory. In Game 3 he hit for 38 more in a 109-101 victory in San Francisco. In Game 4, the Warriors were down eight with 4:44 to go, but went ahead to stay on a Butch Beard layup with under two minutes left. The Finals sweep was only the third in NBA history. Barry, averaging 29.5 points and carrying the Warriors throughout, won a unanimous vote as *Sport* magazine's MVP for the series.

Golden State won 59 games the following season (11 more than their title season), but were knocked out in the seven-game Conference Finals against Phoenix. They never got that close again. Barry played his last two seasons, in quiet fashion, with the Houston Rockets, finishing his career in 1980.

After two lackluster seasons coaching Fort Wayne in the Continental Basketball Association (CBA) in 1993 and 1994, he traveled to New Jersey of the United States Basketball League (USBL). In 1999 the team went 23-6 and swept its three post-season games against Tampa Bay, Pennsylvania, and Connecticut to win the USBL championship.

In his 14-year pro career Barry was a four-time ABA All-Star and eight-time NBA All-Star. He was elected to the Basketball Hall of Fame in 1986 and named to the NBA's 50th

Anniversary All-Time Team in 1996.

Between the ABA and NBA combined, Barry scored 25,279 points. His career line of 24.8 points, 6.7 rebounds, and 4.9 assists is one of the most balanced ever at the forward position.

Barry had three sons (Brent, Jon, Drew) who made the NBA, and another (Richard) who played in the CBA and Europe. His father-in-law Bruce Hale played in the BAA and NBA and was a noted coach.

Elgin Baylor

Forward, Minneapolis, 1958-59 through 1959-60; LA Lakers, 1960-72

Born: September 16, 1934 in Washington, D.C. 6-5, 225 High School: Phelps Vocational (Washington, D.C.), then Spingarn (Washington, D.C.) College: The College of Idaho; Seattle University

Elgin Baylor, who began his NBA career in 1958, is sometimes referred to as the first player with hang time. "Elgin Baylor invented modern basketball," says Bob Ryan. With his drives and double-pumps and off-balance shots, Baylor brought the NBA its first airborne presence.

When he scored 64 points on November 8, 1959, he broke Joe Fulks' record of 63. On November 15, 1960 he broke his own record with 71 points in Madison Square Garden. He had 34 points in the first half, and with Los Angeles leading by 17 points entering the fourth quarter, Baylor's rookie teammate Jerry West kept feeding him. With about 90 seconds remaining in the game, Baylor broke his record of 64 and left the floor with 71 points as the Garden crowd gave him a rousing ovation. Teammate "Hot" Rod Hundley recalled that Bob Short gave every member of the team cufflinks with a '71.

The 61 points he dropped on the Celtics in Boston Garden on April 14, 1962 is still a Finals record. Red Auerbach even had Bill Russell guard Baylor that day, but nothing worked. (It took Michael Jordan three overtime periods to get 63 in a first-round playoff game against the Celtics 24 years later.)

Nearly 30 years after his retirement, Baylor is still in fourth place in all-time regular season scoring (27.4) and playoff scoring (27.0). No one standing 6-foot-5 ever put up the line Baylor did in his third season: 34.8 points and 19.8 rebounds. He was voted to the All-NBA first team 10 times in his first 11 years between 1959 and 1969.

Baylor was born in 1934. At his birth, the story goes, his father, John Baylor, took out his pocket watch to check the time of his fifth child's arrival. It was an Elgin watch, and Baylor's father decided to name the boy after his most prized possession.

Baylor joined the team at Phelps Vocational High in Washington, D.C. and made all-city his first two years. But he quit to get away from all the attention and worked for a year in a furniture store. He listened to his mother—who wanted him to exploit his athletic gifts—and returned to Spingarn High, a black academic school. He set a District of Columbia scoring record with 68 points.

Baylor, now 20, followed a high school friend to the College of Idaho, where he played football. When the football coach (also the basketball coach) saw Baylor on the court, he wound up playing the full 26 games, averaging 31 points and 19 rebounds. The school began to de-emphasize sports and Baylor

transferred to Seattle University. Under NCAA rules, a transfer student had to sit out a year of varsity competition. Baylor spent the winter playing for an AAU team, the West Side Fords, leading the league with 33 points a game.

In his first year with the varsity he was third in the country with a 29.7 average, led the country in rebounds, and guided his school to a record of 22-3. The next year he scored 32.5, second only to Cincinnati's Oscar Robertson. Seattle lost the 1958 NCAA Final against Kentucky, 84-72. Baylor had 25 points (on just 9-of-32 shooting) and 19 rebounds. He was named Tournament MVP. Overall, he averaged 31.3 points over three college seasons. When Leo Leavitt of the Globetrotters saw him in the spring of 1958, he said, "Baylor is better than Chamberlain or Russell already. He can do more things than either. And he's got speed, stamina, strength, and competitive spirit."

Baylor then passed up his final year at college, as the Minneapolis Lakers made him the first pick overall in the 1958 draft. The Globetrotters also sought his services. He got married in the summer of 1958 (with Wilt Chamberlain as his best man) and his new bride didn't want to be a basketball widow while he practiced globetrotting. That helped him to make up his mind and he signed with the Lakers for $20,000.

The NBA Rookie of the Year in 1959, Baylor scored 55 points in one game. He was co-MVP of the All-Star Game, recording 24 points and 11 rebounds. His 24.9 scoring average was fourth in the league. Because of Baylor, a team that had finished 19-53 before he arrived made it all the way to the NBA Finals against Boston. Lakers president Bob Short was blunt: without Baylor, he said, the club would have gone bankrupt.

Knicks' guard Richie Guerin played in the record-setting game and later in the game that Wilt Chamberlain scored 100, just over a year later. "By far, Elgin's was the better performance, and that 71-point game remains the greatest individual effort I have ever seen," said Guerin. "In Wilt's game, they set out to get him the record. There was nothing artificial about Elgin's 71. He got all the points in a natural flow." He also got 25 rebounds, 11 more than anyone else in the game.

Professional basketball was new to Los Angeles and fans immediately fell for Baylor's brand of grace and scoring punch. In his first three California seasons he averaged 34.8, 38.2, and 34.0. In his first five years in the league he averaged above 32 points per game. He'd also set league records with his 64- and 71-point outbursts.

The Lakers became the first NBA team to gross more than $1 million in a regular season. An attendance study showed that Baylor's presence in the game was good for an additional 2,000 more people in the arena, or $6,000 in the till. That translated to $200,000 for a season or $600,000 for his first three seasons in Los Angeles.

Baylor courageously fought and overcame knee problems from the middle of his career until the end. He played only 48 games in the 1961-62 season, but that was due to an Army commitment. Bothered by pain, he turned to the bandages and heavy canvas-elastic knee braces popular at the time. His movements restricted, in three consecutive games during the 1963-64 season he scored 8, then 10, then 13 points. Rumors flew that he was near the end. When asked about it, Baylor showed

a temper than surprised everyone who knew him: "I have no time for gravediggers," he fumed. He stuck it out and played 78 of 80 games that year, his average "dropping" to 25.4 per game.

He went to the Mayo Clinic in Rochester, Minnesota for a diagnosis, but doctors couldn't figure out his problem. Five minutes into the first playoff game in the 1965 season he took a jumper, but there was a popping sound when his feet touched down. He had ripped off the upper portion of his left kneecap. The following season his minutes were reduced and he fell below 20 points per game (16.6) for the first time in his career. A year later he strained ligaments in his right knee, was put in a hip-to-ankle cast, and missed a month.

The Baylor-West tandem combined for 52 points per game in 1961, 69 per game in 1962, 61 in 1963, 54 in 1964, and 58 in 1965. It was simply the best 1-2 scoring punch in NBA history. But even the high-voltage connection of Baylor-West didn't generate the juice to propel the team to a championship. In seven seasons—1959, 1962, 1963, 1965, 1966, 1968, and 1969—the Lakers fell to the Celtics in the Finals. Three of those Finals, 1962, 1966, and 1969, took an agonizing seven games. None was more painful than the 1962 series, when Baylor posted a playoff average of 38.6 points and West chipped in with 31.5. The Lakers held a 3-games-to-2 lead, only to lose Game 6 at home, 118-105. At the end of regulation in Game 7, the Lakers' Frank Selvy took a pass from Rod Hundley and missed a 12-foot jumper. Had the shot fallen, the Lakers would have won. Instead, Boston regrouped in overtime and won 110-107.

In 1970-71, his penultimate season, Baylor tore an Achilles tendon and played just two games. He retired, at 37, after playing just nine games of the 1972 season. He was then the fourth-highest scorer in NBA history and second-highest rebounder (next to Bob Pettit) among all NBA forwards.

Despite 14 NBA seasons without a title, the Baylor legacy remains. With his ability to hang in the air and score inside and out, Baylor is the precursor to stars like Julius Erving and Michael Jordan. The 27.4 points-per-game average is fourth best all-time, behind only Jordan (30.12), Chamberlain (30.06), and Shaquille O'Neal (27.6). He is one of 14 players in NBA history to register 20,000 points and 10,000 rebounds. His 11,453 rebounds are first in Lakers' history.

Baylor was inducted into the Hall of Fame in 1976 and coached the New Orleans Jazz from 1975 through 1979. Since 1986 he has been the vice president of basketball operations with the Los Angeles Clippers. He was voted to the NBA's 35th Anniversary Team in 1980 and the 50th Anniversary Team in 1996.

Walt Bellamy

Center, Chicago, 1961-63; Baltimore, 1963-65, New York, 1965-68, Detroit, 1968-70, Atlanta, 1970-74, New Orleans, 1974
Born: July 24, 1939 in New Bern, N.C. 6-11, 245 High School: J.T. Barber, New Bern, N.C. College: Indiana

Walt Bellamy is hardly mentioned when the names of the great centers are rattled off. This is hard to figure, since "The Big Bell" was one of the most consistent scorers and rebounders the game has ever seen. The burly pivot man

snatched 1,000 rebounds a staggering nine times in his career. His 14,241 rebounds place him eighth all-time.

Bellamy is one of those odd NBA players whose rookie season was his best. He didn't disappoint in his first campaign, scoring 31.6 points per game while grabbing 19 rebounds. He also topped the league in field goal percentage (.519) and easily took Rookie of the Year honors. But Bellamy's season was overlooked, since 1962 was the Year of Chamberlain. Wilt Chamberlain averaged 50.4 points and 25.7 rebounds for the Philadelphia Warriors. That gap between the first and second scorer remains the largest in NBA history.

In that season and the 12 that followed, Bellamy never played less than 74 games, and in eight different seasons played every game. In 1969, his eighth NBA season, he set an all-time record by playing in 88 games, an oddity that resulted when the Knicks traded him to Detroit in December 1968. Despite a good jumper, and agility that allowed him to drive around most NBA centers, Bellamy's career accomplishments got short shrift and were drowned out by the frequent headlines about Bill Russell, Wilt Chamberlain, Willis Reed, Wes Unseld, and Kareem Abdul-Jabbar.

Bellamy grew up in New Bern, North Carolina. He was 6-foot-1 by the time he was 14, but his best game was football. As a senior, playing end, he led Barber High to the state championship and won all-state recognition. But he also had begun playing basketball on the playgrounds and high school coach Simon Coates discovered him.

Cates introduced him to Indiana coach Branch McCracken, who worked on getting Bellamy to be a more aggressive player. He was an All-American in 1961 and left the Bloomington campus with the school's single-game scoring record of 42 points (the previous record was 41, set 17 years earlier) and a record field goal percentage (.517). Bellamy was also a member of the legendary 1960 U.S. Olympic team in Rome. With Oscar Robertson, Jerry West, and Jerry Lucas, the United States went 8-0, with the closest contest being an 81-57 thrashing of the Soviet Union.

The 6-foot-11 center was clearly the best pivot man available in the 1961 draft and in any other season New York, which had the league's worst record in 1961 (21-58), would have been allowed to pick first. But league owners voted to follow an unprecedented procedure, allowing a new franchise, the Chicago Packers, to choose first. They chose Bellamy.

Bellamy amazed everyone his rookie season. Not only was his 31.6 average second to Chamberlain's 50.4, but his 2,495 points were 356 more than Chicago's second and third high scorers combined, Bob Leonard and Andy Johnson. Bellamy also finished third in the league (behind Chamberlain and Russell) with 19 rebounds a game. In his first of four All-Star Games he scored 23 points and grabbed 17 rebounds.

After the 1961-62 season few noticed and fewer cared that the Packers' Windy City franchise was renamed the Zephyrs. When the team was moved to Baltimore a year later and dubbed the Bullets, "Bells" continued his scoring ways and in each of his first four years averaged more than 24 points a game. During the 1963-64 season his coach Slick Leonard frequently got on him for standing around. Despite Bellamy's 27 point, 17 rebound output, Leonard frequently,

and publicly, vented his frustration on Bellamy. Finally, Buddy Jeannette took over and made Bellamy captain. Bellamy played in his fourth All-Star Game in as many years and led the Bullets past the Hawks and to the Conference Finals, where they lost to Los Angeles in six games. But Baltimore traded him to New York for Johnny Green, John Egan, and Jim Barnes on November 2, 1965.

Converting more than 50 percent of his shots and sharing the rebounding and scoring load with Willis Reed, Bellamy helped New York out of the Eastern Division cellar and into unfamiliar territory, as they reached the playoffs in 1967 and 1968. With Bellamy in the pivot, however, Reed played forward, which wasn't his natural position. Moreover, New York general manager Eddie Donovan wanted Dave DeBusschere, the rugged Pistons forward so highly regarded in Detroit that he had been named player-coach in 1964, at 24 the youngest ever to hold that position. On December 19, 1968, Donovan made the bold move, offering guard Howard Komives and Bellamy to the Pistons for DeBusschere.

In February of 1970 Bellamy was traded to the Atlanta Hawks, where he would contribute the same high field goal percentage and double-digit points and rebounds that were his career trademarks. He finished his career with his fifth team, the New Orleans Jazz, in 1975.

Bellamy finished with 20,941 points and 14,241 rebounds, one of only 14 members of the 20,000-point, 10,000-rebound club. He was left off the NBA's 50th Anniversary All-Time Team, an outcome that surprised Wes Unseld and prompted him to ask, "Do you know what Bellamy did?"

It was not Bellamy's first slight. Incredibly, it took 18 years after his retirement for the four-time all-star to make the Hall of Fame.

Dave Bing

Guard, Detroit, 1966-67 through 1974-75; Washington, 1975-76 through 1976-77; Boston, 1976-77 through 1977-78
Born: November 24, 1943 in Washington, D.C. 6-3, 185 High School: Spingarn (Washington, D.C.) College: Syracuse

In a letter recommending Dave Bing for the Hall of Fame in 1983, Syracuse coach Jim Boeheim wrote, "Dave is certainly the best college player that I've been associated with in my twenty years in the college game." Bing, an All-American his senior year, did not disappoint at the pro level, either.

The Pistons lost a coin flip to the Knicks, who selected Cazzie Russell first in the 1966 draft. Since Russell had starred at the University of Michigan, the Detroit fans at Cobo Arena serenaded Bing with chants of "We want Cazzie!" The jeers soon stopped. They shouted "Bingo" whenever Bing hit a jumper. The NBA Rookie of the Year in the 1966-67 season, he averaged 20 points, 5 rebounds, and 4 assists. But Bing's Pistons had the next-to-worst record (30-51) in the NBA. The die was cast; Bing would flourish, but his teams would not.

In his second season he led the league in scoring (27.1), the first guard to do so since Max Zaslofsky, who led the circuit with 21 points per game for the Chicago Stags in 1948. Bing's high game was 54 points. He also learned to hone his passing

skills. In the playoffs the Pistons played a tough six games against the Celtics and Bing averaged 28 points. In Game 6 Bing had 37 points in the second half—at one point 16 in a row—and 44 for the night, but the Pistons were eliminated.

With his gliding, graceful style and his one-on-one abilities, Bing was a crowd-pleaser. "We had only 120,000 customers the year before Dave came," said George Maskin, the Pistons' publicity director. "When Dave came we went to 200,000."

While the league's best teams—New York, Boston, Los Angeles, Milwaukee, and Los Angeles—always presented formidable opposition for the hapless Pistons, Bing had immense competition in the backcourt, too. The 1960s and '70s may have been the most guard-rich era of NBA history. Oscar Robertson and Jerry West were in their primes. So were Sam Jones, Hal Greer, and Len Wilkens. Walt Frazier and Earl Monroe were just hitting their strides. So Bing was selected All-NBA first team just two times (1968, 1971) in a 12-year career.

Bing was traded to the Washington Bullets in August 1975. He won the All-Star Game MVP in 1976 when he scored 16 points. His scoring, however, was down to 10 points a game, and he was waived by the Bullets and signed as a free agent by Boston in September 1977. No amount of Celtics' mystique could keep the team from a 30-52 record in 1978, and Bing retired after the season.

He was elected to the Hall of Fame in 1989 and voted to the NBA 50th Anniversary All-Time Team in 1996. Along with great players like Elgin Baylor, Karl Malone, John Stockton, and Bob Lanier, Dave Bing never won an NBA championship. After retiring, he founded Bing Steel.

Larry Bird

Forward, Boston, 1979-80 through 1991-92
Born: December 7, 1956 in West Baden, Ind. 6-9, 220 High School: Springs Valley (French Lick, Ind.) College: Indiana, then Northwood Institute, then Indiana State

Larry Bird is arguably the most complete forward who ever played. No forward ever possessed the full bag of skills—rebounding, passing, perimeter shooting—that Bird did. A look at Bird's lifetime line of 24 points, 10 rebounds, and 6 assists tells a story: Bird could beat you with a 3-point shot, a tough rebound in traffic, or a quick pass. The nonstatistical intangibles also favor Bird. From his rookie year on he was the leader of the Celtics. With Bird, the Celtics played in five Finals between 1981 and 1987 and won three of them.

With Magic Johnson, Bird will be recalled for putting his stamp on 1980s basketball with a team-oriented pass-first, shoot-second philosophy. Bird was a great offensive player, but, like Johnson, was more concerned with winning than he was with individual achievements.

Bird grew up in the French Lick-West Baden area of Indiana. There were six siblings and the family grew up poor, but small town living suited him. When he joined the Celtics he would later refer to himself as the "hick from French Lick." The first time Bird remembered feeling any love for the game he was 13. He didn't watch games on television, but by high school his coach, Jim Jones, was drilling him extensively on his own game—working on his shooting and ballhandling. Wanting to catch up to his older brothers, Mark and Mike,

honed his competitive instincts.

Indiana coach Bobby Knight visited Bird on three separate occasions and offered him a scholarship. Larry's mother, Georgia, wanted him to go to Indiana State in nearby Terre Haute. His father, Joe, wanted him to go with Bobby Knight and Indiana University.

Bird finally agreed by to commit to Indiana by his senior year, in spring 1974. But Bird—arriving on the Bloomington campus with $75 in his pocket—was overwhelmed by the size of the campus and hitchhiked home after three weeks.

For a year he took a job in French Lick driving a garbage truck, and hung out with pals. In 1975 his father, having problems with drinking and with inconsistent employment, took his own life. Bird transferred into Indiana State for the 1975-76 season but was not eligible to play. Right off he was a major contributor, averaging 32.8 points and 13.1 rebounds in his first year on the court. He was All-American his second and third years, and led the Sycamores to the title game against Michigan and Earvin Johnson in 1979.

Indiana State was undefeated (29-0) and became the first school ever to make it to the Final Four in its first trip to the NCAA tournament. Though he had 19 points and 13 rebounds, Bird connected on just seven of 21 shots, and Johnson and his mates played better and won, 75-64.

Red Auerbach had drafted Bird on June 9, 1978 in one of his gutsy moves. He gambled, spending the sixth pick of the first round on Bird. The gamble was that Bird, a "junior eligible," had the option to sign with the team or finish his senior year and go back into a second draft. Auerbach would attempt to sell Bird on the Celtics' legacy. "I felt that the reputation of the Celtics was such that every player would want to play here," he said. After much haggling with Bird's agent Bob Wolff, the Celtics paid $650,000, the most ever for a rookie.

In camp that first year Cedric Maxwell looked at Bird and made a sarcastic crack to Curtis Rowe, "Hey, Curtis, here's our savior." He was sometimes called "The Great White Hope." Bird endured the remarks about his ability—"too slow, can't run, can't jump." In Bird's first year Boston was 61-21, up from 29-53 the year before. He led the team in scoring and rebounding.

After five years with Boston, Bird had led the Celtics to two Championships. Boston's victory over Los Angeles in the 1984 Finals reestablished the league's most historic rivalry. In 1985, Los Angeles returned the favor, with Kareem Abdul-Jabbar taking the Finals MVP trophy that Bird had earned the year before. In 1986 Bird won his third consecutive league MVP—something done by only Bill Russell and Wilt Chamberlain before him—and second Finals MVP. It was the last championship Boston won.

Bird's rebounding declined in 1987 and 1988, though it was fairly astounding that he averaged 28 and 30 points in those years, despite visiting an orthopedic therapist for his back after every game. Bird's spinal condition dated to when he was 26, in 1983. He was in severe pain the morning after he had laid gravel around his French Lick basketball court. Doctors discovered he had disk problems that were congenital.

In 1988, Detroit beat Boston in the Conference Finals. He missed all but six games of the 1988-89 season with bone mass

in both heels that were imbedded in the tendon. His legs were never the same again. In Bird's last four years, Boston reached the second round of the playoffs only once.

He couldn't walk in the opening ceremonies of the 1992 Olympics, since the ceremony lasted four hours and he could no longer bear the weight on his back for such a long period. After playing with the Barcelona "Dream Team" that won the gold, Bird announced his retirement on August 18, 1992. I would like to have played a little bit longer, maybe a year or two more, but there was no way possible I was going to be able to do that."

A 12-time all-star, Bird was also selected All-NBA first team nine straight years, from 1980 through 1988. A member of the NBA Championship Teams of 1981, 1984 and 1986, Bird was named to the NBA's 50th Anniversary All-Time Team in 1996.

After serving as a special assistant to the Celtics from 1992 through 1997, Bird became head coach of the Indiana Pacers for the 1997-98 season. He won Coach of the Year and led Indiana to the Eastern Conference Finals, where they lost to Chicago in seven games. In 1999-2000 the Pacers went 56-26 and beat Milwaukee, Philadelphia, and then New York to reach the Finals. But Indiana couldn't contain Shaquille O'Neal and lost in six games. Bird stepped down as coach after the playoffs. Three years later, on July 11, 2003 he was named Pacers President of Basketball Operations.

Kobe Bryant

Guard, LA Lakers 1996-97 to present
Born: August 23, 1978 in Philadelphia 6-7, 210 High School: Lower Merion (Ardmore, Pennsylvania)

Following the 2003 season, Kobe Bryant was charged with a single count of felony sexual assault stemming from an alleged incident at a Colorado resort. A conviction would bring a sentence of four years to life in prison or 20 years to life on probation. Bryant denied the charges but admitted he had consensual sex with an employee of the resort. Regardless of the outcome of the case, the charges will result in the loss of millions of dollars in endorsement revenue for one of the NBA's highest-profile stars.

Before these charges put Bryant's basketball future in doubt, it could have been argued that of all the players to be tagged "Next Jordan," Bryant came the closest. Since bypassing college and coming into the league at 18 years old, he has steadily improved. Now, just 25, he is among the most talented guards in the league and still capable of improving.

Bryant's reputation certainly preceded him. The son of Joe 'Jelly Bean' Bryant, who played on three NBA teams between 1975 and 1983, Kobe was the all-time leading scorer in Southeastern Pennsylvania high school history with 2,883 points, breaking the marks of Wilt Chamberlain (2,359 points) and former St. Joseph's star Carlin Warley (2,441 points). It wasn't merely a solo show either: Bryant led his high school to a 77-13 record in his last three seasons.

He became the youngest player to appear in an NBA game on November 3, 1996 when he made his pro debut at the age of 18 years, 2 months, 11 days, and was named to the All-Rookie Team after averaging 7.6 points in 71 games. In 1998, he became the youngest All-Star in NBA history, scoring a

team-high 18 points and 6 rebounds. Los Angeles was guard rich with Eddie Jones and Nick Van Exxel. But by his third season, in 1999, Bryant had shown his scoring ability, posting 19.9 points a game and leading the team in assists.

The offense, defense and leadership have climbed steadily since then. He was won NBA All-Defensive First Team honors and All-NBA First Team honors. More importantly, the marriage of Bryant and Shaqulle O'Neal flourished after a strained beginning. Phil Jackson took over as coach for the 1999-2000 season and since then the Bryant-O'Neal pairing has been the most potent in the league. In the last four years the duo has combined for 52, 57, 52 and 58 points per game respectively, making them one of the greatest one-two punches in league history. They also led the Lakers to three consecutive Championships from 1999-2000 to 2001-02. In 2003 Bryant averaged 30 points for the first time and was close to winning the scoring title, but Orlando's Tracy McGrady prevailed. Winning scoring titles will be a constant challenge for Bryant because O'Neal is a career 57 percent shooter with the third highest ppg in league history.

Bryant's playoff scoring average has exceeded his regular season average. In 2003 he topped out at 33 points per game but his field goal percentage dipped to 43 percent compared to his career average of 46.

Wilt Chamberlain

Center, Philadelphia, 1959-60 through 1961-62; San Francisco, 1962-63 to 1964-65; Philadelphia, 1965-66 through 1967-68; LA Lakers, 1968-69 through 1972-73 Born: August 21, 1936 in Philadelphia 7-1, 275 Died: October 12, 1999 High School: Overbrook (Philadelphia) College: Kansas

If you want to consider numerical records, it seems that one player holds most of the keys to the kingdom.

Wilt Chamberlain holds the single-game records for most points, 100; rebounds, 55; field goals, 36. He holds the playoff record for most rebounds, 41 (April 5, 1957 vs. Boston); most points by a rookie, 53 (March 14, 1960 vs. Syracuse). His single-season records include most points, 4029 (1962); rebounds, 2,149 (1961); most games with 50 or more points, 45 (1962); minutes played, 3,882 (1962); highest points-per-game average, 50.4; most consecutive field goals made, 35 (February 17 through February 28, 1967). He holds the career record for most games with 50 or more points, 118; most rebounds, 23,924; most consecutive seasons leading the league in scoring, 7; highest rebounds per-game average, 22.9.

It just never ends.

Wilt Chamberlain had scored 78 points for the Philadelphia Warriors in a triple-overtime game on December 8, 1961.

His coach, Frank McGuire, didn't expect Wilt's NBA record to last long.

"He'll get 100 points some day," said McGuire. Less than three months later McGuire's prediction became true when Wilt scored 100 points against the Knicks at Hershey, Pennsylvania, where the Warriors played a few games each year. Just 4,124 people turned out for the game. Part of that audience was there to see a preliminary game between NFL teams, the Eagles and the Colts. New York's regular center, Phil Jordan,

was out with the flu, and 6-foot-11 Darrall Imhoff, who was known for his rugged defense, started in the middle. Chamberlain had 23 in the first quarter as Imhoff got into foul trouble. After one call Imhoff protested, "Why don't you just give him 100 points and we'll go home?"

Shooting mostly finger rolls, fadeaways, and dunks, Chamberlain had 41 points at half-time. He finished the third quarter with 69 points. Imhoff fouled out in the fourth quarter, leaving 6-foot-9 forward Cleveland Buckner and 6-foot-7 Willie Naulls to contend with Wilt. He broke his own mark of 78 with just under eight minutes remaining. Since the Warriors were far ahead, they decided to feed Wilt to get him the 100. The Knicks tried to stop it, holding the ball for the full 24 seconds on offense and fouling other Warriors before they could feed Chamberlain. So the Warriors started fouling the Knicks to get the ball back quicker. For more than two minutes Wilt didn't score. But then he rallied and stuffed in points 97 and 98 with 1:19 left. With 46 seconds remaining he took a pass and stuffed it again. He was mobbed by some 200 fans and players from both teams shook his hand. He had scored 31 in the fourth quarter and Warriors guard Guy Rodgers had gotten 20 assists. Besides shooting 36 for 73 from the field, Wilt shot 28 for 32 from the free throw line. The next night the two teams played again at Madison Square Garden and when Imhoff left the game he received a standing ovation, because he had held Wilt to a mere 54 points.

That 1961-62 campaign was the year that Chamberlain averaged 50.4 points per game. Much was made of Kobe Bryant's nine consecutive games with 40 or more points in 2003. Try this nine-game run by Chamberlain in the 1961-62 season: 78, 61, 55, 54, 52, 43, 50, 57, and 55. Eight of those games were above 50!

The real rivalry of the time was between Wilt and Bill Russell. While they often socialized and even shared Thanksgiving dinner together, Wilt and Russell were known for their fierce rivalry on the floor. The Celtics and Russell usually came out on top. In 1967 that changed, as the 76ers beat the Celtics in five games and went on to win the title by beating San Francisco four games to two. It was the first time in Wilt's career that he didn't win the scoring title, with the honor going to Rick Barry that season. But Chamberlain led the league in rebounds per game (24) and averaged 24 points and 8 assists.

Two years later Russell and Chamberlain met again in the Finals. In Game 7 Chamberlain took himself out after bruising his shin with five minutes left. When he asked Lakers coach Butch Van Breda Kolff to put him back in, Van Breda Kolff refused. The Celtics won by two points with Chamberlain on the bench.

Chamberlain won his second championship with the 1972 Lakers, a team that won a record 33 consecutive games. In the Finals they avenged their loss to the Knicks, who had beaten them to win the 1970 championship.

When he retired after the 1973 season, Chamberlain was the all-time leader in total points (31,419), points per game (30.1), rebounds (23,924), and rebounds per game (22.9). He had won 11 rebounding titles and seven scoring titles. He had also missed 5,805 free throws, nearly six per game.

He died October 12, 1999.

Tom Chambers

Forward, San Diego, 1981-82 through 1982-83; Seattle, 1983-84 through 1987-88; Phoenix, 1988-89 through 1992-93; Utah, 1993-94 through 1994-95; played in Israel 1995-96; Charlotte, 1996-97; Philadelphia, 1997-98
Born: June 21, 1959 in Ogden, Ut. 6-10, 230 High School: Fairview (Boulder, Colo.) College: Utah

There are many NBA players with impressive career distinctions who are nonetheless overlooked in an accounting of the game's history. One such player is Tom Chambers. Though he averaged 20-plus points five times and amassed 20,049 points in his career, Chambers, perhaps because none of the six teams he played for won titles, didn't get the notoriety of other players with similar numbers. He flourished during the years when Karl Malone was the most dominant forward in the Western Conference, so the best he could manage was being selected to the All-NBA second team in 1989 and 1990.

Drafted by the San Diego Clippers in the first round (eighth pick overall) in the 1981 draft, Chambers put up the kind of numbers that good players on poor teams often do. After averaging 17 points per game as a 33-minute player with the Clippers, Chambers was traded to Seattle where he enjoyed some of his best years as a pro. The lithe forward averaged between 18 and 23 points per game over the next five seasons, while playing in all 82 games three times. A leaper and scorer, Chambers was one of the most athletic power forwards of his time.

His coming-out party was the 1987 All-Star Game (his first of four all-star selections), when he scored 34 points before his hometown fans. Despite winning only 39 games, Seattle made it to the Conference Finals after beating Dallas and Houston. With Chambers, Xavier McDaniel and Dale Ellis, the team had three 20-point scorers. Alton Lister chipped in double-digit points and rebounds. But they were swept by the Lakers, who went on to beat the Celtics in the Finals. Chambers averaged 23 points in the playoffs and posted a 25.8 post-season average in 1988. Two months later the unrestricted free agent was signed by Phoenix, the second five-year stop in his career.

He posted a 26-point average his first year in Phoenix and the Suns won 55 games. Sweeping Denver and then Seattle, the Suns then were swept by the Lakers in the Conference Finals. The next year looked like a carbon copy, with Chambers averaging 27 points and the Suns getting through the first two rounds, only to be beaten by Portland in the Conference Finals.

By 1993 Chambers had a diminished role on a team whose big stars included Kevin Johnson and Charles Barkley. Their 62-20 record was the league's best and the Suns won 13 playoff games while losing 11. But 13 is still two wins short and Phoenix, which squandered its home court advantage by losing three games at home, lost to Chicago in six games.

Utah signed Chambers as an unrestricted free agent in 1993 and he played two years for the Jazz without distinction. He did, however, register his 20,000th point in 1995. He played in Israel for the 1995-96 season and made a comeback with the Charlotte Hornets during the 1996-97 season before being signed again by the Suns in the summer of 1997. He played his final game with Philadelphia during the 1997-98 season, his 16th in the NBA.

Maurice Cheeks

Guard, Philadelphia, 1978-79 through 1988-89; San Antonio, 1989-90; New York, 1990, 1990-91; Atlanta, 1991-92; New Jersey, 1992-93
Born: September 8, 1956 in Chicago 6-1, 180 High School: Du Sable (Chicago) College: West Texas State.

Maurice Cheeks was the textbook example of what a point guard should be. He had a career assists-to-turnover ratio of better than 3 to 1 and still ranks sixth among career leaders in assists with 7,393. The man called "Mo" was at his best on Philadelphia, where he played the first 11 years of his career. He was the prudent economical point guard for the 76ers squads that made it to three NBA Finals and an Eastern Conference Final between 1980 and 1983. Cheeks was assists leader on the 1983 champion 76ers. He is Philadelphia's career assists leader with 6,212 and all-time Philadelphia steals leader with 1,942.

Perhaps it was size that kept this solid performer from West Texas State from being drafted higher. He was selected in the second round (36th pick overall) in the 1978 draft. From the start Cheeks' game was balanced, not impulsive. Despite playing on teams that included all-time greats like Julius Erving and Moses Malone and a great streak shooter in Andrew Toney, Cheeks was the team leader, always in charge of distributing the ball. There was very little that was rash about his game. As a bonus, Cheeks was an exceptional shooter and defender. Over the first nine years of his career, Cheeks hit better than 50 percent of his shots from the floor. For his career he shot .523, an exceptional mark at any position and extraordinary for a guard. For four consecutive years, 1983 through 1986, Cheeks was selected NBA All-Defensive first team, and the following year he was selected second team.

The four-time all-star was the assists leader on a team that went to the NBA Finals three times in four years. With Cheeks quarterbacking in 1983, the Sixers, who now had Malone to fill a long-running vacancy in the middle, sailed through the playoffs with a 12-1 record, including a sweep of the defending champion Lakers in the Finals. Clutch player that he was, Cheeks raised his scoring to 16 points per game in the post-season that year.

He was traded to San Antonio in 1989, then to New York in 1990. He shot 10-for-10 in Game 5 to help eliminate Boston in the first round and get the Knicks to the semi-finals of the Eastern Conference. From there it was on to Atlanta and New Jersey, where he ended his 15-year career in 1993.

Bob Cousy

Guard, Boston, 1950-51 through 1962-63; Cincinnati, 1969-70
Born: August 9, 1928 in New York 6-1, 175 High School: Andrew Jackson (Queens, N.Y.) College: Holy Cross

Right from the start, Bob Cousy brought splash and panache to the league. Cousy may not be the greatest ever at creating, maybe not even the first. But Cousy's razzle-dazzle was more consistent than anyone else's. The behind-the-back-dribble, the misdirection passes, the mid-air deception with the ball going behind the back from right hand to left and then into

the basket, the blind pass over the shoulder, the running out of the clock with several defenders pursuing him—these elements comprised the lasting legacy of Cousy.

The press got caught up in his maneuvers and labeled him "The Magician" and "The Houdini of the Hardwood." But Cousy was lectured by coach Red Auerbach that a good pass was a completed pass, not a fancy one that bounced off a teammate's head or shoulders.

Despite the occasional misfires, Cousy was the NBA's assists leader from 1953 through 1960. Starting with his second season, he averaged between 18 and 21 points for 10 years in a row. Beginning in 1952, his second season, he was All-NBA first team 10 years in a row, tied with Jerry West and Michael Jordan for most by a guard in NBA history. As great players are now often labeled "the next Jordan," Cousy's stature was similar in his time. When a new player came along showing some razzle-dazzle with the ball, the players and press would say, "He thinks he's another Cousy."

Cousy was the only child of immigrant parents who came to the United States several months before Bob was born on August 9, 1928. His mother was born in the United States, brought up in France, and could not speak English. His father was from Alsace-Lorraine. The family spoke only French at home and it was the only language Cousy knew when he began attending grade school. Cousy would carry a speech defect—it showed in his rolling Rs and his trouble with Ls—into his adult years.

The Cousy family moved to St. Albans in Long Island when Bob was 11 years old. In his freshman year at Andrew Jackson High, when he was 14 years old and 5-foot-8, he was cut from the junior varsity. Three years later he was the most celebrated player in New York City and one of the most sought after players in the country. He scored 28 points in his first game for Andrew Jackson and in his senior year won the New York City High School scoring championship, was named to the all-scholastic team, and boosted Jackson to the Queens Division championship.

Cousy had his choice of colleges. He had promised his grandmother he'd attend a Catholic college and ended up narrowing his selection to Boston College and Holy Cross. He went with Holy Cross since Boston College had no dormitory. He was a part-timer his freshman year when Holy Cross won the 1947 NCAA championship. He didn't have a strong season until his senior year, when he was All-American.

He almost missed playing in Boston. Since Cousy was a favorite in the Boston area, he expected to be a territorial draft choice of the Celtics. The Holy Cross star was a local favorite, but not to Boston coach Red Auerbach. "Am I supposed to worry about the local yokels or win?" Auerbach asked Walter Brown, Boston's owner. "Just win," Brown replied. Boston desperately needed a big man and Auerbach drafted 6-11 Charlie Share from Bowling Green.

Cousy was picked up by the Tri-Cities Black Hawks. Before playing a single game, he was traded to the Chicago Stags, a team whose franchise soon went bankrupt. When the Stags folded, their players were dispersed. The three most sought after Stags included scorer Max Zaslofsky, playmaker Andy Phillip, and Cousy. Boston, New York and Philadelphia were the three

clubs to pick from a hat and all of them wanted 1948 scoring champion Zaslofsky. The Knicks got Zaslofsky, Philadelphia picked Phillip, and Boston owner Walter Brown groused that he was "stuck" with Bob Cousy.

When he arrived for the 1950-51 season, Cousy was given little chance of success by the "experts." They claimed that the 6-foot-1, 175-pounder was too small and too given to razzle-dazzle and would give away more points with turnovers and porous defense.

Boston made the playoffs and posted winning records in each of Cousy's first six seasons, from 1951 through 1956. Cousy topped the league in assists in four of those years. In addition, he worked to instill pride in the league's players about competing in the NBA.

College ball had a greater share of the public attention than NBA ball, but to Cousy the NBA was "the big league." He demanded that the league pay top dollar to bring in the best referees. He wanted teams to stay in first-class hotels, so the players wouldn't look like bushers. He wanted small town teams to be replaced by teams in larger cities. He rapidly became the best ambassador and symbol of the fledgling league. To the press he was the easiest and best interview. His time was sought for endorsements and personal appearances like no other player's.

Known more as a playmaker, Cousy would finish no lower than third in league scoring between 1953 and 1955. In 1953 his 19.8 points were behind only Philadelphia's Neil Johnston and Minneapolis' George Mikan.

By now, Auerbach was saying, "We got stuck with the greatest player in the league when we drew his name out of a hat." Boston, however, was still losing close games due to its smallish frontcourt.

They needed a player who could get the ball off the boards and wreak havoc on defense.

The drafting of Bill Russell would change all of that.

Now the frontcourt was Heinsohn, Loscutoff, and Russell, and the two leading scorers were Sharman and Cousy, who also won league MVP honors in 1957. It began a run of success in which the Celtics would win 11 NBA titles in 13 seasons.

With Cousy, who retired in 1963, they notched six in seven years.

He still holds several records, such as his 19 assists in one half against Minneapolis in 1959. In 1953 he set a playoff record of free throws attempted—32 (since topped by Shaquille O'Neal with 39) and made—30—against Syracuse. For 10 consecutive years, from 1952 through 1961, he was selected All-NBA first team. He was named to the All-Star team in each of his 13 years and was MVP of the game in 1954 and 1957.

Following his retirement in 1963, Cousy coached Boston College for six seasons (117-38, .755), taking its team as far as the NIT Finals in 1969, when BC lost to Temple, 89-76. Then it was five years with the Cincinnati Royals and Kansas City-Omaha Kings from 1970 (when he played seven games) to 1974. Today he is a broadcaster for the Celtics.

Cousy is still the Celtics all-time assists leader with 6945. He was selected for the NBA's 25th Anniversary (1970), 35th Anniversary (1980), and 50th Anniversary All-Time Team (1996).

Dave Cowens

Center, Boston, 1970-71 through 1979-80; retired 1980-81 through 1981-82; Milwaukee, 1982-83
Born: October 25, 1948 in Newport, Ky. 6-9, 230 High School: Newport (Ky.) Central Catholic College: Florida State

Dave Cowens had the thankless job of being the Celtics' first full-time center to follow Bill Russell, who retired after the 1969 season. In his first NBA season Cowens' play was wildly enthusiastic, with frequent emphasis on the wild part. Sharing Rookie of the Year honors with Portland's Geoff Petrie, Cowens was better known for more dubious distinctions over the 1970-71 season, such as leading the league with 350 personal fouls and getting himself disqualified from 15 games. Cowens never shied away from contact.

With Cowens—a running, hustling, nonstop 6-foot-9 "small" center with a mop of red hair who outraced most of his opponents up court—the Celtics had a center who played the rebounding *and* running part of the fast break, filling the lanes with Jo Jo White and John Havlicek.

Cowens did not play high school ball until his junior season, preferring baseball and swimming (mostly the 100-yard backstroke and 200-yard freestyle). In the summer between his sophomore and junior years he grew five inches, and a new coach persuaded him to give basketball a try. By his senior season he led Newport Central Catholic High (in Newport, Kentucky) to the state championship tournament and earned a scholarship to Florida State. He averaged 19 points and 17 rebounds there, but he drew little national publicity since the school was on NCAA probation and prohibited from playing in tournaments.

Boston got the fourth draft pick in the 1970 sweepstakes, their highest pick in 24 years, and selected Cowens. Auerbach's first idea was to use Cowens at forward or as an interim center until a permanent replacement for Russell could be found. After all, Cowens was equally comfortable playing with his back to the basket or facing the basket. But after witnessing Cowens' strength and jumping ability, Auerbach and coach Tommy Heinsohn changed their minds.

After his randy rookie season, in which Boston improved from 34 wins in 1970 to 44 wins, Cowens helped the Celts to 56 wins and the Atlantic Division title in his second year. He averaged 19 points and scored 14 points and grabbed 20 rebounds in the All-Star Game. He enjoyed some stellar games—32 points and 21 rebounds against Baltimore, 26 points and 20 rebounds to eliminate Atlanta from the playoffs. But New York eliminated the Celtics in five games. Cowens didn't play well, except for the lone Boston win when he got 23 points and 16 rebounds. Jerry Lucas rained shots from 20-25 feet out and Cowens didn't want to leave the post to play him.

But 1973 would be his best year. Cowens raised his points (20.5) and rebounds (16.2) for the third straight season. While Cowens couldn't always match Abdul-Jabbar or Chamberlain in the pivot, they were no match for him when he ran them around on the perimeter. Some of Cowens' great battles came against the league's two other great "small" centers, Wes Unseld and Willis Reed. Boston won 68 games and Cowens was named league MVP, as well as MVP of the All-Star Game with 15 points and 13 rebounds.

The Celtics finished 11 games ahead of the Knicks in the Atlantic Division. Boston, always a hockey town first, had its best attendance ever. The Celtics were having a dream season until Havlicek, the team's leading scorer, separated his shoulder in the playoffs and the Knicks beat them in the Conference Finals.

The following year belonged to Boston. The Celtics topped New York in the Conference Finals and faced Milwaukee in the Finals. In Game 7, in a series notable for both teams losing all their home games, Boston had to win on the road. Cowens had shot 6-for-15 in Game 6, while Abdul-Jabbar hit a 15-foot baseline hook with seconds remaining to give the Bucks a 1-point victory in double-overtime. Cowens, who according to Bob Ryan made redemption for bad games "a biblical thing," posted 28 points and 14 rebounds as Boston won Game 7, 102-87.

Boston won its fourth consecutive Atlantic Division title—and reached its fourth consecutive Conference Finals—in 1975. In 1976, Cowens battled Bob McAdoo in the semifinals, the second time the two met in the post-season. Buffalo's lithe thoroughbred McAdoo ran Cowens ragged on the perimeter, while Cowens pounded McAdoo inside. After dispatching the Braves, Boston, led by series MVP Jo Jo White, bested Phoenix in a memorable six-game Final. Game 5, a triple overtime Celtics victory at the Garden, is regarded by some as the greatest game ever played. Now Red Auerbach had a ready reply for the skeptics who said, "Just let's see you win one without Russell." The Celtics and the Knicks were the only teams to win two titles in the 1970s.

Traded for Quinn Buckner in September 1982, Cowens played his last year for Milwaukee in 1983, having come back from a two-year retirement to play his 11th season. The seven-time all-star had coached Boston during the 1978-79 season, taking over for Satch Sanders after 14 games. Cowens was elected to the Hall of Fame in 1990.

From 1994 through 1996 Cowens was an assistant coach with the San Antonio Spurs, and then took over the head coaching reigns for Charlotte beginning in the 1996-97 season. He guided the Hornets to the playoffs in 1997 and 1998, before resigning on March 7, 1999 and being replaced by another great Celtic, Paul Silas.

Aside from being voted to the NBA 50th Anniversary All-Time Team in 1996, Cowens holds other impressive distinctions. Rugged defense got him picked for the NBA All-Defensive first team in 1976, and he still shares a single-game playoff mark with 20 defensive rebounds, which he accomplished twice, in 1975 and 1977.

Terry Cummings

Forward, San Diego, 1982-83 through 1983-84; Milwaukee, 1984-85 through 1988-89; San Antonio, 1989-90 through 1994-95; Milwaukee, 1995-96; Seattle, 1996-97; Philadelphia, 1997-98; New York, 1998; Golden State, 1998-99 through 1999-2000.
Born: March 15, 1961 in Chicago 6-9, 250 High School: Carver (Chicago) College: DePaul

Terry Cummings came into the NBA in the manner he left De Paul—as a high-scoring and rebounding forward. The San Diego Clippers selected him second overall in the 1982 draft.

He thanked them by winning Rookie of the Year honors, averaging 24 points and 11 rebounds. He went on to average 20 points in seven of his first eight seasons. Rarely missing games, shooting around 50 percent, he was one of the more steady power forwards of the 1980s.

Just before his third season, he was involved in a blockbuster trade. Cummings, Craig Hodges, and Ricky Pierce were sent to Milwaukee for Marques Johnson, Harvey Catchings, Junior Bridgeman, and cash. Milwaukee won the Central Division title with a 59-23 season. Cummings was a force in the playoffs, averaging 28 points and 9 rebounds, but the season ended abruptly, with the Bucks being swept by Philadelphia in the Conference semi-finals. The next season the Bucks won 57, riding Cummings, Sidney Moncrief, Paul Pressey, and Ricky Pierce to the Conference Finals. But the Central Division champs were swept again, this time by Boston. Over the next three years the team exited in the first and second rounds and Cummings was dealt to San Antonio following the 1989 season.

Cummings left a good team hitting its declining years for a better one. The combination of Cummings and David Robinson produced 56 wins in 1990, 55 in 1991, and 47 in 1992. The post-season formula never worked, however, even when they won 55 games (with Cummings now a part-time performer) in 1994, and a league-best 62 in 1995. San Antonio lost to Houston in the Western Conference Finals in six games, as Hakeem Olajuwon emphatically outplayed David Robinson.

Over the last three seasons Cummings continued his part-time role with Milwaukee, Seattle, Philadelphia, New York, and Golden State. By the end of his career a pattern was set: when a good team sought scoring and rebounding help at the power forward position for a stretch run, Cummings got a call. The 18-year veteran and two-time all-star, who overcame playing with a heart murmur since the beginning of his career, posted more than 19,000 points and 8,000 rebounds.

Billy Cunningham

Forward, Philadelphia, 1965-66 through 1975-76
Born: June 3, 1942 in Brooklyn, N.Y. 6-7, 210 High School: Erasmus Hall (Brooklyn, N.Y.) College: North Carolina

"Billy C" the coach is more memorable than Billy Cunningham the player to early '80s basketball fans who watched him stalk the sidelines during the best years of the Philadelphia 76ers. The association is a good one, since he posted a 454-196 (.698) lifetime record from 1977 through 1985, for a .698 percentage. In the playoffs he coached his charges to a 66-39 (.629) record. But Cunningham was also a shooter, leaper, and driver who had so many moves that 76ers teammate Wali Jones said that Cunningham and Jerry West "were the only two whites who play like brothers."

Cunningham admitted as much, explaining that playing in Brooklyn schoolyards had helped develop the "black" style that Jones later referred to. "There's a hoop every two blocks in Brooklyn and there's always somebody there—and there's nothing else much," he recalled. He could drive, come up against a blocker, bring the ball down, pump, and put it back up again.

Cunningham would later become known as the "Kangaroo Kid." Said Bob Ryan, "He was a phenomenal driver and slasher; a quintessential Brooklyn player who you picture playing on a court with the rim bent, net missing, and wind blowing, so it made no sense shooting from the outside anyway. So you take it to the hoop." The first emperor of flight, Elgin Baylor, once said "All of us [leapers] were black except Cunningham, and you'd better check on him." He used his flight time effectively when driving to the hoop and was able to raise his scoring average each of his first five seasons in the NBA.

After stardom at Erasmus High in Brooklyn, Cunningham's college career at North Carolina began in 1961, Dean Smith's first year. He averaged 25 points and 15 rebounds for the Tarheels, and was an All-American as a senior. He participated in the 1964 Olympic trials but failed to make the team.

Cunningham was selected by Philadelphia seventh overall in the 1965 draft and received a signing bonus of $15,000. In just his second season he was a key player off the bench, scoring 19 points a game in limited playing time and helping the 76ers and their vaunted front line of Chet Walker, Luke Jackson, and Wilt Chamberlain to a 68-13 record. In the clinching Game 6, Cunningham had 13 fourth-quarter points off the bench to topple Rick Barry and the Golden State Warriors.

After 1967, Philadelphia never got out of the first round of playoffs over the remainder of Cunningham's career. In his 11 pro seasons—nine in the NBA and two in the ABA after being signed as a free agent by the Carolina Cougars—he was a six-time all-star. A balanced line of 24 points, 12 rebounds, and 6 assists helped him carry off MVP honors with Carolina in 1973 before returning to Philadelphia in 1974. A horrific knee injury forced him to retire 20 games into the 1975-76 season.

Despite his gaudy record as an eight-year NBA coach, Cunningham, like his predecessor Gene Shue, found out how difficult the job was. His first season was with the 1977-78 76ers, a team that achieved legendary status for selfish play. World (who had changed his name from Lloyd) B. Free, George McGinnis, Doug Collins, and several others constantly harped about too little playing time and too few shots attempted. Some cursed at Cunningham when he substituted for them. Already given to fits of temper, Cunningham was typically near the top of the coaching ranks in technical fouls.

After leading Philadelphia to NBA Finals in 1980 and 1982 and a Conference Final in 1981, Cunningham got his in 1983 after the 76ers picked up Moses Malone to fill a scoring and rebounding void in the pivot. He left coaching in 1985, the same year that he was elected to the Hall of Fame. He reemerged as part owner of the Miami Heat from 1987 through 1995. In 1996 he was named to the NBA's 50th Anniversary All-Time Team.

Bob Dandridge

Forward, Milwaukee, 1969-70 through 1976-77; Washington, 1977-78 through 1980-81; Milwaukee, 1981-82 Born: November 15, 1947 in Richmond, Va. 6-6, 195 High School: Maggie Walker (Richmond, Va.) College: Norfolk State

Bob Dandridge was a steady front court player for two teams winning their first NBA championships. A scorer with a smooth outside touch, Dandridge averaged 18 points and 8 rebounds when the Bucks won the title in 1971. In his first year with the Washington Bullets in 1978, he contributed 19 points

a game to aid the front line of Wes Unseld and Elvin Hayes as Washington got by Seattle in seven games.

Dandridge had averaged 32.3 points a game in his senior year at Norfolk State, so it was a surprise that he was drafted by Milwaukee as late as the fourth round in 1969.

Besides his scoring, Dandridge was a clutch player, improving his playoff average to 20 points a game. The small forward credited Oscar Robertson, who joined the team in Dandridge's second season, with improving his running game. He said he had never received passes like the ones he got from Robertson. As Jabbar said, "Bobby was deadly from 15 to 20 feet and Oscar could spot him the moment he came open."

With Robertson, Alcindor, John McGlocklin and Greg Smith, Dandridge helped Milwaukee to a league-best 66-16 record. In the playoffs they went 12-2, sweeping the Bullets in the Finals.

A four-time all-star, Dandridge gave Washington a perimeter touch to go with the inside presence that Unseld and Hayes provided. The 1978 team finished an unimpressive 44-38 but came back from a 3-2 deficit in games to win the Finals. They surrendered the title to Seattle in five games in 1979.

Dandridge played just 79 games over his last three seasons and retired in 1982, playing his last season back at Milwaukee. He finished with 15,530 points and a lifetime average of 18.5 per game.

Mel Daniels

Center, Minnesota (ABA), 1967-68; Indiana (ABA), 1968-69 through 1973-74; Memphis (ABA), 1974-75; New York Nets, 1976-77
Born: July 20, 1944 in Detroit 6-9, 225 High School: Pershing (Detroit) Junior College: Burlington (Ia.) Junior College; New Mexico

While his name is not mentioned in the roll call of great centers, Mel Daniels had an astounding ABA career. It was full of awards: a Rookie of the Year, two league MVPs, three championships, three rebounding titles, four All-ABA first team selections, and an All-Star Game MVP.

Selected by the Minnesota Muskies in the first round of the 1967 draft, Daniels got busy with a league-leading 16 rebounds and 22 points per game. After the season, Daniels was traded to the Indiana Pacers for a first-round pick, two other players, and cash. He upped his totals with Indiana, winning the rebounding title again in 1969 and the league MVP. In one game against the Nets he had 37 points and 26 rebounds in the second half, finishing with 56 points and 31 rebounds. In the game he set ABA records for most field goals in a quarter (10), half (16), and game (25).

The following season Indiana won its first championship. The Pacers were a league-best 59-25 and had the most solid frontcourt in the league, with Roger Brown and Bob Netolicky each averaging over 20 points per game. With his smooth jumper Daniels chipped in 19 points and 18 rebounds, finishing second in boarding to Denver's Spencer Haywood. Brown averaged an incredible 46 points over the last three games of the Finals, as the Pacers bested the Los Angeles Stars in six games. In 1971 Daniels grabbed his third rebounding title and his second MVP, but Indiana lost to Utah in seven in the Western

Division Finals. Indiana finished just 47-37 in 1972, way behind league-best Kentucky at 68-16. In the playoffs Indian caught fire, however, rolling past Denver and Utah in seven, before besting New York and star Rick Barry in six. Daniels finished second in rebounding to Artis Gilmore and now had three rebounding titles and two runner-ups in five years.

After the 1974 season Daniels and Freddie Lewis were traded to the Memphis Sounds. There, Daniels' numbers and minutes continued the decline started during the 1974 season in Indiana. The seven-time all-star—who still holds Indiana's team record for rebounds in a season, set in 1970-71 with 1475—fell to single digits in points and rebounds for the first time in his eight-year career. The Memphis franchise was transferred to Baltimore for the 1975-76 campaign. But the Baltimore Claws never played a game, folding prior to the season. So Daniels was without a team for a full year. He was signed by the New York Nets in October 1976 but waived less than two months later. His NBA career lasted 11 games.

Daniels was an assistant coach at Indiana State, beginning in Larry Bird's last college season, when the team was 33-1, and continuing through the 1982 season. Thereafter he was a Pacers assistant coach from 1984 through 1989. In November 1989 he had one of the briefest interim head-coaching stints ever, taking over the 0-7 Pacers from Jack Ramsey, losing two games, and then being replaced four days later by George Irvine. He was USBL Coach of the Year in 1993. He is currently a director of player personnel and assistant coach for the Pacers.

Adrian Dantley

Forward, Buffalo, 1976-77; Indiana, 1977; LA Lakers 1977, 1978-79; Utah, 1979-80 through 1985-86; Detroit, 1986-87 to 1988-89; Dalls, 1989, 1989-90; Milwaukee, 1990-91
Born: February 28, 1956 in Washington, D.C. 6-5, 210 High School: De Matha Catholic (Hyattsville, Md.) College: Notre Dame

Adrian Dantley, scoring machine and two-time All-American at Notre Dame, played with four different teams in his first four years of the NBA. At various times in his first eight pro seasons Dantley would lead the NBA in minutes, field goals, free throws (five times), points (twice), and scoring (twice). In 1984 Dantley, who had powerful low-post moves despite his size, would become only the third player in the history of the league (other than Chamberlain and Robertson) to score 30-plus points per game in *four straight* seasons. Since then, Michael Jordan did it in seven consecutive years, from 1987 through 1993.

In his 15-year career, Dantley also had the dubious distinction of scoring 20 points per game with four different teams. The 6-foot-5 small forward belied his position. With more low post moves and feints than any forward of his time excepting Kevin McHale, Dantley nonetheless earned frequent flyer miles in seven different cities. Before achieving NBA stardom, Dantley played in the 1976 Montreal Olympics. His 19.3 average is the all-time record for any American competing in the Olympics.

He was selected by the Buffalo Braves after his junior season at Notre Dame and immediately made an impact, averaging 20 points and winning the Rookie of the Year Award in 1977. The

Braves traded him and forward Mike Bantom for Billy Knight before the 1977-78 season. He played with the Pacers a couple of months before being traded to Los Angeles with Dave Robisch for James Edwards and Earl Tatum. He played in Los Angeles for a year and a half before being traded—a month before Magic Johnson's arrival—to the Utah Jazz in exchange for Spencer Haywood.

Dantley's seven-year body of work in Utah was a marvel to behold. Before Karl Malone became Utah's iron man, Dantley put up consecutive scoring averages of 28, 31, 30, 31, 31, 27 and 30. In 1984 he tied Wilt Chamberlain's record for 28 free throws in a game; in the playoffs that year, he posted an all-world 32 points a game. His field-goal percentages were 56 percent or higher in six of those years, "falling" to 53 percent in 1985. After missing 60 games to injury in 1983, he earned NBA Comeback Player of the Year the following season when he led the league in scoring. He and George Gervin battled for scoring honors, with Dantley leading the league in scoring twice and finishing third on three other occasions. He was traded to Detroit before the 1986-87 season.

Several weeks before his 33rd birthday, Dantley was averaging 19 points a game, but was shipped to Dallas, with a first draft choice, for forward Mark Aguirre. Four months later the Pistons were capturing their first of two consecutive Championships without Dantley. Dantley blamed Isiah Thomas for going to management and engineering the trade. He played well with Dallas in a limited role the following year and was signed as a free agent by Milwaukee for one last season. Following his NBA career he played for Breeze Milan in Italy, showing that he could still light it up by shooting nearly 60 percent and averaging 27 points per game.

Despite 23,000 points and 54-percent accuracy from the floor, being one of the best ever at his position and having a deserved reputation as a scoring machine, Dantley was overlooked when the NBA 50th Anniversary All-Time Team was announced in 1996.

Walter Davis

Guard, Phoenix, 1977-78 through 1987-88; Denver, 1988-89 to 1990-91; Portland, 1991; Denver, 1991-92
Born: September 9, 1954 in Pineville, N.C. 6-6, 200 High School: South Mecklenburg Charlotte, N.C. College: North Carolina

In 1977, Walter Davis' rookie year, he and Paul Westphal were known as the "Guns of the Suns." Together they were the top one-two punch in the league, averaging 49.4 points a game. In one game against the Celtics they scored 83 points. Davis was the only rookie selected for the All-Star Game. Posting marks of 24 points and 6 rebounds per game, Davis walked off with Rookie of the Year honors. He would soon be known as "The Greyhound" for his speed on the court. Though his career ended in 1992, he is still the Suns' all-time leading scorer.

Davis grew up in Pineville, N.C., the youngest of 13 children. Three of his older brothers taught him how to play. While walking barefoot between his freshman and sophomore years, he stepped in a hole full of broken glass and severed his Achilles tendon. A doctor said there was a chance he might not play again, but he spent the entire summer in a cast and was soon

well enough to compete. Playing for South Mecklenburg High, Davis was the star on a team that won the state championship three years in a row.

Davis wanted to go to North Carolina, just as his idol Charlie Scott had. In four years at Chapel Hill, the Tar Heels won 98 games and lost 23, wining two ACC tournaments, two regular-season ACC championships, and finishing as runner-up to Marquette for the national championship when Davis was a senior. Davis played the game with a broken finger on his shooting hand. He also played on the gold medal-winning 1976 U.S. Olympic team in Montreal.

After interviewing Davis, Suns officials were as impressed with his character as they were with his ability. With a smooth stroke from the outside, he finished fifth in the league in scoring that year and shot over 50 percent from the field. Phoenix won 49 games, up 15 wins from the year before. It was first of four consecutive all-star seasons for the Greyhound.

Davis was far less flamboyant on offense than Julius Erving, David Thompson, and other great scorers of his time, but he always got his points and shot .511 for his career. In his rookie season he was matched against Erving twice and outscored him both times, 35-19 and 29-12. In a special poll of the players conducted by *The New York Times*, Davis was second only to Maurice Lucas in the voting for top Western Division forward, outpolling Rick Barry and Bobby Jones.

After 11 seasons with Phoenix, during six of which he averaged between 20 and 24 points per game, the Greyhound headed to Denver. In January 1991 he was traded to Portland. Waived in the off-season, Davis was signed by Denver and finished out his career with the Nuggets. The six-time all-star finished with a lifetime 18.9 points-per-game average and 19,521 points, 30th place on the all-time scoring list of NBA and ABA players.

Dave DeBusschere

Forward, Detroit, 1962-63 to 1968; New York Knicks, 1968-69 through 1973-74
Born: October 16, 1940 in Detroit 6-6, 235 Died: May 14, 2003 High School: Austin Catholic (Detroit) College Detroit

On the New York Knicks championship teams of 1970 and 1973, Dave DeBusschere was less renowned than the other team leaders, Willis Reed and Walt Frazier. On May 8, 1970, the Knicks fought for the title in Game 7 against the Lakers, with Wilt Chamberlain, Jerry West and Elgin Baylor. The story for the Knicks that night was whether Reed would play and, later, Frazier's miraculous line against West: 36 points, 19 assists, and 7 rebounds. DeBusschere's 17 points and 18 rebounds were, for him, merely routine and drew no mention.

Never unnoticed was what he contributed to the Knicks' identity. Like the Knicks as a whole, DeBusschere was rugged, smart, a defender first and foremost, and team-oriented. DeBusschere was the cornerstone of a dogged, helping defense that was first in the league in *points against* in 1970, 1971, and 1973. The sound that originated in the $5 seats and came rolling down to the court at Madison Square Garden was "dee-fense, dee-fense." That sound was for DeBusschere as much as any player on the Knicks. The DeBusschere defense was con-

spicuous the night of May 8, 1970, as the Knicks held the Lakers—with, to that point, the three greatest playoff scorers in history—to 42 points in the first half. New York led 69-42 at the intermission and ran off to an easy 113-99 victory.

He was the star of Austin High, a 23-0 state championship team. After an undersold Detroit College career in which he averaged 25 points and 19 rebounds, DeBusschere was Detroit's territorial pick in the first round and the Pistons signed him for $15,000. Baseball's Chicago White Sox also signed him for a $70,000 bonus. He played with both teams for two years and then gave up baseball to become player-coach of the Pistons. As a pitcher, he pitched in 36 games in 1962 and 1963, finishing with a record of 3-4 before being placed on the restricted list for more than three years. The Pale Hose released him on December 23, 1968. In three years of coaching the Pistons his mark was 69-143. He was three times an all-star in his six years with Detroit and, at 24, the youngest player-coach in the history of the league.

That December date was four days after the Knicks acquired DeBusschere in a trade for center Walt Bellamy and guard Howard Komives. In the history of the Knicks, the acquisition of DeBusschere will always be referred to as "the trade." With DeBusschere now anchoring the power forward spot, Bill Bradley could move from guard, where he was too slow, to small forward. With Bellamy gone, Reed didn't have to split minutes in the pivot. Frazier now owned the backcourt.

Like clockwork, DeBusschere put up 15 points and 11 rebounds per game in his six years in New York. During that stretch, the Knicks played in three NBA Finals and three Conference Finals. His assignment was guarding the best forwards in the league—Rick Barry, Elgin Baylor, Elvin Hayes, Bob Love, Chet Walker, Gus Johnson, Billy Cunningham, and Connie Hawkins. Like the other New York starters, he had a solid perimeter game. They took their second championship in 1973, taking the Lakers in five games.

DeBusschere, a seven-time all-star, retired after the 1974 season. He was the general manager of the Knicks from May 1982 through January 1986. He was elected to the Hall of Fame in 1983. In 1996, DeBusschere was one of five Knicks from the 1970 and 1973 championship teams to be selected to the NBA 50th Anniversary All-Time Team. He became commissioner of the ABA in 1975 and was a key player in 1976's merger with the NBA. He died suddenly in May 2003.

Clyde Drexler

Guard, Portland, 1983-84 to 1995; Houston, 1995, 1995-96 through 1997-98
Born: June 22, 1962 in New Orleans 6-7, 222 High School: Sterling (Houston) College: Houston

Clyde Drexler retired after 15 years, 1,086 games and 22,195 points, good enough for 20th place on the all-time scoring list of ABA and NBA players. He was one of the great open-court players in NBA history, soaring to the basket. "Clyde the Glide" finally played on a title team when he joined Hakeem Olajuwon and the Houston Rockets in his 12th NBA season. Twice prior, in the 1990 Finals vs. Detroit and the 1992 Finals against Chicago, his teams came up short. When he finished up in spring 1998, Drexler was the fifth highest scoring guard in NBA

history. His career line is 20 points, 6 rebounds and 5 assists.

Known for his spectacular dunks—including one triple-pump job that a *Sports Illustrated* writer said was "the greatest of the century"—Drexler was straight from the Houston fraternity known as "Phi Slamma Jamma." He played on the team with Hakeem Olajuwon that surprised many observers by losing to North Carolina State in the NCAA Finals in 1983. He left after his junior year.

Drexler was picked 14th overall in the 1983 draft. Right out of the gate he was at odds with first NBA coach, Jack Ramsay. Drexler thought that Houston Cougars' coach Guy Lewis' physical practices and running style had prepared him well for the NBA. But Ramsay pointed out the flaws in his game—defense, judgment, and outside shooting. The Houston program had given Drexler freedom on and off the court. Said Drexler of Ramsay, "Sometimes it seems like he's holding me back." He pushed for more playing time, while Ramsay wanted him to reduce his assist-to-turnover ration from 2-1 to 4-1.

Drexler increased his scoring average in each of his first six seasons and played in the 1986 All-Star Game, Ramsay's last year as coach. In 1989 Drexler scored a personal best 27.2 points per game. While one teammate said, "Clyde is Michael Jordan without the publicity," another said, "Clyde is Michael Jordan without the training in the fundamentals."

At several notable times in his career he played like the second best guard on the floor. The first was in the 1990 Finals, when Isiah Thomas led a disciplined, physical bad-boy Detroit team past Portland, four games to one. In the 1991 Conference Finals Portland lost to the Lakers. In the 1992 Finals, Drexler came up against Michael Jordan and the Bulls, who won in six games. Before the series there was talk of Drexler being "the NBA's second greatest player" and close to Jordan for the No. 1 spot. This prediction proved empty, however: Jordan averaged 36 points on 53-percent shooting to Drexler's 25 points on 41-percent shooting. That summer Drexler played in the Barcelona Olympics on the "Dream Team."

In 1997, in the Western Conference Finals, Utah's John Stockton took control of the last minutes of Game 6, hitting a 3-pointer to send the Jazz past Houston to the Finals. In the first round of the 1998 playoffs, Houston was playing on its home court with a 2-to-1 lead at home against Utah. But the Rockets lost by margins of 22 and 14 points in Games 4 and 5. Hakeem Olajuwon played a strong series, but Drexler had a swan song to forget, hitting just 31 percent of his shots.

In between, Drexler did finally get his title. Many argue that if the Houston Rockets hadn't made the Otis Thorpe-for-Drexler deal in February 1995, they would not have won their second consecutive title. Drexler gave Houston a fast-break guard who also provided rebounding to replace Thorpe. He also brought a passion born of frustration from two previous Finals. Houston would face five elimination games in the 1995 post-season. But Drexler, then 32, in his 12th season, played with youthful vigor, averaging 22 points, 10 rebounds, and 7 assists in a sweep of Orlando.

Drexler was one of the best ever at soaring to the basket and finishing the fast break. He was a 10-time All Star, although he made the All-NBA first team only once. He was voted to the NBA's 50th Anniversary All-Time Team in 1996.

After retiring in 1998, Drexler coached his alma mater, Houston, to a 19-39 record over two seasons, and then moved to a job as an assistant coach with the Denver Nuggets.

Joe Dumars

Guard, Detroit, 1985-86 through 1998-99
Born: May 24, 1963 in Shreveport, La. 6-3, 195 High School: Natchitoches Central, La. College: McNeese State

Joe Dumars was at his all-around best when Detroit played its best. The 6-foot-3 guard drew the unenviable task of guarding Michael Jordan in several head-to-head Chicago-Detroit series of the late 1980s and early '90s. Dumars even named his first son "Jordan." While Jordan couldn't be shut down, Dumars was the linchpin of "The Jordan Rules," a defensive plan scripted by coach Chuck Daly to bounce Michael around most every time he touched the ball. Detroit's grinding defense forced Jordan's teammates to carry more of the scoring load. For three years they couldn't, and in two of those years, 1989 (when Dumars won the Finals MVP) and 1990, Detroit won the NBA title.

Joe Dumars was the 18th pick in the 1985 draft. Detroit's star was on the rise and in 1986 the Pistons made the playoffs for the first of seven straight seasons. Dumars assumed a more important role, increasing his scoring average for his first six years in the league. In the two title seasons, he averaged 17 points, 5 assists, and made the NBA All-Defensive first team. Detroit overcame its chief rival Chicago in post-season play in 1988 (five games), 1989 (six), and 1990 (seven). As the Bulls extended the series with each passing year, so too Detroit bolstered its defensive prowess with players like Dennis Rodman, Rick Mahorn, and John Salley to go with mainstays Isiah Thomas, Bill Laimbeer, and Dumars. Those Pistons teams were among the greatest defensive units ever, finishing third in the NBA in points against in 1988, second in 1989, and first in 1990.

In the 1989 Finals Dumars averaged 27 points. With the Pistons trailing in the third quarter of Game 3, he scored 17 straight points and 21 for the quarter in one of the truly memorable performances in Finals history. Dumars won the MVP in a Finals sweep of Los Angeles.

Dumars was also selected NBA All-Defensive first team in 1992 and 1993, but by then Detroit was in decline. In 1994 he played on "Dream Team II" in the world championships.

For his last few years Dumars was the leader of a bad team, tutoring Detroit guard Grant Hill. In 1994 he still had enough in the tank to hit 10 3-pointers in a game and tie an NBA record. By then he was regarded as a throwback, a player trying to understand the current crop of players whom he called "the dunking and contract generation." Dumars won the J. Walter Kennedy Citizenship Award in 1994 and was the first winner of the NBA Sportsmanship Award in 1996.

Dumars, then 36, retired after the 1999 season. In 14 years—all with Detroit—Dumars had played 1,018 games, more than any other player in Pistons' history. In addition to being Detroit's all-time leader in games, Dumars had team records for 3-pointers (990) and was second all-time in points (16,041), second in assists (4,612), and second in steals (902). He scored 40 or more points 13 times for Detroit. He is currently the team's vice president of player personnel.

Tim Duncan

Center, San Antonio, 1997-98 through present
Born: April 25, 1976 in St. Croix, Virgin Islands 7-0, 255
High School: St. Dunstan's Episcopal High, Virgin Islands
College: Wake Forest

In a very short time, Tim Duncan has won almost every pro award there is to win.

He was Rookie of the Year, has been All-NBA first team in six consecutive seasons, NBA All-Defensive first team five times, and a five-time all-star and has won back-to-back MVPs. His stellar career follows four years at Wake Forest, where he got better in steady increments and was All-American and College Player of the Year in 1997. That year, as a senior, he was the Division I rebounding champ, averaging 14.7 a game. In four years he snatched 1570 boards, the highest Division I total in a four-year career since 1973.

Selected first overall by the San Antonio Spurs in the 1997 draft, Duncan played like a veteran right out of the blocks, averaging 21 points, 12 rebounds, and 2.5 blocks. His season high was 35 points; he twice scored 34, and his 57 double-doubles (double digits in points and rebounds in the same game) led the NBA. His addition to the Spurs helped take the scoring, rebounding, and defensive burden off David Robinson. The team went from 20 wins (Robinson missed nearly the entire 1996-97 season with an injury) to 56 wins. The season ended with San Antonio losing to Utah in five games in the Conference semi-finals.

In a strike-shortened 50-game schedule in 1999, San Antonio finished 37-13 and then went 15-2 in the post-season, sweeping Los Angeles and Portland on the way to a throttling of New York in the Finals. With Duncan and Robinson combining to stifle the Knicks' Ewing-less inside game, blocking 26 shots between them, the Spurs won in five games. Duncan recorded 33 points and 16 rebounds in Game 1, 25 and 15 in Game 2, 28 and 18 in Game 4, and 31 and 9 in Game 5. The Spurs held the undersized Knicks to an anemic 80 points per game on 39-percent shooting. Scoring 26 points per game and averaging 14 assists, Duncan won the Finals MVP. Following the season Duncan nixed the chance to play with Grant Hill in Orlando and, in July 2000, signed a three-year $32.6 million deal, with an option for a fourth year.

In 2003, in the Conference Finals, Duncan played masterfully, including 37 points and 16 rebounds in Game 6 to eliminate the Lakers, who had won three consecutive titles. For the series he connected on 57 percent of his shots and averaged 28 points and 17 rebounds. He then took the Finals MVP again as he led the Spurs past New Jersey in six games.

Alex English

Forward, Milwaukee, 1976-77 through 1977-78; Indiana, 1978-80; Denver, 1980-81 through 1990-91.
Born: January 5, 1954 in Columbia, S.C. 6-7, 190 High School: Dreher (Columbia, S.C.) College: South Carolina

For eight consecutive seasons, from 1982 through 1989, Alex English averaged more than 25 points per game. During that time he was not a "gunner," a term used as far back as the

'50s for a player who shot too much and missed more than he made. In every one of those eight years he shot between 49 percent and 55 percent from the field. When he retired after the 1990-91 season he had 25,613 points—14th best in NBA history—and a 51-percent field-goal percentage.

Milwaukee made English its second-round pick, 23rd overall, in the 1976 draft. By his second year with the Bucks he had doubled his minutes and points and shot 62 percent in the playoffs for a team that reached the Western Conference semifinals. That quintet—with Junior Bridgeman, Brian Winters, Marques Johnson, and Dave Meyers—was not given a chance to mesh, because English, a free agent, was signed by Indiana following the 1978 season. After a year and a half with Indiana, English was traded to Denver for George McGinnis on February 1, 1980.

In Denver English flourished. He made the All-Star team eight years in a row, from 1982 through 1989. In 11 seasons in Denver—in eight of which the Nuggets made the playoffs—English would establish himself as one of the most consistent scorers in the game's history.

In his first nine years in Denver English was also one of the league's irrepressible iron men, playing in 731 of a possible 738 games. He won the scoring title (28.4) in 1982. With teammates like David Thompson, Dan Issel and Kiki Vandeweghe early on and Calvin Natt, Fat Lever and Michael Adams in later years, Denver twice won 50 games and finished above .500 seven times.

With English averaging 30 points in the post-season, the Nuggets made it to the Western Conference Finals in 1985 before losing to Los Angeles in five games. They made it as far as the Western Conference semis in 1986 and 1988.

Dallas signed English as an unrestricted free agent in August 1990 and he retired after the 1990-91 season. He is still Denver's all-time leader in points (21,645) and assists (3,679). Post-NBA, he played with Depi Napoli of the Italian League.

Julius Erving

Forward, Virginia (ABA), 1971-72 through 1972-73; New York (ABA), 1973-74 through 1975-76; Philadelphia, 1976-77 through 1986-87

Born: February 22, 1950 in Roosevelt, N.Y. 6-7, 210 High School: Roosevelt (N.Y.) College: Massachusetts

Julius Erving continued a style of play begun by Elgin Baylor more than a decade before. Erving soared even higher, and there may never have been a better player at going to the basket. Erving jumped over defenders for stuffs, went around them, even hung in the air while weighing various creative options. "Julius was the best player I've ever seen in the open court, and that includes Jordan," said Billy Cunningham, who coached him in Philadelphia and played against him in the ABA.

Following his junior season at the University of Massachusetts, Erving decided to go pro. Playing in the Yankee Conference, he was still relatively unknown across the country. He first signed a contract for $500,000 for four years with the Virginia Squires. Each year he received $75,000 in cash with $50,000 deferred, to be paid out in seven years.

"It was in training camp where Julius first got the nickname

'Doctor'," recalls Red Kerr, Virginia general manager. "Willie Sojourner would say, 'There's the doctor digging into his bag again,' whenever Julius came up with a new dunk. Then he became Doctor J as the other players picked it up."

Those who missed his first five seasons in the ABA missed seeing the vintage Julius Erving. He unveiled his entire repertoire of skills for a league that needed a superstar for its survival. With a head of hair that would have made Billy Preston envious, Erving established a high-flying standard. "A young Julius Erving was like Thomas Edison—he was inventing something new every night," said Kerr.

The NBA powers held a curmudgeonly attitude toward their red, white, and blue rivals. With Erving on their side, the ABA could boast, "This guy's as good as any one of yours."

In 1972, his rookie year, Erving averaged 16 rebounds a game and then 32 points, 20 rebounds, and 7 assists in the playoffs.

Erving averaged 27 points his first year in Virginia and led the league his second year with a 31.9 average. He was unhappy with his contract, which deferred too much of his money and the Nets got him for George Carter, the draft rights to Kermit Washington and cash in August 1973. He led the Long Island franchise to a title in his very first year, leading the league in scoring and walking off with MVP honors. He carried them to a second title in 1976, averaging 29 per game. That closed the book on his inimitable ABA career: two MVPs, two championships, three scoring titles, 28.7 points and 12 rebounds per game.

The ABA then merged with the NBA before the 1976-77 season. Nets' owner Roy Boe needed cash to pay the $3.2 million "entry" charge into the new league, plus an additional $480,000 to New York for playing in "the Knicks territory." The Philadelphia 76ers offered him $3 million for Erving and Boe took it to pay his bill.

Erving promptly averaged 27 points in his first NBA season and scored 30 points to win the All-Star Game MVP. In his next seven years, he ended up playing in four Finals. In 1977, when the starting lineups for the Portland Trailblazers included five former ABA players, Philadelphia lost in six games, after winning the first two. In 1980 and 1982 they met the same result against the Los Angeles Lakers. Then Moses Malone joined the 76ers for the 1982-83 season. Philadelphia won 65 games and roared through the playoffs with a 12-1 record, including a sweep of Los Angeles in the Finals, to win the Championship.

Erving retired after the 1987 season, finishing with career averages of 24 points, 8 rebounds and 4 assists. With his ABA and NBA totals combined, he had 30,026 points, making him, at his retirement, the highest scoring forward in history. (Karl Malone surpassed Erving's total early in the 1999-2000 season.) Erving played on three championship teams in the ABA and NBA and a combined 16 All-Star teams.

Erving was elected to the Hall of Fame in 1993. He was picked for the NBA's 35th Anniversary Team (1980) and 50th Anniversary All-Time Team (1996).

He became a television broadcaster after his career and was an executive vice president with the Orlando Magic starting with the 1997-98 season.

Patrick Ewing

Center, New York, 1985-86 through 1999-2000; Seattle, 2000-01; Orlando, 2001-02
Born: August 5, 1962 in Kingston, Jamaica 7-0, 255 High School: Cambridge (Mass.) Rindge and Latin School College: Georgetown

Patrick Ewing finished his career in 13th place on the all-time scoring list and is one of 14 players to score 20,000 points and grab 10,000 rebounds. His ownership of New York's all-time scoring (23,665) and rebounding (10,579) records are just two benchmarks that will ensure his election to the Hall of Fame. He has appeared in an NBA Final (1994) and been selected for the All-Star team 11 times. If Ewing—a give-no-quarter warrior—hasn't been the greatest center since his first year in 1985, he's been one of the greatest, along with Kareem Abdul-Jabbar and Moses Malone, Hakeem Olajuwon and Shaquille O'Neal, Tim Duncan and David Robinson. The controversy surrounding Ewing's 15 years in New York has to do with a missing piece: he never played on an NBA Championship team.

In four years at Georgetown University Ewing led the Hoyas to the final game of the Final Four three times. In 1982 they lost to North Carolina on Jordan's jumper with 17 seconds remaining. In 1984 he was voted the NCAA Tournament Outstanding Player as Georgetown bested Kentucky in the semis and Houston, with then Hakeem Olajuwon, in the Finals. That same near he was the third leading scorer and leading shot blocker on the gold medal-winning 1984 U.S. Olympic team in Los Angeles. In 1985, Villanova connected on 22 of its 28 field goal attempts to effect one of the biggest upset winners in tournament history with a 66-64 victory over Georgetown. Ewing was voted College Player of the Year.

Ewing is the answer to that perennial trivia question, "Who was the first pick in the NBA's first draft lottery?" The Georgetown center was selected first overall in the 1985 NBA draft, and Knicks general manager Dave DeBusschere pumped his fist with joy upon learning that New York had the first pick. Ewing won Rookie of the Year honors in 1986 and was selected to the All-Star Game, but did not play. Missing 51 games to injuries over his first two seasons lessened his impact.

His fifth season was Ewing's career best, as he led New York to the second round of playoffs for the second straight year. He averaged 29 points, 11 rebounds, and 4 blocks in 1990 and finished fourth in the MVP voting. For the only time in his career he was All-NBA first team. For a brief moment, he could be compared to Hakeem Olajuwon as the game's best pivot man.

The following season Ewing's scoring (27 points per game) and rebounding (11) averages were high, but he lost 10 points off his regular season average as Chicago humiliated New York in three games. In 1992 he was selected to play on the "Dream Team" in Barcelona and won his second gold medal. In 1994 the Knicks won 57 and Ewing set a NBA Finals record for 30 blocks in a series (a record broken by Tim Duncan, who had 32 against New Jersey in the 2003 Finals) and tied a record for 8 blocks in one game. He shot an anemic 36 percent from the field in the seven-game series, while Houston won the championship and Olajuwon earned the MVP award and Finals MVP awards.

Five years later the Knicks returned to the Finals, but an injury kept Ewing sidelined for the New York's last nine games of the Conference Finals (when they beat Indiana) and Finals (when they lost to San Antonio).

It appeared, however, that with a healthy Ewing the Knicks would not only make it back to the Finals but might win a title. A March 2000 game against Los Angeles was telling, however. Ewing, 37, thought it was his job to match league MVP Shaquille O'Neal basket for basket. O'Neal scored 43 and Ewing, on 6-for-19 shooting, tallied 12. In the games prior he had been most valuable as a rebounder and defender, leaving the scoring to Allen Houston and Latrell Sprewell and averaging 15 points and 10 rebounds. The Lakers won easily and observers had to wonder if Ewing had yet learned what his NBA endgame should look like.

But Ewing rightly pointed out that he did shoot less in his last years. He averaged 17.2 field goal attempts per game in 1997, 15.5 attempts in 1998, 14.9 in 1999, and 12.5 in 2000.

As union president, Ewing's disdain for the media was reaffirmed during the 1999-2000 lockout that lopped 32 games off the NBA season. He took a hard-line, pro-union stance and was criticized in the press.

Before the 2000-2001 season he was traded to the Seattle SuperSonics and then, in July of 2001, he was signed as a free agent by Orlando. He retired after the 2002 season, taking as assistant coaching job with Washington, then moved to Houston. Ewing is one of just 13 players in NBA history to post 20,000 points and 10,000 rebounds.

Walt Frazier

Guard, New York Knicks, 1967-68 through 1976-77; Cleveland, 1977-78 through 1979-80
Born: March 29, 1945 in Atlanta 6-4, 205 High School: David Howard (Atlanta) College: Southern Illinois

It's easy for Walt Frazier to remember the highlight of his career. "I'd have to say it was that seventh game against the Lakers," he recalls. That night in 1970 Frazier led New York to its first Championship and in the process laid down a line for the ages: 36 points, 19 assists (tying an NBA playoff record), 7 rebounds, and 5 steals. It was enough to deal the Lakers, including Jerry West, Wilt Chamberlain and Elgin Baylor, a 113-99 defeat.

Frazier soaked up all the adulation and sumptuous nightlife that New York had to offer. He was a stylish dresser and drove about Manhattan in a pink Rolls Royce. He boldly announced his lifestyle with a color magazine spread of his round bed and ceiling mirror and signed a then-gaudy $400,000 contract to match that lifestyle. New York trainer Danny Whelan called him "Clyde" because he had a love for wide-brimmed hats, like the one worn by the bank-robber Clyde Barrow in *Bonnie and Clyde*. Teammate Bill Hosket once said Frazier's hands were so fast that he could "steal the hubcaps off moving cars."

A prep school quarterback, Frazier turned down scholarships to Kansas and Indiana. He learned how to play defense under Jack Hartman at Southern Illinois. In his senior year he led his team to the NIT championship and was selected tournament MVP. A 17-point, 10-rebound-a-game guard, Frazier was picked fifth overall by the Knicks in the 1967 draft.

With the Knicks then giving Bill Bradley minutes at guard,

Frazier's time was limited. It all changed in December 1968, when center Walt Bellamy and guard Howard Komives were dealt to Detroit for power forward Dave DeBusschere. Bradley moved to small forward and Frazier, teaming with Dick Barnett in the backcourt, went from a 20-minute player in his rookie season to a 35-minute player in his second year.

Henceforth Frazier controlled the tempo on a Knicks squad that won 320 and lost 172 (.650) from 1969 through 1974. With Frazier bringing the ball up court, the Knicks won two championships (1970, 1973) and made it to the Finals one other time (1972). Frazier led the Knicks in assists in all 10 of his New York seasons and led the team in scoring in five of them. He also made the NBA All-Defensive first team every year between 1969 and 1975. A powerfully built 6-4, 205-pounder, Frazier had six or more rebounds per game every year from 1969 through 1976. "The ball belongs to Walt Frazier," opined Willis Reed, New York's captain. "He just lets us play with it."

After the 1976 season, when DeBusschere had already retired and Reed's knees had betrayed him, Frazier and Bradley were the last remaining pieces from those stellar 1970s New York squads. In October 1977 Frazier was traded to Cleveland for guard Jim Cleamons. Frazier's famous quip—that he couldn't find a place in Cleveland to park his Rolls—seemed to capture his indifference toward the last three years of his career in a new city, away from the excitement and celebrity he had known. Foot injuries kept him to just 66 games over his last three years.

The Knicks later retired his No. 10. He is still the team's all-time assists leader with 4,791 and finished with career averages of 19 points, 6 rebounds, and 6 assists per game. In post-season play, he raised each of those figures. Frazier was the best all-around player on his Knicks teams and, in the mind of many, the greatest ever to wear the uniform. He was elected to the Hall of Fame in 1987, and in 1996 was named to NBA's 50th Anniversary All-Time Team. Michael Jordan (with 10) and Gary Payton (7) are the only two guards in league history to be named to the NBA's All-Defensive first team as many times as Frazier.

Joe Fulks

Forward-Center, Philadelphia, 1946-47 through 1953-54 Born: October 26, 1921 in Birmingham, Ky. Died: March 21, 1976 6-5, 190 High School: Birmingham, Ky., then Kuttawa, Ky. College: Murray State

Joe Fulks is credited with being one of pro basketball's pioneers. He had an over-the-head jumper when everyone else was using a standing set shot. He wasn't the first jump shooter, but definitely one of the innovators. He employed turn-around jumpers, could shoot with either hand on the run, or even change his shot in mid-air in response to defenders. His .302 field-goal percentage shows that he was an errant shooter, but he used his jumper—which earned him the name "Jumpin' Joe"—to become a dominant scorer for the Philadelphia Warriors.

Fulks left Murray State College after just two years, spent three years in the military, and was already 25 when he was signed by the Warriors of the Basketball Association of America (BAA), an 11-team league founded the previous summer. To his teammates, Fulks was a man of few words and a kind of competitive hillbilly whose Kentucky twang could scarcely be

understood. A teammate, guard Petey Rosenberg, had first noticed Fulks when he was playing for a U.S. Marines team in Hawaii during the war. Rosenberg was impressed with Fulks' shooting and fired off a letter to Philadelphia owner Ed Gottlieb, who followed up on the recommendation.

He led the league in scoring in 1946-47, averaging 23 points a game. The Cleveland Rebels' Ed Sadowski was a distant second, averaging just 16.5. Fulks' feat was staggering, considering that the shot clock did not come about until 1954; stall tactics were rampant throughout the league, and the mean scoring average was 68 points a game.

The wiry Fulks was known as a "gunner." "He could shoot from anywhere," Red Auerbach once said. He fit the definition of what the league and Gottlieb wanted—a high-scoring player with a singular flair. He attempted 26 shots per game in 1946-47, 1557 in all. The total was higher than the team's next two top scorers—Angelo Musie and Howie Dellmar—combined. Then again, his .305 percentage was tops on the Warriors.

Philadelphia was 35 and 25, finishing 14 games behind the league-best Washington Capitols, coached by the 29-year-old Red Auerbach. But the odd playoff bracketing left Washington (49-11), the best in the Eastern Division, playing Chicago (39-22), the best in the West, in the first round. Chicago won in six games. While Auerbach groused about the idiocy of the playoff system, Philadelphia moved on, beating St. Louis in the quarter-finals and New York in the semi-finals.

When Fulks scored 37 points to lead Philadelphia past Chicago in Game 1 of the Finals, an AP writer called it "the greatest shooting exhibition ever seen on the [Market Square] arena floor." Fulks then scored 26, 24, and 34 in Games 3, 4 and 5 and the Warriors took the Championship in five games. Fulks and his mates each took home a $2,000 bonus and a ring.

The following year Fulks led the league in scoring again (22 ppg), but this time the Bullets closed out the Warriors in six games. Fulks would never make the Finals again. His greatest game came on February 10, 1949 in Philadelphia, when he hit for a then NBA record 63 points against five different Indianapolis Jets defenders. That performance, on a Philly team that averaged only 85 points a game, led to his being a unanimous selection on the All-Star Team. George Mikan's previous record of 48 points had stood only 11 days. Fulks' record stood for more than 10 years. Fulks had been selected to the All-BAA first team in each of his first three seasons.

Fulks retired at the age of 32 following the 1954 season. He struggled in the years following the end of his career, but was settled in a job as director of recreation at the Kentucky State Penitentiary in March 1976 when, late one evening, he became embroiled in an argument with the son of a woman he was dating. After a long night of drinking, the son pulled out a shotgun and shot Fulks dead. The son was paroled after serving two years of a 4-1/2-year sentence for reckless homicide.

Kevin Garnett

Forward, Minnesota, 1995-96 to present Born May 19, 1976 in Mauldin, S.C. 6-11, 220 High School: Mauldin (S.C.) then Farragut Academy (Chicago) College: Did not attend

Kevin Garnett has played eight years in the NBA and is just

27 years old. It is almost trite to say that he has improved every year. In 2003 he peaked. A 122-panel member of writers and broadcasters selected him to the All-NBA First Team for the second time. His points reached 23 a game, to go with 13 rebounds and six assists.

It marked the fourth consecutive season in which Garnett posted at least 20 points, 10 rebounds, and five assists per game, joining Larry Bird as the only players in league history to achieve that feat. Garnett also posted a franchise-record and league-best 68 double-doubles, in addition to tallying an NBA-high six triple-doubles. He became the first player since Bird in 1989-90 to rank among the league's top 15 in all three categories. He also led Minnesota in scoring 60 times, rebounding on 69 occasions and in assists 35 times

With Garnett leading the way, the Wolves won 50 games for the third time in four years. Garnett came of age in still other ways. He was named MVP of the 52nd NBA All-Star Game on Feb. 9 in Atlanta, after tallying 37 points, nine rebounds, and five steals in the West's 155-145 double-overtime victory.

Compared with what came before Garnett, the results are astounding. In the four years before Garnett's arrival, the Wolves had lost 60 games and then 56 games in his rookie season.

George Gervin

Guard-Forward, Virginia (AB), 1972-74; San Antonio (ABA), 1974-76; San Antonio Spurs, 1976-85, Chicago, 1985-1986,

Born: April 27, 1952 in Detroit 6-7, 185 High School: Martin Luther King, Detroit College: Long Beach State, then Eastern Michigan

Comically thin at 6-foot-8 and 183 pounds, George Gervin was a slithery scoring machine who won four professional scoring titles. Only Michael Jordan (10) and Wilt Chamberlain (7) won more. Known for a stunning variety of moves, the wiry Gervin could score from downtown or with creative drives down the lane and from the baseline. The most memorable of these was his delicate "finger roll" shot, which he could guide into the basket from two feet or 10 and anywhere in between. Nothing ever seemed to fluster Gervin; he played with such a relaxed style that teammate Fatty Taylor dubbed him "The Iceman."

A star in the ABA with the San Antonio Spurs, his four scoring championships nonetheless came with San Antonio between 1978 and 1982, after the team had been incorporated into the NBA. In fact, he was the first NBA guard ever to win the scoring title in three straight years. Michael Jordan, with seven straight titles, is still the only backcourt man to eclipse Gervin.

Gervin's father, Booker Gervin Sr., deserted his wife and six children in Detroit's Eastside ghetto when George was only three. His mother, Geraldine, worked hard to keep the family clothed and fed. After being cut from his high school team as a sophomore, Gervin fell under the influence of an assistant coach, Willie Meriweather, who tutored George on the junior varsity squad. Gervin coaxed the key to the gym out of the school janitor and stayed up all hours shooting hoops.

Because his grades at Martin Luther King High were horrible, he was not eligible to play for the varsity until the last four games of his junior year. In those games he scored 28, 29, 30, and 27 points. He grew four inches to 6-foot-6 after his junior

year and became a starter, averaging 31 points and 21 rebounds per game, with a high game of 53 points.

Two weeks after getting into Long Beach State with coach Jerry Tarkanian, Gervin became homesick and transferred to Eastern Michigan University, where he had to sit out his freshman year. The next year he scored 29.5 points per game, but trouble flared in the College Division NCAA semi-final game against Roanoke College. Gervin had been roughed up under the basket. When he threw an elbow at Jay Piccola, he was called for a flagrant foul and was ejected. He then walked to Roanoke's bench, where Piccola thought he would shake hands. Instead Gervin threw a right hand and knocked him out cold. He was thrown off the team and lost any chance of playing in the 1972 Olympics. Since he couldn't play ball and his grades were poor, he quit school and ended up playing semipro ball with the Pontiac Chaparrals of the original Continental Basketball Association. Playing for just $500 a month, he was discovered by Red Kerr, a former NBA star then scouting for the Virginia Squires. With just a year and a half of high school ball, a year and a half of college, and seven months in semi-pro ball, Gervin, 19, became a pro.

Gervin was selected by the ABA's Virginia Squires in the first round of the special circumstance draft in 1973. He played parts of two seasons with Virginia, making the All-Star Game in his second season. Gervin and Julius Erving played as teammates for 30 games during the 1972-73 season, but the team, with Gervin at forward, was taking a licking off the boards and was only 15-15 during those games. Gervin was sold to San Antonio for $225,000 on January 30, 1974.

Gervin averaged 21, 23 and 23 points over his three years with San Antonio in the ABA, but his scoring catapulted when the Spurs franchise became part of the establishment NBA. Despite a widely held view that flashy stars like Gervin would not perform well in the NBA, with its better defenders, he played in the All-Star Game in all but one of his 10 NBA seasons. He not only averaged more points (26.2) in the NBA than he had in the ABA (21.9), but beginning in 1978 he dominated the league scoring leaders.

On the final day of the season, April 9, Gervin (26.77 points per game) and Denver's David Thompson (26.57) were vying for the scoring title. Playing in Detroit, Thompson's teammates fed him all afternoon. He set an NBA record with 32 points at the quarter, 53 at the half, then cooled off but still finished with 73. Gervin knew he needed 58 points against the New Orleans Jazz that night. He registered 20 in the first quarter, 33 in the second quarter—breaking Thompson's scoring record, which lasted all of seven hours—and finished with 63 to top Thompson, 27.22 to 27.15.

Gervin didn't require any last-game heroics to win his 1979, 1980, and 1982 scoring titles. In 1980 he received 400,000 votes for the All-Star Game, leading all NBA players. The Iceman shot over smaller guards and seemingly beat forwards off the dribble at will.

He was traded to Chicago for forward David Greenwood in October 1985. Gervin played 82 games for the Bulls in his final season, but Michael Jordan missed 64 of those games with a foot injury, so Air never came under the influence of Ice. Gervin played in Italy the following season (still averaging 26

points at age 35) and two years later finished his pro career as a 20-point scorer with the Quad City Thunder of the CBA.

Between the ABA and NBA he scored 26,595 points. He is the Spurs all-time scoring leading with 19,383 points. While many great ABA players scored less when they got to the NBA, Gervin proved his mettle by scoring more. This may be the best argument for his inclusion on the NBA 50th Anniversary All-Time Team, a distinction he earned in 1996, the same year he was voted into the Hall of Fame. He works as a community relations representative with the Spurs. His brother, Derrick, played in the NBA for two seasons.

Artis Gilmore

Center, Kentucky (ABA), 1971-72 through 1975-76; Chicago, 1976-77 through 1981-82; San Antonio, 1982-83 through 1986-87; Chicago, 1987; Boston, 1988; Bologna Arimo (Italy) 1988-89
Born: September 21, 1949 in Hempstead, N.Y. 7-2, 265 High School: Roulhac (Chipley, Fla.), then Carver (Dothan, Ala.) Junior College: Gardner-Webb Junior College (N.C.) College: Jacksonville

Artis Gilmore was one of the strongest players who ever walked on a court. He holds numerous ABA records and won a title with the Kentucky Colonels in 1975. His 16,330 rebounds place him fourth behind Wilt Chamberlain, Bill Russell, and Kareem Abdul-Jabbar.

For years, he kept a painting in his home of a shot by Jabbar that he blocked in a 1972 exhibition game between Milwaukee and Kentucky. But he never got to Jabbar's level. The kind of respect accorded other great pivot men wasn't showered on Gilmore, probably the greatest center in ABA history. He was one of three members of the 20,000-point, 10,000-rebound club who didn't make the NBA 50th Anniversary All-Time Team in 1996. The other two were Walt Bellamy and Dan Issel.

Gilmore was one of nine children growing up in rural Chipley, Florida. He averaged an astounding 38 points per game in high school, scoring 75 in one game. After attending Gardner-Webb Junior College for two years, Gilmore led the Jacksonville University Dolphins to the championship game in 1970, losing to UCLA 80-69. He got 16 rebounds and 19 points, but connected on only 9 of 29 shots. He was still selected for the All-Tournament team. He still holds the NCAA career record for average rebounds per game with 22.7, and led Division 1 with 22.2 rebounds per game in 1970 and 23.2 per game in 1971.

When Kentucky general manager Mike Storen was considering who to draft first in 1971, someone said of Gilmore, "All he does is play defense." While the point was inaccurate—he averaged 24.3 points per game over four years in college—the GM was steadfast. "Wait a minute," Storen said. "The guy is at least seven-foot-two and if all he does is play defense, that's an awful lot, since all defense does is win games." Wanting to sign Gilmore before the NBA draft, Storen claimed he would pay $3 million to get Gilmore, a figure no other ABA team could match, and then paid him half that much. Gilmore, seeking security, accepted a 10-year deal worth about $1.5 million.

Possessed of a 9-foot-7 flat-footed reach, Gilmore repaid the huge contract with a huge rookie season. Leading the league in

four statistical categories (minutes, 44 per game; field-goal percentage, .598; total rebounds, 1491; and rebounds per game, 17.8), Gilmore was named ABA All-Star first team for the first of five consecutive years, won the Rookie of the Year award, and was the league's MVP. In his next four years he followed suit, winning the rebounding title three times (and total rebounds every season); leading in minutes twice and in field goal percentage once; making ABA All-Star first team four times; and winning another MVP in 1974. He didn't miss a single game in his first five seasons, appearing in all 420 regular season contests.

Kentucky was not one of the teams absorbed in the NBA merger in 1976. Gilmore, however, was selected by the Bulls in the ABA dispersal draft in August 1976. He continued to post high rebound, field goal, and points-per-game averages. He also continued his consecutive game streak— in his first eight years of professional basketball (5 ABA, 3 NBA), Gilmore didn't miss a game, playing in 666 straight contests.

He proved his fitness in NBA battles, making six All-Star squads with San Antonio, where he was traded in 1982, and the Bulls, whom he joined in 1987. After being waived by Chicago, he was back with Boston in 1988, where he ended his career. He still holds the career field-goal percentage record (.599) for players with 2000 or more field goals. He scored 24,041 points and grabbed 16,330 rebounds; the two totals combined are good enough for sixth place in history. Despite these impressive markers, Gilmore, who retired in 1988, still has not been elected to the Basketball Hall of Fame.

Gail Goodrich

Guard, LA Lakers, 1965-66 through 1967-68; Phoenix, 1968-69 through 1969-70; LA Lakers, 1970-71 through 1975-76; New Orleans, 1976-77 through 1978-79
Born: April 23, 1943 in Los Angeles 6-1, 175 High School: Los Angeles Poly technic College: UCLA

A 6-foot-1 guard, Gail Goodrich was given the nickname "Stumpy" by Los Angeles teammate Elgin Baylor. The name wasn't derisive. Goodrich overcame his size with quickness, a smooth, left-handed stroke from the perimeter, a fast-breaking style, and a small guard post-up game second to none. Over a seven-year period from 1969-65 he averaged between 20 and 26 points for Phoenix and Los Angeles. Goodrich was teamed with Jerry West for four seasons and the duo formed one of the highest scoring backcourts ever, regularly scoring 50 points between them. He led the Lakers in scoring from 1972 through 1975.

At the age of two, Goodrich suffered from rheumatic fever, which severely weakens the body. By the time he was ready to play basketball at Polytechnic High in Los Angeles, he was 5-foot-2 and 93 pounds. His mother, Jean—an athlete who had competed in high school basketball, track, volleyball, and baseball and toured with the Hollywood All-Stars, a women's softball team—and father, Gail, helped him to develop his ability and the right mindset. His mother encouraged him and he always tagged along when his father, a player on the USC team in the 1930s, officiated games.

He played with Walt Hazzard (later Mahdi Abdul-Rahmad); the tandem led UCLA to a 30-0 record and actually began the school's phenomenal string of nine titles in 10 years with a National Championship in 1964. In the championship game

Goodrich scored 27 points and Kenny Washington 26 as the Bruins beat Duke, 98-83, to give John Wooden his first national title. In his senior year, Goodrich averaged 26 points and was a consensus All-American, leading the Bruins to their second straight NCAA championship.

A territorial choice of the Lakers in the 1965 draft, Goodrich was a part-time player for three seasons, starting behind Jerry West, Walt Hazzard, and later Archie Clark. He demanded to be traded and was selected by the Phoenix Suns in the May 1968 expansion draft.

He was the Suns' star right out of the gate, averaging 24 points and 6 assists for the 1968-69 season and making the All Star Team. He averaged an even 20 a game in 1970-71. Two weeks after the Lakers' crushing loss to New York in the 1970 Finals, team owner Jack Kent Cooke decided he wanted Goodrich back. Goodrich, who was having contract problems with Phoenix, was traded to the Lakers for journeyman center Mel Counts.

With West and Goodrich, the Lakers won 48 games in 1971, a record 69 in 1972 (including an astounding 33 straight), 60 in 1973, and 47 in 1974. Goodrich learned the value of off-season conditioning, especially distance running, instead of working out a week before training camp, as many players did.

The duo peaked in 1972, combining for 51.7 points per game and leading the Lakers to their first title in Los Angeles. Goodrich was often the open man, pumping jumpers while defenders keyed on West, who led the league in assists with 9.7 per game. Regarded as one of the best teams ever, the Lakers defeated the Knicks in a five-game Final, avenging their seven-game defeat two years before.

The Lakers returned to the Finals in 1973 and lost to New York in five games. Chamberlain did not return after the season and West retired in 1974. Goodrich continued to score and made the All-Star Team in 1974 and 1975, but the Lakers, who had been to three Finals in four years, finished in the basement of the Pacific Division with 30 wins in 1975. Following a contract dispute, Goodrich was signed by New Orleans after the 1976 season. Los Angeles got two first-round draft picks for him and used the 1979 pick to sign Magic Johnson. Goodrich teamed with Pete Maravich in New Orleans. An Achilles tendon injury in his first game kept him from being a scoring threat. He returned for two more seasons, but with Maravich responsible for much of the offense, he was never again a dominant scorer.

Goodrich retired after the 1978-79 season, his 14th in the NBA. He had 19,181 points and averaged 18.6 per game. By anyone's reckoning, he must be considered one of the greatest small guards ever to play. The five-time all-star was elected to the Hall of Fame in 1996.

Hal Greer

Guard, Syracuse, 1958-59 through 1962-63; Philadelphia, 1963-64 through 1972-73
Born: June 26, 1936 in Huntington, WV 6-2, 175 High School: Douglass (Huntington, WV) College: Marshall

It's easy to picture Hal Greer driving hard right and nailing a 15-foot pull-up jumper. His other signature was using that jump while taking free throws. Besides his speed—"I must be

quick; the day I slow down I'm finished"—the essence of the Greer career was consistency. He averaged between 19 and 24 points a game over 11 straight seasons, beginning in 1961.

The youngest of nine siblings growing up in Huntington, Virginia, Greer was a quarterback on the Douglass High football team and guard on the basketball team. He led the latter to the black high school state championship in his senior year, and dozens of scholarship offers poured in. His older brother, J.D., who was taller and heftier than Hal, used to say that his kid brother was "the greatest in the Greer family." "I guess that's why I have so much desire to excel," said Hal. The first black player ever to attend Marshall College in West Virginia, he used a fast-breaking style to become a potent offensive player, connecting on 55 percent of his shots and leading his team to a 50-21 record in three varsity seasons.

Syracuse coach Paul Seymour, heeding the strong recommendation of Greer's college coach Jules Rivlin, drafted Greer in the second round, 14th overall, in the 1958 draft. By his third season he was an all-star for the first of 10 times. Greer increased his minutes, points, rebounds, and assists over each of his first four years, twice playing in the All-Star Game.

The Syracuse Nationals moved to Philadelphia and changed their name to the 76ers for the 1963-64 season. The team got a jolt by signing Wilt Chamberlain in January 1965. The 76ers lost to Boston in a seven-game Conference Finals, but Greer averaged 24.6 points per game over the 11 games in the post-season. Only Chamberlain outscored him. He also averaged 7 rebounds and 5 assists.

Two years later, Philadelphia set an NBA record with 68 wins and 13 losses. Greer was second in scoring and assists to Chamberlain. The team completed its record-breaking season by tearing through Cincinnati, Boston, and San Francisco in the Finals. Greer was the leading playoff scorer, enjoying a personal best post-season average of 28 points per game.

In 1968 Greer was selected to the All-Star Game and won the game MVP, going 8-for-8 from the field and scoring 21 points. He startled everyone by scoring 19 of his points on 7-for-7 shooting in the third quarter. Greer ended his career in 1973, playing for a 9-73 76ers squad that was perhaps the worst in NBA history.

Greer recorded his 20,000th point in 1971. For his steady contribution to his teams and his amazingly consistent play, he was elected to the Hall of Fame in 1981and to the NBA 50th Anniversary All-Time Team in 1996.

He remains the Philadelphia 76ers' all-time leading scorer with 21,586 points. Despite tough competition at the guard position from Bob Cousy, Oscar Robertson, Jerry West—and later Walt Frazier and Earl Monroe—Greer made All-NBA second team seven times.

Cliff Hagan

Forward, St. Louis, 1956-57 through 1965-66; Dallas (ABA), 1967-68 through 1969-70
Born: December 9, 1931 in Owensboro, Ky. 6-4, 215 High School: Owensboro College: Kentucky

A five-time all-star, Cliff Hagan played with Bob Pettit and Clyde Lovellette on the St. Louis Hawks to form one of the great front lines of all time. Rugged beyond his 6-foot-4 stature

and known for his clutch play in big games, Hagan helped the Hawks to an NBA title in 1958 and Finals appearances in three other seasons. He played on Kentucky's 1951 title team that beat Kansas State, 68-58. In 1970 he was still playing with the Dallas Chaparrals of the ABA.

Hagan was a star even before reaching the pros, having led the Kentucky Wildcats to the title in 1951. Playing under Adolph Rupp, the Cats were 86-5 in the Hagan years. Employing a sweeping hook to offset his size disadvantage, Hagan got the nickname "Li'l Abner" (from Al Capp's comic Dogpatch character) because he was a Kentucky native and because of his strength.

Drafted by Boston in the third round of the 1953 draft, Hagan, a second lieutenant, only saw action at Andrews' Air Force Base, serving out a military commitment during the 1954-55 and 1955-56 seasons.

In April 1956 his draft rights, and Ed Macauley's, were packaged to the Hawks for the rights to Bill Russell in one of the NBA's most historic trades. Years later, Celtics' owner Walter Brown sent a note to Hagan saying, "Trading you away was the biggest boner of my life." The sentiment was exceedingly odd, since with Russell the Celtics won 11 NBA titles in 13 years.

Hagan was nearly 25 when he played his first NBA game and was only a part-timer on the 1956-57 Hawks' squad. He got his chance to play when Bob Pettit broke his wrist in a game against Boston.

Hagan then flourished and helped St. Louis to push Boston to seven games and two overtimes before losing in the Finals, 125-123. In 1958 he was a major contributor. Finishing seventh in the league in scoring—Pettit finished third—and second in field-goal percentage, he made his first of five consecutive All-Star squads and helped the Hawks to a Western Division title. Riding a 50-point game by Pettit in Game 6, the Hawks toppled the champion Celtics in the Finals. Hagan and Pettit combined for a 52 post-season points per game, with Hagan contributing 28 per game.

In 1960 the Hawks won their third straight Western Division crown and pushed Boston through another long Final before losing, 122-103, in Game 7. Hagan was again a major contributor, averaging 20-plus points and 10 rebounds for his third straight regular season and post-season. With the help of Richie Guerin and Len Wilkens and the continued strong play of Pettit and Hagan, St. Louis got to the Western Conference Finals in 1963 and 1964, losing to Los Angeles and San Francisco.

They are still remembered as the only team to beat Boston between 1957 and 1966, keeping the Celtics' run of titles to eight instead of 10. In June 1967, Hagan, then 35, was signed as a player and head coach by the Dallas Chaparrals of the ABA. In his three years with the Dallas club he compiled a record of 109-90, but was replaced in January of 1970.

For his five All-Star Game appearances, his being a part of one of the great teams of the late 1950s and early '60s, and his solid career line of 18 points and 7 rebounds per game, Cliff Hagan is recalled as a player who played bigger than his 6-foot-4 size, and bigger still in big games. He was elected to the Hall of Fame in 1977.

John Havlicek

Forward-Guard, Boston, 1962-63 through 1977-78
Born: April 8, 1940 in Martins Ferry, Ohio 6-5, 205 High School: Bridgeport (Ohio). College: Ohio State

Built as slightly as a matador but as durably as a marathoner, John Havlicek was one of the greatest Celtics in their run of championships in the 1960s and 1970s. His brilliant 16-year career bridged several Boston eras. Havlicek's first season was Bob Cousy's last; he played with Tommy Heinsohn, Sam Jones and Bill Russell, but also with Dave Cowens, Jo Jo White and Paul Silas. He missed being a teammate of Larry Bird's by one year.

Havlicek played on eight Boston championship teams from 1963 to 1976 and is the all-time leading scorer for the storied franchise, with 26,395 points. He played 1,270 games, sixth highest in NBA history. Havlicek was an all-around player—a shooter who could nail a perimeter jumper and run Boston's fabled fast break to perfection; a five-time NBA first-team defender; and a swingman who could play four different positions on the court.

He was known as "Hondo." Mel Nowell, a teammate at Ohio State, gave him the name because Havlicek liked Western novels and bore a resemblance to John Wayne, the star of the movie *Hondo*.

People would ask Havlicek where his incredible stamina came from. "When I was a kid, I lived on Route 40," he recalls. "That was probably the first national highway and they had markers every mile or so. I used to play games with myself running between them. I didn't have a bicycle and I had to run to keep up with the other kids.

His running was put to good use at Bridgeport High, not only for basketball. He was the finest T-option quarterback in the state and could throw a football 80 yards. So Woody Hayes had an interest him at Ohio State.

So did Ohio State's basketball coach, Fred Taylor. Havlicek reportedly said to Taylor, "There's only one basketball and you've got plenty of guys who can shoot it. I'm going to make this team on the other end of the floor." As a sophomore in 1960 Havlicek played on the same Ohio State squad that included Jerry Lucas and Larry Siegfried. They won the national championship that year by beating California, 75-55.

Havlicek averaged just 14.6 points in his four college seasons, but was such a ball hound on the defensive end that Red Auerbach made him the Celtics' first pick in the 1962 draft. Paul Brown also drafted him for the Cleveland Browns. The NFL paid better, so Havlicek chose the Browns and the car that was included in the signing. He had talent as a receiver, but the Browns were stacked with guys like Gary Collins, Mel Renfro, and others. He was the final cut.

He averaged about 30 minutes during each of his first five years, four of them resulting in Boston championships. Auerbach, who had instituted the sixth man idea in the 1950s with Frank Ramsey, found Havlicek a perfect fit for that role. Havlicek was a "swing man" capable of playing forward and guard.

In 1965, Havlicek became a permanent part of Celtics' lore. Boston was in a cliffhanger against Philadelphia in Game 7 of

the Eastern Conference Finals. With five seconds left, the Celtics led the Sixers by one point, but the Sixers had the ball out of bounds beneath their own basket. Mindful that if the play was set for Chamberlain the Celtics would foul to put him on the line, Philadelphia coach Dolph Schayes called Chet Walker's number in the huddle. With the 5-second clock running down, Greer sent a looping pass toward Walker, but Havlicek anticipated the play and jumped and tipped the ball free to Sam Jones, who ran out the clock. Boston announcer Johnny Most's gravelly voice screamed, "Havlicek stole the ball, he stole the ball!" The play was instrumental in sending the team to its seventh consecutive title.

When Bill Russell came back to Boston Garden to collect his things after his last championship and retirement in 1969, he said to Havlicek, "It's your team now; you're the leader." Havlicek, who had already played on six championship teams with Russell, ended up playing on two more without the legendary center.

After his sixth-man tenure, Havlicek became a 40-minute player, leading the league with 45 minutes per game in 1971 and 46 in 1972. He and MVP Dave Cowens led Boston to a 68-14 record in 1973, but Havlicek separated his shoulder in the Conference Finals and the Knicks became the first team ever to win a Game 7 in Boston. A year later, in a tightly played Final series in which each team won just a single home game, Boston topped Milwaukee in seven. Havlicek scored nine points in overtime to tie a record in Game 6. But Kareem Abdul-Jabbar's 15-foot hook from the baseline with seconds left won the game. Boston took Game 7 in Milwaukee, 102-87. Averaging 27 points, 6 rebounds and 6 assists, Havlicek took Finals MVP honors.

In 1976, with Hondo now 36, the Celtics took Phoenix in six games for Boston's second title in the post-Russell era. The series included perhaps the greatest game ever played, a triple-overtime win by Boston in Game 5.

Havlicek retired after the 1978 season, having played in 13 straight All-Star Games. In the regular season, he is the 12th all-time leading scorer; in the playoffs; sixth. At the beginning of Havlicek's career, with anti-Boston sentiment prevalent throughout the league, detractors had challenged Auerbach, "Let's see you win without Russell." With Havlicek he won twice.

Havlicek was elected to Hall of Fame in 1983, his first year of eligibility. He was selected for both the NBA's 35th and 50th Anniversary All-Time Teams.

Connie Hawkins

Forward-Center, Pittsburgh Rens (ABL), 1961-62; Harlem Globetrotters, 1963-1964 to 1966-1967; Pittsburgh (ABA), 1967-1968; Minnesota (ABA), 1968-1969; Phoenix, 1969-1970 through 1973-1974; LA Lakers, 1974-1975; Atlanta 1975-1976

Born: July 17, 1942 6-8, 215 High School: High School Boys (Brooklyn, NY) College: Iowa

Connie Hawkins will be recalled for his inimitable fluid moves and creativity on the court. "The Hawk" was a playground legend in Brooklyn, a legend at Boys High, and then was thrown out of Iowa while still a freshman, after he was suspected of consorting with gamblers. Undeterred, he played

on and competed in the inaugural seasons of two leagues—the ill-fated American Basketball League (ABL) in 1961-62 and the American Basketball Association (ABA) in 1967, where he was the MVP that first year. He would become a four-time NBA All Star.

One of six children, Hawkins' father left the family when he was 10. His mother was blind and on welfare and basketball provided a financial incentive for Hawkins. He led Boys High to consecutive titles, games played before 18,000 fans at the old Madison Square Garden on Eighth Avenue. The recruiting battle for his services promised a way out. Given nearly 250 scholarship offers, Hawkins was recruited by Iowa but never played a game there. He was suspected of having introduced players, like Roger Brown, to Jack Molinas, who was later convicted and sent to jail for gambling on games. Hawkins had borrowed $200 from Molinas on one occasion but repaid it. Hawkins was unofficially guilty by association. The suspicion followed him for years, keeping him from playing in the Eastern League, a forerunner of the CBA, and from the NBA for nearly a decade.

At 19, Hawkins signed a $5000 contract to play with the Pittsburgh Rens of the ABL for the 1961-1962 season. He averaged 27 points and 13 rebounds, leading the league in scoring and easily taking league MVP honors. When the ABL folded midway through the 1962-1963 season, he signed on with the Harlem Globetrotters for $125 a week.

By 1967 he was no longer with the Trotters. He was playing with an industrial league team named the Porky Chedwicks of the YMHA. The team charged customers 50 cents a night. Hawkins' talents were rusting. He was married (and looking after his wife's brother who was mentally retarded), had no children, no money, and he was living in a poor section of Pittsburgh.

George Mikan was commissioner of the American Basketball Association for its startup 1967-1968 season. After investigating Hawkins, Roger Brown, Tony Jackson, Charlie Williams, and Doug Moe, he decided to let them play, saying "I'm proud to say that I'm the one who brought those guys back into pro basketball." The Pittsburgh Pipers gave Hawkins a $5,000 bonus, a $15,000 salary and a $25,000 salary for the following year.

Mikan wanted Hawkins to score 50 a game to bring attention to the ABA. But Hawkins' perspective on the game was different, saying, "Let's move the ball around and let everyone touch it." Hawkins made a sweep of the league's inaugural awards, with the scoring title (26.8), All Star first team, and League MVP. Then he carried the Pipers through the playoffs. In the Finals the New Orleans Bucaneers led three games to two on their home court. Hawkins scored 41 to tie the series at three games apiece. Pittsburgh then won 122-113 at home before a crowd of more than 11,000 in Game Seven (they usually played before 2,000). Hawkins got 20 points, 16 rebounds, and 9 assists.

Pittsburgh was transferred to Minnesota the following year and Hawkins upped his average to 30 points a game. Hawkins then won a court settlement with the NBA for more than $1 million and Commissioner J. Walter Kennedy lifted the ban against him. In effect, the league said they would allow Hawkins to play if he would drop the $6 million suit brought by his Pittsburgh lawyer David Litman. The Phoenix Suns won

a coin flip to determine who would get his services and signed him to $100,000 a year for three years.Hawkins made the All-NBA first team for the 1969-70 season and made the first of four consecutive All-Star games.

He was already 27 when he began with the Suns, with his most spectacular years behind him. Since 1992 Hawkins has worked as a community service representative with the Phoenix Suns.

Elvin Hayes

Forward-Center, San Diego, 1968-69 through 1970-71; Houston, 1971-72; Baltimore, 1972-73; Capital Bullets, 1973-74; Washington, 1974-75 through 1980-81; Houston, 1981-82 through 1983-84
Born: November 17, 1945 in Rayville, La. 6-9, 235 High School: Eula D. Britton (Rayville, La.) College: Houston

Elvin Hayes was that rarest of players—one who dominated the NBA in his first year. He had achieved legendary status as a college senior, when his Houston Cougars upset the UCLA Bruins and broke their streak of 47 consecutive victories. Hayes got 39 points and 15 rebounds that night, before 52,693 fans at the Astrodome. His free throws with 28 seconds left gave Houston the 71-69 victory. Much was made of how he outplayed Lew Alcindor, who, while playing with a scratched retina, got only 15 points and had four of his shots blocked by Hayes. He averaged 37 points and 19 rebounds that season.

Once in the NBA, Hayes would post 12 consecutive 20-point, 10-rebound seasons.

Elvin was the youngest of six children born to Chris Hayes, a boiler supervisor, and his wife, Savannah, in Rayville, Louisiana. Chris Hayes died when Elvin was in the ninth grade; by then the kid had tacked up a tin can in the yard and begun tossing a rubber ball through it. He scored and rebounded mightily in high school, and scholarship offers poured in from every school in the Southwest Conference and quite a few others. He chose little-known Houston. "If I don't succeed, nobody will know," he reasoned. He never regretted his decision.

Impressed by the three-time All-American's preternatural senior season at Houston and his four-year college average of 31 points and 17 rebounds, the San Diego Rockets made Hayes the first overall pick in the 1968 NBA Draft. Few players in NBA history had the enormous impact in their first season that Hayes did. The man now known as the "Big E" was instant "O," leading the league in five categories, including minutes (he still holds the record for most minutes played by a rookie, 3695, or 45.1 per game), points, and points per game (28.4). He led the league in total rebounds in his second year.

But in Hayes' four years with the Rockets (who moved to Houston for the 1971-72 season), the team failed to play .500 ball. Hayes could play big forward or center and his repertoire included a devastating turn-around from the baseline and from the left and right of the lane. But he had problems with teammates and coaches. His conflict with his first coach, Jack McMahon, ended up with McMahon being fired.

When the Rockets moved to Houston for the 1971-72 season, Hayes' fourth, the problems followed. Hayes refused to enter a game as a substitute and failed to show up at a practice. Despite his posting 25.2 points and 14.6 rebounds, the Rockets were still losing.

In June 1972, the Rockets traded him to the Baltimore Bullets in exchange for Jack Marin. The Baltimore franchise moved to Washington the following season. A change of scenery hardly affected Hayes' sighting of the rim. He scored his 10,000th point in his fifth season; only Wilt Chamberlain and Oscar Robertson had done it in less time. Now teamed with stocky center Wes Unseld, Hayes played forward, and became a more complete player with Unseld at his side.

The Bullets' big twosome played in three Finals in the 1970s. Hayes' fine performance (25 points, 11 rebounds) in the 1975 playoffs wasn't enough to keep Washington from being swept by the Golden State Warriors, with Rick Barry. Three years later, the Bullets were back again and trailing Seattle, three games to two. But with Unseld leading the way, Washington triumphed in seven games. In all 10 of his playoff seasons, Hayes averaged double-digits in points and rebounds.

The Bullets never threatened after that and traded Hayes, then 35, to Houston for 1981 and 1983 second-round draft picks. In his last season, 1984, Hayes still played in 81 games.

Ever a workhorse, Hayes missed just nine games in 16 NBA seasons. He is fifth in games played (1303), seventh in points (27,313) and fifth in rebounds (16,279). He was a 12-time all-star, making the squad every year from 1969 through 1980. The only players with more or as many consecutive 20-point, 10-rebound seasons are Hakeem Olajuwon (13) and Kareem Abdul-Jabbar (12). He was elected to the Hall of Fame in 1990 and to the NBA 50th Anniversary All-Time Team in 1996.

Spencer Haywood

Forward-Center Denver (ABA), 1969-70; Seattle, 1970-71 through 1974-75; New York Knicks, 1975-76 to 1979; New Orleans, 1979; LA Lakers 1979-80; 1980-81 to 1981-82 Venezia (Italian League); Washington, 1981-82 to 1982-83
Born: April 22, 1949 in Silver City, Miss. 6-9, 225 High Schools: McNair (Belzoni, MS), Pershing (Detroit) Junior College: Trinidad State Junior College (Colo.) College: Detroit

Spencer Haywood's pro basketball career spanned three decades. He played two positions with six different teams, and competed in three pro leagues. In 1969 he upset the NCAA's sacrosanct "four-year rule" by completing his sophomore year at the University of Detroit and leaving to make money for his family. Thus the term "going hardship" was born. The ABA tendered Haywood a contract without having to outbid the establishment NBA. Lawsuits followed, but Haywood won, with the courts ruling in 1971 that he had the right to turn pro whenever he wanted. It was concluded that, although the "four-year rule" was a convention of long standing, it had no basis in law. Through it all—from the turbulent '60s to the hegemony of Bird and Magic in the early 1980s, Haywood was a pioneering, anti-establishment player, a five-time all-star, and a record-setter in the courts and on them.

Haywood knew about hardship before the term was used to describe his condition in 1969. Born in Silver City, Mississippi in 1949, he grew up without a father, who died the year before he was born. His mother raised six sons and four daughters in a six-room frame abode on the $10 a week she earned scrub-

bing floors and a $10-a-month relief stipend. Spencer, like the other children, began working early—mowing lawns, cutting hair, and picking cotton at the rate of $6 per 300 pounds.

He ended up living in Chicago with a brother, Andy, who noticed Spencer's skill on the playgrounds. Andy sent him to a friend playing for Bowling Green University and living in Detroit during the summer. Heywood was introduced to Will Robinson, basketball coach at Pershing High in Detroit. Robinson took a liking to Spencer and became his guardian. Haywood made the All-State team for two years, led Pershing to a state championship, and became an All-American high school player.

He had hoped to enroll at the University of Tennessee and become the first black player in the Southeastern Conference. "I was thinking of being a crusader," he said. But poor high school grades and failure on an entrance exam disqualified him. Nor could he play at Tennessee State University or hundreds of other colleges. He gained entry to Trinidad Junior College in Colorado, where he "really buckled down to studies and basketball."

Haywood held a B-average and became a Junior College All-American and a member of the 1968 U.S. Olympic team. At 19, he was the youngest American ever on a U.S. basketball team at the games. The United States finished 9-0, captured the gold medal, and Haywood, teaming with future NBA stars like Charlie Scott and Jo Jo White, led the squad with 16 points per game while shooting 72 percent from the field. Approached by NBA and ABA scouts, Haywood listened to Robinson, who wanted him to go to the University of Detroit, where Robinson had been promised the head coaching job after Bob Calihan retired. When Calihan left a year later, the university hired Jim Harding as coach. "We were suckered," Haywood said. "There was no way I was going to play for Harding. After one year at Detroit, Haywood decided he would leave.

At the end of his year with Detroit Haywood was an All-American, led Division 1 with 22 rebounds per game, and averaged 32 points. He signed a lucrative contract with the ABA's Denver Rockets that was supposed to pay him $450,000 over three years.

Few athletes ever took a pro league by storm in their rookie year as Haywood did in 1969-70. Just 20, he played every game (84) and led the ABA in six offensive categories, including minutes (3,808), field goals made (986), rebounds (1,637), points (2,519), rebounds per game (19.5), and points per game (30). He won every conceivable award, including Rookie of the Year, Most Valuable Player, and All-Star Game MVP. Though Denver lost to Los Angeles in the Western Finals, Haywood averaged a stratospheric 37 points and 20 rebounds in 12 playoff games.

Haywood learned that the contract he signed had loopholes. His deal with the Rockets was structured so that he'd receive $50,000 per season, then $15,000 annually for 20 years once Haywood reached 40. It was subsequently renegotiated to total $1.9 million over six years, but, again, the majority of the money was deferred many years. Haywood wanted to be paid over five years and hired Al Ross as his agent. He was moody to begin the 1970-71 season, broke his hand, was sidelined, and left the club. He signed a six-year deal $1.5-million deal, all cash, with Seattle in the NBA.

In and out of courts, Haywood played only 33 games with Seattle, as opposing teams played under protest, claiming he was an illegal player since he was still under contract with Denver and his class hadn't yet graduated. When the furor died down, Haywood settled in to play four all-star seasons with Seattle.

He was traded to New York in 1975. There he was supposed to revive a sagging franchise, which had lost several key players from its championship years to retirement. Bob McAdoo joined the team two years later. But the combination of Earl Monroe, McAdoo, and Haywood didn't bring New York close to a title and Haywood was traded to New Orleans for Joe Meriweather at the beginning of the 1979 season. Then the Lakers traded Adrian Dantley to get him. In Los Angeles he was a reliable bench player, averaging 10 points per game, and helped the Lakers win the 1980 title. After the season he was waived and signed by Washington for his last two years. He averaged 24 points for two seasons in Italy before retiring.

Playing a combined total of 14 ABA and NBA seasons, Haywood averaged 20 points and 10 rebounds a game.

Tom Heinsohn

Forward, Boston, 1956-57 through 1964-65
Born: August 26, 1934 in Jersey City, N.J. 6-7, 218 High School: St. Michael's (Union City, N.J.) College: Holy Cross

In nine seasons with the Boston Celtics, Tommy Heinsohn was a steady rebounder and scorer and one of the greatest clutch players in the league. In Game 7 of the 1957 Finals against the St. Louis Hawks, with Boston seeking its first championship, Heinsohn scored 39 points to lead the Celtics to a 125-123 double-overtime victory. He would play on seven more championship squads in the next eight years.

When Red Auerbach retired from coaching in 1966, the first person he asked to coach the team was Heinsohn. Tommy declined, suggesting that Red make Bill Russell the coach, which he did.

In his nine NBA seasons Heinsohn took 19,903 shots, or almost two for every three minutes he was on the court. This propensity to shoot was not unnoticed by his teammates, who called him, variously, "Tommy Gun," "Gunner," and "Ack-Ack." He usually scored on line drive set shots, but it was a hook—with either hand—that became his signature.

Pursued by 42 colleges, Heinsohn said he selected Holy Cross because they leveled with him. They told him that if he took pre-med courses, he'd be too busy to play basketball. Getting married while he was still in college, he nonetheless won the varsity club award for being the best student athlete in college and made the dean's list four years in a row. An irrepressible front-line presence over his college career, Heinsohn averaged 22 points and 16 rebounds. The Celtics made the local college star a territorial pick in the 1956 draft.

During his first season he and Bob Cousy, another Holy Cross graduate, became close friends. Heinsohn was the team's third-highest scorer (16.2), behind Bill Sharman and Cousy, and their third-highest rebounder (9.8) behind Bill Russell, who joined the team 24 games into the season, and Jim Loscutoff. Now the Celtics had a rugged front-line, correcting a weakness that went back to the beginning of Cousy's career.

In 1957 his playoff averages were 23 points and 12

rebounds, far above his regular season averages of 16 points and 9 rebounds. Five times in his nine-year career he either led Boston in scoring or finished second.

In a Celtics constellation rich with stars, Heinsohn could get lost. Among all the Celtics' stars, Heinsohn got short shrift in the press. "I'd rather be on a winner with a dozen stars than on a loser with none," was his reply.

When Red Auerbach needed to blow off steam, Heinsohn was the whipping boy. A practical joker, Heinsohn put up with Auerbach's venting and once paid Red back by giving him a cigar that exploded. To relax, Heinsohn would make charcoal caricatures of teammates before games. He also kept the team loose by mimicking certain teammates and being the butt of jokes. When Heinsohn scored 36 points against Syracuse one Christmas night, Cousy joked, "Tom didn't know what to give himself for Christmas, so he made up his mind to get a lot of shots."

In his nine years Heinsohn led Boston in scoring three times and was second twice. He was just 30 when he retired because of a foot injury in 1965, and turned to selling insurance, as he had in the off-season during his career. After turning down the opportunity to be Auerbach's coaching successor for the 1966-67 season, he succeeded Russell, who had brought Boston two championships in his three years as player-coach, in 1969-70. Many around the league doubted Boston's ability to win after Russell's retirement. In nine years at the helm, Heinsohn led the Celtics to five 50-win seasons, winning Coach of the Year after the team finished with a 68-14 record in 1973 and guiding Boston to Championships in 1974 and 1976. All told, his Celtics played to a record of 427-263 (.619).

Heinsohn was elected to the Hall of Fame in 1985. He is now a broadcaster with the Boston Celtics.

Bailey Howell

Forward, Detroit, 1959-60 through 1963-64; Baltimore, 1964-65 through 1965-66; Boston, 1966-67 through 1969-70; Philadelphia, 1970-71
Born: January 20, 1937 in Middleton, Tenn. 6-7, 220 High School: Middleton (Tenn.) College: Mississippi State

The term "garbage man" was used more than once to describe the pesky inside game of Bailey Howell. It was not a pejorative term; in fact, it was paying homage. Howell scored a load of "hustle points" in close, often following up on a fast break or fighting through traffic around the basket to get a put-back or tip-in. Always a strong scorer and rebounder, he contributed mightily to the 1968 and 1969 Boston championships.

Howell grew up in Middleton, Tennessee, a town of about 350 people 70 miles east of Memphis. He was 15 miles from the nearest movie theater in Bolivar. His family might be found at church three times a week—a prayer meeting on Wednesday night and two services on Sunday.

Howell had many college offers but settled on Mississippi State. He and his family liked the new coach, Babe McCarthy. In his sophomore season, 1957, Howell led all of the NCAA major college division with a .568 field-goal percentage. Two years later he was All-America.

Detroit chose Howell in the first round of the 1959 draft. Only Wilt Chamberlain, Bob Ferry, and Bob Boozer were picked ahead of him. Detroit won 30, lost 45 and was promptly eliminated by Minneapolis in a two-game playoff. But Howell was learning the ropes from teammates like forwards Ed Conlin and Earl Lloyd (who had been the first black player to play in an NBA game in 1950). He had a strong rookie season, averaging 17.8 points and 10.5 rebounds. In his second year he upped those totals to 23.6 points and 14.4 rebounds, personal bests, and was selected for his first of six All-Star Games. In 1964 the team landed in the basement with a 23-57 record. After the season the Pistons moved Howell (and Ferry and Ohl) in a seven-player deal with Baltimore.

After the 1966 season he was traded to Boston for center Mel Counts. Boston was coming off eight straight championships between 1959 and 1966. But Tommy Heinsohn had retired in 1965 and the Celtics were still looking for more scoring and rebounding on the front line. Howell provided it for the 1966-67 season, finishing second on the team in scoring to John Havlicek and second in rebounding to Bill Russell. But Philadelphia won 68 games, steamrolled Boston in five in the Conference Finals, and won the NBA title.

Howell was again his team's second-leading scorer for the 1967-68 season, but Philadelphia's dominance continued as it won the Eastern Division, finishing eight games ahead of the Celtics. The 76ers raced to a 3-1 lead in the playoffs, but Boston rose from the dead and stunned them in seven games. In the Finals, Howell scored 30 points and snatched 11 rebounds in Game 6 to help dispatch the Lakers.

For the 1968-69 season Howell again finished second in team rebounding and scoring, averaging 20 points and 9 rebounds. Boston finished fourth in the division but rallied past Philadelphia and New York in the playoffs for the right to meet Los Angeles, now with Chamberlain, in the Finals. After falling behind 2-0 in games, and then 3-2, Boston won the last two games, including Game 7 at the Los Angeles Forum, 108-106.

Following the 1970 season, the Buffalo Braves selected Howell in the expansion draft. Before he played a game for the Braves he was traded to the 76ers, where he finished his career in 1971, playing all 82 games for the second straight season before retiring. His lifetime averages were 19 points and 10 rebounds per game. The six-time all-star's 950 games were fourth best all time, and he finished in the top 10 in 11 all-time statistical categories, including points and rebounds. He was elected to the Hall of Fame in 1997.

Lou Hudson

Forward-Guard, St. Louis, 1966-67 through 1967-68; Atlanta, 1968-69 through 1976-77; LA Lakers, 1977-78 through 1978-79
Born: July 11, 1944 in Greensboro, N.C. 6-5, 210 High School: Dudley Senior (Greensboro, N.C.) College: Minnesota

"Sweet" Lou Hudson, who played in six consecutive All-Star Games as a member of the Atlanta Hawks from 1969 through 1974, was one of the league's steadiest scorers.

Four times in his career he averaged over 25 points per game, though he labored in near-anonymity for a mediocre Atlanta team that never once made a post-season splash. He finished his 13-year career with a 20-point per game average.

Hudson gave up baseball by the ninth grade and quit playing quarterback by high school. His speed and mobility, not to mention scoring and rebounding ability, brought Dudley High several state titles, including the state's Negro high school championship.

From there Hudson played under coach John Kundla (who coached the Minneapolis Lakers to six championships) at the University of Minnesota.

The Hawks, then in St. Louis, made Hudson the fourth pick overall in the 1966 draft. He made an immediate impact, averaging 18 points and finishing runner-up to Dave Bing for Rookie of the Year. The Hawks were in their post-Bob Pettit era, but had Lenny Wilkens at guard, Bill Bridges, and Paul Silas for boards.

An obligation to the U.S. Army limited Hudson to 46 games in the 1967-68 season, but the Hawks, playing their last campaign in St. Louis, won the Western Division with a 56-26 record. Playing out of shape most of the year, Hudson dipped to 13 points a game but contributed 22 per contest in the playoffs.

The 1968-69 season began a great six-year run for Hudson. He averaged between 22 and 27 points per game on 50-percent shooting and made the All-Star Team every year. Teammates thought he didn't shoot enough. At 6-foot-5, 210 pounds, Hudson was an ideal swingman, and coach Richie Guerin, wanting to put the ball in his hands more often, made him a guard.

In a 1970 game Hudson hit for a personal high, 57 points. When Joe Caldwell left for the ABA, Hudson was back at forward for the 1970-71 season; becoming an all-star at that position. Pete Maravich was the Hawks' third pick in the 1970 draft and the team decided to showcase him, signing him to a long-term deal worth about $2 million. Despite sharing the scoring load with Pistol Pete, Hudson averaged 26.8, 24.7, and 27.1 points over the next three years.

Following the 1977 season, Hudson's 11th as a Hawk, he was traded to Los Angeles. He played two seasons and retired in 1979. He averaged 20 points on 49 percent shooting for his career.

Dan Issel

Forward-Center, Kentucky Colonels (ABA), 1970-71 through 1974-75 (ABA); Baltimore Claws (ABA), 1975 (did not play); Denver, 1975-76 through 1984-85
Born: October 25, 1948 in Batavia, Ill. 6-9, 240 High School: Batavia (Ill.) College: Kentucky

Dan Issel was the leading scorer in the history of the University of Kentucky. In his senior year, as an All-American, he averaged an astounding 34 points and 13 rebounds. He kept it up with the ABA's Kentucky Colonels, leading the league in scoring in his rookie year.

At 6-foot-9, 240 pounds, he was able to play pivot and power forward and always scored at both positions. Issel was never a flashy player during his six ABA and nine NBA seasons, and garnered few headlines compared to other stars. His career ended when Michael Jordan's began; in 1985. By then he had 27,482 points, still seventh best in history, and 11,133 rebounds.

In 1970 the ABA held its first draft and Dallas selected Issel.

The former Kentucky star said that the only way he could play in the ABA would be if it was in Louisville. The Kentucky Colonels immediately acquired the rights to Issel. He signed a $1.4 million contract over five years before they had their first draft. He scored 30 points a game, leading the league, and shared Rookie of the Year honors with Virginia's Charlie Scott.

After the season, according to Issel, the Phoenix Suns offered to triple his salary if he would jump to the NBA. But he stayed in Kentucky and averaged 31, 27, and 26 points over the next three seasons. The 1973 Finals also ended with a disappointing seven-game defeat to Indiana. In 1974 it was a four-game seep at the hands of the New York Nets in the Eastern Division Finals. The Colonels, now with center Artis Gilmore, had two excellent low post players, while the rest of the league was playing fast-break ball. Oddly, the first time Issel's average dipped below 20 points, with coach Hubie Brown at the helm in 1975, was the year that he played on his only title team.

With Issel and Gilmore providing the scoring and inside muscle, the Colonels went through the playoffs winning 12 of 15 after posting an Eastern Division best 58-26 regular season record. They bested Indiana in a five-game Final. But title or no, owner John Brown sold the Colonels because they were losing money. Issel wanted to use his no-trade clause to block the deal, but the team was not going to survive.

His new team was the Baltimore Claws, but the franchise was underfinanced and could not afford the $350,000 it owed John Brown for Issel. So Brown arranged for Issel to be traded to Denver, for Dave Robisch and a large amount of money. Now he was a Nugget. Issel had been in Baltimore for 10 days and cashed one check, which bounced. The Claws never played an official ABA game, collapsing after three exhibition contests.

In nine NBA seasons with Denver, Issel played in seven All-Star Games. He could drain shots from 20 feet and averaged 20 points in seven different NBA seasons. He was a savvy performer; if guarded closely, his patented move was a head fake and a drive to the hoop. He still played both center and forward, but preferred forward. His weakness remained his defense.

He and Alex English made Denver an explosive offensive team, but Denver gave every bit as much on defense as much as they took on offense. In 1985, Issel's last season, Denver finally made it to the Western Conference Finals before losing to the Lakers in five.

When he retired in 1985 Issel ranked fourth on the all-time scoring list with 27,482 points, behind only Abdul-Jabbar, Wilt Chamberlain, and Julius Erving. He was not named for the NBA 50th Anniversary All-Time Team, although he was elected to the Hall of Fame in 1993.

Allen Iverson

Guard, Philadelphia, 1996-97 through present
Born: June 7, 1975 in Hampton, Va. 6-0, 165 High School: Bethel (Hampton, Va.) College: Georgetown

Allen Iverson, an All-American at Georgetown, left college in 1996 to turn pro after his sophomore season. He has been a lightning rod as an NBA player, attracting such unsavory labels as "selfish," "disruptive," and "uncoachable." None of his detractors doubt his talent, however. In just seven NBA seasons he has won a Rookie of the Year, been selected All-NBA first

team twice, led the league in scoring three times and won an MVP award. In his second All-Star Game, in 2000, he scored 26 points and handed out 9 assists and in the 2002 game was named MVP.

With a lethal quickness that reminds many veteran aficionados of a young Nate Archibald, Iverson simply blows by opposing guards.

In 1993, Iverson was to serve four months of jail time for his role in a Hampton, Virginia, bowling-alley brawl. But his sentence was eventually commuted. From there, Iverson's persona—with his cornrows, abundant jewelry, and more tattoos than any three sailors combined—was not one that won mainstream approval. Still, Philadelphia made him the first pick overall in the 1996 draft.

Playing the point guard, Iverson had an impact right off the bat. His boundless talent and energy were evident and before long he was regarded as the quickest, most fearless player in the league. He not only went around defenders—and risked bodily harm suspending his 165-pound frame at the rim—but he became the 76ers' man in a pinch, taking the last shot, even if it meant an off-balance jumper.

He had game, but the game of wild shot-making and an unguardable crossover dribble looked undisciplined to some veterans. Charles Barkley weighed in on Iverson, calling him "Allen-Me-Myself-and-Iverson" and "the playground rookie of the year."

Despite rampant criticism, Iverson's 23.5 average was high among all rookies and sixth in the league overall. He also led rookies in assists, steals, and minutes. In an April game against Cleveland he scored 50 points, making him the second youngest player ever to score 50 (Rick Barry was 49 days younger than Iverson when he turned the trick for the San Francisco Warriors in 1965). He also had five straight games of 40 points or more late in the season.

Larry Brown, who coached Philadelphia from 1997-98 to the end of the 2002-03 season, switched Iverson from the point to shooting guard. Now Iverson, who led the league with 337 turnovers in his first year, could forget about thinking pass first and focus on scoring. His field-goal percentage jumped to .461 from .416. Iverson applauded the move to two-guard. "It's a lot easier to play the two," said Iverson. "I give coach Brown a lot of credit for not just deciding that I was going to be a certain type of point guard no matter what. He found a way that puts me in the position to do what I do best and to help the team the most."

In his third season Iverson won the scoring title, though his average spoke volumes about the diminished fire-power in the NBA. His 26.8 points per game was the lowest for an NBA leader since Paul Arizin's 25.6 average in the 1956-57 season. Iverson's 41.2 percent accuracy was the lowest for the scoring champ in 48 years, when George Mikan shot 40.7 percent in the 1949-50 season. Iverson signed a contract extension in 1999, inking a six-year $70.9 million agreement that would keep him in Philadelphia through 2005.

Iverson, nicknamed "The Answer," carried the 76ers to the 1999 playoffs, the first time since 1991 that Philadelphia saw post-season action. Though guarded by the 6-foot-7 Penny Hardaway, Iverson scored 30 in one game and 33 in another to lead Philadelphia past Orlando in four games. In 2000, the 76ers again reached the second round, beating Charlotte in four games in the opening series. They fell behind Indiana 3-0 before winning two straight games and losing in six to the NBA finalists.

In his fourth season Iverson upped his scoring average to 28.4, finishing runner-up to Shaquille O'Neal. The following year, in 2001, Iverson led the league in scoring with a 31.1 average, won the MVP and carried Philadelphia to the Finals against Los Angeles. After winning the first game, Philadelphia lost the following four. During that summer Iverson faced numerous felony charges after allegedly threatening two men with a gun. All the charges were dropped, however, due to inconsistencies in the court testimony of the accusers.

Iverson's lifetime playoff scoring average of 30.6 points per game is second all-time behind Michael Jordan's 33.4

Dennis Johnson

Guard, Seattle, 1976-77 through 1979-80; Phoenix, 1980-81 through 1982-83; Boston, 1983-84 through 1989-90
Born: September 18, 1954 in San Pedro, Ca. 6-4, 202
High School: Dominguez (Compton, Ca.) Junior College: Los Angeles Harbor College: Pepperdine

Of all those eligible for the Hall of Fame but not yet in, Dennis Johnson may be the most deserving of election. The man with the freckled face who dribbled upcourt with a serene, "I've-got-this-under-control" gait, was one of the shrewdest players ever. Teammate Larry Bird called Johnson "the smartest [player] I ever played with." Johnson, who played on three championship teams, could hurt you on both ends of the court.

Johnson played two years at Los Angeles Harbor Junior College before moving on to Pepperdine, where he once had 17 assists in a game. Following his junior season Seattle picked him in the second-round, just 29th overall in the NBA Draft. He got steadily better with Seattle, helping the Sonics to the Finals in 1978 and 1979. In 1978 they surrendered a 3-2 lead in games and lost to Washington. The following year Seattle zoomed past Washington in five games, with Johnson upping his totals to 21 points, 6 rebounds, and 4 assists in the post-season.

In 1980 the SuperSonics made it to the Western Conference Finals before falling to Los Angeles in five games. Following the playoffs Johnson was traded to Phoenix for Paul Westphal. He played well for Phoenix, making his only appearance on the All-NBA first team, and Phoenix won a Pacific Division crown in 1981. But in Johnson's three years the team never got past the first round of the playoffs. His liberation came with a trade to Boston in 1983 for Rick Robey.

It was one of Red Auerbach's greatest deals. Robey, a front-line player and pal of Larry Bird's, never averaged more than 5.6 points over three seasons with Phoenix, while Johnson became another name belonging on the long list of great Celtics trade heists. He helped deliver two titles in the next three seasons.

A five-time all-star, Johnson was also selected for the NBA All-Defensive first team six times (1979-83 and 1987). The only guards with more defensive awards are Michael Jordan (9), Gary Payton (9), and Walt Frazier (7). Like Frazier, Johnson will be recalled as a rounded, heady, clutch player who was essential to the championship teams on which he played.

Kevin Johnson

Guard, Cleveland, 1987-88; Phoenix, 1988-89 through 1999-2000
Born: March 4, 1966 in Sacramento, Ca. 6-1, 190 High School: Sacramento College: California

The formula for Kevin Johnson never failed. Excepting his rookie season (when he was a part-time player), whenever he was healthy enough to play 65 or more games, he delivered anywhere from 19 to 22 points and 9 to 12 assists per game. The combination of assists and scoring (on 49-percent career shooting) made him one of the best point guards of his or any time. In March 2000 he came back from a five-month retirement, thinking his 34-year-old legs would hold up and allow him to play as before. But by August 2000 he retired for good.

At his best, Johnson could break down defenses on the drive and either score or find teammates left open as defenses collapsed to stop him. He also had a perimeter game. Whenever great small guards are mentioned the roll call includes Bob Cousy, Nate Archibald, Isiah Thomas, John Stockon, and, now, Allen Iverson. The list might be lengthened to include the 6-foot-1, 190-pound Johnson.

Johnson was chosen in the 1986 baseball draft by the Oakland Athletics, but he stuck with basketball. Following his four seasons at California, Cleveland chose him seventh overall in the 1987 draft. But Cleveland had Mark Price and didn't need to hold Johnson. Halfway through his rookie season he was traded to Phoenix and Cleveland got Larry Nance in return. Johnson took off in Phoenix, averaging 20-plus points and 10-plus assists for three consecutive seasons, the only guard in the NBA to do so. He finished no lower than fourth in assists, usually behind John Stockton and Magic Johnson.

In his fourth season Johnson shot a personal best 52 percent from the field, averaged 19.7 points, and missed by .3 points from posting his fourth straight year with 20 points and ten rebounds. He was already second in Phoenix history in assists behind Alvan Adams.

Injuries first undercut him in 1993, when he missed 33 games, most of them due to hamstring problems. When he was healthy he delivered 16 points and 8 assists and, with MVP Charles Barkley, helped the Suns to reach the Finals against Chicago. With the Suns down 2-0 in games, Johnson set a finals record by playing 62 minutes—all but one minute of a triple overtime win. With Phoenix facing elimination in Chicago (where downtown store windows were boarded in anticipation of a celebration) Johnson posted 25 points and 8 assists in a 108-98 Phoenix win. Phoenix then lost Game 6.

Johnson made his third All-Star appearance in 1994. Johnson felt snubbed that he wasn't originally chosen for a spot on the United States' "Dream Team II" in the World Championships, but did make the team when Isiah Thomas went down with an injury and helped lead the team to gold.

With Johnson in and out of the line-up between 1995 and 1998, the Suns only got out of the first round of playoffs once. After the 1996 season, his career average of 9.55 assists was fourth all time among players with 400 or more games.

Johnson missed 32 games in 1998 and saw his scoring dip to single digits for the first time since his rookie season. He missed all of the abbreviated 1999 season and came out of retirement to play just six games in 2000. After Phoenix was eliminated from the playoffs by Los Angeles, Johnson retired. He is Phoenix's all-time assists leader with 6,711. His career averages are 17.9 points and 9 assists.

Earvin "Magic" Johnson

Guard, LA Lakers, 1979-80 through 1990-91; 1991-92 through 1994-95 voluntary retired list; 1995-96 (32 games)
Born: August 14, 1959 in Lansing, Mich. 6-9, 255 High School: Everett (Lansing) College: Michigan State

Earving "Magic" Johnson was a member of five NBA Championship Teams (1980, 1982, 1985, 1987, 1988), and a gold medal-winning U.S. Olympic Team (1992), and retired as the Los Angeles Lakers all-time assists leader with 10,141. He provided several of the most indelible images in basketball history.

We can still see him grabbing a rebound and beginning his end-to-end gallop. Pushing the ball, he would sometimes take it all the way to the hoop with a double-pump off glass, a swift dunk, or—better for his fans—look one way and pass the other to a streaking teammate on the wing. Another lasting image is of Johnson, all 6-foot-9 of him, backing down an opposing guard, looking over him for an open teammate, dribbling with one hand and directing traffic with the other. With his great height he revolutionized the guard position. No one since has continued the revolution.

A native of Lansing, Michigan, Johnson got his nickname during his sophomore year at Everett High School. It came following a 36-point, 18-rebound, 16-assist game that a sportswriter dubbed as Magic. In two years of college Johnson offered a tantalizing glimpse of what he would become as a pro: an all-around player who directed offenses and led his teams to victory. As a sophomore he was an All-American and led the Michigan State Spartans past the previously undefeated Indiana State Sycamores and Larry Bird, 75-64, in the NCAA Tournament title game. Johnson had 24 points, 7 rebounds and 5 assists, and was named Outstanding Player of the Tournament.

Johnson was selected by the Lakers first overall in the 1979 draft. While Larry Bird won Rookie of the Year for the 1979-80 season, it was Johnson who led Los Angeles to the Finals. Abdul-Jabbar was having a stellar series when he went down with the ankle injury in Game 5. Johnson, a rookie, had to jump center against Darryl Dawkins. With a dazzling array of drives, hooks, and jumpers, Johnson, who played center, forward and guard during the game, poured in 42 points, dished out 15 assists, and grabbed 7 rebounds. It was one of the great individual performances of all time, as Los Angeles won 123-106 and Johnson, at 20 years old, walked off with the Finals MVP award. It was the first of five NBA titles that Johnson orchestrated for Los Angeles.

The next season, Johnson missed 45 games due to a knee injury, but the Lakers took back the Championship in 1982. Philadelphia was the victim, again in six games, with Johnson grabbing his second Finals MVP. After losing to the Boston Celtics in the 1984 Finals, the Lakers regained the title by defeating the Celtics in 6 games in 1985, becoming the first

team ever to beat Boston in a Final on the Celtics' home court. Jabbar won the Finals MVP this time, but Johnson's play was against solid.

In 1986-87 Johnson took on a greater part of the Lakers' scoring load and sportswriters began describing him as "new and improved." He shot 52 percent from the field, averaged a career-best 23.9 points, and led the league in assists (12.2) for the fourth time in five seasons. Leading L.A. to a sixth straight Pacific Division title, he won his first MVP. But for Johnson the 1987 Finals against Boston may have been his greatest, as the Lakers won in six games and Johnson won his third Finals MVP. The Lakers defended their Championship in a seven-game final against Detroit in 1988, Magic's fifth and last title.

Johnson's announcement in November 1991, before the start of the 1991-92 season, shocked the world. He was infected with HIV, the virus that causes AIDs. He would miss that season and the following three, being placed on the NBA's voluntarily retired list. He did return briefly in 1992, playing in the All-Star Game and winning the game's MVP award, his second, by scoring 25 points and getting 9 assists. His stellar performance changed attitudes about the capabilities of people with the virus. That summer Johnson would be heard from again, playing for the U.S. Olympic "Dream Team" that won the gold in Barcelona.

Johnson continued to follow a rugged physical regimen, playing organized basketball. He was a broadcaster from 1992 through 1994 and assumed the duties of vice president of the Lakers for the 1994-95 season. In March 1994 he took over as Lakers coach, but stepped down at the end of the season after the Lakers went 5-11. On January 29, 1996, Johnson, now 36, was activated from retirement by the Lakers after more than a four-year absence from regular season play. Many guards would have been happy with a line of 15 points, 6 rebounds, and 7 assists. But after a defeat to Houston in the first round of playoffs, Johnson retired for good on May 14, 1996. He finished with 10,141 assists and 17,707 points.

Later in the year he was voted to the NBA 50th Anniversary All-Time Team.

Neil Johnston

Center, Philadelphia, 1951-52 through 1958-59
Born: February 4, 1929 in Chillicothe, Ohio Died: September 27, 1978 6-8, 210 High School: Chillicothe College: Ohio State

Almost forgotten today, Neil Johnston is nevertheless in distinguished company. He is one of only six players in NBA history—along with George Mikan, Wilt Chamberlain, Bob McAdoo, George Gervin, and Michael Jordan—who won three or more consecutive scoring titles. Johnston accomplished the feat from 1953-55 as a hook-shot artist playing center for the Philadelphia Warriors. When his streak ended in 1956, he still averaged 22 points and 13 rebounds and helped lead the Warriors to their first NBA title. After the six-time all-star's career ended, he coached Philadelphia and then Pittsburgh, in Abe Saperstein's American Basketball League, and Wilmington, in the Eastern league.

After two years at Ohio State, Johnston signed a pro baseball contract with the Phillies organization, becoming ineligible for

his final two years at OSU. But in three seasons with Terre Haute and Wilmington, the 6-foot-8 right-hander was just 24-33, including a 3-9 record in his last season. He told manager Jim Ward that he was ready to give pro basketball a try. Though newly married, Johnston agreed to a tryout in Hershey, Pennsylvania from the Philadelphia Warriors' owner and coach, Eddie Gottlieb.

From his second year in the league, Johnston began a trend that lasted most of his career. Not only did he lead the league in points per game, but also in points scored. Since defenders tried in vain to block his sweeping hook, he was fouled often, and led the league both in free throws attempted and free throws made from 1953 through 1955. His field-goal percentage was high for his time, and he led the circuit three times and routinely finished in the top five in accuracy. He was often near the top in rebounding, too, and led the league in caroms in 1955. In the Warriors' 1956 title season, he averaged 20 points, 14 rebounds, and 5 assists on the team's run through the playoffs.

A knee injury felled Johnston in 1958 and he could no longer get the lift for his hook shot or play physically inside. The game was also changing, with centers getting taller. "As a kid growing up, one of the saddest things I ever saw as a spectator—or ever was a part of—was when Neil's career was winding down and [Bill] Russell's was just starting," Guokas recalls. "In Convention Hall in 1958, Neil took a hook shot—and he used to be able to get that shot off on *anybody*. But Russell had the long arms, and I remember Neil coming across the lane and Russell blocking the shot, and Neil crumbled. He had injured his knee, and he looked so surprised to see that . . . His career was effectively over after that."

The following two seasons he coached Philadelphia and a new center named Chamberlain. While the Warriors were 95-59 over Johnston's two seasons, Chamberlain's impression was that Johnston was just handed the job by Gottlieb and lacked knowledge as a coach. In 1966 Johnston coached Wilmington to a title in the Eastern Professional Basketball League.

Despite his prolific scoring, Johnston was overlooked, in part because he had the misfortune to follow one prolific scorer in the pivot, George Mikan, and precede another, Wilt Chamberlain. That might explain why it took until 1989, 30 years after his retirement, and 11 years after his death, for him to get elected to the Hall of Fame.

Bobby Jones

Forward, Denver 1975-76 (ABA); Denver, 1976-77 through 1977-78; Philadelphia, 1978-79 through 1985-86
Born: December 18, 1951 in Charlotte, N.C. 6-9, 210 High School: South Mecklenburg (Charlotte, N.C.) College: North Carolina

Once, during an ABA game, Bobby Jones told an official that a mistake had been made on a foul, and that it was actually on him, his fifth. "Jones never says anything to us, so I got to think he was right, and I changed it," the referee said. "Watching Bobby Jones on the basketball court is like watching an honest man in a liars' poker game," said Larry Brown. Aside from being known for his unfailingly clean play, Jones is one of the few players who could be mentioned among the all-time greats on the strength of defense alone.

Even a stalwart defender like Bill Russell was also noted for his ferocious rebounding. Dennis Rodman, too, though known for defensive ability, led the league in rebounding seven times. But Bobby Jones, one of the great defensive forwards ever, was known for little else than defense. He earned that reputation early on, as a member of the ABA's Denver Nuggets.

"As a kid, I never wanted to play basketball or any sport," Jones recalls. "I wasn't a good athlete and all I wanted to do was be with my friends or sit home and watch television." His older brother Kirby was the athlete in the family, and Bobby often refused to play backyard basketball with his brother and father. To avoid their needling, he finally joined in. Kirby became a high school all-star and played at Oklahoma, where dad had been a member of the national championship runner-up team in 1949. In the sixth grade Bobby was cajoled into playing for a church team and in the seventh grade went out for the junior high team. Though left-handed, he began shooting with his right hand, because that's what everyone else did.

By the 10th grade he was a 6-foot-6 reed, playing next to his brother on the high school team. He preferred track, however, because "I could practice by myself and spend as little time as I wanted, then go home." As a sophomore he won the state high-jump title, then finished second to another North Carolina kid, Bob McAdoo. As a senior, Jones set the state record by jumping 6-8. He was Charlotte's basketball player of the year as a junior and senior, leading South Mecklenburg High to the state playoffs both years. In his junior year the team lost to McAdoo's Greensboro High, but won the championship the next year.

Colleges made offers and Jones, while still viewing basketball as merely a seasonal diversion, thought he could use it to go to school for free. He decided on North Carolina. After his sophomore season—during which McAdoo transferred in, averaged 20 points and 10 rebounds and then turned pro—Jones met his future wife, Tess West. Doctors discovered he had a heart condition and prescribed rest. But since one player had left the tryout camp for the Olympics team, coach Dean Smith recommended Jones. He was on the 1972 U.S. squad that lost the gold medal to the U.S.S.R. in Munich.

After he made All-American as a senior, Houston picked him in the NBA and his ABA rights moved with the Carolina Cougars to St. Louis. But Brown wanted Jones, and St. Louis traded his draft rights to the Nuggets for the draft rights to Marvin Barnes.

In 1976, his second season, Jones played in the All-Star Game, scoring 24 points and grabbing 10 rebounds. After two ABA seasons, he played his first NBA season and averaged 15.1 points per game, his personal best. Aside from playing in his first NBA All-Star Game in 1977, he earned his first of eight consecutive NBA All-Defensive first team awards. Even Dennis Rodman would amass only seven. He was an all-star again in 1978 and led the league in field-goal percentage (.578), a record for forwards. He also held the ABA single-season record, posting a .605 mark in 1975. He was also the only forward in the NBA with more than 100 steals and 100 blocks.

Jones had a seizure in college, another during his first year in the pros, and one in his third year, when he was finally diagnosed with epilepsy. The medication he took jeopardized his career. He also took medication for a heart problem. No one knew why his heart shot up to 200 beats per minute when he went into a game.

Following the 1978 season Jones was traded with Ralph Sampson to Philadelphia for George McGinnis. Philadelphia wanted defense, not scoring, and now Jones played alongside Julius Erving. With Denver, Jones, considered the ABA's best defensive forward, had faced off against Erving, then with the New York Nets, in the last ABA Finals in 1976. While Erving praised Jones' defense, Erving's six-game scoring totals in that series were 45, 48, 31, 34, 37, and 31—an average of 38 points per game (plus 14 rebounds) on 60-percent shooting. With Jones and Erving at forward, Philadelphia played in three NBA Finals. After losing in six games to Los Angeles in 1980 and 1982, Philadelphia acquired Moses Malone and swept the Lakers in 1983.

Winning the NBA's Sixth Man Award, Jones was instrumental on the 1983 team. Philadelphia won 65 games and then sailed through the playoffs at a 12-1 clip. By 1986, his last season, Philadelphia had fallen off the pace being set by the Celtics in the east. Still a 50-percent shooter in the regular season and playoffs, Jones played his last game against Milwaukee in the Eastern Conference semi-finals in 1986. He was 34.

Sam Jones

Guard, Boston, 1957-58 through 1968-69
Born: June 24, 1933 in Wilmington, N.C. 6-4, 205 High School: Laurinburg Institute (N.C.) College: North Carolina Central

Sam Jones was a reliable shooter and playmaker on pro basketball's greatest dynasty. One of his lasting contributions is the bank shot, which he developed in high school "because I couldn't make a layup," he says. "I used to spend hours in practice aiming at the strips [of tape] on the backboard." With repetition, he could bank the ball correctly at a higher percentage. He understood that there was great allowance for error if you bank the ball than there is if you shoot it directly.

"Sam has two speeds," Bill Russell once said, "fast and real fast." That speed helped the Celtics in the post-Sharman and then the post-Cousy era. Jones played on 10 Boston title teams between 1958 and 1969, second only to Bill Russell's 11 in NBA history.

Since the Celtics had won the title (their first) in 1957, they held the last pick in the draft. Coach Red Auerbach was looking for a sleeper. A former Celtic, Bones McKinney, was coaching at Wake Forest, and he recommended Sam Jones, a modern-sized 6-foot-4 guard from North Carolina Central, an obscure NAIA Negro college in Wilson, North Carolina. Auerbach took McKinney's advice. Jones, who had received only two college offers to play basketball, was honored but frightened by the Celtics' interest, thinking he'd never get playing time on the Championship squad. He nearly followed a standing offer to teach high school, but when the school balked at his demand for an extra $500, he made basketball his career. Consigned to the bench behind Bob Cousy and Bill Sharman in 1958, Jones barely played 10 minutes per night on the floor.

As the Celtics' titles increased, so did Jones' playing time. He was a 10-point per game scorer in his second year, then 15 when he succeeded Sharman as the shooting guard for the

1960-61 season. He successively jumped to 18, 20, and then 26 points a night, the latter in the year following Cousy's retirement. By then he was a three-time all-star, shouldering a greater scoring burden on a young team.

He also became one of Auerbach's go-to guys in a big spot. Auerbach would sit Jones down when, early in his career, he would make yet another speedy, but aimless, dash up the floor. But he came to rely on him for scoring punch later. In the 1960 Finals against St. Louis, Jones scored eight straight baskets and the Celtics won, 122-103. He scored 34 points in 22 minutes against Philadelphia in 1961. He scored 44 against Syracuse in 1962. He scored 37 points in Game 7 of the Division Finals against the 76ers in 1965 and averaged 29.1 for the series. That season he became the first player in Celtic history to score 2000 points. He also led the team with a .452 shooting percentage, and his 25.9 points per contest were fourth best in the league.

Jones' last year was also Russell's last. After falling behind two games to one to the Lakers, the Celtics trailed 88-87 on their home court with seconds to go in Game 4 of the 1969 Finals. Near the top of the key Jones stumbled and began falling backwards as he came around a triple pick—the Celtics' "Ohio play," so-called because it was brought to Boston by John Havlicek and Larry Siegfried—but threw the ball up with three seconds left. The shot was as ugly as the delivery, bouncing off the rim before falling through to give Boston a 89-88 victory. Jones was on his rear as the shot fell through.

The Lakers took Game 5, 117-104, and Boston needed consecutive wins to claim its 11th championship. They won Game 6 at home, but had to travel to the Forum in Los Angeles for Game 7. There they scratched out a 108-106 victory.

Post-Celtics, Jones became coach of Federal City College in Washington, D.C., a job he held for four years. He also coached a year at his alma mater, North Carolina Central, in 1973-74. He was elected to the Hall of Fame in 1984 and voted to both the NBA's 25th and 50th Anniversary All-Time Teams.

Michael Jordan

Guard, Chicago, 1984-1985 through 1992-93; retired list 1993 through March 18, 1995; Chicago, 1995-1999; Washington, 2001-02 through 2002-03
Born February 17, 1963 in Brooklyn, N.Y. 6-6, 216 High School: Emsley Laney (Wilmington, N.C.) College: North Carolina

Michael Jordan's achievements, taken in the aggregate, comprise an insurmountable Olympus of basketball distinctions. Due to the sheer magnitude and variety of his accomplishments, and his year-to-year consistency of excellence, a strong case can be made that he is the greatest basketball player of all time.

In 1987, in just his third season, Jordan became the first guard ever to score 3,000 points (3,041) and led the league with a 37.1 scoring average. That same season he became the first player ever to record 100 blocks (125) and 200 steals (236) in the same season. The following year he won the scoring title and again surpassed 200 steals (259) and 100 blocks (131). He won the NBA Defensive Player of the Year Award, and the pattern of all-around excellence he established in those early seasons would not vary throughout his career.

On nine occasions, Jordan would win the scoring title *and*

make the NBA's All-Defensive first team, making him the greatest two-way player in the league's history. No other player had achieved that feat more than four times. To pile on another distinction, in nine separate seasons he made both All-NBA first team and NBA All-Defensive first team. In light of this, it is legitimate to ask if there has ever been or will ever be a basketball talent as full-blown as Jordan.

Jordan's athletic endowments included quickness, a lightning-fast first step, and airborne ability that allowed him to create his own shot almost any time he wanted to. In addition, he used his hang time to get into the lane and score, or draw a foul. These talents aided his defense and increased his incredible variety of offensive options. When he entered the league in 1984, he relied mostly on penetration and short jumpers. He soon developed a better perimeter and back-to-the-basket game. He could post-up even tall guards and shoot over them with such improbable fadeaway jumpers that he seemed to be falling over backwards, his back parallel with the floor.

His drive and appetite for competition were legendary. His former coach Doug Collins said that Jordan "lived for practice." He once took the court and asked defensive coach Johnny Bach, "What have you got for me today?" Bach liked to prepare different kinds of double-teams to stop Jordan and Jordan would challenge himself to find ways to beat them.

When the Bulls made Michael Jordan a first-round pick in the 1984 NBA draft, they had no way of knowing what he would become. He was twice College Player of the Year (1983, 1984) and in 1982 hit the jumper with 17 seconds remaining that beat Georgetown and made North Carolina national champions. Despite those achievements, other players had enjoyed college careers as great or greater than his and it didn't appear that he would become the greatest player of all time.

The fourth child of Deloris Peoples and James Jordan, Michael Jeffrey Jordan was born in Brooklyn, New York on February 17, 1963, while his father was attending a General Electric training school. Soon after, his parents moved the family to Wilmington, North Carolina, not far from the tiny village of Wallace, where James grew up.

A sharecropper's son, James began as a forklift operator at GE, moving on to dispatcher and retiring as a supervisor. Deloris worked for a drive-through window at the United Carolina Banks, advanced to head teller and retired as head of customer service. According to Deloris, the children—James, Ronald, Deloris, Larry, Michael, and Roslyn—"grew up normal like everybody else." Their lives were organized around the kids' sports—baseball, football, and track.

Michael was the most outgoing of the children. From his father he took his sense of humor and love of mischief. Jordan's outlet was sports and he tested people there, too. Black kids played basketball in Wilmington and white kids played baseball, as if it were ordained that way. Not for Jordan. He was one of the few black kids on the baseball team and didn't back down to anyone's taunts. Nor would he back down when a white girl called him a "nigger." He crushed a popsicle on her head and was suspended from school. He was suspended another time for leaving the school grounds and practicing his jump shot and a third time for fighting a boy who erased the white lines Michael was drawing to form basepaths on the school infield.

He threw two no-hitters in Little League and fared even better in the Babe Ruth League. "My favorite childhood memory, my greatest accomplishment, was when I got the Most Valuable Player award when my team won the state baseball championship," he once related.

His hyper-competitive skills were further honed on the basketball court his father built on the property. He measured himself in losing efforts against his older brother Larry, who stood a few inches taller than Michael for several years. The two pounded on each other, and from these contests Jordan developed a passion for competition.

As a sophomore at Laney High he was cut from the varsity team. He made the varsity his junior year, joining his older brother Larry. He requested number 23, because that was roughly half the number 45 that Larry wore. He had an impressive junior season playing forward, but college scouts weren't beating a path to his door. His name was nowhere on a list of the top 300 college prospects published before his senior year in high school. In the summer before his senior year he attended a camp conducted by Bobby Cremins (later head coach at Georgia Tech) at Appalachian State University. Cremins didn't even know that Jordan was in the camp and couldn't believe it when Jordan told him several years later.

His mother recalls that Michael "hated the University of North Carolina" growing up. When Jordan started to visit colleges, however, his mother liked it that Dean Smith talked about education at UNC. Jordan showed his stuff in a game in his freshman year. He connected on 11 of 15 shots and got four steals and a block. There were still significant obstacles. Doctors considered removing his tonsils because of a severe throat problem. The decision not to operate on the eve of the first game of the ACC Tournament was crucial, since Jordan's 18 points helped UNC beat Georgia Tech. The team was on a roll that continued into the NCAA Finals.

With less than a minute to play against Georgetown in the championship game, Sleepy Floyd hit a runner in the lane to put the Hoyas ahead, 62-61. Dean Smith called time out with 32 seconds left. Thinking that Georgetown would probably be keying on James Worthy and Sam Perkins, Carolina's two biggest scoring threats, Smith called a play for his freshman. As the team broke huddle, the coach said, "Make it, Michael." Jordan, who had had a premonition of hitting the winning shot, was going to get his chance before 61,000 people at the New Orleans Superdome.

Left open for a second, Jordan caught a cross-court pass from Jimmy Black as two defenders scrambled to get to him. Jordan dropped in a 17-footer, "a rainbow," he called it, as if he were shooting in practice. The Tar Heels had their title 16 seconds later. Averaging 20 points per game in both his sophomore and junior seasons, Jordan was twice selected first-team All-America. After his junior year, he left college for the pros, without a degree in his cultural geography major.

Before joining a lowly Bulls squad that won 27 games and lost 55 before his arrival, Jordan took home the gold from the 1984 Olympics. The United States swept its games, winning by an average of 32 points.

In his first NBA season Jordan averaged 28 points, 7 rebounds and 6 assists, the first rookie since Larry Bird to lead his team in all three major categories. He also won Rookie of the Year. He missed all but 18 games to a broken foot the following season. It was after the break that he began protecting his feet by tying on a sturdy new pair of sneakers before every game.

He returned in time for the playoffs in April against the Champions to be, the Boston Celtics. Jordan gave the keepers of tradition a glimpse of the new world order, scoring 63 points in Game 1, but "Michael and the Jordanaires" lost in double-overtime. Boston swept the swept the series, 3-0, en route to its 16th title. Jordan's total broke Elgin Baylor's record of 61, scored in regulation time, in the Finals against Boston on April 14, 1962.

The 1986-87 season was Jordan's best individual campaign. He led the league in seven offensive categories and won his first scoring title, averaging 37.1 points per game. From 1987 through 1998, Jordan won each of 10 scoring titles he was eligible for (he did not qualify due to retirement in 1994 and 1995).

The Bulls did not reach the NBA Finals in any of Jordan's first six seasons. When Phil Jackson took over as coach in 1989, he had said that Jordan could still be the first option on offense but would have to make better use of his teammates to win an NBA title.

Jackson opted for assistant Tex Winter's "Triangle Offense," a spread-out attack that would make use of more players' skills with proper spacing and crisp passing. The contributions of Scottie Pippen, Horace Grant, John Paxson, and B. J. Armstrong increased. After another loss to the Pistons in the 1990 Conference Finals, the playoff frustration ended in 1991. The Bulls dumped their hated Motown rivals in four straight and bested Los Angeles in five in the Finals. In the Finals Jordan outdueled five-time champion Magic Johnson, averaging 31 points on 54-percent shooting and adding 6 rebounds and 11 assists. As Jordan clutched the Championship trophy that had eluded him for six years, a world television audience watched him cry uncontrollably.

His mission in 1992 was to win consecutive titles to prove that the 1991 team was no fluke. New York, playing inspired physical defense under new coach Pat Riley, battled Chicago to a seven-game Conference Final. Jordan settled that series with 42 points in a 110-81 blowout at Chicago Stadium. The Bulls then ousted Cleveland in six. Against Portland in Game 1 of the Finals, Jordan was on fire, hitting six consecutive 3-pointers and finishing with a record 35 points in the first half. Chicago won, 122-89. Nine days later, in Game 6, the Bulls trailed by 15 points entering the fourth quarter. With Jordan resting on the bench for nearly seven minutes, Scottie Pippen and the reserves wreaked havoc on defense and led a furious rally. Jordan returned with five minutes left and finished with 14 fourth-quarter points to seal the deal, 97-93. He was awarded his second straight Finals MVP award.

The highest highs and lowest lows of Jordan's life rushed together in 1993. After Chicago dropped two playoff games to New York, he left Madison Square Garden with his father, James, and headed for Atlantic City for some gambling. The press stirred the dust, conjecturing about how a man whose team was down two games could be relaxed enough to gamble. Jordan threatened to sue anyone who maintained, as a *New York Times* story did, that he was in Bally's Casino at 2 a.m. He

had left at 11:04 p.m. with his father, he said.

Jordan struck back with silence, granting no interviews, except a recorded puff piece with his friend Ahmad Rashad, an NBC broadcaster. Casino gambling is legal and he wasn't betting on Bulls games, so why should he be persecuted in the press? Circling the wagons, the Bulls ousted the Knicks four straight, with Jordan scoring 54 points in Game 4. In the Finals against Phoenix, Jordan scored 73 points over the first two contests to put Chicago ahead by two. "It's all about history now," he said. "We're here to make history." By "history" he meant being the first team since the Boston Celtics in 1966 to win three consecutive championships. After dropping Game 3 in three overtimes, 129-121, Jordan scorched the Suns for 55 points in Game 4. But despite Jordan's 41 points, the Suns won Game 5 and Chicago had to return to Phoenix.

In Game 6 the Bulls led by eight points entering the fourth quarter, but Phoenix fought all the way back and was leading, 98-94. The Bulls had just nine fourth-quarter points, all scored by Jordan. Phoenix had a four-point lead and the ball with 40 seconds left when Jordan rebounded a miss and went coast to coast to make it 98-96. With the 24-second clock about to expire, Dan Majerle air-balled a 15-footer from the baseline, leaving 14.1 seconds on the game clock. With 3.9 seconds left, John Paxson nailed a 3-pointer for a 99-98 Chicago lead. Horace Grant then blocked Kevin Johnson's last-second shot attempt. Jordan had his third straight Finals MVP and, with his 33 points in Game 6, had set a record with 41 points per game in the series.

Jordan should have been on top of the world. But he felt suffocated by the unceasing media inspection of his life, and had already spoken with his father about retiring. About a month later, on July 22, his father attended a funeral in Atkinson, North Carolina. Then no one heard from him for weeks. On August 13, the check of dental records of a body found in a McColl, South Carolina creek showed that it was James Jordan. He had been killed with a single shot through the chest. Apparently, the elder Jordan had grown tired, parked the red Lexus Michael had bought him on the side of the road, and closed his eyes. A trial in Lumberton, North Carolina in February 1996 confirmed that the motive of killer Daniel Green and accomplice Larry Demery was robbery.

Not happy with exposing his gambling "dark side" three months before, the media now found more opportunities for wild conjecture. Speculation was rife—in print, and on a popular spots radio station in New York—that the sins of the son had been visited on the father: James Jordan's death was payback for the son's unpaid gambling debts. When he announced his retirement from the game in October 1993, Jordan denounced the media for its lack of feeling. His responses to their questions were curt. He had "nothing more to prove" in basketball, he said.

Before the press conference, Jackson had gathered the team privately, asking each player to make a statement to Jordan. Pippen thanked him for his leadership and Paxson said how grateful he was to have played by his side. Toni Kukoc surprised Jordan the most. The reserved Croatian was so upset that he broke into tears. For his part, Jordan said he was content that "Pops" had seen his last game.

He couldn't give up competition altogether, however, and tried his first love, baseball. But the lithe 6-foot-6, 216-pound frame that aided his NBA skywalking didn't help a whit in hitting a baseball for the Birmingham Barons, the Chicago White Sox Double-A affiliate. The quip in baseball is that you had better bat your weight. Hitting .202 over two seasons, Jordan hadn't even done that.

Despite the predictions of friends like Rashad—who said he would never play basketball again—Jordan suited up for several Bulls practices, and anticipation reached a fever pitch that he would leave green grass behind for drafty arenas.

With the terse statement "I'm back," Jordan returned on March 19, 1995 against Indiana. But he was out of sync; despite scoring 55 in a game against the Knicks, Jordan was misfiring on nearly 60 percent of his shots. Against Orlando in the second round of the playoffs, he turned the ball over with seconds remaining in Game 1 and cost his team the game. Orlando won in six.

That summer, while filming the movie *Space Jam*, Jordan used a court built by Warner Brothers to get himself in championship condition. He was 32 and had been away from competitive basketball for 21 months, from June 1993 through March 1995. Could he regain his old form and lead his team to a title?

The Chicago Bulls made history in 1995-96 as Jordan led them to 72 wins, eclipsing the previous record of 69 held by the 1972 Lakers. Chicago sailed through the playoffs, crushing Orlando in four straight and then topping Seattle in a six-game Finals. Jordan averaged 30.7 points for the playoffs and led the Bulls to a 15-3 post-season finish. The team's record for the entire season was 87-13. Jordan won his fourth Finals MVP in as many attempts.

The fantasy continued during the 1996-97 season. The Bulls won 69 more games, with a loss at home against New York depriving them of consecutive 70-win seasons. Jordan walked off with his ninth scoring title. In the Finals against Utah, he won Game 1 by hitting an 18-foot buzzer-beater over Byron Russell. He finished with 31 points, 8 assists, and 4 rebounds. The Bulls won Game 2, 97-85, as Jordan scored 38 points and added 13 rebounds and 9 assists. Chicago dropped Games 3 and 4 at Utah and faced the prospect of returning home, down 3-2.

In one of the most gutty performances ever, Jordan played Game 5 despite suffering a viral condition that left him bedridden with a splitting headache and nausea the entire day. Treated with medication and fluids, an exhausted Jordan willed himself to 38 points—including a game-clinching 3-pointer with under a minute left—as Chicago won, 90-88.

In Game 6 clincher at the United Center in Chicago, Jordan scored 39 points and grabbed 11 rebounds in a 90-86 win. Chicago had its fifth title and Jordan, averaging 32.5 for the series, took home his fifth Finals MVP award.

In 1998, Chicago was put to the test. Whispers of "fatigue" began to circulate around the 35-year-old Jordan, who nevertheless won his third All-Star Game MVP (he had scored 40 in the 1988 game to win his first, and won his second in 1996). The Bulls won 62 regular season games. In three full seasons since coming out of retirement, Jordan had now led his team to

a 203-43 record (.825), the best three-year mark of any team in NBA history. He averaged 28.7 points (his first full season below 30 since his rookie year) in winning his 10th scoring title and was selected for the All-Defensive first team for a record ninth time. In a *USA Today* survey, 493 players, coaches, trainers, and general managers selected their choices for league MVP. Of the 309 (63 percent) who returned their ballots, Jordan was chosen Most Valuable Player on 253—an amazing 82 percent. Karl Malone, the previous year's winner, ranked a distant second with 35 votes (11 percent).

The Bulls narrowly escaped a Conference Finals defeat against Indiana. Jordan guaranteed victory, but with four minutes to go, the Bulls trailed by seven points. They pulled it out, however, and Jordan finished with 28 in an 88-83 victory. In the process, he became the all-time playoff scoring leader, finishing the game with 5,786 points in 173 post-season contests (33.4 points per game). The previous record belonged to Kareem Abdul-Jabbar.

For the second consecutive season the Bulls played Utah in the Finals. This time the Jazz had home-court advantage. In Game 6, with the Bulls holding a 3-2 edge, the Jazz led 86-83 with 41.9 seconds remaining after a John Stockton 3-pointer. Jordan, who scored the Bulls' final eight points of the game, hit a layup and then, with Karl Malone posting Dennis Rodman down low and 18.9 seconds on the clock, came from behind Malone and stole the ball. He calmly dribbled down court, then drove hard right on Byron Russell. As Russell slipped, Jordan planted, slid left, and nailed a 15-footer with 5.2 seconds remaining. A 3-point attempt by Stockton fell short and the Bulls won, 87-86, capturing their sixth NBA championship in eight years. Jordan posted 45 points in the final game, the 23rd time in his career he had scored that many in the playoffs. He was awarded his sixth (and last) Finals MVP.

Jordan retired after the season with 29,277 points, behind only Kareem Abdul-Jabbar and Wilt Chamberlain. At age 35, Jordan had won a scoring title (the previous oldest winner was Jerry West, who was 31 when he won in 1972). He also won his fifth MVP award. At season's close he had the all-time highest points per game average, 31.5, and playoff points per game average, 33.4. His nine times on the NBA All-Defensive first team are the most ever by a guard. And he had won an NBA championship with the last shot he ever attempted.

Despite those markers, after sitting out three seasons and working in the Washington Wizards' front office, Jordan returned to play for the 2001-02 season. After they had finished dead last with 19 wins and 63 defeats in 2001, Jordan carried them to 37 wins the following year. He averaged nearly 23 points a game and only injuries that caused him to miss 22 games kept Washington from the post-season. The 2002-03 season didn't deliver on the promise of the one before. Jordan played in all 82 contests but the team could merely duplicate its 37 wins of the year before and after one loss in New York Jordan publicly criticized his teammates. Again the Wizards missed the playoffs.

For his part, Jordan retired with the highest points per game averages in the regular season (30.1) and in the playoffs (33.4) of all-time. His ten scoring titles, including seven consecutive, are also tops all-time.

Jason Kidd

Guard, Dallas, 1994-1996; Phoenix, 1996-2001; New Jersey, 2001-present
Born: March 23, 1973 in San Francisco, Cal, 6-4, 212 High School: St. Joseph of Notre Dame (Alameda, Cal.) College: California

If any doubts remained about the kind of impact player Jason Kidd could be, he has erased them in the last two years. In 2001, Jason Kidd became the Nets' most important trade acquisition since they stole Julius Erving from the Virginia Squires in 1973.

After being traded by Dallas to Phoenix in 1996, Kidd would become a fixture on the All-NBA First Team in years to come, winning the honor four consecutive years (1999-2002). He led the league in assists three consecutive years, joining Bob Cousy, Oscar Robertson and John Stockton as the only others to do it. His 9.4 assists per game average trail only Magic Johnson, Robertson and Stockton in league history. Before he was 30, his numbers at least had earned a place among the greats.

The last two years he has shown the league more than numbers. The Nets were 26-56 in 2001, 30 games out of first place in the Atlantic Division.

Then Kidd ran every chance he got.

He was relentless in shoving the ball down opponents' throats, seeming to revive the kind of fast-break style that the Celtics and Lakers employed in previous decades. Averaging nearly 10 assists a game, Kidd took advantage of the athletic skills of mates like Kenyon Martin, Kerry Kittles and Richard Jefferson.

The team won 52 games, doubling the previous year's total, and won the division title. Once they squeaked past Indiana in a five-gamer, they picked up steam, dumping Charlotte in five and beating Boston three straight to win in six. With no one to stop Shaquille O'Neal's prodigious strength in the pivot, New Jersey was swept in the Finals. But it was the franchise's first Finals appearance in the NBA. Not since the Nets played in the ABA, in 1976, had they reached the round of champions. In a close vote, Kidd was barely beaten by San Antonio's Tim Duncan for league MVP honors.

New Jersey won the division again in 2003. Kidd led the league with 8.9 assists per game and while the team lost three fewer games than the year before, their playoff showing was even stronger. After sweeping Boston (making it seven straight post-season wins against them) and Detroit, they faced San Antonio for the title. Here Kidd and the team seemed to be running in mud against a stifling Spurs' defense.

While he would average 20 points, eight rebounds, and eight assists for the 20-game duration of the playoffs, Kidd's shooting fell to 36 percent for the Final series and none of his teammates played consistently enough to make up the slack. San Antonio won in six in a Final that rivaled the 1994 Houston-New York affair for tenacious defense and errant shooting.

After prolonged controversy about whether he would remain with New Jersey or leave for San Antonio, Kidd agreed to a six-year $99 million deal to stay with the Nets.

Bernard King

Forward New Jersey Nets, 1977-78 through 1978-79; Utah Jazz, 1979-80; Golden State Warriors, 1980-81 through 1981-82; New York Knicks, 1982-83 through 1986-87; Washington Bullets, 1987-88 through 1991-92; New Jersey Nets, 1992-93
Born: December 4, 1956 in Brooklyn, N.Y. 6-7, 205 High School: Fort Hamilton (Brooklyn, N.Y.) College: Tennessee

"There was a time," said Bob Ryan, "when the surest way to get two points was to throw the ball to Bernard King." Ryan is referring to King's 1983-84 and 1984-85 seasons in New York, when King was about as close to automatic as a small forward has even been. He averaged 26.3 points and 32.9 points in those years. King's base of operations was eight to 15 feet out, with his back to the basket, preferably to the left of the hoop. His game was to catch, twirl, and shoot, with a release as quick as any in the game. He shot 57 percent from the field in 1984, and his average of 35 points in 12 playoff games carried the Knicks to Game 7 of the Eastern Conference semi-final against Boston. He won the scoring title the following year, averaging 33 points per game.

King rarely had trouble scoring points and shooting for a high percentage. In his freshman year at Tennessee he averaged 26 points and led the nation with a .622 field-goal percentage. After his junior season, the New Jersey Nets chose him seventh overall in the 1977 draft. After making the All-Rookie team in his first season, and posting a second consecutive 20-point season his second year, he was traded to Utah for center Rich Kelley. He played just 19 games for the Jazz in 1980 and was dealt to Golden State, where he posted two more 20-point seasons. The Knicks signed him as a free agent after the 1982 campaign, but the Warriors matched the offer and traded him to New York for Micheal Ray Richardson.

New York had never had a player average 30 points per game, and had never had a player who poured in 50 points in back-to-back games, as King did against San Antonio and Dallas in 1984 (he scored 50 or more five times in all). On Christmas Day in 1984 he went off for 60 points against the New Jersey Nets. In three seasons with New York he scored 40 or more 23 times.

King also provided the Knicks with their most memorable post-season moments in more than a decade. Playing with two dislocated fingers in the first-round playoffs against the Pistons in 1984, King still posted 213 points in the five-game series—his five-game scoring average of 42.6 remained a record until Michael Jordan wiped it out with a 226-point (45.2) five-game performance against Cleveland in 1988. King was so reliable in that series that coach Hubie Brown started Game 1 against Detroit by calling King's number ("power right") 13 straight times. The 13 trips down the court produced 26 points, and New York went on to win, 94-93. Game 5 saw Isiah Thomas score 16 points in 90 seconds to rally the Pistons back from a huge fourth-quarter deficit and send the game into overtime. King then took over and New York won the game, 127-123, and the series.

Before the next series, M. L Carr of the Celtics vowed that King "won't get 40 against us." King scored 46 in one game and averaged 29 for the series. Despite his efforts, New York succumbed to a superior Boston team, lead by MVP Larry

Bird, in seven games.

He did all this before wrecking his knee with an anterior cruciate ligament injury in March 1985, which caused him to miss the next 185 regular season games. He eventually returned to the Knicks for the final six games of the 1987 season, and represented the Washington Bullets in the 1991 All-Star Game.

As a scorer, King was so automatic that many consider him to be the greatest offensive player in the 50-year history of the New York Knicks. Despite missing two entire seasons to injuries (1986 and 1992), he played until 36, finishing his 14th and last campaign with the New Jersey Nets in 1993. The four-time all-star (with Golden State, New York, and Washington) scored 19,655 points, at a career clip of 22.5 per game. His brother, Albert, played in the NBA from 1981-1992.

Bill Laimbeer

Center, Cleveland, 1980-81 to 1982; Detroit, 1982-83 through 1993-94
Born: May 19, 1957 in Boston 6-11, 260 High School: Palos Verdes (Ca.) Junior College: Owens Technical (Toledo, Ohio) College: Notre Dame

Bill Laimbeer was once described as having "the vertical leap of an anchor." His perimeter game consisted of tippy-toes jumpers and one of the sweetest touches of any big man, even from the 3-point line. He was also a physical player, leading with his elbows, hip-checking drivers, taking tough offensive fouls, and getting involved in scraps with the opposing team. Whatever NBA opponents thought of Laimbeer—and there were many who claimed his tactics where designed to cause injury—they couldn't deny his accomplishments, and would have loved to see him wearing their team's uniform.

Laimbeer twice led the league in total rebounds and was a key component in the Detroit "Bad Boys" teams, a scrappy, pugnacious bunch that went to three consecutive Finals and won NBA titles in 1989 and 1990. When Laimbeer said that the Pistons were the "Oakland Raiders" of the NBA, Oakland owner Al Davis was so flattered at the comparison that he sent along Raiders t-shirts to all 12 Pistons.

Laimbeer played without distinction at Notre Dame from 1975-76 through 1978-1979. No wonder, then, that he was drafted 65th overall in the 1979 draft. Following a year with Brescia, in Italy, he played nearly two seasons with Cleveland before being traded to Detroit on February 16, 1982. Once with the Pistons, Laimbeer asserted himself under the boards, beginning a seven-year run in which he finished among the NBA's top 10 rebounders. He finished second in 1985 and led the league in 1986.

The Pistons—with Laimbeer, Adrian Dantley and Dennis Rodman in the front court, Isiah Thomas and Joe Dumars in the backcourt, with Vinnie Johnson off the bench—finally emerged from the shadow cast by the Celtics in the Eastern Conference in 1988. After beating Chicago in five games—with Laimbeer hitting 13 consecutive shots in the final game—Detroit bested Boston.

In the 1988 Finals against Los Angeles, a questionable foul called on Laimbeer with seconds left and the Lakers trailing put Kareem Abdul-Jabbar on the line, where he hit two shots to win Game 6 and knot the series. The Lakers won the final game; if

not for that borderline call in Game 6, Detroit would have won three consecutive NBA finals.

After that, the Pistons hit their stride, winning 63 games and beating Los Angeles four straight in the 1989 Finals. Detroit won 59 the following year and, although tested by Chicago in the Conference Finals, used superior team defense—a rough, team-oriented approach that ran Jordan off picks, floored him when he drove the lane—that came to be known as "the Jordan Rules." Laimbeer was at the core of that interior defense, stealing passes, blocking shots, and bodying players who drove the lane.

For the second consecutive year they found the Finals easier than the Conference Finals. After splitting the first two games at the Palace of Auburn Hills, Detroit had to face possible elimination in Portland, where they hadn't won since October 1974, in Bill Walton's second professional game. They swept three straight and took the series in five.

Following the 1990 Finals, the Bad Boys era was essentially over, ending with a four-game sweep at the hands of the Bulls in the 1991 Conference Finals. Laimbeer missed his first game to an injury in the 1992 season. By then, he was relaxing more as a player, and spending more time boating and fishing away from the court. Through 1993 he had missed only seven games in 12 seasons with the Pistons and only nine games in his 13 NBA seasons. But injuries caught up with him the following year. After just 11 games, he announced his retirement on December 1, 1993.

Laimbeer was the 19th player in NBA history to score 10,000 points and grab 10,000 rebounds. He is still the Pistons' all-time leading rebounder with 9,430. Of players eligible for the Hall of Fame but not yet in, Bill Laimbeer is among those most deserving.

In June 2002, Laimbeer was hired to coach the last-place Detroit Shock of the WNBA. He took the team to the championship in 2003 and was named Coach of the Year.

Bob Lanier

Center, Detroit, 1970-71 to 1979-80; Milwaukee, 1980-81 through 1983-84
Born: September 10, 1948 in Buffalo, N.Y. 6-11, 265 High School: Bennett High School (Buffalo, N.Y.) College: St. Bonaventure

Bob Lanier was a 1970 All-American, carrying St. Bonaventure, a small Division I school in Olean, New York, to the NCAA semi-finals. A knee injury kept him from playing in the contest against Jacksonville University, and Artis Gilmore and his mates prevailed, 91-83. Lanier's college averages of 28 points and 16 rebounds, on 58-percent shooting, helped make him Detroit's number pick in the 1970 NBA Draft. When he left college, his coach, Larry Weise, said of him, "I've never known a more unselfish player. It may sound trite, but I would call him the complete basketball player." He is still recalled as having as soft a touch from the perimeter as any big man in basketball history.

After signing Lanier to a $1.3 million five-year deal, the Pistons weren't pleased with him at first. He was playing with a big brace around his right knee, following surgery to repair an injury sustained in the 1970 NCAA Tournament. Detroit fans booed him for his lack of speed and for not utilizing his 6-foot-11, 290-pound bulk around the basket. Rumors had him being traded to Buffalo, where he grew up. But he still made the All-Rookie team, sharing the pivot with center Otto Moore.

Once assured that he wasn't going to be traded, Lanier worked out furiously to get in shape for his second year. He dropped down to 270 pounds and increased his mobility. He averaged 26 points and 14 rebounds that year and played in his first of eight All-Star Games. Over seven consecutive seasons in Detroit, from 1972 to 1978, Lanier averaged better than 20 points and 10 rebounds a game. He shot field goals at better than 50 percent and made free throws at better than 75 percent. He was a big man with a perimeter game, a lefthander with a sweet touch from 20 feet on in.

He was named the All-Star Game MVP, with 24 points and 10 rebounds, in 1974. He finished third in the MVP voting that year behind Kareem Abdul-Jabbar and Bob McAdoo. Over the years he played with Dave Bing, Jimmy Walker, Howard Porter, and M. L. Carr. But the Pistons made the playoffs just four times in Lanier's 10 years, reaching the second round only twice.

The 31-year-old center's chances of getting deep into the playoffs improved dramatically when he was traded to Milwaukee for center Kent Benson and a first-round draft choice in February 1980. Milwaukee topped the Midwest Division with 49 wins. Suddenly, Lanier didn't need to carry the scoring burden, with teammates like Marques Johnson, Sidney Moncrief, Junior Bridgeman, and Brian Winters. The team lost a seven-game playoff to Seattle in 1980 and then lost to a superior Philadelphia team in 1981 and in 1982. In 1983 the Bucks stunned Boston with a sweep before Philadelphia, on its way to a title, beat them in the Eastern Conference Finals in five games.

In 1984, Lanier's 14th and last season, he had his best shot at a title. The Bucks topped both Atlanta and New Jersey in five-game series before Boston exacted revenge for the year before, trouncing them in five games in the Conference Finals.

Lanier finished with better than 19,000 points and 9,000 rebounds, and twice averaged above 25 points a season. He was elected to the Hall of Fame in 1991.

Jerry Lucas

Forward-Center, Cincinnati, 1963-64 through 1968-69; San Francisco, 1969-70 through 1970-71; New York Knicks, 1971-72 through 1973-74
Born: March 30, 1940 in Middletown, Ohio 6-8, 235 High School: Middletown College: Ohio State

Jerry Lucas distinguished himself at every level of play—high school, college, Olympics, and professional. After leading his Middletown High team to 76 straight victories and two state titles in Ohio, he was recruited by more than 150 schools. One college offered a full scholarship, including room and board, tuition and extras for four years. The school was also willing to guarantee his father, who made $6,500 a year as a press man, a $15,000 job. To top it off, they offered to pay the mortgage on the family home, provide a scholarship for Jerry's younger brother Roy when he reached college age, and provide Jerry with a new car and liberal expense account. Another college, hearing of this bid, offered him all that plus a fully furnished home after he got married.

Lucas turned them both down and chose Ohio State. "Ohio State was the only college which emphasized the classes it had to offer," he said. "Everyone else talked nothing but basketball. I went on the condition that I would have an academic scholarship." An unusual sentiment for an athlete, perhaps, but Lucas was no ordinary jock. He later coauthored *The Memory Book* and was noted for having recalled the first 500 pages of the New York Telephone Directory before a national television audience. "I knew every play of every team in the league," he once said. "I had them all memorized."

Lucas will go down as one of the great rebounders in NBA history. In his first year he had to make the change from a back-to-the-basket center, as he was in college, to forward, which required a wider range of movements and shots.

As a sophomore in 1960, Lucas led Ohio State to a win over California in the NCAA Finals. Playing with teammates John Havlicek and Larry Siegfried, Lucas scored 16 points and grabbed 10 rebounds to key a 75-55 win. He led all Division I players with a .637 field-goal percentage. That summer he left for the Rome Olympics. With Jerry West and Oscar Robertson on the team, and Robertson and Lucas each averaging 17 ppg, the United States took the gold by winning eight straight. The closest margin of victory was 24 points—an 81-57 victory over the Soviet Union. Twice named College Player of the Year, Lucas won an unprecedented three straight field goal titles and finished with a record .624 field-goal percentage. Kareem Abdul-Jabbar (.639) later broke his record at UCLA.

Pepper Wilson, the Cincinnati Royals' general manager, offered Lucas $100,000 for three years, the best contract offer for a rookie since the one tendered to Wilt Chamberlain. Lucas turned them down, since he was not scheduled to graduate until December 1962, after the NBA season had started. George Steinbrenner, then president of the Cleveland Pipers of the American Basketball League, got Lucas to accept a four-year deal for less cash, offering instead a portfolio of stocks and investments. Steinbrenner knew that Lucas valued his studies and was willing to delay the start of the ABL season to coincide with Lucas' graduation. He thought that Lucas would help Cleveland show a profit and would help other teams by being a drawing card. But the league folded on December 31 and Lucas never played a game in the ABL.

He agreed to terms with Cincinnati, and immediately gave the Royals good value, averaging 17 points and 17 rebounds and winning the Rookie of the Year Award in 1964.

Lucas became synonymous with boards. One of the great position rebounders, he studied the various ways in which a ball could glance off the rim and how far it would subsequently travel. Only four players ever recorded 40 rebounds in an NBA game: Wilt Chamberlain (13 times), Bill Russell (eight times) and Nate Thurmond and Jerry Lucas, once each.

He won the All-Star Game MVP in 1965, scoring 25 points. In two seasons, 1965 and 1966, he averaged 20 points and 20 rebounds per game. The only other players ever to accomplish 20-20 seasons were Chamberlain, Thurmond, and Bob Pettit. Over the four years from 1965 through 1968, Lucas averaged 19.8 rebounds. But even with teammates like Oscar Robertson, Jack Twyman Happy Hairston, Wayne Embry, Tom Van Arsdale, and Adrian Smith, Cincinnati could not get past the first round of playoffs.

Eventually, Lucas threatened to quit basketball if the Royals didn't let him go. He was traded to the Warriors in October 1969, and broke his hand a month later in a game against Los Angeles. He finished that season and the next with the Warriors, playing in his seventh and last All-Star Game in 1971.

After the 1971 season the Knicks traded Cazzie Russell to get the veteran rebounder. The timing could not have been better for New York: Willis Reed missed 71 games the following year due to knee injuries and Lucas chipped in 17 points and 13 rebounds a game. Despite playoff averages of 19 points and 11 rebounds from Lucas, the Knicks lost in five games to the Lakers in the 1972 Finals. In 1973, Lucas and the Knicks repaid Los Angeles, winning the championship series in five games.

Lucas, 34, retired after the 1974 season. He was elected to the Hall of Fame in 1979. His book on memory sold two million copies and he launched a company that published mnemonic and other learning materials for children. He was named to the NBA 50th Anniversary All-Time Team in 1996.

Ed Macauley

Center-Forward St. Louis, 1949-50; Boston, 1950-51 through 1955-56; St. Louis, 1956-57 through 1958-59
Born: March 22, 1928 in St. Louis 6-8, 190 High School: St. Louis University High College: St. Louis

"Easy Ed" Macauley was known for never getting too excited, for effortless performances, and for fluid movement. If he had strength to go along with his speed and grace, the Celtics might have won a title with Macauley playing center and forward in the early 1950s. He was traded to the St. Louis Hawks and helped the Hawks to win a championship in 1958 and become a perennial contender in the Finals. When he retired from the pro game after his 10-year career, his 11,234 points were fourth all-time, trailing only Dolph Schayes, Bob Cousy, and George Mikan.

Macauley won national fame as an All-American at St. Louis University in his junior year. The St. Louis Bombers of the Basketball Association of America paid him $15,000 in his first year, record compensation for a rookie at that time. But the club went belly up following a 26-42 season. Ned Irish, the president of the Knicks, offered $125,000 to buy the franchise, just so he could get Macauley. But Red Auerbach blocked the deal, demanding that Boston get the first choice since the Celtics had finished last in the Eastern Division (22-46) in the 1949-50 season. The league agreed and Macauley went to Boston. The Celtics' record jumped to 39-30, as Macauley finished third in the league in scoring (20.4), behind only Mikan and Alex Groza. He earned the Outstanding Player award in the All-Star Game, the league's first, by scoring 20 points.

With Bill Sharman joining the team for the 1951-52 season, Boston had what might be called the first "modern" backcourt—a pure shooter in Sharman and a point guard in Cousy—to help Macauley carry the scoring load. Macauley finished among the league's top 10 scorers in each of his six seasons in Boston. His .486 field-goal percentage in 1954 not only led the league, but was a league record.

Macauley was also instrumental in changing the game. Danny Biasone's plan for a 24-second clock encountered wide-

spread opposition and didn't look like it would get accepted. But at a luncheon in Boston, Macauley stood up and said, "Make us shoot the ball within a set number of seconds and you'll see a better game." His words were instrumental in making other players and coaches come around. In the summer of 1954 the 24-second rule was put into effect.

In the mid-1950s Boston was consistently getting beaten in the first and second rounds of the playoffs. Macauley was giving away 50 to 75 pounds to other big men; while the Celtics had no trouble scoring, they "couldn't get the ball," in the words of Auerbach. Not could they hope to deny other teams without a strong man in the middle. On April 29, 1956, they traded Cliff Hagan and Macauley to the Hawks for St. Louis' draft pick, center Bill Russell. The trade benefited Macauley, who actually had told the Celtics he would have to retire from the game unless he was traded to St. Louis. His home was there, his son was gravely ill, and he had business interests in the city.

In his first year with the Hawks, Macauley scored over 1,000 points for his eighth straight year. The fit was right, since St. Louis had Bob Pettit, Jack Coleman and Charlie Share to do the rebounding. The Hawks finished just 34-38 in 1957 but took Boston to seven games in the Finals before losing in double overtime. In 1958 St. Louis won the Western Division title and beat Boston in six games in the Finals. Macauley, a seven-time all-star, played only 14 games the following season before retiring.

St. Louis University wanted the popular Macauley to coach, but Hawks' owner Ben Kerner offered him $20,000 a year for three years to take over the team's coaching and executive vice president duties. Kerner was known for firing his coaches. Macauley lasted two years, winning the Western Division title twice. He packed it in following a seventh-game Finals loss to Boston on April 9, 1960, and was elected to the Hall of Fame that year.

Karl Malone

Forward, Utah, 1985-86 through 2002-03
Born: July 24, 1963 in Summerfield, La. 6-9, 256 High School: Summerfield (La.) College: Louisiana Tech

The Iron Horse of the NBA, Karl Malone has missed just five games (and played 1,434) in 18 years. On December 5, 2000, he took a pass from John Stockton, made a whirling scoop shot in the lane, and passed Wilt Chamberlain's total of 31,419 points to become the No. 2 scorer of all-time, behind Kareem Abdul-Jabbar. The two-time MVP (1997, 1999) has a career average of 25.4 points per game, in tenth place all-time. He was All-NBA first team 11 years in a row from 1989 through 1999 and chosen for the NBA All-Defensive first team three times. Many consider Malone the greatest power forward who ever played. When he steams in from the wing on a fast break, few dare to get in the way of his 6-foot-9, 270-pound frame.

Malone was just the 13th pick overall in the first round of the 1985 draft. His scoring average climbed from 14.9 points in his first year to 31 by his fifth. He went on to average more than 25 points in 11 consecutive seasons and in 12 of 13 seasons between 1987-88 and 1999-2000.

Always a good mid-range shooter, Malone eventually added distance to his step-back jumper. Malone and Stockton are one of the best one-two punches ever, worthy of being mentioned

with Bob Cousy and Bill Russell, Elgin Baylor and Jerry West, Michael Jordan and Scottie Pippen. Throughout the 2002-03 season, as they continued to pick and roll their way to the Hall of Fame, the twosome remained as inseparable as Abbott and Costello. Neither would have been as good without the other.

The downside is that despite their having played together for 13 years, Malone and Stockton never won an NBA title. Through no fault of theirs, Utah's strength in the middle was usually lacking. Stockton and Malone played together from 1986 to 2003. Over that span they won more than 60 games three times, more than 55 games seven times, and more than 50 games 10 times. No duo has been that steady, that long.

On several occasions Stockton and Malone have not played their post-season A-games at the same time. While Stockton had a post-season to remember in 1997—averaging 16 points and nearly 10 assists per game, making more than half his shots and hitting the jumper against Houston that put the Jazz in the Finals—Malone drew criticism for his poor showing. He had connected on 55 percent of his shots and averaged 27 points in the regular season and dropped to 44 percent and 24 points in the playoffs. He shot an abysmal 60 percent from the foul line.

In the 1998 playoffs Malone turned it around, averaging 25 points and 10 rebounds on 50 percent shooting. With Utah facing elimination in Game 5, the Mailman delivered on the road, hitting for 39 points and leading the Jazz to an 83-81 victory. He followed that with 31 points in Game 6. But Stockton had a poor series, averaging just 10 points to go with his 9 assists.

Although he's made a lower percentage of his field goals in the playoffs than in the regular season, Malone's career playoff averages of 26 points and 11 rebounds are still high. Like Stockton, Malone played on consecutive gold medal-winning Olympic Teams in 1992 and 1996. And like his longtime teammate, he was named to the NBA 50th Anniversary All-Time Team in 1996.

Malone's 36,374 points put him in striking distance of Kareem Abdul-Jabbar's all-time record of 38,387. In July 2003, Malone signed with the Los Angeles Lakers.

Moses Malone

Center, Utah, 1974-75 (ABA); St. Louis, 1975-76 (ABA); Houston, 1976-77 through 1981-82; Philadelphia, 1982-83 through 1985-86; Washington, 1986-87 through 1987-88; Atlanta, 1988-89 through 1990-91; Milwaukee, 1991-92 through 1992-93; Philadelphia, 1993-94; San Antonio, 1994-95
Born: March 23, 1955 in Petersburg, Va. 6-10, 260 High School: Petersburg (Va.) College: did not attend

Moses Malone had a pro career of 21 years, longer than any NBA-ABA player except Robert Parish. Malone was an inside force with 17,834 boards and a great scorer with 29,580 points. In basketball history only Wilt Chamberlain, Kareem Abdul-Jabbar, and Karl Malone have a greater sum of points and rebounds. Add to that distinction six rebounding titles (including eight offensive rebounding titles), three MVPs and a Finals MVP, and Malone was simply one of the greatest—and most unsung—players in league history.

Malone has been called the greatest offensive rebounder in NBA history. He began his boardwork at Petersburg High,

where he was so dominant as an inside player that his teammates would not give him the ball. He solved this problem by going to the boards to rebound their missed shots, once grabbing 45 rebounds in a game.

In 1974, when Malone was 19, the ABA's Utah Stars drafted him in the third round out of high school. He was sold to the St. Louis Sprits a year later and selected by the Portland Trailblazers in the ABA dispersal draft. Before playing a game with Portland, he was traded to the Buffalo Braves for a 1978 first-round draft choice. In turn, Buffalo traded him a week later, in October 1976, to Houston, for first-round draft choices in 1977 and 1978.

When he got to the Rockets in 1976, he provided a good portion of their offense on put-backs. When Malone led the league with 17.6 rebounds per game in 1979, he hauled down 38 percent of his team's rebounds, the largest percentage of a team's boards ever claimed by a single player.

During Malone's six seasons in Houston, he led the team to one NBA Final. Houston won only 40 games in 1980-81, but beat Los Angeles, San Antonio, and Kansas City before facing Boston for the title. Malone crowed, "Me and four guys from Petersburg High could beat the Celtics." Although the Rockets slowed their game down and kept passing to Malone, his shots (48 percent in the playoffs) did not fall with the same regularity as they had during the regular season (52 percent), and the Celtics won in six.

Philadelphia signed Malone as a veteran free agent before the 1982-83 season. He joined a team with Julius Erving, Andrew Toney and Mo Cheeks, a squad that had come close in 1980 and 1982 but had yet to win the championship. Malone's 25 points and 15 rebounds earned him his third MVP. His numbers improved in the playoffs and the result wasn't that different from Moses "fo'-fo'-fo'" prediction of three series sweeps. Milwaukee managed to win one game, but the 76ers swept New York and Los Angeles for a 12-1 playoff run. Malone was awarded the Finals MVP. That balanced team, which finished 65-17, is recognized as one of the best ever.

Following the 1986 season, Malone and Terry Catledge (and some 1988 first-round draft choices) were traded to Washington for Jeff Ruland and Cliff Robinson. Malone had two solid 20-point, 11-rebound seasons with Washington and was an all-star in both seasons. Following the 1987-88 campaign, the Atlanta Hawks signed him as an unrestricted free agent. In his first two seasons in Atlanta he led the team in rebounding and was second in scoring. By the end of the 1991 season, he was a 12-time all-star. In addition, between 1979 and 1989, he had 11 consecutive seasons of 20 points and 10 rebounds.

In 1991, Malone, now 36, was signed by the Milwaukee Bucks, and then by Philadelphia two years later. While other stars of the 1980s and 1990s—including some whose best years were clearly behind them—went to Barcelona to play on the first all-professional U.S. Olympic team, Malone was overlooked. After being waived by Philadelphia in June 1994, he finished his career with the San Antonio Spurs in 1994-95, appearing in only 17 games.

Among his many records, Malone has the career mark for consecutive games without a disqualification—1,212 games

between 1978 and 1995. He held the career record for most free throws made (8,531) until his namesake, Karl Malone, surpassed him in 2001. He still holds the career record for most offensive rebounds (6,731); the single-season mark for most offensive rebounds (587); the single-game mark for most offensive rebounds (21); and the single-game playoff mark for most offensive rebounds (15). He was named to the NBA's 50th Anniversary All-Time Team in 1996 and elected to the Hall of Fame in 2001.

Pete Maravich

Guard, Atlanta, 1970-71 through 1973-74; New Orleans, 1974-75 through 1978-79; Utah 1979-80; Boston, 1980 Born: June 22, 1947 in Aliquippa, Pa. Died: January 5, 1988 6-5, 200 High School: Daniels (Clemson, S.C.), then Needham Broughton (Raleigh, N.C.), then Edwards Military Institute (Salemburg, N.C.) College: Louisiana State

Pete Maravich is recalled for his unsurpassed ball-handling and dazzling passing. "Pistol Pete"—a name bestowed upon him by his father for his push shots that originated at the hip—left behind an insuperable legacy of showmanship. With his mad bombing and riveting array of dribbling and passing feats, he is regarded by immortal razzle-dazzlers such as Isiah Thomas and Magic Johnson as "the greatest showman" the NBA ever saw.

The Pistol played only 10 years in the NBA, never on a champion. As he drew more blame for playing on losing teams, Maravich affectionately recalled his childhood days, long before he was paid millions to play, when it was only his love of ball-tricks and dribbling that beckoned him to hit the courts 12 hours a day. His father, Press Maravich, played in the BAA's first year with the Pittsburgh Ironmen.

It was not uncommon to see Maravich leap at the free throw line and pass between his legs to a teammate on the wing. Another maneuver saw him breaking upcourt, letting the dribble get away and then fanning at it like a handball player whiffing the air with his hand. He'd then hit the ball with the last wave of his hand, slapping it to a teammate.

Maravich played nine of his 10 seasons with two perennial disappointments, New Orleans and Atlanta. "I wish I had good players all my life," he said in 1976. "Can you imagine if I had been on Washington, or Boston, or Los Angeles? I'd already have two championships under my belt, and they'd be saying I was the greatest player of all time."

Maravich grew up in Clemson, South Carolina, and legends rapidly grew up around his basketball prowess. He would dribble a ball while riding a bicycle and while walking into town. At the age of eight he allegedly won half the games of H-O-R-S-E that he played against the Clemson Tigers players. He started basketball at seven, after watching his father shooting hoops. He worked hours a day on shooting and dribbling. He once hustled bets against kids who didn't believe he could spin a ball on his index finger for an hour. "I'd play 12 hours a day out on the playground," Maravich recalled. "I just couldn't stop. When I got home, I'd have my TV dribble—learn to dribble the ball as low as I could, while still watching the television." A writer noted that while Maravich was watching the tube, the ball seemed less than one-eighth of an inch from the floor on the dribble, and that the space between the ball and floor was so

small he couldn't even see it bouncing.

When Maravich was a high-school freshman he could dump college stars in one-on-one contests. His passing feats included behind-the-back deliveries that passed through both his and his opponent's legs. He could pass full-court behind-the-back.

He then took his homespun legend to Louisiana State, where, in mop top and floppy socks, he posted many NCAA career records, including points per game (44.2), most points (3,667), and most games with 50 or more points (28; his high was 66 points against Tulane). He was the first point-a-minute career scorer in college history. The three-time All-American still holds nearly a dozen other scoring records, including a scoring average of 44.5 in 1970. It didn't hurt that his father was the college coach, giving Pete free reign and watching him with the same awe that fans did. Even so, Maravich scored more in three varsity seasons than anyone else had scored in four, before or since.

When he was healthy, his brief NBA career was almost as impressive. The Atlanta Hawks selected Maravich third in the 1970 draft. After four years with the Hawks—three of them playoff seasons—Atlanta traded him to the New Orleans Jazz for Dean Meminger and Bob Kaufman, plus first-round draft picks in 1974 and 1975 and second-round picks in 1975 and 1976. Five times he averaged more than 25 points per game. In 1977, he led the league with a 31.1 scoring average.

In New Orleans, there was some promise that Maravich and Gail Goodrich, a scorer who poured in points in droves with Jerry West on the 1972 championship Lakers, would mesh. But Goodrich was hurt in 1977, missed 55 games, and was never again the potent player he'd been five years before. The duo had little playing time to mesh. In the six years Maravich played for the Jazz, the team never had a playoff-caliber squad. He was waived by the Jazz (newly relocated to Utah) on January 17, 1980, and signed as a free agent by the Celtics five days later.

For the first time in seven seasons Maravich saw playoff time, contributing six points per game off the bench. But he never played another NBA game after the 1980 season. No doubt he was tired of all the remarks about not winning, or even coming close to, an NBA championship. He was neither the first nor last great player to play his entire career without a title. If he had stuck it out with the Celtics, Maravich would have been a member of Boston's 1981 championship team.

After retiring at the age of 32, Maravich found peace away from the game, if only for a short while. He died of a heart attack while playing pickup basketball in a church gymnasium. He was 40 years old. He had been elected to the Hall of Fame in 1987. In 1996 Maravich was posthumously named to the NBA's 50th Anniversary All-Time Team.

Bob McAdoo

Center-Forward, Buffalo, 1972-73 through 1975, 1976; New York Knicks, 1976-77 through 1977-78, 1979; Boston, 1979; Detroit, 1979-80, 1981; New Jersey, 1981; LA Lakers, 1981-82 through 1984-85; Philadelphia, 1985-86
Born: September 25, 1951 in Greensboro, N.C. 6-9, 225 High School: Ben Smith (Greensboro, N.C.) Junior College: Vincennes University, Ind. College: North Carolina

At his best, Bob McAdoo scored with metronomic

regularity. He was a 6-foot-9 beanpole who bounded around the perimeter, pouring in jumper after jumper while the league's larger centers strained to keep up with him. Bill Russell once called him "the greatest shooter of all time, period. Forget that bit about the 'greatest shooting big man.'"

Shooting over 50 percent for his career, McAdoo scored more than 50 points in a game six times and averaged over 30 for a season three times. He's one of only six players (the others being George Mikan, Neil Johnston, Wilt Chamberlain, George Gervin, and Michael Jordan) to win three or more consecutive scoring titles. Averaging 30.6, 34.5, and 31.1 from his second through fourth seasons (1974 through 1976), McAdoo won the scoring title each year. In the process he twice carried the Buffalo Braves further than they had a right to go—to six-game playoffs against Boston in 1974 and '76. The year in between he averaged 34.5, and then 37.4 in the playoffs, copping league MVP honors.

After leading the Tar Heels to the Final Four in his junior season, McAdoo went hardship, leaving the University of North Carolina. Buffalo made him the second pick overall in the 1972 draft. He was Rookie of the Year in 1973. The Braves, who had won just 21 games the year before he arrived and 22 in his rookie season, won 42, 49, and 46 during his unstoppable second through fourth campaigns. But McAdoo was never completely happy in Buffalo. To get him and Tom McMillen in December 1976, the Knicks gave up John Gianelli and cash. After McAdoo left, Buffalo dropped to 30 and then 27 wins.

New York was a new town, but no one had to explain the location of a new basket to McAdoo. In parts of three seasons with the Knicks he averaged better than 24 and 26 points a game and between nine and 13 boards. For the Knicks, the timing could not have been better; they had lost the scoring punch from their title teams of the early '70s. McAdoo and Earl Monroe, with help from Spencer Haywood, carried the scoring load for a rebuilding New York team.

When McAdoo failed to bring the Knicks back to their championship level, they traded him to Boston in February 1979 for three first-round draft picks. He would call Boston, Detroit, and New Jersey home over the next two years. But the most rewarding part of his career came after he was traded to the Lakers in December 1981.

At first he couldn't get enough playing time on a Lakers squad that featured not only Abdul-Jabbar and Magic Johnson, but Jamaal Wilkes, Norm Nixon, Michael Cooper, and, later, James Worthy. But in four seasons with the Lakers McAdoo played in three Finals, helping the team to titles in 1982 and 1985.

There had always been talk about his being a scorer and not a winner, about his lackadaisical defense, and about how he fell short of being the savior for three or four different franchises. He turned the talk off; in his 11th NBA season, McAdoo had his first title. In 1985 he helped the Lakers avenge their Finals loss from the year before, as they beat Boston in six games.

He finished his NBA career in Philadelphia in 1986, after 14 seasons. But his pro career was not over. At the age of 35 he began a nomadic sojourn in the Italian League, spending two years with Tracer Milan before moving to Philips Milano,

Filanto Forli, and Teamsystem Fabriano. Playing in 20 to 39 games a season, his scoring average ranged from 19 to 33 points per game. When he retired at the age of 41, he had played 21 years of pro basketball and averaged better than 20 points per game in 13 of them.

In September 1995 McAdoo became an assistant coach for Miami and his old Lakers coach, Pat Riley. The five-time all-star finished with averages of 22 points and 9 rebounds, while shooting .503 from the field. Inexplicably, it took 14 years for McAdoo to be elected to the Hall of Fame, an honor bestowed in 2000.

George McGinnis

Forward, Indiana (ABA), 1971-72 through 1974-75; Philadelphia, 1975-76 through 1977-78; Denver, 1978-79, 1980; Indiana, 1980, 1980-81 through 1981-82
Born: August 12, 1950 in Indianapolis, Ind. 6-8, 235 High School: George Washington (Indianapolis, Ind.) College: Indiana

As both an ABA and NBA star, George McGinnis was a chiseled but limber big forward, a kind of forerunner to Karl Malone. Physically gifted, McGinnis could rebound ferociously, beat players off the dribble, and hit the open man. The first time Bill Sharman, then coaching the Lakers, saw the man known as "Big George," he gushed, "My God, he's a six-foot-eight, two-hundred-and-forty-five-pound Earl Monroe."

He began and ended his pro career in Indianapolis, starting with its ABA franchise in 1972 and finishing with its NBA team a decade later. But his stardom was with the ABA Pacers, a team that played in five of the league's nine finals from 1968-76. That franchise—which Mel Daniels liked to call "the Celtics of the ABA"—retired three numbers: Daniels' number 34, Roger Brown's 35, and McGinnis' 30. McGinnis still holds Pacers team records for points in a game, 58; rebounds in a game, 37; and scoring average, 29.8 in 1974-75.

McGinnis grew up in Indianapolis, born to a father, Burnie, who was 6-foot-7, and a mother, Willie, who was 5-foot-10. Burnie was stern, but quick to praise his son. George sought his adulation in sports. His coach at Washington High, Bob Springer, claimed that McGinnis was "the best football player I had ever seen." Michigan State was just one of the 300 schools that recruited him. One scout said he was already good enough for the NFL.

But basketball was his strongest suit. In 1968, as a Washington High School senior, McGinnis averaged 32.5 points per game to break Oscar Robertson's Indiana high school record, leading his team to a 31-0 record and the state championship.

When his father, a carpenter, fell off a construction scaffold and was killed, McGinnis' longing to play college ball subsided. But his mother convinced him to attend Indiana University. In his lone varsity season, as a sophomore, McGinnis led the Big Ten in scoring with 29.9 points per game. He also grabbed 14.7 rebounds. His basketball aptitude assured, he signed a three-year deal for $50,000 annually with the Indiana Pacers at the close of his sophomore year. He also received a $45,000 bonus, plus other perks, like $20,000 to buy three cars.

Teaming with a starting lineup of Roger Brown, Freddie

Lewis, Rick Mount, and Mel Daniels, McGinnis and the Pacers finished second in the Western Division with a 47-37 record, but topped Denver and Utah to reach the 1972 Finals. In the Finals they overcame the New York Nets and the shooting of Rick Barry and John Roche and won the title in six games.

The following year McGinnis upped his scoring to 27 and his rebounds to 12 per game. With 47 wins, Indiana was again second behind Utah in the West, and fourth best overall. But McGinnis' 27 points in Game 7 of a nip-and-tuck series lifted the Pacers over the Kentucky Colonels and earned McGinnis the playoffs' Most Valuable Player award.

In both 1974 and 1975 McGinnis was selected for the ABA All-Star first team. In 1975 Hubie Brown's Kentucky team beat Indiana in five games in the Finals. McGinnis averaged 32 points, 16 rebounds, and 8 assists for the playoffs, capping off a season in which he led the league in points per game (29.8) and placed second in steals (2.6 per game), third in assists (6.3), and fourth in 3-point shooting. His play was acknowledged as he shared the MVP award with Julius Erving. But his stellar ABA career was over.

In 1973 the Philadelphia 76ers drafted McGinnis, then a two-year pro with Indiana, in the second round (22nd overall) of the NBA draft.

But in August 1974, the Knicks got permission from the 76ers to negotiate with McGinnis for 30 days. They sought a power forward to replace Dave DeBusschere, who had just retired. The Knicks offered Earl Monroe, a top draft pick, and cash to Philadelphia for the right to sign McGinnis. But McGinnis turned down the Knicks' offer.

The Knicks tried again in October 1974 under the same 30-day agreement, again without success. McGinnis instead inked a two-year deal with Indiana, with the proviso that he could buy his freedom for $86,750 after one year. The Knicks came calling a year later, but 76ers general manager Pat Williams said "No, we want McGinnis in Philadelphia."

The Knicks negotiated with the forward anyway, this time offering a $500,000 bonus. McGinnis accepted and New York signed him on May 30, 1975. New Commissioner Larry O'Brien revoked the Knicks' contract, took a No. 1 draft choice away from them, and even ordered them to pay Philadelphia's legal fees. On July 15, 1975, the 76ers signed him to a new deal worth $3.2 million over six years.

It was June 1976 when four ABA teams—Indiana, New York, San Antonio, and Denver—were absorbed into the NBA. Julius Erving, the greatest player in the history of the ABA, joined Philadelphia. With Erving, McGinnis, Collins, and World B. Free, the 76ers had a potent, if disjointed, offense. Both that potency and disjointedness were exposed when Philadelphia matched up with the Portland Trailblazers, a quintet known for team play, in the 1977 Finals. After winning the first two games at the Spectrum, Philadelphia, and particularly McGinnis, played an awful series. Portland swept the next four games and McGinnis shot 37 percent from the field, averaging only 14.2 points per game.

Philadelphia traded McGinnis to Denver in 1978. In return the Sixers got forward Bobby Jones. In Denver, McGinnis put up impressive numbers for the last time in his career. But in his second season with the Nuggets he was traded to Indiana for

Alex English and a first-round draft pick. English would become a lethal scorer for his decade in Denver and would win election to the Hall of Fame in 1997. McGinnis retired after the 1982 season at the age of 31. He averaged 25 points for his four ABA seasons and 17 points for his seven NBA seasons.

Tracy McGrady

Guard, Toronto, 1997-98 through 1999-2000; Orlando, 2000-01 to present
Born May 24, 1979 in Bartow, Fla. 6-8, 210 High School: Auburndale (Tampa, Fla.) then Mount Zion Christian Academy (Durham, N.C.)

Could it really be that the two most versatile players in the NBA never attended college? Not quite 24 when he turned the feat, Tracy McGrady won the 2003 scoring title with a 32.1 points a game, the highest average since Michael Jordan's 32.6 in 1993.

Still at Auburndale High, the story goes that McGrady went to the annual Adidas ABCD camp in Teaneck, New Jersey. During the senior all-star game, he dribbled down the left wing on a fast break and encountered James Felton, a 6-foot-9 forward from NJ, already committed to St Johns, between him and the basket. Tracy went up, cupped the ball in his right hand and executed a windmill dunk over James.

The gym went nuts.

Said McGrady, "After I made that Dunk, I had chills run through my body; it's like the moment I knew I had finally arrived". The recruiting newsletter Hoop Scoop praised Tracy as "the sleeper of the decade." He hadn't even been included in the top 500 prospects list before the summer.

As Tracy was set to commit to Kentucky and Rick Pitino, a call came from NBA Super scout Marty Blake asking for a high school schedule. NBA Teams wanted to go out to Mount Zion Christian Academy, his new high school, and watch Tracy play. He had already played all five positions in high school, and thus made himself eligible for the NBA draft on June 25, 1997.

"I considered college," McGrady said later, "but my dream is to make it to the top, and I had a chance to do that earlier."

Any questions about whether he would get drafted were answered in the first round, as Isiah Thomas and the Toronto Raptors made him their No. 9 pick. It would turn out that he had joined some select high school company. In 1995, the Minnesota Timberwolves picked Kevin Garnett right out of high school at No. 5. In 1996, Kobe Bryant was chosen at No. 13 by the Charlotte Hornets and dealt to the Lakers, and the Portland Trail Blazers took Jermaine O'Neal at No. 17.

By McGrady's second year the Raptors had drafted his cousin Vince Carter.

In his second season McGrady played the role of sixth man. It was also the last season he would see single-digit scoring. In his third year he led the Raptors in blocks (1.91) and was 2nd on the team in scoring, behind Carter, at 15.4 ppg.

Following the 2000 season, he became a free agent. He was acquired by Orlando in a sign and trade deal with the Raptors in exchange for a future conditional draft pick. Now he spread his wings.

He made his first All-Star appearance and won the NBA Most Improved Player Award. He led the Magic in most every statistical category, including a 26.8 ppg average and helped them to the playoffs.

He has been voted All-NBA first team the last two seasons and will probably reach 10,000 points scored before he is 25. Though his teams have been eliminated in the first round for four consecutive years, McGrady has posted 30-plus points per game over the last three post-seasons.

Kevin McHale

Forward-Center, Celtics, 1980-81 through 1992-93
Born: December 19, 1957 in Hibbing, Minn. 6-10, 225 High School: Hibbing (Minn.) College: Minnesota

Kevin McHale possessed the most varied arsenal of moves of any low-post forward in NBA history. McHale's ball fakes, feints, and footwork could make any post defender look ungainly. Forwards who muscled him inside were ripe for McHale's clever picking: he could step back and hit a fadeaway. A hyper-aggressive defender might leap at one of his ball fakes, only to find McHale ducking under him with a scoop shot as he flew by.

The story of how the Celtics got McHale is another memorable bit of Celtic lore. In 1980 Boston dealt its No. 1 and No. 13 picks to Golden State for Robert Parish and a first-round pick, the third pick overall. While Red Auerbach and others in the organization wanted Joe Barry Carroll, Golden State chose him first. Utah chose Darrell Griffith second. Then the Celtics scooped up McHale. In essence, in a single stroke Boston got two-thirds of its vaunted front line, Robert Parish and Kevin McHale—who, with Larry Bird, formed a frontcourt that stayed together for 12 years and is probably the greatest ever—for Joe Barry Carroll and Ricky Brown. A poll of general managers said it was the most lopsided deal in NBA history.

After a solid but unspectacular four years at Minnesota, McHale joined Boston as a 20-minute-a-game sixth man for the 1980-81 season, when Boston won the title. He increased his scoring and rebounding in each of his first five years, and blocked shots as well as any forward in the league. In his fourth season McHale, now a 30-minute-a-game player, won the Sixth Man award as Boston won its 15th title. After playing four years without missing a game, he missed just three in 1985, when he again won the Sixth Man award.

The Celtics would get to the NBA Finals five times and to the Eastern Conference Finals three other times between 1980 and 1988. Only the Los Angeles Lakers, on balance perhaps the most talented team in league history, kept Boston from winning more titles. During this time McHale peaked. In 1986-87 and 1987-88 he led the circuit in field-goal percentage, hitting 60 percent of his shots two years in a row. For three straight years, 1986 through 1988, he was named to the NBA All-Defensive first team, and in three other years he made the second team.

McHale's .554 field-goal percentage is ninth best in league history. It is first among forwards, besting the .550 recorded by Bobby Jones. A seven-time all-star, McHale saw his No. 32 raised to the rafters of Boston Garden in 1994. In 1996 he was voted to the NBA's 50th Anniversary All-Time Team, and in 1999 he was elected to the Hall of Fame. He is vice president of basketball operations with the Minnesota Timberwolves.

George Mikan

Center, Chicago (NBL), 1946-47; Chicago (PBLA), 1947; Minneapolis (NBL) 1947-48; Minneapolis (BAA), 1948-49; Minneapolis, 1949-50 through 1953-54; 1955-56
Born: June 18, 1924 in Joliet, Ill. 6-10, 245 High School: Joliet Catholic (Ill.), then Quigley Prep (Chicago) College: DePaul

'Mr. Basketball' George Mikan was the NBA's first dominant big man.

The Associated Press named him the top player of the half-century in 1950; he received 139 of the 380 votes cast and edged out Stanford's star of the 1930s, Hank Luisettti, who received 123 votes. As a scorer and shot blocker, Mikan led his teams to seven championships in eight years in the National Basketball League (1947, 1948), Basketball Association of America (1949), and NBA (1950, 1952, 1953, 1954). As a gate attraction, he and the Minneapolis Lakers were responsible for making the league a financial success. So dominant was Mikan that the old Madison Square Garden marquee on 50th Street and Eight Avenue once read, "Knicks versus Mikan tonight."

The nearsighted Mikan, a Clark Kent look-alike with his quarter-inch-thick glasses and the number 99 across his chest, was the leading vote-getter for the all-league team seven years in a row—the equivalent of today's MVP award. Mikan's teams played in 22 playoff series and won an amazing 21 of them.

The start of his career was hardly auspicious. As a child he was constantly teased about his height, and his only skills were piano playing and shooting marbles, for which he won a trip to Chicago to have his picture taken with Babe Ruth. Father Gilbert Burns, his coach at Catholic High in Joliet, thinking basketball and glasses didn't fit together, cut him from the team because he saw Mikan squinting. At Notre Dame, coach George Keogan complained that big George was "too awkward, lacking in talent and [wearing] glasses."

Mikan did make the team at DePaul, where coach Ray Meyer worked him hard and taught him how to take advantage of his height. Besides pitching for the school baseball team and being recruited by several baseball clubs, on the hardwood he made All-American from 1944 through 1946, leading the conference in scoring his last two years. Scoring 120 points in three games, Mikan led DePaul to the NIT championship in 1945. He signed a five-year deal for $60,000 with the NBL's Chicago Gears.

The largest player of his time at 6-foot-10, 245 pounds, Mikan used height and bulk to dominate near the basket. He faced constant double- and triple-teaming and took a constant beating. Once told that opposing players claimed he was "getting away with murder," Mikan replied, *"I get away with murder?"* Pointing to the welts on his arms and legs he said, "What do you think these are, cherry blossoms?" Over his career he sustained a broken leg, two wrist fractures, a broken nose, innumerable finger breaks, the loss of several teeth, and a collection of cuts, slashes and punctures that required 166 stitches.

He employed a sweeping hook in the lane, a shot he made right- and left-handed. Playing for the Chicago Gears, he led the NBL in scoring in 1947. Chicago joined the PBLA the following year and when the league folded within a month, Mikan was awarded to the Lakers in November 1947. He won the

scoring title that year and again the following season, a year in which the Lakers were transferred to the Basketball Association of America. Mikan closed out his only regular season in the BAA by scoring 48 and 51 points in consecutive games against New York, 53 against Baltimore, and 46 against Rochester. The scoring explosion ensured that Mikan took the scoring title over runner-up Joe Fulks.

The BAA and NBL merged for the 1949-50 season, but for Mikan nothing changed. He scored 30 or more points 25 times in the NBA's first season. He played on his fourth straight championship team and won his fourth straight scoring title. Over the next five years, the Lakers won four titles. In 1951 they finished with the league's best mark at 51-17, but Mikan fractured his ankle as the season ended. They got by Indianapolis in a best-of-three series, but lost three games to one to Rochester in the Western Conference Finals. They then ran off three straight titles, besting New York in 1952 and 1953 and in Syracuse in 1954.

With no shot clock to hurry them, his teammates waited patiently for Mikan to get open underneath. It often took them 30 seconds or more to get off a shot, but Mikan hit consistently with his patented running hook and used his size, and elbows, to make room for a variety of close shots. In 1951, league officials widened the lane from six feet to 12 feet. The rule may as well have been called "The Mikan Rule," since its intent was to counter his inside scoring. The man who had won five consecutive scoring titles finished second to Paul Arizin (25.4 to 23.8) in 1952. He still led the league in rebounding. Mikan, who had just turned 30, announced his reirement in June 1954.

He was the Lakers' general manager and coached for a while, but the team urged him to make a comeback. He did return for the 1955-56 season, but played only 37 games and retired, this time for good. Mikan went on to become the first commissioner of the upstart ABA. He was elected to the Hall of Fame in 1959 and to the NBA 50th Anniversary All-Time Team in 1996. His son, Larry, played briefly in the NBA in 1970-71 in Cleveland.

Reggie Miller

Guard, Indiana, 1987-88 through present
Born: August 24, 1965 in Riverside, Cal. 6-7, 202 High School: Riverside Polytechnic (Cal.) College: UCLA

Reggie Miller owns most every Pacers record under the sun. His 23,505 points and his 1390 steals are first in team history. He also holds the league record with 2,330 career 3-pointers and led the league with 167 treys in 1993. Aside from these distinctions, there are three All-NBA third team selections, but no first- or second-team honors. In 16 years, all with Indiana, he has been an all-star just five times. He has no NBA championship ring and has made only one trip to the Finals, in 2000. But it is Miller's reputation as a playoff assassin that separates him from many of the league's 348 players and earns him his notoriety. In one Indiana playoff comeback against New York, he posted 26 points in the fourth quarter.

For Reggie Miller's parents, survival, not basketball, was the first preoccupation of his upbringing. Miller was born in 1965 with pronated hips that caused severely splayed feet, one foot pointing east and the other west. He also was born with an open chest cavity, and doctors told his parents that he would

never walk unassisted. He wore leg braces for his first four years and was only mobile with crutches or a wheelchair. For the open chest cavity the prescription was to eat liver twice a day, every day, until he was five.

Miller was surrounded with athletics as a boy. His sister is arguably the best woman basketball player ever. His brother Darrell caught for the California Angels. Sister Tammy played volleyball at Cal State-Fullerton. Reggie distinguished himself as a pitcher early, but in his sophomore year at Riverside Poly High he was playing basketball. He was full of himself when he scored 39 points one game, but that night Cheryl scored 105 for the girl's team. She attended USC and he attended UCLA.

Over his college career Miller scored 2,095 points, third all-time at UCLA. A three-time John Wooden Award winner, he also led the Bruins to their first Pac-10 Conference title in many a moon. But Miller would ultimately bear the blame for not leading the team to a national title. He was attacked in the press, and when he bristled at the criticism, a negative image resulted that hurt his draft status. When Indiana chose him 11th in the draft, boos could be heard from those who wanted Steve Alford, Indiana University's sharpshooter, instead.

Miller broke Larry Bird's rookie record with 61 three-pointers. By his third season he was an all-star, averaging 24.6 points and leading the league with a .918 free-throw percentage. From 1990 through 1993, the Pacers were out in the first round of playoffs, despite Miller's averaging between 20 and 31 points in the post-season.

The hotly contested 1994 and 1995 series with the Knicks established Indiana as a force in the East. After losing to New York in '94, the Pacers endured another seven-game Conference Finals loss to Orlando in 1995. He played on the U.S. team world championship team in 1994 and won a gold medal at the 1996 Olympics in Atlanta.

A sure bet for the Hall of Fame, Miller scored his 20,000th point early in the 2000-01 season, becoming the 29th player in NBA history to achieve that distinction. He moved into 19th place on the all-time scoring list in 2003.

Sidney Moncrief

Guard, Milwaukee, 1979-80 through 1988-89; Atlanta, 1990-91
Born: September 21, 1957 in Little Rock, Ark. 6-3, 183
High School: Hall (Little Rock, Ark.) College: Arkansas

Sidney Moncrief was one of the best all-around guards of the 1980s. His calling card was defense and he earned NBA Defensive Player of the Year awards in 1983 and 1984 and was All-Defensive first team every year from 1983 through 1986, when the Bucks were winning the Central Division title most every season.

Moncrief impressed throughout his Arkansas career. As a freshman he led the nation with a .665 field-goal percentage. As a senior he contributed 22 points and 10 rebounds a game to the Razorbacks and was named All-American.

Milwaukee made him the fifth pick overall in the 1979 draft. His talents expanded, and he became known as a player who could win a game with a steal, a pass, or a bucket. With Moncrief quarterbacking, Milwaukee won between 49 and 60 games each season from 1980 through 1987. The team's high-

water mark came in his second season when, with Marques Johnson, Junior Bridgeman, and Bob Lanier, the Bucks won 60 games. It may be that no team in NBA history was as consistently good without reaching an NBA Finals.

The Bucks' perennial nemesis was a superior 76ers squad. Milwaukee lost playoff series to Philadelphia three years in a row—in seven games in 1981, six in 1982, and five in 1983. Milwaukee lost to Boston in 1984, the team's last year with Lanier, and was swept by the 76ers in 1985. In 1986 the Bucks returned the favor, sweeping Philly. But Boston pulverized them in four straight in the Eastern Finals. The 1987 playoffs also ended with a loss to the Celtics, this time in seven games.

For most of those years Moncrief, a five-time all-star, upped his totals every post-season. His defense drew praise from Milwaukee coach Don Nelson, who called him "probably the top defensive guard in the NBA."

Moncrief retired after the 1989 season, but came back for another go-round, this time with the Atlanta Hawks, in October 1990. He helped the Hawks in a part-time role and retired after the 1991 season. He was head coach of Arkansas-Little Rock in 1999-00 and has been an assistant coach in Dallas since 2000-01.

Earl Monroe

Guard, Baltimore, 1967-68 through 1970-71, 1971; New York Knicks, 1971-72 through 1979-80
Born: November 21, 1944 in Philadelphia, Pa. 6-3, 190
High School: John Bartram (Philadelphia) College: Winston-Salem State (N.C.)

Earl "The Pearl" Monroe was one of the most exciting players to ever step onto the court. He didn't have the speed or jumping ability to create thrills in a flash. His style had a build-up, and created an anticipation that usually lasted about 15 to 20 seconds. While Jordan and Erving could score in an eye-blink, Monroe had to work for every edge. His symphony on offense had a beginning, often spin-dribbling side to side; a middle, pump faking and twirling in the lane; and an end, a shot, usually below the foul line, which he barely got off. Amazing to tell, Monroe generally shot better with players draped all over him and with hands in his face than he did when he was wide open.

Fans wanting to see Monroe's team—whether on the playgrounds of Philadelphia, or at Winston-Salem, or with the Baltimore Bullets—were more interested in the sheer imagination of Earl's movements than in the final score. One such fan was Woody Allen, who was going to use a one-on-one sequence of himself vs. Monroe in his 1977 Oscar winner, *Annie Hall*. Thinking the sequence wasn't funny enough, Allen cut it from the film. But he always liked the euphony of the name Earl Monroe, and in his futuristic comedy, *Sleeper*, he named himself Miles Monroe.

Monroe was a soccer and baseball player growing up and didn't get acquainted with basketball until he was 14. The story goes that the coach at Audenried junior high in Philadelphia asked him if he could play, and the gawky 6-foot-3 youth ended up as the team's starting center. He then learned the game over the next two years, without coaching, on Philadelphia streets.

His graduate-level indoctrination came in Philly's Baker

League, the city's equivalent of Harlem's Rucker Tournament. He later recalled that Guy Rodgers was his main influence. Oddly, Rodgers' minimalist style contrasted with the one that later suited Monroe.

Monroe was confident enough about his game that he wanted to join the American Basketball League after he finished high school. But the league disbanded in less than two years. Convinced by a friend to visit an all-black college, Winston-Salem State in North Carolina, Monroe decided on attending the school and was coached by Clarence "Big House" Gaines. By 1990 Gaines would be the second coach in college history to win 800 games. Monroe didn't start as a freshman; he'd vent his anger about it, and Gaines would call Monroe's mother and Earl would straighten out. Monroe grew to love him.

By his senior year, Monroe's moves had him spinning in his own orbit. In 1967, Monroe's senior year, Winston-Salem became the first black school to win an NCAA Division II title. It was mostly thanks to Monroe, who averaged 41.5 points per game, leading the nation in scoring and his team to a 31-1 record. His shooting was phenomenal; he hit 61 percent of his shots for the year and averaged 53 points over the season's first seven games. When a local sportswriter tallied his points and called them "Earl's Pearls," the fans picked up on it and screamed "Earl the Pearl." He also earned sobriquets like "Magic" and "Black Jesus."

The Bullets selected Monroe second overall (Jimmy Walker was picked first) in the 1967 draft. In his first season he averaged 24 points, won Rookie of the Year, and raised the team from a cellar-dwelling 20-61 record the year before to a respectable 36-46. He was unhappy with his contract, expecting about $110,000 per year for two years but getting less. He upped his average to 25.8 the next year and the Bullets took the Eastern Division title with 57 wins. The team spent its first pick in 1968 on Wes Unseld, who grabbed 18 rebounds a game and won Rookie of the Year and Most Valuable Player for the 1968-69 season. Now the Bullets had muscle inside, plus a swooping, powerful forward in Gus Johnson and perimeter accuracy with Jack Marin and Kevin Loughery.

Three games into the 1971-72 season Monroe, after a dispute with the Bullets' management, left Baltimore for New York. Stories abounded about whether Monroe's individual style could be fit into the Knicks' team game. Publicly, Monroe did everything to embrace his new mates, but privately he bristled.

Monroe was getting less minutes due to his creaking knees and scoring less with his new mates. His 1972 and 1973 averages of 11.9 and 15.5 points were new lows for him. But in 1973 his field-goal percentage in the playoffs catapulted to 53 percent, up from 41 the year before, and the Knicks avenged their 1972 Finals loss to the Lakers by dunking them in five games. Monroe scored 23 against Gail Goodrich in the clincher and earned his only championship ring.

Monroe came into the league wanting to score 20,000—the equivalent of 25 points a night, eighty games a year, for ten years. But being sent to the Knicks made him recalibrate to fit in with an array of stars.

He played seven more years with the Knicks, getting his scoring above 20 points for two of those years. But Reed, DeBusschere, and Bradley retired, and Frazier, his backcourt mate of six years, was traded before the 1977-78 season. The team was bringing in talented players like Spencer Haywood and Bob McAdoo, but the chemistry of those early '70s New York championship teams had been irrevocably altered. Monroe retired in 1980, after his ninth season with New York and 13th overall. It took until 1990—10 years after his retirement—for Monroe to land in the Hall of Fame. In 1996 he was named to the NBA's 50th Anniversary All-Time Team.

Alonzo Mourning

Center, Charlotte, 1992-93 through 1994-95; Miami, 1995-96 through 2002-03
Born: February 8, 1970 in Chesapeake, Va. 6-10, 261 High School: Indian River (Chesapeake, Va.) College: Georgetown

The news in October 2000 that Alonzo Mourning was ill with a serious kidney disease sent shock waves through the NBA. Mourning had played just eight years, and not only his career but his life was threatened. Considering that his numbers were as good or better at age 30 than they had been when he was younger, Mourning, it seemed, had many good years remaining. A "small" center, the 6-foot-10, 261-pounder was tough in the tradition of other small pivot men like Willis Reed, Dave Cowens, and Wes Unseld. He was NBA Defensive Player of the Year in consecutive years, 1999 and 2000. Despite his size, he nonetheless led the league in blocks both years.

As yet another star center at Georgetown University, following in the giant footsteps of Patrick Ewing and Dikembe Mutombo, Alonzo Mourning raised eyebrows early with his feisty play. A ferocious interior player who would once be described as having "almost as many tantrums as points," Mourning, as a senior, was Big East Player of the Year, Defensive Player of the Year, and NCAA Tournament MVP in 1992. He was the second player in Georgetown history (after Ewing) to amass more than 2,000 career points and 1,000 rebounds. His career average of 3.78 blocks per game was second only to Mutombo. He graduated with a degree in sociology.

Charlotte's first-round pick and number two overall in the 1992 draft, Mourning was selected right after Shaquille O'Neal. Coupled with Larry Johnson on the Hornets' front line, Mourning was an immediate force, averaging 21 points, 10 rebounds, and 3.5 blocks per game while earning runner-up honors for Rookie of the Year and helping the Hornets to 44 wins and a first-round playoff victory over Boston. He drained the clinching shot, a 20-footer at the buzzer, to send his team into the second round against New York.

Mourning was selected for his first of five all-star teams the following season. On November 3, 1995, in the middle of a contract dispute with Charlotte, Mourning had a lengthy late-night phone conversation with Miami coach Pat Riley. Soon after, the Georgetown alumnus agreed to a trade, and Glen Rice went to Charlotte. In Miami, Mourning got scoring help from Tim Hardaway and Rex Chapman. He set a personal and team record with 22 rebounds in a January game. In the first round of the playoffs the Heat played the Bulls (72-10), who lambasted them three straight, by an average margin of 23 points. In the first game Mourning tied a team playoff record with 30 points.

In 1998-99 Mourning averaged 20 points, 11 rebounds, led the league in blocks (3.91), and finished second to Karl Malone

in the MVP voting. The next year Mourning again led the league in blocked shots and finished third in the MVP voting. In what had become an annual, and very hard-played, rite of passage, New York overcame a three-two deficit against Miami in the Conference semi-finals, winning the last two games by point margins of two and one and beating the Heat for the third time in four years. Mourning played a physical series, but got little help from teammates like Tim Hardaway.

While Mourning has never developed a varied offensive repertoire around the hoop, he nevertheless averaged 21 points per game scorer through his first eight seasons. During that span he also connected on 53 percent of his shots and grabbed 10 boards a night. He twice led the league in blocks, consistently getting more rejections than taller centers like O'Neal and Ewing. He was also a member of two gold medal-winning teams, the U.S. World Championship team in 1994 and the U.S. Olympic team in 2000.

Mourning first received treatment for his illness, focal glomerulosclerosis, in October 2000, to see whether medicine could forestall the need for dialysis or a kidney transplant. The disease attacks small filters in the kidney that remove waste from the blood, causing protein to spill into the urine and scar the kidney. The disease tends to affect younger men, with more prevalence in African Americans. Treatment leads to remission in about 50 percent of patients, at best

For his career, Mourning has averaged 20.3 points and 9.80 rebounds per game, but in his 2001 his numbers dropped off to 13.6 and 7.80 and 15.7 and 8.40 in the 2002 campaign. In September 2002, shortly before training camp, Mourning was advised by doctors to skip the 2002-03 season because test results indicated his condition had worsened. Nonetheless, following the 2003 season, the free agent center signed a four-year, $20 million contract with the Nets.

Chris Mullin

Forward, Golden State, 1985-86 through 1996-97; Indiana, 1997-98 through 1999-2000; Golden State 2000-01
Born: July 30, 1963 in New York 6-7, 215 High School: Power Memorial (New York), then Xaverian (Brooklyn, New York) College: St. John's

Chris Mullin won the John Wooden Award as the nation's top college player in 1985. He shared Big East Conference Player of the Year with Georgetown's Patrick Ewing and led St. John's to the NCAA's Final Four. Mullin had the reputation of being able to win a game in many ways—with a perimeter shot or a 3-pointer, a clutch free throw, a pass in traffic. On the strength of his college career Mullin was drafted in the first round, seventh pick overall, by the Golden State Warriors.

Before he did any of that he was the prototypical gym rat at Xaverian High in Brooklyn. He got a key to the gym and would turn up shooting at all hours for shoot-arounds. Mullin wore No. 17, a reminder of the all-around player he strived to be. The jersey number was the same as that of his boyhood legend, John Havlicek. It didn't take long for him to adapt to the pro game, in which even small forwards were taller and faster. From a part-time role and 14 points a game, he went to 15, 20, 26, 25, 25, 25, and 25 points over the next seven seasons. In five of those first seven seasons Mullin shot 88 or 89 percent from the free throw line. He led Golden State in scoring for six straight years, 1988 through 1993. In 1991 he had a career playoff high, hitting 16 of 21 field goal attempts against the Lakers in the Conference semi-finals.

The left-handed Mullin was already a four-time all-star when he was named to the All-NBA first team in 1992. That same year he was selected to play on the U.S. Olympic "Dream Team" in Barcelona. Playing in all eight Olympic games, Mullin was no tag-along. He hit 62 percent of his field goals and led the team in 3-pointers made (14) and 3-point percentage (54). He finished fourth on the team in scoring, behind Charles Barkley, Michael Jordan, and Karl Malone. Mullin also won an Olympic gold medal with the 1984 team.

For all his success, however, during his years with Golden State Mullin was alone, a New Yorker transplanted to the West Coast. He ate junk food, drank beer and ballooned from 210 to 240 pounds. He was suspended in December 1987 for missing a workout, and two days later he voluntarily entered an alcohol rehabilitation program in Southern California.

Mullin spent a month in the hospital and returned to work out with Mark Grabow, the team's conditioning coach. "After he worked out for 90 minutes, I told him to shoot 10 free throws," Grabow said. "He hadn't touched a basketball in 30 days but made 91 in a row." Mullin became a workout zealot, visiting the Oakland Coliseum court at all hours and even on game days.

He trimmed down to 210 pounds and pared his body fat from 15 to 6 percent, lower than the NBA average. Mullin led the NBA in minutes played for the 1990-91 and 1991-92 seasons, averaging 40 and 41 per contest while missing just one of 164 games. In 1993 he joined Wilt Chamberlain as the only Warrior to average more than 25 points per game in five straight seasons. But he tore the collateral ligament in his right thumb in a January game and ended up missing 36 games. He then tore a ligament in his right hand to begin the next season and missed 20 games. It got worse in the 1994-95 season, as Mullin fractured a bone in his left leg. Later, after he passed out at home, he was diagnosed with vasovagal syncope, a non-life-threatening condition that causes blackouts. He missed 57 games. After a torn ligament in his right ring finger, he missed 27 more games the following season.

In the 1997 season, his 12th with Golden State, Mullin appeared in 79 games. After the season he was traded to Indiana. In 1998 (against Chicago, when Mullin was 34) and 1999 (against New York), the Pacers reached the Conference Finals. In 2000 they made the NBA Finals, but Mullin played a total of 12 minutes and contributed just four points.

Back with Golden State, Mullin's 2000-01 season was his 16th and last. His career line reads 18.2 points per game on 51 percent shooting from the field and 86 percent from the free throw line.

Norm Nixon

Guard, LA Lakers, 1977-78 through 1982-83; San Diego 1983-84 (moved to LA for 1984-85) through 1988-89
Born: October 10, 1955 in Macon, Ga. 6-2, 175 High School: Southwest (Macon, Ga.) College: Duquesne

Norm Nixon was the Lakers' point guard in the 1977-78 season, but he moved to shooting guard when Magic Johnson

joined the team in 1979. The Lakers went on to win two titles in three years with Nixon in the backcourt. A three-time all-star, Nixon, like Mo Cheeks and others who played next to bigger stars, was bound to be overlooked. But the record shows that the wiry Nixon was quick, perennially among the league's best playmakers, and an excellent defender.

The Lakers chose Nixon in the first round, 22nd overall, in the 1977 draft, picking him after Kenny Carr (sixth) and Brad Davis (15th). Nixon soon flourished, becoming a full-time player, making the NBA All-Rookie Team, and leading the Lakers in assists and steals over his first two years. He also set a club rookie record with 14 assists on November 20, 1977.

Although some veterans complained that Magic Johnson was handling the ball too much when he came on board in 1979, Nixon was not one of them. Even with Johnson, Nixon was the team assists leader for the 1979-80 and 1980-81 seasons. In 1980 Los Angeles finished 60-22, the second best record to Boston. In the post-season the Lakers sailed past Phoenix and Seattle in five games and beat Philadelphia in a six-game Final. Nixon was a playoff workhorse, averaging 40.5 minutes and posting 17 points and 8 assists per game.

In the 1980-81 season the defending champions melted down. Johnson tore up his knee, missed 45 games, and returned late in the season. The Lakers finished 54-28. Before the playoffs, Nixon, talking to a writer about the sacrifices he'd made for Johnson, added: "Anyway, 15 years from now everyone will have forgotten Magic." The story ran the day the series opened, and a 40-42 Houston team upset Los Angeles in the Forum for a 1-0 lead in a three-game miniseries. In Houston for the second game, Johnson lashed back. "If Norm Nixon feels that strongly about having the ball, we'll get him a ball, put his name on it, and he can keep it under his arm during the game," he said. The two talked before the second game, which the Lakers won. But team divisions surfaced before Game 3 in the locker room over quotes attributed to Johnson in the paper. The team went out and lost, 87-86, when Johnson, who'd already missed 13 of 15 shots, put up a running, last-second air ball on a play designed for Jabbar.

In 1982, Nixon's first all-star season, the Lakers blanked Phoenix and San Antonio in four games before beating Philadelphia in the Finals. Nixon improved his averages to 20 points and eight rebounds in the post-season.

During 1982-83, Nixon had been convinced that the organization, especially Jerry West (with whom he had differences when he coached), was out to get him. His suspicion was well-founded, since the Lakers had put a private detective on his tail to check out drug rumors. Nixon spotted the tail and the story wound up in the newspapers. The rumors about him were never substantiated.

After the season, his sixth with Los Angeles, he was traded to the San Diego Clippers in exchange for the draft rights to Byron Scott. In San Diego there was no slacking off for Nixon. For the fourth time in his career he played a full 82 games, averaging 17 points and a personal best 11.1 assists, finishing just behind Magic in a tie for second with Isiah Thomas in that category. In 1985 he finished fourth in assists and in 1986, eighth. All told he finished in the top five in assists seven times and in the top 10 on nine occasions. He made the All-Star Game for

the third and final time in 1987 but did not play, and missed the entire 1987-88 season with an Achilles tendon injury.

Nixon finished his NBA career in 1989 before playing his last pro season with Scavolini Pesaro in Italy. His lifetime line was 15.7 points and 8.3 assists per game on 48 percent shooting. He was better in the playoffs, with 17.7 points and 8 assists. His single game assists high was 21, and his 6,386 assists were ninth in league history when he retired.

Hakeem Olajuwon

Center, Houston, 1984-85 through 2000-01; Toronto, 2001-02
Born: January 21, 1963 in Lagos, Nigeria 7-0, 255 High School: Muslim Teachers College (Lagos) College: Houston

Hakeem Olajuwon was one of the most versatile centers in NBA history. When Olajuwon went to Pete Newell's Big Man Camp, Newell looked at his footwork and asked, "Who taught you that?" Olajuwon said, "Nobody, that's my footwork." Unlike most American athletes who learn eye-hand coordination, Olajuwon learned eye-foot coordination, from having played soccer in Nigeria. Before the 1994 Finals, *New York Times* columnist Harvey Araton wrote, "He has the feet of a dancer and the touch of a surgeon." That was just before "The Dream" outplayed Patrick Ewing, David Robinson and Shaquille O'Neal in succession over the next 13 months of playoffs. In the 1994 playoffs he averaged 29 points, 11 rebounds and 4 blocks, shooting 52 percent from the field. In 1995, he improved to 33 points, 10 rebounds, 3 blocks, and 53 percent from the field. He won consecutive Finals MVPs, one of only three players—along with Michael Jordan and Shaquille O'Neal—to accomplish the feat.

Less noted was how the most productive scoring seasons of his came when he was 30, 31, and 32 years old, in his ninth, 10th and 11th seasons. Olajuwon's play in the third millennium did match his bust-out performance of the 1994 and 1995 post-season, when he led the Houston Rockets to consecutive Championships. But the 18-year veteran retired as the all-time leader in blocks (3,830) and is in the top 20 in points, rebounds and steals.

Akeem Olajuwon (he added the 'H' to his first name in 1991) first started piling up distinctions at the University of Houston. He was Outstanding Player of the 1983 NCAA Tournament, though Houston lost to North Carolina State, 54-52, on a last-second putback by Lorenzo Charles. Up until then Olajuwon had dominated, scoring 20 points and grabbing 18 rebounds. The following year Olajuwon led all Division I players in field-goal percentage (.675), rebounds (13.5), and blocked shots (5.6). But in the NCAA Finals the Cougars succumbed again, this time to Georgetown, 84-75. It was no surprise when the Houston Rockets made Olajuwon the first pick overall in the 1984 draft.

Making the All-Rookie team for the 1984-85 season, he averaged 21 points and 11 rebounds, the first of 12 successive years in which he averaged more than 20 points and 10 rebounds. Houston shot up to 48 wins and a playoff berth that first year, up from 29 wins the season before. In Olajuwon's second year the Rockets posted 51 wins and, after beating Los Angeles in five games in the Western Conference Finals, earned a chance to play

for the Championship against Boston. With Houston behind three games to one, Olajuwon set a Finals record with eight blocked shots on June 5, 1986. But the Celtics closed out the series in six games, winning 114-97 in Boston.

Houston didn't return to the Finals for another eight years. Olajuwon won the MVP in 1994, but the Rockets fell behind three games to two against New York in the Finals. With seconds remaining in Game 6 at Houston, John Starks broke free for a 3-point attempt that might have won the title for New York. But Olajuwon deflected the shot and Houston had an 86-84 win. The Rockets had better control of Game 7, winning 90-84.

Olajuwon had brought the city its first title in a major sport. Before he was awarded the Finals MVP trophy, he just sat courtside and let the realization of the championship wash over him. Several weeks before, he had invited his teammates out to center court to celebrate with him when he accepted the MVP trophy.

The following season, Houston, now with Clyde Drexler, swept the Orlando Magic in the Finals. That same year—1996—saw the Nigerian-born center named to the NBA's 50th Anniversary All-Time Team. The naturalized U.S. citizen also played on the gold medal-winning U.S. Olympic team. During the 1996-97 season, it was discovered that Olajuwon had a heart condition. An indomitable competitor, he nevertheless played in all but four of Houston's games.

Olajuwon finished up his 18-year career with the Toronto Raptors but was forced to retire on November 9, 2002, with a back injury after the 2001-02 season. His 26,946 points put him in tenth place all-time.

Shaquille O'Neal

Center, Orlando, 1992-93 through 1995-96; LA Lakers, 1996-97 to present
Born: March 6, 1972 in Newark, N.J. 7-1, 338 High School: Cole (San Antonio, Tex.) College: Louisiana State

In November 1996, a Bronx cheer could be heard across the fruited plain when Shaquille O'Neal, just 24 and with only four seasons under his belt, was selected as one of the league's 50 greatest all-time players. Seven years later, the derisive comments have stopped. At 31, O'Neal's body of work now includes two scoring titles (1995, 2000), four All-NBA first team selections (1998, 2000, 2001, 2002), an MVP (2000), and an NBA title and Finals MVP that same year (he also was Finals MVP in 2001 and 2002). When O'Neal is on the low blocks, and begins backing in, defenders scatter like tenpins. He has also learned to hit turnarounds from the baseline. His strength in the pivot compares favorably with Wilt Chamberlain's and his career average of 27.6 points per game is the third highest of all-time, trailing only Michael Jordan and Chamberlain.

His first and middle names, Shaquille Rashaun, mean "Little Warrior" in Arabic.

After the 2000 Finals, when he averaged 38 points (on .611 shooting) and 17 rebounds, he seemed anything but little and very much the warrior. Indiana's interior defense, like that of 28 other NBA teams, simply could not deal with his size (7-foot-1, 338 pounds) and agility in the post. His performance during the year and in the post-season quieted his early critics, who

contended that his game was limited and that he was an over-hyped, overrated marketing tool of the NBA, leading the league only in rap albums, feature films, and martial arts video games.

O'Neal was born in Newark, New Jersey, in 1972. His father, Philip Harrison, wanting to move his family out of the inner city, joined the army. He was sent overseas before he married Lucille O'Neal, who decided to give her infant son a "unique" name. Shaquille would become an army brat, traveling from base to base around the globe. His father, a drill sergeant who stood 6-foot-5 and 250 pounds, took no nonsense, even from his kids, who answered him "Yes sir" and "No sir."

O'Neal was already over six feet tall at the time he entered junior high. The family was stationed in Germany, where there was some anti-American feeling in the early and mid-1980s, and Shaquille, who got teased about his height and grades, got into fights. His father cured him of that. "He wore me out with a paddle," O'Neal recalls. "I told him the world had too many followers," said the father. "What he needed to be was a leader."

A basketball clinic at the base was being run by Dale Brown, Louisiana State University's head coach. "What rank are you?" were the first words Brown uttered looking at the 6-foot-6 boy. "I don't have a rank, sir," O'Neal replied. "I'm just 13." A couple of years later O'Neal wrote Brown a letter, telling him he was back in the United States and would be going to Robert G. Cole High School at Fort Sam Houston military base in San Antonio. He was 6-foot-9 and 240, the letter announced, and just entering his junior year.

In November, before his senior year started at Cole, O'Neal signed a letter of intent to play at LSU. "That decision to attend LSU was his alone," said his father. He averaged 32 points, 22 rebounds, and 8 blocks and was a *Parade* All-American in his last year as a high-schooler, and Cole won the state championship. Defenders were starting to hold and bang him, even hanging on to him when he went up for short layups and banks.

O'Neal came of age in college ball during his sophomore year. LSU lost in the NCAA tournament to Connecticut, 79-62, but O'Neal won just about every imaginable award. He was a consensus first-team All-American, as well as Southeast Conference Player of the Year. He was named Player of the Year by AP, UPI, and *Sports Illustrated*. In 28 games he had averaged 27.6 points, 14.7 rebounds, and had a 62.8 shooting percentage. His 140 blocks—five per game—set a national record for a sophomore.

By his junior year O'Neal was not enjoying college ball. Double and triple-teams were the rule, and coaches were sending players off the bench to foul him schoolyard-style, even with kidney shots. His scoring was down to 24 points a game, but he led the nation with 14 rebounds per game and 157 blocks, nearly six per game.

All the hits he was taking took their toll. He was ejected, along with several other players, for fighting in the first game of the SEC tournament against Tennessee. With O'Neal suspended for the next game, LSU lost to Kentucky, but still got a tournament bid. In the first game LSU beat Brigham Young University. O'Neal had 30 points, 11 rebounds, and set an NCAA tournament record with 11 blocks. But Indiana eliminated LSU despite O'Neal's 36 points and 12 boards.

O'Neal contemplated leaving college early. Like Chamberlain, who had left Kansas after his junior year 34 years before, O'Neal was tired of the rough play.

Drafted first overall by Orlando in 1992, he inked a mammoth seven-year deal for $39.9 million, by far the most money given to a rookie player in any sport. Orlando had about $14 million available to begin with, but manipulated the salary cap to get him signed. At least four players had their contracts restructured to free up money.

The year before O'Neal arrived, Orlando's record was 21-61. With him on the roster for the 1992-93 season, the Magic improved to 41-41. Shaq won Rookie of the Year, made the All-Star Team, and averaged 23 points and 14 rebounds, while making 56 percent of his shots. He led the league in field-goal percentage (.599) in 1994, and the next season won the scoring title, with 29.3 points per game, and made his third straight All-Star Game appearance. In four seasons in Orlando he brought the Magic to an NBA Finals (1995) and an Eastern Conference Finals (1996).

O'Neal now had something in common with Wilt Chamberlain in addition to horrific free-throw shooting. After three years of college without ever reaching a Final and years in the pros of not taking his team to a title, O'Neal was getting a reputation as a player who couldn't win. He was a free agent in '96 and Los Angeles signed him to a seven-year, $121-million deal. That year brought two other goodies to his doorstep: he played for the gold medal-winning 1996 U.S. Olympic team in Atlanta and was selected for the NBA's 50th Anniversary All-Time Team.

He soon fell victim to what was starting to be called "hack-a-Shaq" tactics. Charlotte's Matt Gieger fractured O'Neal's right thumb in a preseason game, which caused Shaq to miss 21 games.

In March 1999 O'Neal announced that he would not be playing in the 2000 Olympics in Sydney. He cited a lack of respect from the NBA front office for not getting referees to call fouls for all the hacking he received. O'Neal cited injuries to his abdominal muscles—one of which caused him to miss 21 games in 1998—caused by players draping themselves on him as he went up strong with the ball. Two of three doctors he'd sought recommended surgery. San Antonio swept the Lakers out of the post-season in 1999; it was the fifth time in six playoff seasons that a team with O'Neal in the pivot had been booted out in straight sets.

The streak ended in 2000. After much finger-pointing among the players and unfulfilled promise, Phil Jackson came out of retirement and took the helm for the Lakers. Personally, Shaq had one of his best seasons rebounding and won his second scoring title (29.7 ppg).

The title didn't come easy, though. Los Angeles was pushed to the brink by Sacramento before winning Game 5. The Lakers had an easier time with Phoenix, winning a best-of-seven in five games. Against Portland they were again pushed to the brink, trailing by 15 points entering the fourth quarter in Game 7 of the Conference Finals. But Portland got cold and Kobe Bryant and O'Neal led the Lakers to an 89-84 victory. In the Finals, the best Indiana could do was send the series back to Los Angeles for a sixth game, which was won by the Lakers, 116-111.

In 2001 the Lakers plowed through everyone in the post-season, compiling a 15-1 record, losing only the opener to Philadelphia in the Finals, who they then dunked four straight. In 2002 they encountered more resistance, finishing 15-4, but still swept New Jersey in the Finals. They joined the Bulls, Celtics, and Minneapolis Lakers as the league's only "three-peaters." O'Neal had now won five consecutive field goal percentage titles making him the first pivot man since Chamberlain (1965-69) to do it.

The title run ended at the hands of the Spurs in 2003, despite Shaq posting playoffs numbers of 27 points and 15 rebounds per game.

Robert Parish

Center, Golden State, 1976-77 through 1979-80; Boston, 1980-81 through 1993-94; Charlotte, 1994-95 through 1995-96; Chicago, 1996-97

Born: August 30, 1953 in Shreveport, La. 7-0, 230 High School: Woodlawn (Shreveport, La.) College: Centenary

Robert Parish played 21 years, competing against Bill Walton in 1977 and Shaquille O'Neal in 1997. In Boston he was known as "The Chief," but who thought Robert Parish would be a warrior on the boards for more than two decades? He was never selected All-NBA first team and was a one-time selection for both the second and third teams. He might be regarded as the Don Sutton of basketball: never the best player at his position, but nonetheless reliable and steady for an awfully long time.

Parish owns several distinctions, including the NBA records for most years and most games, 1,611. With Parish in the pivot—and with coach Bill Fitch's willingness to use him in the post and as part of Boston's running game—Boston won the 1981 NBA title. The Celtics reached four more Finals in the 1980s, winning two of them.

Parish had two notable attributes that made him more than just a player with longevity. "He had the great turn-around jump shot and incredible ability to run the floor," says Bob Ryan.

Golden State drafted the 7-foot center from Centenary in the first round, selecting him eighth overall. Who recalls that Golden State won a league-best 59 games the year before Parish arrived? But Phoenix, on route to a surprisingly competitive 1976 showdown against Boston, beat the Warriors in seven in the Western Conference Finals. From there Golden State went steadily south in the standings, even as Parish came into his own as an NBA center. "I got tired of taking the blame for losing," said Parish of his four years with the Warriors.

Boston owned the No. 1 and No. 13 picks in the 1980 draft and offered them to Golden State in exchange for the No. 3 pick and Parish. Holding the No. 3, Boston watched and waited as Golden State selected Joe Barry Carroll and Utah went for Darrell Griffith. Then the Celtics selected Kevin McHale. In essence, Boston walked off with Parish and McHale—two-thirds (along with Larry Bird) of "The Big Three," considered the greatest frontline ever assembled and teammates for 13 years—for Carroll and Rickey Brown. All things considered, it might have been the most significant transaction in basketball history.

In practices, Fitch ran Parish hard. With Golden State he had been perceived as a laconic, emotionless player, but now Parish was part of Fitch's running game, a game that Warriors coach Al Attles hadn't had. Parish flourished, averaging 19 points and 10 rebounds and making the All-Star Team, as Boston, with rookie McHale and Bird, won its 14th title in 1981. Parish was an all-star for the next six seasons, and in eight of his next 10 years, over which span Boston would capture two more Championships.

Parish's nickname, "The Chief," was bestowed by teammate Cedric Maxwell, who thought that the big center reminded him of Chief Bromden, the mountain-sized asylum inmate from *One Flew Over the Cuckoo's Nest*. Parish seemed to have the same placid, cigar-store Indian demeanor as the fictional chief. By comparison with Bird and McHale, Parish got less of the credit for Boston's success. He was surely one of the most underrated centers of his time, perhaps ever.

Parish earned respect from his mates for his consistent play and steady manner. He always kept his body clock on Eastern time, getting up at the same hour each day, no matter what city he'd be in. Since he normally rose at 7 a.m. in Boston, on the West Coast he rose at 4 a.m. It was his way of stabilizing a nomadic, city-to-city life.

Parish played well until 1994, when he was 40, in his last year with Boston. Thereafter, he played two seasons with Charlotte and one more with Chicago, finishing up in 1997. It was in 1996 that he broke Kareem Abdul-Jabbar's record of 1560 games played. That same year he was included on the NBA's 50th Anniversary All-Time Team. Playing 43 games and about nine minutes a night as a Bulls' reserve in 1997, Parish won his fourth Championship. He announced his retirement on August 25, 1997, five days before his 44th birthday.

Gary Payton

Guard, Seattle, 1990-91 through 2003; Milwaukee, 2003
Born: July 23, 1968 in Oakland, Ca. 6-4, 180 High School: Skyline (Oakland, CA) College: Oregon State

Gary Payton went through his Oregon State career as if he were climbing a staircase. His points, assists, and field-goal percentage steadily increased from year to year. No wonder that OSU retired his uniform number and that Seattle picked him second overall (New Jersey made Derrick Coleman the top selection) in the 1990 draft.

Once the Sonics had Payton, Seattle's win total began to climb—first to 41, then 47, 55, 63, 57, 64, 57, and 61, before falling back to 25 wins over the strike season and 45 in 2000. Over that time, Payton piled up distinctions as one of the league's premier point guards. Most notable are his seven consecutive seasons (1994 to 2000) on the NBA All-Defensive first team and being named NBA Defensive Player of the Year in 1996, the first guard since Michael Jordan (1988) to win the award. His ability to put the clamp on opposing guards has earned him the nickname "The Glove." He led the league in steals in 1996.

A six-time all-star, Payton has been an iron man, missing only two games in his first 10 years as a pro—one due to injury in 1992 and the other due to suspension in 1996. The suspension ended a consecutive game streak of 354.

Payton played poorly in the 1993 playoffs, when Seattle lost to Phoenix in a seven-game Conference Finals. In 1996 he improved dramatically, outplaying John Stockton in the Conference Finals and helping Seattle into the championship round against Chicago. Falling behind three games to none, Seattle won two by margins of 21 and 11 before losing in Chicago, 87-75. After the season he signed a seven-year, $85-million deal.

Oddly, Payton became more adept at the perimeter game and increased his points per game (from 7.2 to 20.6) and field-goal percentage (.450 to .509) for his first five years in the league, only to see his field-goal percentage in sharp decline over the eight years since. In 1999-2000 he shot below 45 percent for the second straight year. He did lead the league in total assists, with 732, and three pointers, 177.

Payton was a member of two gold medal-winning U.S. Olympic Teams, in 1996 and 2000. Payton, a nine-time All Star, was selected All-NBA First Team Defense for nine consecutive years (1994-2002).

No one expected that the Bucks would trade three-time all star Ray Allen, 27, for Gary Payton, 34, but that was the move made on February 20, 2003. After the Bucks were eliminated by New Jersey in six playoff games. After the season, Payton signed with the Los Angeles Lakers, who needed a reliable point guard.

Bob Pettit

Forward, Center Milwaukee 1954-55; St. Louis 1955-56 through 1964-65
Born: December 12, 1932 in Baton Rouge, La. 6-9, 215 High School: Baton Rouge College: Louisiana State

Bob Pettit was so ungainly that he didn't make his high school team until his junior season. But you wouldn't have known that once he turned pro. Pettit was the first rookie ever to make the NBA's All-League Team. In 1958, the "Bayou Bomber" hit for 50 points in Game 6 of the Finals and led the Hawks past the Celtics, the only interruption to Boston's run of titles from 1957 through 1966. Over his first nine NBA seasons, he never finished below fourth in either rebounding or scoring. When Pettit retired in 1965, he was the NBA's all-time scoring leader with 20,880 points.

Pettit had the dubious distinction of being cut from his high school baseball and football teams. He was 5-foot-9 as a freshman at Baton Rouge High School and his awkward play got him cut from the team. Then his father nailed up a basket in the backyard, and Pettit practiced around the clock. By his senior year he had grown to 6-foot-7; he scored 31 points per game and led his school to a Louisiana state title, the Bulldogs' first since 1932. Pettit mistakenly thought his success owed only to his stature. "I could stand in front of the basket and no one could reach the ball," he said.

After his freshman year at LSU, he met Ray Meyer, who had coached George Mikan at DePaul. Pettit studied movies of Mikan, with Meyer at his side. He averaged 25 points his sophomore year and by his senior season was an All-American, posting 31 points and 17 rebounds per game. Pettit's 785 points that year would have won him even more fame, but Furman's Frank Selvy scored 1209 and Bevo Francis, with the

help of 84- and 113-point games (he had scored 116 in a game the previous year), scored 1254 for a second-division school.

The Milwaukee Hawks (who moved to St. Louis for the 1955-56 season) chose Pettit in the first round. He rejected owner Ben Kerner's initial offer of $9000 and weighed several offers from AAU industrial teams. He settled for a first-year salary of $11,000 with the Hawks.

Despite a 27-point college average, Pettit was surrounded by larger, more physical centers in the pros. Coach Red Holzman solved the problem by switching him to forward. Pettit was eternally grateful to Holzman, he said, because "he wasn't strong enough" to play center in the NBA.

In 1958-59 Pettit rewrote the league's record book by setting eight marks: most points (2,105), highest scoring average (29.2), most field goals (719), most free throws attempted (879) and made (667), and most 50-point games (3). During the 1961-62 season he became the fourth player to reach 15,000 points. Dolph Schayes, Paul Arizin, and Cousy got there ahead of him, but Pettit reached the milestone in fewer games than any of them. He had an amazing All-Star Game, posting 25 points and 27 rebounds, netting his third All-Star MVP award (the others were in 1956 and 1958). In 1959 he tied for MVP voting with rookie Elgin Baylor and handed the trophy to Baylor, saying, "Take it, I have two already."

By 1965, Pettit was plagued by back and leg injuries. Just 32, he retired at season's end. No other player had scored 20,000 points, and he was also the first to tally 20,000 points and 10,000 rebounds. The total of his career points (26 per game) and rebounds (16) is 42, a sum second only to Wilt Chamberlain's 30 points and 22 rebounds. In 11 All-Star Games he averaged 20 points and 16 rebounds.

Ten times Pettit was voted All-NBA First Team; only Cousy was selected as many times. He was elected to the Hall of Fame in 1970, and named to the NBA's 25th 35th, and 50th Anniversary Teams.

Scottie Pippen

Forward, Chicago, 1987-88 through 1997-98; Houston, 1998-99; Portland, 1999-2000 to present
Born: September 25, 1965 in Hamburg, Ark. 6-7, 210 High School: Hamburg (Ark.) College: Central Arkansas

In 16 years as a pro, Scottie Pippen may have established the most varied portfolio of skills of any forward who ever played. At his best, he could soar and finish drives. He got assists at a clip more befitting a guard than a forward. He could turn games around with his harassing, intimidating defense. He has made the NBA All-Defensive first team eight times, a distinction he shares with only one other forward, Bobby Jones. Playing on all six Chicago Championship teams in the 1990s, Pippen provided a complement to Michael Jordan's stellar play and leadership.

Central Arkansas is hardly a college that comes to mind when fans talk of basketball factories. But that is where Pippen began in 1983, steadily improving to a 20-points-per-game performer in his senior year. He was drafted fifth overall by Seattle in 1987. The Sonics then followed their prudent selection of Pippen with a supreme act of imprudence. Bulls' general manager Jerry Krause got Pippen for Chicago's eighth pick, Olden

Polynice, and an exchange of draft picks. There's no telling what Seattle, which won 60 games three times in the 1990s, might have done had they kept Pippen.

For many fans, Pippen's eternal identity may be as an accessory to Michael Jordan. As graceful and beautiful a player as Pippen can be, he couldn't carry the Bulls to victory in 1994, when Jordan was retired. Game 3 of that series included an unsightly, perhaps unprecedented, "spoiled star" incident that reflected badly on Pippen. He refused to reenter the game after Phil Jackson, with 1.8 seconds remaining, called a play in which Toni Kukoc would take the last shot. Kukoc nailed the game-winner, but Pippen's action couldn't be ignored. Bill Cartwright berated him in the locker room for his sulking behavior.

In January 1999, Pippen was traded to Houston for Roy Rogers and a conditional second-round draft pick. Playing alongside Charles Barkley and Hakeem Olajuwon in Houston, Pippen played terribly in the first round of playoffs. He connected on only 33 percent of his shots for the series as Los Angeles won in four games. He was dealt to Portland after the season for five players. In the 2000 Western Conference Finals versus the Lakers, the Blazers carried a 15-point lead into the fourth quarter of Game 7, but Pippen didn't scored in the fourth, and the Lakers rallied to win, 89-84.

Although Pippen is a complementary player—"a vice president but not a president," as Gary Payton once put it—he was a most necessary complement for the six titles that Chicago won in the '90s. Even more than a player who contributed from 17 to 20 points a game, Pippen, despite playing the forward position, led Chicago in assists for eight straight years. He led the league in steals in 1995, getting 2.9 per game. When coach Bach used to say, "We unleash the Dobermans" on defense, he had in mind Jordan and Pippen.

When it came to scoring points, however, the morning wire reports didn't lie. In the playoffs, when defenses routinely become chest-to-chest-tough in a half-court offense, Pippen's field-goal percentage goes south. In 1996, he hit 39 percent from the field. In 1999, with Houston, his shooting plummeted to a tragic 33 percent. With Portland in 2000 he hit just 42 percent and in 2002 41 percent.

Like Jordan, Pippen twice won gold medals with the U.S. Olympic basketball team, in 1992 and 1996. In the latter year, he was named to the NBA's 50th Anniversary All-Time Team.

Willis Reed

Center-Forward, New York Knicks, 1964-65 through 1973-74
Born: June 25, 1942 in Hico, La. 6-9, 225 High School: West Side (Lillie, La.) College: Grambling State

Willis Reed is one of those people who, for one night, got to live out a fairy tale. There was no more memorable entry into a basketball game than Willis Reed's lumbering walk from the Madison Square Garden tunnel to the floor for Game 7 of the NBA Finals against Los Angeles. It was May 8, 1970. Reed had fallen and sustained a deep thigh bruise in Game 5 of the series and missed Game 6. Wilt Chamberlain flattened New York on the Forum floor with 45 points and 27 rebounds, making a rotating army of defenders seem like Lilliputians. Los Angeles waltzed, 135-113.

In the first minute of Game 7 Reed hit New York's first two shots—the only two he would hit all night—but his mere presence on the court lifted his mates. Chamberlain played 48 minutes, scored 21 points and grabbed 24 rebounds. But Reed's appearance—not to mention 27 minutes of bulky physical interior defense against Chamberlain—made a difference. Walt Frazier owned the game, scoring 36 points, passing for 19 assists, and grabbing 7 rebounds. Dave DeBusschere chipped in 17 boards and New York held its own inside. In the end the Knicks prevailed 113-99 over Chamberlain, Jerry West, and Elgin Baylor, the three highest scorers in playoff history to that point.

More than 30 years later, Willis Reed remains a symbol of courage. Although he played a brief 10 years, and just 650 games, he was the embodiment of determination and muscle on a team that was one of the smartest ever assembled. Reed leaned on Chamberlain and Kareem Abdul-Jabbar and, while giving away four or five inches in height, drove them from under the basket to the outer boundaries of their offensive range.

Reed was a force before he came to New York. His hunger for excellence began in rural Louisiana. He flourished at Grambling State, an NAIA team, and was eventually elected to its Hall of Fame. He graduated with a degree in physical education, which would later incline him toward teaching, and a minor in biology.

The Knicks picked forward Jim "Bad News" Barnes in the first round and made Reed their first pick of the second round. Barnes would never thrive in the NBA; Reed was a pro star immediately. Right off, he led New York in minutes, points, and rebounds, made the All-Star Team, and won the Rookie of the Year award. But at the start of the 1965-66 season, Walt Bellamy, who had averaged 31 points a game and led the league in field-goal percentage in his rookie year, came to New York in exchange for Barnes, Johnny Green, and John Egan, and the pivot belonged to him. Reed moved over to power forward. The Knicks weren't winning in those days; the league's doormat for more than a decade, they finished 30-52 that season. Reed's minutes declined, and his numbers—19 points and 14 rebounds per game in his rookie year—slid to 15 points and 11 rebounds.

At the beginning of the 1968-69 season the Knicks were still plodding, but then a key trade liberated Reed and changed the fortunes of the team for years. In December, the Knicks moved guard Howard Komives and Bellamy to Detroit for Dave DeBusschere. Back in the pivot, Reed responded with his best year—21 points and 14 rebounds per game.

Reed owned the softest outside touch of any big man in the league and could hit his lefty jumper shot from up to 18 feet. He set picks for his mates and used his bulk to rugged effect on the interior. On defense, Bradley described him as "the big man backing up our mistakes. If your man slips through you for a backdoor, Willis is there."

Before winning the NBA Finals in 1970, New York had to get past Baltimore in a classic series in the first round. In Game 5 Reed played one of the great clutch games ever, scoring 36 points and grabbing 36 rebounds to give New York a 101-80 victory. The Knicks won in seven. After they'd beaten Los Angeles, 113-99, and taken the 1970 Finals, Reed had won it all. He earned a clean sweep of the Most Valuable Player awards—All-Star Game, regular season, and Finals.

Despite a low six-figure salary, a Harlem liquor store, and other investments that provided Reed considerable wealth in the early 1970s, Reed's lifestyle was not overly elaborate. He liked to hunt, and purchased a 276-acre dairy farm in Pennsylvania for the purpose. He rented a modest, two-bedroom, $285 apartment in Rego Park, Queens.

In 1971, Reed averaged 21 points and 14 rebounds for the regular season but fell off to 15 points (on 41 percent shooting) and 12 rebounds in a surprisingly poor post-season performance, for him and the Knicks.

Playing on creaky knees afflicted by tendonitis, Reed could not push off or leap the following year. He suited up for only 11 regular season games over the 1971-72 season and missed the entire playoffs. The Knicks reached the Finals against L.A. and notched their second championship, this time on L.A.'s court, 102-93. Averaging just 13 points and 8 rebounds, Reed still captured his second Finals Most Valuable Player.

Reed played 19 games the following year, plus 11 more in the playoffs before calling it quits. His retirement marked the end of an era for New York, as Bill Bradley, Jerry Lucas, and Dave DeBusschere left soon after. Four years after his retirement, Reed returned as the Knicks coach. Fired early in his second season, he coached Creighton for four years. In the late 1980s he landed with New Jersey and finished his NBA coaching career with an 82-124 mark. He was elected to the Hall of Fame in 1982 and to the NBA 50th Anniversary All-Time Team in 1996.

Mitch Richmond

Guard, Golden State, 1988-89 through 1990-91; Sacramento, 1991-92 through 1999-2000
Born: June 30, 1964 in Ft. Lauderdale, Fla. 6-5, 220 High School: Boyd Anderson (Ft. Lauderdale, Fla.) Junior College: Moberly (Missouri) Area Junior College College: Kansas State

A six-time All Star, Mitch Richmond began his career with the Golden State Warriors, who made him the fifth overall pick of the 1988 draft. He was a steady scoring machine for 12 years. In 1998, he became just the fourth player in NBA history to average 21 points or more in each of his first ten seasons (the other three were Oscar Robertson, Kareem Abdul-Jabbar, and Michael Jordan). During the 2000-2001season he became the 30th player in NBA-ABA history to score 20,000 points. His unflagging play led Golden State teammate Chris Mullin to tag him with the nickname "Rock."

While Richmond's childhood hero was Julius Erving, he didn't play organized basketball until he was a high school sophomore in Florida. "I didn't think about going out for the team," he said, "mainly because I was only six feet tall when I was a tenth grader and only a pretty good player." By graduation, he was 6-foot-5. But his grade point averaged was under 2.0, so he had to attend the Moberly Area Junior College in Missouri, where his coach Dana Altman switched him—not without a fight from Richmond—from power forward to guard and stressed the importance of hitting the books.

The duo then transferred to Kansas State. Altman became assistant to coach Lon Kruger. Richmond's personal passage

from college to the pros was seamless. Playing 79 games his rookie season, he averaged 22 points and won Rookie of the Year honors.

Teaming with Tim Hardaway and Chris Mullin from 1989 through 1991, Richmond and the Warriors could score with anyone. Golden State finished in the top four in team scoring three years in a row and led the league in 1990. The problem is that the threesome played, like the rest of the team, as veritable toreadors on defense, leaving Golden State last in the league in defense and next-to-last two other years.

The 1989 and 1991 teams made it to the second round of the playoffs and the trio gained in popularity. A San Francisco newspaper ran a contest to give the threesome a nickname, letting them select the winner. They settled on Run TMC, a play on their first names and a popular rap group.

After the 1990-91 season Richmond was traded to Sacramento for forward Billy Owens. Beginning in 1993, he was selected for the All-Star team for six straight years. He won the MVP at the 1995 All-Star Game in Phoenix, connecting on 10 of 13 shots and getting 23 points. He also played on both the 1988 and 1996 U.S. Olympic basketball teams.

In May 1998, Richmond, then 33, was traded with Otis Thorpe to Washington for Chris Webber. After three years with Washington he was waived and signed as a free agent by the Lakers in July 2001. He played his last year in Los Angeles, appearing in 64 games, then just two in the post-season, but had his first championship ring in 14 years.

Richmond finished his career with 20,497 points and a 21-point career average.

Oscar Robertson

Guard, Cincinnati, 1960-61 through 1969-70; Milwaukee, 1970-71 through 1973-74
Born: November 24, 1938 in Charlotte, Tenn. 6-5, 205 High School: Crispus Attucks (Indianapolis, Ind.) College: Cincinnati

Excepting Wilt Chamberlain and Michael Jordan, it is hard to think of a player in NBA history with more impressive statistics than Oscar Robertson. The best known of his numerical markers is his "triple-double" (a phrase coined by the late Lakers' PR man Bruce Jolesch) in 1962, his second season, at the age of 23. But what is less known and more impressive, is likely Robertson's unsurpassable achievement is averaging a triple-double over the *first five years* of his career. From 1961 through 1965, the player known as "The Big O" averaged 30.2 points, 10.4 rebounds and 10.6 assists. For all those years, however, Cincinnati was a dismal 12-18 (.400) in playoff contests. The Royals twice made it to the second round, but lost to Boston each time.

Beginning his career two years before Bob Cousy retired, Robertson, with Jerry West, ushered in a new era of guard play. Guards became larger, more physical, and better defenders. A husky 6-foot-5 and 200-plus pounds, Robertson was in a select group: the only other 6-foot-5 guards at the time were Tom Gola and John Havlicek. From 1961 through 1969 he had a lock on the All-NBA first team, making it all nine years. He was voted to 12 consecutive All-Star Teams from 1961 through 1972—winning the game's MVP in 1961, his rookie year,

when he scored 23 points to go with 14 assists and 9 rebounds. He repeated as MVP in the 1964 classic (26 points, 8 assists, 14 rebounds) and in 1969 (24 points, 5 assists, 6 rebounds).

As staggering as Robertson's individual exploits were in the pro game, he had done just as well at Cincinnati University. From 1958 through 1960 he was All-American three times, Division I scoring champ three times, and College Player of the year three times. He did encounter some racial problems at college. During his sophomore year he was not allowed to stay with his teammates at the Shamrock Hotel in Houston. "If that happens again," he told a friend, "I'll take the first bus [home] to Indianapolis." Thereafter the team stayed at fraternity houses and dormitories when it played in the South. His father's grandfather, a former slave who died in 1954, lived to the age of 116. Robertson's close contact with his great-grandfather, who had lived in pre-Civil War days, may have increased his sensitivity about racial relations.

After being selected first pick overall by Cincinnati in the 1960 draft, Robertson played in the Rome Olympics before joining the Royals. He and Jerry West co-captained the undefeated United States team. The Royals had to bid against the Harlem Globetrotters to get Robertson, offering him $100,000 for three years.

In his first season he won Rookie of the Year and became only the second rookie to win the All-Star Game MVP, following his stellar performance in the West's 153-131 victory. The attendance at Royals games was greater in the first quarter of the 1960-61 season than it was the entire season before.

Because he strove to be perfect in all parts of the game, Robertson soon became known as "basketball's Willie Mays." Few guards of the early 1960s were as large as the Big O. He used his burly frame to back defenders down and punish them. He didn't settle for a 17-footer when he could get a 15-footer, or a 15-footer when he could elbow his way to a 12-footer. In six seasons he averaged 30 or more points; in three he averaged double-digits in rebounds, and five times he averaged double-digits in assists.

On April 21, 1970, Robertson was traded to the Milwaukee Bucks for guard Flynn Robinson and forward Charlie Paulik. In his first full season with Milwaukee, he provided the leadership, and 19 points and 8 assists per game, teaming with MVP Kareem Abdul-Jabbar to lead the Bucks to their first and only NBA Championship. Robertson's enduring reputation is that of a complete player. A 12-time all-star, when he retired he was the all-time leader in assists, and was first in total points among all backcourt players. As a leader of the NBA Players Association he helped to bring free agency to professional sports.

Robertson was elected to the Hall of Fame in 1980. He was named to the NBA's 35th Anniversary All-Time Team in 1980 and its 50th Anniversary All-Time Team in 1996.

David Robinson

Center, 1987-88 through 2002-03 (did not play 1987-88 through 1988-89, military obligation)
Born: August 9, 1965 in Key West, Fla. 7-1, 235 High School: Osbourn Park (Manassas, Va.) College: Navy

David Robinson had a stellar career in all phases of the game. Though the celebrated "Admiral" from Navy didn't play in his

first NBA contest until he was 24, he scooped up all manner of awards as if following orders. He was Rookie of the Year in 1990; All-NBA first team in 1991, 1992, 1995, and 1996; and All-NBA second team in two other years. He won a scoring title in 1993 and the league MVP in 1995. On the other end of the court, he was NBA All-Defensive first team in 1991, 1992, 1995, and 1996, and second team on four other occasions. He led the league with a gaudy 4.49 blocks per game in 1992.

Despite those spoils, amassed over 11 years, up until 1999 Robinson hadn't even brought his team to the Finals, much less won a title. He had heard about his post-season failures from NBA scribes and sports newscasters more frequently than he heard reveille during his four-year Navy hitch.

Robinson played only a year of high school basketball before entering the Naval Academy, at 6-foot-6 and 175 pounds. He grew seven inches in college. As one writer put it, he was always faster than everyone else. Now he was bigger than everyone else, too.

San Antonio made Robinson its first pick overall in the 1987 draft. But he still had a two-year commitment to the Navy and lived on the base. NBA regulations included a seldom-invoked "military clause." A player drafted by the league who still had military time to serve before playing could reenter the draft when he returned from the service, if he had not previously signed a contract. Thus Robinson had a good deal of leverage over the Spurs.

On a flight to San Antonio he told his agent that he wanted to introduce a new clause in his contract. The clause stated that if two players in the league made more than Robinson, the average annual salaries of their long-term contracts would be divided by two, and this figure would become Robinson's new salary. If the Spurs chose not to match that figure, he would be granted free agency at the end of the year. San Antonio agreed, and the NBA ratified the deal in November 1987.

Robinson was a member of the U.S. Olympic basketball team in 1988, when the Soviet Union beat the U.S. in the semis, 82-76, and then Yugoslavia for the gold. Robinson was America's second leading scorer with 13 points a game and led the squad in rebounds and blocks. Robinson played for the gold medal-winning U.S. Olympic teams in 1992 and 1996. He is the only man to play on three U.S. Olympic hoops teams.

At the advent of his rookie year in 1989-90, some were saying that Robinson would be "the next Russell." They turned out to be wrong in at least two ways: Robinson would score a lot more than Russell, but he wouldn't be leading the Spurs to 11 Finals in 13 years. Even so, his impact was immediate. San Antonio was 21-61 a year before his arrival and 56-26 when the Admiral joined the team. He posted 24 points and 12 rebounds a game, numbers that would be only slightly better than his career averages 14 years later.

At the beginning of the 1995 season he signed a six-year, $66 million deal. Despite San Antonio's investment, the word was that in the playoffs Robertson had a way of disappearing. In the 1994-95 season San Antonio won 62 and lost 20, the best record in the NBA, and Robinson, averaging 28 points, 11 rebounds and three blocks, won the MVP. But in the post-season he morphed into a 44-percent shooter, down from his regular season mark of 53 percent. The culmination of his

subpar efforts came in the Conference Finals when Hakeem Olajuwon outplayed him, thoroughly, on the way to Houston's second consecutive title.

In 1996 it was more of the same. The team won 59 games, second best in the conference to Seattle. This time San Antonio faltered in the second round, getting outplayed by the Jazz in six games. They lost three of those games by an average of 29 points.

The addition of Tim Duncan, the No. 1 draft pick in 1997, changed the complexion of the team. Now Robinson had a teammate who could shoulder some of the scoring load. The two formed the best front-line duo in decades, maybe ever. In the 1999 Finals, Robinson and Duncan combined for 44 points, 26 rebounds, 5 assists, and 5 blocks per game. Their defense held New York to an average of 80 points on 39-percent shooting. The Spurs' inside game overpowered the Knicks, four games to one. At the center of San Antonio's celebration was a beaming, and very relieved, David Robinson, earning his first championship in his 10th NBA season. San Antonio won 53 games the next year, but a knee injury to Duncan hurt the Spurs' chances of defending their title, and they lost to Phoenix in the first round.

In 2001 the Spurs reached the Conference Finals but were swept by Los Angeles, losing the last two games by margins 39 and 29 points. Robinson and Duncan were healthy, but the Lakers were in the midst of a three-year run in which Shaquille O'Neal had his way with every NBA center. In 2002, the Lakers trounced the Spurs again.

During the 2002-03 campaign Robinson announced he'd retire after the season. His goal was to exit with one more title, an objective he successfully achieved when San Antonio defeated New Jersey in a 6-game Final series. If his farewell game, Robinson contributed 13 points and 17 rebounds in an 88-77 victory.

Robinson retired with more than 20,000 points and 10,000 rebounds and posted career averages of 21 points, 11 rebounds and three blocks per game. He was voted to the NBA's 50th Anniversary All-Time Team in 1996.

Guy Rodgers

Guard, Philadelphia, 1958-59 through 1961-62; San Francisco, 1962-63 through 1965-66; Chicago, 1966-67, 67; Cincinnati, 1967-68; Milwaukee, 1968-69 through 1969-70
Born: September 1, 1935 in Philadelphia, Pa. 6-0, 185
Died: February 19, 2001 High School: Northeast (Philadelphia, Pa.) College: Temple

A muscular 6-foot, 185-pound guard, Guy Rodgers set up Wilt Chamberlain for the six most titanic offensive seasons in the history of basketball. Rodgers had played with Wilt in Philadelphia playgrounds while Chamberlain was attending Overbrook High. From 1960 through 1965, when the two teamed for the Philadelphia and later the San Francisco Warriors, Rodgers finished either first or second in assists in the NBA. Over those six years, when Chamberlain averaged an otherworldly 40.6 points, Guy Rodgers posted 8.1 assists per game. He racked up 28 assists in a game in 1963, tying the league record set by Bob Cousy. In his career, which covered 1959 through 1970, Rodgers played with Chamberlain, Nate

Thurmond, and then Lew Alcindor. When he retired after the 1970 season he had 6,917 assists, then third behind Cousy and Oscar Robertson.

With speed and deft dribbling, Rodgers could break any press and feed his teammates with the best of them. Rodgers was a star in high school, and at Temple University he teamed in the backcourt with Hal Lear. He was twice an All-American and won the Most Valuable Player trophy at the 1957 Holiday Festival Tournament in Madison Square Garden. He scored 1767 points to become the Owls' all-time leader. He also set the school assists record for one game (15) and season (185).

When he was a sophomore, his coach, Harry Litwack, rose at a luncheon and began comparing the maturing playmaker with Bob Cousy. Red Auerbach interrupted Litwack. "Everybody's another Cousy," the feisty coach shouted. "Everywhere I hear about someone's being another Cousy. Well, there isn't anyone who comes close." By the time Rodgers was a senior, Auerbach had a different appraisal. "If anyone has a chance to become another Cousy, it might be Rodgers," he said.

A territorial draft pick of the Philadelphia Warriors, Rodgers was chosen fifth overall in 1958. It was a precarious time for black players, since an unspoken quota system seemed to prevail, one that seemingly allowed no more than four blacks per team. The Warriors already had four blacks—Guy Rodgers, Andy Johnson, Woody Sauldsberry and Wilt Chamberlain. Shortly after Rodgers arrived, Sauldsberry was traded, giving additional impetus to the suspicion of a quota system for black players. Despite the unsettling racial undertones, Rodgers attended to the task at hand and increased his points, assists, and rebounds in each of his first three seasons. In his second year Wilt Chamberlain joined the Warriors. In 1962 Chamberlain averaged 50.4 points per game.

Rodgers was tough beyond his size. In 1964, the only year that he played in the Finals, the Warriors played a knock-down, drag-out, seven-game series with St. Louis for the Western Division title. In the seventh game Rodgers was knocked out cold. "I was trying for a rebound," he said," and my feet flew out from under me. My head hit the floor with terrific force. After that everything was very fuzzy." Rodgers rested for five minutes and returned. He scored 19 points, made 8 assists, and the Warriors won the Western Division.

In the Finals against Boston, Rodgers dislocated his thumb in the opening game. Playing with a cast, he scored 10 points and led both teams in assists in Game 3. The next night he scored 16 points in the last 12 minutes and 23 for the game. Hank Luisetti was watching and said, "It was one of the great guard exhibitions of all time." The Warriors wasted his heroics, though, losing in five games.

The left-handed Rodgers was hardly a complete offensive player. Like Cousy, he connected on just 38 percent of his field goal attempts for his career.

After playing his first eight years with the Warriors, Rodgers was lost to Chicago in the 1966 expansion draft. Thus, when Alex Hannum went to the Philadelphia 76ers for the 1966-67 season, Rodgers had already lost the chance to go with him and wound up missing the party when Philly finished 68-13 and rolled to a championship.

Rodgers played out his last four seasons with Chicago,

Cincinnati, and Milwaukee. Given his third-place ranking in all-time assists when he retired in 1970, it seems odd to many that Rodgers has not been elected to the Hall of Fame.

Dennis Rodman

Forward, Detroit, 1986-87 through 1992-93; San Antonio, 1993-94 through 1994-95; Chicago, 1995-96 through 1987-88; LA Lakers, 1998-99; Dallas, 1999-2000
Born: May 13, 1961 in Trenton, N.J. 6-7, 220 High School: South Oak Cliff (Dallas, Tex.) Junior College: Cooke County (Tex.) Junior College College: Southeastern Oklahoma State

Dennis Rodman's 13-year career played out as a three-act spectacle—quiet in the beginning, wonderfully impressive through its middle years, and utterly bizarre at its conclusion. He wanted to be a part of teams, but he also hankered to play a complete basketball game in the nude. He worked out vigorously, even lifting weights and mounting an exercise bike after games, but frequently missed practices. He craved basketball's dirtiest work, clawing for every rebound and playing physical defense, but off the court was inclined to get into full drag, wearing dresses and make-up around downtown Chicago with a different hair color each day of the week.

While playing on five champions, not to mention winning seven consecutive rebounding titles and appearing seven times on the NBA's All-Defensive first team, Rodman barely managed to integrate all his warring tendencies. If his teams played badly, however, and a strong leader didn't emerge, Rodman would lose interest and show persistent indifference and bad behavior—like undressing in the huddle, coming late for games, and even turning his back on the team by not showing up at all.

Dennis Rodman grew up in the Oak Cliff projects section of Dallas. For fun, he and other teenage kids in the neighborhood would walk through a sewage tunnel and emerge several miles later at the annual Dallas State Fair. He thinks the experience is a metaphor for his life—passing through dark, even foul, moments and successfully emerging.

Little went smooth in Rodman's youth. His father, Philander Rodman, was in the Air Force and stationed in New Jersey, where Dennis was born, but the family moved to Dallas when his father stopped coming home. Rodman never saw him again, and grew up with his mother and two younger sisters. Both sisters wound up exceeding six feet in height and became college All-Americans in basketball. At 20, Rodman was making $6.50 as a janitor on the graveyard shift at Dallas-Fort Worth Airport.

He had only played basketball for part of his sophomore season in high school when he was pulled aside at a Cooke County Junior College tryout in Texas and offered a scholarship. After one semester, in which he averaged 17 points and 13 rebounds, he flunked out of school and went back to his aimless existence of hanging out in Dallas.

The assistant coach for Southeastern Oklahoma of the NAIA had seen Rodman play and thought he could make it. Unannounced, the assistant showed up at his door, and Dennis happened to be home. He averaged 26 points and 16 rebounds over his four college seasons and Detroit made him its second-round pick, the 27th overall, in the 1986 draft. Rodman was 25

when he played his first pro game. His minutes, rebounds, and defensive prowess increased steadily, and in his third season, 1989, he led the league in field-goal percentage (.595) and was selected for his first of seven NBA All-Defensive first team awards. He was also an essential cog in the Pistons' "Bad Boy" machine that plowed through two Conference Finals and three consecutive Finals.

Rodman represented Detroit's defense and muscle. His coach, Chuck Daly, called him "the most unselfish player in the history of the NBA. He can win six to ten games by himself with his defense and rebounding." The team's close-knit structure suited Rodman: Daly was the father he never had, and Isiah Thomas, Bill Laimbeer, and Rick Mahorn were his surrogate family.

After Detroit's first title in 1989, Mahorn was drafted by Minnesota. Rodman and John Salley took over his power forward spot. Following the second title season in 1990, the team's identity changed. In the 1991 playoffs the Pistons continued to level opponents—as exemplified by Rodman shoving Scottie Pippen into the photographers after a layup. But the team had averaged 100 games from 1987 through 1991, and little more than swagger remained. This time, the Bulls pasted them in four straight.

Daly left to coach New Jersey and Pistons mainstays were traded or retired. Rodman ignored the new coach, Ron Rothstein, and turned up late—or not at all—for practices. His sitting on the floor, shoes off, during timeouts became a symbol of his indifference toward the team. He was also embroiled in a very public divorce. Even so, Rodman won his first of seven consecutive rebounding titles (second only to Chamberlain's 11) in 1991-92, getting 18.7 per game, the highest figure since Wilt's 19.2 in 1972. He also led the league in offensive rebounds six times.

His seven rebounding titles exceed the number of any non-center in NBA history. Not only was he winning rebounding titles, but he was blowing out the competition. In 1992 he had 18.7 rebounds to runner-up Kevin Willis's 15.5; in 1993, 18.3 to Shaquille O'Neal's 13.9; in 1994 he surpassed O'Neal 17.3 to 13.2; in 1995, he outdistanced Dikembe Mutombo 16.8 to 12.5; in 1996 he surpassed David Robinson 14.9 to 12.2; in 1997 he finished at 16.1 to Mutombo's 11.6; and in 1998 it was 15 for Rodman and 13.6 for Jason Williams.

Off the court, Rodman was becoming increasingly unpredictable. One day police found him with a loaded rifle in his lap at 5 a.m. in the parking lot of the Palace of Auburn Hills. He was traded to San Antonio in October 1993, and coach John Lucas allowed him to do as he chose, provided he came to games and got rebounds. He did both, leading the league in boards, not to mention tattoos and body piercings. Then Nike aired its infamous commercial, in which Santa Claus chides Rodman for missing practices and being late for games. "But I led the league in rebounds," Rodman replies, whereupon Santa agrees to give him the shoes he wants for Christmas. "Rodman has made a mockery of the NBA," fumed Wayne Embry, "and we publicize him. That just galls me."

Rodman's suspension in the 1994 playoffs versus Utah was a big reason that the Spurs came up short. The next year, San Antonio lost to Houston in six games in the Western Conference Finals. With Hakeem Olajuwon outplaying David Robinson, Rodman was again a disruptive force on his team, showing up late before games. During huddles he removed his shoes and sat off to the side or stood out of earshot, conveying his disinterest in what coach Bob Hill had to say. Hill benched him for one game of the Los Angeles series and didn't start him in a single game in the Houston series.

A trade to Chicago in October 1995 (Will Perdue went to San Antonio) meant three more Championships for Rodman and three more rebounding titles. The nonconformist Phil Jackson accepted Rodman, likening his antics to a tribe member who takes a different path from his fellows. Michael Jordan's strong grip on the team ensured that Rodman would not disrupt its chemistry. The rebounds-for-titles bargain was cut, and the tattooed forward enjoyed some of his finest moments.

After retiring from the Bulls, the 37-year-old Rodman was signed by the Lakers as a free agent and played 23 games, grabbing 11 rebounds per contest in the spring of 1999. But reverting to his usual insubordinate behavior, he quickly wore out his welcome, and Los Angeles waived him in the spring of 1999. He played 12 games with Dallas before being waived in March 2000.

Despite his legacy of disruptive, boorish, and self-promoting behavior, Dennis Rodman is unmistakably a Hall-of-Fame-caliber player. He remains one of the best defensive forwards and the very best rebounding forward in basketball history.

Bill Russell

Center, Boston, 1956-57 through 1968-69
Born: February 12, 1934 in Monroe, La. 6-9, 220 High School: McClymonds (Oakland, Cal.) College: San Francisco

Bill Russell is credited with revolutionizing basketball by playing intimidating defense, sweeping the boards, and making the outlet pass to initiate the Boston Celtics' fast break. With Russell the blocked shot was a weapon. "Russell introduced a new sound to basketball," said Red Auerbach, "the sound of his footsteps." In Russell's 13 years the Celtics won 11 championships, a record unmatched in basketball history.

Russell was an unexceptional high school player. Baseball Hall of Famer Frank Robinson, who played with Russell on the McClymonds High basketball team in Oakland, once remarked of him, "He couldn't even put the ball in the basket when he dunked." The story goes that Russell, while having one of his rare good games, was noticed by Hal Dejulio, a former University of San Francisco player. Dejulio touted Russell to San Francisco coach Phil Wolpert, and Wolpert reluctantly took him to play for the Dons.

Russell made a genius out of Hal Dejulio. He led the University of San Francisco to back-to-back NCAA titles in 1955 and 1956. In 1955 he was named the Outstanding Player of the Tournament, scoring 23 points and had 25 rebounds in the championship game, a 77-63 victory over LaSalle. Defensive specialist K.C. Jones (who would also be Russell's teammate in the Olympics and on the Boston Celtics) held Iowa's All-American guard Tom Gola scoreless for a 21-minute stretch and outscored him, 24-16. In 1956, Iowa was the Dons' victim. Russell scored 26 and grabbed 27 rebounds in an 83-71 win.

Before the 1956 draft, Russell announced that he would play in the fall for the U.S. Olympic team in Melbourne, Australia before turning pro. The United States finished 8-0 in Melbourne, and its closest game was an 85-55 laugher against the Soviet Union. In the Finals the U.S. played the Russians again and won by the nearly identical score of 89-55. Russell was the team's leading scorer, but his participation in the games meant that whichever NBA team drafted him would have to wait until early December to begin using his services. Also, Russell reportedly was seeking the rather pricey salary of $25,000 a year, with the option of signing with the Harlem Globetrotters, who had made him an offer of $50,000 a year to play for them.

Boston had the sixth pick in the 1956 draft, and landing Russell took some of Auerbach's best trading tactics. He made a call to Ben Kerner, owner of the St. Louis Hawks, who had the second draft pick and whose needs were painfully obvious. Kerner wanted another drawing card in addition to his star, Bob Pettit, in order to keep the franchise going. Moreover, the Hawks at the time remained the only all-white team in the NBA, and Kerner also objected to Russell's $25,000 salary demand. The Minneapolis Lakers owned the No. 3 draft pick, and word was that the club intended to draft Russell.

Auerbach offered the Hawks his NBA all-star "Easy" Ed Macauley, a St. Louis University grad. Kerner wanted more, and asked for the draft rights to Kentucky guard Cliff Hagan, who had just completed two years in the military and was about to enter the NBA. Auerbach agreed.

Spinning another ball, Auerbach needed to know what Rochester intended to do with its No. 1 selection. He didn't want to give away the farm for St. Louis' second pick, only to have Rochester select Russell. Celtics owner Walter Brown was friendly with Rochester boss Les Harrison and gave him a call. Two factors already favored the Celtics: the Royals were strong up front with 6-foot-7 forward Maurice Stokes, and they, too, were put off by Russell's $25,000-a-year requirement. Brown provided still further incentive for Rochester to leave Russell alone: If Harrison passed on Russell, Brown would arrange for the Ice Capades to come to Rochester and fill his building two weeks a year. Elated, Harrison said, "You give me the Ice Capades and I'll give you my word we won't take Russell."

The Rochester Royals drafted Sihugo Green, a guard out of Duquesne. St. Louis picked Russell and traded him to Boston. Hoping to replace George Mikan, who had brought the franchise six championships and had just retired in the spring of 1956, Minneapolis was closed out, missing Russell by a single pick. Russell went to Walter Brown's office and signed for $19,500, taking a cut because of the time he missed due to the Olympics.

He joined the Celtics on December 22, but still led the team in rebounds despite missing 24 games. Led by Cousy, Bill Sharman, and rookie Tommy Heinsohn, Boston made it to the NBA Finals and faced the St. Louis Hawks. In the deciding seventh game, the Celtics won the title in double-overtime, 125-123, as Russell scored 19 points and pulled down 32 rebounds. He averaged 24 rebounds for the post-season.

After the Hawks won the championship in 1958, behind Pettit's 50 points in the final game (and Russell's injured ankle),

the Celtics took the championship back in 1959. They didn't let go, winning the title for eight consecutive years. Their victims through 1966 were Minneapolis-Los Angeles (five times), St. Louis (thrice), and San Francisco. The great players they stranded in search of titles included Jerry West and Elgin Baylor, Oscar Robertson and Wilt Chamberlain. Whether Russell was better than them all has proved fertile ground for debate.

The Celtics' general manager, Auerbach offered the coaching job to Heinsohn for the 1966-67 season. Heinsohn refused, claming that only Russell could coach Russell. Before accepting the post, Russell offered it to Frank Ramsey, who had retired in 1964. Ramsey refused and Russell became the first black coach in a major professional sport.

Russell assumed the role of player-coach, and Russell the coach didn't go lightly on Russell the player. He played 81 games and 40 minutes a night to help the Celtics record 60 wins for the 1966-67 season. He averaged 21 rebounds a game, second only to Chamberlain's 24. Chamberlain and the 76ers set a record by winning 68 games and evicted Boston in five in the Eastern Division Finals.

The following year Philadelphia landed atop the Eastern Division with 62 wins, eight more than Boston. The Sixers jumped out to a 3-1 lead against the Celtics in the Division Finals. But Philly had lost Billy Cunningham in Game 4 with a broken right wrist, and Boston won Game 5 on the road and Game 6 at home. Game 7 in Philadelphia was exceptionally bizarre. In a year that saw Wilt Chamberlain so concerned with assists that he would check his totals at the scorer's table at half-time, he simply refused to shoot in the second half. He took only two shots—both on offensive rebounds—as his team-mates laid bricks all around. But Chamberlain kept on passing. He out-rebounded Russell, 34 to 26. But the Sixers' offense sputtered and Boston won, 100-96, on Philadelphia's court. The outcome did little to allay Russell's suspicion that Chamberlain, great as he was, lacked a killer instinct.

Russell and Chamberlain confronted each other again in the 1969 Finals, and again it went seven games. Boston won 108-106. Russell played the entire 48 minutes and had 21 rebounds. Chamberlain shot 7-for-8 and had 18 points and 27 rebounds. But he hurt his knee with the Lakers down by nine with five minutes left. He needed a breather, then asked coach Butch van Breda Kolff to put him back in. Van Breda Kolff ignored him. When Chamberlain asked a second time, the coach said, "We're playing better without you." The Lakers had rallied with Mel Counts on the floor (though he shot only 4-for-13 and was called for traveling in the last two minutes) and Van Breda Kolff kept the backup center in the game. Russell criticized Chamberlain publicly, saying, "In a game like that, they would have had to carry me out to get me off the floor." The remark stung Chamberlain and caused a rift between the two men.

No one had an inkling that Russell was retiring, but a *Sports Illustrated* article came out that summer in which Russell announced that he was packing it in. He had sold his story, but never told the Celtics, whom he coached to two championships in three years. Russell returned to the game to coach Seattle for the 1973-74 season. He stayed on the bench for four years, leaving after the 1977 season. While the team hovered around

the .500 mark, he helped build the Supersonics into a squad that reached the Finals in 1978 and won the championship in 1979. He would return to coaching once more, with Sacramento for part of the 1987-88 season.

Russell won five MVPs in an eight-year span from 1958 through 1965. He was voted All-NBA first team three times (compared to Chamberlain's seven times). He was an all-star for 12 consecutive years (1958 through 1969) and won the MVP of the 1963 classic with 19 points and 24 rebounds. He was elected to the Hall of Fame in 1975. In 1980 the Professional Basketball Writers Association of America declared him the greatest player in the history of the NBA. He was selected for the league's 25th, 35th and 50th Anniversary All-Time Teams.

He still holds a plethora of rebounding records. He remains the Celtics' all-time leader with 21,620 boards and still has the most ever in the playoffs, 4,104. In 1959 he established a Finals record for rebounds per game with 29.5; two years earlier, he had set a rookie rebound record in the Finals with an average of 22.9. He shares a Finals record with 40 rebounds in a game, something he did twice. With Russell, however, the individual feats blur. His most memorable number is 11 of 13. He led his teams to that many titles in that many years. No player has approached that.

Dolph Schayes

Forward, Syracuse 1948-49 (NBL); Syracuse 1949-50 through 1962-63; Philadelphia, 1963-64
Born: May 19, 1928 in New York 6-8, 220 High School: DeWitt Clinton (Bronx, N.Y.) College: NYU

Dolph Schayes was basketball's Iron Man in the 1950s, once playing in 706 consecutive games. During one stretch from 1949 until just after Christmas in 1961, when a broken cheek-bone forced him out of action, Schayes missed only three games. Known as the "Rainbow Kid" around the league because of his high-arching set shots, Schayes posted double-digits in points and rebounds over 11 consecutive seasons starting in 1951. In his practices, he'd fit a 14-inch basket inside the regulation 18-inch hoop to improve his free throw accuracy. Twice in his career he hit 90 percent of his free throws and three times led the league at the charity stripe. In 1950 he set a record with 35 rebounds in a game. A year later he grabbed 1,080, the first player to notch 1,000.

Schayes was the first player in league history to reach 15,000 points. He was known as "Mr. Nat," having played all 16 of his seasons (1949-64) with the Syracuse Nationals franchise (including one season in Philadelphia after the team moved). A six-time All-NBA first team player, Schayes had unlimited range on the perimeter and was consistently among the league's leading scorers and rebounders for more than a decade. He played in 12 straight All-Star Games from 1951 through 1962.

When Schayes graduated New York University in 1948 there were two pro leagues competing for players. He received bids from each. He wanted to go with the Knicks, who then belonged to the BAA, but a league rule prevented them from paying a rookie more than $5,000. Syracuse, at that time in the older National Basketball League (NBL), offered $7,500. Schayes accepted Syracuse's offer.

Syracuse never failed to make the playoffs in the Dolph Schayes era. Schayes broke his arm and played wearing a cast against Minneapolis in the 1954 Finals. His inspirational presence was not enough, however, as the Lakers won the seesaw series in seven games. It was the second close call for Syracuse, which had lost to Minneapolis in six games in the 1950 Finals. In 1955 the Nats won their only NBA title, beating the Fort Wayne Pistons in seven games as Schayes averaged 19 points and 13 rebounds.

By the time Schayes, who was then making $25,000, retired 24 games into the 1963-64 season, the Syracuse franchise had moved to Philadelphia. He had 19,247 points, second in NBA history at that time to Bob Pettit.

Schayes became Philadelphia's coach from 1964 through 1966, winning Coach of the Year in his last season as the 76ers, led by Wilt Chamberlain, won 55 and lost 25. But in the Eastern Division Finals the Sixers lost to Boston in five games, and Alex Hannum replaced Schayes as Philly's coach. Schayes coached the Buffalo Braves in 1971 and was replaced after one game in 1972. Again his timing was poor: it was the pre-Bob McAdoo era in Buffalo. He later served as the NBA's supervisor of officials.

Schayes was elected to the Hall of Fame in 1972. He had already been selected for the league's 25th Anniversary Team in 1970s and was named to the NBA's 50th Anniversary All-Time Team in 1996. His son, Danny, played 18 years with seven different NBA teams and retired in 1999.

Bill Sharman

Guard, Washington, 1950-51; Boston, 1951-52 through 1960-61
Born: May 25, 1926 in Abilene, Tex. 6-1, 190 High School: Narbonne (Lomita, Cal.) then Porterville (Cal.) College: Southern California

Bill Sharman was a sharp-shooting guard for the Boston Celtics from 1951 through 1961. He played on four Boston title teams and formed, with Bob Cousy, what has been called "the first modern backcourt." There were no clearly delineated "one" and "two" guards as such in the 1950s. But in essence, Cousy was the playmaker and Sharman the shotmaker. Sharman was the best mid-range shooter of his time. Between them, they averaged 35 to 40 points per game for nearly a decade. No other team had a backcourt tandem remotely like them.

When the league average was around 35-percent accuracy, Sharman was hitting between 40 and 45 percent of his shots, finishing in the top 10 in field-goal percentage six times. An all-star for eight consecutive years from 1953 through 1960, he also led the league in free-throw percentage five times in a row and seven times in nine years. His .883 free-throw percentage is sixth best all-time.

Sharman's boyhood hero was Stanford's Hank Luisetti, who popularized the one-handed push shot. An all-around athlete at Narbonne and then Porterville high schools, Sharman won letters in baseball, football, and basketball. He tossed the shot and javelin, ran hurdles on the track team, and was an undefeated amateur boxer when he hung up the gloves. He graduated high school the day after his 18th birthday; a day later he won the Central California tennis championship. The next day he got married and joined the Navy after a 24-hour honeymoon.

More than a dozen colleges would have taken Sharman on a football scholarship, but he sacrificed football to protect his baseball future. He entered Southern California on the GI Bill in 1946, but three months later he had a basketball scholarship. As a senior he scored 446 points, breaking Luisetti's Pacific Coast Conference record for points in a season. Two years earlier he had broken Luisetti's 12-game conference record of 232 points when he scored 25 points against UCLA in the season's last game to finish with 238.

An All-American in 1950, Sharman left college before getting his degree, enticed by a $12,000 bonus to sign with baseball's Brooklyn Dodgers. After signing, he was selected by the NBA's Washington Caps and became a two-sport pro. After the Washington franchise folded in January 1951, Sharman was selected by Fort Wayne in the 1951 NBA dispersal draft. He didn't report to Fort Wayne, but went home and waited for the start of the baseball season. The Dodgers brought him up for a look in 1951, just before the season ended. The Dodgers of the early 1950s were a team laden with future Hall of Famers, however, and when they returned Sharman to the minors in 1952, he reluctantly quit. The Celtics acquired him as a throw-in, with forward Bob Brannum, in exchange for center Charlie Share.

Starting with the 1951-52 season, Sharman teamed with Cousy to give Boston the NBA's premier backcourt. It was Cousy the dazzling passer and fast-breaker and Sharman the pure shooter. In 1953 the ex-Dodger held the league record with 11 straight field goals. The record stood for seven years until George Yardley broke it with 12 straight.

Sharman not only won the free throw title seven times, but broke 90 percent efficiency three times. In 1953-54 he set a record by hitting 50 free throws in a row. He then missed one and hit 29 more, for a string of 79 of 80. The following year he hit 55 in a row without missing. In the 1958-59 playoffs he ran off 56 in a row and made 57 of 59 overall. That same year he set another NBA regular season record, finishing with a 93.2 success rate at the charity stripe.

By the time he retired in 1961 Bill Sharman was 11th lifetime in field-goal percentage; the 10 men ahead of him were all frontcourt players.

His 42.9 percent shooting was the best in history among the guards. Sharman left Boston at the end of the 1961 season, accepting a three-year contract to coach the Los Angeles Jets in the new American Basketball League. With a record of 24-15, the team folded halfway through the inaugural season. Two weeks later Sharman ended up with the Cleveland Pipers, who he guided to an ABL championship.

In 1971, he coached the Utah Stars of the ABA to a title, besting Kentucky in seven games in the Finals. The following season he won Coach of the Year, leading the Los Angeles Lakers to an NBA title, giving him championships in three different leagues.

Sharman was elected to the Hall of Fame in 1975. He coached the Lakers through the 1976 season before becoming general manager of the team through 1982. He later became vice president of the Los Angeles Clippers, president of the Lakers, and then a consultant to the Lakers. In 1996 he was voted to the NBA's 50th Anniversary All-Time Team.

John Stockton

Guard, Utah, 1984-85 through 2002-03
Born: March 26, 1962 in Spokane, Wash. 6-1, 175 High School: Gonzaga Prep School (Spokane, Wash.) College: Gonzaga

After 19 seasons, John Stockton's career has assumed a legendary status. Stockton assisted shooters 15,806 times, more than 5,000 ahead of runner-up Mark Jackson. He led the league in assists nine years in a row. Less known, Stockton hit 52 percent of his shots and scored 19,711 points. He is the NBA's all-time steals leader (a statistic kept only since the 1973-74 season) with 3,265. With Karl Malone, Stockton—an iron man who played the full 82-game slate 13 times and is No. 2 on the all-time games-played list at 1,504—has formed the game's most lasting and perhaps greatest one-two punch.

How Stockton was still around at 16th in the first round of the 1984 draft is anyone's guess. He finished his college career at Gonzaga University as the school's all-time assist leader (554) and sixth leading scorer. He averaged 20.9 points and 7.2 assists as a senior. After the draft, the story goes, Stockton took home Utah's game films and came to camp knowing where Darrell Griffith and Adrian Dantley liked to receive the ball. At first a back-up point guard, Stockton beat out Rickey Green in his third year. The job was his thereafter.

In his first 14 seasons he played in 1,062 games and missed only four. In 16 years he had played in 1,258 games and missed only 22. He missed 18 games in the 1997-98 season, the only extended injury time in his career. When he passed Moses Malone with 1,456 games, he moved into third place on the all-time list behind Robert Parish and Kareem Abdul-Jabbar.

The symbiotic Stockton-Malone relationship has produced two trips to the NBA Finals, but a championship has eluded them. Stockton and Malone were together long enough to produce about 48,000 points.

Stockton's greatest highlights came in the 1997 playoffs. He controlled the late minutes of the Conference Finals versus Houston, hitting a 3-pointer that won Game 6 and sent the Jazz to the Finals. He duplicated those heroics in Game 4 of the Finals, hitting a 3-pointer, then stealing the ball from Jordan and hitting Malone with a floor-length pass that sealed the game. Though Stockton hit 50 percent of his shots and averaged 15 points and 9 assists against the Bulls, Chicago won in six games. In 1998 he didn't play as well in the Finals, averaging just 10 points and 9 assists against Jordan and company.

Aside from his disappointment in NBA title games, Stockton did play on two championship teams, the gold medal-winning U.S. Olympic squads in 1992 and 1996. He was named to the NBA 50th Anniversary All-Time Team in 1996. He retired at the end of the 2002-03 season.

Isiah Thomas

Guard, Detroit, 1981-82 through 1993-94
Born: April 30, 1961 in Chicago, Ill. 6-1, 182 High School: St. Joseph's (Westchester, Ill.) College: Indiana

Isiah 'Zeke' Thomas was the pivotal player on one of basketball's greatest teams, Detroit's "Bad Boy" Pistons. The "Bad Boys" fought their way to the NBA Finals in 1988, 1989, and

1990, winning the last two against Los Angeles and Portland. In the 1990 series Thomas was Finals MVP. Even before that series, he had established himself as one of the great big-game performers and streak shooters in history and perhaps the greatest small guard of all-time. He could use his singular dribbling ability and speed to break down most any defender and score on the drive or get free for a jumper.

For a long time Thomas did not have a reputation as a consistent performer. During the 1986-87 season, Detroit coach Chuck Daly said Thomas' "threshold of boredom in the game is very low." As if to prove Daly prophetic, Thomas, with the 1987 Conference Finals tied at two games apiece and his team up by a point with five seconds left, had his looping inbound pass stolen by Larry Bird, who fed Dennis Johnson for the winning basket. The Celtics won in seven games and went to the Finals against the Lakers. If not for that moment, the Pistons might have played in four consecutive NBA Finals from 1987 to 1990. The intercepted pass probably turned around Thomas' career, giving him renewed determination, which in turn helped him and his team to an esteemed place in NBA history.

Isiah Lord Thomas III was the oldest of nine children. He lived in a Chicago ghetto and his father, a janitor, left when he was six years old. He did not blame his father. He understood why an intelligent man—who had learned to read blueprints and became the first black foreman at International Harvester, but had no outlet for his skill after the local plant closed—would leave when he couldn't make use of his intelligence.

Thomas traveled hours by train and bus to attend a suburban catholic high school in Westchester, Illinois. There he learned to get by academically and play well enough to earn a scholarship to Indiana University. As a sophomore he led the Hoosiers to an NCAA title in 1981 and won Outstanding Player in the Tournament. On the strength of that performance Detroit chose him in the first round, second overall, in the 1981 draft.

He made the All-Star team as a rookie and in each of the next 11 years. He won the All-Star Game MVP twice, scoring 21 points and getting 15 assists in 1984 and 30 points and 10 assists in 1986. Throughout, he stayed in touch with his father until the summer of 1987, when his dad died at the age of 64. "He was proud of me," Thomas said. "But he never wanted me to be a basketball player. He always wanted me to be a politician."

Thomas had already built a reputation for rapid-fire brilliance. In the 1984 opening round against the Knicks, he brought his team back from certain defeat, scoring 16 points in the last 94 seconds of regulation to send the game into overtime.

In 1988 Detroit ended the Celtics' dominance of the Eastern Conference. The Pistons prevailed in a six-game Conference Finals and the Celtics reached 100 points only once. Detroit then took a 3-2 lead in the Finals against Los Angeles, and was leading in the third quarter of Game 6 when Thomas sprained his ankle and fell to the floor in pain. Instead of nursing the ankle he essentially played on one foot, scoring a Finals record 25 points in the quarter on an assortment of drives and jumpers, many of them off the wrong foot. Detroit led with seconds remaining, but lost on a Byron Scott runner and Kareem Abdul-Jabbar's two free throws.

The following year Detroit stormed through the playoffs at a 15-2 clip (sweeping Boston and Milwaukee, beating Chicago 4-2, and sweeping Los Angeles in the Finals) and Thomas had his first title in eight NBA seasons. In 1990 the Pistons repeated, beating Portland four games to one. Thomas scored 28 points per game and was awarded Finals MVP.

Thomas underwent wrist surgery and played only 48 games the following year. The Bulls ended the Bad Boys' reign by sweeping them in the Conference Finals. In two of the next three seasons the Pistons didn't make the playoffs, and they were eliminated in the first round in the other year. Perhaps more painful was Thomas' being snubbed for the Olympic "Dream Team" in 1992. (He was selected for the U.S. Olympic team in 1980, but that team boycotted the Games.) Thomas announced his retirement in May 1994. His 9,061 assists are fifth on the NBA all-time list, and he is Detroit's career leader with 18,822 points. He was chosen for the NBA 50th Anniversary All-Time in 1996, and in 2000 was elected to the Hall of Fame.

Three days after his retirement, Thomas became part-owner and executive vice-president of the new Toronto Raptors. Failing in his attempt to gain full ownership of the team, he left to become a broadcaster and then bought the Continental Basketball Association for $10 million in 1999. The following year, Thomas became coach of the Indiana Pacers, and was forced by the NBA to divest his interest in the CBA. He was fired by the Pacers in August 2003.

David Thompson

Guard, Denver, 1975-76 (ABA); Denver, 1976-77 through 1981-82; Seattle, 1982-83 through 1983-84
Born: July 13, 1954 in Boiling Springs, N.C. 6-4, 195 High School: Crest High School (Shelby, N.C.) College: North Carolina State

David Thompson scored 73 points on the last day of the 1977-78 season. It remains the highest total in NBA history by any player not named Chamberlain. From his time at college, when he dethroned UCLA in 1974 and brought a national title to North Carolina State, Thompson was a skywalker of the first magnitude. At the 1976 ABA All-Star Game he took on Julius Erving in a legendary slam-dunk competition, years before the NBA ever made it a staple of its own All-Star weekend. A major magazine would declare the slam-dunk contest "the best half-time invention since the rest room."

What Thompson's career lacked, and what stratospheric players like Michael Jordan and Julius Erving had, was longevity. His outstanding offensive attributes were mostly gone before his 27th birthday and his nine-year pro career was history before he turned 30. Like Herb Score in baseball or Gale Sayers in football, Thompson gave us a glimpse of how great he could have been had his fortunes been different. But due to injuries, and bouts with drugs and alcohol, no one ever saw the full picture.

David Thompson was one of 11 children. His father was a Shelby, North Carolina, truck driver, and young David helped out in the Baptist church where his father was a deacon. Before he starred for the Wolfpack, he was a North Carolina legend as a leaper, slashing driver and accurate shooter. He turned down several multimillion-dollar offers after his sophomore and junior seasons because his mother wanted him to graduate. The Wolfpack's record in his three All-American seasons was 79-7, and he ushered in a new world order with his aerial show over

Bill Walton and the Bruins in 1974. He became known as "The Skywalker," the guard with a 44-inch vertical leap. The 1974 tournament MVP, he was the prize thoroughbred in a 1975 bidding battle between the ABA and NBA. The ABA won out, with the Denver Nuggets signing him for three years at a league-high $450,000 per year.

Thompson won Rookie of the Year, and helped the Nuggets to a 60-24 record and the 1976 ABA Finals, the league's last before it merged with the NBA. The franchise had moved into the 17,000-seat McNichols Arena and averaged more than 13,000 fans per game, the fourth best in all of pro basketball and far and away the best in the ABA. The move to the NBA hardly slowed Thompson. In the 1977 All-Star Game, the first after the merger, Thompson could look around and see that five of the 10 starters were old ABA mates, no longer deemed inferior to the NBA players. Thompson scored 18 points on 7-for-9 shooting and grabbed 7 rebounds. The next year Thompson led the West All-Stars with 20 points, and in 1979 he scored 26, leading the West to victory and notching the MVP—making him the first and last player to win an All-Star MVP in both pro leagues. In four NBA All-Star Games he averaged 19 points, connecting on an otherworldly 67 percent of his shots.

Thompson was now an unstoppable offensive force, equally adept at scoring on spectacular slams, suspended-in-midair drives, or jumpers. He shot well over 50 percent for his career. In 1978 he signed a five-year $4 million deal contract that made him the highest paid player in basketball history. He posted his best offensive season that year, averaging 27.2 points per game. He lost the scoring title to George Gervin, 27.22 to 27.15, the closest differential ever recorded.

But problems had already begun for Thompson. "It started at the end of my rookie season," Thompson later recalled in his memoir, *Tall Tales*. "After the exhibition games, the regular season and the playoffs, we had played almost 100 games. One day I was very tired and I started telling a teammate about that. He said, 'Hey, I've got something that will help you.' Then he started putting some lines of cocaine on the table. It gave me a lift, but it later ruined my life."

In 1983 Thompson got into a scuffle at Studio 54, slid down a flight of stairs, and ripped up the ligaments in his left knee. His career was essentially over. Thompson played only 94 games over his last two years and retired in 1984 at the age of 29. "I had a chance to be the greatest basketball player ever and I blew it because of drugs," he admitted. Thompson now speaks at basketball clinics for the Charlotte Hornets and instructs kids' groups about drugs. In 1996, 12 years after his retirement, he was elected to the Basketball Hall of Fame.

Nate Thurmond

Center, San Francisco, 1963-64 through 1970-71; Golden State, 1971-1972 through 1973-74; Chicago, 1974-75, 1975; Cleveland, 1975-76 through 1976-77
Born: July 25, 1941 in Akron, Ohio 6-11, 235 High School: Akron Central Hower (Akron, OH) College: Bowling Green

Nate Thurmond's career line is the quintessence of balance: 14,437 points and 14,464 rebounds, 15 points and 15 rebounds per game. If Nate "The Great" Thurmond were playing now, broadcasters on sports highlight shows would be talk-

ing endlessly about his "double-doubles." The term was not used in the basketball lexicon of Thurmond's time, but the feat it describes is what the big man did game in, game out, for every season from 1965 through 1974. If he graced the game today Thurmond would also be getting ink for being the "best all-around center in the league," which is what guards Dick Barnett and Jerry West were calling him in 1968. That same year Knicks coach Dick McGuire said, "Nate Thurmond is the most valuable property in the league." Thurmond himself was aware of this; he once confessed, "My goal is to become the best all-around big man ever." He was most noted for his defense. No less than Kareem Abdul-Jabbar said that Thurmond was the toughest defender he ever played against.

When Thurmond graduated grade school he was already 6-foot-1, and his older brother Ben was leading him away from baseball and toward basketball. By the time he was a sophomore at Akron Central Hower in Ohio he was 6-foot-4 and the tallest kid on the team. His coach, Joe Siegfirth, put him at forward. "I wasn't too strong then," Thurmond recalls, remembering how smaller, wider bodies muscled him under the basket. He thus developed a shot from 15 to 18 feet. By the time he was a junior he had risen to 6-foot-8, but stayed at forward, giving way to his stronger teammate (and future Baltimore Bullets great), Gus Johnson. By his senior year Thurmond had bulked up a little and began playing in the pivot.

Among the 20 scholarships offered to him, Thurmond settled on Bowling Green. He had to learn how to use his height on offense. He played a gentle game, as if he was afraid of hurting anyone, so coach Harold Anderson reminded him to be aggressive. In 1963, his senior year, he was chosen All-American.

The San Francisco Warriors grabbed him in the first round, third overall (behind Art Heyman and Rod Thorn) in the 1963 draft. He was offered a $2000 signing bonus and a salary of $14,000. At 6-foot-11 Thurmond was big for his time, but in training camp he met a bigger teammate—the 7-foot-1 Wilt Chamberlain. But Wilt became a mentor, teaching Thurmond how to exploit his height. Wilt played the pivot, Thurmond forward, and the Warriors got to the NBA Finals against Boston, losing in five games.

At the All-Star break in 1965 the Warriors unloaded Chamberlain and his $200,000 salary to Philadelphia. Thurmond moved to the pivot and posted 17 points and 18 rebounds per game. His liberation was hardly San Francisco's: the Warriors won 17 and lost 63, 14 games worse than any other team in the league. When Thurmond snatched 42 rebounds against Detroit in a November 1965 game, he became one of only four players—the others are Chamberlain, Bill Russell, and Jerry Lucas—ever to get 40 in a game.

Now Thurmond honed his all-around game. On November 4, 1967, he became the first player ever to hold Chamberlain scoreless for a game. Even so, Thurmond's coaches—first Alex Hannum and then Bill Sharman—said that his game was too soft.

In 1967, Thurmond hurt his leg and missed the final 31 games of the season and all of the playoffs. At the time of his injury, Thurmond was enjoying his best season, averaging 21 points and 22 rebounds a game. Only three others had ever accomplished the 20-20 feat— Chamberlain, Bob Pettit, and

Jerry Lucas. A doctor fitted him with a built-up sneaker to mitigate his back troubles, caused by one hip being lower than the other.

He started the 1968-69 season by receiving a three-season $95,000-per-year deal from the Warriors. Again, he posted gargantuan numbers of 22 points and 20 rebounds per game. Following the 1974 season, Thurmond was traded to the Bulls for center Clifford Ray and a first-round draft pick. It was the first year that blocks were recorded and Thurmond, at 32, averaged 2.9 per game.

Thurmond retired after the 1977 season and was inducted into the Hall of Fame in 1985. He was named to the NBA's 50th Anniversary All-Time Team in 1996.

Wes Unseld

Center-Forward, Baltimore, 1968-69 through 1972-73; Capital Bullets, 1973-74; 1974-75 through 1980-81
Born: March 14, 1946 in Louisville, Ky. 6-7, 245 High School: Seneca (Louisville, Ky.) College: Louisville

Without being a dominant scorer, Wes Unseld led his teams to the NBA Finals four times in the nine seasons from 1971 through 1979. His was a game of rebounds and granite picks and outlet passes that don't ever show up in a box score. "Unseld was the consummate team player; his only objective was to win," says Mitch Kupchak, the Lakers' general manager, who was Unseld's teammate. "Statistics were never important to him. You can't begin to imagine what he did to make his teammates better."

Red Auerbach, Bob Ryan and Hubie Brown all called him the greatest outlet passer who ever played. "No man in history ever began more fast breaks with 50-foot outlet passes than Wes Unseld did," says Ryan.

The Baltimore Bullets selected Unseld second overall in the 1968 draft. Only Elvin Hayes, his future teammate, was picked ahead of him. He had a reputation as an irrepressible rebounder at Louisville and he continued boarding as a center for Baltimore. He led the Bullets to a 57-25 record and an Eastern Division title in his first year. That, plus 14 points and 18 rebounds per game, was enough to get him Rookie of the Year and Most Valuable Player honors, the first player to earn both distinctions since Wilt Chamberlain in 1960. Baltimore was swept in the semi-finals and lost in seven in 1970, both times at the hands of New York.

In 1971 Baltimore toppled New York in the Eastern Conference Finals and met Milwaukee for the title. Unseld posted averages of 15 points and 19 rebounds in the championship series, but he was giving away seven inches in the pivot to Kareem Abdul-Jabbar, who logged 27 points and 19 rebounds a game and took home the MVP award as Milwaukee swept Baltimore in four.

Unseld made the All-Star team for the fifth time in 1975, leading Washington (the Bullets had moved from Baltimore before the 1973-74 season) to its sixth division title in seven years. In the Finals the team was swept by Golden State.

The two-Finals-two-sweeps ledger was improved in 1978, when the Bullets faced Seattle and came back after being down 3-to-2. They won Game 6 by 35 points and got key contributions from Charles Johnson and Kupchak to outlast Seattle in Game 7, 105-99. Unseld was awarded series MVP. "He went 40 to 46 minutes, setting picks, and doing all the little things you need done," said teammate Phil Chenier. "He was the established leader of that team."

Seattle returned the favor the following season, beating the Bullets in five games. Two years later, following the 1980-81 season, Unseld retired. In 13 years he averaged 11 points and 14 rebounds per game. He was vice president of the Bullets the following season and then, after a five-year hiatus, an assistant coach, before taking over the head coaching duties for the 1987-88 season. That season was the only one he posted a .500 record in his seven years at the helm; his coaching record was 202-345 (.369).

Starting in 1995, Unseld became the team's vice president for a year, and was then general manager from 1996-97 until stepping down for health reasons in June 2003. He was elected to the Hall of Fame in 1987 and was selected for the NBA's 50th Anniversary Team in 1996.

Chet Walker

Forward-Guard, Syracuse, 1962-63; Philadelphia, 1963-64 through 1968-69; Chicago, 1969-70 through 1974-75
Born: February 22, 1940 in Benton Harbor, Mich. 6-7, 220 High School: Benton Harbor College: Bradley

Chet Walker's reputation was enormous even before his 13 pro seasons got under way. His tag was "Chet the Jet," bestowed for his speed and his celebrated one-on-one skills. At Bradley he set the world on fire, being named All-Missouri Conference three times and consensus All-American twice. In 1960 he scored 50 points in a game against California. Averaging 24.4 points, 12.8 rebounds, and connecting on 55 percent of his shots, Walker led the Braves to a top-10 ranking and a three-year mark of 69-14.

A seven-time all-star, Walker player on the 1967 Philadelphia 76ers, one of the greatest teams of all-time. He began, though, with the Sixers' earlier incarnation, the Syracuse Nats, who chose him in the second round, 14th overall, in the 1962 draft. Chosen ahead of him were three future Hall of Famers—Jerry Lucas, Dave DeBusschere, and John Havlicek—and other stars like Zelmo Beaty. Walker saved his rookie best for the playoffs in 1963, averaging 15 points and 9 rebounds, in the Nats' last season before the franchise moved to Philly.

Walker's six years in Philadelphia would include three all-star seasons. For Philadelphia's 1967 Championship season, Walker averaged 19 points and 8 rebounds per game. The result was 68 wins and a staggering per-game average of 125 points. The Sixers capped an incredible year by defeating San Francisco in the Finals. Walker was an all-star for the third time in four years and scored 15 points in the All-Star Game. He had his best playoff showing with 22 points and 8 rebounds a game.

Walker played the full 82 games in each of the next two seasons, but Philadelphia, which traded Chamberlain in 1968-69, didn't reach the Finals again until nearly a decade later. After the 1969 season Walker, still just 29, was traded to Chicago.

Chicago was a gritty team, with stars like Bob Love and top-notch defenders like Norm Van Lier and Jerry Sloan. In six seasons with the Bulls Walker posted some of his personal bests, including four straight 20-point seasons and two more over

19 a game. He had a league-leading 86 percent mark from the free throw line in 1971, but went even higher in his last two seasons, 1974 and 1975. He still had enough in the tank to score a personal high 56 points against the Kansas City Royals in 1972.

Walker retired after playing 76 games that season, and then 13 more in the playoffs. He left with his reputation intact, that of a forward equally adept at scoring on the drive or from the perimeter.

Bill Walton

Center, Portland, 1974-75 through 1978-79; San Diego from 1979-80 through 1983-84; LA Clippers, 1984-85; Boston, 1985-86 through 1986-87
Born: November 5, 1952 in La Mesa, Cal. 6-11, 235 High School: Helix (La Mesa, Cal.) College: UCLA

Bill Walton owned what may have been the most complete, albeit short-lived package of skills of any pivot man in history. Like Kareem Abdul-Jabbar before him, Walton was a John Wooden disciple, schooled in a philosophy of team play. He could shoot, defend, pass, rebound, make great outlet passes—his talent quotient was optimal and his game had no shortcomings. "If you were grading a player for every fundamental skill," Wooden said, "Walton would rank the highest of any center who ever played."

A distinguished panel of 50 coaches, former players, writers, and broadcasters selected Bill Walton as one of the 50 greatest players of all time. He might also have been voted one of the 10 most injured. His physical mishaps didn't keep the basketball world from seeing his greatness, but they did keep him from displaying it more frequently. No other great player in NBA history was compromised more often by injuries. In Walton's 14 NBA seasons, from 1975 through 1988, he was only able to play in 468 of a possible 1,148 games. On average he played 33 games per year and missed 49. In four entire seasons he has no statistical record because he did not play a game. Three of those seasons occurred between the ages of 26 and 29. When he did play, he averaged 28 minutes per game. He has endured no less than 30 operations to his feet.

Those who saw Walton at his best affirm that his career would have been legendary had he played more often. Evidence abounds. He was College Player of the Year from 1972 through 1974, his sophomore through senior years. In 1972 and 1973 he was voted the Most Outstanding Player of the NCAA Tournament. He is UCLA's career rebounding leader (1,370) and third in scoring average (20.3). Walton's UCLA teams won their first 73 games, part of the Bruins' 88-game winning streak, until upset by Notre Dame in 1974. UCLA was 86-4 during the Walton years.

He still holds the NCAA career tournament record for highest field-goal percentage, shooting at a 68.6 clip (1972 through 1974). His 1972 and 1973 teams won the NCAA title, while North Carolina State, led by David Thompson, upset UCLA in Walton's senior season.

But those are just a few of his achievements. Walton's college career was as notable for his views as it was for his athletic distinctions. Professors, students, and other athletes knew him, and lauded him, as much for his social and political conscious-

ness as for his athletic endowments. He was as likely to be found at an anti-war or pro-environment rally as on the basketball court.

Portland took Walton first in the draft. When injuries plagued Walton during his first two NBA seasons, some writers and sportscasters, amazingly, attributed them to his vegetarianism, political activism, or lifestyle. A summer knee operation kept him from running, and Walton played his rookie season in subpar physical condition. Team physician Bob Cook said that his unending string of injuries owed to his being rushed back into action before he was ready because of his value to the team. The stress on muscles, bones, and ligaments that were unhealed and fatigued got him into an injury cycle. He played just 35 games his first season.

A week before his second training camp he broke his foot on a lawn sprinkler while playing catch with a Frisbee. The toll of his first two seasons included several broken noses, a broken leg, a broken foot, a broken wrist, and several dislocated fingers. He managed 51 games in his second season and improved to 16 points and 13 rebounds per game.

Portland finished under .500 in Walton's first two seasons, but a game against Philadelphia early in his third proved a harbinger of things to come. The Trailblazers scorched the 76ers, 146-104, in a November contest. At one point Julius Erving drove, hung in the air, switched the ball from one hand to the other, and double-pumped. Walton hung with him and smashed the shot away. Playing just 32 minutes, Walton was 10-for-13 from the field and scored 26 points. He also led his team with 16 rebounds and 6 assists.

Six months later, after sweeping Los Angeles in the Western Conference Finals, Portland would have to wait nine days before playing Philadelphia in the Finals. It appeared that Erving, McGinnis, Doug Collins, World B. Free and company would win the title despite their tendencies to play as individuals. The Sixers took the first two games in Philadelphia, the second by a convincing 107-89 score. In Games 3 and 4 Portland won by margins of 22 and 32 points. The Trailblazers triumphed in the next two games and won their first and last NBA title. It was the first time in the 31-year history of the league that a team won four straight games in the final round after losing the first two. Walton won the Outstanding Player Award for the series, then given by *SPORT* magazine, and he received a car.

In 1978 Portland won 58 games, nine more than the year before, but played without Walton, who appeared in only 58 games due to an injury. Walton still managed to win the league's MVP award, but Seattle eliminated Portland in the first round. Injured the entire 1979 season, Walton would never play another game for the Blazers. After the season he was signed by San Diego as a veteran free agent.

In five seasons in San Diego Walton would play just 102 games. He played only 14 games in 1980 and missed the 1981 and 1982 seasons entirely. The team moved to Los Angeles for the 1984-85 season, but Walton, in his 11th season, was no longer the same player. Averaging 25 minutes a night, he registered 10 points and 9 rebounds per game. Before the 1986 season, the Celtics gave up Cedric Maxwell, a star from their 1981 and 1984 title teams, and a first-round draft pick for Walton.

He joined a Boston team with seeking its third title in the

1980s and 16th overall. Walton played back-up to Robert Parish as Boston won a league-leading 67 games. The team then tore through the post-season at a 15-3 clip and won its last NBA title. Walton won the league's Sixth Man Award.

But the cycle of injuries continued for Walton, who appeared in only 10 games the following year.

Despite his absentee seasons and time spent recuperating, Walton was elected to the Hall of Fame in 1993, his first year of eligibility. Three years later he was selected for the NBA's 50th Anniversary All-Time Team. He currently enjoys a second act as a popular, if notoriously opinionated, basketball broadcaster.

Jerry West

Guard, LA Lakers, 1960-61 through 1973-74
Born: May 28, 1938 in Cheylan, W. Va. 6-2, 185 High School: East Bank (W. Va.) College: West Virginia

Hoops fans of the 1960s and early 1970s remember Jerry West as an unstoppable scorer. If only a few minutes remained and No. 44 was coming downcourt against any defender, it was time to check the scoreboard to see if the lead was safe. Time and again he would back a defender down and shoot over him, releasing his shot with that perfect form. West could wipe out a 10-point lead in a four-minute spurt like no other player. His wiry build and long arms gave him a seemingly effortless grace.

For his endgame exploits West was aptly named "Mr. Clutch." His 29.1 career playoff scoring average is second only to Michael Jordan's 33.4. He was selected for the All-Defensive first team from 1970 through 1973 (the award wasn't given until 1969). His career is the story of stellar play—he was All-NBA first team 10 times between 1962 and 1973—and heart-breaking losses. In no less than six playoffs, West's Lakers would run out of gas against the deeper talent of the Boston Celtics.

West's older brother David, who was later killed in Korea, taught him the fundamentals of basketball. In his senior year, he helped the Consolidated East Bank High School Team to an undefeated season and a state championship by scoring 927 points in 27 games. The mayor changed the name of the town from East Bank to West Bank for one day, in honor of West. After that, scouts and coaches descended on the town of Cheylan to lure him into a college.

The spotlight was uncomfortable for West, who was the son of an electrician and grew up in a town with no post office, 35 miles from Charleston, West Virginia. When he arrived at the University of West Virginia, he was dubbed "the hick from Cabin Creek," which eventually became "Zeke from Cabin Creek." West never won a Division I scoring title, but tied an NCAA record by scoring 160 points in the 1959 tournament. He scored 28 points and grabbed 12 rebounds in the Finals, but West Virginia lost to California, 71-70. West received the tournament MVP and led all players with averages of 32 points and 14.6 rebounds per game.

With Oscar Robertson, West was co-captain of the U.S. team that went undefeated to take home the gold in the 1960 Rome Olympics. The Minneapolis Lakers (who moved to Los Angeles before the start of the 1960-61 season) made West their first pick; he was second overall in the draft. He signed for two years at $20,000 per year. He averaged 17 points and 7 rebounds in his rookie season, and was selected to his first of 14 consecutive All-Star Games. In his second year he averaged 31 points per game, and the West-Elgin Baylor duo often scored a combined 75 to 85 points a night. West frequently played hurt and suffered through a sinus condition that resulted from breaking his nose four times.

In each of his first eight seasons West averaged more points in the playoffs than he had during the regular season. Yet even with Baylor and West scoring more than 50,000 points between them and forming what is undoubtedly the greatest one-two punch in NBA history, they would suffer seven losses in the Finals between 1962 and 1970. Six of those seven losses were to the Celtics (the other was to New York), and four of the series went an agonizing seven games. Even when West averaged 40.6 points, as he did in the 1965 post-season, it was not enough.

At 31, West became the oldest player in NBA history to win a scoring title when he led the league with a 31.2 average in 1970 (Jordan later won scoring titles at 33, 34, and 35 years of age). In 1972 the Lakers shattered the Bucks' record of 19 consecutive wins by running off 33 wins in a row from November 5, 1971 through January 7, 1972. They averaged 121 points a game and finished with a 69-13 record. The defense allowed just 108.7 points per game, giving them an average winning margin of 12.3 points per game, the highest in the league that year. On average, West and Gail Goodrich combined for 52 points a night.

They stormed through the playoffs, trouncing Chicago four-zip before avenging their loss to Milwaukee in 1971 by besting the Bucks, with Abdul-Jabbar and Robertson, four games to two. In the Finals they settled accounts with the Knicks, paying them back for the 1970 defeat. After New York took the opener, the Lakers clobbered them in four straight. For the season they went 81-16. Ironically, West had the worst post-season of his career, shooting only 37 percent from the field. In 1973, the Knicks took back the Championship with a five-game victory. West retired after playing just 31 games of the 1974 season.

West coached the Lakers from 1977 through 1979, posting a record of 145-101 (.589). He was a consultant and general manager with Los Angeles from 1979 through 1994, before becoming the team's executive VP in 1995, a position he retired from in 2000. On April 30, 2002, he accepted a position as president of basketball operations with the Memphis Grizzlies.

West was elected to the Hall of Fame in 1980, the same year he was named to the league's 35th Anniversary Team. In 1996 he was voted to the NBA's 50th Anniversary All-Time Team. His 27 points per game average is sixth best all-time, and his 29.1 points per game in the playoffs is the second highest in NBA history.

Jo Jo White

Guard, Boston, 1969-70 through 1977-78, 1979; Golden State, 1979, 1979-80; Kansas City, 1980-81
Born: November 16, 1946 in St. Louis, Mo. 6-3, 190 High School: Vashon (St. Louis, Mo.) and then McKinley (St. Louis, Mo.) College: Kansas

The Celtics owned the ninth pick in the 1969 draft, and since Bill Russell had just retired, most people expected they'd select a center. Red Auerbach had other ideas. He chose Jo Jo

White, a 6-foot-3 guard from Kansas, reasoning that he had potential to be a star, a playmaker good enough to allow John Havlicek to return to playing forward, where he was most effective. The following year Boston selected Dave Cowens, from Florida, and Auerbach had a team that could go into battle in the 1970s. White was a key scorer for Boston. His repertoire included running a speedy fast break and unleashing one of the best off-the-dribble pull-up jumpers in the league. In the playoffs he significantly increased his scoring, from 17.2 to 21.5 points per game. A seven-time all-star, White was Most Valuable Player in the 1976 Finals.

Growing up in St. Louis, White was the seventh child of a Baptist minister. His father forbid him to follow his inclination to play football and Jo Jo opted for basketball instead. By the time he graduated McKinley High School, he was All-America and the recipient of 67 scholarship offers. He chose Kansas, and was again named All-America in both his junior and senior seasons.

Prior to graduation, White played for the 1968 U.S. Olympic team in Mexico City. In Kansas' slow-down offense, White had averaged just 15.3 points per game that season, far less than the 43.9 posted by Pete Maravich at Louisiana State and the 38.2 scored by Calvin Murphy at Niagara. But neither Maravich nor Murphy made the team. White's job was to quarterback and keep the Americans' Olympic record unblemished against strong teams like Yugoslavia and Russia. In the team's first meeting against Yugoslavia, White spearheaded the American attack with ball-hawking, a running game, and pinpoint passes. He scored 24 as the U.S. won, 73-58. The Americans again faced Yugoslavia in the final game, winning 65-50. White ended up scoring 11.6 points in nine undefeated Olympic games, second only to Spencer Haywood's 16.1

White was a part-timer in his first year with Boston, playing only 60 games due to a military commitment. He averaged 12.2 points and made the NBA All-Rookie team, but was often unimpressive. In January 1971 he was made a starter and responded by averaging 21 points, making the all-star team for the first of seven consecutive seasons. White would average between 18 and 23 points and 5 and 6 assists over the next six years. From 1973 to 1977 he played the full 82 games each year.

White adapted to Boston's signature offense—the fast break. He ran the break and had a deadly line-drive pull-up jumper, a shot whose accuracy increased come playoff time. He connected on 83 percent of his free throws. With White at the helm, Boston won the Atlantic Division title five years in a row, from 1972 through 1976. They twice won 60 or more, peaking with 68 wins in 1973.

White's clutch performances in the playoffs were undersold. Five times he averaged 20 points or better, and in 1976 he was the NBA Finals Most Valuable Player, ringing up 22.7 points and 5 assists per game in leading Boston to its second championship of the decade. Boston and New York were the only teams to win two titles in the decade of parity that followed, and preceded, such NBA dynasties as the Celtics, Lakers, and Bulls.

John Havlicek's retirement in 1978 signaled the end of an era, and White was traded to Golden State the following year.

He played his last NBA season with Kansas City in 1981. He retired at the age of 34, but came back to play one year in the CBA, seven years later. He currently serves as Director of Special Projects and Community Relations for the Celtics.

Lenny Wilkens

Guard, St. Louis, 1960-61 through 1967-68; Seattle, 1968-69 through 1971-72; Cleveland, 1972-73 through 1973-74; Portland, 1974-75
Born: October 28, 1937 in Brooklyn, N.Y. 6-1, 180 High School: Boys (Brooklyn, N.Y.) College: Providence

As a coach, Lenny Wilkens has won 1,292 games, more than anyone in NBA history. Wilkens the player was a slick NBA guard who, in an 11-year stretch from 1963 to 1973, was selected for the All-Star team nine times. His was a precision game—using his speed to break down a defense and taking what was available. Wilkens played on four undistinguished teams in his 15 pro seasons—St. Louis, Seattle, Cleveland, and Portland—and was the quarterback on all of them.

A lean 6-foot-1, Wilkens got his start on the courts of the Bedford-Stuyvesant section of Brooklyn. While he lacked the bulk and flashier moves of his playground peers, he made the Boys High team with a brainy style of play that would follow him through his NBA career. His ball-handling, defense, and consistent if unspectacular scoring was good enough for Providence, where he started at guard for four seasons. In his freshman year he steered the team to a 23-0 record. In his junior season he led the Friars to the semi-finals of the NIT, and in his senior year they made the Finals before losing to Bradley. Wilkens was named tournament MVP. He graduated with a degree in economics.

In the 1960 draft the St. Louis Hawks selected Wilkens in the first round, fifth overall. With Wilkens, St. Louis won the four-team Western Division in the 1960-61 season (there were just eight teams overall), finishing 51-28 and then beating Los Angeles in the Western Finals and meeting Boston for the title. Wilkens played a larger role in the playoffs, increasing his minutes, points, and rebounds. But St. Louis, despite its high-scoring front line of Pettit, Cliff Hagan, and Clyde Lovellette, went down in five games.

In 1962 he played only 20 games, serving 18 months in the U.S. Army Quartermasters Corps from May 1961 through November 1962. Before the 1968-69 season he was traded to Seattle, joining a team that was one year old and had tallied only 23 wins. With Wilkens at the helm the Sonics increased their win totals to 30, then 36, 38, and finally 47. Those last three totals came with Wilkens acting as player-coach. Appearing in the All-Star Game with numbing regularity, Wilkens scored 21 points and took the classic's MVP honors in 1971. He was a bonafide if unheralded force in the league, finishing no lower than second in assists from 1969 through 1973 and capturing the assists title, over Walt Frazier, in 1970. Wilkens, then 34, was traded to Cleveland in 1972.

Cleveland was another fledgling squad, having finished in the basement of the Central Division with just 23 wins the year before his arrival. He played two solid years with the Cavaliers before becoming player-coach with Portland in his 15th, and last, season as a player. After Wilkens' two sub-.500 years with

Portland, Jack Ramsay took over and—with a healthy Bill Walton—delivered the city its first and last NBA title.

By 1978 Wilkens was back coaching and took Seattle all the way to the Finals. In all he coached eight years in Seattle, winning 50 or more games four times. Beginning in the 1986-87 season he took over a Cleveland team on the rise. But his seven Cleveland years, which included three 50-win seasons and frequent forays into the playoffs, were perennially spoiled by Chicago, which beat the Cavs four times in the post-season. In 1992, Wilkens' next-to-last year in Cleveland before moving to Atlanta, the Cavaliers made it to the Eastern Conference Finals. Chicago eliminated them in six games.

His seven-year tenure in Atlanta produced three more 50-win campaigns. No victory was sweeter than the one on January 6, 1995, when the Hawks defeated the Bullets at the Omni and Wilkens lit up a cigar in celebration of his 939th career win, one more than Boston legend Red Auerbach. Wilkens coached three seasons in Toronto (he was fired in April 2003) and increased his NBA record to 1,292. He also holds the record for most coaching losses (1,114).

Wilkens was voted to the NBA's 50th Anniversary All-Time Team in 1996. In 1998 he was elected to the Hall of Fame as a coach and joined John Wooden as the only men inducted as players and as coaches. He'd been elected as a player in 1988.

Dominique Wilkins

Forward-Guard, Atlanta, 1982-83 through 1992-93, 1994; LA Clippers, 1994; Boston, 1994-95; San Antonio, 1996-97; Orlando, 1998-99
Born: January 12, 1960 in Paris, France 6-8, 224 High School: Washington (N.C.) College: Georgia

Dominique Wilkins played in 1,047 regular season NBA games and only 56 playoff games. There are few ratios like that in the history of the league, and that may account for much of the league's indifference—such as failing to name him to the NBA's 50th Anniversary All-Time Team—toward his career. Known as the "Human Highlight Film" for his hang time, double-clutching drives and miraculous 360-degree spins, Wilkins is Atlanta's all-time leading scorer with 23,292 points and finished with 26,668 points (11th place overall), averaging 24.8 points (11th). But there is a widespread, and perhaps justified, belief that scoring points ought to contribute to victories. In only three of his 15 NBA seasons did Wilkins' teams get past the first round of the playoffs.

Twice an All-American at Georgia, Wilkins left after his junior season and was chosen by Utah as the third pick overall of the 1982 draft. Several months later, Utah traded him to Atlanta for John Drew, Freeman Williams, and cash. Over his first four NBA seasons, Wilkins played in all but five of the Hawks' games, and his average climbed from 18 to 30 points per game. He won a scoring title in 1986 and averaged 29 and 31 points per game the following two seasons, but by then Michael Jordan had made the scoring title his private possession.

Wilkins would end up finishing second to Jordan in scoring three times between 1987 and 1993. The Hawks traded Wilkins and a first-round draft pick to the Los Angeles Clippers for Danny Manning in February 1994. The following year he

played for a Boston squad that won all of 35 games. In 1996 he ventured to Greece and scored 21 points a game to help Panathinaikos win a championship. Now 37, he returned to the San Antonio Spurs for the 1996-97 season and led the team in scoring. His last stop was Italy, where he played for Teamsystem Bologna of the Italian League during the 1997-98 season. After his retirement, he became an executive VP with the Atlanta Hawks.

Along with Alex English and Dan Issel, Wilkins was one of three 25,000-point scorers left off the NBA's 50th Anniversary All-Time Team in 1996. His brother, Gerald, played in the NBA for 13 seasons.

Gus Williams

Guard, Golden State, 1975-76 through 1976-77; Seattle, 1977-78 through 1983-84; Washington, 1984-85 through 1985-86; Atlanta, 1986-87
Born: August 10, 1953 in New York, N.Y. 6-2, 175 High School: Mt. Vernon, New York College: USC

Gus Williams came to Seattle from Golden State in 1977, in time for the team's most memorable seasons. Playing alongside Dennis Johnson in the backcourt, he led the SuperSonics to the Finals in 1978 (they lost in seven games to Washington) and to the championship in 1979, when they ran roughshod over the Bullets and won the title in five games. A super-fast, showy guard, Williams led a powerful Seattle team in scoring in five of his first six seasons, and was the among the league leaders in scoring and steals.

When Williams was just six years old, growing up in Mt. Vernon, New York, the sixth sibling in his household was born and his father died soon after. Williams learned basketball on the playgrounds, "playing from sunup to sundown." He didn't make the high school team until his junior year and then played in just a few games with the varsity at the end of the season. He had intended to quit playing his senior year and get a job. "My brother-in-law, Bill Taylor, coached me in the recreational league," Williams says, "and told me to go back and try again. My senior year I started on the high school team and made All-American."

Williams went to USC and was coached there by Bob Boyd, who stressed good position defense—training that would benefit Williams in years to come. Golden State made Williams its second pick in the second round of the 1975 draft, shortly after the Warriors won their only NBA title. He was a 20-minute-a-game player in his rookie season, but that doesn't tell the whole story. The 6-foot-2, 175-pound guard made an impression early on, outrunning and outmaneuvering opponents. He made the All-Rookie team and was the fourth leading scorer on a team whose potent offense led the league, spearheaded by such great shooters as Rick Barry, Phil Smith, and Jamaal Wilkes. Williams' quick hands and ability to anticipate plays made him sixth in the league in steals, remarkable for a part-time player.

Still not a full-time player, Williams became a free agent after the 1977 season and the Sonics picked him up. In Seattle, Williams would play more minutes, take more shots, and score between 18 and 23 points per game in his six seasons. Williams' first season resulted in 47 Seattle wins and a march to the

Finals, where, after leading 3-2, the Sonics lost Game 6 in a blowout at Washington and then a 105-99 decision in Game 7 at home.

Seattle won 52 games in 1978-79, second only to Washington's 54. The Sonics were down 3-2 to Phoenix in the Western Conference Finals, but won Games 6 and 7 to face Washington in the Finals. After losing Game 1, Seattle stopped the Bullets in four straight. The Sonics were led by their guards, with Williams averaging 26.6 points overall in the playoffs.

Seattle won 56 games in 1980 and made the playoffs for the third straight year. In the six times that Sonics played in the post-season between 1978 and 1984, Gus Williams was their leading scorer each time, averaging between 18 and 32 points, while connecting on 50 percent of his shots. For his career, Williams' accuracy (.475 to .461) and points per game (19.5 to 17.1) was greater in the playoffs than in the regular season.

By the mid-'80s Seattle had fallen back to about .500, and then to 31-51 in 1985. They needed to rebuild, and traded Williams. He spent two years in Washington and one last season in Atlanta in 1987. His brother, Ray, also played in the NBA from 1977-78.

James Worthy

Forward, LA Lakers, 1982-83 through 1993-94
Born: February 27, 1961 in Gastonia, N.C. 6-9, 225 High School: Ashbrook (Gastonia, N.C.) College: North Carolina

With James Worthy at forward, the Los Angeles Lakers played in five NBA Finals and won three of them. Worthy was a sleek, at times unstoppable offensive player. Often drawing the league's best defensive forwards to guard him, he was too quick off the dribble for them to guard him with any real success. On the wing he gathered in many of Magic Johnson's passes and finished the break with a quick dunk. While Worthy was merely the third greatest player on those 1985, 1987, and 1988 Los Angeles Championship squads, he was still the leading scorer.

He had highlights aplenty. In Game 5 of the 1985 Finals he scored 33 points, and in the title-clinching Game 6 he tallied 28, to go with Jabbar's 29, as the Lakers beat the Celtics, 111 to 100. It was the first time that the Celtics had been eliminated from the Finals on their own court. In the 1988 Finals against the Pistons, Worthy had a career performance in Game 7. He netted 36 points (15-22 from the field) while logging 16 rebounds and 10 assists to give the Lakers what Pat Riley had promised: back-to-back titles. Worthy was awarded the Finals MVP.

In 1982, his third year at North Carolina, Worthy was a first-team All-American and the NCAA Tournament's Most Outstanding Player as the Tar Heels bested Georgetown, 63-62, before 61,612 spectator at the New Orleans Superdome in the title game. The 6-foot-9 "small" forward was first pick overall for the Lakers in the 1982 draft and eased his way into a lineup that had won titles in two of the three previous seasons.

There were moments in the 1984 Finals against Boston—a series that Los Angeles squandered with ill-considered passes, missed free throws, and mistakes in managing the shot clock—when Worthy showed he was not yet a prime-time performer. In the overtime period of the crucial fourth game, Worthy could have tied the game with 10 seconds left in overtime, but he missed a free throw. A series that could have been 3-1 in the Lakers' favor was now tied. In Game 7 the Celtics' Cedric Maxwell told his mates, "Get on my back, boys," and then exploited Worthy's low-post defense, carrying Boston to its 15th NBA title. Although Worthy was a star in college, he would have to acquire some big-league seasoning to become an all-star and big-game performer in the NBA.

The Lakers were back in the Finals in 1985. By now the McHale-Worthy match-up, never much publicized, was an interesting study in contrasts. Worthy loved to get the ball on the wing, try to draw McHale to him, and then drive by for a layup or quick jam. McHale, on the other hand, sought to post Worthy and use his array of back-to-the-basket low-post maneuvers to take his high-percentage shots. This time Los Angeles won in six games. Worthy shot a startling 62 percent from the field and averaged 21.5 ppg in the playoffs.

As if that had been his baptism in the pro game, Worthy, the man with the sleepy, half-mast eyes, was quietly consistent and often magnificent thereafter. From 1986 through 1992 he played on seven consecutive all-star squads, and his post-season field-goal accuracy and points per game routinely bettered his regular season totals. Averaging 22 points in the 1988 Finals, Worthy received the only one of five Lakers' Finals MVPs in the '80s not won by Earvin Johnson or Kareem Abdul-Jabbar.

Worthy retired following the 1994 season with a career average of 17.6 points per game and with an impressive accuracy rating of .521 from the floor. In 1996 he was voted to the NBA's 50th Anniversary All-Time Team. He was elected to the Hall of Fame in 2003.

The International Game

Magic Johnson, 1992
Jubilation follows 117-85 win over
Croatia, giving the first
U.S. Dream Team the gold
medal at the 1992
Barcelona Olympic Games.

Chapter 44   The Olympic Games

By Alex Sachere

From the time basketball was introduced into the Olympic Games, it has been a case of the United States taking the lead and the rest of the world playing catch-up. And all signs indicate that while the U.S. remains in the lead at the dawn of the 21st century, the rest of the world is indeed catching up.

From improved play by national teams in global events like the 2000 Olympics in Sydney to the ever-growing presence of foreign-born players in the ranks of the NBA and Division I college basketball, it is becoming more and more evident that basketball is no longer just "America's Game," as it was dubbed by a television network in the 1980s, but rather a global game. This is only fitting, given that the sport's inventor, Dr. James Naismith, was not an American but a Canadian, and that within a few years of basketball's invention in 1891, it had been exported from its birthplace of Springfield, Mass., and was being played halfway around the world in Japan.

A demonstration sport at the 1904 Olympics in St. Louis, basketball first became a medal sport in Berlin in 1936, when the United States beat Canada 19-8 for the first

The Basket Heard Round the World, 1972
Alexander Belov's two-pointer in the gold medal game of the 1972 Olympics gave the Russians a controversial 51-50 win over the U.S.

gold medal. The United States won its first 62 games in Olympic competition (plus one forfeit) before suffering a controversial, last-second 51-50 defeat at the hands of the Soviet Union in the 1972 gold medal game in Munich. While that result was hotly disputed because the ending of the game was replayed not once but three times, it marked the first indication that the rest of the world was beginning to catch up to the United States in basketball. Of course, the best American players, those in the NBA, were prohibited from competing in the Olympics or other major international events, which were deemed for "amateur" players only, so it was a much older and more experienced team from the Soviet Union that defeated the American collegians in 1972.

The United States regained the gold at Tokyo in 1976, then came two boycott-marred Olympics—the United States not competing in Moscow in 1980, the Soviet Union sitting out the 1984 Olympics in Los Angeles. In 1988, the United States—still forced to send a team of collegians against other countries' older and more experienced players—lost to the

Soviet Union 82-76 in Seoul and had to settle for a bronze medal. By now it was clear that the Soviet Union—and Yugoslavia as well—had caught up with the United States, at least the teams the U.S. was sending to the Olympics.

That all changed in 1989, when the Federation Internationale de Basketball—FIBA, the sport's global governing body—voted to repeal the ban on American pros and open its events such as the Olympics and the World Championships to all competitors. FIBA knew it was once again placing the rest of the world at a significant competitive disadvantage against the United States, but it passed the resolution by an overwhelming 56-13 margin anyway.

"We see this as a triumphant entry into the 21st century," said Boris Stankovic of Yugoslavia, the secretary general of FIBA who spearheaded the move to open competition. "It is a dream come true."

Stankovic's dream was for the rest of the world to catch up to the very best basketball the United States had to offer, not just the best college all-stars it could muster. "The first reason I

want this is technical, to improve the skills of our players," said Stankovic. "Our feeling is that only by playing with the best players in the world can everyone else make progress. The second reason is moral. We now have a very hypocritical situation. We have 172 countries in our organization representing 200 million basketball players, but we do not have the best 300 players in the world because they are 'professionals.' People are being paid all over the world. To leave out the best 300 players because they have the name of professionals is hypocritical.

"We accept the fact that the Olympics and World Championships will be dominated by the United States, but that difference will be less every year. And one of these years, other countries will be competitive with the NBA. In 1936, the U.S. was represented by AAU players. They dominated for a while, but the world caught up. Then the U.S. changed to college players, and they dominated for a while, but the world caught up. Now NBA players are dominating, but one day—not in my lifetime, but one day—the world will catch up."

While the United States has won all three gold medals since the advent of open competition, the rest of the world clearly is getting more competitive, and this despite the breakups of the Soviet Union and Yugoslavia, Europe's two greatest basketball powers. In the 2000 Olympics in Sydney, the United States barely survived to win an 85-83 squeaker over Lithuania in the semi-finals, then defeated France 85-75 for the gold medal, results that left American ace Vince Carter impressed by the competition.

"Basketball has evolved," said Carter, one of the NBA's high-flying marquee players. "It's come a long way. We give respect to France and Lithuania. They pushed us to the end."

"What this Olympics demonstrated," said NBA Commissioner David Stern following the Sydney Games, "is that the competitive level of international basketball has improved—more so than casual observers of the game understood."

Yet even the most casual basketball observers recognize how much the game has evolved. The two-handed set shot has been replaced by the one-handed jumper; the two-handed chest pass has given way to one-handed bullets, sometimes delivered while the passer looks away from his target. Basketball has taken to the air; the game is played above the rim as well as below it. Players today display greater athleticism than ever before, and the rules of the game have been modified to allow their skills to flourish. Shot clocks speed up play at virtually every level of the game, preventing the stalling and foul-filled contests that nearly doomed the professional game in the early 1950s. Defenses are more intricate and elaborate than ever as coaches combine man-to-man and zone principles in an effort to offset more talented offensive players. The layout of the basketball floor itself has changed with the widening of the foul lane and the introduction of the three-point field goal, both designed to relieve congestion around the basket, keep the game fluid and offset the dominance of oversized centers, the 7-foot-plus "air-craft carriers," as the late Al McGuire dubbed them.

How much has the game evolved? The first Olympic gold medal was decided not on any basketball floor, but on an outdoor dirt court at the 1936 Olympics in Berlin, Germany. Long before that, however, basketball had been a presence at the

Summer Olympics.

In 1904, less than 13 years after the game's invention, basketball had become so popular in the United States that the organizing committee for the Olympic Games in St. Louis made it a demonstration sport, meaning exhibitions were held but no medals were awarded. Similar demonstrations were held at Paris in 1924 and Amsterdam in 1928, but even though the 10th Olympiad was held in the United States, basketball was ignored for the 1932 Games in Los Angeles in favor of lacrosse and college football as demonstration sports.

That snub lit a fire under basketball's leaders, in both the United States and abroad. One of the problems was that the sport was being played under different rules in different countries, so in 1932 representatives from 10 European nations gathered in Geneva and agreed to adopt uniform rules, based largely on those used in the United States although modified somewhat to better fit the European style of play. With the support of the International YMCA (the sport had been invented by Naismith at the Springfield Y, and the group played a major role in spurring its early growth) as well as the Amateur Athletic Union and the National Collegiate Athletic Association, that gathering led to the creation of an international governing body—the Federation Internationale de Basketball Amateur (the word "amateur" later would be dropped from the organization's name, although it remains in its acronym). FIBA oversaw the translation of basketball rules into more than 30 languages and claimed more than 10 million participants worldwide, which was enough to induce the organizing committee for the 1936 Olympics in Berlin to petition the International Olympic Committee for the addition of men's basketball as a medal sport.

Twenty two nations from five continents competed for the first Olympic basketball gold medal: Belgium, Brazil, Canada, Chile, China, Czechoslovakia, Egypt, Estonia, France, Germany, Hungary, Italy, Japan, Latvia, Mexico, Peru, the Philippines, Poland, Switzerland, Turkey, the United States, and Uruguay. A 23rd nation, Spain, originally entered a team, but it was forced to withdraw due to a civil war in the country. Naismith, the sport's inventor who by then was in his 60s, was invited to attend the inaugural competition and tossed up the opening ball in the gold medal game, which fittingly pitted his native country, Canada, against his adopted land, the United States.

That inaugural competition turned out to be anything but competitive. As a new sport whose popularity was yet to be proven, basketball was denied an indoor venue and instead relegated to an outdoor tennis stadium with a clay playing surface. The United States was by far the power of the field; half its players were members of the Universal Studios team that had won the Olympic Trials, with six other players coming from the AAU's Phillips Petroleum team and one, Ralph Bishop, from the University of Washington. In an attempt to make the event more competitive, the European-dominated FIBA had tried to ban players taller than 6-foot-3 after the Olympics had begun, but the United States, which would have lost three team members, protested vehemently and the ban proposal was withdrawn.

The captain of that first U.S. Olympic team was Francis Johnson, who had starred for the AAU champion McPherson Globe Oilers. He noted that the German basketballs used in

the competition "weren't balanced properly, so if you threw them through the air they would just wobble. They were also too light, and when you would go to shoot outdoors, the wind would catch them and move them over three feet or so. This made accuracy rather difficult."

Nonetheless, the United States dominated play, outscoring its first three opponents 133-61, then beating Canada in a gold medal game memorable not for the play but the playing conditions. Two days of rain caused organizers to move the gold medal game to the Court of Honour, which at least had some permanent seats for fans. But it also had a brick border circling the playing surface that held the rain, turning the court into a muddy wading pool. "We skidded and slid around," recalled one of the American players, Sam Balter. "There was no way the ball could be dribbled." The United States led 15-4 at halftime, then sloshed its way through a 4-4 second half to a 19-8 victory. Joe Fortenberry, a 6-foot-8 center who averaged a team-high 14.5 points per game in the tournament, led the way for the United States with eight points, personally matching the total scored by the Canadian team. Mexico took home the bronze medal by beating Poland 26-12.

Thankfully for all involved, the basketball competition was moved indoors to Wembley Arena for the 1948 Olympics in London (there were no Olympics in 1940 or 1944 because of World War II). The United States was comprised of five players from the AAU champion Phillips 66ers, including 7-foot center Bob Kurland, one of the early dominant big men; the starting five of the NCAA champion Kentucky Wildcats, including All-Americans Ralph Beard and Alex Groza; plus two additional players each from the AAU and college ranks. Phillips had beaten Kentucky 53-49 in the finals of the U.S. Olympic trials.

Among the added players was Don Barksdale, a former All-American at UCLA who was then playing for the AAU's Oakland Bittners and became the first African-American to compete for the United States in basketball. Barksdale, who later would become the first African-American to play in an NBA All-Star Game, was a brilliant all-around athlete who was an AAU champion in the triple jump.

The Americans were coached by Bud Browning of the Phillips 66ers, with Adolph Rupp of Kentucky as his assistant. "One game we would start the Kentucky five, and the next game it would be the Phillips 66 players," said Barksdale. "The U.S. was so far ahead of anybody else in basketball that we had only one tough game." The Americans survived a 59-57 scare against Argentina early in the competition and then rolled to victory, beating its eight opponents by an average of 33.5 points per game and taking the gold medal with a 65-21 victory over France. Groza was the team's only double-digit scorer at 11.1 points per game, but six other players tallied at least 7.0 ppg apiece.

The competition was not without its unusual moments, one of which involved Kurland. A Chinese player, finding his path to the basket blocked by the massive pivotman, bounced the ball between Kurland's legs, ran around him and picked up the ball behind him for a layup. Ireland managed to score just 17 points per game, and Iraq twice lost by margins of more than 100 points. Brazil won the bronze medal with a 52-47

decision over Mexico even though it lost one of its players, Alfredo Rodrigues de Motta, when he had to go to the locker room after his pants ripped.

At the 1952 Olympics in Helsinki, the U.S. team consisted of seven members of the Kansas Jayhawks, led by 6-foot-9 Clyde Lovellette, and seven AAU players—five from the Peoria Caterpillars and two, one of whom was Kurland, from the Phillips 66ers. Opponents decided that their best chance against the mighty Americans was to slow down the pace of the game and hope for some breaks that might enable them to win a low-scoring contest. Brazil came close, bowing 57-53, and Argentina also put up a fight before losing 85-75.

But the matchup fans the wanted to see was between the United States and the Soviet Union, which had joined the Olympic competition after dominating European basketball for several years with a team led by Otar Korkiya, Styapas Butautos, and Ilmar Kullam. The fans got their wish, not once but twice. In the semi-final round, the Soviets attempted to run with the Americans but were crushed 86-58. So when they met again in the gold medal game, the Soviets decided to try freezing the ball—FIBA did not yet use a shot clock in its events. After 10 minutes, the Americans led by just 4-2, and at halftime the score was 17-15 in favor of the United States. After a basket by Lovellette widened the margin to 31-25 with five minutes to play, it became the Americans' turn to stall. The Soviets became frustrated, one player actually sitting down on the floor until ordered to stand up by his coach. They could do nothing but foul, and the United States emerged from the ragged game with a 36-25 victory and their third gold medal. Lovellette led the team with 14.1 points per game.

Uruguay won the bronze medal, but it did not come easily. In the semi-final round, Uruguay was reduced to three players because of excessive fouling and lost to France 68-66, getting into a pair of fights with referee Vincent Farrell in the closing seconds that resulted in two Uruguayan players being banned from further competition. When Uruguay met the Soviet Union, three Soviet players required first aid for injuries received in the hard-fought game. And Uruguay's 68-59 victory over neighboring Argentina for the bronze medal was marred by an all-out brawl involving 25 players, just part of a foul-filled game that resulted in Uruguay being left with only four players at the end and Argentina three.

The remoteness of Melbourne, Australia reduced the field for the 1956 Olympic basketball competition to 15 teams, and once again the United States dominated. The Americans were led by teammates from the NCAA champion University of San Francisco, 6-foot-9 center Bill Russell and guard K.C. Jones, both defensive standouts. The Americans, whose roster also included five members of the Phillips 66ers, won all eight games by at least 30 points apiece and scored over 100 in half of them, coasting to the gold by an average score of 99-46. Russell scored 22 points in the 89-55 victory over the Soviets and their 7-foot-2 center, Janis Krumins, in the gold medal game, while Uruguay again took the bronze, this time beating France 71-62. Four Americans averaged in double figures for the tournament, topped by Russell at 14.1 ppg.

After these games, a 30-second clock was adopted by FIBA for international events such as the Olympics, mirroring the

NBA's 24-second clock.

As good as the 1956 Olympic team was, the squad the United States sent to the 1960 Olympics in Rome was even stronger, probably the greatest amateur basketball team ever assembled. Ten of its 12 members went on to play in the NBA, four have been inducted into the basketball Hall of Fame—Walt Bellamy, Jerry Lucas, Oscar Robertson, and Jerry West—and four more were NBA All-Stars—Bob Boozer, Terry Dischinger, Darrall Imhoff and Adrian Smith. Another All-Star and Hall of Famer, John Havlicek, was only selected as an alternate. The coach was yet another Hall of Famer, the legendary Pete Newell.

Against this galaxy of stars, the Soviet Union sent up a team whose six-man nucleus had played together for four years. But even though the United States players were together as a unit for less than a month, their superior talent proved far too much for the Soviets or anyone else to overcome, despite the continued strides being made all around the world. The Americans averaged nearly 102 points per game and allowed just 60, with Robertson and Lucas averaging 17.0 ppg apiece and West, Dischinger and Smith also scoring in double figures.

For the first time, there was no single elimination medal round, but rather four teams advanced to a round-robin final. Joining the United States were the Soviet Union, Brazil and Italy. The U.S. breezed to an 81-57 victory over the Soviets in the opening matchup, then topped Italy 112-81 and Brazil 90-63 to secure the gold medal with a 3-0 mark. In the latter game, the Americans raced to a 41-14 lead and coasted home. The Soviet Union bounced back from its opening loss to edge Brazil 64-62 and beat Italy 78-70 to win the silver medal, while Brazil took the bronze by virtue of a 78-75 decision over Italy.

It was a similar, if somewhat less dramatic, case of American talent vs. global experience at the 1964 Olympics in Tokyo, and once again talent won out. The United States team, again a mixture of collegians and AAU players, was led by Jerry Shipp of the Phillips 66ers at 12.4 points per game and Princeton's Bill Bradley at 10.1 ppg. Point guard duties were shared by Walt Hazzard and Larry Brown, with Luke Jackson, Jim "Bad News" Barnes and George Wilson providing muscle up front and Pogo Joe Caldwell adding a heaping measure of athleticism.

Yugoslavia pressed the Americans in the preliminary round before succumbing 69-61. In the gold medal game, the United States faced the Soviet Union, which was undefeated to that point and had five players on its roster who had competed in Rome four years earlier, including Krumins and Aleksandr Petrov. The Soviets were primed for an upset. "There will be a surprise for everyone. We are fed up with second," declared their coach, Aleksandr Gomelsky, the "Father of Basketball" in the Soviet Union who was enshrined in the Hall of Fame in 1995.

It was not to be. The Soviet Union took a 16-13 lead in the first 10 minutes but could not stay with the United States after that. The Americans asserted control with an 18-4 spurt and went on to win 73-59. Brazil, another experienced team, beat Puerto Rico 76-60 for the bronze.

By the 1968 Olympics in Mexico City, there was a growing feeling that American domination may be coming to an end. For one thing, the Americans had lost to both the Soviet Union and Yugoslavia in pre-Olympic games held in Europe. Several

top college players, notably Kareem Abdul-Jabbar and Elvin Hayes, had declined invitations to try out for the United States team, Hayes saying he wanted to focus on preparing for his NBA debut and Abdul-Jabbar citing his studies at UCLA and talk of an Olympic boycott by black athletes. And in addition to their experience, the Soviets had a significant advantage in size, boasting a pair of 7-footers, Sergei Kovalenko and Vladimir Andreev; the United States' biggest man was 19-year-old Spencer Haywood, a 6-foot-9 center who had just completed one season at Trinidad Junior College in Colorado.

The United States team, which also included college stars Jo Jo White and Charlie Scott and several AAU and armed forces players, struggled but survived, beating Puerto Rico by five points and Brazil by a dozen to earn a berth in the gold medal game. This time, however, the opponent was not the Soviet Union but Yugoslavia, which posted a dramatic 63-62 victory over the Soviets in the semi-finals thanks to a steal and a pair of clinching free throws by Vladimir Cvetkovic with four seconds to play. The Yugoslavs were no match for the Americans in the final, losing 65-50 as Haywood made a name for himself by scoring a game-high 22 points to finish the tournament with a team-high 16.1 points per game. The Soviet Union, instead of its customary silver medal, took home a bronze by beating Brazil 70-53.

The cracks that some had seen in American dominance prior to the 1968 Olympics loomed even larger four years later, when the games were held in Munich. With the decline in prominence of AAU ball, 11 of the 12 U.S. team members came from the college ranks, but in addition to being a far younger and less experienced team than many of its opponents, the United States did not even have all its best college players at its disposal as stars such as All-American center Bill Walton elected to stay home. Even so, the Americans extended their Olympic winning streak to 63 games (including one forfeit) and made it to a gold medal matchup against the Soviet Union before bowing in one of the most controversial games ever.

The Soviets outplayed the younger Americans for most of the game and held a 44-36 lead with five minutes remaining. But fueled by a pair of baskets by guard Kevin Joyce, the U.S. rallied and closed to within one at 49-48. That's when Doug Collins stole the ball in the closing seconds and drove to the hoop, where he was fouled by Zurab Sakandelidze. Collins, who went on to a successful career as an NBA player, coach and TV commentator, recalls the play this way: "We were down by one with about 10 seconds to go, but I was able to steal a pass and was heading for a layup when I was fouled with three seconds left. I slid under the basket and hit my head on the basket support. I was unconscious for a few seconds, and when I went to the foul line I still felt groggy. But I think that helped me. I didn't feel the pressure. I made two shots, and we were ahead by one."

The Soviets put the ball in play and went the length of the court, but Sergei Belov's basket came after the final buzzer and the Americans celebrated what they thought was a 50-49 victory. But it was not to be. Referee Renato Righetto of Brazil had noticed a commotion at the scorer's table, where he determined that the Soviet coach, Vladimir Kondrashin, had been trying to request a timeout, and after conferring with time-

keeper Andre Chopard, he ordered that one second be put back on the clock.

So, the Soviets had a second chance. They threw the ball inbounds, a shot bounced off the backboard and the buzzer sounded. Again, the Americans headed off the court with what they thought was a victory.

Once again, however, it was premature. R. William Jones of Britain, the secretary general of FIBA, intervened and ruled that Kondrashin had requested the timeout when Collins was still at the free throw line, and so three seconds should have been put back on the clock instead of one. Jones ordered the teams back onto the floor, and this time Ivan Edeshko threw a court-length pass to Aleksandr Belov, who muscled his way past defenders Kevin Joyce and James Forbes and laid it in at the buzzer to give the Soviet Union a 51-50 victory.

Now it was the Americans' turn to protest, their contention being that an off-court official such as Jones had no authority to intervene in the conduct of a game in progress and overrule an on-court official, referee Reghetto. The appeal was denied by a five-man judicial panel by the slimmest of margins, with the chair of the committee, Terrence Hepp of Hungary, voting along with representatives from Poland and Cuba, while representatives of Italy and Puerto Rico voted in favor of upholding the protest. So, by a 3-2 vote, the outcome stood. The Soviet Union had ended the United States' dominance of Olympic basketball, stopping a winning streak that went back to the very first game played in Berlin in 1936.

"It was a very bittersweet experience for me, to be a member of the first U.S. men's basketball team to lose in the Olympics, but I still don't believe that we lost," said Collins. "It was something that was out of our hands. I see it today as clearly as if it's happening on a video replay. The Russians got two chances to win it, and they finally put one in and won 51-50. After being so happy about the two free throws I had made, I was the most dejected person in the world. Every Olympic year really brings that experience into focus.

"I think the one thing I regret more than anything else is not having that feeling you get standing on the platform, getting the gold medal around your neck and listening to the national anthem. I feel we were robbed of that, and that to me is something I really feel badly about."

It was, in light of the circumstances, a bitter pill for the Americans to swallow. When the medals were handed out the next day, the United States team elected to boycott the ceremony rather than accept silver medals when they felt they deserved gold. The Soviet Union players received gold medals and the Cubans, who had edged Italy 66-65, received bronze, but the silver medals were never awarded. Kenny Davis, the lone AAU player on the American team, went even further: in his will he forbade any family member from ever accepting a silver medal in his name.

Adding further insult, United States coach Hank Iba, coaching in his third Olympics, had his pocket picked and lost $370 at 2 a.m. while he was signing the official protest, the one that was eventually denied.

While it will forever be remembered for its controversial ending, the fact remains that for most of that gold medal game, the Soviet Union had outplayed the United States. Clearly, the

time when a group of American collegians could be put together in a month or two and defeat older, more experienced European teams that had been playing together for years was coming to an end. If it hadn't happened in 1972, it surely would have happened soon after.

"For many of us, that was truly the first realization that Americans were not the only people playing basketball," observed Chuck Daly, the Hall of Fame coach who would guide the original Dream Team to gold at the 1992 Olympics in Barcelona, after the event was opened up to American professionals. "In the other Olympics, we had taken it for granted that we would win. But 1972 sticks in my mind because that Olympics showed us that we were not invincible. Our dominance had been broken, and the world was catching up."

The much-anticipated rematch between the United States and the Soviet Union at the 1976 Olympics in Montreal never came about. The veteran Soviet team, featuring many of the same players who had dethroned the Americans, was beaten 89-84 in the semi-finals by a Yugoslavian team led by Kresimir Cosic (a former All-American at Brigham Young University), Dragan Kicanovic and Drazen Dalipagic. The Americans also nearly didn't make the gold medal game, surviving an early scare at the hands of a Puerto Rican team led by Butch Lee, who starred for Marquette University but was not sent to the U.S. Olympic Trials. So he returned to his birthplace, made the team there and scored 35 points on 15-for-18 shooting against the United States, which managed to eke out a 95-94 victory.

In the gold medal game, the United States raced out to a 44-22 lead over Yugoslavia and went on to win 95-74. Adrian Dantley scored 30 points and finished the tournament with a team-high 19.3 points per game, the highest scoring average by an American player in any Olympics. The American team, for the first time comprised entirely of players from the college ranks, had a decidedly North Carolina flavor thanks to players Phil Ford, Walter Davis, Tom LaGarde, and Mitch Kupchak and coach Dean Smith. The Soviet Union bounced back from its semi-final loss and defeated Canada 100-72 for the bronze medal.

Women's basketball was added to the Olympic medal competition in 1976, and the Soviet team, which had not lost a game in five years and had not lost in international tournament competition since 1958, breezed to the gold medal in round-robin play. Juliana Semanova, their 6-foot-10-1/2, 284-pound center and a future Hall of Famer, averaged 19.4 points and 12.4 rebounds per game, even though she spent more than half the time on the bench in the Soviet Union's five lopsided victories. The United States, with a team featuring Ann Meyers, Lucy Harris and Nancy Lieberman, all Hall of Famers, was awarded the silver medal by virtue of a 95-79 victory over Bulgaria, even though both teams posted 3-2 records.

The next two Olympics had their fields cut by political boycotts, the United States being among those who chose not to compete in Moscow in 1980 and the Soviet Union and several other Eastern bloc nations electing not to participate in Los Angeles in 1984.

Despite the home-country advantage, the Soviet Union's men's team could manage only a bronze medal in 1980, suffering a 10-point overtime loss to Yugoslavia in the semi-finals

before bouncing back to beat Spain 117-94. Yugoslavia, with Dalipagic averaging 24.4 points per game, Kicanovic contributing 23.6 ppg and Cosic playing a solid all-around game, went 8-0 to win the gold medal, beating an Italian team led by Dino Meneghin 86-77 in the final.

In addition to the United States, five other countries—Argentina, Canada, China, Mexico and Puerto Rico—qualified for the Olympic basketball competition but did not compete in protest of the Soviet Union's invasion of Afghanistan. Twelve U.S. college stars, including Isiah Thomas, Mark Aguirre and Michael Brooks, played a six-game exhibition series under coach Dave Gavitt against pickup teams of NBA players in the summer of 1980 and compiled a 5-1 record.

The Soviet women, meanwhile, coasted to the gold by an average victory margin of 44 points per game, compiling a 6-0 record. Semenova averaged 21.8 points and 12.5 rebounds per game and teamed with 6-foot-3 Olga Sukharnova to dominate the boards. Bulgaria finished second and Yugoslavia was third.

The Americans, both the men and the women, dominated the field in Los Angeles in 1984.

The United States men's team was a strong one led by Michael Jordan (17.1 points per game), Patrick Ewing, Chris Mullin, Sam Perkins and Alvin Robertson. Future NBA star Charles Barkley was not selected for the team that was coached by Indiana's Bob Knight, who preferred one of his own players, Steve Alford (who vindicated his coach by averaging 10.3 points per game and ranking second on the team with 26 assists). The team's top playmaker was Leon Wood, who went on to a short career in the NBA as a player and a longer one as a referee. The only team given any chance against them, defending champion Yugoslavia, lost to Spain in the semi-finals.

The Americans, who beat their eight opponents by 32.3 points per game, pounded Spain 96-65 to win the gold medal. Yugoslavia, led by Dalipagic and future NBA star Drazen Petrovic, beat Canada 88-82 to take the bronze.

On the women's side, the United States won its first gold medal with a team led by Hall of Famers Anne Donovan, Cheryl Miller, and Denise Curry plus Teresa Edwards, Lynette Woodard, and Pam McGee. The Americans breezed to the title with an 85-55 victory over Korea in the finals.

The 1988 Olympics in Seoul finally offered the American men a chance to avenge their defeat at the hands of the Soviet Union 16 years earlier. While the United States had a team of collegians that included David Robinson, Danny Manning and little-known Dan Majerle, who emerged as the team's leading scorer at 14.1 points per game, the Soviet Union had a much more experienced team as well as possibly its most talented squad ever. The Soviet Union roster featured three players who would eventually play in the NBA, Sarunas Marciulionis, Alexander Volkov and Arvydas Sabonis, the latter a 7-foot-3, 300-pounder with soft hands, great passing skills and a shooting touch that extended to three-point range. The Soviets had several other strong players, including Sergei Tarakanov, Valeri Tikhonenko, Rimas Kurtinaitis and Tiit Sokk, all of whom were considered to be of NBA caliber.

The two met in the semi-finals and the Soviet Union dominated from the start, building an early 10-point lead and

maintaining it most of the way until the Americans, who were without the services of the injured Hersey Hawkins, their best outside shooter, closed at the end to make the final score 82-76. The Soviet Union went on to avenge a 97-92 loss in the preliminary round by beating powerful Yugloslavia, which included Petrovic and future NBA players Toni Kukoc, Vlade Divac, Dino Radja and Zarko Paspalj, 76-63 in the gold medal game. The United States took the bronze with a 78-49 win over Australia. Brazil's Oscar Schmidt, meanwhile, set an Olympic record by scoring 55 points in a game against Spain.

The American women fared better, winning the gold medal with a 77-70 victory over Yugoslavia in the championship game. Donovan and Edwards returned to lead a United States team that also included Teresa Weatherspoon and Cynthia Cooper, two future WNBA stars, on its roster.

That 1988 competition turned out to be the end of an era in Olympic basketball. On April 7, 1989 FIBA voted in favor of open competition, lifting the ban against NBA players competing for the United States team. That paved the way for the original Dream Team, composed almost exclusively of NBA stars, to represent the United States in 1992. Meanwhile, political developments in Eastern Europe also had a significant impact on Olympic basketball, as the breakup of the Soviet Union and Yugoslavia into numerous smaller republics took away what had been the United States' two premier rivals.

Stankovic, the Yugoslavian-born secretary general of FIBA, pushed hard for the inclusion of NBA stars in the Olympics even though he knew it all but erased any battle for the gold medal. He looked at the long-term picture and viewed open competition as vital for the global growth of the sport; essential, in fact, if other countries ever were to catch up to the U.S.

"Remember that from 1936 to 1972, the target for all other nations in Olympic basketball was second place," said Stankovic when the decision was announced in 1989. "Since 1972 it has not been so, and it will be the same pattern now. Right now the United States is certainly the strongest, but the world will catch up."

The short-term impact was to send U.S. basketball officials scrambling to revamp their entire approach to the Olympics, with an eye on Barcelona and 1992. Since 1964, an organization called the Basketball Federation of the USA had been an overseeing body, but in 1974 that group gave way to the Amateur Basketball Association of the USA, which included representatives from all amateur levels of the sport. With the FIBA vote in 1989, ABAUSA changed its name to USA Basketball and welcomed the NBA as an active member. Indeed, once it became clear that USA Basketball's primary challenge was to integrate NBA players into the 1992 Olympic effort, it became equally clear that this could best be achieved by NBA executives, who quickly began playing key roles in USA Basketball's activities.

FIBA's vote for open competition opened the floodgates to a wave of speculation regarding the direction of the U.S. Olympic effort. What should the makeup of the team be? How fair would it be if opening the door to NBA players also effectively closed it to the "amateur" players who had represented the nation for decades? On the other hand, if the Olympics were indeed now an open competition, how fair would it be to

deny places on the team to NBA players of superior talent and experience, just so the traditional amateur ranks could be represented? And how should the team be selected? Since 1936 there had been an Olympic Trials competition involving teams of invited players, sometimes competing as a unit (such as the AAU or collegiate champion), sometimes competing on All-Star teams. At the conclusion of the Trials, a selection committee would meet and name the Olympic players, plus alternates. But did it make sense for perennial NBA All-Stars to be put through trials? After all, if anybody didn't know what Michael Jordan could do at this point, a week-long series of exhibitions wasn't going to enlighten them.

Before these questions even could be raised, there was the issue of whether NBA stars would be interested in competing in the first place. Many, such as Jordan in 1984, already had been through the Olympic experience. Would they be willing to give up much of their limited off-season to compete in the 1992 Olympics? And would they be willing to risk injury to do so? Many thought the answer would be no, but they turned out to be dead wrong. NBA officials, led by Deputy Commissioner Russ Granik, who was also a vice president of USA Basketball, and Rod Thorn, at the time the league's Vice President of Operations, began putting out feelers to players and agents to gauge interest. They found most to be very interested right off the bat, and the others quickly came around after it became obvious just how big this Olympic basketball competition was going to be. Nobody wanted to miss a landmark event like this.

Once it became clear that NBA players wanted to be involved, USA Basketball officials faced the thorny issue of team makeup. Based on talent and experience, all 12 places on the team clearly would go to NBA players. But that didn't sit well with members of the amateur basketball community, who had carried the banner in previous Olympiads. So it was decided to reserve at least one place on the team for a college player, as a representative of the amateur ranks.

Next came the question of how to select the team. "The Olympic Trials worked when it was a college team, because there's always somebody out there at some school that you don't know about," explained C.M. Newton, the athletic director at the University of Kentucky and the chair of a 13-member selection committee made up of basketball people from the pro and college ranks. "Dan Majerle is a perfect example; he didn't have much of a national reputation when he made the 1988 Olympic team out of Central Michigan. We felt that this time, with a predominantly pro team, there would be no one out there that we wouldn't know. So what we did, essentially, is take the last two NBA seasons, plus college seasons, and use them as our Olympic Trials."

But before selecting the players, a coach had to be chosen. For a team dominated by NBA players, it made sense to go with an experienced NBA head coach with a winning background. And for a team of All-Stars, it made sense to go with a so-called "player's coach," one whose success was predicated to a large extent by his ability to get his players to want to play together and give their best for him. And for all the attention the team would receive, it also made sense to go with a coach who was accomplished at dealing with the media and comfortable being in the spotlight. USA Basketball turned to Chuck Daly, the

dapper dandy who had recently led the Detroit Pistons of "Bad Boys" fame to a pair of NBA titles. The thinking was that if Daly could work with such diverse personalities as Isiah Thomas, Dennis Rodman, Joe Dumars and Bill Laimbeer and lead them to consecutive NBA titles, he ought to be able to handle the group that would become known as the Dream Team.

"What tipped the choice in my favor?" said Daly. "I think that the committee looked first at where I'd come from. I was a lifer. I'd coached at every level—high school, collegiate and professional. I'd crossed all the boundaries in terms of coaching. I think, next, they looked at our accomplishments in Detroit, the fact that our team had won two NBA championships and been in a third NBA Finals. I had been successful; but I don't think our record was the paramount reason I was selected. There was some discussion about my being a guy who can deal with players, a player's coach. Well, sometimes yes, sometimes no, but I think that's part of being a successful professional coach today. In this day and age, the people aspect of coaching is paramount."

For assistant coaches, USA Basketball selected Lenny Wilkens, a long-time NBA head coach and a former standout playmaker; Mike Krzyzewski, the highly successful coach of Duke University; and P.J. Carlesimo, the energetic coach who had led Seton Hall to the NCAA title game and would go on to coach Portland and Golden State in the NBA.

Choosing the players was a rotisserie fan's dream, but also a potential nightmare. With so much talent at the selection committee's disposal, chemistry entered into the equation more than ever before. As Daly himself said, "With all the great players in the NBA, not to mention the college ranks, how do you pick a 12-man team? No matter who you choose, some outstanding individuals were going to be left off. Picking this team was an impossible task."

To make Daly's life easier from a practical standpoint, he was largely taken out of the process, playing only an advisory role to the selection committee, which made the actual choices. But before any choices were publicly announced, two NBA officials on the committee, Granik and Thorn, approached those players and asked whether they would accept if invited. "Each player who was contacted said, 'Yes,' and I felt that was really strong," said Newton. "When we were going into this, a lot of people said we would never get this guy to play or that guy to play. But every player just jumped right on it."

On September 13, 1991, on a nationally televised broadcast, the first 10 members of the Dream Team were announced: forwards Charles Barkley, Larry Bird, Karl Malone, Chris Mullin and Scottie Pippen, centers Patrick Ewing and David Robinson, and guards Magic Johnson, Michael Jordan and John Stockton. All were NBA All-Stars; even Johnson, who had retired from the league prior to the 1991-92 season after learning he had tested positive for the HIV virus that leads to AIDS, would come back to earn MVP honors in the 1992 NBA All-Star Game in Orlando. Two spots were held open until the completion of the 1991-92 NBA and college seasons so players who might come on strong could be added to the squad. On May 11, 1992, those final two slots were filled with Clyde Drexler and Christian Laettner, the latter getting the nod over Shaquille O'Neal as the lone college player on the team

because he could play forward as well as center.

Indeed, a hallmark of this team was versatility, with numerous players capable of playing more than one position. Barkley and Bird could play either forward spot, while Drexler, Johnson, Jordan, Mullin and Pippen all could play guard or small forward. Pippen and Jordan handled the ball well enough to play point guard should Johnson and/or Stockton get hurt, as both would before the end of the Olympics. And Malone and Laettner could fill in at center if needed.

Daly suspected talent would not be a problem for the United States team. "The biggest challenge of the Olympics is not necessarily going to be the European teams or the Asiatic team or the African team. The challenge is going to be our own people," he predicted. "How do we bring this team together in spirit and in thinking, as well as from a technical basketball standpoint? Will there be a clash of wills, of egos, among these stars? Will they be supporting of each other and willing to modulate their individual personalities in order to blend as a team and achieve our ultimate goal? That's going to be the challenge."

Because the United States had not won the gold medal in 1988, it was not assured a berth in the field at the Olympics. It had to win a place by competing in the Basketball Tournament of the Americas in Portland, Oregon, against other teams from North, Central and South America. That meant the team would have to get together on June 21, shortly after the completion of the NBA Finals, and then stay together for most of the next seven weeks, through the gold medal game on Saturday, August 8. After that, players would have little more than a month off before they had to report to their NBA training camps, so they were giving up the bulk of their off-season.

That's why USA Basketball went out of its way to make the trip as attractive as possible for the participating players. They were invited to bring along their families. They flew on a special charter. Their initial training camp was held at a swanky resort in La Jolla, just north of San Diego, and then their pre-Olympic camp was held in the posh enclave of Monte Carlo, with the players staying at a luxury hotel complete with its own casino. At the Olympics in Barcelona they stayed not in the dormitory-like Olympic Village, where most of the athletes stayed, but in a new, first-class downtown hotel just off Las Ramblas, Barcelona's lively main drag.

The team went through six days of practice in La Jolla, including scrimmages against a developmental team of collegians that included such stars as Grant Hill, Chris Webber, Allan Houston and Penny Hardaway. Perhaps the best thing that happened to the Dream Team was that it got outplayed and outscored 62-54 in one of those 20-minute scrimmages. "Afterwards I found out that our players were more than a little upset by the way they had played, and I was pleased by that reaction," declared Daly.

They took it out on their opponents in the pre-Olympic qualifying tournament, routing Cuba 136-57, Panama 112-52, Argentina 128-87, Puerto Rico 119-81 and Venezuela 127-80. "The U.S. team is from another planet," raved Venezuela's coach, Julio Toro, summing up the ease with which the Americans earned their trip to Barcelona. But their opponents didn't seem to mind; they loved being on the same court as these legends, and posed with the Dream Team for two-team

pictures before every game.

"Without any doubt, not just for us but for everyone playing in this tournament, it is great to play with Michael Jordan and Magic Johnson. I am so overwhelmed with joy," said Argentina's point guard, Marcelo Milanesio, who during his game against the United States was seen frantically waving to a teammate on the bench to take a picture of him guarding Johnson.

After about 10 days off, the players regrouped at Newark Airport for the charter that would fly them to Nice, then on to Monte Carlo by bus. By now, Daly's fears about jealousies among the players largely had been allayed.

"What was most interesting for me those two weeks was the bonding that took place among the players," he said of the pre-Olympic camp and tournament. "They really came together and enjoyed themselves on and off the court, more so than you might imagine for such high-profile stars."

As for their talent, even Daly was impressed by what he had seen. "I don't think you can even sense how great these players really are," he said. "I've been in the league some 15 years now and I still marvel, even in these games which were not very competitive, at some of the things these people are capable of doing. We really are seeing the greatest players in the history of the game, and it's a joy to be a part of it."

Daly, and a few select others fortunate to be present at a closed scrimmage, got an eyeful in Monte Carlo as the team tuned up for the Olympics. Daly had split the team in half, with Johnson leading one unit and Jordan the other, and their competitiveness really came to the fore. "We were leading 14-2 and I let Michael know about it," said Johnson. "I told him this wasn't Chicago Stadium and that he'd better get into the show or it's all over. I don't know why I said that. All of a sudden he said, 'I'm bringing us back,' and he did. Singlehandedly."

Johnson had made the mistake of tugging on Superman's cape with his trash-talking, and Jordan made him pay. He crouched into his defensive stance and shut Johnson down, then took it out on him at the other end. "I pushed him to his level, the highest he can go," Johnson said later. "I didn't like it at the time, but at the same time, I did enjoy it. It was really something. Your mind says you want to stop him, but the other side of it says you have no chance. He just starts jumping over you. Every time I looked up, he had his shoes on my No. 15. It was as good a demonstration of basketball as I've ever seen in my life, everything a basketball player could want."

By the time it was over, Jordan had brought his team back to win 40-36 and the Bulls star was exultant, racing around the court and singing the "Sometimes I Dream…" refrain from his "Be Like Mike" commercials.

The rest of the world got to share the dream in Barcelona, where the Americans quickly became the stars of the show. Wherever they went they were followed by hundreds of fans, many of whom waited outside the team's hotel or outside the basketball arena in the working class suburb of Badalona just to catch a glimpse of their heroes. All the games involving the Dream Team were sellouts, with the gold medal game ranking with the opening and closing ceremonies as the hottest tickets of the fortnight. More than 1,000 members of the media turned out on July 25 for a pre-tournament press conference,

held in a vast auditorium at the main press center. And when coaches and players went to the Olympic Village to pick up their credentials, other athletes rushed out to see them and get autographs and the situation almost got out of control before the players could get back to the safety of their team bus.

The players coped with the attention in different ways. Jordan took to the golf course, usually playing with Daly, Carlesimo and Thorn and often logging 36 holes, even on game days. Bird and Mullin, among others, spent countless hours working out. Many stayed with their families, doing what sightseeing they could but otherwise enjoying family time at the hotel. Because he's only 6-foot-1, Stockton was one of the few who could easily blend into the Olympic crowd, so he would often go out with his family to tour Barcelona. Barkley, never one to shy from attention, frequently left the hotel at night and became something of a Pied Piper along Las Ramblas as he bounced from one night spot to another. Others stayed in the hotel and played cards, often till 3 or 4 in the morning.

Many of the players marched in the opening ceremonies, where once again their unique status was confirmed. Other athletes, not just Americans but from other teams, frequently broke ranks and ran over to see the Dream Team members, snapping photographs and shaking hands. Scenes like that justified USA Basketball's decision to have the team stay at the new Ambassador Hotel, on a relatively quiet side street off Las Ramblas, rather than in the Olympic Village, where they never would have had time to themselves.

Finally, on Sunday, July 26, the United States played its first game, routing a much smaller team from Angola 116-48, outscoring the Angolans by an amazing 46-1 count during one stretch of the first half. During the game an elbow was thrown by Barkley at a skinny Angolan player when the two became entangled while heading upcourt. It wasn't much of an elbow by NBA standards, but it became a rallying point for those, mostly back in the United States, who felt NBA players should not be competing against so-called amateurs in the Olympics. In Barcelona, however, it wasn't much of an issue, and neither was the presence of the NBA stars. After all, professionals had been competing for other countries for years.

The Americans faced their first real test in their next game, against Croatia. "I only let Michael play nine holes today because I wanted him to be ready," quipped Daly. Jordan and Pippen, his Bulls teammate, were more than ready, since the star of the Croatian team, Toni Kukoc, was being hotly recruited by the Bulls, who even delayed renegotiating Pippen's contract in their effort to land the European star. With that extra incentive, Jordan and especially Pippen wanted to show Kukoc a thing or two, and Daly sagely took advantage of it. He started the game with Pippen guarding Kukoc, and when Pippen came out, Jordan took over for him. "I never saw that kind of defense before," Kukoc, who managed just four points on 2-for-11 shooting, said later. "From the first moment, Scottie was all over me."

With Kukoc all but erased from the game, the Americans breezed to a 103-70 victory over one of Europe's best teams, even though Johnson had suffered a hamstring injury 8-1/2 minutes into the game. Though Johnson would be sidelined for a couple of games and Stockton was already out with an injury

suffered in the pre-Olympic tournament, it was clear the Dream Team had little to worry about en route to the gold.

The U.S. went on to win all eight of their games by an average of 43.8 points per game, beating Lithuania, with Arvydas Sabonis and Sarunas Marciulionis, 127-76 in the semi-finals and then defeating Croatia in a rematch 117-85 for the gold medal. Barkley finished as the team's top scorer with 18.0 points per game, and nine other players (all but Stockton, injured for much of the Olympics, and Laettner, the collegian) tallied at least 8.0 ppg. Daly made good on his pre-tournament goal of never calling a timeout, not even when Croatia grabbed a 25-23 lead midway through the first half of the final game. The Americans were that good. "Dream Team is a lot of name to live up to," said Daly, "but if anything, the 1992 U.S. Olympic men's basketball team exceeded all hopes and expectations."

With all the attention focused on the Dream Team, the United States women's team found itself overshadowed, and overmatched, by a Unified Team comprised of players from many of the former Soviet republics. Even though six of its players had competed at the Olympics four years earlier, the Americans were beaten by the Unified Team 79-73 in the semi-finals. The Unified Team went on to capture the gold medal with a 76-66 victory over China, while the United States came home with a bronze following an 88-74 win over Cuba.

This result led to a major rethinking by USA Basketball, which was determined to give its women's team every opportunity for a better showing at the 1996 Olympics in Atlanta. Boosted by the organizational and marketing support of the NBA, USA Basketball committed to hiring a coaching staff and bringing together the best women players in the nation more than a year before the Olympics, instead of just months, as had been the practice.

Tara VanDerveer, the highly successful coach at Stanford, took a one-year leave of absence and was hired as the national team coach in 1995. Tryouts were held and a team of 11 players began working out together at the Olympic Training Center in Colorado Springs, Colo. The idea was for these 11 to practice and compete as a unit for an extended period of time and hopefully form an experienced core for the 1996 Olympic team.

The 11 players were all former U.S. college stars, many of whom had played professionally in Europe or Asia. The exception was Rebecca Lobo, who was coming off a 1994-95 season in which she had led the University of Connecticut to a 35-0 record and an NCAA championship. Joining her were Jennifer Azzi and Katy Steding, who had played under VanDerveer at Stanford; former Tennessee stars Nikki McCray and Carla McGhee; Sheryl Swoopes, who had led Texas Tech to the NCAA title in 1993; former Virginia standout Dawn Staley, and veterans of the overseas pro ranks Ruthie Bolton, Teresa Edwards, Lisa Leslie and Katrina McClain.

In late October, the team began an exhibition tour against top U.S. college teams as well as national and Olympic teams from others countries. It went undefeated in 51 games over the next nine months, including 10 nationally televised appearances—unprecedented exposure for women's college basketball. Center Venus Lacy, a former Louisiana Tech star with pro experience, was added in May to complete the roster for the Olympic team, and the squad stretched its record to 52-0 by

beating Italy's Olympic team in an exhibition on July 13.

The United States women headed to Atlanta on a roll and proved unstoppable. Leslie, who once scored 101 points in one half of a game while in high school, poured in 35 points against Japan and led the team with 19.5 points per game. McClain averaged 8.3 rebounds per game and Edwards dished 8.0 assists per game. The Americans won all eight of their games and avenged a loss to Brazil in the 1994 World Championships with a 111-87 victory in the gold medal game. Australia beat Ukraine for the bronze.

The six games played by the United States women at the Georgia Dome drew crowds in excess of 30,000, and the success and popularity of the team spawned not one but two professional leagues in the United States: the American Basketball League began play in the winter of 1996-97 and the Women's National Basketball Association, backed by the NBA, began play in the summer of 1997. The ABL folded midway through its second season, but the better-financed and marketed WNBA lives on.

The United States men's team, this time composed entirely of NBA players, lived up to the high expectations of the home fans in Atlanta by winning its eight games by a margin of 31 points per game en route to the gold under the guidance of Wilkens, the NBA's winningest coach and an aide to Daly four years earlier. The team included five members of the original Dream Team—Barkley, Malone, Pippen, Robinson and Stockton, plus newcomers Penny Hardaway, Grant Hill, Reggie Miller, Hakeem Olajuwon, Shaquille O'Neal, Gary Payton and Mitch Richmond. Olajuwon, a native of Nigeria, had obtained citizenship papers and filed a special petition in order to represent the United States.

The Americans struggled a bit in their opener, starting slowly before pulling away from Argentina 96-68 behind Robinson's 18 points. Following an 87-54 win over Angola, Team USA beat a solid Lithuanian squad that once again featured Sabonis and Marciulionis, 104-82. The Americans then set a record for most points scored in an Olympic game as Pippen tallied 24 and Miller netted five three-pointers in a 133-70 rout of China. Wins over Croatia 102-71 and Brazil 98-75 propelled the Americans into the medal round, where they beat Australia 101-73 and then Yugoslavia 95-69. A record crowd of 34,600 watched Robinson score 28 points, Miller 20 and Hardaway 17 in the championship game. Nine players averaged between 8.4 and 12.4 points per game on the deep American squad, with Barkley the leading scorer as he was in 1992. He also led the team with 6.6 rebounds per game, while Payton was the top playmaker at 4.5 assists per game.

Signs that the rest of the world was catching up to the NBA stars now representing the United States became evident at the 2000 Olympics in Sydney, where the American men once again took the gold medal. This time, however, it wasn't easy.

"Nobody can tell us we didn't earn it, that's what makes it even more special," declared Allan Houston after the United States beat France 85-75 for the gold medal after having survived an 85-83 nail-biter against Lithuania in the semi-finals. "It wasn't a cakewalk," echoed Ray Allen. We earned it and played some tough teams. A lot of people assumed that we would automatically win the gold, and we did, but it wasn't easy.

"This wasn't a day at the beach, where just because we're from the United States other teams aren't going to say, 'Well, they're better, and they get the game,'" said Rudy Tomjanovich, coach of Team USA. "They came out and battled. I have so much respect for how the foreign teams played. When you put five guys together on a team, if they've got their chemistry together and they're working, anything can happen."

The American team had just two players with Olympic experience, Payton and Hardaway. Joining them were many of the younger stars of the NBA: Shareef Abdur-Rahim, Ray Allen, Vin Baker, Vince Carter, Kevin Garnett, Allan Houston, Jason Kidd, Antonio McDyess. Completing the team were two veterans, Alonzo Mourning and Steve Smith.

Things began easily enough for the Americans at the Sydney SuperDome, with victories over China 119-72 and Italy 93-61. Then came Lithuania, a team led by former University of Maryland star Sarunas Jasikevicius. In a game marked by 55 fouls and 76 free throws, the Americans led by as many as 14 points late in the first half, fell behind 50-49 with 17:54 to play, came back to again lead by 14 at 70-56 with 7:54 left, then saw Lithuania close to within five before hanging on to win 85-76. The Americans bounced back to pound New Zealand 102-56, then erased an early 20-10 deficit to beat France 106-94 and advance to the medal round. The game against France saw the most spectacular play of the Olympics when the acrobatic, 6-foot-6 Carter leaped over France's 7-foot-2 center Frederic Weis for a dunk.

Kidd had 10 points, eight assists and seven rebounds and Garnett had 16 points and 11 rebounds as the United States beat Russia 85-70 in the quarter-finals, setting up a rematch against Lithuania. This one was even closer than the first, going right down to the buzzer. The United States led 48-36 at half-time, but Lithuania opened the second half with a 20-6 run for the first of eight second-half lead changes. Lithuania held an 81-80 advantage before Carter's floater with 31 seconds to play put the United States back on top. Kidd made the first of two free throws with 10 seconds left to make it 85-83, but missed the second. The ball squirted loose and in the scramble for the rebound, McDyess dove to the floor to force a jump ball with Ramunas Siskauskas. Lithuania controled the tap and Jasikevicius, the game's leading scorer with 27 points who had previously hit 5-of-10 three-pointers, managed to launch a hurried 23-footer at the buzzer. But his shot, which would have handed the United States its first defeat since NBA players became part of its Olympic team, fell short and to the left of the rim, and the Americans escaped with a two-point victory. "Unfortunately, I just had time to throw up a prayer," said Jasikevicius, who went on to play professionally in Europe. "That was a one-in-a-million shot."

Meanwhile, France upset host Australia 76-52 in the other semi-final to set up another rematch against the Americans. This one also was a struggle as the Americans saw a 46-32 half-time lead wither to 76-72 with 4:26 left to play. But an 8-2 spurt, capped by a Carter double-clutch dunk, stretched the lead out to 10 points with 1:40 remaining and the United States went on to win 85-75 for the gold medal. It was, however, the lowest margin of victory in any of the U.S. gold medal games. Lithuania beat Australia 89-71 for the bronze.

Every player on the United States team averaged at least 5.5 points per game, with Carter leading the way at 14.8. Garnett was the team's top rebounder at 9.1 per game, and Kidd led the way in assists with a 4.4 average.

The United States women defended their gold medal successfully, playing their best game of the tournament to beat host Australia 76-54 in the final. "I'm glad they decided to save the best for last," said coach Nell Fortner. "It was a game where we knew that if we gave Australia an inch, they'd take advantage of it."

So the Americans never gave their hosts an inch, taking the lead for good at the 17:05 mark of the first half, going into halftime ahead 43-30 and breaking the game wide open with an 11-2 run that made it 64-47 with 9:29 to go. Lisa Leslie and Natalie Williams each had 14 points and nine rebounds to lead a balanced effort by the U.S. team, which included six players from the 1996 Olympic squad: Edwards, Bolton (now Ruthie Bolton-Holifield), Staley, McCray, Swoopes and Leslie. Joining them were Williams, Yolanda Griffith, Chamique Holdsclaw, DeLisha Milton, Katie Smith and Kara Wolters. Leslie led the team with 15.8 points per game, Griffith was the top rebounder at 8.8 rpg and Staley led the way in assists at 3.6 apg.

It was the fourth gold medal for Edwards, who also won a bronze in 1992 and tied a record set by Teofilo Cruz Downs of Puerto Rico by appearing in her fifth Olympics. The 36-year-old Edwards retired as the United States' career leader in games played (32), assists (143) and steals (59) in Olympic competition.

"For a long time, I have said a prayer on the podium during the national anthem," she said when it was all over. "I truly love what I do. I love this game. I know that I was born to play basketball. I think I've left a mark, etched something somewhere that people will remember me by when they talk about women's basketball. That's what you should strive to do in a career."

OLYMPIC STATISTICS

OVERALL OLYMPIC MEDAL STANDINGS

	Gold	Silver	Bronze	Total
MEN				
United States	12	1	1	14
Soviet Union	2	4	3	9
Yugoslavia	1	4	1	6
Brazil	0	0	3	3
Lithuania	0	0	3	3
Uruguay	0	0	2	2
France	0	2	0	2
Canada	0	1	0	1
Croatia	0	1	0	1
Cuba	0	0	1	1
Italy	0	1	0	1
Mexico	0	0	1	1
Spain	0	1	0	1
WOMEN				
United States	4	1	1	6
Soviet Union	2	0	1	3
Australia	0	1	1	2
Brazil	0	1	1	2
Bulgaria	0	1	1	2
Yugoslavia	0	1	1	2
Unified Team	1	0	0	1
China	0	1	0	1
South Korea	0	1	0	1
Canada	0	0	1	1

BERLIN 1936

MEN
Final: USA 19, Canada 8
Consolation: Mexico 26, Poland 12
USA Team Members:
BALTER, Samuel J. Jr.
BISHOP, Ralph English
FORTENBERRY, Joseph Cephis
GIBBONS, John Haskell
JOHNSON, Francis Lee
KNOWLES, Carl Stanley
LUBIN, Frank John
MOLLNER, Arthur Owen
PIPER, Donald Arthur
RAGLAND, Jack Williamson
SCHMIDT, Willard Theodore
SHY, Carl L.
SWANSON, Duane Alexander
WHEATLEY, William John
Final Standings:
Gold: United States
Silver: Canada
Bronze: Mexico
4. Poland, 5. Philippines, 6. Uruguay, 7. Italy, 8. Peru, 9. Brazil

LONDON 1948

Final: USA 65, France 21
Consolation: Brazil 52, Mexico 47
USA Team Members:
BARKER, Clifford Eugene
BARKSDALE, Donald Argee
BEARD, Ralph Milton Jr.
BECK, Lewis William Jr.
BORYLA, Vincent Joseph
CARPENTER, Gordon
GROZA, Alexander John
JONES, Wallace Clayton
KURLAND, Robert Albert
LUMPP, Raymond George
PITTS, Robert C.
RENICK, John (Jesse) Bernard
ROBINSON, Robert L.Jackson
ROLLINS, Kenneth Herman
Final Standings:
Gold: United States
Silver: France
Bronze: Brazil
4. Mexico, 5. Uruguay, 6. Chile, 7. Czechoslovakia, 8. Korea, 9. Canada, 10. Peru, 11. Belgium, 12. Philippines, 13. Cuba, 14. Islamic Republic of Iran, 15. Argentina, 16. Hungary, 17. Italy, 18. China, 19. Egypt, 20. Great Britain, 21. Switzerland, 22. Iraq, 23. Ireland

HELSINKI 1952

MEN
Final: USA 36, Soviet Union 25
Consolation: Uruguay 68, Argentina 59
USA Team Members:
BONTEMPS, Ronald Yngve
FRIEBERGER, Marcus Ross
GLASGOW, Victor Wayne
HOAG, Charles Monroe
HOUGLAND, William Marion
KELLER, John Frederick
KELLEY, Melvin Dean
KENNEY, Robert Earl
KURLAND, Robert Albert
LIENHARD, William Barner
LOVELETTE, Clyde Edward
MCCABE, Frank Reilly
PIPPIN, Daniel Luther
WILLIAMS, Howard Earl
Final Standings:
Gold: United States
Silver: Soviet Union
Bronze: Uruguay
4. Argentina, 5. Chile, 6. Brazil, 7. Bulgaria, 8. France, 9. Canada

MELBOURNE 1956

MEN
Final: USA 89, Soviet Union 55
Consolation: Uruguay 71, France 62
USA Team Members:
BOUSHKA, Richard James
CAIN, Carl Cecil
DARLING, Charles Frick
EVANS, William Best
FORD, Gilbert
HALDORSSON, Burdette Eliele
HOUGLAND, William Marion
JEANGERARD, Robert Eugene
JONES, Kenneth C.
RUSSELL, William Fenton
TOMSIC, Ronald Paul
WALSH, James Patrick
Final Standings:
Gold: United States
Silver: Soviet Union
Bronze: Uruguay
4. France, 5. Bulgaria, 6. Brazil, 7. Philippines, 8. Chile, 9. Canada, 10. Japan, 11. Formosa, 12. Australia, 13. Singapore, 14. Korea, 15. Thailand

ROME 1960

MEN
Round-Robin Final Group: USA (3-0), Soviet Union (2-1), Brazil (1-2), Italy (0-3)
USA Team Members:
ARNETTE, Jay Hoyland
BELLAMY, Walter Jones Jr.
BOOZER, Robert Lewis
DISCHINGER, Terence Gilbert
HALDORSSON, Burdette Eliele
IMHOFF, Darrall Tucker
KELLEY, Allen Earl
LANE, Lester E.
LUCAS, Jeremy Ray
ROBERTSON, Oscar Palmer
SMITH, Adrian Howard
WEST, Jeremy Alan
Final Standings:
Gold: United States
Silver: Soviet Union
Bronze: Brazil
4. Italy, 5. Czechoslovakia, 6. Yugoslavia, 7. Poland, 8. Uruguay, 9. Hungary, 10. France, 11. Philippines, 12. Mexico, 13. Puerto Rico, 14. Spain, 15. Japan, 16. Bulgaria

TOKYO 1964

MEN

Final: USA 73, Soviet Union 59
Consolation: Brazil 76, Puerto Rico 60
USA Team Members:
BARNES, James
BRADLEY, William Warren
BROWN, Lawrence Harvey
CALDWELL, Joseph Louis
COUNTS, Melvin Grant
DAVIES, Richard Allen
HAZZARD, Walter Raphael
JACKSON, Lucius Brown
MCCAFFREY, John Paul
MULLINS, Jeffry Vincent
SHIPP, Jeremy Franklin
WILSON, George
Final Standings:
Gold: United States
Silver: Soviet Union
Bronze: Brazil
4. Puerto Rico, 5. Italy, 6. Poland, 7. Yugoslavia,
8. Uruguay, 9. Australia, 10. Japan, 11. Finland,
12. Mexico, 13. Hungary, 14. Canada, 15. Peru,
16. Korea

MEXICO CITY 1968

MEN

Final: USA 65, Yugoslavia 50
Consolation: Soviet Union 70, Brazil 53
USA Team Members:
BARRETT, Michael Thomas
CLAWSON, John Richard
DEE, Donald Francis
FOWLER, Calvin Bernard
HAYWOOD, Spencer
HOSKETT, Wilmer Frederick
KING, James
SAULTERS, Glynn
SCOTT, Charles Thomas
SILLIMAN, Michael Barnwell
SPAIN, John Kenneth
WHITE, Joseph Henry
Final Standings:
Gold: United States
Silver: Yugoslavia
Bronze: Soviet Union
4. Brazil, 5. Mexico, 6. Poland, 7. Spain, 8. Italy,
9. Puerto Rico, 10. Bulgaria, 11. Cuba,
12. Panama, 13. Philippines, 14. Korea,
15. Senegal, 16. Morocco

MUNICH 1972

MEN

Final: Soviet Union 51, USA 50
Consolation: Cuba 66, Italy 65
USSR Team Members:
BELOV, Aleksandr
BELOV, Sergei
BOLOSHEV, Aleksandr
DVORNY, Ivan
EDESHKO, Ivan
KORKIYA, Mikhail
KOVALENKO, Sergei
PAULAUSKAS, Modestas
POLIVODA, Anatoli
SAKANDELIDZE, Zurab
VOLNOV, Gennadi
ZHARMUKHAMEDOV, Alzhan
Final Standings:
Gold: Soviet Union
Silver: United States
Bronze: Cuba
4. Italy, 5. Yugoslavia, 6. Puerto Rico, 7. Brazil,
8. Czechoslovakia, 9. Australia, 10. Poland,
11. Spain, 12. Federal Republic of Germany,
13. Philippines, 14. Japan, 15. Senegal, 16. Egypt

MONTREAL 1976

MEN

Final: USA 95, Yugoslavia 74
Consolation: Soviet Union 100, Canada 72
USA Team Members:
ARMSTRONG, Michael Taylor (Tate)
BUCKNER, William Quinn
CARR, Kenneth Alan
DANTLEY, Adrian Delano
DAVIS, Walter Paul
FORD, Philip Jackson, Jr.
GRUNFELD, Ernest
HUBBARD, Phillip Gregory
KUPCHAK, Mitchell
LAGARDE, Thomas Joseph
MAY, Scott Glenn
SHEPPARD, Steven
Final Standings:
Gold: United States
Silver: Yugoslavia
Bronze: Soviet Union
4. Canada, 5. Italy, 6. Czechoslovakia, 7. Cuba,
8. Australia, 9. Puerto Rico, 10. Mexico, 11. Japan,
12. Egypt

WOMEN

Round-Robin: Soviet Union (5-0), USA (3-2),
Bulgaria (3-2), Czechoslovakia (2-3), Japan (2-3),
Canada (0-5)
USSR Team Members:
BARISHEVA-KOROSTELEVA, Olga
DAUNENE, Tamara
FERYABNIKOVA, Nelli
KLIMOVA, Natalya
KURVYAKOVA, Raisa
OVECHKINA, Tatiana
RUPSHENE, Angelia
SEMENOVA, Uljana
SHUVAEVA-OLKHOVA, Nadezhda
SUKHARNOVA, Olga
ZAKHAROVA, Nadezhda
ZAKHAROVA-NADIROVA, Tatiana
Final Standings: Bulgaria
Gold: Soviet Union
Silver: United States
Bronze: Bulgaria
4. Czechoslovakia, 5. Japan, 6. Canada

MOSCOW 1980

MEN

Final: Yugoslavia 86, Italy 77
Consolation: Soviet Union 117, Spain 94
Yugoslavia Team Members:
COSIC, Kresimir
DALIPAGIC, Drazen
DELIBASIC, Mirza
JERKOV, Zeljko
KICANOVIC, Dragan
KNEGO, Andro
KRSTULOVIC, Duje
NAKIC-VOJNOVIC, Mihovil
RADOVANOVIC, Ratko
SKROCE, Branko
SLAVNIC, Zoran
ZIZIC, Rajko
Final Standings:
Gold: Yugoslavia
Silver: Italy
Bronze: Soviet Union
4. Spain, 5. Brazil, 6. Cuba, 7. Poland, 8. Australia,
9. Czechoslovakia, 10. Sweden, 11. Senegal,
12. India

WOMEN

Final: Soviet Union 104, Bulgaria 73
Consolation: Yugoslavia 68, Hungary 65
USSR Team Members:
BARISHEVA-KOROSTELEVA, Olga
BESSELENE, Vida
FERYABNIKOVA, Nelli
IVINSKAIA, Tatiana
OVECHKINA, Tatiana
ROGOZHINA, Liudmila
RUPSHENE, Angelia
SEMENOVA, Uljana
SHARMAI, Liubov
SHUVAEVA-OLKHOVA, Nadezhda
SUKHARNOVA, Olga
ZAKHAROVA-NADIROVA, Tatiana
Final Standings:
Gold: Soviet Union
Silver: Bulgaria
Bronze: Yugoslavia
4. Hungary, 5. Cuba, 6. Italy

LOS ANGELES 1984

MEN

Final: USA 96, Spain 65
Consolation: Yugoslavia 88, Canada 82
USA Team Members:
ALFORD, Steven Todd
EWING, Patrick Aloysius
FLEMING, Vernon
JORDAN, Michael
KLEINE, Joseph William
KONCAK, Jon Francis
MULLIN, Christopher Paul
PERKINS, Samuel Bruce
ROBERTSON, Alvin Cyrrale
TISDALE, Wayman Lawrence
TURNER, Jeffrey Stephen
WOOD, Leonard III
Final Standings:
Gold: United States
Silver: Spain
Bronze: Yugoslavia
4. Canada, 5. Italy, 6. Uruguay, 7. Australia,
8. Federal Republic of Germany, 9. Brazil,
10. China, 11. France, 12. Egypt

WOMEN

Final: USA 85, Korea 55
Consolation: China 63, Canada 57
USA Team Members:
BOSWELL, Catherine La Ora
CURRY, Denise Marie
DONOVAN, Anne Theresa
EDWARDS, Teresa
HENRY, Ludi "Lea"
LAWRENCE, Janice Faye
MCGEE, Pamela Denise
MENKEN-SCHAUDT, Carol Jean
MILLER, Cheryl Deann
MULKEY, Kimberly Duane
NOBLE, Cindy Jo.
WOODARD, Lynette
Final Standings:
Gold: United States
Silver: Korea
Bronze: China
4. Canada, 5. Australia, 6. Yugoslavia

SEOUL 1988
MEN
Final: Soviet Union 76, Yugoslavia 63
Consolation: USA 78, Australia 49
USSR Team Members:
BELOSTENNYI, Aleksandr
GOBOROV, Valeri
KHOMICHUS, Valdemaras
KURTINAITIS, Rimas
MARCHULENIS, Raimundas
MIGLIENIKS, Igors
PANKRASHKIN, Viktor
SABONIS, Arvidas Romas
SOOK, Tiit
TARAKANOV, Sergei
TIKHONENKO, Valeri
VOLKOV, Aleksandr
Final Standings:
Gold: Soviet Union
Silver: Yugoslavia
Bronze: United States
4. Australia, 5. Brazil, 6. Canada, 7. Puerto Rico,
8. Spain, 9. Korea, 10. Central African Republic,
11. China, 12. Egypt

WOMEN
Final: USA 77, Yugoslavia 70
Consolation: Soviet Union 68, Australia 53
USA Team Members:
BROWN, Cynthia Louise
BULLETT, Victoria
COOPER, Cynthia Lynne
DONOVAN, Anne Theresa
EDWARDS, Teresa
ETHRIDGE, Mary Camille
GILLOM, Jennifer
GORDON, Bridgette C.
LLOYD, Andrea Lane
MCCLAIN, Katrina Felicia
MCCONNELL, Suzanne
WEATHERSPOON, Teresa G.
Final Standings:
Gold: United States
Silver: Yugoslavia
Bronze: Soviet Union
SEOUL 1988
Gold: United States
Silver: Yugoslavia
Bronze: Soviet Union
4. Australia, 5. Bulgaria, 6. China, 7. S.Korea,
8. Czechoslovakia

BARCELONA 1992
MEN
Final: USA 117, Croatia 85
Consolation: Lithuania 82, Unified Team 78
USA Team Members:
BARKLEY, Charles
BIRD, Larry
DREXLER, Clyde
EWING, Patrick Aloysius
JOHNSON, Magic
JORDAN, Michael
LAETTNER, Christian D.
MALONE, Karl
MULLIN, Christopher Paul
PIPPEN, Scottie
ROBINSON, David Maurice
STOCKTON, John Houston
Final Standings:
Gold: United States
Silver: Croatia
Bronze: Lithuania
4. Unified Team, 5. Brazil, 6. Australia,
7. Federal Republic of Germany, 8. Puerto Rico,
9. Spain, 10. Angola, 11. Venezuela, 12. China

WOMEN
Final: Unified Team 76, China 66
Consolation: USA 88, Cuba 74
Unified Team Members:
BARANOVA, Elena
BOUNATIANTS, Elen
CHVAIBOVITCH, Elena
GUERLITS, Irina
KHOUDACHOVA, Elena
MINKH, Irina
SOUMNIKOVA, Irina
TKACHENKO, Marina
TORNIKIDOU, Elena
ZABOLOUEVA, Svetlana
ZASSOULSKAIA, Natalia
ZHIRKO, Elena
Final Standings:
Gold: Unified Team
Silver: China
Bronze: United States
4. Cuba, 5. Spain, 6. Czechoslovakia, 7. Brazil,
8. Italy

ATLANTA 1996
MEN
Final: USA 95, Yugoslavia 69
Consolation: Lithuania 80, Australia 74
USA Team Members:
BARKLEY, Charles
HARDAWAY, Anfernee
HILL, Grant
MALONE, Karl
MILLER, Reggie
O'NEAL, Shaquille
OLAJUWON, Hakeem
PAYTON, Gary
PIPPEN, Scottie
RICHMOND, Mitchell J.
ROBINSON, David Maurice
STOCKTON, John Houston
Final Standings:
Gold: United States
Silver: Yugoslavia
Bronze: Lithuania
4. Australia, 5. Greece, 6. Brazil, 7. Croatia,
8. China, 9. Argentina, 10. Puerto Rico, 11. Angola,
12. Korea

WOMEN
Final: USA 111, Brazil 87
Consolation: Australia 66, Ukraine 56
USA Team Members:
AZZI, Jennifer
BOLTON, Ruthie
EDWARDS, Teresa
LACEY, Venus
LESLIE, Lisa
LOBO, Rebecca
MCCLAIN, Katrina Felicia
MCCRAY, Nikki
MCGHEE, Carla
STALEY, Dawn
STEDING, Katy
SWOOPES, Sheryl
Final Standings:
Gold: United States
Silver: Brazil
Bronze: Australia
4. Ukraine, 5. Russia, 6. Cuba, 7. Japan, 8. Italy,
9. China, 10. Korea, 11. Canada, 12. Congo

SYDNEY 2000
MEN
Final: USA 85, France 75
Consolation: Lithuania 89, Australia 71
USA Team Members:
ABDUR-RAHIM, Shareef
ALLEN, Ray
BAKER, Vin
CARTER, Vince
GARNETT, Kevin
HARDAWAY, Tim
HOUSTON, Allan
KIDD, Jason
MCDYESS, Antonio
MOURNING, Alonzo
PAYTON, Gary
SMITH, Steve
Final Standings:
Gold: United States
Silver: France
Bronze: Lithuania
4. Australia, 5. Italy, 6. Yugoslavia, 7. Canada,
8. Russia, 9. Spain, 10. China, 11. New Zealand,
12. Angola

WOMEN
Final: USA 76, Australia 54
Consolation: Brazil 84, Korea 73
USA Team Members:
BOLTON, Ruthie
EDWARDS, Teresa
GRIFFITH, Yolanda
HOLDSCLAW, Chamique
LESLIE, Lisa
MCCRAY, Nikki
MILTON, Delisha
SMITH, Katie
STALEY, Dawn
SWOOPES, Sheryl
WILLIAMS, Natalie
WOLTERS, Kara
Final Standings:
Gold: United States
Silver: Australia
Bronze: Brazil
4. S.Korea, 5. France, 6. Russia, 7. Poland,
8. Slovakia, 9. Cuba, 10. Canada,
11. New Zealand, 12. Senegal

Chapter 45

FIBA World Championships

The World Basketball Championships, organized by The Federation Internationale de Basketball Amateur (FIBA), are held for men and women in four-year intervals that fall mid-way between Olympic years. Through 1990, the tournament was restricted to amateur players but, following the acceptance of professionals into the 1992 Olympics, FIBA opened its doors to NBA players for the 1994 events.

The men's tournament was inaugurated in 1950 in Buenos Aires, Argentina, where the host team upset the favored Americans in a controversial final. South America remained the site for the next four tournaments (Brazil twice, Chile and Uruguay) but, since 1970, the tournament has gained prominence as it moved around the world, stopping three times in Europe (Yugoslavia, Spain, Greece), twice each in continental North America (Canada, USA) and South America (Colombia, Brazil), as well as once each in Puerto Rico and the Philippines.

The nations of Yugoslavia, the Soviet Union and USA have combined to win 11 of the 14 men's titles (including the last 10), with Yugoslavia the most successful nation, winning five titles and finishing second twice, followed by the Soviet Union and USA with three each. Brazil, a two-time winner, and Argentina are the only other winners.

For the first seven tournaments, the medals were awarded based on the results of a round robin, a format that often resulted in placings being determined by sometimes-complicated tie-breaking procedures. In 1978 the format was changed so that the top teams from a preliminary round advanced to a medal round to determine the medal winners.

The women's tournament began in 1953 in Chile. It has been dominated by the USA and the former Soviet Union, with the USA winning seven titles and the USSR six. Brazil is the only other nation to win gold.

Here is a tournament-by-tournament recap:

Vlade Divac & Predrag Stojakovic, 2002
Yugoslavian stars hold world championship trophy aloft after 84-77 victory over Argentina in 2002 final. The United States finished sixth.

MEN
1950—Buenos Aires, Argentina
The United States and Argentina were undefeated in the tournament when they met in the final. A wildly enthusiastic crowd of more than 25,000 packed the stadium and was delighted to watch seven USA players foul out of the game.

The USA, represented by the AAU Denver Chevrolets, played the final minute with just four players. Argentina scored 32 points from the foul line (compared to 14 for the USA) to win 64-50. Chile defeated Brazil to place third.
1954—Rio de Janeiro, Brazil
The United States once again met the host nation in the final. But this time the crowd, numbering 35,000, was silenced early as the USA, represented by the three-time AAU champion Peoria Caterpillars, took a 35-19 half-time lead en route to defeating Brazil 62-41. Top scorer was Ed Solomon with 14 points. Bertram Born added 12 and Joe Stratton had 11.

In earning its first world title, the USA had a perfect 9-0 record, winning by more than an average of 25 points a game. Born led the team by averaging 11.2 points per game. The Philippines defeated France to take third place.
1959—Santiago, Chile
Originally scheduled to be held in 1958, the tournament was postponed until January 1959 when construction of a new stadium fell behind schedule. The scheduling change placed the

tournament in the middle of the American season, so the USA withdraw but then decided to send a team comprised of "volunteers" from the Air Force.

The makeshift USA team got into position to successfully defend its 1954 title but ran into a very strong Brazil team. The gold-medal game proved no contest, an 81-67 victory for Brazil. The Americans' only other loss in the tournament came at the hands of the Soviet Union, 62-37, marking the Soviets first ever basketball win over the USA. A very strong Soviet team, however, was declared ineligible for the final round because, for political reasons, it refused to play Formosa (now Taiwan).

1963—Rio de Janeiro, Brazil

Brazil emerged as the first two-time winner of the world title when the tournament returned to Rio de Janeiro. The Brazilians went undefeated for the tournament and wrapped things up by defeating the USA 85-81 in the final game.

The Americans, comprised of a team of AAU and college players, had a disappointing tournament, finishing out of the medals with a 6-3 record that included losses to Yugoslavia and the Soviet Union. Yugoslavia and the Soviet Union played for the silver medal, with Yugoslavia winning 69-67 to claim its first of eight consecutive world championship medals.

1967—Montevideo, Uruguay

The fifth world tournament is remembered as the Big Chill. It was held in an 18,000-seat concrete and steel stadium (the "Cylinder") that had no heat and where the temperature remained below 40-degrees. To combat the cold, teams were issued blankets and electric heaters for the benches.

Perhaps it was fitting, therefore, that the Soviet Union emerged from the deep freeze to claim its first world title. The Soviets, along with Yugoslavia and the United States, took 4-1 records into the final day of the round robin. The Soviet Union beat Yugoslavia and, when Brazil upset the USA, the Soviets took home the gold cup that had been renamed in honor of Dr. James Naismith. Yugoslavia, Brazil and the United States finished with 4-2 records, and through tiebreakers, Yugoslavia placed second and Brazil third, leaving the USA out of the medals for a second straight tournament.

1970—Ljubljana, Yugoslavia

Led by Kresimir Cosic, a sophomore at Brigham Young University, Yugoslavia rode the enthusiasm of their home crowd to the nation's first world title after finishing second in 1967 and '63. Cosic, a 6-foot-11 center had led, Yugoslavia to an Olympic silver medal in 1968 and was at the top of his game as Yugoslavia went 8-1 in the tournament, including 5-1 in the final round.

Brazil and the Soviet Union each went 4-2 in the final round, but Brazil was awarded the gold on a tiebreaker. It was another poor showing for the Americans. After placing fourth in the previous two tournaments, they fell to fifth after losses to Italy, Yugoslavia and Brazil. The team included high school senior Bill Walton.

1974—San Juan, Puerto Rico

Although represented by a young, inexperienced team, the United States went into the final game against the Soviet Union with an 8-0 record and a shot at the gold medal. The Soviets, however, were represented by a team that included five members from their 1972 Olympic gold medal winning squad.

Experience proved an important factor as the Americans got into early foul trouble. Still, they were tied 55-55 at the half. But the Soviets pulled ahead in the second half and, with the aid of 37 points from the foul line, won 105-94.

The loss meant that the USA, Soviet Union and Yugoslavia all finished with one loss and, after the tie-breaking procedure was applied, the gold went to the Soviets and Yugoslavia took the silver.

1978—Manila, Philippines

A change in format saw the introduction of a medal round to determine the winners. Yugoslavia met the Soviet Union in the first gold-medal game, with Yugoslavia winning 82-81 in overtime. The bronze-medal game was just as close as Italy beat Brazil 86-85.

The tournament was held in October, which meant the United States couldn't send a team of college players so Athletes in Action was selected as its representative. The USA lost four games and placed fifth.

1982—Cali, Colombia

A spirited USA team almost pulled off a major upset when they rode five straight wins into a gold-medal showdown with the Soviet Union. The Americans led by two at the half, fell behind early in the third but, with nine seconds to play, closed the gap to one point, 95-94. They had a chance to steal the win as the clock ran out buy a jump shot from short range bounced off the rim.

In a wide-open bronze-medal game, defending champion Yugoslavia beat Spain 119-117 to keep its medalling streak intact at six consecutive world tournaments.

1986—Madrid, Spain

After a 32-year wait, the USA won its second world title with a college team that featured such future NBA stars as David Robinson, Kenny Smith and Charles Smith. Coached by Arizona's Lute Olson, the USA defeated Brazil 96-80 to reach the gold-medal showdown with the Soviet Union.

The USA led 48-38 at the half and, with less than eight minutes left in the game, was ahead 18, 78-60. But the Soviet's, behind 7-foot-2 Arvidas Sabonis closed the gap to two points with 50 seconds remaining. But the USA dug in for an 87-85 victory. Kenny Smith had 23 points and Robinson added 20.

1990—Buenos Aires, Argentina

Argentine fans may not have realized it at the time, but they were treated to a tournament that featured a host of future NBA stars. The gold-medal winning Yugoslavian team had five would-be NBA players, including Vlade Divac, Drazen Petrovic and Toni Kukoc. A young American team, under coach Mike Krzyzewski, showcased Alonzo Mourning, Kenny Anderson and Christian Laettner.

Yugoslavia and the USA faced off in a semi-final to see who would advance to the gold-medal game against the Soviet Union, with the more experienced Yugoslav side winning 99-91. The gold-medal game, won easily 92-75 by Yugoslavia, marked the end of an era for both finalists. The breakup of the Soviet Union and Yugoslavia federations meant that the 1994 event would instead field teams from Russia and Croatia. In the bronze-medal game, the USA came from behind to win in overtime, 107-105.

1994—Toronto, Canada

Following the precedent set in the 1992 Olympics, the world tournament opened its doors to NBA professionals. To no one's surprise, this rule change resulted in the USA dominating the tournament, compiling an 8-0 record and winning by an average of 37 points per game.

In the gold-medal game, the USA team, showcasing the likes of Shaquille O'Neal and Reggie Miller, romped to a ridiculously easy 137-91 victory over Russia. The Americans, who came under some fire for showboating, topped 100 points in seven of their eight games. Croatia defeated Greece 78-60 to earn the bronze medal.

1998—Athens, Greece

After dazzling the field in 1994, the USA arrived at Athens with a rag-tag team of collegians and minor-league pros due to an NBA labor dispute. Yet, despite the absence of the NBA stars, coach Rudy Tomjanovich took his team to the semi-finals, where it lost to Russia 66-64. The USA had led by 10 points with less than three minutes to go.

Yugoslavia was forced to play without star center Vlade Divac, but still managed to take the gold medal by defeating Russia 64-62 in the final. The USA earned bronze by hammering Greece 84-61.

2002—Indianapolis, USA

With the tournament coming to the United States for the first time, the USA team was heavily favored to recapture the gold. The team, comprised of NBA players—but lacking many of the big stars—proved to be a major disappointment, placing sixth, its worst finish ever at the world tournament.

The gold medal was won by defending champion Yugoslavia. Led by Dejan Bodiroga's 27 points in the final game, Yugoslavia overcame an eight-point deficit in the closing minutes to force overtime before pulling away to a 84-77 victory over Argentina. Germany got 29 points from NBA star Dirk Nowitzki in the bronze-medal game to defeat New Zealand 117-94 to earn its first-ever world championship medal.

WOMEN

1953—Santiago, Chile

The inaugural women's world championship was played on a wooden platform in Chile's 35,000-seat national stadium. The USA proved to be the class of the field, compiling a 4-1 record to win the gold medal. The only blemish was a 29-23 loss to Brazil. They reached the final game of the tournament tied with Chile in the standings but defeated Chile 49-36 to clinch the title. France earned the bronze.

1957—Rio de Janeiro, Brazil

With a team of AAU All-Americans under coach John Head, the USA easily defended its title, running up a 6-0 record in the final round. The Americans were considered co-favorites with the Soviet Union, the four-time European champion making its world championship debut.

The two giants of the sport met in the final game of the round robin, with the gold medal on the line. It was the first time they met in international competition. The USSR took a three-point lead into the half but the USA rebounded to win 51-48 to launch what would become a bitter rivalry over the ensuing decades

1959—Moscow, USSR

The much-anticipated rematch between the USSR and the USA did not materialize because, with the Cold War raging, the USA skipped the Moscow tournament. In the Americans' absence, the Soviets had an easy time, compiling a 7-0 record to win their first of five consecutive world titles.

With the exception of a loss to the USSR, Bulgaria had a perfect record to win the silver, ahead of Czechoslovakia.

1964—Lima, Peru

Postponed a year because of construction delays, the 1964 tournament included all the top nations. But the highly-anticipated showdown between the USA and USSR was anticlimactic.

The USA had already lost to Bulgaria and Czechoslovakia before meeting the USSR. It was no contest. The Soviets humbled the Americans 71-37 and romped to the gold medal with a 6-0 record. Czechoslovakia earned the bronze and any hope for a USA medal was lost when Bulgaria beat the USA 46-42 to take the bronze.

1967—Prague, Czechoslovakia

By the time of the 1967 tournament it was clear that the USSR was virtually unbeatable for the gold medal and the rest of the field was playing for silver and bronze. And the tournament unfolded as scripted, albeit with two surprises: South Korea won the bronze with a 4-1 record and the USA placed 11th.

The only real drama of the tournament came with the silver medal at stake, where South Korea was an overwhelming underdog against the host nation. But the Koreans stunned the Czechs 74-71 in a game that still ranks among the top upsets in tournament history.

1971—Sao Paulo, Brazil

The Soviet Union, already far and away the top women's team in the world, unveiled a new weapon—18-year old Uljana Semenova who, at 6-foot-11 towered over every other player in the tournament. To no one's surprise, the Soviets again went undefeated (6-0) to claim their fourth consecutive title.

Czechoslovakia won the silver and Brazil earned the bronze. The tournament had originally been scheduled for 1970 in Chile but had to be rescheduled after Chile rescinded its offer to host the event.

1975—Cali, Colombia

The Soviets remained at the height of their power and extended their world-championship winning streak to 30 games in taking their fifth consecutive gold medal. They won by an average of 34.6 points in the final round. Overall, since entering their first world tournament in 1957, the Soviets' record was a remarkable 35-1.

Japan emerged as a surprise silver medallist, their first ever world championship medal. Czechoslovakia extended its medal streak to six tournaments by winning the bronze.

1979—Seoul, South Korea

The 1979 tournament was marred by a political boycott by the Soviet Union and five other communist nations. Without the powerful eastern-bloc nations, the USA was able to win its first gold medal since 1957.

The championship was decided in a final-day showdown against Canada. Canada, the surprise of the tournament, was a

perfect 5-0 and could claim gold by either winning outright or losing by no more than 13 points (due to the tiebreaker formula). But the US won 77-61 to take the gold and, after tiebreakers were applied, relegate Canada to the bronze behind South Korea.

1983—Sao Paulo, Brazil

The Communist nations returned and the USSR reclaimed the gold medal, but not before receiving a major scare from the USA. The Americans had served notice in a one-point preliminary round loss to the USSR that they would be formidable opponent.

When they met in the medal round, with the gold medal at stake, the final seconds were ticking away in a tied game when Elena Chausova fired a desperation shot that connected to give the USSR an 84-82 victory. The USA had to settle for silver, with China taking the bronze.

1986—Moscow, USSR

The Soviets had a 38-game world championship winning streak and six gold medals to show off to a partisan crowd as the 1986 tournament opened. But at the end, they were left holding silver after a humbling loss to the USA.

The Americans ended Soviet domination of the sport by taking a 56-43 half-time lead and cruising to a 108-88 victory. They celebrated in customary USA fashion by cutting down the nets, a ceremony that greatly displeased their hosts. In the bronze medal game, Canada defeated Czechoslovakia 64-59.

1990—Kuala Lumpur, Malaysia

The USA picked up where the USSR had left off—dominating the tournament to repeat as gold medallists. Under coach Theresa Grentz, the USA went a perfect 8-0.

In the gold-medal game, Katrina McClain scored 23 points as the USA defeated Yugoslavia 88-78. For the first time in any of the world championships it entered, the USSR failed to win a medal. Cuba won the bronze by defeating Czechoslovakia 83-61.

1994—Sydney, Australia

For the first time in tournament history, a team other than the USA or USSR won the coveted gold medal. Brazil, led by high-scoring duo of Hortencia Marcari and Maria Paula de Silva, won the gold, its first medal of any kind at the world championships, by defeating China 96-87.

Brazil had advanced to the final by defeating the USA 110-107 in a semi-final in which Katrina McClain had 29 points and 19 rebounds. The USA won the bronze by beating Australia 100-95.

1998—Berlin, Germany

The USA was back in top form, posting a perfect 9-0 record to reclaim the gold medal. The final game pitted the USA against Russia and the USA had to come back from a nine-point half-time deficit to win 71-65.

The Americans were led by Lisa Leslie's 20 points and Dawn Staley's 12 assists. In the bronze medal game, Australia earned its first-ever medal by defeating China 96-84.

2002—China

If there were any doubts about its status as the No. 1 women's basketball power, the USA erased them in the 2002 tournament. The Americans dominated both offensively and defensively to win a tournament-record seventh gold medal.

Their only scare came in the final where they battled a resilient Russian team to the final whistle before emerging with a 79-74 win. In the consolation final, Australia repeated as the bronze medallist by easily defeating South Korea 91-63.

WORLD CHAMPIONSHIPS AT A GLANCE

WORLD CHAMPIONSHIPS, MEN

Year	Round	Winner	Loser	Score	Site
2002	Final	Yugoslavia	Argentina	84-77	Indianapolis, USA
	Consolation	Germany	New Zealand	117-94	
1998	Final	Russia	Yugoslavia	62-64 †	Athens, Greece
	Consolation	USA	Greece	84-61 †	
1994	Final	USA	Russia	137-91	Toronto, Canada
	Consolation	Croatia	Greece	78-60	
1990	Final	Yugoslavia	USSR	92-75	Buenos Aires, Brazil
	Consolation	USA	Puerto Rico	107-105	
1986	Final	USA	USSR	87-85	Madrid, Spain
	Consolation	Yugoslavia	Brazil		
1982	Final	USSR	USA	95-94	Cali, Colombia
	Consolation	Yugoslavia	Spain	119-117	
1978	Final	Yugoslavia	USSR	82-81(OT)	Manila, Phillipines
	Consolation	Brazil	Italy	86-85	

Year	Gold	Silver	Bronze	Site
1974	USSR	Yugoslavia	USA	San Juan, Puerto Rico
1970	Yugoslavia	Brazil	USSR	Ljubliana, Yugoslavia
1967	USSR	Brazil	Yugoslavia	Montivedo, Uruguay
1963	Brazil	Yugoslavia	USSR	Rio de Janeiro, Brazil
1959	Brazil	USA	Chile	Santiago, Chile
1954	USA	Brazil	Phillipines	Rio de Janeiro, Brazil
1950	Argentina	USA	Chile	Rio de Janeiro, Brazil

WORLD CHAMPIONSHIPS, WOMEN

Year	Round	Winner	Loser	Score	Site
2002	Final	USA	Russia	79-74	China
	Consolation	Australia	Korea	91-63	
1998	Final	USA	Russia	71-65	Berlin, Germany
	Consolation	Australia	Brazil	72-67	
1994	Final	Brazil	China	96-84	Sydney, Australia
	Consolation	USA	Australia	100-95	
1990	Final	USA	Yugoslavia	88-78	Kuala Lumpur, Malaysia
	Consolation	Cuba	Czechoslovakia	83-61	
1986	Final	USA	USSR	108-88	Moscow, Soviet Union
	Consolation	Canada	Czechoslovakia	64-59	
1983	Final	USSR	USA	84-82	Sao Paulo, Brazil
	Consolation	China	Korea	71-63	

Year	Gold	Silver	Bronze	Site
1979	USA (5-1) *	Korea (5-1)	Canada (5-1)	Seoul, South Korea
1975	USSR (6-0)	Japan (5-1)	Czechoslovakia (4-2)	Cali, Colombia
1971	USSR (6-0)	Czechoslovakia (4-2)	Brazil (4-2)	Sao Paulo, Brazil
1967	USSR (5-0)	Korea (4-1)	Czechoslovakia (3-2)	Prague, Czechoslovakia
1964	USSR (6-0)	Czechoslovakia (5-1)	Bulgaria (4-2)	Lima, Peru
1959	USSR (7-0)	Bulgaria (6-1)	Czechoslovakia (5-2)	Moscow, Soviet Union
1957	USA (6-0)	USSR (5-1)	Czechoslovakia (4-2)	Rio de Janeiro, Brazil
1953	USA (4-1)	Chile (3-2)	France (3-2)	Santiago, Chile

* U.S., Korea and Canada all finished 5-1 and the final standings were determined by point differential between tied teams.

YEAR BY YEAR, TOP 10 NATIONS, MEN

2002 Indianapolis, USA
1 Yugoslavia
2 Argentina
3 Germany
4 New Zealand
5 Spain
6 USA
7 Puerto Rico
8 Brazil
9 Turkey
10 Russia

1998 Athens, Greece
1 Yugoslavia
2 Russia
3 USA
4 Greece
5 Spain
6 Italy
7 Lithuania
8 Argentina
9 Australia
10 Brazil

1994 Toronto, Canada
1 USA
2 Russia
3 Croatia
4 Greece
5 Australia
6 Puerto Rico
7 Canada
8 China
9 Argentina
10 Spain

1990 Buenos Aires, Brazil
1 Yugoslavia
2 Soviet Union
3 USA
4 Puerto Rico
5 Brazil
6 Greece
7 Australia
8 Argentina
9 Italy
10 Spain

1986 Madrid, Spain
1 USA
2 Soviet Union
3 Yugoslavia
4 Brazil
5 Spain
6 Italy
7 Israel
8 Canada
9 China
10 Greece

1982 Cali, Colombia
1 Soviet Union
2 USA
3 Yugoslavia
4 Spain
5 Australia
6 Canada
7 Colombia
8 Brazil
9 Panama
10 Czechoslovakia

1978 Manila, Phillipines
1 Yugoslavia
2 Soviet Union
3 Italy
4 Italy
5 USA
6 Canada
7 Australia
8 Philippines
9 Czechoslovakia
10 Puerto Rico

1974 San Juan, Puerto Rico
1 Soviet Union
2 Yugoslavia
3 USA
4 Cuba
5 Spain
6 Brazil
7 Puerto Rico
8 Canada
9 Mexico
10 Czechoslovakia

1970 Ljubliana, Yugoslavia
1 Yugoslavia
2 Brazil
3 Soviet Union
4 Italy
5 USA
6 Czechoslovakia
7 Uruguay
8 Cuba
9 Panama
10 Canada

1967 Montivedo, Uruguay
1 Soviet Union
2 Brazil
3 Yugoslavia
4 USA
5 Poland
6 Argentina
7 Uruguay
8 Mexico
9 Italy
10 Peru

1963 Rio de Janeiro, Brazil
1 Brazil
2 Yugoslavia
3 Soviet Union
4 USA
5 France
6 Puerto Rico
7 Italy
8 Argentina
9 Mexico
10 Uruguay

1959 Santiago, Chile
1 Brazil
2 USA
3 Chile
4 Formosa
5 Puerto Rico
6 Soviet Union
7 Bulgaria
8 Philippines
9 Uruguay
10 Argentina

1954 Rio de Janeiro, Brazil
1 USA
2 Brazil
3 Philippines
4 France
5 Formosa
6 Uruguay
7 Canada
8 Israel
9 Paraguay
10 Chile

1950 Buenos Aires, Argentina
1 Argentina
2 USA
3 Chile
4 Brazil
5 Egypt
6 France
7 Peru
8 Ecuador
9 Spain
10 Yugoslavia

YEAR BY YEAR, TOP 10 NATIONS, WOMEN

2002 China
1 USA
2 Russia
3 Australia
4 Korea
5 Spain
6 China
7 Brazil
8 France
9 Cuba
10 Argentina

1998 Berlin, Germany
1 USA
2 Russia
3 Australia
4 Brazil
5 Spain
6 Lithuania
7 Cuba
8 Slovak Republic
9 Japan
10 Hungary

1994 Sydney, Australia
1 Brazil
2 China
3 USA
4 Australia
5 Slovak Republic
6 Cuba
7 Canada
8 Spain
9 France
10 Korea

1990 Kuala Lumpur, Malaysia
1 USA
2 Yugoslavia
3 Cuba
4 Czechoslovakia
5 Soviet Union
6 Australia
7 Canada
8 Bulgaria
9 China
10 Brazil

1986 Moscow, USSR
1 USA
2 Soviet Union
3 Canada
4 Czechoslovakia
5 China
6 Cuba
7 Bulgaria
8 Hungary
9 Australia
10 Korea

1983 Sao Paulo, Brazil
1 Soviet Union
2 USA
3 China
4 Korea
5 Brazil
6 Bulgaria
7 Poland
8 Yugoslavia
9 Canada
10 Cuba

1979 Seoul, South Korea
1 USA
2 Korea
3 Canada
4 Australia
5 Italy
6 Japan
7 France
8 Netherlands
9 Brazil
10 Bolivia

1975 Cali, Colombia
1 Soviet Union
2 Japan
3 Czechoslovakia
4 Italy
5 Korea
6 Mexico
7 Colombia
8 USA
9 Hungary
10 Australia

1971 Sao Paulo, Brazil
1 Soviet Union
2 Czechoslovakia
3 Brazil
4 Korea
5 Japan
6 France
7 Cuba
8 USA
9 Australia
10 Canada

1967 Prague, Czechoslovakia
1 Soviet Union
2 Korea
3 Czechoslovakia
4 German Democratic Republic
5 Japan
6 Yugoslavia
7 Bulgaria
8 Brazil
9 Italy
10 Australia

1964 Lima, Peru
1 Soviet Union
2 Czechoslovakia
3 Bulgaria
4 USA
5 Brazil
6 Yugoslavia
7 Peru
8 Korea
9 Japan
10 France

1959 Moscow, USSR
1 Soviet Union
2 Bulgaria
3 Czechoslovakia
4 Yugoslavia
5 Poland
6 Romania
7 Hungary
8 Korea

1957 Rio de Janeiro, Brazil
1 USA
2 Soviet Union
3 Czechoslovakia
4 Brazil
5 Hungary
6 Paraguay
7 Chile
8 Mexico
9 Argentina
10 Australia

1953 Santiago, Chile
1 USA
2 Chile
3 France
4 Brazil
5 Paraguay
6 Argentina
7 Peru
8 Mexico
9 Switzerland
10 Cuba

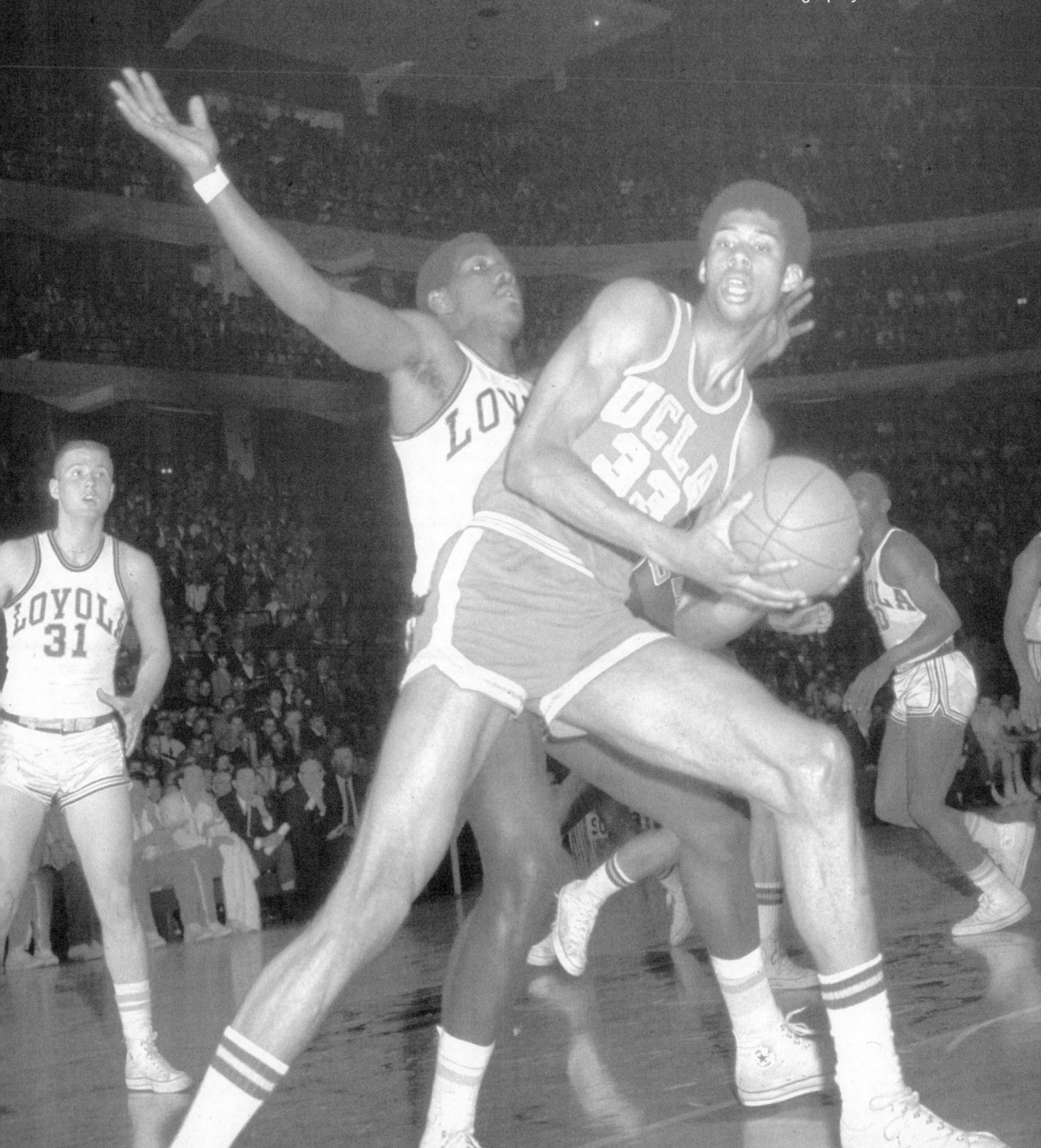

Kareem Abdul-Jabbar, 1969
Absolutely dominant in leading the UCLA Bruins from 1967 to 1969, the then-Lew Alcindor was named the Final Four's Most Outstanding Player all three seasons and gets *Total Basketball*'s nod as the No. 1 college player of all time.

Chapter 46

College Basketball: The Formative Years

By Peter C. Bjarkman

College basketball has enjoyed several defining moments that have drastically reshaped future directions for the sport. None of these crossroads were more vital than the pair that occurred almost simultaneously near the end of the 1930s (during the 1937 and 1938 seasons), on the very eve of the hardwood sport's half-century anniversary. First came a revolutionary rule change canceling the center jump after each successful basket. By eliminating both the stoppage of action and the repetitive marches to center court after each score, college games could truly become, for the first time, the action-filled, high-scoring spectacles we celebrate today. A second defining event was the establishment of postseason national tournament competitions to provide the winter-long season with meaningful direction and also a climactic purpose. Both landmark events together contributed heavily to a burgeoning new audience for college basketball, one that has continued to surge nonstop across the more than half a century that has followed.

Basketball's first five-plus decades were not without their own brand of raw excitement, a bevy of attractive campus stars, and an ever-expanding and sometimes even quite rabid fan following. But the decades before Hank Luisetti at Stanford or Adolph Rupp at Kentucky witnessed largely an era of narrow regional interests, an epoch of domineering coaches (Meanwell in Wisconsin, Lambert at Purdue, Carlson at Pittsburgh, Notre Dame's George Keogan, and above all Phog Allen in Kansas) who always held a far bigger piece of the spotlight than did their constantly changing players, and a period of constant rules-shifting that chipped away at the stability and thus the broad appeal of the sport. College basketball was indeed nearly as popular as its fall rival gridiron sport in some corners of the land—especially in the isolated heartland sectors of Kentucky, Kansas and Indiana; in the big city mecca of New York, where Ned Irish was already ballyhooing intersectional matches between popular local teams and attractive clubs from the provinces as early as 1931; and in certain isolated pockets of basketball fanaticism far out on the Pacific coast.

Clair Bee, 1950
Chalktalk with an attentive audience at Long Island University

In brief, the flavor of the sport was largely provincial in nature. If Buck Freeman's "Wonder Five" outfit at St. John's was the rage of New York City at the close of the Roaring Twenties, they were certainly never winter-season front-page news anywhere else across the land. Baron Rupp would not become a household name for sports fans in most quarters of the nation until well after World War II, despite his 80% winning percentage throughout the decade of the 1930s. Small campus arenas and cramped gymnasiums in most parts of the country meant that the biggest college cage stars—like Paul Endacott at Kansas or Vic Hanson with Syracuse or Johnny Wooden at Purdue—performed their nightly magic in relative obscurity. While professional baseball heroes like Babe Ruth and collegiate footballers like Red Grange achieved substantial and even reverential attention in the sporting press (Ruth logged more ink than any of the nation's presidents during his heyday), few newspapers outside of those located in the campus towns themselves covered basketball action on any kind of semi-regular basis.

While numerous rule changes and constant shifting of regional styles of play worked against an identifiable spectacle with which basketball fans could readily relate, some of the

changes during the '30s were indeed moving the game rapidly toward a fan-friendlier spectacle. Basketball in the teens, '20s and early '30s—even the more popular collegiate variety—was a slow-paced game with little sustained action and painfully little scoring. Dominant teams like the St. John's Wonder Five club of the 1929, 1930 and 1931 seasons often achieved their successes largely because of their deadly strategies (deadly for both fans and the opposition teams) of stalling on offense, holding the ball at the far end of the court (there was no backcourt rule to prevent such a tactic), and deftly passing back and forth for long stretches of time until the perfect uncontested setshot or layup eventually became available.

Fans who witnessed a watershed January 1931 benefit tripleheader in Madison Square Garden were thus "entertained" by scores of 21-18 (Columbia surprising Fordham), 16-14 (Manhattan edging NYU), and 17-9 (the latter score resulting from St. John's painstaking slowdown tactics against CCNY, which brought a game-long cascade of resounding boos and catcalls from the 16,000 fans). Realizing the game needed a drastic overhaul in order to retain existing audiences and attract new ones, the lords of the college sport reacted in 1932 by instituting a center line painted at midcourt and a rule requiring the ball to be moved into the frontcourt within 10 seconds time. Three seasons later (1935) a three-second legislation banning offensive players from camping under the basket was also belatedly adopted.

But it was not until the eve of the 1937-38 college season that the biggest obstacle to offense-oriented basketball was finally removed. This came with the liberating deletion of the constantly repeated center jump. Since the game clock had continued to run throughout such pauses in the action after each field goal, as much as 12 minutes of playing time was still being lost out of each individual game. Once the new rule was in effect, offenses immediately opened up their attacks; overnight, game scores more than doubled almost everywhere. Basketball was finally ready to greet its modern epoch, and it was the collegiate players, coaches and game officials who would lead the way into the thrill-packed future.

The center jump rule adjustment indeed had a most far-reaching effect on the pace and thus the nature of modern basketball play. Even before Stanford's Hank Luisetti broke loose with an incredible 50-point outburst in Cleveland (versus Duquesne) little more than a month into the new season, St. John's and Illinois had already availed themselves of the streamlined game with a record-setting scoring performance of their own during the first Madison Square Garden doubleheader of the year. Illinois won that contest, 60-45, behind a hot-handed guard named Lou Boudreau, an eventual member of baseball's Hall of Fame. Such scoring had previously been ruled out by dead time alone—time wasted while players walked repeatedly back and forth between center jumps, with the scoreboard clock eating up potential minutes of play. Now the sport could leap forward from the slow-paced game of cross-court passing and offensive positioning envisioned by Dr. Naismith himself (Naismith had ruled out "running" and didn't conceive of dribbling) to the spontaneous, action-packed freelance type of run-and-gun action we have come to expect today.

The college version of Naismith's sport is of course nearly as old as the indoor cage game itself. Both men and women played the first reported intercollegiate contests in the very shadows of Naismith's trial run at the Springfield YMCA. While a rough-and-tumble men's version may have been what the good doctor had intended to design, women (especially women college students) overnight found the new sport's appeal equally alluring. Some of the earliest organized college competitions, in fact, are reported to have taken place among all-female teams. And within a year of Naismith's invention, a Springfield neighbor, Lithuanian-born physical education instructor Senda Berenson, was both organizing women's games at nearby Smith College in Holyoke and also publishing the first set of Spalding Guidebook rules for inspired female competitors.

Women had thus enthusiastically adopted the sport literally within weeks of its original 1891 debut. Not only did Naismith invite female students to join games at the Springfield YMCA that very first winter, but one of those pioneering women participants (Maude Sherman) soon became his wife. Full-fledged collegiate women's games also date back to the same year or two when male college play was first launched, and coeds at Stanford and Cal-Berkeley are alleged to have staged a primitive contest (complete with bloomers and long black hose for uniforms) as early as the winter of 1896. The earliest documented women's matches may thus actually predate (or at least approximate) the very first male campus contests.

It would be Berenson's early rules, of course, that would send the women's version in quite a different direction from the game that the men were playing. Berenson gained much of the credit for such segregationist tactics by adapting Naismith's rules to fit Victorian notions of female daintiness—players were to stand demurely in one of three fixed regions of the court and were barred from snatching the ball from opponents. Other versions of "women's rules" also appeared in places like nearby Mount Holyoke College and far away Sophie Newcomb College (located in New Orleans and later a part of Tulane University). One far-reaching rule change for women competitors was actually the result of a mistake in interpreting a set of explanations provided by Naismith. Requesting a written set of rules from the game's originator, Newcomb College instructor Clara Baer misread an accompanying diagram enclosed by Naismith that merely suggested zones on the floor where players might stand to commence play. Designing her own version called "basquette," Baer incorporated the longstanding and long-rued legislation that echoed Berenson's Smith College guidelines and prevented frontcourt and backcourt players from stepping out of their fixed zones. By thus restricting running and barring roughhousing, these adopted standards for girls' basketball included all the era's popular assumptions about the fragility of women. The inevitable result was not surprisingly a static version of women's "basquette" that would prevail for almost three quarters of the coming century.

Naismith's original notion of basketball play was itself a far cry from the rapid action, star-oriented, and highly competitive entertainment spectacle we embrace today. Naismith, in fact, had a very different notion in mind when he invented the game for the sole purpose of entertaining and exercising his group of bored and often rowdy future YMCA secretaries (that is, instructors and administrators). The 13 rules with which he

started are still to no small degree present in basketball's modern versions. The ball has to be moved around the court by passing and not by carrying or kicking; running (traveling) with the sphere is illegal and so is tackling, swatting, or otherwise assaulting the player who possesses it. The entire contest turns on throwing the ball into the raised basket, and the elevation of the goal prevents defenders from easily blocking it with their bodies (Naismith of course did not envision today's seven-footers or rubber-legged leapers). But the intention of play was far different in Naismith's mind than it is in the minds of today's players, coaches and enthusiastic spectators. Winning a contest was an afterthought, much subordinated to more important altruistic notions of camaraderie, healthful competition and physical exercise, and good clean fun for all participants. Any notion of a spectator spectacle was completely foreign and even something of an anathema to the game's founding father.

Today college basketball sits near the pinnacle of the American sporting scene. No event—not even the heavily hyped Super Bowl nor the nostalgically revered World Series—captures as large or as intense an audience as the postseason NCAA tournament that is now known in every corner of America simply as March Madness. Despite setbacks over the years—in particular a devastating game-fixing scandal in the early 1950s that nearly compromised altogether the sport's integrity—the game has lurched steadily forward and has even been a rapid-growth industry ever since its miraculous recovery from the near-death experience of those very betting scandals. Along the way have also arisen some of the greatest legends and most intriguing personalities of American sports history.

Basketball, quite unlike all other spectator sports, can precisely pinpoint its moment of origin. The bare facts of Naismith's single-handed invention of the sport remain an often retold staple of American sports history. But the origin of college competitions is not quite as clear-cut, and this is especially true when it comes to documenting the very first legitimate collegiate game.

There are indeed several candidates for what might have been the earliest college game. The best case, perhaps, can be made for the Iowa-versus-Chicago and Yale-versus-Penn contests of 1896 and 1897. Each of these prototypical affairs has its special claims for pioneering bragging rights. Yet each also owns a feature or two that would convince many to set it aside as a mere historical curiosity and not the sought-after landmark event. On January 16, 1896, Naismith's Springfield colleague Alonzo Stagg (later of football fame and already coaching an undergraduate cage team he had patched together) brought his Chicago University squad to Iowa City for their first contest against outside competition. Stagg's boys prevailed, 15-12, yet in true Naismith spirit the contingent of Iowa athletes (all enrolled at the state university in that city) were official representatives of the Iowa City YMCA and not of the University of Iowa. While this was likely the first five-on-five contest—even the true beginning of five-man basketball—it must be dismissed as representing a genuine "intercollegiate" competition. Although the Yale-Penn match of March 1897 lags behind the Iowa City game by more than a full year, it nonetheless boasts the distinction of being a five-versus-five affair between two universities, with Yale breezing to victory by a slightly more

modern-looking tally of 32-10.

On February 9, 1895—11 months prior to the Iowa City game—Hamline College of Minnesota fell to the Minnesota State School of Agriculture by a yawn-producing 9-3 score. Teams were clearly both comprised of collegians in this time contest, but squads in this case were nine-man units. A similar nine-versus-nine affair also transpired on March 23, 1895, out east in Pennsylvania, with Haverford besting Temple, 6-4. Both losing outfits were, by coincidence, organized and coached by original Naismith students (Ray Kaighn at Hamline and Charles Williams at Temple), who had together participated in the famed first Springfield YMCA exhibition back in 1891.

There were other sporadic starts and these included both men's and women's competitions. There had been games reported as early as 1893 involving college contingents in Iowa and Minnesota, all of them again involving Naismith's own Springfield disciples. Women's teams representing Stanford and California reputedly met sometime in the winter of 1896, as reportedly did squads from Smith and Vassar. And the crack Yale University team accomplished the first extended barnstorming excursion during the winter of 1899-1900, trekking to Chicago and back during the Christmas holidays, winning several games on route, but having a handful of others wiped out by last-minute cancellations. It is Yale, then, which stakes the ablest claim for trailblazing in the college sport. In addition to the Eli's landmark contest with Penn and their partially aborted Midwestern junket—both inaugural events—Yale's position as pacesetter is also backed by bold experimentations with a new method of offensive attack known as the dribble.

Serious college competition took shape, however, only with the first organized conference competitions. The Ivy League (nee Eastern League) and Big Ten Conference (nee Western Conference) progenitors were among the bold pioneers. The first winter season of a new century witnessed vanguard primitive attempts at such leagues, all clustered in the nation's northeastern sector. Connecticut's "big three" of Yale, Trinity and Wesleyan formed the first formalized circuit, which would loosely be called the Triangle League. Later that same winter the New England League took shape with Dartmouth, Holy Cross, Amherst College, Williams College, and Trinity College joining forces; the Eastern League, comprised initially of Columbia, Cornell, Harvard, Princeton, and Yale, was soon to follow.

Identification with one confederation obviously did not preclude affiliation with still another, as the dual memberships of Trinity and Yale vividly attest. Yale would claim the first title in what would eventually call itself the Ivy League. The Western Conference, in turn, had been formed for football competitions back in 1895, but the future Big Ten also took up basketball play in 1905, with the seven gridiron schools (Minnesota, the first year's winner, plus Wisconsin, Indiana, Chicago, Illinois, Purdue, and Iowa) competing in the initial winter's round-robin of cage play.

Basketball's opening decades also boast some oversized heroes who have today been largely and unjustifiably forgotten by fans and historians of the game. H. O. "Pat" Page (an innovator of guard play) and John Schommer (the first prototype center) provided backbone for the Joseph Raycroft-coached University of Chicago teams that proved nearly invincible at

the end of the century's first decade. The speedy Page was twice an All-American, later a coaching legend himself for both his alma mater and Butler University of Indianapolis, and a clear choice as 1910 national player of the year. Schommer earned his lasting fame as inventor of the modern-style backboard, but earlier preceded Page by precisely one season as the nation's top player, averaging 10 points per game—enough to pace Western Conference athletes in scoring three winters running. Vic Hanson achieved legendary status at Syracuse while pacing the Orangemen to a 48-7 three-year mark and a consensus 1926 national championship; his play, a decade and a half after Page's and Schommer's, was remarkable enough to earn a spot on sportswriter Grantland Rice's mid-century All-Time All-American squad. Christian Steinmetz of Wisconsin was a still earlier nonpareil who accomplished rare offensive feats, garnering the game's first 1,000-point career total (1903-05) and cutting loose for a then-remarkable single-game outburst of 44 points against Beloit. A Clemson player named J. O. Erwin outdid even Steinmetz with a yet-more-remarkable one-night scoring explosion (58 points), which incredibly has lasted unscathed to the present day as a school mark. Strangely enough, it occurred in Clemson's first-ever varsity intercollegiate game.

The distinctive flavor of college play across the first five decades was largely one of stark regionalism. The game evolved somewhat differently in different parts of the land and rarely did teams from different regions collide to test different coaching styles and different strategies for offensive and defensive play. One such landmark collision came when Adolph Rupp and his emerging Kentucky University team first ventured into New York City in 1935 to meet Howard Cann-coached NYU (18-1 that season) at Madison Square Garden. Local-leaning officials blithely allowed NYU's frontcourt brutes "King Kong" Klein and "Slim" Terjesen to shove and batter Wildcats center LeRoy "Cowboy" Edwards under the home-team bucket while Rupp's men were repeatedly whistled for blocking fouls at the other end. The results, and Rupp's outrage, were typical of such rare and almost always one-sided intersectional collisions.

As the game evolved in fits and starts, its seminal figures were almost exclusively innovative coaches like Rupp and Cann, who shaped the nature of playing tactics both with their own teams and throughout their own regions. Most fell into two camps—one favoring plodding and more scientific play while both shooting and defending the ball and the other advocating a much more wide-open racehorse style of offensive game. Despite regional leanings, there were proponents of both styles spread out widely across all sectors of the country.

Joseph Raycroft was one far-sighted mentor who exercised an early and major influence in the Midwest. Raycroft also broke ground by drawing a regular salary for his services. His talented and impeccably trained University of Chicago team won 78 of 90 matches during the new century's first decade, peaking with a 21-2 record that earned a "mythical" national championship during the 1908 season. That title was earned by a first-ever national playoff held between consensus East and West regional champions. The East Coast selection fell easily to Pennsylvania, with its all-star forward Charles Keinath (a renowned fancy dribbler); after losing their first three matches

the Quakers won a string of 22, which included eight Eastern League games. Chicago earned a spot in the best-of-three event against Penn by capturing a playoff with Western Conference co-champion Wisconsin. The final tally was 18-16 when Pat Page hit a last-minute shot while surrounded by three defenders. Page was again the hero of the national series, making a shot from under his legs to seal a 21-18 win on the home floor and also pacing a 16-15 victory in Philadelphia. There were three unbeatable elements behind the powerhouse Chicago Maroons team of the century's first decade: the deadly combination of a paid coach (Raycroft), a quick ball-handling guard (All-American Page), and a lanky and athletic center (All-American Schommer).

A decade later Walter "Doc" Meanwell was developing a popular and successful style of play up the road from Chicago at the University of Wisconsin. Meanwell thundered onto the scene in the Western Conference with two unbeaten campaigns (1912, 1914) and an overall 44-1 ledger during his first three seasons on the job. Unlike many of his colleagues in the young coaching profession, Meanwell himself had never played the still relatively novel game of basketball. But that shortcoming was seemingly no obstacle to his emergence as one of the game's most innovative first-generation mentors. Meanwell despised the dribble, advocated tight man-on-man defense, and taught an offensive system based on short-pass patterns and patient selection of unmolested shots. Another "Doc" who nursed the game in new directions earned an actual medical degree at Pittsburgh in 1920, yet found his true calling only when he took over the school's basketball program two years later. Henry Carlson earned his own special niche with his invention of the "Figure 8" offensive weave pattern (he called it a "continuity attack") and with the two "mythical" national championships which this playing style eventually bought for his team in 1928 and 1930. But he is perhaps best remembered for his early experiments with fundamentals of the offensive stall. Doc Carlson could not tolerate zone defenses, and on several occasions had his team hold the ball for much of the game in order to counter such "tactless" zone play.

Carlson was as much a showman as he was a chalkboard innovator, and his colorful sideline displays would often bring memorable responses from opposition arena crowds witnessing his team on the road. He was known to throw peanuts into the stands to hostile road crowds while his visiting Panthers slowed down their offense against hated zone defenses. On one occasion he was struck on the head with an umbrella wielded by a matronly patron at Washington and Jefferson, and on still another he had a bucket of ice water poured on his head from the stands behind the Pittsburgh bench by enraged West Virginia partisans (he had been shouting "This burns me up!" at the game officials just before his unexpected shower).

In addition to Chicago, Wisconsin and Pittsburgh, other regions were soon equal hotbeds of experimentation and landmark innovation. New York City was one such early cradle, and its most influential coach—despite Nat Holman at CCNY, Ed Kelleher at Fordham, and Cann at NYU—was James "Buck" Freeman with his "Wonder Five" four-year team at St. John's. The Wonder Five emerged on the scene in 1928, the first of many subsequent fabled New York City collegiate clubs. It was

Freeman's team more than any other than truly put New York (and thus East Coast) cage play back on the map at the close of the 1920s and dawn of the '30s. With its four Jewish starters—Jack "Rip" Gerson, Max Posnack, Allie Schuckman, and Mac Kinsbrunner—and their fifth teammate Matty Begovich, the Roman Catholic college would make plenty of news on the hardwoods over the next several seasons.

As unseasoned freshman the Wonder Five upset CCNY, captured 18 of 22 contests, and averaged better than 36 points while holding opponents to less than 10 points per contest. With a 23-2 ledger as sophomores their nearly error-free ball-control game had already become a marvel of the region. The 10-point margin of victory they maintained through the 1928-29 season was truly marvelous for an era when most teams only scored around 30 points per contest. As juniors, their unbreakable pattern continued: domination of the New York scene, patient offense and air-tight defense (both based on a strategy of keeping the ball away from opponents), and a 24-1 ledger at season's end. The Wonder Five's senior year would prove even better, as Freeman's outfit would pile up 21 more victories against stiffer opposition, run its winning streak to 27 before being tripped for the only time all winter by NYU, and set new standards for defensive stinginess. In the end the team's four-year record stood at 86-8, but the legacies of the Wonder Five were greater than the mere tally of victories and losses. One such legacy was cultivating a new popularity for the cage sport, which would make huge crowds at Madison Square Garden for college games a staple of the coming decade. A second was the introduction of the 10-second backcourt rule preventing excessive stalling, a legislation made necessary by the action-killing ball-holding techniques that Freeman's teams had built into an all-too-effective and unassailable art form.

Doc Meanwell's archrival, in both Western Conference (Big Ten) competitions and theoretical approaches to basketball strategy, was Ward "Piggy" Lambert, the head man at Purdue from the opening storm clouds of World War I through the closing salvos of World War II. Lambert advocated a more wide-open, racehorse style of play that was the antithesis of Meanwell's dribble-free and painfully patient passing offenses. While his 371 career wins at Purdue would not be surpassed until 1997 (by Gene Keady), Lambert's teams already reached their peak in the early '30s with a lineup that featured home-grown three-time All-American John Wooden in the backcourt and towering Charles "Stretch" Murphy under the basket. Murphy established an important prototype, that of the sure-handed rebounder who could clear defensive boards and fire the necessary outlet passes to fuel Lambert's fast-breaking attack. But perhaps the ultimate credit for a modern fast-break-style game goes not so much to Lambert as to a pair of even more run-and-gun-crazy proponents at Rhode Island State and George Washington University almost a full decade later. It is Bill Reinhart, Red Auerbach's earliest mentor, who perhaps deserves chief kudos for fostering racehorse basketball in its present form. With only moderately talented George Washington teams in the late '30s, Reinhart nonetheless fashioned the classic attack (three players charging down the lanes at full speed) that provided the modern blueprint. And somewhat earlier the colorful Frank Keaney already had his Rhode

Island State teams using the same strategy to balloon their scoring average above a point per minute by 1927, achieving 1000 points for the season in 1937, 70 points per game by 1939, and 2000 total points with the 1945 campaign.

All these innovations and pioneers aside, nowhere was the game more deeply entrenched or more carefully nurtured across its first half-century than on the plains of Kansas by Forrest "Phog" Allen, disciple and colleague of the game's transplanted inventor. Allen had taken over at Kansas for Naismith himself, who had arrived at Lawrence in 1899, introduced his game there, and then served for a handful of winters (1899-1909) as the first varsity coach. In fact, for many years Allen continued to have the game's father (who remained a professor of physical education until his retirement in 1937) residing in his own backyard. But Allen envisioned and soon developed a very different game from the one Naismith had imagined. When chided by his mentor that basketball was not an activity that one coached, a young Allen countered that at least you could teach the boys "to pass at angles and run in curves." He taught much more, lessons that almost immediately lifted Kansas to its first lofty heights in only his third and fourth seasons on the job. Allen's 1922 and 1923 squads posted the first undefeated records in the Missouri Valley Conference as well as a pair of consensus national championships; they featured All-American guard Paul Endacott, a 5-foot-10 firebrand who controlled center jumps and shone as a defensive specialist.

Ironically, it was not Endacott but a less-heralded player from his 1923 championship team who would turn out to be one of Phog Allen's greatest pupils. Adolph Rupp played only sparingly for Allen, but took over the coaching reins at Kentucky in 1930 as an unknown replacement for John Maurer and was soon building a legend of his own that would first rival and then surpass that of his master. His very first club went 15-3 to match the career .825 winning percentage he would post over the following four-plus decades. Rupp had great teams even in his first decade, such as the one starring "Cowboy" Edwards that went to New York in 1935 and established the attractiveness (and often blatant unfairness and one-sidedness) of intersectional competitions.

While Allen and Rupp built their great teams in the hinterlands in the 1920s and '30s, the first large crowds were flocking to the game's meccas on the East Coast. The first inkling of the sport's robust appeal came in 1920, when 10,000 fans packed New York's 168th Street Regimental Armory to see the year's best attractions—NYU, at 11-1 and featuring future coach Howard Cann as its star player, and City University, at 13-2—lock horns in an exciting 39-21 match that fell to the Violet. Big arenas and field houses were springing up elsewhere as well, especially in the Midwest in places like Iowa City, where the state university had constructed a 16,000-seater in the mid 1920s. The Palestra opened in Philadelphia on January 1, 1927 (it was built for the then lofty price of $750,000), and only weeks later drew 10,000 to watch Penn battle Princeton. Such crowds soon meant more visibility and renown for the game's recognizable stars—Endacott at Kansas, Hanson for three seasons during the mid 1920s at Syracuse, Purdue's "Stretch" Murphy and John Wooden, Indiana's Branch McCracken, Wisconsin's Harold "Bud" Foster, and Montana State's John

"Cat" Thompson out west.

Before it could truly enter the modern age basketball had to shape, hone and regularize its rules. A telling moment came in 1929 with what would later be referred to as "The Last Great Dribble Debate," which featured some of the game's largest personalities of the time. Controversy surrounding the act of dribbling was nothing new to the sport. The strategy had almost immediately entered the game as part and parcel of efforts during the first few winters to relax Naismith's original strictures against running with the ball. Pivoting (moving one foot) was first ruled not to be a traveling violation, but soon it was discovered that action picked up if a man with the ball being tightly guarded could be allowed to escape by tossing the ball into the air and recapturing it (the "air dribble"). Yale's team reportedly expanded the strategy as a serious weapon by also bouncing the sphere while moving toward the goal. Such methods of escaping the defense seemed to many to be a vast improvement, yet soon the early basketball establishment was radically divided over both the advisability and appropriateness of dribbling the ball. Several new dribbling legislations would go in and out of favor during the next several decades (one of them being that the dribbler could not also shoot the ball at the basket).

So heated was the battle that the national Association of Basketball Coaches was finally created specifically to protect the sport against the encroachments of the anti-dribbling forces. There is a most delightful story surrounding the meeting of coaches to resolve the dribbling issue one last time in the late '20s. Wisconsin's Doc Meanwell had led a final onslaught by conservatives in 1929 to kill the dribble by limiting players to a single legal bounce. Meanwell, who believed that the pro-style game of continuous passing made dribbles unnecessary and even unaesthetic, presented one side of the argument to the annual NABC meeting and received a 9-8 vote in his favor. The coaches' group then adjourned to watch a pro game featuring Cleveland's Rosenblums and the Original Celtics, a match that seemed to argue for Meanwell's version of the game that might be played with passing and shooting exclusively. Then Nat Holman, who was already coaching the CCNY team while still playing for these same Celtics, asked for a reconvening of the group. In an impassioned speech he pointed out that college youngsters were not prepared to play like pros and needed the dribble as a strategy. The vote was retaken and this time the forces loyal to Holman and other dribble supporters finally held sway.

Basketball's newfound audience, spawned by the rule modifications and strategy innovations of the decades between the two world wars, would be first fully exploited in New York City. What had become widely known as "The City Game" was booming by the time the '20s flip-flopped into the '30s. Howard Cann rebuilt sagging fortunes at NYU and peaked with his 1934 victory over Holman's CCNY club in a clash of unbeaten teams. Freeman's Wonder Five captured the public's imagination as well as most of the games played during the same epoch. Clair Bee was already building relentless winners at LIU with 26-1, 24-2 and 25-0 ledgers in 1934, 1935 and 1936. And Nat Holman had taken over on a part-time basis for CCNY while continuing his professional barnstorming career (mostly with the Original Celtics and Brooklyn, Syracuse and

Chicago ABL clubs) as a sidelight, thus transferring his own polished pro style of play to his well-schooled college charges. The "Holman Wheel" was a patient offensive scheme in which all five players cut and swerved through endless loops around the basket until the uncontested shot could be found. Holman's teams only thrice lost as many as six games in a single season throughout the entire span between 1920 and 1940; more important, the Holman trademark offensive strategy was soon a much-imitated favorite everywhere throughout the northeastern quadrant of the country. It was Holman's system if not Holman's teams that soon ruled the New York roundball scene.

It took an innovative genius of another sort, however, to exploit fully this great new surge of basketball interest. He would arrive in the form of a far-sighted dreamer named Edward "Ned" Irish, a budding sports journalist who was at first merely enamored with covering the cage sport, but who soon became obsessed with the notion of being college basketball's original promoter par excellence. Legend is mixed with fact when it comes to Irish's first insights into the marketing potential of the college hoops sport. It is widely reported that he initially stumbled upon the idea for larger venues when he tore his own trousers while trying to crawl through a window and into a stuffy Manhattan College gymnasium so that he could cover a sold-out city series game. The tale may indeed be entirely apocryphal, yet the details of his subsequent steps are very much a matter of record. Soon Irish was taking time off from sports writing to schedule and promote doubleheaders that matched local schools with showcase teams from other regions. His first triumph arrived with a $20,000 gate and 16,188 attendees for a twin bill featuring a stellar card that included St. John's versus Pennsylvania's Westminster College and NYU facing Notre Dame. The landmark date was December 29, 1934. Earlier Irish had also assisted New York *World Telegram* sportswriter Dan Daniel in staging an all-local-team triple bill in January 1931 that featured Columbia, Fordham, Manhattan, NYU, St. John's, and CCNY.

Ned Irish had flung open doors for the college game (even if he once had to crawl through windows himself) with his unprecedented doubleheaders and tripleheaders in Madison Square Garden. It was with Irish and these Garden extravaganzas that basketball went big-time, making New York City a center-stage venue for the increasingly popular sport. The twin bills ballooned to eight per year over the next several seasons and brought to town such novel acts from the provinces as Kentucky with "Cowboy" Edwards and Stanford with Hank Luisetti, along with other marquee intersectional attractions like the teams from Colorado, Oklahoma A&M, Notre Dame, Loyola-Chicago, and Bradley. They also brought a steady stream of overflow crowds to witness the action. With a handful of big-ticket events, a minor sport was transformed almost overnight into a five-star spectacle.

The new Garden attractions were from the start an exciting venue for pitched battles between the city's top teams and the best that the rest of the nation had to offer. It was these clashes between regions with distinct playing styles, played out on New York's grandest stage, that would first break down the game's stark regionalisms and bring basketball—especially among the collegians—into its modern era on the eve of the Second World

War. One such entrenched regionalism about to evaporate was West Coast one-handed gunning versus East Coast two-handed set shooting. The moment for dramatic confrontation came in late December of 1936, with one of the most memorable single games of the sport's history, certainly "the" most important single game in the first half-century of college competitions. Clair Bee's long-unbeaten LIU Blackbirds (with their invincible lineup of Ben Kramer, Art Hillhouse, Jules Bender, Willie Schwartz, and Leo Merson) would be forced to stake their reputation and test their merit against a touring Stanford club and Hank Luisetti's notorious one-hand push shot. With its 43-game victory streak squarely on the line, LIU found itself paralyzed by Luisetti and the free-lancing Stanford attack designed by Johnny Bunn. The West Coast star turned 18,000 heads in the grandstands and dozens more on press row with his 15 points (the final score was only 45-31), most of which came on a volley of unstoppable running one-handers. In a single evening Stanford earned a number-one ranking, Luisetti created a New York fan and media frenzy, and the college cage game was changed forever.

Angelo "Hank" Luisetti was the game's first true matinee idol—darkly handsome, unassuming although charismatic, entirely unselfish on the basketball court, and loaded with supreme athletic talent. He excelled in every phase of the game—rebounding, passing, dribbling, defending, running the floor and shooting on the dead run. He was also a remarkable team player and an innovator touched by the unpredictable winds of rare good fortune, much of the latter provided by his perfectly timed East Coast visits. While he certainly didn't invent the one-handed toss, he nonetheless gave it full legitimacy and currency. Luisetti enjoyed his defining moment when he gunned down Clair Bee's team in the Garden and took the New York media by storm in the process. Shortly thereafter he would increase the legend with an eye-opening 50-point game in Cleveland Arena against overwhelmed Duquesne, on a night when his teammates returned every pass and forced him to shoot often. The outburst against Duquesne was truly remarkable, coming as it did in the era of low scores, and it was achieved by a reluctant star who would have much preferred sharing the offensive burden with his overly cooperative teammates.

Luisetti's lasting influence on the East Coast version of the game was soon almost everywhere evident. Even entrenched conservatives like Nat Holman soon gave in to the winds of change, and coaches who had earlier sworn, like Holman, that they would never allow one-handed shooting on their teams were soon exploiting the new style and stuffing their lineups with players enamored of the new offensive maneuver. A dozen seasons later Holman would be caught boasting that with Tony Lavelli's hook shots for Yale, Paul Arizin's jumpers for Villanova, and the running push shot of his own star Irwin Dambrot, the East could hold its own with any sector when it came to sharp one-handed shooters.

Luisetti's shooting opened one door for the college game. A second door was cracked with the significant rule changes of 1937 and 1938 involving the archaic center jump. The game was still slow (by modern standards), low scoring, and dominated by two-handed set-shots. But the main fetters had already been removed once continuous action and shooting on the run were encouraged. More significantly, a considerable amount of playing time had now been put back on the scoreboard clock. This was the clock-time earlier lost while players and officials trudged back to center court for new jump-ups after each score, all with the game clock relentlessly ticking away.

Another spinoff of Irish's suddenly popular Madison Square Garden spectacles was the annual postseason tournament. It was an idea that seemed to be long overdue when it first arrived with the six-team affair sponsored by the Metropolitan Basketball Writers and staged at the Garden to cap the 1938 season. The inaugural National Invitational Tournament reflected its organizers' desire to for a strong East-West flavor, with Colorado, Oklahoma A&M, Temple, and Bradley joining the host schools from LIU and NYU; it also succeeded wildly both at the gate and on the playing floor. But the idea for such tournaments was not new and indeed stretched back as far as 1904, when Hiram College, Wheaton College, and Latter Day Saints University (today Brigham Young) met at the St. Louis World's Fair for what was ambitiously billed as an Olympic World's College Basket Ball Championship. Other attempts had been made by the college coaches to institute a year-end championship, and the first truly national tournament was the NAIA event, which originated in Kansas City in 1937 as replacement for a national AAU playoff that had been relocated to Detroit. The showcase small school affair, which preceded the NIT by a full year, offered a field of 32 teams and a full week of nearly round-the-clock playoff showdowns.

By the close of the 1930s, with war clouds looming everywhere on the near horizon, college basketball had finally come of age. The game had been modernized by both modifications to the playing structure and bold innovations among the gifted athletes themselves. For the first time there was a distinctly national flavor to the sport, with teams from east, west, north, and south now frequently meeting head-on to test regional supremacies. Large audiences flocked into packed venues (especially those in New York or Philadelphia and in the large field houses on many Midwestern campuses), and the game was welcoming its first nationally recognized stars, players such as Luisetti of Stanford, Wintermute of Oregon, Jaworski of Rhode Island, Torgoff of Long Island, and Nowak of Notre Dame. Optimism for the sport's future was everywhere in the air, and basketball's long-anticipated moment in the sun seemed to sit visibly on the horizon.

Chapter 47

The History of NCAA Basketball, 1939-2003

By Roland Lazenby, Michael Douchant
and Ken Shouler

College basketball has come a long way since 5,000 spectators attended the inaugural NCAA Tournament Final. What follows is a year-by-year review of college basketball, focusing on the NCAA Tournament, since 1939.

1939

Smelling the success of the National Invitational Tournament founded a year earlier in New York, the National Association of Basketball Coaches organized the first NCAA tournament to close the 1938-39 season.

The NCAA's original format divided the country into eight districts, each with a regional selection committee sending a team to the eight-team field. This format lasted for 12 years. While the NIT took many of its teams from the pool of independent schools, most of the NCAA's entries were affiliated with conferences. The first NCAA field included Brown with a 17-3 record, Villanova, 19-4, Ohio State, 14-6, Oklahoma, 11-8, Texas, 19-4, Wake Forest, 18-5, and Utah State from the old Skyline Conference. Oregon entered with a 26-5 record.

The four eastern division teams met March 17 at the Palestra in Philadelphia, where the inclusion of Villanova helped draw a crowd. The western divisions began three days later in San Francisco and attracted only 3,000. The Oregon Ducks were an early trendsetter, playing an ambitious schedule and using a dominant inside game. Coach Howard Hobson's team was tall by 1939 standards, with 6-foot-8 Slim Wintermute at center, and two 6-foot-4 forwards, Laddie Gale and John Dick. Their fans nicknamed them "The Tall Firs."

With their height and the experience their schedule brought them, the Firs moved past Texas, 56-41, and Oklahoma, 55-37 in the West. In the East, Ohio State coach Harold Olsen's Buckeyes hadn't shown much offensive flair. Only four times in a 20-game schedule had they scored more than 50 points. Yet they awakened offensively in the tournament and out-distanced Wake Forest 64-52 in the first round, as guard Dick Baker scored 25 points. State's captain, Jim Hull, took over in the second round, scoring 28 points as the Buckeyes eliminated Villanova, 53-36.

Patton Gym at Northwestern University in Evanston, Illinois, was the site of that first NCAA championship on Friday, March 27, 1939. The game drew about 5,000 spectators who saw 5-foot-8 guard Bobby Anet push Oregon to the first NCAA championship. The Firs led 21-16 at the half, then used their inside advantage to win, 46-33.

The championship trophy was broken during the game when Anet crashed into the trophy table going after a loose ball.

Bill Walton and John Wooden, 1972
Wooden's UCLA Bruins' 88-game win streak may well last forever.

The coaches' association lost $2,531 on its first tournament, the only deficit in the history of the event. The NCAA agreed to run the tournament the following season.

1940

History marked the 1939-40 college basketball season with a neat crease, folding one era while ushering in another. Dr. James Naismith died on November 28, 1939. While his passing marked an end to the formative years of the game, the modern era was born quietly three months later on February 28,

1940, when a New York station, W2XBS (later WNBC), first televised a college basketball game. It was a double-header from Madison Square Garden matching Pitt against Fordham and NYU against Georgetown. There were only a few hundred TV sets in America at the time, many of them in New York.

The 1940 NCAA tournament produced some surprises as Indiana, coached by Branch McCracken, and Kansas, coached by Phog Allen, battled their way to the Finals. Indiana had finished second in the Big Ten behind Purdue, despite two wins over the Boilermakers. When Purdue declined the invitation to the NCAA tournament, the Hoosiers agreed to go.

Kansas, meanwhile, had won a playoff from Oklahoma and Missouri to take the Big Six title, but the Jayhawks weren't considered prime contenders. The top team in the country was thought to be Southern Cal with Ralph Vaughn and a 19-2 record. The Trojans had hammered Oregon State, 62-26, in the Pacific Coast playoff. In the first round of the NCAA West, Southern Cal defeated Colorado, winner of the NIT just days earlier. Despite the Trojans' momentum, Kansas stopped them in the West semi-finals, 43-42. USC led by a point with 17 seconds to play, but Howard Engleman scored to give Kansas the upset. Ralph Miller, who would go on to coaching greatness at Oregon State, scored 10 points for Kansas.

In the East, Indiana's fast-break offense ran a weave drill through the competition. First the Hoosiers dispatched little Springfield College, 48-24. Then they eliminated Duquesne, another NIT finals team.

The NCAA Finals were held in Kansas City's Municipal Auditorium, giving a home-crowd advantage to the Jayhawks, whose campus was an hour away. (The crowd was estimated at a little over 9,000 in the 10,000-seat auditorium.) But Indiana dominated, 60-42. Marv Huffman scored 12 for the Hoosiers and was named the outstanding player, the first selected by the NCAA. Huffman and teammates Jay McCreary and Bill Menke were selected to the first all-tournament team, along with Engleman and Bob Allen of Kansas. The second NCAA tournament made a profit of $9,590. The two schools in the championship each received $750.

1941

The 1940-41 season celebrated basketball's 50th birthday. The Wisconsin Badgers entered the NCAA tournament with a 12-game winning streak and a home-court advantage. Wisconsin's first-round opponent was Dartmouth, with All-American Gus Broberg, who scored 20 points and kept Dartmouth ahead until the last minute, when Wisconsin sophomore John Kotz hit two free throws to give the Badgers a 51-50 win. All-American center Gene Englund scored 18 points for Wisconsin.

The Badgers' opponent in the East semi-finals was Pittsburgh, another of Doc Carlson's methodical teams that had eased past North Carolina and George Glamack, 26-20. In a match of methodologies, Foster's team worked a precise 36-30 win before 14,000 screaming fans. For the third year in a row, the Big Ten had a team in the NCAA Finals, and again the eastern teams had been shut out.

In the West, a fast-breaking Washington State team had beaten Stanford in the Pacific Coast playoffs and kept that pace through the NCAA's opening rounds. Led by 6-foot-7 center Paul Lindeman, Washington State beat Creighton, 48-39, in the first round and faced Arkansas in the semi-finals at Kansas City. The Razorbacks were considered heavy favorites to win the third NCAA championship with high-scoring guard Johnny Adams, but Washington State's fast break rolled to the win, 64-53.

The Badgers took their leather knee pads, striped socks and quaint control offense to the finals in Kansas City, where sportswriters were predicting that Washington State's fast break would blow right by them. But Foster's cautious offense and stifling defense turned the game into a battle of centers. Englund overpowered the taller Lindeman, as State's offense went scoreless for nine minutes in the first half. When State's offense again struggled in the second half, Wisconsin's plodding attack settled the issue, 39-34.

Kotz scored 12 points in the final and was named the outstanding player. North Carolina's prolific scorer George Glamack (he had scored 45 points during a regular-season game), knocked in 31 points during the tournament's first consolation game, setting an NCAA playoff scoring record that would last almost a decade.

1942

The 1941-42 college basketball season was marked by the eeriness of Pearl Harbor and America's gathering of forces to fight World War II. As much as possible, college basketball maintained business-as-usual right up to tournament time.

The NCAA tournament brought together a collection of first-rate teams. From the West came once-beaten Colorado and young-but-talented Stanford. Elsewhere, sportswriters were raving over the Illinois Whiz Kids and Dartmouth with George Munroe. And a grand tradition was born as Adolph Rupp's Kentucky Wildcats made their first appearance in the tournament. They would make the field 30 more times over the next 44 years, winning five championships. Their role in the '42 tournament was that of spoiler. In the East first round, played in New Orleans before only 3,000 spectators, Kentucky ended the season of sophomore All-American Andy Phillip and the Illinois Whiz Kids, 46-44. There would be no Big Ten team in the Finals for the first time in the NCAA's short history.

With the Illini finished, Dartmouth and Munroe charged to the top in the East and whacked Rupp's team in the semi-finals, 47-28. In the West, Everett Dean's Stanford team had compiled a 25-4 regular-season record, but the Indians struggled in their opening-round game against Rice. After building a substantial first-half lead, they fell behind late. Freshman forward Jim Pollard stepped forward with 26 points to lead the Cardinals, 53-47.

A classic confrontation was anticipated in the West semi-final between Stanford and Colorado. On the talent of Bob Doll and Leason McCloud, Colorado had put together a string of wins against the country's top teams, losing only to Wyoming, 40-39. But the Buffalos' magic came unglued against Stanford. Pollard scored 17 points, and the Indians advanced to the finals, 46-35.

Dean, who had coached at Indiana for 14 years before leaving for Stanford in 1938, was poised to claim the championship

when bad luck struck. Pollard caught the flu and couldn't play in the Final. But substitute Jack Dana scored 14, and Howie Dallmar (who was named outstanding player) led Stanford with 15 points as the Cardinal downed Dartmouth, 53-38.

Despite the tight tournament scores, the college game was opening up, with Frank Keaney's "point-a-minute" Rhode Island team leading the way. At the head of Keaney's fast break was Stanley "Stutz" Modzelewski, whose 1,730 points over a four-year career broke Hank Luisetti's NCAA scoring record of 1,596 that had stood for six years. West Texas State's Price Brookfield also set a new single-season scoring record: 520 points.

1943

World war leaned heavily on college basketball in 1943, as it did all of American society. The military siphoned off many of the game's bright young players. With wartime travel restrictions, most schools played games closer to home. Cross-country and intersectional rivalries were put on hold and replaced by games with nearby YMCAs and AAU teams.

"It was wartime, and if you played ball then, you were either 4-F, you were a freshman, or you were in medical, or dental, or engineering school," recalled Utah's Arnie Ferrin. "They were the only people still in school." Many of the country's best teams formed at military bases, where college athletes were sent for training after being drafted. Some colleges with military training programs on their campuses or bases nearby benefited from the upheaval. The war also placed a premium on good freshmen and sophomores, who were too young or too tall to be drafted. At DePaul, 6-foot-10 freshman center George Mikan led coach Ray Meyer's first team to the NCAA semifinals. And 6-foot-9 sophomore Harry Boykoff helped St. John's, now coached by former Celtic Joe Lapchick, to the NIT title over Toledo, 48-27.

The Whiz Kids at the University of Illinois with Andy Phillip dominated the Big Ten, leaving some calling them the best team in the nation. Yet Illinois declined an invitation to the NCAA tournament. In the place of the Illini, Meyer's DePaul team was selected. With Mikan scoring 20, the Blue Demons from Chicago dispatched Dartmouth, 45-35, in the first round of the East Regionals. In the other bracket, John Mahnken led the Georgetown Hoyas over NYU, 55-36.

Eyeing the financial success of the NIT in Madison Square Garden, the NCAA tournament directors decided to move their East Regionals and the national championship game to the Garden in 1943. The invitation to NYU, the first New York school to appear in the NCAA tournament, drew a city crowd of 16,500 on March 24. But NYU's offense fizzled in a 55-36 loss to Georgetown.

The East final in the Garden was a faceoff of freshman centers: DePaul's Mikan vs. Georgetown's Mahnken. Mikan would go on to greatness in the NBA, but for a night in the NCAA tournament Mahnken prevailed, scoring 17 points to Mikan's 11, as Georgetown won, 53-49.

University of Texas' All-American guard John Hargis set a new tournament record by scoring 30 as the Longhorns eased by Washington, 59-55, in the West's opening round in Kansas City. Wyoming faced Oklahoma in the other West opener and

trailed until the fourth quarter when center Milo Komenich led the Cowboys to a 53-50 comeback win. In the West finals, Wyoming fell behind Texas early, as Hargis scored another 29 points. But the Texas star got into foul trouble late, allowing the Cowboys to sneak into the national championship game, 58-54.

With no home team in the championship, the Madison Square Garden crowd dwindled to 13,000 for the NCAA finals, but it was still much larger than the crowds in Kansas City in previous years. The Garden chilled both teams into a low-scoring first half (Wyoming led, 18-16, at intermission). Georgetown took a five point lead in the third quarter. The Cowboys caught up, and the game remained close until the last 90 seconds, when Wyoming scored nine straight points to claim the championship, 46-34.

Shooting the one-hander, Kenny Sailors scored 16 points in the championship and was named the outstanding player. Hargis of Texas scored 59 points in two games, a tournament record. Wyoming later beat NIT champion St. John's in the Red Cross Classic, a war-effort benefit, 52-47.

1944

NCAA tournament officials faced the challenge of keeping competition alive in 1944 amid the homefront chaos created by the American war effort. As a result, the field was a hodge-podge.

Region 7 sent no representative because the Skyline Conference had suspended play. So the Big Six Conference sent two schools, Iowa State and Missouri, a 9-8 team. With an impressive 26-6 record, Washington won the northern division of the Pacific Coast Conference, and California, at 7-3, won the southern. But travel restrictions meant the two divisions couldn't have a playoff. Instead, the committee selected Pepperdine, 21-11.

To round out the West field, the NCAA offered a bid to Utah, but coach Vadal Peterson and his Utes declined, electing instead to go to the NIT because they wanted to see New York. In their place, the NCAA invited Arkansas. In the East bracket, the Region 4 selection committee opted to send an inferior Big Ten team, Ohio State with 14 wins and six losses. DePaul with Mikan was overlooked with a 20-3 record that included a win over Ohio State. Region 2 sent Temple at 13-8.

Somehow, the Region 3 committee chose little Catholic University in Washington, D.C., which Dartmouth promptly dismissed, 63-38, in the first round. Over four years, Dartmouth had run up a 74-10 record. By 1944, the Indians, with military training on campus, had picked up several stars from other colleges, including Dick McGuire from St. John's; Harry Leggat from NYU; and Cornell veteran Bob Gale.

In the other East first-round game, Ohio State and star Arnie Risen brushed aside Temple, 57-47. The Buckeyes, however, were no match for All-American McGuire and Dartmouth in the regional finals. Dartmouth center and team captain, Audley Brindley, scored 28 points as the Indians advanced to the championship game, 60-53.

The West Regional, meanwhile, had been thrown into chaos when the University of Arkansas team was involved in an auto accident driving to the tournament in Kansas City. Two players

were injured, forcing the Razorbacks to withdraw. Desperate for a replacement, tournament officials looked around and found Utah, which had just been dumped by Kentucky, 46-38, in the first round of the NIT. The Utes had to pass through Kansas City on their train ride home to Salt Lake City, so they agreed to stop over and play in the tournament.

"We didn't practice; didn't have a scouting report; no preparation," recalled Utah's Arnie Ferrin. "We just started playing." With only nine players, including a starting five that averaged 18 years of age, Utah showed remarkable composure. In that era, almost no coaching was allowed during games. "During timeouts you could not go to the bench," Ferrin recalled. "When you took a timeout, the players sat down on the floor and talked about what was happening and made the decision right there. You saw the coach before the game and at half-time. If he had a message for you during the game, he'd send in a substitute so you could take a timeout."

Right off the train, the young Utes sliced through the West Regionals, ousting Missouri, 45-35, then Iowa State, 40-31. Suddenly Peterson's team was headed back to New York on the train to play for the NCAA championship. If anything, the Finals brought out the best in the war-weary New Yorkers. One of the Utes was 5-foot-7 guard Wat Misaka, a Japanese-American, whose hustling made him a favorite of the 15,000 spectators. But it was the 6-foot-3, silky-smooth Ferrin who led Utah to the championship. He scored 18 points in regulation to give the Utes what appeared to be a 36-34 victory. Then Dartmouth's Dick McGuire hit a bankshot from half court just before the buzzer to send the game into overtime, the first extra period in NCAA tournament history. "McGuire was running down the left sideline around midcourt and threw the ball," Ferrin recalled. "He was just inside halfcourt. It was a left-handed shot, and he banked it off the board."

At the close of overtime, Ferrin's teammate, Herb Wilkinson, pitched up a one-hander from the top of the key to give Utah the title, 42-40. Ferrin, with 22 of his team's 42 points, was named the outstanding player. A week later, the Utes beat NIT champion St. John's in the Red Cross benefit, 43-36, thus making their storybook comeback and their championship season complete.

Without question, Western teams were ruling the college game. "If you want to identify a reason for their early success, my opinion would be that New York was too heavy into the set shot," Ferrin said. "We played more wide open and used the one-handed jump shot. Our game was a faster, more productive game because of our style. That was a very obvious difference between Eastern and Western basketball."

1945

The 1944-45 basketball season brought the maturing of the game's two dominating young big men, DePaul's George Mikan and Oklahoma A&M's Bob Kurland; both hovering at 6-foot-10, both eager to prove that tall boys could play the game, if not with grace, at least with guile and power. Their defensive domination, particularly that of Kurland, led to a rewriting of the goaltending rule.

When they entered college in 1942, basketball was still the domain of the little man. But after watching Kurland and Mikan for four years, college coaches saw the way to victory. Today, Kurland takes immense pride in being one of the first players to change the public's perception of big men. "We opened the door to the idea that the big man could play the game," Kurland said. "which in our day was, by Eastern standards, played by guys 5-foot-10, 5-foot-11, who were quick, took the set shot and so forth. We opened the door for what the game is today."

With "Foothills" Kurland at center, the Oklahoma A&M (later to become Oklahoma State) Aggies of coach Henry Iba would win back-to-back NCAA championships in the 1945 and '46 seasons. For Mikan and DePaul, locked out of the NCAA by the Big Ten, the 1945 season would bring an NIT championship, a 71-54 win over Bowling Green. Mikan scored 53 points against Rhode Island in the NIT semi-finals as the Blue Demons set 10 team scoring records. Twice the country's top college scorer, Mikan would go on to a storied professional career. Kurland, on the other hand, turned down substantial pro offers to remain an amateur after college. He played with the Phillips Petroleum Company team in AAU competition and represented the United States in the 1948 and '52 Olympics.

When he came to college as a thin, awkward freshman in 1942, Kurland walked with a pronounced stoop, as if he were trying to shrug his body into a smaller frame. He was 6-foot-9 and weighed 175. "You have to remember that Henry Iba had never had and there were almost no coaches who'd ever had people as tall as I was," Kurland said. "So the early coaches really were pioneers in discovering skills that were required in playing a post type of game."

Knowing that Kurland's strength was defense, Iba devised a strategy in which the big center simply goaltended opponents shots, which was allowed under the rules of 1944. (Goaltending involves striking the ball on its downward flight or while it is in the cylinder of the basket.) According to 1944 rules, a defensive player could hit or catch a shot on its downward flight to the basket. Today a defensive player can only hit a shot as it rises. "There were other people who could goaltend," Kurland explained, "but we were the first team to sit down and deliberately devise a strategy and to play a defense that included goaltending as its central theme.

"We developed a technique where it was literally a zone defense with me knocking the ball down. We were very effective at it. People in many cases would beat themselves psychologically, and that was a bad thing for the game. But it was a way of winning, and it was within the rules." Kurland and the goaltending defense carried the Aggies to a 27-6 record for 1943-44. After the season, Kurland's effectiveness forced the NCAA to change its goaltending rule. No longer were players allowed to knock away shots when the ball was on its downward flight to the basket. To balance that measure, the rules committee also decided that players should be allowed five fouls, instead of four, before fouling out.

Many observers mistakenly thought the new goaltending rule would diminish Kurland's presence in the game. Just the opposite happened. The Aggies ground out 23 wins against four losses during the 1944-45 regular season, then whipped Utah and Arkansas to gain the Finals of the NCAA tourna-

ment. Howard Cann's NYU team emerged in the East, blasting by Tufts, 59-44, in the first round to the delight of the Madison Square Garden crowd. The NYU Violets featured highscoring forward Sid Tannenbaum and freshman Dolph Schayes at center. Then they beat Ohio State, setting up a match with Kurland and Iba's control game for the national title.

For the first time, the NCAA had a Fnal in the Garden featuring a New York team. Cann's Violets and Iba's Cowboys engaged in a classic of possession basketball. With each team frightened of taking bad shots, the lead stayed close. Iba told reporters afterward that he was proud of the way his team worked the ball into Kurland, who scored 22 points. That was enough as Iba claimed his first NCAA championship, 49-45.

The outcome set up the meeting the basketball world had been waiting for: Kurland and A&M versus Mikan and DePaul, the NIT champions, in the Red Cross benefit game. Unfortunately, both big men were held down by foul troubles (Mikan was disqualified with only 14 minutes gone in the game). Kurland scored 14 and Mikan 9, as A&M won, 52-44. Kurland and Mikan never had the opportunity for a rematch, despite being the college game's dominant seniors the next season.

1946

During the season, George Mikan led the nation in scoring, averaging a little better than 23 points a game, but DePaul was not invited to either tournament at season's end. Bob Kurland was again the centerpiece in Hank Iba's grand defensive machine at Oklahoma A&M. He averaged 19 points in the Cowboys' controlled offense. Only in the last regular game of the season, against St. Louis University in Kurland's hometown, did Iba turn his center loose offensively. Kurland scored 58 points.

With a 28-2 record, the Aggies entered the NCAA tournament as the favorite. They oozed experience. "In '45 and '46 we had guys that were in the war and had been shot at," Kurland explained. "Some of them had been in Iwo Jima and Italy, and these were not boys. These were guys that didn't rattle. These were men playing a boys' game."

Kurland scored 20 in the first round as A&M strode past Baylor, 44-29. In the second round, he powered in 29 more in a 52-35 victory over California. In the East, Madison Square Garden fans saw their NYU favorites downed by North Carolina, 57-49, in the first round. Then North Carolina beat Ohio State in overtime to gain the Finals against A&M. The Tar Heels were led by forward John Dillon and a skinny, talkative center, a 27-year-old ex-serviceman, Horace "Bones" McKinney.

With the 6-foot-6 McKinney playing tough defense, the Tar Heels almost upset Iba's masterpiece. After dogging Kurland much of the game, McKinney fouled out in the second half with five points, as did Kurland minutes later. The game came down to a frantic final moment, when the Aggies, ahead 41-40, had to inbound the ball against the pressing Carolina defense. A&M was successful and scored to claim a second championship, 43-40.

Kurland had scored 72 points in three tournament games and was named the Most Outstanding Player for the second

consecutive year. "I have great admiration," Kurland said, "for men like Henry Iba and Ray Meyer, who were brave enough to take odd people or strange giants like myself and had the courage to put their careers on the line in trying to teach us how to play. You can't measure our performance to today's performance or tomorrow's performance. That's foolish. But the thing I take pride in is, we opened the door for the big man and caused people to think."

1947

In 1946-47, the Holy Cross Crusaders didn't have a home gym, and they didn't have a starter over 6-foot-4 (center George Kaftan was just that height). But they did have Doggie Julian as a coach, and they had a whiz-bang, fast-break weave drill as their offense. And when the season was over, they had an NCAA championship.

Young Bob Cousy was a reserve guard on the Holy Cross bench, but he wasn't the big story in '47. The headlines belonged to Kaftan, a ball of rebounding and inside-scoring presence. On the strength of his play, Holy Cross entered the NCAA tournament with a 24-3 record, despite having played most games on the road or in Boston Garden. Nursing a 20-game winning streak at tournament time, the Crusaders were considered something of a favorite in the East.

Their opponent in the NCAA finals was Oklahoma. At 22-6, the Sooners had entered the tournament with the Big 6 championship. They beat favored Texas, 55-54, in the West regional final when role player Ken Pryor hit a long set shot with 10 seconds left in overtime.

The Sooners and Holy Cross then played for the championship in Madison Square Garden. Gerry Tucker scored 22 as Oklahoma stayed at the heels of the Crusaders. With three minutes left, Holy Cross led, 48-45, but then exploded to win the championship, 58-47. Kaftan with 18 points in the finals was named the outstanding player.

The season brought the return of more war-seasoned players to the lineups: Arnie Ferrin at Utah, Andy Phillip at Illinois, Alex Groza at Kentucky; Kenny Sailors and Milo Komenich at Wyoming, and Danny Kraus at Georgetown.

1948

Kentucky next emerged as the college game's dominant team. The proof is sad and ironic, but the Wildcats of 1948 and '49 were even better than their impressive record. Over two seasons, they won 68 games and lost just five. Coach Adolph Rupp's teams capped this run with back-to-back NCAA championships. But their accomplishments were later tarnished with the revelation that several Kentucky players had taken money from gamblers to shave points in key games.

The war had shaken up millions of lives, including those of the Kentucky players, many of whom were veterans just home from the conflict. Rupp, meanwhile, had used the circumstances to make Kentucky one of the most dynamic sports programs in America. Before the 1945-46 season, the Army had invited Rupp to develop a recreation program for the forces in Europe. While overseas, he recruited the best players among the servicemen soon to be returning from the war. Among his finds were Dale Barnstable and Jim Line, both of whom starred in

service leagues in Europe.

Joe B. Hall, who succeeded Rupp as Kentucky's head coach, was a freshman at the school during those post-war years. "It was a time," Hall said, "when veterans were flooding the colleges, so you had a backlog of about four years of athletes who had been in the service." Basketball had become "a kind of a salvation for Kentucky," Hall explained. "The small rural communities on the high school level did not play football in the state of Kentucky. Many of the schools were so inaccessible back up in the hollows that they just couldn't get that many kids together to have a football team. Basketball became a way of life in the Kentucky mountains and in eastern Kentucky."

A man of overbearing pride, Rupp had played for Phog Allen at Kansas in the 1930s. He was named Kentucky's coach in 1930 and by the opening of the 1947-48 season, his trophy case lacked only an NCAA championship. His teams had won five straight Southeastern Conference championships from 1944 to 1948 and the 1946 NIT Championship. For the 1947-48 team, Rupp had Alex Groza, greyhound guard Ralph Beard, and forward Wallace "Wah Wah" Jones. Beyond those three, Kentucky was deep in talent with Cliff Barker, Barnstable, Jim Line and Ken Rollins. Rupp had recruited Groza as a skinny high school senior in 1944. The younger brother of pro football player Lou, Groza appeared briefly in Kentucky uniform during the 1944-45 season before going into the service his freshman year. Two years later, he returned to the Wildcats as a mature physical specimen well on his way to becoming an imposing inside player.

"Groza was the big man," Hall recalled, "and certainly one of the finest in the country. He was only 6-foot-7, but he was a scoring machine. He understood the game, and he wasn't intimidated ... That team had tremendous maturity, because they had a lot of army veterans, including Groza. Cliff Barker was 28-years-old and had been in a German prisoner-of-war camp for 18 months, and if that doesn't lend maturity to a ball club, then I don't know what would."

The Wildcats regularly ran up 70 points or more in an era when most games were settled with scores in the 50s. It was, assistant coach Harry Lancaster once said, "a beautiful team. They had the finest fast break I have ever seen, before or since. It was just magnificent the way Groza got the ball off the board." Groza, who averaged 14.7 points a game, usually hit Wah Wah Jones or Ken Rollins with the outlet pass, and they in turn would find Beard streaking to the basket. "I've often said that Ralph Beard could step on the floor today and be an outstanding basketball player without changing skills at all," Hall said. "He was such a competitor, a defensive ball-hawk and outstanding scorer, just a tremendous athlete. He had the greatest quickness of anyone I've ever seen on the basketball floor. Beard had ups and downs because he had games that the opposition really concentrated on stopping him. Many teams felt that if they could stop Ralph Beard, they could stop Kentucky."

The 5-foot-10 Beard, who averaged 10.8 points a game over his career, could hit the deep set shot, a two-hander from over his head, and a one-handed jumper. And if he missed, the 6-foot-4 Jones, who came to Kentucky to play football for Bear Bryant, was an offensive rebounding specialist.

Their regular-season record in 1947-48 was 29-2, the two being one-point losses to Notre Dame and Temple. By NCAA tournament time, most sportswriters figured that the only club among the NCAA's field of eight capable of beating them was defending champion Holy Cross.

But in the East Regional finals, the Wildcats shut down Bob Cousy and Holy Cross to advance, 60-52. Kentucky ran out to an early 17-point lead and rapped the Baylor Bears in the NCAA finals, 58-42, giving Rupp his first NCAA championship. Groza, who scored 14, was named the tournament's most outstanding player.

After the college season ended, the Kentucky dream continued to the '48 Olympics, played in London, where the Kentucky squad combined with the Phillips Oilers of the AAU, including Bob Kurland, to form the U.S. team. With Groza and Kurland in the same lineup, the Americans easily outclassed the world competition for the gold medal.

1949

The Associated Press introduced its nationwide poll at the outset of the 1948-49 season, and as expected, the Wildcats ruled it. Known as the "Fabulous Five," the 1949 team could have been the first in history to win both the NCAA and NIT, but they lost in the 1949 NIT while attempting to keep the point spread where the bookies wanted it. At the 1952 trial of three Kentucky players, a New York judge lambasted Rupp's personal relationship with a bookmaker and the Kentucky program's "ruthless exploitation of athletes." The university later conducted an internal investigation that cleared the coach, but his reputation remained besmirched despite an impressive career won-loss record.

An early-season loss to St. Louis in the Sugar Bowl tournament convinced the Baron that his team needed to concentrate on getting the ball to Groza. With that adjustment, the Kentucky inside game became dominant, until the team entered the NIT, where it was upset by Loyola-Illinois in the quarter-finals, 67-56. Two years later, it would be revealed that the Wildcats lost the game while trying to shave points. But those developments were known only to the players and a small circle of gamblers in late 1949. Kentucky entered the NCAA tournament and made quick work of the opposition. Villanova fell first, 85-72, in the East opener. Then Kentucky humiliated a strong Illinois team, 76-47, in the East finals.

In the West, Hank Iba's Oklahoma A&M team moved through his brand of controlled paces. The Aggies nipped Wyoming, 40-39, then powered past Oregon State, 55-30. The 1949 finals was a battle of coaching wits—Rupp against Iba. The site had been shifted to Seattle, giving Rupp's team the discomfort of a 3,000-mile train ride from the East regionals at Madison Square Garden. The score remained tight late in the game when Groza, who had scored 25 of his team's 46 points, fouled out. The Aggies, however, missed key shots down the stretch, and the Wildcats won, 46-36, to give Rupp his second NCAA championship. Groza, named the outstanding player for the second year in a row, joined Beard and Jones on UPI's All-America first team.

After the season, Groza, Beard and Jones formed the nucleus of a new pro team, the Indianapolis Olympians. With stock ownership in the team, the wealth and fame of the three young

Kentuckians would grow, until 1951 when it was revealed Groza and Beard had accepted bribes during college. They were subsequently banned for life from the NBA and forced to sell their stock. Their team eventually folded as a result of the negative publicity.

The players confessed they had accepted $500 each to trim points in the 1949 NIT game. They later implicated several of their Kentucky teammates in the scandal. And the New York judge who imposed suspended sentences on Groza and Beard decried the fact that Rupp had allowed Ed Curd, a Lexington bookmaker, to travel with the team and fraternize with the players at a New York nightclub. Some players even claimed that Rupp frequently phoned his bookie before Kentucky games, but that allegation was never substantiated.

With the scandal, University of Kentucky President Herman L. Donovan ordered an internal investigation of the program. "From all we could learn," Donovan said after reviewing the results, "Coach Rupp is an honorable man who did not knowingly violate the athletic rules."

1950

Nat Holman's CCNY teams had always been good, but in 1950 the Beavers became the best. They accomplished what no other college team could; they won both the NCAA and NIT tournaments.

In their excitement, the CCNY student body developed a cheer for the Beavers: "Allagaroo-garoo-gara; Allagaroo-garoo-gara; eeyah-eeyah; sis boom ba, team, team, team." As the Beavers moved along their improbable march that spring of 1950, the Allagaroo cheer rang through the canyons of Manhattan. But from the height of this euphoria, Holman and his team tumbled dramatically several months later when it was revealed that several key players were among those involved in the point-shaving scandal that rocked the college game.

The Beavers were the epitomy of the city-slick brand of ball that evolved in New York in the 1940s. Sadly, just as that style of play came to prominence, the gambling investigations virtually wiped out the city's thriving basketball culture. The major programs at Long Island University, CCNY, Manhattan and NYU never recovered from the scandal. Fortuitously, a New York newspaper had commented early in the 1949-50 season that CCNY might well become the greatest team that New York City had ever produced. Arguably, it was. "I think our team would do pretty good today," Irwin Dambrot, the team's senior star who later became a New York dentist, said in 1989. "We were the best of our era."

Not only did the Beavers have talent, but they had a coach. Nat Holman had what you might call the complete basketball experience. As a playmaking guard, he was a key member of pro basketball's original Celtics. He took the coaching job at CCNY in 1920 and continued his professional barnstorming career on the side for another 14 years. He was a legend in New York. A snappy dresser, he lectured and wrote extensively on the game. His career record stood at 359-127 as he headed into the 1950 season.

"Nat Holman was a very strong disciplinarian," Dambrot said. "When he talked, he wanted silence. When he showed somebody on the team a movement, he wanted no one to

move. Everybody would just have to freeze and pay very, very close attention. Directly and indirectly, he demanded a lot of respect."

When it came to offense, he believed in precise motion in the half-court game, and a controlled fast break when the conditions allowed. CCNY ran lots of give-and-gos. He liked to have all five players rotating in and out of the pivot. That suited the 1950 starting five because all of them had played center in high school. The pivot man had to be versatile and a solid passer, able to hit his teammates as they cut off of him toward the basket. It was literally a game of hot potato, Dambrot recalled. "The ball would move, everybody would move. So if a defensive man turned his head, you were gone. We went in for back-door layups all the time."

At the same time, Holman taught defense and fundamentals with passion. "If you didn't box out, he'd pull you right out of the game," Dambrot said. Like LIU's Clair Bee, Holman developed a scouting report on each opponent and prepared his team for each game. In 1949-50, Holman had the makings of a truly great team. Ed Warner, who would become disabled in an auto accident later in life, was the real talent of the bunch, Dambrot said. "When he got there, we just got better and better and better." A 6-foot-4 forward, Warner had long arms that allowed him to play as if he were 6-foot-8. Plus he could handle the ball.

At 6-foot-6, Ed Roman played the pivot when it wasn't being occupied by someone else in Holman's rotating attack. Roman was a little beefy at 220 pounds, but he was a fine all-around shooter and passer. He had range to his shot and liked to take it from the corner. Plus he could hook with either hand. Dambrot was the other scorer, averaging a little better than 10 points a game. A left-hander, he was one of the city's early jump shooters, having fashioned himself after former LIU center Dick Holub.

The guards, Floyd Layne and Al "Fats" Roth, both averaged about six points a game. At 6-foot-3, Layne had the height to be a good multi-purpose player. Layne would survive the scandals at CCNY and later became head coach at the college. Roth earned the name "Fats." At 200 pounds, he had the bulk to push his way through picks. The other major factor would be 6-foot-5 senior reserve forward Norm Mager, who scored 14 against Bradley in the national championship game.

With their talent, they were clearly the city's favorites in 1949. "New York basketball in those days was unreal," Dambrot said. "There would be 18,000 fans in Madison Square Garden packed to the rafters."

The Beavers finished the regular season 17-5, just enough to get a bid to the NIT. In the first round, they drew defending champion San Francisco and made short work of the Dons, 65-46, as Warner scored 26. In the second round, they faced NCAA defending champion Kentucky. "Just play your game," Holman told them. They won 89-50, issuing Adolph Rupp's team its worst beating in his 42 years of coaching. Bill Spivey, Kentucky's 7-foot center, had opened the game by blocking several of Roman's shots. But Holman shifted Warner into the post, and he was too quick for the big man. "We just ran them off the court and made every shot," Dambrot recalled. "They just couldn't handle our fast break."

The Kentucky legislature considered a resolution that the

capitol's flag be lowered to half staff to mark the catastrophe. It served as extra motivation for CCNY, one of the first integrated teams in the East, that third-ranked Kentucky usually scheduled no team with black players. In the NIT's third round, the Beavers outlasted Duquesne, 62-52. But the opponent in the championship was top-ranked Bradley, and the sportswriters predicted that midnight would strike on CCNY's "Cinderella." As the AP's top team, the Braves had three All America candidates in forward Paul Unruh and guards Gene Melchiorre and Bill Mann. However, the Beavers' Warner usurped the all-star attention by scoring 87 points in four NIT games, including 16 in the final, to earn MVP honors. In the process, he led CCNY to the upset championship, 69-61.

The real star, though, was the Beavers' defense. "Against Bradley, they were destroying us the first half," Dambrot said. "It was like a snake pit they were so good. At one point we were down 10 to 12 points, but we closed to three by the half and won it from there."

Holman had been ill with a high fever during the Final, but the victory cured him. "The team just seemed to arrive in the Kentucky game," he told reporters. "I don't think they've been lucky. They've just been hot. They simply found themselves. And if they stay hale and hearty, I think we can beat anybody and that includes Bradley again."

As the best team in New York, the Beavers received the bid to the eight-team NCAA field, where both Bradley and CCNY again played their way to the finals (again held in the Garden). CCNY got there by edging Ohio State and North Carolina State in the East regionals. Bradley advanced through the West with victories over UCLA and Baylor.

The second meeting of CCNY and Bradley in the NCAA finals had the fans and press chirping. In the closing moments, with CCNY leading by a point, Dambrot blocked a Melchiorre shot. The Beavers then scored an easy layup and took the NCAA championship, 71-68.

Chanting "Allagaroo," students and fans mobbed the streets in celebration. The college shut down classes the next day and the players were introduced at a celebration. College President Harry N. Wright told the crowd, "This is one of the proudest days of my life. This team came here to study, not to play basketball. I am proud of the team and what it has done for the college. I want to point out that they are given no scholarships to play ball, and they have not been imported to play ball. I am particularly proud of their high scholastic rating."

The New York Times reported that Mager, one of the heroes of both final games, missed the celebration because he was taking a mid-term exam. The jubilation carried right through to the next February when abruptly several CCNY players were arrested as part of the point shaving scandal. The investigation into gambling in college basketball revealed that between 1946 and 1950, 86 games in 23 cities had been fixed by 37 players. The players represented 22 colleges, but it was widely believed that the probe could have pinpointed dozens of others. The scandal brought an end to NCAA games in the Garden, as critics blamed the rabid atmosphere there for feeding the corruption.

Clair Bee at LIU was distraught. Several of his players were caught in the scandal. "Public confidence in college basketball is shattered," he said, "and the fault is partly mine. I was a win-'em-all coach who, by resorting to established practices, helped to create the emotional climate that led to the worst scandal in the history of sports."

In response, LIU's program was disbanded for six years. "We have flunked," Bee told other coaches. "We have not done the job that was expected for us in training the young people. I am not bitter. I am hurt, hurt desperately. When I was told that three of my boys had sold themselves, it was deep bereavement. I am not ashamed to say that I wept. It was then that something died within me."

As for CCNY, the investigation revealed that grade records had been falsified to allow its talented basketball recruits admission to the university, enough of an embarrassment to silence the Allagaroo cheers.

1951

If anything, the 1950-51 college basketball season was eventful. The NCAA tournament expanded its field to 16 teams. And Adolph Rupp's Kentucky Wildcats won their third NCAA championship, making Kentucky the first school and Rupp the first coach to capture three titles. But those tarts lost their sweetness in an atmosphere of uncertainty, as each day through the spring of 1951 newspaper headlines told of the expanding gambling investigation.

On the positive side, Duke's Dick Groat, who went on to baseball fame, scored 831 points, the single-season NCAA record, while Temple's Bill Mlkvy finished with a record scoring average—29.2 points per game. But Kentucky remained as the game's big story. Rupp had dug into his supply of All-Americans and come up with a young team seemingly poised at the edge of a dynasty. Two freshmen—Cliff Hagan and Frank Ramsey—had emerged as top-flight talents. At the heart of the team was junior center Bill Spivey. "I remember when he first came in to try out at Kentucky in the spring of his senior year in high school," Joe B. Hall said of Spivey. "He was 7 feet tall and weighed something under 170 pounds. One of the first things they did was get some weight on him. The year that Spivey was recruited, coach Rupp took the team on tour in Europe, but coach Harry Lancaster was back at the university working with Spivey. He was watching his diet more than he was watching his playing. Coach Lancaster would send reports to coach Rupp overseas about Spivey's weight. When Lancaster reported that Spivey had broken the 200-pound mark, coach Rupp wired back, "I know he can eat, but can he play?"

The answer was affirmative. Spivey developed a hook shot and showed a knack for rebounding and blocking shots. With Hagan and Ramsey, he gave the Wildcats a three-pronged attack that speared another NCAA title.

Having ended its relationship with Madison Square Garden, the NCAA selected Minneapolis, Minnesota, as the site of the 1951 finals. With its 16-team format, the tournament headed off in a new direction. Under the new rules, the selection committee would take the teams with the best won-lost percentages in the 10 major conferences. In addition, six teams would be tapped with at-large bids.

The draw of that first 16-game tournament laid the groundwork for tradition. Kentucky met cross-state rival Louisville in

the opening round of the East. The Cardinals successfully shut down Spivey, but forward Shelby Linville scored 23 points, a career best, and the Wildcats advanced, 79-68. In the second round, Rupp's team faced St. John's, the only New York school not implicated in the scandal. The Redmen featured a competitive little guard by the name of Al McGuire, younger brother of Dick. He scored five points and watched his Redmen go down, 59-43.

Kentucky's real test in the tournament came in the East finals against Illinois and forward Don Sunderlage. The Illini led by seven at the half, 39-32,. Then Spivey took over. He scored 28 points with 16 rebounds before fouling out in the fourth period. The game tightened, and with 10 seconds left Linville hit a 10-footer to give the Cats a 76-74 lead. Sunderlage's last hook shot missed at the buzzer, and once again Rupp was in the finals.

There they met Kansas State, coached by Jack Gardner. A balanced team with a deep bench, State held a two-point lead over Kentucky at the half. But then Kansas State went through an eight-minute stretch of the second half without scoring. That was enough for Kentucky to win going away, 68-58. Spivey scored 22 points with 21 rebounds for the Final, yet NCAA officials decided not to select an outstanding player.

The Kentucky dream abruptly ended there. Spivey became embroiled in the gambling scandal and was indicted for perjury. He maintained his innocence, and the case resulted in a hung jury. But Spivey's college career was finished, and the suggestion of impropriety dampened his pro prospects as well. Times were only going to get rougher for Rupp.

1952

When the 1951-52 season opened, Phog Allen—who would be known as "the Father of Basketball Coaching" and be selected to the Naismith Memorial Basketball Hall of Fame—was searching desperately for the one thing that had eluded him in nearly five decades of coaching: the NCAA championship. An outspoken and opinionated man, Allen had been particularly critical of the "sinful" atmosphere of college basketball in Madison Square Garden. With the scandal having run its course and taken its toll, Allen's Kansas team moved to the fore in the college game. The main reason for the Jayhawks' advancement was 6-foot-9 senior center Clyde Lovellette. He played a beefy inside game that made him college basketball's most accomplished performer. It also brought Allen his much desired NCAA championship.

Lovellette finished his senior year by setting the all-time NCAA scoring record, 1,888 points. His last two points of the season, in the NCAA finals against St. John's, allowed him to ease past the record of 1,886 points, set just days earlier by Duke's Dick Groat. Lovellette weighed more than 270 pounds by the close of his college career, leading the newspapers to dub him "Man Mountain." Allen designed an offense around his star and encouraged him to shoot freely and often. "He is closer to the basket than anyone else on the floor," Allen explained to reporters, "so I'd rather see him go for it than anyone else."

In the opening round game of the 1952 Midwest Regional, Lovellette scored 31 points against TCU. In the second round against St. Louis, he scored 44 points, setting a new tournament single-game scoring record. On the strength of that effort, Kansas strode to the finals in Seattle.

The Jayhawks' opponent, St. John's, had ousted top-ranked Kentucky in the second round of the East Regionals, 64-57, then dumped second-ranked Illinois and star center Johnny "Red" Kerr in the national semi-finals, 61-59.

In the national championship game in Seattle, the Redmen were carried by center Bob Zawoluk, who scored 20 points. But St. John's was no match for Lovellette's inside mastery. He muscled in 33 points as the Jayhawks prevailed easily, 80-63. For the first time since 1939, the NCAA selected an all-tournament team: Lovellette, Zawoluk, Kerr, Ron MacGilvray of St. John's and Dean Kelley of Kansas. Lovellette was named the outstanding player after setting tournament records for points (141) and rebounds (69). Also on the Kansas roster was a little-used substitute guard named Dean Smith.

1953

Deep. Quick. Big. Sharp-shooting. All the customary basketball adjectives applied to Indiana's 1952-53 Hoosiers, who ran up a 23-3 record on their way to winning the NCAA championship over defending champion Kansas.

They had a strong inside game in 6-foot-9 sophomore center Don Schlundt, who could score with either hand. They had an outside game in junior Bob "Slick" Leonard, a 6-foot-3 guard who could drop shots in from the perimeter. And they had the specialists, a 6-foot-5 rebounder in Charlie Kraak, and a defensive hawk in 6-foot-3 Dick Farley. To go with all that, they had a system, coach Branch McCracken's high-speed, up-tempo offense. That was the only way McCracken wanted to approach the game. His thoughts were to get the ball off the defensive boards and head the other way, the sooner, the better. To make sure his players had the wind to go with the game plan, he ran them four miles a day, beginning with the first day of classes in the fall.

His penchant for the fastbreak may seem strange considering McCracken played at Indiana in the late 1920s for coach Everett Dean, who was known for his controlled, half-court offenses. In Dean's system, McCracken led the team in scoring and earned All-America honors. But after college, McCracken became the coach at Ball State, where he developed his own philosophies and teams that were known for their running and gunning. When Dean decided to move to Stanford before the 1939 season, Indiana hired McCracken to replace him, and he brought the running game with him to Bloomington.

In just his second season, the "Big Bear" watched his Hoosiers, who had finished second in the Big Ten, beat Kansas for the 1940 NCAA championship. McCracken continued to rack up winning seasons after that, but heading into the 1952-53 season, his Indiana teams had never won a Big Ten championship, mostly because McCracken had trouble recruiting a big center to outmuscle league opponents. Ultimately, the coach's solution to the big-man problem was to grow one. When McCracken first recruited Don Schlundt out of South Bend, the center was 6-foot-6. But by his sophomore year at Indiana, Schlundt had grown to 6-foot-9. McCracken's bushy eyebrows arched with his smile as he watched Schlundt develop that fall. "He was always making his moves in the post," Charlie Kraak

said of Schlundt. "He could move pretty well. Once you hit him with the pass, he almost always got his shot off. He used the board a lot. He had a great touch."

And it had been developed just in time. The 1952-53 season brought an offensive explosion to college basketball, as more and more teams adopted fast-paced offensive schemes. Another major reason for the outburst was the NCAA's tampering with the free-throw rules in an attempt to cut down on excessive fouling. The changes had just the opposite effect, with the number of free-throws ballooning. It was not uncommon for a team to have 25 to 40 foul calls per game. Scores soared with the changes, from the 60s to the 80s, 90s, even beyond 100.

As a result, the season became a shootout with most major scoring records falling. Furman, led by Frank Selvy (who scored 100 points in one game), averaged 90.2 points per game and made 44.4 percent of its shots, both national records. Johnny O'Brien at Seattle set a new NCAA career scoring record: 2,537 points. Indiana would set no less than a dozen Big Ten scoring records. Schlundt himself would set four new records, including most points in a career. And he was just a sophomore.

The Hoosiers at last claimed the league championship and headed into NCAA tournament play with a 19-3 record. They barely escaped De Paul, 82-80, in the face of the Blue Demons' frantic defense. Indiana then beat 10th-ranked Notre Dame and advanced to the Final Four in Kansas City's Municipal Auditorium. In the semi-finals against LSU, Schlundt scored 29 and Leonard added 22, more than enough to offset a 29-point game by LSU sophomore Bob Pettit, as Indiana advanced, 80-67.

Suddenly, the NCAA had a rematch of its 1940 championship game. McCracken's Hoosiers faced Phog Allen's Kansas Jayhawks. The defending national champions featuring B.H. Born, Dean Kelley and Harold Patterson (Lovellette had graduated). It was a classic, a one-point nail-biter that took Allen and McCracken to the edge of their competitiveness. The teams went the distance with barely a basket separating them. The game was marred by at least one controversy and some technical fouls. With Kansas leading 53-52, Born banged into Charlie Kraak and was called for the foul. The scoring official ruled Born out of the game on fouls, but when Phog Allen protested that Born had only four fouls, the scorer agreed and changed his decision. That brought Indiana's McCracken off the bench.

Schlundt, Kraak and Leonard all drew technicals, and the two teams were never more than three points apart in the final period. The score was tied at 68 when Leonard went to the line with 27 seconds to go. "I wanted to make the shots as much as anything I've ever wanted in my life," he said later. "In fact, I had to make them." Usually a proficient free-throw shooter, Leonard missed his first but made the second, leaving the Hoosiers playing defense with a one-point lead. Kansas struggled on offense and had to settle for a late shot by substitute center Jerry Alberts. It missed, and the celebration began in Bloomington.

Schlundt had scored 30 points in Indiana's winning effort, but the NCAA named Born of Kansas as Most Outstanding Player, the first time a player for a losing team had received the award.

1954

The gambling probe had led to more woes at the University of Kentucky in 1952. Subsequent investigations had turned up additional charges of illegal payments to athletes, academic irregularities, and recruiting violations. As punishment, the NCAA and Southeastern Conference suspended the Wildcats, so they played no games during the 1952-53 season, choosing instead to practice and play intrasquad scrimmages.

Rupp may have been effectively barred from competing, but he wasn't about to stop building his team. "I will never be satisfied," Rupp is reported to have said, "until the men who suspended us hand us the national championship trophy." To that end, he ran practice three or four times per week during the season of probation. The scandal had taken its toll on the program, and he wasn't about to let it sink further. At the end of the 1952 season, Kentucky had only nine varsity players on scholarship. Although the Wildcats were on probation, Rupp restocked the program with young talent. "Coach Rupp brought in 12 to 15 freshmen," team captain Frank Ramsey recalled. "We had a tremendous group. We practiced three or four times a week." Four times during the 1952-53 season, beginning in December and ending in February, Rupp set up intrasquad scrimmages and invited Kentucky's basketball-crazy public. The four events drew a little more than 36,000 people. One scrimmage was held the night of an ice storm, the worst weather of the winter, and still 6,000 fans showed up.

Already a master motivator and strategist, Rupp used the adverse circumstances to build his team's mental toughness for the next year. "I think he felt the judge in New York had taken some very unwarranted potshots at him," Ramsey said when asked about Rupp's desire for vindication.

When Rupp's players returned to competition in 1954, they did so with a vengeance. Running the break to perfection, the Wildcats hammered out a 25-0 record with an average margin of victory of 27 points. "I hold no love for Kentucky," St. Louis University coach Ed Hickey said in December 1953 after Kentucky beat his team, 71-59. "But they're the sweetest-operating team to watch that I've ever seen. And that Frank Ramsey—I've said it before and I say it again—is the best college player in the country."

To go with Rupp's motivation, they had talent and experience. At 6-foot-4, Cliff Hagan was the center, with a smooth hook shot and a solid rebounding game. A 19.2 point-per-game career scorer, he had been a consensus All American in 1952 and would repeat the honors for 1953-54. Ramsey, too, had gotten All America notice in '52. A 6-foot-3 guard, he had quickness to go with his size and scored frequently in Rupp's fast-breaking offense, averaging 14.7 points per game. His outside shooting was good enough, but his quickness was his weapon. If he saw an opening, he was gone. Lou Tsioropoulos, at 6-foot-5, was the frontcourt defensive whiz, and 5-foot-10 guard Billy Evans, a junior, filled the same role in the backcourt. Phil Grawemeyer played the big forward, and Gayle Rose and Linville Puckett were the top subs.

Their break was a thing of beauty, and when they needed it, they could flash into a demoralizing full-court press. The only problem was, they didn't need it too often. Ramsey explained: "We had sat out a year, and we were coming back with that

great Kentucky tradition, with coach Adolph Rupp and our system. We were very confident in our system and our ability to execute it. "When Hagan took a hook shot, I knew that thing was going in. When we had a tough opponent like Tom Gola or Bob Pettit, I knew Lou Tsioropoulos would shut 'em down, or Billy Evans would shut 'em down."

In December, they steamrolled the Temple Owls, 86-59, as Hagan set a new Southeastern Conference single-game scoring record with 51 points. After drubbing Xavier, Wake Forest and St. Louis, the Wildcats opened their first UK Inviational on December 21. With the gambling scandal shutting down much of New York basketball, particularly in Madison Square Garden, there was a movement across the country "to return the game to the college campuses." The holiday tournament in Lexington was part of that movement, and Rupp didn't cheat the fans with low-grade competition.

In the first round, Kentucky ran right by a good Duke team, 85-69, and in the Final, they faced LaSalle with Tom Gola, the defending NIT champions. LaSalle would go on to win the NCAA tournament that spring, but the Wildcats stuffed them rather easily, 73-60. The streak continued from there, with Minnesota, Georgia Tech, DePaul, Tulane and Vanderbilt all falling by healthy margins. Ramsey said he doesn't recall just when the bad news hit Lexington. "At that time," he said, "there was a rule nobody was aware of until January or February stating that graduate students were ineligible for the NCAA tournament."

The NCAA informed Kentucky that Ramsey, Hagan and Tsioropoulos would all be ineligible for postseason play. Each of the three had graduated during the probation year, then come back to play their final season as graduate students. Across Kentucky there was a feeling that the NCAA was adding one extra punishment for the gambling scandal. "And the rest of these boys were in high school when those things happened," Ramsey told reporters. "Why'd they take it out on us?"

Stuffing their disappointment, the Wildcats ripped through the rest of their schedule, with no team coming closer than 15 points. Kentucky and LSU with Bob Pettit also finished the SEC schedule undefeated. To determine who would go to the NCAA tournament, the two schools faced off in Nashville. The Wildcats fell behind in the third quarter, but they went to their full-court press. That effort produced the necessary turnovers, while Tsioropoulos shut down Pettit, and Kentucky won, 63-56, for their 25th victory and the SEC championship.

Afterward, Rupp and the players voted not to accept the NCAA tournament bid, allowing LSU to go instead. As a result, the Wildcats never entered the tournament, leaving Tom Gola and LaSalle an open road to the title. The Philadelphia school struggled only once in the tournament, in the opening round against Fordham. Down by a bucket with four seconds left, Gola took an inbounds pass and drew a crowd of defenders. Instead of forcing a shot, Gola rifled a pass to teammate Fran O'Malley under the basket for a score at the buzzer to send the game into overtime. Once there LaSalle prevailed, 76-74. Gola finished with 28 points, but he was just getting started.

The next round brought an 88-81 win over NC State, an NCAA record for total points scored in a game. Gola had 26 rebounds to go with his 26 points. Navy was the next victim,

64-48, as Gola turned in 24 rebounds and 22 points. He slowed somewhat in the national semi-finals at Kansas City with only 19 points against Penn State, but LaSalle had little trouble with the Nittany Lions.

The championship, the first to be nationally televised, became a matter of unranked teams. Bradley had snaked through the West, defeating Oklahoma City, Colorado, Oklahoma A&M, and Southern Cal in turn. Gola and LaSalle struggled in the first half and trailed 43-42 at intermission. But in the second half, coach Ken Loeffler shifted from his man-to-man defense to a zone, and LaSalle claimed the championship easily, 92-76.

Gola, a consensus All-American, was named the tournament's outstanding player. The AP still voted Kentucky the top ranking in its poll. UPI, however, took its poll from the coaches, many of whom detested Rupp. Three of the 35 coaches voting failed to even mention Kentucky on the ballot. The Wildcats still collected enough points to finish second.

The measures taken against Kentucky were stern, but they helped college basketball overcome its darkest challenge. Within a decade, gambling scandal would strike the sport again, and would again be met with strong measures.

1955

Many of basketball's greatest players have been prolific scorers or flashy ball-handlers. Bill Russell was neither. He was simply the most successful athlete in the history of the game. He led the University of San Francisco to two NCAA championships in 1955 and '56, then helped the U.S. team to the gold medal in the 1956 Olympics in Australia. From there, he ran through an unparalleled professional career as the heart of a Boston Celtics team that won 11 NBA titles in 13 seasons.

Not a bad run for a guy who struggled to get playing time on his high school team. It seems that even the greatest players have a knock, and the one against Russell was that he couldn't shoot. And, frankly, he wasn't a great passer, either. He scored adequately enough, but he came along in the 1950s when the basketball ideal was a deadeye swisher. The jump shot was coming into vogue, and coaches everywhere seemed infatuated by acrobatic gunners. Russell, on the other hand, was the first of a new breed, the athletic big man. (At 6-foot-9, he could run the 440-yard dash in 49 seconds.) His shot-blocking skills were revolutionary, and his rebounding abilities controlled any game he played in. But far more important, he had a heart and a will dedicated solely to winning.

As Bob Cousy, his former teammate on the Boston Celtics, once said, "Bill Russell was the ultimate team player." Russell, Cousy explained, was willing to forego the ego thrill of scoring to concentrate on the defense and rebounding that made his team successful.

At McClymonds High in Oakland, Russell caught the attention of Hal DeJulio, an alumnus of the University of San Francisco, who asked coach Phil Woolpert to give him a tryout. The coach agreed, and after taking a look at Russell, offered a scholarship. The coach wasn't completely sold on the big youngster, but Russell had height and a degree of agility.

At San Francisco, Russell met life-long friend and teammate K.C. Jones. Like himself, Russell found that Jones believed in

defense almost out of desperation. Woolpert, too, was a defensive fanatic, and the three of them put together one of the most fearsome defensive units in the history of college basketball. The chief weapon was Russell's shot-blocking. "Heck," he once told reporters, "I'd rather block a shot any day than score. It seems to do more for team morale."

One of his first varsity appearances was against Pete Newell's University of California team featuring center Bob McKeen. Early on, Russell blocked McKeen's shot, reportedly leading Newell to exclaim on the sideline, "Now where did he come from?" It would be a question asked often around college basketball over the next two seasons as Russell's intimidation lifted San Francisco to the top of the rankings. Between December 1954 and March 1956, the Dons set what was then an NCAA record by winning 56 straight games.

In December 1954, Russell and his teammates faced eighth-ranked UCLA in the first round of a Los Angeles holiday tournament. Although his team was projected to lose big, Russell played UCLA's Wille Naulls tightly. San Francisco eventually lost, 47-40, but the game changed the way the Dons looked at themselves, Jones said. "Almost overnight, we became arrogantly confident, and we just rode that confidence." After that game, Woolpert shuffled the starting lineup, moving Hal Perry, a black, in at guard in place of Bill Bush, a white, meaning San Francisco would start more blacks than whites. To say the least, it was a unusual situation for the 1950s. "The beauty of it," Jones recalled, "was that Bill Bush said, 'That's well and good.' There was no hassle about him being demoted. He said, 'This is best for the team, and I'll do it coming off the bench.'"

With Perry and Jones at guard and Russell at center, Woolpert's lineup featured two seniors, 6-foot-5 Jerry Mullen and 6-foot-3 Stan Buchanan, at forwards. Mullen averaged nearly 14 points per game, but Buchanan had few offensive skills. He spent his time boxing out and playing defense. "He just ran and hustled and did the best he could," Jones said of Buchanan. "That's what we all did. If we happened to score, fine. Our defense was so good, it took pressure off us offensively."

The Dons would not lose another game for two years. They rolled through their schedule in the winter of 1955 with a defense that dismantled opponents. Woolpert explained it this way: "If your opponents can't shoot, they can't score." In the backcourt, Jones and Perry were a high-pressure duo. "We just had this approach of getting up and getting all over people," Jones explained. Having Russell at center allowed them to gamble defensively. If somebody broke through the defense, Russell usually blocked the shot or intimidated the shooter into missing.

He was fueled by a natural high-octane intensity that made him a quick leaper. And he was ambidextrous. His left hand shut down many right-handed shooters. In fact, much of the offense came from fast break opportunities created by Russell's defense, Jones said. "If Russell blocked the shot, we tried to determine which way it was gonna go. And then we were off to the races."

About the only relief opponents got was when it came time for him to shoot. But during his early years at San Francisco, offensive goaltending was within the rules, and Russell often used his jumping ability to "guide" errant shots into the basket. He did that often enough to lead the team in scoring, averaging better than 21 points per game.

With a 23-1 regular season record, USF entered the West Regionals in 1955 and sliced up West Texas State, 89-66, and Utah, 78-59. Only in the regional final were they tested, when Oregon State and 7-foot-3 center Swede Holbrook pushed them to the final whistle before falling, 57-56.

Oregon State adopted a strategy of double-teaming Russell while leaving Buchanan unguarded. Buchanan lacked confidence as a shooter and passed up several open shots until Woolpert ordered him to take them. To his teammate's relief, Buchanan hit a couple of baseline jumpers, forcing Oregon State to shift strategy. That created just enough of an opening for the Dons to escape.

At the Final Four in Kansas City, Russell scored 24 as San Francisco beat Colorado, 62-50. Third-ranked LaSalle and Tom Gola were the opponents in the Finals, having returned there by thrashing West Virginia, Princeton, Canisius in the East, before edging Iowa in the national semis.

Gola and his teammates, the defending national champions, were the favorites of the eastern basketball establishment. "At the time, nobody had heard of Bill Russell," Gola recalled. "The West Coast was not a prominent factor in NCAA basketball ... In fact, I had never seen Bill Russell until we met in the lobby of the hotel [in Kansas City during the NCAA finals]. He was coming in, and I was going out. I'll be honest with you. I've always said that Bill Russell is a great athlete. But in those days, I didn't think he could shoot, and I don't think he shot that well in the pros except for that little hook shot. But he had a defensive ability that nobody could match. In those days, there was no such thing as offensive goaltending, so when somebody took a shot, he could jump up and guide it into the basket. He would get maybe 20 points a game just steering in all the shots."

The press promoted a giant showdown between Russell and the 6-foot-5 Gola, but at the pre-game meal, Woolpert informed Jones that he would be playing Gola. Jones recalled his shock at the news. But Woolpert knew Jones was a strong leaper, and he figured if Gola got by Jones, Russell would always be there. Woolpert didn't want the task of guarding Gola to take Russell way from the basket.

The National Championship was tight for a half, as both teams performed in a dull trance. But in the second half Woolpert's strategy began to pay off as the Dons steadily outdistanced LaSalle to win, 77-63. Jones had 24 points, and Russell, who was named the Most Outstanding Player, had 23 with 25 rebounds. Gola finished with 16 but didn't score in the first 21 minutes of the game. "The guy who hurt us that night was K.C. Jones, with 24 points," Gola said, "and K.C. was not known for his shooting ability. Russell guarded Alonzo Lewis and also sagged off back into the pivot on me. Alonzo just couldn't hit his shots. If he had, it would have been nip-and tuck all the way. But that was one of those things. There's always a guy on the team who sacrifices, who plays good defense, who moves the ball, and that was K.C. He was the catalyst for those San Francisco. teams."

1956

Playmaker Hal Perry returned with Russell and Jones for the 1955-56 season. Junior forward Carl Boldt moved into the starting lineup, as did 6-foot-7 sophomore Mike Farmer.

Another sophomore, guard Gene Brown, joined the Dons' rotation. The only drawback was K.C. Jones' eligibility. An appendicitis attack had caused him to miss a season, and he had been granted an extra year of play. But his eligibility extended only through the regular season. He would be unable to play in the tournament.

Over the off-season, the NCAA had adopted what became known as the "Russell rule," widening the free throw lane in an effort to keep him farther away from the basket. It had little effect. "This is a hungry team," Woolpert said just before the season. His Dons would run through 25 wins during the regular season, leaving believers sprawled in their path. "They're the best college team I've ever seen," said St. John's coach Joe Lapchick. The greatness was mostly Russell's, said Bill Logan of Iowa, "You jump as high as you can and you're still only high enough to tap Russell on the shoulder." "Yes it's Russell," Woolpert replied, "but it's more than just him. Why, this is the finest college basketball team I've ever seen."

Any doubters remaining in the East ended their holdout early in the season. San Francisco appeared in the ECAC Holiday Festival in Madison Square Garden and blew away some of the best teams in the country. LaSalle fell the first night, 79-62, as Russell wiped 22 rebounds off the boards and scored 26. The next night the Dons did in Holy Cross and Tom Heinsohn, Russell's future teammate on the Boston Celtics, 67-51. Again Russell grabbed 22 rebounds and scored 24. The final night they beat UCLA with Willie Naulls, 70-53. Later in the season, they visited Pete Newell's California team, and the former San Francisco coach was ready with a slowdown. The Dons still won easily, 33-24, for their 40th straight victory.

By tournament time, their winning streak was 51 games, and it continued there. Jones, of course, was through with his eligibility and had to watch the game from the bench. But Brown filled in nicely. In order, San Francisco turned aside UCLA a second time, and Utah in the West Regional and Southern Methodist in the national semis, with Russell scoring 22 in each game.

The national championship, played in Northwestern University's new arena in Evanston, Illinois, brought San Francisco face to face with fourth-ranked Iowa and All-American Carl "Sugar" Cain. The Hawkeyes had left tournament victims Morehead State, Kentucky and Temple in their wake, but they were no match for Russell and company. San Francisco claimed its second championship, 83-71, and with it a $12,500 winner's share from the NCAA.

Russell scored 26 points in the final but wasn't named Most Outstanding Player. That award went to Temple's Hal Lear, who broke the tournament's single-game scoring record with a 48-point performance in the consolation game against Southern Methodist.

With Russell and Jones graduated, the Dons extended their number of wins to 60 straight into the 1956-57 season before losing to Illinois, 62-33. Over the 58 games of his last two years at San Francisco, Russell had averaged 20.7 boards.

1957

Serious students of Southern basketball have often noted in jest that Everett Case is the father of basketball at the University of North Carolina. The humor in this remark comes from the fact that Case coached at rival North Carolina State.

In the late 1940s and early '50s, Case's Wolfpack teams regularly drubbed the sickly Tar Heels, thus causing much anguish among the Carolina faithful. At one point, State won 15 straight games from the Heels. Finally, in August, 1952, UNC officials had had enough. To compete with Case, they hired Frank McGuire away from St. John's, where he had compiled a 106-36 record. At Carolina, McGuire would prove to be more than a remedy for the Wolfpack ailment.

Within five seasons, he would coach North Carolina to what was then the best record in the history of college basketball, a 32-0 undefeated season that culminated in the 1957 national championship. The secret to McGuire's success would be his ability to lure players from the New York playgrounds to the little academic community in Chapel Hill. McGuire already had the first of his recruiting successes in hand even before he decided to take the Carolina job, that being 6-foot-5 Lennie Rosenbluth, a willowy Jewish kid with a clear shooting conscience. McGuire dressed his northern players in blazers, schooled them in his basketball, and turned them loose on the Atlantic Coast Conference. They didn't overwhelm Case's State teams, but they held their own. By 1956, they had found a footing and finished the regular season 17-4, only to lose to Wake Forest in the ACC semi-finals. McGuire was bitterly disappointed by the loss, but it seems his anger was one of the motivating factors for the 1956-57 season, Rosenbluth's senior year.

In January of 1957, the Tar Heels moved into the top ranking in the polls in particularly sweet fashion, an 83-57 victory over Case's Wofpack on N.C. State's home floor at Reynolds Coliseum. With a 17-0 record, they went to Maryland and found themselves down by four with two minutes left. "You've been gracious winners, now be gracious losers," McGuire told them. But Kearns scored twice, and they escaped in double overtime.

In the ACC Tournament, Rosenbluth scored a record 106 points in three games, including a key three-point play to carry them past Wake Forest. He would score another 91 points in the East Regional, where the Heels earned the trip to the Final Four with comfortable wins over Yale, Canisius and Syracuse. Carolina arrived at the Final Four in Kansas City's Municipal Auditorium with a 30-0 record and the top ranking in both the AP and UPI polls. The newspapers were gleeful over what appeared to be an impending collision with second-ranked Kansas, led by 7-foot-2 sophomore Wilt Chamberlain.

Just about everybody figured the Jayhawks and their agile young giant would dash Carolina's dreams. For that story line to develop, Carolina still had to get past seventh-ranked Michigan State and Johnny Green in the semi-finals in a three-overtime thriller. From a 29-29 tie at the half, the game moved to a 58-58 close at regulation. With 11 seconds left in the first overtime, the Spartans held a 64-62 lead and a chance to win at the free-throw line. But Green missed the free throws. Brennan rebounded the missed shot, drove the length of the floor and scored to send the game into its second extra period. After both teams managed two points, the third overtime began at 66 all. Finally, Rosenbluth hit two shots, and Kearns added two free throws, enough to outlast Michigan State, 74-70. In less than

24 hours, they would meet Kansas for the title.

Phog Allen, the great recruiter, had been denied the pleasure of coaching his greatest recruit, Chamberlain, when before the season he was forced to retire at age 70. Dick Harp, Allen's assistant, took over and guided Kansas through a grand season. Chamberlain had averaged nearly 30 points, and the Jayhawks had lost only once, an upset to Iowa State. After a first-round bye, their trip through the Midwest Regional had carried them past Southern Methodist and Oklahoma City, as "Wilt the Stilt" scored 36 and 30 points. They were more than happy to take a homecourt advantage in Kansas City, and eliminated San Francisco (Bill Russell and K.C. Jones had graduated) in the national semi-finals by a whopping 80-56, as Chamberlain scored 32.

Carolina's match with Kansas would require the second triple overtime in two days. "In the '50s," Kearns explained, "we played the tournament games on consecutive nights, Fridays and Saturdays, instead of on Saturday and Monday like it is today. In the semi-finals we played Michigan State and that game was three overtimes, and then we played Kansas in the Finals for three overtimes. We played six overtimes in two days. That was like playing three and a half games in two days. We only had 10 players and I think only seven played over the last 17 or 18 games, so we all played virtually the whole game every game. For the last 21 or 22 games, I played every minute of every game."

McGuire had a plan to deflate the tension from the championship game. He sent the 5-foot-10 Kearns out to jump center against Chamberlain. Rosenbluth recalled, "With Tommy jumping center against Wilt, we all had a little chuckle, and it just took all the tension out of the game." Of the opening tip, Kearns said, "I really didn't know anything about the plan for me to jump center against Wilt until coach McGuire said something to me five minutes before the game. I just passed it off, however. After the player introductions, we sat on the bench and he said, 'Tommy, you're going out to jump against Wilt.' I was just as surprised as anybody." The biggest surprise was that Kearns won the tip. "I got it," he recalled. "But I think Wilt was taken aback, as I think the whole team was. It set a tone for the game, and we jumped off to a very big lead as a result."

The Jayhawks shot terribly (27 percent for the first half) and the Heels superbly (65 percent). Even so, Carolina ended the first half with only a 29-22 lead. In the second, Chamberlain shook loose from the zone, and the Jayhawks moved into position to claim the title. Carolina was tired, and its frontcourt had gotten into foul trouble trying to shut down Chamberlain. But for some reason, Harp went to the stall with a three-point lead and 10 minutes left.

With 1:45 left in regulation, Rosenbluth fouled out having scored 20. Only a late basket by senior Bob Young allowed the Heels to tie it at the end of regulation, 46 all. The first overtime, produced a single basket by each team and the second overtime was scoreless.

With under 10 seconds left in the third overtime and Kansas holding 53-52 lead, Carolina's Quigg was fouled in the act of shooting and awarded two shots. After McGuire called timeout, Quigg calmly made both, then sealed the championship, 54-53, by slapping away the Jayhawks' inbounds pass as time expired. Carolina had completed the perfect season, 32-0, the most wins ever crammed into an undefeated NCAA championship season.

Chamberlain was named the tournament's Most Outstanding Player but would never make another visit to the Final Four. Kansas didn't reach the tournament his junior year, and he played with the Harlem Globetrotters his senior year. McGuire and Rosenbluth flew off for an appearance on the *Ed Sullivan Show*. As for the rest of the Heels, they returned to Raleigh-Durham Airport and found a crowd of 10,000 waiting to celebrate. Fans there had seen the games broadcast on local television, and it wouldn't be too long before ACC basketball would pioneer college sports television.

1958

College basketball entered the 1957-58 season, stocked with a wealth of future NBA stars. Oscar Robertson, a Cincinnati sophomore, led the nation in scoring with a 35.1 average. Elgin Baylor, also averaging more than 30 points per game, carried the University of Seattle to the national championship game. Jerry West was the firepower in West Virginia's arsenal, shooting the Mountaineers to the top ranking in both the UPI and AP polls, but his team was again upset in the first round of the NCAA tournament. Wilt Chamberlain also scored better than 30 per game, yet the Jayhawks were bounced out of championship competition by cross-state rival, Kansas State, coached by Tex Winter.

For all their ability, none of the aforementioned players could find a path to take their teams to the national title. Instead, the limelight was taken once again by the Baron in the brown suit, Kentucky's Adolph Rupp, who guided a collection of unheralded players to the school's fourth NCAA championship.

His team was ranked ninth in the AP poll, but the UPI poll, voted by Rupp's fellow coaches, made no mention of the Wildcats. "I know I have plenty of enemies," he told reporters, "but I'd rather be the most-hated winning coach in the country than the most-popular losing one." Whereas Rupp's powerhouse 1949 team had been called the "Fabulous Five," he took to calling the '58 unit the "Fiddlin' Five," sometimes with affection, sometimes not.

With a string of undefeated Southeastern Conference seasons in his wake, Rupp and his followers considered a 12-2 finish nothing more than ho-hum. But in the Mideast Regional, played on Kentucky's home floor, the Wildcats bullied Miami of Ohio, 94-70, and a good Notre Dame team, 89-56. Suddenly, the press began to recognize that Kentucky's Vern Hatton and John Cox weren't such bad players after all. But it was the team's special sixth man—a continued "home-court advantage"—that made the difference in the Final Four. The championship was played in Louisville's Freedom Hall, where Kentucky basketball mania ruled the proceedings.

The national semi-final against Temple and All-American guard Guy Rodgers was a thriller. Kentucky and the Owls had met once during the regular season, a match that took three overtimes before Kentucky won on a 47-foot shot by Hatton at the buzzer. The NCAA confrontation was just as tight. Temple led 60-59 with 15 seconds left, but Rodgers missed a free throw for Temple and Hatton made a layup seconds later for a 61-60 win.

The Baron's boys met Seattle and Elgin Baylor for the national championship. It was a tantalizing matchup: Baylor, a great African-American player with an unknown team, against Rupp's lilly-white dynasty. Baylor, who had transferred to Seattle from Idaho, had grown up on the playgrounds of Washington, D.C. Although he played far from the eye of eastern media, it hadn't taken him long to garner national recognition.

A then-record NCAA crowd, 18,803, squeezed into Freedom Hall for the game, and the Kentuckians present weren't disappointed. Rupp outwitted Seattle coach John Castellani, who had assigned Baylor to guard Kentucky forward John Crigler. The Baron simply directed that the ball go to Crigler and that Crigler drive against Baylor. The Seattle star was called for three personal fouls in the first 10 minutes of play, which brought the raised eyebrows of more than a few observers and complaints of home cooking from Seattle fans.

Despite that, Seattle led by three at the half. And with Baylor showing a superhuman caution, the Chieftains held a 61-60 lead midway through the second half. But then Hatton and Cox started scoring and pushed Kentucky to Rupp's fourth championship in 11 seasons, 84-72. Baylor scored 25 points in the championship (he made only nine of 32 attempts from the floor) and was named the outstanding player. Oscar Roberston had scored 56 points, an NCAA record, in a regional consolation game against Arkansas.

1959

College basketball's superstars—Oscar Robertson of Cincinnati and Jerry West of West Virginia—finally carried their teams to the Final Four in 1959, but the championship trophy was claimed by California, a team of modest talent but superior coaching.

Coach Pete Newell armed his California Bears with a clawing, pressure defense. That, and a steady, controlled offense were enough to overcome first Robertson, then West, two of the all-time great basketball talents. With the college game's overall level of play obviously improving, the 1959 season marked the beginning of the NCAA tournament's third decade. Television had yet to distend the popularity of the game, but there were signs of steady growth. More than 15 million people had paid to see college games in 1958 and 1959. Big college programs and tournament committees across the country began looking for larger arenas to accommodate the crowds.

The '59 finals were again held in Louisville's Freedom Hall, and the pressure for tickets was even greater because the University of Louisville Cardinals were surprise participants in the Final Four after beating Eastern Kentucky, second-ranked Kentucky and third-ranked Michigan State to claim the Mideast Regional crown. However, the real story of the '59 season was California's successive dismissals of Cincinnati and West Virginia.

As a junior, Oscar Roberston won the nation's scoring title (32.6 ppg) for the second consecutive time while leading Cincinnati through the Midwest Regional. He did all chores: ball handling, scoring, rebounding. Coach George Smith's Bearcats sat poised at the edge of a dynasty. Cincinnati would make five straight appearances in the Final Four. But for all his greatness, Robertson would never win college championship.

Jerry West played much the same role for West Virginia, a do-it-all superman of rebounding, scoring and ball handling. Incredibly, the 6-foot-3 West played forward for the Moutaineers. In 1958, 6-foot-10 center Lloyd Sharrar had helped West Virginia to a top ranking in the polls. But Sharrar had graduated, and the burden fell on West for '59. He responded with a remarkable feat in the East Regionals.

West Virginia beat Dartmouth, 82-68, in the first round, then fell into deep trouble against St. Joseph's in a second round game in Charlotte, North Carolina. With 13 minutes to go in the game, St. Joseph's led, 67-49, only to watch West score 21 points in nine minutes. When the smoke cleared, West had 36 points in carrying the Mountaineers to a 95-92 miracle win. Reaching once more into their bag of dreams, they stretched past Boston University in the East finals, 86-82, to earn their first trip to the Final Four. There, they doused the hopes of hometown favorite Louisville, 94-79, and waited for the Cincinnati/California survivor.

The Bears featured 6-foot-10 Darrall Imhoff at center and flanked him with defensive specialists Bob Dalton and Jack Grout. Newell's pressure worked perfectly, as Cal's defense held Robertson to 19 points and Imhoff's hook shot anchored the offense for a 64-58 win.

The Bears used that same steadiness in the Final to take a 12-point lead against West Virginia in the second half, but once again West turned on his magic. The Mountaineers raced back, but ran out of time. They never regained the lead, losing 71-70.

"I had my hands on the ball about midcourt with no time left on the clock," West recalled, "and I said, 'If I could have just gotten one more shot ...' But it wasn't to be."

West, who had scored 160 points in five games, was named the outstanding player. He had scored 28 in the final, but California had allowed West Virginia only 55 shots.

1960

When Fred Taylor became coach of the Ohio State Buckeyes in the late 1950s, he sought help from the master coach of the era, Pete Newell, whose University of California Bears had just won the 1959 NCAA championship.

Taylor learned his lessons well. The classroom began as Newell's off-season clinic, but the final grade wasn't handed out until the next March, when Newell's Bears and Taylor's Buckeyes played for the national title at the Cow Palace in San Francisco.

Newell recalls that Taylor first approached him during a clinic in Moorehead, Minnesota. "Freddie had taken over the year before at Ohio State," Newell said, "and they had the worst defensive record in Big Ten history. He comes to my clinic and says, 'Pete, I really want to talk to you. I'd like to pick your brain on defense. Will you help us?' I said fine. So I spend about three hours every afternoon going over just defense with Fred. In December the next year, I'm playing against Jerry West's team [West Virginia] in the L.A. Classic. And Fred's assistant comes to me. He's got a list of questions a foot long that he says Fred needs answers to. I answer all his questions, and later in the season Fred meets me somewhere, and he's got a few more questions. What do you think happens? I end up playing Ohio State in the NCAA finals and he beats me with

some of the defensive things we talked about."

"What coach Taylor learned paid off," said Indiana coach Bobby Knight, who was a substitute on Ohio State's 1960 team, "because as the '60 season wore on, we became a better and better defensive team." The heart of Taylor's exceptional team in 1960 was a talented group of sophomores, including Jerry Lucas, John Havlicek and Mel Nowell. Lucas, a fluid 6-foot-8 center, could shoot, run the break, and pass like a point guard. To go with the sophomores, Taylor had veterans Larry Siegfried and Joe Roberts. Together, they comprised one of the finest shooting teams in college basketball history.

"Larry had been the leading scorer for Ohio State the year before with a 20-point average," Havlicek said of Siegfried, "and Joe Roberts was a seasoned veteran. He was a great rebounder. Siegfried had great confidence and, of course, Jerry never played like a sophomore. He always played beyond his years."

Gaining more confidence as their defense improved, the Buckeyes charged to the Big Ten championship with only three regular season losses. "When we played Indiana tough on their home floor, we knew we could play with just about anyone in the country," Havlicek said. "As sophomores, we really didn't fear anything. We just went out and played as hard as we could." From the momentum of their conference title, the third-ranked Buckeyes sliced apart their competition in the Mideast Regional: Western Kentucky, 98-79, and Georgia Tech, 86-69.

The Final Four brought more of the same. In addition to Newell's California team, the games in San Francisco that year featured Cincinnati with Oscar Robertson, whose talent encompassed all of the game, from playground razzle-dazzle to team strategy. He seemed to see everything on the court and understand it. After two years of missing the national championship, he and his Cincinnati teammates were very hungry.

The Bearcats had come into the NCAA tournament with a 26-1 record and the top ranking in the Associated Press poll. But in San Francisco, they met Newell's team for the second year in a row, which was ranked tops in the UPI poll. Newell's highly structured club held Robertson to 18 points and knocked off Cincinnati, 77-69, giving many observers the idea that the Bears would win their second straight championship.

Ohio State, however, had become a complete team. Newell's tutoring on defense had helped the Buckeyes work out their problems, thus freeing their bountiful offense. In the semifinals, they faced NYU, which featured Tom "Satch" Sanders, who would later join Havlicek as a teammate on the great Boston Celtics teams of the 1960s. The Buckeyes humbled NYU, 76-54, setting up the matchup of student versus the master, California against Ohio State for the national championship.

The Buckeyes killed the Bears with blistering shooting, hitting 15 of their first 16 shots, taking a 37-19 half-time lead. In the lockerroom, a stunned Newell mentioned to his players that they needed to get more defensive rebounds. Star center Darrall Imhoff reportedly answered, "Coach, there have only been three, and I got all of 'em."

"The final ball game was really over at half-time," Havlicek said. "That first half may have been the most awesome half a team ever had in a championship game."

Although California cut the lead to eight points for a time

in the second half, Ohio State surged ahead again and won, 75-55. Nearly 30 years later, Newell said he still didn't regret giving Taylor the help. "Believe it or not, we had a defensive plan," Newell said. "But they beat us with their quickness, especially Mel Nowell [who scored 15 points on six of seven from the field]. That was the only time I felt our defense was a step slow."

Lucas led five Buckeyes in double figures with 16 points and 10 rebounds, enough to earn him the tournament's Most Outstanding Player Award.

1961

For 1960-61, the basketball world was the Buckeyes' oyster, or so it seemed throughout much of the regular season as they dominated both the UPI and AP polls. But their surprise Ohio neighbors at the University of Cincinnati were just as good, finishing at the number two spot in both polls. Bearcat coach George Smith had moved up to the athletic director's post, and Ed Jucker, his assistant, had taken over. Oscar Robertson had graduated, but his presence had attracted a number of other talents to the program: Paul Hogue, Tom Thacker, Tony Yates, Bob Wiesenhahn and Carl Bouldin.

With a run-and-gun offense, Cincinnati and Robertson had reached the top ranking in the nation and fought their way to the Final Four in 1959 and '60. The excitement of the Robertson teams had drawn a throng of supporters to Bearcats games. "The fans had loved watching Robertson and his teams run up and down the floor," Jucker said. But each year at the Final Four, Cincinnati had lost to Newell's California teams that featured uncompromising defense and patient, controlled offense.

Watching from the bench as an assistant, Jucker had come to admire Newell's style. So once he became head coach, Jucker decided that he, too, would downshift Cincinnati's attack into a low-gear, patient offense, while emphasizing defense. At the time, he wasn't even thinking about trying to match the success of the Robertson years, Jucker said. "The control game was really to survive, for myself, the players and the program."

At best he figured, his team might win 15 games. Never in his wildest imagination did Jucker think his team would take two straight NCAA championships and come within a free-throw of a third one. "I was interested in being competitive," Jucker said. "I figured if we could hang in there and keep the games close we would create enough excitement to keep most of our fans."

His new approach brought arched eyebrows from nearly everyone the first few weeks of the 1960-61 season, Jucker said. The fans didn't like it, and the players weren't convinced either. "We lost two conference games and three of the first eight we played," the coach recalled. "Those first eight ball games were almost unbearable because the kids were looking at me tongue-in-cheek. The fans were booing. It wasn't easy."

Jucker, however, was determined to sell the players on what he called the "science of percentage basketball," or in simpler terms, working for good shots. "The closer you are to the basket, the easier it is to score," was the point he drummed into his players. He wanted his teams to control the ball and wait for the other team to make a mistake. "On defense, we try to pressure opponents into a pattern they are not used to playing,"

Jucker explained to reporters at the time. "We want them to play another game, a game they don't know."

The change was a calculated risk, but the stakes were fairly certain. "I knew I was asking for trouble," the coach conceded later. "If it didn't work, I was dead." With the pressures of modern college basketball, some new coaches today might not be so bold. But Jucker was the old school type. In addition to serving as the assistant basketball coach, he was a professor in the school's physical education department and head coach of the Cincinnati's highly successful baseball team, (where had coached Sandy Koufax).

There were two primary obstacles to Jucker's success. First, Robertson had moved across town to star for the Cincinnati Royals in the NBA. He took thousands of Bearcats fans with him. Robertson remained supportive of his old college, but his presence in the city was a reminder of the old style. The second major problem was his players, Jucker said. "They all wanted to be Oscar Robertson. But I finally convinced them that if we all played as one, they could add up to an Oscar Robertson. Some would shoot, some would dribble, all would play defense. In the end, we didn't have an All-American. But we had an All-American team."

As might be imagined, the toughest to convince were those who had played with Robertson under the old system, specifically seniors Bob Wiesenhahn and Carl Bouldin. Wiesenhahn, a rugged 6-foot-4, 215-pound forward, shared playing time as a junior, but came on as a starter to lead the team in scoring with a 17.1 average for the '61 season. Bouldin, a 6-foot-1 guard, was the team's best outside shooter, but Jucker didn't go much for outside shooting. "It took them a while to adjust," Jucker said, "but they did." It helped that Bouldin was an all-around athlete who had pitched for Jucker's baseball team and would go on to a solid career in the majors.

A major key to the Bearcats' eventual turnaround was veteran, junior Paul Hogue, a bulky 6-foot-9 center. Bespectacled and easy going, Hogue had a favorite expression, "Everything's jelly," Jucker recalled. "Meaning everything is fine, sweet." With Hogue at center, it would eventually prove to be. A power rebounder and excellent defensive player, Hogue also possessed good offensive skills, including a short jumper and a half hook. As much as the veterans, the newcomers played a large part in the Bearcats' eventual success. At 6-foot-2, sophomore forward Tom Thacker was the one Cincinnati athlete who could play above the rim. In fact, he came to be known as "the tallest 6-foot-2-inch player in basketball" because of his leaping ability. The other newcomer, playmaker Tony Yates, was a sophomore in name only. An Army veteran, Yates was older than the others and played like it. "He was a leader and a great defensive player," Jucker said. "Being older, he had the experience. He was good with the other players. When they made mistakes, he gave 'em a pat on the back. He was the coach on the floor."

Paired with Bouldin in the backcourt, Yates also had fewer scoring opportunites. "I seldom allowed them to shoot," Jucker said of his guards. "They didn't like it. But at the end of the season, they did pretty well."

If the guards wanted to score, their opportunities came from the Bearcats' trapping press. But there was no reaching for the ball. Jucker didn't want the fouls. The press was there to force

mistakes and bad passes that could be stolen. And if scoring wasn't a job for the guards, ball-handling was. Jucker despised turnovers. "The pride we had in ball-handling, that was a way of life," the coach said. "If somebody turned over the ball, it was almost a time out. We wanted to find out what's going on here."

The Bearcats' early problems featured a 17-point loss to St. Louis and a 19-point defeat by Bradley. Fortunately, they got a key win over Dayton and established their confidence. After opening at 5-3, they lost no more games. And by NCAA tournament time, Cincinnati was ranked second in the country.

Ohio State was riding a 32-game winning streak and ranked first in both polls. Led by Lucas and Havlicek, Ohio State won the Mideast Regional over Kentucky while Cincinnati battled in the Midwest. The Bearcats had an easy second-round game, deleting Texas Tech, 78-55. But the regional final against Kansas State was another matter. With 10 minutes left in the game, Cincinnati trailed by seven. Yet somehow, its deliberate offense generated a flurry of baskets and outdistanced Kansas State down the stretch, 69-64.

The semi-finals of the 1961 Final Four in Kansas City featured two blowouts. Ohio State beat St. Joseph's, 95-69, and Cincinnati numbed Utah, 82-67. But the Finals offered one of those dream-time matchups for college basketball. Number one against number two, and both teams from Ohio. The Buckeyes were listed as solid favorites.

Jucker, as usual, wanted to stay in the game until half-time, keep it close, then win at the end. Ohio State coach Fred Taylor figured that forcing Hogue into foul trouble was the way to go. As it turned out, both coaches got their way. State led, 39-38, at the half, and Hogue had three fouls. But the Cincinnati center stayed in the game the second half, and while he only finished with nine points and seven rebounds, he made Lucas work for his shots. The Ohio State center finished with 27 points and 12 rebounds, but the Bearcats crashed the boards and stopped State's fast break. It was enough, as Jucker had hoped, to put them in position to win. With a minute left, the Bearcats led 61-59, but State's Bobby Knight (the future Indiana coach was a sub for Ohio State) made a layup that sent it to overtime.

In the extra period, Yates made two free throws to give Cincinnati the lead, 66-64. And after OSU's Larry Siegfried missed a free throw, Jucker sent his team into a stall with a 66-65 lead. From there, the discipline paid off. State fouled, and Yates made the key free throws. Cincinnati rode that format to its first championship, 70-65. "We did nothing special," Jucker told reporters afterward. "All we did was a job. Each person did a job. No all-Americans—just a bunch of great defenders, shooters and hustlers." Back home, the fans had forgotten their worries about the run-and-gun days. Cincinnati Councilman Gordon Rich called the victory "the greatest event that has ever happened in the city of Cincinnati. This is the greatest team in the world."

1962

Strangely, college basketball saw its 1961 circumstances repeated in 1962, with only a few changes in the script. Ohio State was again the top-ranked team in both polls, with only Siegfried and Rickie Hoyt gone from the '61 team.

College basketball had again been rocked by point-shaving scandals, as players and teams across the country were caught up in the investigation. But the atmosphere seemed to have little effect on the Buckeyes' march to the top. They nailed Western Kentucky, 93-73, in the second round of the Mideast regional, then pushed past third-ranked Kentucky, 74-64. Cincinnati, on the other hand, had some major changes. Eventually Wiesenhahn and Bouldin would be replaced in the lineup by sophomores Ron Bonham and George Wilson, but not until they gained some maturity.

A 6-foot-5, 200-pound forward out of Indiana, Bonham had a smooth offensive style. "One of the greatest pure shooters I've ever seen," Jucker said. He wasn't fast but had a quick first step. He was best at shooting off the screen. But as a young player, he wanted his shot a little farther out. Jucker, of course, demanded an inside focus. Wilson, on the other hand, was a 6-foot-8 center/forward out of Chicago, also highly recruited. He had good jumping ability and his own style on offense. The team, however, was focused on Hogue's power game. Both sophomores had trouble accepting that, Jucker said. Then came the Holiday Festival at Madison Square Garden in New York. Both young players wanted badly to appear before the big city crowd.

Jucker had them start the game on the bench. When you're ready to play the way I want you to play, just whisper to me, Jucker recalled telling both players. "It wasn't long before they whispered," the coach said. "They started every game after that." And Cincinnati resumed its championship drive. The Bearcats had two early-season losses, then battled past Bradley and Drake to win the Missouri Valley Conference and a bid to the NCAAs. That was enough to earn Cincinnati the number two ranking in the polls. In the Midwest Regional, Cincinnati pushed aside Creighton, 66-46, and Colorado, 73-46.

But the Final Four in Louisville brought an end to Cincinnati's easy run. John Wooden's first Final Four team, the 1962 UCLA Bruins, with Walt Hazzard, John Green and Gary Cunningham, pushed the Bearcats to the brink of elimination. Cincinnati ran out to an early lead, but UCLA came back, setting up a second half of changing leads. Finally, Tom Thacker scored with 10 seconds left to give the Bearcats a shot at their second title. Hogue had the best game of his college career, scoring 36 points with 19 rebounds.

In the other bracket, Ohio State beat Wake Forest, 84-68, but Lucas injured his knee with eight minutes left in the game. With Lucas hobbled, Cincinnati easily claimed a second championship, 71-59. And most observers, including Ohio State coach Fred Taylor, agreed that even a healthy Lucas probably wouldn't have changed the outcome. Cincinnati had become the best team in college basketball.

"The key again was our ability to get the ball in to Hogue," Jucker told reporters, "and our control of the boards. I also thought our defense was terrific. This was real satisfying victory. We have a dedicated team and we proved to the world it is the greatest." With 22 points and 19 rebounds in the Final, Hogue was named the tournament's Most Outstanding Player.

1963

The Cincinnati machine needed only a few adjustments in 1963. George Wilson shifted to center, senior Larry Shingleton

moved in at guard, and the Bearcats rolled on.

The roles shifted again, but the approach was the same. Wilson was a rebounding terror and averaged 15 points a game. Bonham did much of the shooting and led the team with a 21 point scoring average. Yates (who went on to become the head coach at Cincinnati two decades later) became known as the premier defensive player in the country. Thacker averaged almost 16 points and 10 rebounds per game. As a team, they marched to the top of both polls, with a defense that created nightmares for opponents. "I saw Cincinnati beat Kansas," Tulsa coach Joe Swank said early in the 1962-63 season, "and they just looked invincible. I couldn't sleep after I watched them play."

They entered the NCAA tournament with a single loss and seemed headed for a third straight championship. The only thing that stopped them was a little five-man team from Loyola of Chicago. Ultimately, the NCAA championship would come down to a confrontation between the country's highest scoring team, Loyola, averaging 91.8 points per game, and its stingiest defensive team, Cincinnati, giving up just 52.9 points per game.

Loyola coach George Ireland had a high-scoring but finely disciplined team that featured All-American guard Jerry Harkness. In the frontcourt, Ireland worked 6-foot-7 Leslie Hunter and 6-foot-6 Vic Rouse, giving the Ramblers a blend of speed and power.

Behind Bonham, who had been named All-American, Cincinnati took a strong lead in the championship game and appeared a shoo-in for an unprecedented third straight championship. At the midpoint of the second half, the Bearcats led 45-30. But then a stretch of fouling chilled their momentum. Loyola closed the gap with its potent offense, and Cincinnati responded with missed shots and turnovers. Finally, the game came down to a 53-52 Cincinnati lead with seconds left and Shingleton at the line for one and one. He made the first but missed the second, giving Harkness just enough time to rebound, drive the length of the floor and score to send the game into overtime.

Once there, the teams traded baskets until the last second when Rouse rebounded a miss and banked it back in to give the Ramblers the title, 60-58. "Our game plan worked for us 99 out of 100 times," Yates said afterward. "On this night, it didn't."

Sitting in his South Carolina retirement home years later, Jucker offered a matter-of-fact appraisal. "We got into foul trouble and missed our free throws," the coach said. "It was as simple as that. I guess that's what makes the sport so great." Spoken like a coach not afraid to make a decision. And certainly not afraid to live with the results.

1964

When observers talk about the "genius" of John Wooden, they point out that he won NCAA championships with all types of teams. Tall ones. Mid-sized ones. Even short ones. Probably none of his teams cements his reputation more than his first championship club, the 1963-64 UCLA Bruins. The short ones.

Asked to list what he considered the very best teams in the history of college basketball, University of Louisville coach Denny Crum included the '63-64 Bruins. Crum, who played

for Wooden and later served as his assistant, pointed to the strength of the backcourt with Walt Hazzard and Gail Goodrich. "Talk about two great guards," Crum said. "That team didn't have the size, but they were relentless with the zone press, which was relatively new to college teams. As the game wore on, they started anticipating passes and moves. They might be down 15 points, and, all of a sudden, boom, they'd be right back in the game and just beat you with their quickness."

Hazzard, who later coached at UCLA, said the team drew its strength from a specialized chemistry. "We went 30-0," Hazzard said, "and we had no starter larger than 6-foot-5. The chemistry of that ball club was incredible. First, the architect was Coach Wooden, the philosopher of basketball. He found five players who liked his style, who were extremely competitive and were winners, and accepted their roles with pride. My role was the leader, the spirit of the team," Hazzard said. "I had come from a great basketball tradition in high school [Overbrook] in Philadelphia, where I had been a scorer. At UCLA, I became the playmaker and offensive quarterback. I accepted that role.

"I knew I could have been the leading scorer, but Gail Goodrich was a great scorer. If he missed five in a row, that was no big deal to him. He would just hit the next five. He was a hungry guy, who liked to score points. The other players on the team realized that in the fast-break situations, if he was the guy in the middle, he was gonna take the shot.

"Jack Hirsch, a 6-foot-3 forward, was our top defender, always assigned to the other team's top scorer. He had the instincts, the tenacity. He knew how to shut a guy down. In junior college he had averaged 38 points a game, but at UCLA he was the defender. Fred Slaughter, our 6-foot-5 center, weighed about 250 pounds. He was ideal for the high-post offense John Wooden ran. Even with that size, he was the high school 100-yard dash champion in Kansas. He played up front on our press, but when the ball crossed half court, he'd still beat everybody back. "

In retrospect, it was the team that epitomized Wooden's brilliance, Hazzard said. "He took the strengths of his individual players and adjusted his system to maximize those abilities. Keith Erickson, at 6-foot-5, was our fifth man on the 2-2-1 press. He was a great player, and athlete with great reactions, a great rebounder with excellent timing. Above all, he was a fierce competitior. To that, Wooden added his two players off the bench, Kenny Washington and Doug McIntosh. Coach Wooden just fit all these pieces together to make a great team."

Wooden's "brilliance" had yet to be discovered in the early 1960s. In a dozen years at UCLA he had become a bit frustrated by the program's lack of national success. "I wanted to win a national championship very much," Wooden recalled, "and I think it's quite possible that, prior to winning one in 1964, I might have wanted it so much I hurt my players in one or two instances."

After a stint in the Navy during World War II and two years at Indiana State, Wooden had come to UCLA in 1949 and immediately turned a loser into a winner. But his teams fought for more than a dozen years to rise above regional competition. For much of that period, UCLA had a tiny gym. And although he won, Wooden's ability as a coach was held in question in the

West, where Phil Woolpert at San Francisco and Pete Newell at California were winning with disciplined, patient offenses. Beyond that, Wooden showed a countenance of pious discipline that didn't endear him to other coaches.

"The Wooden teams were all different but all alike in the regimen," said broadcaster Curt Gowdy said. "They ran those high-post offenses. I noticed little things about them, how they'd hold their arms up in the free throw lane ready for the rebound, how they'd always banked their side shots. When they'd practice they had a drill where they'd come down, bounce to the baseline and shoot a little bank shot outside the baseline. I asked Wooden about that. He just thought it was an easier way to shoot than aiming straight for the hoop. His teams had beautiful skills fundamentally.

"Wooden was a deceiving man in that he mildly rolled up his program during the games," Gowdy said. "In practice he was tough. When he was a player he was tough. He would drive and crash into the bleachers on layups and played the game hard. His teams played that way." That toughness translated into persistence as Wooden worked the pieces into place. Heading into the '60s, he increased his player rotation to where he was working a first unit of seven or eight men. And he studied various forms of the full-court press, which he had used off and on during his years at UCLA.

The big breakthrough came in the signing of Hazzard, who was considered a blue-chipper out of high school. His 1962 team featured Hazzard, Slaughter at center, forwards Gary Cunningham and Pete Blackman, and guard John Green. They went to the Final Four and took champion Cincinnati to the wire before losing by a basket in the semi-finals.

The 1963 season brought Gail Goodrich, Keith Erickson, Fred Goss and Jack Hirsch into a unit with Hazzard and Slaughter. "A lot of people don't realize that that team was very good the year before," Wooden said of his '62-63 team. "I had instituted the 2-2-1 zone press, and we won the conference championship. We were knocked off in the regionals by Arizona State. They had a tremendously hot-shooting team. They just hit everything they shot, and we got behind early and couldn't catch up."

By the '64 season, Wooden had added sixth man Kenny Washington. With a solid store of talent, his team received a bit more pre-season publicity than usual. But most of the publications and their experts agreed that UCLA didn't have enough height to challenge for the national championship. The team, however, was a thing of beauty in its spare precision. The Bruins generated their offense like lightning off their press. Hirsch and Goodrich were on the front line, pressuring the inbounds pass. Slaughter and Hazzard were the second line, the center with his speed and jumping ability there for the steal, and Hazzard the scorer to convert the turnover into automatic offense. The safety valve was Erickson. This unit stripped and dismantled taller, slower opponents like a band of L.A. car thieves working over a parked car.

"Our five starters on that team had different personalities," Wooden said. "Keith Erickson was a great athlete. I've coached better basketball players, but never a better athlete. And to play that number five position in the press, he was just tremendous. I've never seen anyone come close to being his equal. And other

players filled their roles in the zone press. In the one and four positions in the press, I prefer left-handers. And just by chance, I had left-handers in Gail Goodrich and Jack Hirsch. In the four position, I like a ball-handler, and I put Hazzard there. In the number two position, I had Fred Slaughter, not tall, but big and quick-of-foot. I had two quality substitutes, Kenny Washington and Doug McIntosh. I didn't think they were that good at the beginning of the year, but they came along very well and enabled us to have the type of rotation we needed. The players complemented each other extremely well, and they got to the point where being behind didn't mean anything to them. They knew they were going to get one of those spurts through our press, and they expected it. They expected a spurt in each half, and for the most part we got them."

Wooden instructed his players not to go for steals. "If you go for steals, you'll foul," he told them. Instead, the Bruins' press aimed at forcing opponents to make mistakes, particularly bad passes. Most important, the press offered a means of draining the opponent's confidence.

The final ingredient was conditioning. Wooden told his players he wanted them to be in better shape than each of their opponents. As Wooden has said many times, he was a practice coach. And practice was where he brought these elements together. He drilled them until all their conscious thoughts became almost natural reactions.

After an impressive opening win over Brigham Young, the Bruins moved into the national eye that December of '63. In the Los Angeles Classic, they took apart second-ranked Michigan with Cazzie Russell, 93-80. "The greatest game I've ever seen my team play," Wooden told reporters afterward. The next night of the holiday tournament, UCLA whipped a solid Illinois team, enough of a performance to lift Wooden's team to number two in the national polls behind Kentucky. It was just the kind of recognition the coach had hungered for.

In January, Kentucky stumbled while UCLA whipped Washington State and moved to the top spot in the polls. From there, they whisked their way, despite a few tight spots, through an undefeated 26-game regular season. Having been number one for 12 straight weeks, the Bruins entered the West Regional in Kansas City brimming with confidence. The rest of the country, however, wasn't convinced. Most observers considered Duke the favorite.

The Bruins played to this thinking as their momentum sputtered. They struggled past Seattle, 95-90, and San Francisco, 76-72, surviving on the strength of their conditioning and the wits of their press. Sensing success, Wooden tightened his intensity and cracked the whip, driving Hazzard particularly hard in practice, then retreating into his tightly controlled mindset at game time.

"I didn't believe in artificial motivational things; maybe with some individual now and then," Wooden explained. "For example, I might try to get Hazzard mad at me because, when he'd get mad at me, he'd show me. But if I tried to get Gail Goodrich mad at me, he'd go into a shell. You have to learn the personalities of the players. But generally speaking, I don't agree with the emotional approach. I think for every peak, there is a valley. If you were standing in the hallway of our dressing room when we came out for warmups, you never had to worry about

being run over. I wanted our team to walk out slowly and warm up and not expend a lot of energy. I wanted to save that energy for the game. I didn't want a lot of cheering and yelling in the dressing room. I wanted peace and quiet so we could consider things and analyze things. I think there's the tendency by many coaches to get players overly motivated. Once in a while it works, but I think for every time it works, there may be a couple of times it affects them adversely."

Unusual as it seemed, Wooden was doing it exactly his way. For the second time in three seasons, he was taking a team to the Final Four. The grand event at the Municipal Auditorium in Kansas City also featured Duke, Kansas State and Michigan. In the semi-final, Kansas State set up its zone defense against UCLA and relied on 29 points from star Willie Murrell to take a lead. But as they had frequently during the season, the Bruins came from behind to win, 90-84. Leading the charge was Erickson with 28 points. In the other bracket, Duke had returned as the East champion and faced Russell and Michigan from the Mideast. The Blue Devils prevailed, 91-80, setting up a match of UCLA's speed against Duke's height.

Coach Vic Bubas mixed balanced scorer Jeff Mullins with a pair of 6-foot-10 frontcourt players, Jay Buckley and Hack Tison. Duke's height helped them to an early lead, but Wooden called a timeout and sent Doug McIntosh and Washington into the game. As often happened with opponents who faced the press, the Duke players watched their confidence drain away. "They led us 19-to-7, but it only took us two or three minutes to catch up," Wooden recalled. "And we had a 12-point lead at the half. But the lead wasn't the thing; it was the look they had on their faces. They looked whipped."

With Washington scoring quickly, the Bruins raced off to 16 points, and eventually, a big chunk of basketball history. Duke could never catch up and finally expired, 98-83.

It was the first time Washington had played a college game before his father, who was in the Marines. He finished with 26 points. "Washington came in and did a tremendous job," Wooden said. "Most everyone felt Duke would win the game. In the hotel Saturday afternoon before the game that night, a group of coaches were talking and some of them said, 'Johnny, Duke's a remarkable team—remarkable and big. You've got a nice team, but it's amazing you've won 29.' There was a Czech coach there who had spent some time during the year at different schools around the country, and somebody asked him, 'What do you think about the game?' In broken English, he said, 'UCLA win.' And they asked him, 'How can you say that, Duke's a big team?' He said, 'Yeah, UCLA is team,' and he held up his hand to represent our team. That's about as nice a compliment as a coach can get. And that year, we really played as a team."

To go with Washington's 26, Goodrich had scored 27. But in acknowledgement of Wooden's team notions, Hazzard, the quarterback running the offense, was named the tournament's Most Outstanding Player.

1965

UCLA's Hazzard, Slaughter, and Hirsch had completed their eligibility and did not return for 1965. Just how sorely they would be missed was apparent in the season opener as Illinois

deflated UCLA, 110-83. However, the '65 unit—Goodrich at playmaker, McIntosh at center, Goss at the other guard, sophomores Edgar Lacey and Mike Lynn at forwards, and Washington as sixth man—quickly found its stride. The Bruins lost another game, later in the season, this time at Iowa. But that would be it.

In the West Region, UCLA numbed Brigham Young, 100-76, then outlasted San Francisco, 101-93, in the Finals to earn a third trip to the Final Four. This time the event was in Portland, Oregon, where UCLA faced Wichita State in the semi-finals. With Goodrich scoring 28 and Lacey 24, the Bruins breezed, 108-89. Cazzie Russell and Michigan had eliminated Bill Bradley and Princeton in the other semi-final, 93-76, despite Bradley's 29 points.

The media mentioned a showdown in the finals, because Erickson had pulled a groin muscle. But there was something about a national championship that motivated Kenny Washington. He scored 17 to help the cause. But the real effort came from Goodrich, who scored 42 points and powered Wooden's team to its second championship, 91-80. "We were too quick for Michigan, even with Erickson hurt with a pulled groin muscle," Wooden said. "Kenny Washington came in, and, for the second national championship in a row, just played a beautiful game. And Goodrich had taken over as the leader, the way Hazzard had done the year before."

Earlier in the evening, Bradley had mesmerized the Portland audience, his opponents and his teammates by scoring 58 points in the consolation game against Wichita State. The Princeton senior had captured the fans' fancy by carrying his underdog team to the Final Four and was named outstanding player over Goodrich. "Bradley got his 50-some points in the consolation game against Wichita State," Wooden pointed out. "If you check the records, I think you will find that Goodrich got 42 in that championship Final and played only half the game. I'm not saying that Goodrich is a better basketball player than Bill Bradley. I have nothing but great respect for Bill Bradley because I thought he was one of the all-time greats. But I did feel that, in that particular tournament, Goodrich was the most valuable player."

The prize for Goodrich, however, was the championship, and that was sweet enough. For Wooden, it was only the second of what would become many layers of icing on the cake. "After the first win, I never wanted one as badly," he said of the national championships. "And, you know, they seemed to flow. Someone asked me, 'How come it took you 15 years to win your first one at UCLA?' I said, 'I'm a slow learner, but when I learn something, I get it down pretty good.'"

1966

Lew Alcindor matriculated as a student at UCLA in the fall of 1965, and a few months later the talented freshman team engaged the varsity in a pre-season scrimmage. At the time, the Bruins were ranked number one in the country. With no disrespect intended, the freshmen defeated their elders, 75-60, a score that was reported nationwide.

Sportswriters kept the game in mind that March when the NCAA playoffs began. Figuring Alcindor and his mates would dominate college basketball for the next three years, the press

dubbed the 1966 event the "Last Chance Tournament," suggesting that it would be the last chance for some other college team to win the championship for quite some time.

The press, history shows, was only a bit short-sighted in its prophesying. Instead of retaining the title for three years, John Wooden's teams kept it for seven straight seasons. So the 1966 tournament was a last chance of sorts. In picking a team to seize the opportunity in 1966, the national polls figured the likes of Kentucky or Duke or Kansas or Michigan or Cincinnati. Anybody but the little team that could, the Texas Western Miners.

The United States was in the throes of racial strife in 1965-66, as ghettoes flared up in protest. As circumstance would have it, the 1966 NCAA championship in Cole Field House at the University of Maryland offered a mirror of the nation's racial polarization. There, Adolph Rupp's all-white Kentucky team was pitted against Don Haskins' Miners, a club whose eight primary players were black.

Texas Western (now Texas-El Paso) had a storybook season from start to finish. The only blemish was a late-season loss to Seattle. Led by 6-foot-8, 240-pound Dave Lattin, the Miners entered the Midwest Regional with a 23-1 record and a third-place ranking in the national polls. But Haskins held out most of his starters in their first-round game against Oklahoma City because of curfew violations. After Western fell behind by 15 points, he inserted them and watched them work comeback magic, salvaging an 89-74 victory. From there, the Miners survived a 78-76 overtime match against Cincinnati as Lattin scored 29. The next night against fourth-ranked Kansas, the menu was again overtime, this time a double helping. Kansas' Jo Jo White made a 32-foot shot at the close of the first overtime, but the referee disallowed it, pointing to where White had stepped on the sideline. The second overtime was just as tight until Western's Willie Cager won it, 81-80, with a last-second shot.

The Miners were joined at the Final Four by second-ranked Duke, top-ranked Kentucky and surprise entry Utah, with Jerry Chambers. Most sportswriters gave the Duke/Kentucky semi-final clash the top billing. The Blue Devils with Bob Verga and Jack Marin, were the third Vic Bubas team to make the Final Four in as many years.

Rupp, on the other hand, had brought Kentucky back after an absence of seven years. With no starter taller than 6-foot-5, the Wildcats were dubbed "Rupp's Runts." Their lineup included Larry Conley and Pat Riley. The Baron had reluctantly moved them to a 1-3-1 zone defense, although he wouldn't admit that's what it was.

They escaped Duke in the semi-finals, 83-79, setting up the meeting with Haskins' defense-minded Miners, who had beaten Utah, 85-78. Keyed by the press nickname for the tournament, Rupp sensed this would be his last chance at a fifth title, and he wanted it badly. "It was just a tremendous, cohesive team," Rupp said of his Runts years afterward. "Losing to Haskins that year was possibly the biggest disappointment of my life, because that was my finest coaching effort." With their pressing defense, the Miners dominated from the start and won easily, 72-65. Haskins had drunk from the championship cup just before the long drought settled in. The next decade would

belong to Wooden.

Utah's Jerry Chambers was named tournament's outstanding player although his team lost both Final Four games. He scored 143 points in four tournament games, a record.

1967

Many basketball fans will recall that during his college days, before he converted to Islam, Kareem Abdul-Jabbar went by his given name, Lew Alcindor. In those days before the name change, sportswriters referred to him as Big Lew. But to John Wooden, his coach at UCLA, he was just plain Lewis.

In Wooden's opinion, Alcindor was the most valuable college player ever. The coach emphasized that most valuable didn't necessarily mean most talented or most outstanding. It simply meant that Alcindor was the kind of gifted versatile player who could take a team beyond the sum of its players. Without doubt, he was the best college-age center in history, the kind of player to whom all the adjectives apply. Complete. Well-schooled. Intelligent. Dominating. He was the single player around which a dynasty could be built.

There was, of course, one other major reason the Alcindor teams were dominant. They had the best coach. Perhaps more than anyone, John Wooden set the age of modern college basketball in motion. His UCLA teams popularized the sport and attracted national television. Beyond that, his zone press foreshadowed the age of high-tech defenses. All the same, Wooden was very much a coach from the old school, given to wearing horn-rimmed glasses and quoting inspirational verse. Because of that, when writers described him, they reached for idyllic images, of one-room Indiana school houses and church deacons (Wooden was a deacon in his Santa Monica, California church). He was once described as "the only basketball coach from the Old Testament."

This image cloaked the fact that Wooden was an intense competitor. With his great eye for detail, he focused those competitive energies into a laserlike precision, which he used to cut the hearts out of opponents. In the dozen seasons between 1964 and 1975, his teams won 10 NCAA championships. This competitiveness as a coach was an extension of his intensity as a player. He had been an all-state high school performer in Indiana, and later a three-time All-America at Purdue under coach Piggy Lambert.

His understanding of the game grew from the lessons Lambert taught him about up-tempo basketball. After a stint in the Navy during World War II, Wooden coached two years at Indiana State, then moved on to UCLA in 1947. It was an unheralded urban school in those days with a losing basketball team and a small gym. But Wooden quickly turned that around. He did it with his knack for precision, particularly in his practices.

"I am not a strategic coach," he once said. "I am a practice coach." Each session was organized tightly to run his players through a barrage of drills, conditioning, and scrimmaging. He always saved the scrimmaging for the end so that his players would learn to function when they seemed the most tired.

Like a computer-aided-design system, his mind seemed to view the game from every angle. Quite often he would watch his practices from the upper seats in a gymnasium to get a view of the entire floor. As Marv Harshman, the former Washington State coach once said, John Wooden made adjustments during a game better than anyone. It was his complete view of the game that aided these adjustments. In the early 1960s, Wooden hired one of his former players, Jerry Norman, as an assistant. Wooden had never been much of a recruiter. In that respect, Norman was the perfect addition to the program. He could handle the face-to-face work, the selling of the program to recruits, which Wooden was reluctant to do. Norman also urged Wooden toward the zone press, which the UCLA coach had used in one form or another over the years. That combination led to UCLA's first national championship in 1964.

The timing couldn't have been better. Lew Alcindor was a junior at Power Memorial High in New York and the most-coveted high school player since Wilt Chamberlain a decade earlier. An only child, Alcindor was quiet and bookish. His mother, Cora, was a singer, and his father studied at the Julliard School of Music while working at a variety of jobs to support the family.

As Power Memorial kept winning, the pressure of his college selection mounted on Alcindor. "I'll trade two first round draft picks for him right now," quipped coach Gene Shue of the Baltimore Bullets. Alcindor's high school coach, Jack Donohue, had announced that his player's recruitment would be tightly controlled. College coaches weren't allowed to so much as speak to the 7-foot-1 Alcindor, who spent his time perusing the hundreds of recruiting brochures and pamphlets sent him by colleges.

Those circumstances aided Wooden and Norman. They brought every resource to luring Alcindor to UCLA. One after another, the school's black luminaries—Jackie Robinson, Willie Naulls and Ralph Bunch—made their pitch to Alcindor. The bright, sensitive young center listened to their reasoning and accepted it.

On May 4, 1965, Alcindor announced his decision at a press conference in the Power Memorial gym. "This fall, I'll be attending UCLA," he told the 80 reporters present. His transition from New York City to Los Angeles, from high school to college, was difficult. He had been protected by his mother, and once away from her, was hit with an almost debilitating homesickness, leaving him wishing, as he told reporters, that UCLA could be transported to Times Square.

The cure for this was his focus on basketball. To develop his presence around the basket, Alcindor spent much of his freshman year working with Jay Carty, a 6-foot-8 graduate student from Oregon State. Also on the freshman team were Lucius Allen, a gazelle of a shooting guard from Kansas; Lynn Shackelford, a forward with a deadeye from the corner; and Kenny Heitz, a 6-foot-3 guard/forward.

With Alcindor scoring 31 points, this group humiliated the UCLA varsity, the defending national champions, in a pre-season scrimmage and went on to win every game on the freshman schedule. Wooden used praise sparingly. But even he conceded early that Alcindor was awesome. "At times, he even frightens me," the coach told reporters.

Their sophomore season, 1966-67, the young Bruins continued their display of power. The four sophomores were paired with junior guard Mike Warren (who would later star in the TV

series *Hill Street Blues*) in a starting unit that made a mockery of competition. Alcindor ran through a variety of dunks and bank shots in his first varsity game, against Southern Cal, and set a school record with 56 points, as the Bruins won, 105-90. Wooden had set Alcindor in a low-post offense that maximized the advantage of his skills and height. On defense, his rebounds and strong outlet passes keyed a quick break. When the zones became a little too tight around Alcindor, Shackelford loosened things with shots deep from the corner.

The only obstacle in their path to a perfect season was the stall game. Southern Cal employed it about midway through the season. The Trojans led 17-14 at the half and took the game to overtime, but the Bruins escaped there, 40-35. Beyond that, UCLA's progress was unimpeded. They entered the NCAA tournament undefeated in 26 games and continued apace, defeating Wyoming, 109-60, and Pacific, 80-64, to set up a meeting with Houston and junior All-American Elvin Hayes, "the Big E," in the national semi-finals in Louisville, Kentucky.

It would be the first of three highly publicized meetings between the two teams during the Alcindor era. Hayes, an outspoken 6-foot-8 forward, commented before the game that the UCLA center was overrated. The rest of the basketball world, however, was trying to decide if there was a realistic way to stop him. Bob Boyd, the coach at Southern Cal, said the slowdown game was the only chance. Red Auerbach of the Boston Celtics thought opposing teams might want to clog the middle, but then he thought better of it, because that would only lead to excessive fouling. Double-teaming was thought to be a logical choice, but Pete Newell, the guru of coaching, said that would be a waste because Alcindor would score anyway.

Houston coach Guy Lewis decided the best thing was to go directly at Alcindor with the idea of getting him in foul trouble. That worried Wooden and Norman, who spent the days before the game reminding Shackelford and Heitz that they would have to do their share of the muscle work inside. The Cougars came out strong and even opened a slight lead early in the game, with their big, muscled lineup crashing the boards. But Alcindor committed no fouls, and at times seemed almost bored. Then Shackelford hit on a long-range shot, and the UCLA press forced a turnover. From there, the Bruins opened a lead and went on to win with ease, 73-58. Hayes was less than gracious in defeat, claiming his teammates had choked and repeating his opinions that Alcindor was overrated. "He's not aggressive enough on the boards, particularly on offense," Hayes said. "Defensively, he just stands around. He's not all they really put him up to be."

Alcindor made little comment as he as his teammates focused on the national championship game against Dayton, the Cinderella team with 6-foot-6 center Dan Sadlier. The Flyers fell behind early, 20-4, and UCLA coasted to the national championship, 79-64. The victory matched the 30-0 record of Wooden's 1964 team and provided the Bruins' their third national title in four years.

Alcindor was the obvious choice as tournament's Most Outstanding Player. He had averaged 29 points over the season by making 66.7 percent of his field-goal attempts, an NCAA record. Allen, Warren and Shackelford had all averaged in double figures.

Despite his overwhelming success, the young center's life had its complications. Typical of many college students of the time, he had begun experimenting with drugs, primarily marijuana. And he was miserably short of cash and considered transferring to the University of Michigan, where boosters had hinted of financial rewards. But UCLA booster Sam Gilbert provided relief by purchasing Alcindor's game tickets. Financially secure, Alcindor remained at UCLA.

1968

For 1968, the NCAA outlawed dunking, an apparent attempt to neutralize Alcindor, yet it only made him more powerful, because the slam was the only shot he found difficult to defend. With opponents forced to shoot from short range, he spent much of his time swatting their attempts to the hinterlands.

"Kareem was amazing," Wooden recalled in 1987. "As a freshman the year before, he was largely instrumental in beating our varsity. I think he amazed a lot of people in his early career, and I think a lot of them got so interested in watching him that they forgot to play on occasion. But he was a very unselfish player, and he made every player on our team much better at each end of the court."

Wooden found himself with something of a talent traffic jam for the 1967-68 season, as Edgar Lacey and Mike Lynn, starters from the '66 team, returned after missing a year because of injury (Lacey) and suspension (Lynn). The team switched to a high post/low post offense that required some adjustments, as Lynn and Lacey alternated at the high post. In the opening game, Purdue and Rick Mount pushed the Bruins to 71 all before UCLA reserve Bill Sweek scored at the buzzer to preserve the win streak. It would continue through 47 games, until UCLA met Houston and Hayes in the Astrodome.

The NCAA ban on dunking had little effect on Hayes, whose offense relied heavily on his jumper. His scoring soared up to 36.8 points a game his senior season, up from 28.4 as a junior. He also averaged 18.9 rebounds a game.

With their pressing defense generating easy offense, the Cougars ran up buckets of points. "We had 18 games in a row where we scored over 100 points," Lewis said. "That's a record that stood until the age of the three pointer. We set another record by scoring 158 against Valparaiso coached by Gene Bartow. He didn't know what to say afterward. Elvin scored 62 in that game."

After their loss to UCLA in 1967, the Cougars ran through 17 straight wins. They were ranked number two in the country heading into the Jan. 20 game against the top-ranked Bruins. The anticipation for the meeting had been building since June, with writers, fans and students all talking about the game. A television syndication covering 49 states had been hastily assembled. The hype grew so heavy that Lewis refused to allow his players to mention UCLA by name.

"We've been ripe for an upset because we can't get our minds off UCLA," the coach, breaking his own rule, explained to a reporter. "I had sent a scout out to take a look at UCLA on the west coast before our meeting in January," Lewis recalled. "He came back and told me, 'No college team can beat this team.' I told my players that, and they just laughed and told me, 'We'll

beat them, Coach.'"

Nothing illustrated the growth in college ball more than the Houston program itself. Two years earlier, the Cougars had played their games in a gym that seated 2,500. The Astrodome was a giant facilty, meant for baseball and football. To convert to basketball, the Astrodome spent $10,000. The floor of the Los Angeles Sports Arena was trucked in from the west coast and set in the vast expanse of green Astroturf. It was a strange sight, with the nearest seat 100 feet from the playing area. But television zeroed in, and so did the 52,693 fans in attendance, then an NCAA record. The last tickets, which included standing room only, had sold out 10 days before the event.

Lewis had a brilliant career at Houston. His teams won 586 games and made five trips to the Final Four Yet he had no trouble identifying the biggest event of them all. "The UCLA game in the dome not only helped us at Houston," Lewis said. "It helped basketball. It proved basketball was a national product. That was the greatest game I was ever in, ever coached in."

The Bruins were slowed by injuries. Guard Mike Warren was recovering from the flu. And Alcindor had suffered a painful eye injury. Both played. Hayes opened the game with a turnaround jumper, and Houston never trailed. At one point in the first half, the Cougars led 37-28, the biggest lead ever on an Alcindor team. While the rest of the Cougars played a 1-3 zone, Hayes matched Alcindor in a man-to-man.

But with 12 minutes left in the second half, Hayes drew his fourth foul. And two minutes later, Warren scored to tie the game at 54. Pressing throughout much of the game, UCLA would tie it twice more. Then Houston's Don Chaney scored with two minutes left to give the Cougars a 69-65 lead. UCLA's Lucius Allen made a layup to move it to 69-67 with 72 seconds left. Then Alcindor fouled Ken Spain, and the Houston center missed the free throw. Flustered a bit, Spain then fouled Allen, who hit both free throws to tie the score at 69.

At 28 seconds UCLA's Jim Nielsen fouled Hayes. He made both foul shots, his 38th and 39th points, for a 71-69 lead. But the Bruins flubbed their last opportunity with a bad pass. Hayes ran some time off the clock then passed the ball to Reynolds, who tossed it toward the Astrodome ceiling.

"I don't think it was a great basketball game," Wooden recalled, "but it was a great spectacle in which Elvin Hayes had one of the greatest individual performances I've ever seen. But, generally speaking, individual performances don't win basketball games. We felt that we were a better basketball team, and we sincerely hoped we would play them again, and when we did, we were ready."

The loss burned slowly and deeply with the UCLA players. In the aftermath, Lacey quit the team. The talented forward had been angered at his benching during stretches of the game. With Lacey gone, Wooden reverted to the low-post offense with Alcindor as the single center. Their defensive teeth were their 2-2-1 and 1-2-1-1 zone presses. With that set of tools, the Bruins hammered their competition on the way to a rematch with Houston in the national semi-finals at the Final Four in the Los Angeles Sports Arena.

"We went out there with high expectations," Lewis said of the trip to the Final Four. But UCLA was ready with a box and one defense. Shackelford was assigned to cover Hayes. Alcindor

led five scorers in double figures with 19 points and 18 rebounds. Hayes finished with 10 points, and Houston was drubbed, 101-69, as UCLA advanced to another championship. "It was devastating, there's no question about that," Lewis said of the loss. "People often mention the box and one as the reason we lost. Elvin was so sick in that game. I think they would have won that game regardless. But the box and one wouldn't have contained Elvin if he was feeling all right. But Elvin was really the only shooter I had on that team. Theodis Lee was a streak shooter, but he was off that night."

"Houston was a great basketball team," Wooden said. "They had a lot of talent, and Hayes was a great individual player. Early in the second half, we led them by 44 points, and we could have won by a lot more than we did. Our starting five all scored something like 14 to 18 points. Our players still felt from the loss to them in the Astrodome earlier in the year. We felt we were a better basketball team, and from the time they beat us they were the number-one ranked team, as far as the polls were concerned. The players really wanted that one."

North Carolina with Charlie Scott and Larry Miller had ousted Ohio State in the other semi-final, but the Tar Heels didn't have the talent to stay with UCLA. Alcindor scored 34 points with 16 rebounds to claim his second MVP award, and Wooden picked up his fourth championship, 78-55.

1969

The supporting cast changed considerably for Alcindor's third varsity season, as Warren graduated and Lucius Allen left school. Sophomores Curtis Rowe and Sidney Wicks moved into the picture at forward, and Wooden acquired junior college transfer John Vallely for the backcourt, where he was teamed with Heitz.

The Bruins won their first 23 games, then hit a bump with two overtime wins over Cal and Southern Cal before losing their first game, the season finale, to the Trojans a night later. Their momentum resumed with big wins in the first two games of the NCAA tournament, 53-38 over a stalling New Mexico State and 90-52 over Santa Clara.

But they played poorly against Drake in the national semi-finals in Louisville. John Vallely scored 29 points while Drake played a strong man-to-man defense against Alcindor. The Bruins escaped 85-82. For the national championship, they met Rick Mount and Purdue, who had pounded North Carolina, 92-65, in the other semi-final.

Alcindor was never more dominating than his final college game, scoring 37 points on 15 of 20 from the floor with 20 rebounds as UCLA won its fifth championship, 92-72. He was named MVP for an unprecedented third time. "Purdue had Rick Mount, a great player," Wooden said, "and I had Kenny Heitz, a 6-3 guard play him. Kenny did a tremendous job of controlling Mount until we had the game well in hand. All our team wanted to see Kareem finish his college career with an outstanding game, and he did in every aspect."

1970

UCLA's sixth championship surprised the world of college basketball in 1970. With the graduation of Lew Alcindor (later, Kareem Abdul Jabbar), many observers had assumed the com-

petition would revert to a BA (Before Alcindor) climate. Instead, the Bruins subset of talent found room to flourish. Their game wasn't the dominating style of the Alcindor years. They had to work for their wins. They got them all the same.

Guard John Vallely and forward Curtis Rowe were the returning starters, but Sidney Wicks was the emergent leader at forward. Wooden's new look featured yet another strong front-line, this time with slashing inside power moves and aggressive rebounding. Wicks and Rowe were aligned with high-post center Steve Patterson, and all three registered ample numbers of points and rebounds. Wicks led the three by averaging nearly 19 points and 12 rebounds per game.

Moving into guard slot opposite Vallely was sophomore Henry Bibby from North Carolina, who could drill jumpshots.

Despite the relatively low expectations of many observers, the tone of Wooden's 1970 team was decidedly cocky. Nonchalant was another term used frequently to describe their play. They blasted by many teams, but struggled with mediocre Minnesota and Princeton. Past the midpoint of the season, Oregon whipped UCLA 78-65, then three games later Southern Cal nipped the Bruins in Pauley Pavilion, 87-86.

After a bit of intra-team confrontation and soul searching, they headed into the NCAA tournament's West Regional (where no other team was ranked in the top 10) as the number two team in the nation at 24-2. The nation's talent seemed to be jammed into the Mideast Regional, where top-ranked Kentucky with Dan Issel, ninth-ranked Notre Dame with Austin Carr, and Jacksonville with Artis Gilmore would have to battle with solid Iowa and Western Kentucky teams.

The traffic tie-up was resolved with a shootout. All three of the big teams—Kentucky, Notre Dame and Jacksonville—were high scoring. But Jacksonville was the least regarded, it being a low-profile program with what was considered a soft schedule. The Dolphins, however, were fairly convincing with a 106-100 upset of Kentucky that sent them to the Final Four, held again in College Park, Maryland. The team to emerge in the east was St. Bonaventure. Despite a knee injury to Bob Lanier, The Bonnies kept their national semi-final against Jacksonville reasonably close before losing 91-83.

Using mostly his five starters, Wooden negotiated his way through the West regional, whipping Jerry Tarkanian's Long Beach State team, 88-65, and Utah State, 101-79. In the Midwest, New Mexico State had tripped Drake, but proved to be little trouble for the Bruins in College Park, losing 93-77.

The national championship game was an interesting match of inside power, with Gilmore and Jacksonville taking the early advantage. Wicks matched up against the 7-foot-2 Gilmore, and after a defensive adjustment, UCLA took the lead just before the close of the first half. The second half was all Bruins, and although the final score was 80-69, the game wasn't that close. Wicks, with 17 points and 18 rebounds, was named the Outstanding Player. "Every time somebody mentions three in a row, they say Lew did it," Rowe told reporters. "Now we just proved four other men from that team could play basketball."

For all its success, UCLA's basketball program was laced with a basic unhappiness generated by the circumstances. First, Wooden had drawn a broad collection of talented high school players to his program, and many of them were forced to settle into the obscurity of his second and third teams. Also, the period of the late '60s and early '70s brought a movement of unrest and protest to college campuses across America, particularly at UCLA. Athletes were challenged to be more than athletes, and some felt the need to make political statements. Although a firm disciplinarian, Wooden reluctantly acknowledged the players need for expression and adjusted to it.

Still, he was hurt deeply when departing substitute Bill Seibert used the team banquet to attack the coach, the program and what Seibert saw as a double standard-treatment for subs as opposed to that of the starters. Wooden and assistant coaches Gary Cunningham and Denny Crum, both former players who had joined the staff in '69, attempted to resolve the situation, but there were fears that the discontent would dampen the Bruins' efforts for 1971.

1971

The 1971 UCLA Bruins became known for their seemingly uninspired play. That didn't seem to matter, however, as they won on the sheer force of their talent. Sidney Wicks, Curtis Rowe and Steve Patterson returned as seniors. Henry Bibby, the junior, shifted to playmaker. He was joined by senior Kenny Booker with another senior, Terry Schofield, serving as sixth man. There were a few close games, but only one loss, 89-82, to Notre Dame in South Bend at mid-season, where Austin Carr scored 46 points while Wooden could find no way to stop him.

Then the Bruins tiptoed through a string of narrow wins and come-from-behind victories over Southern Cal, Oregon, Oregon State, Washington and Washington State. Regardless, they entered the NCAA tournament at 25-1. The Bruins blasted Brigham Young in the first round. But in the next game, Jerry Tarkanian's Long Beach State team froze UCLA with a zone and took an 11-point lead. Larry Farmer and John Ecker came off the bench to lift the team, 57-55, to yet another Final Four, this time at the Astrodome in Houston.

In the national semis, Henry Bibby took charge in defeating Kansas, the Midwest winners who featured Dave Robisch, 68-60. Again, the Mideast Regional had been a traffic jam of talent with Western Kentucky, Jacksonville, Ohio State, Kentucky and undefeated, second-ranked Marquette (26-0), all of them top 10 teams. Western Kentucky emerged, after Ohio State knocked off Al McGuire's dream team with Dean Meminger.

In the East, 6-foot-8 All-American Howard Porter and Villanova ended the dreams of undefeated Penn, setting up a national semi-finals showdown in Houston between the Wildcats and Western Kentucky. The Astrodome crowd of 31,428 saw a double-overtime death match. WKU's Jerry Dunn knotted the regulation at 74 by missing a one and one. Porter tied the first overtime at 85 with a baseline jumper, then continued the strain to deliver Villanova, 92-89.

In the championship game, Wooden used a zone press to slow down Villanova's running game. Then with Bibby and Schofield launching bombs over the Wildcat zone, the UCLA coach slowed the tempo. The second half dragged with the Bruins' stall, until Villanova worked a couple of steals and cut UCLA's lead to four. Patterson, however, was having the game of his career, finishing with 29 points. The Wildcats closed within three with just over two minutes left but could get no closer, and

the Bruins gave Wooden his fifth straight title, 68-62.

Porter, with 25 points in the final, was named the Oustanding Player. However, he later acknowledged that he had signed a pro contract during the season, and Villanova's tournament success and his performances were vacated from the record books. A sign of the growing influence of big media, each of the Final Four teams received $60,000 in TV revenues.

1972

The next wave of talented sophomores crested in the UCLA program in 1972. They would play two full seasons and win two national championships before they tasted defeat. Never had a college basketball team, not even one of John Wooden's, enjoyed such success.

The key figure, of course, was the fiery red-headed center, Bill Walton, the 6-foot-11 son of a San Diego social worker. Off the court, he was a radical student in a radical age. On the court, he was the picture of precision, the ultimate passing center, schooled and polished in every phase of the game. It was fortunate that he was a team player, for Wooden and his assistants had assembled a team to go with him. The other starting sophomores were Keith Wilkes, the silky smooth forward, and Greg Lee. Junior Larry Farmer had moved into the lineup after being a key reserve the year before. Henry Bibby, the senior guard, was the only returning starter. Swen Nater, another big, strong sophomore center, served as Walton's backup for three years, then was taken in the first round of the NBA draft.

This group set an NCAA record for obliterating opponents, with an average margin of victory of 30.3 points over 30 games. They scored more than 100 points in their first seven games against Iowa, Iowa State, Notre Dame, Texas A&M, and Texas. The ninth game of the season, Oregon State came close at 78-72, but from there the Bruins zoomed off again, leaving 17 more teams in their wake to enter the NCAA West Regional 26-0. At Provo, Utah they zapped Weber State and Long Beach and headed back home for the Final Four at the Los Angeles Sports Arena.

Former Wooden assistant Denny Crum had left the program for Louisville. His Cardinals faced the Bruins in the semifinals. As Crum would say later, his team played hard but stood no chance. Wooden paddled his former assistant, 96-77. Walton, whom Crum had recruited for the Bruins, scored 33.

In the other semi-final, Robert McAdoo and second-ranked North Carolina faced Hugh Durham's Florida State team, a Cinderella. The Seminoles had upset Minnesota, then defeated Kentucky in what would prove to be the last game coached by Adolph Rupp. Durham had a gifted scorer in Ron King, and the coach put him to work early against the Tar Heels. Carolina shot poorly and struggled early, but then came back from a 23-point deficit, only to lose 79-75. The Seminoles had earned the right to challenge UCLA.

With King lofting deadeye jumpers, Florida State took an early lead until Walton began scoring. When the UCLA center slipped into foul trouble the second half, State again crept close. Walton returned sporadically and played gingerly but still collected 24 points and 24 rebounds to earn Outstanding Player honors, as the Bruins presented Wooden his eighth title and yet another 30-0 season.

1973

To prove it was no fluke, the Walton gang went out and did it again in 1972-73. Henry Bibby had moved on to the NBA, and Larry Hollyfield moved into the lineup. On January 25, 1973, UCLA beat Loyola of Chicago for the Bruins' 60th straight victory, tying San Francisco's record in 1955-56. Two nights later, the Bruins beat Notre Dame and would ring the number all the way up to 75 by the end of the season. A few teams came as close as six points, but not many.

The run continued at the Final Four in St. Louis, where Bobby Knight's young Indiana team fell 70-59 in the semis. N.C. State, the other great undefeated team with David Thompson, was on NCAA restriction and wasn't allowed to play. In the other semi, Gene Bartow's Memphis State team with Larry Finch, Ronnie Robinson and Larry Kenon upset Providence 98-85. The Friars featured Ernie DiGregorio and Marvin Barnes, but they weren't able to overcome Bartow's high-scoring lineup.

The Finals became a showcase of Walton's inside offensive prowess, as he made 21 of 22 field goal attempts for 44 points and 13 rebounds. His performance loosened a game that had been tied at 39 at half-time. UCLA glided over the last 20 minutes to an 87-66 win for Wooden's seventh consecutive championship and ninth overall.

"What stands out in my mind," Walton would later recall of his performance against Memphis, "was it was a situation where we had to play great ... We knew that they had a good powerful front line but not a particularly tall front line and we just came out trying to go to the hoop with that ball and I was feeling great and the ball was really moving around. People talk a lot about scoring all the points and things like that. But it was really our team offense that had to click perfectly for it. I had 21 baskets in that game. Our starting guards, Greg Lee and Larry Hollyfield, between had 22 assists between them—Lee with 13 and Hollyfield with 9. Most of those were right to me. We had the kind of offense that really thrived on passing that ball. In college you don't face a lot of guys who are real tall 6-foot-7, 6-foot-10, but most of them are forwards you find in the NBA so they were trying to deny me the ball and I could just fake out and Greg would come with and just go in back door Greg would go up there I would catch it and put it in"

Walton was named Outstanding Player for the second consecutive year. Larry Finch of Memphis State had averaged 26.8 points over four tournament games.

1974

Some long-time observers claim that the 1973-74 campaign played out as the game's greatest season. The on-court struggles were legendary, elevated almost to the level of myth. Bill Walton's UCLA team, two-time defending champions, flexed its muscle early, then stumbled. N.C. State shook loose the shackles of NCAA restriction and engaged in a fierce ACC struggle with Maryland, from which the Wolfpack emerged to claim the national championship.

Such a turn of events seemed highly unlikely to UCLA fans heading into the 1973-74 season. The team of super sophomores had become super juniors and seemed poised at the verge

of divination for their senior season. Solid, stable Larry Farmer had graduated. Keith Wilkes, Bill Walton and Greg Lee were joined by fellow senior Tommy Curtis at guard. Junior Dave Meyers added a strong element of hustle to the lineup.

Coach John Wooden took all comers in challenges to the crown and agreed to play both Maryland and NC State early in the season. The Bruins warmed up by blasting Arkansas, 101-79, in the season opener, then entertained Maryland at Pauley Pavilion for what was the Terps' first game.

Having come to Maryland for the 1970 season, Coach Lefty Driesell had claimed (much to his later regret) that he was building the "UCLA of the East." His Terps had won the NIT in 1972, but lost to Providence in the 1973 East Regional Finals. Arguably, his 1974 edition was his greatest team with center Len Elmore, forward Tom McMillen and guard John Lucas, all of whom would earn All-American honors during their college careers.

They almost pulled UCLA from the throne in Pauley Pavilion. Going into the closing minutes, the Bruins led 65-57, but the Terps rushed back to 65-64. John Lucas had a shot to win it, but Meyers blocked the attempt and the win streak lived a little longer. After a win over Southern Methodist, Wooden's Bruins played N.C. State in St. Louis, a game sought by State Coach Norm Sloan. Coming off probation and a riding a 29-game win streak, Sloan was eager to test his team's mettle. He, too, had a grand collection of players. The heart of the team was 6-foot-4 David Thompson, blessed with a 42-inch vertical leap. He was aided by 5-foot-6 playmaker Monte Towe and 7-foot-4 center Tom Burleson.

Walton picked up four fouls early on and watched from the bench as his team struggled to 54 all. But the Wolfpack's dreams were dashed late in the second half when Walton's return boosted UCLA to a convincing 84-66 win. The Bruins seemed in position to roll to yet another title. But they were caught up in the times. The mood in the country was nasty, with Watergate and Vietnam creating constant debate. The fiery Walton's emotions were a lightning rod for those controversies. UCLA took on the air of the counterculture and reflected the disillusionment felt by students across the country. Perhaps those distractions cracked their concentration. Perhaps the players buckled under the pressure of their win streak.

Whatever the cause, the Walton team ran through 13 games that season pushing their win streak to an incredible 88 games before heading to South Bend to play undefeated Notre Dame, coached by Digger Phelps. With three minutes left in the game, things seemed business as usual. UCLA led, 70-59. That's when Adrian Dantley and his teammates magically blitzed UCLA with 12 straight points and won, 71-70. The streak had died of a sudden, unexpected heart attack.

Having felt their mortality, Walton's Bruins felt it again four games later in a 61-57 loss to Oregon State, then again the next game to mediocre Oregon, 56-51. Losing their top ranking in the polls, they resumed their pace after that, pausing only at the close of the regular season with a close win over Stanford. Then came a three-overtime screamer against Dayton in the first round of the West Regional, which they won finally, 111-100. In the regional finals they whipped San Francisco soundly and headed to the Final Four in Greensboro, North Carolina.

There they encountered N.C. State again. The Wolfpack was ranked number one in both polls after surviving an overtime scare of its own in the ACC tournament finals. In overtime, they had escaped Maryland, 103-100, a game immediately billed as the greatest in the league's history. In the East Regional on their home floor, Reynolds Coliseum, State had turned away fourth-ranked Providence and eighth-ranked Pitt, but Thompson had been knocked cold in a brutal fall against the Panthers in the final. He lay in a motionless heap that left the home crowd aghast, but returned from the hospital toward the end of the game, a development that brought relieved cheers from Pack supporters.

The semi-final pairing of UCLA and State was immediately pronounced the true championship. In the other bracket, Al McGuire's Marquette team with Maurice Lucas had come out of the Mideast Regional, where Michigan had upset Notre Dame. From a weak Midwest Regional, Kansas had survived Oral Roberts in overtime. Their Final Four meeting was settled by Marquette rather easily, 64-51.

The other semi-final was nothing less than a masterpiece. Wilkes found foul trouble early, and Walton compensated with 29 points and 13 rebounds. Thompson countered for State with 28 and 10. Both coaches played conservatively, using only seven men. At the half, the score was 35 all. At the end of regulation, 65 all. The first overtime ended in a knot at 67. Then UCLA shoved off with a 7-point lead in the second overtime, and it seemed settled. Somehow, the Pack found the fuel for one final, miraculous acceleration and blew past the Bruins at the wire, 80-77, a victory that led to long, loud celebration back in Raleigh.

"Those are the days you never forget," Walton would say later. "You forget the great days like the Memphis State game and winning championships in ABA and winning High School championships but the ones you can never get out of your mind are the ones you lose when should have won. You can't take anything away from NC State they did beat us and they won the championship. But I do feel we beat ourselves in that game. We had it won we did not play as nearly as well in that game as we had played. Our team really started playing poorly the last 2 months of that season after we won 88 straight we lost 4 of our last 10 or whatever. But we lost four games to teams we didn't think we should have lost to. We had a chance to win a lot of games and we should have won 105 in a row if we'd won them all. And really should have won them. But NC State had a lot of talent and David Thompson; they had a game breaker, a guy that could make the big play at the end of a game as if it was slow. We had them and had a seven-point lead in the overtime. We made the turnovers. ... I should have put the game away for us but I missed some shots, and some of them were just right in there close."

In the championship round, Thompson scored another 21 to lead State to a 76-64 victory over Marquette

1975

North Carolina State's victory in the 1974 Final Four had broken the 11-year spell John Wooden and UCLA had cast over college basketball. For the 1974-75 season, the NCAA tournament was expanded to 32 teams, creating a sense of hope

for colleges across the country. For the first time in years, Wooden didn't have an Alcindor or a Walton waiting in the wings. A number of ambitious coaches were sizing up each other, wondering who would be the next to seize the championship mantle.

But Wooden, in a quick surprise, whisked an odd collection of players into the Final Four, captured his tenth title and retired. Seldom in any occupation has a man dominated with such precision, then stepped aside with such panache. Over the course of the season, Wooden's team had slipped a step out of the spotlight. Dave Meyers was the only returning starter. He was teamed with a set of sophomores, Marques Johnson and Richard Washington, to create a solid frontcourt. Junior Andre McCarter was the playmaker, and Pete Trgovich moved into the other guard slot.

Despite a demoralizing 22-point loss to Washington, this collection of Bruins made their way to the Final Four in San Diego. There they faced Denny Crum's Louisville Cardinals, who had earned their second trip to the Final Four in the four years since Crum had left Wooden's program. The Cards, with Wesley Cox and Junior Bridgeman, had come out of the Midwest Regionals, where they had defeated Maryland, 96-82.

It seemed that Crum finally had a club that could beat his old coach. In the national semis, the Cards led by four with 48 seconds left. But in a critical sequence, Dave Meyers tried twice to score, and Louisville's Bill Bunton blocked both shots. UCLA's Washington retrieved the second rejection and shot, and Bunton blocked it, too, but was called for the foul. Washington made both free throws, then UCLA tied the game moments later when Marques Johnson picked off a pass and scored. In overtime, Louisville led by one with seconds left when Johnson dished to Washington at the baseline. His shot killed the Cards, 75-74.

At the press conference after the game, Wooden announced his retirement at the close of the season. Their opponents in the final, Joe B. Hall's Kentucky Wildcats, were downcast at the news. They knew the Bruins would play emotionally in Wooden's last game. "I felt wrung out," Wooden explained. "I went to the dressing room and told my players [of his plans]. I congratulated them on an outstanding win and told them this would be my last game. This shocked them all of course. Then I went to the press room and made the statement that this would be my last game. There were those who felt that I did it to hype up my team to play Kentucky. I never did it to hype up my team."

The Kentucky lineup was studded with 6-foot-5 All-American Kevin Grevey; 6-foot-10 freshmen Rick Robey and Mike Phillips; and Jack "Goose" Givens. The Wildcats kept it close until just under seven minutes to go in the national championship game, with UCLA leading 76-75, when Meyers was called for a charging foul, then a technical. Wooden rushed onto the court in anger and had to be restrained. Kentucky, however, missed the shots and moments later turned over possession. The Bruins moved out to the win, 92-85.

"They were big and strong, but we were quick," Wooden said, summing up his swan song. With little fanfare, the UCLA coach left the game he had dominated for most of two decades. In 27 seasons at the school, he had won 620 games and lost 147, for an .808 winning percentage.

1976

It was NCAA 1976, AW—after Wooden, that is. With a handful of top teams posting their best records ever, and with personal statistical marks being set, it was a wild and wooly scene. Wooden was away and the cats did play. Replacing Wooden—the philosopher-coach of 27 years with the peerless record of 10 championships—was another philosopher coach: Bobby Knight, the 35-year-old leader of Indiana by way of West Point.

It was a year when Indiana finished 32-0, tying a record for victories by an undefeated team set by the 1957 North Carolina Tar Heels. Indiana didn't run up victories against cream puff competition either. In 14 of Indiana's games outside the Big Ten, their opponents won more than 75 percent of their games.

When a reporter mentioned how tough the IU's competition was, Knight was unimpressed. "I don't think a team should really give a damn who it's playing against," Knight explained. "It doesn't make any difference who you play, how good they are, how poor you are. It's not a game against an opponent; it's a game against your potential. If it is going to be a good team, every time it goes on the floor it is going to try to play against its potential. When it walks off the floor, it need not look up at the scoreboard to know if it has played up to its potential or not. It needs only to reflect back on the performance, both individually and collectively, relative to potential, to determine the success of the venture. I think that's the whole essence of athletics."

Victory is also part of that essence, and many teams set school records for winning during the 1975-76 season. Aside from Indiana's 32-0, Rutgers, behind Tom Young, was 31-2; Western Michigan led by Eldon Miller, was 25-3; and North Texas State, with Bill Blakeley in the huddle, was 22-4, after bottoming out at 6-20 the year before. All of these colleges posted historical bests. For Rutgers, it was the first time they finished in the Top 20 in a wire-service poll.

Other teams and players made historic marks. Illinois had lost 13 straight against Purdue until the Illini whipped the Boilermakers, 71-63. Purdue and Wisconsin teamed to sink all 47 of their free throw attempts in a February game. Minnesota's Mychal Thompson established a Big Ten Conference standard with 12 blocked shots in a game against Ohio State. St. Joseph's set a dubious marker: an NCAA-record eight of their players fouled out in a defeat against Xavier. Tennessee's Ernie Grunfeld (25.3) and Bernard King (25.2) became one of only four sets of teammates in NCAA history to each average more than 25 points a game in a single season. But when King suffered a broken right thumb, half of the "Ernie and Bernie Show" was stymied and Grunfeld's 36 points weren't enough to prevent an 81-75 defeat against the Virginia Military Institute in the first round of the Eastern Regional.

In the tournament, the Hoosiers managed to keep a perfect record despite trailing in the second half of three of their five tournament games. But Indiana played big when it counted. Forward Scott May and center Kent Benson combined for 40.8 points and 16.5 rebounds per game, giving IU an averaged margin of victory of 13.2 points.

Indiana got other help. Guard Bob Wilkerson did not score

in the Final, but in the semi-final against UCLA he collected 19 rebounds and seven assists in a 65-61 victory.

His backcourt mate Quinn Buckner contributed 16 points and eight rebounds in the Final. In the Final against Michigan, who had beaten Rutgers 86-70 in the other national semi-final, Indiana trailed 35-29 at the half. Worse, they were playing without Wilkerson, who suffered a concussion early in the game.

But IU shot the lights out in the last 20 minutes. May, Benson, and Buckner combined for 36 or Indiana's first 38 points in the second stanza and the team shot 60 percent for the half against the Wolverines. They made up 24 points and won going away, 86-68. Three Indiana players—forward Tom Abernathy, Benson, and May—were selected for the All-Tournament Team and Benson was awarded Most Outstanding Player.

1977

College basketball and network television found the ingredients for a potent chemistry with the 1977 NCAA tournament. The reaction was a starburst. At its center was the key, albeit volatile, element: Marquette Coach Al McGuire.

McGuire wasn't the whole story in '77. It was also the year the dunk returned to college ball after a nine-year absence. And Dean Smith and North Carolina made the four Corners offense famous, or infamous.

McGuire, though, presented the year's best story. Schooled in the streets of Queens, New York, Al was the younger, less talented brother of Dick McGuire. Al played at St. John's and then, in the early 1950s, played in the same New York Knicks backcourt with his brother. He got his first head coaching at Belmont Abbey, a small college in North Carolina. There he emerged as a feisty, eccentric competitor. He got the job at Marquette and focused the full force of his competitiveness on building an independent power.

At Marquette, he had inherited a 20-game loser and turned it into a 20-game winner. He had a knack for attracting tough city players to Wisconsin, although he was never a great recruiter. He took all that inner-city energy and harnessed it into the picture of precision basketball, teethed with a spirit-breaking defense.

By 1977, he had won the NIT and been to eight NCAA tournaments, rising to the Finals in 1974 before losing to NC State and *wunderkind* David Thompson. But, as McGuire often explained, he felt basketball; he didn't live it and breathe it. He was never a hoops junkie. So early in the '77 season, while his team was struggling and appeared headed nowhere, he grew weary of the grind and announced his retirement, effective at the close of the campaign. What happened from there was pure storybook. The Warriors came alive, hit a winning streak, and rode it into basketball history. When it was over, McGuire was an overnight sensation, a media star created by the moment, and Marquette was the NCAA champion.

It was, after all, the first year of massive media coverage for the Final Four. Carolina's Dean Smith recalled being overwhelmed by the number of reporters when he arrived at the event, held in Atlanta's Omni. Heading into the NCAA tournament, Johnny Orr's Michigan Wolverines appeared to be the chosen ones. They were top-ranked and had been to the Finals

the previous year. With forward John Robinson, center Phil Hubbard, and guards Rickey Green and Steve Grote, Orr had a team of pure power. Yet they sensed their power a little too much, grew a tad overconfident, and were upset in the Mideast Regionals by Cornbread Maxwell and UNC-Charlotte.

North Carolina also had a grand team with Walter Davis, Phil Ford, Mike O'Koren, Tommy LaGarde and Rich Yonakor, but injuries to Ford and LaGarde left the Heels limping into the Final Four. To compensate for their injuries, they had come to rely on Smith's stall game, the "four corners."

The competition in Atlanta was among the best in tournament history. The champion of the West Regional was Jerry Tarkanian's Nevada-Las Vegas team with Reggie Theus. Matched against Carolina in the semis, the Runnin' Rebels opened a 10-point lead, then watched Yonakor and O'Koren snatch it back with a burst of offense. Holding a slim lead, Smith called for the four corners with more than 15 minutes left in the game. The Heels held on, made their free throws, and somehow won, 84-83.

In the other semi, McGuire's team with guard Butch Lee, center Bernard Toone and Jerome Whitehead, squeezed through a tight, low-scoring match with North Carolina-Charlotte. At the buzzer, Whitehead scored in close, and the officials had to think it over. Finally, they ruled the shot good and Marquette the winner, 51-49.

Smith had coached well to overcome his team's injuries, but in the Final, luck left him. The game appeared to be a runaway at the half, as Marquette led Carolina, 39-27. But the Tar Heels worked their way back and nosed into the lead, 45-43, with just under 14 minutes left. Realizing his troops were outmanned and weary, Smith called for the four corners. But McGuire was waiting; his players sagged back on defense to protect against the backdoor play. Shortly, the Warriors regained the lead and gladly stepped to the free-throw line when Carolina was forced to foul.

The Warriors then showed their own delay game and won, 67-59. McGuire wept on the bench before the TV audience, a show of emotion that captured the hearts of millions of viewers. Suddenly network executives realized this NCAA tournament packed quite a bit of drama. Butch Lee, with 19 points, was named the tournament's outstanding player, and McGuire left coaching to become an analyst for NBC.

1978

The NCAA tournament came into its 40th birthday with a healthy mix of competition. There were newcomers in Indiana State, led by junior Larry Bird, and Michigan State, led by freshman Earvin Johnson. But the development of their fortunes was a year away.

The 1978 Final Four would be the domain of the Kentucky Wildcats and Coach Joe B. Hall, who had been a substitute on Adolph Rupp's 1949 championship team. Hall had served as Rupp's assistant in later years, then took on the unenviable task of succeeding the legend. Hall's record as a coach was superior by any standards except those of Kentucky fanatics. He had taken his team to the NCAA championship game in '75, losing to Wooden's last UCLA squad. He had won the NIT the next year, then lost in the regional Finals in '77.

Finally, things were aligned in Hall's favor in '78. His lineup featured the inside power of Rick Robey and Mike Phillips, the scoring finesse of All-American forward Jack "Goose" Givens and the guard play of sophomore Kyle Macy, a transfer from Purdue. They entered the Mideast Regional ranked number one in the country with a 25-2 record. Third-ranked Marquette also was there, but the Warriors were upset in the first round by Miami of Ohio. With that, the Wildcats' real test came in the regional finals against Michigan State. In a snail's game, Kentucky squeezed by, 52-49, leaving some to argue that the NCAA championship had been settled in the regionals.

In the East, a young Duke team with Mike Gminski, Gene Banks and Jim Spanarkel struggled past Rhode Island and Penn before blasting Villanova to gain the Final Four in St. Louis. Notre Dame rode through the Midwest in a scoring whirlwind blown up by Kelly Tripucka and Duck Williams. Their victims, by large margins, were Houston, Utah and DePaul. In the West, it was Eddie Sutton's Arkansas bunch, with Sidney Moncrief and Ron Brewer, that prevailed over Weber State, UCLA and Fullerton State.

Gminski made 13 of 17 from the floor to score 29 points in pushing Duke past Notre Dame in one semi-final. Duke guard John Harrell made two free throws in the closing seconds to preserve the win, 90-86. In the other semi-final, Kentucky fell back on its defense to defeat the small, determined Razorbacks. Forced to abandon their man-to-man because of foul trouble, the Razorbacks switched back to their pressure in the second half and pulled close before losing, 64-59. Givens led Kentucky with 23 points and 9 rebounds. High-jumping senior sub James Lee had 13 points.

In the championship, Givens and Kentucky shredded the Duke zone. The All-American forward hit 18 of 27 from the floor, including a string of line-drive jumpers, for 41 points. The Blue Devils rushed on strong in the last two minutes when Hall pulled his starters with an 11-point lead. He put them back in, and Kentucky held on for its fifth national title, 94-88.

Givens was named Most Outstanding Player and joined Robey, Gminski, Spanarkel, and Brewer on the All-Tournament team.

1979

The 1978-79 college basketball season unraveled like a script. The primary plot linked the emergence of Larry Bird and Earvin "Magic" Johnson. Bird was basketball's debatable phenomenon that season as Indiana State's Sycamores ripped through the regular schedule undefeated. Some thought he was a great, great player headed for the Hall of Fame. Others thought his fame sprang from the Sycamore's second-rate schedule.

As with all great debates, only the first round would be settled in college basketball, and that not coming until the NCAA finals that March in Salt Lake City, Utah.

The yang to Bird's yin, Magic Johnson, was riding with his Michigan State teammates through an up-and-down season in the Big Ten. When it was over, they would have six losses and a share of the league crown, which was enough to get them into the NCAA tournament. The field had been expanded to 40 teams to accommodate the burgeoning number of competitive

college programs. Critics claimed the new format would be awkward. But it created opportunity for more teams.

One of the first to seize it was the University of Pennsylvania. Somehow the Quakers survived the East Regional. Their opponents in the national semi-finals were the chosen ones, Johnson and the Spartans, who had blown away Lamar, LSU and Notre Dame in the Mideast Regional. In the Midwest, Indiana State and Bird had made quick work of Virginia Tech and Oklahoma before nipping Arkansas and Sidney Moncrief in the regional finals.

In the West, Ray Meyer's DePaul Blue Demons came out on top, vanquishing Southern Cal, Marquette and second-ranked UCLA. The strange collection of teams in Utah produced some fairly good basketball, if you leave out Michigan State's 101-67 bombardment of Penn in the semis.

The other game matched Indiana State against Mark Aguirre and DePaul, which proved to be a classic. Meyer chose to go the whole distance with his five starters. Indiana State Coach Bill Hodges offered more rest to Bird, guard Carl Nicks, and their mates. Bird, however, was beyond rest as he registered one of the all-time stellar performances: He made 16 of 19 field goal attempts for 35 points and 16 rebounds. Even so, DePaul guard Gary Garland scored and gave the Blue Demons a 73-71 lead with about five minutes to play. Meyer called for the freeze moments later when DePaul got the ball back. With less than a minute left, Indiana State's Bob Heaton scored off a Nicks' assist to give the Sycamores a 75-74 lead. Aguirre then missed an 18-footer, and State added a free throw to win, 76-74.

With a 33-game unbeaten streak and the top ranking in their back pockets, the Sycamores faced one last obstacle. Building on five impressive tournament victories, Michigan State had jelled around Johnson's multiple talents. But there was more. Coach Jud Heathcote had positioned Greg Kelser, Ron Charles, Mike Brkovich and Terry Donnelly around Johnson. Jay Vincent came off the bench.

In the Finals, Heathcote solved the Bird riddle with a match-up zone. The Indiana State star was snared every way he turned. Hassled into missing 14 of 21 shots, he scored only 19. And while Michigan State found foul trouble early, the Sycamores made only 10 of 22 free throws. The Spartans led by a dozen in the first half, and in the second, when Indiana State threatened, Donnelly repelled the comeback with five long-range jump shots.

Johnson with 24 points and 7 rebounds in the Final was named the Outstanding Player. Mark Aguirre, Bird, DePaul center Gary Garland and Kelser made up the rest of the All-Tournament Team. A sophomore, Johnson would claim hardship status after the season and enter the NBA draft.

1980

It's easy to see why Louisville coach Denny Crum expected great things of himself and his teams. He had played for and served as an assistant coach to UCLA's John Wooden. Charged with ideas and motivation from the master, Crum had come to Louisville in 1971 and promptly directed the Cardinals to the 1972 Final Four, where Louisville convincingly lost to Wooden and UCLA. Not to be deterred, Crum brought his team back in 1975. But again UCLA and Wooden were his undoing in the

national semi-finals.

Finally, in 1980 Crum got his chance at the big prize. Wooden had been retired for five years, and the Cardinals were loaded with talent, including All-America guard Darrell Griffith ("Dr. Dunkenstein"), forward Derek Smith, guard Jerry Eaves and center Rodney McCray. Unranked at the start of the season, the Cardinals ran off an 18-game winning streak and made believers of their doubters. Heading into the NCAA tournament, they were 28-3 and ranked third in the national polls.

The Cardinals almost lost to Kansas State in the Midwest Regional. But super-sub Tony Branch drilled a deep jumper in the final seconds of overtime to keep them alive, 71-69. That scare was followed by another overtime, against Texas A&M, but Louisville again survived, 66-55. From there, LSU fell to the Cardinals, 86-66, in the regional Final.

Louisville met a collection of second-rung teams at the 1980 Final Four in Indianapolis. The NCAA tournament had expanded to a 40-team format, which meant that teams no longer had to be dominant during the regular season; they just had to be good enough to get in the tournament. From there, anything could happen.

The 1980 Final Four read like a list of survivors: UCLA with nine losses and a fourth-place finish in the PAC-10; Purdue with eight losses; and Iowa with nine defeats and a fourth-place tie in the Big 10. In the national semi-finals against Iowa, Louisville jumped to a lead when the Hawkeyes' Ronnie Lester aggravated a knee injury from earlier in the tournament. In the second half, Griffith was at his best, hitting 14 of 21 from the floor to finish with 34 points. The Hawkeyes kept it close, but Crum's team moved into the Finals confidently, 80-72.

Crum was determined to win the title, even if it meant cajoling and badgering his team from the sidelines. Finally, his team had reached the national championship game, only to find his old nemesis—UCLA—waiting. Larry Brown had succeeded Gary Cunningham as coach at UCLA. The Bruins had managed only 17 wins during the season with a young lineup (Rod Foster, Kiki Vandeweghe, James Wilkes, Mike Holton and Mike Sanders). But they matured in the West Regional with a first-round win over Old Dominion. Then they took on top-ranked DePaul, Ray Meyer's 26-1 dream team with Mark Aguirre and freshman Terry Cummings. With balanced scoring, UCLA broke open a close game and earned the upset, 77-71. Next, they stretched past a strong Ohio State team featuring Clark Kellog and Herb Williams, 72-68. Then they eliminated Clemson, 85-74, to reach the Final Four.

In Indianapolis, the Bruins beat local favorite Purdue, led by 7-foot-1 All-American Joe Barry Carroll and coached by Lee Rose, who had taken UNC-Charlotte to the Final Four in '77. Vandeweghe paced UCLA with 24 on 9 of 12 from the floor. In the end, Brown's team played patiently and advanced, 67-62.

In the championship game, the Bruins almost worked the UCLA jinx on Crum's team again. They led by two at the half, and Crum was furious, calling his players chokers. "He really chewed us out," recalled Derek Smith. Before the second half began, Crum apologized to his players and told them to go out and have fun. The UCLA lead grew to five with just under seven minutes left. One last time Crum pushed his players to wake up. They did and blitzed to the title over the last few min-

utes, 59-54. Griffith led the champions with 23 points, but it was Eaves with several key late baskets that spurred the turnaround. Denny Crum had given the basketball-hungry Louisville crowd its first national championship.

Darrell Griffith was named most outstanding player and Rodney McCray also was voted to the All-Tournament Team. Carroll, Vandeweghe, and UCLA's Rod Foster were also selected.

1981

Expanding on trends from 1980, the expanded NCAA tournament format brought an even greater flurry of upsets in 1981, creating a new pastime for TV broadcasters: Counting the carcasses. Arkansas over Louisville, James Madison over Georgetown, Kansas State over powerful Oregon State and Steve Johnson. And again DePaul, again top-ranked, again featuring Mark Aguirre, with a 27-1 record. This time St. Joseph's was the culprit, 49-48.

Yet even in the turmoil, basketball's tradition and power found a home. Bobby Knight's Indiana Hoosiers became the first team to win the title with as many as nine losses. Although the Final Four games were settled with large margins of victory, the field hardly held any patsies. Virginia, with Ralph Sampson, Lee Raker and Jeff Lamp, had spent much of the year ranked No. 1 and had defeated North Carolina twice. The Cavaliers advanced through the East with wins over Villanova, Tennessee and Brigham Young. Danny Ainge and Fred Roberts led BYU to the regional finals in Atlanta, but the 7-foot-4 Sampson, the consensus national player of the year, awakened there from his tournament slump as Virginia won handily, 74-60.

North Carolina found its footing in the West. The Heels had an incredible front line in James Worthy, Sam Perkins and Al Wood, all future first-round NBA draft picks. They beat Pittsburgh, Utah with Tom Chambers and Danny Vraines, and Kansas State to reach the Final Four.

Somehow, the Hoosiers had won the Big Ten championship despite their record. Then they exploded in the Mideast Regional with a burst of power, dumping Maryland, Alabama-Birmingham and St. Joe's. The Final Four setting was just right for Knight, Philadelphia's Spectrum, where he had won the title in 1976.

Out of the Midwest came Dale Brown's Louisiana State Tigers, powered by forward Rudy Macklin, guard Howard Carter and center Greg Cook. In their first tournament victory, 100-78, over Lamar, Macklin had 31 points and 16 rebounds. The Tigers then bumped Arkansas, 72-56, and claimed the regional title over Wichita State with Antoine Carr and Cliff Levingston, 96-85.

But Brown's Tigers lost their snarl in the national semis in Philly. The tamers were the Hoosiers—Isiah Thomas, Landon Turner, Jim Thomas and Ray Tolbert. LSU seemed in control in the first half, until Knight used his particular brand of motivation with his players at intermission. Indiana roared out in the second half, scored 40 points, and won going away, 67-49.

The other semi-final between the Atlantic Coast powers, Carolina and Virginia, was a tight game early. But the Heels had Sampson suffocated in a zone, and Al Wood fell into a scoring trance and had the game of his life, 14 of 19 from the floor for 39 points. His effort blew apart a game that had been tied

at 37 early in the second half. Carolina had a surprisingly easy time of it, 78-65.

The atmosphere of the games was shattered that Monday by news that President Ronald Reagan had been shot and wounded. Officials from the NCAA, the two schools in the Finals and NBC discussed postponing the game, but decided to proceed upon learning the President was out of danger. It was Dean Smith's sixth trip to the Final Four and third shot at a national championship. The Heels held an early, tenuous edge over the Hoosiers, but Indiana eased to a one-point lead at the half. From there, the Hoosier advantage grew to the comfortable realm, as Isiah moved Indiana through the Carolina defense. From an 11-point edge, Knight's team coasted to the championship, 63-50.

Isiah Thomas was named outstanding player. He was joined on the All-Tournament team by teammates Jim Thomas and Landon Turner, Wood from Carolina, and Lamp from Virginia. Virginia defeated LSU in the last consolation game played at the Final Four.

1982

The critics made much of the numbers. Six times Dean Smith had led his North Carolina Tar Heels to the Final Four without claiming the title. Finally, Smith's team ended that dry spell in dramatic fashion, with a 63-62 victory over Georgetown in the 1982 NCAA finals. Veteran broadcaster Curt Gowdy said it was the game, more than any other, that lifted the Final Four to the top level of televised entertainment, equal to that of the World Series and Super Bowl.

Held at the Superdome in New Orleans, the 1982 championship game broke attendance records with 61,612 spectators. Millions more caught it on television. North Carolina entered the tournament number one and somehow managed to maintain that status despite a close call or two. The Heels' lineup featured James Worthy, Matt Doherty and Sam Perkins in the frontcourt, freshman Michael Jordan at off guard and Jimmy Black at the point.

The Carolina firepower, however, didn't seem to deter second-round foe James Madison from Virginia, a team that had upset Ohio State in the first round. The Tar Heels struggled to a 31-29 lead at the half and struggled to hold on to that margin to advance, 52-50. In the regional semi-finals in Raleigh, North Carolina, Alabama served Carolina its next round of troubles before succumbing, 74-69. After a 10-point win over Villanova in the regional finals, the Heels were set to give Smith his much-wanted prize.

In the Midwest, the unranked Houston Cougars made a run. With starters Michael Young, Rob Williams, Larry Micheaux, Lynden Rose and Clyde Drexler, Coach Guy Lewis pulled Akeem Olajuwan and Reid Gettys off the bench to form a potent rotation. By 1983, the Cougars would become known as Phi Slama Jama, the dunking fraternity. For 1982, however, they were just another hot Cinderella, burning Alcorn State, Tulsa, Missouri and Boston College on their way to New Orleans.

Louisville's path in the Mideast was cleared when Alabama-Birmingham upset Virginia and Ralph Sampson. Denny Crum's 20th-ranked Cards polished off Middle Tennessee State, sixth-ranked Minnesota and UAB on the way to their second

Final Four appearance in three years. Louisville had no dominant player, just the solid leadership of Jerry Eaves, Rodney McCray and Derek Smith.

The NCAA tournament selection committee had sent Georgetown to the West Regional, and that worked for coach John Thompson's team. The Hoyas had added freshman center Patrick Ewing to a roster that included All-American guard Eric "Sleepy" Floyd. The victims, in succession, were Wyoming, Fresno State and fourth-ranked Oregon State.

In the national semi-finals against Houston, Sam Perkins took charge with 25 points and 10 rebounds, while the Tar Heels held the Cougars' Rob Williams scoreless from the floor. North Carolina never trailed and advanced to the championship round, 68-63.

The Georgetown-Louisville matchup was a defensive collision. The Hoyas had the most pressure and the most points, 50-46, setting up a special meeting Finals: Dean Smith vs. John Thompson. Two friends and America's Olympic coaches from 1976 facing each other for the championship both wanted dearly. In addition, Carolina's Worthy and Georgetown's Floyd were both All-Americans, both from little Gastonia, North Carolina, both the stalwarts of their teams.

The familiarity made for a heavy tension at game time. In the early going, Ewing swatted away four Carolina shots. All four were ruled goaltending. The Heels scored their first eight points without putting the ball through the hoop. From there, the game settled into the coaches' cat-and-mouse. The Hoyas grabbed a lead, then Carolina evened it at 18. Worthy came alive with 18 first-half points. The lead became a pendulum. Georgetown held it at the half, 32-31.

The swinging continued throughout the final 20 minutes. At the six-minute mark, Carolina eased ahead, 57-56, on a pair of Worthy free throws. The pace became agony after that. Somewhere under two minutes, Georgetown pulled to 61-60 when Ewing swished a 14-foot jumper. After Carolina missed on its next possession, Floyd scored on a short jumper, and the Hoyas had the lead, 62-61, with just under a minute left. Carolina worked for a good shot, and, with 15 seconds, Doherty passed to Jordan for a 16-foot jumper from near the left sideline. The ensuing swish marked the first great feat of what would become the Jordan legend.

Down 63-62 with adequate time, Georgetown attacked immediately with guard Fred Brown working the ball at the edge of the Carolina defense. He thought he saw Floyd out of the corner of his eye, but the shadowy form in white was Carolina's Worthy. The Tar Heel senior was surprised, then elated, to receive the ball and he headed downcourt, where he was fouled. Worthy missed both free throws with two seconds left, but it didn't matter. Carolina had its championship. In one of the finer moments in all of sports, Thompson stepped onto the court and hugged a disconsolate Brown. Worthy was named the tournament's Most Outstanding Player. Perkins and Jordan were named to the All-Tournament team, along with Georgetown's Floyd and Ewing.

"As you know, Michael was up and down his freshman year, as any freshman would be," Dean Smith recalled later. "But his best game in his whole freshman year was the Finals against Georgetown. If he hadn't made that shot, it would still have

been the best game he played all year." Worthy had 28 points (on 13 of 17 shooting) and Jordan had 16 points and led the Heels with nine rebounds.

Of Jordan's final shot, Smith said, "We missed a foul shot, and we're one down with 32 seconds. Usually, I don't like to take a timeout there. We should know what to do. But I called a timeout. I expected Georgetown to come back to the zone and jam it in. I said, 'Doherty, take a look for James or Sam, and, Jimmy, the cross-court pass will be there to Michael.' As it turned out, Michael's whole side of the court is wide open because they're chasing James. If Michael had missed, Sam would've been the hero because he'd have had the rebound."

1983

Phi Slama Jama. Never has a nickname been more appropriate to a basketball team, yet more misleading.

Sportswriter Thomas Bonk, then with the *Houston Post*, came up with that tag for the University of Houston Cougars after watching them indulge in a dunkfest during a 112-58 blowout of Pacific in January 1983. At the time, the Cougars were just beginning a 26-game winning streak. As they stuffed one opponent after another that winter of 1983 on their way to the top ranking in the national polls, Phi Slama Jama grew from a sportswriter's fancy into a dominant force.

The name was appropriate because it headlined the tremendous talent of the Houston players and the style of Coach Guy Lewis, who loved the dunk. He loved it so much that Houston became the first team to keep stats on dunks. Yet the flip side of this hype was the suggestion that the Cougars trafficked solely on their leaping ability and athleticism. In reality, they were a finely balanced team: Fierce defensively, overwhelming offensively, and determined enough to overcome their substantial inexperience.

In the minds of many college basketball fans, Phi Slama Jama was a team so fat in confidence and talent that it was upset by underdog North Carolina State in the NCAA finals. But in reality, State was rich in experience while Houston lacked it at the key positions. Technically, you could say the Cougars fell victim to the poor free throw shooting that plagued them much of the 1982-83 season. But when he looks back on it, Guy Lewis sees fate as a far bigger factor than the technicalities. "It was meant to be," he says of N.C. State's incredible run to the 1983 NCAA championship.

Fate, however, can't rub out the fact that the Cougars were one of the best teams, albeit a flawed one, in the history of the game. They had Clyde "The Glide" Drexler at small forward and Akeem "The Dream" (later to be Hakeem) Olajuwon at center.

The only major flaw for Phi Slama Jama was at point guard. Houston had reached the Final Four in 1982, with junior Rob Williams playing the point. Over the '82 season, Williams led the Cougars in scoring and the Southwest Conference in assists. But at the end of the year, he decided to declare hardship status and turn professional.

"There's no doubt in my mind," Lewis says, "that if Rob Williams had stayed in school, no one would have stopped us the next year." After Houston demolished his Lamar team in November, Coach Pat Foster remarked, "They could win with

a nun at point guard." It made for a nice quote, but Guy Lewis knew that few teams had ever won a championship without a proven ball-handler and floor leader. Fortunately, Alvin Franklin, a freshman, was a determined worker. He made steady progress learning the position.

Enough of flaws, though. What made this team so good was its strength in the frontcourt. There, the veteran leadership came from two players: Larry Micheaux, a 6-foot-9 senior power forward, and Drexler, a 6-foot-6 junior. A Houston native, Drexler averaged nearly 16 points and nine rebounds a game. Because of Drexler's strength, Lewis felt comfortable using a double low post offense with Drexler as one of the posts, whenever Houston happened to be in a half-court game, which wasn't often. Typical of Lewis teams, Phi Slama Jama featured a plethora of presses. Zone presses. Man presses. Drexler figured prominently in all of them.

The other element in the frontcourt was Olajuwon, a sophomore center. A native of Lagos, Nigeria, Olajuwon had played plenty of soccer but little basketball during his schooldays in Africa. The neophyte center entered the 1982-83 season still unsure of the game. The Cougars had suffered an early season loss to Syracuse, then dropped a game to Virginia in Japan in late December. But from there, Lewis's team did little but gather momentum. With Franklin gaining confidence at point guard and Olajuwon finding his footing in the post, the Cougars ripped through the remainder of the schedule and polished off TCU in the conference tournament finals. At 27-2, they entered the tournament and whipped Maryland (with Len Bias), Memphis State (with Keith Lee) and Villanova.

For the second time in two years, Houston was headed back to the Final Four; this time the championship would be played in the rarefied air of Albuquerque, New Mexico. The semifinals pitted the Cougars against Louisville, featuring Milt Wagner, Rodney and Scooter McCray and Lancaster Gordon. The second-ranked Cards had picked their way through a patch of overtimes to win the Mideast Regional. They outdistanced Tennessee before struggling with Arkansas and Joe Kleine. In the finals, the Cardinals whipped cross-state rival, Kentucky, 80-68, in overtime.

Houston versus the high-flying Cards provided perhaps the most inspiring athletic display ever witnessed by a Final Four crowd. Louisville seemed in command until the midpoint of second half, when Phi Slama Jama bounded to a new plane, wiping away the Cards' eight-point lead in the process. Once trailing 57-49, the Cougars went on a 21-1 tear over the next five minutes and 46 seconds to take a 70-58 lead. From there, they cruised to victory, 94-81. Olajuwon turned in 21 points, 22 rebounds and eight blocked shots. Drexler also scored 21 and Young 16.

In the national championship game, they faced North Carolina State, the Cinderella. Coach Jim Valvano's team had begun its improbable march in the Atlantic Coast Conference tournament. There, the Wolfpack had upset North Carolina and Virginia (with Ralph Sampson) to gain a berth in the NCAAs with a 20-10 record.

Seniors Dereck Whittenburg, Thurl Bailey and Sidney Lowe led the Wolfpack in the NCAA West Regional. In their first-round game against Pepperdine, Valvano's charges found them-

selves down by six with 1:10 left in overtime. Intentionally fouling and watching their opponents die at the line, State's veterans worked a miraculous comeback to beat Pepperdine, 69-67.

Then they dazzled sixth-ranked Nevada-Las Vegas when Bailey tapped in a missed jumper by Whittenburg just before the final buzzer to win, 71-70. After blowing out Utah, N.C. State again faced Virginia and Ralph Sampson in the regional finals, the same team they had defeated in the ACC finals. The Cavaliers were up by seven in the second half, but State kept close. Virginia held a 63-62 lead in the final minute, until the Wolfpack's sophomore forward, Lorenzo Charles, was fouled and made two free throws. Virginia got two shots at winning it, but missed both. Valvano's only "easy" win came in the national semi-finals with a 67-60 win over Georgia.

Suddenly a team that seemed headed nowhere in March was playing for the national championship. Still, just about everybody figured the Final for a blowout. "North Carolina State's best chance is a bus wreck," wrote Charlie Smith of the *Tulsa World*. "Make it Houston 78, N.C. State 53," projected Billy Reed of the *Louisville Courier-Journal*.

Rather than a blowout, the game developed as a tight squeeze, just tight enough for Valvano and the Pack to work one more trick. "If we get the opening tip, we won't take a shot till Tuesday morning," Valvano joked in a press conference before the game.

Instead, the Pack played almost arrogantly in the first half, opening with a dunk and scoring frequently and controlling the game. They moved to an eight-point lead at the half and coasted there. But in the back of their minds was the display Houston had put on in the second half against Louisville. Lewis reminded his players at intermission of their credo: The team with the most dunks wins.

The Cougars opened the second half with a 15-2 run and seemed poised to dash off to the championship. Then, with about nine minutes left, Lewis decided to slow the pace. "I went in it for a couple of minutes trying to rest my team," Lewis explained. "The altitude in Albuquerque left us gasping. All my players were just worn out." Lewis also hoped the spread offense would pull State out of its tightly packed zone and open up the back door.

That didn't happen. N.C. State tied the score at 52 heading into the final two minutes, and Lewis opted for still more stalling. "At the end," he said, "we were just trying to make a free throw and survive." That didn't happen either. Just about everybody on the team missed clutch free throws. Whittenburg with about a minute left fouled Franklin. The freshman guard missed his one-and-one opportunity. N.C. State rebounded and had a shot at the national title with 44 seconds left. Valvano opted to take the game's last shot. State worked 17 passes on the wings while the clock ticked down. Finally, Whittenburg launched an off-balance air ball from just inside 30 feet. But Lorenzo Charles rose up from near the basket, where Olajuwon had failed to box him out, and slammed home the winner at the buzzer.

It was the second dunk of the game for State, the first shot and the last being slams, and it fulfilled Lewis's prophesy. The team with the most dunks would win. Phi Slama Jama had recorded just one. As Valvano and the State crowd erupted, dis-

appointment fell over the Cougars. Phi Slama Jama had suffered a death by dunk, 54-52. Olajuwon with 20 points was named the tournament's Most Outstanding Player.

But there was no consolation for the Cougars.

Rounding out the All-Tournament Team were Bailey, Lowe, Wagner, and Whittenburg.

1984

Like many of the very best college basketball teams, the 1983-84 Georgetown Hoyas had a greatness born of failure, having suffered that painfully close loss to North Carolina in the 1982 NCAA Finals, when center Patrick Ewing was a freshman. Then they struggled through a rebuilding season his sophomore year, all the while carrying with them the sting of the championship loss to North Carolina.

"Winning is a big satisfaction, and losing is a big disappointment," Georgetown Coach John Thompson said when asked to reflect on the '82 loss. "The higher you climb, the more you feel the disappointment when you don't get it." Thompson used this disappointment as the motivation to drive his team to the national championship in April 1984.

Early on it was obvious that Georgetown had one of the finest teams in the country, with Ewing at center, freshman Reggie Williams at forward, Bill Martin as sixth man, and David Wingate at shooting guard. Michael Jackson played the point, and freshman Michael Graham was the resident bruiser at power forward. Senior guards Gene Smith and Fred Brown came off the bench. From the fierceness of the full-court pressure to Ewing's shot blocking, the Hoyas were a defensive team. Thompson's time with the Celtics in the 1960s had brought him close to Red Auerbach. And like the Celtics coach, Thompson had come to believe in defense.

Charged by this intensity, the Hoyas bolted through the regular season with a 26-3 record and rolled through the Big East Tournament, sending Providence, St. John's and Syracuse reeling. Ewing was named the tournament's MVP, mainly because his shotblocking had dominated the field.

With a 29-3 record, the Hoyas entered the West Regional and immediately found trouble in SMU's stall game. With seconds left, the score was tied at 34. And Gene Smith, a mediocre foul shooter, was at the free throw line with a one-and-one. In the huddle before the shot, Ewing told his teammates, "We're not going home, and that's it."

When Smith missed the free throw, Ewing muscled past the Mustang's Larry Davis to rebound and score on the putback for a 36-34 Hoya lead. After a final exchange, the game ended, 37-36, Georgetown. From there the Hoyas controlled both Nevada-Las Vegas and Dayton to claim a seat for the Final Four in Seattle.

In retrospect, the 1983-84 season could best be described as the year of the big man. Kentucky had the Twin Towers of Melvin Turpin and Sam Bowie. Houston featured Akeem Olajuwon. And Georgetown put forth Ewing. Although the NCAA tournament had expanded to 54 teams, the dominant centers prevailed. Turpin, Bowie, and Olajuwon all joined Ewing in leading their teams to the Final Four in Seattle. The press coverage predicted the championship would settle the question of who was the most dominating big man in college

basketball.

In the first semi-final in Seattle, Houston beat Virginia, the Cinderella team playing in the season after Ralph Sampson's graduation, in overtime, 49-47. In the second game, Georgetown faced Kentucky. In an informal poll, most of the coaches at the National Association of Basketball Coaches Convention, held each year at the Final Four, figured Kentucky's Twin Towers would be too much for Ewing. But the Hoyas taught the basketball world another defensive lesson that afternoon with an astounding turnaround. Ewing was called for three fouls in the first 11 minutes as Kentucky raced to a 27-15 lead. With their center on the bench, the Hoyas jumpstarted their dreaded full-court press and narrowed the gap to 29-22 by half-time. With three minutes left in the half, Turpin had scored on a jumper. Kentucky wouldn't score again for another 13 minutes, as Georgetown suffocated the Wildcats.

There were more than 300 coaches in the audience at Seattle's Kingdome. The second half left many of them stunned. "No one had ever seen anything like it," said Miami coach Bill Foster. "Incredible." The most stunned of all was Kentucky Coach Joe Hall. "I can't explain it," he said afterward. "What happened is beyond me." Kentucky had failed to score on its first 14 possessions of the second half. For the half, the Wildcats made 3 of 33 attempts or 9 percent, an NCAA record low. The five starters missed all 21 shots they attempted in the second half. The Hoyas had moved to a 34-29 lead before Winston Bennett scored for Kentucky. Then Georgetown ran off another 11 points for a 45-31 lead. After a few more depressing minutes, it ended, 53-40. "They took everything away from me," Melvin Turpin lamented afterward. "Every time I turned around they were in my face."

With such an emotional victory, the fear for Georgetown was that the championship game with Houston would seem anticlimatic. The Cougars jumped out to a 10-2 lead, then watched Georgetown close the gap and take over. Olajuwon was called for his third foul just before the half. Then just 23 seconds into the last half, with the Hoyas leading 40-30, he was whistled for a fourth.

Houston closed to 51-47, then to 57-54, but could get no closer. With Reggie Williams providing critical scoring down the stretch, the two powers raced toward a 84-75 close. Finishing with 19 points, Williams led five Hoyas in double figures. Patrick Ewing, with 10 points and nine rebounds, was named the Most Outstanding Player. Others named to the All-Tournament Team were Olajuwon, Graham, and Houston's Alvi Franklin and Michael Young.

1985

The questions popped up in the first moments after Georgetown's victory in the 1984 title game. Would the Hoyas become the first team since UCLA to repeat as champions? The analysts thought so. "Georgetown has assembled the greatest amount of talent in college basketball since the Wooden era," wrote Al McGuire, "and for the first time in years I think there is an odds on chance for a repeat."

Over the summer, however, Hoya coach John Thompson decided that power forward Michael Graham wasn't taking his studies seriously enough and planned to hold the power for-

ward out for the season. Angered, Graham left the program. The loss of the intimidator was a blow. Even so, the Hoyas rolled with a power across college basketball in 1984-85.

Most of the war was fought in the Big East, where St. John's with Chris Mullin and Villanova with Eddie Pinckney and Harold Pressley had strong teams. Both of those schools joined Georgetown and Memphis State from the Metro Conference at the Final Four at Rupp Arena in Lexington, Kentucky, the first time in history that three teams from one conference had reached the big event. The team least expected to win was Villanova which had entered the tournament with a mediocre 19-10 record.

So much for expectations. Memphis State, coached by Dana Kirk, had survived in the Midwest Regional with a pair of squeakers, 59-57 over Boston College, and 63-61 over Oklahoma. Keith Lee and William Bedford gave the Tigers height along the front line, and Andre Turner ran things from the point. But Villanova had little trouble advancing, 52-45. St. John's had players aplenty in Mullin and frontliners Bill Wennington and Walter Berry. For rebounding and defense, Coach Lou Carnesecca added Willie Glass at forward. For confidence, they had a 66-65 win over Georgetown during the regular season that had propelled them briefly into the top ranking. But at the Final Four, it did them little good. Georgetown's David Wingate allowed Mullin a puny 8 points. Reggie Williams and Ewing rammed in 20 and 16 points respectively as the Hoyas advanced to the national championship game, 77-59.

When it was over, Carnesecca compared Georgetown to the great San Francisco dynasty with Bill Russell. "We tried everything," the St. John's coach said. "But when a club like Georgetown is executing and performing at that level of proficiency, there's very little you can do." The prospect of Villanova playing Georgetown for the title produced mostly guffaws. One Lexington columnist suggested that the NCAA not even bother to hold the Final. Asked what his team would have to do to win, Villinova coach Rollie Massimino replied, "We're going to have to play a perfect game ... And that may not be enough. We can't turn the ball over too much against their various pressure defenses. And we have to shoot in the 50 percent range." Considering that the Hoyas had held most of their opponents to near 40 percent shooting, Massimino seemed to be wishing for a lot. Yet if his team had shot a mere 50 percent, Villanova would have lost the championship by 14 points.

The Wildcats had to shoot nearly 80 percent to win by a hair. In the second half, Villanova shot 90 percent from the floor. Guard Harold Jensen was 5 for 5 from long range. To go with the shooting, guard Gary McLain gave Massimino errorless ball-handling. And the Wildcats' match-up zone smartly squeezed Georgetown's offense outside. The inside, meanwhile, was a standoff with Ed Pinckney, Harold Pressley and Dwayne McClain battling Ewing and company.

There were other factors that figured in the outcome. The Hoyas had to get the lead early and keep it to prevent Villanova from slowing the tempo. Reggie Williams ran off a string of jumpers to stake Georgetown to a 20-14 advantage, but a nagging ankle injury cut into his playing time. With him on the bench, Villanova worked its way back to take a 29-28 lead at the half. The Hoyas' uneasiness stretched into the second half,

as Villanova extended its advantage first to 36-30, then to 53-48. Georgetown kept pressing, though, and finally it worked, forcing a run of turnovers. Suddenly, the Hoyas took the lead, 54-53, and had the ball with four minutes remaining. The Georgetown crowd roared as third guard Horace Broadnax brought the ball up the floor. But the Hoyas opted not to play against the Villanova zone, and the Cats eased out of it momentarily. Then came the key turnover. Hoya forward Bill Martin's pass glanced off Broadnax' foot, and Villanova scooped up the loose ball. The momentum shifted again, and the Hoyas could never recover.

The crowd of 23,000 in Lexington's Rupp Arena witnessed a miracle. Villanova whipped Georgetown, 66-64, one of the most unexpected outcomes in tournament history. The Wildcats had hit a tournament record 78.6 percent from the floor. In the second half alone, Villanova shot 90 percent of their field goals, many of them long jumpers over the Hoyas' scrambling defense. Pinckney was named the tournament's outstanding player with 16 points, six rebounds and five assists in the title game. Teammates Gary and Dwayne McLain and Harold Jensen also made the team, as did Patrick Ewing.

1986

It appeared to be a terribly bad luck when Louisville's senior guard, Milt Wagner, broke his right foot two games into the 1984-85 season. But that injury turned out to be a very positive thing. Without it, there's a good possibility Louisville would not have won the 1986 championship. Wagner spent the rest of the '85 season watching from the bench, then resumed his career just in time for the Cardinals' golden season.

Wagner's injury brought another benefit to coach Denny Crum's team. The other starting guard, Jeff Hall, had to spend more time handling the ball. The 6-foot-4 Hall had always been considered a fine perimeter shooter, but the extra ball-handling work only improved his game and the team's balance. With Wagner and Hall as the senior guards, the 1985-86 Cards were an experienced group.

The other stalwart was 6-foot-7 senior forward Billy Thompson, out of Camden, N.J. He could play above the rim, but Thompson was also a zinger of a passer. His junior year, Thompson had led Louisville in scoring, rebounds and assists. The other forward, sophomore Herbert Crook, also 6-foot-7, was underrated. A superb offensive rebounder, he was thin and quick and nearly impossible to box out. And when he got the offensive rebound, he usually knew how to score with it. Into this foundation of experience, Crum set his prize recruit out of Georgia, 6-foot-9 freshman center Pervis Ellison, a shotblocker with his long arms and excellent timing. It was a group of players perfectly matched to the coach's system. They had the athleticism to play both of Crum's trademarks: tough man-to-man defense and up-tempo offense. Beyond that, they had an unusual amount of poise. After all, Wagner's nickname was "Ice," and before the season was over, Ellison would come to be known as "Never Nervous" Pervis.

The Cards won the first two games they played in the Big Apple NIT, the early season tournament, then headed for the semi-finals in New York. There Louisville lost close games to two very fine teams, Kansas and St. John's, both ranked in the Top 20.

Despite the loss, Crum remained confident. He knew Wagner was struggling to get back into form after the season off. Indeed, other people saw the potential as well. Tulsa Coach J.D. Barnett commented that Louisville belonged in the Western Division of the NBA after the Cards thunked and dunked his team in the second round of the pre-season tournament.

With a 2-2 record, the Cards returned home and picked up five straight wins, including a 65-63 thriller over Indiana. The game became a shooting match between Wagner and Indiana's Steve Alford. Wagner's 22 points marked the first sign that he was coming back to form. Later in the season, Louisville suffered a close loss to 13th-ranked Kentucky, but the freshman Ellison had played well. Among the impressed was Kentucky Coach Eddie Sutton, who said, "They have the type squad, if they continue to improve—and I think they will—that may very well be in Dallas [for the Final Four]."

After moving through a series of ups and downs, the Cards beat fourth-ranked Syracuse in Louisville, 83-73, as Wagner hit for 24 points. "One thing about Milt," Syracuse guard Pearl Washington said afterward. "When he gets his points, they're honest. Just jumpers. Pure jumpers. For my money, he's the best shooter in the country."

Still, the Cardinals were very much a work in progress. After a 71-69 loss to seventh-ranked Kansas on the road, they stood at 11-6 and appeared to be mediocre.

However, Louisville's tough schedule (a practice Crum picked up from Wooden) was deceiving. They ran off four straight wins from there, including a 91-72 topping of UCLA. "I told everyone at the start of the year," Crum reminded reporters, "that this team would have its ups and downs and probably wouldn't have a great record, but that we had the potential to be an outstanding team by the end of the year. I still feel that way. We're not bad right now. Tell me who else had played five Top 10 teams on the road."

Despite his optimism, fan discontent remained high. The home crowd had taken to booing Thompson, but the story changed dramatically from there. They ran off 11 straight wins, capturing the Metro Conference tournament title in the process with an 88-79 win over Memphis State. In the title game, Wagner scored 31. But Ellison's 21 points and 13 rebounds earned the freshman the Most Valuable Player award. It would be a scenario the Cards would repeat within days. "We are capable of being a Final Four team," Wagner told reporters. "We've got us a true center for the first time."

Louisville opened the NCAA tournament with big wins over Drexel and Bradley. But the West Region semi-final in Houston presented an imposing obstruction, a North Carolina team that featured Brad Daugherty, Kenny Smith, Joe Wolf and Jeff Lebo. Four times Crum had played against one of Dean Smith's Carolina teams in the past, and four times Crum had lost. The fifth, however, was the charm. Louisville surged to win, 94-79. "Our guys have all the confidence in the world," Wagner said afterward.

Auburn, with Chuck Person and Chris Morris, was the obstacle in the region final. Again, the Cards took control of a tight game late in the second half. Usually a stubborn man-to-man disciple, Crum resorted to a zone defense to cool down

Auburn's potent offense. Riding a 15-game winning streak, Louisville entered the Final Four in Dallas, where LSU, Duke and Kansas were vying for the prize. The trip to the big event would be Louisville's fourth in seven years. Wagner had played on three of those four teams. "I'm on a mission," he told reporters. In the national semi-finals, he scored 22 to lead his teammates past Dale Brown's LSU Tigers, 88-77. Duke squeezed past Kansas in the other bracket, setting up a meeting between the Cards, at 31-7, and the Atlantic Coast Conference champions with a 37-2 record.

Using his quickness, Duke's All-American guard Johnny Dawkins posed big problems for Louisville. With eight minutes to go, the Blue Devils led, 58-55, when Crum decided to switch Jeff Hall, who was not known for his quickness, to cover Dawkins, who had scored 22 points. Over the last eight minutes Hall held him to just two free throws. The Cards got the lead, 64-63, with just under three minutes to go, and down the stretch Ellison earned his "Never Nervous" tag, scoring on an offensive rebound and sinking key free throws. He finished with 25 points and 11 rebounds to earn the Most Outstanding Player award, only the second freshman to do so in NCAA tournament history (the first was Utah's Arnie Ferrin during World War II).

"It's unbelievable that a freshman can handle that kind of pressure and play as well as he did," Crum said. "Ellison was terrific," Duke coach Mike Krzyzewski told reporters. "He played a sensational game. He was a true force inside both offensively and defensively."

1987

For years, Bobby Knight had disdained the idea of recruiting junior college players for his Indiana teams. But the world of college basketball began to change in the 1980s after the NCAA adopted Proposition 48, the academic guidelines for athletic scholarships. Whether Proposition 48 was positive or negative for college athletics was much debated, but there was little question as to its effect. It prevented a large number of educationally disadvantaged athletes, the majority of whom were black, from gaining scholarships to Division I colleges and universities.

Many of the athletes denied admission chose to continue their studies at the nation's vast network of junior colleges. For nearly a half century, the JUCOs had been a proving ground for both players and coaches, many of whom went on to major and colleges and universities. But with Proposition 48, JUCO players became even more important to college programs.

Always desperate for the top players, many coaches were eager to bring in JUCO transfers to bolster their programs. Despite his reluctance, Knight finally joined this trend in 1986. To the great delight of Hoosier fans, the result was a championship combination: a pair of JUCOs to align with All-American Steve Alford. They brought Knight his third and Indiana's fifth national title with a sizzling late-game victory over Syracuse in the 1987 NCAA finals.

The junior college players, Dean Garrett and Keith Smart, joined Alford, Rick Calloway, and Daryl Thomas to give Indiana a veteran roster. Best of all, the Hoosiers could shoot, which was more important than ever in 1986-87. It was the

year of the 3-pointer, a controversial new rule that had some coaches fuming and some smiling the entire season. Dr. Edward Steitz, the long-time chairman of the rules committee, had engineered the change to offset the various zone defenses that had rendered college basketball boring. The abruptness of the change left some coaches—Louisville's Denny Crum, for example—without time to recruit players who could drill jump-shots from the 19-foot, 6-inch 3-point range. The teams that did emerge had long-range shooters in residence: Steve Alford at Indiana and Gerald Paddio and Freddie Banks at UNLV. Ultimately, the 3-pointer played a major role in determining the national championship, as Alford hit seven of 10 attempts in the Finals.

Coach Jerry Tarkanian's Nevada-Las Vegas club quickly employed the 3-pointer and gunned their way to the top seed in the West Regional. The Runnin' Rebels offered more than shooting, however, with senior Armen Gilliam in the front-court. In the regionals, the Rebels gunned down Idaho State, 95-70, Kansas State, 80-61, and Wyoming, 92-78, before fighting it out with a nifty Iowa team (coached by Dr. Tom Davis and led by Kevin Gamble) in the regional finals. Gilliam tallied 27 points and 10 rebounds as UNLV won a tight one, 84-81.

The Hoosiers, meanwhile, came out smoking in the Midwest Regional, drilling Fairfield, 92-58, in the first round, then sending home Auburn, 107-90 (Smart had 20 points, nine rebounds and 15 assists). From there, however, the regionals were a sweat, as Knight's team played the Duke Blue Devils, coached by his friend and former player, Krzyzewski. Duke had lost Dawkins and company from the season before but was still pesky in the semi-finals before losing 88-82. And Dale Brown (he and Knight didn't like each other) was waiting with another Cinderella team in the regional finals hoping to sneak into the Final Four. But Alford led four teammates in double figures with 20 points, and Indiana snipped Brown's hopes, 77-76.

The seasons brought another great show for the Big East Conference with emergence of both Providence and Syracuse. Providence, coached by Rick Pitino, was a surprise force in the Southeast Regional. The Friars were led by senior guard Billy Donovan and Delray Brooks, a transfer from Knight's Indiana. Donovan got the Friars' tour rolling with 35 points and 12 assists in an opening round win over Alabama-Birmingham. Then Providence threw cold milk on another Cinderella, Austin Peay, 90-87, in overtime and dumped second-seeded Alabama 103-82. But the real delight for Providence was whipping Big East rival Georgetown, 88-73, in the Southeast finals. For all the Providence joy, a pallor was cast over the regionals by death of Pitino's six-month-old son, Daniel Paul, after a long illness.

Syracuse coach Jim Boeheim's team came alive on the emergence of guard Sherman Douglas, and the maturation of center Rony Seikaly. It didn't hurt that the Orangemen played the first two rounds of the East Regional on their home floor, the massive Carrier Dome. Syracuse won two straight tournament games for first time in 10 appearances, downing Georgia Southern, 79-73, (as Sherman Douglas scored 27 points), and a good Western Kentucky team, 104-86, (Greg Monroe scored 20 for the Orange).

Then they beat Florida, 87-81, in the regional semi-finals and traveled on to the Final Four in New Orleans with a 79-75

win over N.C. State in the regional finals.

The semi-final in New Orleans was a Big East matchup, Orange versus Friars. But Syracuse pretty much solved the riddle early and coasted, 77-63, with all five starters in double figures. Howard Triche had 12 points and 11 rebounds. Derrick Coleman had 12 and 12. The atmosphere in the other semi-final was anything but sleepy. Tarkanian had put together a sleek unit at UNLV—the nation's top-ranked club much of the year—and nervously chewed his towel as the Runnin' Rebels pitched and pulled their way through a classic shootout with the Hoosiers.

Freddie Banks scored 38 including an incredible 3-point performance and Gilliam slipped in 32 for Vegas. Alford matched that with 33 for Indiana, but he had more help from his teammates, as Calloway, Garrett and Smart all rang up double figures. At the end, Indiana pushed away, 97-93.

The Indiana/Syracuse final was an odd, tight game that twisted the fans in knots. Knight played nine Hoosiers, but only four scored: Daryl Thomas had 20 with seven rebounds; Alford knocked in 23 points with five assists, two steals and three turnovers, (including seven of 10 from three-point range); Keith Smart scored 21 with six assists, two turnovers and two steals.

It almost wasn't enough against Syracuse's balance. Douglas led with 20 points and seven assists, and Seikaly was aggressive inside with 18 points and 10 rebounds. The Hoosiers had a 34-33 lead at the half, and that pace persisted. "I thought we were too tired to win it," Knight recalled. "We had had such a tough game with Vegas on Saturday." Going into the closing seconds, Syracuse was up, 73-72, until Smart launched a sweet jumper from the left baseline to give Indiana a 74-73 lead. The Orange first fumbled the notion of a timeout, then flubbed the inbound pass as the clock ran down.

Indiana had made seven of 11 three point attempts in the final, for 63.6 percent accuracy, much better than their 30 of 63 from two-point range for 48.4 percent.

"We didn't have a set play," Knight said of the winning shot. 'We wanted to run our offense and try to screen off the goal. I didn't want a shot taken until 10 seconds were left. We went inside to Thomas, and he made a great play getting the ball back outside to Smart. He got an open 16-foot shot from the baseline, and he drilled it.

"I keep saying this wasn't a great team, but there was a great quality to this team with its ability to make points. They went through tight games with Duke, LSU and Vegas and made almost every play that had to be made."

Smart was named Most Outstanding Player.

1988

They kept their scoreboards blinking and their opponents humble. The 1987-88 University of Oklahoma Sooners pinned a new look on the face of the college game. On defense they pressed and undressed opponents as no team had ever done before. On offense, they played without conscience, throwing down three pointers and jams with equal delight. The Sooners did all this while exhibiting a brashness seldom seen in amateur athletics. Other coaches might agonize about making the competition look too bad. But Oklahoma coach Billy Tubbs gloried in running up the score.

Early in the season, the Sooners ran weave drills past Georgia State, 124-81. Late in the game, State coach Bob Reinhart sent a player down to ask Tubbs to ease up. The Oklahoma coach responded by sending his team back into the full-court press. "Damn guy wanted mercy," Tubbs said later. For all their style, Tubbs' bunch began the season in relative obscurity—only two writers picked them in a preseason poll to win the Big Eight Conference title—but they got everybody's attention early.

Through their first 13 games, all wins, they averaged 117.2 points, second only in organized American basketball to the NBA's Denver Nuggets with 118.6. Most of the scores read like Australian rules football: Texas A&M 104-80; Penn State 93-59; Loyola-Chicago 123-73; Sam Houston State 111-69; Centenary 152-84; Virginia 109-61; Dayton 151-99; Oral Roberts 144-93; Illinois State 107-56; Austin Peay 109-69; Oklahoma State 108-80.

The slaughters forced a variety of publications to send feature writers to Norman to find out what was going on. Tubbs explained the secret was not offense, but that his pressing defense generated points in a hurry. But underneath those technicalities, the story was all personality. Billy Tubbs really seemed intent on redefining sportsmanship.

"One coach whined a little but I don't concern myself with it," Tubbs replied when asked about the scores. "My philosophy is that we're going to play hard every minute of the game, and there's no compromise on that."

Pinning the blame on his players really didn't work either, though. As center Stacey King explained, the team was just an extension of Tubbs' personality. "I might feel sorry for these teams getting blown out by 40 or 50," guard Ricky Grace told reporters, "but I've been around Coach too long. He says, 'Remember where nice guys finish.'"

He had to have 100 points a game, Tubbs told his players. And he wanted them to set records. Lots of 'em. Which they did.

The most impressive was the NCAA record for most points in a season: heading into the Final Four in Kansas City, the Sooners had scored 3,847 in 37 games. There were also NCAA records for most points against a Division I team, 152 vs. Centenary; and most steals, 34 vs. Centenary (Guard Mookie Blaylock set an individual steals record in that game with 13). To go with those, they set more than three dozen Big Eight Conference records for scoring, steals, blocked shots, assists, free throw attempts, you name it.

Always known as a football powerhouse, Oklahoma had begun to take on a new sports look after Tubbs left Lamar to take the coaching job there in 1980. After an initial losing season, he produced seven straight 20-win seasons, seven straight NCAA tournament appearances and three Big Eight championships. His program had been highlighted by stars Wayman Tisdale and Daryl Kennedy. But they had moved on by 1987-88, and Tubbs found quick replacements in junior college players, forward Harvey Grant and guards Blaylock and Grace.

The guards had been paired at Midland (Texas) Junior College. Grace had selected Oklahoma in 1986, while Blaylock played one more season for Midland, where he earned All-America honors. Paired together, they executed just as they had

at Midland. Although only six feet, Blaylock preferred to play shooting guard on offense while the 6-foot-1 Grace handled the ball. But on defense, it was Blaylock who delighted in reducing opposing point guards to nervous wrecks. He stole and stole again.

Grant, the other JUCO, had also considered attending Kansas after playing at Independence (Kansas) Junior College, where he, too, earned first-team All-America honors. A 6-foot-8 senior, Grant had started his career at Clemson with twin brother, Horace, but transferred when Horace got most of the playing time. Grant moved nicely into the role of leading scorer for the Sooners, spending most of the season averaging better than 23 points and 12 rebounds per game. His repertoire of shots featured 17-footers as well as the inside moves.

This inside game was a crucial pairing with the Oklahoma press. Tubbs' team had to make baskets to run the press, and Grant gave them plenty. But perhaps the Sooners' real strength was the fact that Grant wasn't their only inside force. The development of 6-foot-10 junior center Stacey King was the major factor. Teaming with Grant, the left-handed King averaged 22.5 points over 1987-88 while shooting 54 percent from the floor. His game featured a deft turnaround bank shot and a variety of short hooks. On defense, he was a natural shot-blocker, setting a Big Eight season record with 87.

In the Big Eight tournament, the Sooners ripped off three straight wins and doused Kansas State and Mitch Richmond in the finals to claim the conference title.

Everybody, it seemed, figured the Sooners a juggernaut to a national championship. But few people outside Oklahoma liked it. "Oklahoma's lust to run up the score is hard to watch," an Atlanta newspaper declared. Thriving on their high profile and laughing at their critics, Tubbs and his Sooners took a 34-3 record into the NCAA tournament. In order, they ripped Tennessee-Chattanooga, Auburn, Louisville, and Villanova on their way to the Final Four.

The event marked the 50th anniversary of the Final Four. To celebrate the occasion, the tournament returned to Kansas City, where so many of the great finals of the past had been held. There was a banquet for retired coaches and former players. And there were exhibits of memorabilia from the previous 49 years. In the semi-finals, Oklahoma faced second-ranked Arizona, and as many predicted, the Sooners easily dispatched Lute Olson's team. In the other bracket, Kansas and forward Danny Manning were the Cinderellas, upsetting Duke and Danny Ferry for the chance to play the Sooners for the national championship in Kemper Arena.

Kansas, with a 26-11 record, had lost twice to Oklahoma. And just about everybody figured the third meeting would be a cinch. But on its 50th anniversary, the NCAA tournament offered a championship game to stir America's underdog soul.

The first half was a bag of surprises as the Kansas players surged on the momentum of their emotion. They played beyond their abilities and couldn't seem to miss, shooting 64 percent from the field for the game, and well beyond 70 percent during much of the crucial early going. Manning provided an offensive core on which his teammates could build. And Kansas Coach Larry Brown blunted the effect of Oklahoma's withering pressure and speed with a series of deft substitutions.

The first half was probably the tightest in tournament history as the Jayhawks came out and ran with Oklahoma through its gasping pace. Throughout, the two teams traded points and turnovers furiously, and in the process, the Jayhawks sought to keep the tempo a few miles-per-hour off the Sooners' regular pace. Probably the most important first-half development was that Oklahoma's fabled pressure defense failed to crack the Jayhawks, and their confidence mounted. The half-time score of this 50th anniversary game was fittingly enough 50-50.

Still, at the end of the first half, the pace remained in Oklahoma's favor. But in the second half, Harvey Grant for some reason dropped off his coverage of Kansas' Chris Piper to help Stacey King cover Manning. When that happened, Piper became the open outlet for the Jayhawks' passing, and Kansas cracked the Sooner defense. Suddenly, the game went from a 100-point to a 75-point contest, very much in Kansas' favor. The second biggest factor was Oklahoma's poor shot selection in the second half. Ricky Grace had a particularly poor game, taking one bad shot after another. He continued to loft from outside instead of going inside to Grant and King. When Oklahoma didn't score, it couldn't apply its pressure defense.

Manning picked up his third foul early in the second half. But when Oklahoma didn't go inside, they missed an opportunity to force him into foul trouble. Which meant the Jayhawks' stamina was no longer a factor. Kansas faltered slightly midway in the second half when substitute Scooter Barry (son of Hall of Famer Rick) missed an inside shot and moments later had the ball stolen in open court. But even that trauma was resolved in the closing minutes as Barry hit a key free throw to preserve the win.

Manning and the University of Kansas upset top-ranked Oklahoma, 83-79. Manning finished with 31 points, 18 rebounds and five steals and was named the Most Outstanding Player.

1989

The proliferation of parity and the wisdom of expanding the post-season field to 62 teams was never more evident than it was in 1989. All of the Final Four teams would not have qualified for the NCAA Tournament prior to 1975 when, for the first time, more than one league member could be invited—champion Michigan (finished in third place in Big Ten Conference), Seton Hall (lost in Big East Tournament semi-finals after finishing runner-up to Georgetown in regular-season standings), Duke (lost in ACC Tournament final after finishing in three-way tie for second place behind North Carolina State in regular-season standings) and Illinois (runner-up in Big Ten to Indiana).

The roster Michigan's interim coach Steve Fisher inherited at the start of the playoffs included four future NBA first-round draft choices—Terry Mills, Glen Rice, Rumeal Robinson and Loy Vaught.

The season was full of record-setting magnificence and more than a few surprises. One of the all-time biggest upsets occurred when NCAA champion-to-be Michigan lost on a neutral court to obscure Alaska-Anchorage, 70-66, during the Wolverines' pre-Big Ten competition slate. Illinois became the only school to defeat the NCAA champion-to-be twice in one season by at

least 12 points when the Illini swept Michigan.

Other oddities abounded. Wake Forest's lone victory in one nine-game stretch in ACC competition was a 75-71 decision over Duke when the Blue Devils were ranked No. 1 in the nation. North Carolina failed to have an All-ACC first-team selection for the first time in 27 years. Duke's Danny Ferry established an ACC and school single-game record by pouring in 58 points at Miami (Fla.). Freshman teammate Christian Laettner, who would become national player of the year as a senior, went scoreless against Miami.

Loyola Marymount junior Hank Gathers became the only player to lead the nation in scoring (32.7 points per game) in a season he shot better than 60 percent from the floor (60.8). Gathers collected 41 points and a school-record 29 rebounds in 30 minutes in a 181-150 victory over U.S. International that set an NCAA record for most total points. Later, the Lions combined with Gonzaga to establish an NCAA standard for most points in a half by both teams (86 apiece in the second half for a total of 172) in a 147-136 Loyola Marymount triumph.

Kentucky's NCAA-record streak of consecutive non-losing seasons was stopped at 60 when the Wildcats compiled a 13-19 mark in Eddie Sutton's last year as their coach. They lost their home opener, 85-82, to a rag-tag squad from Northwestern (La.) State that finished the campaign with a 13-16 mark.

The tournament got underway with a compelling story. No. 16 seed Princeton pushed No. 1 seed Georgetown to the limit in the East Regional before the patient and precise Tigers bowed, 50-49, when a last-second shot was blocked. Seton Hall (31-7) made for its own compelling story. Seton Hall finished in the Top 20 of a final wire-service poll for the first time since 1953. Come tournament time, however, the Pirates rolled over South West Missouri State and Evansville before handing Bobby Knight's Indiana teams its worst NCAA tournament defeat in history, 78-65. They then dusted off UNLV (already victorious over number-one ranked Arizona) by employing a stifling defense to start a 33-8 run that turned a close one into an 84-61 route.

In the national semi-final against Duke, Seton Hall fell behind 26-8 in the first 11 minutes. Darryl Walker, the Pirates Senior center remembers thinking, "We weren't going to go down like that." Walker and frontcourt mate Andrew Gaze combined for 37 points, and guard Gerald Greene poured in 17. In the process they got four fouls on Duke center Christian Laettner and another four on his back-up Alaa Abdelnaby. A 38-33 half-time deficit was turned into a 95-78 blowout.

Ranked third in the Southeast, Michigan won by less than 10 points against Xavier (Ohio), South Alabama, and North Carolina. They then had a laugher against Virginia, 102-65. But against Illinois they won by the slightest of margins, 83-81, when Sean Higgins rebounded a missed three-pointer and put it back up with a second left.

That margin would be even smaller in the Final against Seton Hall. With over eight minutes the Wolverines were up by ten points when John Morton caught fire, tallying 17 points in eight minutes and tying the game on a three-pointer with 24 seconds left. Glen Rice, the tournament high scorer, then missed with two seconds remaining to send the game into overtime.

Seton Hall led by three with a 1:35 remaining when Morton missed in the lane and Michigan's Terry Mills hit to make it a one-point game, 79-78. After another Morton miss, Rumeal Robinson drove and a questionable foul was called on Seton Hall. Robinson, an inconsistent 65-percent free throw shooter hit both and Michigan won, 80-79.

Michigan became the NCAA titlist to win its two Final Four games by the fewest total of points (three). In the first overtime final since 1963, Seton Hall guard John Morton had the highest scoring output (35 points with 17 in the last eight minutes of regulation to help the Pirates erase a 12-point deficit) of any player for the losing team in a championship game. They had trailed by 18 points midway through the first half (26-8).

Rice, the Final Four Most Outstanding Player, set records for most three-point baskets and points in a playoff series (27 treys and 184 points in six games). The senior forward hit 12 of 17 from three-point range on his way to a total of 66 points in Southeast Regional semi-final and final victories over North Carolina (92-87) and Virginia (102-65). Rice's liberal use of the three-pointer enabled him to become the only player from a national champion to average more than 25 points per game in a title season (25.6) since David Thompson finished with a 26-point average for North Carolina State in 1974.

1990

In 1985, Paul Westhead, the former Laker coach, was named the head coach at little Loyola Marymount in Los Angeles and soon transformed the Lions into a high-scoring, high-ranking team. He did this largely on the skills of two Philadelphia high school stars, Hank Gathers and Bo Kimble.

Gathers and Kimble first had gone to Southern Cal, then transferred to Loyola Marymount in 1987. By the 1988-89 season, the 6-foot-7 Gathers was leading the nation in both rebounding (13.7) and scoring (32.7), and the Lions were the highest scoring team (112.5 points per game) in major college basketball. Westhead worried little about defense. Instead, he had his players rush upcourt to take three-pointers. Their 9.3 treys per game was also tops in the nation for 1988-89. This non-stop approach left many opponents gasping. The Lions finished 20-11 and made a brief appearance in the NCAA tournament.

But for 1989-90, Kimble and Gathers joined three other returning starters to push Loyola into the top 20. The Lions averaged better than 122 points per game, and Kimble, blasting away from three-point range, led the nation in scoring with a 35.7 average. But the bright prospects for the season dimmed unexpectedly when Gathers collapsed during a mid-season game. Doctors examined him, prescribed a heart medication and determined that he was fit to continue playing. Gathers, a spirited competitor, was determined to keep pace with Loyola's non-stop offense. But when he returned to action, he wasn't the same rebounding and scoring machine. There were reports that his medication slowed him down. Gathers then reportedly trimmed back the dosage in an effort to keep pace. In early March during a West Coast Conference tournament game against Portland on Loyola's home floor, Gathers again collapsed. Attempts to revive him failed, and he was pronounced dead.

The news stunned college basketball. Gathers' teammates

were devastated. But rather than end their season, the Lions decided to play on. "We had a lot to deal with quickly," Kimble told reporters. "It was hard on everyone. But we knew Hank would have wanted us to play in the NCAAs. At the memorial service [in the school's Gersten Pavilion] I looked over and saw that his coffin was in the paint. I knew then we would have to find a way to win for him." Kimble announced that he would shoot his first free throw in each tournament game left-handed in honor of Gathers (who had experimented with shooting his free throws left-handed). "It may sound corny," Kimble explained, "but it makes me feel like I've got a little bit of Hank inside me. It gives me strength."

Although the Lions were seeded only 11th in the West Regional, they beat sixth-seeded New Mexico State in the first round, 111-92, as the 6-foot-5 Kimble scored 45 points and pulled down 18 rebounds. Next, they blasted defending national champion Michigan, 149-115, setting an NCAA tournament record for points scored. (St. Joseph's owned the previous record, scoring 127 points in four overtimes against Utah in 1961.) Against the Wolverines, the Lions' Jeff Fryer made 11 of 15 three-point attempts and scored 41 points.

The emotion carried them all the way to the West Regional final against top-ranked Nevada-Las Vegas, a brash, high-scoring team. "They're living a dream," UNLV guard Greg Anthony said of the Lions before the game. "It's time someone woke them up." The Runnin' Rebels took the lead early and outran the Lions, 131-101.

Despite the inevitable loss, Loyola's run through the West Regional had been a fitting tribute to Gathers. His family later filed suit against Westhead and the university. But no one claimed the coach's and team's emotions weren't genuine.

Basketball has been marked by other tragedies, including:

• Len Bias, the University of Maryland star who died just hours after being taken as the second player in the 1986 NBA draft by the Boston Celtics. Not known for his drug use, Bias reportedly ingested a large amount of cocaine, claimed he was invincible, then collapsed and died. "That's the cruelest thing I ever heard," Larry Bird said when told of Bias' death.

• On February 8, 1965, Utah State's Wayne Estes scored 48 points against Denver. After the game, Estes began walking back to his room with three friends. On the way, the group encountered an auto accident. Walking by the scene, Estes brushed against a high-voltage power wire knocked loose by the collision. He was electrocuted by the 2,300-volt charge. Utah State's all-time leading scorer, he would later be named to the All-America team posthumously.

• Maurice Stokes, a 6-foot-7 center out of St. Francis College, was selected by the Rochester Royals in the first round of the 1955 NBA draft. He averaged 17 points and 16 rebounds over his first season to earn the Rookie-of-the-Year award. The Royals moved to Cincinnati for the 1956-57 season, and Stokes was one of their stars, averaging better than 17 points and 18 rebounds per game. In the last regular-season game, Stokes tripped and fell to the floor, hitting his head. He was out cold for three minutes. He recovered over the next few days and attempted to play in the Royals' first playoff game.

But afterward, he became terribly ill. Doctors examined him and determined he had encephalitis, which caused brain dam-

age and left him paralyzed. He would never be able to move or speak again, doctors predicted. The tragedy left Stokes destitute. But teammate Jack Twyman had himself named Stokes' guardian and began raising funds for his care. He eventually worked out a means of communicating in which Stokes would blink his eyelids in reply to questions. Twyman talked the NBA into holding a benefit game for Stokes, which raised $10,000. The event soon became an annual affair. In 1967, Stokes made an appearance at the game in New York and received an overwhelming ovation. Spurred on by the support of his fellow players, Stokes proved doctors wrong by learning to speak and regaining limited movement in his hands. His fight ended with his death in 1970. But his battle and Twyman's efforts remain an inspiration to pro basketball players and fans.

Twyman, by the way, was one of pro basketball's greatest shooting forwards. An All-American at the University of Cincinnati, Twyman went on to play for the Royals and became the sixth NBA player to score 15,000 career points. An iron man, he played in 609 consecutive games and was elected to the Hall of Fame in 1982.

Beyond the Gathers tragedy, college basketball was marked by the emergence of Tarkanian's UNLV Rebels in 1990. For years, Tarkanian had been at odds with the NCAA. The governing body of college athletics viewed the Nevada-Las Vegas coach as a renegade and had attempted in the 1977 to force the school to suspend Tarkanian for two seasons for rule violations. But Tarkanian blunted the NCAA's efforts with a lawsuit that dragged on for 13 years. During that time, UNLV teams racked up wins and Tarkanian persisted in his renegade ways. He specialized in talented but sometimes troubled athletes, some of whom had questionable academic credentials. Tarkanian viewed it as part of his mission to offer these athletes another chance to play basketball and get an education. "Education is for everybody," he once explained. "Nothing bothers me more than when someone says they don't belong in college. Why not give a kid the chance to improve, so he can have an opportunity when he gets out?"

But taking chances on troubled athletes sometimes backfired on Tarkanian. He often inherited their problems. Virtually consumed by basketball, he acquired the image of a win-at-all-costs coach. His nickname "Tark the Shark" confirmed it. In his early years at UNLV, few of his players graduated. "Number one, if all of our kids went to class and we lost, I'd be fired," he said. "There's no question about that. My job, I understand, is to win." Win, he did.

In seven years at Riverside City College and Pasadena City College, Tarkanian's teams went 212-26 and won five California junior college championships. From there, he moved to Long Beach State, where his teams posted a 116-17 record over five years and made four appearances in the NCAA tournament. He was hired at UNLV for the 1973-74 season, and within months the NCAA had placed Long Beach on three years' probation. Those troubles soon followed Tarkanian to Las Vegas. In 1977, the NCAA placed the school on two years' probation and ordered Tarkanian suspended. He obtained the state court injunction that allowed him to keep coaching.

By 1989-90, the case had gone all the way to the Supreme Court, and Tarkanian's UNLV teams had run up a 414-97

record. The school unabashedly gloried in the "Tark the Shark" identity. The atmosphere at the Thomas & Mack Center, where UNLV played its home games, was something to behold. The arena featured a giant shark in a tank. Each game was introduced by fireworks and a laser light show that helped to overwhelm opponents.

After years of coming close, the 59-year-old Tarkanian finally put together a championship-caliber team for 1989-90. Guards Greg Anthony and Anderson Hunt gave the Runnin' Rebels both quickness and shooting. Forward Stacey Augmon was an excellent defensive player with Olympic experience. Center David Butler was 6-foot-10 and averaged 15 points a game. To go with them, Tarkanian brought in Larry Johnson, the nation's top junior college player. A power forward, the 6-foot-7 Johnson had almost no body fat on his 250-pound frame.

Many sports publications predicted that Tarkanian's team would win the national championship. But at the height of his success, Tarkanian was also reaching the depth of his trouble. The NCAA investigators were probing the school's recruitment of troubled New York playground star Lloyd Daniels. And the Supreme Court had recently sided with the NCAA, opening questions about Tarkanian's future. When he wasn't coaching, he was wondering how the NCAA would resolve the 13-year-old issue of his suspension. Observers figured UNLV was headed for probation.

The bald, sad-eyed Tarkanian (he was of Armenian descent) carried the image of a world-class worrier. Since his days as a high school coach, he had superstitiously chewed a wet towel during tense moments of games. Yet his Rebels gave him precious little time to chew about during the 1989-90 season. Rather than becoming distracted by the NCAA actions, the players seemed to draw motivation from it. They grew stronger with each game and rolled to the Final Four in Denver's McNichols Arena as the obvious favorite.

In the national semi-finals, Georgia Tech with freshman sensation Kenny Anderson and three-point artist Dennis Scott gave UNLV some first-half trouble. But the Rebels snuffed Georgia Tech with defense. For the first time in his career, a Tarkanian team was headed to the national championship game. Waiting there were the Duke Blue Devils, setting up one of the more intriguing match-ups in tournament history: Tarkanian with his renegade team against highly respected Duke, steeped in an image of academic responsibility.

The Blue Devils had played in seven previous Final Fours and never claimed a championship. Coach Mike Krzyzewski hoped the eighth time would end the drought.

Duke had a core of three seniors: center Alaa Abdelnaby, guard Phil Henderson and forward Robert Brickey. Beyond that, however, the Devils were young, with three freshmen and two sophomores in the top eight players. The offense, in fact, relied on freshman point guard Bobby Hurley. When the Blue Devils lost, they usually lost big, as evidenced by 19- and 12-point defeats at the hands of ACC rival North Carolina.

The important factor for Duke was the coach, tournament-tough Krzyzewski. He had coached teams to the Final Four in four out of the five seasons since 1986. His teams played defense and showed a knack for making the big shot. Most

observers, however, figured Duke wouldn't get past Nolan Richardson's talented Arkansas team in the national semi-finals. But Duke's experience and defense were too much for the Razorbacks.

In the championship game, UNLV made quick work of Duke. Tarkanian's guards harassed Hurley into numerous turnovers. First the lead was 21-11, then 47-35 at the half. UNLV was up 57-47 with 16 minutes left and settled the issue by scoring 18 unanswered points over the next three minutes. Tarkanian's Runnin' Rebels blasted their way to the title, 103-73, the largest margin of victory in tournament history. Johnson, who played only 30 minutes, led the assault with 22 points, 11 rebounds and four steals. Anderson, who made 12 of 16 from the floor to finish with 29 points, was named the tournament's Outstanding Player.

"It was scary just watching them," Duke's Abdelnaby said. "They engulfed us."

Reporters asked a smiling Tarkanian if the victory was sweet revenge against the NCAA. "I don't look at this as sweet revenge," he said. "Just sweet."

1991

There was much speculation in the press that after leading UNLV to the national championship, forward Larry Johnson would promptly renounce his amateur status to enter the NBA draft. Such a move made good sense. As one of the top picks, Johnson would sign a fat pro contract. Plus UNLV seemed headed for certain NCAA probation.

Johnson, however, elected to stay in school. He explained that he wanted to earn a four-year degree and lead the Runnin' Rebels to another title.

It would be quite a feat. No team had repeated as NCAA champs since UCLA and Bill Walton did it in 1972 and '73. Not long after Johnson announced his intentions to stay, the NCAA hit UNLV with a year's probation as a result of the settlement of Tarkanian's suit. Johnson and his teammates complained bitterly and pointed out that the probation prevented their team from defending the title. In response, NCAA executive director Richard Schultz pulled a surprise move and postponed the probation for one season. Never in its history had the NCAA granted such a postponement. Given a reprieve, the Runnin' Rebels then set out to dominate the college game. They were a powerful force during the regular season, crushing opponents by an average margin of 29.4 points per game. They stacked up leads of 30, 40, even 50 points each game until Tarkanian pulled his starters and played the subs. Their winning streak (dating back to the previous season) grew to 25, then 30.

Each win brought more declarations that the Rebels were the greatest team of all time. California-Irvine coach Bill Mulligan, who had coached against John Wooden's great teams at UCLA, was a Vegas booster. "I know Wooden says his teams could beat Vegas," Mulligan said. "But he had guys starting who couldn't play on this Vegas team. I've been coaching for 35 years, and to me, this is the best college basketball team I've ever seen." New Mexico State coach Neil McCarthy agreed. "I get tired of talking about Vegas because it's demoralizing in a way," he told Steve Wieberg of *USA Today*. "They're a great, great

basketball team, and I would match them up against anybody that's played on a collegiate level. I've seen the USF [San Francisco] teams, the Indianas and the UCLAs. That's not to take anything away from those great champions, but the game has changed a little bit the last few years. Vegas epitomizes excellence in just about every department."

To many observers, the Rebels seemed a sure bet to power their way to a second national championship, finishing the season with a 36-0 record and a 46-game winning streak. Tarkanian, ever the worrier, didn't agree. "We're certainly not unbeatable," he said. UNLV's dominance did little to lessen Duke's humiliation.

"It was devastating," Bobby Hurley said of the 1990 title game. Hurley told reporters of his recurring off-season dream: He's in a swimming pool surrounded by sharks. But after dreaming frequently, the young point guard said he grew used to swimming with the sharks. At least in his dreams. Hurley seemed to gain maturity over his sophomore campaign, and some observers felt the Blue Devils were a stronger team despite the fact that Abdelnaby, Henderson and Brickey had completed their eligibility. Freshman forward Grant Hill, the son of Dallas Cowboy great and former Yale star Calvin Hill, was only a freshman, but he was a slashing, driving player and a solid defender. Those skills went a long way toward eliminating Duke's deficiencies. Also stepping to the fore were guard Thomas Hill (no relation to Grant), backup center Antonio Lang and small forward Brian Davis. They and Greg Koubek, the team's only senior, gave Kryzyzewski the depth he needed.

But the Devils still played "young." They finished the regular season with only six losses, then played their way to the ACC tournament finals, where they suffered yet another humiliation, a 96-74 loss to North Carolina. With a 26-7 record, Duke entered the Midwest Regional and quickly recovered. In order, they turned aside Northeast Louisiana, Iowa, Connecticut and St. John's to reach the Final Four in Indianapolis, giving the 44-year-old Krzyzewski his fourth consecutive appearance and fifth in six years.

UCLA had been to 10 straight Final Fours from 1967-76, and Cincinnati had made five straight, from 1959-63. Although Krzyzewski's team had never won the title, he was the tournament's winningest active coach, with a 25-7 record in NCAA play. "It's because he's got his system down to a science" center Christian Laettner said of his coach. "He knows what he's doing every day and every week, and it's all geared toward playing well in March. You need a certain talent level, but he brought the talent here. And he knows what to do with it."

Krzyzewski had jokingly sworn before the 1990 championship that he would grow a beard and change his name if Duke lost. But afterward he did neither, choosing instead to go back to the system that had served him well. There was no doubt that he hungered for another shot at the Rebels. That came when Vegas won the West Regional. It would be Duke and UNLV in the national semi-finals, a dream rematch if there ever was one.

The other semi-final wasn't bad either. Dean Smith had coached North Carolina through the East Regional. And his former assistant coach, Roy Williams, had directed the Kansas Jayhawks through the Southeast, where they upset second-ranked Arkansas. Their teams played alike and battled to a near standstill. Kansas was led by senior Mark Randall in the frontcourt and sophomore Adonis Jordan at the point. Carolina relied on a depth of talented players, led by senior Rick Fox. Down the stretch, the Jayhawks pulled ahead and won. In one of the NCAA tournament's ugliest moments, official Pete Pavia ejected Smith with just seconds left in the game. Many editorialists said the ejection was uncalled for. (Smith was out of his coaching box in a low-key protest of the officiating.) Smith, a Hall of Famer, was escorted off the floor by security guards.

The other semi-final offered no such theatrics, but held plenty of intensity. Krzyzewski hadn't looked at the film of Duke's 1990 championship debacle. But after his team won the Midwest Regional, he viewed the massacre. Then he spent the week preparing his team, and just before the semi-final on Saturday he let them watch the gruesome evidence. He wanted them motivated but he didn't want them to feel the pressure of Duke's nine trips to the Final Four without a championship. "We're not in it for what past Duke teams have done or not done," he told them. "You're in it for yourselves."

And they played like it. The Vegas challenge was substantial. Senior center George Ackles had moved into the starting line-up, and the Rebels hadn't missed a beat. With four seniors and a junior, their starting five reeked of experience. Duke's primary goal was to keep it close and hope that either UNLV point guard Greg Anthony or Johnson got into foul trouble. The plan called for a double-team of Johnson and a strong effort at cutting off the Vegas fast break. Most important, Duke's players had to get confidence early, which they did, jumping to a 15-6 lead. From there, Laettner kept them going with 20 first-half points. (He would finish with 28 and seven rebounds.) That, in turn, infused the rest of the roster. Freshman Grant Hill played excellent defense and scored 11 points with five rebounds. And Hurley swam with the sharks, scoring 12 points (including critical three-of-four shooting from three-point range) and getting seven assists. The Rebels, meanwhile, helped the Duke effort by making only nine of 15 free-throw attempts.

With 3:51 to go in the game and UNLV leading 74-71, Anthony picked up his fifth foul on a charging call. Tarkanian inserted reserve forward Everic Gray, which left the Rebels without a driver at the wheel. Duke caught, then passed Vegas. In the final seconds, Laettner hit two free throws for a 79-77 lead. Johnson had the ball with time on the clock, but he passed it to Anderson Hunt, who took a three-pointer and missed. Duke halted the UNLV winning streak at 45 games.

"We had the ball in the hands of our best player in the open court and he gave it up," Tarkanian lamented afterward. "I'll never have a group of players like this again," he added. "You only get a team like this once in your career. This was a very special group of kids."

Duke, meanwhile, celebrated deliriously. The game had worked just like their coach had told them. "We talked about it all week," Grant Hill said. "We had played a tough schedule; we'd been in a lot of close games. We knew that UNLV had been winning almost every game by 20 or 30 points. Coach told us that would be our advantage. If we could get to the final minute close, they'd fold."

In the championship, Duke cooled red-hot Kansas in the

first half. The Blue Devils shot 59 percent from the floor. Then they pulled away with a 13-4 run midway through the second half. They led 61-47 with 8:30 to play, but the Jayhawks closed to within five points. Duke answered with another run, pushing the score to 70-59 with a little over a minute to go. From there, the Blue Devils claimed their first title, 72-65.

"We wanted to give Coach this one. He's earned it," said Hurley, who finished with 12 points and five assists. Laettner led Duke with 18 points and was named the tournament's outstanding player. Sophomore reserve guard Billy McCaffrey scored 16.

Krzyzewski said it was nice that his players said they won the championship for him. But he added, "Kids shouldn't play for coaches. They should play to play together and to have fun." There was little doubt that it had been fun. "It's nice," Krzyzewski said, "to say we finally played well in April."

1992

It was a year when the consensus All-Americans were Ohio State's Jimmy Jackson, Southern Cal's Harold Miner, Georgetown's Alonzo Mourning, Louisiana State's Shaquille O'Neal and Duke's Christian Laettner.

There was also a constant buzz about the Michigan Wolverines freshmen, the quintet known as the "Fab Five:" Chris Webber, Jalen Rose, Juwan Howard, Ray Jackson and Jimmy King. But the story of the entire season was about one University: Duke

Duke (35-2) became the first team since North Carolina in 1982 to be ranked number one all season and win the championship. By reaching the title game in its third consecutive year it matched the records established by UCLA, Cincinnati, and Ohio State. The year marked coach Mike Krzyzewski's fifth consecutive trip to the Final Four. He did the unthinkable and temporarily passed UCLA legend John Wooden (47-10, .8246) for the top spot in all-time NCAA playoff winning percentage (minimum of 20 games). Moreover, Duke became the first school since UCLA (1967-73) to repeat as national champions.

Early in the tournament, Duke enjoyed easy wins over Campbell and Iowa. The next victim was Seton Hall, 81-69. But Kentucky, their opponent in the East Regional final at the Philadelphia Spectrum, would be the furthest thing from easy. The game was played at an extraordinarily high level. Kentucky hit 57 percent of its shots, led by Jamal Mashburn with 28 points (and 10 rebounds) and guard Sean Woods with 21. Duke was accurate 65 percent of the time. Christian Laettner scored 31 and Bobby Hurley added 22. Duke led at halftime, 50-45. After regulation it was tied at 93. Woods' bank shot made it 103-102 with two seconds left. Grant Hill then heaved a pass some 75 feet, from the baseline to the opposite foul line. Laettner took the pass, dribbled once and shot a turnaround that went through as time expired, giving Duke a 104-103 victory. Laettner had connected on all 10 of his field goals and all 10 of his free throws. The game would go down as one of the most exciting playoff games ever.

Next was the national semi-finals and Duke trailed Indiana at halftime, 42-37. Hurley poured in 26 and Duke squeaked by Indiana, 81-78. To get to the semi-final Michigan needed an overtime win against Ohio State. Against Cincinnati they had

another close one, winning 76-72, despite Nick Van Exel's game-leading 21 points.

Compared to the overtime game for the ages against the Wildcats, the Final in Minneapolis was actually anti-climatic. Though Michigan led the lackluster game at the half, 31-30, Laettner dominated the second half with 14 points and 19 for the game. Sophomore Grant Hill was outstanding, logging 18 points, 10 rebounds, and five assists. Duke won easily, 71-51.

Bobby Hurley was named Most Outstanding Player, but dissenters believed that Duke teammate Grant Hill deserved the honor instead. In the two Final Four games, Hill had more field goals than Hurley (14 to 10), outshot him from the floor (61 percent to 41.7), blocked more shots (5 to 0), out-rebounded him (16 to 3) and accumulated just as many assists (11 each). Moreover, Hurley's 3 of 12 field-goal shooting in the final against Michigan was the worst marksmanship from the floor for a Final Four Most Outstanding Player in a championship game since Elgin Baylor of runner-up Seattle went 9 of 32 against Kentucky in 1958.

Guard Jalen Rose became the only freshman to finish with the highest season scoring average for a team reaching the NCAA Tournament championship game. He averaged 17.6 points per game for national runner-up Michigan. Rose and Chris Webber became the only set of freshman teammates to be named to an NCAA All-Tournament team.

1993

Despite the overwhelming success of 1982, the University of North Carolina faithful saw their team close out the decade with another string of near misses, as one talented Tar Heel team after another failed to climb out of the NCAA tourney regionals.

Happily, the '90s finally brought more rounds of sweet success. First came a return to the Final Four in 1991, where the Heels came head to head with Kansas in the national semi-finals at Indianapolis only to lose. The Tar Heels' next march to the top came two seasons later when the 1993 team used a blue-collar mindset to reach the national championship game. The setting, magically enough, was once again New Orleans.

Hard-nosed forward George Lynch provided the rebounding and leadership. Sophomore guard Donald Williams offered up a sweet perimeter shot. Center Eric Montross had the interior size and post game. Derrick Phelps was the heady junior point guard while Brian Reese turned in a great season at small forward. Henrik Rodl, Kevin Salvidori, and Pat Sullivan all made key contributions as well.

Early in the season, the Heels lost a one-point game to the University of Michigan's Fab Five, but that more than anything gave them confidence that they could play with the best teams in the country. By January, they had run their record to 17-1, and the sense that this could be a special season was settling across Chapel Hill. The key complicating factor would prove to be the health of point guard Phelps, who was first injured during the ACC regular season. Phelps took a bad fall against Virginia in the ACC tournament semi-finals and was unavailable for the championship game, which Carolina lost to Georgia Tech. He returned, however, for the Heels roll in the NCAAs.

The avenue this time was the East Regional, where Carolina bounced Arkansas and Cincinnati, where Williams hit a last-minute bucket to beat the Razorbacks, then followed that up with a big performance in overtime to nail the Bearcats. Lynch had set the outcome with a 21-point, 14-rebound performance. Once again, the matchup in the national semi-finals was against Roy Williams' Kansas club, but this time the Tar Heels didn't let the game get away from them, mainly because Lynch refused to let that happen.

The senior forward had felt that Carolina was the better team in 1991 but had failed to exhibit the determination. This time, he made sure the Heels were brimming with it.

Mainly, Carolina coach Dean Smith wanted to make sure that his team avoided the open-court game that Kansas had gotten them into in 1991. The Carolina coach wanted it to be a battle in the post, with Montross taking on the Jayhawks' Greg Ostertag.

Working off the low screens in Carolina's offense, Montross powered inside to outscore Ostertag 23-2, the primary difference in Carolina's 78-68 win. Once again, Phelps had to shrug off painful injury to return to the game to preserve the lead down the stretch.

In the national championship game on Monday night, the Heels faced a rematch with Michigan's Fab Five, the team that had given them their one-point loss at a tournament in Hawaii early in the season. In the West regional. Michigan had survived overtime against UCLA, then whipped George Washington and Temple on the way to the Final Four. The Wolverines' opponent in the national semi-finals was Kentucky, led by Jamal Mashburn. The Wolverines needed overtime again to advance 81-78, to meet Dean Smith's team for the national title.

In the hours before the event, Michigan forward Chris Webber offered the opinion that he and teammate Juwan Howard obviously gave the Wolverines the dominant front-court in the game. Lynch's answer was to screw his determination even tighter, telling his teammates in the huddle just before tipoff, "Let's win this one for coach Smith." Michigan, though, took an early eight-point lead, prompting Smith to switch to a 3-2 zone, which helped ignite a Tar Heel run that first tied the game then sent Carolina to a 42-36 halftime lead. Much of the offense was provided by Donald Williams, who was on his way to putting down a Final Four record 10 three pointers in two games.

Michigan surged in the second half and took a 65-61 lead. Williams responded with a 12-footer and another trey to pull closer. Then Phelps hit a twisting layup to give Carolina a 68-67 edge with just over three minutes left. Lynch and Montross both scored to push that margin to five points with a minute left. The Wolverines, however, charged right back, cutting it to 73-71, and trouble loomed when Pat Sullivan missed a late free throw for Carolina. Webber rebounded and was soon snared in a Carolina trap when his teammates headed upfloor without looking to help him bring it up. In deep trouble, Webber called for time, one of those classic Final Four moments. Unfortunately, the Wolverines had burned their timeouts, meaning that the Heels buried the win in a run of technical free throws. Like that, Dean Smith had national title number two, 77-71.

1994

After missing the NCAA Finals for the first time in four years in 1993, Duke was back at it again in 1994. The cast of characters were a combination of the old and the new, but mostly new. The new Blue Devils were led by senior Grant Hill, a consensus All-American in 1994, along with California's Jason Kidd, Connecticut's Donyell Marshall, Purdue's Glenn Robinson, and Louisville's Clifford Rozier. Robinson, with an average of 30.1 points, to go with 10 rebounds, was chosen National Player of the Year. He was the first Big Ten player to lead the country in scoring since Purdue's Dave Schellhase in 1966.

But this was a basketball season when most everyone was cut down by the Arkansas Razorbacks. Arkansas was led by a couple of sophomores, Corliss Williamson (20.4 ppg) and Scotty Thurman (15.9). The dapper coach Nolan Richardson led his charges to a 31-3 mark, sharing Coach of the Year honors with Purdue's Gene Keady (29-5), St. Louis' Charlie Spoonhour (23-6) and Missouri's Norm Stewart (28-4).

Boasting a roster with 11 different players who had a season high in scoring of more than 10 points, Arkansas ended a SEC dry spell in the NCAA playoffs. Despite having an average of three first-round NBA draft choices annually in 15 years since 1979, no current member of the 12-team SEC reached the NCAA Tournament championship game in that span although every school participated in the playoffs at least once.

Arkansas' title vindicated Richardson, who probably would have been dismissed in 1987 after his second season with the Hogs if they didn't rally from a 21-point second-half deficit in the NIT to edge Arkansas State, 67-64, in overtime. But that wasn't the most strain he faced that year because his 16-year-old daughter, Yvonne, died of leukemia. "The people who barbecued me ran out of sauce," said Richardson, who was also a leading figure in a national controversy concerning alleged racial injustices. Richardson became one of a kind: the only coach to win national championships in junior college (1980 with Western Texas), the NIT (1981 with Tulsa) and the NCAA.

If pressure had a habit of finding Richardson, it must be said he transferred to the makeup of his team. Arkansas in 1994 will forever be known as a defense-driven team, a team that wrought such havoc on the defensive end that they became known as "40 minutes of hell." Arkansas led 34-33 at halftime and even a 13-0 run by Duke in the second half couldn't put the Razorbacks out of sorts. Pressure was also intense on Arkansas swingman Scotty Thurman with the shot clock winding down and the score tied with 50.7 seconds remaining when he lofted a three-point attempt over Duke's Antonio Lang that hit nothing but net. Thurman attributed his ability to get off such a high arc shot to an age-old drill shooting over a defender with a broomstick his coach at Ruston (La.) High School employed during practices. "He made a great play," Duke guard Chris Collins said of Thurman after the Razorbacks' 76-72 victory. "The national championship, less than a minute left, tie game—he made a great shot."

Final Four Most Outstanding Player Williamson briefly surpassed Bill Walton's playoff field-goal shooting record (68.6

percent) before missing his first five shots in the final against Duke's Cherokee Parks and finishing the game 10 of 24 from the floor.

1995

If anyone doubted how big college basketball had become, CBS television removed the doubts. In 1995 they paid $1.725 billion for the broadcast rights to the tournament through 2002. The consensus All-Americans were UCLA's Ed O'Bannon, Arizona's Damon Stoudamire. Maryland's Joe Smith, North Carolina's Jerry Stackhouse, and Michigan State's Shawn Respert. But this season's story was not about high finance or individual excellence.

It was about the return to glory for UCLA. UCLA, the all-time leader in championships with 11, hadn't won since 1975. As great as the Bruins were—winning 10 of 12 titles from 1964 through 1975—they were starting to slip through the cracks of history. Jim Harrick coached the Bruins to a 31-2 mark and earned a share of the Coach of the Year honors.

In the Finals UCLA had to face defending champ Arkansas, with the components of their "40 minutes of hell" defense from the previous year still in place.

UCLA playmaker deluxe Tyus Edney, a senior who had logged seven assists per game in quarterbacking the Bruins' attack all year, played only three minutes in the Final because of a sprained right wrist. But his replacement, Cameron Dollar, played like a million dollars. "I was definitely tight and tense at the beginning," said Dollar, who committed just one turnover. "Then I got going and it turned out to be just another game, like any other day in the playground."

Edney played the role of Wizard of Westwood II with a series of breathtaking drives and baskets in the first five playoff games, including a length-of-the-court game-winner against Missouri in the second round. UCLA led by a single digit, 40-39, at the half. But forward Ed O'Bannon collected 30 points and 17 rebounds. UCLA dusted the Razorbacks off the backboards, 50-31. The result was an 89-78 victory over Arkansas.

O'Bannon logged one of the best title game performances in history. He became only the third different player to amass at least 30 points and 15 rebounds in a championship game, joining Clyde Lovellette (Kansas '52) and Lew Alcindor (UCLA '68 & '69). During a crucial five-game stretch in February, O'Bannon averaged 27.8 points and nine rebounds per game. Toby Bailey became the only freshman to score more than 25 points in a national championship game when he tallied 26 after managing just two in the semi-finals against Oklahoma State. UCLA became the only champion other than Kentucky '51 to have six players finish the season with scoring averages higher than nine points per game.

1996

UCLA had won its eleventh NCAA championship in 1995. By then it might easily have been forgotten who was runner-up to the Bruins. It's understandable: like UCLA, they hadn't won since the 1970s and so their once proud tradition was lost to a new generation of fans. Of late the Kentucky Wildcats had near misses aplenty.

But there would be no warming up this year. Rick Pitino's 'Cats clawed to a 34-2 mark and ended up winning their sixth national championship. For a moment, Kentucky's air of invincibility dissipated when the Wildcats' 27-game winning streak was shattered by Mississippi State in the SEC Tournament final. But UK quickly regrouped, and the Big Blue showed clearly in the NCAA playoffs that it was the nation's premier team.

Kentucky's dominance in the Midwest Regional led some observers to again believe the Wildcats were untouchable. Consider: they blew out San Jose State, 110-72, then Virginia Tech, 84-60. The Next victim was Utah, 101-79, followed by Wake Forest 83-63. The average margin of victory was 24 points.

But two rugged games at the Final Four revealed that the principal difference between the Wildcats and the remainder of the field was roster depth brimming with high school All-Americans. UK, entering the Final Four with an opportunity to become the first NCAA kingpin to win all of its playoff games by at least 20 points, won both Final Four games by a single-digit margin. Massachusetts and Syracuse cut double-digit second-half deficits to two against the 'Cats before faltering as they captured their first NCAA title since 1978.

National player of the year Marcus Camby finished with 25 points and eight rebounds in the semi-finals for UMass, but at one point he went almost 16 minutes without a field goal to impede its "refuse to lose" motto. "I want us to play mother-in-law defense: constant nagging and harassment," said Pitino before the game. And so they did. Kentucky prevailed, 81-74, behind Tony Delk's 20 points.

In the Final, Kentucky shot with two barrels. Freshman Ron Mercer gave Kentucky a big boost with 20 points and Delk hit for 24 and tied a championship game record with seven three-pointers. The Wildcats won, 76-67, despite shooting 38 percent from the floor, the lowest for a winner in 33 years. Delk was the Final Four Most Outstanding Player.

1997

Kentucky made the Finals again in 1997, but without the same result. There was a new winner in town—a school that had never won before. The Arizona Wildcats finished 25-9—not usually the kind of team that ends up cutting down the nets following the Final Four. But coach Lute Olson's troops dug out the tough games to win.

Arizona was so ordinary for so much of the season that they came within four points of finishing 9-9 in the Pacific-10 Conference. Nonetheless, they beat the three winningest programs in the history of major-college basketball (No. 1 seeds Kansas, North Carolina and Kentucky) in its last three playoff games to capture the NCAA crown. The Wildcats are the only team to win an NCAA crown after finishing as low as fifth place in its league.

It wasn't smooth sailing for Arizona in the tournament either. Leading scorer Michael Dickerson struggled during the tourney, shooting 5 of 28 from three-point range. The Wildcats overcame 10-point second-half deficits against South Alabama and the College of Charleston in the first two rounds. In the Southeast Regional final against Providence, two technical fouls with 6:50 remaining helped push Arizona to a 12-point cush-

ion before the Wildcats blew that lead and nearly lost when the Friars missed a last-second shot in regulation.

Simon and backcourtmate Mike Bibby combined for two-thirds of UA's points in a 66-58 victory over North Carolina in the national semi-finals to snap the Tar Heels' 16-game winning streak.

Arizona, capitalizing on a 34-9 edge in free throws made, prevailed in the Final against Kentucky, 84-79, despite not making a field goal in overtime. Bibby and Simon combined for 49 points. Bibby, who committed eight turnovers in the final, is the first freshman point guard to lead a team to a crown since the NCAA made freshmen eligible in the 1972-73 campaign. Bibby became the highest-scoring freshman at the Final Four for an NCAA titlist with a total of 39 points. Speed killed UK, however, as Arizona's quickness among perimeter players negated Kentucky's vaunted press and also pressured Kentucky's 30 three-point attempts.

Neither team gained a double-digit lead in the championship game. The score was tied 16 times, and there were 18 lead changes. "I think we just wanted it more in the end," said Miles Simon, the Final Four Most Outstanding Player who had missed UA's first 11 games because of academic difficulties. "Their legs were tired. We played with great heart." Lute Olson, making his fourth Final Four appearance, had been the only coach to go winless at the Final Four among the first 25 to reach the national semi-finals at least three times.

"I'm very proud of the toughness of this group that no one thought should be here and no one thought could do it," said Olson, who had endured three first-round ousters in a four-year span from 1992 through 1995.

The playoff storyline was a good one with an overtime Final, but the aesthetics of Arizona's NCAA title underscored a serious erosion for college basketball teams tending to fundamentals. The Wildcats became the first champion since the national tourney went to four regionals in 1956 to shoot less than 40 percent from the floor in both the national semi-finals and final. The national numbers weren't pretty, either, as teams across the country combined to hit 43.5 percent of their field-goal attempts, continuing a decline from an all-time high of 48.1 percent in 1983-84.

1998

Kentucky was back for a third straight Final in 1998. Their new coach was Tubby Smith, who had come over from the University of Georgia after Rick Pitino had departed to coach the Boston Celtics. The change in leadership didn't slow Kentucky: they ran up a 35-4 record and finished in first place in the SEC East Division by three games with a 14-2 record.

This Wildcat bunch was known as the "Rally Cats." To get to the Final Four they had to come back from a 17-point deficit with 9 1/2 minutes remaining to beat Duke, 86-84, in the South Regional final. Duke, losing its first regional final in coach Mike K's eight trips that far, reeled off 17 unanswered points in the first half but played the last 5:21 without a time-out and was unable to break UK's momentum. The tournament rivalry between the two teams had been cemented six years earlier when Christian Laettner beat Kentucky with a last second shot.

A harbinger of the Duke-Kentucky contest came three months before. Duke was ranked No. 1 in mid-December when the Blue Devils blew a 17-point, second-half lead and bowed at Michigan, 81-73. They won 14 games by 30 points or more, but squandered the same 17-point cushion in the South Regional final against Kentucky.

Kentucky not only had a new coach in Smith, but its roster was without a couple of outstanding players (Ron Mercer and Antoine Walker) who could have been eligible if they hadn't left early for the NBA. UK was 33-0 when leading with two minutes remaining.

Oddly, Kentucky and Utah reached the Final although neither team had a player named a first-, second- or third-team All-American on the AP honor squad. This was a no-name, defensive oriented Kentucky team. With their best players of the previous two seasons in the pros, they had to rely on players like Jeff Sheppard and Heshimu Evans. In Kentucky's national semi-final, teammate Nazr Mohammed, a center who shed more than 60 pounds since attending high school, scored 17 second-half points against Stanford to help erase his 0-for-6 free-throw shooting in the 1997 final vs. Arizona. Kentucky needed an overtime to take Stanford 86-85. Utah made its first Final Four appearance in 32 years while Stanford made its first in 56 years.

No team ever had rallied from a double-digit half-time deficit to win the NCAA championship game until Kentucky erased Utah's 41-31 edge at intermission. The Utes had built their half-time cushion by out-rebounding UK, 24-6, but they ran out of gas and missed 11 consecutive field-goal attempts in the last five minutes. The Wildcats also benefited from an experienced roster that combined for 49 points and 21 rebounds in a title-game defeat to Arizona the previous year. Kentucky's Jeff Sheppard scored a career-high 27 points against Stanford in a national semi-final overtime victory. Against Rick Majerus' Utes he added 16 more and was chosen Most Outstanding Player.

1999

The regular season had belonged to Duke. While celebrating the Blue Devils, not nearly as many observers took notice of what the Connecticut Huskies were doing. Rarely has a team dominated a college season as thoroughly as the Blue Devils. They went unbeaten in the ACC regular season and won the ACC tournament. In the AP poll (of sportswriters and broadcasters taken on March 8, before the tournament) they were voted number one on 69 of 70 ballots. The lone dissenting vote went for Michigan State. Duke's record stood at 32-1, their only blemish being a two-point loss at Cincinnati in the sixth game of the season.

Before taking on Connecticut in the Finals, they had run their record to 37-1, the most victories ever by any NCAA team. Moreover, they had won their previous five tournament games by an average of 25 points. In addition, no team that lost in the Finals was ever favored by a spread as large: 9-1/2 points.

None of this seemed to intimidate Connecticut. They entered the tournament at 29-2 and then cut through Texas-San Antonio (91-66), New Mexico (78-56), Iowa (78-68), and Gonzaga (64-58) to reach the Final Four. Against Ohio State,

they led by just a point at the half but won 64-58 behind 24 points from their most versatile offensive player and season high-scorer Richard Hamilton.

Now they had to face Duke, a team that had shot 51 percent for the year and held opponents to 39 percent accuracy. The Huskies would nearly reverse those numbers. Finding themselves in a tight game, Duke seemed to rush, hoisting the first shot available. Still, they led 39-37 at the half. Connecticut's reserves outscored Duke's vaunted bench and again Hamilton led the Huskies with 27 points. Duke center Elton Brand had 13 rebounds but he would only take eight shots for the game, making five of them. Guard Trajan Langon hit for 25 points, but no other Blue Devil was hot and the team hit a season low only 41 percent. The Huskies connected on 52 percent of their attempts. Duke whittled a five-point lead down to one, but a pair of free throw by guard Khalid El-Amin sealed the deal and Connecticut won, 77-74.

Connecticut became the first team to win the national championship in its first Final Four appearance since Texas Western in 1966. The national championship matchup between UConn and Duke marked the first time since 1965 that the only two teams ranked No. 1 in the nation throughout the entire year went on to meet in the NCAA Final. Richard Hamilton was chosen the Most Outstanding Player.

2000

Following the 1999 season, Duke lost four players to the NBA draft, three of them underclassmen. Drafted in the first round were Elton Brand (1), Trajan Langdon (11), Corey Maggette (13) and William Avery (14). While Duke ranked first in losing underclassmen to the draft in 1999, they didn't come close to ranking first in early entry candidates sent to the pros since 1976. Depleting the college ranks of talent had become an epidemic, making it increasingly difficult to coach a winner.

The year 2000 slowed that trend and remarkable results followed. In fact, it was in large part because Michigan State's senior point guard Mateen Cleaves stayed in college that State won the NCAA title and his own notoriety soared. When he broke a foot in preseason and missed his team's first 12 games, the decision to make the NBA wait looked like the wrong one. Cleaves showed he still had his stride after the injury, setting a Big Ten Conference record with a national-high 20 assists in a 114-63 mauling of Michigan.

Cleaves' stay-in-school decision still looked like a bad one when the Spartans, playing in the second-round of the tournament against Syracuse, trailed by 10 points at the half. Cleaves cursed a blue streak in chewing out his teammates at halftime. The Spartans won the second half battle and won going away, 75-58. After a 75-64 win against Iowa State, they had advanced to the national semi-finals. A convincing 53-41 win over a pugnacious Wisconsin team put them in the Finals against the Florida Gators.

Coach Billy Donovan's Gators (24-7) were underrated all year. In a pre-tournament poll they ranked 13th. Known for their tenacious, helping defense, the Gators had beaten Duke

(29-5), Oklahoma State (27-7), and then North Carolina (22-13) in the national semi-finals. It was Michigan, however, who played the greater defense, holding Florida to 43 percent shooting. The Spartans led 43-32 at intermission. State shot the lights out, hitting 56 percent of their attempts. Cleaves twisted his ankle in the second half, when the Gators had closed the lead to six. Cleaves thought the ankle was broken, but after missing four minutes and receiving treatment from the trainers, he returned with 12 minutes remaining. He didn't score another point and finished with 18, but his teammates, especially Morris Peterson with 19 points, increased the score. The Spartans won, 89-76, to win their first national title since 1979, when Earvin Johnson led them to victory over Indiana State.

2001

Duke had been ousted by Florida in the 2000 NCAA tournament. The defeat came after junior Shane Battier had promised coach Mike Krzyzewski a national title. Now a senior, Battier, voted Player of the Year, was back with a vengeance. Bolstered by sophomore guard Jason Williams, Duke ran off a 29-4 record and a No. 1 ranking in the polls. They could play defense but were better known for sudden offense, becoming the first school to have more than 400 three-point field goals in a single season.

After easy wins against Monmouth, Missouri, UCLA, and USC, Duke found themselves in the national semi-final against Maryland, against whom they had shown both their best and worst tendencies. The Blue Devils last loss of the season came against Maryland, 91-80. Earlier in the year they pulled out a miraculous finish at Maryland, winning 98-96 in overtime after being behind by ten points with a minute left.

So which Duke team would show up in the Final Four? After falling behind 39-17 in the first half, the Duke team that could perform miracles arrived. Mike Dunleavy hit three consecutive three-pointers in a 45-second span of the second half after Krzyzewski told his squad to quit calling plays and just go out and play the game. They ran off a 78-45 finish to finish the Terrapins, 95-84. Overcoming the 22-point deficit was the biggest comeback in Final Four history.

In the other semi-final, Arizona thumped the defending champs Michigan State, 80-61. Guard Jason Gardner led with 21 points. Lute Olson was back in the Finals, after winning it all in 1997.

In the Finals, Duke led at the half 35-33, with Dunleavy and Battier leading the way. Dunleavy scored 32 points—including five for nine from three-point territory. Battier logged 18 points and grabbed 11 rebounds and Duke won 82-72. Richard Jefferson posted 19 points for Arizona and center Loren Woods had 22 points and 11 rebounds to earn a spot on the All-Final Four team, with teammate Jefferson, and Battier, Dunleavy and Williams from Duke.

For Duke (35-4), 2001 was a time of more records. They became the first team in NCAA history to earn a No. 1 seed in four consecutive years en route to establishing an all-time record for victories in a four-year span (133). Duke became the first team since Indiana's undefeated squad 25 years earlier to reach the Final Four with two NCAA consensus first-team All-Americas (Williams and Battier).

It was Duke's third NCAA title since 1991. At tournament's end, they also held the highest all-time winning percentage in tournament history (for teams with a minimum of 30 games played). After the season, here were the first four teams:

Duke	73-22	.768
UCLA	78-28	.736
Michigan St.	33-14	.702
Kentucky	87-37	.702

2002

It was a year when bright lights were shining. Bobby Knight returned to college coaching by reviving Texas Tech's program. He took the Red Raiders to the NCAA playoffs and produced the largest average increase in home attendance from the previous season. They averaged 13,743 in 17 home games, an increase of 4,186.

History making streaks were being set or broken. North Carolina's sterling streak of top-three ACC finishes (37), 20-win seasons (31) and consecutive NCAA Tournament appearances (27) ended as the Tar Heels suffered their most defeats in school history (8-20 record). St. John's suffered its worst loss in 79 years (97-55 at Duke). Duke became the first school to rank No. 1 in the final AP poll four consecutive years.

Showing some of his brilliance and downside, Duke guard Jason Williams hit seven second-half three-pointers but missed all six of his free throws when the Blue Devils' 22-game winning streak was ended at Florida State, 77-76. In the Sweet Sixteen against Indiana, he duplicated this inconsistency. His chance at a four-point play to tie the game failed when he missed a free throw and Indiana won.

It was a season of a near-Cinderella team as Indiana, under new coach Mike Davis, came close to a national title. They came back against Duke, beating the Blue Devils 74-73 to advance to the elite eight. So there was little surprise among the faithful when they overcame a 12-point deficit in the Final against Maryland and led with 9:53 remaining. Maryland (32-4) had folded in legendary fashion the year before, giving up a 22-point lead to Duke, the largest blown advantage in Final Four history.

But guard Juan Dixon did not let it happen. In the next minute he hit a three-pointer and a fadeaway and gave the Terrapins a lead they would never relinquish. They won 64-52, holding the Hoosiers to 34 percent shooting. Coach Roy Williams and Maryland had its first title. Maryland won the 2002 national title in the school's 2002nd game of all-time. In beating Indiana, they became the only team to defeat five former NCAA championship schools in the same tournament.

Maryland's Juan Dixon became the first player in NCAA history to accumulate 2,000 points, 300 steals and 200 three-point field goals. Dixon also led Maryland with 33 points in the semi-final against Kansas, giving them a 97-88 win. He was the obvious choice for most outstanding player in the tournament, along with teammates Lonny Baxter and Chris Wilcox and Indiana's Kyle Hornsby and Dane Fife.

2003

For the second year in a row, a tournament team that had often sniffed success but never won finally got their first NCAA title. Syracuse was 29-5 before the Final against Kansas, but none of that would have mattered, especially to coach Jim Boeheim, if his team had lost its third try at a championship.

Syracuse hit 10 of 13 three-point field-goal attempts—including six of eight by freshman Gerry McNamara—in the first half of the championship game against Kansas to run out to a 53-42 led at the half. From there they held on. The Jayhawks cut an 18-point deficit to three but hit only one of their first 12 free throws in the second half en route to setting a championship game record for most missed foul shots with 18. Leading by three, Syracuse freshman Hakim Warrick missed two free throws that would have clinched the game with 13.5 seconds left. But the 6-foot-8 forward, known as the "The Helicopter" for his 7-foot armspan, redeemed himself by coming from nowhere to swat a 3-point attempt by Michael Lee that would have tied it with 1.5 seconds left. Then Kirk Hinrich, the Jayhawks' best long-range shooter, threw up an airball at the buzzer.

In 1976 Jim Boeheim had signed as head coach for $28,000. Now, 27 years later, it was the chance for Boeheim to bury the awful memory of 16 years before when Keith Smart's baseline 17-footer with four seconds left gave Indiana a 74-73 victory. He also lost to Kentucky, 76-67, in the 1996 Final. His record stands at 653 wins, 22nd all-time, with a .742 winning percentage that ranks third among active Division I coaches. His 27-year run makes him the longest-tenured coach at the same school.

Freshman Carmelo Anthony paced the Orangemen with 20 points and 10 rebounds in the Final. Anthony was named Final Four most outstanding player.

Chapter 48

The Tournaments

The NCAA Tournament

By Michael Douchant

When college basketball ushers in another NCAA Tournament, we are reminded anew how the playoffs are akin to walking a tightrope, playing Russian roulette, or participating in a crapshoot. When March arrives, it's time for Madness while witnessing postseason competition fraught with sentiment and punctuated by compelling drama. In every region of the country, the playoffs become a zany period with surprises galore.

Selection Sunday when the NCAA Division I Basketball Committee announces the bracket is anything but a peaceful Sabbath for devotees of "on the bubble" at-large teams all across the country. The nerve-wracking tension includes all fans during the competition as the zest for pressurized basketball in a one-loss-and-you're-out format spirals to its zenith at the NCAA semifinals and championship game known as the "Final Four".

It's difficult to believe now, but the Final Four hasn't eternally been the final word in national postseason competition. The initial reference to "Final Four" in an NCAA publication was an offhand comment in the national preview-review of the *1975 Official Collegiate Basketball Guide*. The first time Final Four was capitalized occurred a mere quarter century ago in the 1978 NCAA guide.

In the last quarter of the 20th Century, the reference emerged as a two-word icon of American sports, ascending to a spotlight previously reserved for marquee events such as the Super Bowl, World Series, Indianapolis 500, Kentucky Derby and major New Year's college football bowl games. No sporting event duplicates the Final Four's ambiance moments before tipoff of the first game of the Saturday doubleheader when four groups of loyalists in the same facility are consumed with hope that they are just two evenings away from witnessing firsthand their school capture a national title.

The fanfare created by March Madness, when alumni all across the country don their school sweaters and "return" to college, is contagious. What is the genesis of this exhilaration? Well, not everyone was so enthusiastic in the early years.

Actually, the NCAA's crown jewel wasn't the NCAA's idea and was literally dumped into the governing body's lap by the National Association of Basketball Coaches. A collection of New York sportswriters staged the first major college tournament, the National Invitation Tournament in 1938 in New York. But a group of NABC members, especially coaches from the Midwest, felt if there was to be national tourney, it should be sponsored by a collegiate organization and not scribes, particularly those with a "biased" Eastern influence.

Harold Olsen, a former Wisconsin player and coach at Ohio State, is given much of the credit for bringing the NCAA Tournament to the American sports scene. The first NCAA Tournament was conducted in 1939, sponsored not by the NCAA but by the NABC. Oddly, Olsen's Ohio State team reached the final of the eight-team event (one from each district) before losing to Oregon, 46-33.

Total attendance for the inaugural NCAA playoff was a paltry 15,025, and the venture produced $2,531 worth of red ink. Because the NABC was out of funds, it asked the NCAA to assume responsibility.

TV ratings and revenue increased exponentially over the decades. The 1992 NCAA championship game between Duke and Michigan was the most-watched basketball game in television history at the time. An estimated 53 million viewers took in all or part of the final in the United States' TV homes covered by the Nielsen ratings. CBS estimated an additional 10 percent of the total audience watched the 1992 final away from home—in taverns, dormitories and other venues Nielsen doesn't survey. That's more than 100 times the initial viewing audience estimated at 500,000 in 1946, when the championship game (Oklahoma State defeated North Carolina, 43-40) was televised locally for the first time in New York by WCBS-TV. Eight years later, the first NCAA final was televised nationally for a broadcast rights fee of $7,500. The staggering dollars CBS put on the table since the early 1990s to gain contract extensions from the NCAA make previous deals pale in comparison.

The rapid growth of "The Big Show" since television became a vital factor and the revenue a school can generate are incredible. Each Final Four participant in 1990 received more than $1.47 million, a whopping increase of about 2,870 percent in just 20 years. Media purists frequently bemoan the cosmetic appearance of games conducted in cavernous domed stadiums, but the magnitude of the playoffs is such the NCAA doesn't have much of an option. The NCAA eventually decided to abandon intimate settings and establish a minimum seating capacity of 30,000 for Final Four sites.

As time passed, some believe the NCAA Tournament lost perspective and embraced a trip-to-the-bank mentality. That is a 180-degree contrast from when Stanford coach Everett Dean took home a meager check for $93.75 to cover his team's stay in Kansas City after the Cardinal (they were the Indians then) won the 1942 title. But the early years represented an era when the NCAA playoffs had more naivete and was, above all, an opportunity to compete against the best squads across the nation.

Differing views notwithstanding, there is no doubt that March has become a showcase month for college athletics. It's an invigorating time for college enthusiasts as they watch the countdown to coronation unfold.

NCAA MEN'S DIVISION I CHAMPIONSHIP RESULTS

Year	Champion (Coach)	Score	Runner-up (Coach)	Third Place	Fourth Place	Most Outstanding Player	Site of Finals
1939	Oregon (Howard Hobson)	46-33	Ohio State (Harold Olsen)	*Oklahoma	*Villanova	Jimmy Hull, Ohio State	Evanston, IL
1940	Indiana (Branch McCracken)	60-42	Kansas (Phog Allen)	*Duquesne	*Southern Cal	Marvin Huffman, Indiana	Kansas City
1941	Wisconsin (Bud Foster)	39-34	Washington State (Jack Friel)	*Pittsburgh	*Arkansas	John Kotz, Wisconsin	Kansas City
1942	Stanford (Everett Dean)	53-38	Dartmouth (Ozzie Cowles)	*Colorado	*Kentucky	Howie Dallmar, Stanford	Kansas City
1943	Wyoming (Everett Shelton)	46-34	Georgetown (Elmer Ripley)	*Texas	*DePaul	Ken Sailors, Wyoming	New York City
1944	Utah (Vadal Peterson)	42-40 (OT)	Dartmouth (Earl Brown)	*Iowa State	*Ohio State	Arnie Ferrin, Utah	New York City
1945	Oklahoma State (Henry Iba)	49-45	NYU (Howard Cann)	*Arkansas	*Ohio State	Bob Kurland, Okla. State	New York City
1946	Oklahoma State (Henry Iba)	43-40	North Carolina (Ben Carnevale)	Ohio State	California	Bob Kurland, Okla. State	New York City
1947	Holy Cross (Doggie Julian)	58-47	Oklahoma (Bruce Drake)	Texas	CCNY	George Kaftan, Holy Cross	New York City
1948	Kentucky (Adolph Rupp)	58-42	Baylor (Bill Henderson)	Holy Cross	Kansas State	Alex Groza, Kentucky	New York City
1949	Kentucky (Adolph Rupp)	46-36	Oklahoma State (Henry Iba)	Illinois	Oregon State	Alex Groza, Kentucky	Seattle
1950	CCNY (Nat Holman)	71-68	Bradley (Forddy Anderson)	N.C. State	Baylor	Irwin Dambrot, CCNY	New York City
1951	Kentucky (Adolph Rupp)	68-58	Kansas State (Jack Gardner)	Illinois	Okla. State	Bill Spivey, Kentucky	Minneapolis
1952	Kansas (Phog Allen)	80-63	St. John's (Frank McGuire)	Illinois	Santa Clara	Clyde Lovellette, Kansas	Seattle
1953	Indiana (Branch McCracken)	69-68	Kansas (Phog Allen)	Washington	Louisiana St.	B.H. Born, Kansas	Kansas City
1954	La Salle (Ken Loeffler)	92-76	Bradley (Forddy Anderson)	Penn State	Southern Cal	Tom Gola, La Salle	Kansas City
1955	San Francisco (Phil Woolpert)	77-63	La Salle (Ken Loeffler)	Colorado	Iowa	Bill Russell, San Francisco	Kansas City
1956	San Francisco (Phil Woolpert)	83-71	Iowa (Bucky O'Connor)	Temple	SMU	Hal Lear, Temple	Evanston, IL
1957	North Carolina (Frank McGuire)	54-53 (3OT)	Kansas (Dick Harp)	San Francisco	Michigan State	Wilt Chamberlain, Kansas	Kansas City
1958	Kentucky (Adolph Rupp)	84-72	Seattle (John Castellani)	Temple	Kansas State	Elgin Baylor, Seattle	Louisville, KY
1959	California (Pete Newell)	71-70	West Virginia (Fred Schaus)	Cincinnati	Louisville	Jerry West, West Virginia	Louisville, KY
1960	Ohio State (Fred Taylor)	75-55	California (Pete Newell)	Cincinnati	New York Univ.	Jerry Lucas, Ohio State	San Francisco
1961	Cincinnati (Ed Jucker)	70-65 (OT)	Ohio State (Fred Taylor)	St. Joseph's	Utah	Jerry Lucas, Ohio State	Kansas City
1962	Cincinnati (Ed Jucker)	71-59	Ohio State (Fred Taylor)	Wake Forest	UCLA	Paul Hogue, Cincinnati	Louisville, KY
1963	Loyola, Ill. (George Ireland)	60-58 (OT)	Cincinnati (Ed Jucker)	Duke	Oregon State	Art Heyman, Duke	Louisville, KY
1964	UCLA (John Wooden)	98-83	Duke (Vic Bubas)	Michigan	Kansas State	Walt Hazzard, UCLA	Kansas City
1965	UCLA (John Wooden)	91-80	Michigan (Dave Strack)	Princeton	Wichita State	Bill Bradley, Princeton	Portland, OR
1966	Texas Western (Don Haskins)	72-65	Kentucky (Adolph Rupp)	Duke	Utah	Jerry Chambers, Utah	College Park, MD
1967	UCLA (John Wooden)	79-64	Dayton (Don Donoher)	Houston	North Carolina	Lew Alcindor, UCLA	Louisville, KY
1968	UCLA (John Wooden)	78-55	North Carolina (Dean Smith)	Ohio State	Houston	Lew Alcindor, UCLA	Los Angeles
1969	UCLA (John Wooden)	92-72	Purdue (George King)	Drake	North Carolina	Lew Alcindor, UCLA	Louisville, KY
1970	UCLA (John Wooden)	80-69	Jacksonville (Joe Williams)	New Mexico St.	St. Bonaventure	Sidney Wicks, UCLA	College Park, MD
1971	UCLA (John Wooden)	68-62	Villanova (Jack Kraft)	Western Ky.	Kansas	Howard Porter, Villanova	Houston
1972	UCLA (John Wooden)	81-76	Florida State (Hugh Durham)	North Carolina	Louisville	Bill Walton, UCLA	Los Angeles
1973	UCLA (John Wooden)	87-66	Memphis State (Gene Bartow)	Indiana	Providence	Bill Walton, UCLA	St. Louis
1974	N.C. State (Norman Sloan)	76-64	Marquette (Al McGuire)	UCLA	Kansas	David Thompson, N.C. State	Greensboro, NC
1975	UCLA (John Wooden)	92-85	Kentucky (Joe B. Hall)	Louisville	Syracuse	Richard Washington, UCLA	San Diego
1976	Indiana (Bob Knight)	86-68	Michigan (Johnny Orr)	UCLA	Rutgers	Kent Benson, Indiana	Philadelphia
1977	Marquette (Al McGuire)	67-59	North Carolina (Dean Smith)	UNLV	UNC Charlotte	Butch Lee, Marquette	Atlanta
1978	Kentucky (Joe B. Hall)	94-88	Duke (Bill E. Foster)	Arkansas	Notre Dame	Jack Givens, Kentucky	St. Louis
1979	Michigan State (Jud Heathcote)	75-64	Indiana State (Bill Hodges)	DePaul	Penn	Magic Johnson, Michigan St.	Salt Lake City
1980	Louisville (Denny Crum)	59-54	UCLA (Larry Brown)	Purdue	Iowa	Darrell Griffith, Louisville	Indianapolis
1981	Indiana (Bob Knight)	63-50	North Carolina (Dean Smith)	Virginia	Louisiana St.	Isiah Thomas, Indiana	Philadelphia
1982	North Carolina (Dean Smith)	63-62	Georgetown (John Thompson)	*Houston	*Louisville	James Worthy, N. Carolina	New Orleans
1983	N.C. State (Jim Valvano)	54-52	Houston (Guy Lewis)	*Louisville	*Georgia	Hakeem Olajuwon, Houston	Albuquerque, NM
1984	Georgetown (John Thompson)	84-75	Houston (Guy Lewis)	*Kentucky	*Virginia	Patrick Ewing, Georgetown	Seattle
1985	Villanova (Rollie Massimino)	66-64	Georgetown (John Thompson)	*St. John's	*Memphis State	Ed Pinckney, Villanova	Lexington, KY
1986	Louisville (Denny Crum)	72-69	Duke (Mike Krzyzewski)	*Kansas	*Louisiana St.	Pervis Ellison, Louisville	Dallas
1987	Indiana (Bob Knight)	74-73	Syracuse (Jim Boeheim)	*Providence	*UNLV	Keith Smart, Indiana	New Orleans
1988	Kansas (Larry Brown)	83-79	Oklahoma (Billy Tubbs)	*Arizona	*Duke	Danny Manning, Kansas	Kansas City
1989	Michigan (Steve Fisher)	80-79 (OT)	Seton Hall (P.J. Carlesimo)	*Duke	*Illinois	Glen Rice, Michigan	Seattle
1990	UNLV (Jerry Tarkanian)	103-73	Duke (Mike Krzyzewski)	*Arkansas	*Georgia Tech	Anderson Hunt, UNLV	Denver
1991	Duke (Mike Krzyzewski)	72-65	Kansas (Roy Williams)	*N. Carolina	*UNLV	Christian Laettner, Duke	Indianapolis
1992	Duke (Mike Krzyzewski)	71-51	Michigan (Steve Fisher)	*Cincinnati	*Indiana	Bobby Hurley, Duke	Minneapolis
1993	North Carolina (Dean Smith)	77-71	Michigan (Steve Fisher)	*Kansas	*Kentucky	Donald Williams, N. Carolina	New Orleans
1994	Arkansas (Nolan Richardson)	76-72	Duke (Mike Krzyzewski)	*Arizona	*Florida	Corliss Williamson, Arkansas	Charlotte
1995	UCLA (Jim Harrick)	89-78	Arkansas (Nolan Richardson)	*N. Carolina	*Okla. State	Ed O'Bannon, UCLA	Seattle
1996	Kentucky (Rick Pitino)	76-67	Syracuse (Jim Boeheim)	*Massachusetts	*Miss. State	Tony Delk, Kentucky	E. Rutherford, NJ
1997	Arizona (Lute Olson)	84-79 (OT)	Kentucky (Rick Pitino)	*Minnesota	*North Carolina	Miles Simon, Arizona	Indianapolis
1998	Kentucky (Tubby Smith)	78-69	Utah (Rick Majerus)	*North Carolina	*Stanford	Jeff Sheppard, Kentucky	San Antonio
1999	Connecticut (Jim Calhoun)	77-74	Duke (Mike Krzyzewski)	*Michigan State	*Ohio State	Richard Hamilton, Connecticut	St. Petersburg
2000	Michigan State (Tom Izzo)	89-76	Florida (Billy Donovan)	*North Carolina	*Wisconsin	Mateen Cleaves, Michigan State	Indianapolis
2001	Duke (Mike Krzyzewski)	82-72	Arizona (Lute Olson)	*Maryland	*Michigan State	Shane Battier, Duke	Minneapolis
2002	Maryland (Gary Williams)	64-52	Indiana (Mike Davis)	*Kansas	*Oklahoma	Juan Dixon, Maryland	Atlanta
2003	Syracuse (Jim Boeheim)	81-78	Kansas (Roy Williams)	*Marquette	*Texas	Carmelo Anthony, Syracuse	New Orleans

*Tied for third position because there was no consolation game.

NCAA MEN'S DIVISION I CHAMPIONSHIP APPEARANCE RECORDS

Most NCAA Tournament Championships By School (through 2003)

UCLA (11), Kentucky (7), Indiana (5), Duke (3), North Carolina (3), Cincinnati (2), Kansas (2), Louisville (2), North Carolina State (2), Oklahoma State (2), San Francisco (2), Michigan State

Most Final Four Appearances By School

North Carolina (15), UCLA (15), Duke (13), Kentucky (13), Kansas (12), Ohio State (9), Indiana (8), Louisville (7), Arkansas (6), Cincinnati (6), Michigan (6).

Most Final Four Victories By School

UCLA (25), Kentucky (17), Duke (14), Indiana (12), North Carolina (11), Kansas (9), Cincinnati (7), Michigan (7), Ohio State (7), Georgetown (5), Louisville (5), North Carolina State (5), Oklahoma State (5), San Francisco

Most Final Four Games By School

UCLA (28), North Carolina (24), Duke (24), Kentucky (23), Kansas (21), Ohio St (15), Indiana (15), Louisville (12), Michigan (12), Cincinnati (11)

Consecutive Final Four Appearances by School

UCLA, 10, 1967-76, Cincinnati, 5,1959-63, Duke, 5, 1988-92, Houston, 3, 1982-84, Kentucky, 3, 1996-98, Michigan State, 3, 1999-01, North Carolina, 3, 1967-69, Ohio State, 3, 1944-46, Ohio State, 3, 1960-62, San Francisco, 1955-57

NCAA MEN'S DIVISION II CHAMPIONSHIP RESULTS

Year	Winner	Score	Runner-up	Third Place	Fourth Place
1957	Wheaton (IL)	89-65	Kentucky Wesleyan	Mount St Mary's (MD)	Cal St-Los Angeles
1958	S Dakota	75-53	St. Michael's	Evansville	Wheaton (IL)
1959	Evansville	83-67	SW Missouri St	N Carolina A&T	Cal St-Los Angeles
1960	Evansville	90-69	Chapman	Kentucky Wesleyan	Cornell College
1961	Wittenberg	42-38	SE Missouri St	S Dakota St	Mount St Mary's (MD)
1962	Mount St Mary's (MD)	58-57 (OT)	Cal St-Sacramento	Southern Illinois	Nebraska Wesleyan
1963	S Dakota St	44-42	Wittenberg	Oglethorpe	Southern Illinois
1964	Evansville	72-59	Akron	N Carolina A&T	Northern Iowa
1965	Evansville	85-82 (OT)	Southern Illinois	N Dakota	St Michael's
1966	Kentucky Wesleyan	54-51	Southern Illinois	Akron	N Dakota
1967	Winston-Salem	77-74	SW Missouri St	Kentucky Wesleyan	Illinois St
1968	Kentucky Wesleyan	63-52	Indiana St	Trinity (TX)	Ashland
1969	Kentucky Wesleyan	75-71	SW Missouri St	**Vacated	Ashland
1970	Philadelphia Textile	76-65	Tennessee St	UC-Riverside	Buffalo St
1971	Evansville	97-82	Old Dominion	**Vacated	Kentucky Wesleyan
1972	Roanoke	84-72	Akron	Tennessee St	Eastern Mich
1973	Kentucky Wesleyan	78-76 (OT)	Tennessee St	Assumption	Brockport St
1974	Morgan St	67-52	SW Missouri St	Assumption	New Orleans
1975	Old Dominion	76-74	New Orleans	Assumption	TN-Chattanooga
1976	Puget Sound	83-74	TN-Chattanooga	Eastern Illinois	Old Dominion
1977	TN-Chattanooga	71-62	Randolph-Macon	N Alabama	Sacred Heart
1978	Cheyney	47-40	WI-Green Bay	Eastern Illinois	Central Florida
1979	N Alabama	64-50	WI-Green Bay	Cheyney	Bridgeport
1980	Virginia Union	80-74	New York Tech	Florida Southern	N Alabama
1981	Florida Southern	73-68	Mount St Mary's (MD)	Cal Poly-SLO	WI-Green Bay
1982	District of Columbia	73-63	Florida Southern	Kentucky Wesleyan	Cal St-Bakersfield
1983	Wright St	92-73	District of Columbia	*Cal St-Bakersfield	*Morningside
1984	Central Missouri St	81-77	St. Augustine's	*Kentucky Wesleyan	*N Alabama
1985	Jacksonville St	74-73	S Dakota St	*Kentucky Wesleyan	*Mount St. Mary's (MD)
1986	Sacred Heart	93-87	SE Missouri St	*Cheyney	*Florida Southern
1987	Kentucky Wesleyan	92-74	Gannon	*Delta St	*Eastern Montana
1988	Lowell	75-72	AK-Anchorage	Florida Southern	Troy St
1989	N Carolina Central	73-46	SE Missouri St	UC-Riverside	Jacksonville St
1990	Kentucky Wesleyan	93-79	Cal St-Bakersfield	N Dakota	Morehouse
1991	N Alabama	79-72	Bridgeport (CT)	*Cal St-Bakersfield	*Virginia Union
1992	Virginia Union	100-75	Bridgeport (CT)	*Cal St-Bakersfield	*California (PA)
1993	Cal St-Bakersfield	85-72	Troy St (AL)	*New Hampshire Coll	*Wayne St (MI)
1994	Cal St-Bakersfield	92-86	Southern Indiana	*New Hampshire Coll	*Washburn
1995	Southern Indiana	71-63	UC-Riverside	*Norfolk St	*Indiana (PA)
1996	Fort Hays St	70-63	Northern Kentucky	*California (PA)	*Virginia Union
1997	Cal St-Bakersfield	57-56	Northern Kentucky	*Lynn	*Salem-Teikyo
1998	UC-Davis	83-77	Kentucky Wesleyan	*St. Rose	*Virginia Union
1999	Kentucky Wesleyan	75-60	Metropolitan St	*Truman St	*Florida Southern
2000	Metropolitan State, Colo.	97-79	Kentucky Wesleyan	*Mo. Southern St.	*Seattle Pacific
2001	Kentucky Wesleyan	72-63	Washburn	*Western Washington	*Tampa
2002	Metro State	80-72	Kentucky Wesleyan	*Indiana-Pa.	*Shaw
2003	Northeastern St.	75-64	Kentucky Wesleyan	*Bowie State	*Queens

*Indicates tied for third.
**Student-athletes representing American International in 1969 and Southwestern Louisiana in 1971 were declared ineligible subsequent to the tournament. Under NCAA rules, the teams' and ineligible student-athletes' records were deleted, and the teams' places in the final standings were vacated.

NCAA MEN'S DIVISION III CHAMPIONSHIP RESULTS

Year	Winner	Score	Runner-up	Third Place	Fourth Place
1975	LeMoyne-Owen	57-54	Glassboro St	Augustana (IL)	Brockport St
1976	Scranton	60-57	Wittenberg	Augustana (IL)	Plattsburgh St
1977	Wittenberg	79-66	Oneonta St	Scranton	Hamline
1978	North Park	69-57	Widener	Albion	Stony Brook
1979	North Park	66-62	Potsdam St	Franklin & Marshall	Centre
1980	North Park	83-76	Upsala	Wittenberg	Longwood
1981	Potsdam St	67-65 (OT)	Augustana (IL)	Ursinus	Otterbein
1982	Wabash	83-62	Potsdam St	Brooklyn	Cal St-Stanislaus
1983	Scranton	64-63	Wittenberg	Roanoke	WI-Whitewater
1984	WI-Whitewater	103-86	Clark (MA)	DePauw	Upsala
1985	North Park	72-71	Potsdam St	Nebraska Wesleyan	Widener
1986	Potsdam St	76-73	LeMoyne-Owen	Nebraska Wesleyan	Jersey City St
1987	North Park	106-100	Clark (MA)	Wittenberg	Stockton St
1988	Ohio Wesleyan	92-70	Scranton	Nebraska Wesleyan	Hartwick
1989	WI-Whitewater	94-86	Trenton St	Southern Maine	Centre
1990	Rochester	43-42	DePauw	Washington (MD)	Calvin
1991	WI-Platteville	81-74	Franklin & Marshall	Otterbein	Ramapo (NJ)
1992	Calvin	62-49	Rochester	WI-Platteville	Jersey City St
1993	Ohio Northern	71-68	Augustana	Mass-Dartmouth	Rowan
1994	Lebanon Valley Coll	66-59 (OT)	New York University	Wittenberg	St Thomas (MN)
1995	WI-Platteville	69-55	Manchester	Rowan	Trinity (CT)
1996	Rowan	100-93	Hope (MI)	Illinois Wesleyan	Franklin & Marshall
1997	Illinois Wesleyan	89-86	Nebraska Wesleyan	Williams	Alvernia
1998	WI-Platteville	69-56	Hope (MI)	Williams	Wilkes
1999	WI-Platteville	76-75 (2 OT)	Hampden-Sydney	William Paterson	Connecticut Coll.
2000	Calvin	79-74	WI-Eau Claire	Salem St.	Franklin & Marshall
2001	Catholic	76-62	Wm. Paterson	Illinois Wesleyan	Ohio Northern
2002	Otterbein	102-83	Elizabethtown	Carthage	Rochester
2003	Williams	67-65	Gustavus Adolphus	Wooster (30-3)	Hampden-Sydney

The Men's and Women's Invitation Tournaments

By Morgan G. Brenner

In college basketball, a successful season is defined by a bid, either automatic or at-large, to a national championship tournament conducted by the athletic association of which the school is a member—i.e., the NCAA (National Collegiate Athletic Association) or NAIA (National Association of Intercollegiate Athletics). For those teams that do not receive a bid to the association tournament, a reasonably successful season is validated by a bid to the National Invitation Tournament or the Women's National Invitation Tournament.

What follows is a history of the two major postseason invitational events that have operated since 1938 for men and 1969 for women.

The National Invitation Tournament

The National Invitation Tournament is basketball's oldest major college postseason "national championship" tournament. For many years it was arguably *the* premier college basketball postseason event. It is not related to the women's tournament of similar name.

The first NIT was held in 1938—one year after what became the NAIA tournament began its still-continuing run in 1937, and one year prior to the first NCAA postseason event in 1939. It is, however, the longest continuously running "national championship" tournament since the NAIA took a hiatus in 1944 because of World War II travel restrictions that apparently did not apply to the NIT.

It should be noted that on its Internet website history page and in various "histories" in tournament programs and other publications, the NIT claims, inaccurately, that it is the "oldest tournament in college basketball," was the "first postseason tournament to be played in the country," and "started what today is known as March Madness."

The NIT was the brainchild of the Metropolitan (New York) Basketball Writers Association. However, its creation was not front-page news. *The New York Times* gave it about four column inches on an inside sports page in the February 2, 1938 edition. The headline read BEST U.S. COLLEGE QUINTETS TO BE MATCHED IN WRITER'S GARDEN TOURNAMENT IN MARCH, and the lead stated, "Plans for a nation-wide intercollegiate invitation tournament to be held in this city in March were discussed at the Metropolitan Basketball Writers Association luncheon yesterday at the Hotel Lincoln."

The article added that on opening night (March 9) the two leading metropolitan squads would meet teams from other parts of the east; that the winners would play in the next round (March 14) against two "standout aggregations" from other sections of the country; and that the championship and consolation games would be played on March 16. The two metropolitan teams were New York University and Long Island University. However, only one other eastern representative, Temple, the eventual winner, was chosen, with Bradley, Colorado, and Oklahoma State (then A&M) representing the rest of the country.

Timing for the first NIT could not have been more propitious. For the 1937-38 season, the center-jump after each

basket (while the clock kept running as players repositioned themselves) was eliminated, which resulted in a faster game and an increase in scoring.

The inaugural event was considered an artistic and financial success, with 39,883 fans paying their way into old Madison Square Garden over the three nights, with a close-to-sellout crowd of 14,497 for the Final and consolation games.

The NIT may have been the result of the extremely successful college basketball double-headers at the Garden, promoted by Edward "Ned" Irish, a local sportswriter who later left his newspaper career to become the Garden's full-time college basketball promoter. While basketball had drawn well for games involving local colleges, Irish's efforts brought schools from throughout the country into New York and created even greater enthusiasm, probably leading to the writer's NIT "brainstorm," which, some claim, was encouraged by Irish.

In 1940, responsibility for the tournament was transferred from the Writer's Association to the created-for-the-purpose Metropolitan Intercollegiate Basketball Committee, then a consortium of 10 area colleges. Known since 1948 as the Metropolitan Intercollegiate Basketball Association (MIBA), the group is comprised of representatives of five New York area colleges: Fordham, Manhattan, New York, St. John's, and Wagner. Although it exists solely for the operation of the tournament, the MIBA maintains an office with several full-time employees, including executive director John J. "Jack" Powers, former coach and athletics director at Manhattan College.

From 1938 through 1976, all games were played at New York's Madison Square Garden—originally at located at 49th Street and, since 1968, at the 33rd Street (Pennsylvania Station) site, where its opening that year was celebrated with expansion to 16 teams. In 1977, then executive director Peter A. Carlesimo (who served in that capacity from 1977 through 1988) and the tournament committee instituted a plan, still in use, that provided for games prior to the quarter-finals and then in the semi-finals to be played at a participant's home court. Almost immediately, attendance at the school sites justified the move.

In the NIT's first three years (1938-40), six teams competed, with the designated "top two" teams receiving first-round byes to the round of four. From 1941 through 1948, the tourney was an eight-team field. From 1949 through 1964 and again in 1976, 12 teams competed, with four of them receiving first-round byes. In 1965, 1966, and 1967, 14 teams received invitations with two of them receiving byes. From 1968 through 1978, 16-teams competed (except for 12 teams in 1976). In 1979, the NIT assumed its current configuration as a 32-team tournament.

Except for the first-round byes to the designated top teams in the years when the number of teams was not a multiple of eight, the tournament always has been officially unseeded. While many publications refer to seedings, the NIT does not admit to them. And, in the years when there was a first-round bye, the teams having a bye were not designated as 1, 2, 3, or 4 seeds.

For the most part, NIT teams have been NCAA Division I schools. However, before the NCAA began divisional classification in 1957, several "small" NCAA schools were invited. Probably the biggest surprise was the championship won by Southern Illinois with Walt Frazier in 1967—the only NIT title

ever taken by a Division II school.

While the NAIA tournament was the first such event to have participation by a black college—in 1953, when Tennessee State broke the barrier—the NCAA followed suit by including several historically black schools in its inaugural Division II tournament in 1957. The first black college to participate in the NIT was Alcorn State in 1979. However, it should be noted that, until the mid '70s, most of the historically black colleges were NCAA Division II.

The NCAA began its tournament one year after the NIT debuted. The NCAA tourney did not immediately enjoy equal prestige, however, and the two organizations competed for the better teams, for virtually all of the major colleges were NCAA members. Many schools found the allure of a week in New York City far more attractive than several days in a less impressive site for the early rounds of the NCAA tournament. On 14 occasions, teams played in both events in the same year, the most notable instance being in 1950, when City College of New York became the only team to win both tournaments in the same year. Following are the schools that participated in both tournaments in the same year with their finish in each.

YEAR	SCHOOL	FINISH IN NIT	FINISH IN NCAA
1940	Colorado	8	1
	Duquesne	3	2
1944	Utah	1	8
1949	Kentucky	1	8
1950	Bradley	2	2
	City College	1	1
1951	Arizona	16	8
	Brigham Young	8	1
	North Carolina State	8	8
	St. John's (NY)	6	3
1952	Dayton	12	2
	Duquesne	8	4
	St. John's (NY)	2	8
	St. Louis	8	8

From 1943 through 1948 and again in 1950, the NCAA scheduled its tournament in Madison Square Garden two weeks or so after the NIT. Fans loved both events, as evidenced by almost equal attendance on "Finals Night."

Over the years the NCAA, aware that its tournament would suffer if the NIT prospered, adopted various measures to reduce the competition, including expansion. The apparent "last straw" was Marquette's rejecting an NCAA bid in 1970 and then winning the NIT. By the mid '70s, NCAA clout won out, with schools required to accept an NCAA tournament bid if tendered—relegating the NIT to an event of also-rans, as echoed by the rather unkind but reasonably accurate version of its acronym, the "Not Invited Tournament."

In addition to the NCAA's strong-arm tactics, there was another reason for the status loss by the NIT—money. Starting in 1979, the NCAA initiated the practice of charging exorbitant fees for the rights to nationally televise the games of its annual tournament. Schools were left with no choice. A first-round loss in NCAA would mean more to a school, both financially and to its basketball reputation, than an appearance in the NIT.

The effect on the NIT was dramatic—after 1979, none of its teams were ranked by the major polls (the lone exceptions were UNLV in 1993, when the school was ineligible for the NCAA tournament, and New Mexico in 1990, which was ignored by the NCAA). Even newspaper coverage was reduced, with *The New York Times* relegating the NIT to an inside page as NCAA tournament previews occupied the front page of the sports section. Eventually, to avoid going head-to-head with its rival, in the early 1980s the NIT moved its semi-finals and finals to midweek of the week between the NCAA quarter-finals and the Final Four—although it did pick up national television coverage, including selected games in the early rounds. Yet despite the NIT's attempts to stay competitive, attendance from the mid '70s on was about 12- to 13,000 per game, some 5,000 under capacity. Some Finals drew under five figures.

Nevertheless, the NIT continues and prospers. In its 66 years—1938 to 2003—almost 1,200 teams, led by more than 450 coaches and representing approximately 250 schools, have participated in this venerable and fabled tournament. The NIT may have lost some of its original glamor, but its example was indirectly responsible for the NCAA tournament and, moreover, it provides an attractive event for the schools not invited to the NCAA event. Large, enthusiastic crowds for the tournament's on-campus games are a good indicator of the NIT's continuing popularity.

The MIBA also conducts the Preseason NIT, which began in 1985. The Finals are held during Thanksgiving week, and the event has come to symbolize of the opening of the college basketball season. It is conducted in same basic format as its postseason cousin: 16 teams with on-campus sites until the semi-finals. NCAA rules allow one team from a conference in a year and restrict team participation to once every four years.

MEN'S NIT RESULTS

Year	Champion	Runnerup	Score	MVP	Winning Coach	Runner Up Coach
1938	Temple	Colorado	60–36	Don Shields, Temple	James Usilton	Frosty Cox
1939	Long Island Univ.	Loyola of Chicago	44–32	Bill Lloyd, St. John's	Clair Bee	Lennie Sachs
1940	Colorado	Duquesne	51–40	Bob Doll, Colorado	Frosty Cox	Chick Davies
1941	Long Island Univ.	Ohio University	56–42	Frankie Baumholtz, Ohio Univ.	Clair Bee	Dutch Trautwein
1942	West Virginia	Western Kentucky	47–45	Rudy Baric, West Virginia	Dyke Raese	Ed Diddle
1943	St. John's	Toledo	48–27	Harry Boykoff, St. John's	Joe Lapchick	Berle Friddle
1944	St. John's	DePaul	47–39	Bill Kotsores, St. John's	Joe Lapchick	Ray Meyer
1945	DePaul	Bowling Green State	71–54	George Mikan, DePaul	Ray Meyer	Harold Anderson
1946	Kentucky	Rhode Island	46–45	Ernie Calverley, Rhode Island	Adolph Rupp	Frank Keaney
1947	Utah	Kentucky	49–45	Vern Gardner, Utah	Vadal Peterson	Adolph Rupp
1948	St. Louis	New York University	65–52	Ed Macauley, St. Louis	Eddie Hickey	Howard Cann
1949	San Francisco	Loyola of Chicago	48–47	Don Lofgran, San Francisco	Pete Newell	Tom Haggerty
1950	CCNY	Bradley	69–61	Ed Warner, CCNY	Nat Holman	Forddy Anderson
1951	Brigham Young	Dayton	62–43	Roland Minson, Brigham Young	Stan Watts	Tom Blackburn
1952	La Salle	Dayton	75–64	Tom Gola and Norm Grekin, La Salle	Ken Loeffler	Tom Blackburn
1953	Seton Hall	St. John's	58–46	Walter Dukes, Seton Hall	Honey Russell	Dusty DeStefano
1954	Holy Cross	Duquesne	71–62	Togo Palazzi, Holy Cross	Buster Sheary	Dudey Moore

MEN'S NIT RESULTS

Year	Champion	Runnerup	Score	MVP	Winning Coach	Runner Up Coach
1955	Duquesne	Dayton	70–58	Maurice Stokes, St. Francis (Pa.)	Dudey Moore	Tom Blackburn
1956	Louisville	Dayton	93–80	Charlie Tyra, Louisville	Peck Hickman	Tom Blackburn
1957	Bradley	Memphis State	84–83	Win Wilfong, Memphis State	Chuck Orsborn	Bob Vanatta
1958	Xavier	Dayton	78–74 (OT)	Hank Stein, Xavier	Jim McCafferty	Tom Blackburn
1959	St. John's	Bradley	76–71 (OT)	Tony Jackson, St. John's	Joe Lapchick	Chuck Orsborn
1960	Bradley	Providence	88–72	Lenny Wilkens, Providence	Chuck Orsborn	Joe Mullaney
1961	Providence	St. Louis	62–59	Vin Ernst, Providence	Joe Mullaney	John Benington
1962	Dayton	St. John's	73–67	Bill Chmielewski, Dayton	Tom Blackburn	Joe Lapchick
1963	Providence	Canisius	81–66	Ray Flynn, Providence	Joe Mullaney	Bob MacKinnon
1964	Bradley	New Mexico	86–54	Lavern Tart, Bradley	Chuck Orsborn	Bob King
1965	St. John's	Villanova	55–51	Ken McIntyre, St. John's	Joe Lapchick	Jack Kraft
1966	Brigham Young	New York Univ.	97–84	Bill Melchionni, Villanova	Stan Watts	Lou Rossini
1967	Southern Illinois	Marquette	71–56	Walt Frazier, Southern Illinois	Jack Hartman	Al McGuire
1968	Dayton	Kansas	61–48	Don May, Dayton	Don Donoher	Ted Owens
1969	Temple	Boston College	89–76	Terry Driscoll, Boston College	Harry Litwack	Bob Cousy
1970	Marquette	St. John's	65–53	Dean Meminger, Marquette	Al McGuire	Lou Carnesecca
1971	North Carolina	Georgia Tech	84–66	Bill Chamberlain, N. Carolina	Dean Smith	Whack Hyder
1972	Maryland	Niagara	100–69	Tom McMillen, Maryland	Lefty Driesell	Frank Layden
1973	Virginia Tech	Notre Dame	92–91 (OT)	John Shumate, Notre Dame	Don DeVoe	Digger Phelps
1974	Purdue	Utah	97–81	Mike Sojourner, Utah	Fred Schaus	Bill E. Foster
1975	Princeton	Providence	80–69	Ron Lee, Oregon	Pete Carril	Dave Gavitt
1976	Kentucky	UNC Charlotte	71–67	Cedric Maxwell, UNC Charlotte	Joe B. Hall	Lee Rose
1977	St. Bonaventure	Houston	94–91	Greg Sanders, St. Bonaventure	Jim Satalin	Guy Lewis
1978	Texas	N.C. State	101–93	Jim Krivacs and Ron Baxter, Texas	Abe Lemons	Norman Sloan
1979	Indiana	Purdue	53–52	Butch Carter and Ray Tolbert, Indiana	Bob Knight	Lee Rose
1980	Virginia	Minnesota	58–55	Ralph Sampson, Virginia	Terry Holland	Jim Dutcher
1981	Tulsa	Syracuse	86–84 (OT)	Greg Stewart, Tulsa	Nolan Richardson	Jim Boeheim
1982	Bradley	Purdue	67–58	Mitchell Anderson, Bradley	Dick Versace	Gene Keady
1983	Fresno State	DePaul	69–60	Ron Anderson, Fresno State	Boyd Grant	Ray Meyer
1984	Michigan	Notre Dame	83–63	Tim McCormick, Michigan	Bill Frieder	Digger Phelps
1985	UCLA	Indiana	65–62	Reggie Miller, UCLA	Walt Hazzard	Bob Knight
1986	Ohio State	Wyoming	73–63	Brad Sellers, Ohio State	Eldon Miller	Jim Brandenburg
1987	Southern Miss.	La Salle	84–80	Randolph Keys, Southern Miss.	M.K. Turk	Speedy Morris
1988	Connecticut	Ohio State	72–67	Phil Gamble, Connecticut	Jim Calhoun	Gary Williams
1989	St. John's	St. Louis	73–65	Jayson Williams, St. John's	Lou Carnesecca	Rich Grawer
1990	Vanderbilt	St. Louis	74–72	Scott Draud, Vanderbilt	Eddie Fogler	Rich Grawer
1991	Stanford	Oklahoma	78–72	Adam Keefe, Stanford	Mike Montgomery	Billy Tubbs
1992	Virginia	Notre Dame	81–76	Bryant Stith, Virginia	Jeff Jones	John MacLeod
1993	Minnesota	Georgetown	62–61	Voshon Lenard, Minnesota	Clem Haskins	John Thompson
1994	Villanova	Vanderbilt	80–73	Doremus Bennerman, Siena	Steve Lappas	Jan van Breda Kolff
1995	Virginia Tech	Marquette	65–64 (OT)	Shawn Smith, Virginia Tech	Bill C. Foster	Mike Deane
1996	Nebraska	St. Joseph's	60–56	Erick Strickland, Nebraska	Danny Nee	Phil Martelli
1997	Michigan	Florida State	82–73	Robert Traylor, Michigan	Steve Fisher	Pat Kennedy
1998	Minnesota	Penn State	79–72	Kevin Clark, Minnesota	Clem Haskins	Jerry Dunn
1999	California	Clemson	61–60	Sean Lampley, California	Ben Braun	Larry Shyatt
2000	Wake Forest	Notre Dame	71-61	Robert O'Kelley, Wake Forest	Dave Odom	Matt Doherty
2001	Tulsa	Alabama	79-60	Marcus Hill, Tulsa	Buzz Peterson	Mark Gottfried
2002	Memphis	South Carolina	72-62	Dajuan Wagner, Memphis	John Calipari	Dave Odom
2003	St. John's	Georgetown	70-67	Marcus Hatten, St. John's	Mike Jarvis	Craig Esherick

National Women's Invitational Tournament / Women's National Invitation Tournament

College basketball's national invitation tournaments for women have a two-life history with two sponsors, two formats, and two slightly different and somewhat confusing names. The National Women's Invitational Tournament (NWIT), the original tourney, operated from 1969 through 1996. The new version, the Women's National Invitation Tournament (WNIT), began in 1998. There was no women's invitational tournament in 1997.

Beginning in 1969, the same year in which the first Association for Intercollegiate Athletics for Women (AIAW) Invitational Tournament was held, the NWIT was the oldest, longest running women's college basketball tournament until it ceased operations after the 1996 edition, because the sponsors could not and/or would not meet the requirements imposed by the NCAA for postseason play.

Always an eight-team seeded event, the National Women's Invitational Tournament was not associated with the more widely known men's event of similar name. Sponsored by the Amarillo, Texas, chamber of commerce and conducted by its sports committee, the tournament presented big-time basket-

ball in a delightful small-town atmosphere. Held in the Amarillo Civic Center, it featured half-time entertainment by local musical organizations, kiddie basketball teams and gymnastic troupes, drawings and raffles, team "hosts" and "boosters," and a cadre of local volunteer workers, many of whom were involved for most of the years that the tournament operated. While the NWIT may not have had the glamor and glitz of New York City and Madison Square Garden, it had a charm and allure that players and coaches remember fondly.

For the first three years, tournament games were played with six-member teams. Two players were allowed to be "rovers" over the entire court; the others (forwards or guards) were restricted to either the front or backcourt, respectively. In 1972, the five-member, full-court game as it is played today was instituted.

In the NWIT's early years, most of the participants were the smaller schools, including junior colleges, from west of the Mississippi, but many of them had well-established reputations from the Amateur Athletic Union (AAU) women's tournament, which for many years was the nation's premier (and often the only) women's basketball national championship event. Wayland Baptist made the most appearances—10—while John F. Kennedy (Nevada; defunct) and Belmont (Tenn.) had seven;

Ranger (Tex.), a junior college, and Illinois State, six; and Temple Junior College (Tex.) and Drake, five.

By the late 1970s, after the bigger schools began women's basketball and after the National Junior College Athletic Association (NJCAA) started its women's tournament in 1975, the NWIT teams were the four-year schools that did not qualify for the then reasonably well-established AIAW event, which continued through 1982 and competed with the new NCAA tournament in its last year.

Wayland Baptist of Plainview, Texas, now an NAIA school, dominated the AIAW era of the NWIT. In tournament terms, Wayland's domination of the event was surpassed only by UCLA's 1964-75 championship run in the men's NCAA Division I tournament. From 1969 through 1977, The Flying Queens won nine straight NWIT titles, the first five under Harley Redin and the last four under Dean Weese. During that stretch, they won 268 games and lost a mere 40, for an awesome winning percentage of .870.

Although City College of New York holds a special place in basketball history as the only school to have won both the men's NCAA Division I and the NIT championships in the same year, consider that Wayland Baptist took both the NWIT and the AAU women's championships in 1970, 1971, 1974, and 1975, and just missed another double with an AAU finish of second in 1976. (For the record, The Flying Queens finished third in the AAU event in 1969, fourth in 1972, and, of all things, 16th in 1973.) For good measure, from 1974 to 1976 the Queens also participated in the AIAW event (three national tournaments in the same year!), finishing fifth, fifth, and third.

In 1969 and 1970, five of the eight NWIT teams also played in the AAU tourney, with John F. Kennedy finishing fourth in the NWIT and second in the AAU in 1969 and Ouachita Baptist garnering a third place in the NWIT and a second place in the AAU in 1970. In 1971, 1972, and 1973 four of the eight NWIT schools also appeared in the AAU tourney. For 1974 and 1975, dual participation shrunk to two schools, and in 1976, Wayland Baptist was the only double participant.

In addition to Wayland Baptist from 1974 to 1976, other schools that participated in the NWIT and the AIAW in the same year were Kansas State, 1970, seventh in the NWIT and eighth in the AIAW; Temple Junior College, 1974, fourth in the NWIT and eighth in the AIAW JC division; and Mississippi College, 1977, third in the NWIT and 12th in the AIAW large school division. Note that no school won the NWIT and the AIAW (or NCAA) tournaments in the same year.

The NCAA era, as expected, featured women's NCAA Division I schools, with no one winning more than one title.

After the NCAA began its tournament in 1982, Amarillo was able to attract only the NCAA non-qualifiers. Interestingly, no NAIA schools ever participated in the NWIT.

The NWIT saw its share of outstanding players, including Nancy Lieberman Cline of Old Dominion, Ann Myers (Drysdale) of UCLA, and Judy Spolestra of Oregon State (all MVPs), and Ellen Mosher (Parsons), Carol Booth and Juliene Simpson (both of John F. Kennedy), and Tara Van Derveer (UCLA), among others.

In spite of the fact that the "association tournaments" took most of the ranked teams, the NWIT managed to attract a few. The first women's "national poll" was for the 1977 season, and the NWIT landed four of the elite teams: Wayland Baptist (no. 7), UCLA (13), Old Dominion (14), and Mississippi College (18). In succeeding years, teams ranked by the AP that participated in the NWIT were as follows:

1978: Old Dominion (12), Texas (15)
1979: South Carolina (15)
1984: Tennessee: Chattanooga (20)
1985: Texas Tech (19)
1993: UNLV (24; USAToday Poll)

In 1998, the Women's National Invitation Tournament, sponsored by Triple Crown Sports (which also conducts the preseason NIT), was instituted under a format totally different from the NWIT. The new sponsor began operations in 1982 to organize and produce adult slow-pitch softball tournaments. Since then it expanded to work with youth soccer, roller hockey, baseball, and girl's fast-pitch softball in addition to the two basketball tournaments. Many of the events have been franchised to regional owners.

The new format provided for a 16-team unseeded event, growing to 32 teams in 1999 and 2000, for schools that do not receive an invitation to the NCAA Division I tournament. The schools are bracketed in four reasonable geographic sections to produce a Final Four. All games, including the championship, are played at the home site of one of the teams.

Both the NWIT and its successor, the WNIT, have made a profound and lasting contribution to women's college basketball. Although it can be argued that the women's game might have survived and prospered without these tournaments, it certainly is better because of them. Through 2003, more than 150 schools have participated in either the NWIT and/or the WNIT. For many good teams that did not qualify for "the big dance," it was an awfully nice alternative.

WOMEN'S NIT RESULTS

Year	Champion	Runner-Up	Year	Champion	Runner-Up	Year	Champion	Runner-Up
1969	Wayland Baptist	Ouachita Baptist	1981	Georgia	Arizona State	1993	Arkansas State	Southern Methodist
1970	Wayland Baptist	Midwestern Okla. St.	1982	Oregon State	Florida State	1994	Oklahoma	Arkansas State
1971	Wayland Baptist	Parsons	1983	New Orleans	Memphis	1995	Texas A&M	Northwestern State
1972	Wayland Baptist	John F. Kennedy	1984	Vanderbilt	Tenn.-Chattanooga	1996	Arizona	Northwestern Univ.
1973	Wayland Baptist	John F. Kennedy	1985	Louisiana State	Florida	1997	no tournament	
1974	Wayland Baptist	John F. Kennedy	1986	Idaho	Northwestern State	1998	Penn State	Baylor
1975	Wayland Baptist	UCLA	1987	Arkansas	California	1999	Arkansas	Wisconsin
1976	Wayland Baptist	UCLA	1988	DePaul	Purdue	2000	Wisconsin	Florida
1977	Wayland Baptist	UCLA	1989	Oregon	San Diego State	2001	Ohio State	New Mexico
1978	Old Dominion	Texas	1990	Kentucky	Toledo	2002	Oregon State	Houston
1979	South Carolina	Drake	1991	Santa Clara	Indiana	2003	Auburn	Baylor
1980	Oregon State	North Carolina	1992	Georgia Tech	Hawaii			

Chapter 49

College Awards, Honors and Records

Total Basketball's look at the Top 20 Programs, Coaches, Players and Teams

By Michael Douchant

Who and what are the best in college basketball history? There is excellence everywhere one turns ... so many star players to choose from ... so many divergent opinions on a seemingly endless list of standout coaches ... so many entertaining teams ... so many inspiring games and moments ... so many potent programs ...

Citing qualifications for determining the greatest this and the greatest that is a no-win situation. Nothing provokes disagreements among ardent hoop fans more than a healthy argument about "Who's the best?" In order to whittle the illustrious field of candidates to a manageable number, however, there must be criteria. The list would be infinite if one made these kind of judgments by anything other than numbers, awards and participation with championship-caliber teams. Following are Solomon-like decisions in a variety of Top 20 categories.

TOP 20 PROGRAMS

Take any combination of categories (victories, national team records, winning streaks, final Top 20 polls, conference championships, total of All-Americans, etc.) and one program has consistently stood above them all: The University of Kentucky!

Surprisingly, excellence wasn't linked to Kentucky at the beginning of its hoop program. Believe it or not, the mighty Wildcats lost their first six games against Georgetown. The nemesis was Georgetown College (Ky.), not Georgetown University (D.C.). Basketball at UK reportedly started in 1903 when W.W.H. Mustaine called together some students, took up a collection totaling $3 for a ball and told them to start playing. There was no official coach the first seven seasons when managers guided the squad to a 21-35 record (.375). Over the years, UK's program evolved to the pressure point that, it has so many fans, it seems as if it is managed by three million "coaches."

Although Kentucky was late in embracing African-American players, it's difficult for any program to measure up to the success enjoyed by the Wildcats' fans in Big Blue Heaven since an inauspicious start. Here is an assessment of the nation's premier programs:

1. Kentucky—Winningest program in NCAA history registered one of the nation's top five records in six of the previous seven decades, finishing ninth in the 1980s ... Set NCAA record with 60 consecutive non-losing seasons (1928-88) ... Only school to twice win at least 30 games overall in three consecutive campaigns. No other major college has achieved the 30-win trifecta once ... Average record in a 15-year span from 1944-59 was an incredible 27-3. The Wildcats won 92.3 percent of their SEC games in that stretch (156-13) ... Most NCAA Tournament appearances of any school ... Paces SEC with 47 regular-season championships and 25 postseason league tournament titles ... Boasts highest total of All-American selections (61) than any school since 1929 ... Won 51 consecutive games in SEC competition from 1950 until 1955 when Georgia Tech broke the Wildcats' NCAA-record of 129 straight homecourt triumphs.

2. North Carolina—Second-winningest program in NCAA history sustained only one losing mark in a 30-year stretch from 1920-21 through 1949-50 ... Posted one of nation's top six records in each of the previous three decades, including the best mark in the 1980s ... Assembled its NCAA-record 31-year streak of 20-win seasons through 2000-01 despite having only six players average at least 20 points per game in a single campaign during that span ... Won more than 70 percent of its national postseason tournament games ... Concluded 20th Century with 35 consecutive finishes no lower than third place in the vaunted ACC ... Paces ACC with most regular-season (23) and postseason tournament (15) championships ... Captured eight Southern Conference Tournaments before joining the ACC ... Runner-up to Kentucky for most All-American choices (56) since 1929 ... Holds NCAA record for most consecutive Top 20 finishes in final polls with 19 from 1971 through 1989. The Tar Heels finished no lower than 16th in that span.

3. Kansas—Third-winningest program in NCAA history after becoming the nation's winningest school in the 1990s when the Jayhawks finished no lower than 13th in final national polls in nine consecutive seasons ... Only school to reach the Final Four under five different coaches—Phog Allen (1940, 1952 and 1953), Dick Harp (1957), Ted Owens (1971 and 1974), Larry Brown (1986 and 1988) and Roy Williams (1991, 1993, 2002 and 2003) ... Won 34 straight games in Missouri Valley competition from 1922 to 1924.

4. UCLA—After losing 42 consecutive contests in its intracity rivalry with Southern California, the Bruins became one of the nation's five winningest programs by percentage on the strength of 54 straight winning seasons ... Nation's best record in back-to-back decades (1960s and 1970s). Supplied an amazing total of 19 All-Americans in the '70s ... Only school to win at least three consecutive national championships. The Bruins' first of seven consecutive NCAA titles from 1967-73 featured a team that is the only champion since World War II not to have a senior on its roster. UCLA, the only school to

have two separate streaks of at least 10 consecutive playoff appearances, has participated in more NCAA tourneys (38) than any school other than Kentucky ... Captured league championship every year in the 1970s en route to a total of 25 undisputed Pacific-10 Conference titles ... Total of nine undefeated and one-loss seasons ... Won 50 straight games in Pacific-8 Conference competition from 1970 to 1974.

5. Indiana—Four of five NCAA Tournament titles came in different decades ... Tied with Kentucky for most different individuals (36) named an All-American since 1929 ... Holds Big Ten record for consecutive victories in conference competition with 37 from 1974 to 1977 ... Last school to go undefeated (32-0 in 1975-76) ... Participated in a national postseason tournament 26 consecutive years through 2003.

6. Duke—One of four schools with more than 1,700 victories ... Incurred only one losing record in a 45-year span from 1927-28 through 1971-72 ... Only school to win more than three-fourths of its NCAA Tournament games through 2003 ... Finished no lower than 17th in 11 consecutive final national polls from 1984 through 1994 and among the top 10 in six straight polls from 1961 through 1966 ... Duke became the first school to rank No. 1 in a final AP poll four consecutive years (1999 through 2002).

7. St. John's—Only school in the 20th Century with as many as 50 national postseason tournament appearances ... One of the 20 winningest programs by percentage in six consecutive decades (1930s through 1980s) ... Holds NIT record with six titles.

8. Purdue—Won 50 of its first 60 meetings with archrival Indiana ... Streak of 23 consecutive winning seasons ended in 1942-43 ... Leads Big Ten with 21 regular-season titles.

9. Ohio State—Only school to reach the Final Four three consecutive years on two separate occasions (1944 through 1946 and 1960 through 1962) ... Ohio State '60, the only team to lead the nation in scoring offense and win the NCAA championship in the same season, is also the only champion to win all of its tournament games by more than 15 points ... One of only seven schools to win more than 60 percent of its games in both the NCAA Tournament and NIT.

10. Louisville—Ranks third in the nation for most national postseason tournament appearances with 43 through 2003 ... Finished among the Top 20 of final national polls in seven consecutive seasons from 1977 through 1983 ... Established Metro Conference records with 12 regular-season titles and 11 league tournament championships ... Ranked among the nation's 15 winningest programs in three decades (1950s, '70s and '80s).

11. Illinois—One of only five schools to boast as many as 28 different individuals named an All-American since 1929, including nine in the 1940s and 10 in the 1950s ... Probably would have cracked list of Top 10 programs in history if the Illini ever had a team reach the NCAA Tournament championship game ... Finished among the Top 20 of final national polls in seven consecutive seasons from 1984 through 1990 and six straight from 1951 through 1956 ... Ranked among the nation's 15 winningest programs by percentage in three decades (1940s, 1950s and 1980s).

12. Marquette—One of only 14 schools with as many as 17 different individuals named an All-American ... UCLA was the only school to have a better record in the 1970s than Marquette, which flourished despite having three key frontcourt players leave school early to turn pro in consecutive seasons—Jim Chones (drafted in '72), Larry McNeill ('73) and Maurice Lucas ('74). The Warriors finished in the Top 10 of a final wire-service poll all 10 years that decade.

13. Syracuse—One of only seven schools to win more than 1,600 games ... Frequently leads the nation in home attendance ... Finished among the Top 20 in nine consecutive final national polls from 1984 through 1992 ... Ranked among the nation's 15 winningest programs by percentage each of the previous three decades ... Two Helms Foundation national championships (1918 and 1926).

14. North Carolina State—Won five consecutive Southern Conference regular-season and league tournament titles from 1947 through 1951 ... Won 10 ACC Tournaments ... Captured seven Southern Conference Tournaments before joining the ACC ... Only ACC school to compile back-to-back undefeated league records (1973 and 1974).

15. Kansas State—Captured 11 Big Eight Conference regular-season titles in 18 years from 1956 through 1973 ... One of only 12 schools with at least 20 Top 20 finishes in final national polls since 1949, including eight consecutive from 1957 through 1964.

16. Michigan—One of only five schools to win more than two-thirds of its games in both the NCAA Tournament and NIT (minimum of 20 decisions).

17. Temple—One of only seven schools to win more than 1,600 games ... Made more national postseason tournament appearances (39 through 2003) than marquee schools Duke, Indiana and Kansas ... So dominant in the inaugural NIT final against Colorado that coach James Usilton removed the Owls' starters after six minutes of the second half ... Holds series edge over each of the other Philadelphia Big Five schools ... Captured more Atlantic 10 Conference regular-season crowns than any member with eight.

18. Notre Dame—Ranks among top eight in the nation for most All-Americans since 1929, including eight in the 1930s and 10 in the 1940s ... Finished among the Top 20 of final national polls in eight consecutive seasons from 1974 through 1981 ... Two Helms Foundation national championships (1927 and 1936).

19. Villanova—One of only four schools with more than

40 national postseason tournament appearances through 2003.

20. Cincinnati—One of only nine schools with more than 20 Top 20 rankings in final polls since 1949. The Bearcats finished with that lofty status in six consecutive seasons from 1958 through 1963 ... North Carolina and UCLA were the only schools to boast more All-Americans than the Bearcats (10) in the 1960s ... Won all four Great Midwest Conference Tournament titles.

TOP 20 COACHES

There are 20 coaches in history with tenures at least 30 years at one school. Insofar as players have had at most four seasons of eligibility, one could build a case that coaches enjoy a significant edge over players in long-term impact on the sport. How in the world does one attempt to pare down a "greatest" list?

There are two "musts" to be included among the Top 20 of the best 100 mentors: National postseason tournament success (reaching the NCAA Final Four or capturing an NIT title) and longstanding success (winning more than two-thirds of their games while coaching at least 20 years in college).

The longevity criteria eliminates former college luminaries such as Vic Bubas, Everett Case and Fred Schaus from consideration for the Top 20 along with, at least for now, current headliners like Rick Majerus, Rick Pitino, Tubby Smith and Roy Williams.

1. John Wooden (664-162 record from 1947-75 with Indiana State and UCLA, .804)

Classic example of why schools and fans should exercise a little more patience. Legendary coach lost his first five playoff games at UCLA by an average of 11.4 points and compiled an anemic 3-9 record from 1950 through 1963 before the Bruins won an unprecedented 10 national titles in 12 years from 1964 through 1975, including seven straight from 1967 through 1973. His 1962 team finished fourth in the NCAA Tournament and his 1974 squad finished third. Six-time national coach of the year won 13 conference titles in his last 14 years. Posted the nation's best record in back-to-back decades (1960s and 1970s).

2. Dean Smith (879-254 from 1962-97 with North Carolina, .776)

Only coach to direct teams to Final Fours in four different decades. He made 11 Final Four appearances (1967-68-69-72-77-81-82-91-93-95-97). All-time winningest major-college coach overall and in NCAA Tournament competition (65 victories). Three-time national coach of the year reached NCAA Final Four 11 times—1967 (fourth), 1968 (runner-up), 1969 (fourth), 1972 (third), 1977 (runner-up), 1981 (runner-up), 1982 (champion), 1991 (tied for third), 1993 (champion), 1995 (tied for third) and 1997 (tied for third). Coach of 1971 NIT champion and 1973 third-place team. Captured 13 ACC Tournament championships with North Carolina. Posted the nation's best record in the 1980s.

3. Adolph Rupp (876-190 from 1931-72 with Kentucky, .822)

Coached teams to four NCAA titles (1948, 1949, 1951 and

1958). His 1942 squad finished tied for third in the 1942 NCAA Tournament and his 1966 team was runner-up to Texas Western. Directed Kentucky to 1946 NIT title and to NIT championship game again in 1947. His 1944 UK team finished fourth at NIT. Coach of 1933 Kentucky team that was selected as national champion by the Helms Foundation. Held NCAA career record for most victories until it was broken by Dean Smith. Coached UK to a SEC-record 24 conference and 13 league tournament titles. "If winning isn't important, why do they keep score?" said Rupp, who posted the nation's best record in back-to-back decades (1940s and 1950s). He reached the 400-, 500-, 600-, 700- and 800-win plateaus faster than any coach in major-college history.

4. Clair Bee (412-87 from 1929-51 with Rider and LIU, .826)

Unbeaten LIU team won 1939 NIT. Lost fewer than four games seven times in nine years from 1934-42 en route to becoming the Blackbirds' all-time winningest coach. LIU went an eye-popping 218-20 (.916) during that nine-year stretch. "Play as a team and eliminate all thoughts of personal glory," Bee said. He reached the 200- and 300-win plateaus faster than any coach in major-college history. From 1934-35 until 1957-58, the Blackbirds had a homecourt winning streak of 139 games at the Brooklyn College of Pharmacy gymnasium. "In the first half of the century, Bee was basketball," said Bob Knight, who was befriended by Bee when Knight was at Army and Bee at a local military school. "There wasn't a thing he did that didn't affect the game, and there wasn't a thing that affected the game that he didn't do. He was one of the most singularly brilliant minds ever involved with athletics, and one of the greatest analytical basketball minds we've ever had. He had such a clear, brilliant grasp of what had to be done. He was a coach in the truest sense of the word."

5. Hank Iba (767-338 from 1930-70 with Northwest Missouri State, Colorado and Oklahoma State; .694)

Only coach with six or more NCAA playoff appearances to reach the regional finals every time. Oklahoma State won two national titles, was national runner-up once, finished fourth once, and was regional runners-up on four occasions in eight playoff appearances under Iba from 1945-65. Reached Final Four on four occasions—1945 (1st), 1946 (1st), 1949 (2nd) and 1951 (4th)—after directing Oklahoma A&M to three NIT semi-finals—1938 (3rd), 1940 (3rd) and 1944 (4th). The engaging Iba, hailed as the patriarch of basketball's first family of coaches, had seven of his former Oklahoma State players eventually coach teams into the NCAA playoffs. Five generations of major-college coaches emanate from Iba, encompassing those coaches who were either players or assistant coaches for Iba or later generations of coaches with ties to the sage. At last count, it is believed a total of more than 50 coaches who can trace their coaching lineage to Iba have made participated in the NCAA Tournament. "Mr. Iba's system was so sound and he inspired such confidence that there was never any question in my mind that his philosophy offered the best opportunity to be successful," current Oklahoma State coach Eddie Sutton said. "The things he gave us are as valid today as they were 40 years ago."

6. Phog Allen (746-264 from 1906-09 and 1913-56 with Baker, Haskell, Central Missouri State and Kansas; .739)

Total of 21 league champions. Had 17 consecutive undisputed first-division finishes with Kansas in the Big Six Conference from 1930 through 1946. "The team with a great defense coupled with a good offense will almost always defeat the team with a good defense and a great offense," Allen said.

7. Mike Krzyzewski (663-234 from 1976-2003 with Army and Duke, .739)

Five-time national coach of the year guided Duke to back-to-back NCAA Tournament titles in 1991 and 1992. Reached NCAA Final Four seven times in nine years from 1986 through 1994 before returning for an eighth time in 1999. Duke's all-time winningest coach had four ACC Tournament champions in the 20th Century. Elevated ranking above mentor Bob Knight is contingent upon not returning to another dismal stint comparable to 1980-83 when he averaged 16 defeats annually.

8. Bob Knight (806-314 from 1966-2003 with Army, Indiana and Texas Tech; .720)

Four-time national coach of the year reached NCAA Final Four five times—1973 (third), 1976 (champion), 1981 (champion), 1987 (champion) and 1992 (tied for third). Coach of six NIT semi-finalists captured 1974 Collegiate Commissioners Association Tournament championship. Winningest coach in Big Ten Conference history. Of the three coaches to win basketball championships at every major level (the NCAA, NIT and Summer Olympics), he is the only one to capture the "Triple Crown" in a span of less than 10 years.

9. Jerry Tarkanian (784-205 from 1969-92 and 1995-2002 with Long Beach State, UNLV and Fresno State; .793)

Coach of 1990 NCAA champion reached NCAA Final Four four times in 15 years from 1977-91. Coach of seven Big West Tournament champions—1983, 1985, 1986, 1987, 1989, 1990 and 1991. All-time winningest coach for Long Beach State and UNLV.

10. Al McGuire (405-143 from 1958-77 with Belmont Abbey and Marquette, .739)

Marquette's all-time winningest coach guided school to the NIT title in 1970 and NCAA championship in 1977. His 1974 Marquette squad finished runner-up to North Carolina State in the NCAA Tournament and his 1967 team lost to Southern Illinois in the NIT final.

11. Denny Crum (675-295 from 1972-2001 with Louisville, .696)

Reached NCAA Final Four six times—1972 (fourth), 1975 (third), 1980 (champion), 1982 (tied for third), 1983 (tied for third) and 1986 (champion). Coach of 1985 NIT fourth-place team. Louisville's all-time winningest coach directed the Cardinals to 11 Metro Conference Tournament champions—1978, 1980, 1981, 1983, 1986, 1988, 1989, 1990, 1993, 1994 and 1995. Holds NCAA record by winning at least 20 games each of his first 13 seasons as a head coach.

12. Frank Keaney (387-117 from 1921-48 with Rhode Island, .768)

Never sustained more than eight defeats in a single season in his 27 years at Rhode Island on his way to becoming the school's all-time winningest coach. His "worse" record in his last 22 campaigns was a 16-7 mark in his swan song in 1947-48. Ranks eighth all-time in winning percentage.

13. Ward "Piggy" Lambert (371-152 from 1917 and 1919-45 with Purdue, .709)

Directed Purdue to six Big Ten titles and five co-championships and holds the conference record for longevity. He was succeeded by assistant Mel Tabue with seven games remaining in his final season, which marked the school's first losing league mark (4-8) since 1919.

14. Joe Lapchick (335-130 from 1937-47 and 1957-65 with St. John's, .720)

Led the Redmen to four NIT titles (1943, 1944, 1959 and 1965). Didn't reach double figures in defeats in a single college season until his 18th campaign.

15. Frank McGuire (549-236 from 1948-61 and 1965-80 with St. John's, North Carolina and South Carolina; .699)

First coach to win more than 100 games for three colleges—St. John's (103), North Carolina (164) and South Carolina (283). Directed North Carolina to an undefeated record (32-0) en route to the 1957 NCAA Tournament title. Guided St. John's to back-to-back NIT third-place finishes in 1950 and 1951.

16. Lute Olson (691-244 from 1974-2003 with Long Beach State, Iowa and Arizona; .739)

Named national coach of the year by NABC in 1980. Reached NCAA Final Four five times—1980 (fourth with Iowa), 1988 (tied for third with Arizona), 1994 (tied for third with Arizona), 1997 (first with Arizona) and 2001 (runner-up with Arizona). Guided UA to NCAA playoffs every year since the field expanded to at least 64 teams in 1985.

17. Lou Carnesecca (526-200 from 1966-70 and 1974-92 with St. John's, .725)

Two-time national coach of the year guided St. John's to the 1985 NCAA Final Four. The school's all-time winningest coach directed the Redmen to three NIT semi-finalists—1970 (runner-up), 1975 (fourth place) and 1989 (champion).

18. Ray Meyer (724-354 from 1943-84 with DePaul, .672)

Four-time national coach of the year guided three teams to the NIT championship game (1944-45-83), winning the title in 1945. His 1948 squad finished fourth at the NIT. DePaul's all-time winningest coach twice took teams to NCAA Final Four—1943 (T3rd) and 1979 (3rd). Shares the longest coaching tenure (42 years) at one school with Western Kentucky's Ed Diddle.

19. John Thompson (596-239 from 1973-99 with Georgetown, .714)

Three-time national coach of year reached NCAA Final

Four three times in a four-year span—1982 (runner-up), 1984 (champion) and 1985 (runner-up). Georgetown's all-time winningest coach had two NIT semi-finalists—1978 (fourth) and 1993 (runner-up)—and six Big East Conference Tournament champions—1980, 1982, 1984, 1985, 1987 and 1989.

20. Hec Edmundson (508-204 from 1917-47 with Idaho and Washington, .713)

In an 18-year span from 1927-28 through 1944-45, he notched 20-win seasons 11 times. Washington was the only school in the 1930s to post more than 200 victories. He is the Huskies' all-time winningest coach.

TOP 20 PLAYERS

Michael Jordan, a mere five years after failing to earn a spot on his high school varsity basketball team in Wilmington, N.C., as a sophomore, became unanimous national college player of the year at North Carolina.

You take the risk of making a colossal blunder by doing anything reflecting a mite negatively on His Airness. But a question lingers: Where does MJ rank among the 100 players who had the most impact while in college?

One could assemble a compelling argument that Jordan is the greatest team sport athlete of all time. At first glance, the prospect of not including him among the top 10 to 20 collegians in history resembles the futility of his chances to legitimately earn a spot on the Chicago White Sox major league roster. He quickly discovered that the single most difficult thing to do in any professional team sport is to consistently make contact with 90-mile-per-hour fastballs and wicked sliders (hit .202 with 114 strikeouts in 127 games for Birmingham in the AA Southern League in 1994).

Similarly, it is a copout to simply accept the instant visibility of an icon such as Jordan and automatically cite him among the most influential players in college history. Jordan's prolific pro career featuring 10 scoring titles, six NBA championships and multiple MVP awards somewhat distorts his collegiate impact. Notwithstanding the appeal of Jordan's game-winning basket as a freshman in the closing seconds of the 1982 national final against Georgetown, a closer examination of the raw facts shows that other players were more efficient more often at the collegiate level.

In order to whittle the illustrious field to a manageable number, candidates for most influential had to play a minimum of three major-college seasons to be included among the Top 20. Such restrictive criteria eliminates many underrated junior college jewels and all-time greats such as Georgia Tech guard Kenny Anderson, Seattle forward Elgin Baylor (one of three seasons was at small-school level), Kansas center Wilt Chamberlain, Massachusetts forward Julius Erving, Memphis State guard Penny Hardaway, Detroit forward-center Spencer Haywood, LSU guard Chris Jackson, Michigan State guard Magic Johnson, California guard Jason Kidd, Georgia Tech guard Stephon Marbury, North Carolina forward Bob McAdoo, Indiana forward George McGinnis, Purdue forward Glenn Robinson, Indiana guard Isiah Thomas and Michigan forward Chris Webber.

Jordan's 33.4-point NBA playoff scoring average in his 13

seasons with the Chicago Bulls more than doubled the NCAA Tournament scoring average he compiled for North Carolina. Jordan averaged 16.5 points per NCAA playoff game with the Tar Heels, scoring 20 or more in only two of 10 postseason games from 1982 through 1984. Most fans don't remember his inauspicious playoff debut when he garnered a meager six points, one rebound, no assists and no steals in 37 minutes of a 52-50 opening-round victory against James Madison in the East Regional. He was Carolina's third-best player at the time behind Sam Perkins and James Worthy.

Jordan's final NCAA Tournament appearance before he left school early to dominate the NBA was nothing to write home about, either. The college player of the year was restricted to six points in the first 35 minutes of the 1984 East Regional semifinals against Indiana and finished with 13 points, one rebound, one assist and one steal in 26 foul-plagued minutes when the top-ranked Tar Heels were eliminated (72-68).

Of course, the celestial Jordan seemed to progress every year with the Bulls while most of his "human" counterparts were fortunate to maintain their game. Few, if any, of them, come close to being in the same league with him in their pro days.

But Jordan's incomparable NBA career followed much more of a down-to-earth college stint. Among the standouts not included among the Top 20 players in the following list but who probably had equally distinguished college careers as Jordan in terms of sustained impact include Terry Dischinger (Purdue), Tim Duncan (Wake Forest), Bailey Howell (Mississippi State), Dan Issel (Kentucky), Rick Mount (Purdue), Calvin Murphy (Niagara), Shaquille O'Neal (LSU), David Robinson (Navy), Ralph Sampson (Virginia), Lionel Simmons (La Salle), Wayman Tisdale (Oklahoma), Wes Unseld (Louisville) and Jimmy Walker (Providence).

Again, Jordan is the greatest of all time if you include his pro career. But he averaged a modest 17.7 points and five rebounds per game with Carolina. Naturally, it's somewhat contrived to rank him No. 23, but no one else deserves to be linked to that number, anyway. Here is a thought-provoking assessment of the most influential college basketball players while they were in school (minimum of two varsity seasons):

1. Lew Alcindor, C, UCLA (88-2 record, .978; 26.4 ppg, 15.5 rpg, 63.9 FG%)

The only individual selected the Final Four's Most Outstanding Player three times averaged 25.7 points and 18.8 rebounds and shot 64.1 percent from the floor in six Final Four games from 1967 through 1969. Alcindor, who later changed his name to Kareem Abdul-Jabbar, is the only player to couple three unanimous first-team All-America seasons with three NCAA titles. Of the 10 different individuals to average more than 23 points per game for a national champion a total of 12 times, Alcindor achieved the feat all three of his seasons with the Bruins. He is also the only player to hit better than 70 percent of his field-goal attempts in two NCAA title games.

UCLA '67, the first varsity season for Alcindor, set the record for largest average margin of victory for a champion when the Bruins started a dazzling streak of 10 consecutive Final Four appearances. They won their 12 NCAA playoff games with Alcindor manning the middle by an average margin

of 21.5 points. The three Alcindor-led UCLA teams rank among the seven NCAA champions with average margins of victory in a tournament of more than 19 points per game. He led the nation in field-goal percentage in 1967 and 1969 and finished fourth in 1968. Ranked among the nation's leading scorers in 1967 (2nd), 1968 (12th) and 1969 (29th). Ranked among the nation's leading rebounders in 1967 (4th), 1968 (9th) and 1969 (16th). Both of UCLA's defeats with Alcindor manning the middle were by two points. It's no wonder a perceptive scribe wrote that the acronym NCAA took on a new meaning during the Alcindor Era—"No Chance Against Alcindor."

2. Oscar Robertson, F-G, Cincinnati (79-9, .898; 33.8 ppg, 15.2 rpg, 53.5 FG%)

Averaged at least 29 points and 10 rebounds per game each of his three years in the NCAA tourney. Led the country in scoring all three varsity seasons. First player to lead the nation's scorers in both his sophomore and junior seasons. Ranked among the nation's top 20 in rebound percentage and field-goal percentage all three seasons. Also ranked among the leaders in free-throw percentage in 1958 (33rd) and 1959 (35th). Had six games of at least 50 points, including a school-record 62 against North Texas State and 56 when he personally outscored Seton Hall (118-54).

3. Jerry Lucas, C, Ohio State (78-6, .929; 24.3 ppg, 17.2 rpg, 62.4 FG%)

Final Four Most Outstanding Player in 1960 and 1961. Three-time Big Ten Conference MVP led the nation in field-goal percentage all three seasons from 1960 through 1962. Paced the country in rebounding in 1961 and 1962 after finishing 11th in 1960. Ranked among the nation's leading scorers in 1960 (8th), 1961 (11th) and 1962 (38th) and 43rd in free-throw percentage in 1962. Lucas departed with the three best single-season rebounding totals in Big Ten history. He became the first player ever to gain five individual national statistical titles in a career (two for rebounding and three for shooting). Had 20 games with at least 20 rebounds.

4. Larry Bird, F, Indiana State (81-13, .862; 30.3 ppg, 13.3 rpg, 53.3 FG%, 82.2 FT%)

Indiana transfer ranked among the nation's top three scorers in 1977 (3rd), 1978 (2nd) and 1979 (2nd). Two-time MVC Player of the Year ranked among the nation's top seven rebounders in 1977 and 1979. Had eight games with at least 44 points, including a school-record 49 against Wichita State.

5. Bill Walton, C, UCLA (86-4, .956; 20.3 ppg, 15.7 rpg, 65.1 FG%)

Averaged 28.8 points and 17.8 rebounds per game at the Final Four in 1972 and 1973. His championship game-record 44 points against Memphis State in 1973 when he hit 21 of 22 field-goal attempts will probably never be duplicated. Ranked among the nation's top four in field-goal percentage in 1972 (4th), 1973 (2nd) and 1974 (2nd). Ranked among the nation's top 10 rebounders all three seasons. He joined Oscar Robertson (Cincinnati '58) as the only players in history to be named

national player of the year in their first season of varsity competition. Walton was headliner of the first major-college team in history to compile back-to-back perfect-record seasons. Walton, who paced three consecutive league champions in scoring and rebounding, is the only player to be a three-time first-team NCAA unanimous All-American and first-team Academic All-American. He shot an NCAA Tournament-record 68.6 percent from the floor in 12 playoff games.

6. Pete Maravich, G, Louisiana State (49-35, .583; 44.2 ppg, 6.4 rpg, 5.1 apg)

All-time leading scorer in Division I holds NCAA records for most 50-point games (10) and most 40-point games (56). Dazzling ballhandler never scored fewer than 30 points in back-to-back games and tallied under 20 just once (17 at Tennessee as a sophomore) in his three varsity seasons. The son of LSU coach Press Maravich was outscored in just one regular-season game by a teammate en route to three consecutive national scoring titles. "Pistol Pete" scored an amazing 48.2 percent of LSU's points in his three-year career en route to setting a bevy of NCAA scoring records. It's mind-boggling to think about how many points the three-time SEC Player of the Year would have scored if there had been a three-point arc at the time.

7. David Thompson, F, North Carolina State (79-7, .919; 26.8 ppg, 8.1 rpg, 55.3 FG%)

Three-time ACC Player of the Year ranked among the nation's leading scorers in 1973 (17th), 1974 (5th) and 1975 (3rd). Incredible leaper ranked 19th in the nation in field-goal percentage in 1973. He had a total of 33 30-point games, including a school-record 57 against Buffalo State.

8. Elvin Hayes, F-C, Houston (81-12, .871; 31 ppg, 17.2 rpg, 53.6 FG%)

He is the only player to lead an NCAA tournament in scoring by more than 60 points (167 points in five games in 1968). Hayes became the only player in tournament history to collect more than 40 points and 25 rebounds in the same game when he amassed 49 points and 27 rebounds in a 94-76 decision over Loyola of Chicago in the first round of the '68 Midwest Regional. He holds the records for most rebounds in a playoff series (97 in five games as a senior in 1968) and career (222 in 13 games). He had five tourney games with at least 24 rebounds, including the first three playoff contests in 1968, before being held to five in a 101-69 national semi-final loss against UCLA. Hayes also holds the record for most playoff field goals in a career with 152. Ranked among the nation's top six rebounders in 1966 (5th), 1967 (6th) and 1968 (3rd). Ranked among the nation's leading scorers in 1966 (11th), 1967 (4th) and 1968 (3rd). Had 52 games with at least 30 points and 25 contests with a minimum of least 20 rebounds.

9. Bill Bradley, F, Princeton (62-21, .747; 30.2 ppg, 12.1 rpg, 51.3 FG%, 87.6 FT%)

The former U.S. Senator (D-N.J.) and presidential candidate for 2000 holds the record for most points in a single Final Four game (58 against Wichita State in 1965 national third-place game). He scored 39 points in the second half of the con-

solation game. The Rhodes Scholar was the only player to have a double-digit season scoring average (30.5 points per game) for Princeton's Final Four team. Bradley also holds the career playoff record for highest free-throw percentage (minimum of 50 attempts). He was 89 of 96 from the foul line (90.6 percent) from 1963 through 1965. In five of his nine playoff games, Bradley made at least 10 free throws while missing no more than one attempt from the charity stripe. He made 16 of 16 free throws against St. Joseph's in the first round of the 1963 East Regional and 13 of 13 foul shots against Providence in the 1965 East Regional final to become the only player to twice convert more than 12 free throws without a miss in playoff games. He led the nation in free-throw percentage in 1965 after finishing 2nd in 1963 and 14th in 1964. Ranked among the nation's top five scorers in 1963 (5th), 1964 (4th) and 1965 (3rd). Set a mark for most points in an Ivy League contest when he poured in 51 against Harvard. He is the only Princeton player to score 40 or more points in a game, a feat he achieved 11 times. Bradley led three consecutive Ivy League champions in scoring and rebounding.

10. Bill Russell, C, San Francisco (71-8, .899; 20.7 ppg, 20.3 rpg, 51.6 FG%)

Grabbed an incredible 50 rebounds at the 1956 Final Four (23 against SMU in the semi-finals and 27 against Iowa in the championship game). No other player has retrieved more than 41 missed shots in two Final Four games or more than 21 in the final. One of six players to average more than 20 points and 20 rebounds per game in his career. Ranked among the nation's leading rebounders in 1954 (7th), 1955 (4th) and 1956 (4th). Ranked among the nation's leaders in field-goal percentage in 1954 (15th), 1955 (7th) and 1956 (9th).

11. Tom Gola, F-C, La Salle (101-17, .856; 20.9 ppg, 18.7 rpg)

The only individual to earn NCAA Final Four Most Outstanding Player and NIT Most Valuable Player awards in his career. Ranked among the nation's top rebounders in 1952 (9th), 1953 (19th), 1954 (3rd) and 1955 (6th). Ranked among the nation's leading scorers all four seasons—1952 (41st), 1953 (55th), 1954 (21st) and 1955 (18th). Also finished 22nd in the nation in free-throw percentage in 1953. Concluded his career with 2,462 points and 2,201 rebounds. His total of points and rebounds (4,663) is the highest in NCAA history.

12. George Mikan, C, DePaul (81-17, .827; 19.1 ppg)

Led the nation in scoring in 1945 and 1946. NIT Most Valuable Player in 1945. Leading scorer in NIT in 1944 and 1945 when he averaged 28.2 points in six games. Set a school single-game scoring record that still exists (53 points vs. Rhode Island State in NIT). Had 13 games with at least 30 points.

13. Jerry West, F-G, West Virginia (81-12, .871; 24.8 ppg, 13.3 rpg, 50.8 FG%)

He is the only player to score at least 25 points in eight consecutive tournament games. West is also the only player to rank among the top five in scoring average in both the NCAA Tournament (30.6 points per game) and NBA playoffs (29.1

ppg). He had 62 contests with at least 20 points. Ranked among the nation's leading scorers in 1958 (65th), 1959 (5th) and 1960 (4th). Ranked among the nation's top 25 in field-goal percentage in 1958 and 1959 and in rebound percentage in 1960.

14. Cazzie Russell, F, Michigan (65-17, .793; 27.1 ppg, 8.5 rpg, 50.5 FG%, 82.8 FT%)

Averaged at least 24 points per game each of his three years in the NCAA tourney. Two-time Big Ten MVP ranked among the nation's leading scorers in 1964 (24th), 1965 (10th) and 1966 (3rd). Ranked among the nation's top 35 in free-throw percentage all three seasons. Set a school record for most points in a regulation game with 48 against Northwestern. He had 23 outings with at least 30 points.

15. Bob Pettit, F-C, Louisiana State (59-15, .797; 27.4 ppg, 14.6 rpg)

Of the more than nearly 50 different players to score more than 225 points in the NCAA playoffs and/or average over 25 points per tournament game (minimum of six games), he is the only one to score more than 22 points in every postseason contest (six games in 1953 and 1954). He was perhaps the most consistent big scorer in NCAA Tournament history with a single-digit differential between his high game (36 points) and his low game (27). Pettit wasn't named to the 1953 All-Tournament team despite leading the Tigers to the Final Four and averaging 30.5 points per game in four NCAA playoff contests. He averaged the same number of points in two tourney games the next year. Ranked among the nation's leaders in scoring in 1952 (3rd), 1953 (9th) and 1954 (2nd), field-goal percentage in 1953 (9th) and 1954 (13th) and rebounding in 1954 (11th).

16. Bernard King, F, Tennessee (61-20, .753; 25.8 ppg, 13.2 rpg, 59 FG%)

Led the nation in field-goal percentage as a freshman in 1975. Ranked among the nation's top 12 scorers all three seasons. Three-time SEC Player of the Year ranked among the nation's top 10 rebounders as a sophomore and junior. He had five games with at least 40 points. Probably would have placed higher if he didn't forgo his final year of eligibility.

17. Austin Carr, G, Notre Dame (61-24, .718; 34.6 ppg, 7.3 rpg, 52.8 FG%, 81.4 FT%)

Carr averaged 47.2 ppg in his last six NCAA playoff contests to finish with a tourney record 41.3-point average. Ranked second in the nation in scoring in 1970 and 1971. Ranked 25th in the nation in field-goal percentage in 1970 and among the nation's leaders in free-throw percentage in 1970 (25th) and 1971 (29th). Accounted for 18 of the 20 times in Irish history when a player scored 45 or more points, including a school-record 61 against Ohio University.

18. Bob Lanier, C, St. Bonaventure (65-12, .844; 27.6 ppg, 15.7 rpg, 57.6 FG%)

Ranked among the nation's leading scorers in 1968 (11th), 1969 (8th) and 1970 (9th). Also ranked among the nation's top

15 in rebounding while ranking among the top 21 in field-goal percentage all three seasons. Boasts the top five single-game rebound totals in Bonnies history plus four of the top five single-game scoring outputs, including a school-record 51 against Seton Hall.

19. Adrian Dantley, F, Notre Dame (68-19, .782; 25.8 ppg, 9.8 rpg, 56.2 FG%, 80 FT%)

Ranked among the nation's top four scorers in 1975 (2nd) and 1976 (4th). Ranked 17th in the nation in free-throw percentage in 1974 and 18th in field-goal percentage in 1976. Averaged 25.4 points and 8.3 rebounds in eight NCAA Tournament games. Scored a career-high 49 points against Air Force.

20. Rick Barry, F, Miami, Fla. (65-16, .802; 29.8 ppg, 16.5 rpg, 52.2 FG%, 84.7 FG%)

Led the nation in scoring in 1965 after finishing 4th in 1964. Ranked among the nation's leading rebounders in 1963 (18th), 1964 (11th) and 1965 (4th). Ranked among the nation's top 20 in free-throw percentage all three seasons. Barry was able to stay ahead of Utah State's Wayne Estes in the 1965 scoring race by amassing six 50-point games, including a national-high and school record 59 against Rollins. Barry finished that season with an amazing average of 55.7 points and rebounds per contest. He hauled down a school-record 29 rebounds against Oklahoma City and retrieved 27 missed shots to equal Rollins' entire team total.

TOP 20 TEAMS

UCLA boasts four undefeated squads under legendary coach John Wooden, but he deemed another as his best.

"It would be hard to pick a team over the 1968 team," Wooden said. "I will say it would be the most difficult team to prepare for and play against offensively and defensively. It created so many problems. It had such great balance.

"We had the big center (Lew Alcindor before he changed his name to Kareem Abdul-Jabbar), who is the most valuable player of all time. Mike Warren was a three-year starter who may have been the most intelligent floor leader ever, going eight complete games once without a turnover. Lucius Allen was a very physical, talented individual who was extremely quick. Lynn Shackleford was a great shooter out of the corner who didn't allow defenses to sag on Jabbar. Mike Lynn didn't have power, but he had as fine a pair of hands around the boards as I have ever seen."

The roster for UCLA's 1968 national champion included six players with double-digit season scoring averages, but senior forward Edgar Lacey dropped off the team with an 11.9-point average following a dispute with Wooden after a highly-publicized mid-season defeat against Houston before 52,693 fans at the Astrodome. Lacey, assigned to defend Cougars star Elvin Hayes early in the game, was annoyed with Wooden for singling him out following Hayes' 29-point first-half outburst. Lacey, the leading rebounder for the Bruins' 1965 NCAA titlist when he was an All-Tournament team selection, missed the 1966-67 campaign because of a fractured left kneecap. Houston, entering the tourney undefeated, lost in the national

semi-finals against UCLA (101-69) when Hayes, averaging 37.6 points per game entering the Final Four, was restricted to 10 as the Bruins neutralized him by employing a "diamond-and-one" defense with Lynn Shackelford assigned to cover Hayes.

Still, any lineup blessed with Alcindor's inside artistry will be one of the greatest of all-time. The following Top 20 team rankings claim UCLA supplied five of the six best squads in history:

1. UCLA '68 (29-1 record)

Coach: John Wooden (20th of 27 seasons with Bruins).
Key Players: C Lew Alcindor (26.2 ppg, 16.5 rpg, 61.3 FG%); G Lucius Allen (15.1 ppg, 6 rpg); G Mike Warren (12.1 ppg, 3.7 rpg); F Lynn Shackelford (10.7 ppg, 5 rpg, 84.8 FT%); F Mike Lynn (10.3 ppg, 5.2 rpg); G Ken Heitz (5.3 ppg); F Jim Nielsen (4.6 ppg, 3.3 rpg); G Bill Sweek (3.6 ppg).
Only Defeat: At Houston (2-point margin).

Comment: The Bruins almost lost their season opener on the road when Purdue, Wooden's alma mater, opened its new arena. But they "Sweeked" past the Boilermakers, 73-71, on backup guard Bill Sweek's 24-footer in the closing seconds after future All-American guard Rick Mount missed the front end of a one-and-one free-throw opportunity for the Boilermakers.

2. UCLA '67 (30-0)

Coach: John Wooden (19th of 27 seasons with Bruins).
Key Players: C Lew Alcindor (29 ppg, 15.5 rpg, 66.7 FG%); G Lucius Allen (15.5 ppg, 5.8 rpg); G Mike Warren (12.7 ppg, 4.5 rpg); F Lynn Shackelford (11.4 ppg, 5.9 rpg, 82.1 FT%); F-G Ken Heitz (6.1 ppg, 3.2 rpg, 50.6 FG%); G Bill Sweek (4.7 ppg, 2.8 rpg); F-C Jim Nielsen (4.6 ppg, 3.4 rpg, 51.9 FG%); G Don Saffer (2.9 ppg).

Comment: Lew Alcindor scored 56 points in his varsity debut against Southern California. Alcindor's opening-game outburst was topped just once all season—by his school-record 61 against Washington State. He finished his sophomore season ranked among the top seven in the country in field-goal shooting (first at 66.7 percent), scoring (second at 29 points per game) and rebounding (seventh at 15.5 per game). His scoring average is still the highest in Pacific-10 Conference history. The Bruins, starting four sophomores and one junior, won the national championship by a record average of 23.75 points. They won 26 of their 30 games by at least 15 points with the only contest in doubt being a 40-35 overtime triumph at Southern California in mid-season.

3. UCLA '69 (29-1)

Coach: John Wooden (21st of 27 seasons with Bruins).
Key Players: C Lew Alcindor (24 ppg, 14.7 rpg, 63.5 FG%); F Curtis Rowe (12.9 ppg, 7.9 rpg, 50.2 FG%); G John Vallely (11 ppg, 3.3 rpg); F Sidney Wicks (7.5 ppg, 5.1 rpg); F Lynn Shackelford (7 ppg, 4 rpg); G Ken Heitz (6.5 ppg, 2.3 rpg); G Bill Sweek (6.3 ppg, 50.6 FG%); C Steve Patterson (5 ppg, 3.9 rpg, 52.7 FG%).
Only Defeat: At Southern California (2).

Comment: Southern California ended UCLA's 41-game winning streak, 46-44. It was one of only two defeats for the Bruins during Lew Alcindor's three-year varsity career with

both of the setbacks by two points. Alcindor, climaxing a streak when he became the only individual to earn three consecutive Final Four Most Outstanding Player awards, collected 37 points and 20 rebounds in his final college game, a victory against Purdue (92-72).

4. UCLA '72 (30-0)

Coach: John Wooden (24th of 27 seasons with Bruins).
Key Players: C Bill Walton (21.1 ppg, 15.5 rpg, 64 FG%); G Henry Bibby (15.7 ppg, 3.5 rpg, 80.6 FT%); F Keith Wilkes (13.5 ppg, 8.2 rpg, 53.1 FG%); F Larry Farmer (10.7 ppg, 5.5 rpg); G Greg Lee (8.7 ppg, 82.4 FT%); F Larry Hollyfield (7.3 ppg, 3.3 rpg, 51.4 FG%); C Swen Nater (6.7 ppg, 4.8 rpg, 53.5 FG%); G Tommy Curtis (4.1 ppg); G Andy Hill (2.7 ppg); F Vince Carson (2.4 ppg, 2.6 rpg).

Summary: UCLA won the national championship by an average of 18 points. Although the Bill Walton-led Bruins trailed Florida State by a season-high seven points in the first half and the final margin of the championship game was just five (81-76), the outcome never seemed in doubt. Excluding a six-point triumph at Oregon State, they won every other game by at least 13 points. Walton joined Oscar Robertson (Cincinnati '58) as the only players in history to be named national player of the year in their first season of varsity competition. UCLA set an NCAA single-season record for highest average scoring margin (30.3). Incredibly, the Bruins' average halftime margin (17.4) was greater than any other team over an entire game excluding North Carolina's 17.7.

5. Indiana '76 (32-0)

Coach: Bob Knight (5th of first 29 seasons with Hoosiers).
Key Players: F Scott May (23.5 ppg, 7.7 rpg, 52.7 FG%); C Kent Benson (17.3 ppg, 8.8 rpg, 57.8 FG%); F Tom Abernethy (10 ppg, 5.3 rpg, 56.1 FG%); G Quinn Buckner (8.9 ppg, 2.8 rpg, 2 spg); G-F Bobby Wilkerson (7.8 ppg, 4.9 rpg, 5.3 apg); G Wayne Radford (4.7 ppg, 56.3 FG%); G Jim Crews (3.3 ppg, 85.7 FT%); G Jim Wisman (2.5 ppg); F Rich Valavicius (2.4 ppg).

Summary: Indiana tied North Carolina '57 for the all-time record for victories by an undefeated team (32-0). The Hoosiers' schedule was one of the most difficult of any NCAA kingpin. In 14 games outside the rigorous Big Ten, their opponents combined to win more than three-fourths of their games excluding the contests with Indiana. IU's Scott May and Kent Benson combined for 40.8 points and 16.5 rebounds per game for team winning national championship by an average of 13.2 points. The Hoosiers kept a perfect record intact despite trailing in the second half of three of their five tournament games, including Mideast Regional contests against Alabama and Marquette accounting for two of the 11 contests they won by single-digit margins. The closest result was a two-point triumph at Ohio State in their Big Ten Conference opener.

6. UCLA '73 (30-0)

Coach: John Wooden (25th of 27 seasons with Bruins).
Key Players: C Bill Walton (20.4 ppg, 16.9 rpg, 5.6 apg, 65 FG%); F Keith Wilkes (14.8 ppg, 7.3 rpg, 52.5 FG%); F Larry Farmer (12.2 ppg, 5 rpg, 51.1 FG%); G Larry Hollyfield (10.7

ppg, 2.9 rpg); G Tommy Curtis (6.4 ppg, 51.2 FG%); F Dave Meyers (4.9 ppg, 2.9 rpg); G Greg Lee (4.6 ppg); C Swen Nater (3.2 ppg, 3.3 rpg); G-F Pete Trgovich (3.1 ppg).

Summary: UCLA, spearheaded by center Bill Walton, became the first major college in history to compile back-to-back perfect-record seasons. "Walton might have been a better all-around player (than Lew Alcindor)," Bruins coach John Wooden said. "If you were grading a player for every fundamental skill, Walton would rank the highest of any center who ever played."

UCLA won the national championship by an average of 16 points. Walton, aided by Greg Lee's tourney-high 14 assists, erupted for a championship game-record 44 points in an 87-66 triumph over Memphis State in the final. It was UCLA's fifth title-game victory in seven years over a Final Four newcomer. Walton had been outscored by fellow center Steve Downing, 26-14, in a 70-59 victory against Indiana in the national semifinals. The Bruins won 26 of their 30 games by a double-digit margin with the closest results being six-point victories against league rivals Oregon State and Stanford.

7. North Carolina State '74 (30-1)

Coach: Norman Sloan (8th of 14 seasons with Wolfpack).
Key Players: F David Thompson (26 ppg, 7.9 rpg, 54.7 FG%); C Tom Burleson (18.1 ppg, 12.2 rpg, 51.6 FG%); G Monte Towe (12.8 ppg, 51.7 FG%, 3.8 apg, 81.1 FT%); G Moe Rivers (12.1 ppg, 2.9 rpg); F Phil Spence (6 ppg, 6.3 rpg); F Tim Stoddard (5.5 ppg, 4.5 rpg); F Steve Nuce (4.4 ppg, 3.2 rpg); F Greg Hawkins (2.8 ppg); G Mark Moeller (2.7 ppg, 91.3 FT%).
Only Defeat: UCLA at St. Louis (18).

Summary: North Carolina State, unbeaten in 27 games the previous season when it was ineligible to participate in the national tournament because of an NCAA probation, defeated Marquette in the championship game (76-64). The final in N.C. State's home state at Greensboro was anticlimatic after the Wolfpack avenged an 18-point loss to UCLA earlier in the season on a neutral court (St. Louis) by ending the Bruins' 38-game playoff winning streak (80-77 in double overtime). N.C. State erased an 11-point deficit midway through the second half and a seven-point deficit in the second extra session behind David Thompson's 28 points and 10 rebounds to halt UCLA's string of seven consecutive NCAA championships. Thompson became the only undergraduate non-center to average more than 23 points per game for a national champion (26 ppg). N.C. State traveled a thorny path during the season to the NCAA title, defeating nine teams that, at the time, were ranked among the nation's top five.

8. Indiana '75 (31-1)

Coach: Bob Knight (4th of 29 seasons with Hoosiers).
Key Players: F Steve Green (16.6 ppg, 58.2 FG%); F Scott May (16.3 ppg, 6.6 rpg, 51 FG%); C Kent Benson (15 ppg, 8.9 rpg, 54.1 FG%); G Quinn Buckner (11.8 ppg, 3.8 rpg); F Tom Abernethy (4.2 ppg, 3 rpg, 52.6 FG%).
Only Defeat: Kentucky in Mideast Regional final (2).

Summary: Indiana's Bob Knight had one of the all-time greatest coaching staffs. His four assistants all eventually became head coaches for at least two different major colleges—

Dave Bliss, Bob Donewald, Mike Krzyzewski and Bob Weltlich. The Hoosiers, undefeated entering the tourney (29-0), lost the Mideast Regional final against Kentucky (92-90) despite Kent Benson's 33 points and tourney-high 23 rebounds. Knight said he made a mistake by playing an offensive player (John Laskowski) substantially more minutes (33 to 3) than defensive standout Tom Abernethy. Kentucky guards Jimmy Dan Conner and Mike Flynn combined to outscore Indiana counterparts Quinn Buckner and Bobby Wilkerson, 39-22. It was IU's only setback in a 68-game stretch from March 15, 1974, until December 1, 1976.

9. Georgetown '84 (34-3)
Coach: John Thompson (12th of 27 seasons with Hoyas).
Key Players: C Patrick Ewing (16.4 ppg, 10 rpg, 3.6 bpg, 65.8 FG%); G-F David Wingate (11.2 ppg, 3.6 rpg); G Michael Jackson (10.1 ppg, 4.4 apg, 50.9 FG%); G-F Reggie Williams (9.1 ppg, 3.5 rpg); F Bill Martin (8.9 ppg, 5.9 rpg, 50.9 FG%); F Michael Graham (4.9 ppg, 4 rpg, 56.1 FG%); G Horace Broadnax (4.8 ppg, 85.3 FG%); G Gene Smith (3.7 ppg, 2.1 rpg, 1.9 spg, 51.1 FG%); G Fred Brown (3.2 ppg, 2.6 rpg); C-F Ralph Dalton (2.8 ppg, 2.2 rpg, 56.9 FG%).
Only Defeats: At DePaul (2), Villanova (2 in 2OT), and St. John's (4).

Summary: Georgetown became the first Eastern school in 30 years to win an NCAA title. Ewing, the Hoyas' leading scorer on the season, tied the all-time low scoring total for a Final Four Most Outstanding Player with 18 points in two games (fifth on the team), but he was the key component in Georgetown's suffocating defense. The Hoyas led the nation in field-goal percentage defense (39.5 percent) and exhibited their tenacity in the national semi-finals when they harassed Kentucky into shooting a dismal 9.1 percent in the second half (3 of 33) en route to a 53-40 victory. Georgetown's Michael Jackson, a 6-1 guard averaging 1.4 rebounds per game entering the Final Four, retrieved 10 missed shots against Kentucky's formidable frontline to help the Hoyas overcome a seven-point halftime deficit in the national semi-finals.

10. North Carolina '82 (32-2)
Coach: Dean Smith (21st of 36 seasons with Tar Heels).
Key Players: F James Worthy (15.6 ppg, 6.3 rpg, 57.3 FG%); C Sam Perkins (14.3 ppg, 7.8 rpg, 1.7 bpg, 57.8 FG%); G Michael Jordan (13.5 ppg, 4.4 rpg, 53.4 FG%); F Matt Doherty (9.3 ppg, 3 rpg, 51.9 FG%); G Jimmy Black (7.6 ppg, 6.3 apg, 1.7 spg, 51.3 FG%); G Jim Braddock (1.9 ppg, 83.3 FT%); F Chris Brust (1.7 ppg, 62.2 FG%); G Buzz Peterson (1.2 ppg).
Only Defeats: Wake Forest (7) and at Virginia (16).

Summary: Freshman guard Michael Jordan swished a 16-foot jumper from the left side with 16 seconds remaining to provide the title contest's final points as North Carolina edged Georgetown, 63-62. Georgetown guard Fred Brown's errant pass directly to Tar Heels forward James Worthy prevented the Hoyas from attempting a potential game-winning shot in the closing seconds. Worthy, the Final Four Most Outstanding Player, hit 20 of 27 field-goal attempts in two Final Four games. He scored a career-high 28 points in the championship game. Jordan's heroics came after an inauspicious playoff debut when

he collected six points, one rebound, no assists and no steals in 37 minutes of a 52-50 opening-round victory against James Madison in the East Regional.

11. Kentucky '54 (25-0)
Coach: Adolph Rupp (23rd of 41 seasons with Wildcats).
Key Players: F-C Cliff Hagan (24 ppg, 13.5 rpg); G Frank Ramsey (19.6 ppg, 8.8 rpg); F Lou Tsioropoulos (14.5 ppg, 9.6 rpg); F-G Billy Evans (8.4 ppg, 7.2 rpg); G Gayle Rose (6.7 ppg); F-C Phil Grawemeyer (5.9 ppg, 6.1 rpg); G Linville Puckett (5.1 ppg, 2.2 rpg).

Comment: After a one-year schedule boycott, UK's undefeated squad (25-0) declined a bid to the NCAA playoffs because its three fifth-year (postgraduate) stars—Cliff Hagan, Frank Ramsey and Lou Tsioropoulos—were ineligible. The Wildcats defeated national champion-to-be La Salle by 13 points in the UK Invitation Tournament final on their way to being ranked 1st by AP and 2nd by UPI. They had just two games tighter than a 12-point decision (77-71 over Xavier and 63-56 over LSU). Sandwiched between those two contests were 16 victories by an average margin of 33.7 points. Kentucky, coached by Adolph Rupp, finished among the top 10 in team offense and won at least 25 games for the eighth consecutive season in which it participated (barred from playing in 1952-53 as the result of an NCAA ruling regarding improper payments to players). Hagan and Ramsey combined for 43.6 points per game and either one or both of them led the Wildcats in scoring in each of their 25 contests.

12. UNLV '91 (34-1)
Coach: Jerry Tarkanian (18th of 19 seasons with Rebels).
Key Players: F Larry Johnson (22.7 ppg, 10.9 rpg, 3 apg, 2.1 spg, 66.2 FG%, 81.8 FT%); G Anderson Hunt (17.2 ppg, 2.9 apg, 39.9 3FG%); F Stacey Augmon (16.5 ppg, 7.3 rpg, 3.6 apg, 2.2 spg, 58.7 FG%); G Greg Anthony (11.6 ppg, 2.5 rpg, 8.9 apg, 2.4 spg, 39.5 3FG%); C George Ackles (8.2 ppg, 5.7 rpg, 2.2 bpg, 53.9 FG%); F Evric Gray (6.8 ppg, 3.7 rpg, 42.9 3FG%); C Elmore Spencer (6.4 ppg, 4 rpg, 2.5 bpg, 52.2 FG%).
Only Defeat: Duke in NCAA Tournament national semi-finals (2).

Summary: Defending champion UNLV, the first team to enter the NCAA Tournament undefeated since Indiana State in 1979, was upset by Duke in the national semi-finals. Still, the Rebels will go down as one of the greatest teams in history if only because they're the only squad to have at least four teammates score a minimum of 1,500 points—Stacey Augmon (2,011), Greg Anthony (1,738), Anderson Hunt (1,632) and Larry Johnson (1,617). They accounted for four of the six-man All-Big West Conference first-team picks.

13. San Francisco '56 (29-0)
Coach: Phil Woolpert (6th of nine seasons with Dons).
Key Players: C Bill Russell (20.6 ppg, 21 rpg, 51.3 FG%); G K.C. Jones (9.8 ppg, 5.2 rpg); G Hal Perry (9.1 ppg, 2 rpg); F Carl Boldt (8.6 ppg, 5 rpg); F Mike Farmer (8.4 ppg, 7.8 rpg); G Gene Brown (7.1 ppg, 4.4 rpg); F Mike Preaseau (4.1 ppg, 3.1 rpg); G Warren Baxter (2.2 ppg).

Comment: USF won the national championship by an average of 14 points after winning all but two of its regular-season

games by double-digit margins. Bill Russell became the only player to grab more than 41 rebounds at a Final Four (50) and more than 21 in a championship game (Final Four-record 27 against Iowa). K.C. Jones was ineligible for the playoffs because he had played one game two years earlier before an appendectomy ended his season, but USF still became the first undefeated champion in NCAA history (29-0/coached by Phil Woolpert).

14. Ohio State '60 (25-3)

Coach: Fred Taylor (2nd of 18 seasons with Buckeyes).
Key Players: C Jerry Lucas (26.3 ppg, 16.4 rpg, 63.7 FG%); G Larry Siegfried (13.3 ppg, 3.8 rpg); G Mel Nowell (13.1 ppg, 2.6 rpg); F John Havlicek (12.2 ppg, 7.3 rpg); F Joe Roberts (11 ppg, 6.9 rpg); F Richard Furry (5.1 ppg, 3.3 rpg); F-G Bob Knight (3.7 ppg, 2 rpg); C Howard Nourse (3.1 ppg, 2.7 rpg, 51.1 FG%); G Gary Gearhart (2.6 ppg); G Richie Hoyt (2.5 ppg).

Only Defeats: At Utah (5), at Kentucky (3), and at Indiana (16).

Comment: Sophomore Jerry Lucas had the largest-ever margin over the national runner-up in field-goal shooting. Lucas hit 63.7 percent of his shots compared to 57.6 percent for Cincinnati's Paul Hogue. The Buckeyes became the only NCAA titlist to win all of their tournament games by more than 15 points. Lucas and OSU's four other starters—sophomores John Havlicek and Mel Nowell, senior Joe Roberts and junior Larry Siegfried—were all high school centers. They each scored in double figures in the NCAA final before eventually playing at least two seasons in the NBA or ABA or both.

15. Duke '92 (34-2)

Coach: Mike Krzyzewski (12th of first 23 seasons with Blue Devils).
Key Players: C Christian Laettner (21.5 ppg, 7.9 rpg, 2.1 spg, 57.5 FG%, 81.5 FT%, 55.7 3FG%); G Thomas Hill (14.6 ppg, 3.4 rpg, 53.4 FG%, 40.7 3FG%); F-G Grant Hill (14 ppg, 5.7 rpg, 4.1 apg, 61.1 FG%); G Bobby Hurley (13.2 ppg, 7.6 apg, 42.1 3FG%); F Brian Davis (11.2 ppg, 4.5 rpg); F Antonio Lang (6.4 ppg, 4.1 rpg, 56.2 FG%); C Cherokee Parks (5 ppg, 2.4 rpg, 57.1 FG%); G Marty Clark (2.9 ppg, 54.1 FG%); C Erik Meek (2.5 ppg, 57.9 FG%).
Only Defeats: At North Carolina (2) and Wake Forest (4).

Summary: Christian Laettner hit a dramatic decisive last-second shot against Kentucky in overtime after receiving a long inbounds pass in the East Regional final. The game is acknowledged as one of the most suspenseful in NCAA history. Laettner became the NCAA Tournament's all-time leading scorer and teammate Bobby Hurley became the tourney's all-time leader in assists as the Blue Devils became the first school since UCLA (1967-73) to repeat as national champion. Hurley took up the slack with 26 points when Laettner was limited to eight points in an 81-78 decision over Indiana in the national semi-finals. Laettner closed out his college career with a game-high 19 points in the championship game against Michigan, which became the only school ever to lead an NCAA final at halftime and end up losing the game by at least 20 points. Duke coach Mike Krzyzewski did the unthinkable and temporarily passed UCLA legend John Wooden (47-10, .8246) for the top spot in all-time NCAA playoff winning percentage (minimum of 20 games). Hurley was selected Final Four Most Outstanding Player although dissenters believed that Duke

teammate Grant Hill deserved the honor instead. In the two Final Four games, Hill had more field goals than Hurley (14 to 10), outshot him from the floor (61 percent to 41.7), blocked more shots (5 to 0), outrebounded him (16 to 3) and accumulated just as many assists (11 each). Moreover, Hurley's 3 of 12 field-goal shooting in the final against Michigan was the worst marksmanship from the floor for a Final Four Most Outstanding Player in a championship game since Elgin Baylor of runner-up Seattle went 9 of 32 against Kentucky in 1958. It was the second consecutive year for the Final Four Most Outstanding Player to come from Duke and manage just three baskets and shoot less than 50 percent from the floor in the title game. In 1991, Laettner hit 3 of 8 field-goal attempts against Kansas. Duke became the 18th NCAA Tournament champion to win at least two playoff games by fewer than six points when the Blue Devils edged Kentucky (104-103 in overtime) and Indiana (81-78 in national semi-finals).

16. Houston '83 (31-3)

Coach: Guy Lewis (27th of 30 seasons with Cougars).
Key Players: F-G Michael Young (17.3 ppg, 5.7 rpg, 51.3 FG%); F Clyde Drexler (15.9 ppg, 8.8 rpg, 53.6 FG%); C Hakeem Olajuwon (13.9 ppg, 11.4 rpg, 61.1 FG%); F Larry Micheaux 13.8 ppg, 6.8 rpg, 58.8 FG%); F-G Benny Anders (5.9 ppg); G Alvin Franklin (4.8 ppg); G David Rose (3.5 ppg); G Reid Gettys (3.4 ppg, 54.8 FG%).
Only Defeats: At Syracuse (5), Virginia at Tokyo (9) and North Carolina State in NCAA Tournament final (2).

Summary: Hakeem Olajuwon, who collected 41 points and 40 rebounds (tourney-high 22 vs. Louisville and 18 vs. N.C. State) for national runner-up Houston in two Final Four games, is the only Final Four Most Outstanding Player since 1972 not to play for the championship team. Swingman Clyde Drexler set a SWC record with 11 steals against Syracuse.

17. UCLA '64 (30-0)

Coach: John Wooden (16th of 27 seasons with Bruins).
Key Players: G Gail Goodrich (21.5 ppg, 5.2 rpg); G Walt Hazzard (18.6 ppg, 4.7 rpg); F Jack Hirsch (14 ppg, 7.6 rpg, 52.8 FG%); F Keith Erickson (10.7 ppg, 9.1 rpg); C Fred Slaughter (7.9 ppg, 8.1 rpg); F-G Kenny Washington (6.1 ppg, 4.2 rpg); C Doug McIntosh (3.6 ppg, 4.4 rpg, 51.9 FG%).

Comment: Undefeated UCLA won its first of 10 NCAA titles in 12 years, a stretch of dominance that many believe ranks among the greatest achievements in the history of competitive sports. The Bruins entered the season without a Final Four victory despite finishing in a final Top 20 wire-service poll eight times in the previous 14 years under coach John Wooden. Gail Goodrich, a 6-1 junior, became the shortest undergraduate to average more than 20 points per game for an NCAA titlist (21.5 ppg).

18. San Francisco '55 (28-1)

Coach: Phil Woolpert (5th of nine seasons with Dons).
Key Players: C Bill Russell (21.4 ppg, 20.5 rpg, 54.1 FG%); F Jerry Mullen (13.6 ppg, 7.1 rpg); G K.C. Jones (10.6 ppg, 5.1 rpg); G Hal Perry (6.9 ppg); F Stan Buchanan (5.2 ppg, 3.2 rpg); F Bob Wiebusch (3.6 ppg, 2.1 rpg).

Only Defeat: At UCLA (7).

Comment: Any time the ball neared USF's goal, Bill Russell was there to guide the ball through the net, grab the rebound and score or pass to a teammate. The first of San Francisco's back-to-back champions survived a scare in a West Regional and won by one point at Oregon State (57-56). The Beavers would have avenged a 26-point defeat earlier in the season against the Dons if they hadn't missed a last-second shot. A 60-34 verdict over Oregon State was the first of USF's 60 consecutive victories, the longest winning streak in major-college history until UCLA won 88 games in a row from 1971-74.

19. North Carolina '57 (32-0)

Coach: Frank McGuire (5th of nine seasons with Tar Heels).
Key Players: F Lennie Rosenbluth (28 ppg, 8.8 rpg); F Pete Brennan (14.7 ppg, 10.4 rpg); G Tommy Kearns (12.8 ppg, 3.1 rpg); C Joe Quigg (10.3 ppg, 8.6 rpg); G Bob Cunningham (7.2 ppg, 6.7 rpg).

Comment: An NCAA championship game frequently misconstrued as an enormous upset was Carolina's 54-53 triple-overtime victory against Wilt Chamberlain-led Kansas. After all, the Tar Heels were undefeated (32-0), winning 22 games by at least nine points, and their top three scorers wound up playing in the NBA albeit briefly—forwards Lennie Rosenbluth and Pete Brennan and guard Tommy Kearns. Rosenbluth was the team's leading scorer in 27 of its 32 contests, although the Heels won the NCAA final after he fouled out with 1:45 remaining in regulation.

20. Kentucky '49 (32-2)

Coach: Adolph Rupp (19th of 41 seasons with Wildcats).
Key Players: C Alex Groza (20.5 ppg); G Ralph Beard (10.9 ppg); F-C Wallace Jones (9.7 ppg); G-F Cliff Barker (7.3 ppg); F-G Dale Barnstable (6.1 ppg); F Jim Line (5.7 ppg, 84.3 FT%); F-G Walt Hirsch (4.6 ppg).
Only Defeats: Neutral courts vs. St. Louis (2-point margin) and Loyola of Chicago (11).

Comment: Despite returning seven of his top eight scorers from an NCAA titlist, UK coach Adolph Rupp experimented with the Wildcats' lineup until he achieved the chemistry he sought. Cliff Barker was moved from forward to guard and forward Dale Barnstable also played some guard. After an early-season defeat to St. Louis on a last-second tip-in, Kentucky won all of its games until bowing in the NIT to eventual finalist Loyola of Chicago. A couple of years later, Alex Groza, Ralph Beard and Barnstable admitted in sworn testimony that they accepted $1,500 in bribes to throw the NIT game against Loyola. There was also testimony that bribes from gamblers were accepted to shave points in other contests. Each received a suspended sentence in return for cooperating with federal officials and were banned by the NBA. Groza is the only player to appear at a minimum of two Final Fours and be the game-high scorer in every Final Four contest in which he competed.

MEN

United Press International

Awarded from 1955 to 1996 as selected by a panel of college basketball writers.

1955 Tom Gola, La Salle
1956 Bill Russell, San Francisco
1957 Chet Forte, Columbia
1958 Oscar Robertson, Cincinnati
1959 Oscar Robertson, Cincinnati
1960 Oscar Robertson, Cincinnati
1961 Jerry Lucas, Ohio St
1962 Jerry Lucas, Ohio St
1963 Art Heyman, Duke
1964 Gary Bradds, Ohio St
1965 Bill Bradley, Princeton
1966 Cazzie Russell, Michigan
1967 Lew Alcindor, UCLA
1968 Elvin Hayes, Houston
1969 Lew Alcindor, UCLA
1970 Pete Maravich, LSU
1971 Austin Carr, Notre Dame
1972 Bill Walton, UCLA
1973 Bill Walton, UCLA
1974 Bill Walton, UCLA
1975 David Thompson, North Carolina St.
1976 Scott May, Indiana
1977 Marques Johnson, UCLA
1978 Butch Lee, Marquette
1979 Larry Bird, Indiana St.
1980 Mark Aguirre, DePaul
1981 Ralph Sampson, Virginia
1982 Ralph Sampson, Virginia
1983 Ralph Sampson, Virginia
1984 Michael Jordan, North Carolina
1985 Chris Mullin, St. John's (N.Y.)
1986 Walter Berry, St John's (N.Y.)
1987 David Robinson, Navy
1988 Hersey Hawkins, Bradley
1989 Danny Ferry, Duke
1990 Lionel Simmons, La Salle
1991 Shaquille O'Neal, LSU
1992 Jim Jackson, Ohio St.
1993 Calbert Cheaney, Indiana
1994 Glenn Robinson, Purdue
1995 Joe Smith, Maryland
1996 Marcus Camby, Massachusetts

The Associated Press Adolph Rupp Trophy,

Awarded annually by The Associated Press to the college basketball player of the year as selected by a 72-member national panel.

1961 Jerry Lucas, Ohio St.
1962 Jerry Lucas, Ohio St.
1963 Art Heyman, Duke
1964 Gary Bradds, Ohio St
1965 Bill Bradley, Princeton
1966 Cazzie Russell, Michigan
1967 Lew Alcindor, UCLA
1968 Elvin Hayes, Houston
1969 Lew Alcindor, UCLA
1970 Pete Maravich, LSU
1971 Austin Carr, Notre Dame
1972 Bill Walton, UCLA
1973 Bill Walton, UCLA
1974 David Thompson, North Carolina St.
1975 David Thompson, North Carolina St.
1976 Scott May, Indiana
1977 Marques Johnson, UCLA
1978 Butch Lee, Marquette
1979 Larry Bird, Indiana St.
1980 Mark Aguirre, DePaul
1981 Ralph Sampson, Virginia
1982 Ralph Sampson, Virginia
1983 Ralph Sampson, Virginia
1984 Michael Jordan, North Carolina
1985 Patrick Ewing, Georgetown
1986 Walter Berry, St John's (N.Y.)
1987 David Robinson, Navy
1988 Hersey Hawkins, Bradley
1989 Scan Elliott, Arizona
1990 Lionel Simmons, La Salle

1991 Shaquille O'Neal, LSU
1992 Christian Laettner, Duke
1993 Calbert Cheaney, Indiana
1994 Glenn Robinson, Purdue
1995 Joe Smith, Maryland
1996 Marcus Camby, Massachusetts
1997 Tim Duncan, Wake Forest
1998 Antawn Jamison, North Carolina
1999 Elton Brand, Duke
2000 Kenyon Martin, Cincinnati
2001 Shane Battier, Duke
2002 Jason Williams, Duke
2003 David West, Xavier

U.S. Basketball Writers Association Oscar Robertson Award

Awarded annually by the U.S. Basketball Writers Association to the nation's top Division I player.

1959 Oscar Robertson, Cincinnati
1960 Oscar Robertson, Cincinnati
1961 Jerry Lucas, Ohio St
1962 Jerry Lucas, Ohio St
1963 Art Heyman, Duke
1964 Walt Hazzard, UCLA
1965 Bill Bradley, Princeton
1966 Cazzie Russell, Michigan
1967 Lew Alcindor, UCLA
1968 Elvin Hayes, Houston
1969 Lew Alcindor, UCLA
1970 Pete Maravich, LSU
1971 Sidney Wicks, UCLA
1972 Bill Walton, UCLA
1973 Bill Walton, UCLA
1974 Bill Walton, UCLA
1975 David Thompson, North Carolina St.
1976 Adrian Dantley, Notre Dame
1977 Marques Johnson, UCLA
1978 Phil Ford, North Carolina
1979 Larry Bird, Indiana St.
1980 Mark Aguirre, DePaul
1981 Ralph Sampson, Virginia
1982 Ralph Sampson, Virginia
1983 Ralph Sampson, Virginia
1984 Michael Jordan, North Carolina
1985 Chris Mullin, St. John's (N.Y.)
1986 Walter Berry, St John's (N.Y.)
1987 David Robinson, Navy
1988 Hersey Hawkins, Bradley
1989 Danny Ferry, Duke
1990 Lionel Simmons, La Salle
1991 Larry Johnson, UNLV
1992 Christian Laettner, Duke
1993 Calbert Cheaney, Indiana
1994 Glenn Robinson, Purdue
1995 Ed O'Bannon, UCLA
1996 Marcus Camby, Massachusetts
1997 Tim Duncan, Wake Forest
1998 Antawn Jamison, North Carolina
1999 Elton Brand, Duke
2000 Kenyon Martin, Cincinnati
2001 Shane Rattier, Duke
2002 Jason Williams, Duke
2003 David West, Xavier

John R. Wooden Award

Awarded annually by the Los Angeles Athletic Club to the player of the year as selected by a vote of more than 1,000 sportswriters and sportscasters.

1977 Marques Johnson, UCLA
1978 Phil Ford, North Carolina
1979 Larry Bird, Indiana St.
1980 Darrell Griffith, Louisville
1981 Danny Ainge, Brigham Young
1982 Ralph Sampson, Virginia
1983 Ralph Sampson, Virginia
1984 Michael Jordan, North Carolina
1985 Chris Mullin, St John's (N.Y.)
1986 Waller Berry, St John's (N.Y.)
1987 David Rabinson, Navy
1988 Danny Manning, Kansas
1989 Sean Elliott, Arizona
1990 Lionel Simmons, La Salle
1991 Larry Johnson, UNLV

1992 Christian Laettner, Duke
1993 Calbert Cheaney, Indiana
1994 Glenn Robinson, Purdue
1995 Ed O'Bannon, UCLA
1996 Marcus Camby, Massachusetts
1997 Trm Duncan, Wake Forest
1998 Antawn Jamison, North Carolina
1999 Elton Brand, Duke
2000 Kenyon Martin, Cincinnati
2001 Shane Battier, Duke
2002 Jason Williams, Duke
2003 T.J. Ford, Texas

National Association of Basketball Coaches Award

Awarded annually to the outstanding college player as selected by a poll of college coaches.

1975 David Thompson, North Carolina St.
1976 Scott May, Indiana
1977 Marques Johnson, UCLA
1978 Phil Ford, North Carolina
1979 Larry Bird, Indiana St.
1980 Michael Brooks, La Salle
1981 Danny Ainge, Brigham Young
1982 Ralph Sampson, Virginia
1983 Ralph Sampson, Virginia
1984 Michael Jordan, North Carolina
1985 Patrick Ewing, Georgetown
1986 Waller Berry, St John's (N.Y.)
1987 David Rabinson, Navy
1988 Danny Manning, Kansas
1989 Sean Elliott, Arizona
1990 Lionel Simmons, La Salle
1991 Larry Johnson, UNLV
1992 Christian Laettner, Duke
1993 Calbert Cheaney, Indiana
1994 Glenn Robinson, Purdue
1995 Shawn Respert, Michigan St.
1996 Marcus Camby, Massachusetts
1997 Trm Duncan, Wake Forest
1998 Antawn Jamison, North Carolina
1999 Elton Brand, Duke
2000 Kenyon Martin, Cincinnati
2001 Jason Williams, Duke
2002 Jason Williams, Duke
2003 Drew Gooden, Kansas

Naismith Award

Awarded annually by the Atlanta Tipoff Club to the outstanding player of the year as selected by a board of selectors comprising coaches, journalists and analysts.

1969 Lew Alcindor, UCLA
1970 Pete Maravich, LSU
1971 Austin Carr, Notre Dame
1972 Bill Walton, UCLA
1973 Bill Walton, UCLA
1974 Bill Walton, UCLA
1975 David Thompson, North Carolina St.
1976 Scott May, Indiana
1977 Marques Johnson, UCLA
1978 Butch Lee, Marquelte
1979 Larry Bird, Indiana St.
1980 Mark Aguirre, DePaul
1981 Ralph Sampson, Virginia
1982 Ralph Sampson, Virginia
1983 Ralph Sampson, Virginia
1984 Michael Jordan, North Carolina
1985 Patrick Ewing, Georgetown
1986 Johnny Dawkins, Duke
1987 David Rabinson, Navy
1988 Danny Manning, Kansas
1989 Danny Ferry, Duke
1990 Lionel Simmons, La Salle
1991 Larry Johnson, UNLV
1992 Christian Laettner, Duke
1993 Calbert Cheaney, Indiana
1994 Glenn Robinson, Purdue
1995 Joe Smith, Maryland
1996 Marcus Camby, Massachusetts
1997 Tim Duncan, Wake Forest
1998 Antawn Jamiso n, North Carolina
1999 Elton Brand, Duke

COLLEGIATE OUTSTANDING PLAYER AWARDS

2000 Kenyon Martin, Cincinnati
2001 Shane Rattier, Duke
2002 Jason Williams, Duke
2003 T.J. Ford, Texas

Frances Pomeroy Naismith Award

Awarded annually by the Naismith Memorial Basketball Hall of Fame and the National Association of Basketball Coaches to the nation's most outstanding senior six-foot and under.

1969 Billy Keller, Purdue
1970 John Rinka, Kenyon
1971 Charlie Johnson, California
1972 Scott Martin, Oklahoma
1973 Bobby Sherwin, Army
1974 Mike Rabinson, Michigan St.
1975 Monty Towe, North Carolina St.
1976 Frank Algia, St John's (N.Y.)
1977 Jeff Jonas, Utah
1978 Mike Schib, Susquehanna
1979 Alton Byrd, Columbia
1980 Jm Sweeney, Boston College
1981 Terry Adolph, West Texas A&M
1982 Jack Moore, Nebraska
1983 Ray McCallum, Ball St.
1984 Ricky Stokes, Virginia
1985 Bubba Jennings, Texas Tech
1986 Jim Les, Bradley
1987 Tyrone Bogues, Wake Forest
1988 Jerry Johnson, Fla. Southern
1989 Tim Hardaway, UTEP
1990 Boo Harvey, St John's (N.Y.)
1991 Keith Jennings, East Tenn St.
1992 Tony Bennett, Wis.-Green Bay
1993 Sam Crawford, New Mexico St.
1994 Greg Brown, Evansville
1995 Tyus Edney, UCLA
1996 Eddie Benton, Vermont
1997 Kent McCausland, Iowa
1998 Earl Boykins, Eastern Michigan
1999 Shawnta Rogers, George Washington
2000 Scoonie Penn, Ohio St.
2001 Rashad Phillips, Detriot
2002 Steve Lagan, Cincinnati
2003 Jason Gardner, Arizona

WOMEN

The Associated Press Player of the Year

Awarded annually by The Associated Press to the college basketball player of the year.

1995 Rebecca Lobo, Connecticut
1996 Jennifer Rizzotti, Connecticut
1997 Kara Wolters, Connecticut
1998 Chamique Holdsclaw, Tennessee
1999 Chamique Holdsclaw, Tennessee
2000 Tamika Catchings, Tennessee
2001 Ruth Riley, Notre Dame
2002 Sue Bird, Connecticut
2003 Diana Taurasi, Connecticut

The U.S. Basketball Writers Association Player of the Year

Awarded annually by the U.S. Basketball Writers Association to the nation's top player.

1994 Lisa Leslie, Southern California
1998 Chamique Holdsclaw, Tennessee
1999 Chamique Holdsclaw, Tennessee
2000 Tamika Catchings, Tennessee
2001 Ruth Riley, Notre Dame
2002 Sue Bird, Connecticut
2003 Diana Taurasi, Connecticut

Naismith Trophy

First presented in 1983 by the Atlanta Tip-Off Club and voted on by a panel of media and coaches. Named after Dr. James Naismith, inventor of basketball. Goes to the Player of the Year.

1983 Anne Donovan, Old Dominion
1984 Cheryl Miller, Southern California
1985 Cheryl Miller, Southern California
1986 Cheryl Miller, Southern California
1987 Clarissa Davis, Texas
1988 Sue Wicks, Rutgers
1989 Clarissa Davis, Texas
1990 Jennifer Azzi, Stanford
1991 Dawn Staley, Virginia
1992 Dawn Staley, Virginia
1993 Sheryl Swoopes, Texas Tech
1994 Lisa Leslie, Southern California
1995 Rebecca Lobo, Connecticut
1996 Saudia Roundtree, Georgia
1997 Kate Starbird, Stanford
1998 Chamique Holdsclaw, Tennessee
1999 Chamique Holdsclaw, Tennessee
2000 Tamika Catchings, Tennessee
2001 Ruth Riley, Notre Dame
2002 Sue Bird, Connecticut
2003 Diana Taurasi, Connecticut

Wade Trophy

First presented in 1978 by the National Association for Girls and Women in Sport (NAGWS). Named after former Delta State head coach Margaret Wade. Presented to the outstanding collegiate women's basketball player. Selected from the Kodak all-America team seniors. The criteria include being a member of the Kodak all-America team, a senior, a leader, community service and sportsmanship.

1978 Carol Blazejowski, Montclair St.
1979 Nancy Lieberman, Old Dominion
1980 Nancy Lieberman, Old Dominion
1981 Lynette Woodard, Kansas
1982 Pam Kelly, Louisiana Tech
1983 LaTaunya Pollard, Long Beach St.
1984 Janice Lawrence, Louisiana Tech
1985 Cheryl Miller, Southern California
1986 Kamie Ethridge, Texas
1987 Shelly Pennefather, Villanova
1988 Teresa Weatherspoon, Louisiana Tech
1989 Clarissa Davis, Texas
1990 Jennifer Azzi, Stanford
1991 Daedra Charles, Tennessee
1992 Susan Robinson, Penn St.
1993 Karen Jennings, Nebraska
1994 Carol Ann Shudlick, Minnesota
1995 Rebecca Lobo, Connecticut
1996 Jennifer Rizzotti, Connecticut
1997 DeLisha Milton, Florida
1998 Ticha Penicheiro, Old Dominion
1999 Stephanie White-McCarty, Purdue
2000 Edwina Brown, Texas
2001 Jackie Stiles, Southwest Mo. St.
2002 Sue Bird, Connecticut
2003 Diana Taurasi, Connecticut

Frances Pomeroy Naismith Award

First presented in 1984 to the outstanding female senior collegian 5-6 or under in height. Nominated and selected by the WBCA and presented by the Naismith Memorial Basketball Hall of Fame.

1984 Kim Mulkey, Louisiana Tech
1985 Maria Stack, Georgia
1986 Kamie Ethridge, Texas
1987 Rhonda Windham, Southern California
1988 Suzie McConnell, Penn St.

1989 Paulette Backstrom, Bowling Green
1990 Julie Dabrowski, New Hampshire
1991 Shanya Evans, Providence
1992 Rosemary Kosiorek, West Virginia
1993 Dena Evans, Virginia
1994 Nicole Levesque, Wake Forest
1995 Amy Dodrill, Johns Hopkins
1996 Jennifer Rizzotti, Connecticut
1997 Jennifer Howard, North Carolina St.
1998 Angie Arnold, Johns Hopkins
1999 Becky Hammon, Colorado St.
2000 Helen Darling, Penn St.
2001 Niele Ivey, Notre Dame
2002 Sheila Lambert, Baylor
2003 Kara Lawson, Diana Taurasi, Connecticut

Women's Basketball Coaches Association

Awarded annually by the WBCA to the female college basketball player of the year.

1983   Anne Donovan, Old Dominion
1984   Janice Lawrence, La. Tech
1985   Cheryl Miller, USC
1986   Cheryl Miller, USC
1987   Katrina McClain, Georgia
1988   Michelle Edwards, Iowa
1989   Clarissa Davis, Texas
1990   Venus Lacy, La. Tech
1991   Dawn Staley, Virgina
1992   Dawn Staley, Virgina
1993   Sheryl Swoopes, Texas Tech
1994   Lisa Leslie, USC
1995   Rebecca Lobo, Connecticut
1996   Saudia Roundtree, Georgia
1997   Kate Starbird, Stanford
1998   Chamique Holdsclaw, Tennessee
1999   Chamique Holdsclaw, Tennessee
2000   Tamika Catchings, Tennessee
2001   Ruth Riley, Notre Dame
2002   Sue Bird, Connecticut
2003   Diana Taurasi, Connecticut

Broderick Award

Awarded annually to the outstanding female college player as selected by a national panel of women's collegiate athletic directors.

1977   Lucy Harris, Delta St.
1978   Ann Meyers, UCLA
1979   Nancy Lieberman, Old Dominion
1980   Nancy Lieberman, Old Dominion
1981   Lynette Woodard, Kansas
1982   Pam Kelly, La. Tech
1983   Anne Donovan, Old Dominion
1984   Cheryl Miller, USC
1985   Cheryl Miller, USC
1986   Kamie Ethridge, Texas
1987   Katrina McClain, Georgia
1988   Teresa Weatherspoon, La. Tech
1989   Bridgette Gordon, Tennessee
1990   Jennifer Azzi, Stanford
1991   Dawn Staley, Virginia
1992   Dawn Staley, Virginia
1993   Sheryl Swoopes, Texas Tech
1994   Lisa Leslie, USC
1995   Rebecca Lobo, Connecticut
1996   Jennifer Rizzotti, Connecticut
1997   Chamique Holdsclaw, Tennessee
1998   Chamique Holdsclaw, Tennessee
1999   Stephanie White-McCarty, Purdue
2000   Shea Ralph, Connecticut
2001   Jackie Stiles, Southwest Missouri State
2002   Sue Bird, Connecticut
2003   Diana Taurasi, Connecticut

Scoring Average

Season	Player	School	Ht.	Cl.	G	FG	FT	3FG	Pts.	Avg.
1948	Murray Wier	Iowa	5'9	Sr.	19	152	95	—	399	21.0
1949	Tony Lavelli	Yale	6'3	Sr.	30	228	215	—	671	22.4
1950	Paul Arizin	Villanova	6'3	Sr.	29	260	215	—	735	25.3
1951	Bill Mlkvy	Temple	6'4	Sr.	25	303	125	—	731	29.2
1952	Clyde Iovelletle	Kansas	6'9	Sr.	28	315	165	—	795	28.4
1953	Frank Selvy	Furman	6'3	Jr.	25	272	194	—	738	29.5
1954	Frank Selvy	Furman	6'3	Sr.	29	427	355	—	1,209	41.7
1955	Darrell Floyd	Furman	6'1	Jr.	25	344	209	—	897	35.9
1956	Darrell Floyd	Furman	6'1	Sr.	28	339	268	—	946	33.8
1957	Giady Wallace	South Carolina	6'4	Sr.	29	336	234	—	906	31.2
1958	Oscar Robertson	Cincinnati	6'5	So.	28	352	280	—	984	35.1
1959	Oscar Robertson	Cincinnati	6'5	Jr.	30	331	316	—	978	32.6
1960	Oscar Robertson	Cincinnati	6'5	Sr.	30	369	273	—	1,011	33.7
1961	Frank Burgess	Gonzaga	6'1	Sr.	26	304	234	—	842	32.4
1962	Billy McGill	Utah	6'9	Sr.	26	394	221	—	1,009	38.8
1963	Nick Werkman	Seton Hal	6'3	Jr.	22	221	208	—	650	29.5
1964	Howard Komives	Bolwing Green	6'1	Sr.	23	292	260	—	844	36.7
1965	Rick Barry	Miami (Fla)	6'7	Sr.	26	340	293	—	973	37.4
1966	Dave Schellhase	Purdue	64	Sr.	24	284	213	—	781	32.5
1967	Jim Walker	Providence	6'3	Sr.	28	323	205	—	851	30.4
1968	Pete Maravich	ISU	6'5	So.	26	432	274	—	1,138	43.8
1969	Pete Maravich	ISU	6'5	Jr.	26	433	282	—	1,148	44.2
1970	Pete Maravich	ISU	6'5	Sr.	31	522	337	—	1,381	44.5
1971	Johnny Neumann	Mississippi	6'6	So.	23	366	191	—	923	40.1
1972	Dwight Lamar	La-Lafayette	6'1	Jr.	29	429	196	—	1,054	36.3
1973	William Averitt	Fepperdine	6'1	Sr.	25	352	144	—	848	33.9
1974	Larry Fogle	Canisius	6'5	So.	25	326	183	—	835	33.4
1975	Bob McCurdy	Richmond	6'7	Sr.	26	321	213	—	855	32.9
1976	Marshal Rodgers	Tex.-Pan American	6'2	Sr.	25	361	197	—	919	36.8
1977	Freeman Williams	Portland St	6'4	Jr.	26	417	176	—	1,010	38.8
1978	Freeman Williams	Portland St	6'4	Sr.	27	410	149	—	969	35.9
1979	Lawrence Butler	Idaho St	6'3	Sr.	27	310	192	—	812	30.1
1980	Tony Murphy	Southern U	6'3	Sr.	29	377	178	—	932	32.1
1981	Zam Fredrick	South Carolina	6'2	Sr.	27	300	181	—	781	28.9
1982	Harry Kelly	Texas Southern	6'7	Jr.	29	336	190	—	862	29.7
1983	Harry Kelly	Texas Southern	6'7	Sr.	29	333	169	—	835	28.8
1984	Joe Jakubick	Akron	6'5	Sr.	27	304	206	—	814	30.1
1985	Xavier McDaniel	Wichita St	6'8	Sr.	31	351	142	—	844	27.2
1986	Terrance Bailey	Wagner	6'2	Jr.	29	321	212	—	854	29.4
1987	Kevin Houston	Army	5'11	Sr.	29	311	268	63	953	32.9
1988	Hersey Hawkins	Bradley	6'3	Sr.	31	377	284	87	1,125	36.3
1989	Hank Gathers	Loyola Marymount	6'7	Jr.	31	419	177	0	1,015	32.7
1990	Bo Kimble	Loyola Maiymount	6'5	Sr.	32	404	231	92	1,131	35.3
1991	Kevin Bradshaw	US Int'l	6'6	Sr.	28	358	278	60	1,054	37.6
1992	Brett Roberts	Morehead St	6'8	Sr.	29	278	193	66	815	28.1
1993	Greg Guy	Tex-Pan American	6'1	Jr.	19	189	111	67	556	29.3
1994	Glenn Robinson	Purdue	6'8	Jr.	34	368	215	79	1,030	30.3
1995	Kurt Thomas	TCU	6'9	Sr.	27	288	202	3	781	28.9
1996	Kevin Granger	Texas Southern	6'3	Sr.	24	194	230	30	648	27.0
1997	Charles Jones	Long Island	6'3	Jr.	30	338	118	109	903	30.1
1998	Charles Janes	Long Island	6'3	Sr.	30	326	101	116	869	29.0
1999	Alvin Young	Niagara	6'3	Sr.	29	253	157	65	728	25.1
2000	Courtney Alexander	Fresno St	6'6	Sr.	27	252	107	58	669	24.8
2001	Ronnie McCollum	Centenary (La)	6'4	Sr.	27	244	214	85	787	29.1
2002	Jason Conley	Virginia Military	6'5	Fr.	28	285	171	79	820	29.3
2003-	Ruben Douglas	New Mexico (10-18)	6'4	Sr.	28	218	253	94	783	28.0

SCORING

POINTS

Game
100—Frank Selvy, Furman vs. Newberry, Feb. 13, 1954 (41 FGs, 18 FTs)
Season
1,381—Pete Maravich, LSU, 1970 (522 FGs, 337 FTs, 1 games)
Career
3,667—Pete Maravich, LSU, 1968-70 (1,387 FGs, 893 FTs, 83 games)

POINTS VS. DIVISION I OPPONENT

Game
72—Kevin Bradshaw, U.S. Int'l vs. Loyola Marymount, Jan. 5, 1991

AVERAGE PER GAME

Season
44.5—Pete Maravich, LSU, 1970 (1,381 in 31)
Career
44.2—Pete Maravich, LSU, 1968-70 (3,667 in 83)

COMBINED POINTS, TWO TEAMMATES

Game
125—Frank Selvy (100) and Darrell Floyd (25), Furman vs. Newberry, Feb. 13, 1954

COMBINED POINTS, TWO TEAMMATES VS. DIVISION I OPPONENT

Game
92—Kevin Bradshaw (72) and Isaac Brown (20), U.S. Int'l vs. Loyola Marymount, Jan. 5, 1991

COMBINED POINTS, TWO OPPOSING PLAYERS ON DIVISION I TEAMS

Game
115—Pete Maravich (64), LSU and Dan Issel (51), Kentucky, Feb. 21, 1970

GAMES SCORING AT LEAST 50 POINTS

Season
10—Pete Maravich, LSU, 1970
Season—Consecutive Games
3—Pete Maravich, LSU, Feb. 10 to Feb. 15, 1969
Career
28—Pete Maravich, LSU, 1968-70

GAMES SCORING AT LEAST 40 POINTS

Career
56—Pete Maravich, LSU, 1968-70

GAMES SCORING IN DOUBLE FIGURES

Career
132—Danny Manning, Kansas, 1985-88

CONSECUTIVE GAMES SCORING IN DOUBLE FIGURES

Career
115—Lionel Simmons, La Salle, 1987-90

FIELD GOALS

Game
41—Frank Selvy, Furman vs. Newberry, Feb. 13, 1954 (66 attempts)
Season
522—Pete Maravich, LSU, 1970 (1,168 attempts)
Career
1, 3 87—Pete Maravich, LSU, 1968-70 (3,166 attempts)

CONSECUTIVE FIELD GOALS

Game
16—Doug Grayson, Kent St. vs. North Carolina, Dec. 6, 1967 (18 of 19)
Season
25—Ray Voelkel, American, 1978 (during nine games, Nov. 24-Dec. 16)

FIELD-GOAL ATTEMPTS

Game
71—Jay Handlan, Wash. & Lee vs. Furman, Feb. 17, 1951 (30 made)
Season
1,168—Pete Maravich, LSU, 1970 (522 made)
Career
3,166—Pete Maravich, LSU, 1968-70 (1,387 made)

FIELD-GOAL PERCENTAGE

Game
(Min. 15 made) 100%—Clifford Rozier, Louisville vs. Eastern Ky., Dec. 11, 1993 (15 of 15)
(Min. 20 made) 9 5 . 5%—Bill Walton, UCLA vs. Memphis, March 26, 1973 (21 of 22)
*Season
74 .6%—Steve Johnson, Oregon St., 1981 (235 of 315)
*Based on qualifiers for national championship.
Career
(Min. 400 made and 4 made per game) 67.8 %—Steve Johnson, Oregon St., 1976-81 (828 of 1,222)

THREE-POINT FIELD GOALS

THREE-POINT FIELD GOALS

Game
15—Keith Veney, Marshall vs. Morehead St., Dec. 14, 1996 (25 attempts)
Season
158—Darrin Fitzgerald, Butler, 1987 (362 attempts)
Career
413—Curtis Staples, Virginia, 1995-98 (1,079 attempts)

THREE-POINT FIELD GOALS MADE PER GAME

Season
5.6—Darrin Fitzgerald, Butler, 1987 (158 in 28)
Career
(Min. 200 made) 4.6—Timothy Pollard, Mississippi Val., 1988-89 (256 in 56)

CONSECUTIVE THREE-POINT FIELD GOALS

Game
11—Gary Bossert, Niagara vs. Siena, Jan. 7, 1987
Season
15—Todd Leslie, Northwestern, 1990 (during four games, Dec. 15 - 2 8)

CONSECUTIVE GAMES MAKING A THREE-POINT FIELD GOAL

Season
38—Steve Kerr, Arizona, Nov. 27, 1987, to April 2, 1988
Career
88—Cory Bradford, Illinois, Nov. 10, 1998 to Feb. 10, 2001

THREE-POINT FIELD-GOAL ATTEMPTS

Game
27—Bruce Seals, Manhattan vs. Canisius, Jan. 31, 2000 (9 made)
Season
362—Darrin Fitzgerald, Butler, 1987 (158 made)
Career
1,079—Curtis Staples, Virgina, 1995-98 (413 made)

THREE-POINT FIELD-GOAL ATTEMPTS PER GAME

Season
12.9—Darrin Fitzgerald, Butler, 1987 (362 in 28)
Career
9.1—Keith Veney, Lamar & Marshall, 1993-94, 1996-97 (1,014 in 111)

THREE-POINT FIELD-GOAL PERCENTAGE

Game
(Min. 9 made) 100%—Mark Poag, Old Dominion vs. VMI, Nov. 25, 1997 (9 of 9); Markus Wilson, Evansville vs. Tenn.-Martin, Nov. 18, 1998 (9 of 9)
(Min. 12 made) 85.7%—Gary Bossert, Niagara vs. Siena, Jan. 7, 1987 (12 of 14)

Season
(Min. 50 made) 63.4%—Glenn Tropf, Holy Cross, 1988 (52 of 82)
(Min. 100 made) 57.3%—Steve Kerr, Arizona, 1988 (114 of 199)
Career
(Min. 200 made and 1.5 made per game) 49.7%—Tony Bennett, Wis.-Green Bay, 1989-92 (290 of 584)
(Min. 300 made) 45.5%—Shawn Respert, Michigan St., 1992-95 (331 of 728)

FREE THROWS

Game
30—Pete Maravich, LSU vs. Oregon St., Dec. 22, 1969 (31 attempts)
Season
355—Frank Selvy, Furman, 1954 (444 attempts)
Career
(3 yrs.) 8 93—Pete Maravich, LSU, 1968-70 (1,152 attempts)
(4 yrs.) 905—Dickie Hemric, Wake Forest, 1952-55 (1,359 attempts)

CONSECUTIVE FREE THROWS

Game
24—Arlen Clark, Oklahoma St. vs. Colorado, March 7, 1959 (24 of 24)
Season
73—Gary Buchanan, Villanova, 2000-01 (during 21 games, Nov. 17-Feb. 12)
Career
73—Gary Buchanan, Villanova, 2000-01 (during 21 games, Nov. 17-Feb. 12)

FREE-THROW ATTEMPTS

Game
36—Ed Tooley, Brown vs. Amherst, Dec. 4, 1954 (23 made)
Season
444—Frank Selvy, Furman, 1954 (355 made)
Career
*(3 yrs.)*1,15 2—Pete Maravich, LSU, 1968-70 (893 made)
(4 yrs.) 1,359—Dickie Hemric, Wake Forest, 1952-55 (905 made)

FREE-THROW PERCENTAGE

Game
(Min. 24 made) 100% —Arlen Clark, Oklahoma St. vs. Colorado, March 7, 1959 (24 of 24)
*Season
95.9%—Craig Collins, Penn St., 1985 (94 of 98)
*Based on qualifiers for national championship.
Career
(Min. 300 made and 2 made per game) 90.9 % — Greg Starrick, Kentucky & Southern Ill., 1969, 1970-72 (341 of 375)
(Min. 600 made) 88.5%—Ron Perry, Holy Cross, 1976-80 (680 of 768)
(Min. 2.5 made per game) 92.3%—Dave Hildahl, Portland St., 1979-81 (131 of 142)

REBOUNDS

Game
51—Bill Chambers, William & Mary vs. Virginia, Feb. 14, 1953
(Since 1973) 35—Larry Abney, Fresno St. vs. Southern Methodist, Feb. 17, 2000
Season
734—Walt Dukes, Seton Hall, 1953 (33 games)
(Since 1973) 597—Marvin Barnes, Providence, 1974 (32 games)
Career
(3 yrs.) 1,751—Paul Silas, Creighton, 1962-64 (81 games)
(4 yrs.) 2,201 —Tom Gola, La Salle,1952-55 (118 games)
(Since 1973) 1,570—Tim Duncan, Wake Forest, 1994-97 (128 games)

AVERAGE PER GAME
Season
25.6—Charlie Slack, Marshall, 1955 (538 in 21)
(Since 1973) 20.4—Kermit Washington, American, 1973 (511 in 25)
Career
(Min. 800) 22.7—Artis Gilmore, Jacksonville, 1970-71 (1,224 in 54)
(4 yrs.) 21.8—Charlie Slack, Marshall, 1953-56 (1,916 in 88)
(Since 1973) 15.2—Glenn Mosley, Seton Hall, 1974-77 (1,263 in 83)

ASSISTS

Game
22—Tony Fairley, Charleston So. vs. Armstrong Atlan-tic, Feb. 9, 1987; Avery Johnson, Southern U. vs. Texas Southern, Jan. 25, 1988; Sherman Douglas, Syracuse vs. Providence, Jan. 28, 1989
Season
406—Mark Wade, UNLV, 1987 (38 games)
Career
1,076—Bobby Hurley, Duke, 1990-93 (140 games)

AVERAGE PER GAME
Season
13.3—Avery Johnson, Southern U., 1988 (399 in 30)
Career
(Min. 600) 12.0—Avery Johnson, Southern U., 1987-88 (732 in 61)
(4 yrs.) 8 .4—Chris Corchiani, North Carolina St., 1988-91 (1,038 in 1 2 4)

BLOCKED SHOTS

Game
14—David Robinson, Navy vs. UNC Wilmington, Jan. 4, 1986; Shawn Bradley, Brigham Young vs. Eastern Ky., Dec. 7, 1990; Roy Rogers, Alabama vs. Georgia, Feb. 10, 1996; Loren Woods, Arizona vs. Oregon, Feb. 3, 2000
Season
207—David Robinson, Navy, 1986 (35 games)
Career
535—Wojciech Myrda, La.-Monroe, 1999-2002 (115 games)

AVERAGE PER GAME
Season
6.4—Adonal Foyle, Colgate, 1997 (180 in 28)
Career
(Min. 225) 5.9—Keith Closs, Central Conn. St., 1995-96 (317 in 54)
(4 yrs.) 4.7—Wojciech Myrda, La.-Monroe, 1999-2002 (535 in 115)

STEALS

Game
13—Mookie Blaylock, Oklahoma vs. Centenary (La.), Dec. 12, 1987; and vs. Loyola Marymount, Dec. 17, 1988
Season
160—Desmond Cambridge, Alabama A&M, 2002 (29 games)
Career
385—John Linehan, Providence, 1998-2002 (122 games)

AVERAGE PER GAME
Season
5.5—Desmond Cambridge, Alabama A&M, 2002 (160 in 29)
Career
(Min. 225) 3.9—Desmond Cambridge, Alabama A&M, 1999-2002 (330 in 84)
(4 yrs.) 3.2—Eric Murdock, Providence, 1988-91 (376 in 117)

FOULS

SHORTEST PLAYING TIME BEFORE BEING DISQUALIFIED
Game
1:38—Mike Pflugner, Butler vs. Ill.-Chicago, March 2, 1996

GAMES

GAMES PLAYED (Since 1947-48)
Season
40—Mark Alarie, Tommy Amaker, Johnny Dawkins, Danny Ferry and Billy King, Duke,1986; Larry Johnson, UNLV, 1990; Anthony Epps, Jamaal Magloire, Ron Mercer and Wayne Turner, Kentucky, 1997
Career
151—Wayne Turner, Kentucky, 1996-99

GENERAL

ACHIEVED 2,000 POINTS AND 2,000 REBOUNDS
Career
Tom Gola, LaSalle, 1952-55 (2,462 points and 2,201 rebounds)
Joe Holup, George Washington, 1953-56 (2,226 points and 2,030 rebounds)

AVERAGED 20 POINTS AND 20 REBOUNDS
Career
Bill Russell, San Francisco, 1954-56 (20.7 points and 20.3 rebounds)
Paul Silas, Creighton, 1962-64 (20.5 points and 21.6 rebounds)
Julius Erving, Massachusetts, 1970-71 (26.3 points and 20.2 rebounds)
Artis Gilmore, Jacksonville, 1970-71 (24.3 points and 22.7 rebounds)
Kermit Washington, American, 1971-73 (20.1 points and 20.2 rebounds)

NCAA DIVISION I TEAM RECORDS

Note: Where records involve both teams, each team must be an NCAA Division I member institution.

SINGLE-GAME RECORDS

POINTS
186—Loyola Marymount vs. U.S. Int'l (140), Jan. 5, 1991

POINTS BY LOSING TEAM
150—U.S. Int'l vs. Loyola Marymount (181), Jan. 31, 1989

POINTS, BOTH TEAMS
331—Loyola Marymount (181) vs. U.S. Int'l (150), Jan. 31, 1989

MARGIN OF VICTORY
117—Long Island (179) vs. Medgar Evers (62), Nov. 26, 1997

MARGIN OF VICTORY VS. DIVISION I OPPONENT
91—Tulsa (141) vs. Prairie View (50), Dec. 7, 1995

POINTS IN A HALF
98—Long Island vs. Medgar Evers, Nov. 26,1997 (2nd)

POINTS IN A HALF VS. DIVISION I OPPONENT
97—Oklahoma vs. U.S. Int'l, Nov. 29, 1989 (1st)

POINTS IN A HALF, BOTH TEAMS
172—Loyola Marymount (86) vs. Gonzaga (86), Feb. 18, 1989 (2nd)

LEAD BEFORE OPPONENT SCORES AT START OF A GAME
34-0—Seton Hall vs. Kean, Nov. 29, 1998

LEAD BEFORE DIVISION I OPPONENT SCORES AT START OF A GAME
3 2-0—Connecticut vs. New Hampshire, Dec.12, 1990

DEFICIT OVERCOME TO WIN GAME
32—Duke (74) vs. Tulane (72), Dec. 30, 1950 (trailed 22-54 with 2:00 left in the first half)

SECOND-HALF DEFICIT OVERCOME TO WIN GAME
31—Duke (74) vs. Tulane (72), Dec. 30, 1950 (trailed 27-58 with 19:00 left in the second half); Kentucky (99) vs. LSU (95), Feb. 15, 1994 (trailed 37-68 with 15:34 left in the second half)

HALFTIME DEFICIT OVERCOME TO WIN GAME
29—Duke (74) vs. Tulane (72), Dec. 30, 1950 (trailed 27-56 at halftime)

DEFICIT BEFORE SCORING OVERCOME TO WIN GAME
28—New Mexico St. (117) vs. Bradley (109), Jan. 27, 1977 (trailed 0-28 with 13:49 left in first half)

FEWEST POINTS ALLOWED (Since 1938)
6—Tennessee (11) vs. Temple, Dec. 15, 1973; Kentucky (75) vs. Arkansas St., Jan. 8, 1945

FEWEST POINTS ALLOWED (Since 1986)
2 1—Coastal Caro. (61) vs. Georgia So., Jan. 2, 1997

FEWEST POINTS, BOTH TEAMS (Since 1938)
17—Tennessee (11) vs. Temple (6), Dec. 15, 1973

FIELD GOALS
76—Long Island vs. Medgar Evers, Nov. 26, 1997 (124 attempts)

FIELD GOALS VS. DIVISION I OPPONENT
74—Houston vs. Valparaiso, Feb. 24, 1968 (112 attempts)

FIELD GOALS, BOTH TEAMS
130—Loyola Marymount (67) vs. U.S. Int'l (63), Jan. 31, 1989

FIELD GOALS IN A HALF
42—Oklahoma vs. U.S. Int'l, Nov. 29, 1989 (90 attempts) (1st)

FIELD-GOAL ATTEMPTS
147—Oklahoma vs. U.S. Int'l, Nov. 29, 1989 (70 made)

FIELD-GOAL ATTEMPTS, BOTH TEAMS
245—Loyola Marymount (124) vs. U.S. Int'l (121), Jan. 7, 1989

FIELD-GOAL ATTEMPTS IN A HALF
90—Oklahoma vs. U.S. Int'l, Nov. 29, 1989 (42 made) (1st)

FEWEST FIELD GOALS (Since 1938)
2—Duke vs. North Carolina St., March 8, 1968 (11 attempts); Arkansas St. vs. Kentucky, Jan. 8, 1945

FEWEST FIELD-GOAL ATTEMPTS (Since 1938)
9—Pittsburgh vs. Penn St., March 1, 1952 (3 made)

FIELD-GOAL PERCENTAGE
(Min. 15 made) 83.3%—Maryland vs. South Carolina, Jan. 9, 1971 (15 of 18)
(Min. 30 made) 81.4%—New Mexico vs. Oregon St., Nov. 30, 1985 (35 of 43)

FIELD-GOAL PERCENTAGE, HALF
94.1%—North Carolina vs. Virginia, Jan. 7, 1978 (16 of 17) (2nd)

THREE-POINT FIELD GOALS
28—Troy St. vs. George Mason, Dec. 10, 1994 (74 attempts)

THREE-POINT FIELD GOALS, BOTH TEAMS
44—Troy St. (28) vs. George Mason (16), Dec. 10, 1994

CONSECUTIVE THREE-POINT FIELD GOALS MADE WITHOUT A MISS
11—Niagara vs. Siena, Jan. 7, 1987; Eastern Ky. vs. UNC Asheville, Jan. 14, 1987

THREE-POINT FIELD-GOAL ATTEMPTS WITHOUT MAKING ONE
22—Canisius vs. St. Bonaventure, Jan. 21, 1995

NUMBER OF DIFFERENT PLAYERS TO SCORE A THREE-POINT FIELD GOAL, ONE TEAM
9—Dartmouth vs. Boston College, Nov. 30, 1993

THREE-POINT FIELD-GOAL ATTEMPTS
74—Troy St. vs. George Mason, Dec. 10, 1994 (28 made)

THREE-POINT FIELD-GOAL ATTEMPTS, BOTH TEAMS
108—Troy St. (74) vs. George Mason (34), Dec. 10, 1994

THREE-POINT FIELD-GOAL PERCENTAGE
(Min. 10 made) 91.7%—Drexel vs. Delaware, Dec. 3, 2000 (11 of 12)
(Min. 15 made) 83.3%—Eastern Ky. vs. UNC Asheville, Jan. 14, 1987 (15 of 18)

THREE-POINT FIELD-GOAL PERCENTAGE, BOTH TEAMS
(Min. 10 made) 83.3%—Lafayette (7 of 8) vs. Marist (3 of 4), Dec. 6, 1986 (10 of 12)
(Min. 15 made) 76.2%—Florida (10 of 14) vs. California (6 of 7), Dec. 27, 1986 (16 of 21)
(Min. 20 made) 72.4%—Princeton (12 of 15) vs. Brown (9 of 14), Feb. 20, 1988 (21 of 29)

FREE THROWS MADE
56—TCU vs. Eastern Mich., Dec. 21, 1999 (70 attempts)

FREE THROWS MADE, BOTH TEAMS
88—Morehead St. (53) vs. Cincinnati (35), Feb. 11, 1956 (111 attempts)

FREE-THROW ATTEMPTS
79—Northern Ariz. vs. Arizona, Jan. 26, 1953 (46 made)

FREE-THROW ATTEMPTS, BOTH TEAMS
130—Northern Ariz. (79) vs. Arizona (51), Jan. 26, 1953 (78 made)

FEWEST FREE THROWS MADE
0—Many teams

FEWEST FREE-THROW ATTEMPTS
0—Many teams

FREE-THROW PERCENTAGE
(Min. 32 made) 100.0%—UC Irvine vs. Pacific (Cal.), Feb. 21, 1981 (34 of 34); Samford vs. UCF, Dec. 20, 1990 (34 of 34)
(Min. 35 made) 97.2%—Vanderbilt vs. Mississippi St., Feb. 26, 1986 (35 of 36); Butler vs. Dayton, Feb. 21, 1991 (35 of 36); Marquette vs. Memphis, Jan. 23, 1993 (35 of 36)
(Min. 40 made) 95.5%—UNLV vs. San Diego St., Dec. 11, 1976 (42 of 44)

FREE-THROW PERCENTAGE, BOTH TEAMS
100%—Purdue (25 of 25) vs. Wisconsin (22 of 22), Feb. 7, 1976 (47 of 47)

REBOUNDS
108—Kentucky vs. Mississippi, Feb. 8, 1964

REBOUNDS, BOTH TEAMS
152—Indiana (95) vs. Michigan (57), March 11, 1961

REBOUND MARGIN
84—Arizona (102) vs. Northern Ariz. (18), Jan. 6, 1951

ASSISTS (INCLUDING OVERTIMES)
44—Colorado vs. George Mason, Dec. 2, 1995 (ot)

ASSISTS (REGULATION)
41—North Carolina vs. Manhattan, Dec. 27, 1985; Weber St. vs. Northern Ariz., March 2, 1991

ASSISTS, BOTH TEAMS (INCLUDING OVERTIMES)
67—Colorado (44) vs. George Mason (23), Dec. 2, 1995 (ot)

ASSISTS, BOTH TEAMS (REGULATION)
65—Dayton (34) vs. UCF (31), Dec. 3, 1988

BLOCKED SHOTS
21—Georgetown vs. Southern (N.O.), Dec. 1, 1993

BLOCKED SHOTS, BOTH TEAMS
29—Rider (17) vs. Fairleigh Dickinson (12), Jan. 9, 1989

STEALS
39—Long Island vs. Medgar Evers, Nov. 26, 1997

STEALS VS. DIVISION I OPPONENT
34—Oklahoma vs. Centenary (La.), Dec. 12, 1987

STEALS, BOTH TEAMS
44—Oklahoma (34) vs. Centenary (La.) (10), Dec. 12, 1987

FOULS
50—Arizona vs. Northern Ariz., Jan. 26, 1953

FOULS, BOTH TEAMS
84—Arizona (50) vs. Northern Ariz. (34), Jan. 26, 1953

PLAYERS DISQUALIFIED
8—St. Joseph's vs. Xavier, Jan. 10, 1976

PLAYERS DISQUALIFIED, BOTH TEAMS
12—UNLV (6) vs. Hawaii (6), Jan. 19, 1979 (ot); Arizona (7) vs. West Tex. A&M (5), Feb. 14, 1952

OVERTIME PERIODS
7—Cincinnati (75) vs. Bradley (73), Dec. 21, 1981

POINTS IN ONE OVERTIME PERIOD
26—Vermont vs. Hartford, Jan. 24, 1998

POINTS IN ONE OVERTIME PERIOD, BOTH TEAMS
45—Va. Commonwealth (23) vs. Texas A&M (22), Dec. 2, 2000

POINTS IN OVERTIME PERIODS
49—Middle Tenn. vs. Tennessee Tech, Feb. 12, 2000 (4 ot)

POINTS IN OVERTIME PERIODS, BOTH TEAMS
94—Middle Tenn. (49) vs. Tennessee Tech (45), Feb. 12, 2000 (4 ot)

WINNING MARGIN IN OVERTIME GAME
21—Nicholls St. (86) vs. Sam Houston St. (65), Feb. 4, 1999 (23-2 in the ot)

SEASON RECORDS

POINTS
4,012—Oklahoma, 1988 (39 games)

POINTS PER GAME
122.4—Loyola Marymount, 1990 (3,918 in 32)

SCORING MARGIN AVERAGE
30.3—UCLA, 1972 (94.6 offense, 64.3 defense)

GAMES AT LEAST 100 POINTS
28—Loyola Marymount, 1990

CONSECUTIVE GAMES AT LEAST 100 POINTS
12—UNLV, 1977; Loyola Marymount, 1990

FIELD GOALS
1,533—Oklahoma, 1988 (3,094 attempts)

FIELD GOALS PER GAME
46.3—UNLV, 1976 (1,436 in 31)

FIELD-GOAL ATTEMPTS
3,094—Oklahoma, 1988 (1,533 made)

FIELD-GOAL ATTEMPTS PER GAME
98.5—Oral Roberts, 1973 (2,659 in 27)

FIELD-GOAL PERCENTAGE
57.2%—Missouri, 1980 (936 of 1,635)

THREE-POINT FIELD GOALS
407—Duke, 2001 (1,057 attempts)

THREE-POINT FIELD GOALS PER GAME
11.1—Troy St., 1996 (300 in 27)

THREE-POINT FIELD-GOAL ATTEMPTS
1,057—Duke, 2001 (407 made)

THREE-POINT FIELD-GOAL ATTEMPTS PER GAME
34.0—Mississippi Val., 1997 (985 in 29)

THREE-POINT FIELD-GOAL PERCENTAGE
(Min. 100 made) 50.8%—Indiana, 1987 (130 of 256)
(Min. 150 made) 50.0%—Mississippi Val., 1987 (161 of 322)
(Min. 200 made) 49.2%—Princeton, 1988 (211 of 429)

CONSECUTIVE GAMES SCORING A THREE-POINT FIELD GOAL (Multiple Seasons)
505—UNLV, Nov. 26, 1986, to present; Vanderbilt, Nov. 28, 1986, to present

FREE THROWS
865—Bradley, 1954 (1,263 attempts)

FREE THROWS PER GAME
28.9—Morehead St., 1956 (838 in 29)

CONSECUTIVE FREE THROWS
49—Indiana St., 1991 (during two games, Feb. 13-18)

FREE-THROW ATTEMPTS
1,263—Bradley, 1954 (865 made)

FREE-THROW ATTEMPTS PER GAME
41.0—Bradley, 1953 (1,107 in 27)

FREE-THROW PERCENTAGE
82.2%—Harvard, 1984 (535 of 651)

REBOUNDS
2,109—Kentucky, 1951 (34 games)

REBOUNDS PER GAME
70.0—Connecticut, 1955 (1,751 in 25)

REBOUND MARGIN AVERAGE
25.0—Morehead St., 1957 (64.3 offense, 39.3 defense)
(Since 1973) 18.5—Manhattan, 1973 (56.5, 38.0)

ASSISTS
926—UNLV, 1990 (40 games)

ASSISTS PER GAME
24.7—UNLV, 1991 (863 in 35)

BLOCKED SHOTS
309—Georgetown, 1989 (34 games)

BLOCKED SHOTS PER GAME
9.1—Georgetown, 1989 (309 in 34)

STEALS
486—Oklahoma, 1988 (39 games)

STEALS PER GAME
14.9—Long Island, 1998 (478 in 32)

FOULS
966—Providence, 1987 (34 games)

FOULS PER GAME
29.3—Indiana, 1952 (644 in 22)

FEWEST FOULS
253—Air Force, 1962 (23 games)

FEWEST FOULS PER GAME
11.0—Air Force, 1962 (253 in 23)

LOWEST SCORING AVERAGE PER GAME ALLOWED (Since 1982)
(Since 1938) 25.7—Oklahoma St., 1939 (693 in 27)
(Since 1948) 32.5—Oklahoma St., 1948 (1,006 in 31)
(Since 1965) 47.1—Fresno St., 1982 (1,412 in 30)

LOWEST FIELD-GOAL PERCENTAGE ALLOWED (Since 1978)
35.2—Stanford, 2000 (667 of 1,893)

OVERTIME GAMES
8—Western Ky., 1978 (won 5, lost 3); Portland, 1984 (won 4, lost 4); Valparaiso, 1993 (won 4, lost 4)

CONSECUTIVE OVERTIME GAMES
4—Jacksonville, 1982 (won 3, lost 1); Illinois St., 1985 (won 3, lost 1); Dayton, 1988 (won 1, lost 3)

OVERTIME WINS
6—Chattanooga, 1989 (6-0); Wake Forest, 1984 (6-1)

OVERTIME HOME WINS
5—Cincinnati, 1967 (5-0)

OVERTIME ROAD WINS
4—Delaware, 1973 (4-0); Arizona St., 1981 (4-0); Cal St. Fullerton, 1989 (4-0); New Mexico St., 1994 (4-0)

OVERTIME PERIODS
14—Bradley, 1982 (3-3)

CONSECUTIVE OVERTIME WINS—ALL-TIME
11—Louisville, Feb. 10, 1968-March 29, 1975; Massachusetts, March 21, 1991-Feb. 28, 1996; Virginia, Dec. 5, 1991-Feb. 8, 1996

GENERAL RECORDS

GAMES IN A SEASON
45—Oregon, 1945 (30-15)

GAMES IN A SEASON (Since 1948)
40—Duke, 1986 (37-3); UNLV, 1990 (35-5); Kentucky, 1997 (35-5)

VICTORIES IN A SEASON
37—Duke, 1986 (37-3) & 1999 (37-2); UNLV, 1987 (37-2)

VICTORIES IN FIRST SEASON IN DIVISION I
29—Seattle, 1953 (29-4)

WON-LOST PERCENTAGE IN FIRST SEASON IN DIVISION I
.931—Md.-East. Shore, 1974 (27-2)

VICTORIES IN A PERFECT SEASON
32—North Carolina, 1957; Indiana, 1976

CONSECUTIVE VICTORIES IN A SEASON
34—UNLV, 1991 (34-1)

CONSECUTIVE VICTORIES
88—UCLA, from Jan. 30, 1971, through Jan. 17, 1974 (ended Jan. 19, 1974, at Notre Dame, 71-70; last UCLA defeat before streak also came at Notre Dame, 89-82)

CONSECUTIVE HOME-COURT VICTORIES
129—Kentucky, from Jan. 4, 1943, to Jan. 8, 1955 (ended by Georgia Tech, 59-58)

CONSECUTIVE REGULAR-SEASON VICTO-RIES (National Postseason Tournaments Not Included)
76—U CLA, 1971-74

DEFEATS IN A SEASON
28—Prairie View, 1992 (0-28)

CONSECUTIVE DEFEATS IN A SEASON
28—Prairie View, 1992 (0-28)

CONSECUTIVE DEFEATS
37—Citadel, from Jan. 16, 1954, to Dec. 12, 1955

NCAA DIVISION I TEAM RECORDS

CONSECUTIVE HOME-COURT DEFEATS
32—New Hampshire, from Feb. 9, 1988, to Feb. 2, 1991 (ended vs. Holy Cross, 72-56)

CONSECUTIVE ROAD DEFEATS (including only games at the opponents' home sites)
64—Tex.-Pan American, from Nov. 25, 1995, to Jan. 8, 2000 (ended vs. Oral Roberts, 79-62)

CONSECUTIVE NON-HOME DEFEATS (including games at the opponents' home sites and at neutral sites)
56—Sacramento St., from Nov. 22, 1991, to Jan. 5, 1995 [ended at Loyola (Ill.), 68-56]

CONSECUTIVE 30-WIN SEASONS
3—Kentucky, 1947-49 and 1996-98

CONSECUTIVE 25-WIN SEASONS
10—U CLA, 19 6 7 -76; UNLV, 19 8 3 - 9 2

CONSECUTIVE 20-WIN SEASONS
31—North Carolina, 1971-2001

CONSECUTIVE WINNING SEASONS
54—UCLA, 1949-2002

CONSECUTIVE NON-LOSING SEASONS (Includes .500 Re c o r d)
60—Kentucky, 1928-52, 54-88# (2 .500 seasons)
#Kentucky did not play basketball during the 1953 season.

CONSECUTIVE NON-LOSING SEASONS (Includes .500 Record) - CURRENT
54—UCLA, 1949-2002

UNBEATEN TEAMS (Since 1938; Number Of Victories In Parentheses)
1939 Long Island (24)†
1940 Seton Hall (19)††
1944 Army (15)††
1954 Kentucky (25)††
1956 San Francisco (29)*
1957 North Carolina (32)*
1964 UCLA (30)*
1967 UCLA (30)*
1972 UCLA (30)*
1973 UCLA (30)*
1973 North Carolina St. (27)††
1976 Indiana (32)*
*NCAA champion; †NIT champion; † †not in either tournament

UNBEATEN IN REGULAR SEASON BUT LOST IN NCAA (*) OR NIT (†)
1939 Loyola (Ill.) (20; 21-1)†
1941 Seton Hall (19; 20-2)†
1951 Columbia (21; 21-1)*
1961 Ohio St. (24; 27-1)*
1968 Houston (28; 31-2)*
1968 St. Bonaventure (22; 23-2)*
1971 Marquette (26; 28-1)*
1971 Pennsylvania (26; 28-1)*
1975 Indiana (29; 31-1)*
1976 Rutgers (28; 31-2)*
1979 Indiana St. (27; 33-1)*
1979 Alcorn St. (25; 28-1)†
1991 UNLV (30; 34-1)*

30-GAME WINNERS (Since 1938)
37—Duke, 1986 & 1999; UNLV, 1987.
36—Kentucky, 1948.
3 5 — Arizona, 1988; Duke, 2001; Georgetown,19 8 5 ; Kansas, 1986 & 1998; Kentucky, 1997 & 1998; Massachusetts, 1996; UNLV, 1990; Oklahoma, 1988.
34 — Arkansas, 1991; Connecticut, 1999; Duke,1992; Georgetown, 1984; Kansas,19 97; Kentucky,1947 & 1996; UNLV, 1991; North Carolina, 1993 &1998.
33—Indiana St., 1979; Louisville, 1980; Michigan St., 1999; UNLV, 1986.
32—Arkansas, 1978 & 1995; Bradley, 1950, 1951 & 1986; Connecticut, 1996 & 1998; Duke, 1991 & 1998; Houston, 1984; Indiana, 1976; Iowa St., 2000; Kentucky, 1949, 1951 & 1986; Louisville, 1983 & 1986; Marshall, 1947; Maryland, 2002; Michigan St., 2000; North Carolina, 1957, 1982 & 1987; Temple, 1987 & 1988; Tulsa, 2000.
31—Arkansas, 1994; Cincinnati, 2002; Connecticut, 1990; Duke, 2002; Houston, 1968 & 1983; Illinois, 1989; Indiana, 1975 & 1993; LSU, 1981; Memphis, 1985; Michigan, 1993; Minnesota, 1997; Oklahoma, 1985 & 2002; Oklahoma St., 1946; Rutgers, 1976; St. John's (N.Y.), 1985 & 1986; Seton Hall, 1953 & 1989; Stanford, 2001; Syracuse, 1987; UCLA, 1995; Wyoming, 1943.
30—A r i z o n a , 1998; Arkansas, 1990; California, 1946; Georgetown, 1982; Indiana, 19 87; Iowa, 1987; Kansas, 1990; Kentucky, 1978 & 1993; La Salle, 1990; Massachusetts, 1992; Michigan, 1989; Navy, 1986; North Carolina, 1946; North Carolina St., 1951 & 1974; Oklahoma, 1989; Oregon, 1945; Stanford 1998; Syracuse, 1989; Texas Tech, 1996; UCLA, 1964, 1967, 1972 & 1973; Utah, 1991 & 1998; Virginia, 1982; Western Ky., 1938.

RECORDS, SINGLE SEASON

Wins

Team	Season	Won	Lost	Pct.
UNLV	1987	37	2	.949
Duke	1999	37	2	.949
Duke	1986	37	3	.925
Kentucky	1948	36	3	.923
Massachusetts	1996	35	2	.946
Georgetown	1985	35	3	.921
Arizona	1988	35	3	.921
Kansas	1986	35	4	.897
Oklahoma	1988	35	4	.897
Kansas	1998	35	4	.897
Kentucky	1998	35	4	.897
Duke	2001	35	4	.897
UNLV	1990	35	5	.875
Kentucky	1997	35	5	.875
UNLV	1991	34	1	.971

Chapter 50

10 NCAA Records That Will Never Be Broken

By Michael Douchant

The 2003-04 season marked the 30th anniversary of the most amazing record in NCAA history. UCLA's 88-game winning streak ended at Notre Dame, 71-70, on January 19, 1974, when guard Dwight Clay's fallaway jump shot from the right baseline with 29 seconds remaining climaxed a 12-0 spurt in the last three minutes for the Irish.

Bruins All-American center Bill Walton, who had injured his back two weeks earlier, hadn't played in 12 days but still went 12 for 13 from the floor. UCLA coach John Wooden, believing his squad was more prepared than any opponent, wasn't fond of calling timeouts and five consecutive turnovers by his team enabled Notre Dame to get back into the game.

UCLA compiled a 149-2 record at Pauley Pavilion under Wooden, but its streak of Pacific-8 Conference victories ended at 50 when the Bruins bowed at Oregon State, 61-57. It was OSU's lone victory over UCLA in a 26-game stretch of their series from 1967 through 1979. The Bruins then succumbed at Oregon, 56-51, to give them back-to-back defeats for the first time since 1966. They seemed to be afflicted somewhat by the dreaded disease known as "senioritis" in coaching circles.

"When you have the same group for three years, they're a little more difficult to work with. They don't mean to be, but they are," Wooden said of the Walton Gang. "I can't find fault with my team, but I failed to motivate them. And I'm not talking about won-lost record. In many games we won, I didn't think we displayed intensity and didn't play up to our potential."

The last undefeated squad was Indiana in 1975-76. It's almost inconceivable that a school could go 2-1/2 consecutive seasons without a loss. What are other team and individual standards of excellence that will be impossible to duplicate, let alone exceed? UCLA dominates the most illustrious of the following sizing up of the 10 records most likely never to be broken:

1. UCLA's 88-game winning streak (under coach John Wooden from Jan. 30, 1971, to Jan. 19, 1974).

UCLA sandwiched 88 consecutive victories between January defeats at Notre Dame (89-82 in 1971 and 71-70 at 1974). The streak began inauspiciously when five of the first eight triumphs were by fewer than five points. Then, the Bruins went ballistic and finished the streak with an average margin of victory of 23.4 points, including an NCAA single-season record of 30.3 in 1971-72.

They won 49 home games by 29.6 points per game, 25 road games by 23.4 ppg and 14 neutral contests by 13.6 ppg. Here is a further breakdown of UCLA's winning margins during the streak: 0-10 points—17 games; 11-20 points—25 games; 21-30 points—20 games; 31-40 points—17 games; 41-50 points—four games, and more than 50 points—five games.

Twelve different UCLA players led the Bruins in scoring during the streak, including 45 times by All-American center Bill Walton.

UCLA	Opponent		High Scorer	
74	UC Santa Barbara	61	Curtis Rowe	18
64	at Southern California	60	Sidney Wicks	24
69	at Oregon	68	Sidney Wicks	20
67	at Oregon State	65	Curtis Rowe	22
94	Oregon State	64	Sidney Wicks	25
74	Oregon	67	Sidney Wicks	28
57	at Washington State	53	Sidney Wicks	16
71	at Washington	69	Henry Bibby	21
103	California	69	Curtis Rowe	23
107	Stanford	72	Steve Patterson	20
73	Southern California	62	Curtis Rowe	15
91	Brigham Young*	73	Henry Bibby	15
57	Long Beach State*	55	Sidney Wicks	18
68	Kansas*	60	Sidney Wicks	21
68	Villanova*	62	Steve Patterson	29
105	The Citadel	49	Henry Bibby	26
106	Iowa	72	Henry Bibby	32
110	Iowa State	81	Bill Walton	24
117	Texas A&M	53	Bill Walton	23
114	Notre Dame	56	Henry Bibby	28
119	Texas Christian	81	Bill Walton	31
115	Texas	65	Bill Walton	28
79	Ohio State	53	Bill Walton	14
78	at Oregon State	72	Henry Bibby	17
93	at Oregon	68	Bill Walton	30
118	Stanford	79	Bill Walton	32
82	California	43	Bill Walton	20
92	Santa Clara	57	Keith Wilkes	16
108	Denver	61	Larry Farmer	19
92	at Loyola of Chicago	64	Henry Bibby/Bill Walton	18
57	at Notre Dame	32	Henry Bibby	15
81	Southern California	56	Bill Walton	22
89	Washington State	58	Bill Walton	25
109	Washington	70	Bill Walton	27
100	at Washington	83	Bill Walton	31
85	at Washington State	55	Larry Hollyfield/Keith Wilkes	16
92	Oregon	70	Bill Walton	37
91	Oregon State	72	Bill Walton	26
85	at California	71	Bill Walton	24
102	at Stanford	73	Greg Lee	16
79	at Southern California	66	Bill Walton	20
90	Weber State*	58	Henry Bibby	16
73	Long Beach State*	57	Henry Bibby	23
96	Louisville*	77	Bill Walton	33
81	Florida State*	76	Bill Walton	24
94	Wisconsin	53	Bill Walton	26
73	Bradley	38	Bill Walton	16
81	Pacific	48	Keith Wilkes	18
98	UC Santa Barbara	67	Bill Walton	30
89	Pittsburgh	73	Keith Wilkes	20
82	Notre Dame	56	Keith Wilkes	18
85	Drake*	72	Bill Walton	29
71	Illinois*	64	Bill Walton	22
64	Oregon	38	Larry Farmer/Keith Wilkes	14
87	Oregon State	61	Keith Wilkes	19
82	at Stanford	67	Larry Farmer/Larry Hollyfield/Bill Walton	18
69	at California	50	Larry Farmer/Keith Wilkes	18
92	San Francisco	64	Bill Walton	22
101	Providence	77	Larry Farmer	21
87	at Loyola of Chicago	73	Bill Walton	32
82	at Notre Dame	63	Keith Wilkes	20
79	at Southern California	56	Bill Walton	20
88	at Washington State	50	Bill Walton	17
76	at Washington	67	Bill Walton	29
93	Washington	62	Bill Walton	26
96	Washington State	64	Bill Walton	29
72	at Oregon	61	Keith Wilkes	18
73	at Oregon State	67	Bill Walton	21
90	California	65	Keith Wilkes/Bill Walton	15
51	Stanford	45	Bill Walton	23
76	Southern California	56	Bill Walton	17
98	Arizona State	81	Bill Walton	28
54	San Francisco	39	Larry Farmer	13
70	Indiana*	59	Tommy Curtis	22
87	Memphis State*	66	Bill Walton	44
101	Arkansas	79	Bill Walton	23

65	Maryland	64	Bill Walton	18
77	Southern Methodist	60	Bill Walton	25
84	North Carolina State*	66	Keith Wilkes	27
110	Ohio University	63	Bill Walton	25
111	St. Bonaventure	59	Dave Meyers	16
86	Wyoming	58	Keith Wilkes/Bill Walton	18
90	Michigan	70	Bill Walton	20
100	at Washington	48	Bill Walton	18
55	at Washington State	45	Keith Wilkes	13
92	California	56	Keith Wilkes	24
66	Stanford	52	Keith Wilkes	21
68	Iowa*	44	Ralph Drollinger/Keith Wilkes	12

*Neutral court games.

2. Frank Selvy's 100-point game
(for Furman vs. Newberry on Feb. 13, 1954).

Selvy scored 100 points vs. Newberry (S.C.) on his way to becoming the first three-year player to reach 2,000 points, finishing with 2,538. Selvy (41.7 ppg) and Darrell Floyd (24.3) combined for 66 points per game during the season and are the highest-scoring duo in major-college history. Selvy scored 50 or more in seven games en route to becoming the first player to score 1,000 points in a single season (1,209) and average 30 or more for a career (32.5 ppg).

Making Selvy's 100-point outburst even more amazing was the fact his mother, watching her son play for the initial time, was among several hundred fans from his hometown of Corbin, Ky., who made the trip to Greenville, S.C., to watch the game. An early indication that something special was in the offing came less than three minutes into the game when Newberry's Bobby Bailey, who helped hold Selvy to a season-low 25 points two weeks earlier, fouled out.

Selvy's last three field goals in a 41-of-66 shooting performance from the floor came in the game's closing 30 seconds, and the crowning moment was his final basket. "It (the 100-point game) was something that was just meant to be," Selvy said. "My last basket was from past halfcourt just before the final buzzer."

He played every minute of every game during his senior season.

FURMAN (149)	FG	FT-A	PTS.	NEWBERRY (95)	FG	FT-A	PTS.
A.D. Bennett	0	1-1	1	Boland	0	0-0	0
Darrell Floyd	12	1-1	25	Warner	2	0-4	4
Fred Fraley	3	0-2	6	Leitner	6	4-7	16
Bob Poole	0	0-0	0	Bailey	0	1-2	1
Bob Thomas	5	1-1	11	Blanko	14	7-10	35
Al Kyber	0	0-2	0	Cone	1	0-0	2
Charles Ruth	0	0-0	0	Roth	0	3-4	3
Brock Gordon	0	0-0	0	McKlven	1	0-0	2
Frank Selvy	41	18-22	100	Davis	13	6-7	32
Kenny Deardorff	1	1-1	3				
Sylvester Wright	0	0-0	0				
Harry Jones	0	1-1	1				
Joe Gilreath	1	0-0	2				
TOTALS	63	23-31	149		37	21-34	95

Halftime: Furman 77-44.

3. UCLA's 38-game winning streak in NCAA Tournament
(under coach John Wooden from 1964 to 1974).

Here is a look at UCLA's NCAA Tournament hit list during the Bruins' wonder years when they won nine national championships from 1964 through 1973 before losing to North Carolina State (80-77 in double overtime) at the 1974 Final Four:

Opponent	Score	High Scorer	
Seattle	95-90	Walt Hazzard	26
San Francisco	76-72	Walt Hazzard	23
Kansas State	90-84	Keith Erickson	28
Duke*	98-83	Gail Goodrich	27
Brigham Young	100-76	Gail Goodrich	40
San Francisco	101-93	Gail Goodrich	30
Wichita State	108-89	Gail Goodrich	28
Michigan*	91-80	Gail Goodrich	42
Wyoming	109-60	Lew Alcindor	29
Pacific	80-64	Lew Alcindor	38
Houston	73-58	Lynn Shackelford	22
Dayton*	79-64	Lew Alcindor	20
New Mexico State	58-49	Lew Alcindor	28
Santa Clara	87-66	Lew Alcindor	22
Houston	101-69	Lew Alcindor/Mike Lynn/	
		Lucious Allen	19
North Carolina*	78-55	Lew Alcindor	34
New Mexico State	53-38	Lew Alcindor	16
Santa Clara	90-52	Lew Alcindor	17
Drake	85-82	John Vallely	29
Purdue*	92-72	Lew Alcindor	37
Long Beach State	88-65	Henry Bibby/Sidney Wicks	20
Utah State	101-79	Curtis Rowe/Sidney Wicks	26
New Mexico State	93-77	John Vallely	23
Jacksonville*	80-69	Curtis Rowe	19

Brigham Young	91-73	Henry Bibby	15
Long Beach State	57-55	Sidney Wicks	18
Kansas	68-60	Sidney Wicks	21
Villanova*	68-62	Steve Patterson	29
Weber State	90-58	Henry Bibby	16
Long Beach State	73-57	Henry Bibby	23
Louisville	96-77	Bill Walton	33
Florida State*	81-76	Bill Walton	24
Arizona State	98-81	Bill Walton	28
San Francisco	54-39	Larry Farmer	13
Indiana	70-59	Tommy Curtis	22
Memphis State*	87-66	Bill Walton	44
Dayton**	111-100	Dave Meyers	28
San Francisco	83-60	Jamaal Wilkes	27

*NCAA Tournament title games.
**Triple overtime.

4. Pete Maravich's career scoring average of 44.2 points per game with a total of 28 contests scoring at least 50 points
(for LSU from 1967-68 through 1969-70).

"Pistol Pete" set NCAA single-season records for most points (1,381) and highest average (44.5), finishing his career with NCAA career marks for most points (3,667) and highest average (44.2). He also established an NCAA record for most successful free throws in a game when he converted 30 of 31 foul shots at Oregon State. Maravich, who broke Oscar Robertson's NCAA career scoring mark with 13 regular-season games remaining, is the only player in NCAA Division I history to score more than 1,000 points and average over 40 points per game in each of three seasons.

Maravich's statistics would have been even more staggering if there had been a three-point basket at the time. He had 56 games with at least 40 points in his three-year career, including a school- and SEC-record 69 in a 106-104 postgame brawl-marred defeat at Alabama when he was hampered by leg ailments. No other player has had more than 21 games with a minimum of 40. He averaged more than 50 points per game in a 10-game stretch spanning the last three games of 1968-69 and the first seven games of 1969-70. Incredibly, Maravich improved his field-goal accuracy and assists average each year. Combining scoring and assists, Maravich was responsible for a whopping 59.4 percent of LSU's offense during his career.

Maravich never scored fewer than 30 points in back-to-back games and tallied under 20 just once (17 at Tennessee as a sophomore) in his three varsity seasons. The son of LSU coach Press Maravich was outscored in just one regular-season game by a teammate.

Maravich tallied more than 50 points in four outings against both SEC power Kentucky and intrastate independent rival Tulane. The Tigers lost all six times to Kentucky by double-digit margins despite his firepower. Here is a breakdown of how he amassed a 44.1-point career scoring average and modest 28-26 record in 54 games against SEC competition:

SEC Opponent	High Average	Low Game	Game	W-L
Alabama	48.8 ppg	69	30	4-2
Auburn	49 ppg	55	44	3-3
Florida	44 ppg	52	32	4-2
Georgia	46 ppg	58	37	5-1
Kentucky	52 ppg	64	44	0-6
Mississippi	42.3 ppg	53	31	3-3
Mississippi State	47.3 ppg	58	33	6-0
Tennessee	23 ppg	30	17	1-5
Vanderbilt	44.7 ppg	61	35	2-4

NOTE: LSU guard Chris Jackson is the only player to compile single-game scoring outbursts higher than Maravich in SEC competition against Mississippi (55 points), Florida (53) and Tennessee (50).

Best estimates are that Maravich would have averaged eight three-point goals per game if the arc had been around during his college playing days, which would have increased his scoring average to in excess of 50 ppg. Following is a game-by-game summary of Pistol Pete's career showing how his prolific scoring produced so many records:

Sophomore (1967-68) Record: 14-12; 8-10 in SEC					
Opponent	FG-A	FT-A	REB	PTS	LSU-OPP
Tampa	20-50	8-9	16	48	97-81
at Texas	15-34	12-16	5	42	87-74
Loyola (New Orleans)	22-43	7-11	9	51	90-56
at Wisconsin*	16-40	10-13	9	42	94-96
Florida State*	17-41	8-10	5	42	100-130
Mississippi	17-34	12-13	11	46	81-68
Mississippi State	22-40	14-16	8	58	111-87
Alabama	10-30	10-11	6	30	81-70
Auburn	20-38	15-17	9	55	76-72
at Florida	9-22	14-17	10	32	90-97
at Georgia	14-37	14-17	11	42	79-76
at Tulane	20-42	12-15	5	52	100-91
Clemson	14-29	5-6	6	33	104-81
Kentucky	19-51	14-17	11	52	95-121
Vanderbilt	22-57	10-15	6	54	91-99

at Kentucky	16-38	12-15	8	44	96-109
Tennessee	9-34	3-3	6	21	67-87
at Auburn	18-47	13-13	6	49	69-74
Florida (OT)	17-48	13-15	7	47	93-92
Georgia	20-47	11-18	4	51	73-78
at Alabama	24-52	11-13	12	59	99-89
at Mississippi State	13-38	8-12	7	34	94-83
Tulane	21-47	13-15	5	55	99-92
at Mississippi	13-26	14-16	4	40	85-87
at Tennessee	7-18	3-4	3	17	71-74
at Vanderbilt	17-39	8-11	6	42	86-11

*Milwaukee Classic.

Junior (1968-69) Record: 13-13; 7-11 in SEC

Opponent	FG-A	FT-A	REB	PTS	LSU-OPP
at Loyola (New Orleans)	22-34	8-9	7	52	109-82
at Clemson	10-32	18-22	4	38	86-85
Tulane (2 OT)	20-48	15-20	7	55	99-101
Florida (OT)	17-32	11-15	8	45	93-89
Georgia	18-33	11-16	10	47	98-89
Wyoming**	14-34	17-24	6	45	84-78
at Oklahoma City**	19-36	2-5	8	40	101-85
Duquesne**	18-36	17-21	2	53	94-91
at Alabama	19-49	4-4	10	42	82-85
at Vanderbilt	15-30	8-13	4	38	92-94
at Auburn	16-41	14-18	5	46	71-90
Kentucky	20-48	12-14	11	52	96-108
Tennessee	8-18	5-8	4	21	68-81
Pittsburgh	13-34	14-18	8	40	120-79
Mississippi (OT)	11-33	9-13	11	31	81-84
Mississippi State	14-32	5-6	11	33	95-71
Alabama	15-30	8-12	5	38	81-75
at Tulane	25-51	16-20	10	66	94-110
at Florida	14-41	22-27	6	50	79-95
Auburn	20-44	14-15	3	54	93-81
Vanderbilt	14-33	7-8	8	35	83-85
at Kentucky	21-53	3-7	5	45	89-103
at Tennessee	8-18	4-8	3	20	63-87
at Mississippi	21-39	7-11	3	49	76-78
at Mississippi State	20-49	15-19	4	55	99-89
at Georgia (2 OT)	21-48	16-25	6	58	90-80

**All-College Tournament at Oklahoma City.

Senior (1969-70) Record: 22-10; 13-5 in SEC

Opponent	FG-A	FT-A	REB	PTS	LSU-OPP
Oregon State	14-32	15-19	5	43	94-72
Loyola (New Orleans)	17-36	9-10	6	43	100-87
Vanderbilt	26-54	9-10	10	61	109-86
at Tulane	17-42	12-19	4	46	97-91
Southern California	18-43	14-16	6	50	98-101
at Clemson	22-30	5-8	6	49	111-103
at Oregon State	9-23	30-31	1	48	76-68
at UCLA	14-42	10-12	4	38	84-133
St. John's***	20-44	13-16	8	53	80-70
Yale***	13-28	8-11	5	34	94-97
Alabama	22-42	11-18	7	55	90-83
Auburn	18-46	8-11	6	44	70-79
at Kentucky	21-44	13-15	5	55	96-109
Tennessee	12-23	5-7	4	29	71-59
Mississippi	21-46	11-15	5	53	109-86
Mississippi State	21-40	7-9	3	49	109-91
at Florida	20-38	12-16	9	52	97-75
at Alabama	26-57	17-21	5	69	104-106
Tulane	18-45	13-15	4	49	127-114
Florida	16-35	6-10	3	38	94-85
at Vanderbilt	14-46	10-13	5	38	99-89
at Auburn	18-46	10-15	8	46	70-64
Georgia	17-34	3-6	2	37	88-86
Kentucky	23-42	18-22	4	64	105-121
at Tennessee	10-24	10-13	7	30	87-88
at Mississippi	13-43	9-14	9	35	103-90
at Mississippi State	22-44	11-13	5	55	97-87
at Georgia	16-37	9-10	3	41	99-88
Georgetown (NIT)	6-16	8-12	6	20	83-80
Oklahoma (NIT)	14-33	9-13	8	37	97-94
Marquette (NIT)	4-13	12-16	1	20	79-101

Army (NIT)DNP & ankle & hip injuries 68-75
***Rainbow Classic at Honolulu.

Career Scoring Site-of-Game Breakdown

	G	PTS	AVG
Home (25-12 mark)	37	1667	45.1
Neutral (5-3)	8	304	38
Road (19-19)	38	1696	44.6

Marks of Ownership

Three different Rhode Island State players in a six-year span set the major-college single-season scoring average record in the late 1930s and early 1940s. Pete Maravich's record of 44.5 ppg in 1969-70 might never be eclipsed. Following is a look at how long players have held the NCAA Division I single-season scoring average standard (through 2002-03):

Player, School	Years	Record (Season)
Hank Luisetti, Stanford	1	17.1 ppg (1936-37)
Chester Jaworski, Rhode Island St.	1	22.6 ppg (1938-39)
Stan Modzelewski, Rhode Island St.	3	23.1 ppg (1939-40)
George Senesky, St. Joseph's	1	23.4 ppg (1942-43)
Ernie Calverley, Rhode Island St.	7	26.7 ppg (1943-44)
Bill Mlkvy, Temple	2	29.2 ppg (1950-51)
Frank Selvy, Furman	15	41.7 ppg (1953-54)
Pete Maravich, Louisiana St.	34	44.5 ppg (1969-70)

5. Bill Walton's NCAA Tournament championship game field-goal accuracy of 95.5 percent (21 of 22 for UCLA vs. Memphis State in 1973).

Walton, aided by Greg Lee's tourney-high 14 assists, erupted for a championship game-record 44 points in an 87-66 triumph over Memphis State in the 1973 NCAA Tournament final at St. Louis. Walton had been outscored by fellow center Steve Downing, 26-14, in a 70-59 victory against Indiana in the national semi-finals.

UCLA (87)	MIN.	FG-A	FT-A	REB.	A	PF	PTS.
Keith Wilkes	39	8-14	0-0	7	1	2	16
Larry Farmer	33	1-4	0-0	2	0	2	2
Bill Walton	33	21-22	2-5	13	2	4	44
Greg Lee	34	1-1	3-3	3	14	2	5
Larry Hollyfield	30	4-7	0-0	3	9	4	8
Tommy Curtis	11	1-4	2-2	3	0	1	4
Dave Meyers	10	2-7	0-0	3	0	1	4
Swen Nater	7	1-1	0-0	3	0	2	2
Gary Franklin	1	1-2	0-1	1	0	0	2
Vince Carson	1	0-0	0-0	0	0	0	0
Bob Webb	1	0-0	0-0	0	0	0	0
Team Totals	200	40-62	7-11	40	26	18	87

FG%–.645. FT%–.636. Blocks–5. Turnovers–17 (Walton 6, Wilkes 4). Steals–2.

MEMPHIS STATE (66)	MIN.	FG-A	FT-A	REB.	A	PF	PTS.
Billy Buford	38	3-7	1-2	3	1	1	7
Larry Kenon	34	8-16	4-4	8	3	3	20
Ronnie Robinson	33	3-6	0-1	7	1	4	6
Bill Laurie	21	0-1	0-0	0	2	0	0
Larry Finch	38	9-21	11-13	1	2	2	29
Wes Westfall	10	0-1	0-0	0	0	5	0
Bill Cook	18	1-4	2-2	0	2	1	4
Doug McKinney	1	0-0	0-0	0	0	0	0
Clarence Jones	4	0-0	0-0	0	0	0	0
Jerry Tetzlaff	1	0-0	0-2	0	0	1	0
Jim Liss	1	0-1	0-0	0	0	0	0
Ken Andrews	1	0-0	0-0	0	0	0	0
Team Totals	200	24-57	18-24	21	11	17	66

FG%–.421. FT%–.750. Blocks–1. Turnovers–8. Steals–0.
Halftime: Tied 39-39.

6. UCLA's streak of 13 consecutive undisputed conference championships (from 1967 through 1979 in Pacific-8/Pacific-10).

The Bruins' composite conference record while capturing 13 straight regular-season league titles was an amazing 171-15 (.919). They were undefeated in conference competition five times in the first seven years of that streak. UCLA had three different coaches during the last five seasons of its domination.

Year	School (League Record)	Head Coach
1967	UCLA (14-0)	John Wooden
1968	UCLA (14-0)	John Wooden
1969	UCLA (13-1)	John Wooden
1970	UCLA (12-2)	John Wooden
1971	UCLA (14-0)	John Wooden
1972	UCLA (14-0)	John Wooden
1973	UCLA (14-0)	John Wooden
1974	UCLA (12-2)	John Wooden
1975	UCLA (12-2)	John Wooden
1976	UCLA (12-2)	Gene Bartow
1977	UCLA (11-3)	Gene Bartow
1978	UCLA (14-0)	Gary Cunningham
1979	UCLA (15-3)	Gary Cunningham

7. Jerry Tarkanian's streak of nine consecutive seasons with at least 28 victories (with UNLV from 1982-83 through 1990-91).

Embattled Tarkanian was forced out at UNLV after the 1991-92 campaign, but not before the Rebels captured their 10th consecutive PCAA/Big West Conference championship. Tarkanian's 307 victories in his last 10 seasons with them is by far the most successful 10-year stretch in major-college history. He won at least 28 games the first nine of those campaigns until going 26-2 when the Rebels were on probation and prohibited from competing in postseason play, including the Big West Tournament.

Tarkanian departed after becoming the only coach in history to compile back-to-back undefeated conference records for two different schools in the same league. He achieved the feat earlier with Long Beach State in 1970 and 1971 when the alliance was known as the Pacific Coast Athletic Association.

Season	School	Overall	League	Finish	Postseason
1982-83	UNLV	28-3	15-1	1st (PCAA)	NCAA (0-1)
1983-84	UNLV	29-6	16-2	1st (PCAA)	NCAA (2-1)
1984-85	UNLV	28-4	17-1	1st (PCAA)	NCAA (1-1)
1985-86	UNLV	33-5	16-2	1st (PCAA)	NCAA (2-1)
1986-87	UNLV	37-2	18-0	1st (PCAA)	NCAA (4-1)
1987-88	UNLV	28-6	15-3	1st (PCAA)	NCAA (1-1)
1988-89	UNLV	29-8	16-2	1st (Big West)	NCAA (3-1)
1989-90	UNLV	35-5	16-2	T1st (Big West)	NCAA (6-0)
1990-91	UNLV	34-1	18-0	1st (Big West)	NCAA (4-1)

8. Artis Gilmore's career rebounding average of 22.7 per game (for Jacksonville in 1969-70 and 1970-71)

Gilmore, a junior college transfer, led Division I in rebounding in 1970 and 1971 en route to becoming the only player in major-college history to average more than 22 points and 22 rebounds per game in his career. He finished with 24.3 points and 22.7 rebounds per outing in powering the Dolphins to a 49-6 record during his tenure.

The only time when Gilmore retrieved fewer than 10 missed shots was in New Orleans against Loyola (La.) at the end of a streak of four consecutive road games in his junior season. Here is a game-by-game summary of Gilmore's scoring and rebounding totals:

Junior (27-2 in 1969-70)

Date	Opponent	PTS.	REB.
D. 1	East Tennessee State	35	18
D. 2	Morehead State	31	26
D. 9	Mercer	34	32
D. 13	Biscayne (Fla.)	24	30
D. 18	Georgetown*	11	21
D. 22	Harvard	29	26
D. 26	vs. Arizona	32	17
D. 27	at Evansville	37	22
J. 2	at Hawaii	23	28
J. 5	at Hawaii	13	21
J. 9	Richmond	38	29
J. 10	Miami	13	23
J. 16	Virgin Islands	18	26
J. 27	at Florida State	21	19
J. 30	St. Peter's	46	30
F. 2	Iona	29	26
F. 5	at East Carolina	27	19
F. 6	at Richmond	27	21
F. 13	at Oklahoma City	27	15
F. 14	at Loyola (La.)	16	8
F. 18	Florida State	19	21
F. 24	Oklahoma City	25	18
F. 26	at Georgia Tech	27	10
M. 4	at Miami	19	10
M. 7	vs. Western Kentucky	30	19
M. 12	vs. Iowa	30	17
M. 14	vs. Kentucky	24	20
M. 19	vs. St. Bonaventure	29	21
M. 21	vs. UCLA	19	16

*Forfeit at 1:26 of first half.

Senior (22-4 in 1970-71)

Date	Opponent	PTS.	REB.
D. 1	Biscayne (Fla.)	50	29
D. 3	at St. Peter's	28	34
D. 7	George Washington	40	29
D. 8	Florida State	31	26
D. 12	at Richmond	28	19
D. 23	at Western Kentucky	29	18
D. 29	vs. Creighton	15	23
D. 30	vs. Wake Forest	13	21
J. 9	Miami	21	22
J. 11	Oklahoma City	15	17
J. 13	Manhattan	12	16
J. 20	Furman	18	18
J. 23	at Mercer	19	20
J. 25	South Alabama	15	19
J. 27	Florida State	15	28
F. 4	at South Alabama	25	17
F. 6	at Oklahoma City	18	19
F. 8	Loyola (La.)	24	28
F. 11	at William & Mary	2	14
F. 13	at Bradley	24	20
F. 15	at Florida State	22	25
F. 20	Valdosta (Ga.) State	26	24
F. 22	East Carolina	25	28
F. 27	at Houston	22	15
M. 2	at Miami	21	10
M. 13	vs. Western Kentucky	12	22

9. Kentucky's 129-game homecourt winning streak (under coach Adolph Rupp from Jan. 4, 1943, to Jan. 8, 1955)

Kentucky, two nights after losing to Ohio State, 45-40, in its first game in 1943, started a streak that went 11 years without dropping a homecourt game until bowing to Georgia Tech, 59-58, on Jan. 8, 1954. The setback also snapped a 70-game winning streak in SEC competition.

The first 84 of Kentucky's 129 consecutive homecourt victories were in Alumni Gym. The remainder were in Memorial Coliseum.

UK's average margin of victory during the streak was 31 points. Vanderbilt was involved in two of the three closest games—one-point loss in '43 and four-point setback in '50. The only other contest settled by fewer than five points during the streak was a 38-35 verdict against DePauw (Ind.) in 1944.

Date/Home Game	UK	Visiting Team	
Jan. 4, 1943	64	Ft. Knox	43
Jan. 26, 1943	39	Vanderbilt	38
Feb. 6, 1943	67	Alabama	41
Feb. 8, 1943	48	Xavier	36
Feb. 13, 1943	53	Tennessee	29
Feb. 15, 1943	58	Georgia Tech	31
Dec. 1, 1943	51	Ft. Knox	18
Dec. 4, 1943	54	Berea (Naval V-12)	40
Dec. 18, 1943	58	Cincinnati	30
Jan. 15, 1944	61	Wright Field	28
Jan. 31, 1944	76	Ft. Knox A.R.C.	48
Feb. 5, 1944	38	DePauw (Ind.)	35
Feb. 7, 1944	51	Illinois	40
Feb. 26, 1944	51	Ohio University	35
Dec. 2, 1944	56	Ft. Knox	23
Dec. 4, 1944	56	Berea (Ky.)	32
Dec. 9, 1944	66	Cincinnati	24
Dec. 23, 1944	53	Ohio State	48
Jan. 6, 1945	59	Ohio University	46
Jan. 8, 1945	75	Arkansas State	6
Jan. 13, 1945	66	Michigan State	35
Jan. 29, 1945	73	Georgia	37
Feb. 3, 1945	51	Georgia Tech	32
Feb. 17, 1945	40	Tennessee	34
Dec. 1, 1945	59	Ft. Knox	36
Dec. 7, 1945	51	Western Ontario	42
Dec. 8, 1945	71	Western Ontario	28
Dec. 15, 1945	67	Cincinnati	31
Dec. 18, 1945	67	Arkansas	42
Dec. 21, 1945	43	Oklahoma	33
Jan. 5, 1946	57	Ohio University	48
Jan. 7, 1946	81	Ft. Benning	25
Jan. 28, 1946	54	Georgia Tech	26
Feb. 5, 1946	59	Michigan State	51
Feb. 16, 1946	54	Tennessee	34
Feb. 23, 1946	83	Xavier	40
Nov. 28, 1946	78	Indiana Central	36
Nov. 30, 1946	64	Tulane	35
Dec. 2, 1946	68	Ft. Knox	31
Dec. 9, 1946	65	Idaho	35
Dec. 14, 1946	83	Texas A&M	18
Dec. 16, 1946	62	Miami of Ohio	49
Dec. 23, 1946	75	Baylor	34
Dec. 28, 1946	96	Wabash (O.)	24
Jan. 4, 1947	46	Ohio University	36
Jan. 11, 1947	70	Dayton	29
Jan. 25, 1947	71	Xavier	34
Jan. 27, 1947	86	Michigan State	36
Feb. 10, 1947	81	Georgia	40
Feb. 15, 1947	61	Tennessee	46
Feb. 17, 1947	63	Alabama	33
Feb. 22, 1947	83	Georgia Tech	46
Nov. 9, 1947	80	Indiana Central	41
Dec. 1, 1947	80	Ft. Knox	41
Dec. 5, 1947	72	Tulsa	18
Dec. 6, 1947	71	Tulsa	22

Date			
Dec. 17, 1947	79	Xavier	37
Jan. 3, 1948	98	Western Ontario	41
Jan. 24, 1948	70	Cincinnati	43
Feb. 14, 1948	69	Tennessee	42
Feb. 16, 1948	63	Alabama	33
Feb. 20, 1948	79	Vanderbilt	43
Feb. 21, 1948	78	Georgia Tech	54
Nov. 29, 1948	74	Indiana Central	38
Dec. 10, 1948	81	Tulsa	27
Dec. 13, 1948	76	Arkansas	39
Feb. 8, 1949	71	Tennessee	56
Feb. 12, 1949	96	Xavier	50
Feb. 14, 1949	74	Alabama	32
Feb. 16, 1949	85	Mississippi	31
Feb. 19, 1949	78	Georgia Tech	32
Feb. 21, 1949	95	Georgia	40
Feb. 26, 1949	70	Vanderbilt	37
Dec. 3, 1949	84	Indiana Central	61
Dec. 10, 1949	90	Western Ontario	18
Jan. 9, 1950	83	North Carolina	44
Jan. 28, 1950	88	Georgia	56
Feb. 11, 1950	79	Tennessee	52
Feb. 13, 1950	77	Alabama	57
Feb. 15, 1950	90	Mississippi	50
Feb. 18, 1950	97	Georgia Tech	62
Feb. 23, 1950	58	Xavier	53
Feb. 25, 1950	70	Vanderbilt	66
Dec. 1, 1950	73	West Texas State	43
Dec. 9, 1950	70	Purdue	52
Dec. 14, 1950	85	Florida	37
Dec. 16, 1950	68	Kansas	39
Jan. 5, 1951	79	Auburn	35
Jan. 8, 1951	63	DePaul	55
Jan. 13, 1951	65	Alabama	48
Jan. 15, 1951	69	Notre Dame	44
Feb. 9, 1951	75	Georgia Tech	42
Feb. 13, 1951	78	Xavier	51
Feb. 17, 1951	86	Tennessee	61
Feb. 23, 1951	88	Georgia	41
Feb. 24, 1951	89	Vanderbilt	57
Mar. 13, 1951	97	Loyola of Chicago	61
Dec. 8, 1951	96	Washington & Lee	46
Dec. 17, 1951	81	St. John's	40
Dec. 20, 1951	98	DePaul	60
Dec. 26, 1951	84	UCLA	53
Jan. 5, 1952	57	Louisiana State	47
Jan. 7, 1952	83	Xavier	50
Jan. 12, 1952	99	Florida	52
Feb. 4, 1952	103	Tulane	54
Feb. 6, 1952	81	Mississippi	61
Feb. 9, 1952	93	Georgia Tech	42
Feb. 11, 1952	110	Mississippi State	66
Feb. 16, 1952	95	Tennessee	40

Date			
Feb. 21, 1952	75	Vanderbilt	45
Dec. 5, 1953	86	Temple	59
Dec. 14, 1953	101	Wake Forest	69
Dec. 21, 1953	85	Duke	69
Dec. 22, 1953	73	La Salle	60
Dec. 28, 1953	74	Minnesota	59
Jan. 4, 1953	77	Xavier	71
Jan. 9, 1953	105	Georgia Tech	53
Jan. 11, 1953	81	DePaul	63
Jan. 16, 1953	94	Tulane	43
Feb. 4, 1953	106	Georgia	55
Feb. 13, 1953	88	Mississippi	62
Feb. 15, 1953	81	Mississippi State	49
Feb. 18, 1953	90	Tennessee	63
Feb. 22, 1953	100	Vanderbilt	64
Dec. 4, 1953	74	Louisiana State	58
Dec. 18, 1953	79	Temple	61
Dec. 21, 1953	70	Utah	65
Dec. 22, 1953	63	La Salle	54
Dec. 30, 1953	82	St. Louis	65

NOTE: Kentucky was barred from playing competitive basketball during the 1952-53 season because of NCAA probation.

10. Bill Chambers' 51 rebounds in a single game
(for William & Mary vs. Virginia on Feb. 14, 1953).

Chambers, standing a mere 6-4, grabbed an NCAA-record 51 rebounds for William & Mary in a 105-84 victory against Virginia on Valentine's Day. Chambers later became his alma mater's all-time winningest coach in a nine-year coaching career with the Tribe from 1957-58 through 1965-66.

WILLIAM & MARY (105)

Player	FG	FT-A	PTS.
Mahoney	5	6-11	16
Savage	0	0-4	0
Berry	1	1-2	3
Harris	10	0-1	20
Chambers	16	5-6	37
Hume	6	4-7	16
Drake	0	0-0	0
Hoitsma	4	5-6	13
Team	42	21-37 (.568)	105

VIRGINIA (84)

Player	FG	FT-A	PTS.
ROACH	2	2-5	6
Burlage	1	3-4	5
Cooke	2	1-1	5
Esckilsen	6	1-5	13
Gamble	2	5-6	9
Wilkinson	10	8-8	28
Dohner	7	2-2	16
Casey	1	0-0	2
Team	31	22-31 (.710)	84

The MVPs

Opposite Page: Wilt Chamberlain, a four-time NBA Most Valuable Player whose records for points in a game—100—and average points over a season—50.4—will surely never fall.

Left: Bill Russell, who won the MVP award five times while leading the Boston Celtics to 11 championships in 13 seasons and whose mano-a-mano rivalry with Chamberlain may have been the greatest in the history of team sports.

Lower right: Kareem Abdul-Jabbar (with Chamberlain on defense), named MVP a record six times and author of a record 38,387 points in 20 seasons.

Following page: Michael Jordan, five times MVP during the regular season, six times MVP of the Finals, whose 30.12 point per game lifetime average edges Wilt and his 30.06 by a whisker.

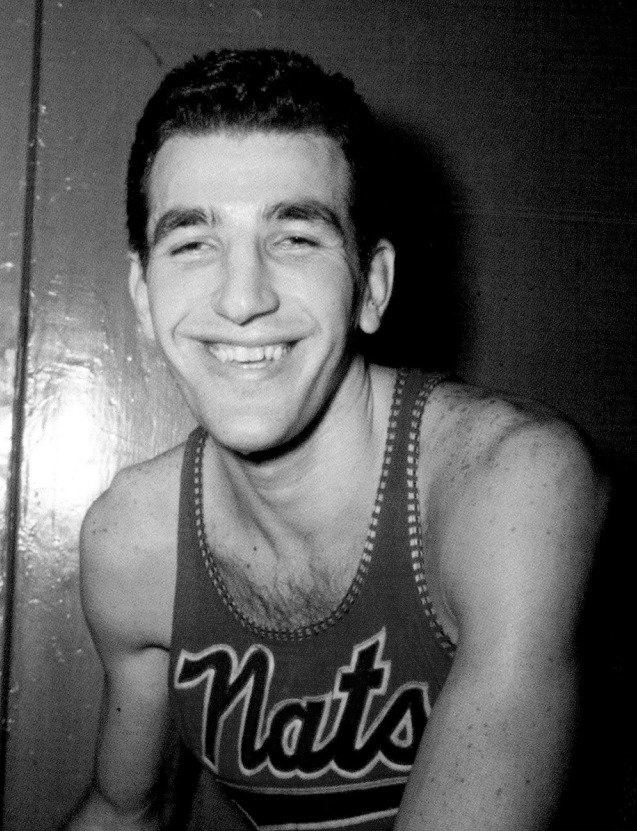

The Early Giants

Top left: George Mikan, the game's first true superstar whose size (6-foot-10, 245 pounds) and athleticism permitted the Minneapolis Lakers to dominate in the late '40s and early '50s.

Lower left: Dolph Schayes, the game's Iron Man of the 1950s, a 12-time All-NBA selection in his 16 seasons with the Syracuse Nationals.

Top right: Neil Johnston, the first to perfect the hook shot, a four-time first-team All-NBA and three-time scoring champ for the old Philadelphia Warriors.

The All-Time Greats

Top left: Bob Pettit, first and twice the NBA's MVP; 10 times a first-team All-NBA choice, No. 3 on the all-time rebounding list and No. 7 in scoring.

Lower left: Oscar Robertson, nine times a first-team All-NBA choice, so great in every facet of the game that over the first five seasons of his career he *averaged* a triple double—points, rebounds and assists in double digits.

Lower right: Jerry West and Elgin Baylor, the Lakers' gold dust twins, each with 10 first-team All-NBA nods and No. 6 and No. 4 rankings respectively on the all-time scoring list.

Opposite page: Bob Cousy, an utter magician in the backcourt and 10 times an All-NBA first team selection.

The All-Time Greats

Opposite page: Karl Malone, two-time MVP, first team All-NBA a record 11 times and now, after 18 seasons as the ultimate Utah star, a Laker.

Top left: Earvin 'Magic' Johnson, the regular season and NBA Finals MVP three times each, nine times a first-team All-NBA choice who possessed an innate sense of joy that helped revitalize the game in the 1980s.

Lower right: Larry Bird, arch-rival and alter ego to Magic, three times the regular season MVP—plus twice more in the Finals—and named nine times to the All-NBA first team.

The Modern Giants

Above: Moses Malone, a force in the pro game (the ABA) at the tender age of 18, three times the NBA MVP.

Right page, clockwise from top left: David Robinson, 10 times an All-NBA selection to go with his one MVP;
Hakeem Olajuwon (battling arch-enemy Patrick Ewing), 12 times named to an All-NBA team and an MVP once during the season and twice in the Finals;
Shaquille O'Neal (7-foot-1, 300 pounds) and Tim Duncan (7-foot, 248 pounds), the dominant big men in the game today, which may be why their teams have shared the past five NBA titles. O'Neal's haul: one regular-season MVP, three times in the Finals, and five times a first-team All-NBA selection.
Duncan's: two regular-season MVPs, one in the Finals, and six first-team All-NBA berths.

The Pioneers

Top left: Hank Luisetti, pioneer of the one-handed set shot while at Stanford in the 1930s and the game's first matinee idol after snapping the 43-game win streak of Clair Bee's Long Island University Blackbirds at Madison Square Garden one fateful December day in 1936.

Top right: Kenny Sailors, early architect of the jump shot while trying desperately to shoot over older, taller brother Bud on their Hillsdale, Wyoming farm in the summer of 1933.

Lower left: Clair Bee, instructing star player Sherman White in later years at LIU, was the game's first great defensive strategist, developing the 1-3-1 zone defense; he also had a hand in the adoption of the three-second rule and 24-second shot clock and, in his spare time, penned the Chip Hilton series of sports stories for kids.

The Pioneers, Part II

Top left: Nat 'Sweetwater' Clifton, the first African American to sign with an NBA team, the New York Knickerbockers in May 1950.

Top right: Chuck Cooper, the first African American to be drafted by an NBA team, the Boston Celtics in April 1950.

Lower right: Earl Lloyd, basketball's Jackie Robinson, the first African American to play in an NBA game—it was Halloween night, 1950, one day before Clifton and Cooper hit the floor for the first time—and, as of September 2003, a member of the Naismith Memorial Basketball Hall of Fame.

Following pages, from left: Ray Felix, the first African American to win an NBA award, as 1953-54 rookie of the year;
Reece 'Goose' Tatum, the original Clown Prince of Basketball, for 13 years the star attraction of the Harlem Globetrotters—and hero of the team's two late-1940s wins over the NBA champion Minneapolis Lakers.

The Pioneers, Part III

Top: Earl 'The Pearl' Monroe, whose whirling-dervish, high-intensity game fused artistry to basketball and set the stage for its cultural ascendancy.

Lower left: Maurice Stokes, the NBA's first African American star, whose career was cut tragically short in 1958 after three consecutive All-NBA seasons.

Bottom right: Frank Ramsay, the Original Sixth Man, whose success when thrown on the floor by Red Auerbach after the Celtics sagged early, set a lasting trend.

The Little Big Men

Above: Hal Greer (6-foot-2), seven times All-NBA in 15 ultra-consistent seasons.

Following page: Top left: Nate 'Tiny' Archibald (6-foot-1), the only man in history to lead in scoring and assists in the same season (1972-73);

Top right: John Stockton (6-foot-1), who retired with 50% more career assists than the No. 2 guy;

Lower right: Bill Sharman (6-foot-1), seven-time All-NBA as Bob Cousy's sharp-shooting backcourt mate;

Lower left: Allen Iverson (6-foot), already owner of a scoring title, an MVP award, five All-NBA selections and more tattoos than a port full of sailors.

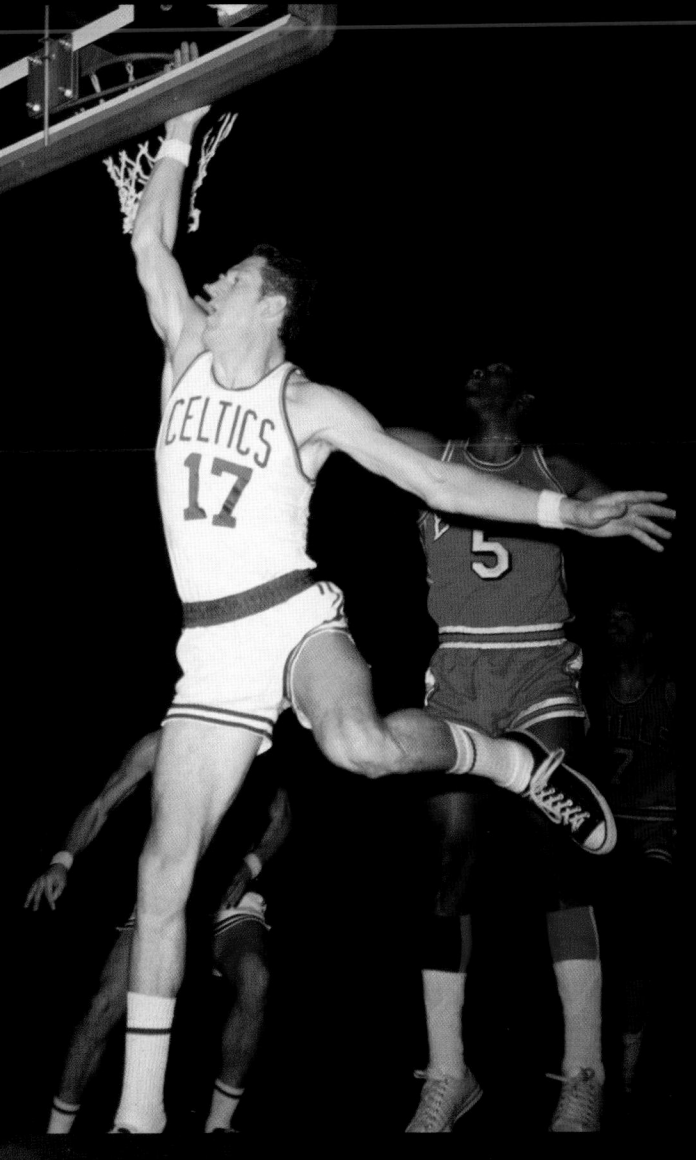

The All-Stars

Top left: Rick Barry, five times a first-team All-NBA selection, once Superman for a *SPORT* magazine photo shoot.

Top right: John Havlicek, swingman extraordinaire and 11 times All-NBA.

Bottom: Elvin Hayes, six times All-NBA.

The All-Stars, Part II

Top left: George Gervin, four scoring titles, seven All-NBA selections.

Top right: Charles Barkley, 11 All-NBA selections, plus an MVP.

Lower right: Julius 'Dr. J' Erving, seven All-NBA selections and a legacy of gravity-defying derring-do.

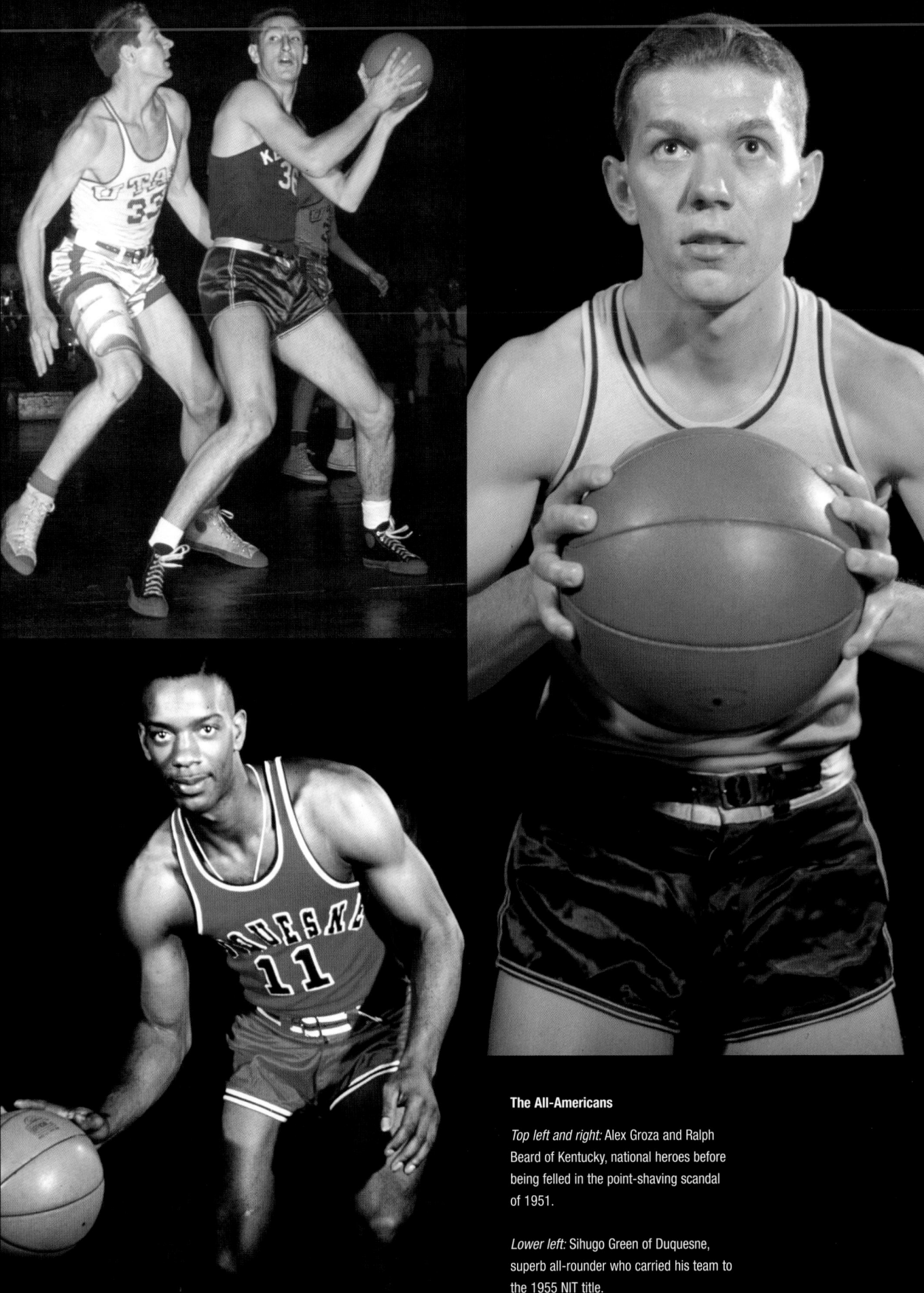

The All-Americans

Top left and right: Alex Groza and Ralph Beard of Kentucky, national heroes before being felled in the point-shaving scandal of 1951.

Lower left: Sihugo Green of Duquesne, superb all-rounder who carried his team to the 1955 NIT title.

The All-Americans, Part II

Left: 'Pistol' Pete Maravich of LSU, still the leading single season and career college scorer.

Lower right: Tom Gola of La Salle, only player to earn Most Outstanding Player awards in both the NCAA Final Four and NIT tournaments.

Opposite page, top: Bill Bradley of Princeton, Rhodes scholar, erstwhile U.S. senator and Most Outstanding Player of the Final Four in 1965.

Opposite page, bottom: Jerry Lucas of Ohio State, Most Outstanding Player of the Final Four in both 1960 and 1961.

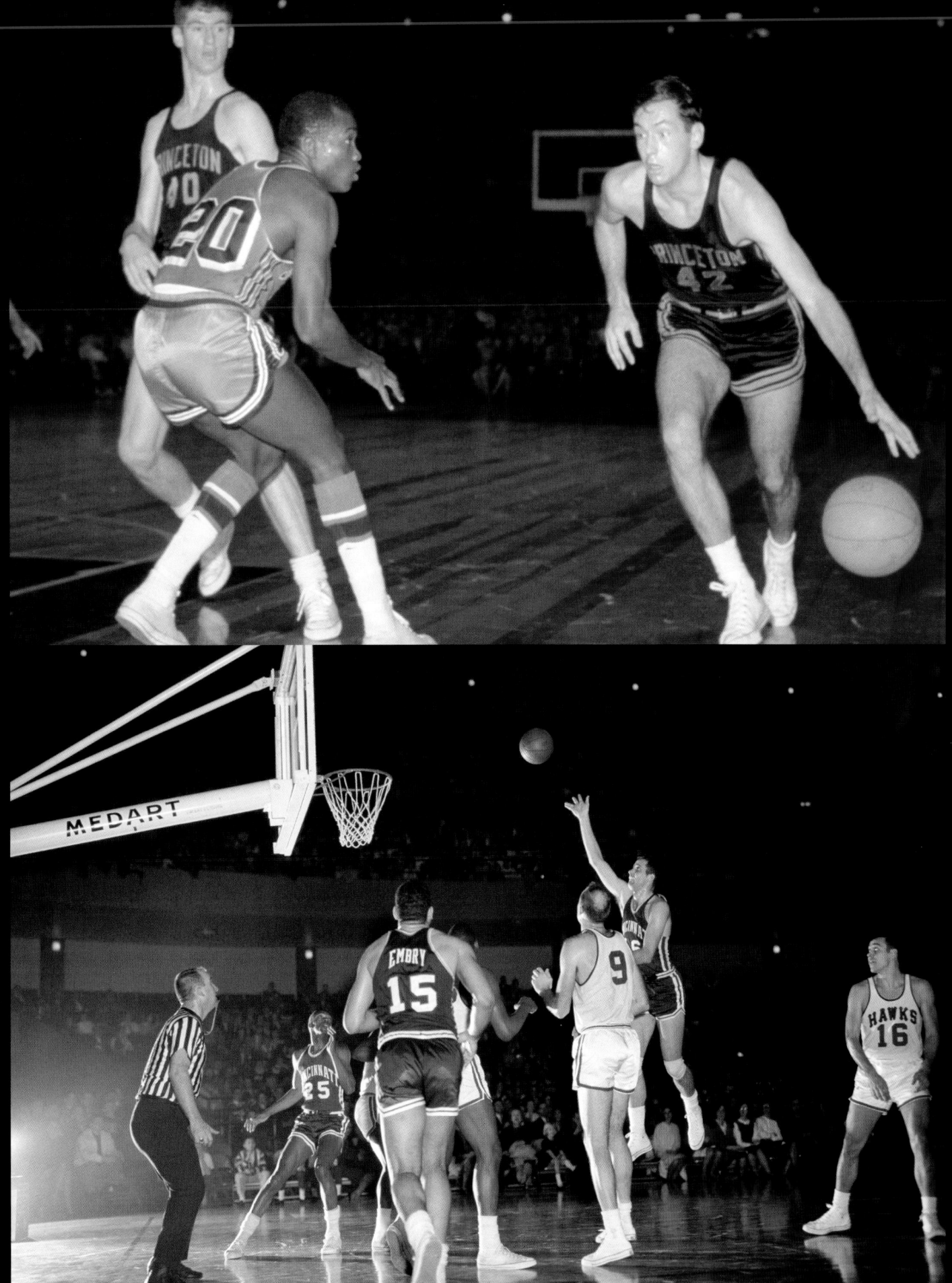

The Modern Warriors

Top left: Kevin Garnett, worth every penny to the Timberwolves.

Top right: Kobe Bryant, part of a dominant one-two punch with Shaq on three consecutive NBA championship teams.

Bottom: Tracy McGrady, fulfilled promise with scoring title in 2002-2003.

Wes Unseld, 1969
Emerging from a bunker during tour of U.S. combat positions in South Vietnam following astonishing 1968-69 season, in which he was named the NBA's MVP.

Chapter 51

History By The Numbers

By Sean Lahman

The pages that follow contain the most exhaustive statistical record of professional basketball that has ever been compiled. In addition to thousands of pieces of data that has never before been published, the *Total Basketball* Player Register includes a new statistic called Points Created that will revolutionize the way the game is analyzed.

The Player Register comprises the yearly records for more than 4,000 men who have played professional basketball. Individual statistics are presented for every player who stepped onto the court in the National Basketball Association (NBA), the American Basketball Association (ABA), the Basketball Association of America (BAA), and the National Basketball League (NBL).

By including statistics from the NBL and the BAA, *Total Basketball* is paying homage to two organizations that have been largely ignored. Their merger in 1949 gave birth to the NBA, but their roots extend to 1937 for the NBL, and 1946 for the BAA. The NBL was the first league to recognize the value of statistics. Up to 1939, only two statistics were recorded at the end of each game—the number of free throws and the number of field goals made by each player. From those numbers one could also derive points per game, but that's about as far as you could go. Then, for the 1939 season, the NBL began to record the number of shots attempted, giving us field goal and free throw percentage as an analytical measure. The NBL also began to count the number of personal fouls committed by each player. The concept of assists was introduced by the BAA in 1946, and continued as an official NBA statistic beginning in 1949.

The NBA began measuring rebounds in 1950 and added minutes played in 1951. The next major development occurred with the arrival of the ABA, the colorful league that not only sent four teams to the modern NBA, but also changed the way the game is played. The three-point shot was popularized by the ABA in 1967, but was not adopted by the NBA until 1979. The ABA invented two new statistics in 1972—steals and blocked shots. The NBA added those items to their official record the following year. They also added offensive rebounds in 1973, and four years later began counting turnovers.

This register treats the NBA and ABA as equals. You will find not only complete year-by-year statistics for every ABA player, plus career totals, but we have added a career total line that shows the combined career statistics for the many players who competed in both leagues. This addition provides a true measure of the accomplishments of such star performers as Julius Erving and Artis Gilmore.

Because the post-season has become such a large part of the professional game, we have included year-by-year breakdowns

for every player who has participated in NBA and ABA playoff games—an innovation unique to *Total Basketball*. Separate career totals are provided for regular season and post-season performances. In addition—and another unique feature of *Total Basketball*—are team "splits", where available, for players who saw action for more than one team in a season. For example, if a player was traded from Los Angeles to Detroit in mid-season, we show his statistics from the Lakers and Pistons on separate lines. Where the split is not available, the totals appear on one line, with the team names abbreviated.

Other unique features of the register are inclusion of categories for Minutes Per Game (MPG) and Points Created, which is represented here as Points Created per Minute (PCM). MPG has become increasingly significant in recent years and, we believe, no register could call itself comprehensive without its inclusion. Points Created is an exciting way to analyze each player's contribution and is described in greater detail in the following chapter.

The names in the register are listed alphabetically according to the most common surname of each player. So a player such as Kareem Abdul-Jabbar, who entered the league as Lew Alcindor, is listed only once, under Abdul-Jabbar. We also use the most common first name (so look for Bill Russell, not William Russell) or a common nickname (so look for Penny Hardaway, not Anfernee Hardaway).

In the body of the statistics you will occasionally see a bold-faced number. This indicates a league-leading statistic for that season or, in the case of the total lines, for a career. In a situation where a player has played for two teams in a season in which he led the league, his total for each team is bold-faced with the addition of the two numbers providing the leading total.

Basketball seasons typically span two calendar years. The schedule begins in October or November and carries over to the following spring. The standard practice is to label a season with both its start and end year. For example, the season that started in November 1985 and ended in April 1986 is referred to as the 85-86 season.

The following abbreviations are used for statistical data in this register:

GP	games played	TRB	total rebounds
GS	games started	AST	assists
MIN	minutes played	PF	personal fouls
PTS	points scored	DQ	disqualifications
FGM	field goals made	STL	steals
FGA	field goals attempted	BLK	blocks
FG%	field goal percent	TO	turnovers
3PM	three point shots made	MPG	minutes played per game
3PA	three point shots attempted	PPG	points scored per game
3P%	three point shooting percentage	RPG	rebounds per game
FTM	free throws made	APG	assists per game
FTA	free throws attempted	PCM	points created per minute
FT%	free throw shooting percentage	A	American Basketball Association
ORB	offensive rebounds	N	National Basketball League
DRB	defensive rebounds		

Chapter 52

The Magic Number: Points Created

By Bob Bellotti

The System

Points Created™ is a formula that can be used to calculate a player or team's overall performance. It comprises points, rebounds, assists, steals, blocked shots, missed field goals, missed free throws, turnovers, and personal fouls. Essentially, Points Created adds the good things a player does and subtracts the bad things. Using these categories—and the Value of Ball Possession as a weight—a single number results: the points a player creates.

The system can be used on any level of basketball in any league where statistics are kept. It can be used to evaluate players and teams for one or more games, a season, and a career.

The Value of Ball Possession

The VBP is shorthand for points scored (or allowed) per possession, and it is the reason Points Created works. It effectively measures offensive and defensive efficiency. Because the VBP changes from year to year, the equation for computing the points a player or team creates also changes annually. Each category (points, rebounds, assists, etc.) is weighted based on the index for each season. This helps to compare players from different eras because the system weighs the prevailing factors that affect play in each era.

A ball possession is any action that result in the ball changing hands from one team to another when a specific event occurs—rebounds, made field goals, turnovers, some made free throws, and some blocked shots. Therefore, adding all rebounds, made field goals and turnovers, and calculating the possession changes caused by made free throws and blocks, yields the formula for ball possessions:

Ball possessions formula: Rebounds + Field Goals Made + Turnovers + (Free Throws Made / 2) + (Blocked Shots / 2)

The VBP is calculated by dividing points by ball possessions:

Value of Ball Possession (Points per possession) formula: Points / Ball Possessions

For the 2002-03 season, the VBP was .908, which means that teams averaged .908 points per possession, or 90.8 points for every 100 possessions.

Offenses have become more efficient over the years. For example, in the 1950s teams routinely averaged between 71 and 80 points per 100 possessions. Starting around 1968, the VBP rose above 80 points and in 1979-80 it topped 90 points for the first time and got as high as 93.7 in 1989-90. Since then, the VBP has declined slightly along with the league-wide drop in scoring.

The chart below shows the correlation between VBP and the NBA's average field goal percentage.

Year	Average FG%	Points scored per 100 possessions
1952-53	37.0	72.4
1962-63	44.1	79.1
1972-73	45.6	85.8
1982-83	48.5	90.2
1992-93	47.3	93.3
2002-03	44.2	90.8

Based on the VBP, each category is assigned a value, or weight. Each weight is explained in the following paragraphs:

Points are taken at face value. A point scored is a point created.

A rebound—the act of gaining possession of the ball—equals the prevailing VBP. In 2002-03, each possession was worth .908. Therefore, each rebound had that same value.

A steal also gains possession of the ball and therefore is worth the VBP.

A blocked shot ends a possession, with the swatted ball being recovered by either team and recorded as a rebound in the stat sheet. Because rebounds are counted separately, the value of a block is the same as a ball possession (e.g., .908).

A turnover has the opposite effect of a rebound or steal; it loses a possession. Thus, it is worth the negative value of a ball possession, (e.g., -.908).

Like a turnover, a missed field goal attempt (two- or three-pointer) always causes the loss of a possession and is worth the negative value of a possession. But what about offensive rebounds, you say? Well, technically an offensive rebound begins the next possession and we include offensive glasswork in the rebounding category.

Points Created distinguishes between missed field goals and missed free throws, because the latter results in a change of possession approximately half the time. Thus, a missed foul shots equals the negative VBP divided by two (e.g., -.908 / 2, or .454).

An assist turns a ball possession into two points, or occasionally, three points. As a result, an assist is worth the difference between the VBP and two points—1.092 last year (2.0 minus .908).

Finally, personal fouls are valued at half of a possession (e.g., .454 in 2002-03). Many ratings systems do not penalize for fouls, using the argument that "good" and "bad" fouls even out. But players must be penalized for personal fouls because most often they lead directly to one or two points for the opposing team. NBA players make about 75% of their free throws, totaling about 19 points a game. If you do not penalize a team for its fouls, how can you account for those 19 points?

How accurate is Points Created? Here's one measure: the

NBA's MVP in any given year has ranked in the top 4 in Points Created in 23 of the past 24 seasons. In 2002-03, for example, MVP Tim Duncan ranked third in the league, slightly behind Shaquille O'Neal and Kevin Garnett.

The players with the top 50 career PC ratings are, as represented by Points Created per Minute:

Points Created Top 50 Career List

Regular Season only (minimum 500 games)

Rank	Player	PCM	Rank	Player	PCM
1.	Wilt Chamberlain	.832	26.	George Gervin	.614
2.	Magic Johnson	.782	26.	Clyde Drexler	.614
3.	Kareem Abdul-Jabbar	.759	28.	Robert Parish	.607
4.	Shaquille O'Neal	.749	29.	Alex English	.603
5.	Larry Bird	.743	30.	Alvan Adams	.602
6.	Michael Jordan	.736	31.	Alonzo Mourning	.599
7.	Oscar Robertson	.735	32.	Adrian Dantley	.597
8.	David Robinson	.725	33.	Brad Daugherty	.594
9.	Charles Barkley	.723	34.	Rick Barry	.591
10.	Bob Pettit	.705	35.	Grant Hill	.588
11.	Hakeem Olajuwon	.701	36.	Tom Boerwinkle	.586
12.	Karl Malone	.687	36.	Dave Cowens	.586
13.	Elgin Baylor	.673	38.	Willis Reed	.584
14.	Jerry West	.671	39.	Bailey Howell	.581
15.	Bob Lanier	.663	40.	Clyde Lovellette	.574
16.	Moses Malone	.657	41.	George McGinnis	.572
17.	Dan Issel	.649	41.	Dominique Wilkins	.572
18.	Bill Russell	.641	41.	Bob Cousy	.572
19.	Jerry Lucas	.638	44.	Wes Unseld	.571
19.	Bob McAdoo	.638	45.	Fat Lever	.571
21.	Artis Gilmore	.635	46.	Jack Sikma	.565
22.	Patrick Ewing	.624	47.	Dolph Schayes	.564
23.	Chris Webber	.623	48.	Cliff Hagan	.563
24.	Walt Bellamy	.622	49.	Walter Davis	.562
25.	Billy Cunningham	.615	50.	Walt Frazier	.561

Admittedly, the system has one weakness. Although Points Created uses all available statistical categories, it has no means of including an area for which statistics aren't recorded—man-to-man defense or defensive "stops," as the pros call them. This hole in generally accepted basketball record keeping is significant—it means there is no account of many defensive plays.

The consequence of using incomplete defensive statistics is that Points Created ratings should be adjusted to one degree or another for players who either are very strong or very weak man-to-man defenders. Fortunately, most players' defensive abilities fall somewhere between the very good and very bad. So, the gap in defensive statistics does not seriously undermine most players' ratings. Stops are only one defensive contribution, along with steals, blocks, defensive rebounds, and defensive fouls, all of which are recorded and reflected in Points Created.

The Formulas

Two Points Created formulas exist. The first is a basic version. Because the current VBP is nearly 1.0, the weights in this version are rounded to 1.0, making it easy to calculate Points Created from a boxscore. The equation looks like this:

Points Created Basic Formula

(Points + Rebounds + Assists + Steals + Blocked Shots) − (Missed Field Goals + Turnovers) − (Missed Free Throws / 2) − (Personal fouls / 2).

The complex formula is more precise and is what I use for analyses. It looks like this:

Points Created Complex Formula

((Points) + ((Rebounds + Steals + Blocked Shots) * VBP) + (Assists * (2 − VBP)) − ((Missed Field Goals + Turnovers) * VBP) − ((Missed Free Throws / 2) * VBP) − (Personal Fouls * VBP / 2))

Here's an example of the simplified formula. In 2002-03 Tracy McGrady accumulated: 2,407 points, 488 rebounds, 411 assists, 124 steals, 59 blocks, equaling 3,489 positive actions

McGrady also had: 984 missed field goals, 195 turnovers, 156 personal fouls, 150 missed free throws, equaling 1,332 negative actions (after dividing fouls and missed free throws by 2)

The difference between McGrady's positive and negative totals is 2,157 points created.

Points Created can be expressed as both per-game and per-minute figures, which make for better comparisons and easier understanding. McGrady, for instance, created an average of 28.8 points per game in 2002-03 (2,157 divided by 75 games). The per-game equation is:

Points Created per Game
Points Created / Games Played

The per-minute equation is the most exact, the best for comparing players, and the one used in *Total Basketball*'s Player Register. McGrady created 0.730 points per minute (2,157 divided by 2,954 minutes), the league's fourth-best mark (behind O'Neal 0.787, Garnett 0.768, and Duncan 0.739). The per-minute equation is:

Points Created per minute
Points Created / Minutes Played

Think of Points Created per minute in terms of a baseball batting average, except that a good basketball "batting average" is .450 and above. The following chart may help you interpret the PCM ratings.

PCM Rating	Category
Above .650	Superstar category. Normally, only a handful of players each season reach this level of performance.
.550-.650	All-Star. All-Stars are in this range, or either just below or above it.
.450-.550	Good players who are sometimes outstanding fall into this category.
.350-.450	Regulars. Solid players who are either starters or among a team's first seven or eight regulars.
.200-.350	Poor. Players in this category are frequently rookies, or veterans whose skills are declining.
Below .200	Awful. Players in this category are living life on the edge. Most are soon traded or released.

When calculating Points Created for leagues in which blocked shots, steals, and turnovers aren't recorded, you can omit those categories from the formula without losing the inherent logic of the system. Thus, the equation becomes an offshoot of the ones above.

Points Created Formula without Steals, Blocks, and Turnovers

((Points) + (Rebounds * VBP) + (Assists * (2 − VBP)) − (Missed Field Goals * VBP) − ((Missed Free Throws / 2) * VBP) − (Personal Fouls * VBP / 2))

' Points Created is a trademark of Bellotti Basketball

Chapter 53 The Player Register

• ABDELNABY, Alaa

Alaa Abdelnaby

Born: June 24, 1968. Cairo, Egypt. Height: 6'10". Weight: 240 lbs. Drafted: 1990 College: Duke

YEAR	TEAM	GP	GS	MIN	PTS	FGM	FGA	FG%	3PM	3PA	3P%	FTM	FTA	FT%	ORB	DRB	TRB	AST	PF	DQ	STL	BLK	TO	MPG	PPG	RPG	APG	PCM
90-91	Portland	43	0	290	135	55	116	.474	0	0	.000	25	44	.568	27	62	89	12	39	0	4	12	22	6.7	3.1	2.1	0.3	.487
91-92	Portland	71	1	934	432	178	361	.493	0	0	.000	76	101	.752	81	179	260	30	132	1	25	17	64	13.2	6.1	3.7	0.4	.474
92-93	Milwaukee	12	0	159	64	26	56	.464	0	1	.000	12	16	.750	12	25	37	10	24	0	6	4	13	13.3	5.3	3.1	0.8	.411
92-93	Boston	63	52	1152	514	219	417	.525	0	0	.000	76	100	.760	114	186	300	17	165	0	19	22	82	18.3	8.2	4.8	0.3	.435
93-94	Boston	13	0	159	64	24	55	.436	0	0	.000	16	25	.640	12	34	46	3	20	0	2	3	17	12.2	4.9	3.5	0.2	.357
94-95	Sacramento	51	0	476	254	117	220	.532	0	2	.000	20	35	.571	34	72	106	13	102	1	15	12	41	9.3	5.0	2.1	0.3	.426
94-95	Philadelphia	3	0	30	2	1	11	.091	0	0	.000	0	0	.000	3	5	8	0	2	0	0	0	5	10.0	0.7	2.7	0.0	-.183
NBA Season Totals		256	53	3200	1465	620	1236	.502	0	3	.000	225	321	.701	283	563	846	85	484	2	71	70	244	12.5	5.7	3.3	0.3	....
90-91	Portland	5	0	13	4	2	6	.333	0	0	.000	0	0	.000	1	2	3	0	0	0	0	0	0	2.6	0.8	0.6	0.0	.236
91-92	Portland	8	0	25	12	5	10	.500	0	0	.000	2	4	.500	0	4	4	2	4	0	0	0	2	3.1	1.5	0.5	0.3	.343
92-93	Boston	4	4	68	22	11	24	.458	0	0	.000	0	0	.000	2	11	13	1	7	0	0	1	9	17.0	5.5	3.3	0.3	.181
NBA Playoff Totals		17	4	106	38	18	40	.450	0	0	.000	2	4	.500	3	17	20	3	11	0	0	1	11	6.2	2.2	1.2	0.2	....

• ABDUL-AZIZ, Zaid

Zaid (The Kangaroo) Abdul-Aziz aka.: Donald A. Smith

Born: Apr. 7, 1946. Brooklyn, NY, United States. Height: 6'9". Weight: 235 lbs. Drafted: 1968 College: Iowa State

YEAR	TEAM	GP	GS	MIN	PTS	FGM	FGA	FG%	3PM	3PA	3P%	FTM	FTA	FT%	ORB	DRB	TRB	AST	PF	DQ	STL	BLK	TO	MPG	PPG	RPG	APG	PCM
68-69	Cincinnati	20	....	108	38	18	43	.419	....	....	....	2	7	.286	....	....	31	4	17	0	....	....	....	5.4	1.9	1.6	0.2	.356
68-69	Milwaukee	29	....	837	320	126	347	.363	....	....	....	68	106	.642	....	....	378	33	98	3	....	....	....	28.9	11.0	13.0	1.1	.517
69-70	Milwaukee	80	....	1637	593	237	546	.434	....	....	....	119	185	.643	....	....	603	62	167	2	....	....	....	20.5	7.4	7.5	0.8	.500
70-71	Seattle	61	....	1276	665	263	597	.441	....	....	....	139	188	.739	....	....	468	42	118	0	....	....	....	20.9	10.9	7.7	0.7	.593
71-72	Seattle	58	....	1780	798	322	751	.429	....	....	....	154	214	.720	....	....	654	124	178	1	....	....	....	30.7	13.8	11.3	2.1	.579
72-73	Houston	48	....	900	417	149	375	.397	....	....	....	119	162	.735	....	....	304	53	108	2	....	....	....	18.8	8.7	6.3	1.1	.533
73-74	Houston	79	....	2459	865	336	732	.459	....	....	....	193	240	.804	259	664	923	166	227	3	80	104	....	31.1	10.9	11.7	2.1	.564
74-75	Houston	65	....	1450	629	235	538	.437	....	....	....	159	203	.783	154	334	488	84	128	1	37	74	....	22.3	9.7	7.5	1.3	.558
75-76	Seattle	27	....	223	86	35	75	.467	....	....	....	16	29	.552	30	46	76	16	29	0	8	15	....	8.3	3.2	2.8	0.6	.525
76-77	Buffalo	22	....	195	83	25	74	.338	....	....	....	33	43	.767	41	49	90	7	21	0	3	9	....	8.9	3.8	4.1	0.3	.579
77-78	Boston	2	....	24	8	3	13	.231	....	....	....	2	3	.667	6	9	15	3	4	0	1	1	3	12.0	4.0	7.5	1.5	.529
77-78	Houston	14	....	134	55	20	47	.426	....	....	....	15	20	.750	13	22	35	7	25	0	2	2	8	9.6	3.9	2.5	0.5	.397
NBA Season Totals		505	....	11023	4557	1769	4138	.428	....	....	....	1019	1400	.728	503	1124	4065	601	1120	12	131	205	11	21.8	9.0	8.0	1.2	....
69-70	Milwaukee	7	....	82	30	11	19	.579	....	....	....	8	10	.800	....	....	26	4	5	0	....	....	....	11.7	4.3	3.7	0.6	.576
74-75	Houston	6	....	68	26	12	31	.387	....	....	....	2	5	.400	7	10	17	3	5	0	1	3	....	11.3	4.3	2.8	0.5	.358
75-76	Seattle	5	....	60	36	14	20	.700	....	....	....	8	11	.727	4	17	21	2	2	0	0	5	....	12.0	7.2	4.2	0.4	.817
NBA Playoff Totals		18	....	210	92	37	70	.529	....	....	....	18	26	.692	11	27	64	9	12	0	1	8	....	11.7	5.1	3.6	0.5	....

• ABDUL-JABBAR, Kareem

Kareem Abdul-Jabbar aka.: Ferdinand Lewis Alcindor Jr.

Born: Apr. 16, 1947. New York, NY, United States. Height: 7'2". Weight: 225 lbs. Drafted: 1969 College: UCLA HOF: 1995

YEAR	TEAM	GP	GS	MIN	PTS	FGM	FGA	FG%	3PM	3PA	3P%	FTM	FTA	FT%	ORB	DRB	TRB	AST	PF	DQ	STL	BLK	TO	MPG	PPG	RPG	APG	PCM
69-70	Milwaukee	82	....	3534	**2361**	**938**	1810	.518	....	....	....	485	743	.653	....	....	1190	337	283	8	....	....	....	43.1	28.8	14.5	4.1	.787
70-71	Milwaukee	82	....	3288	**2596**	**1063**	1843	.577	....	....	....	470	681	.690	....	....	1311	272	264	4	....	....	....	40.1	**31.7**	16.0	3.3	.961
71-72	Milwaukee	81	....	3583	**2822**	**1159**	**2019**	.574	....	....	....	504	732	.689	....	....	1346	370	235	1	....	....	....	44.2	**34.8**	16.6	4.6	.966
72-73	Milwaukee	76	....	3254	2292	982	1772	.554	....	....	....	328	460	.713	....	....	1224	379	208	0	....	....	....	42.8	30.2	16.1	5.0	.907
73-74	Milwaukee	81	....	3548	2191	**948**	1759	.539	....	....	....	295	420	.702	287	891	1178	386	238	2	112	283	....	43.8	27.0	14.5	4.8	.787
74-75	Milwaukee	65	....	2747	1949	812	1584	.513	....	....	....	325	426	.763	194	718	912	264	205	2	65	212	....	42.3	30.0	14.0	4.1	.816
75-76	LA Lakers	82	....	**3379**	2275	914	1728	.529	....	....	....	447	636	.703	272	**1111**	**1383**	413	292	6	119	**338**	....	41.2	27.7	**16.9**	5.0	.896
76-77	LA Lakers	82	....	3016	2152	**888**	1533	**.579**	....	....	....	376	536	.701	266	**824**	**1090**	319	262	4	101	**261**	....	36.8	26.2	13.3	3.9	.901
77-78	LA Lakers	62	....	2265	1600	663	1205	.550	....	....	....	274	350	.783	186	615	801	269	182	1	103	185	211	36.5	25.8	12.9	4.3	.920
78-79	LA Lakers	80	....	3157	1903	777	1347	.577	....	....	....	349	474	.736	207	818	1025	431	230	3	76	**316**	280	39.5	23.8	12.8	5.4	.864
79-80	LA Lakers	82	....	3143	2034	835	1383	.604	0	1	.000	364	476	.765	190	696	886	371	216	2	81	**280**	295	38.3	24.8	10.8	4.5	.846
80-81	LA Lakers	80	....	2976	2095	836	1457	.574	0	1	.000	423	552	.766	197	624	821	272	244	4	59	228	248	37.2	26.2	10.3	3.4	.820
81-82	LA Lakers	76	76	2677	1818	753	1301	.579	0	3	.000	312	442	.706	172	487	659	225	224	0	63	207	228	35.2	23.9	8.7	3.0	.762
82-83	LA Lakers	79	79	2554	1722	722	1228	.588	0	2	.000	278	371	.749	167	425	592	200	220	1	61	170	198	32.3	21.8	7.5	2.5	.747
83-84	LA Lakers	80	80	2622	1717	716	1238	.578	0	1	.000	285	394	.723	169	418	587	211	211	1	55	143	224	32.8	21.5	7.3	2.6	.698
84-85	LA Lakers	79	79	2630	1735	723	1207	.599	0	1	.000	289	395	.732	162	460	622	249	238	3	63	162	198	33.3	22.0	7.9	3.2	.758
85-86	LA Lakers	79	79	2629	1846	755	1338	.564	0	2	.000	336	439	.765	133	345	478	280	248	2	67	130	205	33.3	23.4	6.1	3.5	.714
86-87	LA Lakers	78	78	2441	1366	560	993	.564	1	3	.333	245	343	.714	152	371	523	203	245	2	49	97	187	31.3	17.5	6.7	2.6	.602
87-88	LA Lakers	80	80	2308	1165	480	903	.532	0	1	.000	205	269	.762	118	360	478	135	216	1	48	92	160	28.9	14.6	6.0	1.7	.525
88-89	LA Lakers	74	74	1695	748	313	659	.475	0	3	.000	122	165	.739	103	231	334	74	196	1	38	85	96	22.9	10.1	4.5	1.0	.431
NBA Season Totals		1560	625	**57446**	**38387**	**15837**	**28307**	.559	1	18	.056	6712	9304	.721	2975	9394	17440	5660	**4657**	48	1160	3189	2530	36.8	24.6	11.2	3.6	....
69-70	Milwaukee	10	....	435	352	139	245	.567	....	....	....	74	101	.733	....	....	168	41	25	1	....	....	....	43.5	35.2	16.8	4.1	.988
70-71	Milwaukee	14	....	577	372	152	295	.515	....	....	....	68	101	.673	....	....	238	35	45	0	....	....	....	41.2	26.6	17.0	2.5	.797
71-72	Milwaukee	11	....	510	316	139	318	.437	....	....	....	38	54	.704	....	....	200	56	35	0	....	....	....	46.4	28.7	18.2	5.1	.737
72-73	Milwaukee	6	....	276	137	59	138	.428	....	....	....	19	35	.543	....	....	97	17	26	0	....	....	....	46.0	22.8	16.2	2.8	.557
73-74	Milwaukee	16	....	758	515	224	402	.557	....	....	....	67	91	.736	67	186	253	78	41	0	20	39	....	47.4	32.2	15.8	4.9	.845

YEAR	TEAM	GP	GS	MIN	PTS	FGM	FGA	FG%	3PM	3PA	3P%	FTM	FTA	FT%	ORB	DRB	TRB	AST	PF	DQ	STL	BLK	TO	MPG	PPG	RPG	APG	PCM
76-77	LA Lakers	11	....	467	381	147	242	.607	....	....	....	87	120	.725	51	144	195	45	42	0	19	38	....	42.5	34.6	17.7	4.1	1.041
77-78	LA Lakers	3	....	134	81	38	73	.521	....	....	....	5	9	.556	14	27	41	11	14	1	2	12	14	44.7	27.0	13.7	3.7	.677
78-79	LA Lakers	8	....	367	228	88	152	.579	....	....	....	52	62	.839	18	83	101	38	26	0	8	33	29	45.9	28.5	12.6	4.8	.811
79-80	LA Lakers	15	....	618	479	198	346	.572	0	0	.000	83	105	.790	51	130	181	46	51	0	17	58	55	41.2	31.9	12.1	3.1	.881
80-81	LA Lakers	3	....	134	80	30	65	.462	0	0	.000	20	28	.714	13	37	50	12	14	0	3	8	11	44.7	26.7	16.7	4.0	.722
81-82	LA Lakers	14	14	493	285	115	221	.520	0	0	.000	55	87	.632	33	86	119	51	45	0	14	45	41	35.2	20.4	8.5	3.6	.676
82-83	LA Lakers	15	15	588	406	163	287	.568	0	1	.000	80	106	.755	25	90	115	42	61	1	17	55	50	39.2	27.1	7.7	2.8	.722
83-84	LA Lakers	21	21	767	502	206	371	.555	0	0	.000	90	120	.750	56	117	173	79	71	2	23	45	45	36.5	23.9	8.2	3.8	.741
84-85	LA Lakers	19	19	610	416	168	300	.560	0	0	.000	80	103	.777	50	104	154	76	67	1	23	36	52	32.1	21.9	8.1	4.0	.791
85-86	LA Lakers	14	14	489	362	157	282	.557	0	0	.000	48	61	.787	26	57	83	49	54	0	15	24	42	34.9	25.9	5.9	3.5	.698
86-87	LA Lakers	18	18	559	345	124	234	.530	0	1	.000	97	122	.795	39	84	123	36	56	0	8	35	40	31.1	19.2	6.8	2.0	.645
87-88	LA Lakers	24	24	718	338	141	304	.464	0	2	.000	56	71	.789	49	82	131	36	81	1	15	37	46	29.9	14.1	5.5	1.5	.428
88-89	LA Lakers	15	15	351	167	68	147	.463	0	0	.000	31	43	.721	13	46	59	19	43	0	5	11	22	23.4	11.1	3.9	1.3	.392
NBA Playoff Totals		**237**	140	**8851**	5762	**2356**	4422	.533	0	4	.000	1050	1419	.740	505	1273	2481	767	**797**	7	189	**476**	447	37.3	24.3	10.5	3.2	....

• ABDUL-RAHMAN, Mahdi

Mahdi Abdul-Rahman aka.: Walter Raphael Hazzard Jr.

Born: Apr. 15, 1942. Philadelphia, PA, United States. Height: 6'2". Weight: 185 lbs. Drafted: 1964 College: UCLA

YEAR	TEAM	GP	GS	MIN	PTS	FGM	FGA	FG%	3PM	3PA	3P%	FTM	FTA	FT%	ORB	DRB	TRB	AST	PF	DQ	STL	BLK	TO	MPG	PPG	RPG	APG	PCM
64-65	LA Lakers	66	....	919	280	117	306	.382	....	....	....	46	71	.648	....	....	111	140	132	0	....	....	....	13.9	4.2	1.7	2.1	.362
65-66	LA Lakers	80	....	2198	1098	458	1003	.457	....	....	....	182	257	.708	....	....	219	393	224	0	....	....	....	27.5	13.7	2.7	4.9	.547
66-67	LA Lakers	79	....	1642	731	301	706	.426	....	....	....	129	177	.729	....	....	231	323	203	1	....	....	....	20.8	9.3	2.9	4.1	.536
67-68	Seattle	79	....	2666	1894	733	1662	.441	....	....	....	428	553	.774	....	....	332	493	246	3	....	....	....	33.7	24.0	4.2	6.2	.698
68-69	Atlanta	80	....	2420	898	345	869	.397	....	....	....	208	294	.707	....	....	266	474	264	6	....	....	....	30.3	11.2	3.3	5.9	.449
69-70	Atlanta	82	....	2757	1253	493	1056	.467	....	....	....	267	330	.809	....	....	329	561	264	2	....	....	....	33.6	15.3	4.0	6.8	.556
70-71	Atlanta	82	....	2877	1349	517	1126	.459	....	....	....	315	415	.759	....	....	300	514	276	2	....	....	....	35.1	16.5	3.7	6.3	.524
71-72	Buffalo	72	....	2389	1137	450	998	.451	....	....	....	237	303	.782	....	....	213	406	230	2	....	....	....	33.2	15.8	3.0	5.6	.494
72-73	Buffalo	9	....	134	53	25	60	.417	....	....	....	3	6	.500	....	....	10	17	19	0	....	....	....	14.9	5.9	1.1	1.9	.310
72-73	Golden State	46	....	629	208	82	196	.418	....	....	....	44	51	.863	....	....	78	112	91	0	....	....	....	13.7	4.5	1.7	2.4	.418
73-74	Seattle	49	....	571	186	76	180	.422	....	....	....	34	45	.756	18	39	57	122	78	0	26	6	....	11.7	3.8	1.2	2.5	.435
NBA Season Totals		724	....	19202	9087	3597	8162	.441	....	....	....	1893	2502	.757	18	39	2146	3555	2027	16	26	6	....	26.5	12.6	3.0	4.9	....
64-65	LA Lakers	7	....	118	53	19	57	.333	....	....	....	15	20	.750	....	....	18	30	18	0	....	....	....	16.9	7.6	2.6	4.3	.557
65-66	LA Lakers	14	....	340	166	70	142	.493	....	....	....	26	42	.619	....	....	41	44	40	0	....	....	....	24.3	11.9	2.9	3.1	.510
66-67	LA Lakers	3	....	86	20	6	25	.240	....	....	....	8	10	.800	....	....	8	16	11	0	....	....	....	28.7	6.7	2.7	5.3	.294
68-69	Atlanta	11	....	360	154	53	135	.393	....	....	....	48	61	.787	....	....	33	43	38	0	....	....	....	32.7	14.0	3.0	3.9	.394
69-70	Atlanta	7	....	255	150	65	130	.500	....	....	....	20	32	.625	....	....	24	54	23	0	....	....	....	36.4	21.4	3.4	7.7	.624
70-71	Atlanta	5	....	202	70	25	76	.329	....	....	....	20	25	.800	....	....	25	27	22	1	....	....	....	40.4	14.0	5.0	5.4	.331
72-73	Golden State	11	....	215	72	30	84	.357	....	....	....	12	12	1.000	....	....	20	28	24	0	....	....	....	19.5	6.5	1.8	2.5	.300
NBA Playoff Totals		58	....	1576	685	268	649	.413	....	....	....	149	202	.738	....	....	169	242	176	1	....	....	....	27.2	11.8	2.9	4.2	....

• ABDUL-RAUF, Mahmoud

Mahmoud Abdul-Rauf aka.: Chris Wayne Jackson

Born: Mar. 9, 1969. Gulfport, MS, United States. Height: 6'1". Weight: 162 lbs. Drafted: 1990 College: Louisiana State

YEAR	TEAM	GP	GS	MIN	PTS	FGM	FGA	FG%	3PM	3PA	3P%	FTM	FTA	FT%	ORB	DRB	TRB	AST	PF	DQ	STL	BLK	TO	MPG	PPG	RPG	APG	PCM
90-91	Denver	67	19	1505	942	417	1009	.413	24	100	.240	84	98	.857	34	87	121	206	149	2	55	4	107	22.5	14.1	1.8	3.1	.400
91-92	Denver	81	11	1538	837	356	845	.421	31	94	.330	94	108	.870	22	92	114	192	130	0	44	4	113	19.0	10.3	1.4	2.4	.369
92-93	Denver	81	81	2710	1553	633	1407	.450	70	197	.355	217	232	.935	51	174	225	344	179	0	84	8	186	33.5	19.2	2.8	4.2	.454
93-94	Denver	80	78	2617	1437	588	1279	.460	42	133	.316	219	229	**.956**	27	141	168	362	150	1	82	10	152	32.7	18.0	2.1	4.5	.467
94-95	Denver	73	43	2082	1165	472	1005	.470	83	215	.386	138	156	.885	32	105	137	263	126	0	77	9	117	28.5	16.0	1.9	3.6	.469
95-96	Denver	57	53	2029	1095	414	955	.434	121	309	.392	146	157	**.930**	26	112	138	389	117	0	64	3	114	35.6	19.2	2.4	6.8	.505
96-97	Sacramento	75	51	2131	1031	411	924	.445	94	246	.382	115	136	.846	16	106	122	189	174	3	56	6	120	28.4	13.7	1.6	2.5	.340
97-98	Sacramento	31	0	530	227	103	273	.377	5	31	.161	16	16	1.000	6	31	37	58	31	0	16	1	19	17.1	7.3	1.2	1.9	.287
00-01	Vancouver	41	0	486	266	120	246	.488	4	14	.286	22	29	.759	5	20	25	76	50	0	9	1	26	11.9	6.5	0.6	1.9	.451
NBA Season Totals		586	336	15628	8553	3514	7943	.442	474	1339	.354	1051	1161	.905	219	868	1087	2079	1106	6	487	46	954	26.7	14.6	1.9	3.5	....
93-94	Denver	12	12	339	155	57	154	.370	12	37	.324	29	31	.935	3	15	18	30	29	0	5	1	14	28.3	12.9	1.5	2.5	.276
94-95	Denver	3	2	76	40	12	33	.364	2	12	.167	14	14	1.000	2	3	5	5	8	0	2	0	8	25.3	13.3	1.7	1.7	.275
NBA Playoff Totals		15	14	415	195	69	187	.369	14	49	.286	43	45	.956	5	18	23	35	37	0	7	1	22	27.7	13.0	1.5	2.3	....

• ABDUL-WAHAD, Tariq

Tariq Abdul-Wahad aka.: Olivier Michael Saint-Jean

Born: Nov. 3, 1974. Maisons Alfort, France. Height: 6'6". Weight: 223 lbs. Drafted: 1997 College: Michigan

YEAR	TEAM	GP	GS	MIN	PTS	FGM	FGA	FG%	3PM	3PA	3P%	FTM	FTA	FT%	ORB	DRB	TRB	AST	PF	DQ	STL	BLK	TO	MPG	PPG	RPG	APG	PCM
97-98	Sacramento	59	16	959	376	144	357	.403	4	19	.211	84	125	.672	44	72	116	51	81	0	35	13	65	16.3	6.4	2.0	0.9	.283
97-98	Sacramento	49	49	1205	454	177	407	.435	6	21	.286	94	136	.691	72	114	186	50	121	0	50	16	70	24.6	9.3	3.8	1.0	.327
99-00	Orlando	46	46	1205	563	223	515	.433	2	21	.095	115	151	.762	77	162	239	72	116	1	53	16	87	26.2	12.2	5.2	1.6	.422
99-00	Denver	15	10	373	134	51	131	.389	1	2	.500	31	42	.738	24	28	52	26	31	0	6	12	19	24.9	8.9	3.5	1.7	.314
00-01	Denver	29	12	420	111	43	111	.387	4	10	.400	21	36	.583	14	45	59	22	54	0	14	13	34	14.5	3.8	2.0	0.8	.214
01-02	Denver	20	12	417	135	55	145	.379	1	2	.500	24	32	.750	39	39	78	22	51	1	18	9	24	20.9	6.8	3.9	1.1	.298
01-02	Dallas	4	0	24	0	0	2	.000	0	0	.000	0	1	.000	2	4	6	2	5	0	2	1	3	6.0	0.0	1.5	0.5	.129
02-03	Dallas	14	0	204	57	27	58	.466	0	1	.000	3	6	.500	14	26	40	21	26	0	6	3	7	14.6	4.1	2.9	1.5	.376
NBA Season Totals		236	145	4807	1830	720	1726	.417	18	76	.237	372	529	.703	286	490	776	266	485	2	184	83	309	20.4	7.8	3.3	1.1	....
98-99	Sacramento	5	5	99	43	15	33	.455	0	1	.000	13	16	.813	6	13	19	4	8	0	4	4	3	19.8	8.6	3.8	0.8	.484
02-03	Dallas	8	0	79	25	9	30	.300	0	2	.000	7	8	.875	11	11	22	7	6	0	0	0	1	9.9	3.1	2.8	0.9	.373
NBA Playoff Totals		13	5	178	68	24	63	.381	0	3	.000	20	24	.833	17	24	41	11	14	0	4	4	13.7	5.2	3.2	0.8	....	

• ABDUR-RAHIM, Shareef

Shareef Abdur-Rahim

Born: Dec. 11, 1976. Marietta, GA, United States. Height: 6'9". Weight: 225 lbs. Drafted: 1996 College: California

YEAR	TEAM	GP	GS	MIN	PTS	FGM	FGA	FG%	3PM	3PA	3P%	FTM	FTA	FT%	ORB	DRB	TRB	AST	PF	DQ	STL	BLK	TO	MPG	PPG	RPG	APG	PCM
96-97	Vancouver	80	71	2802	1494	550	1214	.453	7	27	.259	387	519	.746	216	339	555	175	199	0	79	79	224	35.0	18.7	6.9	2.2	.487
97-98	Vancouver	82	82	2950	1829	653	1347	.485	21	51	.412	502	640	.784	227	354	581	213	201	0	89	76	254	36.0	22.3	7.1	2.6	.583
98-99	Vancouver	50	50	2021	1152	386	893	.432	11	36	.306	369	439	.841	114	260	374	172	137	1	69	55	**186**	40.4	23.0	7.5	3.4	.533
99-00	Vancouver	82	82	3223	1663	594	1277	.465	29	96	.302	446	551	.809	218	607	825	271	244	1	89	87	249	39.3	20.3	10.1	3.3	.578

YEAR	TEAM	GP	GS	MIN	PTS	FGM	FGA	FG%	3PM	3PA	3P%	FTM	FTA	FT%	ORB	DRB	TRB	AST	PF	DQ	STL	BLK	TO	MPG	PPG	RPG	APG	PCM
00-01	Vancouver	81	81	3241	1663	604	1280	.472	12	64	.188	443	531	.834	175	560	735	250	238	1	90	77	231	40.0	20.5	9.1	3.1	.552
01-02	Atlanta	77	77	2980	1636	598	1297	.461	21	70	.300	419	523	.801	198	498	696	239	214	2	98	81	250	38.7	21.2	9.0	3.1	.566
02-03	Atlanta	81	81	3083	1608	566	1183	.478	21	60	.350	455	541	.841	175	502	677	242	240	2	87	39	210	38.1	19.9	8.4	3.0	.552
NBA Season Totals		533	524	20300	11045	3951	8491	.465	122	404	.302	3021	3744	.807	1323	3120	4443	1562	1473	7	601	494	1604	38.1	20.7	8.3	2.9	....

• ABERNETHY, Tom

Thomas Craig Abernethy

Born: May 6, 1954. South Bend, IN, United States.   Height: 6'7".   Weight: 220 lbs.   Drafted: 1976   College: Indiana

YEAR	TEAM	GP	GS	MIN	PTS	FGM	FGA	FG%	3PM	3PA	3P%	FTM	FTA	FT%	ORB	DRB	TRB	AST	PF	DQ	STL	BLK	TO	MPG	PPG	RPG	APG	PCM
76-77	LA Lakers	70	....	1378	439	169	349	.484	....	....	....	101	134	.754	113	178	291	98	118	1	49	10	....	19.7	6.3	4.2	1.4	.422
77-78	LA Lakers	73	....	1317	493	201	404	.498	....	....	....	91	111	.820	105	160	265	101	122	1	55	22	51	18.0	6.8	3.6	1.4	.472
78-79	Golden State	70	....	1219	422	176	342	.515	....	....	....	70	94	.745	74	142	216	79	133	1	39	13	35	17.4	6.0	3.1	1.1	.409
79-80	Golden State	67	....	1222	362	153	318	.481	0	1	.000	56	82	.683	62	129	191	87	118	0	35	12	40	18.2	5.4	2.9	1.3	.345
80-81	Golden State	10	....	39	4	1	3	.333	0	0	.000	2	3	.667	1	7	8	1	5	0	1	0	2	3.9	0.4	0.8	0.1	.177
80-81	Indiana	29	....	259	59	24	56	.429	0	1	.000	11	19	.579	19	21	40	18	29	0	6	3	6	8.9	2.0	1.4	0.6	.277
NBA Season Totals		319	....	5434	1779	724	1472	.492	0	2	.000	331	443	.747	374	637	1011	384	525	3	185	60	134	17.0	5.6	3.2	1.2	....
76-77	LA Lakers	11	....	214	64	21	50	.420	....	....	....	22	27	.815	12	28	40	22	16	0	7	2	....	19.5	5.8	3.6	2.0	.418
77-78	LA Lakers	2	....	12	4	1	4	.250	....	....	....	2	2	1.000	2	0	2	1	2	0	0	0	0	6.0	2.0	1.0	0.5	.281
NBA Playoff Totals		13	....	226	68	22	54	.407	....	....	....	24	29	.828	14	28	42	23	18	0	7	2	0	17.4	5.2	3.2	1.8	....

• ABLE, Forest

Forest Edward (Frosty) Able

Born: July 27, 1932.   Height: 6'3".   Weight: 180 lbs.   Drafted: 1956   College: Western Kentucky

YEAR	TEAM	GP	GS	MIN	PTS	FGM	FGA	FG%	3PM	3PA	3P%	FTM	FTA	FT%	ORB	DRB	TRB	AST	PF	DQ	STL	BLK	TO	MPG	PPG	RPG	APG	PCM
56-57	Syracuse	1	....	1	0	0	2	.000	....	....	....	0	0	.000	....	....	1	1	1	0	....	....	....	1.0	0.0	1.0	1.0	.135
NBA Season Totals		1	....	1	0	0	2	.000	....	....	....	0	0	.000	....	....	1	1	1	0	....	....	....	1.0	0.0	1.0	1.0	

• ABRAMOVIC, John

John (Brooms) Abramovic Jr.

Born: Feb. 9, 1919. Etna, PA, United States. Died: June 9, 2000.   Height: 6'3".   Weight: 195 lbs.   Drafted: —   College: Salem

YEAR	TEAM	GP	GS	MIN	PTS	FGM	FGA	FG%	3PM	3PA	3P%	FTM	FTA	FT%	ORB	DRB	TRB	AST	PF	DQ	STL	BLK	TO	MPG	PPG	RPG	APG	PCM
46-47	Pittsburgh	47	....	....	527	202	834	.242	....	....	....	123	178	.691	....	....	....	35	161	....	....	....	....	11.2	....	0.7	....
47-48	Syracuse-N	35	....	....	186	72	....	....	....	....	....	42	54	**.778**	....	....	....	....	96	....	....	....	....	5.3	....	....	....
47-48	St. Louis	4	....	....	4	1	10	.100	....	....	....	2	4	.500	....	....	....	1	5	....	....	....	....	1.0	....	0.3	....
47-48	Baltimore	5	....	....	2	0	11	.000	....	....	....	2	3	.667	....	....	....	1	5	....	....	....	....	0.4	....	0.2	....
NBA Season Totals		56	....	....	533	203	855	.237	....	....	....	127	185	.686	....	....	....	37	171	....	....	....	....	9.5	....	0.7	....
NBL Season Totals		35	....	....	186	72	....	....	....	....	....	42	54		....	....	....	....	96	....	....	....	....	5.3	....	....	
Career Totals		91	....	....	719	275	855		....	....	....	169	239		....	....	....	37	267	....	....	....	....	7.9	....	0.4	
47-48	Syracuse-N	3	....	....	12	5	....	....	....	....	....	2	3	.667	....	....	....	....	....	....	....	....	....	4.0	....	....	
NBL Playoff Totals		3	....	....	12	5	....	....	....	....	....	2	3		....	....	....	....	....	....	....	....	....	4.0	....	....	

• ACKERMAN, Don

Donald D. (Buddy) Ackerman

Born: Sept. 4, 1930. New York, NY, United States.   Height: 6'   Weight: 183 lbs.   Drafted: 1953   College: Long Island University

YEAR	TEAM	GP	GS	MIN	PTS	FGM	FGA	FG%	3PM	3PA	3P%	FTM	FTA	FT%	ORB	DRB	TRB	AST	PF	DQ	STL	BLK	TO	MPG	PPG	RPG	APG	PCM
53-54	New York	28	....	220	43	14	63	.222	....	....	....	15	28	.536	....	....	15	23	43	0	....	....	....	7.9	1.5	0.5	0.8	.130
NBA Season Totals		28	....	220	43	14	63	.222	....	....	....	15	28	.536	....	....	15	23	43	0	....	....	....	7.9	1.5	0.5	0.8	....
53-54	New York	4	....	20	2	1	3	.333	....	....	....	0	0	.000	....	....	4	1	7	0	....	....	....	5.0	0.5	1.0	0.3	.111
NBA Playoff Totals		4	....	20	2	1	3	.333	....	....	....	0	0	.000	....	....	4	1	7	0	....	....	....	5.0	0.5	1.0	0.3	

• ACRES, Mark

Mark Richard Acres

Born: Nov. 15, 1962. Inglewood, CA, United States.   Height: 6'11".   Weight: 220 lbs.   Drafted: 1985   College: Oral Roberts

YEAR	TEAM	GP	GS	MIN	PTS	FGM	FGA	FG%	3PM	3PA	3P%	FTM	FTA	FT%	ORB	DRB	TRB	AST	PF	DQ	STL	BLK	TO	MPG	PPG	RPG	APG	PCM
87-88	Boston	79	5	1151	287	108	203	.532	0	0	.000	71	111	.640	105	165	270	42	198	2	29	27	55	14.6	3.6	3.4	0.5	.334
88-89	Boston	62	0	632	137	55	114	.482	1	1	1.000	26	48	.542	59	87	146	19	94	0	19	6	25	10.2	2.2	2.4	0.3	.292
89-90	Orlando	80	50	1691	362	138	285	.484	3	4	.750	83	120	.692	154	277	431	67	248	4	36	25	72	21.1	4.5	5.4	0.8	.329
90-91	Orlando	68	0	1313	285	109	214	.509	1	3	.333	66	101	.653	140	219	359	25	218	4	25	25	41	19.3	4.2	5.3	0.4	.334
91-92	Orlando	68	6	926	208	78	151	.517	1	3	.333	51	67	.761	97	155	252	22	140	1	25	15	34	13.6	3.1	3.7	0.3	.357
92-93	Houston	6	0	23	6	2	9	.222	1	2	.500	1	2	.500	2	4	6	0	2	0	0	0	2	3.8	1.0	1.0	0.0	.078
92-93	Washington	12	7	246	58	24	40	.600	0	0	.000	10	14	.714	24	37	61	5	32	0	3	6	11	20.5	4.8	5.1	0.4	.352
NBA Season Totals		375	68	5982	1343	514	1016	.506	7	13	.538	308	463	.665	581	944	1525	180	932	11	137	104	240	16.0	3.6	4.1	0.5	....
87-88	Boston	17	0	158	37	14	26	.538	0	1	.000	9	18	.500	14	22	36	2	33	0	1	1	6	9.3	2.2	2.1	0.1	.242
88-89	Boston	2	0	2	0	0	1	.000	0	1	.000	0	0	.000	0	1	1	0	0	0	0	0	0	1.0	0.0	0.5	0.0	.000
NBA Playoff Totals		19	0	160	37	14	27	.519	0	2	.000	9	18	.500	14	23	37	2	33	0	1	1	6	8.4	1.9	1.9	0.1	....

• ACTON, Bud

Charles R. (Bud) Acton

Born: Jan. 11, 1942.   Height: 6'6".   Weight: 210 lbs.   Drafted: —   College: Hillsdale (MI)

YEAR	TEAM	GP	GS	MIN	PTS	FGM	FGA	FG%	3PM	3PA	3P%	FTM	FTA	FT%	ORB	DRB	TRB	AST	PF	DQ	STL	BLK	TO	MPG	PPG	RPG	APG	PCM
67-68	San Diego	23	....	195	77	29	74	.392	....	....	....	19	29	.655	....	....	47	11	35	0	....	....	....	8.5	3.3	2.0	0.5	.379
NBA Season Totals		23	....	195	77	29	74	.392	....	....	....	19	29	.655	....	....	47	11	35	0	....	....	....	8.5	3.3	2.0	0.5	

• ADAMS, Alvan

Alvan Leigh (Double A, The Oklahoma Kid) Adams

Born: July 19, 1954. Lawrence, KS, United States.   Height: 6'9".   Weight: 210 lbs.   Drafted: 1975   College: Oklahoma

YEAR	TEAM	GP	GS	MIN	PTS	FGM	FGA	FG%	3PM	3PA	3P%	FTM	FTA	FT%	ORB	DRB	TRB	AST	PF	DQ	STL	BLK	TO	MPG	PPG	RPG	APG	PCM
75-76	Phoenix	80	....	2656	1519	629	1341	.469	....	....	....	261	355	.735	215	512	727	450	274	6	121	116	....	33.2	19.0	9.1	5.6	.711
76-77	Phoenix	72	....	2278	1296	522	1102	.474	....	....	....	252	334	.754	180	472	652	322	260	4	95	87	....	31.6	18.0	9.1	4.5	.692

YEAR	TEAM	GP	GS	MIN	PTS	FGM	FGA	FG%	3PM	3PA	3P%	FTM	FTA	FT%	ORB	DRB	TRB	AST	PF	DQ	STL	BLK	TO	MPG	PPG	RPG	APG	PCM
77-78	Phoenix	70	....	1914	1082	434	895	.485	....	....	....	214	293	.730	158	407	565	225	242	8	86	63	231	27.3	15.5	8.1	3.2	.634
78-79	Phoenix	77	....	2364	1369	569	1073	.530	....	....	....	231	289	.799	220	485	705	360	246	4	110	63	277	30.7	17.8	9.2	4.7	.726
79-80	Phoenix	75	....	2168	1118	465	875	.531	0	2	.000	188	236	.797	158	451	609	322	237	4	108	55	218	28.9	14.9	8.1	4.3	.679
80-81	Phoenix	75	....	2054	1115	458	870	.526	0	0	.000	199	259	.768	157	389	546	344	226	2	106	69	225	27.4	14.9	7.3	4.6	.699
81-82	Phoenix	79	75	2393	1196	507	1027	.494	0	1	.000	182	233	.781	138	448	586	356	269	7	114	78	198	30.3	15.1	7.4	4.5	.622
82-83	Phoenix	80	75	2447	1135	477	981	.486	1	3	.333	180	217	.829	161	387	548	376	287	7	114	74	240	30.6	14.2	6.9	4.7	.570
83-84	Phoenix	70	13	1452	670	269	582	.462	0	4	.000	132	160	.825	118	201	319	219	195	1	73	32	119	20.7	9.6	4.6	3.1	.546
84-85	Phoenix	82	69	2136	1202	476	915	.520	0	0	.000	250	283	.883	153	347	500	308	254	2	115	48	197	26.0	14.7	6.1	3.8	.666
85-86	Phoenix	78	45	2005	841	341	679	.502	0	2	.000	159	203	.783	148	329	477	324	272	7	103	46	203	25.7	10.8	6.1	4.2	.559
86-87	Phoenix	68	40	1690	756	311	618	.503	0	1	.000	134	170	.788	91	247	338	223	207	3	62	37	136	24.9	11.1	5.0	3.3	.518
87-88	Phoenix	82	25	1646	611	251	506	.496	1	2	.500	108	128	.844	118	247	365	183	245	3	82	41	139	20.1	7.5	4.5	2.2	.468
NBA Season Totals		988	342	27203	13910	5709	11464	.498	2	15	.133	2490	3160	.788	2015	4922	6937	4012	3214	58	1289	809	2183	27.5	14.1	7.0	4.1	....
75-76	Phoenix	19	....	668	341	137	303	.452	....	....	....	67	82	.817	54	137	191	98	60	1	24	20	....	35.2	17.9	10.1	5.2	.662
77-78	Phoenix	2	....	71	32	15	33	.455	....	....	....	2	2	1.000	8	8	16	4	8	0	2	1	9	35.5	16.0	8.0	2.0	.366
78-79	Phoenix	12	....	372	154	66	139	.475	....	....	....	22	31	.710	25	65	90	53	41	1	11	12	36	31.0	12.8	7.5	4.4	.520
79-80	Phoenix	8	....	251	129	56	99	.566	0	0	.000	17	19	.895	18	59	77	46	24	1	7	10	24	31.4	16.1	9.6	5.8	.765
80-81	Phoenix	7	....	218	74	27	60	.450	0	0	.000	20	28	.714	11	30	41	26	20	0	4	1	19	31.1	10.6	5.9	3.7	.386
81-82	Phoenix	7	7	233	118	48	92	.522	0	0	.000	22	28	.786	19	32	51	26	22	0	14	10	21	33.3	16.9	7.3	3.7	.611
82-83	Phoenix	3	3	84	35	15	32	.469	0	0	.000	5	7	.714	3	15	18	14	15	0	2	5	5	28.0	11.7	6.0	4.7	.541
83-84	Phoenix	17	0	312	142	53	126	.421	0	0	.000	36	53	.679	27	60	87	42	53	0	17	11	34	18.4	8.4	5.1	2.5	.519
84-85	Phoenix	3	3	79	51	23	46	.500	0	0	.000	5	6	.833	4	13	17	11	8	0	7	1	6	26.3	17.0	5.7	3.7	.694
NBA Playoff Totals		78	13	2288	1076	440	930	.473	0	0	.000	196	256	.766	169	419	588	320	251	3	88	71	154	29.3	13.8	7.5	4.1	....

• ADAMS, Don

Donald L. Adams

Born: Nov. 27, 1947. Atlanta, GA, United States. Height: 6'6". Weight: 210 lbs. Drafted: 1970 College: Northwestern

70-71	San Diego	82	....	2374	937	391	957	.409	....	....	....	155	212	.731	....	....	581	173	344	11	....	....	....	29.0	11.4	7.1	2.1	.411
71-72	Houston	3	....	41	13	6	19	.316	....	....	....	1	2	.500	....	....	8	3	7	1	....	....	....	13.7	4.3	2.7	1.0	.211
71-72	Atlanta	70	....	2030	818	307	779	.394	....	....	....	204	273	.747	....	....	494	137	259	5	....	....	....	29.0	11.7	7.1	2.0	.419
72-73	Atlanta	4	....	76	23	8	38	.211	....	....	....	7	8	.875	....	....	22	5	11	0	....	....	....	19.0	5.8	5.5	1.3	.220
72-73	Detroit	70	....	1798	652	257	640	.402	....	....	....	138	176	.784	....	....	419	112	220	0	....	....	....	25.7	9.3	6.0	1.6	.389
73-74	Detroit	74	....	2298	759	303	742	.408	....	....	....	153	201	.761	133	315	448	141	242	2	110	12	....	31.1	10.3	6.1	1.9	.350
74-75	St. Louis-A	16	....	342	101	42	98	.429	0	1	.000	17	22	.773	21	47	68	54	38	....	13	2	27	21.4	6.3	4.3	3.4	.446
74-75	Detroit	51	....	1376	299	127	315	.403	....	....	....	45	78	.577	63	181	244	75	179	1	69	20	....	27.0	5.9	4.8	1.5	.249
75-76	St. Louis-A	20	....	725	261	99	251	.394	0	2	.000	63	83	.759	44	72	116	88	80	....	38	7	52	36.3	13.1	5.8	4.4	.389
75-76	Buffalo	56	....	704	174	67	170	.394	....	....	....	40	57	.702	38	107	145	73	128	1	30	7	....	12.6	3.1	2.6	1.3	.328
76-77	Buffalo	77	....	1710	561	216	526	.411	....	....	....	129	173	.746	130	241	371	150	201	0	74	16	....	22.2	7.3	4.8	1.9	.397
NBA Season Totals		487	....	12407	4236	1682	4186	.402	....	....	....	872	1180	.739	364	844	2732	869	1591	21	283	55	....	25.5	8.7	5.6	1.8	....
ABA Season Totals		36	....	1067	362	141	349	.404	0	3	.000	80	105	.762	65	119	184	142	118	....	51	9	79	29.6	10.1	5.1	3.9	....
Career Totals		523	....	13474	4598	1823	4535	.402	0	3	.000	952	1285	.741	429	963	2916	1011	1709	21	334	64	79	25.8	8.8	5.6	1.9	....
71-72	Atlanta	6	....	188	56	20	56	.357	....	....	....	16	23	.696	....	....	38	12	25	1	....	....	....	31.3	9.3	6.3	2.0	.306
73-74	Detroit	7	....	256	64	28	73	.384	....	....	....	8	14	.571	17	34	51	20	26	0	6	1	....	36.6	9.1	7.3	2.9	.307
74-75	St. Louis-A	10	....	301	90	35	82	.427	0	0	.000	20	28	.714	12	35	47	46	32	....	17	11	28	30.1	9.0	4.7	4.6	.410
75-76	Buffalo	9	....	122	36	15	36	.417	....	....	....	6	7	.857	8	19	27	13	23	0	2	0	....	13.6	4.0	3.0	1.4	.375
NBA Playoff Totals		22	....	566	156	63	165	.382	....	....	....	30	44	.682	25	53	116	45	74	1	8	1	....	25.7	7.1	5.3	2.0	....
ABA Playoff Totals		10	....	301	90	35	82	.427	0	0	.000	20	28	.714	12	35	47	46	32	....	17	11	28	30.1	9.0	4.7	4.6	....
Career Playoff Totals		32	....	867	246	98	247	.397	0	0	.000	50	72	.694	37	88	163	91	106	1	25	12	28	27.1	7.7	5.1	2.8	....

• ADAMS, George

George Adams

Born: May 15, 1949. Kings Mountain, NC, United States. Height: 6'5". Weight: 210 lbs. Drafted: 1972 College: Gardner-Webb

72-73	San Diego-A	60	....	865	373	153	312	.490	2	7	.286	65	83	.783	75	130	205	64	97	0	....	....	67	14.4	6.2	3.4	1.1	.501
73-74	San Diego-A	80	....	1433	585	253	506	.500	1	7	.143	78	103	.757	124	217	341	127	111	....	44	23	119	17.9	7.3	4.3	1.6	.521
74-75	San Diego-A	75	....	1605	694	310	622	.498	1	3	.333	73	86	.849	114	213	327	126	164	....	44	36	106	21.4	9.3	4.4	1.7	.479
ABA Season Totals		215	....	3903	1652	716	1440	.497	4	17	.235	216	272	.794	313	560	873	317	372	0	88	59	292	18.2	7.7	4.1	1.5	....
72-73	San Diego-A	3	....	23	8	4	8	.500	0	0	.000	0	0	.000	3	3	6	3	1	0	....	....	2	7.7	2.7	2.0	1.0	.550
73-74	San Diego-A	6	....	161	72	30	58	.517	0	1	.000	12	16	.750	13	15	28	12	13	....	4	4	14	26.8	12.0	4.7	2.0	.487
ABA Playoff Totals		9	....	184	80	34	66	.515	0	1	.000	12	16	.750.	16	18	34	15	14	0	4	4	16	20.4	8.9	3.8	1.7	....

• ADAMS, Howard

Howard O'Neale Adams

Born: Jan. 21, 1919. El Paso, AR, United States. Height: 6'3". Weight: 195 lbs. Drafted: — College: Arkansas

42-43	Oshkosh-N	13	....	....	9	4	....	....	....	....	....	1	....	....	....	....	....	....	....	....	....	....	....	....	0.7	....	....	....
NBL Season Totals		13	....	....	9	4	....	....	....	....	....	1	....	....	....	....	....	....	....	....	....	....	....	....	0.7	....	....	....

• ADAMS, Michael

Michael Adams

Born: Jan. 19, 1963. Hartford, CT, United States. Height: 5'10". Weight: 162 lbs. Drafted: 1985 College: Boston College

85-86	Sacramento	18	0	139	40	16	44	.364	0	3	.000	8	12	.667	2	4	6	22	9	0	9	1	11	7.7	2.2	0.3	1.2	.260
86-87	Washington	63	0	1303	453	160	393	.407	28	102	.275	105	124	.847	38	85	123	244	88	0	85	6	82	20.7	7.2	2.0	3.9	.437
87-88	Denver	82	75	2778	1137	416	927	.449	139	**379**	.367	166	199	.834	40	183	223	503	138	0	168	16	148	33.9	13.9	2.7	6.1	.489
88-89	Denver	77	77	2787	1424	468	1082	.433	**166**	**466**	.356	322	393	.819	71	212	283	490	149	0	166	11	177	36.2	18.5	3.7	6.4	.552
89-90	Denver	79	74	2690	1221	398	989	.402	**158**	**432**	.366	267	314	.850	49	176	225	495	133	0	121	3	142	34.1	15.5	2.8	6.3	.484
90-91	Denver	66	66	2346	1752	560	1421	.394	167	**564**	.296	465	529	.879	58	198	256	693	162	1	147	6	238	35.5	26.5	3.9	10.5	.743
91-92	Washington	78	78	2795	1408	485	1233	.393	125	386	.324	313	360	.869	58	252	310	594	162	1	145	9	211	35.8	18.1	4.0	7.6	.532
92-93	Washington	70	70	2499	1035	365	831	.439	68	212	.321	237	277	.856	52	188	240	526	146	0	100	4	175	35.7	14.8	3.4	7.5	.493
93-94	Washington	70	67	2337	849	285	698	.408	55	191	.288	224	270	.830	37	146	183	480	140	0	96	6	168	33.4	12.1	2.6	6.9	.433

YEAR	TEAM	GP	GS	MIN	PTS	FGM	FGA	FG%	3PM	3PA	3P%	FTM	FTA	FT%	ORB	DRB	TRB	AST	PF	DQ	STL	BLK	TO	MPG	PPG	RPG	APG	PCM
94-95	Charlotte	29	0	443	188	67	148	.453	29	81	.358	25	30	.833	6	23	29	95	41	0	23	1	26	15.3	6.5	1.0	3.3	.489
95-96	Charlotte	21	3	329	114	37	83	.446	14	41	.341	26	35	.743	5	17	22	67	25	0	21	4	25	15.7	5.4	1.0	3.2	.445
NBA Season Totals		653	510	20446	9621	3257	7849	.415	949	2857	.332	2158	2543	.849	416	1484	1900	4209	1193	2	1081	67	1403	31.3	14.7	2.9	6.4	....
86-87	Washington	3	1	82	19	8	25	.320	2	9	.222	1	3	.333	0	7	7	10	6	0	7	0	5	27.3	6.3	2.3	3.3	.226
87-88	Denver	11	11	406	147	47	130	.362	17	54	.315	36	41	.878	9	27	36	64	19	0	18	2	23	36.9	13.4	3.3	5.8	.388
88-89	Denver	2	1	75	47	15	36	.417	10	22	.455	7	8	.875	5	12	17	9	6	0	3	0	8	37.5	23.5	8.5	4.5	.600
89-90	Denver	3	3	105	39	13	34	.382	6	20	.300	7	8	.875	0	6	6	18	10	0	4	0	8	35.0	13.0	2.0	6.0	.335
94-95	Charlotte	1	0	11	4	2	5	.400	0	2	.000	0	0	.000	0	1	1	2	0	0	0	0	0	11.0	4.0	1.0	2.0	.386
NBA Playoff Totals		20	16	679	256	85	230	.370	35	107	.327	51	60	.850	14	53	67	103	41	0	32	2	44	34.0	12.8	3.4	5.2	....

• ADAMS, Ray
Raymond Adams

Born: 1914.   Height: 6'2".   Weight: 185 lbs.   Drafted: —   College: DePaul

YEAR	TEAM	GP	GS	MIN	PTS	FGM	FGA	FG%	3PM	3PA	3P%	FTM	FTA	FT%	ORB	DRB	TRB	AST	PF	DQ	STL	BLK	TO	MPG	PPG	RPG	APG	PCM
37-38	Oshkosh-N	12	....	....	62	26	....	....	....	....	....	10	....	....	....	....	....	....	....	....	....	....	....	....	5.2	....	....	....
38-39	Oshkosh-N	24	....	....	110	42	....	....	....	....	....	26	....	....	....	....	....	....	....	....	....	....	....	....	4.6	....	....	....
39-40	Oshkosh-N	1	....	....	3	1	....	....	....	....	....	1	....	....	....	....	....	....	....	....	....	....	....	....	3.0	....	....	....
40-41	Chicago-N	20	....	....	60	23	....	....	....	....	....	14	....	....	....	....	....	....	....	....	....	....	....	....	3.0	....	....	....
NBL Season Totals		57	....	....	235	92	....	....	....	....	....	51	....	....	....	....	....	....	....	....	....	....	....	....	4.1	....	....	....
37-38	Oshkosh-N	5	....	....	17	5	....	....	....	....	....	7	....	....	....	....	....	....	....	....	....	....	....	....	3.4	....	....	....
38-39	Oshkosh-N	5	....	....	9	3	....	....	....	....	....	3	....	....	....	....	....	....	....	....	....	....	....	....	1.8	....	....	....
NBL Playoff Totals		10	....	....	26	8	....	....	....	....	....	10	....	....	....	....	....	....	....	....	....	....	....	....	2.6	....	....	....

• ADAMS, Sparky
Sparky Adams

Born: 1917.   Height: 6'1".   Weight: 185 lbs.   Drafted: —   College: Marquette

YEAR	TEAM	GP	GS	MIN	PTS	FGM	FGA	FG%	3PM	3PA	3P%	FTM	FTA	FT%	ORB	DRB	TRB	AST	PF	DQ	STL	BLK	TO	MPG	PPG	RPG	APG	PCM
38-39	Sheboygan-N	1	....	....	8	3	....	....	....	....	....	2	....	....	....	....	....	....	....	....	....	....	....	....	8.0	....	....	....
39-40	Sheboygan-N	26	....	....	119	43	....	....	....	....	....	33	....	....	....	....	....	....	....	....	....	....	....	....	4.6	....	....	....
NBL Season Totals		27	....	....	127	46	....	....	....	....	....	35	....	....	....	....	....	....	....	....	....	....	....	....	4.7	....	....	....
39-40	Sheboygan-N	3	....	....	5	2	....	....	....	....	....	1	....	....	....	....	....	....	....	....	....	....	....	....	1.7	....	....	....
NBL Playoff Totals		3	....	....	5	2	....	....	....	....	....	1	....	....	....	....	....	....	....	....	....	....	....	....	1.7	....	....	....

• ADAMS, Willie
Willie Adams

Born: —.   Height: 5'11".   Weight: 160 lbs.   Drafted: —   College: —

YEAR	TEAM	GP	GS	MIN	PTS	FGM	FGA	FG%	3PM	3PA	3P%	FTM	FTA	FT%	ORB	DRB	TRB	AST	PF	DQ	STL	BLK	TO	MPG	PPG	RPG	APG	PCM
37-38	Fort Wayne-N	16	....	....	58	21	....	....	....	....	....	16	....	....	....	....	....	....	....	....	....	....	....	....	3.6	....	....	....
NBL Season Totals		16	....	....	58	21	....	....	....	....	....	16	....	....	....	....	....	....	....	....	....	....	....	....	3.6	....	....	....

• ADDISON, Rafael
Rafael Addison

Born: July 22, 1964. Jersey City, NJ, United States.   Height: 6'7".   Weight: 215 lbs.   Drafted: 1986   College: Syracuse

YEAR	TEAM	GP	GS	MIN	PTS	FGM	FGA	FG%	3PM	3PA	3P%	FTM	FTA	FT%	ORB	DRB	TRB	AST	PF	DQ	STL	BLK	TO	MPG	PPG	RPG	APG	PCM
86-87	Phoenix	62	12	711	359	146	331	.441	16	50	.320	51	64	.797	41	65	106	45	75	1	27	7	56	11.5	5.8	1.7	0.7	.383
91-92	New Jersey	76	8	1175	444	187	432	.433	14	49	.286	56	76	.737	65	100	165	68	109	1	28	28	46	15.5	5.8	2.2	0.9	.334
92-93	New Jersey	68	15	1164	428	182	411	.443	7	34	.206	57	70	.814	45	87	132	53	125	0	23	11	61	17.1	6.3	1.9	0.8	.262
94-95	Detroit	79	16	1776	656	279	586	.476	24	83	.289	74	99	.747	67	175	242	109	236	2	53	25	79	22.5	8.3	3.1	1.4	.331
95-96	Charlotte	53	0	516	171	77	165	.467	0	9	.000	17	22	.773	25	65	90	30	74	0	9	9	27	9.7	3.2	1.7	0.6	.308
96-97	Charlotte	41	3	355	128	49	122	.402	8	20	.400	22	28	.786	19	26	45	34	52	0	8	3	16	8.7	3.1	1.1	0.8	.300
NBA Season Totals		379	54	5697	2186	920	2047	.449	69	245	.282	277	359	.772	262	518	780	339	671	4	148	83	285	15.0	5.8	2.1	0.9	....
91-92	New Jersey	1	0	9	5	2	7	.286	1	2	.500	0	0	.000	0	0	0	1	0	0	0	0	0	9.0	5.0	0.0	1.0	.158
92-93	New Jersey	5	0	53	17	7	21	.333	0	0	.000	3	3	1.000	3	3	6	5	3	0	3	0	3	10.6	3.4	1.2	1.0	.254
NBA Playoff Totals		6	0	62	22	9	28	.321	1	2	.500	3	3	1.000	3	3	6	6	3	0	3	0	3	10.3	3.7	1.0	1.0	....

• ADELMAN, Rick
Richard Leonard Adelman

Born: June 16, 1946. Lynwood, CA, United States.   Height: 6'1".   Weight: 175 lbs.   Drafted: 1968   College: Loyola (CA)

YEAR	TEAM	GP	GS	MIN	PTS	FGM	FGA	FG%	3PM	3PA	3P%	FTM	FTA	FT%	ORB	DRB	TRB	AST	PF	DQ	STL	BLK	TO	MPG	PPG	RPG	APG	PCM
68-69	San Diego	77	....	1448	485	177	449	.394	....	....	....	131	204	.642	....	....	216	238	158	1	....	....	....	18.8	6.3	2.8	3.1	.427
69-70	San Diego	35	....	717	260	96	247	.389	....	....	....	68	91	.747	....	....	81	113	90	0	....	....	....	20.5	7.4	2.3	3.2	.384
70-71	Portland	81	....	2303	1023	378	895	.422	....	....	....	267	369	.724	....	....	282	380	214	2	....	....	....	28.4	12.6	3.5	4.7	.486
71-72	Portland	80	....	2445	809	329	753	.437	....	....	....	151	201	.751	....	....	229	413	209	2	....	....	....	30.6	10.1	2.9	5.2	.408
72-73	Portland	76	....	1822	501	214	525	.408	....	....	....	73	102	.716	....	....	157	294	155	2	....	....	....	24.0	6.6	2.1	3.9	.343
73-74	Chicago	55	....	618	182	64	170	.376	....	....	....	54	76	.711	16	53	69	56	63	0	36	1	....	11.2	3.3	1.3	1.0	.289
74-75	Chicago	12	....	340	114	43	104	.413	....	....	....	28	39	.718	6	20	26	35	31	0	16	1	....	28.3	9.5	2.2	2.9	.313
74-75	New Orleans	28	....	613	175	67	159	.421	....	....	....	41	59	.695	13	42	55	69	58	1	47	6	....	21.9	6.3	2.0	2.5	.310
74-75	Omaha	18	....	121	30	13	28	.464	....	....	....	4	5	.800	6	8	14	8	12	0	7	1	....	6.7	1.7	0.8	0.4	.271
NBA Season Totals		462	....	10427	3579	1381	3330	.415	....	....	....	817	1146	.713	41	123	1129	1606	990	8	106	9	....	22.6	7.7	2.4	3.5	....
68-69	San Diego	6	....	187	70	24	53	.453	....	....	....	22	37	.595	....	....	15	29	18	0	....	....	....	31.2	11.7	2.5	4.8	.418
73-74	Chicago	9	....	108	39	16	34	.471	....	....	....	7	11	.636	1	9	10	7	5	0	7	0	....	12.0	4.3	1.1	0.8	.337
74-75	Omaha	6	....	34	12	3	9	.333	....	....	....	6	8	.750	1	1	2	3	9	0	1	0	....	5.7	2.0	0.3	0.5	.216
NBA Playoff Totals		21	....	329	121	43	96	.448	....	....	....	35	56	.625	2	10	27	39	32	0	8	0	....	15.7	5.8	1.3	1.9	....

• AGUIRRE, Mark

Mark Anthony Aguirre

Born: Dec. 10, 1959. Chicago, IL, United States. Height: 6'6". Weight: 232 lbs. Drafted: 1981 College: DePaul

YEAR TEAM	GP	GS	MIN	PTS	FGM	FGA	FG%	3PM	3PA	3P%	FTM	FTA	FT%	ORB	DRB	TRB	AST	PF	DQ	STL	BLK	TO	MPG	PPG	RPG	APG	PCM
81-82 Dallas	51	20	1468	955	381	820	.465	25	71	.352	168	247	.680	89	160	249	164	152	0	37	22	133	28.8	18.7	4.9	3.2	.533
82-83 Dallas	81	75	2784	1979	767	1589	.483	16	76	.211	429	589	.728	191	317	508	332	247	5	80	26	259	34.4	24.4	6.3	4.1	.625
83-84 Dallas	79	79	2900	2330	**925**	**1765**	.524	15	56	.268	465	621	.749	161	308	469	358	246	5	80	22	284	36.7	29.5	5.9	4.5	.694
84-85 Dallas	80	79	2699	2055	794	1569	.506	27	85	.318	440	580	.759	188	289	477	249	250	3	60	24	256	33.7	25.7	6.0	3.1	.630
85-86 Dallas	74	73	2501	1670	668	1327	.503	16	56	.286	318	451	.705	177	268	445	339	229	6	62	14	252	33.8	22.6	6.0	4.6	.601
86-87 Dallas	80	80	2663	2056	787	1590	.495	53	150	.353	429	557	.770	181	246	427	254	243	4	84	30	216	33.3	25.7	5.3	3.2	.642
87-88 Dallas	77	77	2610	1932	746	1571	.475	52	172	.302	388	504	.770	182	252	434	278	223	1	70	57	200	33.9	25.1	5.6	3.6	.628
88-89 Dallas	44	44	1529	953	373	829	.450	29	99	.293	178	244	.730	90	145	235	189	128	0	29	29	141	34.8	21.7	5.3	4.3	.512
88-89 Detroit	36	32	1068	558	213	441	.483	22	75	.293	110	149	.738	56	95	151	89	101	2	16	7	68	29.7	15.5	4.2	2.5	.444
89-90 Detroit	78	40	2005	1099	438	898	.488	31	93	.333	192	254	.756	117	188	305	145	201	2	34	19	125	25.7	14.1	3.9	1.9	.457
90-91 Detroit	78	13	2006	1104	420	909	.462	24	78	.308	240	317	.757	134	240	374	139	209	2	47	20	125	25.7	14.2	4.8	1.8	.477
91-92 Detroit	75	12	1582	851	339	787	.431	15	71	.211	158	230	.687	67	169	236	126	171	0	51	11	105	21.1	11.3	3.1	1.7	.402
92-93 Detroit	51	15	1056	503	187	422	.443	30	83	.361	99	129	.767	43	109	152	104	100	1	17	7	66	20.7	9.9	3.0	2.0	.414
93-94 LA Clippers	39	0	859	413	163	348	.468	37	93	.398	50	72	.694	28	88	116	104	98	2	21	8	70	22.0	10.6	3.0	2.7	.430
NBA Season Totals	923	639	27730	18458	7201	14865	.484	392	1258	.312	3664	4944	.741	1704	2874	4578	2870	2598	33	688	296	2300	30.0	20.0	5.0	3.1	....
83-84 Dallas	10	9	350	220	88	184	.478	0	5	.000	44	57	.772	21	55	76	32	34	2	5	5	27	35.0	22.0	7.6	3.2	.566
84-85 Dallas	4	4	164	116	44	89	.494	1	2	.500	27	32	.844	16	14	30	16	16	1	3	0	15	41.0	29.0	7.5	4.0	.598
85-86 Dallas	10	10	345	247	105	214	.491	2	6	.333	35	55	.636	21	50	71	54	28	1	9	0	23	34.5	24.7	7.1	5.4	.679
86-87 Dallas	4	4	130	85	31	62	.500	0	4	.000	23	30	.767	11	13	24	8	15	1	8	0	9	32.5	21.3	6.0	2.0	.584
87-88 Dallas	17	17	558	367	147	294	.500	13	34	.382	60	86	.698	34	66	100	59	49	0	14	9	41	32.8	21.6	5.9	3.5	.599
88-89 Detroit	17	17	462	214	89	182	.489	8	29	.276	28	38	.737	26	49	75	28	38	0	8	3	20	27.2	12.6	4.4	1.6	.425
89-90 Detroit	20	3	439	219	86	184	.467	8	24	.333	39	52	.750	31	60	91	27	51	0	10	3	30	22.0	11.0	4.6	1.4	.445
90-91 Detroit	15	2	397	234	90	178	.506	12	33	.364	42	51	.824	17	44	61	29	41	0	12	1	20	26.5	15.6	4.1	1.9	.529
91-92 Detroit	5	0	113	45	16	48	.333	1	5	.200	12	16	.750	4	5	9	12	9	0	2	1	13	22.6	9.0	1.8	2.4	.187
NBA Playoff Totals	102	66	2958	1747	696	1435	.485	45	142	.317	310	417	.743	181	356	537	265	281	5	71	22	198	29.0	17.1	5.3	2.6	....

• AHEARN, Jake

Jake Ahearn

Born: 1917. Height: 6'2". Weight: 185 lbs. Drafted: — College: St. John's (NY)

YEAR TEAM	GP	GS	MIN	PTS	FGM	FGA	FG%	3PM	3PA	3P%	FTM	FTA	FT%	ORB	DRB	TRB	AST	PF	DQ	STL	BLK	TO	MPG	PPG	RPG	APG	PCM
40-41 Detroit-N	15	....	....	79	32	....	....	....	....	....	15	....	....	....	....	....	....	....	....	....	....	....	....	5.3	....	....	....
NBL Season Totals	15	....	....	79	32	....	....	....	....	....	15	....	....	....	....	....	....	....	....	....	....	....	....	5.3	....	....	....
40-41 Detroit-N	3	....	....	8	3	....	....	....	....	....	2	....	....	....	....	....	....	....	....	....	....	....	....	2.7	....	....	....
NBL Playoff Totals	3	....	....	8	3	....	....	....	....	....	2	....	....	....	....	....	....	....	....	....	....	....	....	2.7	....	....	....

• AINGE, Danny

Daniel Ray Ainge

Born: Mar. 17, 1959. Eugene, OR, United States. Height: 6'4". Weight: 175 lbs. Drafted: 1981 College: Brigham Young

YEAR TEAM	GP	GS	MIN	PTS	FGM	FGA	FG%	3PM	3PA	3P%	FTM	FTA	FT%	ORB	DRB	TRB	AST	PF	DQ	STL	BLK	TO	MPG	PPG	RPG	APG	PCM
81-82 Boston	53	1	564	219	79	221	.357	5	17	.294	56	65	.862	25	31	56	87	86	1	37	3	53	10.6	4.1	1.1	1.6	.316
82-83 Boston	80	76	2048	791	357	720	.496	5	29	.172	72	97	.742	83	131	214	251	259	2	109	6	96	25.6	9.9	2.7	3.1	.401
83-84 Boston	71	3	1154	384	166	361	.460	6	22	.273	46	56	.821	29	87	116	162	143	2	41	4	71	16.3	5.4	1.6	2.3	.337
84-85 Boston	75	73	2564	971	419	792	.529	15	56	.268	118	136	.868	76	192	268	399	228	4	122	6	150	34.2	12.9	3.6	5.3	.454
85-86 Boston	80	78	2407	855	353	701	.504	26	73	.356	123	136	.904	47	188	235	405	204	4	94	7	128	30.1	10.7	2.9	5.1	.440
86-87 Boston	71	66	2499	1053	410	844	.486	85	192	.443	148	165	.897	49	193	242	400	189	3	101	14	142	35.2	14.8	3.4	5.6	.473
87-88 Boston	81	81	3018	1270	482	982	.491	**148**	357	.415	158	180	.878	59	190	249	503	203	1	115	17	154	37.3	15.7	3.1	6.2	.480
88-89 Boston	45	28	1349	714	271	589	.460	58	155	.374	114	128	.891	37	117	154	215	108	0	52	1	81	30.0	15.9	3.4	4.8	.525
88-89 Sacramento	28	26	1028	567	209	462	.452	58	150	.387	91	112	.813	34	67	101	187	78	1	41	7	64	36.7	20.3	3.6	6.7	.549
89-90 Sacramento	75	68	2727	1342	506	1154	.438	108	289	.374	222	267	.831	69	257	326	453	238	2	113	18	188	36.4	17.9	4.3	6.0	.490
90-91 Portland	80	0	1710	890	337	714	.472	102	251	.406	114	138	.826	45	160	205	285	195	2	63	13	104	21.4	11.1	2.6	3.6	.529
91-92 Portland	81	6	1595	784	299	676	.442	78	230	.339	108	131	.824	40	108	148	202	148	0	73	12	73	19.7	9.7	1.8	2.5	.451
92-93 Phoenix	80	0	2163	947	337	730	.462	150	372	.403	123	145	.848	49	165	214	260	175	3	69	8	112	27.0	11.8	2.7	3.3	.431
93-94 Phoenix	68	1	1555	606	224	537	.417	80	244	.328	78	94	.830	28	103	131	180	140	0	57	8	82	22.9	8.9	1.9	2.6	.352
94-95 Phoenix	74	1	1374	571	194	422	.460	78	214	.364	105	130	.808	25	84	109	210	155	1	46	7	81	18.6	7.7	1.5	2.8	.416
NBA Season Totals	1042	508	27755	11964	4643	9905	.469	1002	2651	.378	1676	1980	.846	695	2073	2768	4199	2549	26	1133	131	1579	26.6	11.5	2.7	4.0	....
81-82 Boston	10	0	129	50	19	45	.422	2	4	.500	10	13	.769	6	7	13	11	21	0	2	1	11	12.9	5.0	1.3	1.1	.244
82-83 Boston	7	7	201	66	28	72	.389	2	5	.400	8	11	.727	2	12	14	25	24	0	5	1	6	28.7	9.4	2.0	3.6	.270
83-84 Boston	19	0	253	91	41	90	.456	2	9	.222	7	10	.700	4	12	16	38	36	0	9	2	13	13.3	4.8	0.8	2.0	.320
84-85 Boston	21	21	687	231	97	208	.466	7	16	.438	30	39	.769	20	38	58	121	76	1	32	1	32	32.7	11.0	2.8	5.8	.396
85-86 Boston	18	18	652	280	107	193	.554	14	34	.412	52	60	.867	22	54	76	93	57	0	41	1	31	36.2	15.6	4.2	5.2	.537
86-87 Boston	20	19	762	295	116	238	.487	32	73	.438	31	36	.861	13	39	52	92	62	0	24	4	41	38.1	14.8	2.6	4.6	.374
87-88 Boston	17	17	670	198	71	184	.386	19	57	.333	37	42	.881	15	38	53	109	64	2	9	1	41	39.4	11.6	3.1	6.4	.295
90-91 Portland	16	0	277	128	47	105	.448	11	36	.306	23	28	.821	1	27	28	31	33	0	12	4	24	17.3	8.0	1.8	1.9	.390
91-92 Portland	21	0	449	222	81	169	.479	21	52	.404	39	47	.830	8	32	40	49	58	1	15	1	25	21.4	10.6	1.9	2.3	.425
92-93 Phoenix	24	0	591	195	64	170	.376	33	80	.413	34	39	.872	20	40	60	56	61	0	12	2	22	24.6	8.1	2.5	2.3	.294
93-94 Phoenix	10	0	230	86	27	59	.458	17	40	.425	15	21	.714	7	16	23	21	26	0	6	1	5	23.0	8.6	2.3	2.1	.381
94-95 Phoenix	10	0	137	60	19	38	.500	12	26	.462	10	11	.909	2	8	10	10	15	0	5	0	6	13.7	6.0	1.0	1.0	.392
NBA Playoff Totals	193	82	5038	1902	717	1571	.456	172	432	.398	296	357	.829	120	323	443	656	533	4	172	19	257	26.1	9.9	2.3	3.4	....

• AITCH, Matthew

Matthew Alexander Aitch

Born: Sept. 21, 1944. St. Louis, MO, United States. Height: 6'7". Weight: 230 lbs. Drafted: 1967 College: Michigan State

YEAR TEAM	GP	GS	MIN	PTS	FGM	FGA	FG%	3PM	3PA	3P%	FTM	FTA	FT%	ORB	DRB	TRB	AST	PF	DQ	STL	BLK	TO	MPG	PPG	RPG	APG	PCM
67-68 Indiana-A	45	....	637	252	100	247	.405	0	2	.000	52	77	.675	....	....	160	18	69	1	....	....	37	14.2	5.6	3.6	0.4	.384
ABA Season Totals	45	....	637	252	100	247	.405	0	2	.000	52	77	.675	....	....	160	18	69	1	....	....	37	14.2	5.6	3.6	0.4	....
67-68 Indiana-A	2	....	4	4	2	4	.500	0	0	.000	0	0	.000	....	....	0	0	0	0	....	....	1	2.0	2.0	0.0	0.0	.585
ABA Playoff Totals	2	....	4	4	2	4	.500	0	0	.000	0	0	.000	....	....	0	0	0	0	....	....	1	2.0	2.0	0.0	0.0	....

YEAR	TEAM	GP	GS	MIN	PTS	FGM	FGA	FG%	3PM	3PA	3P%	FTM	FTA	FT%	ORB	DRB	TRB	AST	PF	DQ	STL	BLK	TO	MPG	PPG	RPG	APG	PCM

• AJAX, Warren

Warren Ajax

Born: 1921.   Height: 6'2".   Weight: 170 lbs.   Drafted: —   College: Minnesota

YEAR	TEAM	GP	GS	MIN	PTS	FGM	FGA	FG%	3PM	3PA	3P%	FTM	FTA	FT%	ORB	DRB	TRB	AST	PF	DQ	STL	BLK	TO	MPG	PPG	RPG	APG	PCM
47-48	Minneapolis-N	3	....	....	1	0	....	....	....	....	....	1	2	.500	....	....	....	....	1	....	....	....	....	....	0.3	....	....	....
NBL Season Totals		3	....	....	1	0	....	....	....	....	....	1	2	....	....	....	....	....	1	....	....	....	....	....	0.3	....	....	....

• AKIN, Henry

Henry T. Akin

Born: July 31, 1944. Detroit, MI, United States.   Height: 6'10".   Weight: 225 lbs.   Drafted: 1966   College: Morehead State

YEAR	TEAM	GP	GS	MIN	PTS	FGM	FGA	FG%	3PM	3PA	3P%	FTM	FTA	FT%	ORB	DRB	TRB	AST	PF	DQ	STL	BLK	TO	MPG	PPG	RPG	APG	PCM
66-67	New York	50	....	453	192	83	230	.361	....	....	....	26	37	.703	....	....	120	25	82	0	....	....	....	9.1	3.8	2.4	0.5	.361
67-68	Seattle	36	....	259	112	46	137	.336	....	....	....	20	31	.645	....	....	57	14	48	1	....	....	....	7.2	3.1	1.6	0.4	.302
68-69	Kentucky-A	2	....	25	4	1	4	.250	0	2	.000	2	3	.667	0	4	4	1	0	0	....	....	4	12.5	2.0	2.0	0.5	.223
NBA Season Totals		86	....	712	304	129	367	.351	....	....	....	46	68	.676	....	....	177	39	130	1	....	....	....	8.3	3.5	2.1	0.5	....
ABA Season Totals		2	....	25	4	1	4	.250	0	2	.000	2	3	.667	0	4	4	1	0	0	....	....	4	12.5	2.0	2.0	0.5	....
Career Totals		88	....	737	308	130	371	.350	0	2	.000	48	71	.676	0	4	181	40	130	1	....	....	4	8.4	3.5	2.1	0.5	....
66-67	New York	2	....	16	3	1	7	.143	....	....	....	1	2	.500	....	....	8	0	3	0	....	....	....	8.0	1.5	4.0	0.0	.188
NBA Playoff Totals		2	....	16	3	1	7	.143	....	....	....	1	2	.500	....	....	8	0	3	0	....	....	....	8.0	1.5	4.0	0.0	....

• ALARIE, Mark

Mark Steven Alarie

Born: Dec. 11, 1963. Phoenix, AZ, United States.   Height: 6'8".   Weight: 217 lbs.   Drafted: 1986   College: Duke

YEAR	TEAM	GP	GS	MIN	PTS	FGM	FGA	FG%	3PM	3PA	3P%	FTM	FTA	FT%	ORB	DRB	TRB	AST	PF	DQ	STL	BLK	TO	MPG	PPG	RPG	APG	PCM
86-87	Denver	64	25	1110	503	217	443	.490	2	9	.222	67	101	.663	73	141	214	74	138	1	22	28	58	17.3	7.9	3.3	1.2	.436
87-88	Washington	63	0	769	327	144	300	.480	4	18	.222	35	49	.714	70	90	160	39	107	1	10	12	50	12.2	5.2	2.5	0.6	.377
88-89	Washington	74	5	1141	498	206	431	.478	13	38	.342	73	87	.839	103	152	255	63	160	1	25	22	59	15.4	6.7	3.4	0.9	.439
89-90	Washington	82	10	1893	860	371	785	.473	10	49	.204	108	133	.812	151	223	374	142	219	2	60	39	98	23.1	10.5	4.6	1.7	.454
90-91	Washington	42	1	587	244	99	225	.440	5	21	.238	41	48	.854	41	76	117	45	88	1	15	8	42	14.0	5.8	2.8	1.1	.377
NBA Season Totals		325	41	5500	2432	1037	2184	.475	34	135	.252	324	418	.775	438	682	1120	363	712	6	132	109	307	16.9	7.5	3.4	1.1	....
86-87	Denver	3	0	41	20	9	15	.600	0	0	.000	2	2	1.000	0	5	5	1	9	0	2	2	4	13.7	6.7	1.7	0.3	.389
87-88	Washington	1	0	4	3	1	2	.500	1	2	.500	0	0	.000	0	1	1	0	0	0	0	0	0	4.0	3.0	1.0	0.0	.750
NBA Playoff Totals		4	0	45	23	10	17	.588	1	2	.500	2	2	1.000	0	6	6	1	9	0	2	2	4	11.3	5.8	1.5	0.3	....

• ALCORN, Gary

Gary R. Alcorn

Born: Oct. 8, 1936.   Height: 6'9".   Weight: 225 lbs.   Drafted: 1959   College: Fresno State

YEAR	TEAM	GP	GS	MIN	PTS	FGM	FGA	FG%	3PM	3PA	3P%	FTM	FTA	FT%	ORB	DRB	TRB	AST	PF	DQ	STL	BLK	TO	MPG	PPG	RPG	APG	PCM
59-60	Detroit	58	....	670	230	91	312	.292	....	....	....	48	84	.571	....	....	279	22	123	4	....	....	....	11.6	4.0	4.8	0.4	.360
60-61	LA Lakers	20	....	174	31	12	40	.300	....	....	....	7	8	.875	....	....	50	2	47	1	....	....	....	8.7	1.6	2.5	0.1	.184
NBA Season Totals		78	....	844	261	103	352	.293	....	....	....	55	92	.598	....	....	329	24	170	5	....	....	....	10.8	3.3	4.2	0.3	....

• ALEKSINAS, Chuck

Charles Aleksinas

Born: Feb. 26, 1959. Litchfield, CT, United States.   Height: 6'11".   Weight: 260 lbs.   Drafted: 1982   College: Connecticut

YEAR	TEAM	GP	GS	MIN	PTS	FGM	FGA	FG%	3PM	3PA	3P%	FTM	FTA	FT%	ORB	DRB	TRB	AST	PF	DQ	STL	BLK	TO	MPG	PPG	RPG	APG	PCM
84-85	Golden State	74	4	1114	377	161	337	.478	0	1	.000	55	75	.733	87	183	270	36	171	1	15	15	74	15.1	5.1	3.6	0.5	.335
NBA Season Totals		74	4	1114	377	161	337	.478	0	1	.000	55	75	.733	87	183	270	36	171	1	15	15	74	15.1	5.1	3.6	0.5	....

• ALEXANDER, Cory

Cory Lynn Alexander

Born: June 22, 1973. Waynesboro, VA, United States.   Height: 6'1".   Weight: 185 lbs.   Drafted: 1995   College: Virginia

YEAR	TEAM	GP	GS	MIN	PTS	FGM	FGA	FG%	3PM	3PA	3P%	FTM	FTA	FT%	ORB	DRB	TRB	AST	PF	DQ	STL	BLK	TO	MPG	PPG	RPG	APG	PCM
95-96	San Antonio	60	0	560	168	63	155	.406	26	66	.394	16	25	.640	9	33	42	121	94	0	27	2	66	9.3	2.8	0.7	2.0	.297
96-97	San Antonio	80	6	1454	577	194	490	.396	94	252	.373	95	129	.736	29	94	123	254	148	0	82	16	144	18.2	7.2	1.5	3.2	.385
97-98	San Antonio	37	3	501	165	60	145	.414	20	64	.313	25	37	.676	7	40	47	71	53	2	25	5	48	13.5	4.5	1.3	1.9	.321
97-98	Denver	23	19	797	323	111	255	.435	46	112	.411	55	65	.846	10	89	99	138	45	0	45	6	64	34.7	14.0	4.3	6.0	.495
98-99	Denver	36	4	778	261	97	260	.373	30	105	.286	37	44	.841	7	67	74	119	77	0	35	5	69	21.6	7.3	2.1	3.3	.323
99-00	Denver	29	2	329	82	28	98	.286	9	35	.257	17	22	.773	8	34	42	58	39	0	24	2	28	11.3	2.8	1.4	2.0	.298
00-01	Orlando	26	0	227	52	18	56	.321	4	16	.250	12	18	.667	0	25	25	36	29	0	16	0	25	8.7	2.0	1.0	1.4	.248
NBA Season Totals		291	34	4646	1628	571	1459	.391	229	650	.352	257	340	.756	70	382	452	797	485	2	254	36	444	16.0	5.6	1.6	2.7	....
95-96	San Antonio	9	0	70	26	10	24	.417	1	5	.200	5	7	.714	4	5	9	9	8	0	2	0	6	7.8	2.9	1.0	1.0	.320
NBA Playoff Totals		9	0	70	26	10	24	.417	1	5	.200	5	7	.714	4	5	9	9	8	0	2	0	6	7.8	2.9	1.0	1.0	....

• ALEXANDER, Courtney

Courtney Jason Alexander

Born: Apr. 27, 1977. Bridgeport, CT, United States.   Height: 6'5".   Weight: 205 lbs.   Drafted: 2000   College: Fresno State

YEAR	TEAM	GP	GS	MIN	PTS	FGM	FGA	FG%	3PM	3PA	3P%	FTM	FTA	FT%	ORB	DRB	TRB	AST	PF	DQ	STL	BLK	TO	MPG	PPG	RPG	APG	PCM
00-01	Dallas	38	6	472	160	62	178	.348	3	10	.300	33	45	.733	20	43	63	21	76	1	16	3	21	12.4	4.2	1.7	0.6	.200
00-01	Washington	27	18	910	458	177	395	.448	14	36	.389	90	105	.857	22	58	80	41	63	0	29	2	54	33.7	17.0	3.0	1.5	.356
01-02	Washington	56	28	1325	549	223	474	.470	5	18	.278	98	121	.810	43	105	148	86	113	0	35	7	60	23.7	9.8	2.6	1.5	.356
02-03	New Orleans	66	7	1360	523	193	505	.382	19	57	.333	118	146	.808	39	79	118	79	125	0	31	6	68	20.6	7.9	1.8	1.2	.247
NBA Season Totals		187	59	4067	1690	655	1552	.422	41	121	.339	339	417	.813	124	285	409	227	377	1	111	18	203	21.7	9.0	2.2	1.2	....
02-03	New Orleans	5	0	39	18	7	16	.438	1	1	1.000	3	4	.750	2	2	4	1	6	0	2	0	1	7.8	3.6	0.8	0.2	.315
NBA Playoff Totals		5	0	39	18	7	16	.438	1	1	1.000	3	4	.750	2	2	4	1	6	0	2	0	1	7.8	3.6	0.8	0.2	....

YEAR	TEAM	GP	GS	MIN	PTS	FGM	FGA	FG%	3PM	3PA	3P%	FTM	FTA	FT%	ORB	DRB	TRB	AST	PF	DQ	STL	BLK	TO	MPG	PPG	RPG	APG	PCM

• ALEXANDER, Gary

Gary R. Alexander

Born: Nov. 1, 1969. Jacksonville, FL, United States.   Height: 6'7".   Weight: 240 lbs.   Drafted: —   College: South Florida

YEAR	TEAM	GP	GS	MIN	PTS	FGM	FGA	FG%	3PM	3PA	3P%	FTM	FTA	FT%	ORB	DRB	TRB	AST	PF	DQ	STL	BLK	TO	MPG	PPG	RPG	APG	PCM
93-94	Miami	4	0	12	2	1	2	.500	0	0	.000	0	2	.000	1	2	3	1	3	0	0	0	1	3.0	0.5	0.8	0.3	.142
93-94	Cleveland	7	0	43	17	7	12	.583	0	0	.000	3	7	.429	6	6	12	1	7	0	3	0	7	6.1	2.4	1.7	0.1	.367
NBA Season Totals		11	0	55	19	8	14	.571	0	0	.000	3	9	.333	7	8	15	2	10	0	3	0	8	5.0	1.7	1.4	0.2	....

• ALEXANDER, Merle

Merle Alexander

Born: 1907.   Height: 6'6".   Weight: 185 lbs.   Drafted: —   College: none

YEAR	TEAM	GP	GS	MIN	PTS	FGM	FGA	FG%	3PM	3PA	3P%	FTM	FTA	FT%	ORB	DRB	TRB	AST	PF	DQ	STL	BLK	TO	MPG	PPG	RPG	APG	PCM
38-39	Indianapolis-N	2	....	....	0	0	....	....	....	....	....	0	....	....	....	....	....	....	....	....	....	....	....	0.0	....	....	....	
NBL Season Totals		2	....	....	0	0	....	....	....	....	....	0	....	....	....	....	....	....	....	....	....	....	....	0.0	....	....	....	

• ALEXANDER, Victor

Victor Joe Alexander

Born: Aug. 31, 1969. Detroit, MI, United States.   Height: 6'9".   Weight: 265 lbs.   Drafted: 1991   College: Iowa State

YEAR	TEAM	GP	GS	MIN	PTS	FGM	FGA	FG%	3PM	3PA	3P%	FTM	FTA	FT%	ORB	DRB	TRB	AST	PF	DQ	STL	BLK	TO	MPG	PPG	RPG	APG	PCM
91-92	Golden State	80	28	1350	589	243	459	.529	0	1	.000	103	149	.691	106	230	336	32	176	0	45	62	88	16.9	7.4	4.2	0.4	.481
92-93	Golden State	72	59	1753	809	344	667	.516	10	22	.455	111	162	.685	132	288	420	93	218	2	34	53	122	24.3	11.2	5.8	1.3	.480
93-94	Golden State	69	39	1318	602	266	502	.530	2	13	.154	68	129	.527	114	194	308	66	168	0	28	32	83	19.1	8.7	4.5	1.0	.465
94-95	Golden State	50	29	1237	502	230	447	.515	6	25	.240	36	60	.600	87	204	291	60	145	2	28	29	75	24.7	10.0	5.8	1.2	.436
01-02	Detroit	15	0	97	40	18	51	.353	0	2	.000	4	8	.500	7	22	29	6	6	0	0	1	5	6.5	2.7	1.9	0.4	.359
NBA Season Totals		286	155	5755	2542	1101	2126	.518	18	63	.286	322	508	.634	446	938	1384	257	713	4	135	177	373	20.1	8.9	4.8	0.9	....
91-92	Golden State	4	0	24	7	3	5	.600	0	0	.000	1	1	1.000	1	5	6	1	8	0	2	0	2	6.0	1.8	1.5	0.3	.336
01-02	Detroit	1	0	3	0	0	1	.000	0	0	.000	0	0	.000	0	1	1	0	0	0	0	0	0	3.0	0.0	1.0	0.0	.000
NBA Playoff Totals		5	0	27	7	3	6	.500	0	0	.000	1	1	1.000	1	6	7	1	8	0	2	0	2	5.4	1.4	1.4	0.2	....

• ALFORD, Steve

Stephen Todd Alford

Born: Nov. 23, 1964. Franklin, IN, United States.   Height: 6'2".   Weight: 183 lbs.   Drafted: 1987   College: Indiana

YEAR	TEAM	GP	GS	MIN	PTS	FGM	FGA	FG%	3PM	3PA	3P%	FTM	FTA	FT%	ORB	DRB	TRB	AST	PF	DQ	STL	BLK	TO	MPG	PPG	RPG	APG	PCM
87-88	Dallas	28	0	197	59	21	55	.382	1	8	.125	16	17	.941	3	20	23	23	23	0	17	3	11	7.0	2.1	0.8	0.8	.358
88-89	Dallas	9	0	38	7	3	11	.273	0	2	.000	1	2	.500	0	3	3	9	3	0	1	0	1	4.2	0.8	0.3	1.0	.266
88-89	Golden State	57	3	868	359	145	313	.463	20	53	.377	49	59	.831	10	59	69	83	54	0	44	3	46	15.2	6.3	1.2	1.5	.377
89-90	Dallas	41	0	302	168	63	138	.457	7	22	.318	35	37	.946	2	23	25	39	22	0	15	3	16	7.4	4.1	0.6	1.0	.507
90-91	Dallas	34	0	236	151	59	117	.504	7	23	.304	26	31	.839	10	14	24	22	11	0	8	1	17	6.9	4.4	0.7	0.6	.542
NBA Season Totals		169	3	1641	744	291	634	.459	35	108	.324	127	146	.870	25	119	144	176	113	0	85	10	91	9.7	4.4	0.9	1.0	....
87-88	Dallas	4	0	12	6	3	8	.375	0	2	.000	0	0	.000	1	1	2	2	0	0	0	0	1	3.0	1.5	0.5	0.5	.367
88-89	Golden State	6	0	52	25	9	22	.409	4	9	.444	3	4	.750	2	2	4	5	7	0	2	0	1	8.7	4.2	0.7	0.8	.369
89-90	Dallas	3	0	42	23	8	18	.444	2	6	.333	5	5	1.000	1	2	3	8	4	0	1	0	3	14.0	7.7	1.0	2.7	.505
NBA Playoff Totals		13	0	106	54	20	48	.417	6	17	.353	8	9	.889	4	5	9	15	11	0	3	0	5	8.2	4.2	0.7	1.2	....

• ALLEN, Bill

Bill Allen

Born: 1945.   Height: 6'8".   Weight: 205 lbs.   Drafted: —   College: New Mexico State

YEAR	TEAM	GP	GS	MIN	PTS	FGM	FGA	FG%	3PM	3PA	3P%	FTM	FTA	FT%	ORB	DRB	TRB	AST	PF	DQ	STL	BLK	TO	MPG	PPG	RPG	APG	PCM
67-68	Anaheim-A	38	....	857	300	120	280	.429	2	2	1.000	58	99	.586	....	....	269	23	121	5	....	....	38	22.6	7.9	7.1	0.6	.409
ABA Season Totals		38	....	857	300	120	280	.429	2	2	1.000	58	99	.586	....	....	269	23	121	5	....	....	38	22.6	7.9	7.1	0.6	....

• ALLEN, Bob

Robert J. Allen

Born: July 17, 1946.   Height: 6'9".   Weight: 205 lbs.   Drafted: 1968   College: Marshall

YEAR	TEAM	GP	GS	MIN	PTS	FGM	FGA	FG%	3PM	3PA	3P%	FTM	FTA	FT%	ORB	DRB	TRB	AST	PF	DQ	STL	BLK	TO	MPG	PPG	RPG	APG	PCM
68-69	San Francisco	27	....	232	48	14	43	.326	....	....	....	20	36	.556	....	....	56	10	27	0	....	....	....	8.6	1.8	2.1	0.4	.277
NBA Season Totals		27	....	232	48	14	43	.326	....	....	....	20	36	.556	....	....	56	10	27	0	....	....	....	8.6	1.8	2.1	0.4	....
68-69	San Francisco	3	....	19	4	0	4	.000	....	....	....	4	7	.571	....	....	6	0	2	0	....	....	....	6.3	1.3	2.0	0.0	.189
NBA Playoff Totals		3	....	19	4	0	4	.000	....	....	....	4	7	.571	....	....	6	0	2	0	....	....	....	6.3	1.3	2.0	0.0	....

• ALLEN, Jerome

Jerome Byron Allen

Born: Jan. 28, 1973. Philadelphia, PA, United States.   Height: 6'4".   Weight: 184 lbs.   Drafted: 1995   College: Pennsylvania

YEAR	TEAM	GP	GS	MIN	PTS	FGM	FGA	FG%	3PM	3PA	3P%	FTM	FTA	FT%	ORB	DRB	TRB	AST	PF	DQ	STL	BLK	TO	MPG	PPG	RPG	APG	PCM
95-96	Minnesota	41	0	362	108	36	105	.343	10	33	.303	26	36	.722	5	20	25	49	42	0	21	5	33	8.8	2.6	0.6	1.2	.242
96-97	Indiana	51	1	692	164	57	147	.388	23	59	.390	27	47	.574	13	52	65	109	67	0	27	0	56	13.6	3.2	1.3	2.1	.274
96-97	Denver	25	0	251	64	21	74	.284	7	34	.206	15	25	.600	12	21	33	43	17	0	4	4	13	10.0	2.6	1.3	1.7	.295
NBA Season Totals		117	1	1305	336	114	326	.350	40	126	.317	68	108	.630	30	93	123	201	126	0	52	9	102	11.2	2.9	1.1	1.7	....

• ALLEN, Lucius

Lucius Oliver Allen Jr.

Born: Sept. 26, 1947. Kansas City, KS, United States.   Height: 6'2".   Weight: 175 lbs.   Drafted: 1969   College: UCLA

YEAR	TEAM	GP	GS	MIN	PTS	FGM	FGA	FG%	3PM	3PA	3P%	FTM	FTA	FT%	ORB	DRB	TRB	AST	PF	DQ	STL	BLK	TO	MPG	PPG	RPG	APG	PCM
69-70	Seattle	81	....	1817	794	306	692	.442	....	....	....	182	249	.731	....	....	211	342	201	0	....	....	....	22.4	9.8	2.6	4.2	.498
70-71	Milwaukee	61	....	1162	433	178	398	.447	....	....	....	77	110	.700	....	....	152	161	108	0	....	....	....	19.0	7.1	2.5	2.6	.428
71-72	Milwaukee	80	....	2316	1080	441	874	.505	....	....	....	198	259	.764	....	....	254	333	214	2	....	....	....	29.0	13.5	3.2	4.2	.512
72-73	Milwaukee	80	....	2693	1237	547	1130	.484	....	....	....	143	200	.715	....	....	279	426	188	1	....	....	....	33.7	15.5	3.5	5.3	.504
73-74	Milwaukee	72	....	2388	1268	526	1062	.495	....	....	....	216	274	.788	89	202	291	374	215	2	137	22	....	33.2	17.6	4.0	5.2	.575
74-75	Milwaukee	10	....	342	167	68	164	.415	....	....	....	31	37	.838	9	22	31	53	23	0	14	1	....	34.2	16.7	3.1	5.3	.468
74-75	LA Lakers	56	....	2011	1093	443	1006	.440	....	....	....	207	269	.770	81	166	247	319	194	4	122	28	....	35.9	19.5	4.4	5.7	.537
75-76	LA Lakers	76	....	2388	1119	461	1004	.459	....	....	....	197	254	.776	64	150	214	357	241	2	101	20	....	31.4	14.7	2.8	4.7	.468
76-77	LA Lakers	78	....	2482	1139	472	1035	.456	....	....	....	195	252	.774	58	193	251	405	183	0	116	19	....	31.8	14.6	3.2	5.2	.494

YEAR	TEAM	GP	GS	MIN	PTS	FGM	FGA	FG%	3PM	3PA	3P%	FTM	FTA	FT%	ORB	DRB	TRB	AST	PF	DQ	STL	BLK	TO	MPG	PPG	RPG	APG	PCM
77-78	Kansas City	77	....	2147	920	373	846	.441	....	....	....	174	220	.791	66	163	229	360	180	0	93	28	216	27.9	11.9	3.0	4.7	.433
78-79	Kansas City	31	....	413	157	69	174	.397	....	....	....	19	33	.576	14	32	46	44	52	0	21	6	31	13.3	5.1	1.5	1.4	.289
NBA Season Totals		702	....	20159	9407	3884	8385	.463	....	....	....	1639	2157	.760	381	928	2205	3174	1799	11	604	124	247	28.7	13.4	3.1	4.5	....
70-71	Milwaukee	14	....	312	102	41	81	.506	....	....	....	20	28	.714	....	....	40	52	30	0	....	....	6	22.3	7.3	2.9	3.7	.465
71-72	Milwaukee	11	....	386	197	78	166	.470	....	....	....	41	54	.759	....	....	38	42	30	0	....	....	6	35.1	17.9	3.5	3.8	.474
72-73	Milwaukee	6	....	203	94	36	89	.404	....	....	....	22	28	.786	....	....	16	21	15	0	....	....	6	33.8	15.7	2.7	3.5	.380
76-77	LA Lakers	7	....	186	77	32	82	.390	....	....	....	13	19	.684	7	25	32	24	18	0	11	3	....	26.6	11.0	4.6	3.4	.421
78-79	Kansas City	5	....	73	36	15	32	.469	....	....	....	6	6	1.000	2	5	7	3	7	0	2	1	5	14.6	7.2	1.4	0.6	.348
NBA Playoff Totals		43	....	1160	506	202	450	.449	....	....	....	102	135	.756	9	30	133	142	100	0	13	4	5	27.0	11.8	3.1	3.3	....

• ALLEN, Malik
Malik Allen

Born: June 27, 1978. Willingboro, NJ, United States.   Height: 6'10".   Weight: 255 lbs.   Drafted: —   College: Villanova

YEAR	TEAM	GP	GS	MIN	PTS	FGM	FGA	FG%	3PM	3PA	3P%	FTM	FTA	FT%	ORB	DRB	TRB	AST	PF	DQ	STL	BLK	TO	MPG	PPG	RPG	APG	PCM
01-02	Miami	12	2	161	52	22	51	.431	0	1	.000	8	10	.800	15	23	38	5	16	0	3	8	2	13.4	4.3	3.2	0.4	.408
02-03	Miami	80	73	2318	767	335	790	.424	0	4	.000	97	121	.802	134	291	425	54	234	1	37	78	128	29.0	9.6	5.3	0.7	.289
NBA Season Totals		92	75	2479	819	357	841	.424	0	5	.000	105	131	.802	149	314	463	59	250	1	40	86	130	26.9	8.9	5.0	0.6	....

• ALLEN, Randy
James Randall Allen

Born: Jan. 26, 1965. Milton, FL, United States.   Height: 6'8".   Weight: 220 lbs.   Drafted: —   College: Florida State

YEAR	TEAM	GP	GS	MIN	PTS	FGM	FGA	FG%	3PM	3PA	3P%	FTM	FTA	FT%	ORB	DRB	TRB	AST	PF	DQ	STL	BLK	TO	MPG	PPG	RPG	APG	PCM
95-96	Sacramento	7	0	43	17	8	19	.421	0	1	.000	1	2	.500	3	4	7	0	7	0	1	1	2	6.1	2.4	1.0	0.0	.222
96-97	Sacramento	63	6	746	235	106	239	.444	0	7	.000	23	43	.535	49	89	138	23	102	0	16	19	25	11.8	3.7	2.2	0.4	.290
NBA Season Totals		70	6	789	252	114	258	.442	0	8	.000	24	45	.533	52	93	145	23	109	0	17	20	27	11.3	3.6	2.1	0.3	....

• ALLEN, Ray
Walter Ray Allen

Born: July 20, 1975. Merced, CA, United States.   Height: 6'5".   Weight: 205 lbs.   Drafted: 1996   College: Connecticut

YEAR	TEAM	GP	GS	MIN	PTS	FGM	FGA	FG%	3PM	3PA	3P%	FTM	FTA	FT%	ORB	DRB	TRB	AST	PF	DQ	STL	BLK	TO	MPG	PPG	RPG	APG	PCM
96-97	Milwaukee	82	81	2532	1102	390	908	.430	117	298	.393	205	249	.823	97	229	326	210	218	0	75	10	148	30.9	13.4	4.0	2.6	.382
97-98	Milwaukee	82	82	3287	1602	563	1315	.428	134	368	.364	342	391	.875	127	278	405	356	244	2	111	12	262	40.1	19.5	4.9	4.3	.429
98-99	Milwaukee	50	50	1719	856	303	673	.450	74	208	.356	176	195	.903	57	155	212	178	117	0	53	7	122	34.4	17.1	4.2	3.6	.464
99-00	Milwaukee	82	82	3070	1809	642	1411	.455	172	407	.423	353	398	.887	83	276	359	308	187	1	110	19	183	37.4	22.1	4.4	3.8	.527
00-01	Milwaukee	82	82	3129	1806	642	1309	.480	202	467	.433	348	392	.888	101	327	428	374	192	2	124	20	204	38.2	22.0	5.2	4.6	.585
01-02	Milwaukee	69	67	2525	1503	530	1148	.462	**229**	528	.434	214	245	.873	81	231	312	271	157	0	88	18	159	36.6	21.8	4.5	3.9	.550
02-03	Milwaukee	47	46	1683	1003	351	803	.437	**123**	311	.395	178	195	.913	45	173	218	164	149	2	57	11	117	35.8	21.3	4.6	3.5	.505
02-03	Seattle	29	29	1197	710	247	560	.441	**78**	222	.351	138	150	.920	49	114	163	170	71	2	46	3	81	41.3	24.5	5.6	5.9	.579
NBA Season Totals		523	519	19142	10391	3654	8127	.450	1129	2809	.402	1954	2215	.882	640	1783	2423	2031	1335	9	664	100	1276	36.6	19.9	4.6	3.9	....
98-99	Milwaukee	3	3	120	67	25	47	.532	9	19	.474	8	13	.615	8	14	22	13	9	0	3	1	11	40.0	22.3	7.3	4.3	.575
99-00	Milwaukee	5	5	186	110	40	90	.444	10	26	.385	20	22	.909	10	23	33	13	10	0	8	0	9	37.2	22.0	6.6	2.6	.551
00-01	Milwaukee	18	18	768	452	158	331	.477	57	119	.479	79	86	.919	19	55	74	108	44	0	24	10	43	42.7	25.1	4.1	6.0	.587
NBA Playoff Totals		26	26	1074	629	223	468	.476	76	164	.463	107	121	.884	37	92	129	134	63	0	35	11	63	41.3	24.2	5.0	5.2	....

• ALLEN, Willie
Willie Allen

Born: Feb. 8, 1949.   Height: 6'6".   Weight: 230 lbs.   Drafted: 1971   College: Miami (FL)

YEAR	TEAM	GP	GS	MIN	PTS	FGM	FGA	FG%	3PM	3PA	3P%	FTM	FTA	FT%	ORB	DRB	TRB	AST	PF	DQ	STL	BLK	TO	MPG	PPG	RPG	APG	PCM
71-72	Florida-A	7	....	30	13	4	13	.308	0	0	.000	5	6	.833	4	10	14	4	11	0	....	....	6	4.3	1.9	2.0	0.6	.554
ABA Season Totals		7	....	30	13	4	13	.308	0	0	.000	5	6	.833	4	10	14	4	11	0	....	....	6	4.3	1.9	2.0	0.6	....

• ALLISON, Odis
Odis Allison Jr.

Born: Oct. 2, 1949.   Height: 6'6".   Weight: 195 lbs.   Drafted: 1971   College: UNLV

YEAR	TEAM	GP	GS	MIN	PTS	FGM	FGA	FG%	3PM	3PA	3P%	FTM	FTA	FT%	ORB	DRB	TRB	AST	PF	DQ	STL	BLK	TO	MPG	PPG	RPG	APG	PCM
71-72	Golden State	36	....	166	67	17	78	.218	....	....	....	33	61	.541	....	....	45	10	34	0	....	....	....	4.6	1.9	1.3	0.3	.227
NBA Season Totals		36	....	166	67	17	78	.218	....	....	....	33	61	.541	....	....	45	10	34	0	....	....	....	4.6	1.9	1.3	0.3	....

• ALLUMS, Darrell
Darrell Wilbert Allums Jr.

Born: Sept. 12, 1958. Los Angeles, CA, United States.   Height: 6'9".   Weight: 220 lbs.   Drafted: 1980   College: UCLA

YEAR	TEAM	GP	GS	MIN	PTS	FGM	FGA	FG%	3PM	3PA	3P%	FTM	FTA	FT%	ORB	DRB	TRB	AST	PF	DQ	STL	BLK	TO	MPG	PPG	RPG	APG	PCM
80-81	Dallas	22	....	276	59	23	67	.343	0	1	.000	13	22	.591	19	46	65	25	51	2	5	8	22	12.5	2.7	3.0	1.1	.253
NBA Season Totals		22	....	276	59	23	67	.343	0	1	.000	13	22	.591	19	46	65	25	51	2	5	8	22	12.5	2.7	3.0	1.1	....

• ALSTON, Derrick
Derrick Samuel Alston

Born: Aug. 20, 1972. Bronx, NY, United States.   Height: 6'11".   Weight: 225 lbs.   Drafted: 1994   College: Duquesne

YEAR	TEAM	GP	GS	MIN	PTS	FGM	FGA	FG%	3PM	3PA	3P%	FTM	FTA	FT%	ORB	DRB	TRB	AST	PF	DQ	STL	BLK	TO	MPG	PPG	RPG	APG	PCM
94-95	Philadelphia	64	1	1032	299	120	258	.465	0	4	.000	59	120	.492	98	121	219	33	107	1	39	35	51	16.1	4.7	3.4	0.5	.342
95-96	Philadelphia	73	41	1614	452	198	387	.512	1	3	.333	55	112	.491	127	175	302	61	191	1	56	52	58	22.1	6.2	4.1	0.8	.343
96-97	Atlanta	2	0	11	0	0	5	.000	0	0	.000	0	2	.000	3	1	4	0	0	0	0	0	0	5.5	0.0	2.0	0.0	-.169
NBA Season Totals		139	42	2657	751	318	650	.489	1	7	.143	114	234	.487	228	297	525	94	298	2	95	87	109	19.1	5.4	3.8	0.7	....

YEAR	TEAM	GP	GS	MIN	PTS	FGM	FGA	FG%	3PM	3PA	3P%	FTM	FTA	FT%	ORB	DRB	TRB	AST	PF	DQ	STL	BLK	TO	MPG	PPG	RPG	APG	PCM

• ALSTON, Rafer

Rafer Alston

Born: July 24, 1976. New York, NY, United States.   Height: 6'2".   Weight: 171 lbs.   Drafted: 1998   College: Fresno State

YEAR	TEAM	GP	GS	MIN	PTS	FGM	FGA	FG%	3PM	3PA	3P%	FTM	FTA	FT%	ORB	DRB	TRB	AST	PF	DQ	STL	BLK	TO	MPG	PPG	RPG	APG	PCM
99-00	Milwaukee	27	0	361	60	27	95	.284	3	14	.214	3	4	.750	5	18	23	70	29	0	12	0	29	13.4	2.2	0.9	2.6	.184
00-01	Milwaukee	37	2	288	77	30	84	.357	8	30	.267	9	13	.692	4	27	31	68	27	0	13	0	20	7.8	2.1	0.8	1.8	.386
01-02	Milwaukee	50	7	600	177	66	191	.346	27	71	.380	18	29	.621	10	62	72	143	42	0	32	2	40	12.0	3.5	1.4	2.9	.427
02-03	Toronto	47	4	979	366	139	335	.415	51	130	.392	37	54	.685	21	86	107	192	120	0	38	15	86	20.8	7.8	2.3	4.1	.411
NBA Season Totals		161	13	2228	680	262	705	.372	89	245	.363	67	100	.670	40	193	233	473	218	0	95	17	175	13.8	4.2	1.4	2.9	....
99-00	Milwaukee	4	0	16	0	0	3	.000	0	1	.000	0	2	.000	0	0	0	1	0	0	0	0	1	4.0	0.0	0.0	0.3	-.216
00-01	Milwaukee	5	0	8	0	0	1	.000	0	0	.000	0	0	.000	0	0	0	1	0	0	0	0	2	1.6	0.0	0.0	0.2	-.199
NBA Playoff Totals		9	0	24	0	0	4	.000	0	1	.000	0	2	.000	0	0	0	2	0	0	0	0	3	2.7	0.0	0.0	0.2	....

• ALTERMAN, Chink

Leonard (Chink) Alterman

Born: 1922.   Height: 6'3".   Weight: 185 lbs.   Drafted: —   College: Denver

YEAR	TEAM	GP	GS	MIN	PTS	FGM	FGA	FG%	3PM	3PA	3P%	FTM	FTA	FT%	ORB	DRB	TRB	AST	PF	DQ	STL	BLK	TO	MPG	PPG	RPG	APG	PCM
48-49	Denver-N	50	....	....	196	67	....	....	....	....	....	62	100	.620	....	....	....	....	126	....	....	....	....	....	3.9	....	....	....
NBL Season Totals		50	....	....	196	67	....	....	....	....	....	62	100		....	....	....	....	126	....	....	....	....	....	3.9	....	....	....

• ALUMA, Peter

Peter Aluma

Born: Apr. 23, 1973. Lagos, Nigeria.   Height: 6'10".   Weight: 260 lbs.   Drafted: —   College: Liberty

YEAR	TEAM	GP	GS	MIN	PTS	FGM	FGA	FG%	3PM	3PA	3P%	FTM	FTA	FT%	ORB	DRB	TRB	AST	PF	DQ	STL	BLK	TO	MPG	PPG	RPG	APG	PCM
98-99	Sacramento	2	0	5	2	1	2	.500	0	0	.000	0	0	.000	1	1	2	0	4	0	1	1	2	2.5	1.0	1.0	0.0	.222
NBA Season Totals		2	0	5	2	1	2	.500	0	0	.000	0	0	.000	1	1	2	0	4	0	1	1	2	2.5	1.0	1.0	0.0	....

• ALVAREZ, Al

Al Alvarez

Born: 1912.   Height: 6'   Weight: 160 lbs.   Drafted: —   College: Toledo

YEAR	TEAM	GP	GS	MIN	PTS	FGM	FGA	FG%	3PM	3PA	3P%	FTM	FTA	FT%	ORB	DRB	TRB	AST	PF	DQ	STL	BLK	TO	MPG	PPG	RPG	APG	PCM
41-42	Toledo-N	4	....	....	21	8	....	....	....	....	....	5	....	....	....	....	....	....	....	....	....	....	....	....	5.3	....	....	....
NBL Season Totals		4	....	....	21	8	....	....	....	....	....	5	....	....	....	....	....	....	....	....	....	....	....	....	5.3	....	....	....

• ALWIN, Bob

Bob Alwin

Born: 1920.   Height: 5'10".   Weight: 145 lbs.   Drafted: —   College: Wisconsin

YEAR	TEAM	GP	GS	MIN	PTS	FGM	FGA	FG%	3PM	3PA	3P%	FTM	FTA	FT%	ORB	DRB	TRB	AST	PF	DQ	STL	BLK	TO	MPG	PPG	RPG	APG	PCM
42-43	Oshkosh-N	4	....	....	21	7	....	....	....	....	....	7	....	....	....	....	....	....	....	....	....	....	....	....	5.3	....	....	....
NBL Season Totals		4	....	....	21	7	....	....	....	....	....	7	....	....	....	....	....	....	....	....	....	....	....	....	5.3	....	....	....

• AMADEN, Ralph

Ralph Amaden

Born: 1917.   Height: 6'4".   Weight: 200 lbs.   Drafted: —   College: Marquette

YEAR	TEAM	GP	GS	MIN	PTS	FGM	FGA	FG%	3PM	3PA	3P%	FTM	FTA	FT%	ORB	DRB	TRB	AST	PF	DQ	STL	BLK	TO	MPG	PPG	RPG	APG	PCM
40-41	Sheboygan-N	11	....	....	24	6	....	....	....	....	....	12	....	....	....	....	....	....	....	....	....	....	....	....	2.2	....	....	....
NBL Season Totals		11	....	....	24	6	....	....	....	....	....	12	....	....	....	....	....	....	....	....	....	....	....	....	2.2	....	....	....
40-41	Sheboygan-N	5	....	....	10	2	....	....	....	....	....	6	....	....	....	....	....	....	....	....	....	....	....	....	2.0	....	....	....
NBL Playoff Totals		5	....	....	10	2	....	....	....	....	....	6	....	....	....	....	....	....	....	....	....	....	....	....	2.0	....	....	....

• AMAECHI, John

John Ekwugha Amaechi

Born: Nov. 26, 1970. Boston, MA, United States.   Height: 6'10".   Weight: 270 lbs.   Drafted: —   College: Penn State

YEAR	TEAM	GP	GS	MIN	PTS	FGM	FGA	FG%	3PM	3PA	3P%	FTM	FTA	FT%	ORB	DRB	TRB	AST	PF	DQ	STL	BLK	TO	MPG	PPG	RPG	APG	PCM
95-96	Cleveland	28	3	357	77	29	70	.414	0	0	.000	19	33	.576	13	39	52	9	49	1	6	11	34	12.8	2.8	1.9	0.3	.144
99-00	Orlando	80	53	1684	836	306	700	.437	1	6	.167	223	291	.766	62	204	266	95	161	1	35	37	139	21.1	10.5	3.3	1.2	.391
00-01	Orlando	82	36	1710	650	237	592	.400	0	7	.000	176	279	.631	77	191	268	74	175	1	28	29	124	20.9	7.9	3.3	0.9	.274
01-02	Utah	54	0	586	175	54	166	.325	0	0	.000	67	105	.638	52	57	109	29	64	0	7	10	55	10.9	3.2	2.0	0.5	.211
02-03	Utah	50	1	474	99	37	118	.314	0	0	.000	25	52	.481	26	51	77	21	50	1	14	7	34	9.5	2.0	1.5	0.4	.151
NBA Season Totals		294	93	4811	1837	663	1646	.403	1	13	.077	510	760	.671	230	542	772	228	499	4	90	94	386	16.4	6.2	2.6	0.8	....
95-96	Cleveland	1	0	2	0	0	1	.000	0	0	.000	0	0	.000	0	0	0	0	0	0	0	0	0	2.0	0.0	0.0	0.0	-.470
00-01	Orlando	4	0	29	9	3	8	.375	0	0	.000	3	4	.750	1	2	3	3	2	0	3	2	0	7.3	2.3	0.8	0.8	.471
02-03	Utah	2	0	16	4	1	4	.250	0	0	.000	2	4	.500	0	1	1	0	4	0	0	0	0	8.0	2.0	0.5	0.0	-.034
NBA Playoff Totals		7	0	47	13	4	13	.308	0	0	.000	5	8	.625	1	3	4	3	6	0	3	2	0	6.7	1.9	0.6	0.4	....

• AMAYA, Ashraf

Ashraf Amaya

Born: Nov. 23, 1971. Oak Park, IL, United States.   Height: 6'8".   Weight: 230 lbs.   Drafted: —   College: Southern Illinois

YEAR	TEAM	GP	GS	MIN	PTS	FGM	FGA	FG%	3PM	3PA	3P%	FTM	FTA	FT%	ORB	DRB	TRB	AST	PF	DQ	STL	BLK	TO	MPG	PPG	RPG	APG	PCM
95-96	Vancouver	54	34	1104	339	121	252	.480	0	1	.000	97	149	.651	114	189	303	33	151	3	22	10	59	20.4	6.3	5.6	0.6	.376
96-97	Washington	31	0	144	40	12	40	.300	1	1	1.000	15	28	.536	19	33	52	3	29	0	7	3	9	4.6	1.3	1.7	0.1	.326
NBA Season Totals		85	34	1248	379	133	292	.455	1	2	.500	112	177	.633	133	222	355	36	180	3	29	13	68	14.7	4.5	4.2	0.4	....

• ANDEREGG, Bob

Robert H. Anderegg

Born: Aug. 24, 1937. Monroe, WI, United States.   Height: 6'3".   Weight: 200 lbs.   Drafted: 1959   College: Michigan State

YEAR	TEAM	GP	GS	MIN	PTS	FGM	FGA	FG%	3PM	3PA	3P%	FTM	FTA	FT%	ORB	DRB	TRB	AST	PF	DQ	STL	BLK	TO	MPG	PPG	RPG	APG	PCM
59-60	New York	33	....	373	133	55	143	.385	....	....	....	23	42	.548	....	....	69	29	32	0	....	....	....	11.3	4.0	2.1	0.9	.363
NBA Season Totals		33	....	373	133	55	143	.385	....	....	....	23	42	.548	....	....	69	29	32	0	....	....	....	11.3	4.0	2.1	0.9	....

YEAR	TEAM	GP	GS	MIN	PTS	FGM	FGA	FG%	3PM	3PA	3P%	FTM	FTA	FT%	ORB	DRB	TRB	AST	PF	DQ	STL	BLK	TO	MPG	PPG	RPG	APG	PCM

• ANDERSEN, Chris
Chris Andersen

Born: July 7, 1978. Iola, TX, United States. Height: 6'10". Weight: 230 lbs. Drafted: — College: Blinn College

YEAR	TEAM	GP	GS	MIN	PTS	FGM	FGA	FG%	3PM	3PA	3P%	FTM	FTA	FT%	ORB	DRB	TRB	AST	PF	DQ	STL	BLK	TO	MPG	PPG	RPG	APG	PCM
01-02	Denver	24	1	262	72	25	74	.338	0	4	.000	22	28	.786	38	38	76	7	35	0	7	28	13	10.9	3.0	3.2	0.3	.403
02-03	Denver	59	3	907	305	114	285	.400	0	1	.000	77	140	.550	109	165	274	32	90	1	30	60	60	15.4	5.2	4.6	0.5	.431
NBA Season Totals		83	4	1169	377	139	359	.387	0	5	.000	99	168	.589	147	203	350	39	125	1	37	88	73	14.1	4.5	4.2	0.5	....

• ANDERSON, Andrew
Andrew Emil Anderson

Born: July 6, 1945. Buffalo, NY, United States. Height: 6'2". Weight: 184 lbs. Drafted: 1967 College: Canisius

YEAR	TEAM	GP	GS	MIN	PTS	FGM	FGA	FG%	3PM	3PA	3P%	FTM	FTA	FT%	ORB	DRB	TRB	AST	PF	DQ	STL	BLK	TO	MPG	PPG	RPG	APG	PCM
67-68	Oakland-A	77	....	1894	730	279	756	.369	9	44	.205	163	225	.724	....	....	167	118	190	1	....	....	120	24.6	9.5	2.2	1.5	.267
68-69	Miami-A	33	....	718	332	118	263	.449	0	6	.000	96	120	.800	48	53	101	42	71	1	....	....	51	21.8	10.1	3.1	1.3	.420
68-69	Oakland-A	3	....	24	12	5	9	.556	0	0	.000	2	3	.667	3	1	4	3	5	0	....	....	2	8.0	4.0	1.3	1.0	.536
69-70	Los Angeles-A	49	....	1533	700	292	677	.431	1	11	.091	115	155	.742	110	89	199	125	122	1	....	....	89	31.3	14.3	4.1	2.6	.400
69-70	Miami-A	32	....	617	307	109	253	.431	0	2	.000	89	113	.788	30	26	56	39	74	0	....	....	54	19.3	9.6	1.8	1.2	.379
ABA Season Totals		194	....	4786	2081	803	1958	.410	10	63	.159	465	616	.755	191	169	527	327	462	3	....	....	316	24.7	10.7	2.7	1.7	....
68-69	Miami-A	12	....	244	97	35	81	.432	1	3	.333	26	35	.743	....	....	23	16	21	0	....	....	23	20.3	8.1	1.9	1.3	.339
69-70	Los Angeles-A	16	....	307	128	50	134	.373	0	2	.000	28	31	.903	....	....	37	0	....	0	....	....	17	19.2	8.0	2.3	0.0	....
ABA Playoff Totals		28	....	551	225	85	215	.395	1	5	.200	54	66	.818	....	....	60	16	21	0	....	....	40	19.7	8.0	2.1	0.6	....

• ANDERSON, Art
Art Anderson

Born: 1916. Height: 6'6". Weight: 190 lbs. Drafted: — College: Augustana (IL)

YEAR	TEAM	GP	GS	MIN	PTS	FGM	FGA	FG%	3PM	3PA	3P%	FTM	FTA	FT%	ORB	DRB	TRB	AST	PF	DQ	STL	BLK	TO	MPG	PPG	RPG	APG	PCM
40-41	Wingfoots-N	12	....	....	8	2	....	....	....	....	....	4	....	....	....	....	....	....	....	....	....	....	....	0.7	....	....	....
NBL Season Totals		12	....	....	8	2	....	....	....	....	....	4	....	....	....	....	....	....	....	....	....	....	....	0.7	....	....	....

• ANDERSON, Carl
Carl (Buttercup) Anderson

Born: 1913. Height: 6'3". Weight: 215 lbs. Drafted: 1961 College: USC

YEAR	TEAM	GP	GS	MIN	PTS	FGM	FGA	FG%	3PM	3PA	3P%	FTM	FTA	FT%	ORB	DRB	TRB	AST	PF	DQ	STL	BLK	TO	MPG	PPG	RPG	APG	PCM
38-39	Indianapolis-N	3	....	....	0	0	....	....	....	....	....	0	....	....	....	....	....	....	....	....	....	....	....	0.0	....	....	....
40-41	Hammond-N	2	....	....	0	0	....	....	....	....	....	0	....	....	....	....	....	....	....	....	....	....	....	0.0	....	....	....
NBL Season Totals		5	....	....	0	0	....	....	....	....	....	0	....	....	....	....	....	....	....	....	....	....	....	0.0	....	....	....

• ANDERSON, Cliff
Clifford V. Anderson

Born: Sept. 7, 1944. Height: 6'2". Weight: 200 lbs. Drafted: 1967 College: St. Joseph's (PA)

YEAR	TEAM	GP	GS	MIN	PTS	FGM	FGA	FG%	3PM	3PA	3P%	FTM	FTA	FT%	ORB	DRB	TRB	AST	PF	DQ	STL	BLK	TO	MPG	PPG	RPG	APG	PCM
67-68	LA Lakers	18	....	94	26	7	29	.241	....	....	....	12	28	.429	....	....	11	17	18	1	....	....	....	5.2	1.4	0.6	0.9	.256
68-69	LA Lakers	35	....	289	135	44	108	.407	....	....	....	47	82	.573	....	....	44	31	58	0	....	....	....	8.3	3.9	1.3	0.9	.400
69-70	Denver-A	3	....	22	6	2	4	.500	0	0	.000	2	6	.333	1	3	4	4	3	0	....	....	3	7.3	2.0	1.3	1.3	.422
70-71	Cleveland	23	....	171	79	19	59	.322	....	....	....	41	60	.683	....	....	37	16	22	1	....	....	....	7.4	3.4	1.6	0.7	.450
70-71	Philadelphia	5	....	27	7	1	6	.167	....	....	....	5	7	.714	....	....	11	4	7	0	....	....	....	5.4	1.4	2.2	0.8	.476
NBA Season Totals		81	....	581	247	71	202	.351	....	....	....	105	177	.593	....	....	103	68	105	2	....	....	....	7.2	3.0	1.3	0.8	....
ABA Season Totals		3	....	22	6	2	4	.500	0	0	.000	2	6	.333	1	3	4	4	3	0	....	....	3	7.3	2.0	1.3	1.3	....
Career Totals		84	....	603	253	73	206	.354	0	0	.000	107	183	.585	1	3	107	72	108	2	....	....	3	7.2	3.0	1.3	0.9	....
68-69	LA Lakers	3	....	10	4	2	5	.400	....	....	....	0	0	.000	....	....	1	0	1	0	....	....	....	3.3	1.3	0.3	0.0	.191
NBA Playoff Totals		3	....	10	4	2	5	.400	....	....	....	0	0	.000	....	....	1	0	1	0	....	....	....	3.3	1.3	0.3	0.0	....

• ANDERSON, Dan
Daniel Edward (Danny) Anderson

Born: Jan. 1, 1951. Height: 6'2". Weight: 185 lbs. Drafted: 1974 College: USC

YEAR	TEAM	GP	GS	MIN	PTS	FGM	FGA	FG%	3PM	3PA	3P%	FTM	FTA	FT%	ORB	DRB	TRB	AST	PF	DQ	STL	BLK	TO	MPG	PPG	RPG	APG	PCM
74-75	Portland	43	....	453	120	47	105	.448	....	....	....	26	30	.867	8	21	29	81	44	0	16	1	....	10.5	2.8	0.7	1.9	.370
75-76	Portland	52	....	614	227	88	181	.486	....	....	....	51	61	.836	15	47	62	85	58	0	20	2	....	11.8	4.4	1.2	1.6	.437
NBA Season Totals		95	....	1067	347	135	286	.472	....	....	....	77	91	.846	23	68	91	166	102	0	36	3	....	11.2	3.7	1.0	1.7	....

• ANDERSON, Dan
Daniel W. Anderson

Born: Feb. 15, 1943. Minneapolis, MN, United States. Height: 6'10". Weight: 230 lbs. Drafted: 1965 College: Augsburg

YEAR	TEAM	GP	GS	MIN	PTS	FGM	FGA	FG%	3PM	3PA	3P%	FTM	FTA	FT%	ORB	DRB	TRB	AST	PF	DQ	STL	BLK	TO	MPG	PPG	RPG	APG	PCM
67-68	New Jersey-A	78	....	2626	1149	463	938	.494	0	0	.000	223	320	.697	303	553	856	92	329	10	....	....	131	33.7	14.7	11.0	1.2	.532
68-69	Kentucky-A	8	....	94	20	7	22	.318	0	0	.000	6	8	.750	8	17	25	6	19	1	....	....	8	11.8	2.5	3.1	0.8	.281
68-69	Minnesota-A	29	....	628	261	112	228	.491	0	0	.000	37	50	.740	98	120	218	26	72	1	....	....	30	21.7	9.0	7.5	0.9	.544
68-69	New York-A	25	....	677	277	101	233	.433	0	0	.000	75	91	.824	79	138	217	34	83	7	....	....	43	27.1	11.1	8.7	1.4	.512
ABA Season Totals		140	....	4025	1707	683	1421	.481	0	0	.000	341	469	.727	488	828	1316	158	503	19	....	....	212	28.8	12.2	9.4	1.1	....
68-69	Minnesota-A	5	....	38	15	6	13	.462	0	0	.000	3	4	.750	....	....	10	5	8	0	....	....	2	7.6	3.0	2.0	1.0	.511
ABA Playoff Totals		5	....	38	15	6	13	.462	0	0	.000	3	4	.750	....	....	10	5	8	0	....	....	2	7.6	3.0	2.0	1.0	....

• ANDERSON, Derek
Derek Lamont Anderson

Born: July 18, 1974. Louisville, KY, United States. Height: 6'5". Weight: 194 lbs. Drafted: 1997 College: Kentucky

YEAR	TEAM	GP	GS	MIN	PTS	FGM	FGA	FG%	3PM	3PA	3P%	FTM	FTA	FT%	ORB	DRB	TRB	AST	PF	DQ	STL	BLK	TO	MPG	PPG	RPG	APG	PCM
97-98	Cleveland	66	13	1839	770	239	586	.408	17	84	.202	275	315	.873	55	132	187	227	136	0	86	13	125	27.9	11.7	2.8	3.4	.416
98-99	Cleveland	38	13	978	409	125	314	.398	21	69	.304	138	165	.836	20	89	109	145	73	0	48	4	82	25.7	10.8	2.9	3.8	.437
99-00	LA Clippers	64	58	2201	1080	377	860	.438	55	178	.309	271	309	.877	80	178	258	220	149	2	90	11	167	34.4	16.9	4.0	3.4	.441

YEAR	TEAM	GP	GS	MIN	PTS	FGM	FGA	FG%	3PM	3PA	3P%	FTM	FTA	FT%	ORB	DRB	TRB	AST	PF	DQ	STL	BLK	TO	MPG	PPG	RPG	APG	PCM
00-01	San Antonio	82	82	2859	1269	413	993	.416	101	253	.399	342	402	.851	75	288	363	301	188	1	120	14	165	34.9	15.5	4.4	3.7	.443
01-02	Portland	70	27	1860	757	247	612	.404	85	228	.373	178	208	.856	47	142	189	216	113	1	68	8	87	26.6	10.8	2.7	3.1	.408
02-03	Portland	76	76	2555	1057	355	832	.427	116	331	.350	231	269	.859	53	211	264	325	141	1	90	16	128	33.6	13.9	3.5	4.3	.437
NBA Season Totals		396	269	12292	5342	1756	4197	.418	395	1143	.346	1435	1668	.860	330	1040	1370	1434	800	5	502	66	754	31.0	13.5	3.5	3.6	....
97-98	Cleveland	4	0	103	43	10	22	.455	0	0	.000	23	26	.885	0	9	9	11	10	0	5	1	12	25.8	10.8	2.3	2.8	.396
00-01	San Antonio	7	7	194	54	16	61	.262	6	22	.273	16	21	.762	3	16	19	17	10	0	3	0	15	27.7	7.7	2.7	2.4	.164
01-02	Portland	3	0	76	44	13	30	.433	2	6	.333	16	18	.889	3	4	7	7	1	0	2	0	6	25.3	14.7	2.3	2.3	.495
02-03	Portland	2	2	22	2	1	4	.250	0	1	.000	0	1	1.000	1	0	1	0	1	0	0	0	1	11.0	1.0	0.5	0.0	-.074
NBA Playoff Totals		16	9	395	143	40	117	.342	8	29	.276	55	66	.833	7	29	36	35	22	0	10	1	34	24.7	8.9	2.3	2.2	....

• ANDERSON, Dwight

Dwight Anthony Anderson

Born: Dec. 28, 1960. Dayton, OH, United States.   Height: 6'3".   Weight: 185 lbs.   Drafted: 1982   College: USC

YEAR	TEAM	GP	GS	MIN	PTS	FGM	FGA	FG%	3PM	3PA	3P%	FTM	FTA	FT%	ORB	DRB	TRB	AST	PF	DQ	STL	BLK	TO	MPG	PPG	RPG	APG	PCM
82-83	Denver	5	0	33	21	7	14	.500	0	0	.000	7	10	.700	0	2	2	3	7	0	1	0	5	6.6	4.2	0.4	0.6	.354
NBA Season Totals		5	0	33	21	7	14	.500	0	0	.000	7	10	.700	0	2	2	3	7	0	1	0	5	6.6	4.2	0.4	0.6	....

• ANDERSON, Eric

Eric Walfred Anderson

Born: May 26, 1970. Chicago, IL, United States.   Height: 6'9".   Weight: 220 lbs.   Drafted: —   College: Indiana

YEAR	TEAM	GP	GS	MIN	PTS	FGM	FGA	FG%	3PM	3PA	3P%	FTM	FTA	FT%	ORB	DRB	TRB	AST	PF	DQ	STL	BLK	TO	MPG	PPG	RPG	APG	PCM
92-93	New York	16	0	44	21	5	18	.278	0	0	.000	11	13	.846	6	8	14	3	14	0	3	1	5	2.8	1.3	0.9	0.2	.380
93-94	New York	11	0	39	21	7	17	.412	2	2	1.000	5	14	.357	6	11	17	2	9	0	0	1	2	3.5	1.9	1.5	0.2	.523
NBA Season Totals		27	0	83	42	12	35	.343	2	2	1.000	16	27	.593	12	19	31	5	23	0	3	2	7	3.1	1.6	1.1	0.2	....
92-93	New York	2	0	6	2	1	2	.500	0	0	.000	0	0	.000	0	1	1	0	2	0	0	0	1	3.0	1.0	0.5	0.0	.022
NBA Playoff Totals		2	0	6	2	1	2	.500	0	0	.000	0	0	.000	0	1	1	0	2	0	0	0	1	3.0	1.0	0.5	0.0	....

• ANDERSON, Gene

Gene Anderson

Born: 1917.   Height: 6'2".   Weight: 190 lbs.   Drafted: —   College: Purdue

YEAR	TEAM	GP	GS	MIN	PTS	FGM	FGA	FG%	3PM	3PA	3P%	FTM	FTA	FT%	ORB	DRB	TRB	AST	PF	DQ	STL	BLK	TO	MPG	PPG	RPG	APG	PCM
39-40	Wingfoots-N	25	....	....	108	47	....	....	....	....	....	....	14	....	....	....	....	....	....	....	....	....	....	....	4.3	....	....	....
40-41	Wingfoots-N	23	....	....	114	43	....	....	....	....	....	....	28	....	....	....	....	....	....	....	....	....	....	....	5.0	....	....	....
41-42	Wingfoots-N	23	....	....	108	45	....	....	....	....	....	....	18	....	....	....	....	....	....	....	....	....	....	....	4.7	....	....	....
NBL Season Totals		71	....	....	330	135	....	....	....	....	....	....	60	....	....	....	....	....	....	....	....	....	....	....	4.6	....	....	....
41-42	Wingfoots-N	3	....	....	17	8	....	....	....	....	....	....	1	....	....	....	....	....	....	....	....	....	....	....	5.7	....	....	....
NBL Playoff Totals		3	....	....	17	8	....	....	....	....	....	....	1	....	....	....	....	....	....	....	....	....	....	....	5.7	....	....	....

• ANDERSON, Greg

Gregory Wayne (Cadillac) Anderson

Born: June 22, 1964. Houston, TX, United States.   Height: 6'10".   Weight: 230 lbs.   Drafted: 1987   College: Houston

YEAR	TEAM	GP	GS	MIN	PTS	FGM	FGA	FG%	3PM	3PA	3P%	FTM	FTA	FT%	ORB	DRB	TRB	AST	PF	DQ	STL	BLK	TO	MPG	PPG	RPG	APG	PCM
87-88	San Antonio	82	45	1984	957	379	756	.501	1	5	.200	198	328	.604	161	352	513	79	228	1	54	122	139	24.2	11.7	6.3	1.0	.522
88-89	San Antonio	82	56	2401	1127	460	914	.503	0	3	.000	207	403	.514	255	421	676	61	221	2	102	103	180	29.3	13.7	8.2	0.7	.511
89-90	Milwaukee	60	28	1291	529	219	432	.507	0	0	.000	91	170	.535	112	261	373	24	176	3	32	54	78	21.5	8.8	6.2	0.4	.459
90-91	Milwaukee	26	0	247	70	27	73	.370	0	1	.000	16	28	.571	26	49	75	3	29	0	8	9	21	9.5	2.7	2.9	0.1	.313
90-91	New Jersey	1	0	18	8	4	4	1.000	0	0	.000	0	0	.000	4	2	6	1	4	0	2	0	1	18.0	8.0	6.0	1.0	.763
90-91	Denver	41	2	659	214	85	193	.440	0	0	.000	44	87	.506	67	170	237	12	107	3	25	36	62	16.1	5.2	5.8	0.3	.419
91-92	Denver	82	82	2793	945	389	854	.456	0	4	.000	167	268	.623	337	604	941	78	263	3	88	65	205	34.1	11.5	11.5	1.0	.449
93-94	Detroit	77	47	1624	491	201	370	.543	1	3	.333	88	154	.571	183	388	571	51	234	4	55	68	92	21.1	6.4	7.4	0.7	.496
94-95	Atlanta	51	0	622	148	57	104	.548	0	0	.000	34	71	.479	62	126	188	17	103	0	23	32	31	12.2	2.9	3.7	0.3	.410
95-96	San Antonio	46	7	344	54	24	47	.511	0	1	.000	6	25	.240	29	71	100	10	66	0	9	25	23	7.5	1.2	2.2	0.2	.312
96-97	San Antonio	82	48	1659	322	130	262	.496	0	1	.000	62	93	.667	157	291	448	34	225	2	63	67	74	20.2	3.9	5.5	0.4	.353
97-98	Atlanta	50	0	398	88	36	81	.444	0	5	.000	16	41	.390	39	79	118	15	85	0	19	8	15	8.0	1.8	2.4	0.3	.331
NBA Season Totals		680	315	14040	4953	2011	4090	.492	2	23	.087	929	1668	.557	1432	2814	4246	385	1741	18	480	589	921	20.6	7.3	6.2	0.6	....
87-88	San Antonio	3	3	95	38	17	36	.472	0	0	.000	4	9	.444	6	15	21	3	10	1	2	4	10	31.7	12.7	7.0	1.0	.341
89-90	Milwaukee	4	0	101	33	13	19	.684	0	0	.000	7	14	.500	6	18	24	0	19	2	1	4	4	25.3	8.3	6.0	0.0	.382
94-95	Atlanta	3	0	39	5	1	5	.200	0	0	.000	3	4	.750	1	12	13	2	9	0	2	2	0	13.0	1.7	4.3	0.7	.375
95-96	San Antonio	6	0	34	1	0	5	.000	0	0	.000	0	2	.500	2	7	9	0	5	0	2	1	4	5.7	0.2	1.5	0.0	.029
97-98	Atlanta	1	0	4	0	0	0	.000	0	0	.000	0	2	.000	0	2	2	0	1	0	0	1	1	4.0	0.0	2.0	0.0	.114
NBA Playoff Totals		17	3	273	77	31	65	.477	0	0	.000	15	31	.484	15	54	69	5	44	3	7	12	19	16.1	4.5	4.1	0.3	....

• ANDERSON, J.J.

Mitchell Keith (J.J.) Anderson

Born: Sept. 23, 1960. Chicago, IL, United States.   Height: 6'8".   Weight: 195 lbs.   Drafted: 1982   College: Bradley

YEAR	TEAM	GP	GS	MIN	PTS	FGM	FGA	FG%	3PM	3PA	3P%	FTM	FTA	FT%	ORB	DRB	TRB	AST	PF	DQ	STL	BLK	TO	MPG	PPG	RPG	APG	PCM
82-83	Philadelphia	13	0	48	17	8	22	.364	0	1	.000	1	3	.333	4	8	12	1	6	0	1	0	5	3.7	1.3	0.9	0.1	.189
82-83	Utah	52	2	1154	463	182	357	.510	0	3	.000	99	172	.576	115	167	282	66	147	1	62	21	73	22.2	8.9	5.4	1.3	.469
83-84	Utah	48	0	311	122	55	130	.423	0	3	.000	12	29	.414	38	25	63	22	28	0	15	9	19	6.5	2.5	1.3	0.5	.380
84-85	Utah	44	0	457	149	61	149	.409	0	2	.000	27	45	.600	29	53	82	21	70	0	29	9	31	10.4	3.4	1.9	0.5	.287
NBA Season Totals		157	2	1970	751	306	658	.465	0	9	.000	139	249	.558	186	253	439	110	251	1	107	39	128	12.5	4.8	2.8	0.7	....
83-84	Utah	5	0	13	11	5	8	.625	1	1	1.000	0	0	.000	3	1	4	0	2	0	0	1	0	2.6	2.2	0.8	0.0	.918
NBA Playoff Totals		5	0	13	11	5	8	.625	1	1	1.000	0	0	.000	3	1	4	0	2	0	0	1	0	2.6	2.2	0.8	0.0	....

• ANDERSON, Jerome

Jerome Anderson

Born: Oct. 9, 1953. Mullens, WV, United States. Height: 6'5". Weight: 195 lbs. Drafted: 1975 College: West Virginia

YEAR	TEAM	GP	GS	MIN	PTS	FGM	FGA	FG%	3PM	3PA	3P%	FTM	FTA	FT%	ORB	DRB	TRB	AST	PF	DQ	STL	BLK	TO	MPG	PPG	RPG	APG	PCM
75-76	Boston	22	....	126	61	25	45	.556	....	....	....	11	16	.688	4	9	13	6	25	0	3	3	....	5.7	2.8	0.6	0.3	.389
76-77	Indiana	27	....	164	66	26	59	.441	....	....	....	14	20	.700	9	3	12	10	26	0	6	2	....	6.1	2.4	0.4	0.4	.277
NBA Season Totals		49	....	290	127	51	104	.490	....	....	....	25	36	.694	13	12	25	16	51	0	9	5	....	5.9	2.6	0.5	0.3	....
75-76	Boston	4	....	5	2	1	3	.333	....	....	....	0	0	.000	1	0	1	1	1	0	0	0	....	1.3	0.5	0.3	0.3	.371
NBA Playoff Totals		4	....	5	2	1	3	.333	....	....	....	0	0	.000	1	0	1	1	1	0	0	0	....	1.3	0.5	0.3	0.3	....

• ANDERSON, Kenny

Kenneth Anderson

Born: Oct. 9, 1970. Queens, NY, United States. Height: 6' Weight: 168 lbs. Drafted: 1991 College: Georgia Tech

YEAR	TEAM	GP	GS	MIN	PTS	FGM	FGA	FG%	3PM	3PA	3P%	FTM	FTA	FT%	ORB	DRB	TRB	AST	PF	DQ	STL	BLK	TO	MPG	PPG	RPG	APG	PCM
91-92	New Jersey	64	13	1086	450	187	480	.390	3	13	.231	73	98	.745	38	89	127	203	68	0	67	9	96	17.0	7.0	2.0	3.2	.416
92-93	New Jersey	55	55	2010	927	370	850	.435	7	25	.280	180	232	.776	51	175	226	449	140	1	96	11	154	36.5	16.9	4.1	8.2	.515
93-94	New Jersey	82	82	3135	1538	576	1381	.417	40	132	.303	346	423	.818	89	233	322	784	201	0	158	15	262	38.2	18.8	3.9	9.6	.553
94-95	New Jersey	72	70	2689	1267	411	1031	.399	97	294	.330	348	414	.841	73	177	250	680	184	1	103	14	223	37.3	17.6	3.5	9.4	.530
95-96	New Jersey	31	28	1042	473	143	380	.376	36	99	.364	151	188	.803	37	64	101	247	73	0	52	8	59	33.6	15.3	3.3	8.0	.534
95-96	Charlotte	38	36	1302	577	206	454	.454	56	157	.357	109	150	.727	26	76	102	328	105	1	59	6	87	34.3	15.2	2.7	8.6	.536
96-97	Portland	82	81	3081	1436	485	1137	.427	132	366	.361	334	435	.768	91	272	363	584	222	2	162	15	197	37.6	17.5	4.4	7.1	.526
97-98	Portland	45	40	1472	567	204	527	.387	47	133	.353	112	145	.772	36	98	134	245	99	1	61	1	113	32.7	12.6	3.0	5.4	.376
97-98	Boston	16	16	386	179	64	147	.435	10	27	.370	41	49	.837	3	36	39	100	36	0	26	0	29	24.1	11.2	2.4	6.3	.581
98-99	Boston	34	33	1010	412	161	357	.451	6	24	.250	84	101	.832	24	79	103	193	78	1	33	2	71	29.7	12.1	3.0	5.7	.465
99-00	Boston	82	82	2593	1149	434	986	.440	85	220	.386	196	253	.775	55	170	225	420	230	4	139	8	130	31.6	14.0	2.7	5.1	.461
00-01	Boston	33	28	849	246	88	227	.388	11	33	.333	59	71	.831	16	57	73	134	62	0	44	2	52	25.7	7.5	2.2	4.1	.348
01-02	Boston	76	76	2430	731	312	716	.436	9	33	.273	98	132	.742	57	218	275	403	210	4	141	10	119	32.0	9.6	3.6	5.3	.401
02-03	Seattle	38	1	689	233	102	232	.440	0	5	.000	29	35	.829	17	70	87	121	63	0	40	1	33	18.1	6.1	2.3	3.2	.438
02-03	New Orleans	23	1	446	139	61	150	.407	1	2	.500	16	22	.727	14	31	45	77	43	0	18	4	42	19.4	6.0	2.0	3.3	.320
NBA Season Totals		771	642	24220	10324	3804	9055	.420	540	1563	.345	2176	2748	.792	627	1845	2472	4968	1814	15	1199	106	1667	31.4	13.4	3.2	6.4	....
91-92	New Jersey	3	0	24	8	3	9	.333	0	0	.000	2	2	1.000	1	2	3	3	1	0	1	0	1	8.0	2.7	1.0	1.0	.332
93-94	New Jersey	4	4	181	63	19	54	.352	3	10	.300	22	33	.667	2	10	12	27	11	0	9	0	9	45.3	15.8	3.0	6.8	.337
96-97	Portland	4	4	169	68	22	46	.478	5	19	.263	19	20	.950	2	15	17	19	10	0	7	1	11	42.3	17.0	4.3	4.8	.437
01-02	Boston	16	16	560	192	82	197	.416	0	0	.000	28	35	.800	13	37	50	76	58	1	21	0	28	35.0	12.0	3.1	4.8	.322
02-03	New Orleans	5	0	51	11	4	12	.333	0	0	.000	3	3	1.000	0	2	2	9	6	0	3	0	4	10.2	2.2	0.4	1.8	.230
NBA Playoff Totals		32	24	985	342	130	318	.409	8	29	.276	74	93	.796	18	66	84	134	86	1	41	1	53	30.8	10.7	2.6	4.2	....

• ANDERSON, Kim

Keith Kim Anderson

Born: May 12, 1955. Sedalia, MO, United States. Height: 6'7". Weight: 200 lbs. Drafted: 1978 College: Missouri

YEAR	TEAM	GP	GS	MIN	PTS	FGM	FGA	FG%	3PM	3PA	3P%	FTM	FTA	FT%	ORB	DRB	TRB	AST	PF	DQ	STL	BLK	TO	MPG	PPG	RPG	APG	PCM
78-79	Portland	21	....	224	63	24	77	.312	....	....	....	15	28	.536	17	28	45	15	42	0	4	5	21	10.7	3.0	2.1	0.7	.165
NBA Season Totals		21	....	224	63	24	77	.312	....	....	....	15	28	.536	17	28	45	15	42	0	4	5	21	10.7	3.0	2.1	0.7	....

• ANDERSON, Michael

Michael Levin Anderson

Born: Mar. 23, 1966. Philadelphia, PA, United States. Height: 5'11". Weight: 184 lbs. Drafted: 1988 College: Drexel

YEAR	TEAM	GP	GS	MIN	PTS	FGM	FGA	FG%	3PM	3PA	3P%	FTM	FTA	FT%	ORB	DRB	TRB	AST	PF	DQ	STL	BLK	TO	MPG	PPG	RPG	APG	PCM
88-89	San Antonio	36	12	730	204	73	175	.417	1	7	.143	57	82	.695	44	45	89	153	64	0	44	3	83	20.3	5.7	2.5	4.3	.385
NBA Season Totals		36	12	730	204	73	175	.417	1	7	.143	57	82	.695	44	45	89	153	64	0	44	3	83	20.3	5.7	2.5	4.3	....

• ANDERSON, Nick

Nelison Anderson

Born: Jan. 20, 1968. Chicago, IL, United States. Height: 6'6". Weight: 205 lbs. Drafted: 1989 College: Illinois

YEAR	TEAM	GP	GS	MIN	PTS	FGM	FGA	FG%	3PM	3PA	3P%	FTM	FTA	FT%	ORB	DRB	TRB	AST	PF	DQ	STL	BLK	TO	MPG	PPG	RPG	APG	PCM
89-90	Orlando	81	9	1785	931	372	753	.494	1	17	.059	186	264	.705	107	209	316	124	140	0	69	34	138	22.0	11.5	3.9	1.5	.486
90-91	Orlando	70	42	1971	990	400	857	.467	17	58	.293	173	259	.668	92	294	386	106	145	0	74	44	112	28.2	14.1	5.5	1.5	.474
91-92	Orlando	60	59	2203	1196	482	1042	.463	30	85	.353	202	303	.667	98	286	384	163	132	0	97	33	126	36.7	19.9	6.4	2.7	.500
92-93	Orlando	79	76	2920	1574	594	1324	.449	88	249	.353	298	402	.741	122	355	477	265	200	1	128	56	166	37.0	19.9	6.0	3.4	.512
93-94	Orlando	81	81	2811	1277	504	1054	.478	101	314	.322	168	250	.672	113	363	476	294	148	1	134	33	162	34.7	15.8	5.9	3.6	.508
94-95	Orlando	76	76	2588	1200	439	923	.476	179	431	.415	143	203	.704	85	250	335	314	124	0	125	22	144	34.1	15.8	4.4	4.1	.506
95-96	Orlando	77	77	2717	1134	400	904	.442	168	430	.391	166	240	.692	92	323	415	279	135	0	121	46	139	35.3	14.7	5.4	3.6	.469
96-97	Orlando	63	61	2163	757	288	725	.397	143	405	.353	38	94	.404	66	238	304	182	160	1	120	32	88	34.3	12.0	4.8	2.9	.364
97-98	Orlando	58	44	1701	890	343	754	.455	77	214	.360	127	199	.638	98	199	297	119	98	1	72	23	87	29.3	15.3	5.1	2.1	.496
98-99	Orlando	47	39	1581	701	253	640	.395	96	277	.347	99	162	.611	51	226	277	91	72	0	64	15	83	33.6	14.9	5.9	1.9	.405
99-00	Sacramento	72	72	2094	781	306	782	.391	132	397	.332	37	76	.487	83	256	339	123	118	0	94	16	95	29.1	10.8	4.7	1.7	.350
00-01	Sacramento	21	0	169	38	14	57	.246	10	39	.256	0	0	.000	3	22	25	13	13	0	10	4	7	8.0	1.8	1.2	0.6	.217
01-02	Memphis	15	0	219	60	21	76	.276	13	48	.271	5	9	.556	1	32	33	14	17	0	6	6	14	14.6	4.0	2.2	0.9	.201
NBA Season Totals		800	636	24922	11529	4416	9891	.446	1055	2964	.356	1642	2461	.667	1011	3053	4064	2087	1502	4	1114	364	1361	31.2	14.4	5.1	2.6	....
93-94	Orlando	3	3	120	43	13	34	.382	8	20	.400	9	12	.750	2	8	10	10	8	0	5	2	5	40.0	14.3	3.3	3.3	.338
94-95	Orlando	21	21	814	298	107	239	.448	41	107	.383	43	63	.683	21	79	100	65	49	0	33	10	30	38.8	14.2	4.8	3.1	.389
95-96	Orlando	11	11	418	156	55	127	.433	18	63	.286	28	45	.622	16	39	55	21	22	0	21	5	21	38.0	14.2	5.0	1.9	.356
96-97	Orlando	5	5	130	28	12	36	.333	4	15	.267	0	2	.000	3	26	29	3	8	0	3	9	6	26.0	5.6	5.8	0.6	.283
98-99	Orlando	4	4	152	83	29	79	.367	11	42	.262	14	19	.737	7	20	27	9	12	1	9	0	10	38.0	20.8	6.8	2.3	.422
99-00	Sacramento	5	5	132	36	11	34	.324	7	20	.350	7	8	.875	4	13	17	2	9	0	1	3	4	26.4	7.2	3.4	0.4	.214
NBA Playoff Totals		49	49	1766	644	227	549	.413	89	267	.333	101	149	.678	53	185	238	110	108	1	72	29	76	36.0	13.1	4.9	2.2	....

• ANDERSON, Richard

Richard Andrew Anderson

Born: Nov. 19, 1960. San Pedro, CA, United States. Height: 6'10". Weight: 240 lbs. Drafted: 1982 College: Cal State Santa Barbara

YEAR	TEAM	GP	GS	MIN	PTS	FGM	FGA	FG%	3PM	3PA	3P%	FTM	FTA	FT%	ORB	DRB	TRB	AST	PF	DQ	STL	BLK	TO	MPG	PPG	RPG	APG	PCM
82-83	San Diego	78	5	1274	403	174	431	.404	7	19	.368	48	69	.696	111	161	272	120	170	2	57	26	94	16.3	5.2	3.5	1.5	.355
83-84	Denver	78	17	1380	663	272	638	.426	3	19	.158	116	150	.773	136	270	406	193	183	0	46	28	109	17.7	8.5	5.2	2.5	.560

YEAR TEAM	GP	GS	MIN	PTS	FGM	FGA	FG%	3PM	3PA	3P%	FTM	FTA	FT%	ORB	DRB	TRB	AST	PF	DQ	STL	BLK	TO	MPG	PPG	RPG	APG	PCM
86-87 Houston	51	0	312	144	59	139	.424	4	16	.250	22	29	.759	24	55	79	33	37	0	7	3	20	6.1	2.8	1.5	0.6	.476
87-88 Houston	12	0	53	32	11	26	.423	6	15	.400	4	5	.800	9	8	17	4	4	0	1	0	1	4.4	2.7	1.4	0.3	.676
87-88 Portland	62	3	1297	416	160	413	.387	42	135	.311	54	72	.750	82	204	286	108	133	1	50	16	62	20.9	6.7	4.6	1.7	.382
88-89 Portland	72	3	1082	371	145	348	.417	49	141	.348	32	38	.842	62	169	231	98	100	1	44	12	58	15.0	5.2	3.2	1.4	.417
89-90 Charlotte	54	2	604	231	88	211	.417	37	100	.370	18	23	.783	33	94	127	55	64	0	20	9	27	11.2	4.3	2.4	1.0	.435
NBA Season Totals	407	30	6002	2260	909	2206	.412	148	445	.333	294	386	.762	457	961	1418	611	691	4	225	94	371	14.7	5.6	3.5	1.5	....
83-84 Denver	4	0	37	16	6	15	.400	0	1	.000	4	6	.667	1	8	9	5	6	0	0	1	1	9.3	4.0	2.3	1.3	.476
86-87 Houston	5	0	5	5	1	3	.333	1	2	.500	2	2	1.000	1	0	1	0	1	0	0	0	1	1.0	1.0	0.2	0.0	.535
87-88 Portland	3	0	63	32	11	24	.458	6	14	.429	4	4	1.000	5	8	13	1	11	0	2	1	2	21.0	10.7	4.3	0.3	.458
88-89 Portland	3	0	35	5	2	6	.333	1	4	.250	0	0	.000	0	0	0	4	2	0	0	1	0	11.7	1.7	0.0	1.3	.159
NBA Playoff Totals	15	0	140	58	20	48	.417	8	21	.381	10	12	.833	7	16	23	10	20	0	2	3	4	9.3	3.9	1.5	0.7	....

• ANDERSON, Ron

Ronald Gene Anderson

Born: Oct. 15, 1958. Chicago, IL, United States. Height: 6'7". Weight: 215 lbs. Drafted: 1984 College: Fresno State

YEAR TEAM	GP	GS	MIN	PTS	FGM	FGA	FG%	3PM	3PA	3P%	FTM	FTA	FT%	ORB	DRB	TRB	AST	PF	DQ	STL	BLK	TO	MPG	PPG	RPG	APG	PCM
84-85 Cleveland	36	7	520	210	84	195	.431	1	2	.500	41	50	.820	39	49	88	34	40	0	9	7	32	14.4	5.8	2.4	0.9	.360
85-86 Cleveland	17	3	207	86	37	74	.500	0	1	.000	12	16	.750	5	21	26	8	20	0	1	0	7	12.2	5.1	1.5	0.5	.327
85-86 Indiana	60	27	1469	621	273	554	.493	2	8	.250	73	111	.658	125	123	248	136	105	0	55	6	78	24.5	10.4	4.1	2.3	.445
86-87 Indiana	63	0	721	363	139	294	.473	0	5	.000	85	108	.787	73	78	151	54	65	0	31	3	57	11.4	5.8	2.4	0.9	.492
87-88 Indiana	74	1	1097	542	217	436	.498	0	2	.000	108	141	.766	89	127	216	78	98	0	41	6	74	14.8	7.3	2.9	1.1	.489
88-89 Philadelphia	82	12	2618	1330	566	1152	.491	2	11	.182	196	229	.856	167	239	406	139	166	1	71	23	123	31.9	16.2	5.0	1.7	.455
89-90 Philadelphia	78	3	2089	926	379	841	.451	3	21	.143	165	197	.838	81	214	295	143	143	0	72	13	78	26.8	11.9	3.8	1.8	.405
90-91 Philadelphia	82	13	2340	1198	512	1055	.485	9	43	.209	165	198	.833	103	264	367	115	163	1	65	13	98	28.5	14.6	4.5	1.4	.447
91-92 Philadelphia	82	11	2432	1123	469	1008	.465	42	127	.331	143	163	.877	96	182	278	135	128	0	86	11	107	29.7	13.7	3.4	1.6	.389
92-93 Philadelphia	69	0	1263	561	225	544	.414	39	120	.325	72	89	.809	62	122	184	93	75	0	31	5	62	18.3	8.1	2.7	1.3	.370
93-94 New Jersey	11	2	176	44	15	43	.349	4	12	.333	10	12	.833	8	18	26	6	9	0	5	2	1	16.0	4.0	2.4	0.5	.279
93-94 Washington	10	0	180	52	20	43	.465	3	14	.214	9	11	.818	8	19	27	11	7	0	3	1	9	18.0	5.2	2.7	1.1	.327
NBA Season Totals	664	79	15112	7056	2936	6239	.471	105	366	.287	1079	1325	.814	856	1456	2312	952	1019	2	470	90	726	22.8	10.6	3.5	1.4	....
84-85 Cleveland	2	0	9	0	0	3	.000	0	0	.000	0	0	.000	1	2	3	0	0	0	0	0	0	4.5	0.0	1.5	0.0	.000
86-87 Indiana	4	0	24	4	2	4	.500	0	0	.000	0	0	.000	2	1	3	0	2	0	0	0	0	6.0	1.0	0.8	0.0	.167
88-89 Philadelphia	3	0	109	62	29	51	.569	0	1	.000	4	5	.800	7	9	16	13	10	0	1	2	2	36.3	20.7	5.3	4.3	.607
89-90 Philadelphia	10	0	256	112	40	93	.430	3	5	.600	29	30	.967	6	31	37	14	22	0	4	0	15	25.6	11.2	3.7	1.4	.355
90-91 Philadelphia	8	0	223	88	35	88	.398	1	5	.200	17	19	.895	9	12	21	19	24	0	6	0	12	27.9	11.0	2.6	2.4	.272
NBA Playoff Totals	27	0	621	266	106	239	.444	4	11	.364	50	54	.926	25	55	80	46	58	0	11	2	29	23.0	9.9	3.0	1.7	....

• ANDERSON, Shandon

Shandon Rodriguez Anderson

Born: Dec. 31, 1973. Atlanta, GA, United States. Height: 6'6". Weight: 208 lbs. Drafted: 1996 College: Georgia

YEAR TEAM	GP	GS	MIN	PTS	FGM	FGA	FG%	3PM	3PA	3P%	FTM	FTA	FT%	ORB	DRB	TRB	AST	PF	DQ	STL	BLK	TO	MPG	PPG	RPG	APG	PCM
96-97 Utah	65	0	1066	386	147	318	.462	24	47	.511	68	99	.687	52	127	179	49	113	0	27	8	72	16.4	5.9	2.8	0.8	.323
97-98 Utah	82	2	1602	681	269	500	.538	7	32	.219	136	185	.735	86	141	227	89	145	0	66	18	90	19.5	8.3	2.8	1.1	.424
98-99 Utah	50	2	1072	427	162	363	.446	14	41	.341	89	125	.712	49	83	132	56	89	0	39	10	66	21.4	8.5	2.6	1.1	.333
99-00 Houston	82	82	2700	1009	368	778	.473	79	225	.351	194	253	.767	91	293	384	239	182	0	96	32	194	32.9	12.3	4.7	2.9	.399
00-01 Houston	82	82	2396	710	263	590	.446	46	170	.271	138	188	.734	72	261	333	189	202	0	82	40	131	29.2	8.7	4.1	2.3	.335
01-02 New York	82	6	1596	411	149	373	.399	39	141	.277	74	107	.692	57	192	249	76	134	1	48	15	97	19.5	5.0	3.0	0.9	.257
02-03 New York	82	9	1731	687	248	537	.462	52	140	.371	139	190	.732	64	190	254	87	177	1	73	20	114	21.1	8.4	3.1	1.1	.363
NBA Season Totals	525	183	12163	4311	1606	3459	.464	261	796	.328	838	1147	.731	471	1287	1758	785	1042	2	431	143	764	23.2	8.2	3.3	1.5	....
96-97 Utah	18	0	296	83	29	66	.439	5	12	.417	20	28	.714	20	28	48	13	28	0	11	1	13	16.4	4.6	2.7	0.7	.302
97-98 Utah	20	0	378	134	53	103	.515	3	11	.273	25	37	.676	26	37	63	19	30	0	5	1	30	18.9	6.7	3.2	1.0	.332
98-99 Utah	11	0	297	104	37	77	.481	6	14	.429	24	34	.706	8	33	41	13	34	2	6	3	14	27.0	9.5	3.7	1.2	.321
NBA Playoff Totals	49	0	971	321	119	246	.484	14	37	.378	69	99	.697	54	98	152	45	92	2	22	5	57	19.8	6.6	3.1	0.9	....

• ANDERSON, Willie

Willie Lloyd (Chill) Anderson Jr.

Born: Jan. 8, 1967. Greenville, SC, United States. Height: 6'7". Weight: 190 lbs. Drafted: 1988 College: Georgia

YEAR TEAM	GP	GS	MIN	PTS	FGM	FGA	FG%	3PM	3PA	3P%	FTM	FTA	FT%	ORB	DRB	TRB	AST	PF	DQ	STL	BLK	TO	MPG	PPG	RPG	APG	PCM
88-89 San Antonio	81	79	2738	1508	640	1285	.498	4	21	.190	224	289	.775	152	265	417	372	295	8	150	62	259	33.8	18.6	5.1	4.6	.542
89-90 San Antonio	82	81	2788	1288	532	1082	.492	7	26	.269	217	290	.748	115	257	372	364	252	3	111	58	197	34.0	15.7	4.5	4.4	.477
90-91 San Antonio	75	75	2592	1083	453	991	.457	7	35	.200	170	213	.798	68	283	351	358	226	4	79	46	165	34.6	14.4	4.7	4.8	.435
91-92 San Antonio	57	55	1889	744	312	685	.455	13	56	.232	107	138	.775	62	238	300	302	151	2	54	51	143	33.1	13.1	5.3	5.3	.466
92-93 San Antonio	38	7	560	183	80	186	.430	1	8	.125	22	28	.786	7	50	57	79	52	0	14	6	46	14.7	4.8	1.5	2.1	.304
93-94 San Antonio	80	79	2488	955	394	837	.471	22	68	.324	145	171	.848	68	174	242	347	187	1	71	46	152	31.1	11.9	3.0	4.3	.409
94-95 San Antonio	38	11	556	185	76	162	.469	3	19	.158	30	41	.732	15	40	55	52	71	1	26	10	38	14.6	4.9	1.4	1.4	.307
95-96 Toronto	49	42	1564	606	232	527	.440	29	95	.305	113	132	.856	35	151	186	149	171	5	58	51	118	31.9	12.4	3.8	3.0	.360
95-96 New York	27	2	496	136	56	133	.421	5	25	.200	19	31	.613	13	47	60	48	59	0	17	8	24	18.4	5.0	2.2	1.8	.279
96-97 Miami	28	1	303	83	29	64	.453	8	19	.421	17	20	.850	15	27	42	34	36	0	14	4	20	10.8	3.0	1.5	1.2	.349
NBA Season Totals	555	432	15974	6771	2804	5952	.471	99	372	.266	1064	1353	.786	550	1532	2082	2105	1500	24	594	342	1162	28.8	12.2	3.8	3.8	....
89-90 San Antonio	10	10	375	205	87	168	.518	2	5	.400	29	36	.806	16	38	54	52	40	2	9	4	26	37.5	20.5	5.4	5.2	.535
90-91 San Antonio	4	4	159	76	33	68	.485	2	10	.200	8	13	.615	2	17	19	19	16	0	6	2	13	39.8	19.0	4.8	4.8	.421
92-93 San Antonio	10	0	219	95	37	82	.451	6	11	.545	15	17	.882	4	19	23	28	23	0	9	2	12	21.9	9.5	2.3	2.8	.419
93-94 San Antonio	4	4	106	33	14	37	.378	1	1	1.000	4	7	.571	3	5	8	12	7	0	5	2	4	26.5	8.3	2.0	3.0	.287
94-95 San Antonio	11	0	97	20	9	20	.450	0	1	.000	2	3	.667	5	7	12	10	12	0	5	0	8	8.8	1.8	1.1	0.9	.233
95-96 New York	4	0	64	21	7	22	.318	1	6	.167	6	7	.857	2	7	9	1	10	0	4	0	6	16.0	5.3	2.3	0.3	.146
96-97 Miami	9	0	120	33	11	30	.367	2	8	.250	9	10	.900	2	15	17	5	20	0	4	2	12	13.3	3.7	1.9	0.6	.176
NBA Playoff Totals	52	18	1140	483	198	427	.464	14	42	.333	73	93	.785	34	108	142	127	128	2	42	12	81	21.9	9.3	2.7	2.4	....

YEAR TEAM	GP	GS	MIN	PTS	FGM	FGA	FG%	3PM	3PA	3P%	FTM	FTA	FT%	ORB	DRB	TRB	AST	PF	DQ	STL	BLK	TO	MPG	PPG	RPG	APG	PCM

• ANDERZUNAS, Wally
Walter Charles Anderzunas

Born: Jan. 11, 1946. Died: May 28, 1989.   Height: 6'7".   Weight: 220 lbs.   Drafted: 1969   College: Creighton

YEAR TEAM	GP	GS	MIN	PTS	FGM	FGA	FG%	3PM	3PA	3P%	FTM	FTA	FT%	ORB	DRB	TRB	AST	PF	DQ	STL	BLK	TO	MPG	PPG	RPG	APG	PCM
69-70 Cincinnati	44	....	370	159	65	166	.392	....	....	....	29	46	.630	....	....	82	9	47	1	....	....	....	8.4	3.6	1.9	0.2	.336
NBA Season Totals	44	....	370	159	65	166	.392	....	....	....	29	46	.630	....	....	82	9	47	1	....	....	....	8.4	3.6	1.9	0.2	

• ANDRES, Ernie
Ernest Henry (Junie) Andres

Born: Jan. 11, 1918. Jeffersonville, IN, United States.   Height: 6'1".   Weight: 200 lbs.   Drafted: —   College: Indiana

YEAR TEAM	GP	GS	MIN	PTS	FGM	FGA	FG%	3PM	3PA	3P%	FTM	FTA	FT%	ORB	DRB	TRB	AST	PF	DQ	STL	BLK	TO	MPG	PPG	RPG	APG	PCM
39-40 Indianapolis-N	27	....	....	292	**130**	....	....	....	....	....	32	....	....	....	....	....	....	....	....	....	....	....	....	10.8	....	....	....
45-46 Indianapolis-N	3	....	....	48	20	....	....	....	....	....	8	....	....	....	....	....	....	....	....	....	....	....	....	16.0	....	....	....
46-47 Indianapolis-N	44	....	....	346	140	....	....	....	....	....	66	88	.750	....	....	87	....	....	....	....	....	....	....	7.9	....	....	....
47-48 Indianapolis-N	47	....	....	259	106	....	....	....	....	....	47	75	.627	....	....	86	....	....	....	....	....	....	....	5.5	....	....	....
NBL Season Totals	121	....	....	945	396	....	....	....	....	....	153	163	....	....	....	173	....	....	....	....	....	....	....	7.8	....	....	....
46-47 Indianapolis-N	5	....	....	33	14	....	....	....	....	....	5	6	.833	....	....	....	....	....	....	....	....	....	....	6.6	....	....	....
47-48 Indianapolis-N	4	....	....	5	1	....	....	....	....	....	3	3	1.000	....	....	....	....	....	....	....	....	....	....	1.3	....	....	....
NBL Playoff Totals	9	....	....	38	15	....	....	....	....	....	8	9	....	....	....	....	....	....	....	....	....	....	....	4.2	....	....	....

• ANIELAK, Don
Donald Robert Anielak

Born: Nov. 1, 1930.   Height: 6'7".   Weight: 190 lbs.   Drafted: 1954   College: Southwest Missouri State

YEAR TEAM	GP	GS	MIN	PTS	FGM	FGA	FG%	3PM	3PA	3P%	FTM	FTA	FT%	ORB	DRB	TRB	AST	PF	DQ	STL	BLK	TO	MPG	PPG	RPG	APG	PCM
54-55 New York	1	....	10	3	0	4	.000	....	....	....	3	4	.750	....	....	2	0	0	0	....	....	....	10.0	3.0	2.0	0.0	.112
NBA Season Totals	1	....	10	3	0	4	.000	....	....	....	3	4	.750	....	....	2	0	0	0	....	....	....	10.0	3.0	2.0	0.0	

• ANSLEY, Michael
Michael Antonio Ansley

Born: Feb. 8, 1967. Birmingham, AL, United States.   Height: 6'7".   Weight: 225 lbs.   Drafted: 1989   College: Alabama

YEAR TEAM	GP	GS	MIN	PTS	FGM	FGA	FG%	3PM	3PA	3P%	FTM	FTA	FT%	ORB	DRB	TRB	AST	PF	DQ	STL	BLK	TO	MPG	PPG	RPG	APG	PCM
89-90 Orlando	72	5	1221	626	231	465	.497	0	0	.000	164	227	.722	187	175	362	40	152	0	24	17	50	17.0	8.7	5.0	0.6	.556
90-91 Orlando	67	1	877	379	144	263	.548	0	0	.000	91	127	.717	122	131	253	25	125	0	27	7	34	13.1	5.7	3.8	0.4	.519
91-92 Philadelphia	8	0	32	15	5	11	.455	0	0	.000	5	6	.833	2	2	4	2	6	0	0	0	3	4.0	1.9	0.5	0.3	.289
91-92 Charlotte	2	0	13	6	3	7	.429	0	0	.000	0	0	.000	0	2	2	0	1	0	0	0	0	6.5	3.0	1.0	0.0	.283
NBA Season Totals	149	6	2143	1026	383	746	.513	0	0	.000	260	360	.722	311	310	621	67	284	0	51	24	87	14.4	6.9	4.2	0.4	....

• ANSTEY, Chris
Christopher John Anstey

Born: Jan. 1, 1975. Melbourne, Australia.   Height: 7'   Weight: 249 lbs.   Drafted: 1997   College: Catholic Regional College (AUS)

YEAR TEAM	GP	GS	MIN	PTS	FGM	FGA	FG%	3PM	3PA	3P%	FTM	FTA	FT%	ORB	DRB	TRB	AST	PF	DQ	STL	BLK	TO	MPG	PPG	RPG	APG	PCM
97-98 Dallas	41	8	680	240	92	231	.398	3	16	.188	53	74	.716	53	104	157	35	95	1	31	27	41	16.6	5.9	3.8	0.9	.378
98-99 Dallas	41	4	470	134	50	139	.360	0	7	.000	34	48	.708	35	62	97	27	98	1	18	13	26	11.5	3.3	2.4	0.7	.268
99-00 Chicago	73	11	1007	439	161	364	.442	1	6	.167	116	147	.789	90	190	280	65	180	4	29	25	80	13.8	6.0	3.8	0.9	.457
NBA Season Totals	155	23	2157	813	303	734	.413	4	29	.138	203	269	.755	178	356	534	127	373	6	78	65	147	13.9	5.2	3.4	0.8	....

• ANTHONY, Greg
Gregory C. (G-Money) Anthony

Born: Nov. 15, 1967. Las Vegas, NV, United States.   Height: 6'   Weight: 176 lbs.   Drafted: 1991   College: UNLV

YEAR TEAM	GP	GS	MIN	PTS	FGM	FGA	FG%	3PM	3PA	3P%	FTM	FTA	FT%	ORB	DRB	TRB	AST	PF	DQ	STL	BLK	TO	MPG	PPG	RPG	APG	PCM
91-92 New York	82	1	1510	447	161	435	.370	8	55	.145	117	158	.741	33	103	136	314	170	0	59	9	98	18.4	5.5	1.7	3.8	.350
92-93 New York	70	35	1699	459	174	419	.415	4	30	.133	107	159	.673	42	128	170	398	141	0	113	12	105	24.3	6.6	2.4	5.7	.437
93-94 New York	80	36	1994	628	225	571	.394	48	160	.300	130	168	.774	43	146	189	365	163	1	114	13	128	24.9	7.9	2.4	4.6	.394
94-95 New York	61	2	943	372	128	293	.437	56	155	.361	60	76	.789	7	57	64	160	99	1	50	7	55	15.5	6.1	1.0	2.6	.419
95-96 Vancouver	69	68	2096	967	324	781	.415	90	271	.332	229	297	.771	29	145	174	476	137	1	116	11	159	30.4	14.0	2.5	6.9	.515
96-97 Vancouver	65	44	1863	616	199	507	.393	88	238	.370	130	178	.730	25	159	184	407	122	0	129	4	130	28.7	9.5	2.8	6.3	.461
97-98 Seattle	80	0	1021	419	150	349	.430	66	159	.415	53	80	.663	18	93	111	205	97	0	64	3	88	12.8	5.2	1.4	2.6	.475
98-99 Portland	50	0	806	319	104	251	.414	49	125	.392	62	89	.697	14	49	63	100	75	0	66	3	55	16.1	6.4	1.3	2.0	.400
99-00 Portland	82	3	1548	514	169	416	.406	88	233	.378	88	114	.772	17	116	133	208	143	0	59	9	85	18.9	6.3	1.6	2.5	.352
00-01 Portland	58	0	856	282	97	253	.383	65	159	.409	23	35	.657	21	40	61	82	63	0	40	3	43	14.8	4.9	1.1	1.4	.296
01-02 Chicago	36	35	961	302	113	287	.394	29	90	.322	47	70	.671	16	72	88	203	72	1	49	4	36	26.7	8.4	2.4	5.6	.415
01-02 Milwaukee	24	3	553	172	70	188	.372	19	73	.260	13	21	.619	6	38	44	79	42	0	28	1	36	23.0	7.2	1.8	3.3	.294
NBA Season Totals	757	227	15850	5497	1914	4750	.403	610	1748	.349	1059	1445	.733	271	1146	1417	2997	1324	4	887	79	1040	20.9	7.3	1.9	4.0	....
91-92 New York	12	0	213	63	19	46	.413	5	12	.417	20	33	.606	4	13	17	41	28	0	16	1	13	17.8	5.3	1.4	3.4	.386
92-93 New York	15	0	240	59	24	60	.400	3	14	.214	8	14	.571	4	26	30	52	26	0	13	1	11	16.0	3.9	2.0	3.5	.403
93-94 New York	25	3	436	122	45	128	.352	18	61	.295	14	24	.583	9	18	27	59	55	0	19	8	31	17.4	4.9	1.1	2.4	.232
94-95 New York	11	0	135	47	15	38	.395	7	23	.304	10	11	.909	2	8	10	15	27	0	2	2	6	12.3	4.3	0.9	1.4	.265
97-98 Seattle	9	0	118	32	12	40	.300	5	19	.263	3	8	.375	3	7	10	10	17	1	5	1	11	13.1	3.6	1.1	1.1	.099
98-99 Portland	13	0	225	67	18	55	.327	8	31	.258	23	34	.676	4	10	14	32	25	0	13	1	9	17.3	5.2	1.1	2.5	.314
99-00 Portland	15	0	213	60	19	52	.365	10	31	.323	12	16	.750	2	14	16	25	27	0	13	4	12	14.2	4.0	1.1	1.7	.293
00-01 Portland	2	0	17	5	2	6	.333	1	3	.333	0	0	.000	0	0	0	0	2	0	1	0	1	8.5	2.5	0.0	0.0	.030
NBA Playoff Totals	102	3	1597	455	154	425	.362	57	194	.294	90	140	.643	28	96	124	234	207	1	82	18	94	15.7	4.5	1.2	2.3	....

• ANTHONY, Paul
Paul Anthony

Born: 1924.   Height: 6'5".   Weight: 195 lbs.   Drafted: —   College: Washington & Jefferson

YEAR TEAM	GP	GS	MIN	PTS	FGM	FGA	FG%	3PM	3PA	3P%	FTM	FTA	FT%	ORB	DRB	TRB	AST	PF	DQ	STL	BLK	TO	MPG	PPG	RPG	APG	PCM
46-47 Tri-Cities-N	1	....	....	0	0	....	....	....	....	....	0	0	.000	....	....	....	....	....	....	....	....	....	....	0.0	....	....	....
47-48 Tri-Cities-N	1	....	....	0	0	....	....	....	....	....	0	0	.000	....	....	....	....	0	....	....	....	....	....	0.0	....	....	....
NBL Season Totals	2	....	....	0	0	....	....	....	....	....	0	0	....	....	....	....	....	0	....	....	....	....	....	0.0	....	....	....

ANTON, Clyde
Clyde Anton

Born: 1915. Height: — Weight: — Drafted: — College: none

YEAR TEAM	GP	GS	MIN	PTS	FGM	FGA	FG%	3PM	3PA	3P%	FTM	FTA	FT%	ORB	DRB	TRB	AST	PF	DQ	STL	BLK	TO	MPG	PPG	RPG	APG	PCM
37-38 Columbus-N	7	....	....	10	4	....	....	....	....	....	2	....	....	....	....	....	....	....	....	....	....	....	1.4	....	....	....	
NBL Season Totals	7	....	....	10	4	....	....	....	....	....	2	....	....	....	....	....	....	....	....	....	....	....	1.4	....	....	....	

ARCENEAUX, Stacey
Stacey Arceneaux   aka.: Robert L. Stacey

Born: Feb. 17, 1936. Height: 6'4". Weight: 210 lbs. Drafted: — College: Iowa State

YEAR TEAM	GP	GS	MIN	PTS	FGM	FGA	FG%	3PM	3PA	3P%	FTM	FTA	FT%	ORB	DRB	TRB	AST	PF	DQ	STL	BLK	TO	MPG	PPG	RPG	APG	PCM
61-62 St. Louis	7	....	110	50	22	56	.393	....	....	....	6	13	.462	....	....	32	4	10	0	....	....	....	15.7	7.1	4.6	0.6	.424
NBA Season Totals	7	....	110	50	22	56	.393	....	....	....	6	13	.462	....	....	32	4	10	0	....	....	....	15.7	7.1	4.6	0.6	

ARCHIBALD, Gerry
Gerald (Gerry) Archibald

Born: Aug. 22, 1908. Died: Nov.1990. Height: 6' Weight: 170 lbs. Drafted: — College: none

YEAR TEAM	GP	GS	MIN	PTS	FGM	FGA	FG%	3PM	3PA	3P%	FTM	FTA	FT%	ORB	DRB	TRB	AST	PF	DQ	STL	BLK	TO	MPG	PPG	RPG	APG	PCM
37-38 Warren-N	7	....	....	5	2	....	....	....	....	....	1	....	....	....	....	....	....	....	....	....	....	....	0.7	....	....	....	
38-39 Cleveland-N	2	....	....	0	0	....	....	....	....	....	0	....	....	....	....	....	....	....	....	....	....	....	0.0	....	....	....	
NBL Season Totals	9	....	....	5	2	....	....	....	....	....	1	....	....	....	....	....	....	....	....	....	....	....	0.6	....	....	....	

ARCHIBALD, Nate
Nathaniel (Tiny) Archibald   HOF: 1991

Born: Sept. 2, 1948. New York, NY, United States. Height: 6'1". Weight: 160 lbs. Drafted: 1970 College: Texas (El Paso)

YEAR TEAM	GP	GS	MIN	PTS	FGM	FGA	FG%	3PM	3PA	3P%	FTM	FTA	FT%	ORB	DRB	TRB	AST	PF	DQ	STL	BLK	TO	MPG	PPG	RPG	APG	PCM
70-71 Cincinnati	82	....	2867	1308	486	1095	.444	....	....	....	336	444	.757	....	....	242	450	218	2	....	....	....	35.0	16.0	3.0	5.5	.476
71-72 Cincinnati	76	....	3272	2145	734	1511	.486	....	....	....	677	824	.822	....	....	222	701	198	3	....	....	....	43.1	28.2	2.9	9.2	.707
72-73 Omaha	80	....	3681	2719	1028	2106	.488	....	....	....	663	783	.847	....	....	223	910	207	2	....	....	....	46.0	34.0	2.8	11.4	.784
73-74 Omaha	35	....	1272	617	222	492	.451	....	....	....	173	211	.820	21	64	85	266	76	0	56	7	....	36.3	17.6	2.4	7.6	.563
74-75 Omaha	82	....	3244	2170	759	1664	.456	....	....	....	652	748	.872	48	174	222	557	187	0	119	7	....	39.6	26.5	2.7	6.8	.649
75-76 Kansas City	78	....	3184	1935	717	1583	.453	....	....	....	501	625	.802	67	146	213	615	169	0	126	15	....	40.8	24.8	2.7	7.9	.613
76-77 New York	34	....	1277	697	250	560	.446	....	....	....	197	251	.785	22	58	80	254	77	1	59	11	....	37.6	20.5	2.4	7.5	.572
78-79 Boston	69	....	1662	760	259	573	.452	....	....	....	242	307	.788	25	78	103	324	132	2	55	6	200	24.1	11.0	1.5	4.7	.430
79-80 Boston	80	....	2864	1131	383	794	.482	4	18	.222	361	435	.830	59	138	197	671	218	2	106	10	240	35.8	14.1	2.5	8.4	.499
80-81 Boston	80	....	2820	1106	382	766	.499	0	9	.000	342	419	.816	36	140	176	618	201	1	75	18	264	35.3	13.8	2.2	7.7	.464
81-82 Boston	68	51	2167	858	308	652	.472	6	16	.375	236	316	.747	25	91	116	541	131	1	52	3	177	31.9	12.6	1.7	8.0	.472
82-83 Boston	66	18	1811	695	235	553	.425	5	24	.208	220	296	.743	25	66	91	409	110	1	38	4	165	27.4	10.5	1.4	6.2	.411
83-84 Milwaukee	46	46	1038	340	136	279	.487	4	18	.222	64	101	.634	16	60	76	160	78	0	33	0	78	22.6	7.4	1.7	3.5	.341
NBA Season Totals	876	115	31159	16481	5899	12628	.467	19	85	.224	4664	5760	.810	344	1015	2046	6476	2002	15	719	81	1124	35.6	18.8	2.3	7.4	
74-75 Omaha	6	....	242	121	43	118	.364	....	....	....	35	43	.814	2	9	11	32	18	0	4	0	....	40.3	20.2	1.8	5.3	.380
79-80 Boston	9	....	332	128	45	89	.506	1	2	.500	37	42	.881	3	8	11	71	28	1	10	0	38	36.9	14.2	1.2	7.9	.408
80-81 Boston	17	....	630	266	95	211	.450	0	5	.000	76	94	.809	6	22	28	107	39	0	13	0	50	37.1	15.6	1.6	6.3	.385
81-82 Boston	8	8	277	85	30	70	.429	0	4	.000	25	28	.893	1	16	17	52	21	0	5	2	23	34.6	10.6	2.1	6.5	.340
82-83 Boston	7	0	161	67	22	68	.324	1	6	.167	22	29	.759	3	7	10	44	12	0	2	0	11	23.0	9.6	1.4	6.3	.411
NBA Playoff Totals	47	8	1642	667	235	556	.423	2	17	.118	195	236	.826	15	62	77	306	118	1	34	2	122	34.9	14.2	1.6	6.5	....

ARCHIBALD, Robert
Robert Archibald

Born: Mar. 29, 1980. Paisley, Scotland. Height: 6'11". Weight: 250 lbs. Drafted: 2002 College: Illinois

YEAR TEAM	GP	GS	MIN	PTS	FGM	FGA	FG%	3PM	3PA	3P%	FTM	FTA	FT%	ORB	DRB	TRB	AST	PF	DQ	STL	BLK	TO	MPG	PPG	RPG	APG	PCM
02-03 Memphis	12	0	72	19	6	20	.300	0	0	.000	7	18	.389	6	11	17	3	9	0	0	3	7	6.0	1.6	1.4	0.3	.171
NBA Season Totals	12	0	72	19	6	20	.300	0	0	.000	7	18	.389	6	11	17	3	9	0	0	3	7	6.0	1.6	1.4	0.3	....

ARD, Jim
Jimmie Lee Ard

Born: Sept. 19, 1948. Harvey, IL, United States. Height: 6'8". Weight: 215 lbs. Drafted: 1970 College: Cincinnati

YEAR TEAM	GP	GS	MIN	PTS	FGM	FGA	FG%	3PM	3PA	3P%	FTM	FTA	FT%	ORB	DRB	TRB	AST	PF	DQ	STL	BLK	TO	MPG	PPG	RPG	APG	PCM
70-71 New York-A	73	....	1027	427	174	382	.455	0	3	.000	79	132	.598	112	225	337	40	119	1	....	....	108	14.1	5.8	4.6	0.5	.496
71-72 New York-A	71	....	1145	397	159	353	.450	2	8	.250	77	127	.606	124	244	368	34	150	2	....	....	98	16.1	5.6	5.2	0.5	.437
72-73 New York-A	42	....	426	140	53	140	.379	0	4	.000	34	50	.680	48	100	148	14	50	0	....	....	29	10.1	3.3	3.5	0.3	.424
73-74 Memphis-A	27	....	502	174	66	164	.402	2	2	1.000	40	51	.784	48	111	159	41	44	....	16	25	42	18.6	6.4	5.9	1.5	.497
74-75 Boston	59	....	719	226	89	266	.335	....	....	....	48	65	.738	59	140	199	40	96	2	13	32	....	12.2	3.8	3.4	0.7	.337
75-76 Boston	81	....	853	285	107	294	.364	....	....	....	71	100	.710	96	193	289	48	141	2	12	36	....	10.5	3.5	3.6	0.6	.415
76-77 Boston	63	....	969	241	96	254	.378	....	....	....	49	76	.645	77	219	296	53	128	1	18	28	....	15.4	3.8	4.7	0.8	.365
77-78 Boston	1	....	9	1	0	1	.000	....	....	....	1	2	.500	1	3	4	1	1	0	0	0	....	9.0	1.0	4.0	1.0	.431
77-78 Chicago	14	....	116	18	8	16	.500	....	....	....	2	3	.667	8	24	32	7	18	0	0	0	14	8.3	1.3	2.3	0.5	.227
NBA Season Totals	218	....	2666	771	300	831	.361	....	....	....	171	246	.695	241	579	820	149	384	5	43	96	14	12.2	3.5	3.8	0.7	....
ABA Season Totals	213	....	3100	1138	452	1039	.435	4	17	.235	230	360	.639	332	680	1012	129	363	3	16	25	277	14.6	5.3	4.8	0.6	....
Career Totals	431	....	5766	1909	752	1870	.402	4	17	.235	401	606	.662	573	1259	1832	278	747	8	59	121	291	13.4	4.4	4.3	0.6	....
70-71 New York-A	6	....	98	47	16	29	.552	0	0	.000	15	22	.682	11	18	29	3	15	1	....	....	6	16.3	7.8	4.8	0.5	.557
71-72 New York-A	13	....	117	31	14	32	.438	0	2	.000	3	10	.300	....	....	28	4	19	....	....	....	6	9.0	2.4	2.2	0.3	.281
74-75 Boston	5	....	14	2	1	8	.125	....	....	....	0	0	.000	2	0	2	1	5	0	0	1	....	2.8	0.4	0.4	0.2	-.232
75-76 Boston	16	....	110	37	13	29	.448	....	....	....	11	14	.786	10	16	26	8	29	0	1	3	....	6.9	2.3	1.6	0.5	.373
NBA Playoff Totals	21	....	124	39	14	37	.378	....	....	....	11	14	.786	12	16	28	9	34	0	1	4	....	5.9	1.9	1.3	0.4	....
ABA Playoff Totals	19	....	215	78	30	61	.492	0	2	.000	18	32	.563	11	18	57	7	34	1	....	....	12	11.3	4.1	3.0	0.4	....
Career Playoff Totals	40	....	339	117	44	98	.449	0	2	.000	29	46	.630	23	34	85	16	68	1	1	4	12	8.5	2.9	2.1	0.4	....

• ARENAS, Gilbert

Gilbert Jay Arenas

Born: Jan. 6, 1982. Los Angeles, CA, United States. Height: 6'3". Weight: 191 lbs. Drafted: 2001 College: Arizona

YEAR TEAM	GP	GS	MIN	PTS	FGM	FGA	FG%	3PM	3PA	3P%	FTM	FTA	FT%	ORB	DRB	TRB	AST	PF	DQ	STL	BLK	TO	MPG	PPG	RPG	APG	PCM
01-02 Golden State	47	30	1155	511	174	384	.453	39	113	.345	124	160	.775	41	91	132	174	115	3	69	11	97	24.6	10.9	2.8	3.7	.473
02-03 Golden State	82	82	2868	1497	509	1180	.431	109	313	.348	370	468	.791	97	289	386	514	260	3	124	17	290	35.0	18.3	4.7	6.3	.524
NBA Season Totals	129	112	4023	2008	683	1564	.437	148	426	.347	494	628	.787	138	380	518	688	375	6	193	28	387	31.2	15.6	4.0	5.3	....

• ARIZIN, Paul

Paul Joseph (Pitchin' Paul) Arizin

Born: Apr. 9, 1928. Philadelphia, PA, United States. Height: 6'4". Weight: 190 lbs. Drafted: 1950 College: Villanova HOF: 1978

YEAR TEAM	GP	GS	MIN	PTS	FGM	FGA	FG%	3PM	3PA	3P%	FTM	FTA	FT%	ORB	DRB	TRB	AST	PF	DQ	STL	BLK	TO	MPG	PPG	RPG	APG	PCM
50-51 Philadelphia	65	....	....	1121	352	864	.407	....	....	....	417	526	.793	....	....	640	138	284	18	....	....	....	....	17.2	9.8	2.1	....
51-52 Philadelphia	66	....	**2939**	**1674**	**548**	1222	**.448**	....	....	....	**578**	**707**	.818	....	....	745	170	250	5	....	....	....	**44.5**	**25.4**	11.3	2.6	.615
54-55 Philadelphia	72	....	**2953**	1512	**529**	**1325**	.399	....	....	....	454	585	.776	....	....	675	210	270	5	....	....	....	**41.0**	21.0	9.4	2.9	.519
55-56 Philadelphia	72	....	2724	1741	617	1378	.448	....	....	....	507	626	.810	....	....	539	189	282	11	....	....	....	37.8	24.2	7.5	2.6	.607
56-57 Philadelphia	71	....	2767	**1817**	**613**	1451	.422	....	....	....	591	**713**	.829	....	....	561	150	274	13	....	....	....	39.0	**25.6**	7.9	2.1	.597
57-58 Philadelphia	68	....	2377	1406	483	1229	.393	....	....	....	440	544	.809	....	....	503	135	235	7	....	....	....	35.0	20.7	7.4	2.0	.537
58-59 Philadelphia	70	....	2799	1851	632	1466	.431	....	....	....	587	722	.813	....	....	637	119	264	7	....	....	....	40.0	26.4	9.1	1.7	.608
59-60 Philadelphia	72	....	2618	1606	593	1400	.424	....	....	....	420	526	.798	....	....	621	165	263	6	....	....	....	36.4	22.3	8.6	2.3	.585
60-61 Philadelphia	79	....	2935	1832	650	1529	.425	....	....	....	532	639	.833	....	....	681	188	**335**	11	....	....	....	37.2	23.2	8.6	2.4	.595
61-62 Philadelphia	78	....	2785	1706	611	1490	.410	....	....	....	484	601	.805	....	....	527	201	307	18	....	....	....	35.7	21.9	6.8	2.6	.542
NBA Season Totals	713	....	24897	16266	5628	13354	.421	....	....	....	5010	6189	.810	....	....	6129	1665	2764	101	....	....	....	34.9	22.8	8.6	2.3	....
50-51 Philadelphia	2	....	....	41	14	27	.519	....	....	....	13	16	.813	....	....	20	3	10	1	....	....	....	....	20.5	10.0	1.5	....
51-52 Philadelphia	3	....	120	77	24	53	.453	....	....	....	29	33	.879	....	....	38	8	17	2	....	....	....	40.0	25.7	12.7	2.7	.719
55-56 Philadelphia	10	....	409	289	103	229	.450	....	....	....	83	99	.838	....	....	84	29	31	1	....	....	....	40.9	28.9	8.4	2.9	.673
56-57 Philadelphia	2	....	22	9	3	8	.375	....	....	....	3	5	.600	....	....	8	1	3	0	....	....	....	11.0	4.5	4.0	0.5	.483
57-58 Philadelphia	8	....	309	188	66	169	.391	....	....	....	56	72	.778	....	....	62	16	26	1	....	....	....	38.6	23.5	7.8	2.0	.528
59-60 Philadelphia	9	....	371	237	84	195	.431	....	....	....	69	79	.873	....	....	86	33	29	0	....	....	....	41.2	26.3	9.6	3.7	.659
60-61 Philadelphia	3	....	125	67	22	67	.328	....	....	....	23	33	.697	....	....	26	12	17	2	....	....	....	41.7	22.3	8.7	4.0	.457
61-62 Philadelphia	12	....	459	278	95	253	.375	....	....	....	88	102	.863	....	....	80	26	44	1	....	....	....	38.3	23.2	6.7	2.2	.493
NBA Playoff Totals	49	....	1815	1186	411	1001	.411	....	....	....	364	439	.829	....	....	404	128	177	8	....	....	....	37.0	24.2	8.2	2.6	....

• ARLAUCKAS, Joe

Joseph Arlauckas

Born: July 20, 1965. Rochester, NY, United States. Height: 6'9". Weight: 230 lbs. Drafted: 1987 College: Niagara

YEAR TEAM	GP	GS	MIN	PTS	FGM	FGA	FG%	3PM	3PA	3P%	FTM	FTA	FT%	ORB	DRB	TRB	AST	PF	DQ	STL	BLK	TO	MPG	PPG	RPG	APG	PCM
87-88 Sacramento	9	0	85	34	14	43	.326	0	0	.000	6	8	.750	6	7	13	8	16	0	3	4	4	9.4	3.8	1.4	0.9	.259
NBA Season Totals	9	0	85	34	14	43	.326	0	0	.000	6	8	.750	6	7	13	8	16	0	3	4	4	9.4	3.8	1.4	0.9	....

• ARMSTRONG, B.J.

Benjamin Roy (The Kid) Armstrong Jr.

Born: Sept. 9, 1967. Detroit, MI, United States. Height: 6'2". Weight: 175 lbs. Drafted: 1989 College: Iowa

YEAR TEAM	GP	GS	MIN	PTS	FGM	FGA	FG%	3PM	3PA	3P%	FTM	FTA	FT%	ORB	DRB	TRB	AST	PF	DQ	STL	BLK	TO	MPG	PPG	RPG	APG	PCM
89-90 Chicago	81	0	1291	452	190	392	.485	3	6	.500	69	78	.885	19	83	102	199	105	0	46	6	81	15.9	5.6	1.3	2.5	.379
90-91 Chicago	82	0	1731	720	304	632	.481	15	30	.500	97	111	.874	25	124	149	301	118	0	70	4	107	21.1	8.8	1.8	3.7	.452
91-92 Chicago	82	3	1875	809	335	697	.481	35	87	.402	104	129	.806	19	126	145	266	88	0	46	5	90	22.9	9.9	1.8	3.2	.429
92-93 Chicago	82	74	2492	1009	408	818	.499	63	139	**.453**	130	151	.861	27	122	149	330	169	0	66	6	82	30.4	12.3	1.8	4.0	.409
93-94 Chicago	82	82	2770	1212	479	1007	.476	60	135	.444	194	227	.855	28	142	170	323	147	1	80	9	131	33.8	14.8	2.1	3.9	.402
94-95 Chicago	82	82	2577	1150	418	894	.468	108	253	.427	206	233	.884	25	161	186	244	159	0	84	8	107	31.4	14.0	2.3	3.0	.402
95-96 Golden State	82	64	2262	1012	340	727	.468	98	207	.473	234	279	.839	22	162	184	401	147	0	68	6	131	27.6	12.3	2.2	4.9	.487
96-97 Golden State	49	17	1020	389	148	327	.453	25	90	.278	68	79	.861	7	67	74	126	56	0	25	2	54	20.8	7.9	1.5	2.6	.362
97-98 Golden State	4	0	59	17	6	19	.316	0	1	.000	5	7	.714	4	3	7	6	6	0	4	0	7	14.8	4.3	1.8	1.5	.197
97-98 Charlotte	62	0	772	244	99	194	.510	9	34	.265	37	43	.860	12	57	69	144	68	0	25	0	37	12.5	3.9	1.1	2.3	.430
98-99 Charlotte	10	1	178	57	21	43	.488	6	8	.750	9	10	.900	1	15	16	27	16	0	3	0	10	17.8	5.7	1.6	2.7	.381
98-99 Orlando	22	0	180	48	19	45	.422	1	7	.143	9	11	.818	1	22	23	34	15	0	9	0	15	8.2	2.2	1.0	1.5	.390
99-00 Chicago	27	18	583	201	83	186	.446	13	29	.448	22	25	.880	2	45	47	78	34	0	7	1	40	21.6	7.4	1.7	2.9	.325
NBA Season Totals	747	341	17790	7320	2850	5981	.477	436	1026	.425	1184	1383	.856	192	1129	1321	2479	1128	1	533	47	892	23.8	9.8	1.8	3.3	....
89-90 Chicago	16	0	217	64	21	62	.339	0	4	.000	22	24	.917	3	17	20	29	22	0	10	0	12	13.6	4.0	1.3	1.8	.286
90-91 Chicago	17	0	273	93	35	70	.500	3	5	.600	20	25	.800	5	22	27	43	13	0	19	1	13	16.1	5.5	1.6	2.5	.475
91-92 Chicago	22	0	434	161	63	139	.453	5	17	.294	30	38	.789	2	22	24	47	33	0	14	0	18	19.7	7.3	1.1	2.1	.323
92-93 Chicago	19	19	643	217	88	168	.524	21	41	.512	20	22	.909	6	22	28	62	49	0	19	2	14	33.8	11.4	1.5	3.3	.338
93-94 Chicago	10	10	360	153	55	106	.519	7	12	.583	36	44	.818	2	22	24	25	21	0	8	0	9	36.0	15.3	2.4	2.5	.392
94-95 Chicago	10	10	288	103	36	79	.456	13	29	.448	18	22	.818	4	14	18	27	21	0	6	0	6	28.8	10.3	1.8	2.7	.335
97-98 Charlotte	9	0	146	37	16	42	.381	2	5	.400	3	4	.750	2	8	10	18	11	0	6	0	6	16.2	4.1	1.1	2.0	.249
98-99 Orlando	2	0	3	0	0	1	.000	0	0	.000	0	0	.000	0	0	0	1	1	0	0	0	1	1.5	0.0	0.0	0.5	-.371
NBA Playoff Totals	105	39	2364	828	314	667	.471	51	113	.451	149	179	.832	24	127	151	252	171	0	82	3	79	22.5	7.9	1.4	2.4	....

• ARMSTRONG, Bob

Robert Armstrong

Born: 1920. Height: 6'1". Weight: 180 lbs. Drafted: — College: Glenville State

YEAR TEAM	GP	GS	MIN	PTS	FGM	FGA	FG%	3PM	3PA	3P%	FTM	FTA	FT%	ORB	DRB	TRB	AST	PF	DQ	STL	BLK	TO	MPG	PPG	RPG	APG	PCM
45-46 Youngstown-N	1	....	....	0	0	....	....	....	....	....	0	0	.000	....	....	....	....	....	....	....	....	....	....	0.0	....	....	....
NBL Season Totals	1	....	....	0	0	....	....	....	....	....	0	0	....	....	....	....	....	....	....	....	....	....	....	0.0	....	....	....

• ARMSTRONG, Bob

T. Robert Armstrong

Born: June 17, 1933. Detroit, MI, United States. Height: 6'8". Weight: 220 lbs. Drafted: 1955 College: Michigan State

YEAR TEAM	GP	GS	MIN	PTS	FGM	FGA	FG%	3PM	3PA	3P%	FTM	FTA	FT%	ORB	DRB	TRB	AST	PF	DQ	STL	BLK	TO	MPG	PPG	RPG	APG	PCM
56-57 Philadelphia	19	....	110	28	11	37	.297	....	....	....	6	12	.500	....	....	39	3	13	0	....	....	....	5.8	1.5	2.1	0.2	.312
NBA Season Totals	19	....	110	28	11	37	.297	....	....	....	6	12	.500	....	....	39	3	13	0	....	....	....	5.8	1.5	2.1	0.2	....

• ARMSTRONG, Brandon

Brandon Simone Armstrong

Born: June 16, 1980. San Francisco, CA, United States. Height: 6'5". Weight: 188 lbs. Drafted: 2001 College: Pepperdine

YEAR	TEAM	GP	GS	MIN	PTS	FGM	FGA	FG%	3PM	3PA	3P%	FTM	FTA	FT%	ORB	DRB	TRB	AST	PF	DQ	STL	BLK	TO	MPG	PPG	RPG	APG	PCM
01-02	New Jersey	35	0	196	64	27	85	.318	5	17	.294	5	10	.500	10	6	16	8	26	0	7	1	8	5.6	1.8	0.5	0.2	.105
02-03	New Jersey	17	0	69	24	9	27	.333	1	6	.167	5	6	.833	0	4	4	2	8	0	3	1	5	4.1	1.4	0.2	0.1	.123
NBA Season Totals		52	0	265	88	36	112	.321	6	23	.261	10	16	.625	10	10	20	10	34	0	10	2	13	5.1	1.7	0.4	0.2	....

• ARMSTRONG, Curly

Paul Carlyle (Curly) Armstrong

Born: Nov. 1, 1918. Died: June6, 1983. Height: 5'11". Weight: 170 lbs. Drafted: — College: Indiana

YEAR	TEAM	GP	GS	MIN	PTS	FGM	FGA	FG%	3PM	3PA	3P%	FTM	FTA	FT%	ORB	DRB	TRB	AST	PF	DQ	STL	BLK	TO	MPG	PPG	RPG	APG	PCM
41-42	Fort Wayne-N	24	....	....	198	69	....	....	....	....	....	60	....	....	....	....	....	....	....	....	....	....	....	....	8.3	....	....	....
42-43	Fort Wayne-N	23	....	....	183	67	....	....	....	....	....	49	....	....	....	....	....	....	....	....	....	....	....	....	8.0	....	....	....
45-46	Fort Wayne-N	6	....	....	7	3	....	....	....	....	....	1	....	....	....	....	....	....	....	....	....	....	....	....	1.2	....	....	....
46-47	Fort Wayne-N	44	....	....	388	127	....	....	....	....	....	134	195	.687	....	....	....	....	145	....	....	....	....	....	8.8	....	....	....
47-48	Fort Wayne-N	53	....	....	435	148	....	....	....	....	....	139	206	.675	....	....	....	....	180	....	....	....	....	....	8.2	....	....	....
48-49	Fort Wayne	52	....	....	380	131	428	.306	....	....	....	118	169	.698	....	....	....	105	152	....	....	....	....	....	7.3	....	2.0	....
49-50	Fort Wayne	63	....	....	458	144	516	.279	....	....	....	170	241	.705	....	....	....	170	217	....	....	....	....	....	7.3	....	2.7	....
50-51	Fort Wayne	38	....	....	202	72	232	.310	....	....	....	58	90	.644	....	....	89	77	97	2	....	....	....	....	5.3	2.3	2.0	....
NBA Season Totals		153	....	....	1040	347	1176	.295	....	....	....	346	500	.692	....	....	89	352	466	2	....	....	....	....	6.8	0.6	2.3	....
NBL Season Totals		150	....	....	1211	414	....	....	....	....	....	383	401	....	....	....	....	....	325	....	....	....	....	....	8.1	....	....	....
Career Totals		303	....	....	2251	761	1176	....	....	....	....	729	901	....	....	....	89	352	791	2	....	....	....	....	7.4	0.3	1.2	....
41-42	Fort Wayne-N	6	....	....	71	25	....	....	....	....	....	21	....	....	....	....	....	....	....	....	....	....	....	....	11.8	....	....	....
42-43	Fort Wayne-N	6	....	....	59	20	....	....	....	....	....	19	....	....	....	....	....	....	....	....	....	....	....	....	9.8	....	....	....
45-46	Fort Wayne-N	3	....	....	11	5	....	....	....	....	....	1	2	.500	....	....	....	....	....	....	....	....	....	....	3.7	....	....	....
46-47	Fort Wayne-N	8	....	....	71	24	....	....	....	....	....	23	31	.742	....	....	....	....	....	....	....	....	....	....	8.9	....	....	....
47-48	Fort Wayne-N	4	....	....	37	13	....	....	....	....	....	11	16	.688	....	....	....	....	....	....	....	....	....	....	9.3	....	....	....
49-50	Fort Wayne	3	....	....	9	4	22	.182	....	....	....	1	4	.250	....	....	....	6	6	....	....	....	....	....	3.0	....	2.0	....
50-51	Fort Wayne	3	....	....	15	7	19	.368	....	....	....	1	1	1.000	....	....	7	5	8	0	....	....	....	....	5.0	2.3	1.7	....
NBA Playoff Totals		6	....	....	24	11	41	.268	....	....	....	2	5	.400	....	....	7	11	14	0	....	....	....	....	4.0	1.2	1.8	....
NBL Playoff Totals		27	....	....	249	87	....	....	....	....	....	75	49	....	....	....	....	....	....	....	....	....	....	....	9.2	....	....	....
Career Playoff Totals		33	....	....	273	98	41	....	....	....	....	77	54	....	....	....	7	11	14	0	....	....	....	....	8.3	0.2	0.3	....

• ARMSTRONG, Darrell

Darrell Eugene Armstrong

Born: June 22, 1968. Gastonia, NC, United States. Height: 6' Weight: 170 lbs. Drafted: — College: Fayetteville State

YEAR	TEAM	GP	GS	MIN	PTS	FGM	FGA	FG%	3PM	3PA	3P%	FTM	FTA	FT%	ORB	DRB	TRB	AST	PF	DQ	STL	BLK	TO	MPG	PPG	RPG	APG	PCM
94-95	Orlando	3	0	8	10	3	8	.375	2	6	.333	2	2	1.000	1	0	1	3	3	0	1	0	1	2.7	3.3	0.3	1.0	1.003
95-96	Orlando	13	0	41	42	16	32	.500	6	12	.500	4	4	1.000	0	2	2	5	4	0	6	0	7	3.2	3.2	0.2	0.4	.764
96-97	Orlando	67	0	1010	411	132	345	.383	55	181	.304	92	106	.868	35	41	76	175	114	1	61	9	101	15.1	6.1	1.1	2.6	.378
97-98	Orlando	48	17	1236	442	156	380	.411	25	68	.368	105	123	.854	65	94	159	236	96	1	58	5	110	25.8	9.2	3.3	4.9	.440
98-99	Orlando	50	15	1502	690	230	522	.441	69	189	.365	161	178	.904	53	127	180	335	90	0	108	4	158	30.0	13.8	3.6	6.7	.582
99-00	Orlando	82	82	2590	1330	484	1119	.433	137	403	.340	225	247	.911	65	205	270	501	137	1	169	9	248	31.6	16.2	3.3	6.1	.544
00-01	Orlando	75	75	2767	1189	413	1002	.412	143	403	.355	220	249	.884	94	249	343	524	155	2	135	13	200	36.9	15.9	4.6	7.0	.512
01-02	Orlando	82	79	2730	1015	347	828	.419	139	398	.349	182	205	.888	83	236	319	453	166	2	157	10	175	33.3	12.4	3.9	5.5	.466
02-03	Orlando	82	23	2351	769	263	643	.409	78	232	.336	165	188	.878	91	204	295	323	167	1	135	13	160	28.7	9.4	3.6	3.9	.403
NBA Season Totals		502	291	14235	5898	2044	4879	.419	654	1892	.346	1156	1302	.888	487	1158	1645	2555	932	8	830	63	1160	28.4	11.7	3.3	5.1	....
96-97	Orlando	5	0	143	57	20	42	.476	6	18	.333	11	13	.846	3	18	21	17	6	0	8	1	7	28.6	11.4	4.2	3.4	.506
98-99	Orlando	4	4	163	59	17	46	.370	9	24	.375	16	16	1.000	6	14	20	25	16	1	9	0	25	40.8	14.8	5.0	6.3	.352
00-01	Orlando	4	4	167	53	17	45	.378	7	19	.368	12	13	.923	5	17	22	19	10	0	8	2	11	41.8	13.3	5.5	4.8	.376
01-02	Orlando	4	4	158	61	20	42	.476	4	17	.235	17	21	.810	3	8	11	13	14	0	5	0	7	39.5	15.3	2.8	3.3	.350
02-03	Orlando	7	1	226	66	20	44	.455	6	18	.333	20	22	.909	7	10	17	26	22	0	6	0	17	32.3	9.4	2.4	3.7	.297
NBA Playoff Totals		24	13	857	296	94	219	.429	32	96	.333	76	85	.894	24	67	91	100	68	1	36	3	67	35.7	12.3	3.8	4.2	....

• ARMSTRONG, Scott

Scott (Scotty) Armstrong

Born: Oct. 12, 1913. Died: Aug.20, 1997. Height: 6'4". Weight: 190 lbs. Drafted: — College: Butler

YEAR	TEAM	GP	GS	MIN	PTS	FGM	FGA	FG%	3PM	3PA	3P%	FTM	FTA	FT%	ORB	DRB	TRB	AST	PF	DQ	STL	BLK	TO	MPG	PPG	RPG	APG	PCM
37-38	Fort Wayne-N	17	....	....	147	56	....	....	....	....	....	35	....	....	....	....	....	....	....	....	....	....	....	....	8.6	....	....	....
38-39	Oshkosh-N	27	....	....	166	65	....	....	....	....	....	36	....	....	....	....	....	....	....	....	....	....	....	....	6.1	....	....	....
39-40	Indianapolis-N	28	....	....	113	42	....	....	....	....	....	29	....	....	....	....	....	....	....	....	....	....	....	....	4.0	....	....	....
41-42	Indianapolis-N	22	....	....	91	32	....	....	....	....	....	27	....	....	....	....	....	....	....	....	....	....	....	....	4.1	....	....	....
NBL Season Totals		94	....	....	517	195	....	....	....	....	....	127	....	....	....	....	....	....	....	....	....	....	....	....	5.5	....	....	....
38-39	Oshkosh-N	5	....	....	25	10	....	....	....	....	....	5	....	....	....	....	....	....	....	....	....	....	....	....	5.0	....	....	....
NBL Playoff Totals		5	....	....	25	10	....	....	....	....	....	5	....	....	....	....	....	....	....	....	....	....	....	....	5.0	....	....	....

• ARMSTRONG, Tate

Michel Taylor Armstrong

Born: Oct. 5, 1955. Moultrie, GA, United States. Height: 6'3". Weight: 175 lbs. Drafted: 1977 College: Duke

YEAR	TEAM	GP	GS	MIN	PTS	FGM	FGA	FG%	3PM	3PA	3P%	FTM	FTA	FT%	ORB	DRB	TRB	AST	PF	DQ	STL	BLK	TO	MPG	PPG	RPG	APG	PCM
77-78	Chicago	66	....	716	284	131	280	.468	....	....	....	22	27	.815	24	44	68	74	42	0	23	0	59	10.8	4.3	1.0	1.1	.341
78-79	Chicago	26	....	259	66	28	70	.400	....	....	....	10	13	.769	7	13	20	31	22	0	10	0	21	10.0	2.5	0.8	1.2	.229
NBA Season Totals		92	....	975	350	159	350	.454	....	....	....	32	40	.800	31	57	88	105	64	0	33	0	80	10.6	3.8	1.0	1.1	....

YEAR	TEAM	GP	GS	MIN	PTS	FGM	FGA	FG%	3PM	3PA	3P%	FTM	FTA	FT%	ORB	DRB	TRB	AST	PF	DQ	STL	BLK	TO	MPG	PPG	RPG	APG	PCM

• ARNDT, Fred

Fred Arndt

Born: —.   Height: —   Weight: —   Drafted: —   College: —

YEAR	TEAM	GP	GS	MIN	PTS	FGM	FGA	FG%	3PM	3PA	3P%	FTM	FTA	FT%	ORB	DRB	TRB	AST	PF	DQ	STL	BLK	TO	MPG	PPG	RPG	APG	PCM
37-38	Whiting-N	2	....	....	2	1	....	....	....	....	....	0	....	....	....	....	....	....	....	....	....	....	....	....	1.0	....	....	....
NBL Playoff Totals		2	....	....	2	1	....	....	....	....	....	0	....	....	....	....	....	....	....	....	....	....	....	....	1.0	....	....	....

• ARNELLE, Jesse

Hugh Jesse Arnelle

Born: Dec. 30, 1933. New Rochelle, NY, United States.   Height: 6'5".   Weight: 220 lbs.   Drafted: 1955   College: Penn State

YEAR	TEAM	GP	GS	MIN	PTS	FGM	FGA	FG%	3PM	3PA	3P%	FTM	FTA	FT%	ORB	DRB	TRB	AST	PF	DQ	STL	BLK	TO	MPG	PPG	RPG	APG	PCM
55-56	Fort Wayne	31	....	409	147	52	164	.317	....	....	....	43	69	.623	....	....	170	18	60	0	....	....	....	13.2	4.7	5.5	0.6	.442
NBA Season Totals		31	....	409	147	52	164	.317	....	....	....	43	69	.623	....	....	170	18	60	0	....	....	....	13.2	4.7	5.5	0.6	....

• ARNETTE, Jay

Jay Hoyland Arnette

Born: Dec. 19, 1938. Austin, TX, United States.   Height: 6'2".   Weight: 175 lbs.   Drafted: 1960   College: Texas

YEAR	TEAM	GP	GS	MIN	PTS	FGM	FGA	FG%	3PM	3PA	3P%	FTM	FTA	FT%	ORB	DRB	TRB	AST	PF	DQ	STL	BLK	TO	MPG	PPG	RPG	APG	PCM
63-64	Cincinnati	48	....	501	184	71	196	.362	....	....	....	42	54	.778	....	....	54	71	105	2	....	....	....	10.4	3.8	1.1	1.5	.339
64-65	Cincinnati	63	....	662	238	91	245	.371	....	....	....	56	75	.747	....	....	62	68	125	1	....	....	....	10.5	3.8	1.0	1.1	.296
65-66	Cincinnati	3	....	14	2	1	6	.167	....	....	....	0	0	.000	....	....	0	0	3	0	....	....	....	4.7	0.7	0.0	0.0	-.221
NBA Season Totals		114	....	1177	424	163	447	.365	....	....	....	98	129	.760	....	....	116	139	233	3	....	....	....	10.3	3.7	1.0	1.2	....
63-64	Cincinnati	8	....	79	29	11	31	.355	....	....	....	7	8	.875	....	....	10	9	21	1	....	....	....	9.9	3.6	1.3	1.1	.299
64-65	Cincinnati	1	....	2	0	0	1	.000	....	....	....	0	0	.000	....	....	0	1	1	0	....	....	....	2.0	0.0	0.0	1.0	.040
NBA Playoff Totals		9	....	81	29	11	32	.344	....	....	....	7	8	.875	....	....	10	10	22	1	....	....	....	9.0	3.2	1.1	1.1	....

• ARNZEN, Bob

Robert Louis Arnzen

Born: Nov. 3, 1947. Covington, KY, United States.   Height: 6'5".   Weight: 205 lbs.   Drafted: 1969   College: Notre Dame

YEAR	TEAM	GP	GS	MIN	PTS	FGM	FGA	FG%	3PM	3PA	3P%	FTM	FTA	FT%	ORB	DRB	TRB	AST	PF	DQ	STL	BLK	TO	MPG	PPG	RPG	APG	PCM
69-70	New York-A	13	....	98	40	19	48	.396	0	1	.000	2	6	.333	12	10	22	5	11	0	....	....	8	7.5	3.1	1.7	0.4	.339
70-71	Cincinnati	55	....	594	301	128	277	.462	....	....	....	45	52	.865	....	....	152	24	54	0	....	....	....	10.8	5.5	2.8	0.4	.513
72-73	Indiana-A	23	....	111	46	20	38	.526	0	3	.000	6	8	.750	11	12	23	3	12	0	....	....	0	4.8	2.0	1.0	0.1	.428
73-74	Indiana-A	20	....	149	56	24	48	.500	1	1	1.000	7	9	.778	10	10	20	3	11	....	3	2	8	7.5	2.8	1.0	0.2	.338
NBA Season Totals		55	....	594	301	128	277	.462	....	....	....	45	52	.865	....	....	152	24	54	0	....	....	....	10.8	5.5	2.8	0.4	....
ABA Season Totals		56	....	358	142	63	134	.470	1	5	.200	15	23	.652	33	32	65	11	34	0	3	2	16	6.4	2.5	1.2	0.2	....
Career Totals		111	....	952	443	191	411	.465	1	5	.200	60	75	.800	33	32	217	35	88	0	3	2	16	8.6	4.0	2.0	0.3	....
72-73	Indiana-A	7	....	13	7	3	6	.500	0	2	.000	1	1	1.000	0	0	0	0	1	0	....	....	0	1.9	1.0	0.0	0.0	.296
ABA Playoff Totals		7	....	13	7	3	6	.500	0	2	.000	1	1	1.000	0	0	0	0	1	0	....	....	0	1.9	1.0	0.0	0.0	....

• ARNZEN, Stan

Stan Arnzen

Born: 1914.   Height: 5'11".   Weight: 170 lbs.   Drafted: —   College: Morehead State

YEAR	TEAM	GP	GS	MIN	PTS	FGM	FGA	FG%	3PM	3PA	3P%	FTM	FTA	FT%	ORB	DRB	TRB	AST	PF	DQ	STL	BLK	TO	MPG	PPG	RPG	APG	PCM
37-38	Cincinnati-N	5	....	....	23	10	....	....	....	....	....	3	....	....	....	....	....	....	....	....	....	....	....	....	4.6	....	....	....
NBL Season Totals		5	....	....	23	10	....	....	....	....	....	3	....	....	....	....	....	....	....	....	....	....	....	....	4.6	....	....	....

• ARROYO, Carlos

Carlos Arroyo

Born: July 30, 1979. Fajardo, Puerto Rico.   Height: 6'2".   Weight: 202 lbs.   Drafted: —   College: Florida International

YEAR	TEAM	GP	GS	MIN	PTS	FGM	FGA	FG%	3PM	3PA	3P%	FTM	FTA	FT%	ORB	DRB	TRB	AST	PF	DQ	STL	BLK	TO	MPG	PPG	RPG	APG	PCM
01-02	Toronto	17	0	96	30	13	29	.448	0	0	.000	4	6	.667	3	9	12	21	12	0	6	0	12	5.6	1.8	0.7	1.2	.391
01-02	Denver	20	1	275	81	36	82	.439	0	2	.000	9	12	.750	9	19	28	49	18	0	5	1	11	13.8	4.1	1.4	2.5	.379
02-03	Utah	44	0	287	121	50	109	.459	3	7	.429	18	22	.818	11	15	26	53	28	0	12	1	30	6.5	2.8	0.6	1.2	.414
NBA Season Totals		81	1	658	232	99	220	.450	3	9	.333	31	40	.775	23	43	66	123	58	0	23	2	53	8.1	2.9	0.8	1.5	....
02-03	Utah	3	0	27	9	3	9	.333	0	0	.000	3	4	.750	2	0	2	5	2	0	0	0	0	9.0	3.0	0.7	1.7	.351
NBA Playoff Totals		3	0	27	9	3	9	.333	0	0	.000	3	4	.750	2	0	2	5	2	0	0	0	0	9.0	3.0	0.7	1.7	....

• ARTEST, Ron

Ronald William Artest

Born: Nov. 13, 1979. Queensbridge, NY, United States.   Height: 6'6".   Weight: 244 lbs.   Drafted: 1999   College: St. John's (NY)

YEAR	TEAM	GP	GS	MIN	PTS	FGM	FGA	FG%	3PM	3PA	3P%	FTM	FTA	FT%	ORB	DRB	TRB	AST	PF	DQ	STL	BLK	TO	MPG	PPG	RPG	APG	PCM
99-00	Chicago	72	63	2238	866	309	759	.407	60	191	.314	188	279	.674	62	246	308	202	159	0	119	39	166	31.1	12.0	4.3	2.8	.374
00-01	Chicago	76	74	2363	907	327	815	.401	43	148	.291	210	280	.750	59	235	294	228	254	7	152	45	159	31.1	11.9	3.9	3.0	.369
01-02	Chicago	27	26	823	421	152	351	.433	36	91	.396	81	129	.628	40	91	131	77	108	6	75	23	69	30.5	15.6	4.9	2.9	.485
01-02	Indiana	28	24	819	306	117	285	.411	17	79	.215	55	75	.733	33	107	140	50	109	4	66	16	49	29.3	10.9	5.0	1.8	.375
02-03	Indiana	69	67	2316	1068	362	846	.428	71	211	.336	273	371	.736	101	261	362	198	242	7	159	50	145	33.6	15.5	5.2	2.9	.465
NBA Season Totals		272	254	8559	3568	1267	3056	.415	227	720	.315	807	1134	.712	295	940	1235	755	872	24	571	173	588	31.5	13.1	4.5	2.8	....
01-02	Indiana	5	5	167	59	22	54	.407	6	13	.462	9	13	.692	6	24	30	16	19	1	13	3	9	33.4	11.8	6.0	3.2	.423
02-03	Indiana	6	6	252	114	35	90	.389	12	31	.387	32	40	.800	11	24	35	13	25	2	15	6	16	42.0	19.0	5.8	2.2	.395
NBA Playoff Totals		11	11	419	173	57	144	.396	18	44	.409	41	53	.774	17	48	65	29	44	3	28	9	25	38.1	15.7	5.9	2.6	....

• ARTHURS, John

John Charles Arthurs

Born: Aug. 15, 1947.   Height: 6'4".   Weight: 185 lbs.   Drafted: 1969   College: Tulane

YEAR	TEAM	GP	GS	MIN	PTS	FGM	FGA	FG%	3PM	3PA	3P%	FTM	FTA	FT%	ORB	DRB	TRB	AST	PF	DQ	STL	BLK	TO	MPG	PPG	RPG	APG	PCM
69-70	Milwaukee	11	....	86	35	12	35	.343	....	....	....	11	15	.733	....	....	14	17	15	0	....	....	....	7.8	3.2	1.3	1.5	.439
NBA Season Totals		11	....	86	35	12	35	.343	....	....	....	11	15	.733	....	....	14	17	15	0	....	....	....	7.8	3.2	1.3	1.5	....

• ASKEW, Vincent

Vincent Jerome Askew

Born: Feb. 28, 1966. Memphis, TN, United States. Height: 6'6". Weight: 210 lbs. Drafted: 1987 College: Memphis State

YEAR	TEAM	GP	GS	MIN	PTS	FGM	FGA	FG%	3PM	3PA	3P%	FTM	FTA	FT%	ORB	DRB	TRB	AST	PF	DQ	STL	BLK	TO	MPG	PPG	RPG	APG	PCM
87-88	Philadelphia	14	2	234	52	22	74	.297	0	0	.000	8	11	.727	6	16	22	33	12	0	10	6	13	16.7	3.7	1.6	2.4	.235
90-91	Golden State	7	0	85	33	12	25	.480	0	0	.000	9	11	.818	7	4	11	13	21	1	2	0	6	12.1	4.7	1.6	1.9	.359
91-92	Golden State	80	10	1496	498	193	379	.509	1	10	.100	111	160	.694	89	144	233	188	128	1	47	23	88	18.7	6.2	2.9	2.4	.431
92-93	Sacramento	9	0	76	27	8	17	.471	0	0	.000	11	15	.733	7	4	11	5	11	0	2	1	8	8.4	3.0	1.2	0.6	.297
92-93	Seattle	64	4	1053	384	144	291	.495	2	6	.333	94	134	.701	55	95	150	117	124	2	38	18	64	16.5	6.0	2.3	1.8	.406
93-94	Seattle	80	3	1690	727	273	567	.481	6	31	.194	175	211	.829	60	124	184	194	145	0	73	19	72	21.1	9.1	2.3	2.4	.457
94-95	Seattle	71	1	1721	703	248	504	.492	31	94	.330	176	238	.739	65	116	181	176	191	1	49	13	85	24.2	9.9	2.5	2.5	.395
95-96	Seattle	69	2	1725	584	215	436	.493	29	86	.337	125	163	.767	65	153	218	163	178	0	47	15	97	25.0	8.5	3.2	2.4	.359
96-97	New Jersey	1	0	7	0	0	0	.000	0	0	.000	0	0	.000	0	0	0	0	1	0	0	0	0	7.0	0.0	0.0	0.0	-.067
96-97	Indiana	41	0	822	233	79	183	.432	7	24	.292	68	86	.791	25	73	98	90	122	5	17	6	41	20.0	5.7	2.4	2.2	.294
96-97	Denver	1	0	9	6	2	3	.667	0	0	.000	2	2	1.000	0	0	0	0	0	0	0	0	4	9.0	6.0	0.0	0.0	.149
97-98	Portland	30	5	443	66	19	54	.352	0	2	.000	28	39	.718	21	47	68	38	39	0	19	5	36	14.8	2.2	2.3	1.3	.234
NBA Season Totals		467	27	9361	3313	1215	2533	.480	76	253	.300	807	1070	.754	400	776	1176	1017	972	10	304	106	514	20.0	7.1	2.5	2.2	....
90-91	Golden State	6	0	41	15	6	15	.400	0	0	.000	3	6	.500	5	6	11	2	6	0	2	0	0	6.8	2.5	1.8	0.3	.407
91-92	Golden State	4	0	30	2	1	8	.125	0	0	.000	0	0	.000	3	1	4	5	3	0	0	0	2	7.5	0.5	1.0	1.3	.044
92-93	Seattle	12	0	103	62	23	41	.561	0	0	.000	16	23	.696	10	9	19	9	12	0	1	1	7	8.6	5.2	1.6	0.8	.573
93-94	Seattle	5	0	95	36	10	28	.357	0	1	.000	16	19	.842	2	4	6	9	10	0	2	0	2	19.0	7.2	1.2	1.8	.303
94-95	Seattle	4	0	93	30	12	29	.414	4	5	.800	2	3	.667	11	4	15	8	14	1	3	0	3	23.3	7.5	3.8	2.0	.318
95-96	Seattle	19	0	345	71	24	70	.343	6	23	.261	17	28	.607	5	36	41	26	50	0	13	8	28	18.2	3.7	2.2	1.4	.170
NBA Playoff Totals		50	0	707	216	76	191	.398	10	29	.345	54	79	.684	36	60	96	59	95	1	21	9	42	14.1	4.3	1.9	1.2	....

• ASKINS, Keith

Keith Bernard Askins

Born: Dec. 15, 1967. Athens, AL, United States. Height: 6'7". Weight: 197 lbs. Drafted: — College: Alabama

YEAR	TEAM	GP	GS	MIN	PTS	FGM	FGA	FG%	3PM	3PA	3P%	FTM	FTA	FT%	ORB	DRB	TRB	AST	PF	DQ	STL	BLK	TO	MPG	PPG	RPG	APG	PCM
90-91	Miami	39	1	266	86	34	81	.420	6	25	.240	12	25	.480	30	38	68	19	46	0	16	13	12	6.8	2.2	1.7	0.5	.429
91-92	Miami	59	4	843	219	84	205	.410	25	73	.342	26	37	.703	65	77	142	38	109	0	40	15	47	14.3	3.7	2.4	0.6	.274
92-93	Miami	69	1	935	227	88	213	.413	22	65	.338	29	40	.725	74	124	198	31	141	2	31	29	35	13.6	3.3	2.9	0.4	.300
93-94	Miami	37	0	319	85	36	88	.409	4	21	.190	9	10	.900	33	49	82	13	57	0	11	1	22	8.6	2.3	2.2	0.4	.285
94-95	Miami	50	5	854	229	81	207	.391	21	78	.269	46	57	.807	86	112	198	39	109	0	35	17	25	17.1	4.6	4.0	0.8	.359
95-96	Miami	75	14	1897	458	157	391	.402	99	237	.418	45	57	.789	113	211	324	121	271	6	48	61	83	25.3	6.1	4.3	1.6	.296
96-97	Miami	78	30	1773	384	138	319	.433	69	172	.401	39	58	.672	86	185	271	75	196	4	53	19	62	22.7	4.9	3.5	1.0	.258
97-98	Miami	46	12	681	111	39	122	.320	21	74	.284	12	19	.632	28	73	101	29	107	3	27	12	28	14.8	2.4	2.2	0.6	.172
98-99	Miami	33	13	415	53	20	62	.323	8	29	.276	5	8	.625	10	34	44	10	58	0	17	3	13	12.6	1.6	1.3	0.3	.108
NBA Season Totals		486	80	7983	1852	677	1688	.401	275	774	.355	223	311	.717	525	903	1428	375	1094	15	278	170	327	16.4	3.8	2.9	0.8	....
91-92	Miami	3	0	48	13	5	11	.455	3	5	.600	0	2	.000	4	5	9	3	7	0	1	0	1	16.0	4.3	3.0	1.0	.309
93-94	Miami	1	0	6	0	0	1	.000	0	0	.000	0	0	.000	1	0	1	0	0	0	0	0	2	6.0	0.0	1.0	0.0	-.306
95-96	Miami	3	0	48	13	4	11	.364	2	6	.333	3	3	1.000	3	5	8	2	9	0	1	0	4	16.0	4.3	2.7	0.7	.188
96-97	Miami	12	0	146	30	10	23	.435	6	12	.500	4	4	1.000	11	17	28	7	26	0	3	2	3	12.2	2.5	2.3	0.6	.282
97-98	Miami	4	0	58	5	2	7	.286	1	5	.200	0	0	.000	1	6	7	1	9	0	2	0	1	14.5	1.3	1.8	0.3	.081
98-99	Miami	4	0	27	0	0	4	.000	0	3	.000	0	0	.000	2	2	4	0	5	0	2	1	0	6.8	0.0	1.0	0.0	.016
NBA Playoff Totals		27	0	333	61	21	57	.368	12	31	.387	7	9	.778	22	35	57	13	56	0	9	3	11	12.3	2.3	2.1	0.5	....

• ASMONGA, Don

Donald A. Asmonga

Born: Feb. 15, 1928. Height: 6'2". Weight: 185 lbs. Drafted: — College: California (PA)

YEAR	TEAM	GP	GS	MIN	PTS	FGM	FGA	FG%	3PM	3PA	3P%	FTM	FTA	FT%	ORB	DRB	TRB	AST	PF	DQ	STL	BLK	TO	MPG	PPG	RPG	APG	PCM
53-54	Baltimore	7	....	46	5	2	15	.133	....	....	....	1	1	1.000	....	....	1	5	12	1	....	....	....	6.6	0.7	0.1	0.7	-.029
NBA Season Totals		7	....	46	5	2	15	.133	....	....	....	1	1	1.000	....	....	1	5	12	1	....	....	....	6.6	0.7	0.1	0.7	....

• ATHA, Dick

Richard E. Atha

Born: Sept. 21, 1931. Otterbein, IN, United States. Height: 6'2". Weight: 190 lbs. Drafted: 1953 College: Indiana State

YEAR	TEAM	GP	GS	MIN	PTS	FGM	FGA	FG%	3PM	3PA	3P%	FTM	FTA	FT%	ORB	DRB	TRB	AST	PF	DQ	STL	BLK	TO	MPG	PPG	RPG	APG	PCM
55-56	New York	25	....	288	93	36	88	.409	....	....	....	21	27	.778	....	....	42	32	39	0	....	....	....	11.5	3.7	1.7	1.3	.375
57-58	Detroit	18	....	160	44	17	47	.362	....	....	....	10	12	.833	....	....	24	19	24	0	....	....	....	8.9	2.4	1.3	1.1	.339
NBA Season Totals		43	....	448	137	53	135	.393	....	....	....	31	39	.795	....	....	66	51	63	0	....	....	....	10.4	3.2	1.5	1.2	....

• ATKINS, Chucky

Kenneth Lavon (Chucky) Atkins

Born: Aug. 14, 1974. Orlando, FL, United States. Height: 5'11". Weight: 160 lbs. Drafted: — College: South Florida

YEAR	TEAM	GP	GS	MIN	PTS	FGM	FGA	FG%	3PM	3PA	3P%	FTM	FTA	FT%	ORB	DRB	TRB	AST	PF	DQ	STL	BLK	TO	MPG	PPG	RPG	APG	PCM
99-00	Orlando	82	0	1626	782	314	741	.424	57	163	.350	97	133	.729	20	106	126	306	137	1	52	3	142	19.8	9.5	1.5	3.7	.421
00-01	Detroit	81	75	2363	971	380	952	.399	121	339	.357	90	130	.692	28	145	173	330	184	2	67	5	149	29.2	12.0	2.1	4.1	.341
01-02	Detroit	79	62	2284	957	368	790	.466	138	336	.411	83	120	.692	31	127	158	263	177	1	72	11	128	28.9	12.1	2.0	3.3	.380
02-03	Detroit	65	7	1398	462	168	465	.361	86	242	.355	40	49	.816	21	75	96	175	108	0	27	4	77	21.5	7.1	1.5	2.7	.269
NBA Season Totals		307	144	7671	3172	1230	2948	.417	402	1080	.372	310	432	.718	100	453	553	1074	606	4	218	23	496	25.0	10.3	1.8	3.5	....
01-02	Detroit	10	10	294	113	43	118	.364	14	39	.359	13	17	.765	5	19	24	34	25	0	6	1	14	29.4	11.3	2.4	3.4	.287
02-03	Detroit	17	3	312	103	32	91	.352	18	49	.367	21	26	.808	2	18	20	26	39	0	17	0	18	18.4	6.1	1.2	1.5	.241
NBA Playoff Totals		27	13	606	216	75	209	.359	32	88	.364	34	43	.791	7	37	44	60	64	0	23	1	32	22.4	8.0	1.6	2.2	....

• ATTLES, Al

Alvin A. Attles Jr.

Born: Nov. 7, 1936. Newark, NJ, United States. Height: 6' Weight: 175 lbs. Drafted: 1960 College: North Carolina A&T

YEAR	TEAM	GP	GS	MIN	PTS	FGM	FGA	FG%	3PM	3PA	3P%	FTM	FTA	FT%	ORB	DRB	TRB	AST	PF	DQ	STL	BLK	TO	MPG	PPG	RPG	APG	PCM
60-61	Philadelphia	77	....	1544	541	222	543	.409	....	....	....	97	162	.599	....	....	214	174	235	5	....	....	....	20.1	7.0	2.8	2.3	.363
61-62	Philadelphia	75	....	2468	844	343	724	.474	....	....	....	158	267	.592	....	....	355	333	279	8	....	....	....	32.9	11.3	4.7	4.4	.437
62-63	San Francisco	71	....	1876	735	301	630	.478	....	....	....	133	206	.646	....	....	205	184	253	7	....	....	....	26.4	10.4	2.9	2.6	.389
63-64	San Francisco	70	....	1883	763	289	640	.452	....	....	....	185	275	.673	....	....	236	197	249	4	....	....	....	26.9	10.9	3.4	2.8	.416

YEAR	TEAM	GP	GS	MIN	PTS	FGM	FGA	FG%	3PM	3PA	3P%	FTM	FTA	FT%	ORB	DRB	TRB	AST	PF	DQ	STL	BLK	TO	MPG	PPG	RPG	APG	PCM
64-65	San Francisco	73	....	1733	679	254	662	.384	....	....	....	171	274	.624	....	....	239	205	242	7	....	....	....	23.7	9.3	3.3	2.8	.386
65-66	San Francisco	79	....	2053	882	364	724	.503	....	....	....	154	252	.611	....	....	322	225	265	7	....	....	....	26.0	11.2	4.1	2.8	.479
66-67	San Francisco	69	....	1764	512	212	467	.454	....	....	....	88	151	.583	....	....	321	269	265	13	....	....	....	25.6	7.4	4.7	3.9	.429
67-68	San Francisco	67	....	1992	654	252	540	.467	....	....	....	150	216	.694	....	....	276	390	284	9	....	....	....	29.7	9.8	4.1	5.8	.489
68-69	San Francisco	51	....	1516	419	162	359	.451	....	....	....	95	149	.638	....	....	181	306	183	3	....	....	....	29.7	8.2	3.5	6.0	.437
69-70	San Francisco	45	....	676	231	78	202	.386	....	....	....	75	113	.664	....	....	74	142	103	0	....	....	....	15.0	5.1	1.6	3.2	.420
70-71	San Francisco	34	....	321	68	22	54	.407	....	....	....	24	41	.585	....	....	40	58	59	2	....	....	....	9.4	2.0	1.2	1.7	.337
NBA Season Totals		711	....	17826	6328	2499	5545	.451	....	....	....	1330	2106	.632	....	....	2463	2483	2417	65	....	....	....	25.1	8.9	3.5	3.5	....
60-61	Philadelphia	3	....	110	29	12	26	.462	....	....	....	5	14	.357	....	....	12	9	14	0	....	....	....	36.7	9.7	4.0	3.0	.272
61-62	Philadelphia	12	....	338	73	28	76	.368	....	....	....	17	31	.548	....	....	55	27	54	4	....	....	....	28.2	6.1	4.6	2.3	.251
63-64	San Francisco	12	....	386	146	58	144	.403	....	....	....	30	56	.536	....	....	37	30	54	5	....	....	....	32.2	12.2	3.1	2.5	.294
66-67	San Francisco	15	....	237	46	20	46	.435	....	....	....	6	16	.375	....	....	62	38	45	1	....	....	....	15.8	3.1	4.1	2.5	.416
67-68	San Francisco	10	....	277	73	25	62	.403	....	....	....	23	30	.767	....	....	53	70	49	2	....	....	....	27.7	7.3	5.3	7.0	.533
68-69	San Francisco	6	....	109	15	7	21	.333	....	....	....	1	4	.250	....	....	18	21	17	0	....	....	....	18.2	2.5	3.0	3.5	.316
70-71	San Francisco	4	....	47	13	4	7	.571	....	....	....	5	7	.714	....	....	8	11	13	0	....	....	....	11.8	3.3	2.0	2.8	.498
NBA Playoff Totals		62	....	1504	395	154	382	.403	....	....	....	87	158	.551	....	....	245	206	246	12	....	....	....	24.3	6.4	4.0	3.3	....

• AUBUCHON, Chet

Chester J. Aubuchon Jr.

Born: May 8, 1916. Gary, IN, United States. Height: 5'10". Weight: 137 lbs. Drafted: — College: Michigan State

YEAR	TEAM	GP	GS	MIN	PTS	FGM	FGA	FG%	3PM	3PA	3P%	FTM	FTA	FT%	ORB	DRB	TRB	AST	PF	DQ	STL	BLK	TO	MPG	PPG	RPG	APG	PCM
46-47	Detroit	30	....	....	65	23	91	.253	....	....	....	19	35	.543	....	....	....	20	46	....	....	....	....	....	2.2	....	0.7	....
NBA Season Totals		30	....	....	65	23	91	.253	....	....	....	19	35	.543	....	....	....	20	46	....	....	....	....	....	2.2	....	0.7	....

• AUGMON, Stacey

Stacey Orlando (The Plastic Man) Augmon

Born: Aug. 1, 1968. Pasadena, CA, United States. Height: 6'6". Weight: 205 lbs. Drafted: 1991 College: UNLV

YEAR	TEAM	GP	GS	MIN	PTS	FGM	FGA	FG%	3PM	3PA	3P%	FTM	FTA	FT%	ORB	DRB	TRB	AST	PF	DQ	STL	BLK	TO	MPG	PPG	RPG	APG	PCM
91-92	Atlanta	82	82	2505	1094	440	899	.489	1	6	.167	213	320	.666	191	229	420	201	161	0	124	27	180	30.5	13.3	5.1	2.5	.448
92-93	Atlanta	73	66	2112	1021	397	792	.501	0	4	.000	227	307	.739	141	146	287	170	141	1	91	18	161	28.9	14.0	3.9	2.3	.450
93-94	Atlanta	82	82	2605	1212	439	861	.510	1	7	.143	333	436	.764	178	216	394	187	179	0	149	45	148	31.8	14.8	4.8	2.3	.500
94-95	Atlanta	76	76	2362	1053	397	876	.453	7	26	.269	252	346	.728	157	211	368	197	163	0	100	47	152	31.1	13.9	4.8	2.6	.437
95-96	Atlanta	77	49	2294	976	362	738	.491	1	4	.250	251	317	.792	137	167	304	137	188	1	106	31	139	29.8	12.7	3.9	1.8	.406
96-97	Detroit	20	3	292	90	31	77	.403	0	0	.000	28	41	.683	14	35	49	15	29	0	10	10	28	14.6	4.5	2.5	0.8	.280
96-97	Portland	40	7	650	189	74	143	.517	0	0	.000	41	56	.732	33	56	89	41	58	0	32	7	36	16.3	4.7	2.2	1.0	.339
97-98	Portland	71	23	1445	403	154	372	.414	1	7	.143	94	156	.603	104	131	235	88	144	0	57	32	78	20.4	5.7	3.3	1.2	.297
98-99	Portland	48	21	874	208	78	174	.448	0	2	.000	52	76	.684	47	78	125	58	81	0	57	18	30	18.2	4.3	2.6	1.2	.334
99-00	Portland	59	0	692	203	83	175	.474	0	2	.000	37	55	.673	42	74	116	53	69	0	27	11	38	11.7	3.4	2.0	0.9	.351
00-01	Portland	66	23	1182	311	127	266	.477	0	4	.000	57	87	.655	60	99	159	98	105	0	48	21	48	17.9	4.7	2.4	1.5	.334
01-02	Charlotte	77	3	1320	357	140	328	.427	0	3	.000	77	101	.762	59	166	225	103	115	0	56	12	54	17.1	4.6	2.9	1.3	.343
02-03	New Orleans	70	3	862	212	79	192	.411	0	7	.000	54	72	.750	26	93	119	69	80	0	27	9	40	12.3	3.0	1.7	1.0	.284
NBA Season Totals		841	438	19195	7329	2801	5893	.475	11	72	.153	1716	2370	.724	1189	1701	2890	1417	1513	2	884	288	1132	22.8	8.7	3.4	1.7	....
92-93	Atlanta	3	3	93	36	14	31	.452	0	0	.000	8	12	.667	3	5	8	5	7	0	4	0	4	31.0	12.0	2.7	1.7	.299
93-94	Atlanta	11	11	324	119	46	89	.517	0	0	.000	27	38	.711	13	16	29	28	26	0	7	2	15	29.5	10.8	2.6	2.5	.352
94-95	Atlanta	3	1	52	21	6	14	.429	0	0	.000	9	12	.750	3	4	7	5	8	0	3	0	2	17.3	7.0	2.3	1.7	.407
95-96	Atlanta	10	10	314	103	35	72	.486	0	1	.000	33	40	.825	9	27	36	27	26	0	11	6	17	31.4	10.3	3.6	2.7	.367
96-97	Portland	4	0	35	7	2	6	.333	0	0	.000	3	4	.750	1	0	1	3	6	0	1	0	1	8.8	1.8	0.3	0.8	.118
97-98	Portland	4	0	28	5	2	4	.500	0	0	.000	1	2	.500	1	2	3	1	2	0	2	1	2	7.0	1.3	0.8	0.3	.234
98-99	Portland	13	0	176	35	10	28	.357	0	1	.000	15	18	.833	10	23	33	5	15	0	8	3	3	13.5	2.7	2.5	0.4	.301
99-00	Portland	7	0	34	9	4	12	.333	0	0	.000	1	2	.500	0	2	2	0	6	0	0	0	0	4.9	1.3	0.3	0.0	.011
00-01	Portland	2	0	28	10	4	10	.400	0	0	.000	2	2	1.000	1	3	4	4	3	0	1	0	1	14.0	5.0	2.0	2.0	.402
01-02	Charlotte	9	0	152	48	16	41	.390	0	0	.000	16	21	.762	7	20	27	13	21	1	10	1	12	16.9	5.3	3.0	1.4	.338
02-03	New Orleans	4	0	69	17	5	15	.333	0	0	.000	7	8	.875	1	9	10	3	8	0	3	0	3	17.3	4.3	2.5	0.8	.235
NBA Playoff Totals		70	25	1305	410	144	322	.447	0	2	.000	122	159	.767	49	111	160	94	128	1	50	13	60	18.6	5.9	2.3	1.3	....

• AUSTIN, Isaac

Isaac Edward Austin

Born: Aug. 18, 1969. Gridley, CA, United States. Height: 6'10". Weight: 255 lbs. Drafted: 1991 College: Arizona State

YEAR	TEAM	GP	GS	MIN	PTS	FGM	FGA	FG%	3PM	3PA	3P%	FTM	FTA	FT%	ORB	DRB	TRB	AST	PF	DQ	STL	BLK	TO	MPG	PPG	RPG	APG	PCM
91-92	Utah	31	0	112	61	21	46	.457	0	0	.000	19	30	.633	11	24	35	5	20	0	2	2	9	3.6	2.0	1.1	0.2	.505
92-93	Utah	46	3	306	129	50	112	.446	0	1	.000	29	44	.659	38	41	79	6	60	1	8	14	23	6.7	2.8	1.7	0.1	.377
93-94	Philadelphia	14	0	201	72	29	66	.439	0	1	.000	14	23	.609	25	44	69	17	29	0	5	10	17	14.4	5.1	4.9	1.2	.500
96-97	Miami	82	17	1881	792	321	639	.502	0	3	.000	150	226	.664	136	342	478	101	244	4	45	43	164	22.9	9.7	5.8	1.2	.441
97-98	Miami	52	25	1371	659	252	532	.474	0	3	.000	155	228	.680	119	211	330	87	162	5	43	34	120	26.4	12.7	6.3	1.7	.476
97-98	LA Clippers	26	25	895	396	154	339	.454	0	5	.000	88	135	.652	80	147	227	88	69	0	18	22	88	34.4	15.2	8.7	3.4	.484
98-99	Orlando	49	49	1259	477	185	453	.408	2	7	.286	105	157	.669	83	154	237	89	125	1	47	35	114	25.7	9.7	4.8	1.8	.350
99-00	Washington	59	23	1173	397	151	352	.429	1	4	.250	94	137	.686	64	218	282	74	128	0	17	38	107	19.9	6.7	4.8	1.3	.364
00-01	Vancouver	52	16	845	226	96	270	.356	6	24	.250	28	40	.700	50	172	222	58	94	0	20	23	54	16.3	4.3	4.3	1.1	.326
01-02	Memphis	21	8	306	76	36	92	.391	0	3	.000	4	4	1.000	11	60	71	13	36	0	9	5	11	14.6	3.6	3.4	0.6	.295
NBA Season Totals		432	166	8349	3285	1295	2901	.446	9	51	.176	686	1024	.670	617	1413	2030	538	967	11	214	226	707	19.3	7.6	4.7	1.2	....
92-93	Utah	1	0	3	2	1	2	.500	0	0	.000	0	0	.000	0	1	1	0	1	0	0	1	0	3.0	2.0	1.0	0.0	.822
96-97	Miami	15	0	287	98	36	81	.444	1	4	.250	25	31	.806	16	50	66	6	35	0	6	7	22	19.1	6.5	4.4	0.4	.336
98-99	Orlando	4	4	112	26	9	23	.391	0	2	.000	8	12	.667	7	9	16	8	14	0	4	3	8	28.0	6.5	4.0	2.0	.248
NBA Playoff Totals		20	4	402	126	46	106	.434	1	6	.167	33	43	.767	23	60	83	14	50	0	10	11	30	20.1	6.3	4.2	0.7	....

• AUSTIN, Johnny

John W. Austin

Born: Aug. 31, 1944. Washington, DC, United States. Height: 6' Weight: 170 lbs. Drafted: 1966 College: Boston College

YEAR TEAM	GP	GS	MIN	PTS	FGM	FGA	FG%	3PM	3PA	3P%	FTM	FTA	FT%	ORB	DRB	TRB	AST	PF	DQ	STL	BLK	TO	MPG	PPG	RPG	APG	PCM
66-67 Baltimore	4	....	61	23	5	22	.227	....	....	....	13	16	.813	....	....	7	4	12	0	....	....	....	15.3	5.8	1.8	1.0	.227
67-68 New Jersey-A	41	....	692	317	108	279	.387	0	11	.000	101	140	.721	....	....	64	58	110	0	....	....	57	16.9	7.7	1.6	1.4	.338
NBA Season Totals	4	....	61	23	5	22	.227	....	....	....	13	16	.813	....	....	7	4	12	0	....	....	....	15.3	5.8	1.8	1.0	....
ABA Season Totals	41	....	692	317	108	279	.387	0	11	.000	101	140	.721	....	....	64	58	110	0	....	....	57	16.9	7.7	1.6	1.4	....
Career Totals	45	....	753	340	113	301	.375	0	11	.000	114	156	.731	....	....	71	62	122	0	....	....	57	16.7	7.6	1.6	1.4	....

• AUSTIN, Ken

Ken Austin

Born: July 15, 1961. Los Angeles, CA, United States. Height: 6'9". Weight: 205 lbs. Drafted: 1983 College: Rice

YEAR TEAM	GP	GS	MIN	PTS	FGM	FGA	FG%	3PM	3PA	3P%	FTM	FTA	FT%	ORB	DRB	TRB	AST	PF	DQ	STL	BLK	TO	MPG	PPG	RPG	APG	PCM
83-84 Detroit	7	0	28	12	6	13	.462	0	0	.000	0	0	.000	2	1	3	1	7	0	1	1	3	4.0	1.7	0.4	0.1	.184
NBA Season Totals	7	0	28	12	6	13	.462	0	0	.000	0	0	.000	2	1	3	1	7	0	1	1	3	4.0	1.7	0.4	0.1	....

• AUSTING, Carl

Carl Austing

Born: Apr. 25, 1910. Died: Mar.25, 1992. Height: 6'4". Weight: 180 lbs. Drafted: — College: Cincinnati

YEAR TEAM	GP	GS	MIN	PTS	FGM	FGA	FG%	3PM	3PA	3P%	FTM	FTA	FT%	ORB	DRB	TRB	AST	PF	DQ	STL	BLK	TO	MPG	PPG	RPG	APG	PCM
37-38 Cincinnati-N	5	....	....	37	16	....	....	....	....	....	5	....	....	....	....	....	....	....	....	....	....	....	....	7.4	....	....	....
NBL Season Totals	5	....	....	37	16	....	....	....	....	....	5	....	....	....	....	....	....	....	....	....	....	....	....	7.4	....	....	....

• AVENT, Anthony

Anthony (A.A.) Avent

Born: Oct. 18, 1969. Rocky Mount, NC, United States. Height: 6'9". Weight: 235 lbs. Drafted: 1991 College: Seton Hall

YEAR TEAM	GP	GS	MIN	PTS	FGM	FGA	FG%	3PM	3PA	3P%	FTM	FTA	FT%	ORB	DRB	TRB	AST	PF	DQ	STL	BLK	TO	MPG	PPG	RPG	APG	PCM
92-93 Milwaukee	82	78	2285	806	347	802	.433	0	2	.000	112	172	.651	180	332	512	91	237	0	57	73	139	27.9	9.8	6.2	1.1	.354
93-94 Milwaukee	33	20	695	245	92	228	.404	0	0	.000	61	79	.772	60	94	154	33	60	0	16	20	43	21.1	7.4	4.7	1.0	.367
93-94 Orlando	41	20	676	144	58	170	.341	0	0	.000	28	44	.636	84	100	184	32	87	0	17	11	41	16.5	3.5	4.5	0.8	.274
94-95 Orlando	71	3	1066	258	105	244	.430	0	0	.000	48	75	.640	97	196	293	41	170	1	28	50	50	15.0	3.6	4.1	0.6	.356
95-96 Vancouver	71	32	1586	415	179	466	.384	0	0	.000	57	77	.740	108	247	355	69	202	3	30	42	107	22.3	5.8	5.0	1.0	.262
98-99 Utah	5	0	44	9	4	13	.308	0	0	.000	1	2	.500	8	4	12	1	6	0	2	0	7	8.8	1.8	2.4	0.2	.119
99-00 LA Clippers	49	3	377	81	29	96	.302	0	0	.000	23	32	.719	23	51	74	11	62	1	16	15	24	7.7	1.7	1.5	0.2	.195
NBA Season Totals	352	156	6729	1958	814	2019	.403	0	2	.000	330	481	.686	560	1024	1584	278	824	5	166	211	411	19.1	5.6	4.5	0.8	....
93-94 Orlando	2	0	40	19	6	13	.462	0	0	.000	7	8	.875	8	3	11	1	2	0	0	0	1	20.0	9.5	5.5	0.5	.536
94-95 Orlando	7	0	40	9	3	7	.429	0	1	.000	3	4	.750	4	4	8	0	11	0	0	1	2	5.7	1.3	1.1	0.0	.155
NBA Playoff Totals	9	0	80	28	9	20	.450	0	1	.000	10	12	.833	12	7	19	1	13	0	0	1	3	8.9	3.1	2.1	0.1	....

• AVERITT, Bird

William Rodney (Bird) Averitt

Born: July 22, 1952. Hopkinsville, KY, United States. Height: 6'1". Weight: 170 lbs. Drafted: 1973 College: Pepperdine

YEAR TEAM	GP	GS	MIN	PTS	FGM	FGA	FG%	3PM	3PA	3P%	FTM	FTA	FT%	ORB	DRB	TRB	AST	PF	DQ	STL	BLK	TO	MPG	PPG	RPG	APG	PCM
73-74 San Antonio-A	74	....	1639	851	343	912	.376	9	50	.180	156	224	.696	44	77	121	132	166	....	63	6	137	22.1	11.5	1.6	1.8	.315
74-75 Kentucky-A	84	....	2031	1100	422	1014	.416	7	47	.149	249	320	.778	51	134	185	319	212	....	87	13	232	24.2	13.1	2.2	3.8	.476
75-76 Kentucky-A	78	....	2272	1398	546	1274	.429	40	128	.313	266	346	.769	55	158	213	297	208	....	106	22	221	29.1	17.9	2.7	3.8	.502
76-77 Buffalo	75	....	1136	589	234	619	.378	....	....	....	121	169	.716	20	58	78	134	127	2	30	5	....	15.1	7.9	1.0	1.8	.353
77-78 New Jersey	21	....	409	174	69	188	.367	....	....	....	36	45	.800	7	26	33	68	37	1	17	1	55	19.5	8.3	1.6	3.2	.300
77-78 Buffalo	34	....	676	322	129	296	.436	....	....	....	64	96	.667	10	40	50	128	86	2	22	8	88	19.9	9.5	1.5	3.8	.386
NBA Season Totals	130	....	2221	1085	432	1103	.392	....	....	....	221	310	.713	37	124	161	330	250	5	69	14	143	17.1	8.3	1.2	2.5	....
ABA Season Totals	236	....	5942	3349	1311	3200	.410	56	225	.249	671	890	.754	150	369	519	748	586	....	256	41	590	25.2	14.2	2.2	3.2	....
Career Totals	366	....	8163	4434	1743	4303	.405	56	225	.249	892	1200	.743	187	493	680	1078	836	5	325	55	733	22.3	12.1	1.9	2.9	....
73-74 San Antonio-A	6	....	104	53	19	51	.373	0	3	.000	15	19	.789	0	11	11	2	11	....	1	4	9	17.3	8.8	1.8	0.3	.296
74-75 Kentucky-A	14	....	265	138	56	154	.364	1	5	.200	25	31	.806	5	17	22	30	32	....	7	0	24	18.9	9.9	1.6	2.1	.328
75-76 Kentucky-A	10	....	358	199	80	198	.404	2	13	.154	37	42	.881	7	15	22	61	31	....	12	2	30	35.8	19.9	2.2	6.1	.461
ABA Playoff Totals	30	....	727	390	155	403	.385	3	21	.143	77	92	.837	12	43	55	93	74	....	20	6	63	24.2	13.0	1.8	3.1	....

• AVERY, William

William Avery

Born: Aug. 8, 1979. Augusta, GA, United States. Height: 6'2". Weight: 197 lbs. Drafted: 1999 College: Duke

YEAR TEAM	GP	GS	MIN	PTS	FGM	FGA	FG%	3PM	3PA	3P%	FTM	FTA	FT%	ORB	DRB	TRB	AST	PF	DQ	STL	BLK	TO	MPG	PPG	RPG	APG	PCM
99-00 Minnesota	59	1	484	154	56	181	.309	18	63	.286	24	36	.667	8	32	40	88	60	0	14	2	42	8.2	2.6	0.7	1.5	.241
00-01 Minnesota	55	0	463	154	55	144	.382	16	59	.271	28	36	.778	5	24	29	75	48	0	13	4	45	8.4	2.8	0.5	1.4	.286
01-02 Minnesota	28	0	258	71	26	90	.289	6	35	.171	13	19	.684	4	20	24	36	17	0	7	0	19	9.2	2.5	0.9	1.3	.205
NBA Season Totals	142	1	1205	379	137	415	.330	40	157	.255	65	91	.714	17	76	93	199	125	0	34	6	106	8.5	2.7	0.7	1.4	....
00-01 Minnesota	2	0	12	7	3	6	.500	1	2	.500	0	0	.000	0	1	1	2	0	0	0	1	0	6.0	3.5	0.5	1.0	.692
NBA Playoff Totals	2	0	12	7	3	6	.500	1	2	.500	0	0	.000	0	1	1	2	0	0	0	1	0	6.0	3.5	0.5	1.0	....

• AWTREY, Dennis

Dennis Wade Awtrey

Born: Feb. 22, 1948. Hollywood, CA, United States. Height: 6'10". Weight: 235 lbs. Drafted: 1970 College: Santa Clara

YEAR TEAM	GP	GS	MIN	PTS	FGM	FGA	FG%	3PM	3PA	3P%	FTM	FTA	FT%	ORB	DRB	TRB	AST	PF	DQ	STL	BLK	TO	MPG	PPG	RPG	APG	PCM
70-71 Philadelphia	70	....	1292	504	200	421	.475	....	....	....	104	157	.662	....	....	430	89	211	7	....	....	....	18.5	7.2	6.1	1.3	.520
71-72 Philadelphia	58	....	794	245	98	222	.441	....	....	....	49	76	.645	....	....	248	51	141	3	....	....	....	13.7	4.2	4.3	0.9	.425
72-73 Philadelphia	3	....	37	7	3	7	.429	....	....	....	1	4	.250	....	....	14	2	8	0	....	....	....	12.3	2.3	4.7	0.7	.355
72-73 Chicago	79	....	1650	371	143	298	.480	....	....	....	85	149	.570	....	....	433	222	226	0	....	....	....	20.9	4.7	5.5	2.8	.448
73-74 Chicago	68	....	756	184	65	123	.528	....	....	....	54	94	.574	49	125	174	86	128	3	22	14	....	11.1	2.7	2.6	1.3	.410
74-75 Phoenix	82	....	2837	810	339	722	.470	....	....	....	132	195	.677	242	462	704	342	227	2	60	52	....	34.6	9.9	8.6	4.2	.477
75-76 Phoenix	74	....	1376	359	142	304	.467	....	....	....	75	109	.688	93	200	293	159	153	1	21	22	....	18.6	4.9	4.0	2.1	.416
76-77 Phoenix	72	....	1760	411	160	373	.429	....	....	....	91	126	.722	111	245	356	182	170	1	23	31	....	24.4	5.7	4.9	2.5	.371

YEAR	TEAM	GP	GS	MIN	PTS	FGM	FGA	FG%	3PM	3PA	3P%	FTM	FTA	FT%	ORB	DRB	TRB	AST	PF	DQ	STL	BLK	TO	MPG	PPG	RPG	APG	PCM
77-78	Phoenix	81	....	1623	293	112	264	.424	....	....	....	69	109	.633	97	205	302	163	153	0	19	25	130	20.0	3.6	3.7	2.0	.276
78-79	Boston	23	....	247	50	17	44	.386	....	....	....	16	20	.800	13	34	47	20	37	0	3	6	44	10.7	2.2	2.0	0.9	.163
78-79	Seattle	40	....	499	79	27	63	.429	....	....	....	25	36	.694	29	75	104	49	69	0	13	7	8	12.5	2.0	2.6	1.2	.339
79-80	Chicago	26	....	560	86	27	60	.450	0	0	.000	32	50	.640	29	86	115	40	66	0	12	15	26	21.5	3.3	4.4	1.5	.298
80-81	Seattle	47	....	607	102	44	93	.473	0	0	.000	14	20	.700	33	75	108	54	85	0	12	8	33	12.9	2.2	2.3	1.1	.266
81-82	Portland	10	3	121	15	5	15	.333	0	0	.000	5	9	.556	7	7	14	8	28	1	1	2	6	12.1	1.5	1.4	0.8	.081
NBA Season Totals		733	3	14159	3516	1382	3009	.459	0	0	.000	752	1154	.652	703	1514	3342	1467	1702	18	186	182	247	19.3	4.8	4.6	2.0	....
70-71	Philadelphia	7	....	144	53	21	36	.583	....	....	....	11	15	.733	....	....	27	5	25	1	....	....	....	20.6	7.6	3.9	0.7	.393
72-73	Chicago	7	....	268	63	26	48	.542	....	....	....	11	22	.500	....	....	77	31	26	1	....	....	....	38.3	9.0	11.0	4.4	.484
73-74	Chicago	10	....	158	30	12	28	.429	....	....	....	6	10	.600	11	29	40	13	21	0	6	2	....	15.8	3.0	4.0	1.3	.346
75-76	Phoenix	19	....	286	60	21	45	.467	....	....	....	18	33	.545	17	46	63	25	38	1	5	9	....	15.1	3.2	3.3	1.3	.347
77-78	Phoenix	2	....	24	3	1	4	.250	....	....	....	1	1	1.000	2	0	2	3	0	0	1	0	1	12.0	1.5	1.0	1.5	.229
78-79	Seattle	16	....	153	28	10	16	.625	....	....	....	8	13	.615	15	27	42	11	34	0	5	4	9	9.6	1.8	2.6	0.7	.359
NBA Playoff Totals		61	....	1033	237	91	177	.514	....	....	....	55	94	.585	45	102	251	88	144	3	17	15	10	16.9	3.9	4.1	1.4	....

• BABIC, Milos

Milos Babic

Born: Nov. 23, 1968. Kraljevo, Yugoslavia.   Height: 7'   Weight: 240 lbs.   Drafted: 1990   College: Tennessee Tech

YEAR	TEAM	GP	GS	MIN	PTS	FGM	FGA	FG%	3PM	3PA	3P%	FTM	FTA	FT%	ORB	DRB	TRB	AST	PF	DQ	STL	BLK	TO	MPG	PPG	RPG	APG	PCM
90-91	Cleveland	12	0	52	19	6	19	.316	0	0	.000	7	12	.583	6	3	9	4	7	0	1	1	5	4.3	1.6	0.8	0.3	.214
91-92	Miami	9	0	35	18	6	13	.462	0	0	.000	6	8	.750	2	9	11	6	0	0	1	0	5	3.9	2.0	1.2	0.7	.671
NBA Season Totals		21	0	87	37	12	32	.375	0	0	.000	13	20	.650	8	12	20	10	7	0	2	1	10	4.1	1.8	1.0	0.5	....

• BACH, Johnny

John William Bach

Born: July 10, 1924. Brooklyn, NY, United States.   Height: 6'2".   Weight: 180 lbs.   Drafted: 1948   College: Fordham

YEAR	TEAM	GP	GS	MIN	PTS	FGM	FGA	FG%	3PM	3PA	3P%	FTM	FTA	FT%	ORB	DRB	TRB	AST	PF	DQ	STL	BLK	TO	MPG	PPG	RPG	APG	PCM
48-49	Boston	34	....	....	119	34	119	.286	....	....	....	51	75	.680	....	....	....	25	24	....	....	....	....		3.5	....	0.7	....
NBA Season Totals		34	....	....	119	34	119	.286	....	....	....	51	75	.680	....	....	....	25	24	....	....	....	....		3.5	....	0.7	....

• BACON, Henry

William Henry Bacon

Born: July 5, 1948. Louisville, KY, United States.   Height: 6'3".   Weight: 205 lbs.   Drafted: 1972   College: Louisville

YEAR	TEAM	GP	GS	MIN	PTS	FGM	FGA	FG%	3PM	3PA	3P%	FTM	FTA	FT%	ORB	DRB	TRB	AST	PF	DQ	STL	BLK	TO	MPG	PPG	RPG	APG	PCM
72-73	San Diego-A	47	....	425	166	60	164	.366	2	10	.200	44	73	.603	40	42	82	38	72	1	....	....	64	9.0	3.5	1.7	0.8	.336
ABA Season Totals		47	....	425	166	60	164	.366	2	10	.200	44	73	.603	40	42	82	38	72	1	....	....	64	9.0	3.5	1.7	0.8	....
72-73	San Diego-A	2	....	16	10	4	9	.444	2	3	.667	0	2	.000	4	2	6	1	0	0	....	....	2	8.0	5.0	3.0	0.5	.694
ABA Playoff Totals		2	....	16	10	4	9	.444	2	3	.667	0	2	.000	4	2	6	1	0	0	....	....	2	8.0	5.0	3.0	0.5	....

• BAECHTOLD, Jim

James E. Baechtold

Born: Dec. 9, 1927. McKeesport, PA, United States.   Height: 6'4".   Weight: 205 lbs.   Drafted: 1952   College: Eastern Kentucky

YEAR	TEAM	GP	GS	MIN	PTS	FGM	FGA	FG%	3PM	3PA	3P%	FTM	FTA	FT%	ORB	DRB	TRB	AST	PF	DQ	STL	BLK	TO	MPG	PPG	RPG	APG	PCM
52-53	Baltimore	64	....	1893	661	242	621	.390	....	....	....	177	240	.738	....	....	219	154	203	8	....	....	....	29.6	10.3	3.4	2.4	.341
53-54	New York	70	....	1627	474	170	465	.366	....	....	....	134	177	.757	....	....	183	117	195	5	....	....	....	23.2	6.8	2.6	1.7	.283
54-55	New York	72	....	2536	1003	362	898	.403	....	....	....	279	339	.823	....	....	307	218	202	0	....	....	....	35.2	13.9	4.3	3.0	.396
55-56	New York	70	....	1738	769	268	695	.386	....	....	....	233	291	.801	....	....	220	163	156	2	....	....	....	24.8	11.0	3.1	2.3	.421
56-57	New York	45	....	462	216	75	197	.381	....	....	....	66	88	.750	....	....	80	33	39	0	....	....	....	10.3	4.8	1.8	0.7	.440
NBA Season Totals		321	....	8256	3123	1117	2876	.388	....	....	....	889	1135	.783	....	....	1009	685	795	15	....	....	....	25.7	9.7	3.1	2.1	....
52-53	Baltimore	2	....	86	38	16	30	.533	....	....	....	6	11	.545	....	....	8	11	9	0	....	....	....	43.0	19.0	4.0	5.5	.496
53-54	New York	4	....	106	35	12	29	.414	....	....	....	11	13	.846	....	....	10	11	19	1	....	....	....	26.5	8.8	2.5	2.8	.347
54-55	New York	3	....	115	48	17	45	.378	....	....	....	14	15	.933	....	....	14	14	13	0	....	....	....	38.3	16.0	4.7	4.7	.432
NBA Playoff Totals		9	....	307	121	45	104	.433	....	....	....	31	39	.795	....	....	32	36	41	1	....	....	....	34.1	13.4	3.6	4.0	....

• BAER, Carl

Carl Baer

Born: —.   Height: 6'5".   Weight: —   Drafted: —   College: —

YEAR	TEAM	GP	GS	MIN	PTS	FGM	FGA	FG%	3PM	3PA	3P%	FTM	FTA	FT%	ORB	DRB	TRB	AST	PF	DQ	STL	BLK	TO	MPG	PPG	RPG	APG	PCM
45-46	Youngstown-N	1	....	....	0	0	....	....	....	....	....	0	0	.000	....	....	....	....	....	....	....	....	....	0.0	....	....	....	....
NBL Season Totals		1	....	....	0	0	....	....	....	....	....	0	0		....	....	....	....	....	....	....	....	....	0.0	....	....	....	....

• BAGARIC, Dalibor

Bagaric Bagaric

Born: Feb. 7, 1980. Croatia.   Height: 7'1".   Weight: 255 lbs.   Drafted: 2000   College: none

YEAR	TEAM	GP	GS	MIN	PTS	FGM	FGA	FG%	3PM	3PA	3P%	FTM	FTA	FT%	ORB	DRB	TRB	AST	PF	DQ	STL	BLK	TO	MPG	PPG	RPG	APG	PCM
00-01	Chicago	35	0	259	47	17	65	.262	0	1	.000	13	28	.464	22	34	56	10	44	0	9	16	21	7.4	1.3	1.6	0.3	.163
01-02	Chicago	50	0	638	185	72	178	.404	0	1	.000	41	70	.586	55	107	162	23	108	0	17	24	46	12.8	3.7	3.2	0.5	.305
02-03	Chicago	10	0	76	19	8	26	.308	0	0	.000	3	4	.750	7	13	20	4	11	0	3	3	5	7.6	1.9	2.0	0.4	.272
NBA Season Totals		95	0	973	251	97	269	.361	0	2	.000	57	102	.559	84	154	238	37	163	0	29	43	72	10.2	2.6	2.5	0.4	....

• BAGLEY, John

John Edward (Bags) Bagley

Born: Apr. 23, 1960. Bridgeport, CT, United States.   Height: 6'   Weight: 185 lbs.   Drafted: 1982   College: Boston College

YEAR	TEAM	GP	GS	MIN	PTS	FGM	FGA	FG%	3PM	3PA	3P%	FTM	FTA	FT%	ORB	DRB	TRB	AST	PF	DQ	STL	BLK	TO	MPG	PPG	RPG	APG	PCM
82-83	Cleveland	68	3	990	386	161	373	.432	0	14	.000	64	84	.762	17	79	96	167	74	0	54	5	116	14.6	5.7	1.4	2.5	.375
83-84	Cleveland	76	19	1712	673	257	607	.423	2	17	.118	157	198	.793	49	107	156	333	113	1	78	4	167	22.5	8.9	2.1	4.4	.408
84-85	Cleveland	81	65	2401	804	338	693	.488	3	26	.115	125	167	.749	54	237	291	697	132	0	129	5	211	29.6	9.9	3.6	8.6	.556
85-86	Cleveland	78	77	2472	911	366	865	.423	9	37	.243	170	215	.791	76	199	275	735	165	1	122	10	242	31.7	11.7	3.5	9.4	.522
86-87	Cleveland	72	67	2182	768	312	732	.426	31	103	.301	113	136	.831	55	197	252	379	114	0	91	7	166	30.3	10.7	3.5	5.3	.408
87-88	New Jersey	82	74	2774	981	393	896	.439	47	161	.292	148	180	.822	61	196	257	479	162	0	110	10	205	33.8	12.0	3.1	5.8	.394
88-89	New Jersey	68	20	1642	500	200	481	.416	11	54	.204	89	123	.724	36	108	144	391	117	0	72	5	156	24.1	7.4	2.1	5.8	.394

780 • BAILEY Total Basketball

YEAR	TEAM	GP	GS	MIN	PTS	FGM	FGA	FG%	3PM	3PA	3P%	FTM	FTA	FT%	ORB	DRB	TRB	AST	PF	DQ	STL	BLK	TO	MPG	PPG	RPG	APG	PCM
89-90	Boston	54	17	1095	230	100	218	.459	1	18	.056	29	39	.744	26	63	89	296	77	0	40	4	92	20.3	4.3	1.6	5.5	.394
91-92	Boston	73	59	1742	524	223	506	.441	10	42	.238	68	95	.716	38	123	161	480	123	1	57	4	146	23.9	7.2	2.2	6.6	.446
92-93	Boston	10	0	97	23	9	25	.360	0	1	.000	5	6	.833	1	6	7	20	11	0	2	0	17	9.7	2.3	0.7	2.0	.169
93-94	Atlanta	3	0	13	2	0	2	.000	0	0	.000	2	2	1.000	0	1	1	3	2	0	0	0	0	4.3	0.7	0.3	1.0	.263
NBA Season Totals		665	401	17120	5802	2359	5398	.437	114	473	.241	970	1245	.779	413	1316	1729	3980	1090	3	755	54	1518	25.7	8.7	2.6	6.0	....
84-85	Cleveland	4	4	168	51	22	56	.393	0	3	.000	7	10	.700	1	15	16	40	7	0	10	0	17	42.0	12.8	4.0	10.0	.391
89-90	Boston	5	0	70	19	8	15	.533	0	1	.000	3	4	.750	3	1	4	17	9	0	4	1	9	14.0	3.8	0.8	3.4	.369
91-92	Boston	10	10	308	111	42	95	.442	1	4	.250	26	37	.703	8	19	27	85	17	0	9	1	35	30.8	11.1	2.7	8.5	.460
NBA Playoff Totals		19	14	546	181	72	166	.434	1	8	.125	36	51	.706	12	35	47	142	33	0	23	2	61	28.7	9.5	2.5	7.5	....

• BAILEY, Carl

Carl Bailey

Born: Apr. 23, 1958. Birmingham, AL, United States. Height: 7' Weight: 210 lbs. Drafted: 1980 College: Tuskegee

YEAR	TEAM	GP	GS	MIN	PTS	FGM	FGA	FG%	3PM	3PA	3P%	FTM	FTA	FT%	ORB	DRB	TRB	AST	PF	DQ	STL	BLK	TO	MPG	PPG	RPG	APG	PCM
81-82	Portland	1	0	7	2	1	1	1.000	0	0	.000	0	0	.000	0	0	0	0	2	0	0	0	2	7.0	2.0	0.0	0.0	-.109
NBA Season Totals		1	0	7	2	1	1	1.000	0	0	.000	0	0	.000	0	0	0	0	2	0	0	0	2	7.0	2.0	0.0	0.0	....

• BAILEY, Gus

Augustus Bailey

Born: Feb. 18, 1951. Gibson, NC, United States. Died: Nov.28, 1988. Height: 6'5". Weight: 185 lbs. Drafted: 1974 College: Texas (El Paso)

YEAR	TEAM	GP	GS	MIN	PTS	FGM	FGA	FG%	3PM	3PA	3P%	FTM	FTA	FT%	ORB	DRB	TRB	AST	PF	DQ	STL	BLK	TO	MPG	PPG	RPG	APG	PCM
74-75	Houston	47	....	446	122	51	126	.405	....	....	....	20	41	.488	23	59	82	59	52	0	17	16	....	9.5	2.6	1.7	1.3	.369
75-76	Houston	30	....	262	70	28	77	.364	....	....	....	14	28	.500	20	30	50	41	33	1	14	8	....	8.7	2.3	1.7	1.4	.372
77-78	New Orleans	48	....	449	155	59	139	.424	....	....	....	37	67	.552	44	38	82	40	46	0	18	15	34	9.4	3.2	1.7	0.8	.373
78-79	New Orleans	2	....	9	4	2	7	.286	....	....	....	0	0	.000	2	0	2	2	1	0	0	0	1	4.5	2.0	1.0	1.0	.240
79-80	Washington	20	....	180	38	16	35	.457	1	1	1.000	5	13	.385	6	22	28	26	18	0	7	4	12	9.0	1.9	1.4	1.3	.344
NBA Season Totals		147	....	1346	389	156	384	.406	1	1	1.000	76	149	.510	95	149	244	168	150	1	56	43	47	9.2	2.6	1.7	1.1	....
74-75	Houston	8	....	116	45	18	36	.500	....	....	....	9	10	.900	6	13	19	16	12	0	6	2	....	14.5	5.6	2.4	2.0	.506
NBA Playoff Totals		8	....	116	45	18	36	.500	....	....	....	9	10	.900	6	13	19	16	12	0	6	2	....	14.5	5.6	2.4	2.0	....

• BAILEY, James

James L. (Jammin' James) Bailey

Born: May 21, 1957. Dublin, GA, United States. Height: 6'9". Weight: 220 lbs. Drafted: 1979 College: Rutgers

YEAR	TEAM	GP	GS	MIN	PTS	FGM	FGA	FG%	3PM	3PA	3P%	FTM	FTA	FT%	ORB	DRB	TRB	AST	PF	DQ	STL	BLK	TO	MPG	PPG	RPG	APG	PCM
79-80	Seattle	67	....	726	312	122	271	.450	0	0	.000	68	101	.673	71	126	197	28	116	1	21	54	80	10.8	4.7	2.9	0.4	.433
80-81	Seattle	82	....	2539	1145	444	889	.499	1	2	.500	256	361	.709	192	415	607	98	332	11	74	143	221	31.0	14.0	7.4	1.2	.471
81-82	Seattle	10	0	180	66	31	65	.477	0	0	.000	4	11	.364	17	31	48	13	42	2	3	7	19	18.0	6.6	4.8	1.3	.345
81-82	New Jersey	67	0	1288	593	230	440	.523	0	0	.000	133	213	.624	110	233	343	52	228	3	39	76	121	19.2	8.9	5.1	0.8	.485
82-83	New Jersey	6	0	50	20	9	18	.500	0	0	.000	2	2	1.000	3	3	6	2	15	0	1	1	6	8.3	3.3	1.0	0.3	.182
82-83	Houston	69	39	1715	976	376	756	.497	0	1	.000	224	320	.700	168	300	468	65	256	7	42	59	193	24.9	14.1	6.8	0.9	.516
83-84	Houston	73	0	1174	646	254	517	.491	0	1	.000	138	192	.719	104	190	294	79	197	8	33	40	102	16.1	8.8	4.0	1.1	.524
84-85	New York	74	28	1297	385	156	349	.447	0	1	.000	73	108	.676	122	222	344	39	286	10	30	50	104	17.5	5.2	4.6	0.5	.305
85-86	New York	48	36	1245	533	202	443	.456	0	4	.000	129	167	.772	102	232	334	50	207	12	33	40	101	25.9	11.1	7.0	1.0	.428
86-87	New Jersey	34	2	542	282	112	239	.469	0	0	.000	58	80	.725	48	89	137	20	119	5	12	23	54	15.9	8.3	4.0	0.6	.423
87-88	Phoenix	65	0	869	288	109	241	.452	0	4	.000	70	89	.787	73	137	210	42	180	1	17	28	72	13.4	4.4	3.2	0.6	.331
NBA Season Totals		595	105	11625	5246	2045	4228	.484	1	13	.077	1155	1644	.703	1010	1978	2988	488	1978	60	305	521	1073	19.5	8.8	5.0	0.8	....
79-80	Seattle	12	....	138	55	21	44	.477	0	0	.000	13	20	.650	8	17	25	5	22	0	9	9	9	11.5	4.6	2.1	0.4	.415
81-82	New Jersey	2	0	26	4	1	3	.333	0	0	.000	2	2	1.000	2	4	6	1	5	0	2	1	3	13.0	2.0	3.0	0.5	.248
NBA Playoff Totals		14	0	164	59	22	47	.468	0	0	.000	15	22	.682	10	21	31	6	27	0	11	10	12	11.7	4.2	2.2	0.4	....

• BAILEY, John

John Garfield (Toby) Bailey Jr.

Born: Nov. 19, 1975. Los Angeles, CA, United States. Height: 6'6". Weight: 213 lbs. Drafted: 1998 College: UCLA

YEAR	TEAM	GP	GS	MIN	PTS	FGM	FGA	FG%	3PM	3PA	3P%	FTM	FTA	FT%	ORB	DRB	TRB	AST	PF	DQ	STL	BLK	TO	MPG	PPG	RPG	APG	PCM
98-99	Phoenix	27	10	249	78	34	86	.395	1	5	.200	9	13	.692	24	30	54	13	24	0	9	2	11	9.2	2.9	2.0	0.5	.328
99-00	Phoenix	46	2	449	163	58	140	.414	2	10	.200	45	65	.692	26	46	72	30	55	0	13	4	24	9.8	3.5	1.6	0.7	.326
NBA Season Totals		73	12	698	241	92	226	.407	3	15	.200	54	78	.692	50	76	126	43	79	0	22	6	35	9.6	3.3	1.7	0.6	....
99-00	Phoenix	5	0	15	4	1	4	.250	0	0	.000	2	4	.500	1	1	2	2	1	0	0	0	0	3.0	0.8	0.4	0.4	.261
NBA Playoff Totals		5	0	15	4	1	4	.250	0	0	.000	2	4	.500	1	1	2	2	1	0	0	0	0	3.0	0.8	0.4	0.4	....

• BAILEY, Thurl

Thurl Lee (Big T.) Bailey

Born: Apr. 7, 1961. Washington, DC, United States. Height: 6'11". Weight: 215 lbs. Drafted: 1983 College: North Carolina State

YEAR	TEAM	GP	GS	MIN	PTS	FGM	FGA	FG%	3PM	3PA	3P%	FTM	FTA	FT%	ORB	DRB	TRB	AST	PF	DQ	STL	BLK	TO	MPG	PPG	RPG	APG	PCM
83-84	Utah	81	54	2009	692	302	590	.512	0	0	.000	88	117	.752	115	349	464	129	193	1	38	122	105	24.8	8.5	5.7	1.6	.469
84-85	Utah	80	68	2481	1212	507	1034	.490	1	1	1.000	197	234	.842	153	372	525	138	215	2	51	105	152	31.0	15.2	6.6	1.7	.501
85-86	Utah	82	13	2358	1196	483	1077	.448	0	7	.000	230	277	.830	148	345	493	153	160	0	42	114	148	28.8	14.6	6.0	1.9	.499
86-87	Utah	81	2	2155	1116	463	1036	.447	0	2	.000	190	236	.805	145	287	432	102	150	0	38	88	122	26.6	13.8	5.3	1.3	.467
87-88	Utah	82	10	2804	1604	633	1286	.492	1	3	.333	337	408	.826	134	397	531	158	186	1	49	125	189	34.2	19.6	6.5	1.9	.544
88-89	Utah	82	3	2777	1595	615	1272	.483	2	5	.400	363	440	.825	115	332	447	138	185	0	48	91	205	33.9	19.5	5.5	1.7	.491
89-90	Utah	82	33	2583	1162	470	977	.481	0	8	.000	222	285	.779	116	294	410	137	175	2	32	100	139	31.5	14.2	5.0	1.7	.425
90-91	Utah	82	22	2486	1017	399	872	.458	0	3	.000	219	271	.808	101	306	407	124	160	0	53	91	131	30.3	12.4	5.0	1.5	.403
91-92	Utah	13	0	327	122	39	101	.386	0	1	.000	44	55	.800	23	55	78	19	31	0	5	15	21	25.2	9.4	6.0	1.5	.418
91-92	Minnesota	71	18	1777	829	329	735	.448	0	1	.000	171	215	.795	99	308	407	59	129	1	30	102	85	25.0	11.7	5.7	0.8	.482
92-93	Minnesota	70	3	1276	525	203	446	.455	0	0	.000	119	142	.838	53	162	215	61	88	0	20	47	63	18.2	7.5	3.1	0.9	.404
93-94	Minnesota	79	3	1297	583	232	455	.510	0	2	.000	119	149	.799	66	149	215	54	93	0	20	58	55	16.4	7.4	2.7	0.7	.462
98-99	Utah	43	0	543	181	78	175	.446	0	2	.000	25	34	.735	36	58	94	26	78	0	9	28	27	12.6	4.2	2.2	0.6	.327
NBA Season Totals		928	229	24873	11834	4753	10056	.473	4	35	.114	2324	2863	.812	1304	3414	4718	1298	1843	7	435	1086	1442	26.8	12.8	5.1	1.4	....
83-84	Utah	11	10	340	117	50	97	.515	0	2	.000	17	21	.810	15	46	61	10	33	0	2	11	16	30.9	10.6	5.5	0.9	.355
84-85	Utah	10	10	375	169	62	152	.408	0	0	.000	45	55	.818	21	71	92	27	30	0	5	18	21	37.5	16.9	9.2	2.7	.488

YEAR	TEAM	GP	GS	MIN	PTS	FGM	FGA	FG%	3PM	3PA	3P%	FTM	FTA	FT%	ORB	DRB	TRB	AST	PF	DQ	STL	BLK	TO	MPG	PPG	RPG	APG	PCM
85-86	Utah	4	4	147	64	28	77	.364	0	1	.000	8	11	.727	11	21	32	13	13	0	2	2	5	36.8	16.0	8.0	3.3	.366
86-87	Utah	5	0	151	78	30	63	.476	0	0	.000	18	18	1.000	14	16	30	9	12	1	3	6	12	30.2	15.6	6.0	1.8	.506
87-88	Utah	11	0	449	255	99	203	.488	0	1	.000	57	68	.838	21	42	63	18	32	0	6	23	21	40.8	23.2	5.7	1.6	.498
88-89	Utah	3	2	122	36	12	34	.353	0	0	.000	12	15	.800	10	15	25	3	11	0	1	4	9	40.7	12.0	8.3	1.0	.260
89-90	Utah	5	5	190	105	43	88	.489	0	0	.000	19	24	.792	8	24	32	7	19	1	5	6	5	38.0	21.0	6.4	1.4	.498
90-91	Utah	9	0	228	68	23	64	.359	0	0	.000	22	25	.880	11	21	32	9	27	1	3	6	12	25.3	7.6	3.6	1.0	.230
98-99	Utah	11	0	115	37	17	33	.515	0	0	.000	3	4	.750	5	10	15	2	19	0	3	6	8	10.5	3.4	1.4	0.2	.264
NBA Playoff Totals		69	31	2117	929	364	811	.449	0	4	.000	201	241	.834	116	266	382	98	196	3	30	82	109	30.7	13.5	5.5	1.4	....

• BAIRD, Frank

Frank A. Baird

Born: 1912.　Height: 5'11".　Weight: 160 lbs.　Drafted: —　College: Butler

YEAR	TEAM	GP	GS	MIN	PTS	FGM	FGA	FG%	3PM	3PA	3P%	FTM	FTA	FT%	ORB	DRB	TRB	AST	PF	DQ	STL	BLK	TO	MPG	PPG	RPG	APG	PCM
37-38	Indianapolis-N	12	....	....	50	21	....	....	....	....	....	8	....	....	....	....	....	....	....	....	....	....	....	....	4.2	....	....	....
38-39	Indianapolis-N	23	....	....	181	81	....	....	....	....	....	19	....	....	....	....	....	....	....	....	....	....	....	....	7.9	....	....	....
39-40	Indianapolis-N	16	....	....	72	28	....	....	....	....	....	16	....	....	....	....	....	....	....	....	....	....	....	....	4.5	....	....	....
41-42	Indianapolis-N	11	....	....	15	7	....	....	....	....	....	1	....	....	....	....	....	....	....	....	....	....	....	....	1.4	....	....	....
NBL Season Totals		62	....	....	318	137	....	....	....	....	....	44	....	....	....	....	....	....	....	....	....	....	....	....	5.1	....	....	....
41-42	Indianapolis-N	2	....	....	0	0	....	....	....	....	....	0	....	....	....	....	....	....	....	....	....	....	....	....	0.0	....	....	....
NBL Playoff Totals		2	....	....	0	0	....	....	....	....	....	0	....	....	....	....	....	....	....	....	....	....	....	....	0.0	....	....	....

• BAKER, Bob

Robert Baker

Born: —.　Height: —　Weight: —　Drafted: —　College: —

YEAR	TEAM	GP	GS	MIN	PTS	FGM	FGA	FG%	3PM	3PA	3P%	FTM	FTA	FT%	ORB	DRB	TRB	AST	PF	DQ	STL	BLK	TO	MPG	PPG	RPG	APG	PCM
45-46	Indianapolis-N	6	....	....	15	6	....	....	....	....	....	3	....	....	....	....	....	....	....	....	....	....	....	....	2.5	....	....	....
NBL Season Totals		6	....	....	15	6	....	....	....	....	....	3	....	....	....	....	....	....	....	....	....	....	....	....	2.5	....	....	....

• BAKER, Jimmie

Jimmie Baker Jr.

Born: Dec. 25, 1953. Philadelphia, PA, United States.　Height: 6'9".　Weight: 220 lbs.　Drafted: 1975　College: Hawaii

YEAR	TEAM	GP	GS	MIN	PTS	FGM	FGA	FG%	3PM	3PA	3P%	FTM	FTA	FT%	ORB	DRB	TRB	AST	PF	DQ	STL	BLK	TO	MPG	PPG	RPG	APG	PCM
75-76	Kentucky-A	5	....	40	6	3	15	.200	0	0	.000	0	2	.000	4	10	14	4	11	....	0	3	6	8.0	1.2	2.8	0.8	.161
ABA Season Totals		5	....	40	6	3	15	.200	0	0	.000	0	2	.000	4	10	14	4	11	....	0	3	6	8.0	1.2	2.8	0.8	

• BAKER, Mark

LaMark Anthony Baker

Born: Nov. 11, 1969. Dayton, OH, United States.　Height: 6'1".　Weight: 175 lbs.　Drafted: —　College: Ohio State

YEAR	TEAM	GP	GS	MIN	PTS	FGM	FGA	FG%	3PM	3PA	3P%	FTM	FTA	FT%	ORB	DRB	TRB	AST	PF	DQ	STL	BLK	TO	MPG	PPG	RPG	APG	PCM
98-99	Toronto	1	0	2	0	0	1	.000	0	0	.000	0	0	.000	0	0	0	0	0	0	0	0	1	2.0	0.0	0.0	0.0	-.889
NBA Season Totals		1	0	2	0	0	1	.000	0	0	.000	0	0	.000	0	0	0	0	0	0	0	0	1	2.0	0.0	0.0	0.0	....

• BAKER, Norm

Norman Henry Baker

Born: Feb. 17, 1923. Canada.　Height: 6'　Weight: 180 lbs.　Drafted: —　College: none

YEAR	TEAM	GP	GS	MIN	PTS	FGM	FGA	FG%	3PM	3PA	3P%	FTM	FTA	FT%	ORB	DRB	TRB	AST	PF	DQ	STL	BLK	TO	MPG	PPG	RPG	APG	PCM
46-47	Chicago	4	....	....	0	0	1	.000	....	....	....	0	0	.000	....	....	0	0	....	....	....	....	....	0.0	....	0.0	....	
NBA Season Totals		4	....	....	0	0	1	.000	....	....	....	0	0	.000	....	....	0	0	....	....	....	....	....	0.0	....	0.0	....	

• BAKER, Vin

Vincent Lamont Baker

Born: Nov. 23, 1971. Lake Wales, FL, United States.　Height: 6'11".　Weight: 232 lbs.　Drafted: 1993　College: Hartford

YEAR	TEAM	GP	GS	MIN	PTS	FGM	FGA	FG%	3PM	3PA	3P%	FTM	FTA	FT%	ORB	DRB	TRB	AST	PF	DQ	STL	BLK	TO	MPG	PPG	RPG	APG	PCM
93-94	Milwaukee	82	63	2560	1105	435	869	.501	1	5	.200	234	411	.569	277	344	621	163	231	3	60	114	164	31.2	13.5	7.6	2.0	.498
94-95	Milwaukee	82	82	3361	1451	594	1229	.483	7	24	.292	256	432	.593	289	557	846	296	277	5	86	116	221	41.0	17.7	10.3	3.6	.516
95-96	Milwaukee	82	82	3319	1729	699	1429	.489	10	48	.208	321	479	.670	263	545	808	212	272	3	68	91	213	40.5	21.1	9.9	2.6	.535
96-97	Milwaukee	78	78	3159	1637	632	1251	.505	15	54	.278	358	521	.687	267	537	804	211	275	8	81	112	242	40.5	21.0	10.3	2.7	.565
97-98	Seattle	82	82	2944	1574	631	1164	.542	1	7	.143	311	526	.591	286	370	656	152	278	7	91	86	172	35.9	19.2	8.0	1.9	.554
98-99	Seattle	34	31	1162	468	198	437	.453	0	3	.000	72	160	.450	86	125	211	56	121	2	32	34	76	34.2	13.8	6.2	1.6	.347
99-00	Seattle	79	75	2849	1311	514	1129	.455	2	8	.250	281	412	.682	227	378	605	148	288	6	47	66	213	36.1	16.6	7.7	1.9	.415
00-01	Seattle	76	27	2129	927	347	822	.422	1	16	.063	232	321	.723	179	251	430	90	264	2	38	73	158	28.0	12.2	5.7	1.2	.369
01-02	Seattle	55	41	1710	774	315	649	.485	1	8	.125	143	226	.633	168	182	350	72	197	4	22	36	127	31.1	14.1	6.4	1.3	.396
02-03	Boston	52	9	942	270	99	207	.478	0	4	.000	72	107	.673	90	108	198	29	146	1	22	30	61	18.1	5.2	3.8	0.6	.311
NBA Season Totals		702	570	24135	11246	4464	9186	.486	38	177	.215	2280	3595	.634	2132	3397	5529	1429	2349	41	547	758	1647	34.4	16.0	7.9	2.0	....
97-98	Seattle	10	10	371	158	71	134	.530	0	0	.000	16	38	.421	41	53	94	18	38	1	18	15	22	37.1	15.8	9.4	1.8	.508
99-00	Seattle	5	4	177	70	30	75	.400	0	1	.000	10	17	.588	16	22	38	10	19	0	5	2	16	35.4	14.0	7.6	2.0	.308
01-02	Seattle	5	4	144	66	29	58	.500	1	1	1.000	7	9	.778	11	14	25	4	23	1	3	6	4	28.8	13.2	5.0	0.8	.416
NBA Playoff Totals		20	18	692	294	130	267	.487	1	2	.500	33	64	.516	68	89	157	32	80	2	26	23	42	34.6	14.7	7.9	1.6	....

• BAKERAITIS, Art

Art Bakeraitis

Born: 1925.　Height: 6'4".　Weight: 210 lbs.　Drafted: —　College: Bay City JC

YEAR	TEAM	GP	GS	MIN	PTS	FGM	FGA	FG%	3PM	3PA	3P%	FTM	FTA	FT%	ORB	DRB	TRB	AST	PF	DQ	STL	BLK	TO	MPG	PPG	RPG	APG	PCM
48-49	Detroit-N	13	....	....	60	18	....	....	....	....	....	24	37	.649	....	....	....	....	....	....	....	....	....	....	4.6	....	....	....
NBL Season Totals		13	....	....	60	18	....	....	....	....	....	24	37	.649	....	....	....	....	....	....	....	....	....	....	4.6	....	....	....

YEAR	TEAM	GP	GS	MIN	PTS	FGM	FGA	FG%	3PM	3PA	3P%	FTM	FTA	FT%	ORB	DRB	TRB	AST	PF	DQ	STL	BLK	TO	MPG	PPG	RPG	APG	PCM

• BALL, —
Ball

Born: —.   Height: —   Weight: —   Drafted: —   College: —

40-41	Chicago-N	6	....	....	3	1	....	....	....	....	....	1	....	....	....	....	....	....	....	....	....	....	....	0.5	....	....	....
NBL Season Totals		6	....	....	3	1	....	....	....	....	....	1	....	....	....	....	....	....	....	....	....	....	....	0.5	....	....	....

• BALL, Cedric
Cedric Glenn Ball

Born: Apr. 16, 1968. Worcester, MA, United States.   Height: 6'8".   Weight: 210 lbs.   Drafted: —   College: North Carolina (Charlotte)

90-91	LA Clippers	7	0	26	8	3	8	.375	0	0	.000	2	2	1.000	5	6	11	0	5	0	0	2	2	3.7	1.1	1.6	0.0	.433
NBA Season Totals		7	0	26	8	3	8	.375	0	0	.000	2	2	1.000	5	6	11	0	5	0	0	2	2	3.7	1.1	1.6	0.0	....

• BALLARD, Greg
Gregory Ballard

Born: Jan. 29, 1955. Los Angeles, CA, United States.   Height: 6'7".   Weight: 215 lbs.   Drafted: 1977   College: Oregon

77-78	Washington	76	....	936	372	142	334	.425	....	....	....	88	114	.772	102	164	266	62	90	1	30	13	61	12.3	4.9	3.5	0.8	.470
78-79	Washington	82	....	1552	639	260	559	.465	....	....	....	119	172	.692	143	307	450	116	167	3	58	30	98	18.9	7.8	5.5	1.4	.512
79-80	Washington	82	....	2438	1277	545	1101	.495	16	47	.340	171	227	.753	240	398	638	159	197	2	90	36	131	29.7	15.6	7.8	1.9	.577
80-81	Washington	82	....	2610	1271	549	1186	.463	7	32	.219	166	196	.847	167	413	580	195	194	1	118	39	115	31.8	15.5	7.1	2.4	.524
81-82	Washington	79	79	2946	1486	621	1307	.475	9	22	.409	235	283	.830	136	497	633	250	204	0	137	22	119	37.3	18.8	8.0	3.2	.553
82-83	Washington	78	78	2840	1401	603	1274	.473	13	37	.351	182	233	.781	123	385	508	262	176	2	135	25	156	36.4	18.0	6.5	3.4	.508
83-84	Washington	82	82	2701	1188	510	1061	.481	2	15	.133	166	208	.798	140	348	488	290	214	1	94	35	139	32.9	14.5	6.0	3.5	.486
84-85	Washington	82	77	2664	1072	469	978	.480	14	46	.304	120	151	.795	150	381	531	208	221	0	100	33	107	32.5	13.1	6.5	2.5	.459
85-86	Golden State	75	14	1792	662	272	570	.477	17	35	.486	101	126	.802	132	285	417	83	174	0	65	8	53	23.9	8.8	5.6	1.1	.440
86-87	Golden State	82	7	1579	579	248	564	.440	15	40	.375	68	91	.747	99	241	340	108	167	0	50	15	74	19.3	7.1	4.1	1.3	.393
88-89	Seattle	2	0	15	6	1	8	.125	0	1	.000	4	4	1.000	2	5	7	0	3	0	0	0	0	7.5	3.0	3.5	0.0	.307
NBA Season Totals		802	337	22073	9953	4220	8942	.472	93	275	.338	1420	1805	.787	1434	3424	4858	1733	1807	10	877	256	1053	27.5	12.4	6.1	2.2	....
77-78	Washington	19	....	243	74	21	63	.333	....	....	....	32	41	.780	27	52	79	18	29	0	9	3	14	12.8	3.9	4.2	0.9	.445
78-79	Washington	19	....	312	137	53	101	.525	....	....	....	31	41	.756	34	58	92	17	28	0	9	6	20	16.4	7.2	4.8	0.9	.557
79-80	Washington	2	....	73	22	9	28	.321	0	0	.000	4	7	.571	2	12	14	7	8	0	1	1	8	36.5	11.0	7.0	3.5	.202
81-82	Washington	7	7	268	93	36	100	.360	0	0	.000	21	25	.840	22	41	63	22	20	1	14	3	12	38.3	13.3	9.0	3.1	.408
83-84	Washington	4	4	168	66	27	59	.458	0	1	.000	12	13	.923	7	17	24	14	12	0	7	3	8	42.0	16.5	6.0	3.5	.413
84-85	Washington	4	0	65	30	11	24	.458	0	2	.000	8	9	.889	4	10	14	6	7	0	3	0	5	16.3	7.5	3.5	1.5	.488
86-87	Golden State	10	0	179	59	26	48	.542	4	10	.400	3	4	.750	18	22	40	19	16	0	8	0	9	17.9	5.9	4.0	1.9	.487
NBA Playoff Totals		65	11	1308	481	183	423	.433	4	13	.308	111	140	.793	114	212	326	103	120	1	51	16	76	20.1	7.4	5.0	1.6	....

• BALTIMORE, Herschel
Herschel David Baltimore

Born: June 21, 1921. Died: Jan.1, 1968.   Height: 6'4".   Weight: 195 lbs.   Drafted: —   College: Penn State

46-47	St. Louis	58	....	....	138	53	263	.202	....	....	....	32	69	.464	....	....	....	16	98	....	....	....	....	2.4	....	0.3	....
NBA Season Totals		58	....	....	138	53	263	.202	....	....	....	32	69	.464	....	....	....	16	98	....	....	....	....	2.4	....	0.3	....
46-47	St. Louis	3	....	....	4	2	10	.200	....	....	....	0	1	.000	....	....	....	0	3	....	....	....	....	1.3	....	0.0	....
NBA Playoff Totals		3	....	....	4	2	10	.200	....	....	....	0	1	.000	....	....	....	0	3	....	....	....	....	1.3	....	0.0	....

• BANKS, Gene
Eugene Lavon (Tinkerbell) Banks

Born: May 15, 1959. Philadelphia, PA, United States.   Height: 6'7".   Weight: 215 lbs.   Drafted: 1981   College: Duke

81-82	San Antonio	80	4	1700	767	311	652	.477	0	8	.000	145	212	.684	157	254	411	147	199	2	55	17	104	21.3	9.6	5.1	1.8	.493
82-83	San Antonio	81	82	2722	1206	505	919	.550	0	5	.000	196	278	.705	222	390	612	279	229	3	78	21	170	33.6	14.9	7.6	3.4	.546
83-84	San Antonio	80	66	2600	1049	424	747	.568	1	6	.167	200	270	.741	204	378	582	254	256	5	105	23	168	32.5	13.1	7.3	3.2	.528
84-85	San Antonio	82	41	2091	778	289	493	.586	1	3	.333	199	257	.774	133	312	445	234	220	3	65	13	139	25.5	9.5	5.4	2.9	.510
85-86	Chicago	82	33	2139	895	356	688	.517	0	19	.000	183	255	.718	178	182	360	251	212	4	81	10	139	26.1	10.9	4.4	3.1	.474
86-87	Chicago	63	39	1822	610	249	462	.539	0	5	.000	112	146	.767	115	193	308	170	173	3	52	17	113	28.9	9.7	4.9	2.7	.408
NBA Season Totals		468	265	13074	5305	2134	3961	.539	2	46	.043	1035	1418	.730	1009	1709	2718	1335	1289	20	436	101	833	27.9	11.3	5.8	2.9	....
81-82	San Antonio	9	0	146	64	30	65	.462	0	1	.000	4	10	.400	21	22	43	9	12	0	4	3	6	16.2	7.1	4.8	1.0	.505
82-83	San Antonio	11	11	398	175	76	150	.507	0	0	.000	23	35	.657	27	49	76	50	25	1	11	1	21	36.2	15.9	6.9	4.5	.520
84-85	San Antonio	1	0	10	0	0	1	.000	0	0	.000	0	0	.000	0	0	0	1	3	0	0	0	2	10.0	0.0	0.0	1.0	-.313
85-86	Chicago	3	0	69	22	10	18	.556	0	2	.000	2	4	.500	4	6	10	5	10	0	1	0	4	23.0	7.3	3.3	1.7	.302
86-87	Chicago	3	3	79	31	13	22	.591	0	0	.000	5	8	.625	3	5	8	2	13	1	0	0	2	26.3	10.3	2.7	0.7	.290
NBA Playoff Totals		27	14	702	292	129	256	.504	0	3	.000	34	57	.596	55	82	137	67	63	2	16	4	35	26.0	10.8	5.1	2.5	....

• BANKS, Walker
Walker Burrell Banks Jr.

Born: Aug. 26, 1947.   Height: 6'10".   Weight: 205 lbs.   Drafted: 1970   College: Western Kentucky

70-71	Pittsburgh-A	16	....	154	41	17	34	.500	0	0	.000	7	17	.412	19	30	49	8	34	0	....	....	16	9.6	2.6	3.1	0.5	.381
ABA Season Totals		16	....	154	41	17	34	.500	0	0	.000	7	17	.412	19	30	49	8	34	0	....	....	16	9.6	2.6	3.1	0.5	....

• BANNISTER, Ken
Kenneth (The Animal) Bannister

Born: Apr. 1, 1960. Baltimore, MD, United States.   Height: 6'9".   Weight: 235 lbs.   Drafted: 1984   College: St. Augustine

84-85	New York	75	50	1404	509	209	445	.470	0	0	.000	91	192	.474	108	222	330	39	279	**16**	38	40	143	18.7	6.8	4.4	0.5	.285
85-86	New York	70	15	1405	601	235	479	.491	0	1	.000	131	249	.526	89	233	322	42	208	5	42	24	126	20.1	8.6	4.6	0.6	.364
88-89	LA Clippers	9	2	130	74	22	36	.611	0	1	.000	30	53	.566	6	27	33	3	17	0	7	2	8	14.4	8.2	3.7	0.3	.594

YEAR	TEAM	GP	GS	MIN	PTS	FGM	FGA	FG%	3PM	3PA	3P%	FTM	FTA	FT%	ORB	DRB	TRB	AST	PF	DQ	STL	BLK	TO	MPG	PPG	RPG	APG	PCM
89-90	LA Clippers	52	1	589	206	77	161	.478	0	1	.000	52	110	.473	39	73	112	18	92	1	17	7	42	11.3	4.0	2.2	0.3	.279
90-91	LA Clippers	47	3	339	111	43	81	.531	0	1	.000	25	65	.385	34	62	96	9	73	0	5	7	24	7.2	2.4	2.0	0.2	.327
NBA Season Totals		**253**	**71**	**3867**	**1501**	**586**	**1202**	**.488**	**0**	**4**	**.000**	**329**	**669**	**.492**	**276**	**617**	**893**	**111**	**669**	**22**	**109**	**80**	**343**	**15.3**	**5.9**	**3.5**	**0.4**	**....**

• BANTOM, Mike

Michael Allen Bantom

Born: Dec. 3, 1951. Philadelphia, PA, United States. Height: 6'9". Weight: 200 lbs. Drafted: 1973 College: St. Joseph's (PA)

YEAR	TEAM	GP	GS	MIN	PTS	FGM	FGA	FG%	3PM	3PA	3P%	FTM	FTA	FT%	ORB	DRB	TRB	AST	PF	DQ	STL	BLK	TO	MPG	PPG	RPG	APG	PCM
73-74	Phoenix	76	....	1982	769	314	787	.399	....	....	....	141	213	.662	172	347	519	163	289	**15**	50	47	....	26.1	10.1	6.8	2.1	.425
74-75	Phoenix	82	....	2239	1021	418	907	.461	....	....	....	185	259	.714	211	342	553	159	273	8	62	47	....	27.3	12.5	6.7	1.9	.496
75-76	Phoenix	7	....	68	21	8	26	.308	....	....	....	5	5	1.000	7	16	23	3	13	1	2	2	....	9.7	3.0	3.3	0.4	.340
75-76	Seattle	66	....	1503	555	212	450	.471	....	....	....	131	194	.675	133	235	368	102	208	3	26	26	....	22.8	8.4	5.6	1.5	.444
76-77	Seattle	44	....	795	332	137	281	.488	....	....	....	58	84	.690	83	103	186	52	113	3	35	21	....	18.1	7.5	4.2	1.2	.462
76-77	New York	33	....	1114	614	224	474	.473	....	....	....	166	226	.735	101	184	285	50	120	4	28	28	....	33.8	18.6	8.6	1.5	.560
77-78	Indiana	82	....	2775	1258	502	1047	.479	....	....	....	254	342	.743	184	426	610	238	333	13	100	50	221	33.8	15.3	7.4	2.9	.482
78-79	Indiana	81	....	2528	1191	482	1036	.465	....	....	....	227	338	.672	225	425	650	223	316	8	99	62	194	31.2	14.7	8.0	2.8	.515
79-80	Indiana	77	....	2330	908	384	760	.505	1	3	.333	139	209	.665	192	264	456	279	268	7	85	49	193	30.3	11.8	5.9	3.6	.463
80-81	Indiana	76	....	2375	1061	431	882	.489	0	6	.000	199	281	.708	150	277	427	240	284	9	80	85	198	31.3	14.0	5.6	3.2	.465
81-82	Indiana	39	37	1037	458	178	406	.438	1	3	.333	101	153	.660	87	127	214	68	139	5	38	24	86	26.6	11.7	5.5	1.7	.394
81-82	Philadelphia	43	1	979	380	156	306	.510	1	3	.333	67	114	.588	87	139	226	46	133	0	25	37	65	22.8	8.8	5.3	1.1	.423
NBA Season Totals		**706**	**38**	**19725**	**8568**	**3446**	**7362**	**.468**	**3**	**15**	**.200**	**1673**	**2418**	**.692**	**1632**	**2885**	**4517**	**1623**	**2489**	**76**	**630**	**478**	**957**	**27.9**	**12.1**	**6.4**	**2.3**	**....**
75-76	Seattle	6	....	114	58	22	38	.579	....	....	....	14	20	.700	9	14	23	8	27	1	4	2	....	19.0	9.7	3.8	1.3	.517
80-81	Indiana	2	....	51	29	12	16	.750	0	0	.000	5	7	.714	5	3	8	1	10	0	1	1	6	25.5	14.5	4.0	0.5	.483
81-82	Philadelphia	21	0	399	91	36	91	.396	0	0	.000	19	42	.452	39	38	77	24	60	1	15	9	24	19.0	4.3	3.7	1.1	.248
NBA Playoff Totals		**29**	**0**	**564**	**178**	**70**	**145**	**.483**	**0**	**0**	**.000**	**38**	**69**	**.551**	**53**	**55**	**108**	**33**	**97**	**2**	**20**	**12**	**30**	**19.4**	**6.1**	**3.7**	**1.1**	**....**

• BARBER, John

John Barber

Born: June 27, 1927. Height: 6'6". Weight: 210 lbs. Drafted: 1956 College: Los Angeles State

YEAR	TEAM	GP	GS	MIN	PTS	FGM	FGA	FG%	3PM	3PA	3P%	FTM	FTA	FT%	ORB	DRB	TRB	AST	PF	DQ	STL	BLK	TO	MPG	PPG	RPG	APG	PCM
56-57	St. Louis	5	....	5	7	2	8	.250	....	....	....	3	6	.500	....	....	6	0	4	0	....	....	....	1.0	1.4	1.2	0.0	.878
NBA Season Totals		**5**	**....**	**5**	**7**	**2**	**8**	**.250**	**....**	**....**	**....**	**3**	**6**	**.500**	**....**	**....**	**6**	**0**	**4**	**0**	**....**	**....**	**....**	**1.0**	**1.4**	**1.2**	**0.0**	**....**

• BARDO, Steve

Stephen Dean Bardo

Born: Apr. 5, 1968. Henderson, KY, United States. Height: 6'5". Weight: 190 lbs. Drafted: 1990 College: Illinois

YEAR	TEAM	GP	GS	MIN	PTS	FGM	FGA	FG%	3PM	3PA	3P%	FTM	FTA	FT%	ORB	DRB	TRB	AST	PF	DQ	STL	BLK	TO	MPG	PPG	RPG	APG	PCM
91-92	San Antonio	1	0	1	0	0	0	.000	0	0	.000	0	0	.000	1	0	1	0	0	0	0	0	0	1.0	0.0	1.0	0.0	.929
92-93	Dallas	23	0	175	51	19	62	.306	1	6	.167	12	17	.706	10	27	37	29	28	0	8	3	16	7.6	2.2	1.6	1.3	.322
95-96	Detroit	9	0	123	22	9	23	.391	0	4	.000	4	6	.667	2	20	22	15	17	1	4	1	5	13.7	2.4	2.4	1.7	.297
NBA Season Totals		**33**	**0**	**299**	**73**	**28**	**85**	**.329**	**1**	**10**	**.100**	**16**	**23**	**.696**	**13**	**47**	**60**	**44**	**45**	**1**	**12**	**4**	**21**	**9.1**	**2.2**	**1.8**	**1.3**	**....**

• BARKER, Cliff

Clifford Eugene Barker

Born: Jan. 15, 1921. Yorktown, IN, United States. Died: Mar.17, 1998. Height: 6'2". Weight: 185 lbs. Drafted: — College: Kentucky

YEAR	TEAM	GP	GS	MIN	PTS	FGM	FGA	FG%	3PM	3PA	3P%	FTM	FTA	FT%	ORB	DRB	TRB	AST	PF	DQ	STL	BLK	TO	MPG	PPG	RPG	APG	PCM
49-50	Indianapolis	49	....	....	279	102	274	.372	....	....	....	75	106	.708	....	....	....	109	99	....	....	....	....	....	5.7	....	2.2	....
50-51	Indianapolis	56	....	....	152	51	202	.252	....	....	....	50	77	.649	....	....	100	115	98	0	....	....	....	....	2.7	1.8	2.1	....
51-52	Indianapolis	44	....	494	126	48	161	.298	....	....	....	30	51	.588	....	....	81	70	56	0	....	....	....	11.2	2.9	1.8	1.6	.336
NBA Season Totals		**149**	**....**	**494**	**557**	**201**	**637**	**.316**	**....**	**....**	**....**	**155**	**234**	**.662**	**....**	**....**	**181**	**294**	**253**	**0**	**....**	**....**	**....**	**3.3**	**3.7**	**1.2**	**2.0**	**....**
49-50	Indianapolis	6	....	....	34	12	31	.387	....	....	....	10	15	.667	....	....	....	13	10	....	....	....	....	....	5.7	....	2.2	....
50-51	Indianapolis	3	....	....	8	4	19	.211	....	....	....	0	3	.000	....	....	15	10	10	0	....	....	....	....	2.7	5.0	3.3	....
NBA Playoff Totals		**9**	**....**	**....**	**42**	**16**	**50**	**.320**	**....**	**....**	**....**	**10**	**18**	**.556**	**....**	**....**	**15**	**23**	**20**	**0**	**....**	**....**	**....**	**....**	**4.7**	**1.7**	**2.6**	**....**

• BARKER, Tom

Thomas Kevin Barker

Born: Mar. 11, 1955. Harlingen, TX, United States. Height: 6'11". Weight: 225 lbs. Drafted: 1976 College: Hawaii

YEAR	TEAM	GP	GS	MIN	PTS	FGM	FGA	FG%	3PM	3PA	3P%	FTM	FTA	FT%	ORB	DRB	TRB	AST	PF	DQ	STL	BLK	TO	MPG	PPG	RPG	APG	PCM
76-77	Atlanta	59	....	1354	476	182	436	.417	....	....	....	112	164	.683	111	290	401	60	223	11	33	41	....	22.9	8.1	6.8	1.0	.408
78-79	Houston	5	....	16	8	3	6	.500	....	....	....	2	2	1.000	2	4	6	0	5	0	0	0	1	3.2	1.6	1.2	0.0	.472
78-79	Boston	12	....	131	53	21	48	.438	....	....	....	11	15	.733	12	18	30	6	26	0	4	4	13	10.9	4.4	2.5	0.5	.339
78-79	New York	22	....	329	102	44	102	.431	....	....	....	14	20	.700	31	52	83	9	45	0	6	7	20	15.0	4.6	3.8	0.4	.320
NBA Season Totals		**98**	**....**	**1830**	**639**	**250**	**592**	**.422**	**....**	**....**	**....**	**139**	**201**	**.692**	**156**	**364**	**520**	**75**	**299**	**11**	**43**	**52**	**34**	**18.7**	**6.5**	**5.3**	**0.8**	**....**

• BARKLEY, Charles

Charles Wade (Round Mound of Rebound) Barkley

Born: Feb. 20, 1963. Leeds, AL, United States. Height: 6'5". Weight: 250 lbs. Drafted: 1984 College: Auburn

YEAR	TEAM	GP	GS	MIN	PTS	FGM	FGA	FG%	3PM	3PA	3P%	FTM	FTA	FT%	ORB	DRB	TRB	AST	PF	DQ	STL	BLK	TO	MPG	PPG	RPG	APG	PCM
84-85	Philadelphia	82	60	2347	1148	427	783	.545	1	6	.167	293	400	.733	266	437	703	155	301	5	95	80	205	28.6	14.0	8.6	1.9	.605
85-86	Philadelphia	80	80	2952	1603	595	1041	.572	17	75	.227	396	578	.685	354	672	1026	312	**333**	8	173	125	**352**	36.9	20.0	12.8	3.9	.741
86-87	Philadelphia	68	62	2740	1564	557	937	.594	21	104	.202	429	564	.761	**390**	604	994	331	252	5	119	104	320	40.3	23.0	**14.6**	4.9	.810
87-88	Philadelphia	80	80	3170	2264	753	1283	.587	44	157	.280	714	**951**	.751	**385**	566	951	254	278	6	100	103	304	39.6	28.3	11.9	3.2	.818
88-89	Philadelphia	79	79	3088	2037	700	1208	.579	35	162	.216	602	799	.753	**403**	583	986	325	262	3	126	67	253	39.1	25.8	12.5	4.1	.829
89-90	Philadelphia	79	79	3085	1989	706	1177	.600	20	92	.217	557	744	.749	361	548	909	307	250	2	148	50	245	39.1	25.2	11.5	3.9	.803
90-91	Philadelphia	67	67	2498	1849	665	1167	.570	44	155	.284	475	658	.722	258	422	680	284	173	2	110	33	208	37.3	27.6	10.1	4.2	.837
91-92	Philadelphia	75	75	2881	1730	622	1126	.552	32	137	.234	454	653	.695	271	559	830	308	196	2	136	44	233	38.4	23.1	11.1	4.1	.739
92-93	Phoenix	76	76	2859	1944	716	1376	.520	67	220	.305	445	582	.765	237	691	928	385	197	0	119	74	236	37.6	25.6	12.2	5.1	.843
93-94	Phoenix	65	65	2298	1402	518	1046	.495	48	178	.270	318	452	.704	198	529	727	296	160	1	101	37	208	35.4	21.6	11.2	4.6	.742
94-95	Phoenix	68	66	2382	1561	554	1141	.486	74	219	.338	379	507	.748	203	553	756	276	201	3	110	45	150	35.0	23.0	11.1	4.1	.782
95-96	Phoenix	71	71	2632	1649	580	1160	.500	49	175	.280	440	566	.777	243	578	821	262	208	3	114	56	220	37.1	23.2	11.6	3.7	.741
96-97	Houston	53	53	2009	1016	335	692	.484	58	205	.283	288	415	.694	212	504	716	248	153	2	69	25	148	37.9	19.2	13.5	4.7	.714

YEAR	TEAM	GP	GS	MIN	PTS	FGM	FGA	FG%	3PM	3PA	3P%	FTM	FTA	FT%	ORB	DRB	TRB	AST	PF	DQ	STL	BLK	TO	MPG	PPG	RPG	APG	PCM
97-98	Houston	68	41	2243	1036	361	744	.485	18	84	.214	296	397	.746	241	553	794	217	187	2	71	28	150	33.0	15.2	11.7	3.2	.655
98-99	Houston	42	40	1526	676	240	502	.478	4	25	.160	192	267	.719	167	349	516	192	89	0	43	13	100	36.3	16.1	12.3	4.6	.657
99-00	Houston	20	18	620	289	106	222	.477	6	26	.231	71	110	.645	71	138	209	63	48	0	14	4	44	31.0	14.5	10.5	3.2	.612
NBA Season Totals		1073	1012	39330	23757	8435	15605	.541	538	2020	.266	6349	8643	.735	4260	8286	12546	4215	3288	44	1648	888	3376	36.7	22.1	11.7	3.9	....
84-85	Philadelphia	13	2	408	194	75	139	.540	4	6	.667	40	63	.635	52	92	144	26	49	0	23	15	35	31.4	14.9	11.1	2.0	.651
85-86	Philadelphia	12	12	497	300	104	180	.578	1	15	.067	91	131	.695	60	129	189	67	52	2	27	15	65	41.4	25.0	15.8	5.6	.830
86-87	Philadelphia	5	5	210	123	43	75	.573	1	8	.125	36	45	.800	27	36	63	12	21	0	4	8	22	42.0	24.6	12.6	2.4	.673
88-89	Philadelphia	3	3	135	81	29	45	.644	1	5	.200	22	31	.710	8	27	35	16	9	0	5	2	11	45.0	27.0	11.7	5.3	.768
89-90	Philadelphia	10	10	419	247	88	162	.543	6	18	.333	65	108	.602	66	89	155	43	36	0	8	7	30	41.9	24.7	15.5	4.3	.758
90-91	Philadelphia	8	8	326	199	74	125	.592	2	20	.100	49	75	.653	31	53	84	48	23	0	15	3	25	40.8	24.9	10.5	6.0	.772
92-93	Phoenix	24	24	1026	638	230	482	.477	10	45	.222	168	218	.771	93	233	326	102	73	0	39	25	50	42.8	26.6	13.6	4.3	.752
93-94	Phoenix	10	10	425	276	110	216	.509	14	40	.350	42	55	.764	34	96	130	48	26	0	25	9	27	42.5	27.6	13.0	4.8	.797
94-95	Phoenix	10	10	390	257	91	182	.500	9	35	.257	66	90	.733	39	95	134	32	28	0	13	11	25	39.0	25.7	13.4	3.2	.785
95-96	Phoenix	4	4	164	102	31	70	.443	3	12	.250	37	47	.787	18	36	54	15	15	0	4	4	6	41.0	25.5	13.5	3.8	.745
96-97	Houston	16	16	605	286	86	198	.434	11	38	.289	103	134	.769	64	128	192	54	52	1	19	7	43	37.8	17.9	12.0	3.4	.601
97-98	Houston	4	0	87	36	12	23	.522	0	2	.000	12	21	.571	5	16	21	4	12	1	5	0	6	21.8	9.0	5.3	1.0	.448
98-99	Houston	4	4	157	94	36	68	.529	2	7	.286	20	30	.667	13	42	55	15	12	0	6	2	8	39.3	23.5	13.8	3.8	.773
NBA Playoff Totals		123	108	4849	2833	1009	1965	.513	64	251	.255	751	1048	.717	510	1072	1582	482	408	4	193	108	353	39.4	23.0	12.9	3.9	....

• BARKLEY, Erick

Erick Barkley

Born: Feb. 21, 1978. Queens, NY, United States. Height: 6'1". Weight: 177 lbs. Drafted: 2000 College: St. John's (NY)

YEAR	TEAM	GP	GS	MIN	PTS	FGM	FGA	FG%	3PM	3PA	3P%	FTM	FTA	FT%	ORB	DRB	TRB	AST	PF	DQ	STL	BLK	TO	MPG	PPG	RPG	APG	PCM
00-01	Portland	8	0	38	19	8	22	.364	3	8	.375	0	0	.000	0	3	3	6	2	0	2	0	5	4.8	2.4	0.4	0.8	.320
01-02	Portland	19	4	228	58	24	68	.353	1	7	.143	9	10	.900	5	13	18	34	29	0	17	1	12	12.0	3.1	0.9	1.8	.278
NBA Season Totals		27	4	266	77	32	90	.356	4	15	.267	9	10	.900	5	16	21	40	31	0	19	1	17	9.9	2.9	0.8	1.5	....

• BARKSDALE, Don

Don Angelo Barksdale

Born: Mar. 31, 1923. Oakland, CA, United States. Died: Mar.8, 1993. Height: 6'6". Weight: 200 lbs. Drafted: — College: UCLA

YEAR	TEAM	GP	GS	MIN	PTS	FGM	FGA	FG%	3PM	3PA	3P%	FTM	FTA	FT%	ORB	DRB	TRB	AST	PF	DQ	STL	BLK	TO	MPG	PPG	RPG	APG	PCM
51-52	Baltimore	62	....	2014	781	272	804	.338	....	....	....	237	343	.691	....	....	601	137	230	13	....	....	....	32.5	12.6	9.7	2.2	.441
52-53	Baltimore	65	....	2298	899	321	829	.387	....	....	....	257	401	.641	....	....	597	166	273	13	....	....	....	35.4	13.8	9.2	2.6	.446
53-54	Boston	63	....	1358	461	156	415	.376	....	....	....	149	225	.662	....	....	345	117	213	4	....	....	....	21.6	7.3	5.5	1.9	.420
54-55	Boston	72	....	1790	754	267	699	.382	....	....	....	220	338	.651	....	....	545	129	225	7	....	....	....	24.9	10.5	7.6	1.8	.487
NBA Season Totals		262	....	7460	2895	1016	2747	.370	....	....	....	863	1307	.660	....	....	2088	549	941	37	....	....	....	28.5	11.0	8.0	2.1	....
53-54	Boston	6	....	106	30	11	36	.306	....	....	....	8	11	.727	....	....	27	7	23	2	....	....	....	17.7	5.0	4.5	1.2	.295
54-55	Boston	7	....	122	54	18	40	.450	....	....	....	18	21	.857	....	....	35	10	17	1	....	....	....	17.4	7.7	5.0	1.4	.563
NBA Playoff Totals		13	....	228	84	29	76	.382	....	....	....	26	32	.813	....	....	62	17	40	3	....	....	....	17.5	6.5	4.8	1.3	....

• BARLE, Louis

Louis Peter (Fats) Barle

Born: June 23, 1916. Gilbert, MN, United States. Died: Dec.30, 1996. Height: 6'1". Weight: 200 lbs. Drafted: — College: Minnesota (Duluth)

YEAR	TEAM	GP	GS	MIN	PTS	FGM	FGA	FG%	3PM	3PA	3P%	FTM	FTA	FT%	ORB	DRB	TRB	AST	PF	DQ	STL	BLK	TO	MPG	PPG	RPG	APG	PCM
39-40	Oshkosh-N	27	....	....	148	54	....	....	....	....	....	40	....	....	....	....	....	....	....	....	....	....	....	....	5.5	....	....	....
40-41	Oshkosh-N	24	....	....	118	45	....	....	....	....	....	28	....	....	....	....	....	....	....	....	....	....	....	....	4.9	....	....	....
41-42	Oshkosh-N	24	....	....	123	55	....	....	....	....	....	13	....	....	....	....	....	....	....	....	....	....	....	....	5.1	....	....	....
42-43	Oshkosh-N	4	....	....	8	3	....	....	....	....	....	2	....	....	....	....	....	....	....	....	....	....	....	....	2.0	....	....	....
NBL Season Totals		79	....	....	397	157	....	....	....	....	....	83	....	....	....	....	....	....	....	....	....	....	....	....	5.0	....	....	....
39-40	Oshkosh-N	8	....	....	48	17	....	....	....	....	....	14	....	....	....	....	....	....	....	....	....	....	....	....	6.0	....	....	....
40-41	Oshkosh-N	5	....	....	12	4	....	....	....	....	....	4	....	....	....	....	....	....	....	....	....	....	....	....	2.4	....	....	....
41-42	Oshkosh-N	5	....	....	33	15	....	....	....	....	....	3	....	....	....	....	....	....	....	....	....	....	....	....	6.6	....	....	....
NBL Playoff Totals		18	....	....	93	36	....	....	....	....	....	21	....	....	....	....	....	....	....	....	....	....	....	....	5.2	....	....	....

• BARNES, Harry

Harry J. Barnes

Born: July 25, 1945. Height: 6'3". Weight: 205 lbs. Drafted: 1968 College: Northeastern

YEAR	TEAM	GP	GS	MIN	PTS	FGM	FGA	FG%	3PM	3PA	3P%	FTM	FTA	FT%	ORB	DRB	TRB	AST	PF	DQ	STL	BLK	TO	MPG	PPG	RPG	APG	PCM
68-69	San Diego	22	....	126	43	18	64	.281	....	....	....	7	13	.538	....	....	26	5	25	0	....	....	....	5.7	2.0	1.2	0.2	.152
NBA Season Totals		22	....	126	43	18	64	.281	....	....	....	7	13	.538	....	....	26	5	25	0	....	....	....	5.7	2.0	1.2	0.2	....

• BARNES, Jim

V. James (Bad News) Barnes

Born: Apr. 13, 1941. Tuckerman, AR, United States. Died: Sept.14, 2002. Height: 6'8". Weight: 210 lbs. Drafted: 1964 College: Texas Western

YEAR	TEAM	GP	GS	MIN	PTS	FGM	FGA	FG%	3PM	3PA	3P%	FTM	FTA	FT%	ORB	DRB	TRB	AST	PF	DQ	STL	BLK	TO	MPG	PPG	RPG	APG	PCM
64-65	New York	75	....	2586	1159	454	1070	.424	....	....	....	251	379	.662	....	....	729	93	312	8	....	....	....	34.5	15.5	9.7	1.2	.461
65-66	New York	7	....	263	110	40	90	.444	....	....	....	30	42	.714	....	....	72	9	33	0	....	....	....	37.6	15.7	10.3	1.3	.458
65-66	Baltimore	66	....	1928	798	308	728	.423	....	....	....	182	268	.679	....	....	683	85	250	10	....	....	....	29.2	12.1	10.3	1.3	.506
66-67	LA Lakers	80	....	1398	562	217	497	.437	....	....	....	128	187	.684	....	....	450	47	266	5	....	....	....	17.5	7.0	5.6	0.6	.447
67-68	LA Lakers	42	....	713	261	101	235	.430	....	....	....	59	88	.670	....	....	211	27	134	4	....	....	....	17.0	6.2	5.0	0.6	.407
67-68	Chicago	37	....	712	314	120	264	.455	....	....	....	74	103	.718	....	....	204	28	128	3	....	....	....	19.2	8.5	5.5	0.8	.468
68-69	Chicago	10	....	111	56	23	59	.390	....	....	....	10	19	.526	....	....	30	1	15	0	....	....	....	11.1	5.6	3.0	0.1	.379
68-69	Boston	49	....	595	249	92	202	.455	....	....	....	65	92	.707	....	....	194	27	107	2	....	....	....	12.1	5.1	4.0	0.6	.495
69-70	Boston	77	....	1049	451	178	434	.410	....	....	....	95	128	.742	....	....	350	52	229	4	....	....	....	13.6	5.9	4.5	0.7	.454
70-71	Baltimore	11	....	100	37	15	28	.536	....	....	....	7	11	.636	....	....	16	8	23	0	....	....	....	9.1	3.4	1.5	0.7	.371
NBA Season Totals		454	....	9455	3997	1548	3607	.429	....	....	....	901	1317	.684	....	....	2939	377	1497	36	....	....	....	20.8	8.8	6.5	0.8	....
65-66	Baltimore	3	....	93	39	16	32	.500	....	....	....	7	13	.538	....	....	28	3	15	2	....	....	....	31.0	13.0	9.3	1.0	.471
66-67	LA Lakers	3	....	50	19	7	19	.368	....	....	....	5	5	1.000	....	....	12	2	7	0	....	....	....	16.7	6.3	4.0	0.7	.372
67-68	Chicago	5	....	57	6	3	12	.250	....	....	....	0	0	.000	....	....	21	1	13	0	....	....	....	11.4	1.2	4.2	0.2	.203
NBA Playoff Totals		11	....	200	64	26	63	.413	....	....	....	12	18	.667	....	....	61	6	35	2	....	....	....	18.2	5.8	5.5	0.5	....

• BARNES, Marvin

Marvin Jerome (Good News, The Magnificent) Barnes

Born: July 27, 1952. Providence, RI, United States. Height: 6'8". Weight: 210 lbs. Drafted: 1974 College: Providence

YEAR	TEAM	GP	GS	MIN	PTS	FGM	FGA	FG%	3PM	3PA	3P%	FTM	FTA	FT%	ORB	DRB	TRB	AST	PF	DQ	STL	BLK	TO	MPG	PPG	RPG	APG	PCM
74-75	St. Louis-A	77	....	3076	1849	777	1561	.498	0	3	.000	295	440	.670	419	783	1202	250	328	....	96	137	307	39.9	24.0	15.6	3.2	.744
75-76	St. Louis-A	67	....	2487	1616	681	1355	.503	3	11	.273	251	339	.740	263	462	725	149	273	....	124	134	230	37.1	24.1	10.8	2.2	.670
76-77	Detroit	53	....	989	510	202	452	.447	....	....	....	106	156	.679	69	184	253	45	139	1	38	33	....	18.7	9.6	4.8	0.8	.488
77-78	Detroit	12	....	269	120	53	118	.449	....	....	....	14	29	.483	28	63	91	19	43	2	7	11	29	22.4	10.0	7.6	1.6	.480
77-78	Buffalo	48	....	1377	566	226	543	.416	....	....	....	114	153	.745	107	241	348	117	198	7	57	72	106	28.7	11.8	7.3	2.4	.466
78-79	Boston	38	....	796	309	133	271	.491	....	....	....	43	66	.652	57	120	177	53	144	3	38	39	68	20.9	8.1	4.7	1.4	.422
79-80	San Diego	20	....	287	64	24	60	.400	0	0	.000	16	32	.500	34	43	77	18	52	0	5	12	18	14.4	3.2	3.9	0.9	.311
NBA Season Totals		171	....	3718	1569	638	1444	.442	0	0	.000	293	436	.672	295	651	946	252	576	13	145	167	221	21.7	9.2	5.5	1.5	....
ABA Season Totals		144	....	5563	3465	1458	2916	.500	3	14	.214	546	779	.701	682	1245	1927	399	601	....	220	271	537	38.6	24.1	13.4	2.8	....
Career Totals		315	....	9281	5034	2096	4360	.481	3	14	.214	839	1215	.691	977	1896	2873	651	1177	13	365	438	758	29.5	16.0	9.1	2.1	....
74-75	St. Louis-A	10	....	444	308	124	249	.498	0	1	.000	60	77	.779	53	88	141	16	45	....	20	19	38	44.4	30.8	14.1	1.6	.704
ABA Playoff Totals		10	....	444	308	124	249	.498	0	1	.000	60	77	.779	53	88	141	16	45	....	20	19	38	44.4	30.8	14.1	1.6	....

• BARNETT, Dick

Richard (Skull, Fall Back Baby) Barnett

Born: Oct. 2, 1936. Gary, IN, United States. Height: 6'4". Weight: 190 lbs. Drafted: 1959 College: Tennessee State

YEAR	TEAM	GP	GS	MIN	PTS	FGM	FGA	FG%	3PM	3PA	3P%	FTM	FTA	FT%	ORB	DRB	TRB	AST	PF	DQ	STL	BLK	TO	MPG	PPG	RPG	APG	PCM
59-60	Syracuse	57	....	1235	706	289	701	.412	....	....	....	128	180	.711	....	....	155	160	98	0	....	....	....	21.7	12.4	2.7	2.8	.530
60-61	Syracuse	78	....	2070	1320	540	1194	.452	....	....	....	240	337	.712	....	....	283	218	169	0	....	....	....	26.5	16.9	3.6	2.8	.583
62-63	LA Lakers	80	....	2544	1437	547	1162	.471	....	....	....	343	421	.815	....	....	242	224	189	3	....	....	....	31.8	18.0	3.0	2.8	.514
63-64	LA Lakers	78	....	2620	1433	541	1197	.452	....	....	....	351	454	.773	....	....	250	238	233	3	....	....	....	33.6	18.4	3.2	3.1	.488
64-65	LA Lakers	74	....	2026	1020	375	908	.413	....	....	....	270	338	.799	....	....	200	159	209	1	....	....	....	27.4	13.8	2.7	2.1	.421
65-66	New York	75	....	2589	1729	631	1344	.469	....	....	....	467	605	.772	....	....	310	259	235	6	....	....	....	34.5	23.1	4.1	3.5	.611
66-67	New York	67	....	1969	1139	454	949	.478	....	....	....	231	295	.783	....	....	226	161	185	2	....	....	....	29.4	17.0	3.4	2.4	.518
67-68	New York	81	....	2488	1461	559	1159	.482	....	....	....	343	440	.780	....	....	238	242	222	0	....	....	....	30.7	18.0	2.9	3.0	.537
68-69	New York	82	....	2953	1442	565	1220	.463	....	....	....	312	403	.774	....	....	251	291	239	4	....	....	....	36.0	17.6	3.1	3.5	.442
69-70	New York	82	....	2772	1220	494	1039	.475	....	....	....	232	325	.714	....	....	221	298	220	0	....	....	....	33.8	14.9	2.7	3.6	.408
70-71	New York	82	....	2843	1273	540	1184	.456	....	....	....	193	278	.694	....	....	238	225	232	1	....	....	....	34.7	15.5	2.9	2.7	.367
71-72	New York	79	....	2256	964	401	918	.437	....	....	....	162	215	.753	....	....	153	198	229	4	....	....	....	28.6	12.2	1.9	2.5	.334
72-73	New York	51	....	514	192	88	226	.389	....	....	....	16	30	.533	....	....	41	50	52	0	....	....	....	10.1	3.8	0.8	1.0	.268
73-74	New York	5	....	58	22	10	26	.385	....	....	....	2	3	.667	1	3	4	6	2	0	1	0	....	11.6	4.4	0.8	1.2	.300
NBA Season Totals		971	....	28937	15358	6034	13227	.456	....	....	....	3290	4324	.761	1	3	2812	2729	2514	24	1	0	....	29.8	15.8	2.9	2.8	....
59-60	Syracuse	3	....	64	30	12	38	.316	....	....	....	6	7	.857	....	....	14	4	4	0	....	....	....	21.3	10.0	4.7	1.3	.375
60-61	Syracuse	8	....	226	124	49	112	.438	....	....	....	26	36	.722	....	....	36	12	25	0	....	....	....	28.3	15.5	4.5	1.5	.465
62-63	LA Lakers	13	....	370	219	71	151	.470	....	....	....	77	97	.794	....	....	38	21	35	0	....	....	....	28.5	16.8	2.9	1.6	.512
63-64	LA Lakers	5	....	154	69	21	52	.404	....	....	....	27	32	.844	....	....	8	17	16	0	....	....	....	30.8	13.8	1.6	3.4	.414
64-65	LA Lakers	10	....	287	175	72	150	.480	....	....	....	31	39	.795	....	....	30	33	25	0	....	....	....	28.7	17.5	3.0	3.3	.579
67-68	New York	6	....	211	143	61	117	.521	....	....	....	21	29	.724	....	....	27	21	24	1	....	....	....	35.2	23.8	4.5	3.5	.627
68-69	New York	10	....	402	167	65	163	.399	....	....	....	37	54	.685	....	....	35	27	32	0	....	....	....	40.2	16.7	3.5	2.7	.312
69-70	New York	19	....	714	321	131	280	.468	....	....	....	59	76	.776	....	....	39	64	64	0	....	....	....	37.6	16.9	2.1	3.4	.364
70-71	New York	12	....	455	234	95	199	.477	....	....	....	44	63	.698	....	....	38	36	33	0	....	....	....	37.9	19.5	3.2	3.0	.431
71-72	New York	12	....	131	51	23	49	.469	....	....	....	5	12	.417	....	....	8	10	19	0	....	....	....	10.9	4.3	0.7	0.8	.272
72-73	New York	4	....	17	6	3	6	.500	....	....	....	0	0	.000	....	....	0	2	5	0	....	....	....	4.3	1.5	0.0	0.5	.210
NBA Playoff Totals		102	....	3031	1539	603	1317	.458	....	....	....	333	445	.748	....	....	273	247	282	1	....	....	....	29.7	15.1	2.7	2.4	....

• BARNETT, Jim

James Franklin Barnett

Born: July 7, 1944. Greenville, SC, United States. Height: 6'4". Weight: 170 lbs. Drafted: 1966 College: Oregon

YEAR	TEAM	GP	GS	MIN	PTS	FGM	FGA	FG%	3PM	3PA	3P%	FTM	FTA	FT%	ORB	DRB	TRB	AST	PF	DQ	STL	BLK	TO	MPG	PPG	RPG	APG	PCM
66-67	Boston	48	....	383	198	78	211	.370	....	....	....	42	62	.677	....	....	53	41	61	0	....	....	....	8.0	4.1	1.1	0.9	.395
67-68	San Diego	47	....	1068	442	179	456	.393	....	....	....	84	118	.712	....	....	155	134	101	0	....	....	....	22.7	9.4	3.3	2.9	.423
68-69	San Diego	80	....	2346	1163	465	1093	.425	....	....	....	233	310	.752	....	....	362	339	240	2	....	....	....	29.3	14.5	4.5	4.2	.513
69-70	San Diego	80	....	2105	1189	450	998	.451	....	....	....	289	366	.790	....	....	305	287	222	3	....	....	....	26.3	14.9	3.8	3.6	.553
70-71	Portland	78	....	2371	1444	559	1283	.436	....	....	....	326	402	.811	....	....	376	323	190	1	....	....	....	30.4	18.5	4.8	4.1	.590
71-72	Golden State	80	....	2200	992	374	915	.409	....	....	....	244	292	.836	....	....	250	309	189	0	....	....	....	27.5	12.4	3.1	3.9	.450
72-73	Golden State	82	....	2215	971	394	844	.467	....	....	....	183	217	.843	....	....	255	301	150	1	....	....	....	27.0	11.8	3.1	3.7	.482
73-74	Golden State	77	....	1689	884	350	755	.464	....	....	....	184	226	.814	76	146	222	209	146	1	56	11	....	21.9	11.5	2.9	2.7	.526
74-75	New Orleans	45	....	1238	586	215	480	.448	....	....	....	156	188	.830	45	83	128	137	109	1	35	16	....	27.5	13.0	2.8	3.0	.457
74-75	New York	28	....	538	183	70	172	.407	....	....	....	43	50	.860	15	36	51	39	51	0	12	0	....	19.2	6.5	1.8	1.4	.296
75-76	New York	71	....	1026	418	164	371	.442	....	....	....	90	114	.789	48	40	88	90	86	0	24	3	....	14.5	5.9	1.2	1.3	.362
76-77	Philadelphia	16	....	231	66	28	64	.438	....	....	....	10	18	.556	7	7	14	23	28	0	4	0	....	14.4	4.1	0.9	1.4	.249
NBA Season Totals		732	....	17410	8536	3326	7642	.435	....	....	....	1884	2363	.797	191	312	2259	2232	1573	9	131	30	....	23.8	11.7	3.1	3.0	....
66-67	Boston	5	....	26	14	6	21	.286	....	....	....	2	2	1.000	....	....	4	1	5	0	....	....	....	5.2	2.8	0.8	0.2	.171
68-69	San Diego	6	....	51	25	9	23	.391	....	....	....	7	8	.875	....	....	3	7	5	0	....	....	....	8.5	4.2	0.5	1.2	.420
71-72	Golden State	5	....	197	108	39	91	.429	....	....	....	30	41	.732	....	....	20	26	20	0	....	....	....	39.4	21.6	4.0	5.2	.490
72-73	Golden State	11	....	336	143	60	147	.408	....	....	....	23	27	.852	....	....	39	39	28	0	....	....	....	30.5	13.0	3.5	3.5	.395
74-75	New York	3	....	59	31	13	21	.619	....	....	....	5	5	1.000	5	3	8	5	6	0	1	1	....	19.7	10.3	2.7	1.7	.579
NBA Playoff Totals		30	....	669	321	127	303	.419	....	....	....	67	83	.807	5	3	74	78	64	0	1	1	....	22.3	10.7	2.5	2.6	....

• BARNETT, Nathaniel

Nathaniel Barnett Jr.

Born: Jan. 29, 1953. Height: 6'3". Weight: 175 lbs. Drafted: 1975 College: Akron

YEAR	TEAM	GP	GS	MIN	PTS	FGM	FGA	FG%	3PM	3PA	3P%	FTM	FTA	FT%	ORB	DRB	TRB	AST	PF	DQ	STL	BLK	TO	MPG	PPG	RPG	APG	PCM
75-76	Indiana-A	12	....	73	27	12	26	.462	0	1	.000	3	8	.375	3	5	8	8	22	....	3	1	8	6.1	2.3	0.7	0.7	.253
ABA Season Totals		12	....	73	27	12	26	.462	0	1	.000	3	8	.375	3	5	8	8	22	....	3	1	8	6.1	2.3	0.7	0.7	....

• BARNETT, Shannie

Shannie Barnett

Born: 1919. Height: 6'3". Weight: 175 lbs. Drafted: — College: none

YEAR TEAM	GP	GS	MIN	PTS	FGM	FGA	FG%	3PM	3PA	3P%	FTM	FTA	FT%	ORB	DRB	TRB	AST	PF	DQ	STL	BLK	TO	MPG	PPG	RPG	APG	PCM
42-43 Toledo-N	4	....	....	14	5	....	....	....	....	....	4	....	....	....	....	....	....	....	....	....	....	....	....	3.5	....	....	....
NBL Season Totals	4	....	....	14	5	....	....	....	....	....	4	....	....	....	....	....	....	....	....	....	....	....	....	3.5	....	....	....

• BARNHILL, John

John Anthony (Rabbit) Barnhill

Born: Mar. 20, 1938. Evansville, IN, United States. Height: 6'1". Weight: 180 lbs. Drafted: 1959 College: Tennessee State

YEAR TEAM	GP	GS	MIN	PTS	FGM	FGA	FG%	3PM	3PA	3P%	FTM	FTA	FT%	ORB	DRB	TRB	AST	PF	DQ	STL	BLK	TO	MPG	PPG	RPG	APG	PCM
62-63 St. Louis	77	....	2692	901	360	838	.430	....	....	....	181	255	.710	....	....	359	322	168	0	....	....	....	35.0	11.7	4.7	4.2	.409
63-64 St. Louis	74	....	1367	486	208	505	.412	....	....	....	70	115	.609	....	....	157	145	107	0	....	....	....	18.5	6.6	2.1	2.0	.362
64-65 St. Louis	41	....	777	287	121	312	.388	....	....	....	45	70	.643	....	....	91	76	56	0	....	....	....	19.0	7.0	2.2	1.9	.351
65-66 St. Louis	31	....	691	262	104	243	.428	....	....	....	54	86	.628	....	....	91	83	58	0	....	....	....	22.3	8.5	2.9	2.7	.420
65-66 Detroit	45	....	926	337	139	363	.383	....	....	....	59	98	.602	....	....	112	113	76	0	....	....	....	20.6	7.5	2.5	2.5	.369
66-67 Baltimore	53	....	1214	440	187	447	.418	....	....	....	66	103	.641	....	....	157	136	80	0	....	....	....	22.9	8.3	3.0	2.6	.391
67-68 San Diego	75	....	1883	744	295	700	.421	....	....	....	154	234	.658	....	....	173	259	143	1	....	....	....	25.1	9.9	2.3	3.5	.415
68-69 Baltimore	30	....	504	191	76	175	.434	....	....	....	39	65	.600	....	....	53	71	63	0	....	....	....	16.8	6.4	1.8	2.4	.393
69-70 Indiana-A	77	....	2374	879	325	824	.394	71	272	.261	158	238	.664	60	113	173	312	196	2	....	....	157	30.8	11.4	2.2	4.1	.353
70-71 Denver-A	24	....	684	274	101	255	.396	18	72	.250	54	73	.740	20	34	54	77	55	1	....	....	40	28.5	11.4	2.3	3.2	.375
70-71 Indiana-A	43	....	619	216	80	241	.332	14	75	.187	42	61	.689	27	35	62	83	51	0	....	....	39	14.4	5.0	1.4	1.9	.336
71-72 Indiana-A	19	....	194	68	28	87	.322	4	35	.114	8	15	.533	8	11	19	16	16	0	....	....	12	10.2	3.6	1.0	0.8	.210
NBA Season Totals	426	....	10054	3648	1490	3583	.416	....	....	....	668	1026	.651	....	....	1193	1205	751	1	....	....	....	23.6	8.6	2.8	2.8	....
ABA Season Totals	163	....	3871	1437	534	1407	.380	107	454	.236	262	387	.677	115	193	308	488	318	3	....	....	248	23.7	8.8	1.9	3.0	....
Career Totals	589	....	13925	5085	2024	4990	.406	107	454	.236	930	1413	.658	115	193	1501	1693	1069	4	....	....	248	23.6	8.6	2.5	2.9	....
62-63 St. Louis	11	....	314	77	31	77	.403	....	....	....	15	22	.682	....	....	27	36	28	0	....	....	....	28.5	7.0	2.5	3.3	.292
63-64 St. Louis	5	....	61	26	12	23	.522	....	....	....	2	5	.400	....	....	5	5	8	0	....	....	....	12.2	5.2	1.0	1.0	.380
64-65 St. Louis	4	....	36	6	2	11	.182	....	....	....	2	4	.500	....	....	7	2	3	0	....	....	....	9.0	1.5	1.8	0.5	.139
68-69 Baltimore	1	....	10	2	1	2	.500	....	....	....	0	0	.000	....	....	2	1	3	0	....	....	....	10.0	2.0	2.0	1.0	.275
69-70 Indiana-A	14	....	317	85	28	88	.318	8	35	.229	21	41	.512	5	28	33	25	41	0	....	....	16	22.6	6.1	2.4	1.8	.203
NBA Playoff Totals	21	....	421	111	46	113	.407	....	....	....	19	31	.613	....	....	41	44	42	0	....	....	....	20.0	5.3	2.0	2.1	....
ABA Playoff Totals	14	....	317	85	28	88	.318	8	35	.229	21	41	.512	5	28	33	25	41	0	....	....	16	22.6	6.1	2.4	1.8	....
Career Playoff Totals	35	....	738	196	74	201	.368	8	35	.229	40	72	.556	5	28	74	69	83	0	....	....	16	21.1	5.6	2.1	2.0	....

• BARNHILL, Norton

Norton Barnhill

Born: July 15, 1953. Winston-Salem, NC, United States. Height: 6'4". Weight: 205 lbs. Drafted: 1976 College: Washington State

YEAR TEAM	GP	GS	MIN	PTS	FGM	FGA	FG%	3PM	3PA	3P%	FTM	FTA	FT%	ORB	DRB	TRB	AST	PF	DQ	STL	BLK	TO	MPG	PPG	RPG	APG	PCM
76-77 Seattle	4	....	10	4	2	6	.333	....	....	....	0	0	.000	2	1	3	1	5	0	0	0	....	2.5	1.0	0.8	0.3	.212
NBA Season Totals	4	....	10	4	2	6	.333	....	....	....	0	0	.000	2	1	3	1	5	0	0	0	....	2.5	1.0	0.8	0.3	....

• BARNHORST, Leo

Leo A. (Barney) Barnhorst

Born: May 11, 1924. Height: 6'4". Weight: 190 lbs. Drafted: 1949 College: Notre Dame

YEAR TEAM	GP	GS	MIN	PTS	FGM	FGA	FG%	3PM	3PA	3P%	FTM	FTA	FT%	ORB	DRB	TRB	AST	PF	DQ	STL	BLK	TO	MPG	PPG	RPG	APG	PCM
49-50 Chicago	67	....	....	438	174	499	.349	....	....	....	90	129	.698	....	....	....	140	192	....	....	....	....	....	6.5	....	2.1	....
50-51 Indianapolis	68	....	....	546	232	671	.346	....	....	....	82	119	.689	....	....	296	218	197	1	....	....	....	....	8.0	4.4	3.2	....
51-52 Indianapolis	66	....	2344	820	349	897	.389	....	....	....	122	187	.652	....	....	430	255	196	3	....	....	....	35.5	12.4	6.5	3.9	.415
52-53 Indianapolis	71	....	2871	967	402	1034	.389	....	....	....	163	259	.629	....	....	483	277	245	8	....	....	....	40.4	13.6	6.8	3.9	.379
53-54 Bal/FtW	72	....	2064	461	199	588	.338	....	....	....	63	88	.716	....	....	297	226	203	4	....	....	....	28.7	6.4	4.1	3.1	.294
NBA Season Totals	344	....	7279	3232	1356	3689	.368	....	....	....	520	782	.665	....	....	1506	1116	1033	16	....	....	....	21.2	9.4	4.4	3.2	....
49-50 Chicago	2	....	....	22	8	25	.320	....	....	....	6	6	1.000	....	....	....	4	10	....	....	....	....	....	11.0	....	2.0	....
50-51 Indianapolis	3	....	....	34	13	35	.371	....	....	....	8	10	.800	....	....	9	12	7	0	....	....	....	....	11.3	3.0	4.0	....
51-52 Indianapolis	2	....	85	31	14	34	.412	....	....	....	3	7	.429	....	....	9	8	7	0	....	....	....	42.5	15.5	4.5	4.0	.348
52-53 Indianapolis	2	....	79	30	12	33	.364	....	....	....	6	9	.667	....	....	22	5	10	0	....	....	....	39.5	15.0	11.0	2.5	.410
53-54 Fort Wayne	4	....	60	23	10	19	.526	....	....	....	3	5	.600	....	....	5	6	10	0	....	....	....	15.0	5.8	1.3	1.5	.394
NBA Playoff Totals	13	....	224	140	57	146	.390	....	....	....	26	37	.703	....	....	45	35	44	0	....	....	....	17.2	10.8	3.5	2.7	....

• BARR, John

John E. Barr

Born: Aug. 18, 1918. Height: 6'3". Weight: 205 lbs. Drafted: — College: Penn State

YEAR TEAM	GP	GS	MIN	PTS	FGM	FGA	FG%	3PM	3PA	3P%	FTM	FTA	FT%	ORB	DRB	TRB	AST	PF	DQ	STL	BLK	TO	MPG	PPG	RPG	APG	PCM
46-47 St. Louis	58	....	....	295	124	438	.283	....	....	....	47	79	.595	....	....	....	54	164	....	....	....	....	....	5.1	....	0.9	....
NBA Season Totals	58	....	....	295	124	438	.283	....	....	....	47	79	.595	....	....	....	54	164	....	....	....	....	....	5.1	....	0.9	....

• BARR, Mike

Michael J. Barr

Born: Oct. 19, 1950. Canton, OH, United States. Height: 6'3". Weight: 180 lbs. Drafted: — College: Duquesne

YEAR TEAM	GP	GS	MIN	PTS	FGM	FGA	FG%	3PM	3PA	3P%	FTM	FTA	FT%	ORB	DRB	TRB	AST	PF	DQ	STL	BLK	TO	MPG	PPG	RPG	APG	PCM
72-73 Virginia-A	79	....	2076	720	289	612	.472	1	4	.250	141	188	.750	76	151	227	254	220	4	....	....	185	26.3	9.1	2.9	3.2	.382
73-74 Virginia-A	45	....	652	199	82	171	.480	2	5	.400	33	43	.767	22	49	71	82	80	....	27	4	60	14.5	4.4	1.6	1.8	.366
74-75 St. Louis-A	54	....	1341	300	136	269	.506	0	2	.000	28	41	.683	20	75	95	176	117	....	67	14	100	24.8	5.6	1.8	3.3	.301
75-76 St. Louis-A	56	....	1048	300	124	240	.517	6	16	.375	46	55	.836	29	80	109	174	76	....	64	7	83	18.7	5.4	1.9	3.1	.428
76-77 Kansas City	73	....	1224	285	122	279	.437	....	....	....	41	57	.719	33	97	130	175	96	0	52	18	....	16.8	3.9	1.8	2.4	.337
NBA Season Totals	73	....	1224	285	122	279	.437	....	....	....	41	57	.719	33	97	130	175	96	0	52	18	....	16.8	3.9	1.8	2.4	....
ABA Season Totals	234	....	5117	1519	631	1292	.488	9	27	.333	248	327	.758	147	355	502	686	493	4	158	25	428	21.9	6.5	2.1	2.9	....
Career Totals	307	....	6341	1804	753	1571	.479	9	27	.333	289	384	.753	180	452	632	861	589	4	210	43	428	20.7	5.9	2.1	2.8	....

YEAR	TEAM	GP	GS	MIN	PTS	FGM	FGA	FG%	3PM	3PA	3P%	FTM	FTA	FT%	ORB	DRB	TRB	AST	PF	DQ	STL	BLK	TO	MPG	PPG	RPG	APG	PCM
72-73	Virginia-A	5	....	84	15	5	18	.278	0	0	.000	5	6	.833	2	4	6	10	8	0	....	....	10	16.8	3.0	1.2	2.0	.187
73-74	Virginia-A	5	....	186	47	20	44	.455	0	0	.000	7	7	1.000	7	16	23	18	16	....	12	4	15	37.2	9.4	4.6	3.6	.322
74-75	St. Louis-A	10	....	369	74	33	66	.500	1	1	1.000	7	11	.636	8	28	36	44	38	....	13	1	12	36.9	7.4	3.6	4.4	.290
ABA Playoff Totals		20	....	639	136	58	128	.453	1	1	1.000	19	24	.792	17	48	65	72	62	0	25	5	37	32.0	6.8	3.3	3.6	....

• BARR, Moe

Thomas L. Barr

Born: June 19, 1944.   Height: 6'4".   Weight: 195 lbs.   Drafted: —   College: Duquesne

YEAR	TEAM	GP	GS	MIN	PTS	FGM	FGA	FG%	3PM	3PA	3P%	FTM	FTA	FT%	ORB	DRB	TRB	AST	PF	DQ	STL	BLK	TO	MPG	PPG	RPG	APG	PCM
70-71	Cincinnati	31	....	145	61	25	62	.403	....	....	....	11	13	.846			20	28	27	0				4.7	2.0	0.6	0.9	.454
NBA Season Totals		31	....	145	61	25	62	.403	....	....	....	11	13	.846			20	28	27	0				4.7	2.0	0.6	0.9	....

• BARRETT, Ernie

Ernie Drew Barrett

Born: Aug. 27, 1929. Pratt, KS, United States.   Height: 6'3".   Weight: 180 lbs.   Drafted: 1951   College: Kansas State

YEAR	TEAM	GP	GS	MIN	PTS	FGM	FGA	FG%	3PM	3PA	3P%	FTM	FTA	FT%	ORB	DRB	TRB	AST	PF	DQ	STL	BLK	TO	MPG	PPG	RPG	APG	PCM
53-54	Boston	59	....	641	134	60	191	.314	....	....	....	14	25	.560			100	55	116	2				10.9	2.3	1.7	0.9	.215
55-56	Boston	72	....	1451	507	207	533	.388	....	....	....	93	118	.788			243	174	184	4				20.2	7.0	3.4	2.4	.400
NBA Season Totals		131	....	2092	641	267	724	.369	....	....	....	107	143	.748			343	229	300	6				16.0	4.9	2.6	1.7	....
53-54	Boston	6	....	63	8	3	20	.150	....	....	....	2	2	1.000			6	4	14	0				10.5	1.3	1.0	0.7	.006
55-56	Boston	3	....	43	11	4	13	.308	....	....	....	3	3	1.000			7	4	7	0				14.3	3.7	2.3	1.3	.274
NBA Playoff Totals		9	....	106	19	7	33	.212	....	....	....	5	5	1.000			13	8	21	0				11.8	2.1	1.4	0.9	....

• BARRETT, Mike

Michael Thomas (Bird Man) Barrett

Born: Sept. 5, 1943. Montgomery, WV, United States.   Height: 6'2".   Weight: 155 lbs.   Drafted: —   College: West Virginia Tech

YEAR	TEAM	GP	GS	MIN	PTS	FGM	FGA	FG%	3PM	3PA	3P%	FTM	FTA	FT%	ORB	DRB	TRB	AST	PF	DQ	STL	BLK	TO	MPG	PPG	RPG	APG	PCM
69-70	Washington-A	84	....	2262	1252	479	1126	.425	62	180	.344	232	305	.761	139	157	296	259	243	2	....	....	223	26.9	14.9	3.5	3.1	.491
70-71	Virginia-A	84	....	2754	1152	458	988	.464	28	103	.272	208	274	.759	130	142	272	425	202	3	....	....	255	32.8	13.7	3.2	5.1	.489
72-73	San Diego-A	19	....	284	96	37	101	.366	4	20	.200	18	35	.514	8	16	24	46	28	0	....	....	39	14.9	5.1	1.3	2.4	.319
ABA Season Totals		187	....	5300	2500	974	2215	.440	94	303	.310	458	614	.746	277	315	592	730	473	5	....	....	517	28.3	13.4	3.2	3.9	....
69-70	Washington-A	7	....	270	185	73	150	.487	11	31	.355	28	33	.848	....	....	23	19	....	0	....	....	19	38.6	26.4	3.3	2.7	....
70-71	Virginia-A	12	....	456	202	70	177	.395	13	44	.295	49	59	.831	15	11	26	55	32	0	....	....	30	38.0	16.8	2.2	4.6	.408
71-72	Virginia-A	1	....	1	0	0	1	.000	0	1	.000	0	0	.000	0	0	0	0	1	0	....	....	0	1.0	0.0	0.0	0.0	-1.32
ABA Playoff Totals		20	....	727	387	143	328	.436	24	76	.316	77	92	.837	15	11	49	74	33	0	....	....	49	36.4	19.4	2.5	3.7	....

• BARROS, Dana

Dana Bruce Barros

Born: Apr. 13, 1967. Boston, MA, United States.   Height: 5'11".   Weight: 163 lbs.   Drafted: 1989   College: Boston College

YEAR	TEAM	GP	GS	MIN	PTS	FGM	FGA	FG%	3PM	3PA	3P%	FTM	FTA	FT%	ORB	DRB	TRB	AST	PF	DQ	STL	BLK	TO	MPG	PPG	RPG	APG	PCM
89-90	Seattle	81	25	1630	782	299	738	.405	95	238	.399	89	110	.809	35	97	132	205	97	0	53	1	122	20.1	9.7	1.6	2.5	.364
90-91	Seattle	66	0	750	418	154	311	.495	32	81	.395	78	85	.918	17	54	71	111	40	0	23	1	53	11.4	6.3	1.1	1.7	.543
91-92	Seattle	75	1	1331	619	238	493	.483	83	186	**.446**	60	79	.759	17	64	81	125	84	0	51	4	53	17.7	8.3	1.1	1.7	.410
92-93	Seattle	69	2	1243	541	214	474	.451	64	169	.379	49	59	.831	18	89	107	151	78	0	63	3	55	18.0	7.8	1.6	2.2	.425
93-94	Philadelphia	81	70	2519	1075	412	878	.469	135	354	.381	116	145	.800	28	168	196	424	96	0	107	5	170	31.1	13.3	2.4	5.2	.467
94-95	Philadelphia	82	82	3318	1686	571	1165	.490	197	425	.464	347	386	.899	27	247	274	619	159	1	149	4	246	40.5	20.6	3.3	7.5	.562
95-96	Boston	80	25	2328	1038	379	805	.471	150	368	.408	130	147	.884	21	171	192	306	116	1	58	3	120	29.1	13.0	2.4	3.8	.440
96-97	Boston	24	8	708	300	110	253	.435	43	105	.410	37	43	.860	5	43	48	81	34	0	26	6	38	29.5	12.5	2.0	3.4	.387
97-98	Boston	80	15	1686	784	281	609	.461	100	246	.407	122	144	.847	28	125	153	286	124	0	83	6	104	21.1	9.8	1.9	3.6	.506
98-99	Boston	50	16	1156	464	168	371	.453	64	160	.400	64	73	.877	16	89	105	208	64	1	52	5	88	23.1	9.3	2.1	4.2	.474
99-00	Boston	72	0	1139	517	196	435	.451	59	144	.410	66	76	.868	13	86	99	133	80	0	31	4	76	15.8	7.2	1.4	1.8	.409
00-01	Detroit	60	0	1079	478	183	412	.444	44	105	.419	68	80	.850	6	88	94	110	63	0	30	2	60	18.0	8.0	1.6	1.8	.388
01-02	Detroit	29	20	582	193	74	192	.385	24	71	.338	21	27	.778	1	56	57	78	37	0	14	2	33	20.1	6.7	2.0	2.7	.323
NBA Season Totals		849	264	19469	8895	3279	7136	.460	1090	2652	.411	1247	1454	.858	232	1377	1609	2837	1072	3	740	46	1208	22.9	10.5	1.9	3.3	....
90-91	Seattle	3	0	25	23	9	13	.692	2	5	.400	3	4	.750	1	3	4	5	1	0	3	0	3	8.3	7.7	1.3	1.7	1.096
91-92	Seattle	7	0	96	52	21	40	.525	10	17	.588	0	0	.000	1	6	7	8	11	0	4	0	6	13.7	7.4	1.0	1.1	.442
92-93	Seattle	16	0	136	55	22	47	.468	5	16	.313	6	8	.750	0	12	12	12	6	0	5	0	8	8.5	3.4	0.8	0.8	.361
01-02	Detroit	4	0	6	2	1	3	.333	0	1	.000	0	0	.000	0	1	1	2	0	0	0	0	1	1.5	0.5	0.0	0.3	.063
NBA Playoff Totals		30	0	263	132	53	103	.515	17	39	.436	9	12	.750	2	21	23	26	20	0	12	0	17	8.8	4.4	0.8	0.9	....

• BARRY, Brent

Brent Robert Barry

Born: Dec. 31, 1971. Hempstead, NY, United States.   Height: 6'6".   Weight: 185 lbs.   Drafted: 1995   College: Oregon State

YEAR	TEAM	GP	GS	MIN	PTS	FGM	FGA	FG%	3PM	3PA	3P%	FTM	FTA	FT%	ORB	DRB	TRB	AST	PF	DQ	STL	BLK	TO	MPG	PPG	RPG	APG	PCM
95-96	LA Clippers	79	44	1898	800	283	597	.474	123	296	.416	111	137	.810	38	130	168	230	196	2	95	22	119	24.0	10.1	2.1	2.9	.422
96-97	LA Clippers	59	0	1094	442	155	379	.409	56	173	.324	76	93	.817	30	80	110	154	88	1	51	15	77	18.5	7.5	1.9	2.6	.403
97-98	LA Clippers	41	36	1341	561	190	444	.428	78	195	.400	103	122	.844	27	116	143	132	88	0	50	23	94	32.7	13.7	3.5	3.2	.399
97-98	Miami	17	0	259	70	23	62	.371	12	34	.353	12	12	1.000	2	26	28	21	30	0	14	4	9	15.2	4.1	1.6	1.2	.298
98-99	Chicago	37	30	1181	412	141	356	.396	52	172	.302	78	105	.743	39	105	144	116	98	2	42	11	72	31.9	11.1	3.9	3.1	.345
99-00	Seattle	80	74	2726	945	327	707	.463	164	399	.411	127	157	.809	50	322	372	291	228	4	103	31	142	34.1	11.8	4.7	3.6	.415
00-01	Seattle	67	20	1778	589	198	401	.494	109	229	**.476**	84	103	.816	33	178	211	225	126	1	80	14	86	26.5	8.8	3.1	3.4	.442
01-02	Seattle	81	81	3041	1164	401	790	.508	164	387	.424	198	234	.846	58	383	441	426	182	3	147	37	165	37.5	14.4	5.4	5.3	.525
02-03	Seattle	75	68	2481	774	264	577	.458	118	293	.403	128	161	.795	48	253	301	384	199	1	113	15	142	33.1	10.3	4.0	5.1	.429
NBA Season Totals		536	353	15799	5757	1982	4313	.460	876	2178	.402	917	1120	.819	325	1593	1918	1979	1235	14	695	172	906	29.5	10.7	3.6	3.7	....
96-97	LA Clippers	3	0	84	35	11	27	.407	5	11	.455	8	9	.889	1	6	7	10	10	0	4	0	4	28.0	11.7	2.3	3.3	.383
99-00	Seattle	5	3	155	42	12	33	.364	8	20	.400	10	14	.714	3	10	13	15	20	2	3	3	7	31.0	8.4	2.6	3.0	.254
01-02	Seattle	5	5	149	39	14	34	.412	7	16	.438	4	4	1.000	6	17	23	14	12	0	3	4	9	29.8	7.8	4.6	2.8	.334
NBA Playoff Totals		13	8	388	116	37	94	.394	20	47	.426	22	27	.815	10	33	43	39	42	2	10	7	20	29.8	8.9	3.3	3.0	....

• BARRY, Drew

Drew William Barry

Born: Feb. 17, 1973. Oakland, CA, United States. Height: 6'5". Weight: 191 lbs. Drafted: 1996 College: Georgia Tech

YEAR	TEAM	GP	GS	MIN	PTS	FGM	FGA	FG%	3PM	3PA	3P%	FTM	FTA	FT%	ORB	DRB	TRB	AST	PF	DQ	STL	BLK	TO	MPG	PPG	RPG	APG	PCM
97-98	Atlanta	27	0	256	56	18	38	.474	9	21	.429	11	13	.846	5	30	35	49	28	0	10	1	30	9.5	2.1	1.3	1.8	.359
98-99	Seattle	17	0	183	37	10	32	.313	8	24	.333	9	13	.692	3	17	20	29	24	0	7	1	12	10.8	2.2	1.2	1.7	.281
99-00	Golden State	8	0	85	22	9	18	.500	3	9	.333	1	2	.500	0	8	8	17	14	0	2	0	6	10.6	2.8	1.0	2.1	.344
99-00	Atlanta	8	0	74	19	6	15	.400	4	9	.444	3	3	1.000	0	4	4	16	9	0	0	0	7	9.3	2.4	0.5	2.0	.290
NBA Season Totals		60	0	598	134	43	103	.417	24	63	.381	24	31	.774	8	59	67	111	75	0	19	2	55	10.0	2.2	1.1	1.9	....
97-98	Atlanta	2	0	5	0	0	1	.000	0	1	.000	0	0	.000	0	1	1	0	0	0	0	0	0	2.5	0.0	0.5	0.0	.000
NBA Playoff Totals		2	0	5	0	0	1	.000	0	1	.000	0	0	.000	0	1	1	0	0	0	0	0	0	2.5	0.0	0.5	0.0	....

• BARRY, Jon

Jon Alan Barry

Born: July 25, 1969. Oakland, CA, United States. Height: 6'4". Weight: 195 lbs. Drafted: 1992 College: Georgia Tech

YEAR	TEAM	GP	GS	MIN	PTS	FGM	FGA	FG%	3PM	3PA	3P%	FTM	FTA	FT%	ORB	DRB	TRB	AST	PF	DQ	STL	BLK	TO	MPG	PPG	RPG	APG	PCM
92-93	Milwaukee	47	0	552	206	76	206	.369	21	63	.333	33	49	.673	10	33	43	68	57	0	35	3	42	11.7	4.4	0.9	1.4	.289
93-94	Milwaukee	72	7	1242	445	158	382	.414	32	115	.278	97	122	.795	36	110	146	168	110	0	102	17	86	17.3	6.2	2.0	2.3	.422
94-95	Milwaukee	52	0	602	191	57	134	.425	16	48	.333	61	80	.763	15	34	49	85	54	0	30	4	42	11.6	3.7	0.9	1.6	.354
95-96	Golden State	68	0	712	257	91	185	.492	44	93	.473	31	37	.838	17	46	63	85	51	1	33	11	41	10.5	3.8	0.9	1.3	.413
96-97	Atlanta	58	8	965	285	100	246	.407	48	124	.387	37	46	.804	26	73	99	115	56	0	55	3	58	16.6	4.9	1.7	2.0	.346
97-98	LA Lakers	49	1	374	121	38	104	.365	18	61	.295	27	29	.931	8	29	37	51	33	0	24	3	20	7.6	2.5	0.8	1.0	.375
98-99	Sacramento	43	0	736	213	59	138	.428	24	79	.304	71	84	.845	25	71	96	112	61	1	53	5	47	17.1	5.0	2.2	2.6	.448
99-00	Sacramento	62	1	1281	495	161	346	.465	66	154	.429	107	116	.922	38	121	159	150	104	1	75	7	85	20.7	8.0	2.6	2.4	.454
00-01	Sacramento	62	2	1010	316	103	255	.404	46	132	.348	64	73	.877	16	78	94	130	66	0	28	6	53	16.3	5.1	1.5	2.1	.353
01-02	Detroit	82	6	1986	739	255	522	.489	121	258	.469	108	116	.931	42	192	234	274	134	0	94	20	111	24.2	9.0	2.9	3.3	.477
02-03	Detroit	80	0	1473	555	191	424	.450	87	214	.407	86	100	.860	33	147	180	206	104	0	63	14	81	18.4	6.9	2.3	2.6	.458
NBA Season Totals		675	25	10933	3823	1289	2942	.438	523	1341	.390	722	852	.847	266	934	1200	1444	830	3	592	93	666	16.2	5.7	1.8	2.1	....
96-97	Atlanta	2	0	9	0	0	3	.000	0	3	.000	0	0	.000	0	0	0	0	0	0	0	0	0	4.5	0.0	0.0	0.0	-.311
97-98	LA Lakers	7	0	18	0	0	8	.000	0	5	.000	0	0	.000	0	2	2	0	1	0	1	0	0	2.6	0.0	0.3	0.0	-.280
98-99	Sacramento	5	0	112	40	12	34	.353	5	19	.263	11	12	.917	3	7	10	9	9	0	6	1	9	22.4	8.0	2.0	1.8	.296
99-00	Sacramento	5	0	102	39	9	21	.429	7	12	.583	14	16	.875	2	10	12	12	7	0	3	0	4	20.4	7.8	2.4	2.4	.462
00-01	Sacramento	7	0	55	16	7	17	.412	2	7	.286	0	0	.000	3	0	3	4	7	0	1	0	3	7.9	2.3	0.4	0.6	.167
01-02	Detroit	10	0	176	80	29	61	.475	17	38	.447	5	8	.625	4	16	20	21	14	0	5	1	19	17.6	8.0	2.0	2.1	.413
02-03	Detroit	14	0	173	70	23	54	.426	15	33	.455	9	9	1.000	5	19	24	20	14	0	8	1	7	12.4	5.0	1.7	1.4	.468
NBA Playoff Totals		50	0	645	245	80	198	.404	46	117	.393	39	45	.867	17	54	71	66	52	0	24	3	42	12.9	4.9	1.4	1.3	....

• BARRY, Rick

Richard Francis Dennis Barry III

Born: Mar. 28, 1944. Elizabeth, NJ, United States. Height: 6'7". Weight: 205 lbs. Drafted: 1965 College: Miami (FL) HOF: 1987

YEAR	TEAM	GP	GS	MIN	PTS	FGM	FGA	FG%	3PM	3PA	3P%	FTM	FTA	FT%	ORB	DRB	TRB	AST	PF	DQ	STL	BLK	TO	MPG	PPG	RPG	APG	PCM
65-66	San Francisco	80	....	2990	2059	745	1698	.439	....	....	....	569	660	.862	....	....	850	173	297	2	....	....	....	37.4	25.7	10.6	2.2	.681
66-67	San Francisco	78	....	3175	**2775**	**1011**	**2240**	.451	....	....	....	**753**	852	.884	....	....	714	282	258	1	....	....	....	40.7	**35.6**	9.2	3.6	.807
68-69	Oakland-A	35	....	1361	1190	392	767	.511	3	10	.300	403	454	**.888**	82	247	329	136	124	1	....	....	141	38.9	**34.0**	9.4	3.9	.904
69-70	Washington-A	52	....	1849	1442	517	1036	.499	8	39	.205	400	463	.864	130	233	363	178	174	1	....	....	184	35.6	27.7	7.0	3.4	.762
70-71	New York-A	59	....	2502	1734	632	1348	.469	19	86	.221	451	507	**.890**	105	296	401	294	205	1	....	....	202	42.4	29.4	6.8	5.0	.691
71-72	New York-A	80	....	3616	2518	902	1969	.458	73	237	.308	**641**	730	**.878**	155	447	602	327	261	2	....	....	263	**45.2**	31.5	7.5	4.1	.642
72-73	Golden State	82	....	3075	1832	737	1630	.452	....	....	....	358	397	**.902**	....	....	728	399	245	2	....	....	....	37.5	22.3	8.9	4.9	.658
73-74	Golden State	80	....	2918	2009	796	1746	.456	....	....	....	417	464	.899	103	437	540	484	265	4	169	40	....	36.5	25.1	6.8	6.1	.714
74-75	Golden State	80	....	3235	2450	1028	**2217**	.464	....	....	....	394	436	**.904**	92	364	456	492	225	0	**228**	33	....	40.4	30.6	5.7	6.2	.703
75-76	Golden State	81	....	3122	1701	707	1624	.435	....	....	....	287	311	**.923**	74	422	496	496	215	1	202	27	....	38.5	21.0	6.1	6.1	.578
76-77	Golden State	79	....	2904	1723	682	1551	.440	....	....	....	359	392	.916	73	349	422	475	194	2	172	58	....	36.8	21.8	5.3	6.0	.613
77-78	Golden State	82	....	3024	1898	760	1686	.451	....	....	....	378	409	**.924**	75	374	449	446	188	1	158	45	221	36.9	23.1	5.5	5.4	.619
78-79	Houston	80	....	2566	1082	461	1000	.461	....	....	....	160	169	**.947**	40	237	277	502	195	0	95	38	200	32.1	13.5	3.5	6.3	.486
79-80	Houston	72	....	1816	866	325	771	.422	73	221	.330	143	153	**.935**	53	183	236	268	182	0	80	28	151	25.2	12.0	3.3	3.7	.465
NBA Season Totals		794	....	28825	18395	7252	16163	.449	73	221	.330	3818	4243	.900	510	2366	5168	4017	2264	13	1104	269	572	36.3	23.2	6.5	5.1	....
ABA Season Totals		226	....	9328	6884	2443	5120	.477	103	372	.277	1895	2154	**.880**	472	1223	1695	935	764	5	....	....	790	41.3	30.5	7.5	4.1	....
Career Totals		1020	....	38153	25279	9695	21283	.456	176	593	.297	5713	6397	**.893**	982	3589	6863	4952	3028	18	1104	269	1362	37.4	24.8	6.7	4.9	....
66-67	San Francisco	15	....	614	521	197	489	.403	....	....	....	127	157	.809	....	....	113	58	49	0	....	....	....	40.9	34.7	7.5	3.9	.679
69-70	Washington-A	7	....	302	281	108	203	.532	3	9	.333	62	68	.912	....	....	70	23	....	0	....	....	26	43.1	40.1	10.0	3.3	....
70-71	New York-A	6	....	287	202	70	135	.519	14	27	.519	48	59	.814	17	53	70	24	23	0	....	....	33	47.8	33.7	11.7	4.0	.771
71-72	New York-A	18	....	749	554	203	429	.473	23	61	.377	125	146	.856	....	....	117	69	67	....	....	....	61	41.6	30.8	6.5	3.8	.663
72-73	Golden State	11	....	292	180	65	164	.396	....	....	....	50	55	.909	....	....	54	24	41	1	....	....	....	26.5	16.4	4.9	2.2	.510
74-75	Golden State	17	....	726	479	189	426	.444	....	....	....	101	110	.918	22	72	94	103	51	1	50	15	....	42.7	28.2	5.5	6.1	.619
75-76	Golden State	13	....	532	312	126	289	.436	....	....	....	60	68	.882	20	64	84	84	40	1	38	14	....	40.9	24.0	6.5	6.5	.601
76-77	Golden State	10	....	415	284	122	262	.466	....	....	....	40	44	.909	25	34	59	47	32	0	17	7	....	41.5	28.4	5.9	4.7	.607
78-79	Houston	2	....	65	24	8	25	.320	....	....	....	8	8	1.000	2	6	8	9	8	0	0	2	2	32.5	12.0	4.0	4.5	.342
79-80	Houston	6	....	79	33	12	33	.364	3	12	.250	6	6	1.000	0	6	6	15	11	0	1	1	10	13.2	5.5	1.0	2.5	.299
NBA Playoff Totals		74	....	2723	1833	719	1688	.426	3	12	.250	392	448	.875	69	182	418	340	232	3	106	39	12	36.8	24.8	5.6	4.6	....
ABA Playoff Totals		31	....	1338	1037	381	767	.497	40	97	.412	235	273	.861	17	53	257	116	90	0	....	....	120	43.2	33.5	8.3	3.7	....
Career Playoff Totals		105	....	4061	2870	1100	2455	.448	43	109	.394	627	721	.870	86	235	675	456	322	3	106	39	132	38.7	27.3	6.4	4.3	....

• BARTELS, Ed

Edward John Bartels

Born: Oct. 8, 1925. Height: 6'5". Weight: 195 lbs. Drafted: — College: North Carolina State

YEAR	TEAM	GP	GS	MIN	PTS	FGM	FGA	FG%	3PM	3PA	3P%	FTM	FTA	FT%	ORB	DRB	TRB	AST	PF	DQ	STL	BLK	TO	MPG	PPG	RPG	APG	PCM
49-50	Denver	13	....	....	59	21	82	.256	....	....	....	17	31	.548	....	....	....	20	27	....	....	....	....	....	4.5	....	1.5	....
49-50	New York	2	....	....	4	1	4	.250	....	....	....	2	3	.667	....	....	....	0	2	....	....	....	....	....	2.0	....	0.0	....
50-51	Washington	17	....	....	72	24	97	.247	....	....	....	24	46	.522	....	....	84	12	54	0	....	....	....	....	4.2	4.9	0.7	....
NBA Season Totals		32	....	....	135	46	183	.251	....	....	....	43	80	.538	....	....	84	32	83	0	....	....	....	....	4.2	2.6	1.0	....

YEAR	TEAM	GP	GS	MIN	PTS	FGM	FGA	FG%	3PM	3PA	3P%	FTM	FTA	FT%	ORB	DRB	TRB	AST	PF	DQ	STL	BLK	TO	MPG	PPG	RPG	APG	PCM

• BARTOLOME, Vic

Victor Bartolome

Born: Sept. 29, 1948. Height: 7' Weight: 230 lbs. Drafted: 1970 College: Oregon State

YEAR	TEAM	GP	GS	MIN	PTS	FGM	FGA	FG%	3PM	3PA	3P%	FTM	FTA	FT%	ORB	DRB	TRB	AST	PF	DQ	STL	BLK	TO	MPG	PPG	RPG	APG	PCM
71-72	Golden State	38	....	165	34	15	59	.254	....	....	....	4	5	.800	....	....	60	3	22	0	....	....	....	4.3	0.9	1.6	0.1	.250
NBA Season Totals		38	....	165	34	15	59	.254	....	....	....	4	5	.800	....	....	60	3	22	0	....	....	....	4.3	0.9	1.6	0.1	....

• BASICH, Pete

Pete Basich

Born: 1917. Height: 5'9". Weight: 145 lbs. Drafted: — College: Michigan State

YEAR	TEAM	GP	GS	MIN	PTS	FGM	FGA	FG%	3PM	3PA	3P%	FTM	FTA	FT%	ORB	DRB	TRB	AST	PF	DQ	STL	BLK	TO	MPG	PPG	RPG	APG	PCM
37-38	Columbus-N	1	....	....	3	1	....	....	....	....	....	1	....	....	....	....	....	....	....	....	....	....	...	3.0	....	....	....	....
NBL Season Totals		1	....	....	3	1	....	....	....	....	....	1	....	....	....	....	....	....	....	....	....	....	...	3.0	....	....	....	....

• BASKERVILLE, Jerry

Jerry W. Baskerville

Born: Nov. 10, 1951. Philadelphia, PA, United States. Height: 6'7". Weight: 190 lbs. Drafted: — College: Temple

YEAR	TEAM	GP	GS	MIN	PTS	FGM	FGA	FG%	3PM	3PA	3P%	FTM	FTA	FT%	ORB	DRB	TRB	AST	PF	DQ	STL	BLK	TO	MPG	PPG	RPG	APG	PCM
75-76	Philadelphia	21	....	105	26	8	26	.308	....	....	....	10	16	.625	13	15	28	3	32	0	6	5	....	5.0	1.2	1.3	0.1	.207
NBA Season Totals		21	....	105	26	8	26	.308	....	....	....	10	16	.625	13	15	28	3	32	0	6	5	....	5.0	1.2	1.3	0.1	....

• BASSETT, Tim

Eugene Timothy Bassett

Born: Apr. 1, 1951. Washington, DC, United States. Height: 6'8". Weight: 225 lbs. Drafted: 1973 College: Georgia

YEAR	TEAM	GP	GS	MIN	PTS	FGM	FGA	FG%	3PM	3PA	3P%	FTM	FTA	FT%	ORB	DRB	TRB	AST	PF	DQ	STL	BLK	TO	MPG	PPG	RPG	APG	PCM
73-74	San Diego-A	82	....	1854	565	233	499	.467	0	4	.000	99	167	.593	252	343	595	109	185	....	57	35	87	22.6	6.9	7.3	1.3	.466
74-75	San Diego-A	72	....	1998	573	244	518	.471	3	4	.750	82	146	.562	210	316	526	117	159	....	45	36	97	27.8	8.0	7.3	1.6	.414
75-76	New York	84	....	1790	405	173	396	.437	1	6	.167	58	98	.592	185	346	531	65	247	....	47	41	97	21.3	4.8	6.3	0.8	.348
76-77	New York	76	....	2442	687	293	739	.396	....	....	....	101	177	.571	175	466	641	109	246	10	95	53	....	32.1	9.0	8.4	1.4	.344
77-78	New Jersey	65	....	1474	348	149	384	.388	....	....	....	50	97	.515	142	262	404	63	181	5	62	33	78	22.7	5.4	6.2	1.0	.327
78-79	New Jersey	82	....	1508	321	116	313	.371	....	....	....	89	131	.679	174	244	418	99	219	1	44	29	107	18.4	3.9	5.1	1.2	.319
79-80	New Jersey	7	....	92	24	8	22	.364	0	0	.000	8	12	.667	7	11	18	4	14	0	5	0	4	13.1	3.4	2.6	0.6	.269
79-80	San Antonio	5	....	72	10	4	12	.333	0	0	.000	2	3	.667	4	11	15	10	13	0	3	0	5	14.4	2.0	3.0	2.0	.266
NBA Season Totals		235	....	5588	1390	570	1470	.388	0	0	.000	250	420	.595	502	994	1496	285	673	16	209	115	194	23.8	5.9	6.4	1.2	....
ABA Season Totals		238	....	5642	1543	650	1413	.460	4	14	.286	239	411	.582	647	1005	1652	291	591	....	149	112	281	23.7	6.5	6.9	1.2	....
Career Totals		473	....	11230	2933	1220	2883	.423	4	14	.286	489	831	.588	1149	1999	3148	576	1264	16	358	227	475	23.7	6.2	6.7	1.2	....
73-74	San Diego-A	6	....	244	88	40	77	.519	0	0	.000	8	12	.667	47	42	89	20	18	....	3	7	13	40.7	14.7	14.8	3.3	.598
75-76	New York-A	13	....	312	82	37	81	.457	0	1	.000	8	11	.727	38	55	93	9	46	....	6	7	11	24.0	6.3	7.2	0.7	.365
78-79	New Jersey	2	....	17	6	2	5	.400	....	....	....	2	2	1.000	2	0	2	0	4	0	0	1	8.5	3.0	1.0	0.0	.142
79-80	San Antonio	3	....	19	2	1	2	.500	0	0	.000	0	0	.000	1	0	1	0	7	0	0	1	6.3	0.7	0.3	0.0	-.109
NBA Playoff Totals		5	....	36	8	3	7	.429	0	0	.000	2	2	1.000	3	0	3	0	11	0	0	2	7.2	1.6	0.6	0.0	....
ABA Playoff Totals		19	....	556	170	77	158	.487	0	1	.000	16	23	.696	85	97	182	29	64	....	9	14	24	29.3	8.9	9.6	1.5	....
Career Playoff Totals		24	....	592	178	80	165	.485	0	1	.000	18	25	.720	88	97	185	29	75	0	9	14	26	24.7	7.4	7.7	1.2	....

• BASTON, Maceo

Maceo Baston

Born: May 29, 1975. Corsicana, TX, United States. Height: 6'9". Weight: 215 lbs. Drafted: 1998 College: Michigan

YEAR	TEAM	GP	GS	MIN	PTS	FGM	FGA	FG%	3PM	3PA	3P%	FTM	FTA	FT%	ORB	DRB	TRB	AST	PF	DQ	STL	BLK	TO	MPG	PPG	RPG	APG	PCM
02-03	Toronto	16	0	106	40	15	25	.600	0	0	.000	10	12	.833	4	19	23	0	16	0	4	11	6	6.6	2.5	1.4	0.0	.489
NBA Season Totals		16	0	106	40	15	25	.600	0	0	.000	10	12	.833	4	19	23	0	16	0	4	11	6	6.6	2.5	1.4	0.0	....

• BATEER, Mengke

Mengke Bateer

Born: Nov. 20, 1975. Beijing, China. Height: 6'11". Weight: 290 lbs. Drafted: — College: none

YEAR	TEAM	GP	GS	MIN	PTS	FGM	FGA	FG%	3PM	3PA	3P%	FTM	FTA	FT%	ORB	DRB	TRB	AST	PF	DQ	STL	BLK	TO	MPG	PPG	RPG	APG	PCM
01-02	Denver	27	10	408	139	53	132	.402	4	12	.333	29	37	.784	32	64	96	22	94	3	10	5	32	15.1	5.1	3.6	0.8	.286
02-03	San Antonio	12	0	45	9	4	17	.235	1	3	.333	0	2	.000	2	8	10	4	14	0	0	0	6	3.8	0.8	0.8	0.3	-.046
NBA Season Totals		39	10	453	148	57	149	.383	5	15	.333	29	39	.744	34	72	106	26	108	3	10	5	38	11.6	3.8	2.7	0.7	....

• BATES, Billy Ray

Billy Ray (Dunk) Bates

Born: May 31, 1956. Kosciusko, MS, United States. Height: 6'4". Weight: 210 lbs. Drafted: 1978 College: Kentucky State

YEAR	TEAM	GP	GS	MIN	PTS	FGM	FGA	FG%	3PM	3PA	3P%	FTM	FTA	FT%	ORB	DRB	TRB	AST	PF	DQ	STL	BLK	TO	MPG	PPG	RPG	APG	PCM
79-80	Portland	16	....	235	180	72	146	.493	8	19	.421	28	39	.718	13	16	29	31	26	0	14	2	21	14.7	11.3	1.8	1.9	.647
80-81	Portland	77	....	1560	1062	439	902	.487	14	54	.259	170	199	.854	71	86	157	196	120	0	82	6	146	20.3	13.8	2.0	2.5	.562
81-82	Portland	75	0	1229	832	327	692	.473	12	41	.293	166	211	.787	53	55	108	111	100	0	41	5	90	16.4	11.1	1.4	1.5	.495
82-83	Washington	15	3	277	118	53	129	.411	2	5	.400	10	20	.500	10	8	18	14	18	0	13	3	12	18.5	7.9	1.2	0.9	.260
82-83	LA Lakers	4	0	27	5	2	16	.125	0	0	.000	1	2	.500	1	0	1	0	1	0	1	0	0	6.8	1.3	0.3	0.0	-.249
NBA Season Totals		187	3	3328	2197	893	1885	.474	36	119	.303	375	471	.796	148	165	313	352	265	0	151	16	269	17.8	11.7	1.7	1.9	....
79-80	Portland	3	....	104	75	31	59	.525	2	7	.286	11	14	.786	2	8	10	12	13	0	5	1	15	34.7	25.0	3.3	4.0	.543
80-81	Portland	3	....	115	85	35	62	.565	1	1	1.000	14	17	.824	3	4	7	13	11	0	5	1	11	38.3	28.3	2.3	4.3	.609
NBA Playoff Totals		6	....	219	160	66	121	.545	3	8	.375	25	31	.806	5	12	17	25	24	0	10	2	26	36.5	26.7	2.8	4.2	....

• BATISTE, Mike

Michael Batiste

Born: Nov. 21, 1977. Long Beach, CA, United States. Height: 6'8". Weight: 225 lbs. Drafted: — College: Arizona State

YEAR	TEAM	GP	GS	MIN	PTS	FGM	FGA	FG%	3PM	3PA	3P%	FTM	FTA	FT%	ORB	DRB	TRB	AST	PF	DQ	STL	BLK	TO	MPG	PPG	RPG	APG	PCM
02-03	Memphis	75	2	1249	481	197	467	.422	18	81	.222	69	88	.784	82	175	257	52	120	1	42	16	69	16.7	6.4	3.4	0.7	.363
NBA Season Totals		75	2	1249	481	197	467	.422	18	81	.222	69	88	.784	82	175	257	52	120	1	42	16	69	16.7	6.4	3.4	0.7	....

YEAR	TEAM	GP	GS	MIN	PTS	FGM	FGA	FG%	3PM	3PA	3P%	FTM	FTA	FT%	ORB	DRB	TRB	AST	PF	DQ	STL	BLK	TO	MPG	PPG	RPG	APG	PCM

• BATTERMAN, Buck
Buck Batterman

Born: 1918.   Height: 6'3".   Weight: 195 lbs.   Drafted: —   College: Wisconsin (Oshkosh)

YEAR	TEAM	GP	GS	MIN	PTS	FGM	FGA	FG%	3PM	3PA	3P%	FTM	FTA	FT%	ORB	DRB	TRB	AST	PF	DQ	STL	BLK	TO	MPG	PPG	RPG	APG	PCM
39-40	Oshkosh-N	17	....	....	20	6	....	....	....	....	....	8	....	....	....	....	....	....	....	....	....	....	....	....	1.2	....	....	....
NBL Season Totals		17	....	....	20	6	....	....	....	....	....	8	....	....	....	....	....	....	....	....	....	....	....	....	1.2	....	....	....
39-40	Oshkosh-N	2	....	....	1	0	....	....	....	....	....	1	....	....	....	....	....	....	....	....	....	....	....	....	0.5	....	....	....
NBL Playoff Totals		2	....	....	1	0	....	....	....	....	....	1	....	....	....	....	....	....	....	....	....	....	....	....	0.5	....	....	....

• BATTIE, Tony
Demetrius Antonio Battie

Born: Feb. 11, 1976. Dallas, TX, United States.   Height: 6'11".   Weight: 230 lbs.   Drafted: 1997   College: Texas Tech

YEAR	TEAM	GP	GS	MIN	PTS	FGM	FGA	FG%	3PM	3PA	3P%	FTM	FTA	FT%	ORB	DRB	TRB	AST	PF	DQ	STL	BLK	TO	MPG	PPG	RPG	APG	PCM
97-98	Denver	65	49	1506	544	234	525	.446	3	14	.214	73	104	.702	138	213	351	60	199	6	54	69	98	23.2	8.4	5.4	0.9	.386
98-99	Boston	50	15	1121	335	147	283	.519	0	3	.000	41	61	.672	96	204	300	53	159	1	29	71	45	22.4	6.7	6.0	1.1	.454
99-00	Boston	82	4	1505	541	219	459	.477	1	8	.125	102	151	.675	152	258	410	63	249	4	47	70	67	18.4	6.6	5.0	0.8	.448
00-01	Boston	40	25	845	260	108	201	.537	0	3	.000	44	69	.638	73	160	233	16	126	3	27	60	37	21.1	6.5	5.8	0.4	.450
01-02	Boston	74	73	1819	510	211	390	.541	0	2	.000	88	130	.677	184	297	481	35	219	3	60	67	51	24.6	6.9	6.5	0.7	.425
02-03	Boston	67	62	1683	487	199	369	.539	1	5	.200	88	118	.746	148	285	433	49	197	2	33	81	48	25.1	7.3	6.5	0.7	.437
NBA Season Totals		378	228	8479	2677	1118	2227	.502	5	35	.143	436	633	.689	791	1417	2208	276	1149	19	250	418	346	22.4	7.1	5.8	0.7	....
01-02	Boston	16	16	443	97	42	86	.488	0	0	.000	13	21	.619	39	82	121	13	51	1	10	30	11	27.7	6.1	7.6	0.8	.408
02-03	Boston	10	10	213	66	31	55	.564	0	3	.000	4	8	.500	13	36	49	5	42	1	4	14	7	21.3	6.6	4.9	0.5	.391
NBA Playoff Totals		26	26	656	163	73	141	.518	0	3	.000	17	29	.586	52	118	170	18	93	2	14	44	18	25.2	6.3	6.5	0.7	....

• BATTIER, Shane
Shane Courtney Battier

Born: Sept. 9, 1979. Birmingham, MI, United States.   Height: 6'8".   Weight: 220 lbs.   Drafted: 2001   College: Duke

YEAR	TEAM	GP	GS	MIN	PTS	FGM	FGA	FG%	3PM	3PA	3P%	FTM	FTA	FT%	ORB	DRB	TRB	AST	PF	DQ	STL	BLK	TO	MPG	PPG	RPG	APG	PCM
01-02	Memphis	78	78	3097	1125	412	961	.429	103	276	.373	198	283	.700	180	238	418	216	215	2	121	81	155	39.7	14.4	5.4	2.8	.371
02-03	Memphis	78	47	2383	756	275	569	.483	86	216	.398	120	145	.828	128	217	345	105	207	0	102	88	68	30.6	9.7	4.4	1.3	.387
NBA Season Totals		156	125	5480	1881	687	1530	.449	189	492	.384	318	428	.743	308	455	763	321	422	2	223	169	223	35.1	12.1	4.9	2.1	....

• BATTLE, John
John Sidney (Cricket, Pickle) Battle

Born: Nov. 9, 1962. Washington, DC, United States.   Height: 6'2".   Weight: 175 lbs.   Drafted: 1985   College: Rutgers

YEAR	TEAM	GP	GS	MIN	PTS	FGM	FGA	FG%	3PM	3PA	3P%	FTM	FTA	FT%	ORB	DRB	TRB	AST	PF	DQ	STL	BLK	TO	MPG	PPG	RPG	APG	PCM
85-86	Atlanta	64	0	639	277	101	222	.455	0	7	.000	75	103	.728	12	50	62	74	80	0	23	3	45	10.0	4.3	1.0	1.2	.366
86-87	Atlanta	64	8	804	381	144	315	.457	0	10	.000	93	126	.738	16	44	60	124	76	0	29	5	58	12.6	6.0	0.9	1.9	.419
87-88	Atlanta	67	1	1227	713	278	613	.454	16	41	.390	141	188	.750	26	87	113	158	84	0	31	5	74	18.3	10.6	1.7	2.4	.471
88-89	Atlanta	82	0	1672	779	287	628	.457	11	34	.324	194	238	.815	30	110	140	197	125	0	42	9	107	20.4	9.5	1.7	2.4	.402
89-90	Atlanta	60	48	1477	654	275	544	.506	2	13	.154	102	135	.756	27	72	99	154	115	0	28	3	90	24.6	10.9	1.7	2.6	.361
90-91	Atlanta	79	2	1863	1078	397	862	.461	14	49	.286	270	316	.854	34	125	159	217	145	0	45	6	111	23.6	13.6	2.0	2.7	.472
91-92	Cleveland	76	2	1637	779	316	659	.480	2	17	.118	145	171	.848	19	93	112	159	116	0	36	5	91	21.5	10.3	1.5	2.1	.380
92-93	Cleveland	41	0	497	223	83	200	.415	1	6	.167	56	72	.778	4	25	29	54	39	0	9	5	21	12.1	5.4	0.7	1.3	.335
93-94	Cleveland	51	1	814	338	130	273	.476	5	19	.263	73	97	.753	7	32	39	83	66	0	22	1	41	16.0	6.6	0.8	1.6	.338
94-95	Cleveland	28	0	280	116	43	114	.377	11	31	.355	19	26	.731	3	8	11	37	28	0	8	1	17	10.0	4.1	0.4	1.3	.268
NBA Season Totals		612	62	10910	5338	2054	4430	.464	62	227	.273	1168	1472	.793	178	646	824	1257	874	0	273	43	655	17.8	8.7	1.3	2.1	....
85-86	Atlanta	6	0	27	11	4	11	.364	0	1	.000	3	4	.750	0	4	4	2	5	0	2	0	3	4.5	1.8	0.7	0.3	.246
86-87	Atlanta	8	0	78	53	15	34	.441	2	5	.400	21	23	.913	2	8	10	8	13	0	1	0	7	9.8	6.6	1.3	1.0	.521
87-88	Atlanta	12	0	166	81	32	67	.478	0	2	.000	17	25	.680	2	18	20	26	14	0	2	0	11	13.8	6.8	1.7	2.2	.459
88-89	Atlanta	5	0	118	49	20	46	.435	0	6	.000	9	12	.750	5	8	13	16	13	0	2	0	5	23.6	9.8	2.6	3.2	.371
90-91	Atlanta	5	0	107	58	16	44	.364	2	5	.400	24	25	.960	4	6	10	11	11	0	1	0	9	21.4	11.6	2.0	2.2	.373
91-92	Cleveland	15	0	202	89	34	82	.415	0	2	.000	21	23	.913	4	8	12	15	11	0	5	1	18	13.5	5.9	0.8	1.0	.269
92-93	Cleveland	1	0	6	0	0	1	.000	0	0	.000	0	0	.000	0	1	1	1	2	0	0	0	2	6.0	0.0	1.0	1.0	-.289
93-94	Cleveland	1	0	8	0	0	1	.000	0	0	.000	0	0	.000	1	1	1	2	0	0	0	0	0	8.0	0.0	1.0	1.0	.021
94-95	Cleveland	2	0	7	4	2	3	.667	0	1	.000	0	0	.000	0	0	0	1	1	0	0	0	0	3.5	2.0	0.0	0.5	.522
NBA Playoff Totals		55	0	719	345	123	289	.426	4	22	.182	95	112	.848	17	54	71	81	72	0	13	1	55	13.1	6.3	1.3	1.5	....

• BATTLE, Kenny
Kenneth R. Battle

Born: Oct. 10, 1964. Aurora, IL, United States.   Height: 6'6".   Weight: 210 lbs.   Drafted: 1989   College: Illinois

YEAR	TEAM	GP	GS	MIN	PTS	FGM	FGA	FG%	3PM	3PA	3P%	FTM	FTA	FT%	ORB	DRB	TRB	AST	PF	DQ	STL	BLK	TO	MPG	PPG	RPG	APG	PCM
89-90	Phoenix	59	8	729	242	93	170	.547	1	4	.250	55	82	.671	44	80	124	38	94	2	35	11	30	12.4	4.1	2.1	0.6	.391
90-91	Phoenix	16	4	263	96	38	86	.442	0	2	.000	20	29	.690	21	32	53	15	25	0	19	6	18	16.4	6.0	3.3	0.9	.408
90-91	Denver	40	4	682	243	95	196	.485	3	22	.136	50	64	.781	62	61	123	47	83	0	41	12	36	17.1	6.1	3.1	1.2	.417
91-92	Boston	8	0	46	14	3	4	.750	0	0	.000	8	8	1.000	3	6	9	0	4	0	1	0	2	5.8	1.8	1.1	0.0	.465
91-92	Golden State	8	0	46	18	8	13	.615	0	1	.000	2	4	.500	1	6	7	4	6	0	1	2	5	5.8	2.3	0.9	0.5	.464
92-93	Boston	3	1	29	14	6	13	.462	0	1	.000	2	2	1.000	7	4	11	2	2	0	1	0	2	9.7	4.7	3.7	0.7	.621
NBA Season Totals		134	17	1795	627	243	482	.504	4	30	.133	137	189	.725	138	189	327	106	214	2	98	31	90	13.4	4.7	2.4	0.8	....
89-90	Phoenix	8	0	34	9	4	13	.308	0	0	.000	1	1	1.000	1	4	5	0	5	0	0	0	2	4.3	1.1	0.6	0.0	.030
NBA Playoff Totals		8	0	34	9	4	13	.308	0	0	.000	1	1	1.000	1	4	5	0	5	0	0	0	2	4.3	1.1	0.6	0.0	....

• BATTON, Dave
David Robert Batton

Born: Mar. 26, 1956. Baltimore, MD, United States.   Height: 6'10".   Weight: 240 lbs.   Drafted: 1978   College: Notre Dame

YEAR	TEAM	GP	GS	MIN	PTS	FGM	FGA	FG%	3PM	3PA	3P%	FTM	FTA	FT%	ORB	DRB	TRB	AST	PF	DQ	STL	BLK	TO	MPG	PPG	RPG	APG	PCM
82-83	Washington	54	5	558	178	85	191	.445	0	3	.000	8	17	.471	45	74	119	29	56	0	15	13	27	10.3	3.3	2.2	0.5	.346
83-84	San Antonio	4	0	31	10	5	10	.500	0	0	.000	0	0	.000	1	3	4	3	5	0	0	3	4	7.8	2.5	1.0	0.8	.291
NBA Season Totals		58	5	589	188	90	201	.448	0	3	.000	8	17	.471	46	77	123	32	61	0	15	16	31	10.2	3.2	2.1	0.6	....

• BATTS, Lloyd
Lloyd Batts

Born: May 9, 1951. Chicago, IL, United States. Height: 6'4". Weight: 185 lbs. Drafted: 1974 College: Cincinnati

YEAR TEAM	GP	GS	MIN	PTS	FGM	FGA	FG%	3PM	3PA	3P%	FTM	FTA	FT%	ORB	DRB	TRB	AST	PF	DQ	STL	BLK	TO	MPG	PPG	RPG	APG	PCM
74-75 Virginia-A	58	....	1317	598	249	680	.366	42	147	.286	58	94	.617	71	126	197	106	104	....	73	6	89	22.7	10.3	3.4	1.8	.339
ABA Season Totals	58	....	1317	598	249	680	.366	42	147	.286	58	94	.617	71	126	197	106	104	....	73	6	89	22.7	10.3	3.4	1.8	....

• BAUM, Johnny
John Baum

Born: June 17, 1946. Philadelphia, PA, United States. Height: 6'5". Weight: 200 lbs. Drafted: 1969 College: Temple

YEAR TEAM	GP	GS	MIN	PTS	FGM	FGA	FG%	3PM	3PA	3P%	FTM	FTA	FT%	ORB	DRB	TRB	AST	PF	DQ	STL	BLK	TO	MPG	PPG	RPG	APG	PCM
69-70 Chicago	3	....	13	6	3	11	.273	....	....	....	0	0	.000	....	....	4	0	1	0	....	....	....	4.3	2.0	1.3	0.0	.157
70-71 Chicago	62	....	543	286	123	293	.420	....	....	....	40	58	.690	....	....	125	31	55	0	....	....	....	8.8	4.6	2.0	0.5	.463
71-72 New York-A	44	....	551	247	103	170	.606	0	0	.000	41	52	.788	54	81	135	17	75	0	....	....	24	12.5	5.6	3.1	0.4	.523
72-73 New York-A	75	....	1071	549	221	438	.505	0	2	.000	107	143	.748	75	126	201	31	99	0	....	....	76	14.3	7.3	2.7	0.4	.474
73-74 Indiana-A	13	....	113	36	17	36	.472	0	0	.000	2	4	.500	12	13	25	2	17	....	6	2	6	8.7	2.8	1.9	0.2	.312
73-74 Memphis-A	47	....	1106	374	163	364	.448	0	0	.000	48	57	.842	69	107	176	60	84	....	30	14	41	23.5	8.0	3.7	1.3	.345
NBA Season Totals	65	....	556	292	126	304	.414	....	....	....	40	58	.690	....	....	129	31	56	0	....	....	....	8.6	4.5	2.0	0.5	....
ABA Season Totals	179	....	2841	1206	504	1008	.500	0	2	.000	198	256	.773	210	327	537	110	275	0	36	16	147	15.9	6.7	3.0	0.6	....
Career Totals	244	....	3397	1498	630	1312	.480	0	2	.000	238	314	.758	210	327	666	141	331	0	36	16	147	13.9	6.1	2.7	0.6	....
70-71 Chicago	2	....	5	0	0	0	.000	....	....	....	0	0	.000	....	....	1	0	2	0	....	....	....	2.5	0.0	0.5	0.0	.000
71-72 New York-A	17	....	302	128	59	107	.551	0	0	.000	10	16	.625	....	....	72	7	34	....	....	....	21	17.8	7.5	4.2	0.4	.461
72-73 New York-A	5	....	191	94	41	78	.526	0	0	.000	12	17	.706	10	11	21	4	20	0	....	....	8	38.2	18.8	4.2	0.8	.381
73-74 Indiana-A	11	....	107	40	17	32	.531	0	0	.000	6	6	1.000	8	12	20	2	12	....	5	1	5	9.7	3.6	1.8	0.2	.387
NBA Playoff Totals	2	....	5	0	0	0	.000	....	....	....	0	0	.000	....	....	1	0	2	0	....	....	....	2.5	0.0	0.5	0.0	....
ABA Playoff Totals	33	....	600	262	117	217	.539	0	0	.000	28	39	.718	18	23	113	13	66	0	5	1	34	18.2	7.9	3.4	0.4	....
Career Playoff Totals	35	....	605	262	117	217	.539	0	0	.000	28	39	.718	18	23	114	13	68	0	5	1	34	17.3	7.5	3.3	0.4	....

• BAUMHOLTZ, Frankie
Frank Conrad Baumholtz

Born: Oct. 7, 1918. Midvale, OH, United States. Died: Dec.14, 1997. Height: 5'10". Weight: 170 lbs. Drafted: — College: Ohio University

YEAR TEAM	GP	GS	MIN	PTS	FGM	FGA	FG%	3PM	3PA	3P%	FTM	FTA	FT%	ORB	DRB	TRB	AST	PF	DQ	STL	BLK	TO	MPG	PPG	RPG	APG	PCM
45-46 Youngstown-N	26	....	....	274	99	....	....	....	....	....	76	107	.710	....	....	....	....	....	....	....	....	....	....	10.5	....	....	....
46-47 Cleveland	45	....	....	631	255	856	.298	....	....	....	121	156	.776	....	....	....	54	93	....	....	....	....	....	14.0	....	1.2	....
NBA Season Totals	45	....	....	631	255	856	.298	....	....	....	121	156	.776	....	....	....	54	93	....	....	....	....	....	14.0	....	1.2	....
NBL Season Totals	26	....	....	274	99	....	....	....	....	....	76	107	....	....	....	....	....	....	....	....	....	....	....	10.5	....	....	....
Career Totals	71	....	....	905	354	856	....	....	....	....	197	263	....	....	....	....	54	93	....	....	....	....	....	12.7	....	0.8	....

• BAXTER, Lonny
Lonny Leroy Baxter

Born: Jan. 27, 1979. Silver Spring, MD, United States. Height: 6'8". Weight: 260 lbs. Drafted: 2002 College: Maryland

YEAR TEAM	GP	GS	MIN	PTS	FGM	FGA	FG%	3PM	3PA	3P%	FTM	FTA	FT%	ORB	DRB	TRB	AST	PF	DQ	STL	BLK	TO	MPG	PPG	RPG	APG	PCM
02-03 Chicago	55	0	682	262	96	206	.466	0	2	.000	70	103	.680	65	100	165	16	135	1	9	22	46	12.4	4.8	3.0	0.3	.351
NBA Season Totals	55	0	682	262	96	206	.466	0	2	.000	70	103	.680	65	100	165	16	135	1	9	22	46	12.4	4.8	3.0	0.3	....

• BAYLOR, Elgin
Elgin Gay Baylor

Born: Sept. 16, 1934. Washington, DC, United States. Height: 6'5". Weight: 225 lbs. Drafted: 1958 College: Seattle HOF: 1977

YEAR TEAM	GP	GS	MIN	PTS	FGM	FGA	FG%	3PM	3PA	3P%	FTM	FTA	FT%	ORB	DRB	TRB	AST	PF	DQ	STL	BLK	TO	MPG	PPG	RPG	APG	PCM
58-59 Minneapolis	70	....	2855	1742	605	1482	.408	....	....	....	532	685	.777	....	....	1050	287	270	4	....	....	....	40.8	24.9	15.0	4.1	.725
59-60 Minneapolis	70	....	2873	2074	755	1781	.424	....	....	....	564	770	.732	....	....	1150	243	234	2	....	....	....	41.0	29.6	16.4	3.5	.802
60-61 LA Lakers	73	....	3133	2538	931	2166	.430	....	....	....	676	863	.783	....	....	1447	371	279	3	....	....	....	42.9	34.8	19.8	5.1	.952
61-62 LA Lakers	48	....	2129	1836	680	1588	.428	....	....	....	476	631	.754	....	....	892	222	155	1	....	....	....	44.4	38.3	18.6	4.6	.927
62-63 LA Lakers	80	....	3370	2719	1029	2273	.453	....	....	....	661	790	.837	....	....	1146	386	226	1	....	....	....	42.1	34.0	14.3	4.8	.881
63-64 LA Lakers	78	....	3164	1983	756	1778	.425	....	....	....	471	586	.804	....	....	936	347	235	1	....	....	....	40.6	25.4	12.0	4.4	.697
64-65 LA Lakers	74	....	3056	2009	763	1903	.401	....	....	....	483	610	.792	....	....	950	280	235	0	....	....	....	41.3	27.1	12.8	3.8	.677
65-66 LA Lakers	65	....	1975	1079	415	1034	.401	....	....	....	249	337	.739	....	....	621	224	157	0	....	....	....	30.4	16.6	9.6	3.4	.636
66-67 LA Lakers	70	....	2706	1862	711	1658	.429	....	....	....	440	541	.813	....	....	898	215	211	1	....	....	....	38.7	26.6	12.8	3.1	.723
67-68 LA Lakers	77	....	3029	2002	757	1709	.443	....	....	....	488	621	.786	....	....	941	355	232	0	....	....	....	39.3	26.0	12.2	4.6	.751
68-69 LA Lakers	76	....	3064	1881	730	1632	.447	....	....	....	421	567	.743	....	....	805	408	204	0	....	....	....	40.3	24.8	10.6	5.4	.695
69-70 LA Lakers	54	....	2213	1298	511	1051	.486	....	....	....	276	357	.773	....	....	559	292	132	1	....	....	....	41.0	24.0	10.4	5.4	.700
70-71 LA Lakers	2	....	57	20	8	19	.421	....	....	....	4	6	.667	....	....	11	2	6	0	....	....	....	28.5	10.0	5.5	1.0	.331
71-72 LA Lakers	9	....	239	106	42	97	.433	....	....	....	22	27	.815	....	....	57	18	20	0	....	....	....	26.6	11.8	6.3	2.0	.491
NBA Season Totals	846	....	33863	23149	8693	20171	.431	....	....	....	5763	7391	.780	....	....	11463	3650	2596	14	....	....	....	40.0	27.4	13.5	4.3	....
58-59 Minneapolis	13	....	556	331	122	303	.403	....	....	....	87	113	.770	....	....	156	43	52	0	....	....	....	42.8	25.5	12.0	3.3	.605
59-60 Minneapolis	9	....	408	301	111	234	.474	....	....	....	79	94	.840	....	....	128	31	38	0	....	....	....	45.3	33.4	14.2	3.4	.792
60-61 LA Lakers	12	....	540	457	170	352	.483	....	....	....	117	142	.824	....	....	183	55	44	1	....	....	....	45.0	38.1	15.3	4.6	.925
61-62 LA Lakers	13	....	571	502	186	425	.438	....	....	....	130	168	.774	....	....	230	47	45	1	....	....	....	43.9	38.6	17.7	3.6	.910
62-63 LA Lakers	13	....	562	424	160	362	.442	....	....	....	104	126	.825	....	....	177	58	48	0	....	....	....	43.2	32.6	13.6	4.5	.795
63-64 LA Lakers	5	....	221	121	45	119	.378	....	....	....	31	40	.775	....	....	58	28	17	0	....	....	....	44.2	24.2	11.6	5.6	.600
64-65 LA Lakers	1	....	5	0	0	2	.000	....	....	....	0	0	.000	....	....	0	1	0	0	....	....	....	5.0	0.0	0.0	1.0	-.061
65-66 LA Lakers	14	....	586	375	145	328	.442	....	....	....	85	105	.810	....	....	197	52	38	0	....	....	....	41.9	26.8	14.1	3.7	.728
66-67 LA Lakers	3	....	121	71	28	76	.368	....	....	....	15	20	.750	....	....	39	9	6	0	....	....	....	40.3	23.7	13.0	3.0	.581
67-68 LA Lakers	15	....	633	428	176	376	.468	....	....	....	76	112	.679	....	....	218	60	41	0	....	....	....	42.2	28.5	14.5	4.0	.764
68-69 LA Lakers	18	....	640	277	107	278	.385	....	....	....	63	100	.630	....	....	166	74	56	0	....	....	....	35.6	15.4	9.2	4.1	.500
69-70 LA Lakers	18	....	667	336	138	296	.466	....	....	....	60	81	.741	....	....	173	83	50	1	....	....	....	37.1	18.7	9.6	4.6	.616
NBA Playoff Totals	134	....	5510	3623	1388	3151	.440	....	....	....	847	1101	.769	....	....	1725	541	435	3	....	....	....	41.1	27.0	12.9	4.0	....

YEAR	TEAM	GP	GS	MIN	PTS	FGM	FGA	FG%	3PM	3PA	3P%	FTM	FTA	FT%	ORB	DRB	TRB	AST	PF	DQ	STL	BLK	TO	MPG	PPG	RPG	APG	PCM

• BAYNE, Howard   Howard Edgar Bayne

Born: July 28, 1942.   Height: 6'6".   Weight: 235 lbs.   Drafted: 1966   College: Tennessee

YEAR	TEAM	GP	GS	MIN	PTS	FGM	FGA	FG%	3PM	3PA	3P%	FTM	FTA	FT%	ORB	DRB	TRB	AST	PF	DQ	STL	BLK	TO	MPG	PPG	RPG	APG	PCM
67-68	Kentucky-A	69	....	1181	338	130	361	.360	1	7	.143	77	143	.538	....	....	456	71	199	6	....	....	117	17.1	4.9	6.6	1.0	.422
ABA Season Totals		69	....	1181	338	130	361	.360	1	7	.143	77	143	.538	....	....	456	71	199	6	....	....	117	17.1	4.9	6.6	1.0	....
67-68	Kentucky-A	5	....	85	12	3	19	.158	0	1	.000	6	11	.545	....	....	23	5	12	0	....	....	7	17.0	2.4	4.6	1.0	.195
ABA Playoff Totals		5	....	85	12	3	19	.158	0	1	.000	6	11	.545	....	....	23	5	12	0	....	....	7	17.0	2.4	4.6	1.0	....

• BAZAREVICH, Sergei   Sergei Bazarevich

Born: Mar. 16, 1965. Russia.   Height: 6'2".   Weight: 168 lbs.   Drafted: —   College: none

YEAR	TEAM	GP	GS	MIN	PTS	FGM	FGA	FG%	3PM	3PA	3P%	FTM	FTA	FT%	ORB	DRB	TRB	AST	PF	DQ	STL	BLK	TO	MPG	PPG	RPG	APG	PCM
94-95	Atlanta	10	0	74	30	11	22	.500	1	6	.167	7	9	.778	1	6	7	14	10	0	1	1	7	7.4	3.0	0.7	1.4	.416
NBA Season Totals		10	0	74	30	11	22	.500	1	6	.167	7	9	.778	1	6	7	14	10	0	1	1	7	7.4	3.0	0.7	1.4	....

• BEACH, Ed   Edward Leon Beach Jr.

Born: Jan. 25, 1929.   Height: 6'3".   Weight: 200 lbs.   Drafted: 1950   College: West Virginia

YEAR	TEAM	GP	GS	MIN	PTS	FGM	FGA	FG%	3PM	3PA	3P%	FTM	FTA	FT%	ORB	DRB	TRB	AST	PF	DQ	STL	BLK	TO	MPG	PPG	RPG	APG	PCM
50-51	Min/Tri	12	....	....	22	8	38	.211	....	....	....	6	9	.667	....	....	25	3	14	0	....	....	....	1.8	2.1	0.3	....	....
NBA Season Totals		12	....	....	22	8	38	.211	....	....	....	6	9	.667	....	....	25	3	14	0	....	....	....	1.8	2.1	0.3	....	....

• BEARD, Al   Albert Beard

Born: Apr. 27, 1942. Fort Valley, GA, United States.   Height: 6'9".   Weight: 200 lbs.   Drafted: —   College: Norfolk State

YEAR	TEAM	GP	GS	MIN	PTS	FGM	FGA	FG%	3PM	3PA	3P%	FTM	FTA	FT%	ORB	DRB	TRB	AST	PF	DQ	STL	BLK	TO	MPG	PPG	RPG	APG	PCM
67-68	New Jersey-A	12	....	118	30	12	23	.522	0	0	.000	6	11	.545	....	....	46	0	39	1	....	....	12	9.8	2.5	3.8	0.0	.346
ABA Season Totals		12	....	118	30	12	23	.522	0	0	.000	6	11	.545	....	....	46	0	39	1	....	....	12	9.8	2.5	3.8	0.0	....

• BEARD, Butch   Alfred (Butch) Beard Jr.

Born: May 4, 1947. Hardinsburg, KY, United States.   Height: 6'3".   Weight: 185 lbs.   Drafted: 1969   College: Louisville

YEAR	TEAM	GP	GS	MIN	PTS	FGM	FGA	FG%	3PM	3PA	3P%	FTM	FTA	FT%	ORB	DRB	TRB	AST	PF	DQ	STL	BLK	TO	MPG	PPG	RPG	APG	PCM
69-70	Atlanta	72	....	941	501	183	392	.467	....	....	....	135	163	.828	....	....	140	121	124	0	....	....	....	13.1	7.0	1.9	1.7	.541
71-72	Cleveland	68	....	2434	1048	394	849	.464	....	....	....	260	342	.760	....	....	276	456	213	2	....	....	....	35.8	15.4	4.1	6.7	.527
72-73	Seattle	73	....	1403	482	191	435	.439	....	....	....	100	140	.714	....	....	174	247	139	0	....	....	....	19.2	6.6	2.4	3.4	.447
73-74	Golden State	79	....	2134	805	316	617	.512	....	....	....	173	234	.739	136	253	389	300	241	11	105	9	....	27.0	10.2	4.9	3.8	.514
74-75	Golden State	82	....	2521	1048	408	773	.528	....	....	....	232	279	.832	116	200	316	345	297	9	132	11	....	30.7	12.8	3.9	4.2	.498
75-76	Cleveland	15	....	255	97	35	90	.389	....	....	....	27	37	.730	14	29	43	45	36	0	10	2	....	17.0	6.5	2.9	3.0	.464
75-76	New York	60	....	1449	503	193	406	.475	....	....	....	117	155	.755	89	178	267	173	180	2	71	6	....	24.2	8.4	4.5	2.9	.451
76-77	New York	70	....	1082	371	148	293	.505	....	....	....	75	109	.688	50	113	163	144	137	0	57	5	....	15.5	5.3	2.3	2.1	.440
77-78	New York	79	....	1979	745	308	614	.502	....	....	....	129	160	.806	76	188	264	339	201	2	117	3	150	25.1	9.4	3.3	4.3	.486
78-79	New York	7	....	85	22	11	26	.423	....	....	....	0	0	.000	1	9	10	19	13	0	7	0	10	12.1	3.1	1.4	2.7	.352
NBA Season Totals		605	....	14283	5622	2187	4495	.487	....	....	....	1248	1619	.771	482	970	2042	2189	1581	26	499	36	160	23.6	9.3	3.4	3.6	....
69-70	Atlanta	9	....	146	81	31	65	.477	....	....	....	19	26	.731	....	....	26	8	19	0	....	....	....	16.2	9.0	2.9	0.9	.490
74-75	Golden State	17	....	448	154	60	146	.411	....	....	....	34	53	.642	23	49	72	53	64	1	24	2	....	26.4	9.1	4.2	3.1	.374
77-78	New York	6	....	160	54	24	48	.500	....	....	....	6	10	.600	7	14	21	27	22	0	10	2	11	26.7	9.0	3.5	4.5	.445
NBA Playoff Totals		32	....	754	289	115	259	.444	....	....	....	59	89	.663	30	63	119	88	105	1	34	4	11	23.6	9.0	3.7	2.8	....

• BEARD, Ralph   Ralph Milton Beard Jr.

Born: Dec. 2, 1927. Hardinsburg, KY, United States.   Height: 5'10".   Weight: 175 lbs.   Drafted: 1949   College: Kentucky

YEAR	TEAM	GP	GS	MIN	PTS	FGM	FGA	FG%	3PM	3PA	3P%	FTM	FTA	FT%	ORB	DRB	TRB	AST	PF	DQ	STL	BLK	TO	MPG	PPG	RPG	APG	PCM
49-50	Indianapolis	60	....	....	895	340	936	.363	....	....	....	215	282	.762	....	....	....	233	132	....	....	....	....	14.9	....	3.9	....	....
50-51	Indianapolis	66	....	....	1111	409	1110	.368	....	....	....	293	378	.775	....	....	251	318	96	0	....	....	....	16.8	3.8	4.8	....	....
NBA Season Totals		126	....	....	2006	749	2046	.366	....	....	....	508	660	.770	....	....	251	551	228	0	....	....	....	15.9	2.0	4.4	....	....
49-50	Indianapolis	5	....	....	66	22	70	.314	....	....	....	22	28	.786	....	....	....	22	11	....	....	....	....	13.2	....	4.4	....	....
50-51	Indianapolis	3	....	....	66	27	61	.443	....	....	....	12	17	.706	....	....	12	13	6	0	....	....	....	22.0	4.0	4.3	....	....
NBA Playoff Totals		8	....	....	132	49	131	.374	....	....	....	34	45	.756	....	....	12	35	17	0	....	....	....	16.5	1.5	4.4	....	....

• BEASLEY, Charles   Charles P. Beasley

Born: Sept. 23, 1945. Shawnee, OK, United States.   Height: 6'5".   Weight: 190 lbs.   Drafted: 1967   College: Southern Methodist

YEAR	TEAM	GP	GS	MIN	PTS	FGM	FGA	FG%	3PM	3PA	3P%	FTM	FTA	FT%	ORB	DRB	TRB	AST	PF	DQ	STL	BLK	TO	MPG	PPG	RPG	APG	PCM
67-68	Dallas-A	78	....	2969	1036	374	758	.493	3	13	.231	285	327	**.872**	....	....	295	290	202	3	....	....	189	38.1	13.3	3.8	3.7	.404
68-69	Dallas-A	75	....	1719	602	220	506	.435	1	15	.067	161	192	.839	22	136	158	208	158	0	....	....	129	22.9	8.0	2.1	2.8	.377
69-70	Dallas-A	80	....	2150	834	292	667	.438	19	72	.264	231	262	.882	32	173	205	280	222	2	....	....	179	26.9	10.4	2.6	3.5	.418
70-71	Florida-A	5	....	23	11	5	11	.455	0	2	.000	1	2	.500	0	1	1	2	2	0	....	....	1	4.6	2.2	0.2	0.4	.356
70-71	Texas-A	43	....	486	150	52	125	.416	7	24	.292	39	47	.830	13	32	45	80	67	0	....	....	44	11.3	3.5	1.0	1.9	.398
ABA Season Totals		281	....	7347	2633	943	2067	.456	30	126	.238	717	830	.864	67	342	704	860	651	5	....	....	542	26.1	9.4	2.5	3.1	....
67-68	Dallas-A	8	....	345	146	55	115	.478	0	2	.000	36	43	.837	....	....	20	28	27	0	....	....	24	43.1	18.3	2.5	3.5	.381
68-69	Dallas-A	7	....	198	62	22	53	.415	1	5	.200	17	23	.739	2	11	13	24	13	0	....	....	17	28.3	8.9	1.9	3.4	.332
68-69	Dallas-A	5	....	110	45	18	36	.500	1	4	.250	8	9	.889	4	6	10	23	....	1	....	....	5	22.0	9.0	2.0	4.6	....
70-71	Texas-A	3	....	45	11	4	14	.286	1	7	.143	2	3	.667	1	6	7	5	8	0	....	....	1	15.0	3.7	2.3	1.7	.244
ABA Playoff Totals		23	....	698	264	99	218	.454	3	18	.167	63	78	.808	7	23	50	80	48	1	....	....	47	30.3	11.5	2.2	3.5	....

• BEASLEY, John

John Michael Beasley

Born: Feb. 5, 1944. Texarkana, TX, United States. Height: 6'9". Weight: 225 lbs. Drafted: 1966 College: Texas A&M

YEAR	TEAM	GP	GS	MIN	PTS	FGM	FGA	FG%	3PM	3PA	3P%	FTM	FTA	FT%	ORB	DRB	TRB	AST	PF	DQ	STL	BLK	TO	MPG	PPG	RPG	APG	PCM
67-68	Dallas-A	77	....	2840	1515	622	1264	.492	0	2	.000	271	322	.842	278	704	982	112	245	3	....	....	107	36.9	19.7	12.8	1.5	.636
68-69	Dallas-A	78	....	3050	1505	585	1200	.488	3	10	.300	332	402	.826	248	582	830	110	259	5	....	....	136	39.1	19.3	10.6	1.4	.549
69-70	Dallas-A	84	....	3066	1539	626	1254	.499	3	8	**.375**	284	347	.818	303	703	1006	132	278	4	....	....	175	36.5	18.3	12.0	1.6	.609
70-71	Texas-A	83	....	2691	1316	532	1070	.497	16	58	.276	236	285	.828	303	462	765	147	206	0	....	....	109	32.4	15.9	9.2	1.8	.584
71-72	Dallas-A	12	....	268	108	42	85	.494	0	2	.000	24	29	.828	30	60	90	13	26	0	....	....	12	22.3	9.0	7.5	1.1	.561
71-72	Utah-A	58	....	617	225	90	199	.452	8	23	.348	37	46	.804	70	130	200	26	81	0	....	....	24	10.6	3.9	3.4	0.4	.477
72-73	Utah-A	71	....	934	519	214	417	.513	29	89	.326	62	70	.886	82	182	264	43	142	0	....	....	39	13.2	7.3	3.7	0.6	.593
73-74	Utah-A	43	....	481	182	75	181	.414	22	64	.344	10	11	.909	45	75	120	19	57	....	7	10	21	11.2	4.2	2.8	0.4	.397
ABA Season Totals		506	....	13947	6909	2786	5670	.491	81	256	.316	1256	1512	.831	1359	2898	4257	602	1294	12	7	10	623	27.6	13.7	8.4	1.2	....
67-68	Dallas-A	8	....	332	170	63	133	.474	1	2	.500	43	51	.843	29	72	101	10	21	0	....	....	15	41.5	21.3	12.6	1.3	.589
68-69	Dallas-A	7	....	240	122	46	94	.489	0	1	.000	30	34	.882	26	47	73	8	27	0	....	....	12	34.3	17.4	10.4	1.1	.580
68-69	Dallas-A	6	....	219	108	50	86	.581	0	2	.000	8	9	.889	21	43	64	19	....	1	....	....	9	36.5	18.0	10.7	3.2	....
70-71	Texas-A	4	....	115	46	20	52	.385	2	8	.250	4	5	.800	16	26	42	6	9	0	....	....	7	28.8	11.5	10.5	1.5	.497
71-72	Utah-A	9	....	168	42	18	34	.529	1	6	.167	5	5	1.000	13	39	52	9	21	0	....	....	2	18.7	4.7	5.8	1.0	.443
72-73	Utah-A	8	....	102	49	22	37	.595	2	8	.250	3	4	.750	8	15	23	5	14	0	....	....	2	12.8	6.1	2.9	0.6	.539
73-74	Utah-A	9	....	98	23	9	29	.310	2	9	.222	3	4	.750	6	15	21	5	13	....	0	2	5	10.9	2.6	2.3	0.6	.240
ABA Playoff Totals		51	....	1274	560	228	465	.490	8	36	.222	96	112	.857	119	257	376	62	105	1	0	2	52	25.0	11.0	7.4	1.2	....

• BEATY, Frank

Frank Beaty

Born: 1922. Height: 6'2". Weight: 205 lbs. Drafted: — College: Rochester Tech

YEAR	TEAM	GP	GS	MIN	PTS	FGM	FGA	FG%	3PM	3PA	3P%	FTM	FTA	FT%	ORB	DRB	TRB	AST	PF	DQ	STL	BLK	TO	MPG	PPG	RPG	APG	PCM
46-47	Rochester-N	6	....	....	1	0	....	....	....	....	....	1	4	.250	....	....	....	....	....	....	....	....	....	....	0.2	....	....	....
NBL Season Totals		6	....	....	1	0	....	....	....	....	....	1	4	....	....	....	....	....	....	....	....	....	....	....	0.2	....	....	....
46-47	Rochester-N	2	....	....	2	1	....	....	....	....	....	0	2	.000	....	....	....	....	....	....	....	....	....	....	1.0	....	....	....
NBL Playoff Totals		2	....	....	2	1	....	....	....	....	....	0	2	....	....	....	....	....	....	....	....	....	....	....	1.0	....	....	....

• BEATY, Zelmo

Zelmo (Big Z) Beaty Jr.

Born: Oct. 25, 1939. Hillister, TX, United States. Height: 6'9". Weight: 225 lbs. Drafted: 1962 College: Prairie View A&M

YEAR	TEAM	GP	GS	MIN	PTS	FGM	FGA	FG%	3PM	3PA	3P%	FTM	FTA	FT%	ORB	DRB	TRB	AST	PF	DQ	STL	BLK	TO	MPG	PPG	RPG	APG	PCM
62-63	St. Louis	80	....	1918	814	297	677	.439	....	....	....	220	307	.717	....	....	665	85	**312**	12	....	....	....	24.0	10.2	8.3	1.1	.513
63-64	St. Louis	59	....	1922	774	287	647	.444	....	....	....	200	270	.741	....	....	633	79	262	**11**	....	....	....	32.6	13.1	10.7	1.3	.496
64-65	St. Louis	80	....	2916	1351	505	1047	.482	....	....	....	341	477	.715	....	....	966	111	328	11	....	....	....	36.5	16.9	12.1	1.4	.561
65-66	St. Louis	80	....	3072	1656	616	1301	.473	....	....	....	424	559	.758	....	....	1086	125	**344**	15	....	....	....	38.4	20.7	13.6	1.6	.630
66-67	St. Louis	48	....	1661	853	328	694	.473	....	....	....	197	260	.758	....	....	515	60	189	3	....	....	....	34.6	17.8	10.7	1.3	.568
67-68	St. Louis	82	....	3068	1733	639	1310	.488	....	....	....	455	573	.794	....	....	959	174	295	6	....	....	....	37.4	21.1	11.7	2.1	.654
68-69	Atlanta	72	....	2578	1546	588	1251	.470	....	....	....	370	506	.731	....	....	798	131	272	7	....	....	....	35.8	21.5	11.1	1.8	.636
70-71	Utah-A	76	....	2915	1744	661	1192	**.555**	2	4	.500	420	531	.791	407	783	1190	148	299	5	....	....	196	38.4	22.9	15.7	1.9	.784
71-72	Utah-A	84	....	3133	1980	729	1353	.539	0	7	.000	522	630	.829	355	755	1110	125	315	9	....	....	223	37.3	23.6	13.2	1.5	.754
72-73	Utah-A	82	....	2804	1348	521	1002	.520	0	1	.000	306	381	.803	261	540	801	125	269	3	....	79	197	34.2	16.4	9.8	1.5	.577
73-74	Utah-A	77	....	2476	1028	417	796	.524	0	1	.000	194	244	.795	170	445	615	128	229	....	62	64	110	32.2	13.4	8.0	1.7	.508
74-75	LA Lakers	69	....	1213	380	136	310	.439	....	....	....	108	135	.800	93	234	327	74	130	1	45	29	....	17.6	5.5	4.7	1.1	.436
NBA Season Totals		570	....	18348	9107	3396	7237	.469	....	....	....	2315	3087	.750	93	234	5949	839	2132	66	45	29	....	32.2	16.0	10.4	1.5	....
ABA Season Totals		319	....	11328	6100	2328	4343	.536	2	13	.154	1442	1786	.807	1193	2523	3716	526	1112	17	62	143	726	35.5	19.1	11.6	1.6	....
Career Totals		889	....	29676	15207	5724	11580	.494	2	13	.154	3757	4873	.771	1286	2757	9665	1365	3244	83	107	172	726	33.4	17.1	10.9	1.5	....
62-63	St. Louis	11	....	307	113	43	97	.443	....	....	....	27	36	.750	....	....	84	11	47	3	....	....	....	27.9	10.3	7.6	1.0	.417
63-64	St. Louis	12	....	436	172	63	121	.521	....	....	....	46	77	.597	....	....	114	12	56	1	....	....	....	36.3	14.3	9.5	1.0	.450
64-65	St. Louis	4	....	154	77	29	59	.492	....	....	....	19	25	.760	....	....	55	1	19	1	....	....	....	38.5	19.3	13.8	0.3	.570
65-66	St. Louis	10	....	418	190	73	148	.493	....	....	....	44	58	.759	....	....	131	22	38	1	....	....	....	41.8	19.0	13.1	2.2	.575
66-67	St. Louis	9	....	318	143	46	104	.442	....	....	....	51	65	.785	....	....	89	12	34	0	....	....	....	35.3	15.9	9.9	1.3	.513
67-68	St. Louis	6	....	239	129	43	92	.467	....	....	....	43	55	.782	....	....	81	15	26	1	....	....	....	39.8	21.5	13.5	2.5	.659
68-69	Atlanta	11	....	473	247	102	236	.432	....	....	....	43	64	.672	....	....	142	25	47	0	....	....	....	43.0	22.5	12.9	2.3	.538
70-71	Utah-A	18	....	698	418	157	293	.536	0	0	.000	104	123	.846	95	168	263	43	75	2	....	....	28	38.8	23.2	14.6	2.4	.765
71-72	Utah-A	11	....	443	221	74	134	.552	0	0	.000	73	88	.830	56	98	154	24	43	0	....	....	31	40.3	20.1	14.0	2.2	.689
72-73	Utah-A	10	....	387	159	58	105	.552	0	0	.000	43	52	.827	31	85	116	14	36	0	....	....	25	38.7	15.9	11.6	1.4	.559
73-74	Utah-A	13	....	472	193	80	159	.503	0	0	.000	33	40	.825	42	99	141	21	38	....	18	12	26	36.3	14.8	10.8	1.6	.532
NBA Playoff Totals		63	....	2345	1071	399	857	.466	....	....	....	273	380	.718	....	....	696	98	267	7	....	....	....	37.2	17.0	11.0	1.6	....
ABA Playoff Totals		52	....	2000	991	369	691	.534	0	0	.000	253	303	.835	224	450	674	102	192	2	18	12	110	38.5	19.1	13.0	2.0	....
Career Playoff Totals		115	....	4345	2062	768	1548	.496	0	0	.000	526	683	.770	224	450	1370	200	459	9	18	12	110	37.8	17.9	11.9	1.7	....

• BECK, Byron

A. Byron Beck

Born: Jan. 25, 1945. Ellensburg, WA, United States. Height: 6'9". Weight: 225 lbs. Drafted: 1967 College: Denver

YEAR	TEAM	GP	GS	MIN	PTS	FGM	FGA	FG%	3PM	3PA	3P%	FTM	FTA	FT%	ORB	DRB	TRB	AST	PF	DQ	STL	BLK	TO	MPG	PPG	RPG	APG	PCM
67-68	Denver-A	71	....	1623	669	275	570	.482	0	2	.000	119	159	.748	....	....	559	38	219	6	....	....	72	22.9	9.4	7.9	0.5	.508
68-69	Denver-A	71	....	2289	1030	423	843	.502	2	3	.667	182	238	.765	272	507	779	77	248	9	....	....	92	32.2	14.5	11.0	1.1	.566
69-70	Denver-A	79	....	2454	1017	440	841	.523	0	2	.000	137	174	.787	250	514	764	112	293	12	....	....	137	31.1	12.9	9.7	1.4	.536
70-71	Denver-A	84	....	2849	1142	490	1033	.474	4	14	.286	158	182	.868	280	604	884	177	273	7	....	....	160	33.9	13.6	10.5	2.1	.529
71-72	Denver-A	66	....	1816	814	337	669	.504	0	3	.000	140	166	.843	171	357	528	136	213	7	....	....	96	27.5	12.3	8.0	2.1	.569
72-73	Denver-A	77	....	2303	1092	466	879	.530	2	7	.286	158	198	.798	203	334	537	107	267	9	....	....	126	29.9	14.2	7.0	1.4	.514
73-74	Denver-A	82	....	1979	970	425	823	.516	0	1	.000	120	141	.851	164	253	417	76	233	....	48	8	83	24.1	11.8	5.1	0.9	.487

YEAR	TEAM	GP	GS	MIN	PTS	FGM	FGA	FG%	3PM	3PA	3P%	FTM	FTA	FT%	ORB	DRB	TRB	AST	PF	DQ	STL	BLK	TO	MPG	PPG	RPG	APG	PCM
74-75	Denver-A	84	....	1818	849	384	745	.515	0	1	.000	81	97	.835	127	216	343	106	270	....	59	14	76	21.6	10.1	4.1	1.3	.453
75-76	Denver-A	80	....	1586	770	334	646	.517	5	11	.455	97	116	.836	123	231	354	116	192	....	48	20	91	19.8	9.6	4.4	1.5	.531
76-77	Denver	53	....	480	250	107	246	.435	....	....	....	36	44	.818	45	51	96	33	59	1	15	1	....	9.1	4.7	1.8	0.6	.461
NBA Season Totals		53	....	480	250	107	246	.435	....	....	....	36	44	.818	45	51	96	33	59	1	15	1	....	9.1	4.7	1.8	0.6	....
ABA Season Totals		694	....	18717	8353	3574	7049	.507	13	44	.295	1192	1471	.810	1590	3016	5165	945	2208	50	155	42	933	27.0	12.0	7.4	1.4	....
Career Totals		747	....	19197	8603	3681	7295	.505	13	44	.295	1228	1515	.811	1635	3067	5261	978	2267	51	170	43	933	25.7	11.5	7.0	1.3	....
67-68	Denver-A	5	....	160	57	23	50	.460	0	0	.000	11	15	.733	29	26	55	5	21	1	....	....	7	32.0	11.4	11.0	1.0	.473
68-69	Denver-A	7	....	214	110	48	95	.505	0	1	.000	14	17	.824	....	....	63	9	23	0	....	....	13	30.6	15.7	9.0	1.3	.574
69-70	Denver-A	12	....	439	191	77	176	.438	1	4	.250	36	47	.766	36	108	144	19	41	0	....	....	24	36.6	15.9	12.0	1.6	.522
71-72	Denver-A	7	....	264	139	56	115	.487	1	4	.250	26	28	.929	28	44	72	14	29	0	....	....	15	37.7	19.9	10.3	2.0	.578
72-73	Denver-A	4	....	130	69	28	63	.444	0	0	.000	13	17	.765	19	20	39	5	16	0	....	....	9	32.5	17.3	9.8	1.3	.532
74-75	Denver-A	13	....	278	162	69	134	.515	0	0	.000	24	28	.857	21	29	50	18	44	....	4	3	21	21.4	12.5	3.8	1.4	.530
75-76	Denver-A	13	....	276	112	42	95	.442	0	1	.000	28	34	.824	19	37	56	11	41	....	4	1	16	21.2	8.6	4.3	0.8	.384
76-77	Denver	5	....	29	8	3	9	.333	....	....	....	2	2	1.000	2	4	6	1	5	0	0	0	....	5.8	1.6	1.2	0.2	.241
NBA Playoff Totals		5	....	29	8	3	9	.333	....	....	....	2	2	1.000	2	4	6	1	5	0	0	0	....	5.8	1.6	1.2	0.2	....
ABA Playoff Totals		61	....	1761	840	343	728	.471	2	10	.200	152	186	.817	152	264	479	81	215	1	8	4	105	28.9	13.8	7.9	1.3	....
Career Playoff Totals		66	....	1790	848	346	737	.469	2	10	.200	154	188	.819	154	268	485	82	220	1	8	4	105	27.1	12.8	7.3	1.2	....

• BECK, Corey
Corey Laveon Beck

Born: May 27, 1971. Memphis, TN, United States. Height: 6'1". Weight: 190 lbs. Drafted: — College: Arkansas

YEAR	TEAM	GP	GS	MIN	PTS	FGM	FGA	FG%	3PM	3PA	3P%	FTM	FTA	FT%	ORB	DRB	TRB	AST	PF	DQ	STL	BLK	TO	MPG	PPG	RPG	APG	PCM
95-96	Charlotte	5	0	33	5	2	8	.250	0	0	.000	1	2	.500	3	4	7	5	8	0	1	0	4	6.6	1.0	1.4	1.0	.127
97-98	Charlotte	59	14	738	191	73	159	.459	2	4	.500	43	59	.729	27	63	90	98	100	0	33	7	71	12.5	3.2	1.5	1.7	.298
98-99	Detroit	8	0	30	10	4	8	.500	0	0	.000	2	2	1.000	3	2	5	0	5	0	2	0	2	3.8	1.3	0.6	0.0	.289
98-99	Charlotte	16	0	150	35	14	31	.452	1	1	1.000	6	13	.462	3	20	23	20	21	0	7	2	11	9.4	2.2	1.4	1.3	.322
NBA Season Totals		88	14	951	241	93	206	.451	3	5	.600	52	76	.684	36	89	125	123	134	0	43	9	88	10.8	2.7	1.4	1.4	....
97-98	Charlotte	6	0	26	15	6	12	.500	1	2	.500	2	2	1.000	1	0	1	0	4	0	4	0	3	4.3	2.5	0.2	0.0	.366
NBA Playoff Totals		6	0	26	15	6	12	.500	1	2	.500	2	2	1.000	1	0	1	0	4	0	4	0	3	4.3	2.5	0.2	0.0	

• BECK, Ernie
Ernest Joseph Beck

Born: Dec. 11, 1931. Philadelphia, PA, United States. Height: 6'4". Weight: 190 lbs. Drafted: 1953 College: Pennsylvania

YEAR	TEAM	GP	GS	MIN	PTS	FGM	FGA	FG%	3PM	3PA	3P%	FTM	FTA	FT%	ORB	DRB	TRB	AST	PF	DQ	STL	BLK	TO	MPG	PPG	RPG	APG	PCM
53-54	Philadelphia	15	....	422	112	39	142	.275	....	....	....	34	43	.791	....	....	50	34	29	0	....	....	....	28.1	7.5	3.3	2.3	.248
55-56	Philadelphia	67	....	1007	348	136	351	.387	....	....	....	76	106	.717	....	....	196	79	86	0	....	....	....	15.0	5.2	2.9	1.2	.385
56-57	Philadelphia	72	....	1743	501	195	508	.384	....	....	....	111	157	.707	....	....	312	190	155	1	....	....	....	24.2	7.0	4.3	2.6	.381
57-58	Philadelphia	71	....	1974	714	272	683	.398	....	....	....	170	203	.837	....	....	307	190	173	2	....	....	....	27.8	10.1	4.3	2.7	.408
58-59	Philadelphia	70	....	1017	369	163	418	.390	....	....	....	43	65	.662	....	....	176	89	124	0	....	....	....	14.5	5.3	2.5	1.3	.360
59-60	Philadelphia	66	....	809	255	114	294	.388	....	....	....	27	32	.844	....	....	127	72	90	0	....	....	....	12.3	3.9	1.9	1.1	.332
60-61	St. Louis	7	....	62	19	7	21	.333	....	....	....	5	5	1.000	....	....	12	13	6	0	....	....	....	8.9	2.7	1.7	1.9	.505
60-61	Syracuse	3	....	20	7	3	8	.375	....	....	....	1	2	.500	....	....	11	2	1	0	....	....	....	6.7	2.3	3.7	0.7	.664
NBA Season Totals		371	....	7054	2325	929	2425	.383	....	....	....	467	613	.762	....	....	1191	669	664	3	....	....	....	19.0	6.3	3.2	1.8	....
55-56	Philadelphia	10	....	250	84	31	72	.431	....	....	....	22	31	.710	....	....	51	22	32	1	....	....	....	25.0	8.4	5.1	2.2	.413
56-57	Philadelphia	2	....	89	31	14	38	.368	....	....	....	3	3	1.000	....	....	10	5	4	0	....	....	....	44.5	15.5	5.0	2.5	.285
57-58	Philadelphia	8	....	156	52	23	61	.377	....	....	....	6	9	.667	....	....	32	13	16	0	....	....	....	19.5	6.5	4.0	1.6	.367
59-60	Philadelphia	4	....	22	8	4	9	.444	....	....	....	0	1	.000	....	....	6	3	1	0	....	....	....	5.5	2.0	1.5	0.8	.533
NBA Playoff Totals		24	....	517	175	72	180	.400	....	....	....	31	44	.705	....	....	99	43	53	1	....	....	....	21.5	7.3	4.1	1.8	....

• BECKER, Arthur
Arthur C. (Beck) Becker

Born: Jan. 12, 1942. Akron, OH, United States. Height: 6'7". Weight: 205 lbs. Drafted: 1964 College: Arizona State

YEAR	TEAM	GP	GS	MIN	PTS	FGM	FGA	FG%	3PM	3PA	3P%	FTM	FTA	FT%	ORB	DRB	TRB	AST	PF	DQ	STL	BLK	TO	MPG	PPG	RPG	APG	PCM
67-68	Houston-A	76	....	2689	1427	563	1204	.468	4	12	.333	297	362	.820	252	461	713	95	321	12	....	....	154	35.4	18.8	9.4	1.3	.535
68-69	Houston-A	78	....	2429	1046	423	888	.476	0	3	.000	200	240	.833	175	422	597	103	304	9	....	....	156	31.1	13.4	7.7	1.3	.465
69-70	Indiana-A	82	....	1504	729	309	593	.521	0	1	.000	111	137	.810	110	269	379	45	249	8	....	....	61	18.3	8.9	4.6	0.5	.495
70-71	Denver-A	29	....	803	440	183	365	.501	1	2	.500	73	87	.839	80	129	209	31	107	4	....	....	36	27.7	15.2	7.2	1.1	.561
70-71	Indiana-A	51	....	840	440	187	376	.497	4	6	.667	62	69	.899	71	146	217	22	153	1	....	....	41	16.5	8.6	4.3	0.4	.506
71-72	Denver-A	84	....	2193	1035	435	954	.456	0	3	.000	165	195	.846	167	304	471	113	271	5	....	....	132	26.1	12.3	5.6	1.3	.450
72-73	Dallas-A	6	....	50	20	7	12	.583	0	0	.000	6	6	1.000	4	8	12	0	3	0	....	....	4	8.3	3.3	2.0	0.0	.499
72-73	New York-A	8	....	46	23	9	16	.563	0	1	.000	5	5	1.000	1	5	6	1	3	0	....	....	1	5.8	2.9	0.8	0.1	.475
ABA Season Totals		414	....	10554	5160	2116	4408	.480	9	28	.321	919	1101	.835	860	1744	2604	410	1411	39	....	....	585	25.5	12.5	6.3	1.0	....
67-68	Houston-A	3	....	94	51	18	43	.419	0	0	.000	15	18	.833	....	....	16	5	10	0	....	....	2	31.3	17.0	5.3	1.7	.468
69-70	Indiana-A	15	....	227	93	36	69	.522	0	0	.000	21	24	.875	15	43	58	5	36	1	....	....	5	15.1	6.2	3.9	0.3	.456
71-72	Denver-A	7	....	94	34	14	31	.452	0	1	.000	6	9	.667	....	....	12	4	18	0	....	....	7	13.4	4.9	1.7	0.6	.264
ABA Playoff Totals		25	....	415	178	68	143	.476	0	1	.000	42	51	.824	15	43	86	14	64	1	....	....	14	16.6	7.1	3.4	0.6	....

• BECKER, Moe
Morris R. (Moe) Becker

Born: Feb. 24, 1917. Died: Jan.9, 1996. Height: 6'1". Weight: 185 lbs. Drafted: — College: Duquesne

YEAR	TEAM	GP	GS	MIN	PTS	FGM	FGA	FG%	3PM	3PA	3P%	FTM	FTA	FT%	ORB	DRB	TRB	AST	PF	DQ	STL	BLK	TO	MPG	PPG	RPG	APG	PCM
45-46	Youngstown-N	30	....	....	270	115	....	....	....	....	....	40	69	.580	....	....	....	....	....	....	....	....	....	9.0	....	....	....	
46-47	Pittsburgh	17	....	....	108	46	229	.201	....	....	....	16	30	.533	....	....	....	14	50	....	....	....	....	6.4	....	0.8		
46-47	Boston	6	....	....	13	5	22	.227	....	....	....	3	4	.750	....	....	....	1	15	....	....	....	....	2.2	....	0.2		
46-47	Detroit	20	....	....	41	19	107	.178	....	....	....	3	10	.300	....	....	....	15	33	....	....	....	....	2.1	....	0.8		
NBA Season Totals		43	....	....	162	70	358	.196	....	....	....	22	44	.500	....	....	....	30	98	....	....	....	....	3.8	....	0.7		
NBL Season Totals		30	....	....	270	115	....	....	....	....	....	40	69	....	....	....	....	....	....	....	....	....	....	9.0	....	....		
Career Totals		73	....	....	432	185	358	....	....	....	....	62	113	....	....	....	....	30	98	....	....	....	....	5.9	....	0.4		

BECKER, Tom
Tom Becker

Born: 1923. Height: 6'1". Weight: 180 lbs. Drafted: — College: —

YEAR TEAM	GP	GS	MIN	PTS	FGM	FGA	FG%	3PM	3PA	3P%	FTM	FTA	FT%	ORB	DRB	TRB	AST	PF	DQ	STL	BLK	TO	MPG	PPG	RPG	APG	PCM
44-45 Cleveland-N	1	....	....	0	0	....	....	....	....	....	0	....	....	....	....	....	....	....	....	....	....	....	....	0.0	....	....	....
NBL Season Totals	1	....	....	0	0	....	....	....	....	....	0	....	....	....	....	....	....	....	....	....	....	....	....	0.0	....	....	....

BEDELL, Bob
Robert George Bedell

Born: June 26, 1944. Los Angeles, CA, United States. Height: 6'7". Weight: 205 lbs. Drafted: 1966 College: Stanford

YEAR TEAM	GP	GS	MIN	PTS	FGM	FGA	FG%	3PM	3PA	3P%	FTM	FTA	FT%	ORB	DRB	TRB	AST	PF	DQ	STL	BLK	TO	MPG	PPG	RPG	APG	PCM
67-68 Anaheim-A	76	....	1492	792	325	736	.442	0	4	.000	142	190	.747	....	....	506	79	203	5	....	....	111	19.6	10.4	6.7	1.0	.576
68-69 Dallas-A	42	....	479	232	92	221	.416	0	2	.000	48	84	.571	42	74	116	30	76	1	....	....	35	11.4	5.5	2.8	0.7	.432
69-70 Dallas-A	80	....	1536	779	285	677	.421	2	10	.200	207	246	.841	153	301	454	126	192	3	....	....	145	19.2	9.7	5.7	1.6	.571
70-71 Texas-A	71	....	970	454	176	441	.399	9	42	.214	93	113	.823	138	172	310	85	124	0	....	....	79	13.7	6.4	4.4	1.2	.551
ABA Season Totals	269	....	4477	2257	878	2075	.423	11	58	.190	490	633	.774	333	547	1386	320	595	9	....	....	370	16.6	8.4	5.2	1.2	....
68-69 Dallas-A	7	....	148	94	38	70	.543	0	1	.000	18	23	.783	23	26	49	6	25	1	....	....	12	21.1	13.4	7.0	0.9	.693
68-69 Dallas-A	6	....	69	25	10	27	.370	0	1	.000	5	6	.833	6	12	18	4	....	1	....	....	9	11.5	4.2	3.0	0.7	....
70-71 Texas-A	3	....	33	6	2	17	.118	0	7	.000	2	3	.667	3	8	11	5	9	0	....	....	3	11.0	2.0	3.7	1.7	.145
ABA Playoff Totals	16	....	250	125	50	114	.439	0	9	.000	25	32	.781	32	46	78	15	34	2	....	....	24	15.6	7.8	4.9	0.9	....

BEDFORD, William
William Bedford

Born: Dec. 14, 1963. Memphis, TN, United States. Height: 7' Weight: 225 lbs. Drafted: 1986 College: Memphis State

YEAR TEAM	GP	GS	MIN	PTS	FGM	FGA	FG%	3PM	3PA	3P%	FTM	FTA	FT%	ORB	DRB	TRB	AST	PF	DQ	STL	BLK	TO	MPG	PPG	RPG	APG	PCM
86-87 Phoenix	50	18	979	334	142	358	.397	0	1	.000	50	86	.581	79	167	246	57	125	1	18	37	85	19.6	6.7	4.9	1.1	.327
87-88 Detroit	38	0	298	101	44	101	.436	0	0	.000	13	23	.565	27	38	65	4	47	0	8	17	19	7.8	2.7	1.7	0.1	.308
89-90 Detroit	42	0	246	118	54	125	.432	1	6	.167	9	22	.409	15	43	58	4	39	0	3	17	21	5.9	2.8	1.4	0.1	.345
90-91 Detroit	60	4	562	272	106	242	.438	5	13	.385	55	78	.705	55	76	131	32	76	0	2	36	30	9.4	4.5	2.2	0.5	.468
91-92 Detroit	32	0	363	114	50	121	.413	0	1	.000	14	22	.636	24	39	63	12	56	0	6	18	16	11.3	3.6	2.0	0.4	.268
92-93 San Antonio	16	0	66	25	9	27	.333	1	1	1.000	6	12	.500	1	9	10	0	15	0	0	1	2	4.1	1.6	0.6	0.0	.103
NBA Season Totals	238	30	2514	964	405	974	.416	7	22	.318	147	243	.605	201	372	573	109	358	1	37	126	173	10.6	4.1	2.4	0.5	....
89-90 Detroit	5	0	19	4	1	6	.167	0	0	.000	2	2	1.000	0	2	2	0	4	0	0	1	0	3.8	0.8	0.4	0.0	.013
90-91 Detroit	8	3	65	19	5	24	.208	0	2	.000	9	14	.643	9	13	22	4	14	0	2	4	4	8.1	2.4	2.8	0.5	.293
91-92 Detroit	1	0	9	6	3	6	.500	0	0	.000	0	0	.000	0	2	2	0	1	0	1	0	0	9.0	6.0	2.0	0.0	.615
NBA Playoff Totals	14	3	93	29	9	36	.250	0	2	.000	11	16	.688	9	17	26	4	19	0	3	5	4	6.6	2.1	1.9	0.3	....

BEENDERS, Hank
Henry G. Beenders

Born: June 2, 1916. Haarlem, Netherlands. Height: 6'6". Weight: 185 lbs. Drafted: — College: Long Island University

YEAR TEAM	GP	GS	MIN	PTS	FGM	FGA	FG%	3PM	3PA	3P%	FTM	FTA	FT%	ORB	DRB	TRB	AST	PF	DQ	STL	BLK	TO	MPG	PPG	RPG	APG	PCM
46-47 Providence	58	....	....	713	266	1016	.262	....	....	....	181	257	.704	....	....	....	37	196	....	....	....	....	12.3	....	0.6	....	
47-48 Providence	21	....	....	143	53	200	.265	....	....	....	37	58	.638	....	....	....	6	68	....	....	....	....	6.8	....	0.3	....	
47-48 Philadelphia	24	....	....	60	23	69	.333	....	....	....	14	24	.583	....	....	....	7	31	....	....	....	....	2.5	....	0.3	....	
48-49 Boston	8	....	....	19	6	28	.214	....	....	....	7	9	.778	....	....	....	3	9	....	....	....	....	2.4	....	0.4	....	
NBA Season Totals	111	....	....	935	348	1313	.265	....	....	....	239	348	.687	....	....	....	53	304	....	....	....	....	8.4	....	0.5	....	
47-48 Philadelphia	12	....	....	23	8	35	.229	....	....	....	7	13	.538	....	....	....	4	15	....	....	....	....	1.9	....	0.3	....	
NBA Playoff Totals	12	....	....	23	8	35	.229	....	....	....	7	13	.538	....	....	....	4	15	....	....	....	....	1.9	....	0.3	....	

BEERY, Don
Don Beery

Born: 1920. Height: 6' Weight: 180 lbs. Drafted: — College: none

YEAR TEAM	GP	GS	MIN	PTS	FGM	FGA	FG%	3PM	3PA	3P%	FTM	FTA	FT%	ORB	DRB	TRB	AST	PF	DQ	STL	BLK	TO	MPG	PPG	RPG	APG	PCM
41-42 Fort Wayne-N	11	....	....	8	3	....	....	....	....	....	2	....	....	....	....	....	....	....	....	....	....	....	....	0.7	....	....	....
NBL Season Totals	11	....	....	8	3	....	....	....	....	....	2	....	....	....	....	....	....	....	....	....	....	....	....	0.7	....	....	....
41-42 Fort Wayne-N	2	....	....	2	1	....	....	....	....	....	0	....	....	....	....	....	....	....	....	....	....	....	....	1.0	....	....	....
NBL Playoff Totals	2	....	....	2	1	....	....	....	....	....	0	....	....	....	....	....	....	....	....	....	....	....	....	1.0	....	....	....

BEHAGEN, Ron
Ronald Michael Behagen

Born: Jan. 14, 1951. New York, NY, United States. Height: 6'9". Weight: 185 lbs. Drafted: 1973 College: Minnesota

YEAR TEAM	GP	GS	MIN	PTS	FGM	FGA	FG%	3PM	3PA	3P%	FTM	FTA	FT%	ORB	DRB	TRB	AST	PF	DQ	STL	BLK	TO	MPG	PPG	RPG	APG	PCM
73-74 Omaha	80	....	2059	876	357	827	.432	....	....	....	162	212	.764	188	379	567	134	291	0	56	37	....	25.7	11.0	7.1	1.7	.470
74-75 Omaha	81	....	2205	865	333	834	.399	....	....	....	199	264	.754	146	446	592	153	301	8	60	42	....	27.2	10.7	7.3	1.9	.436
75-76 New Orleans	66	....	1733	760	308	691	.446	....	....	....	144	179	.804	190	363	553	139	222	6	67	26	....	26.3	11.5	8.4	2.1	.551
76-77 New Orleans	60	....	1170	516	213	509	.418	....	....	....	90	126	.714	144	287	431	83	166	1	14	19	....	19.5	8.6	7.2	1.4	.547
77-78 Atlanta	26	....	571	285	117	249	.470	....	....	....	51	70	.729	53	120	173	34	97	3	30	12	57	22.0	11.0	6.7	1.3	.517
77-78 Houston	3	....	33	14	7	11	.636	....	....	....	0	1	.000	2	5	7	2	6	0	0	1	3	11.0	4.7	2.3	0.7	.400
77-78 Indiana	51	....	1131	572	222	544	.408	....	....	....	128	176	.727	146	187	333	65	160	1	32	19	112	22.2	11.2	6.5	1.3	.451
78-79 Detroit	1	....	1	0	0	0	.000	....	....	....	0	0	.000	0	0	0	0	1	0	0	0	1	1.0	0.0	0.0	0.0	-1.35
78-79 New York	5	....	38	12	5	12	.417	....	....	....	2	2	1.000	2	9	11	2	8	0	2	0	4	7.6	2.4	2.2	0.4	.327
78-79 Kansas City	9	....	126	54	23	50	.460	....	....	....	8	11	.727	11	20	31	5	27	0	2	1	6	14.0	6.0	3.4	0.6	.373
79-80 Washington	6	....	64	23	9	23	.391	0	0	.000	5	6	.833	6	8	14	7	14	0	0	4	4	10.7	3.8	2.3	1.2	.373
NBA Season Totals	388	....	9131	3977	1594	3750	.425	0	0	.000	789	1047	.754	888	1824	2712	624	1293	19	290	160	187	23.5	10.3	7.0	1.6	....
74-75 Omaha	6	....	108	47	22	43	.512	....	....	....	3	3	1.000	4	25	29	6	28	2	1	2	....	18.0	7.8	4.8	1.0	.452
79-80 Washington	2	....	14	4	2	7	.286	0	0	.000	0	0	.000	1	1	2	3	4	0	0	0	1	7.0	2.0	1.0	1.5	.133
NBA Playoff Totals	8	....	122	51	24	50	.480	0	0	.000	3	3	1.000	5	26	31	9	32	2	1	2	1	15.3	6.4	3.9	1.1	....

YEAR	TEAM	GP	GS	MIN	PTS	FGM	FGA	FG%	3PM	3PA	3P%	FTM	FTA	FT%	ORB	DRB	TRB	AST	PF	DQ	STL	BLK	TO	MPG	PPG	RPG	APG	PCM

• BEHNKE, Elmer
Elmer H. Behnke

Born: Feb. 3, 1929. Rockford, IL, United States. Height: 6'7". Weight: 210 lbs. Drafted: 1951 College: Bradley

YEAR	TEAM	GP	GS	MIN	PTS	FGM	FGA	FG%	3PM	3PA	3P%	FTM	FTA	FT%	ORB	DRB	TRB	AST	PF	DQ	STL	BLK	TO	MPG	PPG	RPG	APG	PCM
51-52	Milwaukee	4	....	55	16	6	22	.273	....	....	....	4	7	.571	....	....	17	4	13	1	....	....	....	13.8	4.0	4.3	1.0	.294
NBA Season Totals		4	....	55	16	6	22	.273	....	....	....	4	7	.571	....	....	17	4	13	1	....	....	....	13.8	4.0	4.3	1.0	....

• BEHR, Bill
Bill Behr

Born: 1919. Height: 6'2". Weight: 190 lbs. Drafted: — College: none

YEAR	TEAM	GP	GS	MIN	PTS	FGM	FGA	FG%	3PM	3PA	3P%	FTM	FTA	FT%	ORB	DRB	TRB	AST	PF	DQ	STL	BLK	TO	MPG	PPG	RPG	APG	PCM
40-41	Hammond-N	20	....	....	70	28	....	....	....	....	....	14	....	....	....	....	....	....	....	....	....	....	....	....	3.5	....	....	....
NBL Season Totals		20	....	....	70	28	....	....	....	....	....	14	....	....	....	....	....	....	....	....	....	....	....	....	3.5	....	....	....

• BELL, Byron
Byron Bell

Born: 1914. Height: 6'3". Weight: 180 lbs. Drafted: — College: Wisconsin

YEAR	TEAM	GP	GS	MIN	PTS	FGM	FGA	FG%	3PM	3PA	3P%	FTM	FTA	FT%	ORB	DRB	TRB	AST	PF	DQ	STL	BLK	TO	MPG	PPG	RPG	APG	PCM
38-39	Oshkosh-N	1	....	....	4	1	....	....	....	....	....	2	....	....	....	....	....	....	....	....	....	....	....	....	4.0	....	....	....
NBL Season Totals		1	....	....	4	1	....	....	....	....	....	2	....	....	....	....	....	....	....	....	....	....	....	....	4.0	....	....	....

• BELL, Charlie
Charles Bell

Born: Mar. 12, 1979. Flint, MI, United States. Height: 6'3". Weight: 200 lbs. Drafted: — College: Michigan State

YEAR	TEAM	GP	GS	MIN	PTS	FGM	FGA	FG%	3PM	3PA	3P%	FTM	FTA	FT%	ORB	DRB	TRB	AST	PF	DQ	STL	BLK	TO	MPG	PPG	RPG	APG	PCM
01-02	Phoenix	5	0	42	8	3	11	.273	0	6	.000	2	2	1.000	2	2	4	2	3	0	0	0	5	8.4	1.6	0.8	0.4	.016
01-02	Dallas	2	0	2	0	0	0	.000	0	0	.000	0	0	.000	0	1	1	0	0	0	0	0	0	1.0	0.0	0.5	0.0	.453
NBA Season Totals		7	0	44	8	3	11	.273	0	6	.000	2	2	1.000	2	3	5	2	3	0	0	0	5	6.3	1.1	0.7	0.3	....

• BELL, Dennis
Dennis R. Bell

Born: June 2, 1951. Cincinnati, OH, United States. Height: 6'5". Weight: 185 lbs. Drafted: 1973 College: Drake

YEAR	TEAM	GP	GS	MIN	PTS	FGM	FGA	FG%	3PM	3PA	3P%	FTM	FTA	FT%	ORB	DRB	TRB	AST	PF	DQ	STL	BLK	TO	MPG	PPG	RPG	APG	PCM
73-74	New York	1	....	4	0	0	1	.000	....	....	....	0	0	.000	0	0	0	0	0	0	0	0	....	4.0	0.0	0.0	0.0	-.213
74-75	New York	52	....	465	156	68	181	.376	....	....	....	20	36	.556	48	57	105	25	54	0	22	9	....	8.9	3.0	2.0	0.5	.318
75-76	New York	10	....	76	19	8	21	.381	....	....	....	3	7	.429	4	10	14	3	11	0	6	1	....	7.6	1.9	1.4	0.3	.222
NBA Season Totals		63	....	545	175	76	203	.374	....	....	....	23	43	.535	52	67	119	28	65	0	28	10	....	8.7	2.8	1.9	0.4	....
74-75	New York	3	....	27	2	1	8	.125	....	....	....	0	5	.000	0	4	4	0	6	0	0	0	....	9.0	0.7	1.3	0.0	-.194
NBA Playoff Totals		3	....	27	2	1	8	.125	....	....	....	0	5	.000	0	4	4	0	6	0	0	0	....	9.0	0.7	1.3	0.0	....

• BELL, Raja
Raja Bell

Born: Sept. 19, 1976. St. Croix, Virgin Islands. Height: 6'5". Weight: 204 lbs. Drafted: — College: Florida International

YEAR	TEAM	GP	GS	MIN	PTS	FGM	FGA	FG%	3PM	3PA	3P%	FTM	FTA	FT%	ORB	DRB	TRB	AST	PF	DQ	STL	BLK	TO	MPG	PPG	RPG	APG	PCM
00-01	Philadelphia	5	0	30	5	2	7	.286	1	3	.333	0	0	.000	0	1	1	0	1	0	1	0	2	6.0	1.0	0.2	0.0	.002
01-02	Philadelphia	74	12	890	254	103	240	.429	12	44	.273	36	48	.750	31	80	111	71	109	0	21	4	48	12.0	3.4	1.5	1.0	.261
02-03	Dallas	75	32	1173	230	93	211	.441	21	51	.412	23	34	.676	47	98	145	57	134	1	52	8	43	15.6	3.1	1.9	0.8	.227
NBA Season Totals		154	44	2093	489	198	458	.432	34	98	.347	59	82	.720	78	179	257	128	244	1	74	12	93	13.6	3.2	1.7	0.8	....
00-01	Philadelphia	15	0	124	34	12	27	.444	2	8	.250	8	14	.571	4	9	13	7	20	0	15	0	5	8.3	2.3	0.9	0.5	.300
01-02	Philadelphia	3	0	8	2	1	3	.333	0	2	.000	0	0	.000	1	0	1	0	0	0	0	0	0	2.7	0.7	0.3	0.0	.137
02-03	Dallas	17	7	305	97	40	73	.548	6	13	.462	11	20	.550	13	38	51	27	41	0	5	0	6	17.9	5.7	3.0	1.6	.391
NBA Playoff Totals		35	7	437	133	53	103	.515	8	23	.348	19	34	.559	18	47	65	34	61	0	20	0	11	12.5	3.8	1.9	1.0	....

• BELL, Whitey
William Hoyet (Whitey, Popeye) Bell

Born: Sept. 13, 1932. Monticello, KY, United States. Height: 6' Weight: 180 lbs. Drafted: — College: North Carolina State

YEAR	TEAM	GP	GS	MIN	PTS	FGM	FGA	FG%	3PM	3PA	3P%	FTM	FTA	FT%	ORB	DRB	TRB	AST	PF	DQ	STL	BLK	TO	MPG	PPG	RPG	APG	PCM
59-60	New York	31	....	449	168	70	185	.378	....	....	....	28	43	.651	....	....	87	55	59	0	....	....	....	14.5	5.4	2.8	1.8	.417
60-61	New York	5	....	45	15	7	18	.389	....	....	....	1	3	.333	....	....	7	1	7	0	....	....	....	9.0	3.0	1.4	0.2	.217
NBA Season Totals		36	....	494	183	77	203	.379	....	....	....	29	46	.630	....	....	94	56	66	0	....	....	....	13.7	5.1	2.6	1.6	....

• BELLAMY, Walt
Walter Jones (Bells) Bellamy

HOF: 1993

Born: July 24, 1939. New Bern, NC, United States. Height: 6'11". Weight: 225 lbs. Drafted: 1961 College: Indiana

YEAR	TEAM	GP	GS	MIN	PTS	FGM	FGA	FG%	3PM	3PA	3P%	FTM	FTA	FT%	ORB	DRB	TRB	AST	PF	DQ	STL	BLK	TO	MPG	PPG	RPG	APG	PCM
61-62	Chicago	79	....	3344	2495	973	1875	**.519**	....	....	....	549	853	.644	....	....	1500	210	281	6	....	....	....	42.3	31.6	19.0	2.7	.894
62-63	Chicago	80	....	3306	2233	840	1595	.527	....	....	....	553	821	.674	....	....	1309	233	283	7	....	....	....	41.3	27.9	16.4	2.9	.827
63-64	Baltimore	80	....	3394	2159	811	1582	.513	....	....	....	537	825	.651	....	....	1361	126	300	7	....	....	....	42.4	27.0	17.0	1.6	.749
64-65	Baltimore	80	....	3301	1981	733	1441	.509	....	....	....	515	752	.685	....	....	1166	191	260	2	....	....	....	41.3	24.8	14.6	2.4	.720
65-66	Baltimore	8	....	268	152	56	124	.452	....	....	....	40	67	.597	....	....	102	18	32	2	....	....	....	33.5	19.0	12.8	2.3	.662
65-66	New York	72	....	3084	1668	639	1249	.512	....	....	....	390	622	.627	....	....	1152	217	262	7	....	....	....	42.8	23.2	16.0	3.0	.701
66-67	New York	79	....	3010	1499	565	1084	.521	....	....	....	369	580	.636	....	....	1064	206	275	5	....	....	....	38.1	19.0	13.5	2.6	.660
67-68	New York	82	....	2695	1372	511	944	.541	....	....	....	350	529	.662	....	....	961	164	259	3	....	....	....	32.9	16.7	11.7	2.0	.674
68-69	New York	35	....	1136	533	204	402	.507	....	....	....	125	202	.619	....	....	385	77	123	1	....	....	....	32.5	15.2	11.0	2.2	.612
68-69	Detroit	53	....	2023	994	359	701	.512	....	....	....	276	416	.663	....	....	716	99	197	4	....	....	....	38.2	18.8	13.5	1.9	.633
69-70	Detroit	56	....	1173	560	210	384	.547	....	....	....	140	249	.562	....	....	397	55	163	3	....	....	....	20.9	10.0	7.1	1.0	.595
69-70	Atlanta	23	....	855	357	141	287	.491	....	....	....	75	124	.605	....	....	310	88	97	2	....	....	....	37.2	15.5	13.5	3.8	.626
70-71	Atlanta	82	....	2908	1202	433	879	.493	....	....	....	336	556	.604	....	....	1060	230	271	4	....	....	....	35.5	14.7	12.9	2.8	.612
71-72	Atlanta	82	....	3187	1526	593	1089	.545	....	....	....	340	581	.585	....	....	1049	262	255	2	....	....	....	38.9	18.6	12.8	3.2	.655
72-73	Atlanta	74	....	2802	1193	455	901	.505	....	....	....	283	526	.538	....	....	964	179	244	1	....	....	....	37.9	16.1	13.0	2.4	.583

YEAR	TEAM	GP	GS	MIN	PTS	FGM	FGA	FG%	3PM	3PA	3P%	FTM	FTA	FT%	ORB	DRB	TRB	AST	PF	DQ	STL	BLK	TO	MPG	PPG	RPG	APG	PCM
73-74	Atlanta	77	....	2440	1011	389	801	.486	....	....	....	233	383	.608	264	476	740	189	232	2	52	48	....	31.7	13.1	9.6	2.5	.551
74-75	New Orleans	1	....	14	6	2	2	1.000	....	....	....	2	2	1.000	0	5	5	0	2	0	0	0	....	14.0	6.0	5.0	0.0	.672
NBA Season Totals		1043	....	38940	20941	7914	15340	.516	....	....	....	5113	8088	.632	264	481	14241	2544	3536	58	52	48	....	37.3	20.1	13.7	2.4	....
64-65	Baltimore	10	....	427	209	74	158	.468	....	....	....	61	92	.663			151	34	38	0	....	....	....	42.7	20.9	15.1	3.4	.646
66-67	New York	4	....	157	73	28	54	.519	....	....	....	17	29	.586			66	12	15	0	....	....	....	39.3	18.3	16.5	3.0	.691
67-68	New York	6	....	277	120	45	107	.421	....	....	....	30	48	.625			96	21	22	0	....	....	....	46.2	20.0	16.0	3.5	.565
69-70	Atlanta	9	....	368	151	59	126	.468	....	....	....	33	46	.717			140	35	32	0	....	....	....	40.9	16.8	15.6	3.9	.638
70-71	Atlanta	5	....	216	104	41	69	.594	....	....	....	22	29	.759			72	10	16	0	....	....	....	43.2	20.8	14.4	2.0	.664
71-72	Atlanta	6	....	247	111	42	86	.488	....	....	....	27	43	.628			82	11	20	0	....	....	....	41.2	18.5	13.7	1.8	.570
72-73	Atlanta	6	....	247	82	34	86	.395	....	....	....	14	31	.452			73	13	17	0	....	....	....	41.2	13.7	12.2	2.2	.406
NBA Playoff Totals		46	....	1939	850	323	686	.471	....	....	....	204	318	.642			680	136	160	0	....	....	....	42.2	18.5	14.8	3.0	....

● BELLINGHAM, Ray

Ray Bellingham

Born: 1916.　Height: 6'8".　Weight: 200 lbs.　Drafted: —　College: Westminster (PA)

YEAR	TEAM	GP	GS	MIN	PTS	FGM	FGA	FG%	3PM	3PA	3P%	FTM	FTA	FT%	ORB	DRB	TRB	AST	PF	DQ	STL	BLK	TO	MPG	PPG	RPG	APG	PCM
45-46	Youngstown-N	1	....	....	1	0	....	....	....	....	....	1	....	....	....	....	....	....	....	....	....	....	....	....	1.0	....	....	....
NBL Season Totals		1	....	....	1	0	....	....	....	....	....	1	....	....	....	....	....	....	....	....	....	....	....	....	1.0	....	....	....

● BEMORAS, Irv

Irving Bemoras

Born: Nov. 18, 1930.　Height: 6'3".　Weight: 185 lbs.　Drafted: 1953　College: Illinois

YEAR	TEAM	GP	GS	MIN	PTS	FGM	FGA	FG%	3PM	3PA	3P%	FTM	FTA	FT%	ORB	DRB	TRB	AST	PF	DQ	STL	BLK	TO	MPG	PPG	RPG	APG	PCM
53-54	Milwaukee	69	....	1496	509	185	505	.366	....	....	....	139	208	.668			214	79	152	2	....	....	....	21.7	7.4	3.1	1.1	.306
56-57	St. Louis	62	....	983	318	124	385	.322	....	....	....	70	103	.680			127	46	76	0	....	....	....	15.9	5.1	2.0	0.7	.239
NBA Season Totals		131	....	2479	827	309	890	.347	....	....	....	209	311	.672			341	125	228	2	....	....	....	18.9	6.3	2.6	1.0	....
56-57	St. Louis	3	....	20	9	3	8	.375	....	....	....	3	3	1.000			6	1	4	0	....	....	....	6.7	3.0	2.0	0.3	.475
NBA Playoff Totals		3	....	20	9	3	8	.375	....	....	....	3	3	1.000			6	1	4	0	....	....	....	6.7	3.0	2.0	0.3	....

● BENBOW, Leon

Leon Benbow

Born: July 23, 1950. Columbia, SC, United States.　Height: 6'4".　Weight: 185 lbs.　Drafted: 1974　College: Jacksonville

YEAR	TEAM	GP	GS	MIN	PTS	FGM	FGA	FG%	3PM	3PA	3P%	FTM	FTA	FT%	ORB	DRB	TRB	AST	PF	DQ	STL	BLK	TO	MPG	PPG	RPG	APG	PCM
74-75	Chicago	39	....	252	85	35	94	.372	....	....	....	15	18	.833	14	24	38	25	41	0	11	6	....	6.5	2.2	1.0	0.6	.306
75-76	Chicago	76	....	1586	543	219	551	.397	....	....	....	105	140	.750	65	111	176	158	186	1	62	11	....	20.9	7.1	2.3	2.1	.312
NBA Season Totals		115	....	1838	628	254	645	.394	....	....	....	120	158	.759	79	135	214	183	227	1	73	17	....	16.0	5.5	1.9	1.6	....
74-75	Chicago	2	....	5	5	2	4	.500	....	....	....	1	2	.500	1	0	1	2	0	0	0	0	....	2.5	2.5	0.5	1.0	1.203
NBA Playoff Totals		2	....	5	5	2	4	.500	....	....	....	1	2	.500	1	0	1	2	0	0	0	0	....	2.5	2.5	0.5	1.0	....

● BENDER, Jonathan

Jonathan Rene Bender

Born: Jan. 30, 1981. Picayune, MS, United States.　Height: 6'11".　Weight: 202 lbs.　Drafted: 1999　College: none (HS: Picayune Memorial, MS)

YEAR	TEAM	GP	GS	MIN	PTS	FGM	FGA	FG%	3PM	3PA	3P%	FTM	FTA	FT%	ORB	DRB	TRB	AST	PF	DQ	STL	BLK	TO	MPG	PPG	RPG	APG	PCM
99-00	Indiana	24	0	130	64	23	70	.329	2	12	.167	16	24	.667	4	17	21	3	18	0	1	5	7	5.4	2.7	0.9	0.1	.238
00-01	Indiana	59	7	574	193	66	186	.355	11	41	.268	50	68	.735	14	60	74	32	73	0	7	28	42	9.7	3.3	1.3	0.5	.244
01-02	Indiana	78	17	1647	581	198	460	.430	45	125	.360	140	181	.773	64	180	244	62	147	1	19	49	96	21.1	7.4	3.1	0.8	.317
02-03	Indiana	46	2	819	303	112	254	.441	19	53	.358	60	84	.714	42	91	133	42	86	0	8	56	42	17.8	6.6	2.9	0.9	.379
NBA Season Totals		207	26	3170	1141	399	970	.411	77	231	.333	266	357	.745	124	348	472	139	324	1	35	138	187	15.3	5.5	2.3	0.7	....
99-00	Indiana	9	0	21	12	4	6	.667	1	1	1.000	3	6	.500	0	3	3	0	2	0	1	0	0	2.3	1.3	0.3	0.0	.550
00-01	Indiana	1	0	4	0	0	1	.000	0	0	.000	0	0	.000	0	0	0	1	0	0	0	0	0	4.0	0.0	0.0	0.0	-.337
01-02	Indiana	5	0	46	6	3	6	.500	0	1	.000	0	0	.000	0	4	4	2	6	0	2	3	5	9.2	1.2	0.8	0.4	.139
02-03	Indiana	3	0	34	17	5	15	.333	3	9	.333	4	6	.667	3	4	7	0	2	0	0	2	0	11.3	5.7	2.3	0.0	.420
NBA Playoff Totals		18	0	105	35	12	28	.429	4	11	.364	7	12	.583	3	11	14	2	11	0	3	5	5	5.8	1.9	0.8	0.1	....

● BENJAMIN, Benoit

Lenard Benoit Benjamin

Born: Nov. 22, 1964. Monroe, LA, United States.　Height: 7'　Weight: 250 lbs.　Drafted: 1985　College: Creighton

YEAR	TEAM	GP	GS	MIN	PTS	FGM	FGA	FG%	3PM	3PA	3P%	FTM	FTA	FT%	ORB	DRB	TRB	AST	PF	DQ	STL	BLK	TO	MPG	PPG	RPG	APG	PCM
85-86	LA Clippers	79	37	2088	878	324	661	.490	1	3	.333	229	307	.746	161	439	600	79	286	5	64	206	142	26.4	11.1	7.6	1.0	.554
86-87	LA Clippers	72	61	2230	828	320	713	.449	0	2	.000	188	263	.715	134	452	586	135	251	7	60	187	187	31.0	11.5	8.1	1.9	.474
87-88	LA Clippers	66	59	2171	860	340	693	.491	0	8	.000	180	255	.706	112	418	530	172	203	2	50	225	224	32.9	13.0	8.0	2.6	.519
88-89	LA Clippers	79	62	2585	1299	491	907	.541	0	2	.000	317	426	.744	164	532	696	157	221	4	57	221	237	32.7	16.4	8.8	2.0	.624
89-90	LA Clippers	71	58	2313	959	362	688	.526	0	1	.000	235	321	.732	156	501	657	159	217	3	59	187	185	32.6	13.5	9.3	2.2	.585
90-91	LA Clippers	39	38	1337	581	229	465	.492	0	0	.000	123	169	.728	95	374	469	74	110	1	26	91	137	34.3	14.9	12.0	1.9	.588
90-91	Seattle	31	27	899	401	157	313	.502	0	0	.000	87	126	.690	62	192	254	45	74	0	28	54	96	29.0	12.9	8.2	1.5	.528
91-92	Seattle	63	61	1941	879	354	740	.478	0	2	.000	171	249	.687	130	383	513	76	185	1	39	118	176	30.8	14.0	8.1	1.2	.484
92-93	Seattle	31	6	448	209	81	163	.497	0	0	.000	47	67	.701	27	86	113	12	73	0	17	35	43	14.5	6.7	3.6	0.4	.482
92-93	LA Lakers	28	0	306	126	52	108	.481	0	0	.000	22	37	.595	24	72	96	10	61	0	14	13	36	10.9	4.5	3.4	0.4	.425
93-94	New Jersey	77	74	1817	718	283	589	.480	0	0	.000	152	214	.710	135	364	499	44	198	2	35	90	100	23.6	9.3	6.5	0.6	.466
94-95	New Jersey	61	57	1598	675	271	531	.510	0	0	.000	133	175	.760	94	346	440	38	151	3	23	64	122	26.2	11.1	7.2	0.6	.476
95-96	Vancouver	13	10	404	181	71	161	.441	0	0	.000	39	56	.696	31	72	103	16	40	1	10	15	34	31.1	13.9	7.9	1.2	.433
95-96	Milwaukee	70	58	1492	547	223	429	.520	0	3	.000	101	138	.732	110	326	436	48	184	0	35	70	112	21.3	7.8	6.2	0.7	.472
96-97	Toronto	4	3	44	13	5	12	.417	0	0	.000	3	4	.750	3	6	9	1	5	0	1	0	2	11.0	3.3	2.3	0.3	.277
97-98	Philadelphia	14	0	197	63	22	41	.537	0	0	.000	19	30	.633	18	35	53	3	26	0	4	4	13	14.1	4.5	3.8	0.2	.385
98-99	Philadelphia	6	0	33	4	2	7	.286	0	0	.000	0	0	.000	3	5	8	1	6	0	0	3	5	5.5	0.7	1.3	0.2	.074
99-00	Cleveland	3	0	8	2	1	3	.333	0	0	.000	0	0	.000	0	1	1	0	1	0	0	1	0	2.7	0.7	0.3	0.0	.193
NBA Season Totals		807	614	21911	9223	3588	7224	.497	1	21	.048	2046	2837	.721	1459	4604	6063	1070	2292	27	522	1581	1849	27.2	11.4	7.5	1.3	....

Total Basketball

YEAR	TEAM	GP	GS	MIN	PTS	FGM	FGA	FG%	3PM	3PA	3P%	FTM	FTA	FT%	ORB	DRB	TRB	AST	PF	DQ	STL	BLK	TO	MPG	PPG	RPG	APG	PCM
90-91	Seattle	5	5	163	69	20	41	.488	0	0	.000	29	32	.906	7	26	33	1	17	1	3	13	11	32.6	13.8	6.6	0.2	.470
91-92	Seattle	9	4	161	55	23	41	.561	0	1	.000	9	18	.500	10	36	46	5	20	0	5	13	8	17.9	6.1	5.1	0.6	.510
93-94	New Jersey	4	4	108	21	7	17	.412	0	0	.000	7	8	.875	5	16	21	1	16	0	2	8	5	27.0	5.3	5.3	0.3	.268
NBA Playoff Totals		18	13	432	145	50	99	.505	0	1	.000	45	58	.776	22	78	100	7	53	1	10	34	24	24.0	8.1	5.6	0.4	....

• BENNETT, Corey

Corey Benjamin

Born: Feb. 24, 1978. Compton, CA, United States. Height: 6'6". Weight: 200 lbs. Drafted: 1998 College: Oregon State

YEAR	TEAM	GP	GS	MIN	PTS	FGM	FGA	FG%	3PM	3PA	3P%	FTM	FTA	FT%	ORB	DRB	TRB	AST	PF	DQ	STL	BLK	TO	MPG	PPG	RPG	APG	PCM
98-99	Chicago	31	1	320	118	44	117	.376	3	14	.214	27	40	.675	15	25	40	10	46	0	11	8	21	10.3	3.8	1.3	0.3	.224
99-00	Chicago	48	10	862	370	145	350	.414	31	89	.348	49	82	.598	21	67	88	54	122	2	31	22	74	18.0	7.7	1.8	1.1	.271
00-01	Chicago	65	5	857	307	115	302	.381	21	81	.259	56	83	.675	38	62	100	69	128	2	28	16	63	13.2	4.7	1.5	1.1	.255
02-03	Atlanta	9	0	152	40	13	43	.302	2	13	.154	12	16	.750	10	21	31	10	20	0	1	2	6	16.9	4.4	3.4	1.1	.251
NBA Season Totals		153	16	2191	835	317	812	.390	57	197	.289	144	221	.652	84	175	259	143	316	4	71	48	164	14.3	5.5	1.7	0.9	....

• BENNETT, Elmer

Elmer James Bennett

Born: Feb. 13, 1970. Evanston, IL, United States. Height: 6' Weight: 170 lbs. Drafted: 1992 College: Notre Dame

YEAR	TEAM	GP	GS	MIN	PTS	FGM	FGA	FG%	3PM	3PA	3P%	FTM	FTA	FT%	ORB	DRB	TRB	AST	PF	DQ	STL	BLK	TO	MPG	PPG	RPG	APG	PCM
94-95	Cleveland	4	0	18	15	6	11	.545	0	2	.000	3	4	.750	0	1	1	3	3	0	4	0	3	4.5	3.8	0.3	0.8	.750
95-96	Philadelphia	8	0	66	11	4	17	.235	0	0	.000	3	4	.750	1	4	5	8	6	0	1	1	7	8.3	1.4	0.6	1.0	.060
96-97	Houston	4	0	16	10	2	6	.333	1	3	.333	5	6	.833	0	1	1	4	1	0	2	0	0	4.0	2.5	0.3	1.0	.776
96-97	Denver	5	0	59	12	4	13	.308	2	6	.333	2	4	.500	0	3	3	7	6	0	2	0	10	11.8	2.4	0.6	1.4	.046
NBA Season Totals		21	0	159	48	16	47	.340	3	11	.273	13	18	.722	1	9	10	22	16	0	9	1	20	7.6	2.3	0.5	1.0	....

• BENNETT, Mario

Mario Marcell Bennett

Born: Aug. 1, 1973. Denton, TX, United States. Height: 6'6". Weight: 235 lbs. Drafted: 1995 College: Arizona State

YEAR	TEAM	GP	GS	MIN	PTS	FGM	FGA	FG%	3PM	3PA	3P%	FTM	FTA	FT%	ORB	DRB	TRB	AST	PF	DQ	STL	BLK	TO	MPG	PPG	RPG	APG	PCM
95-96	Phoenix	19	14	230	85	29	64	.453	0	1	.000	27	42	.643	21	28	49	6	46	0	11	11	11	12.1	4.5	2.6	0.3	.375
97-98	LA Lakers	45	4	354	177	80	135	.593	1	2	.500	16	44	.364	60	66	126	18	61	0	19	11	23	7.9	3.9	2.8	0.4	.642
98-99	Chicago	3	0	19	7	2	6	.333	0	0	.000	3	4	.750	2	3	5	0	4	0	1	0	1	6.3	2.3	1.7	0.0	.298
99-00	LA Clippers	1	0	3	0	0	3	.000	0	0	.000	0	0	.000	1	1	2	0	1	0	0	0	0	3.0	0.0	2.0	0.0	-.454
NBA Season Totals		68	18	606	269	111	208	.534	1	3	.333	46	90	.511	84	98	182	24	112	0	31	22	35	8.9	4.0	2.7	0.4	....
95-96	Phoenix	2	0	8	4	2	4	.500	0	0	.000	0	0	.000	2	1	3	0	0	0	0	0	2	4.0	2.0	1.5	0.0	.383
97-98	LA Lakers	4	0	10	4	1	2	.500	0	0	.000	2	2	1.000	2	4	6	0	2	0	0	1	0	2.5	1.0	1.5	0.0	.858
NBA Playoff Totals		6	0	18	8	3	6	.500	0	0	.000	2	2	1.000	4	5	9	0	2	0	0	1	2	3.0	1.3	1.5	0.0	....

• BENNETT, Mel

Melvin P. Bennett

Born: Jan. 4, 1955. Pittsburgh, PA, United States. Height: 6'7". Weight: 200 lbs. Drafted: — College: Pittsburgh

YEAR	TEAM	GP	GS	MIN	PTS	FGM	FGA	FG%	3PM	3PA	3P%	FTM	FTA	FT%	ORB	DRB	TRB	AST	PF	DQ	STL	BLK	TO	MPG	PPG	RPG	APG	PCM
75-76	Virginia-A	75	....	2193	904	329	819	.402	0	2	.000	246	403	.610	249	277	526	97	266	....	77	47	176	29.2	12.1	7.0	1.3	.390
76-77	Indiana	67	....	911	314	101	294	.344	....	....	....	112	187	.599	110	127	237	70	155	0	37	33	....	13.6	4.7	3.5	1.0	.365
77-78	Indiana	31	....	285	74	23	81	.284	....	....	....	28	45	.622	49	44	93	22	54	1	11	7	31	9.2	2.4	3.0	0.7	.305
80-81	Utah	28	....	313	105	26	60	.433	0	2	.000	53	81	.654	33	60	93	15	56	0	3	11	31	11.2	3.8	3.3	0.5	.388
81-82	Cleveland	3	0	23	5	2	4	.500	0	0	.000	1	6	.167	1	2	3	0	2	0	1	0	4	7.7	1.7	1.0	0.0	-.003
NBA Season Totals		129	0	1532	498	152	439	.346	0	2	.000	194	319	.608	193	233	426	107	267	1	52	51	66	11.9	3.9	3.3	0.8	....
ABA Season Totals		75	....	2193	904	329	819	.402	0	2	.000	246	403	.610	249	277	526	97	266	....	77	47	176	29.2	12.1	7.0	1.3	....
Career Totals		204	0	3725	1402	481	1258	.382	0	4	.000	440	722	.609	442	510	952	204	533	1	129	98	242	18.3	6.9	4.7	1.0	....

• BENNETT, Spider

Willis (Spider) Bennett

Born: Aug. 4, 1943. Lakewood, NJ, United States. Height: 6'3". Weight: 190 lbs. Drafted: — College: Winston-Salem

YEAR	TEAM	GP	GS	MIN	PTS	FGM	FGA	FG%	3PM	3PA	3P%	FTM	FTA	FT%	ORB	DRB	TRB	AST	PF	DQ	STL	BLK	TO	MPG	PPG	RPG	APG	PCM
68-69	Dallas-A	46	....	823	352	116	311	.373	2	11	.182	118	179	.659	44	70	114	69	125	8	....	....	114	17.9	7.7	2.5	1.5	.342
68-69	Houston-A	13	....	170	88	31	74	.419	4	14	.286	22	37	.595	18	15	33	15	40	1	....	....	31	13.1	6.8	2.5	1.2	.429
ABA Season Totals		59	....	993	440	147	385	.382	6	25	.240	140	216	.648	62	85	147	84	165	9	....	....	145	16.8	7.5	2.5	1.4	....

• BENNETT, Tony

Anthony Guy Bennett

Born: June 1, 1969. Green Bay, WI, United States. Height: 6' Weight: 175 lbs. Drafted: 1992 College: Wisconsin (Green Bay)

YEAR	TEAM	GP	GS	MIN	PTS	FGM	FGA	FG%	3PM	3PA	3P%	FTM	FTA	FT%	ORB	DRB	TRB	AST	PF	DQ	STL	BLK	TO	MPG	PPG	RPG	APG	PCM
92-93	Charlotte	75	2	857	276	110	260	.423	26	80	.325	30	41	.732	12	51	63	136	110	0	30	0	53	11.4	3.7	0.8	1.8	.306
93-94	Charlotte	74	5	983	248	105	263	.399	27	75	.360	11	15	.733	16	74	90	163	84	0	39	1	37	13.3	3.4	1.2	2.2	.330
94-95	Charlotte	3	0	46	14	6	13	.462	2	9	.222	0	0	.000	0	2	2	4	6	0	0	0	3	15.3	4.7	0.7	1.3	.172
NBA Season Totals		152	7	1886	538	221	536	.412	55	164	.335	41	56	.732	28	127	155	303	200	0	69	1	93	12.4	3.5	1.0	2.0	....
92-93	Charlotte	8	0	86	30	12	25	.480	4	8	.500	2	2	1.000	1	8	9	13	8	0	2	1	5	10.8	3.8	1.1	1.6	.402
NBA Playoff Totals		8	0	86	30	12	25	.480	4	8	.500	2	2	1.000	1	8	9	13	8	0	2	1	5	10.8	3.8	1.1	1.6	....

• BENNETT, Wesley

Wesley Bennett

Born: Mar. 13, 1913. Nashville, TN, United States. Height: 6'3". Weight: 175 lbs. Drafted: — College: Westminster (PA)

YEAR	TEAM	GP	GS	MIN	PTS	FGM	FGA	FG%	3PM	3PA	3P%	FTM	FTA	FT%	ORB	DRB	TRB	AST	PF	DQ	STL	BLK	TO	MPG	PPG	RPG	APG	PCM
37-38	Wingfoots-N	15	....	....	87	28	....	....	....	....	....	31	....	....	....	....	....	....	....	....	....	....	....	....	5.8	....	....	....
38-39	Wingfoots-N	22	....	....	109	36	....	....	....	....	....	37	....	....	....	....	....	....	....	....	....	....	....	....	5.0	....	....	....
NBL Season Totals		37	....	....	196	64	....	....	....	....	....	68	....	....	....	....	....	....	....	....	....	....	....	....	5.3	....	....	....
37-38	Wingfoots-N	5	....	....	25	10	....	....	....	....	....	5	....	....	....	....	....	....	....	....	....	....	....	....	5.0	....	....	....
NBL Playoff Totals		5	....	....	25	10	....	....	....	....	....	5	....	....	....	....	....	....	....	....	....	....	....	....	5.0	....	....	....

• BENNETT, Winston

Winston George (Steady Bee) Bennett III

Born: Feb. 9, 1965. Louisville, KY, United States. Height: 6'7". Weight: 210 lbs. Drafted: 1988 College: Kentucky

YEAR	TEAM	GP	GS	MIN	PTS	FGM	FGA	FG%	3PM	3PA	3P%	FTM	FTA	FT%	ORB	DRB	TRB	AST	PF	DQ	STL	BLK	TO	MPG	PPG	RPG	APG	PCM
89-90	Cleveland	55	34	990	338	137	286	.479	0	0	.000	64	96	.667	84	104	188	54	133	1	23	10	61	18.0	6.1	3.4	1.0	.332
90-91	Cleveland	27	13	334	115	40	107	.374	0	0	.000	35	47	.745	30	34	64	28	50	0	8	2	19	12.4	4.3	2.4	1.0	.314
91-92	Cleveland	52	45	831	193	79	209	.378	0	1	.000	35	50	.700	62	99	161	38	121	1	19	9	31	16.0	3.7	3.1	0.7	.237
91-92	Miami	2	0	2	2	1	2	.500	0	0	.000	0	0	.000	1	0	1	0	1	0	0	0	0	1.0	1.0	0.5	0.0	.768
NBA Season Totals		136	92	2157	648	257	604	.425	0	1	.000	134	193	.694	177	237	414	120	305	2	50	21	111	15.9	4.8	3.0	0.9	....
89-90	Cleveland	5	5	135	50	23	47	.489	0	0	.000	4	6	.667	14	7	21	5	11	0	3	1	4	27.0	10.0	4.2	1.0	.344
NBA Playoff Totals		5	5	135	50	23	47	.489	0	0	.000	4	6	.667	14	7	21	5	11	0	3	1	4	27.0	10.0	4.2	1.0	....

• BENOIT, David

David Benoit

Born: May 9, 1968. Lafayette, LA, United States. Height: 6'8". Weight: 220 lbs. Drafted: — College: Alabama

YEAR	TEAM	GP	GS	MIN	PTS	FGM	FGA	FG%	3PM	3PA	3P%	FTM	FTA	FT%	ORB	DRB	TRB	AST	PF	DQ	STL	BLK	TO	MPG	PPG	RPG	APG	PCM
91-92	Utah	77	2	1161	434	175	375	.467	3	14	.214	81	100	.810	105	191	296	34	124	0	19	44	69	15.1	5.6	3.8	0.4	.420
92-93	Utah	82	27	1717	664	258	592	.436	34	98	.347	114	152	.750	116	276	392	43	201	2	45	43	90	20.9	8.1	4.8	0.5	.379
93-94	Utah	55	18	1070	358	139	361	.385	12	59	.203	68	88	.773	89	171	260	23	115	0	23	37	39	19.5	6.5	4.7	0.4	.351
94-95	Utah	71	67	1841	740	285	587	.486	38	115	.330	132	157	.841	96	272	368	58	183	1	45	47	78	25.9	10.4	5.2	0.8	.423
95-96	Utah	81	63	1961	661	255	581	.439	64	192	.333	87	112	.777	90	293	383	82	166	2	43	49	73	24.2	8.2	4.7	1.0	.372
97-98	New Jersey	53	0	799	282	102	269	.379	41	119	.345	37	44	.841	42	99	141	17	120	0	26	16	37	15.1	5.3	2.7	0.3	.279
97-98	Orlando	24	0	324	138	50	139	.360	14	51	.275	24	30	.800	18	44	62	8	37	0	9	4	12	13.5	5.8	2.6	0.3	.319
00-01	Utah	49	2	446	178	71	147	.483	5	13	.385	31	39	.795	20	61	81	22	75	0	6	6	28	9.1	3.6	1.7	0.4	.348
NBA Season Totals		492	179	9319	3455	1335	3051	.438	211	661	.319	574	722	.795	576	1407	1983	287	1021	5	216	246	426	18.9	7.0	4.0	0.6	....
91-92	Utah	13	9	257	89	36	84	.429	6	13	.462	11	11	1.000	18	32	50	6	30	0	6	5	10	19.8	6.8	3.8	0.5	.328
92-93	Utah	5	5	136	37	13	41	.317	2	9	.222	9	13	.692	7	17	24	5	17	0	3	6	2	27.2	7.4	4.8	1.0	.260
93-94	Utah	16	5	357	115	48	122	.393	3	16	.188	16	25	.640	23	44	67	10	31	0	7	11	16	22.3	7.2	4.2	0.6	.288
94-95	Utah	5	5	167	59	21	45	.467	11	25	.440	6	9	.667	7	21	28	4	10	0	2	4	10	33.4	11.8	5.6	0.8	.342
95-96	Utah	14	5	259	87	33	70	.471	14	28	.500	7	9	.778	6	31	37	7	17	0	1	3	14	18.5	6.2	2.6	0.5	.294
00-01	Utah	4	0	61	23	7	19	.368	2	6	.333	7	7	1.000	1	6	7	2	6	0	0	2	2	15.3	5.8	1.8	0.5	.295
NBA Playoff Totals		57	29	1237	410	158	381	.415	38	97	.392	56	74	.757	62	151	213	34	111	0	19	31	54	21.7	7.2	3.7	0.6	....

• BENSON, Al

Al Benson

Born: 1914. Height: 6'6". Weight: 220 lbs. Drafted: — College: none

YEAR	TEAM	GP	GS	MIN	PTS	FGM	FGA	FG%	3PM	3PA	3P%	FTM	FTA	FT%	ORB	DRB	TRB	AST	PF	DQ	STL	BLK	TO	MPG	PPG	RPG	APG	PCM
40-41	Detroit-N	8	....	....	16	7	....	....	....	....	....	2	....	....	....	....	....	....	....	....	....	....	....	....	2.0	....	....	....
40-41	Hammond-N	2	....	....	0	0	....	....	....	....	....	0	....	....	....	....	....	....	....	....	....	....	....	....	0.0	....	....	....
NBL Season Totals		10	....	....	16	7	....	....	....	....	....	2	....	....	....	....	....	....	....	....	....	....	....	....	1.6	....	....	....
40-41	Detroit-N	2	....	....	2	1	....	....	....	....	....	0	....	....	....	....	....	....	....	....	....	....	....	....	1.0	....	....	....
NBL Playoff Totals		2	....	....	2	1	....	....	....	....	....	0	....	....	....	....	....	....	....	....	....	....	....	....	1.0	....	....	....

• BENSON, Kent

Michael Kent (Benny) Benson

Born: Dec. 27, 1954. New Castle, IN, United States. Height: 6'10". Weight: 235 lbs. Drafted: 1977 College: Indiana

YEAR	TEAM	GP	GS	MIN	PTS	FGM	FGA	FG%	3PM	3PA	3P%	FTM	FTA	FT%	ORB	DRB	TRB	AST	PF	DQ	STL	BLK	TO	MPG	PPG	RPG	APG	PCM
77-78	Milwaukee	69	....	1288	532	220	473	.465	....	....	....	92	141	.652	89	206	295	99	177	1	69	54	117	18.7	7.7	4.3	1.4	.455
78-79	Milwaukee	82	....	2132	1006	413	798	.518	....	....	....	180	245	.735	187	397	584	204	280	4	89	81	156	26.0	12.3	7.1	2.5	.594
79-80	Milwaukee	56	....	1389	492	213	431	.494	0	1	.000	66	97	.680	96	237	333	127	178	1	54	74	106	24.8	8.8	5.9	2.3	.476
79-80	Detroit	17	....	502	206	86	187	.460	1	4	.250	33	44	.750	30	90	120	51	68	3	19	18	51	29.5	12.1	7.1	3.0	.459
80-81	Detroit	59	....	1956	924	364	770	.473	0	4	.000	196	254	.772	124	276	400	172	184	1	72	67	189	33.2	15.7	6.8	2.9	.486
81-82	Detroit	75	72	2467	940	405	802	.505	3	11	.273	127	158	.804	219	434	653	159	214	2	66	98	158	32.9	12.5	8.7	2.1	.503
82-83	Detroit	21	15	599	208	85	182	.467	0	1	.000	38	50	.760	53	102	155	49	61	0	14	17	36	28.5	9.9	7.4	2.3	.462
83-84	Detroit	82	58	1734	579	248	451	.550	0	1	.000	83	101	.822	117	292	409	130	230	4	71	53	82	21.1	7.1	5.0	1.6	.481
84-85	Detroit	72	35	1401	478	201	397	.506	0	3	.000	76	94	.809	103	221	324	93	207	4	53	44	65	19.5	6.6	4.5	1.3	.444
85-86	Detroit	72	41	1344	469	201	415	.484	1	2	.500	66	83	.795	118	258	376	80	196	3	58	51	58	18.7	6.5	5.2	1.1	.486
86-87	Utah	73	2	895	329	140	316	.443	2	7	.286	47	58	.810	80	151	231	39	138	0	39	28	44	12.3	4.5	3.2	0.5	.418
87-88	Cleveland	2	0	12	5	2	2	1.000	0	0	.000	1	2	.500	0	1	1	0	2	0	1	1	2	6.0	2.5	0.5	0.0	.378
NBA Season Totals		680	223	15719	6168	2578	5224	.493	7	34	.206	1005	1327	.757	1216	2665	3881	1203	1935	23	605	586	1064	23.1	9.1	5.7	1.8	....
77-78	Milwaukee	9	....	103	28	11	23	.478	....	....	....	6	11	.545	5	10	15	3	20	0	5	3	6	11.4	3.1	1.7	0.3	.241
83-84	Detroit	5	5	129	38	16	37	.432	0	0	.000	6	10	.600	9	21	30	7	14	0	5	7	3	25.8	7.6	6.0	1.4	.418
84-85	Detroit	9	1	142	63	25	46	.543	0	0	.000	13	15	.867	9	27	36	4	27	0	8	2	6	15.8	7.0	4.0	0.4	.503
85-86	Detroit	4	0	55	8	4	10	.400	0	0	.000	0	0	.000	3	10	13	0	11	0	0	2	1	13.8	2.0	3.3	0.0	.188
86-87	Utah	2	0	3	0	0	0	.000	0	0	.000	0	0	.000	0	0	0	0	0	0	0	0	1	1.5	0.0	0.0	0.0	-.310
NBA Playoff Totals		29	6	432	137	56	116	.483	0	0	.000	25	36	.694	26	68	94	14	72	0	18	14	17	14.9	4.7	3.2	0.5	....

• BERCE, Gene

Eugene D. Berce

Born: Nov. 22, 1926. Height: 5'11". Weight: 175 lbs. Drafted: 1948 College: Marquette

YEAR	TEAM	GP	GS	MIN	PTS	FGM	FGA	FG%	3PM	3PA	3P%	FTM	FTA	FT%	ORB	DRB	TRB	AST	PF	DQ	STL	BLK	TO	MPG	PPG	RPG	APG	PCM
48-49	Oshkosh-N	58	....	....	341	120	....	....	....	....	....	101	153	.660	....	....	....	....	137	....	....	....	....	....	5.9	....	....	....
49-50	Tri-Cities	3	....	....	10	5	16	.313	....	....	....	0	5	.000	....	....	....	0	6	....	....	....	....	....	3.3	....	0.0	....
NBA Season Totals		3	....	....	10	5	16	.313	....	....	....	0	5	.000	....	....	....	0	6	....	....	....	....	....	3.3	....	0.0	....
NBL Season Totals		58	....	....	341	120	....	....	....	....	....	101	153	....	....	....	....	....	137	....	....	....	....	....	5.9	....	....	....
Career Totals		61	....	....	351	125	16	....	....	....	....	101	158	....	....	....	....	0	143	....	....	....	....	....	5.8	....	0.0	....
48-49	Oshkosh-N	7	....	....	48	8	....	....	....	....	....	32	39	.821	....	....	....	....	....	....	....	....	....	....	6.9	....	....	....
NBL Playoff Totals		7	....	....	48	8	....	....	....	....	....	32	39	....	....	....	....	....	....	....	....	....	....	....	6.9	....	....	....

YEAR	TEAM	GP	GS	MIN	PTS	FGM	FGA	FG%	3PM	3PA	3P%	FTM	FTA	FT%	ORB	DRB	TRB	AST	PF	DQ	STL	BLK	TO	MPG	PPG	RPG	APG	PCM

• BERENS, Beanie
Beanie Berens

Born: 1913.　Height: 6'5".　Weight: 190 lbs.　Drafted: —　College: Ohio University

YEAR	TEAM	GP	GS	MIN	PTS	FGM	FGA	FG%	3PM	3PA	3P%	FTM	FTA	FT%	ORB	DRB	TRB	AST	PF	DQ	STL	BLK	TO	MPG	PPG	RPG	APG	PCM
37-38	Columbus-N	1	....	....	1	0	....	....	....	....	....	1													1.0	....	....	....
NBL Season Totals		1	....	....	1	0	....	....	....	....	....	1													1.0	....	....	....

• BERETTA, Fred
Fred Beretta

Born: 1917.　Height: —　Weight: —　Drafted: —　College: Purdue

YEAR	TEAM	GP	GS	MIN	PTS	FGM	FGA	FG%	3PM	3PA	3P%	FTM	FTA	FT%	ORB	DRB	TRB	AST	PF	DQ	STL	BLK	TO	MPG	PPG	RPG	APG	PCM
40-41	Non-Skids-N	9	....	....	2	1	....	....	....	....	....	0													0.2	....	....	....
NBL Season Totals		9	....	....	2	1	....	....	....	....	....	0													0.2	....	....	....

• BERGEN, Gary
Gary Dean Bergen

Born: July 16, 1932. Independence, MO, United States.　Height: 6'8".　Weight: 210 lbs.　Drafted: 1956　College: Utah

YEAR	TEAM	GP	GS	MIN	PTS	FGM	FGA	FG%	3PM	3PA	3P%	FTM	FTA	FT%	ORB	DRB	TRB	AST	PF	DQ	STL	BLK	TO	MPG	PPG	RPG	APG	PCM
56-57	New York	6	....	40	8	3	11	.273				2	2	1.000	....	....	8	1	4	0	....	....	....	6.7	1.3	1.3	0.2	.194
NBA Season Totals		6	....	40	8	3	11	.273				2	2	1.000	....	....	8	1	4	0	....	....	....	6.7	1.3	1.3	0.2	

• BERGH, Larry
Larry Clifford Bergh

Born: Apr. 2, 1945.　Height: 6'8".　Weight: 210 lbs.　Drafted: 1969　College: Tuskegee

YEAR	TEAM	GP	GS	MIN	PTS	FGM	FGA	FG%	3PM	3PA	3P%	FTM	FTA	FT%	ORB	DRB	TRB	AST	PF	DQ	STL	BLK	TO	MPG	PPG	RPG	APG	PCM
69-70	Pittsburgh-A	20	....	255	121	49	120	.408	0	1	.000	23	33	.697	36	49	85	18	52	2	....	....	14	12.8	6.1	4.3	0.9	.498
ABA Season Totals		20	....	255	121	49	120	.408	0	1	.000	23	33	.697	36	49	85	18	52	2	....	....	14	12.8	6.1	4.3	0.9	

• BERRY, Connie
Connie Mack (Warhouse) Berry

Born: Apr. 19, 1915. Spartanburg, SC, United States. Died: June 24, 1980.　Height: 6'3".　Weight: 210 lbs.　Drafted: —　College: North Carolina State

YEAR	TEAM	GP	GS	MIN	PTS	FGM	FGA	FG%	3PM	3PA	3P%	FTM	FTA	FT%	ORB	DRB	TRB	AST	PF	DQ	STL	BLK	TO	MPG	PPG	RPG	APG	PCM
39-40	Oshkosh-N	26	....	....	179	65	....	....	....	....	....	49													6.9	....	....	....
40-41	Oshkosh-N	23	....	....	94	40	....	....	....	....	....	14													4.1	....	....	....
41-42	Oshkosh-N	24	....	....	124	53	....	....	....	....	....	18													5.2	....	....	....
42-43	Oshkosh-N	5	....	....	15	5	....	....	....	....	....	5													3.0	....	....	....
43-44	Oshkosh-N	11	....	....	39	16	....	....	....	....	....	7													3.5	....	....	....
44-45	Chicago-N	18	....	....	28	11	....	....	....	....	....	6													1.6	....	....	....
45-46	Chicago-N	6	....	....	2	1	....	....	....	0	.000	0													0.3	....	....	....
NBL Season Totals		113	....	....	481	191	....	....	....	0		99	0												4.3	....	....	....
39-40	Oshkosh-N	8	....	....	66	28	....	....	....	....	....	10													8.3	....	....	....
40-41	Oshkosh-N	5	....	....	12	5	....	....	....	....	....	2													2.4	....	....	....
41-42	Oshkosh-N	5	....	....	15	5	....	....	....	....	....	5													3.0	....	....	....
43-44	Oshkosh-N	3	....	....	15	6	....	....	....	....	....	3													5.0	....	....	....
44-45	Chicago-N	3	....	....	0	0	....	....	....	....	....	0													0.0	....	....	....
NBL Playoff Totals		24	....	....	108	44	....	....	....	....		20													4.5	....	....	....

• BERRY, Ricky
Ricky Alan Berry

Born: Oct. 6, 1964. Lansing, MI, United States. Died: Aug. 14, 1989.　Height: 6'8".　Weight: 205 lbs.　Drafted: 1988　College: San Jose State

YEAR	TEAM	GP	GS	MIN	PTS	FGM	FGA	FG%	3PM	3PA	3P%	FTM	FTA	FT%	ORB	DRB	TRB	AST	PF	DQ	STL	BLK	TO	MPG	PPG	RPG	APG	PCM
88-89	Sacramento	64	21	1406	706	255	567	.450	65	160	.406	131	166	.789	57	140	197	80	197	4	37	22	83	22.0	11.0	3.1	1.3	.394
NBA Season Totals		64	21	1406	706	255	567	.450	65	160	.406	131	166	.789	57	140	197	80	197	4	37	22	83	22.0	11.0	3.1	1.3	

• BERRY, Walter
Walter Berry

Born: May 14, 1964. New York, NY, United States.　Height: 6'8".　Weight: 215 lbs.　Drafted: 1986　College: St. John's (NY)

YEAR	TEAM	GP	GS	MIN	PTS	FGM	FGA	FG%	3PM	3PA	3P%	FTM	FTA	FT%	ORB	DRB	TRB	AST	PF	DQ	STL	BLK	TO	MPG	PPG	RPG	APG	PCM
86-87	Portland	7	0	19	13	6	8	.750	0	0	.000	1	1	1.000	4	3	7	1	8	0	2	0	0	2.7	1.9	1.0	0.1	.887
86-87	San Antonio	56	45	1567	988	401	758	.529	0	3	.000	186	287	.648	132	170	302	104	188	2	36	40	151	28.0	17.6	5.4	1.9	.538
87-88	San Antonio	73	56	1922	1272	540	960	.563	0	0	.000	192	320	.600	176	219	395	110	207	2	55	63	161	26.3	17.4	5.4	1.5	.609
88-89	New Jersey	29	17	556	259	108	231	.468	0	0	.000	43	63	.683	32	83	115	20	69	0	10	13	41	19.2	8.9	4.0	0.7	.386
88-89	Houston	40	14	799	350	146	270	.541	1	2	.500	57	80	.713	54	98	152	57	114	1	19	35	48	20.0	8.8	3.8	1.4	.474
NBA Season Totals		205	132	4863	2882	1201	2227	.539	1	5	.200	479	751	.638	398	573	971	292	586	5	122	151	401	23.7	14.1	4.7	1.4	
87-88	San Antonio	3	0	94	66	27	50	.540	0	1	.000	12	15	.800	13	8	21	6	10	0	5	2	11	31.3	22.0	7.0	2.0	.646
88-89	Houston	4	0	57	33	13	26	.500	0	0	.000	7	8	.875	3	6	9	5	8	0	2	1	6	14.3	8.3	2.3	1.3	.485
NBA Playoff Totals		7	0	151	99	40	76	.526	0	1	.000	19	23	.826	16	14	30	11	18	0	7	3	17	21.6	14.1	4.3	1.6	

• BESHORE, Del
Delmer Beshore

Born: Nov. 29, 1956. Mechanicsburg, PA, United States.　Height: 5'11".　Weight: 165 lbs.　Drafted: —　College: California (PA)

YEAR	TEAM	GP	GS	MIN	PTS	FGM	FGA	FG%	3PM	3PA	3P%	FTM	FTA	FT%	ORB	DRB	TRB	AST	PF	DQ	STL	BLK	TO	MPG	PPG	RPG	APG	PCM
78-79	Milwaukee	1	....	1	0	0	0	.000	....	....	....	0	0	.000	0	0	0	0	0	0	0	0	0	1.0	0.0	0.0	0.0	.000
79-80	Chicago	68	....	869	244	88	250	.352	10	26	.385	58	87	.667	16	47	63	139	105	0	58	5	102	12.8	3.6	0.9	2.0	.242
NBA Season Totals		69	....	870	244	88	250	.352	10	26	.385	58	87	.667	16	47	63	139	105	0	58	5	102	12.6	3.5	0.9	2.0	

• BEST, Travis
Travis Eric Best

Born: July 12, 1972. Springfield, MA, United States.　Height: 5'11".　Weight: 182 lbs.　Drafted: 1995　College: Georgia Tech

YEAR	TEAM	GP	GS	MIN	PTS	FGM	FGA	FG%	3PM	3PA	3P%	FTM	FTA	FT%	ORB	DRB	TRB	AST	PF	DQ	STL	BLK	TO	MPG	PPG	RPG	APG	PCM
95-96	Indiana	59	1	571	221	69	163	.423	8	25	.320	75	90	.833	11	33	44	97	80	0	20	3	65	9.7	3.7	0.7	1.6	.337
96-97	Indiana	76	46	2064	754	274	620	.442	57	155	.368	149	197	.756	36	130	166	318	221	3	98	5	152	27.2	9.9	2.2	4.2	.366

YEAR	TEAM	GP	GS	MIN	PTS	FGM	FGA	FG%	3PM	3PA	3P%	FTM	FTA	FT%	ORB	DRB	TRB	AST	PF	DQ	STL	BLK	TO	MPG	PPG	RPG	APG	PCM
97-98	Indiana	82	0	1547	535	201	480	.419	21	70	.300	112	131	.855	28	94	122	281	193	3	85	5	115	18.9	6.5	1.5	3.4	.373
98-99	Indiana	49	0	1043	346	127	305	.416	22	59	.373	70	83	.843	19	61	80	169	111	2	42	4	62	21.3	7.1	1.6	3.4	.362
99-00	Indiana	82	0	1691	733	271	561	.483	35	93	.376	156	190	.821	16	126	142	272	204	1	76	5	107	20.6	8.9	1.7	3.3	.452
00-01	Indiana	77	21	2457	918	347	788	.440	37	97	.381	187	226	.827	38	184	222	473	246	10	110	11	127	31.9	11.9	2.9	6.1	.451
01-02	Indiana	44	3	954	302	116	264	.439	13	34	.382	57	65	.877	10	60	70	175	101	3	57	6	59	21.7	6.9	1.6	4.0	.395
01-02	Chicago	30	18	793	279	112	254	.441	8	25	.320	47	51	.922	10	71	81	149	72	3	32	1	40	26.4	9.3	2.7	5.0	.436
02-03	Miami	72	52	1807	603	231	583	.396	36	109	.330	105	123	.854	26	121	147	255	174	6	44	7	106	25.1	8.4	2.0	3.5	.309
NBA Season Totals		571	141	12927	4691	1748	4018	.435	237	667	.355	958	1156	.829	194	880	1074	2189	1402	31	564	47	833	22.6	8.2	1.9	3.8	....
95-96	Indiana	5	0	84	29	11	22	.500	1	6	.167	6	7	.857	3	8	11	9	10	0	6	0	10	16.8	5.8	2.2	1.8	.353
97-98	Indiana	16	0	280	97	27	72	.375	5	18	.278	38	43	.884	1	15	16	31	36	0	11	3	19	17.5	6.1	1.0	1.9	.288
98-99	Indiana	11	0	150	46	16	46	.348	2	10	.200	12	13	.923	7	10	17	21	34	1	4	1	14	13.6	4.2	1.5	1.9	.228
99-00	Indiana	23	0	463	204	77	179	.430	13	30	.433	37	44	.841	15	42	57	66	61	1	19	4	25	20.1	8.9	2.5	2.9	.437
00-01	Indiana	4	4	163	39	17	39	.436	1	3	.333	4	4	1.000	6	13	19	37	15	1	4	0	6	40.8	9.8	4.8	9.3	.421
NBA Playoff Totals		59	4	1140	415	148	358	.413	22	67	.328	97	111	.874	32	88	120	164	156	3	44	8	74	19.3	7.0	2.0	2.8	....

• BETOURNE, Don
Donald Betourne

Born: 1915. Height: 6'1". Weight: 200 lbs. Drafted: — College: St. Viator

YEAR	TEAM	GP	GS	MIN	PTS	FGM	FGA	FG%	3PM	3PA	3P%	FTM	FTA	FT%	ORB	DRB	TRB	AST	PF	DQ	STL	BLK	TO	MPG	PPG	RPG	APG	PCM
37-38	Kankakee-N	12	....	....	76	30	....	....	....	....	....	16													6.3	....	....	....
NBL Season Totals		12	....	....	76	30						16													6.3			

• BIALOSUKNIA, Wesley
Wesley John Bialosuknia

Born: June 8, 1945. Poughkeepsie, NY, United States. Height: 6'2". Weight: 185 lbs. Drafted: 1967 College: Connecticut

YEAR	TEAM	GP	GS	MIN	PTS	FGM	FGA	FG%	3PM	3PA	3P%	FTM	FTA	FT%	ORB	DRB	TRB	AST	PF	DQ	STL	BLK	TO	MPG	PPG	RPG	APG	PCM
67-68	Oakland-A	70	....	1224	608	238	570	.418	29	73	.397	103	132	.780	....	....	89	57	101	1	....	....	62	17.5	8.7	1.3	0.8	.342
ABA Season Totals		70	....	1224	608	238	570	.418	29	73	.397	103	132	.780	....	....	89	57	101	1	....	....	62	17.5	8.7	1.3	0.8	....

• BIANCHI, Al
Alfred A. Bianchi

Born: Mar. 26, 1932. Long Island City, NY, United States. Height: 6'3". Weight: 185 lbs. Drafted: 1954 College: Bowling Green

YEAR	TEAM	GP	GS	MIN	PTS	FGM	FGA	FG%	3PM	3PA	3P%	FTM	FTA	FT%	ORB	DRB	TRB	AST	PF	DQ	STL	BLK	TO	MPG	PPG	RPG	APG	PCM
56-57	Syracuse	68	....	1577	563	199	567	.351				165	239	.690	....	....	227	106	198	5	....	....	....	23.2	8.3	3.3	1.6	.310
57-58	Syracuse	69	....	1421	570	215	625	.344				140	205	.683	....	....	221	114	188	4	....	....	....	20.6	8.3	3.2	1.7	.341
58-59	Syracuse	72	....	1779	719	285	756	.377				149	206	.723	....	....	199	159	260	8	....	....	....	24.7	10.0	2.8	2.2	.334
59-60	Syracuse	69	....	1256	531	211	576	.366				109	155	.703	....	....	179	169	231	5	....	....	....	18.2	7.7	2.6	2.4	.395
60-61	Syracuse	52	....	667	296	118	342	.345				60	87	.690	....	....	105	93	137	5	....	....	....	12.8	5.7	2.0	1.8	.387
61-62	Syracuse	80	....	1925	826	336	847	.397				154	221	.697	....	....	281	263	232	5	....	....	....	24.1	10.3	3.5	3.3	.442
62-63	Syracuse	61	....	1159	524	202	476	.424				120	164	.732	....	....	134	170	165	2	....	....	....	19.0	8.6	2.2	2.8	.463
63-64	Philadelphia	78	....	1437	623	257	684	.376				109	141	.773	....	....	147	149	248	6	....	....	....	18.4	8.0	1.9	1.9	.333
64-65	Philadelphia	60	....	1116	404	175	486	.360				54	76	.711	....	....	95	140	178	10	....	....	....	18.6	6.7	1.6	2.3	.299
65-66	Philadelphia	78	....	1312	494	214	560	.382				66	98	.673	....	....	134	134	232	4	....	....	....	16.8	6.3	1.7	1.7	.295
NBA Season Totals		687	....	13649	5550	2212	5919	.374				1126	1592	.707	....	....	1722	1497	2069	54	....	....	....	19.9	8.1	2.5	2.2	....
56-57	Syracuse	5	....	97	32	12	38	.316				8	12	.667	....	....	15	8	16	1	....	....	....	19.4	6.4	3.0	1.6	.272
57-58	Syracuse	2	....	37	11	4	12	.333				3	8	.375	....	....	7	2	4	0	....	....	....	18.5	5.5	3.5	1.0	.258
58-59	Syracuse	9	....	192	82	34	74	.459				14	22	.636	....	....	29	25	41	4	....	....	....	21.3	9.1	3.2	2.8	.451
59-60	Syracuse	2	....	18	0	0	8	.000				0	0	.000	....	....	3	3	2	0	....	....	....	9.0	0.0	1.5	1.5	-.045
60-61	Syracuse	7	....	90	42	17	46	.370				8	9	.889	....	....	7	5	20	1	....	....	....	12.9	6.0	1.0	0.7	.261
61-62	Syracuse	5	....	184	71	27	69	.391				17	20	.850	....	....	26	18	17	0	....	....	....	36.8	14.2	5.2	3.6	.395
62-63	Syracuse	5	....	77	34	15	34	.441				4	7	.571	....	....	8	2	17	0	....	....	....	15.4	6.8	1.6	0.4	.257
63-64	Philadelphia	5	....	68	27	12	29	.414				3	4	.750	....	....	4	4	12	0	....	....	....	13.6	5.4	0.8	0.8	.246
64-65	Philadelphia	11	....	308	104	45	118	.381				14	21	.667	....	....	16	30	45	2	....	....	....	28.0	9.5	1.5	2.7	.251
65-66	Philadelphia	5	....	64	45	18	43	.419				9	12	.750	....	....	10	4	19	1	....	....	....	12.8	9.0	2.0	0.8	.461
NBA Playoff Totals		56	....	1135	448	184	471	.391				80	115	.696	....	....	125	101	193	9	....	....	....	20.3	8.0	2.2	1.8	....

• BIANCO, Johnny
John Bianco

Born: 1922. Height: 6'4". Weight: 195 lbs. Drafted: — College: St. John's (NY)

YEAR	TEAM	GP	GS	MIN	PTS	FGM	FGA	FG%	3PM	3PA	3P%	FTM	FTA	FT%	ORB	DRB	TRB	AST	PF	DQ	STL	BLK	TO	MPG	PPG	RPG	APG	PCM
46-47	Toledo-N	10	....	....	10	4	....	....	....	....	....	2	6	.333	....	....	....	....	....	....	....	....	....	1.0	....	....	....	....
NBL Season Totals		10	....	....	10	4	....	....	....	....	....	2	6	....	....	....	....	....	....	....	....	....	....	1.0	....	....	....	....

• BIASATTI, Hank
Henry Arcado Biasatti

Born: Jan. 14, 1922. Beano, Italy. Died: Jan.14, 1996. Height: 5'11". Weight: 175 lbs. Drafted: 1947 College: Assumption (ONT)

YEAR	TEAM	GP	GS	MIN	PTS	FGM	FGA	FG%	3PM	3PA	3P%	FTM	FTA	FT%	ORB	DRB	TRB	AST	PF	DQ	STL	BLK	TO	MPG	PPG	RPG	APG	PCM
46-47	Toronto	6	....	....	6	2	5	.400	....	....	....	2	4	.500	....	....	0	3	....	....	....	....	....	1.0	....	0.0	....	
NBA Season Totals		6	....	....	6	2	5	.400	....	....	....	2	4	.500	....	....	0	3	....	....	....	....	....	1.0	....	0.0	....	

• BIBBY, Henry
Charles Henry Bibby

Born: Nov. 24, 1949. Franklinton, NC, United States. Height: 6'1". Weight: 185 lbs. Drafted: 1972 College: UCLA

YEAR	TEAM	GP	GS	MIN	PTS	FGM	FGA	FG%	3PM	3PA	3P%	FTM	FTA	FT%	ORB	DRB	TRB	AST	PF	DQ	STL	BLK	TO	MPG	PPG	RPG	APG	PCM
72-73	New York	55	....	475	229	78	205	.380				73	86	.849			82	64	67	0	....	....		8.6	4.2	1.5	1.2	.482
73-74	New York	66	....	986	493	210	465	.452				73	88	.830	48	85	133	91	123	0	65	2		14.9	7.5	2.0	1.4	.441
74-75	New York	47	....	876	427	179	400	.448				69	96	.719	29	58	87	105	96	0	29	3		18.6	9.1	1.9	2.2	.435
74-75	New Orleans	28	....	524	250	91	219	.416				68	93	.731	18	32	50	76	61	0	25	0		18.7	8.9	1.8	2.7	.446
75-76	New Orleans	79	....	1772	732	266	622	.428				200	251	.797	58	121	179	225	165	0	62	3		22.4	9.3	2.3	2.8	.420
76-77	Philadelphia	81	....	2639	825	302	702	.430				221	282	.784	86	187	273	356	200	2	108	5		32.6	10.2	3.4	4.4	.382
77-78	Philadelphia	82	....	2518	743	286	659	.434				171	219	.781	62	189	251	464	207	0	91	6	156	30.7	9.1	3.1	5.7	.395

YEAR	TEAM	GP	GS	MIN	PTS	FGM	FGA	FG%	3PM	3PA	3P%	FTM	FTA	FT%	ORB	DRB	TRB	AST	PF	DQ	STL	BLK	TO	MPG	PPG	RPG	APG	PCM
78-79	Philadelphia	82	....	2538	1002	368	869	.423	....	....	....	266	335	.794	72	172	244	371	199	0	72	7	197	31.0	12.2	3.0	4.5	.376
79-80	Philadelphia	82	....	2035	739	251	626	.401	11	52	.212	226	286	.790	65	143	208	307	161	0	62	6	148	24.8	9.0	2.5	3.7	.369
80-81	San Diego	73	....	1112	335	118	306	.386	32	95	.337	67	98	.684	25	49	74	200	85	0	47	2	73	15.2	4.6	1.0	2.7	.337
NBA Season Totals		675	....	15475	5775	2149	5073	.424	43	147	.293	1434	1834	.782	463	1036	1581	2259	1364	2	561	34	574	22.9	8.6	2.3	3.3	....
72-73	New York	6	....	43	20	8	18	.444	....	....	....	4	8	.500	....	....	2	3	5	0	....	....	....	7.2	3.3	0.3	0.5	.295
73-74	New York	10	....	89	42	16	45	.356	....	....	....	10	12	.833	5	5	10	11	15	0	3	0	....	8.9	4.2	1.0	1.1	.351
76-77	Philadelphia	19	....	691	211	83	197	.421	....	....	....	45	59	.763	28	43	71	75	59	0	24	2	....	36.4	11.1	3.7	3.9	.329
77-78	Philadelphia	10	....	289	86	33	82	.402	....	....	....	20	22	.909	9	21	30	48	25	0	12	0	22	28.9	8.6	3.0	4.8	.356
78-79	Philadelphia	9	....	231	72	26	67	.388	....	....	....	20	30	.667	8	11	19	42	26	0	4	0	22	25.7	8.0	2.1	4.7	.287
79-80	Philadelphia	18	....	400	135	45	124	.363	5	13	.385	40	50	.800	15	29	44	52	35	0	7	0	27	22.2	7.5	2.4	2.9	.305
NBA Playoff Totals		72	....	1743	566	211	533	.396	5	13	.385	139	181	.768	65	109	176	231	165	0	50	2	71	24.2	7.9	2.4	3.2	....

• BIBBY, Mike

Michael Bibby

Born: May 13, 1978. Cherry Hill, NJ, United States.   Height: 6'1".   Weight: 190 lbs.   Drafted: 1998   College: Arizona

YEAR	TEAM	GP	GS	MIN	PTS	FGM	FGA	FG%	3PM	3PA	3P%	FTM	FTA	FT%	ORB	DRB	TRB	AST	PF	DQ	STL	BLK	TO	MPG	PPG	RPG	APG	PCM
98-99	Vancouver	50	50	1758	662	260	605	.430	15	74	.203	127	169	.751	30	106	136	325	122	0	78	5	146	35.2	13.2	2.7	6.5	.403
99-00	Vancouver	82	82	3155	1190	459	1031	.445	77	212	.363	195	250	.780	73	233	306	665	171	0	132	15	247	38.5	14.5	3.7	8.1	.469
00-01	Vancouver	82	82	3190	1301	525	1157	.454	108	285	.379	143	188	.761	47	257	304	685	148	1	107	12	248	38.9	15.9	3.7	8.4	.489
01-02	Sacramento	80	80	2659	1098	446	985	.453	51	138	.370	155	193	.803	37	185	222	403	133	0	87	15	134	33.2	13.7	2.8	5.0	.431
02-03	Sacramento	55	55	1835	875	329	700	.470	56	137	.409	161	187	.861	34	113	147	285	93	0	72	8	127	33.4	15.9	2.7	5.2	.483
NBA Season Totals		349	349	12597	5126	2019	4478	.451	307	846	.363	781	987	.791	221	894	1115	2363	667	1	476	55	902	36.1	14.7	3.2	6.8	....
01-02	Sacramento	16	16	661	324	114	257	.444	25	59	.424	71	86	.826	14	46	60	80	30	0	23	3	37	41.3	20.3	3.8	5.0	.463
02-03	Sacramento	12	12	404	152	57	135	.422	11	39	.282	27	34	.794	8	23	31	60	31	1	14	5	18	33.7	12.7	2.6	5.0	.392
NBA Playoff Totals		28	28	1065	476	171	392	.436	36	98	.367	98	120	.817	22	69	91	140	61	1	37	8	55	38.0	17.0	3.3	5.0	....

• BIEDENBACH, Ed

Edward Joseph (Eddie) Biedenbach

Born: Aug. 12, 1945.   Height: 6'1".   Weight: 175 lbs.   Drafted: 1968   College: North Carolina State

YEAR	TEAM	GP	GS	MIN	PTS	FGM	FGA	FG%	3PM	3PA	3P%	FTM	FTA	FT%	ORB	DRB	TRB	AST	PF	DQ	STL	BLK	TO	MPG	PPG	RPG	APG	PCM
68-69	Phoenix	7	....	18	4	0	6	.000	....	....	....	4	6	.667	....	....	2	3	1	0	....	....	....	2.6	0.6	0.3	0.4	.161
NBA Season Totals		7	....	18	4	0	6	.000	....	....	....	4	6	.667	....	....	2	3	1	0	....	....	....	2.6	0.6	0.3	0.4	....

• BIELKE, Don

Donald P. Bielke

Born: —.   Height: 6'7".   Weight: 240 lbs.   Drafted: 1954   College: Valparaiso

YEAR	TEAM	GP	GS	MIN	PTS	FGM	FGA	FG%	3PM	3PA	3P%	FTM	FTA	FT%	ORB	DRB	TRB	AST	PF	DQ	STL	BLK	TO	MPG	PPG	RPG	APG	PCM
55-56	Fort Wayne	7	....	38	14	5	9	.556	....	....	....	4	7	.571	....	....	9	1	9	0	....	....	....	5.4	2.0	1.3	0.1	.381
NBA Season Totals		7	....	38	14	5	9	.556	....	....	....	4	7	.571	....	....	9	1	9	0	....	....	....	5.4	2.0	1.3	0.1	....

• BIGELOW, Bob

Robert S. Bigelow

Born: Dec. 26, 1953. Boston, MA, United States.   Height: 6'7".   Weight: 215 lbs.   Drafted: 1975   College: Pennsylvania

YEAR	TEAM	GP	GS	MIN	PTS	FGM	FGA	FG%	3PM	3PA	3P%	FTM	FTA	FT%	ORB	DRB	TRB	AST	PF	DQ	STL	BLK	TO	MPG	PPG	RPG	APG	PCM
75-76	Kansas City	31	....	163	56	16	47	.340	....	....	....	24	33	.727	9	20	29	9	18	0	4	1	....	5.3	1.8	0.9	0.3	.325
76-77	Kansas City	29	....	162	85	35	70	.500	....	....	....	15	17	.882	8	19	27	8	17	0	3	1	....	5.6	2.9	0.9	0.3	.488
77-78	Kansas City	1	....	7	2	1	1	1.000	....	....	....	0	0	.000	2	3	5	0	2	0	0	0	0	7.0	2.0	5.0	0.0	.786
77-78	Boston	4	....	17	6	3	12	.250	....	....	....	0	0	.000	1	3	4	0	1	0	0	0	0	4.3	1.5	1.0	0.0	.070
78-79	San Diego	29	....	413	85	36	90	.400	....	....	....	13	21	.619	15	31	46	25	37	0	12	2	17	14.2	2.9	1.6	0.9	.200
NBA Season Totals		94	....	762	234	91	220	.414	....	....	....	52	71	.732	35	76	111	42	75	0	19	4	17	8.1	2.5	1.2	0.4	....

• BIGGS, Max

Max Biggs

Born: 1926.   Height: 6'   Weight: 190 lbs.   Drafted: —   College: Purdue

YEAR	TEAM	GP	GS	MIN	PTS	FGM	FGA	FG%	3PM	3PA	3P%	FTM	FTA	FT%	ORB	DRB	TRB	AST	PF	DQ	STL	BLK	TO	MPG	PPG	RPG	APG	PCM
46-47	Sheboygan-N	4	....	....	2	1	....	....	....	....	....	0	0	.000	....	....	....	....	....	....	....	....	....	0.5	....	....	....	....
NBL Playoff Totals		4	....	....	2	1	....	....	....	....	....	0	0		....	....	....	....	....	....	....	....	....	0.5	....	....	....	....

• BILLINGY, Lionel

Lionel (Big Train) Billingy

Born: 1952.   Height: 6'9".   Weight: 215 lbs.   Drafted: 1974   College: Duquesne

YEAR	TEAM	GP	GS	MIN	PTS	FGM	FGA	FG%	3PM	3PA	3P%	FTM	FTA	FT%	ORB	DRB	TRB	AST	PF	DQ	STL	BLK	TO	MPG	PPG	RPG	APG	PCM
74-75	Virginia-A	46	....	1022	393	150	351	.427	0	2	.000	93	143	.650	107	173	280	49	112	....	40	10	122	22.2	8.5	6.1	1.1	.436
ABA Season Totals		46	....	1022	393	150	351	.427	0	2	.000	93	143	.650	107	173	280	49	112	....	40	10	122	22.2	8.5	6.1	1.1	....

• BILLUPS, Chauncey

Chauncey Ray Billups

Born: Sept. 25, 1976. Denver, CO, United States.   Height: 6'3".   Weight: 202 lbs.   Drafted: 1997   College: Colorado

YEAR	TEAM	GP	GS	MIN	PTS	FGM	FGA	FG%	3PM	3PA	3P%	FTM	FTA	FT%	ORB	DRB	TRB	AST	PF	DQ	STL	BLK	TO	MPG	PPG	RPG	APG	PCM
97-98	Boston	51	44	1296	565	177	454	.390	64	189	.339	147	180	.817	40	73	113	217	118	1	77	2	117	25.4	11.1	2.2	4.3	.422
97-98	Toronto	29	26	920	328	103	295	.349	43	136	.316	79	86	.919	22	55	77	97	54	1	30	2	55	31.7	11.3	2.7	3.3	.303
98-99	Denver	45	41	1488	624	191	495	.386	85	235	.362	157	172	.913	24	72	96	173	115	0	58	14	98	33.1	13.9	2.1	3.8	.370
99-00	Denver	13	5	305	112	34	101	.337	7	41	.171	37	44	.841	8	26	34	39	27	0	10	2	24	23.5	8.6	2.6	3.0	.322
00-01	Minnesota	77	33	1790	713	248	587	.422	73	194	.376	144	171	.842	32	126	158	260	178	2	51	11	111	23.2	9.3	2.1	3.4	.392
01-02	Minnesota	82	54	2356	1027	348	823	.423	124	315	.394	207	234	.885	35	191	226	450	169	1	66	17	138	28.7	12.5	2.8	5.5	.490
02-03	Detroit	74	74	2327	1199	366	870	.421	149	380	.392	318	362	.878	38	235	273	287	136	0	63	15	134	31.4	16.2	3.7	3.9	.503
NBA Season Totals		371	277	10482	4568	1467	3625	.405	545	1490	.366	1089	1249	.872	199	778	977	1523	797	5	355	63	677	28.3	12.3	2.6	4.1	....

YEAR	TEAM	GP	GS	MIN	PTS	FGM	FGA	FG%	3PM	3PA	3P%	FTM	FTA	FT%	ORB	DRB	TRB	AST	PF	DQ	STL	BLK	TO	MPG	PPG	RPG	APG	PCM
00-01	Minnesota	3	0	26	3	1	6	.167	0	1	.000	1	1	1.000	1	4	5	2	5	0	0	0	1	8.7	1.0	1.7	0.7	.079
01-02	Minnesota	3	3	134	66	23	51	.451	6	15	.400	14	20	.700	1	14	15	17	14	1	3	1	9	44.7	22.0	5.0	5.7	.442
02-03	Detroit	14	14	485	252	71	190	.374	26	84	.310	84	90	.933	4	43	47	66	38	0	9	2	34	34.6	18.0	3.4	4.7	.449
NBA Playoff Totals		20	17	645	321	95	247	.385	32	100	.320	99	111	.892	6	61	67	85	57	1	12	3	44	32.3	16.1	3.4	4.3	....

• BING, Dave
David Bing

Born: Nov. 24, 1943. Washington, DC, United States.   Height: 6'3".   Weight: 180 lbs.   Drafted: 1966   College: Syracuse   HOF: 1990

YEAR	TEAM	GP	GS	MIN	PTS	FGM	FGA	FG%	3PM	3PA	3P%	FTM	FTA	FT%	ORB	DRB	TRB	AST	PF	DQ	STL	BLK	TO	MPG	PPG	RPG	APG	PCM
66-67	Detroit	80	....	2762	1601	664	1522	.436	....	....	....	273	370	.738	....	....	359	330	217	2	....	....	....	34.5	20.0	4.5	4.1	.534
67-68	Detroit	79	....	3209	**2142**	835	**1893**	.441	....	....	....	472	668	.707	....	....	373	509	254	2	....	....	....	40.6	**27.1**	4.7	6.4	.632
68-69	Detroit	77	....	3039	1800	678	1594	.425	....	....	....	444	623	.713	....	....	382	546	256	3	....	....	....	39.5	23.4	5.0	7.1	.595
69-70	Detroit	70	....	2334	1604	575	1295	.444	....	....	....	454	580	.783	....	....	299	418	196	0	....	....	....	33.3	22.9	4.3	6.0	.668
70-71	Detroit	82	....	3065	2213	799	1710	.467	....	....	....	**615**	**772**	.797	....	....	364	408	228	4	....	....	....	37.4	27.0	4.4	5.0	.666
71-72	Detroit	45	....	1936	1016	369	891	.414	....	....	....	278	354	.785	....	....	186	317	138	3	....	....	....	43.0	22.6	4.1	7.0	.513
72-73	Detroit	82	....	3361	1840	692	1545	.448	....	....	....	456	560	.814	....	....	298	637	229	1	....	....	....	41.0	22.4	3.6	7.8	.580
73-74	Detroit	81	....	3124	1520	582	1336	.436	....	....	....	356	438	.813	108	173	281	555	216	1	109	17	....	38.6	18.8	3.5	6.9	.521
74-75	Detroit	79	....	3222	1499	578	1333	.434	....	....	....	343	424	.809	86	200	286	610	222	3	116	26	....	40.8	19.0	3.6	7.7	.518
75-76	Washington	82	....	2945	1326	497	1113	.447	....	....	....	332	422	.787	94	143	237	492	262	0	118	23	....	35.9	16.2	2.9	6.0	.479
76-77	Washington	64	....	1516	678	271	597	.454	....	....	....	136	176	.773	54	89	143	275	150	1	61	5	....	23.7	10.6	2.2	4.3	.495
77-78	Boston	80	....	2256	1088	422	940	.449	....	....	....	244	296	.824	76	136	212	300	247	2	79	18	216	28.2	13.6	2.7	3.8	.409
NBA Season Totals		901	....	32769	18327	6962	15769	.441	....	....	....	4403	5683	.775	418	741	3420	5397	2615	22	483	89	216	36.4	20.3	3.8	6.0	....
67-68	Detroit	6	....	254	169	68	166	.410	....	....	....	33	45	.733	....	....	24	29	21	0	....	....	....	42.3	28.2	4.0	4.8	.518
73-74	Detroit	7	....	312	132	55	131	.420	....	....	....	22	30	.733	6	20	26	42	20	0	3	1	....	44.6	18.9	3.7	6.0	.403
74-75	Detroit	3	....	134	48	20	47	.426	....	....	....	8	13	.615	3	8	11	29	12	0	5	0	....	44.7	16.0	3.7	9.7	.450
75-76	Washington	7	....	209	96	34	76	.447	....	....	....	28	35	.800	6	12	18	28	18	0	7	2	....	29.9	13.7	2.6	4.0	.462
76-77	Washington	8	....	55	32	14	32	.438	....	....	....	4	4	1.000	3	3	6	5	5	0	0	1	....	6.9	4.0	0.8	0.6	.458
NBA Playoff Totals		31	....	964	477	191	452	.423	....	....	....	95	127	.748	18	43	85	133	76	0	15	4	....	31.1	15.4	2.7	4.3	....

• BINION, Joe
Joe Binion

Born: Mar. 26, 1961. Rochester, NY, United States.   Height: 6'8".   Weight: 235 lbs.   Drafted: 1984   College: North Carolina A&T

YEAR	TEAM	GP	GS	MIN	PTS	FGM	FGA	FG%	3PM	3PA	3P%	FTM	FTA	FT%	ORB	DRB	TRB	AST	PF	DQ	STL	BLK	TO	MPG	PPG	RPG	APG	PCM
86-87	Portland	11	0	51	14	4	10	.400	0	0	.000	6	10	.600	8	10	18	1	5	0	2	2	3	4.6	1.3	1.6	0.1	.451
NBA Season Totals		11	0	51	14	4	10	.400	0	0	.000	6	10	.600	8	10	18	1	5	0	2	2	3	4.6	1.3	1.6	0.1	....

• BIRCH, Paul
Paul (Polly) Birch

Born: Jan. 14, 1910. Homestead, PA, United States. Died: June5, 1982.   Height: 6'1".   Weight: 190 lbs.   Drafted: —   College: Duquesne

YEAR	TEAM	GP	GS	MIN	PTS	FGM	FGA	FG%	3PM	3PA	3P%	FTM	FTA	FT%	ORB	DRB	TRB	AST	PF	DQ	STL	BLK	TO	MPG	PPG	RPG	APG	PCM
38-39	Pittsburgh-N	22	....	....	221	85	....	....	....	....	....	51	....	....	....	....	....	....	....	....	....	....	....	....	10.0			
41-42	Fort Wayne-N	8	....	....	42	16	....	....	....	....	....	10	....	....	....	....	....	....	....	....	....	....	....	....	5.3			
42-43	Fort Wayne-N	23	....	....	78	29	....	....	....	....	....	20	....	....	....	....	....	....	....	....	....	....	....	....	3.4			
43-44	Fort Wayne-N	22	....	....	71	27	....	....	....	....	....	17	....	....	....	....	....	....	....	....	....	....	....	....	3.2			
44-45	Fort Wayne-N	28	....	....	65	29	....	....	....	....	....	7	....	....	....	....	....	....	....	....	....	....	....	....	2.3			
45-46	Youngstown-N	31	....	....	96	35	....	....	....	....	....	26	....	....	....	....	....	....	....	....	....	....	....	....	3.1			
NBL Season Totals		134	....	....	573	221	....	....	....	....	....	131	....	....	....	....	....	....	....	....	....	....	....	....	4.3			
41-42	Fort Wayne-N	6	....	....	37	15	....	....	....	....	....	7	....	....	....	....	....	....	....	....	....	....	....	....	6.2			
42-43	Fort Wayne-N	6	....	....	8	3	....	....	....	....	....	2	....	....	....	....	....	....	....	....	....	....	....	....	1.3			
43-44	Fort Wayne-N	5	....	....	16	7	....	....	....	....	....	2	....	....	....	....	....	....	....	....	....	....	....	....	3.2			
44-45	Fort Wayne-N	3	....	....	7	2	....	....	....	....	....	3	....	....	....	....	....	....	....	....	....	....	....	....	2.3			
NBL Playoff Totals		20	....	....	68	27	....	....	....	....	....	14	....	....	....	....	....	....	....	....	....	....	....	....	3.4			

• BIRD, Jerry
Jerry Lee Bird

Born: Feb. 2, 1935. Corbin, KY, United States.   Height: 6'6".   Weight: 210 lbs.   Drafted: 1956   College: Kentucky

YEAR	TEAM	GP	GS	MIN	PTS	FGM	FGA	FG%	3PM	3PA	3P%	FTM	FTA	FT%	ORB	DRB	TRB	AST	PF	DQ	STL	BLK	TO	MPG	PPG	RPG	APG	PCM
58-59	New York	11	....	45	25	12	32	.375	....	....	....	1	1	1.000	....	....	12	4	7	0	....	....	....	4.1	2.3	1.1	0.4	.474
NBA Season Totals		11	....	45	25	12	32	.375	....	....	....	1	1	1.000	....	....	12	4	7	0	....	....	....	4.1	2.3	1.1	0.4	....

• BIRD, Larry
Larry Joe Bird

Born: Dec. 7, 1956. West Baden, IN, United States.   Height: 6'9".   Weight: 220 lbs.   Drafted: 1978   College: Indiana State   HOF: 1998

YEAR	TEAM	GP	GS	MIN	PTS	FGM	FGA	FG%	3PM	3PA	3P%	FTM	FTA	FT%	ORB	DRB	TRB	AST	PF	DQ	STL	BLK	TO	MPG	PPG	RPG	APG	PCM
79-80	Boston	82	....	2955	1745	693	1463	.474	58	143	.406	301	360	.836	216	636	852	370	279	4	143	53	262	36.0	21.3	10.4	4.5	.681
80-81	Boston	82	....	3239	1741	719	1503	.478	20	74	.270	283	328	.863	191	704	895	451	239	2	161	63	287	39.5	21.2	10.9	5.5	.663
81-82	Boston	77	58	2923	1761	711	1414	.503	11	52	.212	328	380	.863	200	637	837	447	244	0	143	66	254	38.0	22.9	10.9	5.8	.749
82-83	Boston	79	79	2982	1867	747	1481	.504	22	77	.286	351	418	.840	193	677	870	458	197	0	148	71	237	37.7	23.6	11.0	5.8	.790
83-84	Boston	79	77	3028	1908	758	1542	.492	18	73	.247	374	421	**.888**	181	615	796	520	197	0	144	69	237	38.3	24.2	10.1	6.6	.773
84-85	Boston	80	77	3161	2295	918	1760	.522	56	131	.427	403	457	.882	164	678	842	531	208	0	129	98	248	**39.5**	28.7	10.5	6.6	.861
85-86	Boston	82	81	3113	2115	796	1606	.496	82	**194**	.423	441	492	**.896**	190	615	805	557	182	0	166	51	262	38.0	25.8	9.8	6.8	.821
86-87	Boston	74	73	3005	2076	786	1497	.525	90	225	.400	414	455	**.910**	124	558	682	566	185	3	135	70	237	**40.6**	28.1	9.2	7.6	.838
87-88	Boston	76	75	2965	2275	881	1672	.527	98	237	.414	415	453	.916	108	595	703	467	157	0	125	57	213	39.0	29.9	9.3	6.1	.867
88-89	Boston	6	6	189	116	49	104	.471	0	0	.000	18	19	.947	1	36	37	29	18	0	6	5	11	31.5	19.3	6.2	4.8	.643
89-90	Boston	75	75	2944	1820	718	1517	.473	65	195	.333	319	343	**.930**	90	622	712	562	173	2	106	61	240	39.3	24.3	9.5	7.5	.739
90-91	Boston	60	60	2277	1164	462	1017	.454	77	198	.389	163	183	.891	53	456	509	431	118	0	108	58	186	38.0	19.4	8.5	7.2	.658
91-92	Boston	45	45	1662	908	353	758	.466	52	128	.406	150	162	.926	46	388	434	306	82	0	42	33	126	36.9	20.2	9.6	6.8	.705
NBA Season Totals		897	706	34443	21791	8591	17334	.496	649	1727	.376	3960	4471	.886	1757	7217	8974	5695	2279	11	1556	755	2800	38.4	24.3	10.0	6.3	....
79-80	Boston	9	....	372	192	83	177	.469	4	15	.267	22	25	.880	22	79	101	42	30	0	14	8	33	41.3	21.3	11.2	4.7	.590
80-81	Boston	17	....	750	373	147	313	.470	3	8	.375	76	85	.894	49	189	238	103	53	0	39	17	62	44.1	21.9	14.0	6.1	.689
81-82	Boston	12	12	490	214	88	206	.427	1	6	.167	37	45	.822	33	117	150	67	43	0	23	17	38	40.8	17.8	12.5	5.6	.600
82-83	Boston	6	6	240	123	49	116	.422	1	4	.250	24	29	.828	20	55	75	41	15	0	13	3	19	40.0	20.5	12.5	6.8	.681

YEAR	TEAM	GP	GS	MIN	PTS	FGM	FGA	FG%	3PM	3PA	3P%	FTM	FTA	FT%	ORB	DRB	TRB	AST	PF	DQ	STL	BLK	TO	MPG	PPG	RPG	APG	PCM
83-84	Boston	23	23	961	632	229	437	.524	7	17	.412	167	190	.879	62	190	252	136	71	0	54	27	87	41.8	27.5	11.0	5.9	.800
84-85	Boston	20	20	815	520	196	425	.461	7	25	.280	121	136	.890	53	129	182	115	54	0	34	19	57	40.8	26.0	9.1	5.8	.691
85-86	Boston	18	18	770	466	171	331	.517	23	56	.411	101	109	.927	34	134	168	148	55	0	37	11	47	42.8	25.9	9.3	8.2	.784
86-87	Boston	23	23	1015	622	216	454	.476	14	41	.341	176	193	.912	41	190	231	165	55	1	27	19	71	44.1	27.0	10.0	7.2	.724
87-88	Boston	17	17	763	417	152	338	.450	12	32	.375	101	113	.894	29	121	150	115	45	0	36	14	49	44.9	24.5	8.8	6.8	.630
89-90	Boston	5	5	207	122	44	99	.444	5	19	.263	29	32	.906	7	39	46	44	10	0	5	5	18	41.4	24.4	9.2	8.8	.709
90-91	Boston	10	10	396	171	62	152	.408	3	21	.143	44	51	.863	8	64	72	65	28	0	13	3	19	39.6	17.1	7.2	6.5	.516
91-92	Boston	4	2	107	45	21	42	.500	0	5	.000	3	4	.750	2	16	18	21	7	0	1	2	6	26.8	11.3	4.5	5.3	.544
NBA Playoff Totals		164	136	6886	3897	1458	3090	.472	80	249	.321	901	1012	.890	360	1323	1683	1062	466	1	296	145	506	42.0	23.8	10.3	6.5	....

• BIRDSONG, Otis

Otis Lee (Bird) Birdsong

Born: Dec. 9, 1955. Winter Haven, FL, United States.   Height: 6'3".   Weight: 190 lbs.   Drafted: 1977   College: Houston

YEAR	TEAM	GP	GS	MIN	PTS	FGM	FGA	FG%	3PM	3PA	3P%	FTM	FTA	FT%	ORB	DRB	TRB	AST	PF	DQ	STL	BLK	TO	MPG	PPG	RPG	APG	PCM
77-78	Kansas City	73	....	1878	1156	470	955	.492	....	....	....	216	310	.697	70	105	175	174	179	1	74	12	146	25.7	15.8	2.4	2.4	.484
78-79	Kansas City	82	....	2839	1778	741	1456	.509	....	....	....	296	408	.725	176	178	354	281	255	2	125	17	197	34.6	21.7	4.3	3.4	.546
79-80	Kansas City	82	....	2885	1858	781	1546	.505	10	36	.278	286	412	.694	170	161	331	202	226	2	136	22	180	35.2	22.7	4.0	2.5	.522
80-81	Kansas City	71	....	2593	1747	710	1306	.544	10	35	.286	317	455	.697	119	139	258	233	172	2	93	18	170	36.5	24.6	3.6	3.3	.578
81-82	New Jersey	37	22	1025	524	225	480	.469	0	10	.000	74	127	.583	30	67	97	124	74	0	30	5	63	27.7	14.2	2.6	3.4	.418
82-83	New Jersey	62	54	1885	936	426	834	.511	2	6	.333	82	145	.566	53	97	150	239	155	0	85	16	112	30.4	15.1	2.4	3.9	.455
83-84	New Jersey	69	57	2168	1365	583	1147	.508	5	20	.250	194	319	.608	74	96	170	266	180	2	86	17	173	31.4	19.8	2.5	3.9	.496
84-85	New Jersey	56	45	1842	1155	495	968	.511	4	21	.190	161	259	.622	60	88	148	232	145	1	84	7	118	32.9	20.6	2.6	4.1	.522
85-86	New Jersey	77	74	2395	1214	542	1056	.513	8	22	.364	122	210	.581	88	114	202	261	228	8	85	17	177	31.1	15.8	2.6	3.0	.412
86-87	New Jersey	7	6	127	44	19	42	.452	0	1	.000	6	9	.667	3	4	7	17	16	0	3	0	9	18.1	6.3	1.0	2.4	.259
87-88	New Jersey	67	59	1882	730	337	736	.458	9	25	.360	47	92	.511	73	94	167	222	143	2	54	11	127	28.1	10.9	2.5	3.3	.322
88-89	Boston	13	0	108	37	18	36	.500	1	3	.333	0	2	.000	4	9	13	9	10	0	3	1	12	8.3	2.8	1.0	0.7	.268
NBA Season Totals		696	317	21627	12544	5347	10562	.506	49	179	.274	1801	2748	.655	920	1152	2072	2260	1783	20	858	143	1484	31.1	18.0	3.0	3.2	....
78-79	Kansas City	5	....	168	105	39	76	.513	....	....	....	27	38	.711	8	10	18	9	13	0	10	0	10	33.6	21.0	3.6	1.8	.518
79-80	Kansas City	3	....	112	66	30	62	.484	0	3	.000	6	14	.429	11	12	23	7	5	0	4	0	6	37.3	22.0	7.7	2.3	.516
80-81	Kansas City	8	....	234	124	56	98	.571	1	1	1.000	11	18	.611	8	13	21	27	13	1	12	0	20	29.3	15.5	2.6	3.4	.504
82-83	New Jersey	2	0	37	13	6	16	.375	0	1	.000	1	2	.500	1	1	2	9	3	0	3	0	1	18.5	6.5	1.0	4.5	.423
83-84	New Jersey	11	11	387	167	71	171	.415	0	1	.000	25	48	.521	7	19	26	41	38	0	20	1	22	35.2	15.2	2.4	3.7	.291
85-86	New Jersey	3	3	132	69	29	55	.527	0	3	.000	11	19	.579	5	7	12	10	14	0	6	3	9	44.0	23.0	4.0	3.3	.428
88-89	Boston	3	1	20	2	1	5	.200	0	2	.000	0	0	.000	0	2	2	1	3	0	1	1	3	6.7	0.7	0.7	0.3	-.056
NBA Playoff Totals		35	15	1090	546	232	483	.480	1	11	.091	81	139	.583	40	64	104	104	89	1	56	5	71	31.1	15.6	3.0	3.0	....

• BIRK, Emmet

Emmet C. Birk

Born: Mar. 12, 1914. Died: Nov.6, 2000.   Height: 6'1".   Weight: 185 lbs.   Drafted: —   College: North Dakota

YEAR	TEAM	GP	GS	MIN	PTS	FGM	FGA	FG%	3PM	3PA	3P%	FTM	FTA	FT%	ORB	DRB	TRB	AST	PF	DQ	STL	BLK	TO	MPG	PPG	RPG	APG	PCM
38-39	Oshkosh-N	1	....	....	0	0	....	....	....	....	....	0	....	....	....	....	....	....	....	....	....	....	....	0.0	....	....	....	
NBL Season Totals		1	....	....	0	0	....	....	....	....	....	0	....	....	....	....	....	....	....	....	....	....	....	0.0	....	....	....	

• BIRR, Jim

Jim (Crash) Birr

Born: 1916.   Height: 6'3".   Weight: 215 lbs.   Drafted: —   College: Indiana

YEAR	TEAM	GP	GS	MIN	PTS	FGM	FGA	FG%	3PM	3PA	3P%	FTM	FTA	FT%	ORB	DRB	TRB	AST	PF	DQ	STL	BLK	TO	MPG	PPG	RPG	APG	PCM
38-39	Indianapolis-N	24	....	....	182	77	....	....	....	....	....	28	....	....	....	....	....	....	....	....	....	....	....	....	7.6	....	....	....
39-40	Indianapolis-N	3	....	....	21	10	....	....	....	....	....	1	....	....	....	....	....	....	....	....	....	....	....	....	7.0	....	....	....
45-46	Indianapolis-N	3	....	....	6	3	....	....	....	....	....	0	0	.000	....	....	....	....	....	....	....	....	....	....	2.0	....	....	....
NBL Season Totals		30	....	....	209	90	....	....	....	....	....	29	0	....	....	....	....	....	....	....	....	....	....	....	7.0	....	....	....

• BISHOP, Gale

Gale Bishop

Born: June 4, 1922. Sumas, WA, United States.   Height: 6'3".   Weight: 195 lbs.   Drafted: —   College: Washington State

YEAR	TEAM	GP	GS	MIN	PTS	FGM	FGA	FG%	3PM	3PA	3P%	FTM	FTA	FT%	ORB	DRB	TRB	AST	PF	DQ	STL	BLK	TO	MPG	PPG	RPG	APG	PCM
48-49	Philadelphia	56	....	....	467	170	523	.325	....	....	....	127	195	.651	....	....	92	137	....	....	....	....	....	....	8.3	....	1.6	....
NBA Season Totals		56	....	....	467	170	523	.325	....	....	....	127	195	.651	....	....	92	137	....	....	....	....	....	....	8.3	....	1.6	....
48-49	Philadelphia	2	....	....	18	7	26	.269	....	....	....	4	8	.500	....	....	2	3	....	....	....	....	....	....	9.0	....	1.0	....
NBA Playoff Totals		2	....	....	18	7	26	.269	....	....	....	4	8	.500	....	....	2	3	....	....	....	....	....	....	9.0	....	1.0	....

• BISHOP, Ralph

Ralph Bishop

Born: Oct. 1, 1915. Brooklyn, NY, United States.   Height: 6'4".   Weight: 190 lbs.   Drafted: 1947   College: Washington

YEAR	TEAM	GP	GS	MIN	PTS	FGM	FGA	FG%	3PM	3PA	3P%	FTM	FTA	FT%	ORB	DRB	TRB	AST	PF	DQ	STL	BLK	TO	MPG	PPG	RPG	APG	PCM
48-49	Denver-N	12	....	....	22	10	....	....	....	....	....	2	3	.667	....	....	....	....	15	....	....	....	....	....	1.8	....	....	....
NBL Season Totals		12	....	....	22	10	....	....	....	....	....	2	3		....	....	....	....	15	....	....	....	....	....	1.8	....	....	....

• BLAB, Uwe

Uwe Konstantine Blab

Born: Mar. 26, 1962. Munich, Germany.   Height: 7'1".   Weight: 252 lbs.   Drafted: 1985   College: Indiana

YEAR	TEAM	GP	GS	MIN	PTS	FGM	FGA	FG%	3PM	3PA	3P%	FTM	FTA	FT%	ORB	DRB	TRB	AST	PF	DQ	STL	BLK	TO	MPG	PPG	RPG	APG	PCM
85-86	Dallas	48	0	409	124	44	94	.468	0	0	.000	36	67	.537	25	66	91	17	65	0	3	12	29	8.5	2.6	1.9	0.4	.300
86-87	Dallas	30	0	160	53	20	51	.392	0	0	.000	13	28	.464	11	25	36	13	33	0	4	9	15	5.3	1.8	1.2	0.4	.296
87-88	Dallas	73	1	658	162	58	132	.439	0	0	.000	46	65	.708	52	82	134	35	108	1	8	29	51	9.0	2.2	1.8	0.5	.278
88-89	Dallas	37	0	208	68	24	52	.462	0	0	.000	20	25	.800	11	33	44	12	36	0	3	13	15	5.6	1.8	1.2	0.3	.373
89-90	Golden State	40	33	481	83	33	87	.379	0	0	.000	17	31	.548	28	71	99	24	93	0	1	22	32	12.0	2.1	2.5	0.6	.192
89-90	San Antonio	7	0	50	15	6	11	.545	0	0	.000	3	6	.500	1	8	9	1	9	0	0	0	5	7.1	2.1	1.3	0.1	.190
NBA Season Totals		235	34	1966	505	185	427	.433	0	0	.000	135	222	.608	128	285	413	102	344	1	19	85	147	8.4	2.1	1.8	0.4	....

YEAR	TEAM	GP	GS	MIN	PTS	FGM	FGA	FG%	3PM	3PA	3P%	FTM	FTA	FT%	ORB	DRB	TRB	AST	PF	DQ	STL	BLK	TO	MPG	PPG	RPG	APG	PCM
85-86	Dallas	1	0	6	4	2	3	.667	0	0	.000	0	0	.000	0	1	1	0	1	0	0	0	0	6.0	4.0	1.0	0.0	.589
86-87	Dallas	1	0	10	3	1	1	1.000	0	0	.000	1	4	.250	1	2	3	0	4	0	1	1	2	10.0	3.0	3.0	0.0	.253
87-88	Dallas	3	0	8	2	0	2	.000	0	0	.000	2	2	1.000	1	0	1	1	1	0	0	0	1	2.7	0.7	0.3	0.3	.092
89-90	San Antonio	2	0	5	3	0	1	.000	0	0	.000	3	6	.500	0	2	2	0	0	0	0	0	0	2.5	1.5	1.0	0.0	.506
NBA Playoff Totals		7	0	29	12	3	7	.429	0	0	.000	6	12	.500	2	5	7	1	6	0	1	1	3	4.1	1.7	1.0	0.1	....

• BLACK, Charlie

Charles Bradford (Hawk) Black Jr.

Born: June 15, 1921. Arco, ID, United States. Died: Dec.22, 1992.   Height: 6'5".   Weight: 200 lbs.   Drafted: —   College: Kansas

YEAR	TEAM	GP	GS	MIN	PTS	FGM	FGA	FG%	3PM	3PA	3P%	FTM	FTA	FT%	ORB	DRB	TRB	AST	PF	DQ	STL	BLK	TO	MPG	PPG	RPG	APG	PCM
47-48	Anderson-N	58	....	....	445	148	....	....	....	....	....	149	249	.598			....	196	....	....	....	....	....	7.7	....	....	....
48-49	Indianapolis	41	....	....	437	157	546	.288	....	....	....	123	229	.537		....	115	183	....	....	....	....	....	10.7	....	2.8	....
48-49	Fort Wayne	17	....	....	130	46	145	.317	....	....	....	38	62	.613		....	25	64	....	....	....	....	....	7.6	....	1.5	....
49-50	Fort Wayne	36	....	....	382	125	435	.287	....	....	....	132	209	.632		....	75	140	....	....	....	....	....	10.6	....	2.1	....
49-50	Anderson	29	....	....	279	101	378	.267	....	....	....	77	112	.688		....	88	133	....	....	....	....	....	9.6	....	3.0	....
51-52	Milwaukee	13	....	117	17	6	31	.194	....	....	....	5	12	.417		....	31	9	31	2	....	....	....	9.0	1.3	2.4	0.7	.165
NBA Season Totals		136	....	117	1245	435	1535	.283	....	....		375	624	.601		....	31	312	551	2	....	....	....	0.9	9.2	0.2	2.3	....
NBL Season Totals		58	....	....	445	148			....	....		149	249	....		....		196	....	....	....	....	....	7.7	....	....	....
Career Totals		194	....	117	1690	583	1535		....	....		524	873	....		....	31	312	747	2	....	....	....	0.6	8.7	0.2	1.6	....
47-48	Anderson-N	6	....	....	66	28	....	....				10	22	.455			....	....	....	....	....	....	11.0	....	....	....
49-50	Anderson	8	....	....	57	18	61	.295				21	29	.724		....	17	38	....		....	....	....	7.1	....	2.1	....
NBA Playoff Totals		8	....	....	57	18	61	.295				21	29	.724		....	17	38	....		....	....	....	7.1	....	2.1	....
NBL Playoff Totals		6	....	....	66	28						10	22				....	....			....	....	....	11.0	....	....	....
Career Playoff Totals		14	....	....	123	46	61					31	51			....	17	38	....		....	....	....	8.8	....	1.2	....

• BLACK, Norman

Norman Augustus Black

Born: Nov. 12, 1957. Baltimore, MD, United States.   Height: 6'5".   Weight: 185 lbs.   Drafted: —   College: St. Joseph's (PA)

YEAR	TEAM	GP	GS	MIN	PTS	FGM	FGA	FG%	3PM	3PA	3P%	FTM	FTA	FT%	ORB	DRB	TRB	AST	PF	DQ	STL	BLK	TO	MPG	PPG	RPG	APG	PCM
80-81	Detroit	3	....	28	8	3	10	.300	0	0	.000	2	8	.250	0	2	2	2	2	0	1	0	1	9.3	2.7	0.7	0.7	.071
NBA Season Totals		3	....	28	8	3	10	.300	0	0	.000	2	8	.250	0	2	2	2	2	0	1	0	1	9.3	2.7	0.7	0.7	....

• BLACK, Tom

Thomas Donald Black

Born: July 9, 1941.   Height: 6'10".   Weight: 220 lbs.   Drafted: 1964   College: South Dakota State

YEAR	TEAM	GP	GS	MIN	PTS	FGM	FGA	FG%	3PM	3PA	3P%	FTM	FTA	FT%	ORB	DRB	TRB	AST	PF	DQ	STL	BLK	TO	MPG	PPG	RPG	APG	PCM
70-71	Seattle	55	....	773	273	111	268	.414	....	....	....	51	73	.699	....	....	225	42	116	1	....	....	....	14.1	5.0	4.1	0.8	.414
70-71	Cincinnati	16	....	100	26	10	33	.303	....	....	....	6	15	.400	....	....	34	2	20	0	....	....	....	6.3	1.6	2.1	0.1	.253
NBA Season Totals		71	....	873	299	121	301	.402	....	....	....	57	88	.648	....	....	259	44	136	1	....	....	....	12.3	4.2	3.6	0.6	....

• BLACKLIDGE, Thermon

Thermon (Blackie) Blacklidge

Born: Mar. 19, 1920. Moselle, MS, United States. Died: July6, 1972.   Height: 6'3".   Weight: 185 lbs.   Drafted: —   College: Delta State

YEAR	TEAM	GP	GS	MIN	PTS	FGM	FGA	FG%	3PM	3PA	3P%	FTM	FTA	FT%	ORB	DRB	TRB	AST	PF	DQ	STL	BLK	TO	MPG	PPG	RPG	APG	PCM
41-42	Sheboygan-N	11	....	....	51	17	....	....	....	....	....	17	....	....	....	....	....	....	....	....	....	....	....	4.6	....	....	....
NBL Season Totals		11	....	....	51	17			....	....	....	17			....	....	....	....	....	....	....	....	....	4.6	....	....	....

• BLACKMAN, Rolando

Rolando Antonio Blackman

Born: Feb. 26, 1959. Panama City, Panama.   Height: 6'6".   Weight: 190 lbs.   Drafted: 1981   College: Kansas State

YEAR	TEAM	GP	GS	MIN	PTS	FGM	FGA	FG%	3PM	3PA	3P%	FTM	FTA	FT%	ORB	DRB	TRB	AST	PF	DQ	STL	BLK	TO	MPG	PPG	RPG	APG	PCM
81-82	Dallas	82	16	1979	1091	439	855	.513	1	4	.250	212	276	.768	97	157	254	105	122	0	46	30	115	24.1	13.3	3.1	1.3	.472
82-83	Dallas	75	62	2349	1326	513	1042	.492	3	15	.200	297	381	.780	108	185	293	185	116	0	37	29	120	31.3	17.7	3.9	2.5	.501
83-84	Dallas	81	81	3025	1815	721	1320	.546	1	11	.091	372	458	.812	124	249	373	288	127	0	56	37	170	37.3	22.4	4.6	3.6	.576
84-85	Dallas	81	80	2834	1598	625	1230	.508	6	20	.300	342	413	.828	107	193	300	289	96	0	61	16	162	35.0	19.7	3.7	3.6	.517
85-86	Dallas	82	81	2787	1762	677	1318	.514	4	29	.138	404	483	.836	88	203	291	271	138	0	79	25	189	34.0	21.5	3.5	3.3	.555
86-87	Dallas	80	80	2758	1676	626	1264	.495	5	15	.333	419	474	.884	96	182	278	266	142	0	64	21	176	34.5	21.0	3.5	3.3	.525
87-88	Dallas	71	69	2580	1325	497	1050	.473	0	5	.000	331	379	.873	82	164	246	262	112	0	64	18	142	36.3	18.7	3.5	3.7	.461
88-89	Dallas	78	78	2946	1534	594	1249	.476	30	85	.353	316	370	.854	70	203	273	288	137	0	65	20	164	37.8	19.7	3.5	3.7	.450
89-90	Dallas	80	80	2934	1552	626	1256	.498	13	43	.302	287	340	.844	88	192	280	289	128	0	77	21	176	36.7	19.4	3.5	3.6	.468
90-91	Dallas	80	80	2965	1590	634	1316	.482	40	114	.351	282	326	.865	63	193	256	301	153	0	69	19	160	37.1	19.9	3.2	3.8	.457
91-92	Dallas	75	74	2527	1374	535	1161	.461	65	169	.385	239	266	.898	78	161	239	204	134	0	50	22	150	33.7	18.3	3.2	2.7	.430
92-93	New York	60	33	1434	580	239	539	.443	31	73	.425	71	90	.789	23	79	102	157	129	1	22	10	66	23.9	9.7	1.7	2.6	.322
93-94	New York	55	1	969	400	161	369	.436	30	84	.357	48	53	.906	23	70	93	76	100	0	25	6	44	17.6	7.3	1.7	1.4	.327
NBA Season Totals		980	815	32087	17623	6887	13969	.493	229	667	.343	3620	4309	.840	1047	2231	3278	2981	1634	1	715	274	1834	32.7	18.0	3.3	3.0	....
83-84	Dallas	10	10	397	239	93	175	.531	0	0	.000	53	63	.841	15	26	41	40	15	0	6	4	24	39.7	23.9	4.1	4.0	.552
84-85	Dallas	4	4	169	131	47	92	.511	1	2	.500	36	38	.947	11	15	26	19	8	0	2	2	14	42.3	32.8	6.5	4.8	.708
85-86	Dallas	10	10	371	208	83	167	.497	0	1	.000	42	53	.792	15	20	35	32	26	1	8	1	20	37.1	20.8	3.5	3.2	.456
86-87	Dallas	4	4	153	94	36	73	.493	0	1	.000	22	24	.917	4	10	14	17	7	0	2	0	8	38.3	23.5	3.5	4.3	.529
87-88	Dallas	17	17	672	307	126	261	.483	0	3	.000	55	62	.887	26	29	55	77	28	0	15	3	25	39.5	18.1	3.2	4.5	.434
89-90	Dallas	3	3	127	60	24	54	.444	2	5	.400	10	10	1.000	2	7	9	13	7	0	6	2	13	42.3	20.0	3.0	4.3	.364
92-93	New York	15	0	214	63	22	64	.344	4	15	.267	15	18	.833	4	13	17	16	22	0	3	2	21	14.3	4.2	1.1	1.1	.141
93-94	New York	6	0	34	8	3	11	.273	2	4	.500	0	0	.000	1	2	3	3	6	0	0	0	1	5.7	1.3	0.5	0.5	.088
NBA Playoff Totals		69	48	2137	1110	434	897	.484	9	31	.290	233	268	.869	78	122	200	217	119	1	42	14	126	31.0	16.1	2.9	3.1	....

YEAR	TEAM	GP	GS	MIN	PTS	FGM	FGA	FG%	3PM	3PA	3P%	FTM	FTA	FT%	ORB	DRB	TRB	AST	PF	DQ	STL	BLK	TO	MPG	PPG	RPG	APG	PCM

• BLACKWELL, Alex

Robert Alexander Blackwell

Born: June 27, 1970. Toms River, NJ, United States.　Height: 6'6".　Weight: 250 lbs.　Drafted: —　College: Monmouth

YEAR	TEAM	GP	GS	MIN	PTS	FGM	FGA	FG%	3PM	3PA	3P%	FTM	FTA	FT%	ORB	DRB	TRB	AST	PF	DQ	STL	BLK	TO	MPG	PPG	RPG	APG	PCM
92-93	LA Lakers	27	0	109	34	14	42	.333	0	3	.000	6	8	.750	10	13	23	7	14	0	4	2	5	4.0	1.3	0.9	0.3	.278
NBA Season Totals		27	0	109	34	14	42	.333	0	3	.000	6	8	.750	10	13	23	7	14	0	4	2	5	4.0	1.3	0.9	0.3	....

• BLACKWELL, Cory

Cory Blackwell

Born: Mar. 27, 1963. Chicago, IL, United States.　Height: 6'6".　Weight: 210 lbs.　Drafted: 1984　College: Wisconsin

YEAR	TEAM	GP	GS	MIN	PTS	FGM	FGA	FG%	3PM	3PA	3P%	FTM	FTA	FT%	ORB	DRB	TRB	AST	PF	DQ	STL	BLK	TO	MPG	PPG	RPG	APG	PCM
84-85	Seattle	60	0	551	202	87	237	.367	0	2	.000	28	55	.509	42	54	96	26	55	0	25	3	42	9.2	3.4	1.6	0.4	.233
NBA Season Totals		60	0	551	202	87	237	.367	0	2	.000	28	55	.509	42	54	96	26	55	0	25	3	42	9.2	3.4	1.6	0.4	....

• BLACKWELL, James

James Blackwell

Born: Feb. 25, 1968. Mount Kisco, NY, United States.　Height: 6'　Weight: 190 lbs.　Drafted: —　College: Dartmouth

YEAR	TEAM	GP	GS	MIN	PTS	FGM	FGA	FG%	3PM	3PA	3P%	FTM	FTA	FT%	ORB	DRB	TRB	AST	PF	DQ	STL	BLK	TO	MPG	PPG	RPG	APG	PCM
94-95	Charlotte	4	0	19	4	2	3	.667	0	0	.000	0	0	.000	0	3	3	5	1	0	1	0	2	4.8	1.0	0.8	1.3	.515
94-95	Boston	9	0	61	14	6	10	.600	0	0	.000	2	3	.667	2	6	8	6	7	0	3	0	3	6.8	1.6	0.9	0.7	.334
NBA Season Totals		13	0	80	18	8	13	.615	0	0	.000	2	3	.667	2	9	11	11	8	0	4	0	5	6.2	1.4	0.8	0.8	....

• BLACKWELL, Nate

Nathaniel Blackwell

Born: Feb. 15, 1965. Philadelphia, PA, United States.　Height: 6'4".　Weight: 170 lbs.　Drafted: 1987　College: Temple

YEAR	TEAM	GP	GS	MIN	PTS	FGM	FGA	FG%	3PM	3PA	3P%	FTM	FTA	FT%	ORB	DRB	TRB	AST	PF	DQ	STL	BLK	TO	MPG	PPG	RPG	APG	PCM
87-88	San Antonio	10	0	112	37	15	41	.366	2	11	.182	5	6	.833	2	4	6	18	16	0	3	0	8	11.2	3.7	0.6	1.8	.223
NBA Season Totals		10	0	112	37	15	41	.366	2	11	.182	5	6	.833	2	4	6	18	16	0	3	0	8	11.2	3.7	0.6	1.8	....

• BLANEY, George

George R. Blaney

Born: Nov. 12, 1939. Jersey City, NJ, United States.　Height: 6'1".　Weight: 175 lbs.　Drafted: 1961　College: Holy Cross

YEAR	TEAM	GP	GS	MIN	PTS	FGM	FGA	FG%	3PM	3PA	3P%	FTM	FTA	FT%	ORB	DRB	TRB	AST	PF	DQ	STL	BLK	TO	MPG	PPG	RPG	APG	PCM
61-62	New York	36	....	363	117	54	142	.380	....	....	....	9	17	.529	....	....	36	45	34	0	....	....	....	10.1	3.3	1.0	1.3	.316
NBA Season Totals		36	....	363	117	54	142	.380	....	....	....	9	17	.529	....	....	36	45	34	0	....	....	....	10.1	3.3	1.0	1.3	....

• BLANKS, Lance

Lance Blanks

Born: Sept. 9, 1966. Del Rio, TX, United States.　Height: 6'4".　Weight: 190 lbs.　Drafted: —　College: Texas

YEAR	TEAM	GP	GS	MIN	PTS	FGM	FGA	FG%	3PM	3PA	3P%	FTM	FTA	FT%	ORB	DRB	TRB	AST	PF	DQ	STL	BLK	TO	MPG	PPG	RPG	APG	PCM
90-91	Detroit	38	0	214	64	26	61	.426	2	16	.125	10	14	.714	4	16	20	26	35	0	9	2	19	5.6	1.7	0.5	0.7	.243
91-92	Detroit	43	0	189	64	25	55	.455	6	16	.375	8	11	.727	9	13	22	19	26	0	14	1	13	4.4	1.5	0.5	0.4	.346
92-93	Minnesota	61	2	642	161	65	150	.433	11	43	.256	20	32	.625	18	50	68	72	61	1	16	5	31	10.5	2.6	1.1	1.2	.278
NBA Season Totals		142	2	1045	289	116	266	.436	19	75	.253	38	57	.667	31	79	110	117	122	1	39	8	63	7.4	2.0	0.8	0.8	....
91-92	Detroit	1	0	10	2	1	2	.500	0	0	.000	0	0	.000	0	1	1	3	2	0	3	0	1	10.0	2.0	1.0	3.0	.614
NBA Playoff Totals		1	0	10	2	1	2	.500	0	0	.000	0	0	.000	0	1	1	3	2	0	3	0	1	10.0	2.0	1.0	3.0	....

• BLANTON, Ricky

Ricky Wayne Blanton

Born: Apr. 21, 1966. Miami, FL, United States.　Height: 6'7".　Weight: 215 lbs.　Drafted: 1989　College: Louisiana State

YEAR	TEAM	GP	GS	MIN	PTS	FGM	FGA	FG%	3PM	3PA	3P%	FTM	FTA	FT%	ORB	DRB	TRB	AST	PF	DQ	STL	BLK	TO	MPG	PPG	RPG	APG	PCM
92-93	Chicago	2	0	13	6	3	7	.429	0	0	.000	0	0	.000	2	1	3	1	1	0	2	0	1	6.5	3.0	1.5	0.5	.508
NBA Season Totals		2	0	13	6	3	7	.429	0	0	.000	0	0	.000	2	1	3	1	1	0	2	0	1	6.5	3.0	1.5	0.5	....

• BLAYLOCK, Mookie

Daron Oshay (Mookie) Blaylock

Born: Mar. 20, 1967. Garland, TX, United States.　Height: 6'　Weight: 180 lbs.　Drafted: 1989　College: Oklahoma

YEAR	TEAM	GP	GS	MIN	PTS	FGM	FGA	FG%	3PM	3PA	3P%	FTM	FTA	FT%	ORB	DRB	TRB	AST	PF	DQ	STL	BLK	TO	MPG	PPG	RPG	APG	PCM
89-90	New Jersey	50	17	1267	505	212	571	.371	18	80	.225	63	81	.778	42	98	140	210	110	0	82	14	110	25.3	10.1	2.8	4.2	.355
90-91	New Jersey	72	70	2585	1017	432	1039	.416	14	91	.154	139	176	.790	67	182	249	441	180	0	169	40	209	35.9	14.1	3.5	6.1	.407
91-92	New Jersey	72	67	2548	996	429	993	.432	12	54	.222	126	177	.712	101	168	269	492	182	1	170	40	151	35.4	13.8	3.7	6.8	.469
92-93	Atlanta	80	78	2820	1069	414	964	.429	118	315	.375	123	169	.728	89	191	280	671	156	0	203	23	184	35.3	13.4	3.5	8.4	.524
93-94	Atlanta	81	81	2915	1118	444	1079	.411	114	341	.334	116	159	.730	117	307	424	789	144	0	212	44	194	36.0	13.8	5.2	9.7	.600
94-95	Atlanta	80	80	3069	1373	509	1198	.425	199	555	.359	156	214	.729	117	276	393	616	164	3	200	26	240	38.4	17.2	4.9	7.7	.532
95-96	Atlanta	81	81	2893	1268	455	1123	.405	231	623	.371	127	170	.747	110	222	332	478	151	1	212	17	186	35.7	15.7	4.1	5.9	.487
96-97	Atlanta	78	78	3056	1354	501	1159	.432	221	**604**	.366	131	174	.753	114	299	413	463	141	0	**212**	20	187	39.2	17.4	5.3	5.9	.516
97-98	Atlanta	70	69	2700	921	368	938	.392	90	334	.269	95	134	.709	81	260	341	469	122	0	183	21	175	38.6	13.2	4.9	6.7	.435
98-99	Atlanta	48	48	1763	640	247	651	.379	77	251	.307	69	91	.758	45	179	224	278	61	0	99	9	115	36.7	13.3	4.7	5.8	.423
99-00	Golden State	73	72	2459	822	327	837	.391	101	301	.336	95	105	.705	55	215	270	489	122	0	146	22	143	33.7	11.3	3.7	6.7	.444
00-01	Golden State	69	59	2352	760	317	801	.396	73	225	.324	53	76	.697	71	201	272	462	134	1	163	20	128	34.1	11.0	3.9	6.7	.450
01-02	Golden State	35	0	599	119	50	146	.342	15	42	.357	4	8	.500	8	44	52	114	20	0	24	4	37	17.1	3.4	1.5	3.3	.309
NBA Season Totals		889	800	31026	11962	4705	11499	.409	1283	3816	.336	1269	1724	.736	1017	2642	3659	5972	1687	6	2075	300	2059	34.9	13.5	4.1	6.7	....
91-92	New Jersey	4	4	148	38	17	55	.309	1	6	.167	3	4	.750	5	11	16	31	16	0	15	2	7	37.0	9.5	4.0	7.8	.352
92-93	Atlanta	3	3	99	27	9	25	.360	4	12	.333	5	6	.833	2	11	13	13	9	0	3	4	11	33.0	9.0	4.3	4.3	.300
93-94	Atlanta	11	11	415	143	48	141	.340	22	64	.344	25	30	.833	16	39	55	98	22	0	24	5	32	37.7	13.0	5.0	8.9	.480
94-95	Atlanta	3	3	121	54	18	49	.367	11	28	.393	7	11	.636	7	6	13	17	6	0	4	0	9	40.3	18.0	4.3	5.7	.378
95-96	Atlanta	10	10	426	171	61	145	.421	33	84	.393	16	24	.667	13	30	43	64	15	0	22	8	29	42.6	17.1	4.3	6.4	.447
96-97	Atlanta	10	10	441	164	61	154	.396	28	85	.329	14	21	.667	12	58	70	65	15	0	21	2	35	44.1	16.4	7.0	6.5	.432
97-98	Atlanta	4	4	153	59	22	53	.415	8	27	.296	7	12	.583	6	14	20	33	8	0	9	1	9	38.3	14.8	5.0	8.3	.521
98-99	Atlanta	9	9	358	113	44	135	.326	18	51	.353	7	15	.467	6	30	36	36	11	0	18	2	30	39.8	12.6	4.0	4.0	.242
NBA Playoff Totals		54	54	2161	769	280	757	.370	125	357	.350	84	123	.683	67	199	266	357	102	0	116	24	162	40.0	14.2	4.9	6.6	....

• BLEVINS, Leon

Leon Gravette Blevins

Born: June 25, 1926. Height: 6'2". Weight: 160 lbs. Drafted: 1950 College: Arizona

YEAR	TEAM	GP	GS	MIN	PTS	FGM	FGA	FG%	3PM	3PA	3P%	FTM	FTA	FT%	ORB	DRB	TRB	AST	PF	DQ	STL	BLK	TO	MPG	PPG	RPG	APG	PCM
50-51	Indianapolis	3	....	....	2	1	4	.250	....	....	....	0	1	.000	....	....	2	1	3	0	....	....	....	....	0.7	0.7	0.3	....
NBA Season Totals		3	....	....	2	1	4	.250	....	....	....	0	1	.000	....	....	2	1	3	0	....	....	....	....	0.7	0.7	0.3	....

• BLOCK, John

John William Block Jr.

Born: Apr. 16, 1944. Los Angeles, CA, United States. Height: 6'9". Weight: 207 lbs. Drafted: 1966 College: USC

YEAR	TEAM	GP	GS	MIN	PTS	FGM	FGA	FG%	3PM	3PA	3P%	FTM	FTA	FT%	ORB	DRB	TRB	AST	PF	DQ	STL	BLK	TO	MPG	PPG	RPG	APG	PCM
66-67	LA Lakers	22	....	118	64	20	52	.385	....	....	....	24	34	.706	....	....	45	5	20	0	....	....	....	5.4	2.9	2.0	0.2	.580
67-68	San Diego	52	....	1805	1048	366	865	.423	....	....	....	316	394	.802	....	....	571	71	189	3	....	....	....	34.7	20.2	11.0	1.4	.601
68-69	San Diego	78	....	2489	1195	448	1061	.422	....	....	....	299	400	.748	....	....	703	141	249	0	....	....	....	31.9	15.3	9.0	1.8	.518
69-70	San Diego	82	....	2152	1193	453	1025	.442	....	....	....	287	367	.782	....	....	609	137	275	2	....	....	....	26.2	14.5	7.4	1.7	.568
70-71	San Diego	73	....	1464	702	245	584	.420	....	....	....	212	270	.785	....	....	442	98	193	2	....	....	....	20.1	9.6	6.1	1.3	.543
71-72	Milwaukee	79	....	1524	672	233	530	.440	....	....	....	206	275	.749	....	....	410	95	213	4	....	....	....	19.3	8.5	5.2	1.2	.496
72-73	Philadelphia	48	....	1558	858	311	706	.441	....	....	....	236	302	.781	....	....	442	94	173	0	....	....	....	32.5	17.9	9.2	2.0	.580
72-73	Omaha	25	....	483	224	80	180	.444	....	....	....	64	76	.842	....	....	120	19	69	0	....	....	....	19.3	9.0	4.8	0.8	.472
73-74	Omaha	82	....	1777	714	275	634	.434	....	....	....	164	206	.796	129	260	389	94	229	2	68	35	....	21.7	8.7	4.7	1.1	.412
74-75	New Orleans	4	....	57	27	9	29	.310	....	....	....	9	10	.900	6	12	18	7	11	0	4	1	....	14.3	6.8	4.5	1.8	.495
74-75	Chicago	50	....	882	405	150	317	.473	....	....	....	105	134	.784	63	151	214	44	110	0	38	31	....	17.6	8.1	4.3	0.9	.495
75-76	Chicago	2	....	7	4	2	4	.500	....	....	....	0	2	.000	0	2	2	0	2	0	1	0	....	3.5	2.0	1.0	0.0	.326
NBA Season Totals		597	....	14316	7106	2592	5987	.433	....	....	....	1922	2470	.778	198	425	3965	805	1733	13	111	67	....	24.0	11.9	6.6	1.3	....
66-67	LA Lakers	1	....	1	0	0	0	.000	....	....	....	0	0	.000	....	....	0	0	0	0	....	....	....	1.0	0.0	0.0	0.0	.000
68-69	San Diego	5	....	97	62	24	45	.533	....	....	....	14	18	.778	....	....	14	3	18	0	....	....	....	19.4	12.4	2.8	0.6	.520
71-72	Milwaukee	11	....	156	55	20	52	.385	....	....	....	15	18	.833	....	....	55	6	15	0	....	....	....	14.2	5.0	5.0	0.5	.474
74-75	Chicago	4	....	34	13	6	15	.400	....	....	....	1	3	.333	2	4	6	0	5	0	4	0	....	8.5	3.3	1.5	0.0	.219
NBA Playoff Totals		21	....	288	130	50	112	.446	....	....	....	30	39	.769	2	4	75	9	38	0	4	0	....	13.7	6.2	3.6	0.4	....

• BLOEDORN, Charles

Charles (Chuck) Bloedorn

Born: 1912. Height: 6' Weight: 180 lbs. Drafted: — College: Bowling Green

YEAR	TEAM	GP	GS	MIN	PTS	FGM	FGA	FG%	3PM	3PA	3P%	FTM	FTA	FT%	ORB	DRB	TRB	AST	PF	DQ	STL	BLK	TO	MPG	PPG	RPG	APG	PCM
37-38	Wingfoots-N	18	....	....	132	58	....	....	....	....	....	16	....	....	....	....	....	....	....	....	....	....	....	....	7.3	....	....	....
38-39	Wingfoots-N	25	....	....	204	79	....	....	....	....	....	46	....	....	....	....	....	....	....	....	....	....	....	....	8.2	....	....	....
39-40	Wingfoots-N	11	....	....	20	9	....	....	....	....	....	2	....	....	....	....	....	....	....	....	....	....	....	....	1.8	....	....	....
NBL Season Totals		54	....	....	356	146	....	....	....	....	....	64	....	....	....	....	....	....	....	....	....	....	....	....	6.6	....	....	....
37-38	Wingfoots-N	5	....	....	33	14	....	....	....	....	....	5	....	....	....	....	....	....	....	....	....	....	....	....	6.6	....	....	....
NBL Playoff Totals		5	....	....	33	14	....	....	....	....	....	5	....	....	....	....	....	....	....	....	....	....	....	....	6.6	....	....	....

• BLOOM, Mike

Meyer Bloom

Born: Jan. 14, 1915. New York, NY, United States. Died: June5, 1993. Height: 6'6". Weight: 190 lbs. Drafted: — College: Temple

YEAR	TEAM	GP	GS	MIN	PTS	FGM	FGA	FG%	3PM	3PA	3P%	FTM	FTA	FT%	ORB	DRB	TRB	AST	PF	DQ	STL	BLK	TO	MPG	PPG	RPG	APG	PCM
47-48	Baltimore	34	....	....	379	128	471	.272	....	....	....	123	172	.715	....	....	....	24	79	....	....	....	....	....	11.1	....	0.7	....
47-48	Boston	14	....	....	129	46	169	.272	....	....	....	37	57	.649	....	....	....	14	37	....	....	....	....	....	9.2	....	1.0	....
48-49	Minneapolis	24	....	....	55	13	92	.141	....	....	....	29	40	.725	....	....	....	15	22	....	....	....	....	....	2.3	....	0.6	....
48-49	Chicago	21	....	....	71	22	89	.247	....	....	....	27	34	.794	....	....	....	17	31	....	....	....	....	....	3.4	....	0.8	....
NBA Season Totals		93	....	....	634	209	821	.255	....	....	....	216	303	.713	....	....	....	70	169	....	....	....	....	....	6.8	....	0.8	....
47-48	Boston	3	....	....	36	11	42	.262	....	....	....	14	19	.737	....	....	....	2	10	....	....	....	....	....	12.0	....	0.7	....
48-49	Chicago	1	....	....	0	0	0	.000	....	....	....	0	0	.000	....	....	....	0	1	....	....	....	....	....	0.0	....	0.0	....
NBA Playoff Totals		4	....	....	36	11	42	.262	....	....	....	14	19	.737	....	....	....	2	11	....	....	....	....	....	9.0	....	0.5	....

• BLOUNT, Corie

Corie Kasoun Blount

Born: Jan. 4, 1969. Monrovia, CA, United States. Height: 6'9". Weight: 240 lbs. Drafted: 1993 College: Cincinnati

YEAR	TEAM	GP	GS	MIN	PTS	FGM	FGA	FG%	3PM	3PA	3P%	FTM	FTA	FT%	ORB	DRB	TRB	AST	PF	DQ	STL	BLK	TO	MPG	PPG	RPG	APG	PCM
93-94	Chicago	67	8	690	198	76	174	.437	0	0	.000	46	75	.613	76	118	194	56	93	0	19	33	54	10.3	3.0	2.9	0.8	.419
94-95	Chicago	68	9	889	238	100	210	.476	0	2	.000	38	67	.567	107	133	240	60	146	0	26	33	61	13.1	3.5	3.5	0.9	.382
95-96	LA Lakers	57	2	715	183	79	167	.473	0	2	.000	25	44	.568	69	101	170	42	109	2	25	35	46	12.5	3.2	3.0	0.7	.360
96-97	LA Lakers	58	18	1009	241	92	179	.514	1	3	.333	56	83	.675	113	163	276	35	121	2	22	25	52	17.4	4.2	4.8	0.6	.378
97-98	LA Lakers	70	3	1029	253	107	187	.572	0	4	.000	39	78	.500	114	184	298	37	157	2	29	25	49	14.7	3.6	4.3	0.5	.396
98-99	LA Lakers	14	3	162	32	13	33	.394	0	1	.000	6	12	.500	24	22	46	2	27	0	1	4	6	11.6	2.3	3.3	0.1	.258
98-99	Cleveland	20	0	368	68	23	67	.343	0	0	.000	22	42	.524	34	71	105	10	47	0	18	12	15	18.4	3.4	5.3	0.5	.318
99-00	Phoenix	38	1	446	107	44	89	.494	0	2	.000	19	33	.576	52	61	113	10	78	0	15	7	28	11.7	2.8	3.0	0.3	.297
00-01	Phoenix	30	6	387	54	23	47	.489	0	0	.000	8	15	.533	35	50	85	8	75	2	13	5	18	12.9	1.8	2.8	0.3	.209
00-01	Golden State	38	0	918	259	107	247	.433	2	8	.250	43	68	.632	146	169	315	51	90	1	29	17	55	24.2	6.8	8.3	1.3	.449
01-02	Philadelphia	72	21	1427	259	115	251	.458	0	1	.000	29	45	.644	149	219	368	44	176	1	49	26	52	19.8	3.6	5.1	0.6	.316
02-03	Chicago	50	3	836	150	65	134	.485	0	0	.000	20	35	.571	68	137	205	50	121	1	33	19	43	16.7	3.0	4.1	1.0	.328
NBA Season Totals		582	74	8876	2042	844	1785	.473	3	23	.130	351	597	.588	987	1428	2415	405	1240	11	279	241	479	15.3	3.5	4.1	0.7	....
94-95	Chicago	8	0	20	0	0	3	.000	0	1	.000	0	0	.000	1	4	5	0	5	0	0	0	1	2.5	0.0	0.6	0.0	-.070
96-97	LA Lakers	3	0	8	3	1	1	1.000	0	0	.000	1	2	.500	0	2	2	1	2	0	0	0	0	2.7	1.0	0.7	0.3	.567
97-98	LA Lakers	12	0	209	31	12	24	.500	0	0	.000	7	11	.636	24	40	64	7	27	1	6	4	3	17.4	2.6	5.3	0.6	.375
99-00	Phoenix	9	0	162	44	17	31	.548	0	0	.000	10	18	.556	25	31	56	3	36	0	6	6	13	18.0	4.9	6.2	0.3	.398
01-02	Philadelphia	5	0	88	7	2	8	.250	0	0	.000	3	4	.750	10	4	14	2	9	0	2	2	4	17.6	1.4	2.8	0.4	.135
NBA Playoff Totals		37	0	487	85	32	67	.478	0	1	.000	21	35	.600	60	81	141	13	79	1	14	12	21	13.2	2.3	3.8	0.4	....

• BLOUNT, Mark

Mark D. Blount

Born: Nov. 30, 1975. Dobbs Ferry, NY, United States.   Height: 7'   Weight: 230 lbs.   Drafted: 1997   College: Pittsburgh

YEAR	TEAM	GP	GS	MIN	PTS	FGM	FGA	FG%	3PM	3PA	3P%	FTM	FTA	FT%	ORB	DRB	TRB	AST	PF	DQ	STL	BLK	TO	MPG	PPG	RPG	APG	PCM
00-01	Boston	64	50	1098	248	101	200	.505	0	0	.000	46	66	.697	97	134	231	32	183	0	39	76	62	17.2	3.9	3.6	0.5	.326
01-02	Boston	44	0	415	94	32	76	.421	0	0	.000	30	37	.811	26	59	85	10	59	0	16	19	23	9.4	2.1	1.9	0.2	.297
02-03	Denver	54	24	885	281	105	267	.393	0	0	.000	71	99	.717	62	121	183	35	112	1	22	51	70	16.4	5.2	3.4	0.6	.314
02-03	Boston	27	7	518	120	45	80	.563	0	0	.000	30	40	.750	49	76	125	21	75	1	20	17	33	19.2	4.4	4.6	0.8	.366
NBA Season Totals		189	81	2916	743	283	623	.454	0	0	.000	177	242	.731	234	390	624	98	429	2	97	163	188	15.4	3.9	3.3	0.5	....
01-02	Boston	4	0	38	6	2	4	.500	0	0	.000	2	2	1.000	3	4	7	1	7	0	2	2	1	9.5	1.5	1.8	0.3	.294
02-03	Boston	10	0	144	31	12	22	.545	0	0	.000	7	10	.700	12	24	36	2	20	0	11	8	8	14.4	3.1	3.6	0.2	.391
NBA Playoff Totals		14	0	182	37	14	26	.538	0	0	.000	9	12	.750	15	28	43	3	27	0	13	10	9	13.0	2.6	3.1	0.2	....

• BLUME, Ray

Bernard Ray Blume

Born: Sept. 23, 1958. Valdosta, GA, United States.   Height: 6'4".   Weight: 185 lbs.   Drafted: 1981   College: Oregon State

YEAR	TEAM	GP	GS	MIN	PTS	FGM	FGA	FG%	3PM	3PA	3P%	FTM	FTA	FT%	ORB	DRB	TRB	AST	PF	DQ	STL	BLK	TO	MPG	PPG	RPG	APG	PCM
81-82	Chicago	49	2	546	226	102	222	.459	4	18	.222	18	28	.643	14	27	41	68	57	0	23	2	54	11.1	4.6	0.8	1.4	.310
NBA Season Totals		49	2	546	226	102	222	.459	4	18	.222	18	28	.643	14	27	41	68	57	0	23	2	54	11.1	4.6	0.8	1.4	....

• BOBB, Nelson

Nelson Bobb

Born: Feb. 25, 1924. Philadelphia, PA, United States.   Height: 6'   Weight: 170 lbs.   Drafted: —   College: Temple

YEAR	TEAM	GP	GS	MIN	PTS	FGM	FGA	FG%	3PM	3PA	3P%	FTM	FTA	FT%	ORB	DRB	TRB	AST	PF	DQ	STL	BLK	TO	MPG	PPG	RPG	APG	PCM
49-50	Philadelphia	57	....	....	242	80	248	.323	....	....	....	82	131	.626	....	....	....	46	97	....	....	....	....	4.2	....	0.8	....	
50-51	Philadelphia	53	....	....	148	52	158	.329	....	....	....	44	79	.557	....	....	101	82	83	1	....	....	....	2.8	1.9	1.5	....	
51-52	Philadelphia	62	....	1192	319	110	306	.359	....	....	....	99	167	.593	....	....	147	168	182	9	....	....	....	19.2	5.1	2.4	2.7	.346
52-53	Philadelphia	55	....	1286	343	119	318	.374	....	....	....	105	162	.648	....	....	157	192	161	7	....	....	....	23.4	6.2	2.9	3.5	.372
NBA Season Totals		227	....	2478	1052	361	1030	.350	....	....	....	330	539	.612	....	....	405	488	523	17	....	....	....	10.9	4.6	1.8	2.1	....
49-50	Philadelphia	2	....	....	2	1	3	.333	....	....	....	0	0	.000	....	....	....	1	3	....	....	....	....	1.0	....	0.5	....	
50-51	Philadelphia	1	....	....	0	0	0	.000	....	....	....	0	0	.000	....	....	0	2	2	0	....	....	....	0.0	0.0	2.0	....	
51-52	Philadelphia	3	....	29	4	1	3	.333	....	....	....	2	5	.400	....	....	2	1	4	0	....	....	....	9.7	1.3	0.7	0.3	.097
NBA Playoff Totals		6	....	29	6	2	6	.333	....	....	....	2	5	.400	....	....	2	4	9	0	....	....	....	4.8	1.0	0.3	0.7	....

• BOCKHORN, Bucky

Arlen Dale (Bucky) Bockhorn

Born: July 8, 1933. Campbell Hill, IL, United States.   Height: 6'4".   Weight: 200 lbs.   Drafted: 1958   College: Dayton

YEAR	TEAM	GP	GS	MIN	PTS	FGM	FGA	FG%	3PM	3PA	3P%	FTM	FTA	FT%	ORB	DRB	TRB	AST	PF	DQ	STL	BLK	TO	MPG	PPG	RPG	APG	PCM
58-59	Cincinnati	71	....	2251	726	294	771	.381	....	....	....	138	196	.704	....	....	460	206	215	6	....	....	....	31.7	10.2	6.5	2.9	.385
59-60	Cincinnati	75	....	2103	791	323	812	.398	....	....	....	145	194	.747	....	....	382	256	249	8	....	....	....	28.0	10.5	5.1	3.4	.436
60-61	Cincinnati	79	....	2669	992	420	1059	.397	....	....	....	152	208	.731	....	....	434	338	282	9	....	....	....	33.8	12.6	5.5	4.3	.422
61-62	Cincinnati	80	....	3062	1260	531	1234	.430	....	....	....	198	251	.789	....	....	376	366	280	5	....	....	....	38.3	15.8	4.7	4.6	.431
62-63	Cincinnati	80	....	2612	933	375	954	.393	....	....	....	183	242	.756	....	....	322	261	260	6	....	....	....	32.7	11.7	4.0	3.3	.352
63-64	Cincinnati	70	....	1670	580	242	587	.412	....	....	....	96	126	.762	....	....	205	173	227	4	....	....	....	23.9	8.3	2.9	2.5	.349
64-65	Cincinnati	19	....	424	148	60	157	.382	....	....	....	28	39	.718	....	....	55	45	52	1	....	....	....	22.3	7.8	2.9	2.4	.347
NBA Season Totals		474	....	14791	5430	2245	5574	.403	....	....	....	940	1256	.748	....	....	2234	1645	1565	39	....	....	....	31.2	11.5	4.7	3.5	....
61-62	Cincinnati	4	....	157	68	27	62	.435	....	....	....	14	16	.875	....	....	19	20	11	0	....	....	....	39.3	17.0	4.8	5.0	.476
62-63	Cincinnati	12	....	407	135	56	135	.415	....	....	....	23	31	.742	....	....	45	39	44	1	....	....	....	33.9	11.3	3.8	3.3	.331
63-64	Cincinnati	10	....	301	97	41	108	.380	....	....	....	15	20	.750	....	....	39	39	40	1	....	....	....	30.1	9.7	3.9	3.9	.350
NBA Playoff Totals		26	....	865	300	124	305	.407	....	....	....	52	67	.776	....	....	103	98	95	2	....	....	....	33.3	11.5	4.0	3.8	....

• BOEHLER, Bruce

Bruce Boehler

Born: 1917.   Height: 5'11".   Weight: 195 lbs.   Drafted: —   College: Akron

YEAR	TEAM	GP	GS	MIN	PTS	FGM	FGA	FG%	3PM	3PA	3P%	FTM	FTA	FT%	ORB	DRB	TRB	AST	PF	DQ	STL	BLK	TO	MPG	PPG	RPG	APG	PCM
45-46	Cleveland-N	5	....	....	8	4	....	....	....	....	....	0	0	.000	....	....	....	....	....	....	....	....	....	1.6	....	....	....	
NBL Season Totals		5	....	....	8	4	....	....	....	....	....	0	0		....	....	....	....	....	....	....	....	....	1.6	....	....	....	

• BOERWINKLE, Tom

Thomas F. Boerwinkle

Born: Aug. 23, 1945. Cleveland, OH, United States.   Height: 7'   Weight: 265 lbs.   Drafted: 1968   College: Tennessee

YEAR	TEAM	GP	GS	MIN	PTS	FGM	FGA	FG%	3PM	3PA	3P%	FTM	FTA	FT%	ORB	DRB	TRB	AST	PF	DQ	STL	BLK	TO	MPG	PPG	RPG	APG	PCM
68-69	Chicago	80	....	2365	781	318	831	.383	....	....	....	145	222	.653	....	....	889	178	317	11	....	....	....	29.6	9.8	11.1	2.2	.481
69-70	Chicago	81	....	2335	846	348	775	.449	....	....	....	150	226	.664	....	....	1016	229	255	4	....	....	....	28.8	10.4	12.5	2.8	.632
70-71	Chicago	82	....	2370	882	357	736	.485	....	....	....	168	232	.724	....	....	1133	397	275	3	....	....	....	28.9	10.8	13.8	4.8	.775
71-72	Chicago	80	....	2022	556	219	500	.438	....	....	....	118	180	.656	....	....	897	281	253	4	....	....	....	25.3	7.0	11.2	3.5	.629
72-73	Chicago	8	....	176	30	9	24	.375	....	....	....	12	20	.600	....	....	54	40	22	0	....	....	....	22.0	3.8	6.8	5.0	.547
73-74	Chicago	46	....	602	158	58	119	.487	....	....	....	42	60	.700	53	160	213	94	80	0	16	18	....	13.1	3.4	4.6	2.0	.587
74-75	Chicago	80	....	1175	337	132	271	.487	....	....	....	73	95	.768	105	275	380	272	163	0	25	45	....	14.7	4.2	4.8	3.4	.660
75-76	Chicago	74	....	2045	648	265	530	.500	....	....	....	118	177	.667	263	529	792	283	263	0	47	52	....	27.6	8.8	10.7	3.8	.628
76-77	Chicago	82	....	1070	302	134	273	.491	....	....	....	34	63	.540	101	211	312	189	147	0	19	19	....	13.0	3.7	3.8	2.3	.552
77-78	Chicago	22	....	227	56	23	50	.460	....	....	....	10	13	.769	14	45	59	44	36	0	3	4	26	10.3	2.5	2.7	2.0	.440
NBA Season Totals		635	....	14387	4596	1863	4109	.453	....	....	....	870	1288	.675	536	1220	5745	2007	1811	22	110	138	26	22.7	7.2	9.0	3.2	....
69-70	Chicago	5	....	177	88	40	79	.506	....	....	....	8	13	.615	....	....	72	16	19	0	....	....	....	35.4	17.6	14.4	3.2	.703
70-71	Chicago	7	....	169	43	19	41	.463	....	....	....	5	7	.714	....	....	67	31	17	0	....	....	....	24.1	6.1	9.6	4.4	.644
71-72	Chicago	1	....	8	0	0	3	.000	....	....	....	0	0	.000	....	....	6	3	0	0	....	....	....	8.0	0.0	6.0	3.0	.750
72-73	Chicago	4	....	30	9	4	6	.667	....	....	....	1	1	1.000	....	....	9	11	7	0	....	....	....	7.5	2.3	2.3	2.8	.819
73-74	Chicago	2	....	7	2	0	1	.000	....	....	....	2	2	1.000	0	1	1	0	2	0	0	0	....	3.5	1.0	0.5	0.0	.164

YEAR	TEAM	GP	GS	MIN	PTS	FGM	FGA	FG%	3PM	3PA	3P%	FTM	FTA	FT%	ORB	DRB	TRB	AST	PF	DQ	STL	BLK	TO	MPG	PPG	RPG	APG	PCM
74-75	Chicago	13	....	377	106	43	98	.439	....	....	....	20	25	.800	56	109	165	55	48	2	4	10	....	29.0	8.2	12.7	4.2	.637
76-77	Chicago	3	....	17	2	1	5	.200	....	....	....	0	0	.000	2	8	10	7	1	0	0	1	....	5.7	0.7	3.3	2.3	.865
NBA Playoff Totals		35	....	785	250	107	233	.459	....	....	....	36	48	.750	58	118	330	123	94	2	4	11	....	22.4	7.1	9.4	3.5	....

• BOGDANSKI, Ed
Ed Bogdanski

Born: 1921.   Height: 6'4".   Weight: 220 lbs.   Drafted: —   College: DePaul

YEAR	TEAM	GP	GS	MIN	PTS	FGM	FGA	FG%	3PM	3PA	3P%	FTM	FTA	FT%	ORB	DRB	TRB	AST	PF	DQ	STL	BLK	TO	MPG	PPG	RPG	APG	PCM
47-48	Indianapolis-N	19	....	....	32	15	....	....	....	....	....	2	11	.182	....	....	....	....	....	....	....	....	....	....	1.7	....	....	....
NBL Season Totals		19	....	....	32	15	....	....	....	....	....	2	11		....	....	....	....	....	....	....	....	....	....	1.7	....	....	....

• BOGUES, Muggsy
Tyrone Curtis (Muggsy) Bogues

Born: Jan. 9, 1965. Baltimore, MD, United States.   Height: 5'3".   Weight: 136 lbs.   Drafted: 1987   College: Wake Forest

YEAR	TEAM	GP	GS	MIN	PTS	FGM	FGA	FG%	3PM	3PA	3P%	FTM	FTA	FT%	ORB	DRB	TRB	AST	PF	DQ	STL	BLK	TO	MPG	PPG	RPG	APG	PCM
87-88	Washington	79	14	1628	393	166	426	.390	3	16	.188	58	74	.784	35	101	136	404	138	1	127	3	103	20.6	5.0	1.7	5.1	.407
88-89	Charlotte	79	21	1755	423	178	418	.426	1	13	.077	66	88	.750	53	112	165	620	141	1	111	7	126	22.2	5.4	2.1	7.8	.532
89-90	Charlotte	81	65	2743	763	326	664	.491	5	26	.192	106	134	.791	48	159	207	867	168	1	166	3	146	33.9	9.4	2.6	10.7	.544
90-91	Charlotte	81	46	2299	568	241	524	.460	0	12	.000	86	108	.796	58	158	216	669	160	2	137	3	122	28.4	7.0	2.7	8.3	.501
91-92	Charlotte	82	69	2790	730	317	671	.472	2	27	.074	94	120	.783	58	177	235	743	156	0	170	6	156	34.0	8.9	2.9	9.1	.484
92-93	Charlotte	81	80	2833	808	331	730	.453	6	27	.222	140	168	.833	51	247	298	711	179	0	161	5	154	35.0	10.0	3.7	8.8	.490
93-94	Charlotte	77	77	2746	835	354	751	.471	2	12	.167	125	155	.806	78	235	313	780	147	1	133	2	169	35.7	10.8	4.1	10.1	.543
94-95	Charlotte	78	78	2629	862	348	730	.477	6	30	.200	160	180	.889	51	206	257	675	151	0	103	0	133	33.7	11.1	3.3	8.7	.515
95-96	Charlotte	6	0	77	14	6	16	.375	1	4	.000	2	2	1.000	6	1	7	19	4	0	2	0	6	12.8	2.3	1.2	3.2	.334
96-97	Charlotte	65	65	1880	522	204	443	.460	60	144	.417	54	64	.844	25	116	141	469	114	0	82	2	111	28.9	8.0	2.2	7.2	.451
97-98	Charlotte	2	0	16	6	2	5	.400	0	0	.000	2	2	1.000	0	1	1	4	2	0	2	0	1	8.0	3.0	0.5	2.0	.532
97-98	Golden State	59	31	1554	341	139	318	.437	4	16	.250	59	66	.894	30	101	131	327	56	0	65	3	106	26.3	5.8	2.2	5.5	.379
98-99	Golden State	36	5	714	183	76	154	.494	0	6	.000	31	36	.861	16	57	73	134	44	0	43	1	47	19.8	5.1	2.0	3.7	.424
99-00	Toronto	80	5	1731	410	157	358	.439	17	51	.333	79	87	.908	25	110	135	299	119	0	65	4	59	21.6	5.1	1.7	3.7	.363
00-01	Toronto	3	0	34	0	0	2	.000	0	1	.000	0	0	.000	0	3	3	5	3	0	2	0	4	11.3	0.0	1.0	1.7	.096
NBA Season Totals		889	556	25429	6858	2845	6210	.458	106	382	.277	1062	1284	.827	534	1784	2318	6726	1582	6	1369	39	1443	28.6	7.7	2.6	7.6	....
87-88	Washington	1	0	2	0	0	0	.000	0	0	.000	0	0	.000	0	0	0	2	0	0	0	0	1	2.0	0.0	0.0	2.0	.602
92-93	Charlotte	9	9	346	88	39	82	.476	0	2	.000	10	14	.714	6	30	36	70	21	0	24	0	17	38.4	9.8	4.0	7.8	.436
94-95	Charlotte	4	4	145	34	14	45	.311	1	3	.333	5	5	1.000	3	3	6	25	8	0	4	0	9	36.3	8.5	1.5	6.3	.198
96-97	Charlotte	2	2	58	32	11	19	.579	6	7	.857	4	4	1.000	1	2	3	5	3	0	1	0	6	29.0	16.0	1.5	2.5	.459
99-00	Toronto	3	2	87	16	6	21	.286	3	9	.333	1	3	.333	3	3	6	5	4	0	4	0	4	29.0	5.3	2.0	1.7	.121
NBA Playoff Totals		19	17	638	170	70	167	.419	10	21	.476	20	26	.769	13	38	51	107	36	0	33	0	37	33.6	8.9	2.7	5.6	....

• BOHANNON, Etdrick
Etdrick Bohannon

Born: May 29, 1973. San Bernardino, CA, United States.   Height: 6'9".   Weight: 220 lbs.   Drafted: —   College: Auburn-Montgomery

YEAR	TEAM	GP	GS	MIN	PTS	FGM	FGA	FG%	3PM	3PA	3P%	FTM	FTA	FT%	ORB	DRB	TRB	AST	PF	DQ	STL	BLK	TO	MPG	PPG	RPG	APG	PCM
97-98	Indiana	5	0	11	0	0	4	.000	0	0	.000	0	0	.000	2	4	6	1	3	0	0	2	3	2.2	0.0	1.2	0.2	.057
98-99	Washington	2	0	4	0	0	0	.000	0	0	.000	0	0	.000	0	0	0	0	0	0	0	0	0	2.0	0.0	0.0	0.0	.000
99-00	New York	2	0	5	3	0	0	.000	0	0	.000	3	4	.750	1	0	1	0	1	0	0	0	2	2.5	1.5	0.5	0.0	.237
99-00	LA Clippers	11	0	113	26	7	13	.538	0	0	.000	12	20	.600	12	18	30	5	24	0	2	6	8	10.3	2.4	2.7	0.5	.343
00-01	Cleveland	6	0	19	8	2	4	.500	0	0	.000	4	4	1.000	3	4	7	0	4	0	0	2	1	3.2	1.3	1.2	0.0	.610
NBA Season Totals		26	0	152	37	9	21	.429	0	0	.000	19	28	.679	18	26	44	6	32	0	2	10	14	5.8	1.4	1.7	0.2	....

• BOL, Manute
Manute Bol

Born: Oct. 16, 1962. Gogrial, Sudan.   Height: 7'6".   Weight: 200 lbs.   Drafted: 1985   College: Bridgeport

YEAR	TEAM	GP	GS	MIN	PTS	FGM	FGA	FG%	3PM	3PA	3P%	FTM	FTA	FT%	ORB	DRB	TRB	AST	PF	DQ	STL	BLK	TO	MPG	PPG	RPG	APG	PCM
85-86	Washington	80	60	2090	298	128	278	.460	0	1	.000	42	86	.488	123	354	477	23	255	5	28	**397**	64	26.1	3.7	6.0	0.3	.394
86-87	Washington	82	12	1552	251	103	231	.446	0	1	.000	45	67	.672	84	278	362	11	189	1	20	302	57	18.9	3.1	4.4	0.1	.405
87-88	Washington	77	4	1136	176	75	165	.455	0	1	.000	26	49	.531	72	203	275	13	160	0	11	208	39	14.8	2.3	3.6	0.2	.392
88-89	Golden State	80	4	1763	314	127	344	.369	20	91	.220	40	66	.606	116	346	462	27	226	2	11	**345**	80	22.0	3.9	5.8	0.3	.403
89-90	Golden State	75	20	1310	146	56	169	.331	9	48	.188	25	49	.510	33	243	276	36	194	3	13	238	53	17.5	1.9	3.7	0.5	.321
90-91	Philadelphia	82	6	1522	155	65	164	.396	1	14	.071	24	41	.585	66	284	350	20	184	0	16	247	66	18.6	1.9	4.3	0.2	.329
91-92	Philadelphia	71	2	1267	110	49	128	.383	0	9	.000	12	26	.462	54	168	222	22	139	1	11	205	43	17.8	1.5	3.1	0.3	.281
92-93	Philadelphia	58	23	855	126	52	127	.409	10	32	.313	12	19	.632	44	149	193	18	87	0	14	119	52	14.7	2.2	3.3	0.3	.336
93-94	Miami	8	0	61	2	1	12	.083	0	3	.000	0	0	.000	1	10	11	0	4	0	0	6	5	7.6	0.3	1.4	0.0	.018
93-94	Washington	2	0	6	0	0	0	.000	0	0	.000	0	0	.000	0	1	1	1	1	0	0	1	0	3.0	0.0	0.5	0.5	.410
93-94	Philadelphia	4	0	49	6	3	7	.429	0	0	.000	0	0	.000	2	4	6	0	8	0	2	9	0	12.3	1.5	1.5	0.0	.291
94-95	Golden State	5	2	81	15	6	10	.600	3	5	.600	0	0	.000	1	11	12	0	10	0	0	9	1	16.2	3.0	2.4	0.0	.313
NBA Season Totals		624	133	11692	1599	665	1635	.407	43	205	.210	226	403	.561	596	2051	2647	171	1457	12	126	2086	460	18.7	2.6	4.2	0.3	....
85-86	Washington	5	5	152	23	10	17	.588	0	0	.000	3	8	.375	16	22	38	1	15	0	3	29	4	30.4	4.6	7.6	0.2	.458
86-87	Washington	3	0	43	8	4	10	.400	0	1	.000	0	2	.000	5	4	9	0	6	0	0	5	0	14.3	2.7	3.0	0.0	.273
87-88	Washington	5	0	44	9	4	7	.571	0	0	.000	1	1	1.000	7	5	12	0	5	0	0	2	1	8.8	1.8	2.4	0.0	.363
88-89	Golden State	8	0	148	18	7	36	.194	2	22	.091	2	7	.286	5	26	31	1	21	0	2	29	3	18.5	2.3	3.9	0.1	.236
90-91	Philadelphia	8	0	109	24	9	18	.500	0	0	.000	6	9	.667	4	15	19	1	14	0	1	12	5	13.6	3.0	2.4	0.1	.311
NBA Playoff Totals		29	5	496	82	34	88	.386	2	23	.087	12	27	.444	37	72	109	3	61	0	6	77	13	17.1	2.8	3.8	0.1	....

• BOLGER, Ed
William J. Bolger

Born: Aug. 21, 1931.   Height: 6'5".   Weight: 205 lbs.   Drafted: 1953   College: Georgetown

YEAR	TEAM	GP	GS	MIN	PTS	FGM	FGA	FG%	3PM	3PA	3P%	FTM	FTA	FT%	ORB	DRB	TRB	AST	PF	DQ	STL	BLK	TO	MPG	PPG	RPG	APG	PCM
53-54	Baltimore	20	....	202	56	24	59	.407	....	....	....	8	13	.615	....	....	36	11	27	0	....	....	....	10.1	2.8	1.8	0.6	.295
NBA Season Totals		20	....	202	56	24	59	.407	....	....	....	8	13	.615	....	....	36	11	27	0	....	....	....	10.1	2.8	1.8	0.6	....

YEAR	TEAM	GP	GS	MIN	PTS	FGM	FGA	FG%	3PM	3PA	3P%	FTM	FTA	FT%	ORB	DRB	TRB	AST	PF	DQ	STL	BLK	TO	MPG	PPG	RPG	APG	PCM

• BOLSTORFF, Doug
F. Douglas Bolstorff

Born: Oct. 29, 1931.   Height: 6'4".   Weight: 195 lbs.   Drafted: 1957   College: Minnesota

YEAR	TEAM	GP	GS	MIN	PTS	FGM	FGA	FG%	3PM	3PA	3P%	FTM	FTA	FT%	ORB	DRB	TRB	AST	PF	DQ	STL	BLK	TO	MPG	PPG	RPG	APG	PCM
57-58	Detroit	3	....	21	4	2	5	.400	....	....	....	0	0	.000	....	....	0	0	1	0	....	....	....	7.0	1.3	0.0	0.0	.069
NBA Season Totals		3	....	21	4	2	5	.400	....	....	....	0	0	.000	....	....	0	0	1	0	....	....	....	7.0	1.3	0.0	0.0	....

• BOLYARD, Bob
Robert (Bob) Bolyard

Born: 1920.   Height: 6'   Weight: 182 lbs.   Drafted: 1947   College: Toledo

YEAR	TEAM	GP	GS	MIN	PTS	FGM	FGA	FG%	3PM	3PA	3P%	FTM	FTA	FT%	ORB	DRB	TRB	AST	PF	DQ	STL	BLK	TO	MPG	PPG	RPG	APG	PCM
46-47	Anderson-N	38	....	....	184	73	....	....	....	....	....	38	50	.760	....	....	....	....	76		....	....	....		4.8	....	....	....
47-48	Sheboygan-N	56	....	....	194	72	....	....	....	....	....	50	73	.685	....	....	....	....	87		....	....	....		3.5	....	....	....
48-49	Sheboygan-N	64	....	....	308	98	....	....	....	....	....	112	150	.747	....	....	....	....	129		....	....	....		4.8	....	....	....
NBL Season Totals		158	....	....	686	243	....	....	....	....	....	200	273	....	....	....	....	....	292		....	....	....		4.3	....	....	....
48-49	Sheboygan-N	2	....	....	9	2	....	....	....	....	....	5	6	.833	....	....	....	....			....	....	....		4.5	....	....	....
NBL Playoff Totals		2	....	....	9	2	....	....	....	....	....	5	6	....	....	....	....	....			....	....	....		4.5	....	....	....

• BON SALLE, George
George H. Bon Salle

Born: July 1, 1935. Chicago, IL, United States.   Height: 6'8".   Weight: 220 lbs.   Drafted: 1957   College: Illinois

YEAR	TEAM	GP	GS	MIN	PTS	FGM	FGA	FG%	3PM	3PA	3P%	FTM	FTA	FT%	ORB	DRB	TRB	AST	PF	DQ	STL	BLK	TO	MPG	PPG	RPG	APG	PCM
61-62	Chicago	3	....	9	4	2	8	.250	....	....	....	0	0	.000	....	....	2	0	0	0	....	....	....	3.0	1.3	0.7	0.0	.097
NBA Season Totals		3	....	9	4	2	8	.250	....	....	....	0	0	.000	....	....	2	0	0	0	....	....	....	3.0	1.3	0.7	0.0	....

• BOND, Phil
Phillip Damone Bond

Born: July 27, 1954. Louisville, KY, United States.   Height: 6'2".   Weight: 175 lbs.   Drafted: 1977   College: Louisville

YEAR	TEAM	GP	GS	MIN	PTS	FGM	FGA	FG%	3PM	3PA	3P%	FTM	FTA	FT%	ORB	DRB	TRB	AST	PF	DQ	STL	BLK	TO	MPG	PPG	RPG	APG	PCM
77-78	Houston	7	....	21	4	2	6	.333	....	....	....	0	0	.000	1	3	4	2	1	0	1	0	2	3.0	0.6	0.6	0.3	.235
NBA Season Totals		7	....	21	4	2	6	.333	....	....	....	0	0	.000	1	3	4	2	1	0	1	0	2	3.0	0.6	0.6	0.3	....

• BOND, Walter
Walter Bond

Born: Feb. 1, 1969. Chicago, IL, United States.   Height: 6'5".   Weight: 200 lbs.   Drafted: —   College: Minnesota

YEAR	TEAM	GP	GS	MIN	PTS	FGM	FGA	FG%	3PM	3PA	3P%	FTM	FTA	FT%	ORB	DRB	TRB	AST	PF	DQ	STL	BLK	TO	MPG	PPG	RPG	APG	PCM
92-93	Dallas	74	38	1578	590	227	565	.402	7	42	.167	129	167	.772	52	144	196	122	223	3	75	18	111	21.3	8.0	2.6	1.6	.285
93-94	Utah	56	4	559	176	63	156	.404	19	54	.352	31	40	.775	20	41	61	31	90	1	16	12	17	10.0	3.1	1.1	0.6	.259
94-95	Detroit	5	0	51	10	3	12	.250	1	4	.250	3	4	.750	1	4	5	7	10	0	1	0	3	10.2	2.0	1.0	1.4	.130
94-95	Utah	18	0	239	97	36	72	.500	14	37	.378	11	16	.688	7	20	27	17	37	0	5	4	14	13.3	5.4	1.5	0.9	.344
NBA Season Totals		153	42	2427	873	329	805	.409	41	137	.299	174	227	.767	80	209	289	177	360	4	97	34	145	15.9	5.7	1.9	1.2	....
93-94	Utah	4	0	13	1	0	2	.000	0	1	.000	1	2	.500	0	1	1	0	4	0	1	0	0	3.3	0.3	0.3	0.0	-.099
NBA Playoff Totals		4	0	13	1	0	2	.000	0	1	.000	1	2	.500	0	1	1	0	4	0	1	0	0	3.3	0.3	0.3	0.0	....

• BONEY, Dexter
Dexter Lyndell Boney

Born: Apr. 27, 1970. Wilmington, DE, United States.   Height: 6'4".   Weight: 185 lbs.   Drafted: —   College: UNLV

YEAR	TEAM	GP	GS	MIN	PTS	FGM	FGA	FG%	3PM	3PA	3P%	FTM	FTA	FT%	ORB	DRB	TRB	AST	PF	DQ	STL	BLK	TO	MPG	PPG	RPG	APG	PCM
96-97	Phoenix	8	0	48	19	6	19	.316	1	6	.167	6	8	.750	3	3	6	0	3	0	2	1	1	6.0	2.4	0.8	0.0	.250
NBA Season Totals		8	0	48	19	6	19	.316	1	6	.167	6	8	.750	3	3	6	0	3	0	2	1	1	6.0	2.4	0.8	0.0	....

• BONHAM, Ron
Ronald D. (Muncie Mortar) Bonham

Born: May 31, 1942. Muncie, IN, United States.   Height: 6'5".   Weight: 192 lbs.   Drafted: 1964   College: Cincinnati

YEAR	TEAM	GP	GS	MIN	PTS	FGM	FGA	FG%	3PM	3PA	3P%	FTM	FTA	FT%	ORB	DRB	TRB	AST	PF	DQ	STL	BLK	TO	MPG	PPG	RPG	APG	PCM
64-65	Boston	37	....	369	274	91	220	.414	....	....	....	92	112	.821	....	....	78	19	33	0	....	....	....	10.0	7.4	2.1	0.5	.645
65-66	Boston	39	....	312	204	76	207	.367	....	....	....	52	61	.852	....	....	35	11	29	0	....	....	....	8.0	5.2	0.9	0.3	.408
67-68	Indiana-A	42	....	426	245	80	210	.381	0	2	.000	85	105	.810	....	....	57	14	36	0	....	....	32	10.1	5.8	1.4	0.3	.417
NBA Season Totals		76	....	681	478	167	427	.391	....	....	....	144	173	.832	....	....	113	30	62	0	....	....	....	9.0	6.3	1.5	0.4	....
ABA Season Totals		42	....	426	245	80	210	.381	0	2	.000	85	105	.810	....	....	57	14	36	0	....	....	32	10.1	5.8	1.4	0.3	....
Career Totals		118	....	1107	723	247	637	.388	0	2	.000	229	278	.824	....	....	170	44	98	0	....	....	32	9.4	6.1	1.4	0.4	....
64-65	Boston	4	....	13	14	5	12	.417	....	....	....	4	5	.800	....	....	1	0	1	0	....	....	....	3.3	3.5	0.3	0.0	.663
65-66	Boston	5	....	16	17	7	11	.636	....	....	....	3	9	.333	....	....	3	0	2	0	....	....	....	3.2	3.4	0.6	0.0	.818
67-68	Indiana-A	3	....	30	13	4	15	.267	0	0	.000	5	6	.833	....	....	6	3	4	0	....	....	2	10.0	4.3	2.0	1.0	.343
NBA Playoff Totals		9	....	29	31	12	23	.522	....	....	....	7	14	.500	....	....	4	0	3	0	....	....	....	3.2	3.4	0.4	0.0	....
ABA Playoff Totals		3	....	30	13	4	15	.267	0	0	.000	5	6	.833	....	....	6	3	4	0	....	....	2	10.0	4.3	2.0	1.0	....
Career Playoff Totals		12	....	59	44	16	38	.421	0	0	.000	12	20	.600	....	....	10	3	7	0	....	....	2	4.9	3.7	0.8	0.3	....

• BONN, Herb
Herbert (Herb) Bonn

Born: 1914.   Height: 6'   Weight: 195 lbs.   Drafted: —   College: Duquesne

YEAR	TEAM	GP	GS	MIN	PTS	FGM	FGA	FG%	3PM	3PA	3P%	FTM	FTA	FT%	ORB	DRB	TRB	AST	PF	DQ	STL	BLK	TO	MPG	PPG	RPG	APG	PCM
37-38	Pittsburgh-N	8	....	....	58	24	....	....	....	....	....	10	....	....	....	....	....	....	....	....	....	....	....	7.3	....	....	....
38-39	Pittsburgh-N	7	....	....	28	12	....	....	....	....	....	4	....	....	....	....	....	....	....	....	....	....	....	4.0	....	....	....
NBL Season Totals		15	....	....	86	36	....	....	....	....	....	14	....	....	....	....	....	....	....	....	....	....	....	5.7	....	....	....

YEAR	TEAM	GP	GS	MIN	PTS	FGM	FGA	FG%	3PM	3PA	3P%	FTM	FTA	FT%	ORB	DRB	TRB	AST	PF	DQ	STL	BLK	TO	MPG	PPG	RPG	APG	PCM

• BONNER, Anthony
Anthony Bonner

Born: June 8, 1968. St. Louis, MO, United States. Height: 6'8". Weight: 215 lbs. Drafted: 1990 College: St. Louis

YEAR	TEAM	GP	GS	MIN	PTS	FGM	FGA	FG%	3PM	3PA	3P%	FTM	FTA	FT%	ORB	DRB	TRB	AST	PF	DQ	STL	BLK	TO	MPG	PPG	RPG	APG	PCM
90-91	Sacramento	34	6	750	250	103	230	.448	0	0	.000	44	76	.579	59	102	161	49	62	0	39	5	41	22.1	7.4	4.7	1.4	.391
91-92	Sacramento	79	18	2287	740	294	658	.447	1	4	.250	151	241	.627	192	293	485	125	194	0	94	26	134	28.9	9.4	6.1	1.6	.368
92-93	Sacramento	70	35	1764	601	229	499	.459	0	7	.000	143	241	.593	188	267	455	96	183	1	86	17	105	25.2	8.6	6.5	1.4	.421
93-94	New York	73	38	1402	374	162	288	.563	0	0	.000	50	105	.476	150	194	344	88	175	3	76	13	88	19.2	5.1	4.7	1.2	.403
94-95	New York	58	23	1126	221	88	193	.456	1	5	.200	44	67	.657	113	149	262	80	159	0	48	23	81	19.4	3.8	4.5	1.4	.318
95-96	Orlando	4	0	43	13	5	15	.333	0	0	.000	3	7	.429	6	13	19	4	11	0	3	0	3	10.8	3.3	4.8	1.0	.434
NBA Season Totals		318	120	7372	2199	881	1883	.468	2	16	.125	435	737	.590	708	1018	1726	442	784	4	346	84	452	23.2	6.9	5.4	1.4	
93-94	New York	13	7	118	27	10	22	.455	0	0	.000	7	13	.538	15	13	28	2	22	0	5	0	13	9.1	2.1	2.2	0.2	.201
94-95	New York	6	0	38	15	6	11	.545	0	1	.000	3	6	.500	4	4	8	2	6	0	1	1	3	6.3	2.5	1.3	0.3	.389
95-96	Orlando	4	0	16	3	1	3	.333	0	0	.000	1	2	.500	2	0	2	1	3	0	0	0	0	4.0	0.8	0.5	0.3	.136
NBA Playoff Totals		23	7	172	45	17	36	.472	0	1	.000	11	21	.524	21	17	38	5	31	0	6	1	16	7.5	2.0	1.7	0.2	

• BONNIWELL, Al
Al Bonniwell

Born: 1911. Height: 6'2". Weight: 185 lbs. Drafted: — College: Dartmouth

YEAR	TEAM	GP	GS	MIN	PTS	FGM	FGA	FG%	3PM	3PA	3P%	FTM	FTA	FT%	ORB	DRB	TRB	AST	PF	DQ	STL	BLK	TO	MPG	PPG	RPG	APG	PCM
37-38	Non-Skids-N	15	....		91	36	....	....	....	....	....	19	....	....	....	....	....	....	....	....	....	....	....		6.1	....	....	....
38-39	Non-Skids-N	24	....		106	49	....	....	....	....	....	8	....	....	....	....	....	....	....	....	....	....	....		4.4	....	....	....
NBL Season Totals		39	....		197	85	....		....		....	27	....		....	....	....	....	....	....	....	....	....		5.1	....	....	....
37-38	Non-Skids-N	2	....		1	0	....	....	....	....	....	1	....	....	....	....	....	....	....	....	....	....	....		0.5	....	....	....
38-39	Non-Skids-N	5	....		13	5	....	....	....	....	....	3	....	....	....	....	....	....	....	....	....	....	....		2.6	....	....	....
NBL Playoff Totals		7	....		14	5	....		....		....	4	....		....	....	....	....	....	....	....	....	....		2.0	....	....	....

• BOOKER, Butch
Harold (Butch) Booker

Born: July 20, 1945. Height: 6'10". Weight: 230 lbs. Drafted: 1969 College: Cheyney State

YEAR	TEAM	GP	GS	MIN	PTS	FGM	FGA	FG%	3PM	3PA	3P%	FTM	FTA	FT%	ORB	DRB	TRB	AST	PF	DQ	STL	BLK	TO	MPG	PPG	RPG	APG	PCM
69-70	Miami-A	12	....	221	70	30	61	.492	0	1	.000	10	18	.556	44	47	91	6	23	0			13	18.4	5.8	7.6	0.5	.521
ABA Season Totals		12	....	221	70	30	61	.492	0	1	.000	10	18	.556	44	47	91	6	23	0	....	....	13	18.4	5.8	7.6	0.5	

• BOOKER, Melvin
Melvin Jermaine Booker

Born: Aug. 20, 1972. Pascagoula, MS, United States. Height: 6'1". Weight: 185 lbs. Drafted: — College: Missouri

YEAR	TEAM	GP	GS	MIN	PTS	FGM	FGA	FG%	3PM	3PA	3P%	FTM	FTA	FT%	ORB	DRB	TRB	AST	PF	DQ	STL	BLK	TO	MPG	PPG	RPG	APG	PCM
95-96	Houston	11	0	131	44	16	50	.320	3	19	.158	9	11	.818	1	8	9	21	18	0	5	1	12	11.9	4.0	0.8	1.9	.212
96-97	Denver	5	0	21	5	2	4	.500	1	2	.500	0	0	.000	0	1	1	3	0	0	0	0	7	4.2	1.0	0.2	0.6	.036
96-97	Golden State	16	4	409	117	44	101	.436	11	35	.314	18	20	.900	7	21	28	50	28	0	3	2	21	25.6	7.3	1.8	3.1	.280
NBA Season Totals		32	4	561	166	62	155	.400	15	56	.268	27	31	.871	8	30	38	74	46	0	8	3	40	17.5	5.2	1.2	2.3	

• BOONE, Ron
Ronald Bruce Boone

Born: Sept. 6, 1946. Oklahoma City, OK, United States. Height: 6'2". Weight: 200 lbs. Drafted: 1968 College: Idaho State

YEAR	TEAM	GP	GS	MIN	PTS	FGM	FGA	FG%	3PM	3PA	3P%	FTM	FTA	FT%	ORB	DRB	TRB	AST	PF	DQ	STL	BLK	TO	MPG	PPG	RPG	APG	PCM
68-69	Dallas-A	78	....	2682	1478	520	1197	.434	2	15	.133	436	537	.812	155	239	394	279	303	8	....	....	355	34.4	18.9	5.1	3.6	.515
69-70	Dallas-A	84	....	2340	1163	423	980	.432	17	55	.309	300	382	.785	124	242	366	272	265	5	....	....	282	27.9	13.8	4.4	3.2	.496
70-71	Texas-A	42	....	1313	854	345	755	.457	25	65	.385	139	180	.772	112	199	311	142	133	4	....	....	154	31.3	20.3	7.4	3.4	.667
70-71	Utah-A	44	....	1163	693	265	640	.414	24	73	.329	139	177	.785	110	143	253	114	165	3	....	....	118	26.4	15.8	5.8	2.6	.559
71-72	Utah-A	84	....	2040	1092	404	962	.420	13	65	.200	271	341	.795	163	230	393	233	274	2	....	....	215	24.3	13.0	4.7	2.8	.638
72-73	Utah-A	84	....	2585	1557	566	1136	.498	10	40	.250	415	479	.866	173	252	425	353	308	7	....	....	276	30.8	18.5	5.1	4.2	.638
73-74	Utah-A	84	....	3098	1480	587	1188	.494	6	26	.231	300	343	.875	157	278	435	417	289	....	123	22	316	36.9	17.6	5.2	5.0	.539
74-75	Utah-A	84	....	3414	2117	872	1776	.491	10	33	.303	363	422	.860	141	265	406	372	265	....	126	34	335	40.6	25.2	4.8	4.4	.570
75-76	St. Louis-A	62	....	2325	1300	547	1128	.485	14	35	.400	192	219	.877	94	153	247	312	198	....	127	13	219	37.5	21.0	4.0	5.0	.537
75-76	Utah-A	16	....	636	419	166	339	.490	2	8	.250	85	99	.859	21	51	72	75	45	....	27	2	57	39.8	26.2	4.5	4.7	.607
76-77	Kansas City	82	....	3021	1818	747	1577	.474				324	384	.844	128	193	321	338	258	1	119	19	....	36.8	22.2	3.9	4.1	.538
77-78	Kansas City	82	....	2653	1448	563	1271	.443				322	377	.854	112	157	269	311	233	3	105	11	303	32.4	17.7	3.3	3.8	.424
78-79	LA Lakers	82	....	1583	608	259	569	.455				90	104	.865	53	92	145	154	171	1	66	11	148	19.3	7.4	1.8	1.9	.305
79-80	LA Lakers	6	....	106	34	14	40	.350	0	0	.000	6	7	.857	7	4	11	7	13	0	5	0	13	17.7	5.7	1.8	1.2	.137
79-80	Utah	75	....	2286	970	391	875	.447	19	50	.380	169	189	.894	50	166	216	302	219	3	92	3	188	30.5	12.9	2.9	4.0	.379
80-81	Utah	52	....	1146	406	160	371	.431	11	39	.282	75	94	.798	17	67	84	161	126	0	33	8	109	22.0	7.8	1.6	3.1	.295
NBA Season Totals		379	....	10795	5284	2134	4703	.454	30	89	.337	986	1155	.854	367	679	1046	1273	1020	8	420	52	761	28.5	13.9	2.8	3.4	
ABA Season Totals		662	....	21596	12153	4695	10101	.465	123	415	.296	2640	3179	.830	1250	2052	3302	2569	2245	29	403	71	2327	32.6	18.4	5.0	3.9	
Career Totals		1041	....	32391	17437	6829	14804	.461	153	504	.304	3626	4334	.837	1617	2731	4348	3842	3265	37	823	123	3088	31.1	16.8	4.2	3.7	
68-69	Dallas-A	7	....	196	97	38	85	.447	0	4	.000	21	25	.840	10	12	22	27	25	1	....	....	20	28.0	13.9	3.1	3.9	.479
68-69	Dallas-A	6	....	193	110	46	97	.474	3	8	.375	15	21	.714	11	38	49	54		2	....	....	22	32.2	18.3	8.2	9.0	
70-71	Utah-A	18	....	569	309	113	256	.441	9	27	.333	74	86	.860	50	60	110	94	71	1	....	....	56	31.6	17.2	6.1	5.2	.636
71-72	Utah-A	11	....	209	126	50	105	.476	1	5	.200	25	29	.862	10	14	24	26	30	0	....	....	24	19.0	11.5	2.2	2.4	.540
72-73	Utah-A	10	....	360	169	68	135	.504	0	3	.000	33	34	.971	17	26	43	47	41	1	....	....	39	36.0	16.9	4.3	4.7	.501
73-74	Utah-A	18	....	747	308	137	289	.474	0	7	.000	34	37	.919	48	60	108	109	54	....	30	4	47	41.5	17.1	6.0	6.1	.496
74-75	Utah-A	6	....	219	142	54	127	.425	0	0	.000	34	38	.895	9	15	24	41	22	....	14	6	27	36.5	23.7	4.0	6.8	.605
78-79	LA Lakers	8	....	226	94	37	77	.481	....	....	....	20	21	.952	7	8	15	14	28	0	9	0	14	28.3	11.8	1.9	1.8	.307
NBA Playoff Totals		8	....	226	94	37	77	.481	....	....	....	20	21	.952	7	8	15	14	28	0	9	0	14	28.3	11.8	1.9	1.8	
ABA Playoff Totals		76	....	2493	1261	506	1094	.463	13	54	.241	236	270	.874	155	225	380	398	243	5	44	10	235	32.8	16.6	5.0	5.2	
Career Playoff Totals		84	....	2719	1355	543	1171	.464	13	54	.241	256	291	.880	162	233	395	412	271	5	53	10	249	32.4	16.1	4.7	4.9	

• BOOTH, Calvin

Calvin L. Booth

Born: May 7, 1976. Reynoldsburg, OH, United States. Height: 6'11". Weight: 230 lbs. Drafted: 1999 College: Penn State

YEAR TEAM	GP	GS	MIN	PTS	FGM	FGA	FG%	3PM	3PA	3P%	FTM	FTA	FT%	ORB	DRB	TRB	AST	PF	DQ	STL	BLK	TO	MPG	PPG	RPG	APG	PCM
99-00 Washington	11	0	143	42	16	46	.348	0	0	.000	10	14	.714	15	17	32	7	23	0	3	14	6	13.0	3.8	2.9	0.6	.344
00-01 Washington	40	22	640	181	74	168	.440	0	0	.000	33	45	.733	53	121	174	23	91	1	17	81	36	16.0	4.5	4.4	0.6	.449
00-01 Dallas	15	7	293	112	46	84	.548	0	0	.000	20	33	.606	24	48	72	19	55	0	12	30	17	19.5	7.5	4.8	1.3	.530
01-02 Seattle	15	15	279	93	35	82	.427	0	0	.000	23	24	.958	20	34	54	16	47	1	6	13	16	18.6	6.2	3.6	1.1	.351
02-03 Seattle	47	0	573	138	52	119	.437	0	2	.000	34	47	.723	32	77	109	12	74	0	11	33	22	12.2	2.9	2.3	0.3	.296
NBA Season Totals	128	44	1928	566	223	499	.447	0	2	.000	120	163	.736	144	297	441	77	290	2	49	171	97	15.1	4.4	3.4	0.6	....
00-01 Dallas	10	0	137	38	15	37	.405	0	0	.000	8	9	.889	16	12	28	2	29	0	7	6	4	13.7	3.8	2.8	0.2	.293
NBA Playoff Totals	10	0	137	38	15	37	.405	0	0	.000	8	9	.889	16	12	28	2	29	0	7	6	4	13.7	3.8	2.8	0.2	....

• BOOTH, Keith

Keith Eugene Booth

Born: Oct. 9, 1974. Baltimore, MD, United States. Height: 6'6". Weight: 226 lbs. Drafted: 1997 College: Maryland

YEAR TEAM	GP	GS	MIN	PTS	FGM	FGA	FG%	3PM	3PA	3P%	FTM	FTA	FT%	ORB	DRB	TRB	AST	PF	DQ	STL	BLK	TO	MPG	PPG	RPG	APG	PCM
97-98 Chicago	6	0	17	10	2	6	.333	0	1	.000	6	6	1.000	2	2	4	1	3	0	0	0	3	2.8	1.7	0.7	0.2	.410
98-99 Chicago	39	4	432	120	49	151	.325	1	10	.100	21	42	.500	25	68	93	38	60	0	22	11	39	11.1	3.1	2.4	1.0	.261
NBA Season Totals	45	4	449	130	51	157	.325	1	11	.091	27	48	.563	27	70	97	39	63	0	22	11	42	10.0	2.9	2.2	0.9	....

• BOOZER, Bob

Robert Lewis (Bullet Bob) Boozer

Born: Apr. 26, 1937. Omaha, NE, United States. Height: 6'8". Weight: 215 lbs. Drafted: 1959 College: Kansas State

YEAR TEAM	GP	GS	MIN	PTS	FGM	FGA	FG%	3PM	3PA	3P%	FTM	FTA	FT%	ORB	DRB	TRB	AST	PF	DQ	STL	BLK	TO	MPG	PPG	RPG	APG	PCM
60-61 Cincinnati	79	....	1573	666	250	603	.415	....	....	....	166	247	.672	....	....	488	109	193	1	....	....	....	19.9	8.4	6.2	1.4	.508
61-62 Cincinnati	79	....	2488	1083	410	936	.438	....	....	....	263	372	.707	....	....	804	130	275	3	....	....	....	31.5	13.7	10.2	1.6	.526
62-63 Cincinnati	79	....	2488	1132	440	992	.444	....	....	....	252	353	.714	....	....	878	102	299	8	....	....	....	31.5	14.3	11.1	1.3	.545
63-64 Cincinnati	32	....	727	352	139	334	.416	....	....	....	74	119	.622	....	....	178	33	83	0	....	....	....	22.7	11.0	5.6	1.0	.453
63-64 New York	49	....	1652	856	329	762	.432	....	....	....	198	257	.770	....	....	418	63	148	1	....	....	....	33.7	17.5	8.5	1.3	.509
64-65 New York	80	....	2139	1136	424	963	.440	....	....	....	288	375	.768	....	....	604	108	183	0	....	....	....	26.7	14.2	7.6	1.4	.568
65-66 LA Lakers	78	....	1847	955	365	754	.484	....	....	....	225	289	.779	....	....	548	87	196	0	....	....	....	23.7	12.2	7.0	1.1	.587
66-67 Chicago	80	....	2451	1436	538	1104	.487	....	....	....	360	461	.781	....	....	679	90	212	0	....	....	....	30.6	18.0	8.5	1.1	.616
67-68 Chicago	77	....	2988	1655	622	1265	.492	....	....	....	411	535	.768	....	....	756	121	229	1	....	....	....	38.8	21.5	9.8	1.6	.586
68-69 Chicago	79	....	2872	1716	661	1375	.481	....	....	....	394	489	.806	....	....	614	156	218	2	....	....	....	36.4	21.7	7.8	2.0	.586
69-70 Seattle	82	....	2549	1249	493	1005	.491	....	....	....	263	320	.822	....	....	717	110	237	2	....	....	....	31.1	15.2	8.7	1.3	.558
70-71 Milwaukee	80	....	1775	728	290	645	.450	....	....	....	148	181	.818	....	....	435	128	216	0	....	....	....	22.2	9.1	5.4	1.6	.471
NBA Season Totals	874	....	25549	12964	4961	10738	.462	....	....	....	3042	3998	.761	....	....	7119	1237	2489	18	....	....	....	29.2	14.8	8.1	1.4	....
61-62 Cincinnati	4	....	143	73	32	57	.561	....	....	....	9	12	.750	....	....	42	3	16	0	....	....	....	35.8	18.3	10.5	0.8	.577
62-63 Cincinnati	12	....	381	159	57	138	.413	....	....	....	45	63	.714	....	....	96	18	44	0	....	....	....	31.8	13.3	8.0	1.5	.441
65-66 LA Lakers	10	....	181	67	26	65	.400	....	....	....	15	20	.750	....	....	50	7	20	0	....	....	....	18.1	6.7	5.0	0.7	.411
66-67 Chicago	3	....	105	59	24	38	.632	....	....	....	11	14	.786	....	....	35	1	8	0	....	....	....	35.0	19.7	11.7	0.3	.691
67-68 Chicago	5	....	190	94	33	73	.452	....	....	....	28	38	.737	....	....	44	12	13	0	....	....	....	38.0	18.8	8.8	2.4	.539
70-71 Milwaukee	14	....	283	104	41	85	.482	....	....	....	22	29	.759	....	....	74	17	35	0	....	....	....	20.2	7.4	5.3	1.2	.463
NBA Playoff Totals	48	....	1283	556	213	456	.467	....	....	....	130	176	.739	....	....	341	58	136	0	....	....	....	26.7	11.6	7.1	1.2	....

• BOOZER, Carlos

Carlos Boozer

Born: Nov. 20, 1981. Juneau, AK, United States. Height: 6'9". Weight: 258 lbs. Drafted: 2002 College: Duke

YEAR TEAM	GP	GS	MIN	PTS	FGM	FGA	FG%	3PM	3PA	3P%	FTM	FTA	FT%	ORB	DRB	TRB	AST	PF	DQ	STL	BLK	TO	MPG	PPG	RPG	APG	PCM
02-03 Cleveland	81	54	2049	810	331	618	.536	0	1	.000	148	192	.771	202	407	609	106	224	2	59	50	103	25.3	10.0	7.5	1.3	.538
NBA Season Totals	81	54	2049	810	331	618	.536	0	1	.000	148	192	.771	202	407	609	106	224	2	59	50	103	25.3	10.0	7.5	1.3	....

• BORIS, —

Boris

Born: —. Height: — Weight: — Drafted: — College: —

YEAR TEAM	GP	GS	MIN	PTS	FGM	FGA	FG%	3PM	3PA	3P%	FTM	FTA	FT%	ORB	DRB	TRB	AST	PF	DQ	STL	BLK	TO	MPG	PPG	RPG	APG	PCM
38-39 Hammond-N	1	....	....	6	2	....	....	....	....	....	2	....	....	....	....	....	....	....	....	....	....	....	....	6.0	....	....	....
NBL Season Totals	1	....	....	6	2	....	....	....	....	....	2	....	....	....	....	....	....	....	....	....	....	....	....	6.0	....	....	....

• BORNHEIMER, Jake

Jacob Bornheimer

Born: June 29, 1927. New Brunswick, NJ, United States. Died: Sept.10, 1986. Height: 6'5". Weight: 200 lbs. Drafted: — College: Muhlenberg

YEAR TEAM	GP	GS	MIN	PTS	FGM	FGA	FG%	3PM	3PA	3P%	FTM	FTA	FT%	ORB	DRB	TRB	AST	PF	DQ	STL	BLK	TO	MPG	PPG	RPG	APG	PCM
48-49 Philadelphia	15	....	....	88	34	109	.312	....	....	....	20	29	.690	....	....	....	13	47	....	....	....	....	....	5.9	....	0.9	....
49-50 Philadelphia	60	....	....	254	88	305	.289	....	....	....	78	117	.667	....	....	....	40	111	....	....	....	....	....	4.2	....	0.7	....
NBA Season Totals	75	....	....	342	122	414	.295	....	....	....	98	146	.671	....	....	....	53	158	....	....	....	....	....	4.6	....	0.7	....
48-49 Philadelphia	2	....	....	20	7	17	.412	....	....	....	6	9	.667	....	....	....	2	11	....	....	....	....	....	10.0	....	1.0	....
49-50 Philadelphia	2	....	....	2	1	3	.333	....	....	....	0	0	.000	....	....	....	0	2	....	....	....	....	....	1.0	....	0.0	....
NBA Playoff Totals	4	....	....	22	8	20	.400	....	....	....	6	9	.667	....	....	....	2	13	....	....	....	....	....	5.5	....	0.5	....

• BORRELL, Lazaro

Lazaro Borrell

Born: Sept. 20, 1972. Cuba. Height: 6'8". Weight: 220 lbs. Drafted: — College: none

YEAR TEAM	GP	GS	MIN	PTS	FGM	FGA	FG%	3PM	3PA	3P%	FTM	FTA	FT%	ORB	DRB	TRB	AST	PF	DQ	STL	BLK	TO	MPG	PPG	RPG	APG	PCM
99-00 Seattle	17	6	167	62	28	63	.444	0	3	.000	6	11	.545	14	26	40	10	9	0	6	3	6	9.8	3.6	2.4	0.6	.442
NBA Season Totals	17	6	167	62	28	63	.444	0	3	.000	6	11	.545	14	26	40	10	9	0	6	3	6	9.8	3.6	2.4	0.6	....
99-00 Seattle	2	1	26	10	4	7	.571	0	0	.000	2	4	.500	3	8	11	1	2	0	0	0	1	13.0	5.0	5.5	0.5	.601
NBA Playoff Totals	2	1	26	10	4	7	.571	0	0	.000	2	4	.500	3	8	11	1	2	0	0	0	1	13.0	5.0	5.5	0.5	....

YEAR	TEAM	GP	GS	MIN	PTS	FGM	FGA	FG%	3PM	3PA	3P%	FTM	FTA	FT%	ORB	DRB	TRB	AST	PF	DQ	STL	BLK	TO	MPG	PPG	RPG	APG	PCM

• BORREVIK, Slats

Wally (Slats) Borrevik

Born: 1921. Height: 6'7". Weight: 205 lbs. Drafted: — College: Oregon

YEAR	TEAM	GP	GS	MIN	PTS	FGM	FGA	FG%	3PM	3PA	3P%	FTM	FTA	FT%	ORB	DRB	TRB	AST	PF	DQ	STL	BLK	TO	MPG	PPG	RPG	APG	PCM
47-48	Anderson-N	15	....	....	38	13	....	....	....	....	....	12	25	.480	....	....	....	....	....	....	....	....	....	....	2.5	....	....	....
47-48	Flint-N	5	....	....	14	6	....	....	....	....	....	2	7	.286	....	....	....	....	....	....	....	....	....	....	2.8	....	....	....
47-48	Tri-Cities-N	30	....	....	36	14	....	....	....	....	....	8	23	.348	....	....	....	....	....	....	....	....	....	....	1.2	....	....	....
NBL Season Totals		50	....	....	88	33	....	....	....	....	....	22	55	....	....	....	....	....	....	....	....	....	....	....	1.8	....	....	....
47-48	Tri-Cities-N	5	....	....	13	4	....	....	....	....	....	5	7	.714	....	....	....	....	....	....	....	....	....	....	2.6	....	....	....
NBL Playoff Totals		5	....	....	13	4	....	....	....	....	....	5	7	....	....	....	....	....	....	....	....	....	....	....	2.6	....	....	....

• BORSAVAGE, Ike

Costic F. (Ike) Borsavage

Born: July 25, 1924. Height: 6'8". Weight: 220 lbs. Drafted: 1950 College: Temple

YEAR	TEAM	GP	GS	MIN	PTS	FGM	FGA	FG%	3PM	3PA	3P%	FTM	FTA	FT%	ORB	DRB	TRB	AST	PF	DQ	STL	BLK	TO	MPG	PPG	RPG	APG	PCM
50-51	Philadelphia	24	....	....	64	26	74	.351	....	....	....	12	18	.667	....	....	24	4	34	1	....	....	....	....	2.7	1.0	0.2	....
NBA Season Totals		24	....	....	64	26	74	.351	....	....	....	12	18	.667	....	....	24	4	34	1	....	....	....	....	2.7	1.0	0.2	....

• BORYLA, Vince

Vincent Joseph (Moose) Boryla

Born: Mar. 11, 1927. East Chicago, IN, United States. Height: 6'5". Weight: 210 lbs. Drafted: — College: Denver

YEAR	TEAM	GP	GS	MIN	PTS	FGM	FGA	FG%	3PM	3PA	3P%	FTM	FTA	FT%	ORB	DRB	TRB	AST	PF	DQ	STL	BLK	TO	MPG	PPG	RPG	APG	PCM
49-50	New York	59	....	....	612	204	600	.340	....	....	....	204	267	.764	....	....	....	95	203	....	....	....	....	....	10.4	....	1.6	....
50-51	New York	66	....	....	982	352	867	.406	....	....	....	278	332	.837	....	....	249	182	244	6	....	....	....	....	14.9	3.8	2.8	....
51-52	New York	42	....	1440	500	202	522	.387	....	....	....	96	115	.835	....	....	219	90	121	2	....	....	....	34.3	11.9	5.2	2.1	.343
52-53	New York	66	....	2200	673	254	686	.370	....	....	....	165	201	.821	....	....	233	166	226	8	....	....	....	33.3	10.2	3.5	2.5	.294
53-54	New York	52	....	1522	420	175	525	.333	....	....	....	70	81	.864	....	....	130	77	128	0	....	....	....	29.3	8.1	2.5	1.5	.206
NBA Season Totals		285	....	5162	3187	1187	3200	.371	....	....	....	813	996	.816	....	....	831	610	922	16	....	....	....	18.1	11.2	2.9	2.1	....
49-50	New York	5	....	....	75	23	52	.442	....	....	....	29	32	.906	....	....	....	7	25	....	....	....	....	....	15.0	....	1.4	....
50-51	New York	14	....	....	217	83	193	.430	....	....	....	51	56	.911	....	....	52	37	42	1	....	....	....	....	15.5	3.7	2.6	....
52-53	New York	11	....	397	117	44	116	.379	....	....	....	29	34	.853	....	....	35	20	35	2	....	....	....	36.1	10.6	3.2	1.8	.255
53-54	New York	3	....	66	27	8	14	.571	....	....	....	11	13	.846	....	....	2	1	12	1	....	....	....	22.0	9.0	0.7	0.3	.310
NBA Playoff Totals		33	....	463	436	158	375	.421	....	....	....	120	135	.889	....	....	89	65	114	4	....	....	....	14.0	13.2	2.7	2.0	....

• BOSAK, John

John Bosak

Born: 1922. Height: 6'3". Weight: 185 lbs. Drafted: — College: none

YEAR	TEAM	GP	GS	MIN	PTS	FGM	FGA	FG%	3PM	3PA	3P%	FTM	FTA	FT%	ORB	DRB	TRB	AST	PF	DQ	STL	BLK	TO	MPG	PPG	RPG	APG	PCM
46-47	Youngstown-N	10	....	....	24	11	....	....	....	....	....	2	5	.400	....	....	....	....	....	....	....	....	....	....	2.4	....	....	....
NBL Season Totals		10	....	....	24	11	....	....	....	....	....	2	5	....	....	....	....	....	....	....	....	....	....	....	2.4	....	....	....

• BOSTIC, Jim

James Bostic

Born: Jan. 28, 1953. Brooklyn, NY, United States. Height: 6'7". Weight: 225 lbs. Drafted: 1975 College: New Mexico State

YEAR	TEAM	GP	GS	MIN	PTS	FGM	FGA	FG%	3PM	3PA	3P%	FTM	FTA	FT%	ORB	DRB	TRB	AST	PF	DQ	STL	BLK	TO	MPG	PPG	RPG	APG	PCM
77-78	Detroit	4	....	48	26	12	22	.545	....	....	....	2	5	.400	8	8	16	3	5	0	0	0	3	12.0	6.5	4.0	0.8	.594
NBA Season Totals		4	....	48	26	12	22	.545	....	....	....	2	5	.400	8	8	16	3	5	0	0	0	3	12.0	6.5	4.0	0.8	....

• BOSTON, Lawrence

Lawrence D. Boston

Born: May 18, 1956. Cleveland, OH, United States. Height: 6'8". Weight: 225 lbs. Drafted: 1978 College: Maryland

YEAR	TEAM	GP	GS	MIN	PTS	FGM	FGA	FG%	3PM	3PA	3P%	FTM	FTA	FT%	ORB	DRB	TRB	AST	PF	DQ	STL	BLK	TO	MPG	PPG	RPG	APG	PCM
79-80	Washington	13	....	125	56	24	52	.462	0	0	.000	8	13	.615	19	20	39	2	25	0	4	2	8	9.6	4.3	3.0	0.2	.422
NBA Season Totals		13	....	125	56	24	52	.462	0	0	.000	8	13	.615	19	20	39	2	25	0	4	2	8	9.6	4.3	3.0	0.2	....

• BOSWELL, Tom

Tommy G. Boswell

Born: Oct. 2, 1953. Montgomery, AL, United States. Height: 6'9". Weight: 220 lbs. Drafted: 1975 College: South Carolina

YEAR	TEAM	GP	GS	MIN	PTS	FGM	FGA	FG%	3PM	3PA	3P%	FTM	FTA	FT%	ORB	DRB	TRB	AST	PF	DQ	STL	BLK	TO	MPG	PPG	RPG	APG	PCM
75-76	Boston	35	....	275	96	41	93	.441	....	....	....	14	24	.583	26	45	71	16	70	1	2	1	....	7.9	2.7	2.0	0.5	.350
76-77	Boston	70	....	1083	446	175	340	.515	....	....	....	96	135	.711	111	195	306	85	237	9	27	8	....	15.5	6.4	4.4	1.2	.503
77-78	Boston	65	....	1149	463	185	357	.518	....	....	....	93	123	.756	117	171	288	71	204	5	25	14	98	17.7	7.1	4.4	1.1	.427
78-79	Denver	79	....	2201	840	321	603	.532	....	....	....	198	284	.697	248	290	538	242	263	4	50	51	182	27.9	10.6	6.8	3.1	.503
79-80	Denver	18	....	522	203	72	135	.533	1	2	.500	58	70	.829	40	74	114	46	56	1	5	8	40	29.0	11.3	6.3	2.6	.468
79-80	Utah	61	....	1555	700	274	478	.573	4	8	.500	148	203	.729	106	222	328	115	214	8	24	29	140	25.5	11.5	5.4	1.9	.474
83-84	Utah	38	0	261	73	28	52	.538	1	1	1.000	16	21	.762	28	36	64	16	58	1	9	0	11	6.9	1.9	1.7	0.4	.368
NBA Season Totals		366	0	7046	2821	1096	2058	.533	6	11	.545	623	860	.724	676	1033	1709	591	1102	29	142	111	471	19.3	7.7	4.7	1.6	....
75-76	Boston	3	....	3	2	1	2	.500	....	....	....	0	0	....	0	1	1	0	2	0	0	0	....	1.0	0.7	0.3	0.0	.381
76-77	Boston	9	....	81	20	8	18	.444	....	....	....	4	6	.667	10	10	20	7	18	0	1	0	....	9.0	2.2	2.2	0.8	.345
78-79	Denver	3	....	120	52	21	35	.600	....	....	....	10	13	.769	14	13	27	16	10	0	3	5	6	40.0	17.3	9.0	5.3	.644
83-84	Utah	5	0	55	8	3	4	.750	0	0	.000	2	5	.400	2	4	6	2	12	0	0	1	4	11.0	1.6	1.2	0.4	.091
NBA Playoff Totals		20	0	259	82	33	59	.559	0	0	.000	16	24	.667	26	28	54	25	42	0	4	6	10	13.0	4.1	2.7	1.3	....

• BOSWELL, Wyatt

Wyatt (Sonny) Boswell

Born: 1915. Died: Oct.19, 1964.   Height: 6'1".   Weight: 180 lbs.   Drafted: —   College: none (HS: Scott, OH)

YEAR TEAM	GP	GS	MIN	PTS	FGM	FGA	FG%	3PM	3PA	3P%	FTM	FTA	FT%	ORB	DRB	TRB	AST	PF	DQ	STL	BLK	TO	MPG	PPG	RPG	APG	PCM
42-43 Chicago-N	22	....	....	229	88	....	....	....	....	....	53	....	....	....	....	....	....	....	....	....	....	....	10.4	....	....	....
NBL Season Totals	22	....	....	229	88	....	....	....	....	....	53	....	....	....	....	....	....	....	....	....	....	....	10.4	....	....	....
42-43 Chicago-N	3	....	....	30	13	....	....	....	....	....	4	....	....	....	....	....	....	....	....	....	....	....	10.0	....	....	....
NBL Playoff Totals	3	....	....	30	13	....	....	....	....	....	4	....	....	....	....	....	....	....	....	....	....	....	10.0	....	....	....

• BOUDREAU, Louis

Louis Boudreau Jr.

Born: July 17, 1917. Harvey, IL, United States.   Height: 5'11".   Weight: 170 lbs.   Drafted: —   College: Illinois

YEAR TEAM	GP	GS	MIN	PTS	FGM	FGA	FG%	3PM	3PA	3P%	FTM	FTA	FT%	ORB	DRB	TRB	AST	PF	DQ	STL	BLK	TO	MPG	PPG	RPG	APG	PCM
38-39 Hammond-N	23	....	....	189	78	....	....	....	....	....	33	....	....	....	....	....	....	....	....	....	....	....	8.2	....	....	....
NBL Season Totals	23	....	....	189	78	....	....	....	....	....	33	....	....	....	....	....	....	....	....	....	....	....	8.2	....	....	....

• BOUMTJE-BOUMTJE, Ruben

Ruben Bertrand Boumtje-Boumtje

Born: May 20, 1978. Edda, Cameroon.   Height: 7'   Weight: 257 lbs.   Drafted: 2001   College: Georgetown

YEAR TEAM	GP	GS	MIN	PTS	FGM	FGA	FG%	3PM	3PA	3P%	FTM	FTA	FT%	ORB	DRB	TRB	AST	PF	DQ	STL	BLK	TO	MPG	PPG	RPG	APG	PCM
01-02 Portland	33	1	245	39	13	32	.406	0	0	.000	13	25	.520	21	34	55	4	38	0	3	16	14	7.4	1.2	1.7	0.1	.236
02-03 Portland	2	0	5	0	0	1	.000	0	0	.000	0	0	.000	1	0	1	1	0	0	1	0	0	2.5	0.0	0.5	0.5	.400
NBA Season Totals	35	1	250	39	13	33	.394	0	0	.000	13	25	.520	22	34	56	5	38	0	4	16	14	7.1	1.1	1.6	0.1	....

• BOVEN, Don

Donald E. Boven

Born: Mar. 6, 1925. Kalamazoo, MI, United States.   Height: 6'4".   Weight: 210 lbs.   Drafted: 1949   College: Western Michigan

YEAR TEAM	GP	GS	MIN	PTS	FGM	FGA	FG%	3PM	3PA	3P%	FTM	FTA	FT%	ORB	DRB	TRB	AST	PF	DQ	STL	BLK	TO	MPG	PPG	RPG	APG	PCM
49-50 Waterloo	62	....	....	656	208	558	.373	....	....	....	240	349	.688	....	....	....	137	255	....	....	....	....	10.6	....	2.2	....
51-52 Milwaukee	66	....	1982	656	200	668	.299	....	....	....	256	350	.731	....	336	177	271	**18**	....	....	....	....	30.0	9.9	5.1	2.7	.333
52-53 Mil/Bal/FtW	67	....	1373	451	153	427	.358	....	....	....	145	209	.694	....	217	79	227	13	....	....	....	....	20.5	6.7	3.2	1.2	.295
NBA Season Totals	195	....	3355	1763	561	1653	.339	....	....	....	641	908	.706	....	553	393	753	31	....	....	....	....	17.2	9.0	2.8	2.0	....
52-53 Fort Wayne	8	....	111	23	7	28	.250	....	....	....	9	16	.563	....	16	2	22	0	....	....	....	....	13.9	2.9	2.0	0.3	.103
NBA Playoff Totals	8	....	111	23	7	28	.250	....	....	....	9	16	.563	....	16	2	22	0	....	....	....	....	13.9	2.9	2.0	0.3	....

• BOWDLER, Cal

James Calloway Bowdler II

Born: Mar. 31, 1977. Sharps, VA, United States.   Height: 6'10".   Weight: 245 lbs.   Drafted: 1999   College: Old Dominion

YEAR TEAM	GP	GS	MIN	PTS	FGM	FGA	FG%	3PM	3PA	3P%	FTM	FTA	FT%	ORB	DRB	TRB	AST	PF	DQ	STL	BLK	TO	MPG	PPG	RPG	APG	PCM
99-00 Atlanta	46	0	423	122	49	115	.426	0	1	.000	24	38	.632	22	63	85	14	46	1	14	9	21	9.2	2.7	1.8	0.3	.305
00-01 Atlanta	44	0	375	140	53	114	.465	1	5	.200	33	40	.825	30	47	77	4	45	0	10	21	11	8.5	3.2	1.8	0.1	.409
01-02 Atlanta	52	0	584	162	61	174	.351	1	5	.200	39	47	.830	38	72	110	11	64	1	18	15	11	11.2	3.1	2.1	0.2	.272
NBA Season Totals	142	0	1382	424	163	403	.404	2	11	.182	96	125	.768	90	182	272	29	155	2	42	45	43	9.7	3.0	1.9	0.2	....

• BOWEN, Bruce

Bruce Bowen

Born: June 14, 1971. Merced, CA, United States.   Height: 6'7".   Weight: 185 lbs.   Drafted: —   College: Cal State Fullerton

YEAR TEAM	GP	GS	MIN	PTS	FGM	FGA	FG%	3PM	3PA	3P%	FTM	FTA	FT%	ORB	DRB	TRB	AST	PF	DQ	STL	BLK	TO	MPG	PPG	RPG	APG	PCM
96-97 Miami	1	0	1	0	0	0	.000	0	0	.000	0	0	.000	0	0	0	0	0	0	0	1	0	1.0	0.0	0.0	0.0	.932
97-98 Boston	61	9	1305	340	122	298	.409	20	59	.339	76	122	.623	79	95	174	81	174	0	87	29	55	21.4	5.6	2.9	1.3	.292
98-99 Boston	30	1	494	70	26	93	.280	7	26	.269	11	24	.458	15	37	52	28	51	2	21	9	13	16.5	2.3	1.7	0.9	.151
99-00 Philadelphia	42	0	311	59	26	73	.356	1	2	.500	6	12	.500	14	22	36	16	37	0	9	5	5	7.4	1.4	0.9	0.4	.177
99-00 Miami	27	2	567	137	46	121	.380	26	56	.464	19	31	.613	13	47	60	18	81	0	14	10	14	21.0	5.1	2.2	0.7	.194
00-01 Miami	82	72	2685	623	211	581	.363	103	307	.336	98	161	.609	45	200	245	132	269	8	83	53	74	32.7	7.6	3.0	1.6	.210
01-02 San Antonio	59	59	1700	412	155	398	.389	56	148	.378	46	96	.479	42	120	162	88	116	0	62	55	66	28.8	7.0	2.7	1.5	.223
02-03 San Antonio	82	82	2567	583	223	479	.466	101	229	**.441**	36	89	.404	59	180	239	113	195	0	66	42	72	31.3	7.1	2.9	1.4	.238
NBA Season Totals	384	225	9630	2224	809	2043	.396	314	827	.380	292	535	.546	267	701	968	476	923	10	342	174	299	25.1	5.8	2.5	1.2	....
99-00 Miami	10	0	157	35	10	27	.370	5	22	.227	10	16	.625	1	9	10	8	27	1	7	4	6	15.7	3.5	1.0	0.8	.172
00-01 Miami	3	3	58	12	5	16	.313	2	8	.250	0	0	.000	1	1	2	2	8	0	2	2	2	19.3	4.0	0.7	0.7	.075
01-02 San Antonio	10	10	345	68	25	61	.410	11	25	.440	7	14	.500	9	24	33	14	28	0	11	7	7	34.5	6.8	3.3	1.4	.217
02-03 San Antonio	24	24	750	166	54	145	.372	35	80	.438	23	42	.548	14	55	69	39	52	0	20	17	15	31.3	6.9	2.9	1.6	.235
NBA Playoff Totals	47	37	1310	281	94	249	.378	53	135	.393	40	72	.556	25	89	114	63	115	1	40	30	30	27.9	6.0	2.4	1.3	....

• BOWEN, Ryan

Ryan Cleo Bowen

Born: Nov. 20, 1975. Fort Madison, IA, United States.   Height: 6'7".   Weight: 215 lbs.   Drafted: 1998   College: Iowa

YEAR TEAM	GP	GS	MIN	PTS	FGM	FGA	FG%	3PM	3PA	3P%	FTM	FTA	FT%	ORB	DRB	TRB	AST	PF	DQ	STL	BLK	TO	MPG	PPG	RPG	APG	PCM
99-00 Denver	52	0	589	131	46	117	.393	1	9	.111	38	53	.717	75	39	114	20	95	0	39	13	14	11.3	2.5	2.2	0.4	.300
00-01 Denver	57	0	696	191	80	144	.556	4	11	.364	27	44	.614	62	51	113	30	95	0	37	12	24	12.2	3.4	2.0	0.5	.345
01-02 Denver	75	21	1686	364	147	307	.479	1	12	.083	69	92	.750	134	165	299	52	171	1	75	41	41	22.5	4.9	4.0	0.7	.313
02-03 Denver	62	31	997	223	97	197	.492	2	7	.286	27	41	.659	78	79	157	54	82	0	65	29	43	16.1	3.6	2.5	0.9	.337
NBA Season Totals	246	52	3968	909	370	765	.484	8	39	.205	161	230	.700	349	334	683	156	443	1	216	95	122	16.1	3.7	2.8	0.6	....

YEAR	TEAM	GP	GS	MIN	PTS	FGM	FGA	FG%	3PM	3PA	3P%	FTM	FTA	FT%	ORB	DRB	TRB	AST	PF	DQ	STL	BLK	TO	MPG	PPG	RPG	APG	PCM

• BOWENS, Tommie
Tommie Lee (Tom) Bowens Jr.

Born: July 7, 1940. Okolona, MS, United States.   Height: 6'8".   Weight: 220 lbs.   Drafted: —   College: Grambling

YEAR	TEAM	GP	GS	MIN	PTS	FGM	FGA	FG%	3PM	3PA	3P%	FTM	FTA	FT%	ORB	DRB	TRB	AST	PF	DQ	STL	BLK	TO	MPG	PPG	RPG	APG	PCM
67-68	Denver-A	67	....	1287	410	177	453	.391	1	2	.500	55	90	.611	....	....	374	41	159	3	....	....	83	19.2	6.1	5.6	0.6	.356
68-69	New York-A	76	....	1550	455	186	453	.411	0	3	.000	83	128	.648	159	296	455	52	236	6	....	....	111	20.4	6.0	6.0	0.7	.358
69-70	New Orleans-A	68	....	753	267	110	251	.438	0	0	.000	47	62	.758	73	105	178	41	147	2	....	....	51	11.1	3.9	2.6	0.6	.367
ABA Season Totals		211	....	3590	1132	473	1157	.409	1	5	.200	185	280	.661	232	401	1007	134	542	11	....	....	245	17.0	5.4	4.8	0.6	....
67-68	Denver-A	5	....	94	30	14	31	.452	0	1	.000	2	2	1.000	....	....	25	5	17	1	....	....	6	18.8	6.0	5.0	1.0	.377
ABA Playoff Totals		5	....	94	30	14	31	.452	0	1	.000	2	2	1.000	....	....	25	5	17	1	....	....	6	18.8	6.0	5.0	1.0	....

• BOWERS, Harold
Harold Bowers

Born: 1912.   Height: 5'10".   Weight: 165 lbs.   Drafted: —   College: Earlham

YEAR	TEAM	GP	GS	MIN	PTS	FGM	FGA	FG%	3PM	3PA	3P%	FTM	FTA	FT%	ORB	DRB	TRB	AST	PF	DQ	STL	BLK	TO	MPG	PPG	RPG	APG	PCM
37-38	Cincinnati-N	2	....	....	9	4	....	....	....	....	....	1	....	....	....	....	....	....	....	....	....	....	....	....	4.5	....	....	....
NBL Season Totals		2	....	....	9	4	....	....	....	....	....	1	....	....	....	....	....	....	....	....	....	....	....	....	4.5	....	....	....

• BOWIE, Anthony
Anthony Lee (A.B.) Bowie

Born: Nov. 9, 1963. Tulsa, OK, United States.   Height: 6'6".   Weight: 190 lbs.   Drafted: 1986   College: Oklahoma

YEAR	TEAM	GP	GS	MIN	PTS	FGM	FGA	FG%	3PM	3PA	3P%	FTM	FTA	FT%	ORB	DRB	TRB	AST	PF	DQ	STL	BLK	TO	MPG	PPG	RPG	APG	PCM
88-89	San Antonio	18	5	438	155	72	144	.500	1	5	.200	10	15	.667	25	31	56	29	43	1	18	4	22	24.3	8.6	3.1	1.6	.340
89-90	Houston	66	0	918	284	119	293	.406	6	21	.286	40	54	.741	36	82	118	96	80	0	42	5	59	13.9	4.3	1.8	1.5	.303
91-92	Orlando	52	26	1721	758	312	633	.493	17	44	.386	117	136	.860	70	175	245	163	101	1	55	38	109	33.1	14.6	4.7	3.1	.460
92-93	Orlando	77	45	1761	618	268	569	.471	15	48	.313	67	84	.798	36	158	194	175	131	0	54	14	85	22.9	8.0	2.5	2.3	.352
93-94	Orlando	70	0	948	320	139	289	.481	1	18	.056	41	49	.837	29	91	120	102	81	0	32	12	56	13.5	4.6	1.7	1.5	.370
94-95	Orlando	77	4	1261	427	177	369	.480	12	40	.300	61	73	.836	54	85	139	159	138	1	47	21	85	16.4	5.5	1.8	2.1	.365
95-96	Orlando	74	4	1078	308	128	272	.471	12	31	.387	40	46	.870	40	83	123	105	112	0	34	10	52	14.6	4.2	1.7	1.4	.312
97-98	New York	27	3	224	75	32	59	.542	3	4	.750	8	9	.889	9	17	26	11	25	1	6	2	8	8.3	2.8	1.0	0.4	.331
NBA Season Totals		461	87	8349	2945	1247	2628	.475	67	211	.318	384	466	.824	299	722	1021	840	711	4	288	106	476	18.1	6.4	2.2	1.8	....
89-90	Houston	2	0	4	0	0	1	.000	0	0	.000	0	0	.000	0	0	0	1	0	0	0	0	0	2.0	0.0	0.0	0.0	-.351
93-94	Orlando	2	0	13	0	0	1	.000	0	0	.000	0	0	.000	0	0	0	3	0	0	0	0	0	6.5	0.0	0.0	0.0	-.176
94-95	Orlando	17	0	118	55	21	42	.500	5	7	.714	8	9	.889	4	8	12	18	23	0	1	1	8	6.9	3.2	0.7	1.1	.413
95-96	Orlando	12	1	152	30	13	27	.481	0	0	.000	4	4	1.000	3	14	17	14	16	0	3	2	5	12.7	2.5	1.4	1.2	.264
97-98	New York	7	0	23	4	2	4	.500	0	0	.000	0	0	.000	0	0	0	1	4	0	1	0	1	3.3	0.6	0.0	0.1	.062
NBA Playoff Totals		40	1	310	89	36	75	.480	5	7	.714	12	13	.923	7	22	29	33	47	0	5	3	14	7.8	2.2	0.7	0.8	....

• BOWIE, Sam
Samuel Paul Bowie

Born: Mar. 17, 1961. Lebanon, PA, United States.   Height: 7'1".   Weight: 235 lbs.   Drafted: 1984   College: Kentucky

YEAR	TEAM	GP	GS	MIN	PTS	FGM	FGA	FG%	3PM	3PA	3P%	FTM	FTA	FT%	ORB	DRB	TRB	AST	PF	DQ	STL	BLK	TO	MPG	PPG	RPG	APG	PCM
84-85	Portland	76	62	2216	758	299	557	.537	0	0	.000	160	225	.711	207	449	656	215	278	9	55	203	175	29.2	10.0	8.6	2.8	.576
85-86	Portland	38	34	1132	448	167	345	.484	0	0	.000	114	161	.708	93	234	327	99	142	4	21	96	87	29.8	11.8	8.6	2.6	.559
86-87	Portland	5	5	163	80	30	66	.455	0	0	.000	20	30	.667	14	19	33	9	19	0	1	10	15	32.6	16.0	6.6	1.8	.427
88-89	Portland	20	0	412	171	69	153	.451	5	7	.714	28	49	.571	36	70	106	36	43	0	7	33	32	20.6	8.6	5.3	1.8	.504
89-90	New Jersey	68	54	2207	998	347	834	.416	10	31	.323	294	379	.776	206	484	690	91	211	5	38	121	122	32.5	14.7	10.1	1.3	.535
90-91	New Jersey	62	51	1916	801	314	723	.434	4	22	.182	169	231	.732	176	304	480	147	175	4	43	90	143	30.9	12.9	7.7	2.4	.472
91-92	New Jersey	71	61	2179	1062	421	947	.445	8	25	.320	212	280	.757	203	375	578	186	212	2	41	120	149	30.7	15.0	8.1	2.6	.546
92-93	New Jersey	79	65	2092	717	287	638	.450	2	6	.333	141	181	.779	158	398	556	127	226	3	32	128	119	26.5	9.1	7.0	1.6	.458
93-94	LA Lakers	25	7	556	223	75	172	.436	1	4	.250	72	83	.867	27	104	131	47	65	0	4	28	43	22.2	8.9	5.2	1.9	.468
94-95	LA Lakers	67	10	1225	306	118	267	.442	2	11	.182	68	89	.764	72	216	288	118	182	4	21	80	94	18.3	4.6	4.3	1.8	.386
NBA Season Totals		511	349	14098	5564	2127	4702	.452	32	106	.302	1278	1708	.748	1192	2653	3845	1075	1553	31	263	909	979	27.6	10.9	7.5	2.1	....
84-85	Portland	9	9	259	66	26	59	.441	0	0	.000	14	25	.560	16	60	76	21	36	2	4	21	12	28.8	7.3	8.4	2.3	.458
88-89	Portland	3	1	67	31	12	28	.429	1	2	.500	6	8	.750	10	8	18	3	8	0	0	7	3	22.3	10.3	6.0	1.0	.524
91-92	New Jersey	4	4	112	37	14	33	.424	1	2	.500	8	12	.667	8	11	19	9	19	0	3	3	5	28.0	9.3	4.8	2.3	.329
92-93	New Jersey	3	3	71	10	4	9	.444	0	0	.000	2	2	1.000	2	10	12	2	9	0	6	1	4	23.7	3.3	4.0	0.7	.243
94-95	LA Lakers	10	0	135	21	8	30	.267	0	0	.000	5	5	1.000	13	20	33	3	25	0	1	9	6	13.5	2.1	3.3	0.3	.197
NBA Playoff Totals		29	17	644	165	64	159	.403	2	4	.500	35	52	.673	49	109	158	38	97	2	14	41	30	22.2	5.7	5.4	1.3	....

• BOWLING, Orbie
Orbie Lee (Gomer) Bowling

Born: Mar. 21, 1939. KY, United States.   Height: 6'10".   Weight: 215 lbs.   Drafted: 1963   College: Tennessee

YEAR	TEAM	GP	GS	MIN	PTS	FGM	FGA	FG%	3PM	3PA	3P%	FTM	FTA	FT%	ORB	DRB	TRB	AST	PF	DQ	STL	BLK	TO	MPG	PPG	RPG	APG	PCM
67-68	Kentucky-A	11	....	90	21	9	28	.321	0	0	.000	3	12	.250	....	....	29	1	16	0	....	....	6	8.2	1.9	2.6	0.1	.223
ABA Season Totals		11	....	90	21	9	28	.321	0	0	.000	3	12	.250	....	....	29	1	16	0	....	....	6	8.2	1.9	2.6	0.1	....

• BOWMAN, Art
Art Bowman

Born: —.   Height: —   Weight: —   Drafted: —   College: St. Joseph's (IN)

YEAR	TEAM	GP	GS	MIN	PTS	FGM	FGA	FG%	3PM	3PA	3P%	FTM	FTA	FT%	ORB	DRB	TRB	AST	PF	DQ	STL	BLK	TO	MPG	PPG	RPG	APG	PCM
40-41	Hammond-N	8	....	....	9	4	....	....	....	....	....	1	....	....	....	....	....	....	....	....	....	....	....	....	1.1	....	....	....
NBL Season Totals		8	....	....	9	4	....	....	....	....	....	1	....	....	....	....	....	....	....	....	....	....	....	....	1.1	....	....	....

YEAR	TEAM	GP	GS	MIN	PTS	FGM	FGA	FG%	3PM	3PA	3P%	FTM	FTA	FT%	ORB	DRB	TRB	AST	PF	DQ	STL	BLK	TO	MPG	PPG	RPG	APG	PCM

• BOWMAN, Ira
Ira Bowman

Born: June 11, 1973. Newark, NJ, United States.   Height: 6'5".   Weight: 195 lbs.   Drafted: —   College: Pennsylvania

YEAR	TEAM	GP	GS	MIN	PTS	FGM	FGA	FG%	3PM	3PA	3P%	FTM	FTA	FT%	ORB	DRB	TRB	AST	PF	DQ	STL	BLK	TO	MPG	PPG	RPG	APG	PCM
99-00	Philadelphia	11	0	20	5	2	2	1.000	0	0	.000	1	2	.500	0	2	2	1	0	0	1	0	1	1.8	0.5	0.2	0.1	.373
00-01	Atlanta	3	0	19	0	0	2	.000	0	0	.000	1	1	2	7	0	0	0	1	6.3	0.0	0.7	2.3	.359
01-02	Philadelphia	3	0	29	10	5	7	.714	0	1	.000	0	0	.000	0	1	1	1	3	0	2	0	0	9.7	3.3	0.3	0.3	.367
NBA Season Totals		17	0	68	15	7	11	.636	0	1	.000	1	2	.500	1	4	5	9	3	0	3	0	2	4.0	0.9	0.3	0.5	....
99-00	Philadelphia	7	0	11	0	0	2	.000	0	1	.000	0	2	.000	0	0	0	2	0	0	0	0	0	1.6	0.0	0.0	0.3	-.049
NBA Playoff Totals		7	0	11	0	0	2	.000	0	1	.000	0	2	.000	0	0	0	2	0	0	0	0	0	1.6	0.0	0.0	0.3	....

• BOWMAN, Nate
Nathaniel (Nate the Skate) Bowman

Born: Mar. 19, 1943. Fort Worth, TX, United States. Died: Dec.11, 1984.   Height: 6'10".   Weight: 230 lbs.   Drafted: 1965   College: Wichita State

YEAR	TEAM	GP	GS	MIN	PTS	FGM	FGA	FG%	3PM	3PA	3P%	FTM	FTA	FT%	ORB	DRB	TRB	AST	PF	DQ	STL	BLK	TO	MPG	PPG	RPG	APG	PCM
66-67	Chicago	9	....	65	22	8	21	.381	....	....	....	6	8	.750	....	....	28	2	18	0	....	....	....	7.2	2.4	3.1	0.2	.437
67-68	New York	42	....	272	114	52	134	.388	....	....	....	10	15	.667	....	....	113	20	69	0	....	....	....	6.5	2.7	2.7	0.5	.490
68-69	New York	67	....	607	193	82	226	.363	....	....	....	29	61	.475	....	....	220	53	142	4	....	....	....	9.1	2.9	3.3	0.8	.404
69-70	New York	81	....	744	237	98	235	.417	....	....	....	41	79	.519	....	....	257	46	189	2	....	....	....	9.2	2.9	3.2	0.6	.395
70-71	Buffalo	44	....	483	136	58	148	.392	....	....	....	20	38	.526	....	....	173	41	91	2	....	....	....	11.0	3.1	3.9	0.9	.429
71-72	Pittsburgh-A	18	....	217	43	19	53	.358	0	1	.000	5	9	.556	32	55	87	13	48	2	....	....	17	12.1	2.4	4.8	0.7	.375
NBA Season Totals		243	....	2171	702	298	764	.390	....	....	....	106	201	.527	....	....	791	162	509	8	....	....	....	8.9	2.9	3.3	0.7	....
ABA Season Totals		18	....	217	43	19	53	.358	0	1	.000	5	9	.556	32	55	87	13	48	2	....	....	17	12.1	2.4	4.8	0.7	....
Career Totals		261	....	2388	745	317	817	.388	0	1	.000	111	210	.529	32	55	878	175	557	10	....	....	17	9.1	2.9	3.4	0.7	....
67-68	New York	1	....	6	0	0	4	.000	....	....	....	0	0	.000	....	....	3	0	1	0	....	....	....	6.0	0.0	3.0	0.0	-.200
68-69	New York	10	....	62	11	4	15	.267	....	....	....	3	3	1.000	....	....	32	3	16	0	....	....	....	6.2	1.1	3.2	0.3	.409
69-70	New York	18	....	128	43	18	47	.383	....	....	....	7	10	.700	....	....	44	6	34	0	....	....	....	7.1	2.4	2.4	0.3	.364
NBA Playoff Totals		29	....	196	54	22	66	.333	....	....	....	10	13	.769	....	....	79	9	51	0	....	....	....	6.8	1.9	2.7	0.3	....

• BOYCE, Donnie
Donald Nathaniel Boyce

Born: Sept. 2, 1973. Chicago, IL, United States.   Height: 6'5".   Weight: 196 lbs.   Drafted: 1995   College: Colorado

YEAR	TEAM	GP	GS	MIN	PTS	FGM	FGA	FG%	3PM	3PA	3P%	FTM	FTA	FT%	ORB	DRB	TRB	AST	PF	DQ	STL	BLK	TO	MPG	PPG	RPG	APG	PCM
95-96	Atlanta	8	0	41	24	9	23	.391	4	8	.500	2	4	.500	5	5	10	3	2	0	3	1	6	5.1	3.0	1.3	0.4	.480
96-97	Atlanta	22	2	154	55	21	63	.333	2	16	.125	11	22	.500	7	8	15	13	17	0	10	4	15	7.0	2.5	0.7	0.6	.193
NBA Season Totals		30	2	195	79	30	86	.349	6	24	.250	13	26	.500	12	13	25	16	19	0	13	5	21	6.5	2.6	0.8	0.5	....
95-96	Atlanta	1	0	2	0	0	2	.000	0	2	.000	0	0	.000	0	0	0	0	0	0	0	0	0	2.0	0.0	0.0	0.0	-.940
NBA Playoff Totals		1	0	2	0	0	2	.000	0	2	.000	0	0	.000	0	0	0	0	0	0	0	0	0	2.0	0.0	0.0	0.0	....

• BOYD, Dennis
Dennis Boyd

Born: May 21, 1954. Portsmouth, VA, United States.   Height: 6'1".   Weight: 175 lbs.   Drafted: 1977   College: Detroit

YEAR	TEAM	GP	GS	MIN	PTS	FGM	FGA	FG%	3PM	3PA	3P%	FTM	FTA	FT%	ORB	DRB	TRB	AST	PF	DQ	STL	BLK	TO	MPG	PPG	RPG	APG	PCM
78-79	Detroit	5	....	40	6	3	12	.250	....	....	....	0	0	.000	0	2	2	7	5	0	0	0	6	8.0	1.2	0.4	1.4	-.005
NBA Season Totals		5	....	40	6	3	12	.250	....	....	....	0	0	.000	0	2	2	7	5	0	0	0	6	8.0	1.2	0.4	1.4	....

• BOYD, Freddie
Fred L. Boyd

Born: June 13, 1950. Bakersfield, CA, United States.   Height: 6'2".   Weight: 180 lbs.   Drafted: 1972   College: Oregon State

YEAR	TEAM	GP	GS	MIN	PTS	FGM	FGA	FG%	3PM	3PA	3P%	FTM	FTA	FT%	ORB	DRB	TRB	AST	PF	DQ	STL	BLK	TO	MPG	PPG	RPG	APG	PCM
72-73	Philadelphia	82	....	2351	860	362	923	.392	....	....	....	136	200	.680	....	....	210	301	184	1	....	....	....	28.7	10.5	2.6	3.7	.339
73-74	Philadelphia	75	....	1818	713	286	712	.402	....	....	....	141	195	.723	16	77	93	249	173	1	60	9	....	24.2	9.5	1.2	3.3	.341
74-75	Philadelphia	66	....	1362	465	205	495	.414	....	....	....	55	115	.478	16	73	89	161	134	0	43	4	....	20.6	7.0	1.3	2.4	.290
75-76	Philadelphia	6	....	33	5	2	6	.333	....	....	....	1	2	.500	0	2	2	5	0	1	0	....	5.5	0.8	0.3	0.3	.091
75-76	New Orleans	30	....	584	172	72	165	.436	....	....	....	28	49	.571	4	26	30	78	54	0	27	7	....	19.5	5.7	1.0	2.6	.299
76-77	New Orleans	47	....	1212	467	194	406	.478	....	....	....	79	98	.806	19	71	90	147	78	0	44	6	....	25.8	9.9	1.9	3.1	.402
77-78	New Orleans	21	....	363	102	44	110	.400	....	....	....	14	22	.636	2	17	19	48	23	0	9	3	21	17.3	4.9	0.9	2.3	.257
NBA Season Totals		327	....	7723	2784	1165	2817	.414	....	....	....	454	681	.667	57	266	533	986	651	2	184	29	21	23.6	8.5	1.6	3.0	....

• BOYD, Ken
Ken Boyd

Born: Mar. 25, 1952. Frederick, MD, United States.   Height: 6'5".   Weight: 195 lbs.   Drafted: 1974   College: Boston University

YEAR	TEAM	GP	GS	MIN	PTS	FGM	FGA	FG%	3PM	3PA	3P%	FTM	FTA	FT%	ORB	DRB	TRB	AST	PF	DQ	STL	BLK	TO	MPG	PPG	RPG	APG	PCM
74-75	New Orleans	6	....	25	19	7	13	.538	....	....	....	5	11	.455	3	2	5	2	2	0	3	0	....	4.2	3.2	0.8	0.3	.681
NBA Season Totals		6	....	25	19	7	13	.538	....	....	....	5	11	.455	3	2	5	2	2	0	3	0	....	4.2	3.2	0.8	0.3	....

• BOYKINS, Earl
Earl Antoine Boykins

Born: June 2, 1976. Cleveland, OH, United States.   Height: 5'5".   Weight: 135 lbs.   Drafted: —   College: Eastern Michigan

YEAR	TEAM	GP	GS	MIN	PTS	FGM	FGA	FG%	3PM	3PA	3P%	FTM	FTA	FT%	ORB	DRB	TRB	AST	PF	DQ	STL	BLK	TO	MPG	PPG	RPG	APG	PCM
98-99	New Jersey	5	0	51	21	10	21	.476	1	5	.200	0	0	.000	1	3	4	6	3	0	1	0	7	10.2	4.2	0.8	1.2	.290
98-99	Cleveland	17	0	170	44	20	58	.345	2	13	.154	2	3	.667	6	7	13	27	17	0	5	0	13	10.0	2.6	0.8	1.6	.216
99-00	Orlando	1	0	8	6	3	4	.750	0	0	.000	0	0	.000	0	1	1	3	0	0	0	0	0	8.0	6.0	1.0	3.0	1.160
99-00	Cleveland	25	0	253	132	53	112	.473	8	20	.400	18	23	.783	11	14	25	45	23	0	12	1	17	10.1	5.3	1.0	1.8	.529
00-01	LA Clippers	10	0	149	65	25	63	.397	1	8	.125	14	17	.824	4	7	11	32	9	0	5	0	9	14.9	6.5	1.1	3.2	.450
01-02	LA Clippers	68	2	761	280	110	275	.400	13	42	.310	47	61	.770	27	27	54	145	44	0	20	2	44	11.2	4.1	0.8	2.1	.384
02-03	Golden State	68	0	1321	600	199	464	.429	29	77	.377	173	200	.865	35	53	88	221	75	0	38	4	73	19.4	8.8	1.3	3.3	.459
NBA Season Totals		194	2	2713	1148	420	997	.421	54	165	.327	254	304	.836	85	111	196	479	171	0	81	7	163	14.0	5.9	1.0	2.5	....

YEAR	TEAM	GP	GS	MIN	PTS	FGM	FGA	FG%	3PM	3PA	3P%	FTM	FTA	FT%	ORB	DRB	TRB	AST	PF	DQ	STL	BLK	TO	MPG	PPG	RPG	APG	PCM

• BOYKOFF, Harry

Harry J. (Big Hesh, Heshie, Big Boy) Boykoff

Born: July 24, 1922. Brooklyn, NY, United States. Died: Feb.20, 2001. Height: 6'10". Weight: 225 lbs. Drafted: — College: St. John's (NY)

YEAR	TEAM	GP	GS	MIN	PTS	FGM	FGA	FG%	3PM	3PA	3P%	FTM	FTA	FT%	ORB	DRB	TRB	AST	PF	DQ	STL	BLK	TO	MPG	PPG	RPG	APG	PCM
47-48	Toledo-N	59	....	....	574	225	....	....	....	....	....	124	161	.770	....	....	....	....	**219**	....	....	....	....	9.7	....	....	....
48-49	Waterloo-N	61	....	....	777	293	....	....	....	....	....	191	265	.721	....	....	....	....	233	....	....	....	....	12.7	....	....	....
49-50	Waterloo	61	....	....	779	288	698	.413	....	....	....	203	262	.775	....	....	149	229	....	....	....	....	12.8	....	2.4	....
50-51	Bos/Tri	48	....	....	326	126	336	.375	....	....	....	74	100	.740	....	....	220	60	197	12	....	....	....	6.8	4.6	1.3	....
NBA Season Totals		109	....	....	1105	414	1034	.400	....	....	....	277	362	.765	....	....	220	209	426	12	....	....	....	10.1	2.0	1.9	....
NBL Season Totals		120	....	....	1351	518	....	....	....	....	....	315	426	....	....	....	....	....	452	....	....	....	....	11.3	....	....	....
Career Totals		229	....	....	2456	932	1034	....	....	....	....	592	788	....	....	....	220	209	878	12	....	....	....	10.7	1.0	0.9	....

• BOYNES, Winford

Winford Gladstone Boynes III

Born: May 17, 1957. Greenville, SC, United States. Height: 6'6". Weight: 185 lbs. Drafted: 1978 College: San Francisco

YEAR	TEAM	GP	GS	MIN	PTS	FGM	FGA	FG%	3PM	3PA	3P%	FTM	FTA	FT%	ORB	DRB	TRB	AST	PF	DQ	STL	BLK	TO	MPG	PPG	RPG	APG	PCM
78-79	New Jersey	69	....	1176	645	256	595	.430	....	....	....	133	169	.787	60	95	155	75	117	1	43	7	117	17.0	9.3	2.2	1.1	.369
79-80	New Jersey	64	....	1102	546	221	467	.473	0	4	.000	104	136	.765	51	82	133	95	132	1	59	19	96	17.2	8.5	2.1	1.5	.415
80-81	Dallas	44	....	757	287	121	313	.387	0	0	.000	45	55	.818	24	51	75	37	79	1	23	16	70	17.2	6.5	1.7	0.8	.201
NBA Season Totals		177	....	3035	1478	598	1375	.435	0	4	.000	282	360	.783	135	228	363	207	328	3	125	42	283	17.1	8.4	2.1	1.2	....

• BRACEY, Steve

Stephen Henry Bracey

Born: Aug. 1, 1950. Brooklyn, NY, United States. Height: 6'1". Weight: 175 lbs. Drafted: 1972 College: Tulsa

YEAR	TEAM	GP	GS	MIN	PTS	FGM	FGA	FG%	3PM	3PA	3P%	FTM	FTA	FT%	ORB	DRB	TRB	AST	PF	DQ	STL	BLK	TO	MPG	PPG	RPG	APG	PCM
72-73	Atlanta	70	....	1050	457	192	395	.486	....	....	....	73	110	.664	....	....	107	125	125	0	....	....	....	15.0	6.5	1.5	1.8	.427
73-74	Atlanta	*75	....	1463	551	241	520	.463	....	....	....	69	96	.719	26	120	146	231	157	0	60	5	....	19.5	7.3	1.9	3.1	.427
74-75	Golden State	42	....	340	133	54	130	.415	....	....	....	25	38	.658	10	28	38	52	41	0	14	1	....	8.1	3.2	0.9	1.2	.404
NBA Season Totals		187	....	2853	1141	487	1045	.466	....	....	....	167	244	.684	36	148	291	408	323	0	74	6	....	15.3	6.1	1.6	2.2	....
72-73	Atlanta	6	....	123	59	24	47	.511	....	....	....	11	16	.688	....	....	13	20	13	0	....	....	....	20.5	9.8	2.2	3.3	.533
74-75	Golden State	4	....	14	10	3	7	.429	....	....	....	4	4	1.000	0	1	1	3	1	0	3	0	....	3.5	2.5	0.3	0.8	.747
NBA Playoff Totals		10	....	137	69	27	54	.500	....	....	....	15	20	.750	0	1	14	23	14	0	3	0	....	13.7	6.9	1.4	2.3	....

• BRADDS, Gary

Gary Lee (Tex) Bradds

Born: July 26, 1942. Jamestown, OH, United States. Died: July15, 1983. Height: 6'8". Weight: 210 lbs. Drafted: 1964 College: Ohio State

YEAR	TEAM	GP	GS	MIN	PTS	FGM	FGA	FG%	3PM	3PA	3P%	FTM	FTA	FT%	ORB	DRB	TRB	AST	PF	DQ	STL	BLK	TO	MPG	PPG	RPG	APG	PCM
64-65	Baltimore	41	....	335	137	46	111	.414	....	....	....	45	63	.714	....	....	84	19	36	0	....	....	....	8.2	3.3	2.0	0.5	.460
65-66	Baltimore	3	....	15	7	2	6	.333	....	....	....	3	4	.750	....	....	8	1	1	0	....	....	....	5.0	2.3	2.7	0.3	.705
67-68	Oakland-A	49	....	1052	619	199	440	.452	0	4	.000	221	283	.781	....	....	289	51	131	1	....	....	81	21.5	12.6	5.9	1.0	.607
68-69	Oakland-A	75	....	2249	1399	517	1041	.497	1	7	.143	364	444	.820	198	379	577	88	244	6	....	....	175	30.0	18.7	7.7	1.2	.625
69-70	Washington-A	60	....	1239	801	292	608	.480	0	5	.000	217	262	.828	93	243	336	54	181	1	....	....	122	20.7	13.4	5.6	0.9	.632
70-71	Carolina-A	7	....	114	44	17	45	.378	0	1	.000	10	18	.556	13	28	41	2	15	0	....	....	12	16.3	6.3	5.9	0.3	.418
70-71	Texas-A	19	....	207	99	35	82	.427	0	1	.000	29	40	.725	26	37	63	12	26	0	....	....	13	10.9	5.2	3.3	0.6	.538
NBA Season Totals		44	....	350	144	48	117	.410	....	....	....	48	67	.716	....	....	92	20	37	0	....	....	....	8.0	3.3	2.1	0.5	....
ABA Season Totals		210	....	4861	2962	1060	2216	.478	1	18	.056	841	1047	.803	330	687	1306	207	597	8	....	....	403	23.1	14.1	6.2	1.0	....
Career Totals		254	....	5211	3106	1108	2333	.475	1	18	.056	889	1114	.798	330	687	1398	227	634	8	....	....	403	20.5	12.2	5.5	0.9	....
64-65	Baltimore	1	....	5	6	2	3	.667	....	....	....	2	2	1.000	....	....	2	0	0	0	....	....	....	5.0	6.0	2.0	0.0	1.354
68-69	Oakland-A	16	....	517	328	121	253	.478	0	0	.000	86	103	.835	....	....	162	15	66	1	....	....	34	32.3	20.5	10.1	0.9	.648
69-70	Washington-A	6	....	116	57	25	61	.410	1	1	1.000	6	12	.500	....	....	17	3	....	0	....	....	11	19.3	9.5	2.8	0.5	....
NBA Playoff Totals		1	....	5	6	2	3	.667	....	....	....	2	2	1.000	....	....	2	0	0	0	....	....	....	5.0	6.0	2.0	0.0	....
ABA Playoff Totals		22	....	633	385	146	314	.465	1	1	1.000	92	115	.800	....	....	179	18	66	1	....	....	45	28.8	17.5	8.1	0.8	....
Career Playoff Totals		23	....	638	391	148	317	.467	1	1	1.000	94	117	.803	....	....	181	18	66	1	....	....	45	27.7	17.0	7.9	0.8	....

• BRADLEY, Alex

Alex Bradley III

Born: Oct. 30, 1959. Bradenton, FL, United States. Height: 6'6". Weight: 215 lbs. Drafted: 1981 College: Villanova

YEAR	TEAM	GP	GS	MIN	PTS	FGM	FGA	FG%	3PM	3PA	3P%	FTM	FTA	FT%	ORB	DRB	TRB	AST	PF	DQ	STL	BLK	TO	MPG	PPG	RPG	APG	PCM
81-82	New York	39	0	331	137	54	103	.524	0	1	.000	29	48	.604	31	34	65	11	37	0	12	5	27	8.5	3.5	1.7	0.3	.389
NBA Season Totals		39	0	331	137	54	103	.524	0	1	.000	29	48	.604	31	34	65	11	37	0	12	5	27	8.5	3.5	1.7	0.3	....

• BRADLEY, Alonzo

Alonzo Bradley

Born: Oct. 16, 1953. Utica, MS, United States. Height: 6'6". Weight: 190 lbs. Drafted: 1977 College: Texas Southern

YEAR	TEAM	GP	GS	MIN	PTS	FGM	FGA	FG%	3PM	3PA	3P%	FTM	FTA	FT%	ORB	DRB	TRB	AST	PF	DQ	STL	BLK	TO	MPG	PPG	RPG	APG	PCM
77-78	Houston	43	....	798	303	130	304	.428	....	....	....	43	59	.729	24	75	99	54	83	1	16	6	56	18.6	7.0	2.3	1.3	.282
78-79	Houston	34	....	245	96	37	88	.420	....	....	....	22	33	.667	13	33	46	17	33	0	5	1	17	7.2	2.8	1.4	0.5	.329
79-80	Houston	22	....	96	41	17	48	.354	1	1	1.000	6	9	.667	2	4	6	3	9	0	3	0	9	4.4	1.9	0.3	0.1	.113
NBA Season Totals		99	....	1139	440	184	440	.418	1	1	1.000	71	101	.703	39	112	151	74	125	1	24	7	82	11.5	4.4	1.5	0.7	....
78-79	Houston	1	....	1	0	0	0	.000	....	....	....	0	0	.000	0	0	0	0	0	0	0	0	0	1.0	0.0	0.0	0.0	.000
79-80	Houston	4	....	15	16	6	9	.667	1	1	1.000	3	5	.600	1	2	3	1	2	0	1	0	0	3.8	4.0	0.8	0.3	1.079
NBA Playoff Totals		5	....	16	16	6	9	.667	1	1	1.000	3	5	.600	1	2	3	1	2	0	1	0	0	3.2	3.2	0.6	0.2	....

• BRADLEY, Bill

William Bradley

Born: 1941. Height: 5'11". Weight: 165 lbs. Drafted: — College: Tennessee State

YEAR	TEAM	GP	GS	MIN	PTS	FGM	FGA	FG%	3PM	3PA	3P%	FTM	FTA	FT%	ORB	DRB	TRB	AST	PF	DQ	STL	BLK	TO	MPG	PPG	RPG	APG	PCM
67-68	Kentucky-A	58	....	521	218	82	258	.318	3	18	.167	51	56	.911	....	....	47	54	40	0	....	....	50	9.0	3.8	0.8	0.9	.298
ABA Season Totals		58	....	521	218	82	258	.318	3	18	.167	51	56	.911	....	....	47	54	40	0	....	....	50	9.0	3.8	0.8	0.9	....
67-68	Kentucky-A	2	....	9	6	2	2	1.000	0	0	.000	2	2	1.000	....	....	1	1	3	0	....	....	0	4.5	3.0	0.5	0.5	.751
ABA Playoff Totals		2	....	9	6	2	2	1.000	0	0	.000	2	2	1.000	....	....	1	1	3	0	....	....	0	4.5	3.0	0.5	0.5	....

• BRADLEY, Bill

William Warren (Dollar Bill) Bradley

Born: July 28, 1943. Crystal City, MO, United States. Height: 6'5". Weight: 205 lbs. Drafted: 1965 College: Princeton HOF: 1983

YEAR	TEAM	GP	GS	MIN	PTS	FGM	FGA	FG%	3PM	3PA	3P%	FTM	FTA	FT%	ORB	DRB	TRB	AST	PF	DQ	STL	BLK	TO	MPG	PPG	RPG	APG	PCM
67-68	New York	45	....	874	360	142	341	.416	....	....	....	76	104	.731	....	....	113	137	138	2	....	....	....	19.4	8.0	2.5	3.0	.446
68-69	New York	82	....	2413	1020	407	948	.429	....	....	....	206	253	.814	....	....	350	302	295	4	....	....	....	29.4	12.4	4.3	3.7	.443
69-70	New York	67	....	2098	971	413	897	.460	....	....	....	145	176	.824	....	....	239	268	219	0	....	....	....	31.3	14.5	3.6	4.0	.451
70-71	New York	78	....	2300	970	413	912	.453	....	....	....	144	175	.823	....	....	260	280	245	3	....	....	....	29.5	12.4	3.3	3.6	.420
71-72	New York	78	....	2780	1177	504	1085	.465	....	....	....	169	199	.849	....	....	250	315	254	4	....	....	....	35.6	15.1	3.2	4.0	.405
72-73	New York	82	....	2998	1319	575	1252	.459	....	....	....	169	194	.871	....	....	301	367	273	5	....	....	....	36.6	16.1	3.7	4.5	.430
73-74	New York	82	....	2813	1150	502	1112	.451	....	....	....	146	167	.874	59	194	253	242	278	2	42	21	....	34.3	14.0	3.1	3.0	.354
74-75	New York	79	....	2787	1048	452	1036	.436	....	....	....	144	165	.873	65	186	251	247	283	5	74	18	....	35.3	13.3	3.2	3.1	.329
75-76	New York	82	....	2709	914	392	906	.433	....	....	....	130	148	.878	47	187	234	247	256	2	68	18	....	33.0	11.1	2.9	3.0	.309
76-77	New York	67	....	1027	288	127	274	.464	....	....	....	34	42	.810	27	76	103	128	122	0	25	8	....	15.3	4.3	1.5	1.9	.331
NBA Season Totals		742	....	22799	9217	3927	8763	.448	....	....	....	1363	1623	.840	198	643	2354	2533	2363	27	209	65	....	30.7	12.4	3.2	3.4	....
67-68	New York	6	....	64	33	12	28	.429	....	....	....	9	13	.692	....	....	6	2	7	0	....	....	....	10.7	5.5	1.0	0.3	.360
68-69	New York	10	....	419	160	65	141	.461	....	....	....	30	39	.769	....	....	73	40	38	1	....	....	....	41.9	16.0	7.3	4.0	.440
69-70	New York	19	....	616	235	100	233	.429	....	....	....	35	43	.814	....	....	72	60	59	1	....	....	....	32.4	12.4	3.8	3.2	.356
70-71	New York	12	....	368	126	56	132	.424	....	....	....	14	19	.737	....	....	41	43	40	0	....	....	....	30.7	10.5	3.4	3.6	.341
71-72	New York	16	....	594	259	106	227	.467	....	....	....	47	56	.839	....	....	47	54	66	1	....	....	....	37.1	16.2	2.9	3.4	.377
72-73	New York	17	....	587	238	99	221	.448	....	....	....	40	50	.800	....	....	57	45	59	1	....	....	....	34.5	14.0	3.4	2.6	.348
73-74	New York	12	....	425	151	63	159	.396	....	....	....	25	29	.862	8	20	28	13	39	1	7	3	....	35.4	12.6	2.3	1.1	.211
74-75	New York	3	....	88	20	9	24	.375	....	....	....	2	2	1.000	4	5	9	6	5	0	2	0	....	29.3	6.7	3.0	2.0	.223
NBA Playoff Totals		95	....	3161	1222	510	1165	.438	....	....	....	202	251	.805	12	25	333	263	313	5	9	3	....	33.3	12.9	3.5	2.8	....

• BRADLEY, Charles

Charles Warnell Bradley

Born: May 16, 1959. Havre De Grace, MD, United States. Height: 6'5". Weight: 215 lbs. Drafted: 1981 College: Wyoming

YEAR	TEAM	GP	GS	MIN	PTS	FGM	FGA	FG%	3PM	3PA	3P%	FTM	FTA	FT%	ORB	DRB	TRB	AST	PF	DQ	STL	BLK	TO	MPG	PPG	RPG	APG	PCM
81-82	Boston	51	1	339	152	55	122	.451	0	1	.000	42	62	.677	12	26	38	22	61	0	14	6	36	6.6	3.0	0.7	0.4	.286
82-83	Boston	51	5	532	184	69	176	.392	0	3	.000	46	90	.511	30	48	78	28	84	0	32	27	41	10.4	3.6	1.5	0.5	.276
83-84	Seattle	8	0	39	11	3	7	.429	0	0	.000	5	7	.714	0	3	3	5	6	0	0	1	8	4.9	1.4	0.4	0.6	.133
NBA Season Totals		110	6	910	347	127	305	.416	0	4	.000	93	159	.585	42	77	119	55	151	0	46	34	85	8.3	3.2	1.1	0.5	....
81-82	Boston	7	0	18	4	2	8	.250	0	0	.000	0	2	.000	1	4	5	1	6	0	1	0	4	2.6	0.6	0.7	0.1	-.127
82-83	Boston	2	0	4	0	0	0	.000	0	0	.000	0	0	.000	0	0	0	0	0	0	0	0	0	2.0	0.0	0.0	0.0	.000
NBA Playoff Totals		9	0	22	4	2	8	.250	0	0	.000	0	2	.000	1	4	5	1	6	0	1	0	4	2.4	0.4	0.6	0.1	....

• BRADLEY, Dudley

Dudley Leroy Bradley

Born: Mar. 19, 1957. Baltimore, MD, United States. Height: 6'6". Weight: 195 lbs. Drafted: 1979 College: North Carolina

YEAR	TEAM	GP	GS	MIN	PTS	FGM	FGA	FG%	3PM	3PA	3P%	FTM	FTA	FT%	ORB	DRB	TRB	AST	PF	DQ	STL	BLK	TO	MPG	PPG	RPG	APG	PCM
79-80	Indiana	82	....	2027	688	275	609	.452	2	5	.400	136	174	.782	69	154	223	252	194	1	211	48	164	24.7	8.4	2.7	3.1	.417
80-81	Indiana	82	....	1867	657	265	559	.474	2	16	.125	125	178	.702	70	123	193	188	236	2	186	37	123	22.8	8.0	2.4	2.3	.391
81-82	Phoenix	64	3	937	325	125	281	.445	1	4	.250	74	100	.740	30	57	87	80	115	0	78	10	70	14.6	5.1	1.4	1.3	.320
82-83	Chicago	58	11	683	201	82	159	.516	1	5	.200	36	45	.800	27	78	105	106	91	0	49	10	58	11.8	3.5	1.8	1.8	.437
84-85	Washington	73	24	1232	358	142	299	.475	20	64	.313	54	79	.684	34	100	134	173	152	0	96	21	88	16.9	4.9	1.8	2.4	.378
85-86	Washington	70	7	842	195	73	209	.349	17	68	.250	32	56	.571	24	71	95	107	101	0	85	3	42	12.0	2.8	1.4	1.5	.304
86-87	Milwaukee	68	2	900	212	76	213	.357	13	50	.260	47	58	.810	31	71	102	66	118	2	105	8	34	13.2	3.1	1.5	1.0	.293
87-88	Milwaukee	2	0	5	0	0	1	.000	0	1	.000	0	0	.000	0	1	1	1	2	0	0	0	0	2.5	0.0	0.5	0.5	.027
87-88	New Jersey	63	15	1432	423	156	364	.429	37	101	.366	74	97	.763	25	101	126	150	170	1	114	43	88	22.7	6.7	2.0	2.4	.336
88-89	Atlanta	38	0	267	72	28	86	.326	8	31	.258	8	16	.500	7	25	32	24	41	0	16	2	15	7.0	1.9	0.8	0.6	.200
NBA Season Totals		600	62	10192	3131	1222	2780	.440	101	345	.293	586	803	.730	317	781	1098	1147	1220	6	940	182	682	17.0	5.2	1.8	1.9	....
80-81	Indiana	2	....	19	9	3	9	.333	1	1	1.000	2	2	1.000	1	1	2	2	4	0	2	0	5	9.5	4.5	1.0	1.0	.157
81-82	Phoenix	7	0	24	5	2	8	.250	0	0	.000	1	1	1.000	0	1	1	5	3	0	1	1	5	3.4	0.7	0.1	0.7	.069
84-85	Washington	4	0	41	14	5	9	.556	1	5	.200	3	4	.750	2	4	6	6	5	0	2	0	5	10.3	3.5	1.5	1.5	.407
85-86	Washington	5	0	82	33	12	29	.414	3	10	.300	6	9	.667	2	3	5	7	14	0	5	0	7	16.4	6.6	1.0	1.4	.239
86-87	Milwaukee	12	0	46	9	4	11	.364	0	6	.000	1	2	.500	0	0	0	2	9	0	3	0	1	3.8	0.8	0.0	0.2	.040
NBA Playoff Totals		30	0	212	70	26	66	.394	5	22	.227	13	18	.722	5	9	14	22	35	0	13	1	23	7.1	2.3	0.5	0.7	....

• BRADLEY, Jim

James Arthur Bradley

Born: Mar. 16, 1952. East Chicago, IN, United States. Died: Feb.20, 1982. Height: 6'8". Weight: 215 lbs. Drafted: 1974 College: Northern Illinois

YEAR	TEAM	GP	GS	MIN	PTS	FGM	FGA	FG%	3PM	3PA	3P%	FTM	FTA	FT%	ORB	DRB	TRB	AST	PF	DQ	STL	BLK	TO	MPG	PPG	RPG	APG	PCM
73-74	Kentucky-A	35	....	884	291	130	309	.421	0	2	.000	31	44	.705	67	147	214	49	106	....	37	27	55	25.3	8.3	6.1	1.4	.369
74-75	Kentucky-A	56	....	922	364	144	327	.440	0	4	.000	76	103	.738	101	183	284	68	112	....	27	30	73	16.5	6.5	5.1	1.2	.507
75-76	Denver-A	7	....	107	32	15	38	.395	0	0	.000	2	3	.667	4	26	30	11	26	....	5	5	5	15.3	4.6	4.3	1.6	.359
ABA Season Totals		98	....	1913	687	289	674	.429	0	6	.000	109	150	.727	172	356	528	128	244	....	69	62	133	19.5	7.0	5.4	1.3	....
73-74	Kentucky-A	8	....	162	60	27	69	.391	0	0	.000	6	11	.545	10	29	39	8	21	....	3	5	13	20.3	7.5	4.9	1.0	.342
74-75	Kentucky-A	4	....	20	1	0	7	.000	0	0	.000	1	2	.500	3	4	7	3	3	....	1	0	2	5.0	0.3	1.8	0.8	.128
ABA Playoff Totals		12	....	182	61	27	76	.355	0	0	.000	7	13	.538	13	33	46	11	24	....	4	5	15	15.2	5.1	3.8	0.9	....

YEAR	TEAM	GP	GS	MIN	PTS	FGM	FGA	FG%	3PM	3PA	3P%	FTM	FTA	FT%	ORB	DRB	TRB	AST	PF	DQ	STL	BLK	TO	MPG	PPG	RPG	APG	PCM

• BRADLEY, Joe

Joseph L. Bradley

Born: Sept. 24, 1928. Washington, OK, United States. Died: June 5, 1987. Height: 6'3". Weight: 175 lbs. Drafted: — College: Oklahoma A&M

YEAR	TEAM	GP	GS	MIN	PTS	FGM	FGA	FG%	3PM	3PA	3P%	FTM	FTA	FT%	ORB	DRB	TRB	AST	PF	DQ	STL	BLK	TO	MPG	PPG	RPG	APG	PCM
49-50	Chicago	46	....	....	87	36	134	.269	....	....	....	15	38	.395	....	....	....	36	51	....	....	....	....	....	1.9	....	0.8	....
NBA Season Totals		46	....	....	87	36	134	.269	....	....	....	15	38	.395	....	....	....	36	51	....	....	....	....	....	1.9	....	0.8	....

• BRADLEY, Michael

Michael Thomas Bradley

Born: Apr. 18, 1979. Worcester, MA, United States. Height: 6'10". Weight: 245 lbs. Drafted: 2001 College: Villanova

YEAR	TEAM	GP	GS	MIN	PTS	FGM	FGA	FG%	3PM	3PA	3P%	FTM	FTA	FT%	ORB	DRB	TRB	AST	PF	DQ	STL	BLK	TO	MPG	PPG	RPG	APG	PCM
01-02	Toronto	26	0	117	30	13	25	.520	0	2	.000	4	8	.500	7	17	24	3	10	0	0	6	6	4.5	1.2	0.9	0.1	.323
02-03	Toronto	67	11	1314	338	151	314	.481	1	6	.167	35	67	.522	162	247	409	67	125	0	16	32	76	19.6	5.0	6.1	1.0	.409
NBA Season Totals		93	11	1431	368	164	339	.484	1	8	.125	39	75	.520	169	264	433	70	135	0	16	38	82	15.4	4.0	4.7	0.8	....
01-02	Toronto	1	0	3	0	0	0	.000	0	0	.000	0	0	.000	0	1	1	1	1	0	0	0	0	3.0	0.0	1.0	1.0	.516
NBA Playoff Totals		1	0	3	0	0	0	.000	0	0	.000	0	0	.000	0	1	1	1	1	0	0	0	0	3.0	0.0	1.0	1.0	....

• BRADLEY, Shawn

Shawn Paul Bradley

Born: Mar. 22, 1972. Landstuhl, Germany. Height: 7'5". Weight: 235 lbs. Drafted: 1993 College: Brigham Young

YEAR	TEAM	GP	GS	MIN	PTS	FGM	FGA	FG%	3PM	3PA	3P%	FTM	FTA	FT%	ORB	DRB	TRB	AST	PF	DQ	STL	BLK	TO	MPG	PPG	RPG	APG	PCM
93-94	Philadelphia	49	45	1385	504	201	491	.409	0	3	.000	102	168	.607	98	208	306	98	170	3	45	147	147	28.3	10.3	6.2	2.0	.403
94-95	Philadelphia	82	59	2365	778	315	693	.455	0	3	.000	148	232	.638	243	416	659	53	**338**	**18**	54	274	139	28.8	9.5	8.0	0.6	.455
95-96	Philadelphia	12	11	334	105	43	97	.443	0	0	.000	19	25	.760	34	72	106	8	42	0	8	38	31	27.8	8.8	8.8	0.7	.461
95-96	New Jersey	67	57	1995	839	344	776	.443	1	4	.250	150	221	.679	187	345	532	55	244	5	41	250	147	29.8	12.5	7.9	0.8	.491
96-97	New Jersey	40	38	1228	479	199	456	.436	0	5	.000	81	122	.664	118	207	325	20	122	4	23	160	64	30.7	12.0	8.1	0.5	.488
96-97	Dallas	33	32	1060	482	207	449	.461	0	3	.000	68	106	.642	103	183	286	32	115	3	17	88	69	32.1	14.6	8.7	1.0	.490
97-98	Dallas	64	46	1822	731	300	711	.422	1	3	.333	130	180	.722	164	354	518	60	214	9	51	214	96	28.5	11.4	8.1	0.9	.509
98-99	Dallas	49	33	1294	420	167	348	.480	0	4	.000	86	115	.748	130	262	392	40	153	2	35	159	56	26.4	8.6	8.0	0.8	.536
99-00	Dallas	77	54	1901	647	266	555	.479	1	5	.200	114	149	.765	160	337	497	60	260	7	71	190	74	24.7	8.4	6.5	0.8	.493
00-01	Dallas	82	35	2001	579	219	447	.490	1	6	.167	140	178	.787	160	448	608	38	256	6	36	**228**	88	24.4	7.1	7.4	0.5	.494
01-02	Dallas	53	16	757	215	78	163	.479	0	1	.000	59	64	.922	53	123	176	20	128	3	28	64	25	14.3	4.1	3.3	0.4	.422
02-03	Dallas	81	39	1731	543	201	375	.536	0	1	.000	141	175	.806	151	325	476	54	242	5	65	170	67	21.4	6.7	5.9	0.7	.522
NBA Season Totals		689	465	17873	6322	2540	5561	.457	4	38	.105	1238	1735	.714	1601	3280	4881	538	2284	65	474	1982	1003	25.9	9.2	7.1	0.8	....
00-01	Dallas	10	10	256	64	27	51	.529	0	0	.000	10	13	.769	24	47	71	5	37	1	4	30	10	25.6	6.4	7.1	0.5	.450
01-02	Dallas	7	0	25	6	3	6	.500	0	0	.000	0	0	.000	1	4	5	0	9	0	0	1	1	3.6	0.9	0.7	0.0	.149
02-03	Dallas	17	7	246	49	20	50	.400	0	1	.000	9	12	.750	23	42	65	5	48	2	3	14	15	14.5	2.9	3.8	0.3	.264
NBA Playoff Totals		34	17	527	119	50	107	.467	0	1	.000	19	25	.760	48	93	141	10	94	3	7	45	26	15.5	3.5	4.1	0.3	....

• BRADTKE, Mark

Mark Bradtke

Born: Sept. 27, 1968. Adelaide, SA, Australia. Height: 6'10". Weight: 265 lbs. Drafted: — College: none (HS: Redcliff, AUS)

YEAR	TEAM	GP	GS	MIN	PTS	FGM	FGA	FG%	3PM	3PA	3P%	FTM	FTA	FT%	ORB	DRB	TRB	AST	PF	DQ	STL	BLK	TO	MPG	PPG	RPG	APG	PCM
96-97	Philadelphia	36	0	251	59	25	58	.431	0	0	.000	9	13	.692	26	42	68	7	34	0	5	5	11	7.0	1.6	1.9	0.2	.321
NBA Season Totals		36	0	251	59	25	58	.431	0	0	.000	9	13	.692	26	42	68	7	34	0	5	5	11	7.0	1.6	1.9	0.2	....

• BRAGG, Marques

Marques Bragg

Born: Mar. 24, 1970. East Orange, NJ, United States. Height: 6'8". Weight: 230 lbs. Drafted: — College: Providence

YEAR	TEAM	GP	GS	MIN	PTS	FGM	FGA	FG%	3PM	3PA	3P%	FTM	FTA	FT%	ORB	DRB	TRB	AST	PF	DQ	STL	BLK	TO	MPG	PPG	RPG	APG	PCM
95-96	Minnesota	53	0	369	131	54	120	.450	0	0	.000	23	41	.561	38	41	79	8	71	0	17	8	27	7.0	2.5	1.5	0.2	.293
NBA Season Totals		53	0	369	131	54	120	.450	0	0	.000	23	41	.561	38	41	79	8	71	0	17	8	27	7.0	2.5	1.5	0.2	....

• BRAMLETT, A.J.

Aaron Jordan Bramlett

Born: Jan. 10, 1977. Dekalb, IL, United States. Height: 6'10". Weight: 227 lbs. Drafted: 1999 College: Arizona

YEAR	TEAM	GP	GS	MIN	PTS	FGM	FGA	FG%	3PM	3PA	3P%	FTM	FTA	FT%	ORB	DRB	TRB	AST	PF	DQ	STL	BLK	TO	MPG	PPG	RPG	APG	PCM
99-00	Cleveland	8	0	61	8	4	21	.190	0	0	.000	0	0	.000	12	10	22	0	13	0	1	0	3	7.6	1.0	2.8	0.0	.079
NBA Season Totals		8	0	61	8	4	21	.190	0	0	.000	0	0	.000	12	10	22	0	13	0	1	0	3	7.6	1.0	2.8	0.0	....

• BRANCH, Adrian

Adrian Francis Branch

Born: Nov. 17, 1963. Washington, DC, United States. Height: 6'7". Weight: 185 lbs. Drafted: 1985 College: Maryland

YEAR	TEAM	GP	GS	MIN	PTS	FGM	FGA	FG%	3PM	3PA	3P%	FTM	FTA	FT%	ORB	DRB	TRB	AST	PF	DQ	STL	BLK	TO	MPG	PPG	RPG	APG	PCM
86-87	LA Lakers	32	0	219	138	48	96	.500	0	2	.000	42	54	.778	23	30	53	16	39	0	16	3	26	6.8	4.3	1.7	0.5	.591
87-88	New Jersey	20	3	308	133	56	134	.418	1	5	.200	20	23	.870	20	28	48	16	41	1	16	11	28	15.4	6.7	2.4	0.8	.327
88-89	Portland	67	4	811	498	202	436	.463	7	31	.226	87	120	.725	63	69	132	60	99	0	45	3	67	12.1	7.4	2.0	0.9	.479
89-90	Minnesota	11	0	91	65	25	61	.410	1	1	1.000	14	22	.636	8	12	20	4	14	0	6	0	8	8.3	5.9	1.8	0.4	.462
NBA Season Totals		130	7	1429	834	331	727	.455	9	39	.231	163	219	.744	114	139	253	96	193	1	83	17	129	11.0	6.4	1.9	0.7	....
86-87	LA Lakers	11	0	42	14	4	21	.190	0	1	.000	6	12	.500	3	7	10	5	10	0	2	0	5	3.8	1.3	0.9	0.5	.062
88-89	Portland	1	0	5	2	0	3	.000	0	0	.000	2	2	1.000	0	2	2	2	0	0	0	0	0	5.0	2.0	2.0	2.0	.642
NBA Playoff Totals		12	0	47	16	4	24	.167	0	1	.000	8	14	.571	3	9	12	7	10	0	2	0	5	3.9	1.3	1.0	0.6	....

• BRAND, Elton

Elton Tyron Brand

Born: Mar. 11, 1979. Cortland, NY, United States. Height: 6'8". Weight: 275 lbs. Drafted: 1999 College: Duke

YEAR	TEAM	GP	GS	MIN	PTS	FGM	FGA	FG%	3PM	3PA	3P%	FTM	FTA	FT%	ORB	DRB	TRB	AST	PF	DQ	STL	BLK	TO	MPG	PPG	RPG	APG	PCM
99-00	Chicago	81	80	2999	1627	630	1306	.482	0	2	.000	367	536	.685	**348**	462	810	155	259	3	66	132	228	37.0	20.1	10.0	1.9	.566
00-01	Chicago	74	74	2906	1490	578	1215	.476	0	2	.000	334	472	.708	285	461	746	240	243	4	71	118	219	39.3	20.1	10.1	3.2	.569

YEAR	TEAM	GP	GS	MIN	PTS	FGM	FGA	FG%	3PM	3PA	3P%	FTM	FTA	FT%	ORB	DRB	TRB	AST	PF	DQ	STL	BLK	TO	MPG	PPG	RPG	APG	PCM
01-02	LA Clippers	80	80	3021	1453	532	1010	.527	0	0	.000	389	524	.742	**396**	529	925	191	254	3	80	163	173	37.8	18.2	11.6	2.4	.647
02-03	LA Clippers	62	61	2453	1146	451	899	.502	0	1	.000	244	356	.685	283	420	703	157	204	3	71	158	161	39.6	18.5	11.3	2.5	.598
NBA Season Totals		297	295	11379	5716	2191	4430	.495	0	5	.000	1334	1888	.707	1312	1872	3184	743	960	13	288	571	781	38.3	19.2	10.7	2.5	

• BRANDON, Terrell

Thomas Terrell Brandon

Born: May 20, 1970. Portland, OR, United States.   Height: 5'11".   Weight: 180 lbs.   Drafted: 1991   College: Oregon

YEAR	TEAM	GP	GS	MIN	PTS	FGM	FGA	FG%	3PM	3PA	3P%	FTM	FTA	FT%	ORB	DRB	TRB	AST	PF	DQ	STL	BLK	TO	MPG	PPG	RPG	APG	PCM
91-92	Cleveland	82	9	1605	605	252	601	.419	1	23	.043	100	124	.806	49	113	162	316	107	0	81	22	139	19.6	7.4	2.0	3.9	.421
92-93	Cleveland	82	8	1622	725	297	621	.478	13	42	.310	118	143	.825	37	142	179	302	122	1	79	27	107	19.8	8.8	2.2	3.7	.519
93-94	Cleveland	73	10	1548	606	230	548	.420	7	32	.219	139	162	.858	38	121	159	277	108	0	84	16	110	21.2	8.3	2.2	3.8	.446
94-95	Cleveland	67	41	1961	889	341	762	.448	48	121	.397	159	186	.855	35	151	186	363	118	0	107	14	141	29.3	13.3	2.8	5.4	.493
95-96	Cleveland	75	75	2570	1449	510	1096	.465	91	235	.387	338	381	.887	47	201	248	487	146	1	132	33	143	34.3	19.3	3.3	6.5	.615
96-97	Cleveland	78	78	2868	1519	575	1313	.438	101	271	.373	268	297	.902	48	253	301	490	177	1	138	30	179	36.8	19.5	3.9	6.3	.533
97-98	Milwaukee	50	48	1784	841	339	731	.464	31	93	.333	132	156	.846	23	153	176	387	120	1	111	17	145	35.7	16.8	3.5	7.7	.550
98-99	Milwaukee	15	14	505	203	85	208	.409	7	28	.250	26	31	.839	11	42	53	104	25	0	24	3	36	33.7	13.5	3.5	6.9	.465
98-99	Minnesota	21	20	712	298	127	299	.425	5	19	.263	39	47	.830	16	65	81	205	57	0	39	7	38	33.9	14.2	3.9	9.8	.594
99-00	Minnesota	71	71	2587	1212	486	1042	.466	53	132	.402	187	208	.899	44	194	238	629	158	1	134	30	184	36.4	17.1	3.4	8.9	.584
00-01	Minnesota	78	78	2821	1250	511	1134	.451	33	91	.363	195	224	.871	60	238	298	583	138	1	161	21	155	36.2	16.0	3.8	7.5	.549
01-02	Minnesota	32	28	962	397	155	365	.425	4	23	.174	83	84	.988	17	76	93	264	49	1	52	6	43	30.1	12.4	2.9	8.3	.593
NBA Season Totals		724	480	21545	9994	3908	8720	.448	394	1110	.355	1784	2043	.873	425	1749	2174	4407	1325	7	1142	226	1420	29.8	13.8	3.0	6.1	
91-92	Cleveland	12	0	157	47	22	55	.400	0	3	.000	3	4	.750	4	18	22	30	17	0	3	1	11	13.1	3.9	1.8	2.5	.344
92-93	Cleveland	8	0	132	51	20	46	.435	2	5	.400	9	9	1.000	4	13	17	17	6	0	7	3	14	16.5	6.4	2.1	2.1	.411
93-94	Cleveland	3	0	56	26	12	19	.632	0	0	.000	2	3	.667	1	3	4	5	1	0	1	0	1	18.7	8.7	1.3	1.7	.495
95-96	Cleveland	3	3	125	58	21	47	.447	3	9	.333	13	15	.867	1	8	9	24	10	0	4	1	11	41.7	19.3	3.0	8.0	.449
98-99	Minnesota	4	4	161	77	31	69	.449	3	5	.600	12	13	.923	2	28	30	28	11	0	9	2	14	40.3	19.3	7.5	7.0	.578
99-00	Minnesota	4	4	162	78	32	63	.508	4	11	.364	10	11	.909	4	19	23	34	11	0	3	0	8	40.5	19.5	5.8	8.5	.604
00-01	Minnesota	4	4	153	61	27	62	.435	4	9	.444	3	3	1.000	2	15	17	25	10	0	4	2	8	38.3	15.3	4.3	6.3	.432
NBA Playoff Totals		38	15	946	398	165	361	.457	16	42	.381	52	58	.897	18	104	122	163	66	0	31	9	67	24.9	10.5	3.2	4.3	

• BRANNUM, Bob

Robert Warren (Beeb, The Tank) Brannum

Born: May 28, 1925.   Height: 6'5".   Weight: 215 lbs.   Drafted: —   College: Michigan State

YEAR	TEAM	GP	GS	MIN	PTS	FGM	FGA	FG%	3PM	3PA	3P%	FTM	FTA	FT%	ORB	DRB	TRB	AST	PF	DQ	STL	BLK	TO	MPG	PPG	RPG	APG	PCM
48-49	Sheboygan-N	64	....	....	507	169	....	....	....	....	....	169	261	.648	....	....	232	....	....	....	....	....	....	....	7.9	....	....	....
49-50	Sheboygan	59	....	....	713	234	718	.326	....	....	....	245	355	.690	....	....	....	205	279	....	....	....	....	....	12.1	....	3.5	....
51-52	Boston	66	....	1324	405	149	404	.369	....	....	....	107	171	.626	406	76	235	9	....	....	....	20.1	6.1	6.2	1.2	.381
52-53	Boston	71	....	1900	486	188	541	.348	....	....	....	110	185	.595	537	147	287	17	....	....	....	26.8	6.8	7.6	2.1	.356
53-54	Boston	71	....	1729	409	140	453	.309	....	....	....	129	206	.626	509	144	280	10	....	....	....	24.4	5.8	7.2	2.0	.351
54-55	Boston	71	....	1623	442	176	465	.378	....	....	....	90	127	.709	492	127	232	6	....	....	....	22.9	6.2	6.9	1.8	.402
NBA Season Totals		338	....	6576	2455	887	2581	.344	....	....	....	681	1044	.652	....	1944	699	1313	42	....	....	....	19.5	7.3	5.8	2.1	
NBL Season Totals		64	....	....	507	169	....	....	....	....	....	169	261	....	....	....	232	....	....	....	....	....	....	7.9	....	....	....
Career Totals		402	....	6576	2962	1056	2581	....	....	....	....	850	1305	....	....	1944	699	1545	42	....	....	....	16.4	7.4	4.8	1.7	
48-49	Sheboygan-N	2	....	....	16	7	....	....	....	....	....	2	3	.667	....	....	....	....	....	....	....	....	....	8.0	....	....	....
49-50	Sheboygan	3	....	....	43	15	43	.349	....	....	....	13	20	.650	....	....	11	16	....	....	....	....	....	14.3	....	3.7	....
51-52	Boston	3	....	48	9	4	12	.333	....	....	....	1	6	.167	10	3	16	2	....	....	....	16.0	3.0	3.3	1.0	.142
52-53	Boston	6	....	83	31	12	23	.522	....	....	....	7	11	.636	21	10	23	2	....	....	....	13.8	5.2	3.5	1.7	.497
53-54	Boston	6	....	136	28	11	38	.289	....	....	....	6	11	.545	45	10	29	2	....	....	....	22.7	4.7	7.5	1.7	.306
54-55	Boston	7	....	225	63	26	61	.426	....	....	....	11	19	.579	79	13	32	2	....	....	....	32.1	9.0	11.3	1.9	.432
NBA Playoff Totals		25	....	492	174	68	177	.384	....	....	....	38	67	.567	....	155	47	116	8	....	....	....	19.7	7.0	6.2	1.9	
NBL Playoff Totals		2	....	....	16	7	....	....	....	....	....	2	3	....	....	....	....	....	....	....	....	....	....	8.0	....	....	....
Career Playoff Totals		27	....	492	190	75	177	....	....	....	....	40	70	....	....	155	47	116	8	....	....	....	18.2	7.0	5.7	1.7	

• BRANSON, Brad

Bradley Alexander Branson

Born: Sept. 24, 1958. Harvey, IL, United States.   Height: 6'10".   Weight: 220 lbs.   Drafted: 1980   College: Southern Methodist

YEAR	TEAM	GP	GS	MIN	PTS	FGM	FGA	FG%	3PM	3PA	3P%	FTM	FTA	FT%	ORB	DRB	TRB	AST	PF	DQ	STL	BLK	TO	MPG	PPG	RPG	APG	PCM
81-82	Cleveland	10	3	176	53	21	52	.404	0	0	.000	11	12	.917	14	19	33	6	17	0	5	4	13	17.6	5.3	3.3	0.6	.280
82-83	Indiana	62	2	680	338	131	308	.425	0	1	.000	76	108	.704	73	100	173	46	81	0	27	26	43	11.0	5.5	2.8	0.7	.504
NBA Season Totals		72	5	856	391	152	360	.422	0	1	.000	87	120	.725	87	119	206	52	98	0	32	30	56	11.9	5.4	2.9	0.7	

• BRANSON, Jesse

Herman Jesse Branson

Born: Jan. 7, 1942. Burlington, NC, United States.   Height: 6'7".   Weight: 195 lbs.   Drafted: 1965   College: Elon

YEAR	TEAM	GP	GS	MIN	PTS	FGM	FGA	FG%	3PM	3PA	3P%	FTM	FTA	FT%	ORB	DRB	TRB	AST	PF	DQ	STL	BLK	TO	MPG	PPG	RPG	APG	PCM
65-66	Philadelphia	5	....	14	5	1	6	.167	....	....	....	3	4	.750	....	....	9	1	4	0	....	....	....	2.8	1.0	1.8	0.2	.528
67-68	New Orleans-A	78	....	1892	1086	376	877	.429	2	9	.222	332	473	.702	....	....	541	67	248	3	....	....	115	24.3	13.9	6.9	0.9	.548
NBA Season Totals		5	....	14	5	1	6	.167	....	....	....	3	4	.750	....	....	9	1	4	0	....	....	....	2.8	1.0	1.8	0.2	
ABA Season Totals		78	....	1892	1086	376	877	.429	2	9	.222	332	473	.702	....	....	541	67	248	3	....	....	115	24.3	13.9	6.9	0.9	
Career Totals		83	....	1906	1091	377	883	.427	2	9	.222	335	477	.702	....	....	550	68	252	3	....	....	115	23.0	13.1	6.6	0.8	
67-68	New Orleans-A	17	....	402	193	61	155	.394	0	3	.000	71	87	.816	....	....	102	20	62	0	....	....	31	23.6	11.4	6.0	1.2	.474
ABA Playoff Totals		17	....	402	193	61	155	.394	0	3	.000	71	87	.816	....	....	102	20	62	0	....	....	31	23.6	11.4	6.0	1.2	

YEAR	TEAM	GP	GS	MIN	PTS	FGM	FGA	FG%	3PM	3PA	3P%	FTM	FTA	FT%	ORB	DRB	TRB	AST	PF	DQ	STL	BLK	TO	MPG	PPG	RPG	APG	PCM

• BRASCO, Jim
James J. (Jim) Brasco

Born: Feb. 3, 1931. Height: 6'1". Weight: 170 lbs. Drafted: 1952 College: New York University

52-53	Syracuse	10	....	111	33	11	48	.229	....	....	....	11	14	.786	....	....	15	12	18	1	....	....	....	11.1	3.3	1.5	1.2	.223
52-53	Milwaukee	20	....	248	77	25	94	.266	....	....	....	27	34	.794	....	....	24	21	30	2	....	....	....	12.4	3.9	1.2	1.1	.233
NBA Season Totals		30	....	359	110	36	142	.254	....	....	....	38	48	.792	....	....	39	33	48	3	....	....	....	12.0	3.7	1.3	1.1	....

• BRATZ, Mike
Michael Louis Bratz

Born: Oct. 17, 1955. Lompoc, CA, United States. Height: 6'2". Weight: 185 lbs. Drafted: 1977 College: Stanford

77-78	Phoenix	80	....	933	374	159	395	.403	....	....	....	56	68	.824	42	73	115	123	104	1	39	5	88	11.7	4.7	1.4	1.5	.340
78-79	Phoenix	77	....	1297	623	242	533	.454	....	....	....	139	170	.818	55	86	141	179	151	0	64	7	139	16.8	8.1	1.8	2.3	.418
79-80	Phoenix	82	....	1589	700	269	687	.392	21	86	.244	141	162	.870	50	117	167	223	165	0	93	9	131	19.4	8.5	2.0	2.7	.382
80-81	Cleveland	80	....	2595	802	319	817	.390	**57**	**169**	.337	107	132	.811	66	132	198	452	194	1	136	17	160	32.4	10.0	2.5	5.7	.353
81-82	San Antonio	81	3	1616	625	230	565	.407	46	138	.333	119	152	.783	40	126	166	438	180	0	65	11	138	20.0	7.7	2.0	5.4	.486
82-83	Chicago	15	0	140	39	14	42	.333	1	8	.125	10	13	.769	3	16	19	23	20	0	7	0	14	9.3	2.6	1.3	1.5	.282
83-84	Golden State	82	0	1428	561	213	521	.409	15	51	.294	120	137	.876	41	102	143	252	155	0	84	6	107	17.4	6.8	1.7	3.1	.407
84-85	Golden State	56	6	746	287	106	250	.424	6	26	.231	69	82	.841	11	47	58	122	76	1	47	4	56	13.3	5.1	1.0	2.2	.390
85-86	Sacramento	33	0	269	70	26	70	.371	4	14	.286	14	18	.778	2	21	23	39	43	0	13	0	17	8.2	2.1	0.7	1.2	.248
NBA Season Totals		586	9	10613	4081	1578	3880	.407	150	492	.305	775	934	.830	310	720	1030	1851	1091	3	548	59	850	18.1	7.0	1.8	3.2	....
77-78	Phoenix	2	....	9	2	1	5	.200	....	....	....	0	0	.000	0	0	0	1	0	0	0	0	0	4.5	1.0	0.0	0.5	-.042
78-79	Phoenix	15	....	293	159	57	115	.496	....	....	....	45	59	.763	10	11	21	30	42	0	15	3	29	19.5	10.6	1.4	2.0	.423
79-80	Phoenix	8	....	169	104	43	84	.512	9	23	.391	9	10	.900	6	14	20	16	20	0	9	0	13	21.1	13.0	2.5	2.0	.529
81-82	San Antonio	9	0	180	43	15	52	.288	5	18	.278	8	10	.800	2	12	14	48	20	0	9	0	12	20.0	4.8	1.6	5.3	.337
85-86	Sacramento	3	0	15	7	3	6	.500	0	0	.000	1	1	1.000	2	2	4	1	0	0	0	0	2	5.0	2.3	1.3	0.3	.476
NBA Playoff Totals		37	0	666	315	119	262	.454	14	41	.341	63	80	.788	20	39	59	96	82	0	33	3	56	18.0	8.5	1.6	2.6	....

• BRAUN, Carl
Carl August Braun

Born: Sept. 25, 1927. Brooklyn, NY, United States. Height: 6'5". Weight: 180 lbs. Drafted: — College: Colgate

47-48	New York	47	....	....	671	276	854	.323	....	....	....	119	183	.650	....	....	....	61	102	....	....	....	....	14.3	....	1.3	....
48-49	New York	57	....	....	810	299	906	.330	....	....	....	212	279	.760	....	....	....	173	144	....	....	....	....	14.2	....	3.0	....
49-50	New York	67	....	....	1031	373	1024	.364	....	....	....	285	374	.762	....	....	....	247	188	....	....	....	....	15.4	....	3.7	....
52-53	New York	70	....	2316	977	323	807	.400	....	....	....	331	401	.825	....	233		243	287	14	....	....	....	33.1	14.0	3.3	3.5	.421
53-54	New York	72	....	2373	1062	354	884	.400	....	....	....	354	429	.825	....	246		209	259	6	....	....	....	33.0	14.8	3.4	2.9	.426
54-55	New York	71	....	2479	1074	400	1032	.388	....	....	....	274	342	.801	....	295		274	208	3	....	....	....	34.9	15.1	4.2	3.9	.427
55-56	New York	72	....	2316	1112	396	1064	.372	....	....	....	320	382	.838	....	259		298	215	0	....	....	....	32.2	15.4	3.6	4.1	.460
56-57	New York	72	....	2345	1001	378	993	.381	....	....	....	245	303	.809	....	259		256	195	1	....	....	....	32.6	13.9	3.6	3.6	.410
57-58	New York	71	....	2475	1173	426	1018	.418	....	....	....	321	378	.849	....	330		393	183	2	....	....	....	34.9	16.5	4.6	5.5	.563
58-59	New York	72	....	1959	754	287	684	.420	....	....	....	180	218	.826	....	251		349	178	3	....	....	....	27.2	10.5	3.5	4.8	.510
59-60	New York	54	....	1514	699	285	659	.432	....	....	....	129	154	.838	....	168		270	127	2	....	....	....	28.0	12.9	3.1	5.0	.543
60-61	New York	15	....	218	85	37	79	.468	....	....	....	11	14	.786	....	31		48	29	0	....	....	....	14.5	5.7	2.1	3.2	.568
61-62	Boston	48	....	414	176	78	207	.377	....	....	....	20	27	.741	....	50		71	49	0	....	....	....	8.6	3.7	1.0	1.5	.432
NBA Season Totals		788	....	18409	10625	3912	10211	.383	....	....	....	2801	3484	.804	....	2122		2892	2164	34	....	....	....	23.4	13.5	2.7	3.7	....
47-48	New York	3	....	....	30	12	41	.293	....	....	....	6	10	.600	....	....		2	6	....	....	....	....	10.0	....	0.7	....
48-49	New York	6	....	....	116	33	102	.324	....	....	....	50	62	.806	....	....		19	22	....	....	....	....	19.3	....	3.2	....
49-50	New York	5	....	....	85	28	68	.412	....	....	....	29	38	.763	....	....		19	21	....	....	....	....	17.0	....	3.8	....
52-53	New York	11	....	374	148	47	145	.324	....	....	....	54	67	.806	....	44		31	46	2	....	....	....	34.0	13.5	4.0	2.8	.340
53-54	New York	4	....	125	71	18	52	.346	....	....	....	35	40	.875	....	12		9	22	2	....	....	....	31.3	17.8	3.0	2.3	.459
54-55	New York	3	....	103	54	18	44	.409	....	....	....	18	20	.900	....	14		16	11	0	....	....	....	34.3	18.0	4.7	5.3	.583
58-59	New York	2	....	62	32	12	32	.375	....	....	....	8	9	.889	....	4		10	4	0	....	....	....	31.0	16.0	2.0	5.0	.493
61-62	Boston	6	....	42	25	11	28	.393	....	....	....	3	4	.750	....	7		2	3	0	....	....	....	7.0	4.2	1.2	0.3	.430
NBA Playoff Totals		40	....	706	561	179	512	.350	....	....	....	203	250	.812	....	81		108	135	4	....	....	....	17.7	14.0	2.0	2.7	....

• BREAUX, Tim
Timothy Breaux

Born: Sept. 19, 1970. Baton Rouge, LA, United States. Height: 6'7". Weight: 215 lbs. Drafted: — College: Wyoming

94-95	Houston	42	2	340	128	45	121	.372	6	25	.240	32	49	.653	16	18	34	15	25	0	11	4	17	8.1	3.0	0.8	0.4	.244
95-96	Houston	54	4	570	161	59	161	.366	15	46	.326	28	45	.622	22	38	60	24	42	0	11	8	32	10.6	3.0	1.1	0.4	.188
97-98	Milwaukee	6	0	30	10	4	11	.364	1	3	.333	1	2	.500	0	2	2	2	1	0	2	1	1	5.0	1.7	0.3	0.3	.284
NBA Season Totals		102	6	940	299	108	293	.369	22	74	.297	61	96	.635	38	58	96	41	68	0	24	13	50	9.2	2.9	0.9	0.4	....

• BREMER, J.R.
Ernest Lenell (J.R.) Bremer

Born: Sept. 19, 1980. Cleveland, OH, United States. Height: 6'2". Weight: 185 lbs. Drafted: — College: St. Bonaventure

02-03	Boston	64	41	1502	528	171	464	.369	101	286	.353	85	111	.766	18	127	145	164	80	1	38	3	59	23.5	8.3	2.3	2.6	.338
NBA Season Totals		64	41	1502	528	171	464	.369	101	286	.353	85	111	.766	18	127	145	164	80	1	38	3	59	23.5	8.3	2.3	2.6	....
02-03	Boston	10	0	146	47	16	56	.286	8	32	.250	7	8	.875	0	15	15	12	12	0	3	0	8	14.6	4.7	1.5	1.2	.185
NBA Playoff Totals		10	0	146	47	16	56	.286	8	32	.250	7	8	.875	0	15	15	12	12	0	3	0	8	14.6	4.7	1.5	1.2	....

YEAR TEAM	GP	GS	MIN	PTS	FGM	FGA	FG%	3PM	3PA	3P%	FTM	FTA	FT%	ORB	DRB	TRB	AST	PF	DQ	STL	BLK	TO	MPG	PPG	RPG	APG	PCM

• BRENNAN, Pete
Peter Joseph Brennan

Born: Sept. 23, 1936. Brooklyn, NY, United States.   Height: 6'6".   Weight: 205 lbs.   Drafted: 1958   College: North Carolina

YEAR TEAM	GP	GS	MIN	PTS	FGM	FGA	FG%	3PM	3PA	3P%	FTM	FTA	FT%	ORB	DRB	TRB	AST	PF	DQ	STL	BLK	TO	MPG	PPG	RPG	APG	PCM
58-59 New York	16	....	136	40	13	43	.302	....	....	....	14	25	.560	....	....	31	6	15	0	....	....	....	8.5	2.5	1.9	0.4	.283
NBA Season Totals	16	....	136	40	13	43	.302	....	....	....	14	25	.560	....	....	31	6	15	0	....	....	....	8.5	2.5	1.9	0.4	....
58-59 New York	2	....	6	4	2	7	.286	....	....	....	0	1	.000	....	....	5	0	4	0	....	....	....	3.0	2.0	2.5	0.0	.353
NBA Playoff Totals	2	....	6	4	2	7	.286	....	....	....	0	1	.000	....	....	5	0	4	0	....	....	....	3.0	2.0	2.5	0.0	....

• BRENNAN, Tom
Thomas F. Brennan

Born: Aug. 6, 1930.   Height: 6'3".   Weight: 195 lbs.   Drafted: 1958   College: Villanova

YEAR TEAM	GP	GS	MIN	PTS	FGM	FGA	FG%	3PM	3PA	3P%	FTM	FTA	FT%	ORB	DRB	TRB	AST	PF	DQ	STL	BLK	TO	MPG	PPG	RPG	APG	PCM
54-55 Philadelphia	11	....	52	10	5	11	.455	....	....	....	0	0	.000	....	....	5	2	5	0	....	....	....	4.7	0.9	0.5	0.2	.190
NBA Season Totals	11	....	52	10	5	11	.455	....	....	....	0	0	.000	....	....	5	2	5	0	....	....	....	4.7	0.9	0.5	0.2	....

• BRENNER, Irv
Irving Brenner

Born: May 31, 1913.   Died: Jan.20, 1991.   Height: 6'4".   Weight: 200 lbs.   Drafted: —   College: Duquesne

YEAR TEAM	GP	GS	MIN	PTS	FGM	FGA	FG%	3PM	3PA	3P%	FTM	FTA	FT%	ORB	DRB	TRB	AST	PF	DQ	STL	BLK	TO	MPG	PPG	RPG	APG	PCM
44-45 Pittsburgh-N	14	....	....	64	28	....	....	....	....	....	8	....	....	....	....	....	....	....	....	....	....	....	....	4.6	....	....	....
45-46 Youngstown-N	22	....	....	67	26	....	....	....	....	....	15	....	....	....	....	....	....	....	....	....	....	....	....	3.0	....	....	....
46-47 Youngstown-N	1	....	....	2	1	....	....	....	....	....	0	0	.000	....	....	....	....	....	....	....	....	....	....	2.0	....	....	....
NBL Season Totals	37	....	....	133	55	....	....	....	....	....	23	0	....	....	....	....	....	....	....	....	....	....	....	3.6	....	....	....

• BREUER, Randy
Randall W. Breuer

Born: Oct. 11, 1960. Lake City, MN, United States.   Height: 7'3".   Weight: 230 lbs.   Drafted: 1983   College: Minnesota

YEAR TEAM	GP	GS	MIN	PTS	FGM	FGA	FG%	3PM	3PA	3P%	FTM	FTA	FT%	ORB	DRB	TRB	AST	PF	DQ	STL	BLK	TO	MPG	PPG	RPG	APG	PCM
83-84 Milwaukee	57	8	472	168	68	177	.384	0	0	.000	32	46	.696	48	61	109	17	98	1	11	38	34	8.3	2.9	1.9	0.3	.314
84-85 Milwaukee	78	0	1083	413	162	317	.511	0	0	.000	89	127	.701	92	164	256	40	179	4	21	82	62	13.9	5.3	3.3	0.5	.450
85-86 Milwaukee	82	63	1792	685	272	570	.477	0	1	.000	141	198	.712	159	299	458	114	214	2	50	116	123	21.9	8.4	5.6	1.4	.485
86-87 Milwaukee	76	10	1467	600	241	497	.485	0	0	.000	118	202	.584	129	221	350	47	229	9	56	61	99	19.3	7.9	4.6	0.6	.415
87-88 Milwaukee	81	73	2258	968	390	788	.495	0	0	.000	188	286	.657	191	360	551	103	198	3	46	107	105	27.9	12.0	6.8	1.3	.499
88-89 Milwaukee	48	4	513	200	86	179	.480	0	0	.000	28	51	.549	51	84	135	22	59	0	9	37	29	10.7	4.2	2.8	0.5	.468
89-90 Milwaukee	30	8	554	204	86	186	.462	0	0	.000	32	51	.627	43	84	127	13	63	0	9	33	27	18.5	6.8	4.2	0.4	.395
89-90 Minnesota	51	47	1325	518	212	510	.416	0	1	.000	94	142	.662	111	179	290	84	133	2	33	75	66	26.0	10.2	5.7	1.6	.418
90-91 Minnesota	73	44	1505	429	197	435	.453	0	1	.000	35	79	.443	114	231	345	73	132	1	35	80	66	20.6	5.9	4.7	1.0	.379
91-92 Minnesota	67	25	1176	363	161	344	.468	0	1	.000	41	77	.532	98	183	281	89	117	0	27	99	40	17.6	5.4	4.2	1.3	.475
92-93 Atlanta	12	0	107	32	15	31	.484	0	0	.000	2	5	.400	10	18	28	6	12	0	2	3	5	8.9	2.7	2.3	0.5	.398
93-94 Sacramento	26	3	247	19	8	26	.308	0	1	.000	3	14	.214	15	41	56	8	30	0	6	19	8	9.5	0.7	2.2	0.3	.240
NBA Season Totals	681	285	12499	4599	1898	4060	.467	0	4	.000	803	1278	.628	1061	1925	2986	616	1464	22	305	750	664	18.4	6.8	4.4	0.9	....
83-84 Milwaukee	12	0	66	25	11	26	.423	0	0	.000	3	5	.600	6	11	17	4	18	0	0	6	2	5.5	2.1	1.4	0.3	.387
84-85 Milwaukee	8	0	104	44	15	26	.577	0	0	.000	14	21	.667	9	15	24	0	15	0	2	2	8	13.0	5.5	3.0	0.0	.405
85-86 Milwaukee	14	14	318	118	46	86	.535	0	0	.000	26	38	.684	20	40	60	11	38	1	11	18	13	22.7	8.4	4.3	0.8	.440
86-87 Milwaukee	12	2	156	40	16	33	.485	0	0	.000	8	12	.667	9	22	31	4	32	1	7	9	4	13.0	3.3	2.6	0.3	.332
87-88 Milwaukee	4	0	47	19	9	16	.563	0	0	.000	1	6	.167	2	10	12	1	7	0	1	2	1	11.8	4.8	3.0	0.3	.447
88-89 Milwaukee	9	1	162	39	17	32	.531	0	0	.000	5	13	.385	9	31	40	5	17	0	2	6	2	18.0	4.3	4.4	0.6	.380
92-93 Atlanta	1	0	17	2	1	4	.250	0	0	.000	0	0	.000	1	1	2	1	2	0	0	1	0	17.0	2.0	2.0	1.0	.126
NBA Playoff Totals	60	17	870	287	115	223	.516	0	0	.000	57	95	.600	56	130	186	26	129	2	23	44	30	14.5	4.8	3.1	0.4	....

• BREWER, Jamison
Jamison Rudy Brewer

Born: Nov. 19, 1980. East Point, GA, United States.   Height: 6'4".   Weight: 184 lbs.   Drafted: 2001   College: Auburn

YEAR TEAM	GP	GS	MIN	PTS	FGM	FGA	FG%	3PM	3PA	3P%	FTM	FTA	FT%	ORB	DRB	TRB	AST	PF	DQ	STL	BLK	TO	MPG	PPG	RPG	APG	PCM
01-02 Indiana	13	0	43	4	2	5	.400	0	1	.000	0	0	.000	2	6	8	9	3	0	2	0	3	3.3	0.3	0.6	0.7	.375
02-03 Indiana	10	0	80	22	9	17	.529	0	2	.000	4	9	.444	5	4	9	18	11	0	2	1	6	8.0	2.2	0.9	1.8	.407
NBA Season Totals	23	0	123	26	11	22	.500	0	3	.000	4	9	.444	7	10	17	27	14	0	4	1	9	5.3	1.1	0.7	1.2	....
01-02 Indiana	2	0	6	1	0	2	.000	0	0	.000	1	2	.500	2	2	4	1	3	0	0	0	1	3.0	0.5	2.0	0.5	.198
NBA Playoff Totals	2	0	6	1	0	2	.000	0	0	.000	1	2	.500	2	2	4	1	3	0	0	0	1	3.0	0.5	2.0	0.5	....

• BREWER, Jim
James Turner (Brew, Papa) Brewer

Born: Dec. 3, 1951. Maywood, IL, United States.   Height: 6'9".   Weight: 210 lbs.   Drafted: 1973   College: Minnesota

YEAR TEAM	GP	GS	MIN	PTS	FGM	FGA	FG%	3PM	3PA	3P%	FTM	FTA	FT%	ORB	DRB	TRB	AST	PF	DQ	STL	BLK	TO	MPG	PPG	RPG	APG	PCM
73-74 Cleveland	82	....	1862	500	210	548	.383	....	....	....	80	123	.650	207	317	524	149	192	1	46	35	....	22.7	6.1	6.4	1.8	.392
74-75 Cleveland	82	....	1991	685	291	639	.455	....	....	....	103	159	.648	205	304	509	128	150	2	77	43	....	24.3	8.4	6.2	1.6	.443
75-76 Cleveland	82	....	2913	940	400	874	.458	....	....	....	140	214	.654	298	593	891	209	214	0	94	89	....	35.5	11.5	10.9	2.5	.485
76-77 Cleveland	81	....	2672	689	296	657	.451	....	....	....	97	178	.545	275	487	762	195	214	3	94	82	....	33.0	8.5	9.4	2.4	.423
77-78 Cleveland	80	....	1798	396	175	390	.449	....	....	....	46	100	.460	182	313	495	98	178	1	60	48	104	22.5	5.0	6.2	1.2	.363
78-79 Cleveland	55	....	1301	251	114	259	.440	....	....	....	23	48	.479	125	245	370	74	136	2	48	56	77	23.7	4.6	6.7	1.3	.374
78-79 Detroit	25	....	310	57	27	60	.450	....	....	....	3	15	.200	34	71	105	13	38	0	13	10	20	12.4	2.3	4.2	0.5	.375
79-80 Portland	67	....	1016	194	90	184	.489	0	5	.000	14	29	.483	101	156	257	75	129	2	42	43	47	15.2	2.9	3.8	1.1	.387
80-81 LA Lakers	78	....	1107	217	101	197	.513	0	2	.000	15	40	.375	127	154	281	55	158	2	43	58	47	14.2	2.8	3.6	0.7	.372
81-82 LA Lakers	71	9	966	170	81	175	.463	1	6	.167	7	19	.368	106	158	264	42	127	1	39	46	36	13.6	2.4	3.7	0.6	.365
NBA Season Totals	703	9	15936	4099	1785	3983	.448	1	13	.077	528	925	.571	1660	2798	4458	1038	1536	14	556	510	331	22.7	5.8	6.3	1.5	....
75-76 Cleveland	13	....	489	114	44	101	.436	....	....	....	26	48	.542	40	100	140	37	34	0	13	12	....	37.6	8.8	10.8	2.8	.416
76-77 Cleveland	3	....	113	23	11	27	.407	....	....	....	1	1	1.000	11	25	36	5	11	0	4	4	....	37.7	7.7	12.0	1.7	.365
77-78 Cleveland	1	....	9	0	0	1	.000	....	....	....	0	2	.000	0	0	0	0	2	0	0	0	0	9.0	0.0	0.0	0.0	-.292
79-80 Portland	3	....	67	21	10	10	1.000	0	0	.000	1	3	.333	6	10	16	3	6	0	5	2	1	22.3	7.0	5.3	1.0	.606

YEAR	TEAM	GP	GS	MIN	PTS	FGM	FGA	FG%	3PM	3PA	3P%	FTM	FTA	FT%	ORB	DRB	TRB	AST	PF	DQ	STL	BLK	TO	MPG	PPG	RPG	APG	PCM
80-81	LA Lakers	3	....	7	0	0	0	.000	0	0	.000	0	0	.000	0	1	1	0	1	0	0	0	0	2.3	0.0	0.3	0.0	.065
81-82	LA Lakers	8	0	57	6	3	6	.500	0	0	.000	0	0	.000	4	7	11	4	5	0	2	6	4	7.1	0.8	1.4	0.5	.334
NBA Playoff Totals		31	0	742	164	68	145	.469	0	0	.000	28	54	.519	61	143	204	49	59	0	24	24	5	23.9	5.3	6.6	1.6	....

• BREWER, Ron

Ronald Charles (Boot) Brewer

Born: Sept. 16, 1955. Fort Smith, AR, United States. Height: 6'4". Weight: 180 lbs. Drafted: 1978 College: Arkansas

YEAR	TEAM	GP	GS	MIN	PTS	FGM	FGA	FG%	3PM	3PA	3P%	FTM	FTA	FT%	ORB	DRB	TRB	AST	PF	DQ	STL	BLK	TO	MPG	PPG	RPG	APG	PCM
78-79	Portland	81	....	2454	1078	434	878	.494	....	....	....	210	256	.820	88	141	229	165	181	3	102	79	154	30.3	13.3	2.8	2.0	.403
79-80	Portland	82	....	2815	1286	548	1182	.464	6	32	.188	184	219	.840	54	160	214	216	154	0	98	48	164	34.3	15.7	2.6	2.6	.370
80-81	Portland	29	....	548	217	95	246	.386	1	3	.333	26	34	.765	13	20	33	55	42	0	34	9	38	18.9	7.5	1.1	1.9	.276
80-81	San Antonio	46	....	904	425	180	385	.468	0	4	.000	65	80	.813	21	32	53	93	53	0	27	25	55	19.7	9.2	1.2	2.0	.392
81-82	San Antonio	25	0	595	444	182	361	.504	3	10	.300	77	88	.875	13	37	50	67	37	0	23	7	35	23.8	17.8	2.0	2.7	.623
81-82	Cleveland	47	0	1724	913	387	833	.465	5	21	.238	134	172	.779	42	69	111	121	114	0	59	23	89	36.7	19.4	2.4	2.6	.382
82-83	Cleveland	21	18	563	240	98	245	.400	0	3	.000	44	51	.863	9	28	37	27	27	0	20	6	25	26.8	11.4	1.8	1.3	.277
82-83	Golden State	53	34	1401	597	246	562	.438	7	15	.467	98	119	.824	50	57	107	69	96	0	70	19	74	26.4	11.3	2.0	1.3	.318
83-84	Golden State	13	3	210	65	27	58	.466	0	1	.000	11	17	.647	5	8	13	6	10	0	6	5	7	16.2	5.0	1.0	0.5	.243
83-84	San Antonio	40	5	782	348	152	345	.441	3	13	.231	41	50	.820	17	33	50	44	54	0	18	16	32	19.6	8.7	1.3	1.1	.300
84-85	San Antonio	9	0	81	33	13	34	.382	0	0	.000	7	7	1.000	1	2	3	6	8	0	1	1	4	9.0	3.7	0.3	0.7	.210
84-85	New Jersey	11	0	245	114	49	84	.583	0	2	.000	16	18	.889	8	10	18	11	15	0	5	5	6	22.3	10.4	1.6	1.0	.431
85-86	Chicago	4	0	18	7	3	9	.333	0	0	.000	1	1	1.000	0	0	0	0	1	0	0	0	2	4.5	1.8	0.0	0.0	-.050
85-86	Cleveland	40	3	552	204	83	215	.386	5	17	.294	33	37	.892	14	39	53	40	43	0	17	6	20	13.8	5.1	1.3	1.0	.280
NBA Season Totals		501	63	12892	5971	2497	5437	.459	30	121	.248	947	1149	.824	335	636	971	920	835	3	480	249	705	25.7	11.9	1.9	1.8	....
78-79	Portland	3	....	94	53	22	39	.564	....	....	....	9	13	.692	4	7	11	8	7	0	1	9	5	31.3	17.7	3.7	2.7	.596
79-80	Portland	3	....	106	57	26	61	.426	0	3	.000	5	9	.556	1	2	3	6	10	0	3	1	7	35.3	19.0	1.0	2.0	.241
80-81	San Antonio	7	....	118	80	29	61	.475	1	3	.333	21	29	.724	0	5	5	13	6	0	1	6	6	16.9	11.4	0.7	1.9	.543
84-85	New Jersey	3	0	93	36	15	30	.500	0	1	.000	6	8	.750	1	4	5	5	7	0	3	0	3	31.0	12.0	1.7	1.7	.299
NBA Playoff Totals		16	0	411	226	92	191	.482	1	7	.143	41	59	.695	6	18	24	32	30	0	8	16	21	25.7	14.1	1.5	2.0	....

• BREZEC, Primoz

Primoz Brezec

Born: Oct. 2, 1979. Postojna, Slovakia. Height: 7'2". Weight: 252 lbs. Drafted: 2000 College: none

YEAR	TEAM	GP	GS	MIN	PTS	FGM	FGA	FG%	3PM	3PA	3P%	FTM	FTA	FT%	ORB	DRB	TRB	AST	PF	DQ	STL	BLK	TO	MPG	PPG	RPG	APG	PCM
01-02	Indiana	22	4	160	43	14	29	.483	0	0	.000	15	25	.600	16	12	28	6	28	0	0	7	6	7.3	2.0	1.3	0.3	.281
02-03	Indiana	22	1	111	42	15	38	.395	0	1	.000	12	20	.600	13	10	23	4	16	0	2	4	7	5.0	1.9	1.0	0.2	.311
NBA Season Totals		44	5	271	85	29	67	.433	0	1	.000	27	45	.600	29	22	51	10	44	0	2	11	13	6.2	1.9	1.2	0.2	....

• BRIAN, Frankie

Frank Sands (Flash) Brian

Born: May 1, 1923. Zachary, LA, United States. Height: 6'1". Weight: 180 lbs. Drafted: — College: Louisiana State

YEAR	TEAM	GP	GS	MIN	PTS	FGM	FGA	FG%	3PM	3PA	3P%	FTM	FTA	FT%	ORB	DRB	TRB	AST	PF	DQ	STL	BLK	TO	MPG	PPG	RPG	APG	PCM
47-48	Anderson-N	59	....	....	651	248	....	....	....	....	....	155	210	.738	....	....	....	....	148	....	....	....	....	....	11.0	....	....	....
48-49	Anderson-N	64	....	....	633	216	....	....	....	....	....	201	256	**.785**	....	....	....	....	144	....	....	....	....	....	9.9	....	....	....
49-50	Anderson	64	....	....	1138	368	1156	.318	....	....	....	402	488	.824	....	....	....	189	192	....	....	....	....	....	17.8	....	3.0	....
50-51	Tri-Cities	68	....	....	1144	363	1127	.322	....	....	....	418	508	.823	....	....	244	266	215	4	....	....	....	....	16.8	3.6	3.9	....
51-52	Fort Wayne	66	....	2672	1051	342	972	.352	....	....	....	367	433	.848	....	....	232	233	220	6	....	....	....	40.5	15.9	3.5	3.5	.362
52-53	Fort Wayne	68	....	1910	726	245	699	.351	....	....	....	236	297	.795	....	....	133	142	205	8	....	....	....	28.1	10.7	2.0	2.1	.303
53-54	Fort Wayne	64	....	973	401	132	352	.375	....	....	....	137	182	.753	....	....	79	92	100	2	....	....	....	15.2	6.3	1.2	1.4	.378
54-55	Fort Wayne	71	....	1381	691	237	623	.380	....	....	....	217	255	.851	....	....	127	142	133	0	....	....	....	19.5	9.7	1.8	2.0	.441
55-56	Fort Wayne	37	....	680	228	78	263	.297	....	....	....	72	88	.818	....	....	88	74	62	0	....	....	....	18.4	6.2	2.4	2.0	.318
NBA Season Totals		438	....	7616	5379	1765	5192	.340	....	....	....	1849	2251	.821	....	....	903	1138	1127	20	....	....	....	17.4	12.3	2.1	2.6	....
NBL Season Totals		123	....	....	1284	464	....	....	....	....	....	356	466	....	....	....	....	....	292	....	....	....	....	....	10.4	....	....	....
Career Totals		561	....	7616	6663	2229	5192	....	....	....	....	2205	2717	....	....	....	903	1138	1419	20	....	....	....	13.6	11.9	1.6	2.0	....
47-48	Anderson-N	6	....	....	47	18	....	....	....	....	....	11	16	.688	....	....	....	....	....	....	....	....	....	....	7.8	....	....	....
48-49	Anderson-N	7	....	....	79	26	....	....	....	....	....	27	32	.844	....	....	....	....	0	....	....	....	....	....	11.3	....	....	....
49-50	Anderson	8	....	....	95	26	96	.271	....	....	....	43	48	.896	....	....	....	19	24	....	....	....	....	....	11.9	....	2.4	....
51-52	Fort Wayne	2	....	81	17	6	24	.250	....	....	....	5	6	.833	....	....	6	9	10	0	....	....	....	40.5	8.5	3.0	4.5	.199
52-53	Fort Wayne	8	....	146	45	13	42	.310	....	....	....	19	25	.760	....	....	9	11	23	1	....	....	....	18.3	5.6	1.1	1.4	.233
53-54	Fort Wayne	4	....	106	41	15	36	.417	....	....	....	11	16	.688	....	....	12	10	7	0	....	....	....	26.5	10.3	3.0	2.5	.408
54-55	Fort Wayne	11	....	269	127	48	120	.400	....	....	....	31	38	.816	....	....	22	27	26	0	....	....	....	24.5	11.5	2.0	2.5	.411
55-56	Fort Wayne	10	....	166	69	26	68	.382	....	....	....	17	21	.810	....	....	12	17	15	0	....	....	....	16.6	6.9	1.2	1.7	.361
NBA Playoff Totals		43	....	768	394	134	386	.347	....	....	....	126	154	.818	....	....	61	93	105	1	....	....	....	17.9	9.2	1.4	2.2	....
NBL Playoff Totals		13	....	....	126	44	....	....	....	....	....	38	48	....	....	....	....	....	0	....	....	....	....	....	9.7	....	....	....
Career Playoff Totals		56	....	768	520	178	386	....	....	....	....	164	202	....	....	....	61	93	105	1	....	....	....	13.7	9.3	1.1	1.7	....

• BRICKOWSKI, Frank

Francis Anthony (Brick) Brickowski

Born: Aug. 14, 1959. Bayville, NY, United States. Height: 6'9". Weight: 240 lbs. Drafted: 1981 College: Penn State

YEAR	TEAM	GP	GS	MIN	PTS	FGM	FGA	FG%	3PM	3PA	3P%	FTM	FTA	FT%	ORB	DRB	TRB	AST	PF	DQ	STL	BLK	TO	MPG	PPG	RPG	APG	PCM
84-85	Seattle	78	9	1115	385	150	305	.492	0	4	.000	85	127	.669	76	184	260	100	171	1	34	15	101	14.3	4.9	3.3	1.3	.396
85-86	Seattle	40	2	311	78	30	58	.517	0	0	.000	18	27	.667	16	38	54	21	74	2	11	7	24	7.8	2.0	1.4	0.5	.259
86-87	LA Lakers	37	0	404	146	53	94	.564	0	0	.000	40	59	.678	40	57	97	12	105	4	14	4	26	10.9	3.9	2.6	0.3	.361
86-87	San Antonio	7	0	83	30	10	30	.333	0	4	.000	10	11	.909	8	11	19	5	13	0	6	2	7	11.9	4.3	2.7	0.7	.347
87-88	San Antonio	70	68	2227	1119	425	805	.528	1	5	.200	268	349	.768	167	316	483	266	275	**11**	74	36	210	31.8	16.0	6.9	3.8	.557
88-89	San Antonio	64	60	1822	875	337	654	.515	0	2	.000	201	281	.715	148	258	406	131	252	10	102	35	166	28.5	13.7	6.3	2.0	.503
89-90	San Antonio	78	12	1438	517	211	387	.545	0	2	.000	95	141	.674	89	238	327	105	226	4	66	37	94	18.4	6.6	4.2	1.3	.453
90-91	Milwaukee	75	73	1912	942	372	706	.527	0	2	.000	198	248	.798	129	297	426	131	255	4	86	43	158	25.5	12.6	5.7	1.7	.522
91-92	Milwaukee	65	60	1556	740	306	584	.524	3	6	.500	125	163	.767	98	246	344	122	223	11	60	23	111	23.9	11.4	5.3	1.9	.504
92-93	Milwaukee	66	64	2075	1115	456	836	.545	8	26	.308	195	268	.728	120	285	405	196	235	8	80	44	205	31.4	16.9	6.1	3.0	.544
93-94	Milwaukee	43	40	1441	653	251	521	.482	3	18	.167	148	191	.775	53	226	279	165	165	3	52	16	125	33.5	15.2	6.5	3.8	.480

YEAR	TEAM	GP	GS	MIN	PTS	FGM	FGA	FG%	3PM	3PA	3P%	FTM	FTA	FT%	ORB	DRB	TRB	AST	PF	DQ	STL	BLK	TO	MPG	PPG	RPG	APG	PCM
93-94	Charlotte	28	6	653	282	117	233	.502	1	2	.500	47	63	.746	32	93	125	57	77	3	28	11	56	23.3	10.1	4.5	2.0	.450
95-96	Seattle	63	8	986	339	123	252	.488	32	79	.405	61	86	.709	26	125	151	58	185	4	26	8	76	15.7	5.4	2.4	0.9	.287
96-97	Boston	17	2	255	81	32	73	.438	7	20	.350	10	14	.714	6	28	34	15	42	1	5	4	19	15.0	4.8	2.0	0.9	.234
NBA Season Totals		731	404	16278	7302	2873	5538	.519	55	170	.324	1501	2028	.740	1008	2402	3410	1384	2298	66	644	285	1378	22.3	10.0	4.7	1.9	....
87-88	San Antonio	3	3	113	58	22	44	.500	1	1	1.000	13	19	.684	7	15	22	14	12	0	6	2	9	37.7	19.3	7.3	4.7	.563
89-90	San Antonio	10	0	161	79	31	54	.574	0	0	.000	17	26	.654	16	28	44	11	31	0	8	1	15	16.1	7.9	4.4	1.1	.534
90-91	Milwaukee	3	3	110	55	24	45	.533	0	2	.000	7	14	.500	5	21	26	3	16	1	1	2	6	36.7	18.3	8.7	1.0	.449
95-96	Seattle	21	3	206	41	16	38	.421	6	22	.273	3	4	.750	2	28	30	11	55	1	7	5	20	9.8	2.0	1.4	0.5	.128
NBA Playoff Totals		37	9	590	233	93	181	.514	7	25	.280	40	63	.635	30	92	122	39	114	2	22	10	50	15.9	6.3	3.3	1.1	....

• BRIDGEMAN, Junior

Ulysses Lee (Junior, J.B., The Torch) Bridgeman

Born: Sept. 17, 1953. East Chicago, IN, United States. Height: 6'5". Weight: 210 lbs. Drafted: 1975 College: Louisville

75-76	Milwaukee	81	....	1646	700	286	651	.439	....	....	....	128	161	.795	113	181	294	157	235	3	52	21	....	20.3	8.6	3.6	1.9	.427
76-77	Milwaukee	82	....	2410	1179	491	1094	.449	....	....	....	197	228	.864	129	287	416	205	221	3	82	26	....	29.4	14.4	5.1	2.5	.474
77-78	Milwaukee	82	....	1876	1118	476	947	.503	....	....	....	166	205	.810	114	176	290	175	202	1	72	30	172	22.9	13.6	3.5	2.1	.528
78-79	Milwaukee	82	....	1963	1269	540	1067	.506	....	....	....	189	228	.829	113	184	297	163	184	2	88	41	139	23.9	15.5	3.6	2.0	.577
79-80	Milwaukee	81	....	2316	1423	594	1243	.478	5	27	.185	230	266	.865	104	197	301	237	216	3	94	20	170	28.6	17.6	3.7	2.9	.519
80-81	Milwaukee	77	....	2215	1290	537	1102	.487	3	21	.143	213	241	.884	78	211	289	234	182	2	88	28	146	28.8	16.8	3.8	3.0	.528
81-82	Milwaukee	41	4	924	511	209	433	.483	4	9	.444	89	103	.864	37	88	125	109	91	0	28	3	66	22.5	12.5	3.0	2.7	.494
82-83	Milwaukee	70	5	1855	1007	421	856	.492	1	13	.077	164	196	.837	44	202	246	207	155	0	40	9	119	26.5	14.4	3.5	3.0	.494
83-84	Milwaukee	81	10	2431	1220	509	1094	.465	6	31	.194	196	243	.807	80	252	332	265	224	2	53	14	146	30.0	15.1	4.1	3.3	.440
84-85	LA Clippers	80	15	2042	1115	460	990	.465	14	39	.359	181	206	.879	55	175	230	171	128	0	47	18	112	25.5	13.9	2.9	2.1	.442
85-86	LA Clippers	58	14	1161	510	199	451	.441	6	18	.333	106	119	.891	29	94	123	108	81	1	31	8	70	20.0	8.8	2.1	1.9	.373
86-87	Milwaukee	34	4	418	175	79	171	.462	1	6	.167	16	20	.800	14	38	52	35	50	0	10	2	14	12.3	5.1	1.5	1.0	.354
NBA Season Totals		849	52	21257	11517	4801	10099	.475	40	164	.244	1875	2216	.846	910	2085	2995	2066	1969	17	685	220	1154	25.0	13.6	3.5	2.4	....
75-76	Milwaukee	3	....	67	25	9	20	.450	....	....	....	7	11	.636	4	7	11	5	10	0	1	0	....	22.3	8.3	3.7	1.7	.369
77-78	Milwaukee	9	....	178	94	44	91	.484	....	....	....	6	8	.750	6	12	18	11	31	0	9	2	8	19.8	10.4	2.0	1.2	.389
79-80	Milwaukee	5	....	124	51	20	56	.357	0	1	.000	11	15	.733	4	15	19	17	17	0	5	2	14	24.8	10.2	3.8	3.4	.310
80-81	Milwaukee	7	....	183	98	42	91	.462	1	1	1.000	13	16	.813	6	9	15	23	27	0	6	0	11	26.1	14.0	2.1	3.3	.404
82-83	Milwaukee	9	4	308	152	61	130	.469	2	5	.400	28	30	.933	21	24	45	28	26	1	10	2	19	34.2	16.9	5.0	3.1	.462
83-84	Milwaukee	16	4	499	230	88	193	.456	1	9	.111	53	65	.815	12	52	64	44	37	1	6	5	22	31.2	14.4	4.0	2.8	.413
NBA Playoff Totals		49	8	1359	650	264	581	.454	4	16	.250	118	145	.814	53	119	172	128	148	2	37	11	74	27.7	13.3	3.5	2.6	....

• BRIDGES, Bill

William C. Bridges

Born: Apr. 4, 1939. Hobbs, NM, United States. Height: 6'6". Weight: 228 lbs. Drafted: 1961 College: Kansas

62-63	St. Louis	27	....	374	164	66	160	.413	....	....	....	32	51	.627	....	....	144	23	58	0	....	....	....	13.9	6.1	5.3	0.9	.537
63-64	St. Louis	80	....	1949	682	268	675	.397	....	....	....	146	224	.652	....	....	680	181	269	6	....	....	....	24.4	8.5	8.5	2.3	.503
64-65	St. Louis	79	....	2362	910	362	938	.386	....	....	....	186	275	.676	....	....	853	187	276	3	....	....	....	29.9	11.5	10.8	2.4	.514
65-66	St. Louis	78	....	2677	1011	377	927	.407	....	....	....	257	364	.706	....	....	951	208	333	11	....	....	....	34.3	13.0	12.2	2.7	.525
66-67	St. Louis	79	....	3130	1373	503	1106	.455	....	....	....	367	523	.702	....	....	1190	222	325	12	....	....	....	39.6	17.4	15.1	2.8	.612
67-68	St. Louis	82	....	3197	1279	466	1009	.462	....	....	....	347	484	.717	....	....	1102	253	**366**	12	....	....	....	39.0	15.6	13.4	3.1	.572
68-69	Atlanta	80	....	2930	941	351	775	.453	....	....	....	239	353	.677	....	....	1132	298	290	3	....	....	....	36.6	11.8	14.2	3.7	.584
69-70	Atlanta	82	....	3269	1217	443	932	.475	....	....	....	331	451	.734	....	....	1181	345	292	6	....	....	....	39.9	14.8	14.4	4.2	.621
70-71	Atlanta	82	....	3140	975	382	834	.458	....	....	....	211	330	.639	....	....	1233	240	317	7	....	....	....	38.3	11.9	15.0	2.9	.552
71-72	Atlanta	14	....	546	133	51	134	.381	....	....	....	31	44	.705	....	....	190	40	50	1	....	....	....	39.0	9.5	13.6	2.9	.446
71-72	Philadelphia	64	....	2210	847	328	645	.509	....	....	....	191	272	.702	....	....	861	158	219	5	....	....	....	34.5	13.2	13.5	2.5	.619
72-73	Philadelphia	10	....	376	140	47	125	.376	....	....	....	46	65	.708	....	....	122	23	35	0	....	....	....	37.6	14.0	12.2	2.3	.481
72-73	LA Lakers	72	....	2491	705	286	597	.479	....	....	....	133	190	.700	....	....	782	196	261	0	....	....	....	34.6	9.8	10.9	2.7	.480
73-74	LA Lakers	65	....	1812	548	216	513	.421	....	....	....	116	164	.707	193	306	499	148	219	3	58	31	....	27.9	8.4	7.7	2.3	.428
74-75	LA Lakers	17	....	307	56	20	57	.351	....	....	....	16	30	.533	46	48	94	27	46	1	7	5	....	18.1	3.3	5.5	1.6	.358
74-75	Golden State	15	....	108	31	15	36	.417	....	....	....	1	4	.250	18	22	40	4	19	0	4	0	....	7.2	2.1	2.7	0.3	.393
NBA Season Totals		926	....	30878	11012	4181	9463	.442	....	....	....	2650	3824	.693	257	376	11054	2553	3375	70	69	36	....	33.3	11.9	11.9	2.8	....
62-63	St. Louis	11	....	204	102	41	96	.427	....	....	....	20	27	.741	....	....	86	9	31	0	....	....	....	18.5	9.3	7.8	0.8	.600
63-64	St. Louis	12	....	240	64	26	83	.313	....	....	....	12	19	.632	....	....	84	24	46	0	....	....	....	20.0	5.3	7.0	2.0	.390
64-65	St. Louis	4	....	145	52	21	59	.356	....	....	....	10	15	.667	....	....	67	9	19	1	....	....	....	36.3	13.0	16.8	2.3	.525
65-66	St. Louis	10	....	421	203	86	170	.506	....	....	....	31	43	.721	....	....	149	28	47	2	....	....	....	42.1	20.3	14.9	2.8	.629
66-67	St. Louis	9	....	369	141	48	128	.375	....	....	....	45	67	.672	....	....	169	22	36	2	....	....	....	41.0	15.7	18.8	2.4	.583
67-68	St. Louis	6	....	216	94	38	75	.507	....	....	....	18	25	.720	....	....	77	14	23	0	....	....	....	36.0	15.7	12.8	2.3	.605
68-69	Atlanta	11	....	442	172	69	156	.442	....	....	....	34	48	.708	....	....	178	37	48	2	....	....	....	40.2	15.6	16.2	3.4	.600
69-70	Atlanta	9	....	381	104	44	110	.400	....	....	....	16	27	.593	....	....	154	29	37	1	....	....	....	42.3	11.6	17.1	3.2	.506
70-71	Atlanta	5	....	229	49	23	58	.397	....	....	....	3	9	.333	....	....	104	5	17	0	....	....	....	45.8	9.8	20.8	1.0	.455
72-73	LA Lakers	17	....	582	152	57	136	.419	....	....	....	38	49	.776	....	....	158	29	68	2	....	....	....	34.2	8.9	9.3	1.7	.376
73-74	LA Lakers	5	....	144	30	12	41	.293	....	....	....	6	13	.462	14	16	30	6	19	0	7	0	....	28.8	6.0	6.0	1.2	.185
74-75	Golden State	14	....	148	22	10	23	.435	....	....	....	2	7	.286	13	36	49	7	23	0	9	4	....	10.6	1.6	3.5	0.5	.330
NBA Playoff Totals		113	....	3521	1185	475	1135	.419	....	....	....	235	349	.673	27	52	1305	219	414	10	16	4	....	31.2	10.5	11.5	1.9	....

• BRIGHTMAN, Al

Horace Albert Brightman

Born: Sept. 22, 1923. Died: June10, 1992. Height: 6'2". Weight: 195 lbs. Drafted: — College: Long Beach State

46-47	Boston	58	....	....	567	223	870	.256	....	....	....	121	193	.627	....	....	....	60	115	....	....	....	....	....	9.8	....	1.0	....
NBA Season Totals		58	....	....	567	223	870	.256	....	....	....	121	193	.627	....	....	....	60	115	....	....	....	....	....	9.8	....	1.0	....

YEAR	TEAM	GP	GS	MIN	PTS	FGM	FGA	FG%	3PM	3PA	3P%	FTM	FTA	FT%	ORB	DRB	TRB	AST	PF	DQ	STL	BLK	TO	MPG	PPG	RPG	APG	PCM

• BRINDLEY, Aud
Audley Brindley

Born: Dec. 31, 1923. Mineola, NY, United States. Died: Nov.19, 1958.   Height: 6'4".   Weight: 175 lbs.   Drafted: —   College: Dartmouth

YEAR	TEAM	GP	GS	MIN	PTS	FGM	FGA	FG%	3PM	3PA	3P%	FTM	FTA	FT%	ORB	DRB	TRB	AST	PF	DQ	STL	BLK	TO	MPG	PPG	RPG	APG	PCM
46-47	New York	12	....	....	34	14	49	.286	....	....	....	6	7	.857	....	....	....	1	16	....	....	....	....	....	2.8	....	0.1	....
NBA Season Totals		12	....	....	34	14	49	.286	....	....	....	6	7	.857	....	....	....	1	16	....	....	....	....	....	2.8	....	0.1	....
46-47	New York	3	....	....	10	3	6	.500	....	....	....	4	6	.667	....	....	....	0	4	....	....	....	....	....	3.3	....	0.0	....
NBA Playoff Totals		3	....	....	10	3	6	.500	....	....	....	4	6	.667	....	....	....	0	4	....	....	....	....	....	3.3	....	0.0	....

• BRISKER, John
John Brisker

Born: June 15, 1947. Detroit, MI, United States. Died: Apr.1978.   Height: 6'5".   Weight: 210 lbs.   Drafted: —   College: Toledo

YEAR	TEAM	GP	GS	MIN	PTS	FGM	FGA	FG%	3PM	3PA	3P%	FTM	FTA	FT%	ORB	DRB	TRB	AST	PF	DQ	STL	BLK	TO	MPG	PPG	RPG	APG	PCM
69-70	Pittsburgh-A	77	....	2173	1617	627	1361	.461	34	116	.293	329	398	.827	198	243	441	133	236	4	....	....	203	28.2	21.0	5.7	1.7	.638
70-71	Pittsburgh-A	79	....	3089	2315	898	**1972**	.455	89	264	.337	430	519	.829	299	467	766	226	273	3	....	....	320	39.1	29.3	9.7	2.9	.710
71-72	Pittsburgh-A	49	....	2065	1417	563	1228	.458	43	137	.314	248	286	.867	154	293	447	203	156	1	....	....	210	42.1	28.9	9.1	4.1	.662
72-73	Seattle	70	....	1633	898	352	809	.435	....	....	....	194	236	.822	....	....	319	150	169	1	....	....	....	23.3	12.8	4.6	2.1	.527
73-74	Seattle	35	....	717	438	178	396	.449	....	....	....	82	100	.820	59	87	146	56	70	0	28	6	....	20.5	12.5	4.2	1.6	.563
74-75	Seattle	21	....	276	162	60	141	.426	....	....	....	42	49	.857	15	18	33	19	33	0	7	3	....	13.1	7.7	1.6	0.9	.456
NBA Season Totals		126	....	2626	1498	590	1346	.438	....	....	....	318	385	.826	74	105	498	225	272	1	35	9	....	20.8	11.9	4.0	1.8	
ABA Season Totals		205	....	7327	5349	2088	4561	.458	166	517	.321	1007	1203	.837	651	1003	1654	562	665	8	....	....	733	35.7	26.1	8.1	2.7	
Career Totals		331	....	9953	6847	2678	5907	.453	166	517	.321	1325	1588	.834	725	1108	2152	787	937	9	35	9	733	30.1	20.7	6.5	2.4	

• BRISTOW, Allan
Allan Mercer (Disco) Bristow Jr.

Born: Aug. 23, 1951. Richmond, VA, United States.   Height: 6'7".   Weight: 210 lbs.   Drafted: 1973   College: Virginia Tech

YEAR	TEAM	GP	GS	MIN	PTS	FGM	FGA	FG%	3PM	3PA	3P%	FTM	FTA	FT%	ORB	DRB	TRB	AST	PF	DQ	STL	BLK	TO	MPG	PPG	RPG	APG	PCM
73-74	Philadelphia	55	....	643	258	108	270	.400	....	....	....	42	57	.737	68	99	167	92	68	1	29	1	....	11.7	4.7	3.0	1.7	.517
74-75	Philadelphia	72	....	1101	447	163	393	.415	....	....	....	121	153	.791	111	143	254	99	101	0	25	2	....	15.3	6.2	3.5	1.4	.476
75-76	San Antonio-A	47	....	882	328	125	271	.461	0	1	.000	78	92	.848	68	106	174	121	81	....	24	2	63	18.8	7.0	3.7	2.6	.504
76-77	San Antonio	82	....	2017	936	365	747	.489	....	....	....	206	258	.798	119	229	348	240	195	1	89	2	....	24.6	11.4	4.2	2.9	.532
77-78	San Antonio	82	....	1481	666	257	538	.478	....	....	....	152	208	.731	99	158	257	194	150	0	69	4	148	18.1	8.1	3.1	2.4	.478
78-79	San Antonio	74	....	1324	472	174	354	.492	....	....	....	124	149	.832	80	167	247	231	154	0	56	15	111	17.9	6.4	3.3	3.1	.506
79-80	Utah	82	....	2304	953	377	785	.480	2	7	.286	197	243	.811	170	342	512	341	211	2	88	6	180	28.1	11.6	6.2	4.2	.532
80-81	Utah	82	....	2001	713	271	611	.444	5	18	.278	166	198	.838	103	327	430	383	190	1	63	3	172	24.4	8.7	5.2	4.7	.507
81-82	Dallas	82	54	2035	573	218	499	.437	3	18	.167	134	164	.817	119	220	339	448	222	2	65	6	164	24.8	7.0	4.1	5.5	.446
82-83	Dallas	37	0	371	104	44	99	.444	6	13	.462	10	14	.714	24	35	59	70	46	0	6	1	30	10.0	2.8	1.6	1.9	.381
NBA Season Totals		648	54	13277	5122	1977	4296	.460	16	56	.286	1152	1444	.798	893	1720	2613	2098	1337	7	490	40	805	20.5	7.9	4.0	3.2	
ABA Season Totals		47	....	882	328	125	271	.461	0	1	.000	78	92	.848	68	106	174	121	81	....	24	2	63	18.8	7.0	3.7	2.6	
Career Totals		695	54	14159	5450	2102	4567	.460	16	57	.281	1230	1536	.801	961	1826	2787	2219	1418	7	514	42	868	20.4	7.8	4.0	3.2	
75-76	San Antonio-A	7	....	97	45	13	35	.371	0	1	.000	19	24	.792	9	5	14	12	14	....	5	0	8	13.9	6.4	2.0	1.7	.440
76-77	San Antonio	2	....	28	8	3	9	.333	....	....	....	2	9	.222	3	1	4	7	6	0	2	0	....	14.0	4.0	2.0	3.5	.308
77-78	San Antonio	5	....	51	22	9	15	.600	....	....	....	4	6	.667	4	7	11	7	10	0	2	0	5	10.2	4.4	2.2	1.4	.517
78-79	San Antonio	13	....	163	56	20	49	.408	....	....	....	16	21	.762	12	15	27	28	17	0	9	5	11	12.5	4.3	2.1	2.2	.478
NBA Playoff Totals		20	....	242	86	32	73	.438	....	....	....	22	36	.611	19	23	42	42	33	0	13	5	16	12.1	4.3	2.1	2.1	
ABA Playoff Totals		7	....	97	45	13	35	.371	0	1	.000	19	24	.792	9	5	14	12	14	....	5	0	8	13.9	6.4	2.0	1.7	
Career Playoff Totals		27	....	339	131	45	108	.417	0	1	.000	41	60	.683	28	28	56	54	47	0	18	5	24	12.6	4.9	2.1	2.0	

• BRITT, Tyrone
Tyrone Britt

Born: Apr. 18, 1944.   Height: 6'4".   Weight: 190 lbs.   Drafted: —   College: Johnson C. Smith

YEAR	TEAM	GP	GS	MIN	PTS	FGM	FGA	FG%	3PM	3PA	3P%	FTM	FTA	FT%	ORB	DRB	TRB	AST	PF	DQ	STL	BLK	TO	MPG	PPG	RPG	APG	PCM
67-68	San Diego	11	....	84	28	13	34	.382	....	....	....	2	3	.667	....	....	15	12	10	0	....	....	....	7.6	2.5	1.4	1.1	.396
NBA Season Totals		11	....	84	28	13	34	.382	....	....	....	2	3	.667	....	....	15	12	10	0	....	....	....	7.6	2.5	1.4	1.1	

• BRITT, Wayman
Wayman P. Britt

Born: Aug. 31, 1952. Wilson Mills, NC, United States.   Height: 6'2".   Weight: 185 lbs.   Drafted: 1976   College: Michigan

YEAR	TEAM	GP	GS	MIN	PTS	FGM	FGA	FG%	3PM	3PA	3P%	FTM	FTA	FT%	ORB	DRB	TRB	AST	PF	DQ	STL	BLK	TO	MPG	PPG	RPG	APG	PCM
77-78	Detroit	7	....	16	9	3	10	.300	....	....	....	3	4	.750	1	3	4	2	3	0	1	0	1	2.3	1.3	0.6	0.3	.430
NBA Season Totals		7	....	16	9	3	10	.300	....	....	....	3	4	.750	1	3	4	2	3	0	1	0	1	2.3	1.3	0.6	0.3	

• BRITTAIN, Mike
Michael James Brittain

Born: June 21, 1963. Clearwater, FL, United States.   Height: 7'   Weight: 235 lbs.   Drafted: 1985   College: South Carolina

YEAR	TEAM	GP	GS	MIN	PTS	FGM	FGA	FG%	3PM	3PA	3P%	FTM	FTA	FT%	ORB	DRB	TRB	AST	PF	DQ	STL	BLK	TO	MPG	PPG	RPG	APG	PCM
85-86	San Antonio	32	2	219	54	22	43	.512	0	0	.000	10	19	.526	10	39	49	5	54	1	3	12	19	6.8	1.7	1.5	0.2	.239
86-87	San Antonio	6	0	29	9	4	9	.444	0	0	.000	1	2	.500	2	2	4	2	3	0	1	0	2	4.8	1.5	0.7	0.3	.256
NBA Season Totals		38	2	248	63	26	52	.500	0	0	.000	11	21	.524	12	41	53	7	57	1	4	12	21	6.5	1.7	1.4	0.2	
85-86	San Antonio	1	0	2	2	1	2	.500	0	0	.000	0	0	.000	1	0	1	0	0	0	0	0	1	0	2.0	2.0	1.0	0.0	1.465
NBA Playoff Totals		1	0	2	2	1	2	.500	0	0	.000	0	0	.000	1	0	1	0	0	0	0	0	1	0	2.0	2.0	1.0	0.0	

• BRITTON, Dave
David Britton

Born: Aug. 29, 1958. New York, NY, United States.   Height: 6'4".   Weight: 180 lbs.   Drafted: 1980   College: Texas A&M

YEAR	TEAM	GP	GS	MIN	PTS	FGM	FGA	FG%	3PM	3PA	3P%	FTM	FTA	FT%	ORB	DRB	TRB	AST	PF	DQ	STL	BLK	TO	MPG	PPG	RPG	APG	PCM
80-81	Washington	2	....	9	4	2	3	.667	0	0	.000	0	0	.000	0	2	2	3	2	0	1	0	2	4.5	2.0	1.0	1.5	.706
NBA Season Totals		2	....	9	4	2	3	.667	0	0	.000	0	0	.000	0	2	2	3	2	0	1	0	2	4.5	2.0	1.0	1.5	

• BROGAN, Jim
James Riley Brogan

Born: Feb. 24, 1958. Ardmore, PA, United States. Height: 6'4". Weight: 185 lbs. Drafted: — College: West Virginia Wesleyan

YEAR	TEAM	GP	GS	MIN	PTS	FGM	FGA	FG%	3PM	3PA	3P%	FTM	FTA	FT%	ORB	DRB	TRB	AST	PF	DQ	STL	BLK	TO	MPG	PPG	RPG	APG	PCM
81-82	San Diego	63	19	1027	400	165	364	.453	9	32	.281	61	84	.726	61	59	120	156	123	2	49	13	82	16.3	6.3	1.9	2.5	.399
82-83	San Diego	58	0	466	219	91	213	.427	3	13	.231	34	43	.791	33	29	62	66	79	0	26	9	41	8.0	3.8	1.1	1.1	.413
NBA Season Totals		121	19	1493	619	256	577	.444	12	45	.267	95	127	.748	94	88	182	222	202	2	75	22	123	12.3	5.1	1.5	1.8	....

• BROKAW, Gary
Gary George Brokaw

Born: Jan. 11, 1954. New Brunswick, NJ, United States. Height: 6'4". Weight: 178 lbs. Drafted: 1974 College: Notre Dame

YEAR	TEAM	GP	GS	MIN	PTS	FGM	FGA	FG%	3PM	3PA	3P%	FTM	FTA	FT%	ORB	DRB	TRB	AST	PF	DQ	STL	BLK	TO	MPG	PPG	RPG	APG	PCM
74-75	Milwaukee	73	....	1639	594	234	514	.455	....	....	....	126	184	.685	36	111	147	221	176	3	31	18	....	22.5	8.1	2.0	3.0	.387
75-76	Milwaukee	75	....	1468	633	237	519	.457	....	....	....	159	227	.700	26	99	125	246	138	1	37	17	....	19.6	8.4	1.7	3.3	.471
76-77	Milwaukee	41	....	891	365	130	324	.401	....	....	....	105	137	.766	10	54	64	111	85	0	22	23	....	21.7	8.9	1.6	2.7	.369
76-77	Cleveland	39	....	596	282	112	240	.467	....	....	....	58	82	.707	12	47	59	117	79	2	14	13	....	15.3	7.2	1.5	3.0	.522
77-78	Buffalo	13	....	130	54	18	43	.419	....	....	....	18	24	.750	3	9	12	20	11	0	3	5	12	10.0	4.2	0.9	1.5	.417
NBA Season Totals		241	....	4724	1928	731	1640	.446	....	....	....	466	654	.713	87	320	407	715	489	6	107	76	12	19.6	8.0	1.7	3.0	....
75-76	Milwaukee	3	....	108	63	23	37	.622	....	....	....	17	18	.944	0	11	11	24	10	0	3	3	....	36.0	21.0	3.7	8.0	.770
76-77	Cleveland	3	....	44	20	9	19	.474	....	....	....	2	6	.333	3	1	4	12	7	0	2	1	....	14.7	6.7	1.3	4.0	.539
NBA Playoff Totals		6	....	152	83	32	56	.571	....	....	....	19	24	.792	3	12	15	36	17	0	5	4	....	25.3	13.8	2.5	6.0	....

• BROOKFIELD, Price
Emery Price Brookfield

Born: May 11, 1920. Floydada, TX, United States. Height: 6'4". Weight: 185 lbs. Drafted: — College: West Texas State

YEAR	TEAM	GP	GS	MIN	PTS	FGM	FGA	FG%	3PM	3PA	3P%	FTM	FTA	FT%	ORB	DRB	TRB	AST	PF	DQ	STL	BLK	TO	MPG	PPG	RPG	APG	PCM
46-47	Chicago-N	42	....	....	188	82	....	....	....	....	....	24	33	.727	....	....	....	....	53	....	....	....	....	....	4.5	....	....	....
47-48	Anderson-N	49	....	....	191	82	....	....	....	....	....	27	40	.675	....	....	....	....	56	....	....	....	....	....	3.9	....	....	....
48-49	Indianapolis	54	....	....	442	176	638	.276	....	....	....	90	125	.720	....	....	....	136	145	....	....	....	....	....	8.2	....	2.5	....
49-50	Rochester	7	....	....	34	11	23	.478	....	....	....	12	13	.923	....	....	....	1	7	....	....	....	....	....	4.9	....	0.1	....
NBA Season Totals		61	....	....	476	187	661	.283	....	....	....	102	138	.739	....	....	....	137	152	....	....	....	....	....	7.8	....	2.2	....
NBL Season Totals		91	....	....	379	164	....	....	....	....	....	51	73	....	....	....	....	....	109	....	....	....	....	....	4.2	....	....	....
Career Totals		152	....	....	855	351	661	....	....	....	....	153	211	....	....	....	....	137	261	....	....	....	....	....	5.6	....	0.9	....
46-47	Chicago-N	11	....	....	61	29	....	....	....	....	....	3	7	.429	....	....	....	....	....	....	....	....	....	....	5.5	....	....	....
47-48	Anderson-N	6	....	....	43	17	....	....	....	....	....	9	12	.750	....	....	....	....	....	....	....	....	....	....	7.2	....	....	....
NBL Playoff Totals		17	....	....	104	46	....	....	....	....	....	12	19	....	....	....	....	....	....	....	....	....	....	....	6.1	....	....	....

• BROOKINS, Clarence
Clarence Brookins

Born: 1946. Height: 6'4". Weight: 190 lbs. Drafted: 1968 College: Temple

YEAR	TEAM	GP	GS	MIN	PTS	FGM	FGA	FG%	3PM	3PA	3P%	FTM	FTA	FT%	ORB	DRB	TRB	AST	PF	DQ	STL	BLK	TO	MPG	PPG	RPG	APG	PCM
70-71	Florida-A	8	....	59	21	8	26	.308	0	1	.000	5	12	.417	8	4	12	1	5	0	....	....	0	7.4	2.6	1.5	0.1	.213
ABA Season Totals		8	....	59	21	8	26	.308	0	1	.000	5	12	.417	8	4	12	1	5	0	....	....	0	7.4	2.6	1.5	0.1	....

• BROOKS, Kevin
Kevin Brooks

Born: Oct. 12, 1969. Beaufort, SC, United States. Height: 6'6". Weight: 200 lbs. Drafted: 1991 College: Southwestern Louisiana

YEAR	TEAM	GP	GS	MIN	PTS	FGM	FGA	FG%	3PM	3PA	3P%	FTM	FTA	FT%	ORB	DRB	TRB	AST	PF	DQ	STL	BLK	TO	MPG	PPG	RPG	APG	PCM
91-92	Denver	37	0	270	105	43	97	.443	2	11	.182	17	21	.810	13	26	39	11	19	0	8	2	19	7.3	2.8	1.1	0.3	.310
92-93	Denver	55	2	571	227	93	233	.399	6	26	.231	35	40	.875	22	59	81	34	46	0	10	2	39	10.4	4.1	1.5	0.6	.279
93-94	Denver	34	0	190	85	36	99	.364	4	23	.174	9	10	.900	5	16	21	3	19	0	0	2	14	5.6	2.5	0.6	0.1	.156
NBA Season Totals		126	2	1031	417	172	429	.401	12	60	.200	61	71	.859	40	101	141	48	84	0	18	6	72	8.2	3.3	1.1	0.4	....
93-94	Denver	2	0	5	5	2	7	.286	0	1	.000	1	2	.500	1	1	2	0	0	0	0	0	0	2.5	2.5	1.0	0.0	.358
NBA Playoff Totals		2	0	5	5	2	7	.286	0	1	.000	1	2	.500	1	1	2	0	0	0	0	0	0	2.5	2.5	1.0	0.0	....

• BROOKS, Mike
Michael Anthony Brooks

Born: Aug. 17, 1958. Philadelphia, PA, United States. Height: 6'7". Weight: 220 lbs. Drafted: 1980 College: LaSalle

YEAR	TEAM	GP	GS	MIN	PTS	FGM	FGA	FG%	3PM	3PA	3P%	FTM	FTA	FT%	ORB	DRB	TRB	AST	PF	DQ	STL	BLK	TO	MPG	PPG	RPG	APG	PCM
80-81	San Diego	82	....	2479	1202	488	1018	.479	0	6	.000	226	320	.706	210	232	442	208	234	2	99	31	164	30.2	14.7	5.4	2.5	.471
81-82	San Diego	82	73	2750	1276	537	1066	.504	0	7	.000	202	267	.757	207	417	624	236	285	7	113	39	197	33.5	15.6	7.6	2.9	.515
82-83	San Diego	82	26	2457	1002	402	830	.484	5	15	.333	193	277	.697	239	282	521	262	297	6	112	39	180	30.0	12.2	6.4	3.2	.478
83-84	San Diego	47	30	1405	530	213	445	.479	0	5	.000	104	151	.689	142	200	342	88	125	1	50	14	80	29.9	11.3	7.3	1.9	.450
86-87	Indiana	10	0	148	33	13	37	.351	0	0	.000	7	10	.700	9	19	28	11	19	0	9	0	11	14.8	3.3	2.8	1.1	.246
87-88	Denver	16	0	133	43	20	49	.408	0	0	.000	3	4	.750	19	25	44	13	21	1	4	1	13	8.3	2.7	2.8	0.8	.400
NBA Season Totals		319	129	9372	4086	1673	3445	.486	5	33	.152	735	1029	.714	826	1175	2001	818	981	17	387	124	645	29.4	12.8	6.3	2.6	....
87-88	Denver	4	0	11	3	1	3	.333	1	2	.500	0	0	.000	1	3	4	2	1	0	0	0	0	2.8	0.8	1.0	0.5	.594
NBA Playoff Totals		4	0	11	3	1	3	.333	1	2	.500	0	0	.000	1	3	4	2	1	0	0	0	0	2.8	0.8	1.0	0.5	....

• BROOKS, Scott
Scott William Brooks

Born: July 31, 1965. French Camp, CA, United States. Height: 5'11". Weight: 165 lbs. Drafted: — College: California (Irvine)

YEAR	TEAM	GP	GS	MIN	PTS	FGM	FGA	FG%	3PM	3PA	3P%	FTM	FTA	FT%	ORB	DRB	TRB	AST	PF	DQ	STL	BLK	TO	MPG	PPG	RPG	APG	PCM
88-89	Philadelphia	82	6	1372	428	156	371	.420	55	153	.359	61	69	.884	19	75	94	306	116	0	69	3	66	16.7	5.2	1.1	3.7	.431
89-90	Philadelphia	72	1	975	319	119	276	.431	31	79	.392	50	57	.877	15	49	64	207	105	0	47	0	36	13.5	4.4	0.9	2.9	.420
90-91	Minnesota	80	0	980	424	159	370	.430	45	135	.333	61	72	.847	28	44	72	204	122	1	53	5	48	12.3	5.3	0.9	2.6	.469
91-92	Minnesota	82	0	1082	417	167	374	.447	32	90	.356	51	63	.810	27	72	99	205	82	0	66	7	49	13.2	5.1	1.2	2.5	.476
92-93	Houston	82	0	1516	519	183	385	.475	41	99	.414	112	135	.830	22	77	99	243	136	0	79	3	74	18.5	6.3	1.2	3.0	.406
93-94	Houston	73	0	1225	381	142	289	.491	23	61	.377	74	85	.871	10	92	102	149	98	0	51	2	58	16.8	5.2	1.4	2.0	.365
94-95	Houston	28	0	186	96	35	65	.538	8	17	.471	18	21	.857	1	12	13	22	14	0	8	1	14	6.6	3.4	0.5	0.8	.488

YEAR	TEAM	GP	GS	MIN	PTS	FGM	FGA	FG%	3PM	3PA	3P%	FTM	FTA	FT%	ORB	DRB	TRB	AST	PF	DQ	STL	BLK	TO	MPG	PPG	RPG	APG	PCM
94-95	Dallas	31	0	622	245	91	210	.433	17	52	.327	46	58	.793	13	40	53	94	42	0	26	3	34	20.1	7.9	1.7	3.0	.407
95-96	Dallas	69	0	716	352	134	293	.457	25	62	.403	59	69	.855	11	30	41	100	53	0	42	3	41	10.4	5.1	0.6	1.4	.449
96-97	New York	38	0	251	57	19	39	.487	5	12	.417	14	15	.933	6	12	18	29	35	1	21	0	15	6.6	1.5	0.5	0.8	.299
97-98	Cleveland	43	0	312	79	28	66	.424	5	11	.455	18	20	.900	6	24	30	49	25	0	18	3	13	7.3	1.8	0.7	1.1	.384
NBA Season Totals		680	7	9237	3317	1233	2738	.450	287	771	.372	564	664	.849	158	527	685	1608	828	2	480	30	448	13.6	4.9	1.0	2.4	....
88-89	Philadelphia	3	0	21	5	1	6	.167	1	2	.500	2	2	1.000	0	4	4	5	4	0	0	0	1	7.0	1.7	1.3	1.7	.316
89-90	Philadelphia	9	0	99	21	6	19	.316	3	7	.429	6	9	.667	2	6	8	16	13	0	3	0	7	11.0	2.3	0.9	1.8	.223
92-93	Houston	12	0	197	47	16	42	.381	5	13	.385	10	13	.769	1	9	10	31	21	0	9	0	13	16.4	3.9	0.8	2.6	.255
93-94	Houston	5	0	23	11	5	6	.833	1	1	1.000	0	1	.000	1	1	2	3	3	0	0	0	0	4.6	2.2	0.4	0.6	.580
96-97	New York	4	0	7	3	1	2	.500	0	0	.000	1	1	1.000	0	0	0	0	0	0	0	0	0	1.8	0.8	0.0	0.0	.295
97-98	Cleveland	1	0	8	2	0	1	.000	0	0	.000	2	2	1.000	0	0	0	2	1	0	0	0	0	8.0	2.0	0.0	2.0	.350
NBA Playoff Totals		34	0	355	89	29	76	.382	10	23	.435	21	28	.750	4	20	24	57	42	0	12	0	21	10.4	2.6	0.7	1.7	....

• BROWN, —
Brown

Born: —. Height: — Weight: — Drafted: — College: —

YEAR	TEAM	GP	GS	MIN	PTS	FGM	FGA	FG%	3PM	3PA	3P%	FTM	FTA	FT%	ORB	DRB	TRB	AST	PF	DQ	STL	BLK	TO	MPG	PPG	RPG	APG	PCM
38-39	Hammond-N	1	....	....	2	1	....	....	....	....	....	0	....	....	....	....	....	....	....	....	....	....	....	....	2.0	....	....	....
NBL Season Totals		1	....	....	2	1	....	....	....	....	....	0	....	....	....	....	....	....	....	....	....	....	....	....	2.0	....	....	....

• BROWN, Bill
Bill Brown

Born: —. Height: 6'3". Weight: — Drafted: — College: Maryland

YEAR	TEAM	GP	GS	MIN	PTS	FGM	FGA	FG%	3PM	3PA	3P%	FTM	FTA	FT%	ORB	DRB	TRB	AST	PF	DQ	STL	BLK	TO	MPG	PPG	RPG	APG	PCM
41-42	Toledo-N	4	....	....	10	3	....	....	....	....	....	4	....	....	....	....	....	....	....	....	....	....	....	....	2.5	....	....	....
43-44	Cleveland-N	1	....	....	0	0	....	....	....	....	....	0	....	....	....	....	....	....	....	....	....	....	....	....	0.0	....	....	....
48-49	Oshkosh-N	10	....	....	36	13	....	....	....	....	....	10	17	.588	....	....	....	....	21	....	....	....	....	....	3.6	....	....	....
NBL Season Totals		15	....	....	46	16	....	....	....	....	....	14	17	....	....	....	....	....	21	....	....	....	....	....	3.1	....	....	....

• BROWN, Bob
Robert Edward Brown

Born: Nov. 12, 1923. Height: 6'4". Weight: 205 lbs. Drafted: — College: Miami (OH)

YEAR	TEAM	GP	GS	MIN	PTS	FGM	FGA	FG%	3PM	3PA	3P%	FTM	FTA	FT%	ORB	DRB	TRB	AST	PF	DQ	STL	BLK	TO	MPG	PPG	RPG	APG	PCM
45-46	Indianapolis-N	3	....	....	5	1	....	....	....	....	....	3	....	....	....	....	....	....	....	....	....	....	....	....	1.7	....	....	....
48-49	Providence	20	....	....	108	37	111	.333	....	....	....	34	47	.723	....	....	....	14	67	....	....	....	....	....	5.4	....	0.7	....
49-50	Denver	62	....	....	724	276	764	.361	....	....	....	172	252	.683	....	....	....	101	269	....	....	....	....	....	11.7	....	1.6	....
NBA Season Totals		82	....	....	832	313	875	.358	....	....	....	206	299	.689	....	....	....	115	336	....	....	....	....	....	10.1	....	1.4	....
NBL Season Totals		3	....	....	5	1	....	....	....	....	....	3	....	....	....	....	....	....	....	....	....	....	....	....	1.7	....	....	....
Career Totals		85	....	....	837	314	875	....	....	....	....	209	299	....	....	....	....	115	336	....	....	....	....	....	9.8	....	1.4	....

• BROWN, Chucky
Clarence (Chucky, Wild Thing) Brown

Born: Feb. 29, 1968. New York, NY, United States. Height: 6'7". Weight: 214 lbs. Drafted: 1989 College: North Carolina State

YEAR	TEAM	GP	GS	MIN	PTS	FGM	FGA	FG%	3PM	3PA	3P%	FTM	FTA	FT%	ORB	DRB	TRB	AST	PF	DQ	STL	BLK	TO	MPG	PPG	RPG	APG	PCM
89-90	Cleveland	75	35	1339	545	210	447	.470	0	7	.000	125	164	.762	83	148	231	50	148	0	33	26	68	17.9	7.3	3.1	0.7	.371
90-91	Cleveland	74	51	1485	627	263	502	.524	0	4	.000	101	144	.701	78	135	213	80	130	0	26	24	96	20.1	8.5	2.9	1.1	.380
91-92	Cleveland	6	0	50	15	5	10	.500	0	0	.000	5	8	.625	2	4	6	3	7	0	3	0	2	8.3	2.5	1.0	0.5	.309
91-92	LA Lakers	36	2	381	135	55	118	.466	0	3	.000	25	41	.610	29	47	76	23	41	0	9	7	29	10.6	3.8	2.1	0.6	.349
92-93	New Jersey	77	20	1186	391	160	331	.483	0	5	.000	71	98	.724	88	144	232	51	112	0	20	23	54	15.4	5.1	3.0	0.7	.360
93-94	Dallas	1	0	10	3	1	1	1.000	0	0	.000	1	1	1.000	0	1	1	0	2	0	0	0	0	10.0	3.0	1.0	0.0	.300
94-95	Houston	41	14	814	249	105	174	.603	1	3	.333	38	62	.613	64	125	189	30	105	0	11	14	29	19.9	6.1	4.6	0.7	.404
95-96	Houston	82	82	2019	705	300	555	.541	1	8	.125	104	150	.693	134	307	441	89	163	0	47	38	90	24.6	8.6	5.4	1.1	.432
96-97	Phoenix	10	0	83	34	13	26	.500	0	0	.000	8	11	.727	3	13	16	4	14	0	0	2	4	8.3	3.4	1.6	0.4	.377
96-97	Milwaukee	60	1	674	170	65	128	.508	1	6	.167	39	59	.661	38	94	132	24	86	1	9	20	18	11.2	2.8	2.2	0.4	.328
97-98	Atlanta	77	8	1202	387	161	372	.433	2	8	.250	63	87	.724	57	126	183	55	100	0	23	13	54	15.6	5.0	2.4	0.7	.289
98-99	Charlotte	48	21	1192	407	176	373	.472	15	40	.375	40	59	.678	36	138	174	57	106	0	16	19	38	24.8	8.5	3.6	1.2	.329
99-00	San Antonio	30	27	602	190	82	176	.466	1	3	.333	25	31	.806	11	66	77	41	53	0	8	10	28	20.1	6.3	2.6	1.4	.305
99-00	Charlotte	33	2	494	144	66	152	.434	1	7	.143	11	21	.524	24	66	90	25	61	1	12	8	17	15.0	4.4	2.7	0.8	.294
00-01	Golden State	6	0	74	24	9	20	.450	0	2	.000	6	10	.600	3	15	18	5	10	0	3	1	2	12.3	4.0	3.0	0.8	.423
00-01	Cleveland	20	2	265	78	31	75	.413	0	1	.000	16	24	.667	5	31	36	6	27	0	6	6	6	13.3	3.9	1.8	0.3	.253
01-02	Sacramento	18	0	92	21	10	27	.370	0	0	.000	1	2	.500	10	23	33	6	12	0	2	4	5	5.1	1.2	1.8	0.3	.403
NBA Season Totals		694	265	11962	4125	1712	3487	.491	22	97	.227	679	972	.699	665	1483	2148	549	1177	2	228	215	540	17.2	5.9	3.1	0.8	....
91-92	LA Lakers	3	0	44	19	8	19	.421	0	1	.000	3	6	.500	3	8	11	2	3	0	0	2	1	14.7	6.3	3.7	0.7	.438
92-93	New Jersey	4	0	62	24	9	22	.409	0	0	.000	6	7	.857	3	6	9	1	2	0	3	3	2	15.5	6.0	2.3	0.3	.382
94-95	Houston	21	1	326	94	34	76	.447	1	2	.500	25	37	.676	20	45	65	7	46	2	9	2	12	15.5	4.5	3.1	0.3	.291
95-96	Houston	8	8	168	65	25	45	.556	0	0	.000	15	18	.833	6	18	24	5	17	0	3	0	4	21.0	8.1	3.0	0.6	.379
97-98	Atlanta	4	0	50	16	7	15	.467	1	2	.500	1	2	.500	1	5	6	4	5	0	0	0	2	12.5	4.0	1.5	1.0	.279
01-02	Sacramento	1	0	1	0	0	0	.000	0	0	.000	0	0	.000	0	1	1	0	1	0	0	0	0	1.0	0.0	1.0	0.0	.453
NBA Playoff Totals		41	9	651	218	83	177	.469	2	5	.400	50	70	.714	33	83	116	19	74	2	15	7	21	15.9	5.3	2.8	0.5	....

• BROWN, Damone
Damone Lamar Brown

Born: June 28, 1979. Buffalo, NY, United States. Height: 6'9". Weight: 200 lbs. Drafted: 2001 College: Syracuse

YEAR	TEAM	GP	GS	MIN	PTS	FGM	FGA	FG%	3PM	3PA	3P%	FTM	FTA	FT%	ORB	DRB	TRB	AST	PF	DQ	STL	BLK	TO	MPG	PPG	RPG	APG	PCM
01-02	Philadelphia	17	0	66	23	8	21	.381	0	1	.000	7	8	.875	2	2	4	2	11	0	1	1	9	3.9	1.4	0.2	0.1	.080
02-03	Toronto	5	3	115	28	11	35	.314	0	2	.000	6	8	.750	3	12	15	3	14	0	1	0	6	23.0	5.6	3.0	0.6	.098
NBA Season Totals		22	3	181	51	19	56	.339	0	3	.000	13	16	.813	5	14	19	5	25	0	2	1	15	8.2	2.3	0.9	0.2	....

• BROWN, Darrell

Darrell H. Brown

Born: Mar. 14, 1923. Height: 6'2". Weight: 175 lbs. Drafted: 1948 College: Humboldt State

YEAR	TEAM	GP	GS	MIN	PTS	FGM	FGA	FG%	3PM	3PA	3P%	FTM	FTA	FT%	ORB	DRB	TRB	AST	PF	DQ	STL	BLK	TO	MPG	PPG	RPG	APG	PCM
48-49	Baltimore	3	....	....	4	2	6	.333	....	....	....	0	2	.000	....	....	....	0	3	....	....	....	....	....	1.3	....	0.0	....
NBA Season Totals		3	....	....	4	2	6	.333	....	....	....	0	2	.000	....	....	....	0	3	....	....	....	....	....	1.3	....	0.0	....

• BROWN, Dee

DeCovan Kadell (Dee-lightful) Brown

Born: Nov. 29, 1968. Jacksonville, FL, United States. Height: 6'1". Weight: 160 lbs. Drafted: 1990 College: Jacksonville

YEAR	TEAM	GP	GS	MIN	PTS	FGM	FGA	FG%	3PM	3PA	3P%	FTM	FTA	FT%	ORB	DRB	TRB	AST	PF	DQ	STL	BLK	TO	MPG	PPG	RPG	APG	PCM
90-91	Boston	82	5	1945	712	284	612	.464	7	34	.206	137	157	.873	41	141	182	344	161	0	83	14	139	23.7	8.7	2.2	4.2	.421
91-92	Boston	31	20	883	363	149	350	.426	5	22	.227	60	78	.769	15	64	79	164	74	0	33	7	59	28.5	11.7	2.5	5.3	.413
92-93	Boston	80	48	2254	874	328	701	.468	26	82	.317	192	242	.793	45	201	246	461	203	2	138	31	136	28.2	10.9	3.1	5.8	.515
93-94	Boston	77	76	2867	1192	490	1021	.480	30	96	.313	182	219	.831	63	237	300	347	207	3	156	47	123	37.2	15.5	3.9	4.5	.460
94-95	Boston	79	69	2792	1236	437	977	.447	126	327	.385	236	277	.852	63	186	249	301	181	0	110	49	142	35.3	15.6	3.2	3.8	.428
95-96	Boston	65	23	1591	695	246	617	.399	68	220	.309	135	158	.854	36	100	136	146	119	0	80	12	72	24.5	10.7	2.1	2.2	.365
96-97	Boston	21	2	522	160	61	166	.367	20	65	.308	18	22	.818	8	40	48	67	45	0	31	7	23	24.9	7.6	2.3	3.2	.325
97-98	Boston	41	10	811	280	109	255	.427	43	113	.381	19	28	.679	10	52	62	53	76	1	44	6	33	19.8	6.8	1.5	1.3	.293
97-98	Toronto	31	2	908	378	137	307	.446	65	158	.411	39	43	.907	14	76	90	101	47	0	38	17	40	29.3	12.2	2.9	3.3	.446
98-99	Toronto	49	0	1377	549	187	495	.378	**135**	**349**	.387	40	55	.727	15	88	103	143	75	0	56	8	80	28.1	11.2	2.1	2.9	.342
99-00	Toronto	38	12	673	264	93	258	.360	67	187	.358	11	16	.688	9	45	54	86	62	1	24	5	39	17.7	6.9	1.4	2.3	.323
00-01	Orlando	7	0	155	48	16	44	.364	12	32	.375	4	5	.800	0	11	11	12	10	0	4	0	7	22.1	6.9	1.6	1.7	.247
01-02	Orlando	7	0	65	7	3	20	.150	1	12	.083	0	0	.000	0	9	9	2	4	0	3	1	4	9.3	1.0	1.3	0.3	.002
NBA Season Totals		608	267	16843	6758	2540	5823	.436	605	1697	.357	1073	1300	.825	319	1250	1569	2227	1264	7	800	204	897	27.7	11.1	2.6	3.7	....
90-91	Boston	11	0	284	134	53	108	.491	0	5	.000	28	34	.824	9	36	45	41	32	0	11	6	22	25.8	12.2	4.1	3.7	.514
91-92	Boston	6	0	120	48	22	44	.500	0	3	.000	4	6	.667	3	9	12	31	16	2	1	4	7	20.0	8.0	2.0	5.2	.514
92-93	Boston	4	3	133	45	15	41	.366	1	7	.143	14	14	1.000	2	4	6	15	11	0	2	4	6	33.3	11.3	1.5	3.8	.280
94-95	Boston	4	4	172	75	26	62	.419	9	26	.346	14	16	.875	6	14	20	19	13	1	5	1	7	43.0	18.8	5.0	4.8	.420
99-00	Toronto	3	0	19	0	0	4	.000	0	3	.000	0	0	.000	0	2	2	2	4	0	2	0	1	6.3	0.0	0.7	0.7	-.028
00-01	Orlando	3	0	54	18	6	13	.462	6	11	.545	0	0	.000	0	3	3	4	3	0	2	0	1	18.0	6.0	1.0	1.3	.340
NBA Playoff Totals		31	7	782	320	122	272	.449	16	55	.291	60	70	.857	20	68	88	112	79	3	23	15	44	25.2	10.3	2.8	3.6	....

• BROWN, Devin

Devin Brown

Born: Dec. 30, 1978. Height: 6'5". Weight: 235 lbs. Drafted: — College: Texas-San Antonio

YEAR	TEAM	GP	GS	MIN	PTS	FGM	FGA	FG%	3PM	3PA	3P%	FTM	FTA	FT%	ORB	DRB	TRB	AST	PF	DQ	STL	BLK	TO	MPG	PPG	RPG	APG	PCM
02-03	San Antonio	7	0	22	12	5	10	.500	0	0	.000	2	2	1.000	4	3	7	2	3	0	0	0	5	3.1	1.7	1.0	0.3	.459
02-03	Denver	3	2	71	18	7	25	.280	0	1	.000	4	6	.667	4	7	11	5	11	0	4	1	4	23.7	6.0	3.7	1.7	.171
NBA Season Totals		10	2	93	30	12	35	.343	0	1	.000	6	8	.750	8	10	18	7	14	0	4	1	9	9.3	3.0	1.8	0.7	....

• BROWN, Ernest

Ernest Brown

Born: May 17, 1979. Bronx, NY, United States. Height: 7' Weight: 244 lbs. Drafted: 2000 College: Indian Hills CC

YEAR	TEAM	GP	GS	MIN	PTS	FGM	FGA	FG%	3PM	3PA	3P%	FTM	FTA	FT%	ORB	DRB	TRB	AST	PF	DQ	STL	BLK	TO	MPG	PPG	RPG	APG	PCM
01-02	Miami	3	0	21	3	1	6	.167	0	0	.000	1	4	.250	1	5	6	0	4	0	0	1	3	7.0	1.0	2.0	0.0	-.051
NBA Season Totals		3	0	21	3	1	6	.167	0	0	.000	1	4	.250	1	5	6	0	4	0	0	1	3	7.0	1.0	2.0	0.0	....

• BROWN, Fred

Fred (Downtown) Brown

Born: Aug. 7, 1948. Milwaukee, WI, United States. Height: 6'3". Weight: 182 lbs. Drafted: 1971 College: Iowa

YEAR	TEAM	GP	GS	MIN	PTS	FGM	FGA	FG%	3PM	3PA	3P%	FTM	FTA	FT%	ORB	DRB	TRB	AST	PF	DQ	STL	BLK	TO	MPG	PPG	RPG	APG	PCM
71-72	Seattle	33	....	359	140	59	180	.328	....	....	....	22	29	.759	....	....	37	60	44	0	....	....	....	10.9	4.2	1.1	1.8	.316
72-73	Seattle	79	....	2320	1063	471	1035	.455	....	....	....	121	148	.818	....	....	318	438	226	5	....	....	....	29.4	13.5	4.0	5.5	.536
73-74	Seattle	82	....	2501	1351	578	1226	.471	....	....	....	195	226	.863	114	287	401	414	276	6	136	18	....	30.5	16.5	4.9	5.0	.594
74-75	Seattle	81	....	2669	1700	737	1537	.480	....	....	....	226	272	.831	113	230	343	284	227	2	187	14	....	33.0	21.0	4.2	3.5	.569
75-76	Seattle	76	....	2516	1757	742	1522	.488	....	....	....	273	314	.869	111	206	317	207	186	0	143	18	....	33.1	23.1	4.2	2.7	.596
76-77	Seattle	72	....	2098	1236	534	1114	.479	....	....	....	168	190	.884	68	164	232	176	140	1	124	19	....	29.1	17.2	3.2	2.4	.508
77-78	Seattle	72	....	1965	1192	508	1042	.488	....	....	....	176	196	.898	61	127	188	240	145	0	110	25	166	27.3	16.6	2.6	3.3	.539
78-79	Seattle	77	....	1961	1075	446	951	.469	....	....	....	183	206	.888	38	134	172	260	142	0	119	23	162	25.5	14.0	2.2	3.4	.495
79-80	Seattle	80	....	1701	960	404	843	.479	39	88	**.443**	113	135	.837	35	120	155	174	117	0	65	17	104	21.3	12.0	1.9	2.2	.477
80-81	Seattle	78	....	1986	1206	505	1035	.488	23	64	.359	173	208	.832	53	122	175	233	141	0	88	13	133	25.5	15.5	2.2	3.0	.517
81-82	Seattle	82	2	1785	922	393	863	.455	25	77	.325	111	129	.860	42	98	140	238	111	0	69	4	98	21.8	11.2	1.7	2.9	.444
82-83	Seattle	80	1	1432	814	371	714	.520	14	32	.438	58	72	.806	32	65	97	242	98	0	59	13	112	17.9	10.2	1.2	3.0	.539
83-84	Seattle	71	1	1129	602	258	506	.510	9	34	.265	77	86	.895	14	48	62	194	84	0	49	2	71	15.9	8.5	0.9	2.7	.509
NBA Season Totals		963	4	24422	14018	6006	12568	.478	110	295	.373	1896	2211	.858	681	1601	2637	3160	1937	14	1149	166	846	25.4	14.6	2.7	3.3	....
74-75	Seattle	8	....	240	165	69	139	.496	....	....	....	27	32	.844	12	24	36	23	19	0	17	1	....	30.0	20.6	4.5	2.9	.634
75-76	Seattle	6	....	236	171	68	133	.511	....	....	....	35	44	.795	12	16	28	17	20	0	13	0	....	39.3	28.5	4.7	2.8	.620
77-78	Seattle	22	....	575	381	153	341	.449	....	....	....	75	90	.833	16	31	47	53	47	0	23	2	31	26.1	17.3	2.1	2.4	.495
78-79	Seattle	17	....	260	142	64	142	.451	....	....	....	14	17	.824	8	14	22	35	23	0	9	4	16	15.3	8.4	1.3	2.1	.446
79-80	Seattle	15	....	313	188	80	182	.440	10	34	.294	18	21	.857	16	22	38	32	23	0	2	1	23	20.9	12.5	2.5	2.1	.432
81-82	Seattle	8	0	158	95	43	89	.483	2	5	.400	7	10	.700	6	9	15	18	5	0	5	0	9	19.8	11.9	1.9	2.3	.497
82-83	Seattle	2	0	30	6	2	9	.222	0	0	.000	2	2	1.000	0	3	3	5	3	0	1	0	0	15.0	3.0	1.5	2.5	.248
83-84	Seattle	5	0	88	49	20	47	.426	1	3	.333	8	11	.727	2	5	7	10	4	0	4	0	3	17.6	9.8	1.4	2.0	.441
NBA Playoff Totals		83	0	1900	1197	499	1082	.461	13	42	.310	186	227	.819	72	124	196	193	144	0	74	8	82	22.9	14.4	2.4	2.3	....

• BROWN, George

George Raff Brown

Born: Oct. 30, 1935. Height: 6'6". Weight: 190 lbs. Drafted: 1957 College: Wayne State (MI)

YEAR	TEAM	GP	GS	MIN	PTS	FGM	FGA	FG%	3PM	3PA	3P%	FTM	FTA	FT%	ORB	DRB	TRB	AST	PF	DQ	STL	BLK	TO	MPG	PPG	RPG	APG	PCM
57-58	Minneapolis	1	....	6	1	0	2	.000	....	....	....	1	2	.500	....	....	1	0	1	0	....	....	....	6.0	1.0	1.0	0.0	-.076
NBA Season Totals		1	....	6	1	0	2	.000	....	....	....	1	2	.500	....	....	1	0	1	0	....	....	....	6.0	1.0	1.0	0.0	....

YEAR	TEAM	GP	GS	MIN	PTS	FGM	FGA	FG%	3PM	3PA	3P%	FTM	FTA	FT%	ORB	DRB	TRB	AST	PF	DQ	STL	BLK	TO	MPG	PPG	RPG	APG	PCM

• BROWN, Gerald
Gerald Brown

Born: July 28, 1975. Los Angeles, CA, United States.   Height: 6'4".   Weight: 210 lbs.   Drafted: —   College: Pepperdine

YEAR	TEAM	GP	GS	MIN	PTS	FGM	FGA	FG%	3PM	3PA	3P%	FTM	FTA	FT%	ORB	DRB	TRB	AST	PF	DQ	STL	BLK	TO	MPG	PPG	RPG	APG	PCM
98-99	Phoenix	33	0	236	80	33	89	.371	3	10	.300	11	14	.786	5	17	22	31	21	0	5	1	22	7.2	2.4	0.7	0.9	.251
NBA Season Totals		33	0	236	80	33	89	.371	3	10	.300	11	14	.786	5	17	22	31	21	0	5	1	22	7.2	2.4	0.7	0.9	....
98-99	Phoenix	1	0	1	2	1	1	1.000	0	0	.000	0	0	.000	0	0	0	0	0	0	0	0	0	1.0	2.0	0.0	0.0	2.000
NBA Playoff Totals		1	0	1	2	1	1	1.000	0	0	.000	0	0	.000	0	0	0	0	0	0	0	0	0	1.0	2.0	0.0	0.0	....

• BROWN, Harold
Harold V. (Brownie) Brown

Born: Oct. 2, 1923. Died: Sept.1980.   Height: 6'   Weight: 155 lbs.   Drafted: —   College: Evansville

YEAR	TEAM	GP	GS	MIN	PTS	FGM	FGA	FG%	3PM	3PA	3P%	FTM	FTA	FT%	ORB	DRB	TRB	AST	PF	DQ	STL	BLK	TO	MPG	PPG	RPG	APG	PCM
46-47	Detroit	54	....	....	264	95	383	.248	....	....	....	74	117	.632	....	....	....	39	122	....	....	....	....	....	4.9	....	0.7	
NBA Season Totals		54	....	....	264	95	383	.248	....	....	....	74	117	.632	....	....	....	39	122	....	....	....	....	....	4.9	....	0.7	

• BROWN, Hillery
Hillery Brown

Born: July 30, 1912. Chicago, IL, United States. Died: Feb.8, 1991.   Height: 6'3".   Weight: 190 lbs.   Drafted: —   College: none

YEAR	TEAM	GP	GS	MIN	PTS	FGM	FGA	FG%	3PM	3PA	3P%	FTM	FTA	FT%	ORB	DRB	TRB	AST	PF	DQ	STL	BLK	TO	MPG	PPG	RPG	APG	PCM
42-43	Chicago-N	23	....	....	94	36	....	....	....	....	....	22	....	....	....	....	....	....	....	....	....	....	....	....	4.1	....		
NBL Season Totals		23	....	....	94	36	....	....	....	....	....	22	....	....	....	....	....	....	....	....	....	....	....	....	4.1	....		
42-43	Chicago-N	3	....	....	6	2	....	....	....	....	....	2	....	....	....	....	....	....	....	....	....	....	....	....	2.0	....		
NBL Playoff Totals		3	....	....	6	2	....	....	....	....	....	2	....	....	....	....	....	....	....	....	....	....	....	....	2.0	....		

• BROWN, Jim
Jim Brown

Born: 1912.   Height: 6'1".   Weight: 190 lbs.   Drafted: —   College: Temple

YEAR	TEAM	GP	GS	MIN	PTS	FGM	FGA	FG%	3PM	3PA	3P%	FTM	FTA	FT%	ORB	DRB	TRB	AST	PF	DQ	STL	BLK	TO	MPG	PPG	RPG	APG	PCM
40-41	Detroit-N	22	....	....	103	42	....	....	....	....	....	19	....	....	....	....	....	....	....	....	....	....	....	....	4.7	....		
NBL Season Totals		22	....	....	103	42	....	....	....	....	....	19	....	....	....	....	....	....	....	....	....	....	....	....	4.7	....		
40-41	Detroit-N	3	....	....	15	7	....	....	....	....	....	1	....	....	....	....	....	....	....	....	....	....	....	....	5.0	....		
NBL Playoff Totals		3	....	....	15	7	....	....	....	....	....	1	....	....	....	....	....	....	....	....	....	....	....	....	5.0	....		

• BROWN, John
John Young Brown

Born: Dec. 14, 1951. Frankfurt, Germany.   Height: 6'7".   Weight: 220 lbs.   Drafted: 1973   College: Missouri

YEAR	TEAM	GP	GS	MIN	PTS	FGM	FGA	FG%	3PM	3PA	3P%	FTM	FTA	FT%	ORB	DRB	TRB	AST	PF	DQ	STL	BLK	TO	MPG	PPG	RPG	APG	PCM
73-74	Atlanta	77	....	1715	717	277	632	.438	....	....	....	163	217	.751	177	264	441	114	239	10	29	16	....	22.3	9.3	5.7	1.5	.464
74-75	Atlanta	73	....	1986	815	315	684	.461	....	....	....	185	250	.740	180	254	434	133	228	7	54	15	....	27.2	11.2	5.9	1.8	.452
75-76	Atlanta	75	....	1758	592	215	486	.442	....	....	....	162	209	.775	146	257	403	126	235	7	45	16	....	23.4	7.9	5.4	1.7	.414
76-77	Atlanta	77	....	1405	441	160	350	.457	....	....	....	121	150	.807	75	161	236	103	217	7	46	7	....	18.2	5.7	3.1	1.3	.350
77-78	Atlanta	75	....	1594	549	192	405	.474	....	....	....	165	200	.825	137	166	303	105	280	18	55	8	113	21.3	7.3	4.0	1.4	.354
78-79	Chicago	77	....	1265	388	152	317	.479	....	....	....	84	98	.857	83	155	238	104	180	5	18	10	92	16.4	5.0	3.1	1.4	.335
79-80	Utah	4	....	24	4	0	7	.000	0	0	.000	4	4	1.000	5	4	9	4	4	0	0	0	5	6.0	1.0	2.3	1.0	.161
79-80	Atlanta	28	....	361	108	37	98	.378	0	0	.000	34	44	.773	21	41	62	14	66	0	3	4	25	12.9	3.9	2.2	0.5	.204
NBA Season Totals		486	....	10108	3614	1348	2979	.453	0	0	.000	918	1172	.783	824	1302	2126	703	1449	54	250	76	235	20.8	7.4	4.4	1.4	....
77-78	Atlanta	2	....	6	0	0	0	.000	....	....	....	0	0	.000	0	0	0	1	0	0	0	2	3.0	0.0	0.0	0.0	-.365
79-80	Atlanta	5	....	58	10	4	13	.308	0	1	.000	2	2	1.000	2	8	10	1	9	0	1	1	5	11.6	2.0	2.0	0.2	.090
NBA Playoff Totals		7	....	64	10	4	13	.308	0	1	.000	2	2	1.000	2	8	10	1	10	0	1	1	7	9.1	1.4	1.4	0.1	....

• BROWN, Kedrick
Albert Kedrick Brown

Born: Mar. 18, 1981. Zachary, LA, United States.   Height: 6'7".   Weight: 222 lbs.   Drafted: 2001   College: Okaloosa-Walton CC

YEAR	TEAM	GP	GS	MIN	PTS	FGM	FGA	FG%	3PM	3PA	3P%	FTM	FTA	FT%	ORB	DRB	TRB	AST	PF	DQ	STL	BLK	TO	MPG	PPG	RPG	APG	PCM
01-02	Boston	29	5	245	63	23	70	.329	5	27	.185	12	20	.600	11	39	50	15	18	0	18	7	7	8.4	2.2	1.7	0.5	.354
02-03	Boston	51	5	666	145	61	171	.357	3	39	.077	20	32	.625	45	95	140	20	68	0	34	13	23	13.1	2.8	2.7	0.4	.270
NBA Season Totals		80	10	911	208	84	241	.349	8	66	.121	32	52	.615	56	134	190	35	86	0	52	20	30	11.4	2.6	2.4	0.4	....
01-02	Boston	2	0	3	5	2	2	1.000	1	1	1.000	0	0	.000	0	0	0	0	0	0	0	1	0	1.5	2.5	0.0	0.0	1.969
02-03	Boston	3	0	11	3	1	4	.250	0	0	.000	1	2	.500	2	0	2	0	0	0	1	1	0	3.7	1.0	0.7	0.0	.231
NBA Playoff Totals		5	0	14	8	3	6	.500	1	1	1.000	1	2	.500	2	0	2	0	0	0	1	1	0	2.8	1.6	0.4	0.0	....

• BROWN, Kwame
Kwame Brown

Born: Mar. 10, 1982. Charleston, SC, United States.   Height: 6'11".   Weight: 240 lbs.   Drafted: 2001   College: none (HS: Glynn Academy, GA)

YEAR	TEAM	GP	GS	MIN	PTS	FGM	FGA	FG%	3PM	3PA	3P%	FTM	FTA	FT%	ORB	DRB	TRB	AST	PF	DQ	STL	BLK	TO	MPG	PPG	RPG	APG	PCM
01-02	Washington	57	3	818	258	94	243	.387	0	1	.000	70	99	.707	63	135	198	43	105	2	16	26	43	14.4	4.5	3.5	0.8	.352
02-03	Washington	80	20	1774	593	224	502	.446	0	3	.000	145	217	.668	128	298	426	58	159	1	50	80	110	22.2	7.4	5.3	0.7	.397
NBA Season Totals		137	23	2592	851	318	745	.427	0	4	.000	215	316	.680	191	433	624	101	264	3	66	106	153	18.9	6.2	4.6	0.7	....

• BROWN, Larry
Lawrence Harvey Brown

Born: Sept. 14, 1940. Brooklyn, NY, United States.   Height: 5'9".   Weight: 160 lbs.   Drafted: 1963   College: North Carolina

YEAR	TEAM	GP	GS	MIN	PTS	FGM	FGA	FG%	3PM	3PA	3P%	FTM	FTA	FT%	ORB	DRB	TRB	AST	PF	DQ	STL	BLK	TO	MPG	PPG	RPG	APG	PCM
67-68	New Orleans-A	78	....	2807	1045	330	901	.366	19	89	.213	366	450	.813	....	....	249	**506**	220	1	....	....	**355**	36.0	13.4	3.2	**6.5**	.443
68-69	Oakland-A	77	....	2381	925	308	706	.436	8	35	.229	301	379	.794	62	173	235	**544**	230	6	....	....	**331**	30.9	12.0	3.1	**7.1**	.535
69-70	Washington-A	82	....	2766	1124	376	854	.440	10	39	.256	362	439	.825	52	194	246	**580**	257	4	....	....	**356**	33.7	13.7	3.0	**7.1**	.522

YEAR	TEAM	GP	GS	MIN	PTS	FGM	FGA	FG%	3PM	3PA	3P%	FTM	FTA	FT%	ORB	DRB	TRB	AST	PF	DQ	STL	BLK	TO	MPG	PPG	RPG	APG	PCM
70-71	Denver-A	34	....	813	287	85	236	.360	5	19	.263	112	136	.824	11	51	62	208	96	4	....	....	115	23.9	8.4	1.8	6.1	.513
70-71	Virginia-A	29	....	530	159	42	104	.404	1	2	.500	74	89	.831	13	34	47	122	49	0	....	....	73	18.3	5.5	1.6	4.2	.505
71-72	Denver-A	76	....	2012	689	243	556	.437	5	25	.200	198	244	.811	53	113	166	549	207	1	....	....	217	26.5	9.1	2.2	7.2	.529
ABA Season Totals		376	....	11309	4229	1384	3357	.412	48	209	.230	1413	1737	.813	191	565	1005	2509	1059	16	....	....	1447	30.1	11.2	2.7	**6.7**	
67-68	New Orleans-A	17	....	696	284	90	212	.425	4	18	.222	100	122	.820	....	....	59	129	58	0	....	....	77	40.9	16.7	3.5	7.6	.502
68-69	Oakland-A	16	....	534	224	74	173	.428	0	3	.000	76	90	.844	....	....	52	87	49	0	....	....	59	33.4	14.0	3.3	5.4	.479
69-70	Washington-A	7	....	269	97	33	73	.452	1	5	.200	30	34	.882	....	....	35	68		1	....	....	25	38.4	13.9	5.0	9.7	....
71-72	Denver-A	7	....	211	65	21	50	.420	0	3	.000	23	24	.958	....	....	10	36	25	0	....	....	14	30.1	9.3	1.4	5.1	.366
ABA Playoff Totals		47	....	1710	670	218	508	.429	5	29	.172	229	270	.848	....	....	156	320	132	1	....	....	175	36.4	14.3	3.3	6.8	....

• BROWN, Leon

Leon (Stretch) Brown

Born: Oct. 12, 1919.   Height: 6'3".   Weight: 190 lbs.   Drafted: —   College: Wyoming

YEAR	TEAM	GP	GS	MIN	PTS	FGM	FGA	FG%	3PM	3PA	3P%	FTM	FTA	FT%	ORB	DRB	TRB	AST	PF	DQ	STL	BLK	TO	MPG	PPG	RPG	APG	PCM
46-47	Cleveland	5	....	....	0	0	3	.000	....	....	....	0	0	.000	....	....	....	0	2	....	....	....	...	0.0	....	0.0	....	
NBA Season Totals		5	....	....	0	0	3	.000	....	....	....	0	0	.000	....	....	....	0	2	....	....	....	....	0.0	....	0.0	....	

• BROWN, Lewis

Lewis Brown

Born: Feb. 19, 1955. Los Angeles, CA, United States.   Height: 6'11".   Weight: 225 lbs.   Drafted: 1977   College: UNLV

YEAR	TEAM	GP	GS	MIN	PTS	FGM	FGA	FG%	3PM	3PA	3P%	FTM	FTA	FT%	ORB	DRB	TRB	AST	PF	DQ	STL	BLK	TO	MPG	PPG	RPG	APG	PCM
80-81	Washington	2	....	5	2	0	3	.000	0	0	.000	2	5	.400	1	1	2	0	2	0	0	0	1	2.5	1.0	1.0	0.0	-.420
NBA Season Totals		2	....	5	2	0	3	.000	0	0	.000	2	5	.400	1	1	2	0	2	0	0	0	1	2.5	1.0	1.0	0.0	

• BROWN, Marcus

Marcus James Brown

Born: Apr. 3, 1974. West Memphis, AR, United States.   Height: 6'3".   Weight: 185 lbs.   Drafted: 1996   College: Murray State

YEAR	TEAM	GP	GS	MIN	PTS	FGM	FGA	FG%	3PM	3PA	3P%	FTM	FTA	FT%	ORB	DRB	TRB	AST	PF	DQ	STL	BLK	TO	MPG	PPG	RPG	APG	PCM
96-97	Portland	21	0	184	82	28	70	.400	13	32	.406	13	19	.684	4	11	15	20	26	0	8	2	13	8.8	3.9	0.7	1.0	.329
99-00	Detroit	6	0	45	10	4	14	.286	0	7	.000	2	2	1.000	3	4	7	3	8	0	0	0	3	7.5	1.7	1.2	0.5	.093
NBA Season Totals		27	0	229	92	32	84	.381	13	39	.333	15	21	.714	7	15	22	23	34	0	8	2	16	8.5	3.4	0.8	0.9	

• BROWN, Marshall

Marshall Brown

Born: 1918.   Height: 6'3".   Weight: 170 lbs.   Drafted: —   College: Texas Tech

YEAR	TEAM	GP	GS	MIN	PTS	FGM	FGA	FG%	3PM	3PA	3P%	FTM	FTA	FT%	ORB	DRB	TRB	AST	PF	DQ	STL	BLK	TO	MPG	PPG	RPG	APG	PCM
45-46	Cleveland-N	10	....	....	36	12	....	....	....	....	....	12	....	....	....	....	....	....	....	....	....	....	....	3.6	....	....	....	
NBL Season Totals		10	....	....	36	12	....	....	....	....	....	12	....	....	....	....	....	....	....	....	....	....	....	3.6	....	....	....	

• BROWN, Mike

Michael (Bear) Brown

Born: July 19, 1963. Newark, NJ, United States.   Height: 6'9".   Weight: 257 lbs.   Drafted: 1985   College: George Washington

YEAR	TEAM	GP	GS	MIN	PTS	FGM	FGA	FG%	3PM	3PA	3P%	FTM	FTA	FT%	ORB	DRB	TRB	AST	PF	DQ	STL	BLK	TO	MPG	PPG	RPG	APG	PCM
86-87	Chicago	62	3	818	258	106	201	.527	0	0	.000	46	72	.639	71	143	214	24	129	2	20	7	62	13.2	4.2	3.5	0.4	.354
87-88	Chicago	46	27	591	197	78	174	.448	0	1	.000	41	71	.577	66	93	159	28	85	0	11	4	37	12.8	4.3	3.5	0.6	.358
88-89	Utah	66	16	1051	300	104	248	.419	0	0	.000	92	130	.708	92	166	258	41	133	0	25	17	79	15.9	4.5	3.9	0.6	.320
89-90	Utah	82	0	1397	512	177	344	.515	1	2	.500	157	199	.789	111	262	373	47	187	0	32	28	90	17.0	6.2	4.5	0.6	.444
90-91	Utah	82	2	1391	390	129	284	.454	0	0	.000	132	178	.742	109	228	337	49	166	0	29	24	82	17.0	4.8	4.1	0.6	.349
91-92	Utah	82	1	1783	632	221	488	.453	0	1	.000	190	285	.667	187	289	476	81	196	1	42	34	107	21.7	7.7	5.8	1.0	.420
92-93	Utah	82	21	1541	465	176	409	.430	0	1	.000	113	164	.689	147	244	391	64	190	1	32	32	98	18.8	5.7	4.8	0.8	.343
93-94	Minnesota	82	40	1921	299	111	260	.427	0	2	.000	77	118	.653	119	328	447	72	218	4	51	29	74	23.4	3.6	5.5	0.9	.280
94-95	Minnesota	27	0	213	35	10	40	.250	0	1	.000	15	27	.556	9	36	45	10	35	0	7	0	16	7.9	1.3	1.7	0.4	.137
95-96	Philadelphia	9	1	162	26	9	16	.563	0	0	.000	8	17	.471	14	23	37	3	24	1	3	2	6	18.0	2.9	4.1	0.3	.253
96-97	Phoenix	6	1	83	16	5	12	.417	0	0	.000	6	10	.600	9	16	25	5	9	0	1	2	2	13.8	2.7	4.2	0.8	.397
NBA Season Totals		626	112	10951	3130	1126	2476	.455	1	8	.125	877	1271	.690	934	1828	2762	424	1372	9	253	170	653	17.5	5.0	4.4	0.7	....
86-87	Chicago	1	0	3	0	0	1	.000	0	0	.000	0	0	.000	0	0	0	0	1	0	1	0	1	3.0	0.0	0.0	0.0	-.466
87-88	Chicago	1	0	4	1	0	0	.000	0	0	.000	1	2	.500	0	0	0	1	0	0	1	0	0	4.0	1.0	0.0	1.0	.634
88-89	Utah	2	1	11	0	0	2	.000	0	0	.000	0	0	.000	0	2	2	0	3	0	0	0	0	5.5	0.0	1.0	0.0	-.127
89-90	Utah	5	0	67	18	7	15	.467	0	0	.000	4	5	.800	5	5	10	3	11	0	1	1	5	13.4	3.6	2.0	0.6	.218
90-91	Utah	9	0	223	86	27	56	.482	0	0	.000	32	38	.842	20	46	66	5	36	1	3	1	12	24.8	9.6	7.3	0.6	.443
91-92	Utah	16	0	274	92	30	75	.400	0	0	.000	32	41	.780	22	43	65	11	43	0	2	2	16	17.1	5.8	4.1	0.7	.318
92-93	Utah	5	0	93	33	13	25	.520	0	0	.000	7	11	.636	4	12	16	2	9	0	0	1	5	18.6	6.6	3.2	0.4	.313
96-97	Phoenix	4	0	27	11	2	5	.400	0	0	.000	7	8	.875	2	2	4	1	6	0	0	0	1	6.8	2.8	1.0	0.3	.326
97-98	Phoenix	1	0	1	0	0	0	.000	0	0	.000	0	0	.000	0	0	0	0	0	0	0	0	0	1.0	0.0	0.0	0.0	.000
NBA Playoff Totals		44	1	703	241	79	179	.441	0	0	.000	83	105	.790	53	110	163	23	109	1	8	5	40	16.0	5.5	3.7	0.5	....

• BROWN, Myron

Julian Myron Brown

Born: Nov. 3, 1969. McKees Rocks, PA, United States.   Height: 6'3".   Weight: 180 lbs.   Drafted: 1991   College: Slippery Rock

YEAR	TEAM	GP	GS	MIN	PTS	FGM	FGA	FG%	3PM	3PA	3P%	FTM	FTA	FT%	ORB	DRB	TRB	AST	PF	DQ	STL	BLK	TO	MPG	PPG	RPG	APG	PCM
91-92	Minnesota	4	0	20	9	4	6	.667	1	3	.333	0	0	.000	0	3	3	6	2	0	1	0	4	5.0	2.3	0.8	1.5	.632
NBA Season Totals		4	0	20	9	4	6	.667	1	3	.333	0	0	.000	0	3	3	6	2	0	1	0	4	5.0	2.3	0.8	1.5	....

• BROWN, P.J.

Collier (P.J., Big Cat) Brown Jr.

Born: Oct. 14, 1969. Detroit, MI, United States.   Height: 6'11".   Weight: 225 lbs.   Drafted: 1992   College: Louisiana Tech

YEAR	TEAM	GP	GS	MIN	PTS	FGM	FGA	FG%	3PM	3PA	3P%	FTM	FTA	FT%	ORB	DRB	TRB	AST	PF	DQ	STL	BLK	TO	MPG	PPG	RPG	APG	PCM
93-94	New Jersey	79	54	1950	450	167	402	.415	1	6	.167	115	152	.757	188	305	493	93	177	1	71	93	71	24.7	5.7	6.2	1.2	.397
94-95	New Jersey	80	63	2466	651	254	570	.446	4	24	.167	139	207	.671	178	309	487	135	262	8	69	135	80	30.8	8.1	6.1	1.7	.372
95-96	New Jersey	81	81	2942	915	354	798	.444	3	15	.200	204	265	.770	215	345	560	165	249	6	79	100	130	36.3	11.3	6.9	2.0	.374
96-97	Miami	80	71	2592	761	300	656	.457	0	2	.000	161	220	.732	239	431	670	92	283	7	85	98	112	32.4	9.5	8.4	1.2	.408
97-98	Miami	74	74	2362	707	278	590	.471	0	0	.000	151	197	.766	235	400	635	103	264	9	66	98	96	31.9	9.6	8.6	1.4	.438

YEAR	TEAM	GP	GS	MIN	PTS	FGM	FGA	FG%	3PM	3PA	3P%	FTM	FTA	FT%	ORB	DRB	TRB	AST	PF	DQ	STL	BLK	TO	MPG	PPG	RPG	APG	PCM
98-99	Miami	50	50	1611	571	229	477	.480	0	0	.000	113	146	.774	115	231	346	66	166	2	46	48	69	32.2	11.4	6.9	1.3	.413
99-00	Miami	80	80	2302	764	322	671	.480	0	1	.000	120	159	.755	216	384	600	145	264	4	65	61	100	28.8	9.6	7.5	1.8	.450
00-01	Charlotte	80	79	2811	676	249	561	.444	0	4	.000	178	209	.852	257	485	742	127	260	6	78	92	108	35.1	8.5	9.3	1.6	.401
01-02	Charlotte	80	80	2563	669	250	527	.474	0	0	.000	169	197	.858	273	513	786	107	222	1	59	78	85	32.0	8.4	9.8	1.3	.461
02-03	New Orleans	78	78	2609	832	319	601	.531	0	3	.000	194	232	.836	243	458	701	147	201	3	67	80	98	33.4	10.7	9.0	1.9	.502
NBA Season Totals		762	710	24208	6996	2722	5853	.465	8	55	.145	1544	1984	.778	2159	3861	6020	1180	2348	46	685	883	949	31.8	9.2	7.9	1.5	....
93-94	New Jersey	4	1	56	12	2	9	.222	0	0	.000	8	8	1.000	4	4	8	3	13	0	0	2	3	14.0	3.0	2.0	0.8	.166
96-97	Miami	15	15	451	122	42	103	.408	0	0	.000	38	53	.717	48	81	129	10	40	0	9	20	16	30.1	8.1	8.6	0.7	.405
97-98	Miami	5	5	190	46	19	37	.514	0	0	.000	8	22	.364	15	29	44	4	22	1	7	3	6	38.0	9.2	8.8	0.8	.323
98-99	Miami	5	5	144	51	21	45	.467	0	1	.000	9	10	.900	14	17	31	5	17	0	2	2	3	28.8	10.2	6.2	1.0	.387
99-00	Miami	10	10	308	75	35	82	.427	0	0	.000	5	6	.833	26	56	82	11	42	3	8	4	11	30.8	7.5	8.2	1.1	.325
00-01	Charlotte	10	10	385	80	28	67	.418	0	0	.000	24	29	.828	41	59	100	11	31	1	12	14	12	38.5	8.0	10.0	1.1	.372
01-02	Charlotte	9	9	331	92	32	75	.427	0	0	.000	28	37	.757	29	57	86	14	37	3	6	12	8	36.8	10.2	9.6	1.6	.406
02-03	New Orleans	6	6	193	61	21	44	.477	0	0	.000	19	25	.760	20	26	46	6	22	0	7	3	5	32.2	10.2	7.7	1.0	.416
NBA Playoff Totals		64	61	2058	539	200	462	.433	0	1	.000	139	190	.732	197	329	526	64	224	8	51	60	64	32.2	8.4	8.2	1.0	....

• BROWN, Randy

Randy Brown

Born: May 22, 1968. Chicago, IL, United States.   Height: 6'2".   Weight: 190 lbs.   Drafted: 1991   College: New Mexico State

YEAR	TEAM	GP	GS	MIN	PTS	FGM	FGA	FG%	3PM	3PA	3P%	FTM	FTA	FT%	ORB	DRB	TRB	AST	PF	DQ	STL	BLK	TO	MPG	PPG	RPG	APG	PCM
91-92	Sacramento	56	0	535	192	77	169	.456	0	6	.000	38	58	.655	26	43	69	59	68	0	35	12	45	9.6	3.4	1.2	1.1	.364
92-93	Sacramento	75	34	1726	567	225	486	.463	2	6	.333	115	157	.732	75	137	212	196	206	4	108	34	120	23.0	7.6	2.8	2.6	.368
93-94	Sacramento	61	2	1041	273	110	251	.438	0	4	.000	53	87	.609	40	72	112	133	132	2	63	14	73	17.1	4.5	1.8	2.2	.305
94-95	Sacramento	67	2	1086	317	124	287	.432	14	47	.298	55	82	.671	24	84	108	133	153	0	99	19	80	16.2	4.7	1.6	2.0	.330
95-96	Chicago	68	0	671	185	78	192	.406	1	11	.091	28	46	.609	17	49	66	73	88	0	57	12	34	9.9	2.7	1.0	1.1	.299
96-97	Chicago	72	3	1057	341	140	333	.420	4	22	.182	57	84	.679	34	77	111	133	116	0	81	17	58	14.7	4.7	1.5	1.8	.357
97-98	Chicago	71	6	1147	288	116	302	.384	0	5	.000	56	78	.718	34	60	94	151	118	0	71	12	64	16.2	4.1	1.3	2.1	.280
98-99	Chicago	39	32	1139	342	132	319	.414	0	10	.000	78	103	.757	27	105	132	149	93	1	68	8	80	29.2	8.8	3.4	3.8	.354
99-00	Chicago	59	55	1625	379	157	435	.361	3	6	.500	62	84	.738	23	121	144	202	120	1	61	15	105	27.5	6.4	2.4	3.4	.238
00-01	Boston	54	35	1238	223	100	237	.422	0	3	.000	23	40	.575	23	76	99	154	132	1	62	10	56	22.9	4.1	1.8	2.9	.247
01-02	Boston	1	0	6	0	0	1	.000	0	0	.000	0	0	.000	0	0	0	2	1	0	0	1	0	6.0	0.0	0.0	2.0	.289
02-03	Phoenix	32	0	262	41	16	43	.372	0	0	.000	9	12	.750	3	23	26	35	36	0	17	2	17	8.2	1.3	0.8	1.1	.238
NBA Season Totals		655	169	11533	3148	1275	3055	.417	24	120	.200	574	831	.691	326	847	1173	1420	1263	9	722	156	732	17.6	4.8	1.8	2.2	....
95-96	Chicago	16	0	112	44	16	28	.571	3	6	.500	9	12	.750	3	7	10	7	18	0	5	1	7	7.0	2.8	0.6	0.4	.346
96-97	Chicago	17	0	98	21	9	30	.300	0	0	.000	3	5	.600	3	7	10	6	22	0	8	2	4	5.8	1.2	0.6	0.4	.118
97-98	Chicago	14	0	71	9	2	12	.167	0	0	.000	5	6	.833	3	6	9	9	6	0	2	0	7	5.1	0.6	0.6	0.6	.142
NBA Playoff Totals		47	0	281	74	27	70	.386	3	6	.500	17	23	.739	9	20	29	22	46	0	15	3	18	6.0	1.6	0.6	0.5	....

• BROWN, Raymond

Raymond Brown

Born: July 5, 1965. Atlanta, GA, United States.   Height: 6'8".   Weight: 220 lbs.   Drafted: —   College: Idaho

YEAR	TEAM	GP	GS	MIN	PTS	FGM	FGA	FG%	3PM	3PA	3P%	FTM	FTA	FT%	ORB	DRB	TRB	AST	PF	DQ	STL	BLK	TO	MPG	PPG	RPG	APG	PCM
89-90	Utah	16	0	56	16	8	28	.286	0	0	.000	0	2	.000	10	5	15	4	11	0	0	0	6	3.5	1.0	0.9	0.3	.069
NBA Season Totals		16	0	56	16	8	28	.286	0	0	.000	0	2	.000	10	5	15	4	11	0	0	0	6	3.5	1.0	0.9	0.3	....
89-90	Utah	3	0	6	0	0	0	.000	0	0	.000	0	0	.000	0	0	0	0	2	0	0	0	0	2.0	0.0	0.0	0.0	-.156
NBA Playoff Totals		3	0	6	0	0	0	.000	0	0	.000	0	0	.000	0	0	0	0	2	0	0	0	0	2.0	0.0	0.0	0.0	....

• BROWN, Rickey

Rickey Darnell Brown

Born: Aug. 20, 1958. Madison County, MS, United States.   Height: 6'10".   Weight: 215 lbs.   Drafted: 1980   College: Mississippi State

YEAR	TEAM	GP	GS	MIN	PTS	FGM	FGA	FG%	3PM	3PA	3P%	FTM	FTA	FT%	ORB	DRB	TRB	AST	PF	DQ	STL	BLK	TO	MPG	PPG	RPG	APG	PCM
80-81	Golden State	45	....	580	182	83	162	.512	0	0	.000	16	21	.762	52	114	166	21	103	4	9	14	32	12.9	4.0	3.7	0.5	.391
81-82	Golden State	82	11	1260	470	192	418	.459	0	0	.000	86	122	.705	136	228	364	19	243	4	36	29	82	15.4	5.7	4.4	0.2	.376
82-83	Golden State	50	7	743	276	118	245	.482	0	2	.000	40	65	.615	56	122	178	16	126	0	8	21	60	14.9	5.5	3.6	0.3	.328
82-83	Atlanta	26	0	305	123	49	104	.471	0	1	.000	25	40	.625	35	53	88	9	46	1	5	5	21	11.7	4.7	3.4	0.3	.411
83-84	Atlanta	68	.3	785	236	94	201	.468	0	0	.000	48	65	.738	67	114	181	29	161	4	18	23	54	11.5	3.5	2.7	0.4	.307
84-85	Atlanta	69	5	814	195	78	192	.406	0	0	.000	39	68	.574	76	147	223	25	117	0	19	22	48	11.8	2.8	3.2	0.4	.306
NBA Season Totals		340	26	4487	1482	614	1322	.464	0	3	.000	254	381	.667	422	778	1200	119	796	13	95	114	297	13.2	4.4	3.5	0.4	....
82-83	Atlanta	2	0	15	3	1	3	.333	0	0	.000	1	2	.500	0	3	3	0	3	0	0	0	0	7.5	1.5	1.5	0.0	.140
83-84	Atlanta	5	0	83	30	10	21	.476	0	0	.000	10	12	.833	5	14	19	2	19	0	0	1	5	16.6	6.0	3.8	0.4	.314
NBA Playoff Totals		7	0	98	33	11	24	.458	0	0	.000	11	14	.786	5	17	22	2	22	0	0	1	5	14.0	4.7	3.1	0.3	....

• BROWN, Roger

Roger A. Brown

Born: May 22, 1942. Brooklyn, NY, United States. Died: Mar.4, 1997.   Height: 6'5".   Weight: 205 lbs.   Drafted: —   College: Dayton

YEAR	TEAM	GP	GS	MIN	PTS	FGM	FGA	FG%	3PM	3PA	3P%	FTM	FTA	FT%	ORB	DRB	TRB	AST	PF	DQ	STL	BLK	TO	MPG	PPG	RPG	APG	PCM
67-68	Indiana-A	76	....	2974	1492	544	1286	.423	14	54	.259	390	517	.754	....	....	647	327	296	10	....	....	265	39.1	19.6	8.5	4.3	.545
68-69	Indiana-A	75	....	2658	1573	563	1169	.482	5	16	.313	442	563	.785	223	287	510	345	281	11	....	....	215	35.4	21.0	6.8	4.6	.644
69-70	Indiana-A	84	....	3495	1935	719	1444	.498	40	120	.333	457	562	.813	178	442	620	392	308	3	....	....	229	41.6	23.0	7.4	4.7	.605
70-71	Indiana-A	82	....	3364	1690	610	1266	.482	63	223	.283	407	512	.795	176	393	569	395	289	5	....	....	232	41.0	20.6	6.9	4.8	.576
71-72	Indiana-A	78	....	2987	1444	532	1112	.478	57	185	.308	323	401	.805	163	339	502	306	227	6	....	....	214	38.3	18.5	6.4	3.9	.530
72-73	Indiana-A	72	....	2177	909	332	700	.474	42	118	.356	203	247	.822	111	237	348	204	181	3	....	....	120	30.2	12.6	4.8	2.8	.466
73-74	Indiana-A	82	....	2527	969	379	829	.457	56	155	.361	155	200	.775	112	278	390	232	248	....	56	60	125	30.8	11.8	4.8	2.8	.418
74-75	Indiana-A	10	....	133	46	20	46	.435	3	12	.250	3	4	.750	12	11	23	13	19	....	7	1	14	13.3	4.6	2.3	1.3	.368
74-75	Memphis-A	7	....	209	82	30	82	.366	8	24	.333	14	16	.875	11	20	31	21	12	....	3	5	11	29.9	11.7	4.4	3.0	.385
74-75	Utah-A	39	....	930	358	131	293	.447	24	64	.375	72	94	.766	33	85	118	80	68	....	37	15	69	23.8	9.2	3.0	2.1	.396
ABA Season Totals		605	....	21454	10498	3860	8227	.469	312	971	.321	2466	3116	.791	1019	2092	3758	2315	1929	38	103	81	1494	35.5	17.4	6.2	3.8	....
67-68	Indiana-A	3	....	129	65	26	57	.456	0	3	.000	13	21	.619	....	....	31	20	14	2	....	....	12	43.0	21.7	10.3	6.7	.614
68-69	Indiana-A	17	....	668	459	169	329	.514	1	5	.200	120	155	.774	....	....	143	57	86	6	....	....	49	39.3	27.0	8.4	3.4	.685
69-70	Indiana-A	15	....	693	428	151	318	.475	18	51	.353	108	131	.824	41	110	151	84	58	2	....	....	48	46.2	28.5	10.1	5.6	.686
70-71	Indiana-A	11	....	477	240	88	194	.454	10	33	.303	54	69	.783	26	58	84	53	42	1	....	....	22	43.4	21.8	7.6	4.8	.552

YEAR	TEAM	GP	GS	MIN	PTS	FGM	FGA	FG%	3PM	3PA	3P%	FTM	FTA	FT%	ORB	DRB	TRB	AST	PF	DQ	STL	BLK	TO	MPG	PPG	RPG	APG	PCM
71-72	Indiana-A	20	....	845	409	160	329	.486	15	34	.441	74	90	.822	47	74	121	81	65	0	....	....	35	42.3	20.5	6.1	4.1	.499
72-73	Indiana-A	17	....	584	214	82	160	.513	13	29	.448	37	49	.755	20	54	74	41	58	0	....	....	24	34.4	12.6	4.4	2.4	.384
73-74	Indiana-A	13	....	452	183	67	151	.444	9	27	.333	40	49	.816	23	52	75	48	44	....	9	13	11	34.8	14.1	5.8	3.7	.459
74-75	Indiana-A	14	....	182	62	22	52	.423	2	8	.250	16	19	.842	8	18	26	21	24	....	4	8	6	13.0	4.4	1.9	1.5	.384
ABA Playoff Totals		**110**	....	**4030**	**2060**	**765**	1590	.481	68	190	.358	462	583	.792	165	366	705	405	391	**11**	13	21	207	36.6	18.7	6.4	3.7	....

• BROWN, Roger

W. Roger Brown

Born: Feb. 23, 1950. Chicago, IL, United States.   Height: 6'11".   Weight: 225 lbs.   Drafted: 1971   College: Kansas

YEAR	TEAM	GP	GS	MIN	PTS	FGM	FGA	FG%	3PM	3PA	3P%	FTM	FTA	FT%	ORB	DRB	TRB	AST	PF	DQ	STL	BLK	TO	MPG	PPG	RPG	APG	PCM
72-73	Carolina-A	62	....	579	146	59	129	.457	0	0	.000	28	51	.549	62	116	178	25	120	2	....	....	46	9.3	2.4	2.9	0.4	.356
72-73	LA Lakers	1	....	5	1	0	0	.000	....	....	....	1	3	.333	....	....	0	0	1	0	....	....	....	5.0	1.0	0.0	0.0	-.057
73-74	San Antonio-A	2	....	26	10	5	6	.833	0	0	.000	0	0	.000	3	3	6	1	4	....	0	0	2	13.0	5.0	3.0	0.5	.528
73-74	Virginia-A	61	....	964	220	93	254	.366	0	0	.000	34	56	.607	142	204	346	45	125	....	23	62	78	15.8	3.6	5.7	0.7	.381
75-76	Denver-A	37	....	291	74	28	61	.459	2	2	1.000	16	24	.667	25	50	75	22	63	....	8	22	17	7.9	2.0	2.0	0.6	.358
75-76	Detroit	29	....	454	72	29	72	.403	....	....	....	14	18	.778	47	83	130	12	76	1	6	25	....	15.7	2.5	4.5	0.4	.278
76-77	Detroit	43	....	322	60	21	56	.375	....	....	....	18	26	.692	31	59	90	12	68	4	15	18	....	7.5	1.4	2.1	0.3	.274
79-80	Chicago	4	....	37	2	1	3	.333	0	0	.000	0	0	.000	2	8	10	1	4	0	0	3	0	9.3	0.5	2.5	0.3	.304
NBA Season Totals		**77**	....	**818**	**135**	**51**	131	.389	0	0	.000	33	47	.702	80	150	230	25	149	5	21	46	0	10.6	1.8	3.0	0.3	....
ABA Season Totals		**162**	....	**1860**	**450**	**185**	450	.411	2	2	1.000	78	131	.595	232	373	605	93	312	2	31	84	143	11.5	2.8	3.7	0.6	....
Career Totals		**239**	....	**2678**	**585**	**236**	581	.406	2	2	1.000	111	178	.624	312	523	835	118	461	7	52	130	143	11.2	2.4	3.5	0.5	....
72-73	Carolina-A	7	....	40	11	5	7	.714	0	0	.000	1	1	1.000	4	7	11	1	6	0	....	....	3	5.7	1.6	1.6	0.1	.437
73-74	Virginia-A	5	....	50	20	9	19	.474	0	0	.000	2	3	.667	8	6	14	2	6	....	0	2	1	10.0	4.0	2.8	0.4	.454
75-76	Detroit	9	....	51	10	4	9	.444	....	....	....	2	4	.500	7	7	14	2	10	0	0	1	....	5.7	1.1	1.6	0.2	.291
76-77	Detroit	2	....	5	0	0	1	.000	....	....	....	0	0	.000	0	0	0	0	0	0	0	1	....	2.5	0.0	0.0	0.0	-.173
NBA Playoff Totals		**11**	....	**56**	**10**	**4**	10	.400	....	....	....	2	4	.500	7	7	14	2	10	0	0	2	....	5.1	0.9	1.3	0.2	....
ABA Playoff Totals		**12**	....	**90**	**31**	**14**	26	.538	0	0	.000	3	4	.750	12	13	25	3	12	0	0	2	4	7.5	2.6	2.1	0.3	....
Career Playoff Totals		**23**	....	**146**	**41**	**18**	36	.500	0	0	.000	5	8	.625	19	20	39	5	22	0	0	4	4	6.3	1.8	1.7	0.2	....

• BROWN, Stan

Stanley Brown

Born: June 27, 1929.   Height: 6'3".   Weight: 200 lbs.   Drafted: —   College: none

YEAR	TEAM	GP	GS	MIN	PTS	FGM	FGA	FG%	3PM	3PA	3P%	FTM	FTA	FT%	ORB	DRB	TRB	AST	PF	DQ	STL	BLK	TO	MPG	PPG	RPG	APG	PCM
47-48	Philadelphia	19	....		50	19	71	.268	....	....	....	12	19	.632	....	....		1	16	....	....	....	....		2.6		0.1	....
51-52	Philadelphia	15	....	141	54	22	63	.349	....	....	....	10	18	.556	....	....	17	9	32	0	....	....	....	9.4	3.6	1.1	0.6	.243
NBA Season Totals		**34**	....	**141**	**104**	**41**	134	.306	....	....	....	22	37	.595	....	....	17	10	48	0	....	....	....	4.1	3.1	0.5	0.3	....

• BROWN, Tierre

Tierre Brown

Born: June 3, 1979. Iowa, LA, United States.   Height: 6'2".   Weight: 189 lbs.   Drafted: —   College: McNeese State

YEAR	TEAM	GP	GS	MIN	PTS	FGM	FGA	FG%	3PM	3PA	3P%	FTM	FTA	FT%	ORB	DRB	TRB	AST	PF	DQ	STL	BLK	TO	MPG	PPG	RPG	APG	PCM
01-02	Houston	40	1	403	123	49	115	.426	4	12	.333	21	28	.750	12	30	42	70	26	0	19	3	40	10.1	3.1	1.1	1.8	.364
02-03	Cleveland	15	0	168	65	27	59	.458	0	1	.000	11	14	.786	8	22	30	39	9	0	13	0	22	11.2	4.3	2.0	2.6	.549
NBA Season Totals		**55**	**1**	**571**	**188**	**76**	174	.437	4	13	.308	32	42	.762	20	52	72	109	35	0	32	3	62	10.4	3.4	1.3	2.0	....

• BROWN, Tony

Anthony William Brown

Born: July 29, 1960. Chicago, IL, United States.   Height: 6'6".   Weight: 185 lbs.   Drafted: 1982   College: Arkansas

YEAR	TEAM	GP	GS	MIN	PTS	FGM	FGA	FG%	3PM	3PA	3P%	FTM	FTA	FT%	ORB	DRB	TRB	AST	PF	DQ	STL	BLK	TO	MPG	PPG	RPG	APG	PCM
84-85	Indiana	82	26	1586	544	214	465	.460	0	6	.000	116	171	.678	146	142	288	159	212	3	59	12	115	19.3	6.6	3.5	1.9	.368
85-86	Chicago	10	0	132	45	18	41	.439	0	2	.000	9	13	.692	5	11	16	14	16	0	5	1	4	13.2	4.5	1.6	1.4	.349
86-87	New Jersey	77	67	2339	873	358	810	.442	5	20	.250	152	206	.738	84	135	219	259	273	12	89	14	154	30.4	11.3	2.8	3.4	.313
88-89	Houston	14	0	91	36	14	45	.311	2	9	.222	6	8	.750	7	8	15	5	14	0	3	0	7	6.5	2.6	1.1	0.4	.168
88-89	Milwaukee	29	0	274	92	36	73	.493	2	7	.286	18	23	.783	15	14	29	21	28	0	12	4	9	9.4	3.2	1.0	0.7	.258
89-90	Milwaukee	61	10	635	219	88	206	.427	5	20	.250	38	56	.679	39	33	72	41	79	0	32	4	49	10.4	3.6	1.2	0.7	.255
90-91	LA Lakers	7	0	27	5	2	3	.667	1	1	1.000	0	0	.000	0	4	4	3	8	0	0	0	4	3.9	0.7	0.6	0.4	.131
90-91	Utah	23	0	267	78	28	77	.364	2	11	.182	20	23	.870	24	15	39	13	39	0	4	0	12	11.6	3.4	1.7	0.6	.208
91-92	LA Clippers	22	0	254	103	39	89	.438	7	22	.318	18	29	.621	9	19	28	16	31	0	12	1	13	11.5	4.7	1.3	0.7	.316
91-92	Seattle	35	2	401	168	63	160	.394	12	41	.293	30	37	.811	23	33	56	32	51	0	18	4	21	11.5	4.8	1.6	0.9	.345
NBA Season Totals		**360**	**105**	**6006**	**2163**	**860**	1969	.437	36	139	.259	407	566	.719	352	414	766	563	751	15	234	40	388	16.7	6.0	2.1	1.6	....
88-89	Milwaukee	6	0	69	11	4	11	.364	0	1	.000	3	4	.750	2	5	7	6	9	1	2	0	1	11.5	1.8	1.2	1.0	.199
89-90	Milwaukee	2	0	13	3	1	3	.333	1	1	1.000	0	0	.000	0	0	0	0	3	0	2	0	0	6.5	1.5	0.0	0.0	.123
90-91	Utah	4	0	29	9	4	8	.500	1	2	.500	0	0	.000	2	1	3	1	2	0	0	0	1	7.3	2.3	0.8	0.3	.251
91-92	Seattle	5	0	22	9	2	6	.333	1	4	.250	4	7	.571	0	2	2	2	3	0	0	0	0	4.4	1.8	0.4	0.4	.295
NBA Playoff Totals		**17**	**0**	**133**	**32**	**11**	28	.393	3	8	.375	7	11	.636	4	8	12	9	17	1	4	0	2	7.8	1.9	0.7	0.5	....

• BROWN, William

William (Rookie) Brown

Born: 1925.   Height: 6'4".   Weight: 190 lbs.   Drafted: 1948   College: Howard

YEAR	TEAM	GP	GS	MIN	PTS	FGM	FGA	FG%	3PM	3PA	3P%	FTM	FTA	FT%	ORB	DRB	TRB	AST	PF	DQ	STL	BLK	TO	MPG	PPG	RPG	APG	PCM
48-49	Dayton-N	10	....	....	48	19	....	....	....	....	....	10	20	.500	....	....	....	....	....	....	....	....	....	4.8	....	....	....
48-49	Waterloo-N	43	....	....	113	41	....	....	....	....	....	31	48	.646	....	....	....		55	....	....	....	....	2.6	....	....	....
NBL Season Totals		**53**	....	....	**161**	**60**	....	....	....	....	....	41	68	....	....	....	....		55	....	....	....	....	3.0	....	....	....

YEAR TEAM	GP	GS	MIN	PTS	FGM	FGA	FG%	3PM	3PA	3P%	FTM	FTA	FT%	ORB	DRB	TRB	AST	PF	DQ	STL	BLK	TO	MPG	PPG	RPG	APG	PCM

• BROWNE, Jim — James (Stretch) Browne

Born: Jan. 1, 1930. Midlothian, IL, United States. Height: 6'10". Weight: 235 lbs. Drafted: — College: none (HS: Tilden, IL)

YEAR TEAM	GP	GS	MIN	PTS	FGM	FGA	FG%	3PM	3PA	3P%	FTM	FTA	FT%	ORB	DRB	TRB	AST	PF	DQ	STL	BLK	TO	MPG	PPG	RPG	APG	PCM
48-49 Chicago	4	....	....	3	1	2	.500	....	....	....	1	2	.500	....	....	....	0	4	....	....	....	....	....	0.8	....	0.0	....
49-50 Denver	31	....	....	47	17	48	.354	....	....	....	13	27	.481	....	....	....	8	16	....	....	....	....	....	1.5	....	0.3	....
NBA Season Totals	35	....	....	50	18	50	.360	....	....	....	14	29	.483	....	....	....	8	20	....	....	....	....	....	1.4	....	0.2	....

• BRUNDY, Stanley — Stanley Dwayne Brundy

Born: Nov. 13, 1967. New Orleans, LA, United States. Height: 6'6". Weight: 210 lbs. Drafted: 1989 College: DePaul

YEAR TEAM	GP	GS	MIN	PTS	FGM	FGA	FG%	3PM	3PA	3P%	FTM	FTA	FT%	ORB	DRB	TRB	AST	PF	DQ	STL	BLK	TO	MPG	PPG	RPG	APG	PCM
89-90 New Jersey	16	0	128	37	15	30	.500	0	0	.000	7	18	.389	15	11	26	3	24	0	6	5	6	8.0	2.3	1.6	0.2	.303
NBA Season Totals	16	0	128	37	15	30	.500	0	0	.000	7	18	.389	15	11	26	3	24	0	6	5	6	8.0	2.3	1.6	0.2	

• BRUNKHORST, Brian — Brian J. (Bronk) Brunkhorst

Born: June 12, 1945. Owen, WI, United States. Height: 6'6". Weight: 208 lbs. Drafted: 1968 College: Marquette

YEAR TEAM	GP	GS	MIN	PTS	FGM	FGA	FG%	3PM	3PA	3P%	FTM	FTA	FT%	ORB	DRB	TRB	AST	PF	DQ	STL	BLK	TO	MPG	PPG	RPG	APG	PCM
68-69 Los Angeles-A	3	....	56	25	6	11	.545	0	0	.000	13	17	.765	6	7	13	3	8	0	....	....	5	18.7	8.3	4.3	1.0	.538
ABA Season Totals	3	....	56	25	6	11	.545	0	0	.000	13	17	.765	6	7	13	3	8	0	....	....	5	18.7	8.3	4.3	1.0	

• BRUNS, George — George William Bruns

Born: Aug. 30, 1946. Brooklyn, NY, United States. Height: 6' Weight: 160 lbs. Drafted: — College: Manhattan

YEAR TEAM	GP	GS	MIN	PTS	FGM	FGA	FG%	3PM	3PA	3P%	FTM	FTA	FT%	ORB	DRB	TRB	AST	PF	DQ	STL	BLK	TO	MPG	PPG	RPG	APG	PCM
72-73 New York-A	13	....	236	86	31	66	.470	2	4	.500	22	27	.815	1	7	8	36	26	0	....	....	20	18.2	6.6	0.6	2.8	.370
ABA Season Totals	13	....	236	86	31	66	.470	2	4	.500	22	27	.815	1	7	8	36	26	0	....	....	20	18.2	6.6	0.6	2.8	
72-73 New York-A	2	....	7	1	0	1	.000	0	0	.000	1	2	.500	0	0	0	1	3	0	....	....	2	3.5	0.5	0.0	0.5	-.085
ABA Playoff Totals	2	....	7	1	0	1	.000	0	0	.000	1	2	.500	0	0	0	1	3	0	....	....	2	3.5	0.5	0.0	0.5	

• BRUNSON, Rick — Rick Daniel Brunson

Born: June 14, 1972. Syracuse, NY, United States. Height: 6'4". Weight: 190 lbs. Drafted: — College: Temple

YEAR TEAM	GP	GS	MIN	PTS	FGM	FGA	FG%	3PM	3PA	3P%	FTM	FTA	FT%	ORB	DRB	TRB	AST	PF	DQ	STL	BLK	TO	MPG	PPG	RPG	APG	PCM
97-98 Portland	38	10	622	162	49	141	.348	22	61	.361	42	62	.677	14	42	56	100	55	0	25	3	53	16.4	4.3	1.5	2.6	.290
98-99 New York	17	0	95	17	6	21	.286	0	5	.000	5	18	.278	3	7	10	19	8	0	9	0	12	5.6	1.0	0.6	1.1	.228
99-00 New York	37	0	289	71	29	70	.414	2	13	.154	11	18	.611	3	24	27	49	35	0	9	1	31	7.8	1.9	0.7	1.3	.255
00-01 Boston	7	0	142	26	10	35	.286	2	11	.182	4	9	.444	2	7	9	24	16	0	7	1	9	20.3	3.7	1.3	3.4	.195
00-01 New York	15	0	66	20	8	19	.421	0	3	.000	4	6	.667	3	9	12	7	5	0	1	0	8	4.4	1.3	0.8	0.5	.291
01-02 Portland	59	2	520	125	45	113	.398	6	11	.545	29	41	.707	23	45	68	114	51	0	25	2	47	8.8	2.1	1.2	1.9	.390
02-03 Chicago	17	0	196	60	23	50	.460	4	6	.667	10	12	.833	4	15	19	36	20	0	10	3	17	11.5	3.5	1.1	2.1	.400
NBA Season Totals	190	12	1930	481	170	449	.379	36	110	.327	105	166	.633	52	149	201	349	190	0	86	10	177	10.2	2.5	1.1	1.8	
98-99 New York	9	0	18	6	2	5	.400	0	0	.000	2	2	1.000	1	0	1	2	3	0	0	0	4	2.0	0.7	0.1	0.2	.086
99-00 New York	3	0	4	0	0	1	.000	0	0	.000	0	0	.000	0	0	1	2	0	1	0	0	0	1.3	0.0	0.0	0.3	.046
00-01 New York	2	0	4	3	0	1	.000	0	0	.000	3	4	.750	0	0	0	0	0	0	0	0	1	2.0	1.5	0.0	0.0	.189
01-02 Portland	2	0	2	0	0	0	.000	0	0	.000	0	0	.000	0	0	0	0	0	0	0	0	0	1.0	0.0	0.0	0.0	.000
NBA Playoff Totals	16	0	28	9	2	7	.286	0	0	.000	5	6	.833	1	0	1	3	5	0	1	0	5	1.8	0.6	0.1	0.2	

• BRYANT, Em — Emmette Bryant

Born: Nov. 4, 1938. Chicago, IL, United States. Height: 6'1". Weight: 175 lbs. Drafted: 1964 College: DePaul

YEAR TEAM	GP	GS	MIN	PTS	FGM	FGA	FG%	3PM	3PA	3P%	FTM	FTA	FT%	ORB	DRB	TRB	AST	PF	DQ	STL	BLK	TO	MPG	PPG	RPG	APG	PCM
64-65 New York	77	....	1332	377	145	436	.333	....	....	....	87	133	.654	....	167	167	212	3	....	....	....	17.3	4.9	2.2	2.2	.292
65-66 New York	71	....	1193	498	212	449	.472	....	....	....	74	101	.733	....	170	216	215	4	....	....	....	16.8	7.0	2.4	3.0	.514
66-67 New York	63	....	1593	546	236	577	.409	....	....	....	74	114	.649	....	273	218	231	4	....	....	....	25.3	8.7	4.3	3.5	.406
67-68 New York	77	....	968	283	112	291	.385	....	....	....	59	86	.686	....	133	134	173	0	....	....	....	12.6	3.7	1.7	1.7	.338
68-69 Boston	80	....	1388	459	197	488	.404	....	....	....	65	100	.650	....	192	176	264	9	....	....	....	17.4	5.7	2.4	2.2	.329
69-70 Boston	71	....	1617	555	210	520	.404	....	....	....	135	181	.746	....	269	231	201	5	....	....	....	22.8	7.8	3.8	3.3	.414
70-71 Buffalo	73	....	2137	727	288	684	.421	....	....	....	151	203	.744	....	262	352	266	7	....	....	....	29.3	10.0	3.6	4.8	.410
71-72 Buffalo	54	....	1223	277	101	220	.459	....	....	....	75	125	.600	....	127	206	167	5	....	....	....	22.6	5.1	2.4	3.8	.347
NBA Season Totals	566	....	11451	3722	1501	3665	.410	....	....	....	720	1043	.690	....	1593	1700	1729	37	....	....	....	20.2	6.6	2.8	3.0	
66-67 New York	4	....	76	21	5	21	.238	....	....	....	11	11	1.000	....	9	9	16	0	....	....	....	19.0	5.3	2.3	2.3	.261
67-68 New York	5	....	75	12	4	13	.308	....	....	....	4	5	.800	....	14	7	13	0	....	....	....	15.0	2.4	2.8	1.4	.251
68-69 Boston	18	....	607	198	79	193	.409	....	....	....	40	53	.755	....	88	54	75	0	....	....	....	33.7	11.0	4.9	3.0	.333
NBA Playoff Totals	27	....	758	231	88	227	.388	....	....	....	55	69	.797	....	111	70	104	0	....	....	....	28.1	8.6	4.1	2.6	

• BRYANT, Joe — Joseph Washington (Jellybean) Bryant

Born: Oct. 19, 1954. Philadelphia, PA, United States. Height: 6'9". Weight: 185 lbs. Drafted: 1975 College: LaSalle

YEAR TEAM	GP	GS	MIN	PTS	FGM	FGA	FG%	3PM	3PA	3P%	FTM	FTA	FT%	ORB	DRB	TRB	AST	PF	DQ	STL	BLK	TO	MPG	PPG	RPG	APG	PCM
75-76 Philadelphia	75	....	1203	558	233	552	.422	....	....	....	92	147	.626	97	181	278	61	165	0	44	23	....	16.0	7.4	3.7	0.8	.414
76-77 Philadelphia	61	....	612	267	107	240	.446	....	....	....	53	70	.757	45	72	117	48	84	1	36	13	....	10.0	4.4	1.9	0.8	.432
77-78 Philadelphia	81	....	1236	491	190	436	.436	....	....	....	111	144	.771	103	177	280	129	185	1	56	24	113	15.3	6.1	3.5	1.6	.438
78-79 Philadelphia	70	....	1064	533	205	478	.429	....	....	....	123	170	.724	96	163	259	103	171	1	49	9	112	15.2	7.6	3.7	1.5	.458
79-80 San Diego	81	....	2328	754	294	682	.431	5	34	.147	161	217	.742	171	345	516	144	258	4	102	39	170	28.7	9.3	6.4	1.8	.369
80-81 San Diego	82	....	2359	953	379	791	.479	2	15	.133	193	244	.791	146	294	440	189	264	6	72	34	172	28.8	11.6	5.4	2.3	.416
81-82 San Diego	75	49	1988	884	341	701	.486	8	30	.267	194	247	.785	79	195	274	189	250	1	78	29	180	26.5	11.8	3.7	2.5	.403
82-83 Houston	81	56	2055	812	344	768	.448	8	36	.222	116	165	.703	88	189	277	186	258	4	82	30	178	25.4	10.0	3.4	2.3	.334
NBA Season Totals	606	105	12845	5252	2093	4648	.450	23	115	.200	1043	1404	.743	825	1616	2441	1049	1635	16	519	201	925	21.2	8.7	4.0	1.7	

YEAR	TEAM	GP	GS	MIN	PTS	FGM	FGA	FG%	3PM	3PA	3P%	FTM	FTA	FT%	ORB	DRB	TRB	AST	PF	DQ	STL	BLK	TO	MPG	PPG	RPG	APG	PCM
75-76	Philadelphia	3	....	43	23	9	12	.750	....	....	....	5	7	.714	3	10	13	1	11	1	1	1	....	14.3	7.7	4.3	0.3	.631
76-77	Philadelphia	10	....	74	29	12	31	.387	....	....	....	5	8	.625	2	13	15	7	13	0	6	2	....	7.4	2.9	1.5	0.7	.360
77-78	Philadelphia	10	....	122	50	21	47	.447	....	....	....	8	11	.727	7	18	25	9	22	0	6	1	5	12.2	5.0	2.5	0.9	.410
78-79	Philadelphia	7	....	35	21	10	26	.385	....	....	....	1	2	.500	0	1	1	4	8	0	1	0	2	5.0	3.0	0.1	0.6	.200
NBA Playoff Totals		30	....	274	123	52	116	.448	....	....	....	19	28	.679	12	42	54	21	54	1	14	4	7	9.1	4.1	1.8	0.7	....

• BRYANT, Kobe

Kobe Bean Bryant

Born: Aug. 23, 1978. Philadelphia, PA, United States. Height: 6'6". Weight: 200 lbs. Drafted: 1996 College: none (HS: Lower Merion, PA)

YEAR	TEAM	GP	GS	MIN	PTS	FGM	FGA	FG%	3PM	3PA	3P%	FTM	FTA	FT%	ORB	DRB	TRB	AST	PF	DQ	STL	BLK	TO	MPG	PPG	RPG	APG	PCM
96-97	LA Lakers	71	6	1103	539	176	422	.417	51	136	.375	136	166	.819	47	85	132	91	102	0	49	23	114	15.5	7.6	1.9	1.3	.389
97-98	LA Lakers	79	1	2056	1220	391	913	.428	75	220	.341	363	457	.794	79	163	242	199	180	1	74	40	158	26.0	15.4	3.1	2.5	.493
98-99	LA Lakers	50	50	1896	996	362	779	.465	27	101	.267	245	292	.839	53	211	264	190	153	3	72	50	157	37.9	19.9	5.3	3.8	.502
99-00	LA Lakers	66	62	2524	1485	554	1183	.468	46	144	.319	331	403	.821	108	308	416	323	220	4	106	62	182	38.2	22.5	6.3	4.9	.594
00-01	LA Lakers	68	68	2783	1938	701	1510	.464	61	200	.305	475	557	.853	104	295	399	338	222	3	114	43	220	40.9	28.5	5.9	5.0	.629
01-02	LA Lakers	80	80	3063	2019	749	1597	.469	33	132	.250	488	589	.829	112	329	441	438	228	1	118	35	223	38.3	25.2	5.5	5.5	.626
02-03	LA Lakers	82	82	3402	**2461**	**868**	1924	.451	124	324	.383	601	713	.843	106	458	564	481	218	0	181	67	288	41.5	30.0	6.9	5.9	.692
NBA Season Totals		496	349	16827	10658	3801	8328	.456	417	1257	.332	2639	3177	.831	609	1849	2458	2060	1323	12	714	320	1342	33.9	21.5	5.0	4.2	....
96-97	LA Lakers	9	0	133	74	21	55	.382	6	23	.261	26	30	.867	1	10	11	11	23	0	3	2	14	14.8	8.2	1.2	1.2	.326
97-98	LA Lakers	11	0	220	96	31	76	.408	3	14	.214	31	45	.689	7	14	21	16	28	0	3	8	11	20.0	8.7	1.9	1.5	.328
98-99	LA Lakers	8	8	315	158	61	142	.430	8	23	.348	28	35	.800	13	42	55	37	24	1	15	10	31	39.4	19.8	6.9	4.6	.498
99-00	LA Lakers	22	22	857	465	174	394	.442	22	64	.344	95	126	.754	26	72	98	97	89	1	32	32	55	39.0	21.1	4.5	4.4	.483
00-01	LA Lakers	16	16	694	471	168	358	.469	11	34	.324	124	151	.821	29	87	116	97	53	0	25	12	51	43.4	29.4	7.3	6.1	.667
01-02	LA Lakers	19	19	833	506	187	431	.434	22	58	.379	110	145	.759	28	83	111	87	65	1	27	17	54	43.8	26.6	5.8	4.6	.512
02-03	LA Lakers	12	12	531	385	137	317	.432	25	62	.403	86	104	.827	16	45	61	62	35	0	14	1	42	44.3	32.1	5.1	5.2	.558
NBA Playoff Totals		97	77	3583	2155	779	1773	.439	97	278	.349	500	636	.786	120	353	473	407	317	3	119	82	258	36.9	22.2	4.9	4.2	....

• BRYANT, Mark

Mark Craig Bryant

Born: Apr. 25, 1965. Glen Ridge, CA, United States. Height: 6'9". Weight: 245 lbs. Drafted: 1988 College: Seton Hall

YEAR	TEAM	GP	GS	MIN	PTS	FGM	FGA	FG%	3PM	3PA	3P%	FTM	FTA	FT%	ORB	DRB	TRB	AST	PF	DQ	STL	BLK	TO	MPG	PPG	RPG	APG	PCM
88-89	Portland	56	32	803	280	120	247	.486	0	0	.000	40	69	.580	65	114	179	33	144	3	20	7	39	14.3	5.0	3.2	0.6	.339
89-90	Portland	58	0	562	168	70	153	.458	0	0	.000	28	50	.560	54	92	146	13	93	0	18	9	23	9.7	2.9	2.5	0.2	.339
90-91	Portland	53	0	781	272	99	203	.488	0	1	.000	74	101	.733	65	125	190	27	120	0	15	12	32	14.7	5.1	3.6	0.5	.394
91-92	Portland	56	0	800	230	95	198	.480	0	3	.000	40	60	.667	87	114	201	41	105	0	26	8	28	14.3	4.1	3.6	0.7	.391
92-93	Portland	80	24	1396	476	186	370	.503	0	1	.000	104	148	.703	132	192	324	41	226	1	37	23	64	17.5	6.0	4.1	0.5	.373
93-94	Portland	79	10	1441	442	185	384	.482	0	1	.000	72	104	.692	117	198	315	37	187	0	32	29	63	18.2	5.6	4.0	0.5	.337
94-95	Portland	49	0	658	244	101	192	.526	1	2	.500	41	63	.651	55	106	161	28	109	1	19	16	39	13.4	5.0	3.3	0.6	.417
95-96	Houston	71	9	1587	611	242	446	.543	0	2	.000	127	177	.718	131	220	351	52	234	4	31	19	85	22.4	8.6	4.9	0.7	.402
96-97	Phoenix	41	18	1018	380	152	275	.553	0	0	.000	76	108	.704	67	145	212	47	136	4	22	5	45	24.8	9.3	5.2	1.1	.411
97-98	Phoenix	70	22	1110	291	109	225	.484	0	1	.000	73	95	.768	92	152	244	46	180	3	36	15	56	15.9	4.2	3.5	0.7	.325
98-99	Chicago	45	29	1204	407	168	348	.483	0	1	.000	71	110	.645	92	140	232	48	149	2	34	16	68	26.8	9.0	5.2	1.1	.338
99-00	Cleveland	75	50	1712	424	174	346	.503	0	0	.000	76	94	.809	126	226	352	61	250	5	31	31	87	22.8	5.7	4.7	0.8	.298
00-01	Dallas	18	1	101	19	8	20	.400	0	0	.000	3	5	.600	4	17	21	3	29	1	1	2	5	5.6	1.1	1.2	0.2	.145
01-02	San Antonio	30	3	206	56	25	55	.455	0	0	.000	6	8	.750	25	19	44	10	38	1	7	2	6	6.9	1.9	1.5	0.3	.312
02-03	Philadelphia	11	0	77	12	5	17	.294	0	0	.000	2	2	1.000	7	9	16	1	12	0	1	1	5	7.0	1.1	1.5	0.1	.111
02-03	Denver	3	0	14	1	0	1	.000	0	0	.000	1	2	.500	1	1	2	2	4	0	0	0	2	4.7	0.3	0.7	0.7	.000
02-03	Boston	2	0	9	0	0	1	.000	0	0	.000	0	0	.000	0	2	2	1	2	0	0	0	0	4.5	0.0	1.0	0.5	.121
NBA Season Totals		797	198	13479	4313	1739	3481	.500	1	12	.083	834	1196	.697	1120	1872	2992	491	2018	25	330	195	647	16.9	5.4	3.8	0.6	....
89-90	Portland	13	0	160	42	18	33	.545	0	0	.000	6	8	.750	9	20	29	3	27	1	3	2	12	12.3	3.2	2.2	0.2	.239
90-91	Portland	14	0	137	34	10	22	.455	0	0	.000	14	16	.875	14	18	32	2	25	0	2	1	4	9.8	2.4	2.3	0.1	.301
91-92	Portland	12	0	116	23	10	29	.345	0	0	.000	3	4	.750	11	18	29	1	22	0	3	0	9	9.7	1.9	2.4	0.1	.147
92-93	Portland	4	4	83	39	17	37	.459	0	0	.000	5	5	1.000	10	8	18	0	14	0	0	3	6	20.8	9.8	4.5	0.0	.335
93-94	Portland	4	1	64	10	5	17	.294	0	2	.000	0	0	.000	6	6	12	2	7	0	2	2	3	16.0	2.5	3.0	0.5	.154
94-95	Portland	2	0	6	2	1	2	.500	0	0	.000	0	2	.000	1	1	2	0	1	0	0	0	0	3.0	1.0	1.0	0.0	.255
95-96	Houston	8	0	145	54	21	35	.600	0	0	.000	12	15	.800	7	20	27	4	21	0	1	2	3	18.1	6.8	3.4	0.5	.408
96-97	Phoenix	4	0	36	11	4	10	.400	0	0	.000	3	3	1.000	1	3	4	0	4	0	0	0	2	9.0	2.8	1.0	0.0	.150
97-98	Phoenix	4	1	93	40	17	34	.500	0	0	.000	6	12	.500	9	14	23	1	16	1	4	2	3	23.3	10.0	5.8	0.3	.422
00-01	Dallas	4	0	34	2	1	2	.500	0	0	.000	0	0	.000	3	3	6	0	6	0	1	0	1	8.5	0.5	1.5	0.0	.112
01-02	San Antonio	9	4	91	21	9	20	.450	0	0	.000	3	6	.500	8	4	12	1	14	0	1	2	1	10.1	2.3	1.3	0.1	.188
02-03	Boston	1	0	2	0	0	0	.000	0	0	.000	0	0	.000	0	0	0	0	0	0	0	0	0	2.0	0.0	0.0	0.0	.000
NBA Playoff Totals		79	10	967	278	113	241	.469	0	2	.000	52	71	.732	79	115	194	14	157	2	17	14	44	12.2	3.5	2.5	0.2	....

• BRYANT, Wallace

Wallace Gordon Bryant Jr.

Born: July 14, 1959. Madrid, Spain. Height: 7' Weight: 245 lbs. Drafted: 1982 College: San Francisco

YEAR	TEAM	GP	GS	MIN	PTS	FGM	FGA	FG%	3PM	3PA	3P%	FTM	FTA	FT%	ORB	DRB	TRB	AST	PF	DQ	STL	BLK	TO	MPG	PPG	RPG	APG	PCM
83-84	Chicago	29	0	317	118	52	133	.391	0	0	.000	14	33	.424	37	43	80	13	48	0	9	11	17	10.9	4.1	2.8	0.4	.324
84-85	Dallas	56	35	860	164	67	148	.453	0	0	.000	30	44	.682	74	167	241	84	110	1	21	24	45	15.4	2.9	4.3	1.5	.401
85-86	Dallas	9	8	154	28	11	30	.367	0	0	.000	6	11	.545	9	24	33	11	26	2	3	2	7	17.1	3.1	3.7	1.2	.237
85-86	LA Clippers	8	0	64	13	4	18	.222	0	0	.000	5	8	.625	8	12	20	4	12	0	2	3	2	8.0	1.6	2.5	0.5	.292
NBA Season Totals		102	43	1395	323	134	329	.407	0	0	.000	55	96	.573	128	246	374	112	196	3	35	40	71	13.7	3.2	3.7	1.1	....
84-85	Dallas	2	1	36	2	0	1	.000	0	0	.000	2	2	1.000	1	6	7	1	5	0	1	1	2	18.0	1.0	3.5	0.5	.176
NBA Playoff Totals		2	1	36	2	0	1	.000	0	0	.000	2	2	1.000	1	6	7	1	5	0	1	1	2	18.0	1.0	3.5	0.5	....

• BRYN, Torgeir

Torgeir Bryn

Born: Aug. 8, 1964. Oslo, Norway. Height: 6'9". Weight: 250 lbs. Drafted: — College: SW Texas State

YEAR	TEAM	GP	GS	MIN	PTS	FGM	FGA	FG%	3PM	3PA	3P%	FTM	FTA	FT%	ORB	DRB	TRB	AST	PF	DQ	STL	BLK	TO	MPG	PPG	RPG	APG	PCM
89-90	LA Clippers	3	0	10	4	0	2	.000	0	0	.000	4	6	.667	0	2	2	0	5	0	2	1	1	3.3	1.3	0.7	0.0	.259
NBA Season Totals		3	0	10	4	0	2	.000	0	0	.000	4	6	.667	0	2	2	0	5	0	2	1	1	3.3	1.3	0.7	0.0	....

YEAR	TEAM	GP	GS	MIN	PTS	FGM	FGA	FG%	3PM	3PA	3P%	FTM	FTA	FT%	ORB	DRB	TRB	AST	PF	DQ	STL	BLK	TO	MPG	PPG	RPG	APG	PCM

• BUCCI, George

George P. (The King) Bucci Jr.

Born: July 9, 1953. Cornwall, NY, United States.   Height: 6'3".   Weight: 200 lbs.   Drafted: 1975   College: Manhattan

75-76	New York-A	33	....	237	128	50	124	.403	0	4	.000	28	41	.683	15	22	37	15	19	....	12	3	22	7.2	3.9	1.1	0.5	.411
ABA Season Totals		33	....	237	128	50	124	.403	0	4	.000	28	41	.683	15	22	37	15	19	....	12	3	22	7.2	3.9	1.1	0.5	....
75-76	New York-A	2	....	9	8	3	7	.429	1	1	1.000	1	2	.500	0	0	0	0	2	....	0	0	0	4.5	4.0	0.0	0.0	.344
ABA Playoff Totals		2	....	9	8	3	7	.429	1	1	1.000	1	2	.500	0	0	0	0	2	....	0	0	0	4.5	4.0	0.0	0.0	

• BUCKHALTER, Joe

Joseph Buckhalter

Born: Aug. 1, 1937.   Height: 6'7".   Weight: 210 lbs.   Drafted: 1958   College: Tennessee State

61-62	Cincinnati	63	....	728	373	153	334	.458	....	....	....	67	108	.620	....	....	262	43	123	1	....	....	....	11.6	5.9	4.2	0.7	.583
62-63	Cincinnati	2	....	12	2	0	5	.000	....	....	....	2	2	1.000	....	....	3	0	1	0	....	....	....	6.0	1.0	1.5	0.0	.002
NBA Season Totals		65	....	740	375	153	339	.451	....	....	....	69	110	.627	....	....	265	43	124	1	....	....	....	11.4	5.8	4.1	0.7	
61-62	Cincinnati	4	....	60	34	16	38	.421	....	....	....	2	3	.667	....	....	22	4	14	0	....	....	....	15.0	8.5	5.5	1.0	.550
NBA Playoff Totals		4	....	60	34	16	38	.421	....	....	....	2	3	.667	....	....	22	4	14	0	....	....	....	15.0	8.5	5.5	1.0	

• BUCKNALL, Steve

Steven Lee Bucknall

Born: Mar. 17, 1966. London, Great Britain.   Height: 6'6".   Weight: 215 lbs.   Drafted: —   College: North Carolina

| 89-90 | LA Lakers | 18 | 0 | 75 | 23 | 9 | 33 | .273 | 0 | 1 | .000 | 5 | 6 | .833 | 5 | 2 | 7 | 10 | 10 | 0 | 2 | 1 | 11 | 4.2 | 1.3 | 0.4 | 0.6 | .067 |
| **NBA Season Totals** | | 18 | 0 | 75 | 23 | 9 | 33 | .273 | 0 | 1 | .000 | 5 | 6 | .833 | 5 | 2 | 7 | 10 | 10 | 0 | 2 | 1 | 11 | 4.2 | 1.3 | 0.4 | 0.6 | .... |

• BUCKNER, Cleveland

Cleveland Buckner

Born: Aug. 17, 1938. Yazoo City, MS, United States.   Height: 6'9".   Weight: 210 lbs.   Drafted: 1961   College: Jackson State

61-62	New York	62	....	696	399	158	367	.431	....	....	....	83	133	.624	....	....	236	39	114	1	....	....	....	11.2	6.4	3.8	0.6	.580
62-63	New York	6	....	27	12	5	10	.500	....	....	....	2	4	.500	....	....	4	5	6	0	....	....	....	4.5	2.0	0.7	0.8	.522
NBA Season Totals		68	....	723	411	163	377	.432	....	....	....	85	137	.620	....	....	240	44	120	1	....	....	....	10.6	6.0	3.5	0.6	

• BUCKNER, Greg

Gregory Derayle Buckner

Born: Sept. 16, 1976. Hopkinsville, KY, United States.   Height: 6'4".   Weight: 210 lbs.   Drafted: 1998   College: Clemson

99-00	Dallas	48	1	923	275	111	233	.476	10	26	.385	43	63	.683	56	118	174	55	148	1	38	20	36	19.2	5.7	3.6	1.1	.353
00-01	Dallas	37	9	820	229	84	192	.438	2	7	.286	59	81	.728	60	97	157	49	118	2	33	9	27	22.2	6.2	4.2	1.3	.339
01-02	Dallas	44	16	885	253	104	198	.525	5	16	.313	40	58	.690	67	106	173	48	124	1	31	19	27	20.1	5.8	3.9	1.1	.377
02-03	Philadelphia	75	5	1513	450	185	398	.465	15	55	.273	65	81	.802	72	144	216	96	203	0	72	16	62	20.2	6.0	2.9	1.3	.318
NBA Season Totals		204	31	4141	1207	484	1021	.474	32	104	.308	207	283	.731	255	465	720	248	593	4	174	64	152	20.3	5.9	3.5	1.2	
00-01	Dallas	5	0	75	30	11	23	.478	1	3	.333	7	10	.700	8	13	21	3	12	0	5	0	2	15.0	6.0	4.2	0.6	.498
01-02	Dallas	7	0	105	27	12	25	.480	0	1	.000	3	4	.750	13	13	26	4	15	0	3	1	3	15.0	3.9	3.7	0.6	.351
02-03	Philadelphia	10	0	112	26	10	31	.323	2	9	.222	4	4	1.000	3	14	17	3	18	0	1	2	3	11.2	2.6	1.7	0.3	.156
NBA Playoff Totals		22	0	292	83	33	79	.418	3	13	.231	14	18	.778	24	40	64	10	45	0	9	3	8	13.3	3.8	2.9	0.5	

• BUCKNER, Quinn

William Quinn Buckner

Born: Aug. 20, 1954. Phoenix, IL, United States.   Height: 6'3".   Weight: 190 lbs.   Drafted: 1976   College: Indiana

76-77	Milwaukee	79	....	2095	681	299	689	.434	....	....	....	83	154	.539	91	173	264	372	291	5	192	21	....	26.5	8.6	3.3	4.7	.400
77-78	Milwaukee	82	....	2072	759	314	671	.468	....	....	....	131	203	.645	78	169	247	456	287	6	188	19	230	25.3	9.3	3.0	5.6	.482
78-79	Milwaukee	81	....	1757	581	251	553	.454	....	....	....	79	125	.632	57	153	210	468	224	1	156	17	211	21.7	7.2	2.6	5.8	.489
79-80	Milwaukee	67	....	1690	719	306	655	.467	2	5	.400	105	143	.734	69	169	238	383	202	1	135	4	147	25.2	10.7	3.6	5.7	.546
80-81	Milwaukee	82	....	2384	1092	471	956	.493	1	6	.167	149	203	.734	88	210	298	384	271	3	197	3	238	29.1	13.3	3.6	4.7	.485
81-82	Milwaukee	70	70	2156	906	396	822	.482	4	15	.267	110	168	.655	77	173	250	328	218	2	174	3	182	30.8	12.9	3.6	4.7	.448
82-83	Boston	72	56	1565	570	248	561	.442	0	4	.000	74	117	.632	62	125	187	275	195	2	108	5	158	21.7	7.9	2.6	3.8	.390
83-84	Boston	79	0	1249	324	138	323	.427	0	6	.000	48	74	.649	41	96	137	214	187	0	84	3	103	15.8	4.1	1.7	2.7	.316
84-85	Boston	75	6	858	180	74	193	.383	0	1	.000	32	50	.640	26	61	87	148	142	0	63	2	68	11.4	2.4	1.2	2.0	.269
85-86	Indiana	32	3	419	117	49	104	.471	0	1	.000	19	27	.704	9	42	51	86	80	0	40	3	54	13.1	3.7	1.6	2.7	.368
NBA Season Totals		719	135	16245	5929	2546	5527	.461	7	38	.184	830	1264	.657	598	1371	1969	3114	2097	20	1337	80	1391	22.6	8.2	2.7	4.3	
77-78	Milwaukee	9	....	257	101	43	86	.500	....	....	....	15	23	.652	3	24	27	62	30	0	18	1	39	28.6	11.2	3.0	6.9	.477
79-80	Milwaukee	7	....	165	43	18	53	.340	0	1	.000	7	11	.636	6	10	16	31	20	0	15	0	13	23.6	6.1	2.3	4.4	.307
80-81	Milwaukee	7	....	183	63	26	60	.433	0	0	.000	11	16	.688	5	15	20	35	26	1	11	0	14	26.1	9.0	2.9	5.0	.391
82-83	Boston	7	0	98	32	16	37	.432	0	2	.000	0	2	.000	1	9	10	2	18	1	1	0	5	14.0	4.6	1.4	0.3	.119
83-84	Boston	23	0	268	76	32	79	.405	0	1	.000	12	22	.545	12	23	35	28	52	0	13	0	18	11.7	3.3	1.5	1.2	.229
84-85	Boston	15	0	86	31	13	22	.591	0	0	.000	5	8	.625	2	5	7	12	24	0	6	0	6	5.7	2.1	0.5	0.8	.342
NBA Playoff Totals		68	0	1057	346	148	337	.439	0	4	.000	50	82	.610	29	86	115	170	170	2	64	1	95	15.5	5.1	1.7	2.5	

• BUDD, Dave

David L. Budd

Born: Oct. 28, 1938. Woodbury, NJ, United States.   Height: 6'6".   Weight: 205 lbs.   Drafted: 1960   College: Wake Forest

60-61	New York	61	....	1075	399	156	361	.432	....	....	....	87	134	.649	....	....	297	45	171	2	....	....	....	17.6	6.5	4.9	0.7	.411
61-62	New York	79	....	1370	514	188	431	.436	....	....	....	138	231	.597	....	....	345	86	162	4	....	....	....	17.3	6.5	4.4	1.1	.437
62-63	New York	78	....	1725	739	294	596	.493	....	....	....	151	202	.748	....	....	395	87	204	3	....	....	....	22.1	9.5	5.1	1.1	.474

YEAR	TEAM	GP	GS	MIN	PTS	FGM	FGA	FG%	3PM	3PA	3P%	FTM	FTA	FT%	ORB	DRB	TRB	AST	PF	DQ	STL	BLK	TO	MPG	PPG	RPG	APG	PCM
63-64	New York	73	....	1031	340	128	297	.431	....	....	....	84	115	.730	....	....	276	57	130	1	....	....	....	14.1	4.7	3.8	0.8	.417
64-65	New York	62	....	1188	513	196	407	.482	....	....	....	121	170	.712	....	....	310	62	147	1	....	....	....	19.2	8.3	5.0	1.0	.497
NBA Season Totals		353	....	6389	2505	962	2092	.460	....	....	....	581	852	.682	....	....	1623	337	814	11	....	....	....	18.1	7.1	4.6	1.0	

• BUDKO, Walt

Walter Budko Jr.

Born: June 30, 1925. Brooklyn, NY, United States.   Height: 6'5".   Weight: 220 lbs.   Drafted: 1948   College: Columbia

YEAR	TEAM	GP	GS	MIN	PTS	FGM	FGA	FG%	3PM	3PA	3P%	FTM	FTA	FT%	ORB	DRB	TRB	AST	PF	DQ	STL	BLK	TO	MPG	PPG	RPG	APG	PCM
48-49	Baltimore	60	....	....	692	224	644	.348	....	....	....	244	309	.790	....	....	....	99	201	....	....	....	....	11.5	....	1.7		
49-50	Baltimore	66	....	....	595	198	652	.304	....	....	....	199	263	.757	....	....	....	146	259	....	....	....	....	9.0	....	2.2		
50-51	Baltimore	64	....	....	496	165	464	.356	....	....	....	166	223	.744	....	....	452	135	203	7	....	....	....	7.8	7.1	2.1		
51-52	Philadelphia	63	....	1126	254	97	240	.404	....	....	....	60	89	.674	....	....	232	91	196	10	....	....	....	17.9	4.0	3.7	1.4	.315
NBA Season Totals		253	....	1126	2037	684	2000	.342	....	....	....	669	884	.757	....	....	684	471	859	17	....	....	....	4.5	8.1	2.7	1.9	
48-49	Baltimore	3	....	....	37	11	26	.423	....	....	....	15	19	.789	....	....	....	4	16	....	....	....	....	12.3	....	1.3		
51-52	Philadelphia	3	....	58	16	6	14	.429	....	....	....	4	7	.571	....	....	12	5	11	0	....	....	....	19.3	5.3	4.0	1.7	.350
NBA Playoff Totals		6	....	58	53	17	40	.425	....	....	....	19	26	.731	....	....	12	9	27	0	....	....	....	9.7	8.8	2.0	1.5	

• BUECHLER, Jud

Judson Donald Buechler

Born: June 19, 1968. San Diego, CA, United States.   Height: 6'6".   Weight: 220 lbs.   Drafted: 1990   College: Arizona

YEAR	TEAM	GP	GS	MIN	PTS	FGM	FGA	FG%	3PM	3PA	3P%	FTM	FTA	FT%	ORB	DRB	TRB	AST	PF	DQ	STL	BLK	TO	MPG	PPG	RPG	APG	PCM
90-91	New Jersey	74	10	859	232	94	226	.416	1	4	.250	43	66	.652	61	80	141	51	79	0	33	15	30	11.6	3.1	1.9	0.7	.307
91-92	New Jersey	2	0	29	8	4	8	.500	0	0	.000	0	0	.000	2	0	2	2	2	0	2	1	1	14.5	4.0	1.0	1.0	.318
91-92	San Antonio	11	0	140	33	15	30	.500	0	0	.000	3	9	.333	6	16	22	11	18	0	8	3	6	12.7	3.0	2.0	1.0	.320
91-92	Golden State	15	0	121	29	10	33	.303	0	1	.000	9	12	.750	10	18	28	10	11	0	9	3	8	8.1	1.9	1.9	0.7	.344
92-93	Golden State	70	9	1287	437	176	403	.437	20	59	.339	65	87	.747	81	114	195	94	98	0	47	19	56	18.4	6.2	2.8	1.3	.358
93-94	Golden State	36	0	218	106	42	84	.500	12	29	.414	10	20	.500	13	19	32	16	24	0	8	1	11	6.1	2.9	0.9	0.4	.444
94-95	Chicago	57	0	605	217	90	183	.492	15	48	.313	22	39	.564	36	62	98	50	64	0	24	12	29	10.6	3.8	1.7	0.9	.402
95-96	Chicago	74	0	740	278	112	242	.463	40	90	.444	14	22	.636	45	66	111	56	70	0	34	7	37	10.0	3.8	1.5	0.8	.387
96-97	Chicago	76	0	703	139	58	158	.367	18	54	.333	5	14	.357	45	81	126	60	50	0	23	21	30	9.3	1.8	1.7	0.8	.303
97-98	Chicago	74	0	608	198	85	176	.483	25	65	.385	3	6	.500	24	53	77	49	47	0	22	15	22	8.2	2.7	1.0	0.7	.377
98-99	Detroit	50	0	1056	274	100	240	.417	61	148	.412	13	18	.722	29	104	133	57	83	0	37	13	21	21.1	5.5	2.7	1.1	.301
99-00	Detroit	58	5	657	130	55	156	.353	18	83	.217	2	7	.286	30	61	91	33	50	1	25	16	13	11.3	2.2	1.6	0.6	.240
00-01	Detroit	57	3	737	193	76	164	.463	32	77	.416	9	12	.750	20	74	94	39	83	0	21	10	25	12.9	3.4	1.6	0.7	.282
01-02	Phoenix	6	0	54	6	2	6	.333	2	6	.333	0	0	.000	2	6	8	3	7	0	1	0	1	9.0	1.0	1.3	0.5	.180
01-02	Orlando	60	2	630	105	42	112	.375	19	54	.352	2	4	.500	27	81	108	29	46	0	20	8	14	10.5	1.8	1.8	0.5	.257
NBA Season Totals		720	29	8444	2385	961	2221	.433	263	718	.366	200	316	.633	431	835	1266	560	732	1	314	144	304	11.7	3.3	1.8	0.8	
94-95	Chicago	10	0	104	20	9	21	.429	0	2	.000	2	4	.500	11	9	20	5	15	0	4	3	3	10.4	2.0	2.0	0.5	.275
95-96	Chicago	17	0	127	46	18	38	.474	8	21	.381	2	4	.500	2	8	10	6	13	0	7	0	8	7.5	2.7	0.6	0.4	.275
96-97	Chicago	18	0	138	33	13	31	.419	4	12	.333	3	5	.600	9	14	23	5	15	0	3	1	1	7.7	1.8	1.3	0.3	.274
97-98	Chicago	16	0	64	11	4	11	.364	3	5	.600	0	0	.000	4	7	11	3	7	0	3	1	1	4.0	0.7	0.7	0.2	.273
98-99	Detroit	5	0	84	8	3	15	.200	2	8	.250	0	0	.000	4	9	13	3	6	0	3	1	3	16.8	1.6	2.6	0.6	.124
99-00	Detroit	3	0	34	6	2	7	.286	2	5	.400	0	0	.000	0	4	4	1	4	0	0	1	0	11.3	2.0	1.3	0.3	.155
01-02	Orlando	2	0	10	0	0	0	.000	0	0	.000	0	0	.000	0	1	1	1	0	0	1	0	0	5.0	0.0	0.5	0.5	.291
NBA Playoff Totals		71	0	561	124	49	123	.398	19	53	.358	7	13	.538	30	52	82	24	60	0	21	7	16	7.9	1.7	1.2	0.3	

• BUEHLER, Ken

Ken Buehler

Born: 1919.   Height: 6'2".   Weight: 180 lbs.   Drafted: —   College: Wisconsin (Milwaukee)

YEAR	TEAM	GP	GS	MIN	PTS	FGM	FGA	FG%	3PM	3PA	3P%	FTM	FTA	FT%	ORB	DRB	TRB	AST	PF	DQ	STL	BLK	TO	MPG	PPG	RPG	APG	PCM
42-43	Sheboygan-N	22	....	....	165	62	....	....	....	....	....	41	....	....	....	....	....	....	....	....	....	....	....	....	7.5	....		
45-46	Sheboygan-N	3	....	....	16	7	....	....	....	....	....	2	....	....	....	....	....	....	....	....	....	....	....	....	5.3	....		
46-47	Fort Wayne-N	8	....	....	11	4	....	....	....	....	....	3	10	.300	....	....	....	....	....	....	....	....	....	....	1.4	....		
NBL Season Totals		33	....	....	192	73	....	....	....	....	....	46	10		....	....	....	....	....	....	....	....	....	....	5.8	....		

• BUFORD, Rodney

Rodney Alan Buford

Born: Nov. 2, 1977. Milwaukee, WI, United States.   Height: 6'5".   Weight: 189 lbs.   Drafted: 1999   College: Creighton

YEAR	TEAM	GP	GS	MIN	PTS	FGM	FGA	FG%	3PM	3PA	3P%	FTM	FTA	FT%	ORB	DRB	TRB	AST	PF	DQ	STL	BLK	TO	MPG	PPG	RPG	APG	PCM
99-00	Miami	34	0	386	147	62	151	.411	7	29	.241	16	22	.727	10	38	48	21	44	0	10	8	9	11.4	4.3	1.4	0.6	.306
00-01	Philadelphia	47	0	573	248	104	241	.432	16	38	.421	24	29	.828	16	58	74	17	68	0	17	6	29	12.2	5.3	1.6	0.4	.300
01-02	Memphis	63	21	1769	591	258	593	.435	17	70	.243	58	80	.725	52	220	272	71	110	1	42	12	63	28.1	9.4	4.3	1.1	.307
NBA Season Totals		144	21	2728	986	424	985	.430	40	137	.292	98	131	.748	78	316	394	109	222	1	69	26	101	18.9	6.8	2.7	0.8	
99-00	Miami	1	0	16	11	4	8	.500	1	2	.500	2	2	1.000	0	1	1	1	3	0	0	0	0	16.0	11.0	1.0	1.0	.500
00-01	Philadelphia	15	0	72	21	8	24	.333	3	6	.500	2	2	1.000	5	7	12	3	15	0	4	1	4	4.8	1.4	0.8	0.2	.207
NBA Playoff Totals		16	0	88	32	12	32	.375	4	8	.500	4	4	1.000	5	8	13	4	18	0	4	1	4	5.5	2.0	0.8	0.3	

• BULLARD, Matt

Matthew Gordon Bullard

Born: June 5, 1967. W.D.Moin./Ames, IA, United States.   Height: 6'10".   Weight: 215 lbs.   Drafted: —   College: Iowa

YEAR	TEAM	GP	GS	MIN	PTS	FGM	FGA	FG%	3PM	3PA	3P%	FTM	FTA	FT%	ORB	DRB	TRB	AST	PF	DQ	STL	BLK	TO	MPG	PPG	RPG	APG	PCM
90-91	Houston	18	0	63	39	14	31	.452	0	3	.000	11	17	.647	6	8	14	2	10	0	3	0	4	3.5	2.2	0.8	0.1	.475
91-92	Houston	80	7	1278	512	205	447	.459	64	166	.386	38	50	.760	73	150	223	75	129	1	26	21	56	16.0	6.4	2.8	0.9	.392
92-93	Houston	79	4	1356	575	213	494	.431	91	243	.374	58	74	.784	66	156	222	110	129	0	30	11	55	17.2	7.3	2.8	1.4	.410
93-94	Houston	65	0	725	226	78	226	.345	50	154	.325	20	26	.769	23	61	84	64	67	0	14	6	26	11.2	3.5	1.3	1.0	.273
95-96	Atlanta	46	0	460	174	66	162	.407	26	72	.361	16	20	.800	18	42	60	18	50	0	17	11	23	10.0	3.8	1.3	0.4	.301
96-97	Houston	71	12	1025	320	114	284	.401	67	183	.366	25	34	.735	13	104	117	67	68	0	21	18	36	14.4	4.5	1.6	0.9	.302
97-98	Houston	67	24	1190	466	175	389	.450	96	231	.416	20	27	.741	25	121	146	60	104	0	31	24	40	17.8	7.0	2.2	0.9	.363
98-99	Houston	41	0	413	117	43	114	.377	24	62	.387	7	10	.700	9	33	42	18	28	0	13	4	14	10.1	2.9	1.0	0.4	.242
99-00	Houston	56	27	1024	382	139	340	.409	79	177	.446	25	30	.833	13	125	138	63	85	0	19	13	36	18.3	6.8	2.5	1.1	.341

YEAR	TEAM	GP	GS	MIN	PTS	FGM	FGA	FG%	3PM	3PA	3P%	FTM	FTA	FT%	ORB	DRB	TRB	AST	PF	DQ	STL	BLK	TO	MPG	PPG	RPG	APG	PCM
00-01	Houston	61	5	1000	354	129	305	.423	86	213	.404	10	14	.714	22	108	130	42	76	0	10	9	12	16.4	5.8	2.1	0.7	.329
01-02	Charlotte	31	0	350	105	39	115	.339	16	57	.281	11	12	.917	10	37	47	16	29	0	2	2	12	11.3	3.4	1.5	0.5	.215
NBA Season Totals		615	79	8884	3270	1215	2907	.418	599	1561	.384	241	314	.768	278	945	1223	535	775	1	186	119	314	14.4	5.3	2.0	0.9	....
92-93	Houston	12	0	169	61	20	42	.476	15	28	.536	6	6	1.000	4	19	23	13	11	0	4	5	9	14.1	5.1	1.9	1.1	.418
93-94	Houston	10	0	55	16	4	19	.211	2	10	.200	6	8	.750	2	8	10	0	6	0	1	2	0	5.5	1.6	1.0	0.0	.191
95-96	Atlanta	4	0	51	14	4	12	.333	4	8	.500	2	4	.500	0	6	6	0	6	0	0	2	2	12.8	3.5	1.5	0.0	.164
96-97	Houston	2	0	7	6	2	2	1.000	2	2	1.000	2	2	1.000	0	1	2	0	1	0	0	0	0	3.5	3.0	1.0	0.0	1.057
97-98	Houston	5	4	70	17	6	18	.333	3	10	.300	2	2	1.000	3	5	8	5	5	0	1	0	0	14.0	3.4	1.6	1.0	.248
98-99	Houston	2	0	8	7	2	2	1.000	1	1	1.000	2	2	1.000	0	0	0	1	0	0	0	0	0	4.0	3.5	0.0	0.5	1.014
NBA Playoff Totals		35	4	360	121	38	95	.400	27	59	.458	18	22	.818	10	39	49	19	29	0	6	9	11	10.3	3.5	1.4	0.5	....

• BUNCE, Larry

Lawrence Melvin Bunce

Born: July 29, 1945. Tacoma, WA, United States.   Height: 7'   Weight: 240 lbs.   Drafted: 1967   College: Utah State

YEAR	TEAM	GP	GS	MIN	PTS	FGM	FGA	FG%	3PM	3PA	3P%	FTM	FTA	FT%	ORB	DRB	TRB	AST	PF	DQ	STL	BLK	TO	MPG	PPG	RPG	APG	PCM
67-68	Anaheim-A	71	....	2266	856	300	716	.419	0	1	.000	256	352	.727	....	....	589	75	189	8	....	....	132	31.9	12.1	8.3	1.1	.428
68-69	Dallas-A	24	....	423	155	50	113	.442	0	0	.000	55	76	.724	36	91	127	15	62	2	....	....	30	17.6	6.5	5.3	0.6	.453
68-69	Denver-A	23	....	225	93	22	59	.373	0	0	.000	49	70	.700	17	41	58	2	44	1	....	....	21	9.8	4.0	2.5	0.1	.380
68-69	Houston-A	11	....	156	38	14	31	.452	0	0	.000	10	19	.526	21	26	47	2	22	0	....	....	9	14.2	3.5	4.3	0.2	.338
ABA Season Totals		129	....	3070	1142	386	919	.420	0	1	.000	370	517	.716	74	158	821	94	317	11	....	....	192	23.8	8.9	6.4	0.7	....

• BUNCH, Greg

Darnell Greg Bunch

Born: May 15, 1956. San Bernardino, CA, United States.   Height: 6'6".   Weight: 190 lbs.   Drafted: 1978   College: Cal State Fullerton

YEAR	TEAM	GP	GS	MIN	PTS	FGM	FGA	FG%	3PM	3PA	3P%	FTM	FTA	FT%	ORB	DRB	TRB	AST	PF	DQ	STL	BLK	TO	MPG	PPG	RPG	APG	PCM
78-79	New York	12	....	97	28	9	26	.346	....	....	....	10	12	.833	9	8	17	4	10	0	3	3	5	8.1	2.3	1.4	0.3	.288
NBA Season Totals		12	....	97	28	9	26	.346	....	....	....	10	12	.833	9	8	17	4	10	0	3	3	5	8.1	2.3	1.4	0.3	....

• BUNT, Dick

Richard J. Bunt

Born: July 13, 1930.   Height: 6'   Weight: 170 lbs.   Drafted: 1952   College: New York University

YEAR	TEAM	GP	GS	MIN	PTS	FGM	FGA	FG%	3PM	3PA	3P%	FTM	FTA	FT%	ORB	DRB	TRB	AST	PF	DQ	STL	BLK	TO	MPG	PPG	RPG	APG	PCM
52-53	New York	14	....	145	38	11	52	.212	....	....	....	16	23	.696	....	....	12	7	17	0	....	....	....	10.4	2.7	0.9	0.5	.119
52-53	Baltimore	12	....	126	54	18	55	.327	....	....	....	18	25	.720	....	....	16	10	23	0	....	....	....	10.5	4.5	1.3	0.8	.323
NBA Season Totals		26	....	271	92	29	107	.271	....	....	....	34	48	.708	....	....	28	17	40	0	....	....	....	10.4	3.5	1.1	0.7	....
52-53	Baltimore	1	....	1	0	0	0	.000	....	....	....	0	0	.000	....	....	0	0	0	0	....	....	....	1.0	0.0	0.0	0.0	.000
NBA Playoff Totals		1	....	1	0	0	0	.000	....	....	....	0	0	.000	....	....	0	0	0	0	....	....	....	1.0	0.0	0.0	0.0	....

• BUNTIN, Bill

William Buntin

Born: May 5, 1942. Detroit, MI, United States. Died: May 9, 1968.   Height: 6'7".   Weight: 250 lbs.   Drafted: 1965   College: Michigan

YEAR	TEAM	GP	GS	MIN	PTS	FGM	FGA	FG%	3PM	3PA	3P%	FTM	FTA	FT%	ORB	DRB	TRB	AST	PF	DQ	STL	BLK	TO	MPG	PPG	RPG	APG	PCM
65-66	Detroit	42	....	713	324	118	299	.395	....	....	....	88	143	.615	....	....	252	36	119	4	....	....	....	17.0	7.7	6.0	0.9	.498
NBA Season Totals		42	....	713	324	118	299	.395	....	....	....	88	143	.615	....	....	252	36	119	4	....	....	....	17.0	7.7	6.0	0.9	....

• BUNTING, Bill

William Carl Bunting

Born: Aug. 26, 1947. New Bern, NC, United States.   Height: 6'8".   Weight: 200 lbs.   Drafted: 1969   College: North Carolina

YEAR	TEAM	GP	GS	MIN	PTS	FGM	FGA	FG%	3PM	3PA	3P%	FTM	FTA	FT%	ORB	DRB	TRB	AST	PF	DQ	STL	BLK	TO	MPG	PPG	RPG	APG	PCM
69-70	Carolina-A	57	....	701	271	96	248	.387	0	0	.000	79	106	.745	73	96	169	34	106	3	....	....	48	12.3	4.8	3.0	0.6	.381
70-71	New York-A	39	....	687	190	65	151	.430	0	0	.000	60	69	.870	64	78	142	34	94	2	....	....	51	17.6	4.9	3.6	0.9	.341
70-71	Virginia-A	33	....	436	142	49	94	.521	0	0	.000	44	55	.800	40	51	91	24	63	1	....	....	23	13.2	4.3	2.8	0.7	.408
71-72	Virginia-A	16	....	115	20	4	15	.267	0	1	.000	12	17	.706	3	12	15	3	11	0	....	....	5	7.2	1.3	0.9	0.2	.173
ABA Season Totals		145	....	1939	623	214	508	.421	0	1	.000	195	247	.789	180	237	417	95	274	6	....	....	127	13.4	4.3	2.9	0.7	....
70-71	Virginia-A	6	....	35	18	5	10	.500	0	0	.000	8	12	.667	2	4	6	1	4	0	....	....	1	5.8	3.0	1.0	0.2	.480
ABA Playoff Totals		6	....	35	18	5	10	.500	0	0	.000	8	12	.667	2	4	6	1	4	0	....	....	1	5.8	3.0	1.0	0.2	....

• BURDEN, Ticky

Luther D. (Ticky) Burden

Born: Feb. 28, 1953. Haines City, FL, United States.   Height: 6'2".   Weight: 185 lbs.   Drafted: 1975   College: Utah

YEAR	TEAM	GP	GS	MIN	PTS	FGM	FGA	FG%	3PM	3PA	3P%	FTM	FTA	FT%	ORB	DRB	TRB	AST	PF	DQ	STL	BLK	TO	MPG	PPG	RPG	APG	PCM
75-76	Virginia-A	71	....	2181	1413	561	1247	.450	8	36	.222	283	369	.767	108	94	202	131	188	....	103	9	181	30.7	19.9	2.8	1.8	.461
76-77	New York	61	....	608	347	148	352	.420	....	....	....	51	85	.600	26	40	66	62	88	0	47	1	....	10.0	5.7	1.1	1.0	.404
77-78	New York	2	....	15	2	1	2	.500	....	....	....	0	0	.000	0	0	0	1	1	0	1	0	0	7.5	1.0	0.0	0.5	.179
NBA Season Totals		63	....	623	349	149	354	.421	....	....	....	51	85	.600	26	40	66	63	89	0	48	1	0	9.9	5.5	1.0	1.0	....
ABA Season Totals		71	....	2181	1413	561	1247	.450	8	36	.222	283	369	.767	108	94	202	131	188	....	103	9	181	30.7	19.9	2.8	1.8	....
Career Totals		134	....	2804	1762	710	1601	.443	8	36	.222	334	454	.736	134	134	268	194	277	0	151	10	181	20.9	13.1	2.0	1.4	....

• BURKE, Pat

Patrick John Burke

Born: Dec. 14, 1973. Cape Coral, FL, United States.   Height: 6'11".   Weight: 250 lbs.   Drafted: —   College: Auburn

YEAR	TEAM	GP	GS	MIN	PTS	FGM	FGA	FG%	3PM	3PA	3P%	FTM	FTA	FT%	ORB	DRB	TRB	AST	PF	DQ	STL	BLK	TO	MPG	PPG	RPG	APG	PCM
02-03	Orlando	62	8	783	267	113	296	.382	1	7	.143	40	58	.690	57	89	146	23	99	1	19	25	47	12.6	4.3	2.4	0.4	.259
NBA Season Totals		62	8	783	267	113	296	.382	1	7	.143	40	58	.690	57	89	146	23	99	1	19	25	47	12.6	4.3	2.4	0.4	....
02-03	Orlando	6	0	43	17	6	10	.600	0	0	.000	5	6	.833	1	10	11	1	9	0	1	0	4	7.2	2.8	1.8	0.2	.400
NBA Playoff Totals		6	0	43	17	6	10	.600	0	0	.000	5	6	.833	1	10	11	1	9	0	1	0	4	7.2	2.8	1.8	0.2	....

• BURKMAN, Roger

Roger Allen Burkman

Born: May 22, 1958. Indianapolis, IN, United States. Height: 6'5". Weight: 175 lbs. Drafted: 1981 College: Louisville

YEAR	TEAM	GP	GS	MIN	PTS	FGM	FGA	FG%	3PM	3PA	3P%	FTM	FTA	FT%	ORB	DRB	TRB	AST	PF	DQ	STL	BLK	TO	MPG	PPG	RPG	APG	PCM
81-82	Chicago	6	0	30	5	0	4	.000	0	1	.000	5	6	.833	2	4	6	5	6	0	6	2	3	5.0	0.8	1.0	0.8	.454
NBA Season Totals		6	0	30	5	0	4	.000	0	1	.000	5	6	.833	2	4	6	5	6	0	6	2	3	5.0	0.8	1.0	0.8	....

• BURLESON, Tom

Tommy Loren Burleson

Born: Feb. 24, 1952. Crossnore, NC, United States. Height: 7'2". Weight: 225 lbs. Drafted: 1974 College: North Carolina State

YEAR	TEAM	GP	GS	MIN	PTS	FGM	FGA	FG%	3PM	3PA	3P%	FTM	FTA	FT%	ORB	DRB	TRB	AST	PF	DQ	STL	BLK	TO	MPG	PPG	RPG	APG	PCM
74-75	Seattle	82	....	1888	826	322	772	.417	....	....	....	182	265	.687	155	417	572	115	221	1	64	153	....	23.0	10.1	7.0	1.4	.494
75-76	Seattle	82	....	2647	1283	496	1032	.481	....	....	....	291	388	.750	258	484	742	180	273	1	70	150	....	32.3	15.6	9.0	2.2	.569
76-77	Seattle	82	....	1803	796	288	652	.442	....	....	....	220	301	.731	184	367	551	93	259	1	74	117	....	22.0	9.7	6.7	1.1	.508
77-78	Kansas City	76	....	1525	653	228	525	.434	....	....	....	197	248	.794	170	312	482	131	259	6	62	81	122	20.1	8.6	6.3	1.7	.554
78-79	Kansas City	56	....	927	435	157	342	.459	....	....	....	121	169	.716	84	197	281	50	183	3	26	58	62	16.6	7.8	5.0	0.9	.531
79-80	Kansas City	37	....	272	95	36	104	.346	0	3	.000	23	40	.575	23	49	72	20	49	0	8	13	26	7.4	2.6	1.9	0.5	.317
80-81	Atlanta	31	....	363	102	41	99	.414	0	0	.000	20	41	.488	44	50	94	12	73	2	8	19	25	11.7	3.3	3.0	0.4	.294
NBA Season Totals		446	....	9425	4190	1568	3526	.445	0	3	.000	1054	1452	.726	918	1876	2794	601	1317	14	312	591	235	21.1	9.4	6.3	1.3	....
74-75	Seattle	9	....	364	186	78	152	.513	....	....	....	30	40	.750	30	66	96	13	29	0	7	18	....	40.4	20.7	10.7	1.4	.558
75-76	Seattle	6	....	208	125	45	75	.600	....	....	....	35	46	.761	15	42	57	10	25	1	6	8	....	34.7	20.8	9.5	1.7	.693
NBA Playoff Totals		15	....	572	311	123	227	.542	....	....	....	65	86	.756	45	108	153	23	54	1	13	26	....	38.1	20.7	10.2	1.5	....

• BURMASTER, Jack

John H. Burmaster

Born: Dec. 23, 1926. Height: 6'3". Weight: 190 lbs. Drafted: 1948 College: Illinois

YEAR	TEAM	GP	GS	MIN	PTS	FGM	FGA	FG%	3PM	3PA	3P%	FTM	FTA	FT%	ORB	DRB	TRB	AST	PF	DQ	STL	BLK	TO	MPG	PPG	RPG	APG	PCM
48-49	Oshkosh-N	64	....	....	360	140	....	....	....	....	....	80	128	.625	....	....	....	....	168	....	....	....	....	....	5.6	....	....	....
49-50	Sheboygan	61	....	....	598	237	711	.333	....	....	....	124	182	.681	....	....	....	179	237	....	....	....	....	....	9.8	....	2.9	....
NBA Season Totals		61	....	....	598	237	711	.333	....	....	....	124	182	.681	....	....	....	179	237	....	....	....	....	....	9.8	....	2.9	....
NBL Season Totals		64	....	....	360	140	....	....	....	....	....	80	128	....	....	....	....	....	168	....	....	....	....	....	5.6	....	....	....
Career Totals		125	....	....	958	377	711	....	....	....	....	204	310	....	....	....	....	179	405	....	....	....	....	....	7.7	....	1.4	....
48-49	Oshkosh-N	7	....	....	44	14	....	....	....	....	....	16	24	.667	....	....	....	....	....	....	....	....	....	....	6.3	....	....	....
49-50	Sheboygan	3	....	....	36	16	31	.516	....	....	....	4	4	1.000	....	....	....	8	7	....	....	....	....	....	12.0	....	2.7	....
NBA Playoff Totals		3	....	....	36	16	31	.516	....	....	....	4	4	1.000	....	....	....	8	7	....	....	....	....	....	12.0	....	2.7	....
NBL Playoff Totals		7	....	....	44	14	....	....	....	....	....	16	24	....	....	....	....	....	....	....	....	....	....	....	6.3	....	....	....
Career Playoff Totals		10	....	....	80	30	31	....	....	....	....	20	28	....	....	....	....	8	7	....	....	....	....	....	8.0	....	0.8	....

• BURNS, David

David Earl Burns

Born: July 3, 1958. Dallas, TX, United States. Height: 6'2". Weight: 180 lbs. Drafted: 1981 College: St. Louis

YEAR	TEAM	GP	GS	MIN	PTS	FGM	FGA	FG%	3PM	3PA	3P%	FTM	FTA	FT%	ORB	DRB	TRB	AST	PF	DQ	STL	BLK	TO	MPG	PPG	RPG	APG	PCM
81-82	New Jersey	3	0	34	7	2	5	.400	0	0	.000	3	6	.500	0	2	2	4	4	0	1	0	5	11.3	2.3	0.7	1.3	.103
81-82	Denver	6	1	53	16	5	11	.455	0	0	.000	6	9	.667	1	2	3	11	13	0	2	0	8	8.8	2.7	0.5	1.8	.230
NBA Season Totals		9	1	87	23	7	16	.438	0	0	.000	9	15	.600	1	4	5	15	17	0	3	0	13	9.7	2.6	0.6	1.7	....

• BURNS, Evers

Evers Allen Burns

Born: Aug. 24, 1971. Baltimore, MD, United States. Height: 6'8". Weight: 260 lbs. Drafted: 1993 College: Maryland

YEAR	TEAM	GP	GS	MIN	PTS	FGM	FGA	FG%	3PM	3PA	3P%	FTM	FTA	FT%	ORB	DRB	TRB	AST	PF	DQ	STL	BLK	TO	MPG	PPG	RPG	APG	PCM
93-94	Sacramento	23	0	143	56	22	55	.400	0	0	.000	12	23	.522	13	17	30	9	33	0	6	3	7	6.2	2.4	1.3	0.4	.312
NBA Season Totals		23	0	143	56	22	55	.400	0	0	.000	12	23	.522	13	17	30	9	33	0	6	3	7	6.2	2.4	1.3	0.4	....

• BURNS, Jim

James B. Burns

Born: Sept. 21, 1945. Height: 6'3". Weight: 195 lbs. Drafted: 1967 College: Northwestern

YEAR	TEAM	GP	GS	MIN	PTS	FGM	FGA	FG%	3PM	3PA	3P%	FTM	FTA	FT%	ORB	DRB	TRB	AST	PF	DQ	STL	BLK	TO	MPG	PPG	RPG	APG	PCM
67-68	Dallas-A	33	....	392	155	52	137	.380	0	2	.000	51	89	.573	....	....	60	24	52	0	....	....	42	11.9	4.7	1.8	0.7	.319
67-68	Chicago	3	....	11	4	2	7	.286	....	....	....	0	0	.000	....	....	2	1	1	0	....	....	....	3.7	1.3	0.7	0.3	.219
NBA Season Totals		3	....	11	4	2	7	.286	....	....	....	0	0	.000	....	....	2	1	1	0	....	....	....	3.7	1.3	0.7	0.3	....
ABA Season Totals		33	....	392	155	52	137	.380	0	2	.000	51	89	.573	....	....	60	24	52	0	....	....	42	11.9	4.7	1.8	0.7	....
Career Totals		36	....	403	159	54	144	.375	0	2	.000	51	89	.573	....	....	62	25	53	0	....	....	42	11.2	4.4	1.7	0.7	....

• BURRELL, Scott

Scott David Burrell

Born: Jan. 12, 1971. New Haven, CT, United States. Height: 6'7". Weight: 218 lbs. Drafted: 1993 College: Connecticut

YEAR	TEAM	GP	GS	MIN	PTS	FGM	FGA	FG%	3PM	3PA	3P%	FTM	FTA	FT%	ORB	DRB	TRB	AST	PF	DQ	STL	BLK	TO	MPG	PPG	RPG	APG	PCM
93-94	Charlotte	51	16	767	244	98	234	.419	2	6	.333	46	70	.657	46	86	132	62	88	0	37	16	46	15.0	4.8	2.6	1.2	.342
94-95	Charlotte	65	62	2014	750	277	593	.467	96	235	.409	100	144	.694	96	272	368	161	187	1	75	40	85	31.0	11.5	5.7	2.5	.442
95-96	Charlotte	20	20	693	263	92	206	.447	37	98	.378	42	56	.750	26	72	98	47	76	2	27	13	42	34.7	13.2	4.9	2.4	.366
96-97	Charlotte	28	2	482	151	45	131	.344	19	55	.345	42	53	.792	24	55	79	39	60	0	14	11	25	17.2	5.4	2.8	1.4	.318
96-97	Golden State	29	0	457	145	54	141	.383	22	61	.361	15	23	.652	25	54	79	35	60	0	14	8	29	15.8	5.0	2.7	1.2	.299
97-98	Chicago	80	3	1096	416	159	375	.424	51	144	.354	47	64	.734	80	118	198	65	131	1	64	37	48	13.7	5.2	2.5	0.8	.411
98-99	New Jersey	32	10	706	212	75	208	.361	28	72	.389	34	42	.810	32	87	119	45	82	2	40	11	23	22.1	6.6	3.7	1.4	.332
99-00	New Jersey	74	9	1336	451	165	419	.394	82	232	.353	39	50	.780	65	191	256	72	173	1	67	44	38	18.1	6.1	3.5	1.0	.385
00-01	Charlotte	4	0	41	17	7	15	.467	2	6	.333	1	4	.250	1	2	3	1	8	0	3	0	0	10.3	4.3	0.8	0.3	.277
NBA Season Totals		383	122	7592	2649	972	2322	.419	339	909	.373	366	506	.723	395	937	1332	527	865	7	341	180	336	19.8	6.9	3.5	1.4	....

YEAR	TEAM	GP	GS	MIN	PTS	FGM	FGA	FG%	3PM	3PA	3P%	FTM	FTA	FT%	ORB	DRB	TRB	AST	PF	DQ	STL	BLK	TO	MPG	PPG	RPG	APG	PCM
97-98	Chicago	21	0	261	80	32	73	.438	6	20	.300	10	11	.909	11	32	43	10	33	0	19	3	11	12.4	3.8	2.0	0.5	.334
00-01	Charlotte	2	0	12	5	2	3	.667	0	1	.000	1	2	.500	0	3	3	1	0	0	2	0	0	6.0	2.5	1.5	0.5	.770
NBA Playoff Totals		23	0	273	85	34	76	.447	6	21	.286	11	13	.846	11	35	46	11	33	0	21	3	11	11.9	3.7	2.0	0.5	....

• BURRIS, Art
Arthur C. Burris

Born: Apr. 7, 1924. Height: 6'5". Weight: 220 lbs. Drafted: 1950 College: Tennessee

YEAR	TEAM	GP	GS	MIN	PTS	FGM	FGA	FG%	3PM	3PA	3P%	FTM	FTA	FT%	ORB	DRB	TRB	AST	PF	DQ	STL	BLK	TO	MPG	PPG	RPG	APG	PCM
50-51	Fort Wayne	33	....	....	77	28	113	.248	....	....	....	21	36	.583	....	....	106	27	51	0	....	....	....		2.3	3.2	0.8	....
51-52	FtW/Mil	41	....	514	110	42	156	.269	....	....	....	26	39	.667	....	....	99	27	49	3	....	....		12.5	2.7	2.4	0.7	.218
NBA Season Totals		74	....	514	187	70	269	.260	....	....	....	47	75	.627	....	....	205	54	100	3	....	....	....	6.9	2.5	2.8	0.7	

• BURROUGH, Junior
Thomas Harold (Junior) Burrough

Born: Jan. 18, 1973. Charlotte, NC, United States. Height: 6'8". Weight: 242 lbs. Drafted: 1995 College: Virginia

YEAR	TEAM	GP	GS	MIN	PTS	FGM	FGA	FG%	3PM	3PA	3P%	FTM	FTA	FT%	ORB	DRB	TRB	AST	PF	DQ	STL	BLK	TO	MPG	PPG	RPG	APG	PCM
95-96	Boston	61	3	495	189	64	170	.376	0	0	.000	61	93	.656	45	64	109	15	74	0	15	10	43	8.1	3.1	1.8	0.2	.285
NBA Season Totals		61	3	495	189	64	170	.376	0	0	.000	61	93	.656	45	64	109	15	74	0	15	10	43	8.1	3.1	1.8	0.2	....

• BURROW, Bob
Robert Brantley Burrow

Born: June 29, 1934. Malvern, AR, United States. Height: 6'7". Weight: 228 lbs. Drafted: 1956 College: Kentucky

YEAR	TEAM	GP	GS	MIN	PTS	FGM	FGA	FG%	3PM	3PA	3P%	FTM	FTA	FT%	ORB	DRB	TRB	AST	PF	DQ	STL	BLK	TO	MPG	PPG	RPG	APG	PCM
56-57	Rochester	67	....	1028	404	137	366	.374	....	....	....	130	211	.616	....	....	293	41	165	2	....	....	....	15.3	6.0	4.4	0.6	.400
57-58	Minneapolis	14	....	171	55	22	70	.314	....	....	....	11	33	.333	....	....	64	6	15	0	....	....	....	12.2	3.9	4.6	0.4	.356
NBA Season Totals		81	....	1199	459	159	436	.365	....	....	....	141	244	.578	....	....	357	47	180	2	....	....	....	14.8	5.7	4.4	0.6	

• BURTON, Ed
Edward Burton

Born: Aug. 13, 1939. Height: 6'6". Weight: 225 lbs. Drafted: — College: Michigan State

YEAR	TEAM	GP	GS	MIN	PTS	FGM	FGA	FG%	3PM	3PA	3P%	FTM	FTA	FT%	ORB	DRB	TRB	AST	PF	DQ	STL	BLK	TO	MPG	PPG	RPG	APG	PCM
61-62	New York	8	....	28	15	7	14	.500	....	....	....	1	4	.250	....	....	5	1	3	0	....	....	....	3.5	1.9	0.6	0.1	.440
64-65	St. Louis	7	....	42	18	7	20	.350	....	....	....	4	7	.571	....	....	13	2	13	0	....	....	....	6.0	2.6	1.9	0.3	.341
NBA Season Totals		15	....	70	33	14	34	.412	....	....	....	5	11	.455	....	....	18	3	16	0	....	....	....	4.7	2.2	1.2	0.2	

• BURTON, Willie
Willie Ricardo Burton

Born: May 26, 1968. Detroit, MI, United States. Height: 6'8". Weight: 210 lbs. Drafted: 1990 College: Minnesota

YEAR	TEAM	GP	GS	MIN	PTS	FGM	FGA	FG%	3PM	3PA	3P%	FTM	FTA	FT%	ORB	DRB	TRB	AST	PF	DQ	STL	BLK	TO	MPG	PPG	RPG	APG	PCM
90-91	Miami	76	26	1928	915	341	773	.441	4	30	.133	229	293	.782	111	151	262	107	275	6	72	24	144	25.4	12.0	3.4	1.4	.346
91-92	Miami	68	50	1585	762	280	622	.450	6	15	.400	196	245	.800	76	168	244	123	186	2	46	37	122	23.3	11.2	3.6	1.8	.415
92-93	Miami	26	8	451	204	54	141	.383	5	15	.333	91	127	.717	22	48	70	16	58	0	13	16	49	17.3	7.8	2.7	0.6	.316
93-94	Miami	53	1	697	371	124	283	.438	3	15	.200	120	158	.759	50	86	136	39	96	0	18	20	53	13.2	7.0	2.6	0.7	.455
94-95	Philadelphia	53	31	1564	812	243	606	.401	106	275	.385	220	267	.824	49	115	164	96	167	3	32	19	122	29.5	15.3	3.1	1.8	.358
96-97	Atlanta	24	2	380	148	39	116	.336	13	46	.283	57	68	.838	11	30	41	11	55	0	8	3	26	15.8	6.2	1.7	0.5	.214
97-98	San Antonio	13	0	43	27	8	21	.381	3	9	.333	8	12	.667	3	6	9	1	7	0	2	2	1	3.3	2.1	0.7	0.1	.515
98-99	Charlotte	3	0	18	4	1	7	.143	0	1	.000	2	4	.500	4	2	6	0	2	0	0	0	1	6.0	1.3	2.0	0.0	.074
NBA Season Totals		316	118	6666	3243	1090	2569	.424	140	406	.345	923	1174	.786	326	606	932	393	846	11	191	121	518	21.1	10.3	2.9	1.2	....
93-94	Miami	2	0	11	2	1	4	.250	0	2	.000	0	0	.000	0	0	0	0	3	0	0	0	1	5.5	1.0	0.0	0.0	-.277
NBA Playoff Totals		2	0	11	2	1	4	.250	0	2	.000	0	0	.000	0	0	0	0	3	0	0	0	1	5.5	1.0	0.0	0.0	....

• BURTT, Steve
Steven Dwayne Burtt

Born: Nov. 5, 1962. New York, NY, United States. Height: 6'2". Weight: 185 lbs. Drafted: 1984 College: Iona

YEAR	TEAM	GP	GS	MIN	PTS	FGM	FGA	FG%	3PM	3PA	3P%	FTM	FTA	FT%	ORB	DRB	TRB	AST	PF	DQ	STL	BLK	TO	MPG	PPG	RPG	APG	PCM
84-85	Golden State	47	0	418	197	72	188	.383	0	1	.000	53	77	.688	10	18	28	20	76	0	21	4	33	8.9	4.2	0.6	0.4	.197
87-88	LA Clippers	19	0	312	171	62	138	.449	0	4	.000	47	69	.681	6	21	27	38	56	0	10	5	40	16.4	9.0	1.4	2.0	.341
91-92	Phoenix	31	2	361	187	74	160	.463	1	6	.167	38	54	.704	10	24	34	59	58	0	16	4	34	11.6	6.0	1.1	1.9	.428
92-93	Washington	4	0	35	29	10	26	.385	1	3	.333	8	10	.800	2	1	3	6	5	0	2	0	4	8.8	7.3	0.8	1.5	.518
NBA Season Totals		101	2	1126	584	218	512	.426	2	14	.143	146	210	.695	28	64	92	123	195	0	49	13	111	11.1	5.8	0.9	1.2	....
91-92	Phoenix	8	0	104	50	16	38	.421	0	2	.000	18	21	.857	3	9	12	14	18	0	5	0	8	13.0	6.3	1.5	1.8	.415
NBA Playoff Totals		8	0	104	50	16	38	.421	0	2	.000	18	21	.857	3	9	12	14	18	0	5	0	8	13.0	6.3	1.5	1.8	....

• BUSE, Don
Donald R. (Boo) Buse

Born: Aug. 10, 1950. Huntingburg, IN, United States. Height: 6'4". Weight: 190 lbs. Drafted: 1972 College: Evansville

YEAR	TEAM	GP	GS	MIN	PTS	FGM	FGA	FG%	3PM	3PA	3P%	FTM	FTA	FT%	ORB	DRB	TRB	AST	PF	DQ	STL	BLK	TO	MPG	PPG	RPG	APG	PCM
72-73	Indiana-A	77	....	1484	413	163	360	.453	5	24	.208	82	109	.752	96	114	210	223	143	0	....	....	66	19.3	5.4	2.7	2.9	.400
73-74	Indiana-A	77	....	1877	424	170	427	.398	36	107	.336	48	70	.686	85	169	254	258	109	....	146	20	75	24.4	5.5	3.3	3.4	.352
74-75	Indiana-A	80	....	2369	517	216	500	.432	38	123	.309	47	59	.797	84	188	272	335	149	0	166	15	95	29.6	6.5	3.4	4.2	.341
75-76	Indiana-A	84	....	**3380**	1051	400	887	.451	72	208	.346	179	220	.814	90	232	322	**689**	194	....	**346**	31	159	**40.2**	12.5	3.8	**8.2**	.463
76-77	Indiana	81	....	2947	646	266	639	.416	....	....	....	114	145	.786	66	204	270	**685**	129	0	**281**	16	....	36.4	8.0	3.3	**8.5**	.430
77-78	Phoenix	82	....	2547	686	287	626	.458	....	....	....	112	136	.824	59	190	249	391	144	0	185	14	123	31.1	8.4	3.0	4.8	.408
78-79	Phoenix	82	....	2544	640	285	576	.495	....	....	....	70	91	.769	44	173	217	356	149	0	156	18	98	31.0	7.8	2.6	4.3	.376
79-80	Phoenix	81	....	2499	626	261	589	.443	19	79	.241	85	128	.664	70	163	233	320	111	0	132	10	89	30.9	7.7	2.9	4.0	.348
80-81	Indiana	58	....	1095	297	114	287	.397	19	58	.328	50	65	.769	19	65	84	140	61	0	74	8	41	18.9	5.1	1.4	2.4	.339
81-82	Indiana	82	78	2529	797	312	685	.455	**73**	189	.386	100	123	.813	46	177	223	407	176	0	164	27	98	30.8	9.7	2.7	5.0	.432
82-83	Portland	41	1	643	194	72	182	.396	9	35	.257	41	46	.891	19	35	54	115	60	0	44	2	25	15.7	4.7	1.3	2.8	.403

YEAR	TEAM	GP	GS	MIN	PTS	FGM	FGA	FG%	3PM	3PA	3P%	FTM	FTA	FT%	ORB	DRB	TRB	AST	PF	DQ	STL	BLK	TO	MPG	PPG	RPG	APG	PCM
83-84	Kansas City	76	10	1327	381	150	352	.426	18	59	.305	63	80	.788	29	87	116	303	62	0	86	1	84	17.5	5.0	1.5	4.0	.446
84-85	Kansas City	65	14	939	218	82	203	.404	31	87	.356	23	30	.767	21	40	61	203	75	0	38	1	46	14.4	3.4	0.9	3.1	.356
NBA Season Totals		648	103	17070	4485	1829	4139	.442	169	507	.333	658	844	.780	373	1134	1507	2920	967	0	1160	97	604	26.3	6.9	2.3	4.5	....
ABA Season Totals		318	....	9110	2405	949	2174	.437	151	462	.327	356	458	.777	355	703	1058	1505	595	0	658	66	395	28.6	7.6	3.3	4.7	....
Career Totals		966	103	26180	6890	2778	6313	.440	320	969	.330	1014	1302	.779	728	1837	2565	4425	1562	0	1818	163	999	27.1	7.1	2.7	4.6	....
72-73	Indiana-A	14	....	163	45	16	45	.356	0	7	.000	13	21	.619	12	13	25	17	30	0	....	....	10	11.6	3.2	1.8	1.2	.264
73-74	Indiana-A	14	....	331	73	30	68	.441	7	22	.318	6	9	.667	17	20	37	36	21	....	30	1	12	23.6	5.2	2.6	2.6	.311
74-75	Indiana-A	18	....	576	100	39	103	.379	6	26	.231	16	30	.533	16	42	58	80	42	....	45	5	17	32.0	5.6	3.2	4.4	.276
75-76	Indiana-A	3	....	138	37	15	33	.455	3	9	.333	4	4	1.000	3	11	14	26	7	....	7	0	7	46.0	12.3	4.7	8.7	.429
77-78	Phoenix	2	....	76	8	4	11	.364	....	....	....	0	0	.000	0	5	5	4	3	0	4	0	1	38.0	4.0	2.5	2.0	.159
78-79	Phoenix	15	....	512	118	47	116	.405	....	....	....	24	33	.727	17	38	55	52	31	0	23	5	15	34.1	7.9	3.7	3.5	.306
79-80	Phoenix	8	....	236	68	28	64	.438	5	13	.385	7	11	.636	8	13	21	44	15	0	6	0	13	29.5	8.5	2.6	5.5	.371
80-81	Indiana	2	....	35	5	1	8	.125	1	4	.250	2	2	1.000	0	5	5	7	4	0	3	0	2	17.5	2.5	2.5	3.5	.283
82-83	Portland	5	0	31	7	2	8	.250	0	0	.000	3	4	.750	0	2	2	7	2	0	0	0	2	6.2	1.4	0.4	1.4	.256
83-84	Kansas City	3	0	50	21	7	16	.438	3	6	.500	4	6	.667	0	3	3	11	5	0	1	1	3	16.7	7.0	1.0	3.7	.460
NBA Playoff Totals		35	0	940	227	89	223	.399	9	23	.391	40	56	.714	25	66	91	125	60	0	37	6	36	26.9	6.5	2.6	3.6	....
ABA Playoff Totals		49	....	1208	255	100	249	.402	16	64	.250	39	64	.609	48	86	134	159	100	0	**82**	6	46	24.7	5.2	2.7	3.2	....
Career Playoff Totals		84	0	2148	482	189	472	.400	25	87	.287	79	120	.658	73	152	225	284	160	0	119	12	82	25.6	5.7	2.7	3.4	....

• BUSH, Jerry

Gerard Bush

Born: 1914. Height: 6'3". Weight: 200 lbs. Drafted: — College: St. John's (NY)

YEAR	TEAM	GP	GS	MIN	PTS	FGM	FGA	FG%	3PM	3PA	3P%	FTM	FTA	FT%	ORB	DRB	TRB	AST	PF	DQ	STL	BLK	TO	MPG	PPG	RPG	APG	PCM
38-39	Non-Skids-N	24	....	....	126	50	....	....	....	....	....	26	....	....	....	....	....	....	....	....	....	....	....	....	5.3	....	....	....
39-40	Non-Skids-N	27	....	....	162	63	....	....	....	....	....	36	....	....	....	....	....	....	....	....	....	....	....	....	6.0	....	....	....
40-41	Non-Skids-N	22	....	....	91	29	....	....	....	....	....	33	....	....	....	....	....	....	....	....	....	....	....	....	4.1	....	....	....
42-43	Fort Wayne-N	23	....	....	110	39	....	....	....	....	....	32	....	....	....	....	....	....	....	....	....	....	....	....	4.8	....	....	....
43-44	Fort Wayne-N	22	....	....	132	55	....	....	....	....	....	22	....	....	....	....	....	....	....	....	....	....	....	....	6.0	....	....	....
44-45	Fort Wayne-N	28	....	....	154	62	....	....	....	....	....	30	....	....	....	....	....	....	....	....	....	....	....	....	5.5	....	....	....
45-46	Fort Wayne-N	34	....	....	153	61	....	....	....	....	....	31	43	.721	....	....	....	....	....	....	....	....	....	....	4.5	....	....	....
46-47	Anderson-N	15	....	....	88	39	....	....	....	....	....	10	19	.526	....	....	....	....	....	....	....	....	....	....	5.9	....	....	....
46-47	Fort Wayne-N	21	....	....	66	26	....	....	....	....	....	14	21	.667	....	....	....	....	....	....	....	....	....	....	3.1	....	....	....
47-48	Toledo-N	22	....	....	65	25	....	....	....	....	....	15	19	.789	....	....	....	....	20	....	....	....	....	....	3.0	....	....	....
NBL Season Totals		238	....	....	1147	449	....	....	....	....	....	249	102	....	....	....	....	....	20	....	....	....	....	....	4.8	....	....	....
38-39	Non-Skids-N	5	....	....	30	8	....	....	....	....	....	14	....	....	....	....	....	....	....	....	....	....	....	....	6.0	....	....	....
39-40	Non-Skids-N	8	....	....	31	13	....	....	....	....	....	5	....	....	....	....	....	....	....	....	....	....	....	....	3.9	....	....	....
40-41	Non-Skids-N	2	....	....	4	1	....	....	....	....	....	2	....	....	....	....	....	....	....	....	....	....	....	....	2.0	....	....	....
42-43	Fort Wayne-N	6	....	....	34	14	....	....	....	....	....	6	....	....	....	....	....	....	....	....	....	....	....	....	5.7	....	....	....
43-44	Fort Wayne-N	5	....	....	31	12	....	....	....	....	....	7	....	....	....	....	....	....	....	....	....	....	....	....	6.2	....	....	....
44-45	Fort Wayne-N	7	....	....	38	14	....	....	....	....	....	10	....	....	....	....	....	....	....	....	....	....	....	....	5.4	....	....	....
45-46	Fort Wayne-N	4	....	....	13	3	....	....	....	....	....	7	12	.583	....	....	....	....	....	....	....	....	....	....	3.3	....	....	....
NBL Playoff Totals		37	....	....	181	65	....	....	....	....	....	51	12	....	....	....	....	....	....	....	....	....	....	....	4.9	....	....	....

• BUSTION, David

David C. (Stretch) Bustion

Born: Aug. 30, 1949. Gadsden, AL, United States. Height: 6'8". Weight: 215 lbs. Drafted: 1972 College: Denver

YEAR	TEAM	GP	GS	MIN	PTS	FGM	FGA	FG%	3PM	3PA	3P%	FTM	FTA	FT%	ORB	DRB	TRB	AST	PF	DQ	STL	BLK	TO	MPG	PPG	RPG	APG	PCM
72-73	Denver-A	47	....	355	158	58	133	.436	0	0	.000	42	59	.712	39	62	101	21	82	0	....	....	54	7.6	3.4	2.1	0.4	.451
ABA Season Totals		47	....	355	158	58	133	.436	0	0	.000	42	59	.712	39	62	101	21	82	0	....	....	54	7.6	3.4	2.1	0.4	....
72-73	Denver-A	1	....	11	10	2	7	.286	0	0	.000	6	7	.857	0	1	1	1	3	0	....	....	1	11.0	10.0	1.0	1.0	.519
ABA Playoff Totals		1	....	11	10	2	7	.286	0	0	.000	6	7	.857	0	1	1	1	3	0	....	....	1	11.0	10.0	1.0	1.0	....

• BUTCHER, Donnie

Donnis Butcher

Born: Feb. 8, 1936. Williamsport, KY, United States. Height: 6'2". Weight: 200 lbs. Drafted: 1961 College: Pikeville

YEAR	TEAM	GP	GS	MIN	PTS	FGM	FGA	FG%	3PM	3PA	3P%	FTM	FTA	FT%	ORB	DRB	TRB	AST	PF	DQ	STL	BLK	TO	MPG	PPG	RPG	APG	PCM
61-62	New York	47	....	479	138	48	155	.310	....	....	....	42	69	.609	....	....	79	51	63	0	....	....	....	10.2	2.9	1.7	1.1	.299
62-63	New York	68	....	1193	475	172	424	.406	....	....	....	131	194	.675	....	....	180	138	164	1	....	....	....	17.5	7.0	2.6	2.0	.415
63-64	New York	26	....	418	116	37	115	.322	....	....	....	42	66	.636	....	....	67	66	53	0	....	....	....	16.1	4.5	2.6	2.5	.378
63-64	Detroit	52	....	1553	447	165	392	.421	....	....	....	117	190	.616	....	....	262	178	196	4	....	....	....	29.9	8.6	5.0	3.4	.378
64-65	Detroit	71	....	1157	412	143	353	.405	....	....	....	126	204	.618	....	....	200	122	183	4	....	....	....	16.3	5.8	2.8	1.7	.393
65-66	Detroit	15	....	285	108	45	96	.469	....	....	....	18	34	.529	....	....	33	30	40	1	....	....	....	19.0	7.2	2.2	2.0	.380
NBA Season Totals		279	....	5085	1696	610	1535	.397	....	....	....	476	757	.629	....	....	821	585	699	10	....	....	....	18.2	6.1	2.9	2.1	....

• BUTLER, Al

Elbert J. Butler

Born: July 9, 1938. Rochester, NY, United States. Height: 6'2". Weight: 175 lbs. Drafted: 1961 College: Niagara

YEAR	TEAM	GP	GS	MIN	PTS	FGM	FGA	FG%	3PM	3PA	3P%	FTM	FTA	FT%	ORB	DRB	TRB	AST	PF	DQ	STL	BLK	TO	MPG	PPG	RPG	APG	PCM
61-62	Boston	5	....	47	31	13	29	.448	....	....	....	5	6	.833	....	....	13	4	9	0	....	....	....	9.4	6.2	2.6	0.8	.630
61-62	New York	54	....	1969	796	336	725	.463	....	....	....	124	176	.705	....	....	324	201	147	0	....	....	....	36.5	14.7	6.0	3.7	.463
62-63	New York	74	....	1488	738	297	676	.439	....	....	....	144	187	.770	....	....	170	156	145	3	....	....	....	20.1	10.0	2.3	2.1	.462
63-64	New York	76	....	1379	658	260	616	.422	....	....	....	138	187	.738	....	....	168	157	167	3	....	....	....	18.1	8.7	2.2	2.1	.449
64-65	Baltimore	25	....	172	59	24	73	.329	....	....	....	11	15	.733	....	....	21	12	25	0	....	....	....	6.9	2.4	0.8	0.5	.239
NBA Season Totals		234	....	5055	2282	930	2119	.439	....	....	....	422	571	.739	....	....	696	530	493	6	....	....	....	21.6	9.8	3.0	2.3	....

• BUTLER, Caron

James Caron Butler

Born: Mar. 13, 1980. Racine, WI, United States.   Height: 6'7".   Weight: 217 lbs.   Drafted: 2002   College: Connecticut

YEAR	TEAM	GP	GS	MIN	PTS	FGM	FGA	FG%	3PM	3PA	3P%	FTM	FTA	FT%	ORB	DRB	TRB	AST	PF	DQ	STL	BLK	TO	MPG	PPG	RPG	APG	PCM
02-03	Miami	78	78	2858	1201	429	1032	.416	34	107	.318	309	375	.824	135	262	397	213	230	3	137	31	192	36.6	15.4	5.1	2.7	.382
NBA Season Totals		78	78	2858	1201	429	1032	.416	34	107	.318	309	375	.824	135	262	397	213	230	3	137	31	192	36.6	15.4	5.1	2.7	....

• BUTLER, Charlie

Charles Butler

Born: 1921.   Height: 6'2".   Weight: 165 lbs.   Drafted: —   College: Notre Dame

YEAR	TEAM	GP	GS	MIN	PTS	FGM	FGA	FG%	3PM	3PA	3P%	FTM	FTA	FT%	ORB	DRB	TRB	AST	PF	DQ	STL	BLK	TO	MPG	PPG	RPG	APG	PCM
45-46	Chicago-N	10	....	....	23	8	....	....	....	....	....	7	....	....	...	...	...	...	...	...	....	....	....	...	2.3	...	...	...
46-47	Syracuse-N	3	....	....	5	2	....	...	....	....	....	1	1	1.000	...	...	...	...	...	...	....	....	....	...	1.7	...	...	...
46-47	Youngstown-N	32	....	....	258	85	....	...	....	....	....	88	144	.611	...	...	...	...	...	...	....	....	....	...	8.1	...	...	...
NBL Season Totals		45	....	....	286	95	....	...	....	....	....	96	145	....	...	...	...	...	...	...	....	....	....	...	6.4	...	...	...

• BUTLER, Greg

Gregory Edward (G-Man) Butler

Born: Mar. 11, 1966. Inglewood, CA, United States.   Height: 6'11".   Weight: 240 lbs.   Drafted: 1988   College: Stanford

YEAR	TEAM	GP	GS	MIN	PTS	FGM	FGA	FG%	3PM	3PA	3P%	FTM	FTA	FT%	ORB	DRB	TRB	AST	PF	DQ	STL	BLK	TO	MPG	PPG	RPG	APG	PCM
88-89	New York	33	0	140	56	20	48	.417	0	3	.000	16	20	.800	9	19	28	2	28	0	1	2	17	4.2	1.7	0.8	0.1	.216
89-90	New York	13	0	33	6	3	12	.250	0	0	.000	0	2	.000	3	6	9	1	8	0	0	0	3	2.5	0.5	0.7	0.1	-.013
90-91	LA Clippers	9	0	37	14	5	19	.263	0	0	.000	4	6	.667	8	8	16	1	9	0	0	0	4	4.1	1.6	1.8	0.1	.218
NBA Season Totals		55	0	210	76	28	79	.354	0	3	.000	20	28	.714	20	33	53	4	45	0	1	2	24	3.8	1.4	1.0	0.1	....

• BUTLER, Mike

Michael Edward Butler

Born: Oct. 22, 1946. Memphis, TN, United States.   Height: 6'2".   Weight: 170 lbs.   Drafted: 1968   College: Memphis State

YEAR	TEAM	GP	GS	MIN	PTS	FGM	FGA	FG%	3PM	3PA	3P%	FTM	FTA	FT%	ORB	DRB	TRB	AST	PF	DQ	STL	BLK	TO	MPG	PPG	RPG	APG	PCM
68-69	New Orleans-A	77	....	1315	576	207	528	.392	50	162	.309	112	133	.842	26	89	115	171	130	0	....	....	113	17.1	7.5	1.5	2.2	.403
69-70	New Orleans-A	83	....	1728	818	298	800	.373	87	300	.290	135	161	.839	10	109	119	134	193	1	....	....	103	20.8	9.9	1.4	1.6	.317
70-71	Utah-A	71	....	1414	727	271	646	.420	32	125	.256	153	168	.911	24	107	131	186	142	0	....	....	107	19.9	10.2	1.8	2.6	.489
71-72	Utah-A	14	....	97	37	14	36	.389	3	9	.333	6	7	.857	4	6	10	13	18	0	....	....	12	6.9	2.6	0.7	0.9	.337
ABA Season Totals		245	....	4554	2158	790	2010	.393	172	596	.289	406	469	.866	64	311	375	504	483	1	....	....	335	18.6	8.8	1.5	2.1	....
68-69	New Orleans-A	11	....	237	100	30	107	.280	14	53	.264	26	29	.897	....	....	29	17	26	0	....	....	14	21.5	9.1	2.6	1.5	.278
70-71	Utah-A	10	....	77	48	19	33	.576	2	8	.250	8	9	.889	2	9	11	6	8	0	....	....	9	7.7	4.8	1.1	0.6	.639
ABA Playoff Totals		21	....	314	148	49	140	.350	16	61	.262	34	38	.895	2	9	40	23	34	0	....	....	23	15.0	7.0	1.9	1.1	....

• BUTLER, Mitchell

Mitchell Leon Butler

Born: Dec. 15, 1970. Los Angeles, CA, United States.   Height: 6'5".   Weight: 210 lbs.   Drafted: —   College: UCLA

YEAR	TEAM	GP	GS	MIN	PTS	FGM	FGA	FG%	3PM	3PA	3P%	FTM	FTA	FT%	ORB	DRB	TRB	AST	PF	DQ	STL	BLK	TO	MPG	PPG	RPG	APG	PCM
93-94	Washington	75	19	1321	518	207	418	.495	0	5	.000	104	180	.578	106	119	225	77	131	1	54	20	90	17.6	6.9	3.0	1.0	.382
94-95	Washington	76	5	1554	597	214	508	.421	46	141	.326	123	185	.665	43	127	170	91	155	0	61	10	106	20.4	7.9	2.2	1.2	.285
95-96	Washington	61	3	858	237	88	229	.384	13	60	.217	48	83	.578	29	89	118	67	104	0	41	12	67	14.1	3.9	1.9	1.1	.242
96-97	Portland	49	1	465	148	52	125	.416	12	39	.308	32	50	.640	19	34	53	30	55	1	13	2	29	9.5	3.0	1.1	0.6	.246
97-98	Cleveland	18	0	206	37	15	47	.319	1	6	.167	6	10	.600	6	16	22	18	26	0	8	0	7	11.4	2.1	1.2	1.0	.168
98-99	Cleveland	31	1	418	168	67	139	.482	11	29	.379	23	32	.719	13	31	44	22	41	0	15	4	29	13.5	5.4	1.4	0.7	.326
01-02	Portland	11	0	90	29	10	23	.435	1	3	.333	8	12	.667	6	8	14	5	10	0	0	1	5	8.2	2.6	1.3	0.5	.282
NBA Season Totals		321	29	4912	1734	653	1489	.439	84	283	.297	344	552	.623	222	424	646	310	522	2	192	49	333	15.3	5.4	2.0	1.0	....
96-97	Portland	2	0	4	2	1	2	.500	0	0	.000	0	0	.000	0	1	1	0	0	0	0	0	0	2.0	1.0	0.5	0.0	.500
NBA Playoff Totals		2	0	4	2	1	2	.500	0	0	.000	0	0	.000	0	1	1	0	0	0	0	0	0	2.0	1.0	0.5	0.0	....

• BUTLER, Rasual

Rasual Butler

Born: May 23, 1979. Philadelphia, PA, United States.   Height: 6'7".   Weight: 205 lbs.   Drafted: 2002   College: LaSalle

YEAR	TEAM	GP	GS	MIN	PTS	FGM	FGA	FG%	3PM	3PA	3P%	FTM	FTA	FT%	ORB	DRB	TRB	AST	PF	DQ	STL	BLK	TO	MPG	PPG	RPG	APG	PCM
02-03	Miami	72	28	1514	540	207	572	.362	50	171	.292	76	104	.731	29	157	186	93	105	0	21	43	77	21.0	7.5	2.6	1.3	.269
NBA Season Totals		72	28	1514	540	207	572	.362	50	171	.292	76	104	.731	29	157	186	93	105	0	21	43	77	21.0	7.5	2.6	1.3	....

• BYRD, Walter

Walter Byrd

Born: 1942.   Height: 6'7".   Weight: 205 lbs.   Drafted: —   College: Temple

YEAR	TEAM	GP	GS	MIN	PTS	FGM	FGA	FG%	3PM	3PA	3P%	FTM	FTA	FT%	ORB	DRB	TRB	AST	PF	DQ	STL	BLK	TO	MPG	PPG	RPG	APG	PCM
69-70	Miami-A	22	....	109	33	14	43	.326	0	1	.000	5	17	.294	8	17	25	6	22	0	....	....	8	5.0	1.5	1.1	0.3	.200
ABA Season Totals		22	....	109	33	14	43	.326	0	1	.000	5	17	.294	8	17	25	6	22	0	....	....	8	5.0	1.5	1.1	0.3	....

• BYRNES, Marty

Martin William Byrnes

Born: Apr. 30, 1956. Syracuse, NY, United States.   Height: 6'7".   Weight: 215 lbs.   Drafted: 1978   College: Syracuse

YEAR	TEAM	GP	GS	MIN	PTS	FGM	FGA	FG%	3PM	3PA	3P%	FTM	FTA	FT%	ORB	DRB	TRB	AST	PF	DQ	STL	BLK	TO	MPG	PPG	RPG	APG	PCM
78-79	Phoenix	43	....	734	291	109	223	.489	....	....	....	73	100	.730	49	48	97	61	69	0	15	2	77	17.1	6.8	2.3	1.4	.335
78-79	New Orleans	36	....	530	189	78	166	.470	....	....	....	33	54	.611	41	53	94	43	42	0	12	8	40	14.7	5.3	2.6	1.2	.369
79-80	LA Lakers	32	....	194	63	25	50	.500	0	0	.000	13	15	.867	9	18	27	13	32	0	5	1	22	6.1	2.0	0.8	0.4	.254
80-81	Dallas	72	....	1360	561	216	451	.479	9	20	.450	120	157	.764	74	103	177	113	126	0	29	17	58	18.9	7.8	2.5	1.6	.402
82-83	Indiana	80	12	1436	391	157	374	.420	6	26	.231	71	95	.747	75	116	191	179	149	1	41	6	72	18.0	4.9	2.4	2.2	.323
NBA Season Totals		263	12	4254	1495	585	1264	.463	15	46	.326	310	421	.736	248	338	586	409	418	1	102	34	269	16.2	5.7	2.2	1.6	....
79-80	LA Lakers	4	....	8	6	1	3	.333	0	0	.000	4	6	.667	1	0	1	1	0	0	0	0	1	2.0	1.5	0.3	0.3	.548
NBA Playoff Totals		4	....	8	6	1	3	.333	0	0	.000	4	6	.667	1	0	1	1	0	0	0	0	1	2.0	1.5	0.3	0.3	....

• BYRNES, Tommy
Thomas P. Byrnes

Born: Feb. 19, 1923. Teaneck, NJ, United States. Died: Jan.9, 1981. Height: 6'3". Weight: 175 lbs. Drafted: — College: Seton Hall

YEAR TEAM	GP	GS	MIN	PTS	FGM	FGA	FG%	3PM	3PA	3P%	FTM	FTA	FT%	ORB	DRB	TRB	AST	PF	DQ	STL	BLK	TO	MPG	PPG	RPG	APG	PCM
46-47 New York	60	....	....	453	175	583	.300	....	....	....	103	160	.644	....	....	....	35	90	....	....	....	....	....	7.6	....	0.6	....
47-48 New York	47	....	....	299	117	410	.285	....	....	....	65	103	.631	....	....	....	17	56	....	....	....	....	....	6.4	....	0.4	....
48-49 New York	35	....	....	200	77	270	.285	....	....	....	46	81	.568	....	....	....	54	53	....	....	....	....	....	5.7	....	1.5	....
48-49 Indianapolis	22	....	....	212	83	255	.325	....	....	....	46	68	.676	....	....	....	48	31	....	....	....	....	....	9.6	....	2.2	....
49-50 Baltimore	53	....	....	327	120	397	.302	....	....	....	87	124	.702	....	....	....	88	76	....	....	....	....	....	6.2	....	1.7	....
50-51 Baltimore	16	....	....	90	35	100	.350	....	....	....	20	28	.714	....	....	27	21	28	0	....	....	....	....	5.6	1.7	1.3	....
50-51 Was/Tri	32	....	....	131	48	175	.274	....	....	....	35	56	.625	....	....	45	48	58	0	....	....	....	....	4.1	1.4	1.5	....
NBA Season Totals	265	....	....	1712	655	2190	.299	....	....	....	402	620	.648	....	....	72	311	392	0	....	....	....	....	6.5	0.3	1.2	....
46-47 New York	5	....	....	24	11	46	.239	....	....	....	2	11	.182	....	....	....	0	2	....	....	....	....	....	4.8	....	0.0	....
47-48 New York	3	....	....	26	11	27	.407	....	....	....	4	12	.333	....	....	....	2	7	....	....	....	....	....	8.7	....	0.7	....
NBA Playoff Totals	8	....	....	50	22	73	.301	....	....	....	6	23	.261	....	....	....	2	9	....	....	....	....	....	6.3	....	0.3	....

• BYTZURA, Michael
Michael John Bytzura

Born: June 18, 1922. Died: Jan.24, 1989. Height: 6'1". Weight: 170 lbs. Drafted: — College: Long Island University

YEAR TEAM	GP	GS	MIN	PTS	FGM	FGA	FG%	3PM	3PA	3P%	FTM	FTA	FT%	ORB	DRB	TRB	AST	PF	DQ	STL	BLK	TO	MPG	PPG	RPG	APG	PCM
44-45 Cleveland-N	30	....	....	261	113	....	....	....	....	....	35	....	....	....	....	....	....	....	....	....	....	....	....	8.7	....	....	....
45-46 Cleveland-N	33	....	....	191	78	....	....	....	....	....	35	65	.538	....	....	....	....	....	....	....	....	....	....	5.8	....	....	....
46-47 Pittsburgh	60	....	....	210	87	356	.244	....	....	....	36	72	.500	....	....	....	31	108	....	....	....	....	....	3.5	....	0.5	....
NBA Season Totals	60	....	....	210	87	356	.244	....	....	....	36	72	.500	....	....	....	31	108	....	....	....	....	....	3.5	....	0.5	....
NBL Season Totals	63	....	....	452	191	....	....	....	....	....	70	65	....	....	....	....	....	....	....	....	....	....	....	7.2	....	....	....
Career Totals	123	....	....	662	278	356	....	....	....	....	106	137	....	....	....	....	31	108	....	....	....	....	....	5.4	....	0.3	....
44-45 Cleveland-N	2	....	....	11	4	....	....	....	....	....	3	....	....	....	....	....	....	....	....	....	....	....	....	5.5	....	....	....
NBL Playoff Totals	2	....	....	11	4	....	....	....	....	....	3	....	....	....	....	....	....	....	....	....	....	....	....	5.5	....	....	....

• CABLE, Barney
Byrum William (Barney) Cable

Born: July 29, 1935. Height: 6'7". Weight: 175 lbs. Drafted: 1958 College: Bradley

YEAR TEAM	GP	GS	MIN	PTS	FGM	FGA	FG%	3PM	3PA	3P%	FTM	FTA	FT%	ORB	DRB	TRB	AST	PF	DQ	STL	BLK	TO	MPG	PPG	RPG	APG	PCM
58-59 Detroit	31	....	271	109	43	126	.341	....	....	....	23	29	.793	....	....	88	12	30	0	....	....	....	8.7	3.5	2.8	0.4	.421
59-60 Detroit	7	....	116	48	22	60	.367	....	....	....	4	10	.400	....	....	48	6	19	0	....	....	....	16.6	6.9	6.9	0.9	.462
59-60 Syracuse	50	....	599	214	87	230	.378	....	....	....	40	57	.702	....	....	177	33	74	1	....	....	....	12.0	4.3	3.5	0.7	.411
60-61 Syracuse	75	....	1642	605	266	574	.463	....	....	....	73	108	.676	....	....	469	85	246	1	....	....	....	21.9	8.1	6.3	1.1	.442
61-62 Chicago	15	....	498	206	82	217	.378	....	....	....	42	59	.712	....	....	83	31	55	1	....	....	....	33.2	13.7	5.5	2.1	.352
61-62 St. Louis	52	....	1363	522	223	532	.419	....	....	....	76	122	.623	....	....	480	84	156	3	....	....	....	26.2	10.0	9.2	1.6	.498
62-63 St. Louis	42	....	662	255	107	216	.495	....	....	....	41	63	.651	....	....	129	42	86	0	....	....	....	15.8	6.1	3.1	1.0	.421
62-63 Chicago	19	....	541	153	66	164	.402	....	....	....	21	33	.636	....	....	109	41	49	0	....	....	....	28.5	8.1	5.7	2.2	.346
63-64 Baltimore	71	....	1125	260	116	290	.400	....	....	....	28	42	.667	....	....	301	47	166	3	....	....	....	15.8	3.7	4.2	0.7	.308
NBA Season Totals	362	....	6817	2372	1012	2409	.420	....	....	....	348	523	.665	....	....	1884	381	881	9	....	....	....	18.8	6.6	5.2	1.1	....
59-60 Syracuse	3	....	63	14	5	14	.357	....	....	....	4	8	.500	....	....	28	1	12	0	....	....	....	21.0	4.7	9.3	0.3	.374
60-61 Syracuse	8	....	185	62	26	65	.400	....	....	....	10	17	.588	....	....	61	7	29	1	....	....	....	23.1	7.8	7.6	0.9	.398
NBA Playoff Totals	11	....	248	76	31	79	.392	....	....	....	14	25	.560	....	....	89	8	41	1	....	....	....	22.5	6.9	8.1	0.7	....

• CABLE, Howard
Howard (Soup) Cable

Born: 1913. Height: 6'3". Weight: 200 lbs. Drafted: — College: Akron

YEAR TEAM	GP	GS	MIN	PTS	FGM	FGA	FG%	3PM	3PA	3P%	FTM	FTA	FT%	ORB	DRB	TRB	AST	PF	DQ	STL	BLK	TO	MPG	PPG	RPG	APG	PCM
37-38 Non-Skids-N	15	....	....	129	42	....	....	....	....	....	**45**	....	....	....	....	....	....	....	....	....	....	....	....	8.6	....	....	....
38-39 Non-Skids-N	24	....	....	262	99	....	....	....	....	....	64	....	....	....	....	....	....	....	....	....	....	....	....	10.9	....	....	....
39-40 Non-Skids-N	25	....	....	214	77	....	....	....	....	....	60	....	....	....	....	....	....	....	....	....	....	....	....	8.6	....	....	....
40-41 Non-Skids-N	15	....	....	94	30	....	....	....	....	....	34	....	....	....	....	....	....	....	....	....	....	....	....	6.3	....	....	....
41-42 Toledo-N	5	....	....	29	10	....	....	....	....	....	9	....	....	....	....	....	....	....	....	....	....	....	....	5.8	....	....	....
NBL Season Totals	84	....	....	728	258	....	....	....	....	....	212	....	....	....	....	....	....	....	....	....	....	....	....	8.7	....	....	....
37-38 Non-Skids-N	2	....	....	22	6	....	....	....	....	....	10	....	....	....	....	....	....	....	....	....	....	....	....	11.0	....	....	....
38-39 Non-Skids-N	5	....	....	41	12	....	....	....	....	....	17	....	....	....	....	....	....	....	....	....	....	....	....	8.2	....	....	....
39-40 Non-Skids-N	8	....	....	42	11	....	....	....	....	....	20	....	....	....	....	....	....	....	....	....	....	....	....	5.3	....	....	....
40-41 Non-Skids-N	2	....	....	22	7	....	....	....	....	....	8	....	....	....	....	....	....	....	....	....	....	....	....	11.0	....	....	....
NBL Playoff Totals	17	....	....	127	36	....	....	....	....	....	55	....	....	....	....	....	....	....	....	....	....	....	....	7.5	....	....	....

• CAFFEY, Jason
Jason Andre Caffey

Born: June 12, 1973. Mobile, AL, United States. Height: 6'8". Weight: 255 lbs. Drafted: 1995 College: Alabama

YEAR TEAM	GP	GS	MIN	PTS	FGM	FGA	FG%	3PM	3PA	3P%	FTM	FTA	FT%	ORB	DRB	TRB	AST	PF	DQ	STL	BLK	TO	MPG	PPG	RPG	APG	PCM
95-96 Chicago	57	0	545	182	71	162	.438	0	1	.000	40	68	.588	51	60	111	24	91	3	12	7	46	9.6	3.2	1.9	0.4	.266
96-97 Chicago	75	19	1405	549	205	385	.532	0	1	.000	139	211	.659	135	166	301	89	149	0	25	9	98	18.7	7.3	4.0	1.2	.423
97-98 Chicago	51	8	710	268	100	199	.503	0	1	.000	68	103	.660	76	97	173	36	92	1	13	17	46	13.9	5.3	3.4	0.7	.425
97-98 Golden State	29	6	713	315	126	267	.472	0	1	.000	63	97	.649	84	87	171	31	89	3	12	3	58	24.6	10.9	5.9	1.1	.393
98-99 Golden State	35	32	876	308	123	277	.444	0	1	.000	62	98	.633	79	126	205	18	113	1	24	9	75	25.0	8.8	5.9	0.5	.308
99-00 Golden State	71	56	2159	852	323	675	.479	0	2	.000	206	345	.597	189	293	482	119	269	11	62	20	170	30.4	12.0	6.8	1.7	.387
00-01 Milwaukee	70	33	1460	500	179	367	.488	0	0	.000	142	211	.673	135	218	353	53	184	8	38	25	77	20.9	7.1	5.0	0.8	.398
01-02 Milwaukee	23	0	283	99	36	72	.500	0	1	.000	27	43	.628	24	26	50	12	39	0	4	5	19	12.3	4.3	2.2	0.5	.321
02-03 Milwaukee	51	16	894	295	113	248	.456	0	0	.000	69	106	.651	68	108	176	38	122	3	19	15	56	17.5	5.8	3.5	0.7	.315
NBA Season Totals	462	170	9045	3368	1276	2652	.481	0	8	.000	816	1282	.637	841	1181	2022	420	1148	30	209	110	645	19.6	7.3	4.4	0.9	....

YEAR	TEAM	GP	GS	MIN	PTS	FGM	FGA	FG%	3PM	3PA	3P%	FTM	FTA	FT%	ORB	DRB	TRB	AST	PF	DQ	STL	BLK	TO	MPG	PPG	RPG	APG	PCM
96-97	Chicago	17	5	167	41	15	33	.455	0	0	.000	11	14	.786	25	17	42	15	27	0	3	3	12	9.8	2.4	2.5	0.9	.358
00-01	Milwaukee	18	0	297	68	24	63	.381	0	0	.000	20	31	.645	31	43	74	14	44	0	3	5	15	16.5	3.8	4.1	0.8	.282
NBA Playoff Totals		35	5	464	109	39	96	.406	0	0	.000	31	45	.689	56	60	116	29	71	0	6	8	27	13.3	3.1	3.3	0.8	....

• CAGE, Michael

Michael Jerome (John Shaft) Cage

Born: Jan. 28, 1962. West Memphis, AR, United States.   Height: 6'9".   Weight: 224 lbs.   Drafted: 1984   College: San Diego State

YEAR	TEAM	GP	GS	MIN	PTS	FGM	FGA	FG%	3PM	3PA	3P%	FTM	FTA	FT%	ORB	DRB	TRB	AST	PF	DQ	STL	BLK	TO	MPG	PPG	RPG	APG	PCM
84-85	LA Clippers	75	41	1610	533	216	398	.543	0	0	.000	101	137	.737	126	266	392	51	164	1	41	32	83	21.5	7.1	5.2	0.7	.423
85-86	LA Clippers	78	12	1566	521	204	426	.479	0	3	.000	113	174	.649	168	249	417	81	176	1	62	34	109	20.1	6.7	5.3	1.0	.426
86-87	LA Clippers	80	76	2922	1255	457	878	.521	0	3	.000	341	467	.730	354	568	922	131	221	1	99	67	168	36.5	15.7	11.5	1.6	.581
87-88	LA Clippers	72	70	2660	1046	360	766	.470	0	1	.000	326	474	.688	371	567	938	110	194	1	91	58	158	36.9	14.5	**13.0**	1.5	.561
88-89	Seattle	80	71	2536	825	314	630	.498	0	4	.000	197	265	.743	276	489	765	126	184	1	92	52	128	31.7	10.3	9.6	1.6	.503
89-90	Seattle	82	82	2595	798	325	645	.504	0	0	.000	148	212	.698	306	515	821	70	232	1	79	45	90	31.6	9.7	10.0	0.9	.476
90-91	Seattle	82	55	2141	522	226	445	.508	0	3	.000	70	112	.625	177	381	558	89	194	0	85	58	82	26.1	6.4	6.8	1.1	.411
91-92	Seattle	82	69	2461	720	307	542	.566	0	5	.000	106	171	.620	266	462	728	92	237	0	99	55	82	30.0	8.8	8.9	1.1	.489
92-93	Seattle	82	66	2156	499	219	416	.526	0	1	.000	61	130	.469	268	391	659	69	183	0	76	46	57	26.3	6.1	8.0	0.8	.439
93-94	Seattle	82	42	1708	378	171	314	.545	0	1	.000	36	74	.486	164	280	444	45	179	0	77	38	49	20.8	4.6	5.4	0.5	.389
94-95	Cleveland	82	21	2040	407	177	340	.521	0	2	.000	53	88	.602	203	361	564	56	149	1	61	67	57	24.9	5.0	6.9	0.7	.403
95-96	Cleveland	82	80	2631	490	220	396	.556	0	1	.000	50	92	.543	288	441	729	53	215	0	87	79	57	32.1	6.0	8.9	0.6	.398
96-97	Philadelphia	82	24	1247	151	66	141	.468	0	0	.000	19	41	.463	112	208	320	43	118	0	48	42	16	15.2	1.8	3.9	0.5	.344
97-98	New Jersey	79	17	1201	106	43	84	.512	0	1	.000	20	36	.556	115	193	308	32	105	1	45	44	24	15.2	1.3	3.9	0.4	.324
99-00	New Jersey	20	7	242	27	12	24	.500	0	0	.000	3	3	1.000	33	48	81	9	30	0	8	8	4	12.1	1.4	4.1	0.5	.400
NBA Season Totals		1140	733	29716	8278	3317	6445	.515	0	25	.000	1644	2476	.664	3227	5419	8646	1057	2581	8	1050	725	1164	26.1	7.3	7.6	0.9	....
88-89	Seattle	8	0	175	57	24	40	.600	0	1	.000	9	22	.409	22	24	46	5	14	0	7	3	8	21.9	7.1	5.8	0.6	.455
90-91	Seattle	5	0	80	25	6	14	.429	0	0	.000	13	17	.765	9	12	21	2	12	0	3	2	3	16.0	5.0	4.2	0.4	.421
91-92	Seattle	9	4	197	39	19	34	.559	0	0	.000	1	1	1.000	18	33	51	4	22	0	6	8	8	21.9	4.3	5.7	0.4	.366
92-93	Seattle	19	2	378	91	42	80	.525	0	0	.000	7	18	.389	47	64	111	10	43	1	13	7	16	19.9	4.8	5.8	0.5	.392
93-94	Seattle	5	5	93	14	6	16	.375	0	0	.000	2	6	.333	10	17	27	4	15	0	4	5	3	18.6	2.8	5.4	0.8	.330
94-95	Cleveland	4	0	81	16	8	18	.444	0	1	.000	0	2	.000	8	10	18	3	9	0	2	4	1	20.3	4.0	4.5	0.8	.324
95-96	Cleveland	3	3	101	19	8	14	.571	0	0	.000	3	5	.600	13	15	28	2	5	0	2	5	0	33.7	6.3	9.3	0.7	.446
NBA Playoff Totals		53	14	1105	261	113	216	.523	0	2	.000	35	71	.493	127	175	302	30	120	1	37	34	39	20.8	4.9	5.7	0.6	....

• CALABRESE, Gerry

Gerald A. Calabrese

Born: Feb. 4, 1925.   Height: 6'1".   Weight: 175 lbs.   Drafted: 1950   College: St. John's (NY)

YEAR	TEAM	GP	GS	MIN	PTS	FGM	FGA	FG%	3PM	3PA	3P%	FTM	FTA	FT%	ORB	DRB	TRB	AST	PF	DQ	STL	BLK	TO	MPG	PPG	RPG	APG	PCM
50-51	Syracuse	46	....	....	201	70	197	.355	....	....	....	61	88	.693	....	....	65	65	80	0	....	....	....	....	4.4	1.4	1.4	....
51-52	Syracuse	58	....	937	291	109	317	.344	....	....	....	73	103	.709	....	....	84	83	107	0	....	....	....	16.2	5.0	1.4	1.4	.279
NBA Season Totals		104	....	937	492	179	514	.348	....	....	....	134	191	.702	....	....	149	148	187	0	....	....	....	9.0	4.7	1.4	1.4	....
51-52	Syracuse	6	....	53	24	10	24	.417	....	....	....	4	4	1.000	....	....	8	4	18	0	....	....	....	8.8	4.0	1.3	0.7	.349
NBA Playoff Totals		6	....	53	24	10	24	.417	....	....	....	4	4	1.000	....	....	8	4	18	0	....	....	....	8.8	4.0	1.3	0.7	....

• CALDWELL, Adrian

Adrian Bernard Caldwell

Born: July 4, 1966. Falls County, TX, United States.   Height: 6'8".   Weight: 265 lbs.   Drafted: —   College: Lamar

YEAR	TEAM	GP	GS	MIN	PTS	FGM	FGA	FG%	3PM	3PA	3P%	FTM	FTA	FT%	ORB	DRB	TRB	AST	PF	DQ	STL	BLK	TO	MPG	PPG	RPG	APG	PCM
89-90	Houston	51	0	331	97	42	76	.553	0	0	.000	13	28	.464	36	73	109	7	69	0	11	18	31	6.5	1.9	2.1	0.1	.403
90-91	Houston	42	0	343	77	35	83	.422	0	1	.000	7	17	.412	43	57	100	8	35	0	19	10	29	8.2	1.8	2.4	0.2	.330
94-95	Houston	7	0	30	5	1	4	.250	0	0	.000	3	6	.500	1	9	10	0	6	0	1	0	1	4.3	0.7	1.4	0.0	.245
95-96	Indiana	51	1	327	110	46	83	.554	0	0	.000	18	36	.500	42	68	110	6	73	0	9	5	36	6.4	2.2	2.2	0.1	.372
96-97	New Jersey	18	0	204	29	10	35	.286	0	2	.000	9	17	.529	20	36	56	5	27	0	8	1	13	11.3	1.6	3.1	0.3	.212
96-97	Philadelphia	27	0	365	72	30	57	.526	0	0	.000	12	33	.364	38	73	111	7	60	1	8	7	16	13.5	2.7	4.1	0.3	.326
97-98	Dallas	1	0	3	0	0	0	.000	0	0	.000	0	0	.000	0	0	0	0	0	0	0	0	0	3.0	0.0	0.0	0.0	.000
NBA Season Totals		197	1	1603	390	164	338	.485	0	3	.000	62	137	.453	180	316	496	33	270	1	56	41	126	8.1	2.0	2.5	0.2	....
89-90	Houston	1	0	1	0	0	0	.000	0	0	.000	0	0	.000	0	0	0	0	0	0	0	0	0	1.0	0.0	0.0	0.0	.000
95-96	Indiana	1	0	3	2	1	1	1.000	0	0	.000	0	0	.000	0	1	1	0	0	0	0	0	0	3.0	2.0	1.0	0.0	.980
NBA Playoff Totals		2	0	4	2	1	1	1.000	0	0	.000	0	0	.000	0	1	1	0	0	0	0	0	0	2.0	1.0	0.5	0.0	....

• CALDWELL, Jim

James W. Caldwell Jr.

Born: Jan. 28, 1943. Durham, NC, United States.   Height: 6'10".   Weight: 240 lbs.   Drafted: 1965   College: Georgia Tech

YEAR	TEAM	GP	GS	MIN	PTS	FGM	FGA	FG%	3PM	3PA	3P%	FTM	FTA	FT%	ORB	DRB	TRB	AST	PF	DQ	STL	BLK	TO	MPG	PPG	RPG	APG	PCM
67-68	Kentucky-A	58	....	1582	490	200	469	.426	1	6	.167	89	144	.618	....	....	543	136	205	9	....	....	102	27.3	8.4	9.4	2.3	.486
67-68	New Jersey-A	12	....	261	56	23	66	.348	0	0	.000	10	22	.455	....	....	85	11	29	1	....	....	19	21.8	4.7	7.1	0.9	.332
67-68	New York	2	....	7	0	0	1	.000	....	....	....	0	0	.000	....	....	1	1	1	0	....	....	....	3.5	0.0	0.5	0.5	.115
68-69	Kentucky-A	65	....	1235	422	167	381	.438	1	9	.111	87	129	.674	133	290	423	130	211	3	....	....	97	19.0	6.5	6.5	2.0	.519
NBA Season Totals		2	....	7	0	0	1	.000	....	....	....	0	0	.000	....	....	1	1	1	0	....	....	....	3.5	0.0	0.5	0.5	....
ABA Season Totals		135	....	3078	968	390	916	.426	2	15	.133	186	295	.631	133	290	1051	277	445	13	....	....	218	22.8	7.2	7.8	2.1	....
Career Totals		137	....	3085	968	390	917	.425	2	15	.133	186	295	.631	133	290	1052	278	446	13	....	....	218	22.5	7.1	7.7	2.0	....
67-68	Kentucky-A	5	....	175	58	22	51	.431	0	0	.000	14	20	.700	17	42	59	14	25	0	....	....	12	35.0	11.6	11.8	2.8	.494
68-69	Kentucky-A	7	....	63	11	4	15	.267	0	0	.000	3	7	.429	....	....	21	5	11	0	....	....	1	9.0	1.6	3.0	0.7	.299
ABA Playoff Totals		12	....	238	69	26	66	.394	0	0	.000	17	27	.630	17	42	80	19	36	0	....	....	13	19.8	5.8	6.7	1.6	....

• CALDWELL, Joe

Joe Louis (Pogo) Caldwell

Born: Nov. 1, 1941. Texas City, TX, United States.   Height: 6'5".   Weight: 195 lbs.   Drafted: 1964   College: Arizona State

YEAR	TEAM	GP	GS	MIN	PTS	FGM	FGA	FG%	3PM	3PA	3P%	FTM	FTA	FT%	ORB	DRB	TRB	AST	PF	DQ	STL	BLK	TO	MPG	PPG	RPG	APG	PCM
64-65	Detroit	66	....	1543	709	290	776	.374	....	....	....	129	210	.614	....	....	441	118	171	3	....	....	....	23.4	10.7	6.7	1.8	.469
65-66	Detroit	33	....	716	346	143	338	.423	....	....	....	60	88	.682	....	....	190	65	63	0	....	....	....	21.7	10.5	5.8	2.0	.538
65-66	St. Louis	46	....	1141	655	268	600	.447	....	....	....	119	166	.717	....	....	246	61	140	3	....	....	....	24.8	14.2	5.3	1.3	.516

YEAR	TEAM	GP	GS	MIN	PTS	FGM	FGA	FG%	3PM	3PA	3P%	FTM	FTA	FT%	ORB	DRB	TRB	AST	PF	DQ	STL	BLK	TO	MPG	PPG	RPG	APG	PCM
66-67	St. Louis	81	....	2256	1116	458	1076	.426	....	....	....	200	308	.649	....	....	442	166	230	4	....	....	....	27.9	13.8	5.5	2.0	.461
67-68	St. Louis	79	....	2641	1293	564	1219	.463	....	....	....	165	290	.569	....	....	338	240	208	1	....	....	....	33.4	16.4	4.3	3.0	.453
68-69	Atlanta	81	....	2720	1281	561	1106	.507	....	....	....	159	296	.537	....	....	303	320	231	1	....	....	....	33.6	15.8	3.7	4.0	.477
69-70	Atlanta	82	....	2857	1727	674	1329	.507	....	....	....	379	551	.688	....	....	407	287	255	3	....	....	....	34.8	21.1	5.0	3.5	.575
70-71	Carolina-A	72	....	3008	1678	685	1528	.448	6	30	.200	302	541	.558	216	273	489	301	237	3	....	....	249	41.8	23.3	6.8	4.2	.520
71-72	Carolina-A	61	....	2145	1032	434	922	.471	5	20	.250	159	318	.500	157	186	343	259	208	5	....	....	164	35.2	16.9	5.6	4.2	.482
72-73	Carolina-A	77	....	2739	1283	555	1118	.496	1	6	.167	172	405	.425	189	206	395	352	252	4	166	....	246	35.6	16.7	5.1	4.6	.475
73-74	Carolina-A	79	....	2654	1135	502	1027	.489	3	17	.176	128	258	.496	177	235	412	350	255	....	170	35	242	33.6	14.4	5.2	4.4	.479
74-75	St. Louis-A	25	....	841	364	161	326	.494	3	7	.429	39	87	.448	44	67	111	128	78	....	49	10	74	33.6	14.6	4.4	5.1	.479
NBA Season Totals		468	....	13874	7127	2958	6444	.459	....	....	....	1211	1909	.634	....	....	2367	1257	1298	15	....	....	....	29.6	15.2	5.1	2.7	....
ABA Season Totals		314	....	11387	5492	2337	4921	.475	18	80	.225	800	1609	.497	783	967	1750	1390	1030	12	385	45	975	36.3	17.5	5.6	4.4	....
Career Totals		782	....	25261	12619	5295	11365	.466	18	80	.225	2011	3518	.572	783	967	4117	2647	2328	27	385	45	975	32.3	16.1	5.3	3.4	....
65-66	St. Louis	10	....	315	187	78	169	.462	....	....	....	31	49	.633	....	....	55	16	29	0	....	....	....	31.5	18.7	5.5	1.6	.507
66-67	St. Louis	9	....	217	110	42	105	.400	....	....	....	26	39	.667	....	....	39	13	27	1	....	....	....	24.1	12.2	4.3	1.4	.417
67-68	St. Louis	6	....	148	32	15	46	.326	....	....	....	2	15	.133	....	....	21	15	10	0	....	....	....	24.7	5.3	3.5	2.5	.222
68-69	Atlanta	11	....	404	162	65	134	.485	....	....	....	32	69	.464	....	....	55	37	40	1	....	....	....	36.7	14.7	5.0	3.4	.399
69-70	Atlanta	9	....	393	225	93	198	.470	....	....	....	39	60	.650	....	....	45	38	34	1	....	....	....	43.7	25.0	5.0	4.2	.485
72-73	Carolina-A	12	....	467	187	80	163	.491	3	8	.375	24	50	.480	35	33	68	40	35	0	....	....	44	38.9	15.6	5.7	3.3	.407
73-74	Carolina-A	4	....	105	38	16	34	.471	0	2	.000	6	12	.500	18	9	27	13	14	....	8	0	12	26.3	9.5	6.8	3.3	.495
NBA Playoff Totals		45	....	1477	716	293	652	.449	....	....	....	130	232	.560	....	....	215	119	140	3	....	....	....	32.8	15.9	4.8	2.6	....
ABA Playoff Totals		16	....	572	225	96	197	.487	3	10	.300	30	62	.484	53	42	95	53	49	0	8	0	56	35.8	14.1	5.9	3.3	....
Career Playoff Totals		61	....	2049	941	389	849	.458	3	10	.300	160	294	.544	53	42	310	172	189	3	8	0	56	33.6	15.4	5.1	2.8	....

• CALHOUN, Bill

William C. Calhoun

Born: Nov. 4, 1927. San Francisco, CA, United States. Height: 6'3". Weight: 180 lbs. Drafted: — College: San Francisco City

YEAR	TEAM	GP	GS	MIN	PTS	FGM	FGA	FG%	3PM	3PA	3P%	FTM	FTA	FT%	ORB	DRB	TRB	AST	PF	DQ	STL	BLK	TO	MPG	PPG	RPG	APG	PCM
47-48	Rochester-N	42	....	....	80	31	....	....	....	....	....	18	34	.529	....	....	....	....	32	....	....	....	....	....	1.9	....	....	....
48-49	Rochester	56	....	....	367	146	408	.358	....	....	....	75	131	.573	....	....	....	125	97	....	....	....	....	....	6.6	....	2.2	....
49-50	Rochester	62	....	....	560	207	549	.377	....	....	....	146	203	.719	....	....	....	115	100	....	....	....	....	....	9.0	....	1.9	....
50-51	Rochester	66	....	....	511	175	506	.346	....	....	....	161	228	.706	....	....	199	99	87	1	....	....	....	....	7.7	3.0	1.5	....
51-52	Baltimore	55	....	1594	383	129	409	.315	....	....	....	125	183	.683	....	....	252	117	84	0	....	....	....	29.0	7.0	4.6	2.1	.291
52-53	Syr/Mil	62	....	2148	571	180	534	.337	....	....	....	211	292	.723	....	....	277	156	136	4	....	....	....	34.6	9.2	4.5	2.5	.296
53-54	Milwaukee	72	....	2370	594	190	545	.349	....	....	....	214	292	.733	....	....	274	189	151	3	....	....	....	32.9	8.3	3.8	2.6	.295
54-55	Milwaukee	69	....	2109	454	144	480	.300	....	....	....	166	236	.703	....	....	290	235	181	4	....	....	....	30.6	6.6	4.2	3.4	.293
NBA Season Totals		442	....	8221	3440	1171	3431	.341	....	....	....	1098	1565	.702	....	....	1292	1036	836	12	....	....	....	18.6	7.8	2.9	2.3	....
NBL Season Totals		42	....	....	80	31	....	....	....	....	....	18	34	....	....	....	....	....	32	....	....	....	....	....	1.9	....	....	....
Career Totals		484	....	8221	3520	1202	3431	....	....	....	....	1116	1599	....	....	....	1292	1036	868	12	....	....	....	17.0	7.3	2.7	2.1	....
47-48	Rochester-N	8	....	....	24	11	....	....	....	....	....	2	3	.667	....	....	....	....	....	....	....	....	....	....	3.0	....	....	....
48-49	Rochester	4	....	....	39	13	30	.433	....	....	....	13	18	.722	....	....	....	14	6	....	....	....	....	....	9.8	....	3.5	....
50-51	Rochester	14	....	....	61	20	48	.417	....	....	....	21	28	.750	....	....	41	20	19	0	....	....	....	....	4.4	2.9	1.4	....
NBA Playoff Totals		18	....	....	100	33	78	.423	....	....	....	34	46	.739	....	....	41	34	25	0	....	....	....	....	5.6	2.3	1.9	....
NBL Playoff Totals		8	....	....	24	11	....	....	....	....	....	2	3	....	....	....	....	....	....	....	....	....	....	....	3.0	....	....	....
Career Playoff Totals		26	....	....	124	44	78	....	....	....	....	36	49	....	....	....	41	34	25	0	....	....	....	....	4.8	1.6	1.3	....

• CALHOUN, Corky

David L. (Corky) Calhoun

Born: Nov. 1, 1950. Waukegan, IL, United States. Height: 6'7". Weight: 210 lbs. Drafted: 1972 College: Pennsylvania

YEAR	TEAM	GP	GS	MIN	PTS	FGM	FGA	FG%	3PM	3PA	3P%	FTM	FTA	FT%	ORB	DRB	TRB	AST	PF	DQ	STL	BLK	TO	MPG	PPG	RPG	APG	PCM
72-73	Phoenix	82	....	2025	493	211	450	.469	....	....	....	71	96	.740	....	....	338	76	214	2	....	....	....	24.7	6.0	4.1	0.9	.278
73-74	Phoenix	77	....	2207	634	268	581	.461	....	....	....	98	129	.760	115	292	407	135	253	4	71	30	....	28.7	8.2	5.3	1.8	.339
74-75	Phoenix	13	....	108	38	12	32	.375	....	....	....	14	15	.933	14	19	33	4	20	0	6	2	....	8.3	2.9	2.5	0.3	.414
74-75	LA Lakers	57	....	1270	284	120	286	.420	....	....	....	44	62	.710	95	141	236	75	160	1	49	23	....	22.3	5.0	4.1	1.3	.279
75-76	LA Lakers	76	....	1816	409	172	368	.467	....	....	....	65	83	.783	117	224	341	85	216	4	62	35	....	23.9	5.4	4.5	1.1	.292
76-77	Portland	70	....	743	236	85	183	.464	....	....	....	66	85	.776	40	104	144	35	123	1	24	8	....	10.6	3.4	2.1	0.5	.342
77-78	Portland	79	....	1370	416	175	365	.479	....	....	....	66	76	.868	73	142	215	87	141	3	42	15	63	17.3	5.3	2.7	1.1	.339
78-79	Indiana	81	....	1332	378	153	335	.457	....	....	....	72	86	.837	64	174	238	104	189	1	37	19	57	16.4	4.7	2.9	1.3	.338
79-80	Indiana	7	....	30	8	4	9	.444	0	0	.000	0	2	.000	7	3	10	0	6	0	2	0	1	4.3	1.1	1.4	0.0	.327
NBA Season Totals		542	....	10901	2896	1200	2609	.460	0	0	.000	496	634	.782	525	1099	1962	601	1322	16	293	132	121	20.1	5.3	3.6	1.1	....
76-77	Portland	12	....	94	28	13	25	.520	....	....	....	2	3	.667	6	8	14	4	16	0	4	2	....	7.8	2.3	1.2	0.3	.287
77-78	Portland	6	....	109	34	15	29	.517	....	....	....	4	7	.571	6	8	14	3	6	0	2	1	3	18.2	5.7	2.3	0.5	.307
NBA Playoff Totals		18	....	203	62	28	54	.519	....	....	....	6	10	.600	12	16	28	7	22	0	6	3	3	11.3	3.4	1.6	0.4	....

• CALIHAN, Robert

Robert J. Calihan

Born: Aug. 2, 1918. Perry, IA, United States. Height: 6'3". Weight: 200 lbs. Drafted: — College: Detroit

YEAR	TEAM	GP	GS	MIN	PTS	FGM	FGA	FG%	3PM	3PA	3P%	FTM	FTA	FT%	ORB	DRB	TRB	AST	PF	DQ	STL	BLK	TO	MPG	PPG	RPG	APG	PCM
40-41	Detroit-N	23	....	....	181	69	....	....	....	....	....	43	....	....	....	....	....	....	....	....	....	....	....	....	7.9	....	....	....
45-46	Chicago-N	31	....	....	270	109	....	....	....	....	....	52	77	.675	....	....	....	....	....	....	....	....	....	....	8.7	....	....	....
46-47	Chicago-N	44	....	....	484	196	....	....	....	....	....	92	132	.697	....	....	....	....	124	....	....	....	....	....	11.0	....	....	....
47-48	Flint-N	56	....	....	806	273	....	....	....	....	....	260	371	.701	....	....	....	....	145	....	....	....	....	....	14.4	....	....	....
48-49	Syracuse-N	11	....	....	69	28	....	....	....	....	....	13	21	.619	....	....	....	....	33	....	....	....	....	....	6.3	....	....	....
NBL Season Totals		165	....	....	1810	675	....	....	....	....	....	460	601	....	....	....	....	....	302	....	....	....	....	....	11.0	....	....	....
40-41	Detroit-N	3	....	....	21	10	....	....	....	....	....	1	....	....	....	....	....	....	....	....	....	....	....	....	7.0	....	....	....
46-47	Chicago-N	11	....	....	135	57	....	....	....	....	....	21	37	.568	....	....	....	....	....	....	....	....	....	....	12.3	....	....	....
48-49	Syracuse-N	6	....	....	59	21	....	....	....	....	....	17	23	.739	....	....	....	....	....	....	....	....	....	....	9.8	....	....	....
NBL Playoff Totals		20	....	....	215	88	....	....	....	....	....	39	60	....	....	....	....	....	....	....	....	....	....	....	10.8	....	....	....

YEAR TEAM	GP	GS	MIN	PTS	FGM	FGA	FG%	3PM	3PA	3P%	FTM	FTA	FT%	ORB	DRB	TRB	AST	PF	DQ	STL	BLK	TO	MPG	PPG	RPG	APG	PCM

• CALIP, Demetrius
Demetrius Calip

Born: Nov. 18, 1969. Flint, MI, United States. Height: 6'1". Weight: 165 lbs. Drafted: — College: Michigan

YEAR TEAM	GP	GS	MIN	PTS	FGM	FGA	FG%	3PM	3PA	3P%	FTM	FTA	FT%	ORB	DRB	TRB	AST	PF	DQ	STL	BLK	TO	MPG	PPG	RPG	APG	PCM
91-92 LA Lakers	7	0	58	11	4	18	.222	1	5	.200	2	3	.667	1	4	5	12	8	0	1	0	5	8.3	1.6	0.7	1.7	.131
NBA Season Totals	7	0	58	11	4	18	.222	1	5	.200	2	3	.667	1	4	5	12	8	0	1	0	5	8.3	1.6	0.7	1.7	....

• CALLAHAN, Tom
Thomas Francis Callahan

Born: June 2, 1921. Height: 6'1". Weight: 180 lbs. Drafted: — College: Rockhurst

YEAR TEAM	GP	GS	MIN	PTS	FGM	FGA	FG%	3PM	3PA	3P%	FTM	FTA	FT%	ORB	DRB	TRB	AST	PF	DQ	STL	BLK	TO	MPG	PPG	RPG	APG	PCM
46-47 Providence	13	....	....	17	6	29	.207	....	....	....	5	12	.417	....	....	....	4	9	....	....	....	....	....	1.3	....	0.3	....
NBA Season Totals	13	....	....	17	6	29	.207	....	....	....	5	12	.417	....	....	....	4	9	....	....	....	....	....	1.3	....	0.3	....

• CALLOWAY, Rick
Richard Marlon Calloway

Born: Dec. 12, 1966. Cincinnati, OH, United States. Height: 6'6". Weight: 180 lbs. Drafted: — College: Kansas

YEAR TEAM	GP	GS	MIN	PTS	FGM	FGA	FG%	3PM	3PA	3P%	FTM	FTA	FT%	ORB	DRB	TRB	AST	PF	DQ	STL	BLK	TO	MPG	PPG	RPG	APG	PCM
90-91 Sacramento	64	0	678	205	75	192	.391	0	2	.000	55	79	.696	25	53	78	61	98	1	22	7	51	10.6	3.2	1.2	1.0	.230
NBA Season Totals	64	0	678	205	75	192	.391	0	2	.000	55	79	.696	25	53	78	61	98	1	22	7	51	10.6	3.2	1.2	1.0	....

• CALVERLEY, Ernie
Ernest A. Calverley

Born: Jan. 30, 1924. Pawtucket, RI, United States. Height: 5'10". Weight: 145 lbs. Drafted: — College: Rhode Island

YEAR TEAM	GP	GS	MIN	PTS	FGM	FGA	FG%	3PM	3PA	3P%	FTM	FTA	FT%	ORB	DRB	TRB	AST	PF	DQ	STL	BLK	TO	MPG	PPG	RPG	APG	PCM
46-47 Providence	59	....	....	845	323	1102	.293	....	....	....	199	283	.703	....	....	....	202	191	....	....	....	....	....	14.3	....	3.4	....
47-48 Providence	47	....	....	559	226	835	.271	....	....	....	107	161	.665	....	....	....	119	168	....	....	....	....	....	11.9	....	2.5	....
48-49 Providence	59	....	....	557	218	696	.313	....	....	....	121	160	.756	....	....	....	251	183	....	....	....	....	....	9.4	....	4.3	....
NBA Season Totals	165	....	....	1961	767	2633	.291	....	....	....	427	604	.707	....	....	....	572	542	....	....	....	....	....	11.9	....	3.5	....

• CALVIN, Mack
Mack Calvin

Born: July 27, 1947. Fort Worth, TX, United States. Height: 6' Weight: 165 lbs. Drafted: 1969 College: USC

YEAR TEAM	GP	GS	MIN	PTS	FGM	FGA	FG%	3PM	3PA	3P%	FTM	FTA	FT%	ORB	DRB	TRB	AST	PF	DQ	STL	BLK	TO	MPG	PPG	RPG	APG	PCM
69-70 Los Angeles-A	84	....	2955	1414	441	1047	.421	3	25	.120	529	642	.824	95	199	294	478	289	6	....	....	261	35.2	16.8	3.5	5.7	.514
70-71 Florida-A	81	....	3394	2201	744	1728	.431	17	59	.288	696	805	.865	107	176	283	619	263	5	....	....	356	41.9	27.2	3.5	7.6	.658
71-72 Florida-A	82	....	2977	1726	552	1253	.441	11	48	.229	611	701	.872	116	158	274	481	270	4	....	....	261	36.3	21.0	3.3	5.9	.582
72-73 Carolina-A	84	....	2228	1467	478	944	.506	11	28	.393	500	582	.859	97	118	215	301	219	3	....	....	247	26.5	17.5	2.6	3.6	.645
73-74 Carolina-A	83	....	2592	1496	498	1078	.462	10	43	.233	490	560	.875	78	165	243	347	244	....	135	7	234	31.2	18.0	2.9	4.2	.567
74-75 Denver-A	74	....	2463	1444	483	996	.485	3	16	.188	475	530	.896	36	174	210	570	206	....	140	8	279	33.3	19.5	2.8	7.7	.687
75-76 Virginia-A	45	....	1658	872	306	717	.427	7	26	.269	253	285	.888	38	90	128	271	122	....	71	1	192	36.8	19.4	2.8	6.0	.514
76-77 LA Lakers	12	....	207	95	27	82	.329	....	....	....	41	48	.854	6	10	16	21	16	0	11	1	....	17.3	7.9	1.3	1.8	.364
76-77 San Antonio	35	....	606	309	93	237	.392	....	....	....	123	146	.842	11	20	31	104	58	0	23	1	....	17.3	8.8	0.9	3.0	.486
76-77 Denver	29	....	625	323	100	225	.444	....	....	....	123	144	.854	19	30	49	115	53	0	27	1	....	21.6	11.1	1.7	4.0	.570
77-78 Denver	77	....	988	467	147	333	.441	....	....	....	173	206	.840	11	73	84	148	87	0	46	5	108	12.8	6.1	1.1	1.9	.447
79-80 Utah	48	....	772	306	100	227	.441	1	11	.091	105	117	.897	13	71	84	134	72	0	27	0	58	16.1	6.4	1.8	2.8	.450
80-81 Cleveland	21	....	128	52	13	39	.333	1	5	.200	25	35	.714	2	10	12	28	13	0	5	0	17	6.1	2.5	0.6	1.3	.378
NBA Season Totals	222	....	3326	1552	480	1143	.420	2	16	.125	590	696	.848	62	214	276	550	299	0	139	8	183	15.0	7.0	1.2	2.5	....
ABA Season Totals	533	....	18267	10620	3502	7763	.451	62	245	.253	3554	4105	.866	567	1080	1647	3067	1613	18	346	16	1830	34.3	19.9	3.1	5.8	....
Career Totals	755	....	21593	12172	3982	8906	.447	64	261	.245	4144	4801	.863	629	1294	1923	3617	1912	18	485	24	2013	28.6	16.1	2.5	4.8	....
69-70 Los Angeles-A	17	....	593	392	133	294	.452	4	7	.571	122	156	.782	....	....	63	101	....	0	....	....	55	34.9	23.1	3.7	5.9	....
70-71 Florida-A	6	....	255	164	62	120	.517	1	3	.333	39	46	.848	5	11	16	42	10	0	....	....	27	42.5	27.3	2.7	7.0	.682
71-72 Florida-A	4	....	154	85	28	65	.431	0	1	.000	29	33	.879	....	....	16	21	13	....	....	....	14	38.5	21.3	4.0	5.3	.536
72-73 Carolina-A	12	....	370	218	72	154	.468	2	9	.222	72	88	.818	12	22	34	52	35	0	....	....	33	30.8	18.2	2.8	4.3	.565
73-74 Carolina-A	4	....	143	97	34	74	.459	2	7	.286	27	32	.844	8	11	19	13	14	....	5	0	12	35.8	24.3	4.8	3.3	.599
74-75 Denver-A	13	....	444	233	76	163	.466	3	8	.375	78	82	.951	6	35	41	68	50	....	23	1	39	34.2	17.9	3.2	5.2	.549
76-77 Denver	6	....	112	62	19	40	.475	....	....	....	24	29	.828	1	8	9	13	13	0	1	0	....	18.7	10.3	1.5	2.2	.524
77-78 Denver	12	....	135	65	19	42	.452	....	....	....	27	29	.931	3	5	8	21	11	0	7	0	11	11.3	5.4	0.7	1.8	.491
NBA Playoff Totals	18	....	247	127	38	82	.463	....	....	....	51	58	.879	4	13	17	34	24	0	8	0	11	13.7	7.1	0.9	1.9	....
ABA Playoff Totals	56	....	1959	1189	405	870	.466	12	35	.343	367	437	.840	31	79	189	297	122	0	28	1	180	35.0	21.2	3.4	5.3	....
Career Playoff Totals	74	....	2206	1316	443	952	.465	12	35	.343	418	495	.844	35	92	206	331	146	0	36	1	191	29.8	17.8	2.8	4.5	....

• CAMBRIDGE, Dexter
Dexter Ryan Cambridge

Born: Jan. 29, 1970. Eleuthra, Bahamas. Height: 6'7". Weight: 224 lbs. Drafted: — College: Texas

YEAR TEAM	GP	GS	MIN	PTS	FGM	FGA	FG%	3PM	3PA	3P%	FTM	FTA	FT%	ORB	DRB	TRB	AST	PF	DQ	STL	BLK	TO	MPG	PPG	RPG	APG	PCM
92-93 Dallas	53	13	885	370	151	312	.484	0	4	.000	68	99	.687	88	79	167	58	128	1	24	6	64	16.7	7.0	3.2	1.1	.375
NBA Season Totals	53	13	885	370	151	312	.484	0	4	.000	68	99	.687	88	79	167	58	128	1	24	6	64	16.7	7.0	3.2	1.1	....

• CAMBY, Marcus
Marcus D. Camby

Born: Mar. 22, 1974. Hartford, CT, United States. Height: 6'11". Weight: 220 lbs. Drafted: 1996 College: Massachusetts

YEAR TEAM	GP	GS	MIN	PTS	FGM	FGA	FG%	3PM	3PA	3P%	FTM	FTA	FT%	ORB	DRB	TRB	AST	PF	DQ	STL	BLK	TO	MPG	PPG	RPG	APG	PCM
96-97 Toronto	63	38	1897	935	375	778	.482	2	14	.143	183	264	.693	131	263	394	97	214	7	66	130	132	30.1	14.8	6.3	1.5	.502
97-98 Toronto	63	58	2002	765	308	747	.412	0	2	.000	149	244	.611	203	263	466	111	200	1	68	230	132	31.8	12.1	7.4	1.8	.463
98-99 New York	46	0	945	329	136	261	.521	0	0	.000	57	103	.553	102	151	253	12	131	2	29	74	39	20.5	7.2	5.5	0.3	.460
99-00 New York	59	11	1548	601	226	471	.480	1	2	.500	148	221	.670	174	287	461	49	204	5	43	116	72	26.2	10.2	7.8	0.8	.519
00-01 New York	63	63	2127	759	304	580	.524	1	8	.125	150	225	.667	196	527	723	52	205	4	66	136	63	33.8	12.0	11.5	0.8	.572
01-02 New York	29	29	1007	322	130	290	.448	0	1	.000	62	99	.626	89	233	322	33	107	3	34	50	42	34.7	11.1	11.1	1.1	.474
02-03 Denver	29	9	616	221	93	227	.410	2	5	.400	33	50	.660	75	133	208	47	69	1	20	40	27	21.2	7.6	7.2	1.6	.536
NBA Season Totals	352	208	10142	3932	1572	3354	.469	6	32	.188	782	1206	.648	970	1857	2827	401	1130	23	326	776	507	28.8	11.2	8.0	1.1	....

YEAR	TEAM	GP	GS	MIN	PTS	FGM	FGA	FG%	3PM	3PA	3P%	FTM	FTA	FT%	ORB	DRB	TRB	AST	PF	DQ	STL	BLK	TO	MPG	PPG	RPG	APG	PCM
98-99	New York	20	3	509	207	81	143	.566	0	1	.000	45	73	.616	51	102	153	6	76	2	24	38	15	25.5	10.4	7.7	0.3	.570
99-00	New York	16	0	386	77	29	86	.337	0	1	.000	19	31	.613	35	77	112	6	51	1	8	23	12	24.1	4.8	7.0	0.4	.316
00-01	New York	4	4	141	25	10	26	.385	0	0	.000	5	13	.385	4	28	32	7	18	1	2	9	2	35.3	6.3	8.0	1.8	.308
NBA Playoff Totals		40	7	1036	309	120	255	.471	0	2	.000	69	117	.590	90	207	297	19	145	4	34	70	29	25.9	7.7	7.4	0.5	....

• CAMIC, Joe

Joseph (The Rankin Razor) Camic

Born: 1922. Height: 6'5". Weight: 195 lbs. Drafted: — College: Duquesne

YEAR	TEAM	GP	GS	MIN	PTS	FGM	FGA	FG%	3PM	3PA	3P%	FTM	FTA	FT%	ORB	DRB	TRB	AST	PF	DQ	STL	BLK	TO	MPG	PPG	RPG	APG	PCM
47-48	Tri-Cities-N	60	....	....	333	129	....	....	....	....	....	75	113	.664	....	....	....	....	187	....	....	....	....	....	5.6	....	....	....
48-49	Hammond-N	31	....	....	202	71	....	....	....	....	....	60	97	.619	....	....	....	....	....	....	....	....	....	....	6.5	....	....	....
48-49	Tri-Cities-N	31	....	....	91	32	....	....	....	....	....	27	47	.574	....	....	....	....	....	....	....	....	....	....	2.9	....	....	....
NBL Season Totals		122	....	....	626	232	....	....	....	....	....	162	257	....	....	....	....	....	187	....	....	....	....	....	5.1	....	....	....
47-48	Tri-Cities-N	6	....	....	31	11	....	....	....	....	....	9	12	.750	....	....	....	....	....	....	....	....	....	....	5.2	....	....	....
48-49	Hammond-N	2	....	....	19	7	....	....	....	....	....	5	5	1.000	....	....	....	....	....	....	....	....	....	....	9.5	....	....	....
NBL Playoff Totals		8	....	....	50	18	....	....	....	....	....	14	17	....	....	....	....	....	....	....	....	....	....	....	6.3	....	....	....

• CAMPBELL, Elden

Elden Jerome (Big E) Campbell

Born: July 23, 1968. Los Angeles, CA, United States. Height: 6'11". Weight: 215 lbs. Drafted: 1990 College: Clemson

YEAR	TEAM	GP	GS	MIN	PTS	FGM	FGA	FG%	3PM	3PA	3P%	FTM	FTA	FT%	ORB	DRB	TRB	AST	PF	DQ	STL	BLK	TO	MPG	PPG	RPG	APG	PCM
90-91	LA Lakers	52	0	380	144	56	123	.455	0	0	.000	32	49	.653	40	56	96	10	71	1	11	38	16	7.3	2.8	1.8	0.2	.451
91-92	LA Lakers	81	47	1876	578	220	491	.448	0	2	.000	138	223	.619	155	268	423	59	203	1	53	159	73	23.2	7.1	5.2	0.7	.415
92-93	LA Lakers	79	13	1551	606	238	520	.458	0	3	.000	130	204	.637	127	205	332	48	165	0	59	99	71	19.6	7.7	4.2	0.6	.434
93-94	LA Lakers	76	74	2253	934	373	808	.462	0	2	.000	188	273	.689	167	352	519	86	241	2	64	146	99	29.6	12.3	6.8	1.1	.469
94-95	LA Lakers	73	59	2076	913	360	785	.459	0	1	.000	193	290	.666	168	277	445	92	246	4	69	132	95	28.4	12.5	6.1	1.3	.466
95-96	LA Lakers	82	82	2699	1143	447	888	.503	0	5	.000	249	349	.713	162	461	623	182	**300**	4	88	212	139	32.9	13.9	7.6	2.2	.545
96-97	LA Lakers	77	77	2516	1148	442	942	.469	1	4	.250	263	370	.711	207	408	615	126	276	6	46	117	131	32.7	14.9	8.0	1.6	.493
97-98	LA Lakers	81	28	1784	816	289	624	.463	1	2	.500	237	342	.693	143	312	455	78	209	1	35	102	113	22.0	10.1	5.6	1.0	.498
98-99	LA Lakers	17	1	325	126	44	101	.436	0	0	.000	38	62	.613	38	58	96	8	51	2	1	16	22	19.1	7.4	5.6	0.5	.405
98-99	Charlotte	32	32	1134	490	178	364	.489	0	1	.000	134	207	.647	88	213	301	61	108	1	38	57	58	35.4	15.3	9.4	1.9	.540
99-00	Charlotte	78	77	2538	987	370	829	.446	0	6	.000	247	358	.690	168	422	590	129	269	6	56	150	127	32.5	12.7	7.6	1.7	.452
00-01	Charlotte	78	78	2337	1022	367	834	.440	0	6	.000	288	406	.709	157	451	608	104	280	1	60	140	144	30.0	13.1	7.8	1.3	.486
01-02	Charlotte	77	74	2155	1074	384	794	.484	0	2	.000	306	384	.797	133	397	530	102	264	4	60	137	138	28.0	13.9	6.9	1.3	.554
02-03	New Orleans	41	1	685	295	101	247	.409	0	1	.000	93	115	.809	34	108	142	42	102	2	24	31	42	16.7	7.2	3.5	1.0	.427
02-03	Seattle	15	0	184	48	16	48	.333	0	0	.000	16	21	.762	13	26	39	9	27	0	9	8	8	12.3	3.2	2.6	0.6	.314
NBA Season Totals		939	643	24493	10324	3885	8398	.463	2	35	.057	2552	3653	.699	1800	4014	5814	1136	2812	35	673	1544	1276	26.1	11.0	6.2	1.2	....
90-91	LA Lakers	14	0	138	57	25	38	.658	0	0	.000	7	15	.467	8	21	29	3	23	1	6	8	6	9.9	4.1	2.1	0.2	.494
91-92	LA Lakers	4	2	117	40	14	37	.378	0	0	.000	12	18	.667	9	16	25	6	14	0	3	6	4	29.3	10.0	6.3	1.5	.373
92-93	LA Lakers	5	5	178	70	29	69	.420	0	0	.000	12	24	.500	17	25	42	7	15	0	6	12	12	35.6	14.0	8.4	1.4	.406
94-95	LA Lakers	10	10	376	157	64	132	.485	0	0	.000	29	44	.659	26	47	73	16	44	2	4	30	15	37.6	15.7	7.3	1.6	.449
95-96	LA Lakers	4	4	129	48	20	39	.513	0	1	.000	8	16	.500	3	29	32	8	17	1	1	9	10	32.3	12.0	8.0	2.0	.441
96-97	LA Lakers	9	9	278	106	37	93	.398	1	1	1.000	31	38	.816	14	25	39	9	30	0	7	13	14	30.9	11.8	4.3	1.0	.317
97-98	LA Lakers	13	0	180	68	23	51	.451	0	0	.000	22	34	.647	17	28	45	8	27	0	3	12	13	13.8	5.2	3.5	0.6	.423
99-00	Charlotte	4	4	150	57	22	47	.468	0	1	.000	13	14	.929	9	24	33	4	16	0	2	4	8	37.5	14.3	8.3	1.0	.394
00-01	Charlotte	10	10	287	121	42	106	.396	0	0	.000	37	49	.755	27	52	79	7	37	1	5	11	17	28.7	12.1	7.9	0.7	.416
01-02	Charlotte	9	9	254	122	49	110	.445	0	1	.000	24	34	.706	14	46	60	16	34	0	6	23	17	28.2	13.6	6.7	1.8	.510
NBA Playoff Totals		82	53	2087	846	325	722	.450	1	4	.250	195	286	.682	144	313	457	84	257	5	43	128	116	25.5	10.3	5.6	1.0	....

• CAMPBELL, Fred

Fred Campbell

Born: 1920. Height: 5'11". Weight: 175 lbs. Drafted: — College: Southern Illinois

YEAR	TEAM	GP	GS	MIN	PTS	FGM	FGA	FG%	3PM	3PA	3P%	FTM	FTA	FT%	ORB	DRB	TRB	AST	PF	DQ	STL	BLK	TO	MPG	PPG	RPG	APG	PCM
46-47	Detroit-N	39	....	....	268	105	....	....	....	....	....	58	81	.716	....	....	....	....	68	....	....	....	....	....	6.9	....	....	....
48-49	Detroit-N	10	....	....	18	5	....	....	....	....	....	8	11	.727	....	....	....	....	....	....	....	....	....	....	1.8	....	....	....
NBL Season Totals		49	....	....	286	110	....	....	....	....	....	66	92	....	....	....	....	....	68	....	....	....	....	....	5.8	....	....	....

• CAMPBELL, Ken

Kenton Campbell

Born: 1926. Newton, OH, United States. Height: 6'4". Weight: 198 lbs. Drafted: — College: Kentucky

YEAR	TEAM	GP	GS	MIN	PTS	FGM	FGA	FG%	3PM	3PA	3P%	FTM	FTA	FT%	ORB	DRB	TRB	AST	PF	DQ	STL	BLK	TO	MPG	PPG	RPG	APG	PCM
48-49	Hammond-N	14	....	....	70	29	....	....	....	....	....	12	18	.667	....	....	....	....	18	....	....	....	....	....	5.0	....	....	....
NBL Season Totals		14	....	....	70	29	....	....	....	....	....	12	18	....	....	....	....	....	18	....	....	....	....	....	5.0	....	....	....

• CAMPBELL, Tony

Anthony (Top Cat, T.C.) Campbell

Born: May 7, 1962. Teaneck, NJ, United States. Height: 6'7". Weight: 215 lbs. Drafted: 1984 College: Ohio State

YEAR	TEAM	GP	GS	MIN	PTS	FGM	FGA	FG%	3PM	3PA	3P%	FTM	FTA	FT%	ORB	DRB	TRB	AST	PF	DQ	STL	BLK	TO	MPG	PPG	RPG	APG	PCM
84-85	Detroit	56	0	625	316	130	262	.496	0	1	.000	56	70	.800	41	48	89	24	107	1	28	3	67	11.2	5.6	1.6	0.4	.339
85-86	Detroit	82	1	1292	648	294	608	.484	2	9	.222	58	73	.795	83	153	236	45	164	0	62	7	82	15.8	7.9	2.9	0.5	.409
86-87	Detroit	40	0	332	138	57	145	.393	0	3	.000	24	39	.615	21	37	58	19	40	0	12	1	32	8.3	3.5	1.5	0.5	.262
87-88	LA Lakers	13	1	242	143	57	101	.564	1	3	.333	28	39	.718	8	19	27	15	41	0	11	2	26	18.6	11.0	2.1	1.2	.441
88-89	LA Lakers	63	2	787	388	158	345	.458	2	21	.095	70	83	.843	53	77	130	47	108	0	37	6	63	12.5	6.2	2.1	0.7	.394
89-90	Minnesota	82	81	3164	1903	723	1581	.457	9	54	.167	448	569	.787	209	242	451	213	260	7	111	31	254	38.6	23.2	5.5	2.6	.463
90-91	Minnesota	77	71	2893	1678	652	1502	.434	16	61	.262	358	446	.803	161	185	346	214	204	0	121	48	193	37.6	21.8	4.5	2.8	.442
91-92	Minnesota	78	41	2441	1307	527	1137	.464	13	37	.351	240	299	.803	141	145	286	229	206	1	84	31	164	31.3	16.8	3.7	2.9	.444
92-93	New York	58	13	1062	449	194	396	.490	2	5	.400	59	87	.678	59	96	155	62	150	0	34	5	52	18.3	7.7	2.7	1.1	.354
93-94	New York	22	11	379	157	63	128	.492	1	3	.333	30	37	.811	28	32	60	31	59	1	20	1	29	17.2	7.1	2.7	1.4	.392
93-94	Dallas	41	3	835	398	164	384	.427	6	25	.240	64	83	.771	48	78	126	51	75	0	30	14	53	20.4	9.7	3.1	1.2	.378
94-95	Cleveland	78	0	1128	469	161	392	.411	15	42	.357	132	159	.830	60	93	153	69	122	0	32	8	62	14.5	6.0	2.0	0.9	.336
NBA Season Totals		690	224	15180	7994	3180	6981	.456	67	264	.254	1567	1984	.790	912	1205	2117	1019	1536	10	582	157	1077	22.0	11.6	3.1	1.5	....

YEAR	TEAM	GP	GS	MIN	PTS	FGM	FGA	FG%	3PM	3PA	3P%	FTM	FTA	FT%	ORB	DRB	TRB	AST	PF	DQ	STL	BLK	TO	MPG	PPG	RPG	APG	PCM
84-85	Detroit	2	0	9	2	1	3	.333	0	0	.000	0	0	.000	0	2	2	1	1	0	0	0	0	4.5	1.0	1.0	0.5	.289
85-86	Detroit	2	0	16	9	4	10	.400	0	0	.000	1	2	.500	0	2	2	0	5	0	0	0	1	8.0	4.5	1.0	0.0	.098
86-87	Detroit	4	0	13	9	3	6	.500	1	1	1.000	2	2	1.000	0	5	5	0	1	0	0	0	0	3.3	2.3	1.3	0.0	.800
87-88	LA Lakers	15	0	94	47	18	42	.429	0	1	.000	11	16	.688	4	6	10	5	16	0	3	0	5	6.3	3.1	0.7	0.3	.294
88-89	LA Lakers	9	1	106	56	19	31	.613	2	4	.500	16	22	.727	4	8	12	6	26	1	3	0	9	11.8	6.2	1.3	0.7	.396
92-93	New York	2	0	33	14	4	10	.400	0	1	.000	6	8	.750	2	2	4	2	7	0	1	0	3	16.5	7.0	2.0	1.0	.249
94-95	Cleveland	4	0	37	23	6	14	.429	1	2	.500	10	12	.833	1	1	2	1	3	0	1	1	3	9.3	5.8	0.5	0.3	.409
NBA Playoff Totals		38	1	308	160	55	116	.474	4	9	.444	46	62	.742	11	26	37	15	59	1	8	1	21	8.1	4.2	1.0	0.4	....

• CAMPION, Ed

Ed Campion

Born: 1915.   Height: 6'2".   Weight: 190 lbs.   Drafted: —   College: DePaul

YEAR	TEAM	GP	GS	MIN	PTS	FGM	FGA	FG%	3PM	3PA	3P%	FTM	FTA	FT%	ORB	DRB	TRB	AST	PF	DQ	STL	BLK	TO	MPG	PPG	RPG	APG	PCM
37-38	Whiting-N	15	....	....	42	19	....	....	....	....	....	4	....	....	....	....	....	....	....	....	....	....	....	....	2.8	....	....	....
38-39	Hammond-N	23	....	....	95	40	....	....	....	....	....	15	....	....	....	....	....	....	....	....	....	....	....	....	4.1	....	....	....
NBL Season Totals		38	....	....	137	59	....	....	....	....	....	19	....	....	....	....	....	....	....	....	....	....	....	....	3.6	....	....	....
37-38	Whiting-N	2	....	....	2	1	....	....	....	....	....	0	....	....	....	....	....	....	....	....	....	....	....	....	1.0	....	....	....
NBL Playoff Totals		2	....	....	2	1	....	....	....	....	....	0	....	....	....	....	....	....	....	....	....	....	....	....	1.0	....	....	....

• CANNON, Larry

Lawrence T. Cannon

Born: Apr. 12, 1947. Philadelphia, PA, United States.   Height: 6'4".   Weight: 195 lbs.   Drafted: 1969   College: LaSalle

YEAR	TEAM	GP	GS	MIN	PTS	FGM	FGA	FG%	3PM	3PA	3P%	FTM	FTA	FT%	ORB	DRB	TRB	AST	PF	DQ	STL	BLK	TO	MPG	PPG	RPG	APG	PCM
69-70	Miami-A	57	....	1503	672	253	660	.383	8	30	.267	158	232	.681	74	67	141	153	133	2	....	....	124	26.4	11.8	2.5	2.7	.352
70-71	Denver-A	80	....	3097	2126	751	1722	.436	18	69	.261	606	763	.794	207	126	333	414	237	6	....	....	346	38.7	26.6	4.2	5.2	.631
71-72	Indiana-A	28	....	478	186	67	175	.383	1	6	.167	51	71	.718	15	18	33	72	61	1	....	....	42	17.1	6.6	1.2	2.6	.346
71-72	Memphis-A	26	....	693	437	161	435	.370	2	8	.250	113	150	.753	43	31	74	78	63	0	....	....	63	26.7	16.8	2.8	3.0	.440
73-74	Indiana-A	3	....	26	7	3	7	.429	0	0	.000	1	3	.333	1	2	3	3	2	0	0	0	3	8.7	2.3	1.0	1.0	.302
73-74	Philadelphia	19	....	335	117	49	127	.386	....	....	....	19	28	.679	16	20	36	52	48	0	7	4	....	17.6	6.2	1.9	2.7	.349
NBA Season Totals		19	....	335	117	49	127	.386	....	....	....	19	28	.679	16	20	36	52	48	0	7	4	....	17.6	6.2	1.9	2.7	....
ABA Season Totals		194	....	5797	3428	1235	2999	.412	29	113	.257	929	1219	.762	340	244	584	720	496	9	0	0	578	29.9	17.7	3.0	3.7	....
Career Totals		213	....	6132	3545	1284	3126	.411	29	113	.257	948	1247	.760	356	264	620	772	544	9	7	4	578	28.8	16.6	2.9	3.6	....

• CARD, Frank

Frank Howard Card

Born: Dec. 28, 1944. Philadelphia, PA, United States.   Height: 6'7".   Weight: 195 lbs.   Drafted: 1967   College: South Carolina State

YEAR	TEAM	GP	GS	MIN	PTS	FGM	FGA	FG%	3PM	3PA	3P%	FTM	FTA	FT%	ORB	DRB	TRB	AST	PF	DQ	STL	BLK	TO	MPG	PPG	RPG	APG	PCM
68-69	Minnesota-A	76	....	1596	591	222	537	.413	1	5	.200	146	244	.598	185	234	419	81	155	2	....	....	110	21.0	7.8	5.5	1.1	.416
69-70	Washington-A	74	....	1820	881	351	666	.527	1	5	.200	178	286	.622	.158	322	480	92	216	3	....	....	149	24.6	11.9	6.5	1.2	.543
70-71	Carolina-A	63	....	1795	781	293	645	.454	1	5	.200	194	298	.651	95	353	448	111	210	8	....	....	161	28.5	12.4	7.1	1.8	.482
70-71	Virginia-A	7	....	70	20	9	17	.529	0	0	.000	2	5	.400	2	7	9	2	2	0	....	....	5	10.0	2.9	1.3	0.3	.303
71-72	Carolina-A	9	....	141	38	10	48	.208	0	1	.000	18	25	.720	12	16	28	7	16	0	....	....	9	15.7	4.2	3.1	0.8	.191
71-72	Denver-A	73	....	1443	562	225	495	.455	0	1	.000	112	172	.651	141	189	330	79	204	4	....	....	115	19.8	7.7	4.5	1.1	.407
72-73	Denver-A	4	....	36	21	6	15	.400	0	0	.000	9	13	.692	4	3	7	0	4	0	....	....	3	9.0	5.3	1.8	0.0	.434
ABA Season Totals		306	....	6901	2894	1116	2423	.461	3	17	.176	659	1043	.632	597	1124	1721	372	807	17	....	....	552	22.6	9.5	5.6	1.2	....
68-69	Minnesota-A	6	....	113	54	23	41	.561	0	1	.000	8	13	.615	....	....	28	6	17	0	....	....	10	18.8	9.0	4.7	1.0	.531
69-70	Washington-A	7	....	197	87	37	61	.607	0	0	.000	13	27	.481	....	....	49	13	....	2	....	....	18	28.1	12.4	7.0	1.9	....
71-72	Denver-A	4	....	28	8	4	8	.500	0	0	.000	0	1	1.000	....	....	7	3	10	0	....	....	1	7.0	2.0	1.8	0.8	.327
ABA Playoff Totals		17	....	338	149	64	110	.582	0	1	.000	21	41	.512	....	....	84	22	27	2	....	....	29	19.9	8.8	4.9	1.3	....

• CARDINAL, Brian

Brian Lee Cardinal

Born: May 2, 1977. Tolono, IL, United States.   Height: 6'8".   Weight: 245 lbs.   Drafted: 2000   College: Purdue

YEAR	TEAM	GP	GS	MIN	PTS	FGM	FGA	FG%	3PM	3PA	3P%	FTM	FTA	FT%	ORB	DRB	TRB	AST	PF	DQ	STL	BLK	TO	MPG	PPG	RPG	APG	PCM
00-01	Detroit	15	0	126	31	10	31	.323	0	5	.000	11	18	.611	8	15	23	3	27	0	7	2	9	8.4	2.1	1.5	0.2	.165
01-02	Detroit	8	0	43	17	6	13	.462	3	7	.429	2	2	1.000	2	4	6	2	5	0	1	0	0	5.4	2.1	0.8	0.3	.394
02-03	Washington	5	0	15	4	1	4	.250	0	1	.000	2	2	1.000	3	2	5	1	0	0	0	0	1	3.0	0.8	1.0	0.2	.400
NBA Season Totals		28	0	184	52	17	48	.354	3	13	.231	15	22	.682	13	21	34	6	32	0	8	2	10	6.6	1.9	1.2	0.2	....

• CAREY, Keith

Keith Carey

Born: 1920.   Height: 6'3".   Weight: 190 lbs.   Drafted: —   College: Alma

YEAR	TEAM	GP	GS	MIN	PTS	FGM	FGA	FG%	3PM	3PA	3P%	FTM	FTA	FT%	ORB	DRB	TRB	AST	PF	DQ	STL	BLK	TO	MPG	PPG	RPG	APG	PCM
47-48	Flint-N	37	....	....	111	33	....	....	....	....	....	45	64	.703	....	....	....	21	....	....	....	....	....	....	3.0	....	....	....
NBL Season Totals		37	....	....	111	33	....	....	....	....	....	45	64	....	....	....	....	21	....	....	....	....	....	....	3.0	....	....	....

• CARL, Howie

Howard Hershey (Hersh) Carl

Born: June 7, 1938. Chicago, IL, United States.   Height: 5'9".   Weight: 160 lbs.   Drafted: 1961   College: DePaul

YEAR	TEAM	GP	GS	MIN	PTS	FGM	FGA	FG%	3PM	3PA	3P%	FTM	FTA	FT%	ORB	DRB	TRB	AST	PF	DQ	STL	BLK	TO	MPG	PPG	RPG	APG	PCM
61-62	Chicago	31	....	382	170	67	201	.333	....	....	....	36	51	.706	....	....	39	57	41	1	....	....	....	12.3	5.5	1.3	1.8	.375
NBA Season Totals		31	....	382	170	67	201	.333	....	....	....	36	51	.706	....	....	39	57	41	1	....	....	....	12.3	5.5	1.3	1.8	....

• CARLISLE, Chet

Chester G. Carlisle

Born: Nov. 2, 1916. Died: Aug.1988.   Height: 6'5".   Weight: 195 lbs.   Drafted: —   College: California

YEAR TEAM	GP	GS	MIN	PTS	FGM	FGA	FG%	3PM	3PA	3P%	FTM	FTA	FT%	ORB	DRB	TRB	AST	PF	DQ	STL	BLK	TO	MPG	PPG	RPG	APG	PCM
46-47 Chicago	51	....	....	256	100	373	.268	....	....	....	56	92	.609	....	....	....	17	136	....	....	....	....	5.0	....	0.3	....	
NBA Season Totals	51	....	....	256	100	373	.268	....	....	....	56	92	.609	....	....	....	17	136	....	....	....	....	5.0	....	0.3	....	
46-47 Chicago	10	....	....	56	20	88	.227	....	....	....	16	28	.571	....	....	....	2	33	....	....	....	....	5.6	....	0.2	....	
NBA Playoff Totals	10	....	....	56	20	88	.227	....	....	....	16	28	.571	....	....	....	2	33	....	....	....	....	5.6	....	0.2	....	

• CARLISLE, Rick

Richard Preston Carlisle

Born: Oct. 27, 1959. Ogdensburg, NY, United States.   Height: 6'5".   Weight: 210 lbs.   Drafted: 1984   College: Virginia

YEAR TEAM	GP	GS	MIN	PTS	FGM	FGA	FG%	3PM	3PA	3P%	FTM	FTA	FT%	ORB	DRB	TRB	AST	PF	DQ	STL	BLK	TO	MPG	PPG	RPG	APG	PCM
84-85 Boston	38	0	179	67	26	67	.388	0	2	.000	15	17	.882	8	13	21	25	21	0	3	0	19	4.7	1.8	0.6	0.7	.276
85-86 Boston	77	1	760	199	92	189	.487	0	10	.000	15	23	.652	22	55	77	104	92	1	19	4	46	9.9	2.6	1.0	1.4	.295
86-87 Boston	42	0	297	80	30	92	.326	5	16	.313	15	20	.750	8	22	30	35	28	0	8	0	25	7.1	1.9	0.7	0.8	.190
87-88 New York	26	0	204	74	29	67	.433	6	17	.353	10	11	.909	6	7	13	32	39	1	11	4	21	7.8	2.8	0.5	1.2	.297
89-90 New Jersey	5	0	21	2	1	7	.143	0	3	.000	0	0	.000	0	0	0	5	7	0	1	1	4	4.2	0.4	0.0	1.0	-.165
NBA Season Totals	188	1	1461	422	178	422	.422	11	48	.229	55	71	.775	44	97	141	201	187	2	42	9	115	7.8	2.2	0.8	1.1	....
85-86 Boston	10	0	54	19	8	15	.533	0	0	.000	3	4	.750	3	2	5	8	9	0	2	0	3	5.4	1.9	0.5	0.8	.373
87-88 New York	2	0	8	2	1	4	.250	0	2	.000	0	0	.000	1	1	2	0	1	0	1	0	0	4.0	1.0	1.0	0.0	.192
NBA Playoff Totals	12	0	62	21	9	19	.474	0	2	.000	3	4	.750	4	3	7	8	10	0	3	0	3	5.2	1.8	0.6	0.7	....

• CARLOS, Don

Don A. Carlos

Born: Mar. 3, 1944. Columbus, OH, United States.   Height: 6'5".   Weight: 210 lbs.   Drafted: 1967   College: Otterbein

YEAR TEAM	GP	GS	MIN	PTS	FGM	FGA	FG%	3PM	3PA	3P%	FTM	FTA	FT%	ORB	DRB	TRB	AST	PF	DQ	STL	BLK	TO	MPG	PPG	RPG	APG	PCM
68-69 Houston-A	56	....	1527	628	207	505	.410	0	3	.000	214	283	.756	122	157	279	159	231	10	....	....	140	27.3	11.2	5.0	2.8	.435
ABA Season Totals	56	....	1527	628	207	505	.410	0	3	.000	214	283	.756	122	157	279	159	231	10	....	....	140	27.3	11.2	5.0	2.8	

• CARLSON, Al

Alvin Harold Carlson

Born: Sept. 17, 1951. Oceanside, CA, United States.   Height: 6'11".   Weight: 235 lbs.   Drafted: —   College: USC

YEAR TEAM	GP	GS	MIN	PTS	FGM	FGA	FG%	3PM	3PA	3P%	FTM	FTA	FT%	ORB	DRB	TRB	AST	PF	DQ	STL	BLK	TO	MPG	PPG	RPG	APG	PCM
75-76 Seattle	28	....	279	72	27	79	.342	....	....	....	18	29	.621	30	43	73	13	39	1	7	11	....	10.0	2.6	2.6	0.5	.299
NBA Season Totals	28	....	279	72	27	79	.342	....	....	....	18	29	.621	30	43	73	13	39	1	7	11	....	10.0	2.6	2.6	0.5	

• CARLSON, Don

Don Vernon (Swede) Carlson

Born: Mar. 22, 1921. Minneapolis, MN, United States.   Height: 6'   Weight: 170 lbs.   Drafted: —   College: Minnesota

YEAR TEAM	GP	GS	MIN	PTS	FGM	FGA	FG%	3PM	3PA	3P%	FTM	FTA	FT%	ORB	DRB	TRB	AST	PF	DQ	STL	BLK	TO	MPG	PPG	RPG	APG	PCM
46-47 Chicago	59	....	....	630	272	845	.322	....	....	....	86	159	.541	....	....	....	59	182	....	....	....	....	10.7	....	1.0	....	
47-48 Minneapolis-N	58	....	....	475	205	....	....	....	....	....	65	109	.596	....	....	....	....	177	....	....	....	....	8.2	....	....	....	
48-49 Minneapolis	55	....	....	508	211	632	.334	....	....	....	86	130	.662	....	....	....	170	180	....	....	....	....	9.2	....	3.1	....	
49-50 Minneapolis	57	....	....	267	99	290	.341	....	....	....	69	95	.726	....	....	....	76	126	....	....	....	....	4.7	....	1.3	....	
50-51 Baltimore	9	....	....	42	17	46	.370	....	....	....	8	16	.500	....	....	15	19	23	0	....	....	....	4.7	1.7	2.1	....	
NBA Season Totals	180	....	....	1447	599	1813	.330	....	....	....	249	400	.623	....	....	15	324	511	0	....	....	....	8.0	0.1	1.8	....	
NBL Season Totals	58	....	....	475	205	....	....	....	....	....	65	109	....	....	....	....	....	177	....	....	....	....	8.2	....	....	....	
Career Totals	238	....	....	1922	804	1813	....	....	....	....	314	509	....	....	....	15	324	688	0	....	....	....	8.1	0.1	1.4	....	
46-47 Chicago	11	....	....	135	54	200	.270	....	....	....	27	44	.614	....	....	....	6	31	....	....	....	....	12.3	....	0.5	....	
47-48 Minneapolis-N	9	....	....	38	17	....	....	....	....	....	4	10	.400	....	....	....	....	....	....	....	....	....	4.2	....	....	....	
48-49 Minneapolis	10	....	....	60	23	95	.242	....	....	....	14	25	.560	....	....	....	28	30	....	....	....	....	6.0	....	2.8	....	
49-50 Minneapolis	10	....	....	54	21	37	.568	....	....	....	12	15	.800	....	....	....	11	19	....	....	....	....	5.4	....	1.1	....	
NBA Playoff Totals	31	....	....	249	98	332	.295	....	....	....	53	84	.631	....	....	....	45	80	....	....	....	....	8.0	....	1.5	....	
NBL Playoff Totals	9	....	....	38	17	....	....	....	....	....	4	10	....	....	....	....	....	....	....	....	....	....	4.2	....	....	....	
Career Playoff Totals	40	....	....	287	115	332	....	....	....	....	57	94	....	....	....	....	45	80	....	....	....	....	7.2	....	1.1	....	

• CARNEVALE, Dan

Dan Carnevale

Born: 1918.   Height: 6'   Weight: 185 lbs.   Drafted: —   College: Canisius

YEAR TEAM	GP	GS	MIN	PTS	FGM	FGA	FG%	3PM	3PA	3P%	FTM	FTA	FT%	ORB	DRB	TRB	AST	PF	DQ	STL	BLK	TO	MPG	PPG	RPG	APG	PCM
37-38 Buffalo-N	9	....	....	26	10	....	....	....	....	....	6	....	....	....	....	....	....	....	....	....	....	....	2.9	....	....	....	
NBL Season Totals	9	....	....	26	10	....	....	....	....	....	6	....	....	....	....	....	....	....	....	....	....	....	2.9	....	....	....	

• CARNEY, Bob

Robert Lee Carney

Born: Aug. 3, 1932.   Height: 6'3".   Weight: 170 lbs.   Drafted: 1954   College: Bradley

YEAR TEAM	GP	GS	MIN	PTS	FGM	FGA	FG%	3PM	3PA	3P%	FTM	FTA	FT%	ORB	DRB	TRB	AST	PF	DQ	STL	BLK	TO	MPG	PPG	RPG	APG	PCM
54-55 Minneapolis	19	....	244	69	24	64	.375	....	....	....	21	40	.525	....	....	45	16	36	0	....	....	....	12.8	3.6	2.4	0.8	.295
NBA Season Totals	19	....	244	69	24	64	.375	....	....	....	21	40	.525	....	....	45	16	36	0	....	....	....	12.8	3.6	2.4	0.8	....
54-55 Minneapolis	7	....	41	10	1	8	.125	....	....	....	8	9	.889	....	....	5	3	7	0	....	....	....	5.9	1.4	0.7	0.4	.225
NBA Playoff Totals	7	....	41	10	1	8	.125	....	....	....	8	9	.889	....	....	5	3	7	0	....	....	....	5.9	1.4	0.7	0.4	....

• CARP, Tony

Tony Carp

Born: 1911. Height: 6'7". Weight: 215 lbs. Drafted: — College: none

YEAR TEAM	GP	GS	MIN	PTS	FGM	FGA	FG%	3PM	3PA	3P%	FTM	FTA	FT%	ORB	DRB	TRB	AST	PF	DQ	STL	BLK	TO	MPG	PPG	RPG	APG	PCM
39-40 Chicago-N	1	....	....	0	0	....	....	....	....	....	0	....	....	....	....	....	....	....	....	....	....	....	....	0.0	....	....	....
NBL Season Totals	1	....	....	0	0	....	....	....	....	....	0	....	....	....	....	....	....	....	....	....	....	....	....	0.0	....	....	....

• CARPENTER, Bob

Robert H. Carpenter

Born: Nov. 6, 1917. Died: Apr.18, 1997. Height: 6'5". Weight: 200 lbs. Drafted: — College: East Texas State

YEAR TEAM	GP	GS	MIN	PTS	FGM	FGA	FG%	3PM	3PA	3P%	FTM	FTA	FT%	ORB	DRB	TRB	AST	PF	DQ	STL	BLK	TO	MPG	PPG	RPG	APG	PCM
40-41 Oshkosh-N	24	....	....	121	40	....	....	....	....	....	41	....	....	....	....	....	....	....	....	....	....	....	....	5.0	....	....	....
45-46 Oshkosh-N	34	....	....	**473**	**186**	....	....	....	....	....	101	144	.701	....	....	....	....	....	....	....	....	....	....	13.9	....	....	....
46-47 Oshkosh-N	44	....	....	513	199	....	....	....	....	....	115	169	.680	....	....	....	....	93	....	....	....	....	....	11.7	....	....	....
47-48 Oshkosh-N	60	....	....	582	211	....	....	....	....	....	160	213	.751	....	....	....	....	120	....	....	....	....	....	9.7	....	....	....
48-49 Hammond-N	23	....	....	241	87	....	....	....	....	....	67	91	.736	....	....	....	....	....	....	....	....	....	....	10.5	....	....	....
48-49 Oshkosh-N	24	....	....	210	73	....	....	....	....	....	64	89	.719	....	....	....	....	....	....	....	....	....	....	8.8	....	....	....
49-50 Fort Wayne	66	....	....	614	212	617	.344	....	....	....	190	256	.742	....	....	....	92	168	....	....	....	....	....	9.3	....	1.4	....
50-51 FtW/Tri	56	....	....	323	109	355	.307	....	....	....	105	128	.820	....	....	229	79	115	2	....	....	....	....	5.8	4.1	1.4	....
NBA Season Totals	122	....	....	937	321	972	.330	....	....	....	295	384	.768	....	....	229	171	283	2	....	....	....	....	7.7	1.9	1.4	....
NBL Season Totals	209	....	....	2140	796	....	....	....	....	....	548	706	....	....	....	....	....	213	....	....	....	....	....	10.2	....	....	....
Career Totals	331	....	....	3077	1117	972	....	....	....	....	843	1090	....	....	....	229	171	496	2	....	....	....	....	9.3	0.7	0.5	....
40-41 Oshkosh-N	5	....	....	55	15	....	....	....	....	....	25	....	....	....	....	....	....	....	....	....	....	....	....	11.0	....	....	....
45-46 Oshkosh-N	5	....	....	53	18	....	....	....	....	....	17	21	.810	....	....	....	....	....	....	....	....	....	....	10.6	....	....	....
46-47 Oshkosh-N	7	....	....	41	17	....	....	....	....	....	7	21	.333	....	....	....	....	....	....	....	....	....	....	5.9	....	....	....
47-48 Oshkosh-N	4	....	....	26	7	....	....	....	....	....	12	14	.857	....	....	....	....	....	....	....	....	....	....	6.5	....	....	....
48-49 Oshkosh-N	7	....	....	80	25	....	....	....	....	....	30	42	.714	....	....	....	....	....	....	....	....	....	....	11.4	....	....	....
49-50 Fort Wayne	4	....	....	32	11	30	.367	....	....	....	10	14	.714	....	....	....	2	6	....	....	....	....	....	8.0	....	0.5	....
NBA Playoff Totals	4	....	....	32	11	30	.367	....	....	....	10	14	.714	....	....	....	2	6	....	....	....	....	....	8.0	....	0.5	....
NBL Playoff Totals	28	....	....	255	82	....	....	....	....	....	91	98	....	....	....	....	....	....	....	....	....	....	....	9.1	....	....	....
Career Playoff Totals	32	....	....	287	93	30	....	....	....	....	101	112	....	....	....	....	2	6	....	....	....	....	....	9.0	....	0.1	....

• CARR, Antoine

Antoine Labotte (The Big Dog) Carr

Born: July 23, 1961. Oklahoma City, OK, United States. Height: 6'9". Weight: 225 lbs. Drafted: 1983 College: Wichita State

YEAR TEAM	GP	GS	MIN	PTS	FGM	FGA	FG%	3PM	3PA	3P%	FTM	FTA	FT%	ORB	DRB	TRB	AST	PF	DQ	STL	BLK	TO	MPG	PPG	RPG	APG	PCM
84-85 Atlanta	62	15	1195	499	198	375	.528	2	6	.333	101	128	.789	79	153	232	80	219	4	29	78	105	19.3	8.0	3.7	1.3	.438
85-86 Atlanta	17	0	258	116	49	93	.527	0	0	.000	18	27	.667	16	36	52	14	51	1	7	15	14	15.2	6.8	3.1	0.8	.457
86-87 Atlanta	65	2	695	342	134	265	.506	1	3	.333	73	103	.709	60	96	156	34	146	1	14	48	39	10.7	5.3	2.4	0.5	.491
87-88 Atlanta	80	2	1483	705	281	517	.544	1	4	.250	142	182	.780	94	195	289	103	272	7	38	83	112	18.5	8.8	3.6	1.3	.490
88-89 Atlanta	78	12	1488	582	226	471	.480	0	1	.000	130	152	.855	106	168	274	91	221	0	31	62	86	19.1	7.5	3.5	1.2	.403
89-90 Atlanta	44	0	803	335	128	248	.516	0	4	.000	79	102	.775	50	99	149	53	128	4	15	34	53	18.3	7.6	3.4	1.2	.428
89-90 Sacramento	33	4	924	614	228	473	.482	0	3	.000	158	196	.806	65	108	173	66	119	2	15	34	73	28.0	18.6	5.2	2.0	.563
90-91 Sacramento	77	48	2527	1551	628	1228	.511	0	3	.000	295	389	.758	163	257	420	191	315	14	45	101	169	32.8	20.1	5.5	2.5	.544
91-92 San Antonio	81	27	1867	881	359	732	.490	1	5	.200	162	212	.764	128	218	346	63	264	5	32	96	113	23.0	10.9	4.3	0.8	.424
92-93 San Antonio	71	46	1947	932	379	705	.538	0	5	.000	174	224	.777	107	281	388	97	264	5	35	87	99	27.4	13.1	5.5	1.4	.497
93-94 San Antonio	34	0	465	198	78	160	.488	0	1	.000	42	58	.724	12	39	51	15	75	0	9	22	14	13.7	5.8	1.5	0.4	.343
94-95 Utah	78	4	1677	746	290	546	.531	1	4	.250	165	201	.821	81	184	265	67	253	4	24	68	86	21.5	9.6	3.4	0.9	.415
95-96 Utah	80	0	1532	580	233	510	.457	0	3	.000	114	144	.792	71	129	200	74	254	4	28	65	80	19.2	7.3	2.5	0.9	.303
96-97 Utah	82	0	1460	603	252	522	.483	0	3	.000	99	127	.780	60	135	195	74	214	2	24	63	74	17.8	7.4	2.4	0.9	.350
97-98 Utah	66	8	1086	378	151	325	.465	0	0	.000	76	98	.776	42	89	131	48	195	3	11	53	46	16.5	5.7	2.0	0.7	.284
98-99 Houston	18	0	152	47	21	52	.404	0	1	.000	5	7	.714	9	22	31	9	31	0	1	10	9	8.4	2.6	1.7	0.5	.290
99-00 Vancouver	21	0	221	67	28	64	.438	0	0	.000	11	14	.786	8	24	32	7	42	0	3	6	9	10.5	3.2	1.5	0.3	.229
NBA Season Totals	987	168	19780	9176	3663	7286	.503	6	46	.130	1844	2364	.780	1151	2233	3384	1086	3063	56	361	925	1181	20.0	9.3	3.4	1.1	....
86-87 Atlanta	9	0	162	104	39	56	.696	0	0	.000	26	32	.813	11	16	27	13	36	1	3	8	10	18.0	11.6	3.0	1.4	.670
87-88 Atlanta	12	0	210	81	36	68	.529	0	1	.000	9	14	.643	12	29	41	15	47	2	4	17	10	17.5	6.8	3.4	1.3	.435
88-89 Atlanta	5	0	81	34	13	21	.619	0	0	.000	8	11	.727	5	3	8	7	13	0	0	4	4	16.2	6.8	1.6	1.4	.420
91-92 San Antonio	3	3	109	59	24	44	.545	1	2	.500	10	16	.625	8	15	23	3	14	1	2	11	4	36.3	19.7	7.7	1.0	.588
92-93 San Antonio	8	8	171	84	39	74	.527	0	0	.000	6	10	.600	13	25	38	9	28	1	3	9	7	21.4	10.5	4.8	1.1	.504
93-94 San Antonio	3	0	37	18	5	11	.455	0	0	.000	8	9	.889	1	0	1	3	7	0	1	2	0	12.3	6.0	0.3	1.0	.426
94-95 Utah	5	0	114	48	14	31	.452	0	0	.000	20	24	.833	3	12	15	7	26	2	3	5	4	22.8	9.6	3.0	1.4	.379
95-96 Utah	18	0	339	109	46	97	.474	0	0	.000	17	25	.680	11	23	34	21	66	2	4	14	16	18.8	6.1	1.9	1.2	.243
96-97 Utah	20	0	280	98	40	83	.482	0	0	.000	18	24	.750	11	29	40	10	64	1	6	9	18	14.0	4.9	2.0	0.5	.252
97-98 Utah	20	0	292	88	41	90	.456	0	0	.000	6	8	.750	16	25	41	11	63	1	1	12	9	14.6	4.4	2.1	0.6	.228
98-99 Houston	4	0	37	8	4	11	.364	0	0	.000	0	0	.000	3	4	7	4	19	1	0	1	4	9.3	2.0	1.8	1.0	.036
NBA Playoff Totals	107	11	1832	731	301	586	.514	1	3	.333	128	173	.740	94	181	275	103	383	12	27	92	86	17.1	6.8	2.6	1.0	....

• CARR, Austin

Austin George Carr

Born: Mar. 10, 1948. Washington, DC, United States. Height: 6'4". Weight: 200 lbs. Drafted: 1971 College: Notre Dame

YEAR TEAM	GP	GS	MIN	PTS	FGM	FGA	FG%	3PM	3PA	3P%	FTM	FTA	FT%	ORB	DRB	TRB	AST	PF	DQ	STL	BLK	TO	MPG	PPG	RPG	APG	PCM
71-72 Cleveland	43	....	1539	911	381	894	.426	....	....	....	149	196	.760	....	....	150	148	99	0	....	....	....	35.8	21.2	3.5	3.4	.456
72-73 Cleveland	82	....	3097	1685	702	1575	.446	....	....	....	281	342	.822	....	....	369	279	185	1	....	....	....	37.8	20.5	4.5	3.4	.473
73-74 Cleveland	81	....	3100	1775	748	1682	.445	....	....	....	279	326	.856	139	150	289	305	189	2	92	14	....	38.3	21.9	3.6	3.8	.476
74-75 Cleveland	41	....	1081	593	252	538	.468	....	....	....	89	106	.840	51	56	107	154	57	0	48	2	....	26.4	14.5	2.6	3.8	.542
75-76 Cleveland	65	....	1282	658	276	625	.442	....	....	....	106	134	.791	67	65	132	122	92	0	37	2	....	19.7	10.1	2.0	1.9	.437
76-77 Cleveland	82	....	2409	1329	558	1221	.457	....	....	....	213	268	.795	120	120	240	220	221	3	57	10	....	29.4	16.2	2.9	2.7	.455
77-78 Cleveland	82	....	2186	1011	414	945	.438	....	....	....	183	225	.813	76	111	187	225	168	1	68	19	148	26.7	12.3	2.3	2.7	.374
78-79 Cleveland	82	....	2714	1394	551	1161	.475	....	....	....	292	358	.816	155	135	290	217	210	1	77	14	172	33.1	17.0	3.5	2.6	.423
79-80 Cleveland	77	....	1595	909	390	839	.465	2	6	.333	127	172	.738	81	84	165	150	120	0	39	3	108	20.7	11.8	2.1	1.9	.427
80-81 Dallas	8	....	77	16	7	28	.250	0	0	.000	2	4	.500	4	5	9	9	10	0	1	0	9	9.6	2.0	1.1	1.1	.027
80-81 Washington	39	....	580	192	80	206	.388	0	7	.000	32	50	.640	18	34	52	49	43	0	14	2	31	14.9	4.9	1.3	1.3	.235
NBA Season Totals	682	....	19660	10473	4359	9714	.449	2	13	.154	1753	2181	.804	711	760	1990	1878	1394	8	433	66	468	28.8	15.4	2.9	2.8	....

YEAR	TEAM	GP	GS	MIN	PTS	FGM	FGA	FG%	3PM	3PA	3P%	FTM	FTA	FT%	ORB	DRB	TRB	AST	PF	DQ	STL	BLK	TO	MPG	PPG	RPG	APG	PCM
75-76	Cleveland	13	....	273	154	66	138	.478	....	....	....	22	36	.611	11	12	23	26	29	0	6	3	....	21.0	11.8	1.8	2.0	.451
76-77	Cleveland	3	....	83	23	11	39	.282	....	....	....	1	3	.333	4	6	10	10	13	0	2	1	....	27.7	7.7	3.3	3.3	.149
77-78	Cleveland	2	....	69	35	10	27	.370	....	....	....	15	16	.938	3	5	8	5	8	0	2	1	4	34.5	17.5	4.0	2.5	.405
NBA Playoff Totals		18	....	425	212	87	204	.426	....	....	....	38	55	.691	18	23	41	41	50	0	10	5	4	23.6	11.8	2.3	2.3	....

• CARR, Chris

Chris Dean Carr

Born: Mar. 12, 1974. Ironton, MI, United States. Height: 6'5". Weight: 207 lbs. Drafted: 1995 College: Southern Illinois

YEAR	TEAM	GP	GS	MIN	PTS	FGM	FGA	FG%	3PM	3PA	3P%	FTM	FTA	FT%	ORB	DRB	TRB	AST	PF	DQ	STL	BLK	TO	MPG	PPG	RPG	APG	PCM
95-96	Phoenix	60	10	590	240	90	217	.415	11	42	.262	49	60	.817	27	75	102	43	77	1	10	5	42	9.8	4.0	1.7	0.7	.331
96-97	Minnesota	55	10	830	337	125	271	.461	31	88	.352	56	73	.767	31	82	113	48	93	0	24	10	39	15.1	6.1	2.1	0.9	.363
97-98	Minnesota	51	40	1165	504	190	452	.420	40	127	.315	84	99	.848	43	112	155	85	129	1	17	11	71	22.8	9.9	3.0	1.7	.337
98-99	Minnesota	11	2	81	23	9	26	.346	3	9	.333	2	4	.500	0	12	12	7	9	0	1	1	4	7.4	2.1	1.1	0.6	.243
98-99	New Jersey	28	2	364	184	67	179	.374	25	66	.379	25	36	.694	23	36	59	16	36	0	7	1	24	13.0	6.6	2.1	0.6	.328
99-00	Golden State	7	0	74	39	11	33	.333	1	8	.125	16	19	.842	5	8	13	3	12	0	0	1	5	10.6	5.6	1.9	0.4	.320
99-00	Chicago	50	2	1092	492	185	463	.400	31	93	.333	91	106	.858	36	124	160	81	101	0	30	14	112	21.8	9.8	3.2	1.6	.329
00-01	Boston	35	0	309	169	53	112	.473	17	37	.459	46	60	.767	11	33	44	11	45	1	4	3	19	8.8	4.8	1.3	0.3	.422
NBA Season Totals		297	66	4505	1988	730	1753	.416	159	470	.338	369	457	.807	176	482	658	294	502	3	93	46	316	15.2	6.7	2.2	1.0	....
95-96	Phoenix	3	0	36	24	9	14	.643	2	3	.667	4	5	.800	3	4	7	4	6	0	2	1	4	12.0	8.0	2.3	1.3	.719
96-97	Minnesota	1	0	8	0	0	2	.000	0	2	.000	0	0	.000	0	2	2	1	0	0	0	0	1	8.0	0.0	2.0	1.0	.017
NBA Playoff Totals		4	0	44	24	9	16	.563	2	5	.400	4	5	.800	3	6	9	5	6	0	2	1	5	11.0	6.0	2.3	1.3	....

• CARR, Cory

Cory Jermaine Carr

Born: Dec. 5, 1975. Fordyce, AR, United States. Height: 6'3". Weight: 210 lbs. Drafted: 1998 College: Texas Tech

YEAR	TEAM	GP	GS	MIN	PTS	FGM	FGA	FG%	3PM	3PA	3P%	FTM	FTA	FT%	ORB	DRB	TRB	AST	PF	DQ	STL	BLK	TO	MPG	PPG	RPG	APG	PCM
98-99	Chicago	42	7	624	171	71	216	.329	5	30	.167	24	32	.750	8	41	49	66	66	0	21	7	46	14.9	4.1	1.2	1.6	.176
NBA Season Totals		42	7	624	171	71	216	.329	5	30	.167	24	32	.750	8	41	49	66	66	0	21	7	46	14.9	4.1	1.2	1.6	....

• CARR, Kenny

Kenneth Alan Carr

Born: Aug. 15, 1955. Washington, DC, United States. Height: 6'7". Weight: 220 lbs. Drafted: 1977 College: North Carolina State

YEAR	TEAM	GP	GS	MIN	PTS	FGM	FGA	FG%	3PM	3PA	3P%	FTM	FTA	FT%	ORB	DRB	TRB	AST	PF	DQ	STL	BLK	TO	MPG	PPG	RPG	APG	PCM
77-78	LA Lakers	52	....	733	323	134	302	.444	....	....	....	55	85	.647	53	155	208	26	127	0	18	14	88	14.1	6.2	4.0	0.5	.368
78-79	LA Lakers	72	....	1149	533	225	450	.500	....	....	....	83	137	.606	70	222	292	60	152	0	38	31	115	16.0	7.4	4.1	0.8	.457
79-80	LA Lakers	5	....	57	16	7	16	.438	0	0	.000	2	2	1.000	5	12	17	1	6	0	2	1	9	11.4	3.2	3.4	0.2	.284
79-80	Cleveland	74	....	1781	913	371	752	.493	0	4	.000	171	261	.655	194	377	571	76	240	3	64	51	148	24.1	12.3	7.7	1.0	.555
80-81	Cleveland	81	....	2615	1230	469	918	.511	0	4	.000	292	409	.714	260	575	835	192	296	3	76	42	235	32.3	15.2	10.3	2.4	.572
81-82	Cleveland	46	42	1482	688	271	524	.517	1	9	.111	145	220	.659	114	280	394	63	180	0	58	16	110	32.2	15.0	8.6	1.4	.496
81-82	Detroit	28	6	444	207	77	168	.458	0	1	.000	53	82	.646	53	84	137	23	69	0	6	6	39	15.9	7.4	4.9	0.8	.460
82-83	Portland	82	26	2331	981	362	717	.505	2	6	.333	255	366	.697	182	407	589	116	306	10	62	42	189	28.4	12.0	7.2	1.4	.452
83-84	Portland	82	57	2455	1283	518	923	.561	0	5	.000	247	367	.673	208	434	642	157	274	3	68	33	205	29.9	15.6	7.8	1.9	.567
84-85	Portland	48	30	1120	498	190	363	.523	0	3	.000	118	164	.720	90	233	323	56	141	0	25	17	101	23.3	10.4	6.7	1.2	.496
85-86	Portland	55	31	1557	613	232	466	.498	0	4	.000	149	217	.687	146	346	492	70	203	5	38	30	105	28.3	11.1	8.9	1.3	.493
86-87	Portland	49	43	1443	528	201	399	.504	0	2	.000	126	169	.746	131	368	499	83	159	1	29	13	103	29.4	10.8	10.2	1.7	.517
NBA Season Totals		674	235	17167	7813	3057	5998	.510	3	38	.079	1696	2479	.684	1506	3493	4999	923	2153	25	484	296	1447	25.5	11.6	7.4	1.4	....
77-78	LA Lakers	2	....	17	6	3	8	.375	....	....	....	0	0	.000	0	4	4	0	2	0	1	0	3	8.5	3.0	2.0	0.0	.147
78-79	LA Lakers	8	....	117	43	19	35	.543	....	....	....	5	8	.625	4	13	17	4	18	0	4	2	11	14.6	5.4	2.1	0.5	.294
82-83	Portland	7	0	171	70	26	60	.433	0	0	.000	18	23	.783	15	36	51	10	26	0	3	5	10	24.4	10.0	7.3	1.4	.471
83-84	Portland	5	5	180	74	31	59	.525	0	0	.000	12	19	.632	11	24	35	6	22	1	2	2	10	36.0	14.8	7.0	1.2	.377
84-85	Portland	9	9	265	116	50	95	.526	0	1	.000	16	20	.800	30	40	70	10	40	2	3	2	23	29.4	12.9	7.8	1.1	.425
85-86	Portland	4	4	143	59	24	42	.571	0	1	.000	11	15	.733	9	44	53	7	18	1	5	1	8	35.8	14.8	13.3	1.8	.608
NBA Playoff Totals		35	18	893	368	153	299	.512	0	2	.000	62	85	.729	69	161	230	37	126	4	18	12	65	25.5	10.5	6.6	1.1	....

• CARR, M.L.

Michael Leon Carr

Born: Jan. 9, 1951. Wallace, NC, United States. Height: 6'6". Weight: 205 lbs. Drafted: 1973 College: Guilford

YEAR	TEAM	GP	GS	MIN	PTS	FGM	FGA	FG%	3PM	3PA	3P%	FTM	FTA	FT%	ORB	DRB	TRB	AST	PF	DQ	STL	BLK	TO	MPG	PPG	RPG	APG	PCM
75-76	St. Louis-A	74	....	2174	906	380	786	.483	9	24	.375	137	206	.665	171	288	459	224	225	....	127	44	162	29.4	12.2	6.2	3.0	.492
76-77	Detroit	82	....	2643	1091	443	931	.476	....	....	....	205	279	.735	211	420	631	181	287	8	165	58	....	32.2	13.3	7.7	2.2	.478
77-78	Detroit	79	....	2556	980	390	857	.455	....	....	....	200	271	.738	202	355	557	185	243	4	147	27	213	32.4	12.4	7.1	2.3	.429
78-79	Detroit	80	....	3207	1497	587	1143	.514	....	....	....	323	435	.743	219	370	589	262	279	2	197	46	256	40.1	18.7	7.4	3.3	.508
79-80	Boston	82	....	1994	914	362	763	.474	12	41	.293	178	241	.739	106	224	330	156	214	1	120	36	139	24.3	11.1	4.0	1.9	.457
80-81	Boston	41	....	655	248	97	216	.449	1	14	.071	53	67	.791	26	57	83	56	74	0	30	18	45	16.0	6.0	2.0	1.4	.365
81-82	Boston	56	27	1296	455	184	409	.450	5	17	.294	82	116	.707	56	94	150	128	136	2	67	21	62	23.1	8.1	2.7	2.3	.362
82-83	Boston	77	0	883	333	135	315	.429	3	19	.158	60	81	.741	51	86	137	71	140	0	48	10	77	11.5	4.3	1.8	0.9	.320
83-84	Boston	60	1	585	185	70	171	.409	3	15	.200	42	48	.875	26	49	75	49	67	0	17	4	48	9.8	3.1	1.3	0.8	.264
84-85	Boston	47	0	397	150	62	149	.416	9	23	.391	17	17	1.000	21	22	43	24	44	0	21	6	24	8.4	3.2	0.9	0.5	.294
NBA Season Totals		604	28	14216	5853	2330	4954	.470	33	129	.256	1160	1555	.746	918	1677	2595	1112	1484	17	812	226	864	23.5	9.7	4.3	1.8	....
ABA Season Totals		74	....	2174	906	380	786	.483	9	24	.375	137	206	.665	171	288	459	224	225	....	127	44	162	29.4	12.2	6.2	3.0	....
Career Totals		678	28	16390	6759	2710	5740	.472	42	153	.275	1297	1761	.737	1089	1965	3054	1336	1709	17	939	270	1026	24.2	10.0	4.5	2.0	....
76-77	Detroit	3	....	112	28	12	31	.387	....	....	....	4	7	.571	9	8	17	6	9	0	1	3	....	37.3	9.3	5.7	2.0	.249
79-80	Boston	9	....	172	82	32	80	.400	2	5	.400	16	24	.667	14	19	33	11	20	0	6	1	7	19.1	9.1	3.7	1.2	.394
80-81	Boston	17	....	288	102	42	101	.416	0	4	.000	18	24	.750	8	17	25	14	32	0	10	6	8	16.9	6.0	1.5	0.8	.265
81-82	Boston	12	12	305	89	37	105	.352	0	4	.000	15	23	.652	21	22	43	28	30	0	11	0	21	25.4	7.4	3.6	2.3	.228
82-83	Boston	3	0	22	6	2	8	.250	0	1	.000	2	2	1.000	1	0	1	0	3	0	2	0	0	7.3	2.0	0.3	0.0	.088
83-84	Boston	16	0	82	38	13	32	.406	2	6	.333	10	11	.909	5	3	8	4	13	0	7	0	3	5.1	2.4	0.5	0.3	.357
84-85	Boston	7	0	24	9	4	15	.267	1	2	.500	0	0	.000	1	1	2	1	4	0	1	0	1	3.4	1.3	0.3	0.1	-.008
NBA Playoff Totals		67	12	1005	354	142	372	.382	5	22	.227	65	91	.714	59	70	129	64	111	0	38	10	40	15.0	5.3	1.9	1.0	....

YEAR	TEAM	GP	GS	MIN	PTS	FGM	FGA	FG%	3PM	3PA	3P%	FTM	FTA	FT%	ORB	DRB	TRB	AST	PF	DQ	STL	BLK	TO	MPG	PPG	RPG	APG	PCM

• CARRIER, Darel
James Darel Carrier

Born: Oct. 26, 1940. Warren County, KY, United States. Height: 6'3". Weight: 185 lbs. Drafted: 1964 College: Western Kentucky

YEAR	TEAM	GP	GS	MIN	PTS	FGM	FGA	FG%	3PM	3PA	3P%	FTM	FTA	FT%	ORB	DRB	TRB	AST	PF	DQ	STL	BLK	TO	MPG	PPG	RPG	APG	PCM
67-68	Kentucky-A	77	....	3192	1765	643	1545	.416	84	235	**.357**	395	479	.825	....	....	352	172	263	7	....	....	228	41.5	22.9	4.6	2.2	.428
68-69	Kentucky-A	73	....	2858	1690	559	1376	.406	125	330	**.379**	447	545	.820	75	208	283	214	227	1	....	....	213	39.2	23.2	3.9	2.9	.468
69-70	Kentucky-A	77	....	2805	1775	608	1458	.417	105	280	**.375**	454	509	**.892**	44	205	249	212	268	8	....	....	213	36.4	23.1	3.2	2.8	.486
70-71	Kentucky-A	84	....	2664	1380	495	1140	.434	63	161	.391	327	377	.867	50	182	232	244	229	2	....	....	199	31.7	16.4	2.8	2.9	.462
71-72	Kentucky-A	23	....	629	326	117	288	.406	16	37	.432	76	88	.864	11	46	57	44	64	0	....	....	38	27.3	14.2	2.5	1.9	.384
72-73	Memphis-A	16	....	190	75	23	60	.383	5	12	.417	24	26	.923	2	12	14	10	21	0	....	....	15	11.9	4.7	0.9	0.6	.289
ABA Season Totals		350	....	12338	7011	2445	5867	.417	398	1055	.377	1723	2024	.851	182	653	1187	896	1072	18	....	....	906	35.3	20.0	3.4	2.6	
67-68	Kentucky-A	5	....	211	115	38	100	.380	8	21	.381	31	36	.861	....	....	25	13	15	0	....	....	11	42.2	23.0	5.0	2.6	.432
68-69	Kentucky-A	7	....	303	168	51	117	.436	14	28	.500	52	64	.813	....	....	21	19	28	1	....	....	18	43.3	24.0	3.0	2.7	.442
69-70	Kentucky-A	12	....	487	258	87	228	.382	14	38	.368	70	79	.886	17	29	46	29	....	1	....	....	34	40.6	21.5	3.8	2.4	
70-71	Kentucky-A	19	....	675	369	130	280	.464	21	58	.362	88	98	.898	11	47	58	69	65	0	....	....	53	35.5	19.4	3.1	3.6	.516
71-72	Kentucky-A	2	....	17	6	3	8	.375	0	1	.000	0	0	.000	....	....	1	1	3	....	....	....	4	8.5	3.0	0.5	0.5	.135
ABA Playoff Totals		45	....	1693	916	309	733	.422	57	146	.390	241	277	.870	28	76	151	131	111	2	....	....	120	37.6	20.4	3.4	2.9	....

• CARRINGTON, Bob
Robert Frederick Carrington

Born: July 3, 1953. Brookline, MA, United States. Height: 6'6". Weight: 195 lbs. Drafted: 1976 College: Boston College

YEAR	TEAM	GP	GS	MIN	PTS	FGM	FGA	FG%	3PM	3PA	3P%	FTM	FTA	FT%	ORB	DRB	TRB	AST	PF	DQ	STL	BLK	TO	MPG	PPG	RPG	APG	PCM
77-78	New Jersey	37	....	1032	386	157	392	.401	....	....	....	72	97	.742	42	70	112	55	132	5	43	12	67	27.9	10.4	3.0	1.5	.253
77-78	Indiana	35	....	621	250	96	197	.487	....	....	....	58	74	.784	28	34	62	62	73	1	22	11	53	17.7	7.1	1.8	1.8	.369
79-80	San Diego	10	....	134	36	15	37	.405	0	2	.000	6	8	.750	6	7	13	3	18	0	4	1	5	13.4	3.6	1.3	0.3	.165
NBA Season Totals		82	....	1787	672	268	626	.428	0	2	.000	136	179	.760	76	111	187	120	223	6	69	24	125	21.8	8.2	2.3	1.5	....

• CARROLL, Joe Barry
Joe Barry Carroll

Born: July 24, 1958. Pine Bluff, AR, United States. Height: 7' Weight: 225 lbs. Drafted: 1980 College: Purdue

YEAR	TEAM	GP	GS	MIN	PTS	FGM	FGA	FG%	3PM	3PA	3P%	FTM	FTA	FT%	ORB	DRB	TRB	AST	PF	DQ	STL	BLK	TO	MPG	PPG	RPG	APG	PCM
80-81	Golden State	82	....	2919	1547	616	1254	.491	0	2	.000	315	440	.716	274	485	759	117	313	10	50	121	246	35.6	18.9	9.3	1.4	.520
81-82	Golden State	76	75	2627	1289	527	1016	.519	0	1	.000	235	323	.728	210	423	633	64	265	8	64	127	205	34.6	17.0	8.3	0.8	.501
82-83	Golden State	79	79	2988	1907	785	1529	.513	0	3	.000	337	469	.719	220	468	688	169	260	7	108	155	284	37.8	24.1	8.7	2.1	.618
83-84	Golden State	80	80	2962	1639	663	1390	.477	0	1	.000	313	433	.723	235	401	636	198	244	9	103	142	272	37.0	20.5	8.0	2.5	.531
85-86	Golden State	79	79	2801	1677	650	1404	.463	0	2	.000	377	501	.752	193	477	670	176	277	**13**	101	143	277	35.5	21.2	8.5	2.2	.561
86-87	Golden State	81	81	2724	1720	690	1461	.472	0	0	.000	340	432	.787	173	416	589	214	255	2	92	123	227	33.6	21.2	7.3	2.6	.590
87-88	Golden State	14	14	408	217	79	209	.378	0	1	.000	59	74	.797	21	72	93	19	46	1	13	25	43	29.1	15.5	6.6	1.4	.416
87-88	Houston	63	16	1596	759	323	715	.452	0	1	.000	113	151	.748	110	286	396	94	149	0	37	81	120	25.3	12.0	6.3	1.5	.485
88-89	New Jersey	64	62	1996	902	363	810	.448	0	0	.000	176	220	.800	118	355	473	105	193	2	71	81	141	31.2	14.1	7.4	1.6	.470
89-90	New Jersey	46	20	1002	403	159	405	.393	0	2	.000	85	107	.794	82	168	250	43	122	4	19	56	64	21.8	8.8	5.4	0.9	.395
89-90	Denver	30	27	719	358	153	354	.432	0	0	.000	52	70	.743	51	142	193	54	70	0	28	59	78	24.0	11.9	6.4	1.8	.522
90-91	Phoenix	11	0	96	37	13	36	.361	0	0	.000	11	12	.917	3	21	24	11	18	0	1	8	12	8.7	3.4	2.2	1.0	.396
NBA Season Totals		705	533	22838	12455	5021	10583	.474	0	13	.000	2413	3232	.747	1690	3714	5404	1264	2212	56	687	1121	1969	32.4	17.7	7.7	1.8	....
86-87	Golden State	10	10	334	189	74	163	.454	0	1	.000	41	51	.804	16	49	65	19	42	2	14	25	31	33.4	18.9	6.5	1.9	.510
87-88	Houston	4	4	116	44	18	47	.383	0	0	.000	8	10	.800	8	11	19	2	12	0	3	1	5	29.0	11.0	4.8	0.5	.253
89-90	Denver	3	3	46	20	9	16	.563	0	0	.000	2	2	1.000	1	8	9	3	6	0	1	5	1	15.3	6.7	3.0	1.0	.586
90-91	Phoenix	2	0	15	8	4	8	.500	0	0	.000	0	1	.000	0	1	1	2	0	0	0	1	1	7.5	4.0	0.5	1.0	.458
NBA Playoff Totals		19	17	511	261	105	234	.449	0	1	.000	51	64	.797	25	69	94	26	60	2	18	32	38	26.9	13.7	4.9	1.4	....

• CARRUTH, Jimmy
Jimmy Dawn Carruth II

Born: Nov. 4, 1969. El Paso, TX, United States. Height: 6'10". Weight: 265 lbs. Drafted: — College: Virginia Tech

YEAR	TEAM	GP	GS	MIN	PTS	FGM	FGA	FG%	3PM	3PA	3P%	FTM	FTA	FT%	ORB	DRB	TRB	AST	PF	DQ	STL	BLK	TO	MPG	PPG	RPG	APG	PCM
96-97	Milwaukee	4	0	21	5	2	3	.667	0	0	.000	1	1	1.000	0	4	4	0	4	0	0	2	1	5.3	1.3	1.0	0.0	.327
NBA Season Totals		4	0	21	5	2	3	.667	0	0	.000	1	1	1.000	0	4	4	0	4	0	0	2	1	5.3	1.3	1.0	0.0	....

• CARSWELL, Frank
Frank Willis (Tex, Wheels) Carswell

Born: Nov. 6, 1919. Palestine, TX, United States. Height: 6' Weight: 185 lbs. Drafted: — College: Rice

YEAR	TEAM	GP	GS	MIN	PTS	FGM	FGA	FG%	3PM	3PA	3P%	FTM	FTA	FT%	ORB	DRB	TRB	AST	PF	DQ	STL	BLK	TO	MPG	PPG	RPG	APG	PCM
47-48	Flint-N	4	....	....	10	4	....	....	....	....	....	2	2	1.000	....	....	....	....	....	....	....	....	....	....	2.5	....	....	....
NBL Season Totals		4	....	....	10	4	....	....	....	....	....	2	2	....	....	....	....	....	....	....	....	....	....	....	2.5	....	....	....

• CARTER, Anthony
Anthony Bernard Carter

Born: June 16, 1975. Milwaukee, WI, United States. Height: 6'1". Weight: 190 lbs. Drafted: — College: Hawaii

YEAR	TEAM	GP	GS	MIN	PTS	FGM	FGA	FG%	3PM	3PA	3P%	FTM	FTA	FT%	ORB	DRB	TRB	AST	PF	DQ	STL	BLK	TO	MPG	PPG	RPG	APG	PCM
99-00	Miami	79	30	1859	498	201	509	.395	3	23	.130	93	124	.750	48	151	199	378	167	0	93	5	173	23.5	6.3	2.5	4.8	.352
00-01	Miami	72	6	1630	461	195	480	.406	6	40	.150	65	103	.631	46	134	180	268	154	1	73	10	119	22.6	6.4	2.5	3.7	.333
01-02	Miami	46	18	1050	198	89	260	.342	1	19	.053	19	36	.528	19	98	117	214	85	2	50	3	72	22.8	4.3	2.5	4.7	.305
02-03	Miami	49	26	912	199	83	233	.356	0	8	.000	33	50	.660	12	71	83	203	70	0	45	5	81	18.6	4.1	1.7	4.1	.320
NBA Season Totals		246	80	5451	1356	568	1482	.383	10	90	.111	210	313	.671	125	454	579	1063	476	3	261	23	445	22.2	5.5	2.4	4.3	....
99-00	Miami	10	3	275	77	32	77	.416	1	6	.167	12	16	.750	8	32	40	56	22	0	12	2	23	27.5	7.7	4.0	5.6	.413
00-01	Miami	3	1	69	18	9	19	.474	0	1	.000	0	0	.000	0	6	6	11	9	0	2	1	10	23.0	6.0	2.0	3.7	.235
NBA Playoff Totals		13	4	344	95	41	96	.427	1	7	.143	12	16	.750	8	38	46	67	31	0	14	3	33	26.5	7.3	3.5	5.2	....

YEAR	TEAM	GP	GS	MIN	PTS	FGM	FGA	FG%	3PM	3PA	3P%	FTM	FTA	FT%	ORB	DRB	TRB	AST	PF	DQ	STL	BLK	TO	MPG	PPG	RPG	APG	PCM

• CARTER, Butch

Clarence Eugene (Butch) Carter Jr.

Born: June 11, 1958. Springfield, OH, United States.   Height: 6'5".   Weight: 180 lbs.   Drafted: 1980   College: Indiana

YEAR	TEAM	GP	GS	MIN	PTS	FGM	FGA	FG%	3PM	3PA	3P%	FTM	FTA	FT%	ORB	DRB	TRB	AST	PF	DQ	STL	BLK	TO	MPG	PPG	RPG	APG	PCM
80-81	LA Lakers	54	....	672	301	114	247	.462	3	10	.300	70	95	.737	34	31	65	52	99	0	23	1	49	12.4	5.6	1.2	1.0	.322
81-82	Indiana	75	0	1035	442	188	402	.468	8	25	.320	58	70	.829	30	49	79	60	110	0	34	11	53	13.8	5.9	1.1	0.8	.308
82-83	Indiana	81	28	1716	849	354	706	.501	17	51	.333	124	154	.805	62	88	150	194	207	5	78	13	122	21.2	10.5	1.9	2.4	.434
83-84	Indiana	73	54	2045	977	413	862	.479	15	46	.326	136	178	.764	70	83	153	206	211	1	128	13	139	28.0	13.4	2.1	2.8	.394
84-85	New York	69	11	1279	548	214	476	.450	11	43	.256	109	134	.813	36	59	95	167	151	1	57	5	110	18.5	7.9	1.4	2.4	.347
85-86	New York	5	0	31	5	2	8	.250	0	1	.000	1	1	1.000	2	1	3	3	6	0	1	0	6	6.2	1.0	0.6	0.6	-.065
85-86	Philadelphia	4	0	36	15	5	16	.313	0	0	.000	5	6	.833	0	1	1	1	8	0	0	0	1	9.0	3.8	0.3	0.3	.046
NBA Season Totals		361	93	6814	3137	1290	2717	.475	54	176	.307	503	638	.788	234	312	546	683	792	7	321	43	480	18.9	8.7	1.5	1.9	....

• CARTER, Fred

Frederick James (Mad Dog) Carter

Born: Feb. 14, 1945. Philadelphia, PA, United States.   Height: 6'3".   Weight: 185 lbs.   Drafted: 1969   College: Mount St. Mary's

YEAR	TEAM	GP	GS	MIN	PTS	FGM	FGA	FG%	3PM	3PA	3P%	FTM	FTA	FT%	ORB	DRB	TRB	AST	PF	DQ	STL	BLK	TO	MPG	PPG	RPG	APG	PCM
69-70	Baltimore	76	....	1219	394	157	439	.358	....	....	....	80	116	.690	....	....	192	121	137	0	....	....	....	16.0	5.2	2.5	1.6	.307
70-71	Baltimore	77	....	1707	799	340	815	.417	....	....	....	119	183	.650	....	....	251	165	165	0	....	....	....	22.2	10.4	3.3	2.1	.408
71-72	Baltimore	2	....	68	15	6	27	.222	....	....	....	3	9	.333	....	....	19	12	7	0	....	....	....	34.0	7.5	9.5	6.0	.313
71-72	Philadelphia	77	....	2147	1059	440	991	.444	....	....	....	179	284	.630	....	....	307	199	235	4	....	....	....	27.9	13.8	4.0	2.6	.432
72-73	Philadelphia	81	....	2993	1617	679	1614	.421	....	....	....	259	368	.704	....	....	485	349	252	8	....	....	....	37.0	20.0	6.0	4.3	.493
73-74	Philadelphia	78	....	3044	1666	706	1641	.430	....	....	....	254	358	.709	82	289	371	443	276	4	113	23	....	39.0	21.4	4.8	5.7	.504
74-75	Philadelphia	77	....	3046	1686	715	1598	.447	....	....	....	256	347	.738	73	267	340	336	257	5	82	20	....	39.6	21.9	4.4	4.4	.479
75-76	Philadelphia	82	....	2992	1549	665	1594	.417	....	....	....	219	312	.702	113	186	299	372	286	5	137	13	....	36.5	18.9	3.6	4.5	.425
76-77	Philadelphia	14	....	237	96	43	101	.426	....	....	....	10	19	.526	10	14	24	21	29	0	11	2	....	16.9	6.9	1.7	1.5	.313
76-77	Milwaukee	47	....	875	390	166	399	.416	....	....	....	58	77	.753	45	48	93	104	96	0	28	7	....	18.6	8.3	2.0	2.2	.386
NBA Season Totals		611	....	18328	9271	3917	9219	.425	....	....	....	1437	2073	.693	323	804	2381	2122	1740	26	371	65	....	30.0	15.2	3.9	3.5	....
69-70	Baltimore	7	....	253	99	41	107	.383	....	....	....	17	28	.607	....	....	31	24	27	0	....	....	....	36.1	14.1	4.4	3.4	.310
70-71	Baltimore	18	....	597	263	108	260	.415	....	....	....	47	73	.644	....	....	82	36	63	1	....	....	....	33.2	14.6	4.6	2.0	.344
75-76	Philadelphia	3	....	125	84	29	67	.433	....	....	....	26	30	.867	4	6	10	15	12	0	4	1	....	41.7	28.0	3.3	5.0	.562
NBA Playoff Totals		28	....	975	446	178	434	.410	....	....	....	90	131	.687	4	6	123	75	102	1	4	1	....	34.8	15.9	4.4	2.7	....

• CARTER, George

George (Dirty Dingus) Carter

Born: Jan. 10, 1944. Buffalo, NY, United States.   Height: 6'4".   Weight: 210 lbs.   Drafted: 1967   College: St. Bonaventure

YEAR	TEAM	GP	GS	MIN	PTS	FGM	FGA	FG%	3PM	3PA	3P%	FTM	FTA	FT%	ORB	DRB	TRB	AST	PF	DQ	STL	BLK	TO	MPG	PPG	RPG	APG	PCM
67-68	Detroit	1	....	5	3	1	2	.500	....	....	....	1	1	1.000	....	....	0	1	0	0	....	....	....	5.0	3.0	0.0	1.0	.681
69-70	Washington-A	67	....	1848	968	397	871	.456	7	13	.538	167	216	.773	157	268	425	94	203	1	....	....	143	27.6	14.4	6.3	1.4	.501
70-71	Virginia-A	81	....	2721	1534	594	1255	.473	0	1	.000	346	437	.792	215	435	650	157	290	2	....	....	183	33.6	18.9	8.0	1.9	.574
71-72	Carolina-A	29	....	738	479	161	349	.461	0	2	.000	157	185	.849	51	100	151	25	72	0	....	....	50	25.4	16.5	5.2	0.9	.583
71-72	Pittsburgh-A	46	....	1885	985	377	878	.429	0	8	.000	231	289	.799	121	234	355	103	148	0	....	....	140	41.0	21.4	7.7	2.2	.468
72-73	New York-A	83	....	2976	1578	569	1249	.456	0	9	.000	440	529	.832	205	310	515	173	308	7	....	....	255	35.9	19.0	6.2	2.1	.484
73-74	Virginia-A	80	....	2815	1546	561	1329	.422	32	93	.344	392	466	.841	189	346	535	136	308	....	67	12	229	35.2	19.3	6.7	1.7	.475
74-75	Memphis-A	82	....	3066	1508	590	1354	.436	10	37	.270	318	400	.795	232	349	581	255	276	....	92	33	198	37.4	18.4	7.1	3.1	.479
75-76	Utah-A	10	....	180	82	25	65	.385	0	0	.000	32	41	.780	11	20	31	15	27	....	5	3	16	18.0	8.2	3.1	1.5	.414
NBA Season Totals		1	....	5	3	1	2	.500	....	....	....	1	1	1.000	....	....	0	1	0	0	....	....	....	5.0	3.0	0.0	1.0	....
ABA Season Totals		478	....	16229	8680	3274	7350	.445	49	163	.301	2083	2563	.813	1181	2062	3243	958	1632	10	164	48	1214	34.0	18.2	6.8	2.0	....
Career Totals		479	....	16234	8683	3275	7352	.445	49	163	.301	2084	2564	.813	1181	2062	3243	959	1632	10	164	48	1214	33.9	18.1	6.8	2.0	....
69-70	Washington-A	3	....	65	26	11	21	.524	0	1	.000	4	5	.800	....	....	18	2	....	0	....	....	5	21.7	8.7	6.0	0.7	....
70-71	Virginia-A	12	....	409	229	88	190	.463	0	2	.000	53	65	.815	43	65	108	29	46	1	....	....	26	34.1	19.1	9.0	2.4	.600
72-73	New York-A	5	....	218	106	36	72	.500	0	0	.000	34	40	.850	16	29	45	13	27	2	....	....	21	43.6	21.2	9.0	2.6	.521
73-74	Virginia-A	5	....	204	104	42	96	.438	1	9	.111	19	22	.864	18	20	38	4	19	....	4	2	21	40.8	20.8	7.6	0.8	.419
74-75	Memphis-A	5	....	223	105	38	82	.463	1	2	.500	28	34	.824	15	22	37	12	20	....	1	1	21	44.6	21.0	7.4	2.4	.451
ABA Playoff Totals		30	....	1119	570	215	461	.466	2	14	.143	138	166	.831	92	136	246	60	112	3	5	3	94	37.3	19.0	8.2	2.0	....

• CARTER, Howard

Howard O'Neal Carter

Born: Oct. 26, 1961. Baton Rouge, LA, United States.   Height: 6'5".   Weight: 215 lbs.   Drafted: 1983   College: Louisiana State

YEAR	TEAM	GP	GS	MIN	PTS	FGM	FGA	FG%	3PM	3PA	3P%	FTM	FTA	FT%	ORB	DRB	TRB	AST	PF	DQ	STL	BLK	TO	MPG	PPG	RPG	APG	PCM
83-84	Denver	55	5	688	342	145	316	.459	5	19	.263	47	61	.770	38	48	86	71	81	0	19	4	44	12.5	6.2	1.6	1.3	.400
84-85	Dallas	11	0	66	9	4	23	.174	0	3	.000	1	1	1.000	1	2	3	4	4	0	1	0	8	6.0	0.8	0.3	0.4	-.152
NBA Season Totals		66	5	754	351	149	339	.440	5	22	.227	48	62	.774	39	50	89	75	85	0	20	4	52	11.4	5.3	1.3	1.1	....
83-84	Denver	5	0	60	15	7	22	.318	1	5	.200	0	0	.000	1	4	5	5	3	0	4	1	5	12.0	3.0	1.0	1.0	.161
NBA Playoff Totals		5	0	60	15	7	22	.318	1	5	.200	0	0	.000	1	4	5	5	3	0	4	1	5	12.0	3.0	1.0	1.0	....

• CARTER, Hugh

Hugh Carter

Born: —.   Height: —   Weight: —   Drafted: —   College: —

YEAR	TEAM	GP	GS	MIN	PTS	FGM	FGA	FG%	3PM	3PA	3P%	FTM	FTA	FT%	ORB	DRB	TRB	AST	PF	DQ	STL	BLK	TO	MPG	PPG	RPG	APG	PCM
41-42	Indianapolis-N	2	....	....	5	2	....	....	....	....	....	1	....	....	....	....	....	....	....	....	....	....	....	....	2.5	....	....	....
NBL Playoff Totals		2	....	....	5	2	....	....	....	....	....	1	....	....	....	....	....	....	....	....	....	....	....	....	2.5	....	....	....

CARTER, Jake
John D. (Jake, Jack) Carter

Born: July 25, 1924.   Height: 6'4".   Weight: 195 lbs.   Drafted: 1948   College: East Texas State

YEAR	TEAM	GP	GS	MIN	PTS	FGM	FGA	FG%	3PM	3PA	3P%	FTM	FTA	FT%	ORB	DRB	TRB	AST	PF	DQ	STL	BLK	TO	MPG	PPG	RPG	APG	PCM
48-49	Hammond-N	62	....	....	454	133	....	....	....	....	....	188	267	.704	....	....	....	....	201	....	....	....	....	....	7.3	....	....	....
49-50	Denver	13	....	....	44	13	45	.289	....	....	....	18	26	.692	....	....	....	16	27	....	....	....	....	....	3.4	....	1.2	....
49-50	Anderson	11	....	....	38	10	30	.333	....	....	....	18	27	.667	....	....	....	8	32	....	....	....	....	....	3.5	....	0.7	....
NBA Season Totals		24	....	....	82	23	75	.307	....	....	....	36	53	.679	....	....	....	24	59	....	....	....	....	....	3.4	....	1.0	....
NBL Season Totals		62	....	....	454	133	....	....	....	....	....	188	267	....	....	....	....	....	201	....	....	....	....	....	7.3	....	....	....
Career Totals		86	....	....	536	156	75	....	....	....	....	224	320	....	....	....	....	24	260	....	....	....	....	....	6.2	....	0.3	....
48-49	Hammond-N	2	....	....	19	7	....	....	....	....	....	5	13	.385	....	....	....	....	....	....	....	....	....	....	9.5	....	....	....
49-50	Anderson	8	....	....	10	3	21	.143	....	....	....	4	6	.667	....	....	....	3	12	....	....	....	....	....	1.3	....	0.4	....
NBA Playoff Totals		8	....	....	10	3	21	.143	....	....	....	4	6	.667	....	....	....	3	12	....	....	....	....	....	1.3	....	0.4	....
NBL Playoff Totals		2	....	....	19	7	....	....	....	....	....	5	13	....	....	....	....	....	....	....	....	....	....	....	9.5	....	....	....
Career Playoff Totals		10	....	....	29	10	21	....	....	....	....	9	19	....	....	....	....	3	12	....	....	....	....	....	2.9	....	0.3	....

CARTER, Reggie
Reginald Carter

Born: Oct. 10, 1957. New York, NY, United States. Died: Dec.24, 1999.   Height: 6'3".   Weight: 175 lbs.   Drafted: 1979   College: St. John's (NY)

YEAR	TEAM	GP	GS	MIN	PTS	FGM	FGA	FG%	3PM	3PA	3P%	FTM	FTA	FT%	ORB	DRB	TRB	AST	PF	DQ	STL	BLK	TO	MPG	PPG	RPG	APG	PCM
80-81	New York	60	....	536	169	59	179	.330	0	3	.000	51	69	.739	30	39	69	76	68	0	22	2	36	8.9	2.8	1.2	1.3	.290
81-82	New York	75	1	923	302	119	280	.425	0	0	.000	64	80	.800	35	60	95	130	124	1	36	6	75	12.3	4.0	1.3	1.7	.311
NBA Season Totals		135	1	1459	471	178	459	.388	0	3	.000	115	149	.772	65	99	164	206	192	1	58	8	111	10.8	3.5	1.2	1.5	....
80-81	New York	1	....	7	0	0	1	.000	0	0	.000	0	0	.000	1	1	2	0	4	0	0	0	1	7.0	0.0	2.0	0.0	-.260
NBA Playoff Totals		1	....	7	0	0	1	.000	0	0	.000	0	0	.000	1	1	2	0	4	0	0	0	1	7.0	0.0	2.0	0.0	....

CARTER, Ron
Ronald Carter Jr.

Born: Aug. 31, 1956. Pittsburgh, PA, United States.   Height: 6'5".   Weight: 190 lbs.   Drafted: 1978   College: Virginia Military Institute

YEAR	TEAM	GP	GS	MIN	PTS	FGM	FGA	FG%	3PM	3PA	3P%	FTM	FTA	FT%	ORB	DRB	TRB	AST	PF	DQ	STL	BLK	TO	MPG	PPG	RPG	APG	PCM
78-79	LA Lakers	46	....	332	144	54	124	.435	....	....	....	36	54	.667	21	24	45	25	54	1	17	7	41	7.2	3.1	1.0	0.5	.306
79-80	Indiana	13	....	117	32	15	37	.405	0	0	.000	2	7	.286	5	14	19	9	19	0	2	3	10	9.0	2.5	1.5	0.7	.203
NBA Season Totals		59	....	449	176	69	161	.429	0	0	.000	38	61	.623	26	38	64	34	73	1	19	10	51	7.6	3.0	1.1	0.6	....
78-79	LA Lakers	2	....	2	0	0	1	.000	....	....	....	0	0	.000	0	0	0	0	0	0	0	0	0	1.0	0.0	0.0	0.0	-.449
NBA Playoff Totals		2	....	2	0	0	1	.000	....	....	....	0	0	.000	0	0	0	0	0	0	0	0	0	1.0	0.0	0.0	0.0	....

CARTER, Vince
Vincent Lamar Carter

Born: Jan. 26, 1977. Daytona Beach, FL, United States.   Height: 6'7".   Weight: 215 lbs.   Drafted: 1998   College: North Carolina

YEAR	TEAM	GP	GS	MIN	PTS	FGM	FGA	FG%	3PM	3PA	3P%	FTM	FTA	FT%	ORB	DRB	TRB	AST	PF	DQ	STL	BLK	TO	MPG	PPG	RPG	APG	PCM
98-99	Toronto	50	49	1760	913	345	766	.450	19	66	.288	204	268	.761	94	189	283	149	140	2	55	77	110	35.2	18.3	5.7	3.0	.503
99-00	Toronto	82	82	3126	2107	788	1696	.465	95	236	.403	436	551	.791	150	326	476	322	263	2	110	92	178	38.1	25.7	5.8	3.9	.613
00-01	Toronto	75	75	2979	2070	762	1656	.460	162	397	.408	384	502	.765	176	240	416	291	205	1	114	82	167	39.7	27.6	5.5	3.9	.618
01-02	Toronto	60	60	2385	1484	559	1307	.428	121	313	.387	245	307	.798	138	175	313	239	191	4	94	43	154	39.8	24.7	5.2	4.0	.512
02-03	Toronto	43	42	1471	884	355	760	.467	45	131	.344	129	160	.806	59	129	188	143	121	2	48	41	74	34.2	20.6	4.4	3.3	.536
NBA Season Totals		310	308	11721	7458	2809	6185	.454	442	1143	.387	1398	1788	.782	617	1059	1676	1144	920	11	421	335	683	37.8	24.1	5.4	3.7	....
99-00	Toronto	3	3	119	58	15	50	.300	1	10	.100	27	31	.871	9	9	18	19	12	0	3	4	8	39.7	19.3	6.0	6.3	.463
00-01	Toronto	12	12	539	327	122	280	.436	25	61	.410	58	74	.784	37	41	78	56	45	1	20	20	27	44.9	27.3	6.5	4.7	.559
NBA Playoff Totals		15	15	658	385	137	330	.415	26	71	.366	85	105	.810	46	50	96	75	57	1	23	24	35	43.9	25.7	6.4	5.0	....

CARTWRIGHT, Bill
James William (Mr. Bill) Cartwright

Born: July 30, 1957. Lodi, CA, United States.   Height: 7'1".   Weight: 245 lbs.   Drafted: 1979   College: San Francisco

YEAR	TEAM	GP	GS	MIN	PTS	FGM	FGA	FG%	3PM	3PA	3P%	FTM	FTA	FT%	ORB	DRB	TRB	AST	PF	DQ	STL	BLK	TO	MPG	PPG	RPG	APG	PCM
79-80	New York	82	....	3150	1781	665	1215	.547	0	0	.000	451	566	.797	194	532	726	165	279	2	48	101	221	38.4	21.7	8.9	2.0	.596
80-81	New York	82	....	2925	1646	619	1118	.554	0	1	.000	408	518	.788	161	452	613	111	259	2	48	83	197	35.7	20.1	7.5	1.4	.562
81-82	New York	72	50	2060	1037	390	694	.562	0	0	.000	257	337	.763	116	305	421	87	208	2	48	65	166	28.6	14.4	5.8	1.2	.513
82-83	New York	82	82	2468	1290	455	804	.566	0	0	.000	380	511	.744	185	405	590	136	315	7	41	127	205	30.1	15.7	7.2	1.7	.576
83-84	New York	77	77	2487	1310	453	808	.561	0	1	.000	404	502	.805	195	454	649	107	262	4	44	97	200	32.3	17.0	8.4	1.4	.593
85-86	New York	2	0	36	12	3	7	.429	0	0	.000	6	10	.600	2	8	10	5	6	0	1	1	6	18.0	6.0	5.0	2.5	.405
86-87	New York	58	50	1989	1016	335	631	.531	0	0	.000	346	438	.790	132	313	445	96	188	2	40	26	128	34.3	17.5	7.7	1.7	.538
87-88	New York	82	4	1676	914	287	528	.544	0	0	.000	340	426	.798	127	257	384	85	234	4	43	43	131	20.4	11.1	4.7	1.0	.565
88-89	Chicago	78	76	2333	966	365	768	.475	0	0	.000	236	308	.766	152	369	521	90	234	2	21	41	187	29.9	12.4	6.7	1.2	.392
89-90	Chicago	71	71	2160	811	292	598	.488	0	0	.000	227	280	.811	137	328	465	145	243	6	38	34	121	30.4	11.4	6.5	2.0	.430
90-91	Chicago	79	79	2273	760	318	649	.490	0	0	.000	124	178	.697	167	319	486	126	167	0	32	15	111	28.8	9.6	6.2	1.6	.386
91-92	Chicago	64	64	1471	512	208	445	.467	0	0	.000	96	159	.604	93	231	324	87	131	0	22	14	77	23.0	8.0	5.1	1.4	.379
92-93	Chicago	63	63	1253	354	141	343	.411	0	0	.000	72	98	.735	83	150	233	83	154	1	20	10	63	19.9	5.6	3.7	1.3	.285
93-94	Chicago	42	41	780	235	98	191	.513	0	0	.000	39	57	.684	43	109	152	57	83	0	8	8	50	18.6	5.6	3.6	1.4	.350
94-95	Seattle	29	19	430	69	27	69	.391	0	0	.000	15	24	.625	25	62	87	10	70	0	6	3	17	14.8	2.4	3.0	0.3	.180
NBA Season Totals		963	676	27491	12713	4656	8868	.525	0	2	.000	3401	4412	.771	1812	4294	6106	1390	2833	32	460	668	1880	28.5	13.2	6.3	1.4	....
80-81	New York	2	....	49	20	6	17	.353	0	0	.000	8	12	.667	4	9	13	1	7	0	1	1	6	24.5	10.0	6.5	0.5	.291
82-83	New York	6	6	172	67	25	43	.581	0	0	.000	17	22	.773	9	25	34	4	25	0	3	7	19	28.7	11.2	5.7	0.7	.373
83-84	New York	12	12	398	209	70	126	.556	0	0	.000	69	80	.863	27	72	99	5	44	0	2	14	26	33.2	17.4	8.3	0.4	.551
87-88	New York	4	0	76	29	9	18	.500	0	0	.000	11	15	.733	8	11	19	6	12	0	0	3	8	19.0	7.3	4.8	1.5	.429
88-89	Chicago	17	17	583	200	72	148	.486	0	0	.000	56	80	.700	33	88	121	20	70	1	9	12	41	34.3	11.8	7.1	1.2	.345
89-90	Chicago	16	16	462	129	50	121	.413	0	0	.000	29	43	.674	25	50	75	16	52	0	5	4	25	28.9	8.1	4.7	1.0	.225
90-91	Chicago	17	17	511	162	70	135	.519	0	0	.000	22	32	.688	25	55	80	32	55	0	9	7	21	30.1	9.5	4.7	1.9	.343
91-92	Chicago	22	22	612	123	55	116	.474	0	0	.000	13	31	.419	29	69	98	38	70	1	11	4	27	27.8	5.6	4.5	1.7	.239

YEAR TEAM	GP	GS	MIN	PTS	FGM	FGA	FG%	3PM	3PA	3P%	FTM	FTA	FT%	ORB	DRB	TRB	AST	PF	DQ	STL	BLK	TO	MPG	PPG	RPG	APG	PCM
92-93 Chicago	19	19	444	120	46	99	.465	0	0	.000	28	36	.778	28	57	85	29	51	1	11	3	13	23.4	6.3	4.5	1.5	.347
93-94 Chicago	9	8	189	41	14	43	.326	0	0	.000	13	16	.813	19	25	44	11	26	0	3	2	6	21.0	4.6	4.9	1.2	.278
NBA Playoff Totals	124	117	3496	1100	417	866	.482	0	0	.000	266	367	.725	207	461	668	162	412	3	54	57	192	28.2	8.9	5.4	1.3	....

• CARTY, Jay

Jay J. Carty Jr.

Born: July 4, 1941. Height: 6'8". Weight: 220 lbs. Drafted: 1962 College: Oregon State

YEAR TEAM	GP	GS	MIN	PTS	FGM	FGA	FG%	3PM	3PA	3P%	FTM	FTA	FT%	ORB	DRB	TRB	AST	PF	DQ	STL	BLK	TO	MPG	PPG	RPG	APG	PCM
68-69 LA Lakers	28	....	192	76	34	89	.382	....	....	....	8	11	.727	....	....	58	11	31	0	....	....	....	6.9	2.7	2.1	0.4	.402
NBA Season Totals	28	....	192	76	34	89	.382	....	....	....	8	11	.727	....	....	58	11	31	0	....	....	....	6.9	2.7	2.1	0.4	....
68-69 LA Lakers	3	....	10	1	0	2	.000	....	....	....	1	3	.333	....	....	2	1	3	0	....	....	....	3.3	0.3	0.7	0.3	.007
NBA Playoff Totals	3	....	10	1	0	2	.000	....	....	....	1	3	.333	....	....	2	1	3	0	....	....	....	3.3	0.3	0.7	0.3	....

• CASH, Cornelius

Cornelius Cash Jr.

Born: Mar. 3, 1952. Macon, MS, United States. Height: 6'8". Weight: 215 lbs. Drafted: 1975 College: Bowling Green

YEAR TEAM	GP	GS	MIN	PTS	FGM	FGA	FG%	3PM	3PA	3P%	FTM	FTA	FT%	ORB	DRB	TRB	AST	PF	DQ	STL	BLK	TO	MPG	PPG	RPG	APG	PCM
76-77 Detroit	6	....	49	21	9	23	.391	....	....	....	3	6	.500	8	8	16	1	8	0	2	1	....	8.2	3.5	2.7	0.2	.390
NBA Season Totals	6	....	49	21	9	23	.391	....	....	....	3	6	.500	8	8	16	1	8	0	2	1	....	8.2	3.5	2.7	0.2	....

• CASH, Sam

Sam Cash

Born: Nov. 13, 1950. Height: 6'8". Weight: 230 lbs. Drafted: 1972 College: California (Riverside)

YEAR TEAM	GP	GS	MIN	PTS	FGM	FGA	FG%	3PM	3PA	3P%	FTM	FTA	FT%	ORB	DRB	TRB	AST	PF	DQ	STL	BLK	TO	MPG	PPG	RPG	APG	PCM
72-73 Memphis-A	7	....	52	20	4	18	.222	0	0	.000	12	17	.706	9	10	19	0	11	0	....	....	5	7.4	2.9	2.7	0.0	.333
ABA Season Totals	7	....	52	20	4	18	.222	0	0	.000	12	17	.706	9	10	19	0	11	0	....	....	5	7.4	2.9	2.7	0.0	....

• CASSELL, Sam

Samuel James Cassell

Born: Nov. 18, 1969. Baltimore, MD, United States. Height: 6'3". Weight: 185 lbs. Drafted: 1993 College: Florida State

YEAR TEAM	GP	GS	MIN	PTS	FGM	FGA	FG%	3PM	3PA	3P%	FTM	FTA	FT%	ORB	DRB	TRB	AST	PF	DQ	STL	BLK	TO	MPG	PPG	RPG	APG	PCM
93-94 Houston	66	6	1122	440	162	388	.418	26	88	.295	90	107	.841	25	109	134	192	136	1	59	7	92	17.0	6.7	2.0	2.9	.419
94-95 Houston	82	1	1882	783	253	593	.427	63	191	.330	214	254	.843	38	173	211	405	209	3	94	14	164	23.0	9.5	2.6	4.9	.490
95-96 Houston	61	0	1682	886	289	658	.439	73	210	.348	235	285	.825	51	137	188	278	166	2	53	4	159	27.6	14.5	3.1	4.6	.483
96-97 Phoenix	22	9	539	325	100	241	.415	19	62	.306	106	124	.855	12	38	50	99	66	4	23	6	59	24.5	14.8	2.3	4.5	.517
96-97 Dallas	16	13	398	197	70	165	.424	15	49	.306	42	50	.840	14	36	50	57	48	2	17	6	42	24.9	12.3	3.1	3.6	.432
96-97 New Jersey	23	22	777	445	167	377	.443	47	120	.392	64	77	.831	21	61	82	149	86	3	37	7	67	33.8	19.3	3.6	6.5	.537
97-98 New Jersey	75	72	2606	1471	510	1156	.441	15	80	.188	436	507	.860	73	155	228	603	262	5	121	20	270	34.7	19.6	3.0	8.0	.565
98-99 New Jersey	4	3	100	72	21	49	.429	1	7	.143	29	31	.935	1	5	6	19	13	1	3	0	12	25.0	18.0	1.5	4.8	.589
98-99 Milwaukee	4	0	99	55	18	44	.409	1	3	.333	18	19	.947	4	5	9	17	9	0	6	0	8	24.8	13.8	2.3	4.3	.531
99-00 Milwaukee	81	81	2899	1506	545	1170	.466	26	90	.289	390	445	.876	69	232	301	729	255	5	102	8	267	35.8	18.6	3.7	9.0	.595
00-01 Milwaukee	76	75	2709	1381	537	1132	.474	30	98	.306	277	323	.858	46	244	290	580	214	5	88	8	220	35.6	18.2	3.8	7.6	.560
01-02 Milwaukee	74	73	2604	1461	554	1197	.463	71	204	.348	282	328	.860	54	258	312	493	208	3	90	12	177	35.2	19.7	4.2	6.7	.583
02-03 Milwaukee	78	77	2700	1536	546	1162	.470	59	163	.362	385	447	.861	57	285	342	450	216	1	88	14	177	34.6	19.7	4.4	5.8	.587
NBA Season Totals	662	432	20117	10558	3772	8332	.453	446	1365	.327	2568	2997	.857	465	1738	2203	4071	1888	35	781	106	1714	30.4	15.9	3.3	6.1	....
93-94 Houston	22	0	478	207	63	160	.394	17	45	.378	64	74	.865	19	40	59	93	62	1	21	5	47	21.7	9.4	2.7	4.2	.462
94-95 Houston	22	0	485	243	74	169	.438	24	60	.400	71	85	.835	8	34	42	89	66	1	21	2	33	22.0	11.0	1.9	4.0	.497
95-96 Houston	8	0	206	83	26	81	.321	8	29	.276	23	29	.793	1	16	17	34	20	0	6	1	18	25.8	10.4	2.1	4.3	.295
97-98 New Jersey	3	1	26	6	3	9	.333	0	0	.000	0	0	.000	1	2	3	5	7	0	0	1	2	8.7	2.0	1.0	1.7	.175
98-99 Milwaukee	3	3	102	46	16	32	.500	0	1	.000	14	16	.875	0	6	6	26	14	1	3	0	7	34.0	15.3	2.0	8.7	.542
99-00 Milwaukee	5	5	178	79	30	72	.417	1	5	.200	18	21	.857	0	17	17	45	19	1	4	0	9	35.6	15.8	3.4	9.0	.511
00-01 Milwaukee	18	18	682	314	110	278	.396	10	30	.333	84	97	.866	12	71	83	120	76	2	19	3	52	37.9	17.4	4.6	6.7	.444
02-03 Milwaukee	6	6	217	103	39	83	.470	11	21	.524	14	15	.933	3	16	19	16	20	0	3	1	17	36.2	17.2	3.2	2.7	.352
NBA Playoff Totals	87	33	2374	1081	361	884	.408	71	191	.372	288	337	.855	44	202	246	428	284	6	77	13	185	27.3	12.4	2.8	4.9	....

• CATCHINGS, Harvey

Harvey Lee Catchings

Born: Sept. 2, 1951. Jackson, MS, United States. Height: 6'9". Weight: 218 lbs. Drafted: 1974 College: Hardin-Simmons

YEAR TEAM	GP	GS	MIN	PTS	FGM	FGA	FG%	3PM	3PA	3P%	FTM	FTA	FT%	ORB	DRB	TRB	AST	PF	DQ	STL	BLK	TO	MPG	PPG	RPG	APG	PCM
74-75 Philadelphia	37	....	528	98	41	74	.554	....	....	....	16	25	.640	49	104	153	21	82	1	10	60	....	14.3	2.6	4.1	0.6	.352
75-76 Philadelphia	75	....	1731	264	103	242	.426	....	....	....	58	96	.604	191	329	520	63	262	6	21	164	....	23.1	3.5	6.9	0.8	.309
76-77 Philadelphia	53	....	864	157	62	123	.504	....	....	....	33	47	.702	64	170	234	30	130	1	23	78	....	16.3	3.0	4.4	0.6	.322
77-78 Philadelphia	61	....	748	174	70	178	.393	....	....	....	34	55	.618	105	145	250	34	124	1	20	67	43	12.3	2.9	4.1	0.6	.417
78-79 Philadelphia	25	....	289	69	28	68	.412	....	....	....	13	17	.765	30	68	98	18	42	1	8	35	38	11.6	2.8	3.9	0.7	.432
78-79 New Jersey	32	....	659	195	74	175	.423	....	....	....	47	61	.770	71	133	204	30	90	2	15	56	51	20.6	6.1	6.4	0.9	.443
79-80 Milwaukee	72	....	1366	233	97	244	.398	0	1	.000	39	62	.629	164	246	410	82	191	1	23	162	65	19.0	3.2	5.7	1.1	.419
80-81 Milwaukee	77	....	1635	327	134	300	.447	0	0	.000	59	92	.641	154	319	473	99	284	7	33	184	108	21.2	4.2	6.1	1.3	.409
81-82 Milwaukee	80	9	1603	229	94	224	.420	0	0	.000	41	69	.594	129	227	356	97	237	3	42	135	96	20.0	2.9	4.5	1.2	.308
82-83 Milwaukee	74	33	1554	242	90	197	.457	0	0	.000	62	92	.674	132	276	408	77	224	4	26	148	81	21.0	3.3	5.5	1.0	.365
83-84 Milwaukee	69	3	1156	144	61	153	.399	0	1	.000	22	42	.524	89	182	271	43	172	3	25	81	55	16.8	2.1	3.9	0.6	.272
84-85 LA Clippers	70	14	1049	203	72	149	.483	0	1	.000	59	89	.663	89	173	262	14	162	0	15	57	56	15.0	2.9	3.7	0.2	.301
NBA Season Totals	725	59	13182	2335	926	2127	.435	0	3	.000	483	747	.647	1267	2372	3639	608	2000	30	261	1227	593	18.2	3.2	5.0	0.8	....
75-76 Philadelphia	3	....	87	17	8	13	.615	....	....	....	1	3	.333	12	16	28	6	11	0	0	9	....	29.0	5.7	9.3	2.0	.437
76-77 Philadelphia	8	....	54	4	2	5	.400	....	....	....	0	3	.000	5	7	12	1	9	0	0	4	....	6.8	0.5	1.5	0.1	.143
77-78 Philadelphia	7	....	26	9	3	8	.375	....	....	....	3	4	.750	3	6	9	0	4	0	1	3	0	3.7	1.3	1.3	0.0	.531
78-79 New Jersey	2	....	26	2	1	6	.167	....	....	....	0	3	.000	5	3	8	1	4	0	0	1	2	13.0	1.0	4.0	0.5	.068
79-80 Milwaukee	6	....	64	6	2	6	.333	0	0	.000	2	4	.500	5	16	21	2	13	0	0	8	2	10.7	1.0	3.5	0.3	.347
80-81 Milwaukee	7	....	109	8	3	16	.188	0	0	.000	2	2	1.000	10	16	26	8	24	0	0	11	7	15.6	1.1	3.7	1.1	.195
81-82 Milwaukee	6	0	26	4	2	3	.667	0	0	.000	0	0	.000	3	4	7	0	9	0	0	3	3	4.3	0.7	1.2	0.0	.207

YEAR	TEAM	GP	GS	MIN	PTS	FGM	FGA	FG%	3PM	3PA	3P%	FTM	FTA	FT%	ORB	DRB	TRB	AST	PF	DQ	STL	BLK	TO	MPG	PPG	RPG	APG	PCM
82-83	Milwaukee	9	0	139	21	9	19	.474	0	0	.000	3	3	1.000	15	23	38	4	18	0	2	10	2	15.4	2.3	4.2	0.4	.371
83-84	Milwaukee	5	0	25	3	1	2	.500	0	0	.000	1	2	.500	2	3	5	1	7	0	0	0	2	5.0	0.6	1.0	0.2	.088
NBA Playoff Totals		53	0	556	74	31	78	.397	0	0	.000	12	24	.500	60	94	154	23	99	0	3	49	18	10.5	1.4	2.9	0.4	....

• CATLEDGE, Terry

Terry DeWayne (Cat Man) Catledge

Born: Aug. 22, 1963. Houston, MS, United States.   Height: 6'8".   Weight: 220 lbs.   Drafted: 1985   College: South Alabama

YEAR	TEAM	GP	GS	MIN	PTS	FGM	FGA	FG%	3PM	3PA	3P%	FTM	FTA	FT%	ORB	DRB	TRB	AST	PF	DQ	STL	BLK	TO	MPG	PPG	RPG	APG	PCM
85-86	Philadelphia	64	7	1092	494	202	431	.469	0	4	.000	90	139	.647	107	165	272	21	127	0	31	8	70	17.1	7.7	4.3	0.3	.408
86-87	Washington	78	77	2149	1025	413	835	.495	0	4	.000	199	335	.594	248	312	560	56	195	1	43	14	148	27.6	13.1	7.2	0.7	.453
87-88	Washington	70	40	1610	746	296	585	.506	0	2	.000	154	235	.655	180	217	397	63	172	0	33	9	98	23.0	10.7	5.7	0.9	.462
88-89	Washington	79	77	2077	822	334	681	.490	1	5	.200	153	254	.602	230	342	572	75	250	5	46	25	119	26.3	10.4	7.2	0.9	.435
89-90	Orlando	74	72	2462	1435	546	1152	.474	2	8	.250	341	486	.702	271	292	563	72	201	0	36	17	178	33.3	19.4	7.6	1.0	.484
90-91	Orlando	51	38	1459	745	292	632	.462	0	5	.000	161	258	.624	168	187	355	58	113	2	34	9	107	28.6	14.6	7.0	1.1	.455
91-92	Orlando	78	67	2430	1154	457	922	.496	0	4	.000	240	346	.694	257	292	549	109	196	2	58	16	140	31.2	14.8	7.0	1.4	.472
92-93	Orlando	21	0	262	99	36	73	.493	0	0	.000	27	34	.794	18	28	46	5	31	1	4	1	25	12.5	4.7	2.2	0.2	.291
NBA Season Totals		515	379	13541	6520	2576	5311	.485	3	32	.094	1365	2087	.654	1479	1835	3314	459	1285	11	285	99	885	26.3	12.7	6.4	0.9	....
85-86	Philadelphia	11	10	293	114	46	117	.393	0	0	.000	22	38	.579	37	38	75	5	34	0	6	8	14	26.6	10.4	6.8	0.5	.341
86-87	Washington	3	3	98	55	23	41	.561	0	0	.000	9	17	.529	7	18	25	0	5	0	3	1	7	32.7	18.3	8.3	0.0	.537
87-88	Washington	5	0	45	11	4	11	.364	0	1	.000	3	4	.750	2	4	6	2	9	0	0	0	2	9.0	2.2	1.2	0.4	.126
NBA Playoff Totals		19	13	436	180	73	169	.432	0	1	.000	34	59	.576	46	60	106	7	48	0	9	9	23	22.9	9.5	5.6	0.4	....

• CATLETT, Sid

Sidny Leon Catlett

Born: Apr. 18, 1948.   Height: 6'6".   Weight: 230 lbs.   Drafted: 1971   College: Notre Dame

YEAR	TEAM	GP	GS	MIN	PTS	FGM	FGA	FG%	3PM	3PA	3P%	FTM	FTA	FT%	ORB	DRB	TRB	AST	PF	DQ	STL	BLK	TO	MPG	PPG	RPG	APG	PCM
71-72	Cincinnati	9	....	40	6	2	9	.222	....	....	....	2	9	.222	....	....	4	1	3	0	....	....	....	4.4	0.7	0.4	0.1	.006
NBA Season Totals		9	....	40	6	2	9	.222	....	....	....	2	9	.222	....	....	4	1	3	0	....	....	....	4.4	0.7	0.4	0.1	....

• CATO, Kelvin

Kelvin T. Cato

Born: Aug. 26, 1974. Atlanta, GA, United States.   Height: 6'11".   Weight: 255 lbs.   Drafted: 1997   College: Iowa State

YEAR	TEAM	GP	GS	MIN	PTS	FGM	FGA	FG%	3PM	3PA	3P%	FTM	FTA	FT%	ORB	DRB	TRB	AST	PF	DQ	STL	BLK	TO	MPG	PPG	RPG	APG	PCM
97-98	Portland	74	8	1007	282	98	229	.428	0	3	.000	86	125	.688	91	161	252	23	164	2	29	94	44	13.6	3.8	3.4	0.3	.394
98-99	Portland	43	0	546	151	58	129	.450	1	1	1.000	34	67	.507	49	101	150	19	100	3	23	56	27	12.7	3.5	3.5	0.4	.420
99-00	Houston	65	32	1581	567	216	402	.537	0	4	.000	135	208	.649	102	287	389	26	175	1	33	124	71	24.3	8.7	6.0	0.4	.471
00-01	Houston	35	13	624	165	64	111	.577	0	0	.000	37	57	.649	47	94	141	11	89	1	13	31	25	17.8	4.7	4.0	0.3	.368
01-02	Houston	75	73	1915	493	190	326	.583	0	1	.000	113	194	.582	176	349	525	29	208	5	40	95	53	25.5	6.6	7.0	0.4	.428
02-03	Houston	73	5	1252	332	133	256	.520	0	4	.000	66	124	.532	132	296	428	20	176	0	38	85	56	17.2	4.5	5.9	0.3	.468
NBA Season Totals		365	131	6925	1990	759	1453	.522	1	13	.077	471	775	.608	597	1288	1885	128	912	12	176	485	276	19.0	5.5	5.2	0.4	....
97-98	Portland	4	0	58	26	9	17	.529	0	1	.000	8	11	.727	3	9	12	1	12	0	1	7	4	14.5	6.5	3.0	0.3	.475
98-99	Portland	8	0	43	6	1	9	.111	0	0	.000	4	10	.400	6	1	7	2	13	0	1	1	2	5.4	0.8	0.9	0.3	-.026
NBA Playoff Totals		12	0	101	32	10	26	.385	0	1	.000	12	21	.571	9	10	19	3	25	0	2	8	6	8.4	2.7	1.6	0.3	....

• CATTAGE, Bobby

Robert Lewis Cattage

Born: Aug. 17, 1958. Huntsville, AL, United States.   Height: 6'9".   Weight: 250 lbs.   Drafted: 1981   College: Auburn

YEAR	TEAM	GP	GS	MIN	PTS	FGM	FGA	FG%	3PM	3PA	3P%	FTM	FTA	FT%	ORB	DRB	TRB	AST	PF	DQ	STL	BLK	TO	MPG	PPG	RPG	APG	PCM
81-82	Utah	49	0	337	150	60	135	.444	0	2	.000	30	41	.732	22	51	73	7	58	0	7	0	20	6.9	3.1	1.5	0.1	.332
85-86	New Jersey	29	1	185	92	28	83	.337	1	5	.200	35	44	.795	15	19	34	4	23	0	6	0	12	6.4	3.2	1.2	0.1	.305
NBA Season Totals		78	1	522	242	88	218	.404	1	7	.143	65	85	.765	37	70	107	11	81	0	13	0	32	6.7	3.1	1.4	0.1	....

• CAUSWELL, Duane

Duane Causwell

Born: May 31, 1968. Queens Village, NY, United States.   Height: 7'   Weight: 240 lbs.   Drafted: 1990   College: Temple

YEAR	TEAM	GP	GS	MIN	PTS	FGM	FGA	FG%	3PM	3PA	3P%	FTM	FTA	FT%	ORB	DRB	TRB	AST	PF	DQ	STL	BLK	TO	MPG	PPG	RPG	APG	PCM
90-91	Sacramento	76	55	1719	525	210	413	.508	0	0	.000	105	165	.636	141	250	391	69	225	4	49	148	99	22.6	6.9	5.1	0.9	.426
91-92	Sacramento	80	77	2291	636	250	455	.549	0	1	.000	136	222	.613	196	384	580	59	281	4	47	215	128	28.6	8.0	7.3	0.7	.437
92-93	Sacramento	55	45	1211	453	175	321	.545	0	1	.000	103	165	.624	112	191	303	35	192	7	32	87	61	22.0	8.2	5.5	0.6	.473
93-94	Sacramento	41	8	674	182	71	137	.518	0	0	.000	40	68	.588	68	118	186	11	109	2	19	49	33	16.4	4.4	4.5	0.3	.405
94-95	Sacramento	58	24	820	209	76	147	.517	0	1	.000	57	98	.582	57	117	174	15	146	4	14	80	35	14.1	3.6	3.0	0.3	.353
95-96	Sacramento	73	26	1044	250	90	216	.417	0	1	.000	70	96	.729	86	162	248	20	173	2	27	58	51	14.3	3.4	3.4	0.3	.329
96-97	Sacramento	46	8	581	118	48	94	.511	2	3	.667	20	37	.541	57	70	127	20	131	5	15	38	32	12.6	2.6	2.8	0.4	.285
97-98	Miami	37	2	363	89	37	89	.416	0	0	.000	15	26	.577	29	70	99	5	73	0	7	27	19	9.8	2.4	2.7	0.1	.311
98-99	Miami	19	1	137	44	20	35	.571	0	0	.000	4	12	.333	14	21	35	2	32	1	0	11	18	7.2	2.3	1.8	0.1	.292
99-00	Miami	25	2	185	66	20	37	.541	0	0	.000	26	38	.684	11	36	47	2	42	0	2	16	10	7.4	2.6	1.9	0.1	.423
00-01	Miami	31	14	384	76	32	85	.376	0	0	.000	12	25	.480	23	60	83	5	67	0	8	18	23	12.4	2.5	2.7	0.2	.196
NBA Season Totals		541	262	9409	2648	1029	2029	.507	2	7	.286	588	952	.618	794	1479	2273	243	1471	29	220	767	509	17.4	4.9	4.2	0.4	....
95-96	Sacramento	2	0	25	5	1	3	.333	0	1	.000	3	4	.750	1	4	5	1	3	0	0	0	2	12.5	2.5	2.5	0.5	.205
97-98	Miami	1	1	5	0	0	0	.000	0	0	.000	0	0	.000	0	2	2	0	0	0	0	0	1	5.0	0.0	2.0	0.0	.183
98-99	Miami	4	0	20	6	1	2	.500	0	0	.000	4	6	.667	0	2	2	1	2	0	1	0	0	5.0	1.5	0.5	0.3	.356
00-01	Miami	1	0	5	0	0	1	.000	0	0	.000	0	0	.000	0	3	3	0	1	0	0	0	0	5.0	0.0	3.0	0.0	.269
NBA Playoff Totals		8	1	55	11	2	6	.333	0	1	.000	7	10	.700	1	11	12	2	6	0	1	0	3	6.9	1.4	1.5	0.3	....

• CAVENALL, Ron

Ronnie Goodall Cavenall

Born: Apr. 30, 1959. Beaumont, TX, United States.   Height: 7'1".   Weight: 230 lbs.   Drafted: —   College: Texas Southern

YEAR	TEAM	GP	GS	MIN	PTS	FGM	FGA	FG%	3PM	3PA	3P%	FTM	FTA	FT%	ORB	DRB	TRB	AST	PF	DQ	STL	BLK	TO	MPG	PPG	RPG	APG	PCM
84-85	New York	53	2	653	78	28	86	.326	0	0	.000	22	39	.564	53	113	166	19	123	2	12	42	42	12.3	1.5	3.1	0.4	.222
88-89	New Jersey	5	0	16	6	2	3	.667	0	0	.000	2	5	.400	0	2	2	0	2	0	0	2	2	3.2	1.2	0.4	0.0	.288
NBA Season Totals		58	2	669	84	30	89	.337	0	0	.000	24	44	.545	53	115	168	19	125	2	12	44	44	11.5	1.4	2.9	0.3	....

• CEBALLOS, Cedric

Cedric Z. (Ice) Ceballos

Born: Aug. 2, 1969. Maui, HI, United States. Height: 6'6". Weight: 190 lbs. Drafted: 1990 College: Cal State Fullerton

YEAR	TEAM	GP	GS	MIN	PTS	FGM	FGA	FG%	3PM	3PA	3P%	FTM	FTA	FT%	ORB	DRB	TRB	AST	PF	DQ	STL	BLK	TO	MPG	PPG	RPG	APG	PCM
90-91	Phoenix	63	0	730	519	204	419	.487	1	6	.167	110	166	.663	77	73	150	35	70	0	22	5	69	11.6	8.2	2.4	0.6	.545
91-92	Phoenix	64	4	730	462	176	365	.482	1	6	.167	109	148	.736	60	92	152	50	52	0	16	11	70	11.4	7.2	2.4	0.8	.547
92-93	Phoenix	74	46	1607	949	381	662	**.576**	0	2	.000	187	258	.725	172	236	408	77	103	1	54	29	104	21.7	12.8	5.5	1.0	.653
93-94	Phoenix	53	43	1602	1010	425	795	.535	0	9	.000	160	221	.724	153	191	344	91	124	0	59	23	95	30.2	19.1	6.5	1.7	.617
94-95	LA Lakers	58	54	2029	1261	497	977	.509	58	146	.397	209	292	.716	169	295	464	105	131	1	60	19	145	35.0	21.7	8.0	1.8	.589
95-96	LA Lakers	78	71	2628	1656	638	1203	.530	51	184	.277	329	409	.804	215	321	536	119	144	0	94	22	164	33.7	21.2	6.9	1.5	.611
96-97	LA Lakers	8	8	279	86	34	83	.410	5	21	.238	13	15	.867	11	42	53	15	19	0	5	6	17	34.9	10.8	6.6	1.9	.324
96-97	Phoenix	42	32	1147	643	248	534	.464	21	81	.259	126	171	.737	91	186	277	49	94	0	28	17	67	27.3	15.3	6.6	1.2	.525
97-98	Phoenix	35	16	626	333	129	258	.500	15	50	.300	60	84	.714	51	98	149	35	59	0	22	8	39	17.9	9.5	4.3	1.0	.548
97-98	Dallas	12	9	364	203	75	157	.478	6	20	.300	47	61	.770	24	48	72	25	29	0	11	8	34	30.3	16.9	6.0	2.1	.515
98-99	Dallas	13	5	352	163	59	140	.421	11	28	.393	34	49	.694	23	62	85	12	23	1	7	5	28	27.1	12.5	6.5	0.9	.423
99-00	Dallas	69	25	2064	1147	447	1002	.446	44	134	.328	209	248	.843	172	290	462	90	165	3	56	24	125	29.9	16.6	6.7	1.3	.498
00-01	Detroit	13	0	166	75	28	71	.394	11	40	.275	8	10	.800	7	19	26	7	19	0	6	3	9	12.8	5.8	2.0	0.5	.350
00-01	Miami	27	0	393	186	73	158	.462	11	33	.333	29	33	.879	27	53	80	13	42	0	10	4	23	14.6	6.9	3.0	0.5	.425
NBA Season Totals		609	313	14717	8693	3414	6824	.500	235	760	.309	1630	2165	.753	1252	2006	3258	723	1074	6	450	184	989	24.2	14.3	5.3	1.2	....
90-91	Phoenix	3	0	24	16	7	12	.583	0	0	.000	2	6	.333	3	2	5	2	0	0	2	0	1	8.0	5.3	1.7	0.7	.717
91-92	Phoenix	8	8	188	108	44	80	.550	0	0	.000	20	30	.667	20	31	51	12	14	0	6	6	11	23.5	13.5	6.4	1.5	.663
92-93	Phoenix	16	3	185	96	40	70	.571	0	0	.000	16	22	.727	13	24	37	13	12	0	5	7	5	11.6	6.0	2.3	0.8	.619
93-94	Phoenix	10	8	212	101	43	93	.462	0	2	.000	15	18	.833	16	28	44	8	9	0	8	2	11	21.2	10.1	4.4	0.8	.461
94-95	LA Lakers	10	10	340	142	48	126	.381	18	50	.360	28	38	.737	11	50	61	18	21	0	12	7	21	34.0	14.2	6.1	1.8	.379
95-96	LA Lakers	4	4	142	76	30	62	.484	5	16	.313	11	12	.917	11	22	33	5	9	0	4	1	8	35.5	19.0	8.3	1.3	.526
96-97	Phoenix	5	0	107	33	11	33	.333	3	12	.250	8	8	1.000	9	17	26	3	12	0	4	3	8	21.4	6.6	5.2	0.6	.312
00-01	Miami	3	0	15	5	2	7	.286	0	0	.000	1	2	.500	3	3	6	1	3	0	0	0	1	5.0	1.7	2.0	0.3	.287
NBA Playoff Totals		59	33	1213	577	225	483	.466	26	80	.325	101	136	.743	86	177	263	62	80	0	41	26	66	20.6	9.8	4.5	1.1	....

• CELESTAND, John

John Celestand

Born: Mar. 6, 1977. Houston, TX, United States. Height: 6'4". Weight: 178 lbs. Drafted: 1999 College: Villanova

YEAR	TEAM	GP	GS	MIN	PTS	FGM	FGA	FG%	3PM	3PA	3P%	FTM	FTA	FT%	ORB	DRB	TRB	AST	PF	DQ	STL	BLK	TO	MPG	PPG	RPG	APG	PCM
99-00	LA Lakers	16	0	185	37	15	45	.333	2	9	.222	5	6	.833	1	10	11	20	22	0	7	0	16	11.6	2.3	0.7	1.3	.124
NBA Season Totals		16	0	185	37	15	45	.333	2	9	.222	5	6	.833	1	10	11	20	22	0	7	0	16	11.6	2.3	0.7	1.3	....

• CERVI, Al

Alfred Nicholas (Digger) Cervi

Born: Feb. 12, 1917. Buffalo, NY, United States. Height: 5'11". Weight: 170 lbs. Drafted: — College: — HOF: 1985

YEAR	TEAM	GP	GS	MIN	PTS	FGM	FGA	FG%	3PM	3PA	3P%	FTM	FTA	FT%	ORB	DRB	TRB	AST	PF	DQ	STL	BLK	TO	MPG	PPG	RPG	APG	PCM
37-38	Buffalo-N	9	....	....	44	19	....	....	....	....	....	6	....	....	....	....	....	....	....	....	....	....	....	....	4.9	....	....	....
45-46	Rochester-N	28	....	....	300	112	....	....	....	....	....	76	108	.704	....	....	....	....	....	....	....	....	....	....	10.7	....	....	....
46-47	Rochester-N	44	....	....	**632**	228	....	....	....	....	....	176	236	.746	....	....	....	....	127	....	....	....	....	....	14.4	....	....	....
47-48	Rochester-N	49	....	....	655	234	....	....	....	....	....	187	242	.773	....	....	....	....	118	....	....	....	....	....	13.4	....	....	....
48-49	Syracuse-N	57	....	....	695	204	....	....	....	....	....	287	382	.751	....	....	....	....	170	....	....	....	....	....	12.2	....	....	....
49-50	Syracuse	56	....	....	573	143	431	.332	....	....	....	287	346	.829	....	....	....	264	223	....	....	....	....	....	10.2	....	4.7	....
50-51	Syracuse	53	....	....	458	132	346	.382	....	....	....	194	237	.819	....	....	152	208	180	9	....	....	....	....	8.6	2.9	3.9	....
51-52	Syracuse	55	....	850	417	99	280	.354	....	....	....	219	248	.883	....	....	87	148	176	7	....	....	....	15.5	7.6	1.6	2.7	.551
52-53	Syracuse	38	....	301	143	31	71	.437	....	....	....	81	100	.810	....	....	22	28	90	2	....	....	....	7.9	3.8	0.6	0.7	.419
NBA Season Totals		202	....	1151	1591	405	1128	.359	....	....	....	781	931	.839	....	....	261	648	669	18	....	....	....	5.7	7.9	1.3	3.2	....
NBL Season Totals		187	....	....	2326	797	....	....	....	....	....	732	968	....	....	....	....	....	415	....	....	....	....	....	12.4	....	....	....
Career Totals		389	....	1151	3917	1202	1128	....	....	....	....	1513	1899	....	....	....	261	648	1084	18	....	....	....	3.0	10.1	0.7	1.7	....
45-46	Rochester-N	7	....	....	70	23	....	....	....	....	....	24	30	.800	....	....	....	....	....	....	....	....	....	....	10.0	....	....	....
46-47	Rochester-N	11	....	....	148	49	....	....	....	....	....	50	68	.735	....	....	....	....	....	....	....	....	....	....	13.5	....	....	....
47-48	Rochester-N	6	....	....	50	18	....	....	....	....	....	14	19	.737	....	....	....	....	....	....	....	....	....	....	8.3	....	....	....
48-49	Syracuse-N	6	....	....	46	12	....	....	....	....	....	22	30	.733	....	....	....	....	....	....	....	....	....	....	7.7	....	....	....
49-50	Syracuse	11	....	....	84	23	68	.338	....	....	....	38	46	.826	....	....	....	52	36	....	....	....	....	....	7.6	....	4.7	....
50-51	Syracuse	7	....	....	78	17	56	.304	....	....	....	44	50	.880	....	....	33	38	31	1	....	....	....	....	11.1	4.7	5.4	....
51-52	Syracuse	7	....	88	36	7	30	.233	....	....	....	22	23	.957	....	....	10	15	23	1	....	....	....	12.6	5.1	1.4	2.1	.427
52-53	Syracuse	2	....	28	18	3	5	.600	....	....	....	12	15	.800	....	....	0	1	12	1	....	....	....	14.0	9.0	0.0	0.5	.443
NBA Playoff Totals		27	....	116	216	50	159	.314	....	....	....	116	134	.866	....	....	43	106	102	3	....	....	....	4.3	8.0	1.6	3.9	....
NBL Playoff Totals		30	....	....	314	102	....	....	....	....	....	110	147	....	....	....	....	....	....	....	....	....	....	....	10.5	....	....	....
Career Playoff Totals		57	....	116	530	152	159	....	....	....	....	226	281	....	....	....	43	106	102	3	....	....	....	2.0	9.3	0.8	1.9	....

• CHAMBERLAIN, Bill

William Martin Chamberlain

Born: Dec. 16, 1949. Height: 6'6". Weight: 188 lbs. Drafted: 1972 College: North Carolina

YEAR	TEAM	GP	GS	MIN	PTS	FGM	FGA	FG%	3PM	3PA	3P%	FTM	FTA	FT%	ORB	DRB	TRB	AST	PF	DQ	STL	BLK	TO	MPG	PPG	RPG	APG	PCM
72-73	Kentucky-A	43	....	566	237	101	248	.407	1	3	.333	34	55	.618	56	51	107	69	81	1	....	....	54	13.2	5.5	2.5	1.6	.408
72-73	Memphis-A	7	....	99	25	11	34	.324	1	5	.200	2	4	.500	5	6	11	7	17	0	....	....	4	14.1	3.6	1.6	1.0	.135
73-74	Phoenix	28	....	367	153	57	130	.438	....	....	....	39	56	.696	33	47	80	37	74	2	20	12	....	13.1	5.5	2.9	1.3	.443
NBA Season Totals		28	....	367	153	57	130	.438	....	....	....	39	56	.696	33	47	80	37	74	2	20	12	....	13.1	5.5	2.9	1.3	....
ABA Season Totals		50	....	665	262	112	282	.397	2	8	.250	36	59	.610	61	57	118	76	98	1	....	....	58	13.3	5.2	2.4	1.5	....
Career Totals		78	....	1032	415	169	412	.410	2	8	.250	75	115	.652	94	104	198	113	172	3	20	12	58	13.2	5.3	2.5	1.4	....

• CHAMBERLAIN, Wilt

Wilton Norman (Wilt the Stilt, The Big Dipper) Chamberlain

Born: Aug. 21, 1936. Philadelphia, PA, United States. Died: Oct.12, 1999. Height: 7'1". Weight: 250 lbs. Drafted: 1959 College: Kansas HOF: 1979

YEAR	TEAM	GP	GS	MIN	PTS	FGM	FGA	FG%	3PM	3PA	3P%	FTM	FTA	FT%	ORB	DRB	TRB	AST	PF	DQ	STL	BLK	TO	MPG	PPG	RPG	APG	PCM
59-60	Philadelphia	72	....	**3338**	**2707**	**1065**	**2311**	.461	....	....	....	577	**991**	.582	....	....	**1941**	168	150	0	....	....	....	**46.4**	**37.6**	**27.0**	2.3	.967
60-61	Philadelphia	79	....	**3773**	**3033**	**1251**	**2457**	**.509**	....	....	....	531	**1054**	.504	....	....	**2149**	148	130	0	....	....	....	**47.8**	**38.4**	**27.2**	1.9	.977
61-62	Philadelphia	80	....	**3882**	**4029**	**1597**	**3159**	.506	....	....	....	**835**	**1363**	.613	....	....	**2052**	192	123	0	....	....	....	**48.5**	**50.4**	**25.7**	2.4	1.131

YEAR	TEAM	GP	GS	MIN	PTS	FGM	FGA	FG%	3PM	3PA	3P%	FTM	FTA	FT%	ORB	DRB	TRB	AST	PF	DQ	STL	BLK	TO	MPG	PPG	RPG	APG	PCM
62-63	San Francisco	80	....	**3806**	**3586**	**1463**	**2770**	**.528**	....	....	....	660	**1113**	.593	....	....	**1946**	275	136	0	....	....	....	**47.6**	**44.8**	**24.3**	3.4	1.101
63-64	San Francisco	80	....	**3689**	**2948**	**1204**	**2298**	.524	....	....	....	540	**1016**	.531	....	....	1787	403	182	0	....	....	....	**46.1**	**36.9**	22.3	5.0	1.009
64-65	San Francisco	38	....	1743	**1480**	**636**	**1275**	**.499**	....	....	....	208	**500**	.416	....	....	893	117	76	0	....	....	....	45.9	**38.9**	23.5	3.1	.963
64-65	Philadelphia	35	....	1558	**1054**	**427**	**808**	**.528**	....	....	....	200	**380**	.526	....	....	780	133	70	0	....	....	....	44.5	**30.1**	22.3	3.8	.917
65-66	Philadelphia	79	....	**3737**	**2649**	**1074**	**1990**	**.540**	....	....	....	501	976	.513	....	....	**1943**	414	171	0	....	....	....	**47.3**	**33.5**	**24.6**	5.2	.991
66-67	Philadelphia	81	....	**3682**	1956	785	1150	**.683**	....	....	....	386	**875**	.441	....	....	**1957**	630	143	0	....	....	....	**45.5**	24.1	**24.2**	7.8	1.013
67-68	Philadelphia	82	....	**3836**	1992	819	1377	**.595**	....	....	....	354	**932**	.380	....	....	**1952**	**702**	160	0	....	....	....	**46.8**	24.3	**23.8**	**8.6**	**.952**
68-69	LA Lakers	81	....	3669	1664	641	1099	**.583**	....	....	....	382	**857**	.446	....	....	**1712**	366	142	0	....	....	....	**45.3**	20.5	**21.1**	4.5	.785
69-70	LA Lakers	12	....	505	328	129	227	.568	....	....	....	70	157	.446	....	....	221	49	31	0	....	....	....	42.1	27.3	18.4	4.1	.870
70-71	LA Lakers	82	....	3630	1696	668	1226	.545	....	....	....	360	669	.538	....	....	**1493**	352	174	0	....	....	....	44.3	20.7	**18.2**	4.3	.742
71-72	LA Lakers	82	....	3469	1213	496	764	**.649**	....	....	....	221	524	.422	....	....	**1572**	329	196	0	....	....	....	42.3	14.8	**19.2**	4.0	.720
72-73	LA Lakers	82	....	3542	1084	426	586	**.727**	....	....	....	232	455	.510	....	....	**1526**	365	191	0	....	....	....	43.2	13.2	**18.6**	4.5	.704
NBA Season Totals		1045	....	47859	31419	12681	23497	.540	....	....	....	6057	11862	.511	....	....	**23924**	4643	2075	0	....	....	....	**45.8**	30.1	**22.9**	4.4	....
59-60	Philadelphia	9	....	415	299	125	252	.496	....	....	....	49	110	.445	....	....	232	19	17	0	....	....	....	46.1	33.2	25.8	2.1	.898
60-61	Philadelphia	3	....	144	111	45	96	.469	....	....	....	21	38	.553	....	....	69	6	10	0	....	....	....	48.0	37.0	23.0	2.0	.846
61-62	Philadelphia	12	....	576	420	162	347	.467	....	....	....	96	151	.636	....	....	319	37	27	0	....	....	....	48.0	35.0	26.6	3.1	.934
63-64	San Francisco	12	....	558	416	175	322	.543	....	....	....	66	139	.475	....	....	302	39	27	0	....	....	....	46.5	34.7	25.2	3.3	.977
64-65	Philadelphia	11	....	536	322	123	232	.530	....	....	....	76	136	.559	....	....	299	48	29	0	....	....	....	48.7	29.3	27.2	4.4	.920
65-66	Philadelphia	5	....	240	140	56	110	.509	....	....	....	28	68	.412	....	....	151	15	10	0	....	....	....	48.0	28.0	30.2	3.0	.895
66-67	Philadelphia	15	....	718	326	132	228	.579	....	....	....	62	160	.388	....	....	437	135	37	0	....	....	....	47.9	21.7	29.1	9.0	.984
67-68	Philadelphia	13	....	631	308	124	232	.534	....	....	....	60	158	.380	....	....	321	85	29	0	....	....	....	48.5	23.7	24.7	6.5	.839
68-69	LA Lakers	18	....	832	250	96	176	.545	....	....	....	58	148	.392	....	....	444	46	46	0	....	....	....	46.2	13.9	24.7	2.6	.662
69-70	LA Lakers	18	....	851	398	158	288	.549	....	....	....	82	202	.406	....	....	399	81	42	0	....	....	....	47.3	22.1	22.2	4.5	.769
70-71	LA Lakers	12	....	554	220	85	187	.455	....	....	....	50	97	.515	....	....	242	53	33	0	....	....	....	46.2	18.3	20.2	4.4	.661
71-72	LA Lakers	15	....	703	220	80	142	.563	....	....	....	60	122	.492	....	....	315	49	47	0	....	....	....	46.9	14.7	21.0	3.3	.636
72-73	LA Lakers	17	....	801	177	64	116	.552	....	....	....	49	98	.500	....	....	383	60	48	0	....	....	....	47.1	10.4	22.5	3.5	.609
NBA Playoff Totals		160	....	7559	3607	1425	2728	.522	....	....	....	757	1627	.465	....	....	3913	673	402	0	....	....	....	**47.2**	22.5	24.5	4.2	....

• CHAMBERS, Jerry

Jerome Purcell Chambers

Born: July 18, 1943. Washington, DC, United States. Height: 6'5". Weight: 185 lbs. Drafted: 1966 College: Utah

YEAR	TEAM	GP	GS	MIN	PTS	FGM	FGA	FG%	3PM	3PA	3P%	FTM	FTA	FT%	ORB	DRB	TRB	AST	PF	DQ	STL	BLK	TO	MPG	PPG	RPG	APG	PCM
66-67	LA Lakers	69	....	1015	516	224	496	.452	....	....	....	68	93	.731	....	....	208	44	143	0	....	....	....	14.7	7.5	3.0	0.6	.444
69-70	Phoenix	79	....	1139	657	283	658	.430	....	....	....	91	125	.728	....	....	219	54	162	3	....	....	....	14.4	8.3	2.8	0.7	.434
70-71	Atlanta	65	....	1168	580	237	526	.451	....	....	....	106	134	.791	....	....	245	61	119	0	....	....	....	18.0	8.9	3.8	0.9	.470
71-72	Buffalo	26	....	369	178	78	180	.433	....	....	....	22	32	.688	....	....	67	23	39	0	....	....	....	14.2	6.8	2.6	0.9	.414
72-73	San Diego-A	43	....	885	512	199	468	.425	2	10	.200	112	130	.862	83	107	190	46	102	0	....	....	55	20.6	11.9	4.4	1.1	.495
73-74	San Antonio-A	38	....	579	224	94	206	.456	0	0	.000	36	48	.750	37	66	103	42	74	....	11	3	28	15.2	5.9	2.7	1.1	.393
NBA Season Totals		239	....	3691	1931	822	1860	.442	....	....	....	287	384	.747	....	....	739	182	463	3	....	....	....	15.4	8.1	3.1	0.8	....
ABA Season Totals		81	....	1464	736	293	674	.435	2	10	.200	148	178	.831	120	173	293	88	176	0	11	3	83	18.1	9.1	3.6	1.1	....
Career Totals		320	....	5155	2667	1115	2534	.440	2	10	.200	435	562	.774	120	173	1032	270	639	3	11	3	83	16.1	8.3	3.2	0.8	....
66-67	LA Lakers	3	....	44	31	12	23	.522	....	....	....	7	7	1.000	....	....	8	1	7	0	....	....	....	14.7	10.3	2.7	0.3	.614
69-70	Phoenix	7	....	73	33	14	37	.378	....	....	....	5	8	.625	....	....	17	7	6	0	....	....	....	10.4	4.7	2.4	1.0	.433
70-71	Atlanta	4	....	22	7	3	9	.333	....	....	....	1	2	.500	....	....	5	0	4	0	....	....	....	5.5	1.8	1.3	0.0	.181
NBA Playoff Totals		14	....	139	71	29	69	.420	....	....	....	13	17	.765	....	....	30	8	17	0	....	....	....	9.9	5.1	2.1	0.6	....

• CHAMBERS, Tom

Thomas Doane Chambers

Born: June 21, 1959. Ogden, UT, United States. Height: 6'9". Weight: 220 lbs. Drafted: 1981 College: Utah

YEAR	TEAM	GP	GS	MIN	PTS	FGM	FGA	FG%	3PM	3PA	3P%	FTM	FTA	FT%	ORB	DRB	TRB	AST	PF	DQ	STL	BLK	TO	MPG	PPG	RPG	APG	PCM
81-82	San Diego	81	58	2682	1392	554	1056	.525	0	2	.000	284	458	.620	211	350	561	146	341	17	58	46	219	33.1	17.2	6.9	1.8	.470
82-83	San Diego	79	79	2665	1391	519	1099	.472	0	8	.000	353	488	.723	218	301	519	192	333	15	79	57	237	33.7	17.6	6.6	2.4	.467
83-84	Seattle	82	44	2570	1483	554	1110	.499	0	12	.000	375	469	.800	219	313	532	133	309	8	47	51	189	31.3	18.1	6.5	1.6	.518
84-85	Seattle	81	60	2923	1739	629	1302	.483	6	22	.273	475	571	.832	164	415	579	209	312	4	70	57	259	36.1	21.5	7.1	2.6	.534
85-86	Seattle	66	26	2019	1223	432	928	.466	13	48	.271	346	414	.836	126	305	431	132	248	6	55	37	191	30.6	18.5	6.5	2.0	.528
86-87	Seattle	82	82	3018	1909	660	1446	.456	54	145	.372	535	630	.849	163	382	545	245	307	9	81	50	271	36.8	23.3	6.6	3.0	.540
87-88	Seattle	82	82	2680	1674	611	1364	.448	33	109	.303	419	519	.807	135	355	490	212	297	4	87	53	205	32.7	20.4	6.0	2.6	.526
88-89	Phoenix	81	81	3002	2085	774	1643	.471	28	86	.326	509	598	.851	143	541	684	231	271	2	87	55	235	37.1	25.7	8.4	2.9	.635
89-90	Phoenix	81	81	3046	2201	810	1617	.501	24	86	.279	557	647	.861	121	450	571	190	260	1	88	47	219	37.6	27.2	7.0	2.3	.637
90-91	Phoenix	76	75	2475	1511	556	1271	.437	20	73	.274	379	459	.826	104	386	490	194	235	3	65	52	175	32.6	19.9	6.4	2.6	.528
91-92	Phoenix	69	66	1943	1128	426	989	.431	18	49	.367	258	311	.830	86	315	401	142	196	1	57	37	104	28.2	16.3	5.8	2.1	.517
92-93	Phoenix	73	0	1723	892	320	716	.447	11	28	.393	241	288	.837	96	249	345	101	212	2	43	22	95	23.6	12.2	4.7	1.4	.466
93-94	Utah	80	0	1838	893	329	748	.440	14	45	.311	221	281	.786	87	239	326	79	232	2	40	32	88	23.0	11.2	4.1	1.0	.405
94-95	Utah	81	4	1240	503	195	427	.457	4	24	.167	109	135	.807	66	147	213	73	173	1	25	30	49	15.3	6.2	2.6	0.9	.383
96-97	Charlotte	12	5	83	19	7	31	.226	2	3	.667	3	4	.750	3	11	14	4	14	0	1	0	10	6.9	1.6	1.2	0.3	-.017
97-98	Philadelphia	1	0	10	6	2	2	1.000	0	0	.000	2	2	1.000	0	2	2	0	2	0	2	0	1	10.0	6.0	2.0	0.0	.783
NBA Season Totals		1107	743	33917	20049	7378	15749	.468	227	740	.307	5066	6274	.807	1942	4761	6703	2283	3742	75	885	626	2547	30.6	18.1	6.1	2.1	....
83-84	Seattle	5	5	191	68	28	59	.475	0	1	.000	12	18	.667	4	29	33	8	23	0	5	3	9	38.2	13.6	6.6	1.6	.335
86-87	Seattle	14	14	498	322	118	263	.449	6	17	.353	80	99	.808	32	58	90	32	51	0	12	13	34	35.6	23.0	6.4	2.3	.530
87-88	Seattle	5	5	168	129	50	91	.549	0	2	.000	29	35	.829	8	23	31	11	24	1	3	1	13	33.6	25.8	6.2	2.2	.649
88-89	Phoenix	12	12	495	312	118	257	.459	9	22	.409	67	78	.859	22	109	131	46	44	0	13	15	39	41.3	26.0	10.9	3.8	.642
89-90	Phoenix	16	16	612	355	117	275	.425	5	19	.263	116	132	.879	20	87	107	31	54	0	7	7	49	38.3	22.2	6.7	1.9	.449
90-91	Phoenix	4	4	142	68	27	66	.409	0	5	.000	14	19	.737	2	21	23	10	12	1	7	5	12	35.5	17.0	5.8	2.5	.393
91-92	Phoenix	7	0	194	109	39	85	.459	4	7	.571	27	32	.844	8	23	31	19	25	1	2	5	15	27.7	15.6	4.4	2.7	.485
92-93	Phoenix	24	1	376	174	64	165	.388	2	5	.400	44	54	.815	23	42	65	12	58	0	6	10	26	15.7	7.3	2.7	0.5	.298
93-94	Utah	16	0	325	93	35	97	.361	0	7	.000	23	29	.793	16	29	45	12	50	1	5	9	8	20.3	5.8	2.8	0.8	.216
94-95	Utah	5	0	60	32	11	22	.500	1	3	.333	9	13	.692	3	10	13	2	18	1	2	0	3	12.0	6.4	2.6	0.4	.412
NBA Playoff Totals		108	57	3061	1662	607	1380	.440	27	88	.307	421	509	.827	138	431	569	183	359	5	62	68	208	28.3	15.4	5.3	1.7	....

• CHAMPION, Mike
Mike O. Champion

Born: Apr. 5, 1964. Everett, WA, United States. Height: 6'10". Weight: 230 lbs. Drafted: — College: Gonzaga

YEAR	TEAM	GP	GS	MIN	PTS	FGM	FGA	FG%	3PM	3PA	3P%	FTM	FTA	FT%	ORB	DRB	TRB	AST	PF	DQ	STL	BLK	TO	MPG	PPG	RPG	APG	PCM
88-89	Seattle	2	0	4	0	0	3	.000	0	1	.000	0	0	.000	0	0	0	0	2	0	0	0	1	2.0	0.0	0.0	0.0	-1.16
NBA Season Totals		2	0	4	0	0	3	.000	0	1	.000	0	0	.000	0	0	0	0	2	0	0	0	1	2.0	0.0	0.0	0.0	....

• CHANDLER, Tyson
Tyson Cleotis Chandler

Born: Oct. 2, 1982. Hanford, CA, United States. Height: 7'1". Weight: 235 lbs. Drafted: 2001 College: none (HS: Dominguez, CA)

YEAR	TEAM	GP	GS	MIN	PTS	FGM	FGA	FG%	3PM	3PA	3P%	FTM	FTA	FT%	ORB	DRB	TRB	AST	PF	DQ	STL	BLK	TO	MPG	PPG	RPG	APG	PCM
01-02	Chicago	71	31	1389	436	151	304	.497	0	0	.000	134	222	.604	114	229	343	54	179	1	28	93	99	19.6	6.1	4.8	0.8	.408
02-03	Chicago	75	68	1826	691	257	484	.531	0	0	.000	177	291	.608	169	345	514	76	220	3	37	106	135	24.3	9.2	6.9	1.0	.488
NBA Season Totals		146	99	3215	1127	408	788	.518	0	0	.000	311	513	.606	283	574	857	130	399	4	65	199	234	22.0	7.7	5.9	0.9	....

• CHANEY, Don
Donald R. (Duck) Chaney

Born: Mar. 22, 1946. Baton Rouge, LA, United States. Height: 6'5". Weight: 210 lbs. Drafted: 1968 College: Houston

YEAR	TEAM	GP	GS	MIN	PTS	FGM	FGA	FG%	3PM	3PA	3P%	FTM	FTA	FT%	ORB	DRB	TRB	AST	PF	DQ	STL	BLK	TO	MPG	PPG	RPG	APG	PCM
68-69	Boston	20	....	209	80	36	113	.319	....	....	....	8	20	.400	....	....	46	19	32	0	....	....	....	10.5	4.0	2.3	1.0	.277
69-70	Boston	63	....	839	312	115	320	.359	....	....	....	82	109	.752	....	....	152	72	118	0	....	....	....	13.3	5.0	2.4	1.1	.336
70-71	Boston	81	....	2289	930	348	766	.454	....	....	....	234	313	.748	....	....	463	235	288	11	....	....	....	28.3	11.5	5.7	2.9	.471
71-72	Boston	79	....	2275	943	373	786	.475	....	....	....	197	255	.773	....	....	395	202	295	7	....	....	....	28.8	11.9	5.0	2.6	.442
72-73	Boston	79	....	2488	1038	414	859	.482	....	....	....	210	267	.787	....	....	449	221	276	6	....	....	....	31.5	13.1	5.7	2.8	.463
73-74	Boston	81	....	2258	845	348	750	.464	....	....	....	149	180	.828	210	168	378	176	247	7	83	62	....	27.9	10.4	4.7	2.2	.402
74-75	Boston	82	....	2208	775	321	750	.428	....	....	....	133	165	.806	171	199	370	181	244	5	122	66	....	26.9	9.5	4.5	2.2	.369
75-76	St. Louis-A	48	....	1475	447	191	457	.418	1	4	.250	64	82	.780	113	121	234	169	170	....	66	36	119	30.7	9.3	4.9	3.5	.354
76-77	LA Lakers	81	....	2408	496	213	522	.408	....	....	....	70	94	.745	120	210	330	308	224	4	140	33	....	29.7	6.1	4.1	3.8	.314
77-78	LA Lakers	9	....	133	31	13	36	.361	....	....	....	5	6	.833	4	7	11	17	14	0	8	3	11	14.8	3.4	1.2	1.9	.249
77-78	Boston	42	....	702	215	91	233	.391	....	....	....	33	39	.846	36	69	105	49	93	0	36	10	50	16.7	5.1	2.5	1.2	.272
78-79	Boston	65	....	1074	384	174	414	.420	....	....	....	36	42	.857	63	78	141	75	167	3	72	11	65	16.5	5.9	2.2	1.2	.294
79-80	Boston	60	....	523	167	67	189	.354	1	6	.167	32	42	.762	31	42	73	38	80	1	31	11	36	8.7	2.8	1.2	0.6	.247
NBA Season Totals		742	....	17406	6216	2513	5738	.438	1	6	.167	1189	1532	.776	635	773	2913	1593	2078	44	492	196	162	23.5	8.4	3.9	2.1	....
ABA Season Totals		48	....	1475	447	191	457	.418	1	4	.250	64	82	.780	113	121	234	169	170	....	66	36	119	30.7	9.3	4.9	3.5	....
Career Totals		790	....	18881	6663	2704	6195	.436	2	10	.200	1253	1614	.776	748	894	3147	1762	2248	44	558	232	281	23.9	8.4	4.0	2.2	....
68-69	Boston	7	....	25	5	1	6	.167	....	....	....	3	4	.750	....	....	4	0	7	0	....	....	....	3.6	0.7	0.6	0.0	.033
71-72	Boston	11	....	271	97	41	81	.506	....	....	....	15	20	.750	....	....	39	22	39	0	....	....	....	24.6	8.8	3.5	2.0	.377
72-73	Boston	12	....	288	90	39	82	.476	....	....	....	12	17	.706	....	....	40	25	41	1	....	....	....	24.0	7.5	3.3	2.1	.334
73-74	Boston	18	....	545	171	65	141	.461	....	....	....	41	50	.820	37	40	77	40	64	0	24	9	....	30.3	9.5	4.3	2.2	.343
74-75	Boston	11	....	294	119	48	105	.457	....	....	....	23	29	.793	24	14	38	21	46	2	21	5	....	26.7	10.8	3.5	1.9	.356
76-77	LA Lakers	11	....	412	88	36	96	.375	....	....	....	16	22	.727	24	28	52	48	32	0	21	3	....	37.5	8.0	4.7	4.4	.290
NBA Playoff Totals		70	....	1835	570	230	511	.450	....	....	....	110	142	.775	85	82	250	156	229	3	66	17	....	26.2	8.1	3.6	2.2	....

• CHANEY, John
John Louie Chaney

Born: Feb. 29, 1920. Height: 6'3". Weight: 185 lbs. Drafted: — College: Louisiana State

YEAR	TEAM	GP	GS	MIN	PTS	FGM	FGA	FG%	3PM	3PA	3P%	FTM	FTA	FT%	ORB	DRB	TRB	AST	PF	DQ	STL	BLK	TO	MPG	PPG	RPG	APG	PCM
46-47	Syracuse-N	42	....	....	362	138	....	....	....	....	....	86	119	.723	....	....	....	....	119	....	....	....	....	....	8.6	....	....	....
47-48	Syracuse-N	40	....	....	292	107	....	....	....	....	....	78	103	.757	....	....	....	....	112	....	....	....	....	....	7.3	....	....	....
48-49	Syracuse-N	59	....	....	223	82	....	....	....	....	....	59	88	.670	....	....	....	....	84	....	....	....	....	....	3.8	....	....	....
49-50	Tri-Cities	6	....	....	28	10	37	.270	....	....	....	8	12	.667	....	....	....	15	13	....	....	....	....	....	4.7	....	2.5	....
49-50	Sheboygan	10	....	....	42	15	49	.306	....	....	....	12	17	.706	....	....	....	5	10	....	....	....	....	....	4.2	....	0.5	....
NBA Season Totals		16	....	....	70	25	86	.291	....	....	....	20	29	.690	....	....	....	20	23	....	....	....	....	....	4.4	....	1.3	....
NBL Season Totals		141	....	....	877	327	....	....	....	....	....	223	310	....	....	....	....	....	315	....	....	....	....	....	6.2	....	....	....
Career Totals		157	....	....	947	352	86	....	....	....	....	243	339	....	....	....	....	20	338	....	....	....	....	....	6.0	....	0.1	....
46-47	Syracuse-N	4	....	....	26	12	....	....	....	....	....	2	6	.333	....	....	....	....	....	....	....	....	....	....	6.5	....	....	....
47-48	Syracuse-N	3	....	....	17	6	....	....	....	....	....	5	11	.455	....	....	....	....	....	....	....	....	....	....	5.7	....	....	....
48-49	Syracuse-N	6	....	....	32	13	....	....	....	....	....	6	8	.750	....	....	....	....	....	....	....	....	....	....	5.3	....	....	....
NBL Playoff Totals		13	....	....	75	31	....	....	....	....	....	13	25	....	....	....	....	....	....	....	....	....	....	....	5.8	....	....	....

• CHAPMAN, Rex
Rex Everett Chapman

Born: Oct. 5, 1967. Bowling Green, KY, United States. Height: 6'4". Weight: 185 lbs. Drafted: 1988 College: Kentucky

YEAR	TEAM	GP	GS	MIN	PTS	FGM	FGA	FG%	3PM	3PA	3P%	FTM	FTA	FT%	ORB	DRB	TRB	AST	PF	DQ	STL	BLK	TO	MPG	PPG	RPG	APG	PCM
88-89	Charlotte	75	44	2219	1267	526	1271	.414	60	191	.314	155	195	.795	74	113	187	176	167	1	70	25	113	29.6	16.9	2.5	2.3	.371
89-90	Charlotte	54	52	1762	945	377	924	.408	47	142	.331	144	192	.750	52	127	179	132	113	0	46	6	103	32.6	17.5	3.3	2.4	.350
90-91	Charlotte	70	68	2100	1102	410	922	.445	48	148	.324	234	282	.830	45	146	191	250	167	1	73	16	133	30.0	15.7	2.7	3.6	.442
91-92	Charlotte	21	11	545	260	108	240	.450	8	27	.296	36	53	.679	9	45	54	86	47	0	14	8	42	26.0	12.4	2.6	4.1	.424
91-92	Washington	1	0	22	10	5	12	.417	0	2	.000	0	0	.000	1	3	4	3	4	0	1	0	3	22.0	10.0	4.0	3.0	.305
92-93	Washington	60	23	1300	749	287	602	.477	43	116	.371	132	163	.810	19	69	88	116	119	1	38	10	78	21.7	12.5	1.5	1.9	.433
93-94	Washington	60	59	2025	1094	431	865	.498	64	165	.388	168	206	.816	57	89	146	185	83	0	59	8	114	33.8	18.2	2.4	3.1	.460
94-95	Washington	45	29	1468	731	254	639	.397	86	274	.314	137	159	.862	23	90	113	128	85	0	67	15	63	32.6	16.2	2.5	2.8	.395
95-96	Miami	56	50	1865	786	289	679	.426	125	337	.371	83	113	.735	22	123	145	166	117	0	45	10	78	33.3	14.0	2.6	3.0	.344
96-97	Phoenix	65	33	1833	898	332	749	.443	110	314	.350	124	149	.832	25	156	181	182	108	1	52	7	98	28.2	13.8	2.8	2.8	.422
97-98	Phoenix	68	67	2263	1082	408	956	.427	120	311	.386	146	187	.781	30	143	173	203	102	0	71	14	116	33.3	15.9	2.5	3.0	.382
98-99	Phoenix	38	35	1183	459	165	459	.359	53	151	.351	76	91	.835	12	92	104	109	46	0	34	9	54	31.1	12.1	2.7	2.9	.316
99-00	Phoenix	53	19	957	348	124	320	.388	41	123	.333	59	78	.756	10	70	80	62	70	0	22	1	38	18.1	6.6	1.5	1.2	.268
NBA Season Totals		666	490	19542	9731	3716	8638	.430	805	2301	.350	1494	1868	.800	379	1266	1645	1798	1228	4	592	129	1033	29.3	14.6	2.5	2.7	....

YEAR	TEAM	GP	GS	MIN	PTS	FGM	FGA	FG%	3PM	3PA	3P%	FTM	FTA	FT%	ORB	DRB	TRB	AST	PF	DQ	STL	BLK	TO	MPG	PPG	RPG	APG	PCM
95-96	Miami	3	3	88	27	12	28	.429	3	13	.231	0	0	.000	0	6	6	5	6	0	3	0	1	29.3	9.0	2.0	1.7	.250
96-97	Phoenix	5	5	191	121	41	83	.494	22	48	.458	17	25	.680	2	14	16	13	14	0	2	0	15	38.2	24.2	3.2	2.6	.462
97-98	Phoenix	2	2	58	18	6	23	.261	0	5	.000	6	7	.857	0	0	0	4	1	0	2	0	2	29.0	9.0	0.0	2.0	.101
98-99	Phoenix	3	3	57	17	6	21	.286	2	6	.333	3	4	.750	2	4	6	6	9	1	1	0	4	19.0	5.7	2.0	2.0	.150
NBA Playoff Totals		13	13	394	183	65	155	.419	27	72	.375	26	36	.722	4	24	28	28	30	1	8	0	22	30.3	14.1	2.2	2.2	....

• CHAPMAN, Wayne

Wayne G. Chapman

Born: June 15, 1945. Owensboro, KY, United States.   Height: 6'6".   Weight: 190 lbs.   Drafted: 1968   College: Western Kentucky

YEAR	TEAM	GP	GS	MIN	PTS	FGM	FGA	FG%	3PM	3PA	3P%	FTM	FTA	FT%	ORB	DRB	TRB	AST	PF	DQ	STL	BLK	TO	MPG	PPG	RPG	APG	PCM
68-69	Kentucky-A	48	....	458	194	68	202	.337	4	13	.308	54	72	.750	29	45	74	38	95	0	....	....	39	9.5	4.0	1.5	0.8	.300
69-70	Kentucky-A	82	....	1519	664	261	654	.399	8	37	.216	134	204	.657	101	151	252	139	250	7	....	....	134	18.5	8.1	3.1	1.7	.372
70-71	Denver-A	47	....	1049	468	184	484	.380	11	48	.229	89	129	.690	43	100	143	107	127	3	....	....	100	22.3	10.0	3.0	2.3	.385
70-71	Indiana-A	22	....	192	88	30	78	.385	4	9	.444	24	29	.828	12	19	31	21	31	0	....	....	15	8.7	4.0	1.4	1.0	.443
71-72	Indiana-A	7	....	76	18	7	18	.389	1	2	.500	3	6	.500	2	3	5	11	10	0	....	....	6	10.9	2.6	0.7	1.6	.255
ABA Season Totals		206	....	3294	1432	550	1436	.383	28	109	.257	304	440	.691	187	318	505	316	513	10	....	....	294	16.0	7.0	2.5	1.5	....
68-69	Kentucky-A	5	....	29	7	3	8	.375	0	0	.000	1	2	.500	....	....	4	2	13	0	....	....	0	5.8	1.4	0.8	0.4	.083
69-70	Kentucky-A	10	....	148	102	37	75	.493	1	6	.167	27	36	.750	8	14	22	12	....	....	....	....	11	14.8	10.2	2.2	1.2	
70-71	Indiana-A	5	....	21	17	6	10	.600	1	3	.333	4	6	.667	4	3	7	2	3	0	....	....	4	4.2	3.4	1.4	0.4	.943
ABA Playoff Totals		20	....	198	126	46	93	.495	2	9	.222	32	44	.727	12	17	33	16	16	0	....	....	13	9.9	6.3	1.7	0.8	

• CHAPPELL, Len

Leonard R. Chappell

Born: Jan. 31, 1941. Portage, PA, United States.   Height: 6'8".   Weight: 240 lbs.   Drafted: 1962   College: Wake Forest

YEAR	TEAM	GP	GS	MIN	PTS	FGM	FGA	FG%	3PM	3PA	3P%	FTM	FTA	FT%	ORB	DRB	TRB	AST	PF	DQ	STL	BLK	TO	MPG	PPG	RPG	APG	PCM
62-63	Syracuse	80	....	1241	710	281	604	.465	....	....	....	148	238	.622	....	....	461	56	171	1	....	....	....	15.5	8.9	5.8	0.7	.631
63-64	Philadelphia	1	....	16	1	0	2	.000	....	....	....	1	2	.500	....	....	4	0	2	0	....	....	....	16.0	1.0	4.0	0.0	.087
63-64	New York	78	....	2489	1349	531	1183	.449	....	....	....	287	401	.716	....	....	767	83	212	1	....	....	....	31.9	17.3	9.8	1.1	.568
64-65	New York	43	....	655	358	145	367	.395	....	....	....	68	100	.680	....	....	140	15	73	0	....	....	....	15.2	8.3	3.3	0.3	.417
65-66	New York	46	....	545	246	100	238	.420	....	....	....	46	78	.590	....	....	127	26	64	1	....	....	....	11.8	5.3	2.8	0.6	.425
66-67	Chicago	19	....	179	94	40	89	.449	....	....	....	14	21	.667	....	....	38	12	31	0	....	....	....	9.4	4.9	2.0	0.6	.472
66-67	Cincinnati	54	....	529	223	92	224	.411	....	....	....	39	60	.650	....	....	151	21	73	0	....	....	....	9.8	4.1	2.8	0.4	.427
67-68	Cincinnati	10	....	65	38	15	30	.500	....	....	....	8	10	.800	....	....	15	5	6	0	....	....	....	6.5	3.8	1.5	0.5	.628
67-68	Detroit	57	....	999	570	220	428	.514	....	....	....	130	184	.707	....	....	346	48	113	1	....	....	....	17.5	10.0	6.1	0.8	.672
68-69	Milwaukee	80	....	2207	1168	459	1011	.454	....	....	....	250	339	.737	....	....	637	95	247	3	....	....	....	27.6	14.6	8.0	1.2	.548
69-70	Milwaukee	75	....	1134	621	243	523	.465	....	....	....	135	211	.640	....	....	276	56	127	1	....	....	....	15.1	8.3	3.7	0.7	.521
70-71	Cleveland	6	....	86	41	18	38	.395	....	....	....	11	14	.786	....	....	18	1	9	0	....	....	....	14.3	6.8	3.0	0.2	.380
70-71	Atlanta	42	....	451	202	71	161	.441	....	....	....	60	74	.811	....	....	133	16	63	2	....	....	....	10.7	4.8	3.2	0.4	.497
71-72	Dallas-A	79	....	1403	606	231	511	.452	0	0	.000	144	193	.746	146	172	318	69	158	2	....	....	63	17.8	7.7	4.0	0.9	.446
NBA Season Totals		591	....	10596	5621	2212	4898	.452	....	....	....	1197	1732	.691	....	....	3113	434	1191	10	....	....	....	17.9	9.5	5.3	0.7	....
ABA Season Totals		79	....	1403	606	231	511	.452	0	0	.000	144	193	.746	146	172	318	69	158	2	....	....	63	17.8	7.7	4.0	0.9	....
Career Totals		670	....	11999	6227	2443	5409	.452	0	0	.000	1341	1925	.697	146	172	3431	503	1349	12	....	....	63	17.9	9.3	5.1	0.8	....
62-63	Syracuse	4	....	53	21	4	21	.190	....	....	....	13	16	.813	....	....	18	3	7	0	....	....	....	13.3	5.3	4.5	0.8	.405
66-67	Cincinnati	4	....	66	22	10	27	.370	....	....	....	2	4	.500	....	....	13	9	14	0	....	....	....	16.5	5.5	3.3	2.3	.352
67-68	Detroit	5	....	21	7	2	7	.286	....	....	....	3	6	.500	....	....	12	0	3	0	....	....	....	4.2	1.4	2.4	0.0	.405
69-70	Milwaukee	9	....	133	69	28	50	.560	....	....	....	13	19	.684	....	....	26	5	10	0	....	....	....	14.8	7.7	2.9	0.6	.534
71-72	Dallas-A	4	....	89	29	12	24	.500	0	0	.000	5	8	.625	8	10	18	3	13	0	....	....	3	22.3	7.3	4.5	0.8	.344
NBA Playoff Totals		22	....	273	119	44	105	.419	....	....	....	31	45	.689	....	....	69	17	34	0	....	....	....	12.4	5.4	3.1	0.8	....
ABA Playoff Totals		4	....	89	29	12	24	.500	0	0	.000	5	8	.625	8	10	18	3	13	0	....	....	3	22.3	7.3	4.5	0.8	....
Career Playoff Totals		26	....	362	148	56	129	.434	0	0	.000	36	53	.679	8	10	87	20	47	0	....	....	3	13.9	5.7	3.3	0.8	....

• CHARLES, Ken

Kenneth M. Charles

Born: July 10, 1951. Trinidad.   Height: 6'3".   Weight: 180 lbs.   Drafted: 1973   College: Fordham

YEAR	TEAM	GP	GS	MIN	PTS	FGM	FGA	FG%	3PM	3PA	3P%	FTM	FTA	FT%	ORB	DRB	TRB	AST	PF	DQ	STL	BLK	TO	MPG	PPG	RPG	APG	PCM
73-74	Buffalo	59	....	693	229	88	185	.476	....	....	....	53	79	.671	25	40	65	54	91	0	31	10	....	11.7	3.9	1.1	0.9	.309
74-75	Buffalo	79	....	1690	600	240	515	.466	....	....	....	120	146	.822	68	96	164	171	165	0	87	20	....	21.4	7.6	2.1	2.2	.367
75-76	Buffalo	81	....	2247	817	328	719	.456	....	....	....	161	205	.785	58	161	219	204	257	5	123	48	....	27.7	10.1	2.7	2.5	.344
76-77	Atlanta	82	....	2487	913	354	855	.414	....	....	....	205	256	.801	41	127	168	295	240	4	141	45	....	30.3	11.1	2.0	3.6	.336
77-78	Atlanta	21	....	520	188	73	184	.397	....	....	....	42	50	.840	6	18	24	82	53	0	25	5	38	24.8	9.0	1.1	3.9	.328
NBA Season Totals		322	....	7637	2747	1083	2458	.441	....	....	....	581	736	.789	198	442	640	806	806	9	407	128	38	23.7	8.5	2.0	2.5	....
73-74	Buffalo	2	....	10	6	3	4	.750	....	....	....	0	0	.000	2	0	2	0	2	0	0	0	....	5.0	3.0	1.0	0.0	.600
74-75	Buffalo	7	....	208	52	22	55	.400	....	....	....	8	11	.727	3	10	13	18	27	1	6	5	....	29.7	7.4	1.9	2.6	.206
75-76	Buffalo	9	....	238	53	22	55	.400	....	....	....	9	13	.692	6	20	26	14	31	1	7	6	....	26.4	5.9	2.9	1.6	.202
NBA Playoff Totals		18	....	456	111	47	114	.412	....	....	....	17	24	.708	11	30	41	32	60	2	13	11	....	25.3	6.2	2.3	1.8	....

• CHARLES, Lorenzo

Lorenzo Emile Charles

Born: Nov. 25, 1963. Brooklyn, NY, United States.   Height: 6'7".   Weight: 225 lbs.   Drafted: 1985   College: North Carolina State

YEAR	TEAM	GP	GS	MIN	PTS	FGM	FGA	FG%	3PM	3PA	3P%	FTM	FTA	FT%	ORB	DRB	TRB	AST	PF	DQ	STL	BLK	TO	MPG	PPG	RPG	APG	PCM
85-86	Atlanta	36	0	273	122	49	88	.557	0	0	.000	24	36	.667	13	26	39	8	37	0	2	6	18	7.6	3.4	1.1	0.2	.361
NBA Season Totals		36	0	273	122	49	88	.557	0	0	.000	24	36	.667	13	26	39	8	37	0	2	6	18	7.6	3.4	1.1	0.2	....
85-86	Atlanta	4	0	15	7	3	4	.750	0	0	.000	1	1	1.000	0	2	2	2	1	0	0	0	0	3.8	1.8	0.5	0.5	.640
NBA Playoff Totals		4	0	15	7	3	4	.750	0	0	.000	1	1	1.000	0	2	2	2	1	0	0	0	0	3.8	1.8	0.5	0.5	....

• CHEANEY, Calbert

Calbert Nathaniel Cheaney

Born: July 17, 1971. Evansville, IN, United States. Height: 6'7". Weight: 209 lbs. Drafted: 1993 College: Indiana

YEAR	TEAM	GP	GS	MIN	PTS	FGM	FGA	FG%	3PM	3PA	3P%	FTM	FTA	FT%	ORB	DRB	TRB	AST	PF	DQ	STL	BLK	TO	MPG	PPG	RPG	APG	PCM
93-94	Washington	65	21	1604	779	327	696	.470	1	23	.043	124	161	.770	88	102	190	126	148	0	63	10	111	24.7	12.0	2.9	1.9	.394
94-95	Washington	78	71	2651	1293	512	1129	.453	96	283	.339	173	213	.812	105	216	321	177	215	0	80	21	148	34.0	16.6	4.1	2.3	.392
95-96	Washington	70	70	2324	1055	426	905	.471	52	154	.338	151	214	.706	67	172	239	154	205	1	67	18	126	33.2	15.1	3.4	2.2	.356
96-97	Washington	79	79	2411	837	369	730	.505	4	30	.133	95	137	.693	70	198	268	114	226	3	77	18	95	30.5	10.6	3.4	1.4	.310
97-98	Washington	82	82	2841	1050	448	981	.457	15	53	.283	139	215	.647	82	242	324	173	264	4	96	36	107	34.6	12.8	4.0	2.1	.322
98-99	Washington	50	18	1266	385	172	415	.414	8	37	.216	33	67	.493	33	108	141	73	146	0	39	16	42	25.3	7.7	2.8	1.5	.242
99-00	Boston	67	19	1309	267	120	273	.440	18	54	.333	9	21	.429	23	115	138	80	158	3	44	14	46	19.5	4.0	2.1	1.2	.210
00-01	Denver	9	5	153	21	10	30	.333	0	0	.000	1	2	.500	5	15	20	9	14	0	4	2	5	17.0	2.3	2.2	1.0	.164
01-02	Denver	68	47	1632	494	224	466	.481	0	4	.000	46	67	.687	57	183	240	110	156	1	34	21	70	24.0	7.3	3.5	1.6	.318
02-03	Utah	81	74	2351	700	325	651	.499	10	25	.400	40	69	.580	73	211	284	163	225	1	65	13	108	29.0	8.6	3.5	2.0	.297
NBA Season Totals		649	486	18542	6881	2933	6276	.467	204	663	.308	811	1166	.696	603	1562	2165	1179	1757	13	569	169	858	28.6	10.6	3.3	1.8	....
96-97	Washington	3	3	120	45	18	41	.439	0	2	.000	9	12	.750	6	5	11	4	10	0	3	2	5	40.0	15.0	3.7	1.3	.267
02-03	Utah	5	5	122	22	10	27	.370	0	0	.000	2	4	.500	3	4	7	8	15	0	2	1	7	24.4	4.4	1.4	1.6	.084
NBA Playoff Totals		8	8	242	67	28	68	.412	0	2	.000	11	16	.688	9	9	18	12	25	0	5	3	12	30.3	8.4	2.3	1.5	....

• CHEEKS, Maurice

Maurice Edward Cheeks

Born: Sept. 8, 1956. Chicago, IL, United States. Height: 6'1". Weight: 180 lbs. Drafted: 1978 College: West Texas State

YEAR	TEAM	GP	GS	MIN	PTS	FGM	FGA	FG%	3PM	3PA	3P%	FTM	FTA	FT%	ORB	DRB	TRB	AST	PF	DQ	STL	BLK	TO	MPG	PPG	RPG	APG	PCM
78-79	Philadelphia	82	....	2409	685	292	572	.510	....	....	....	101	140	.721	63	191	254	431	198	2	174	12	197	29.4	8.4	3.1	5.3	.424
79-80	Philadelphia	79	....	2623	898	357	661	.540	4	9	.444	180	231	.779	75	199	274	556	197	1	183	32	213	33.2	11.4	3.5	7.0	.522
80-81	Philadelphia	81	....	2415	763	310	581	.534	3	8	.375	140	178	.787	67	178	245	560	231	1	193	39	170	29.8	9.4	3.0	6.9	.531
81-82	Philadelphia	79	79	2498	881	352	676	.521	6	22	.273	171	220	.777	51	197	248	667	247	0	209	33	182	31.6	11.2	3.1	8.4	.580
82-83	Philadelphia	79	79	2465	990	404	745	.542	1	6	.167	181	240	.754	53	156	209	543	182	0	184	31	182	31.2	12.5	2.6	6.9	.563
83-84	Philadelphia	75	75	2494	950	386	702	.550	8	20	.400	170	232	.733	44	161	205	478	196	1	171	20	180	33.3	12.7	2.7	6.4	.501
84-85	Philadelphia	78	78	2616	1025	422	741	.570	6	26	.231	175	199	.879	54	163	217	497	184	0	169	24	156	33.5	13.1	2.8	6.4	.535
85-86	Philadelphia	82	82	**3270**	1266	490	913	.537	4	17	.235	282	335	.842	55	180	235	753	160	0	207	28	238	**39.9**	15.4	2.9	9.2	.549
86-87	Philadelphia	68	68	2624	1061	415	788	.527	4	17	.235	227	292	.777	47	168	215	538	109	0	180	15	170	38.6	15.6	3.2	7.9	.545
87-88	Philadelphia	79	79	2871	1086	428	865	.495	3	22	.136	227	275	.825	59	194	253	635	116	0	167	22	158	36.3	13.7	3.2	8.0	.538
88-89	Philadelphia	71	70	2298	824	336	696	.483	1	13	.077	151	195	.774	39	144	183	554	114	0	105	17	114	32.4	11.6	2.6	7.8	.516
89-90	San Antonio	50	49	1766	545	215	450	.478	1	9	.111	114	137	.832	39	128	167	302	46	0	82	5	85	35.3	10.9	3.3	6.0	.437
89-90	New York	31	13	753	244	92	159	.579	3	7	.429	57	65	.877	11	62	73	151	32	0	42	5	37	24.3	7.9	2.4	4.9	.532
90-91	New York	76	64	2147	592	241	483	.499	5	20	.250	105	129	.814	22	151	173	435	138	0	128	10	106	28.3	7.8	2.3	5.7	.441
91-92	Atlanta	56	0	1086	259	115	249	.462	3	6	.500	26	43	.605	29	66	95	185	73	0	83	0	34	19.4	4.6	1.7	3.3	.391
92-93	New Jersey	35	0	510	126	51	93	.548	0	2	.000	24	27	.889	5	37	42	107	35	0	33	2	32	14.6	3.6	1.2	3.1	.442
NBA Season Totals		1101	736	34845	12195	4906	9374	.523	52	204	.255	2331	2938	.793	713	2375	3088	7392	2258	5	2310	295	2254	31.6	11.1	2.8	6.7	....
78-79	Philadelphia	9	....	330	169	66	121	.545	....	....	....	37	56	.661	13	22	35	63	29	0	37	4	29	36.7	18.8	3.9	7.0	.635
79-80	Philadelphia	18	....	675	208	89	174	.511	1	5	.200	29	41	.707	22	52	74	111	43	0	45	4	45	37.5	11.6	4.1	6.2	.442
80-81	Philadelphia	16	....	513	168	68	125	.544	0	3	.000	32	42	.762	4	47	51	116	55	1	40	12	36	32.1	10.5	3.2	7.3	.534
81-82	Philadelphia	21	21	765	301	125	265	.472	1	9	.111	50	65	.769	15	47	62	172	58	0	48	6	49	36.4	14.3	3.0	8.2	.504
82-83	Philadelphia	13	13	483	212	83	165	.503	1	2	.500	45	64	.703	11	28	39	91	23	0	26	2	34	37.2	16.3	3.0	7.0	.515
83-84	Philadelphia	5	5	171	83	35	67	.522	0	1	.000	13	15	.867	2	10	12	19	18	0	13	0	10	34.2	16.6	2.4	3.8	.457
84-85	Philadelphia	13	13	483	198	81	153	.529	0	5	.000	36	42	.857	12	34	46	67	29	0	31	5	34	37.2	15.2	3.5	5.2	.478
85-86	Philadelphia	12	12	519	250	94	182	.516	0	7	.000	62	73	.849	13	43	56	85	18	0	13	3	32	43.3	20.8	4.7	7.1	.545
86-87	Philadelphia	5	5	210	88	35	66	.530	0	1	.000	18	21	.857	1	12	13	44	14	0	9	4	12	42.0	17.6	2.6	8.8	.530
88-89	Philadelphia	3	3	128	53	21	41	.512	0	1	.000	11	13	.846	3	8	11	39	4	0	7	1	3	42.7	17.7	3.7	13.0	.689
89-90	New York	10	10	388	128	50	104	.481	0	4	.000	28	31	.903	12	27	39	85	21	0	17	2	19	38.8	12.8	3.9	8.5	.498
90-91	New York	3	3	101	30	14	23	.609	1	3	.333	1	2	.500	3	6	9	16	9	0	3	1	8	33.7	10.0	3.0	5.3	.383
92-93	New Jersey	5	0	82	22	11	23	.478	0	0	.000	0	1	.000	3	3	6	14	3	0	6	1	7	16.4	4.4	1.2	2.8	.359
NBA Playoff Totals		133	85	4848	1910	772	1509	.512	4	41	.098	362	466	.777	114	339	453	922	324	1	295	45	318	36.5	14.4	3.4	6.9	....

• CHENIER, Phil

Philip Chenier

Born: Oct. 30, 1950. Berkeley, CA, United States. Height: 6'3". Weight: 180 lbs. Drafted: 1971 College: California

YEAR	TEAM	GP	GS	MIN	PTS	FGM	FGA	FG%	3PM	3PA	3P%	FTM	FTA	FT%	ORB	DRB	TRB	AST	PF	DQ	STL	BLK	TO	MPG	PPG	RPG	APG	PCM
71-72	Baltimore	81	....	2481	996	407	981	.415	....	....	....	182	247	.737	....	....	268	205	191	2	....	....	....	30.6	12.3	3.3	2.5	.344
72-73	Baltimore	71	....	2776	1398	602	1332	.452	....	....	....	194	244	.795	....	....	288	301	160	0	....	....	....	39.1	19.7	4.1	4.2	.458
73-74	Washington	76	....	2942	1668	697	1607	.434	....	....	....	274	334	.820	114	274	388	239	135	0	155	67	....	38.7	21.9	5.1	3.1	.481
74-75	Washington	77	....	2869	1681	690	1533	.450	....	....	....	301	365	.825	74	218	292	248	158	3	176	58	....	37.3	21.8	3.8	3.2	.488
75-76	Washington	80	....	2952	1590	654	1355	.483	....	....	....	282	341	.827	84	236	320	255	186	2	158	45	....	36.9	19.9	4.0	3.2	.491
76-77	Washington	78	....	2842	1578	654	1472	.444	....	....	....	270	321	.841	56	243	299	294	166	0	120	39	....	36.4	20.2	3.8	3.8	.482
77-78	Washington	36	....	937	509	200	451	.443	....	....	....	109	138	.790	15	87	102	73	54	0	36	9	68	26.0	14.1	2.8	2.0	.431
78-79	Washington	27	....	385	156	69	158	.437	....	....	....	18	28	.643	3	17	20	31	28	0	4	5	30	14.3	5.8	0.7	1.1	.240
79-80	Washington	20	....	470	202	84	214	.393	3	6	.500	31	41	.756	10	33	43	42	26	0	18	5	28	23.5	10.1	2.2	2.1	.316
79-80	Indiana	23	....	380	124	52	135	.385	2	6	.333	18	26	.692	9	26	35	47	29	0	15	10	25	16.5	5.4	1.5	2.0	.303
80-81	Golden State	9	....	82	29	11	33	.333	1	3	.333	6	6	1.000	1	7	8	7	10	0	0	0	4	9.1	3.2	0.9	0.8	.191
NBA Season Totals		578	....	19116	9931	4120	9271	.444	6	15	.400	1685	2091	.806	366	1141	2063	1742	1143	7	682	238	155	33.1	17.2	3.6	3.0	....
71-72	Baltimore	6	....	153	54	22	59	.373	....	....	....	10	12	.833	....	....	16	5	16	0	....	....	....	25.5	9.0	2.7	0.8	.221
72-73	Baltimore	5	....	211	89	43	85	.506	....	....	....	3	4	.750	....	....	21	17	13	0	....	....	....	42.2	17.8	4.2	3.4	.400
73-74	Washington	7	....	310	157	62	137	.453	....	....	....	33	37	.892	6	37	43	12	19	0	13	8	....	44.3	22.4	6.1	1.7	.432
74-75	Washington	17	....	692	412	155	330	.470	....	....	....	102	114	.895	18	58	76	54	45	1	22	11	....	40.7	24.2	4.5	3.2	.528
75-76	Washington	7	....	265	126	56	128	.438	....	....	....	14	17	.824	6	20	26	11	27	0	6	3	....	37.9	18.0	3.7	1.6	.325
76-77	Washington	9	....	360	225	90	189	.476	....	....	....	45	56	.804	8	32	40	23	16	0	15	4	....	40.0	25.0	4.4	2.6	.524
78-79	Washington	9	....	97	25	10	46	.217	....	....	....	5	11	.455	3	5	8	9	16	0	3	0	6	10.8	2.8	0.9	1.0	-.029
NBA Playoff Totals		60	....	2088	1088	438	974	.450	....	....	....	212	251	.845	41	152	230	131	152	1	59	26	6	34.8	18.1	3.8	2.2	....

• CHESTNUT, George

George Chestnut

Born: 1914. Height: 6'5". Weight: 210 lbs. Drafted: — College: Indiana State

YEAR TEAM	GP	GS	MIN	PTS	FGM	FGA	FG%	3PM	3PA	3P%	FTM	FTA	FT%	ORB	DRB	TRB	AST	PF	DQ	STL	BLK	TO	MPG	PPG	RPG	APG	PCM
37-38 Indianapolis-N	12	....	....	53	15	....	....	....	....	....	23	....	....	....	....	....	....	....	....	....	....	....	....	4.4	....	....	....
39-40 Indianapolis-N	21	....	....	129	38	....	....	....	....	....	53	....	....	....	....	....	....	....	....	....	....	....	....	6.1	....	....	....
NBL Season Totals	33	....	....	182	53	....	....	....	....	....	76	....	....	....	....	....	....	....	....	....	....	....	....	5.5	....	....	....

• CHIEVOUS, Derrick

Derrick Joseph (Band-Aid) Chievous

Born: July 3, 1967. New York, NY, United States. Height: 6'7". Weight: 195 lbs. Drafted: 1988 College: Missouri

YEAR TEAM	GP	GS	MIN	PTS	FGM	FGA	FG%	3PM	3PA	3P%	FTM	FTA	FT%	ORB	DRB	TRB	AST	PF	DQ	STL	BLK	TO	MPG	PPG	RPG	APG	PCM
88-89 Houston	81	1	1539	750	277	634	.437	5	24	.208	191	244	.783	114	142	256	77	161	1	48	11	138	19.0	9.3	3.2	1.0	.367
89-90 Houston	41	0	492	244	90	178	.506	3	8	.375	61	87	.701	28	47	75	27	59	0	23	4	41	12.0	6.0	1.8	0.7	.422
89-90 Cleveland	14	0	99	49	15	42	.357	0	1	.000	19	24	.792	7	8	15	4	11	0	3	1	6	7.1	3.5	1.1	0.3	.330
90-91 Cleveland	18	0	110	43	17	46	.370	0	0	.000	9	16	.563	11	7	18	2	16	0	3	1	5	6.1	2.4	1.0	0.1	.211
NBA Season Totals	154	1	2240	1086	399	900	.443	8	33	.242	280	371	.755	160	204	364	110	247	1	77	17	190	14.5	7.1	2.4	0.7	....
88-89 Houston	4	0	40	18	5	17	.294	0	0	.000	8	10	.800	5	1	6	2	7	0	1	1	3	10.0	4.5	1.5	0.5	.236
89-90 Cleveland	3	0	28	19	6	10	.600	0	0	.000	7	9	.778	2	1	3	2	2	0	1	0	3	9.3	6.3	1.0	0.7	.587
NBA Playoff Totals	7	0	68	37	11	27	.407	0	0	.000	15	19	.789	7	2	9	4	9	0	2	1	6	9.7	5.3	1.3	0.6	....

• CHILCUTT, Pete

Peter Shawn (Chili Pete) Chilcutt

Born: Sept. 14, 1968. Sumter, SC, United States. Height: 6'10". Weight: 230 lbs. Drafted: 1991 College: North Carolina

YEAR TEAM	GP	GS	MIN	PTS	FGM	FGA	FG%	3PM	3PA	3P%	FTM	FTA	FT%	ORB	DRB	TRB	AST	PF	DQ	STL	BLK	TO	MPG	PPG	RPG	APG	PCM
91-92 Sacramento	69	2	817	251	113	250	.452	2	2	1.000	23	28	.821	78	109	187	38	70	0	32	17	41	11.8	3.6	2.7	0.6	.380
92-93 Sacramento	59	9	834	362	165	338	.488	0	0	.000	32	46	.696	80	114	194	64	102	2	22	21	53	14.1	6.1	3.3	1.1	.463
93-94 Sacramento	46	24	974	335	152	328	.463	0	1	.000	31	52	.596	100	171	271	71	116	2	43	28	55	21.2	7.3	5.9	1.5	.463
93-94 Detroit	30	0	391	115	51	120	.425	3	14	.214	10	13	.769	29	71	100	15	48	0	10	11	18	13.0	3.8	3.3	0.5	.356
94-95 Houston	68	17	1347	358	146	328	.445	35	86	.407	31	42	.738	106	211	317	66	117	0	25	43	61	19.8	5.3	4.7	1.0	.372
95-96 Houston	74	0	651	200	73	179	.408	37	98	.378	17	26	.654	51	105	156	26	65	0	19	14	22	8.8	2.7	2.1	0.4	.384
96-97 Vancouver	54	1	662	182	72	165	.436	25	69	.362	13	22	.591	67	89	156	47	52	0	26	17	27	12.3	3.4	2.9	0.9	.419
97-98 Vancouver	82	0	1420	405	156	359	.435	54	130	.415	39	59	.661	77	229	306	104	158	0	53	37	66	17.3	4.9	3.7	1.3	.389
98-99 Vancouver	46	0	697	166	63	172	.366	26	68	.382	14	17	.824	29	88	117	30	52	0	22	12	28	15.2	3.6	2.5	0.7	.269
99-00 Utah	26	0	224	47	22	62	.355	1	10	.100	2	2	1.000	15	28	43	10	31	0	5	4	9	8.6	1.8	1.7	0.4	.208
99-00 Cleveland	6	0	30	0	0	2	.000	0	0	.000	0	0	.000	4	5	9	1	3	0	0	0	0	5.0	0.0	1.5	0.2	.203
99-00 LA Clippers	24	2	347	73	31	63	.492	5	16	.313	6	6	1.000	27	52	79	16	39	2	10	6	11	14.5	3.0	3.3	0.7	.346
NBA Season Totals	584	55	8394	2494	1044	2366	.441	188	494	.381	218	313	.696	663	1272	1935	488	853	6	267	210	391	14.4	4.3	3.3	0.8	....
94-95 Houston	20	15	323	90	31	64	.484	14	36	.389	14	17	.824	15	43	58	18	39	0	7	4	11	16.2	4.5	2.9	0.9	.349
95-96 Houston	1	0	10	2	1	4	.250	0	1	.000	0	2	.000	2	1	3	0	0	0	0	0	1	10.0	2.0	3.0	0.0	.012
NBA Playoff Totals	21	15	333	92	32	68	.471	14	37	.378	14	19	.737	17	44	61	18	39	0	7	4	12	15.9	4.4	2.9	0.9	....

• CHILDRESS, Randolph

Randolph Childress

Born: Sept. 21, 1972. Washington, DC, United States. Height: 6'2". Weight: 188 lbs. Drafted: 1995 College: Wake Forest

YEAR TEAM	GP	GS	MIN	PTS	FGM	FGA	FG%	3PM	3PA	3P%	FTM	FTA	FT%	ORB	DRB	TRB	AST	PF	DQ	STL	BLK	TO	MPG	PPG	RPG	APG	PCM
95-96 Portland	28	0	250	85	25	79	.316	13	47	.277	22	27	.815	1	18	19	32	22	0	8	1	28	8.9	3.0	0.7	1.1	.222
96-97 Portland	19	0	125	29	10	30	.333	3	16	.188	6	8	.750	1	4	5	15	11	0	7	0	13	6.6	1.5	0.3	0.8	.155
96-97 Detroit	4	0	30	10	4	10	.400	2	3	.667	0	0	.000	0	1	1	2	5	0	2	0	5	7.5	2.5	0.3	0.5	.078
NBA Season Totals	51	0	405	124	39	119	.328	18	66	.273	28	35	.800	2	23	25	49	38	0	17	1	46	7.9	2.4	0.5	1.0	....

• CHILDS, Chris

Chris Childs

Born: Nov. 20, 1967. Bakersfield, CA, United States. Height: 6'3". Weight: 195 lbs. Drafted: — College: Boise State

YEAR TEAM	GP	GS	MIN	PTS	FGM	FGA	FG%	3PM	3PA	3P%	FTM	FTA	FT%	ORB	DRB	TRB	AST	PF	DQ	STL	BLK	TO	MPG	PPG	RPG	APG	PCM
94-95 New Jersey	53	11	1021	308	106	279	.380	41	125	.328	55	73	.753	14	55	69	219	116	1	42	3	74	19.3	5.8	1.3	4.1	.346
95-96 New Jersey	78	54	2408	1002	324	778	.416	95	259	.367	259	304	.852	51	194	245	548	246	3	111	8	226	30.9	12.8	3.1	7.0	.477
96-97 New York	65	61	2076	605	211	510	.414	70	181	.387	113	149	.758	22	169	191	398	213	6	78	11	182	31.9	9.3	2.9	6.1	.350
97-98 New York	68	0	1599	429	149	354	.421	27	87	.310	104	126	.825	29	133	162	268	179	2	56	6	102	23.5	6.3	2.4	3.9	.345
98-99 New York	48	0	1297	328	114	267	.427	36	94	.383	64	78	.821	18	115	133	193	156	0	44	1	85	27.0	6.8	2.8	4.0	.319
99-00 New York	71	2	1675	376	146	357	.409	37	104	.356	47	59	.797	17	130	147	285	240	4	36	4	105	23.6	5.3	2.1	4.0	.272
00-01 New York	51	5	1309	245	93	222	.419	20	64	.313	39	46	.848	14	124	138	236	160	2	37	7	98	25.7	4.8	2.7	4.6	.298
00-01 Toronto	26	0	550	117	42	113	.372	12	42	.286	21	25	.840	10	54	64	119	82	1	22	8	58	21.2	4.5	2.5	4.6	.324
01-02 Toronto	69	4	1576	285	97	296	.328	33	120	.275	58	71	.817	18	136	154	351	177	3	56	5	123	22.8	4.1	2.2	5.1	.308
02-03 New Jersey	12	0	106	15	6	20	.300	1	6	.167	2	3	.667	3	2	5	16	17	0	8	1	6	8.8	1.3	0.4	1.3	.178
NBA Season Totals	541	137	13617	3710	1288	3196	.403	372	1082	.344	762	934	.816	196	1112	1308	2633	1586	22	490	54	1059	25.2	6.9	2.4	4.9	....
96-97 New York	10	10	328	104	38	87	.437	9	26	.346	19	23	.826	9	40	49	59	39	1	20	0	28	32.8	10.4	4.9	5.9	.425
97-98 New York	10	0	254	63	24	58	.414	4	13	.308	11	15	.733	5	20	25	33	29	0	6	0	23	25.4	6.3	2.5	3.3	.236
98-99 New York	20	0	494	94	33	93	.355	9	28	.321	19	26	.731	8	39	47	73	64	2	13	1	30	24.7	4.7	2.4	3.7	.238
99-00 New York	16	0	334	87	27	70	.386	9	28	.321	24	28	.857	1	36	37	39	53	1	7	0	14	20.9	5.4	2.3	2.4	.275
00-01 Toronto	12	9	380	109	37	90	.411	15	36	.417	20	23	.870	2	36	38	78	48	2	12	3	35	31.7	9.1	3.2	6.5	.370
01-02 Toronto	5	4	163	59	21	54	.389	8	17	.471	9	10	.900	2	17	19	37	14	0	4	0	20	32.6	11.8	3.8	7.4	.402
NBA Playoff Totals	73	23	1953	516	180	452	.398	54	148	.365	102	125	.816	27	188	215	319	247	6	62	4	150	26.8	7.1	2.9	4.4	....

• CHOLLET, Leroy

Leroy Patrick Chollet

Born: Mar. 5, 1925. New Orleans, LA, United States. Height: 6'2". Weight: 190 lbs. Drafted: — College: Canisius

YEAR TEAM	GP	GS	MIN	PTS	FGM	FGA	FG%	3PM	3PA	3P%	FTM	FTA	FT%	ORB	DRB	TRB	AST	PF	DQ	STL	BLK	TO	MPG	PPG	RPG	APG	PCM
49-50 Syracuse	49	....	....	157	61	179	.341	....	....	....	35	56	.625	....	....	....	37	52	....	....	....	....	....	3.2	....	0.8	....
50-51 Syracuse	14	....	....	24	6	51	.118	....	....	....	12	19	.632	....	....	15	12	29	0	....	....	....	....	1.7	1.1	0.9	....
NBA Season Totals	63	....	....	181	67	230	.291	....	....	....	47	75	.627	....	....	15	49	81	0	....	....	....	....	2.9	0.2	0.8	....

YEAR	TEAM	GP	GS	MIN	PTS	FGM	FGA	FG%	3PM	3PA	3P%	FTM	FTA	FT%	ORB	DRB	TRB	AST	PF	DQ	STL	BLK	TO	MPG	PPG	RPG	APG	PCM
49-50	Syracuse	8	....	....	19	7	26	.269	....	....	....	5	13	.385	....	....	....	4	11	....	....	....	....	....	2.4	....	0.5	....
50-51	Syracuse	7	....	....	13	4	23	.174	....	....	....	5	8	.625	....	....	16	9	16	1	....	....	....	....	1.9	2.3	1.3	....
NBA Playoff Totals		15	....	....	32	11	49	.224	....	....	....	10	21	.476	....	....	16	13	27	1	....	....	....	....	2.1	1.1	0.9	....

• CHONES, Jim

James Bernett Chones

Born: Nov. 30, 1949. Racine, WI, United States. Height: 6'11". Weight: 220 lbs. Drafted: 1973 College: Marquette

YEAR	TEAM	GP	GS	MIN	PTS	FGM	FGA	FG%	3PM	3PA	3P%	FTM	FTA	FT%	ORB	DRB	TRB	AST	PF	DQ	STL	BLK	TO	MPG	PPG	RPG	APG	PCM
72-73	New York-A	82	....	2153	932	395	769	.514	0	1	.000	142	240	.592	143	443	586	95	291	7	....	....	213	26.3	11.4	7.1	1.2	.489
73-74	Carolina-A	83	....	2387	1225	535	1017	.526	0	2	.000	155	252	.615	191	454	645	118	**347**	....	59	131	206	28.8	14.8	7.8	1.4	.548
74-75	Cleveland	72	....	2427	1044	446	916	.487	....	....	....	152	224	.679	156	521	677	132	247	5	49	120	....	33.7	14.5	9.4	1.8	.509
75-76	Cleveland	82	....	2741	1298	563	1258	.448	....	....	....	172	260	.662	197	542	739	163	241	2	42	93	....	33.4	15.8	9.0	2.0	.504
76-77	Cleveland	82	....	2378	1055	450	972	.463	....	....	....	155	212	.731	208	480	688	104	258	3	32	77	....	29.0	12.9	8.4	1.3	.496
77-78	Cleveland	82	....	2906	1230	525	1113	.472	....	....	....	180	250	.720	219	625	844	131	235	4	52	58	180	35.4	15.0	10.3	1.6	.484
78-79	Cleveland	82	....	2850	1102	472	1073	.440	....	....	....	158	215	.735	260	582	842	181	278	4	47	102	189	34.8	13.4	10.3	2.2	.467
79-80	LA Lakers	82	....	2394	869	372	760	.489	0	2	.000	125	169	.740	143	421	564	151	271	5	56	65	172	29.2	10.6	6.9	1.8	.420
80-81	LA Lakers	82	....	2562	882	378	751	.503	0	4	.000	126	193	.653	180	477	657	153	324	4	39	96	156	31.2	10.8	8.0	1.9	.433
81-82	Washington	59	13	867	184	74	171	.433	0	0	.000	36	46	.783	39	146	185	64	114	1	15	32	41	14.7	3.1	3.1	1.1	.326
NBA Season Totals		623	13	19125	7664	3280	7014	.468	0	6	.000	1104	1569	.704	1402	3794	5196	1079	1968	28	332	643	738	30.7	12.3	8.3	1.7	....
ABA Season Totals		165	....	4540	2157	930	1786	.521	0	3	.000	297	492	.604	334	897	1231	213	638	7	59	131	419	27.5	13.1	7.5	1.3	....
Career Totals		788	13	23665	9821	4210	8800	.478	0	9	.000	1401	2061	.680	1736	4691	6427	1292	2606	35	391	774	1157	30.0	12.5	8.2	1.6	....
72-73	New York-A	5	....	74	20	8	23	.348	0	0	.000	4	8	.500	4	23	27	5	8	0	....	....	5	14.8	4.0	5.4	1.0	.418
73-74	Carolina-A	4	....	96	46	21	47	.447	0	0	.000	4	8	.500	6	18	24	3	17	....	2	4	3	24.0	11.5	6.0	0.8	.403
75-76	Cleveland	7	....	242	105	47	114	.412	....	....	....	11	18	.611	14	36	50	6	23	0	1	6	....	34.6	15.0	7.1	0.9	.349
76-77	Cleveland	3	....	99	39	16	27	.593	....	....	....	7	7	1.000	11	20	31	3	9	0	0	1	....	33.0	13.0	10.3	1.0	.564
77-78	Cleveland	2	....	82	30	13	27	.481	....	....	....	4	8	.500	3	12	15	7	7	0	2	1	4	41.0	15.0	7.5	3.5	.403
79-80	LA Lakers	16	....	439	119	48	118	.407	0	0	.000	23	34	.676	32	72	104	28	60	0	8	6	32	27.4	7.4	6.5	1.8	.301
80-81	LA Lakers	3	....	67	24	10	17	.588	0	0	.000	4	8	.500	6	11	17	1	9	0	1	4	3	22.3	8.0	5.7	0.3	.449
81-82	Washington	5	0	30	5	2	9	.222	0	0	.000	1	3	.333	1	5	6	2	8	0	1	2	1	6.0	1.0	1.2	0.4	.116
NBA Playoff Totals		36	0	959	322	136	312	.436	0	0	.000	50	78	.641	67	156	223	47	116	0	13	20	40	26.6	8.9	6.2	1.3	....
ABA Playoff Totals		9	....	170	66	29	70	.414	0	0	.000	8	16	.500	10	41	51	8	25	0	2	4	8	18.9	7.3	5.7	0.9	....
Career Playoff Totals		45	0	1129	388	165	382	.432	0	0	.000	58	94	.617	77	197	274	55	141	0	15	24	48	25.1	8.6	6.1	1.2	....

• CHRIST, Fred

Frederick L. Christ

Born: Aug. 6, 1930. Height: 6'4". Weight: 210 lbs. Drafted: — College: Fordham

YEAR	TEAM	GP	GS	MIN	PTS	FGM	FGA	FG%	3PM	3PA	3P%	FTM	FTA	FT%	ORB	DRB	TRB	AST	PF	DQ	STL	BLK	TO	MPG	PPG	RPG	APG	PCM
54-55	New York	6	....	48	20	5	18	.278	....	....	....	10	11	.909	....	....	8	7	3	0	....	....	....	8.0	3.3	1.3	1.2	.489
NBA Season Totals		6	....	48	20	5	18	.278	....	....	....	10	11	.909	....	....	8	7	3	0	....	....	....	8.0	3.3	1.3	1.2	....

• CHRISTENSEN, Cal

Calvin L. Christensen

Born: July 8, 1927. Height: 6'5". Weight: 210 lbs. Drafted: 1950 College: Toledo

YEAR	TEAM	GP	GS	MIN	PTS	FGM	FGA	FG%	3PM	3PA	3P%	FTM	FTA	FT%	ORB	DRB	TRB	AST	PF	DQ	STL	BLK	TO	MPG	PPG	RPG	APG	PCM
50-51	Tri-Cities	67	....	....	443	134	445	.301	....	....	....	175	245	.714	....	....	523	161	266	**19**	....	....	....	....	6.6	7.8	2.4	....
51-52	Milwaukee	24	....	374	88	29	96	.302	....	....	....	30	57	.526	....	....	82	34	47	2	....	....	....	15.6	3.7	3.4	1.4	.311
52-53	Rochester	59	....	777	212	72	230	.313	....	....	....	68	114	.596	....	....	199	54	148	6	....	....	....	13.2	3.6	3.4	0.9	.309
53-54	Rochester	70	....	1654	412	137	395	.347	....	....	....	138	261	.529	....	....	395	107	196	1	....	....	....	23.6	5.9	5.6	1.5	.323
54-55	Rochester	71	....	1204	352	114	305	.374	....	....	....	124	206	.602	....	....	388	104	174	2	....	....	....	17.0	5.0	5.5	1.5	.443
NBA Season Totals		291	....	4009	1507	486	1471	.330	....	....	....	535	883	.606	....	....	1587	460	831	30	....	....	....	13.8	5.2	5.5	1.6	....
52-53	Rochester	2	....	13	3	0	3	.000	....	....	....	3	4	.750	....	....	4	1	5	0	....	....	....	6.5	1.5	2.0	0.5	.218
53-54	Rochester	6	....	137	32	10	28	.357	....	....	....	12	22	.545	....	....	35	15	16	0	....	....	....	22.8	5.3	5.8	2.5	.396
54-55	Rochester	3	....	30	7	2	8	.250	....	....	....	3	6	.500	....	....	6	0	1	0	....	....	....	10.0	2.3	2.0	0.0	.183
NBA Playoff Totals		11	....	180	42	12	39	.308	....	....	....	18	32	.563	....	....	45	16	22	0	....	....	....	16.4	3.8	4.1	1.5	....

• CHRISTIAN, Bob

Bob Christian

Born: May 11, 1946. Height: 6'10". Weight: 255 lbs. Drafted: 1969 College: Grambling

YEAR	TEAM	GP	GS	MIN	PTS	FGM	FGA	FG%	3PM	3PA	3P%	FTM	FTA	FT%	ORB	DRB	TRB	AST	PF	DQ	STL	BLK	TO	MPG	PPG	RPG	APG	PCM
69-70	Dallas-A	1	....	7	0	0	0	.000	0	0	.000	0	0	.000	0	1	1	0	2	0	....	....	1	7.0	0.0	1.0	0.0	.000
69-70	New York-A	1	....	4	2	1	3	.333	0	0	.000	0	0	.000	1	1	2	0	1	0	....	....	2	4.0	2.0	2.0	0.0	.393
70-71	Atlanta	54	....	524	150	55	127	.433	....	....	....	40	64	.625	....	....	177	30	118	0	....	....	....	9.7	2.8	3.3	0.6	.407
71-72	Atlanta	56	....	485	176	66	142	.465	....	....	....	44	61	.721	....	....	181	28	77	0	....	....	....	8.7	3.1	3.2	0.5	.532
72-73	Atlanta	55	....	759	230	85	155	.548	....	....	....	60	79	.759	....	....	305	47	111	2	....	....	....	13.8	4.2	5.5	0.9	.566
73-74	Phoenix	81	....	1244	386	140	288	.486	....	....	....	106	151	.702	85	254	339	98	191	3	19	32	....	15.4	4.8	4.2	1.2	.451
NBA Season Totals		246	....	3012	942	346	712	.486	....	....	....	250	355	.704	85	254	1002	203	497	5	19	32	....	12.2	3.8	4.1	0.8	....
ABA Season Totals		2	....	11	2	1	3	.333	0	0	.000	0	0	.000	1	2	3	0	3	0	....	....	3	5.5	1.0	1.5	0.0	....
Career Totals		248	....	3023	944	347	715	.485	0	0	.000	250	355	.704	86	256	1005	203	500	5	19	32	3	12.2	3.8	4.1	0.8	....
71-72	Atlanta	6	....	34	7	3	8	.375	....	....	....	1	1	1.000	....	....	7	0	10	0	....	....	....	5.7	1.2	1.2	0.0	.130
NBA Playoff Totals		6	....	34	7	3	8	.375	....	....	....	1	1	1.000	....	....	7	0	10	0	....	....	....	5.7	1.2	1.2	0.0	....

• CHRISTIE, Doug

Douglas Dale Christie

Born: May 9, 1970. Seattle, WA, United States. Height: 6'6". Weight: 200 lbs. Drafted: 1992 College: Pepperdine

YEAR	TEAM	GP	GS	MIN	PTS	FGM	FGA	FG%	3PM	3PA	3P%	FTM	FTA	FT%	ORB	DRB	TRB	AST	PF	DQ	STL	BLK	TO	MPG	PPG	RPG	APG	PCM
92-93	LA Lakers	23	0	332	142	45	106	.425	2	12	.167	50	66	.758	24	27	51	53	53	0	22	5	51	14.4	6.2	2.2	2.3	.406
93-94	LA Lakers	65	34	1515	672	244	562	.434	39	119	.328	145	208	.697	93	142	235	136	186	2	89	28	143	23.3	10.3	3.6	2.1	.399
94-95	New York	12	0	79	15	5	22	.227	1	7	.143	4	5	.800	3	10	13	8	18	1	2	1	13	6.6	1.3	1.1	0.7	.018
95-96	New York	23	0	218	93	35	73	.479	10	19	.526	13	22	.591	8	26	34	25	41	1	12	3	18	9.5	4.0	1.5	1.1	.410
95-96	Toronto	32	17	818	322	115	264	.436	36	87	.414	56	71	.789	26	94	120	92	100	4	58	16	77	25.6	10.1	3.8	2.9	.410

YEAR	TEAM	GP	GS	MIN	PTS	FGM	FGA	FG%	3PM	3PA	3P%	FTM	FTA	FT%	ORB	DRB	TRB	AST	PF	DQ	STL	BLK	TO	MPG	PPG	RPG	APG	PCM
96-97	Toronto	81	81	3127	1176	396	949	.417	147	383	.384	237	306	.775	85	347	432	315	245	6	201	45	203	38.6	14.5	5.3	3.9	.414
97-98	Toronto	78	78	2939	1287	458	1071	.428	100	307	.326	271	327	.829	94	310	404	282	198	3	190	57	226	37.7	16.5	5.2	3.6	.444
98-99	Toronto	50	50	1768	760	252	650	.388	49	161	.304	207	246	.841	59	148	207	187	111	1	113	26	119	35.4	15.2	4.1	3.7	.424
99-00	Toronto	73	73	2264	903	311	764	.407	99	275	.360	182	216	.843	63	222	285	321	167	1	102	43	144	31.0	12.4	3.9	4.4	.446
00-01	Sacramento	81	81	2939	996	311	788	.395	94	250	.376	280	312	.897	95	260	355	289	224	2	**183**	45	154	36.3	12.3	4.4	3.6	.393
01-02	Sacramento	81	81	2798	972	338	735	.460	90	256	.352	206	242	.851	74	300	374	340	209	3	160	25	164	34.5	12.0	4.6	4.2	.440
02-03	Sacramento	80	80	2711	748	267	557	.479	73	185	.395	141	174	.810	61	281	342	376	186	1	180	37	144	33.9	9.4	4.3	4.7	.433
NBA Season Totals		679	575	21508	8086	2777	6541	.425	740	2061	.359	1792	2195	.816	685	2167	2852	2424	1738	25	1312	331	1456	31.7	11.9	4.2	3.6	....
92-93	LA Lakers	5	0	39	9	4	11	.364	1	3	.333	0	0	.000	1	3	4	6	5	0	2	2	4	7.8	1.8	0.8	1.2	.263
94-95	New York	2	0	6	0	0	4	.000	0	0	.000	0	0	.000	0	0	0	0	3	0	0	0	1	3.0	0.0	0.0	0.0	-1.02
99-00	Toronto	3	1	61	12	3	13	.231	3	8	.375	3	6	.500	1	4	5	6	10	0	4	1	4	20.3	4.0	1.7	2.0	.148
00-01	Sacramento	8	8	304	79	25	68	.368	5	17	.294	24	29	.828	7	28	35	26	31	1	20	9	19	38.0	9.9	4.4	3.3	.307
01-02	Sacramento	16	16	644	177	54	132	.409	17	64	.266	52	65	.800	19	73	92	79	64	3	33	9	44	40.3	11.1	5.8	4.9	.372
02-03	Sacramento	12	12	381	109	37	99	.374	6	24	.250	29	31	.935	15	59	74	55	22	0	12	3	22	31.8	9.1	6.2	4.6	.427
NBA Playoff Totals		46	37	1435	386	123	327	.376	32	116	.276	108	131	.824	43	167	210	172	135	4	71	24	94	31.2	8.4	4.6	3.7	....

• CHUBIN, Stephen

Stephen (Chube) Chubin

Born: Feb. 8, 1944. New York, NY, United States. Height: 6'2". Weight: 200 lbs. Drafted: 1966 College: Rhode Island

YEAR	TEAM	GP	GS	MIN	PTS	FGM	FGA	FG%	3PM	3PA	3P%	FTM	FTA	FT%	ORB	DRB	TRB	AST	PF	DQ	STL	BLK	TO	MPG	PPG	RPG	APG	PCM
67-68	Anaheim-A	77	....	2441	1398	439	1057	.415	2	10	.200	518	639	.811	....	....	433	364	292	10	....	....	310	31.7	18.2	5.6	4.7	.614
68-69	Indiana-A	24	....	725	332	101	245	.412	1	6	.167	129	162	.796	40	55	95	125	104	1	....	....	86	30.2	13.8	4.0	5.2	.516
68-69	Los Angeles-A	17	....	490	282	84	215	.391	1	4	.250	113	135	.837	44	37	81	78	57	2	....	....	74	28.8	16.6	4.8	4.6	.601
68-69	Minnesota-A	8	....	54	18	6	21	.286	0	0	.000	6	6	1.000	3	9	12	12	17	0	....	....	14	6.8	2.3	1.5	1.5	.404
68-69	New York-A	28	....	828	445	153	394	.388	1	17	.059	138	169	.817	53	50	103	139	109	3	....	....	112	29.6	15.9	3.7	5.0	.514
69-70	Indiana-A	32	....	381	134	41	93	.441	2	4	.500	50	60	.833	23	18	41	69	73	1	....	....	63	11.9	4.2	1.3	2.2	.440
69-70	Kentucky-A	15	....	139	47	10	34	.294	0	1	.000	27	33	.818	6	7	13	17	24	0	....	....	19	9.3	3.1	0.9	1.1	.317
69-70	New York-A	11	....	232	119	40	118	.339	2	6	.333	37	42	.881	22	13	35	26	29	0	....	....	30	21.1	10.8	3.2	2.4	.419
69-70	Pittsburgh-A	14	....	306	129	36	107	.336	1	3	.333	56	64	.875	23	25	48	5	48	2	....	....	39	21.9	9.2	3.4	0.4	.297
ABA Season Totals		226	....	5596	2904	910	2284	.398	10	51	.196	1074	1310	.820	214	214	861	835	753	19	....	....	747	24.8	12.8	3.8	3.7	....
69-70	Kentucky-A	11	....	55	28	8	17	.471	0	4	.000	12	14	.857	2	1	3	0	....	0	....	....	10	5.0	2.5	0.3	0.0	....
ABA Playoff Totals		11	....	55	28	8	17	.471	0	4	.000	12	14	.857	2	1	3	0	....	0	....	....	10	5.0	2.5	0.3	0.0	....

• CHUCKOVITS, Charles

Charles H. (Chuck) Chuckovits

Born: 1912. Height: 6'1". Weight: 175 lbs. Drafted: — College: Toledo

YEAR	TEAM	GP	GS	MIN	PTS	FGM	FGA	FG%	3PM	3PA	3P%	FTM	FTA	FT%	ORB	DRB	TRB	AST	PF	DQ	STL	BLK	TO	MPG	PPG	RPG	APG	PCM
39-40	Hammond-N	14	....	....	90	30	....	....	....	....	....	30	....	....	....	....	....	....	....	....	....	....	....	....	6.4	....	....	....
41-42	Toledo-N	22	....	....	**406**	**143**	....	....	....	....	....	**120**	....	....	....	....	....	....	....	....	....	....	....	....	18.5	....	....	....
NBL Season Totals		36	....	....	496	173	....	....	....	....	....	150	....	....	....	....	....	....	....	....	....	....	....	....	13.8	....	....	....

• CHURCHFIELD, Ralph

Ralph Churchfield

Born: 1918. Height: 6'5". Weight: 220 lbs. Drafted: — College: Washington & Jefferson

YEAR	TEAM	GP	GS	MIN	PTS	FGM	FGA	FG%	3PM	3PA	3P%	FTM	FTA	FT%	ORB	DRB	TRB	AST	PF	DQ	STL	BLK	TO	MPG	PPG	RPG	APG	PCM
44-45	Pittsburgh-N	20	....	....	67	26	....	....	....	....	....	15	....	....	....	....	....	....	....	....	....	....	....	....	3.4	....	....	....
NBL Season Totals		20	....	....	67	26	....	....	....	....	....	15	....	....	....	....	....	....	....	....	....	....	....	....	3.4	....	....	....

• CHURCHWELL, Robert

Robert Churchwell

Born: Feb. 20, 1972. South Bend, IN, United States. Height: 6'6". Weight: 195 lbs. Drafted: — College: Georgetown

YEAR	TEAM	GP	GS	MIN	PTS	FGM	FGA	FG%	3PM	3PA	3P%	FTM	FTA	FT%	ORB	DRB	TRB	AST	PF	DQ	STL	BLK	TO	MPG	PPG	RPG	APG	PCM
95-96	Golden State	4	0	20	6	3	8	.375	0	0	.000	0	0	.000	0	3	3	1	1	0	0	0	2	5.0	1.5	0.8	0.3	.142
NBA Season Totals		4	0	20	6	3	8	.375	0	0	.000	0	0	.000	0	3	3	1	1	0	0	0	2	5.0	1.5	0.8	0.3	....

• CIHLAR, Hal

Hal Cihlar

Born: 1914. Height: 6'5". Weight: 210 lbs. Drafted: — College: —

YEAR	TEAM	GP	GS	MIN	PTS	FGM	FGA	FG%	3PM	3PA	3P%	FTM	FTA	FT%	ORB	DRB	TRB	AST	PF	DQ	STL	BLK	TO	MPG	PPG	RPG	APG	PCM
43-44	Cleveland-N	4	....	....	1	0	....	....	....	....	....	1	....	....	....	....	....	....	....	....	....	....	....	....	0.3	....	....	....
NBL Season Totals		4	....	....	1	0	....	....	....	....	....	1	....	....	....	....	....	....	....	....	....	....	....	....	0.3	....	....	....

• CLARK, Archie

Archie L. Clark

Born: July 15, 1941. Conway, AR, United States. Height: 6'2". Weight: 175 lbs. Drafted: 1966 College: Minnesota

YEAR	TEAM	GP	GS	MIN	PTS	FGM	FGA	FG%	3PM	3PA	3P%	FTM	FTA	FT%	ORB	DRB	TRB	AST	PF	DQ	STL	BLK	TO	MPG	PPG	RPG	APG	PCM
66-67	LA Lakers	76	....	1763	798	331	732	.452	....	....	....	136	192	.708	....	....	218	205	193	1	....	....	....	23.2	10.5	2.9	2.7	.454
67-68	LA Lakers	81	....	3039	1612	628	1309	.480	....	....	....	356	481	.740	....	....	342	353	235	3	....	....	....	37.5	19.9	4.2	4.4	.534
68-69	Philadelphia	82	....	2144	1107	444	928	.478	....	....	....	219	314	.697	....	....	265	296	188	1	....	....	....	26.1	13.5	3.2	3.6	.536
69-70	Philadelphia	76	....	2772	1499	594	1198	.496	....	....	....	311	396	.785	....	....	301	380	201	2	....	....	....	36.5	19.7	4.0	5.0	.553
70-71	Philadelphia	82	....	3245	1746	662	1334	.496	....	....	....	422	536	.787	....	....	391	440	217	2	....	....	....	39.6	21.3	4.8	5.4	.574
71-72	Philadelphia	1	....	42	29	11	16	.688	....	....	....	7	11	.636	....	....	3	7	3	0	....	....	....	42.0	29.0	3.0	7.0	.767
71-72	Baltimore	76	....	3243	1909	701	1500	.467	....	....	....	507	656	.773	....	....	265	606	191	0	....	....	....	42.7	25.1	3.5	8.0	.613
72-73	Baltimore	39	....	1477	715	302	596	.507	....	....	....	111	137	.810	....	....	129	275	111	1	....	....	....	37.9	18.3	3.3	7.1	.561
73-74	Washington	56	....	1786	733	315	675	.467	....	....	....	103	131	.786	44	97	141	285	122	0	59	6	....	31.9	13.1	2.5	5.1	.454
74-75	Seattle	77	....	2481	1071	455	919	.495	....	....	....	161	193	.834	59	176	235	433	188	4	110	5	....	32.2	13.9	3.1	5.6	.515
75-76	Detroit	79	....	1589	600	250	577	.433	....	....	....	100	116	.862	27	110	137	218	157	0	62	4	....	20.1	7.6	1.7	2.8	.385
NBA Season Totals		725	....	23581	11819	4693	9784	.480	....	....	....	2433	3163	.769	130	383	2427	3498	1806	14	231	15	....	32.5	16.3	3.3	4.8	....
66-67	LA Lakers	3	....	125	77	32	62	.516	....	....	....	13	17	.765	....	....	13	15	11	1	....	....	....	41.7	25.7	4.3	5.0	.604
67-68	LA Lakers	15	....	528	229	88	206	.427	....	....	....	53	69	.768	....	....	47	60	42	0	....	....	....	35.2	15.3	3.1	4.0	.419
68-69	Philadelphia	5	....	185	97	40	77	.519	....	....	....	17	19	.895	....	....	19	22	17	0	....	....	....	37.0	19.4	3.8	4.4	.538

YEAR	TEAM	GP	GS	MIN	PTS	FGM	FGA	FG%	3PM	3PA	3P%	FTM	FTA	FT%	ORB	DRB	TRB	AST	PF	DQ	STL	BLK	TO	MPG	PPG	RPG	APG	PCM
69-70	Philadelphia	5	....	146	68	26	60	.433	....	....	....	16	22	.727	....	....	14	18	10	0	....	....	....	29.2	13.6	2.8	3.6	.435
70-71	Philadelphia	7	....	295	165	66	139	.475	....	....	....	33	45	.733	....	....	29	34	21	0	....	....	....	42.1	23.6	4.1	4.9	.514
71-72	Baltimore	6	....	271	160	55	126	.437	....	....	....	50	59	.847	....	....	24	47	15	0	....	....	....	45.2	26.7	4.0	7.8	.599
72-73	Baltimore	5	....	214	106	46	92	.500	....	....	....	14	18	.778	....	....	17	26	20	1	....	....	....	42.8	21.2	3.4	5.2	.470
73-74	Washington	7	....	162	51	20	59	.339	....	....	....	11	20	.550	3	10	13	15	13	0	5	0	....	23.1	7.3	1.9	2.1	.227
74-75	Seattle	9	....	269	100	41	94	.436	....	....	....	18	20	.900	7	25	32	31	23	0	6	1	....	29.9	11.1	3.6	3.4	.398
75-76	Detroit	9	....	192	72	30	62	.484	....	....	....	12	18	.667	2	19	21	29	25	0	6	0	....	21.3	8.0	2.3	3.2	.429
NBA Playoff Totals		71	....	2387	1125	444	977	.454	....	....	....	237	307	.772	12	54	229	297	197	2	17	1	....	33.6	15.8	3.2	4.2	....

• CLARK, Carlos
Carlos R. Clark

Born: Aug. 10, 1960. Somerville, TN, United States.　Height: 6'4".　Weight: 210 lbs.　Drafted: 1983　College: Mississippi

YEAR	TEAM	GP	GS	MIN	PTS	FGM	FGA	FG%	3PM	3PA	3P%	FTM	FTA	FT%	ORB	DRB	TRB	AST	PF	DQ	STL	BLK	TO	MPG	PPG	RPG	APG	PCM
83-84	Boston	31	0	127	54	19	52	.365	0	2	.000	16	18	.889	7	10	17	17	13	0	8	1	12	4.1	1.7	0.5	0.5	.374
84-85	Boston	62	3	562	169	64	152	.421	0	5	.000	41	53	.774	29	40	69	48	66	0	35	2	43	9.1	2.7	1.1	0.8	.286
NBA Season Totals		93	3	689	223	83	204	.407	0	7	.000	57	71	.803	36	50	86	65	79	0	43	3	55	7.4	2.4	0.9	0.7	....
83-84	Boston	8	0	20	9	4	10	.400	0	0	.000	1	2	.500	1	0	1	1	3	0	1	2	1	2.5	1.1	0.1	0.1	.271
84-85	Boston	3	0	11	8	3	5	.600	0	0	.000	2	2	1.000	2	0	2	3	2	0	1	0	0	3.7	2.7	0.7	1.0	1.019
NBA Playoff Totals		11	0	31	17	7	15	.467	0	0	.000	3	4	.750	3	0	3	4	5	0	2	2	1	2.8	1.5	0.3	0.4	....

• CLARK, Keon
Arian Keon Clark

Born: Apr. 16, 1975. Danville, IL, United States.　Height: 6'11".　Weight: 220 lbs.　Drafted: 1998　College: UNLV

YEAR	TEAM	GP	GS	MIN	PTS	FGM	FGA	FG%	3PM	3PA	3P%	FTM	FTA	FT%	ORB	DRB	TRB	AST	PF	DQ	STL	BLK	TO	MPG	PPG	RPG	APG	PCM
98-99	Denver	28	0	409	93	36	80	.450	0	1	.000	21	37	.568	36	60	96	10	52	0	10	31	21	14.6	3.3	3.4	0.4	.337
99-00	Denver	81	20	1850	694	286	528	.542	1	8	.125	121	176	.688	162	343	505	71	231	1	45	114	125	22.8	8.6	6.2	0.9	.493
00-01	Denver	35	3	752	227	82	199	.412	0	0	.000	63	105	.600	58	128	186	34	101	3	16	44	48	21.5	6.5	5.3	1.0	.363
00-01	Toronto	46	0	968	413	167	320	.522	0	1	.000	79	135	.585	78	170	248	38	143	3	16	110	42	21.0	9.0	5.4	0.8	.544
01-02	Toronto	81	31	2185	915	380	775	.490	0	5	.000	155	230	.674	182	421	603	88	258	4	58	122	140	27.0	11.3	7.4	1.1	.497
02-03	Sacramento	80	11	1781	536	226	451	.501	0	4	.000	84	128	.656	138	313	451	80	227	2	38	150	94	22.3	6.7	5.6	1.0	.444
NBA Season Totals		351	65	7945	2878	1177	2353	.500	1	19	.053	523	811	.645	654	1435	2089	321	1012	13	183	571	470	22.6	8.2	6.0	0.9	....
00-01	Toronto	11	0	103	35	11	30	.367	0	0	.000	13	20	.650	7	16	23	6	16	0	2	3	4	9.4	3.2	2.1	0.5	.347
01-02	Toronto	5	5	174	67	26	48	.542	0	0	.000	15	16	.938	14	26	40	8	19	0	2	8	14	34.8	13.4	8.0	1.6	.456
02-03	Sacramento	12	0	171	55	20	41	.488	0	0	.000	15	21	.714	14	30	44	4	30	0	3	8	13	14.3	4.6	3.7	0.3	.363
NBA Playoff Totals		28	5	448	157	57	119	.479	0	0	.000	43	57	.754	35	72	107	18	65	0	7	19	31	16.0	5.6	3.8	0.6	....

• CLARK, Richard
Richard C. Clark

Born: Jan. 5, 1944. Findlay, OH, United States.　Height: 6'4".　Weight: 190 lbs.　Drafted: —　College: Eastern Kentucky

YEAR	TEAM	GP	GS	MIN	PTS	FGM	FGA	FG%	3PM	3PA	3P%	FTM	FTA	FT%	ORB	DRB	TRB	AST	PF	DQ	STL	BLK	TO	MPG	PPG	RPG	APG	PCM
67-68	Minnesota-A	26	....	414	140	46	150	.307	0	10	.000	48	79	.608	....	....	52	33	49	0	....	....	33	15.9	5.4	2.0	1.3	.247
68-69	Houston-A	32	....	723	218	64	222	.288	1	8	.125	89	124	.718	30	58	88	68	99	0	....	....	73	22.6	6.8	2.8	2.1	.246
ABA Season Totals		58	....	1137	358	110	372	.296	1	18	.056	137	203	.675	30	58	140	101	148	0	....	....	106	19.6	6.2	2.4	1.7	....
67-68	Minnesota-A	10	....	231	56	17	65	.262	1	6	.167	21	28	.750	....	....	33	13	18	0	....	....	13	23.1	5.6	3.3	1.3	.209
ABA Playoff Totals		10	....	231	56	17	65	.262	1	6	.167	21	28	.750	....	....	33	13	18	0	....	....	13	23.1	5.6	3.3	1.3	....

• CLAWSON, John
John Richard Clawson

Born: May 15, 1944. Duluth, MN, United States.　Height: 6'4".　Weight: 200 lbs.　Drafted: —　College: Michigan

YEAR	TEAM	GP	GS	MIN	PTS	FGM	FGA	FG%	3PM	3PA	3P%	FTM	FTA	FT%	ORB	DRB	TRB	AST	PF	DQ	STL	BLK	TO	MPG	PPG	RPG	APG	PCM
68-69	Oakland-A	70	....	1067	331	147	309	.476	0	0	.000	37	54	.685	71	124	195	51	187	1	....	....	73	15.2	4.7	2.8	0.7	.309
ABA Season Totals		70	....	1067	331	147	309	.476	0	0	.000	37	54	.685	71	124	195	51	187	1	....	....	73	15.2	4.7	2.8	0.7	....
68-69	Oakland-A	16	....	313	100	42	95	.442	1	3	.333	15	24	.625	....	....	54	14	60	2	....	....	13	19.6	6.3	3.4	0.9	.279
ABA Playoff Totals		16	....	313	100	42	95	.442	1	3	.333	15	24	.625	....	....	54	14	60	2	....	....	13	19.6	6.3	3.4	0.9	....

• CLAXTON, Charles
Charles Claxton Jr.

Born: Dec. 13, 1970. St. Thomas, Virgin Islands.　Height: 7'　Weight: 265 lbs.　Drafted: 1994　College: Georgia

YEAR	TEAM	GP	GS	MIN	PTS	FGM	FGA	FG%	3PM	3PA	3P%	FTM	FTA	FT%	ORB	DRB	TRB	AST	PF	DQ	STL	BLK	TO	MPG	PPG	RPG	APG	PCM
95-96	Boston	3	0	7	2	1	2	.500	0	0	.000	0	2	.000	2	0	2	0	4	0	0	1	1	2.3	0.7	0.7	0.0	.017
NBA Season Totals		3	0	7	2	1	2	.500	0	0	.000	0	2	.000	2	0	2	0	4	0	0	1	1	2.3	0.7	0.7	0.0	....

• CLAXTON, Speedy
Craig (Speedy) Claxton

Born: May 8, 1978. Queens, NY, United States.　Height: 5'11".　Weight: 166 lbs.　Drafted: 2000　College: Hofstra

YEAR	TEAM	GP	GS	MIN	PTS	FGM	FGA	FG%	3PM	3PA	3P%	FTM	FTA	FT%	ORB	DRB	TRB	AST	PF	DQ	STL	BLK	TO	MPG	PPG	RPG	APG	PCM
01-02	Philadelphia	67	18	1528	480	181	452	.400	4	33	.121	114	136	.838	46	114	160	198	145	1	95	6	95	22.8	7.2	2.4	3.0	.344
02-03	San Antonio	30	0	471	173	67	145	.462	0	11	.000	39	57	.684	22	34	56	75	43	0	22	7	35	15.7	5.8	1.9	2.5	.428
NBA Season Totals		97	18	1999	653	248	597	.415	4	44	.091	153	193	.793	68	148	216	273	188	1	117	13	130	20.6	6.7	2.2	2.8	....
01-02	Philadelphia	5	0	49	12	4	12	.333	0	1	.000	4	6	.667	1	0	1	14	8	0	5	0	3	9.8	2.4	0.2	2.8	.373
02-03	San Antonio	24	0	326	125	46	105	.438	0	0	.000	33	44	.750	7	38	45	45	38	0	16	5	24	13.6	5.2	1.9	1.9	.419
NBA Playoff Totals		29	0	375	137	50	117	.427	0	1	.000	37	50	.740	8	38	46	59	46	0	21	5	27	12.9	4.7	1.6	2.0	....

• CLEAMONS, Jim
James Mitchell Cleamons

Born: Sept. 13, 1949. Lincolnton, NC, United States.　Height: 6'3".　Weight: 185 lbs.　Drafted: 1971　College: Ohio State

YEAR	TEAM	GP	GS	MIN	PTS	FGM	FGA	FG%	3PM	3PA	3P%	FTM	FTA	FT%	ORB	DRB	TRB	AST	PF	DQ	STL	BLK	TO	MPG	PPG	RPG	APG	PCM
71-72	LA Lakers	38	....	201	98	35	100	.350	....	....	....	28	36	.778	....	....	39	35	21	0	....	....	....	5.3	2.6	1.0	0.9	.511
72-73	Cleveland	80	....	1392	459	192	423	.454	....	....	....	75	101	.743	....	....	167	205	108	0	....	....	....	17.4	5.7	2.1	2.6	.417

YEAR	TEAM	GP	GS	MIN	PTS	FGM	FGA	FG%	3PM	3PA	3P%	FTM	FTA	FT%	ORB	DRB	TRB	AST	PF	DQ	STL	BLK	TO	MPG	PPG	RPG	APG	PCM
73-74	Cleveland	81	....	1642	565	236	545	.433	....	....	....	93	133	.699	63	167	230	227	152	1	61	17	....	20.3	7.0	2.8	2.8	.412
74-75	Cleveland	74	....	2691	882	369	768	.480	....	....	....	144	181	.796	97	232	329	381	194	0	84	21	....	36.4	11.9	4.4	5.1	.431
75-76	Cleveland	82	....	2835	1000	413	887	.466	....	....	....	174	218	.798	124	230	354	428	214	2	124	20	....	34.6	12.2	4.3	5.2	.450
76-77	Cleveland	60	....	2045	626	257	592	.434	....	....	....	112	148	.757	99	174	273	308	126	0	66	23	....	34.1	10.4	4.6	5.1	.417
77-78	New York	79	....	2009	511	215	448	.480	....	....	....	81	103	.786	69	143	212	283	142	1	68	17	111	25.4	6.5	2.7	3.6	.357
78-79	New York	79	....	2390	752	311	657	.473	....	....	....	130	171	.760	65	160	225	376	147	1	73	11	142	30.3	9.5	2.8	4.8	.385
79-80	New York	22	....	254	75	30	69	.435	3	8	.375	12	15	.800	10	9	19	40	13	0	13	2	18	11.5	3.4	0.9	1.8	.357
79-80	Washington	57	....	1535	444	184	381	.483	4	23	.174	72	98	.735	43	90	133	248	120	0	44	9	91	26.9	7.8	2.3	4.4	.363
NBA Season Totals		652	....	16994	5412	2242	4870	.460	7	31	.226	921	1204	.765	570	1205	1981	2531	1237	5	533	120	362	26.1	8.3	3.0	3.9	....
71-72	LA Lakers	6	....	17	8	4	7	.571	....	....	....	0	0	.000	....	....	4	4	3	0	....	....	....	2.8	1.3	0.7	0.7	.712
75-76	Cleveland	13	....	503	179	73	184	.397	....	....	....	33	40	.825	23	48	71	61	34	0	8	3	....	38.7	13.8	5.5	4.7	.391
77-78	New York	6	....	127	34	14	36	.389	....	....	....	6	6	1.000	5	8	13	23	13	0	3	0	8	21.2	5.7	2.2	3.8	.330
79-80	Washington	2	....	20	0	0	3	.000	0	0	.000	0	0	.000	0	1	1	1	0	0	1	0	1	10.0	0.0	0.5	0.5	-.036
NBA Playoff Totals		27	....	667	221	91	230	.396	0	0	.000	39	46	.848	28	57	89	89	50	0	12	3	9	24.7	8.2	3.3	3.3	....

• CLEARY, Don

Don Cleary

Born: —. Height: — Weight: — Drafted: — College: —

YEAR	TEAM	GP	GS	MIN	PTS	FGM	FGA	FG%	3PM	3PA	3P%	FTM	FTA	FT%	ORB	DRB	TRB	AST	PF	DQ	STL	BLK	TO	MPG	PPG	RPG	APG	PCM
41-42	Indianapolis-N	2	....		1	0	....	....	....	....	....	1													0.5			
NBL Playoff Totals		2	....		1	0	....	....	....	....	....	1													0.5			

• CLEAVES, Mateen

Mateen (Cleaves) Cleaves

Born: Sept. 7, 1977. Flint, MI, United States. Height: 6'2". Weight: 205 lbs. Drafted: 2000 College: Michigan State

YEAR	TEAM	GP	GS	MIN	PTS	FGM	FGA	FG%	3PM	3PA	3P%	FTM	FTA	FT%	ORB	DRB	TRB	AST	PF	DQ	STL	BLK	TO	MPG	PPG	RPG	APG	PCM
00-01	Detroit	78	8	1268	422	160	400	.400	5	17	.294	97	137	.708	26	106	132	207	153	1	49	1	139	16.3	5.4	1.7	2.7	.305
01-02	Sacramento	32	0	153	70	30	68	.441	2	8	.250	8	9	.889	1	7	8	25	9	0	7	0	27	4.8	2.2	0.3	0.8	.311
02-03	Sacramento	12	0	55	16	6	23	.261	1	1	1.000	3	4	.750	1	7	8	10	6	0	2	0	14	4.6	1.3	0.7	0.8	.085
NBA Season Totals		122	8	1476	508	196	491	.399	8	26	.308	108	150	.720	28	120	148	242	168	1	58	1	180	12.1	4.2	1.2	2.0	....

• CLEMENS, Barry

John Barry Clemens

Born: May 1, 1943. Dayton, OH, United States. Height: 6'6". Weight: 210 lbs. Drafted: 1965 College: Ohio Wesleyan

YEAR	TEAM	GP	GS	MIN	PTS	FGM	FGA	FG%	3PM	3PA	3P%	FTM	FTA	FT%	ORB	DRB	TRB	AST	PF	DQ	STL	BLK	TO	MPG	PPG	RPG	APG	PCM
65-66	New York	70	....	877	376	161	391	.412	....	....	....	54	78	.692	....	....	183	67	113	0	....	....	....	12.5	5.4	2.6	1.0	.418
66-67	Chicago	60	....	986	440	186	444	.419	....	....	....	68	90	.756	....	....	201	39	143	1	....	....	....	16.4	7.3	3.4	0.7	.381
67-68	Chicago	78	....	1631	725	301	670	.449	....	....	....	123	170	.724	....	....	375	98	223	4	....	....	....	20.9	9.3	4.8	1.3	.454
68-69	Chicago	75	....	1444	552	235	628	.374	....	....	....	82	125	.656	....	....	318	125	163	1	....	....	....	19.3	7.4	4.2	1.7	.380
69-70	Seattle	78	....	1487	651	270	595	.454	....	....	....	111	140	.793	....	....	316	116	188	1	....	....	....	19.1	8.3	4.1	1.5	.456
70-71	Seattle	78	....	1286	577	247	526	.470	....	....	....	83	114	.728	....	....	243	92	169	1	....	....	....	16.5	7.4	3.1	1.2	.439
71-72	Seattle	82	....	1447	580	252	484	.521	....	....	....	76	90	.844	....	....	288	64	198	4	....	....	....	17.6	7.1	3.5	0.8	.421
72-73	Cleveland	72	....	1119	471	209	405	.516	....	....	....	53	68	.779	....	....	211	115	136	0	....	....	....	15.5	6.5	2.9	1.6	.492
73-74	Cleveland	71	....	913	388	163	346	.471	....	....	....	62	73	.849	42	124	166	80	136	2	36	2	....	12.9	5.5	2.3	1.1	.441
74-75	Portland	77	....	952	381	168	355	.473	....	....	....	45	60	.750	33	128	161	76	139	0	68	2	....	12.4	4.9	2.1	1.0	.399
75-76	Portland	49	....	443	171	70	143	.490	....	....	....	31	35	.886	27	43	70	33	57	0	27	7	....	9.0	3.5	1.4	0.7	.406
NBA Season Totals		790	....	12585	5312	2262	4987	.454	....	....	....	788	1043	.756	102	295	2532	905	1665	14	131	11	....	15.9	6.7	3.2	1.1	....
66-67	Chicago	3	....	20	6	0	4	.000	....	....	....	6	7	.857	....	....	3	2	3	0	....	....	....	6.7	2.0	1.0	0.7	.301
67-68	Chicago	4	....	45	20	8	16	.500	....	....	....	4	4	1.000	....	....	2	5	6	0	....	....	....	11.3	5.0	0.5	1.3	.418
NBA Playoff Totals		7	....	65	26	8	20	.400	....	....	....	10	11	.909	....	....	5	7	9	0	....	....	....	9.3	3.7	0.7	1.0	....

• CLIFTON, Nathaniel

Nathaniel (Sweetwater, Sweets) Clifton

Born: Oct. 13, 1922. Little Rock, AR, United States. Died: Aug.31, 1990. Height: 6'6". Weight: 220 lbs. Drafted: — College: Xavier (LA)

YEAR	TEAM	GP	GS	MIN	PTS	FGM	FGA	FG%	3PM	3PA	3P%	FTM	FTA	FT%	ORB	DRB	TRB	AST	PF	DQ	STL	BLK	TO	MPG	PPG	RPG	APG	PCM
50-51	New York	65	....	....	562	211	656	.322	....	....	....	140	263	.532	....	....	491	162	269	13	....	....	....	8.6	7.6	2.5	....	
51-52	New York	62	....	2101	658	244	729	.335	....	....	....	170	256	.664	....	....	731	209	227	8	....	....	....	33.9	10.6	11.8	3.4	.472
52-53	New York	70	....	2496	744	272	794	.343	....	....	....	200	343	.583	....	....	761	231	274	6	....	....	....	35.7	10.6	10.9	3.3	.425
53-54	New York	72	....	2179	688	257	699	.368	....	....	....	174	277	.628	....	....	528	176	215	0	....	....	....	30.3	9.6	7.3	2.4	.396
54-55	New York	72	....	2390	944	360	932	.386	....	....	....	224	328	.683	....	....	612	198	221	2	....	....	....	33.2	13.1	8.5	2.8	.460
55-56	New York	64	....	1537	561	213	541	.394	....	....	....	135	191	.707	....	....	386	151	189	4	....	....	....	24.0	8.8	6.0	2.4	.455
56-57	New York	71	....	2231	762	308	818	.377	....	....	....	146	217	.673	....	....	557	164	243	5	....	....	....	31.4	10.7	7.8	2.3	.397
57-58	Detroit	68	....	1435	525	217	597	.363	....	....	....	91	146	.623	....	....	403	76	202	3	....	....	....	21.1	7.7	5.9	1.1	.380
NBA Season Totals		544	....	14369	5444	2082	5766	.361	....	....	....	1280	2021	.633	....	....	4469	1367	1840	41	....	....	....	26.4	10.0	8.2	2.5	....
50-51	New York	14	....	....	100	41	118	.347	....	....	....	18	46	.391	....	....	137	46	62	4	....	....	....	7.1	9.8	3.3	....	
51-52	New York	14	....	462	132	39	133	.293	....	....	....	54	76	.711	....	....	133	34	67	4	....	....	....	33.0	9.4	9.5	2.4	.372
52-53	New York	11	....	405	132	51	129	.395	....	....	....	30	47	.638	....	....	140	39	48	1	....	....	....	36.8	12.0	12.7	3.5	.502
53-54	New York	4	....	125	25	8	27	.296	....	....	....	9	17	.529	....	....	39	6	15	0	....	....	....	31.3	6.3	9.8	1.5	.310
54-55	New York	3	....	110	59	20	52	.385	....	....	....	19	24	.792	....	....	23	13	12	0	....	....	....	36.7	19.7	7.7	4.3	.564
57-58	Detroit	7	....	74	28	11	30	.367	....	....	....	6	8	.750	....	....	23	4	11	0	....	....	....	10.6	4.0	3.3	0.6	.422
NBA Playoff Totals		53	....	1176	476	170	489	.348	....	....	....	136	218	.624	....	....	495	142	215	9	....	....	....	22.2	9.0	9.3	2.7	....

• CLOSS, Bill

William Thomas Closs

Born: Jan. 8, 1922. Edge, TX, United States. Height: 6'5". Weight: 195 lbs. Drafted: — College: Rice

YEAR	TEAM	GP	GS	MIN	PTS	FGM	FGA	FG%	3PM	3PA	3P%	FTM	FTA	FT%	ORB	DRB	TRB	AST	PF	DQ	STL	BLK	TO	MPG	PPG	RPG	APG	PCM
46-47	Indianapolis-N	44	....	....	272	119	....	....	....	....	....	34	63	.540	....	....	....	99	....	....	....	....	....	6.2	....	....	....	
47-48	Indianapolis-N	55	....	....	396	162	....	....	....	....	....	72	123	.585	....	....	....	139	....	....	....	....	....	7.2	....	....	....	
48-49	Anderson-N	64	....	....	516	203	....	....	....	....	....	110	166	.663	....	....	....	148	....	....	....	....	....	8.1	....	....	....	
49-50	Anderson	64	....	....	752	283	898	.315	....	....	....	186	259	.718	....	....	....	160	190	....	....	....	....	11.8	....	2.5	....	

YEAR	TEAM	GP	GS	MIN	PTS	FGM	FGA	FG%	3PM	3PA	3P%	FTM	FTA	FT%	ORB	DRB	TRB	AST	PF	DQ	STL	BLK	TO	MPG	PPG	RPG	APG	PCM
50-51	Philadelphia	65	....	....	570	202	631	.320	....	....	....	166	223	.744	....	....	401	110	156	4	....	....	....		8.8	6.2	1.7	
51-52	Fort Wayne	57	....	1120	347	120	389	.308	....	....	....	107	157	.682	....	....	204	76	125	2	....	....	....	19.6	6.1	3.6	1.3	.300
NBA Season Totals		186	....	1120	1669	605	1918	.315	....	....	....	459	639	.718	....	....	605	346	471	6	....	....	....		6.0	9.0	3.3	1.9
NBL Season Totals		163	....	....	1184	484	....	....	....	....	....	216	352	....	....	....	....	....	386							7.3			
Career Totals		349	....	1120	2853	1089	1918		....	....	....	675	991	....	....	....	605	346	857	6				3.2	8.2	1.7	1.0	
46-47	Indianapolis-N	4	....	....	23	10	....	....	....	....	....	3	6	.500											5.8			
47-48	Indianapolis-N	4	....	....	37	15	....	....	....	....	....	7	13	.538											9.3			
48-49	Anderson-N	7	....	....	85	25	....	....	....	....	....	35	47	.745											12.1			
49-50	Anderson	8	....	....	91	33	109	.303	....	....	....	25	30	.833	....	....	14	27							11.4		1.8	
50-51	Philadelphia	2	....	....	7	2	8	.250	....	....	....	3	5	.600			8	5	5	0					3.5	4.0	2.5	
51-52	Fort Wayne	1	....	21	5	1	6	.167	....	....	....	3	3	1.000			8	4	0	0				21.0	5.0	8.0	4.0	.585
NBA Playoff Totals		11	....	21	103	36	123	.293	....	....	....	31	38	.816	....	....	16	23	32	0				1.9	9.4	1.5	2.1	
NBL Playoff Totals		15	....	....	145	50	....	....	....	....	....	45	66	....											9.7			
Career Playoff Totals		26	....	21	248	86	123		....	....	....	76	104	....	....	....	16	23	32	0				0.8	9.5	0.6	0.9	

• CLOSS, Keith

Keith Mitchell Closs Jr.

Born: Apr. 3, 1976. Hartford, CT, United States.　Height: 7'3".　Weight: 212 lbs.　Drafted: —　College: Central Connecticut State

YEAR	TEAM	GP	GS	MIN	PTS	FGM	FGA	FG%	3PM	3PA	3P%	FTM	FTA	FT%	ORB	DRB	TRB	AST	PF	DQ	STL	BLK	TO	MPG	PPG	RPG	APG	PCM
97-98	LA Clippers	58	1	740	232	93	207	.449	0	0	.000	46	77	.597	63	105	168	19	73	0	12	81	41	12.8	4.0	2.9	0.3	.408
98-99	LA Clippers	15	0	87	32	12	23	.522	0	1	.000	8	10	.800	5	20	25	0	14	1	3	9	6	5.8	2.1	1.7	0.0	.490
99-00	LA Clippers	57	6	820	238	96	197	.487	0	3	.000	46	78	.590	65	114	179	25	80	0	13	73	34	14.4	4.2	3.1	0.4	.405
NBA Season Totals		130	7	1647	502	201	427	.471	0	4	.000	100	165	.606	133	239	372	44	167	1	28	163	81	12.7	3.9	2.9	0.3	

• CLOYD, Paul

Paul V. Cloyd

Born: June 13, 1920.　Height: 6'2".　Weight: 180 lbs.　Drafted: 1947　College: Wisconsin

YEAR	TEAM	GP	GS	MIN	PTS	FGM	FGA	FG%	3PM	3PA	3P%	FTM	FTA	FT%	ORB	DRB	TRB	AST	PF	DQ	STL	BLK	TO	MPG	PPG	RPG	APG	PCM
47-48	Sheboygan-N	60	....	....	555	213	....	....	....	....	....	129	181	.713	....	....	....	123	....	....	....	....	....		9.3			
48-49	Sheboygan-N	56	....	....	336	119	....	....	....	....	....	98	137	.715	....	....	....	75	....	....	....	....	....		6.0			
49-50	Baltimore	3	....	....	5	1	8	.125	....	....	....	3	3	1.000			1	4							1.7		0.3	
49-50	Waterloo	4	....	....	14	6	18	.333	....	....	....	2	5	.400			1	1							3.5		0.3	
NBA Season Totals		7	....	....	19	7	26	.269	....	....	....	5	8	.625	....	....	2	5							2.7		0.3	
NBL Season Totals		116	....	....	891	332	....	....	....	....	....	227	318	....	....	....	....	198							7.7			
Career Totals		123	....	....	910	339	26	....	....	....	....	232	326	....	....	....	2	203	....						7.4		0.0	
48-49	Sheboygan-N	2	....	....	8	3	....	....	....	....	....	2	3	.667											4.0			
NBL Playoff Totals		2	....	....	8	3	....	....	....	....	....	2	3												4.0			

• CLUGGISH, Bob

R. Marion Cluggish

Born: Sept. 18, 1917. Corbin, KY, United States.　Height: 6'10".　Weight: 235 lbs.　Drafted: —　College: Kentucky

YEAR	TEAM	GP	GS	MIN	PTS	FGM	FGA	FG%	3PM	3PA	3P%	FTM	FTA	FT%	ORB	DRB	TRB	AST	PF	DQ	STL	BLK	TO	MPG	PPG	RPG	APG	PCM
46-47	New York	54	....	....	238	93	356	.261	....	....	....	52	91	.571	....	....	22	113	....	....	....	....	....		4.4		0.4	
NBA Season Totals		54	....	....	238	93	356	.261	....	....	....	52	91	.571	....	....	22	113	....	....	....	....	....		4.4		0.4	
46-47	New York	5	....	....	8	4	27	.148	....	....	....	0	2	.000	....	....	0	12	....	....	....	....	....		1.6		0.0	
NBA Playoff Totals		5	....	....	8	4	27	.148	....	....	....	0	2	.000	....	....	0	12	....	....	....	....	....		1.6		0.0	

• CLYDE, Ben

Bennie J. Clyde

Born: June 10, 1951. Albany, GA, United States.　Height: 6'7".　Weight: 198 lbs.　Drafted: 1974　College: Florida State

YEAR	TEAM	GP	GS	MIN	PTS	FGM	FGA	FG%	3PM	3PA	3P%	FTM	FTA	FT%	ORB	DRB	TRB	AST	PF	DQ	STL	BLK	TO	MPG	PPG	RPG	APG	PCM
74-75	Boston	25	....	157	69	31	72	.431	....	....	....	7	9	.778	15	26	41	5	34	1	5	3	....	6.3	2.8	1.6	0.2	.378
NBA Season Totals		25	....	157	69	31	72	.431	....	....	....	7	9	.778	15	26	41	5	34	1	5	3	....	6.3	2.8	1.6	0.2	

• COFER, Doyle

Doyle Cofer

Born: 1924.　Height: 6'4".　Weight: —　Drafted: —　College: Indiana State

YEAR	TEAM	GP	GS	MIN	PTS	FGM	FGA	FG%	3PM	3PA	3P%	FTM	FTA	FT%	ORB	DRB	TRB	AST	PF	DQ	STL	BLK	TO	MPG	PPG	RPG	APG	PCM
48-49	Detroit-N	8	....	....	27	9	....	....	....	....	....	9	23	.391	....	....	....	....	....	....	....	....	....		3.4			
NBL Season Totals		8	....	....	27	9	....	....	....	....	....	9	23	....	....	....	....	....	....	....	....	....	....		3.4			

• COFFEY, Richard

Richard Lee Coffey

Born: Sept. 2, 1965. Aurora, NC, United States.　Height: 6'6".　Weight: 212 lbs.　Drafted: —　College: Minnesota

YEAR	TEAM	GP	GS	MIN	PTS	FGM	FGA	FG%	3PM	3PA	3P%	FTM	FTA	FT%	ORB	DRB	TRB	AST	PF	DQ	STL	BLK	TO	MPG	PPG	RPG	APG	PCM
90-91	Minnesota	52	1	320	68	28	75	.373	0	1	.000	12	22	.545	42	37	79	3	45	0	6	4	5	6.2	1.3	1.5	0.1	.250
NBA Season Totals		52	1	320	68	28	75	.373	0	1	.000	12	22	.545	42	37	79	3	45	0	6	4	5	6.2	1.3	1.5	0.1	

• COFIELD, Fred

Frederick Cofield

Born: Jan. 4, 1962. Ypsilanti, MI, United States.　Height: 6'3".　Weight: 190 lbs.　Drafted: 1985　College: Eastern Michigan

YEAR	TEAM	GP	GS	MIN	PTS	FGM	FGA	FG%	3PM	3PA	3P%	FTM	FTA	FT%	ORB	DRB	TRB	AST	PF	DQ	STL	BLK	TO	MPG	PPG	RPG	APG	PCM
85-86	New York	45	1	469	165	75	184	.408	3	15	.200	12	20	.600	6	40	46	82	65	1	20	3	50	10.4	3.7	1.0	1.8	.288
86-87	Chicago	5	0	27	4	2	11	.182	0	1	.000	0	0	.000	1	4	5	4	1	0	2	0	1	5.4	0.8	1.0	0.8	.186
NBA Season Totals		50	1	496	169	77	195	.395	3	16	.188	12	20	.600	7	44	51	86	66	1	22	3	51	9.9	3.4	1.0	1.7	

• COKER, John

John Michael Coker

Born: Oct. 28, 1971. Richland, WA, United States. Height: 7' Weight: 253 lbs. Drafted: — College: Boise State

YEAR TEAM	GP	GS	MIN	PTS	FGM	FGA	FG%	3PM	3PA	3P%	FTM	FTA	FT%	ORB	DRB	TRB	AST	PF	DQ	STL	BLK	TO	MPG	PPG	RPG	APG	PCM
95-96 Phoenix	5	0	11	8	4	5	.800	0	0	.000	0	0	.000	2	0	2	1	1	0	0	1	0	2.2	1.6	0.4	0.2	.952
98-99 Washington	14	0	98	31	13	31	.419	0	0	.000	5	6	.833	7	15	22	0	17	0	1	2	2	7.0	2.2	1.6	0.0	.280
00-01 Golden State	6	0	32	2	1	8	.125	0	0	.000	0	0	.000	3	2	5	2	4	0	1	0	2	5.3	0.3	0.8	0.3	-.009
NBA Season Totals	25	0	141	41	18	44	.409	0	0	.000	5	6	.833	12	17	29	3	22	0	2	3	4	5.6	1.6	1.2	0.1	....

• COLBURN, Bobby

Bobby Colburn

Born: 1911. Height: 5'10". Weight: 190 lbs. Drafted: — College: Ohio State

YEAR TEAM	GP	GS	MIN	PTS	FGM	FGA	FG%	3PM	3PA	3P%	FTM	FTA	FT%	ORB	DRB	TRB	AST	PF	DQ	STL	BLK	TO	MPG	PPG	RPG	APG	PCM
37-38 Dayton-N	11	....	....	80	32	....	....	....	....	....	16	....	....	....	....	....	....	....	....	....	....	....	....	7.3	....	....	....
NBL Season Totals	11	....	....	80	32	....	....	....	....	....	16	....	....	....	....	....	....	....	....	....	....	....	....	7.3	....	....	....

• COLEMAN, Ben

Benjamin (Big Ben) Coleman

Born: Nov. 14, 1961. Minneapolis, MN, United States. Height: 6'9". Weight: 235 lbs. Drafted: 1984 College: Maryland

YEAR TEAM	GP	GS	MIN	PTS	FGM	FGA	FG%	3PM	3PA	3P%	FTM	FTA	FT%	ORB	DRB	TRB	AST	PF	DQ	STL	BLK	TO	MPG	PPG	RPG	APG	PCM
86-87 New Jersey	68	7	1029	452	182	313	.581	0	1	.000	88	121	.727	99	189	288	37	200	7	32	31	95	15.1	6.6	4.2	0.5	.485
87-88 New Jersey	27	10	657	297	116	240	.483	0	2	.000	65	84	.774	58	115	173	39	110	4	28	16	73	24.3	11.0	6.4	1.4	.452
87-88 Philadelphia	43	14	841	296	110	213	.516	0	1	.000	76	101	.752	58	119	177	23	120	1	15	25	56	19.6	6.9	4.1	0.5	.365
88-89 Philadelphia	58	11	703	295	117	241	.485	0	0	.000	61	77	.792	49	128	177	17	120	0	10	18	46	12.1	5.1	3.1	0.3	.402
89-90 Milwaukee	22	0	305	126	46	97	.474	0	1	.000	34	41	.829	31	56	87	12	54	0	7	7	26	13.9	5.7	4.0	0.5	.435
93-94 Detroit	9	0	77	28	12	25	.480	0	0	.000	4	8	.500	10	16	26	0	9	0	2	2	7	8.6	3.1	2.9	0.0	.405
NBA Season Totals	227	42	3612	1494	583	1129	.516	0	5	.000	328	432	.759	305	623	928	128	613	12	94	99	303	15.9	6.6	4.1	0.6	....
88-89 Philadelphia	3	0	23	14	6	8	.750	0	0	.000	2	2	1.000	2	3	5	0	8	0	1	0	1	7.7	4.7	1.7	0.0	.568
NBA Playoff Totals	3	0	23	14	6	8	.750	0	0	.000	2	2	1.000	2	3	5	0	8	0	1	0	1	7.7	4.7	1.7	0.0	....

• COLEMAN, Derrick

Derrick D. Coleman

Born: June 21, 1967. Mobile, AL, United States. Height: 6'10". Weight: 230 lbs. Drafted: 1990 College: Syracuse

YEAR TEAM	GP	GS	MIN	PTS	FGM	FGA	FG%	3PM	3PA	3P%	FTM	FTA	FT%	ORB	DRB	TRB	AST	PF	DQ	STL	BLK	TO	MPG	PPG	RPG	APG	PCM
90-91 New Jersey	74	68	2602	1364	514	1100	.467	13	38	.342	323	442	.731	269	490	759	163	217	3	71	99	215	35.2	18.4	10.3	2.2	.577
91-92 New Jersey	65	58	2207	1289	483	958	.504	23	76	.303	300	393	.763	203	415	618	205	168	2	54	98	247	34.0	19.8	9.5	3.2	.649
92-93 New Jersey	76	73	2759	1572	564	1226	.460	23	99	.232	421	521	.808	247	605	852	276	210	1	92	126	243	36.3	20.7	11.2	3.6	.680
93-94 New Jersey	77	77	2778	1559	541	1209	.447	38	121	.314	439	567	.774	262	608	870	262	209	2	68	142	208	36.1	20.2	11.3	3.4	.675
94-95 New Jersey	56	54	2103	1146	371	875	.424	28	120	.233	376	490	.767	167	424	591	187	162	2	35	94	174	37.6	20.5	10.6	3.3	.597
95-96 Philadelphia	11	11	294	123	48	118	.407	7	21	.333	20	32	.625	13	59	72	31	30	0	4	10	28	26.7	11.2	6.5	2.8	.425
96-97 Philadelphia	57	54	2102	1032	364	836	.435	32	119	.269	272	365	.745	157	416	573	193	164	1	50	75	182	36.9	18.1	10.1	3.4	.552
97-98 Philadelphia	59	58	2135	1040	356	867	.411	26	98	.265	302	391	.772	149	438	587	145	144	1	46	68	159	36.2	17.6	9.9	2.5	.524
98-99 Charlotte	37	29	1178	486	168	406	.414	7	33	.212	143	190	.753	76	252	328	78	96	1	24	42	90	31.8	13.1	8.9	2.1	.482
99-00 Charlotte	74	64	2347	1239	446	979	.456	51	141	.362	296	377	.785	124	508	632	175	195	2	34	130	173	31.7	16.7	8.5	2.4	.591
00-01 Charlotte	34	3	683	277	97	255	.380	20	51	.392	63	92	.685	46	138	184	39	53	1	10	21	42	20.1	8.1	5.4	1.1	.434
01-02 Philadelphia	58	58	2080	875	331	735	.450	28	83	.337	185	227	.815	167	342	509	98	158	0	42	51	119	35.9	15.1	8.8	1.7	.463
02-03 Philadelphia	64	35	1742	602	223	498	.448	22	67	.328	134	171	.784	151	299	450	87	171	2	53	69	96	27.2	9.4	7.0	1.4	.451
NBA Season Totals	742	642	25010	12604	4506	10062	.448	318	1067	.298	3274	4258	.769	2031	4994	7025	1939	1977	18	583	1025	1976	33.7	17.0	9.5	2.6	....
91-92 New Jersey	4	4	162	89	36	74	.486	1	6	.167	16	21	.762	13	32	45	21	12	0	7	4	11	40.5	22.3	11.3	5.3	.680
92-93 New Jersey	5	5	225	134	50	94	.532	5	12	.417	29	36	.806	13	54	67	23	18	0	6	13	13	45.0	26.8	13.4	4.6	.773
93-94 New Jersey	4	4	173	98	27	68	.397	5	9	.556	39	50	.780	19	38	57	10	12	0	2	5	18	43.3	24.5	14.3	2.5	.595
99-00 Charlotte	4	4	169	81	27	57	.474	5	16	.313	22	28	.786	10	40	50	14	11	1	3	12	13	42.3	20.3	12.5	3.5	.642
00-01 Charlotte	5	0	88	27	9	34	.265	2	8	.250	7	9	.778	9	16	25	6	12	0	4	2	5	17.6	5.4	5.0	1.2	.321
01-02 Philadelphia	5	5	191	64	22	42	.524	4	13	.308	16	20	.800	15	31	46	10	10	0	1	7	5	38.2	12.8	9.2	2.0	.497
02-03 Philadelphia	12	12	449	163	59	118	.500	4	10	.400	41	47	.872	29	67	96	24	36	0	7	16	17	37.4	13.6	8.0	2.0	.466
NBA Playoff Totals	39	34	1457	656	230	487	.472	26	74	.351	170	211	.806	108	278	386	108	111	1	30	59	82	37.4	16.8	9.9	2.8	....

• COLEMAN, E.C.

E.C. Coleman Jr.

Born: Sept. 25, 1950. Flora, MS, United States. Height: 6'8". Weight: 225 lbs. Drafted: 1973 College: Houston Baptist

YEAR TEAM	GP	GS	MIN	PTS	FGM	FGA	FG%	3PM	3PA	3P%	FTM	FTA	FT%	ORB	DRB	TRB	AST	PF	DQ	STL	BLK	TO	MPG	PPG	RPG	APG	PCM
73-74 Houston	58	....	1075	303	128	250	.512	....	....	....	47	74	.635	81	171	252	76	162	4	37	20	....	18.5	5.2	4.3	1.3	.391
74-75 New Orleans	77	....	2176	622	253	568	.445	....	....	....	116	166	.699	189	360	549	105	277	10	82	37	....	28.3	8.1	7.1	1.4	.369
75-76 New Orleans	67	....	1850	491	216	479	.451	....	....	....	59	89	.663	124	295	419	87	227	3	56	30	....	27.6	7.3	6.3	1.3	.332
76-77 New Orleans	77	....	2369	662	290	628	.462	....	....	....	82	112	.732	149	399	548	103	280	9	62	32	....	30.8	8.6	7.1	1.3	.349
77-78 Golden State	72	....	1801	464	212	446	.475	....	....	....	40	55	.727	117	259	376	100	253	4	66	23	94	25.0	6.4	5.2	1.4	.322
78-79 Houston	6	....	39	11	5	7	.714	....	....	....	1	1	1.000	1	6	7	1	11	0	2	0	0	6.5	1.8	1.2	0.2	.345
NBA Season Totals	357	....	9310	2553	1104	2378	.464	....	....	....	345	497	.694	661	1490	2151	472	1210	30	305	142	94	26.1	7.2	6.0	1.3	....

• COLEMAN, Jack

Jack L. Coleman

Born: May 23, 1924. Burgin, KY, United States. Died: Dec.11, 1998. Height: 6'7". Weight: 195 lbs. Drafted: 1949 College: Louisville

YEAR TEAM	GP	GS	MIN	PTS	FGM	FGA	FG%	3PM	3PA	3P%	FTM	FTA	FT%	ORB	DRB	TRB	AST	PF	DQ	STL	BLK	TO	MPG	PPG	RPG	APG	PCM
49-50 Rochester	68	....	....	590	250	663	.377	....	....	....	90	121	.744	....	....	....	153	223	....	....	....	....	....	8.7	....	2.3	....
50-51 Rochester	67	....	....	764	315	749	.421	....	....	....	134	172	.779	....	....	584	197	193	4	....	....	....	....	11.4	8.7	2.9	....
51-52 Rochester	66	....	2606	736	308	742	.415	....	....	....	120	169	.710	....	....	692	208	218	7	....	....	....	39.5	11.2	10.5	3.2	.419
52-53 Rochester	70	....	2625	763	314	748	.420	....	....	....	135	208	.649	....	....	774	231	245	12	....	....	....	37.5	10.9	11.1	3.3	.453
53-54 Rochester	71	....	2377	686	289	714	.405	....	....	....	108	181	.597	....	....	589	158	201	3	....	....	....	33.5	9.7	8.3	2.2	.382
54-55 Rochester	72	....	2482	924	400	866	.462	....	....	....	124	183	.678	....	....	729	232	201	1	....	....	....	34.5	12.8	10.1	3.2	.529
55-56 Rochester	34	....	1369	479	195	473	.412	....	....	....	89	125	.712	....	....	344	147	121	1	....	....	....	40.3	14.1	10.1	4.3	.476
55-56 St. Louis	41	....	1369	478	195	473	.412	....	....	....	88	124	.710	....	....	344	147	121	1	....	....	....	33.4	11.7	8.4	3.6	.475

YEAR	TEAM	GP	GS	MIN	PTS	FGM	FGA	FG%	3PM	3PA	3P%	FTM	FTA	FT%	ORB	DRB	TRB	AST	PF	DQ	STL	BLK	TO	MPG	PPG	RPG	APG	PCM
56-57	St. Louis	72	....	2145	755	316	775	.408	....	....	....	123	161	.764	....	....	645	159	235	7	....	....	....	29.8	10.5	9.0	2.2	.462
57-58	St. Louis	72	....	1506	546	231	560	.413	....	....	....	84	131	.641	....	....	485	117	169	3	....	....	....	20.9	7.6	6.7	1.6	.485
NBA Season Totals		633	....	16479	6721	2813	6763	.416	....	....	....	1095	1575	.695	....	....	5186	1749	1927	39	....	....	....	26.0	10.6	8.2	2.8	
49-50	Rochester	2	....	....	15	7	20	.350	....	....	....	1	1	1.000	....	....	....	4	8	....	....	....	....	....	7.5	....	2.0	....
50-51	Rochester	14	....	....	140	55	139	.396	....	....	....	30	41	.732	....	....	179	66	49	0	....	....	....	....	10.0	12.8	4.7	....
51-52	Rochester	6	....	247	59	24	59	.407	....	....	....	11	18	.611	....	....	73	35	25	1	....	....	....	41.2	9.8	12.2	5.8	.485
52-53	Rochester	3	....	110	22	7	24	.292	....	....	....	8	10	.800	....	....	40	7	13	0	....	....	....	36.7	7.3	13.3	2.3	.383
53-54	Rochester	6	....	238	70	27	54	.500	....	....	....	16	18	.889	....	....	74	12	17	1	....	....	....	39.7	11.7	12.3	2.0	.471
54-55	Rochester	3	....	91	24	11	36	.306	....	....	....	2	9	.222	....	....	28	8	11	0	....	....	....	30.3	8.0	9.3	2.7	.324
55-56	St. Louis	8	....	331	110	44	112	.393	....	....	....	22	35	.629	....	....	79	32	31	0	....	....	....	41.4	13.8	9.9	4.0	.427
56-57	St. Louis	10	....	313	92	36	113	.319	....	....	....	20	34	.588	....	....	88	33	32	1	....	....	....	31.3	9.2	8.8	3.3	.398
57-58	St. Louis	11	....	243	99	38	89	.427	....	....	....	23	40	.575	....	....	60	19	38	1	....	....	....	22.1	9.0	5.5	1.7	.451
NBA Playoff Totals		63	....	1573	631	249	646	.385	....	....	....	133	206	.646	....	....	621	216	224	4	....	....	....	25.0	10.0	9.9	3.4	....

• COLEMAN, Norris

Norris J. Coleman

Born: Sept. 27, 1961. Jacksonville, FL, United States.   Height: 6'8".   Weight: 210 lbs.   Drafted: 1987   College: Kansas

YEAR	TEAM	GP	GS	MIN	PTS	FGM	FGA	FG%	3PM	3PA	3P%	FTM	FTA	FT%	ORB	DRB	TRB	AST	PF	DQ	STL	BLK	TO	MPG	PPG	RPG	APG	PCM
87-88	LA Clippers	29	11	431	153	66	191	.346	1	2	.500	20	36	.556	36	45	81	13	51	1	11	6	17	14.9	5.3	2.8	0.4	.220
NBA Season Totals		29	11	431	153	66	191	.346	1	2	.500	20	36	.556	36	45	81	13	51	1	11	6	17	14.9	5.3	2.8	0.4	

• COLEMAN, Paul

Paul Coleman

Born: 1915.   Height: 6'2".   Weight: 160 lbs.   Drafted: —   College: Buffalo

YEAR	TEAM	GP	GS	MIN	PTS	FGM	FGA	FG%	3PM	3PA	3P%	FTM	FTA	FT%	ORB	DRB	TRB	AST	PF	DQ	STL	BLK	TO	MPG	PPG	RPG	APG	PCM
37-38	Buffalo-N	6	....	....	25	12	....	....	....	....	....	1	....	....	....	....	....	....	....	....	....	....	....	....	4.2	....	....	....
NBL Season Totals		6	....	....	25	12	....	....	....	....	....	1	....	....	....	....	....	....	....	....	....	....	....	....	4.2	....	....	....

• COLEN, Marvin

Marvin (Marv) Colen

Born: 1915.   Height: 6'   Weight: 170 lbs.   Drafted: —   College: Loyola (IL)

YEAR	TEAM	GP	GS	MIN	PTS	FGM	FGA	FG%	3PM	3PA	3P%	FTM	FTA	FT%	ORB	DRB	TRB	AST	PF	DQ	STL	BLK	TO	MPG	PPG	RPG	APG	PCM
39-40	Chicago-N	1	....	....	0	0	....	....	....	....	....	0	....	....	....	....	....	....	....	....	....	....	....	....	0.0	....	....	....
39-40	Sheboygan-N	5	....	....	6	3	....	....	....	....	....	0	....	....	....	....	....	....	....	....	....	....	....	....	1.2	....	....	....
NBL Season Totals		6	....	....	6	3	....	....	....	....	....	0	....	....	....	....	....	....	....	....	....	....	....	....	1.0	....	....	....
39-40	Sheboygan-N	1	....	....	0	0	....	....	....	....	....	0	....	....	....	....	....	....	....	....	....	....	....	....	0.0	....	....	....
NBL Playoff Totals		1	....	....	0	0	....	....	....	....	....	0	....	....	....	....	....	....	....	....	....	....	....	....	0.0	....	....	....

• COLES, Bimbo

Vernell Eufaye (Bimbo) Coles

Born: Apr. 22, 1968. Covington, VA, United States.   Height: 6'1".   Weight: 180 lbs.   Drafted: 1990   College: Virginia Tech

YEAR	TEAM	GP	GS	MIN	PTS	FGM	FGA	FG%	3PM	3PA	3P%	FTM	FTA	FT%	ORB	DRB	TRB	AST	PF	DQ	STL	BLK	TO	MPG	PPG	RPG	APG	PCM
90-91	Miami	82	9	1355	401	162	393	.412	6	34	.176	71	95	.747	56	97	153	232	149	0	65	12	98	16.5	4.9	1.9	2.8	.351
91-92	Miami	81	28	1976	816	295	649	.455	10	52	.192	216	262	.824	69	120	189	366	151	3	73	13	170	24.4	10.1	2.3	4.5	.448
92-93	Miami	81	37	2232	855	318	686	.464	42	137	.307	177	220	.805	58	108	166	373	199	4	80	11	105	27.6	10.6	2.0	4.6	.421
93-94	Miami	76	4	1726	588	233	519	.449	20	99	.202	102	131	.779	50	109	159	263	132	0	75	12	106	22.7	7.7	2.1	3.5	.385
94-95	Miami	68	65	2207	679	261	607	.430	16	76	.211	141	174	.810	46	145	191	416	185	1	99	13	156	32.5	10.0	2.8	6.1	.377
95-96	Miami	52	52	1882	664	231	559	.413	63	172	.366	139	173	.803	38	163	201	296	175	3	63	12	125	36.2	12.8	3.9	5.7	.379
95-96	Golden State	29	3	733	228	87	218	.399	25	82	.305	29	38	.763	11	48	59	126	78	2	31	5	49	25.3	7.9	2.0	4.3	.328
96-97	Golden State	51	13	1183	311	122	314	.389	30	102	.294	37	49	.755	39	79	118	149	96	0	35	7	61	23.2	6.1	2.3	2.9	.282
97-98	Golden State	53	44	1471	423	166	438	.379	13	57	.228	78	88	.886	17	106	123	248	135	2	51	3	90	27.8	8.0	2.3	4.7	.317
98-99	Golden State	48	32	1272	455	183	414	.442	6	25	.240	83	101	.822	21	96	117	222	113	2	45	11	82	26.5	9.5	2.4	4.6	.408
99-00	Atlanta	80	54	1924	645	276	607	.455	8	39	.205	85	104	.817	30	142	172	290	178	1	58	11	103	24.1	8.1	2.2	3.6	.362
00-01	Cleveland	47	0	804	232	91	239	.381	2	16	.125	48	56	.857	9	39	48	138	87	0	27	6	59	17.1	4.9	1.0	2.9	.284
01-02	Cleveland	47	1	693	149	56	146	.384	4	20	.200	33	37	.892	12	43	55	107	59	0	13	4	31	14.7	3.2	1.2	2.3	.279
02-03	Cleveland	21	11	516	102	34	119	.286	7	25	.280	27	34	.794	10	38	48	56	43	0	11	4	18	24.6	4.9	2.3	2.7	.202
02-03	Boston	14	0	175	52	22	49	.449	0	7	.000	8	8	1.000	1	10	11	16	17	0	6	0	10	12.5	3.7	0.8	1.1	.249
NBA Season Totals		830	353	20149	6600	2537	5957	.426	252	943	.267	1274	1570	.811	467	1343	1810	3298	1797	18	732	134	1263	24.3	8.0	2.2	4.0	....
91-92	Miami	3	0	45	23	7	10	.700	1	1	1.000	8	10	.800	2	5	7	6	5	0	3	0	5	15.0	7.7	2.3	2.0	.623
93-94	Miami	5	0	140	69	25	47	.532	1	4	.250	18	23	.783	2	12	14	17	15	0	7	1	11	28.0	13.8	2.8	3.4	.487
02-03	Boston	3	0	10	0	0	4	.000	0	2	.000	0	0	.000	0	1	1	2	1	0	0	0	0	3.3	0.0	0.3	0.7	-.099
NBA Playoff Totals		11	0	195	92	32	61	.525	2	7	.286	26	33	.788	4	18	22	25	21	0	10	1	16	17.7	8.4	2.0	2.3	....

• COLLIER, Jason

Jason Jeffrey Collier

Born: Sept. 8, 1977. Springfield, OH, United States.   Height: 7'   Weight: 260 lbs.   Drafted: 2000   College: Georgia Tech

YEAR	TEAM	GP	GS	MIN	PTS	FGM	FGA	FG%	3PM	3PA	3P%	FTM	FTA	FT%	ORB	DRB	TRB	AST	PF	DQ	STL	BLK	TO	MPG	PPG	RPG	APG	PCM
00-01	Houston	23	0	222	71	27	71	.380	0	1	.000	17	24	.708	12	25	37	6	27	1	2	3	11	9.7	3.1	1.6	0.3	.228
01-02	Houston	25	2	365	106	41	95	.432	0	1	.000	24	32	.750	31	51	82	9	40	0	6	4	13	14.6	4.2	3.3	0.4	.320
02-03	Houston	13	3	104	36	17	36	.472	0	0	.000	2	2	1.000	12	17	29	1	10	0	2	1	2	8.0	2.8	2.2	0.1	.409
NBA Season Totals		61	5	691	213	85	202	.421	0	2	.000	43	58	.741	55	93	148	16	77	1	10	8	26	11.3	3.5	2.4	0.3	....

• COLLINS, Art

Arthur Collins

Born: Apr. 14, 1954. Sandersville, GA, United States.   Height: 6'4".   Weight: 185 lbs.   Drafted: 1976   College: Biscayne

YEAR	TEAM	GP	GS	MIN	PTS	FGM	FGA	FG%	3PM	3PA	3P%	FTM	FTA	FT%	ORB	DRB	TRB	AST	PF	DQ	STL	BLK	TO	MPG	PPG	RPG	APG	PCM
80-81	Atlanta	29	....	395	94	35	99	.354	0	2	.000	24	36	.667	19	22	41	25	35	0	11	1	32	13.6	3.2	1.4	0.9	.154
NBA Season Totals		29	....	395	94	35	99	.354	0	2	.000	24	36	.667	19	22	41	25	35	0	11	1	32	13.6	3.2	1.4	0.9	....

COLLINS, Don

Donald Collins

Born: Nov. 28, 1958. Toledo, OH, United States.   Height: 6'6".   Weight: 190 lbs.   Drafted: 1980   College: Washington State

YEAR	TEAM	GP	GS	MIN	PTS	FGM	FGA	FG%	3PM	3PA	3P%	FTM	FTA	FT%	ORB	DRB	TRB	AST	PF	DQ	STL	BLK	TO	MPG	PPG	RPG	APG	PCM
80-81	Atlanta	47	....	1184	597	230	530	.434	0	3	.000	137	162	.846	96	91	187	115	166	5	69	11	108	25.2	12.7	4.0	2.4	.428
80-81	Washington	34	....	661	334	130	281	.463	0	3	.000	74	110	.673	33	48	81	75	93	1	35	14	68	19.4	9.8	2.4	2.2	.417
81-82	Washington	79	18	1609	790	334	653	.511	1	12	.083	121	169	.716	101	95	196	148	195	3	89	24	134	20.4	10.0	2.5	1.9	.438
82-83	Washington	65	21	1575	765	332	635	.523	0	6	.000	101	136	.743	116	94	210	132	166	1	87	30	143	24.2	11.8	3.2	2.0	.452
83-84	Golden State	61	6	957	440	187	387	.483	1	5	.200	65	89	.730	62	67	129	67	119	1	43	14	79	15.7	7.2	2.1	1.1	.375
84-85	Washington	11	0	91	32	12	34	.353	0	0	.000	8	9	.889	10	9	19	7	5	0	7	4	8	8.3	2.9	1.7	0.6	.403
86-87	Milwaukee	6	0	57	25	10	28	.357	0	0	.000	5	7	.714	11	4	15	2	11	0	2	1	5	9.5	4.2	2.5	0.3	.288
NBA Season Totals		303	45	6134	2983	1235	2548	.485	2	29	.069	511	682	.749	429	408	837	546	755	11	332	98	545	20.2	9.8	2.8	1.8	....
81-82	Washington	7	6	149	43	19	44	.432	0	0	.000	5	7	.714	9	13	22	6	25	1	4	1	11	21.3	6.1	3.1	0.9	.193
84-85	Washington	1	0	2	0	0	0	.000	0	0	.000	0	0	.000	0	0	0	0	0	0	0	0	0	2.0	0.0	0.0	0.0	.000
NBA Playoff Totals		8	6	151	43	19	44	.432	0	0	.000	5	7	.714	9	13	22	6	25	1	4	1	11	18.9	5.4	2.8	0.8	....

COLLINS, Doug

Paul Douglas Collins

Born: July 28, 1951. Christopher, IL, United States.   Height: 6'6".   Weight: 180 lbs.   Drafted: 1973   College: Illinois State

YEAR	TEAM	GP	GS	MIN	PTS	FGM	FGA	FG%	3PM	3PA	3P%	FTM	FTA	FT%	ORB	DRB	TRB	AST	PF	DQ	STL	BLK	TO	MPG	PPG	RPG	APG	PCM
73-74	Philadelphia	25	....	436	199	72	194	.371	....	....	....	55	72	.764	7	39	46	40	65	1	13	2	....	17.4	8.0	1.8	1.6	.333
74-75	Philadelphia	81	....	2820	1453	561	1150	.488	....	....	....	331	392	.844	104	211	315	213	291	6	108	17	....	34.8	17.9	3.9	2.6	.466
75-76	Philadelphia	77	....	2995	1600	614	1196	.513	....	....	....	372	445	.836	126	181	307	191	249	2	110	24	....	38.9	20.8	4.0	2.5	.482
76-77	Philadelphia	58	....	2037	1062	426	823	.518	....	....	....	210	250	.840	64	131	195	271	174	2	70	15	....	35.1	18.3	3.4	4.7	.542
77-78	Philadelphia	79	....	2770	1553	643	1223	.526	....	....	....	267	329	.812	87	143	230	320	228	2	128	25	253	35.1	19.7	2.9	4.1	.503
78-79	Philadelphia	47	....	1595	917	358	717	.499	....	....	....	201	247	.814	36	87	123	191	139	1	52	20	132	33.9	19.5	2.6	4.1	.488
79-80	Philadelphia	36	....	963	495	191	410	.466	0	1	.000	113	124	.911	29	65	94	100	76	0	30	7	83	26.8	13.8	2.6	2.8	.426
80-81	Philadelphia	12	....	329	148	62	126	.492	0	0	.000	24	29	.828	6	23	29	42	23	0	7	4	22	27.4	12.3	2.4	3.5	.423
NBA Season Totals		415	....	13945	7427	2927	5839	.501	0	1	.000	1573	1888	.833	459	880	1339	1368	1245	14	518	114	490	33.6	17.9	3.2	3.3	....
75-76	Philadelphia	3	....	117	58	23	53	.434	....	....	....	12	14	.857	13	8	21	10	9	0	3	1	....	39.0	19.3	7.0	3.3	.487
76-77	Philadelphia	19	....	759	425	177	318	.557	....	....	....	71	96	.740	30	49	79	74	57	0	28	3	....	39.9	22.4	4.2	3.9	.554
77-78	Philadelphia	10	....	342	204	82	165	.497	....	....	....	40	49	.816	8	23	31	27	29	0	3	0	23	34.2	20.4	3.1	2.7	.452
NBA Playoff Totals		32	....	1218	687	282	536	.526	....	....	....	123	159	.774	51	80	131	111	95	0	34	4	23	38.1	21.5	4.1	3.5	....

COLLINS, James

James Edgar Collins

Born: Nov. 5, 1973. Jacksonville, FL, United States.   Height: 6'4".   Weight: 196 lbs.   Drafted: 1997   College: Florida State

YEAR	TEAM	GP	GS	MIN	PTS	FGM	FGA	FG%	3PM	3PA	3P%	FTM	FTA	FT%	ORB	DRB	TRB	AST	PF	DQ	STL	BLK	TO	MPG	PPG	RPG	APG	PCM
97-98	LA Clippers	23	0	103	59	21	55	.382	9	20	.450	8	14	.571	7	7	14	3	13	0	6	3	7	4.5	2.6	0.6	0.1	.360
NBA Season Totals		23	0	103	59	21	55	.382	9	20	.450	8	14	.571	7	7	14	3	13	0	6	3	7	4.5	2.6	0.6	0.1	....

COLLINS, Jarron

Jarron Thomas Collins

Born: Dec. 2, 1978. Northridge, CA, United States.   Height: 6'11".   Weight: 255 lbs.   Drafted: 2001   College: Stanford

YEAR	TEAM	GP	GS	MIN	PTS	FGM	FGA	FG%	3PM	3PA	3P%	FTM	FTA	FT%	ORB	DRB	TRB	AST	PF	DQ	STL	BLK	TO	MPG	PPG	RPG	APG	PCM
01-02	Utah	70	68	1441	450	158	343	.461	0	1	.000	134	181	.740	138	158	296	58	234	4	29	22	56	20.6	6.4	4.2	0.8	.335
02-03	Utah	22	7	421	120	38	86	.442	0	1	.000	44	62	.710	32	28	60	14	70	2	5	6	19	19.1	5.5	2.7	0.6	.235
NBA Season Totals		92	75	1862	570	196	429	.457	0	2	.000	178	243	.733	170	186	356	72	304	6	34	28	75	20.2	6.2	3.9	0.8	....
01-02	Utah	4	4	47	22	10	18	.556	0	0	.000	2	2	1.000	4	3	7	0	11	0	0	0	4	11.8	5.5	1.8	0.0	.266
NBA Playoff Totals		4	4	47	22	10	18	.556	0	0	.000	2	2	1.000	4	3	7	0	11	0	0	0	4	11.8	5.5	1.8	0.0	....

COLLINS, Jason

Jason Paul Collins

Born: Dec. 2, 1978. Northridge, CA, United States.   Height: 7'.   Weight: 260 lbs.   Drafted: —   College: Stanford

YEAR	TEAM	GP	GS	MIN	PTS	FGM	FGA	FG%	3PM	3PA	3P%	FTM	FTA	FT%	ORB	DRB	TRB	AST	PF	DQ	STL	BLK	TO	MPG	PPG	RPG	APG	PCM
01-02	New Jersey	77	9	1407	350	117	278	.421	1	2	.500	115	164	.701	132	169	301	81	173	1	29	47	72	18.3	4.5	3.9	1.1	.333
02-03	New Jersey	81	66	1900	460	140	338	.414	0	4	.000	180	236	.763	136	232	368	87	252	4	47	44	85	23.5	5.7	4.5	1.1	.303
NBA Season Totals		158	75	3307	810	257	616	.417	1	6	.167	295	400	.738	268	401	669	168	425	5	76	91	157	20.9	5.1	4.2	1.1	....
01-02	New Jersey	17	0	227	49	12	33	.364	0	0	.000	25	38	.658	24	17	41	7	48	2	5	6	12	13.4	2.9	2.4	0.4	.204
02-03	New Jersey	20	20	529	117	33	91	.363	0	2	.000	51	61	.836	51	74	125	17	74	2	13	12	18	26.5	5.9	6.3	0.9	.311
NBA Playoff Totals		37	20	756	166	45	124	.363	0	2	.000	76	99	.768	75	91	166	24	122	4	18	18	30	20.4	4.5	4.5	0.6	....

COLLINS, Jimmy

James E. Collins

Born: Nov. 24, 1946.   Height: 6'2".   Weight: 175 lbs.   Drafted: 1970   College: New Mexico State

YEAR	TEAM	GP	GS	MIN	PTS	FGM	FGA	FG%	3PM	3PA	3P%	FTM	FTA	FT%	ORB	DRB	TRB	AST	PF	DQ	STL	BLK	TO	MPG	PPG	RPG	APG	PCM
70-71	Chicago	55	....	478	219	92	214	.430	....	....	....	35	45	.778	....	....	54	60	43	0	....	....	....	8.7	4.0	1.0	1.1	.431
71-72	Chicago	19	....	134	62	26	71	.366	....	....	....	10	11	.909	....	....	12	10	11	0	....	....	....	7.1	3.3	0.6	0.5	.296
NBA Season Totals		74	....	612	281	118	285	.414	....	....	....	45	56	.804	....	....	66	70	54	0	....	....	....	8.3	3.8	0.9	0.9	....
70-71	Chicago	2	....	8	3	0	1	.000	....	....	....	3	3	1.000	....	....	1	0	1	0	....	....	....	4.0	1.5	0.5	0.0	.321
NBA Playoff Totals		2	....	8	3	0	1	.000	....	....	....	3	3	1.000	....	....	1	0	1	0	....	....	....	4.0	1.5	0.5	0.0	....

YEAR TEAM	GP	GS	MIN	PTS	FGM	FGA	FG%	3PM	3PA	3P%	FTM	FTA	FT%	ORB	DRB	TRB	AST	PF	DQ	STL	BLK	TO	MPG	PPG	RPG	APG	PCM

• COLONE, Joe

Joseph F. (Bells) Colone

Born: Jan. 23, 1926.   Height: 6'5".   Weight: 210 lbs.   Drafted: —   College: Bloomsburg State

YEAR TEAM	GP	GS	MIN	PTS	FGM	FGA	FG%	3PM	3PA	3P%	FTM	FTA	FT%	ORB	DRB	TRB	AST	PF	DQ	STL	BLK	TO	MPG	PPG	RPG	APG	PCM
48-49 New York	15	....	....	83	35	113	.310	....	....	....	13	19	.684	....	....	....	9	25	....	....	....	....	....	5.5	....	0.6	....
NBA Season Totals	15	....	....	83	35	113	.310	....	....	....	13	19	.684	....	....	....	9	25	....	....	....	....	....	5.5	....	0.6	....
48-49 New York	4	....	....	17	7	30	.233	....	....	....	3	6	.500	....	....	....	3	13	....	....	....	....	....	4.3	....	0.8	....
NBA Playoff Totals	4	....	....	17	7	30	.233	....	....	....	3	6	.500	....	....	....	3	13	....	....	....	....	....	4.3	....	0.8	....

• COLSON, Sean

Sean Colson

Born: July 1, 1975. Philadelphia, PA, United States.   Height: 6'   Weight: 175 lbs.   Drafted: —   College: North Carolina (Charlotte)

YEAR TEAM	GP	GS	MIN	PTS	FGM	FGA	FG%	3PM	3PA	3P%	FTM	FTA	FT%	ORB	DRB	TRB	AST	PF	DQ	STL	BLK	TO	MPG	PPG	RPG	APG	PCM
00-01 Atlanta	3	0	14	0	0	5	.000	0	1	.000	0	0	.000	0	3	3	3	0	0	0	0	2	4.7	0.0	1.0	1.0	-.020
00-01 Houston	10	0	30	15	6	19	.316	1	4	.250	2	4	.500	2	1	3	7	6	0	1	0	0	3.0	1.5	0.3	0.7	.368
NBA Season Totals	13	0	44	15	6	24	.250	1	5	.200	2	4	.500	2	4	6	10	6	0	1	0	2	3.4	1.2	0.5	0.8	....

• COLTER, Steve

Steve Colter

Born: July 24, 1962. Phoenix, AZ, United States.   Height: 6'3".   Weight: 165 lbs.   Drafted: 1984   College: New Mexico State

YEAR TEAM	GP	GS	MIN	PTS	FGM	FGA	FG%	3PM	3PA	3P%	FTM	FTA	FT%	ORB	DRB	TRB	AST	PF	DQ	STL	BLK	TO	MPG	PPG	RPG	APG	PCM
84-85 Portland	78	22	1462	556	216	477	.453	26	74	.351	98	130	.754	40	110	150	243	142	0	75	9	109	18.7	7.1	1.9	3.1	.416
85-86 Portland	81	51	1868	706	272	597	.456	27	83	.325	135	164	.823	41	136	177	257	188	0	113	10	113	23.1	8.7	2.2	3.2	.403
86-87 Chicago	27	18	473	131	49	142	.345	0	9	.000	33	39	.846	9	33	42	94	38	0	19	6	32	17.5	4.9	1.6	3.5	.332
86-87 Philadelphia	43	13	849	293	120	255	.471	4	8	.500	49	68	.721	14	52	66	116	61	0	37	6	39	19.7	6.8	1.5	2.7	.376
87-88 Philadelphia	12	0	152	37	15	40	.375	0	0	.000	7	9	.778	7	11	18	26	20	0	6	0	11	12.7	3.1	1.5	2.2	.285
87-88 Washington	56	53	1361	447	188	401	.469	3	10	.300	68	86	.791	51	104	155	235	112	0	56	14	78	24.3	8.0	2.8	4.2	.423
88-89 Washington	80	5	1425	534	203	457	.444	3	25	.120	125	167	.749	62	120	182	225	158	0	69	14	64	17.8	6.7	2.3	2.8	.404
89-90 Washington	73	1	977	361	142	297	.478	0	5	.000	77	95	.811	55	121	176	148	98	0	47	10	37	13.4	4.9	2.4	2.0	.514
90-91 Sacramento	19	0	251	58	23	56	.411	5	14	.357	7	10	.700	5	21	26	37	27	0	11	1	11	13.2	3.1	1.4	1.9	.310
94-95 Cleveland	57	7	752	196	67	169	.396	8	35	.229	54	71	.761	13	46	59	101	53	0	30	6	34	13.2	3.4	1.0	1.8	.308
NBA Season Totals	526	170	9570	3319	1295	2891	.448	76	263	.289	653	839	.778	297	754	1051	1482	897	0	463	76	528	18.2	6.3	2.0	2.8	....
84-85 Portland	9	0	166	80	36	75	.480	3	11	.273	5	8	.625	4	12	16	37	24	1	5	0	10	18.4	8.9	1.8	4.1	.487
85-86 Portland	4	4	104	26	12	26	.462	0	1	.000	2	2	1.000	3	12	15	23	13	0	5	1	6	26.0	6.5	3.8	5.8	.438
86-87 Philadelphia	2	0	8	2	1	2	.500	0	0	.000	0	0	.000	0	0	0	2	1	0	0	0	0	4.0	1.0	0.0	1.0	.343
87-88 Washington	5	5	86	32	14	31	.452	0	0	.000	4	7	.571	5	10	15	13	9	0	3	3	5	17.2	6.4	3.0	2.6	.458
94-95 Cleveland	4	0	43	12	5	10	.500	0	1	.000	2	4	.500	1	0	1	2	2	0	1	0	0	10.8	3.0	0.3	0.5	.219
NBA Playoff Totals	24	9	407	152	68	144	.472	3	13	.231	13	21	.619	13	34	47	77	49	1	14	4	21	17.0	6.3	2.0	3.2	....

• COMBS, Glen

Glen Courtney (The Kentucky Rifle) Combs

Born: Oct. 30, 1946. Hazard, KY, United States.   Height: 6'2".   Weight: 185 lbs.   Drafted: 1968   College: Virginia Tech

YEAR TEAM	GP	GS	MIN	PTS	FGM	FGA	FG%	3PM	3PA	3P%	FTM	FTA	FT%	ORB	DRB	TRB	AST	PF	DQ	STL	BLK	TO	MPG	PPG	RPG	APG	PCM
68-69 Dallas-A	72	....	2241	1112	364	868	.419	84	233	.361	300	394	.761	63	132	195	165	218	3	....	....	158	31.1	15.4	2.7	2.3	.402
69-70 Dallas-A	84	....	3260	1868	640	1474	.434	130	370	.351	458	548	.836	61	228	289	342	265	2	....	....	294	38.8	22.2	3.4	4.1	.503
70-71 Texas-A	42	....	1605	859	300	690	.435	46	129	.357	213	272	.783	36	96	132	188	124	2	....	....	132	38.2	20.5	3.1	4.5	.501
70-71 Utah-A	44	....	1599	886	310	682	.455	31	81	.383	235	274	.858	41	119	160	173	162	3	....	....	124	36.3	20.1	3.6	3.9	.527
71-72 Utah-A	84	....	2906	1388	483	1109	.436	**103**	254	**.406**	319	380	.839	52	163	215	306	255	0	....	....	191	34.6	16.5	2.6	3.6	.424
72-73 Utah-A	50	....	1488	661	228	535	.426	51	134	**.381**	154	189	.815	21	63	84	138	142	1	....	....	90	29.8	13.2	1.7	2.8	.358
73-74 Memphis-A	39	....	1369	525	199	448	.444	28	79	.354	99	132	.750	28	63	91	233	99	....	36	3	102	35.1	13.5	2.3	6.0	.437
73-74 Utah-A	37	....	617	291	105	248	.423	24	68	.353	57	80	.713	18	35	53	71	55	....	16	8	44	16.7	7.9	1.4	1.9	.424
74-75 Virginia-A	13	....	190	76	23	67	.343	6	21	.286	24	27	.889	5	6	11	23	13	....	4	2	16	14.6	5.8	0.8	1.8	.343
ABA Season Totals	465	....	15275	7666	2652	6121	.433	503	1369	.367	1859	2296	.810	325	905	1230	1639	1333	11	56	13	1151	32.8	16.5	2.6	3.5	....
68-69 Dallas-A	7	....	278	156	55	138	.399	5	28	.179	41	48	.854	7	10	17	17	18	0	....	....	21	39.7	22.3	2.4	2.4	.389
68-69 Dallas-A	6	....	251	146	56	124	.452	10	32	.313	24	31	.774	4	19	23	31	....	0	....	....	17	41.8	24.3	3.8	5.2	....
70-71 Utah-A	18	....	639	297	109	269	.405	11	31	.355	68	85	.800	29	45	74	64	67	0	....	....	47	35.5	16.5	4.1	3.6	.424
71-72 Utah-A	11	....	317	146	56	116	.483	8	22	.364	26	38	.684	7	13	20	27	37	1	....	....	21	28.8	13.3	1.8	2.5	.377
72-73 Utah-A	9	....	60	24	10	31	.323	0	8	.000	4	5	.800	2	5	7	5	12	0	....	....	9	6.7	2.7	0.8	0.6	.185
ABA Playoff Totals	51	....	1545	769	286	678	.422	34	121	.281	163	207	.787	49	92	141	144	134	1	....	....	115	30.3	15.1	2.8	2.8	....

• COMBS, Leroy

Edwin Leroy Combs

Born: Jan. 1, 1961. Oklahoma City, OK, United States.   Height: 6'8".   Weight: 210 lbs.   Drafted: 1983   College: Oklahoma State

YEAR TEAM	GP	GS	MIN	PTS	FGM	FGA	FG%	3PM	3PA	3P%	FTM	FTA	FT%	ORB	DRB	TRB	AST	PF	DQ	STL	BLK	TO	MPG	PPG	RPG	APG	PCM
83-84 Indiana	48	0	446	218	81	163	.497	0	3	.000	56	91	.615	19	37	56	38	49	0	23	18	48	9.3	4.5	1.2	0.8	.424
NBA Season Totals	48	0	446	218	81	163	.497	0	3	.000	56	91	.615	19	37	56	38	49	0	23	18	48	9.3	4.5	1.2	0.8	....

• COMEAUX, John

John Roosevelt Comeaux

Born: Sept. 15, 1943. Lafayette, LA, United States.   Height: 6'5".   Weight: 193 lbs.   Drafted: 1966   College: Grambling

YEAR TEAM	GP	GS	MIN	PTS	FGM	FGA	FG%	3PM	3PA	3P%	FTM	FTA	FT%	ORB	DRB	TRB	AST	PF	DQ	STL	BLK	TO	MPG	PPG	RPG	APG	PCM
67-68 New Orleans-A	23	....	189	77	27	63	.429	0	0	.000	23	32	.719	....	....	28	11	27	0	....	....	15	8.2	3.3	1.2	0.5	.361
ABA Season Totals	23	....	189	77	27	63	.429	0	0	.000	23	32	.719	....	....	28	11	27	0	....	....	15	8.2	3.3	1.2	0.5	....

• COMEGYS, Dallas

Dallas Alonzo Comegys

Born: Aug. 17, 1964. Philadelphia, PA, United States.   Height: 6'9".   Weight: 205 lbs.   Drafted: 1987   College: DePaul

YEAR TEAM	GP	GS	MIN	PTS	FGM	FGA	FG%	3PM	3PA	3P%	FTM	FTA	FT%	ORB	DRB	TRB	AST	PF	DQ	STL	BLK	TO	MPG	PPG	RPG	APG	PCM
87-88 New Jersey	75	17	1122	418	156	363	.430	0	1	.000	106	150	.707	54	164	218	65	175	3	36	70	113	15.0	5.6	2.9	0.9	.347
88-89 San Antonio	67	10	1119	438	166	341	.487	0	2	.000	106	161	.658	112	122	234	30	160	2	42	63	87	16.7	6.5	3.5	0.4	.395
NBA Season Totals	142	27	2241	856	322	704	.457	0	3	.000	212	311	.682	166	286	452	95	335	5	78	133	200	15.8	6.0	3.2	0.7	....

YEAR TEAM	GP	GS	MIN	PTS	FGM	FGA	FG%	3PM	3PA	3P%	FTM	FTA	FT%	ORB	DRB	TRB	AST	PF	DQ	STL	BLK	TO	MPG	PPG	RPG	APG	PCM

• COMINSKY, Jim
Jim Cominsky

Born: 1920.   Height: 6'2".   Weight: 185 lbs.   Drafted: —   College: DePaul

YEAR TEAM	GP	GS	MIN	PTS	FGM	FGA	FG%	3PM	3PA	3P%	FTM	FTA	FT%	ORB	DRB	TRB	AST	PF	DQ	STL	BLK	TO	MPG	PPG	RPG	APG	PCM
46-47 Rochester-N	5	....	....	4	2	....	....	....	....	....	0	0	.000	....	....	....	....	....	....	....	....	....	....	0.8	....	....	....
NBL Season Totals	5	....	....	4	2	....	....	....	....	....	0	0	....	....	....	....	....	....	....	....	....	....	....	0.8	....	....	....

• COMLEY, Larry
Lawrence Robert Comley

Born: Aug. 17, 1939.   Height: 6'5".   Weight: 210 lbs.   Drafted: 1961   College: Kansas State

YEAR TEAM	GP	GS	MIN	PTS	FGM	FGA	FG%	3PM	3PA	3P%	FTM	FTA	FT%	ORB	DRB	TRB	AST	PF	DQ	STL	BLK	TO	MPG	PPG	RPG	APG	PCM
63-64 Baltimore	12	....	89	25	8	37	.216	....	....	....	9	16	.563	....	....	19	12	11	0	....	....	....	7.4	2.1	1.6	1.0	.280
NBA Season Totals	12	....	89	25	8	37	.216	....	....	....	9	16	.563	....	....	19	12	11	0	....	....	....	7.4	2.1	1.6	1.0	

• CONGDON, Jeffrey
Jeffrey D. (Mutt) Congdon

Born: Oct. 17, 1943. Elkhorn, WI, United States.   Height: 6'1".   Weight: 180 lbs.   Drafted: 1966   College: Brigham Young

YEAR TEAM	GP	GS	MIN	PTS	FGM	FGA	FG%	3PM	3PA	3P%	FTM	FTA	FT%	ORB	DRB	TRB	AST	PF	DQ	STL	BLK	TO	MPG	PPG	RPG	APG	PCM
67-68 Anaheim-A	23	....	622	203	83	213	.390	8	24	.333	29	39	.744	....	....	72	74	47	1	....	....	69	27.0	8.8	3.1	3.2	.350
67-68 Denver-A	41	....	398	159	67	191	.351	5	30	.167	20	25	.800	....	....	34	59	37	0	....	....	50	9.7	3.9	0.8	1.4	.341
68-69 Denver-A	59	....	979	288	107	277	.386	5	31	.161	69	85	.812	14	79	93	135	104	1	....	....	97	16.6	4.9	1.6	2.3	.332
69-70 Denver-A	83	....	2461	812	299	775	.386	63	178	.354	151	192	.786	52	181	233	446	205	3	....	....	205	29.7	9.8	2.8	5.4	.409
70-71 New York-A	42	....	579	160	62	150	.413	4	13	.308	32	37	.865	10	44	54	97	50	0	....	....	51	13.8	3.8	1.3	2.3	.392
70-71 Utah-A	38	....	983	293	116	337	.344	14	75	.187	47	59	.797	27	62	89	155	76	0	....	....	94	25.9	7.7	2.3	4.1	.344
71-72 Dallas-A	20	....	261	80	30	86	.349	3	7	.429	17	20	.850	8	18	26	36	19	0	....	....	13	13.1	4.0	1.3	1.8	.323
ABA Season Totals	306	....	6283	1995	764	2029	.377	102	358	.285	365	457	.799	111	384	601	1002	538	5	....	....	579	20.5	6.5	2.0	3.3	
67-68 Denver-A	3	....	35	19	7	21	.333	2	8	.250	3	7	.429	....	....	4	5	5	0	....	....	3	11.7	6.3	1.3	1.7	.366
68-69 Denver-A	7	....	183	62	20	42	.476	2	0	.000	22	22	1.000	....	....	16	34	21	0	....	....	18	26.1	8.9	2.3	4.9	.474
69-70 Denver-A	12	....	313	126	43	118	.364	16	50	.320	24	32	.750	8	25	33	68	41	0	....	....	25	26.1	10.5	2.8	5.7	.468
70-71 New York-A	4	....	76	21	8	21	.381	0	1	.000	5	5	1.000	2	4	6	11	2	0	....	....	5	19.0	5.3	1.5	2.8	.366
ABA Playoff Totals	26	....	607	228	78	202	.386	18	61	.295	54	66	.818	10	29	59	118	69	0	....	....	51	23.3	8.8	2.3	4.5	

• CONLEY, Gene
Donald Eugene (Long Gene) Conley

Born: Nov. 10, 1930. Muskogee, OK, United States.   Height: 6'8".   Weight: 225 lbs.   Drafted: 1952   College: Washington State

YEAR TEAM	GP	GS	MIN	PTS	FGM	FGA	FG%	3PM	3PA	3P%	FTM	FTA	FT%	ORB	DRB	TRB	AST	PF	DQ	STL	BLK	TO	MPG	PPG	RPG	APG	PCM
52-53 Boston	39	....	461	88	35	108	.324	....	....	....	18	31	.581	....	....	171	19	74	1	....	....	....	11.8	2.3	4.4	0.5	.329
58-59 Boston	50	....	663	209	86	262	.328	....	....	....	37	64	.578	....	....	276	19	117	2	....	....	....	13.3	4.2	5.5	0.4	.383
59-60 Boston	71	....	1330	478	201	539	.373	....	....	....	76	114	.667	....	....	590	32	270	10	....	....	....	18.7	6.7	8.3	0.5	.445
60-61 Boston	75	....	1242	472	183	495	.370	....	....	....	106	153	.693	....	....	550	40	275	15	....	....	....	16.6	6.3	7.3	0.5	.467
62-63 New York	70	....	1544	630	254	651	.390	....	....	....	122	186	.656	....	....	469	70	263	10	....	....	....	22.1	9.0	6.7	1.0	.416
63-64 New York	46	....	551	192	74	189	.392	....	....	....	44	65	.677	....	....	156	21	124	2	....	....	....	12.0	4.2	3.4	0.5	.351
NBA Season Totals	351	....	5791	2069	833	2244	.371	....	....	....	403	613	.657	....	....	2212	201	1123	40	....	....	....	16.5	5.9	6.3	0.6	
58-59 Boston	11	....	157	54	24	66	.364	....	....	....	6	13	.462	....	....	75	7	40	2	....	....	....	14.3	4.9	6.8	0.6	.445
59-60 Boston	13	....	269	84	34	88	.386	....	....	....	16	22	.727	....	....	116	3	59	2	....	....	....	20.7	6.5	8.9	0.2	.409
60-61 Boston	9	....	56	31	12	33	.364	....	....	....	7	12	.583	....	....	31	1	20	0	....	....	....	6.2	3.4	3.4	0.1	.542
NBA Playoff Totals	33	....	482	169	70	187	.374	....	....	....	29	47	.617	....	....	222	11	119	4	....	....	....	14.6	5.1	6.7	0.3	

• CONLEY, Larry
George Larry Conley

Born: Jan. 22, 1944. Ashland, KY, United States.   Height: 6'3".   Weight: 175 lbs.   Drafted: —   College: Kentucky

YEAR TEAM	GP	GS	MIN	PTS	FGM	FGA	FG%	3PM	3PA	3P%	FTM	FTA	FT%	ORB	DRB	TRB	AST	PF	DQ	STL	BLK	TO	MPG	PPG	RPG	APG	PCM
67-68 Kentucky-A	1	....	18	2	1	4	.250	0	0	.000	0	0	.000	....	....	0	0	0	0	....	....	3	18.0	2.0	0.0	0.0	-.027
ABA Season Totals	1	....	18	2	1	4	.250	0	0	.000	0	0	.000	....	....	0	0	0	0	....	....	3	18.0	2.0	0.0	0.0	

• CONLIN, Ed
Edward James Conlin

Born: Sept. 2, 1933.   Height: 6'5".   Weight: 200 lbs.   Drafted: 1955   College: Fordham

YEAR TEAM	GP	GS	MIN	PTS	FGM	FGA	FG%	3PM	3PA	3P%	FTM	FTA	FT%	ORB	DRB	TRB	AST	PF	DQ	STL	BLK	TO	MPG	PPG	RPG	APG	PCM
55-56 Syracuse	66	....	1423	543	211	574	.368	....	....	....	121	178	.680	....	....	326	145	121	1	....	....	....	21.6	8.2	4.9	2.2	.440
56-57 Syracuse	71	....	2250	953	335	896	.374	....	....	....	283	368	.769	....	....	430	205	170	0	....	....	....	31.7	13.4	6.1	2.9	.452
57-58 Syracuse	60	....	1871	901	343	877	.391	....	....	....	215	270	.796	....	....	436	133	168	2	....	....	....	31.2	15.0	7.3	2.2	.490
58-59 Syracuse	57	....	1601	678	261	716	.365	....	....	....	156	211	.739	....	....	303	115	156	6	....	....	....	28.1	11.9	5.3	2.0	.392
58-59 Detroit	15	....	354	177	68	175	.389	....	....	....	41	63	.651	....	....	91	17	32	0	....	....	....	23.6	11.8	6.1	1.1	.469
59-60 Detroit	70	....	1636	781	300	831	.361	....	....	....	181	238	.761	....	....	346	126	158	2	....	....	....	23.4	11.2	4.9	1.8	.438
60-61 Philadelphia	77	....	1294	536	216	599	.361	....	....	....	104	139	.748	....	....	262	123	153	1	....	....	....	16.8	7.0	3.4	1.6	.406
61-62 Philadelphia	70	....	963	322	128	371	.345	....	....	....	66	89	.742	....	....	155	85	118	1	....	....	....	13.8	4.6	2.2	1.2	.313
NBA Season Totals	486	....	11392	4891	1862	5039	.370	....	....	....	1167	1556	.750	....	....	2349	949	1076	13	....	....	....	23.4	10.1	4.8	2.0	
55-56 Syracuse	8	....	197	84	31	85	.365	....	....	....	22	38	.579	....	....	47	9	14	0	....	....	....	24.6	10.5	5.9	1.1	.398
56-57 Syracuse	5	....	164	77	28	71	.394	....	....	....	21	27	.778	....	....	17	15	11	0	....	....	....	32.8	15.4	3.4	3.0	.427
57-58 Syracuse	3	....	113	33	14	45	.311	....	....	....	5	7	.714	....	....	21	4	10	0	....	....	....	37.7	11.0	7.0	1.3	.234
58-59 Detroit	3	....	43	10	4	16	.250	....	....	....	2	4	.500	....	....	7	4	5	0	....	....	....	14.3	3.3	2.3	1.3	.200
59-60 Detroit	2	....	20	8	3	10	.300	....	....	....	2	2	1.000	....	....	4	0	2	0	....	....	....	10.0	4.0	2.0	0.0	.249
60-61 Philadelphia	3	....	42	15	5	17	.294	....	....	....	5	5	1.000	....	....	4	4	4	0	....	....	....	14.0	5.0	1.3	1.3	.294
61-62 Philadelphia	11	....	86	26	9	45	.200	....	....	....	8	13	.615	....	....	20	3	14	0	....	....	....	7.8	2.4	1.8	0.3	.113
NBA Playoff Totals	35	....	665	253	94	289	.325	....	....	....	65	96	.677	....	....	120	39	60	0	....	....	....	19.0	7.2	3.4	1.1	

YEAR TEAM	GP	GS	MIN	PTS	FGM	FGA	FG%	3PM	3PA	3P%	FTM	FTA	FT%	ORB	DRB	TRB	AST	PF	DQ	STL	BLK	TO	MPG	PPG	RPG	APG	PCM

• CONLON, Marty
Martin McBride Conlon

Born: Jan. 19, 1968. Bronx, NY, United States.   Height: 6'10".   Weight: 224 lbs.   Drafted: —   College: Providence

YEAR TEAM	GP	GS	MIN	PTS	FGM	FGA	FG%	3PM	3PA	3P%	FTM	FTA	FT%	ORB	DRB	TRB	AST	PF	DQ	STL	BLK	TO	MPG	PPG	RPG	APG	PCM
91-92 Seattle	45	1	381	120	48	101	.475	0	0	.000	24	32	.750	33	36	69	12	40	0	9	7	27	8.5	2.7	1.5	0.3	.302
92-93 Sacramento	46	0	467	219	81	171	.474	0	4	.000	57	81	.704	48	75	123	37	43	0	13	5	28	10.2	4.8	2.7	0.8	.533
93-94 Charlotte	16	8	378	163	66	109	.606	0	1	.000	31	38	.816	34	55	89	28	36	1	5	7	22	23.6	10.2	5.6	1.8	.547
93-94 Washington	14	1	201	70	29	56	.518	0	1	.000	12	15	.800	19	31	50	6	33	0	4	1	10	14.4	5.0	3.6	0.4	.381
94-95 Milwaukee	82	3	2064	815	344	647	.532	8	29	.276	119	194	.613	160	266	426	110	218	3	42	18	123	25.2	9.9	5.2	1.3	.412
95-96 Milwaukee	74	1	958	395	153	327	.468	5	30	.167	84	110	.764	58	119	177	68	126	1	20	11	81	12.9	5.3	2.4	0.9	.367
96-97 Boston	74	15	1614	574	214	454	.471	2	10	.200	144	171	.842	128	195	323	104	154	2	46	18	111	21.8	7.8	4.4	1.4	.393
97-98 Miami	18	0	209	88	28	62	.452	0	0	.000	32	44	.727	16	30	46	12	27	0	9	5	11	11.6	4.9	2.6	0.7	.464
98-99 Miami	7	0	35	8	3	13	.231	0	0	.000	2	2	1.000	1	4	5	1	6	0	1	0	3	5.0	1.1	0.7	0.1	.006
99-00 LA Clippers	3	0	9	2	1	2	.500	0	0	.000	0	0	.000	1	1	2	0	1	0	0	0	0	3.0	0.7	0.7	0.0	.273
NBA Season Totals	379	29	6316	2454	967	1942	.498	15	75	.200	505	687	.735	498	812	1310	378	684	7	148	73	416	16.7	6.5	3.5	1.0	....
91-92 Seattle	1	0	1	2	0	1	.000	0	0	.000	2	2	1.000	0	1	1	0	0	0	0	0	0	1.0	2.0	1.0	0.0	2.000
97-98 Miami	3	0	46	7	3	7	.429	0	0	.000	1	2	.500	1	3	4	3	7	0	1	1	6	15.3	2.3	1.3	1.0	.064
NBA Playoff Totals	4	0	47	9	3	8	.375	0	0	.000	3	4	.750	1	4	5	3	7	0	1	1	6	11.8	2.3	1.3	0.8	....

• CONNER, Jimmy
Jimmy Dan Conner

Born: Mar. 20, 1953. Lawrenceburg, KY, United States.   Height: 6'4".   Weight: 190 lbs.   Drafted: 1975   College: Kentucky

YEAR TEAM	GP	GS	MIN	PTS	FGM	FGA	FG%	3PM	3PA	3P%	FTM	FTA	FT%	ORB	DRB	TRB	AST	PF	DQ	STL	BLK	TO	MPG	PPG	RPG	APG	PCM
75-76 Kentucky-A	24	....	240	106	42	86	.488	0	3	.000	22	29	.759	12	16	28	38	35	....	11	5	32	10.0	4.4	1.2	1.6	.480
ABA Season Totals	24	....	240	106	42	86	.488	0	3	.000	22	29	.759	12	16	28	38	35	....	11	5	32	10.0	4.4	1.2	1.6	....

• CONNER, Lester
Lester Allen Conner

Born: Sept. 17, 1959. Memphis, TN, United States.   Height: 6'4".   Weight: 180 lbs.   Drafted: 1982   College: Oregon State

YEAR TEAM	GP	GS	MIN	PTS	FGM	FGA	FG%	3PM	3PA	3P%	FTM	FTA	FT%	ORB	DRB	TRB	AST	PF	DQ	STL	BLK	TO	MPG	PPG	RPG	APG	PCM
82-83 Golden State	75	10	1416	369	145	303	.479	0	4	.000	79	113	.699	69	152	221	253	141	1	116	7	98	18.9	4.9	2.9	3.4	.457
83-84 Golden State	82	82	2573	907	360	730	.493	1	6	.167	186	259	.718	132	173	305	401	176	1	162	12	139	31.4	11.1	3.7	4.9	.463
84-85 Golden State	79	49	2258	640	246	546	.451	4	20	.200	144	192	.750	87	159	246	369	136	1	161	13	134	28.6	8.1	3.1	4.7	.414
85-86 Golden State	36	0	413	144	51	136	.375	2	7	.286	40	54	.741	25	37	62	43	23	0	24	1	14	11.5	4.0	1.7	1.2	.392
87-88 Houston	52	3	399	132	50	108	.463	0	7	.000	32	41	.780	20	18	38	59	31	0	38	1	31	7.7	2.5	0.7	1.1	.414
88-89 New Jersey	82	63	2532	843	309	676	.457	13	37	.351	212	269	.788	100	255	355	604	132	1	181	5	180	30.9	10.3	4.3	7.4	.551
89-90 New Jersey	82	61	2355	648	237	573	.414	2	13	.154	172	214	.804	90	175	265	385	182	0	172	8	139	28.7	7.9	3.2	4.7	.392
90-91 New Jersey	35	2	489	145	58	111	.523	0	2	.000	29	42	.690	11	46	57	58	38	0	37	1	28	14.0	4.1	1.6	1.7	.401
90-91 Milwaukee	39	2	519	115	38	96	.396	0	3	.000	39	52	.750	10	45	55	107	37	0	48	1	31	13.3	2.9	1.4	2.7	.424
91-92 Milwaukee	81	9	1420	287	103	239	.431	0	7	.000	81	115	.704	63	121	184	294	86	0	97	10	81	17.5	3.5	2.3	3.6	.433
92-93 LA Clippers	31	0	422	74	28	62	.452	0	0	.000	18	19	.947	16	33	49	65	39	0	34	4	22	13.6	2.4	1.6	2.1	.364
93-94 Indiana	11	0	169	31	14	38	.368	0	3	.000	3	6	.500	10	14	24	31	12	0	14	1	9	15.4	2.8	2.2	2.8	.374
94-95 LA Lakers	2	0	5	2	0	0	.000	0	0	.000	2	2	1.000	0	0	0	0	3	0	1	0	0	2.5	1.0	0.0	0.0	.306
NBA Season Totals	687	281	14970	4337	1639	3618	.453	22	109	.202	1037	1378	.753	633	1228	1861	2669	1036	4	1085	64	906	21.8	6.3	2.7	3.9	....
87-88 Houston	1	0	1	2	0	0	.000	0	0	.000	2	2	1.000	0	1	1	1	0	0	1	0	0	1.0	2.0	1.0	1.0	4.932
90-91 Milwaukee	1	0	7	2	1	1	1.000	0	0	.000	0	1	.000	1	0	1	2	1	0	0	0	1	7.0	2.0	1.0	2.0	.457
92-93 LA Clippers	5	0	64	21	9	12	.750	1	1	1.000	2	2	1.000	3	4	7	10	5	0	3	1	0	12.8	4.2	1.4	2.0	.575
93-94 Indiana	6	0	22	6	2	5	.400	0	0	.000	2	2	1.000	1	3	4	0	2	0	1	0	0	3.7	1.0	0.7	0.0	.314
NBA Playoff Totals	13	0	94	31	12	18	.667	1	1	1.000	6	7	.857	5	8	13	13	8	0	5	1	1	7.2	2.4	1.0	1.0	....

• CONNORS, Chuck
Kevin Joseph Aloysius (Chuck) Connors

Born: Apr. 10, 1921. Brooklyn, NY, United States. Died: Nov.10, 1992.   Height: 6'5".   Weight: 190 lbs.   Drafted: —   College: Seton Hall

YEAR TEAM	GP	GS	MIN	PTS	FGM	FGA	FG%	3PM	3PA	3P%	FTM	FTA	FT%	ORB	DRB	TRB	AST	PF	DQ	STL	BLK	TO	MPG	PPG	RPG	APG	PCM
45-46 Rochester-N	14	....	....	28	11	....	....	....	....	....	6	....	....	....	....	....	....	....	....	....	....	....	2.0	....	....	....
46-47 Boston	49	....	....	227	94	380	.247	....	....	....	39	84	.464	....	....	....	40	129	....	....	....	....	4.6	....	0.8	....
47-48 Boston	4	....	....	12	5	13	.385	....	....	....	2	3	.667	....	....	....	1	5	....	....	....	....	3.0	....	0.3	....
NBA Season Totals	53	....	....	239	99	393	.252	....	....	....	41	87	.471	....	....	....	41	134	....	....	....	....	4.5	....	0.8	....
NBL Season Totals	14	....	....	28	11	....	....	....	....	....	6	....	....	....	....	....	....	....	....	....	....	....	2.0	....	....	....
Career Totals	67	....	....	267	110	393	....	....	....	....	47	87	....	....	....	....	41	134	....	....	....	....	4.0	....	0.6	....

• COOK, Anthony
Anthony Lacquise Cook

Born: Mar. 19, 1967. Los Angeles, CA, United States.   Height: 6'9".   Weight: 205 lbs.   Drafted: 1989   College: Arizona

YEAR TEAM	GP	GS	MIN	PTS	FGM	FGA	FG%	3PM	3PA	3P%	FTM	FTA	FT%	ORB	DRB	TRB	AST	PF	DQ	STL	BLK	TO	MPG	PPG	RPG	APG	PCM
90-91 Denver	58	25	1121	307	118	283	.417	0	3	.000	71	129	.550	134	192	326	26	100	1	35	72	52	19.3	5.3	5.6	0.4	.413
91-92 Denver	22	0	115	34	15	25	.600	0	0	.000	4	6	.667	13	21	34	2	10	0	5	4	2	5.2	1.5	1.5	0.1	.516
93-94 Orlando	2	0	2	0	0	1	.000	0	0	.000	0	0	.000	0	0	0	0	2	0	0	2	1	1.0	0.0	0.0	0.0	.000
93-94 Milwaukee	23	0	201	62	26	53	.491	0	1	.000	10	25	.400	20	36	56	4	22	0	3	12	12	8.7	2.7	2.4	0.2	.392
95-96 Portland	11	0	60	15	7	16	.438	0	2	.000	1	4	.250	5	7	12	2	8	0	0	1	1	5.5	1.4	1.1	0.2	.246
NBA Season Totals	116	25	1499	418	166	378	.439	0	6	.000	86	164	.524	172	256	428	34	140	1	43	91	68	12.9	3.6	3.7	0.3	....

• COOK, Bert
Bert E. Cook

Born: Apr. 26, 1929.   Height: 6'3".   Weight: 185 lbs.   Drafted: 1952   College: Utah State

YEAR TEAM	GP	GS	MIN	PTS	FGM	FGA	FG%	3PM	3PA	3P%	FTM	FTA	FT%	ORB	DRB	TRB	AST	PF	DQ	STL	BLK	TO	MPG	PPG	RPG	APG	PCM
54-55 New York	37	....	424	118	42	133	.316	....	....	....	34	50	.680	....	....	72	33	39	0	....	....	....	11.5	3.2	1.9	0.9	.293
NBA Season Totals	37	....	424	118	42	133	.316	....	....	....	34	50	.680	....	....	72	33	39	0	....	....	....	11.5	3.2	1.9	0.9	....
54-55 New York	1	....	20	8	4	6	.667	....	....	....	0	2	.000	....	....	0	2	3	0	....	....	....	20.0	8.0	0.0	2.0	.356
NBA Playoff Totals	1	....	20	8	4	6	.667	....	....	....	0	2	.000	....	....	0	2	3	0	....	....	....	20.0	8.0	0.0	2.0	....

• COOK, Bobby

Robert Bernard (Cookie) Cook

Born: Apr. 1, 1923.   Height: 5'10".   Weight: 155 lbs.   Drafted: 1948   College: Wisconsin

YEAR TEAM	GP	GS	MIN	PTS	FGM	FGA	FG%	3PM	3PA	3P%	FTM	FTA	FT%	ORB	DRB	TRB	AST	PF	DQ	STL	BLK	TO	MPG	PPG	RPG	APG	PCM
48-49 Sheboygan-N	64	....	....	442	172	....	....	....	....	....	98	136	.721	....	....	....	....	111	....	....	....	....	....	6.9	....	....	....
49-50 Sheboygan	51	....	....	587	222	620	.358	....	....	....	143	181	.790	....	....	....	158	114	....	....	....	....	....	11.5	....	3.1	....
NBA Season Totals	51	....	....	587	222	620	.358	....	....	....	143	181	.790	....	....	....	158	114	....	....	....	....	....	11.5	....	3.1	....
NBL Season Totals	64	....	....	442	172	....	....	....	....	....	98	136	....	....	....	....	....	111	....	....	....	....	....	6.9	....	....	....
Career Totals	115	....	....	1029	394	620	....	....	....	....	241	317	....	....	....	....	158	225	....	....	....	....	....	8.9	....	1.4	....
48-49 Sheboygan-N	2	....	....	19	5	....	....	....	....	....	9	10	.900	....	....	....	....	....	....	....	....	....	....	9.5	....	....	....
49-50 Sheboygan	3	....	....	9	3	10	.300	....	....	....	3	6	.500	....	....	....	6	3	....	....	....	....	....	3.0	....	2.0	....
NBA Playoff Totals	3	....	....	9	3	10	.300	....	....	....	3	6	.500	....	....	....	6	3	....	....	....	....	....	3.0	....	2.0	....
NBL Playoff Totals	2	....	....	19	5	....	....	....	....	....	9	10	....	....	....	....	....	....	....	....	....	....	....	9.5	....	....	....
Career Playoff Totals	5	....	....	28	8	10	....	....	....	....	12	16	....	....	....	....	6	3	....	....	....	....	....	5.6	....	1.2	....

• COOK, Darwin

Darwin Louis Cook

Born: Aug. 6, 1958. Los Angeles, CA, United States.   Height: 6'3".   Weight: 184 lbs.   Drafted: 1980   College: Portland

YEAR TEAM	GP	GS	MIN	PTS	FGM	FGA	FG%	3PM	3PA	3P%	FTM	FTA	FT%	ORB	DRB	TRB	AST	PF	DQ	STL	BLK	TO	MPG	PPG	RPG	APG	PCM
80-81 New Jersey	81	....	1980	904	383	819	.468	6	25	.240	132	180	.733	96	140	236	297	197	4	141	36	178	24.4	11.2	2.9	3.7	.471
81-82 New Jersey	82	17	2090	899	387	803	.482	7	31	.226	118	162	.728	52	103	155	319	196	2	146	24	172	25.5	11.0	1.9	3.9	.426
82-83 New Jersey	82	47	2625	1080	443	986	.449	8	38	.211	186	242	.769	73	167	240	448	213	2	194	48	238	32.0	13.2	2.9	5.5	.450
83-84 New Jersey	82	31	1870	714	304	687	.443	11	46	.239	95	126	.754	51	105	156	356	184	3	164	36	139	22.8	8.7	1.9	4.3	.450
84-85 New Jersey	58	9	1063	473	212	453	.468	2	23	.087	47	54	.870	21	71	92	160	96	0	74	10	75	18.3	8.2	1.6	2.8	.438
85-86 New Jersey	79	33	1965	629	267	627	.426	11	53	.208	84	111	.757	51	126	177	390	172	0	156	22	134	24.9	8.0	2.2	4.9	.420
86-87 Washington	82	2	1420	614	265	622	.426	2	23	.087	82	103	.796	46	99	145	151	136	0	98	17	98	17.3	7.5	1.8	1.8	.367
88-89 San Antonio	36	0	757	346	147	315	.467	6	31	.194	46	56	.821	21	38	59	84	77	0	43	4	61	21.0	9.6	1.6	2.3	.371
88-89 Denver	30	4	386	161	71	163	.436	2	10	.200	17	22	.773	13	35	48	43	44	0	28	6	27	12.9	5.4	1.6	1.4	.388
NBA Season Totals	612	143	14156	5820	2479	5475	.453	55	280	.196	807	1056	.764	424	884	1308	2248	1315	11	1044	203	1122	23.1	9.5	2.1	3.7	....
81-82 New Jersey	2	2	86	28	13	33	.394	0	3	.000	2	6	.333	0	3	3	9	7	0	2	0	9	43.0	14.0	1.5	4.5	.144
82-83 New Jersey	2	2	63	20	9	27	.333	0	1	.000	2	2	1.000	3	3	6	10	8	0	1	0	4	31.5	10.0	3.0	5.0	.220
83-84 New Jersey	11	0	185	81	30	82	.366	4	13	.308	17	24	.708	8	10	18	31	26	0	15	0	21	16.8	7.4	1.6	2.8	.333
84-85 New Jersey	1	0	7	6	3	4	.750	0	0	.000	0	0	.000	0	0	0	1	2	0	0	0	2	7.0	6.0	0.0	1.0	.477
85-86 New Jersey	3	0	77	28	13	29	.448	0	4	.000	2	6	.333	3	4	7	17	11	1	5	2	6	25.7	9.3	2.3	5.7	.413
86-87 Washington	3	0	41	14	6	24	.250	1	2	.500	1	2	.500	4	3	7	3	4	0	4	0	0	13.7	4.7	2.3	1.0	.204
88-89 Denver	3	3	66	31	12	24	.500	1	2	.500	6	6	1.000	2	11	13	11	12	0	3	0	4	22.0	10.3	4.3	3.7	.563
NBA Playoff Totals	25	7	525	208	86	223	.386	6	25	.240	30	46	.652	20	34	54	82	70	1	30	4	46	21.0	8.3	2.2	3.3	....

• COOK, Jeff

Jeffrey James Cook

Born: Oct. 21, 1956. West Covina, CA, United States.   Height: 6'10".   Weight: 215 lbs.   Drafted: 1978   College: Idaho State

YEAR TEAM	GP	GS	MIN	PTS	FGM	FGA	FG%	3PM	3PA	3P%	FTM	FTA	FT%	ORB	DRB	TRB	AST	PF	DQ	STL	BLK	TO	MPG	PPG	RPG	APG	PCM
79-80 Phoenix	66	....	904	362	129	275	.469	0	3	.000	104	129	.806	90	151	241	84	102	0	28	18	73	13.7	5.5	3.7	1.3	.507
80-81 Phoenix	79	....	2192	672	286	616	.464	0	5	.000	100	155	.645	170	297	467	201	236	3	82	54	142	27.7	8.5	5.9	2.5	.400
81-82 Phoenix	76	22	1298	391	151	358	.422	0	2	.000	89	134	.664	112	189	301	100	174	1	37	23	84	17.1	5.1	4.0	1.3	.356
82-83 Phoenix	45	2	551	163	61	142	.430	0	2	.000	41	54	.759	44	85	129	58	89	0	12	13	54	12.2	3.6	2.9	1.3	.359
82-83 Cleveland	30	20	782	212	87	162	.537	0	1	.000	38	50	.760	75	131	206	44	92	3	27	18	48	26.1	7.1	6.9	1.5	.421
83-84 Cleveland	81	21	1950	471	188	387	.486	1	2	.500	94	130	.723	174	310	484	123	282	7	68	47	89	24.1	5.8	6.0	1.5	.382
84-85 Cleveland	18	4	440	109	46	105	.438	0	1	.000	17	27	.630	41	63	104	23	53	0	5	9	16	24.4	6.1	5.8	1.3	.328
84-85 San Antonio	54	1	848	214	92	174	.529	0	0	.000	30	37	.811	81	129	210	39	150	2	25	14	32	15.7	4.0	3.9	0.7	.364
85-86 San Antonio	34	0	356	82	28	67	.418	0	1	.000	26	41	.634	31	50	81	21	64	0	13	11	10	10.5	2.4	2.4	0.6	.337
85-86 Utah	2	0	17	7	3	6	.500	0	0	.000	1	1	1.000	2	3	5	0	1	0	0	0	3	8.5	3.5	2.5	0.0	.330
87-88 Phoenix	33	0	359	51	14	59	.237	0	1	.000	23	28	.821	37	69	106	14	64	1	9	8	13	10.9	1.5	3.2	0.4	.263
NBA Season Totals	518	70	9697	2734	1085	2351	.462	1	18	.056	563	786	.716	857	1477	2334	707	1307	17	306	215	564	18.7	5.3	4.5	1.4	....
79-80 Phoenix	7	....	98	54	16	24	.667	0	0	.000	22	26	.846	5	16	21	7	10	0	4	2	5	14.0	7.7	3.0	1.0	.694
80-81 Phoenix	7	....	206	65	25	54	.463	1	1	1.000	14	19	.737	17	30	47	11	29	1	1	0	10	29.4	9.3	6.7	1.6	.338
81-82 Phoenix	7	0	45	8	4	8	.500	0	0	.000	0	0	.000	6	3	9	7	5	0	2	2	2	6.4	1.1	1.3	1.0	.438
84-85 San Antonio	5	0	98	35	9	18	.500	0	1	.000	17	25	.680	6	23	29	4	23	0	5	6	6	19.6	7.0	5.8	0.8	.491
85-86 Utah	4	0	21	5	1	4	.250	0	0	.000	3	4	.750	1	4	5	2	4	0	0	0	0	5.3	1.3	1.3	0.5	.318
NBA Playoff Totals	30	0	468	167	55	108	.509	1	2	.500	56	74	.757	35	76	111	31	71	1	12	10	23	15.6	5.6	3.7	1.0	....

• COOK, Norm

Norman Cook

Born: Mar. 21, 1955. Chicago, IL, United States.   Height: 6'8".   Weight: 210 lbs.   Drafted: 1976   College: Kansas

YEAR TEAM	GP	GS	MIN	PTS	FGM	FGA	FG%	3PM	3PA	3P%	FTM	FTA	FT%	ORB	DRB	TRB	AST	PF	DQ	STL	BLK	TO	MPG	PPG	RPG	APG	PCM
76-77 Boston	25	....	138	63	27	72	.375	....	....	....	9	17	.529	10	17	27	5	27	0	10	3	....	5.5	2.5	1.1	0.2	.276
77-78 Denver	2	....	10	2	1	3	.333	....	....	....	0	0	.000	1	2	3	1	4	0	0	0	0	5.0	1.0	1.5	0.5	.225
NBA Season Totals	27	....	148	65	28	75	.373	....	....	....	9	17	.529	11	19	30	6	31	0	10	3	0	5.5	2.4	1.1	0.2	....
76-77 Boston	1	....	3	4	2	2	1.000	....	....	....	0	0	.000	0	0	0	0	0	0	0	0	....	3.0	4.0	0.0	0.0	1.333
NBA Playoff Totals	1	....	3	4	2	2	1.000	....	....	....	0	0	.000	0	0	0	0	0	0	0	0	....	3.0	4.0	0.0	0.0	....

• COOK, Ted

Theodore Walter Cook

Born: Feb. 6, 1922. Birmingham, AL, United States. Died: May 2, 1990.   Height: 6'   Weight: 160 lbs.   Drafted: —   College: Alabama

YEAR TEAM	GP	GS	MIN	PTS	FGM	FGA	FG%	3PM	3PA	3P%	FTM	FTA	FT%	ORB	DRB	TRB	AST	PF	DQ	STL	BLK	TO	MPG	PPG	RPG	APG	PCM
47-48 Minneapolis-N	2	....	....	0	0	....	....	....	....	....	0	0	.000	....	....	....	....	....	....	....	....	....	....	0.0	....	....	....
48-49 Hammond-N	5	....	....	1	0	....	....	....	....	....	1	2	.500	....	....	....	....	....	....	....	....	....	....	0.2	....	....	....
48-49 Sheboygan-N	4	....	....	6	1	....	....	....	....	....	4	4	1.000	....	....	....	....	....	....	....	....	....	....	1.5	....	....	....
NBL Season Totals	11	....	....	7	1	....	....	....	....	....	5	6	....	....	....	....	....	....	....	....	....	....	....	0.6	....	....	....

• COOKE, David

David D. Cooke

Born: Sept. 27, 1963. Sacramento, CA, United States.   Height: 6'8".   Weight: 230 lbs.   Drafted: —   College: St. Mary's

YEAR TEAM	GP	GS	MIN	PTS	FGM	FGA	FG%	3PM	3PA	3P%	FTM	FTA	FT%	ORB	DRB	TRB	AST	PF	DQ	STL	BLK	TO	MPG	PPG	RPG	APG	PCM
85-86 Sacramento	6	0	38	9	2	11	.182	0	0	.000	5	10	.500	5	5	10	1	5	0	4	0	2	6.3	1.5	1.7	0.2	.216
NBA Season Totals	6	0	38	9	2	11	.182	0	0	.000	5	10	.500	5	5	10	1	5	0	4	0	2	6.3	1.5	1.7	0.2	....

• COOKE, Joe

Joseph Cooke

Born: Aug. 14, 1948.   Height: 6'3".   Weight: 175 lbs.   Drafted: 1970   College: Indiana

YEAR TEAM	GP	GS	MIN	PTS	FGM	FGA	FG%	3PM	3PA	3P%	FTM	FTA	FT%	ORB	DRB	TRB	AST	PF	DQ	STL	BLK	TO	MPG	PPG	RPG	APG	PCM
70-71 Cleveland	73	....	725	316	134	341	.393	....	....	....	48	59	.814	....	....	114	93	135	2	....	....	....	9.9	4.3	1.6	1.3	.385
NBA Season Totals	73	....	725	316	134	341	.393	....	....	....	48	59	.814	....	....	114	93	135	2	....	....	....	9.9	4.3	1.6	1.3	

• COOPER, Chuck

Charles H. (Chuck) Cooper

Born: Sept. 29, 1926. Died: Feb.5, 1984.   Height: 6'5".   Weight: 210 lbs.   Drafted: 1950   College: Duquesne

HOF: 1977

YEAR TEAM	GP	GS	MIN	PTS	FGM	FGA	FG%	3PM	3PA	3P%	FTM	FTA	FT%	ORB	DRB	TRB	AST	PF	DQ	STL	BLK	TO	MPG	PPG	RPG	APG	PCM
50-51 Boston	66	....	....	615	207	601	.344	....	....	....	201	267	.753	....	....	562	174	219	7	....	....	....		9.3	8.5	2.6	
51-52 Boston	66	....	1976	543	197	545	.361	....	....	....	149	201	.741	....	....	502	134	219	8	....	....	....	29.9	8.2	7.6	2.0	.369
52-53 Boston	70	....	1994	458	157	466	.337	....	....	....	144	190	.758	....	....	439	112	258	11	....	....	....	28.5	6.5	6.3	1.6	.293
53-54 Boston	70	....	1101	234	78	261	.299	....	....	....	78	116	.672	....	....	304	74	150	1	....	....	....	15.7	3.3	4.3	1.1	.317
54-55 Milwaukee	70	....	1749	573	193	569	.339	....	....	....	187	249	.751	....	....	385	151	210	8	....	....	....	25.0	8.2	5.5	2.2	.381
55-56 St. Louis	35	....	574	178	58	172	.337	....	....	....	62	84	.738	....	....	138	61	71	0	....	....	....	16.4	5.1	3.9	1.7	.412
55-56 Fort Wayne	32	....	570	124	43	136	.316	....	....	....	38	49	.776	....	....	101	27	69	0	....	....	....	17.8	3.9	3.2	0.8	.234
NBA Season Totals	409	....	7964	2725	933	2750	.339	....	....	....	859	1156	.743	....	....	2431	733	1196	35	....	....	....	19.5	6.7	5.9	1.8	
50-51 Boston	2	....	....	10	4	12	.333	....	....	....	2	5	.400	....	....	13	3	8	0	....	....	....		5.0	6.5	1.5	
51-52 Boston	3	....	128	33	8	25	.320	....	....	....	17	19	.895	....	....	16	4	17	2	....	....	....	42.7	11.0	5.3	1.3	.240
52-53 Boston	6	....	195	60	19	48	.396	....	....	....	22	27	.815	....	....	39	14	27	2	....	....	....	32.5	10.0	6.5	2.3	.377
53-54 Boston	6	....	108	24	8	16	.500	....	....	....	8	11	.727	....	....	31	4	21	1	....	....	....	18.0	4.0	5.2	0.7	.342
55-56 Fort Wayne	9	....	59	12	5	26	.192	....	....	....	2	3	.667	....	....	17	2	5	0	....	....	....	6.6	1.3	1.9	0.2	.155
NBA Playoff Totals	26	....	490	139	44	127	.346	....	....	....	51	65	.785	....	....	116	27	78	5	....	....	....	18.8	5.3	4.5	1.0	

• COOPER, Duane

Samuel Duane Cooper

Born: June 25, 1969. Benton Harbor, MI, United States.   Height: 6'1".   Weight: 185 lbs.   Drafted: 1992   College: USC

YEAR TEAM	GP	GS	MIN	PTS	FGM	FGA	FG%	3PM	3PA	3P%	FTM	FTA	FT%	ORB	DRB	TRB	AST	PF	DQ	STL	BLK	TO	MPG	PPG	RPG	APG	PCM
92-93 LA Lakers	65	0	645	156	62	158	.392	7	30	.233	25	35	.714	13	37	50	150	66	0	18	2	72	9.9	2.4	0.8	2.3	.293
93-94 Phoenix	23	2	136	48	18	41	.439	1	7	.143	11	15	.733	2	7	9	28	12	0	3	0	21	5.9	2.1	0.4	1.2	.306
NBA Season Totals	88	2	781	204	80	199	.402	8	37	.216	36	50	.720	15	44	59	178	78	0	21	2	93	8.9	2.3	0.7	2.0	
92-93 LA Lakers	2	0	4	0	0	6	.000	0	3	.000	0	0	.000	2	0	2	1	0	0	0	0	0	2.0	0.0	1.0	0.5	-.666
NBA Playoff Totals	2	0	4	0	0	6	.000	0	3	.000	0	0	.000	2	0	2	1	0	0	0	0	0	2.0	0.0	1.0	0.5	....

• COOPER, Joe

Joseph Edward Cooper

Born: Sept. 1, 1957. Houston, TX, United States.   Height: 6'10".   Weight: 230 lbs.   Drafted: 1981   College: Colorado

YEAR TEAM	GP	GS	MIN	PTS	FGM	FGA	FG%	3PM	3PA	3P%	FTM	FTA	FT%	ORB	DRB	TRB	AST	PF	DQ	STL	BLK	TO	MPG	PPG	RPG	APG	PCM
81-82 New Jersey	1	0	11	2	1	2	.500	0	0	.000	0	0	.000	1	1	2	0	2	0	0	0	1	11.0	2.0	2.0	0.0	.098
82-83 LA Lakers	2	0	11	2	1	4	.250	0	0	.000	0	0	.000	2	0	2	0	3	0	1	1	3	5.5	1.0	1.0	0.0	-.105
82-83 Washington	5	0	47	15	5	9	.556	0	0	.000	5	9	.556	4	9	13	2	7	0	0	0	6	9.4	3.0	2.6	0.4	.318
82-83 San Diego	13	4	275	73	31	59	.525	0	0	.000	11	20	.550	36	35	71	15	39	0	8	19	23	21.2	5.6	5.5	1.2	.401
84-85 Seattle	3	1	45	17	7	15	.467	0	0	.000	3	6	.500	3	6	9	2	7	1	2	1	0	15.0	5.7	3.0	0.7	.405
NBA Season Totals	24	5	389	109	45	89	.506	0	0	.000	19	35	.543	46	51	97	19	58	1	11	21	33	16.2	4.5	4.0	0.8	....

• COOPER, Michael

Michael Jerome Cooper

Born: Apr. 15, 1956. Los Angeles, CA, United States.   Height: 6'5".   Weight: 170 lbs.   Drafted: 1978   College: New Mexico

YEAR TEAM	GP	GS	MIN	PTS	FGM	FGA	FG%	3PM	3PA	3P%	FTM	FTA	FT%	ORB	DRB	TRB	AST	PF	DQ	STL	BLK	TO	MPG	PPG	RPG	APG	PCM
78-79 LA Lakers	3	....	7	6	3	6	.500	....	....	....	0	0	.000	0	0	0	0	1	0	1	0	1	2.3	2.0	0.0	0.0	.408
79-80 LA Lakers	82	....	1973	722	303	578	.524	5	20	.250	111	143	.776	101	128	229	221	215	3	86	38	139	24.1	8.8	2.8	2.7	.404
80-81 LA Lakers	81	....	2625	763	321	654	.491	4	19	.211	117	149	.785	121	215	336	332	249	4	133	78	162	32.4	9.4	4.1	4.1	.398
81-82 LA Lakers	76	14	2197	907	383	741	.517	2	17	.118	139	171	.813	84	185	269	230	216	1	120	61	152	28.9	11.9	3.5	3.0	.449
82-83 LA Lakers	82	3	2148	639	266	497	.535	5	21	.238	102	130	.785	82	192	274	315	208	0	115	50	131	26.2	7.8	3.3	3.8	.441
83-84 LA Lakers	82	9	2387	739	273	549	.497	38	121	.314	155	185	.838	53	209	262	482	267	3	113	67	148	29.1	9.0	3.2	5.9	.475
84-85 LA Lakers	82	20	2189	702	276	593	.465	35	123	.285	115	133	.865	56	199	255	429	208	0	93	49	156	26.7	8.6	3.1	5.2	.450
85-86 LA Lakers	82	15	2269	758	274	606	.452	63	163	.387	147	170	.865	44	200	244	466	238	2	89	43	148	27.7	9.2	3.0	5.7	.458
86-87 LA Lakers	82	2	2253	859	322	736	.438	89	231	.385	126	148	.851	58	196	254	373	199	1	78	43	98	27.5	10.5	3.1	4.5	.456
87-88 LA Lakers	61	18	1793	532	189	482	.392	57	178	.320	97	113	.858	50	178	228	289	136	1	66	26	104	29.4	8.7	3.7	4.7	.389
88-89 LA Lakers	80	13	1943	587	213	494	.431	80	210	.381	81	93	.871	33	158	191	314	186	0	72	32	96	24.3	7.3	2.4	3.9	.388
89-90 LA Lakers	80	10	1851	515	191	493	.387	50	157	.318	83	94	.883	59	168	227	215	206	1	67	36	88	23.1	6.4	2.8	2.7	.316
NBA Season Totals	873	94	23635	7729	3014	6429	.469	428	1260	.340	1273	1529	.833	741	2028	2769	3666	2329	16	1033	523	1423	27.1	8.9	3.2	4.2	....
79-80 LA Lakers	16	....	464	145	57	140	.407	0	2	.000	31	36	.861	28	31	59	58	54	0	24	11	29	29.0	9.1	3.7	3.6	.357
80-81 LA Lakers	3	....	102	32	11	20	.550	0	3	.000	10	14	.714	2	8	10	7	7	0	6	0	7	34.0	10.7	3.3	2.3	.339
81-82 LA Lakers	14	0	383	166	70	124	.565	1	2	.500	25	34	.735	19	42	61	62	47	0	24	11	29	27.4	11.9	4.4	4.4	.572
82-83 LA Lakers	15	1	453	141	53	114	.465	1	7	.143	34	41	.829	12	47	59	44	54	1	26	6	23	30.2	9.4	3.9	2.9	.371
83-84 LA Lakers	21	21	723	238	88	191	.461	12	36	.333	50	62	.806	20	62	82	119	80	1	24	20	29	34.4	11.3	3.9	5.7	.438
84-85 LA Lakers	19	0	501	198	71	126	.563	8	26	.308	48	52	.923	12	64	76	93	46	0	21	9	36	26.4	10.4	4.0	4.9	.575
85-86 LA Lakers	14	0	421	136	54	115	.470	19	41	.463	9	11	.818	16	30	46	68	24	0	18	4	21	30.1	9.7	3.3	4.9	.458
86-87 LA Lakers	18	0	522	234	77	159	.484	34	70	.486	46	54	.852	8	51	59	90	46	0	25	14	37	29.0	13.0	3.3	5.0	.547
87-88 LA Lakers	24	0	588	153	54	131	.412	25	62	.403	20	27	.741	15	43	58	66	57	0	19	9	21	24.5	6.4	2.4	2.8	.310

YEAR	TEAM	GP	GS	MIN	PTS	FGM	FGA	FG%	3PM	3PA	3P%	FTM	FTA	FT%	ORB	DRB	TRB	AST	PF	DQ	STL	BLK	TO	MPG	PPG	RPG	APG	PCM
88-89	LA Lakers	15	4	414	115	37	89	.416	21	55	.382	20	24	.833	9	31	40	71	38	0	9	8	17	27.6	7.7	2.7	4.7	.387
89-90	LA Lakers	9	0	173	23	10	35	.286	3	12	.250	0	0	.000	11	13	24	25	21	0	7	4	7	19.2	2.6	2.7	2.8	.246
NBA Playoff Totals		168	26	4744	1581	582	1244	.468	124	316	.392	293	355	.825	152	422	574	703	474	2	203	96	256	28.2	9.4	3.4	4.2	....

• COOPER, Wayne

Artis Wayne (Coop) Cooper

Born: Nov. 16, 1956. Milan, GA, United States.   Height: 6'10".   Weight: 220 lbs.   Drafted: 1978   College: New Orleans

YEAR	TEAM	GP	GS	MIN	PTS	FGM	FGA	FG%	3PM	3PA	3P%	FTM	FTA	FT%	ORB	DRB	TRB	AST	PF	DQ	STL	BLK	TO	MPG	PPG	RPG	APG	PCM
78-79	Golden State	65	....	795	297	128	293	.437	....	....	....	41	61	.672	90	190	280	21	118	0	7	44	52	12.2	4.6	4.3	0.3	.454
79-80	Golden State	79	....	1781	871	367	750	.489	1	4	.250	136	181	.751	202	305	507	42	246	5	20	79	142	22.5	11.0	6.4	0.5	.482
80-81	Utah	71	....	1420	489	213	471	.452	1	3	.333	62	90	.689	166	274	440	52	219	8	18	51	78	20.0	6.9	6.2	0.7	.416
81-82	Dallas	76	38	1818	682	281	669	.420	1	8	.125	119	160	.744	200	350	550	115	285	10	37	106	91	23.9	9.0	7.2	1.5	.469
82-83	Portland	80	60	2099	775	320	723	.443	0	5	.000	135	197	.685	214	397	611	116	318	5	27	136	160	26.2	9.7	7.6	1.5	.439
83-84	Portland	81	38	1662	793	304	663	.459	0	7	.000	185	230	.804	176	300	476	76	247	2	26	106	113	20.5	9.8	5.9	0.9	.520
84-85	Denver	80	78	2031	969	404	856	.472	0	2	.000	161	235	.685	229	402	631	86	304	2	28	197	152	25.4	12.1	7.9	1.1	.551
85-86	Denver	78	78	2112	1021	422	906	.466	3	7	.429	174	219	.795	190	420	610	81	315	6	42	227	117	27.1	13.1	7.8	1.0	.568
86-87	Denver	69	64	1561	549	235	524	.448	0	3	.000	79	109	.725	162	311	473	68	257	5	13	101	76	22.6	8.0	6.9	1.0	.445
87-88	Denver	45	32	865	286	118	270	.437	0	1	.000	50	67	.746	98	172	270	30	145	3	12	94	59	19.2	6.4	6.0	0.7	.458
88-89	Denver	79	72	1864	520	220	444	.495	1	4	.250	79	106	.745	212	407	619	78	302	7	36	211	71	23.6	6.6	7.8	1.0	.527
89-90	Portland	79	0	1176	301	138	304	.454	0	3	.000	25	39	.641	118	221	339	44	211	2	18	95	40	14.9	3.8	4.3	0.6	.402
90-91	Portland	67	1	746	147	57	145	.393	0	1	.000	33	42	.786	54	134	188	22	120	0	7	61	20	11.1	2.2	2.8	0.3	.333
91-92	Portland	35	0	344	77	35	82	.427	0	0	.000	7	11	.636	38	63	101	21	57	0	4	27	14	9.8	2.2	2.9	0.6	.399
NBA Season Totals		984	461	20274	7777	3242	7100	.457	7	48	.146	1286	1747	.736	2149	3946	6095	852	3144	55	295	1535	1185	20.6	7.9	6.2	0.9	....
82-83	Portland	7	7	228	87	36	74	.486	0	0	.000	15	17	.882	24	32	56	9	33	3	2	8	17	32.6	12.4	8.0	1.3	.399
83-84	Cleveland	5	1	104	24	10	27	.370	0	0	.000	4	8	.500	11	9	20	4	14	0	1	4	5	20.8	4.8	4.0	0.8	.218
84-85	Denver	15	12	321	164	67	143	.469	0	0	.000	30	40	.750	34	59	93	20	52	0	8	36	19	21.4	10.9	6.2	1.3	.609
85-86	Denver	8	4	154	63	24	56	.429	0	1	.000	15	22	.682	11	29	40	7	31	2	2	5	11	19.3	7.9	5.0	0.9	.367
86-87	Denver	3	1	41	12	5	12	.417	0	0	.000	2	2	1.000	6	11	17	2	9	0	0	1	1	13.7	4.0	5.7	0.7	.470
87-88	Denver	9	0	96	18	8	23	.348	0	0	.000	2	2	1.000	16	17	33	6	19	0	3	8	4	10.7	2.0	3.7	0.7	.405
88-89	Denver	3	3	44	12	6	12	.500	0	0	.000	0	0	.000	4	9	13	2	10	0	1	2	0	14.7	4.0	4.3	0.7	.427
89-90	Portland	18	0	248	48	19	47	.404	0	0	.000	10	19	.526	25	46	71	5	40	0	5	29	5	13.8	2.7	3.9	0.3	.394
90-91	Portland	3	0	13	2	1	2	.500	0	0	.000	0	0	.000	1	4	5	1	2	0	0	1	1	4.3	0.7	1.7	0.3	.379
91-92	Portland	3	0	27	4	2	4	.500	0	0	.000	0	0	.000	1	7	8	0	4	0	0	3	1	9.0	1.3	2.7	0.0	.355
NBA Playoff Totals		74	28	1276	434	178	400	.445	0	1	.000	78	110	.709	133	223	356	56	214	5	22	96	64	17.2	5.9	4.8	0.8	....

• COPA, Tom

Thomas James Copa

Born: Oct. 30, 1964. Robbinsdale, MN, United States.   Height: 6'10".   Weight: 275 lbs.   Drafted: —   College: Marquette

YEAR	TEAM	GP	GS	MIN	PTS	FGM	FGA	FG%	3PM	3PA	3P%	FTM	FTA	FT%	ORB	DRB	TRB	AST	PF	DQ	STL	BLK	TO	MPG	PPG	RPG	APG	PCM
91-92	San Antonio	33	1	132	48	22	40	.550	0	0	.000	4	13	.308	14	22	36	3	29	0	2	6	7	4.0	1.5	1.1	0.1	.388
NBA Season Totals		33	1	132	48	22	40	.550	0	0	.000	4	13	.308	14	22	36	3	29	0	2	6	7	4.0	1.5	1.1	0.1	....

• COPE, Robert

Robert (Bob) Cope

Born: 1911.   Height: 6'4".   Weight: 190 lbs.   Drafted: —   College: Mt. Union

YEAR	TEAM	GP	GS	MIN	PTS	FGM	FGA	FG%	3PM	3PA	3P%	FTM	FTA	FT%	ORB	DRB	TRB	AST	PF	DQ	STL	BLK	TO	MPG	PPG	RPG	APG	PCM
37-38	Wingfoots-N	15	....	....	71	26	....	....	....	....	....	19	....	....	....	....	....	....	....	....	....	....	....	4.7	....	....	....
NBL Season Totals		15	....	....	71	26	....	....	....	....	....	19	....	....	....	....	....	....	....	....	....	....	....	4.7	....	....	....
37-38	Wingfoots-N	5	....	....	18	7	....	....	....	....	....	4	....	....	....	....	....	....	....	....	....	....	....	3.6	....	....	....
NBL Playoff Totals		5	....	....	18	7	....	....	....	....	....	4	....	....	....	....	....	....	....	....	....	....	....	3.6	....	....	....

• COPELAND, Hollis

Hollis Alphonso Copeland Jr.

Born: Dec. 20, 1955. Trenton, NJ, United States.   Height: 6'6".   Weight: 180 lbs.   Drafted: 1978   College: Rutgers

YEAR	TEAM	GP	GS	MIN	PTS	FGM	FGA	FG%	3PM	3PA	3P%	FTM	FTA	FT%	ORB	DRB	TRB	AST	PF	DQ	STL	BLK	TO	MPG	PPG	RPG	APG	PCM
79-80	New York	75	....	1142	427	182	368	.495	0	2	.000	63	86	.733	70	86	156	80	154	0	61	25	83	15.2	5.7	2.1	1.1	.359
81-82	New York	18	0	118	37	16	38	.421	0	0	.000	5	6	.833	3	2	5	9	19	0	4	2	4	6.6	2.1	0.3	0.5	.201
NBA Season Totals		93	0	1260	464	198	406	.488	0	2	.000	68	92	.739	73	88	161	89	173	0	65	27	87	13.5	5.0	1.7	1.0	....

• COPELAND, Lanard

Lanard Copeland

Born: July 16, 1965. Atlanta, GA, United States.   Height: 6'6".   Weight: 190 lbs.   Drafted: —   College: Georgia State

YEAR	TEAM	GP	GS	MIN	PTS	FGM	FGA	FG%	3PM	3PA	3P%	FTM	FTA	FT%	ORB	DRB	TRB	AST	PF	DQ	STL	BLK	TO	MPG	PPG	RPG	APG	PCM
89-90	Philadelphia	23	0	110	74	31	68	.456	1	5	.200	11	14	.786	4	6	10	9	12	0	1	1	18	4.8	3.2	0.4	0.4	.330
91-92	LA Clippers	10	0	48	16	7	23	.304	0	2	.000	2	2	1.000	1	6	7	5	5	0	2	0	4	4.8	1.6	0.7	0.5	.184
NBA Season Totals		33	0	158	90	38	91	.418	1	7	.143	13	16	.813	5	12	17	14	17	0	3	1	22	4.8	2.7	0.5	0.4	....
89-90	Philadelphia	4	0	9	4	2	6	.333	0	0	.000	0	0	.000	0	1	1	0	1	0	0	0	1	2.3	1.0	0.3	0.0	-.024
NBA Playoff Totals		4	0	9	4	2	6	.333	0	0	.000	0	0	.000	0	1	1	0	1	0	0	0	1	2.3	1.0	0.3	0.0	....

• CORBIN, Tyrone

Tyrone Kennedy Corbin

Born: Dec. 31, 1962. Columbia, SC, United States.   Height: 6'6".   Weight: 210 lbs.   Drafted: 1985   College: DePaul

YEAR	TEAM	GP	GS	MIN	PTS	FGM	FGA	FG%	3PM	3PA	3P%	FTM	FTA	FT%	ORB	DRB	TRB	AST	PF	DQ	STL	BLK	TO	MPG	PPG	RPG	APG	PCM
85-86	San Antonio	16	0	174	64	27	64	.422	0	1	.000	10	14	.714	11	14	25	11	21	0	11	2	13	10.9	4.0	1.6	0.7	.305
86-87	San Antonio	31	15	732	275	113	264	.428	0	0	.000	49	67	.731	52	67	119	80	81	0	38	3	47	23.6	8.9	3.8	2.6	.381
86-87	Cleveland	32	0	438	129	43	117	.368	1	4	.250	42	57	.737	36	60	96	17	48	0	17	2	19	13.7	4.0	3.0	0.5	.316
87-88	Cleveland	54	4	1148	393	158	322	.491	0	3	.000	77	98	.786	79	141	220	56	128	2	42	15	65	21.3	7.3	4.1	1.0	.373
87-88	Phoenix	30	1	591	232	99	203	.488	1	3	.333	33	40	.825	48	82	130	59	53	0	30	3	39	19.7	7.7	4.3	2.0	.483
88-89	Phoenix	77	30	1655	631	245	454	.540	0	2	.000	141	179	.788	176	222	398	118	222	2	82	13	92	21.5	8.2	5.2	1.5	.492
89-90	Minnesota	82	80	3011	1203	521	1083	.481	0	11	.000	161	209	.770	219	385	604	216	288	5	175	41	139	36.7	14.7	7.4	2.6	.461
90-91	Minnesota	82	82	3196	1472	587	1311	.448	2	10	.200	296	371	.798	185	404	589	347	257	3	162	53	205	39.0	18.0	7.2	4.2	.491
91-92	Minnesota	11	8	344	158	57	142	.401	0	1	.000	44	53	.830	24	45	69	33	31	0	12	6	26	31.3	14.4	6.3	3.0	.443

YEAR	TEAM	GP	GS	MIN	PTS	FGM	FGA	FG%	3PM	3PA	3P%	FTM	FTA	FT%	ORB	DRB	TRB	AST	PF	DQ	STL	BLK	TO	MPG	PPG	RPG	APG	PCM
91-92	Utah	69	1	1863	622	246	488	.504	0	3	.000	130	148	.878	139	264	403	107	162	1	70	14	69	27.0	9.0	5.8	1.6	.438
92-93	Utah	82	58	2560	950	385	766	.503	0	5	.000	180	218	.826	194	325	519	173	252	3	108	33	107	31.2	11.6	6.3	2.1	.453
93-94	Utah	82	17	2149	659	268	588	.456	6	29	.207	117	144	.813	150	239	389	122	212	0	99	24	90	26.2	8.0	4.7	1.5	.361
94-95	Atlanta	81	4	1389	502	205	464	.442	14	56	.250	78	114	.684	98	164	262	67	161	1	55	16	73	17.1	6.2	3.2	0.8	.347
95-96	Sacramento	49	2	930	312	117	259	.452	1	12	.083	77	92	.837	55	124	179	61	96	1	47	17	49	19.0	6.4	3.7	1.2	.401
95-96	Miami	22	0	354	101	38	92	.413	2	6	.333	23	28	.821	26	39	65	23	51	0	16	3	18	16.1	4.6	3.0	1.0	.312
96-97	Atlanta	70	65	2305	666	253	600	.422	74	208	.356	86	108	.796	76	218	294	124	176	1	90	7	84	32.9	9.5	4.2	1.8	.290
97-98	Atlanta	79	79	2699	806	328	747	.439	49	141	.348	101	128	.789	78	284	362	173	197	1	105	7	87	34.2	10.2	4.6	2.2	.319
98-99	Atlanta	47	6	1066	352	131	335	.391	38	119	.319	52	80	.650	37	108	145	43	74	0	31	7	43	22.7	7.5	3.1	0.9	.279
99-00	Sacramento	54	5	941	219	88	247	.356	10	44	.227	33	39	.846	40	125	165	60	99	2	36	5	29	17.4	4.1	3.1	1.1	.269
00-01	Toronto	15	1	117	20	9	38	.237	0	5	.000	2	4	.500	3	10	13	4	18	0	2	0	3	7.8	1.3	0.9	0.3	.001
NBA Season Totals		1065	458	27662	9766	3918	8584	.456	198	663	.299	1732	2191	.791	1726	3320	5046	1894	2627	22	1228	271	1297	26.0	9.2	4.7	1.8	....
85-86	San Antonio	1	0	14	0	0	4	.000	0	0	.000	0	0	.000	0	1	1	1	0	0	0	0	0	14.0	0.0	1.0	1.0	-.123
88-89	Phoenix	12	12	310	109	45	86	.523	0	0	.000	19	25	.760	43	42	85	26	37	0	24	4	14	25.8	9.1	7.1	2.2	.551
91-92	Utah	16	0	447	180	69	137	.504	0	2	.000	42	54	.778	39	49	88	17	45	0	12	3	17	27.9	11.3	5.5	1.1	.422
92-93	Utah	5	0	161	59	24	50	.480	0	0	.000	11	17	.647	16	22	38	9	15	0	3	1	7	32.2	11.8	7.6	1.8	.417
93-94	Utah	16	11	413	100	41	106	.387	4	12	.333	14	15	.933	25	54	79	15	31	0	21	3	11	25.8	6.3	4.9	0.9	.306
94-95	Atlanta	3	2	79	34	12	26	.462	2	6	.333	8	9	.889	6	4	10	2	10	0	2	1	2	26.3	11.3	3.3	0.7	.356
95-96	Miami	2	0	34	5	1	5	.200	0	0	.000	3	4	.750	4	3	7	1	3	0	2	0	1	17.0	2.5	3.5	0.5	.234
96-97	Atlanta	10	10	364	106	42	92	.457	13	37	.351	9	9	1.000	12	31	43	20	29	0	4	2	14	36.4	10.6	4.3	2.0	.274
97-98	Atlanta	4	4	113	15	7	25	.280	1	6	.167	0	0	.000	3	12	15	4	10	0	6	1	3	28.3	3.8	3.8	1.0	.139
98-99	Atlanta	9	4	268	69	30	72	.417	6	23	.261	3	4	.750	7	26	33	16	20	0	6	0	8	29.8	7.7	3.7	1.8	.252
99-00	Sacramento	3	0	23	4	2	5	.400	0	2	.000	0	1	.000	1	4	5	3	2	0	0	0	0	7.7	1.3	1.7	1.0	.336
NBA Playoff Totals		81	43	2226	681	273	608	.449	26	88	.295	109	138	.790	156	248	404	114	202	0	80	15	77	27.5	8.4	5.0	1.4	....

• CORCHIANI, Chris

Christopher Corchiani

Born: Mar. 28, 1968. Coral Gables, FL, United States. Height: 6' Weight: 185 lbs. Drafted: 1991 College: North Carolina State

YEAR	TEAM	GP	GS	MIN	PTS	FGM	FGA	FG%	3PM	3PA	3P%	FTM	FTA	FT%	ORB	DRB	TRB	AST	PF	DQ	STL	BLK	TO	MPG	PPG	RPG	APG	PCM
91-92	Orlando	51	1	741	255	77	193	.399	10	37	.270	91	104	.875	18	60	78	141	94	0	45	2	77	14.5	5.0	1.5	2.8	.396
92-93	Orlando	9	0	102	42	13	23	.565	0	3	.000	16	21	.762	1	6	7	16	17	0	6	0	8	11.3	4.7	0.8	1.8	.433
92-93	Washington	1	0	3	2	1	1	1.000	0	0	.000	0	0	.000	0	0	0	0	1	0	0	0	0	3.0	2.0	0.0	0.0	.511
93-94	Boston	51	0	467	117	40	94	.426	11	38	.289	26	38	.684	8	36	44	86	47	0	22	2	36	9.2	2.3	0.9	1.7	.349
NBA Season Totals		112	1	1313	416	131	311	.421	21	78	.269	133	163	.816	27	102	129	243	159	0	73	4	121	11.7	3.7	1.2	2.2	....

• CORLEY, Ken

Kenneth (Ken) Corley

Born: 1921. Height: 6'5". Weight: 210 lbs. Drafted: — College: Oklahoma State Teachers

YEAR	TEAM	GP	GS	MIN	PTS	FGM	FGA	FG%	3PM	3PA	3P%	FTM	FTA	FT%	ORB	DRB	TRB	AST	PF	DQ	STL	BLK	TO	MPG	PPG	RPG	APG	PCM
46-47	Cleveland	3	....	....	0	0	0	.000	....	....	....	0	0	.000	....	....	....	0	0	....	....	....	....	....	0.0	....	0.0	....
NBA Season Totals		3	....	....	0	0	0	.000	....	....	....	0	0	.000	....	....	....	0	0	....	....	....	....	....	0.0	....	0.0	....

• CORLEY, Ray

Raymond Charles Corley

Born: Jan. 1, 1928. Height: 6' Weight: 180 lbs. Drafted: — College: Georgetown

YEAR	TEAM	GP	GS	MIN	PTS	FGM	FGA	FG%	3PM	3PA	3P%	FTM	FTA	FT%	ORB	DRB	TRB	AST	PF	DQ	STL	BLK	TO	MPG	PPG	RPG	APG	PCM
49-50	Syracuse	60	....	....	309	117	370	.316	....	....	....	75	122	.615	....	....	....	109	81	....	....	....	....	....	5.2	....	1.8	....
50-51	Baltimore	16	....	....	48	17	67	.254	....	....	....	14	26	.538	....	....	34	22	26	0	....	....	....	....	3.0	2.1	1.4	....
50-51	Tri-Cities	18	....	....	74	29	85	.341	....	....	....	16	29	.552	....	....	43	38	26	0	....	....	....	....	4.1	2.4	2.1	....
52-53	Fort Wayne	8	....	65	11	3	24	.125	....	....	....	5	6	.833	....	....	5	5	18	0	....	....	....	8.1	1.4	0.6	0.6	-.017
NBA Season Totals		102	....	65	442	166	546	.304	....	....	....	110	183	.601	....	....	82	174	151	0	....	....	....	0.6	4.3	0.8	1.7	....
49-50	Syracuse	6	....	....	17	6	36	.167	....	....	....	5	11	.455	....	....	....	10	5	....	....	....	....	....	2.8	....	1.7	....
NBA Playoff Totals		6	....	....	17	6	36	.167	....	....	....	5	11	.455	....	....	....	10	5	....	....	....	....	....	2.8	....	1.7	....

• CORZINE, Dave

David John Corzine

Born: Apr. 25, 1956. Arlington Heights, IL, United States. Height: 6'11". Weight: 250 lbs. Drafted: 1978 College: DePaul

YEAR	TEAM	GP	GS	MIN	PTS	FGM	FGA	FG%	3PM	3PA	3P%	FTM	FTA	FT%	ORB	DRB	TRB	AST	PF	DQ	STL	BLK	TO	MPG	PPG	RPG	APG	PCM
78-79	Washington	59	....	532	175	63	118	.534	....	....	....	49	63	.778	52	95	147	49	67	0	10	14	53	9.0	3.0	2.5	0.8	.468
79-80	Washington	78	....	826	225	90	216	.417	0	0	.000	45	68	.662	104	166	270	63	120	1	9	31	62	10.6	2.9	3.5	0.8	.411
80-81	San Antonio	82	....	1960	857	366	747	.490	0	3	.000	125	175	.714	228	408	636	117	212	0	42	99	131	23.9	10.5	7.8	1.4	.565
81-82	San Antonio	82	21	2189	832	336	648	.519	1	4	.250	159	213	.746	211	418	629	130	235	3	33	126	139	26.7	10.1	7.7	1.6	.525
82-83	Chicago	82	71	2496	1146	457	920	.497	0	2	.000	232	322	.720	243	474	717	154	242	4	47	109	230	30.4	14.0	8.7	1.9	.532
83-84	Chicago	82	82	2674	1004	385	824	.467	3	9	.333	231	275	.840	169	406	575	202	227	3	58	120	172	32.6	12.2	7.0	2.5	.459
84-85	Chicago	82	50	2062	701	276	568	.486	0	1	.000	149	200	.745	130	292	422	140	189	2	32	64	123	25.1	8.5	5.1	1.7	.405
85-86	Chicago	67	4	1709	640	255	519	.491	3	12	.250	127	171	.743	132	301	433	150	133	0	28	53	107	25.5	9.6	6.5	2.2	.498
86-87	Chicago	82	39	2287	683	294	619	.475	0	5	.000	95	129	.736	199	341	540	209	202	1	38	87	115	27.9	8.3	6.6	2.5	.440
87-88	Chicago	80	32	2328	804	344	715	.481	1	9	.111	115	153	.752	170	357	527	154	149	1	36	95	112	29.1	10.1	6.6	1.9	.449
88-89	Chicago	81	7	1483	479	203	440	.461	2	8	.250	71	96	.740	92	223	315	103	134	0	29	45	89	18.3	5.9	3.9	1.3	.387
89-90	Orlando	6	3	79	22	11	29	.379	0	0	.000	0	2	.000	7	11	18	2	7	0	2	0	8	13.2	3.7	3.0	0.3	.181
90-91	Seattle	28	0	147	47	17	38	.447	0	0	.000	13	22	.591	10	23	33	4	18	0	5	5	3	5.3	1.7	1.2	0.1	.384
NBA Season Totals		891	309	20772	7615	3097	6401	.484	10	53	.189	1411	1889	.747	1747	3515	5262	1477	1935	15	369	848	1344	23.3	8.5	5.9	1.7	....
78-79	Washington	12	....	63	8	4	15	.267	....	....	....	0	0	.000	12	13	25	5	9	0	2	0	4	5.3	0.7	2.1	0.4	.321
79-80	Washington	2	....	9	10	4	5	.800	0	0	.000	2	2	1.000	2	1	3	0	2	0	0	0	3	4.5	5.0	1.5	0.0	.910
80-81	San Antonio	7	....	161	63	27	55	.491	0	0	.000	9	13	.692	12	36	48	16	15	0	4	8	11	23.0	9.0	6.9	2.3	.565
81-82	San Antonio	9	0	258	122	49	106	.462	0	0	.000	24	34	.706	38	47	85	17	30	0	6	9	20	28.7	13.6	9.4	1.9	.555
84-85	Chicago	4	4	77	33	14	21	.667	0	0	.000	5	6	.833	9	13	22	3	14	0	2	1	5	19.3	8.3	5.5	0.8	.537
85-86	Chicago	3	3	103	36	16	29	.552	0	0	.000	4	4	1.000	6	21	27	6	12	0	1	2	6	34.3	12.0	9.0	2.0	.457
86-87	Chicago	3	3	122	27	10	22	.455	0	0	.000	7	9	.778	7	14	21	7	6	0	1	3	7	40.7	9.0	7.0	2.3	.298
87-88	Chicago	10	10	308	61	27	76	.355	0	0	.000	7	13	.538	15	42	57	8	21	0	3	8	12	30.8	6.1	5.7	0.8	.206

YEAR	TEAM	GP	GS	MIN	PTS	FGM	FGA	FG%	3PM	3PA	3P%	FTM	FTA	FT%	ORB	DRB	TRB	AST	PF	DQ	STL	BLK	TO	MPG	PPG	RPG	APG	PCM
88-89	Chicago	16	0	219	65	27	64	.422	0	0	.000	11	17	.647	14	27	41	9	27	0	4	6	11	13.7	4.1	2.6	0.6	.283
90-91	Seattle	2	0	12	5	2	3	.667	0	0	.000	1	1	1.000	0	1	1	0	1	0	0	0	0	6.0	2.5	0.5	0.0	.378
NBA Playoff Totals		68	20	1332	430	180	396	.455	0	0	.000	70	99	.707	115	215	330	71	137	0	23	37	79	19.6	6.3	4.9	1.0	....

• COSTAIN, Ed

Ed Costain

Born: 1923. Height: 6' Weight: 170 lbs. Drafted: — College: none

YEAR	TEAM	GP	GS	MIN	PTS	FGM	FGA	FG%	3PM	3PA	3P%	FTM	FTA	FT%	ORB	DRB	TRB	AST	PF	DQ	STL	BLK	TO	MPG	PPG	RPG	APG	PCM
46-47	Toledo-N	3	....	....	4	2	....	....				0	0	.000			....	....	....		....				1.3			
NBL Season Totals		3	....	....	4	2						0	0				....	....							1.3			

• COSTELLO, Larry

Lawrence Ronald Costello

Born: July 2, 1931. Minoa, NY, United States. Died: Dec.11, 2001. Height: 6'1". Weight: 186 lbs. Drafted: 1954 College: Niagara

YEAR	TEAM	GP	GS	MIN	PTS	FGM	FGA	FG%	3PM	3PA	3P%	FTM	FTA	FT%	ORB	DRB	TRB	AST	PF	DQ	STL	BLK	TO	MPG	PPG	RPG	APG	PCM
54-55	Philadelphia	19	....	463	118	46	139	.331				26	32	.813			49	78	37	0				24.4	6.2	2.6	4.1	.359
56-57	Philadelphia	72	....	2111	547	186	497	.374				175	222	.788			323	236	182	2				29.3	7.6	4.5	3.3	.363
57-58	Syracuse	72	....	2746	1076	378	888	.426				320	378	.847			378	317	246	3				38.1	14.9	5.3	4.4	.463
58-59	Syracuse	70	....	2750	1108	414	948	.437				280	349	.802			365	379	263	7				39.3	15.8	5.2	5.4	.483
59-60	Syracuse	71	....	2469	993	372	822	.453				249	289	.862			388	449	234	4				34.8	14.0	5.5	6.3	.567
60-61	Syracuse	75	....	2167	1084	407	844	.482				270	338	.799			292	413	286	9				28.9	14.5	3.9	5.5	.623
61-62	Syracuse	63	....	1854	867	310	726	.427				247	295	.837			245	359	220	5				29.4	13.8	3.9	5.7	.575
62-63	Syracuse	78	....	2066	858	285	660	.432				288	327	**.881**			237	334	263	4				26.5	11.0	3.0	4.3	.500
63-64	Philadelphia	45	....	1137	529	191	408	.468				147	170	.865			105	167	150	3				25.3	11.8	2.3	3.7	.509
64-65	Philadelphia	64	....	1967	861	309	695	.445				243	277	**.877**			169	275	242	10				30.7	13.5	2.6	4.3	.471
66-67	Philadelphia	49	....	976	380	130	293	.444				120	133	.902			103	140	141	2				19.9	7.8	2.1	2.9	.450
67-68	Philadelphia	28	....	492	201	67	148	.453				67	81	.827			51	68	62	0				17.6	7.2	1.8	2.4	.464
NBA Season Totals		706	....	21198	8622	3095	7068	.438				2432	2891	.841			2705	3215	2326	49				30.0	12.2	3.8	4.6	....
56-57	Philadelphia	2	....	16	6	3	8	.375				0	1	.000			5	2	3	0				8.0	3.0	2.5	1.0	.439
57-58	Philadelphia	3	....	134	34	10	34	.294				14	14	1.000			25	12	6	0				44.7	11.3	8.3	4.0	.357
58-59	Syracuse	9	....	361	159	54	121	.446				51	61	.836			53	54	40	2				40.1	17.7	5.9	6.0	.546
59-60	Syracuse	3	....	122	50	20	47	.426				10	12	.833			14	20	15	1				40.7	16.7	4.7	6.7	.481
60-61	Syracuse	8	....	269	131	42	103	.408				47	55	.855			35	52	39	3				33.6	16.4	4.4	6.5	.586
61-62	Syracuse	5	....	167	73	22	51	.431				29	33	.879			16	28	21	0				33.4	14.6	3.2	5.6	.522
62-63	Syracuse	5	....	134	51	16	37	.432				19	23	.826			4	23	27	2				26.8	10.2	0.8	4.6	.396
63-64	Philadelphia	5	....	36	16	3	14	.214				10	10	1.000			3	4	14	1				7.2	3.2	0.6	0.8	.256
64-65	Philadelphia	10	....	207	55	22	53	.415				11	16	.688			12	20	43	2				20.7	5.5	1.2	2.0	.225
66-67	Philadelphia	2	....	25	17	6	8	.750				5	5	1.000			4	3	2	0				12.5	8.5	2.0	1.5	.856
NBA Playoff Totals		52	....	1471	592	198	476	.416				196	230	.852			171	218	210	11				28.3	11.4	3.3	4.2	....

• COTTON, Bob

Bob Cotton

Born: 1922. Height: 6'7". Weight: 205 lbs. Drafted: — College: —

YEAR	TEAM	GP	GS	MIN	PTS	FGM	FGA	FG%	3PM	3PA	3P%	FTM	FTA	FT%	ORB	DRB	TRB	AST	PF	DQ	STL	BLK	TO	MPG	PPG	RPG	APG	PCM
46-47	Chicago-N	4	....	....	5	1	....	....				3	6	.500			....	....	....						1.3		....	....
NBL Season Totals		4	....	....	5	1	....	....				3	6	....			....	....	....						1.3		....	....

• COTTON, Jack

John J. Cotton

Born: Oct. 15, 1924. Height: 6'7". Weight: 200 lbs. Drafted: — College: Wyoming

YEAR	TEAM	GP	GS	MIN	PTS	FGM	FGA	FG%	3PM	3PA	3P%	FTM	FTA	FT%	ORB	DRB	TRB	AST	PF	DQ	STL	BLK	TO	MPG	PPG	RPG	APG	PCM
48-49	Denver-N	57	....	....	209	71	....	....				67	121	.554			....	....	110						3.7		....	....
49-50	Denver	54	....	....	276	97	332	.292				82	161	.509			....	65	184						5.1		1.2	....
NBA Season Totals		54	....	....	276	97	332	.292				82	161	.509			....	65	184						5.1		1.2	....
NBL Season Totals		57	....	....	209	71	....	....				67	121	....			....	....	110						3.7		....	....
Career Totals		111	....	....	485	168	332	....				149	282	....			....	65	294	....						4.4		0.6	....

• COTTON, James

James Wesley Cotton

Born: Dec. 14, 1975. Los Angeles, CA, United States. Height: 6'5". Weight: 220 lbs. Drafted: 1997 College: Long Beach State

YEAR	TEAM	GP	GS	MIN	PTS	FGM	FGA	FG%	3PM	3PA	3P%	FTM	FTA	FT%	ORB	DRB	TRB	AST	PF	DQ	STL	BLK	TO	MPG	PPG	RPG	APG	PCM
97-98	Seattle	9	0	33	24	8	21	.381	0	4	.000	8	9	.889	2	4	6	0	3	0	1	1	6	3.7	2.7	0.7	0.0	.367
98-99	Seattle	10	0	59	25	6	18	.333	0	3	.000	13	18	.722	2	8	10	0	6	0	3	0	3	5.9	2.5	1.0	0.0	.311
NBA Season Totals		19	0	92	49	14	39	.359	0	7	.000	21	27	.778	4	12	16	0	9	0	4	1	9	4.8	2.6	0.8	0.0	....

• COUGHRAN, John

John Douglas Coughran

Born: Sept. 12, 1951. Pittsburg, CA, United States. Height: 6'7". Weight: 225 lbs. Drafted: 1973 College: California

YEAR	TEAM	GP	GS	MIN	PTS	FGM	FGA	FG%	3PM	3PA	3P%	FTM	FTA	FT%	ORB	DRB	TRB	AST	PF	DQ	STL	BLK	TO	MPG	PPG	RPG	APG	PCM
79-80	Golden State	24	....	160	68	29	81	.358	2	9	.222	8	14	.571	2	17	19	12	24	0	7	1	12	6.7	2.8	0.8	0.5	.213
NBA Season Totals		24	....	160	68	29	81	.358	2	9	.222	8	14	.571	2	17	19	12	24	0	7	1	12	6.7	2.8	0.8	0.5	....

• COUNTS, Mel

Mel Grant (Goose) Counts

Born: Oct. 16, 1941. Coos Bay, OR, United States. Height: 7' Weight: 230 lbs. Drafted: 1964 College: Oregon State

YEAR	TEAM	GP	GS	MIN	PTS	FGM	FGA	FG%	3PM	3PA	3P%	FTM	FTA	FT%	ORB	DRB	TRB	AST	PF	DQ	STL	BLK	TO	MPG	PPG	RPG	APG	PCM
64-65	Boston	54	....	572	258	100	272	.368				58	74	.784			265	19	134	1				10.6	4.8	4.9	0.4	.516
65-66	Boston	67	....	1021	562	221	549	.403				120	145	.828			432	50	207	5				15.2	8.4	6.4	0.7	.601
66-67	Baltimore	25	....	343	159	65	167	.389				29	40	.725			155	30	81	2				13.7	6.4	6.2	1.2	.585
66-67	LA Lakers	31	....	517	264	112	252	.444				40	54	.741			189	22	102	4				16.7	8.5	6.1	0.7	.548
67-68	LA Lakers	82	....	1739	958	390	808	.475				190	254	.748			732	139	309	6				21.2	11.7	8.9	1.7	.703
68-69	LA Lakers	77	....	1866	958	390	867	.450				178	221	.805			600	109	223	5				24.2	12.4	7.8	1.4	.577
69-70	LA Lakers	81	....	2193	1024	434	1017	.427				156	201	.776			683	160	304	7				27.1	12.6	8.4	2.0	.519

YEAR	TEAM	GP	GS	MIN	PTS	FGM	FGA	FG%	3PM	3PA	3P%	FTM	FTA	FT%	ORB	DRB	TRB	AST	PF	DQ	STL	BLK	TO	MPG	PPG	RPG	APG	PCM
70-71	Phoenix	80	....	1669	879	365	799	.457	....	....	....	149	198	.753	....	....	503	136	279	8	....	....	....	20.9	11.0	6.3	1.7	.571
71-72	Phoenix	76	....	906	395	147	344	.427	....	....	....	101	140	.721	....	....	257	96	159	2	....	....	....	11.9	5.2	3.4	1.3	.519
72-73	Philadelphia	7	....	47	10	5	16	.313	....	....	....	0	0	.000	....	....	16	3	8	0	....	....	....	6.7	1.4	2.3	0.4	.304
72-73	LA Lakers	59	....	611	293	127	278	.457	....	....	....	39	58	.672	....	....	237	62	98	0	....	....	....	10.4	5.0	4.0	1.1	.634
73-74	LA Lakers	45	....	499	146	61	167	.365	....	....	....	24	33	.727	56	90	146	54	85	2	20	23	....	11.1	3.2	3.2	1.2	.405
74-75	New Orleans	75	....	1421	520	217	495	.438	....	....	....	86	113	.761	102	339	441	182	196	0	49	43	....	18.9	6.9	5.9	2.4	.544
75-76	New Orleans	30	....	319	90	37	91	.407	....	....	....	16	21	.762	27	73	100	38	74	1	16	8	....	10.6	3.0	3.3	1.3	.436
NBA Season Totals		789	....	13723	6516	2665	6122	.435	....	....	....	1186	1552	.764	185	502	4756	1100	2259	43	85	74	....	17.4	8.3	6.0	1.4	....
64-65	Boston	4	....	30	9	4	15	.267	....	....	....	1	1	1.000	....	....	11	1	10	0	....	....	....	7.5	2.3	2.8	0.3	.213
65-66	Boston	10	....	82	43	14	39	.359	....	....	....	15	17	.882	....	....	40	3	26	0	....	....	....	8.2	4.3	4.0	0.3	.578
66-67	LA Lakers	3	....	29	14	5	19	.263	....	....	....	4	4	1.000	....	....	8	0	6	0	....	....	....	9.7	4.7	2.7	0.0	.235
67-68	LA Lakers	15	....	306	129	54	101	.535	....	....	....	21	31	.677	....	....	133	24	52	1	....	....	....	20.4	8.6	8.9	1.6	.659
68-69	LA Lakers	18	....	442	202	74	192	.385	....	....	....	54	71	.761	....	....	143	26	67	1	....	....	....	24.6	11.2	7.9	1.4	.493
69-70	LA Lakers	14	....	212	85	37	88	.420	....	....	....	11	13	.846	....	....	74	16	48	2	....	....	....	15.1	6.1	5.3	1.1	.477
72-73	LA Lakers	17	....	327	154	61	133	.459	....	....	....	32	41	.780	....	....	104	28	51	1	....	....	....	19.2	9.1	6.1	1.6	.574
73-74	LA Lakers	4	....	34	12	6	12	.500	....	....	....	0	0	.000	2	4	6	2	3	0	2	2	....	8.5	3.0	1.5	0.5	.383
NBA Playoff Totals		85	....	1462	648	255	599	.426	....	....	....	138	178	.775	2	4	519	100	263	5	2	2	....	17.2	7.6	6.1	1.2	....

• COURTIN, Steve

Stephen Edward Courtin

Born: Sept. 21, 1942. Height: 6'1". Weight: 188 lbs. Drafted: 1964 College: St. Joseph's (PA)

64-65	Philadelphia	24	....	317	101	42	103	.408	....	....	....	17	21	.810	....	....	22	22	44	0	....	....	....	13.2	4.2	0.9	0.9	.251
NBA Season Totals		24	....	317	101	42	103	.408	....	....	....	17	21	.810	....	....	22	22	44	0	....	....	....	13.2	4.2	0.9	0.9	....

• COURTNEY, Joe

Joseph Pierre Courtney

Born: Oct. 17, 1969. Jackson, MS, United States. Height: 6'8". Weight: 235 lbs. Drafted: — College: Southern Mississippi

92-93	Chicago	5	0	34	11	4	9	.444	0	0	.000	3	4	.750	2	0	2	1	9	0	2	1	3	6.8	2.2	0.4	0.2	.135
92-93	Golden State	7	0	70	22	9	23	.391	0	0	.000	4	5	.800	2	15	17	2	8	0	3	4	3	10.0	3.1	2.4	0.3	.378
93-94	Phoenix	33	1	168	103	40	78	.513	0	0	.000	23	32	.719	14	13	27	9	23	0	3	6	10	5.1	3.1	0.8	0.3	.518
93-94	Milwaukee	19	0	177	65	27	70	.386	2	3	.667	9	15	.600	14	15	29	6	21	0	7	6	11	9.3	3.4	1.5	0.3	.272
95-96	Cleveland	23	0	200	38	15	35	.429	0	0	.000	8	18	.444	24	25	49	9	35	0	5	6	16	8.7	1.7	2.1	0.4	.245
96-97	Philadelphia	4	0	52	12	6	14	.429	0	0	.000	0	0	.000	5	4	9	0	8	1	0	0	1	13.0	3.0	2.3	0.0	.159
96-97	San Antonio	5	0	48	13	5	16	.313	0	0	.000	3	5	.600	4	3	7	0	6	0	0	0	2	9.6	2.6	1.4	0.0	.077
NBA Season Totals		96	1	749	264	106	245	.433	2	3	.667	50	79	.633	65	75	140	27	110	1	20	23	46	7.8	2.8	1.5	0.3	....

• COUSY, Bob

Robert Joseph (Cooz, Houdini of the Hardwood) Cousy

Born: Aug. 9, 1928. New York, NY, United States. Height: 6'1". Weight: 175 lbs. Drafted: 1950 College: Holy Cross HOF: 1971

50-51	Boston	69	....	....	1078	401	1138	.352	....	....	....	276	365	.756	....	....	474	341	185	2	....	....	....	....	15.6	6.9	4.9	....
51-52	Boston	66	....	2681	1433	512	1388	.369	....	....	....	409	506	.808	....	....	421	441	190	5	....	....	....	40.6	21.7	6.4	6.7	.588
52-53	Boston	71	....	2945	1407	464	**1320**	.352	....	....	....	479	587	.816	....	....	449	**547**	227	4	....	....	....	41.5	19.8	6.3	**7.7**	**.574**
53-54	Boston	72	....	2857	1383	486	1262	.385	....	....	....	411	522	.787	....	....	394	**518**	201	3	....	....	....	39.7	19.2	5.5	**7.2**	**.584**
54-55	Boston	71	....	2747	1504	522	1316	.397	....	....	....	460	570	.807	....	....	424	**557**	165	1	....	....	....	38.7	21.2	6.0	**7.8**	**.662**
55-56	Boston	72	....	2767	1356	440	1223	.360	....	....	....	476	564	.844	....	....	492	**642**	206	2	....	....	....	38.4	18.8	6.8	**8.9**	**.657**
56-57	Boston	64	....	2364	1319	478	1264	.378	....	....	....	363	442	.821	....	....	309	**478**	134	0	....	....	....	36.9	20.6	4.8	**7.5**	**.627**
57-58	Boston	65	....	2222	1167	445	1262	.353	....	....	....	277	326	.850	....	....	322	**463**	136	1	....	....	....	34.2	18.0	5.0	**7.1**	**.597**
58-59	Boston	65	....	2403	1297	484	1260	.384	....	....	....	329	385	.855	....	....	359	**557**	135	0	....	....	....	37.0	20.0	5.5	**8.6**	**.669**
59-60	Boston	75	....	2588	1455	568	1481	.384	....	....	....	319	403	.792	....	....	352	**715**	146	2	....	....	....	34.5	19.4	4.7	**9.5**	**.708**
60-61	Boston	76	....	2468	1378	513	1382	.371	....	....	....	352	452	.779	....	....	331	587	196	0	....	....	....	32.5	18.1	4.4	7.7	.642
61-62	Boston	75	....	2114	1175	462	1181	.391	....	....	....	251	333	.754	....	....	261	584	135	0	....	....	....	28.2	15.7	3.5	7.8	.683
62-63	Boston	76	....	1975	1003	392	988	.397	....	....	....	219	298	.735	....	....	193	515	175	0	....	....	....	26.0	13.2	2.5	6.8	.611
69-70	Cincinnati	7	....	34	5	1	3	.333	....	....	....	3	3	1.000	....	....	5	10	11	0	....	....	....	4.9	0.7	0.7	1.4	.412
NBA Season Totals		924	....	30165	16960	6168	16468	.375	....	....	....	4624	5756	.803	....	....	4786	6955	2242	20	....	....	....	32.6	18.4	5.2	7.5	....
50-51	Boston	2	....	....	28	9	42	.214	....	....	....	10	12	.833	....	....	15	12	8	0	....	....	....	....	14.0	7.5	6.0	....
51-52	Boston	3	....	138	93	26	65	.400	....	....	....	41	44	.932	....	....	12	19	13	1	....	....	....	46.0	31.0	4.0	6.3	.671
52-53	Boston	6	....	270	153	46	120	.383	....	....	....	61	73	.836	....	....	25	37	21	0	....	....	....	45.0	25.5	4.2	6.2	.566
53-54	Boston	6	....	260	126	33	116	.284	....	....	....	60	75	.800	....	....	32	38	20	0	....	....	....	43.3	21.0	5.3	6.3	.486
54-55	Boston	7	....	299	152	53	139	.381	....	....	....	46	48	.958	....	....	43	65	26	0	....	....	....	42.7	21.7	6.1	9.3	.636
55-56	Boston	3	....	124	79	28	56	.500	....	....	....	23	25	.920	....	....	24	26	4	0	....	....	....	41.3	26.3	8.0	8.7	.854
56-57	Boston	10	....	440	202	67	207	.324	....	....	....	68	91	.747	....	....	61	93	27	0	....	....	....	44.0	20.2	6.1	9.3	.548
57-58	Boston	11	....	457	198	67	196	.342	....	....	....	64	75	.853	....	....	71	82	20	0	....	....	....	41.5	18.0	6.5	7.5	.544
58-59	Boston	11	....	460	214	72	221	.326	....	....	....	70	94	.745	....	....	76	119	28	0	....	....	....	41.8	19.5	6.9	10.8	.626
59-60	Boston	13	....	468	199	80	262	.305	....	....	....	39	51	.765	....	....	48	116	27	0	....	....	....	36.0	15.3	3.7	8.9	.486
60-61	Boston	10	....	337	167	50	147	.340	....	....	....	67	88	.761	....	....	43	91	33	1	....	....	....	33.7	16.7	4.3	9.1	.647
61-62	Boston	14	....	474	224	86	241	.357	....	....	....	52	76	.684	....	....	64	123	43	0	....	....	....	33.9	16.0	4.6	8.8	.584
62-63	Boston	13	....	413	183	72	204	.353	....	....	....	39	47	.830	....	....	32	116	44	2	....	....	....	31.8	14.1	2.5	8.9	.541
NBA Playoff Totals		109	....	4140	2018	689	2016	.342	....	....	....	640	799	.801	....	....	546	937	314	4	....	....	....	38.0	18.5	5.0	8.6	....

• COVEN, Bill

Bill Coven

Born: 1920. Height: 6'7". Weight: 220 lbs. Drafted: — College: Baldwin-Wallace

46-47	Rochester-N	13	....	....	24	10	....	....	....	....	....	4	8	.500	....	....	....	....	....	....	....	....	....	....	1.8	....	....	....
NBL Season Totals		13	....	....	24	10	....	....	....	....	....	4	8	....	....	....	....	....	....	....	....	....	....	....	1.8	....	....	....
46-47	Rochester-N	5	....	....	0	0	....	....	....	....	....	0	0	.000	....	....	....	....	....	....	....	....	....	....	0.0	....	....	....
NBL Playoff Totals		5	....	....	0	0	....	....	....	....	....	0	0	....	....	....	....	....	....	....	....	....	....	....	0.0	....	....	....

• COWENS, Dave

David William (Big Red) Cowens

Born: Oct. 25, 1948. Newport, KY, United States. Height: 6'9". Weight: 230 lbs. Drafted: 1970 College: Florida State HOF: 1991

YEAR TEAM	GP	GS	MIN	PTS	FGM	FGA	FG%	3PM	3PA	3P%	FTM	FTA	FT%	ORB	DRB	TRB	AST	PF	DQ	STL	BLK	TO	MPG	PPG	RPG	APG	PCM
70-71 Boston	81	....	3076	1373	550	1302	.422	....	....	....	273	373	.732	....	....	1216	228	**350**	15	....	....	....	38.0	17.0	15.0	2.8	.598
71-72 Boston	79	....	3186	1489	657	1357	.484	....	....	....	175	243	.720	....	....	1203	245	**314**	10	....	....	....	40.3	18.8	15.2	3.1	.639
72-73 Boston	82	....	3425	1684	740	1637	.452	....	....	....	204	262	.779	....	....	1329	333	311	7	....	....	....	41.8	20.5	16.2	4.1	.665
73-74 Boston	80	....	3352	1518	645	1475	.437	....	....	....	228	274	.832	264	993	1257	354	294	7	95	101	....	41.9	19.0	15.7	4.4	.639
74-75 Boston	65	....	2632	1329	569	1199	.475	....	....	....	191	244	.783	229	729	958	296	243	7	87	73	....	40.5	20.4	14.7	4.6	.692
75-76 Boston	78	....	3101	1479	611	1305	.468	....	....	....	257	340	.756	335	911	1246	325	314	10	94	71	....	39.8	19.0	16.0	4.2	.694
76-77 Boston	50	....	1888	818	328	756	.434	....	....	....	162	198	.818	147	550	697	248	181	7	46	49	....	37.8	16.4	13.9	5.0	.656
77-78 Boston	77	....	3215	1435	598	1220	.490	....	....	....	239	284	.842	248	830	1078	351	297	5	102	67	216	41.8	18.6	14.0	4.6	.634
78-79 Boston	68	....	2517	1127	488	1010	.483	....	....	....	151	187	.807	152	500	652	242	263	16	76	51	177	37.0	16.6	9.6	3.6	.529
79-80 Boston	66	....	2159	940	422	932	.453	1	12	.083	95	122	.779	126	408	534	206	216	2	69	61	106	32.7	14.2	8.1	3.1	.509
82-83 Milwaukee	40	34	1014	324	136	306	.444	0	2	.000	52	63	.825	73	201	274	82	137	4	30	15	44	25.4	8.1	6.9	2.1	.436
NBA Season Totals	766	34	29565	13516	5744	12499	.460	1	14	.071	2027	2590	.783	1574	5122	10444	2910	2920	90	599	488	543	38.6	17.6	13.6	3.8	....
71-72 Boston	11	....	441	170	71	156	.455	....	....	....	28	47	.596	....	....	152	33	50	2	....	....	....	40.1	15.5	13.8	3.0	.534
72-73 Boston	13	....	598	285	129	273	.473	....	....	....	27	41	.659	....	....	216	48	54	2	....	....	....	46.0	21.9	16.6	3.7	.623
73-74 Boston	18	....	772	369	161	370	.435	....	....	....	47	59	.797	60	180	240	66	85	2	21	17	....	42.9	20.5	13.3	3.7	.557
74-75 Boston	11	....	479	225	101	236	.428	....	....	....	23	26	.885	49	132	181	46	50	2	18	6	....	43.5	20.5	16.5	4.2	.615
75-76 Boston	18	....	798	378	156	341	.457	....	....	....	66	87	.759	87	209	296	83	85	4	22	13	....	44.3	21.0	16.4	4.6	.655
76-77 Boston	9	....	379	149	66	148	.446	....	....	....	17	22	.773	29	105	134	36	37	3	8	13	....	42.1	16.6	14.9	4.0	.572
79-80 Boston	9	....	301	108	49	103	.476	0	2	.000	10	11	.909	18	48	66	21	37	0	9	7	8	33.4	12.0	7.3	2.3	.438
NBA Playoff Totals	89	....	3768	1684	733	1627	.451	0	2	.000	218	293	.744	243	674	1285	333	398	15	78	56	8	42.3	18.9	14.4	3.7	....

• COX, Chubby

John Arthur (Chubby) Cox III

Born: Dec. 29, 1955. Philadelphia, PA, United States. Height: 6'2". Weight: 180 lbs. Drafted: 1978 College: San Francisco

YEAR TEAM	GP	GS	MIN	PTS	FGM	FGA	FG%	3PM	3PA	3P%	FTM	FTA	FT%	ORB	DRB	TRB	AST	PF	DQ	STL	BLK	TO	MPG	PPG	RPG	APG	PCM
82-83 Washington	7	0	78	29	13	37	.351	0	2	.000	3	6	.500	7	3	10	6	16	0	0	1	9	11.1	4.1	1.4	0.9	.092
NBA Season Totals	7	0	78	29	13	37	.351	0	2	.000	3	6	.500	7	3	10	6	16	0	0	1	9	11.1	4.1	1.4	0.9	....

• COX, Johnny

Johnny W. Cox

Born: Nov. 1, 1936. Neon, KY, United States. Height: 6'4". Weight: 180 lbs. Drafted: 1959 College: Kentucky

YEAR TEAM	GP	GS	MIN	PTS	FGM	FGA	FG%	3PM	3PA	3P%	FTM	FTA	FT%	ORB	DRB	TRB	AST	PF	DQ	STL	BLK	TO	MPG	PPG	RPG	APG	PCM
62-63 Chicago	73	....	1685	573	239	568	.421	....	....	....	95	135	.704	....	....	280	142	149	4	....	....	....	23.1	7.8	3.8	1.9	.375
NBA Season Totals	73	....	1685	573	239	568	.421	....	....	....	95	135	.704	....	....	280	142	149	4	....	....	....	23.1	7.8	3.8	1.9	....

• COX, Wesley

Wesley Cox

Born: Jan. 27, 1955. Louisville, KY, United States. Height: 6'6". Weight: 215 lbs. Drafted: 1977 College: Louisville

YEAR TEAM	GP	GS	MIN	PTS	FGM	FGA	FG%	3PM	3PA	3P%	FTM	FTA	FT%	ORB	DRB	TRB	AST	PF	DQ	STL	BLK	TO	MPG	PPG	RPG	APG	PCM
77-78 Golden State	43	....	453	196	69	173	.399	....	....	....	58	100	.580	42	101	143	12	82	1	21	10	34	10.5	4.6	3.3	0.3	.412
78-79 Golden State	31	....	360	146	53	123	.431	....	....	....	40	92	.435	18	45	63	11	68	0	13	5	43	11.6	4.7	2.0	0.4	.210
NBA Season Totals	74	....	813	342	122	296	.412	....	....	....	98	192	.510	60	146	206	23	150	1	34	15	77	11.0	4.6	2.8	0.3	....

• CRAMER, Bill

Bill Cramer

Born: —. Height: — Weight: — Drafted: — College: —

YEAR TEAM	GP	GS	MIN	PTS	FGM	FGA	FG%	3PM	3PA	3P%	FTM	FTA	FT%	ORB	DRB	TRB	AST	PF	DQ	STL	BLK	TO	MPG	PPG	RPG	APG	PCM
39-40 Indianapolis-N	1	....	....	0	0	....	....	....	....	....	0	....	....	....	....	....	....	....	....	....	....	....	....	0.0	....	....	....
NBL Season Totals	1	....	....	0	0	....	....	....	....	....	0	....	....	....	....	....	....	....	....	....	....	....	....	0.0	....	....	....

• CRAWFORD, Chris

Christopher Lee Crawford

Born: May 13, 1975. Kalamazoo, MI, United States. Height: 6'9". Weight: 235 lbs. Drafted: 1997 College: Marquette

YEAR TEAM	GP	GS	MIN	PTS	FGM	FGA	FG%	3PM	3PA	3P%	FTM	FTA	FT%	ORB	DRB	TRB	AST	PF	DQ	STL	BLK	TO	MPG	PPG	RPG	APG	PCM
97-98 Atlanta	40	0	256	150	46	110	.418	1	3	.333	57	68	.838	20	21	41	9	27	0	12	7	20	6.4	3.8	1.0	0.2	.470
98-99 Atlanta	42	30	784	288	110	255	.431	11	33	.333	57	70	.814	37	53	90	24	106	1	10	13	48	18.7	6.9	2.1	0.6	.243
99-00 Atlanta	55	11	668	252	91	229	.397	7	27	.259	63	81	.778	51	48	99	33	83	1	17	16	37	12.1	4.6	1.8	0.6	.304
00-01 Atlanta	47	22	901	318	122	270	.452	6	22	.273	68	83	.819	28	82	110	37	117	3	21	16	62	19.2	6.8	2.3	0.8	.270
01-02 Atlanta	7	4	131	53	21	45	.467	0	1	.000	11	15	.733	9	16	25	5	21	1	2	5	10	18.7	7.6	3.6	0.7	.346
02-03 Atlanta	5	0	38	24	8	13	.615	1	3	.333	7	8	.875	3	4	7	1	7	0	2	3	2	7.6	4.8	1.4	0.2	.684
NBA Season Totals	196	67	2778	1085	398	922	.432	26	89	.292	263	325	.809	148	224	372	109	361	6	64	60	179	14.2	5.5	1.9	0.6	....
97-98 Atlanta	1	0	4	2	0	0	.000	0	0	.000	2	2	1.000	1	1	2	0	2	0	0	1	2	4.0	2.0	2.0	0.0	.500
98-99 Atlanta	6	5	125	59	16	48	.333	4	14	.286	23	26	.885	6	13	19	5	19	2	1	1	6	20.8	9.8	3.2	0.8	.317
NBA Playoff Totals	7	5	129	61	16	48	.333	4	14	.286	25	28	.893	7	14	21	5	21	2	1	2	8	18.4	8.7	3.0	0.7	....

• CRAWFORD, Freddie

Frederick Russell Crawford Jr.

Born: Dec. 23, 1941. New York, NY, United States. Height: 6'4". Weight: 189 lbs. Drafted: 1964 College: St. Bonaventure

YEAR TEAM	GP	GS	MIN	PTS	FGM	FGA	FG%	3PM	3PA	3P%	FTM	FTA	FT%	ORB	DRB	TRB	AST	PF	DQ	STL	BLK	TO	MPG	PPG	RPG	APG	PCM
66-67 New York	19	....	192	112	44	116	.379	....	....	....	24	38	.632	....	....	48	12	39	0	....	....	....	10.1	5.9	2.5	0.6	.449
67-68 New York	31	....	426	167	65	177	.367	....	....	....	37	59	.627	....	....	83	46	67	0	....	....	....	13.7	5.4	2.7	1.5	.384
67-68 LA Lakers	38	....	756	392	159	330	.482	....	....	....	74	120	.617	....	....	112	95	104	1	....	....	....	19.9	10.3	2.9	2.5	.528
68-69 LA Lakers	81	....	1690	505	211	454	.465	....	....	....	83	154	.539	....	....	215	154	224	1	....	....	....	20.9	6.2	2.7	1.9	.318
69-70 Milwaukee	77	....	1331	587	243	506	.480	....	....	....	101	148	.682	....	....	184	225	181	1	....	....	....	17.3	7.6	2.4	2.9	.503
70-71 Buffalo	15	....	203	88	36	106	.340	....	....	....	16	26	.615	....	....	35	24	18	0	....	....	....	13.5	5.9	2.3	1.6	.361
70-71 Philadelphia	36	....	449	180	74	175	.423	....	....	....	32	72	.444	....	....	69	54	59	0	....	....	....	12.5	5.0	1.9	1.5	.382
NBA Season Totals	297	....	5047	2031	832	1864	.446	....	....	....	367	617	.595	....	....	746	610	692	3	....	....	....	17.0	6.8	2.5	2.1	....

YEAR	TEAM	GP	GS	MIN	PTS	FGM	FGA	FG%	3PM	3PA	3P%	FTM	FTA	FT%	ORB	DRB	TRB	AST	PF	DQ	STL	BLK	TO	MPG	PPG	RPG	APG	PCM
66-67	New York	4	....	112	68	31	73	.425	....	....	....	6	12	.500	....	....	24	16	16	1	....	....	....	28.0	17.0	6.0	4.0	.573
67-68	LA Lakers	15	....	257	91	36	83	.434	....	....	....	19	35	.543	....	....	35	16	41	0	....	....	....	17.1	6.1	2.3	1.1	.303
68-69	LA Lakers	5	....	20	4	2	4	.500	....	....	....	0	1	.000	....	....	3	3	4	0	....	....	....	4.0	0.8	0.6	0.6	.312
69-70	Milwaukee	10	....	208	88	34	88	.386	....	....	....	20	24	.833	....	....	35	37	27	1	....	....	....	20.8	8.8	3.5	3.7	.476
70-71	Philadelphia	1	....	9	7	2	4	.500	....	....	....	3	4	.750	....	....	0	1	1	0	....	....	....	9.0	7.0	0.0	1.0	.618
NBA Playoff Totals		35	....	606	258	105	252	.417	....	....	....	48	76	.632	....	....	97	73	89	2	....	....	....	17.3	7.4	2.8	2.1	....

• CRAWFORD, Jamal

Jamal Crawford

Born: Mar. 20, 1980. Seattle, WA, United States.   Height: 6'6".   Weight: 185 lbs.   Drafted: 2000   College: Michigan

YEAR	TEAM	GP	GS	MIN	PTS	FGM	FGA	FG%	3PM	3PA	3P%	FTM	FTA	FT%	ORB	DRB	TRB	AST	PF	DQ	STL	BLK	TO	MPG	PPG	RPG	APG	PCM
00-01	Chicago	61	8	1050	282	107	304	.352	41	117	.350	27	34	.794	9	80	89	141	68	0	43	14	85	17.2	4.6	1.5	2.3	.268
01-02	Chicago	23	6	481	214	89	187	.476	26	58	.448	10	13	.769	5	29	34	55	18	0	18	5	32	20.9	9.3	1.5	2.4	.413
02-03	Chicago	80	31	1992	858	334	808	.413	86	242	.355	104	129	.806	21	164	185	334	126	0	77	25	134	24.9	10.7	2.3	4.2	.433
NBA Season Totals		164	45	3523	1354	530	1299	.408	153	417	.367	141	176	.801	35	273	308	530	212	0	138	44	251	21.5	8.3	1.9	3.2	....

• CREIGHTON, Jim

Jim Creighton

Born: Apr. 18, 1950. Billings, MT, United States.   Height: 6'8".   Weight: 200 lbs.   Drafted: 1972   College: Colorado

YEAR	TEAM	GP	GS	MIN	PTS	FGM	FGA	FG%	3PM	3PA	3P%	FTM	FTA	FT%	ORB	DRB	TRB	AST	PF	DQ	STL	BLK	TO	MPG	PPG	RPG	APG	PCM
75-76	Atlanta	32	....	172	31	12	43	.279	....	....	....	7	16	.438	13	32	45	4	23	0	2	9	....	5.4	1.0	1.4	0.1	.197
NBA Season Totals		32	....	172	31	12	43	.279	....	....	....	7	16	.438	13	32	45	4	23	0	2	9	....	5.4	1.0	1.4	0.1	....

• CREVIER, Ron

Ronald Joseph Oscar Camille Crevier

Born: Apr. 14, 1958. Montreal, QU, Canada.   Height: 7'   Weight: 235 lbs.   Drafted: 1983   College: Boston College

YEAR	TEAM	GP	GS	MIN	PTS	FGM	FGA	FG%	3PM	3PA	3P%	FTM	FTA	FT%	ORB	DRB	TRB	AST	PF	DQ	STL	BLK	TO	MPG	PPG	RPG	APG	PCM
85-86	Golden State	1	0	1	0	0	1	.000	0	0	.000	0	0	.000	0	0	0	0	0	0	0	0	0	1.0	0.0	0.0	0.0	-.929
85-86	Detroit	2	0	3	0	0	2	.000	0	0	.000	0	2	.000	1	0	1	0	2	0	0	0	0	1.5	0.0	0.5	0.0	-.929
NBA Season Totals		3	0	4	0	0	3	.000	0	0	.000	0	2	.000	1	0	1	0	2	0	0	0	0	1.3	0.0	0.3	0.0	....

• CRISLER, Hal

Harold James Crisler

Born: Dec. 31, 1923. Richmond, CA, United States. Died: Nov.2, 1987.   Height: 6'3".   Weight: 215 lbs.   Drafted: —   College: Iowa State

YEAR	TEAM	GP	GS	MIN	PTS	FGM	FGA	FG%	3PM	3PA	3P%	FTM	FTA	FT%	ORB	DRB	TRB	AST	PF	DQ	STL	BLK	TO	MPG	PPG	RPG	APG	PCM
46-47	Boston	4	....	....	6	2	6	.333	....	....	....	2	2	1.000	....	....	....	0	6	....	....	....	....	....	1.5	....	0.0	....
NBA Season Totals		4	....	....	6	2	6	.333	....	....	....	2	2	1.000	....	....	....	0	6	....	....	....	....	....	1.5	....	0.0	....

• CRISPIN, Joe

Joseph Steven Crispin

Born: July 18, 1979. Pitman, NJ, United States.   Height: 6'   Weight: 185 lbs.   Drafted: —   College: Penn State

YEAR	TEAM	GP	GS	MIN	PTS	FGM	FGA	FG%	3PM	3PA	3P%	FTM	FTA	FT%	ORB	DRB	TRB	AST	PF	DQ	STL	BLK	TO	MPG	PPG	RPG	APG	PCM
01-02	LA Lakers	6	0	27	10	3	12	.250	0	4	.000	4	5	.800	0	1	1	2	2	0	1	0	1	4.5	1.7	0.2	0.3	.133
01-02	Phoenix	15	0	129	69	23	56	.411	15	35	.429	8	8	1.000	2	8	10	24	8	0	4	0	9	8.6	4.6	0.7	1.6	.514
NBA Season Totals		21	0	156	79	26	68	.382	15	39	.385	12	13	.923	2	9	11	26	10	0	5	0	10	7.4	3.8	0.5	1.2	....

• CRISS, Charlie

Charles Washington Criss Jr.

Born: Nov. 6, 1948. Valhalla, NY, United States.   Height: 5'8".   Weight: 165 lbs.   Drafted: —   College: New Mexico State

YEAR	TEAM	GP	GS	MIN	PTS	FGM	FGA	FG%	3PM	3PA	3P%	FTM	FTA	FT%	ORB	DRB	TRB	AST	PF	DQ	STL	BLK	TO	MPG	PPG	RPG	APG	PCM
77-78	Atlanta	77	....	1935	874	319	751	.425	....	....	....	236	296	.797	24	97	121	294	143	0	108	5	146	25.1	11.4	1.6	3.8	.421
78-79	Atlanta	54	....	879	285	109	289	.377	....	....	....	67	86	.779	19	41	60	138	70	0	41	3	81	16.3	5.3	1.1	2.6	.291
79-80	Atlanta	81	....	1794	671	249	578	.431	1	17	.059	172	212	.811	27	89	116	246	133	0	74	4	130	22.1	8.3	1.4	3.0	.347
80-81	Atlanta	66	....	1708	626	220	485	.454	1	21	.048	185	214	.864	26	74	100	283	87	0	61	3	132	25.9	9.5	1.5	4.3	.392
81-82	Atlanta	27	0	552	235	84	210	.400	2	8	.250	65	73	.890	6	32	38	75	40	0	23	2	30	20.4	8.7	1.4	2.8	.377
81-82	San Diego	28	20	840	360	138	288	.479	8	21	.381	76	86	.884	7	37	44	112	56	0	21	4	53	30.0	12.9	1.6	4.0	.389
82-83	Milwaukee	66	0	922	412	169	375	.451	6	31	.194	68	76	.895	14	65	79	127	44	0	27	0	46	14.0	6.2	1.2	1.9	.430
83-84	Milwaukee	6	0	107	30	11	30	.367	1	6	.167	7	11	.636	2	7	9	17	7	0	5	0	4	17.8	5.0	1.5	2.8	.324
83-84	Atlanta	9	0	108	23	9	22	.409	0	0	.000	5	5	1.000	3	8	11	21	4	0	3	0	6	12.0	2.6	1.2	2.3	.361
84-85	Atlanta	4	2	115	18	7	17	.412	0	2	.000	4	6	.667	2	12	14	22	5	0	3	0	11	28.8	4.5	3.5	5.5	.300
NBA Season Totals		418	22	8960	3534	1315	3045	.432	19	106	.179	885	1065	.831	130	462	592	1335	589	0	366	21	639	21.4	8.5	1.4	3.2	....
77-78	Atlanta	2	....	65	27	10	24	.417	....	....	....	7	9	.778	0	4	4	3	5	0	4	1	5	32.5	13.5	2.0	1.5	.286
78-79	Atlanta	9	....	99	33	12	29	.414	....	....	....	9	10	.900	2	3	5	16	5	0	3	0	3	11.0	3.7	0.6	1.8	.375
79-80	Atlanta	5	....	152	70	29	59	.492	1	3	.333	11	12	.917	0	5	5	22	12	0	6	0	11	30.4	14.0	1.0	4.4	.402
82-83	Milwaukee	9	0	116	47	15	34	.441	0	1	.000	17	18	.944	1	13	14	12	12	0	9	0	3	12.9	5.2	1.6	1.3	.476
NBA Playoff Totals		25	0	432	177	66	146	.452	1	4	.250	44	49	.898	3	25	28	53	34	0	22	1	22	17.3	7.1	1.1	2.1	....

• CRITCHFIELD, Russell

Russell Dean (Rusty) Critchfield

Born: June 27, 1946. Salinas, CA, United States.   Height: 5'10".   Weight: 150 lbs.   Drafted: —   College: California

YEAR	TEAM	GP	GS	MIN	PTS	FGM	FGA	FG%	3PM	3PA	3P%	FTM	FTA	FT%	ORB	DRB	TRB	AST	PF	DQ	STL	BLK	TO	MPG	PPG	RPG	APG	PCM
68-69	Oakland-A	47	....	439	161	53	147	.361	0	3	.000	55	84	.655	11	18	29	54	41	0	....	....	33	9.3	3.4	0.6	1.1	.312
ABA Season Totals		47	....	439	161	53	147	.361	0	3	.000	55	84	.655	11	18	29	54	41	0	....	....	33	9.3	3.4	0.6	1.1	....
68-69	Oakland-A	5	....	19	4	1	6	.167	0	0	.000	2	6	.333	....	....	2	7	6	0	....	....	5	3.8	0.8	0.4	1.4	.270
ABA Playoff Totals		5	....	19	4	1	6	.167	0	0	.000	2	6	.333	....	....	2	7	6	0	....	....	5	3.8	0.8	0.4	1.4	....

YEAR	TEAM	GP	GS	MIN	PTS	FGM	FGA	FG%	3PM	3PA	3P%	FTM	FTA	FT%	ORB	DRB	TRB	AST	PF	DQ	STL	BLK	TO	MPG	PPG	RPG	APG	PCM

• CRITE, Winston
Winston Arnel Crite

Born: June 20, 1965. Bakersfield, CA, United States.　Height: 6'7".　Weight: 233 lbs.　Drafted: 1987　College: Texas A&M

YEAR	TEAM	GP	GS	MIN	PTS	FGM	FGA	FG%	3PM	3PA	3P%	FTM	FTA	FT%	ORB	DRB	TRB	AST	PF	DQ	STL	BLK	TO	MPG	PPG	RPG	APG	PCM
87-88	Phoenix	29	0	258	87	34	68	.500	0	0	.000	19	25	.760	27	37	64	15	42	0	5	8	26	8.9	3.0	2.2	0.5	.374
88-89	Phoenix	2	0	6	0	0	3	.000	0	0	.000	0	0	.000	1	0	1	0	1	0	0	0	1	3.0	0.0	0.5	0.0	-.543
NBA Season Totals		31	0	264	87	34	71	.479	0	0	.000	19	25	.760	28	37	65	15	43	0	5	8	27	8.5	2.8	2.1	0.5	....

• CROCKER, Dillard
James Dillard Crocker

Born: Jan. 19, 1925. Niles, MI, United States.　Height: 6'4".　Weight: 205 lbs.　Drafted: —　College: Western Michigan

YEAR	TEAM	GP	GS	MIN	PTS	FGM	FGA	FG%	3PM	3PA	3P%	FTM	FTA	FT%	ORB	DRB	TRB	AST	PF	DQ	STL	BLK	TO	MPG	PPG	RPG	APG	PCM
48-49	Anderson-N	43	....	....	208	70	....	....	....	....	....	68	93	.731	....	....	....	134	....	....	....	....	....	4.8	....	....	....
48-49	Detroit-N	8	....	....	89	31	....	....	....	....	....	27	38	.711	....	....	....	....	....	....	....	....	....	11.1	....	....	....
48-49	Fort Wayne	2	....	....	6	1	4	.250	....	....	....	4	6	.667	....	....	0	3	....	....	....	....	....	3.0	....	0.0	....
49-50	Denver	53	....	....	723	245	840	.292	....	....	....	233	317	.735	....	....	85	223	....	....	....	....	....	13.6	....	1.6	....
51-52	Ind/Mil	38	....	783	293	98	279	.351	....	....	....	97	145	.669	....	111	57	132	7	....	....	....	20.6	7.7	2.9	1.5	.323
52-53	Milwaukee	61	....	776	330	100	284	.352	....	....	....	130	189	.688	....	104	63	199	11	....	....	....	12.7	5.4	1.7	1.0	.334
NBA Season Totals		154	....	1559	1352	444	1407	.316	....	....	....	464	657	.706	....	....	215	205	557	18	....	....	....	10.1	8.8	1.4	1.3	....
NBL Season Totals		51	....	....	297	101	....	....	....	....	....	95	131		....	....	....	134	....	....	....	....	....	5.8	....	....	....
Career Totals		205	....	1559	1649	545	1407		....	....	....	559	788		....	....	215	205	691	18	....	....	....	7.6	8.0	1.0	1.0	....
48-49	Anderson-N	6	....	....	13	5	....	....	....	....	....	3	8	.375	....	....	....	....	....	....	....	....	....	2.2	....	....	....
NBL Playoff Totals		6	....	....	13	5	....	....	....	....	....	3	8		....	....	....	....	....	....	....	....	....	2.2	....	....	....

• CROFT, Bobby
Robert Alexander Croft

Born: Aug. 10, 1947. Canada.　Height: 6'10".　Weight: 200 lbs.　Drafted: 1970　College: Tennessee

YEAR	TEAM	GP	GS	MIN	PTS	FGM	FGA	FG%	3PM	3PA	3P%	FTM	FTA	FT%	ORB	DRB	TRB	AST	PF	DQ	STL	BLK	TO	MPG	PPG	RPG	APG	PCM
70-71	Kentucky-A	33	....	222	95	35	114	.307	0	2	.000	25	42	.595	22	43	65	15	67	1	....	....	17	6.7	2.9	2.0	0.5	.307
70-71	Texas-A	29	....	517	230	91	234	.389	0	0	.000	48	70	.686	61	80	141	26	70	0	....	....	27	17.8	7.9	4.9	0.9	.431
ABA Season Totals		62	....	739	325	126	348	.362	0	2	.000	73	112	.652	83	123	206	41	137	1	....	....	44	11.9	5.2	3.3	0.7	....
70-71	Texas-A	4	....	55	20	7	23	.304	1	1	1.000	5	7	.714	9	5	14	3	6	0	....	....	2	13.8	5.0	3.5	0.8	.342
ABA Playoff Totals		4	....	55	20	7	23	.304	1	1	1.000	5	7	.714	9	5	14	3	6	0	....	....	2	13.8	5.0	3.5	0.8	....

• CROMPTON, Geoff
Jeffrey Crompton

Born: July 4, 1955. Burlington, NC, United States.　Height: 6'11".　Weight: 280 lbs.　Drafted: 1978　College: North Carolina

YEAR	TEAM	GP	GS	MIN	PTS	FGM	FGA	FG%	3PM	3PA	3P%	FTM	FTA	FT%	ORB	DRB	TRB	AST	PF	DQ	STL	BLK	TO	MPG	PPG	RPG	APG	PCM
78-79	Denver	20	....	88	26	10	26	.385	....	....	....	6	12	.500	6	17	23	5	19	0	0	3	12	4.4	1.3	1.2	0.3	.210
80-81	Portland	6	....	33	9	4	8	.500	0	0	.000	1	5	.200	7	11	18	2	4	0	0	2	5	5.5	1.5	3.0	0.3	.532
81-82	Milwaukee	35	1	203	28	11	32	.344	0	0	.000	6	15	.400	10	31	41	13	39	0	6	12	18	5.8	0.8	1.2	0.4	.189
82-83	San Antonio	14	0	148	31	14	34	.412	0	0	.000	3	5	.600	18	30	48	7	25	0	3	5	6	10.6	2.2	3.4	0.5	.362
83-84	Cleveland	7	0	23	5	1	8	.125	0	0	.000	3	6	.500	6	3	9	1	4	0	1	1	4	3.3	0.7	1.3	0.1	.122
NBA Season Totals		82	1	495	99	40	108	.370	0	0	.000	19	43	.442	47	92	139	28	91	0	10	23	45	6.0	1.2	1.7	0.3	....

• CROSBY, Terry
Terry Dale Crosby

Born: Jan. 4, 1957. Toledo, OH, United States.　Height: 6'4".　Weight: 195 lbs.　Drafted: 1979　College: Tennessee

YEAR	TEAM	GP	GS	MIN	PTS	FGM	FGA	FG%	3PM	3PA	3P%	FTM	FTA	FT%	ORB	DRB	TRB	AST	PF	DQ	STL	BLK	TO	MPG	PPG	RPG	APG	PCM
79-80	Kansas City	4	....	28	6	2	4	.500	0	0	.000	2	2	1.000	0	1	1	7	4	0	0	0	5	7.0	1.5	0.3	1.8	.229
NBA Season Totals		4	....	28	6	2	4	.500	0	0	.000	2	2	1.000	0	1	1	7	4	0	0	0	5	7.0	1.5	0.3	1.8	....

• CROSHERE, Austin
Austin Nathan Croshere

Born: May 1, 1975. Los Angeles, CA, United States.　Height: 6'9".　Weight: 235 lbs.　Drafted: 1997　College: Providence

YEAR	TEAM	GP	GS	MIN	PTS	FGM	FGA	FG%	3PM	3PA	3P%	FTM	FTA	FT%	ORB	DRB	TRB	AST	PF	DQ	STL	BLK	TO	MPG	PPG	RPG	APG	PCM
97-98	Indiana	26	0	243	76	32	86	.372	4	13	.308	8	14	.571	10	35	45	8	32	1	9	5	13	9.3	2.9	1.7	0.3	.247
98-99	Indiana	27	0	249	92	32	75	.427	8	29	.276	20	23	.870	16	29	45	10	32	0	7	8	23	9.2	3.4	1.7	0.4	.330
99-00	Indiana	81	14	1885	835	288	653	.441	63	174	.362	196	231	.848	135	381	516	89	203	2	44	60	121	23.3	10.3	6.4	1.1	.502
00-01	Indiana	81	23	1874	822	276	701	.394	70	207	.338	200	231	.866	123	264	387	92	180	1	36	50	136	23.1	10.1	4.8	1.1	.400
01-02	Indiana	76	1	1286	516	185	448	.413	49	145	.338	97	114	.851	74	220	294	77	106	0	26	29	67	16.9	6.8	3.9	1.0	.437
02-03	Indiana	49	0	633	252	86	209	.411	27	69	.391	53	65	.815	40	115	155	56	48	0	6	13	28	12.9	5.1	3.2	1.1	.485
NBA Season Totals		340	38	6170	2593	899	2172	.414	221	637	.347	574	678	.847	398	1044	1442	332	601	4	128	165	388	18.1	7.6	4.2	1.0	....
98-99	Indiana	1	0	1	2	0	1	.000	0	0	.000	2	2	1.000	1	0	1	0	0	0	0	0	0	1.0	2.0	1.0	0.0	2.000
99-00	Indiana	23	2	490	216	64	153	.418	15	37	.405	73	87	.839	31	78	109	19	51	0	9	16	25	21.3	9.4	4.7	0.8	.460
00-01	Indiana	4	0	129	43	14	35	.400	2	10	.200	13	15	.867	5	15	20	6	15	1	4	2	9	32.3	10.8	5.0	1.5	.298
01-02	Indiana	4	0	59	24	8	20	.400	2	6	.333	6	8	.750	4	10	14	2	7	1	1	1	6	14.8	6.0	3.5	0.5	.344
02-03	Indiana	4	0	46	16	5	19	.263	0	6	.000	6	7	.857	8	9	17	3	5	0	0	1	3	11.5	4.0	4.3	0.8	.380
NBA Playoff Totals		36	2	725	301	91	228	.399	19	59	.322	100	119	.840	49	112	161	30	78	2	14	20	43	20.1	8.4	4.5	0.8	....

• CROSS, Jeff
Jeffrey A. Cross

Born: Sept. 1, 1961. Chicago, IL, United States.　Height: 6'10".　Weight: 240 lbs.　Drafted: 1984　College: Maine

YEAR	TEAM	GP	GS	MIN	PTS	FGM	FGA	FG%	3PM	3PA	3P%	FTM	FTA	FT%	ORB	DRB	TRB	AST	PF	DQ	STL	BLK	TO	MPG	PPG	RPG	APG	PCM
85-86	LA Clippers	21	0	128	26	6	24	.250	0	0	.000	14	25	.560	9	21	30	1	38	0	2	3	6	6.1	1.2	1.4	0.0	.114
NBA Season Totals		21	0	128	26	6	24	.250	0	0	.000	14	25	.560	9	21	30	1	38	0	2	3	6	6.1	1.2	1.4	0.0	....

CROSS, Pete
Peter Michael Cross

Born: Mar. 28, 1948. Died: Jan.2, 1977.   Height: 6'9".   Weight: 230 lbs.   Drafted: 1970   College: San Francisco

YEAR TEAM	GP	GS	MIN	PTS	FGM	FGA	FG%	3PM	3PA	3P%	FTM	FTA	FT%	ORB	DRB	TRB	AST	PF	DQ	STL	BLK	TO	MPG	PPG	RPG	APG	PCM
70-71 Seattle	79	....	2194	630	245	554	.442	....	....	....	140	203	.690	....	....	949	113	212	2	....	....	....	27.8	8.0	12.0	1.4	.543
71-72 Seattle	74	....	1424	407	152	355	.428	....	....	....	103	140	.736	....	....	509	63	135	2	....	....	....	19.2	5.5	6.9	0.9	.470
72-73 Omaha	3	....	24	0	0	4	.000	....	....	....	0	0	.000	....	....	4	0	5	0	....	....	....	8.0	0.0	1.3	0.0	-.089
72-73 Seattle	26	....	133	20	6	21	.286	....	....	....	8	18	.444	....	....	57	11	24	0	....	....	....	5.1	0.8	2.2	0.4	.406
NBA Season Totals	182	....	3775	1057	403	934	.431	....	....	....	251	361	.695	....	....	1519	187	376	4	....	....	....	20.7	5.8	8.3	1.0	....

CROSS, Russell
Russell Cross Jr.

Born: Sept. 5, 1961. Chicago, IL, United States.   Height: 6'10".   Weight: 215 lbs.   Drafted: 1983   College: Purdue

YEAR TEAM	GP	GS	MIN	PTS	FGM	FGA	FG%	3PM	3PA	3P%	FTM	FTA	FT%	ORB	DRB	TRB	AST	PF	DQ	STL	BLK	TO	MPG	PPG	RPG	APG	PCM
83-84 Golden State	45	0	354	166	64	112	.571	0	0	.000	38	91	.418	35	47	82	22	58	0	12	7	18	7.9	3.7	1.8	0.5	.482
NBA Season Totals	45	0	354	166	64	112	.571	0	0	.000	38	91	.418	35	47	82	22	58	0	12	7	18	7.9	3.7	1.8	0.5	....

CROSSIN, Chink
Francis P. (Chink) Crossin

Born: July 4, 1924. Died: Jan.10, 1981.   Height: 6'1".   Weight: 165 lbs.   Drafted: 1947   College: Pennsylvania

YEAR TEAM	GP	GS	MIN	PTS	FGM	FGA	FG%	3PM	3PA	3P%	FTM	FTA	FT%	ORB	DRB	TRB	AST	PF	DQ	STL	BLK	TO	MPG	PPG	RPG	APG	PCM
47-48 Philadelphia	39	....	....	71	29	121	.240	....	....	....	13	23	.565	....	....	....	20	28	....	....	....	....	....	1.8	....	0.5	....
48-49 Philadelphia	44	....	....	174	74	212	.349	....	....	....	26	42	.619	....	....	....	55	53	....	....	....	....	....	4.0	....	1.3	....
49-50 Philadelphia	64	....	....	449	185	574	.322	....	....	....	79	101	.782	....	....	....	148	139	....	....	....	....	....	7.0	....	2.3	....
NBA Season Totals	147	....	....	694	288	907	.318	....	....	....	118	166	.711	....	....	....	223	220	....	....	....	....	....	4.7	....	1.5	....
47-48 Philadelphia	10	....	....	40	16	49	.327	....	....	....	8	9	.889	....	....	....	10	18	....	....	....	....	....	4.0	....	1.0	....
48-49 Philadelphia	2	....	....	31	13	31	.419	....	....	....	5	7	.714	....	....	....	3	3	....	....	....	....	....	15.5	....	1.5	....
49-50 Philadelphia	2	....	....	26	9	27	.333	....	....	....	8	9	.889	....	....	....	4	3	....	....	....	....	....	13.0	....	2.0	....
NBA Playoff Totals	14	....	....	97	38	107	.355	....	....	....	21	25	.840	....	....	....	17	24	....	....	....	....	....	6.9	....	1.2	....

CROTTY, John
John Kevin Crotty

Born: July 15, 1969. Orange, NJ, United States.   Height: 6'1".   Weight: 185 lbs.   Drafted: —   College: Virginia

YEAR TEAM	GP	GS	MIN	PTS	FGM	FGA	FG%	3PM	3PA	3P%	FTM	FTA	FT%	ORB	DRB	TRB	AST	PF	DQ	STL	BLK	TO	MPG	PPG	RPG	APG	PCM
92-93 Utah	40	0	243	102	37	72	.514	2	14	.143	26	38	.684	4	13	17	55	29	0	11	0	32	6.1	2.6	0.4	1.4	.433
93-94 Utah	45	0	313	132	45	99	.455	11	24	.458	31	36	.861	11	20	31	77	36	0	15	1	27	7.0	2.9	0.7	1.7	.528
94-95 Utah	80	0	1019	295	93	231	.403	11	36	.306	98	121	.810	27	70	97	205	105	0	39	6	72	12.7	3.7	1.2	2.6	.382
95-96 Cleveland	58	4	617	172	51	114	.447	8	27	.296	62	72	.861	20	34	54	102	60	0	22	6	52	10.6	3.0	0.9	1.8	.350
96-97 Miami	48	0	659	232	79	154	.513	20	49	.408	54	64	.844	15	32	47	102	79	0	18	0	43	13.7	4.8	1.0	2.1	.379
97-98 Portland	26	2	379	96	29	90	.322	6	20	.300	32	34	.941	4	28	32	63	28	0	10	1	42	14.6	3.7	1.2	2.4	.253
98-99 Portland	3	0	19	12	4	8	.500	1	1	1.000	3	3	1.000	0	1	1	5	1	0	2	0	0	6.3	4.0	0.3	1.7	.854
98-99 Seattle	24	0	363	147	47	116	.405	13	35	.371	40	47	.851	8	22	30	58	30	0	9	0	33	15.1	6.1	1.3	2.4	.383
99-00 Detroit	69	0	937	325	106	251	.422	33	80	.413	80	93	.860	17	58	75	128	104	0	27	5	54	13.6	4.7	1.1	1.9	.350
00-01 Utah	31	0	264	65	22	65	.338	4	7	.571	17	19	.895	13	15	28	34	32	0	6	0	19	8.5	2.1	0.9	1.1	.235
01-02 Utah	41	0	802	284	98	208	.471	31	69	.449	57	66	.864	16	59	75	141	77	1	19	1	51	19.6	6.9	1.8	3.4	.423
02-03 Denver	12	0	180	41	14	41	.341	4	13	.308	9	15	.600	1	14	15	29	16	0	3	0	9	15.0	3.4	1.3	2.4	.257
NBA Season Totals	477	6	5795	1903	625	1449	.431	144	375	.384	509	608	.837	136	366	502	999	597	1	181	20	434	12.1	4.0	1.1	2.1	....
92-93 Utah	1	0	3	4	2	2	1.000	0	0	.000	0	0	.000	1	0	1	1	0	0	0	0	0	3.0	4.0	1.0	1.0	2.000
93-94 Utah	8	0	38	12	4	11	.364	2	2	1.000	2	2	1.000	0	3	3	9	6	0	1	0	1	4.8	1.5	0.4	1.1	.403
94-95 Utah	3	0	24	7	2	3	.667	0	0	.000	3	5	.600	0	0	0	6	2	0	1	0	0	8.0	2.3	0.0	2.0	.479
95-96 Cleveland	2	0	9	2	0	0	.000	0	0	.000	2	2	1.000	1	0	1	1	0	0	1	1	1	4.5	1.0	0.5	0.5	.549
96-97 Miami	15	0	125	37	13	33	.394	5	12	.417	6	7	.857	5	6	11	11	15	0	4	0	14	8.3	2.5	0.7	0.7	.189
99-00 Detroit	3	0	51	6	2	10	.200	0	3	.000	2	2	1.000	0	4	4	4	4	0	1	1	4	17.0	2.0	1.3	1.3	.061
00-01 Utah	4	0	19	3	0	3	.000	0	0	.000	3	3	1.000	1	2	3	3	3	0	1	1	0	4.8	0.8	0.8	0.8	.356
NBA Playoff Totals	36	0	269	71	23	62	.371	7	17	.412	18	21	.857	8	15	23	35	30	0	9	3	20	7.5	2.0	0.6	1.0	....

CROW, Bill
William R. Crow

Born: Dec. 9, 1940.   Height: 6'1".   Weight: 180 lbs.   Drafted: —   College: Westminster (UT)

YEAR TEAM	GP	GS	MIN	PTS	FGM	FGA	FG%	3PM	3PA	3P%	FTM	FTA	FT%	ORB	DRB	TRB	AST	PF	DQ	STL	BLK	TO	MPG	PPG	RPG	APG	PCM
67-68 Anaheim-A	1	....	16	3	1	8	.125	0	0	.000	1	4	.250	....	....	2	0	0	0	....	....	1	16.0	3.0	2.0	0.0	-.150
ABA Season Totals	1	....	16	3	1	8	.125	0	0	.000	1	4	.250	....	....	2	0	0	0	....	....	1	16.0	3.0	2.0	0.0	....

CROW, Mark
Mark Harvey (Crow-bar) Crow

Born: Oct. 22, 1954. Edwards AFB, CA, United States.   Height: 6'7".   Weight: 210 lbs.   Drafted: 1977   College: Duke

YEAR TEAM	GP	GS	MIN	PTS	FGM	FGA	FG%	3PM	3PA	3P%	FTM	FTA	FT%	ORB	DRB	TRB	AST	PF	DQ	STL	BLK	TO	MPG	PPG	RPG	APG	PCM
77-78 New Jersey	15	....	154	84	35	80	.438	....	....	....	14	20	.700	14	13	27	8	24	0	5	1	12	10.3	5.6	1.8	0.5	.382
NBA Season Totals	15	....	154	84	35	80	.438	....	....	....	14	20	.700	14	13	27	8	24	0	5	1	12	10.3	5.6	1.8	0.5	....

CROWDER, Corey
Jonathan Corey Crowder

Born: Apr. 13, 1969. Carrollton, GA, United States.   Height: 6'5".   Weight: 214 lbs.   Drafted: —   College: Kentucky Wesleyan

YEAR TEAM	GP	GS	MIN	PTS	FGM	FGA	FG%	3PM	3PA	3P%	FTM	FTA	FT%	ORB	DRB	TRB	AST	PF	DQ	STL	BLK	TO	MPG	PPG	RPG	APG	PCM
91-92 Utah	51	0	328	114	43	112	.384	13	30	.433	15	18	.833	16	25	41	17	35	0	7	2	15	6.4	2.2	0.8	0.3	.253
94-95 San Antonio	7	0	29	6	2	10	.200	0	4	.000	2	6	.333	1	2	3	1	1	0	1	0	2	4.1	0.9	0.4	0.1	-.031
NBA Season Totals	58	0	357	120	45	122	.369	13	34	.382	17	24	.708	17	27	44	18	36	0	8	2	17	6.2	2.1	0.8	0.3	....
91-92 Utah	4	0	12	10	5	9	.556	0	2	.000	0	1	.000	1	1	2	1	1	0	1	0	2	3.0	2.5	0.5	0.3	.613
NBA Playoff Totals	4	0	12	10	5	9	.556	0	2	.000	0	1	.000	1	1	2	1	1	0	1	0	2	3.0	2.5	0.5	0.3	....

YEAR	TEAM	GP	GS	MIN	PTS	FGM	FGA	FG%	3PM	3PA	3P%	FTM	FTA	FT%	ORB	DRB	TRB	AST	PF	DQ	STL	BLK	TO	MPG	PPG	RPG	APG	PCM

• CROWE, George
George Daniel (Big George) Crowe

Born: Mar. 22, 1921. Whiteland, IN, United States. Height: 6'2". Weight: 206 lbs. Drafted: — College: Indiana Central

YEAR	TEAM	GP	GS	MIN	PTS	FGM	FGA	FG%	3PM	3PA	3P%	FTM	FTA	FT%	ORB	DRB	TRB	AST	PF	DQ	STL	BLK	TO	MPG	PPG	RPG	APG	PCM
48-49	Dayton-N	40	....	....	437	164	....	....	....	....	....	109	159	.686	....	....	....	....	....	....	....	....	....	....	10.9	....	....	....
NBL Season Totals		40	....	....	437	164	....	....	....	....	....	109	159		....	....	....	....	....	....	....	....	....	....	10.9	....	....	....

• CROWE, Leo
Leo Crowe

Born: 1912. Height: 5'11". Weight: 170 lbs. Drafted: — College: Notre Dame

YEAR	TEAM	GP	GS	MIN	PTS	FGM	FGA	FG%	3PM	3PA	3P%	FTM	FTA	FT%	MPG	PPG	RPG	APG	PCM
37-38	Indianapolis-N	12	....	....	74	30	....	....	....	....	....	14	....		6.2			
NBL Season Totals		12	....	....	74	30	....	....	....	....	....	14			6.2			

• CROWLEY, Kiernan
Kiernan Crowley

Born: 1916. Height: 5'8". Weight: 155 lbs. Drafted: — College: DePaul

YEAR	TEAM	GP	GS	MIN	PTS	FGM	FGA	FG%	3PM	3PA	3P%	FTM	MPG	PPG	RPG	APG	PCM
38-39	Sheboygan-N	5	....	....	10	3	....	....	....	....	....	4	2.0			
NBL Season Totals		5	....	....	10	3	....	....	....	....	....	4	2.0			

• CRUM, Freddie
Freddie Crum

Born: 1912. Height: 6' Weight: 170 lbs. Drafted: — College: none

YEAR	TEAM	GP	GS	MIN	PTS	FGM	FGA	FG%	3PM	3PA	3P%	FTM	MPG	PPG	RPG	APG	PCM
44-45	Pittsburgh-N	29	....	....	168	69	....	....	....	....	....	30	5.8			
NBL Season Totals		29	....	....	168	69	....	....	....	....	....	30	5.8			

• CUETO, Al
Alfonso Angel Cueto

Born: Aug. 2, 1946. Havana, Cuba. Height: 6'7". Weight: 230 lbs. Drafted: 1969 College: Tulsa

YEAR	TEAM	GP	GS	MIN	PTS	FGM	FGA	FG%	3PM	3PA	3P%	FTM	FTA	FT%	ORB	DRB	TRB	AST	PF	DQ	STL	BLK	TO	MPG	PPG	RPG	APG	PCM
69-70	Miami-A	78	....	1265	471	182	449	.405	5	16	.313	102	144	.708	171	281	452	58	257	12	....	....	95	16.2	6.0	5.8	0.7	.449
70-71	Memphis-A	71	....	974	323	134	333	.402	0	5	.000	55	77	.714	100	179	279	86	166	2	....	....	57	13.7	4.5	3.9	1.2	.426
ABA Season Totals		149	....	2239	794	316	782	.404	5	21	.238	157	221	.710	271	460	731	144	423	14	....	....	152	15.0	5.3	4.9	1.0	....
70-71	Memphis-A	4	....	51	14	6	14	.429	0	0	.000	2	3	.667	6	12	18	3	7	0	....	....	2	12.8	3.5	4.5	0.8	.439
ABA Playoff Totals		4	....	51	14	6	14	.429	0	0	.000	2	3	.667	6	12	18	3	7	0	....	....	2	12.8	3.5	4.5	0.8	....

• CULLEN, Marty
Marty Cullen

Born: —. Height: — Weight: — Drafted: — College: —

YEAR	TEAM	GP	GS	MIN	PTS	FGM	FGA	FG%	3PM	3PA	3P%	FTM	MPG	PPG	RPG	APG	PCM
37-38	Whiting-N	2	....	....	1	0	....	....	....	....	....	1	0.5			
NBL Playoff Totals		2	....	....	1	0	....	....	....	....	....	1	0.5			

• CUMBERLAND, Roscoe
Roscoe (Duke) Cumberland

Born: 1919. Height: 6'2". Weight: 189 lbs. Drafted: — College: Knoxville

YEAR	TEAM	GP	GS	MIN	PTS	FGM	FGA	FG%	3PM	3PA	3P%	FTM	MPG	PPG	RPG	APG	PCM
42-43	Chicago-N	22	....	....	151	53	....	....	....	....	....	45	6.9			
NBL Season Totals		22	....	....	151	53	....	....	....	....	....	45	6.9			
42-43	Chicago-N	3	....	....	19	8	....	....	....	....	....	3	6.3			
NBL Playoff Totals		3	....	....	19	8	....	....	....	....	....	3	6.3			

• CUMMINGS, Pat
Patrick Michael Cummings

Born: July 11, 1956. Johnstown, PA, United States. Height: 6'9". Weight: 230 lbs. Drafted: 1978 College: Cincinnati

YEAR	TEAM	GP	GS	MIN	PTS	FGM	FGA	FG%	3PM	3PA	3P%	FTM	FTA	FT%	ORB	DRB	TRB	AST	PF	DQ	STL	BLK	TO	MPG	PPG	RPG	APG	PCM
79-80	Milwaukee	71	....	900	468	187	370	.505	0	0	.000	94	123	.764	81	157	238	53	141	0	22	17	71	12.7	6.6	3.4	0.7	.522
80-81	Milwaukee	74	....	1084	595	248	460	.539	0	2	.000	99	140	.707	97	195	292	62	192	4	31	19	111	14.6	8.0	3.9	0.8	.529
81-82	Milwaukee	78	7	1132	505	219	430	.509	0	2	.000	67	91	.736	61	184	245	99	227	6	22	8	109	14.5	6.5	3.1	1.3	.402
82-83	Dallas	81	71	2317	1014	433	878	.493	0	1	.000	148	196	.755	225	443	668	144	296	9	57	35	162	28.6	12.5	8.2	1.8	.498
83-84	Dallas	80	80	2492	1045	452	915	.494	0	2	.000	141	190	.742	151	507	658	158	282	2	64	23	144	31.2	13.1	8.2	2.0	.477
84-85	New York	63	63	2069	997	410	797	.514	0	4	.000	177	227	.780	139	379	518	109	247	6	50	17	164	32.8	15.8	8.2	1.7	.487
85-86	New York	31	30	1007	487	195	408	.478	0	2	.000	97	139	.698	92	188	280	47	136	7	27	12	87	32.5	15.7	9.0	1.5	.469
86-87	New York	49	11	1056	423	172	382	.450	0	0	.000	79	110	.718	123	189	312	38	145	2	26	7	83	21.6	8.6	6.4	0.8	.407
87-88	New York	62	9	946	339	140	307	.456	0	1	.000	59	80	.738	82	153	235	37	143	0	20	10	62	15.3	5.5	3.8	0.6	.355
88-89	Miami	53	28	1096	466	197	394	.500	0	2	.000	72	97	.742	84	197	281	47	160	3	29	18	111	20.7	8.8	5.3	0.9	.410
89-90	Miami	37	1	391	175	77	159	.484	0	0	.000	21	37	.568	28	65	93	13	60	1	12	4	33	10.6	4.7	2.5	0.4	.377
90-91	Utah	4	0	26	15	4	6	.667	0	0	.000	7	10	.700	3	2	5	0	8	0	0	0	2	6.5	3.8	1.3	0.0	.415
NBA Season Totals		683	300	14516	6529	2734	5506	.497	0	16	.000	1061	1440	.737	1166	2659	3825	807	2037	40	360	170	1139	21.3	9.6	5.6	1.2	....
79-80	Milwaukee	6	....	57	27	11	17	.647	0	0	.000	5	6	.833	4	12	16	2	9	0	1	0	8	9.5	4.5	2.7	0.3	.480
80-81	Milwaukee	5	....	25	9	3	11	.273	0	0	.000	3	4	.750	3	3	6	0	1	0	1	0	1	5.0	1.8	1.2	0.0	.232
81-82	Milwaukee	6	0	44	9	4	11	.364	0	0	.000	1	2	.500	3	8	11	2	7	0	0	2	4	7.3	1.5	1.8	0.3	.212
83-84	Dallas	10	10	300	108	47	115	.409	0	0	.000	14	15	.933	26	46	72	15	30	0	4	2	9	30.0	10.8	7.2	1.5	.369
87-88	New York	3	0	28	7	2	5	.400	0	0	.000	3	4	.750	2	5	7	3	11	0	0	0	0	9.3	2.3	2.3	1.0	.298
NBA Playoff Totals		30	10	454	160	67	159	.421	0	0	.000	26	31	.839	38	74	112	22	59	0	6	4	22	15.1	5.3	3.7	0.7	....

• CUMMINGS, Terry

Robert Terrell Cummings

Born: Mar. 15, 1961. Chicago, IL, United States. Height: 6'9". Weight: 220 lbs. Drafted: 1982 College: DePaul

YEAR	TEAM	GP	GS	MIN	PTS	FGM	FGA	FG%	3PM	3PA	3P%	FTM	FTA	FT%	ORB	DRB	TRB	AST	PF	DQ	STL	BLK	TO	MPG	PPG	RPG	APG	PCM
82-83	San Diego	70	69	2531	1660	684	1309	.523	0	1	.000	292	412	.709	303	441	744	177	294	10	129	62	203	36.2	23.7	10.6	2.5	.697
83-84	San Diego	81	80	2907	1854	737	1491	.494	0	3	.000	380	528	.720	323	454	777	139	298	6	92	57	219	35.9	22.9	9.6	1.7	.603
84-85	Milwaukee	79	78	2722	1861	759	1532	.495	0	1	.000	343	463	.741	244	472	716	228	264	4	117	67	190	34.5	23.6	9.1	2.9	.686
85-86	Milwaukee	82	82	2669	1627	681	1438	.474	0	2	.000	265	404	.656	222	472	694	193	283	4	121	51	189	32.5	19.8	8.5	2.4	.586
86-87	Milwaukee	82	77	2770	1707	729	1426	.511	0	3	.000	249	376	.662	214	486	700	229	296	3	129	81	172	33.8	20.8	8.5	2.8	.647
87-88	Milwaukee	76	76	2629	1621	675	1392	.485	1	3	.333	270	406	.665	184	369	553	181	274	6	78	46	167	34.6	21.3	7.3	2.4	.544
88-89	Milwaukee	80	78	2824	1829	730	1563	.467	7	15	.467	362	460	.787	281	369	650	198	265	5	106	72	200	35.3	22.9	8.1	2.5	.595
89-90	San Antonio	81	78	2821	1818	728	1532	.475	19	59	.322	343	440	.780	226	451	677	219	286	1	110	52	203	34.8	22.4	8.4	2.7	.608
90-91	San Antonio	67	62	2195	1177	503	1039	.484	7	33	.212	164	240	.683	194	327	521	157	225	5	61	30	134	32.8	17.6	7.8	2.3	.524
91-92	San Antonio	70	67	2149	1210	514	1053	.488	5	13	.385	177	249	.711	247	384	631	102	210	4	58	34	112	30.7	17.3	9.0	1.5	.584
92-93	San Antonio	8	0	76	27	11	29	.379	0	0	.000	5	10	.500	6	13	19	4	17	0	1	1	2	9.5	3.4	2.4	0.5	.289
93-94	San Antonio	59	29	1133	429	183	428	.428	0	2	.000	63	107	.589	132	165	297	50	137	0	31	13	59	19.2	7.3	5.0	0.8	.383
94-95	San Antonio	76	20	1273	520	224	464	.483	0	0	.000	72	123	.585	138	240	378	59	188	1	36	19	99	16.8	6.8	5.0	0.8	.439
95-96	Milwaukee	81	13	1777	645	270	584	.462	1	7	.143	104	160	.650	162	283	445	89	263	2	56	30	73	21.9	8.0	5.5	1.1	.408
96-97	Seattle	45	3	828	370	155	319	.486	3	5	.600	57	82	.695	70	113	183	39	113	0	33	7	45	18.4	8.2	4.1	0.9	.435
97-98	Philadelphia	44	2	656	233	97	212	.458	0	1	.000	39	58	.672	55	93	148	21	102	1	22	5	18	14.9	5.3	3.4	0.5	.364
97-98	New York	30	1	529	234	103	216	.477	0	0	.000	28	40	.700	42	93	135	26	79	0	16	5	33	17.6	7.8	4.5	0.9	.434
98-99	Golden State	50	0	1011	454	186	424	.439	1	1	1.000	81	114	.711	95	160	255	58	168	4	46	10	58	20.2	9.1	5.1	1.2	.438
99-00	Golden State	22	0	398	184	76	177	.429	0	0	.000	32	39	.821	45	62	107	21	74	0	13	8	27	18.1	8.4	4.9	1.0	.428
NBA Season Totals		1183	815	33898	19460	8045	16628	.484	44	149	.295	3326	4711	.706	3183	5447	8630	2190	3836	56	1255	650	2203	28.7	16.4	7.3	1.9	....
84-85	Milwaukee	8	8	311	220	86	149	.577	0	1	.000	48	58	.828	21	49	70	20	33	1	12	7	26	38.9	27.5	8.8	2.5	.712
85-86	Milwaukee	14	14	510	303	130	253	.514	0	0	.000	43	62	.694	33	105	138	42	52	0	20	16	39	36.4	21.6	9.9	3.0	.640
86-87	Milwaukee	12	10	443	267	105	215	.488	0	0	.000	57	83	.687	29	66	95	28	51	1	12	13	15	36.9	22.3	7.9	2.3	.579
87-88	Milwaukee	5	5	193	129	50	89	.562	0	0	.000	29	44	.659	12	27	39	13	16	0	9	3	12	38.6	25.8	7.8	2.6	.665
88-89	Milwaukee	5	4	124	64	25	69	.362	0	1	.000	14	16	.875	19	14	33	7	16	0	3	0	4	24.8	12.8	6.6	1.4	.419
89-90	San Antonio	10	10	375	249	103	195	.528	1	5	.200	42	52	.808	31	63	94	22	39	0	7	4	19	37.5	24.9	9.4	2.2	.650
90-91	San Antonio	4	4	124	59	25	49	.510	0	1	.000	9	18	.500	14	23	37	4	13	0	3	2	9	31.0	14.8	9.3	1.0	.495
91-92	San Antonio	3	3	122	78	34	66	.515	0	1	.000	10	20	.500	15	19	34	7	9	0	4	4	7	40.7	26.0	11.3	2.3	.651
92-93	San Antonio	10	0	138	67	31	70	.443	0	1	.000	5	8	.625	17	22	39	5	27	0	3	1	8	13.8	6.7	3.9	0.5	.396
93-94	San Antonio	4	1	72	32	11	22	.500	0	0	.000	10	12	.833	10	15	25	2	10	0	5	3	4	18.0	8.0	6.3	0.5	.627
94-95	San Antonio	15	2	135	58	18	48	.375	0	1	.000	22	30	.733	12	19	31	4	25	0	5	1	7	9.0	3.9	2.1	0.3	.346
96-97	Seattle	12	6	292	106	45	92	.489	0	0	.000	16	24	.667	28	44	72	14	39	1	11	6	14	24.3	8.8	6.0	1.2	.429
97-98	New York	8	1	120	32	15	34	.441	0	0	.000	2	8	.250	11	24	35	5	23	0	4	2	7	15.0	4.0	4.4	0.6	.316
NBA Playoff Totals		110	68	2959	1664	678	1351	.502	1	11	.091	307	435	.706	252	490	742	173	353	3	98	62	171	26.9	15.1	6.7	1.6	....

• CUMMINGS, Vonteego

Vonteego Marfeek Cummings

Born: Feb. 29, 1976. Thomson, GA, United States. Height: 6'3". Weight: 185 lbs. Drafted: 1999 College: Pittsburgh

YEAR	TEAM	GP	GS	MIN	PTS	FGM	FGA	FG%	3PM	3PA	3P%	FTM	FTA	FT%	ORB	DRB	TRB	AST	PF	DQ	STL	BLK	TO	MPG	PPG	RPG	APG	PCM
99-00	Golden State	75	11	1793	706	265	655	.405	49	151	.325	127	169	.751	57	127	184	247	174	4	91	13	132	23.9	9.4	2.5	3.3	.371
00-01	Golden State	66	11	1495	483	178	517	.344	48	143	.336	79	116	.681	47	90	137	227	160	2	67	14	91	22.7	7.3	2.1	3.4	.304
01-02	Philadelphia	58	1	501	192	78	187	.417	12	46	.261	24	32	.750	14	38	52	60	53	0	18	5	36	8.6	3.3	0.9	1.0	.333
NBA Season Totals		199	23	3789	1381	521	1359	.383	109	340	.321	230	317	.726	118	255	373	534	387	6	176	32	259	19.0	6.9	1.9	2.7	....
01-02	Philadelphia	1	0	1	0	0	0	.000	0	0	.000	0	0	.000	0	0	0	0	0	0	0	0	0	1.0	0.0	0.0	0.0	.000
NBA Playoff Totals		1	0	1	0	0	0	.000	0	0	.000	0	0	.000	0	0	0	0	0	0	0	0	0	1.0	0.0	0.0	0.0	....

• CUNNINGHAM, Billy

William John (The Kangaroo Kid) Cunningham

Born: June 3, 1943. Brooklyn, NY, United States. Height: 6'6". Weight: 210 lbs. Drafted: 1965 College: North Carolina HOF: 1986

YEAR	TEAM	GP	GS	MIN	PTS	FGM	FGA	FG%	3PM	3PA	3P%	FTM	FTA	FT%	ORB	DRB	TRB	AST	PF	DQ	STL	BLK	TO	MPG	PPG	RPG	APG	PCM
65-66	Philadelphia	80	....	2134	1143	431	1011	.426	....	....	....	281	443	.634	....	....	599	207	301	12	....	....	....	26.7	14.3	7.5	2.6	.575
66-67	Philadelphia	81	....	2168	1495	556	1211	.459	....	....	....	383	558	.686	....	....	589	205	260	2	....	....	....	26.8	18.5	7.3	2.5	.699
67-68	Philadelphia	74	....	2076	1400	516	1178	.438	....	....	....	368	509	.723	....	....	562	187	260	3	....	....	....	28.1	18.9	7.6	2.5	.667
68-69	Philadelphia	82	....	3345	2034	739	1736	.426	....	....	....	556	754	.737	....	....	1050	287	**329**	10	....	....	....	40.8	24.8	12.8	3.5	.655
69-70	Philadelphia	81	....	3194	2114	802	1710	.469	....	....	....	510	700	.729	....	....	1101	352	331	15	....	....	....	39.4	26.1	13.6	4.3	.767
70-71	Philadelphia	81	....	3090	1859	702	1519	.462	....	....	....	455	620	.734	....	....	946	395	328	5	....	....	....	38.1	23.0	11.7	4.9	.715
71-72	Philadelphia	75	....	2900	1744	658	1428	.461	....	....	....	428	601	.712	....	....	918	443	295	12	....	....	....	38.7	23.3	12.2	5.9	.749
72-73	Carolina-A	84	....	3248	2028	771	1583	.487	14	49	.286	472	598	.789	240	772	1012	530	309	6	**216**	....	381	38.7	24.1	12.0	6.3	.799
73-74	Carolina-A	32	....	1190	656	253	537	.471	1	8	.125	149	187	.797	86	245	331	150	105	....	59	21	127	37.2	20.5	10.3	4.7	.678
74-75	Philadelphia	80	....	2859	1563	609	1423	.428	....	....	....	345	444	.777	130	596	726	442	270	4	91	35	....	35.7	19.5	9.1	5.5	.643
75-76	Philadelphia	20	....	640	274	103	251	.410	....	....	....	68	88	.773	29	118	147	107	57	1	24	10	....	32.0	13.7	7.4	5.4	.566
NBA Season Totals		654	....	22406	13626	5116	11467	.446	....	....	....	3394	4717	.720	159	714	6638	2625	2431	64	115	45	....	34.3	20.8	10.1	4.0	....
ABA Season Totals		116	....	4438	2684	1024	2120	.483	15	57	.263	621	785	.791	326	1017	1343	680	414	6	275	21	508	38.3	23.1	11.6	5.9	....
Career Totals		770	....	26844	16310	6140	13587	.452	15	57	.263	4015	5502	.730	485	1731	7981	3305	2845	70	390	66	508	34.9	21.2	10.4	4.3	....
65-66	Philadelphia	4	....	69	21	5	31	.161	....	....	....	11	13	.846	....	....	18	10	11	0	....	....	....	17.3	5.3	4.5	2.5	.316
66-67	Philadelphia	15	....	339	225	83	221	.376	....	....	....	59	90	.656	....	....	93	33	53	1	....	....	....	22.6	15.0	6.2	2.2	.576
67-68	Philadelphia	3	....	86	62	24	43	.558	....	....	....	14	17	.824	....	....	22	10	16	1	....	....	....	28.7	20.7	7.3	3.3	.800
68-69	Philadelphia	5	....	217	122	49	117	.419	....	....	....	24	38	.632	....	....	63	12	24	1	....	....	....	43.4	24.4	12.6	2.4	.534
69-70	Philadelphia	5	....	205	146	61	123	.496	....	....	....	24	36	.667	....	....	52	20	19	0	....	....	....	41.0	29.2	10.4	4.0	.712
70-71	Philadelphia	7	....	301	181	67	142	.472	....	....	....	47	67	.701	....	....	108	40	28	0	....	....	....	43.0	25.9	15.4	5.7	.779
72-73	Carolina-A	12	....	472	282	112	223	.502	1	4	.250	57	83	.687	35	107	142	61	48	0	....	....	50	39.3	23.5	11.8	5.1	.728
73-74	Carolina-A	3	....	61	22	9	31	.290	0	2	.000	4	5	.800	4	12	16	6	9	....	4	0	6	20.3	7.3	5.3	2.0	.318
NBA Playoff Totals		39	....	1217	757	289	677	.427	....	....	....	179	261	.686	....	....	356	125	151	3	....	....	....	31.2	19.4	9.1	3.2	....
ABA Playoff Totals		15	....	533	304	121	254	.476	1	6	.167	61	88	.693	39	119	158	67	57	0	4	0	56	35.5	20.3	10.5	4.5	....
Career Playoff Totals		54	....	1750	1061	410	931	.440	1	6	.167	240	349	.688	39	119	514	192	208	3	4	0	56	32.4	19.6	9.5	3.6	....

• CUNNINGHAM, Dick
Dick (Cement Mixer) Cunningham

Born: July 11, 1946. Canton, OH, United States. Height: 6'10". Weight: 245 lbs. Drafted: 1968 College: Murray State

YEAR	TEAM	GP	GS	MIN	PTS	FGM	FGA	FG%	3PM	3PA	3P%	FTM	FTA	FT%	ORB	DRB	TRB	AST	PF	DQ	STL	BLK	TO	MPG	PPG	RPG	APG	PCM
68-69	Milwaukee	77	....	1236	351	141	332	.425	....	....	....	69	106	.651	....	....	438	58	166	2	....	....	....	16.1	4.6	5.7	0.8	.437
69-70	Milwaukee	60	....	416	126	52	141	.369	....	....	....	22	33	.667	....	....	160	28	70	0	....	....	....	6.9	2.1	2.7	0.5	.443
70-71	Milwaukee	76	....	675	201	81	195	.415	....	....	....	39	59	.661	....	....	257	43	90	1	....	....	....	8.9	2.6	3.4	0.6	.483
71-72	Houston	63	....	720	171	67	174	.385	....	....	....	37	53	.698	....	....	243	57	76	0	....	....	....	11.4	2.7	3.9	0.9	.435
72-73	Milwaukee	72	....	692	157	64	156	.410	....	....	....	29	50	.580	....	....	208	34	94	0	....	....	....	9.6	2.2	2.9	0.5	.356
73-74	Milwaukee	8	....	45	6	3	6	.500	....	....	....	0	7	.000	1	15	16	0	5	0	2	2	....	5.6	0.8	2.0	0.0	.266
74-75	Milwaukee	2	....	8	0	0	0	.000	....	....	....	0	0	.000	0	2	2	1	1	0	0	0	....	4.0	0.0	1.0	0.5	.303
NBA Season Totals		358	....	3792	1012	408	1004	.406	....	....	....	196	308	.636	1	17	1324	221	502	3	2	2	....	10.6	2.8	3.7	0.6	....
69-70	Milwaukee	8	....	45	21	10	18	.556	....	....	....	1	2	.500	....	....	12	2	6	0	....	....	....	5.6	2.6	1.5	0.3	.526
70-71	Milwaukee	14	....	89	24	9	21	.429	....	....	....	6	9	.667	....	....	24	1	10	0	....	....	....	6.4	1.7	1.7	0.1	.336
72-73	Milwaukee	5	....	17	2	1	1	1.000	....	....	....	0	0	.000	....	....	3	2	6	0	....	....	....	3.4	0.4	0.6	0.4	.252
NBA Playoff Totals		27	....	151	47	20	40	.500	....	....	....	7	11	.636	....	....	39	5	22	0	....	....	....	5.6	1.7	1.4	0.2	....

• CUNNINGHAM, Harold
Harold Brewer (Cookie) Cunningham

Born: Feb. 4, 1905. Mt. Vernon, OH, United States. Died: Nov.3, 1995. Height: 6'3". Weight: 210 lbs. Drafted: — College: Ohio State

YEAR	TEAM	GP	GS	MIN	PTS	FGM	FGA	FG%	3PM	3PA	3P%	FTM	FTA	FT%	ORB	DRB	TRB	AST	PF	DQ	STL	BLK	TO	MPG	PPG	RPG	APG	PCM
37-38	Columbus-N	11	....	....	81	27	....	....	....	....	....	27	....	....	....	....	....	....	....	....	....	....	....	....	7.4	....	....	....
NBL Season Totals		11	....	....	81	27	....	....	....	....	....	27	....	....	....	....	....	....	....	....	....	....	....	....	7.4	....	....	....

• CUNNINGHAM, William
William Cunningham

Born: Mar. 25, 1974. Augusta, GA, United States. Height: 6'11". Weight: 250 lbs. Drafted: — College: Temple

YEAR	TEAM	GP	GS	MIN	PTS	FGM	FGA	FG%	3PM	3PA	3P%	FTM	FTA	FT%	ORB	DRB	TRB	AST	PF	DQ	STL	BLK	TO	MPG	PPG	RPG	APG	PCM
97-98	Utah	6	2	38	8	4	9	.444	0	0	.000	0	0	.000	4	4	8	1	10	0	2	0	0	6.3	1.3	1.3	0.2	.239
97-98	Philadelphia	1	0	1	0	0	0	.000	0	0	.000	0	0	.000	0	2	2	0	0	0	0	0	0	1.0	0.0	2.0	0.0	1.830
98-99	Toronto	1	0	1	0	0	0	.000	0	0	.000	0	0	.000	0	0	0	0	0	0	0	0	0	1.0	0.0	0.0	0.0	.000
98-99	New Jersey	15	6	161	6	3	18	.167	0	0	.000	0	2	.000	13	15	28	1	30	0	1	11	5	10.7	0.4	1.9	0.1	.066
NBA Season Totals		23	8	201	14	7	27	.259	0	0	.000	0	2	.000	17	21	38	2	40	0	3	11	5	8.7	0.6	1.7	0.1	....

• CURCIC, Radisav
Radisav Curcic

Born: Sept. 26, 1965. Cacak, Yugoslavia. Height: 6'10". Weight: 275 lbs. Drafted: — College: none (HS: Cacak, YUG)

YEAR	TEAM	GP	GS	MIN	PTS	FGM	FGA	FG%	3PM	3PA	3P%	FTM	FTA	FT%	ORB	DRB	TRB	AST	PF	DQ	STL	BLK	TO	MPG	PPG	RPG	APG	PCM
92-93	Dallas	20	0	166	58	16	41	.390	0	0	.000	26	36	.722	17	32	49	12	30	0	7	2	8	8.3	2.9	2.5	0.6	.455
NBA Season Totals		20	0	166	58	16	41	.390	0	0	.000	26	36	.722	17	32	49	12	30	0	7	2	8	8.3	2.9	2.5	0.6	....

• CURE, Armand
Armand Arthur Cure

Born: Aug. 1, 1919. New Bedford, MA, United States. Height: 6' Weight: 198 lbs. Drafted: — College: Rhode Island

YEAR	TEAM	GP	GS	MIN	PTS	FGM	FGA	FG%	3PM	3PA	3P%	FTM	FTA	FT%	ORB	DRB	TRB	AST	PF	DQ	STL	BLK	TO	MPG	PPG	RPG	APG	PCM
46-47	Providence	12	....	....	10	4	15	.267	....	....	....	2	3	.667	....	....	....	0	5	....	....	....	....	....	0.8	....	0.0	....
NBA Season Totals		12	....	....	10	4	15	.267	....	....	....	2	3	.667	....	....	....	0	5	....	....	....	....	....	0.8	....	0.0	....

• CURETON, Earl
Earl (The Twirl) Cureton

Born: Sept. 3, 1957. Detroit, MI, United States. Height: 6'9". Weight: 210 lbs. Drafted: 1979 College: Detroit

YEAR	TEAM	GP	GS	MIN	PTS	FGM	FGA	FG%	3PM	3PA	3P%	FTM	FTA	FT%	ORB	DRB	TRB	AST	PF	DQ	STL	BLK	TO	MPG	PPG	RPG	APG	PCM
80-81	Philadelphia	52	....	528	219	93	205	.454	0	1	.000	33	64	.516	51	104	155	25	68	0	20	23	31	10.2	4.2	3.0	0.5	.476
81-82	Philadelphia	66	8	956	349	149	306	.487	0	2	.000	51	94	.543	90	180	270	32	142	0	31	27	46	14.5	5.3	4.1	0.5	.432
82-83	Philadelphia	73	3	987	249	108	258	.419	0	0	.000	33	67	.493	84	185	269	43	144	1	37	24	73	13.5	3.4	3.7	0.6	.317
83-84	Detroit	73	0	907	193	81	177	.458	0	1	.000	31	59	.525	86	201	287	36	143	3	24	31	58	12.4	2.6	3.9	0.5	.360
84-85	Detroit	81	1	1642	496	207	428	.484	0	3	.000	82	144	.569	169	250	419	83	216	1	56	42	113	20.3	6.1	5.2	1.0	.381
85-86	Detroit	80	19	2017	687	285	564	.505	0	2	.000	117	211	.555	198	306	504	137	239	3	58	58	152	25.2	8.6	6.3	1.7	.424
86-87	Chicago	43	36	1105	297	129	276	.467	0	1	.000	39	73	.534	113	114	227	70	102	2	15	26	9	25.7	6.9	5.3	1.6	.374
86-87	LA Clippers	35	11	868	271	114	234	.487	0	1	.000	43	79	.544	99	126	225	52	86	0	18	30	74	24.8	7.7	6.4	1.5	.396
87-88	LA Clippers	69	11	1128	299	133	310	.429	0	3	.000	33	63	.524	97	174	271	63	135	1	32	36	55	16.3	4.3	3.9	0.9	.345
88-89	Charlotte	82	41	2047	532	233	465	.501	0	1	.000	66	123	.537	188	300	488	130	230	3	50	61	115	25.0	6.5	6.0	1.6	.377
90-91	Charlotte	9	1	159	17	8	24	.333	0	1	.000	1	3	.333	6	30	36	3	16	0	0	3	6	17.7	1.9	4.0	0.3	.174
93-94	Houston	2	0	30	4	2	8	.250	0	0	.000	0	2	.000	4	8	12	0	4	0	0	0	1	15.0	2.0	6.0	0.0	.194
96-97	Toronto	9	0	46	7	3	8	.375	0	0	.000	1	3	.333	4	5	9	4	10	0	0	0	1	5.1	0.8	1.0	0.4	.184
NBA Season Totals		674	131	12420	3620	1545	3263	.473	0	16	.000	530	985	.538	1189	1983	3172	678	1535	14	341	361	734	18.4	5.4	4.7	1.0	....
80-81	Philadelphia	9	....	36	12	6	18	.333	0	0	.000	0	2	.000	1	8	9	2	3	0	1	2	1	4.0	1.3	1.0	0.2	.305
81-82	Philadelphia	12	0	75	32	13	41	.317	0	1	.000	6	9	.667	12	14	26	2	12	0	1	1	5	6.3	2.7	2.2	0.2	.302
82-83	Philadelphia	5	0	25	2	1	4	.250	0	0	.000	0	0	.000	0	5	5	1	5	0	2	0	3	5.0	0.4	1.0	0.2	.070
83-84	Detroit	5	0	93	32	15	31	.484	0	0	.000	2	6	.333	14	19	33	2	9	0	2	1	5	18.6	6.4	6.6	0.4	.452
84-85	Detroit	9	0	133	37	16	34	.471	0	1	.000	5	9	.556	10	31	41	4	20	0	9	2	4	14.8	4.1	4.6	0.4	.436
85-86	Detroit	4	4	126	36	17	31	.548	0	1	.000	2	8	.250	12	18	30	9	14	0	3	0	5	31.5	9.0	7.5	2.3	.392
93-94	Houston	10	0	100	18	8	10	.800	0	0	.000	2	2	1.000	6	23	29	2	20	0	1	2	3	10.0	1.8	2.9	0.2	.358
NBA Playoff Totals		54	4	588	169	76	169	.450	0	3	.000	17	36	.472	55	118	173	22	83	0	19	8	26	10.9	3.1	3.2	0.4	....

• CURLEY, Bill
William Michael Curley

Born: May 29, 1972. Boston, MA, United States. Height: 6'9". Weight: 220 lbs. Drafted: 1994 College: Boston College

YEAR	TEAM	GP	GS	MIN	PTS	FGM	FGA	FG%	3PM	3PA	3P%	FTM	FTA	FT%	ORB	DRB	TRB	AST	PF	DQ	STL	BLK	TO	MPG	PPG	RPG	APG	PCM
94-95	Detroit	53	1	595	143	58	134	.433	0	0	.000	27	36	.750	54	70	124	25	128	3	21	21	27	11.2	2.7	2.3	0.5	.276
97-98	Minnesota	11	1	146	34	16	33	.485	0	1	.000	2	3	.667	11	17	28	4	28	1	3	1	3	13.3	3.1	2.5	0.4	.247
98-99	Minnesota	35	7	372	78	29	72	.403	1	5	.200	19	22	.864	20	31	51	14	83	1	17	9	10	10.6	2.2	1.5	0.4	.206
99-00	Houston	4	0	50	12	6	11	.545	0	0	.000	0	0	.000	4	4	8	0	10	1	2	0	4	12.5	3.0	2.0	0.0	.167

YEAR	TEAM	GP	GS	MIN	PTS	FGM	FGA	FG%	3PM	3PA	3P%	FTM	FTA	FT%	ORB	DRB	TRB	AST	PF	DQ	STL	BLK	TO	MPG	PPG	RPG	APG	PCM
99-00	Golden State	24	0	259	64	23	57	.404	0	1	.000	18	25	.720	14	28	42	14	51	1	11	4	17	10.8	2.7	1.8	0.6	.225
00-01	Dallas	5	0	15	3	1	4	.250	0	1	.000	1	4	.250	0	0	0	0	4	0	1	1	2	3.0	0.6	0.0	0.0	-.189
00-01	Golden State	15	2	177	60	24	43	.558	1	1	1.000	11	15	.733	21	16	37	3	41	1	6	8	14	11.8	4.0	2.5	0.2	.335
NBA Season Totals		147	11	1614	394	157	354	.444	2	9	.222	78	105	.743	124	166	290	60	345	8	61	44	77	11.0	2.7	2.0	0.4	....
97-98	Minnesota	2	0	7	0	0	0	.000	0	0	.000	0	0	.000	0	0	0	0	0	0	0	0	0	3.5	0.0	0.0	0.0	.000
NBA Playoff Totals		2	0	7	0	0	0	.000	0	0	.000	0	0	.000	0	0	0	0	0	0	0	0	0	3.5	0.0	0.0	0.0	....

• CURRAN, Fran

Francis Hugh Curran

Born: Sept. 19, 1925.   Height: 6'   Weight: 175 lbs.   Drafted: —   College: Notre Dame

YEAR	TEAM	GP	GS	MIN	PTS	FGM	FGA	FG%	3PM	3PA	3P%	FTM	FTA	FT%	ORB	DRB	TRB	AST	PF	DQ	STL	BLK	TO	MPG	PPG	RPG	APG	PCM
47-48	Toledo-N	58	....	....	377	129							119	156	.763				....	145						6.5		....	....
48-49	Rochester	57	....	....	207	61	168	.363					85	126	.675				78	118						3.6		1.4	
49-50	Rochester	66	....	....	395	98	235	.417					199	241	.826				71	113						6.0		1.1	
NBA Season Totals		123	....	....	602	159	403	.395					284	367	.774				149	231						4.9		1.2	
NBL Season Totals		58	....	....	377	129							119	156					....	145						6.5			
Career Totals		181	....	....	979	288	403						403	523					149	376						5.4		0.8	
48-49	Rochester	4	....	....	4	1	5	.200					2	2	1.000				3	3						1.0		0.8	
49-50	Rochester	2	....	....	5	2	7	.286					1	1	1.000				0	0						2.5		0.0	
NBA Playoff Totals		6	....	....	9	3	12	.250					3	3	1.000				3	3						1.5		0.5	

• CURRIE, Jim

Jim Currie

Born: 1916.   Height: 6'2".   Weight: 185 lbs.   Drafted: —   College: Northwestern

YEAR	TEAM	GP	GS	MIN	PTS	FGM	FGA	FG%	3PM	3PA	3P%	FTM	FTA	FT%	ORB	DRB	TRB	AST	PF	DQ	STL	BLK	TO	MPG	PPG	RPG	APG	PCM
39-40	Hammond-N	27	....	....	105	38	....	....	....	....	....	....	29													3.9	....	....	....
NBL Season Totals		27	....	....	105	38	....	....	....	....	....	....	29													3.9	....	....	

• CURRY, Dell

Wardell Stephen Curry

Born: June 25, 1964. Harrisonburg, VA, United States.   Height: 6'4".   Weight: 190 lbs.   Drafted: 1986   College: Virginia Tech

YEAR	TEAM	GP	GS	MIN	PTS	FGM	FGA	FG%	3PM	3PA	3P%	FTM	FTA	FT%	ORB	DRB	TRB	AST	PF	DQ	STL	BLK	TO	MPG	PPG	RPG	APG	PCM
86-87	Utah	67	0	636	325	139	326	.426	17	60	.283	30	38	.789	30	48	78	58	86	0	27	4	47	9.5	4.9	1.2	0.9	.357
87-88	Cleveland	79	8	1499	787	340	742	.458	28	81	.346	79	101	.782	43	123	166	149	128	0	94	22	111	19.0	10.0	2.1	1.9	.441
88-89	Charlotte	48	0	813	571	256	521	.491	19	55	.345	40	46	.870	26	78	104	50	68	0	42	4	43	16.9	11.9	2.2	1.0	.545
89-90	Charlotte	67	13	1860	1070	461	990	.466	52	147	.354	96	104	.923	31	137	168	159	148	0	98	26	101	27.8	16.0	2.5	2.4	.457
90-91	Charlotte	76	14	1515	802	337	715	.471	32	86	.372	96	104	.842	47	152	199	166	125	0	75	25	84	19.9	10.6	2.6	2.2	.502
91-92	Charlotte	77	0	2020	1209	504	1038	.486	74	183	.404	127	152	.836	57	202	259	177	156	1	93	20	131	26.2	15.7	3.4	2.3	.516
92-93	Charlotte	80	0	2094	1227	498	1102	.452	95	237	.401	136	157	.866	51	235	286	180	150	1	87	23	128	26.2	15.3	3.6	2.3	.490
93-94	Charlotte	82	0	2173	1335	533	1171	.455	152	378	.402	117	134	.873	71	191	262	221	161	0	98	27	123	26.5	16.3	3.2	2.7	.529
94-95	Charlotte	69	0	1718	935	343	778	.441	154	361	.427	95	111	.856	41	127	168	113	144	1	55	18	97	24.9	13.6	2.4	1.6	.412
95-96	Charlotte	82	29	2371	1192	441	974	.453	164	406	.404	146	171	.854	68	196	264	176	173	2	108	25	131	28.9	14.5	3.2	2.1	.436
96-97	Charlotte	68	20	2078	1008	384	836	.459	126	296	.426	114	142	.803	40	171	211	118	147	0	60	14	95	30.6	14.8	3.1	1.7	.389
97-98	Charlotte	52	1	971	490	194	434	.447	61	145	.421	26	75	101	69	85	2	31	4	52	18.7	9.4	1.9	1.3	.390
98-99	Milwaukee	42	0	864	423	163	336	.485	69	145	.476	28	34	.824	18	67	85	48	42	0	36	3	45	20.6	10.1	2.0	1.1	.430
99-00	Toronto	67	9	1095	507	194	454	.427	95	242	.393	24	32	.750	11	89	100	89	66	0	32	9	40	16.3	7.6	1.5	1.3	.389
00-01	Toronto	71	1	956	429	162	382	.424	62	145	.428	43	51	.843	16	69	85	75	66	0	27	8	39	13.5	6.0	1.2	1.1	.370
01-02	Toronto	56	4	886	360	141	347	.406	45	131	.344	33	37	.892	23	58	81	61	50	0	22	6	41	15.8	6.4	1.4	1.1	.313
NBA Season Totals		1083	99	23549	12670	5090	11146	.457	1245	3098	.402	1245	1476	.843	599	2018	2617	1909	1795	7	985	238	1308	21.7	11.7	2.4	1.8	....
86-87	Utah	2	0	4	0	0	3	.000	0	1	.000	0	0	.000	0	0	0	0	1	0	0	0	0	0.0	0.0	0.0	0.0	-.815
87-88	Cleveland	2	0	17	2	1	4	.250	0	1	.000	0	0	.000	1	0	1	2	1	0	0	1	0	8.5	1.0	0.5	1.0	.161
92-93	Charlotte	9	0	222	99	42	97	.433	6	21	.286	9	11	.818	11	21	32	18	19	0	13	0	13	24.7	11.0	3.6	2.0	.392
94-95	Charlotte	4	0	107	51	16	34	.471	9	21	.429	10	11	.909	5	4	9	6	11	0	0	6	26.8	12.8	2.3	1.5	.352
96-97	Charlotte	3	1	50	14	5	17	.294	4	4	.250	0	1	5	5	5	4	0	1	16.7	4.7	0.3	1.7	.191
97-98	Charlotte	9	0	171	52	21	52	.404	4	16	.250	6	7	.857	6	13	19	10	21	0	7	3	5	19.0	5.8	2.1	1.1	.271
98-99	Milwaukee	3	0	49	9	2	15	.133	1	8	.125	4	4	1.000	0	4	4	1	5	0	3	0	0	16.3	3.0	1.3	0.3	.052
99-00	Toronto	3	0	30	7	2	4	.500	2	3	.667	1	2	.500	1	1	2	1	4	0	2	0	2	10.0	2.3	0.7	0.3	.194
00-01	Toronto	12	0	182	78	27	64	.422	14	37	.378	10	12	.833	2	12	14	10	10	0	6	1	11	15.2	6.5	1.2	0.8	.426
01-02	Toronto	4	0	59	28	10	25	.400	4	5	.800	4	4	1.000	0	5	5	4	4	0	5	2	3	14.8	7.0	1.3	1.0	.426
NBA Playoff Totals		51	1	891	340	126	315	.400	41	117	.350	47	54	.870	27	60	87	57	81	0	40	7	41	17.5	6.7	1.7	1.1	....

• CURRY, Eddy

Eddy Curry Jr.

Born: Dec. 5, 1982. Harvey, IL, United States.   Height: 6'11".   Weight: 285 lbs.   Drafted: 2001   College: none (HS: Thornwood, IL)

YEAR	TEAM	GP	GS	MIN	PTS	FGM	FGA	FG%	3PM	3PA	3P%	FTM	FTA	FT%	ORB	DRB	TRB	AST	PF	DQ	STL	BLK	TO	MPG	PPG	RPG	APG	PCM
01-02	Chicago	72	31	1150	483	189	377	.501	0	0	.000	105	160	.656	111	161	272	25	173	0	16	53	69	16.0	6.7	3.8	0.3	.420
02-03	Chicago	81	48	1571	849	335	573	.585	0	0	.000	179	287	.624	116	237	353	37	226	3	18	62	137	19.4	10.5	4.4	0.5	.503
NBA Season Totals		153	79	2721	1332	524	950	.552	0	0	.000	284	447	.635	227	398	625	62	399	3	34	115	206	17.8	8.7	4.1	0.4	....

• CURRY, Michael

Michael Curry

Born: Aug. 12, 1968. Anniston, AL, United States.   Height: 6'5".   Weight: 210 lbs.   Drafted: —   College: Georgia Southern

YEAR	TEAM	GP	GS	MIN	PTS	FGM	FGA	FG%	3PM	3PA	3P%	FTM	FTA	FT%	ORB	DRB	TRB	AST	PF	DQ	STL	BLK	TO	MPG	PPG	RPG	APG	PCM
93-94	Philadelphia	10	0	43	9	3	14	.214	0	2	.000	3	4	.750	0	1	1	1	6	0	1	0	3	4.3	0.9	0.1	0.1	-.096
95-96	Washington	5	0	34	10	3	10	.300	0	3	.000	4	4	1.000	2	3	5	1	3	0	1	0	1	6.8	2.0	1.0	0.2	.229
95-96	Detroit	41	1	749	201	70	151	.464	20	50	.400	41	58	.707	25	55	80	26	89	1	23	2	25	18.3	4.9	2.0	0.6	.237
96-97	Detroit	81	2	1217	318	99	221	.448	23	77	.299	97	108	.898	23	96	119	43	128	0	31	12	24	15.0	3.9	1.5	0.5	.258
97-98	Milwaukee	82	27	1978	543	196	418	.469	4	9	.444	147	176	.835	26	72	98	137	218	1	56	14	74	24.1	6.6	1.2	1.7	.233
98-99	Milwaukee	50	4	1146	244	90	206	.437	1	15	.067	63	79	.797	19	89	108	78	135	0	42	7	37	22.9	4.9	2.2	1.6	.233
99-00	Detroit	82	3	1611	506	182	379	.480	1	5	.200	141	168	.839	21	83	104	87	209	3	33	5	73	19.6	6.2	1.3	1.1	.234

YEAR	TEAM	GP	GS	MIN	PTS	FGM	FGA	FG%	3PM	3PA	3P%	FTM	FTA	FT%	ORB	DRB	TRB	AST	PF	DQ	STL	BLK	TO	MPG	PPG	RPG	APG	PCM
00-01	Detroit	68	58	1485	356	145	319	.455	4	9	.444	62	73	.849	21	100	121	132	173	0	27	3	61	21.8	5.2	1.8	1.9	.231
01-02	Detroit	82	75	1912	329	125	276	.453	7	26	.269	72	91	.791	15	153	168	127	207	1	47	10	60	23.3	4.0	2.0	1.5	.198
02-03	Detroit	78	77	1556	236	92	229	.402	16	54	.296	36	45	.800	16	111	127	104	163	0	44	4	43	19.9	3.0	1.6	1.3	.172
NBA Season Totals		579	247	11731	2752	1005	2223	.452	76	250	.304	666	806	.826	168	763	931	736	1331	6	305	57	401	20.3	4.8	1.6	1.3	....
95-96	Detroit	3	0	43	6	3	7	.429	0	1	.000	0	0	.000	1	2	3	1	5	0	1	1	0	14.3	2.0	1.0	0.3	.131
96-97	Detroit	2	0	7	2	1	2	.500	0	0	.000	0	1	.000	0	1	1	0	1	0	0	0	0	3.5	1.0	0.5	0.0	.153
98-99	Milwaukee	3	0	59	20	7	12	.583	0	1	.000	6	6	1.000	1	3	4	3	8	0	2	1	2	19.7	6.7	1.3	1.0	.335
99-00	Detroit	3	1	79	28	12	23	.522	0	0	.000	4	6	.667	0	3	3	3	5	0	1	1	2	26.3	9.3	1.0	1.0	.264
01-02	Detroit	10	10	221	57	22	39	.564	5	13	.385	8	11	.727	1	13	14	12	32	0	4	0	5	22.1	5.7	1.4	1.2	.229
02-03	Detroit	15	14	274	41	16	44	.364	3	9	.333	6	7	.857	3	13	16	17	35	0	7	2	5	18.3	2.7	1.1	1.1	.131
NBA Playoff Totals		36	25	683	154	61	127	.480	8	24	.333	24	31	.774	6	35	41	36	86	0	15	5	14	19.0	4.3	1.1	1.0	....

• CVETKOVIC, Rastko

Rastko Cvetkovic

Born: June 22, 1970. Belgrade, Yugoslavia.   Height: 7'1".   Weight: 260 lbs.   Drafted: —   College: none

YEAR	TEAM	GP	GS	MIN	PTS	FGM	FGA	FG%	3PM	3PA	3P%	FTM	FTA	FT%	ORB	DRB	TRB	AST	PF	DQ	STL	BLK	TO	MPG	PPG	RPG	APG	PCM
95-96	Denver	14	0	48	10	5	16	.313	0	1	.000	0	4	.000	4	7	11	3	11	0	2	1	3	3.4	0.7	0.8	0.2	.128
NBA Season Totals		14	0	48	10	5	16	.313	0	1	.000	0	4	.000	4	7	11	3	11	0	2	1	3	3.4	0.7	0.8	0.2	....

• CZARNECKI, Walt

Walt Czarnecki

Born: 1916.   Height: 6'5".   Weight: 215 lbs.   Drafted: —   College: none

YEAR	TEAM	GP	GS	MIN	PTS	FGM	FGA	FG%	3PM	3PA	3P%	FTM	FTA	FT%	ORB	DRB	TRB	AST	PF	DQ	STL	BLK	TO	MPG	PPG	RPG	APG	PCM
46-47	Detroit-N	4	....	....	5	2	....	....	....	....	....	1	7	.143	....	....	....	....	....	....	....	....	....	....	1.3	....	....	....
NBL Season Totals		4	....	....	5	2	....	....	....	....	....	1	7		....	....	....	....	....	....	....	....	....	....	1.3	....	....	....

• DABICH, Mike

Michael Lee (Dabbo) Dabich

Born: Dec. 27, 1942. Lander, WY, United States.   Height: 7'   Weight: 242 lbs.   Drafted: 1966   College: New Mexico State

YEAR	TEAM	GP	GS	MIN	PTS	FGM	FGA	FG%	3PM	3PA	3P%	FTM	FTA	FT%	ORB	DRB	TRB	AST	PF	DQ	STL	BLK	TO	MPG	PPG	RPG	APG	PCM
67-68	Dallas-A	3	....	23	10	4	7	.571	0	0	.000	2	5	.400	....	....	7	1	7	0	....	....	0	7.7	3.3	2.3	0.3	.450
67-68	Oakland-A	7	....	26	10	4	5	.800	0	0	.000	2	4	.500	....	....	6	1	5	0	....	....	5	3.7	1.4	0.9	0.1	.478
ABA Season Totals		10	....	49	20	8	12	.667	0	0	.000	4	9	.444	....	....	13	2	12	0	....	....	5	4.9	2.0	1.3	0.2	....

• DAHL, Harold

Harold Dahl

Born: 1923.   Height: 5'9".   Weight: 190 lbs.   Drafted: —   College: Miami (FL)

YEAR	TEAM	GP	GS	MIN	PTS	FGM	FGA	FG%	3PM	3PA	3P%	FTM	FTA	FT%	ORB	DRB	TRB	AST	PF	DQ	STL	BLK	TO	MPG	PPG	RPG	APG	PCM
43-44	Oshkosh-N	5	....	....	4	1	....	....	....	....	....	2	....	....	....	....	....	....	....	....	....	....	....	....	0.8	....	....	....
NBL Season Totals		5	....	....	4	1	....	....	....	....	....	2	....	....	....	....	....	....	....	....	....	....	....	....	0.8	....	....	....

• DAHLER, Ed

Edward Dahler Jr.

Born: Jan. 31, 1926.   Height: 6'5".   Weight: 190 lbs.   Drafted: 1950   College: Duquesne

YEAR	TEAM	GP	GS	MIN	PTS	FGM	FGA	FG%	3PM	3PA	3P%	FTM	FTA	FT%	ORB	DRB	TRB	AST	PF	DQ	STL	BLK	TO	MPG	PPG	RPG	APG	PCM
51-52	Philadelphia	14	....	112	35	14	38	.368	....	....	....	7	7	1.000	....	....	22	5	16	0	....	....	....	8.0	2.5	1.6	0.4	.307
NBA Season Totals		14	....	112	35	14	38	.368	....	....	....	7	7	1.000	....	....	22	5	16	0	....	....	....	8.0	2.5	1.6	0.4	....

• DAILEY, Quintin

Quintin Dailey

Born: Jan. 22, 1961. Baltimore, MD, United States.   Height: 6'3".   Weight: 180 lbs.   Drafted: 1982   College: San Francisco

YEAR	TEAM	GP	GS	MIN	PTS	FGM	FGA	FG%	3PM	3PA	3P%	FTM	FTA	FT%	ORB	DRB	TRB	AST	PF	DQ	STL	BLK	TO	MPG	PPG	RPG	APG	PCM
82-83	Chicago	76	32	2081	1151	470	1008	.466	5	25	.200	206	282	.730	87	173	260	280	248	7	72	10	205	27.4	15.1	3.4	3.7	.457
83-84	Chicago	82	42	2449	1491	583	1229	.474	4	32	.125	321	396	.811	61	174	235	254	218	4	109	11	221	29.9	18.2	2.9	3.1	.470
84-85	Chicago	79	0	2101	1262	525	1111	.473	7	30	.233	205	251	.817	57	151	208	191	192	0	71	5	150	26.6	16.0	2.6	2.4	.444
85-86	Chicago	35	0	723	569	203	470	.432	0	8	.000	163	198	.823	20	48	68	67	86	0	22	5	67	20.7	16.3	1.9	1.9	.501
86-87	LA Clippers	49	5	924	520	200	491	.407	1	10	.100	119	155	.768	34	49	83	79	113	4	43	8	69	18.9	10.6	1.7	1.6	.351
87-88	LA Clippers	67	7	1282	901	328	755	.434	2	12	.167	243	313	.776	62	92	154	109	128	1	69	4	121	19.1	13.4	2.3	1.6	.488
88-89	LA Clippers	69	51	1722	1114	448	964	.465	1	9	.111	217	286	.759	69	135	204	154	152	0	90	6	124	25.0	16.1	3.0	2.2	.499
89-90	Seattle	30	2	491	247	97	240	.404	1	5	.200	52	66	.788	18	33	51	34	63	0	12	0	33	16.4	8.2	1.7	1.1	.288
90-91	Seattle	30	0	299	184	73	155	.471	0	1	.000	38	62	.613	11	21	32	16	25	0	7	1	18	10.0	6.1	1.1	0.5	.409
91-92	Seattle	11	1	98	31	9	37	.243	0	1	.000	13	16	.813	2	10	12	4	6	0	5	1	10	8.9	2.8	1.1	0.4	.128
NBA Season Totals		528	140	12170	7470	2936	6460	.454	21	133	.158	1577	2025	.779	421	886	1307	1188	1231	16	500	51	1018	23.0	14.1	2.5	2.3	....
84-85	Chicago	4	0	129	61	26	62	.419	1	7	.143	8	11	.727	5	8	13	11	9	0	4	0	5	32.3	15.3	3.3	2.8	.347
NBA Playoff Totals		4	0	129	61	26	62	.419	1	7	.143	8	11	.727	5	8	13	11	9	0	4	0	5	32.3	15.3	3.3	2.8	....

• DALEMBERT, Samuel

Samual Davis Dalembert

Born: May 10, 1981. Port-Au-Prince, Haiti.   Height: 6'11".   Weight: 250 lbs.   Drafted: 2001   College: Seton Hall

YEAR	TEAM	GP	GS	MIN	PTS	FGM	FGA	FG%	3PM	3PA	3P%	FTM	FTA	FT%	ORB	DRB	TRB	AST	PF	DQ	STL	BLK	TO	MPG	PPG	RPG	APG	PCM
01-02	Philadelphia	34	0	178	51	22	50	.440	0	0	.000	7	18	.389	25	43	68	5	30	0	6	13	14	5.2	1.5	2.0	0.1	.442
NBA Season Totals		34	0	178	51	22	50	.440	0	0	.000	7	18	.389	25	43	68	5	30	0	6	13	14	5.2	1.5	2.0	0.1	....

• DALLMAR, Howie

Howard Dallmar

Born: May 24, 1922. San Francisco, CA, United States. Died: Dec.19, 1991.   Height: 6'4".   Weight: 200 lbs.   Drafted: —   College: Stanford

YEAR	TEAM	GP	GS	MIN	PTS	FGM	FGA	FG%	3PM	3PA	3P%	FTM	FTA	FT%	ORB	DRB	TRB	AST	PF	DQ	STL	BLK	TO	MPG	PPG	RPG	APG	PCM
46-47	Philadelphia	60	....	....	528	199	710	.280	....	....	....	130	203	.640	....	....	....	104	141	....	....	....	....	....	8.8	....	1.7	....
47-48	Philadelphia	48	....	....	587	215	781	.275	....	....	....	157	211	.744	....	....	....	**120**	141	....	....	....	....	....	12.2	....	2.5	....
48-49	Philadelphia	38	....	....	293	105	342	.307	....	....	....	83	116	.716	....	....	....	116	104	....	....	....	....	....	7.7	....	3.1	....
NBA Season Totals		146	....	....	1408	519	1833	.283	....	....	....	370	530	.698	....	....	....	340	386	....	....	....	....	....	9.6	....	2.3	....

YEAR	TEAM	GP	GS	MIN	PTS	FGM	FGA	FG%	3PM	3PA	3P%	FTM	FTA	FT%	ORB	DRB	TRB	AST	PF	DQ	STL	BLK	TO	MPG	PPG	RPG	APG	PCM
46-47	Philadelphia	10	....	....	82	26	104	.250	....	....	....	30	40	.750	....	....	....	16	28	....	....	....	....	....	8.2	....	1.6	....
47-48	Philadelphia	13	....	....	106	38	178	.213	....	....	....	30	48	.625	....	....	....	37	55	....	....	....	....	....	8.2	....	2.8	....
48-49	Philadelphia	2	....	....	13	4	18	.222	....	....	....	5	7	.714	....	....	....	4	9	....	....	....	....	....	6.5	....	2.0	....
NBA Playoff Totals		25	....	....	201	68	300	.227	....	....	....	65	95	.684	....	....	....	57	92	....	....	....	....	....	8.0	....	2.3	....

• DAMPIER, Erick

Erick Trevez Dampier

Born: July 14, 1974. Jackson, MS, United States. Height: 6'11". Weight: 265 lbs. Drafted: 1996 College: Mississippi State

YEAR	TEAM	GP	GS	MIN	PTS	FGM	FGA	FG%	3PM	3PA	3P%	FTM	FTA	FT%	ORB	DRB	TRB	AST	PF	DQ	STL	BLK	TO	MPG	PPG	RPG	APG	PCM
96-97	Indiana	72	21	1052	370	131	336	.390	1	1	1.000	107	168	.637	96	198	294	43	153	1	19	73	86	14.6	5.1	4.1	0.6	.385
97-98	Golden State	82	82	2656	971	352	791	.445	0	2	.000	267	399	.669	272	443	715	94	281	6	39	139	172	32.4	11.8	8.7	1.1	.430
98-99	Golden State	50	50	1414	442	161	414	.389	0	0	.000	120	204	.588	164	218	382	54	165	2	26	58	92	28.3	8.8	7.6	1.1	.353
99-00	Golden State	21	12	495	167	70	173	.405	0	0	.000	27	51	.529	48	86	134	19	75	0	8	15	29	23.6	8.0	6.4	0.9	.334
00-01	Golden State	43	26	1038	319	126	314	.401	0	2	.000	67	126	.532	97	153	250	59	123	3	17	58	82	24.1	7.4	5.8	1.4	.339
01-02	Golden State	73	46	1740	554	209	480	.435	0	0	.000	136	211	.645	167	220	387	87	235	4	17	167	156	23.8	7.6	5.3	1.2	.367
02-03	Golden State	82	82	1979	673	259	522	.496	0	2	.000	155	222	.698	248	295	543	58	242	3	27	154	112	24.1	8.2	6.6	0.7	.461
NBA Season Totals		423	319	10374	3496	1308	3030	.432	1	7	.143	879	1381	.636	1092	1613	2705	414	1274	19	153	664	729	24.5	8.3	6.4	1.0	....

• DAMPIER, Louie

Louie (Little Louie) Dampier

Born: Nov. 20, 1944. Indianapolis, IN, United States. Height: 6' Weight: 170 lbs. Drafted: 1967 College: Kentucky

YEAR	TEAM	GP	GS	MIN	PTS	FGM	FGA	FG%	3PM	3PA	3P%	FTM	FTA	FT%	ORB	DRB	TRB	AST	PF	DQ	STL	BLK	TO	MPG	PPG	RPG	APG	PCM
67-68	Kentucky-A	72	....	2961	1487	620	1473	.421	38	142	.268	209	254	.823	....	....	333	256	143	0	....	....	163	41.1	20.7	4.6	3.6	.431
68-69	Kentucky-A	78	....	**3326**	1933	713	**1696**	.420	**199**	**552**	.361	308	380	.811	76	223	299	456	156	1	....	....	251	**42.6**	24.8	3.8	5.8	.532
69-70	Kentucky-A	82	....	3353	2131	743	1864	.399	**198**	**548**	.361	447	538	.831	83	227	310	447	235	2	....	....	274	40.9	26.0	3.8	5.5	.539
70-71	Kentucky-A	84	....	3221	1555	566	1353	.418	103	280	.368	320	376	.851	73	224	297	460	213	2	....	....	244	38.3	18.5	3.5	5.5	.499
71-72	Kentucky-A	83	....	3214	1319	477	1078	.442	84	233	.361	281	336	.836	43	216	259	515	237	1	....	....	211	38.7	15.9	3.1	6.2	.457
72-73	Kentucky-A	80	....	3039	1346	515	1143	.451	54	155	.348	262	334	.784	55	158	213	521	216	0	....	....	188	38.0	16.8	2.7	6.5	.466
73-74	Kentucky-A	84	....	2942	1492	603	1296	.465	48	124	**.387**	238	286	.832	46	155	201	473	152	....	84	18	230	35.0	17.8	2.4	5.6	.518
74-75	Kentucky-A	83	....	2879	1395	598	1195	.500	38	96	.396	161	199	.809	42	169	211	449	140	....	92	53	146	34.7	16.8	2.5	5.4	.511
75-76	Kentucky-A	82	....	2835	1068	455	949	.479	32	87	.368	126	146	.863	35	124	159	467	141	....	60	46	148	34.6	13.0	1.9	5.7	.429
76-77	San Antonio	80	....	1634	530	233	507	.460	....	....	....	64	86	.744	22	54	76	234	93	0	49	15	....	20.4	6.6	1.0	2.9	.352
77-78	San Antonio	82	....	2037	748	336	660	.509	....	....	....	76	101	.752	24	98	122	285	84	0	87	13	98	24.8	9.1	1.5	3.5	.415
78-79	San Antonio	70	....	760	275	123	251	.490	....	....	....	29	39	.744	15	48	63	124	42	0	35	8	42	10.9	3.9	0.9	1.8	.435
NBA Season Totals		232	....	4431	1553	692	1418	.488	....	....	....	169	226	.748	61	200	261	643	219	0	171	36	140	19.1	6.7	1.1	2.8	....
ABA Season Totals		**728**	....	**27770**	**13726**	**5290**	**12047**	.439	**794**	**2217**	.358	2352	2849	.826	453	1496	2282	**4044**	1633	6	236	117	1855	38.1	18.9	3.1	5.6	....
Career Totals		**960**	....	**32201**	**15279**	**5982**	**13465**	.444	**794**	**2217**	.358	2521	3075	.820	514	1696	2543	**4687**	1852	6	407	153	1995	33.5	15.9	2.6	4.9	....
67-68	Kentucky-A	5	....	224	133	46	104	.442	15	37	.405	26	31	.839	....	....	24	23	9	0	....	....	20	44.8	26.6	4.8	4.6	.562
68-69	Kentucky-A	7	....	326	156	50	140	.357	16	55	.291	40	46	.870	....	....	30	28	17	0	....	....	22	46.6	22.3	4.3	4.0	.388
69-70	Kentucky-A	12	....	526	212	73	198	.369	25	76	.329	41	53	.774	11	34	45	81	....	2	....	....	38	43.8	17.7	3.8	6.8	....
70-71	Kentucky-A	19	....	828	322	117	304	.385	22	69	.319	66	89	.742	24	54	78	179	56	2	....	....	54	43.6	16.9	4.1	9.4	.504
71-72	Kentucky-A	6	....	254	79	29	69	.420	11	23	.478	10	16	.625	....	....	19	45	17	....	....	....	16	42.3	13.2	3.2	7.5	.397
72-73	Kentucky-A	12	....	411	161	65	126	.516	10	22	.455	21	30	.700	6	19	25	39	35	1	....	....	19	34.3	13.4	2.1	3.3	.369
73-74	Kentucky-A	8	....	229	107	43	89	.483	7	14	.500	14	18	.778	3	13	16	32	8	....	6	0	19	28.6	13.4	2.0	4.0	.492
74-75	Kentucky-A	15	....	604	254	108	212	.509	5	13	.385	33	38	.868	9	27	36	113	34	....	19	7	29	40.3	16.9	2.4	7.5	.500
75-76	Kentucky-A	10	....	393	160	67	129	.519	8	16	.500	18	20	.900	3	10	13	77	20	....	11	5	16	39.3	16.0	1.3	7.7	.488
76-77	San Antonio	2	....	62	12	4	16	.250	....	....	....	4	4	1.000	0	3	3	9	4	0	1	1	....	31.0	6.0	1.5	4.5	.205
77-78	San Antonio	6	....	129	35	17	37	.459	....	....	....	1	4	.250	1	6	7	15	7	0	4	2	4	21.5	5.8	1.2	2.5	.294
78-79	San Antonio	7	....	55	20	8	14	.571	....	....	....	4	7	.571	1	4	5	8	8	0	3	1	1	7.9	2.9	0.7	1.1	.467
NBA Playoff Totals		15	....	246	67	29	67	.433	....	....	....	9	15	.600	2	13	15	32	19	0	8	4	5	16.4	4.5	1.0	2.1	....
ABA Playoff Totals		94	....	3795	1584	598	1371	.436	**119**	**325**	.366	269	341	.789	56	157	286	**617**	196	5	36	12	233	40.4	16.9	3.0	6.6	....
Career Playoff Totals		109	....	4041	1651	627	1438	.436	119	325	.366	278	356	.781	58	170	301	649	215	5	44	16	238	37.1	15.1	2.8	6.0	....

• DANCKER, Ed

Ed Dancker

Born: 1914. Height: 6'7". Weight: 214 lbs. Drafted: — College: none

YEAR	TEAM	GP	GS	MIN	PTS	FGM	FGA	FG%	3PM	3PA	3P%	FTM	FTA	FT%	ORB	DRB	TRB	AST	PF	DQ	STL	BLK	TO	MPG	PPG	RPG	APG	PCM
38-39	Sheboygan-N	28	....	....	162	63	....	....	....	....	....	36	....	....	....	....	....	....	....	....	....	....	....	....	5.8	....	....	....
39-40	Sheboygan-N	24	....	....	86	31	....	....	....	....	....	24	....	....	....	....	....	....	....	....	....	....	....	....	3.6	....	....	....
40-41	Sheboygan-N	23	....	....	105	39	....	....	....	....	....	27	....	....	....	....	....	....	....	....	....	....	....	....	4.6	....	....	....
41-42	Sheboygan-N	24	....	....	243	98	....	....	....	....	....	47	....	....	....	....	....	....	....	....	....	....	....	....	10.1	....	....	....
42-43	Sheboygan-N	22	....	....	240	96	....	....	....	....	....	48	....	....	....	....	....	....	....	....	....	....	....	....	10.9	....	....	....
43-44	Sheboygan-N	22	....	....	192	70	....	....	....	....	....	52	....	....	....	....	....	....	....	....	....	....	....	....	8.7	....	....	....
44-45	Sheboygan-N	30	....	....	283	111	....	....	....	....	....	61	....	....	....	....	....	....	....	....	....	....	....	....	9.4	....	....	....
45-46	Sheboygan-N	33	....	....	393	162	....	....	....	....	....	69	153	.451	....	....	....	....	....	....	....	....	....	....	11.9	....	....	....
46-47	Sheboygan-N	44	....	....	451	160	....	....	....	....	....	131	187	.701	....	....	....	....	149	....	....	....	....	....	10.3	....	....	....
47-48	Sheboygan-N	58	....	....	296	109	....	....	....	....	....	78	155	.503	....	....	....	....	198	....	....	....	....	....	5.1	....	....	....
48-49	Oshkosh-N	13	....	....	39	16	....	....	....	....	....	7	21	.333	....	....	....	....	39	....	....	....	....	....	3.0	....	....	....
NBL Season Totals		321	....	....	2490	955	....	....	....	....	....	580	516	....	....	....	....	....	386	....	....	....	....	....	7.8	....	....	....
39-40	Sheboygan-N	3	....	....	7	2	....	....	....	....	....	3	....	....	....	....	....	....	....	....	....	....	....	....	2.3	....	....	....
40-41	Sheboygan-N	5	....	....	25	8	....	....	....	....	....	9	....	....	....	....	....	....	....	....	....	....	....	....	5.0	....	....	....
42-43	Sheboygan-N	5	....	....	57	22	....	....	....	....	....	13	....	....	....	....	....	....	....	....	....	....	....	....	11.4	....	....	....
43-44	Sheboygan-N	6	....	....	47	16	....	....	....	....	....	15	....	....	....	....	....	....	....	....	....	....	....	....	7.8	....	....	....
44-45	Sheboygan-N	8	....	....	109	41	....	....	....	....	....	27	....	....	....	....	....	....	....	....	....	....	....	....	13.6	....	....	....
45-46	Sheboygan-N	7	....	....	84	33	....	....	....	....	....	18	30	.600	....	....	....	....	....	....	....	....	....	....	12.0	....	....	....
46-47	Sheboygan-N	5	....	....	39	14	....	....	....	....	....	11	18	.611	....	....	....	....	....	....	....	....	....	....	7.8	....	....	....
NBL Playoff Totals		39	....	....	368	136	....	....	....	....	....	96	48	....	....	....	....	....	....	....	....	....	....	....	9.4	....	....	....

• DANDRIDGE, Bob

Robert L. (Greyhound) Dandridge Jr.

Born: Nov. 15, 1947. Richmond, VA, United States. Height: 6'6". Weight: 195 lbs. Drafted: 1969 College: Norfolk State

YEAR	TEAM	GP	GS	MIN	PTS	FGM	FGA	FG%	3PM	3PA	3P%	FTM	FTA	FT%	ORB	DRB	TRB	AST	PF	DQ	STL	BLK	TO	MPG	PPG	RPG	APG	PCM
69-70	Milwaukee	81	....	2461	1067	434	895	.485	....	....	....	199	264	.754	....	....	625	292	279	1	....	....	....	30.4	13.2	7.7	3.6	.564
70-71	Milwaukee	79	....	2862	1452	594	1167	.509	....	....	....	264	376	.702	....	....	632	277	287	4	....	....	....	36.2	18.4	8.0	3.5	.575
71-72	Milwaukee	80	....	2957	1475	630	1264	.498	....	....	....	215	291	.739	....	....	613	249	297	7	....	....	....	37.0	18.4	7.7	3.1	.534
72-73	Milwaukee	73	....	2852	1474	638	1353	.472	....	....	....	198	251	.789	....	....	600	207	279	2	....	....	....	39.1	20.2	8.2	2.8	.515
73-74	Milwaukee	71	....	2521	1341	583	1158	.503	....	....	....	175	214	.818	117	362	479	201	271	4	111	41	....	35.5	18.9	6.7	2.8	.539
74-75	Milwaukee	80	....	3031	1593	691	1460	.473	....	....	....	211	262	.805	142	409	551	243	**330**	7	122	48	....	37.9	19.9	6.9	3.0	.503
75-76	Milwaukee	73	....	2735	1571	650	1296	.502	....	....	....	271	329	.824	171	369	540	206	263	5	111	38	....	37.5	21.5	7.4	2.8	.577
76-77	Milwaukee	70	....	2501	1453	585	1253	.467	....	....	....	283	367	.771	146	294	440	268	222	1	95	28	....	35.7	20.8	6.3	3.8	.571
77-78	Washington	75	....	2777	1450	560	1190	.471	....	....	....	330	419	.788	137	305	442	287	262	6	101	44	240	37.0	19.3	5.9	3.8	.494
78-79	Washington	78	....	2629	1589	629	1260	.499	....	....	....	331	401	.825	109	338	447	365	259	4	71	57	218	33.7	20.4	5.7	4.7	.608
79-80	Washington	45	....	1457	783	329	729	.451	2	11	.182	123	152	.809	63	183	246	178	112	1	29	36	122	32.4	17.4	5.5	4.0	.496
80-81	Washington	23	....	545	230	101	237	.426	0	1	.000	28	39	.718	19	64	83	60	54	1	16	9	32	23.7	10.0	3.6	2.6	.387
81-82	Milwaukee	11	0	174	52	21	55	.382	0	0	.000	10	17	.588	4	13	17	13	25	0	5	2	11	15.8	4.7	1.5	1.2	.184
NBA Season Totals		839	0	29502	15530	6445	13317	.484	2	12	.167	2638	3382	.780	908	2337	5715	2846	2940	43	661	303	623	35.2	18.5	6.8	3.4	....
69-70	Milwaukee	10	....	399	163	72	142	.507	....	....	....	19	29	.655	....	....	87	57	39	1	....	....	....	39.9	16.3	8.7	5.7	.552
70-71	Milwaukee	14	....	535	269	113	244	.463	....	....	....	43	55	.782	....	....	134	48	45	1	....	....	....	38.2	19.2	9.6	3.4	.564
71-72	Milwaukee	11	....	441	237	100	202	.495	....	....	....	37	50	.740	....	....	97	21	47	1	....	....	....	40.1	21.5	8.8	1.9	.523
72-73	Milwaukee	6	....	204	83	32	76	.421	....	....	....	19	27	.704	....	....	28	7	23	2	....	....	....	34.0	13.8	4.7	1.2	.314
73-74	Milwaukee	16	....	648	308	136	276	.493	....	....	....	36	47	.766	31	91	122	45	65	3	22	10	....	40.5	19.3	7.6	2.8	.482
75-76	Milwaukee	3	....	122	66	24	49	.490	....	....	....	18	20	.900	3	20	23	8	9	0	3	0	....	40.7	22.0	7.7	2.7	.563
77-78	Washington	19	....	746	402	172	359	.479	....	....	....	58	84	.690	35	88	123	74	78	1	30	14	57	39.3	21.2	6.5	3.9	.499
78-79	Washington	19	....	787	439	174	368	.473	....	....	....	91	110	.827	45	95	140	105	71	3	14	15	59	41.4	23.1	7.4	5.5	.558
NBA Playoff Totals		98	....	3882	1967	823	1716	.480	....	....	....	321	422	.761	114	294	754	365	377	12	69	39	116	39.6	20.1	7.7	3.7	....

• DANIELS, Antonio

Antonio Ray Daniels

Born: Mar. 19, 1975. Columbus, OH, United States. Height: 6'4". Weight: 195 lbs. Drafted: 1997 College: Bowling Green

YEAR	TEAM	GP	GS	MIN	PTS	FGM	FGA	FG%	3PM	3PA	3P%	FTM	FTA	FT%	ORB	DRB	TRB	AST	PF	DQ	STL	BLK	TO	MPG	PPG	RPG	APG	PCM
97-98	Vancouver	74	50	1956	579	228	548	.416	11	52	.212	112	170	.659	22	121	143	334	88	0	55	10	163	26.4	7.8	1.9	4.5	.318
98-99	San Antonio	47	0	614	220	83	183	.454	5	17	.294	49	65	.754	13	41	54	106	39	0	30	6	44	13.1	4.7	1.1	2.3	.432
99-00	San Antonio	68	1	1195	420	163	344	.474	22	66	.333	72	101	.713	16	70	86	177	73	0	55	5	58	17.6	6.2	1.3	2.6	.404
00-01	San Antonio	79	23	2060	745	275	588	.468	74	183	.404	121	156	.776	26	137	163	304	120	0	61	14	109	26.1	9.4	2.1	3.8	.410
01-02	San Antonio	82	13	2175	753	269	612	.440	57	196	.291	158	210	.752	23	153	176	228	104	0	48	12	70	26.5	9.2	2.1	2.8	.355
02-03	Portland	67	2	871	251	84	186	.452	18	59	.305	65	76	.855	11	61	72	85	43	0	33	9	32	13.0	3.7	1.1	1.3	.346
NBA Season Totals		417	89	8871	2968	1102	2461	.448	187	573	.326	577	778	.742	111	583	694	1234	467	0	282	56	476	21.3	7.1	1.7	3.0	....
98-99	San Antonio	15	0	106	27	9	21	.429	4	6	.667	5	6	.833	1	9	10	16	7	0	4	0	10	7.1	1.8	0.7	1.1	.322
99-00	San Antonio	4	0	82	29	9	23	.391	2	8	.250	9	13	.692	2	8	10	6	5	0	7	0	6	20.5	7.3	2.5	1.5	.351
00-01	San Antonio	13	8	406	176	63	131	.481	17	46	.370	33	35	.943	4	22	26	38	22	0	7	1	13	31.2	13.5	2.0	2.9	.406
01-02	San Antonio	10	0	224	95	35	77	.455	6	16	.375	19	22	.864	3	24	27	15	13	0	7	3	5	22.4	9.5	2.7	1.5	.425
02-03	Portland	6	1	98	22	9	19	.474	3	5	.600	1	2	.500	3	5	8	12	5	0	1	1	2	16.3	3.7	1.3	2.0	.312
NBA Playoff Totals		48	9	916	349	125	271	.461	32	81	.395	67	78	.859	13	68	81	87	52	0	26	5	36	19.1	7.3	1.7	1.8	....

• DANIELS, Lloyd

Lloyd (Swee'pea) Daniels

Born: Sept. 4, 1967. Brooklyn, NY, United States. Height: 6'7". Weight: 205 lbs. Drafted: — College: Mount San Antonio

YEAR	TEAM	GP	GS	MIN	PTS	FGM	FGA	FG%	3PM	3PA	3P%	FTM	FTA	FT%	ORB	DRB	TRB	AST	PF	DQ	STL	BLK	TO	MPG	PPG	RPG	APG	PCM
92-93	San Antonio	77	10	1573	701	285	644	.443	59	177	.333	72	99	.727	86	130	216	148	144	0	38	30	100	20.4	9.1	2.8	1.9	.392
93-94	San Antonio	65	5	980	370	140	372	.376	44	125	.352	46	64	.719	45	66	111	94	69	0	29	16	59	15.1	5.7	1.7	1.4	.314
94-95	Philadelphia	5	0	63	23	9	27	.333	3	14	.214	2	2	1.000	2	5	7	4	8	0	2	0	8	12.6	4.6	1.4	0.8	.120
94-95	LA Lakers	25	14	541	185	71	182	.390	23	86	.267	20	25	.800	27	29	56	36	40	0	20	10	23	21.6	7.4	2.2	1.4	.290
96-97	Sacramento	5	0	28	6	2	16	.125	2	11	.182	0	0	.000	1	3	4	1	4	0	1	0	3	5.6	1.2	0.8	0.2	-.214
96-97	New Jersey	17	0	282	92	34	103	.330	19	59	.322	5	6	.833	18	21	39	25	29	0	9	3	10	16.6	5.4	2.3	1.5	.279
97-98	Toronto	6	0	82	34	12	29	.414	2	9	.222	8	10	.800	4	3	7	4	4	0	3	2	4	13.7	5.7	1.2	0.7	.334
NBA Season Totals		200	29	3549	1411	553	1373	.403	152	481	.316	153	206	.743	183	257	440	312	298	0	102	61	207	17.7	7.1	2.2	1.6	....
92-93	San Antonio	8	0	74	28	11	30	.367	1	7	.143	5	6	.833	9	6	15	2	8	0	3	0	5	9.3	3.5	1.9	0.3	.275
93-94	San Antonio	4	0	66	22	8	20	.400	4	8	.500	2	2	1.000	2	7	9	3	4	0	0	1	2	16.5	5.5	2.3	0.8	.299
NBA Playoff Totals		12	0	140	50	19	50	.380	5	15	.333	7	8	.875	11	13	24	5	12	0	3	1	7	11.7	4.2	2.0	0.4	....

• DANIELS, Mel

Melvin Joe Daniels

Born: July 20, 1944. Detroit, MI, United States. Height: 6'9". Weight: 220 lbs. Drafted: 1967 College: New Mexico

YEAR	TEAM	GP	GS	MIN	PTS	FGM	FGA	FG%	3PM	3PA	3P%	FTM	FTA	FT%	ORB	DRB	TRB	AST	PF	DQ	STL	BLK	TO	MPG	PPG	RPG	APG	PCM
67-68	Minnesota-A	78	....	2938	1729	**669**	**1640**	.408	1	5	.200	390	678	.575	**502**	**711**	**1213**	109	268	11	....	....	232	37.7	22.2	**15.6**	1.4	.622
68-69	Indiana-A	76	....	2934	1824	712	1496	.476	0	4	.000	400	662	.604	383	**873**	**1256**	116	276	8	....	....	272	38.6	24.0	**16.5**	1.5	.726
69-70	Indiana-A	83	....	3039	1556	613	1295	.473	0	2	.000	330	489	.675	423	1039	1462	131	309	7	....	....	307	36.6	18.7	17.6	1.6	.715
70-71	Indiana-A	82	....	3170	1723	698	1357	.514	1	13	.077	326	480	.679	394	1081	**1475**	178	292	8	....	....	230	38.7	21.0	**18.0**	2.2	.761
71-72	Indiana-A	79	....	2971	1513	598	1184	.505	0	6	.000	317	451	.703	383	914	1297	176	289	7	....	....	239	37.6	19.2	16.4	2.2	.723
72-73	Indiana-A	81	....	3103	1497	587	1217	.482	1	4	.250	322	446	.722	348	899	1247	177	315	8	....	157	275	38.3	18.5	15.4	2.2	.660
73-74	Indiana-A	78	....	2539	1201	492	1117	.440	0	0	.000	217	287	.756	251	655	906	122	283	....	56	92	215	32.6	15.4	11.6	1.6	.563
74-75	Memphis-A	71	....	1646	696	290	644	.450	0	0	.000	116	183	.634	186	452	638	125	248	....	40	102	141	23.2	9.8	9.0	1.8	.576
76-77	New York	11	....	126	39	13	35	.371	....	....	....	13	23	.565	10	24	34	6	29	0	3	11	....	11.5	3.5	3.1	0.5	.312
NBA Season Totals		11	....	126	39	13	35	.371	....	....	....	13	23	.565	10	24	34	6	29	0	3	11	....	11.5	3.5	3.1	0.5	....
ABA Season Totals		628	....	22340	11739	4659	9950	.468	3	34	.088	2418	3676	.658	**2870**	**6624**	**9494**	1134	**2280**	49	96	351	1911	35.6	18.7	15.1	1.8	....
Career Totals		639	....	22466	11778	4672	9985	.468	3	34	.088	2431	3699	.657	**2880**	**6648**	**9528**	1140	**2309**	49	99	362	1911	35.2	18.4	14.9	1.8	....
67-68	Minnesota-A	10	....	409	253	98	226	.434	0	0	.000	57	94	.606	59	102	161	19	35	1	....	....	33	40.9	25.3	16.1	1.9	.667
68-69	Indiana-A	17	....	570	333	127	301	.422	0	1	.000	79	130	.608	75	162	237	22	75	1	....	....	57	33.5	19.6	13.9	1.3	.628
69-70	Indiana-A	15	....	533	290	108	243	.444	0	1	.000	74	111	.667	91	174	265	15	62	1	....	....	48	35.5	19.3	17.7	1.0	.706
70-71	Indiana-A	11	....	457	235	94	194	.485	0	0	.000	47	63	.746	71	140	211	16	38	1	....	....	26	41.5	21.4	19.2	1.5	.703

YEAR	TEAM	GP	GS	MIN	PTS	FGM	FGA	FG%	3PM	3PA	3P%	FTM	FTA	FT%	ORB	DRB	TRB	AST	PF	DQ	STL	BLK	TO	MPG	PPG	RPG	APG	PCM
71-72	Indiana-A	20	....	744	306	121	252	.480	0	3	.000	64	85	.753	89	213	302	28	85	....	....	....	58	37.2	15.3	15.1	1.4	.593
72-73	Indiana-A	18	....	636	286	112	238	.471	0	0	.000	62	81	.765	70	178	248	40	76	2	....	....	39	35.3	15.9	13.8	2.2	.624
73-74	Indiana-A	14	....	498	171	69	172	.401	0	0	.000	33	43	.767	35	125	160	27	50	....	11	14	30	35.6	12.2	11.4	1.9	.452
74-75	Memphis-A	4	....	54	27	11	22	.500	0	0	.000	5	9	.556	4	20	24	1	12	....	1	6	1	13.5	6.8	6.0	0.3	.593
ABA Playoff Totals		109	....	3901	1901	740	1648	.449	0	5	.000	421	616	.683	**494**	**1114**	**1608**	168	**433**	6	12	20	**292**	35.8	17.4	14.8	1.5	....

• DANILOVIC, Sasha

Predrag Danilovic

Born: Feb. 26, 1970. Sarajevo, Bosnia.   Height: 6'5".   Weight: 200 lbs.   Drafted: 1992   College: none

YEAR	TEAM	GP	GS	MIN	PTS	FGM	FGA	FG%	3PM	3PA	3P%	FTM	FTA	FT%	ORB	DRB	TRB	AST	PF	DQ	STL	BLK	TO	MPG	PPG	RPG	APG	PCM
95-96	Miami	19	18	542	255	83	184	.451	34	78	.436	55	72	.764	12	34	46	47	49	0	15	3	36	28.5	13.4	2.4	2.5	.379
96-97	Miami	43	33	1351	486	175	396	.442	63	176	.358	73	94	.777	21	81	102	77	123	2	39	8	95	31.4	11.3	2.4	1.8	.256
96-97	Dallas	13	9	438	216	73	174	.420	22	60	.367	48	57	.842	8	26	34	25	37	0	15	1	22	33.7	16.6	2.6	1.9	.350
NBA Season Totals		75	60	2331	957	331	754	.439	119	314	.379	176	223	.789	41	141	182	149	209	2	69	12	153	31.1	12.8	2.4	2.0	....
95-96	Miami	3	0	60	25	9	18	.500	4	10	.400	3	3	1.000	1	0	1	4	8	0	1	0	3	20.0	8.3	0.3	1.3	.268
NBA Playoff Totals		3	0	60	25	9	18	.500	4	10	.400	3	3	1.000	1	0	1	4	8	0	1	0	3	20.0	8.3	0.3	1.3	....

• DANKO, —

Danko

Born: —.   Height: —   Weight: —   Drafted: —   College: —

YEAR	TEAM	GP	GS	MIN	PTS	FGM	FGA	FG%	3PM	3PA	3P%	FTM	FTA	FT%	ORB	DRB	TRB	AST	PF	DQ	STL	BLK	TO	MPG	PPG	RPG	APG	PCM
40-41	Hammond-N	1	....	....	4	2	....	....	....	....	....	0	....	....	....	....	....	....	....	....	....	....	....	4.0	....	....	....	....
NBL Season Totals		1	....	....	4	2	....	....	....	....	....	0	....	....	....	....	....	....	....	....	....	....	....	4.0	....	....	....	....

• DANTLEY, Adrian

Adrian Delano Dantley

Born: Feb. 28, 1956. Washington, DC, United States.   Height: 6'5".   Weight: 208 lbs.   Drafted: 1976   College: Notre Dame

YEAR	TEAM	GP	GS	MIN	PTS	FGM	FGA	FG%	3PM	3PA	3P%	FTM	FTA	FT%	ORB	DRB	TRB	AST	PF	DQ	STL	BLK	TO	MPG	PPG	RPG	APG	PCM
76-77	Buffalo	77	....	2816	1564	544	1046	.520	....	....	....	476	582	.818	251	336	587	144	215	2	91	15	....	36.6	20.3	7.6	1.9	.590
77-78	Indiana	23	....	948	609	201	403	.499	....	....	....	**207**	**263**	.787	94	122	216	65	76	1	48	17	67	41.2	26.5	9.4	2.8	.670
77-78	LA Lakers	56	....	1985	1088	377	725	.520	....	....	....	**334**	**417**	.801	171	233	404	188	157	1	70	7	162	35.4	19.4	7.2	3.4	.589
78-79	LA Lakers	60	....	1775	1040	374	733	.510	....	....	....	292	342	.854	131	211	342	138	162	0	63	12	156	29.6	17.3	5.7	2.3	.568
79-80	Utah	68	....	2674	1903	730	1267	.576	0	2	.000	443	526	.842	183	333	516	191	211	2	96	14	231	39.3	28.0	7.6	2.8	.692
80-81	Utah	80	....	3417	2452	**909**	1627	.559	2	7	.286	**632**	784	.806	192	317	509	322	245	1	109	18	280	**42.7**	**30.7**	6.4	4.0	.671
81-82	Utah	81	81	3222	2457	904	1586	.570	1	3	.333	**648**	818	.792	231	283	514	324	252	1	95	14	300	39.8	30.3	6.3	4.0	.708
82-83	Utah	22	22	887	676	233	402	.580	0	0	.000	210	248	.847	58	82	140	105	62	2	20	0	81	40.3	30.7	6.4	4.8	.750
83-84	Utah	79	79	2984	**2418**	802	1438	.558	1	4	.250	**813**	**946**	.859	179	269	448	310	201	0	61	4	261	37.8	**30.6**	5.7	3.9	.750
84-85	Utah	55	46	1971	1462	512	964	.531	0	0	.000	438	545	.804	148	175	323	186	133	0	57	8	171	35.8	26.6	5.9	3.4	.675
85-86	Utah	76	75	2744	2267	818	1453	.563	1	11	.091	**630**	**796**	.791	178	217	395	264	206	2	64	4	228	36.1	29.8	5.2	3.5	.731
86-87	Detroit	81	81	2736	1742	601	1126	.534	1	6	.167	539	664	.812	104	228	332	162	193	1	63	7	178	33.8	21.5	4.1	2.0	.543
87-88	Detroit	69	50	2144	1380	444	863	.514	0	2	.000	492	572	.860	84	143	227	171	144	0	39	10	138	31.1	20.0	3.3	2.5	.558
88-89	Detroit	42	42	1341	772	258	495	.521	0	0	.000	256	305	.839	53	111	164	93	99	1	23	6	80	31.9	18.4	3.9	2.2	.513
88-89	Dallas	31	25	1081	628	212	459	.462	0	1	.000	204	263	.776	64	89	153	78	87	0	20	7	81	34.9	20.3	4.9	2.5	.468
89-90	Dallas	45	45	1300	662	231	484	.477	0	2	.000	200	254	.787	78	94	172	80	99	0	20	7	77	28.9	14.7	3.8	1.8	.425
90-91	Milwaukee	10	0	126	57	19	50	.380	1	3	.333	18	26	.692	8	5	13	9	8	0	5	0	6	12.6	5.7	1.3	0.9	.329
NBA Season Totals		955	546	34151	23177	8169	15121	.540	7	41	.171	6832	8351	.818	2207	3248	5455	2830	2550	14	944	150	2497	35.8	24.3	5.7	3.0	....
77-78	LA Lakers	3	....	104	51	20	35	.571	....	....	....	11	17	.647	9	16	25	11	9	0	5	3	6	34.7	17.0	8.3	3.7	.647
78-79	LA Lakers	8	....	236	141	50	89	.562	....	....	....	41	52	.788	10	23	33	11	24	0	6	1	19	29.5	17.6	4.1	1.4	.514
83-84	Utah	11	11	454	354	117	232	.504	0	0	.000	120	139	.863	37	46	83	46	30	0	10	1	38	41.3	32.2	7.5	4.2	.717
84-85	Utah	10	10	398	253	79	151	.523	0	1	.000	95	122	.779	25	50	75	20	39	1	16	0	36	39.8	25.3	7.5	2.0	.572
86-87	Detroit	15	15	500	308	111	206	.539	0	0	.000	86	111	.775	29	39	68	35	36	0	13	0	33	33.3	20.5	4.5	2.3	.547
87-88	Detroit	23	23	804	446	153	292	.524	0	2	.000	140	178	.787	37	70	107	46	50	0	19	1	51	35.0	19.4	4.7	2.0	.492
90-91	Milwaukee	3	0	19	5	1	7	.143	0	0	.000	3	4	.750	2	2	4	0	0	0	0	0	2	6.3	1.7	1.3	0.0	.042
NBA Playoff Totals		73	59	2515	1558	531	1012	.525	0	3	.000	496	623	.796	149	246	395	169	188	1	69	6	185	34.5	21.3	5.4	2.3	....

• D'ANTONI, Mike

Michael Andrew D'Antoni

Born: May 8, 1951. Mullens, WV, United States.   Height: 6'3".   Weight: 185 lbs.   Drafted: 1973   College: Marshall

YEAR	TEAM	GP	GS	MIN	PTS	FGM	FGA	FG%	3PM	3PA	3P%	FTM	FTA	FT%	ORB	DRB	TRB	AST	PF	DQ	STL	BLK	TO	MPG	PPG	RPG	APG	PCM
73-74	Omaha	52	....	989	247	107	266	.402	....	....	....	33	47	.702	24	69	93	123	112	0	75	15	....	19.0	4.8	1.8	2.4	.282
74-75	Omaha	67	....	759	166	69	173	.399	....	....	....	28	36	.778	13	64	77	107	106	0	67	12	....	11.3	2.5	1.1	1.6	.286
75-76	St. Louis-A	50	....	798	173	77	162	.475	0	4	.000	19	26	.731	16	60	76	115	134	....	63	14	47	16.0	3.5	1.5	2.3	.288
75-76	Kansas City	9	....	101	16	7	27	.259	....	....	....	2	2	1.000	4	10	14	16	18	0	10	0	....	11.2	1.8	1.6	1.8	.212
76-77	San Antonio	2	....	9	3	1	3	.333	....	....	....	1	2	.500	0	2	2	2	3	0	0	0	....	4.5	1.5	1.0	1.0	.394
NBA Season Totals		130	....	1858	432	184	469	.392	....	....	....	64	87	.736	41	145	186	248	239	0	152	27	....	14.3	3.3	1.4	1.9	....
ABA Season Totals		50	....	798	173	77	162	.475	0	4	.000	19	26	.731	16	60	76	115	134	....	63	14	47	16.0	3.5	1.5	2.3	....
Career Totals		180	....	2656	605	261	631	.414	0	4	.000	83	113	.735	57	205	262	363	373	0	215	41	47	14.8	3.4	1.5	2.0	....
74-75	Omaha	4	....	42	18	7	14	.500	....	....	....	4	4	1.000	2	5	7	1	6	0	4	1	....	10.5	4.5	1.8	0.3	.395
NBA Playoff Totals		4	....	42	18	7	14	.500	....	....	....	4	4	1.000	2	5	7	1	6	0	4	1	....	10.5	4.5	1.8	0.3	....

• DARCEY, Pete

Henry J. Darcey

Born: Mar. 3, 1930.   Height: 6'7".   Weight: 217 lbs.   Drafted: —   College: Oklahoma A&M

YEAR	TEAM	GP	GS	MIN	PTS	FGM	FGA	FG%	3PM	3PA	3P%	FTM	FTA	FT%	ORB	DRB	TRB	AST	PF	DQ	STL	BLK	TO	MPG	PPG	RPG	APG	PCM
52-53	Milwaukee	12	....	90	11	3	18	.167	....	....	....	5	9	.556	....	....	10	2	29	2	....	....	....	7.5	0.9	0.8	0.2	-.022
NBA Season Totals		12	....	90	11	3	18	.167	....	....	....	5	9	.556	....	....	10	2	29	2	....	....	....	7.5	0.9	0.8	0.2	....

YEAR	TEAM	GP	GS	MIN	PTS	FGM	FGA	FG%	3PM	3PA	3P%	FTM	FTA	FT%	ORB	DRB	TRB	AST	PF	DQ	STL	BLK	TO	MPG	PPG	RPG	APG	PCM

• DARDEN, Jimmy
James W. Darden

Born: June 19, 1922. Died: Apr.29, 1994.   Height: 6'1".   Weight: 170 lbs.   Drafted: 1947   College: Denver

YEAR	TEAM	GP	GS	MIN	PTS	FGM	FGA	FG%	3PM	3PA	3P%	FTM	FTA	FT%	ORB	DRB	TRB	AST	PF	DQ	STL	BLK	TO	MPG	PPG	RPG	APG	PCM
48-49	Denver-N	57	....	....	587	197	....	....				193	259	.745	....	....	....	....	149	....	....	....	....	10.3	....	....	....
49-50	Denver	26	....	....	211	78	243	.321				55	80	.688	....	....	....	67	67	....	....	....	....	8.1	....	2.6	....
NBA Season Totals		26	....	....	211	78	243	.321				55	80	.688	....	....	....	:...	67	67	....	....	....	....	8.1	....	2.6	....
NBL Season Totals		57	....	....	587	197	....	....				193	259	....	....	....	....	....	149	....	....	....	....	10.3	....	....	....
Career Totals		83	....	....	798	275	243	....				248	339	....	....	....	....	67	216	....	....	....	....	9.6	....	0.8	....

• DARDEN, Ollie
Oliver Darden

Born: July 28, 1944. Aberdeen, MS, United States.   Height: 6'7".   Weight: 235 lbs.   Drafted: 1966   College: Michigan

YEAR	TEAM	GP	GS	MIN	PTS	FGM	FGA	FG%	3PM	3PA	3P%	FTM	FTA	FT%	ORB	DRB	TRB	AST	PF	DQ	STL	BLK	TO	MPG	PPG	RPG	APG	PCM
67-68	Indiana-A	77	....	2045	922	371	831	.446	0	1	.000	180	270	.667	....	....	527	69	277	2	....	....	140	26.6	12.0	6.8	0.9	.443
68-69	Kentucky-A	47	....	1221	471	185	435	.425	1	5	.200	100	130	.769	143	237	380	62	167	4	....	....	66	26.0	10.0	8.1	1.3	.466
68-69	New York-A	30	....	726	344	133	279	.477	0	0	.000	78	110	.709	80	134	214	42	107	1	....	....	72	24.2	11.5	7.1	1.4	.538
69-70	Indiana-A	26	....	288	111	47	121	.388	1	4	.250	16	23	.696	22	68	90	13	48	0	....	....	25	11.1	4.3	3.5	0.5	.403
69-70	Kentucky-A	43	....	531	199	79	206	.383	0	1	.000	41	64	.641	71	99	170	33	94	1	....	....	57	12.3	4.6	4.0	0.8	.421
ABA Season Totals		223	....	4811	2047	815	1872	.435	2	11	.182	415	597	.695	316	538	1381	219	693	8	....	....	360	21.6	9.2	6.2	1.0	....
67-68	Indiana-A	3	....	60	35	16	28	.571	0	0	.000	3	5	.600	....	....	27	4	13	0	....	....	4	20.0	11.7	9.0	1.3	.765
68-69	Kentucky-A	7	....	102	63	26	49	.531	1	2	.500	10	15	.667	....	....	31	6	19	0	....	....	7	14.6	9.0	4.4	0.9	.651
69-70	Indiana-A	8	....	21	4	2	6	.333	0	0	.000	0	0	.000	2	2	4	2	3	0	....	....	3	2.6	0.5	0.5	0.3	.238
ABA Playoff Totals		18	....	183	102	44	83	.530	1	2	.500	13	20	.650	2	2	62	12	35	0	....	....	14	10.2	5.7	3.4	0.7	....

• DARE, Yinka
Yinka Dare

Born: Oct. 10, 1972. Kano, Nigeria.   Height: 7'   Weight: 265 lbs.   Drafted: 1994   College: George Washington

YEAR	TEAM	GP	GS	MIN	PTS	FGM	FGA	FG%	3PM	3PA	3P%	FTM	FTA	FT%	ORB	DRB	TRB	AST	PF	DQ	STL	BLK	TO	MPG	PPG	RPG	APG	PCM
94-95	New Jersey	1	0	3	0	0	1	.000	0	0	.000	0	0	.000	0	1	1	0	2	0	0	0	1	3.0	0.0	1.0	0.0	-.625
95-96	New Jersey	58	23	626	164	63	144	.438	0	0	.000	38	62	.613	56	125	181	0	117	3	8	40	70	10.8	2.8	3.1	0.0	.273
96-97	New Jersey	41	2	313	57	19	54	.352	0	0	.000	19	37	.514	35	47	82	3	51	0	4	28	21	7.6	1.4	2.0	0.1	.262
97-98	New Jersey	10	0	60	12	4	18	.222	0	0	.000	4	8	.500	10	7	17	1	9	0	0	2	2	6.0	1.2	1.7	0.1	.165
NBA Season Totals		110	25	1002	233	86	217	.396	0	0	.000	61	107	.570	101	180	281	4	179	3	12	70	94	9.1	2.1	2.6	0.0	....

• DARK, Jesse
Jesse L. (Bo) Dark

Born: Sept. 2, 1951. Richmond, VA, United States.   Height: 6'5".   Weight: 210 lbs.   Drafted: 1974   College: Virginia Commonwealth

YEAR	TEAM	GP	GS	MIN	PTS	FGM	FGA	FG%	3PM	3PA	3P%	FTM	FTA	FT%	ORB	DRB	TRB	AST	PF	DQ	STL	BLK	TO	MPG	PPG	RPG	APG	PCM
74-75	New York	47	....	401	170	74	157	.471	....	....	....	22	40	.550	15	22	37	30	48	0	3	1	....	8.5	3.6	0.8	0.6	.342
NBA Season Totals		47	....	401	170	74	157	.471	....	....	....	22	40	.550	15	22	37	30	48	0	3	1	....	8.5	3.6	0.8	0.6	....
74-75	New York	2	....	11	7	1	6	.167	....	....	....	5	5	1.000	1	0	1	1	2	0	0	0	....	5.5	3.5	0.5	0.5	.353
NBA Playoff Totals		2	....	11	7	1	6	.167	....	....	....	5	5	1.000	1	0	1	1	2	0	0	0	....	5.5	3.5	0.5	0.5	....

• DARNELL, Rick
Rick Darnell

Born: Jan. 1, 1953.   Height: 6'10".   Weight: 215 lbs.   Drafted: —   College: San Jose State

YEAR	TEAM	GP	GS	MIN	PTS	FGM	FGA	FG%	3PM	3PA	3P%	FTM	FTA	FT%	ORB	DRB	TRB	AST	PF	DQ	STL	BLK	TO	MPG	PPG	RPG	APG	PCM
75-76	Virginia-A	11	....	120	26	11	30	.367	0	0	.000	4	7	.571	12	24	36	9	30	....	5	3	14	10.9	2.4	3.3	0.8	.304
ABA Season Totals		11	....	120	26	11	30	.367	0	0	.000	4	7	.571	12	24	36	9	30	....	5	3	14	10.9	2.4	3.3	0.8	....

• DARROW, Jimmy
James K. Darrow

Born: Sept. 25, 1937. Akron, OH, United States. Died: June8, 1987.   Height: 5'10".   Weight: 170 lbs.   Drafted: 1960   College: Bowling Green

YEAR	TEAM	GP	GS	MIN	PTS	FGM	FGA	FG%	3PM	3PA	3P%	FTM	FTA	FT%	ORB	DRB	TRB	AST	PF	DQ	STL	BLK	TO	MPG	PPG	RPG	APG	PCM
61-62	St. Louis	5	....	34	12	3	15	.200	....	....	....	6	7	.857			7	6	9	0	....	....	....	6.8	2.4	1.4	1.2	.338
NBA Season Totals		5	....	34	12	3	15	.200	....	....	....	6	7	.857			7	6	9	0	....	....	....	6.8	2.4	1.4	1.2	....

• DAUGHERTY, Brad
Bradley Lee (Big Dukie, Hooch) Daugherty

Born: Oct. 19, 1965. Black Mountain, NC, United States.   Height: 7'   Weight: 245 lbs.   Drafted: 1986   College: North Carolina

YEAR	TEAM	GP	GS	MIN	PTS	FGM	FGA	FG%	3PM	3PA	3P%	FTM	FTA	FT%	ORB	DRB	TRB	AST	PF	DQ	STL	BLK	TO	MPG	PPG	RPG	APG	PCM
86-87	Cleveland	80	80	2695	1253	487	905	.538	0	0	.000	279	401	.696	152	495	647	304	248	3	49	63	248	33.7	15.7	8.1	3.8	.554
87-88	Cleveland	79	78	2957	1480	551	1081	.510	0	2	.000	378	528	.716	151	514	665	333	235	2	48	56	269	37.4	18.7	8.4	4.2	.551
88-89	Cleveland	78	78	2821	1475	544	1012	.538	1	3	.333	386	524	.737	167	551	718	285	175	1	63	40	226	36.2	18.9	9.2	3.7	.621
89-90	Cleveland	41	40	1438	690	244	509	.479	0	2	.000	202	287	.704	77	296	373	130	108	1	29	22	111	35.1	16.8	9.1	3.2	.544
90-91	Cleveland	76	76	2946	1645	605	1155	.524	0	3	.000	435	579	.751	177	653	830	253	191	2	74	46	213	38.8	21.6	10.9	3.3	.656
91-92	Cleveland	73	73	2643	1566	576	1010	.570	0	2	.000	414	533	.777	191	569	760	262	190	1	65	78	183	36.2	21.5	10.4	3.6	.745
92-93	Cleveland	71	71	2691	1432	520	911	.571	1	2	.500	391	492	.795	164	562	726	312	174	0	53	56	149	37.9	20.2	10.2	4.4	.710
93-94	Cleveland	50	50	1838	848	296	606	.488	0	0	.000	256	326	.785	128	380	508	149	145	1	41	36	110	36.8	17.0	10.2	3.0	.578
NBA Season Totals		548	546	20029	10389	3823	7189	.532	2	14	.143	2741	3670	.747	1207	4020	5227	2028	1466	11	422	397	1509	36.5	19.0	9.5	3.7	....
87-88	Cleveland	5	5	204	79	29	63	.460	0	0	.000	21	31	.677	10	36	46	16	11	0	2	7	16	40.8	15.8	9.2	3.2	.446
88-89	Cleveland	5	5	167	55	17	47	.362	0	1	.000	21	35	.600	12	34	46	12	18	0	6	5	6	33.4	11.0	9.2	2.4	.434
89-90	Cleveland	5	5	186	114	41	70	.586	0	0	.000	32	46	.696	4	44	48	20	12	0	2	4	13	37.2	22.8	9.6	4.0	.722
91-92	Cleveland	17	17	687	366	124	235	.528	0	1	.000	118	145	.814	37	137	174	58	47	0	11	17	37	40.4	21.5	10.2	3.4	.646
92-93	Cleveland	9	9	356	168	64	115	.557	0	0	.000	40	50	.800	26	79	105	31	25	1	6	7	26	39.6	18.7	11.7	3.4	.626
NBA Playoff Totals		41	41	1600	782	275	530	.519	0	2	.000	232	307	.756	89	330	419	137	113	1	27	40	98	39.0	19.1	10.2	3.3	....

• DAUGHTRY, Mack

Mack Daughtry

Born: 1947. Height: 6'3". Weight: 175 lbs. Drafted: 1968 College: Albany State (GA)

YEAR	TEAM	GP	GS	MIN	PTS	FGM	FGA	FG%	3PM	3PA	3P%	FTM	FTA	FT%	ORB	DRB	TRB	AST	PF	DQ	STL	BLK	TO	MPG	PPG	RPG	APG	PCM
70-71	Carolina-A	4	....	43	13	4	10	.400	0	0	.000	5	5	1.000	2	3	5	3	4	0	....	....	0	10.8	3.3	1.3	0.8	.330
ABA Season Totals		4	....	43	13	4	10	.400	0	0	.000	5	5	1.000	2	3	5	3	4	0	....	....	0	10.8	3.3	1.3	0.8	....

• DAVID, Kornel

Kornel David

Born: Oct. 22, 1971. Hungary. Height: 6'9". Weight: 235 lbs. Drafted: — College: —

YEAR	TEAM	GP	GS	MIN	PTS	FGM	FGA	FG%	3PM	3PA	3P%	FTM	FTA	FT%	ORB	DRB	TRB	AST	PF	DQ	STL	BLK	TO	MPG	PPG	RPG	APG	PCM
98-99	Chicago	50	6	902	308	109	243	.449	0	1	.000	90	111	.811	70	103	173	40	88	0	23	17	48	18.0	6.2	3.5	0.8	.368
99-00	Chicago	26	5	443	168	63	148	.426	0	3	.000	42	52	.808	22	51	73	16	49	0	13	2	31	17.0	6.5	2.8	0.6	.301
99-00	Cleveland	6	0	31	11	4	9	.444	0	0	.000	3	4	.750	4	4	8	1	7	0	4	1	2	5.2	1.8	1.3	0.2	.449
00-01	Toronto	17	0	140	42	15	29	.517	0	0	.000	12	13	.923	9	24	33	4	20	0	2	3	7	8.2	2.5	1.9	0.2	.373
00-01	Detroit	10	0	69	20	10	22	.455	0	0	.000	0	0	.000	6	13	19	3	8	0	4	1	4	6.9	2.0	1.9	0.3	.390
NBA Season Totals		109	11	1585	549	201	451	.446	0	4	.000	147	180	.817	111	195	306	64	172	0	46	24	92	14.5	5.0	2.8	0.6	....

• DAVIES, Bob

Robert Edris (Harrisburg Houdini, Li'l Abner) Davies

Born: Jan. 15, 1920. Harrisburg, PA, United States. Died: Apr.22, 1990. Height: 6'1". Weight: 175 lbs. Drafted: — College: Seton Hall HOF: 1970

YEAR	TEAM	GP	GS	MIN	PTS	FGM	FGA	FG%	3PM	3PA	3P%	FTM	FTA	FT%	ORB	DRB	TRB	AST	PF	DQ	STL	BLK	TO	MPG	PPG	RPG	APG	PCM
45-46	Rochester-N	27	....	....	242	86	....	....	....	....	....	70	103	.680	....	....	....	....	....	....	....	....	....	....	9.0	....	....	....
46-47	Rochester-N	32	....	....	462	166	....	....	....	....	....	130	166	**.783**	....	....	....	....	90	....	....	....	....	....	14.4	....	....	....
47-48	Rochester-N	48	....	....	472	176	....	....	....	....	....	120	160	.750	....	....	....	....	111	....	....	....	....	....	9.8	....	....	....
48-49	Rochester	60	....	....	904	317	871	.364	....	....	....	270	348	.776	....	....	....	**321**	197	....	....	....	....	....	15.1	....	**5.4**	....
49-50	Rochester	64	....	....	895	317	887	.357	....	....	....	261	347	.752	....	....	....	294	187	....	....	....	....	....	14.0	....	4.6	....
50-51	Rochester	63	....	....	955	326	877	.372	....	....	....	303	381	.795	....	....	197	287	208	7	....	....	....	....	15.2	3.1	4.6	....
51-52	Rochester	65	....	2394	1052	379	990	.383	....	....	....	294	379	.776	....	....	189	390	269	10	....	....	....	36.8	16.2	2.9	6.0	.472
52-53	Rochester	66	....	2216	1029	339	880	.385	....	....	....	351	466	.753	....	....	195	280	261	7	....	....	....	33.6	15.6	3.0	4.2	.451
53-54	Rochester	72	....	2137	887	288	777	.371	....	....	....	311	433	.718	....	....	194	323	224	4	....	....	....	29.7	12.3	2.7	4.5	.455
54-55	Rochester	72	....	1870	872	326	785	.415	....	....	....	220	293	.751	....	....	205	355	220	2	....	....	....	26.0	12.1	2.8	4.9	.542
NBA Season Totals		462	....	8617	6594	2292	6067	.378	....	....	....	2010	2647	.759	....	....	980	2250	1566	30	....	....	....	18.7	14.3	2.1	4.9	....
NBL Season Totals		107	....	....	1176	428	....	....	....	....	....	320	429	....	....	....	....	....	201	....	....	....	....	....	11.0	....	....	....
Career Totals		569	....	8617	7770	2720	6067	....	....	....	....	2330	3076	....	....	....	980	2250	1767	30	....	....	....	15.1	13.7	1.7	4.0	....
45-46	Rochester-N	7	....	....	86	28	....	....	....	....	....	30	41	.732	....	....	....	....	....	....	....	....	....	....	12.3	....	....	....
46-47	Rochester-N	11	....	....	151	54	....	....	....	....	....	43	63	.683	....	....	....	....	....	....	....	....	....	....	13.7	....	....	....
47-48	Rochester-N	11	....	....	161	56	....	....	....	....	....	49	64	.766	....	....	....	....	....	....	....	....	....	....	14.6	....	....	....
48-49	Rochester	4	....	....	48	19	51	.373	....	....	....	10	13	.769	....	....	....	13	12	....	....	....	....	....	12.0	....	3.3	....
49-50	Rochester	2	....	....	15	4	17	.235	....	....	....	7	8	.875	....	....	....	9	11	....	....	....	....	....	7.5	....	4.5	....
50-51	Rochester	14	....	....	222	79	234	.338	....	....	....	64	80	.800	....	....	43	75	45	1	....	....	....	....	15.9	3.1	5.4	....
51-52	Rochester	6	....	233	119	37	92	.402	....	....	....	45	55	.818	....	....	13	28	18	0	....	....	....	38.8	19.8	2.2	4.7	.495
52-53	Rochester	3	....	91	26	6	29	.207	....	....	....	14	20	.700	....	....	4	14	11	0	....	....	....	30.3	8.7	1.3	4.7	.263
53-54	Rochester	6	....	172	51	17	52	.327	....	....	....	17	23	.739	....	....	12	14	16	0	....	....	....	28.7	8.5	2.0	2.3	.261
54-55	Rochester	3	....	75	25	11	33	.333	....	....	....	3	4	.750	....	....	6	9	11	0	....	....	....	25.0	8.3	2.0	3.0	.263
NBA Playoff Totals		38	....	571	506	173	508	.341	....	....	....	160	203	.788	....	....	78	162	124	1	....	....	....	15.0	13.3	2.1	4.3	....
NBL Playoff Totals		29	....	....	398	138	....	....	....	....	....	122	168	....	....	....	....	....	....	....	....	....	....	....	13.7	....	....	....
Career Playoff Totals		67	....	571	904	311	508	....	....	....	....	282	371	....	....	....	78	162	124	1	....	....	....	8.5	13.5	1.2	2.4	....

• DAVIS, Antonio

Antonio Lee Davis

Born: Oct. 31, 1968. Oakland, CA, United States. Height: 6'9". Weight: 215 lbs. Drafted: 1990 College: Texas (El Paso)

YEAR	TEAM	GP	GS	MIN	PTS	FGM	FGA	FG%	3PM	3PA	3P%	FTM	FTA	FT%	ORB	DRB	TRB	AST	PF	DQ	STL	BLK	TO	MPG	PPG	RPG	APG	PCM
93-94	Indiana	81	4	1732	626	216	425	.508	0	1	.000	194	302	.642	190	315	505	55	189	1	45	84	105	21.4	7.7	6.2	0.7	.487
94-95	Indiana	44	1	1030	335	109	245	.445	0	0	.000	117	174	.672	105	175	280	25	134	2	19	29	66	23.4	7.6	6.4	0.6	.379
95-96	Indiana	82	14	2092	719	236	482	.490	1	2	.500	246	345	.713	188	313	501	43	248	6	33	66	90	25.5	8.8	6.1	0.5	.406
96-97	Indiana	82	28	2335	858	308	641	.480	1	14	.071	241	362	.666	190	408	598	65	260	4	42	84	139	28.5	10.5	7.3	0.8	.422
97-98	Indiana	82	12	2191	785	254	528	.481	0	3	.000	277	398	.696	192	368	560	61	234	6	45	72	107	26.7	9.6	6.8	0.7	.438
98-99	Indiana	49	1	1271	463	164	348	.471	0	0	.000	135	192	.703	116	228	344	33	136	3	22	42	50	25.9	9.4	7.0	0.7	.447
99-00	Toronto	79	78	2479	910	313	712	.440	0	0	.000	284	371	.765	235	461	696	105	267	2	38	100	121	31.4	11.5	8.8	1.3	.464
00-01	Toronto	78	77	2729	1069	375	866	.433	0	1	.000	319	423	.754	274	513	787	106	230	4	22	151	135	35.0	13.7	10.1	1.4	.489
01-02	Toronto	77	77	2977	1113	410	963	.426	0	1	.000	293	358	.818	254	486	740	155	225	3	54	83	159	38.7	14.5	9.6	2.0	.437
02-03	Toronto	53	52	1894	738	261	641	.407	0	0	.000	216	280	.771	130	307	437	131	150	0	23	62	118	35.7	13.9	8.2	2.5	.425
NBA Season Totals		707	344	20730	7616	2646	5851	.452	2	22	.091	2322	3205	.724	1874	3574	5448	779	2073	31	343	773	1090	29.3	10.8	7.7	1.1	....
93-94	Indiana	16	0	401	134	48	89	.539	1	1	1.000	37	66	.561	37	69	106	7	47	0	11	18	22	25.1	8.4	6.6	0.4	.431
94-95	Indiana	17	0	367	101	32	71	.451	0	0	.000	37	59	.627	38	59	97	7	61	0	9	11	23	21.6	5.9	5.7	0.4	.330
95-96	Indiana	5	0	127	39	13	25	.520	0	0	.000	13	15	.867	12	19	31	3	12	0	3	6	10	25.4	7.8	6.2	0.6	.414
97-98	Indiana	16	0	459	147	42	91	.462	0	0	.000	63	94	.670	37	71	108	14	65	5	12	18	25	28.7	9.2	6.8	0.9	.385
98-99	Indiana	13	0	326	103	31	75	.413	0	0	.000	41	62	.661	23	69	92	8	39	0	5	14	20	25.1	7.9	7.1	0.6	.390
99-00	Toronto	3	3	105	39	14	24	.583	0	0	.000	11	14	.786	7	18	25	3	9	0	1	4	4	35.0	13.0	8.3	1.0	.489
00-01	Toronto	12	12	485	197	77	154	.500	0	0	.000	43	53	.811	41	92	133	23	35	0	10	22	21	40.4	16.4	11.1	1.9	.541
01-02	Toronto	5	5	202	85	34	75	.453	0	0	.000	17	28	.607	16	37	53	7	17	0	2	5	10	40.4	17.0	10.6	1.4	.436
NBA Playoff Totals		87	20	2472	845	291	604	.482	1	1	1.000	262	391	.670	211	434	645	72	285	5	53	98	135	28.4	9.7	7.4	0.8	....

YEAR	TEAM	GP	GS	MIN	PTS	FGM	FGA	FG%	3PM	3PA	3P%	FTM	FTA	FT%	ORB	DRB	TRB	AST	PF	DQ	STL	BLK	TO	MPG	PPG	RPG	APG	PCM

• DAVIS, Aubrey
Aubrey D. Davis

Born: Mar. 28, 1921. Height: 6'2". Weight: 175 lbs. Drafted: — College: Oklahoma Baptist

YEAR	TEAM	GP	GS	MIN	PTS	FGM	FGA	FG%	3PM	3PA	3P%	FTM	FTA	FT%	ORB	DRB	TRB	AST	PF	DQ	STL	BLK	TO	MPG	PPG	RPG	APG	PCM
46-47	St. Louis	59	....	....	287	107	381	.281	....	....	....	73	115	.635	....	....	....	14	136	....	....	....	....	....	4.9	....	0.2	....
48-49	Hammond-N	8	....	....	9	3	....	....	....	....	....	3	7	.429	....	....	....	....	5	....	....	....	....	....	1.1	....	....	....
NBA Season Totals		59	....	....	287	107	381	.281	....	....	....	73	115	.635	....	....	....	14	136	....	....	....	....	....	4.9	....	0.2	....
NBL Season Totals		8	....	....	9	3	....	....	....	....	....	3	7		....	....	....	....	5	....	....	....	....	....	1.1	....	....	....
Career Totals		67	....	....	296	110	381		....	....	....	76	122		....	....	....	14	141	....	....	....	....	....	4.4	....	0.2	....
46-47	St. Louis	3	....	....	7	2	6	.333	....	....	....	3	3	1.000	....	....	....	0	3	....	....	....	....	....	2.3	....	0.0	....
NBA Playoff Totals		3	....	....	7	2	6	.333	....	....	....	3	3	1.000	....	....	....	0	3	....	....	....	....	....	2.3	....	0.0	....

• DAVIS, Baron
Baron Davis

Born: Apr. 13, 1979. Los Angeles, CA, United States. Height: 6'3". Weight: 209 lbs. Drafted: 1999 College: UCLA

YEAR	TEAM	GP	GS	MIN	PTS	FGM	FGA	FG%	3PM	3PA	3P%	FTM	FTA	FT%	ORB	DRB	TRB	AST	PF	DQ	STL	BLK	TO	MPG	PPG	RPG	APG	PCM
99-00	Charlotte	82	0	1523	486	182	433	.420	25	111	.225	97	153	.634	48	117	165	309	201	1	97	19	140	18.6	5.9	2.0	3.8	.398
00-01	Charlotte	82	82	3192	1131	409	957	.427	85	274	.310	228	337	.677	129	279	408	598	267	1	170	36	226	38.9	13.8	5.0	7.3	.463
01-02	Charlotte	82	82	3319	1484	559	1341	.417	170	478	.356	196	338	.580	93	256	349	698	241	0	172	47	246	40.5	18.1	4.3	8.5	.499
02-03	New Orleans	50	47	1889	856	332	798	.416	99	283	.350	93	131	.710	56	130	186	320	148	3	91	22	140	37.8	17.1	3.7	6.4	.446
NBA Season Totals		296	211	9923	3957	1482	3529	.420	379	1146	.331	614	959	.640	326	782	1108	1925	857	5	530	124	752	33.5	13.4	3.7	6.5	....
99-00	Charlotte	4	0	57	23	10	23	.435	1	6	.167	2	4	.500	3	3	6	6	6	0	4	0	3	14.3	5.8	1.5	1.5	.359
00-01	Charlotte	10	10	397	178	59	123	.480	20	50	.400	40	56	.714	9	35	44	58	33	0	28	5	22	39.7	17.8	4.4	5.8	.534
01-02	Charlotte	9	9	401	203	71	188	.378	21	62	.339	40	67	.597	16	47	63	71	36	2	32	5	27	44.6	22.6	7.0	7.9	.529
02-03	New Orleans	5	5	194	102	37	83	.446	12	35	.343	16	22	.727	4	14	18	42	20	0	7	2	15	38.8	20.4	3.6	8.4	.542
NBA Playoff Totals		28	24	1049	506	177	417	.424	54	153	.353	98	149	.658	32	99	131	177	95	2	71	12	67	37.5	18.1	4.7	6.3	....

• DAVIS, Ben
Ben Jerome Davis

Born: Dec. 26, 1972. Vero Beach, FL, United States. Height: 6'9". Weight: 240 lbs. Drafted: 1996 College: Arizona

YEAR	TEAM	GP	GS	MIN	PTS	FGM	FGA	FG%	3PM	3PA	3P%	FTM	FTA	FT%	ORB	DRB	TRB	AST	PF	DQ	STL	BLK	TO	MPG	PPG	RPG	APG	PCM
96-97	Phoenix	20	0	98	29	10	26	.385	0	0	.000	9	20	.450	12	15	27	0	16	0	4	1	2	4.9	1.5	1.4	0.0	.301
97-98	New York	7	0	13	4	2	10	.200	0	0	.000	0	0	.000	6	0	6	0	3	0	1	0	0	1.9	0.6	0.9	0.0	.132
98-99	New York	8	0	21	17	7	17	.412	0	0	.000	3	6	.500	9	2	11	3	4	0	0	1	1	2.6	2.1	1.4	0.4	.820
99-00	Phoenix	5	0	22	4	2	6	.333	0	0	.000	0	0	.000	3	6	9	2	2	0	1	1	3	4.4	0.8	1.8	0.4	.405
NBA Season Totals		40	0	154	54	21	59	.356	0	0	.000	12	26	.462	30	23	53	5	25	0	6	2	6	3.9	1.4	1.3	0.1	....

• DAVIS, Bill
William F. Davis

Born: Oct. 3, 1921. Height: 6'3". Weight: 215 lbs. Drafted: — College: Notre Dame

YEAR	TEAM	GP	GS	MIN	PTS	FGM	FGA	FG%	3PM	3PA	3P%	FTM	FTA	FT%	ORB	DRB	TRB	AST	PF	DQ	STL	BLK	TO	MPG	PPG	RPG	APG	PCM
46-47	Chicago	47	....	....	84	35	146	.240	....	....	....	14	41	.341	....	....	....	11	92	....	....	....	....	....	1.8	....	0.2	....
NBA Season Totals		47	....	....	84	35	146	.240	....	....	....	14	41	.341	....	....	....	11	92	....	....	....	....	....	1.8	....	0.2	....
46-47	Chicago	7	....	....	6	2	14	.143	....	....	....	2	5	.400	....	....	....	0	10	....	....	....	....	....	0.9	....	0.0	....
NBA Playoff Totals		7	....	....	6	2	14	.143	....	....	....	2	5	.400	....	....	....	0	10	....	....	....	....	....	0.9	....	0.0	....

• DAVIS, Bob
Robert Davis

Born: Apr. 2, 1950. Height: 6'7". Weight: 215 lbs. Drafted: 1972 College: Weber State

YEAR	TEAM	GP	GS	MIN	PTS	FGM	FGA	FG%	3PM	3PA	3P%	FTM	FTA	FT%	ORB	DRB	TRB	AST	PF	DQ	STL	BLK	TO	MPG	PPG	RPG	APG	PCM
72-73	Portland	9	....	41	16	6	28	.214	....	....	....	4	6	.667	....	....	5	2	5	0	....	....	....	4.6	1.8	0.6	0.2	.017
NBA Season Totals		9	....	41	16	6	28	.214	....	....	....	4	6	.667	....	....	5	2	5	0	....	....	....	4.6	1.8	0.6	0.2	....

• DAVIS, Brad
Bradley Ernest Davis

Born: Dec. 17, 1955. Monaca, PA, United States. Height: 6'3". Weight: 180 lbs. Drafted: 1977 College: Maryland

YEAR	TEAM	GP	GS	MIN	PTS	FGM	FGA	FG%	3PM	3PA	3P%	FTM	FTA	FT%	ORB	DRB	TRB	AST	PF	DQ	STL	BLK	TO	MPG	PPG	RPG	APG	PCM
77-78	LA Lakers	33	....	334	82	30	72	.417	....	....	....	22	29	.759	4	31	35	83	39	1	15	2	36	10.1	2.5	1.1	2.5	.397
78-79	LA Lakers	5	....	65	19	8	11	.727	....	....	....	3	4	.750	0	1	1	9	10	0	2	0	6	13.0	3.8	0.2	1.8	.286
78-79	Indiana	22	....	233	59	23	44	.523	....	....	....	13	19	.684	1	15	16	43	22	0	14	2	11	10.6	2.7	0.7	2.0	.403
79-80	Indiana	5	....	43	7	2	7	.286	0	0	.000	3	4	.750	0	2	2	5	7	0	3	0	3	8.6	1.4	0.4	1.0	.143
79-80	Utah	13	....	225	76	33	56	.589	0	1	.000	10	12	.833	4	11	15	45	21	0	10	1	10	17.3	5.8	1.2	3.5	.482
80-81	Dallas	56	....	1686	626	230	410	.561	3	17	.176	163	204	.799	29	122	151	385	156	2	52	11	123	30.1	11.2	2.7	6.9	.519
81-82	Dallas	82	82	2614	993	397	771	.515	14	49	.286	185	230	.804	35	191	226	509	218	5	73	6	156	31.9	12.1	2.8	6.2	.464
82-83	Dallas	79	78	2323	915	359	628	.572	11	43	.256	186	220	.845	34	164	198	565	176	2	80	11	142	29.4	11.6	2.5	7.2	.573
83-84	Dallas	81	81	2665	896	345	651	.530	7	38	.184	199	238	.836	41	146	187	561	218	4	94	13	162	32.9	11.1	2.3	6.9	.456
84-85	Dallas	82	82	2539	825	310	614	.505	47	115	.409	158	178	.888	39	154	193	581	219	1	91	10	123	31.0	10.1	2.4	7.1	.477
85-86	Dallas	82	43	1971	764	267	502	.532	32	89	.360	198	228	.868	26	120	146	467	174	2	57	15	107	24.0	9.3	1.8	5.7	.535
86-87	Dallas	82	6	1582	577	199	436	.456	32	106	.302	147	171	.860	27	87	114	373	159	0	63	10	115	19.3	7.0	1.4	4.5	.466
87-88	Dallas	75	12	1480	537	208	415	.501	30	74	.405	91	108	.843	18	84	102	303	149	0	51	9	90	19.7	7.2	1.4	4.0	.450
88-89	Dallas	78	4	1395	497	183	379	.483	32	102	.314	99	123	.805	14	94	108	242	151	0	48	18	94	17.9	6.4	1.4	3.1	.406
89-90	Dallas	73	2	1292	470	179	365	.490	35	104	.337	77	100	.770	12	81	93	242	151	2	47	9	88	17.7	6.4	1.3	3.3	.409
90-91	Dallas	80	6	1426	431	159	373	.426	22	85	.259	91	118	.771	13	105	118	230	212	1	45	17	80	17.8	5.4	1.5	2.9	.322
91-92	Dallas	33	0	429	92	38	86	.442	5	18	.278	11	15	.733	4	29	33	66	57	0	11	3	26	13.0	2.8	1.0	2.0	.255
NBA Season Totals		961	396	22302	7866	2970	5820	.510	270	841	.321	1656	2001	.828	301	1437	1738	4709	2139	20	756	146	1372	23.2	8.2	1.8	4.9	....
83-84	Dallas	10	10	304	81	33	73	.452	0	2	.000	15	19	.789	6	13	19	50	18	0	6	0	18	30.4	8.1	1.9	5.0	.308
84-85	Dallas	4	4	113	41	13	26	.500	3	8	.375	12	13	.923	1	7	8	22	11	0	4	1	6	28.3	10.3	2.0	5.5	.472
85-86	Dallas	10	0	163	77	24	44	.545	10	15	.667	19	24	.792	1	18	19	23	22	0	3	0	15	16.3	7.7	1.9	2.3	.472

YEAR	TEAM	GP	GS	MIN	PTS	FGM	FGA	FG%	3PM	3PA	3P%	FTM	FTA	FT%	ORB	DRB	TRB	AST	PF	DQ	STL	BLK	TO	MPG	PPG	RPG	APG	PCM
86-87	Dallas	4	0	75	33	13	23	.565	0	2	.000	7	9	.778	2	7	9	17	4	0	0	0	6	18.8	8.3	2.3	4.3	.558
87-88	Dallas	17	0	295	109	42	70	.600	1	5	.200	24	26	.923	1	19	20	55	34	0	3	5	29	17.4	6.4	1.2	3.2	.420
NBA Playoff Totals		45	14	950	341	125	236	.530	14	32	.438	77	91	.846	11	64	75	167	89	0	16	6	74	21.1	7.6	1.7	3.7	....

• DAVIS, Brian

Brian Keith Davis

Born: June 21, 1970. Atlantic City, NJ, United States. Height: 6'7". Weight: 200 lbs. Drafted: 1992 College: Duke

YEAR	TEAM	GP	GS	MIN	PTS	FGM	FGA	FG%	3PM	3PA	3P%	FTM	FTA	FT%	ORB	DRB	TRB	AST	PF	DQ	STL	BLK	TO	MPG	PPG	RPG	APG	PCM
93-94	Minnesota	68	3	374	131	40	126	.317	1	3	.333	50	68	.735	21	34	55	22	34	0	16	4	20	5.5	1.9	0.8	0.3	.274
NBA Season Totals		68	3	374	131	40	126	.317	1	3	.333	50	68	.735	21	34	55	22	34	0	16	4	20	5.5	1.9	0.8	0.3	....

• DAVIS, Charles

Charles Edward Davis Jr.

Born: Oct. 5, 1958. Nashville, TN, United States. Height: 6'7". Weight: 215 lbs. Drafted: 1981 College: Vanderbilt

YEAR	TEAM	GP	GS	MIN	PTS	FGM	FGA	FG%	3PM	3PA	3P%	FTM	FTA	FT%	ORB	DRB	TRB	AST	PF	DQ	STL	BLK	TO	MPG	PPG	RPG	APG	PCM
81-82	Washington	54	10	575	206	88	184	.478	0	2	.000	30	37	.811	54	79	133	31	89	0	10	13	43	10.6	3.8	2.5	0.6	.367
82-83	Washington	74	10	1161	560	251	534	.470	2	10	.200	56	89	.629	83	130	213	73	122	0	32	22	89	15.7	7.6	2.9	1.0	.410
83-84	Washington	46	0	467	231	103	218	.472	1	9	.111	24	39	.615	34	69	103	30	58	1	14	10	37	10.2	5.0	2.2	0.7	.441
84-85	Washington	4	0	28	7	2	10	.200	0	0	.000	3	4	.750	2	2	4	1	3	0	1	0	2	7.0	1.8	1.0	0.3	.055
84-85	Milwaukee	57	2	746	351	151	346	.436	1	10	.100	48	58	.828	57	92	149	50	110	1	21	5	51	13.1	6.2	2.6	0.9	.378
85-86	Milwaukee	57	7	873	440	188	397	.474	3	24	.125	61	75	.813	60	110	170	55	113	1	26	7	51	15.3	7.7	3.0	1.0	.443
87-88	Milwaukee	5	0	39	12	6	18	.333	0	2	.000	0	0	.000	1	2	3	3	4	0	2	1	5	7.8	2.4	0.6	0.6	.079
87-88	San Antonio	16	0	187	92	42	97	.433	1	15	.067	7	10	.700	15	23	38	17	25	0	0	3	13	11.7	5.8	2.4	1.1	.385
88-89	Chicago	49	3	545	185	81	190	.426	4	15	.267	19	26	.731	47	67	114	31	58	1	11	5	20	11.1	3.8	2.3	0.6	.347
89-90	Chicago	53	0	429	130	58	158	.367	7	25	.280	7	8	.875	25	56	81	18	52	0	10	8	21	8.1	2.5	1.5	0.3	.242
NBA Season Totals		415	32	5050	2214	970	2152	.451	19	112	.170	255	346	.737	378	630	1008	309	634	4	127	74	332	12.2	5.3	2.4	0.7	....
81-82	Washington	6	0	52	16	7	17	.412	0	1	.000	2	2	1.000	1	4	5	3	6	0	1	1	7	8.7	2.7	0.8	0.5	.140
83-84	Washington	3	0	17	14	7	12	.583	0	0	.000	0	0	.000	1	2	3	0	0	0	0	0	1	5.7	4.7	1.0	0.0	.659
84-85	Milwaukee	5	0	51	19	8	20	.400	0	2	.000	3	4	.750	6	4	10	4	2	0	0	0	4	10.2	3.8	2.0	0.8	.319
85-86	Milwaukee	12	0	145	60	21	58	.362	0	1	.000	18	20	.900	9	16	25	6	28	1	4	0	12	12.1	5.0	2.1	0.5	.234
88-89	Chicago	17	0	191	46	19	47	.404	1	6	.167	7	9	.778	16	27	43	5	29	0	4	1	13	11.2	2.7	2.5	0.3	.227
89-90	Chicago	6	0	20	4	2	7	.286	0	1	.000	0	0	.000	3	0	3	1	5	0	0	0	1	3.3	0.7	0.5	0.2	-.005
NBA Playoff Totals		49	0	476	159	64	161	.398	1	11	.091	30	35	.857	36	53	89	19	70	1	9	2	38	9.7	3.2	1.8	0.4	....

• DAVIS, Charlie

Charles Lawrence Davis

Born: Sept. 7, 1949. New York, NY, United States. Height: 6'2". Weight: 160 lbs. Drafted: 1971 College: Wake Forest

YEAR	TEAM	GP	GS	MIN	PTS	FGM	FGA	FG%	3PM	3PA	3P%	FTM	FTA	FT%	ORB	DRB	TRB	AST	PF	DQ	STL	BLK	TO	MPG	PPG	RPG	APG	PCM
71-72	Cleveland	61	....	1144	600	229	569	.402	....	....	....	142	169	.840	....	....	92	123	143	3	....	....	....	18.8	9.8	1.5	2.0	.395
72-73	Cleveland	6	....	86	44	20	41	.488	....	....	....	4	7	.571	....	....	5	10	20	0	....	....	....	14.3	7.3	0.8	1.7	.370
72-73	Portland	69	....	1333	612	243	590	.412	....	....	....	126	161	.783	....	....	111	175	174	0	....	....	....	19.3	8.9	1.6	2.5	.390
73-74	Portland	8	....	90	31	14	40	.350	....	....	....	3	4	.750	2	9	11	11	7	0	2	0	....	11.3	3.9	1.4	1.4	.305
NBA Season Totals		144	....	2653	1287	506	1240	.408	....	....	....	275	341	.806	2	9	219	319	344	3	2	0	....	18.4	8.9	1.5	2.2	....

• DAVIS, Dale

Elliott Lydell (D Square, Double D) Davis

Born: Mar. 25, 1969. Toccoa, GA, United States. Height: 6'11". Weight: 230 lbs. Drafted: 1991 College: Clemson

YEAR	TEAM	GP	GS	MIN	PTS	FGM	FGA	FG%	3PM	3PA	3P%	FTM	FTA	FT%	ORB	DRB	TRB	AST	PF	DQ	STL	BLK	TO	MPG	PPG	RPG	APG	PCM
91-92	Indiana	64	23	1301	395	154	279	.552	0	1	.000	87	152	.572	158	252	410	30	191	2	27	74	51	20.3	6.2	6.4	0.5	.476
92-93	Indiana	82	82	2264	727	304	535	.568	0	0	.000	119	225	.529	291	432	723	69	274	5	63	148	82	27.6	8.9	8.8	0.8	.531
93-94	Indiana	66	64	2292	771	308	582	.529	0	1	.000	155	294	.527	280	438	718	100	214	1	48	106	99	34.7	11.7	10.9	1.5	.513
94-95	Indiana	74	70	2346	786	324	576	.563	0	1	.000	138	259	.533	259	437	696	58	222	2	72	116	126	31.7	10.6	9.4	0.8	.495
95-96	Indiana	78	77	2617	803	334	599	.558	0	0	.000	135	289	.467	252	457	709	76	238	0	56	112	117	33.6	10.3	9.1	1.0	.445
96-97	Indiana	80	76	2589	832	370	688	.538	0	0	.000	92	215	.428	301	471	772	59	233	3	60	77	112	32.4	10.4	9.7	0.7	.454
97-98	Indiana	78	78	2174	626	273	498	.548	0	0	.000	80	172	.465	233	378	611	70	209	1	51	87	70	27.9	8.0	7.8	0.9	.451
98-99	Indiana	50	50	1374	398	161	302	.533	0	0	.000	76	123	.618	155	261	416	22	115	0	20	57	43	27.5	8.0	8.3	0.4	.455
99-00	Indiana	74	72	2127	743	302	602	.502	0	0	.000	139	203	.685	256	473	729	64	203	1	52	94	91	28.7	10.0	9.9	0.9	.532
00-01	Portland	81	43	2162	580	242	487	.497	0	4	.000	96	152	.632	233	373	606	103	199	0	44	76	67	26.7	7.2	7.5	1.3	.440
01-02	Portland	78	77	2447	742	296	580	.510	0	0	.000	150	212	.708	262	426	688	96	193	1	62	83	62	31.4	9.5	8.8	1.2	.479
02-03	Portland	78	78	2283	579	237	438	.541	0	0	.000	105	166	.633	233	331	564	94	189	1	51	70	71	29.3	7.4	7.2	1.2	.413
NBA Season Totals		883	790	25976	7982	3305	6166	.536	0	7	.000	1372	2462	.557	2913	4729	7642	841	2480	17	606	1100	991	29.4	9.0	8.7	1.0	....
91-92	Indiana	3	0	69	8	4	10	.400	0	0	.000	0	0	.000	5	14	19	2	8	0	0	5	1	23.0	2.7	6.3	0.7	.322
92-93	Indiana	4	4	117	17	8	12	.667	0	0	.000	1	4	.250	4	28	32	4	15	0	4	4	3	29.3	4.3	8.0	1.0	.373
93-94	Indiana	16	16	578	123	56	106	.528	0	1	.000	11	36	.306	63	96	159	11	52	0	18	17	30	36.1	7.7	9.9	0.7	.353
94-95	Indiana	17	17	490	135	56	105	.533	0	0	.000	23	47	.489	53	83	136	6	56	0	7	14	22	28.8	7.9	8.0	0.4	.377
95-96	Indiana	5	5	184	36	16	31	.516	0	0	.000	4	11	.364	20	36	56	4	16	0	3	6	10	36.8	7.2	11.2	0.8	.364
97-98	Indiana	16	16	466	141	56	86	.651	0	0	.000	29	64	.453	44	76	120	12	42	0	5	18	21	29.1	8.8	7.5	0.8	.436
98-99	Indiana	13	13	394	118	45	77	.584	0	0	.000	28	50	.560	45	87	132	11	42	0	10	18	21	30.3	9.1	10.2	0.8	.500
99-00	Indiana	23	23	714	190	79	151	.523	0	0	.000	32	59	.542	83	180	263	17	83	4	11	31	18	31.0	8.3	11.4	0.7	.496
00-01	Portland	2	0	20	1	0	2	.000	0	1	.000	1	2	.500	3	1	4	0	7	1	1	0	1	10.0	0.5	2.0	0.0	-.040
01-02	Portland	3	3	70	7	3	11	.273	0	0	.000	1	2	.500	6	14	20	4	16	2	4	3	2	23.3	2.3	6.7	1.3	.273
02-03	Portland	6	6	162	45	14	24	.583	0	0	.000	17	26	.654	20	28	48	9	11	0	5	2	10	27.0	7.5	8.0	1.5	.479
NBA Playoff Totals		108	103	3264	821	337	615	.548	0	2	.000	147	301	.488	346	643	989	80	348	7	68	118	139	30.2	7.6	9.2	0.7	....

• DAVIS, Dwight

Dwight E. (Double D) Davis

Born: Oct. 28, 1949. Houston, TX, United States. Height: 6'8". Weight: 220 lbs. Drafted: 1972 College: Houston

YEAR	TEAM	GP	GS	MIN	PTS	FGM	FGA	FG%	3PM	3PA	3P%	FTM	FTA	FT%	ORB	DRB	TRB	AST	PF	DQ	STL	BLK	TO	MPG	PPG	RPG	APG	PCM
72-73	Cleveland	81	....	2151	762	293	748	.392	....	....	....	176	222	.793	....	....	563	118	297	5	....	....	....	26.6	9.4	7.0	1.5	.392
73-74	Cleveland	76	....	2477	949	376	862	.436	....	....	....	197	274	.719	174	470	644	186	291	6	63	74	....	32.6	12.5	8.5	2.4	.460
74-75	Cleveland	78	....	1964	766	295	666	.443	....	....	....	176	245	.718	108	356	464	150	254	3	45	39	....	25.2	9.8	5.9	1.9	.448

YEAR	TEAM	GP	GS	MIN	PTS	FGM	FGA	FG%	3PM	3PA	3P%	FTM	FTA	FT%	ORB	DRB	TRB	AST	PF	DQ	STL	BLK	TO	MPG	PPG	RPG	APG	PCM
75-76	Golden State	72	....	866	300	111	269	.413	....	....	....	78	113	.690	86	139	225	46	141	0	20	28	....	12.0	4.2	3.1	0.6	.386
76-77	Golden State	33	....	552	159	55	124	.444	....	....	....	49	72	.681	34	61	95	59	93	1	11	8	....	16.7	4.8	2.9	1.8	.360
NBA Season Totals		340	....	8010	2936	1130	2669	.423	....	....	....	676	926	.730	402	1026	1991	559	1076	15	139	149	....	23.6	8.6	5.9	1.6	....
75-76	Golden State	11	....	142	50	16	37	.432	....	....	....	18	22	.818	9	19	28	10	28	1	3	4	....	12.9	4.5	2.5	0.9	.378
NBA Playoff Totals		11	....	142	50	16	37	.432	....	....	....	18	22	.818	9	19	28	10	28	1	3	4	....	12.9	4.5	2.5	0.9	....

• DAVIS, Emanual

Emanual (E-mail) Davis

Born: Aug. 27, 1968. Philadelphia, PA, United States.   Height: 6'4".   Weight: 195 lbs.   Drafted: —   College: Delaware State

YEAR	TEAM	GP	GS	MIN	PTS	FGM	FGA	FG%	3PM	3PA	3P%	FTM	FTA	FT%	ORB	DRB	TRB	AST	PF	DQ	STL	BLK	TO	MPG	PPG	RPG	APG	PCM
96-97	Houston	13	0	230	65	24	54	.444	12	27	.444	5	8	.625	2	20	22	26	20	0	9	2	17	17.7	5.0	1.7	2.0	.300
97-98	Houston	45	0	599	184	63	142	.444	27	72	.375	31	37	.838	10	37	47	59	55	0	17	3	54	13.3	4.1	1.0	1.3	.267
99-00	Seattle	54	2	701	217	80	220	.364	31	103	.301	26	38	.684	15	85	100	70	72	0	38	5	44	13.0	4.0	1.9	1.3	.311
00-01	Seattle	62	39	1290	361	133	318	.418	50	127	.394	45	55	.818	28	126	154	137	101	0	64	12	77	20.8	5.8	2.5	2.2	.336
01-02	Atlanta	28	20	774	185	70	198	.354	29	85	.341	16	18	.889	19	55	74	68	68	0	27	5	52	27.6	6.6	2.6	2.4	.208
02-03	Atlanta	24	1	340	88	32	88	.364	7	29	.241	17	22	.773	5	38	43	36	28	0	12	2	25	14.2	3.7	1.8	1.5	.266
NBA Season Totals		226	62	3934	1100	402	1020	.394	156	443	.352	140	178	.787	79	361	440	396	344	0	167	29	269	17.4	4.9	1.9	1.8	....

• DAVIS, Harry

Harry A. Davis

Born: Jan. 27, 1956. Cleveland, OH, United States.   Height: 6'7".   Weight: 220 lbs.   Drafted: 1978   College: Florida State

YEAR	TEAM	GP	GS	MIN	PTS	FGM	FGA	FG%	3PM	3PA	3P%	FTM	FTA	FT%	ORB	DRB	TRB	AST	PF	DQ	STL	BLK	TO	MPG	PPG	RPG	APG	PCM
78-79	Cleveland	40	....	394	162	66	153	.431	....	....	....	30	43	.698	27	39	66	16	66	1	13	8	24	9.9	4.1	1.7	0.4	.311
79-80	San Antonio	4	....	30	13	6	12	.500	0	0	.000	1	2	.500	2	4	6	0	8	0	1	0	3	7.5	3.3	1.5	0.0	.237
NBA Season Totals		44	....	424	175	72	165	.436	0	0	.000	31	45	.689	29	43	72	16	74	1	14	8	27	9.6	4.0	1.6	0.4	....

• DAVIS, Hubert

Hubert Ira Davis Jr.

Born: May 17, 1970. Winston-Salem, NC, United States.   Height: 6'5".   Weight: 183 lbs.   Drafted: 1992   College: North Carolina

YEAR	TEAM	GP	GS	MIN	PTS	FGM	FGA	FG%	3PM	3PA	3P%	FTM	FTA	FT%	ORB	DRB	TRB	AST	PF	DQ	STL	BLK	TO	MPG	PPG	RPG	APG	PCM
92-93	New York	50	2	815	269	110	251	.438	6	19	.316	43	54	.796	13	43	56	83	71	1	22	4	45	16.3	5.4	1.1	1.7	.273
93-94	New York	56	27	1333	614	238	505	.471	53	132	.402	85	103	.825	23	44	67	165	118	0	40	4	78	23.8	11.0	1.2	2.9	.387
94-95	New York	82	4	1697	820	296	617	.480	131	288	.455	97	120	.808	30	80	110	150	146	1	35	11	90	20.7	10.0	1.3	1.8	.389
95-96	New York	74	14	1773	789	275	566	.486	127	267	.476	112	129	.868	35	88	123	103	120	1	31	8	67	24.0	10.7	1.7	1.4	.366
96-97	Toronto	36	0	623	181	74	184	.402	16	70	.229	17	23	.739	11	29	40	34	40	0	11	2	22	17.3	5.0	1.1	0.9	.196
97-98	Dallas	81	30	2378	898	350	767	.456	101	230	.439	97	116	.836	34	135	169	157	117	0	43	5	89	29.4	11.1	2.1	1.9	.312
98-99	Dallas	50	21	1378	457	174	397	.438	65	144	.451	44	50	.880	3	83	86	89	76	0	21	3	57	27.6	9.1	1.7	1.8	.267
99-00	Dallas	79	15	1817	583	217	464	.468	82	167	**.491**	67	77	.870	17	117	134	141	109	0	24	3	70	23.0	7.4	1.7	1.8	.298
00-01	Dallas	51	7	1261	371	139	314	.443	58	133	.436	35	41	.854	18	91	109	61	92	0	29	1	56	24.7	7.3	2.1	1.2	.247
00-01	Washington	15	11	431	153	57	119	.479	20	38	.526	19	21	.905	10	20	30	49	29	0	6	0	25	28.7	10.2	2.0	3.3	.342
01-02	Washington	51	17	1231	365	146	326	.448	57	126	.452	16	21	.762	7	70	77	107	58	0	28	3	44	24.1	7.2	1.5	2.1	.283
02-03	Detroit	43	1	328	79	31	79	.392	12	36	.333	5	6	.833	6	30	36	29	23	0	5	0	11	7.6	1.8	0.8	0.7	.254
NBA Season Totals		668	149	15065	5579	2107	4589	.459	728	1650	.441	637	761	.837	207	830	1037	1168	999	3	295	44	654	22.6	8.4	1.6	1.7	....
92-93	New York	7	0	96	31	14	25	.560	1	2	.500	2	3	.667	1	5	6	5	8	0	6	0	9	13.7	4.4	0.9	0.7	.257
93-94	New York	23	7	396	121	44	121	.364	10	35	.286	23	32	.719	5	16	21	26	43	0	5	3	23	17.2	5.3	0.9	1.1	.152
94-95	New York	11	0	184	46	17	48	.354	10	27	.370	2	2	1.000	0	7	7	9	20	0	1	5	9	16.7	4.2	0.6	0.8	.113
95-96	New York	8	0	145	53	17	31	.548	10	19	.526	9	11	.818	4	8	12	4	12	0	0	0	7	18.1	6.6	1.5	0.5	.291
NBA Playoff Totals		49	7	821	251	92	225	.409	31	83	.373	36	48	.750	10	36	46	44	83	0	12	8	48	16.8	5.1	0.9	0.9	....

• DAVIS, Jim

James W. Davis

Born: Dec. 18, 1941. Muncie, IN, United States.   Height: 6'9".   Weight: 225 lbs.   Drafted: 1964   College: Colorado

YEAR	TEAM	GP	GS	MIN	PTS	FGM	FGA	FG%	3PM	3PA	3P%	FTM	FTA	FT%	ORB	DRB	TRB	AST	PF	DQ	STL	BLK	TO	MPG	PPG	RPG	APG	PCM
67-68	St. Louis	50	....	394	147	61	139	.439	....	....	....	25	64	.391			123	13	85	2	....		....	7.9	2.9	2.5	0.3	.378
68-69	Atlanta	78	....	1367	684	265	568	.467	....	....	....	154	231	.667			529	97	239	6	....		....	17.5	8.8	6.8	1.2	.625
69-70	Atlanta	82	....	2623	1116	438	943	.464	....	....	....	240	318	.755			796	238	**335**	5	....		....	32.0	13.6	9.7	2.9	.555
70-71	Atlanta	82	....	1864	677	241	503	.479	....	....	....	195	288	.677			546	108	253	5	....		....	22.7	8.3	6.7	1.3	.480
71-72	Atlanta	11	....	119	26	8	33	.242	....	....	....	10	18	.556			36	8	14	0	....		....	10.8	2.4	3.3	0.7	.295
71-72	Houston	12	....	180	62	18	54	.333	....	....	....	26	38	.684			44	5	18	0	....		....	15.0	5.2	3.7	0.4	.342
71-72	Detroit	52	....	684	306	121	251	.482	....	....	....	64	98	.653			196	38	106	1	....		....	13.2	5.9	3.8	0.7	.505
72-73	Detroit	73	....	771	334	131	257	.510	....	....	....	72	114	.632			261	56	126	2	....		....	10.6	4.6	3.6	0.8	.573
73-74	Detroit	78	....	947	324	117	283	.413	....	....	....	90	139	.647	102	191	293	86	158	1	39	30	....	12.1	4.2	3.8	1.1	.468
74-75	Detroit	79	....	1078	321	118	260	.454	....	....	....	85	117	.726	96	189	285	90	129	2	50	36	....	13.6	4.1	3.6	1.1	.443
NBA Season Totals		597	....	10027	3997	1518	3291	.461	....	....	....	961	1425	.674	198	380	3109	739	1463	24	89	66	....	16.8	6.7	5.2	1.2	....
67-68	St. Louis	2	....	9	2	1	3	.333	....	....	....	0	0	.000			3	0	2	0	....		....	4.5	1.0	1.5	0.0	.222
68-69	Atlanta	8	....	52	13	4	15	.267	....	....	....	5	8	.625			17	1	7	0	....		....	6.5	1.6	2.1	0.1	.288
69-70	Atlanta	9	....	117	38	14	37	.378	....	....	....	10	17	.588			30	6	24	1	....		....	13.0	4.2	3.3	0.7	.318
70-71	Atlanta	5	....	119	56	17	36	.472	....	....	....	22	27	.815			22	4	17	1	....		....	23.8	11.2	4.4	0.8	.451
73-74	Detroit	7	....	69	26	11	19	.579	....	....	....	4	6	.667	4	12	16	5	11	0	2	1	....	9.9	3.7	2.3	0.7	.479
74-75	Detroit	2	....	16	7	2	4	.500	....	....	....	3	5	.600	2	2	4	0	1	0	1	0	....	8.0	3.5	2.0	0.0	.464
NBA Playoff Totals		33	....	382	142	49	114	.430	....	....	....	44	63	.698	6	14	92	16	62	2	3	1	....	11.6	4.3	2.8	0.5	....

• DAVIS, Johnny

Johnny Reginald Davis

Born: Oct. 21, 1955. Detroit, MI, United States.   Height: 6'2".   Weight: 170 lbs.   Drafted: 1976   College: Dayton

YEAR	TEAM	GP	GS	MIN	PTS	FGM	FGA	FG%	3PM	3PA	3P%	FTM	FTA	FT%	ORB	DRB	TRB	AST	PF	DQ	STL	BLK	TO	MPG	PPG	RPG	APG	PCM
76-77	Portland	79	....	1451	634	234	531	.441	....	....	....	166	209	.794	62	64	126	148	128	1	41	11	....	18.4	8.0	1.6	1.9	.400
77-78	Portland	82	....	2188	874	343	756	.454	....	....	....	188	227	.828	65	108	173	217	173	0	81	14	148	26.7	10.7	2.1	2.6	.351
78-79	Indiana	79	....	2971	1444	565	1240	.456	....	....	....	314	396	.793	70	121	191	453	177	1	95	22	213	37.6	18.3	2.4	5.7	.440
79-80	Indiana	82	....	2912	1300	496	1159	.428	4	42	.095	304	352	.864	102	124	226	440	178	0	110	23	205	35.5	15.9	2.8	5.4	.419
80-81	Indiana	76	....	2536	1094	426	917	.465	4	33	.121	238	299	.796	56	114	170	480	179	2	95	14	167	33.4	14.4	2.2	6.3	.458
81-82	Indiana	82	70	2664	1396	538	1153	.467	5	27	.185	315	394	.799	72	106	178	346	176	1	76	11	189	32.5	17.0	2.2	4.2	.434

YEAR	TEAM	GP	GS	MIN	PTS	FGM	FGA	FG%	3PM	3PA	3P%	FTM	FTA	FT%	ORB	DRB	TRB	AST	PF	DQ	STL	BLK	TO	MPG	PPG	RPG	APG	PCM
82-83	Atlanta	53	33	1465	685	258	567	.455	5	18	.278	164	206	.796	37	91	128	315	100	0	43	7	117	27.6	12.9	2.4	5.9	.507
83-84	Atlanta	75	72	2079	925	354	800	.443	0	8	.000	217	256	.848	53	86	139	326	146	0	62	6	135	27.7	12.3	1.9	4.3	.404
84-85	Cleveland	76	30	1920	941	337	791	.426	12	46	.261	255	300	.850	35	84	119	426	136	1	43	4	152	25.3	12.4	1.6	5.6	.470
85-86	Cleveland	39	0	612	273	102	237	.430	2	11	.182	67	79	.848	6	30	36	105	44	0	24	4	39	15.7	7.0	0.9	2.7	.420
85-86	Atlanta	27	7	402	144	46	107	.430	1	2	.500	51	59	.864	2	17	19	112	32	0	13	0	38	14.9	5.3	0.7	4.1	.456
NBA Season Totals		750	212	21200	9710	3699	8258	.448	33	187	.176	2279	2777	.821	560	945	1505	3368	1469	6	683	116	1403	28.3	12.9	2.0	4.5	....
76-77	Portland	16	....	436	168	65	133	.489	....	....	....	38	53	.717	10	23	33	52	32	0	28	3	....	27.3	10.5	2.1	3.3	.405
77-78	Portland	6	....	201	86	35	76	.461	....	....	....	16	23	.696	3	7	10	13	15	0	1	2	11	33.5	14.3	1.7	2.2	.283
80-81	Indiana	2	....	74	40	14	35	.400	0	1	.000	12	13	.923	2	6	8	11	6	0	2	0	1	37.0	20.0	4.0	5.5	.512
82-83	Atlanta	3	3	113	51	21	52	.404	0	1	.000	9	10	.900	1	4	5	27	6	0	0	0	5	37.7	17.0	1.7	9.0	.438
83-84	Atlanta	5	5	131	50	22	55	.400	0	0	.000	6	6	1.000	2	8	10	24	10	0	1	0	4	26.2	10.0	2.0	4.8	.358
84-85	Cleveland	3	0	50	28	12	16	.750	0	1	.000	4	5	.800	1	5	6	15	5	0	5	0	2	16.7	9.3	2.0	5.0	.918
85-86	Atlanta	8	0	65	22	9	25	.360	0	0	.000	4	4	1.000	2	4	6	15	6	0	2	0	5	8.1	2.8	0.8	1.9	.357
NBA Playoff Totals		43	8	1070	445	178	392	.454	0	3	.000	89	114	.781	21	57	78	157	80	0	39	5	28	24.9	10.3	1.8	3.7	....

• DAVIS, Lee

Lee Connie Davis

Born: Oct. 11, 1945. Raleigh, NC, United States. Height: 6'8". Weight: 235 lbs. Drafted: 1968 College: North Carolina College

YEAR	TEAM	GP	GS	MIN	PTS	FGM	FGA	FG%	3PM	3PA	3P%	FTM	FTA	FT%	ORB	DRB	TRB	AST	PF	DQ	STL	BLK	TO	MPG	PPG	RPG	APG	PCM
68-69	New Orleans-A	65	....	570	222	88	227	.388	1	4	.250	45	90	.500	74	128	202	18	87	1	....	....	31	8.8	3.4	3.1	0.3	.421
69-70	New Orleans-A	16	....	128	40	16	36	.444	0	0	.000	8	15	.533	9	31	40	2	31	0	....	....	4	8.0	2.5	2.5	0.1	.337
70-71	Memphis-A	75	....	925	457	197	431	.457	0	2	.000	63	117	.538	122	129	251	62	169	3	....	....	67	12.3	6.1	3.3	0.8	.493
71-72	Memphis-A	58	....	550	228	101	231	.437	1	8	.125	25	43	.581	70	108	178	21	90	0	....	....	25	9.5	3.9	3.1	0.4	.448
72-73	Memphis-A	78	....	2111	1037	453	871	.520	0	3	.000	131	209	.627	223	385	608	82	266	7	....	....	96	27.1	13.3	7.8	1.1	.542
73-74	Memphis-A	79	....	1632	631	266	590	.451	1	4	.250	98	152	.645	139	280	419	139	237	....	28	40	104	20.7	8.0	5.3	1.8	.457
74-75	San Diego-A	75	....	1838	891	387	733	.528	4	16	.250	113	169	.669	178	314	492	110	179	....	40	40	92	24.5	11.9	6.6	1.5	.565
75-76	San Diego-A	7	....	51	5	2	11	.182	0	0	.000	1	2	.500	0	5	5	1	12	....	0	0	1	7.3	0.7	0.7	0.1	-.064
ABA Season Totals		453	....	7805	3511	1510	3130	.482	7	37	.189	484	797	.607	815	1380	2195	435	1071	11	68	80	420	17.2	7.8	4.8	1.0	....
68-69	New Orleans-A	9	....	69	32	13	33	.394	0	1	.000	6	11	.545	....	....	32	6	13	0	....	....	5	7.7	3.6	3.6	0.7	.600
70-71	Memphis-A	1	....	2	2	0	2	.000	0	0	.000	2	2	1.000	1	0	1	0	1	0	....	....	0	2.0	2.0	1.0	0.0	.399
ABA Playoff Totals		10	....	71	34	13	35	.371	0	1	.000	8	13	.615	1	0	33	6	14	0	....	....	5	7.1	3.4	3.3	0.6	....

• DAVIS, Mark

Mark Anthony Davis

Born: Apr. 26, 1973. Thibodaux, LA, United States. Height: 6'7". Weight: 210 lbs. Drafted: 1995 College: Texas Tech

YEAR	TEAM	GP	GS	MIN	PTS	FGM	FGA	FG%	3PM	3PA	3P%	FTM	FTA	FT%	ORB	DRB	TRB	AST	PF	DQ	STL	BLK	TO	MPG	PPG	RPG	APG	PCM
95-96	Minnesota	57	0	571	188	55	149	.369	4	13	.308	74	116	.638	56	69	125	47	92	1	40	22	68	10.0	3.3	2.2	0.8	.347
96-97	Philadelphia	75	17	1705	639	251	535	.469	24	93	.258	113	168	.673	138	185	323	135	230	7	85	31	120	22.7	8.5	4.3	1.8	.401
97-98	Philadelphia	71	12	906	282	109	244	.447	0	6	.000	64	101	.634	64	94	158	73	95	1	49	18	92	12.8	4.0	2.2	1.0	.330
98-99	Miami	4	1	35	9	2	6	.333	0	0	.000	5	6	.833	2	5	7	1	12	1	1	0	7	8.8	2.3	1.8	0.3	.048
99-00	Golden State	23	7	464	143	56	137	.409	0	2	.000	31	47	.660	31	53	84	38	52	1	25	4	40	20.2	6.2	3.7	1.7	.315
NBA Season Totals		230	37	3681	1261	473	1071	.442	28	114	.246	287	438	.655	291	406	697	294	481	11	200	75	327	16.0	5.5	3.0	1.3	....

• DAVIS, Mark

Mark Giles Davis

Born: June 8, 1963. Chesapeake, VA, United States. Height: 6'6". Weight: 195 lbs. Drafted: 1985 College: Old Dominion

YEAR	TEAM	GP	GS	MIN	PTS	FGM	FGA	FG%	3PM	3PA	3P%	FTM	FTA	FT%	ORB	DRB	TRB	AST	PF	DQ	STL	BLK	TO	MPG	PPG	RPG	APG	PCM
88-89	Milwaukee	31	0	251	123	48	97	.495	1	9	.111	26	32	.813	15	21	36	14	38	0	13	5	12	8.1	4.0	1.2	0.5	.442
88-89	Phoenix	2	0	7	4	1	5	.200	0	1	.000	2	2	1.000	1	0	1	0	1	0	0	0	0	3.5	2.0	0.5	0.0	.106
NBA Season Totals		33	0	258	127	49	102	.480	1	10	.100	28	34	.824	16	21	37	14	39	0	13	5	12	7.8	3.8	1.1	0.4	....

• DAVIS, Mel

Melvyn Jerome (Killer) Davis

Born: Nov. 9, 1950. New York, NY, United States. Height: 6'6". Weight: 220 lbs. Drafted: 1973 College: St. John's (NY)

YEAR	TEAM	GP	GS	MIN	PTS	FGM	FGA	FG%	3PM	3PA	3P%	FTM	FTA	FT%	ORB	DRB	TRB	AST	PF	DQ	STL	BLK	TO	MPG	PPG	RPG	APG	PCM
73-74	New York	30	....	167	78	33	95	.347	....	....	....	12	16	.750	17	37	54	8	36	0	3	4	....	5.6	2.6	1.8	0.3	.379
74-75	New York	62	....	903	356	154	395	.390	....	....	....	48	70	.686	70	251	321	54	105	0	16	8	....	14.6	5.7	5.2	0.9	.478
75-76	New York	42	....	408	174	76	193	.394	....	....	....	22	29	.759	43	105	148	31	56	0	16	5	....	9.7	4.1	3.5	0.7	.512
76-77	New York	22	....	342	104	41	110	.373	....	....	....	22	31	.710	30	70	100	24	45	0	9	1	....	15.5	4.7	4.5	1.1	.394
76-77	New York	34	....	752	296	127	354	.359	....	....	....	42	60	.700	68	125	193	47	85	0	22	4	....	22.1	8.7	5.7	1.4	.367
NBA Season Totals		190	....	2572	1008	431	1147	.376	....	....	....	146	206	.709	228	588	816	164	327	0	66	22	....	13.5	5.3	4.3	0.9	....
73-74	New York	4	....	12	12	6	12	.500	....	....	....	0	0	.000	2	3	5	0	1	0	0	0	....	3.0	3.0	1.3	0.0	.894
74-75	New York	3	....	28	12	5	12	.417	....	....	....	2	2	1.000	0	4	4	2	2	0	0	0	....	9.3	4.0	1.3	0.7	.389
NBA Playoff Totals		7	....	40	24	11	24	.458	....	....	....	2	2	1.000	2	7	9	2	3	0	0	0	....	5.7	3.4	1.3	0.3	....

• DAVIS, Mickey

Edward J. (Mickey, Mr. Hustle) Davis

Born: June 16, 1950. Rochester, PA, United States. Height: 6'7". Weight: 195 lbs. Drafted: 1972 College: Duquesne

YEAR	TEAM	GP	GS	MIN	PTS	FGM	FGA	FG%	3PM	3PA	3P%	FTM	FTA	FT%	ORB	DRB	TRB	AST	PF	DQ	STL	BLK	TO	MPG	PPG	RPG	APG	PCM
71-72	Pittsburgh-A	23	....	126	64	25	63	.397	0	2	.000	14	20	.700	21	20	41	9	23	0	....	....	17	5.5	2.8	1.8	0.4	.508
72-73	Milwaukee	74	....	1046	380	152	347	.438	....	....	....	76	92	.826	....	....	226	72	119	0	....	....	....	14.1	5.1	3.1	1.0	.412
73-74	Milwaukee	73	....	1012	431	169	335	.504	....	....	....	93	112	.830	78	146	224	87	94	0	27	5	....	13.9	5.9	3.1	1.2	.526
74-75	Milwaukee	75	....	1077	426	174	363	.479	....	....	....	78	88	.886	68	169	237	79	103	0	30	5	....	14.4	5.7	3.2	1.1	.473
75-76	Milwaukee	45	....	411	160	55	152	.362	....	....	....	50	63	.794	25	59	84	37	36	0	13	2	....	9.1	3.6	1.9	0.8	.414
76-77	Milwaukee	19	....	165	81	29	68	.426	....	....	....	23	25	.920	11	18	29	20	11	0	6	4	....	8.7	4.3	1.5	1.1	.542
NBA Season Totals		286	....	3711	1478	579	1265	.458	....	....	....	320	380	.842	182	392	800	295	363	0	76	16	....	13.0	5.2	2.8	1.0	....
ABA Season Totals		23	....	126	64	25	63	.397	0	2	.000	14	20	.700	21	20	41	9	23	0	....	....	17	5.5	2.8	1.8	0.4	....
Career Totals		309	....	3837	1542	604	1328	.455	0	2	.000	334	400	.835	203	412	841	304	386	0	76	16	17	12.4	5.0	2.7	1.0	....

YEAR	TEAM	GP	GS	MIN	PTS	FGM	FGA	FG%	3PM	3PA	3P%	FTM	FTA	FT%	ORB	DRB	TRB	AST	PF	DQ	STL	BLK	TO	MPG	PPG	RPG	APG	PCM
72-73	Milwaukee	6	....	54	14	6	17	.353	....	....	....	2	2	1.000	....	....	12	5	10	0	....	....	....	9.0	2.3	2.0	0.8	.301
73-74	Milwaukee	15	....	245	86	32	65	.492	....	....	....	22	24	.917	8	26	34	12	23	0	4	2	....	16.3	5.7	2.3	0.8	.367
NBA Playoff Totals		21	....	299	100	38	82	.463	....	....	....	24	26	.923	8	26	46	17	33	0	4	2	....	14.2	4.8	2.2	0.8	....

• DAVIS, Mike

Michael A. (Crusher) Davis

Born: July 26, 1946. Brooklyn, NY, United States.   Height: 6'3".   Weight: 185 lbs.   Drafted: 1969   College: Virginia Union

		GP	GS	MIN	PTS	FGM	FGA	FG%	3PM	3PA	3P%	FTM	FTA	FT%	ORB	DRB	TRB	AST	PF	DQ	STL	BLK	TO	MPG	PPG	RPG	APG	PCM
69-70	Baltimore	56	....	1330	669	260	586	.444	....	....	....	149	192	.776	....	....	128	111	174	1	....	....	....	23.8	11.9	2.3	2.0	.394
70-71	Buffalo	73	....	1617	833	317	774	.410	....	....	....	199	262	.760	....	....	187	153	220	7	....	....	....	22.2	11.4	2.6	2.1	.404
71-72	Buffalo	62	....	1068	564	213	501	.425	....	....	....	138	180	.767	....	....	120	82	141	5	....	....	....	17.2	9.1	1.9	1.3	.405
72-73	Memphis-A	38	....	553	254	93	222	.419	6	23	.261	62	87	.713	21	20	41	47	87	2	....	....	36	14.6	6.7	1.1	1.2	.319
72-73	Baltimore	13	....	283	123	50	118	.424	....	....	....	23	25	.920	....	....	35	19	45	4	....	....	....	21.8	9.5	2.7	1.5	.340
NBA Season Totals		204	....	4298	2189	840	1979	.424	....	....	....	509	659	.772	....	....	470	365	580	17	....	....	....	21.1	10.7	2.3	1.8	....
ABA Season Totals		38	....	553	254	93	222	.419	6	23	.261	62	87	.713	21	20	41	47	87	2	....	....	36	14.6	6.7	1.1	1.2	....
Career Totals		242	....	4851	2443	933	2201	.424	6	23	.261	571	746	.765	21	20	511	412	667	19	....	....	36	20.0	10.1	2.1	1.7	....

• DAVIS, Mike

Michael Davis

Born: Aug. 2, 1956. Jacksonville, FL, United States.   Height: 6'10".   Weight: 230 lbs.   Drafted: —   College: Maryland

		GP	GS	MIN	PTS	FGM	FGA	FG%	3PM	3PA	3P%	FTM	FTA	FT%	ORB	DRB	TRB	AST	PF	DQ	STL	BLK	TO	MPG	PPG	RPG	APG	PCM
82-83	New York	8	0	28	14	4	10	.400	0	0	.000	6	10	.600	3	7	10	0	4	0	0	4	0	3.5	1.8	1.3	0.0	.629
NBA Season Totals		8	0	28	14	4	10	.400	0	0	.000	6	10	.600	3	7	10	0	4	0	0	4	0	3.5	1.8	1.3	0.0	....
82-83	New York	1	0	1	0	0	0	.000	0	0	.000	0	0	.000	0	0	0	0	0	0	0	0	0	1.0	0.0	0.0	0.0	.000
NBA Playoff Totals		1	0	1	0	0	0	.000	0	0	.000	0	0	.000	0	0	0	0	0	0	0	0	0	1.0	0.0	0.0	0.0	....

• DAVIS, Monti

Damon William (Monti) Davis

Born: July 26, 1958. Warren, OH, United States.   Height: 6'7".   Weight: 205 lbs.   Drafted: 1980   College: Tennessee State

		GP	GS	MIN	PTS	FGM	FGA	FG%	3PM	3PA	3P%	FTM	FTA	FT%	ORB	DRB	TRB	AST	PF	DQ	STL	BLK	TO	MPG	PPG	RPG	APG	PCM
80-81	Philadelphia	1	....	2	2	1	1	1.000	0	0	.000	0	0	.000	0	1	1	0	0	0	0	0	0	2.0	2.0	1.0	0.0	1.456
80-81	Dallas	1	....	8	1	0	4	.000	0	0	.000	1	5	.200	2	1	3	0	0	0	0	1	0	8.0	1.0	3.0	0.0	-.103
NBA Season Totals		2	....	10	3	1	5	.200	0	0	.000	1	5	.200	2	2	4	0	0	0	0	1	0	5.0	1.5	2.0	0.0	....

• DAVIS, Ralph

Ralph E. Davis

Born: Sept. 7, 1938. Vanceburg, KY, United States.   Height: 6'4".   Weight: 180 lbs.   Drafted: 1960   College: Cincinnati

		GP	GS	MIN	PTS	FGM	FGA	FG%	3PM	3PA	3P%	FTM	FTA	FT%	ORB	DRB	TRB	AST	PF	DQ	STL	BLK	TO	MPG	PPG	RPG	APG	PCM
60-61	Cincinnati	73	....	1210	396	181	451	.401	....	....	....	34	52	.654	....	....	86	177	127	1	....	....	....	16.6	5.4	1.2	2.4	.347
61-62	Chicago	77	....	1992	799	364	881	.413	....	....	....	71	103	.689	....	....	162	247	187	1	....	....	....	25.9	10.4	2.1	3.2	.370
NBA Season Totals		150	....	3202	1195	545	1332	.409	....	....	....	105	155	.677	....	....	248	424	314	2	....	....	....	21.3	8.0	1.7	2.8	....

• DAVIS, Red

James R. (Red) Davis

Born: Apr. 22, 1932.   Height: 6'7".   Weight: 220 lbs.   Drafted: 1954   College: St. John's (NY)

		GP	GS	MIN	PTS	FGM	FGA	FG%	3PM	3PA	3P%	FTM	FTA	FT%	ORB	DRB	TRB	AST	PF	DQ	STL	BLK	TO	MPG	PPG	RPG	APG	PCM
55-56	Rochester	3	....	16	2	0	6	.000	....	....	....	2	2	1.000	....	....	4	1	2	0	....	....	....	5.3	0.7	1.3	0.3	.060
NBA Season Totals		3	....	16	2	0	6	.000	....	....	....	2	2	1.000	....	....	4	1	2	0	....	....	....	5.3	0.7	1.3	0.3	....

• DAVIS, Ricky

Tyree Rickardo Davis

Born: Sept. 23, 1979. Las Vegas, NV, United States.   Height: 6'6".   Weight: 195 lbs.   Drafted: 1998   College: Iowa

		GP	GS	MIN	PTS	FGM	FGA	FG%	3PM	3PA	3P%	FTM	FTA	FT%	ORB	DRB	TRB	AST	PF	DQ	STL	BLK	TO	MPG	PPG	RPG	APG	PCM
98-99	Charlotte	46	1	557	209	81	200	.405	2	12	.167	45	59	.763	40	44	84	58	46	0	30	7	54	12.1	4.5	1.8	1.3	.360
99-00	Charlotte	48	4	570	227	94	187	.503	0	4	.000	39	51	.765	29	54	83	62	39	0	30	8	46	11.9	4.7	1.7	1.3	.448
00-01	Miami	7	0	70	32	12	29	.414	1	1	1.000	7	8	.875	1	6	7	11	7	0	5	2	5	10.0	4.6	1.0	1.6	.476
01-02	Cleveland	82	8	1954	959	376	781	.481	11	35	.314	196	248	.790	63	180	243	178	145	0	69	23	148	23.8	11.7	3.0	2.2	.444
02-03	Cleveland	79	76	3130	1626	602	1470	.410	74	204	.363	348	465	.748	97	293	390	436	180	0	125	36	277	39.6	20.6	4.9	5.5	.456
NBA Season Totals		262	89	6281	3053	1165	2667	.437	88	256	.344	635	831	.764	230	577	807	745	417	0	259	76	530	24.0	11.7	3.1	2.8	....

• DAVIS, Ron

Ronald Howard Davis

Born: May 1, 1954. Phoenix, AZ, United States.   Height: 6'6".   Weight: 198 lbs.   Drafted: 1976   College: Washington State

		GP	GS	MIN	PTS	FGM	FGA	FG%	3PM	3PA	3P%	FTM	FTA	FT%	ORB	DRB	TRB	AST	PF	DQ	STL	BLK	TO	MPG	PPG	RPG	APG	PCM
76-77	Atlanta	7	....	67	20	8	35	.229	....	....	....	4	13	.308	2	5	7	2	9	0	7	0	....	9.6	2.9	1.0	0.3	-.041
80-81	San Diego	64	....	817	374	139	314	.443	2	8	.250	94	158	.595	47	72	119	47	98	0	36	11	64	12.8	5.8	1.9	0.7	.349
81-82	San Diego	7	0	67	23	10	25	.400	0	0	.000	3	6	.500	7	6	13	4	8	0	0	0	5	9.6	3.3	1.9	0.6	.236
NBA Season Totals		78	0	951	417	157	374	.420	2	8	.250	101	177	.571	56	83	139	53	115	0	43	11	69	12.2	5.3	1.8	0.7	....

• DAVIS, Terry

Terry Raymond Davis

Born: June 17, 1967. Danville, VA, United States.   Height: 6'9".   Weight: 225 lbs.   Drafted: —   College: Virginia Union

		GP	GS	MIN	PTS	FGM	FGA	FG%	3PM	3PA	3P%	FTM	FTA	FT%	ORB	DRB	TRB	AST	PF	DQ	STL	BLK	TO	MPG	PPG	RPG	APG	PCM
89-90	Miami	63	9	884	298	122	262	.466	0	1	.000	54	87	.621	93	136	229	25	171	2	25	28	69	14.0	4.7	3.6	0.4	.336
90-91	Miami	55	17	996	300	115	236	.487	1	2	.500	69	124	.556	107	159	266	39	129	2	18	28	39	18.1	5.5	4.8	0.7	.399
91-92	Dallas	68	67	2149	693	256	531	.482	0	5	.000	181	285	.635	228	444	672	57	202	1	26	29	116	31.6	10.2	9.9	0.8	.430
92-93	Dallas	75	74	2462	955	393	863	.455	2	8	.250	167	281	.594	259	442	701	68	199	3	36	28	158	32.8	12.7	9.3	0.9	.410
93-94	Dallas	15	5	286	56	24	59	.407	0	0	.000	8	12	.667	30	44	74	6	27	0	9	1	5	19.1	3.7	4.9	0.4	.310
94-95	Dallas	46	2	580	140	49	113	.434	0	2	.000	42	66	.636	63	93	156	10	76	2	6	3	32	12.6	3.0	3.4	0.2	.290
95-96	Dallas	28	0	501	137	55	108	.509	0	0	.000	27	47	.574	43	74	117	21	66	2	10	4	25	17.9	4.9	4.2	0.8	.337

YEAR	TEAM	GP	GS	MIN	PTS	FGM	FGA	FG%	3PM	3PA	3P%	FTM	FTA	FT%	ORB	DRB	TRB	AST	PF	DQ	STL	BLK	TO	MPG	PPG	RPG	APG	PCM
97-98	Washington	74	66	1705	323	127	256	.496	0	1	.000	69	119	.580	209	271	480	30	193	4	41	24	59	23.0	4.4	6.5	0.4	.335
98-99	Washington	37	34	578	126	49	92	.533	0	0	.000	28	38	.737	50	89	139	10	79	0	11	3	16	15.6	3.4	3.8	0.3	.313
00-01	Denver	19	1	228	33	12	25	.480	0	0	.000	9	22	.409	24	29	53	7	34	0	1	1	5	12.0	1.7	2.8	0.4	.232
NBA Season Totals		480	275	10369	3061	1202	2545	.472	3	19	.158	654	1081	.605	1106	1781	2887	273	1176	16	183	149	524	21.6	6.4	6.0	0.6	....

• DAVIS, Walt

Walter Francis (Buddy) Davis

Born: Jan. 5, 1931. Beaumont, TX, United States. Height: 6'8". Weight: 205 lbs. Drafted: 1952 College: Texas A&M

YEAR	TEAM	GP	GS	MIN	PTS	FGM	FGA	FG%	3PM	3PA	3P%	FTM	FTA	FT%	ORB	DRB	TRB	AST	PF	DQ	STL	BLK	TO	MPG	PPG	RPG	APG	PCM
53-54	Philadelphia	68	....	1568	399	167	455	.367	....	....	....	65	101	.644	....	....	435	58	207	9	....	....	....	23.1	5.9	6.4	0.9	.314
54-55	Philadelphia	61	....	766	175	70	182	.385	....	....	....	35	48	.729	....	....	206	36	100	0	....	....	....	12.6	2.9	3.4	0.6	.324
55-56	Philadelphia	70	....	1097	323	123	333	.369	....	....	....	77	112	.688	....	....	276	56	230	7	....	....	....	15.7	4.6	3.9	0.8	.312
56-57	Philadelphia	65	....	1250	430	178	437	.407	....	....	....	74	106	.698	....	....	306	52	235	9	....	....	....	19.2	6.6	4.7	0.8	.345
57-58	Philadelphia	35	....	376	104	44	129	.341	....	....	....	16	24	.667	....	....	88	18	81	0	....	....	....	10.7	3.0	2.5	0.5	.257
57-58	St. Louis	26	....	287	127	41	115	.357	....	....	....	45	58	.776	....	....	86	11	62	0	....	....	....	11.0	4.9	3.3	0.4	.426
NBA Season Totals		325	....	5344	1558	623	1651	.377	....	....	....	312	449	.695	....	....	1397	231	915	25	....	....	....	16.4	4.8	4.3	0.7	....
55-56	Philadelphia	10	....	69	23	10	22	.455	....	....	....	3	6	.500	....	....	28	3	21	0	....	....	....	6.9	2.3	2.8	0.3	.431
56-57	Philadelphia	2	....	37	12	4	13	.308	....	....	....	4	4	1.000	....	....	14	1	8	0	....	....	....	18.5	6.0	7.0	0.5	.378
57-58	St. Louis	9	....	66	32	11	29	.379	....	....	....	10	12	.833	....	....	27	3	22	0	....	....	....	7.3	3.6	3.0	0.3	.509
NBA Playoff Totals		21	....	172	67	25	64	.391	....	....	....	17	22	.773	....	....	69	7	51	0	....	....	....	8.2	3.2	3.3	0.3	....

• DAVIS, Walter

Walter Paul (Greyhound, Sweet D) Davis

Born: Sept. 9, 1954. Pineville, NC, United States. Height: 6'6". Weight: 193 lbs. Drafted: 1977 College: North Carolina

YEAR	TEAM	GP	GS	MIN	PTS	FGM	FGA	FG%	3PM	3PA	3P%	FTM	FTA	FT%	ORB	DRB	TRB	AST	PF	DQ	STL	BLK	TO	MPG	PPG	RPG	APG	PCM
77-78	Phoenix	81	....	2590	1959	786	1494	.526	....	....	....	387	466	.830	158	326	484	273	242	2	113	20	284	32.0	24.2	6.0	3.4	.694
78-79	Phoenix	79	....	2437	1868	764	1362	.561	....	....	....	340	409	.831	111	262	373	339	250	5	147	26	292	30.8	23.6	4.7	4.3	.734
79-80	Phoenix	75	....	2309	1613	657	1166	.563	0	4	.000	299	365	.819	75	197	272	337	202	2	114	19	240	30.8	21.5	3.6	4.5	.671
80-81	Phoenix	78	....	2182	1402	593	1101	.539	7	17	.412	209	250	.836	63	137	200	302	192	3	97	12	218	28.0	18.0	2.6	3.9	.571
81-82	Phoenix	55	12	1182	794	350	669	.523	3	16	.188	91	111	.820	21	82	103	162	104	1	46	3	110	21.5	14.4	1.9	2.9	.555
82-83	Phoenix	80	79	2491	1521	665	1289	.516	7	23	.304	184	225	.818	63	134	197	397	186	2	117	12	192	31.1	19.0	2.5	5.0	.567
83-84	Phoenix	78	70	2546	1557	652	1274	.512	20	87	.230	233	270	.863	38	164	202	429	202	0	107	12	211	32.6	20.0	2.6	5.5	.561
84-85	Phoenix	23	9	570	345	139	309	.450	3	10	.300	64	73	.877	6	29	35	98	42	0	18	0	51	24.8	15.0	1.5	4.3	.472
85-86	Phoenix	70	62	2239	1523	624	1287	.485	18	76	.237	257	305	.843	54	149	203	361	153	1	99	3	217	32.0	21.8	2.9	5.2	.573
86-87	Phoenix	79	79	2646	1867	779	1515	.514	21	81	.259	288	334	.862	90	154	244	364	184	1	96	5	229	33.5	23.6	3.1	4.6	.594
87-88	Phoenix	68	48	1951	1217	488	1031	.473	36	96	.375	205	231	.887	32	127	159	278	131	0	86	3	129	28.7	17.9	2.3	4.1	.536
88-89	Denver	81	0	1857	1267	536	1076	.498	20	69	.290	175	199	.879	41	110	151	190	187	1	72	5	130	22.9	15.6	1.9	2.3	.518
89-90	Denver	69	0	1635	1207	497	1033	.481	6	46	.130	207	227	.912	46	133	179	155	160	1	59	9	104	23.7	17.5	2.6	2.2	.562
90-91	Denver	39	13	1044	728	316	667	.474	10	33	.303	86	94	.915	52	71	123	84	108	2	62	3	62	26.8	18.7	3.2	2.2	.530
90-91	Portland	32	1	439	196	87	195	.446	1	3	.333	21	23	.913	19	39	58	41	42	0	18	0	26	13.7	6.1	1.8	1.3	.376
91-92	Denver	46	0	741	457	185	403	.459	5	16	.313	82	94	.872	20	50	70	68	69	0	29	1	46	16.1	9.9	1.5	1.5	.459
NBA Season Totals		1033	373	28859	19521	8118	15871	.511	157	577	.272	3128	3676	.851	889	2164	3053	3878	2454	21	1280	133	2541	27.9	18.9	3.0	3.8	....
77-78	Phoenix	2	....	66	50	19	40	.475	....	....	....	12	16	.750	4	13	17	8	8	0	3	0	6	33.0	25.0	8.5	4.0	.722
78-79	Phoenix	15	....	490	332	127	244	.520	....	....	....	78	96	.813	24	45	69	79	41	0	26	5	66	32.7	22.1	4.6	5.3	.649
79-80	Phoenix	8	....	245	166	69	137	.504	0	3	.000	28	38	.737	9	14	23	35	20	0	4	1	20	30.6	20.8	2.9	4.4	.557
80-81	Phoenix	7	....	199	112	51	106	.481	0	1	.000	10	17	.588	7	12	19	22	17	0	7	1	17	28.4	16.0	2.7	3.1	.422
81-82	Phoenix	7	0	173	127	52	116	.448	1	3	.333	22	24	.917	5	17	22	30	19	0	5	1	12	24.7	18.1	3.1	4.3	.610
82-83	Phoenix	3	3	113	78	30	69	.435	1	2	.500	17	21	.810	5	10	15	13	6	0	6	5	5	37.7	26.0	5.0	4.3	.633
83-84	Phoenix	17	17	623	423	175	327	.535	3	11	.273	70	78	.897	15	31	46	109	55	0	29	3	43	36.6	24.9	2.7	6.4	.645
88-89	Denver	3	0	94	77	31	60	.517	0	4	.000	15	15	1.000	2	3	5	4	11	0	3	0	8	31.3	25.7	1.7	1.3	.523
89-90	Denver	3	0	70	42	18	45	.400	0	1	.000	6	6	1.000	4	5	9	6	4	0	1	0	5	23.3	14.0	3.0	2.0	.370
90-91	Portland	13	0	111	43	19	48	.396	0	1	.000	5	6	.833	7	8	15	6	5	0	4	0	7	8.5	3.3	1.2	0.5	.277
NBA Playoff Totals		78	20	2184	1450	591	1192	.496	5	26	.192	263	317	.830	82	158	240	312	186	0	88	16	189	28.0	18.6	3.1	4.0	....

• DAVIS, Warren

Warren Lee (Checkmate) Davis

Born: June 30, 1943. Atlantic City, NJ, United States. Height: 6'6". Weight: 212 lbs. Drafted: 1965 College: North Carolina A&T

YEAR	TEAM	GP	GS	MIN	PTS	FGM	FGA	FG%	3PM	3PA	3P%	FTM	FTA	FT%	ORB	DRB	TRB	AST	PF	DQ	STL	BLK	TO	MPG	PPG	RPG	APG	PCM
67-68	Anaheim-A	54	....	1816	916	343	758	.453	1	7	.143	229	353	.649	221	345	566	75	193	3	....	....	128	33.6	17.0	10.5	1.4	.549
68-69	Los Angeles-A	78	....	2406	994	356	711	.501	0	2	.000	282	433	.651	254	523	777	129	269	3	....	....	183	30.8	12.7	10.0	1.7	.550
69-70	Los Angeles-A	46	....	1502	734	277	560	.495	1	1	1.000	179	232	.772	164	336	500	105	175	3	....	....	154	32.7	16.0	10.9	2.3	.627
69-70	Pittsburgh-A	34	....	1145	427	151	301	.502	0	2	.000	125	186	.672	114	293	407	139	125	2	....	....	120	33.7	12.6	12.0	4.1	.634
70-71	Florida-A	76	....	1995	825	308	686	.449	0	2	.000	209	300	.697	224	415	639	170	254	4	....	....	175	26.3	10.9	8.4	2.2	.551
71-72	Carolina-A	41	....	1348	557	223	464	.481	0	1	.000	111	163	.681	136	234	370	99	162	3	....	....	114	32.9	13.6	9.0	2.4	.510
71-72	Memphis-A	45	....	983	324	114	237	.481	0	1	.000	96	136	.706	114	209	323	81	117	1	....	....	73	21.8	7.2	7.2	1.8	.531
72-73	Memphis-A	73	....	1895	672	250	498	.502	0	0	.000	172	227	.758	153	362	515	146	212	5	....	....	129	26.0	9.2	7.1	2.0	.503
ABA Season Totals		447	....	13090	5449	2022	4215	.480	2	16	.125	1403	2030	.691	1380	2717	4097	944	1507	24	....	....	1076	29.3	12.2	9.2	2.1	....
70-71	Florida-A	6	....	180	78	28	58	.483	0	0	.000	22	29	.759	12	36	48	31	26	1	....	....	16	30.0	13.0	8.0	5.2	.647
ABA Playoff Totals		6	....	180	78	28	58	.483	0	0	.000	22	29	.759	12	36	48	31	26	1	....	....	16	30.0	13.0	8.0	5.2	....

• DAVIS, Willie

Willie Edward Davis

Born: Aug. 9, 1945. Fairfield, TX, United States. Height: 6'8". Weight: 234 lbs. Drafted: 1968 College: North Texas State

YEAR	TEAM	GP	GS	MIN	PTS	FGM	FGA	FG%	3PM	3PA	3P%	FTM	FTA	FT%	ORB	DRB	TRB	AST	PF	DQ	STL	BLK	TO	MPG	PPG	RPG	APG	PCM
70-71	Texas-A	8	....	29	18	7	15	.467	0	0	.000	4	8	.500	7	6	13	2	10	0	....	....	3	3.6	2.3	1.6	0.3	.648
ABA Season Totals		8	....	29	18	7	15	.467	0	0	.000	4	8	.500	7	6	13	2	10	0	....	....	3	3.6	2.3	1.6	0.3	....

• DAWKINS, Darryl

Darryl (Chocolate Thunder) Dawkins

Born: Jan. 11, 1957. Orlando, FL, United States. Height: 6'11". Weight: 251 lbs. Drafted: 1975 College: none (HS: Maynard Evans, FL)

YEAR	TEAM	GP	GS	MIN	PTS	FGM	FGA	FG%	3PM	3PA	3P%	FTM	FTA	FT%	ORB	DRB	TRB	AST	PF	DQ	STL	BLK	TO	MPG	PPG	RPG	APG	PCM
75-76	Philadelphia	37	....	165	90	41	82	.500	....	....	....	8	24	.333	15	34	49	3	40	1	2	9	....	4.5	2.4	1.3	0.1	.462
76-77	Philadelphia	59	....	684	310	135	215	.628	....	....	....	40	79	.506	59	171	230	24	129	1	12	49	....	11.6	5.3	3.9	0.4	.576
77-78	Philadelphia	70	....	1722	820	332	577	.575	....	....	....	156	220	.709	117	438	555	85	268	5	34	125	126	24.6	11.7	7.9	1.2	.622
78-79	Philadelphia	78	....	2035	1018	430	831	.517	....	....	....	158	235	.672	123	508	631	128	295	5	32	143	195	26.1	13.1	8.1	1.6	.580
79-80	Philadelphia	80	....	2541	1178	494	946	.522	0	6	.000	190	291	.653	197	496	693	149	**328**	8	49	142	232	31.8	14.7	8.7	1.9	.523
80-81	Philadelphia	76	....	2088	1065	423	697	.607	0	0	.000	219	304	.720	106	439	545	109	316	9	38	112	220	27.5	14.0	7.2	1.4	.567
81-82	Philadelphia	48	36	1124	528	207	367	.564	0	2	.000	114	164	.695	68	237	305	55	193	5	19	55	96	23.4	11.0	6.4	1.1	.524
82-83	New Jersey	81	82	2093	968	401	669	.599	0	0	.000	166	257	.646	127	293	420	114	**379**	**23**	67	152	284	25.8	12.0	5.2	1.4	.459
83-84	New Jersey	81	80	2417	1357	507	855	.593	2	5	.400	341	464	.735	159	382	541	123	**386**	**22**	60	136	235	29.8	16.8	6.7	1.5	.577
84-85	New Jersey	39	30	972	527	192	339	.566	0	1	.000	143	201	.711	55	126	181	45	171	11	14	35	94	24.9	13.5	4.6	1.2	.471
85-86	New Jersey	51	3	1207	778	284	441	.644	0	1	.000	210	297	.707	85	166	251	77	227	10	16	59	122	23.7	15.3	4.9	1.5	.628
86-87	New Jersey	6	2	106	57	20	32	.625	0	0	.000	17	24	.708	9	10	19	2	25	0	2	3	15	17.7	9.5	3.2	0.3	.391
87-88	Utah	4	0	26	6	1	7	.143	0	0	.000	4	12	.333	2	3	5	1	10	0	0	1	4	6.5	1.5	1.3	0.3	-.194
87-88	Detroit	2	0	7	4	1	2	.500	0	0	.000	2	3	.667	0	0	0	1	4	0	0	1	3	3.5	2.0	0.0	0.5	-.008
88-89	Detroit	14	0	48	27	9	19	.474	0	0	.000	9	18	.500	3	4	7	1	13	0	0	1	4	3.4	1.9	0.5	0.1	.255
NBA Season Totals		726	233	17235	8733	3477	6079	.572	2	15	.133	1777	2593	.685	1125	3307	4432	917	2784	100	345	1023	1630	23.7	12.0	6.1	1.3	....
76-77	Philadelphia	18	....	331	131	50	95	.526	....	....	....	31	47	.660	9	89	98	17	46	1	8	18	....	18.4	7.3	5.4	0.9	.512
77-78	Philadelphia	10	....	180	63	27	53	.509	....	....	....	9	17	.529	6	51	57	10	34	1	3	15	14	18.0	6.3	5.7	1.0	.481
78-79	Philadelphia	9	....	255	144	56	106	.528	....	....	....	32	47	.681	21	61	82	12	42	1	2	16	17	28.3	16.0	9.1	1.3	.632
79-80	Philadelphia	18	....	607	312	126	238	.529	0	3	.000	60	93	.645	44	93	137	33	75	2	13	42	46	33.7	17.3	7.6	1.8	.544
80-81	Philadelphia	16	....	421	221	86	153	.562	0	0	.000	49	68	.721	28	70	98	14	71	2	3	16	36	26.3	13.8	6.1	0.9	.494
81-82	Philadelphia	21	9	460	231	99	178	.556	0	0	.000	33	50	.660	23	75	98	11	94	4	7	35	38	21.9	11.0	4.7	0.5	.463
82-83	New Jersey	2	2	59	36	17	22	.773	0	1	.000	2	2	1.000	2	8	10	2	7	0	4	5	8	29.5	18.0	5.0	1.0	.686
83-84	New Jersey	11	11	340	202	66	118	.559	0	3	.000	70	83	.843	22	46	68	13	52	4	5	10	32	30.9	18.4	6.2	1.2	.543
84-85	New Jersey	3	3	64	25	11	23	.478	0	0	.000	3	4	.750	4	10	14	4	13	1	2	6	7	21.3	8.3	4.7	1.3	.399
85-86	New Jersey	1	0	17	10	4	6	.667	0	0	.000	2	3	.667	1	2	3	3	4	0	0	2	2	17.0	10.0	3.0	3.0	.695
NBA Playoff Totals		109	25	2734	1375	542	992	.546	0	7	.000	291	414	.703	160	505	665	119	438	16	47	165	200	25.1	12.6	6.1	1.1	....

• DAWKINS, Johnny

Johnny Earl Dawkins Jr.

Born: Sept. 28, 1963. Washington, DC, United States. Height: 6'2". Weight: 165 lbs. Drafted: 1986 College: Duke

YEAR	TEAM	GP	GS	MIN	PTS	FGM	FGA	FG%	3PM	3PA	3P%	FTM	FTA	FT%	ORB	DRB	TRB	AST	PF	DQ	STL	BLK	TO	MPG	PPG	RPG	APG	PCM
86-87	San Antonio	81	14	1682	835	334	764	.437	14	47	.298	153	191	.801	56	113	169	290	118	0	67	3	122	20.8	10.3	2.1	3.6	.464
87-88	San Antonio	65	61	2179	1027	405	835	.485	19	61	.311	198	221	.896	66	138	204	480	95	0	88	2	156	33.5	15.8	3.1	7.4	.556
88-89	San Antonio	32	30	1083	454	177	400	.443	0	4	.000	100	112	.893	32	69	101	224	64	0	55	0	112	33.8	14.2	3.2	7.0	.454
89-90	Philadelphia	81	81	2865	1162	465	950	.489	22	66	.333	210	244	.861	48	199	247	601	159	1	121	9	211	35.4	14.3	3.0	7.4	.493
90-91	Philadelphia	4	4	124	63	26	41	.634	1	4	.250	10	11	.909	0	16	16	28	4	0	3	0	8	31.0	15.8	4.0	7.0	.700
91-92	Philadelphia	82	82	2815	988	394	902	.437	36	101	.356	164	186	.882	42	185	227	567	158	0	89	5	180	34.3	12.0	2.8	6.9	.416
92-93	Philadelphia	74	10	1598	655	258	590	.437	26	84	.310	113	142	.796	33	103	136	339	91	0	80	4	118	21.6	8.9	1.8	4.6	.467
93-94	Philadelphia	72	12	1343	475	177	423	.418	37	105	.352	84	100	.840	28	95	123	263	74	0	63	5	108	18.7	6.6	1.7	3.7	.424
94-95	Detroit	50	9	1170	325	125	270	.463	25	73	.342	50	55	.909	28	85	113	205	74	1	52	1	85	23.4	6.5	2.3	4.1	.381
NBA Season Totals		541	303	14859	5984	2361	5175	.456	180	545	.330	1082	1262	.857	333	1003	1336	2997	837	2	618	29	1100	27.5	11.1	2.5	5.5	....
87-88	San Antonio	3	0	53	15	6	23	.261	0	2	.000	3	4	.750	1	2	3	5	2	0	2	0	1	17.7	5.0	1.0	1.7	.129
89-90	Philadelphia	10	10	386	142	53	115	.461	0	7	.000	36	43	.837	5	17	22	93	22	0	17	2	29	38.6	14.2	2.2	9.3	.467
NBA Playoff Totals		13	10	439	157	59	138	.428	0	9	.000	39	47	.830	6	19	25	98	24	0	19	2	30	33.8	12.1	1.9	7.5	....

• DAWKINS, Paul

Paul Lamar Dawkins

Born: June 10, 1957. Saginaw, MI, United States. Height: 6'5". Weight: 190 lbs. Drafted: 1979 College: Northern Illinois

YEAR	TEAM	GP	GS	MIN	PTS	FGM	FGA	FG%	3PM	3PA	3P%	FTM	FTA	FT%	ORB	DRB	TRB	AST	PF	DQ	STL	BLK	TO	MPG	PPG	RPG	APG	PCM
79-80	Utah	57	....	776	316	141	300	.470	1	5	.200	33	48	.688	42	83	125	77	112	0	33	9	74	13.6	5.5	2.2	1.4	.365
NBA Season Totals		57	....	776	316	141	300	.470	1	5	.200	33	48	.688	42	83	125	77	112	0	33	9	74	13.6	5.5	2.2	1.4	....

• DAWSON, Jim

James Dawson

Born: 1922. Height: 6'7". Weight: 210 lbs. Drafted: — College: Texas A&M

YEAR	TEAM	GP	GS	MIN	PTS	FGM	FGA	FG%	3PM	3PA	3P%	FTM	FTA	FT%	ORB	DRB	TRB	AST	PF	DQ	STL	BLK	TO	MPG	PPG	RPG	APG	PCM
46-47	Sheboygan-N	10	....	....	20	8	....	....	....	....	....	4	7	.571	....	....	....	....	....	....	....	....	....	....	2.0	....	....	....
NBL Season Totals		10	....	....	20	8	....	....	....	....	....	4	7	....	....	....	....	....	....	....	....	....	....	....	2.0	....	....	....

• DAWSON, Jimmy

James C. Dawson

Born: Apr. 18, 1945. Oak Park, IL, United States. Height: 6' Weight: 175 lbs. Drafted: 1967 College: Illinois

YEAR	TEAM	GP	GS	MIN	PTS	FGM	FGA	FG%	3PM	3PA	3P%	FTM	FTA	FT%	ORB	DRB	TRB	AST	PF	DQ	STL	BLK	TO	MPG	PPG	RPG	APG	PCM
67-68	Indiana-A	21	....	288	118	46	133	.346	1	7	.143	25	43	.581	....	....	21	32	16	0	....	....	16	13.7	5.6	1.0	1.5	.301
ABA Season Totals		21	....	288	118	46	133	.346	1	7	.143	25	43	.581	....	....	21	32	16	0	....	....	16	13.7	5.6	1.0	1.5	....

• DAWSON, Tony

Tony Dawson

Born: Aug. 25, 1967. Kinston, NC, United States. Height: 6'7". Weight: 215 lbs. Drafted: — College: Florida State

YEAR	TEAM	GP	GS	MIN	PTS	FGM	FGA	FG%	3PM	3PA	3P%	FTM	FTA	FT%	ORB	DRB	TRB	AST	PF	DQ	STL	BLK	TO	MPG	PPG	RPG	APG	PCM
90-91	Sacramento	4	0	17	9	4	7	.571	1	1	1.000	0	0	.000	2	0	2	0	0	0	0	0	1	4.3	2.3	0.5	0.0	.420
94-95	Boston	2	0	13	8	3	8	.375	1	3	.333	1	1	1.000	0	3	3	1	4	0	0	0	2	6.5	4.0	1.5	0.5	.264
NBA Season Totals		6	0	30	17	7	15	.467	2	4	.500	1	1	1.000	2	3	5	1	4	0	0	0	3	5.0	2.8	0.8	0.2	....

• DAY, Todd

Todd Fitzgerald Day

Born: Jan. 7, 1970. Decatur, IL, United States. Height: 6'6". Weight: 188 lbs. Drafted: 1992 College: Arkansas

YEAR	TEAM	GP	GS	MIN	PTS	FGM	FGA	FG%	3PM	3PA	3P%	FTM	FTA	FT%	ORB	DRB	TRB	AST	PF	DQ	STL	BLK	TO	MPG	PPG	RPG	APG	PCM
92-93	Milwaukee	71	37	1931	983	358	828	.432	54	184	.293	213	297	.717	144	147	291	117	222	1	75	48	121	27.2	13.8	4.1	1.6	.414
93-94	Milwaukee	76	39	2127	966	351	845	.415	33	148	.223	231	331	.698	115	195	310	138	221	4	103	52	129	28.0	12.7	4.1	1.8	.387
94-95	Milwaukee	82	81	2717	1310	445	1049	.424	163	418	.390	257	341	.754	95	227	322	134	283	6	104	63	156	33.1	16.0	3.9	1.6	.378
95-96	Milwaukee	8	0	171	73	22	71	.310	5	25	.200	24	26	.923	8	14	22	5	27	1	4	3	11	21.4	9.1	2.8	0.6	.208
95-96	Boston	71	12	1636	849	277	746	.371	95	277	.343	200	261	.766	62	140	202	102	198	1	77	48	99	23.0	12.0	2.8	1.4	.372
96-97	Boston	81	27	2277	1178	398	999	.398	126	348	.362	256	331	.773	109	221	330	117	208	0	108	48	130	28.1	14.5	4.1	1.4	.414
97-98	Miami	5	0	69	30	11	31	.355	2	12	.167	6	9	.667	4	2	6	7	10	0	7	0	3	13.8	6.0	1.2	1.4	.326
99-00	Phoenix	58	1	941	396	130	330	.394	64	165	.388	72	108	.667	31	98	129	65	127	1	44	22	50	16.2	6.8	2.2	1.1	.365
00-01	Minnesota	31	0	345	132	44	118	.373	26	69	.377	18	23	.783	10	27	37	28	52	0	10	7	24	11.1	4.3	1.2	0.9	.283
NBA Season Totals		**483**	**197**	**12214**	**5917**	**2036**	**5017**	**.406**	**568**	**1646**	**.345**	**1277**	**1727**	**.739**	**578**	**1071**	**1649**	**713**	**1348**	**14**	**532**	**291**	**723**	**25.3**	**12.3**	**3.4**	**1.5**	**....**
99-00	Phoenix	9	0	100	42	16	35	.457	5	16	.313	5	10	.500	6	4	10	4	24	0	4	1	4	11.1	4.7	1.1	0.4	.259
NBA Playoff Totals		**9**	**0**	**100**	**42**	**16**	**35**	**.457**	**5**	**16**	**.313**	**5**	**10**	**.500**	**6**	**4**	**10**	**4**	**24**	**0**	**4**	**1**	**4**	**11.1**	**4.7**	**1.1**	**0.4**	**....**

• DAYE, Darren

Darren Keefe Daye

Born: Nov. 30, 1960. Des Moines, IA, United States. Height: 6'8". Weight: 220 lbs. Drafted: 1983 College: UCLA

YEAR	TEAM	GP	GS	MIN	PTS	FGM	FGA	FG%	3PM	3PA	3P%	FTM	FTA	FT%	ORB	DRB	TRB	AST	PF	DQ	STL	BLK	TO	MPG	PPG	RPG	APG	PCM
83-84	Washington	75	0	1174	455	180	408	.441	0	6	.000	95	133	.714	90	98	188	176	154	0	38	12	98	15.7	6.1	2.5	2.3	.402
84-85	Washington	80	8	1573	695	258	504	.512	1	7	.143	178	249	.715	93	179	272	240	164	1	53	19	136	19.7	8.7	3.4	3.0	.513
85-86	Washington	64	4	1075	556	198	399	.496	1	3	.333	159	237	.671	71	112	183	109	121	0	46	11	96	16.8	8.7	2.9	1.7	.491
86-87	Chicago	1	0	7	0	0	0	.000	0	0	.000	0	0	.000	0	1	1	1	2	0	0	0	1	7.0	0.0	1.0	1.0	.020
86-87	Boston	61	2	724	236	101	202	.500	0	0	.000	34	65	.523	37	87	124	75	98	0	25	7	55	11.9	3.9	2.0	1.2	.354
87-88	Boston	47	8	655	283	112	217	.516	0	1	.000	59	87	.678	30	46	76	71	68	0	29	4	42	13.9	6.0	1.6	1.5	.425
NBA Season Totals		**328**	**22**	**5208**	**2225**	**849**	**1730**	**.491**	**2**	**17**	**.118**	**525**	**771**	**.681**	**321**	**523**	**844**	**672**	**607**	**1**	**191**	**53**	**428**	**15.9**	**6.8**	**2.6**	**2.0**	**....**
83-84	Washington	3	0	15	4	1	5	.200	0	0	.000	2	2	1.000	0	0	0	1	2	0	0	1	1	5.0	1.3	0.0	0.3	.028
84-85	Washington	4	4	85	41	17	30	.567	0	0	.000	7	16	.438	6	6	12	14	8	0	3	0	6	21.3	10.3	3.0	3.5	.521
85-86	Washington	4	0	32	8	4	12	.333	0	0	.000	0	2	.000	3	5	8	0	3	0	0	0	5	8.0	2.0	2.0	0.0	.032
86-87	Boston	23	1	240	116	42	72	.583	0	0	.000	32	37	.865	11	21	32	13	33	1	9	3	18	10.4	5.0	1.4	0.6	.452
NBA Playoff Totals		**34**	**5**	**372**	**169**	**64**	**119**	**.538**	**0**	**0**	**.000**	**41**	**57**	**.719**	**20**	**32**	**52**	**28**	**46**	**1**	**12**	**4**	**30**	**10.9**	**5.0**	**1.5**	**0.8**	**....**

• DEANE, Greg

Greg Steven Deane

Born: Dec. 6, 1957. Tulare, CA, United States. Height: 6'4". Weight: 190 lbs. Drafted: 1979 College: Utah

YEAR	TEAM	GP	GS	MIN	PTS	FGM	FGA	FG%	3PM	3PA	3P%	FTM	FTA	FT%	ORB	DRB	TRB	AST	PF	DQ	STL	BLK	TO	MPG	PPG	RPG	APG	PCM
79-80	Utah	7	....	48	10	2	11	.182	1	1	1.000	5	7	.714	2	4	6	6	3	0	0	0	3	6.9	1.4	0.9	0.9	.185
NBA Season Totals		**7**	**....**	**48**	**10**	**2**	**11**	**.182**	**1**	**1**	**1.000**	**5**	**7**	**.714**	**2**	**4**	**6**	**6**	**3**	**0**	**0**	**0**	**3**	**6.9**	**1.4**	**0.9**	**0.9**	**....**

• DEANGELIS, Billy

William R. DeAngelis

Born: Oct. 5, 1946. Height: 6'1". Weight: 180 lbs. Drafted: — College: St. Joseph's (PA)

YEAR	TEAM	GP	GS	MIN	PTS	FGM	FGA	FG%	3PM	3PA	3P%	FTM	FTA	FT%	ORB	DRB	TRB	AST	PF	DQ	STL	BLK	TO	MPG	PPG	RPG	APG	PCM
70-71	New York-A	8	....	47	10	3	6	.500	0	0	.000	4	6	.667	2	4	6	8	16	0	....	....	5	5.9	1.3	0.8	1.0	.315
ABA Season Totals		**8**	**....**	**47**	**10**	**3**	**6**	**.500**	**0**	**0**	**.000**	**4**	**6**	**.667**	**2**	**4**	**6**	**8**	**16**	**0**	**....**	**....**	**5**	**5.9**	**1.3**	**0.8**	**1.0**	**....**

• DEATON, Les

Les Deaton

Born: 1923. Height: 6'4". Weight: 210 lbs. Drafted: — College: Denison

YEAR	TEAM	GP	GS	MIN	PTS	FGM	FGA	FG%	3PM	3PA	3P%	FTM	FTA	FT%	ORB	DRB	TRB	AST	PF	DQ	STL	BLK	TO	MPG	PPG	RPG	APG	PCM
47-48	Sheboygan-N	51	....	....	237	83	....	....	....	....	....	71	119	.597	....	....	....	....	106	....	....	....	....	....	4.6	....	....	....
48-49	Sheboygan-N	6	....	....	13	5	....	....	....	....	....	3	5	.600	....	....	....	....	....	....	....	....	....	....	2.2	....	....	....
48-49	Waterloo-N	26	....	....	55	18	....	....	....	....	....	19	33	.576	....	....	....	....	....	....	....	....	....	....	2.1	....	....	....
NBL Season Totals		**83**	**....**	**....**	**305**	**106**	**....**	**....**	**....**	**....**	**....**	**93**	**157**	**....**	**....**	**....**	**....**	**....**	**106**	**....**	**....**	**....**	**....**	**....**	**3.7**	**....**	**....**	**....**

• DEBNAR, Rudy

Rudy Debnar

Born: May 9, 1916. Died: May1982. Height: 5'11". Weight: 160 lbs. Drafted: — College: Duquesne

YEAR	TEAM	GP	GS	MIN	PTS	FGM	FGA	FG%	3PM	3PA	3P%	FTM	FTA	FT%	ORB	DRB	TRB	AST	PF	DQ	STL	BLK	TO	MPG	PPG	RPG	APG	PCM
41-42	Wingfoots-N	24	....	....	141	56	....	....	....	....	....	29	....	....	....	....	....	....	....	....	....	....	....	....	5.9	....	....	....
45-46	Youngstown-N	31	....	....	162	51	....	....	....	....	....	60	78	.769	....	....	....	....	....	....	....	....	....	....	5.2	....	....	....
NBL Season Totals		**55**	**....**	**....**	**303**	**107**	**....**	**....**	**....**	**....**	**....**	**89**	**78**	**....**	**....**	**....**	**....**	**....**	**....**	**....**	**....**	**....**	**....**	**....**	**5.5**	**....**	**....**	**....**
41-42	Wingfoots-N	3	....	....	0	0	....	....	....	....	....	0	....	....	....	....	....	....	....	....	....	....	....	....	0.0	....	....	....
NBL Playoff Totals		**3**	**....**	**....**	**0**	**0**	**....**	**....**	**....**	**....**	**....**	**0**	**....**	**....**	**....**	**....**	**....**	**....**	**....**	**....**	**....**	**....**	**....**	**....**	**0.0**	**....**	**....**	**....**

• DEBUSSCHERE, Dave

David Albert DeBusschere

Born: Oct. 16, 1940. Detroit, MI, United States. Died: May14, 2003. Height: 6'6". Weight: 220 lbs. Drafted: 1962 College: Detroit HOF: 1983

YEAR	TEAM	GP	GS	MIN	PTS	FGM	FGA	FG%	3PM	3PA	3P%	FTM	FTA	FT%	ORB	DRB	TRB	AST	PF	DQ	STL	BLK	TO	MPG	PPG	RPG	APG	PCM
62-63	Detroit	80	....	2352	1018	406	944	.430	....	....	....	206	287	.718	....	....	694	207	247	2	....	....	....	29.4	12.7	8.7	2.6	.537
63-64	Detroit	15	....	304	129	52	133	.391	....	....	....	25	43	.581	....	....	105	23	32	1	....	....	....	20.3	8.6	7.0	1.5	.514
64-65	Detroit	79	....	2769	1322	508	1196	.425	....	....	....	306	437	.700	....	....	874	253	242	5	....	....	....	35.1	16.7	11.1	3.2	.590
65-66	Detroit	79	....	2696	1297	524	1284	.408	....	....	....	249	378	.659	....	....	916	209	252	5	....	....	....	34.1	16.4	11.6	2.6	.565
66-67	Detroit	78	....	2897	1423	531	1278	.415	....	....	....	361	512	.705	....	....	924	216	297	7	....	....	....	37.1	18.2	11.8	2.8	.568
67-68	Detroit	80	....	3125	1435	573	1295	.442	....	....	....	289	435	.664	....	....	1081	181	304	3	....	....	....	39.1	17.9	13.5	2.3	.563
68-69	Detroit	29	....	1092	472	189	423	.447	....	....	....	94	130	.723	....	....	353	63	111	1	....	....	....	37.7	16.3	12.2	2.2	.534
68-69	New York	47	....	1851	769	317	717	.442	....	....	....	135	198	.682	....	....	535	128	179	5	....	....	....	39.4	16.4	11.4	2.7	.502
69-70	New York	79	....	2627	1152	488	1082	.451	....	....	....	176	256	.688	....	....	790	194	244	2	....	....	....	33.3	14.6	10.0	2.5	.533
70-71	New York	81	....	2891	1263	523	1243	.421	....	....	....	217	312	.696	....	....	901	220	237	2	....	....	....	35.7	15.6	11.1	2.7	.528
71-72	New York	80	....	3072	1233	520	1218	.427	....	....	....	193	265	.728	....	....	901	291	219	1	....	....	....	38.4	15.4	11.3	3.6	.525

YEAR	TEAM	GP	GS	MIN	PTS	FGM	FGA	FG%	3PM	3PA	3P%	FTM	FTA	FT%	ORB	DRB	TRB	AST	PF	DQ	STL	BLK	TO	MPG	PPG	RPG	APG	PCM
72-73	New York	77	....	2827	1258	532	1224	.435	....	....	....	194	260	.746	....	....	787	259	215	1	....	....	....	36.7	16.3	10.2	3.4	.536
73-74	New York	71	....	2699	1282	559	1212	.461	....	....	....	164	217	.756	134	623	757	253	222	2	67	39	....	38.0	18.1	10.7	3.6	.572
NBA Season Totals		875	....	31202	14053	5722	13249	.432	....	....	....	2609	3730	.699	134	623	9618	2497	2801	37	67	39	....	35.7	16.1	11.0	2.9	....
62-63	Detroit	4	....	159	80	25	59	.424	....	....	....	30	44	.682	....	....	63	6	14	1	....	....	....	39.8	20.0	15.8	1.5	.623
67-68	Detroit	6	....	263	116	45	106	.425	....	....	....	26	45	.578	....	....	97	13	23	0	....	....	....	43.8	19.3	16.2	2.2	.546
68-69	New York	10	....	419	163	61	174	.351	....	....	....	41	50	.820	....	....	148	33	43	0	....	....	....	41.9	16.3	14.8	3.3	.499
69-70	New York	19	....	701	305	130	309	.421	....	....	....	45	68	.662	....	....	220	46	63	1	....	....	....	36.9	16.1	11.6	2.4	.506
70-71	New York	12	....	488	197	84	202	.416	....	....	....	29	44	.659	....	....	156	22	40	1	....	....	....	40.7	16.4	13.0	1.8	.474
71-72	New York	16	....	616	266	109	242	.450	....	....	....	48	64	.750	....	....	193	37	51	2	....	....	....	38.5	16.6	12.1	2.3	.537
72-73	New York	17	....	632	265	117	265	.442	....	....	....	31	40	.775	....	....	179	58	57	0	....	....	....	37.2	15.6	10.5	3.4	.521
73-74	New York	12	....	404	144	63	166	.380	....	....	....	18	29	.621	25	74	99	38	36	0	7	4	....	33.7	12.0	8.3	3.2	.407
NBA Playoff Totals		96	....	3682	1536	634	1523	.416	....	....	....	268	384	.698	25	74	1155	253	327	5	7	4	....	38.4	16.0	12.0	2.6	....

• DECLERCQ, Andrew

Andrew DeClercq

Born: Feb. 1, 1973. Detroit, MI, United States.　Height: 6'10".　Weight: 230 lbs.　Drafted: 1995　College: Florida

YEAR	TEAM	GP	GS	MIN	PTS	FGM	FGA	FG%	3PM	3PA	3P%	FTM	FTA	FT%	ORB	DRB	TRB	AST	PF	DQ	STL	BLK	TO	MPG	PPG	RPG	APG	PCM
95-96	Golden State	22	1	203	59	24	50	.480	0	1	.000	11	19	.579	18	21	39	9	30	0	7	5	4	9.2	2.7	1.8	0.4	.347
96-97	Golden State	71	1	1065	375	142	273	.520	0	0	.000	91	151	.603	122	176	298	32	229	3	33	27	78	15.0	5.3	4.2	0.5	.388
97-98	Boston	81	49	1523	439	169	340	.497	0	1	.000	101	168	.601	180	212	392	59	277	3	85	49	81	18.8	5.4	4.8	0.7	.392
98-99	Boston	14	1	258	75	28	57	.491	0	0	.000	19	29	.655	33	30	63	10	51	1	13	9	22	18.4	5.4	4.5	0.7	.346
98-99	Cleveland	33	31	844	296	110	219	.502	0	0	.000	76	112	.679	71	121	192	21	110	2	37	20	32	25.6	9.0	5.8	0.6	.415
99-00	Cleveland	82	31	1831	544	225	443	.508	0	0	.000	94	160	.588	156	283	439	58	275	6	63	66	108	22.3	6.6	5.4	0.7	.367
00-01	Orlando	67	51	903	261	107	193	.554	0	0	.000	47	82	.573	91	145	236	32	198	2	41	33	51	13.5	3.9	3.5	0.5	.384
01-02	Orlando	61	14	633	162	67	149	.450	0	0	.000	28	50	.560	74	89	163	22	130	0	23	24	34	10.4	2.7	2.7	0.4	.320
02-03	Orlando	77	21	1327	365	149	279	.534	0	0	.000	67	104	.644	142	197	339	52	258	5	39	36	84	17.2	4.7	4.4	0.7	.354
NBA Season Totals		508	200	8587	2576	1021	2003	.510	0	2	.000	534	875	.610	887	1274	2161	295	1558	22	341	269	494	16.9	5.1	4.3	0.6	....
00-01	Orlando	4	4	54	20	8	14	.571	0	0	.000	4	8	.500	7	9	16	1	17	1	2	2	2	13.5	5.0	4.0	0.3	.416
01-02	Orlando	2	0	9	0	0	0	.000	0	0	.000	0	2	.000	0	0	0	0	3	0	0	0	1	4.5	0.0	0.0	0.0	-.352
02-03	Orlando	7	6	104	28	12	20	.600	0	0	.000	4	5	.800	8	15	23	2	25	1	2	5	9	14.9	4.0	3.3	0.3	.290
NBA Playoff Totals		13	10	167	48	20	34	.588	0	0	.000	8	15	.533	15	24	39	3	45	2	4	7	12	12.8	3.7	3.0	0.2	....

• DEE, Donald

Donald M. Dee

Born: Aug. 9, 1943. Booneville, MD, United States.　Height: 6'8".　Weight: 210 lbs.　Drafted: 1968　College: St. Mary of the Plains

YEAR	TEAM	GP	GS	MIN	PTS	FGM	FGA	FG%	3PM	3PA	3P%	FTM	FTA	FT%	ORB	DRB	TRB	AST	PF	DQ	STL	BLK	TO	MPG	PPG	RPG	APG	PCM
68-69	Indiana-A	58	....	989	332	138	387	.357	0	1	.000	56	75	.747	104	188	292	33	179	9	....	....	72	17.1	5.7	5.0	0.6	.325
ABA Season Totals		58	....	989	332	138	387	.357	0	1	.000	56	75	.747	104	188	292	33	179	9	....	....	72	17.1	5.7	5.0	0.6	....
68-69	Indiana-A	12	....	41	8	4	13	.308	0	0	.000	0	0	.000	....	....	10	1	10	0	....	....	4	3.4	0.7	0.8	0.1	.139
ABA Playoff Totals		12	....	41	8	4	13	.308	0	0	.000	0	0	.000	....	....	10	1	10	0	....	....	4	3.4	0.7	0.8	0.1	....

• DEES, Archie

Archie William Dees

Born: Feb. 22, 1936. Mt. Carmel, IL, United States.　Height: 6'8".　Weight: 205 lbs.　Drafted: 1958　College: Indiana

YEAR	TEAM	GP	GS	MIN	PTS	FGM	FGA	FG%	3PM	3PA	3P%	FTM	FTA	FT%	ORB	DRB	TRB	AST	PF	DQ	STL	BLK	TO	MPG	PPG	RPG	APG	PCM
58-59	Cincinnati	68	....	1252	559	200	562	.356	....	....	....	159	204	.779	....	....	339	56	114	0	....	....	....	18.4	8.2	5.0	0.8	.441
59-60	Detroit	73	....	1244	707	271	617	.439	....	....	....	165	204	.809	....	....	397	43	188	3	....	....	....	17.0	9.7	5.4	0.6	.573
60-61	Detroit	28	....	308	145	53	135	.393	....	....	....	39	47	.830	....	....	94	17	50	0	....	....	....	11.0	5.2	3.4	0.6	.497
61-62	Chi/StL	21	....	288	137	51	115	.443	....	....	....	35	46	.761	....	....	77	16	33	0	....	....	....	13.7	6.5	3.7	0.8	.519
NBA Season Totals		190	....	3092	1548	575	1429	.402	....	....	....	398	501	.794	....	....	907	132	385	3	....	....	....	16.3	8.1	4.8	0.7	....
59-60	Detroit	2	....	18	11	4	12	.333	....	....	....	3	3	1.000	....	....	4	2	2	0	....	....	....	9.0	5.5	2.0	1.0	.539
NBA Playoff Totals		2	....	18	11	4	12	.333	....	....	....	3	3	1.000	....	....	4	2	2	0	....	....	....	9.0	5.5	2.0	1.0	....

• DEHERE, Terry

Lennox Dominique Dehere

Born: Sept. 12, 1971. New York, NY, United States.　Height: 6'2".　Weight: 190 lbs.　Drafted: 1993　College: Seton Hall

YEAR	TEAM	GP	GS	MIN	PTS	FGM	FGA	FG%	3PM	3PA	3P%	FTM	FTA	FT%	ORB	DRB	TRB	AST	PF	DQ	STL	BLK	TO	MPG	PPG	RPG	APG	PCM
93-94	LA Clippers	64	6	759	342	129	342	.377	23	57	.404	61	81	.753	25	43	68	78	69	0	28	3	64	11.9	5.3	1.1	1.2	.293
94-95	LA Clippers	80	28	1774	835	279	685	.407	48	163	.294	229	292	.784	35	117	152	225	200	0	45	7	160	22.2	10.4	1.9	2.8	.344
95-96	LA Clippers	82	10	2018	1016	315	686	.459	139	316	.440	247	327	.755	41	102	143	350	239	2	54	16	189	24.6	12.4	1.7	4.3	.451
96-97	LA Clippers	73	3	1053	470	148	383	.386	52	160	.325	122	148	.824	15	80	95	158	142	0	27	3	95	14.4	6.4	1.3	2.2	.351
94-95	Sacramento	77	18	1410	489	180	451	.399	50	132	.379	79	99	.798	21	85	106	196	150	0	52	4	92	18.3	6.4	1.4	2.5	.312
98-99	Sacramento	4	0	20	9	4	11	.364	1	5	.200	0	0	.000	2	0	2	1	2	0	2	0	2	5.0	2.3	0.5	0.3	.239
98-99	Vancouver	22	0	271	74	27	74	.365	15	34	.441	5	7	.714	5	17	22	26	28	0	5	3	14	12.3	3.4	1.0	1.2	.229
NBA Season Totals		402	65	7305	3235	1082	2632	.411	328	867	.378	743	954	.779	144	444	588	1034	830	2	213	36	616	18.2	8.0	1.5	2.6	....
96-97	LA Clippers	2	0	5	0	0	1	.000	0	1	.000	0	0	.000	1	0	1	0	1	0	0	0	1	2.5	0.0	0.5	0.0	-.280
NBA Playoff Totals		2	0	5	0	0	1	.000	0	1	.000	0	0	.000	1	0	1	0	1	0	0	0	1	2.5	0.0	0.5	0.0	....

• DEHNER, Louis

Louis (Pick) Dehner

Born: Aug. 29, 1914. Lincoln, IL, United States.　Height: 6'5".　Weight: 190 lbs.　Drafted: —　College: Illinois

YEAR	TEAM	GP	GS	MIN	PTS	FGM	FGA	FG%	3PM	3PA	3P%	FTM	FTA	FT%	ORB	DRB	TRB	AST	PF	DQ	STL	BLK	TO	MPG	PPG	RPG	APG	PCM
38-39	Hammond-N	1	....	....	15	7	....	....	....	....	....	1	....	....	....	....	....	....	....	....	....	....	....	....	15.0	....	....	....
NBL Season Totals		1	....	....	15	7	....	....	....	....	....	1	....	....	....	....	....	....	....	....	....	....	....	....	15.0	....	....	....

• DEHNERT, Red
Henry G. (Red) Dehnert

Born: 1924. Height: 6'3". Weight: 175 lbs. Drafted: — College: Columbia HOF: 1969

YEAR	TEAM	GP	GS	MIN	PTS	FGM	FGA	FG%	3PM	3PA	3P%	FTM	FTA	FT%	ORB	DRB	TRB	AST	PF	DQ	STL	BLK	TO	MPG	PPG	RPG	APG	PCM
46-47	Providence	10	....	....	14	6	15	.400	....	....	....	2	6	.333	....	....	....	0	8	....	....	....	....	....	1.4	....	0.0	....
NBA Season Totals		10	....	....	14	6	15	.400	....	....	....	2	6	.333	....	....	....	0	8	....	....	....	....	....	1.4	....	0.0	....

• DEL NEGRO, Vinny
Vincent Joseph Del Negro

Born: Aug. 9, 1966. Springfield, MA, United States. Height: 6'4". Weight: 185 lbs. Drafted: 1988 College: North Carolina State

YEAR	TEAM	GP	GS	MIN	PTS	FGM	FGA	FG%	3PM	3PA	3P%	FTM	FTA	FT%	ORB	DRB	TRB	AST	PF	DQ	STL	BLK	TO	MPG	PPG	RPG	APG	PCM
88-89	Sacramento	80	2	1556	569	239	503	.475	6	20	.300	85	100	.850	48	123	171	206	160	2	65	14	80	19.5	7.1	2.1	2.6	.399
89-90	Sacramento	76	29	1858	739	297	643	.462	10	32	.313	135	155	.871	39	159	198	250	182	2	64	10	114	24.4	9.7	2.6	3.3	.395
92-93	San Antonio	73	31	1526	543	218	430	.507	6	24	.250	101	118	.856	19	144	163	291	146	0	44	1	95	20.9	7.4	2.2	4.0	.449
93-94	San Antonio	77	56	1949	773	309	634	.487	15	43	.349	140	170	.824	27	134	161	320	168	0	64	1	100	25.3	10.0	2.1	4.2	.434
94-95	San Antonio	75	71	2360	938	372	766	.486	66	162	.407	128	162	.790	28	164	192	226	179	0	61	14	53	31.5	12.5	2.6	3.0	.385
95-96	San Antonio	82	82	2766	1191	478	962	.497	57	150	.380	178	214	.832	36	236	272	315	166	0	85	6	98	33.7	14.5	3.3	3.8	.443
96-97	San Antonio	72	53	2243	886	365	781	.467	44	140	.314	112	129	.868	39	171	210	231	131	0	59	7	94	31.2	12.3	2.9	3.2	.377
97-98	San Antonio	54	38	1721	513	211	479	.441	17	39	.436	74	93	.796	13	139	152	183	113	0	39	6	54	31.9	9.5	2.8	3.4	.312
98-99	Milwaukee	48	7	1093	281	114	270	.422	13	30	.433	40	50	.800	14	88	102	174	62	0	33	3	55	22.8	5.9	2.1	3.6	.345
99-00	Milwaukee	67	0	1211	349	153	325	.471	8	24	.333	35	39	.897	9	98	107	160	81	0	36	0	48	18.1	5.2	1.6	2.4	.343
00-01	Golden State	29	1	396	77	30	90	.333	1	9	.111	16	16	1.000	4	27	31	62	36	0	6	0	15	13.7	2.7	1.1	2.1	.240
00-01	Phoenix	36	0	526	177	76	144	.528	0	4	.000	25	28	.893	8	43	51	64	42	0	20	3	19	14.6	4.9	1.4	1.8	.410
01-02	Phoenix	2	0	6	2	1	4	.250	0	0	.000	0	0	.000	0	0	0	2	0	0	0	0	0	3.0	1.0	0.0	1.0	.245
NBA Season Totals		771	370	19211	7038	2863	6031	.475	243	677	.359	1069	1274	.839	284	1526	1810	2484	1466	4	576	65	825	24.9	9.1	2.3	3.2	....
92-93	San Antonio	8	0	112	40	17	38	.447	2	9	.222	4	4	1.000	6	13	19	24	13	0	1	1	3	14.0	5.0	2.4	3.0	.507
93-94	San Antonio	4	4	93	29	12	27	.444	2	4	.500	3	5	.600	1	6	7	18	6	0	1	0	6	23.3	7.3	1.8	4.5	.354
94-95	San Antonio	15	15	382	131	51	118	.432	9	20	.450	20	24	.833	4	28	32	37	23	0	8	2	16	25.5	8.7	2.1	2.5	.312
95-96	San Antonio	10	10	379	143	57	124	.460	16	27	.593	13	19	.684	4	22	26	29	19	0	13	3	6	37.9	14.3	2.6	2.9	.351
97-98	San Antonio	9	3	283	96	39	81	.481	2	10	.200	16	17	.941	2	22	24	29	30	0	8	0	13	31.4	10.7	2.7	3.2	.326
99-00	Milwaukee	5	0	93	26	13	30	.433	0	2	.000	0	0	.000	0	8	8	9	4	0	3	0	3	18.6	5.2	1.6	1.8	.278
00-01	Phoenix	3	0	26	8	4	7	.571	0	0	.000	0	0	.000	0	2	2	5	2	0	0	0	0	8.7	2.7	0.7	1.7	.451
NBA Playoff Totals		54	32	1368	473	193	425	.454	31	72	.431	56	69	.812	17	101	118	151	97	0	34	6	47	25.3	8.8	2.2	2.8	....

• DELE, Bison
Bison Dele aka.: Brian Carson Williams

Born: Apr. 6, 1969. Fresno, CA, United States. Died: Sept.2002. Height: 6'9". Weight: 235 lbs. Drafted: 1991 College: Arizona

YEAR	TEAM	GP	GS	MIN	PTS	FGM	FGA	FG%	3PM	3PA	3P%	FTM	FTA	FT%	ORB	DRB	TRB	AST	PF	DQ	STL	BLK	TO	MPG	PPG	RPG	APG	PCM
91-92	Orlando	48	2	905	437	171	324	.528	0	0	.000	95	142	.669	115	157	272	33	139	2	41	53	86	18.9	9.1	5.7	0.7	.557
92-93	Orlando	21	0	240	96	40	78	.513	0	1	.000	16	20	.800	24	32	56	5	48	2	14	17	25	11.4	4.6	2.7	0.2	.414
93-94	Denver	80	1	1507	639	251	464	.541	0	3	.000	137	211	.649	138	308	446	50	221	3	49	87	104	18.8	8.0	5.6	0.6	.531
94-95	Denver	63	10	1261	498	196	333	.589	0	0	.000	106	162	.654	98	200	298	53	210	7	38	43	113	20.0	7.9	4.7	0.8	.437
95-96	LA Clippers	65	65	2157	1029	416	766	.543	1	6	.167	196	267	.734	149	343	492	122	226	5	70	55	189	33.2	15.8	7.6	1.9	.506
96-97	Chicago	9	0	138	63	26	63	.413	0	0	.000	11	15	.733	14	19	33	12	20	0	3	5	11	15.3	7.0	3.7	1.3	.421
97-98	Detroit	78	78	2619	1261	531	1040	.511	1	3	.333	198	280	.707	223	472	695	94	252	4	67	55	179	33.6	16.2	8.9	1.2	.507
98-99	Detroit	49	48	1177	513	216	431	.501	0	1	.000	81	118	.686	92	180	272	71	181	3	38	40	111	24.0	10.5	5.6	1.4	.439
NBA Season Totals		413	204	10004	4536	1847	3499	.528	2	14	.143	840	1215	.691	853	1711	2564	440	1297	26	320	355	818	24.2	11.0	6.2	1.1	....
93-94	Denver	12	0	289	111	42	76	.553	0	0	.000	27	41	.659	33	56	89	11	36	0	4	11	17	24.1	9.3	7.4	0.9	.514
94-95	Denver	3	0	44	24	10	18	.556	0	0	.000	4	4	1.000	5	13	18	2	15	1	0	1	10	14.7	8.0	6.0	0.7	.455
96-97	Chicago	19	0	336	116	50	104	.481	0	0	.000	16	31	.516	31	40	71	11	63	1	19	8	14	17.7	6.1	3.7	0.6	.355
98-99	Detroit	5	5	122	53	24	40	.600	0	0	.000	5	9	.556	12	20	32	1	25	1	3	2	7	24.4	10.6	6.4	0.2	.440
NBA Playoff Totals		39	5	791	304	126	238	.529	0	0	.000	52	85	.612	81	129	210	25	139	3	26	22	48	20.3	7.8	5.4	0.6	....

• DELK, Tony
Tony Lorenzo Delk

Born: Jan. 28, 1974. Covington, TN, United States. Height: 6'1". Weight: 189 lbs. Drafted: 1996 College: Kentucky

YEAR	TEAM	GP	GS	MIN	PTS	FGM	FGA	FG%	3PM	3PA	3P%	FTM	FTA	FT%	ORB	DRB	TRB	AST	PF	DQ	STL	BLK	TO	MPG	PPG	RPG	APG	PCM
96-97	Charlotte	61	1	867	332	119	256	.465	52	112	.464	42	51	.824	31	68	99	99	71	1	36	6	67	14.2	5.4	1.6	1.6	.394
97-98	Charlotte	3	0	34	8	3	4	.750	1	1	1.000	1	2	.500	0	2	2	3	8	0	0	0	4	11.3	2.7	0.7	1.0	.129
97-98	Golden State	74	9	1647	773	311	794	.392	41	156	.263	110	149	.738	38	132	170	169	88	0	73	12	104	22.3	10.4	2.3	2.3	.361
98-99	Golden State	36	13	630	246	92	253	.364	16	66	.242	46	71	.648	11	43	54	95	47	0	16	6	45	17.5	6.8	1.5	2.6	.324
99-00	Sacramento	46	1	682	296	120	279	.430	9	40	.225	47	59	.797	36	52	88	55	58	0	35	5	32	14.8	6.4	1.9	1.2	.392
00-01	Phoenix	82	11	2288	1005	383	923	.415	54	168	.321	185	235	.787	76	185	261	160	171	1	75	17	101	27.9	12.3	3.2	2.0	.360
01-02	Phoenix	41	1	877	435	166	416	.399	47	147	.320	56	67	.836	38	86	124	81	60	0	31	4	40	21.4	10.6	3.0	2.0	.425
01-02	Boston	22	16	570	162	60	172	.349	20	67	.299	22	30	.733	20	59	79	51	38	0	22	6	19	25.9	7.4	3.6	2.3	.307
02-03	Boston	67	39	1873	654	233	560	.416	120	304	.395	68	87	.782	41	191	232	146	124	0	72	10	69	28.0	9.8	3.5	2.2	.360
NBA Season Totals		432	91	9468	3911	1487	3657	.407	360	1061	.339	577	751	.768	291	818	1109	859	665	2	360	66	481	21.9	9.1	2.6	2.0	....
96-97	Charlotte	3	1	85	31	13	31	.419	5	13	.385	0	0	.000	5	5	10	6	10	0	2	0	2	28.3	10.3	3.3	2.0	.298
99-00	Sacramento	5	0	101	56	18	41	.439	3	5	.600	17	23	.739	11	7	18	7	11	0	3	0	8	20.2	11.2	3.6	1.4	.464
00-01	Phoenix	4	0	114	47	18	43	.419	4	10	.400	7	11	.636	5	11	16	4	7	0	3	0	5	28.5	11.8	4.0	1.0	.321
01-02	Boston	14	0	227	66	23	65	.354	13	33	.394	7	12	.583	8	26	34	16	13	0	8	5	15	16.2	4.7	2.4	1.1	.292
02-03	Boston	10	10	368	158	54	114	.474	22	49	.449	28	32	.875	5	42	47	36	24	0	12	4	13	36.8	15.8	4.7	3.6	.477
NBA Playoff Totals		36	11	895	358	126	294	.429	47	110	.427	59	78	.756	34	91	125	69	65	0	28	9	43	24.9	9.9	3.5	1.9	....

• DELONG, Nate
Nathan J. DeLong

Born: Jan. 5, 1926. Height: 6'6". Weight: 220 lbs. Drafted: 1950 College: Wisconsin (River Falls)

YEAR	TEAM	GP	GS	MIN	PTS	FGM	FGA	FG%	3PM	3PA	3P%	FTM	FTA	FT%	ORB	DRB	TRB	AST	PF	DQ	STL	BLK	TO	MPG	PPG	RPG	APG	PCM
51-52	Milwaukee	17	....	132	64	20	42	.476	....	....	....	24	35	.686	....	....	31	14	47	3	....	....	....	7.8	3.8	1.8	0.8	.514
NBA Season Totals		17	....	132	64	20	42	.476	....	....	....	24	35	.686	....	....	31	14	47	3	....	....	....	7.8	3.8	1.8	0.8	....

YEAR TEAM	GP	GS	MIN	PTS	FGM	FGA	FG%	3PM	3PA	3P%	FTM	FTA	FT%	ORB	DRB	TRB	AST	PF	DQ	STL	BLK	TO	MPG	PPG	RPG	APG	PCM

• DEMBO, Fennis

Fennis Marx Dembo

Born: Jan. 24, 1966. Mobile, AL, United States.　　Height: 6'5".　　Weight: 215 lbs.　　Drafted: 1988　　College: Wyoming

YEAR TEAM	GP	GS	MIN	PTS	FGM	FGA	FG%	3PM	3PA	3P%	FTM	FTA	FT%	ORB	DRB	TRB	AST	PF	DQ	STL	BLK	TO	MPG	PPG	RPG	APG	PCM
88-89 Detroit	31	0	74	36	14	42	.333	0	4	.000	8	10	.800	8	15	23	5	15	0	1	0	6	2.4	1.2	0.7	0.2	.326
NBA Season Totals	31	0	74	36	14	42	.333	0	4	.000	8	10	.800	8	15	23	5	15	0	1	0	6	2.4	1.2	0.7	0.2	....
88-89 Detroit	2	0	4	2	1	1	1.000	0	0	.000	0	0	.000	0	0	0	0	1	0	0	0	1	2.0	1.0	0.0	0.0	.151
NBA Playoff Totals	2	0	4	2	1	1	1.000	0	0	.000	0	0	.000	0	0	0	0	1	0	0	0	1	2.0	1.0	0.0	0.0	....

• DEMBO, Harold

Harold Dembo

Born: —.　　Height: —　　Weight: —　　Drafted: —　　College: Illinois Wesleyan

YEAR TEAM	GP	GS	MIN	PTS	FGM	FGA	FG%	3PM	3PA	3P%	FTM	FTA	FT%	ORB	DRB	TRB	AST	PF	DQ	STL	BLK	TO	MPG	PPG	RPG	APG	PCM
39-40 Chicago-N	2	....	....	2	1	....	....	....	....	....	0	....	....	....	....	....	....	....	....	....	....	....		1.0	....	....	....
NBL Season Totals	2	....	....	2	1	....	....	....	....	....	0	....	....	....	....	....	....	....	....	....	....	....		1.0	....	....	....

• DEMIC, Larry

Lawrence Curtis Demic

Born: June 27, 1957. Gary, IN, United States.　　Height: 6'9".　　Weight: 225 lbs.　　Drafted: 1979　　College: Arizona

YEAR TEAM	GP	GS	MIN	PTS	FGM	FGA	FG%	3PM	3PA	3P%	FTM	FTA	FT%	ORB	DRB	TRB	AST	PF	DQ	STL	BLK	TO	MPG	PPG	RPG	APG	PCM
79-80 New York	82	....	1872	570	230	528	.436	0	0	.000	110	183	.601	195	288	483	64	306	10	56	30	164	22.8	7.0	5.9	0.8	.302
80-81 New York	76	....	964	314	128	254	.504	0	2	.000	58	92	.630	114	129	243	28	153	1	12	13	61	12.7	4.1	3.2	0.4	.346
81-82 New York	48	0	356	92	39	83	.470	0	1	.000	14	39	.359	29	50	79	14	65	1	4	6	24	7.4	1.9	1.6	0.3	.239
NBA Season Totals	206	0	3192	976	397	865	.459	0	3	.000	182	314	.580	338	467	805	106	524	11	72	49	249	15.5	4.7	3.9	0.5	....
80-81 New York	2	....	37	9	4	5	.800	0	0	.000	1	2	.500	5	2	7	0	3	0	0	1	0	18.5	4.5	3.5	0.0	.366
NBA Playoff Totals	2	....	37	9	4	5	.800	0	0	.000	1	2	.500	5	2	7	0	3	0	0	1	0	18.5	4.5	3.5	0.0	....

• DEMPS, Dell

Dell Demps

Born: Feb. 12, 1970. Long Beach, CA, United States.　　Height: 6'3".　　Weight: 205 lbs.　　Drafted: —　　College: Pacific

YEAR TEAM	GP	GS	MIN	PTS	FGM	FGA	FG%	3PM	3PA	3P%	FTM	FTA	FT%	ORB	DRB	TRB	AST	PF	DQ	STL	BLK	TO	MPG	PPG	RPG	APG	PCM
93-94 Golden State	2	0	11	4	2	6	.333	0	0	.000	0	2	.000	0	0	0	1	1	0	2	0	1	5.5	2.0	0.0	0.5	.087
95-96 San Antonio	16	0	87	53	19	33	.576	1	2	.500	14	17	.824	2	7	9	8	10	0	3	1	13	5.4	3.3	0.6	0.5	.485
96-97 Orlando	2	0	10	2	0	3	.000	0	1	.000	2	2	1.000	0	0	0	0	1	0	1	0	0	5.0	1.0	0.0	0.0	-.033
NBA Season Totals	20	0	108	59	21	42	.500	1	3	.333	16	21	.762	2	7	9	9	12	0	6	1	14	5.4	3.0	0.5	0.5	....

• DEMPSEY, George

George P. Dempsey

Born: July 19, 1929. Philadelphia, PA, United States.　　Height: 6'2".　　Weight: 190 lbs.　　Drafted: 1951　　College: King's (DE)

YEAR TEAM	GP	GS	MIN	PTS	FGM	FGA	FG%	3PM	3PA	3P%	FTM	FTA	FT%	ORB	DRB	TRB	AST	PF	DQ	STL	BLK	TO	MPG	PPG	RPG	APG	PCM
54-55 Philadelphia	48	....	1387	352	127	360	.353	....	....	....	98	141	.695	....	....	236	174	141	1	....	....	....	28.9	7.3	4.9	3.6	.362
55-56 Philadelphia	72	....	1444	340	126	265	.475	....	....	....	88	139	.633	....	....	264	205	146	7	....	....	....	20.1	4.7	3.7	2.8	.425
56-57 Philadelphia	71	....	1147	323	134	302	.444	....	....	....	55	102	.539	....	....	251	136	107	0	....	....	....	16.2	4.5	3.5	1.9	.434
57-58 Philadelphia	67	....	1048	294	112	311	.360	....	....	....	70	105	.667	....	....	214	128	113	0	....	....	....	15.6	4.4	3.2	1.9	.395
58-59 Philadelphia	23	....	284	95	36	75	.480	....	....	....	23	33	.697	....	....	60	32	31	0	....	....	....	12.3	4.1	2.6	1.4	.476
58-59 Syracuse	34	....	410	170	56	140	.400	....	....	....	58	73	.795	....	....	100	36	64	0	....	....	....	12.1	5.0	2.9	1.1	.481
NBA Season Totals	315	....	5720	1574	591	1453	.407	....	....	....	392	593	.661	....	....	1125	711	602	8	....	....	....	18.2	5.0	3.6	2.3	....
55-56 Philadelphia	10	....	134	38	12	30	.400	....	....	....	14	20	.700	....	....	25	13	11	0	....	....	....	13.4	3.8	2.5	1.3	.395
56-57 Philadelphia	2	....	74	25	9	21	.429	....	....	....	7	16	.438	....	....	15	12	5	0	....	....	....	37.0	12.5	7.5	6.0	.501
57-58 Philadelphia	8	....	101	33	14	28	.500	....	....	....	5	9	.556	....	....	18	6	11	0	....	....	....	12.6	4.1	2.3	0.8	.377
58-59 Syracuse	5	....	29	9	3	8	.375	....	....	....	3	4	.750	....	....	6	4	8	0	....	....	....	5.8	1.8	1.2	0.8	.392
NBA Playoff Totals	25	....	338	105	38	87	.437	....	....	....	29	49	.592	....	....	64	35	35	0	....	....	....	13.5	4.2	2.6	1.4	....

• DENNARD, Kenny

Kenneth Stephen Dennard

Born: Oct. 18, 1958. King, NC, United States.　　Height: 6'8".　　Weight: 220 lbs.　　Drafted: 1981　　College: Duke

YEAR TEAM	GP	GS	MIN	PTS	FGM	FGA	FG%	3PM	3PA	3P%	FTM	FTA	FT%	ORB	DRB	TRB	AST	PF	DQ	STL	BLK	TO	MPG	PPG	RPG	APG	PCM
81-82 Kansas City	30	3	607	150	62	121	.512	0	0	.000	26	40	.650	47	86	133	42	81	0	35	8	36	20.2	5.0	4.4	1.4	.373
82-83 Kansas City	22	0	224	28	11	34	.324	0	0	.000	6	9	.667	20	32	52	6	27	0	16	1	4	10.2	1.3	2.4	0.3	.263
83-84 Denver	43	0	413	90	36	99	.364	3	10	.300	15	24	.625	37	64	101	45	83	0	23	8	30	9.6	2.1	2.3	1.0	.319
NBA Season Totals	95	3	1244	268	109	254	.429	3	10	.300	47	73	.644	104	182	286	93	191	0	74	17	70	13.1	2.8	3.0	1.0	....

• DENNING, Blaine

Blaine Denning

Born: Sept. 19, 1930.　　Height: 6'2".　　Weight: 175 lbs.　　Drafted: 1952　　College: Lawrence Tech

YEAR TEAM	GP	GS	MIN	PTS	FGM	FGA	FG%	3PM	3PA	3P%	FTM	FTA	FT%	ORB	DRB	TRB	AST	PF	DQ	STL	BLK	TO	MPG	PPG	RPG	APG	PCM
52-53 Baltimore	1	....	9	5	2	5	.400	....	....	....	1	1	1.000	....	....	4	0	3	0	....	....	....	9.0	5.0	4.0	0.0	.515
NBA Season Totals	1	....	9	5	2	5	.400	....	....	....	1	1	1.000	....	....	4	0	3	0	....	....	....	9.0	5.0	4.0	0.0	....

• DENTON, Randy

Randall Drew Denton

Born: Feb. 18, 1949. Raleigh, NC, United States.　　Height: 6'10".　　Weight: 240 lbs.　　Drafted: 1971　　College: Duke

YEAR TEAM	GP	GS	MIN	PTS	FGM	FGA	FG%	3PM	3PA	3P%	FTM	FTA	FT%	ORB	DRB	TRB	AST	PF	DQ	STL	BLK	TO	MPG	PPG	RPG	APG	PCM
71-72 Carolina-A	39	....	710	333	147	339	.434	0	1	.000	39	55	.709	98	162	260	33	67	0	....	....	50	18.2	8.5	6.7	0.8	.554
71-72 Memphis-A	42	....	1329	662	283	596	.475	0	1	.000	96	113	.850	180	300	480	33	113	1	....	....	61	31.6	15.8	11.4	0.8	.593
72-73 Memphis-A	66	....	2205	1124	472	979	.482	3	8	.375	177	237	.747	276	544	820	98	197	2	....	....	124	33.4	17.0	12.4	1.5	.634
73-74 Memphis-A	79	....	2218	1050	447	902	.496	0	3	.000	156	197	.792	255	522	777	152	225	....	55	35	164	28.1	13.3	9.8	1.9	.625
74-75 Utah-A	75	....	1482	692	300	597	.503	0	0	.000	92	120	.767	154	319	473	90	176	....	29	43	99	19.8	9.2	6.3	1.2	.579

YEAR	TEAM	GP	GS	MIN	PTS	FGM	FGA	FG%	3PM	3PA	3P%	FTM	FTA	FT%	ORB	DRB	TRB	AST	PF	DQ	STL	BLK	TO	MPG	PPG	RPG	APG	PCM
75-76	St. Louis-A	51	....	949	373	166	395	.420	0	1	.000	41	53	.774	87	207	294	49	109	....	25	19	52	18.6	7.3	5.8	1.0	.455
75-76	Utah-A	16	....	591	276	117	239	.490	0	0	.000	42	46	.913	69	156	225	40	71	....	12	13	31	36.9	17.3	14.1	2.5	.641
76-77	Atlanta	45	....	700	239	103	256	.402	....	....	....	33	47	.702	81	137	218	33	100	1	14	16	....	15.6	5.3	4.8	0.7	.405
NBA Season Totals		45	....	700	239	103	256	.402	....	....	....	33	47	.702	81	137	218	33	100	1	14	16	....	15.6	5.3	4.8	0.7	....
ABA Season Totals		368	....	9484	4510	1932	4047	.477	3	14	.214	643	821	.783	1119	2210	3329	495	958	3	121	110	581	25.8	12.3	9.0	1.3	....
Career Totals		413	....	10184	4749	2035	4303	.473	3	14	.214	676	868	.779	1200	2347	3547	528	1058	4	135	126	581	24.7	11.5	8.6	1.3	....
74-75	Utah-A	6	....	236	113	49	92	.533	0	0	.000	15	22	.682	28	52	80	11	18	....	4	2	15	39.3	18.8	13.3	1.8	.623
ABA Playoff Totals		6	....	236	113	49	92	.533	0	0	.000	15	22	.682	28	52	80	11	18	....	4	2	15	39.3	18.8	13.3	1.8	....

• DEPRE, Joe

Joe DePre

Born: Dec. 19, 1947. Westbury, NY, United States.   Height: 6'3".   Weight: 185 lbs.   Drafted: 1970   College: St. John's (NY)

YEAR	TEAM	GP	GS	MIN	PTS	FGM	FGA	FG%	3PM	3PA	3P%	FTM	FTA	FT%	ORB	DRB	TRB	AST	PF	DQ	STL	BLK	TO	MPG	PPG	RPG	APG	PCM
70-71	New York-A	72	....	1707	632	250	488	.512	0	4	.000	132	172	.767	55	120	175	138	262	6	....	....	137	23.7	8.8	2.4	1.9	.367
71-72	New York-A	46	....	562	194	79	201	.393	2	6	.333	34	54	.630	16	33	49	45	80	0	....	....	66	12.2	4.2	1.1	1.0	.243
72-73	New York-A	1	....	12	4	2	4	.500	0	0	.000	0	0	.000	2	0	2	2	1	0	....	....	0	12.0	4.0	2.0	2.0	.479
ABA Season Totals		119	....	2281	830	331	693	.478	2	10	.200	166	226	.735	73	153	226	185	343	6	....	....	203	19.2	7.0	1.9	1.6	....
70-71	New York-A	6	....	171	73	29	55	.527	0	1	.000	15	19	.789	10	8	18	13	32	2	....	....	16	28.5	12.2	3.0	2.2	.396
71-72	New York-A	14	....	74	15	5	24	.208	1	2	.500	4	8	.500	....	8	8	6	13	....	....	....	6	5.3	1.1	0.6	0.4	.062
ABA Playoff Totals		20	....	245	88	34	79	.430	1	3	.333	19	27	.704	10	8	26	19	45	2	....	....	22	12.3	4.4	1.3	1.0	....

• DERLINE, Rod

Rodney G. Derline

Born: Mar. 11, 1952. Elma, WA, United States.   Height: 6'   Weight: 175 lbs.   Drafted: 1974   College: Seattle

YEAR	TEAM	GP	GS	MIN	PTS	FGM	FGA	FG%	3PM	3PA	3P%	FTM	FTA	FT%	ORB	DRB	TRB	AST	PF	DQ	STL	BLK	TO	MPG	PPG	RPG	APG	PCM
74-75	Seattle	58	....	666	327	142	332	.428	....	....	....	43	56	.768	12	47	59	45	47	0	23	4	....	11.5	5.6	1.0	0.8	.362
75-76	Seattle	49	....	339	191	73	181	.403	....	....	....	45	56	.804	8	19	27	26	22	0	11	1	....	6.9	3.9	0.6	0.5	.404
NBA Season Totals		107	....	1005	518	215	513	.419	....	....	....	88	112	.786	20	66	86	71	69	0	34	5	....	9.4	4.8	0.8	0.7	....
74-75	Seattle	6	....	64	42	18	33	.545	....	....	....	6	7	.857	1	12	13	7	6	0	2	0	....	10.7	7.0	2.2	1.2	.708
75-76	Seattle	4	....	41	6	2	10	.200	....	....	....	2	2	1.000	1	3	4	1	4	0	1	0	....	10.3	1.5	1.0	0.3	.049
NBA Playoff Totals		10	....	105	48	20	43	.465	....	....	....	8	9	.889	2	15	17	8	10	0	3	0	....	10.5	4.8	1.7	0.8	....

• DEUTSCH, Dave

David Deutsch

Born: May 13, 1945. Brooklyn, NY, United States.   Height: 6'1".   Weight: 170 lbs.   Drafted: 1966   College: Rochester

YEAR	TEAM	GP	GS	MIN	PTS	FGM	FGA	FG%	3PM	3PA	3P%	FTM	FTA	FT%	ORB	DRB	TRB	AST	PF	DQ	STL	BLK	TO	MPG	PPG	RPG	APG	PCM
66-67	New York	19	....	93	21	6	36	.167	....	....	....	9	20	.450	....	....	21	15	17	0	....	....	....	4.9	1.1	1.1	0.8	.223
NBA Season Totals		19	....	93	21	6	36	.167	....	....	....	9	20	.450	....	....	21	15	17	0	....	....	....	4.9	1.1	1.1	0.8	....
66-67	New York	1	....	7	2	1	5	.200	....	....	....	0	0	.000	....	....	3	1	0	0	....	....	....	7.0	2.0	3.0	1.0	.344
NBA Playoff Totals		1	....	7	2	1	5	.200	....	....	....	0	0	.000	....	....	3	1	0	0	....	....	....	7.0	2.0	3.0	1.0	....

• DEVENZIO, Bill

Bill DeVenzio

Born: 1925.   Height: 6'   Weight: 185 lbs.   Drafted: —   College: Geneva

YEAR	TEAM	GP	GS	MIN	PTS	FGM	FGA	FG%	3PM	3PA	3P%	FTM	FTA	FT%	ORB	DRB	TRB	AST	PF	DQ	STL	BLK	TO	MPG	PPG	RPG	APG	PCM
47-48	Syracuse-N	6	....	....	11	2	....	....	....	....	....	7	9	.778	....	....	....	....	....	....	....	....	....	....	1.8	....	....	....
NBL Season Totals		6	....	....	11	2	....	....	....	....	....	7	9	....	....	....	....	....	....	....	....	....	....	....	1.8	....	....	....

• DEVLIN, Corky

Walter James Devlin

Born: Dec. 21, 1931. Died: Apr.28, 1995.   Height: 6'5".   Weight: 195 lbs.   Drafted: 1955   College: George Washington

YEAR	TEAM	GP	GS	MIN	PTS	FGM	FGA	FG%	3PM	3PA	3P%	FTM	FTA	FT%	ORB	DRB	TRB	AST	PF	DQ	STL	BLK	TO	MPG	PPG	RPG	APG	PCM
55-56	Fort Wayne	69	....	1535	546	200	541	.370	....	....	....	146	192	.760	....	....	171	138	119	0	....	....	....	22.2	7.9	2.5	2.0	.342
56-57	Fort Wayne	71	....	1242	477	190	502	.378	....	....	....	97	143	.678	....	....	146	141	114	0	....	....	....	17.5	6.7	2.1	2.0	.379
57-58	Minneapolis	70	....	1248	473	170	489	.348	....	....	....	133	172	.773	....	....	132	167	104	1	....	....	....	17.8	6.8	1.9	2.4	.398
NBA Season Totals		210	....	4025	1496	560	1532	.366	....	....	....	376	507	.742	....	....	449	446	337	1	....	....	....	19.2	7.1	2.1	2.1	....
55-56	Fort Wayne	10	....	275	97	41	101	.406	....	....	....	15	25	.600	....	....	21	23	21	0	....	....	....	27.5	9.7	2.1	2.3	.306
56-57	Fort Wayne	1	....	25	13	6	8	.750	....	....	....	1	1	1.000	....	....	5	5	5	0	....	....	....	25.0	13.0	5.0	5.0	.786
NBA Playoff Totals		11	....	300	110	47	109	.431	....	....	....	16	26	.615	....	....	26	28	26	0	....	....	....	27.3	10.0	2.4	2.5	....

• DEVOLL, Hal

Hal Devoll

Born: 1923.   Height: 6'6".   Weight: 210 lbs.   Drafted: —   College: Lawrence Tech

YEAR	TEAM	GP	GS	MIN	PTS	FGM	FGA	FG%	3PM	3PA	3P%	FTM	FTA	FT%	ORB	DRB	TRB	AST	PF	DQ	STL	BLK	TO	MPG	PPG	RPG	APG	PCM
48-49	Detroit-N	18	....	....	114	46	....	....	....	....	....	22	32	.688	....	....	....	....	....	....	....	....	....	....	6.3	....	....	....
48-49	Hammond-N	9	....	....	11	4	....	....	....	....	....	3	5	.600	....	....	....	....	4	....	....	....	....	....	1.2	....	....	....
NBL Season Totals		27	....	....	125	50	....	....	....	....	....	25	37	....	....	....	....	....	4	....	....	....	....	....	4.6	....	....	....

• DEWEESE, Bob

Bob DeWeese

Born: 1915.   Height: 5'11".   Weight: 160 lbs.   Drafted: —   College: Gallagher Business School

YEAR	TEAM	GP	GS	MIN	PTS	FGM	FGA	FG%	3PM	3PA	3P%	FTM	FTA	FT%	ORB	DRB	TRB	AST	PF	DQ	STL	BLK	TO	MPG	PPG	RPG	APG	PCM
37-38	Kankakee-N	2	....	....	2	1	....	....	....	....	....	0	....	....	....	....	....	....	....	....	....	....	....	....	1.0	....	....	....
NBL Season Totals		2	....	....	2	1	....	....	....	....	....	0	....	....	....	....	....	....	....	....	....	....	....	....	1.0	....	....	....

YEAR	TEAM	GP	GS	MIN	PTS	FGM	FGA	FG%	3PM	3PA	3P%	FTM	FTA	FT%	ORB	DRB	TRB	AST	PF	DQ	STL	BLK	TO	MPG	PPG	RPG	APG	PCM

• DEZONIE, Hank
Henry E. DeZonie

Born: Feb. 12, 1922.　Height: 6'6".　Weight: 215 lbs.　Drafted: —　College: Clark (GA)

YEAR	TEAM	GP	GS	MIN	PTS	FGM	FGA	FG%	3PM	3PA	3P%	FTM	FTA	FT%	ORB	DRB	TRB	AST	PF	DQ	STL	BLK	TO	MPG	PPG	RPG	APG	PCM
48-49	Dayton-N	18	....	....	224	90	....	....	....	....	....	44	59	.746	....	....	....	....	....	....	....	....	....	12.4	....	....	....	....
50-51	Tri-Cities	5	....	....	17	6	25	.240	....	....	....	5	7	.714	....	....	18	9	6	0	....	....	....	3.4	3.6	1.8	....
NBA Season Totals		5	....	....	17	6	25	.240	....	....	....	5	7	.714	....	....	18	9	6	0	....	....	....	3.4	3.6	1.8	....
NBL Season Totals		18	....	....	224	90	....	....	....	....	....	44	59		....	....	....	....	....	....	....	....	....	12.4	....	....	....	....
Career Totals		23	....	....	241	96	25	....	....	....	....	49	66		....	....	18	9	6	0	....	....	....	10.5	0.8	0.4	....

• DIAL, Derrick
Derrick Jonathon Dial

Born: Dec. 20, 1975. Detroit, MI, United States.　Height: 6'4".　Weight: 184 lbs.　Drafted: 1998　College: Eastern Michigan

YEAR	TEAM	GP	GS	MIN	PTS	FGM	FGA	FG%	3PM	3PA	3P%	FTM	FTA	FT%	ORB	DRB	TRB	AST	PF	DQ	STL	BLK	TO	MPG	PPG	RPG	APG	PCM
99-00	San Antonio	8	0	95	40	17	46	.370	3	12	.250	3	5	.600	14	12	26	5	10	0	1	1	6	11.9	5.0	3.3	0.6	.354
00-01	San Antonio	33	0	207	86	36	83	.434	2	10	.200	12	21	.571	12	26	38	21	22	0	4	6	12	6.3	2.6	1.2	0.6	.412
01-02	New Jersey	25	0	249	73	30	94	.319	0	7	.000	13	18	.722	12	33	45	31	12	0	8	4	13	10.0	2.9	1.8	1.2	.326
01-02	Toronto	7	0	50	28	11	26	.423	1	4	.250	5	6	.833	2	9	11	4	1	0	2	0	3	7.1	4.0	1.6	0.6	.539
NBA Season Totals		73	0	601	227	94	249	.378	6	33	.182	33	50	.660	40	80	120	61	45	0	15	11	34	8.2	3.1	1.6	0.8	....
99-00	San Antonio	2	0	8	5	2	4	.500	0	0	.000	1	2	.500	2	0	2	0	1	0	0	0	0	4.0	2.5	1.0	0.0	.512
NBA Playoff Totals		2	0	8	5	2	4	.500	0	0	.000	1	2	.500	2	0	2	0	1	0	0	0	0	4.0	2.5	1.0	0.0	

• DICKAU, Dan
Daniel David Dickau

Born: Sept. 16, 1978. Portland, OR, United States.　Height: 6'　Weight: 190 lbs.　Drafted: 2002　College: Gonzaga

YEAR	TEAM	GP	GS	MIN	PTS	FGM	FGA	FG%	3PM	3PA	3P%	FTM	FTA	FT%	ORB	DRB	TRB	AST	PF	DQ	STL	BLK	TO	MPG	PPG	RPG	APG	PCM
02-03	Atlanta	50	0	515	183	70	170	.412	22	61	.361	21	26	.808	9	34	43	85	66	0	14	2	53	10.3	3.7	0.9	1.7	.307
NBA Season Totals		50	0	515	183	70	170	.412	22	61	.361	21	26	.808	9	34	43	85	66	0	14	2	53	10.3	3.7	0.9	1.7	....

• DICKERSON, Henry
Henry Dickerson

Born: Nov. 27, 1951. Berkley, WV, United States.　Height: 6'4".　Weight: 190 lbs.　Drafted: —　College: Morris-Harvey

YEAR	TEAM	GP	GS	MIN	PTS	FGM	FGA	FG%	3PM	3PA	3P%	FTM	FTA	FT%	ORB	DRB	TRB	AST	PF	DQ	STL	BLK	TO	MPG	PPG	RPG	APG	PCM
75-76	Detroit	17	....	112	28	9	29	.310	....	....	....	10	16	.625	3	0	3	8	17	1	2	1	....	6.6	1.6	0.2	0.5	.113
76-77	Atlanta	6	....	63	17	6	12	.500	....	....	....	5	8	.625	0	2	2	11	13	0	1	0	....	10.5	2.8	0.3	1.8	.304
NBA Season Totals		23		175	45	15	41	.366	....	....	....	15	24	.625	3	2	5	19	30	1	3	1	....	7.6	2.0	0.2	0.8	....
75-76	Detroit	5	....	15	9	4	9	.444	....	....	....	1	2	.500	4	0	4	3	1	0	1	0	....	3.0	1.8	0.8	0.6	.714
NBA Playoff Totals		5	....	15	9	4	9	.444	....	....	....	1	2	.500	4	0	4	3	1	0	1	0	....	3.0	1.8	0.8	0.6	....

• DICKERSON, Michael
Michael DeAngelo Dickerson

Born: June 25, 1975. Greenville, SC, United States.　Height: 6'5".　Weight: 190 lbs.　Drafted: 1998　College: Arizona

YEAR	TEAM	GP	GS	MIN	PTS	FGM	FGA	FG%	3PM	3PA	3P%	FTM	FTA	FT%	ORB	DRB	TRB	AST	PF	DQ	STL	BLK	TO	MPG	PPG	RPG	APG	PCM
98-99	Houston	50	50	1558	547	215	462	.465	71	164	.433	46	72	.639	26	57	83	95	90	0	27	11	66	31.2	10.9	1.7	1.9	.276
99-00	Vancouver	82	82	3103	1496	554	1270	.436	119	291	.409	269	324	.830	78	201	279	208	226	0	116	45	165	37.8	18.2	3.4	2.5	.385
00-01	Vancouver	70	69	2618	1142	425	1020	.417	86	230	.374	206	270	.763	70	159	229	233	207	0	62	27	162	37.4	16.3	3.3	3.3	.337
01-02	Memphis	4	4	124	43	15	48	.313	8	21	.381	5	6	.833	3	9	12	9	12	0	3	1	8	31.0	10.8	3.0	2.3	.196
02-03	Memphis	6	1	87	29	10	24	.417	4	11	.364	5	5	1.000	1	5	6	8	16	0	5	1	6	14.5	4.8	1.0	1.3	.267
NBA Season Totals		212	206	7490	3257	1219	2824	.432	288	717	.402	531	677	.784	178	431	609	553	551	0	213	85	407	35.3	15.4	2.9	2.6	....
98-99	Houston	4	4	82	17	6	22	.273	3	8	.375	2	4	.500	2	2	4	3	8	0	2	3	2	20.5	4.3	1.0	0.8	.096
NBA Playoff Totals		4	4	82	17	6	22	.273	3	8	.375	2	4	.500	2	2	4	3	8	0	2	3	2	20.5	4.3	1.0	0.8	....

• DICKEY, Clyde
Clyde L. Dickey

Born: Dec. 14, 1951. Fort Wayne, IN, United States.　Height: 6'3".　Weight: 185 lbs.　Drafted: 1974　College: Boise State

YEAR	TEAM	GP	GS	MIN	PTS	FGM	FGA	FG%	3PM	3PA	3P%	FTM	FTA	FT%	ORB	DRB	TRB	AST	PF	DQ	STL	BLK	TO	MPG	PPG	RPG	APG	PCM
74-75	Utah-A	58	....	472	160	71	203	.350	2	15	.133	16	21	.762	12	49	61	47	46	....	14	0	45	8.1	2.8	1.1	0.8	.268
ABA Season Totals		58	....	472	160	71	203	.350	2	15	.133	16	21	.762	12	49	61	47	46	....	14	0	45	8.1	2.8	1.1	0.8	....
74-75	Utah-A	1	....	4	0	0	2	.000	0	0	.000	0	0	.000	0	1	1	0	0	....	0	0	1	4.0	0.0	1.0	0.0	-.222
ABA Playoff Totals		1	....	4	0	0	2	.000	0	0	.000	0	0	.000	0	1	1	0	0	....	0	0	1	4.0	0.0	1.0	0.0	....

• DICKEY, Derrek
Derrek Dickey

Born: Mar. 20, 1951. Cincinnati, OH, United States. Died: June 25, 2002.　Height: 6'7".　Weight: 218 lbs.　Drafted: 1973　College: Cincinnati

YEAR	TEAM	GP	GS	MIN	PTS	FGM	FGA	FG%	3PM	3PA	3P%	FTM	FTA	FT%	ORB	DRB	TRB	AST	PF	DQ	STL	BLK	TO	MPG	PPG	RPG	APG	PCM
73-74	Golden State	66	....	930	281	115	233	.494	....	....	....	51	66	.773	123	216	339	54	112	1	17	15	....	14.1	4.3	5.1	0.8	.513
74-75	Golden State	80	....	1859	614	274	569	.482	....	....	....	66	99	.667	190	360	550	125	199	0	52	19	....	23.2	7.7	6.9	1.6	.471
75-76	Golden State	79	....	1207	502	220	473	.465	....	....	....	62	79	.785	114	235	349	83	141	1	26	11	....	15.3	6.4	4.4	1.1	.507
76-77	Golden State	49	....	856	361	158	345	.458	....	....	....	45	61	.738	100	140	240	63	101	1	20	11	....	17.5	7.4	4.9	1.3	.500
77-78	Golden State	22	....	273	136	60	130	.462	....	....	....	16	17	.941	21	28	49	11	29	0	10	2	18	12.4	6.2	2.2	0.5	.409
77-78	Chicago	25	....	220	68	27	68	.397	....	....	....	14	19	.737	15	33	48	10	27	0	4	2	23	8.8	2.7	1.9	0.4	.257
NBA Season Totals		321	....	5345	1962	854	1818	.470	....	....	....	254	341	.745	563	1012	1575	346	609	3	129	60	41	16.7	6.1	4.9	1.1	....
74-75	Golden State	15	....	257	103	47	78	.603	....	....	....	9	16	.563	20	53	73	11	28	1	8	0	....	17.1	6.9	4.9	0.7	.531
75-76	Golden State	12	....	173	76	31	62	.500	....	....	....	14	17	.824	18	24	42	6	27	0	2	1	....	14.4	6.3	3.5	0.5	.459
NBA Playoff Totals		27	....	430	179	78	140	.557	....	....	....	23	33	.697	38	77	115	17	55	1	10	1	....	15.9	6.6	4.3	0.6	....

• DICKEY, Dick
Richard Lea Dickey

Born: Oct. 26, 1926. Grant County, IN, United States. Height: 6'1". Weight: 175 lbs. Drafted: 1950 College: North Carolina State

YEAR	TEAM	GP	GS	MIN	PTS	FGM	FGA	FG%	3PM	3PA	3P%	FTM	FTA	FT%	ORB	DRB	TRB	AST	PF	DQ	STL	BLK	TO	MPG	PPG	RPG	APG	PCM
51-52	Boston	45	....	440	127	40	136	.294	....	....	....	47	69	.681	....	....	81	50	79	2	....	....	....	9.8	2.8	1.8	1.1	.329
NBA Season Totals		45	....	440	127	40	136	.294	....	....	....	47	69	.681	....	....	81	50	79	2	....	....	....	9.8	2.8	1.8	1.1	....
51-52	Boston	3	....	31	8	1	8	.125	....	....	....	6	7	.857	....	....	3	5	7	0	....	....	....	10.3	2.7	1.0	1.7	.282
NBA Playoff Totals		3	....	31	8	1	8	.125	....	....	....	6	7	.857	....	....	3	5	7	0	....	....	....	10.3	2.7	1.0	1.7	....

• DICKSON, John
John Dickson

Born: Nov. 18, 1945. Searcy, AR, United States. Height: 6'10". Weight: 240 lbs. Drafted: 1967 College: Arkansas State

YEAR	TEAM	GP	GS	MIN	PTS	FGM	FGA	FG%	3PM	3PA	3P%	FTM	FTA	FT%	ORB	DRB	TRB	AST	PF	DQ	STL	BLK	TO	MPG	PPG	RPG	APG	PCM
67-68	New Orleans-A	21	....	100	36	14	39	.359	0	0	.000	8	13	.615	....	....	33	3	11	0	....	....	10	4.8	1.7	1.6	0.1	.395
ABA Season Totals		21	....	100	36	14	39	.359	0	0	.000	8	13	.615	....	....	33	3	11	0	....	....	10	4.8	1.7	1.6	0.1	....
67-68	New Orleans-A	1	....	3	0	0	4	.000	0	0	.000	0	0	.000	....	....	2	0	0	0	....	....	1	3.0	0.0	2.0	0.0	-.553
ABA Playoff Totals		1	....	3	0	0	4	.000	0	0	.000	0	0	.000	....	....	2	0	0	0	....	....	1	3.0	0.0	2.0	0.0	....

• DIENELT, Hans
Hans (Whitey) Dienelt

Born: 1921. Height: 6' Weight: 185 lbs. Drafted: — College: Indiana

YEAR	TEAM	GP	GS	MIN	PTS	FGM	FGA	FG%	3PM	3PA	3P%	FTM	FTA	FT%	ORB	DRB	TRB	AST	PF	DQ	STL	BLK	TO	MPG	PPG	RPG	APG	PCM
46-47	Fort Wayne-N	13	....	....	11	4	....	....	....	....	....	3	4	.750	....	....	....	....	....	....	....	....	....	....	0.8	....	....	....
NBL Season Totals		13	....	....	11	4	....	....	....	....	....	3	4	....	....	....	....	....	....	....	....	....	....	....	0.8	....	....	....
46-47	Fort Wayne-N	1	....	....	1	0	....	....	....	....	....	1	2	.500	....	....	....	....	....	....	....	....	....	....	1.0	....	....	....
NBL Playoff Totals		1	....	....	1	0	....	....	....	....	....	1	2	....	....	....	....	....	....	....	....	....	....	....	1.0	....	....	....

• DIERKING, Connie
Conrad William Dierking

Born: Oct. 2, 1936. Brooklyn, NY, United States. Height: 6'9". Weight: 222 lbs. Drafted: 1958 College: Cincinnati

YEAR	TEAM	GP	GS	MIN	PTS	FGM	FGA	FG%	3PM	3PA	3P%	FTM	FTA	FT%	ORB	DRB	TRB	AST	PF	DQ	STL	BLK	TO	MPG	PPG	RPG	APG	PCM
58-59	Syracuse	64	....	726	293	105	290	.362	....	....	....	83	140	.593	....	....	233	34	148	2	....	....	....	11.3	4.6	3.6	0.5	.406
59-60	Syracuse	71	....	1119	492	192	526	.365	....	....	....	108	188	.574	....	....	456	54	168	3	....	....	....	15.8	6.9	6.4	0.8	.498
63-64	Philadelphia	76	....	1286	496	191	514	.372	....	....	....	114	169	.675	....	....	422	50	221	3	....	....	....	16.9	6.5	5.6	0.7	.410
64-65	Philadelphia	38	....	729	296	121	311	.389	....	....	....	54	83	.651	....	....	239	42	101	3	....	....	....	19.2	7.8	6.3	1.1	.460
64-65	San Francisco	30	....	565	240	97	227	.427	....	....	....	46	85	.541	....	....	196	30	64	1	....	....	....	18.8	8.0	6.5	1.0	.510
65-66	Cincinnati	57	....	782	318	134	322	.416	....	....	....	50	82	.610	....	....	245	43	113	0	....	....	....	13.7	5.6	4.3	0.8	.458
66-67	Cincinnati	77	....	1905	716	291	729	.399	....	....	....	134	180	.744	....	....	603	158	251	7	....	....	....	24.7	9.3	7.8	2.1	.483
67-68	Cincinnati	81	....	2637	1325	544	1164	.467	....	....	....	237	310	.765	....	....	766	191	315	6	....	....	....	32.6	16.4	9.5	2.4	.575
68-69	Cincinnati	82	....	2540	1335	546	1232	.443	....	....	....	243	319	.762	....	....	739	222	305	9	....	....	....	31.0	16.3	9.0	2.7	.582
69-70	Cincinnati	76	....	2448	1272	521	1243	.419	....	....	....	230	306	.752	....	....	624	169	275	7	....	....	....	32.2	16.7	8.2	2.2	.499
70-71	Cincinnati	1	....	23	6	3	16	.188	....	....	....	0	0	.000	....	....	7	1	5	0	....	....	....	23.0	6.0	7.0	1.0	-.007
70-71	Philadelphia	53	....	714	305	122	306	.399	....	....	....	61	89	.685	....	....	227	59	109	1	....	....	....	13.5	5.8	4.3	1.1	.491
NBA Season Totals		706	....	15474	7094	2867	6880	.417	....	....	....	1360	1951	.697	....	....	4757	1053	2075	42	....	....	....	21.9	10.0	6.7	1.5	....
58-59	Syracuse	4	....	34	11	2	12	.167	....	....	....	7	9	.778	....	....	17	2	5	0	....	....	....	8.5	2.8	4.3	0.5	.474
59-60	Syracuse	3	....	32	12	6	20	.300	....	....	....	0	1	.000	....	....	15	1	6	0	....	....	....	10.7	4.0	5.0	0.3	.355
63-64	Philadelphia	5	....	71	33	14	33	.424	....	....	....	5	9	.556	....	....	30	5	10	0	....	....	....	14.2	6.6	6.0	1.0	.595
65-66	Cincinnati	4	....	64	27	9	18	.500	....	....	....	9	10	.900	....	....	15	1	11	0	....	....	....	16.0	6.8	3.8	0.3	.441
66-67	Cincinnati	4	....	151	70	32	75	.427	....	....	....	6	6	1.000	....	....	52	14	13	0	....	....	....	37.8	17.5	13.0	3.5	.588
NBA Playoff Totals		20	....	352	153	63	158	.399	....	....	....	27	35	.771	....	....	129	23	45	0	....	....	....	17.6	7.7	6.5	1.2	....

• DIETRICK, Coby
Coby Joseph Dietrick

Born: July 23, 1948. Riverside, CA, United States. Height: 6'10". Weight: 220 lbs. Drafted: 1970 College: San Jose State

YEAR	TEAM	GP	GS	MIN	PTS	FGM	FGA	FG%	3PM	3PA	3P%	FTM	FTA	FT%	ORB	DRB	TRB	AST	PF	DQ	STL	BLK	TO	MPG	PPG	RPG	APG	PCM
70-71	Memphis-A	37	....	357	143	61	160	.381	0	1	.000	21	34	.618	39	75	114	33	56	0	....	....	37	9.6	3.9	3.1	0.9	.468
71-72	Memphis-A	1	....	9	2	1	2	.500	0	0	.000	0	2	.000	3	4	7	1	1	0	....	....	1	9.0	2.0	7.0	1.0	.786
72-73	Dallas-A	77	....	1347	506	205	489	.419	0	0	.000	96	139	.691	133	244	377	136	224	5	....	88	93	17.5	6.6	4.9	1.8	.460
73-74	San Antonio-A	84	....	2142	583	251	569	.441	0	3	.000	81	114	.711	200	332	532	253	285	....	89	50	151	25.5	6.9	6.3	3.0	.429
74-75	San Antonio-A	82	....	1724	522	222	444	.500	2	4	.500	76	99	.768	191	333	524	168	266	....	82	55	117	21.0	6.4	6.4	2.0	.492
75-76	San Antonio-A	81	....	1467	469	200	403	.496	1	7	.143	68	82	.829	109	240	349	159	257	....	67	43	112	18.1	5.8	4.3	2.0	.446
76-77	San Antonio	82	....	1772	689	285	620	.460	....	....	....	119	166	.717	111	261	372	148	267	8	88	57	....	21.6	8.4	4.5	1.8	.425
77-78	San Antonio	79	....	1876	589	250	543	.460	....	....	....	89	114	.781	73	285	358	217	231	4	81	55	142	23.7	7.5	4.5	2.7	.412
78-79	San Antonio	76	....	1487	497	209	400	.523	....	....	....	79	99	.798	88	227	315	198	206	7	72	38	91	19.6	6.5	4.1	2.6	.499
79-80	Chicago	79	....	1830	545	227	500	.454	1	9	.111	90	118	.763	101	262	363	216	230	2	89	51	111	23.2	6.9	4.6	2.7	.422
80-81	Chicago	82	....	1243	371	146	320	.456	2	6	.333	77	111	.694	79	186	265	118	176	1	48	53	90	15.2	4.5	3.2	1.4	.400
81-82	Chicago	74	0	999	222	92	200	.460	0	1	.000	38	54	.704	63	125	188	87	131	1	49	30	44	13.5	3.0	2.5	1.2	.354
82-83	San Antonio	8	0	34	2	1	5	.200	0	0	.000	0	2	.000	2	6	8	6	6	0	1	0	1	4.3	0.3	1.0	0.8	.253
NBA Season Totals		480	0	9241	2915	1210	2588	.468	3	16	.188	492	664	.741	517	1352	1869	990	1247	23	428	284	479	19.3	6.1	3.9	2.1	....
ABA Season Totals		362	....	7046	2225	940	2067	.455	3	15	.200	342	470	.728	675	1228	1903	750	1089	5	238	236	511	19.5	6.1	5.3	2.1	....
Career Totals		842	0	16287	5140	2150	4655	.462	6	31	.194	834	1134	.735	1192	2580	3772	1740	2336	28	666	520	990	19.3	6.1	4.5	2.1	....
70-71	Memphis-A	2	....	10	4	1	4	.250	0	0	.000	2	2	1.000	2	1	3	1	0	0	....	....	0	5.0	2.0	1.5	0.5	.520
73-74	San Antonio-A	7	....	129	34	13	25	.520	0	2	.000	8	12	.667	7	20	27	8	17	....	2	7	7	18.4	4.9	3.9	1.1	.364
74-75	San Antonio-A	6	....	187	69	30	49	.612	0	2	.000	9	11	.818	12	28	40	22	26	....	6	7	14	31.2	11.5	6.7	3.7	.533
75-76	San Antonio-A	7	....	208	62	27	55	.491	0	0	.000	8	13	.615	16	25	41	15	28	....	7	6	17	29.7	8.9	5.9	2.1	.363
76-77	San Antonio	2	....	64	26	12	23	.522	....	....	....	2	6	.333	4	5	9	5	4	0	1	0	....	32.0	13.0	4.5	2.5	.414
77-78	San Antonio	6	....	96	29	14	27	.519	....	....	....	1	2	.500	8	17	25	4	18	1	5	5	9	16.0	4.8	4.2	0.7	.381

YEAR	TEAM	GP	GS	MIN	PTS	FGM	FGA	FG%	3PM	3PA	3P%	FTM	FTA	FT%	ORB	DRB	TRB	AST	PF	DQ	STL	BLK	TO	MPG	PPG	RPG	APG	PCM
78-79	San Antonio	14	....	281	82	39	88	.443	....	....	....	4	8	.500	26	39	65	26	41	0	12	3	18	20.1	5.9	4.6	1.9	.363
80-81	Chicago	6	....	81	19	8	26	.308	0	3	.000	3	4	.750	3	12	15	4	19	0	2	3	2	13.5	3.2	2.5	0.7	.176
NBA Playoff Totals		28	....	522	156	73	164	.445	0	3	.000	10	20	.500	41	73	114	39	82	1	20	11	29	18.6	5.6	4.1	1.4	....
ABA Playoff Totals		22	....	534	169	71	133	.534	0	4	.000	27	38	.711	37	74	111	46	71	0	15	20	38	24.3	7.7	5.0	2.1	....
Career Playoff Totals		50	....	1056	325	144	297	.485	0	7	.000	37	58	.638	78	147	225	85	153	1	35	31	67	21.1	6.5	4.5	1.7	....

● DIETZ, Bob
Bob Dietz

Born: 1917.　Height: 6'1".　Weight: 164 lbs.　Drafted: —　College: Butler

YEAR	TEAM	GP	GS	MIN	PTS	FGM	FGA	FG%	3PM	3PA	3P%	FTM	FTA	FT%	ORB	DRB	TRB	AST	PF	DQ	STL	BLK	TO	MPG	PPG	RPG	APG	PCM
41-42	Indianapolis-N	15	....	....	97	45	....	....	....	....	....	7	....	....											6.5			
45-46	Indianapolis-N	20	....	....	154	66	....					22	38	.579											7.7			
46-47	Indianapolis-N	39	....	....	140	56	....					28	42	.667					54						3.6			
47-48	Indianapolis-N	37	....	....	121	48	....					25	45	.556					68						3.3			
NBL Season Totals		111	....	....	512	215	....					82	125	....					122						4.6			
46-47	Indianapolis-N	4	....	....	2	1	....					0	1	.000											0.5			
47-48	Indianapolis-N	4	....	....	6	3	....					0	1	.000											1.5			
NBL Playoff Totals		8	....	....	8	4	....					0	2	....											1.0			

● DIGREGORIO, Ernie
Ernest (Ernie D.) DiGregorio

Born: Jan. 15, 1951. N. Providence, RI, United States.　Height: 6'　Weight: 180 lbs.　Drafted: 1973　College: Providence

YEAR	TEAM	GP	GS	MIN	PTS	FGM	FGA	FG%	3PM	3PA	3P%	FTM	FTA	FT%	ORB	DRB	TRB	AST	PF	DQ	STL	BLK	TO	MPG	PPG	RPG	APG	PCM
73-74	Buffalo	81	....	2910	1234	530	1260	.421	....			174	193	**.902**	48	171	219	**663**	242	2	59	9		35.9	15.2	2.7	**8.2**	.498
74-75	Buffalo	31	....	712	241	103	234	.440				35	45	.778	6	39	45	151	62	0	19	0		23.0	7.8	1.5	4.9	.436
75-76	Buffalo	67	....	1364	450	182	474	.384				86	94	.915	15	97	112	265	158	1	37	1		20.4	6.7	1.7	4.0	.386
76-77	Buffalo	81	....	2267	868	365	875	.417				138	146	**.945**	52	132	184	378	150	1	57	3		28.0	10.7	2.3	4.7	.418
77-78	LA Lakers	25	....	332	98	41	100	.410				16	20	.800	5	18	23	71	22	0	6	0	45	13.3	3.9	0.9	2.8	.304
77-78	Boston	27	....	274	106	47	109	.431				12	13	.923	2	25	27	66	22	0	12	1	46	10.1	3.9	1.0	2.4	.404
NBA Season Totals		312	....	7859	2997	1268	3052	.415				461	511	.902	128	482	610	1594	656	4	190	14	91	25.2	9.6	2.0	5.1	....
73-74	Buffalo	6	....	240	82	37	86	.430				8	9	.889	3	13	16	52	14	0	1	0		40.0	13.7	2.7	8.7	.447
75-76	Buffalo	9	....	217	68	30	62	.484				8	8	1.000	1	12	13	45	29	2	5	2		24.1	7.6	1.4	5.0	.418
NBA Playoff Totals		15	....	457	150	67	148	.453				16	17	.941	4	25	29	97	43	2	6	2		30.5	10.0	1.9	6.5	....

● DILL, Craig
Craig H. Dill

Born: Dec. 17, 1944.　Height: 6'11".　Weight: 215 lbs.　Drafted: 1967　College: Michigan

YEAR	TEAM	GP	GS	MIN	PTS	FGM	FGA	FG%	3PM	3PA	3P%	FTM	FTA	FT%	ORB	DRB	TRB	AST	PF	DQ	STL	BLK	TO	MPG	PPG	RPG	APG	PCM
67-68	Pittsburgh-A	65	....	1354	445	187	488	.383	0	3	.000	71	106	.670			378	31	164	3			64	20.8	6.8	5.8	0.5	.342
ABA Season Totals		65	....	1354	445	187	488	.383	0	3	.000	71	106	.670			378	31	164	3			64	20.8	6.8	5.8	0.5	....
67-68	Pittsburgh-A	6	....	15	7	3	8	.375	0	0	.000	1	1	1.000			6	2	5	0			3	2.5	1.2	1.0	0.3	.540
ABA Playoff Totals		6	....	15	7	3	8	.375	0	0	.000	1	1	1.000			6	2	5	0			3	2.5	1.2	1.0	0.3	....

● DILLARD, Duane
Duane Dillard

Born: —.　Height: 6'6".　Weight: —　Drafted: —　College: none

YEAR	TEAM	GP	GS	MIN	PTS	FGM	FGA	FG%	3PM	3PA	3P%	FTM	FTA	FT%	ORB	DRB	TRB	AST	PF	DQ	STL	BLK	TO	MPG	PPG	RPG	APG	PCM
75-76	Utah-A	3	....	19	4	1	3	.333	0	0	.000	2	2	1.000	2	7	9	2	7	....	2	2	5	6.3	1.3	3.0	0.7	.491
ABA Season Totals		3	....	19	4	1	3	.333	0	0	.000	2	2	1.000	2	7	9	2	7	....	2	2	5	6.3	1.3	3.0	0.7	....

● DILLARD, Mickey
Mickey Anthony Dillard

Born: Oct. 15, 1958. Hollywood, FL, United States.　Height: 6'3".　Weight: 170 lbs.　Drafted: 1981　College: Florida State

YEAR	TEAM	GP	GS	MIN	PTS	FGM	FGA	FG%	3PM	3PA	3P%	FTM	FTA	FT%	ORB	DRB	TRB	AST	PF	DQ	STL	BLK	TO	MPG	PPG	RPG	APG	PCM
81-82	Cleveland	33	0	221	73	29	79	.367	0	4	.000	15	23	.652	6	9	15	34	40	0	8	2	17	6.7	2.2	0.5	1.0	.221
NBA Season Totals		33	0	221	73	29	79	.367	0	4	.000	15	23	.652	6	9	15	34	40	0	8	2	17	6.7	2.2	0.5	1.0	....

● DILLE, Bob
Robert Orville (Oscar) Dille

Born: July 2, 1917.　Height: 6'3".　Weight: 190 lbs.　Drafted: —　College: Valparaiso

YEAR	TEAM	GP	GS	MIN	PTS	FGM	FGA	FG%	3PM	3PA	3P%	FTM	FTA	FT%	ORB	DRB	TRB	AST	PF	DQ	STL	BLK	TO	MPG	PPG	RPG	APG	PCM
40-41	Hammond-N	3	....	....	19	8	....	....	....	....	....	3	....	....											6.3			
46-47	Detroit	57	....	....	296	111	563	.197				74	111	.667					40	92					5.2		0.7	
NBA Season Totals		57	....	....	296	111	563	.197				74	111	.667					40	92					5.2		0.7	
NBL Season Totals		3	....	....	19	8	....					3	....	....											6.3			
Career Totals		60	....	....	315	119	563	....				77	111	....					40	92					5.3		0.7	

● DILLON, Hooks
John Turley (Hooks) Dillon

Born: Jan. 8, 1924. Savannah, GA, United States.　Height: 6'3".　Weight: 180 lbs.　Drafted: 1948　College: North Carolina

YEAR	TEAM	GP	GS	MIN	PTS	FGM	FGA	FG%	3PM	3PA	3P%	FTM	FTA	FT%	ORB	DRB	TRB	AST	PF	DQ	STL	BLK	TO	MPG	PPG	RPG	APG	PCM
49-50	Washington	22	....	....	36	10	55	.182				16	22	.727					5	19					1.6		0.2	
NBA Season Totals		22	....	....	36	10	55	.182				16	22	.727					5	19					1.6		0.2	
49-50	Washington	1	....	....	4	1	1	1.000				2	2	1.000					0	2					4.0		0.0	
NBA Playoff Totals		1	....	....	4	1	1	1.000				2	2	1.000					0	2					4.0		0.0	

• DINKINS, Byron
Byron Stewart Dinkins

Born: June 15, 1967. Charlotte, NC, United States. Height: 6'1". Weight: 170 lbs. Drafted: — College: North Carolina (Charlotte)

YEAR	TEAM	GP	GS	MIN	PTS	FGM	FGA	FG%	3PM	3PA	3P%	FTM	FTA	FT%	ORB	DRB	TRB	AST	PF	DQ	STL	BLK	TO	MPG	PPG	RPG	APG	PCM
89-90	Houston	33	0	362	115	44	109	.404	1	9	.111	26	30	.867	13	27	40	75	30	0	19	2	36	11.0	3.5	1.2	2.3	.390
90-91	San Antonio	10	0	144	34	13	33	.394	0	0	.000	8	9	.889	0	11	11	19	12	0	2	0	13	14.4	3.4	1.1	1.9	.205
90-91	Indiana	2	0	5	2	1	1	1.000	0	0	.000	0	0	.000	0	1	1	0	3	0	0	0	0	2.5	1.0	0.5	0.0	.307
NBA Season Totals		45	0	511	151	58	143	.406	1	9	.111	34	39	.872	13	39	52	94	45	0	21	2	49	11.4	3.4	1.2	2.1	....

• DINKINS, Jackie
Jackie Dinkins

Born: Jan. 22, 1950. Died: Mar.1983. Height: 6'5". Weight: 210 lbs. Drafted: 1971 College: Voorhees

YEAR	TEAM	GP	GS	MIN	PTS	FGM	FGA	FG%	3PM	3PA	3P%	FTM	FTA	FT%	ORB	DRB	TRB	AST	PF	DQ	STL	BLK	TO	MPG	PPG	RPG	APG	PCM
71-72	Chicago	18	....	89	45	17	41	.415	....	....	....	11	20	.550	....	....	20	7	10	0	....	....	....	4.9	2.5	1.1	0.4	.464
NBA Season Totals		18	....	89	45	17	41	.415	....	....	....	11	20	.550	....	....	20	7	10	0	....	....	....	4.9	2.5	1.1	0.4	....
71-72	Chicago	1	....	1	2	1	1	1.000	....	....	....	0	0	.000	....	....	0	0	0	0	....	....	....	1.0	2.0	0.0	0.0	2.000
NBA Playoff Totals		1	....	1	2	1	1	1.000	....	....	....	0	0	.000	....	....	0	0	0	0	....	....	....	1.0	2.0	0.0	0.0	....

• DINNEL, Harry
Harry Dinnel

Born: 1941. Torrance, CA, United States. Height: 6'4". Weight: 200 lbs. Drafted: 1963 College: Pepperdine

YEAR	TEAM	GP	GS	MIN	PTS	FGM	FGA	FG%	3PM	3PA	3P%	FTM	FTA	FT%	ORB	DRB	TRB	AST	PF	DQ	STL	BLK	TO	MPG	PPG	RPG	APG	PCM
67-68	Anaheim-A	11	....	87	19	6	19	.316	0	0	.000	7	8	.875	....	....	23	5	14	0	....	....	8	7.9	1.7	2.1	0.5	.309
ABA Season Totals		11	....	87	19	6	19	.316	0	0	.000	7	8	.875	....	....	23	5	14	0	....	....	8	7.9	1.7	2.1	0.5	....

• DINWIDDIE, Bill
William E. (Diamond Bill, Widdie) Dinwiddie

Born: July 15, 1943. Height: 6'7". Weight: 220 lbs. Drafted: — College: New Mexico Highlands

YEAR	TEAM	GP	GS	MIN	PTS	FGM	FGA	FG%	3PM	3PA	3P%	FTM	FTA	FT%	ORB	DRB	TRB	AST	PF	DQ	STL	BLK	TO	MPG	PPG	RPG	APG	PCM
67-68	Cincinnati	67	....	871	344	141	358	.394	....	....	....	62	102	.608	....	....	237	31	122	2	....	....	....	13.0	5.1	3.5	0.5	.382
68-69	Cincinnati	69	....	1028	293	124	352	.352	....	....	....	45	87	.517	....	....	242	55	146	0	....	....	....	14.9	4.2	3.5	0.8	.282
70-71	Boston	61	....	717	300	123	328	.375	....	....	....	54	74	.730	....	....	209	34	90	1	....	....	....	11.8	4.9	3.4	0.6	.411
71-72	Milwaukee	23	....	144	37	16	57	.281	....	....	....	5	9	.556	....	....	32	9	23	0	....	....	....	6.3	1.6	1.4	0.4	.193
NBA Season Totals		220	....	2760	974	404	1095	.369	....	....	....	166	272	.610	....	....	720	129	381	3	....	....	....	12.5	4.4	3.3	0.6	....

• DIOP, DeSagana
DeSagana Diop Diop

Born: Jan. 30, 1982. Dakar, Senegal. Height: 7' Weight: 300 lbs. Drafted: 2001 College: none (HS: Oak Hill Academy, VA)

YEAR	TEAM	GP	GS	MIN	PTS	FGM	FGA	FG%	3PM	3PA	3P%	FTM	FTA	FT%	ORB	DRB	TRB	AST	PF	DQ	STL	BLK	TO	MPG	PPG	RPG	APG	PCM
01-02	Cleveland	18	1	109	25	12	29	.414	0	0	.000	1	5	.200	5	12	17	5	19	0	1	10	12	6.1	1.4	0.9	0.3	.176
02-03	Cleveland	80	1	944	119	54	154	.351	0	0	.000	11	30	.367	63	152	215	43	148	4	33	81	56	11.8	1.5	2.7	0.5	.262
NBA Season Totals		98	2	1053	144	66	183	.361	0	0	.000	12	35	.343	68	164	232	48	167	4	34	91	68	10.7	1.5	2.4	0.5	....

• DISCHINGER, Terry
Terry Gilbert Dischinger

Born: Nov. 21, 1940. Terre Haute, IN, United States. Height: 6'7". Weight: 189 lbs. Drafted: 1962 College: Purdue

YEAR	TEAM	GP	GS	MIN	PTS	FGM	FGA	FG%	3PM	3PA	3P%	FTM	FTA	FT%	ORB	DRB	TRB	AST	PF	DQ	STL	BLK	TO	MPG	PPG	RPG	APG	PCM
62-63	Chicago	57	....	2294	1452	525	1026	.512	....	....	....	402	522	.770	....	....	458	175	188	2	....	....	....	40.2	25.5	8.0	3.1	.657
63-64	Baltimore	80	....	2816	1662	604	1217	.496	....	....	....	454	585	.776	....	....	667	157	321	10	....	....	....	35.2	20.8	8.3	2.0	.611
64-65	Detroit	80	....	2698	1456	568	1153	.493	....	....	....	320	424	.755	....	....	479	198	253	5	....	....	....	33.7	18.2	6.0	2.5	.549
67-68	Detroit	78	....	1936	1025	394	797	.494	....	....	....	237	311	.762	....	....	483	114	247	6	....	....	....	24.8	13.1	6.2	1.5	.567
68-69	Detroit	75	....	1456	658	264	513	.515	....	....	....	130	178	.730	....	....	323	93	230	5	....	....	....	19.4	8.8	4.3	1.2	.489
69-70	Detroit	75	....	1754	858	342	650	.526	....	....	....	174	241	.722	....	....	369	106	213	5	....	....	....	23.4	11.4	4.9	1.4	.517
70-71	Detroit	65	....	1855	769	304	568	.535	....	....	....	161	211	.763	....	....	339	113	189	2	....	....	....	28.5	11.8	5.2	1.7	.463
71-72	Detroit	79	....	2062	746	295	574	.514	....	....	....	156	200	.780	....	....	338	92	289	7	....	....	....	26.1	9.4	4.3	1.2	.367
72-73	Portland	63	....	970	386	161	338	.476	....	....	....	64	96	.667	....	....	190	103	125	1	....	....	....	15.4	6.1	3.0	1.6	.461
NBA Season Totals		652	....	17841	9012	3457	6836	.506	....	....	....	2098	2768	.758	....	....	3646	1151	2055	43	....	....	....	27.4	13.8	5.6	1.8	....
67-68	Detroit	6	....	154	56	21	56	.375	....	....	....	14	19	.737	....	....	29	9	19	0	....	....	....	25.7	9.3	4.8	1.5	.341
NBA Playoff Totals		6	....	154	56	21	56	.375	....	....	....	14	19	.737	....	....	29	9	19	0	....	....	....	25.7	9.3	4.8	1.5	....

• DIUTE, Fred
Fred Homer Diute

Born: Jan. 9, 1929. Height: 6'3". Weight: 210 lbs. Drafted: 1951 College: St. Bonaventure

YEAR	TEAM	GP	GS	MIN	PTS	FGM	FGA	FG%	3PM	3PA	3P%	FTM	FTA	FT%	ORB	DRB	TRB	AST	PF	DQ	STL	BLK	TO	MPG	PPG	RPG	APG	PCM
54-55	Milwaukee	7	....	72	11	2	21	.095	....	....	....	7	12	.583	....	....	13	4	12	0	....	....	....	10.3	1.6	1.9	0.6	.071
NBA Season Totals		7	....	72	11	2	21	.095	....	....	....	7	12	.583	....	....	13	4	12	0	....	....	....	10.3	1.6	1.9	0.6	....

• DIVAC, Vlade
Vlade Divac

Born: Feb. 3, 1968. Prijepolje, Yugoslavia. Height: 6'11". Weight: 243 lbs. Drafted: 1989 College: none (HS: Belgrade, YUG)

YEAR	TEAM	GP	GS	MIN	PTS	FGM	FGA	FG%	3PM	3PA	3P%	FTM	FTA	FT%	ORB	DRB	TRB	AST	PF	DQ	STL	BLK	TO	MPG	PPG	RPG	APG	PCM
89-90	LA Lakers	82	5	1611	701	274	549	.499	0	5	.000	153	216	.708	167	345	512	75	240	2	79	114	107	19.6	8.5	6.2	0.9	.584
90-91	LA Lakers	82	81	2310	921	360	637	.565	5	14	.357	196	279	.703	205	461	666	92	247	3	106	127	148	28.2	11.2	8.1	1.1	.566
91-92	LA Lakers	36	18	979	405	157	317	.495	5	19	.263	86	112	.768	87	160	247	60	114	3	55	35	86	27.2	11.3	6.9	1.7	.499
92-93	LA Lakers	82	69	2525	1050	397	819	.485	21	75	.280	235	341	.689	220	509	729	232	311	7	128	136	213	30.8	12.8	8.9	2.8	.569
93-94	LA Lakers	79	73	2685	1123	453	895	.506	9	47	.191	208	303	.686	282	569	851	307	288	5	92	112	190	34.0	14.2	10.8	3.9	.621
94-95	LA Lakers	80	80	2807	1277	485	957	.507	10	53	.189	297	382	.777	261	568	829	329	305	8	109	174	208	35.1	16.0	10.4	4.1	.659
95-96	LA Lakers	79	79	2470	1020	414	807	.513	3	18	.167	189	295	.641	198	481	679	261	274	5	76	131	198	31.3	12.9	8.6	3.3	.565
96-97	Charlotte	81	80	2840	1024	418	847	.494	11	47	.234	177	259	.683	241	484	725	301	277	6	103	180	194	35.1	12.6	9.0	3.7	.541
97-98	Charlotte	64	41	1805	667	267	536	.498	3	14	.214	130	188	.691	183	335	518	172	179	1	83	94	115	28.2	10.4	8.1	2.7	.571
98-99	Sacramento	50	50	1761	714	262	557	.470	11	43	.256	179	255	.702	140	361	501	215	166	2	44	51	131	35.2	14.3	10.0	4.3	.566
99-00	Sacramento	82	81	2374	1005	384	764	.503	7	26	.269	230	333	.691	174	482	656	244	251	2	103	103	190	29.0	12.3	8.0	3.0	.580
00-01	Sacramento	81	81	2420	974	364	755	.482	4	14	.286	242	350	.691	207	466	673	231	242	5	87	93	192	29.9	12.0	8.3	2.9	.543

YEAR	TEAM	GP	GS	MIN	PTS	FGM	FGA	FG%	3PM	3PA	3P%	FTM	FTA	FT%	ORB	DRB	TRB	AST	PF	DQ	STL	BLK	TO	MPG	PPG	RPG	APG	PCM
01-02	Sacramento	80	80	2420	888	338	716	.472	3	13	.231	209	340	.615	205	466	671	297	229	1	79	94	158	30.3	11.1	8.4	3.7	.549
02-03	Sacramento	80	80	2384	795	305	655	.466	6	25	.240	179	251	.713	157	417	574	274	239	3	83	105	152	29.8	9.9	7.2	3.4	.499
NBA Season Totals		1038	898	31391	12564	4878	9811	.497	98	413	.237	2710	3904	.694	2727	6104	8831	3090	3362	53	1227	1549	2282	30.2	12.1	8.5	3.0	....
89-90	LA Lakers	9	1	175	82	32	44	.727	1	2	.500	17	19	.895	16	32	48	10	27	1	8	15	13	19.4	9.1	5.3	1.1	.698
90-91	LA Lakers	19	19	609	252	97	172	.564	1	6	.167	57	71	.803	49	78	127	21	65	2	27	41	41	32.1	13.3	6.7	1.1	.511
91-92	LA Lakers	4	4	143	39	15	43	.349	0	2	.000	9	10	.900	6	16	22	15	17	1	5	3	18	35.8	9.8	5.5	3.8	.223
92-93	LA Lakers	5	5	167	90	37	74	.500	4	9	.444	12	22	.545	17	30	47	28	22	0	6	12	11	33.4	18.0	9.4	5.6	.723
94-95	LA Lakers	10	10	388	156	57	122	.467	2	9	.222	40	62	.645	34	51	85	31	44	2	8	13	28	38.8	15.6	8.5	3.1	.439
95-96	LA Lakers	4	4	115	36	15	35	.429	1	5	.200	5	8	.625	11	19	30	8	10	0	0	5	8	28.8	9.0	7.5	2.0	.391
96-97	Charlotte	3	3	116	54	21	46	.457	0	3	.000	12	15	.800	13	13	26	10	11	0	3	6	6	38.7	18.0	8.7	3.3	.533
97-98	Charlotte	9	9	345	104	42	87	.483	0	1	.000	20	33	.606	25	73	98	31	34	1	7	14	22	38.3	11.6	10.9	3.4	.475
98-99	Sacramento	5	5	198	81	25	56	.446	1	5	.200	30	36	.833	9	41	50	23	17	0	8	4	19	39.6	16.2	10.0	4.6	.540
99-00	Sacramento	5	5	160	56	20	56	.357	0	2	.000	16	23	.696	9	27	36	14	22	0	7	4	9	32.0	11.2	7.2	2.8	.375
00-01	Sacramento	8	8	225	86	28	80	.350	1	3	.333	29	38	.763	20	47	67	19	25	1	8	12	18	28.1	10.8	8.4	2.4	.475
01-02	Sacramento	16	16	535	216	70	151	.464	2	7	.286	74	98	.755	46	103	149	27	76	6	18	20	37	33.4	13.5	9.3	1.7	.491
02-03	Sacramento	12	12	317	137	51	91	.560	0	0	.000	35	52	.673	30	39	69	27	38	0	8	11	16	26.4	11.4	5.8	2.3	.538
NBA Playoff Totals		109	101	3493	1389	510	1057	.482	13	54	.241	356	487	.731	285	569	854	264	408	14	113	160	246	32.0	12.7	7.8	2.4	....

• DIXON, Juan

Juan Dixon

Born: Oct. 9, 1978. Baltimore, MD, United States.   Height: 6'3".   Weight: 164 lbs.   Drafted: 2002   College: Maryland

YEAR	TEAM	GP	GS	MIN	PTS	FGM	FGA	FG%	3PM	3PA	3P%	FTM	FTA	FT%	ORB	DRB	TRB	AST	PF	DQ	STL	BLK	TO	MPG	PPG	RPG	APG	PCM
02-03	Washington	42	3	647	270	104	271	.384	25	84	.298	37	46	.804	13	59	72	40	54	0	26	3	42	15.4	6.4	1.7	1.0	.289
NBA Season Totals		42	3	647	270	104	271	.384	25	84	.298	37	46	.804	13	59	72	40	54	0	26	3	42	15.4	6.4	1.7	1.0	....

• DJORDJEVIC, Aleksandar

Aleksandar Djordjevic

Born: Aug. 26, 1967. Belgrade, Yugoslavia.   Height: 6'2".   Weight: 198 lbs.   Drafted: —   College: none

YEAR	TEAM	GP	GS	MIN	PTS	FGM	FGA	FG%	3PM	3PA	3P%	FTM	FTA	FT%	ORB	DRB	TRB	AST	PF	DQ	STL	BLK	TO	MPG	PPG	RPG	APG	PCM
96-97	Portland	8	0	61	25	8	16	.500	5	7	.714	4	5	.800	1	4	5	5	3	0	0	0	5	7.6	3.1	0.6	0.6	.345
NBA Season Totals		8	0	61	25	8	16	.500	5	7	.714	4	5	.800	1	4	5	5	3	0	0	0	5	7.6	3.1	0.6	0.6	....

• DODD, Earl

Glenn Earl Dodd

Born: Nov. 1, 1924.   Height: 6'5".   Weight: 175 lbs.   Drafted: 1949   College: Northeast Missouri State

YEAR	TEAM	GP	GS	MIN	PTS	FGM	FGA	FG%	3PM	3PA	3P%	FTM	FTA	FT%	ORB	DRB	TRB	AST	PF	DQ	STL	BLK	TO	MPG	PPG	RPG	APG	PCM
49-50	Denver	9	....	....	15	6	27	.222	....	....	....	3	5	.600	....	....	6	13	....	....	....	....	....	1.7	....	0.7	....
NBA Season Totals		9	....	....	15	6	27	.222	....	....	....	3	5	.600	....	....	6	13	....	....	....	....	....	1.7	....	0.7	....

• DOERNER, Gus

Wilfred (Gus) Doerner

Born: Feb. 27, 1922. Mackey, IN, United States. Died: Dec.10, 2001.   Height: 6'2".   Weight: 195 lbs.   Drafted: —   College: Evansville

YEAR	TEAM	GP	GS	MIN	PTS	FGM	FGA	FG%	3PM	3PA	3P%	FTM	FTA	FT%	ORB	DRB	TRB	AST	PF	DQ	STL	BLK	TO	MPG	PPG	RPG	APG	PCM
42-43	Fort Wayne-N	4	....	....	9	4	....	....	....	....	....	1	....	....	....	....	....	....	....	....	....	....	....	2.3	....	....	....
45-46	Fort Wayne-N	11	....	....	21	8	....	....	....	....	....	5	....	....	....	....	....	....	....	....	....	....	....	1.9	....	....	....
46-47	Indianapolis-N	43	....	....	234	94	....	....	....	....	....	46	82	.561	....	....	....	49	....	....	....	....	....	5.4	....	....	....
NBL Season Totals		58	....	....	264	106	....	....	....	....	....	52	82	....	....	....	....	49	....	....	....	....	....	4.6	....	....	....
46-47	Indianapolis-N	5	....	....	59	23	....	....	....	....	....	13	22	.591	....	....	....	....	....	....	....	....	....	11.8	....	....	....
NBL Playoff Totals		5	....	....	59	23	....	....	....	....	....	13	22	....	....	....	....	....	....	....	....	....	....	11.8	....	....	....

• DOLEAC, Michael

Michael Scott Doleac

Born: June 15, 1977. San Antonio, TX, United States.   Height: 6'11".   Weight: 262 lbs.   Drafted: 1998   College: Utah

YEAR	TEAM	GP	GS	MIN	PTS	FGM	FGA	FG%	3PM	3PA	3P%	FTM	FTA	FT%	ORB	DRB	TRB	AST	PF	DQ	STL	BLK	TO	MPG	PPG	RPG	APG	PCM
98-99	Orlando	49	0	780	304	125	267	.468	0	0	.000	54	80	.675	66	82	148	20	117	1	19	17	26	15.9	6.2	3.0	0.4	.355
99-00	Orlando	81	29	1335	565	242	535	.452	1	2	.500	80	95	.842	89	245	334	63	224	3	29	34	65	16.5	7.0	4.1	0.8	.420
00-01	Orlando	77	21	1398	490	220	527	.417	0	3	.000	50	59	.847	70	203	273	65	239	**10**	37	41	59	18.2	6.4	3.5	0.8	.312
01-02	Cleveland	42	15	705	194	78	187	.417	0	0	.000	38	46	.826	47	121	168	25	98	4	15	11	37	16.8	4.6	4.0	0.6	.308
02-03	New York	75	0	1043	328	146	343	.426	0	0	.000	36	46	.783	65	154	219	42	150	1	16	16	49	13.9	4.4	2.9	0.6	.293
NBA Season Totals		324	65	5261	1881	811	1859	.436	1	5	.200	258	326	.791	337	805	1142	215	828	19	116	119	236	16.2	5.8	3.5	0.7	....
98-99	Orlando	4	0	43	17	5	18	.278	0	1	.000	7	9	.778	5	7	12	0	6	0	0	1	3	10.8	4.3	3.0	0.0	.251
00-01	Orlando	4	0	45	12	6	16	.375	0	0	.000	0	0	.000	4	10	14	1	10	0	3	0	2	11.3	3.0	3.5	0.3	.291
NBA Playoff Totals		8	0	88	29	11	34	.324	0	1	.000	7	9	.778	9	17	26	1	16	0	3	1	5	11.0	3.6	3.3	0.1	....

• DOLHON, Joe

Joseph Dolhon

Born: July 9, 1927. Died: Jan.5, 1981.   Height: 6'   Weight: 175 lbs.   Drafted: —   College: New York University

YEAR	TEAM	GP	GS	MIN	PTS	FGM	FGA	FG%	3PM	3PA	3P%	FTM	FTA	FT%	ORB	DRB	TRB	AST	PF	DQ	STL	BLK	TO	MPG	PPG	RPG	APG	PCM
49-50	Baltimore	64	....	....	443	143	458	.312	....	....	....	157	214	.734	....	....	....	155	193	....	....	....	....	6.9	....	2.4	....
50-51	Baltimore	13	....	....	51	17	56	.304	....	....	....	17	23	.739	....	....	18	19	32	1	....	....	....	3.9	1.4	1.5	....
NBA Season Totals		77	....	....	494	160	514	.311	....	....	....	174	237	.734	....	....	18	174	225	1	....	....	....	6.4	0.2	2.3	....

• DOLL, Bob

Robert W. Doll

Born: Aug. 10, 1919. Steamboat Springs, CO, United States. Died: Sept.18, 1959.   Height: 6'5".   Weight: 195 lbs.   Drafted: —   College: Colorado

YEAR	TEAM	GP	GS	MIN	PTS	FGM	FGA	FG%	3PM	3PA	3P%	FTM	FTA	FT%	ORB	DRB	TRB	AST	PF	DQ	STL	BLK	TO	MPG	PPG	RPG	APG	PCM
46-47	St. Louis	60	....	....	522	194	768	.253	....	....	....	134	206	.650	....	....	....	22	167	....	....	....	....	8.7	....	0.4	....
47-48	St. Louis	42	....	....	446	174	658	.264	....	....	....	98	148	.662	....	....	....	26	107	....	....	....	....	10.6	....	0.6	....
48-49	Denver-N	9	....	....	43	15	....	....	....	....	....	13	28	.464	....	....	....	....	22	....	....	....	....	4.8	....	....	....

YEAR	TEAM	GP	GS	MIN	PTS	FGM	FGA	FG%	3PM	3PA	3P%	FTM	FTA	FT%	ORB	DRB	TRB	AST	PF	DQ	STL	BLK	TO	MPG	PPG	RPG	APG	PCM
48-49	Boston	47	....	....	370	145	438	.331	....	....	....	80	117	.684	....	....	....	117	118	....	....	....	....	....	7.9	....	2.5	....
49-50	Boston	47	....	....	315	120	347	.346	....	....	....	75	114	.658	....	....	....	108	117	....	....	....	....	....	6.7	....	2.3	....
NBA Season Totals		196	....	....	1653	633	2211	.286	....	....	....	387	585	.662	....	....	....	273	509	....	....	....	....	....	8.4	....	1.4	....
NBL Season Totals		9	....	....	43	15	....	....	....	....	....	13	28	....	....	....	....	....	22	....	....	....	....	....	4.8	....	....	....
Career Totals		205	....	....	1696	648	2211	....	....	....	....	400	613	....	....	....	....	273	531	....	....	....	....	....	8.3	....	1.3	....
46-47	St. Louis	3	....	....	20	6	39	.154	....	....	....	8	12	.667	....	....	....	0	11	....	....	....	....	....	6.7	....	0.0	....
47-48	St. Louis	7	....	....	50	18	91	.198	....	....	....	14	26	.538	....	....	....	5	18	....	....	....	....	....	7.1	....	0.7	....
NBA Playoff Totals		10	....	....	70	24	130	.185	....	....	....	22	38	.579	....	....	....	5	29	....	....	....	....	....	7.0	....	0.5	....

• DONALDSON, James

James Lee Donaldson III

Born: Aug. 16, 1957. Heacham, Great Britain.　Height: 7'2".　Weight: 275 lbs.　Drafted: 1979　College: Washington State

YEAR	TEAM	GP	GS	MIN	PTS	FGM	FGA	FG%	3PM	3PA	3P%	FTM	FTA	FT%	ORB	DRB	TRB	AST	PF	DQ	STL	BLK	TO	MPG	PPG	RPG	APG	PCM
80-81	Seattle	68	....	980	359	129	238	.542	0	0	.000	101	170	.594	107	202	309	42	79	0	8	74	68	14.4	5.3	4.5	0.6	.543
81-82	Seattle	82	1	1710	661	255	419	.609	0	0	.000	151	240	.629	138	352	490	51	186	2	27	139	115	20.9	8.1	6.0	0.6	.548
82-83	Seattle	82	11	1789	728	289	496	.583	0	0	.000	150	218	.688	131	370	501	97	171	1	19	101	131	21.8	8.9	6.1	1.2	.549
83-84	San Diego	82	67	2525	969	360	604	.596	0	0	.000	249	327	.761	165	484	649	90	214	1	40	139	172	30.8	11.8	7.9	1.1	.520
84-85	LA Clippers	82	58	2392	929	351	551	**.637**	0	0	.000	227	303	.749	168	500	668	48	217	1	28	130	205	29.2	11.3	8.1	0.6	.517
85-86	LA Clippers	14	14	441	143	43	84	.512	0	0	.000	57	70	.814	28	103	131	12	33	0	5	29	38	31.5	10.2	9.4	0.9	.486
85-86	Dallas	69	64	2241	573	213	375	.568	0	0	.000	147	184	.799	143	521	664	84	156	0	23	110	83	32.5	8.3	9.6	1.2	.485
86-87	Dallas	82	82	3028	889	311	531	.586	0	0	.000	267	329	.812	295	678	973	63	191	0	51	136	107	36.9	10.8	11.9	0.8	.533
87-88	Dallas	81	81	2523	571	212	380	.558	0	0	.000	147	189	.778	247	508	755	66	175	2	40	104	113	31.1	7.0	9.3	0.8	.442
88-89	Dallas	53	53	1746	481	193	337	.573	0	0	.000	95	124	.766	158	412	570	38	111	0	24	81	85	32.9	9.1	10.8	0.7	.499
89-90	Dallas	73	73	2265	665	258	479	.539	0	0	.000	149	213	.700	155	475	630	57	129	0	22	47	117	31.0	9.1	8.6	0.8	.430
90-91	Dallas	82	82	2800	819	327	615	.532	0	0	.000	165	229	.721	201	526	727	69	181	0	34	93	148	34.1	10.0	8.9	0.8	.417
91-92	Dallas	44	32	994	273	107	227	.471	0	0	.000	59	84	.702	97	173	270	31	86	0	8	44	40	22.6	6.2	6.1	0.7	.408
91-92	New York	14	0	81	12	5	18	.278	0	0	.000	2	2	1.000	2	17	19	2	17	0	0	5	7	5.8	0.9	1.4	0.1	.123
92-93	Utah	6	1	94	21	8	14	.571	0	0	.000	5	9	.556	6	23	29	1	13	0	1	7	4	15.7	3.5	4.8	0.2	.418
94-95	Utah	43	40	613	110	44	74	.595	0	0	.000	22	31	.710	19	88	107	14	66	0	6	28	22	14.3	2.6	2.5	0.3	.283
NBA Season Totals		957	659	26222	8203	3105	5442	.571	0	0	.000	1993	2722	.732	2060	5432	7492	765	2025	7	336	1267	1455	27.4	8.6	7.8	0.8	....
81-82	Seattle	8	0	189	54	18	43	.419	0	0	.000	18	24	.750	25	49	74	7	16	0	2	5	10	23.6	6.8	9.3	0.9	.496
82-83	Seattle	2	0	47	24	11	22	.500	0	0	.000	2	3	.667	5	12	17	2	4	0	0	3	0	23.5	12.0	8.5	1.0	.682
85-86	Dallas	10	10	410	109	36	48	.750	0	0	.000	37	40	.925	30	87	117	10	26	0	6	12	10	41.0	10.9	11.7	1.0	.515
86-87	Dallas	3	3	68	16	4	5	.800	0	0	.000	8	9	.889	2	15	17	2	6	0	1	3	2	22.7	5.3	5.7	0.7	.465
87-88	Dallas	17	17	499	158	68	104	.654	0	0	.000	22	37	.595	47	99	146	12	41	0	7	15	29	29.4	9.3	8.6	0.7	.482
89-90	Dallas	3	3	74	22	9	13	.692	0	0	.000	4	5	.800	6	10	16	2	8	0	2	0	4	24.7	7.3	5.3	0.7	.396
91-92	New York	2	0	11	4	2	2	1.000	0	0	.000	0	0	.000	0	4	4	0	2	0	0	1	2	5.5	2.0	2.0	0.0	.533
92-93	Utah	1	0	5	0	0	1	.000	0	0	.000	0	0	.000	0	0	0	0	0	0	0	0	0	5.0	0.0	0.0	0.0	-.187
94-95	Utah	5	5	76	14	5	6	.833	0	0	.000	4	4	1.000	3	6	9	0	8	0	0	3	2	15.2	2.8	1.8	0.0	.246
NBA Playoff Totals		51	38	1379	401	153	244	.627	0	0	.000	95	122	.779	118	282	400	35	111	0	18	42	59	27.0	7.9	7.8	0.7	....

• DONHAM, Bob

Robert E. Donham

Born: Oct. 11, 1926. Died: Sept.21, 1983.　Height: 6'2".　Weight: 190 lbs.　Drafted: 1950　College: Ohio State

YEAR	TEAM	GP	GS	MIN	PTS	FGM	FGA	FG%	3PM	3PA	3P%	FTM	FTA	FT%	ORB	DRB	TRB	AST	PF	DQ	STL	BLK	TO	MPG	PPG	RPG	APG	PCM
50-51	Boston	68	....	....	416	151	298	.507	....	....	....	114	229	.498	....	....	235	139	179	3	....	....	....	....	6.1	3.5	2.0	....
51-52	Boston	66	....	1980	551	201	413	.487	....	....	....	149	293	.509	....	....	330	228	223	9	....	....	....	30.0	8.3	5.0	3.5	.403
52-53	Boston	71	....	1435	451	169	353	.479	....	....	....	113	240	.471	....	....	239	153	213	8	....	....	....	20.2	6.4	3.4	2.2	.392
53-54	Boston	68	....	1451	400	141	315	.448	....	....	....	118	213	.554	....	....	267	186	235	11	....	....	....	21.3	5.9	3.9	2.7	.406
NBA Season Totals		273	....	4866	1818	662	1379	.480	....	....	....	494	975	.507	....	....	1071	706	850	31	....	....	....	17.8	6.7	3.9	2.6	
50-51	Boston	2	....	....	13	4	9	.444	....	....	....	5	12	.417	....	....	8	2	9	1	....	....	....	....	6.5	4.0	1.0	....
51-52	Boston	3	....	112	27	9	19	.474	....	....	....	9	18	.500	....	....	13	17	16	1	....	....	....	37.3	9.0	4.3	5.7	.376
52-53	Boston	6	....	138	33	11	38	.289	....	....	....	11	27	.407	....	....	21	13	24	3	....	....	....	23.0	5.5	3.5	2.2	.223
53-54	Boston	6	....	98	20	7	15	.467	....	....	....	6	19	.316	....	....	12	6	32	4	....	....	....	16.3	3.3	2.0	1.0	.149
NBA Playoff Totals		17	....	348	93	31	81	.383	....	....	....	31	76	.408	....	....	54	38	81	9	....	....	....	20.5	5.5	3.2	2.2	....

• DONOVAN, Billy

William John (Billy the Kid) Donovan

Born: May 30, 1965. Rockville Centre, NY, United States.　Height: 5'11".　Weight: 171 lbs.　Drafted: 1987　College: Providence

YEAR	TEAM	GP	GS	MIN	PTS	FGM	FGA	FG%	3PM	3PA	3P%	FTM	FTA	FT%	ORB	DRB	TRB	AST	PF	DQ	STL	BLK	TO	MPG	PPG	RPG	APG	PCM
87-88	New York	44	0	364	105	44	109	.404	0	7	.000	17	21	.810	5	20	25	87	33	0	16	1	44	8.3	2.4	0.6	2.0	.325
NBA Season Totals		44	0	364	105	44	109	.404	0	7	.000	17	21	.810	5	20	25	87	33	0	16	1	44	8.3	2.4	0.6	2.0	

• DONOVAN, Harry

Henry Harry Donovan

Born: Sept. 10, 1926. Union City, NJ, United States.　Height: 6'2".　Weight: 180 lbs.　Drafted: 1949　College: Muhlenberg

YEAR	TEAM	GP	GS	MIN	PTS	FGM	FGA	FG%	3PM	3PA	3P%	FTM	FTA	FT%	ORB	DRB	TRB	AST	PF	DQ	STL	BLK	TO	MPG	PPG	RPG	APG	PCM
49-50	New York	45	....	....	253	90	275	.327	....	....	....	73	106	.689	....	....	....	38	107	....	....	....	....	....	5.6	....	0.8	....
NBA Season Totals		45	....	....	253	90	275	.327	....	....	....	73	106	.689	....	....	....	38	107	....	....	....	....	....	5.6	....	0.8	....
49-50	New York	3	....	....	2	0	4	.000	....	....	....	2	2	1.000	....	....	....	0	4	....	....	....	....	....	0.7	....	0.0	....
NBA Playoff Totals		3	....	....	2	0	4	.000	....	....	....	2	2	1.000	....	....	....	0	4	....	....	....	....	....	0.7	....	0.0	....

• DOOLING, Keyon

Keyon Latwae Dooling

Born: May 8, 1980. Ft. Lauderdale, FL, United States.   Height: 6'3".   Weight: 196 lbs.   Drafted: 2000   College: Missouri

YEAR	TEAM	GP	GS	MIN	PTS	FGM	FGA	FG%	3PM	3PA	3P%	FTM	FTA	FT%	ORB	DRB	TRB	AST	PF	DQ	STL	BLK	TO	MPG	PPG	RPG	APG	PCM
00-01	LA Clippers	76	1	1237	449	148	362	.409	28	80	.350	125	179	.698	8	81	89	177	107	0	41	11	94	16.3	5.9	1.2	2.3	.341
01-02	LA Clippers	14	0	155	58	22	57	.386	4	14	.286	10	12	.833	0	3	3	12	20	0	4	3	10	11.1	4.1	0.2	0.9	.190
02-03	LA Clippers	55	1	969	350	128	329	.389	50	139	.360	44	57	.772	9	63	72	89	93	0	24	6	60	17.6	6.4	1.3	1.6	.263
NBA Season Totals		145	2	2361	857	298	748	.398	82	233	.352	179	248	.722	17	147	164	278	220	0	69	20	164	16.3	5.9	1.1	1.9	....

• DORSEY, Jacky

Jacky Dorsey

Born: Dec. 18, 1954. Atlanta, GA, United States.   Height: 6'7".   Weight: 230 lbs.   Drafted: 1976   College: Georgia

YEAR	TEAM	GP	GS	MIN	PTS	FGM	FGA	FG%	3PM	3PA	3P%	FTM	FTA	FT%	ORB	DRB	TRB	AST	PF	DQ	STL	BLK	TO	MPG	PPG	RPG	APG	PCM
77-78	Denver	7	....	37	9	3	12	.250	....	....	....	3	5	.600	5	15	20	2	9	0	2	2	3	5.3	1.3	2.9	0.3	.458
77-78	Portland	4	....	51	25	9	19	.474	....	....	....	7	11	.636	6	4	10	3	8	0	0	1	3	12.8	6.3	2.5	0.8	.419
78-79	Houston	20	....	108	56	24	43	.558	....	....	....	8	16	.500	12	11	23	2	25	0	1	2	8	5.4	2.8	1.2	0.1	.393
80-81	Seattle	29	....	253	53	20	70	.286	0	0	.000	13	25	.520	23	65	88	9	47	0	9	1	15	8.7	1.8	3.0	0.3	.261
NBA Season Totals		60	....	449	143	56	144	.389	0	0	.000	31	57	.544	46	95	141	16	89	0	12	6	29	7.5	2.4	2.4	0.3	....
78-79	Houston	1	....	1	0	0	0	.000	....	....	....	0	0	.000	0	0	0	0	0	0	0	0	0	1.0	0.0	0.0	0.0	.000
NBA Playoff Totals		1	....	1	0	0	0	.000	....	....	....	0	0	.000	0	0	0	0	0	0	0	0	0	1.0	0.0	0.0	0.0	....

• DORSEY, Ron

Ron Dorsey

Born: Oct. 10, 1948.   Height: 6'4".   Weight: 200 lbs.   Drafted: 1971   College: Tennessee State

YEAR	TEAM	GP	GS	MIN	PTS	FGM	FGA	FG%	3PM	3PA	3P%	FTM	FTA	FT%	ORB	DRB	TRB	AST	PF	DQ	STL	BLK	TO	MPG	PPG	RPG	APG	PCM
71-72	Carolina-A	1	....	12	4	2	8	.250	0	1	.000	0	2	.000	2	3	5	0	2	0	....	....	1	12.0	4.0	5.0	0.0	.114
ABA Season Totals		1	....	12	4	2	8	.250	0	1	.000	0	2	.000	2	3	5	0	2	0	....	....	1	12.0	4.0	5.0	0.0	

• DOUGLAS, Bruce

Bruce Douglas

Born: Apr. 9, 1964. Quincy, IL, United States.   Height: 6'3".   Weight: 195 lbs.   Drafted: 1986   College: Illinois

YEAR	TEAM	GP	GS	MIN	PTS	FGM	FGA	FG%	3PM	3PA	3P%	FTM	FTA	FT%	ORB	DRB	TRB	AST	PF	DQ	STL	BLK	TO	MPG	PPG	RPG	APG	PCM
86-87	Sacramento	8	1	98	14	7	24	.292	0	1	.000	0	4	.000	5	9	14	17	9	0	9	0	9	12.3	1.8	1.8	2.1	.238
NBA Season Totals		8	1	98	14	7	24	.292	0	1	.000	0	4	.000	5	9	14	17	9	0	9	0	9	12.3	1.8	1.8	2.1	....

• DOUGLAS, John

John David Douglas

Born: June 12, 1956. Town Creek, AL, United States.   Height: 6'2".   Weight: 170 lbs.   Drafted: 1978   College: Kansas

YEAR	TEAM	GP	GS	MIN	PTS	FGM	FGA	FG%	3PM	3PA	3P%	FTM	FTA	FT%	ORB	DRB	TRB	AST	PF	DQ	STL	BLK	TO	MPG	PPG	RPG	APG	PCM
81-82	San Diego	64	9	1031	447	181	389	.465	18	59	.305	67	102	.657	27	63	90	146	147	2	48	9	90	16.1	7.0	1.4	2.3	.370
82-83	San Diego	3	1	12	5	1	6	.167	1	2	.500	2	2	1.000	0	1	1	1	0	0	0	0	0	4.0	1.7	0.3	0.3	.208
NBA Season Totals		67	10	1043	452	182	395	.461	19	61	.311	69	104	.663	27	64	91	147	147	2	48	9	90	15.6	6.7	1.4	2.2	....

• DOUGLAS, Leon

Leon Douglas

Born: Aug. 26, 1954. Leighton, AL, United States.   Height: 6'10".   Weight: 230 lbs.   Drafted: 1976   College: Alabama

YEAR	TEAM	GP	GS	MIN	PTS	FGM	FGA	FG%	3PM	3PA	3P%	FTM	FTA	FT%	ORB	DRB	TRB	AST	PF	DQ	STL	BLK	TO	MPG	PPG	RPG	APG	PCM
76-77	Detroit	82	....	1626	617	245	512	.479	....	....	....	127	229	.555	181	345	526	68	294	10	44	81	....	19.8	7.5	6.4	0.8	.459
77-78	Detroit	79	....	1993	863	321	667	.481	....	....	....	221	345	.641	181	401	582	112	295	6	57	48	198	25.2	10.9	7.4	1.4	.467
78-79	Detroit	78	....	2215	892	342	698	.490	....	....	....	208	328	.634	248	416	664	74	319	13	39	55	187	28.4	11.4	8.5	0.9	.438
79-80	Detroit	70	....	1782	567	221	455	.486	0	1	.000	125	185	.676	171	330	501	121	249	10	30	62	126	25.5	8.1	7.2	1.7	.432
80-81	Kansas City	79	....	1356	472	185	323	.573	0	3	.000	102	186	.548	150	234	384	69	251	2	25	38	87	17.2	6.0	4.9	0.9	.440
81-82	Kansas City	63	17	1093	172	70	140	.500	0	0	.000	32	80	.400	111	179	290	35	210	5	15	38	57	17.3	2.7	4.6	0.6	.265
82-83	Kansas City	5	0	46	4	2	3	.667	0	0	.000	0	2	.000	3	4	7	0	13	0	0	3	1	9.2	0.8	1.4	0.0	.097
NBA Season Totals		456	17	10111	3587	1386	2798	.495	0	4	.000	815	1355	.601	1045	1909	2954	479	1631	46	210	325	656	22.2	7.9	6.5	1.1	....
76-77	Detroit	3	....	57	10	4	13	.308	....	....	....	2	7	.286	4	6	10	3	11	0	1	5	....	19.0	3.3	3.3	1.0	.129
80-81	Kansas City	15	....	318	45	15	32	.469	0	0	.000	15	35	.429	18	47	65	11	47	1	4	3	18	21.2	3.0	4.3	0.7	.189
NBA Playoff Totals		18	....	375	55	19	45	.422	0	0	.000	17	42	.405	22	53	75	14	58	1	5	8	18	20.8	3.1	4.2	0.8	....

• DOUGLAS, Sherman

Sherman Douglas

Born: Sept. 15, 1966. Washington, DC, United States.   Height: 6'   Weight: 180 lbs.   Drafted: 1989   College: Syracuse

YEAR	TEAM	GP	GS	MIN	PTS	FGM	FGA	FG%	3PM	3PA	3P%	FTM	FTA	FT%	ORB	DRB	TRB	AST	PF	DQ	STL	BLK	TO	MPG	PPG	RPG	APG	PCM
89-90	Miami	81	66	2470	1155	463	938	.494	5	31	.161	224	326	.687	70	136	206	619	187	0	145	10	243	30.5	14.3	2.5	7.6	.544
90-91	Miami	73	73	2562	1352	532	1055	.504	4	31	.129	284	414	.686	78	131	209	624	178	2	121	5	270	35.1	18.5	2.9	8.5	.565
91-92	Miami	5	2	98	37	16	31	.516	0	1	.000	5	7	.714	1	5	6	19	10	0	4	0	8	19.6	7.4	1.2	3.8	.405
91-92	Boston	37	0	654	271	101	222	.455	1	9	.111	68	100	.680	12	45	57	153	68	0	21	9	59	17.7	7.3	1.5	4.1	.462
92-93	Boston	79	36	1932	618	264	530	.498	6	29	.207	84	150	.560	65	97	162	508	166	1	49	10	158	24.5	7.8	2.1	6.4	.446
93-94	Boston	78	78	2789	1040	425	919	.462	13	56	.232	177	276	.641	70	123	193	683	171	2	89	11	234	35.8	13.3	2.5	8.8	.451
94-95	Boston	65	43	2048	954	365	769	.475	20	82	.244	204	296	.689	48	122	170	446	152	0	80	2	163	31.5	14.7	2.6	6.9	.497
95-96	Boston	10	4	234	98	36	84	.429	1	7	.143	25	40	.625	6	17	23	39	16	0	2	0	29	23.4	9.8	2.3	3.9	.324
95-96	Milwaukee	69	62	2101	792	309	601	.514	39	103	.379	135	179	.754	49	108	157	397	147	0	61	5	166	30.4	11.5	2.3	5.8	.429
96-97	Milwaukee	79	79	2316	764	306	610	.502	38	114	.333	114	171	.667	57	136	193	427	191	0	78	10	150	29.3	9.7	2.4	5.4	.407
97-98	New Jersey	80	11	1699	639	255	515	.495	14	46	.304	115	172	.669	52	83	135	319	156	2	55	7	112	21.2	8.0	1.7	4.0	.428
98-99	LA Clippers	30	19	842	247	96	219	.438	0	11	.000	55	87	.632	16	42	58	124	54	0	27	3	61	28.1	8.2	1.9	4.1	.310
99-00	New Jersey	20	2	309	120	45	90	.500	5	16	.313	25	28	.893	13	16	29	34	26	0	17	0	24	15.5	6.0	1.5	1.7	.398
00-01	New Jersey	59	7	1094	338	122	303	.403	8	40	.200	86	115	.748	21	53	74	144	93	0	36	4	79	18.5	5.7	1.3	2.4	.284
NBA Season Totals		765	482	21148	8425	3335	6886	.484	154	576	.267	1601	2361	.678	558	1114	1672	4536	1615	7	785	76	1756	27.6	11.0	2.2	5.9	....

YEAR	TEAM	GP	GS	MIN	PTS	FGM	FGA	FG%	3PM	3PA	3P%	FTM	FTA	FT%	ORB	DRB	TRB	AST	PF	DQ	STL	BLK	TO	MPG	PPG	RPG	APG	PCM
91-92	Boston	6	0	65	19	9	25	.360	0	2	.000	1	2	.500	1	3	4	10	8	0	0	0	4	10.8	3.2	0.7	1.7	.164
92-93	Boston	4	4	166	44	17	45	.378	0	3	.000	10	15	.667	12	14	26	38	10	0	4	0	12	41.5	11.0	6.5	9.5	.411
94-95	Boston	4	4	168	60	24	68	.353	4	12	.333	8	11	.727	4	16	20	33	12	0	4	1	17	42.0	15.0	5.0	8.3	.323
97-98	New Jersey	3	2	125	55	23	44	.523	2	5	.400	7	10	.700	1	7	8	25	5	0	6	0	13	41.7	18.3	2.7	8.3	.481
NBA Playoff Totals		17	10	524	178	73	182	.401	6	22	.273	26	38	.684	18	40	58	106	35	0	14	1	46	30.8	10.5	3.4	6.2	....

• DOVE, Sonny
Lloyd (Sonny) Dove

Born: Aug. 16, 1945. Brooklyn, NY, United States. Died: Feb.14, 1983.   Height: 6'7".   Weight: 198 lbs.   Drafted: 1967   College: St. John's (NY)

YEAR	TEAM	GP	GS	MIN	PTS	FGM	FGA	FG%	3PM	3PA	3P%	FTM	FTA	FT%	ORB	DRB	TRB	AST	PF	DQ	STL	BLK	TO	MPG	PPG	RPG	APG	PCM
67-68	Detroit	28	....	162	56	22	75	.293	....	....	....	12	26	.462	....	....	52	11	27	0	....	....	....	5.8	2.0	1.9	0.4	.321
68-69	Detroit	29	....	236	118	47	100	.470	....	....	....	24	36	.667	....	....	62	12	49	0	....	....	....	8.1	4.1	2.1	0.4	.483
69-70	New York-A	80	....	2284	1154	456	987	.462	2	13	.154	240	379	.633	236	307	543	107	295	12	....	....	201	28.6	14.4	6.8	1.3	.482
70-71	New York-A	83	....	2280	1124	467	1006	.464	4	14	.286	186	273	.681	264	412	676	88	304	11	....	....	224	27.5	13.5	8.1	1.1	.519
71-72	New York-A	2	....	9	6	2	5	.400	0	0	.000	2	3	.667	1	1	1	1	4	0	....	....	2	4.5	3.0	0.5	0.5	.352
NBA Season Totals		57	....	398	174	69	175	.394	....	....	....	36	62	.581	....	....	114	23	76	0	....	....	....	7.0	3.1	2.0	0.4	....
ABA Season Totals		165	....	4573	2284	925	1998	.463	6	27	.222	428	655	.653	501	719	1220	196	603	23	....	....	427	27.7	13.8	7.4	1.2	....
Career Totals		222	....	4971	2458	994	2173	.457	6	27	.222	464	717	.647	501	719	1334	219	679	23	....	....	427	22.4	11.1	6.0	1.0	....
67-68	Detroit	2	....	6	4	2	4	.500	....	....	....	0	0	.000	....	....	2	0	0	0	....	....	....	3.0	2.0	1.0	0.0	.667
69-70	New York-A	7	....	281	123	48	97	.495	1	4	.250	26	39	.667	27	44	71	9	....	2	....	....	1	40.1	17.6	10.1	1.3	....
70-71	New York-A	5	....	32	11	5	10	.500	0	0	.000	1	4	.250	4	7	11	1	10	0	....	....	1	6.4	2.2	2.2	0.2	.369
NBA Playoff Totals		2	....	6	4	2	4	.500	....	....	....	0	0	.000	....	....	2	0	0	0	....	....	....	3.0	2.0	1.0	0.0	....
ABA Playoff Totals		12	....	313	134	53	107	.495	1	4	.250	27	43	.628	31	51	82	10	10	2	....	....	1	26.1	11.2	6.8	0.8	....
Career Playoff Totals		14	....	319	138	55	111	.495	1	4	.250	27	43	.628	31	51	84	10	10	2	....	....	1	22.8	9.9	6.0	0.7	....

• DOVER, Jerry
Jerry L. Dover

Born: Oct. 16, 1949.   Height: 5'7".   Weight: 155 lbs.   Drafted: —   College: LeMoyne-Owen

YEAR	TEAM	GP	GS	MIN	PTS	FGM	FGA	FG%	3PM	3PA	3P%	FTM	FTA	FT%	ORB	DRB	TRB	AST	PF	DQ	STL	BLK	TO	MPG	PPG	RPG	APG	PCM
71-72	Memphis-A	4	....	13	8	3	9	.333	2	5	.400	0	0	.000	0	0	0	1	3	0	....	....	0	3.3	2.0	0.0	0.3	.195
ABA Season Totals		4	....	13	8	3	9	.333	2	5	.400	0	0	.000	0	0	0	1	3	0	....	....	0	3.3	2.0	0.0	0.3	....

• DOWELL, Robert
Robert (Duck) Dowell

Born: Aug. 14, 1912. Gilman City, MO, United States.   Height: 6'3".   Weight: 200 lbs.   Drafted: —   College: Northwest Missouri State

YEAR	TEAM	GP	GS	MIN	PTS	FGM	FGA	FG%	3PM	3PA	3P%	FTM	FTA	FT%	ORB	DRB	TRB	AST	PF	DQ	STL	BLK	TO	MPG	PPG	RPG	APG	PCM
37-38	Non-Skids-N	14	....	....	49	15	....	....	....	....	....	19	....	....	....	....	....	....	....	....	....	....	....	3.5	....	....	....	....
NBL Season Totals		14	....	....	49	15	....	....	....	....	....	19	....	....	....	....	....	....	....	....	....	....	....	3.5	....	....	....	....
37-38	Non-Skids-N	2	....	....	2	1	....	....	....	....	....	0	....	....	....	....	....	....	....	....	....	....	....	1.0	....	....	....	....
NBL Playoff Totals		2	....	....	2	1	....	....	....	....	....	0	....	....	....	....	....	....	....	....	....	....	....	1.0	....	....	....	....

• DOWNEY, Bill
William K. Downey

Born: Nov. 11, 1923.   Height: 6'6".   Weight: 210 lbs.   Drafted: —   College: Marquette

YEAR	TEAM	GP	GS	MIN	PTS	FGM	FGA	FG%	3PM	3PA	3P%	FTM	FTA	FT%	ORB	DRB	TRB	AST	PF	DQ	STL	BLK	TO	MPG	PPG	RPG	APG	PCM
47-48	Providence	3	....	....	0	0	2	.000	....	....	....	0	0	.000	....	....	0	0	....	....	....	....	....	0.0	....	0.0	....	....
NBA Season Totals		3	....	....	0	0	2	.000	....	....	....	0	0	.000	....	....	0	0	....	....	....	....	....	0.0	....	0.0	....	....

• DOWNEY, Glynn
Glynn Downey

Born: 1915.   Height: 6'   Weight: 180 lbs.   Drafted: —   College: Purdue

YEAR	TEAM	GP	GS	MIN	PTS	FGM	FGA	FG%	3PM	3PA	3P%	FTM	FTA	FT%	ORB	DRB	TRB	AST	PF	DQ	STL	BLK	TO	MPG	PPG	RPG	APG	PCM
38-39	Indianapolis-N	15	....	....	73	27	....	....	....	....	....	19	....	....	....	....	....	....	....	....	....	....	....	4.9	....	....	....	....
39-40	Hammond-N	22	....	....	115	37	....	....	....	....	....	41	....	....	....	....	....	....	....	....	....	....	....	5.2	....	....	....	....
NBL Season Totals		37	....	....	188	64	....	....	....	....	....	60	....	....	....	....	....	....	....	....	....	....	....	5.1	....	....	....	....

• DOWNING, Steve
Steve Downing

Born: Sept. 9, 1950. Indianapolis, IN, United States.   Height: 6'8".   Weight: 225 lbs.   Drafted: 1973   College: Indiana

YEAR	TEAM	GP	GS	MIN	PTS	FGM	FGA	FG%	3PM	3PA	3P%	FTM	FTA	FT%	ORB	DRB	TRB	AST	PF	DQ	STL	BLK	TO	MPG	PPG	RPG	APG	PCM
73-74	Boston	24	....	137	64	21	64	.328	....	....	....	22	38	.579	14	25	39	11	33	0	5	0	....	5.7	2.7	1.6	0.5	.382
74-75	Boston	3	....	9	0	0	2	.000	....	....	....	0	2	.000	0	2	2	0	0	0	0	0	....	3.0	0.0	0.7	0.0	-.095
NBA Season Totals		27	....	146	64	21	66	.318	....	....	....	22	40	.550	14	27	41	11	33	0	5	0	....	5.4	2.4	1.5	0.4	....
73-74	Boston	1	....	4	2	1	2	.500	....	....	....	0	0	.000	2	0	2	0	1	0	0	0	....	4.0	2.0	2.0	0.0	.606
NBA Playoff Totals		1	....	4	2	1	2	.500	....	....	....	0	0	.000	2	0	2	0	1	0	0	0	....	4.0	2.0	2.0	0.0	....

• DOYLE, Danny
Daniel F. Doyle

Born: Feb. 6, 1940. LongIslandCity, NY, United States.   Height: 6'8".   Weight: 200 lbs.   Drafted: 1961   College: Belmont Abbey

YEAR	TEAM	GP	GS	MIN	PTS	FGM	FGA	FG%	3PM	3PA	3P%	FTM	FTA	FT%	ORB	DRB	TRB	AST	PF	DQ	STL	BLK	TO	MPG	PPG	RPG	APG	PCM
62-63	Detroit	4	....	25	16	6	12	.500	....	....	....	4	5	.800	....	....	8	3	4	0	....	....	....	6.3	4.0	2.0	0.8	.769
NBA Season Totals		4	....	25	16	6	12	.500	....	....	....	4	5	.800	....	....	8	3	4	0	....	....	....	6.3	4.0	2.0	0.8	....

• DOZIER, Terry
Terry Linnard Dozier

Born: June 29, 1966. Baltimore, MD, United States. Height: 6'9". Weight: 210 lbs. Drafted: — College: South Carolina

YEAR TEAM	GP	GS	MIN	PTS	FGM	FGA	FG%	3PM	3PA	3P%	FTM	FTA	FT%	ORB	DRB	TRB	AST	PF	DQ	STL	BLK	TO	MPG	PPG	RPG	APG	PCM
89-90 Charlotte	9	0	92	22	9	27	.333	0	1	.000	4	8	.500	7	8	15	3	10	0	6	2	7	10.2	2.4	1.7	0.3	.182
NBA Season Totals	9	0	92	22	9	27	.333	0	1	.000	4	8	.500	7	8	15	3	10	0	6	2	7	10.2	2.4	1.7	0.3	....

• DREILING, Greg
Gregory Alan Dreiling

Born: Nov. 7, 1963. Wichita, KS, United States. Height: 7'1". Weight: 250 lbs. Drafted: 1986 College: Kansas

YEAR TEAM	GP	GS	MIN	PTS	FGM	FGA	FG%	3PM	3PA	3P%	FTM	FTA	FT%	ORB	DRB	TRB	AST	PF	DQ	STL	BLK	TO	MPG	PPG	RPG	APG	PCM
86-87 Indiana	24	0	128	42	16	37	.432	0	0	.000	10	12	.833	12	31	43	7	42	0	2	2	7	5.3	1.8	1.8	0.3	.365
87-88 Indiana	20	0	74	34	8	17	.471	0	0	.000	18	26	.692	3	14	17	5	19	0	2	4	12	3.7	1.7	0.9	0.3	.387
88-89 Indiana	53	4	396	129	43	77	.558	0	0	.000	43	64	.672	39	53	92	18	100	0	5	11	37	7.5	2.4	1.7	0.3	.319
89-90 Indiana	49	0	307	65	20	53	.377	0	0	.000	25	34	.735	21	66	87	8	69	0	4	14	20	6.3	1.3	1.8	0.2	.279
90-91 Indiana	73	42	1031	259	98	194	.505	0	2	.000	63	105	.600	66	189	255	51	178	1	24	29	58	14.1	3.5	3.5	0.7	.344
91-92 Indiana	60	23	509	117	43	87	.494	1	1	1.000	30	40	.750	22	74	96	25	123	1	10	16	30	8.5	2.0	1.6	0.4	.249
92-93 Indiana	43	0	239	46	19	58	.328	0	4	.000	8	15	.533	26	40	66	8	60	0	5	8	9	5.6	1.1	1.5	0.2	.218
93-94 Dallas	54	19	685	132	52	104	.500	1	1	1.000	27	38	.711	47	123	170	31	159	5	16	24	43	12.7	2.4	3.1	0.6	.282
94-95 Cleveland	58	3	483	110	42	102	.412	0	0	.000	26	41	.634	32	84	116	22	108	1	6	22	23	8.3	1.9	2.0	0.4	.275
96-97 Dallas	40	3	389	80	34	74	.459	1	1	1.000	11	27	.407	19	57	76	11	65	1	8	7	8	9.7	2.0	1.9	0.3	.242
NBA Season Totals	474	94	4241	1014	375	803	.467	3	9	.333	261	402	.649	287	731	1018	186	923	9	82	137	247	8.9	2.1	2.1	0.4	....
90-91 Indiana	5	5	75	14	5	15	.333	0	0	.000	4	6	.667	8	10	18	0	17	0	0	0	3	15.0	2.8	3.6	0.0	.131
91-92 Indiana	1	0	3	0	0	0	.000	0	0	.000	0	0	.000	0	0	0	0	2	0	0	0	0	3.0	0.0	0.0	0.0	-.310
92-93 Indiana	2	0	4	3	1	1	1.000	1	1	1.000	0	0	.000	0	1	1	0	1	0	0	0	0	2.0	1.5	0.5	0.0	.867
94-95 Cleveland	1	0	7	0	0	2	.000	0	0	.000	0	0	.000	0	1	1	0	2	0	0	0	0	7.0	0.0	1.0	0.0	-.268
NBA Playoff Totals	9	5	89	17	6	18	.333	1	1	1.000	4	6	.667	8	12	20	0	22	0	0	0	3	9.9	1.9	2.2	0.0	....

• DREW, Bryce
Bryce Homer Drew

Born: Sept. 21, 1974. Baton Rouge, LA, United States. Height: 6'2". Weight: 185 lbs. Drafted: 1998 College: Valparaiso

YEAR TEAM	GP	GS	MIN	PTS	FGM	FGA	FG%	3PM	3PA	3P%	FTM	FTA	FT%	ORB	DRB	TRB	AST	PF	DQ	STL	BLK	TO	MPG	PPG	RPG	APG	PCM
98-99 Houston	34	0	441	118	47	129	.364	16	49	.327	8	8	1.000	3	29	32	52	61	2	12	4	31	13.0	3.5	0.9	1.5	.206
99-00 Houston	72	5	1293	420	158	413	.383	59	163	.362	45	53	.849	23	80	103	162	79	0	41	1	66	18.0	5.8	1.4	2.3	.308
00-01 Chicago	48	41	1305	302	124	327	.379	40	105	.381	14	19	.737	12	57	69	185	99	1	32	3	68	27.2	6.3	1.4	3.9	.237
01-02 Charlotte	61	0	774	210	78	182	.429	31	73	.425	23	29	.793	14	58	72	101	49	0	32	2	33	12.7	3.4	1.2	1.7	.346
02-03 New Orleans	13	0	79	19	8	27	.296	3	7	.429	0	0	.000	4	9	13	11	2	0	2	0	3	6.1	1.5	1.0	0.8	.301
NBA Season Totals	228	46	3892	1069	415	1078	.385	149	397	.375	90	109	.826	56	233	289	511	290	3	119	10	201	17.1	4.7	1.3	2.2	....
98-99 Houston	1	0	4	2	1	1	1.000	0	0	.000	0	2	.000	1	2	3	2	1	0	0	0	0	4.0	2.0	3.0	2.0	1.389
01-02 Charlotte	2	0	5	2	1	1	1.000	0	0	.000	0	0	.000	0	0	0	2	0	0	0	0	0	2.5	1.0	0.0	1.0	.838
NBA Playoff Totals	3	0	9	4	2	2	1.000	0	0	.000	0	2	.000	1	2	3	4	1	0	0	0	0	3.0	1.3	1.0	1.3	....

• DREW, John
John Edward Drew

Born: Sept. 30, 1954. Vredenburgh, AL, United States. Height: 6'6". Weight: 205 lbs. Drafted: 1974 College: Gardner-Webb

YEAR TEAM	GP	GS	MIN	PTS	FGM	FGA	FG%	3PM	3PA	3P%	FTM	FTA	FT%	ORB	DRB	TRB	AST	PF	DQ	STL	BLK	TO	MPG	PPG	RPG	APG	PCM
74-75 Atlanta	78	....	2289	1442	527	1230	.428	....	....	....	388	544	.713	**357**	479	836	138	274	4	119	39	....	29.3	18.5	10.7	1.8	.669
75-76 Atlanta	77	....	2351	1660	586	1168	.502	....	....	....	488	656	.744	286	374	660	150	261	11	138	30	....	30.5	21.6	8.6	1.9	.729
76-77 Atlanta	74	....	2688	1790	689	1416	.487	....	....	....	412	577	.714	280	395	675	133	275	9	102	29	....	36.3	24.2	9.1	1.8	.635
77-78 Atlanta	70	....	2203	1623	593	1236	.480	....	....	....	437	575	.760	213	298	511	141	247	8	119	27	210	31.5	23.2	7.3	2.0	.654
78-79 Atlanta	79	....	2410	1795	650	1375	.473	....	....	....	495	677	.731	225	297	522	119	332	**19**	128	16	213	30.5	22.7	6.6	1.5	.602
79-80 Atlanta	80	....	2306	1559	535	1182	.453	0	7	.000	489	646	.757	203	268	471	101	313	10	91	23	240	28.8	19.5	5.9	1.3	.513
80-81 Atlanta	67	....	2075	1454	500	1096	.456	0	7	.000	454	577	.787	145	238	383	79	264	9	98	15	194	31.0	21.7	5.7	1.2	.528
81-82 Atlanta	70	51	2040	1298	465	957	.486	4	12	.333	364	491	.741	169	206	375	96	250	6	64	3	175	29.1	18.5	5.4	1.4	.500
82-83 Utah	44	33	1206	932	318	671	.474	0	5	.000	296	392	.755	98	137	235	97	152	8	35	7	136	27.4	21.2	5.3	2.2	.610
83-84 Utah	81	4	1797	1430	511	1067	.479	6	22	.273	402	517	.778	146	192	338	135	208	1	88	2	194	22.2	17.7	4.2	1.7	.626
84-85 Utah	19	16	463	308	107	260	.412	0	4	.000	94	122	.770	36	46	82	35	65	0	22	2	42	24.4	16.2	4.3	1.8	.473
NBA Season Totals	739	104	21828	15291	5481	11658	.470	10	57	.175	4319	5774	.748	2158	2930	5088	1224	2641	85	1004	193	1404	29.5	20.7	6.9	1.7	....
77-78 Atlanta	2	....	79	52	21	49	.429	....	....	....	10	16	.625	9	6	15	3	9	0	1	1	4	39.5	26.0	7.5	1.5	.452
78-79 Atlanta	9	....	275	145	55	131	.420	....	....	....	35	46	.761	20	40	60	7	36	1	9	4	16	30.6	16.1	6.7	0.8	.417
79-80 Atlanta	5	....	150	73	24	63	.381	0	0	.000	25	35	.714	10	20	30	4	21	1	7	0	12	30.0	14.6	6.0	0.8	.338
81-82 Atlanta	2	2	59	23	8	22	.364	0	0	.000	7	12	.583	6	4	10	1	11	1	0	0	5	29.5	11.5	5.0	0.5	.143
83-84 Utah	11	0	172	112	43	85	.506	0	0	.000	26	33	.788	10	15	25	9	26	0	4	0	11	15.6	10.2	2.3	0.8	.488
NBA Playoff Totals	29	2	735	405	151	350	.431	0	0	.000	103	142	.725	55	85	140	24	103	3	21	5	48	25.3	14.0	4.8	0.8	....

• DREW, Larry
Larry Donnell Drew

Born: Apr. 2, 1958. Kansas City, KS, United States. Height: 6'1". Weight: 170 lbs. Drafted: 1980 College: Missouri

YEAR TEAM	GP	GS	MIN	PTS	FGM	FGA	FG%	3PM	3PA	3P%	FTM	FTA	FT%	ORB	DRB	TRB	AST	PF	DQ	STL	BLK	TO	MPG	PPG	RPG	APG	PCM
80-81 Detroit	76	....	1581	504	197	484	.407	4	17	.235	106	133	.797	24	96	120	249	125	0	88	7	167	20.8	6.6	1.6	3.3	.309
81-82 Kansas City	81	19	1973	874	358	757	.473	8	27	.296	150	189	.794	30	119	149	419	150	0	110	1	170	24.4	10.8	1.8	5.2	.484
82-83 Kansas City	75	74	2690	1510	599	1218	.492	2	16	.125	310	378	.820	44	163	207	610	207	1	126	10	270	35.9	20.1	2.8	8.1	.581
83-84 Kansas City	73	73	2363	1194	474	1026	.462	3	10	.300	243	313	.776	33	113	146	558	170	0	121	10	197	32.4	16.4	2.0	7.6	.525
84-85 Kansas City	72	66	2373	1075	457	913	.501	7	28	.250	154	194	.794	39	125	164	484	147	0	93	8	180	33.0	14.9	2.3	6.7	.488
85-86 Sacramento	75	31	1971	890	376	776	.485	10	31	.323	128	161	.795	25	100	125	338	134	0	66	2	135	26.3	11.9	1.7	4.5	.435
86-87 LA Clippers	60	22	1566	741	295	683	.432	12	72	.167	139	166	.837	26	77	103	326	107	0	60	2	150	26.1	12.4	1.7	5.4	.434
87-88 LA Clippers	74	51	2024	765	328	720	.456	26	90	.289	83	108	.769	21	98	119	383	114	0	65	0	155	27.4	10.3	1.6	5.2	.381
89-90 LA Lakers	80	3	1333	418	170	383	.444	32	81	.395	46	60	.767	12	86	98	217	92	0	47	4	96	16.7	5.2	1.2	2.7	.337
90-91 LA Lakers	48	2	496	139	54	125	.432	14	33	.424	17	22	.773	5	29	34	118	40	0	15	1	48	10.3	2.9	0.7	2.5	.362
NBA Season Totals	714	341	18370	8110	3308	7085	.467	118	405	.291	1376	1724	.798	259	1006	1265	3702	1286	1	791	45	1568	25.7	11.4	1.8	5.2	....

YEAR	TEAM	GP	GS	MIN	PTS	FGM	FGA	FG%	3PM	3PA	3P%	FTM	FTA	FT%	ORB	DRB	TRB	AST	PF	DQ	STL	BLK	TO	MPG	PPG	RPG	APG	PCM
83-84	Kansas City	3	3	70	17	7	19	.368	0	0	.000	3	3	1.000	0	4	4	11	5	0	3	0	5	23.3	5.7	1.3	3.7	.245
85-86	Sacramento	3	0	56	31	14	25	.560	1	3	.333	2	2	1.000	0	1	1	14	2	0	5	0	0	18.7	10.3	0.3	4.7	.722
89-90	LA Lakers	9	0	51	12	3	8	.375	1	4	.250	5	6	.833	0	2	2	4	9	0	3	0	4	5.7	1.3	0.2	0.4	.153
90-91	LA Lakers	18	0	116	35	14	33	.424	3	11	.273	4	6	.667	0	8	8	21	17	0	0	0	9	6.4	1.9	0.4	1.2	.258
NBA Playoff Totals		33	3	293	95	38	85	.447	5	18	.278	14	17	.824	0	15	15	50	33	0	11	0	18	8.9	2.9	0.5	1.5	....

• DREXLER, Clyde

Clyde Austin (Clyde the Glide) Drexler

Born: June 22, 1962. New Orleans, LA, United States. Height: 6'7". Weight: 210 lbs. Drafted: 1983 College: Houston

83-84	Portland	82	3	1408	628	252	559	.451	1	4	.250	123	169	.728	112	123	235	153	209	2	107	29	123	17.2	7.7	2.9	1.9	.439
84-85	Portland	80	43	2555	1377	573	1161	.494	8	37	.216	223	294	.759	217	259	476	441	265	3	177	68	224	31.9	17.2	6.0	5.5	.629
85-86	Portland	75	58	2576	1389	542	1142	.475	12	60	.200	293	381	.769	171	250	421	600	270	8	197	46	285	34.3	18.5	5.6	8.0	.644
86-87	Portland	82	82	3114	1782	707	1408	.502	11	47	.234	357	470	.760	227	291	518	566	281	7	204	71	254	38.0	21.7	6.3	6.9	.659
87-88	Portland	81	80	3060	2185	849	1679	.506	11	52	.212	476	587	.811	261	272	533	467	250	2	203	52	235	37.8	27.0	6.6	5.8	.738
88-89	Portland	78	78	3064	2123	829	1672	.496	27	104	.260	438	548	.799	289	326	615	450	269	2	213	54	250	39.3	27.2	7.9	5.8	.728
89-90	Portland	73	73	2683	1703	670	1357	.494	30	106	.283	333	430	.774	208	299	507	432	222	1	145	51	190	36.8	23.3	6.9	5.9	.689
90-91	Portland	82	82	2852	1767	645	1338	.482	61	191	.319	416	524	.794	212	334	546	493	226	2	144	60	230	34.8	21.5	6.7	6.0	.693
91-92	Portland	76	76	2751	1903	694	1476	.470	114	338	.337	401	505	.794	166	334	500	512	229	2	138	70	243	36.2	25.0	6.6	6.7	.728
92-93	Portland	49	49	1671	976	350	816	.429	31	133	.233	245	292	.839	126	183	309	278	159	1	95	37	113	34.1	19.9	6.3	5.7	.627
93-94	Portland	68	68	2334	1303	473	1105	.428	71	219	.324	286	368	.777	154	291	445	333	202	2	98	34	170	34.3	19.2	6.5	4.9	.569
94-95	Portland	41	41	1428	904	305	712	.428	87	240	.363	207	248	.835	84	150	234	208	117	0	74	22	98	34.8	22.0	5.7	5.1	.621
94-95	Houston	35	34	1300	749	266	526	.506	60	168	.357	157	194	.809	68	178	246	154	89	1	62	23	88	37.1	21.4	7.0	4.4	.644
95-96	Houston	52	51	1997	1005	331	764	.433	78	235	.332	265	338	.784	97	276	373	302	153	0	105	24	135	38.4	19.3	7.2	5.8	.579
96-97	Houston	62	62	2271	1114	397	899	.442	119	335	.355	201	268	.750	118	255	373	354	151	0	119	36	155	36.6	18.0	6.0	5.7	.559
97-98	Houston	70	70	2473	1287	452	1059	.427	106	334	.317	277	346	.801	105	241	346	382	193	0	126	42	189	35.3	18.4	4.9	5.5	.535
NBA Season Totals		1086	950	37537	22195	8335	17673	.472	827	2603	.318	4698	5962	.788	2615	4062	6677	6125	3285	33	2207	719	2982	34.6	20.4	6.1	5.6	....
83-84	Portland	5	0	85	36	15	35	.429	0	1	.000	6	7	.857	7	10	17	8	11	0	5	1	7	17.0	7.2	3.4	1.6	.415
84-85	Portland	9	9	339	150	55	134	.410	2	7	.286	38	45	.844	27	28	55	83	37	0	23	9	29	37.7	16.7	6.1	9.2	.586
85-86	Portland	4	4	145	72	26	57	.456	2	5	.400	18	23	.783	9	16	25	26	19	1	6	3	19	36.3	18.0	6.3	6.5	.509
86-87	Portland	4	4	153	96	36	79	.456	1	4	.250	23	29	.793	16	14	30	15	16	1	7	3	6	38.3	24.0	7.5	3.8	.611
87-88	Portland	4	4	170	88	32	83	.386	3	6	.500	21	29	.724	12	16	28	21	14	0	12	2	12	42.5	22.0	7.0	5.3	.474
88-89	Portland	3	3	128	83	35	71	.493	0	2	.000	13	17	.765	13	7	20	25	11	0	6	2	12	42.7	27.7	6.7	8.3	.658
89-90	Portland	21	21	853	449	172	390	.441	9	41	.220	96	124	.774	63	88	151	150	72	2	53	18	67	40.6	21.4	7.2	7.1	.589
90-91	Portland	16	16	633	347	128	269	.476	15	56	.268	76	98	.776	40	89	129	129	56	0	34	16	61	39.6	21.7	8.1	8.1	.674
91-92	Portland	21	21	847	553	198	425	.466	19	81	.235	138	171	.807	60	95	155	147	77	2	31	20	58	40.3	26.3	7.4	7.0	.692
92-93	Portland	3	3	116	57	18	43	.419	5	12	.417	16	20	.800	8	11	19	14	9	0	5	3	3	38.7	19.0	6.3	4.7	.560
93-94	Portland	4	4	157	84	31	73	.425	3	13	.231	19	23	.826	10	31	41	22	7	0	8	2	9	39.3	21.0	10.3	5.5	.655
94-95	Houston	22	22	849	450	155	322	.481	30	99	.303	110	140	.786	45	109	154	111	68	1	33	15	45	38.6	20.5	7.0	5.0	.604
95-96	Houston	8	8	292	133	49	118	.415	9	34	.265	26	34	.765	15	47	62	40	22	0	21	4	20	36.5	16.6	7.8	5.0	.546
96-97	Houston	16	16	623	290	105	241	.436	38	102	.373	42	54	.778	25	64	89	77	52	0	26	7	36	38.9	18.1	5.6	4.8	.475
97-98	Houston	5	5	182	75	21	68	.309	5	26	.192	28	37	.757	9	18	27	23	15	0	8	3	13	36.4	15.0	5.4	4.6	.378
NBA Playoff Totals		145	140	5572	2963	1076	2408	.447	141	489	.288	670	851	.787	359	643	1002	891	486	7	278	108	397	38.4	20.4	6.9	6.1	....

• DRIGGERS, Nate

Nathan Allen Driggers

Born: Oct. 12, 1973. Chicago, IL, United States. Height: 6'5". Weight: 215 lbs. Drafted: — College: Montevallo

96-97	Boston	15	0	132	36	13	43	.302	0	9	.000	10	14	.714	12	10	22	6	10	0	3	2	6	8.8	2.4	1.5	0.4	.208
NBA Season Totals		15	0	132	36	13	43	.302	0	9	.000	10	14	.714	12	10	22	6	10	0	3	2	6	8.8	2.4	1.5	0.4	....

• DRISCOLL, Terry

Edward Cuthbert Driscoll Jr.

Born: Aug. 28, 1947. Winthrop, MA, United States. Height: 6'7". Weight: 215 lbs. Drafted: 1969 College: Boston College

70-71	Detroit	69	....	1255	372	132	318	.415	....	....	....	108	154	.701	....	....	402	54	212	2	....	....	....	18.2	5.4	5.8	0.8	.405
71-72	Baltimore	40	....	313	107	40	104	.385	....	....	....	27	39	.692	....	....	109	23	53	0	....	....	....	7.8	2.7	2.7	0.6	.460
72-73	Baltimore	1	....	5	0	0	1	.000	....	....	....	0	0	.000	....	....	3	0	1	0	....	....	....	5.0	0.0	3.0	0.0	.257
72-73	Milwaukee	59	....	959	323	140	326	.429	....	....	....	43	62	.694	....	....	297	55	143	0	....	....	....	16.3	5.5	5.0	0.9	.429
73-74	Milwaukee	64	....	697	206	88	187	.471	....	....	....	30	46	.652	73	126	199	54	121	0	21	16	....	10.9	3.2	3.1	0.8	.423
74-75	St. Louis-A	30	....	351	112	46	122	.377	0	0	.000	20	27	.741	37	51	88	32	51	....	9	6	28	11.7	3.7	2.9	1.1	.377
74-75	Milwaukee	11	....	52	7	3	13	.231	....	....	....	1	2	.500	7	9	16	3	7	0	1	0	....	4.7	0.6	1.5	0.3	.234
NBA Season Totals		244	....	3281	1015	403	949	.425	....	....	....	209	303	.690	80	135	1026	189	537	2	22	16	....	13.4	4.2	4.2	0.8	'....
ABA Season Totals		30	....	351	112	46	122	.377	0	0	.000	20	27	.741	37	51	88	32	51	....	9	6	28	11.7	3.7	2.9	1.1	....
Career Totals		274	....	3632	1127	449	1071	.419	0	0	.000	229	330	.694	117	186	1114	221	588	2	31	22	28	13.3	4.1	4.1	0.8	....
71-72	Baltimore	1	....	2	3	1	1	1.000	....	....	....	1	1	1.000	....	....	1	0	0	0	....	....	....	2.0	3.0	1.0	0.0	1.932
72-73	Milwaukee	6	....	16	0	0	4	.000	....	....	....	0	0	.000	....	....	0	1	2	0	....	....	....	2.7	0.0	0.0	0.2	-.197
73-74	Milwaukee	9	....	29	12	5	10	.500	....	....	....	2	2	1.000	9	5	14	3	12	0	2	1	....	3.2	1.3	1.6	0.3	.621
NBA Playoff Totals		16	....	47	15	6	15	.400	....	....	....	3	3	1.000	9	5	15	4	14	0	2	1	....	2.9	0.9	0.9	0.3	....

• DRISH, John

John Drish

Born: 1917. Height: — Weight: — Drafted: — College: Illinois

41-42	Chicago-N	8	....	....	23	10	....	....	....	....	....	3	....	....	....	....	....	....	....	....	....	....	....	....	2.9	....	....	....
NBL Season Totals		8	....	....	23	10	....	....	....	....	....	3	....	....	....	....	....	....	....	....	....	....	....	....	2.9	....	....	....

YEAR TEAM	GP	GS	MIN	PTS	FGM	FGA	FG%	3PM	3PA	3P%	FTM	FTA	FT%	ORB	DRB	TRB	AST	PF	DQ	STL	BLK	TO	MPG	PPG	RPG	APG	PCM

• DRO, Bob
Bob Dro

Born: 1918.   Height: 6'   Weight: 190 lbs.   Drafted: —   College: Indiana

YEAR TEAM	GP	GS	MIN	PTS	FGM	FGA	FG%	3PM	3PA	3P%	FTM	FTA	FT%	ORB	DRB	TRB	AST	PF	DQ	STL	BLK	TO	MPG	PPG	RPG	APG	PCM
41-42 Indianapolis-N	15	....	....	46	20	....	....	....	....	....	....	6	....	....	....	....	....	....	....	....	....	....	....	....	3.1	....	....	....
NBL Season Totals	15	....	....	46	20	....	....	....	....	....	....	6	....	....	....	....	....	....	....	....	....	....	....	....	3.1	....	....	....

• DROBNJAK, Predrag
Predrag Drobnjak

Born: Oct. 27, 1975. Bijelo Polje, Yugoslavia.   Height: 6'11".   Weight: 270 lbs.   Drafted: 1997   College: none

YEAR TEAM	GP	GS	MIN	PTS	FGM	FGA	FG%	3PM	3PA	3P%	FTM	FTA	FT%	ORB	DRB	TRB	AST	PF	DQ	STL	BLK	TO	MPG	PPG	RPG	APG	PCM
01-02 Seattle	64	12	1174	437	191	414	.461	0	2	.000	55	73	.753	75	144	219	51	109	0	20	31	51	18.3	6.8	3.4	0.8	.368
02-03 Seattle	82	69	1985	771	325	789	.412	30	85	.353	91	115	.791	111	209	320	86	180	0	48	38	65	24.2	9.4	3.9	1.0	.333
NBA Season Totals	146	81	3159	1208	516	1203	.429	30	87	.345	146	188	.777	186	353	539	137	289	0	68	69	116	21.6	8.3	3.7	0.9	....
01-02 Seattle	3	1	38	10	4	12	.333	0	0	.000	2	4	.500	3	5	8	2	2	0	1	0	1	12.7	3.3	2.7	0.7	.273
NBA Playoff Totals	3	1	38	10	4	12	.333	0	0	.000	2	4	.500	3	5	8	2	2	0	1	0	1	12.7	3.3	2.7	0.7	....

• DROLLINGER, Ralph
Ralph Kim Drollinger

Born: Apr. 20, 1954. La Mesa, CA, United States.   Height: 7'2".   Weight: 250 lbs.   Drafted: 1978   College: UCLA

YEAR TEAM	GP	GS	MIN	PTS	FGM	FGA	FG%	3PM	3PA	3P%	FTM	FTA	FT%	ORB	DRB	TRB	AST	PF	DQ	STL	BLK	TO	MPG	PPG	RPG	APG	PCM
80-81 Dallas	6	....	67	15	7	14	.500	0	0	.000	1	4	.250	5	14	19	14	16	0	1	2	13	11.2	2.5	3.2	2.3	.349
NBA Season Totals	6	....	67	15	7	14	.500	0	0	.000	1	4	.250	5	14	19	14	16	0	1	2	13	11.2	2.5	3.2	2.3	....

• DRUMMOND, Beryl
Beryl Drummond

Born: 1918.   Height: 6'1".   Weight: 185 lbs.   Drafted: —   College: none

YEAR TEAM	GP	GS	MIN	PTS	FGM	FGA	FG%	3PM	3PA	3P%	FTM	FTA	FT%	ORB	DRB	TRB	AST	PF	DQ	STL	BLK	TO	MPG	PPG	RPG	APG	PCM
37-38 Dayton-N	2	....	....	2	1	....	....	....	....	....	0	....	....	....	....	....	....	....	....	....	....	....	1.0	....	....	....	
46-47 Toledo-N	1	....	....	0	0	....	....	....	....	....	0	0	.000	....	....	....	....	....	....	....	....	....	0.0	....	....	....	
NBL Season Totals	3	....	....	2	1	....	....	....	....	....	0	0		....	....	....	....	....	....	....	....	....	0.7	....	....	....	
46-47 Toledo-N	2	....	....	0	0	....	....	....	....	....	0	0	.000	....	....	....	....	....	....	....	....	....	0.0	....	....	....	
NBL Playoff Totals	2	....	....	0	0	....	....	....	....	....	0	0		....	....	....	....	....	....	....	....	....	0.0	....	....	....	

• DUCHARME, Paul
Paul DuCharme

Born: 1917.   Height: 5'11".   Weight: 160 lbs.   Drafted: —   College: Notre Dame

YEAR TEAM	GP	GS	MIN	PTS	FGM	FGA	FG%	3PM	3PA	3P%	FTM	FTA	FT%	ORB	DRB	TRB	AST	PF	DQ	STL	BLK	TO	MPG	PPG	RPG	APG	PCM
40-41 Non-Skids-N	3	....	....	1	0	....	....	....	....	....	1	....	....	....	....	....	....	....	....	....	....	....	0.3	....	....	....	
NBL Season Totals	3	....	....	1	0	....	....	....	....	....	1	....	....	....	....	....	....	....	....	....	....	....	0.3	....	....	....	

• DUCKETT, Dick
Richard J. Duckett

Born: Mar. 25, 1933.   Height: 6'1".   Weight: 185 lbs.   Drafted: 1957   College: St. John's (NY)

YEAR TEAM	GP	GS	MIN	PTS	FGM	FGA	FG%	3PM	3PA	3P%	FTM	FTA	FT%	ORB	DRB	TRB	AST	PF	DQ	STL	BLK	TO	MPG	PPG	RPG	APG	PCM
57-58 Cincinnati	34	....	424	132	54	158	.342	....	....	....	24	27	.889	....	....	56	47	60	0	....	....	....	12.5	3.9	1.6	1.4	.316
NBA Season Totals	34	....	424	132	54	158	.342	....	....	....	24	27	.889	....	....	56	47	60	0	....	....	....	12.5	3.9	1.6	1.4	....

• DUCKWORTH, Kevin
Kevin Jerome Duckworth

Born: Apr. 1, 1964. Harvey, IL, United States.   Height: 7'   Weight: 275 lbs.   Drafted: 1986   College: Eastern Illinois

YEAR TEAM	GP	GS	MIN	PTS	FGM	FGA	FG%	3PM	3PA	3P%	FTM	FTA	FT%	ORB	DRB	TRB	AST	PF	DQ	STL	BLK	TO	MPG	PPG	RPG	APG	PCM
86-87 San Antonio	14	1	122	45	18	45	.400	0	0	.000	9	14	.643	13	18	31	6	27	0	5	3	4	8.7	3.2	2.2	0.4	.360
86-87 Portland	51	0	753	307	112	228	.491	0	1	.000	83	120	.692	63	129	192	23	165	3	16	18	77	14.8	6.0	3.8	0.5	.356
87-88 Portland	78	50	2223	1231	450	907	.496	0	0	.000	331	430	.770	224	352	576	66	280	5	31	32	179	28.5	15.8	7.4	0.8	.507
88-89 Portland	79	79	2662	1432	554	1161	.477	0	2	.000	324	428	.757	246	389	635	60	300	6	56	49	198	33.7	18.1	8.0	0.8	.469
89-90 Portland	82	82	2462	1327	548	1146	.478	0	0	.000	231	312	.740	184	325	509	91	271	2	36	34	172	30.0	16.2	6.2	1.1	.439
90-91 Portland	81	81	2511	1282	521	1084	.481	0	2	.000	240	311	.772	177	354	531	89	251	5	33	34	186	31.0	15.8	6.6	1.1	.432
91-92 Portland	82	82	2222	880	362	786	.461	0	3	.000	156	226	.690	151	346	497	99	264	5	38	37	139	27.1	10.7	6.1	1.2	.378
92-93 Portland	74	55	1762	729	301	687	.438	0	2	.000	127	175	.726	118	269	387	70	222	1	45	39	89	23.8	9.9	5.2	0.9	.383
93-94 Washington	69	52	1485	456	184	441	.417	0	0	.000	88	132	.667	103	222	325	56	223	2	37	35	104	21.5	6.6	4.7	0.8	.288
94-95 Washington	40	22	818	283	118	267	.442	2	10	.200	45	70	.643	65	130	195	20	110	3	21	24	60	20.5	7.1	4.9	0.5	.330
95-96 Milwaukee	8	1	58	9	3	14	.214	0	0	.000	3	6	.500	2	5	7	2	19	0	2	0	2	7.3	1.1	0.9	0.3	-.051
96-97 LA Clippers	26	22	384	104	45	103	.437	3	4	.750	11	16	.688	23	37	60	16	63	1	9	11	34	14.8	4.0	2.3	0.6	.204
NBA Season Totals	684	527	17462	8085	3216	6869	.468	5	24	.208	1648	2240	.736	1369	2576	3945	598	2195	33	329	316	1244	25.5	11.8	5.8	0.9	....
86-87 Portland	4	0	53	14	6	12	.500	0	0	.000	2	5	.400	3	5	8	1	14	0	4	1	6	13.3	3.5	2.0	0.3	.153
87-88 Portland	4	4	151	86	34	70	.486	0	1	.000	18	23	.783	20	24	44	7	14	0	1	2	21	37.8	21.5	11.0	1.8	.499
88-89 Portland	3	3	83	34	14	35	.400	0	0	.000	6	11	.545	8	11	19	2	17	2	1	1	5	27.7	11.3	6.3	0.7	.256
89-90 Portland	15	15	453	197	82	187	.439	0	0	.000	33	46	.717	28	59	87	16	60	2	5	9	33	30.2	13.1	5.8	1.1	.320
90-91 Portland	16	16	511	187	73	182	.401	0	0	.000	41	56	.732	40	67	107	14	53	1	8	8	39	31.9	11.7	6.7	0.9	.287
91-92 Portland	21	21	647	249	107	216	.495	0	0	.000	35	53	.660	40	77	117	41	76	1	11	12	45	30.8	11.9	5.6	2.0	.365
92-93 Portland	4	0	58	18	7	21	.333	0	0	.000	4	4	1.000	4	9	13	3	12	0	0	1	6	14.5	4.5	3.3	0.8	.173
NBA Playoff Totals	67	59	1956	785	323	723	.447	0	1	.000	139	198	.702	143	252	395	84	246	6	30	34	155	29.2	11.7	5.9	1.3	....

• DUDLEY, Charles
Charles (Grasshopper) Dudley

Born: Mar. 5, 1950. Harrisburg, PA, United States.   Height: 6'2".   Weight: 180 lbs.   Drafted: 1972   College: Washington

YEAR TEAM	GP	GS	MIN	PTS	FGM	FGA	FG%	3PM	3PA	3P%	FTM	FTA	FT%	ORB	DRB	TRB	AST	PF	DQ	STL	BLK	TO	MPG	PPG	RPG	APG	PCM
72-73 Seattle	12	....	99	34	10	23	.435	....	....	....	14	16	.875	....	....	6	16	15	0	40	....	....	8.3	2.8	0.5	1.3	.394
74-75 Golden State	67	....	756	274	102	217	.470	....	....	....	70	97	.722	61	84	145	103	105	1	40	2	....	11.3	4.1	2.2	1.5	.478
75-76 Golden State	82	....	1456	521	182	345	.528	....	....	....	157	245	.641	112	157	269	239	170	0	77	2	....	17.8	6.4	3.3	2.9	.532
76-77 Golden State	79	....	1682	569	220	421	.523	....	....	....	129	203	.635	119	177	296	347	169	0	67	6	....	21.3	7.2	3.7	4.4	.559

YEAR	TEAM	GP	GS	MIN	PTS	FGM	FGA	FG%	3PM	3PA	3P%	FTM	FTA	FT%	ORB	DRB	TRB	AST	PF	DQ	STL	BLK	TO	MPG	PPG	RPG	APG	PCM
77-78	Golden State	78	....	1660	392	127	249	.510	....	....	....	138	195	.708	86	201	287	409	181	0	68	2	164	21.3	5.0	3.7	5.2	.488
78-79	Chicago	43	....	684	118	45	125	.360	....	....	....	28	42	.667	25	61	86	116	82	0	32	1	65	15.9	2.7	2.0	2.7	.262
NBA Season Totals		361	....	6337	1908	686	1380	.497	....	....	....	536	798	.672	403	680	1089	1230	722	1	284	13	229	17.6	5.3	3.0	3.4	....
74-75	Golden State	13	....	112	36	10	24	.417	....	....	....	16	28	.571	5	12	17	17	23	0	5	2	....	8.6	2.8	1.3	1.3	.385
75-76	Golden State	13	....	260	90	33	57	.579	....	....	....	24	33	.727	20	16	36	38	29	0	22	1	....	20.0	6.9	2.8	2.9	.490
76-77	Golden State	10	....	236	41	13	37	.351	....	....	....	15	23	.652	17	21	38	69	28	0	7	0	....	23.6	4.1	3.8	6.9	.492
NBA Playoff Totals		36	....	608	167	56	118	.475	....	....	....	55	84	.655	42	49	91	124	80	0	34	3	....	16.9	4.6	2.5	3.4	....

• DUDLEY, Chris

Christen Guilford Dudley

Born: Feb. 22, 1965. Stamford, CT, United States.   Height: 6'11".   Weight: 235 lbs.   Drafted: 1987   College: Yale

YEAR	TEAM	GP	GS	MIN	PTS	FGM	FGA	FG%	3PM	3PA	3P%	FTM	FTA	FT%	ORB	DRB	TRB	AST	PF	DQ	STL	BLK	TO	MPG	PPG	RPG	APG	PCM
87-88	Cleveland	55	1	513	170	65	137	.474	0	0	.000	40	71	.563	74	70	144	23	87	2	13	19	33	9.3	3.1	2.6	0.4	.401
88-89	Cleveland	61	2	544	185	73	168	.435	0	1	.000	39	107	.364	72	85	157	21	82	0	9	23	43	8.9	3.0	2.6	0.3	.340
89-90	Cleveland	37	22	684	184	79	203	.389	0	0	.000	26	77	.338	88	115	203	20	83	1	19	41	48	18.5	5.0	5.5	0.5	.333
89-90	New Jersey	27	8	672	166	67	152	.441	0	0	.000	32	105	.305	86	134	220	19	81	1	22	31	38	24.9	6.1	8.1	0.7	.379
90-91	New Jersey	61	25	1560	434	170	417	.408	0	0	.000	94	176	.534	229	282	511	37	217	6	39	153	79	25.6	7.1	8.4	0.6	.440
91-92	New Jersey	82	21	1902	460	190	472	.403	0	0	.000	80	171	.468	343	396	739	58	275	5	38	179	82	23.2	5.6	9.0	0.7	.474
92-93	New Jersey	71	16	1398	245	94	266	.353	0	0	.000	57	110	.518	215	298	513	16	195	5	17	102	57	19.7	3.5	7.2	0.2	.374
93-94	Portland	6	3	86	14	6	25	.240	0	0	.000	2	4	.500	16	8	24	5	18	0	4	3	2	14.3	2.3	4.0	0.8	.226
94-95	Portland	82	82	2245	447	181	446	.406	0	1	.000	85	183	.464	325	439	764	34	286	6	43	126	82	27.4	5.5	9.3	0.4	.380
95-96	Portland	80	61	1924	404	162	358	.453	0	1	.000	80	157	.510	239	481	720	37	251	4	41	100	80	24.1	5.1	9.0	0.5	.436
96-97	Portland	81	14	1840	317	126	293	.430	0	0	.000	65	137	.474	204	389	593	41	247	3	39	96	81	22.7	3.9	7.3	0.5	.358
97-98	New York	51	22	858	157	58	143	.406	0	0	.000	41	92	.446	108	167	275	21	139	4	13	51	46	16.8	3.1	5.4	0.4	.330
98-99	New York	46	16	685	115	48	109	.440	0	0	.000	19	40	.475	79	114	193	7	116	1	13	38	24	14.9	2.5	4.2	0.2	.297
99-00	New York	47	3	459	55	23	67	.343	0	0	.000	9	27	.333	63	73	136	5	95	2	7	21	18	9.8	1.2	2.9	0.1	.222
00-01	Phoenix	53	33	613	72	29	73	.397	0	0	.000	14	36	.389	64	119	183	18	111	1	14	29	26	11.6	1.4	3.5	0.3	.281
01-02	Portland	43	2	327	48	20	50	.400	0	2	.000	8	15	.533	27	53	80	13	42	0	3	14	14	7.6	1.1	1.9	0.3	.269
02-03	Portland	3	0	11	0	0	1	.000	0	0	.000	0	0	.000	0	2	2	0	3	0	0	0	0	3.7	0.0	0.7	0.0	-.041
NBA Season Totals		886	331	16321	3473	1391	3380	.412	0	5	.000	691	1508	.458	2234	3223	5457	375	2328	41	334	1026	753	18.4	3.9	6.2	0.4	....
87-88	Cleveland	4	0	24	5	2	4	.500	0	0	.000	1	2	.500	4	2	6	2	3	0	0	0	1	6.0	1.3	1.5	0.5	.336
88-89	Cleveland	1	0	4	0	0	1	.000	0	0	.000	0	0	.000	0	0	0	0	1	0	0	0	1	4.0	0.0	0.0	0.0	-.581
91-92	New Jersey	4	0	77	14	5	14	.357	0	0	.000	4	8	.500	13	12	25	3	14	1	2	10	1	19.3	3.5	6.3	0.8	.441
93-94	Portland	4	2	81	9	4	10	.400	0	0	.000	1	2	.500	5	10	15	0	16	0	6	0	1	20.3	2.3	3.8	0.0	.173
94-95	Portland	3	3	59	7	2	3	.667	0	0	.000	3	8	.375	6	9	15	1	8	0	0	1	3	19.7	2.3	5.0	0.3	.224
95-96	Portland	5	0	92	14	5	13	.385	0	0	.000	4	6	.667	9	18	27	1	18	0	2	2	4	18.4	2.8	5.4	0.2	.256
96-97	Portland	4	0	69	12	5	11	.455	0	0	.000	2	6	.333	10	18	28	3	19	1	2	5	0	17.3	3.0	7.0	0.8	.457
97-98	New York	6	3	53	8	3	9	.333	0	0	.000	2	4	.500	6	12	18	0	16	0	2	1	2	8.8	1.3	3.0	0.0	.220
98-99	New York	18	6	294	43	16	38	.421	0	0	.000	11	28	.393	27	55	82	5	63	2	9	8	9	16.3	2.4	4.6	0.3	.250
99-00	New York	5	2	43	4	1	2	.500	0	0	.000	2	2	1.000	5	7	12	2	11	0	1	1	1	8.6	0.8	2.4	0.4	.281
00-01	Phoenix	3	0	26	2	1	2	.500	0	0	.000	0	0	.000	3	4	7	0	1	0	1	1	4	8.7	0.7	2.3	0.0	.198
01-02	Portland	2	0	3	0	0	1	.000	0	0	.000	0	0	.000	0	2	2	0	1	0	0	0	1	1.5	0.0	1.0	0.0	-.151
NBA Playoff Totals		59	16	825	118	44	108	.407	0	0	.000	30	66	.455	88	149	237	17	171	4	25	29	28	14.0	2.0	4.0	0.3	....

• DUEROD, Terry

Terry (Sweet Due) Duerod

Born: July 29, 1956. Royal Oak, MI, United States.   Height: 6'2".   Weight: 180 lbs.   Drafted: 1979   College: Detroit

YEAR	TEAM	GP	GS	MIN	PTS	FGM	FGA	FG%	3PM	3PA	3P%	FTM	FTA	FT%	ORB	DRB	TRB	AST	PF	DQ	STL	BLK	TO	MPG	PPG	RPG	APG	PCM
79-80	Detroit	67	....	1331	624	282	598	.472	15	53	.283	45	66	.682	29	69	98	117	102	0	41	11	80	19.9	9.3	1.5	1.7	.356
80-81	Dallas	18	....	337	168	74	161	.460	2	6	.333	18	27	.667	15	24	39	30	19	0	12	4	25	18.7	9.3	2.2	1.7	.404
80-81	Boston	32	....	114	79	30	73	.411	6	10	.600	13	14	.929	2	3	5	6	8	0	5	0	10	3.6	2.5	0.2	0.2	.371
81-82	Boston	21	0	146	72	34	77	.442	0	1	.000	4	12	.333	6	9	15	12	9	0	3	1	2	7.0	3.4	0.7	0.6	.364
82-83	Golden State	5	0	49	18	9	19	.474	0	0	.000	0	0	.000	0	3	3	5	5	0	2	1	9	9.8	3.6	0.6	1.0	.194
NBA Season Totals		143	0	1977	961	429	928	.462	23	70	.329	80	119	.672	52	108	160	170	143	0	63	17	126	13.8	6.7	1.1	1.2	....
80-81	Boston	10	....	12	8	4	10	.400	0	2	.000	0	0	.000	0	0	0	0	0	0	1	0	1	1.2	0.8	0.0	0.0	.211
NBA Playoff Totals		10	....	12	8	4	10	.400	0	2	.000	0	0	.000	0	0	0	0	0	0	1	0	1	1.2	0.8	0.0	0.0	....

• DUFFY, Bob

Robert Joseph Duffy

Born: Sept. 26, 1940. Cold Spring, NY, United States.   Height: 6'3".   Weight: 185 lbs.   Drafted: 1962   College: Colgate

YEAR	TEAM	GP	GS	MIN	PTS	FGM	FGA	FG%	3PM	3PA	3P%	FTM	FTA	FT%	ORB	DRB	TRB	AST	PF	DQ	STL	BLK	TO	MPG	PPG	RPG	APG	PCM
62-63	St. Louis	42	....	435	154	66	174	.379	....	....	....	22	39	.564			39	83	42	0	....	....	....	10.4	3.7	0.9	2.0	.406
63-64	St. Louis	2	....	6	2	1	3	.333	....	....	....	0	1	.000			1	0	0	0	....	....	....	3.0	1.0	0.5	0.0	.139
63-64	New York	4	....	50	16	5	19	.263	....	....	....	6	8	.750			6	5	0	0	....	....	....	12.5	4.0	1.5	1.3	.302
63-64	Detroit	42	....	606	214	88	207	.425	....	....	....	38	56	.679			54	74	48	0	....	....	....	14.4	5.1	1.3	1.8	.377
64-65	Detroit	4	....	26	14	6	11	.364	....	....	....	6	7	.857			4	5	4	0	....	....	....	6.5	3.5	1.0	1.3	.613
NBA Season Totals		94	....	1123	400	164	414	.396	....	....	....	72	111	.649			104	167	94	0	....	....	....	11.9	4.3	1.1	1.8	....
62-63	St. Louis	5	....	24	14	6	15	.400	....	....	....	2	2	1.000			3	3	3	0	....	....	....	4.8	2.8	0.6	0.6	.487
NBA Playoff Totals		5	....	24	14	6	15	.400	....	....	....	2	2	1.000			3	3	3	0	....	....	....	4.8	2.8	0.6	0.6	....

• DUFFY, Bob

Robert John Duffy

Born: July 5, 1922.   Height: 6'4".   Weight: 175 lbs.   Drafted: —   College: Tulane

YEAR	TEAM	GP	GS	MIN	PTS	FGM	FGA	FG%	3PM	3PA	3P%	FTM	FTA	FT%	ORB	DRB	TRB	AST	PF	DQ	STL	BLK	TO	MPG	PPG	RPG	APG	PCM
46-47	Chicago	11	....	....	11	5	25	.200	....	....	....	1	3	.333	....	....		0	13	....	....	....	....	....	1.0	....	0.0	....
46-47	Boston	6	....	....	8	2	7	.286	....	....	....	4	4	1.000	....	....		0	4	....	....	....	....	....	1.3	....	0.0	....
NBA Season Totals		17	....	....	19	7	32	.219	....	....	....	5	7	.714	....	....		0	17	....	....	....	....	....	1.1	....	0.0	....

YEAR TEAM	GP	GS	MIN	PTS	FGM	FGA	FG%	3PM	3PA	3P%	FTM	FTA	FT%	ORB	DRB	TRB	AST	PF	DQ	STL	BLK	TO	MPG	PPG	RPG	APG	PCM

• DUGGER, Jack

John Richard Dugger

Born: Jan. 13, 1923. Pittsburgh, PA, United States. Died: Feb.23, 1988. Height: 6'3". Weight: 225 lbs. Drafted: — College: Ohio State

YEAR TEAM	GP	GS	MIN	PTS	FGM	FGA	FG%	3PM	3PA	3P%	FTM	FTA	FT%	ORB	DRB	TRB	AST	PF	DQ	STL	BLK	TO	MPG	PPG	RPG	APG	PCM
46-47 Syracuse-N	21	....	....	36	13	....	....	....	....	....	10	19	.526	....	....	....	....	19	....	....	....	....	....	1.7	....	....	....
NBL Season Totals	21	....	....	36	13	....	....	....	....	....	10	19	....	....	....	....	....	19	....	....	....	....	....	1.7	....	....	....

• DUKES, Walter

Walter F. Dukes

Born: June 23, 1930. Rochester, NY, United States. Died: Feb.2001. Height: 7' Weight: 220 lbs. Drafted: 1953 College: Seton Hall

YEAR TEAM	GP	GS	MIN	PTS	FGM	FGA	FG%	3PM	3PA	3P%	FTM	FTA	FT%	ORB	DRB	TRB	AST	PF	DQ	STL	BLK	TO	MPG	PPG	RPG	APG	PCM
55-56 New York	60	....	1290	465	149	370	.403	....	....	....	167	236	.708	....	....	443	39	211	11	....	....	....	21.5	7.8	7.4	0.7	.446
56-57 Minneapolis	71	....	1866	720	228	626	.364	....	....	....	264	383	.689	....	....	794	54	273	10	....	....	....	26.3	10.1	11.2	0.8	.502
57-58 Detroit	72	....	2184	803	278	796	.349	....	....	....	247	366	.675	....	....	954	52	**311**	17	....	....	....	30.3	11.2	13.3	0.7	.472
58-59 Detroit	72	....	2338	933	318	904	.352	....	....	....	297	452	.657	....	....	958	64	**332**	**22**	....	....	....	32.5	13.0	13.3	0.9	.475
59-60 Detroit	66	....	2140	1004	314	871	.361	....	....	....	376	508	.740	....	....	883	80	310	**20**	....	....	....	32.4	15.2	13.4	1.2	.553
60-61 Detroit	73	....	2044	853	286	706	.405	....	....	....	281	400	.703	....	....	1028	139	313	**16**	....	....	....	28.0	11.7	14.1	1.9	.648
61-62 Detroit	77	....	1896	720	256	647	.396	....	....	....	208	291	.715	....	....	803	125	327	**20**	....	....	....	24.6	9.4	10.4	1.6	.545
62-63 Detroit	62	....	913	267	83	255	.325	....	....	....	101	137	.737	....	....	360	55	183	5	....	....	....	14.7	4.3	5.8	0.9	.433
NBA Season Totals	553	....	14671	5765	1912	5175	.369	....	....	....	1941	2773	.700	....	....	6223	608	2260	121	....	....	....	26.5	10.4	11.3	1.1	....
56-57 Minneapolis	5	....	177	68	24	57	.421	....	....	....	20	27	.741	....	....	74	5	26	2	....	....	....	35.4	13.6	14.8	1.0	.523
57-58 Detroit	7	....	286	111	37	101	.366	....	....	....	37	56	.661	....	....	97	4	38	3	....	....	....	40.9	15.9	13.9	0.6	.417
58-59 Detroit	3	....	113	43	15	30	.500	....	....	....	13	17	.765	....	....	40	3	15	1	....	....	....	37.7	14.3	13.3	1.0	.517
59-60 Detroit	2	....	78	48	16	31	.516	....	....	....	16	22	.727	....	....	33	2	9	1	....	....	....	39.0	24.0	16.5	1.0	.749
60-61 Detroit	5	....	152	50	20	53	.377	....	....	....	10	18	.556	....	....	49	11	25	2	....	....	....	30.4	10.0	9.8	2.2	.416
61-62 Detroit	10	....	342	124	39	91	.429	....	....	....	46	61	.754	....	....	138	24	52	5	....	....	....	34.2	12.4	13.8	2.4	.568
62-63 Detroit	3	....	8	3	0	0	.000	....	....	....	3	3	1.000	....	....	1	2	3	0	....	....	....	2.7	1.0	0.3	0.7	.628
NBA Playoff Totals	35	....	1156	447	151	363	.416	....	....	....	145	204	.711	....	....	432	51	168	14	....	....	....	33.0	12.8	12.3	1.5	....

• DUMARS, Joe

Joe Dumars III

Born: May 24, 1963. Shreveport, LA, United States. Height: 6'3". Weight: 190 lbs. Drafted: 1985 College: McNeese State

YEAR TEAM	GP	GS	MIN	PTS	FGM	FGA	FG%	3PM	3PA	3P%	FTM	FTA	FT%	ORB	DRB	TRB	AST	PF	DQ	STL	BLK	TO	MPG	PPG	RPG	APG	PCM
85-86 Detroit	82	45	1957	769	287	597	.481	5	16	.313	190	238	.798	60	59	119	390	200	1	66	11	156	23.9	9.4	1.5	4.8	.419
86-87 Detroit	79	75	2439	931	369	749	.493	9	22	.409	184	246	.748	50	117	167	352	194	1	83	5	174	30.9	11.8	2.1	4.5	.373
87-88 Detroit	82	82	2732	1161	453	960	.472	4	19	.211	251	308	.815	63	137	200	387	155	1	87	15	172	33.3	14.2	2.4	4.7	.411
88-89 Detroit	69	67	2408	1186	456	903	.505	14	29	.483	260	306	.850	57	115	172	390	103	1	63	5	179	34.9	17.2	2.5	5.7	.488
89-90 Detroit	75	71	2578	1335	508	1058	.480	22	55	.400	297	330	.900	60	152	212	368	129	1	63	2	143	34.4	17.8	2.8	4.9	.489
90-91 Detroit	80	80	3046	1629	622	1292	.481	14	45	.311	371	417	.890	62	125	187	443	135	0	89	7	192	38.1	20.4	2.3	5.5	.485
91-92 Detroit	82	82	3192	1635	587	1311	.448	49	120	.408	412	475	.867	82	106	188	375	145	0	71	12	197	38.9	19.9	2.3	4.6	.419
92-93 Detroit	77	77	3094	1809	677	1454	.466	112	299	.375	343	397	.864	63	85	148	308	141	0	78	7	139	40.2	23.5	1.9	4.0	.456
93-94 Detroit	69	69	2591	1410	505	1118	.452	124	320	.388	276	330	.836	35	116	151	261	118	0	63	4	159	37.6	20.4	2.2	3.8	.427
94-95 Detroit	67	67	2544	1214	417	970	.430	103	338	.305	277	344	.805	47	111	158	368	153	0	72	7	221	38.0	18.1	2.4	5.5	.392
95-96 Detroit	67	40	2193	793	255	598	.426	121	298	.406	162	197	.822	28	110	138	265	106	0	43	3	94	32.7	11.8	2.1	4.0	.351
96-97 Detroit	79	79	2923	1158	385	875	.440	166	384	.432	222	256	.867	38	153	191	318	97	0	57	1	126	37.0	14.7	2.4	4.0	.374
97-98 Detroit	72	72	2326	943	329	791	.416	158	426	.371	127	154	.825	14	90	104	253	99	0	44	2	86	32.3	13.1	1.4	3.5	.342
98-99 Detroit	38	38	1116	428	144	350	.411	89	221	.403	51	61	.836	12	56	68	134	51	0	23	2	53	29.4	11.3	1.8	3.5	.360
NBA Season Totals	1018	944	35139	16401	5994	13026	.460	990	2592	.382	3423	4059	.843	671	1532	2203	4612	1826	5	902	83	2091	34.5	16.1	2.2	4.5	....
85-86 Detroit	4	4	147	60	25	41	.610	0	0	.000	10	15	.667	6	7	13	25	16	0	4	0	7	36.8	15.0	3.3	6.3	.486
86-87 Detroit	15	15	473	190	78	145	.538	2	3	.667	32	41	.780	8	11	19	72	26	0	12	1	27	31.5	12.7	1.3	4.8	.408
87-88 Detroit	23	23	804	284	113	247	.457	2	6	.333	56	63	.889	18	32	50	112	50	1	13	2	40	35.0	12.3	2.2	4.9	.343
88-89 Detroit	17	17	620	300	106	233	.455	1	12	.083	87	101	.861	11	33	44	96	31	0	12	1	31	36.5	17.6	2.6	5.6	.464
89-90 Detroit	20	20	754	364	130	284	.458	5	19	.263	99	113	.876	18	26	44	95	37	0	22	0	54	37.7	18.2	2.2	4.8	.409
90-91 Detroit	15	15	588	309	105	245	.429	17	42	.405	82	97	.845	21	29	50	62	33	1	16	1	17	39.2	20.6	3.3	4.1	.457
91-92 Detroit	5	5	221	84	32	68	.471	5	10	.500	15	19	.789	5	3	8	16	11	0	5	1	7	44.2	16.8	1.6	3.2	.304
95-96 Detroit	3	3	123	41	16	35	.457	5	14	.357	4	4	1.000	5	8	13	11	5	0	0	0	7	41.0	13.7	4.3	3.7	.310
96-97 Detroit	5	5	214	69	22	61	.361	6	23	.261	19	20	.950	2	7	9	10	9	0	5	0	6	42.8	13.8	1.8	2.0	.216
98-99 Detroit	5	5	153	51	19	39	.487	10	19	.526	3	3	1.000	1	6	7	13	9	0	2	0	9	30.6	10.2	1.4	2.6	.285
NBA Playoff Totals	112	112	4097	1752	646	1398	.462	53	148	.358	407	476	.855	95	162	257	512	227	2	91	6	205	36.6	15.6	2.3	4.6	....

• DUMAS, Rich

Richard Dumas

Born: 1945. Height: 6'3". Weight: 170 lbs. Drafted: 1968 College: Northeast Oklahoma State

YEAR TEAM	GP	GS	MIN	PTS	FGM	FGA	FG%	3PM	3PA	3P%	FTM	FTA	FT%	ORB	DRB	TRB	AST	PF	DQ	STL	BLK	TO	MPG	PPG	RPG	APG	PCM
68-69 Houston-A	1	....	5	2	1	5	.200	0	0	.000	0	0	.000	0	1	1	0	1	0	....	....	1	5.0	2.0	1.0	0.0	-.201
ABA Season Totals	1	....	5	2	1	5	.200	0	0	.000	0	0	.000	0	1	1	0	1	0	....	....	1	5.0	2.0	1.0	0.0	....

• DUMAS, Richard

Richard Wayne Dumas

Born: May 19, 1969. Tulsa, OK, United States. Height: 6'7". Weight: 200 lbs. Drafted: 1991 College: Oklahoma State

YEAR TEAM	GP	GS	MIN	PTS	FGM	FGA	FG%	3PM	3PA	3P%	FTM	FTA	FT%	ORB	DRB	TRB	AST	PF	DQ	STL	BLK	TO	MPG	PPG	RPG	APG	PCM
92-93 Phoenix	48	32	1320	757	302	576	.524	1	3	.333	152	215	.707	100	123	223	60	127	0	85	39	91	27.5	15.8	4.6	1.3	.542
94-95 Phoenix	15	1	167	82	37	73	.507	0	1	.000	8	16	.500	18	11	29	7	22	0	10	2	9	11.1	5.5	1.9	0.5	.429
95-96 Philadelphia	39	14	739	241	95	203	.468	2	9	.222	49	70	.700	42	57	99	44	79	1	42	6	51	18.9	6.2	2.5	1.1	.310
NBA Season Totals	102	47	2226	1080	434	852	.509	3	13	.231	209	301	.694	160	191	351	111	228	1	137	47	151	21.8	10.6	3.4	1.1	....
92-93 Phoenix	23	20	499	251	107	204	.525	0	2	.000	37	49	.755	36	29	65	24	52	0	21	13	27	21.7	10.9	2.8	1.0	.448
94-95 Phoenix	3	0	5	2	1	4	.250	0	0	.000	0	0	.000	1	0	1	0	0	0	0	0	1	1.7	0.7	0.3	0.0	-.163
NBA Playoff Totals	26	20	504	253	108	208	.519	0	2	.000	37	49	.755	37	29	66	24	52	0	21	13	28	19.4	9.7	2.5	0.9	....

• DUMAS, Tony
Tony Dumas

Born: Aug. 25, 1972. Chicago, IL, United States.   Height: 6'6".   Weight: 190 lbs.   Drafted: 1994   College: Missouri-K.C.

YEAR	TEAM	GP	GS	MIN	PTS	FGM	FGA	FG%	3PM	3PA	3P%	FTM	FTA	FT%	ORB	DRB	TRB	AST	PF	DQ	STL	BLK	TO	MPG	PPG	RPG	APG	PCM
94-95	Dallas	58	0	613	264	96	250	.384	22	73	.301	50	77	.649	32	30	62	57	78	0	13	4	52	10.6	4.6	1.1	1.0	.255
95-96	Dallas	67	12	1284	776	274	655	.418	74	207	.357	154	257	.599	58	57	115	99	128	0	42	13	74	19.2	11.6	1.7	1.5	.393
96-97	Dallas	18	0	227	72	27	77	.351	3	24	.125	15	23	.652	3	11	14	22	36	0	10	1	14	12.6	4.0	0.8	1.2	.170
96-97	Phoenix	6	1	51	14	6	19	.316	1	4	.250	1	2	.500	0	2	2	3	9	0	0	1	1	8.5	2.3	0.3	0.5	.045
97-98	Cleveland	7	0	47	14	6	12	.500	2	4	.500	0	3	.000	1	4	5	5	5	0	0	0	5	6.7	2.0	0.7	0.7	.219
NBA Season Totals		156	13	2222	1140	409	1013	.404	102	312	.327	220	362	.608	94	104	198	186	256	0	65	19	146	14.2	7.3	1.3	1.2	....

• DUNCAN, Andy
Andrew Duncan

Born: Apr. 17, 1922.   Height: 6'6".   Weight: 195 lbs.   Drafted: 1947   College: William & Mary

YEAR	TEAM	GP	GS	MIN	PTS	FGM	FGA	FG%	3PM	3PA	3P%	FTM	FTA	FT%	ORB	DRB	TRB	AST	PF	DQ	STL	BLK	TO	MPG	PPG	RPG	APG	PCM
47-48	Rochester-N	60			519	200						119	199	.598					183						8.7			
48-49	Rochester	55			407	162	391	.414				83	135	.615				51	179						7.4		0.9	
49-50	Rochester	67			310	125	289	.433				60	108	.556				42	160						4.6		0.6	
50-51	Boston	14			29	7	40	.175				15	22	.682			30	8	27	0					2.1	2.1	0.6	
NBA Season Totals		136			746	294	720	.408				158	265	.596			30	101	366	0					5.5	0.2	0.7	
NBL Season Totals		60			519	200						119	199						183						8.7			
Career Totals		196			1265	494	720					277	464				30	101	549	0					6.5	0.2	0.5	
47-48	Rochester-N	11			101	39						23	34	.676											9.2			
48-49	Rochester	4			6	3	13	.231				0	1	.000				2	5						1.5		0.5	
49-50	Rochester	2			6	2	3	.667				2	2	1.000				1	5						3.0		0.5	
NBA Playoff Totals		6			12	5	16	.313				2	3	.667				3	10						2.0		0.5	
NBL Playoff Totals		11			101	39						23	34												9.2			
Career Playoff Totals		17			113	44	16					25	37					3	10						6.6		0.2	

• DUNCAN, Tim
Timothy Theodore Duncan

Born: Apr. 25, 1976. St. Croix, VI, Virgin Islands.   Height: 7'.   Weight: 248 lbs.   Drafted: 1997   College: Wake Forest

YEAR	TEAM	GP	GS	MIN	PTS	FGM	FGA	FG%	3PM	3PA	3P%	FTM	FTA	FT%	ORB	DRB	TRB	AST	PF	DQ	STL	BLK	TO	MPG	PPG	RPG	APG	PCM
97-98	San Antonio	82	82	3204	1731	706	1287	.549	0	10	.000	319	482	.662	274	703	977	224	254	1	55	206	279	39.1	21.1	11.9	2.7	.665
98-99	San Antonio	50	50	1963	1084	418	845	.495	1	7	.143	247	358	.690	159	412	571	121	147	2	45	126	146	39.3	21.7	11.4	2.4	.639
99-00	San Antonio	74	74	2875	1716	628	1281	.490	1	11	.091	459	603	.761	262	656	918	234	210	1	66	165	242	38.9	23.2	12.4	3.2	.710
00-01	San Antonio	82	82	3174	1820	702	1406	.499	7	27	.259	409	662	.618	259	738	997	245	247	0	70	192	242	38.7	22.2	12.2	3.0	.676
01-02	San Antonio	82	82	3329	2089	**764**	1504	.508	1	10	.100	**560**	701	.799	268	**774**	**1042**	307	217	2	61	203	263	40.6	25.5	12.7	3.7	.762
02-03	San Antonio	81	81	3181	1884	714	1392	.513	6	22	.273	450	634	.710	259	784	1043	316	231	2	55	237	248	39.3	23.3	12.9	3.9	.758
NBA Season Totals		451	451	17726	10324	3932	7715	.510	16	87	.184	2444	3440	.710	1481	4067	5548	1447	1306	8	352	1129	1420	39.3	22.9	12.3	3.2	....
97-98	San Antonio	9	9	374	186	73	140	.521	0	1	.000	40	60	.667	20	61	81	17	24	1	5	23	25	41.6	20.7	9.0	1.9	.534
98-99	San Antonio	17	17	733	395	144	282	.511	0	3	.000	107	143	.748	55	140	195	48	50	1	13	45	52	43.1	23.2	11.5	2.8	.636
00-01	San Antonio	13	13	526	317	120	246	.488	1	1	1.000	76	119	.639	54	134	188	49	43	0	14	35	50	40.5	24.4	14.5	3.8	.736
01-02	San Antonio	9	9	380	248	82	181	.453	1	3	.333	83	101	.822	28	102	130	45	22	0	6	39	37	42.2	27.6	14.4	5.0	.827
02-03	San Antonio	24	24	1021	593	218	412	.529	0	7	.000	157	232	.677	96	273	369	127	78	0	15	79	76	42.5	24.7	15.4	5.3	.820
NBA Playoff Totals		72	72	3034	1739	637	1261	.505	2	15	.133	463	655	.707	253	710	963	286	217	2	53	221	240	42.1	24.2	13.4	4.0	....

• DUNLEAVY, Mike
Michael Joseph Dunleavy

Born: Mar. 21, 1954. Brooklyn, NY, United States.   Height: 6'3".   Weight: 180 lbs.   Drafted: 1976   College: South Carolina

YEAR	TEAM	GP	GS	MIN	PTS	FGM	FGA	FG%	3PM	3PA	3P%	FTM	FTA	FT%	ORB	DRB	TRB	AST	PF	DQ	STL	BLK	TO	MPG	PPG	RPG	APG	PCM
76-77	Philadelphia	32		359	154	60	145	.414				34	45	.756	10	24	34	56	64	1	13	2		11.2	4.8	1.1	1.8	.394
77-78	Philadelphia	4		17	8	3	7	.429				2	2	1.000	0	1	1	6	0	0	1	0	3	4.3	2.0	0.3	1.5	.610
77-78	Houston	11		102	45	17	43	.395				11	16	.688	1	8	9	22	12	0	8	1	9	9.3	4.1	0.8	2.0	.465
78-79	Houston	74		1486	589	215	425	.506				159	184	.864	28	100	128	324	168	2	56	5	133	20.1	8.0	1.7	4.4	.485
79-80	Houston	51		1036	410	148	319	.464	3	20	.150	111	134	.828	26	74	100	210	120	2	40	4	112	20.3	8.0	2.0	4.1	.434
80-81	Houston	74		1609	777	310	632	.491	1	16	.063	156	186	.839	28	90	118	268	165	1	64	2	141	21.7	10.5	1.6	3.6	.451
81-82	Houston	70	15	1315	520	206	450	.458	33	86	.384	75	106	.708	24	80	104	227	161	0	45	3	77	18.8	7.4	1.5	3.2	.396
82-83	San Antonio	79	9	1619	613	213	510	.418	67	**194**	**.345**	120	154	.779	18	116	134	437	210	1	74	4	158	20.5	7.8	1.7	5.5	.472
83-84	Milwaukee	17	12	404	191	70	127	.551	19	45	.422	32	40	.800	6	22	28	78	51	0	12	1	36	23.8	11.2	1.6	4.6	.492
84-85	Milwaukee	19	19	433	169	64	135	.474	16	47	.340	25	29	.862	6	25	31	85	55	1	15	3	40	22.8	8.9	1.6	4.5	.492
88-89	Milwaukee	2	0	5	3	1	2	.500	1	2	.500	0	0	.000	0	0	0	0	0	0	0	0	0	2.5	1.5	0.0	0.0	.414
89-90	Milwaukee	5	0	43	17	4	14	.286	2	9	.222	7	8	.875	0	2	2	10	7	0	1	0	8	8.6	3.4	0.4	2.0	.229
NBA Season Totals		438	55	8428	3496	1311	2809	.467	142	419	.339	732	904	.810	147	542	689	1723	1013	8	329	25	717	19.2	8.0	1.6	3.9	....
76-77	Philadelphia	11		68	22	9	25	.360				4	5	.800	1	3	4	9	14	0	3	0		6.2	2.0	0.4	0.8	.227
78-79	Houston	1		10	0	0	2	.000				0	0	.000	0	1	1	0	1	0	0	0	0	10.0	0.0	1.0	0.0	-.135
79-80	Houston	6		45	17	6	12	.500	0	2	.000	5	6	.833	2	3	5	13	11	0	5	0	6	7.5	2.8	0.8	2.2	.533
80-81	Houston	20		472	177	69	152	.454	6	15	.400	33	38	.868	9	33	42	68	59	1	15	1	30	23.6	8.9	2.1	3.4	.364
81-82	Houston	3	0	66	23	9	22	.409	0	4	.000	5	6	.833	0	3	3	9	7	0	2	1	22	22.0	7.7	1.0	3.0	.314
82-83	San Antonio	11	0	174	61	22	65	.338	8	30	.267	9	13	.692	3	10	13	49	22	0	9	1	14	15.8	5.5	1.2	4.5	.416
83-84	Milwaukee	15	15	393	169	59	129	.457	18	50	.360	33	36	.917	10	25	35	46	59	2	17	0	35	26.2	11.3	2.3	3.1	.356
NBA Playoff Totals		67	15	1228	469	174	407	.428	32	101	.317	89	104	.856	25	78	103	194	173	3	51	2	86	18.3	7.0	1.5	2.9	....

• DUNLEAVY, Mike
Michael Joseph Dunleavy Jr.

Born: Sept. 15, 1980. Fort Worth, TX, United States.   Height: 6'9".   Weight: 220 lbs.   Drafted: —   College: Duke

YEAR	TEAM	GP	GS	MIN	PTS	FGM	FGA	FG%	3PM	3PA	3P%	FTM	FTA	FT%	ORB	DRB	TRB	AST	PF	DQ	STL	BLK	TO	MPG	PPG	RPG	APG	PCM
02-03	Golden State	82	3	1305	466	168	417	.403	52	150	.347	78	100	.780	66	148	214	106	120	0	53	19	86	15.9	5.7	2.6	1.3	.362
NBA Season Totals		82	3	1305	466	168	417	.403	52	150	.347	78	100	.780	66	148	214	106	120	0	53	19	86	15.9	5.7	2.6	1.3	....

YEAR	TEAM	GP	GS	MIN	PTS	FGM	FGA	FG%	3PM	3PA	3P%	FTM	FTA	FT%	ORB	DRB	TRB	AST	PF	DQ	STL	BLK	TO	MPG	PPG	RPG	APG	PCM

• DUNN, Pat
Patrick L. Dunn

Born: Mar. 17, 1931. Died: Nov.1975.   Height: 6'2".   Weight: 170 lbs.   Drafted: 1956   College: Utah State

YEAR	TEAM	GP	GS	MIN	PTS	FGM	FGA	FG%	3PM	3PA	3P%	FTM	FTA	FT%	ORB	DRB	TRB	AST	PF	DQ	STL	BLK	TO	MPG	PPG	RPG	APG	PCM
57-58	Philadelphia	28	....	206	70	28	90	.311	....	....	....	14	17	.824	....	....	31	28	20	0	....	....	....	7.4	2.5	1.1	1.0	.362
NBA Season Totals		28	....	206	70	28	90	.311	....	....	....	14	17	.824	....	....	31	28	20	0	....	....	....	7.4	2.5	1.1	1.0	....
57-58	Philadelphia	3	....	8	0	0	4	.000	....	....	....	0	0	.000	....	....	1	1	1	0	....	....	....	2.7	0.0	0.3	0.3	-.160
NBA Playoff Totals		3	....	8	0	0	4	.000	....	....	....	0	0	.000	....	....	1	1	1	0	....	....	....	2.7	0.0	0.3	0.3	....

• DUNN, T.R.
Theodore Roosevelt Dunn

Born: Feb. 1, 1955. Birmingham, AL, United States.   Height: 6'4".   Weight: 192 lbs.   Drafted: 1977   College: Alabama

YEAR	TEAM	GP	GS	MIN	PTS	FGM	FGA	FG%	3PM	3PA	3P%	FTM	FTA	FT%	ORB	DRB	TRB	AST	PF	DQ	STL	BLK	TO	MPG	PPG	RPG	APG	PCM
77-78	Portland	63	....	768	237	100	240	.417	....	....	....	37	56	.661	63	84	147	45	74	0	46	8	38	12.2	3.8	2.3	0.7	.348
78-79	Portland	80	....	1828	614	246	549	.448	....	....	....	122	158	.772	145	199	344	103	166	1	86	23	96	22.9	7.7	4.3	1.3	.375
79-80	Portland	82	....	1841	564	240	551	.436	0	3	.000	84	111	.757	132	192	324	147	145	1	102	31	90	22.5	6.9	4.0	1.8	.379
80-81	Denver	82	....	1427	371	146	354	.412	0	2	.000	79	121	.653	133	168	301	81	141	0	66	29	57	17.4	4.5	3.7	1.0	.347
81-82	Denver	82	80	2519	669	258	504	.512	0	1	.000	153	215	.712	211	348	559	188	210	1	135	36	123	30.7	8.2	6.8	2.3	.428
82-83	Denver	82	80	2640	627	254	527	.482	0	1	.000	119	163	.730	231	384	615	189	218	2	147	25	115	32.2	7.6	7.5	2.3	.408
83-84	Denver	80	74	2705	454	174	370	.470	0	1	.000	106	145	.731	195	379	574	228	233	5	173	32	96	33.8	5.7	7.2	2.9	.379
84-85	Denver	81	81	2290	434	175	358	.489	0	2	.000	84	116	.724	169	216	385	153	213	3	140	14	65	28.3	5.4	4.8	1.9	.329
85-86	Denver	82	82	2401	412	172	379	.454	0	1	.000	68	88	.773	143	234	377	171	228	1	155	16	49	29.3	5.0	4.6	2.1	.313
86-87	Denver	81	53	1932	272	118	276	.428	0	2	.000	36	55	.655	91	174	265	147	160	0	100	21	32	23.9	3.4	3.3	1.8	.273
87-88	Denver	82	1	1534	180	70	156	.449	0	1	.000	40	52	.769	110	130	240	87	152	0	101	11	25	18.7	2.2	2.9	1.1	.275
88-89	Phoenix	34	1	321	33	12	35	.343	0	0	.000	9	12	.750	30	30	60	25	35	0	12	1	7	9.4	1.0	1.8	0.7	.256
89-90	Denver	65	2	657	114	44	97	.454	0	2	.000	26	39	.667	56	82	138	43	67	1	41	4	20	10.1	1.8	2.1	0.7	.343
90-91	Denver	17	3	217	52	21	47	.447	1	4	.250	9	10	.900	20	22	42	24	30	0	12	1	7	12.8	3.1	2.5	1.4	.386
NBA Season Totals		993	457	23080	5033	2030	4443	.457	1	20	.050	972	1341	.725	1729	2642	4371	1631	2072	15	1316	252	820	23.2	5.1	4.4	1.6	....
77-78	Portland	4	....	35	4	2	4	.500	....	....	....	0	0	.000	1	4	5	3	3	0	1	0	1	8.8	1.0	1.3	0.8	.248
78-79	Portland	3	....	52	10	5	11	.455	....	....	....	0	0	.000	2	4	6	4	7	0	5	0	1	17.3	3.3	2.0	1.3	.286
79-80	Portland	3	....	24	6	2	8	.250	0	0	.000	2	2	1.000	1	3	4	4	3	0	1	0	1	8.0	2.0	1.3	1.3	.301
81-82	Denver	3	3	81	19	6	13	.462	0	0	.000	7	8	.875	10	8	18	10	11	0	8	1	5	27.0	6.3	6.0	3.3	.470
82-83	Denver	8	8	300	41	18	41	.439	0	0	.000	5	8	.625	27	51	78	20	21	0	12	3	14	37.5	5.1	9.8	2.5	.342
83-84	Denver	5	5	178	33	14	25	.560	0	0	.000	5	7	.714	20	19	39	8	19	0	10	4	8	35.6	6.6	7.8	1.6	.356
84-85	Denver	15	15	371	68	27	65	.415	0	0	.000	14	19	.737	27	33	60	34	45	0	24	3	10	24.7	4.5	4.0	2.3	.316
85-86	Denver	10	10	276	49	20	46	.435	0	0	.000	9	14	.643	22	31	53	13	34	1	16	0	3	27.6	4.9	5.3	1.3	.297
86-87	Denver	3	0	22	2	1	4	.250	0	0	.000	0	0	.000	1	2	3	2	3	0	1	1	1	7.3	0.7	1.0	0.7	.167
87-88	Denver	11	3	185	26	11	20	.550	0	0	.000	4	8	.500	11	18	29	3	20	0	8	0	4	16.8	2.4	2.6	0.3	.218
88-89	Phoenix	8	0	79	7	3	7	.429	0	0	.000	1	2	.500	7	8	15	1	11	0	5	0	2	9.9	0.9	1.9	0.1	.196
89-90	Denver	3	0	31	0	0	0	.000	0	0	.000	0	0	.000	1	6	7	2	3	0	4	1	1	10.3	0.0	2.3	0.7	.356
NBA Playoff Totals		76	44	1634	265	109	244	.447	0	0	.000	47	68	.691	130	187	317	104	180	1	95	13	51	21.5	3.5	4.2	1.4	....

• DUPEE, Dave
Dave Dupee

Born: 1916.   Height: 6'3".   Weight: 185 lbs.   Drafted: —   College: Wisconsin

YEAR	TEAM	GP	GS	MIN	PTS	FGM	FGA	FG%	3PM	3PA	3P%	FTM	FTA	FT%	ORB	DRB	TRB	AST	PF	DQ	STL	BLK	TO	MPG	PPG	RPG	APG	PCM
38-39	Oshkosh-N	1	....	....	1	0	....	....	....	....	....	1	....	....	....	....	....	....	....	....	....	....	....	1.0	....	....	....	
NBL Season Totals		1	....	....	1	0	....	....	....	....	....	1	....	....	....	....	....	....	....	....	....	....	....	1.0	....	....	....	

• DUREN, John
John Thomas Duren

Born: Oct. 30, 1958. Washington, DC, United States.   Height: 6'3".   Weight: 195 lbs.   Drafted: 1980   College: Georgetown

YEAR	TEAM	GP	GS	MIN	PTS	FGM	FGA	FG%	3PM	3PA	3P%	FTM	FTA	FT%	ORB	DRB	TRB	AST	PF	DQ	STL	BLK	TO	MPG	PPG	RPG	APG	PCM
80-81	Utah	40	....	458	71	33	101	.327	0	1	.000	5	9	.556	8	27	35	54	54	0	18	2	36	11.5	1.8	0.9	1.4	.128
81-82	Utah	79	9	1056	272	121	268	.451	3	11	.273	27	37	.730	14	70	84	157	143	0	20	4	71	13.4	3.4	1.1	2.0	.255
82-83	Indiana	82	24	1433	369	163	360	.453	0	13	.000	43	54	.796	38	69	107	200	203	2	66	5	98	17.5	4.5	1.3	2.4	.270
NBA Season Totals		201	33	2947	712	317	729	.435	3	25	.120	75	100	.750	60	166	226	411	400	2	104	11	205	14.7	3.5	1.1	2.0	....

• DURHAM, Jarrett
Jarrett M. Durham

Born: Aug. 22, 1949.   Height: 6'5".   Weight: 188 lbs.   Drafted: 1971   College: Duquesne

YEAR	TEAM	GP	GS	MIN	PTS	FGM	FGA	FG%	3PM	3PA	3P%	FTM	FTA	FT%	ORB	DRB	TRB	AST	PF	DQ	STL	BLK	TO	MPG	PPG	RPG	APG	PCM
71-72	New York-A	1	....	1	0	0	0	.000	0	0	.000	0	0	.000	0	0	0	0	0	0	....	....	1	1.0	0.0	0.0	0.0	.000
ABA Season Totals		1	....	1	0	0	0	.000	0	0	.000	0	0	.000	0	0	0	0	0	0	....	....	1	1.0	0.0	0.0	0.0	....

• DURHAM, Pat
Patrick Wayne (Bull) Durham

Born: Mar. 10, 1967. Dallas, TX, United States.   Height: 6'7".   Weight: 210 lbs.   Drafted: 1989   College: Colorado State

YEAR	TEAM	GP	GS	MIN	PTS	FGM	FGA	FG%	3PM	3PA	3P%	FTM	FTA	FT%	ORB	DRB	TRB	AST	PF	DQ	STL	BLK	TO	MPG	PPG	RPG	APG	PCM
92-93	Golden State	5	1	78	21	6	25	.240	0	0	.000	9	12	.750	5	9	14	4	6	0	1	1	7	15.6	4.2	2.8	0.8	.151
94-95	Minnesota	59	2	852	302	117	237	.494	5	26	.192	63	96	.656	37	57	94	53	114	0	36	32	47	14.4	5.1	1.6	0.9	.334
NBA Season Totals		64	3	930	323	123	262	.469	5	26	.192	72	108	.667	42	66	108	57	120	0	37	33	54	14.5	5.0	1.7	0.9	....

• DURKEE, Bill
Bill Durkee

Born: 1921.   Height: 6'3".   Weight: 205 lbs.   Drafted: —   College: California

YEAR	TEAM	GP	GS	MIN	PTS	FGM	FGA	FG%	3PM	3PA	3P%	FTM	FTA	FT%	ORB	DRB	TRB	AST	PF	DQ	STL	BLK	TO	MPG	PPG	RPG	APG	PCM
47-48	Minneapolis-N	23	....	....	41	15	....	....	....	....	....	11	24	.458	....	....	....	....	....	....	....	....	....	1.8	....	....	....	
NBL Season Totals		23	....	....	41	15	....	....	....	....	....	11	24	....	....	....	....	....	....	....	....	....	....	1.8	....	....	....	

YEAR TEAM	GP	GS	MIN	PTS	FGM	FGA	FG%	3PM	3PA	3P%	FTM	FTA	FT%	ORB	DRB	TRB	AST	PF	DQ	STL	BLK	TO	MPG	PPG	RPG	APG	PCM

• DURKIN, Bill
Bill Durkin

Born: 1922.   Height: 6'1".   Weight: 160 lbs.   Drafted: —   College: Loyola (IL)

YEAR TEAM	GP	GS	MIN	PTS	FGM	FGA	FG%	3PM	3PA	3P%	FTM	FTA	FT%	ORB	DRB	TRB	AST	PF	DQ	STL	BLK	TO	MPG	PPG	RPG	APG	PCM
44-45 Sheboygan-N	1	....	....	2	1	....	....	....	....	....	0	....	....	....	....	....	....	....	....	....	....	....	2.0	....	....	....
NBL Season Totals	1	....	....	2	1	....	....	....	....	....	0	....	....	....	....	....	....	....	....	....	....	....	2.0	....	....	....

• DURRANT, Devin
Devin George Durrant

Born: Oct. 20, 1960. Provo, UT, United States.   Height: 6'7".   Weight: 200 lbs.   Drafted: 1984   College: Brigham Young

YEAR TEAM	GP	GS	MIN	PTS	FGM	FGA	FG%	3PM	3PA	3P%	FTM	FTA	FT%	ORB	DRB	TRB	AST	PF	DQ	STL	BLK	TO	MPG	PPG	RPG	APG	PCM
84-85 Indiana	59	8	756	300	114	274	.416	0	3	.000	72	102	.706	49	75	124	80	106	0	19	10	77	12.8	5.1	2.1	1.4	.322
85-86 Phoenix	4	0	51	17	8	21	.381	0	0	.000	1	4	.250	2	6	8	5	10	0	3	0	4	12.8	4.3	2.0	1.3	.211
NBA Season Totals	63	8	807	317	122	295	.414	0	3	.000	73	106	.689	51	81	132	85	116	0	22	10	81	12.8	5.0	2.1	1.3	....

• DURRETT, Ken
Kenneth L. Durrett

Born: Dec. 8, 1948. Pittsburgh, PA, United States. Died: Jan.7, 2001.   Height: 6'7".   Weight: 190 lbs.   Drafted: 1971   College: LaSalle

YEAR TEAM	GP	GS	MIN	PTS	FGM	FGA	FG%	3PM	3PA	3P%	FTM	FTA	FT%	ORB	DRB	TRB	AST	PF	DQ	STL	BLK	TO	MPG	PPG	RPG	APG	PCM
71-72 Cincinnati	19	....	233	83	31	79	.392	....	....	....	21	28	.750	....	....	39	14	41	0	....	....	....	12.3	4.4	2.1	0.7	.302
72-73 Omaha	8	....	65	22	8	21	.381	....	....	....	6	8	.750	....	....	14	3	16	0	....	....	....	8.1	2.8	1.8	0.4	.286
73-74 Omaha	45	....	462	214	86	176	.489	....	....	....	42	69	.609	28	50	78	19	68	0	13	5	....	10.3	4.8	1.7	0.4	.401
74-75 Omaha	21	....	175	75	32	78	.410	....	....	....	11	20	.550	14	26	40	8	30	0	5	4	....	8.3	3.6	1.9	0.4	.357
74-75 Philadelphia	27	....	270	90	35	88	.398	....	....	....	20	32	.625	21	41	62	10	42	0	4	4	....	10.0	3.3	2.3	0.4	.319
NBA Season Totals	120	....	1205	484	192	442	.434	....	....	....	100	157	.637	63	117	233	54	197	0	22	13	....	10.0	4.0	1.9	0.5	....

• DUVAL, Dennis
Dennis DuVal

Born: Mar. 31, 1952. Westbury, NY, United States.   Height: 6'3".   Weight: 175 lbs.   Drafted: 1974   College: Syracuse

YEAR TEAM	GP	GS	MIN	PTS	FGM	FGA	FG%	3PM	3PA	3P%	FTM	FTA	FT%	ORB	DRB	TRB	AST	PF	DQ	STL	BLK	TO	MPG	PPG	RPG	APG	PCM
74-75 Washington	37	....	137	60	24	65	.369	....	....	....	12	18	.667	8	15	23	14	34	0	16	2	....	3.7	1.6	0.6	0.4	.319
75-76 Atlanta	13	....	130	36	15	43	.349	....	....	....	6	9	.667	1	7	8	20	15	0	6	2	....	10.0	2.8	0.6	1.5	.261
NBA Season Totals	50	....	267	96	39	108	.361	....	....	....	18	27	.667	9	22	31	34	49	0	22	4	....	5.3	1.9	0.6	0.7	....
74-75 Washington	5	....	14	7	3	9	.333	....	....	....	1	2	.500	0	3	3	3	1	0	0	0	....	2.8	1.4	0.6	0.6	.502
NBA Playoff Totals	5	....	14	7	3	9	.333	....	....	....	1	2	.500	0	3	3	3	1	0	0	0	....	2.8	1.4	0.6	0.6	....

• DWAN, Jack
John Dwan

Born: May 3, 1921. Died: Aug.4, 1993.   Height: 6'4".   Weight: 200 lbs.   Drafted: —   College: Loyola (IL)

YEAR TEAM	GP	GS	MIN	PTS	FGM	FGA	FG%	3PM	3PA	3P%	FTM	FTA	FT%	ORB	DRB	TRB	AST	PF	DQ	STL	BLK	TO	MPG	PPG	RPG	APG	PCM
47-48 Minneapolis-N	55	....	....	306	128	....	....	....	....	....	50	73	.685	....	....	....	....	110	....	....	....	....	5.6	....	....	....
48-49 Minneapolis	60	....	....	276	121	380	.318	....	....	....	34	69	.493	....	....	....	129	157	....	....	....	....	4.6	....	2.2	....
NBA Season Totals	60	....	....	276	121	380	.318	....	....	....	34	69	.493	....	....	....	129	157	....	....	....	....	4.6	....	2.2	....
NBL Season Totals	55	....	....	306	128	....	....	....	....	....	50	73	....	....	....	....	....	110	....	....	....	....	5.6	....	....	....
Career Totals	115	....	....	582	249	380	....	....	....	....	84	142	....	....	....	....	129	267	....	....	....	....	5.1	....	1.1	....
47-48 Minneapolis-N	10	....	....	59	27	....	....	....	....	....	5	9	.556	....	....	....	....	....	....	....	....	....	5.9	....	....	....
48-49 Minneapolis	10	....	....	18	7	29	.241	....	....	....	4	9	.444	....	....	....	9	22	....	....	....	....	1.8	....	0.9	....
NBA Playoff Totals	10	....	....	18	7	29	.241	....	....	....	4	9	.444	....	....	....	9	22	....	....	....	....	1.8	....	0.9	....
NBL Playoff Totals	10	....	....	59	27	....	....	....	....	....	5	9	....	....	....	....	....	....	....	....	....	....	5.9	....	....	....
Career Playoff Totals	20	....	....	77	34	29	....	....	....	....	9	18	....	....	....	....	9	22	....	....	....	....	3.9	....	0.5	....

• DYKEMA, Craig
Craig Dykema

Born: June 11, 1959. Lakewood, CA, United States.   Height: 6'8".   Weight: 190 lbs.   Drafted: 1981   College: Long Beach State

YEAR TEAM	GP	GS	MIN	PTS	FGM	FGA	FG%	3PM	3PA	3P%	FTM	FTA	FT%	ORB	DRB	TRB	AST	PF	DQ	STL	BLK	TO	MPG	PPG	RPG	APG	PCM
81-82 Phoenix	32	0	103	43	17	37	.459	2	4	.500	7	9	.778	3	9	12	15	19	0	2	0	6	3.2	1.3	0.4	0.5	.373
NBA Season Totals	32	0	103	43	17	37	.459	2	4	.500	7	9	.778	3	9	12	15	19	0	2	0	6	3.2	1.3	0.4	0.5	....
81-82 Phoenix	6	0	12	2	1	6	.167	0	0	.000	0	0	.000	0	4	4	1	2	0	0	0	1	2.0	0.3	0.7	0.2	.026
NBA Playoff Totals	6	0	12	2	1	6	.167	0	0	.000	0	0	.000	0	4	4	1	2	0	0	0	1	2.0	0.3	0.7	0.2	....

• DYKER, Gene
Eugene Dyker

Born: Feb. 17, 1930. Died: Jan.1966.   Height: 6'6".   Weight: 225 lbs.   Drafted: 1953   College: DePaul

YEAR TEAM	GP	GS	MIN	PTS	FGM	FGA	FG%	3PM	3PA	3P%	FTM	FTA	FT%	ORB	DRB	TRB	AST	PF	DQ	STL	BLK	TO	MPG	PPG	RPG	APG	PCM
53-54 Milwaukee	11	....	91	16	6	26	.231	....	....	....	4	8	.500	....	....	16	5	21	0	....	....	....	8.3	1.5	1.5	0.5	.118
NBA Season Totals	11	....	91	16	6	26	.231	....	....	....	4	8	.500	....	....	16	5	21	0	....	....	....	8.3	1.5	1.5	0.5	....

• DYKSTRA, Bob
Bob Dykstra

Born: 1922.   Height: 6'9".   Weight: 230 lbs.   Drafted: —   College: Simpson

YEAR TEAM	GP	GS	MIN	PTS	FGM	FGA	FG%	3PM	3PA	3P%	FTM	FTA	FT%	ORB	DRB	TRB	AST	PF	DQ	STL	BLK	TO	MPG	PPG	RPG	APG	PCM
46-47 Detroit-N	14	....	....	58	19	....	....	....	....	....	20	30	.667	....	....	....	....	....	....	....	....	....	4.1	....	....	....
46-47 Sheboygan-N	18	....	....	35	10	....	....	....	....	....	15	28	.536	....	....	....	57	....	....	....	....	....	1.9	....	....	....
47-48 Sheboygan-N	51	....	....	64	19	....	....	....	....	....	26	52	.500	....	....	....	123	....	....	....	....	....	1.3	....	....	....
NBL Season Totals	83	....	....	157	48	....	....	....	....	....	61	110	....	....	....	....	180	....	....	....	....	....	1.9	....	....	....
46-47 Sheboygan-N	4	....	....	8	3	....	....	....	....	....	2	5	.400	....	....	....	....	....	....	....	....	....	2.0	....	....	....
NBL Playoff Totals	4	....	....	8	3	....	....	....	....	....	2	5	....	....	....	....	....	....	....	....	....	....	2.0	....	....	....

• EACKLES, Ledell

Ledell (A-Train) Eackles

Born: Nov. 24, 1966. Baton Rouge, LA, United States. Height: 6'5". Weight: 220 lbs. Drafted: 1988 College: New Orleans

YEAR	TEAM	GP	GS	MIN	PTS	FGM	FGA	FG%	3PM	3PA	3P%	FTM	FTA	FT%	ORB	DRB	TRB	AST	PF	DQ	STL	BLK	TO	MPG	PPG	RPG	APG	PCM
88-89	Washington	80	6	1459	917	318	732	.434	9	40	.225	272	346	.786	100	80	180	123	156	1	41	5	128	18.2	11.5	2.3	1.5	.444
89-90	Washington	78	8	1696	1055	413	940	.439	19	59	.322	210	280	.750	74	101	175	182	157	0	50	4	140	21.7	13.5	2.2	2.3	.431
90-91	Washington	67	17	1616	868	345	762	.453	14	59	.237	164	222	.739	47	81	128	136	121	0	47	10	114	24.1	13.0	1.9	2.0	.375
91-92	Washington	65	25	1463	856	355	759	.468	7	35	.200	139	187	.743	39	139	178	125	145	1	47	7	78	22.5	13.2	2.7	1.9	.457
94-95	Miami	54	6	898	395	143	326	.439	18	41	.439	91	126	.722	33	62	95	72	88	0	19	2	54	16.6	7.3	1.8	1.3	.334
95-96	Washington	55	26	1238	474	161	377	.427	54	128	.422	98	118	.831	44	104	148	86	84	1	28	3	55	22.5	8.6	2.7	1.6	.347
97-98	Washington	42	0	547	218	75	175	.429	16	46	.348	52	59	.881	25	50	75	16	43	0	17	0	29	13.0	5.2	1.8	0.4	.327
NBA Season Totals		441	88	8917	4783	1810	4071	.445	137	408	.336	1026	1338	.767	362	617	979	740	794	3	249	31	598	20.2	10.8	2.2	1.7	....

• EAKINS, Jim

James Scott (Jimbo, Jumbo) Eakins

Born: May 24, 1946. Sacramento, CA, United States. Height: 6'11". Weight: 215 lbs. Drafted: 1968 College: Brigham Young

YEAR	TEAM	GP	GS	MIN	PTS	FGM	FGA	FG%	3PM	3PA	3P%	FTM	FTA	FT%	ORB	DRB	TRB	AST	PF	DQ	STL	BLK	TO	MPG	PPG	RPG	APG	PCM
68-69	Oakland-A	78	....	1671	1011	351	646	.543	0	1	.000	309	430	.719	224	339	563	53	234	4	....	....	141	21.4	13.0	7.2	0.7	.688
69-70	Washington-A	82	....	1214	528	181	364	.497	0	0	.000	166	224	.741	130	282	412	71	184	0	....	....	106	14.8	6.4	5.0	0.9	.578
70-71	Virginia-A	84	....	2235	906	332	645	.515	0	0	.000	242	319	.759	222	556	778	160	282	3	....	....	145	26.6	10.8	9.3	1.9	.594
71-72	Virginia-A	84	....	2718	1030	371	764	.486	0	0	.000	288	377	.764	290	517	807	181	298	6	....	....	189	32.4	12.3	9.6	2.2	.525
72-73	Virginia-A	83	....	2559	1244	430	823	.522	0	1	.000	384	479	.802	234	499	733	262	287	5	....	131	233	30.8	15.0	8.8	3.2	.651
73-74	Virginia-A	84	....	2649	1229	445	856	.520	0	1	.000	339	432	.785	296	510	806	236	265	....	65	98	228	31.5	14.6	9.6	2.8	.636
74-75	Utah-A	84	....	2556	1051	380	756	.503	0	0	.000	291	348	.836	210	394	604	146	259	....	57	85	173	30.4	12.5	7.2	1.7	.499
75-76	New York-A	34	....	463	211	72	143	.503	0	0	.000	67	79	.848	42	78	120	18	71	....	7	20	33	13.6	6.2	3.5	0.5	.513
75-76	Utah-A	16	....	568	203	69	157	.439	0	0	.000	65	71	.915	51	99	150	33	72	....	9	9	41	35.5	12.7	9.4	2.1	.458
75-76	Virginia-A	23	....	636	214	74	177	.418	0	0	.000	66	73	.904	74	95	169	37	77	....	18	41	40	27.7	9.3	7.3	1.6	.435
76-77	Kansas City	82	....	1338	490	151	336	.449	....	....	....	188	222	.847	112	249	361	119	195	1	29	49	....	16.3	6.0	4.4	1.5	.507
77-78	San Antonio	16	....	251	89	30	52	.577	....	....	....	29	34	.853	17	29	46	17	46	0	3	10	24	15.7	5.6	2.9	1.1	.387
77-78	Milwaukee	17	....	155	49	14	34	.412	....	....	....	21	26	.808	12	17	29	12	25	0	4	7	9	9.1	2.9	1.7	0.7	.381
NBA Season Totals		115	....	1744	628	195	422	.462	....	....	....	238	282	.844	141	295	436	148	266	1	36	66	33	15.2	5.5	3.8	1.3	....
ABA Season Totals		652	....	17269	7627	2705	5331	.507	0	3	.000	2217	2832	.783	1773	3369	5142	1197	2029	18	156	384	1329	26.5	11.7	7.9	1.8	....
Career Totals		767	....	19013	8255	2900	5753	.504	0	3	.000	2455	3114	.788	1914	3664	5578	1345	2295	19	192	450	1362	24.8	10.8	7.3	1.8	....
68-69	Oakland-A	16	....	329	189	65	121	.537	0	0	.000	59	83	.711	....	....	102	15	52	0	....	....	26	20.6	11.8	6.4	0.9	.647
69-70	Washington-A	7	....	65	31	14	24	.583	0	0	.000	3	3	1.000	....	....	14	5	....	0	....	....	6	9.3	4.4	2.0	0.7	....
70-71	Virginia-A	12	....	296	124	50	99	.505	0	0	.000	24	32	.750	36	84	120	20	44	1	....	....	16	24.7	10.3	10.0	1.7	.622
71-72	Virginia-A	11	....	325	103	38	80	.475	0	0	.000	27	39	.692	29	67	96	22	36	0	....	....	18	29.5	9.4	8.7	2.0	.474
72-73	Virginia-A	5	....	217	124	48	81	.593	0	0	.000	28	34	.824	20	37	57	18	22	1	....	....	22	43.4	24.8	11.4	3.6	.704
73-74	Virginia-A	5	....	190	100	37	71	.521	0	1	.000	26	33	.788	22	32	54	19	23	....	7	4	20	38.0	20.0	10.8	3.8	.663
74-75	Utah-A	6	....	194	81	35	55	.636	0	0	.000	11	12	.917	16	21	37	7	28	....	9	11	18	32.3	13.5	6.2	1.2	.469
75-76	New York-A	13	....	281	89	30	56	.536	0	0	.000	29	36	.806	30	48	78	11	52	....	6	7	19	21.6	6.8	6.0	0.8	.431
77-78	Milwaukee	3	....	18	2	1	5	.200	....	....	....	0	0	.000	1	0	1	1	2	0	1	0	1	6.0	0.7	0.3	0.3	-.021
NBA Playoff Totals		3	....	18	2	1	5	.200	....	....	....	0	0	.000	1	0	1	1	2	0	1	0	1	6.0	0.7	0.3	0.3	....
ABA Playoff Totals		75	....	1897	841	317	587	.540	0	1	.000	207	272	.761	153	289	558	117	257	2	22	22	145	25.3	11.2	7.4	1.6	....
Career Playoff Totals		78	....	1915	843	318	592	.537	0	1	.000	207	272	.761	154	289	559	118	259	2	23	22	146	24.6	10.8	7.2	1.5	....

• EARL, Acie

Acie Boyd Earl

Born: June 23, 1970. Peoria, IL, United States. Height: 6'10". Weight: 240 lbs. Drafted: 1993 College: Iowa

YEAR	TEAM	GP	GS	MIN	PTS	FGM	FGA	FG%	3PM	3PA	3P%	FTM	FTA	FT%	ORB	DRB	TRB	AST	PF	DQ	STL	BLK	TO	MPG	PPG	RPG	APG	PCM
93-94	Boston	74	8	1149	410	151	372	.406	0	1	.000	108	160	.675	85	162	247	12	178	5	24	53	74	15.5	5.5	3.3	0.2	.300
94-95	Boston	30	3	208	66	26	68	.382	0	0	.000	14	29	.483	19	26	45	2	39	0	6	8	15	6.9	2.2	1.5	0.1	.215
95-96	Toronto	42	7	655	316	117	276	.424	0	3	.000	82	114	.719	51	78	129	27	73	0	18	37	50	15.6	7.5	3.1	0.6	.415
96-97	Toronto	38	0	457	162	59	157	.376	0	5	.000	44	70	.629	33	52	85	18	54	0	12	27	34	12.0	4.3	2.2	0.5	.299
96-97	Milwaukee	9	0	43	26	8	23	.348	0	0	.000	10	14	.714	2	9	11	2	7	0	3	1	2	4.8	2.9	1.2	0.2	.492
NBA Season Totals		193	18	2512	980	361	896	.403	0	9	.000	258	387	.667	190	327	517	61	351	5	63	126	175	13.0	5.1	2.7	0.3	....
94-95	Boston	1	0	10	2	1	3	.333	0	0	.000	0	2	.000	1	1	2	0	4	0	0	1	0	10.0	2.0	2.0	0.0	.012
NBA Playoff Totals		1	0	10	2	1	3	.333	0	0	.000	0	2	.000	1	1	2	0	4	0	0	1	0	10.0	2.0	2.0	0.0	....

• EARLE, Ed

Edwin Earle

Born: Apr. 28, 1927. Height: 6'3". Weight: 190 lbs. Drafted: — College: Loyola (IL)

YEAR	TEAM	GP	GS	MIN	PTS	FGM	FGA	FG%	3PM	3PA	3P%	FTM	FTA	FT%	ORB	DRB	TRB	AST	PF	DQ	STL	BLK	TO	MPG	PPG	RPG	APG	PCM
53-54	Syracuse	2	....	12	4	1	2	.500	....	....	....	2	4	.500	....	....	2	0	0	0	....	....	....	6.0	2.0	1.0	0.0	.333
NBA Season Totals		2	....	12	4	1	2	.500	....	....	....	2	4	.500	....	....	2	0	0	0	....	....	....	6.0	2.0	1.0	0.0	....

• EARLY, Penny

Penny Ann Early

Born: 1943. Height: 5'3". Weight: 114 lbs. Drafted: — College: none

YEAR	TEAM	GP	GS	MIN	PTS	FGM	FGA	FG%	3PM	3PA	3P%	FTM	FTA	FT%	ORB	DRB	TRB	AST	PF	DQ	STL	BLK	TO	MPG	PPG	RPG	APG	PCM
68-69	Kentucky-A	1	....	1	0	0	0	.000	0	0	.000	0	0	.000	....	....	0	0	0	....	....	....	....	1.0	0.0	0.0	0.0	.000
ABA Season Totals		1	....	1	0	0	0	.000	0	0	.000	0	0	.000	....	....	0	0	0	....	....	....	....	1.0	0.0	0.0	0.0	....

• EATON, Mark

Mark E. Eaton

Born: Jan. 24, 1957. Westminster, CA, United States. Height: 7'3". Weight: 275 lbs. Drafted: 1982 College: UCLA

YEAR	TEAM	GP	GS	MIN	PTS	FGM	FGA	FG%	3PM	3PA	3P%	FTM	FTA	FT%	ORB	DRB	TRB	AST	PF	DQ	STL	BLK	TO	MPG	PPG	RPG	APG	PCM
82-83	Utah	81	32	1528	351	146	353	.414	0	1	.000	59	90	.656	86	376	462	112	257	6	24	275	138	18.9	4.3	5.7	1.4	.471
83-84	Utah	82	78	2139	461	194	416	.466	0	1	.000	73	123	.593	148	447	595	113	303	4	25	**351**	98	26.1	5.6	7.3	1.4	.478
84-85	Utah	82	82	2813	794	302	673	.449	0	0	.000	190	267	.712	207	**720**	927	124	312	5	36	**456**	205	34.3	9.7	11.3	1.5	.544
85-86	Utah	80	80	2551	676	277	589	.470	0	0	.000	122	202	.604	172	503	675	101	282	5	33	369	160	31.9	8.5	8.4	1.3	.462
86-87	Utah	79	79	2505	608	234	585	.400	0	0	.000	140	213	.657	211	486	697	105	273	5	43	**321**	142	31.7	7.7	8.8	1.3	.434

YEAR	TEAM	GP	GS	MIN	PTS	FGM	FGA	FG%	3PM	3PA	3P%	FTM	FTA	FT%	ORB	DRB	TRB	AST	PF	DQ	STL	BLK	TO	MPG	PPG	RPG	APG	PCM
87-88	Utah	82	82	2731	571	226	541	.418	0	0	.000	119	191	.623	230	487	717	55	320	8	41	**304**	131	33.3	7.0	8.7	0.7	.374
88-89	Utah	82	82	2914	508	188	407	.462	0	0	.000	132	200	.660	227	616	843	83	290	6	40	315	139	35.5	6.2	10.3	1.0	.416
89-90	Utah	82	82	2281	395	158	300	.527	0	0	.000	79	118	.669	171	430	601	39	238	3	33	201	74	27.8	4.8	7.3	0.5	.389
90-91	Utah	80	80	2580	409	169	292	.579	0	0	.000	71	112	.634	182	485	667	51	298	6	39	188	96	32.3	5.1	8.3	0.6	.362
91-92	Utah	81	81	2023	266	107	240	.446	0	0	.000	52	87	.598	150	341	491	40	239	2	36	205	57	25.0	3.3	6.1	0.5	.339
92-93	Utah	64	57	1104	177	71	130	.546	0	0	.000	35	50	.700	73	191	264	17	143	0	18	79	45	17.3	2.8	4.1	0.3	.327
NBA Season Totals		875	815	25169	5216	2072	4526	.458	0	2	.000	1072	1653	.649	1857	5082	6939	840	2955	50	368	3064	1285	28.8	6.0	7.9	1.0	....
83-84	Utah	11	11	254	50	21	41	.512	0	0	.000	8	17	.471	19	57	76	9	33	1	5	34	16	23.1	4.5	6.9	0.8	.447
84-85	Utah	5	5	158	29	12	34	.353	0	0	.000	5	7	.714	11	34	45	5	19	0	4	29	12	31.6	5.8	9.0	1.0	.415
85-86	Utah	4	4	157	58	28	57	.491	0	0	.000	2	3	.667	13	23	36	10	12	0	1	18	4	39.3	14.5	9.0	2.5	.529
86-87	Utah	5	5	193	54	19	41	.463	0	0	.000	16	25	.640	16	39	55	3	18	0	1	21	4	38.6	10.8	11.0	0.6	.477
87-88	Utah	11	11	461	85	31	65	.477	0	0	.000	23	36	.639	28	75	103	13	48	3	12	34	14	41.9	7.7	9.4	1.2	.357
88-89	Utah	3	3	99	25	8	17	.471	0	0	.000	9	11	.818	11	22	33	1	6	0	1	2	7	33.0	8.3	11.0	0.3	.414
89-90	Utah	5	5	128	19	9	17	.529	0	0	.000	1	5	.200	8	22	30	0	17	0	3	14	4	25.6	3.8	6.0	0.0	.328
90-91	Utah	9	9	255	39	16	31	.516	0	0	.000	7	12	.583	17	39	56	5	41	1	1	13	7	28.3	4.3	6.2	0.6	.265
91-92	Utah	16	16	473	73	26	46	.565	0	0	.000	21	27	.778	30	60	90	4	47	0	7	36	11	29.6	4.6	5.6	0.3	.312
92-93	Utah	5	5	117	22	10	19	.526	0	0	.000	2	4	.500	16	17	33	2	9	0	0	9	2	23.4	4.4	6.6	0.4	.410
NBA Playoff Totals		74	74	2295	454	180	368	.489	0	0	.000	94	147	.639	169	388	557	52	250	5	35	210	81	31.0	6.1	7.5	0.7	....

• EAVES, Jerry

Jerry Lee Eaves

Born: Feb. 8, 1959. Louisville, KY, United States.   Height: 6'4".   Weight: 180 lbs.   Drafted: 1982   College: Louisville

YEAR	TEAM	GP	GS	MIN	PTS	FGM	FGA	FG%	3PM	3PA	3P%	FTM	FTA	FT%	ORB	DRB	TRB	AST	PF	DQ	STL	BLK	TO	MPG	PPG	RPG	APG	PCM
82-83	Utah	82	7	1588	761	280	575	.487	1	8	.125	200	247	.810	34	88	122	210	116	0	51	3	156	19.4	9.3	1.5	2.6	.422
83-84	Utah	80	1	1034	356	132	293	.451	0	6	.000	92	132	.697	29	56	85	200	90	0	33	5	96	12.9	4.5	1.1	2.5	.372
84-85	Atlanta	3	0	37	11	3	6	.500	0	0	.000	5	6	.833	0		0	4	6	0	0	0	4	12.3	3.7	0.0	1.3	.148
86-87	Sacramento	3	0	26	4	1	8	.125	0	0	.000	2	2	1.000	1	0	1	0	6	0	1	0	2	8.7	1.3	0.3	0.0	-.204
NBA Season Totals		168	8	2685	1132	416	882	.472	1	14	.071	299	387	.773	64	144	208	414	218	0	85	8	258	16.0	6.7	1.2	2.5	....
83-84	Utah	11	0	132	55	22	46	.478	1	3	.333	10	13	.769	3	7	10	13	10	0	5	2	7	12.0	5.0	0.9	1.2	.378
NBA Playoff Totals		11	0	132	55	22	46	.478	1	3	.333	10	13	.769	3	7	10	13	10	0	5	2	7	12.0	5.0	0.9	1.2	....

• EBAUGH, Floyd

Floyd Ebaugh

Born: May 30, 1914. Died: June1980.   Height: 6'7".   Weight: 230 lbs.   Drafted: —   College: Nebraska

YEAR	TEAM	GP	GS	MIN	PTS	FGM	FGA	FG%	3PM	3PA	3P%	FTM	FTA	FT%	ORB	DRB	TRB	AST	PF	DQ	STL	BLK	TO	MPG	PPG	RPG	APG	PCM
38-39	Wingfoots-N	22	....	....	38	13	....	....	....	....	....	12	....	....	....	....	....	....	....	....	....	....	....	1.7	....	....	....	....
39-40	Wingfoots-N	28	....	....	127	45	....	....	....	....	....	37	....	....	....	....	....	....	....	....	....	....	....	4.5	....	....	....	....
41-42	Wingfoots-N	23	....	....	142	61	....	....	....	....	....	20	....	....	....	....	....	....	....	....	....	....	....	6.2	....	....	....	....
NBL Season Totals		73	....	....	307	119	....	....	....	....	....	69	....	....	....	....	....	....	....	....	....	....	....	4.2	....	....	....	....
41-42	Wingfoots-N	3	....	....	12	3	....	....	....	....	....	6	....	....	....	....	....	....	....	....	....	....	....	4.0	....	....	....	....
NBL Playoff Totals		3	....	....	12	3	....	....	....	....	....	6	....	....	....	....	....	....	....	....	....	....	....	4.0	....	....	....	....

• EBBEN, Bill

William Edward Ebben

Born: Oct. 7, 1935.   Height: 6'4".   Weight: 190 lbs.   Drafted: 1957   College: Detroit

YEAR	TEAM	GP	GS	MIN	PTS	FGM	FGA	FG%	3PM	3PA	3P%	FTM	FTA	FT%	ORB	DRB	TRB	AST	PF	DQ	STL	BLK	TO	MPG	PPG	RPG	APG	PCM
57-58	Detroit	8	....	50	15	6	28	.214	....	....	....	3	4	.750	....	....	8	4	5	0	....	....	....	6.3	1.9	1.0	0.5	.154
NBA Season Totals		8	....	50	15	6	28	.214	....	....	....	3	4	.750	....	....	8	4	5	0	....	....	....	6.3	1.9	1.0	0.5	....

• EBERHARD, Al

Allen Dean Eberhard

Born: May 10, 1952. Cedar Rapids, IA, United States.   Height: 6'6".   Weight: 225 lbs.   Drafted: 1974   College: Missouri

YEAR	TEAM	GP	GS	MIN	PTS	FGM	FGA	FG%	3PM	3PA	3P%	FTM	FTA	FT%	ORB	DRB	TRB	AST	PF	DQ	STL	BLK	TO	MPG	PPG	RPG	APG	PCM
74-75	Detroit	34	....	277	79	31	85	.365	....	....	....	17	21	.810	18	29	47	16	33	0	13	1	....	8.1	2.3	1.4	0.5	.273
75-76	Detroit	81	....	2066	757	283	683	.414	....	....	....	191	229	.834	139	251	390	83	250	5	87	15	....	25.5	9.3	4.8	1.0	.348
76-77	Detroit	68	....	1219	471	181	380	.476	....	....	....	109	138	.790	76	145	221	50	197	4	45	15	....	17.9	6.9	3.3	0.7	.369
77-78	Detroit	37	....	576	183	71	160	.444	....	....	....	41	61	.672	37	65	102	26	64	0	13	4	22	15.6	4.9	2.8	0.7	.317
NBA Season Totals		220	....	4138	1490	566	1308	.433	....	....	....	358	449	.797	270	490	760	175	544	9	158	35	22	18.8	6.8	3.5	0.8	....
75-76	Detroit	8	....	182	48	17	39	.436	....	....	....	14	19	.737	11	15	26	7	14	0	8	4	....	22.8	6.0	3.3	0.9	.282
76-77	Detroit	3	....	42	7	1	9	.111	....	....	....	5	8	.625	2	7	9	2	6	0	1	0	....	14.0	2.3	3.0	0.7	.149
NBA Playoff Totals		11	....	224	55	18	48	.375	....	....	....	19	27	.704	13	22	35	9	20	0	9	4	....	20.4	5.0	3.2	0.8	....

• EBRON, Roy

Roy Lester Ebron

Born: Aug. 31, 1951. Norfolk, VA, United States.   Height: 6'9".   Weight: 220 lbs.   Drafted: 1974   College: Southwestern Louisiana

YEAR	TEAM	GP	GS	MIN	PTS	FGM	FGA	FG%	3PM	3PA	3P%	FTM	FTA	FT%	ORB	DRB	TRB	AST	PF	DQ	STL	BLK	TO	MPG	PPG	RPG	APG	PCM
73-74	Utah-A	40	....	529	249	103	211	.488	0	1	.000	43	84	.512	79	97	176	19	68	....	16	32	35	13.2	6.2	4.4	0.5	.534
ABA Season Totals		40	....	529	249	103	211	.488	0	1	.000	43	84	.512	79	97	176	19	68	....	16	32	35	13.2	6.2	4.4	0.5	....
73-74	Utah-A	7	....	41	17	6	19	.316	0	1	.000	5	10	.500	10	5	15	2	6	....	0	4	2	5.9	2.4	2.1	0.3	.397
ABA Playoff Totals		7	....	41	17	6	19	.316	0	1	.000	5	10	.500	10	5	15	2	6	....	0	4	2	5.9	2.4	2.1	0.3	....

• EDDIE, Patrick

Patrick Eddie

Born: Dec. 27, 1967. Milwaukee, WI, United States.   Height: 6'11".   Weight: 240 lbs.   Drafted: —   College: Mississippi

YEAR	TEAM	GP	GS	MIN	PTS	FGM	FGA	FG%	3PM	3PA	3P%	FTM	FTA	FT%	ORB	DRB	TRB	AST	PF	DQ	STL	BLK	TO	MPG	PPG	RPG	APG	PCM
91-92	New York	4	0	13	4	2	9	.222	0	0	.000	0	0	.000	0	1	1	0	3	0	0	0	0	3.3	1.0	0.3	0.0	-.228
NBA Season Totals		4	0	13	4	2	9	.222	0	0	.000	0	0	.000	0	1	1	0	3	0	0	0	0	3.3	1.0	0.3	0.0	....

YEAR	TEAM	GP	GS	MIN	PTS	FGM	FGA	FG%	3PM	3PA	3P%	FTM	FTA	FT%	ORB	DRB	TRB	AST	PF	DQ	STL	BLK	TO	MPG	PPG	RPG	APG	PCM

● **EDDLEMAN, Dike** Thomas Dwight (Dike) Eddleman

Born: Dec. 27, 1922. Centralia, IL, United States.　　Height: 6'3".　　Weight: 189 lbs.　　Drafted: —　　College: Illinois

YEAR	TEAM	GP	GS	MIN	PTS	FGM	FGA	FG%	3PM	3PA	3P%	FTM	FTA	FT%	ORB	DRB	TRB	AST	PF	DQ	STL	BLK	TO	MPG	PPG	RPG	APG	PCM
49-50	Tri-Cities	64	....	....	826	332	906	.366	....	....	....	162	260	.623	....	....	....	142	254		....	....	....	....	12.9		6.0	2.2	....
50-51	Tri-Cities	68	....	1040	398	1120		.355	....	....	....	244	349	.699	....	....	410	170	231	5	....	....	....	....	15.3		6.0	2.5	....
51-52	Mil/FtW	65	....	1893	740	269	809	.333	....	....	....	202	329	.614	....	....	267	134	249	9	....	....	....	....	29.1	11.4	4.1	2.1	.309
52-53	Fort Wayne	69	....	1571	615	241	687	.351	....	....	....	133	237	.561	....	....	236	104	220	5	....	....	....	....	22.8	8.9	3.4	1.5	.305
NBA Season Totals		266	....	3464	3221	1240	3522	.352	....	....	....	741	1175	.631	....	....	913	550	954	19	....	....	....	....	13.0	12.1	3.4	2.1	
49-50	Tri-Cities	3	....	....	49	17	45	.378	....	....	....	15	25	.600	....	....	....	7	17		....	....	....	....	16.3			2.3	....
51-52	Fort Wayne	2	....	37	16	6	16	.375	....	....	....	4	7	.571	....	....	7	4	9	1	....	....	....	....	18.5	8.0	3.5	2.0	.399
52-53	Fort Wayne	7	....	63	22	9	23	.391	....	....	....	4	15	.267	....	....	5	2	19	1	....	....	....	....	9.0	3.1	0.7	0.3	.114
NBA Playoff Totals		12	....	100	87	32	84	.381	....	....	....	23	47	.489	....	....	12	13	45	2	....	....	....	....	8.3	7.3	1.0	1.1	....

● **EDELIN, Kenton** Kenton Scott Edelin

Born: May 24, 1962. Heidelburg, Germany.　　Height: 6'8".　　Weight: 205 lbs.　　Drafted: 1984　　College: Virginia

YEAR	TEAM	GP	GS	MIN	PTS	FGM	FGA	FG%	3PM	3PA	3P%	FTM	FTA	FT%	ORB	DRB	TRB	AST	PF	DQ	STL	BLK	TO	MPG	PPG	RPG	APG	PCM
84-85	Indiana	10	1	143	11	4	13	.308	0	0	.000	3	8	.375	8	18	26	10	39	1	5	4	3	14.3	1.1	2.6	1.0	.158
NBA Season Totals		10	1	143	11	4	13	.308	0	0	.000	3	8	.375	8	18	26	10	39	1	5	4	3	14.3	1.1	2.6	1.0	....

● **EDGE, Charles** Charles (Razor) Edge

Born: Feb. 23, 1950. Hampraca, MI, United States.　　Height: 6'6".　　Weight: 210 lbs.　　Drafted: 1973　　College: Lemoyne-Owen

YEAR	TEAM	GP	GS	MIN	PTS	FGM	FGA	FG%	3PM	3PA	3P%	FTM	FTA	FT%	ORB	DRB	TRB	AST	PF	DQ	STL	BLK	TO	MPG	PPG	RPG	APG	PCM
73-74	Memphis-A	78	....	1948	748	312	624	.500	0	1	.000	124	182	.681	250	391	641	70	137	....	64	70	130	25.0	9.6	8.2	0.9	.527
74-75	Indiana-A	77	....	1142	453	195	386	.505	0	3	.000	63	114	.553	164	176	340	39	103	....	53	35	82	14.8	5.9	4.4	0.5	.491
ABA Season Totals		155	....	3090	1201	507	1010	.502	0	4	.000	187	296	.632	414	567	981	109	240	....	117	105	212	19.9	7.7	6.3	0.7	....
74-75	Indiana-A	7	....	42	4	2	8	.250	0	0	.000	0	0	.000	4	5	9	2	6	....	0	0	5	6.0	0.6	1.3	0.3	.148
ABA Playoff Totals		7	....	42	4	2	8	.250	0	0	.000	0	0	.000	4	5	9	2	6	....	0	0	5	6.0	0.6	1.3	0.3	....

● **EDMONDS, Bobby** Bobby Joe Edmonds

Born: Mar. 8, 1941. Indianapolis, IN, United States. Died: Nov.12, 1991.　　Height: 6'6".　　Weight: 220 lbs.　　Drafted: 1964　　College: Tennessee State

YEAR	TEAM	GP	GS	MIN	PTS	FGM	FGA	FG%	3PM	3PA	3P%	FTM	FTA	FT%	ORB	DRB	TRB	AST	PF	DQ	STL	BLK	TO	MPG	PPG	RPG	APG	PCM
67-68	Indiana-A	72	....	1338	577	213	488	.436	1	6	.167	150	229	.655	....	....	374	29	183	4	....	....	123	18.6	8.0	5.2	0.4	.437
69-70	Indiana-A	3	....	12	3	1	5	.200	0	0	.000	1	3	.333	2	2	4	0	1	0	....	....	0	4.0	1.0	1.3	0.0	.143
ABA Season Totals		75	....	1350	580	214	493	.434	1	6	.167	151	232	.651	2	2	378	29	184	4	....	....	123	18.0	7.7	5.0	0.4	....
67-68	Indiana-A	3	....	47	20	6	14	.429	1	2	.500	7	9	.778	....	....	18	2	12	1	....	....	5	15.7	6.7	6.0	0.7	.528
ABA Playoff Totals		3	....	47	20	6	14	.429	1	2	.500	7	9	.778	....	....	18	2	12	1	....	....	5	15.7	6.7	6.0	0.7	....

● **EDMONSON, Keith** Keith Andre Edmonson

Born: Sept. 28, 1960. Gulfport, MS, United States.　　Height: 6'5".　　Weight: 195 lbs.　　Drafted: 1982　　College: Purdue

YEAR	TEAM	GP	GS	MIN	PTS	FGM	FGA	FG%	3PM	3PA	3P%	FTM	FTA	FT%	ORB	DRB	TRB	AST	PF	DQ	STL	BLK	TO	MPG	PPG	RPG	APG	PCM
82-83	Atlanta	32	2	309	112	48	139	.345	0	2	.000	16	27	.593	20	19	39	22	41	0	11	6	19	9.7	3.5	1.2	0.7	.207
83-84	San Antonio	40	0	521	346	135	274	.493	0	0	.000	76	101	.752	40	30	70	27	67	1	22	6	44	13.0	8.7	1.8	0.7	.486
83-84	Denver	15	0	101	64	23	47	.489	0	0	.000	18	25	.720	6	12	18	7	16	0	4	1	17	6.7	4.3	1.2	0.5	.436
NBA Season Totals		87	2	931	522	206	460	.448	0	2	.000	110	153	.719	66	61	127	56	124	1	37	13	80	10.7	6.0	1.5	0.6	....
82-83	Atlanta	1	0	2	2	1	1	1.000	0	0	.000	0	0	.000	1	0	1	1	0	0	0	0	0	2.0	2.0	1.0	1.0	2.000
NBA Playoff Totals		1	0	2	2	1	1	1.000	0	0	.000	0	0	.000	1	0	1	1	0	0	0	0	0	2.0	2.0	1.0	1.0	....

● **EDNEY, Tyus** Tyus Dwayne Edney

Born: Feb. 14, 1973. Gardena, CA, United States.　　Height: 5'10".　　Weight: 152 lbs.　　Drafted: 1995　　College: UCLA

YEAR	TEAM	GP	GS	MIN	PTS	FGM	FGA	FG%	3PM	3PA	3P%	FTM	FTA	FT%	ORB	DRB	TRB	AST	PF	DQ	STL	BLK	TO	MPG	PPG	RPG	APG	PCM
95-96	Sacramento	80	60	2481	860	305	740	.412	53	144	.368	197	252	.782	63	138	201	491	203	2	89	3	192	31.0	10.8	2.5	6.1	.381
96-97	Sacramento	70	20	1376	485	150	391	.384	8	42	.190	177	215	.823	34	79	113	226	98	0	60	2	112	19.7	6.9	1.6	3.2	.361
97-98	Boston	52	7	623	277	93	216	.431	3	10	.300	88	111	.793	20	35	55	139	69	0	51	1	68	12.0	5.3	1.1	2.7	.496
00-01	Indiana	24	0	263	106	35	91	.385	1	6	.167	35	39	.897	5	19	24	54	17	0	17	0	25	11.0	4.4	1.0	2.3	.457
NBA Season Totals		226	87	4743	1728	583	1438	.405	65	202	.322	497	617	.806	122	271	393	910	387	2	217	6	397	21.0	7.6	1.7	4.0	....
95-96	Sacramento	4	4	121	48	18	42	.429	2	8	.250	10	12	.833	2	10	12	11	11	1	8	0	9	30.3	12.0	3.0	2.8	.342
00-01	Indiana	2	0	10	4	2	7	.286	0	1	.000	0	1	.000	0	0	0	3	1	0	1	0	0	5.0	2.0	0.0	1.5	.282
NBA Playoff Totals		6	4	131	52	20	49	.408	2	9	.222	10	13	.769	2	10	12	14	12	1	9	0	9	21.8	8.7	2.0	2.3	....

● **EDWARDS, Bill** William Allen Edwards

Born: Sept. 22, 1971. Middletown, OH, United States.　　Height: 6'8".　　Weight: 215 lbs.　　Drafted: —　　College: Wright State

YEAR	TEAM	GP	GS	MIN	PTS	FGM	FGA	FG%	3PM	3PA	3P%	FTM	FTA	FT%	ORB	DRB	TRB	AST	PF	DQ	STL	BLK	TO	MPG	PPG	RPG	APG	PCM
93-94	Philadelphia	3	0	44	6	2	18	.111	0	5	.000	2	5	.400	5	9	14	4	6	0	3	1	4	14.7	2.0	4.7	1.3	.099
NBA Season Totals		3	0	44	6	2	18	.111	0	5	.000	2	5	.400	5	9	14	4	6	0	3	1	4	14.7	2.0	4.7	1.3	....

● **EDWARDS, Blue** Theodore (Blue) Edwards

Born: Oct. 31, 1965. Washington, DC, United States.　　Height: 6'4".　　Weight: 200 lbs.　　Drafted: 1989　　College: East Carolina

YEAR	TEAM	GP	GS	MIN	PTS	FGM	FGA	FG%	3PM	3PA	3P%	FTM	FTA	FT%	ORB	DRB	TRB	AST	PF	DQ	STL	BLK	TO	MPG	PPG	RPG	APG	PCM
89-90	Utah	82	49	1889	727	286	564	.507	9	30	.300	146	203	.719	69	182	251	145	280	2	76	36	156	23.0	8.9	3.1	1.8	.348
90-91	Utah	62	56	1611	576	244	464	.526	6	24	.250	82	117	.701	51	150	201	108	203	4	57	29	105	26.0	9.3	3.2	1.7	.338
91-92	Utah	81	81	2283	1018	433	830	.522	39	103	.379	113	146	.774	86	212	298	137	236	1	81	46	122	28.2	12.6	3.7	1.7	.417

YEAR	TEAM	GP	GS	MIN	PTS	FGM	FGA	FG%	3PM	3PA	3P%	FTM	FTA	FT%	ORB	DRB	TRB	AST	PF	DQ	STL	BLK	TO	MPG	PPG	RPG	APG	PCM
92-93	Milwaukee	82	81	2729	1382	554	1083	.512	37	106	.349	237	300	.790	123	259	382	214	242	1	129	45	172	33.3	16.9	4.7	2.6	.488
93-94	Milwaukee	82	64	2322	953	382	800	.478	38	106	.358	151	189	.799	104	225	329	171	235	1	83	27	148	28.3	11.6	4.0	2.1	.386
94-95	Boston	31	7	507	220	83	195	.426	11	43	.256	43	48	.896	25	40	65	47	64	0	19	10	40	16.4	7.1	2.1	1.5	.361
94-95	Utah	36	0	605	239	98	198	.495	11	32	.344	32	42	.762	25	40	65	30	79	1	24	6	43	16.8	6.6	1.8	0.8	.304
98-99	Vancouver	82	82	2773	1043	401	956	.419	84	245	.343	157	208	.755	98	248	346	212	243	1	118	46	172	33.8	12.7	4.2	2.6	.334
96-97	Vancouver	61	12	1439	478	182	458	.397	25	89	.281	89	109	.817	49	140	189	114	135	0	38	20	79	23.6	7.8	3.1	1.9	.297
97-98	Vancouver	81	20	1968	872	326	742	.439	40	120	.333	180	215	.837	61	156	217	201	183	0	86	27	138	24.3	10.8	2.7	2.5	.399
98-99	Miami	24	0	283	77	32	72	.444	4	10	.400	9	13	.692	7	26	33	30	23	0	17	5	21	11.8	3.2	1.4	1.3	.329
NBA Season Totals		704	452	18409	7585	3021	6362	.475	304	908	.335	1239	1590	.779	698	1678	2376	1409	1923	11	728	297	1196	26.1	10.8	3.4	2.0	....
89-90	Utah	5	0	94	36	14	26	.538	1	3	.333	7	8	.875	8	10	18	8	16	0	7	2	12	18.8	7.2	3.6	1.6	.419
90-91	Utah	9	9	241	91	37	77	.481	1	2	.500	16	20	.800	7	21	28	16	37	0	8	1	15	26.8	10.1	3.1	1.8	.299
91-92	Utah	16	7	354	129	52	111	.468	2	10	.200	23	32	.719	22	29	51	17	45	0	23	3	25	22.1	8.1	3.2	1.1	.327
94-95	Utah	4	0	33	9	4	12	.333	1	1	1.000	0	0	.000	1	5	6	3	3	0	2	0	3	8.3	2.3	1.5	0.8	.241
NBA Playoff Totals		34	16	722	265	107	226	.473	5	16	.313	46	60	.767	38	65	103	44	101	0	40	6	55	21.2	7.8	3.0	1.3	....

• EDWARDS, Doug

Douglas Edwards

Born: Jan. 21, 1971. Miami, FL, United States. Height: 6'7". Weight: 220 lbs. Drafted: 1993 College: Florida State

YEAR	TEAM	GP	GS	MIN	PTS	FGM	FGA	FG%	3PM	3PA	3P%	FTM	FTA	FT%	ORB	DRB	TRB	AST	PF	DQ	STL	BLK	TO	MPG	PPG	RPG	APG	PCM
93-94	Atlanta	16	0	107	43	17	49	.347	0	1	.000	9	16	.563	7	11	18	8	9	0	2	5	6	6.7	2.7	1.1	0.5	.303
94-95	Atlanta	38	0	212	67	22	48	.458	0	1	.000	23	32	.719	19	29	48	13	30	0	5	4	23	5.6	1.8	1.3	0.3	.330
95-96	Vancouver	31	0	519	93	32	91	.352	0	4	.000	29	38	.763	35	52	87	39	51	2	10	18	28	16.7	3.0	2.8	1.3	.255
NBA Season Totals		85	0	838	203	71	188	.378	0	6	.000	61	86	.709	61	92	153	60	90	2	17	27	57	9.9	2.4	1.8	0.7	....
93-94	Atlanta	1	0	3	0	0	0	.000	0	0	.000	0	0	.000	0	0	0	0	0	0	0	1	0	3.0	0.0	0.0	0.0	.306
NBA Playoff Totals		1	0	3	0	0	0	.000	0	0	.000	0	0	.000	0	0	0	0	0	0	0	1	0	3.0	0.0	0.0	0.0	....

• EDWARDS, Franklin

Franklin Delano Edwards

Born: Feb. 2, 1959. New York, NY, United States. Height: 6'1". Weight: 170 lbs. Drafted: 1981 College: Cleveland State

YEAR	TEAM	GP	GS	MIN	PTS	FGM	FGA	FG%	3PM	3PA	3P%	FTM	FTA	FT%	ORB	DRB	TRB	AST	PF	DQ	STL	BLK	TO	MPG	PPG	RPG	APG	PCM
81-82	Philadelphia	42	3	291	150	65	150	.433	0	9	.000	20	27	.741	10	17	27	45	37	0	16	5	25	6.9	3.6	0.6	1.1	.416
82-83	Philadelphia	81	3	1266	542	228	483	.472	0	8	.000	86	113	.761	23	62	85	221	119	0	81	6	113	15.6	6.7	1.0	2.7	.428
83-84	Philadelphia	60	0	654	202	84	221	.380	0	1	.000	34	48	.708	12	47	59	90	78	1	31	5	48	10.9	3.4	1.0	1.5	.263
84-85	LA Clippers	16	0	198	91	36	66	.545	0	0	.000	19	24	.792	3	11	14	38	10	0	17	0	18	12.4	5.7	0.9	2.4	.549
85-86	LA Clippers	73	19	1491	657	262	577	.454	1	9	.111	132	151	.874	24	62	86	259	87	0	89	4	139	20.4	9.0	1.2	3.5	.422
86-87	Sacramento	8	0	122	28	9	32	.281	0	4	.000	10	14	.714	2	8	10	29	7	0	5	0	17	15.3	3.5	1.3	3.6	.251
87-88	Sacramento	16	11	414	132	54	115	.470	0	2	.000	24	32	.750	4	15	19	92	10	0	10	1	46	25.9	8.3	1.2	5.8	.363
NBA Season Totals		296	36	4436	1802	738	1644	.449	1	33	.030	325	409	.795	78	222	300	774	348	1	249	21	406	15.0	6.1	1.0	2.6	....
81-82	Philadelphia	9	0	32	33	12	20	.600	1	1	1.000	8	9	.889	2	3	5	5	0	0	3	0	2	3.6	3.7	0.6	0.6	1.128
82-83	Philadelphia	12	0	101	40	13	32	.406	0	0	.000	14	17	.824	2	7	9	17	7	0	5	0	6	8.4	3.3	0.8	1.4	.438
NBA Playoff Totals		21	0	133	73	25	52	.481	1	1	1.000	22	26	.846	4	10	14	22	7	0	8	0	8	6.3	3.5	0.7	1.0	....

• EDWARDS, Glen

Glen Edwards

Born: —. Height: — Weight: — Drafted: — College: —

YEAR	TEAM	GP	GS	MIN	PTS	FGM	FGA	FG%	3PM	3PA	3P%	FTM	FTA	FT%	ORB	DRB	TRB	AST	PF	DQ	STL	BLK	TO	MPG	PPG	RPG	APG	PCM
41-42	Toledo-N	3	....	....	5	2	....	....	....	....	....	1	....	....	....	....	....	....	....	....	....	....	....	....	1.7	....	....	....
NBL Season Totals		3	....	....	5	2	....	....	....	....	....	1	....	....	....	....	....	....	....	....	....	....	....	....	1.7	....	....	....

• EDWARDS, James

James Franklin (Buddha) Edwards

Born: Nov. 22, 1955. Seattle, WA, United States. Height: 7' Weight: 225 lbs. Drafted: 1977 College: Washington

YEAR	TEAM	GP	GS	MIN	PTS	FGM	FGA	FG%	3PM	3PA	3P%	FTM	FTA	FT%	ORB	DRB	TRB	AST	PF	DQ	STL	BLK	TO	MPG	PPG	RPG	APG	PCM
77-78	LA Lakers	25	....	723	370	145	316	.459	....	....	....	80	125	.640	44	136	180	29	89	3	17	28	58	28.9	14.8	7.2	1.2	.471
77-78	Indiana	58	....	1682	892	350	777	.450	....	....	....	192	296	.649	153	282	435	56	233	9	36	50	110	29.0	15.4	7.5	1.0	.472
78-79	Indiana	82	....	2546	1366	534	1065	.501	....	....	....	298	441	.676	179	514	693	92	363	16	60	109	164	31.0	16.7	8.5	1.1	.546
79-80	Indiana	82	....	2314	1287	528	1032	.512	0	1	.000	231	339	.681	179	399	578	127	324	**12**	55	104	131	28.2	15.7	7.0	1.5	.572
80-81	Indiana	81	....	2375	1266	511	1004	.509	0	3	.000	244	347	.703	191	380	571	212	304	7	32	128	162	29.3	15.6	7.0	2.6	.581
81-82	Cleveland	77	75	2539	1288	528	1033	.511	0	4	.000	232	339	.684	189	392	581	123	347	17	24	117	162	33.0	16.7	7.5	1.6	.497
82-83	Cleveland	15	8	382	184	73	150	.487	0	0	.000	38	61	.623	37	59	96	13	61	3	7	14	30	25.5	12.3	6.4	0.9	.443
82-83	Phoenix	16	1	285	141	55	113	.487	0	0	.000	31	47	.660	19	40	59	27	49	2	5	5	19	17.8	8.8	3.7	1.7	.471
83-84	Phoenix	72	67	1897	1059	438	817	.536	0	1	.000	183	254	.720	108	240	348	184	254	3	23	30	137	26.3	14.7	4.8	2.6	.526
84-85	Phoenix	70	58	1787	1044	384	766	.501	0	3	.000	276	370	.746	95	292	387	153	237	5	26	52	161	25.5	14.9	5.5	2.2	.549
85-86	Phoenix	52	51	1314	848	318	587	.542	0	0	.000	212	302	.702	79	222	301	74	200	5	23	29	130	25.3	16.3	5.8	1.4	.571
86-87	Phoenix	14	9	304	168	57	110	.518	0	0	.000	54	70	.771	20	40	60	19	42	1	6	7	15	21.7	12.0	4.3	1.4	.546
87-88	Phoenix	43	42	1377	673	254	542	.469	0	1	.000	165	260	.635	97	238	335	73	159	2	14	32	108	32.0	15.7	7.8	1.7	.449
87-88	Detroit	26	2	328	141	48	101	.475	0	0	.000	45	61	.738	22	55	77	5	57	0	2	5	21	12.6	5.4	3.0	0.2	.371
88-89	Detroit	76	1	1254	555	211	422	.500	0	2	.000	133	194	.686	68	163	231	49	226	1	11	31	68	16.5	7.3	3.0	0.6	.374
89-90	Detroit	82	70	2283	1189	462	928	.498	0	3	.000	265	354	.749	112	233	345	63	295	4	23	37	131	27.8	14.5	4.2	0.8	.393
90-91	Detroit	72	70	1903	982	383	792	.484	1	2	.500	215	295	.729	91	186	277	65	249	4	12	30	130	26.4	13.6	3.8	0.9	.364
91-92	LA Clippers	72	11	1437	698	250	538	.465	0	1	.000	198	271	.731	55	147	202	53	236	1	24	33	72	20.0	9.7	2.8	0.7	.360
92-93	LA Lakers	52	0	617	328	122	270	.452	0	0	.000	84	118	.712	30	70	100	41	122	0	10	7	52	11.9	6.3	1.9	0.8	.359
93-94	LA Lakers	45	2	469	210	78	168	.464	0	0	.000	54	79	.684	11	54	65	22	90	0	4	3	32	10.4	4.7	1.4	0.5	.288
94-95	Portland	28	0	266	75	32	83	.386	0	0	.000	11	17	.647	10	33	43	8	44	0	5	8	14	9.5	2.7	1.5	0.3	.194
95-96	Chicago	28	0	274	98	41	110	.373	0	0	.000	16	26	.615	15	25	40	11	61	1	1	8	22	9.8	3.5	1.4	0.4	.134
NBA Season Totals		1168	467	28356	14862	5802	11724	.495	1	21	.048	3257	4666	.698	1804	4200	6004	1499	4042	96	420	867	1929	24.3	12.7	5.1	1.3	....
80-81	Indiana	2	....	56	14	7	24	.292	0	0	.000	0	0	.000	4	10	14	5	8	0	1	1	4	28.0	7.0	7.0	2.5	.201
82-83	Phoenix	3	0	54	28	11	26	.423	0	0	.000	6	6	1.000	6	12	18	4	7	0	1	1	5	18.0	9.3	6.0	1.3	.541
83-84	Phoenix	17	17	463	234	93	189	.492	0	0	.000	48	68	.706	22	69	91	27	62	3	4	11	31	27.2	13.8	5.4	1.6	.443
87-88	Detroit	22	2	308	139	56	110	.509	0	1	.000	27	41	.659	23	45	68	11	55	0	2	10	10	14.0	6.3	3.1	0.5	.433
88-89	Detroit	17	0	317	120	40	85	.471	0	1	.000	40	51	.784	11	25	36	12	53	0	1	8	15	18.6	7.1	2.1	0.7	.281
89-90	Detroit	20	20	536	286	114	231	.494	0	1	.000	58	96	.604	24	47	71	13	74	0	5	11	31	26.8	14.3	3.6	0.7	.355

YEAR	TEAM	GP	GS	MIN	PTS	FGM	FGA	FG%	3PM	3PA	3P%	FTM	FTA	FT%	ORB	DRB	TRB	AST	PF	DQ	STL	BLK	TO	MPG	PPG	RPG	APG	PCM
90-91	Detroit	15	11	345	160	61	150	.407	0	0	.000	38	55	.691	15	22	37	9	43	0	2	3	24	23.0	10.7	2.5	0.6	.218
91-92	LA Clippers	5	0	87	32	10	24	.417	0	0	.000	12	19	.632	5	8	13	3	11	0	1	1	4	17.4	6.4	2.6	0.6	.277
92-93	LA Lakers	3	0	14	6	3	4	.750	0	0	.000	0	0	.000	0	2	2	0	2	0	0	0	1	4.7	2.0	0.7	0.0	.362
94-95	Portland	1	0	4	0	0	1	.000	0	0	.000	0	0	.000	0	0	0	0	0	0	0	0	0	4.0	0.0	0.0	0.0	-.235
95-96	Chicago	6	0	28	11	4	9	.444	0	0	.000	3	4	.750	0	4	4	0	10	0	0	0	1	4.7	1.8	0.7	0.0	.141
NBA Playoff Totals		111	50	2212	1030	399	853	.468	0	3	.000	232	340	.682	110	244	354	84	325	3	17	46	126	19.9	9.3	3.2	0.8	....

• EDWARDS, Jay

Jay Charles Edwards

Born: Jan. 3, 1969. Muncie, IN, United States. Height: 6'4". Weight: 185 lbs. Drafted: 1989 College: Indiana

89-90	LA Clippers	4	0	26	7	3	7	.429	0	2	.000	1	3	.333	1	1	2	4	4	0	1	0	1	6.5	1.8	0.5	1.0	.253
NBA Season Totals		4	0	26	7	3	7	.429	0	2	.000	1	3	.333	1	1	2	4	4	0	1	0	1	6.5	1.8	0.5	1.0	....

• EDWARDS, Kevin

Kevin Durell Edwards

Born: Oct. 30, 1965. Cleveland Heights, OH, United States. Height: 6'3". Weight: 190 lbs. Drafted: 1988 College: DePaul

88-89	Miami	79	62	2349	1094	470	1105	.425	10	37	.270	144	193	.746	85	177	262	349	154	0	139	27	245	29.7	13.8	3.3	4.4	.406
89-90	Miami	78	54	2211	938	395	959	.412	9	30	.300	139	183	.760	77	205	282	252	149	1	125	33	179	28.3	12.0	3.6	3.2	.376
90-91	Miami	79	16	2000	955	380	927	.410	24	84	.286	171	213	.803	80	125	205	240	151	2	129	46	166	25.3	12.1	2.6	3.0	.405
91-92	Miami	81	1	1840	819	325	716	.454	7	32	.219	162	191	.848	56	155	211	170	138	1	99	20	122	22.7	10.1	2.6	2.1	.410
92-93	Miami	40	30	1134	556	216	462	.468	5	17	.294	119	141	.844	48	73	121	120	69	0	68	12	76	28.4	13.9	3.0	3.0	.466
93-94	New Jersey	82	82	2727	1144	471	1028	.458	35	99	.354	167	217	.770	94	187	281	232	150	0	120	34	131	33.3	14.0	3.4	2.8	.393
94-95	New Jersey	14	14	466	196	69	154	.448	18	45	.400	40	42	.952	10	27	37	27	42	0	19	5	35	33.3	14.0	2.6	1.9	.319
95-96	New Jersey	34	33	1007	394	142	390	.364	42	104	.404	68	84	.810	14	61	75	71	67	0	54	7	68	29.6	11.6	2.2	2.1	.259
96-97	New Jersey	32	0	477	190	69	183	.377	15	43	.349	37	43	.860	9	34	43	57	34	0	17	4	48	14.9	5.9	1.3	1.8	.295
97-98	New Jersey	27	5	352	91	37	106	.349	4	11	.364	13	15	.867	11	23	34	26	20	0	21	0	19	13.0	3.4	1.3	1.0	.224
97-98	Orlando	12	0	135	59	20	59	.339	2	4	.500	17	20	.850	9	11	20	13	8	0	5	1	10	11.3	4.9	1.7	1.1	.348
00-01	Vancouver	46	5	634	160	56	170	.329	5	19	.263	43	53	.811	23	59	82	52	46	0	29	8	37	13.8	3.5	1.8	1.1	.258
NBA Season Totals		604	302	15332	6596	2650	6259	.423	176	525	.335	1120	1395	.803	516	1137	1653	1609	1028	4	825	197	1136	25.4	10.9	2.7	2.7	....
91-92	Miami	3	0	55	15	5	13	.385	0	0	.000	5	8	.625	1	6	7	7	3	0	2	0	5	18.3	5.0	2.3	2.3	.291
93-94	New Jersey	4	4	148	49	18	50	.360	0	2	.000	13	14	.929	8	8	16	9	9	0	5	1	9	37.0	12.3	4.0	2.3	.248
NBA Playoff Totals		7	4	203	64	23	63	.365	0	2	.000	18	22	.818	9	14	23	16	12	0	7	1	14	29.0	9.1	3.3	2.3	....

• EDWARDS, Leroy

Leroy (Cowboy, Lefty, Li'l Abner) Edwards

Born: Apr. 11, 1914. Indianapolis, IN, United States. Died: Aug.25, 1971. Height: 6'4". Weight: 200 lbs. Drafted: — College: Kentucky

37-38	Oshkosh-N	13	....	....	**210**	**83**	....	....	....	....	....	44	....	....	....	....	....	....	....	....	....	....	....	....	16.2	....	....	....
38-39	Oshkosh-N	28	....	....	**334**	**124**	....	....	....	....	....	**86**	....	....	....	....	....	....	....	....	....	....	....	....	11.9	....	....	....
39-40	Oshkosh-N	28	....	....	**361**	111	....	....	....	....	....	**139**	....	....	....	....	....	....	....	....	....	....	....	....	12.9	....	....	....
40-41	Oshkosh-N	23	....	....	190	57	....	....	....	....	....	**76**	....	....	....	....	....	....	....	....	....	....	....	....	8.3	....	....	....
41-42	Oshkosh-N	24	....	....	262	85	....	....	....	....	....	92	....	....	....	....	....	....	....	....	....	....	....	....	10.9	....	....	....
42-43	Oshkosh-N	23	....	....	220	74	....	....	....	....	....	72	....	....	....	....	....	....	....	....	....	....	....	....	9.6	....	....	....
43-44	Oshkosh-N	19	....	....	148	48	....	....	....	....	....	52	....	....	....	....	....	....	....	....	....	....	....	....	7.8	....	....	....
44-45	Oshkosh-N	30	....	....	407	125	....	....	....	....	....	157	....	....	....	....	....	....	....	....	....	....	....	....	13.6	....	....	....
45-46	Oshkosh-N	34	....	....	359	120	....	....	....	....	....	**119**	**200**	.595	....	....	....	....	....	....	....	....	....	....	10.6	....	....	....
46-47	Oshkosh-N	44	....	....	414	135	....	....	....	....	....	144	222	.649	....	....	....	....	134	....	....	....	....	....	9.4	....	....	....
47-48	Oshkosh-N	46	....	....	294	76	....	....	....	....	....	142	205	.693	....	....	....	....	146	....	....	....	....	....	6.4	....	....	....
48-49	Oshkosh-N	10	....	....	22	7	....	....	....	....	....	8	20	.400	....	....	....	....	24	....	....	....	....	....	2.2	....	....	....
NBL Season Totals		322	....	....	3221	1045	....	....	....	....	....	1131	647	....	....	....	....	....	304	....	....	....	....	....	10.0	....	....	....
37-38	Oshkosh-N	5	....	....	69	24	....	....	....	....	....	21	....	....	....	....	....	....	....	....	....	....	....	....	13.8	....	....	....
38-39	Oshkosh-N	5	....	....	70	23	....	....	....	....	....	24	....	....	....	....	....	....	....	....	....	....	....	....	14.0	....	....	....
39-40	Oshkosh-N	8	....	....	93	33	....	....	....	....	....	27	....	....	....	....	....	....	....	....	....	....	....	....	11.6	....	....	....
40-41	Oshkosh-N	5	....	....	71	23	....	....	....	....	....	25	....	....	....	....	....	....	....	....	....	....	....	....	14.2	....	....	....
41-42	Oshkosh-N	5	....	....	83	30	....	....	....	....	....	23	....	....	....	....	....	....	....	....	....	....	....	....	16.6	....	....	....
42-43	Oshkosh-N	2	....	....	24	8	....	....	....	....	....	8	....	....	....	....	....	....	....	....	....	....	....	....	12.0	....	....	....
43-44	Oshkosh-N	3	....	....	17	6	....	....	....	....	....	5	....	....	....	....	....	....	....	....	....	....	....	....	5.7	....	....	....
45-46	Oshkosh-N	5	....	....	44	15	....	....	....	....	....	14	21	.667	....	....	....	....	....	....	....	....	....	....	8.8	....	....	....
46-47	Oshkosh-N	6	....	....	17	7	....	....	....	....	....	3	14	.214	....	....	....	....	....	....	....	....	....	....	2.8	....	....	....
47-48	Oshkosh-N	4	....	....	41	13	....	....	....	....	....	15	23	.652	....	....	....	....	....	....	....	....	....	....	10.3	....	....	....
48-49	Oshkosh-N	6	....	....	19	7	....	....	....	....	....	5	11	.455	....	....	....	....	....	....	....	....	....	....	3.2	....	....	....
NBL Playoff Totals		54	....	....	548	189	....	....	....	....	....	170	69	....	....	....	....	....	....	....	....	....	....	....	10.1	....	....	....

• EDWARDS, Tommy

Thomas Edwards

Born: 1911. Height: 5'10". Weight: 170 lbs. Drafted: — College: Ohio University

41-42	Toledo-N	1	....	....	1	0	....	....	....	....	....	1	....	....	....	....	....	....	....	....	....	....	....	....	1.0	....	....	....
NBL Season Totals		1	....	....	1	0	....	....	....	....	....	1	....	....	....	....	....	....	....	....	....	....	....	....	1.0	....	....	....

• EGAN, Johnny

John Francis Egan

Born: Jan. 31, 1939. Hartford, CT, United States. Height: 5'11". Weight: 180 lbs. Drafted: 1961 College: Providence

61-62	Detroit	58	....	696	320	128	301	.425	....	....	....	64	84	.762	....	....	86	102	64	0	....	....	....	12.0	5.5	1.5	1.8	.494
62-63	Detroit	46	....	752	273	110	296	.372	....	....	....	53	69	.768	....	....	59	114	70	0	....	....	....	16.3	5.9	1.3	2.5	.367
63-64	Detroit	24	....	838	267	105	256	.410	....	....	....	57	68	.838	....	....	52	116	77	2	....	....	....	34.9	11.1	2.2	4.8	.355
63-64	New York	42	....	1487	594	229	502	.456	....	....	....	136	175	.777	....	....	129	242	104	1	....	....	....	35.4	14.1	3.1	5.8	.486
64-65	New York	74	....	1664	678	258	529	.488	....	....	....	162	199	.814	....	....	143	252	139	0	....	....	....	22.5	9.2	1.9	3.4	.494
65-66	New York	7	....	58	17	5	16	.313	....	....	....	7	10	.700	....	....	2	14	4	0	....	....	....	8.3	2.4	0.3	2.0	.418
65-66	Baltimore	69	....	1586	674	254	558	.455	....	....	....	166	217	.765	....	....	181	259	163	1	....	....	....	23.0	9.8	2.6	3.8	.510

Total Basketball

YEAR	TEAM	GP	GS	MIN	PTS	FGM	FGA	FG%	3PM	3PA	3P%	FTM	FTA	FT%	ORB	DRB	TRB	AST	PF	DQ	STL	BLK	TO	MPG	PPG	RPG	APG	PCM
66-67	Baltimore	71	....	1743	719	267	624	.428	....	....	....	185	219	.845	....	....	180	275	190	3	....	....	....	24.5	10.1	2.5	3.9	.470
67-68	Baltimore	67	....	930	468	163	415	.393	....	....	....	142	183	.776	....	....	112	134	127	0	....	....	....	13.9	7.0	1.7	2.0	.484
68-69	LA Lakers	82	....	1805	696	246	597	.412	....	....	....	204	240	.850	....	....	147	215	206	1	....	....	....	22.0	8.5	1.8	2.6	.374
69-70	LA Lakers	72	....	1627	529	215	491	.438	....	....	....	99	121	.818	....	....	104	216	171	2	....	....	....	22.6	7.3	1.4	3.0	.329
70-71	Cleveland	26	....	410	105	40	98	.408	....	....	....	25	28	.893	....	....	32	58	31	0	....	....	....	15.8	4.0	1.2	2.2	.327
70-71	San Diego	36	....	414	71	27	80	.338	....	....	....	17	23	.739	....	....	31	54	40	0	....	....	....	11.5	2.0	0.9	1.5	.227
71-72	Houston	38	....	437	110	42	104	.404	....	....	....	26	32	.813	....	....	26	51	55	0	....	....	....	11.5	2.9	0.7	1.3	.253
NBA Season Totals		712	....	14447	5521	2089	4867	.429	....	....	....	1343	1668	.805	....	....	1284	2102	1441	10	....	....	....	20.3	7.8	1.8	3.0	
61-62	Detroit	5	....	106	68	29	62	.468	....	....	....	10	10	1.000	....	....	9	16	8	0	....	....	....	21.2	13.6	1.8	3.2	.619
65-66	Baltimore	3	....	117	48	19	47	.404	....	....	....	10	16	.625	....	....	9	23	14	1	....	....	....	39.0	16.0	3.0	7.7	.455
68-69	LA Lakers	18	....	571	251	94	217	.433	....	....	....	63	80	.788	....	....	44	70	55	0	....	....	....	31.7	13.9	2.4	3.9	.414
69-70	LA Lakers	16	....	162	56	23	43	.535	....	....	....	10	11	.909	....	....	5	22	20	0	....	....	....	10.1	3.5	0.3	1.4	.359
NBA Playoff Totals		42	....	956	423	165	369	.447	....	....	....	93	117	.795	....	....	67	131	97	1	....	....	....	22.8	10.1	1.6	3.1	

• EGGLESTON, Lonnie

Lonnie J. Eggleston

Born: June 8, 1918.   Height: 6'   Weight: 170 lbs.   Drafted: —   College: Oklahoma A&M

48-49	St. Louis	2	....	....	4	1	4	.250	....	....	....	2	3	.667	....	....	....	1	3	....	....	....	....	....	2.0	....	0.5	....
NBA Season Totals		2	....	....	4	1	4	.250	....	....	....	2	3	.667	....	....	....	1	3	....	....	....	....	....	2.0	....	0.5	....

• EHLERS, Bulbs

Edwin S. (Bulbs) Ehlers

Born: Mar. 10, 1923.   Height: 6'3".   Weight: 198 lbs.   Drafted: 1947   College: Purdue

47-48	Boston	40	....	....	286	104	417	.249	....	....	....	78	144	.542	....	....	44	92	....	....	....	....	....	7.2	....	1.1	....
48-49	Boston	59	....	....	514	182	583	.312	....	....	....	150	225	.667	....	....	133	119	....	....	....	....	....	8.7	....	2.3	....
NBA Season Totals		99	....	....	800	286	1000	.286	....	....	....	228	369	.618	....	....	177	211	....	....	....	....	....	8.1	....	1.8	....

• EHLO, Craig

Joel Craig (Mr. Everything) Ehlo

Born: Aug. 11, 1961. Lubbock, TX, United States.   Height: 6'6".   Weight: 180 lbs.   Drafted: 1983   College: Washington State

YEAR	TEAM	GP	GS	MIN	PTS	FGM	FGA	FG%	3PM	3PA	3P%	FTM	FTA	FT%	ORB	DRB	TRB	AST	PF	DQ	STL	BLK	TO	MPG	PPG	RPG	APG	PCM
83-84	Houston	7	0	63	23	11	27	.407	0	0	.000	1	1	1.000	4	5	9	6	13	0	3	0	3	9.0	3.3	1.3	0.9	.268
84-85	Houston	45	0	189	87	34	69	.493	0	3	.000	19	30	.633	8	17	25	26	26	0	11	3	23	4.2	1.9	0.6	0.6	.406
85-86	Houston	36	0	199	98	36	84	.429	3	9	.333	23	29	.793	17	29	46	29	22	0	11	4	14	5.5	2.7	1.3	0.8	.579
86-87	Cleveland	44	15	890	273	99	239	.414	5	29	.172	70	99	.707	55	106	161	92	80	0	40	30	62	20.2	6.2	3.7	2.1	.391
87-88	Cleveland	79	27	1709	563	226	485	.466	22	64	.344	89	132	.674	86	188	274	206	182	0	82	30	111	21.6	7.1	3.5	2.6	.406
88-89	Cleveland	82	4	1867	608	249	524	.475	39	100	.390	71	117	.607	100	195	295	266	161	0	110	19	115	22.8	7.4	3.6	3.2	.443
89-90	Cleveland	81	64	2894	1102	436	940	.464	104	248	.419	126	185	.681	147	292	439	371	226	2	126	23	162	35.7	13.6	5.4	4.6	.446
90-91	Cleveland	82	68	2766	832	344	773	.445	49	149	.329	95	140	.679	142	246	388	376	209	0	121	34	164	33.7	10.1	4.7	4.6	.386
91-92	Cleveland	63	62	2016	776	310	684	.453	69	167	.413	87	123	.707	94	213	307	238	150	0	78	22	107	32.0	12.3	4.9	3.8	.434
92-93	Cleveland	82	73	2559	949	385	785	.490	93	244	.381	86	120	.717	113	290	403	254	170	0	104	22	123	31.2	11.6	4.9	3.1	.442
93-94	Atlanta	82	0	2147	821	316	708	.446	77	221	.348	112	154	.727	71	208	279	273	161	0	136	26	131	26.2	10.0	3.4	3.3	.442
94-95	Atlanta	49	0	1166	477	191	422	.453	51	134	.381	44	71	.620	55	92	147	113	86	0	46	6	74	23.8	9.7	3.0	2.3	.381
95-96	Atlanta	79	8	1758	669	253	591	.428	82	221	.371	81	103	.786	65	191	256	138	138	0	85	9	103	22.3	8.5	3.2	1.7	.372
96-97	Seattle	62	0	848	214	87	248	.351	27	95	.284	13	26	.500	39	71	110	68	71	0	36	4	43	13.7	3.5	1.8	1.1	.232
NBA Season Totals		873	321	21071	7492	2977	6579	.453	621	1684	.369	917	1330	.689	996	2143	3139	2456	1695	2	989	232	1235	24.1	8.6	3.6	2.8	
84-85	Houston	3	0	6	4	1	1	1.000	0	0	.000	2	2	1.000	0	0	0	0	3	0	4	0	0	2.0	1.3	0.0	0.0	1.055
85-86	Houston	10	0	38	20	8	16	.500	0	1	.000	4	5	.800	1	2	3	6	4	0	4	1	3	3.8	2.0	0.3	0.6	.561
87-88	Cleveland	5	1	128	44	17	40	.425	0	8	.000	10	16	.625	3	15	18	17	14	0	5	0	12	25.6	8.8	3.6	3.4	.325
88-89	Cleveland	4	1	97	48	17	39	.436	5	13	.385	9	11	.818	2	4	6	13	10	0	3	1	5	24.3	12.0	1.5	3.3	.418
89-90	Cleveland	5	5	196	69	26	62	.419	5	15	.333	12	19	.632	7	25	32	32	18	0	6	0	12	39.2	13.8	6.4	6.4	.418
91-92	Cleveland	17	14	552	163	63	152	.414	21	51	.412	16	21	.762	22	55	77	77	40	0	21	5	18	32.5	9.6	4.5	4.5	.400
92-93	Cleveland	9	9	289	98	38	91	.418	10	26	.385	12	15	.800	10	21	31	25	19	0	12	4	17	32.1	10.9	3.4	2.8	.322
93-94	Atlanta	11	0	317	125	50	118	.424	8	23	.348	17	24	.708	11	19	30	40	32	0	11	0	13	28.8	11.4	2.7	3.6	.359
94-95	Atlanta	3	0	49	9	2	12	.167	1	6	.167	4	4	1.000	0	7	7	3	0	0	2	0	4	16.3	3.0	2.3	1.0	.153
95-96	Atlanta	9	0	171	36	12	41	.293	7	23	.304	5	7	.714	1	17	18	9	14	0	9	2	9	19.0	4.0	2.0	1.0	.173
NBA Playoff Totals		76	30	1843	616	234	572	.409	57	166	.343	91	124	.734	57	165	222	222	154	0	77	13	93	24.3	8.1	2.9	2.9	

• EICH, —

Eich

Born: —.   Height: —   Weight: —   Drafted: —   College: —

41-42	Wingfoots-N	1	....	....	2	1	....	....	....	....	....	0	....	....	....	....	....	....	....	....	....	....	....	2.0	....	....	....
NBL Season Totals		1	....	....	2	1	....	....	....	....	....	0	....	....	....	....	....	....	....	....	....	....	....	2.0	....	....	....

• EICHHORST, Dick

Richard A. Eichhorst

Born: Oct. 21, 1933.   Height: 6'3".   Weight: 200 lbs.   Drafted: —   College: Southeast Missouri

61-62	St. Louis	1	....	10	2	1	2	.500	....	....	....	0	0	.000	....	....	1	3	1	0	....	....	....	10.0	2.0	1.0	3.0	.527
NBA Season Totals		1	....	10	2	1	2	.500	....	....	....	0	0	.000	....	....	1	3	1	0	....	....	....	10.0	2.0	1.0	3.0	

• EISLEY, Howard

Howard Jonathan Eisley

Born: Dec. 4, 1972. Detroit, MI, United States.   Height: 6'2".   Weight: 177 lbs.   Drafted: 1994   College: Boston College

YEAR	TEAM	GP	GS	MIN	PTS	FGM	FGA	FG%	3PM	3PA	3P%	FTM	FTA	FT%	ORB	DRB	TRB	AST	PF	DQ	STL	BLK	TO	MPG	PPG	RPG	APG	PCM
94-95	Minnesota	34	4	496	113	37	105	.352	8	32	.250	31	40	.775	10	32	42	77	78	0	18	5	41	14.6	3.3	1.2	2.3	.227
94-95	San Antonio	15	0	56	7	3	17	.176	1	5	.200	0	0	.000	2	4	6	18	3	0	1	8	3.7	0.5	0.4	1.2	.190
95-96	Utah	65	0	961	287	104	242	.430	14	62	.226	65	77	.844	22	56	78	146	130	0	29	3	78	14.8	4.4	1.2	2.2	.287
96-97	Utah	82	0	1083	368	139	308	.451	20	72	.278	70	89	.787	20	64	84	198	141	0	44	10	107	13.2	4.5	1.0	2.4	.347
97-98	Utah	82	18	1726	633	229	519	.441	48	118	.407	127	149	.852	25	141	166	346	182	3	54	13	164	21.0	7.7	2.0	4.2	.413

YEAR	TEAM	GP	GS	MIN	PTS	FGM	FGA	FG%	3PM	3PA	3P%	FTM	FTA	FT%	ORB	DRB	TRB	AST	PF	DQ	STL	BLK	TO	MPG	PPG	RPG	APG	PCM
98-99	Utah	50	0	1038	368	140	314	.446	21	50	.420	67	80	.838	12	82	94	185	122	2	30	2	109	20.8	7.4	1.9	3.7	.360
99-00	Utah	82	5	2096	708	282	675	.418	60	163	.368	84	102	.824	23	147	170	347	223	2	59	9	132	25.6	8.6	2.1	4.2	.342
00-01	Dallas	82	40	2426	741	265	675	.393	107	269	.398	104	126	.825	23	174	197	295	218	3	99	12	102	29.6	9.0	2.4	3.6	.320
01-02	New York	39	0	609	171	59	175	.337	14	58	.241	39	49	.796	9	40	49	100	55	0	24	3	53	15.6	4.4	1.3	2.6	.274
02-03	New York	82	76	2241	744	262	628	.417	131	337	.389	89	105	.848	24	162	186	444	222	1	71	9	149	27.3	9.1	2.3	5.4	.399
NBA Season Totals		613	143	12732	4140	1520	3658	.416	424	1166	.364	676	817	.827	170	902	1072	2156	1374	9	428	67	943	20.8	6.8	1.7	3.5	....
95-96	Utah	18	0	202	53	16	42	.381	3	9	.333	18	22	.818	4	18	22	44	29	0	3	2	11	11.2	2.9	1.2	2.4	.370
96-97	Utah	20	0	217	112	38	76	.500	9	19	.474	27	28	.964	4	14	18	40	27	1	3	0	17	10.9	5.6	0.9	2.0	.507
97-98	Utah	20	0	366	112	46	125	.368	8	27	.296	12	13	.923	4	36	40	81	42	0	12	5	31	18.3	5.6	2.0	4.1	.360
98-99	Utah	11	0	241	81	26	71	.366	5	24	.208	24	29	.828	3	17	20	32	27	0	7	3	20	21.9	7.4	1.8	2.9	.295
99-00	Utah	10	0	200	51	17	55	.309	9	19	.474	8	9	.889	1	17	18	19	24	0	6	1	13	20.0	5.1	1.8	1.9	.184
00-01	Dallas	9	0	194	52	19	53	.358	10	26	.385	4	4	1.000	1	11	12	17	18	0	5	1	13	21.6	5.8	1.3	1.9	.189
NBA Playoff Totals		88	0	1420	461	162	422	.384	44	124	.355	93	105	.886	17	113	130	233	167	1	36	12	105	16.1	5.2	1.5	2.6	....

• EKEZIE, Obinna

Obinna Ralph Ekezie

Born: Aug. 22, 1975. Port Harcourt, Nigeria.   Height: 6'9".   Weight: 270 lbs.   Drafted: 1999   College: Maryland

YEAR	TEAM	GP	GS	MIN	PTS	FGM	FGA	FG%	3PM	3PA	3P%	FTM	FTA	FT%	ORB	DRB	TRB	AST	PF	DQ	STL	BLK	TO	MPG	PPG	RPG	APG	PCM
99-00	Vancouver	39	0	351	125	41	88	.466	0	0	.000	43	64	.672	34	58	92	8	61	0	9	4	26	9.0	3.2	2.4	0.2	.358
00-01	Washington	29	0	273	101	32	77	.416	0	0	.000	37	53	.698	31	45	76	9	46	0	5	5	14	9.4	3.5	2.6	0.3	.393
00-01	Dallas	4	0	8	0	0	4	.000	0	0	.000	0	0	.000	0	2	2	0	2	0	0	0	0	2.0	0.0	0.5	0.0	-.337
01-02	LA Clippers	29	1	152	54	13	39	.333	0	0	.000	28	40	.700	12	22	34	3	16	0	2	6	10	5.2	1.9	1.2	0.1	.329
NBA Season Totals		101	1	784	280	86	208	.413	0	0	.000	108	157	.688	77	127	204	20	125	0	16	15	50	7.8	2.8	2.0	0.2	....

• EL-AMIN, Khalid

Khalid El-Amin

Born: Apr. 25, 1979. Minneapolis, MN, United States.   Height: 5'10".   Weight: 200 lbs.   Drafted: 2000   College: Connecticut

YEAR	TEAM	GP	GS	MIN	PTS	FGM	FGA	FG%	3PM	3PA	3P%	FTM	FTA	FT%	ORB	DRB	TRB	AST	PF	DQ	STL	BLK	TO	MPG	PPG	RPG	APG	PCM
00-01	Chicago	50	14	936	314	115	311	.370	28	84	.333	56	72	.778	21	60	81	145	99	0	48	2	54	18.7	6.3	1.6	2.9	.337
NBA Season Totals		50	14	936	314	115	311	.370	28	84	.333	56	72	.778	21	60	81	145	99	0	48	2	54	18.7	6.3	1.6	2.9	....

• ELIASON, Don

Donald Carlton Eliason

Born: July 24, 1918. Owatonna, MN, United States.   Height: 6'2".   Weight: 210 lbs.   Drafted: —   College: Hamline

YEAR	TEAM	GP	GS	MIN	PTS	FGM	FGA	FG%	3PM	3PA	3P%	FTM	FTA	FT%	ORB	DRB	TRB	AST	PF	DQ	STL	BLK	TO	MPG	PPG	RPG	APG	PCM
46-47	Boston	1	....	....	0	0	1	.000	....	....	....	0	0	.000	....	....	....	0	1	....	....	....	....	0.0	0.0	....	0.0	....
NBA Season Totals		1	....	....	0	0	1	.000	....	....	....	0	0	.000	....	....	....	0	1	....	....	....	....	0.0	0.0	....	0.0	....

• ELIE, Mario

Mario Antoine Elie

Born: Nov. 26, 1963. New York, NY, United States.   Height: 6'5".   Weight: 210 lbs.   Drafted: 1985   College: American International

YEAR	TEAM	GP	GS	MIN	PTS	FGM	FGA	FG%	3PM	3PA	3P%	FTM	FTA	FT%	ORB	DRB	TRB	AST	PF	DQ	STL	BLK	TO	MPG	PPG	RPG	APG	PCM
90-91	Philadelphia	3	0	20	6	2	7	.286	1	2	.500	1	2	.500	0	1	1	1	2	0	0	0	3	6.7	2.0	0.3	0.3	-.043
90-91	Golden State	30	0	624	231	77	152	.507	3	8	.375	74	87	.851	46	63	109	44	83	1	19	10	27	20.8	7.7	3.6	1.5	.427
91-92	Golden State	79	32	1677	620	221	424	.521	23	70	.329	155	182	.852	69	158	227	174	159	3	68	15	87	21.2	7.8	2.9	2.2	.440
92-93	Portland	82	7	1757	708	240	524	.458	45	129	.349	183	214	.855	59	157	216	177	145	0	74	20	90	21.4	8.6	2.6	2.2	.430
93-94	Houston	67	8	1606	626	208	466	.446	56	167	.335	154	179	.860	28	153	181	208	124	0	50	8	107	24.0	9.3	2.7	3.1	.416
94-95	Houston	81	13	1896	710	243	487	.499	80	201	.398	144	171	.842	50	146	196	189	158	0	65	12	105	23.4	8.8	2.4	2.3	.397
95-96	Houston	45	16	1385	499	180	357	.504	41	127	.323	98	115	.852	47	108	155	138	93	0	45	11	59	30.8	11.1	3.4	3.1	.412
96-97	Houston	78	77	2687	909	291	585	.497	120	286	.420	207	231	.896	60	175	235	310	200	2	92	12	133	34.4	11.7	3.0	4.0	.392
97-98	Houston	73	59	1988	612	206	456	.452	55	189	.291	145	174	.833	39	117	156	221	115	0	81	8	102	27.2	8.4	2.1	3.0	.346
98-99	San Antonio	47	37	1291	455	156	331	.471	40	107	.374	103	119	.866	36	101	137	89	91	0	46	12	61	27.5	9.7	2.9	1.9	.364
99-00	San Antonio	79	79	2217	590	195	457	.427	74	186	.398	126	149	.846	48	201	249	193	156	0	73	9	130	28.1	7.5	3.2	2.4	.300
00-01	Phoenix	68	67	1506	299	104	246	.423	36	100	.360	55	69	.797	38	117	155	131	112	0	58	12	60	22.1	4.4	2.3	1.9	.271
NBA Season Totals		732	395	18654	6265	2123	4492	.473	574	1572	.365	1445	1692	.854	520	1497	2017	1875	1438	6	671	129	964	25.5	8.6	2.8	2.6	....
90-91	Golden State	9	7	197	84	28	56	.500	1	1	1.000	27	32	.844	17	15	32	13	32	0	5	1	10	21.9	9.3	3.6	1.4	.409
91-92	Golden State	4	2	80	50	23	36	.639	2	2	1.000	2	3	.667	11	11	22	10	11	1	5	0	6	20.0	12.5	5.5	2.5	.782
92-93	Portland	4	0	52	20	5	10	.500	2	2	1.000	8	9	.889	2	4	6	4	1	0	2	1	5	13.0	5.0	1.5	1.0	.431
93-94	Houston	23	0	382	134	42	106	.396	10	32	.313	40	47	.851	9	31	40	38	30	0	8	3	21	16.6	5.8	1.7	1.7	.332
94-95	Houston	22	6	635	201	69	137	.504	28	65	.431	35	44	.795	19	43	62	54	55	0	21	1	21	28.9	9.1	2.8	2.5	.352
95-96	Houston	8	0	233	78	29	66	.439	9	24	.375	11	12	.917	6	16	22	14	17	0	7	3	5	29.1	9.8	2.8	1.8	.322
96-97	Houston	16	16	598	184	54	116	.466	24	60	.400	52	62	.839	19	37	56	61	52	3	14	4	30	37.4	11.5	3.5	3.8	.340
97-98	Houston	5	1	133	33	12	27	.444	3	9	.333	6	9	.667	3	10	13	6	10	0	2	0	5	26.6	6.6	2.6	1.2	.218
98-99	San Antonio	17	17	526	135	43	112	.384	8	30	.267	41	49	.837	9	50	59	50	42	0	22	2	25	30.9	7.9	3.5	2.9	.301
99-00	San Antonio	4	4	115	30	6	22	.273	1	7	.143	17	18	.944	5	12	17	7	4	0	5	0	12	28.8	7.5	4.3	1.8	.260
00-01	Phoenix	4	4	103	36	14	31	.452	2	13	.154	6	8	.750	2	11	13	7	6	0	3	1	2	25.8	9.0	3.3	1.8	.372
NBA Playoff Totals		116	57	3054	985	325	719	.452	90	245	.367	245	293	.836	102	240	342	264	260	4	94	16	142	26.3	8.5	2.9	2.3	....

• ELLEFSON, Ray

E. Ray Ellefson

Born: Nov. 18, 1927. Died: Oct.7, 1994.   Height: 6'8".   Weight: 230 lbs.   Drafted: —   College: West Texas State

YEAR	TEAM	GP	GS	MIN	PTS	FGM	FGA	FG%	3PM	3PA	3P%	FTM	FTA	FT%	ORB	DRB	TRB	AST	PF	DQ	STL	BLK	TO	MPG	PPG	RPG	APG	PCM
48-49	Waterloo-N	7	....	....	16	4	....	....	....	....	....	8	11	.727	....	....	....	....	5	....	....	....	....	2.3	....	....	....	....
48-49	Minneapolis	3	....	....	2	1	5	.200	....	....	....	0	0	.000	....	....	....	0	2	....	....	....	....	0.7	....	0.0	....	
50-51	New York	3	....	....	4	0	4	.000	....	....	....	4	4	1.000	....	....	....	8	0	6	0	....	....	....	1.3	2.7	0.0		
NBA Season Totals		6	....	....	6	1	9	.111	....	....	....	4	4	1.000	....	....	....	8	0	8	0	....	....	....	1.0	1.3	0.0		
NBL Season Totals		7	....	....	16	4	....	....	....	....	....	8	11		....	....	....	....	5	....	....	....	....	2.3	....	....	....	....	
Career Totals		13	....	....	22	5	9	....	....	....	....	12	15		....	....	....	8	0	13	0	....	....	....	1.7	0.6	0.0	....	

• ELLIOT, Denny

Denny Elliot

Born: 1914. Height: 5'9". Weight: 150 lbs. Drafted: — College: Otterbein

YEAR	TEAM	GP	GS	MIN	PTS	FGM	FGA	FG%	3PM	3PA	3P%	FTM	FTA	FT%	ORB	DRB	TRB	AST	PF	DQ	STL	BLK	TO	MPG	PPG	RPG	APG	PCM
37-38	Columbus-N	9	....	....	25	10	....	....	....	....	....	5	....	....	....	....	....	....	....	....	....	....	....	....	2.8	....	....	....
NBL Season Totals		9	....	....	25	10	....	....	....	....	....	5	....	....	....	....	....	....	....	....	....	....	....	....	2.8	....	....	....

• ELLIOTT, Bob

Robert Alan Elliott

Born: Aug. 18, 1955. Ann Arbor, MI, United States. Height: 6'9". Weight: 225 lbs. Drafted: 1977 College: Arizona

YEAR	TEAM	GP	GS	MIN	PTS	FGM	FGA	FG%	3PM	3PA	3P%	FTM	FTA	FT%	ORB	DRB	TRB	AST	PF	DQ	STL	BLK	TO	MPG	PPG	RPG	APG	PCM
78-79	New Jersey	14	....	282	123	41	73	.562	....	....	....	41	56	.732	16	40	56	22	34	2	6	4	27	20.1	8.8	4.0	1.6	.466
79-80	New Jersey	54	....	722	307	101	228	.443	1	4	.250	104	152	.684	67	118	185	53	97	0	29	14	86	13.4	5.7	3.4	1.0	.434
80-81	New Jersey	73	....	1320	550	214	419	.511	1	2	.500	121	202	.599	104	157	261	129	175	3	34	16	117	18.1	7.5	3.6	1.8	.427
NBA Season Totals		141	....	2324	980	356	720	.494	2	6	.333	266	410	.649	187	315	502	204	306	5	69	34	230	16.5	7.0	3.6	1.4	....

• ELLIOTT, Sean

Sean Michael Elliott

Born: Feb. 2, 1968. Tucson, AZ, United States. Height: 6'8". Weight: 205 lbs. Drafted: 1989 College: Arizona

YEAR	TEAM	GP	GS	MIN	PTS	FGM	FGA	FG%	3PM	3PA	3P%	FTM	FTA	FT%	ORB	DRB	TRB	AST	PF	DQ	STL	BLK	TO	MPG	PPG	RPG	APG	PCM
89-90	San Antonio	81	69	2032	810	311	647	.481	1	9	.111	187	216	.866	127	170	297	154	172	0	45	14	113	25.1	10.0	3.7	1.9	.390
90-91	San Antonio	82	82	3044	1301	478	976	.490	20	64	.313	325	402	.808	142	314	456	238	190	2	69	33	148	37.1	15.9	5.6	2.9	.443
91-92	San Antonio	82	82	3120	1338	514	1040	.494	25	82	.305	285	331	.861	143	296	439	214	149	0	84	29	156	38.0	16.3	5.4	2.6	.435
92-93	San Antonio	70	70	2604	1207	451	918	.491	37	104	.356	268	336	.798	85	237	322	265	132	1	68	28	154	37.2	17.2	4.6	3.8	.464
93-94	Detroit	73	73	2409	885	360	791	.455	26	87	.299	139	173	.803	68	195	263	197	174	3	54	27	131	33.0	12.1	3.6	2.7	.333
94-95	San Antonio	81	81	2858	1466	502	1072	.468	136	333	.408	326	404	.807	63	224	287	206	216	2	78	38	154	35.3	18.1	3.5	2.5	.436
95-96	San Antonio	77	77	2901	1537	525	1127	.466	161	392	.411	326	423	.771	69	327	396	211	178	1	69	33	200	37.7	20.0	5.1	2.7	.464
96-97	San Antonio	39	39	1393	582	196	464	.422	42	126	.333	148	196	.755	48	142	190	124	105	1	24	24	90	35.7	14.9	4.9	3.2	.381
97-98	San Antonio	36	36	1012	334	122	303	.403	34	90	.378	56	78	.718	16	108	124	62	92	1	24	14	58	28.1	9.3	3.4	1.7	.275
98-99	San Antonio	50	50	1509	561	208	507	.410	39	119	.328	106	140	.757	35	178	213	117	104	1	26	17	71	30.2	11.2	4.3	2.3	.350
99-00	San Antonio	19	19	391	114	38	106	.358	13	37	.351	25	32	.781	6	41	47	28	34	0	12	2	19	20.6	6.0	2.5	1.5	.262
00-01	San Antonio	52	34	1229	409	147	339	.434	55	129	.426	60	84	.714	17	153	170	81	80	0	23	25	51	23.6	7.9	3.3	1.6	.349
NBA Season Totals		742	712	24502	10544	3852	8290	.465	589	1572	.375	2251	2815	.800	819	2385	3204	1897	1626	12	576	284	1345	33.0	14.2	4.3	2.6	....
89-90	San Antonio	10	10	291	127	53	96	.552	0	1	.000	21	29	.724	11	30	41	18	37	0	9	6	15	29.1	12.7	4.1	1.8	.423
90-91	San Antonio	4	4	132	59	17	40	.425	0	3	.000	25	32	.781	8	14	22	16	9	0	4	1	9	33.0	14.8	5.5	4.0	.484
91-92	San Antonio	3	3	137	59	19	40	.475	5	8	.625	16	18	.889	4	9	13	8	6	0	3	4	6	45.7	19.7	4.3	2.7	.419
92-93	San Antonio	10	10	381	158	59	125	.472	3	14	.214	37	40	.925	8	40	48	36	22	0	8	3	22	38.1	15.8	4.8	3.6	.414
94-95	San Antonio	15	15	574	260	87	200	.435	20	55	.364	66	85	.776	23	49	72	40	38	0	10	7	27	38.3	17.3	4.8	2.7	.397
95-96	San Antonio	10	10	389	155	47	117	.402	10	34	.294	51	64	.797	11	28	39	25	24	0	11	4	30	38.9	15.5	3.9	2.5	.311
98-99	San Antonio	17	17	574	203	68	153	.444	22	55	.400	45	59	.763	11	47	58	45	50	0	9	4	21	33.8	11.9	3.4	2.6	.337
99-00	San Antonio	4	4	119	40	15	40	.375	5	13	.385	5	8	.625	1	21	22	5	13	0	0	2	4	29.8	10.0	5.5	1.3	.283
00-01	San Antonio	12	0	239	57	19	51	.373	8	22	.364	11	11	1.000	3	23	26	14	21	0	5	6	13	19.9	4.8	2.2	1.2	.234
NBA Playoff Totals		85	73	2836	1118	384	862	.445	73	205	.356	277	346	.801	80	261	341	207	220	0	59	37	147	33.4	13.2	4.0	2.4	....

• ELLIS, Bo

Maurice Ellis

Born: Aug. 8, 1954. Chicago, IL, United States. Height: 6'9". Weight: 197 lbs. Drafted: 1977 College: Marquette

YEAR	TEAM	GP	GS	MIN	PTS	FGM	FGA	FG%	3PM	3PA	3P%	FTM	FTA	FT%	ORB	DRB	TRB	AST	PF	DQ	STL	BLK	TO	MPG	PPG	RPG	APG	PCM
77-78	Denver	78	....	1213	338	133	320	.416	....	....	....	72	104	.692	114	190	304	73	208	2	49	47	101	15.6	4.3	3.9	0.9	.341
78-79	Denver	42	....	268	113	42	92	.457	....	....	....	29	36	.806	17	45	62	10	45	0	10	13	21	6.4	2.7	1.5	0.2	.423
79-80	Denver	48	....	502	162	61	136	.449	0	3	.000	40	53	.755	51	65	116	30	67	1	10	24	24	10.5	3.4	2.4	0.6	.408
NBA Season Totals		168	....	1983	613	236	548	.431	0	3	.000	141	193	.731	182	300	482	113	320	3	69	84	146	11.8	3.6	2.9	0.7	....
77-78	Denver	12	....	170	46	17	40	.425	....	....	....	12	15	.800	15	28	43	8	25	0	6	8	14	14.2	3.8	3.6	0.7	.354
78-79	Denver	3	....	24	6	2	6	.333	....	....	....	2	2	1.000	1	3	4	1	2	0	2	1	0	8.0	2.0	1.3	0.3	.371
NBA Playoff Totals		15	....	194	52	19	46	.413	....	....	....	14	17	.824	16	31	47	9	27	0	8	9	14	12.9	3.5	3.1	0.6	....

• ELLIS, Boo

Alexander (Boo) Ellis

Born: Feb. 11, 1936. Height: 6'5". Weight: 185 lbs. Drafted: 1958 College: Niagara

YEAR	TEAM	GP	GS	MIN	PTS	FGM	FGA	FG%	3PM	3PA	3P%	FTM	FTA	FT%	ORB	DRB	TRB	AST	PF	DQ	STL	BLK	TO	MPG	PPG	RPG	APG	PCM
58-59	Minneapolis	72	....	1202	428	163	379	.430	....	....	....	102	144	.708	....	....	380	59	137	0	....	....	....	16.7	5.9	5.3	0.8	.464
59-60	Minneapolis	46	....	671	179	64	185	.346	....	....	....	51	76	.671	....	....	236	27	64	2	....	....	....	14.6	3.9	5.1	0.6	.396
NBA Season Totals		118	....	1873	607	227	564	.402	....	....	....	153	220	.695	....	....	616	86	201	2	....	....	....	15.9	5.1	5.2	0.7	....
58-59	Minneapolis	13	....	255	88	35	80	.438	....	....	....	18	31	.581	....	....	93	16	34	0	....	....	....	19.6	6.8	7.2	1.2	.496
59-60	Minneapolis	3	....	36	8	2	10	.200	....	....	....	4	8	.500	....	....	12	2	3	0	....	....	....	12.0	2.7	4.0	0.7	.302
NBA Playoff Totals		16	....	291	96	37	90	.411	....	....	....	22	39	.564	....	....	105	18	37	0	....	....	....	18.2	6.0	6.6	1.1	....

• ELLIS, Dale

Dale Ellis aka.: Lamar Mundane

Born: Aug. 6, 1960. Marietta, GA, United States. Height: 6'7". Weight: 205 lbs. Drafted: 1983 College: Tennessee

YEAR	TEAM	GP	GS	MIN	PTS	FGM	FGA	FG%	3PM	3PA	3P%	FTM	FTA	FT%	ORB	DRB	TRB	AST	PF	DQ	STL	BLK	TO	MPG	PPG	RPG	APG	PCM
83-84	Dallas	67	2	1059	549	225	493	.456	12	29	.414	87	121	.719	106	144	250	56	118	0	41	9	80	15.8	8.2	3.7	0.8	.466
84-85	Dallas	72	4	1314	667	274	603	.454	42	109	.385	77	104	.740	100	138	238	56	131	1	46	7	58	18.3	9.3	3.3	0.8	.429
85-86	Dallas	72	1	1086	508	193	470	.411	63	173	.364	59	82	.720	86	82	168	37	78	0	40	9	36	15.1	7.1	2.3	0.5	.379
86-87	Seattle	82	76	3073	2041	785	1520	.516	86	**240**	.358	385	489	.787	187	260	447	238	267	2	104	32	238	37.5	24.9	5.5	2.9	.573
87-88	Seattle	75	73	2790	1938	764	1519	.503	107	259	.413	303	395	.767	167	173	340	197	221	1	74	11	173	37.2	25.8	4.5	2.6	.550
88-89	Seattle	82	82	3190	2253	857	1710	.501	162	339	.478	377	462	.816	156	186	342	164	197	0	108	22	221	38.9	27.5	4.2	2.0	.545
89-90	Seattle	55	49	2033	1293	502	1011	.497	96	256	.375	193	236	.818	90	148	238	110	124	3	59	7	121	37.0	23.5	4.3	2.0	.505
90-91	Seattle	30	24	800	451	181	391	.463	27	89	.303	62	84	.738	28	64	92	64	59	0	33	3	48	26.7	15.0	3.1	2.1	.450
90-91	Milwaukee	21	0	624	406	159	327	.486	30	68	.441	58	82	.707	38	43	81	31	53	1	16	5	32	29.7	19.3	3.9	1.5	.500
91-92	Milwaukee	81	11	2191	1272	485	1034	.469	138	329	.419	164	212	.774	92	161	253	104	151	0	57	18	122	27.0	15.7	3.1	1.3	.444
92-93	San Antonio	82	76	2731	1366	545	1092	.499	119	297	.401	157	197	.797	81	231	312	107	179	0	78	18	115	33.3	16.7	3.8	1.3	.418
93-94	San Antonio	77	75	2590	1170	478	967	.494	131	332	.395	83	107	.776	70	185	255	80	141	0	66	11	77	33.6	15.2	3.3	1.0	.373

YEAR	TEAM	GP	GS	MIN	PTS	FGM	FGA	FG%	3PM	3PA	3P%	FTM	FTA	FT%	ORB	DRB	TRB	AST	PF	DQ	STL	BLK	TO	MPG	PPG	RPG	APG	PCM
94-95	Denver	81	3	1996	918	351	774	.453	106	263	.403	110	127	.866	56	166	222	57	142	0	37	9	81	24.6	11.3	2.7	0.7	.342
95-96	Denver	81	52	2626	1204	459	959	.479	150	364	.412	136	179	.760	88	227	315	139	191	1	57	7	97	32.4	14.9	3.9	1.7	.395
96-97	Denver	82	51	2940	1361	477	1151	.414	192	528	.364	215	263	.817	99	194	293	165	178	0	60	7	148	35.9	16.6	3.6	2.0	.341
97-98	Seattle	79	0	1939	934	348	700	.497	127	274	**.464**	111	142	.782	51	133	184	89	128	0	60	5	71	24.5	11.8	2.3	1.1	.412
98-99	Seattle	48	5	1232	495	174	395	.441	94	217	.433	53	70	.757	25	90	115	38	77	1	25	3	45	25.7	10.3	2.4	0.8	.313
99-00	Milwaukee	18	0	324	123	47	101	.465	23	65	.354	6	9	.667	7	27	34	6	23	0	6	0	7	18.0	6.8	1.9	0.3	.305
99-00	Charlotte	24	5	240	55	19	58	.328	14	35	.400	3	4	.750	6	16	22	8	22	0	7	0	13	10.0	2.3	0.9	0.3	.135
NBA Season Totals		1209	589	34778	19004	7323	15275	.479	1719	4266	.403	2639	3365	.784	1533	2668	4201	1746	2480	10	974	183	1783	28.8	15.7	3.5	1.4	....
83-84	Dallas	8	1	178	59	26	80	.325	1	12	.083	6	8	.750	19	23	42	4	17	0	10	2	5	22.3	7.4	5.3	0.5	.280
84-85	Dallas	4	1	68	23	10	23	.435	2	5	.400	1	2	.500	4	3	7	3	3	0	4	0	4	17.0	5.8	1.8	0.8	.276
85-86	Dallas	7	0	67	30	9	22	.409	7	12	.583	5	5	1.000	3	4	7	2	6	0	2	2	4	9.6	4.3	1.0	0.3	.355
86-87	Seattle	14	14	530	353	148	304	.487	13	36	.361	44	54	.815	37	53	90	37	54	1	10	6	33	37.9	25.2	6.4	2.6	.539
87-88	Seattle	5	5	172	104	40	83	.482	3	12	.250	21	29	.724	11	12	23	15	17	0	3	2	12	34.4	20.8	4.6	3.0	.484
88-89	Seattle	8	8	304	183	72	160	.450	15	37	.405	24	33	.727	14	18	32	10	19	1	11	1	21	38.0	22.9	4.0	1.3	.395
92-93	San Antonio	10	10	305	125	51	113	.451	10	32	.313	13	16	.813	9	26	35	11	25	0	4	0	10	30.5	12.5	3.5	1.1	.305
93-94	San Antonio	4	4	114	42	17	43	.395	5	17	.294	3	5	.600	3	7	10	1	6	0	3	0	4	28.5	10.5	2.5	0.3	.209
94-95	Denver	3	0	73	36	10	28	.357	4	13	.308	12	13	.923	6	8	14	3	6	0	2	1	2	24.3	12.0	4.7	1.0	.453
97-98	Seattle	10	0	170	56	20	53	.377	11	26	.423	5	6	.833	4	9	13	6	10	0	2	0	2	17.0	5.6	1.3	0.6	.230
NBA Playoff Totals		73	43	1981	1011	403	909	.443	71	202	.351	134	171	.784	110	163	273	92	163	2	51	14	97	27.1	13.8	3.7	1.3	....

• ELLIS, Harold

Harold Ellis

Born: Oct. 7, 1970. Atlanta, GA, United States.   Height: 6'5".   Weight: 200 lbs.   Drafted: —   College: Morehouse

YEAR	TEAM	GP	GS	MIN	PTS	FGM	FGA	FG%	3PM	3PA	3P%	FTM	FTA	FT%	ORB	DRB	TRB	AST	PF	DQ	STL	BLK	TO	MPG	PPG	RPG	APG	PCM
93-94	LA Clippers	49	16	923	424	159	292	.545	0	4	.000	106	149	.711	94	59	153	31	97	0	73	2	44	18.8	8.7	3.1	0.6	.477
94-95	LA Clippers	69	7	656	252	91	189	.481	1	13	.077	69	117	.590	56	32	88	40	102	0	67	12	48	9.5	3.7	1.3	0.6	.372
97-98	Denver	27	3	344	164	62	111	.559	0	4	.000	40	63	.635	27	23	50	18	53	0	19	4	19	12.7	6.1	1.9	0.7	.446
NBA Season Totals		145	26	1923	840	312	592	.527	1	21	.048	215	329	.653	177	114	291	89	252	0	159	18	111	13.3	5.8	2.0	0.6	....

• ELLIS, Joe

Joseph Franklin Ellis

Born: May 3, 1944.   Height: 6'6".   Weight: 175 lbs.   Drafted: 1966   College: San Francisco

YEAR	TEAM	GP	GS	MIN	PTS	FGM	FGA	FG%	3PM	3PA	3P%	FTM	FTA	FT%	ORB	DRB	TRB	AST	PF	DQ	STL	BLK	TO	MPG	PPG	RPG	APG	PCM
66-67	San Francisco	41	....	333	153	67	164	.409	....	....	....	19	25	.760	....	....	112	27	45	0	....	....	....	8.1	3.7	2.7	0.7	.532
67-68	San Francisco	51	....	624	254	111	302	.368	....	....	....	32	50	.640	....	....	195	37	83	2	....	....	....	12.2	5.0	3.8	0.7	.419
68-69	San Francisco	74	....	1731	889	371	939	.395	....	....	....	147	201	.731	....	....	481	130	258	13	....	....	....	23.4	12.0	6.5	1.8	.484
69-70	San Francisco	76	....	2380	1202	501	1223	.410	....	....	....	200	270	.741	....	....	594	139	281	13	....	....	....	31.3	15.8	7.8	1.8	.458
70-71	San Francisco	80	....	2275	863	356	898	.396	....	....	....	151	203	.744	....	....	511	161	287	6	....	....	....	28.4	10.8	6.4	2.0	.384
71-72	Golden State	78	....	1462	655	280	681	.411	....	....	....	95	132	.720	....	....	389	97	224	4	....	....	....	18.7	8.4	5.0	1.2	.439
72-73	Golden State	74	....	1054	467	199	487	.409	....	....	....	69	93	.742	....	....	282	88	143	2	....	....	....	14.2	6.3	3.8	1.2	.466
73-74	Golden State	50	....	515	140	61	190	.321	....	....	....	18	31	.581	37	85	122	37	76	2	33	9	....	10.3	2.8	2.4	0.7	.269
NBA Season Totals		524	....	10374	4623	1946	4884	.398	....	....	....	731	1005	.727	37	85	2686	716	1397	42	33	9	....	19.8	8.8	5.1	1.4	....
66-67	San Francisco	3	....	6	2	1	4	.250	....	....	....	0	0	.000	....	....	1	2	2	0	....	....	....	2.0	0.7	0.3	0.7	.336
67-68	San Francisco	9	....	104	32	13	44	.295	....	....	....	6	7	.857	....	....	19	7	16	0	....	....	....	11.6	3.6	2.1	0.8	.231
68-69	San Francisco	6	....	161	62	23	79	.291	....	....	....	16	25	.640	....	....	51	3	22	0	....	....	....	26.8	10.3	8.5	0.5	.300
70-71	San Francisco	5	....	91	28	13	42	.310	....	....	....	2	3	.667	....	....	21	0	8	0	....	....	....	18.2	5.6	4.2	0.0	.190
71-72	Golden State	5	....	113	54	21	63	.333	....	....	....	12	17	.706	....	....	21	4	9	0	....	....	....	22.6	10.8	4.2	0.8	.304
72-73	Golden State	10	....	100	24	12	38	.316	....	....	....	0	0	.000	....	....	18	7	18	1	....	....	....	10.0	2.4	1.8	0.7	.174
NBA Playoff Totals		38	....	575	202	83	270	.307	....	....	....	36	52	.692	....	....	131	23	75	1	....	....	....	15.1	5.3	3.4	0.6	....

• ELLIS, LaPhonso

LaPhonso Darnell Ellis

Born: May 5, 1970. East St. Louis, IL, United States.   Height: 6'8".   Weight: 240 lbs.   Drafted: 1992   College: Notre Dame

YEAR	TEAM	GP	GS	MIN	PTS	FGM	FGA	FG%	3PM	3PA	3P%	FTM	FTA	FT%	ORB	DRB	TRB	AST	PF	DQ	STL	BLK	TO	MPG	PPG	RPG	APG	PCM
92-93	Denver	82	82	2749	1205	483	958	.504	2	13	.154	237	317	.748	274	470	744	151	293	8	72	111	156	33.5	14.7	9.1	1.8	.534
93-94	Denver	79	79	2699	1215	483	963	.502	7	23	.304	242	359	.674	220	462	682	167	304	6	63	80	174	34.2	15.4	8.6	2.1	.504
94-95	Denver	6	0	58	24	9	25	.360	0	0	.000	6	6	1.000	7	10	17	4	12	0	1	5	5	9.7	4.0	2.8	0.7	.422
95-96	Denver	45	28	1269	471	189	432	.438	4	22	.182	89	148	.601	93	229	322	74	163	3	36	33	81	28.2	10.5	7.2	1.6	.400
96-97	Denver	55	49	2002	1203	445	1014	.439	95	259	.367	218	282	.773	107	279	386	131	181	7	44	41	116	36.4	21.9	7.0	2.4	.514
97-98	Denver	76	71	2575	1083	410	1007	.407	57	201	.284	206	256	.805	146	398	544	213	226	2	65	49	175	33.9	14.3	7.2	2.8	.421
98-99	Atlanta	20	20	539	204	80	190	.421	1	5	.200	43	61	.705	25	84	109	18	48	1	8	7	34	27.0	10.2	5.5	0.9	.328
99-00	Atlanta	58	8	1309	487	209	464	.450	3	21	.143	66	95	.695	98	192	290	59	133	1	32	25	52	22.6	8.4	5.0	1.0	.393
00-01	Minnesota	82	5	1948	772	298	642	.464	7	22	.318	169	214	.790	199	295	494	93	290	7	67	74	108	23.8	9.4	6.0	1.1	.456
01-02	Miami	66	14	1684	469	189	452	.418	38	124	.306	53	84	.631	107	180	287	56	196	4	30	37	73	25.5	7.1	4.3	0.8	.264
02-03	Miami	55	3	784	277	100	262	.382	27	107	.252	50	66	.758	44	113	157	15	88	0	15	15	31	14.3	5.0	2.9	0.3	.307
NBA Season Totals		624	359	17616	7410	2895	6409	.452	241	797	.302	1379	1888	.730	1320	2712	4032	981	1934	39	433	477	1005	28.2	11.9	6.5	1.6	....
93-94	Denver	12	12	436	177	68	142	.479	3	6	.500	38	54	.704	27	70	97	26	46	2	9	11	19	36.3	14.8	8.1	2.2	.456
00-01	Minnesota	4	0	77	24	9	23	.391	0	1	.000	6	8	.750	7	7	14	0	13	0	1	3	5	19.3	6.0	3.5	0.0	.213
NBA Playoff Totals		16	12	513	201	77	165	.467	3	7	.429	44	62	.710	34	77	111	26	59	2	10	14	24	32.1	12.6	6.9	1.6	....

• ELLIS, LeRon

LeRon Perry Ellis

Born: Apr. 28, 1969. Los Angeles, CA, United States.   Height: 6'9".   Weight: 225 lbs.   Drafted: 1991   College: Syracuse

YEAR	TEAM	GP	GS	MIN	PTS	FGM	FGA	FG%	3PM	3PA	3P%	FTM	FTA	FT%	ORB	DRB	TRB	AST	PF	DQ	STL	BLK	TO	MPG	PPG	RPG	APG	PCM
91-92	LA Clippers	29	0	103	43	17	50	.340	0	0	.000	9	19	.474	12	12	24	1	11	0	6	9	12	3.6	1.5	0.8	0.0	.279
93-94	Charlotte	50	1	680	221	88	182	.484	0	0	.000	45	68	.662	70	118	188	24	83	1	17	25	20	13.6	4.4	3.8	0.5	.448
95-96	Miami	12	1	74	13	5	22	.227	0	0	.000	3	6	.500	5	3	8	4	11	0	2	3	4	6.2	1.1	0.7	0.3	.042
NBA Season Totals		91	2	857	277	110	254	.433	0	0	.000	57	93	.613	87	133	220	29	105	1	25	37	36	9.4	3.0	2.4	0.3	....
91-92	LA Clippers	1	0	2	0	0	0	.000	0	0	.000	0	0	.000	0	0	0	0	0	0	0	0	0	2.0	0.0	0.0	0.0	.000
NBA Playoff Totals		1	0	2	0	0	0	.000	0	0	.000	0	0	.000	0	0	0	0	0	0	0	0	0	2.0	0.0	0.0	0.0	....

YEAR	TEAM	GP	GS	MIN	PTS	FGM	FGA	FG%	3PM	3PA	3P%	FTM	FTA	FT%	ORB	DRB	TRB	AST	PF	DQ	STL	BLK	TO	MPG	PPG	RPG	APG	PCM

• ELLIS, Leroy

Leroy Ellis

Born: Mar. 10, 1940. Far Rockaway, NY, United States. Height: 6'10". Weight: 210 lbs. Drafted: 1962 College: St. John's (NY)

YEAR	TEAM	GP	GS	MIN	PTS	FGM	FGA	FG%	3PM	3PA	3P%	FTM	FTA	FT%	ORB	DRB	TRB	AST	PF	DQ	STL	BLK	TO	MPG	PPG	RPG	APG	PCM
62-63	LA Lakers	80	....	1628	577	222	530	.419	....	....	....	133	202	.658	....	....	518	46	194	1	....	....	....	20.4	7.2	6.5	0.6	.427
63-64	LA Lakers	78	....	1459	512	200	473	.423	....	....	....	112	170	.659	....	....	498	41	192	3	....	....	....	18.7	6.6	6.4	0.5	.439
64-65	LA Lakers	80	....	2026	820	311	700	.444	....	....	....	198	284	.697	....	....	652	49	196	1	....	....	....	25.3	10.3	8.2	0.6	.481
65-66	LA Lakers	80	....	2219	972	393	927	.424	....	....	....	186	256	.727	....	....	735	74	232	3	....	....	....	27.7	12.2	9.2	0.9	.496
66-67	Baltimore	81	....	2938	1203	496	1166	.425	....	....	....	211	286	.738	....	....	970	170	258	3	....	....	....	36.3	14.9	12.0	2.1	.515
67-68	Baltimore	78	....	2719	967	380	800	.475	....	....	....	207	286	.724	....	....	862	158	256	5	....	....	....	34.9	12.4	11.1	2.0	.506
68-69	Baltimore	80	....	1603	575	229	527	.435	....	....	....	117	155	.755	....	....	510	73	168	0	....	....	....	20.0	7.2	6.4	0.9	.469
69-70	Baltimore	72	....	1163	474	194	414	.469	....	....	....	86	116	.741	....	....	376	47	129	0	....	....	....	16.2	6.6	5.2	0.7	.511
70-71	Portland	74	....	2581	1179	485	1095	.443	....	....	....	209	261	.801	....	....	907	235	258	5	....	....	....	34.9	15.9	12.3	3.2	.608
71-72	LA Lakers	74	....	1081	342	138	300	.460	....	....	....	66	95	.695	....	....	310	46	115	0	....	....	....	14.6	4.6	4.2	0.6	.425
72-73	LA Lakers	10	....	156	26	11	40	.275	....	....	....	4	5	.800	....	....	33	3	13	0	....	....	....	15.6	2.6	3.3	0.3	.172
72-73	Philadelphia	69	....	2444	945	410	929	.441	....	....	....	125	156	.801	....	....	744	136	186	0	....	....	....	35.4	13.7	10.8	2.0	.491
73-74	Philadelphia	81	....	2831	799	326	722	.452	....	....	....	147	196	.750	292	598	890	189	224	2	86	87	....	35.0	9.9	11.0	2.3	.466
74-75	Philadelphia	82	....	2183	646	287	623	.461	....	....	....	72	99	.727	195	387	582	117	178	1	44	55	....	26.6	7.9	7.1	1.4	.413
75-76	Philadelphia	29	....	489	139	61	132	.462	....	....	....	17	28	.607	47	75	122	21	62	0	16	9	....	16.9	4.8	4.2	0.7	.359
NBA Season Totals		**1048**	**....**	**27520**	**10176**	**4143**	**9378**	**.442**	**....**	**....**	**....**	**1890**	**2595**	**.728**	**534**	**1060**	**8709**	**1405**	**2661**	**24**	**146**	**151**	**....**	**26.3**	**9.7**	**8.3**	**1.3**	**....**
62-63	LA Lakers	13	....	302	81	27	53	.509	....	....	....	27	33	.818	....	....	85	13	35	0	....	....	....	23.2	6.2	6.5	1.0	.421
63-64	LA Lakers	5	....	144	27	8	27	.296	....	....	....	11	15	.733	....	....	50	4	11	0	....	....	....	28.8	5.4	10.0	0.8	.348
64-65	LA Lakers	11	....	405	158	57	145	.393	....	....	....	44	65	.677	....	....	133	7	37	0	....	....	....	36.8	14.4	12.1	0.6	.442
65-66	LA Lakers	14	....	426	137	56	138	.406	....	....	....	25	39	.641	....	....	133	8	52	1	....	....	....	30.4	9.8	9.5	0.6	.378
68-69	Baltimore	4	....	67	19	8	16	.500	....	....	....	3	5	.600	....	....	18	2	8	0	....	....	....	16.8	4.8	4.5	0.5	.381
69-70	Baltimore	3	....	8	2	0	4	.000	....	....	....	2	2	1.000	....	....	3	0	0	0	....	....	....	2.7	0.7	1.0	0.0	.140
71-72	LA Lakers	13	....	134	39	19	41	.463	....	....	....	1	4	.250	....	....	41	10	9	0	....	....	....	10.3	3.0	3.2	0.8	.460
75-76	Philadelphia	1	....	1	0	0	0	.000	....	....	....	0	0	.000	0	0	0	0	0	0	0	0	....	1.0	0.0	0.0	0.0	.000
NBA Playoff Totals		**64**	**....**	**1487**	**463**	**175**	**424**	**.413**	**....**	**....**	**....**	**113**	**163**	**.693**	**0**	**0**	**463**	**44**	**152**	**1**	**0**	**0**	**....**	**23.2**	**7.2**	**7.2**	**0.7**	**....**

• ELLISON, Pervis

Pervis (Never Nervous Pervis) Ellison

Born: Apr. 3, 1967. Savannah, GA, United States. Height: 6'9". Weight: 210 lbs. Drafted: 1989 College: Louisville

YEAR	TEAM	GP	GS	MIN	PTS	FGM	FGA	FG%	3PM	3PA	3P%	FTM	FTA	FT%	ORB	DRB	TRB	AST	PF	DQ	STL	BLK	TO	MPG	PPG	RPG	APG	PCM
89-90	Sacramento	34	22	866	271	111	251	.442	0	2	.000	49	78	.628	64	132	196	65	132	4	16	57	61	25.5	8.0	5.8	1.9	.379
90-91	Washington	76	30	1942	791	326	636	.513	0	6	.000	139	214	.650	224	361	585	102	268	6	49	157	144	25.6	10.4	7.7	1.3	.543
91-92	Washington	66	64	2511	1322	547	1014	.539	1	3	.333	227	312	.728	217	523	740	190	222	2	62	177	198	38.0	20.0	11.2	2.9	.667
92-93	Washington	49	48	1701	852	341	655	.521	0	4	.000	170	242	.702	138	295	433	117	154	3	45	108	108	34.7	17.4	8.8	2.4	.602
93-94	Washington	47	24	1178	344	137	292	.469	0	3	.000	70	97	.722	77	165	242	70	140	3	25	50	75	25.1	7.3	5.1	1.5	.359
94-95	Boston	55	11	1083	375	152	300	.507	0	2	.000	71	99	.717	124	185	309	34	179	5	22	54	77	19.7	6.8	5.6	0.6	.429
95-96	Boston	69	29	1431	365	145	295	.492	0	0	.000	75	117	.641	151	300	451	62	207	2	39	99	83	20.7	5.3	6.5	0.9	.453
96-97	Boston	6	4	125	15	6	16	.375	0	0	.000	3	5	.600	9	17	26	4	21	1	5	9	7	20.8	2.5	4.3	0.7	.240
97-98	Boston	33	8	447	100	40	70	.571	0	0	.000	20	34	.588	52	57	109	31	90	2	20	31	26	13.5	3.0	3.3	0.9	.405
99-00	Boston	30	5	269	53	19	43	.442	0	0	.000	15	21	.714	29	38	67	13	67	1	10	8	13	9.0	1.8	2.2	0.4	.289
00-01	Seattle	9	0	40	6	2	7	.286	0	0	.000	2	2	1.000	2	10	12	3	13	0	0	2	3	4.4	0.7	1.3	0.3	.221
NBA Season Totals		**474**	**245**	**11593**	**4494**	**1826**	**3579**	**.510**	**1**	**20**	**.050**	**841**	**1221**	**.689**	**1087**	**2083**	**3170**	**691**	**1493**	**29**	**293**	**752**	**795**	**24.5**	**9.5**	**6.7**	**1.5**	**....**
94-95	Boston	4	0	68	24	11	19	.579	0	0	.000	2	2	1.000	11	6	17	2	17	1	2	5	4	17.0	6.0	4.3	0.5	.432
NBA Playoff Totals		**4**	**0**	**68**	**24**	**11**	**19**	**.579**	**0**	**0**	**.000**	**2**	**2**	**1.000**	**11**	**6**	**17**	**2**	**17**	**1**	**2**	**5**	**4**	**17.0**	**6.0**	**4.3**	**0.5**	**....**

• ELMORE, Len

Leonard J. Elmore

Born: Mar. 28, 1952. New York, NY, United States. Height: 6'9". Weight: 220 lbs. Drafted: 1974 College: Maryland

YEAR	TEAM	GP	GS	MIN	PTS	FGM	FGA	FG%	3PM	3PA	3P%	FTM	FTA	FT%	ORB	DRB	TRB	AST	PF	DQ	STL	BLK	TO	MPG	PPG	RPG	APG	PCM
74-75	Indiana-A	77	....	1414	509	218	523	.417	1	1	1.000	72	93	.774	148	247	395	35	241	....	67	91	83	18.4	6.6	5.1	0.5	.362
75-76	Indiana-A	76	....	2591	1112	480	1193	.402	0	3	.000	152	206	.738	242	577	819	122	310	....	136	178	175	34.1	14.6	10.8	1.6	.455
76-77	Indiana	6	....	46	18	7	17	.412	....	....	....	4	5	.800	7	8	15	2	11	0	0	4	....	7.7	3.0	2.5	0.3	.422
77-78	Indiana	69	....	1327	372	142	386	.368	....	....	....	88	132	.667	139	281	420	80	174	4	74	71	76	19.2	5.4	6.1	1.2	.438
78-79	Indiana	80	....	1264	334	139	342	.406	....	....	....	56	78	.718	115	287	402	75	183	3	62	79	72	15.8	4.2	5.0	0.9	.447
79-80	Kansas City	58	....	915	259	104	242	.430	0	0	.000	51	74	.689	74	183	257	64	154	0	41	39	70	15.8	4.5	4.4	1.1	.400
80-81	Milwaukee	72	....	925	206	76	212	.358	0	0	.000	54	75	.720	68	140	208	69	178	3	37	52	43	12.8	2.9	2.9	1.0	.322
81-82	New Jersey	81	70	2100	735	300	652	.460	0	0	.000	135	170	.794	167	274	441	100	280	6	92	92	138	25.9	9.1	5.4	1.2	.392
82-83	New Jersey	74	0	975	248	97	244	.398	0	1	.000	54	84	.643	81	157	238	39	125	2	44	38	81	13.2	3.4	3.2	0.5	.312
83-84	New York	65	5	832	155	64	157	.408	0	0	.000	27	38	.711	62	103	165	30	153	3	29	30	46	12.8	2.4	2.5	0.5	.228
NBA Season Totals		**505**	**75**	**8384**	**2327**	**929**	**2252**	**.413**	**0**	**1**	**.000**	**469**	**656**	**.715**	**713**	**1433**	**2146**	**459**	**1258**	**21**	**379**	**405**	**526**	**16.6**	**4.6**	**4.2**	**0.9**	**....**
ABA Season Totals		**153**	**....**	**4005**	**1621**	**698**	**1716**	**.407**	**1**	**4**	**.250**	**224**	**299**	**.749**	**390**	**824**	**1214**	**157**	**551**	**....**	**203**	**269**	**258**	**26.2**	**10.6**	**7.9**	**1.0**	**....**
Career Totals		**658**	**75**	**12389**	**3948**	**1627**	**3968**	**.410**	**1**	**5**	**.200**	**693**	**955**	**.726**	**1103**	**2257**	**3360**	**616**	**1809**	**21**	**582**	**674**	**784**	**18.8**	**6.0**	**5.1**	**0.9**	**....**
74-75	Indiana-A	18	....	565	191	83	190	.437	0	0	.000	25	37	.676	51	94	145	16	74	....	21	39	26	31.4	10.6	8.1	0.9	.362
75-76	Indiana-A	3	....	68	19	9	30	.300	0	0	.000	1	1	1.000	4	11	15	4	10	....	5	2	2	22.7	6.3	5.0	1.3	.201
79-80	Kansas City	3	....	43	9	4	13	.308	0	0	.000	1	2	.500	6	5	11	1	4	0	3	1	4	14.3	3.0	3.7	0.3	.224
80-81	Milwaukee	4	....	12	0	0	1	.000	0	0	.000	0	0	.000	0	0	0	0	4	0	0	0	1	3.0	0.0	0.0	0.0	-.304
81-82	New Jersey	2	2	76	22	9	16	.563	0	0	.000	4	4	1.000	1	15	16	2	4	0	1	2	2	38.0	11.0	8.0	1.0	.415
82-83	New Jersey	2	0	15	5	2	5	.400	0	0	.000	1	2	.500	5	4	9	1	4	0	1	0	1	7.5	2.5	4.5	0.5	.617
NBA Playoff Totals		**11**	**2**	**146**	**36**	**15**	**35**	**.429**	**0**	**0**	**.000**	**6**	**8**	**.750**	**12**	**24**	**36**	**4**	**16**	**0**	**5**	**3**	**8**	**13.3**	**3.3**	**3.3**	**0.4**	**....**
ABA Playoff Totals		**21**	**....**	**633**	**210**	**92**	**220**	**.418**	**0**	**0**	**.000**	**26**	**38**	**.684**	**55**	**105**	**160**	**20**	**84**	**....**	**26**	**41**	**28**	**30.1**	**10.0**	**7.6**	**1.0**	**....**
Career Playoff Totals		**32**	**2**	**779**	**246**	**107**	**255**	**.420**	**0**	**0**	**.000**	**32**	**46**	**.696**	**67**	**129**	**196**	**24**	**100**	**0**	**31**	**44**	**36**	**24.3**	**7.7**	**6.1**	**0.8**	**....**

• ELSER, Don
Donald Elser

Born: 1913. Height: 6'4". Weight: 220 lbs. Drafted: — College: Notre Dame

YEAR TEAM	GP	GS	MIN	PTS	FGM	FGA	FG%	3PM	3PA	3P%	FTM	FTA	FT%	ORB	DRB	TRB	AST	PF	DQ	STL	BLK	TO	MPG	PPG	RPG	APG	PCM
41-42 Toledo-N	6	....	....	27	10	....	....	....	....	....	7	....	....	....	....	....	....	....	....	....	....	....	....	4.5	....	....	....
NBL Season Totals	6	....	....	27	10	....	....	....	....	....	7	....	....	....	....	....	....	....	....	....	....	....	....	4.5	....	....	....

• ELSTON, Darrell
Darrell Eugene Elston

Born: Aug. 15, 1952. Tipton, IN, United States. Height: 6'4". Weight: 190 lbs. Drafted: 1974 College: North Carolina

YEAR TEAM	GP	GS	MIN	PTS	FGM	FGA	FG%	3PM	3PA	3P%	FTM	FTA	FT%	ORB	DRB	TRB	AST	PF	DQ	STL	BLK	TO	MPG	PPG	RPG	APG	PCM
74-75 Virginia-A	72	....	1869	596	250	613	.408	3	18	.167	93	123	.756	48	115	163	202	166	....	82	9	126	26.0	8.3	2.3	2.8	.297
76-77 Indiana	5	....	40	5	2	14	.143	....	....	....	1	2	.500	1	5	6	2	6	0	1	0	....	8.0	1.0	1.2	0.4	-.023
NBA Season Totals	5	....	40	5	2	14	.143	....	....	....	1	2	.500	1	5	6	2	6	0	1	0	....	8.0	1.0	1.2	0.4	....
ABA Season Totals	72	....	1869	596	250	613	.408	3	18	.167	93	123	.756	48	115	163	202	166	....	82	9	126	26.0	8.3	2.3	2.8	....
Career Totals	77	....	1909	601	252	627	.402	3	18	.167	94	125	.752	49	120	169	204	172	0	83	9	126	24.8	7.8	2.2	2.6	....

• ELY, Melvin
Melvin Ely

Born: May 2, 1978. Harvey, IL, United States. Height: 6'10". Weight: 260 lbs. Drafted: 2002 College: Fresno State

YEAR TEAM	GP	GS	MIN	PTS	FGM	FGA	FG%	3PM	3PA	3P%	FTM	FTA	FT%	ORB	DRB	TRB	AST	PF	DQ	STL	BLK	TO	MPG	PPG	RPG	APG	PCM
02-03 LA Clippers	52	7	801	236	92	186	.495	0	0	.000	52	74	.703	64	110	174	15	95	0	10	32	50	15.4	4.5	3.3	0.3	.330
NBA Season Totals	52	7	801	236	92	186	.495	0	0	.000	52	74	.703	64	110	174	15	95	0	10	32	50	15.4	4.5	3.3	0.3	....

• EMBRY, Wayne
Wayne Richard (Goose, The Wall) Embry

Born: Mar. 26, 1937. Springfield, OH, United States. Height: 6'8". Weight: 240 lbs. Drafted: 1958 College: Miami (OH)

YEAR TEAM	GP	GS	MIN	PTS	FGM	FGA	FG%	3PM	3PA	3P%	FTM	FTA	FT%	ORB	DRB	TRB	AST	PF	DQ	STL	BLK	TO	MPG	PPG	RPG	APG	PCM
58-59 Cincinnati	66	....	1590	750	272	702	.387	....	....	....	206	314	.656	....	....	597	96	232	9	....	....	....	24.1	11.4	9.0	1.5	.546
59-60 Cincinnati	73	....	1594	773	303	690	.439	....	....	....	167	325	.514	....	....	692	83	226	1	....	....	....	21.8	10.6	9.5	1.1	.603
60-61 Cincinnati	79	....	2233	1137	458	1015	.451	....	....	....	221	331	.668	....	....	864	127	286	7	....	....	....	28.3	14.4	10.9	1.6	.617
61-62 Cincinnati	75	....	2623	1484	564	1210	.466	....	....	....	356	516	.690	....	....	977	182	286	6	....	....	....	35.0	19.8	13.0	2.4	.683
62-63 Cincinnati	76	....	2511	1411	534	1165	.458	....	....	....	343	514	.667	....	....	936	177	286	7	....	....	....	33.0	18.6	12.3	2.3	.671
63-64 Cincinnati	80	....	2915	1383	556	1213	.458	....	....	....	271	417	.650	....	....	925	113	**325**	7	....	....	....	36.4	17.3	11.6	1.4	.530
64-65 Cincinnati	74	....	2243	943	352	772	.456	....	....	....	239	371	.644	....	....	741	92	297	10	....	....	....	30.3	12.7	10.0	1.2	.507
65-66 Cincinnati	80	....	1882	605	232	564	.411	....	....	....	141	234	.603	....	....	525	81	287	9	....	....	....	23.5	7.6	6.6	1.0	.375
66-67 Boston	72	....	729	376	147	359	.409	....	....	....	82	144	.569	....	....	294	42	137	0	....	....	....	10.1	5.2	4.1	0.6	.566
67-68 Boston	78	....	1088	495	193	483	.400	....	....	....	109	185	.589	....	....	321	52	174	1	....	....	....	13.9	6.3	4.1	0.7	.443
68-69 Milwaukee	78	....	2355	1023	382	894	.427	....	....	....	259	390	.664	....	....	672	149	302	8	....	....	....	30.2	13.1	8.6	1.9	.488
NBA Season Totals	831	....	21763	10380	3993	9067	.440	....	....	....	2394	3741	.640	....	....	7544	1194	2838	65	....	....	....	26.2	12.5	9.1	1.4	....
61-62 Cincinnati	4	....	128	56	14	30	.467	....	....	....	28	36	.778	....	....	45	8	17	0	....	....	....	32.0	14.0	11.3	2.0	.614
62-63 Cincinnati	12	....	394	201	76	169	.450	....	....	....	49	74	.662	....	....	162	16	55	2	....	....	....	32.8	16.8	13.5	1.3	.617
63-64 Cincinnati	10	....	363	134	53	139	.381	....	....	....	28	45	.622	....	....	124	21	46	3	....	....	....	36.3	13.4	12.4	2.1	.454
64-65 Cincinnati	4	....	123	51	21	48	.438	....	....	....	9	11	.818	....	....	25	8	20	1	....	....	....	30.8	12.8	6.3	2.0	.414
65-66 Cincinnati	5	....	139	39	16	38	.421	....	....	....	7	12	.583	....	....	34	2	23	2	....	....	....	27.8	7.8	6.8	0.4	.287
66-67 Boston	5	....	38	26	12	31	.387	....	....	....	2	4	.500	....	....	13	3	9	0	....	....	....	7.6	5.2	2.6	0.6	.538
67-68 Boston	16	....	162	59	23	59	.390	....	....	....	13	29	.448	....	....	45	6	36	0	....	....	....	10.1	3.7	2.8	0.4	.325
NBA Playoff Totals	56	....	1347	566	215	514	.418	....	....	....	136	211	.645	....	....	448	64	206	8	....	....	....	24.1	10.1	8.0	1.1	....

• ENDRESS, Ned
Ned R. Endress

Born: Mar. 2, 1918. Height: 6'2". Weight: 200 lbs. Drafted: — College: Akron

YEAR TEAM	GP	GS	MIN	PTS	FGM	FGA	FG%	3PM	3PA	3P%	FTM	FTA	FT%	ORB	DRB	TRB	AST	PF	DQ	STL	BLK	TO	MPG	PPG	RPG	APG	PCM
43-44 Cleveland-N	16	....	....	65	25	....	....	....	....	....	15	....	....	....	....	....	....	....	....	....	....	....	....	4.1	....	....	....
44-45 Cleveland-N	29	....	....	170	62	....	....	....	....	....	46	....	....	....	....	....	....	....	....	....	....	....	....	5.9	....	....	....
45-46 Cleveland-N	22	....	....	152	58	....	....	....	....	....	36	74	.486	....	....	....	....	....	....	....	....	....	....	6.9	....	....	....
46-47 Cleveland	16	....	....	14	3	25	.120	....	....	....	8	15	.533	....	....	....	4	13	....	....	....	....	....	0.9	....	0.3	....
NBA Season Totals	16	....	....	14	3	25	.120	....	....	....	8	15	.533	....	....	....	4	13	....	....	....	....	....	0.9	....	0.3	....
NBL Season Totals	67	....	....	387	145	....	....	....	....	....	97	74	....	....	....	....	....	....	....	....	....	....	....	5.8	....	....	....
Career Totals	83	....	....	401	148	25	....	....	....	....	105	89	....	....	....	....	4	13	....	....	....	....	....	4.8	....	0.0	....
43-44 Cleveland-N	2	....	....	3	1	....	....	....	....	....	1	....	....	....	....	....	....	....	....	....	....	....	....	1.5	....	....	....
44-45 Cleveland-N	2	....	....	10	4	....	....	....	....	....	2	....	....	....	....	....	....	....	....	....	....	....	....	5.0	....	....	....
NBL Playoff Totals	4	....	....	13	5	....	....	....	....	....	3	....	....	....	....	....	....	....	....	....	....	....	....	3.3	....	....	....

• ENGDAHL, Warner
Warner (Bud) Engdahl

Born: July 2, 1916. Died: May1985. Height: 6'1". Weight: 210 lbs. Drafted: — College: Wisconsin (Superior)

YEAR TEAM	GP	GS	MIN	PTS	FGM	FGA	FG%	3PM	3PA	3P%	FTM	FTA	FT%	ORB	DRB	TRB	AST	PF	DQ	STL	BLK	TO	MPG	PPG	RPG	APG	PCM
41-42 Oshkosh-N	19	....	....	36	10	....	....	....	....	....	16	....	....	....	....	....	....	....	....	....	....	....	....	1.9	....	....	....
42-43 Oshkosh-N	1	....	....	1	0	....	....	....	....	....	1	....	....	....	....	....	....	....	....	....	....	....	....	1.0	....	....	....
45-46 Oshkosh-N	21	....	....	31	10	....	....	....	....	....	11	....	....	....	....	....	....	....	....	....	....	....	....	1.5	....	....	....
NBL Season Totals	41	....	....	68	20	....	....	....	....	....	28	....	....	....	....	....	....	....	....	....	....	....	....	1.7	....	....	....
41-42 Oshkosh-N	4	....	....	4	2	....	....	....	....	....	0	....	....	....	....	....	....	....	....	....	....	....	....	1.0	....	....	....
45-46 Oshkosh-N	4	....	....	1	0	....	....	....	....	....	1	2	.500	....	....	....	....	....	....	....	....	....	....	0.3	....	....	....
NBL Playoff Totals	8	....	....	5	2	....	....	....	....	....	1	2	....	....	....	....	....	....	....	....	....	....	....	0.6	....	....	....

YEAR	TEAM	GP	GS	MIN	PTS	FGM	FGA	FG%	3PM	3PA	3P%	FTM	FTA	FT%	ORB	DRB	TRB	AST	PF	DQ	STL	BLK	TO	MPG	PPG	RPG	APG	PCM

• ENGLER, Chris

Christopher Aaron Engler

Born: Mar. 1, 1959. Stillwater, MN, United States.   Height: 6'11".   Weight: 245 lbs.   Drafted: 1982   College: Wyoming

YEAR	TEAM	GP	GS	MIN	PTS	FGM	FGA	FG%	3PM	3PA	3P%	FTM	FTA	FT%	ORB	DRB	TRB	AST	PF	DQ	STL	BLK	TO	MPG	PPG	RPG	APG	PCM
82-83	Golden State	54	1	369	81	38	94	.404	0	0	.000	5	16	.313	43	61	104	11	95	1	7	17	22	6.8	1.5	1.9	0.2	.245
83-84	Golden State	46	1	360	80	33	83	.398	0	0	.000	14	23	.609	27	70	97	11	68	0	9	3	23	7.8	1.7	2.1	0.2	.248
84-85	New Jersey	7	0	76	19	7	16	.438	0	0	.000	5	9	.556	10	17	27	0	4	0	2	4	1	10.9	2.7	3.9	0.0	.483
84-85	Chicago	3	0	3	2	1	2	.500	0	0	.000	0	0	.000	1	1	2	0	1	0	0	0	1	1.0	0.7	0.7	0.0	.511
84-85	Milwaukee	1	0	3	0	0	2	.000	0	0	.000	0	0	.000	1	0	1	0	0	0	0	1	0	3.0	0.0	1.0	0.0	.000
86-87	Portland	7	0	17	11	4	8	.500	0	0	.000	3	3	1.000	6	2	8	1	0	0	1	1	2	2.4	1.6	1.1	0.1	.929
86-87	Milwaukee	5	0	48	7	3	12	.250	0	0	.000	1	1	1.000	3	13	16	3	10	0	1	1	0	9.6	1.4	3.2	0.6	.290
86-87	New Jersey	18	0	130	40	16	31	.516	0	0	.000	8	12	.667	14	19	33	4	23	0	3	9	11	7.2	2.2	1.8	0.2	.380
87-88	New Jersey	54	0	399	103	36	88	.409	0	0	.000	31	35	.886	32	66	98	15	73	1	9	6	27	7.4	1.9	1.8	0.3	.288
NBA Season Totals		195	2	1405	343	138	336	.411	0	0	.000	67	99	.677	137	249	386	45	274	2	32	42	87	7.2	1.8	2.0	0.2	....
84-85	Milwaukee	1	0	6	2	1	1	1.000	0	0	.000	0	0	.000	0	2	2	0	2	0	0	0	0	6.0	2.0	2.0	0.0	.489
NBA Playoff Totals		1	0	6	2	1	1	1.000	0	0	.000	0	0	.000	0	2	2	0	2	0	0	0	0	6.0	2.0	2.0	0.0	....

• ENGLESTAD, Wayne

Wayne Edward Englestad

Born: Dec. 6, 1963. Rosemead, CA, United States.   Height: 6'8".   Weight: 245 lbs.   Drafted: —   College: California (Irvine)

YEAR	TEAM	GP	GS	MIN	PTS	FGM	FGA	FG%	3PM	3PA	3P%	FTM	FTA	FT%	ORB	DRB	TRB	AST	PF	DQ	STL	BLK	TO	MPG	PPG	RPG	APG	PCM
88-89	Denver	11	0	50	28	11	29	.379	0	0	.000	6	10	.600	5	11	16	7	12	0	1	0	3	4.5	2.5	1.5	0.6	.487
NBA Season Totals		11	0	50	28	11	29	.379	0	0	.000	6	10	.600	5	11	16	7	12	0	1	0	3	4.5	2.5	1.5	0.6	....

• ENGLISH, A.J.

Albert Jay English

Born: July 11, 1967. Wilmington, DE, United States.   Height: 6'3".   Weight: 175 lbs.   Drafted: 1990   College: Virginia Union

YEAR	TEAM	GP	GS	MIN	PTS	FGM	FGA	FG%	3PM	3PA	3P%	FTM	FTA	FT%	ORB	DRB	TRB	AST	PF	DQ	STL	BLK	TO	MPG	PPG	RPG	APG	PCM
90-91	Washington	70	12	1443	616	251	572	.439	3	31	.097	111	157	.707	66	81	147	177	127	1	25	15	112	20.6	8.8	2.1	2.5	.343
91-92	Washington	81	6	1665	886	366	846	.433	6	34	.176	148	176	.841	74	94	168	143	160	1	32	9	89	20.6	10.9	2.1	1.8	.371
NBA Season Totals		151	18	3108	1502	617	1418	.435	9	65	.138	259	333	.778	140	175	315	320	287	2	57	24	201	20.6	9.9	2.1	2.1	....

• ENGLISH, Alex

Alexander English

Born: Jan. 5, 1954. Columbia, SC, United States.   Height: 6'7".   Weight: 190 lbs.   Drafted: 1976   College: South Carolina   HOF: 1997

YEAR	TEAM	GP	GS	MIN	PTS	FGM	FGA	FG%	3PM	3PA	3P%	FTM	FTA	FT%	ORB	DRB	TRB	AST	PF	DQ	STL	BLK	TO	MPG	PPG	RPG	APG	PCM
76-77	Milwaukee	60	....	648	310	132	277	.477	....	....	....	46	60	.767	68	100	168	25	78	0	17	18	....	10.8	5.2	2.8	0.4	.492
77-78	Milwaukee	82	....	1552	790	343	633	.542	....	....	....	104	143	.727	144	251	395	129	178	1	41	55	139	18.9	9.6	4.8	1.6	.576
78-79	Indiana	81	....	2696	1299	563	1102	.511	....	....	....	173	230	.752	253	402	655	271	214	3	70	78	194	33.3	16.0	8.1	3.3	.571
79-80	Indiana	54	....	1526	806	346	686	.504	0	3	.000	114	140	.814	167	213	380	142	128	0	45	33	124	28.3	14.9	7.0	2.6	.581
79-80	Denver	24	....	875	512	207	427	.485	2	3	.667	96	126	.762	102	123	225	82	78	0	28	29	91	36.5	21.3	9.4	3.4	.602
80-81	Denver	81	....	3093	1929	768	1555	.494	3	5	.600	390	459	.850	273	373	646	290	255	2	106	100	243	38.2	23.8	8.0	3.6	.626
81-82	Denver	82	82	3015	2082	855	1553	.551	0	8	.000	372	443	.840	210	348	558	433	261	2	87	120	262	36.8	25.4	6.8	5.3	.735
82-83	Denver	82	82	2988	**2326**	**959**	**1857**	.516	2	12	.167	406	490	.829	263	338	601	397	235	1	116	126	262	36.4	**28.4**	7.3	4.8	.780
83-84	Denver	82	77	2870	2167	907	1714	.529	1	7	.143	352	427	.824	216	248	464	406	252	3	83	95	221	35.0	26.4	5.7	5.0	.728
84-85	Denver	81	81	2924	2262	**939**	1812	.518	1	5	.200	383	462	.829	203	255	458	344	259	1	101	46	251	36.1	27.9	5.7	4.2	.680
85-86	Denver	81	81	3024	**2414**	**951**	1888	.504	1	5	.200	511	593	.862	192	213	405	320	235	1	73	29	251	37.3	29.8	5.0	4.0	.654
86-87	Denver	82	82	3085	2345	965	1920	.503	4	15	.267	411	487	.844	146	198	344	422	216	0	73	21	213	37.6	28.6	4.2	5.1	.642
87-88	Denver	80	80	2818	2000	843	1704	.495	0	6	.000	314	379	.828	166	207	373	377	193	1	70	23	184	35.2	25.0	4.7	4.7	.618
88-89	Denver	82	82	2990	2175	924	**1881**	.491	2	8	.250	325	379	.858	148	178	326	383	174	0	66	12	197	36.5	26.5	4.0	4.7	.596
89-90	Denver	80	80	2211	1433	635	1293	.491	2	5	.400	161	183	.880	119	167	286	225	130	0	51	23	96	27.6	17.9	3.6	2.8	.557
90-91	Dallas	79	26	1748	763	322	734	.439	0	1	.000	119	140	.850	108	146	254	105	141	0	40	25	103	22.1	9.7	3.2	1.3	.353
NBA Season Totals		1193	753	38063	25613	10659	21036	.507	18	83	.217	4277	5141	.832	2778	3760	6538	4351	3027	15	1067	833	2831	31.9	21.5	5.5	3.6	....
77-78	Milwaukee	9	....	208	121	48	78	.615	....	....	....	25	32	.781	16	26	42	13	20	0	6	7	12	23.1	13.4	4.7	1.4	.650
81-82	Denver	3	3	118	58	26	55	.473	0	0	.000	6	7	.857	8	15	23	17	6	0	3	3	4	39.3	19.3	7.7	5.7	.588
82-83	Denver	7	7	270	181	67	150	.447	0	2	.000	47	53	.887	20	24	44	42	21	0	4	7	21	38.6	25.9	6.3	6.0	.632
83-84	Denver	5	5	203	145	60	102	.588	0	1	.000	25	28	.893	16	24	40	28	17	0	3	2	7	40.6	29.0	8.0	5.6	.798
84-85	Denver	14	14	536	423	163	304	.536	0	1	.000	97	109	.890	36	56	92	63	40	1	17	5	30	38.3	30.2	6.6	4.5	.770
85-86	Denver	10	10	394	273	106	229	.463	0	1	.000	61	71	.859	18	17	35	52	29	0	4	4	28	39.4	27.3	3.5	5.2	.534
86-87	Denver	3	3	76	56	25	49	.510	0	0	.000	6	7	.857	10	4	14	10	9	1	0	0	8	25.3	18.7	4.7	3.3	.596
87-88	Denver	11	11	438	267	116	255	.455	0	3	.000	35	43	.814	31	28	59	48	34	0	7	3	16	39.8	24.3	5.4	4.4	.499
88-89	Denver	3	3	108	78	32	62	.516	0	0	.000	14	16	.875	8	5	13	11	6	0	1	0	14	36.0	26.0	4.3	3.7	.538
89-90	Denver	3	3	76	59	25	44	.568	0	0	.000	9	11	.818	3	6	9	9	6	0	2	1	2	25.3	19.7	3.0	3.0	.742
NBA Playoff Totals		68	59	2427	1661	668	1328	.503	0	8	.000	325	377	.862	166	205	371	293	188	2	47	32	142	35.7	24.4	5.5	4.3	....

• ENGLISH, Claude

Claude W. English

Born: Dec. 26, 1946. Columbus, GA, United States.   Height: 6'4".   Weight: 185 lbs.   Drafted: 1970   College: Rhode Island

YEAR	TEAM	GP	GS	MIN	PTS	FGM	FGA	FG%	3PM	3PA	3P%	FTM	FTA	FT%	ORB	DRB	TRB	AST	PF	DQ	STL	BLK	TO	MPG	PPG	RPG	APG	PCM
70-71	Portland	18	....	70	27	11	42	.262	....	....	....	5	7	.714	....	....	20	6	15	0	....	....	....	3.9	1.5	1.1	0.3	.244
NBA Season Totals		18	....	70	27	11	42	.262	....	....	....	5	7	.714	....	....	20	6	15	0	....	....	....	3.9	1.5	1.1	0.3	....

• ENGLISH, Jo Jo

Stephen (Jo-Jo) English

Born: Feb. 4, 1970. Frankfurt, Germany.   Height: 6'4".   Weight: 195 lbs.   Drafted: —   College: South Carolina

YEAR	TEAM	GP	GS	MIN	PTS	FGM	FGA	FG%	3PM	3PA	3P%	FTM	FTA	FT%	ORB	DRB	TRB	AST	PF	DQ	STL	BLK	TO	MPG	PPG	RPG	APG	PCM
92-93	Chicago	6	0	31	6	3	10	.300	0	3	.000	0	2	.000	2	4	6	1	5	0	3	2	4	5.2	1.0	1.0	0.2	.123
93-94	Chicago	36	0	419	130	56	129	.434	8	17	.471	10	21	.476	9	36	45	38	61	0	8	10	36	11.6	3.6	1.3	1.1	.229
94-95	Chicago	8	0	127	43	15	39	.385	3	12	.250	10	13	.769	1	2	3	7	19	0	7	1	6	15.9	5.4	0.4	0.9	.176
NBA Season Totals		50	0	577	179	74	178	.416	11	32	.344	20	36	.556	12	42	54	46	85	0	18	13	46	11.5	3.6	1.1	0.9	....

YEAR	TEAM	GP	GS	MIN	PTS	FGM	FGA	FG%	3PM	3PA	3P%	FTM	FTA	FT%	ORB	DRB	TRB	AST	PF	DQ	STL	BLK	TO	MPG	PPG	RPG	APG	PCM
93-94	Chicago	7	0	58	14	5	12	.417	1	4	.250	3	6	.500	1	2	3	2	4	0	1	1	1	8.3	2.0	0.4	0.3	.176
NBA Playoff Totals		7	0	58	14	5	12	.417	1	4	.250	3	6	.500	1	2	3	2	4	0	1	1	1	8.3	2.0	0.4	0.3	....

• ENGLISH, Scott

Scott Garrison English

Born: Oct. 20, 1950. Evanston, IL, United States.   Height: 6'6".   Weight: 205 lbs.   Drafted: 1972   College: Texas (El Paso)

YEAR	TEAM	GP	GS	MIN	PTS	FGM	FGA	FG%	3PM	3PA	3P%	FTM	FTA	FT%	ORB	DRB	TRB	AST	PF	DQ	STL	BLK	TO	MPG	PPG	RPG	APG	PCM
72-73	Phoenix	29	....	196	93	36	93	.387	....	....	....	21	29	.724	....	....	44	15	38	0	....	....	....	6.8	3.2	1.5	0.5	.404
73-74	Virginia-A	5	....	48	10	3	15	.200	0	0	.000	4	4	1.000	3	13	16	4	9	....	3	0	9	9.6	2.0	3.2	0.8	.295
74-75	San Diego-A	71	....	1316	490	210	494	.425	1	10	.100	69	89	.775	130	233	363	88	115	....	47	20	88	18.5	6.9	5.1	1.2	.454
NBA Season Totals		29	....	196	93	36	93	.387	....	....	....	21	29	.724	....	....	44	15	38	0	....	....	....	6.8	3.2	1.5	0.5	....
ABA Season Totals		76	....	1364	500	213	509	.418	1	10	.100	73	93	.785	133	246	379	92	124	....	50	20	97	17.9	6.6	5.0	1.2	....
Career Totals		105	....	1560	593	249	602	.414	1	10	.100	94	122	.770	133	246	423	107	162	0	50	20	97	14.9	5.6	4.0	1.0	....

• ENGLUND, Gene

Gene E. Englund

Born: Oct. 21, 1917. Kenosha, WI, United States. Died: Nov.5, 1995.   Height: 6'5".   Weight: 205 lbs.   Drafted: —   College: Wisconsin

YEAR	TEAM	GP	GS	MIN	PTS	FGM	FGA	FG%	3PM	3PA	3P%	FTM	FTA	FT%	ORB	DRB	TRB	AST	PF	DQ	STL	BLK	TO	MPG	PPG	RPG	APG	PCM
41-42	Oshkosh-N	22	....	....	164	61	....	....	....	....	....	42	....	....	....	....	....	....	....	....	....	....	....	7.5	....	....		
42-43	Oshkosh-N	17	....	....	130	41	....	....	....	....	....	48	....	....	....	....	....	....	....	....	....	....	....	7.6	....	....		
43-44	Oshkosh-N	2	....	....	23	9	....	....	....	....	....	5	....	....	....	....	....	....	....	....	....	....	....	11.5	....	....		
45-46	Oshkosh-N	33	....	....	220	78	....	....	....	....	....	64	102	.627	....	....	....	....	....	....	....	....	....	6.7	....	....		
46-47	Oshkosh-N	43	....	....	479	187	....	....	....	....	....	105	151	.695	....	....	121	....	....	....	....	....	....	11.1	....	....		
47-48	Oshkosh-N	58	....	....	734	246	....	....	....	....	....	242	333	.727	....	....	204	....	....	....	....	....	....	12.7	....	....		
48-49	Oshkosh-N	63	....	....	850	284	....	....	....	....	....	282	393	.718	....	....	232	....	....	....	....	....	....	13.5	....	....		
49-50	Boston	24	....	....	196	55	148	.372	....	....	....	86	106	.811	....	....	....	17	97	....	....	....	....	8.2	....	0.7		
49-50	Tri-Cities	22	....	....	164	49	126	.389	....	....	....	66	86	.767	....	....	....	24	70	....	....	....	....	7.5	....	1.1		
NBA Season Totals		46	....	....	360	104	274	.380	....	....	....	152	192	.792	....	....	....	41	167	....	....	....	....	7.8	....	0.9		
NBL Season Totals		238	....	....	2600	906	....	....	....	....	....	788	979	....	....	....	557	....	....	....	....	....	....	10.9	....	....		
Career Totals		284	....	....	2960	1010	274	....	....	....	....	940	1171	....	....	....	....	41	724	....	....	....	....	10.4	....	0.1		
41-42	Oshkosh-N	4	....	....	29	11	....	....	....	....	....	7	....	....	....	....	....	....	....	....	....	....	....	7.3	....	....		
42-43	Oshkosh-N	2	....	....	22	7	....	....	....	....	....	8	....	....	....	....	....	....	....	....	....	....	....	11.0	....	....		
45-46	Oshkosh-N	5	....	....	34	14	....	....	....	....	....	6	15	.400	....	....	....	....	....	....	....	....	....	6.8	....	....		
46-47	Oshkosh-N	7	....	....	98	36	....	....	....	....	....	26	49	.531	....	....	....	....	....	....	....	....	....	14.0	....	....		
47-48	Oshkosh-N	4	....	....	51	20	....	....	....	....	....	11	14	.786	....	....	....	....	....	....	....	....	....	12.8	....	....		
48-49	Oshkosh-N	7	....	....	95	32	....	....	....	....	....	31	37	.838	....	....	....	....	....	....	....	....	....	13.6	....	....		
49-50	Tri-Cities	2	....	....	11	1	5	.200	....	....	....	9	11	.818	....	....	....	1	6	....	....	....	....	5.5	....	0.5		
NBA Playoff Totals		2	....	....	11	1	5	.200	....	....	....	9	11	.818	....	....	....	1	6	....	....	....	....	5.5	....	0.5		
NBL Playoff Totals		29	....	....	329	120	....	....	....	....	....	89	115	....	....	....	....	....	....	....	....	....	....	11.3	....	....		
Career Playoff Totals		31	....	....	340	121	5	....	....	....	....	98	126	....	....	....	....	1	6	....	....	....	....	11.0	....	0.0		

• EPPERSON, Charlie

Charlie Epperson

Born: 1919.   Height: 6'2".   Weight: 180 lbs.   Drafted: —   College: Wisconsin

YEAR	TEAM	GP	GS	MIN	PTS	FGM	FGA	FG%	3PM	3PA	3P%	FTM	FTA	FT%	ORB	DRB	TRB	AST	PF	DQ	STL	BLK	TO	MPG	PPG	RPG	APG	PCM
41-42	Sheboygan-N	9	....	....	49	20	....	....	....	....	....	9	....	....	....	....	....	....	....	....	....	....	....	5.4	....	....		
45-46	Sheboygan-N	1	....	....	0	0	....	....	....	....	....	0	0	.000	....	....	....	....	....	....	....	....	....	0.0	....	....		
NBL Season Totals		10	....	....	49	20	....	....	....	....	....	9	....	....	....	....	....	....	....	....	....	....	....	4.9	....	....		

• EPPS, Ray

Raymond Edward Epps Jr.

Born: Aug. 20, 1956. Amelia, VA, United States.   Height: 6'6".   Weight: 195 lbs.   Drafted: 1977   College: Norfolk State

YEAR	TEAM	GP	GS	MIN	PTS	FGM	FGA	FG%	3PM	3PA	3P%	FTM	FTA	FT%	ORB	DRB	TRB	AST	PF	DQ	STL	BLK	TO	MPG	PPG	RPG	APG	PCM
78-79	Golden State	13	....	72	26	10	23	.435	....	....	....	6	8	.750	0	5	5	2	7	0	1	0	3	5.5	2.0	0.4	0.2	.211
NBA Season Totals		13	....	72	26	10	23	.435	....	....	....	6	8	.750	0	5	5	2	7	0	1	0	3	5.5	2.0	0.4	0.2	....

• ERBAN, Eddie

Ed Erban

Born: 1921. Oshkosh, WI, United States.   Height: 6'4".   Weight: —   Drafted: —   College: Marquette

YEAR	TEAM	GP	GS	MIN	PTS	FGM	FGA	FG%	3PM	3PA	3P%	FTM	FTA	FT%	ORB	DRB	TRB	AST	PF	DQ	STL	BLK	TO	MPG	PPG	RPG	APG	PCM
41-42	Toledo-N	15	....	....	28	8	....	....	....	....	....	12	....	....	....	....	....	....	....	....	....	....	....	1.9	....	....		
43-44	Oshkosh-N	22	....	....	58	19	....	....	....	....	....	20	....	....	....	....	....	....	....	....	....	....	....	2.6	....	....		
44-45	Oshkosh-N	15	....	....	36	13	....	....	....	....	....	10	....	....	....	....	....	....	....	....	....	....	....	2.4	....	....		
45-46	Oshkosh-N	1	....	....	0	0	....	....	....	....	....	0	0	.000	....	....	....	....	....	....	....	....	....	0.0	....	....		
46-47	Syracuse-N	5	....	....	1	0	....	....	....	....	....	1	2	.500	....	....	....	....	....	....	....	....	....	0.2	....	....		
NBL Season Totals		58	....	....	123	40	....	....	....	....	....	43	2	....	....	....	....	....	....	....	....	....	....	2.1	....	....		
43-44	Oshkosh-N	3	....	....	6	2	....	....	....	....	....	2	....	....	....	....	....	....	....	....	....	....	....	2.0	....	....		
45-46	Oshkosh-N	3	....	....	4	2	....	....	....	....	....	0	0	.000	....	....	....	....	....	....	....	....	....	1.3	....	....		
NBL Playoff Totals		6	....	....	10	4	....	....	....	....	....	2	0	....	....	....	....	....	....	....	....	....	....	1.7	....	....		

• ERIAS, Bo

Baltico S. Erias

Born: July 30, 1932. Astoria, NY, United States.   Height: 6'3".   Weight: 220 lbs.   Drafted: 1954   College: Niagara

YEAR	TEAM	GP	GS	MIN	PTS	FGM	FGA	FG%	3PM	3PA	3P%	FTM	FTA	FT%	ORB	DRB	TRB	AST	PF	DQ	STL	BLK	TO	MPG	PPG	RPG	APG	PCM
57-58	Minneapolis	18	....	401	148	59	170	.347	....	....	....	30	47	.638	....	....	83	26	52	1	....	....	....	22.3	8.2	4.6	1.4	.338
NBA Season Totals		18	....	401	148	59	170	.347	....	....	....	30	47	.638	....	....	83	26	52	1	....	....	....	22.3	8.2	4.6	1.4	....

• ERICKSON, Keith

Keith Raymond Erickson

Born: Apr. 19, 1944. San Francisco, CA, United States. Height: 6'5". Weight: 195 lbs. Drafted: 1965 College: UCLA

YEAR	TEAM	GP	GS	MIN	PTS	FGM	FGA	FG%	3PM	3PA	3P%	FTM	FTA	FT%	ORB	DRB	TRB	AST	PF	DQ	STL	BLK	TO	MPG	PPG	RPG	APG	PCM
65-66	San Francisco	64	....	646	233	95	267	.356	....	....	....	43	65	.662	....	....	162	38	91	1	....	....	....	10.1	3.6	2.5	0.6	.352
66-67	Chicago	76	....	1454	587	235	641	.367	....	....	....	117	159	.736	....	....	339	119	199	2	....	....	....	19.1	7.7	4.5	1.6	.399
67-68	Chicago	78	....	2257	948	377	940	.401	....	....	....	194	257	.755	....	....	423	267	276	15	....	....	....	28.9	12.2	5.4	3.4	.453
68-69	LA Lakers	77	....	1974	648	264	629	.420	....	....	....	120	175	.686	....	....	308	194	222	6	....	....	....	25.6	8.4	4.0	2.5	.360
69-70	LA Lakers	68	....	1755	607	258	563	.458	....	....	....	91	122	.746	....	....	304	209	175	3	....	....	....	25.8	8.9	4.5	3.1	.427
70-71	LA Lakers	73	....	2272	823	369	783	.471	....	....	....	85	112	.759	....	....	404	223	241	4	....	....	....	31.1	11.3	5.5	3.1	.420
71-72	LA Lakers	15	....	262	86	40	83	.482	....	....	....	6	7	.857	....	....	39	35	26	0	....	....	....	17.5	5.7	2.6	2.3	.422
72-73	LA Lakers	76	....	1920	687	299	696	.430	....	....	....	89	110	.809	....	....	337	242	190	3	....	....	....	25.3	9.0	4.4	3.2	.428
73-74	Phoenix	66	....	2033	963	393	824	.477	....	....	....	177	221	.801	94	320	414	205	193	3	63	20	....	30.8	14.6	6.3	3.1	.533
74-75	Phoenix	49	....	1469	604	237	557	.425	....	....	....	130	156	.833	70	173	243	170	150	3	50	12	....	30.0	12.3	5.0	3.5	.448
75-76	Phoenix	74	....	1850	744	305	649	.470	....	....	....	134	157	.854	106	226	332	185	196	4	79	6	....	25.0	10.1	4.5	2.5	.460
76-77	Phoenix	50	....	949	321	142	294	.483	....	....	....	37	50	.740	36	108	144	104	122	0	30	7	....	19.0	6.4	2.9	2.1	.394
NBA Season Totals		766	....	18841	7251	3014	6926	.435	....	....	....	1223	1591	.769	306	827	3449	1991	2081	44	222	45	....	24.6	9.5	4.5	2.6	....
66-67	Chicago	3	....	68	24	12	27	.444	....	....	....	0	0	.000	....	....	11	4	12	1	....	....	....	22.7	8.0	3.7	1.3	.307
67-68	Chicago	5	....	183	65	25	65	.385	....	....	....	15	17	.882	....	....	41	11	19	0	....	....	....	36.6	13.0	8.2	2.2	.386
68-69	LA Lakers	18	....	446	127	56	142	.394	....	....	....	15	25	.600	....	....	86	40	64	2	....	....	....	24.8	7.1	4.8	2.2	.320
69-70	LA Lakers	17	....	553	169	71	153	.464	....	....	....	27	35	.771	....	....	77	74	44	0	....	....	....	32.5	9.9	4.5	4.4	.406
70-71	LA Lakers	8	....	313	125	54	99	.545	....	....	....	17	22	.773	....	....	45	22	34	1	....	....	....	39.1	15.6	5.6	2.8	.426
72-73	LA Lakers	17	....	404	147	66	147	.449	....	....	....	15	22	.682	....	....	59	30	52	2	....	....	....	23.8	8.6	3.5	1.8	.339
75-76	Phoenix	19	....	426	215	80	173	.462	....	....	....	55	68	.809	15	52	67	35	61	1	11	4	....	22.4	11.3	3.5	1.8	.472
NBA Playoff Totals		87	....	2393	872	364	806	.452	....	....	....	144	189	.762	15	52	386	216	286	7	11	4	....	27.5	10.0	4.4	2.5	....

• ERTEL, Mark

Mark Ertel

Born: 1919. Height: 6'4". Weight: 196 lbs. Drafted: — College: Notre Dame

YEAR	TEAM	GP	GS	MIN	PTS	FGM	FGA	FG%	3PM	3PA	3P%	FTM	FTA	FT%	ORB	DRB	TRB	AST	PF	DQ	STL	BLK	TO	MPG	PPG	RPG	APG	PCM
41-42	Indianapolis-N	20	....	....	66	20	....	....	....	....	....	26	....	....	....	....	....	....	....	....	....	....	....	....	3.3	....	....	....
NBL Season Totals		20	....	....	66	20	....	....	....	....	....	26	....	....	....	....	....	....	....	....	....	....	....	....	3.3	....	....	....
41-42	Indianapolis-N	2	....	....	3	1	....	....	....	....	....	1	....	....	....	....	....	....	....	....	....	....	....	....	1.5	....	....	....
NBL Playoff Totals		2	....	....	3	1	....	....	....	....	....	1	....	....	....	....	....	....	....	....	....	....	....	....	1.5	....	....	....

• ERVING, Julius

Julius Winfield (Dr. J, The Doctor) Erving II

Born: Feb. 22, 1950. Roosevelt, NY, United States. Height: 6'6". Weight: 200 lbs. Drafted: 1972 College: Massachusetts HOF: 1993

YEAR	TEAM	GP	GS	MIN	PTS	FGM	FGA	FG%	3PM	3PA	3P%	FTM	FTA	FT%	ORB	DRB	TRB	AST	PF	DQ	STL	BLK	TO	MPG	PPG	RPG	APG	PCM
71-72	Virginia-A	84	....	3513	2290	910	1826	.498	3	16	.188	467	627	.745	**476**	843	1319	335	264	0	....	....	**342**	41.8	27.3	15.7	4.0	.807
72-73	Virginia-A	71	....	2993	2268	894	**1804**	.496	5	24	.208	475	612	.776	262	605	867	298	197	1	181	127	326	**42.2**	**31.9**	12.2	4.2	.804
73-74	New York-A	84	....	3398	**2299**	**914**	**1785**	.512	17	43	.395	454	593	.766	263	636	899	434	270	....	190	204	341	40.5	**27.4**	10.7	5.2	.778
74-75	New York-A	84	....	3402	2343	**914**	1806	.506	29	87	.333	486	608	.799	284	630	914	462	256	....	186	157	301	40.5	27.9	10.9	5.5	.796
75-76	New York-A	84	....	3244	**2462**	**949**	**1873**	.507	34	103	.330	530	662	.801	337	588	925	423	221	....	207	160	307	38.6	**29.3**	11.0	5.0	.855
76-77	Philadelphia	82	....	2940	1770	685	1373	.499	....	....	....	400	515	.777	192	503	695	306	251	1	159	113	....	35.9	21.6	8.5	3.7	.669
77-78	Philadelphia	74	....	2429	1528	611	1217	.502	....	....	....	306	362	.845	179	302	481	279	207	0	135	97	237	32.8	20.6	6.5	3.8	.664
78-79	Philadelphia	78	....	2802	1803	715	1455	.491	....	....	....	373	501	.745	198	366	564	357	207	0	133	100	312	35.9	23.1	7.2	4.6	.648
79-80	Philadelphia	78	....	2812	2100	838	1614	.519	4	20	.200	420	534	.787	215	361	576	355	208	0	170	140	281	36.1	26.9	7.4	4.6	.778
80-81	Philadelphia	82	....	2874	2014	794	1524	.521	4	18	.222	422	536	.787	244	413	657	364	233	0	173	147	262	35.0	24.6	8.0	4.4	.779
81-82	Philadelphia	81	81	2789	1974	780	1428	.546	3	11	.273	411	539	.763	220	337	557	319	229	1	161	141	211	34.4	24.4	6.9	3.9	.772
82-83	Philadelphia	72	72	2421	1542	605	1170	.517	2	7	.286	330	435	.759	173	318	491	263	202	1	112	131	194	33.6	21.4	6.8	3.7	.690
83-84	Philadelphia	77	77	2683	1727	678	1324	.512	7	21	.333	364	483	.754	190	342	532	309	217	3	141	139	231	34.8	22.4	6.9	4.0	.686
84-85	Philadelphia	78	78	2535	1561	610	1236	.494	3	14	.214	338	442	.765	172	242	414	233	199	0	135	109	211	32.5	20.0	5.3	3.0	.592
85-86	Philadelphia	74	74	2474	1340	521	1085	.480	9	32	.281	289	368	.785	169	201	370	248	196	3	113	82	215	33.4	18.1	5.0	3.4	.517
86-87	Philadelphia	60	60	1918	1005	400	850	.471	14	53	.264	191	235	.813	115	149	264	191	137	0	76	94	156	32.0	16.8	4.4	3.2	.503
NBA Season Totals		836	442	28677	18364	7237	14276	.507	46	176	.261	3844	4950	.777	2067	3534	5601	3224	2286	9	1508	1293	2310	34.3	22.0	6.7	3.9	....
ABA Season Totals		407	....	16550	11662	4581	9094	.504	88	273	.322	2412	3102	.778	1622	3302	4924	1952	1208	1	764	648	1617	40.7	**28.7**	12.1	4.8	....
Career Totals		1243	442	45227	30026	11818	23370	.506	134	449	.298	6256	8052	.777	3689	6836	10525	5176	3494	10	2272	1941	3927	36.4	**24.2**	8.5	4.2	....
71-72	Virginia-A	11	....	504	366	147	284	.518	1	4	.250	71	85	.835	65	159	224	72	26	0	....	....	55	45.8	33.3	20.4	6.5	1.003
72-73	Virginia-A	5	....	219	148	59	112	.527	0	3	.000	30	40	.750	14	31	45	16	16	0	....	....	17	43.8	29.6	9.0	3.2	.670
73-74	New York-A	14	....	579	390	161	305	.528	5	11	.455	63	85	.741	43	92	135	67	40	....	22	19	51	41.4	27.9	9.6	4.8	.746
74-75	New York-A	5	....	211	137	55	121	.455	0	8	.000	27	32	.844	12	37	49	28	18	....	5	9	19	42.2	27.4	9.8	5.6	.677
75-76	New York-A	13	....	551	451	160	300	.533	4	14	.286	127	158	.804	65	99	164	64	41	....	25	26	39	42.4	34.7	12.6	4.9	.928
76-77	Philadelphia	19	....	758	518	204	390	.523	....	....	....	110	134	.821	41	81	122	85	45	0	41	23	....	39.9	27.3	6.4	4.5	.699
77-78	Philadelphia	10	....	358	218	88	180	.489	....	....	....	42	56	.750	40	57	97	40	30	0	15	18	35	35.8	21.8	9.7	4.0	.688
78-79	Philadelphia	9	....	372	229	89	172	.517	....	....	....	51	67	.761	29	41	70	53	22	0	18	17	38	41.3	25.4	7.8	5.9	.688
79-80	Philadelphia	18	....	694	440	165	338	.488	2	9	.222	108	136	.794	31	105	136	79	56	0	36	37	56	38.6	24.4	7.6	4.4	.678
80-81	Philadelphia	16	....	592	367	143	301	.475	0	1	.000	81	107	.757	52	62	114	54	54	0	22	41	55	37.0	22.9	7.1	3.4	.602
81-82	Philadelphia	21	21	780	461	168	324	.519	1	6	.167	124	165	.752	57	99	156	99	55	0	37	37	67	37.1	22.0	7.4	4.7	.680
82-83	Philadelphia	13	13	493	239	95	211	.450	0	1	.000	49	68	.721	32	67	99	44	42	1	15	27	39	37.9	18.4	7.6	3.4	.501
83-84	Philadelphia	5	5	194	91	36	76	.474	0	1	.000	19	22	.864	9	23	32	25	14	0	8	6	21	38.8	18.2	6.4	5.0	.494
84-85	Philadelphia	13	13	434	222	84	187	.449	0	1	.000	54	63	.857	29	44	73	48	34	0	25	11	37	33.4	17.1	5.6	3.7	.517
85-86	Philadelphia	12	12	433	212	81	180	.450	2	11	.182	48	65	.738	26	44	70	50	32	0	11	16	39	36.1	17.7	5.8	4.2	.473
86-87	Philadelphia	5	5	180	91	34	82	.415	2	6	.333	21	25	.840	14	11	25	17	19	0	7	6	9	36.0	18.2	5.0	3.4	.449
NBA Playoff Totals		141	69	5288	3088	1187	2441	.486	7	36	.194	707	908	.779	360	634	994	594	403	1	235	239	396	37.5	21.9	7.0	4.2	....
ABA Playoff Totals		48	....	2064	1492	582	1122	.519	10	40	.250	318	400	.795	199	418	617	247	141	0	52	54	181	43.0	31.1	12.9	5.1	....
Career Playoff Totals		189	69	7352	4580	1769	3563	.496	17	76	.224	1025	1308	.784	559	1052	1611	841	544	1	287	293	577	38.9	24.2	8.5	4.4	....

YEAR TEAM	GP	GS	MIN	PTS	FGM	FGA	FG%	3PM	3PA	3P%	FTM	FTA	FT%	ORB	DRB	TRB	AST	PF	DQ	STL	BLK	TO	MPG	PPG	RPG	APG	PCM

• ESCHMEYER, Evan
Evan Bruce Eschmeyer

Born: May 30, 1975. New Knoxville, OH, United States. Height: 6'11". Weight: 255 lbs. Drafted: 1999 College: Northwestern

YEAR TEAM	GP	GS	MIN	PTS	FGM	FGA	FG%	3PM	3PA	3P%	FTM	FTA	FT%	ORB	DRB	TRB	AST	PF	DQ	STL	BLK	TO	MPG	PPG	RPG	APG	PCM
99-00 New Jersey	31	5	373	91	38	72	.528	0	0	.000	15	30	.500	40	68	108	21	84	2	8	21	21	12.0	2.9	3.5	0.7	.385
00-01 New Jersey	74	51	1331	251	92	200	.460	0	0	.000	67	102	.657	135	231	366	40	220	5	41	58	53	18.0	3.4	4.9	0.5	.341
01-02 Dallas	31	6	299	62	21	50	.420	0	0	.000	20	33	.606	35	63	98	9	60	1	10	9	16	9.6	2.0	3.2	0.3	.348
02-03 Dallas	17	3	135	17	7	19	.368	0	0	.000	3	4	.750	10	19	29	6	35	1	10	7	6	7.9	1.0	1.7	0.4	.242
NBA Season Totals	153	65	2138	421	158	341	.463	0	0	.000	105	169	.621	220	381	601	76	399	9	69	95	96	14.0	2.8	3.9	0.5	....
01-02 Dallas	3	0	8	0	0	1	.000	0	0	.000	0	0	.000	1	1	2	1	2	0	0	1	0	2.7	0.0	0.7	0.3	.250
02-03 Dallas	5	0	32	6	3	6	.500	0	0	.000	0	0	.000	2	3	5	2	8	0	3	1	0	6.4	1.2	1.0	0.4	.313
NBA Playoff Totals	8	0	40	6	3	7	.429	0	0	.000	0	0	.000	3	4	7	3	10	0	3	2	0	5.0	0.8	0.9	0.4	....

• ESKRIDGE, Jack
John I. Eskridge

Born: Jan. 21, 1924. Height: 6'5". Weight: 200 lbs. Drafted: — College: Kansas

YEAR TEAM	GP	GS	MIN	PTS	FGM	FGA	FG%	3PM	3PA	3P%	FTM	FTA	FT%	ORB	DRB	TRB	AST	PF	DQ	STL	BLK	TO	MPG	PPG	RPG	APG	PCM
48-49 Chicago	3	....	....	0	0	0	.000	....	....	....	0	0	.000	....	....	....	0	1	....	....	....	....		0.0	0.0		....
48-49 Indianapolis	20	....	....	64	25	69	.362	....	....	....	14	20	.700	....	....	....	14	24	....	....	....	....		3.2	0.7		....
NBA Season Totals	23	....	....	64	25	69	.362	....	....	....	14	20	.700	....	....	....	14	25	....	....	....	....		2.8	0.6		....

• ESPOSITO, Vincenzo
Vincenzo (El Diablo) Esposito

Born: Jan. 3, 1969. Caserta, Italy. Height: 6'3". Weight: 198 lbs. Drafted: — College: none

YEAR TEAM	GP	GS	MIN	PTS	FGM	FGA	FG%	3PM	3PA	3P%	FTM	FTA	FT%	ORB	DRB	TRB	AST	PF	DQ	STL	BLK	TO	MPG	PPG	RPG	APG	PCM
95-96 Toronto	30	0	282	116	36	100	.360	13	56	.232	31	39	.795	4	12	16	23	27	0	7	0	39	9.4	3.9	0.5	0.8	.173
NBA Season Totals	30	0	282	116	36	100	.360	13	56	.232	31	39	.795	4	12	16	23	27	0	7	0	39	9.4	3.9	0.5	0.8	....

• EVANS, Billy
William D. Evans

Born: Mar. 3, 1947. Height: 6'. Weight: 170 lbs. Drafted: 1969 College: Boston College

YEAR TEAM	GP	GS	MIN	PTS	FGM	FGA	FG%	3PM	3PA	3P%	FTM	FTA	FT%	ORB	DRB	TRB	AST	PF	DQ	STL	BLK	TO	MPG	PPG	RPG	APG	PCM
69-70 New York-A	53	....	602	102	32	87	.368	0	2	.000	38	70	.543	17	22	39	100	89	1	....	....	47	11.4	1.9	0.7	1.9	.250
ABA Season Totals	53	....	602	102	32	87	.368	0	2	.000	38	70	.543	17	22	39	100	89	1	....	....	47	11.4	1.9	0.7	1.9	....
69-70 New York-A	6	....	27	3	1	2	.500	0	1	.000	1	3	.333	....	....	3	0	0	....	0	....	....		4.5	0.5	0.5	0.0	....
ABA Playoff Totals	6	....	27	3	1	2	.500	0	1	.000	1	3	.333	....	....	3	0	0	....	0	....	....		4.5	0.5	0.5	0.0	....

• EVANS, Bob
Robert W. Evans

Born: May 31, 1925. Indianapolis, IN, United States. Height: 6'2". Weight: 175 lbs. Drafted: 1949 College: Butler

YEAR TEAM	GP	GS	MIN	PTS	FGM	FGA	FG%	3PM	3PA	3P%	FTM	FTA	FT%	ORB	DRB	TRB	AST	PF	DQ	STL	BLK	TO	MPG	PPG	RPG	APG	PCM
49-50 Indianapolis	47	....	....	142	56	200	.280	....	....	....	30	44	.682	....	....	....	55	99	....	....	....	....		3.0	1.2		....
NBA Season Totals	47	....	....	142	56	200	.280	....	....	....	30	44	.682	....	....	....	55	99	....	....	....	....		3.0	1.2		....
49-50 Indianapolis	2	....	....	2	1	4	.250	....	....	....	0	0	.000	....	....	....	0	3	....	....	....	....		1.0	0.0		....
NBA Playoff Totals	2	....	....	2	1	4	.250	....	....	....	0	0	.000	....	....	....	0	3	....	....	....	....		1.0	0.0		....

• EVANS, Brian
Brian Keith Evans

Born: Sept. 13, 1973. Rockford, IL, United States. Height: 6'8". Weight: 220 lbs. Drafted: 1996 College: Indiana

YEAR TEAM	GP	GS	MIN	PTS	FGM	FGA	FG%	3PM	3PA	3P%	FTM	FTA	FT%	ORB	DRB	TRB	AST	PF	DQ	STL	BLK	TO	MPG	PPG	RPG	APG	PCM
96-97 Orlando	14	0	59	20	8	22	.364	4	8	.500	0	0	.000	1	7	8	7	6	0	1	2	1	4.2	1.4	0.6	0.5	.355
97-98 Orlando	44	0	561	206	77	206	.374	12	45	.267	40	48	.833	31	54	85	31	57	0	22	8	22	12.8	4.7	1.9	0.7	.315
97-98 New Jersey	28	1	332	115	46	106	.434	17	42	.405	6	9	.667	18	34	52	24	44	0	7	5	14	11.9	4.1	1.9	0.9	.332
98-99 New Jersey	11	0	121	30	11	34	.324	4	11	.364	4	4	1.000	4	13	17	14	7	0	3	3	2	11.0	2.7	1.5	1.3	.336
98-99 Minnesota	5	0	24	4	2	10	.200	0	2	.000	0	0	.000	2	0	2	1	1	0	2	0	0	4.8	0.8	0.4	0.2	.046
NBA Season Totals	102	1	1097	375	144	378	.381	37	108	.343	50	61	.820	56	108	164	77	115	0	35	18	39	10.8	3.7	1.6	0.8	....
96-97 Orlando	2	0	7	2	1	1	1.000	0	0	.000	0	0	.000	0	0	0	2	0	0	1	0	0	3.5	1.0	0.0	1.0	.724
97-98 New Jersey	3	0	4	0	0	0	.000	0	0	.000	0	0	.000	0	1	1	0	0	0	0	0	0	1.3	0.0	0.3	0.0	.229
NBA Playoff Totals	5	0	11	2	1	1	1.000	0	0	.000	0	0	.000	0	1	1	2	0	0	1	0	0	2.2	0.4	0.2	0.4	....

• EVANS, Earl
Earl Joseph Evans II

Born: Nov. 11, 1955. Port Arthur, TX, United States. Height: 6'8". Weight: 202 lbs. Drafted: 1978 College: UNLV

YEAR TEAM	GP	GS	MIN	PTS	FGM	FGA	FG%	3PM	3PA	3P%	FTM	FTA	FT%	ORB	DRB	TRB	AST	PF	DQ	STL	BLK	TO	MPG	PPG	RPG	APG	PCM
79-80 Detroit	36	....	381	157	63	140	.450	7	18	.389	24	42	.571	26	49	75	37	64	0	14	1	36	10.6	4.4	2.1	1.0	.366
NBA Season Totals	36	....	381	157	63	140	.450	7	18	.389	24	42	.571	26	49	75	37	64	0	14	1	36	10.6	4.4	2.1	1.0	....

• EVANS, Hank
Hank Evans

Born: 1915. Height: 6'3". Weight: 195 lbs. Drafted: — College: none

YEAR TEAM	GP	GS	MIN	PTS	FGM	FGA	FG%	3PM	3PA	3P%	FTM	FTA	FT%	ORB	DRB	TRB	AST	PF	DQ	STL	BLK	TO	MPG	PPG	RPG	APG	PCM
44-45 Pittsburgh-N	28	....	....	238	97	....	....	....	....	....	44	....	....	....	....	....	....	....	....	....	....	....		8.5	....	....	....
NBL Season Totals	28	....	....	238	97	....	....	....	....	....	44	....	....	....	....	....	....	....	....	....	....	....		8.5	....	....	....

• EVANS, Maurice

Maurice Eugene Evans

Born: Nov. 8, 1978. Wichita, KS, United States. Height: 6'5". Weight: 220 lbs. Drafted: — College: Texas

YEAR	TEAM	GP	GS	MIN	PTS	FGM	FGA	FG%	3PM	3PA	3P%	FTM	FTA	FT%	ORB	DRB	TRB	AST	PF	DQ	STL	BLK	TO	MPG	PPG	RPG	APG	PCM
01-02	Minnesota	10	0	45	21	9	19	.474	0	3	.000	3	4	.750	3	1	4	4	9	0	0	0	2	4.5	2.1	0.4	0.4	.302
NBA Season Totals		10	0	45	21	9	19	.474	0	3	.000	3	4	.750	3	1	4	4	9	0	0	0	2	4.5	2.1	0.4	0.4	....

• EVANS, Mike

Michael Leeroyall Evans

Born: Apr. 19, 1955. Goldsboro, NC, United States. Height: 6'1". Weight: 170 lbs. Drafted: 1978 College: Kansas State

YEAR	TEAM	GP	GS	MIN	PTS	FGM	FGA	FG%	3PM	3PA	3P%	FTM	FTA	FT%	ORB	DRB	TRB	AST	PF	DQ	STL	BLK	TO	MPG	PPG	RPG	APG	PCM
79-80	San Antonio	79	....	1246	486	208	464	.448	12	42	.286	58	85	.682	29	78	107	230	194	2	60	9	126	15.8	6.2	1.4	2.9	.362
80-81	Milwaukee	71	....	911	320	134	291	.460	2	14	.143	50	64	.781	22	65	87	167	114	0	34	4	71	12.8	4.5	1.2	2.4	.384
81-82	Milwaukee	14	0	196	56	24	51	.471	0	2	.000	8	12	.667	3	9	12	22	26	1	9	0	15	14.0	4.0	0.9	1.6	.238
81-82	Cleveland	8	0	74	27	11	35	.314	0	4	.000	5	8	.625	2	8	10	20	10	0	4	0	11	9.3	3.4	1.3	2.5	.314
82-83	Denver	42	5	695	263	115	243	.473	0	9	.000	33	41	.805	4	54	58	113	94	3	23	3	71	16.5	6.3	1.4	2.7	.341
83-84	Denver	78	5	1687	629	243	564	.431	32	89	.360	111	131	.847	23	115	138	288	175	2	61	4	117	21.6	8.1	1.8	3.7	.372
84-85	Denver	81	0	1437	816	323	661	.489	57	157	.363	113	131	.863	26	93	119	231	174	2	65	12	130	17.7	10.1	1.5	2.9	.501
85-86	Denver	81	1	1389	773	304	715	.425	39	176	.222	126	149	.846	30	71	101	177	159	1	61	1	122	17.1	9.5	1.2	2.2	.385
86-87	Denver	81	4	1567	817	334	729	.458	53	169	.314	96	123	.780	36	92	128	185	149	1	79	12	105	19.3	10.1	1.6	2.3	.428
87-88	Denver	56	0	656	344	139	307	.453	36	91	.396	30	37	.811	9	39	48	81	78	0	34	6	45	11.7	6.1	0.9	1.4	.418
NBA Season Totals		591	15	9858	4531	1835	4060	.452	231	753	.307	630	781	.807	184	624	808	1514	1173	12	430	51	813	16.7	7.7	1.4	2.6	....
79-80	San Antonio	2	....	12	11	3	8	.375	2	4	.500	3	4	.750	0	2	2	2	2	0	0	0	0	6.0	5.5	1.0	1.0	.760
80-81	Milwaukee	4	....	38	25	9	17	.529	0	2	.000	7	8	.875	0	1	1	6	9	0	0	1	3	9.5	6.3	0.3	1.5	.494
82-83	Denver	8	1	183	86	36	74	.486	3	10	.300	11	17	.647	2	17	19	38	20	0	5	0	22	22.9	10.8	2.4	4.8	.456
83-84	Denver	5	0	77	23	9	28	.321	1	8	.125	4	4	1.000	1	2	3	12	13	0	0	0	8	15.4	4.6	0.6	2.4	.097
84-85	Denver	15	0	281	155	62	143	.434	17	51	.333	14	17	.824	3	29	32	46	39	0	13	3	36	18.7	10.3	2.1	3.1	.428
85-86	Denver	10	0	204	92	30	82	.366	7	29	.241	25	30	.833	6	14	20	25	19	0	10	3	13	20.4	9.2	2.0	2.5	.382
86-87	Denver	3	0	57	18	7	19	.368	2	7	.286	2	2	1.000	2	5	7	8	6	0	3	0	3	19.0	6.0	2.3	2.7	.335
87-88	Denver	11	1	219	116	45	114	.395	12	44	.273	14	15	.933	6	16	22	23	19	0	12	0	12	19.9	10.5	2.0	2.1	.399
NBA Playoff Totals		58	2	1071	526	201	485	.414	44	155	.284	80	97	.825	20	86	106	160	127	0	43	7	97	18.5	9.1	1.8	2.8	....

• EVANS, Reggie

Reggie Evans

Born: May 18, 1980. Pensacola, FL, United States. Height: 6'8". Weight: 245 lbs. Drafted: — College: Iowa

YEAR	TEAM	GP	GS	MIN	PTS	FGM	FGA	FG%	3PM	3PA	3P%	FTM	FTA	FT%	ORB	DRB	TRB	AST	PF	DQ	STL	BLK	TO	MPG	PPG	RPG	APG	PCM
02-03	Seattle	67	60	1365	212	66	140	.471	0	0	.000	80	154	.519	167	278	445	34	173	2	38	11	52	20.4	3.2	6.6	0.5	.345
NBA Season Totals		67	60	1365	212	66	140	.471	0	0	.000	80	154	.519	167	**278**	445	34	173	2	38	11	52	20.4	3.2	6.6	0.5	....

• EVANS, Richard

Richard Jacob (Whitey) Evans

Born: May 31, 1917. Chicago, IL, United States. Height: 6'3". Weight: 200 lbs. Drafted: — College: Iowa

YEAR	TEAM	GP	GS	MIN	PTS	FGM	FGA	FG%	3PM	3PA	3P%	FTM	FTA	FT%	ORB	DRB	TRB	AST	PF	DQ	STL	BLK	TO	MPG	PPG	RPG	APG	PCM
40-41	Hammond-N	4	....	....	12	4	....	....	....	....	....	4	....	....	....	....	....	....	....	....	....	....	....	....	3.0	....	....	....
40-41	Sheboygan-N	1	....	....	0	0	....	....	....	....	....	0	....	....	....	....	....	....	....	....	....	....	....	....	0.0	....	....	....
41-42	Chicago-N	18	....	....	54	17	....	....	....	....	....	20	....	....	....	....	....	....	....	....	....	....	....	....	3.0	....	....	....
42-43	Chicago-N	9	....	....	12	3	....	....	....	....	....	6	....	....	....	....	....	....	....	....	....	....	....	....	1.3	....	....	....
NBL Season Totals		32	....	....	78	24	....	....	....	....	....	30	....	....	....	....	....	....	....	....	....	....	....	....	2.4	....	....	....

• EVARD, Byron

Byron (Boob) Evard

Born: Mar. 27, 1908. Died: Dec.1983. Height: 5'8". Weight: 155 lbs. Drafted: — College: St. Viator

YEAR	TEAM	GP	GS	MIN	PTS	FGM	FGA	FG%	3PM	3PA	3P%	FTM	FTA	FT%	ORB	DRB	TRB	AST	PF	DQ	STL	BLK	TO	MPG	PPG	RPG	APG	PCM
37-38	Fort Wayne-N	10	....	....	16	7	....	....	....	....	....	2	....	....	....	....	....	....	....	....	....	....	....	....	1.6	....	....	....
NBL Season Totals		10	....	....	16	7	....	....	....	....	....	2	....	....	....	....	....	....	....	....	....	....	....	....	1.6	....	....	....

• EWING, Patrick

Patrick Aloysius Ewing

Born: Aug. 5, 1962. Kingston, Jamaica. Height: 7' Weight: 240 lbs. Drafted: 1985 College: Georgetown

YEAR	TEAM	GP	GS	MIN	PTS	FGM	FGA	FG%	3PM	3PA	3P%	FTM	FTA	FT%	ORB	DRB	TRB	AST	PF	DQ	STL	BLK	TO	MPG	PPG	RPG	APG	PCM
85-86	New York	50	50	1771	998	386	814	.474	0	5	.000	226	306	.739	124	327	451	102	191	7	54	103	170	35.4	20.0	9.0	2.0	.559
86-87	New York	63	63	2206	1356	530	1053	.503	0	7	.000	296	415	.713	157	398	555	104	248	5	89	147	227	35.0	21.5	8.8	1.7	.605
87-88	New York	82	82	2546	1653	656	1183	.555	0	3	.000	341	476	.716	245	431	676	125	**332**	5	104	245	287	31.0	20.2	8.2	1.5	.693
88-89	New York	80	80	2896	1815	727	1282	.567	0	6	.000	361	484	.746	213	527	740	188	311	5	117	281	264	36.2	22.7	9.3	2.4	.729
89-90	New York	82	82	3165	2347	922	1673	.551	1	4	.250	502	648	.775	235	658	893	182	325	7	78	327	279	38.6	28.6	10.9	2.2	.812
90-91	New York	81	81	3104	2154	845	1645	.514	0	6	.000	464	623	.745	194	711	905	244	287	3	80	258	292	38.3	26.6	11.2	3.0	.756
91-92	New York	82	82	3150	1970	796	1525	.522	1	6	.167	377	511	.738	228	693	921	156	277	2	88	245	205	38.4	24.0	11.2	1.9	.712
92-93	New York	81	81	3003	1959	779	1550	.503	1	7	.143	400	556	.719	191	**789**	980	151	286	2	74	161	267	37.1	24.2	12.1	1.9	.692
93-94	New York	79	79	2972	1939	745	1503	.496	4	14	.286	445	582	.765	219	666	885	179	275	3	90	217	261	37.6	24.5	11.2	2.3	.707
94-95	New York	79	79	2920	1886	730	1452	.503	6	21	.286	420	560	.750	157	710	867	212	272	3	68	159	253	37.0	23.9	11.0	2.7	.695
95-96	New York	76	76	2783	1711	678	1456	.466	4	28	.143	351	461	.761	157	649	806	160	247	2	68	184	220	36.6	22.5	10.6	2.1	.636
96-97	New York	78	78	2887	1751	655	1342	.488	2	9	.222	439	582	.754	175	659	834	156	250	2	69	189	265	37.0	22.4	10.7	2.0	.646
97-98	New York	26	26	848	540	203	403	.504	0	2	.000	134	186	.720	59	206	265	28	74	0	16	58	78	32.6	20.8	10.2	1.1	.670
98-99	New York	38	38	1300	657	247	568	.435	0	2	.000	163	231	.706	74	303	377	43	105	1	30	100	99	34.2	17.3	9.9	1.1	.542
99-00	New York	62	62	2035	929	361	775	.466	0	2	.000	207	283	.731	140	464	604	58	196	1	36	84	142	32.8	15.0	9.7	0.9	.502
00-01	Seattle	79	79	2107	760	294	684	.430	0	2	.000	172	251	.685	124	461	585	92	229	1	53	91	151	26.7	9.6	7.4	1.2	.423
01-02	Orlando	65	4	901	390	148	333	.444	0	1	.000	94	134	.701	60	203	263	35	129	0	22	45	65	13.9	6.0	4.0	0.5	.471
NBA Season Totals		1183	1122	40594	24815	9702	19241	.504	19	125	.152	5392	7289	.740	2752	8855	11607	2215	4034	49	1136	2894	3525	34.3	21.0	9.8	1.9	....
87-88	New York	4	4	153	75	28	57	.491	0	1	.000	19	22	.864	16	35	51	10	17	0	6	13	11	38.3	18.8	12.8	2.5	.682
88-89	New York	9	9	340	179	70	144	.486	0	0	.000	39	52	.750	23	67	90	20	35	0	9	18	15	37.8	19.9	10.0	2.2	.600
89-90	New York	10	10	395	294	114	219	.521	1	2	.500	65	79	.823	21	84	105	31	41	0	13	20	27	39.5	29.4	10.5	3.1	.777
90-91	New York	3	3	110	50	18	45	.400	0	0	.000	14	18	.778	2	28	30	6	12	0	1	5	11	36.7	16.7	10.0	2.0	.428
91-92	New York	12	12	482	272	109	239	.456	0	1	.000	54	73	.740	33	100	133	27	49	1	7	31	23	40.2	22.7	11.1	2.3	.593
92-93	New York	15	15	604	382	165	322	.512	1	1	1.000	51	80	.638	43	121	164	36	60	2	17	31	39	40.3	25.5	10.9	2.4	.652

YEAR	TEAM	GP	GS	MIN	PTS	FGM	FGA	FG%	3PM	3PA	3P%	FTM	FTA	FT%	ORB	DRB	TRB	AST	PF	DQ	STL	BLK	TO	MPG	PPG	RPG	APG	PCM
93-94	New York	25	25	1032	547	210	481	.437	4	11	.364	123	163	.755	88	205	293	65	94	1	32	76	83	41.3	21.9	11.7	2.6	.580
94-95	New York	11	11	399	209	80	156	.513	1	3	.333	48	70	.686	17	89	106	27	51	1	6	25	30	36.3	19.0	9.6	2.5	.583
95-96	New York	8	8	328	172	65	137	.474	1	2	.500	41	63	.651	11	74	85	15	22	0	1	25	30	41.0	21.5	10.6	1.9	.536
96-97	New York	9	9	357	203	88	167	.527	0	1	.000	27	42	.643	26	69	95	17	30	0	3	22	27	39.7	22.6	10.6	1.9	.597
97-98	New York	4	4	132	56	20	56	.357	0	0	.000	16	27	.593	9	23	32	5	16	0	3	5	10	33.0	14.0	8.0	1.3	.330
98-99	New York	11	11	347	144	58	135	.430	0	0	.000	28	36	.778	14	82	96	6	35	0	7	8	10	31.5	13.1	8.7	0.5	.441
99-00	New York	14	14	461	204	71	170	.418	0	0	.000	62	89	.697	29	104	133	6	48	0	16	20	27	32.9	14.6	9.5	0.4	.468
01-02	Orlando	4	0	68	26	8	25	.320	0	1	.000	10	17	.588	5	17	22	4	12	0	1	4	2	17.0	6.5	5.5	1.0	.427
NBA Playoff Totals		139	135	5208	2813	1104	2353	.469	8	23	.348	597	831	.718	337	1098	1435	275	522	5	122	303	345	37.5	20.2	10.3	2.0	....

• EXEL, Ken

Ken Exel

Born: 1920.   Height: 6'1".   Weight: 178 lbs.   Drafted: —   College: Minnesota

YEAR	TEAM	GP	GS	MIN	PTS	FGM	FGA	FG%	3PM	3PA	3P%	FTM	FTA	FT%	ORB	DRB	TRB	AST	PF	DQ	STL	BLK	TO	MPG	PPG	RPG	APG	PCM
46-47	Oshkosh-N	17	....	....	29	10	....	....	....	....	....	9	24	.375	....	....	....	....	....	....	....	....	....	1.7	....	....	....
46-47	Syracuse-N	10	....	....	23	8	....	....	....	....	....	7	11	.636	....	....	....	....	....	....	....	....	....	2.3	....	....	....
47-48	Minneapolis-N	5	....	....	4	1	....	....	....	....	....	2	6	.333	....	....	....	....	....	....	....	....	....	0.8	....	....	....
NBL Season Totals		32	....	....	56	19	....	....	....	....	....	18	41	....	....	....	....	....	....	....	....	....	....	1.8	....	....	....
46-47	Syracuse-N	1	....	....	0	0	....	....	....	....	....	0	0	.000	....	....	....	....	....	....	....	....	....	0.0	....	....	....
NBL Playoff Totals		1	....	....	0	0	....	....	....	....	....	0	0	....	....	....	....	....	....	....	....	....	....	0.0	....	....	....

• EZERSKY, Johnny

John J. (Easy John) Ezersky

Born: 1921.   Height: 6'3".   Weight: 175 lbs.   Drafted: 1947   College: none

YEAR	TEAM	GP	GS	MIN	PTS	FGM	FGA	FG%	3PM	3PA	3P%	FTM	FTA	FT%	ORB	DRB	TRB	AST	PF	DQ	STL	BLK	TO	MPG	PPG	RPG	APG	PCM
47-48	Tri-Cities-N	5	....	....	23	9	....	....	....	....	....	5	8	.625	....	....	....	....	....	....	....	....	....	4.6	....	....	....
47-48	Providence	25	....	....	253	95	376	.253	....	....	....	63	104	.606	....	....	16	62	....	....	....	....	....	10.1	....	0.6	....
48-49	Providence	11	....	....	53	16	73	.219	....	....	....	21	25	.840	....	....	11	13	....	....	....	....	....	4.8	....	1.0	....
48-49	Baltimore	27	....	....	127	44	149	.295	....	....	....	39	55	.709	....	....	27	36	....	....	....	....	....	4.7	....	1.0	....
48-49	Boston	18	....	....	185	68	185	.368	....	....	....	49	80	.613	....	....	29	49	....	....	....	....	....	10.3	....	1.6	....
49-50	Boston	16	....	....	107	36	136	.265	....	....	....	35	51	.686	....	....	22	39	....	....	....	....	....	6.7	....	1.4	....
49-50	Baltimore	38	....	....	306	107	351	.305	....	....	....	92	132	.697	....	....	64	100	....	....	....	....	....	8.1	....	1.7	....
NBA Season Totals		135	....	....	1031	366	1270	.288	....	....	....	299	447	.669	....	....	169	299	....	....	....	....	....	7.6	....	1.3	....
NBL Season Totals		5	....	....	23	9	....	....	....	....	....	5	8	....	....	....	....	....	....	....	....	....	....	4.6	....	....	....
Career Totals		140	....	....	1054	375	1270	....	....	....	....	304	455	....	....	....	169	299	....	....	....	....	....	7.5	....	1.2	....

• FABEL, Joe

Joseph Fabel

Born: Sept. 4, 1913. Died: Jan.1967.   Height: 6'1".   Weight: 190 lbs.   Drafted: —   College: Pittsburgh

YEAR	TEAM	GP	GS	MIN	PTS	FGM	FGA	FG%	3PM	3PA	3P%	FTM	FTA	FT%	ORB	DRB	TRB	AST	PF	DQ	STL	BLK	TO	MPG	PPG	RPG	APG	PCM
38-39	Pittsburgh-N	1	....	....	6	3	....	....	....	....	....	0	....	....	....	....	....	....	....	....	....	....	....	6.0	....	....	....
46-47	Pittsburgh	30	....	....	63	25	96	.260	....	....	....	13	26	.500	....	....	....	2	64	....	....	....	....	2.1	....	0.1	....
NBA Season Totals		30	....	....	63	25	96	.260	....	....	....	13	26	.500	....	....	....	2	64	....	....	....	....	2.1	....	0.1	....
NBL Season Totals		1	....	....	6	3	....	....	....	....	....	0	....	....	....	....	....	....	....	....	....	....	....	6.0	....	....	....
Career Totals		31	....	....	69	28	96	....	....	....	....	13	26	....	....	....	....	2	64	....	....	....	....	2.2	....	0.1	....

• FAIRCHILD, John

John Russell Fairchild

Born: Apr. 28, 1943. Encinitas, CA, United States.   Height: 6'8".   Weight: 205 lbs.   Drafted: 1965   College: Brigham Young

YEAR	TEAM	GP	GS	MIN	PTS	FGM	FGA	FG%	3PM	3PA	3P%	FTM	FTA	FT%	ORB	DRB	TRB	AST	PF	DQ	STL	BLK	TO	MPG	PPG	RPG	APG	PCM
65-66	LA Lakers	30	....	171	60	23	89	.258	....	....	....	14	20	.700	....	....	45	11	33	0	....	....	....	5.7	2.0	1.5	0.4	.243
67-68	Anaheim-A	62	....	1311	678	271	620	.437	1	4	.250	135	200	.675	....	....	332	63	155	0	....	....	103	21.1	10.9	5.4	1.0	.493
68-69	Denver-A	11	....	135	40	12	34	.353	0	0	.000	16	24	.667	7	11	18	9	8	1	....	....	15	12.3	3.6	1.6	0.8	.296
68-69	Indiana-A	52	....	582	285	101	260	.388	10	29	.345	73	103	.709	42	69	111	28	90	0	....	....	59	11.2	5.5	2.1	0.5	.385
69-70	Indiana-A	3	....	26	3	1	6	.167	0	0	.000	1	2	.500	1	8	9	2	8	0	....	....	1	8.7	1.0	3.0	0.7	.187
69-70	Kentucky-A	7	....	52	19	6	17	.353	3	5	.600	4	8	.500	5	3	8	2	10	0	....	....	7	7.4	2.7	1.1	0.3	.244
NBA Season Totals		30	....	171	60	23	89	.258	....	....	....	14	20	.700	....	....	45	11	33	0	....	....	....	5.7	2.0	1.5	0.4	....
ABA Season Totals		135	....	2106	1025	391	937	.417	14	38	.368	229	337	.680	55	91	478	104	271	1	....	....	185	15.6	7.6	3.5	0.8	....
Career Totals		165	....	2277	1085	414	1026	.404	14	38	.368	243	357	.681	55	91	523	115	304	1	....	....	185	13.8	6.6	3.2	0.7	....
68-69	Indiana-A	9	....	85	46	19	44	.432	4	10	.400	4	6	.667	....	....	21	3	13	0	....	....	4	9.4	5.1	2.3	0.3	.465
ABA Playoff Totals		9	....	85	46	19	44	.432	4	10	.400	4	6	.667	....	....	21	3	13	0	....	....	4	9.4	5.1	2.3	0.3	....

• FALDA, Teddy

Teddy Falda

Born: 1920   Height: 6'   Weight: 180 lbs.   Drafted: —   College: Indiana State

YEAR	TEAM	GP	GS	MIN	PTS	FGM	FGA	FG%	3PM	3PA	3P%	FTM	FTA	FT%	ORB	DRB	TRB	AST	PF	DQ	STL	BLK	TO	MPG	PPG	RPG	APG	PCM
40-41	Hammond-N	3	....	....	2	1	....	....	....	....	....	0	....	....	....	....	....	....	....	....	....	....	....	0.7	....	....	....
NBL Season Totals		3	....	....	2	1	....	....	....	....	....	0	....	....	....	....	....	....	....	....	....	....	....	0.7	....	....	....

• FARBMAN, Phil

Philip M. Farbman

Born: Apr. 3, 1924.   Height: 6'1".   Weight: 185 lbs.   Drafted: —   College: CCNY

YEAR	TEAM	GP	GS	MIN	PTS	FGM	FGA	FG%	3PM	3PA	3P%	FTM	FTA	FT%	ORB	DRB	TRB	AST	PF	DQ	STL	BLK	TO	MPG	PPG	RPG	APG	PCM
48-49	Philadelphia	27	....	....	83	29	85	.341	....	....	....	25	43	.581	....	....	....	18	50	....	....	....	....	3.1	....	0.7	....
48-49	Boston	21	....	....	72	21	78	.269	....	....	....	30	38	.789	....	....	....	18	36	....	....	....	....	3.4	....	0.9	....
NBA Season Totals		48	....	....	155	50	163	.307	....	....	....	55	81	.679	....	....	....	36	86	....	....	....	....	3.2	....	0.8	....

YEAR	TEAM	GP	GS	MIN	PTS	FGM	FGA	FG%	3PM	3PA	3P%	FTM	FTA	FT%	ORB	DRB	TRB	AST	PF	DQ	STL	BLK	TO	MPG	PPG	RPG	APG	PCM

• FARLEY, Dick
Richard L. Farley

Born: Apr. 13, 1932. Died: Oct.1, 1969. Height: 6'4". Weight: 190 lbs. Drafted: 1954　College: Indiana

YEAR	TEAM	GP	GS	MIN	PTS	FGM	FGA	FG%	3PM	3PA	3P%	FTM	FTA	FT%	ORB	DRB	TRB	AST	PF	DQ	STL	BLK	TO	MPG	PPG	RPG	APG	PCM
54-55	Syracuse	69	....	1113	408	136	353	.385	....	....	....	136	201	.677	....	....	167	111	145	1	....	....	....	16.1	5.9	2.4	1.6	.386
55-56	Syracuse	72	....	1429	479	168	451	.373	....	....	....	143	207	.691	....	....	165	151	154	2	....	....	....	19.8	6.7	2.3	2.1	.345
58-59	Detroit	70	....	1280	491	177	448	.395	....	....	....	137	186	.737	....	....	195	124	130	2	....	....	....	18.3	7.0	2.8	1.8	.407
NBA Season Totals		211	....	3822	1378	481	1252	.384	....	....	....	416	594	.700	....	....	527	386	429	5	....	....	....	18.1	6.5	2.5	1.8	
54-55	Syracuse	11	....	168	52	19	56	.339	....	....	....	14	25	.560	....	....	13	20	29	0	....	....	....	15.3	4.7	1.2	1.8	.261
55-56	Syracuse	8	....	169	87	34	72	.472	....	....	....	19	31	.613	....	....	21	28	31	2	....	....	....	21.1	10.9	2.6	3.5	.547
58-59	Detroit	3	....	33	11	5	12	.417	....	....	....	1	1	1.000	....	....	6	3	6	0	....	....	....	11.0	3.7	2.0	1.0	.356
NBA Playoff Totals		22	....	370	150	58	140	.414	....	....	....	34	57	.596	....	....	40	51	66	2	....	....	....	16.8	6.8	1.8	2.3	

• FARMER, Jim
James Hubert Farmer III

Born: Sept. 23, 1964. Dothan, AL, United States. Height: 6'4". Weight: 190 lbs. Drafted: 1987　College: Alabama

YEAR	TEAM	GP	GS	MIN	PTS	FGM	FGA	FG%	3PM	3PA	3P%	FTM	FTA	FT%	ORB	DRB	TRB	AST	PF	DQ	STL	BLK	TO	MPG	PPG	RPG	APG	PCM
87-88	Dallas	30	0	157	61	26	69	.377	0	6	.000	9	10	.900	9	9	18	16	18	0	3	1	21	5.2	2.0	0.6	0.5	.192
88-89	Utah	37	0	412	152	57	142	.401	9	20	.450	29	41	.707	22	33	55	28	41	0	9	0	26	11.1	4.1	1.5	0.8	.276
89-90	Seattle	38	0	400	243	89	203	.438	8	27	.296	57	80	.713	17	26	43	25	44	0	17	1	27	10.5	6.4	1.1	0.7	.408
90-91	Philadelphia	2	0	13	6	2	7	.286	0	1	.000	2	2	1.000	2	3	5	0	0	0	0	0	1	6.5	3.0	2.5	0.0	.390
90-91	Denver	25	1	443	249	99	216	.458	5	22	.227	46	63	.730	27	36	63	38	58	0	13	2	38	17.7	10.0	2.5	1.5	.412
93-94	Denver	4	0	29	4	2	6	.333	0	2	.000	0	0	.000	0	2	2	4	3	0	0	0	5	7.3	1.0	0.5	1.0	.019
NBA Season Totals		136	1	1454	715	275	643	.428	22	78	.282	143	196	.730	77	109	186	111	164	0	42	4	118	10.7	5.3	1.4	0.8	....
87-88	Dallas	3	0	11	4	2	6	.333	0	0	.000	0	0	.000	3	1	4	1	2	0	0	0	2	3.7	1.3	1.3	0.3	.207
88-89	Utah	2	0	3	0	0	2	.000	0	1	.000	0	0	.000	0	0	0	0	0	0	0	0	0	1.5	0.0	0.0	0.0	-.620
NBA Playoff Totals		5	0	14	4	2	8	.250	0	1	.000	0	0	.000	3	1	4	1	2	0	0	0	2	2.8	0.8	0.8	0.2	....

• FARMER, Mike
Don Michael Farmer

Born: Sept. 26, 1936. Oklahoma City, OK, United States. Height: 6'7". Weight: 210 lbs. Drafted: 1958　College: San Francisco

YEAR	TEAM	GP	GS	MIN	PTS	FGM	FGA	FG%	3PM	3PA	3P%	FTM	FTA	FT%	ORB	DRB	TRB	AST	PF	DQ	STL	BLK	TO	MPG	PPG	RPG	APG	PCM
58-59	New York	72	....	1545	435	176	498	.353	....	....	....	83	99	.838	....	....	315	66	152	1	....	....	....	21.5	6.0	4.4	0.9	.291
59-60	New York	67	....	1536	494	212	568	.373	....	....	....	70	83	.843	....	....	385	57	130	1	....	....	....	22.9	7.4	5.7	0.9	.347
60-61	New York	2	....	6	0	0	1	.000	....	....	....	0	0	.000	....	....	2	0	2	0	....	....	....	3.0	0.0	1.0	0.0	.000
60-61	Cincinnati	57	....	1295	429	180	460	.391	....	....	....	69	94	.734	....	....	378	81	128	1	....	....	....	22.7	7.5	6.6	1.4	.421
62-63	St. Louis	80	....	1724	595	239	562	.425	....	....	....	117	139	.842	....	....	369	143	155	0	....	....	....	21.6	7.4	4.6	1.8	.426
63-64	St. Louis	76	....	1361	424	178	438	.406	....	....	....	68	83	.819	....	....	225	109	140	0	....	....	....	17.9	5.6	3.0	1.4	.345
64-65	St. Louis	60	....	1272	409	167	408	.409	....	....	....	75	94	.798	....	....	258	88	123	0	....	....	....	21.2	6.8	4.3	1.5	.374
65-66	St. Louis	9	....	79	30	13	30	.433	....	....	....	4	5	.800	....	....	18	6	10	0	....	....	....	8.8	3.3	2.0	0.7	.427
NBA Season Totals		423	....	8818	2816	1165	2965	.393	....	....	....	486	597	.814	....	....	1950	550	840	3	....	....	....	20.8	6.7	4.6	1.3	....
58-59	New York	2	....	34	12	5	17	.294	....	....	....	2	5	.400	....	....	10	0	7	0	....	....	....	17.0	6.0	5.0	0.0	.198
62-63	St. Louis	11	....	262	67	27	74	.365	....	....	....	13	17	.765	....	....	52	27	27	0	....	....	....	23.8	6.1	4.7	2.5	.349
63-64	St. Louis	11	....	119	46	19	34	.559	....	....	....	8	10	.800	....	....	16	9	10	0	....	....	....	10.8	4.2	1.5	0.8	.446
64-65	St. Louis	1	....	7	4	2	4	.500	....	....	....	0	0	.000	....	....	1	0	1	0	....	....	....	7.0	4.0	1.0	0.0	.407
NBA Playoff Totals		25	....	422	129	53	129	.411	....	....	....	23	32	.719	....	....	79	36	45	0	....	....	....	16.9	5.2	3.2	1.4	....

• FARMER, Tony
Anthony Todd Farmer

Born: Jan. 3, 1970. Los Angeles, CA, United States. Height: 6'9". Weight: 244 lbs. Drafted: —　College: Nebraska

YEAR	TEAM	GP	GS	MIN	PTS	FGM	FGA	FG%	3PM	3PA	3P%	FTM	FTA	FT%	ORB	DRB	TRB	AST	PF	DQ	STL	BLK	TO	MPG	PPG	RPG	APG	PCM
97-98	Charlotte	27	2	169	67	17	53	.321	2	9	.222	31	39	.795	16	16	32	5	23	0	10	4	8	6.3	2.5	1.2	0.2	.355
99-00	Golden State	74	9	1199	465	127	312	.407	8	44	.182	203	265	.766	118	177	295	74	167	1	66	16	82	16.2	6.3	4.0	1.0	.452
NBA Season Totals		101	11	1368	532	144	365	.395	10	53	.189	234	304	.770	134	193	327	79	190	1	76	20	90	13.5	5.3	3.2	0.8	....

• FARROW, Bill
Bill Farrow

Born: 1918. Height: 6'4". Weight: 198 lbs. Drafted: —　College: Kentucky State

YEAR	TEAM	GP	GS	MIN	PTS	FGM	FGA	FG%	3PM	3PA	3P%	FTM	FTA	FT%	ORB	DRB	TRB	AST	PF	DQ	STL	BLK	TO	MPG	PPG	RPG	APG	PCM
46-47	Youngstown-N	32	....	....	182	65	....	....	....	....	....	52	106	.491	....	....	....	135	....	....	....	....	....	....	5.7	....	....	....
48-49	Dayton-N	3	....	....	5	1	....	....	....	....	....	3	3	1.000	....	....	....	....	....	....	....	....	....	....	1.7	....	....	....
NBL Season Totals		35	....	....	187	66	....	....	....	....	....	55	109	....	....	....	....	135	....	....	....	....	....	....	5.3	....	....	....

• FAUGHT, Bob
Robert Edward Faught

Born: Sept. 2, 1921. Height: 6'5". Weight: 185 lbs. Drafted: —　College: Notre Dame

YEAR	TEAM	GP	GS	MIN	PTS	FGM	FGA	FG%	3PM	3PA	3P%	FTM	FTA	FT%	ORB	DRB	TRB	AST	PF	DQ	STL	BLK	TO	MPG	PPG	RPG	APG	PCM
46-47	Cleveland	51	....	....	343	141	478	.295	....	....	....	61	106	.575	....	....	33		97	....	....	....	....	6.7	....	0.6	....	
NBA Season Totals		51	....	....	343	141	478	.295	....	....	....	61	106	.575	....	....	33		97	....	....	....	....	6.7	....	0.6	....	
46-47	Cleveland	3	....	....	25	11	32	.344	....	....	....	3	3	1.000	....	....	1		10	....	....	....	....	8.3	....	0.3	....	
NBA Playoff Totals		3	....	....	25	11	32	.344	....	....	....	3	3	1.000	....	....	1		10	....	....	....	....	8.3	....	0.3	....	

• FECHTMAN, Fred
Fred Fechtman

Born: 1910. Height: 6'8". Weight: 210 lbs. Drafted: —　College: Indiana

YEAR	TEAM	GP	GS	MIN	PTS	FGM	FGA	FG%	3PM	3PA	3P%	FTM	FTA	FT%	ORB	DRB	TRB	AST	PF	DQ	STL	BLK	TO	MPG	PPG	RPG	APG	PCM
37-38	Indianapolis-N	3	....	....	9	4	....	....	....	....	....	1	....	....	....	....	....	....	....	....	....	....	....	....	3.0	....	....	....
NBL Season Totals		3	....	....	9	4	....	....	....	....	....	1	....	....	....	....	....	....	....	....	....	....	....	....	3.0	....	....	....

FEDOR, Dave

Samuel David Fedor

Born: Dec. 10, 1940. Height: 6'6". Weight: 190 lbs. Drafted: 1962 College: Florida State

YEAR TEAM	GP	GS	MIN	PTS	FGM	FGA	FG%	3PM	3PA	3P%	FTM	FTA	FT%	ORB	DRB	TRB	AST	PF	DQ	STL	BLK	TO	MPG	PPG	RPG	APG	PCM
62-63 San Francisco	7	....	27	6	3	10	.300	....	....	....	0	1	.000	....	....	6	1	4	0	....	....	....	3.9	0.9	0.9	0.1	.164
NBA Season Totals	7	....	27	6	3	10	.300	....	....	....	0	1	.000	....	....	6	1	4	0	....	....	....	3.9	0.9	0.9	0.1	....

FEERICK, Bob

Robert Joseph Feerick

Born: Jan. 2, 1920. San Francisco, CA, United States. Died: June 8, 1976. Height: 6'3". Weight: 190 lbs. Drafted: — College: Santa Clara

YEAR TEAM	GP	GS	MIN	PTS	FGM	FGA	FG%	3PM	3PA	3P%	FTM	FTA	FT%	ORB	DRB	TRB	AST	PF	DQ	STL	BLK	TO	MPG	PPG	RPG	APG	PCM
45-46 Oshkosh-N	21	....	....	198	81	....	....	....	....	....	36	44	.818	....	....	....	....	....	....	....	....	....	9.4	....	....	....	
46-47 Washington	55	....	....	926	364	908	**.401**	....	....	....	198	260	.762	....	....	....	69	142	....	....	....	....	16.8	....	1.3	....	
47-48 Washington	48	....	....	775	293	861	**.340**	....	....	....	189	240	**.788**	....	....	....	56	139	....	....	....	....	16.1	....	1.2	....	
48-49 Washington	58	....	....	752	248	708	.350	....	....	....	256	298	**.859**	....	....	....	188	171	....	....	....	....	13.0	....	3.2	....	
49-50 Washington	60	....	....	483	172	500	.344	....	....	....	139	174	.799	....	....	....	127	140	....	....	....	....	8.1	....	2.1	....	
NBA Season Totals	221	....	....	2936	1077	2977	.362	....	....	....	782	972	.805	....	....	....	440	592	....	....	....	....	13.3	....	2.0	....	
NBL Season Totals	21	....	....	198	81	....	....	....	....	....	36	44	....	....	....	....	....	....	....	....	....	....	9.4	....	....	....	
Career Totals	242	....	....	3134	1158	2977	....	....	....	....	818	1016	....	....	....	....	440	592	....	....	....	....	13.0	....	1.8	....	
45-46 Oshkosh-N	5	....	....	42	16	....	....	....	....	....	10	11	.909	....	....	....	....	....	....	....	....	....	8.4	....	....	....	
46-47 Washington	6	....	....	90	35	110	.318	....	....	....	20	27	.741	....	....	....	6	22	....	....	....	....	15.0	....	1.0	....	
48-49 Washington	1	....	....	2	0	0	.000	....	....	....	2	2	1.000	....	....	....	1	1	....	....	....	....	2.0	....	1.0	....	
49-50 Washington	2	....	....	9	3	12	.250	....	....	....	3	4	.750	....	....	....	6	10	....	....	....	....	4.5	....	3.0	....	
NBA Playoff Totals	9	....	....	101	38	122	.311	....	....	....	25	33	.758	....	....	....	13	33	....	....	....	....	11.2	....	1.4	....	
NBL Playoff Totals	5	....	....	42	16	....	....	....	....	....	10	11	....	....	....	....	....	....	....	....	....	....	8.4	....	....	....	
Career Playoff Totals	14	....	....	143	54	122	....	....	....	....	35	44	....	....	....	....	13	33	....	....	....	....	10.2	....	0.9	....	

FEHER, Butch

Raymond G. (Butch) Feher

Born: May 19, 1954. Flint, MI, United States. Height: 6'4". Weight: 185 lbs. Drafted: 1976 College: Vanderbilt

YEAR TEAM	GP	GS	MIN	PTS	FGM	FGA	FG%	3PM	3PA	3P%	FTM	FTA	FT%	ORB	DRB	TRB	AST	PF	DQ	STL	BLK	TO	MPG	PPG	RPG	APG	PCM
76-77 Phoenix	48	....	487	248	86	162	.531	....	....	....	76	99	.768	18	56	74	36	46	0	11	7	....	10.1	5.2	1.5	0.8	.529
NBA Season Totals	48	....	487	248	86	162	.531	....	....	....	76	99	.768	18	56	74	36	46	0	11	7	....	10.1	5.2	1.5	0.8	....

FEICK, Jamie

Jamie Feick

Born: July 3, 1974. Lexington, OH, United States. Height: 6'9". Weight: 255 lbs. Drafted: 1996 College: Michigan State

YEAR TEAM	GP	GS	MIN	PTS	FGM	FGA	FG%	3PM	3PA	3P%	FTM	FTA	FT%	ORB	DRB	TRB	AST	PF	DQ	STL	BLK	TO	MPG	PPG	RPG	APG	PCM
96-97 Charlotte	3	0	10	5	2	4	.500	1	1	1.000	0	2	.000	1	2	3	0	3	0	0	1	0	3.3	1.7	1.0	0.0	.453
96-97 San Antonio	38	0	614	146	54	153	.353	4	13	.308	34	65	.523	81	130	211	26	75	0	16	13	30	16.2	3.8	5.6	0.7	.371
97-98 Milwaukee	45	2	450	102	39	90	.433	4	13	.308	20	41	.488	45	79	124	16	67	0	25	17	23	10.0	2.3	2.8	0.4	.363
98-99 Milwaukee	2	0	3	0	0	1	.000	0	0	.000	0	0	.000	0	2	2	0	0	0	0	0	0	1.5	0.0	1.0	0.0	.296
98-99 New Jersey	26	16	849	177	67	133	.504	0	0	.000	43	60	.717	112	174	286	24	73	0	25	18	34	32.7	6.8	11.0	0.9	.433
99-00 New Jersey	81	17	2241	459	181	423	.428	3	3	1.000	94	133	.707	264	491	755	68	206	2	43	38	59	27.7	5.7	9.3	0.8	.405
00-01 New Jersey	6	0	149	22	8	23	.348	0	0	.000	6	12	.500	12	44	56	5	15	0	8	3	7	24.8	3.7	9.3	0.8	.393
NBA Season Totals	201	35	4316	911	351	827	.424	12	30	.400	197	313	.629	515	922	1437	139	439	2	117	90	153	21.5	4.5	7.1	0.7	....

FEIEREISEL, Ron

Ronald E. Feiereisel

Born: Aug. 6, 1931. Height: 6'3". Weight: 185 lbs. Drafted: 1953 College: DePaul

YEAR TEAM	GP	GS	MIN	PTS	FGM	FGA	FG%	3PM	3PA	3P%	FTM	FTA	FT%	ORB	DRB	TRB	AST	PF	DQ	STL	BLK	TO	MPG	PPG	RPG	APG	PCM
55-56 Minneapolis	10	....	59	30	8	28	.286	....	....	....	14	16	.875	....	....	6	6	9	0	....	....	....	5.9	3.0	0.6	0.6	.383
NBA Season Totals	10	....	59	30	8	28	.286	....	....	....	14	16	.875	....	....	6	6	9	0	....	....	....	5.9	3.0	0.6	0.6	....

FEIGENBAUM, George

George Feigenbaum

Born: July 2, 1929. Height: 6'1". Weight: 185 lbs. Drafted: — College: Kentucky

YEAR TEAM	GP	GS	MIN	PTS	FGM	FGA	FG%	3PM	3PA	3P%	FTM	FTA	FT%	ORB	DRB	TRB	AST	PF	DQ	STL	BLK	TO	MPG	PPG	RPG	APG	PCM
49-50 Baltimore	12	....	....	36	14	57	.246	....	....	....	8	18	.444	....	....	10	15	....	....	....	....	....	3.0	....	0.8	....	
52-53 Milwaukee	5	....	79	16	4	22	.182	....	....	....	8	15	.533	....	....	7	9	14	1	....	....	....	15.8	3.2	1.4	1.8	.151
NBA Season Totals	17	....	79	52	18	79	.228	....	....	....	16	33	.485	....	....	7	19	29	1	....	....	....	4.6	3.1	0.4	1.1	....

FEITL, Dave

Dave Scott Feitl

Born: June 8, 1962. Butler, PA, United States. Height: 6'11". Weight: 235 lbs. Drafted: 1986 College: Texas (El Paso)

YEAR TEAM	GP	GS	MIN	PTS	FGM	FGA	FG%	3PM	3PA	3P%	FTM	FTA	FT%	ORB	DRB	TRB	AST	PF	DQ	STL	BLK	TO	MPG	PPG	RPG	APG	PCM
86-87 Houston	62	1	498	229	88	202	.436	0	1	.000	53	71	.746	39	78	117	22	83	0	9	4	37	8.0	3.7	1.9	0.4	.373
87-88 Golden State	70	19	1128	458	182	404	.450	0	4	.000	94	134	.701	83	252	335	53	146	1	15	9	84	16.1	6.5	4.8	0.8	.423
88-89 Washington	57	36	828	286	116	266	.436	0	1	.000	54	65	.831	69	133	202	36	136	0	17	18	63	14.5	5.0	3.5	0.6	.336
90-91 Houston	52	2	372	137	52	140	.371	0	3	.000	33	44	.750	29	71	100	8	52	0	3	12	26	7.2	2.6	1.9	0.2	.315
91-92 New Jersey	34	0	175	82	33	77	.429	0	0	.000	16	19	.842	21	40	61	6	22	0	2	3	20	5.1	2.4	1.8	0.2	.450
NBA Season Totals	275	58	3001	1192	471	1089	.433	0	9	.000	250	333	.751	241	574	815	125	439	1	46	46	230	10.9	4.3	3.0	0.5	....
86-87 Houston	6	0	8	2	1	0	.000	0	0	.000	2	2	1.000	0	1	1	0	0	0	0	0	0	1.3	0.3	0.2	0.0	.366
91-92 New Jersey	1	0	3	2	1	2	.500	0	0	.000	0	0	.000	0	1	1	0	0	0	0	0	1	3.0	2.0	1.0	0.0	.357
NBA Playoff Totals	7	0	11	4	1	2	.500	0	0	.000	2	2	1.000	0	2	2	0	0	0	0	0	1	1.6	0.6	0.3	0.0	....

• FELIX, Ray
Raymond Darlington Felix

Born: Dec. 10, 1930. New York, NY, United States. Died: July28, 1991.   Height: 6'11".   Weight: 220 lbs.   Drafted: 1953   College: Long Island University

YEAR	TEAM	GP	GS	MIN	PTS	FGM	FGA	FG%	3PM	3PA	3P%	FTM	FTA	FT%	ORB	DRB	TRB	AST	PF	DQ	STL	BLK	TO	MPG	PPG	RPG	APG	PCM
53-54	Baltimore	72	....	2672	1269	410	983	.417	....	....	....	449	704	.638	....	....	958	82	253	5	....	....	....	37.1	17.6	13.3	1.1	.549
54-55	New York	72	....	2024	1038	364	832	.438	....	....	....	310	498	.622	....	....	818	67	286	11	....	....	....	28.1	14.4	11.4	0.9	.596
55-56	New York	72	....	1702	885	277	668	.415	....	....	....	331	469	.706	....	....	623	47	293	13	....	....	....	23.6	12.3	8.7	0.7	.562
56-57	New York	72	....	1622	867	295	709	.416	....	....	....	277	371	.747	....	....	587	36	284	8	....	....	....	22.5	12.0	8.2	0.5	.555
57-58	New York	72	....	1709	879	304	688	.442	....	....	....	271	389	.697	....	....	747	52	283	12	....	....	....	23.7	12.2	10.4	0.7	.622
58-59	New York	72	....	1588	749	260	700	.371	....	....	....	229	321	.713	....	....	569	49	275	9	....	....	....	22.1	10.4	7.9	0.7	.484
59-60	New York	16	....	187	81	31	94	.330	....	....	....	19	33	.576	....	....	80	4	44	0	....	....	....	11.7	5.1	5.0	0.3	.411
59-60	Minneapolis	31	....	696	261	105	261	.402	....	....	....	51	79	.646	....	....	258	29	133	5	....	....	....	22.5	8.4	8.3	0.9	.450
60-61	LA Lakers	78	....	1510	513	189	508	.372	....	....	....	135	193	.699	....	....	539	37	302	12	....	....	....	19.4	6.6	6.9	0.5	.390
61-62	LA Lakers	80	....	1478	432	171	398	.430	....	....	....	90	130	.692	....	....	473	55	266	6	....	....	....	18.5	5.4	5.9	0.7	.387
NBA Season Totals		637	....	15188	6974	2406	5841	.412	....	....	....	2162	3187	.678	....	....	5652	458	2419	81	....	....	....	23.8	10.9	8.9	0.7	....
54-55	New York	3	....	63	17	2	16	.125	....	....	....	13	21	.619	....	....	12	1	6	0	....	....	....	21.0	5.7	4.0	0.3	.182
58-59	New York	2	....	45	26	12	28	.429	....	....	....	2	4	.500	....	....	23	2	12	2	....	....	....	22.5	13.0	11.5	1.0	.633
59-60	Minneapolis	8	....	147	52	17	41	.415	....	....	....	18	25	.720	....	....	53	9	34	1	....	....	....	18.4	6.5	6.6	1.1	.474
60-61	LA Lakers	12	....	339	122	46	109	.422	....	....	....	30	39	.769	....	....	125	10	52	2	....	....	....	28.3	10.2	10.4	0.8	.467
61-62	LA Lakers	13	....	242	84	29	59	.492	....	....	....	26	38	.684	....	....	77	7	39	1	....	....	....	18.6	6.5	5.9	0.5	.452
NBA Playoff Totals		38	....	836	301	106	253	.419	....	....	....	89	127	.701	....	....	290	29	143	6	....	....	....	22.0	7.9	7.6	0.8	....

• FENDLEY, Jake
John Phillip Fendley

Born: June 12, 1929.   Height: 6'   Weight: 180 lbs.   Drafted: 1951   College: Northwestern

YEAR	TEAM	GP	GS	MIN	PTS	FGM	FGA	FG%	3PM	3PA	3P%	FTM	FTA	FT%	ORB	DRB	TRB	AST	PF	DQ	STL	BLK	TO	MPG	PPG	RPG	APG	PCM
51-52	Fort Wayne	58	....	651	183	54	170	.318	....	....	....	75	95	.789	....	....	80	58	118	3	....	....	....	11.2	3.2	1.4	1.0	.281
52-53	Fort Wayne	45	....	380	104	32	80	.400	....	....	....	40	60	.667	....	....	46	36	82	3	....	....	....	8.4	2.3	1.0	0.8	.294
NBA Season Totals		103	....	1031	287	86	250	.344	....	....	....	115	155	.742	....	....	126	94	200	6	....	....	....	10.0	2.8	1.2	0.9	....
51-52	Fort Wayne	1	....	4	2	1	4	.250	....	....	....	0	0	.000	....	....	1	1	2	0	....	....	....	4.0	2.0	1.0	1.0	.289
52-53	Fort Wayne	1	....	2	0	0	0	.000	....	....	....	0	0	.000	....	....	1	0	1	0	....	....	....	2.0	0.0	1.0	0.0	.181
NBA Playoff Totals		2	....	6	2	1	4	.250	....	....	....	0	0	.000	....	....	2	1	3	0	....	....	....	3.0	1.0	1.0	0.5	....

• FENLEY, Warren
William Warren Fenley

Born: Feb. 8, 1922.   Height: 6'3".   Weight: 190 lbs.   Drafted: —   College: Manhattan

YEAR	TEAM	GP	GS	MIN	PTS	FGM	FGA	FG%	3PM	3PA	3P%	FTM	FTA	FT%	ORB	DRB	TRB	AST	PF	DQ	STL	BLK	TO	MPG	PPG	RPG	APG	PCM
46-47	Boston	33	....	....	85	31	138	.225	....	....	....	23	45	.511	....	....	....	16	59	....	....	....	....	....	2.6	....	0.5	....
NBA Season Totals		33	....	....	85	31	138	.225	....	....	....	23	45	.511	....	....	....	16	59	....	....	....	....	....	2.6	....	0.5	....

• FERNSTEN, Eric
Eric Robert Fernsten

Born: Nov. 1, 1953. Oakland, CA, United States.   Height: 6'10".   Weight: 205 lbs.   Drafted: 1975   College: San Francisco

YEAR	TEAM	GP	GS	MIN	PTS	FGM	FGA	FG%	3PM	3PA	3P%	FTM	FTA	FT%	ORB	DRB	TRB	AST	PF	DQ	STL	BLK	TO	MPG	PPG	RPG	APG	PCM
75-76	Cleveland	4	....	9	0	0	2	.000	....	....	....	0	0	.000	0	1	1	0	1	0	0	0	....	2.3	0.0	0.3	0.0	-.143
75-76	Chicago	33	....	259	92	33	84	.393	....	....	....	26	37	.703	25	44	69	19	20	0	7	14	....	7.8	2.8	2.1	0.6	.447
76-77	Chicago	5	....	61	14	3	15	.200	....	....	....	8	11	.727	9	7	16	6	9	0	1	3	....	12.2	2.8	3.2	1.2	.313
79-80	Boston	56	....	431	175	71	153	.464	0	0	.000	33	52	.635	40	56	96	28	43	0	17	12	22	7.7	3.1	1.7	0.5	.456
80-81	Boston	45	....	279	96	38	79	.481	0	0	.000	20	30	.667	29	33	62	10	29	0	6	7	18	6.2	2.1	1.4	0.2	.372
81-82	Boston	43	0	202	57	19	49	.388	0	0	.000	19	30	.633	12	30	42	8	23	0	5	7	13	4.7	1.3	1.0	0.2	.298
83-84	New York	32	0	402	83	29	52	.558	0	0	.000	25	34	.735	29	57	86	11	49	0	16	8	19	12.6	2.6	2.7	0.3	.326
NBA Season Totals		218	0	1643	517	193	434	.445	0	0	.000	131	194	.675	144	228	372	82	174	0	52	51	72	7.5	2.4	1.7	0.4	....
79-80	Boston	5	....	18	6	2	6	.333	0	0	.000	2	3	.667	3	2	5	0	1	0	0	3	2	3.6	1.2	1.0	....	.384
80-81	Boston	8	....	14	2	0	3	.000	0	0	.000	2	3	.667	1	3	4	1	3	0	1	0	0	1.8	0.3	0.5	0.1	.221
81-82	Boston	5	....	11	3	1	2	.500	0	0	.000	1	2	.500	2	0	2	0	0	0	0	1	0	2.2	0.6	0.4	0.0	.398
83-84	New York	2	0	3	2	1	2	.500	0	0	.000	0	0	.000	0	0	0	0	0	0	0	0	0	1.5	1.0	0.0	0.0	.357
NBA Playoff Totals		20	0	46	13	4	13	.308	0	0	.000	5	8	.625	6	5	11	1	4	0	1	4	2	2.3	0.7	0.6	0.1	....

• FERRARI, Al
Albert R. Ferrari

Born: July 6, 1933. New York, NY, United States.   Height: 6'4".   Weight: 190 lbs.   Drafted: 1955   College: Michigan State

YEAR	TEAM	GP	GS	MIN	PTS	FGM	FGA	FG%	3PM	3PA	3P%	FTM	FTA	FT%	ORB	DRB	TRB	AST	PF	DQ	STL	BLK	TO	MPG	PPG	RPG	APG	PCM
55-56	St. Louis	68	....	1611	546	191	534	.358	....	....	....	164	236	.695	....	....	186	163	192	3	....	....	....	23.7	8.0	2.7	2.4	.328
58-59	St. Louis	72	....	1189	413	134	385	.348	....	....	....	145	199	.729	....	....	142	122	155	1	....	....	....	16.5	5.7	2.0	1.7	.340
59-60	St. Louis	71	....	1567	608	216	523	.413	....	....	....	176	225	.782	....	....	162	188	205	7	....	....	....	22.1	8.6	2.3	2.6	.406
60-61	St. Louis	63	....	1031	329	117	328	.357	....	....	....	95	116	.819	....	....	115	143	157	4	....	....	....	16.4	5.2	1.8	2.3	.354
61-62	St. Louis	79	....	2046	591	208	582	.357	....	....	....	175	219	.799	....	....	213	313	278	9	....	....	....	25.9	7.5	2.7	4.0	.352
62-63	Chicago	18	....	138	38	12	37	.324	....	....	....	14	17	.824	....	....	12	14	21	0	....	....	....	7.7	2.1	0.7	0.8	.255
NBA Season Totals		371	....	7582	2525	878	2389	.368	....	....	....	769	1012	.760	....	....	830	943	1008	24	....	....	....	20.4	6.8	2.2	2.5	....
55-56	St. Louis	8	....	264	118	32	85	.376	....	....	....	54	70	.771	....	....	33	24	28	0	....	....	....	33.0	14.8	4.1	3.0	.439
58-59	St. Louis	6	....	173	48	14	40	.350	....	....	....	20	25	.800	....	....	15	15	25	1	....	....	....	28.8	8.0	2.5	2.5	.273
59-60	St. Louis	9	....	142	40	15	38	.395	....	....	....	10	18	.556	....	....	9	15	13	0	....	....	....	15.8	4.4	1.0	1.7	.283
60-61	St. Louis	10	....	157	50	20	44	.455	....	....	....	10	17	.588	....	....	22	21	31	1	....	....	....	15.7	5.0	2.2	2.1	.382
NBA Playoff Totals		33	....	736	256	81	207	.391	....	....	....	94	130	.723	....	....	79	75	97	2	....	....	....	22.3	7.8	2.4	2.3	....

• FERREIRA, Rolando

Rolando Ferreira Jr.

Born: May 24, 1964. Curtiba, Brazil. Height: 7'1". Weight: 240 lbs. Drafted: 1988 College: Houston

YEAR TEAM	GP	GS	MIN	PTS	FGM	FGA	FG%	3PM	3PA	3P%	FTM	FTA	FT%	ORB	DRB	TRB	AST	PF	DQ	STL	BLK	TO	MPG	PPG	RPG	APG	PCM
88-89 Portland	12	0	34	9	1	18	.056	0	0	.000	7	8	.875	4	9	13	1	7	0	0	1	6	2.8	0.8	1.1	0.1	-.059
NBA Season Totals	12	0	34	9	1	18	.056	0	0	.000	7	8	.875	4	9	13	1	7	0	0	1	6	2.8	0.8	1.1	0.1	....

• FERRELL, Duane

Duane Ferrell

Born: Feb. 28, 1965. Baltimore, MD, United States. Height: 6'7". Weight: 209 lbs. Drafted: — College: Georgia Tech

YEAR TEAM	GP	GS	MIN	PTS	FGM	FGA	FG%	3PM	3PA	3P%	FTM	FTA	FT%	ORB	DRB	TRB	AST	PF	DQ	STL	BLK	TO	MPG	PPG	RPG	APG	PCM
88-89 Atlanta	41	0	231	100	35	83	.422	0	0	.000	30	44	.682	19	22	41	10	33	0	7	6	12	5.6	2.4	1.0	0.2	.360
89-90 Atlanta	14	0	29	12	5	14	.357	0	1	.000	2	6	.333	3	4	7	2	3	0	1	0	1	2.1	0.9	0.5	0.1	.309
90-91 Atlanta	78	2	1165	475	174	356	.489	2	3	.667	125	156	.801	97	82	179	55	151	3	33	27	78	14.9	6.1	2.3	0.7	.368
91-92 Atlanta	66	12	1598	839	331	632	.524	11	33	.333	166	218	.761	105	105	210	92	134	0	49	17	99	24.2	12.7	3.2	1.4	.461
92-93 Atlanta	82	15	1736	839	327	696	.470	9	36	.250	176	226	.779	97	94	191	132	160	1	59	17	107	21.2	10.2	2.3	1.6	.396
93-94 Atlanta	72	13	1155	513	184	379	.485	1	9	.111	144	184	.783	62	67	129	65	85	0	44	16	65	16.0	7.1	1.8	0.9	.399
94-95 Indiana	56	1	607	231	83	173	.480	1	6	.167	64	85	.753	50	38	88	31	79	0	26	6	45	10.8	4.1	1.6	0.6	.334
95-96 Indiana	54	6	591	202	80	166	.482	0	8	.000	42	57	.737	32	61	93	30	83	0	23	3	32	10.9	3.7	1.7	0.6	.319
96-97 Indiana	62	18	1115	394	159	337	.472	18	44	.409	58	94	.617	57	84	141	66	120	0	38	6	56	18.0	6.4	2.3	1.1	.310
97-98 Golden State	50	5	461	94	41	111	.369	0	6	.000	12	22	.545	25	22	47	26	50	0	21	6	20	9.2	1.9	0.9	0.5	.174
98-99 Golden State	8	0	46	5	1	14	.071	0	0	.000	3	4	.750	5	1	6	0	4	0	1	1	1	5.8	0.6	0.8	0.0	-.056
NBA Season Totals	583	72	8734	3704	1420	2961	.480	42	146	.288	822	1096	.750	552	580	1132	509	902	4	302	105	516	15.0	6.4	1.9	0.9	....
90-91 Atlanta	5	0	73	24	8	18	.444	0	0	.000	8	12	.667	6	11	17	3	10	0	0	0	2	14.6	4.8	3.4	0.6	.347
92-93 Atlanta	3	0	54	33	14	23	.609	1	3	.333	4	5	.800	1	4	5	1	6	0	0	0	4	18.0	11.0	1.7	0.3	.432
93-94 Atlanta	11	0	187	78	25	63	.397	1	4	.250	27	36	.750	22	9	31	17	24	0	5	3	5	17.0	7.1	2.8	1.5	.415
94-95 Indiana	10	0	85	27	8	24	.333	1	2	.500	10	16	.625	8	3	11	13	10	0	0	2	10	8.5	2.7	1.1	1.3	.248
95-96 Indiana	5	0	69	18	7	19	.368	0	0	.000	4	8	.500	6	3	9	3	10	0	4	0	4	13.8	3.6	1.8	0.6	.171
NBA Playoff Totals	34	0	468	180	62	147	.422	3	9	.333	53	77	.688	43	30	73	37	60	0	9	5	25	13.8	5.3	2.1	1.1	....

• FERRIN, Arnie

C. Arnold Ferrin Jr.

Born: July 29, 1925. Salt Lake City, UT, United States. Height: 6'2". Weight: 180 lbs. Drafted: 1948 College: Utah

YEAR TEAM	GP	GS	MIN	PTS	FGM	FGA	FG%	3PM	3PA	3P%	FTM	FTA	FT%	ORB	DRB	TRB	AST	PF	DQ	STL	BLK	TO	MPG	PPG	RPG	APG	PCM
48-49 Minneapolis	47	....	....	345	130	378	.344	....	....	....	85	128	.664	....	....	....	76	142	....	....	....	....	....	7.3	....	1.6	....
49-50 Minneapolis	63	....	....	340	132	396	.333	....	....	....	76	109	.697	....	....	....	95	147	....	....	....	....	....	5.4	....	1.5	....
50-51 Minneapolis	68	....	....	352	119	373	.319	....	....	....	114	164	.695	....	....	271	107	220	8	....	....	....	....	5.2	4.0	1.6	....
NBA Season Totals	178	....	....	1037	381	1147	.332	....	....	....	275	401	.686	....	....	271	278	509	8	....	....	....	....	5.8	1.5	1.6	....
48-49 Minneapolis	10	....	....	82	26	77	.338	....	....	....	30	45	.667	....	....	....	21	41	....	....	....	....	....	8.2	....	2.1	....
49-50 Minneapolis	12	....	....	82	33	97	.340	....	....	....	16	29	.552	....	....	....	30	51	....	....	....	....	....	6.8	....	2.5	....
50-51 Minneapolis	7	....	....	41	12	36	.333	....	....	....	17	18	.944	....	....	33	16	21	1	....	....	....	....	5.9	4.7	2.3	....
NBA Playoff Totals	29	....	....	205	71	210	.338	....	....	....	63	92	.685	....	....	33	67	113	1	....	....	....	....	7.1	1.1	2.3	....

• FERRY, Bob

Robert Dean Ferry

Born: May 31, 1937. St. Louis, MO, United States. Height: 6'8". Weight: 230 lbs. Drafted: 1959 College: St. Louis

YEAR TEAM	GP	GS	MIN	PTS	FGM	FGA	FG%	3PM	3PA	3P%	FTM	FTA	FT%	ORB	DRB	TRB	AST	PF	DQ	STL	BLK	TO	MPG	PPG	RPG	APG	PCM
59-60 St. Louis	62	....	875	364	144	338	.426	....	....	....	76	119	.639	....	....	233	40	132	2	....	....	....	14.1	5.9	3.8	0.6	.431
60-61 Detroit	79	....	1657	889	350	776	.451	....	....	....	189	255	.741	....	....	500	129	205	1	....	....	....	21.0	11.3	6.3	1.6	.605
61-62 Detroit	80	....	1918	1108	411	939	.438	....	....	....	286	422	.678	....	....	503	145	199	2	....	....	....	24.0	13.9	6.3	1.8	.591
62-63 Detroit	79	....	2479	1072	426	984	.433	....	....	....	220	339	.649	....	....	537	170	246	1	....	....	....	31.4	13.6	6.8	2.2	.450
63-64 Detroit	74	....	1522	782	298	670	.445	....	....	....	186	279	.667	....	....	428	94	174	2	....	....	....	20.6	10.6	5.8	1.3	.550
64-65 Baltimore	77	....	1280	408	143	338	.423	....	....	....	122	199	.613	....	....	355	60	156	2	....	....	....	16.6	5.3	4.6	0.8	.403
65-66 Baltimore	66	....	1229	481	188	457	.411	....	....	....	105	157	.669	....	....	334	111	134	1	....	....	....	18.6	7.3	5.1	1.7	.483
66-67 Baltimore	51	....	991	334	132	315	.419	....	....	....	70	110	.636	....	....	258	92	97	0	....	....	....	19.4	6.5	5.1	1.8	.454
67-68 Baltimore	59	....	841	329	128	311	.412	....	....	....	73	117	.624	....	....	186	61	92	0	....	....	....	14.3	5.6	3.2	1.0	.417
68-69 Baltimore	7	....	36	13	5	14	.357	....	....	....	3	6	.500	....	....	9	4	3	0	....	....	....	5.1	1.9	1.3	0.6	.421
NBA Season Totals	634	....	12828	5780	2225	5142	.433	....	....	....	1330	2003	.664	....	....	3343	906	1438	11	....	....	....	20.2	9.1	5.3	1.4	....
59-60 St. Louis	11	....	56	24	10	19	.526	....	....	....	4	7	.571	....	....	15	0	10	0	....	....	....	5.1	2.2	1.4	0.0	.422
60-61 Detroit	5	....	167	101	30	74	.405	....	....	....	41	49	.837	....	....	63	11	12	0	....	....	....	33.4	20.2	12.6	2.2	.727
61-62 Detroit	9	....	156	100	37	81	.457	....	....	....	26	43	.605	....	....	41	13	20	0	....	....	....	17.3	11.1	4.6	1.4	.635
62-63 Detroit	4	....	143	48	20	45	.444	....	....	....	8	24	.333	....	....	35	11	10	0	....	....	....	35.8	12.0	8.8	2.8	.412
64-65 Baltimore	10	....	67	16	7	16	.438	....	....	....	2	9	.222	....	....	19	8	8	0	....	....	....	6.7	1.6	1.9	0.8	.415
65-66 Baltimore	3	....	82	31	11	20	.550	....	....	....	9	13	.692	....	....	25	3	10	0	....	....	....	27.3	10.3	8.3	1.0	.509
NBA Playoff Totals	42	....	671	320	115	255	.451	....	....	....	90	145	.621	....	....	198	46	70	0	....	....	....	16.0	7.6	4.7	1.1	....

• FERRY, Danny

Daniel John Willard Ferry

Born: Oct. 17, 1966. Hyattsville, MD, United States. Height: 6'10". Weight: 230 lbs. Drafted: 1989 College: Duke

YEAR TEAM	GP	GS	MIN	PTS	FGM	FGA	FG%	3PM	3PA	3P%	FTM	FTA	FT%	ORB	DRB	TRB	AST	PF	DQ	STL	BLK	TO	MPG	PPG	RPG	APG	PCM
90-91 Cleveland	81	2	1661	697	275	643	.428	23	77	.299	124	152	.816	99	187	286	142	230	1	43	25	122	20.5	8.6	3.5	1.8	.362
91-92 Cleveland	68	1	937	346	134	328	.409	17	48	.354	61	73	.836	53	160	213	75	135	0	22	15	48	13.8	5.1	3.1	1.1	.390
92-93 Cleveland	76	1	1461	573	220	459	.479	34	82	.415	99	113	.876	81	198	279	137	171	1	29	48	84	19.2	7.5	3.7	1.8	.454
93-94 Cleveland	70	1	965	350	149	334	.446	14	51	.275	38	43	.884	47	94	141	74	113	0	28	22	42	13.8	5.0	2.0	1.1	.355
94-95 Cleveland	82	6	1290	614	223	500	.446	94	233	.403	74	84	.881	30	113	143	96	131	0	27	22	57	15.7	7.5	1.7	1.2	.400
95-96 Cleveland	82	79	2680	1090	422	919	.459	143	363	.394	103	134	.769	71	238	309	191	233	3	57	37	123	32.7	13.3	3.8	2.3	.360
96-97 Cleveland	82	48	2633	870	341	794	.429	114	284	.401	74	87	.851	82	255	337	151	245	1	56	32	90	32.1	10.6	4.1	1.8	.304
97-98 Cleveland	69	3	1034	291	113	286	.395	33	99	.333	32	40	.800	23	91	114	59	118	0	26	17	55	15.0	4.2	1.7	0.9	.225
98-99 Cleveland	50	10	1058	349	141	296	.476	38	97	.392	29	33	.879	16	86	102	53	113	0	23	10	39	21.2	7.0	2.0	1.1	.287
99-00 Cleveland	63	3	1326	463	189	380	.497	33	75	.440	52	57	.912	55	183	238	67	181	1	22	24	55	21.0	7.3	3.8	1.1	.367
00-01 San Antonio	80	29	1688	448	178	375	.475	70	156	.449	22	30	.733	55	168	223	71	169	1	28	21	50	21.1	5.6	2.8	0.9	.278

YEAR	TEAM	GP	GS	MIN	PTS	FGM	FGA	FG%	3PM	3PA	3P%	FTM	FTA	FT%	ORB	DRB	TRB	AST	PF	DQ	STL	BLK	TO	MPG	PPG	RPG	APG	PCM
01-02	San Antonio	50	2	797	229	76	177	.429	43	99	.434	34	36	.944	15	75	90	48	70	0	16	9	22	15.9	4.6	1.8	1.0	.303
02-03	San Antonio	64	1	600	119	44	124	.355	21	60	.350	10	13	.769	20	55	75	21	55	0	7	9	27	9.4	1.9	1.2	0.3	.168
NBA Season Totals		917	186	18130	6439	2505	5615	.446	677	1724	.393	752	895	.840	647	1903	2550	1185	1964	8	384	291	814	19.8	7.0	2.8	1.3	
91-92	Cleveland	9	0	55	19	7	15	.467	1	3	.333	4	4	1.000	7	9	16	1	7	0	1	1	2	6.1	2.1	1.8	0.1	.441
92-93	Cleveland	8	0	118	39	13	34	.382	4	9	.444	9	10	.900	4	21	25	14	14	0	4	3	7	14.8	4.9	3.1	1.8	.429
93-94	Cleveland	1	0	4	0	0	0	.000	0	0	.000	0	0	.000	0	0	0	1	1	0	0	0	1	4.0	0.0	0.0	1.0	-.073
94-95	Cleveland	4	0	67	38	13	25	.520	8	15	.533	4	6	.667	0	3	3	6	9	0	2	0	0	16.8	9.5	0.8	1.5	.487
95-96	Cleveland	3	3	117	29	14	41	.341	1	16	.063	0	0	.000	1	14	15	9	13	1	3	2	4	39.0	9.7	5.0	3.0	.189
97-98	Cleveland	3	0	10	0	0	2	.000	0	2	.000	0	0	.000	0	1	1	0	1	0	0	0	0	3.3	0.0	0.3	0.0	-.137
00-01	San Antonio	13	11	334	75	27	68	.397	21	46	.457	0	0	.000	8	33	41	17	32	0	4	1	6	25.7	5.8	3.2	1.3	.235
01-02	San Antonio	10	0	155	28	10	33	.303	7	20	.350	1	4	.250	5	15	20	8	19	0	1	1	2	15.5	2.8	2.0	0.8	.149
02-03	San Antonio	16	1	101	20	8	28	.286	4	14	.286	0	0	.000	3	20	23	7	20	0	2	0	5	6.3	1.3	1.4	0.4	.184
NBA Playoff Totals		67	15	961	248	92	246	.374	46	125	.368	18	24	.750	28	116	144	63	116	1	16	8	27	14.3	3.7	2.1	0.9	....

• FIELDS, Bobby
Robert L. Fields

Born: Oct. 20, 1949.   Height: 6'3".   Weight: 175 lbs.   Drafted: 1971   College: LaSalle

YEAR	TEAM	GP	GS	MIN	PTS	FGM	FGA	FG%	3PM	3PA	3P%	FTM	FTA	FT%	ORB	DRB	TRB	AST	PF	DQ	STL	BLK	TO	MPG	PPG	RPG	APG	PCM
71-72	Utah-A	22	....	124	54	22	48	.458	2	7	.286	8	13	.615	16	14	30	20	33	0	....	....	21	5.6	2.5	1.4	0.9	.510
ABA Season Totals		22	....	124	54	22	48	.458	2	7	.286	8	13	.615	16	14	30	20	33	0	....	....	21	5.6	2.5	1.4	0.9	....

• FIELDS, George
George Fields

Born: 1921.   Height: 5'11".   Weight: 170 lbs.   Drafted: —   College: Purdue

YEAR	TEAM	GP	GS	MIN	PTS	FGM	FGA	FG%	3PM	3PA	3P%	FTM	FTA	FT%	ORB	DRB	TRB	AST	PF	DQ	STL	BLK	TO	MPG	PPG	RPG	APG	PCM
45-46	Indianapolis-N	20	....	....	48	20	....	....	....	....	....	8	....	....	....	....	....	....	....	....	....	....	....		2.4			
NBL Season Totals		20	....	....	48	20	....	....	....	....	....	8	....	....	....	....	....	....	....	....	....	....	....		2.4			

• FIELDS, Kenny
Kenneth Henry Fields

Born: Feb. 9, 1962. Iowa City, IA, United States.   Height: 6'5".   Weight: 220 lbs.   Drafted: 1984   College: UCLA

YEAR	TEAM	GP	GS	MIN	PTS	FGM	FGA	FG%	3PM	3PA	3P%	FTM	FTA	FT%	ORB	DRB	TRB	AST	PF	DQ	STL	BLK	TO	MPG	PPG	RPG	APG	PCM
84-85	Milwaukee	51	1	535	195	84	191	.440	0	0	.000	27	36	.750	41	43	84	38	84	2	9	10	31	10.5	3.8	1.6	0.7	.298
85-86	Milwaukee	78	3	1120	499	204	398	.513	0	4	.000	91	132	.689	59	144	203	79	170	3	51	15	78	14.4	6.4	2.6	1.0	.431
86-87	Milwaukee	4	0	22	13	6	8	.750	0	0	.000	1	5	.200	0	2	2	1	3	0	1	0	1	5.5	3.3	0.5	0.3	.491
86-87	LA Clippers	44	17	861	381	153	344	.445	3	12	.250	72	89	.809	63	83	146	60	120	2	31	11	53	19.6	8.7	3.3	1.4	.382
87-88	LA Clippers	7	0	154	52	16	36	.444	0	0	.000	20	26	.769	13	16	29	10	17	0	5	2	19	22.0	7.4	4.1	1.4	.319
NBA Season Totals		184	21	2692	1140	463	977	.474	3	16	.188	211	288	.733	176	288	464	188	394	7	97	38	182	14.6	6.2	2.5	1.0	....
85-86	Milwaukee	12	4	158	89	38	69	.551	1	3	.333	12	23	.522	7	21	28	10	23	0	8	0	16	13.2	7.4	2.3	0.8	.466
NBA Playoff Totals		12	4	158	89	38	69	.551	1	3	.333	12	23	.522	7	21	28	10	23	0	8	0	16	13.2	7.4	2.3	0.8	....

• FILIPCZAK, Adam
Adam Filipczak

Born: 1916.   Height: 5'10".   Weight: 170 lbs.   Drafted: —   College: Wayne State (MI)

YEAR	TEAM	GP	GS	MIN	PTS	FGM	FGA	FG%	3PM	3PA	3P%	FTM	FTA	FT%	ORB	DRB	TRB	AST	PF	DQ	STL	BLK	TO	MPG	PPG	RPG	APG	PCM
40-41	Detroit-N	2	....	....	0	0	....	....	....	....	....	0	....	....	....	....	....	....	....	....	....	....	....		0.0			
NBL Season Totals		2	....	....	0	0	....	....	....	....	....	0	....	....	....	....	....	....	....	....	....	....	....		0.0			

• FILIPEK, Ron
Ronald Stanley Filipek

Born: Feb. 5, 1944.   Height: 6'5".   Weight: 205 lbs.   Drafted: 1967   College: Tennessee Tech

YEAR	TEAM	GP	GS	MIN	PTS	FGM	FGA	FG%	3PM	3PA	3P%	FTM	FTA	FT%	ORB	DRB	TRB	AST	PF	DQ	STL	BLK	TO	MPG	PPG	RPG	APG	PCM
67-68	Philadelphia	19	....	73	43	18	47	.383	....	....	....	7	14	.500	....	....	25	7	12	0	....	....	....	3.8	2.3	1.3	0.4	.557
NBA Season Totals		19	....	73	43	18	47	.383	....	....	....	7	14	.500	....	....	25	7	12	0	....	....	....	3.8	2.3	1.3	0.4	....

• FILLMORE, Greg
Gregory Paul Fillmore

Born: Mar. 7, 1947. Philadelphia, PA, United States.   Height: 7'1".   Weight: 240 lbs.   Drafted: 1970   College: Cheyney State

YEAR	TEAM	GP	GS	MIN	PTS	FGM	FGA	FG%	3PM	3PA	3P%	FTM	FTA	FT%	ORB	DRB	TRB	AST	PF	DQ	STL	BLK	TO	MPG	PPG	RPG	APG	PCM
70-71	New York	39	....	271	103	45	102	.441	....	....	....	13	27	.481	....	....	93	17	80	0	....	....	....	6.9	2.6	2.4	0.4	.417
71-72	New York	10	....	67	15	7	27	.259	....	....	....	1	3	.333	....	....	15	3	17	0	....	....	....	6.7	1.5	1.5	0.3	.088
NBA Season Totals		49	....	338	118	52	129	.403	....	....	....	14	30	.467	....	....	108	20	97	0	....	....	....	6.9	2.4	2.2	0.4	....
70-71	New York	8	....	24	0	0	4	.000	....	....	....	0	0	.000	....	....	8	1	9	0	....	....	....	3.0	0.0	1.0	0.1	.030
NBA Playoff Totals		8	....	24	0	0	4	.000	....	....	....	0	0	.000	....	....	8	1	9	0	....	....	....	3.0	0.0	1.0	0.1	....

• FINCH, Larry
Larry O. Finch

Born: Feb. 16, 1951. Memphis, TN, United States.   Height: 6'2".   Weight: 185 lbs.   Drafted: 1973   College: Memphis State

YEAR	TEAM	GP	GS	MIN	PTS	FGM	FGA	FG%	3PM	3PA	3P%	FTM	FTA	FT%	ORB	DRB	TRB	AST	PF	DQ	STL	BLK	TO	MPG	PPG	RPG	APG	PCM
73-74	Memphis-A	65	....	1154	443	164	399	.411	7	26	.269	108	136	.794	24	50	74	111	162	....	26	1	95	17.8	6.8	1.1	1.7	.303
74-75	Memphis-A	63	....	1888	663	264	593	.445	20	53	.377	115	133	.865	44	99	143	190	164	....	52	6	90	30.0	10.5	2.3	3.0	.333
ABA Season Totals		128	....	3042	1106	428	992	.431	27	79	.342	223	269	.829	68	149	217	301	326	....	78	7	185	23.8	8.6	1.7	2.4	....

• FINKEL, Hank
Henry J. Finkel

Born: Apr. 20, 1942. Union City, NJ, United States.   Height: 7'   Weight: 240 lbs.   Drafted: 1966   College: Dayton

YEAR	TEAM	GP	GS	MIN	PTS	FGM	FGA	FG%	3PM	3PA	3P%	FTM	FTA	FT%	ORB	DRB	TRB	AST	PF	DQ	STL	BLK	TO	MPG	PPG	RPG	APG	PCM
66-67	LA Lakers	27	....	141	41	17	47	.362	....	....	....	7	12	.583	....	....	64	5	39	1	....	....	....	5.2	1.5	2.4	0.2	.401
67-68	San Diego	53	....	1116	615	242	492	.492	....	....	....	131	191	.686	....	....	375	72	175	5	....	....	....	21.1	11.6	7.1	1.4	.634
68-69	San Diego	35	....	332	129	49	111	.441	....	....	....	31	41	.756	....	....	107	21	53	1	....	....	....	9.5	3.7	3.1	0.6	.496
69-70	Boston	80	....	1866	776	310	683	.454	....	....	....	156	233	.670	....	....	613	103	292	13	....	....	....	23.3	9.7	7.7	1.3	.504

YEAR	TEAM	GP	GS	MIN	PTS	FGM	FGA	FG%	3PM	3PA	3P%	FTM	FTA	FT%	ORB	DRB	TRB	AST	PF	DQ	STL	BLK	TO	MPG	PPG	RPG	APG	PCM
70-71	Boston	80	....	1234	521	214	489	.438	....	....	....	93	127	.732	....	....	343	79	196	5	....	....	....	15.4	6.5	4.3	1.0	.462
71-72	Boston	78	....	736	249	103	254	.406	....	....	....	43	74	.581	....	....	251	61	118	4	....	....	....	9.4	3.2	3.2	0.8	.462
72-73	Boston	76	....	496	184	78	173	.451	....	....	....	28	52	.538	....	....	151	26	83	0	....	....	....	6.5	2.4	2.0	0.3	.435
73-74	Boston	60	....	427	148	60	130	.462	....	....	....	28	43	.651	41	94	135	27	62	1	3	7	....	7.1	2.5	2.3	0.5	.472
74-75	Boston	62	....	518	127	52	129	.403	....	....	....	23	43	.535	33	79	112	32	72	0	7	3	....	8.4	2.0	1.8	0.5	.298
NBA Season Totals		551	....	6866	2790	1125	2508	.449	....	....	....	540	816	.662	74	173	2151	426	1090	30	10	10	....	12.5	5.1	3.9	0.8	....
66-67	LA Lakers	1	....	1	0	0	0	.000	....	....	....	0	0	.000	....	....	0	0	0	0	....	....	....	1.0	0.0	0.0	0.0	.000
68-69	San Diego	2	....	12	0	0	3	.000	....	....	....	0	0	.000	....	....	7	0	3	0	....	....	....	6.0	0.0	3.5	0.0	.174
71-72	Boston	8	....	68	20	10	22	.455	....	....	....	0	0	.000	....	....	24	3	11	0	....	....	....	8.5	2.5	3.0	0.4	.427
72-73	Boston	7	....	23	12	6	9	.667	....	....	....	0	0	.000	....	....	6	3	4	0	....	....	....	3.3	1.7	0.9	0.4	.708
73-74	Boston	8	....	46	17	8	18	.444	....	....	....	1	1	1.000	5	5	10	3	9	0	1	0	....	5.8	2.1	1.3	0.4	.361
74-75	Boston	7	....	25	9	3	7	.429	....	....	....	3	5	.600	3	3	6	4	2	0	0	0	....	3.6	1.3	0.9	0.6	.544
NBA Playoff Totals		33	....	175	58	27	59	.458	....	....	....	4	6	.667	8	8	53	13	29	0	1	0	....	5.3	1.8	1.6	0.4	....

• FINLEY, Michael

Michael H. Finley

Born: Mar. 6, 1973. Melrose Park, IL, United States. Height: 6'7". Weight: 215 lbs. Drafted: 1995 College: Wisconsin

YEAR	TEAM	GP	GS	MIN	PTS	FGM	FGA	FG%	3PM	3PA	3P%	FTM	FTA	FT%	ORB	DRB	TRB	AST	PF	DQ	STL	BLK	TO	MPG	PPG	RPG	APG	PCM
95-96	Phoenix	82	72	3212	1233	465	976	.476	61	186	.328	242	323	.749	139	235	374	289	199	1	85	31	131	39.2	15.0	4.6	3.5	.394
96-97	Phoenix	27	18	796	352	141	297	.475	14	55	.255	56	69	.812	34	86	120	68	42	0	18	4	43	29.5	13.0	4.4	2.5	.435
96-97	Dallas	56	36	1994	897	334	774	.432	87	225	.387	142	176	.807	54	198	252	156	96	0	50	20	118	35.6	16.0	4.5	2.8	.393
97-98	Dallas	82	82	**3394**	1763	675	1505	.449	87	244	.357	326	416	.784	149	289	438	405	163	0	132	30	221	**41.4**	21.5	5.3	4.9	.493
98-99	Dallas	50	50	2051	1009	389	876	.444	45	136	.331	186	226	.823	69	194	263	218	96	1	66	15	107	41.0	20.2	5.3	4.4	.472
99-00	Dallas	82	82	**3464**	1855	748	1636	.457	99	247	.401	260	317	.820	122	396	518	438	171	1	109	32	196	**42.2**	22.6	6.3	5.3	.532
00-01	Dallas	82	82	**3443**	1765	711	1552	.458	91	263	.346	252	325	.775	109	316	425	360	174	2	118	32	190	**42.0**	21.5	5.2	4.4	.477
01-02	Dallas	69	69	2755	1424	569	1228	.463	76	224	.339	210	251	.837	90	270	360	230	144	1	65	25	117	39.9	20.6	5.2	3.3	.471
02-03	Dallas	69	69	2642	1331	507	1193	.425	119	322	.370	198	230	.861	107	295	402	205	105	0	76	21	114	38.3	19.3	5.8	3.0	.462
NBA Season Totals		599	560	23751	11629	4539	10037	.452	679	1902	.357	1872	2333	.802	873	2279	3152	2369	1190	6	719	210	1237	39.7	19.4	5.3	4.0	....
00-01	Dallas	10	10	434	197	72	200	.360	17	47	.362	36	44	.818	13	40	53	44	23	0	12	2	24	43.4	19.7	5.3	4.4	.358
01-02	Dallas	8	8	373	197	69	148	.466	14	37	.378	45	50	.900	13	37	50	18	24	0	12	4	15	46.6	24.6	6.3	2.3	.478
02-03	Dallas	20	20	822	366	131	301	.435	47	114	.412	57	66	.864	25	90	115	60	47	0	26	12	31	41.1	18.3	5.8	3.0	.441
NBA Playoff Totals		38	38	1629	760	272	649	.419	78	198	.394	138	160	.863	51	167	218	122	94	0	50	18	70	42.9	20.0	5.7	3.2	....

• FINN, Danny

Daniel Lawrence Finn Jr.

Born: May 27, 1928. Height: 6'1". Weight: 185 lbs. Drafted: — College: St. John's (NY)

YEAR	TEAM	GP	GS	MIN	PTS	FGM	FGA	FG%	3PM	3PA	3P%	FTM	FTA	FT%	ORB	DRB	TRB	AST	PF	DQ	STL	BLK	TO	MPG	PPG	RPG	APG	PCM
52-53	Philadelphia	31	....	1015	369	135	409	.330	....	....	....	99	182	.544	....	....	175	146	124	9	....	....	....	32.7	11.9	5.6	4.7	.403
53-54	Philadelphia	68	....	1562	466	170	495	.343	....	....	....	126	196	.643	....	....	216	265	215	7	....	....	....	23.0	6.9	3.2	3.9	.403
54-55	Philadelphia	43	....	820	207	77	265	.291	....	....	....	53	86	.616	....	....	157	155	114	3	....	....	....	19.1	4.8	3.7	3.6	.393
NBA Season Totals		142	....	3397	1042	382	1169	.327	....	....	....	278	464	.599	....	....	548	566	453	19	....	....	....	23.9	7.3	3.9	4.0	....

• FISH, Matt

Matt Fish

Born: Nov. 18, 1969. Washington, IA, United States. Height: 6'11". Weight: 235 lbs. Drafted: 1992 College: North Carolina (Wilmington)

YEAR	TEAM	GP	GS	MIN	PTS	FGM	FGA	FG%	3PM	3PA	3P%	FTM	FTA	FT%	ORB	DRB	TRB	AST	PF	DQ	STL	BLK	TO	MPG	PPG	RPG	APG	PCM
94-95	LA Clippers	26	8	370	123	49	103	.476	0	1	.000	25	37	.676	32	52	84	17	70	1	16	7	29	14.2	4.7	3.2	0.7	.338
95-96	New York	2	1	17	12	6	10	.600	0	0	.000	0	1	.000	3	0	3	1	3	0	0	1	0	8.5	6.0	1.5	0.5	.658
95-96	Denver	16	0	117	40	15	26	.577	0	0	.000	10	18	.556	7	11	18	7	16	0	3	6	3	7.3	2.5	1.1	0.4	.413
96-97	Washington	5	0	7	2	1	3	.333	0	0	.000	0	0	.000	1	4	5	0	2	0	0	0	2	1.4	0.4	1.0	0.0	.286
96-97	Miami	1	0	1	0	0	0	.000	0	0	.000	0	0	.000	0	0	0	0	0	0	0	0	0	1.0	0.0	0.0	0.0	.000
NBA Season Totals		50	9	512	177	71	142	.500	0	1	.000	35	56	.625	43	67	110	25	91	1	19	14	34	10.2	3.5	2.2	0.5	....

• FISHER, Derek

Derek Lamar Fisher

Born: Aug. 9, 1974. Little Rock, AR, United States. Height: 6'1". Weight: 200 lbs. Drafted: 1996 College: Arkansas-Little Rock

YEAR	TEAM	GP	GS	MIN	PTS	FGM	FGA	FG%	3PM	3PA	3P%	FTM	FTA	FT%	ORB	DRB	TRB	AST	PF	DQ	STL	BLK	TO	MPG	PPG	RPG	APG	PCM
96-97	LA Lakers	80	3	921	309	104	262	.397	22	73	.301	79	120	.658	25	72	97	119	87	0	41	5	72	11.5	3.9	1.2	1.5	.321
97-98	LA Lakers	82	36	1760	474	164	378	.434	31	81	.383	115	152	.757	38	155	193	333	126	1	75	5	123	21.5	5.8	2.4	4.1	.399
98-99	LA Lakers	50	21	1131	296	99	263	.376	38	97	.392	60	79	.759	21	70	91	197	95	0	61	1	77	22.6	5.9	1.8	3.9	.341
99-00	LA Lakers	78	22	1803	491	167	483	.346	52	166	.313	105	145	.724	22	121	143	216	150	1	80	3	75	23.1	6.3	1.8	2.8	.272
00-01	LA Lakers	20	20	709	229	77	187	.412	25	63	.397	50	62	.806	5	54	59	87	50	0	39	2	29	35.5	11.5	3.0	4.4	.370
01-02	LA Lakers	70	35	1974	786	274	666	.411	144	349	.413	94	111	.847	15	131	146	181	121	0	66	9	62	28.2	11.2	2.1	2.6	.360
02-03	LA Lakers	82	82	2829	863	339	775	.437	85	212	.401	100	125	.800	40	199	239	298	195	4	93	15	94	34.5	10.5	2.9	3.6	.326
NBA Season Totals		462	219	11127	3448	1224	3014	.406	397	1041	.381	603	794	.759	166	802	968	1431	824	6	455	40	532	24.1	7.5	2.1	3.1	....
96-97	LA Lakers	6	0	34	8	3	11	.273	0	5	.000	2	3	.667	0	3	3	6	4	0	1	0	6	5.7	1.3	0.5	1.0	.081
97-98	LA Lakers	13	13	278	78	27	68	.397	6	20	.300	18	29	.621	2	23	25	49	33	0	17	0	15	21.4	6.0	1.9	3.8	.353
98-99	LA Lakers	8	8	238	78	28	67	.418	10	29	.345	12	15	.800	6	23	29	39	20	1	8	0	11	29.8	9.8	3.6	4.9	.418
99-00	LA Lakers	21	0	322	99	34	79	.430	12	29	.414	19	25	.760	4	18	22	41	30	0	11	1	9	15.3	4.7	1.0	2.0	.339
00-01	LA Lakers	16	16	576	215	77	159	.484	35	68	.515	26	34	.765	5	56	61	48	44	1	21	1	12	36.0	13.4	3.8	3.0	.407
01-02	LA Lakers	19	19	649	193	60	168	.357	29	81	.358	44	56	.786	10	52	62	52	49	0	19	1	20	34.2	10.2	3.3	2.7	.278
02-03	LA Lakers	12	12	424	153	53	102	.520	29	47	.617	18	22	.818	5	31	36	22	39	1	18	1	18	35.3	12.8	3.0	1.8	.346
NBA Playoff Totals		95	68	2521	824	282	654	.431	121	279	.434	139	184	.755	32	206	238	257	219	3	95	4	91	26.5	8.7	2.5	2.7	....

• FISHER, Richard

Richard B. Fisher

Born: Oct. 27, 1948. Height: 6'5". Weight: 215 lbs. Drafted: 1971 College: Colorado State

YEAR	TEAM	GP	GS	MIN	PTS	FGM	FGA	FG%	3PM	3PA	3P%	FTM	FTA	FT%	ORB	DRB	TRB	AST	PF	DQ	STL	BLK	TO	MPG	PPG	RPG	APG	PCM
71-72	Florida-A	3	....	7	6	3	5	.600	0	0	.000	0	0	.000	3	1	4	2	1	0	....	....	1	2.3	2.0	1.3	0.7	1.366
71-72	Utah-A	9	....	59	31	15	29	.517	0	0	.000	1	1	1.000	11	17	28	3	8	0	....	....	3	6.6	3.4	3.1	0.3	.731
ABA Season Totals		12	....	66	37	18	34	.529	0	0	.000	1	1	1.000	14	18	32	5	9	0	....	....	4	5.5	3.1	2.7	0.4	....

• FITTS, Wilson
Wilson Fitts

Born: 1915. Height: 6'2". Weight: 165 lbs. Drafted: — College: Akron

YEAR	TEAM	GP	GS	MIN	PTS	FGM	FGA	FG%	3PM	3PA	3P%	FTM	FTA	FT%	ORB	DRB	TRB	AST	PF	DQ	STL	BLK	TO	MPG	PPG	RPG	APG	PCM
37-38	Wingfoots-N	12	....	....	22	8	....	....	....	....	....	6	....	....	....	....	....	....	....	....	....	....	....	....	1.8	....	....	....
38-39	Wingfoots-N	19	....	....	39	16	....	....	....	....	....	7	....	....	....	....	....	....	....	....	....	....	....	....	2.1	....	....	....
NBL Season Totals		31	....	....	61	24	....	....	....	....	....	13	....	....	....	....	....	....	....	....	....	....	....	....	2.0	....	....	....
37-38	Wingfoots-N	5	....	....	10	2	....	....	....	....	....	6	....	....	....	....	....	....	....	....	....	....	....	....	2.0	....	....	....
NBL Playoff Totals		5	....	....	10	2	....	....	....	....	....	6	....	....	....	....	....	....	....	....	....	....	....	....	2.0	....	....	....

• FITZGERALD, Bob
Robert Fitzgerald

Born: Mar. 14, 1923. Died: July1983. Height: 6'5". Weight: 190 lbs. Drafted: — College: Fordham

YEAR	TEAM	GP	GS	MIN	PTS	FGM	FGA	FG%	3PM	3PA	3P%	FTM	FTA	FT%	ORB	DRB	TRB	AST	PF	DQ	STL	BLK	TO	MPG	PPG	RPG	APG	PCM
45-46	Rochester-N	10	....	....	33	9	....	....	....	....	....	15	....	....	....	....	....	....	....	....	....	....	....	....	3.3	....	....	....
46-47	Toronto	31	....	....	139	47	241	.195	....	....	....	45	70	.643	....	....	....	26	86	....	....	....	....	....	4.5	....	0.8	....
46-47	New York	29	....	....	82	23	121	.190	....	....	....	36	60	.600	....	....	....	9	67	....	....	....	....	....	2.8	....	0.3	....
47-48	Syracuse-N	1	....	....	0	0	....	....	....	....	....	0	1	.000	....	....	....	....	....	....	....	....	....	....	0.0	....	....	....
48-49	Rochester	18	....	....	19	6	29	.207	....	....	....	7	10	.700	....	....	....	12	26	....	....	....	....	....	1.1	....	0.7	....
NBA Season Totals		78	....	....	240	76	391	.194	....	....	....	88	140	.629	....	....	....	47	179	....	....	....	....	....	3.1	....	0.6	....
NBL Season Totals		11	....	....	33	9	....	....	....	....	....	15	1	....	....	....	....	....	....	....	....	....	....	....	3.0	....	....	....
Career Totals		89	....	....	273	85	391	....	....	....	....	103	141	....	....	....	....	47	179	....	....	....	....	....	3.1	....	0.5	....
45-46	Rochester-N	6	....	....	10	2	....	....	....	....	....	6	10	.600	....	....	....	....	....	....	....	....	....	....	1.7	....	....	....
46-47	New York	5	....	....	5	1	9	.111	....	....	....	3	4	.750	....	....	....	1	3	....	....	....	....	....	1.0	....	0.2	....
48-49	Rochester	1	....	....	0	0	1	.000	....	....	....	0	0	.000	....	....	....	0	1	....	....	....	....	....	0.0	....	0.0	....
NBA Playoff Totals		6	....	....	5	1	10	.100	....	....	....	3	4	.750	....	....	....	1	4	....	....	....	....	....	0.8	....	0.2	....
NBL Playoff Totals		6	....	....	10	2	....	....	....	....	....	6	10	....	....	....	....	....	....	....	....	....	....	....	1.7	....	....	....
Career Playoff Totals		12	....	....	15	3	10	....	....	....	....	9	14	....	....	....	....	1	4	....	....	....	....	....	1.3	....	0.1	....

• FITZGERALD, Dick
Richard Fitzgerald

Born: Nov. 18, 1920. Died: Apr.13, 1968. Height: 6'2". Weight: 175 lbs. Drafted: — College: Seton Hall

YEAR	TEAM	GP	GS	MIN	PTS	FGM	FGA	FG%	3PM	3PA	3P%	FTM	FTA	FT%	ORB	DRB	TRB	AST	PF	DQ	STL	BLK	TO	MPG	PPG	RPG	APG	PCM
46-47	Toronto	60	....	....	277	118	495	.238	....	....	....	41	60	.683	....	....	....	40	89	....	....	....	....	....	4.6	....	0.7	....
47-48	Providence	1	....	....	0	0	3	.000	....	....	....	0	0	.000	....	....	....	0	1	....	....	....	....	....	0.0	....	0.0	....
NBA Season Totals		61	....	....	277	118	498	.237	....	....	....	41	60	.683	....	....	....	40	90	....	....	....	....	....	4.5	....	0.7	....

• FIZER, Marcus
Darnell Marcus Lamar Fizer

Born: Aug. 10, 1978. Detroit, MI, United States. Height: 6'9". Weight: 262 lbs. Drafted: 2000 College: Iowa State

YEAR	TEAM	GP	GS	MIN	PTS	FGM	FGA	FG%	3PM	3PA	3P%	FTM	FTA	FT%	ORB	DRB	TRB	AST	PF	DQ	STL	BLK	TO	MPG	PPG	RPG	APG	PCM
00-01	Chicago	72	13	1580	683	278	646	.430	10	39	.256	117	161	.727	76	237	313	76	175	0	30	19	124	21.9	9.5	4.3	1.1	.349
01-02	Chicago	76	20	1963	938	371	848	.438	7	41	.171	189	283	.668	128	299	427	120	186	1	49	24	131	25.8	12.3	5.6	1.6	.430
02-03	Chicago	38	0	809	445	178	383	.465	1	6	.167	88	134	.657	80	136	216	48	89	0	14	17	57	21.3	11.7	5.7	1.3	.522
NBA Season Totals		186	33	4352	2066	827	1877	.441	18	86	.209	394	578	.682	284	672	956	244	450	1	93	60	312	23.4	11.1	5.1	1.3	....

• FLEISHMAN, Jerry
Jerome Fleishman

Born: Feb. 14, 1922. Height: 6'2". Weight: 190 lbs. Drafted: — College: New York University

YEAR	TEAM	GP	GS	MIN	PTS	FGM	FGA	FG%	3PM	3PA	3P%	FTM	FTA	FT%	ORB	DRB	TRB	AST	PF	DQ	STL	BLK	TO	MPG	PPG	RPG	APG	PCM
46-47	Philadelphia	59	....	....	263	97	372	.261	....	....	....	69	127	.543	....	....	....	40	101	....	....	....	....	....	4.5	....	0.7	....
47-48	Philadelphia	46	....	....	333	119	501	.238	....	....	....	95	138	.688	....	....	....	43	122	....	....	....	....	....	7.2	....	0.9	....
48-49	Philadelphia	59	....	....	323	123	424	.290	....	....	....	77	118	.653	....	....	....	120	137	....	....	....	....	....	5.5	....	2.0	....
49-50	Philadelphia	65	....	....	297	102	353	.289	....	....	....	93	151	.616	....	....	....	118	129	....	....	....	....	....	4.6	....	1.8	....
52-53	Philadelphia	33	....	882	296	100	303	.330	....	....	....	96	140	.686	....	....	152	108	118	7	....	....	....	26.7	9.0	4.6	3.3	.383
NBA Season Totals		262	....	882	1512	541	1953	.277	....	....	....	430	674	.638	....	....	152	429	607	7	....	....	....	3.4	5.8	0.6	1.6	....
46-47	Philadelphia	9	....	....	57	22	70	.314	....	....	....	13	18	.722	....	....	....	3	20	....	....	....	....	....	6.3	....	0.3	....
47-48	Philadelphia	7	....	....	16	5	29	.172	....	....	....	6	8	.750	....	....	....	2	7	....	....	....	....	....	2.3	....	0.3	....
48-49	Philadelphia	2	....	....	20	7	26	.269	....	....	....	6	9	.667	....	....	....	4	5	....	....	....	....	....	10.0	....	2.0	....
49-50	Philadelphia	2	....	....	2	1	3	.333	....	....	....	0	1	.000	....	....	....	3	6	....	....	....	....	....	1.0	....	1.5	....
52-53	New York	2	....	26	10	2	3	.667	....	....	....	6	13	.462	....	....	5	7	7	1	....	....	....	13.0	5.0	2.5	3.5	.645
NBA Playoff Totals		22	....	26	105	37	131	.282	....	....	....	31	49	.633	....	....	5	19	45	1	....	....	....	1.2	4.8	0.2	0.9	....

• FLEMING, Al
Albert Fleming Jr.

Born: Apr. 5, 1954. Chicago, IL, United States. Height: 6'7". Weight: 215 lbs. Drafted: 1976 College: Arizona

YEAR	TEAM	GP	GS	MIN	PTS	FGM	FGA	FG%	3PM	3PA	3P%	FTM	FTA	FT%	ORB	DRB	TRB	AST	PF	DQ	STL	BLK	TO	MPG	PPG	RPG	APG	PCM
77-78	Seattle	20	....	97	40	15	31	.484	....	....	....	10	17	.588	13	17	30	7	16	0	0	5	16	4.9	2.0	1.5	0.4	.417
NBA Season Totals		20	....	97	40	15	31	.484	....	....	....	10	17	.588	13	17	30	7	16	0	0	5	16	4.9	2.0	1.5	0.4	....
77-78	Seattle	5	....	21	7	2	6	.333	....	....	....	3	4	.750	1	3	4	2	5	0	1	0	2	4.2	1.4	0.8	0.4	.274
NBA Playoff Totals		5	....	21	7	2	6	.333	....	....	....	3	4	.750	1	3	4	2	5	0	1	0	2	4.2	1.4	0.8	0.4	....

• FLEMING, Ed
Edward R. Fleming

Born: July 25, 1933. Height: 6'3". Weight: 189 lbs. Drafted: 1955 College: Niagara

YEAR	TEAM	GP	GS	MIN	PTS	FGM	FGA	FG%	3PM	3PA	3P%	FTM	FTA	FT%	ORB	DRB	TRB	AST	PF	DQ	STL	BLK	TO	MPG	PPG	RPG	APG	PCM
55-56	Rochester	71	....	2028	889	306	824	.371	....	....	....	277	372	.745	....	....	489	197	178	1	....	....	....	28.6	12.5	6.9	2.8	.497
56-57	Rochester	51	....	927	357	109	364	.299	....	....	....	139	191	.728	....	....	183	81	94	0	....	....	....	18.2	7.0	3.6	1.6	.378
57-58	Minneapolis	72	....	1686	633	226	655	.345	....	....	....	181	255	.710	....	....	492	139	222	5	....	....	....	23.4	8.8	6.8	1.9	.443
58-59	Minneapolis	71	....	1132	461	162	419	.387	....	....	....	137	190	.721	....	....	281	89	148	1	....	....	....	15.9	6.5	4.0	1.3	.455

YEAR	TEAM	GP	GS	MIN	PTS	FGM	FGA	FG%	3PM	3PA	3P%	FTM	FTA	FT%	ORB	DRB	TRB	AST	PF	DQ	STL	BLK	TO	MPG	PPG	RPG	APG	PCM
59-60	Minneapolis	27	....	413	171	59	141	.418	....	....	....	53	69	.768	....	....	87	38	46	0	....	....	....	15.3	6.3	3.2	1.4	.481
NBA Season Totals		292	....	6186	2511	862	2403	.359	....	....	....	787	1077	.731	....	....	1532	544	688	7	....	....	....	21.2	8.6	5.2	1.9	....
58-59	Minneapolis	13	....	178	76	27	77	.351	....	....	....	22	25	.880	....	....	39	18	32	0	....	....	....	13.7	5.8	3.0	1.4	.433
NBA Playoff Totals		13	....	178	76	27	77	.351	....	....	....	22	25	.880	....	....	39	18	32	0	....	....	....	13.7	5.8	3.0	1.4	....

• FLEMING, Vern

Vern Fleming

Born: Feb. 4, 1962. New York, NY, United States. Height: 6'5". Weight: 185 lbs. Drafted: 1984 College: Georgia

YEAR	TEAM	GP	GS	MIN	PTS	FGM	FGA	FG%	3PM	3PA	3P%	FTM	FTA	FT%	ORB	DRB	TRB	AST	PF	DQ	STL	BLK	TO	MPG	PPG	RPG	APG	PCM
84-85	Indiana	80	65	2486	1126	433	922	.470	0	4	.000	260	339	.767	148	175	323	247	232	4	99	8	200	31.1	14.1	4.0	3.1	.404
85-86	Indiana	80	77	2870	1136	436	862	.506	1	6	.167	263	353	.745	102	284	386	505	230	3	131	5	208	35.9	14.2	4.8	6.3	.496
86-87	Indiana	82	82	2549	980	370	727	.509	2	10	.200	238	302	.788	109	225	334	473	222	3	109	18	164	31.1	12.0	4.1	5.8	.509
87-88	Indiana	80	80	2733	1111	442	845	.523	0	13	.000	227	283	.802	106	258	364	568	225	0	115	11	176	34.2	13.9	4.6	7.1	.550
88-89	Indiana	76	69	2552	1084	419	814	.515	3	23	.130	243	304	.799	85	225	310	494	212	4	77	12	190	33.6	14.3	4.1	6.5	.514
89-90	Indiana	82	82	2876	1176	467	919	.508	12	34	.353	230	294	.782	118	204	322	610	213	1	92	10	205	35.1	14.3	3.9	7.4	.513
90-91	Indiana	69	45	1929	877	356	671	.531	4	18	.222	161	221	.729	83	131	214	369	116	0	76	13	138	28.0	12.7	3.1	5.3	.544
91-92	Indiana	82	6	1737	726	294	610	.482	6	27	.222	132	179	.737	69	140	209	266	134	0	56	7	139	21.2	8.9	2.5	3.2	.436
92-93	Indiana	75	8	1503	710	280	554	.505	7	36	.194	143	197	.726	63	106	169	224	126	1	63	9	120	20.0	9.5	2.3	3.0	.481
93-94	Indiana	55	5	1053	358	147	318	.462	0	4	.000	64	87	.736	27	96	123	173	98	1	40	6	88	19.1	6.5	2.2	3.1	.387
94-95	Indiana	55	1	686	251	93	188	.495	0	7	.000	65	90	.722	20	68	88	109	80	0	27	1	44	12.5	4.6	1.6	2.0	.431
95-96	New Jersey	77	3	1747	590	227	524	.433	3	28	.107	133	177	.751	49	121	170	255	115	0	41	5	123	22.7	7.7	2.2	3.3	.340
NBA Season Totals		893	523	24721	10125	3964	7954	.498	38	210	.181	2159	2826	.764	979	2033	3012	4293	2003	17	926	105	1795	27.7	11.3	3.4	4.8	....
86-87	Indiana	4	4	141	49	13	36	.361	0	1	.000	23	30	.767	9	17	26	24	15	1	4	1	10	35.3	12.3	6.5	6.0	.444
89-90	Indiana	3	3	113	40	16	34	.471	0	2	.000	8	9	.889	4	9	13	18	6	0	2	1	8	37.7	13.3	4.3	6.0	.411
90-91	Indiana	5	0	115	47	18	40	.450	0	1	.000	11	14	.786	10	7	17	23	10	0	1	3	8	23.0	9.4	3.4	4.6	.496
91-92	Indiana	3	0	51	21	10	18	.556	0	0	.000	1	3	.333	0	2	2	6	5	0	3	0	4	17.0	7.0	0.7	2.0	.347
92-93	Indiana	3	3	80	30	12	27	.444	2	4	.500	4	4	1.000	1	4	5	3	6	0	2	1	5	26.7	10.0	1.7	1.0	.240
93-94	Indiana	16	1	247	95	39	76	.513	0	5	.000	17	20	.850	12	9	21	38	27	0	10	1	22	15.4	5.9	1.3	2.4	.395
94-95	Indiana	3	0	8	2	1	3	.333	0	1	.000	0	3	.000	1	1	2	2	0	0	0	0	0	2.7	0.7	0.7	0.7	.340
NBA Playoff Totals		37	11	755	284	109	234	.466	2	14	.143	64	83	.771	37	49	86	114	69	1	22	7	57	20.4	7.7	2.3	3.1	....

• FLICK, Gordon

Gordon Flick

Born: 1921. Height: 6'3". Weight: 200 lbs. Drafted: 1948 College: Drake

YEAR	TEAM	GP	GS	MIN	PTS	FGM	FGA	FG%	3PM	3PA	3P%	FTM	FTA	FT%	ORB	DRB	TRB	AST	PF	DQ	STL	BLK	TO	MPG	PPG	RPG	APG	PCM
43-44	Oshkosh-N	3	....	....	4	2	....	....	....	....	....	0	....	....	....	....	....	....	....	....	....	....	....	....	1.3	....	....	....
48-49	Waterloo-N	2	....	....	4	2	....	....	....	....	....	0	0	.000	....	....	....	....	....	....	....	....	....	....	2.0	....	....	....
NBL Season Totals		5	....	....	8	4	....	....	....	....	....	0	0	....	....	....	....	....	....	....	....	....	....	....	1.6	....	....	....

• FLOWERS, Bruce

Bruce Douglas Flowers

Born: June 13, 1957. Rochester, NY, United States. Height: 6'8". Weight: 225 lbs. Drafted: 1979 College: Notre Dame

YEAR	TEAM	GP	GS	MIN	PTS	FGM	FGA	FG%	3PM	3PA	3P%	FTM	FTA	FT%	ORB	DRB	TRB	AST	PF	DQ	STL	BLK	TO	MPG	PPG	RPG	APG	PCM
82-83	Cleveland	53	5	699	261	110	206	.534	0	2	.000	41	53	.774	71	109	180	47	99	2	19	12	42	13.2	4.9	3.4	0.9	.470
NBA Season Totals		53	5	699	261	110	206	.534	0	2	.000	41	53	.774	71	109	180	47	99	2	19	12	42	13.2	4.9	3.4	0.9	....

• FLOYD, Sleepy

Eric Augustus (Sleepy) Floyd

Born: Mar. 6, 1960. Gastonia, NC, United States. Height: 6'3". Weight: 170 lbs. Drafted: 1982 College: Georgetown

YEAR	TEAM	GP	GS	MIN	PTS	FGM	FGA	FG%	3PM	3PA	3P%	FTM	FTA	FT%	ORB	DRB	TRB	AST	PF	DQ	STL	BLK	TO	MPG	PPG	RPG	APG	PCM
82-83	New Jersey	43	8	494	226	92	216	.426	4	14	.286	38	45	.844	16	26	42	67	56	1	19	9	39	11.5	5.3	1.0	1.6	.379
82-83	Golden State	33	9	754	386	134	311	.431	6	11	.545	112	135	.830	40	55	95	71	78	2	39	8	66	22.8	11.7	2.9	2.2	.434
83-84	Golden State	77	73	2555	1291	484	1045	.463	8	45	.178	315	386	.816	87	184	271	269	216	0	103	31	193	33.2	16.8	3.5	3.5	.439
84-85	Golden State	82	82	2873	1598	610	1372	.445	42	143	.294	336	415	.810	62	140	202	406	226	1	134	41	254	35.0	19.5	2.5	5.0	.450
85-86	Golden State	82	82	2764	1410	510	1007	.506	39	119	.328	351	441	.796	76	221	297	746	199	2	157	16	287	33.7	17.2	3.6	9.1	.645
86-87	Golden State	82	82	3064	1541	503	1030	.488	73	190	.384	462	537	.860	56	212	268	848	199	1	146	18	279	37.4	18.8	3.3	10.3	.644
87-88	Golden State	18	18	680	381	132	301	.439	1	20	.050	116	139	.835	26	65	91	178	46	0	27	2	67	37.8	21.2	5.1	9.9	.634
87-88	Houston	59	55	1834	774	288	668	.431	13	52	.250	185	215	.860	51	154	205	366	144	1	68	10	153	31.1	13.1	3.5	6.2	.464
88-89	Houston	82	82	2788	1162	396	893	.443	109	292	.373	261	309	.845	48	258	306	709	196	1	124	11	254	34.0	14.2	3.7	8.6	.545
89-90	Houston	82	73	2630	1000	362	803	.451	89	234	.380	187	232	.806	46	152	198	600	159	0	94	11	205	32.1	12.2	2.4	7.3	.464
90-91	Houston	82	4	1850	1005	386	939	.411	48	176	.273	185	246	.752	52	107	159	317	122	0	95	17	139	22.6	12.3	1.9	3.9	.468
91-92	Houston	82	3	1662	744	286	704	.406	37	123	.301	135	170	.794	34	116	150	239	128	0	57	21	131	20.3	9.1	1.8	2.9	.377
92-93	Houston	52	10	867	345	124	305	.407	16	56	.286	81	102	.794	14	72	86	132	59	0	32	6	68	16.7	6.6	1.7	2.5	.383
93-94	San Antonio	53	2	737	200	70	209	.335	8	36	.222	52	78	.667	10	60	70	101	71	0	12	8	64	13.9	3.8	1.3	1.9	.219
94-95	New Jersey	48	1	831	197	71	212	.335	25	88	.284	30	43	.698	8	46	54	126	73	0	13	6	53	17.3	4.1	1.1	2.6	.213
NBA Season Totals		957	584	26383	12260	4448	10015	.444	518	1599	.324	2846	3493	.815	626	1868	2494	5175	1972	9	1120	215	2252	27.6	12.8	2.6	5.4	....
86-87	Golden State	10	10	414	214	77	152	.507	13	28	.464	47	51	.922	9	21	30	102	24	0	18	2	35	41.4	21.4	3.0	10.2	.614
87-88	Houston	4	4	154	75	26	61	.426	4	8	.500	19	22	.864	3	4	7	34	10	0	8	0	12	38.5	18.8	1.8	8.5	.490
88-89	Houston	4	4	160	62	22	46	.478	8	15	.533	10	14	.714	3	15	18	26	10	0	8	1	10	40.0	15.5	4.5	6.5	.480
89-90	Houston	4	4	172	74	30	64	.469	3	12	.250	11	17	.647	7	8	15	41	5	0	5	1	15	43.0	18.5	3.8	10.3	.501
90-91	Houston	3	0	41	16	8	24	.333	0	4	.000	0	0	.000	0	2	2	7	4	0	2	1	7	13.7	5.3	0.7	2.3	.117
92-93	Houston	7	0	60	20	6	19	.316	1	3	.333	7	10	.700	1	3	4	8	2	0	2	0	9	8.6	2.9	0.6	1.1	.188
93-94	San Antonio	4	0	37	6	2	8	.250	0	0	.000	2	4	.500	0	1	1	1	3	0	0	0	4	9.3	1.5	0.3	0.3	-.094
NBA Playoff Totals		36	22	1038	467	171	374	.457	29	70	.414	96	118	.814	23	54	77	219	58	0	43	5	92	28.8	13.0	2.1	6.1	....

• FLYNN, Mike

Michael David Flynn

Born: July 31, 1953. Casablanca, Morocco. Height: 6'2". Weight: 180 lbs. Drafted: 1975 College: Kentucky

YEAR	TEAM	GP	GS	MIN	PTS	FGM	FGA	FG%	3PM	3PA	3P%	FTM	FTA	FT%	ORB	DRB	TRB	AST	PF	DQ	STL	BLK	TO	MPG	PPG	RPG	APG	PCM
75-76	Indiana-A	67	....	1097	421	166	439	.378	25	99	.253	64	111	.577	63	70	133	133	112	....	44	9	81	16.4	6.3	2.0	2.0	.340

YEAR	TEAM	GP	GS	MIN	PTS	FGM	FGA	FG%	3PM	3PA	3P%	FTM	FTA	FT%	ORB	DRB	TRB	AST	PF	DQ	STL	BLK	TO	MPG	PPG	RPG	APG	PCM
76-77	Indiana	73	....	1324	601	250	573	.436	....	....	....	101	142	.711	76	111	187	179	106	0	57	6	....	18.1	8.2	2.6	2.5	.471
77-78	Indiana	71	....	955	295	120	267	.449	....	....	....	55	97	.567	47	70	117	142	52	0	41	10	78	13.5	4.2	1.6	2.0	.381
NBA Season Totals		144	....	2279	896	370	840	.440	....	....	....	156	239	.653	123	181	304	321	158	0	98	16	78	15.8	6.2	2.1	2.0	....
ABA Season Totals		67	....	1097	421	166	439	.378	25	99	.253	64	111	.577	63	70	133	133	112	....	44	9	81	16.4	6.3	2.0	2.0	....
Career Totals		211	....	3376	1317	536	1279	.419	25	99	.253	220	350	.629	186	251	437	454	270	0	142	25	159	16.0	6.2	2.1	2.2	....
75-76	Indiana-A	3	....	83	41	15	30	.500	3	8	.375	8	11	.727	5	5	10	10	6	....	3	0	5	27.7	13.7	3.3	3.3	.526
ABA Playoff Totals		3	....	83	41	15	30	.500	3	8	.375	8	11	.727	5	5	10	10	6	....	3	0	5	27.7	13.7	3.3	3.3	....

• FOGLE, Larry

Larry Fogle

Born: Mar. 19, 1953. Brooklyn, NY, United States.   Height: 6'5".   Weight: 205 lbs.   Drafted: 1975   College: Canisius

YEAR	TEAM	GP	GS	MIN	PTS	FGM	FGA	FG%	3PM	3PA	3P%	FTM	FTA	FT%	ORB	DRB	TRB	AST	PF	DQ	STL	BLK	TO	MPG	PPG	RPG	APG	PCM
75-76	New York	2	....	14	2	1	5	.200	....	....	....	0	0	.000	1	2	3	0	4	0	1	0	....	7.0	1.0	1.5	0.0	-.041
NBA Season Totals		2	....	14	2	1	5	.200	....	....	....	0	0	.000	1	2	3	0	4	0	1	0	....	7.0	1.0	1.5	0.0	....

• FOLEY, Jack

John E. (Jack the Shot) Foley

Born: Apr. 19, 1939. Worcester, MA, United States.   Height: 6'3".   Weight: 170 lbs.   Drafted: 1962   College: Holy Cross

YEAR	TEAM	GP	GS	MIN	PTS	FGM	FGA	FG%	3PM	3PA	3P%	FTM	FTA	FT%	ORB	DRB	TRB	AST	PF	DQ	STL	BLK	TO	MPG	PPG	RPG	APG	PCM
62-63	Boston	5	....	46	32	13	26	.500	....	....	....	6	8	.750	....	....	7	0	3	0	....	....	....	9.2	6.4	1.4	0.0	.549
62-63	New York	6	....	37	21	7	25	.280	....	....	....	7	7	1.000	....	....	9	5	5	0	....	....	....	6.2	3.5	1.5	0.8	.485
NBA Season Totals		11	....	83	53	20	51	.392	....	....	....	13	15	.867	....	....	16	5	8	0	....	....	....	7.5	4.8	1.5	0.5	....

• FONTAINE, Isaac

Issac Henry Sedric Fontaine IV

Born: Apr. 16, 1975. Sacramento, CA, United States.   Height: 6'4".   Weight: 210 lbs.   Drafted: —   College: Washington State

YEAR	TEAM	GP	GS	MIN	PTS	FGM	FGA	FG%	3PM	3PA	3P%	FTM	FTA	FT%	ORB	DRB	TRB	AST	PF	DQ	STL	BLK	TO	MPG	PPG	RPG	APG	PCM
01-02	Memphis	6	0	76	11	3	14	.214	1	5	.200	4	6	.667	0	5	5	4	6	0	0	0	4	12.7	1.8	0.8	0.7	.035
NBA Season Totals		6	0	76	11	3	14	.214	1	5	.200	4	6	.667	0	5	5	4	6	0	0	0	4	12.7	1.8	0.8	0.7	....

• FONTAINE, Levi

Levi Fontaine

Born: Nov. 1, 1948.   Height: 6'4".   Weight: 190 lbs.   Drafted: 1970   College: Maryland State

YEAR	TEAM	GP	GS	MIN	PTS	FGM	FGA	FG%	3PM	3PA	3P%	FTM	FTA	FT%	ORB	DRB	TRB	AST	PF	DQ	STL	BLK	TO	MPG	PPG	RPG	APG	PCM
70-71	San Francisco	35	....	210	134	53	145	.366	....	....	....	28	37	.757	....	....	15	22	27	0	....	....	....	6.0	3.8	0.4	0.6	.368
NBA Season Totals		35	....	210	134	53	145	.366	....	....	....	28	37	.757	....	....	15	22	27	0	....	....	....	6.0	3.8	0.4	0.6	....
70-71	San Francisco	2	....	9	5	2	3	.667	....	....	....	1	3	.333	....	....	0	0	2	0	....	....	....	4.5	2.5	0.0	0.0	.269
NBA Playoff Totals		2	....	9	5	2	3	.667	....	....	....	1	3	.333	....	....	0	0	2	0	....	....	....	4.5	2.5	0.0	0.0	

• FORD, Alphonso

Alphonso Gene Ford

Born: Oct. 31, 1971. Greenwood, MS, United States.   Height: 6'1".   Weight: 190 lbs.   Drafted: 1993   College: Mississippi Valley State

YEAR	TEAM	GP	GS	MIN	PTS	FGM	FGA	FG%	3PM	3PA	3P%	FTM	FTA	FT%	ORB	DRB	TRB	AST	PF	DQ	STL	BLK	TO	MPG	PPG	RPG	APG	PCM
93-94	Seattle	6	0	16	16	7	13	.538	1	1	1.000	1	2	.500	0	0	0	1	2	0	2	0	1	2.7	2.7	0.0	0.2	.695
94-95	Philadelphia	5	0	98	19	9	39	.231	0	9	.000	1	2	.500	8	12	20	9	5	0	1	0	8	19.6	3.8	4.0	1.8	.100
NBA Season Totals		11	0	114	35	16	52	.308	1	10	.100	2	4	.500	8	12	20	10	7	0	3	0	9	10.4	3.2	1.8	0.9	....

• FORD, Alton

Alton Ford Jr.

Born: May 29, 1981. Houston, TX, United States.   Height: 6'9".   Weight: 275 lbs.   Drafted: 2001   College: Houston

YEAR	TEAM	GP	GS	MIN	PTS	FGM	FGA	FG%	3PM	3PA	3P%	FTM	FTA	FT%	ORB	DRB	TRB	AST	PF	DQ	STL	BLK	TO	MPG	PPG	RPG	APG	PCM
01-02	Phoenix	53	0	452	164	61	118	.517	0	0	.000	42	57	.737	32	75	107	7	99	0	6	7	32	8.5	3.1	2.0	0.1	.328
02-03	Phoenix	11	0	31	7	3	9	.333	0	0	.000	1	3	.333	0	6	6	1	7	0	0	0	2	2.8	0.6	0.5	0.1	.071
NBA Season Totals		64	0	483	171	64	127	.504	0	0	.000	43	60	.717	32	81	113	8	106	0	6	7	34	7.5	2.7	1.8	0.1	....

• FORD, Bob

Robert Alan Ford

Born: Jan. 26, 1950.   Height: 6'7".   Weight: 228 lbs.   Drafted: 1972   College: Purdue

YEAR	TEAM	GP	GS	MIN	PTS	FGM	FGA	FG%	3PM	3PA	3P%	FTM	FTA	FT%	ORB	DRB	TRB	AST	PF	DQ	STL	BLK	TO	MPG	PPG	RPG	APG	PCM
72-73	Memphis-A	9	....	74	14	5	17	.294	0	0	.000	4	5	.800	2	10	12	4	8	0	....	....	4	8.2	1.6	1.3	0.4	.194
ABA Season Totals		9	....	74	14	5	17	.294	0	0	.000	4	5	.800	2	10	12	4	8	0	....	....	4	8.2	1.6	1.3	0.4	....

• FORD, Chris

Christopher Joseph Ford

Born: Jan. 11, 1949. Atlantic City, NJ, United States.   Height: 6'5".   Weight: 190 lbs.   Drafted: 1972   College: Villanova

YEAR	TEAM	GP	GS	MIN	PTS	FGM	FGA	FG%	3PM	3PA	3P%	FTM	FTA	FT%	ORB	DRB	TRB	AST	PF	DQ	STL	BLK	TO	MPG	PPG	RPG	APG	PCM
72-73	Detroit	74	....	1537	476	208	434	.479	....	....	....	60	93	.645	....	....	266	194	133	1	....	....	....	20.8	6.4	3.6	2.6	.430
73-74	Detroit	82	....	2059	585	264	595	.444	....	....	....	57	77	.740	109	195	304	279	159	1	148	14	....	25.1	7.1	3.7	3.4	.392
74-75	Detroit	80	....	1962	475	206	435	.474	....	....	....	63	95	.663	93	176	269	230	187	0	113	26	....	24.5	5.9	3.4	2.9	.346
75-76	Detroit	82	....	2198	685	301	707	.426	....	....	....	83	115	.722	80	211	291	272	222	0	178	24	....	26.8	8.4	3.5	3.3	.359
76-77	Detroit	82	....	2539	1005	437	918	.476	....	....	....	131	170	.771	96	174	270	337	192	1	179	26	....	31.0	12.3	3.3	4.1	.436
77-78	Detroit	82	....	2582	861	374	777	.481	....	....	....	113	154	.734	117	151	268	381	182	2	166	17	230	31.5	10.5	3.3	4.6	.400
78-79	Detroit	3	....	108	33	13	35	.371	....	....	....	7	8	.875	9	9	18	5	9	1	1	1	10	36.0	11.0	6.0	1.7	.215
78-79	Boston	78	....	2629	1215	525	1107	.474	....	....	....	165	219	.753	115	141	256	369	200	2	114	24	203	33.7	15.6	3.3	4.7	.440
79-80	Boston	73	....	2115	816	330	709	.465	70	164	.427	86	114	.754	77	104	181	215	178	0	111	27	102	29.0	11.2	2.5	2.9	.384
80-81	Boston	82	....	2723	728	314	707	.444	36	109	.330	64	87	.736	72	91	163	295	212	2	100	23	123	33.2	8.9	2.0	3.6	.269
81-82	Boston	76	53	1591	435	188	450	.418	20	63	.317	39	56	.696	52	56	108	142	143	0	42	10	53	20.9	5.7	1.4	1.9	.234
NBA Season Totals		794	53	22043	7314	3160	6874	.460	126	336	.375	868	1188	.731	820	1308	2394	2719	1817	10	1152	192	721	27.8	9.2	3.0	3.4	....

YEAR	TEAM	GP	GS	MIN	PTS	FGM	FGA	FG%	3PM	3PA	3P%	FTM	FTA	FT%	ORB	DRB	TRB	AST	PF	DQ	STL	BLK	TO	MPG	PPG	RPG	APG	PCM
73-74	Detroit	5	....	94	20	8	17	.471	....	....	....	4	6	.667	4	11	15	7	10	0	2	2	....	18.8	4.0	3.0	1.4	.298
74-75	Detroit	3	....	82	12	6	11	.545	....	....	....	0	0	.000	2	11	13	10	8	0	1	0	....	27.3	4.0	4.3	3.3	.328
75-76	Detroit	9	....	276	78	33	81	.407	....	....	....	12	15	.800	6	30	36	40	33	1	11	5	....	30.7	8.7	4.0	4.4	.355
76-77	Detroit	3	....	101	41	18	44	.409	....	....	....	5	9	.556	8	11	19	12	11	0	7	0	....	33.7	13.7	6.3	4.0	.417
79-80	Boston	9	....	279	82	34	79	.430	2	13	.154	12	15	.800	9	16	25	21	35	1	14	6	13	31.0	9.1	2.8	2.3	.273
80-81	Boston	17	....	507	154	66	146	.452	7	25	.280	15	25	.600	13	32	45	46	47	0	14	1	19	29.8	9.1	2.6	2.7	.281
81-82	Boston	12	0	138	47	20	42	.476	2	7	.286	5	7	.714	6	9	15	15	15	0	3	1	3	11.5	3.9	1.3	1.3	.361
NBA Playoff Totals		58	0	1477	434	185	420	.440	11	45	.244	53	77	.688	48	120	168	151	159	2	52	15	35	25.5	7.5	2.9	2.6	....

• FORD, Don

Donald J. Ford

Born: Dec. 31, 1952. Santa Barbara, CA, United States.   Height: 6'9".   Weight: 215 lbs.   Drafted: 1975   College: Cal State Santa Barbara

YEAR	TEAM	GP	GS	MIN	PTS	FGM	FGA	FG%	3PM	3PA	3P%	FTM	FTA	FT%	ORB	DRB	TRB	AST	PF	DQ	STL	BLK	TO	MPG	PPG	RPG	APG	PCM
75-76	LA Lakers	76	....	1838	726	311	710	.438	....	....	....	104	139	.748	118	215	333	111	186	3	50	14	....	24.2	9.6	4.4	1.5	.382
76-77	LA Lakers	82	....	1782	597	262	570	.460	....	....	....	73	102	.716	105	248	353	133	170	0	60	21	....	21.7	7.3	4.3	1.6	.393
77-78	LA Lakers	79	....	1945	612	272	576	.472	....	....	....	68	90	.756	106	247	353	142	210	1	68	46	87	24.6	7.7	4.5	1.8	.379
78-79	LA Lakers	79	....	1540	528	228	450	.507	....	....	....	72	89	.809	83	185	268	101	177	2	51	25	95	19.5	6.7	3.4	1.3	.374
79-80	LA Lakers	52	....	580	155	66	130	.508	0	1	.000	23	28	.821	23	75	98	36	86	0	11	15	31	11.2	3.0	1.9	0.7	.309
79-80	Cleveland	21	....	419	153	65	144	.451	1	2	.500	22	25	.880	21	66	87	29	45	0	11	6	21	20.0	7.3	4.1	1.4	.398
80-81	Cleveland	64	....	996	222	100	224	.446	0	3	.000	22	24	.917	74	90	164	84	100	1	15	12	51	15.6	3.5	2.6	1.3	.283
81-82	Cleveland	21	1	201	23	9	24	.375	0	1	.000	5	6	.833	14	21	35	11	30	0	8	0	15	9.6	1.1	1.7	0.5	.162
NBA Season Totals		474	1	9301	3016	1313	2828	.464	1	7	.143	389	503	.773	544	1147	1691	647	1004	7	274	139	300	19.6	6.4	3.6	1.4	....
76-77	LA Lakers	11	....	333	111	42	98	.429	....	....	....	27	36	.750	22	36	58	37	28	0	17	4	....	30.3	10.1	5.3	3.4	.417
77-78	LA Lakers	1	....	10	0	0	3	.000	....	....	....	0	0	.000	2	3	5	0	2	0	1	0	1	10.0	0.0	5.0	0.0	.088
78-79	LA Lakers	8	....	138	33	16	30	.533	....	....	....	1	3	.333	2	20	22	7	20	0	3	2	4	17.3	4.1	2.8	0.9	.282
NBA Playoff Totals		20	....	481	144	58	131	.443	....	....	....	28	39	.718	26	59	85	44	50	0	21	6	5	24.1	7.2	4.3	2.2	....

• FORD, Jake

Jake Ford

Born: Apr. 29, 1946.   Height: 6'3".   Weight: 180 lbs.   Drafted: 1970   College: Maryland State

YEAR	TEAM	GP	GS	MIN	PTS	FGM	FGA	FG%	3PM	3PA	3P%	FTM	FTA	FT%	ORB	DRB	TRB	AST	PF	DQ	STL	BLK	TO	MPG	PPG	RPG	APG	PCM
70-71	Seattle	5	....	68	34	9	25	.360	....	....	....	16	22	.727	....	....	9	9	11	0	....	....	....	13.6	6.8	1.8	1.8	.455
71-72	Seattle	26	....	181	92	33	66	.500	....	....	....	26	33	.788	....	....	11	26	21	0	....	....	....	7.0	3.5	0.4	1.0	.500
NBA Season Totals		31	....	249	126	42	91	.462	....	....	....	42	55	.764	....	....	20	35	32	0	....	....	....	8.0	4.1	0.6	1.1	....

• FORD, Len

Leonard Guy Ford Jr.

Born: Feb. 18, 1926. Washington, DC, United States. Died: Mar.13, 1972.   Height: 6'4".   Weight: 230 lbs.   Drafted: —   College: Michigan

YEAR	TEAM	GP	GS	MIN	PTS	FGM	FGA	FG%	3PM	3PA	3P%	FTM	FTA	FT%	ORB	DRB	TRB	AST	PF	DQ	STL	BLK	TO	MPG	PPG	RPG	APG	PCM
48-49	Dayton-N	6	....	....	6	2	....	....	....	....	....	2	8	.250	....	....	....	....	....	....	....	....	....	1.0	....	....	....
NBL Season Totals		6	....	....	6	2	....	....	....	....	....	2	8	....	....	....	....	....	....	....	....	....	....	1.0	....	....	....

• FORD, Phil

Phil Jackson Ford Jr.

Born: Feb. 9, 1956. Rocky Mount, NC, United States.   Height: 6'2".   Weight: 175 lbs.   Drafted: 1978   College: North Carolina

YEAR	TEAM	GP	GS	MIN	PTS	FGM	FGA	FG%	3PM	3PA	3P%	FTM	FTA	FT%	ORB	DRB	TRB	AST	PF	DQ	STL	BLK	TO	MPG	PPG	RPG	APG	PCM
78-79	Kansas City	79	....	2723	1260	467	1004	.465	....	....	....	326	401	.813	33	149	182	681	245	3	174	6	324	34.5	15.9	2.3	8.6	.521
79-80	Kansas City	82	....	2621	1328	489	1058	.462	4	23	.174	346	423	.818	29	143	172	610	208	0	136	4	279	32.0	16.2	2.1	7.4	.527
80-81	Kansas City	66	....	2287	1153	424	887	.478	11	36	.306	294	354	.831	26	102	128	580	190	3	99	6	244	34.7	17.5	1.9	8.8	.542
81-82	Kansas City	72	65	1952	713	285	649	.439	7	32	.219	136	166	.819	24	81	105	451	160	0	63	1	194	27.1	9.9	1.5	6.3	.386
82-83	New Jersey	7	7	163	47	20	35	.571	0	1	.000	7	10	.700	2	7	7	38	22	0	6	0	21	23.3	6.7	1.0	5.4	.348
82-83	Milwaukee	70	56	1447	477	193	410	.471	1	8	.125	90	113	.796	18	78	96	252	168	2	46	3	112	20.7	6.8	1.4	3.6	.347
83-84	Houston	81	55	2020	572	236	470	.502	2	15	.133	98	117	.838	28	109	137	410	243	7	59	8	138	24.9	7.1	1.7	5.1	.363
84-85	Houston	25	1	290	44	14	47	.298	0	4	.000	16	18	.889	3	24	27	61	33	0	6	1	18	11.6	1.8	1.1	2.4	.265
NBA Season Totals		482	184	13503	5594	2128	4560	.467	25	119	.210	1313	1602	.820	161	693	854	3083	1269	15	589	29	1330	28.0	11.6	1.8	6.4	....
78-79	Kansas City	5	....	143	39	15	57	.263	....	....	....	9	16	.563	2	10	12	29	14	0	12	0	15	28.6	7.8	2.4	5.8	.223
79-80	Kansas City	3	....	110	52	20	43	.465	3	4	.750	9	11	.818	0	6	6	26	6	0	5	0	12	36.7	17.3	2.0	8.7	.501
80-81	Kansas City	5	....	158	39	15	35	.429	0	1	.000	9	13	.692	1	7	8	29	9	0	5	0	17	31.6	7.8	1.6	5.8	.271
82-83	Milwaukee	2	0	5	6	0	2	.000	0	0	.000	6	6	1.000	0	0	0	1	1	0	0	0	0	2.5	3.0	0.0	0.5	.969
NBA Playoff Totals		15	0	416	136	50	137	.365	3	5	.600	33	46	.717	3	23	26	85	30	0	22	0	44	27.7	9.1	1.7	5.7	....

• FORD, Sherell

Willard Sherell Ford

Born: Aug. 26, 1972. Baton Rouge, LA, United States.   Height: 6'7".   Weight: 210 lbs.   Drafted: 1995   College: Illinois (Chicago)

YEAR	TEAM	GP	GS	MIN	PTS	FGM	FGA	FG%	3PM	3PA	3P%	FTM	FTA	FT%	ORB	DRB	TRB	AST	PF	DQ	STL	BLK	TO	MPG	PPG	RPG	APG	PCM
95-96	Seattle	28	1	139	90	30	80	.375	4	25	.160	26	34	.765	12	12	24	5	27	0	8	1	6	5.0	3.2	0.9	0.2	.412
NBA Season Totals		28	1	139	90	30	80	.375	4	25	.160	26	34	.765	12	12	24	5	27	0	8	1	6	5.0	3.2	0.9	0.2	....

• FORESTIERI, Jack

Jack Forestieri

Born: 1927.   Height: 6'   Weight: 185 lbs.   Drafted: —   College: Notre Dame

YEAR	TEAM	GP	GS	MIN	PTS	FGM	FGA	FG%	3PM	3PA	3P%	FTM	FTA	FT%	ORB	DRB	TRB	AST	PF	DQ	STL	BLK	TO	MPG	PPG	RPG	APG	PCM
47-48	Indianapolis-N	1	....	....	4	1	....	....	....	....	....	2	4	.500	....	....	....	5	....	....	....	....	....	4.0	....	....	....
47-48	Sheboygan-N	4	....	....	1	0	....	....	....	....	....	1	1	1.000	....	....	....	....	....	....	....	....	....	0.3	....	....	....
NBL Season Totals		5	....	....	5	1	....	....	....	....	....	3	5	....	....	....	....	5	....	....	....	....	....	1.0	....	....	....

YEAR	TEAM	GP	GS	MIN	PTS	FGM	FGA	FG%	3PM	3PA	3P%	FTM	FTA	FT%	ORB	DRB	TRB	AST	PF	DQ	STL	BLK	TO	MPG	PPG	RPG	APG	PCM

• FORMAN, Donnie
Donald J. Forman

Born: Jan. 17, 1926.   Height: 5'10".   Weight: 175 lbs.   Drafted: —   College: New York University

48-49	Minneapolis	44	....	....	179	68	231	.294	....	....	....	43	67	.642	....	....	....	74	94	....	....	....	....	....	4.1	....	1.7	....
NBA Season Totals		44	....	....	179	68	231	.294	....	....	....	43	67	.642	....	....	....	74	94	....	....	....	....	....	4.1	....	1.7	....
48-49	Minneapolis	9	....	....	13	3	20	.150	....	....	....	7	11	.636	....	....	....	7	15	....	....	....	....	....	1.4	....	0.8	....
NBA Playoff Totals		9	....	....	13	3	20	.150	....	....	....	7	11	.636	....	....	....	7	15	....	....	....	....	....	1.4	....	0.8	....

• FORREST, Bayard
Bayard Forrest

Born: July 8, 1954. San Jose, CA, United States.   Height: 6'10".   Weight: 235 lbs.   Drafted: 1976   College: Grand Canyon

77-78	Phoenix	64	....	887	271	111	238	.466	....	....	....	49	103	.476	84	166	250	129	105	0	23	34	83	13.9	4.2	3.9	2.0	.486
78-79	Phoenix	75	....	1243	298	118	272	.434	....	....	....	62	115	.539	110	205	315	167	151	1	29	37	105	16.6	4.0	4.2	2.2	.402
NBA Season Totals		139	....	2130	569	229	510	.449	....	....	....	111	218	.509	194	371	565	296	256	1	52	71	188	15.3	4.1	4.1	2.1	....
77-78	Phoenix	1	....	3	2	1	1	1.000	....	....	....	0	0	.000	0	0	0	0	0	0	0	0	0	3.0	2.0	0.0	0.0	.667
78-79	Phoenix	14	....	110	22	10	18	.556	....	....	....	2	10	.200	9	20	29	11	21	0	4	2	10	7.9	1.6	2.1	0.8	.331
NBA Playoff Totals		15	....	113	24	11	19	.579	....	....	....	2	10	.200	9	20	29	11	21	0	4	2	10	7.5	1.6	1.9	0.7	....

• FORTE, Joseph
Joseph Xavier Forte

Born: Mar. 23, 1981. Atlanta, GA, United States.   Height: 6'4".   Weight: 194 lbs.   Drafted: 2001   College: North Carolina

01-02	Boston	8	0	39	6	1	12	.083	0	3	.000	4	4	1.000	1	5	6	6	1	0	2	0	3	4.9	0.8	0.8	0.8	.171
02-03	Seattle	17	0	86	24	10	35	.286	0	3	.000	4	6	.667	4	7	11	11	6	0	4	0	10	5.1	1.4	0.6	0.6	.165
NBA Season Totals		25	0	125	30	11	47	.234	0	6	.000	8	10	.800	5	12	17	17	7	0	6	0	13	5.0	1.2	0.7	0.7	....

• FORTNEY, Ernie
Ernie Fortney

Born: 1914.   Height: 6'4".   Weight: 220 lbs.   Drafted: —   College: Duquesne

38-39	Pittsburgh-N	11	....	....	43	16	....	....	....	....	....	11	....	....	....	....	....	....	....	....	....	....	....	3.9	....	....	....
45-46	Youngstown-N	3	....	....	0	0	....	....	....	....	....	0	0	.000	....	....	....	....	....	....	....	....	....	0.0	....	....	....
NBL Season Totals		14	....	....	43	16	....	....	....	....	....	11	0	....	....	....	....	....	....	....	....	....	....	3.1	....	....	....

• FORTSON, Danny
Daniel Anthony Fortson

Born: Mar. 27, 1976. Philadelphia, PA, United States.   Height: 6'7".   Weight: 260 lbs.   Drafted: 1997   College: Cincinnati

97-98	Denver	80	23	1811	816	276	611	.452	1	3	.333	263	339	.776	182	266	448	76	314	7	44	30	160	22.6	10.2	5.6	1.0	.411
98-99	Denver	50	38	1417	550	191	386	.495	0	3	.000	168	231	.727	**210**	371	581	32	**212**	**9**	31	22	77	28.3	11.0	11.6	0.6	.554
99-00	Boston	55	5	856	419	140	265	.528	0	0	.000	139	189	.735	141	225	366	29	180	4	20	5	67	15.6	7.6	6.7	0.5	.616
00-01	Golden State	6	6	203	100	29	50	.580	0	0	.000	42	54	.778	29	69	98	5	22	1	2	0	10	33.8	16.7	16.3	0.8	.750
01-02	Golden State	77	76	2216	864	309	722	.428	1	4	.250	245	308	.795	290	609	899	127	255	5	44	17	160	28.8	11.2	11.7	1.6	.546
02-03	Golden State	17	0	223	59	20	54	.370	0	1	.000	19	29	.655	28	45	73	12	43	0	9	0	15	13.1	3.5	4.3	0.7	.350
NBA Season Totals		285	148	6726	2808	965	2088	.462	2	11	.182	876	1150	.762	880	1585	2465	281	1026	26	150	74	489	23.6	9.9	8.6	1.0	....

• FOSTER, Fred
Fred J. Foster

Born: Mar. 18, 1946. Springfield, OH, United States. Died: Oct.4, 1985.   Height: 6'5".   Weight: 210 lbs.   Drafted: 1968   College: Miami (OH)

68-69	Cincinnati	56	....	497	191	74	193	.383	....	....	....	43	66	.652	....	....	61	36	49	0	....	....	....	8.9	3.4	1.1	0.6	.311
69-70	Cincinnati	74	....	2077	1098	461	1026	.449	....	....	....	176	243	.724	....	....	310	107	209	2	....	....	....	28.1	14.8	4.2	1.4	.420
70-71	Cincinnati	1	....	21	7	3	8	.375	....	....	....	1	3	.333	....	....	4	0	2	0	....	....	....	21.0	7.0	4.0	0.0	.210
70-71	Philadelphia	66	....	888	362	145	360	.403	....	....	....	72	103	.699	....	....	147	61	113	3	....	....	....	13.5	5.5	2.2	0.9	.350
71-72	Philadelphia	74	....	1699	879	347	837	.415	....	....	....	185	243	.761	....	....	276	90	184	3	....	....	....	23.0	11.9	3.7	1.2	.407
72-73	Detroit	63	....	1460	547	243	627	.388	....	....	....	61	87	.701	....	....	183	94	150	0	....	....	....	23.2	8.7	2.9	1.5	.278
73-74	Cleveland	58	....	649	278	112	288	.389	....	....	....	54	64	.844	43	65	108	62	79	0	19	6	....	11.2	4.8	1.9	1.1	.391
74-75	Cleveland	73	....	1136	503	217	521	.417	....	....	....	69	97	.711	56	54	110	103	130	1	22	2	....	15.6	6.9	1.5	1.4	.342
76-77	Buffalo	59	....	689	228	99	247	.401	....	....	....	30	44	.682	33	43	76	48	92	0	16	0	....	11.7	3.9	1.3	0.8	.254
NBA Season Totals		524	....	9116	4093	1701	4107	.414	....	....	....	691	950	.727	132	162	1275	601	1008	9	57	8	....	17.4	7.8	2.4	1.1	....
70-71	Philadelphia	5	....	49	18	8	19	.421	....	....	....	2	2	1.000	....	....	12	5	6	0	....	....	....	9.8	3.6	2.4	1.0	.449
NBA Playoff Totals		5	....	49	18	8	19	.421	....	....	....	2	2	1.000	....	....	12	5	6	0	....	....	....	9.8	3.6	2.4	1.0	....

• FOSTER, Greg
Gregory Clinton Foster

Born: Oct. 3, 1968. Oakland, CA, United States.   Height: 6'11".   Weight: 240 lbs.   Drafted: 1990   College: Texas (El Paso)

90-91	Washington	54	3	606	236	97	211	.460	0	5	.000	42	61	.689	52	99	151	37	112	1	12	22	43	11.2	4.4	2.8	0.7	.397
91-92	Washington	49	3	548	213	89	193	.461	0	1	.000	35	49	.714	43	102	145	35	83	0	6	12	34	11.2	4.3	3.0	0.7	.417
92-93	Washington	10	0	93	24	11	25	.440	0	0	.000	2	3	.667	8	19	27	11	17	0	0	5	9	9.3	2.4	2.7	1.1	.384
92-93	Atlanta	33	0	205	101	44	95	.463	0	4	.000	13	18	.722	24	32	56	10	41	0	3	9	17	6.2	3.1	1.7	0.3	.440
93-94	Milwaukee	3	0	19	10	4	7	.571	0	0	.000	2	2	1.000	0	3	3	0	3	0	0	1	1	6.3	3.3	1.0	0.0	.454
94-95	Chicago	17	3	299	104	41	86	.477	0	0	.000	22	31	.710	18	36	54	16	54	0	2	8	17	17.6	6.1	3.2	0.9	.312
94-95	Minnesota	61	0	845	281	109	232	.470	7	23	.304	56	80	.700	67	138	205	23	129	0	13	20	55	13.9	4.6	3.4	0.4	.343
95-96	Utah	73	2	803	276	107	244	.439	1	8	.125	61	72	.847	53	125	178	25	120	0	7	22	58	11.0	3.8	2.4	0.3	.314
96-97	Utah	79	12	920	278	111	245	.453	2	3	.667	54	65	.831	56	131	187	31	145	0	10	20	55	11.6	3.5	2.4	0.4	.288
97-98	Utah	78	49	1446	441	186	418	.445	2	9	.222	67	87	.770	85	188	273	51	187	2	15	28	70	18.5	5.7	3.5	0.7	.287
98-99	Utah	42	1	458	116	52	138	.377	1	4	.250	13	21	.619	28	55	83	25	63	1	6	8	24	10.9	2.8	2.0	0.6	.224
99-00	Seattle	60	5	718	203	91	224	.406	3	15	.200	18	28	.643	16	91	107	41	105	0	10	18	28	12.0	3.4	1.8	0.7	.239
00-01	LA Lakers	62	8	451	125	56	133	.421	3	9	.333	10	14	.714	29	83	112	32	76	0	9	12	25	7.3	2.0	1.8	0.5	.337

YEAR	TEAM	GP	GS	MIN	PTS	FGM	FGA	FG%	3PM	3PA	3P%	FTM	FTA	FT%	ORB	DRB	TRB	AST	PF	DQ	STL	BLK	TO	MPG	PPG	RPG	APG	PCM
01-02	Milwaukee	6	0	24	7	2	9	.222	0	4	.000	3	4	.750	0	8	8	1	4	0	0	0	0	4.0	1.2	1.3	0.2	.281
02-03	Toronto	29	9	539	121	47	122	.385	1	4	.250	26	32	.813	30	72	102	13	82	1	1	9	30	18.6	4.2	3.5	0.4	.188
NBA Season Totals		656	95	7974	2538	1047	2382	.440	20	89	.225	424	567	.748	509	1182	1691	351	1221	5	94	194	466	12.2	3.9	2.6	0.5	....
92-93	Atlanta	1	0	5	5	1	3	.333	0	0	.000	3	4	.750	0	1	1	0	0	0	0	0	0	5.0	5.0	1.0	0.0	.720
95-96	Utah	12	0	76	28	11	22	.500	0	0	.000	6	10	.600	6	6	12	2	15	0	1	2	5	6.3	2.3	1.0	0.2	.266
96-97	Utah	20	0	309	84	28	72	.389	2	8	.250	26	30	.867	15	41	56	11	53	0	4	7	11	15.5	4.2	2.8	0.6	.260
97-98	Utah	20	16	335	82	39	86	.453	1	2	.500	3	5	.600	20	47	67	5	55	0	2	5	18	16.8	4.1	3.4	0.3	.208
98-99	Utah	8	0	70	16	8	19	.421	0	0	.000	0	0	.000	1	7	8	1	11	0	1	0	3	8.8	2.0	1.0	0.1	.111
99-00	Seattle	5	0	68	18	7	19	.368	2	5	.400	2	2	1.000	1	10	11	1	14	0	0	1	3	13.6	3.6	2.2	0.2	.147
00-01	LA Lakers	1	0	3	0	0	0	.000	0	0	.000	0	0	.000	0	1	1	0	1	0	0	0	0	3.0	0.0	1.0	0.0	.150
NBA Playoff Totals		67	16	866	233	94	221	.425	5	15	.333	40	51	.784	43	113	156	20	149	0	8	15	40	12.9	3.5	2.3	0.3	....

• FOSTER, James

James Foster

Born: Dec. 16, 1951. Jersey City, NJ, United States. Height: 6'1". Weight: 175 lbs. Drafted: 1974 College: Connecticut

YEAR	TEAM	GP	GS	MIN	PTS	FGM	FGA	FG%	3PM	3PA	3P%	FTM	FTA	FT%	ORB	DRB	TRB	AST	PF	DQ	STL	BLK	TO	MPG	PPG	RPG	APG	PCM
74-75	St. Louis-A	41	....	806	183	78	209	.373	0	6	.000	27	34	.794	19	56	75	143	118	....	39	5	88	19.7	4.5	1.8	3.5	.294
75-76	Denver-A	48	....	352	148	54	145	.372	1	8	.125	39	64	.609	19	23	42	47	78	....	19	4	63	7.3	3.1	0.9	1.0	.314
ABA Season Totals		89	....	1158	331	132	354	.373	1	14	.071	66	98	.673	38	79	117	190	196	....	58	9	151	13.0	3.7	1.3	2.1	....
74-75	St. Louis-A	7	....	52	16	6	16	.375	0	1	.000	4	8	.500	3	3	6	6	9	....	3	0	5	7.4	2.3	0.9	0.9	.257
75-76	Denver-A	2	....	13	13	5	8	.625	0	0	.000	3	7	.429	1	1	2	1	4	....	1	0	3	6.5	6.5	1.0	0.5	.743
ABA Playoff Totals		9	....	65	29	11	24	.458	0	1	.000	7	15	.467	4	4	8	7	13	....	4	0	8	7.2	3.2	0.9	0.8	....

• FOSTER, Jeff

Jeffrey Douglas Foster

Born: Jan. 16, 1977. San Antonio, TX, United States. Height: 6'11". Weight: 236 lbs. Drafted: 1999 College: Southwest Texas State

YEAR	TEAM	GP	GS	MIN	PTS	FGM	FGA	FG%	3PM	3PA	3P%	FTM	FTA	FT%	ORB	DRB	TRB	AST	PF	DQ	STL	BLK	TO	MPG	PPG	RPG	APG	PCM
99-00	Indiana	19	0	86	43	13	23	.565	0	1	.000	17	25	.680	12	20	32	5	18	0	5	1	2	4.5	2.3	1.7	0.3	.701
00-01	Indiana	71	9	1152	249	100	213	.469	2	7	.286	47	91	.516	144	245	389	33	152	3	39	28	52	16.2	3.5	5.5	0.5	.398
01-02	Indiana	82	48	1787	467	177	394	.449	2	15	.133	111	182	.610	206	350	556	70	232	4	71	38	79	21.8	5.7	6.8	0.9	.414
02-03	Indiana	77	2	813	162	64	178	.360	0	2	.000	34	63	.540	118	161	279	51	103	0	28	21	34	10.6	2.1	3.6	0.7	.395
NBA Season Totals		249	59	3838	921	354	808	.438	4	25	.160	209	361	.579	480	776	1256	159	505	7	143	88	167	15.4	3.7	5.0	0.6	....
00-01	Indiana	4	2	52	10	4	9	.444	0	0	.000	2	2	1.000	3	9	12	2	8	0	0	3	4	13.0	2.5	3.0	0.5	.269
01-02	Indiana	5	0	78	20	7	13	.538	2	4	.500	4	9	.444	5	19	24	7	13	0	3	1	9	15.6	4.0	4.8	1.4	.401
02-03	Indiana	6	0	38	14	6	11	.545	0	0	.000	2	2	1.000	4	4	8	2	3	0	0	3	0	6.3	2.3	1.3	0.3	.533
NBA Playoff Totals		15	2	168	44	17	33	.515	2	4	.500	8	13	.615	12	32	44	11	24	0	3	7	13	11.2	2.9	2.9	0.7	....

• FOSTER, Rod

Roderick Allen Foster

Born: Oct. 10, 1960. Birmingham, AL, United States. Height: 6'1". Weight: 160 lbs. Drafted: 1983 College: UCLA

YEAR	TEAM	GP	GS	MIN	PTS	FGM	FGA	FG%	3PM	3PA	3P%	FTM	FTA	FT%	ORB	DRB	TRB	AST	PF	DQ	STL	BLK	TO	MPG	PPG	RPG	APG	PCM
83-84	Phoenix	80	34	1424	664	260	580	.448	22	84	.262	122	155	.787	39	81	120	172	193	0	54	9	112	17.8	8.3	1.5	2.2	.359
84-85	Phoenix	79	1	1318	696	286	636	.450	41	126	.325	83	110	.755	27	53	80	186	171	1	61	0	119	16.7	8.8	1.0	2.4	.377
85-86	Phoenix	48	0	704	202	85	218	.390	9	32	.281	23	32	.719	9	49	58	121	77	0	22	1	62	14.7	4.2	1.2	2.5	.264
NBA Season Totals		207	35	3446	1562	631	1434	.440	72	242	.298	228	297	.768	75	183	258	479	441	1	137	10	293	16.6	7.5	1.2	2.3	....
83-84	Phoenix	16	0	128	29	10	39	.256	0	5	.000	9	9	1.000	6	7	13	18	21	0	5	1	13	8.0	1.8	0.8	1.1	.134
84-85	Phoenix	3	0	56	20	7	25	.280	0	4	.000	6	8	.750	0	3	3	7	4	0	5	0	5	18.7	6.7	1.0	2.3	.191
NBA Playoff Totals		19	0	184	49	17	64	.266	0	9	.000	15	17	.882	6	10	16	25	25	0	10	1	18	9.7	2.6	0.8	1.3	....

• FOTSIS, Antonis

Antonis Fotsis

Born: Apr. 1, 1981. Athens, Greece. Height: 6'10". Weight: 219 lbs. Drafted: 2001 College: none

YEAR	TEAM	GP	GS	MIN	PTS	FGM	FGA	FG%	3PM	3PA	3P%	FTM	FTA	FT%	ORB	DRB	TRB	AST	PF	DQ	STL	BLK	TO	MPG	PPG	RPG	APG	PCM
01-02	Memphis	28	1	319	108	42	104	.404	7	23	.304	17	20	.850	25	37	62	10	22	0	9	11	21	11.4	3.9	2.2	0.4	.335
NBA Season Totals		28	1	319	108	42	104	.404	7	23	.304	17	20	.850	25	37	62	10	22	0	9	11	21	11.4	3.9	2.2	0.4	....

• FOUST, Larry

Lawrence Michael Foust

Born: June 24, 1928. Painesville, OH, United States. Died: Oct.27, 1984. Height: 6'9". Weight: 215 lbs. Drafted: 1950 College: LaSalle

YEAR	TEAM	GP	GS	MIN	PTS	FGM	FGA	FG%	3PM	3PA	3P%	FTM	FTA	FT%	ORB	DRB	TRB	AST	PF	DQ	STL	BLK	TO	MPG	PPG	RPG	APG	PCM
50-51	Fort Wayne	68	....	....	915	327	944	.346	....	....	....	261	396	.659	....	....	681	90	247	6	....	....	....	13.5	10.0	1.3	....	
51-52	Fort Wayne	66	....	2615	1047	390	989	.394	....	....	....	267	394	.678	....	....	**880**	200	245	10	....	....	....	39.6	15.9	13.3	3.0	.525
52-53	Fort Wayne	67	....	2303	958	311	865	.360	....	....	....	336	465	.723	....	....	769	151	267	16	....	....	....	34.4	14.3	11.5	2.3	.505
53-54	Fort Wayne	72	....	2693	1090	376	919	.409	....	....	....	338	475	.712	....	....	967	161	258	4	....	....	....	37.4	15.1	13.4	2.2	.542
54-55	Fort Wayne	70	....	2264	1189	398	818	**.487**	....	....	....	393	513	.766	....	....	700	118	264	9	....	....	....	32.3	17.0	10.0	1.7	.619
55-56	Fort Wayne	72	....	2024	1166	367	821	.447	....	....	....	432	555	.778	....	....	648	127	263	7	....	....	....	28.1	16.2	9.0	1.8	.654
56-57	Fort Wayne	61	....	1533	759	243	617	.394	....	....	....	273	380	.718	....	....	555	71	221	7	....	....	....	25.1	12.4	9.1	1.2	.561
57-58	Minneapolis	72	....	2200	1210	391	982	.398	....	....	....	428	566	.756	....	....	876	108	299	11	....	....	....	30.6	16.8	12.2	1.5	.634
58-59	Minneapolis	72	....	1933	882	301	771	.390	....	....	....	280	366	.765	....	....	627	91	233	5	....	....	....	26.8	12.3	8.7	1.3	.514
59-60	Min/StL	72	....	1964	877	312	766	.407	....	....	....	253	320	.791	....	....	621	96	241	7	....	....	....	27.3	12.2	8.6	1.3	.512
60-61	St. Louis	68	....	1208	552	194	489	.397	....	....	....	164	208	.788	....	....	389	77	185	0	....	....	....	17.8	8.1	5.7	1.1	.523
61-62	St. Louis	57	....	1153	553	204	433	.471	....	....	....	145	178	.815	....	....	328	78	186	3	....	....	....	20.2	9.7	5.8	1.4	.555
NBA Season Totals		817	....	21890	11198	3814	9414	.405	....	....	....	3570	4816	.741	....	....	8041	1368	2909	85	....	....	....	26.8	13.7	9.8	1.7	....
50-51	Fort Wayne	3	....	....	36	14	45	.311	....	....	....	8	10	.800	....	....	37	5	5	0	....	....	....	....	12.0	12.3	1.7	....
51-52	Fort Wayne	2	....	77	30	12	23	.522	....	....	....	6	7	.857	....	....	30	5	8	1	....	....	....	38.5	15.0	15.0	2.5	.607
52-53	Fort Wayne	8	....	332	153	48	121	.397	....	....	....	57	68	.838	....	....	111	6	34	2	....	....	....	41.5	19.1	13.9	0.8	.518
53-54	Fort Wayne	4	....	129	41	11	41	.268	....	....	....	19	25	.760	....	....	38	7	21	2	....	....	....	32.3	10.3	9.5	1.8	.358
54-55	Fort Wayne	11	....	331	172	60	152	.395	....	....	....	52	73	.712	....	....	107	26	43	0	....	....	....	30.1	15.6	9.7	2.4	.579
55-56	Fort Wayne	10	....	289	168	49	130	.377	....	....	....	70	89	.787	....	....	127	14	38	2	....	....	....	28.9	16.8	12.7	1.4	.687
56-57	Fort Wayne	2	....	64	45	13	23	.565	....	....	....	19	23	.826	....	....	25	6	10	0	....	....	....	32.0	22.5	12.5	3.0	.914

YEAR	TEAM	GP	GS	MIN	PTS	FGM	FGA	FG%	3PM	3PA	3P%	FTM	FTA	FT%	ORB	DRB	TRB	AST	PF	DQ	STL	BLK	TO	MPG	PPG	RPG	APG	PCM
58-59	Minneapolis	13	....	404	153	56	134	.418	....	....	....	41	50	.820	....	....	136	12	47	2	....	....	....	31.1	11.8	10.5	0.9	.472
59-60	St. Louis	12	....	205	78	29	74	.392	....	....	....	20	25	.800	....	....	68	11	36	0	....	....	....	17.1	6.5	5.7	0.9	.456
60-61	St. Louis	8	....	89	26	9	20	.450	....	....	....	8	14	.571	....	....	28	2	13	0	....	....	....	11.1	3.3	3.5	0.3	.384
NBA Playoff Totals		73	....	1920	902	301	763	.394	....	....	....	300	384	.781	....	....	707	94	255	9	....	....	....	26.3	12.4	9.7	1.3	....

• FOWDY, Steve

Steve Fowdy

Born: Sept. 16, 1915.　Died: Jan. 23, 1995.　Height: 6'2".　Weight: 180 lbs.　Drafted: —　College: North Dakota

YEAR	TEAM	GP	GS	MIN	PTS	FGM	FGA	FG%	3PM	3PA	3P%	FTM	FTA	FT%	ORB	DRB	TRB	AST	PF	DQ	STL	BLK	TO	MPG	PPG	RPG	APG	PCM
38-39	Hammond-N	1	....	....	0	0	....	....	....	....	....	0	....	....	....	....	....	....	....	....	....	....	....	....	0.0	....	....	....
NBL Season Totals		1	....	....	0	0	....	....	....	....	....	0	....	....	....	....	....	....	....	....	....	....	....	....	0.0	....	....	....

• FOWLER, Calvin

Calvin Bernard Fowler

Born: Feb. 11, 1940. Pittsburgh, PA, United States.　Height: 6'　Weight: 175 lbs.　Drafted: —　College: St. Francis (PA)

YEAR	TEAM	GP	GS	MIN	PTS	FGM	FGA	FG%	3PM	3PA	3P%	FTM	FTA	FT%	ORB	DRB	TRB	AST	PF	DQ	STL	BLK	TO	MPG	PPG	RPG	APG	PCM
69-70	Carolina-A	78	....	1234	343	131	288	.455	7	17	.412	74	119	.622	54	116	170	126	156	2	....	....	77	15.8	4.4	2.2	1.6	.334
ABA Season Totals		78	....	1234	343	131	288	.455	7	17	.412	74	119	.622	54	116	170	126	156	2	....	....	77	15.8	4.4	2.2	1.6	
69-70	Carolina-A	4	....	76	19	6	14	.429	0	1	.000	7	10	.700	....	....	13	0	....	....	....	....	....	19.0	4.8	3.3	0.0	
ABA Playoff Totals		4	....	76	19	6	14	.429	0	1	.000	7	10	.700	....	....	13	0	....	....	....	....	....	19.0	4.8	3.3	0.0	

• FOWLER, Jerry

Jerry A. Fowler

Born: June 20, 1927.　Height: 6'8".　Weight: 230 lbs.　Drafted: —　College: Missouri

YEAR	TEAM	GP	GS	MIN	PTS	FGM	FGA	FG%	3PM	3PA	3P%	FTM	FTA	FT%	ORB	DRB	TRB	AST	PF	DQ	STL	BLK	TO	MPG	PPG	RPG	APG	PCM
51-52	Milwaukee	6	....	41	9	4	13	.308	....	....	....	1	4	.250	....	....	10	2	9	0	....	....	....	6.8	1.5	1.7	0.3	.196
NBA Season Totals		6	....	41	9	4	13	.308	....	....	....	1	4	.250	....	....	10	2	9	0	....	....	....	6.8	1.5	1.7	0.3	....

• FOWLKES, Tremain

Tremain Fowlkes

Born: Apr. 11, 1976. Los Angeles, CA, United States.　Height: 6'8".　Weight: 220 lbs.　Drafted: 1998　College: Fresno State

YEAR	TEAM	GP	GS	MIN	PTS	FGM	FGA	FG%	3PM	3PA	3P%	FTM	FTA	FT%	ORB	DRB	TRB	AST	PF	DQ	STL	BLK	TO	MPG	PPG	RPG	APG	PCM
01-02	LA Clippers	22	17	340	74	25	64	.391	0	0	.000	24	31	.774	32	32	64	17	39	0	11	1	13	15.5	3.4	2.9	0.8	.275
02-03	LA Clippers	37	10	573	164	56	128	.438	2	9	.222	50	59	.847	41	62	103	23	63	0	25	2	20	15.5	4.4	2.8	0.6	.333
NBA Season Totals		59	27	913	238	81	192	.422	2	9	.222	74	90	.822	73	94	167	40	102	0	36	3	33	15.5	4.0	2.8	0.7	....

• FOX, Harold

Harold Fox

Born: Aug. 29, 1949.　Height: 6'2".　Weight: 175 lbs.　Drafted: 1972　College: Jacksonville

YEAR	TEAM	GP	GS	MIN	PTS	FGM	FGA	FG%	3PM	3PA	3P%	FTM	FTA	FT%	ORB	DRB	TRB	AST	PF	DQ	STL	BLK	TO	MPG	PPG	RPG	APG	PCM
72-73	Buffalo	10	....	84	31	12	32	.375	....	....	....	7	8	.875	....	....	8	10	7	0	....	....	....	8.4	3.1	0.8	1.0	.342
NBA Season Totals		10	....	84	31	12	32	.375	....	....	....	7	8	.875	....	....	8	10	7	0	....	....	....	8.4	3.1	0.8	1.0	....

• FOX, Jim

James L. (Foxy) Fox

Born: Apr. 7, 1943. Atlanta, GA, United States.　Height: 6'10".　Weight: 230 lbs.　Drafted: 1965　College: South Carolina

YEAR	TEAM	GP	GS	MIN	PTS	FGM	FGA	FG%	3PM	3PA	3P%	FTM	FTA	FT%	ORB	DRB	TRB	AST	PF	DQ	STL	BLK	TO	MPG	PPG	RPG	APG	PCM
67-68	Cincinnati	31	....	244	100	32	79	.405	....	....	....	36	56	.643	....	....	95	12	34	0	....	....	....	7.9	3.2	3.1	0.4	.538
67-68	Detroit	24	....	380	98	34	82	.415	....	....	....	30	52	.577	....	....	135	17	51	0	....	....	....	15.8	4.1	5.6	0.7	.418
68-69	Detroit	25	....	375	124	45	96	.469	....	....	....	34	53	.642	....	....	139	23	56	1	....	....	....	15.0	5.0	5.6	0.9	.515
68-69	Phoenix	51	....	1979	703	273	581	.470	....	....	....	157	214	.734	....	....	679	143	210	5	....	....	....	38.8	13.8	13.3	2.8	.540
69-70	Phoenix	81	....	2041	1044	413	788	.524	....	....	....	218	283	.770	....	....	570	93	261	7	....	....	....	25.2	12.9	7.0	1.1	.576
70-71	Chicago	82	....	1628	799	280	611	.458	....	....	....	239	321	.745	....	....	598	196	213	0	....	....	....	19.9	9.7	7.3	2.4	.691
71-72	Chicago	10	....	133	60	20	53	.377	....	....	....	20	28	.714	....	....	54	6	21	0	....	....	....	13.3	6.0	5.4	0.6	.545
71-72	Cincinnati	71	....	2047	875	334	735	.454	....	....	....	207	269	.770	....	....	659	80	236	8	....	....	....	28.8	12.3	9.3	1.1	.518
72-73	Seattle	74	....	2439	846	316	613	.515	....	....	....	214	265	.808	....	....	827	176	239	6	....	....	....	33.0	11.4	11.2	2.4	.565
73-74	Seattle	78	....	2179	885	322	673	.478	....	....	....	241	293	.823	244	470	714	227	247	5	56	21	....	27.9	11.3	9.2	2.9	.609
74-75	Seattle	75	....	1766	676	253	540	.469	....	....	....	170	212	.802	128	363	491	137	168	1	48	17	....	23.5	9.0	6.5	1.8	.520
75-76	Milwaukee	70	....	918	272	105	203	.517	....	....	....	62	79	.785	82	153	235	42	129	1	27	16	....	13.1	3.9	3.4	0.6	.408
76-77	New York	71	....	1165	463	184	398	.462	....	....	....	95	114	.833	100	229	329	49	158	1	20	25	....	16.4	6.5	4.6	0.7	.465
NBA Season Totals		743	....	17294	6945	2611	5452	.479	....	....	....	1723	2239	.770	554	1215	5525	1201	2023	35	151	79	....	23.3	9.3	7.4	1.6	....
67-68	Detroit	6	....	90	27	6	19	.316	....	....	....	15	19	.789	....	....	37	3	11	1	....	....	....	15.0	4.5	6.2	0.5	.486
69-70	Phoenix	6	....	174	67	25	69	.362	....	....	....	17	24	.708	....	....	64	8	20	0	....	....	....	29.0	11.2	10.7	1.3	.469
70-71	Chicago	7	....	167	79	33	76	.434	....	....	....	13	19	.684	....	....	66	17	17	1	....	....	....	23.9	11.3	9.4	2.4	.648
74-75	Seattle	8	....	40	12	4	14	.286	....	....	....	4	7	.571	4	5	9	2	6	0	0	1	....	5.0	1.5	1.1	0.3	.240
75-76	Milwaukee	3	....	33	10	4	5	.800	....	....	....	2	2	1.000	2	5	7	3	8	0	0	1	....	11.0	3.3	2.3	1.0	.459
NBA Playoff Totals		30	....	504	195	72	183	.393	....	....	....	51	71	.718	6	10	183	33	62	2	0	2	....	16.8	6.5	6.1	1.1	....

• FOX, Rick

Ulrich Alexander Fox

Born: July 24, 1969. Toronto, ON, Canada.　Height: 6'7".　Weight: 230 lbs.　Drafted: 1991　College: North Carolina

YEAR	TEAM	GP	GS	MIN	PTS	FGM	FGA	FG%	3PM	3PA	3P%	FTM	FTA	FT%	ORB	DRB	TRB	AST	PF	DQ	STL	BLK	TO	MPG	PPG	RPG	APG	PCM
91-92	Boston	81	5	1535	644	241	525	.459	23	70	.329	139	184	.755	73	147	220	126	230	3	78	30	122	19.0	8.0	2.7	1.6	.377
92-93	Boston	71	14	1082	453	184	380	.484	4	23	.174	81	101	.802	55	104	159	113	133	1	61	21	78	15.2	6.4	2.2	1.6	.436
93-94	Boston	82	53	2096	887	340	728	.467	33	100	.330	174	230	.757	105	250	355	217	244	4	81	52	156	25.6	10.8	4.3	2.6	.445
94-95	Boston	53	7	1039	464	169	351	.481	31	75	.413	95	123	.772	61	94	155	139	154	1	52	19	80	19.6	8.8	2.9	2.6	.474
95-96	Boston	81	81	2588	1137	421	928	.454	99	272	.364	196	254	.772	158	292	450	369	290	5	113	41	219	32.0	14.0	5.6	4.6	.483
96-97	Boston	76	75	2650	1174	433	950	.456	101	278	.363	207	263	.787	114	280	394	286	279	4	167	40	175	34.9	15.4	5.2	3.8	.467
97-98	LA Lakers	82	82	2709	983	363	771	.471	86	265	.325	171	230	.743	78	280	358	276	309	4	100	48	205	33.0	12.0	4.4	3.4	.375
98-99	LA Lakers	44	1	944	394	148	330	.448	32	95	.337	66	89	.742	26	63	89	89	114	1	28	10	56	21.5	9.0	2.0	2.0	.353
99-00	LA Lakers	82	1	1473	534	206	498	.414	59	181	.326	63	78	.808	63	135	198	138	203	1	52	26	87	18.0	6.5	2.4	1.7	.334
00-01	LA Lakers	82	77	2291	787	287	646	.444	118	300	.393	95	122	.779	80	245	325	262	225	1	70	29	136	27.9	9.6	4.0	3.2	.392

YEAR	TEAM	GP	GS	MIN	PTS	FGM	FGA	FG%	3PM	3PA	3P%	FTM	FTA	FT%	ORB	DRB	TRB	AST	PF	DQ	STL	BLK	TO	MPG	PPG	RPG	APG	PCM
01-02	LA Lakers	82	82	2289	645	255	605	.421	65	208	.313	70	85	.824	90	299	389	283	244	2	67	21	132	27.9	7.9	4.7	3.5	.364
02-03	LA Lakers	76	75	2181	681	262	621	.422	105	280	.375	52	69	.754	64	259	323	253	215	4	69	14	121	28.7	9.0	4.3	3.3	.360
NBA Season Totals		892	553	22877	8783	3309	7333	.451	756	2147	.352	1409	1828	.771	967	2448	3415	2551	2640	31	938	351	1567	25.6	9.8	3.8	2.9	....
91-92	Boston	8	0	67	29	11	23	.478	3	6	.500	4	4	1.000	3	3	6	4	11	0	2	2	2	8.4	3.6	0.8	0.5	.365
92-93	Boston	4	0	71	17	7	25	.280	1	3	.333	2	2	1.000	8	11	19	5	7	0	2	1	4	17.8	4.3	4.8	1.3	.269
97-98	LA Lakers	13	13	428	142	51	114	.447	21	53	.396	19	23	.826	18	40	58	51	47	2	11	3	21	32.9	10.9	4.5	3.9	.381
98-99	LA Lakers	8	1	181	53	24	60	.400	4	21	.190	1	1	1.000	9	13	22	12	26	1	4	5	14	22.6	6.6	2.8	1.5	.209
99-00	LA Lakers	23	0	331	100	33	73	.452	18	39	.462	16	21	.762	11	27	38	28	68	1	9	0	16	14.4	4.3	1.7	1.2	.270
00-01	LA Lakers	16	16	573	160	58	129	.450	18	57	.316	26	30	.867	13	66	79	57	55	1	31	7	36	35.8	10.0	4.9	3.6	.358
01-02	LA Lakers	19	19	652	186	67	139	.482	15	43	.349	37	49	.755	24	78	102	64	70	0	21	6	45	34.3	9.8	5.4	3.4	.352
02-03	LA Lakers	4	4	79	24	8	18	.444	5	10	.500	3	4	.750	2	4	6	7	15	1	1	1	4	19.8	6.0	1.5	1.8	.240
NBA Playoff Totals		95	53	2382	711	259	581	.446	85	232	.366	108	134	.806	88	242	330	228	299	6	81	25	142	25.1	7.5	3.5	2.4	....

• FOX, Wilbur
Wilbur Fox

Born: 1917.   Height: 6'5".   Weight: 185 lbs.   Drafted: —   College: Akron

YEAR	TEAM	GP	GS	MIN	PTS	FGM	FGA	FG%	3PM	3PA	3P%	FTM	FTA	FT%	ORB	DRB	TRB	AST	PF	DQ	STL	BLK	TO	MPG	PPG	RPG	APG	PCM
39-40	Wingfoots-N	11	....	....	11	3	....	....	....	....	....	5												1.0	....	....	....
NBL Season Totals		11	....	....	11	3	....	....	....	....	....	5												1.0	....	....	....

• FOYLE, Adonal
Adonal David Foyle

Born: Mar. 9, 1975. Canovan, Virgin Islands.   Height: 6'10".   Weight: 250 lbs.   Drafted: 1997   College: Colgate

YEAR	TEAM	GP	GS	MIN	PTS	FGM	FGA	FG%	3PM	3PA	3P%	FTM	FTA	FT%	ORB	DRB	TRB	AST	PF	DQ	STL	BLK	TO	MPG	PPG	RPG	APG	PCM
97-98	Golden State	55	1	656	165	69	170	.406	0	1	.000	27	62	.435	73	111	184	14	94	0	13	52	50	11.9	3.0	3.3	0.3	.321
98-99	Golden State	44	0	614	129	52	121	.430	0	0	.000	25	51	.490	79	115	194	18	90	0	15	43	31	14.0	2.9	4.4	0.4	.379
99-00	Golden State	76	59	1654	420	193	380	.508	0	0	.000	34	90	.378	174	250	424	42	218	2	26	136	71	21.8	5.5	5.6	0.6	.387
00-01	Golden State	58	37	1457	342	156	375	.416	0	0	.000	30	68	.441	156	249	405	48	136	0	31	156	79	25.1	5.9	7.0	0.8	.399
01-02	Golden State	79	36	1485	379	171	385	.444	0	0	.000	37	93	.398	150	234	384	41	179	2	36	168	76	18.8	4.8	4.9	0.5	.396
02-03	Golden State	82	0	1787	440	185	345	.536	0	1	.000	70	104	.673	176	314	490	37	214	3	40	205	73	21.8	5.4	6.0	0.5	.461
NBA Season Totals		394	133	7653	1875	826	1776	.465	0	2	.000	223	468	.476	808	1273	2081	200	931	7	161	760	380	19.4	4.8	5.3	0.5	....

• FRANCIS, Chet
Chet Francis

Born: 1918.   Height: 6'2".   Weight: 180 lbs.   Drafted: —   College: Indiana

YEAR	TEAM	GP	GS	MIN	PTS	FGM	FGA	FG%	3PM	3PA	3P%	FTM	FTA	FT%	ORB	DRB	TRB	AST	PF	DQ	STL	BLK	TO	MPG	PPG	RPG	APG	PCM
45-46	Indianapolis-N	3	....	....	2	1	....	....	....	....	....	0	0	.000										0.7	....	....	....
NBL Season Totals		3	....	....	2	1	....	....	....	....	....	0	0											0.7	....	....	....

• FRANCIS, Steve
Steve D'Shawn Francis

Born: Feb. 21, 1978. Silver Spring, MD, United States.   Height: 6'3".   Weight: 195 lbs.   Drafted: 1999   College: Maryland

YEAR	TEAM	GP	GS	MIN	PTS	FGM	FGA	FG%	3PM	3PA	3P%	FTM	FTA	FT%	ORB	DRB	TRB	AST	PF	DQ	STL	BLK	TO	MPG	PPG	RPG	APG	PCM
99-00	Houston	77	77	2776	1388	497	1117	.445	107	310	.345	287	365	.786	152	257	409	507	231	2	118	29	306	36.1	18.0	5.3	6.6	.528
00-01	Houston	80	79	3194	1591	550	1219	.451	133	336	.396	358	438	.817	190	363	553	517	274	7	141	31	265	39.9	19.9	6.9	6.5	.568
01-02	Houston	57	56	2343	1234	420	1007	.417	68	210	.324	326	422	.773	102	299	401	362	172	2	71	25	221	41.1	21.6	7.0	6.4	.524
02-03	Houston	81	81	3318	1703	571	1312	.435	85	240	.354	476	595	.800	159	340	499	502	251	2	141	41	**299**	41.0	21.0	6.2	6.2	.530
NBA Season Totals		295	293	11631	5916	2038	4655	.438	393	1096	.359	1447	1820	.795	603	1259	1862	1888	928	13	471	126	1091	39.4	20.1	6.3	6.4	....

• FRANK, Tellis
Tellis Joseph Frank Jr.

Born: Apr. 26, 1965. Gary, IN, United States.   Height: 6'10".   Weight: 225 lbs.   Drafted: 1987   College: Western Kentucky

YEAR	TEAM	GP	GS	MIN	PTS	FGM	FGA	FG%	3PM	3PA	3P%	FTM	FTA	FT%	ORB	DRB	TRB	AST	PF	DQ	STL	BLK	TO	MPG	PPG	RPG	APG	PCM
87-88	Golden State	78	29	1597	634	242	565	.428	0	1	.000	150	207	.725	95	235	330	111	267	5	53	23	109	20.5	8.1	4.2	1.4	.362
88-89	Golden State	32	2	245	107	34	91	.374	0	1	.000	39	51	.765	26	35	61	15	59	1	14	6	29	7.7	3.3	1.9	0.5	.349
89-90	Miami	77	39	1762	735	278	607	.458	0	0	.000	179	234	.765	151	234	385	85	282	6	51	27	131	22.9	9.5	5.0	1.1	.380
91-92	Minnesota	10	0	140	46	18	33	.545	0	0	.000	10	15	.667	8	18	26	8	24	0	5	4	5	14.0	4.6	2.6	0.8	.393
93-94	Minnesota	67	11	959	188	67	160	.419	0	2	.000	54	76	.711	83	137	220	57	163	1	35	35	47	14.3	2.8	3.3	0.9	.315
NBA Season Totals		264	81	4703	1710	639	1456	.439	0	4	.000	432	583	.741	363	659	1022	276	795	13	158	95	321	17.8	6.5	3.9	1.0	....

• FRANKEL, Nat
Nathan Frankel

Born: Nov. 3, 1913.   Height: 6'   Weight: 195 lbs.   Drafted: —   College: Brooklyn

YEAR	TEAM	GP	GS	MIN	PTS	FGM	FGA	FG%	3PM	3PA	3P%	FTM	FTA	FT%	ORB	DRB	TRB	AST	PF	DQ	STL	BLK	TO	MPG	PPG	RPG	APG	PCM
39-40	Detroit-N	27	....	....	201	73	....	....	....	....	....	55	....	....				....	....					7.4	....	....	....
46-47	Pittsburgh	6	....	....	16	4	27	.148	....	....	....	8	12	.667				3	6					2.7		0.5	....
NBA Season Totals		6	....	....	16	4	27	.148				8	12	.667				3	6					2.7		0.5	....
NBL Season Totals		27	....	....	201	73						55												7.4			....
Career Totals		33	....	....	217	77	27					63	12					3	6					6.6		0.1	....
39-40	Detroit-N	3	....	....	24	10	....	....	....	....	....	4												8.0			....
NBL Playoff Totals		3	....	....	24	10	....	....	....	....	....	4												8.0			....

• FRANKLIN, William

William Thomas Franklin

Born: Oct. 19, 1949. Norfolk, VA, United States. Height: 6'7". Weight: 220 lbs. Drafted: 1972 College: Purdue

YEAR TEAM	GP	GS	MIN	PTS	FGM	FGA	FG%	3PM	3PA	3P%	FTM	FTA	FT%	ORB	DRB	TRB	AST	PF	DQ	STL	BLK	TO	MPG	PPG	RPG	APG	PCM
72-73 Virginia-A	73	....	990	545	218	524	.416	2	7	.286	107	179	.598	123	166	289	50	157	1	....	....	123	13.6	7.5	4.0	0.7	.487
74-75 San Antonio-A	24	....	179	79	32	85	.376	0	1	.000	15	23	.652	39	43	82	10	37	....	3	2	18	7.5	3.3	3.4	0.4	.536
75-76 San Antonio-A	10	....	95	33	12	22	.545	0	0	.000	9	16	.563	12	17	29	5	16	....	3	3	5	9.5	3.3	2.9	0.5	.476
ABA Season Totals	107	....	1264	657	262	631	.415	2	8	.250	131	218	.601	174	226	400	65	210	1	6	5	146	11.8	6.1	3.7	0.6	....
74-75 San Antonio-A	2	....	10	4	2	5	.400	0	0	.000	0	0	.000	3	2	5	0	2	....	0	0	0	5.0	2.0	2.5	0.0	.489
ABA Playoff Totals	2	....	10	4	2	5	.400	0	0	.000	0	0	.000	3	2	5	0	2	....	0	0	0	5.0	2.0	2.5	0.0	....

• FRANZ, Ronald

Ronald Stephen Franz

Born: Oct. 20, 1945. Kansas City, KS, United States. Height: 6'7". Weight: 205 lbs. Drafted: 1967 College: Kansas

YEAR TEAM	GP	GS	MIN	PTS	FGM	FGA	FG%	3PM	3PA	3P%	FTM	FTA	FT%	ORB	DRB	TRB	AST	PF	DQ	STL	BLK	TO	MPG	PPG	RPG	APG	PCM
67-68 Oakland-A	74	....	2080	930	354	903	.392	25	97	.258	197	285	.691	....	....	469	129	249	11	....	....	173	28.1	12.6	6.3	1.7	.421
68-69 New Orleans-A	73	....	2195	1059	381	850	.448	11	31	.355	286	388	.737	163	355	518	189	233	5	....	....	174	30.1	14.5	7.1	2.6	.534
69-70 New Orleans-A	55	....	1305	632	231	547	.422	7	25	.280	163	259	.629	106	181	287	91	139	3	....	....	117	23.7	11.5	5.2	1.7	.468
70-71 Florida-A	67	....	1596	813	309	637	.485	7	22	.318	188	259	.726	124	196	320	97	178	2	....	....	123	23.8	12.1	4.8	1.4	.516
71-72 Florida-A	74	....	1822	857	342	705	.485	2	11	.182	171	243	.704	109	233	342	94	209	6	....	....	97	24.6	11.6	4.6	1.3	.450
72-73 Dallas-A	37	....	511	276	88	174	.506	1	3	.333	99	135	.733	35	70	105	42	66	0	....	....	49	13.8	7.5	2.8	1.1	.574
72-73 Memphis-A	23	....	403	166	60	129	.465	0	1	.000	46	66	.697	32	55	87	26	46	0	....	....	29	17.5	7.2	3.8	1.1	.449
ABA Season Totals	403	....	9912	4733	1765	3945	.447	53	190	.279	1150	1635	.703	569	1090	2128	668	1120	27	....	....	762	24.6	11.7	5.3	1.7	....
68-69 New Orleans-A	11	....	261	102	38	112	.339	1	7	.143	25	37	.676	....	....	47	18	28	0	....	....	24	23.7	9.3	4.3	1.6	.315
70-71 Florida-A	2	....	40	17	7	21	.333	0	1	.000	3	8	.375	4	6	10	2	4	0	....	....	4	20.0	8.5	5.0	1.0	.315
71-72 Florida-A	4	....	88	27	12	36	.333	0	1	.000	3	8	.375	....	....	25	4	10	....	....	....	4	22.0	6.8	6.3	1.0	.293
ABA Playoff Totals	17	....	389	146	57	169	.337	1	9	.111	31	53	.585	4	6	82	24	42	0	....	....	32	22.9	8.6	4.8	1.4	....

• FRASCELLA, Nick

Nick Frascella

Born: July 6, 1914. Died: Apr.9, 2000. Height: 6'2". Weight: 185 lbs. Drafted: — College: Wooster

YEAR TEAM	GP	GS	MIN	PTS	FGM	FGA	FG%	3PM	3PA	3P%	FTM	FTA	FT%	ORB	DRB	TRB	AST	PF	DQ	STL	BLK	TO	MPG	PPG	RPG	APG	PCM
38-39 Wingfoots-N	18	....	....	53	24	....	....	....	....	....	5	....	....	....	....	....	....	....	....	....	....	....	....	2.9	....	....	....
39-40 Wingfoots-N	13	....	....	15	6	....	....	....	....	....	3	....	....	....	....	....	....	....	....	....	....	....	....	1.2	....	....	....
40-41 Wingfoots-N	1	....	....	0	0	....	....	....	....	....	0	....	....	....	....	....	....	....	....	....	....	....	....	0.0	....	....	....
NBL Season Totals	32	....	....	68	30	....	....	....	....	....	8	....	....	....	....	....	....	....	....	....	....	....	....	2.1	....	....	....

• FRAZIER, Walt

Walter Frazier Jr.

Born: Mar. 29, 1945. Atlanta, GA, United States. Height: 6'4". Weight: 200 lbs. Drafted: 1967 College: Southern Illinois HOF: 1987

YEAR TEAM	GP	GS	MIN	PTS	FGM	FGA	FG%	3PM	3PA	3P%	FTM	FTA	FT%	ORB	DRB	TRB	AST	PF	DQ	STL	BLK	TO	MPG	PPG	RPG	APG	PCM
67-68 New York	74	....	1588	666	256	568	.451	....	....	....	154	235	.655	....	....	313	305	199	2	....	....	....	21.5	9.0	4.2	4.1	.580
68-69 New York	80	....	2949	1403	531	1052	.505	....	....	....	341	457	.746	....	....	499	635	245	2	....	....	....	36.9	17.5	6.2	7.9	.669
69-70 New York	77	....	3040	1609	600	1158	.518	....	....	....	409	547	.748	....	....	465	629	203	1	....	....	....	39.5	20.9	6.0	8.2	.685
70-71 New York	80	....	3455	1736	651	1317	.494	....	....	....	434	557	.779	....	....	544	536	240	1	....	....	....	43.2	21.7	6.8	6.7	.604
71-72 New York	77	....	3126	1788	669	1307	.512	....	....	....	450	557	.808	....	....	513	446	185	0	....	....	....	40.6	23.2	6.7	5.8	.659
72-73 New York	78	....	3181	1648	681	1389	.490	....	....	....	286	350	.817	....	....	570	461	186	0	....	....	....	40.8	21.1	7.3	5.9	.613
73-74 New York	80	....	3338	1643	674	1429	.472	....	....	....	295	352	.838	120	416	536	551	212	2	161	15	....	41.7	20.5	6.7	6.9	.592
74-75 New York	78	....	3204	1675	672	1391	.483	....	....	....	331	400	.828	90	375	465	474	205	2	190	14	....	41.1	21.5	6.0	6.1	.588
75-76 New York	59	....	2427	1126	470	969	.485	....	....	....	186	226	.823	79	321	400	351	163	1	106	9	....	41.1	19.1	6.8	5.9	.558
76-77 New York	76	....	2687	1323	532	1089	.489	....	....	....	259	336	.771	52	241	293	403	194	0	132	9	....	35.4	17.4	3.9	5.3	.535
77-78 Cleveland	51	....	1664	825	336	714	.471	....	....	....	153	180	.850	54	155	209	209	124	1	77	13	112	32.6	16.2	4.1	4.1	.497
78-79 Cleveland	12	....	279	129	54	122	.443	....	....	....	21	27	.778	7	13	20	32	22	0	13	2	22	23.3	10.8	1.7	2.7	.367
79-80 Cleveland	3	....	27	10	4	11	.364	0	1	.000	2	2	1.000	1	2	3	8	2	0	2	1	4	9.0	3.3	1.0	2.7	.494
NBA Season Totals	825	....	30965	15581	6130	12516	.490	0	1	.000	3321	4226	.786	403	1523	4830	5040	2180	12	681	63	138	37.5	18.9	5.9	6.1	....
67-68 New York	4	....	119	38	12	33	.364	....	....	....	14	18	.778	....	....	22	25	12	0	....	....	....	29.8	9.5	5.5	6.3	.525
68-69 New York	10	....	415	212	89	177	.503	....	....	....	34	57	.596	....	....	74	91	30	0	....	....	....	41.5	21.2	7.4	9.1	.684
69-70 New York	19	....	834	304	118	247	.478	....	....	....	68	89	.764	....	....	149	156	53	0	....	....	....	43.9	16.0	7.8	8.2	.556
70-71 New York	12	....	501	271	108	204	.529	....	....	....	55	75	.733	....	....	70	54	45	0	....	....	....	41.8	22.6	5.8	4.5	.563
71-72 New York	16	....	704	388	148	276	.536	....	....	....	92	125	.736	....	....	112	98	48	0	....	....	....	44.0	24.3	7.0	6.1	.640
72-73 New York	17	....	765	373	150	292	.514	....	....	....	73	94	.777	....	....	124	106	52	1	....	....	....	45.0	21.9	7.3	6.2	.585
73-74 New York	12	....	491	270	113	225	.502	....	....	....	44	49	.898	21	74	95	48	41	1	21	4	....	40.9	22.5	7.9	4.0	.593
74-75 New York	3	....	124	71	29	46	.630	....	....	....	13	16	.813	3	17	20	21	4	0	11	0	....	41.3	23.7	6.7	7.0	.763
NBA Playoff Totals	93	....	3953	1927	767	1500	.511	....	....	....	393	523	.751	24	91	666	599	285	2	32	4	....	42.5	20.7	7.2	6.4	....

• FRAZIER, Will

Wilbert B. Frazier

Born: Aug. 24, 1942. Minden, LA, United States. Height: 6'7". Weight: 210 lbs. Drafted: 1965 College: Grambling

YEAR TEAM	GP	GS	MIN	PTS	FGM	FGA	FG%	3PM	3PA	3P%	FTM	FTA	FT%	ORB	DRB	TRB	AST	PF	DQ	STL	BLK	TO	MPG	PPG	RPG	APG	PCM
65-66 San Francisco	2	....	9	1	0	4	.000	....	....	....	1	2	.500	....	....	5	1	1	0	....	....	....	4.5	0.5	2.5	0.5	.246
67-68 Houston-A	76	....	2125	945	358	870	.411	1	2	.500	228	376	.606	....	....	666	104	219	3	....	....	146	28.0	12.4	8.8	1.4	.490
68-69 New York-A	75	....	1370	554	217	512	.424	0	0	.000	120	194	.619	148	268	416	66	200	1	....	....	75	18.3	7.4	5.5	0.9	.449
NBA Season Totals	2	....	9	1	0	4	.000	....	....	....	1	2	.500	....	....	5	1	1	0	....	....	....	4.5	0.5	2.5	0.5	....
ABA Season Totals	151	....	3495	1499	575	1382	.416	1	2	.500	348	570	.611	148	268	1082	170	419	4	....	....	221	23.1	9.9	7.2	1.1	....
Career Totals	153	....	3504	1500	575	1386	.415	1	2	.500	349	572	.610	148	268	1087	171	420	4	....	....	221	22.9	9.8	7.1	1.1	....
67-68 Houston-A	3	....	85	29	13	29	.448	0	1	.000	3	7	.429	....	....	12	4	11	0	....	....	5	28.3	9.7	4.0	1.3	.284
ABA Playoff Totals	3	....	85	29	13	29	.448	0	1	.000	3	7	.429	....	....	12	4	11	0	....	....	5	28.3	9.7	4.0	1.3	....

• FREDERICK, Anthony
Anthony Frederick

Born: Dec. 7, 1964. Los Angeles, CA, United States. Died: May29, 2003. Height: 6'7". Weight: 205 lbs. Drafted: 1986 College: Pepperdine

YEAR	TEAM	GP	GS	MIN	PTS	FGM	FGA	FG%	3PM	3PA	3P%	FTM	FTA	FT%	ORB	DRB	TRB	AST	PF	DQ	STL	BLK	TO	MPG	PPG	RPG	APG	PCM
88-89	Indiana	46	0	313	152	63	125	.504	2	5	.400	24	34	.706	26	26	52	20	59	0	14	6	32	6.8	3.3	1.1	0.4	.386
90-91	Sacramento	35	3	475	177	67	168	.399	0	0	.000	43	60	.717	36	48	84	44	50	0	22	13	39	13.6	5.1	2.4	1.3	.364
91-92	Charlotte	66	26	852	389	161	370	.435	4	17	.235	63	92	.685	75	69	144	71	91	0	40	26	59	12.9	5.9	2.2	1.1	.417
NBA Season Totals		147	29	1640	718	291	663	.439	6	22	.273	130	186	.699	137	143	280	135	200	0	76	45	130	11.2	4.9	1.9	0.9	....

• FREE, World B.
World B. Free aka.: Lloyd B. Free

Born: Dec. 9, 1953. Atlanta, GA, United States. Height: 6'2". Weight: 185 lbs. Drafted: 1975 College: Guilford

YEAR	TEAM	GP	GS	MIN	PTS	FGM	FGA	FG%	3PM	3PA	3P%	FTM	FTA	FT%	ORB	DRB	TRB	AST	PF	DQ	STL	BLK	TO	MPG	PPG	RPG	APG	PCM
75-76	Philadelphia	71	....	1121	590	239	533	.448	....	....	....	112	186	.602	64	61	125	104	107	0	37	6	....	15.8	8.3	1.8	1.5	.434
76-77	Philadelphia	78	....	2253	1268	467	1022	.457	....	....	....	334	464	.720	97	140	237	266	207	2	75	25	....	28.9	16.3	3.0	3.4	.511
77-78	Philadelphia	76	....	2050	1191	390	857	.455	....	....	....	411	562	.731	92	120	212	306	199	0	68	41	198	27.0	15.7	2.8	4.0	.527
78-79	San Diego	78	....	2954	2244	795	1653	.481	....	....	....	**654**	**865**	.756	127	174	301	340	253	8	111	35	296	37.9	28.8	3.9	4.4	.601
79-80	San Diego	68	....	2585	2055	737	1556	.474	9	25	.360	**572**	760	.753	129	109	238	283	195	0	81	32	231	38.0	30.2	3.5	4.2	.603
80-81	Golden State	65	....	2370	1565	516	1157	.446	5	31	.161	528	649	.814	48	111	159	361	183	1	85	11	195	36.5	24.1	2.4	5.6	.544
81-82	Golden State	78	78	2796	1789	650	1452	.448	10	56	.179	479	647	.740	118	130	248	419	222	1	71	8	211	35.8	22.9	3.2	5.4	.511
82-83	Golden State	19	18	700	434	164	364	.451	0	3	.000	106	149	.711	22	22	44	89	66	1	15	3	49	36.8	22.8	2.3	4.7	.448
82-83	Cleveland	54	51	1938	1309	485	1059	.458	15	42	.357	324	434	.747	70	87	157	201	175	3	82	12	157	35.9	24.2	2.9	3.7	.500
83-84	Cleveland	75	71	2375	1669	626	1407	.445	22	69	.319	395	504	.784	89	128	217	226	214	2	94	8	158	31.7	22.3	2.9	3.0	.499
84-85	Cleveland	71	50	2249	1597	609	1328	.459	71	193	.368	308	411	.749	61	150	211	320	163	0	75	16	142	31.7	22.5	3.0	4.5	.575
85-86	Cleveland	75	75	2535	1754	652	1433	.455	71	169	.420	379	486	.780	72	146	218	314	186	1	91	19	173	33.8	23.4	2.9	4.2	.541
86-87	Philadelphia	20	2	285	116	39	123	.317	2	9	.222	36	47	.766	5	14	19	30	26	0	5	4	18	14.3	5.8	1.0	1.5	.217
87-88	Houston	58	0	682	374	143	350	.409	8	35	.229	80	100	.800	14	30	44	60	74	2	20	3	46	11.8	6.4	0.8	1.0	.324
NBA Season Totals		886	345	26893	17955	6512	14294	.456	213	632	.337	4718	6264	.753	1008	1422	2430	3319	2270	21	910	223	1874	30.4	20.3	2.7	3.7	....
75-76	Philadelphia	3	....	62	32	11	28	.393	....	....	....	10	13	.769	1	0	1	5	6	0	3	0	....	20.7	10.7	0.3	1.7	.325
76-77	Philadelphia	15	....	281	179	63	170	.371	....	....	....	53	77	.688	10	22	32	29	33	0	12	8	....	18.7	11.9	2.1	1.9	.436
77-78	Philadelphia	10	....	268	161	51	124	.411	....	....	....	59	81	.728	10	21	31	37	26	0	4	6	26	26.8	16.1	3.1	3.7	.488
84-85	Cleveland	4	4	150	105	41	93	.441	0	4	.000	23	25	.920	4	6	10	31	12	0	6	0	6	37.5	26.3	2.5	7.8	.616
87-88	Houston	2	0	12	0	0	2	.000	0	1	.000	0	0	.000	1	1	2	1	2	0	0	0	3	6.0	0.0	1.0	0.5	-.222
NBA Playoff Totals		34	4	773	477	166	417	.398	0	5	.000	145	196	.740	26	50	76	103	79	0	25	14	35	22.7	14.0	2.2	3.0	....

• FREEMAN, Donnie
Donald E. (Free) Freeman

Born: July 18, 1944. Madison, IL, United States. Height: 6'3". Weight: 185 lbs. Drafted: 1966 College: Illinois

YEAR	TEAM	GP	GS	MIN	PTS	FGM	FGA	FG%	3PM	3PA	3P%	FTM	FTA	FT%	ORB	DRB	TRB	AST	PF	DQ	STL	BLK	TO	MPG	PPG	RPG	APG	PCM
67-68	Minnesota-A	69	....	2431	1124	414	1013	.409	0	6	.000	296	414	.715	....	....	326	190	185	5	....	....	187	35.2	16.3	4.7	2.8	.409
68-69	Miami-A	78	....	2874	1724	651	1346	.484	2	23	.087	420	534	.787	121	164	285	501	229	7	....	....	230	36.8	22.1	3.7	6.4	.625
69-70	Miami-A	79	....	3164	2163	766	1684	.455	5	19	.263	**626**	**762**	.822	132	268	400	291	253	5	....	....	190	40.1	27.4	5.1	3.7	.595
70-71	Texas-A	42	....	1613	992	391	807	.485	0	3	.000	210	270	.778	82	105	187	215	114	1	....	....	94	38.4	23.6	4.5	5.1	.618
70-71	Utah-A	24	....	801	567	205	428	.479	0	4	.000	157	189	.831	66	71	137	117	78	1	....	....	79	33.4	23.6	5.7	4.9	.742
71-72	Dallas-A	72	....	2377	1733	628	1336	.470	2	5	.400	475	576	.825	100	106	206	245	177	0	....	....	176	33.0	24.1	2.9	3.4	.608
72-73	Indiana-A	77	....	2170	1103	412	933	.442	2	6	.333	277	343	.808	103	116	219	195	225	1	....	....	160	28.2	14.3	2.8	2.5	.422
73-74	Indiana-A	66	....	1735	943	383	839	.456	0	2	.000	177	222	.797	91	77	168	165	174	....	48	22	132	26.3	14.3	2.5	2.5	.456
74-75	San Antonio-A	77	....	2381	1195	453	1012	.448	0	5	.000	289	352	.821	107	77	184	202	169	....	65	15	131	30.9	15.5	2.4	2.6	.413
75-76	LA Lakers	64	....	1480	689	263	606	.434	....	....	....	163	199	.819	72	108	180	171	160	1	57	11	....	23.1	10.8	2.8	2.7	.446
NBA Season Totals		64	....	1480	689	263	606	.434	....	....	....	163	199	.819	72	108	180	171	160	1	57	11	....	23.1	10.8	2.8	2.7	....
ABA Season Totals		584	....	19546	11544	4303	9398	.458	11	73	.151	2927	3662	.799	802	984	2112	2121	1604	20	113	37	1379	33.5	19.8	3.6	3.6	....
Career Totals		648	....	21026	12233	4566	10004	.456	11	73	.151	3090	3861	.800	874	1092	2292	2292	1764	21	170	48	1379	32.4	18.9	3.5	3.5	....
67-68	Minnesota-A	10	....	365	158	56	134	.418	0	4	.000	46	63	.730	....	....	50	56	46	4	....	....	39	36.5	15.8	5.0	5.6	.477
68-69	Miami-A	12	....	434	257	98	214	.458	0	1	.000	61	75	.813	....	....	48	50	28	0	....	....	29	36.2	21.4	4.0	4.2	.548
70-71	Texas-A	4	....	144	89	38	84	.452	0	3	.000	13	16	.813	12	12	24	5	9	0	....	....	7	36.0	22.3	6.0	1.3	.504
71-72	Dallas-A	4	....	144	107	45	103	.437	0	0	.000	17	27	.630	10	14	24	10	11	0	....	....	7	36.0	26.8	6.0	2.5	.549
72-73	Indiana-A	18	....	557	281	105	237	.443	0	2	.000	71	89	.798	27	21	48	50	52	0	....	....	40	30.9	15.6	2.7	2.8	.411
73-74	Indiana-A	6	....	158	74	30	69	.435	0	0	.000	14	20	.700	2	8	10	8	14	....	4	0	9	26.3	12.3	1.7	1.3	.314
74-75	San Antonio-A	6	....	166	74	33	72	.458	0	0	.000	8	10	.800	11	3	14	19	16	....	2	0	8	27.7	12.3	2.3	3.2	.391
ABA Playoff Totals		60	....	1968	1040	405	913	.444	0	10	.000	230	300	.767	62	58	218	198	176	4	6	0	139	32.8	17.3	3.6	3.3	....

• FREEMAN, Gary
Gary C. Freeman

Born: July 25, 1948. Height: 6'9". Weight: 210 lbs. Drafted: 1970 College: Oregon State

YEAR	TEAM	GP	GS	MIN	PTS	FGM	FGA	FG%	3PM	3PA	3P%	FTM	FTA	FT%	ORB	DRB	TRB	AST	PF	DQ	STL	BLK	TO	MPG	PPG	RPG	APG	PCM
70-71	Milwaukee	41	....	335	152	62	122	.508	....	....	....	28	38	.737	....	....	98	31	63	0	....	....	....	8.2	3.7	2.4	0.8	.563
70-71	Cleveland	11	....	47	15	7	12	.583	....	....	....	1	2	.500	....	....	8	4	4	0	....	....	....	4.3	1.4	0.7	0.4	.425
NBA Season Totals		52	....	382	167	69	134	.515	....	....	....	29	40	.725	....	....	106	35	67	0	....	....	....	7.3	3.2	2.0	0.7	....

• FREEMAN, Rod
Rodney Lee Freeman

Born: Nov. 5, 1950. Height: 6'7". Weight: 225 lbs. Drafted: 1973 College: Vanderbilt

YEAR	TEAM	GP	GS	MIN	PTS	FGM	FGA	FG%	3PM	3PA	3P%	FTM	FTA	FT%	ORB	DRB	TRB	AST	PF	DQ	STL	BLK	TO	MPG	PPG	RPG	APG	PCM
73-74	Philadelphia	35	....	265	106	39	103	.379	....	....	....	28	41	.683	22	32	54	14	42	0	12	1	....	7.6	3.0	1.5	0.4	.340
NBA Season Totals		35	....	265	106	39	103	.379	....	....	....	28	41	.683	22	32	54	14	42	0	12	1	....	7.6	3.0	1.5	0.4	....

YEAR	TEAM	GP	GS	MIN	PTS	FGM	FGA	FG%	3PM	3PA	3P%	FTM	FTA	FT%	ORB	DRB	TRB	AST	PF	DQ	STL	BLK	TO	MPG	PPG	RPG	APG	PCM

• FREY, Frido
Frido Frey

Born: Oct. 26, 1921. Germany.   Height: 6'2".   Weight: 195 lbs.   Drafted: —   College: Long Island University

YEAR	TEAM	GP	GS	MIN	PTS	FGM	FGA	FG%	3PM	3PA	3P%	FTM	FTA	FT%	ORB	DRB	TRB	AST	PF	DQ	STL	BLK	TO	MPG	PPG	RPG	APG	PCM
46-47	New York	23	....	....	88	28	97	.289	....	....	....	32	56	.571	....	....	....	14	37	....	....	....	....	3.8	....	0.6		
NBA Season Totals		23	....	....	88	28	97	.289	....	....	....	32	56	.571	....	....	....	14	37	....	....	....	....	3.8	....	0.6		
46-47	New York	5	....	....	10	3	19	.158	....	....	....	4	11	.364	....	....	....	7	11	....	....	....	....	2.0	....	1.4		
NBA Playoff Totals		5	....	....	10	3	19	.158	....	....	....	4	11	.364	....	....	....	7	11	....	....	....	....	2.0	....	1.4		

• FRIEND, Larry
Lawrence Friend

Born: Apr. 14, 1935. Chicago, IL, United States. Died: Feb.27, 1998.   Height: 6'4".   Weight: 185 lbs.   Drafted: 1957   College: California

YEAR	TEAM	GP	GS	MIN	PTS	FGM	FGA	FG%	3PM	3PA	3P%	FTM	FTA	FT%	ORB	DRB	TRB	AST	PF	DQ	STL	BLK	TO	MPG	PPG	RPG	APG	PCM
57-58	New York	44	....	569	175	74	226	.327	....	....	....	27	41	.659	....	....	106	47	54	0	....	....	....	12.9	4.0	2.4	1.1	.310
NBA Season Totals		44	....	569	175	74	226	.327	....	....	....	27	41	.659	....	....	106	47	54	0	....	....	....	12.9	4.0	2.4	1.1	....

• FRINK, Pat
Patrick Edward Frink

Born: Feb. 18, 1945.   Height: 6'4".   Weight: 195 lbs.   Drafted: 1968   College: Colorado

YEAR	TEAM	GP	GS	MIN	PTS	FGM	FGA	FG%	3PM	3PA	3P%	FTM	FTA	FT%	ORB	DRB	TRB	AST	PF	DQ	STL	BLK	TO	MPG	PPG	RPG	APG	PCM
68-69	Cincinnati	48	....	363	123	50	147	.340	....	....	....	23	29	.793	....	....	41	55	54	1	....	....	....	7.6	2.6	0.9	1.1	.317
NBA Season Totals		48	....	363	123	50	147	.340	....	....	....	23	29	.793	....	....	41	55	54	1	....	....	....	7.6	2.6	0.9	1.1	....

• FRITSCH, Theodore
Theodore Edward Fritsch

Born: Oct. 31, 1920. Spencer, WI, United States. Died: Oct.5, 1979.   Height: 5'10".   Weight: 210 lbs.   Drafted: —   College: Wisconsin (Stevens Point)

YEAR	TEAM	GP	GS	MIN	PTS	FGM	FGA	FG%	3PM	3PA	3P%	FTM	FTA	FT%	ORB	DRB	TRB	AST	PF	DQ	STL	BLK	TO	MPG	PPG	RPG	APG	PCM
44-45	Oshkosh-N	9	....	....	5	1	....	....	....	....	....	3	....	....	....	....	....	....	....	....	....	....	....	....	0.6	....	....	
46-47	Oshkosh-N	10	....	....	11	5	....	....	....	....	....	1	2	.500	....	....	....	....	....	....	....	....	....	....	1.1	....	....	
NBL Season Totals		19	....	....	16	6	....	....	....	....	....	4	2	....	....	....	....	....	....	....	....	....	....	....	0.8	....	....	
46-47	Oshkosh-N	3	....	....	0	0	....	....	....	....	....	0	0	.000	....	....	....	....	....	....	....	....	....	....	0.0	....	....	
NBL Playoff Totals		3	....	....	0	0	....	....	....	....	....	0	0	....	....	....	....	....	....	....	....	....	....	....	0.0	....	....	

• FRITSCHE, Jim
James A. Fritsche

Born: Dec. 10, 1931.   Height: 6'8".   Weight: 210 lbs.   Drafted: 1953   College: Hamline

YEAR	TEAM	GP	GS	MIN	PTS	FGM	FGA	FG%	3PM	3PA	3P%	FTM	FTA	FT%	ORB	DRB	TRB	AST	PF	DQ	STL	BLK	TO	MPG	PPG	RPG	APG	PCM
53-54	Min/Bal	68	....	1221	281	116	379	.306	....	....	....	49	68	.721	....	....	217	73	103	0	....	....	....	18.0	4.1	3.2	1.1	.245
54-55	Fort Wayne	16	....	151	45	16	48	.333	....	....	....	13	16	.813	....	....	32	4	28	0	....	....	....	9.4	2.8	2.0	0.3	.254
NBA Season Totals		84	....	1372	326	132	427	.309	....	....	....	62	84	.738	....	....	249	77	131	0	....	....	....	16.3	3.9	3.0	0.9	....

• FRYER, Bernie
Bernie W. Fryer

Born: Dec. 25, 1949. Bellingham, WA, United States.   Height: 6'3".   Weight: 185 lbs.   Drafted: 1972   College: Brigham Young

YEAR	TEAM	GP	GS	MIN	PTS	FGM	FGA	FG%	3PM	3PA	3P%	FTM	FTA	FT%	ORB	DRB	TRB	AST	PF	DQ	STL	BLK	TO	MPG	PPG	RPG	APG	PCM
73-74	Portland	80	....	1674	559	226	491	.460	....	....	....	107	135	.793	60	99	159	279	187	1	92	10	....	20.9	7.0	2.0	3.5	.417
74-75	St. Louis-A	9	....	264	70	24	68	.353	0	1	.000	22	28	.786	5	17	22	25	28	....	6	0	17	29.3	7.8	2.4	2.8	.239
74-75	New Orleans	31	....	432	127	47	106	.443	....	....	....	33	43	.767	16	30	46	52	54	0	22	0	....	13.9	4.1	1.5	1.7	.343
NBA Season Totals		111	....	2106	686	273	597	.457	....	....	....	140	178	.787	76	129	205	331	241	1	114	10	....	19.0	6.2	1.8	3.0	....
ABA Season Totals		9	....	264	70	24	68	.353	0	1	.000	22	28	.786	5	17	22	25	28	....	6	0	17	29.3	7.8	2.4	2.8	....
Career Totals		120	....	2370	756	297	665	.447	0	1	.000	162	206	.786	81	146	227	356	269	1	120	10	17	19.8	6.3	1.9	3.0	....

• FUCARINO, Frank
Frank A. Fucarino

Born: July 24, 1920.   Height: 6'2".   Weight: 175 lbs.   Drafted: —   College: Long Island University

YEAR	TEAM	GP	GS	MIN	PTS	FGM	FGA	FG%	3PM	3PA	3P%	FTM	FTA	FT%	ORB	DRB	TRB	AST	PF	DQ	STL	BLK	TO	MPG	PPG	RPG	APG	PCM
46-47	Toronto	28	....	....	140	53	198	.268	....	....	....	34	60	.567	....	....	....	7	38	....	....	....	....	5.0	....	0.3		
NBA Season Totals		28	....	....	140	53	198	.268	....	....	....	34	60	.567	....	....	....	7	38	....	....	....	....	5.0	....	0.3		

• FUETSCH, Herm
Herman Joseph (Dutch) Fuetsch

Born: July 6, 1918.   Height: 6'   Weight: 170 lbs.   Drafted: —   College: none

YEAR	TEAM	GP	GS	MIN	PTS	FGM	FGA	FG%	3PM	3PA	3P%	FTM	FTA	FT%	ORB	DRB	TRB	AST	PF	DQ	STL	BLK	TO	MPG	PPG	RPG	APG	PCM
45-46	Cleveland-N	27	....	....	225	82	....	....	....	....	....	61	75	.813	....	....	....	....	....	....	....	....	....	8.3	....	....		
47-48	Baltimore	42	....	....	109	42	140	.300	....	....	....	25	40	.625	....	....	....	17	39	....	....	....	....	2.6	....	0.4		
NBA Season Totals		42	....	....	109	42	140	.300	....	....	....	25	40	.625	....	....	....	17	39	....	....	....	....	2.6	....	0.4		
NBL Season Totals		27	....	....	225	82	....	....	....	....	....	61	75	....	....	....	....	....	....	....	....	....	....	8.3	....	....		
Career Totals		69	....	....	334	124	140	....	....	....	....	86	115	....	....	....	....	17	39	....	....	....	....	4.8	....	0.2		
47-48	Baltimore	9	....	....	12	3	8	.375	....	....	....	6	8	.750	....	....	....	0	10	....	....	....	....	1.3	....	0.0		
NBA Playoff Totals		9	....	....	12	3	8	.375	....	....	....	6	8	.750	....	....	....	0	10	....	....	....	....	1.3	....	0.0		

• FULKS, Joe
Joseph Franklin (Jumpin' Joe) Fulks

Born: Oct. 26, 1921. Birmingham, KY, United States. Died: Mar.21, 1976.   Height: 6'5".   Weight: 190 lbs.   Drafted: —   College: Murray State   HOF: 1978

YEAR	TEAM	GP	GS	MIN	PTS	FGM	FGA	FG%	3PM	3PA	3P%	FTM	FTA	FT%	ORB	DRB	TRB	AST	PF	DQ	STL	BLK	TO	MPG	PPG	RPG	APG	PCM
46-47	Philadelphia	60	....	....	**1389**	475	**1557**	.305	....	....	....	**439**	601	.730	....	....	....	25	199	....	....	....	....	**23.2**	....	0.4		
47-48	Philadelphia	43	....	....	949	326	**1258**	.259	....	....	....	**297**	390	.762	....	....	....	26	162	....	....	....	....	**22.1**	....	0.6		
48-49	Philadelphia	60	....	....	1560	529	**1689**	.313	....	....	....	502	638	.787	....	....	....	74	262	....	....	....	....	26.0	....	1.2		
49-50	Philadelphia	68	....	....	965	336	1209	.278	....	....	....	293	421	.696	....	....	....	56	240	....	....	....	....	14.2	....	0.8		
50-51	Philadelphia	66	....	....	1236	429	1358	.316	....	....	....	378	442	**.855**	....	....	523	117	247	8	....	....	....	18.7	7.9	1.8		

YEAR	TEAM	GP	GS	MIN	PTS	FGM	FGA	FG%	3PM	3PA	3P%	FTM	FTA	FT%	ORB	DRB	TRB	AST	PF	DQ	STL	BLK	TO	MPG	PPG	RPG	APG	PCM
51-52	Philadelphia	61	....	1904	922	336	1078	.312	....	....	....	250	303	.825	....	....	368	123	255	13	....	....	....	31.2	15.1	6.0	2.0	.370
52-53	Philadelphia	70	....	2085	832	332	960	.346	....	....	....	168	231	.727	....	....	387	138	319	20	....	....	....	29.8	11.9	5.5	2.0	.333
53-54	Philadelphia	61	....	501	150	61	229	.266	....	....	....	28	49	.571	....	....	101	28	90	0	....	....	....	8.2	2.5	1.7	0.5	.198
NBA Season Totals		489	....	4490	8003	2824	9338	.302	....	....	....	2355	3075	.766	....	....	1379	587	1774	41	....	....	....	9.2	16.4	2.8	1.2	....
46-47	Philadelphia	10	....	....	222	74	257	.288	....	....	....	74	94	.787	....	....	....	3	32	....	....	....	....	22.2	....	0.3	....
47-48	Philadelphia	13	....	....	282	92	380	.242	....	....	....	98	121	.810	....	....	....	3	55	....	....	....	....	21.7	....	0.2	....
48-49	Philadelphia	1	....	0	0	0	0	.000	....	....	....	0	0	.000	....	....	....	0	1	....	....	....	....	0.0	....	0.0	....
49-50	Philadelphia	2	....	....	15	5	26	.192	....	....	....	5	10	.500	....	....	....	2	10	....	....	....	....	7.5	....	1.0	....
50-51	Philadelphia	2	....	....	52	16	49	.327	....	....	....	20	27	.741	....	....	16	1	9	0	....	....	....	26.0	8.0	0.5	....
51-52	Philadelphia	3	....	70	17	5	33	.152	....	....	....	7	9	.778	....	....	12	2	13	1	....	....	....	23.3	5.7	4.0	0.7	.041
NBA Playoff Totals		31	....	70	588	192	745	.258	....	....	....	204	261	.782	....	....	28	11	120	1	....	....	....	2.3	19.0	0.9	0.4	....

• FULLER, Carl
Carl Fuller

Born: Jan. 10, 1946. St. Augustine, FL, United States.   Height: 6'9".   Weight: 225 lbs.   Drafted: 1968   College: Bethune-Cookman

YEAR	TEAM	GP	GS	MIN	PTS	FGM	FGA	FG%	3PM	3PA	3P%	FTM	FTA	FT%	ORB	DRB	TRB	AST	PF	DQ	STL	BLK	TO	MPG	PPG	RPG	APG	PCM
70-71	Florida-A	70	....	1151	412	170	372	.457	0	1	.000	72	120	.600	102	228	330	54	209	5	....	....	75	16.4	5.9	4.7	0.8	.414
71-72	Florida-A	6	....	63	21	6	14	.429	0	0	.000	9	15	.600	7	21	28	6	11	0	....	....	7	10.5	3.5	4.7	1.0	.601
ABA Season Totals		76	....	1214	433	176	386	.456	0	1	.000	81	135	.600	109	249	358	60	220	5	....	....	82	16.0	5.7	4.7	0.8	....
70-71	Florida-A	6	....	43	16	6	22	.273	0	2	.000	4	6	.667	3	12	15	4	11	0	....	....	1	7.2	2.7	2.5	0.7	.344
ABA Playoff Totals		6	....	43	16	6	22	.273	0	2	.000	4	6	.667	3	12	15	4	11	0	....	....	1	7.2	2.7	2.5	0.7	....

• FULLER, Homer
Homer Fuller

Born: 1920.   Height: 6'3".   Weight: 220 lbs.   Drafted: —   College: East Texas State

YEAR	TEAM	GP	GS	MIN	PTS	FGM	FGA	FG%	3PM	3PA	3P%	FTM	FTA	FT%	ORB	DRB	TRB	AST	PF	DQ	STL	BLK	TO	MPG	PPG	RPG	APG	PCM
44-45	Oshkosh-N	28	....	....	149	66	....	....	....	....	....	17	....	....	....	....	....	....	....	....	....	....	....	....	5.3	....	....	....
NBL Season Totals		28	....	....	149	66	....	....	....	....	....	17	....	....	....	....	....	....	....	....	....	....	....	....	5.3	....	....	....

• FULLER, Todd
Todd Douglas Fuller

Born: July 25, 1974. Fayetteville, NC, United States.   Height: 6'11".   Weight: 255 lbs.   Drafted: 1996   College: North Carolina State

YEAR	TEAM	GP	GS	MIN	PTS	FGM	FGA	FG%	3PM	3PA	3P%	FTM	FTA	FT%	ORB	DRB	TRB	AST	PF	DQ	STL	BLK	TO	MPG	PPG	RPG	APG	PCM
96-97	Golden State	75	18	949	302	113	265	.426	0	0	.000	76	110	.691	108	141	249	24	146	0	10	20	53	12.7	4.0	3.3	0.3	.330
97-98	Golden State	57	1	613	227	86	205	.420	0	4	.000	55	80	.688	61	135	196	10	89	0	6	16	34	10.8	4.0	3.4	0.2	.400
98-99	Utah	42	2	462	142	56	124	.452	0	0	.000	30	50	.600	28	73	101	6	60	0	6	14	27	11.0	3.4	2.4	0.1	.295
99-00	Charlotte	41	2	399	134	51	122	.418	0	0	.000	32	53	.604	36	74	110	5	46	0	9	8	27	9.7	3.3	2.7	0.1	.339
00-01	Miami	10	0	77	28	10	35	.286	0	0	.000	8	8	1.000	7	11	18	1	10	0	3	2	3	7.7	2.8	1.8	0.1	.261
NBA Season Totals		225	23	2500	833	316	751	.421	0	4	.000	201	301	.668	240	434	674	46	351	0	34	60	144	11.1	3.7	3.0	0.2	....
98-99	Utah	10	0	105	26	10	26	.385	0	0	.000	6	10	.600	8	20	28	0	21	0	0	2	5	10.5	2.6	2.8	0.0	.218
NBA Playoff Totals		10	0	105	26	10	26	.385	0	0	.000	6	10	.600	8	20	28	0	21	0	0	2	5	10.5	2.6	2.8	0.0	....

• FULLER, Tony
Anthony Ike Fuller

Born: Sept. 4, 1958. Detroit, MI, United States.   Height: 6'4".   Weight: 180 lbs.   Drafted: 1980   College: Pepperdine

YEAR	TEAM	GP	GS	MIN	PTS	FGM	FGA	FG%	3PM	3PA	3P%	FTM	FTA	FT%	ORB	DRB	TRB	AST	PF	DQ	STL	BLK	TO	MPG	PPG	RPG	APG	PCM
80-81	Detroit	15	....	248	60	24	66	.364	0	1	.000	12	16	.750	13	29	42	28	25	0	10	1	23	16.5	4.0	2.8	1.9	.268
NBA Season Totals		15	....	248	60	24	66	.364	0	1	.000	12	16	.750	13	29	42	28	25	0	10	1	23	16.5	4.0	2.8	1.9	....

• FUNDERBURKE, Lawrence
Lawrence Funderburke

Born: Dec. 15, 1970. Columbus, OH, United States.   Height: 6'9".   Weight: 230 lbs.   Drafted: 1994   College: Ohio State

YEAR	TEAM	GP	GS	MIN	PTS	FGM	FGA	FG%	3PM	3PA	3P%	FTM	FTA	FT%	ORB	DRB	TRB	AST	PF	DQ	STL	BLK	TO	MPG	PPG	RPG	APG	PCM
97-98	Sacramento	52	1	1094	493	191	390	.490	1	7	.143	110	162	.679	80	154	234	63	56	0	19	15	62	21.0	9.5	4.5	1.2	.474
98-99	Sacramento	47	2	936	420	167	299	.559	1	5	.200	85	120	.708	101	121	222	30	77	0	22	23	52	19.9	8.9	4.7	0.6	.510
99-00	Sacramento	75	1	1026	483	184	352	.523	0	2	.000	115	163	.706	98	136	234	33	91	0	32	20	40	13.7	6.4	3.1	0.4	.513
00-01	Sacramento	59	2	698	288	120	242	.496	0	0	.000	48	77	.623	74	122	196	17	44	0	9	13	32	11.8	4.9	3.3	0.3	.475
01-02	Sacramento	56	1	722	264	115	245	.469	0	3	.000	34	56	.607	76	122	198	32	65	0	11	18	33	12.9	4.7	3.5	0.6	.440
02-03	Sacramento	27	0	229	74	32	72	.444	0	0	.000	10	17	.588	17	38	55	8	25	0	1	11	6	8.5	2.7	2.0	0.3	.381
NBA Season Totals		316	7	4705	2022	809	1600	.506	2	17	.118	402	595	.676	446	693	1139	183	358	0	94	100	225	14.9	6.4	3.6	0.6	....
98-99	Sacramento	3	0	31	10	5	12	.417	0	0	.000	0	0	.000	2	2	4	1	3	0	3	0	3	10.3	3.3	1.3	0.3	.229
99-00	Sacramento	4	0	34	10	4	9	.444	0	0	.000	2	4	.500	4	7	11	0	0	0	1	0	0	8.5	2.5	2.8	0.0	.454
00-01	Sacramento	3	0	17	7	3	8	.375	0	0	.000	1	1	1.000	4	2	6	0	4	0	2	2	1	5.7	2.3	2.0	0.0	.517
01-02	Sacramento	5	0	20	6	2	3	.667	0	0	.000	2	2	1.000	1	1	2	0	5	0	0	0	0	4.0	1.2	0.4	0.0	.232
02-03	Sacramento	6	0	15	9	3	8	.375	0	0	.000	3	4	.750	3	5	8	0	2	0	0	0	1	2.5	1.5	1.3	0.0	.630
NBA Playoff Totals		21	0	117	42	17	40	.425	0	0	.000	8	11	.727	14	17	31	1	14	0	6	2	5	5.6	2.0	1.5	0.0	....

• FUREY, Dick
Dick Furey

Born: 1925.   Height: 6'3".   Weight: 195 lbs.   Drafted: 1947   College: St. Thomas

YEAR	TEAM	GP	GS	MIN	PTS	FGM	FGA	FG%	3PM	3PA	3P%	FTM	FTA	FT%	ORB	DRB	TRB	AST	PF	DQ	STL	BLK	TO	MPG	PPG	RPG	APG	PCM
46-47	Anderson-N	11	....	....	30	11	....	....	....	....	....	8	10	.800	....	....	....	....	....	....	....	....	....	2.7	....	....	....
47-48	Anderson-N	12	....	....	25	10	....	....	....	....	....	5	7	.714	....	....	....	....	....	....	....	....	....	2.1	....	....	....
47-48	Flint-N	1	....	....	2	1	....	....	....	....	....	0	2	.000	....	....	....	....	0	....	....	....	....	2.0	....	....	....
47-48	Tri-Cities-N	1	....	....	2	1	....	....	....	....	....	0	0	.000	....	....	....	....	0	....	....	....	....	2.0	....	....	....
NBL Season Totals		25	....	....	59	23	....	....	....	....	....	13	19	....	....	....	....	....	0	....	....	....	....	2.4	....	....	....

• FURLOW, Terry

Terry L. Furlow

Born: Oct. 18, 1954. Flint, MI, United States. Died: May23, 1980. Height: 6'4". Weight: 190 lbs. Drafted: 1976 College: Michigan State

YEAR	TEAM	GP	GS	MIN	PTS	FGM	FGA	FG%	3PM	3PA	3P%	FTM	FTA	FT%	ORB	DRB	TRB	AST	PF	DQ	STL	BLK	TO	MPG	PPG	RPG	APG	PCM
76-77	Philadelphia	32	....	174	84	34	100	.340	....	....	....	16	18	.889	18	21	39	19	11	0	7	2	....	5.4	2.6	1.2	0.6	.441
77-78	Cleveland	53	....	827	472	192	443	.433	....	....	....	88	99	.889	47	60	107	72	67	0	21	14	80	15.6	8.9	2.0	1.4	.427
78-79	Cleveland	49	....	1110	653	275	569	.483	....	....	....	103	125	.824	44	52	96	103	80	1	40	17	88	22.7	13.3	2.0	2.1	.464
78-79	Atlanta	29	....	576	286	113	235	.481	....	....	....	60	70	.857	32	39	71	81	42	0	18	13	46	19.9	9.9	2.4	2.8	.508
79-80	Atlanta	21	....	404	177	66	161	.410	1	9	.111	44	51	.863	23	19	42	72	19	0	19	9	34	19.2	8.4	2.0	3.4	.472
79-80	Utah	55	....	1718	878	364	765	.476	23	73	.315	127	145	.876	47	105	152	221	79	0	54	14	127	31.2	16.0	2.8	4.0	.464
NBA Season Totals		239	....	4809	2550	1044	2273	.459	24	82	.293	438	508	.862	211	296	507	568	298	1	159	69	375	20.1	10.7	2.1	2.4	....
76-77	Philadelphia	5	....	16	16	6	11	.545	....	....	....	4	4	1.000	3	2	5	0	2	0	1	0	....	3.2	3.2	1.0	0.0	.946
77-78	Cleveland	2	....	50	32	13	27	.481	....	....	....	6	6	1.000	3	2	5	5	1	0	0	0	3	25.0	16.0	2.5	2.5	.534
78-79	Atlanta	9	....	244	136	55	113	.487	....	....	....	26	28	.929	11	21	32	29	15	0	7	2	12	27.1	15.1	3.6	3.2	.550
NBA Playoff Totals		16	....	310	184	74	151	.490	....	....	....	36	38	.947	17	25	42	34	18	0	8	2	15	19.4	11.5	2.6	2.1	....

• GABOR, Bill

William A. (Bullet Bill, The Human Projectile) Gabor

Born: May 13, 1922. Height: 5'11". Weight: 170 lbs. Drafted: 1948 College: Syracuse

YEAR	TEAM	GP	GS	MIN	PTS	FGM	FGA	FG%	3PM	3PA	3P%	FTM	FTA	FT%	ORB	DRB	TRB	AST	PF	DQ	STL	BLK	TO	MPG	PPG	RPG	APG	PCM
48-49	Syracuse-N	58	....	....	355	115	....	....	....	....	....	125	169	.740	....	....	....	....	163	....	....	....	....	....	6.1	....	....	....
49-50	Syracuse	56	....	....	609	226	671	.337	....	....	....	157	228	.689	....	....	....	108	198	....	....	....	....	....	10.9	....	1.9	....
50-51	Syracuse	61	....	....	689	255	745	.342	....	....	....	179	242	.740	....	....	150	125	213	7	....	....	....	....	11.3	2.5	2.0	....
51-52	Syracuse	57	....	1085	488	173	538	.322	....	....	....	142	183	.776	....	....	93	86	188	5	....	....	....	19.0	8.6	1.6	1.5	.299
52-53	Syracuse	69	....	1337	647	215	614	.350	....	....	....	217	284	.764	....	....	104	134	262	11	....	....	....	19.4	9.4	1.5	1.9	.363
53-54	Syracuse	61	....	1211	547	204	551	.370	....	....	....	139	194	.716	....	....	96	162	183	4	....	....	....	19.9	9.0	1.6	2.7	.407
54-55	Syracuse	3	....	47	17	7	22	.318	....	....	....	3	5	.600	....	....	5	11	6	0	....	....	....	15.7	5.7	1.7	3.7	.430
NBA Season Totals		307	....	3680	2997	1080	3141	.344	....	....	....	837	1136	.737	....	....	448	626	1050	27	....	....	....	12.0	9.8	1.5	2.0	....
NBL Season Totals		58	....	....	355	115	....	....	....	....	....	125	169	....	....	....	....	....	163	....	....	....	....	....	6.1	....	....	....
Career Totals		365	....	3680	3352	1195	3141	....	....	....	....	962	1305	....	....	....	448	626	1213	27	....	....	....	10.1	9.2	1.2	1.7	....
48-49	Syracuse-N	6	....	....	36	12	....	....	....	....	....	12	15	.800	....	....	....	....	....	....	....	....	....	....	6.0	....	....	....
49-50	Syracuse	10	....	....	76	25	97	.258	....	....	....	26	31	.839	....	....	....	25	27	....	....	....	....	....	7.6	....	2.5	....
50-51	Syracuse	7	....	....	63	27	72	.375	....	....	....	9	14	.643	....	....	20	18	24	1	....	....	....	....	9.0	2.9	2.6	....
51-52	Syracuse	7	....	80	34	11	33	.333	....	....	....	12	16	.750	....	....	6	10	16	0	....	....	....	11.4	4.9	0.9	1.4	.355
52-53	Syracuse	2	....	28	18	5	12	.417	....	....	....	8	13	.615	....	....	3	2	12	2	....	....	....	14.0	9.0	1.5	1.0	.411
53-54	Syracuse	10	....	196	76	24	83	.289	....	....	....	28	40	.700	....	....	28	19	36	1	....	....	....	19.6	7.6	2.8	1.9	.314
NBA Playoff Totals		36	....	304	267	92	297	.310	....	....	....	83	114	.728	....	....	57	74	115	4	....	....	....	8.4	7.4	1.6	2.1	....
NBL Playoff Totals		6	....	....	36	12	....	....	....	....	....	12	15	....	....	....	....	....	....	....	....	....	....	....	6.0	....	....	....
Career Playoff Totals		42	....	304	303	104	297	....	....	....	....	95	129	....	....	....	57	74	115	4	....	....	....	7.2	7.2	1.4	1.8	....

• GADZURIC, Dan

Daniel Gadzuric

Born: Feb. 2, 1978. Den Haag, Netherlands. Height: 6'11". Weight: 240 lbs. Drafted: 2002 College: UCLA

YEAR	TEAM	GP	GS	MIN	PTS	FGM	FGA	FG%	3PM	3PA	3P%	FTM	FTA	FT%	ORB	DRB	TRB	AST	PF	DQ	STL	BLK	TO	MPG	PPG	RPG	APG	PCM
02-03	Milwaukee	49	30	760	169	70	145	.483	0	1	.000	29	56	.518	66	131	197	9	125	3	22	52	27	15.5	3.4	4.0	0.2	.346
NBA Season Totals		49	30	760	169	70	145	.483	0	1	.000	29	56	.518	66	131	197	9	125	3	22	52	27	15.5	3.4	4.0	0.2	....

• GAINER, Elmer

Elmer R. Gainer

Born: 1919. Height: 6'6". Weight: 195 lbs. Drafted: 1947 College: DePaul

YEAR	TEAM	GP	GS	MIN	PTS	FGM	FGA	FG%	3PM	3PA	3P%	FTM	FTA	FT%	ORB	DRB	TRB	AST	PF	DQ	STL	BLK	TO	MPG	PPG	RPG	APG	PCM
41-42	Fort Wayne-N	24	....	....	100	36	....	....	....	....	....	28	....	....	....	....	....	....	....	....	....	....	....	....	4.2	....	....	....
43-44	Sheboygan-N	22	....	....	50	15	....	....	....	....	....	20	....	....	....	....	....	....	....	....	....	....	....	....	2.3	....	....	....
44-45	Chicago-N	29	....	....	126	44	....	....	....	....	....	38	....	....	....	....	....	....	....	....	....	....	....	....	4.3	....	....	....
45-46	Chicago-N	5	....	....	6	2	....	....	....	....	....	2	....	....	....	....	....	....	....	....	....	....	....	....	1.2	....	....	....
46-47	Anderson-N	43	....	....	213	77	....	....	....	....	....	59	79	.747	....	....	....	....	87	....	....	....	....	....	5.0	....	....	....
47-48	Baltimore	5	....	....	5	1	9	.111	....	....	....	3	6	.500	....	....	....	3	8	....	....	....	....	....	1.0	....	0.6	....
48-49	Waterloo-N	36	....	....	96	33	....	....	....	....	....	30	39	.769	....	....	....	....	64	....	....	....	....	....	2.7	....	....	....
49-50	Waterloo	15	....	....	24	9	35	.257	....	....	....	6	8	.750	....	....	....	7	28	....	....	....	....	....	1.6	....	0.5	....
NBA Season Totals		20	....	....	29	10	44	.227	....	....	....	9	14	.643	....	....	....	10	36	....	....	....	....	....	1.5	....	0.5	....
NBL Season Totals		159	....	....	591	207	....	....	....	....	....	177	118	....	....	....	....	....	151	....	....	....	....	....	3.7	....	....	....
Career Totals		179	....	....	620	217	44	....	....	....	....	186	132	....	....	....	....	10	187	....	....	....	....	....	3.5	....	0.1	....
41-42	Fort Wayne-N	6	....	....	12	1	....	....	....	....	....	10	....	....	....	....	....	....	....	....	....	....	....	....	2.0	....	....	....
43-44	Sheboygan-N	6	....	....	7	2	....	....	....	....	....	3	....	....	....	....	....	....	....	....	....	....	....	....	1.2	....	....	....
44-45	Chicago-N	3	....	....	22	10	....	....	....	....	....	2	....	....	....	....	....	....	....	....	....	....	....	....	7.3	....	....	....
NBL Playoff Totals		15	....	....	41	13	....	....	....	....	....	15	....	....	....	....	....	....	....	....	....	....	....	....	2.7	....	....	....

• GAINES, Bill

William Roosevelt Gaines

Born: Mar. 10, 1946. Height: 6'4". Weight: 185 lbs. Drafted: 1968 College: East Texas State

YEAR	TEAM	GP	GS	MIN	PTS	FGM	FGA	FG%	3PM	3PA	3P%	FTM	FTA	FT%	ORB	DRB	TRB	AST	PF	DQ	STL	BLK	TO	MPG	PPG	RPG	APG	PCM
68-69	Houston-A	1	....	5	2	1	2	.500	0	0	.000	0	0	.000	1	0	1	0	0	0	....	....	1	5.0	2.0	1.0	0.0	.400
ABA Season Totals		1	....	5	2	1	2	.500	0	0	.000	0	0	.000	1	0	1	0	0	0	....	....	1	5.0	2.0	1.0	0.0	....

• GAINES, Corey

Corey Yasuto Gaines

Born: June 1, 1965. Los Angeles, CA, United States. Height: 6'3". Weight: 195 lbs. Drafted: 1988 College: Loyola Marymount

YEAR	TEAM	GP	GS	MIN	PTS	FGM	FGA	FG%	3PM	3PA	3P%	FTM	FTA	FT%	ORB	DRB	TRB	AST	PF	DQ	STL	BLK	TO	MPG	PPG	RPG	APG	PCM
88-89	New Jersey	32	0	337	67	27	64	.422	1	5	.200	12	16	.750	3	16	19	67	27	0	15	1	19	10.5	2.1	0.6	2.1	.311
89-90	Philadelphia	9	0	81	10	4	12	.333	1	2	.500	1	4	.250	1	4	5	26	11	0	4	0	10	9.0	1.1	0.6	2.9	.280
90-91	Denver	10	2	226	83	28	70	.400	5	21	.238	22	26	.846	4	10	14	91	25	0	10	2	23	22.6	8.3	1.4	9.1	.576

YEAR	TEAM	GP	GS	MIN	PTS	FGM	FGA	FG%	3PM	3PA	3P%	FTM	FTA	FT%	ORB	DRB	TRB	AST	PF	DQ	STL	BLK	TO	MPG	PPG	RPG	APG	PCM
93-94	New York	18	0	78	33	9	20	.450	2	5	.400	13	15	.867	3	10	13	30	12	0	2	0	5	4.3	1.8	0.7	1.7	.746
94-95	Philadelphia	11	8	280	55	24	51	.471	2	15	.133	5	11	.455	1	17	18	33	23	0	8	1	14	25.5	5.0	1.6	3.0	.226
NBA Season Totals		80	10	1002	248	92	217	.424	11	48	.229	53	72	.736	12	57	69	247	98	0	39	4	71	12.5	3.1	0.9	3.1	....
93-94	New York	4	0	28	0	0	4	.000	0	1	.000	0	0	.000	0	2	2	2	4	0	0	0	0	7.0	0.0	0.5	0.5	-.054
NBA Playoff Totals		4	0	28	0	0	4	.000	0	1	.000	0	0	.000	0	2	2	2	4	0	0	0	0	7.0	0.0	0.5	0.5	....

• GAINES, David

David (Smokey) Gaines

Born: Feb. 27, 1942. Height: 6'1". Weight: 170 lbs. Drafted: — College: LeMoyne-Owen

YEAR	TEAM	GP	GS	MIN	PTS	FGM	FGA	FG%	3PM	3PA	3P%	FTM	FTA	FT%	ORB	DRB	TRB	AST	PF	DQ	STL	BLK	TO	MPG	PPG	RPG	APG	PCM
67-68	Kentucky-A	3	....	36	10	4	16	.250	1	1	1.000	1	2	.500	....	....	10	0	4	0	....	....	0	12.0	3.3	3.3	0.0	.174
ABA Season Totals		3	....	36	10	4	16	.250	1	1	1.000	1	2	.500	....	....	10	0	4	0	....	....	0	12.0	3.3	3.3	0.0	....

• GALE, Lauren

Lauren (Laddie) Gale

Born: Apr. 22, 1917. Grants Pass, OR, United States. Died: July29, 1996. Height: 6'4". Weight: 190 lbs. Drafted: — College: Oregon HOF: 1977

YEAR	TEAM	GP	GS	MIN	PTS	FGM	FGA	FG%	3PM	3PA	3P%	FTM	FTA	FT%	ORB	DRB	TRB	AST	PF	DQ	STL	BLK	TO	MPG	PPG	RPG	APG	PCM
39-40	Detroit-N	8	....	....	60	22	....	....	....	....	....	16	....	....	....	....	....	....	....	....	....	....	....	....	7.5	....	....	....
NBL Season Totals		8	....	....	60	22	....	....	....	....	....	16	....	....	....	....	....	....	....	....	....	....	....	....	7.5	....	....	....
39-40	Detroit-N	3	....	....	17	6	....	....	....	....	....	5	....	....	....	....	....	....	....	....	....	....	....	....	5.7	....	....	....
NBL Playoff Totals		3	....	....	17	6	....	....	....	....	....	5	....	....	....	....	....	....	....	....	....	....	....	....	5.7	....	....	....

• GALE, Mike

Michael Eugene (Flipper) Gale

Born: July 18, 1950. Philadelphia, PA, United States. Height: 6'4". Weight: 185 lbs. Drafted: 1971 College: Elizabeth City State

YEAR	TEAM	GP	GS	MIN	PTS	FGM	FGA	FG%	3PM	3PA	3P%	FTM	FTA	FT%	ORB	DRB	TRB	AST	PF	DQ	STL	BLK	TO	MPG	PPG	RPG	APG	PCM
71-72	Kentucky-A	78	....	1701	497	201	447	.450	0	3	.000	95	140	.679	100	171	271	200	206	1	....	....	113	21.8	6.4	3.5	2.6	.372
72-73	Kentucky-A	81	....	1854	537	218	463	.471	1	6	.167	100	143	.699	78	163	241	248	207	1	131	....	108	22.9	6.6	3.0	3.1	.374
73-74	Kentucky-A	48	....	1591	478	200	454	.441	2	11	.182	76	104	.731	57	159	216	200	158	....	107	47	125	33.1	10.0	4.5	4.2	.373
73-74	New York-A	32	....	904	257	114	266	.429	0	6	.000	29	36	.806	50	102	152	124	84	....	60	34	53	28.3	8.0	4.8	3.9	.398
74-75	New York-A	72	....	1624	535	228	492	.463	7	23	.304	72	91	.791	97	139	236	165	131	....	88	47	111	22.6	7.4	3.3	2.3	.386
75-76	San Antonio-A	78	....	1782	527	230	506	.455	3	17	.176	64	80	.800	48	159	207	244	145	....	123	40	143	22.8	6.8	2.7	3.1	.373
76-77	San Antonio	82	....	2598	843	353	754	.468	....	....	....	137	167	.820	54	219	273	473	224	3	191	50	....	31.7	10.3	3.3	5.8	.447
77-78	San Antonio	70	....	2091	637	275	581	.473	....	....	....	87	100	.870	57	166	223	376	170	2	159	25	175	29.9	9.1	3.2	5.4	.438
78-79	San Antonio	82	....	2121	659	284	612	.464	....	....	....	91	108	.843	40	146	186	374	192	1	152	40	156	25.9	8.0	2.3	4.6	.416
79-80	San Antonio	67	....	1474	441	171	377	.454	2	13	.154	97	120	.808	34	118	152	312	134	2	123	13	114	22.0	6.6	2.3	4.7	.463
80-81	San Antonio	35	....	636	192	86	164	.524	1	3	.333	19	26	.731	7	45	52	99	56	0	55	2	39	18.2	5.5	1.5	2.8	.415
80-81	Portland	42	....	476	179	71	145	.490	1	4	.250	36	42	.857	9	38	47	70	61	0	39	5	38	11.3	4.3	1.1	1.7	.432
81-82	Golden State	75	70	1793	421	185	373	.496	0	5	.000	51	65	.785	37	152	189	261	173	1	121	28	128	23.9	5.6	2.5	3.5	.355
NBA Season Totals		453	70	11189	3372	1425	3006	.474	4	25	.160	518	628	.825	238	884	1122	1965	1010	9	840	163	650	24.7	7.4	2.5	4.3	....
ABA Season Totals		389	....	9456	2831	1191	2628	.453	13	66	.197	436	594	.734	430	893	1323	1181	931	2	509	168	653	24.3	7.3	3.4	3.0	....
Career Totals		842	70	20645	6203	2616	5634	.464	17	91	.187	954	1222	.781	668	1777	2445	3146	1941	11	1349	331	1303	24.5	7.4	2.9	3.7	....
71-72	Kentucky-A	2	....	31	6	3	14	.214	0	2	.000	0	0	.000	....	....	2	8	2	....	....	....	1	15.5	3.0	1.0	4.0	.199
72-73	Kentucky-A	12	....	291	66	23	58	.397	0	2	.000	20	23	.870	8	22	30	40	41	1	....	....	15	24.3	5.5	2.5	3.3	.295
73-74	New York-A	14	....	367	116	48	110	.436	1	1	1.000	19	20	.950	10	48	58	57	34	....	19	18	24	26.2	8.3	4.1	4.1	.443
74-75	New York-A	3	....	73	23	9	19	.474	2	4	.500	3	6	.500	1	4	5	7	7	....	7	6	1	24.3	7.7	1.7	2.3	.300
75-76	San Antonio-A	7	....	286	103	45	98	.459	0	2	.000	13	17	.765	9	31	40	50	16	....	24	10	23	40.9	14.7	5.7	7.1	.482
76-77	San Antonio	2	....	67	22	9	23	.391	....	....	....	4	7	.571	5	5	10	10	9	1	4	2	....	33.5	11.0	5.0	5.0	.369
77-78	San Antonio	6	....	201	52	25	56	.446	....	....	....	2	4	.500	7	18	25	31	15	0	7	4	17	33.5	8.7	4.2	5.2	.343
78-79	San Antonio	14	....	302	95	38	87	.437	....	....	....	19	22	.864	10	19	29	56	33	0	16	4	16	21.6	6.8	2.1	4.0	.418
79-80	San Antonio	3	....	69	21	8	20	.400	1	4	.250	4	7	.571	1	5	6	16	6	0	5	0	3	23.0	7.0	2.0	5.3	.447
80-81	Portland	3	....	51	8	4	16	.250	0	0	.000	0	0	.000	2	3	5	9	2	0	5	0	2	17.0	2.7	1.7	3.0	.260
NBA Playoff Totals		28	....	690	198	84	202	.416	1	4	.250	29	40	.725	25	50	75	122	65	1	37	10	38	24.6	7.1	2.7	4.4	....
ABA Playoff Totals		38	....	1048	314	128	299	.428	3	11	.273	55	66	.833	28	105	135	162	100	1	50	34	64	27.6	8.3	3.6	4.3	....
Career Playoff Totals		66	....	1738	512	212	501	.423	4	15	.267	84	106	.792	53	155	210	284	165	2	87	44	102	26.3	7.8	3.2	4.3	....

• GALLAGHER, Chad

Chad Austin Gallagher

Born: May 30, 1969. Rockford, IL, United States. Height: 6'10". Weight: 255 lbs. Drafted: 1991 College: Creighton

YEAR	TEAM	GP	GS	MIN	PTS	FGM	FGA	FG%	3PM	3PA	3P%	FTM	FTA	FT%	ORB	DRB	TRB	AST	PF	DQ	STL	BLK	TO	MPG	PPG	RPG	APG	PCM
93-94	Utah	2	0	3	6	3	3	1.000	0	0	.000	0	0	.000	0	0	0	0	2	0	0	0	0	1.5	3.0	0.0	0.0	1.694
NBA Season Totals		2	0	3	6	3	3	1.000	0	0	.000	0	0	.000	0	0	0	0	2	0	0	0	0	1.5	3.0	0.0	0.0	....

• GALLATIN, Harry

Harry J. (The Horse, Farmer) Gallatin

Born: Apr. 26, 1927. Roxana, IL, United States. Height: 6'6". Weight: 210 lbs. Drafted: 1948 College: Northeast Missouri State HOF: 1991

YEAR	TEAM	GP	GS	MIN	PTS	FGM	FGA	FG%	3PM	3PA	3P%	FTM	FTA	FT%	ORB	DRB	TRB	AST	PF	DQ	STL	BLK	TO	MPG	PPG	RPG	APG	PCM
48-49	New York	52	....	....	434	157	479	.328	....	....	....	120	169	.710	....	....	....	63	127	....	....	....	....	....	8.3	....	1.2	....
49-50	New York	68	....	....	803	263	664	.396	....	....	....	277	366	.757	....	....	....	56	215	....	....	....	....	....	11.8	....	0.8	....
50-51	New York	66	....	....	845	293	705	.416	....	....	....	259	354	.732	....	....	800	180	244	4	....	....	....	....	12.8	12.1	2.7	....
51-52	New York	66	....	1931	741	233	527	.442	....	....	....	275	341	.806	....	....	661	115	223	5	....	....	....	29.3	11.2	10.0	1.7	.542
52-53	New York	70	....	2333	865	282	635	.444	....	....	....	301	430	.700	....	....	916	126	224	6	....	....	....	33.3	12.4	13.1	1.8	.560
53-54	New York	72	....	2690	949	258	639	.404	....	....	....	433	552	.784	....	....	**1098**	153	208	2	....	....	....	37.4	13.2	**15.3**	2.1	.572
54-55	New York	72	....	2548	1053	330	859	.384	....	....	....	393	483	.814	....	....	995	176	206	5	....	....	....	35.4	14.6	13.8	2.4	.593
55-56	New York	72	....	2378	1002	322	834	.386	....	....	....	358	455	.787	....	....	740	168	220	6	....	....	....	33.0	13.9	10.3	2.3	.531
56-57	New York	72	....	1943	1079	332	817	.406	....	....	....	415	519	.800	....	....	725	85	202	1	....	....	....	27.0	15.0	10.1	1.2	.644
57-58	Detroit	72	....	1990	1072	340	898	.379	....	....	....	392	498	.787	....	....	749	86	217	5	....	....	....	27.6	14.9	10.4	1.2	.604
NBA Season Totals		682	....	15813	8843	2810	7057	.398	....	....	....	3223	4167	.773	....	....	6684	1208	2086	34	....	....	....	23.2	13.0	9.8	1.8	....
48-49	New York	6	....	....	72	20	56	.357	....	....	....	32	39	.821	....	....	....	10	31	....	....	....	....	....	12.0	....	1.7	....
49-50	New York	5	....	....	65	20	52	.385	....	....	....	25	32	.781	....	....	....	6	23	....	....	....	....	....	13.0	....	1.2	....

YEAR	TEAM	GP	GS	MIN	PTS	FGM	FGA	FG%	3PM	3PA	3P%	FTM	FTA	FT%	ORB	DRB	TRB	AST	PF	DQ	STL	BLK	TO	MPG	PPG	RPG	APG	PCM
50-51	New York	14	....	....	165	49	140	.350	....	....	....	67	87	.770	....	....	163	26	57	3	....	....	....	....	11.8	11.6	1.9	....
51-52	New York	14	....	471	151	50	122	.410	....	....	....	51	66	.773	....	....	134	19	45	1	....	....	....	33.6	10.8	9.6	1.4	.421
52-53	New York	11	....	303	116	36	86	.419	....	....	....	44	59	.746	....	....	120	15	29	0	....	....	....	27.5	10.5	10.9	1.4	.561
53-54	New York	4	....	151	54	16	35	.457	....	....	....	22	31	.710	....	....	61	6	12	0	....	....	....	37.8	13.5	15.3	1.5	.557
54-55	New York	3	....	108	55	19	42	.452	....	....	....	17	22	.773	....	....	44	7	11	0	....	....	....	36.0	18.3	14.7	2.3	.681
57-58	Detroit	7	....	182	90	32	87	.368	....	....	....	26	37	.703	....	....	70	11	27	1	....	....	....	26.0	12.9	10.0	1.6	.555
NBA Playoff Totals		64	....	1215	768	242	620	.390	....	....	....	284	373	.761	....	....	592	100	235	5	....	....	....	19.0	12.0	9.3	1.6	....

• GALLOWAY, Lowell

Lowell Galloway

Born: 1921. Height: 6'4". Weight: 210 lbs. Drafted: — College: Evansville

YEAR	TEAM	GP	GS	MIN	PTS	FGM	FGA	FG%	3PM	3PA	3P%	FTM	FTA	FT%	ORB	DRB	TRB	AST	PF	DQ	STL	BLK	TO	MPG	PPG	RPG	APG	PCM
46-47	Indianapolis-N	31	....	....	46	14	....	....	....	....	....	18	34	.529	....	....	....	....	....	....	....	....	....	....	1.5	....	....	....
NBL Season Totals		31	....	....	46	14	....	....	....	....	....	18	34	....	....	....	....	....	....	....	....	....	....	....	1.5	....	....	....
46-47	Indianapolis-N	3	....	....	5	2	....	....	....	....	....	1	1	1.000	....	....	....	....	....	....	....	....	....	....	1.7	....	....	....
NBL Playoff Totals		3	....	....	5	2	....	....	....	....	....	1	1	....	....	....	....	....	....	....	....	....	....	....	1.7	....	....	....

• GAMBEE, Dave

David P. Gambee

Born: Apr. 16, 1937. Portland, OR, United States. Height: 6'6". Weight: 215 lbs. Drafted: 1958 College: Oregon State

YEAR	TEAM	GP	GS	MIN	PTS	FGM	FGA	FG%	3PM	3PA	3P%	FTM	FTA	FT%	ORB	DRB	TRB	AST	PF	DQ	STL	BLK	TO	MPG	PPG	RPG	APG	PCM
58-59	St. Louis	2	....	7	2	1	1	1.000	....	....	....	0	0	.000	....	....	2	0	2	0	....	....	....	3.5	1.0	1.0	0.0	.393
59-60	St. Louis	42	....	445	208	81	198	.409	....	....	....	46	71	.648	....	....	155	29	62	1	....	....	....	10.6	5.0	3.7	0.7	.539
59-60	Cincinnati	19	....	211	95	36	93	.387	....	....	....	23	35	.657	....	....	74	9	21	0	....	....	....	11.1	5.0	3.9	0.5	.505
60-61	Syracuse	79	....	2090	1085	397	947	.419	....	....	....	291	352	.827	....	....	581	101	276	6	....	....	....	26.5	13.7	7.4	1.3	.529
61-62	Syracuse	80	....	2314	1338	477	1126	.424	....	....	....	384	470	.817	....	....	631	114	275	10	....	....	....	28.9	16.7	7.9	1.4	.571
62-63	Syracuse	60	....	1234	669	235	537	.438	....	....	....	199	238	.836	....	....	289	48	190	2	....	....	....	20.6	11.2	4.8	0.8	.507
63-64	Philadelphia	41	....	927	449	149	378	.394	....	....	....	151	185	.816	....	....	256	35	161	6	....	....	....	22.6	11.0	6.2	0.9	.471
64-65	Philadelphia	80	....	1993	1011	356	864	.412	....	....	....	299	368	.813	....	....	468	113	277	7	....	....	....	24.9	12.6	5.9	1.4	.495
65-66	Philadelphia	72	....	1068	495	168	437	.384	....	....	....	159	187	.850	....	....	273	71	189	3	....	....	....	14.8	6.9	3.8	1.0	.468
66-67	Philadelphia	63	....	757	407	150	345	.435	....	....	....	107	125	.856	....	....	197	42	143	5	....	....	....	12.0	6.5	3.1	0.7	.522
67-68	San Diego	80	....	1755	1071	375	853	.440	....	....	....	321	379	.847	....	....	464	93	253	5	....	....	....	21.9	13.4	5.8	1.2	.597
68-69	Milwaukee	34	....	624	410	150	323	.464	....	....	....	110	133	.827	....	....	179	32	99	4	....	....	....	18.4	12.1	5.3	0.9	.643
68-69	Detroit	25	....	302	169	60	142	.423	....	....	....	49	62	.790	....	....	78	15	60	0	....	....	....	12.1	6.8	3.1	0.6	.505
69-70	San Francisco	73	....	951	526	185	464	.399	....	....	....	156	186	.839	....	....	244	55	172	0	....	....	....	13.0	7.2	3.3	0.8	.492
NBA Season Totals		750	....	14678	7935	2820	6708	.420	....	....	....	2295	2791	.822	....	....	3891	757	2180	49	....	....	....	19.6	10.6	5.2	1.0	....
60-61	Syracuse	8	....	208	100	34	95	.358	....	....	....	32	41	.780	....	....	55	12	33	0	....	....	....	26.0	12.5	6.9	1.5	.453
61-62	Syracuse	5	....	170	56	17	54	.315	....	....	....	22	25	.880	....	....	45	4	22	1	....	....	....	34.0	11.2	9.0	0.8	.337
62-63	Syracuse	5	....	75	32	10	34	.294	....	....	....	12	13	.923	....	....	16	0	14	0	....	....	....	15.0	6.4	3.2	0.0	.263
63-64	Philadelphia	5	....	149	69	24	60	.400	....	....	....	21	27	.778	....	....	29	8	23	1	....	....	....	29.8	13.8	5.8	1.6	.416
64-65	Philadelphia	10	....	132	62	16	48	.333	....	....	....	30	34	.882	....	....	23	6	31	1	....	....	....	13.2	6.2	2.3	0.6	.372
65-66	Philadelphia	5	....	82	30	11	29	.379	....	....	....	8	11	.727	....	....	14	4	14	0	....	....	....	16.4	6.0	2.8	0.8	.306
66-67	Philadelphia	5	....	24	18	6	11	.545	....	....	....	6	6	1.000	....	....	6	2	6	0	....	....	....	4.8	3.6	1.2	0.4	.784
NBA Playoff Totals		43	....	840	367	118	331	.356	....	....	....	131	157	.834	....	....	188	36	143	3	....	....	....	19.5	8.5	4.4	0.8	....

• GAMBLE, Kevin

Kevin Douglas Gamble

Born: Nov. 13, 1965. Springfield, IL, United States. Height: 6'5". Weight: 210 lbs. Drafted: 1987 College: Iowa

YEAR	TEAM	GP	GS	MIN	PTS	FGM	FGA	FG%	3PM	3PA	3P%	FTM	FTA	FT%	ORB	DRB	TRB	AST	PF	DQ	STL	BLK	TO	MPG	PPG	RPG	APG	PCM
87-88	Portland	9	0	19	0	0	3	.000	0	1	.000	0	0	.000	2	1	3	1	2	0	2	0	2	2.1	0.0	0.3	0.1	.007
88-89	Boston	44	6	375	187	75	136	.551	2	11	.182	35	55	.636	11	31	42	34	40	0	14	3	18	8.5	4.3	1.0	0.8	.472
89-90	Boston	71	10	990	362	137	301	.455	3	18	.167	85	107	.794	42	70	112	119	77	1	28	8	43	13.9	5.1	1.6	1.7	.391
90-91	Boston	82	76	2706	1281	548	933	.587	0	7	.000	185	227	.815	85	182	267	256	237	6	100	34	148	33.0	15.6	3.3	3.1	.481
91-92	Boston	82	77	2496	1108	480	908	.529	9	31	.290	139	157	.885	80	206	286	219	200	2	75	37	98	30.4	13.5	3.5	2.7	.450
92-93	Boston	82	58	2541	1093	459	906	.507	52	139	.374	123	149	.826	46	200	246	226	185	1	86	37	82	31.0	13.3	3.0	2.8	.428
93-94	Boston	75	28	1880	864	368	804	.458	25	103	.243	103	126	.817	41	118	159	149	134	0	57	22	75	25.1	11.5	2.1	2.0	.374
94-95	Miami	77	0	1223	566	220	450	.489	39	98	.398	87	111	.784	29	93	122	119	130	0	52	10	46	15.9	7.4	1.6	1.5	.437
95-96	Miami	44	13	1033	305	117	297	.394	38	91	.418	33	38	.868	14	72	86	82	119	2	31	5	31	23.5	6.9	2.0	1.9	.242
95-96	Sacramento	21	0	292	81	35	82	.427	6	23	.261	5	10	.500	7	20	27	18	28	0	4	3	11	13.9	3.9	1.3	0.9	.212
96-97	Sacramento	62	2	953	307	123	286	.430	54	112	.482	7	10	.700	13	94	107	77	76	0	21	17	25	15.4	5.0	1.7	1.2	.328
NBA Season Totals		649	270	14508	6154	2562	5106	.502	228	634	.360	802	990	.810	370	1087	1457	1300	1228	12	470	176	579	22.4	9.5	2.2	2.0	....
88-89	Boston	1	1	29	8	4	11	.364	0	1	.000	0	2	.000	1	0	1	2	1	0	1	0	0	29.0	8.0	1.0	2.0	.141
89-90	Boston	3	0	8	6	3	5	.600	0	0	.000	0	0	.000	1	0	1	2	1	0	0	0	1	2.7	2.0	0.3	0.7	.723
90-91	Boston	11	11	238	66	29	60	.483	0	0	.000	8	12	.667	3	10	13	19	24	0	4	2	7	21.6	6.0	1.2	1.7	.233
91-92	Boston	10	10	335	136	62	131	.473	0	2	.000	12	15	.800	13	29	42	23	26	0	12	6	10	33.5	13.6	4.2	2.3	.387
92-93	Boston	4	4	142	55	23	42	.548	5	12	.417	4	4	1.000	3	6	9	10	11	0	6	1	5	35.5	13.8	2.3	2.5	.374
95-96	Sacramento	2	0	3	0	0	0	.000	0	0	.000	0	0	.000	0	0	0	0	0	0	0	0	0	1.5	0.0	0.0	0.0	.000
NBA Playoff Totals		31	26	755	271	121	249	.486	5	15	.333	24	33	.727	21	45	66	56	63	0	23	9	23	24.4	8.7	2.1	1.8	....

• GANTT, Bob

Robert M. Gantt Jr.

Born: June 22, 1922. Height: 6'4". Weight: 205 lbs. Drafted: — College: Duke

YEAR	TEAM	GP	GS	MIN	PTS	FGM	FGA	FG%	3PM	3PA	3P%	FTM	FTA	FT%	ORB	DRB	TRB	AST	PF	DQ	STL	BLK	TO	MPG	PPG	RPG	APG	PCM
46-47	Washington	23	....	....	71	29	89	.326	....	....	....	13	28	.464	....	....	....	5	45	....	....	....	....	....	3.1	....	0.2	....
NBA Season Totals		23	....	....	71	29	89	.326	....	....	....	13	28	.464	....	....	....	5	45	....	....	....	....	....	3.1	....	0.2	....
46-47	Washington	2	....	....	2	1	3	.333	....	....	....	0	1	.000	....	....	....	0	0	....	....	....	....	....	1.0	....	0.0	....
NBA Playoff Totals		2	....	....	2	1	3	.333	....	....	....	0	1	.000	....	....	....	0	0	....	....	....	....	....	1.0	....	0.0	....

YEAR	TEAM	GP	GS	MIN	PTS	FGM	FGA	FG%	3PM	3PA	3P%	FTM	FTA	FT%	ORB	DRB	TRB	AST	PF	DQ	STL	BLK	TO	MPG	PPG	RPG	APG	PCM

• GANTT, Fred — Fred Gantt

Born: 1922.   Height: 6'3".   Weight: 170 lbs.   Drafted: —   College: Richmond

| 47-48 Sheboygan-N | 6 | .... | .... | 11 | 4 | .... | .... | .... | .... | .... | .... | 3 | 3 | 1.000 | .... | .... | .... | .... | .... | .... | .... | .... | .... | .... | 1.8 | .... | .... | .... |
| **NBL Season Totals** | 6 | .... | .... | 11 | 4 | .... | .... | .... | .... | .... | .... | 3 | 3 | .... | .... | .... | .... | .... | .... | .... | .... | .... | .... | .... | 1.8 | .... | .... | .... |

• GARCES, Ruben — Ruben Garces

Born: Oct. 17, 1973. Colon, Panama.   Height: 6'9".   Weight: 245 lbs.   Drafted: —   College: Providence

00-01 Phoenix	10	0	62	16	7	15	.467	0	0	.000	2	8	.250	12	10	22	4	14	0	2	1	5	6.2	1.6	2.2	0.4	.358
00-01 Golden State	3	0	11	0	0	7	.000	0	0	.000	0	0	.000	4	3	7	1	0	0	1	1	0	3.7	0.0	2.3	0.3	.263
NBA Season Totals	13	0	73	16	7	22	.318	0	0	.000	2	8	.250	16	13	29	5	14	0	3	2	5	5.6	1.2	2.2	0.4	....

• GARCIA, Frank — Frank Garcia

Born: 1918.   Height: 6'   Weight: 175 lbs.   Drafted: —   College: none

43-44 Cleveland-N	7	....	....	23	8	....	....	....	....	....	....	7	....	....	....	....	....	....	....	....	....	....	....	....	3.3	....	....	....
44-45 Cleveland-N	25	....	....	40	16	....	....	....	....	....	....	8	....	....	....	....	....	....	....	....	....	....	....	....	1.6	....	....	....
45-46 Cleveland-N	7	....	....	15	7	....	....	....	....	....	....	1	....	....	....	....	....	....	....	....	....	....	....	....	2.1	....	....	....
NBL Season Totals	39	....	....	78	31	....	....	....	....	....	....	16	....	....	....	....	....	....	....	....	....	....	....	....	2.0	....	....	....
43-44 Cleveland-N	2	....	....	4	2	....	....	....	....	....	....	0	....	....	....	....	....	....	....	....	....	....	....	....	2.0	....	....	....
44-45 Cleveland-N	2	....	....	0	0	....	....	....	....	....	....	0	....	....	....	....	....	....	....	....	....	....	....	....	0.0	....	....	....
NBL Playoff Totals	4	....	....	4	2	....	....	....	....	....	....	0	....	....	....	....	....	....	....	....	....	....	....	....	1.0	....	....	....

• GARDNER, Ben — Ben Gardner

Born: 1921.   Height: 6'3".   Weight: 190 lbs.   Drafted: —   College: Sam Houston State

46-47 Anderson-N	6	....	....	3	0	....	....	....	....	....	....	3	8	.375	....	....	....	....	....	....	....	....	....	....	0.5	....	....	....
46-47 Fort Wayne-N	1	....	....	0	0	....	....	....	....	....	....	0	0	.000	....	....	....	....	....	....	....	....	....	....	0.0	....	....	....
NBL Season Totals	7	....	....	3	0	....	....	....	....	....	....	3	8	....	....	....	....	....	....	....	....	....	....	....	0.4	....	....	....

• GARDNER, Chuck — Charles Rutland Gardner

Born: Sept. 30, 1944. Lincoln, NE, United States.   Height: 6'8".   Weight: 205 lbs.   Drafted: 1966   College: Colorado

| 67-68 Denver-A | 42 | .... | 487 | 197 | 71 | 175 | .406 | 0 | 4 | .000 | 55 | 79 | .696 | .... | .... | 136 | 13 | 74 | 1 | .... | .... | 52 | 11.6 | 4.7 | 3.2 | 0.3 | .407 |
| **ABA Season Totals** | 42 | .... | 487 | 197 | 71 | 175 | .406 | 0 | 4 | .000 | 55 | 79 | .696 | .... | .... | 136 | 13 | 74 | 1 | .... | .... | 52 | 11.6 | 4.7 | 3.2 | 0.3 | .... |

• GARDNER, Earl — Earl Baker Gardner

Born: Sept. 18, 1923.   Height: 6'3".   Weight: 195 lbs.   Drafted: 1948   College: DePauw

48-49 Minneapolis	50	....	....	89	38	101	.376	....	....	....	13	28	.464	....	....	....	19	50	....	....	....	....	....	1.8	....	0.4	....
NBA Season Totals	50	....	....	89	38	101	.376	....	....	....	13	28	.464	....	....	....	19	50	....	....	....	....	....	1.8	....	0.4	....
48-49 Minneapolis	7	....	....	4	1	9	.111	....	....	....	2	4	.500	....	....	....	1	3	....	....	....	....	....	0.6	....	0.1	....
NBA Playoff Totals	7	....	....	4	1	9	.111	....	....	....	2	4	.500	....	....	....	1	3	....	....	....	....	....	0.6	....	0.1	....

• GARDNER, Kenneth — Kenneth Kay Gardner

Born: Sept. 27, 1949.   Height: 6'5".   Weight: 205 lbs.   Drafted: 1971   College: Utah

| 75-76 Utah-A | 9 | .... | 51 | 14 | 6 | 18 | .333 | 0 | 0 | .000 | 2 | 2 | 1.000 | 8 | 5 | 13 | 3 | 9 | .... | 2 | 1 | 1 | 5.7 | 1.6 | 1.4 | 0.3 | .279 |
| **ABA Season Totals** | 9 | .... | 51 | 14 | 6 | 18 | .333 | 0 | 0 | .000 | 2 | 2 | 1.000 | 8 | 5 | 13 | 3 | 9 | .... | 2 | 1 | 1 | 5.7 | 1.6 | 1.4 | 0.3 | .... |

• GARDNER, Vern — Vernon B. Gardner

Born: May 14, 1925. Afton, WY, United States. Died: Aug.26, 1987.   Height: 6'5".   Weight: 200 lbs.   Drafted: 1949   College: Utah

49-50 Philadelphia	63	....	....	853	313	916	.342	....	....	....	227	296	.767	....	....	....	119	236	....	....	....	....	13.5	....	1.9	....
50-51 Philadelphia	61	....	....	327	129	383	.337	....	....	....	69	97	.711	....	237	....	89	149	6	....	....	....	5.4	3.9	1.5	....
51-52 Philadelphia	27	....	507	159	72	194	.371	....	....	....	15	23	.652	....	112	....	37	60	2	....	....	18.8	5.9	4.1	1.4	.346
NBA Season Totals	151	....	507	1339	514	1493	.344	....	....	....	311	416	.748	....	349	....	245	445	8	....	....	3.4	8.9	2.3	1.6	....
49-50 Philadelphia	2	....	....	36	15	44	.341	....	....	....	6	9	.667	....	....	....	2	11	....	....	....	....	18.0	....	1.0	....
50-51 Philadelphia	2	....	....	11	4	8	.500	....	....	....	3	3	1.000	....	4	....	0	8	1	....	....	....	5.5	2.0	0.0	....
51-52 Philadelphia	3	....	77	24	7	19	.368	....	....	....	10	11	.909	....	14	....	3	14	0	....	....	25.7	8.0	4.7	1.0	.311
NBA Playoff Totals	7	....	77	71	26	71	.366	....	....	....	19	23	.826	....	18	....	5	33	1	....	....	11.0	10.1	2.6	0.7	....

• GARFINKEL, Jack — Jack (Dutch) Garfinkel

Born: June 13, 1918.   Height: 6'   Weight: 190 lbs.   Drafted: —   College: St. John's (NY)

45-46 Rochester-N	18	....	....	34	14	....	....	....	....	....	....	6	....	....	....	....	....	....	....	....	....	....	....	....	1.9	....	....	....
46-47 Rochester-N	10	....	....	13	5	....	....	....	....	....	....	3	6	.500	....	....	....	....	....	....	....	....	....	....	1.3	....	....	....
46-47 Boston	40	....	....	179	81	304	.266	....	....	....	....	17	28	.607	....	....	....	58	62	....	....	....	....	....	4.5	....	1.5	....

YEAR	TEAM	GP	GS	MIN	PTS	FGM	FGA	FG%	3PM	3PA	3P%	FTM	FTA	FT%	ORB	DRB	TRB	AST	PF	DQ	STL	BLK	TO	MPG	PPG	RPG	APG	PCM
47-48	Boston	43	....	....	263	114	380	.300	....	....	....	35	46	.761	....	....	....	59	78	....	....	....	....	....	6.1	....	1.4	....
48-49	Boston	9	....	....	34	12	70	.171	....	....	....	10	14	.714	....	....	....	17	19	....	....	....	....	....	3.8	....	1.9	....
NBA Season Totals		92	....	....	476	207	754	.275	....	....	....	62	88	.705	....	....	....	134	159	....	....	....	....	....	5.2	....	1.5	....
NBL Season Totals		28	....	....	47	19	....	....	....	....	....	9	6	....	....	....	....	....	....	....	....	....	....	....	1.7	....	....	....
Career Totals		120	....	....	523	226	754	....	....	....	....	71	94	....	....	....	....	134	159	....	....	....	....	....	4.4	....	1.1	....
45-46	Rochester-N	6	....	....	3	1	....	....	....	....	....	1	2	.500	....	....	....	....	....	....	....	....	....	....	0.5	....	....	....
47-48	Boston	3	....	....	22	7	23	.304	....	....	....	8	10	.800	....	....	....	7	15	....	....	....	....	....	7.3	....	2.3	....
NBA Playoff Totals		3	....	....	22	7	23	.304	....	....	....	8	10	.800	....	....	....	7	15	....	....	....	....	....	7.3	....	2.3	....
NBL Playoff Totals		6	....	....	3	1	....	....	....	....	....	1	2	....	....	....	....	....	....	....	....	....	....	....	0.5	....	....	....
Career Playoff Totals		9	....	....	25	8	23	....	....	....	....	9	12	....	....	....	....	7	15	....	....	....	....	....	2.8	....	0.8	....

• GARLAND, Gary

Gary J. Garland

Born: Oct. 12, 1957. East Orange, NJ, United States.   Height: 6'4".   Weight: 180 lbs.   Drafted: 1979   College: DePaul

YEAR	TEAM	GP	GS	MIN	PTS	FGM	FGA	FG%	3PM	3PA	3P%	FTM	FTA	FT%	ORB	DRB	TRB	AST	PF	DQ	STL	BLK	TO	MPG	PPG	RPG	APG	PCM
79-80	Denver	78	....	1106	334	155	356	.435	6	19	.316	18	26	.692	50	88	138	145	80	1	54	4	70	14.2	4.3	1.8	1.9	.348
NBA Season Totals		78	....	1106	334	155	356	.435	6	19	.316	18	26	.692	50	88	138	145	80	1	54	4	70	14.2	4.3	1.8	1.9	....

• GARLAND, Winston

Winston Kinnard Garland

Born: Dec. 19, 1964. Gary, IN, United States.   Height: 6'2".   Weight: 170 lbs.   Drafted: 1987   College: Southwest Missouri State

YEAR	TEAM	GP	GS	MIN	PTS	FGM	FGA	FG%	3PM	3PA	3P%	FTM	FTA	FT%	ORB	DRB	TRB	AST	PF	DQ	STL	BLK	TO	MPG	PPG	RPG	APG	PCM
87-88	Golden State	67	62	2122	831	340	775	.439	13	39	.333	138	157	.879	68	159	227	429	188	2	116	7	168	31.7	12.4	3.4	6.4	.451
88-89	Golden State	79	79	2661	1145	466	1074	.434	10	43	.233	203	251	.809	101	227	328	505	216	2	175	14	190	33.7	14.5	4.2	6.4	.489
89-90	Golden State	51	4	891	270	108	288	.375	1	10	.100	53	63	.841	31	80	111	157	77	1	48	5	82	17.5	5.3	2.2	3.1	.342
89-90	LA Clippers	28	15	871	304	122	285	.428	11	26	.423	49	59	.831	20	83	103	146	75	0	30	5	78	31.1	10.9	3.7	5.2	.371
90-91	LA Clippers	69	26	1702	564	221	519	.426	4	26	.154	118	157	.752	46	152	198	317	189	3	97	10	117	24.7	8.2	2.9	4.6	.407
91-92	Denver	78	67	2209	846	333	750	.444	9	28	.321	171	199	.859	67	123	190	411	206	1	98	22	172	28.3	10.8	2.4	5.3	.416
92-93	Houston	66	4	1004	391	152	343	.443	6	13	.462	81	89	.910	32	76	108	138	116	0	39	4	66	15.2	5.9	1.6	2.1	.380
94-95	Minnesota	73	58	1931	448	170	410	.415	19	75	.253	89	112	.795	48	120	168	318	184	1	71	13	102	26.5	6.1	2.3	4.4	.313
NBA Season Totals		511	315	13391	4799	1912	4444	.430	73	260	.281	902	1087	.830	413	1020	1433	2421	1251	10	674	80	975	26.2	9.4	2.8	4.7	....
88-89	Golden State	8	8	270	107	41	98	.418	1	3	.333	24	28	.857	14	19	33	29	31	1	13	2	15	33.8	13.4	4.1	3.6	.368
92-93	Houston	12	5	246	77	30	74	.405	0	1	.000	17	17	1.000	6	27	33	31	27	1	16	0	22	20.5	6.4	2.8	2.6	.332
NBA Playoff Totals		20	13	516	184	71	172	.413	1	4	.250	41	45	.911	20	46	66	60	58	2	29	2	37	25.8	9.2	3.3	3.0	....

• GARMAKER, Dick

Richard Eugene Garmaker

Born: Oct. 29, 1932. Hibbing, MN, United States.   Height: 6'3".   Weight: 200 lbs.   Drafted: 1955   College: Minnesota

YEAR	TEAM	GP	GS	MIN	PTS	FGM	FGA	FG%	3PM	3PA	3P%	FTM	FTA	FT%	ORB	DRB	TRB	AST	PF	DQ	STL	BLK	TO	MPG	PPG	RPG	APG	PCM
55-56	Minneapolis	68	....	870	388	138	373	.370	....	....	....	112	139	.806	....	....	132	104	127	0	....	....	....	12.8	5.7	1.9	1.5	.437
56-57	Minneapolis	72	....	2406	1177	406	1015	.400	....	....	....	365	435	.839	....	....	336	190	199	1	....	....	....	33.4	16.3	4.7	2.6	.462
57-58	Minneapolis	68	....	2216	1094	390	988	.395	....	....	....	314	411	.764	....	....	365	183	190	2	....	....	....	32.6	16.1	5.4	2.7	.475
58-59	Minneapolis	72	....	2493	984	350	885	.395	....	....	....	284	368	.772	....	....	325	211	226	3	....	....	....	34.6	13.7	4.5	2.9	.390
59-60	Minneapolis	44	....	1187	513	198	525	.377	....	....	....	117	163	.718	....	....	189	133	126	4	....	....	....	27.0	11.7	4.3	3.0	.429
59-60	New York	26	....	745	336	125	290	.431	....	....	....	86	100	.860	....	....	124	73	60	0	....	....	....	28.7	12.9	4.8	2.8	.494
60-61	New York	71	....	2238	1105	415	943	.440	....	....	....	275	358	.768	....	....	277	220	240	2	....	....	....	31.5	15.6	3.9	3.1	.475
NBA Season Totals		421	....	12155	5597	2022	5019	.403	....	....	....	1553	1974	.787	....	....	1748	1114	1168	12	....	....	....	28.9	13.3	4.2	2.6	....
55-56	Minneapolis	3	....	42	30	7	19	.368	....	....	....	16	17	.941	....	....	8	11	8	0	....	....	....	14.0	10.0	2.7	3.7	.885
56-57	Minneapolis	5	....	187	65	19	69	.275	....	....	....	27	32	.844	....	....	35	17	19	1	....	....	....	37.4	13.0	7.0	3.4	.354
58-59	Minneapolis	13	....	439	189	70	165	.424	....	....	....	49	63	.778	....	....	55	39	44	1	....	....	....	33.8	14.5	4.2	3.0	.423
NBA Playoff Totals		21	....	668	284	96	253	.379	....	....	....	92	112	.821	....	....	98	67	71	2	....	....	....	31.8	13.5	4.7	3.2	....

• GARNER, Bill

William Garner

Born: June 17, 1940. East St. Louis, IL, United States.   Height: 6'10".   Weight: 220 lbs.   Drafted: 1962   College: Portland

YEAR	TEAM	GP	GS	MIN	PTS	FGM	FGA	FG%	3PM	3PA	3P%	FTM	FTA	FT%	ORB	DRB	TRB	AST	PF	DQ	STL	BLK	TO	MPG	PPG	RPG	APG	PCM
67-68	Anaheim-A	53	....	514	81	28	103	.272	0	1	.000	25	50	.500	....	....	119	24	101	4	....	....	....	47	9.7	1.5	2.2	0.5	.182
ABA Season Totals		53	....	514	81	28	103	.272	0	1	.000	25	50	.500	....	....	119	24	101	4	....	....	....	47	9.7	1.5	2.2	0.5	....

• GARNER, Chris

Chris Garner

Born: Feb. 2, 1975. Memphis, TN, United States.   Height: 5'10".   Weight: 156 lbs.   Drafted: —   College: Memphis

YEAR	TEAM	GP	GS	MIN	PTS	FGM	FGA	FG%	3PM	3PA	3P%	FTM	FTA	FT%	ORB	DRB	TRB	AST	PF	DQ	STL	BLK	TO	MPG	PPG	RPG	APG	PCM
97-98	Toronto	38	0	293	53	23	70	.329	4	14	.286	3	7	.429	7	17	24	45	50	0	21	4	27	7.7	1.4	0.6	1.2	.185
00-01	Golden State	8	0	149	19	7	37	.189	0	7	.000	5	6	.833	2	10	12	18	18	0	7	1	9	18.6	2.4	1.5	2.3	.089
NBA Season Totals		46	0	442	72	30	107	.280	4	21	.190	8	13	.615	9	27	36	63	68	0	28	5	36	9.6	1.6	0.8	1.4	....

• GARNETT, Bill

William Patrick Garnett

Born: Apr. 22, 1960. Kansas City, MO, United States.   Height: 6'9".   Weight: 225 lbs.   Drafted: 1982   College: Wyoming

YEAR	TEAM	GP	GS	MIN	PTS	FGM	FGA	FG%	3PM	3PA	3P%	FTM	FTA	FT%	ORB	DRB	TRB	AST	PF	DQ	STL	BLK	TO	MPG	PPG	RPG	APG	PCM
82-83	Dallas	75	13	1411	469	170	319	.533	0	3	.000	129	174	.741	141	265	406	103	245	3	48	70	83	18.8	6.3	5.4	1.4	.507
83-84	Dallas	80	34	1529	411	141	299	.472	0	2	.000	129	176	.733	123	208	331	128	217	4	44	66	64	19.1	5.1	4.1	1.6	.411
84-85	Indiana	65	13	1123	418	149	310	.481	0	2	.000	120	174	.690	98	188	286	67	196	3	28	15	91	17.3	6.4	4.4	1.0	.396
85-86	Indiana	80	2	1197	340	112	239	.469	0	2	.000	116	162	.716	106	169	275	95	174	0	39	22	88	15.0	4.3	3.4	1.2	.378
NBA Season Totals		300	62	5260	1638	572	1167	.490	0	9	.000	494	686	.720	468	830	1298	393	832	10	159	173	326	17.5	5.5	4.3	1.3	....
83-84	Dallas	8	0	74	38	15	30	.500	1	1	1.000	7	8	.875	10	12	22	4	10	0	0	2	1	9.3	4.8	2.8	0.5	.603
NBA Playoff Totals		8	0	74	38	15	30	.500	1	1	1.000	7	8	.875	10	12	22	4	10	0	0	2	1	9.3	4.8	2.8	0.5	....

• GARNETT, Kevin

Kevin Garnett

Born: May 19, 1976. Mauldin, SC, United States. Height: 6'11". Weight: 220 lbs. Drafted: 1995 College: none (HS: Mauldin, SC Farragut Academy, IL)

YEAR	TEAM	GP	GS	MIN	PTS	FGM	FGA	FG%	3PM	3PA	3P%	FTM	FTA	FT%	ORB	DRB	TRB	AST	PF	DQ	STL	BLK	TO	MPG	PPG	RPG	APG	PCM
95-96	Minnesota	80	43	2293	835	361	735	.491	8	28	.286	105	149	.705	175	326	501	145	189	2	86	131	112	28.7	10.4	6.3	1.8	.479
96-97	Minnesota	77	77	2995	1309	549	1100	.499	6	21	.286	205	272	.754	190	428	618	236	199	2	105	163	177	38.9	17.0	8.0	3.1	.529
97-98	Minnesota	82	82	3222	1518	635	1293	.491	3	16	.188	245	332	.738	222	564	786	348	224	1	139	150	189	39.3	18.5	9.6	4.2	.609
98-99	Minnesota	47	47	1780	977	414	900	.460	4	14	.286	145	206	.704	166	323	489	202	152	5	78	83	135	37.9	20.8	10.4	4.3	.636
99-00	Minnesota	81	81	3243	1857	759	1526	.497	30	81	.370	309	404	.765	223	733	956	401	205	1	120	126	268	40.0	22.9	11.8	5.0	.712
00-01	Minnesota	81	81	3202	1784	704	1475	.477	19	66	.288	357	467	.764	219	702	921	401	204	0	111	145	230	39.5	22.0	11.4	5.0	.700
01-02	Minnesota	81	81	3175	1714	659	1401	.470	37	116	.319	359	448	.801	243	738	981	422	184	0	96	126	229	39.2	21.2	12.1	5.2	.713
02-03	Minnesota	82	82	3322	1883	743	1481	.502	20	71	.282	377	502	.751	244	**858**	1102	495	199	0	113	129	229	40.5	23.0	13.4	6.0	.788
NBA Season Totals		611	574	23232	11877	4824	9911	.487	127	413	.308	2102	2780	.756	1682	4672	6354	2650	1556	11	848	1053	1569	38.0	19.4	10.4	4.3	....
96-97	Minnesota	3	3	125	52	24	51	.471	1	1	1.000	3	3	1.000	14	14	28	11	6	0	4	3	4	41.7	17.3	9.3	3.7	.517
97-98	Minnesota	5	5	194	79	36	75	.480	0	0	.000	7	9	.778	17	31	48	20	17	0	4	12	22	38.8	15.8	9.6	4.0	.488
98-99	Minnesota	4	4	170	87	35	79	.443	0	2	.000	17	23	.739	16	32	48	15	10	0	7	8	13	42.5	21.8	12.0	3.8	.599
99-00	Minnesota	4	4	171	75	30	78	.385	2	3	.667	13	16	.813	13	30	43	35	12	0	5	3	11	42.8	18.8	10.8	8.8	.580
00-01	Minnesota	4	4	165	84	27	58	.466	0	3	.000	30	36	.833	10	38	48	17	13	0	4	6	6	41.3	21.0	12.0	4.3	.685
01-02	Minnesota	3	3	130	72	24	56	.429	1	2	.500	23	32	.719	16	40	56	15	11	0	5	5	12	43.3	24.0	18.7	5.0	.764
02-03	Minnesota	6	6	265	162	71	138	.514	3	9	.333	17	28	.607	11	83	94	31	23	1	10	10	18	44.2	27.0	15.7	5.2	.780
NBA Playoff Totals		29	29	1220	611	247	535	.462	7	20	.350	110	147	.748	97	268	365	144	92	1	39	47	86	42.1	21.1	12.6	5.0	....

• GARNETT, Marlon

Marlon Garnett

Born: July 3, 1975. Los Angeles, CA, United States. Height: 6'2". Weight: 186 lbs. Drafted: — College: Santa Clara

YEAR	TEAM	GP	GS	MIN	PTS	FGM	FGA	FG%	3PM	3PA	3P%	FTM	FTA	FT%	ORB	DRB	TRB	AST	PF	DQ	STL	BLK	TO	MPG	PPG	RPG	APG	PCM
98-99	Boston	24	0	205	51	15	51	.294	6	23	.261	15	20	.750	3	18	21	18	18	0	5	1	12	8.5	2.1	0.9	0.8	.205
NBA Season Totals		24	0	205	51	15	51	.294	6	23	.261	15	20	.750	3	18	21	18	18	0	5	1	12	8.5	2.1	0.9	0.8	....

• GARRETT, Calvin

Calvin Eugene Garrett

Born: July 11, 1956. Parsons, TN, United States. Height: 6'7". Weight: 190 lbs. Drafted: 1979 College: Oral Roberts

YEAR	TEAM	GP	GS	MIN	PTS	FGM	FGA	FG%	3PM	3PA	3P%	FTM	FTA	FT%	ORB	DRB	TRB	AST	PF	DQ	STL	BLK	TO	MPG	PPG	RPG	APG	PCM
80-81	Houston	70	....	1638	427	188	415	.453	1	3	.333	50	62	.806	85	179	264	132	167	0	50	10	91	23.4	6.1	3.8	1.9	.302
81-82	Houston	51	22	858	230	105	242	.434	3	10	.300	17	26	.654	27	67	94	76	94	0	32	6	36	16.8	4.5	1.8	1.5	.264
82-83	Houston	4	0	34	10	4	11	.364	0	1	.000	2	2	1.000	3	4	7	3	4	0	0	0	3	8.5	2.5	1.8	0.8	.258
83-84	LA Lakers	41	0	478	188	78	152	.513	2	6	.333	30	39	.769	24	47	71	31	62	2	12	2	33	11.7	4.6	1.7	0.8	.351
NBA Season Totals		166	22	3008	855	375	820	.457	6	20	.300	99	129	.767	139	297	436	242	327	2	94	18	163	18.1	5.2	2.6	1.5	....
80-81	Houston	13	....	117	25	9	21	.429	0	0	.000	7	8	.875	3	12	15	6	10	0	5	1	6	9.0	1.9	1.2	0.5	.250
81-82	Houston	1	0	1	0	0	1	.000	0	1	.000	0	0	.000	0	0	0	0	0	0	0	0	0	1.0	0.0	0.0	0.0	-.921
NBA Playoff Totals		14	0	118	25	9	22	.409	0	1	.000	7	8	.875	3	12	15	6	10	0	5	1	6	8.4	1.8	1.1	0.4	....

• GARRETT, Dean

Dean Heath Garrett

Born: Nov. 27, 1966. Los Angeles, CA, United States. Height: 6'10". Weight: 225 lbs. Drafted: 1988 College: Indiana

YEAR	TEAM	GP	GS	MIN	PTS	FGM	FGA	FG%	3PM	3PA	3P%	FTM	FTA	FT%	ORB	DRB	TRB	AST	PF	DQ	STL	BLK	TO	MPG	PPG	RPG	APG	PCM
96-97	Minnesota	68	47	1665	542	223	389	.573	0	0	.000	96	138	.696	149	346	495	38	158	1	40	95	34	24.5	8.0	7.3	0.6	.535
97-98	Denver	82	82	2632	598	242	565	.428	0	0	.000	114	176	.648	227	417	644	90	197	0	57	133	82	32.1	7.3	7.9	1.1	.368
98-99	Minnesota	49	37	1054	270	116	231	.502	0	0	.000	38	51	.745	99	158	257	28	113	0	30	45	29	21.5	5.5	5.2	0.6	.391
99-00	Minnesota	56	23	604	114	48	108	.444	0	0	.000	18	26	.692	41	99	140	19	94	1	8	40	21	10.8	2.0	2.5	0.3	.307
00-01	Minnesota	70	21	831	177	75	156	.481	0	0	.000	27	39	.692	65	152	217	24	93	0	26	49	25	11.9	2.5	3.1	0.3	.389
01-02	Minnesota	29	0	152	28	14	40	.350	0	0	.000	0	3	.000	13	34	47	4	26	0	5	9	7	5.2	1.0	1.6	0.1	.293
01-02	Golden State	5	0	31	8	4	15	.267	0	0	.000	0	0	.000	3	7	10	1	6	0	2	1	3	6.2	1.6	2.0	0.2	.176
NBA Season Totals		359	210	6969	1737	722	1504	.480	0	0	.000	293	433	.677	597	1213	1810	204	687	2	168	372	201	19.4	4.8	5.0	0.6	....
96-97	Minnesota	3	3	118	38	15	29	.517	0	0	.000	8	10	.800	19	16	35	4	11	0	2	3	1	39.3	12.7	11.7	1.3	.504
98-99	Minnesota	4	3	92	22	10	18	.556	0	0	.000	2	5	.400	9	7	16	5	16	1	2	3	2	23.0	5.5	4.0	1.3	.314
99-00	Minnesota	3	0	16	3	1	2	.500	0	0	.000	1	2	.500	1	1	2	0	2	0	0	1	0	5.3	1.0	0.7	0.0	.216
00-01	Minnesota	3	2	41	13	4	12	.333	0	0	.000	5	6	.833	2	7	9	0	6	0	1	1	0	13.7	4.3	3.0	0.0	.306
NBA Playoff Totals		13	8	267	76	30	61	.492	0	0	.000	16	23	.696	31	31	62	9	35	1	5	8	3	20.5	5.8	4.8	0.7	....

• GARRETT, Dick

Eldo Dick Garrett

Born: Jan. 31, 1947. Height: 6'3". Weight: 185 lbs. Drafted: 1969 College: Southern Illinois

YEAR	TEAM	GP	GS	MIN	PTS	FGM	FGA	FG%	3PM	3PA	3P%	FTM	FTA	FT%	ORB	DRB	TRB	AST	PF	DQ	STL	BLK	TO	MPG	PPG	RPG	APG	PCM
69-70	LA Lakers	73	....	2318	846	354	816	.434	....	....	....	138	162	.852	....	....	235	180	236	5	....	....	....	31.8	11.6	3.2	2.5	.316
70-71	Buffalo	75	....	2375	964	373	902	.414	....	....	....	218	251	.869	....	....	295	264	290	9	....	....	....	31.7	12.9	3.9	3.5	.389
71-72	Buffalo	73	....	1905	786	325	735	.442	....	....	....	136	157	.866	....	....	225	165	225	5	....	....	....	26.1	10.8	3.1	2.3	.371
72-73	Buffalo	78	....	1805	778	341	813	.419	....	....	....	96	110	.873	....	....	209	217	217	4	....	....	....	23.1	10.0	2.7	2.8	.388
73-74	New York	25	....	239	74	32	91	.352	....	....	....	10	13	.769	10	16	26	14	41	0	7	1	....	9.6	3.0	1.0	0.6	.181
73-74	Milwaukee	15	....	87	27	11	35	.314	....	....	....	5	6	.833	5	9	14	9	15	0	3	0	....	5.8	1.8	0.9	0.6	.253
NBA Season Totals		339	....	8729	3475	1436	3392	.423	....	....	....	603	699	.863	15	25	1004	849	1024	23	10	1	....	25.7	10.3	3.0	2.5	....
69-70	LA Lakers	18	....	595	230	101	198	.510	....	....	....	28	32	.875	....	....	52	39	68	2	....	....	....	33.1	12.8	2.9	2.2	.340
73-74	Milwaukee	8	....	46	6	2	7	.286	....	....	....	2	4	.500	1	2	3	7	7	0	2	0	....	5.8	0.8	0.4	0.9	.185
NBA Playoff Totals		26	....	641	236	103	205	.502	....	....	....	30	36	.833	1	2	55	46	75	2	2	0	....	24.7	9.1	2.1	1.8	....

• GARRETT, Rowland

Rowland G. Garrett

Born: July 16, 1950. Canton, MS, United States. Height: 6'6". Weight: 210 lbs. Drafted: 1972 College: Florida State

YEAR	TEAM	GP	GS	MIN	PTS	FGM	FGA	FG%	3PM	3PA	3P%	FTM	FTA	FT%	ORB	DRB	TRB	AST	PF	DQ	STL	BLK	TO	MPG	PPG	RPG	APG	PCM
72-73	Chicago	35	....	211	125	52	118	.441	....	....	....	21	31	.677	....	....	61	8	29	0	....	....	....	6.0	3.6	1.7	0.2	.536
73-74	Chicago	41	....	373	157	68	184	.370	....	....	....	21	32	.656	31	39	70	11	43	0	5	9	....	9.1	3.8	1.7	0.3	.288
74-75	Chicago	70	....	1183	533	228	474	.481	....	....	....	77	97	.794	80	167	247	43	124	0	24	13	....	16.9	7.6	3.5	0.6	.441

YEAR	TEAM	GP	GS	MIN	PTS	FGM	FGA	FG%	3PM	3PA	3P%	FTM	FTA	FT%	ORB	DRB	TRB	AST	PF	DQ	STL	BLK	TO	MPG	PPG	RPG	APG	PCM
75-76	Chicago	14	....	324	152	57	131	.435	....	....	....	38	44	.864	27	48	75	7	32	0	8	4	....	23.1	10.9	5.4	0.5	.446
75-76	Cleveland	41	....	216	117	51	127	.402	....	....	....	15	21	.714	18	24	42	10	36	0	17	3	....	5.3	2.9	1.0	0.2	.376
76-77	Cleveland	29	....	215	98	40	93	.430	....	....	....	18	22	.818	10	30	40	7	30	0	7	3	....	7.4	3.4	1.4	0.2	.372
76-77	Milwaukee	33	....	383	155	66	146	.452	....	....	....	23	29	.793	27	45	72	20	50	0	14	7	....	11.6	4.7	2.2	0.6	.383
NBA Season Totals		263	....	2905	1337	562	1273	.441	....	....	....	213	276	.772	193	353	607	106	344	0	75	39	....	11.0	5.1	2.3	0.4	....
72-73	Chicago	1	....	1	0	0	0	.000	....	....	....	0	0	.000	....	....	0	0	0	0	....	....	....	1.0	0.0	0.0	0.0	.000
73-74	Chicago	2	....	6	0	0	4	.000	....	....	....	0	0	.000	0	1	1	0	1	0	0	0	....	3.0	0.0	0.5	0.0	-.496
74-75	Chicago	12	....	143	44	21	56	.375	....	....	....	2	4	.500	8	21	29	3	27	0	4	4	....	11.9	3.7	2.4	0.3	.209
75-76	Cleveland	4	....	5	2	0	0	.000	....	....	....	2	4	.500	0	0	0	0	0	0	0	0	....	1.3	0.5	0.0	0.0	.228
NBA Playoff Totals		19	....	155	46	21	60	.350	....	....	....	4	8	.500	8	22	30	3	28	0	4	4	....	8.2	2.4	1.6	0.2	....

• GARRICK, Tom

Thomas S. (Chief) Garrick

Born: July 7, 1966. West Warwick, RI, United States.   Height: 6'2".   Weight: 185 lbs.   Drafted: 1988   College: Rhode Island

YEAR	TEAM	GP	GS	MIN	PTS	FGM	FGA	FG%	3PM	3PA	3P%	FTM	FTA	FT%	ORB	DRB	TRB	AST	PF	DQ	STL	BLK	TO	MPG	PPG	RPG	APG	PCM
88-89	LA Clippers	71	20	1499	454	176	359	.490	0	13	.000	102	127	.803	37	119	156	243	141	1	78	9	114	21.1	6.4	2.2	3.4	.391
89-90	LA Clippers	73	22	1721	508	208	421	.494	4	21	.190	88	114	.772	34	128	162	289	151	4	90	7	117	23.6	7.0	2.2	4.0	.387
90-91	LA Clippers	67	0	949	260	100	236	.424	0	22	.000	60	79	.759	40	87	127	223	101	0	62	2	67	14.2	3.9	1.9	3.3	.454
91-92	San Antonio	19	5	374	98	44	93	.473	0	1	.000	10	16	.625	8	33	41	63	33	0	21	1	30	19.7	5.2	2.2	3.3	.354
91-92	Minnesota	15	0	112	29	11	33	.333	1	2	.500	6	8	.750	2	7	9	18	14	0	7	3	11	7.5	1.9	0.6	1.2	.249
91-92	Dallas	6	0	63	10	4	17	.235	0	1	.000	2	2	1.000	2	4	6	17	7	0	8	0	4	10.5	1.7	1.0	2.8	.352
NBA Season Totals		251	47	4718	1359	543	1159	.469	5	60	.083	268	346	.775	123	378	501	853	447	5	266	22	343	18.8	5.4	2.0	3.4	....

• GARRIS, John

John Brasker Garris

Born: June 6, 1959. Bridgeport, CT, United States.   Height: 6'8".   Weight: 205 lbs.   Drafted: 1983   College: Boston College

YEAR	TEAM	GP	GS	MIN	PTS	FGM	FGA	FG%	3PM	3PA	3P%	FTM	FTA	FT%	ORB	DRB	TRB	AST	PF	DQ	STL	BLK	TO	MPG	PPG	RPG	APG	PCM
83-84	Cleveland	33	1	267	131	52	102	.510	0	0	.000	27	34	.794	35	42	77	10	40	0	8	6	10	8.1	4.0	2.3	0.3	.557
NBA Season Totals		33	1	267	131	52	102	.510	0	0	.000	27	34	.794	35	42	77	10	40	0	8	6	10	8.1	4.0	2.3	0.3	....

• GARRIS, Kiwane

Kiwane Garris

Born: Sept. 24, 1974.   Height: 6'2".   Weight: 183 lbs.   Drafted: —   College: Illinois

YEAR	TEAM	GP	GS	MIN	PTS	FGM	FGA	FG%	3PM	3PA	3P%	FTM	FTA	FT%	ORB	DRB	TRB	AST	PF	DQ	STL	BLK	TO	MPG	PPG	RPG	APG	PCM
97-98	Denver	28	0	225	68	22	65	.338	5	14	.357	19	25	.760	3	16	19	28	22	0	7	1	14	8.0	2.4	0.7	1.0	.258
99-00	Orlando	3	0	23	4	2	10	.200	0	1	.000	0	0	.000	0	1	1	2	0	0	0	0	1	7.7	1.3	0.3	0.7	-.047
NBA Season Totals		31	0	248	72	24	75	.320	5	15	.333	19	25	.760	3	17	20	30	22	0	7	1	15	8.0	2.3	0.6	1.0	....

• GARRITY, Patrick

Patrick Joseph Garrity

Born: Aug. 23, 1976. Las Vegas, NV, United States.   Height: 6'9".   Weight: 238 lbs.   Drafted: 1998   College: Notre Dame

YEAR	TEAM	GP	GS	MIN	PTS	FGM	FGA	FG%	3PM	3PA	3P%	FTM	FTA	FT%	ORB	DRB	TRB	AST	PF	DQ	STL	BLK	TO	MPG	PPG	RPG	APG	PCM
98-99	Phoenix	39	9	538	217	85	170	.500	7	18	.389	40	56	.714	26	49	75	18	62	0	8	3	20	13.8	5.6	1.9	0.5	.345
99-00	Orlando	82	1	1479	675	258	585	.441	79	197	.401	80	111	.721	44	166	210	58	197	1	31	19	85	18.0	8.2	2.6	0.7	.336
00-01	Orlando	76	1	1579	628	223	576	.387	97	224	.433	85	98	.867	51	159	210	51	241	3	40	15	68	20.8	8.3	2.8	0.7	.272
01-02	Orlando	80	43	2406	884	327	767	.426	169	396	.427	61	73	.836	77	261	338	99	230	1	61	28	68	30.1	11.1	4.2	1.2	.336
02-03	Orlando	81	53	2585	868	312	744	.419	161	407	.396	83	100	.830	72	234	306	121	255	1	62	20	77	31.9	10.7	3.8	1.5	.297
NBA Season Totals		358	107	8587	3272	1205	2842	.424	513	1242	.413	349	438	.797	270	869	1139	347	985	6	202	85	318	24.0	9.1	3.2	1.0	....
98-99	Phoenix	3	0	52	27	9	17	.529	3	3	1.000	6	6	1.000	6	3	9	1	9	0	1	1	3	17.3	9.0	3.0	0.3	.464
00-01	Orlando	4	0	117	48	17	36	.472	10	20	.500	4	5	.800	1	4	5	2	11	0	0	1	2	29.3	12.0	1.3	0.5	.268
01-02	Orlando	4	4	147	34	12	32	.375	7	18	.389	3	4	.750	4	26	30	9	18	0	2	1	5	36.8	8.5	7.5	2.3	.301
02-03	Orlando	7	1	163	28	10	35	.286	4	17	.235	4	4	1.000	4	14	18	5	24	0	2	3	5	23.3	4.0	2.6	0.7	.099
NBA Playoff Totals		18	5	479	137	48	120	.400	24	58	.414	17	19	.895	15	47	62	17	62	0	5	6	13	26.6	7.6	3.4	0.9	....

• GARVIN, Jim

James D. Garvin

Born: Feb. 5, 1950.   Height: 6'7".   Weight: 200 lbs.   Drafted: 1973   College: Boston University

YEAR	TEAM	GP	GS	MIN	PTS	FGM	FGA	FG%	3PM	3PA	3P%	FTM	FTA	FT%	ORB	DRB	TRB	AST	PF	DQ	STL	BLK	TO	MPG	PPG	RPG	APG	PCM
73-74	Buffalo	6	....	11	2	1	4	.250	....	....	....	0	0	.000	1	4	5	0	1	0	0	0	....	1.8	0.3	0.8	0.0	.298
NBA Season Totals		6	....	11	2	1	4	.250	....	....	....	0	0	.000	1	4	5	0	1	0	0	0	....	1.8	0.3	0.8	0.0	....

• GASOL, Pau

Pau Gasol

Born: July 6, 1980. Barcelona, Spain.   Height: 7'.   Weight: 227 lbs.   Drafted: 2001   College: none

YEAR	TEAM	GP	GS	MIN	PTS	FGM	FGA	FG%	3PM	3PA	3P%	FTM	FTA	FT%	ORB	DRB	TRB	AST	PF	DQ	STL	BLK	TO	MPG	PPG	RPG	APG	PCM
01-02	Memphis	82	79	3007	1441	551	1064	.518	1	5	.200	338	477	.709	238	492	730	223	195	2	41	169	224	36.7	17.6	8.9	2.7	.571
02-03	Memphis	82	82	2947	1555	569	1116	.510	1	10	.100	416	565	.736	192	528	720	229	220	3	34	148	213	35.9	19.0	8.8	2.8	.599
NBA Season Totals		164	161	5954	2996	1120	2180	.514	2	15	.133	754	1042	.724	430	1020	1450	452	415	5	75	317	437	36.3	18.3	8.8	2.8	....

• GATES, Frank

Ben Frank (Needle) Gates

Born: Apr. 12, 1920. Died: July26, 1978.   Height: 6'.   Weight: 160 lbs.   Drafted: —   College: Sam Houston State

YEAR	TEAM	GP	GS	MIN	PTS	FGM	FGA	FG%	3PM	3PA	3P%	FTM	FTA	FT%	ORB	DRB	TRB	AST	PF	DQ	STL	BLK	TO	MPG	PPG	RPG	APG	PCM
46-47	Anderson-N	16	....	....	117	48	....	....	....	....	....	21	36	.583	....	....	....	....	....	....	....	....	....	7.3	....	....	....	....
46-47	Fort Wayne-N	16	....	....	49	20	....	....	....	....	....	9	16	.563	....	....	....	....	....	....	....	....	....	3.1	....	....	....	....
48-49	Anderson-N	64	....	....	378	150	....	....	....	....	....	78	123	.634	....	....	....	....	166	....	....	....	....	5.9	....	....	....	....
49-50	Anderson	64	....	....	287	113	402	.281	....	....	....	61	98	.622	....	....	....	91	147	....	....	....	....	4.5	....	1.4	....	....
NBA Season Totals		64	....	....	287	113	402	.281	....	....	....	61	98	.622	....	....	....	91	147	....	....	....	....	4.5	....	1.4	....	....
NBL Season Totals		96	....	....	544	218						108	175		....	....	166						....	5.7	....			....
Career Totals		160	....	....	831	331	402					169	273					91	313				....	5.2	....	0.6		

YEAR	TEAM	GP	GS	MIN	PTS	FGM	FGA	FG%	3PM	3PA	3P%	FTM	FTA	FT%	ORB	DRB	TRB	AST	PF	DQ	STL	BLK	TO	MPG	PPG	RPG	APG	PCM
46-47	Fort Wayne-N	7	....	....	29	10	....	....	....	....	....	9	17	.529	....	....	....	....	....	....	....	....	....	....	4.1	....	....	....
48-49	Anderson-N	7	....	....	31	13	....	....	....	....	....	5	11	.455	....	....	....	....	....	....	....	....	....	....	4.4	....	....	....
49-50	Anderson	7	....	....	25	9	37	.243	....	....	....	7	10	.700	....	....	....	9	15	....	....	....	....	....	3.6	....	1.3	....
NBA Playoff Totals		7	....	....	25	9	37	.243	....	....	....	7	10	.700	....	....	....	9	15	....	....	....	....	....	3.6	....	1.3	....
NBL Playoff Totals		14	....	....	60	23	....	....	....	....	....	14	28	....	....	....	....	....	....	....	....	....	....	....	4.3	....	....	....
Career Playoff Totals		21	....	....	85	32	37	....	....	....	....	21	38	....	....	....	....	9	15	....	....	....	....	....	4.0	....	0.4	....

• GATES, Pop
William Gates

Born: Aug. 30, 1917. Decatur, AL, United States. Died: Dec.2, 1999.   Height: 6'2".   Weight: 196 lbs.   Drafted: —   College: Clark (GA)   HOF: 1989

YEAR	TEAM	GP	GS	MIN	PTS	FGM	FGA	FG%	3PM	3PA	3P%	FTM	FTA	FT%	ORB	DRB	TRB	AST	PF	DQ	STL	BLK	TO	MPG	PPG	RPG	APG	PCM
46-47	Tri-Cities-N	41	....	....	310	125	....	....	....	....	....	60	115	.522	....	....	....	108	....						7.6	....	....	....
48-49	Dayton-N	40	....	....	448	161	....	....	....	....	....	126	220	.573	....	....	....	....	....						11.2	....	....	....
NBL Season Totals		81	....	....	758	286	....	....	....	....	....	186	335	....	....	....	....	108	....						9.4	....	....	....

• GATLING, Chris
Chris Raymond Gatling

Born: Sept. 3, 1967. Elizabeth, NJ, United States.   Height: 6'10".   Weight: 220 lbs.   Drafted: 1991   College: Old Dominion

YEAR	TEAM	GP	GS	MIN	PTS	FGM	FGA	FG%	3PM	3PA	3P%	FTM	FTA	FT%	ORB	DRB	TRB	AST	PF	DQ	STL	BLK	TO	MPG	PPG	RPG	APG	PCM
91-92	Golden State	54	1	612	306	117	206	.568	0	4	.000	72	109	.661	75	107	182	16	101	0	31	36	43	11.3	5.7	3.4	0.3	.601
92-93	Golden State	70	11	1248	648	249	462	.539	0	6	.000	150	207	.725	129	191	320	40	197	2	44	53	105	17.8	9.3	4.6	0.6	.532
93-94	Golden State	82	23	1296	671	271	461	.588	0	1	.000	129	208	.620	143	254	397	41	223	5	40	63	82	15.8	8.2	4.8	0.5	.606
94-95	Golden State	58	22	1470	796	324	512	**.633**	0	1	.000	148	250	.592	144	299	443	51	184	4	39	52	116	25.3	13.7	7.6	0.9	.634
95-96	Golden State	47	2	862	426	171	308	.555	0	1	.000	84	132	.636	78	164	242	26	135	4	19	29	61	18.3	9.1	5.1	0.6	.527
95-96	Miami	24	0	565	365	155	259	.598	0	0	.000	55	75	.733	51	124	175	17	82	0	17	11	36	23.5	15.2	7.3	0.7	.698
96-97	Dallas	44	1	1191	840	309	580	.533	1	6	.167	221	313	.706	126	222	348	25	125	1	35	31	114	27.1	19.1	7.9	0.6	.665
96-97	New Jersey	3	0	92	51	18	43	.419	0	0	.000	15	16	.938	8	14	22	3	13	0	4	0	6	30.7	17.0	7.3	1.0	.468
97-98	New Jersey	57	16	1359	656	248	545	.455	1	4	.250	159	265	.600	118	216	334	53	152	2	52	29	97	23.8	11.5	5.9	0.9	.452
98-99	New Jersey	18	2	281	84	36	97	.371	0	1	.000	12	24	.500	21	44	65	12	40	0	8	4	29	15.6	4.7	3.6	0.7	.223
98-99	Milwaukee	30	1	494	188	81	168	.482	1	7	.143	25	69	.362	31	83	114	20	78	0	24	6	33	16.5	6.3	3.8	0.7	.359
99-00	Orlando	45	0	1041	598	210	462	.455	7	23	.304	171	245	.698	91	206	297	40	142	0	48	10	105	23.1	13.3	6.6	0.9	.520
99-00	Denver	40	0	770	416	155	340	.456	11	47	.234	95	128	.742	63	142	205	31	104	2	34	13	64	19.3	10.4	5.1	0.8	.507
00-01	Cleveland	74	6	1670	842	329	733	.449	28	92	.304	156	228	.684	99	292	391	61	185	0	52	27	119	22.6	11.4	5.3	0.8	.447
01-02	Miami	54	1	809	345	131	293	.447	1	8	.125	82	117	.701	71	135	206	25	109	1	17	11	58	15.0	6.4	3.8	0.5	.395
NBA Season Totals		700	86	13760	7232	2804	5469	.513	50	201	.249	1574	2386	.660	1248	2493	3741	461	1870	17	464	375	1068	19.7	10.3	5.3	0.7	....
91-92	Golden State	4	0	81	50	18	29	.621	0	0	.000	14	22	.636	9	16	25	0	14	0	2	10	1	20.3	12.5	6.3	0.0	.778
93-94	Golden State	3	1	54	26	8	13	.615	0	0	.000	10	13	.769	7	10	17	4	10	0	2	1	2	18.0	8.7	5.7	1.3	.672
95-96	Miami	3	0	68	18	6	22	.273	0	0	.000	6	12	.500	10	14	24	1	8	1	2	0	8	22.7	6.0	8.0	0.3	.211
97-98	New Jersey	3	1	81	46	19	38	.500	0	0	.000	8	12	.667	6	4	10	2	9	0	2	2	3	27.0	15.3	3.3	0.7	.431
98-99	Milwaukee	2	0	12	0	0	2	.000	0	0	.000	0	2	.000	1	2	3	0	3	0	1	0	2	6.0	0.0	1.5	0.0	-.185
NBA Playoff Totals		15	2	296	140	51	104	.490	0	0	.000	38	61	.623	33	46	79	7	44	1	9	13	16	19.7	9.3	5.3	0.5	....

• GATTISON, Kenny
Kenneth Clay Gattison

Born: May 23, 1964. Wilmington, NC, United States.   Height: 6'8".   Weight: 225 lbs.   Drafted: 1986   College: Old Dominion

YEAR	TEAM	GP	GS	MIN	PTS	FGM	FGA	FG%	3PM	3PA	3P%	FTM	FTA	FT%	ORB	DRB	TRB	AST	PF	DQ	STL	BLK	TO	MPG	PPG	RPG	APG	PCM
86-87	Phoenix	77	14	1104	404	148	311	.476	0	3	.000	108	171	.632	87	183	270	36	178	1	24	33	85	14.3	5.2	3.5	0.5	.366
88-89	Phoenix	2	0	9	1	0	1	.000	0	0	.000	1	2	.500	0	1	1	0	2	0	0	0	0	4.5	0.5	0.5	0.0	-.044
89-90	Charlotte	63	2	941	372	148	269	.550	1	1	1.000	75	110	.682	75	122	197	39	150	1	35	31	69	14.9	5.9	3.1	0.6	.420
90-91	Charlotte	72	6	1552	650	243	457	.532	0	2	.000	164	248	.661	136	243	379	44	211	3	48	67	101	21.6	9.0	5.3	0.6	.468
91-92	Charlotte	82	71	2223	1042	423	799	.529	0	2	.000	196	285	.688	177	403	580	131	273	4	59	69	139	27.1	12.7	7.1	1.6	.537
92-93	Charlotte	75	5	1475	508	203	384	.529	0	3	.000	102	169	.604	108	245	353	68	237	3	48	55	68	19.7	6.8	4.7	0.9	.428
93-94	Charlotte	77	18	1644	592	233	445	.524	0	0	.000	126	195	.646	105	253	358	95	229	3	59	46	77	21.4	7.7	4.6	1.2	.437
94-95	Charlotte	21	0	409	125	47	100	.470	0	1	.000	31	51	.608	21	54	75	17	64	1	7	15	21	19.5	6.0	3.6	0.8	.306
95-96	Vancouver	25	14	570	229	91	190	.479	0	0	.000	47	78	.603	35	79	114	14	75	0	10	11	40	22.8	9.2	4.6	0.6	.334
NBA Season Totals		494	130	9927	3923	1536	2956	.520	1	12	.083	850	1309	.649	744	1583	2327	444	1419	16	290	327	600	20.1	7.9	4.7	0.9	....
92-93	Charlotte	9	0	187	53	22	46	.478	0	0	.000	9	21	.429	19	20	39	11	18	0	5	1	7	20.8	5.9	4.3	1.2	.341
94-95	Charlotte	4	0	58	15	5	8	.625	0	0	.000	5	8	.625	5	7	12	2	16	0	2	0	5	14.5	3.8	3.0	0.5	.239
NBA Playoff Totals		13	0	245	68	27	54	.500	0	0	.000	14	29	.483	24	27	51	13	34	0	7	1	12	18.8	5.2	3.9	1.0	....

• GAUCHAT, Bob
Bob Gauchat

Born: 1921.   Height: 6'   Weight: 180 lbs.   Drafted: —   College: Canisius

YEAR	TEAM	GP	GS	MIN	PTS	FGM	FGA	FG%	3PM	3PA	3P%	FTM	FTA	FT%	ORB	DRB	TRB	AST	PF	DQ	STL	BLK	TO	MPG	PPG	RPG	APG	PCM
46-47	Rochester-N	6	....	....	4	1	....	....	....	....	....	2	2	1.000	....	....	....	....	....						0.7	....	....	....
46-47	Tri-Cities-N	4	....	....	2	0	....	....	....	....	....	2	5	.400	....	....	....	....	....						0.5	....	....	....
NBL Season Totals		10	....	....	6	1	....	....	....	....	....	4	7	....	....	....	....	....	....						0.6	....	....	....
46-47	Rochester-N	2	....	....	0	0	....	....	....	....	....	0	0	.000	....	....	....	....	....						0.0	....	....	....
NBL Playoff Totals		2	....	....	0	0	....	....	....	....	....	0	0	....	....	....	....	....	....						0.0	....	....	....

• GAYDA, Ed
Edward C. Gayda

Born: May 11, 1927.   Height: 6'4".   Weight: 210 lbs.   Drafted: 1950   College: Washington State

YEAR	TEAM	GP	GS	MIN	PTS	FGM	FGA	FG%	3PM	3PA	3P%	FTM	FTA	FT%	ORB	DRB	TRB	AST	PF	DQ	STL	BLK	TO	MPG	PPG	RPG	APG	PCM
50-51	Tri-Cities	14	....	....	54	18	42	.429	....	....	....	18	23	.783	....	....	38	13	32	0	....	....	....	....	3.9	2.7	0.9	....
NBA Season Totals		14	....	....	54	18	42	.429	....	....	....	18	23	.783	....	....	38	13	32	0	....	....	....	....	3.9	2.7	0.9	....

YEAR	TEAM	GP	GS	MIN	PTS	FGM	FGA	FG%	3PM	3PA	3P%	FTM	FTA	FT%	ORB	DRB	TRB	AST	PF	DQ	STL	BLK	TO	MPG	PPG	RPG	APG	PCM

• GAZE, Andrew

Andrew Gaze

Born: July 24, 1965. Melbourne, Australia.　Height: 6'7".　Weight: 205 lbs.　Drafted: —　College: Seton Hall

YEAR	TEAM	GP	GS	MIN	PTS	FGM	FGA	FG%	3PM	3PA	3P%	FTM	FTA	FT%	ORB	DRB	TRB	AST	PF	DQ	STL	BLK	TO	MPG	PPG	RPG	APG	PCM
93-94	Washington	7	0	70	22	8	17	.471	4	8	.500	2	2	1.000	1	6	7	5	9	0	2	1	3	10.0	3.1	1.0	0.7	.306
98-99	San Antonio	19	0	58	21	8	25	.320	5	16	.313	0	0	.000	2	3	5	6	7	0	2	1	4	3.1	1.1	0.3	0.3	.224
NBA Season Totals		26	0	128	43	16	42	.381	9	24	.375	2	2	1.000	3	9	12	11	16	0	4	2	7	4.9	1.7	0.5	0.4	....

• GEARY, Reggie

Reggie Elliot Geary

Born: Aug. 31, 1973. Trenton, NJ, United States.　Height: 6'2".　Weight: 187 lbs.　Drafted: 1996　College: Arizona

YEAR	TEAM	GP	GS	MIN	PTS	FGM	FGA	FG%	3PM	3PA	3P%	FTM	FTA	FT%	ORB	DRB	TRB	AST	PF	DQ	STL	BLK	TO	MPG	PPG	RPG	APG	PCM
96-97	Cleveland	39	0	246	57	22	58	.379	8	21	.381	5	11	.455	4	11	15	36	36	0	13	2	16	6.3	1.5	0.4	0.9	.225
97-98	San Antonio	62	2	685	152	56	169	.331	12	40	.300	28	56	.500	19	48	67	74	95	0	37	12	43	11.0	2.5	1.1	1.2	.204
NBA Season Totals		101	2	931	209	78	227	.344	20	61	.328	33	67	.493	23	59	82	110	131	0	50	14	59	9.2	2.1	0.8	1.1	....
97-98	San Antonio	7	0	46	9	3	7	.429	1	4	.250	2	4	.500	0	2	2	6	10	0	1	0	2	6.6	1.3	0.3	0.9	.158
NBA Playoff Totals		7	0	46	9	3	7	.429	1	4	.250	2	4	.500	0	2	2	6	10	0	1	0	2	6.6	1.3	0.3	0.9	

• GEE, John

John Alexander (Whiz) Gee

Born: Dec. 7, 1915. Syracuse, NY, United States. Died: Jan.23, 1988.　Height: 6'9".　Weight: 225 lbs.　Drafted: —　College: Michigan

YEAR	TEAM	GP	GS	MIN	PTS	FGM	FGA	FG%	3PM	3PA	3P%	FTM	FTA	FT%	ORB	DRB	TRB	AST	PF	DQ	STL	BLK	TO	MPG	PPG	RPG	APG	PCM
46-47	Syracuse-N	24	....	....	156	59	....	....	....	....	....	38	60	.633	....	....	59	....	....	....	....	....	....	....	6.5	....	....	....
NBL Season Totals		24	....	....	156	59	....	....	....	....	....	38	60	....	....	....	59	....	....	....	....	....	....	....	6.5	....	....	....
46-47	Syracuse-N	3	....	....	3	1	....	....	....	....	....	1	4	.250	....	....	....	....	....	....	....	....	....	....	1.0	....	....	....
NBL Playoff Totals		3	....	....	3	1	....	....	....	....	....	1	4	....	....	....	....	....	....	....	....	....	....	....	1.0	....	....	

• GEIGER, Matt

Matthew Allen Geiger

Born: Sept. 10, 1969. Salem, MA, United States.　Height: 7'　Weight: 243 lbs.　Drafted: 1992　College: Georgia Tech

YEAR	TEAM	GP	GS	MIN	PTS	FGM	FGA	FG%	3PM	3PA	3P%	FTM	FTA	FT%	ORB	DRB	TRB	AST	PF	DQ	STL	BLK	TO	MPG	PPG	RPG	APG	PCM
92-93	Miami	48	2	554	214	76	145	.524	0	4	.000	62	92	.674	46	74	120	14	123	6	15	18	38	11.5	4.5	2.5	0.3	.362
93-94	Miami	72	0	1199	521	202	352	.574	1	5	.200	116	149	.779	119	184	303	32	201	2	36	29	58	16.7	7.2	4.2	0.4	.496
94-95	Miami	74	43	1712	617	260	485	.536	4	10	.400	93	143	.650	146	267	413	55	245	5	41	51	111	23.1	8.3	5.6	0.7	.406
95-96	Charlotte	77	50	2349	866	357	666	.536	3	8	.375	149	205	.727	201	448	649	60	290	11	46	63	139	30.5	11.2	8.4	0.8	.451
96-97	Charlotte	49	13	1044	437	171	350	.489	6	20	.300	89	127	.701	100	158	258	38	153	1	20	27	69	21.3	8.9	5.3	0.8	.423
97-98	Charlotte	78	42	1839	885	358	709	.505	1	11	.091	168	236	.712	196	325	521	78	191	1	68	87	109	23.6	11.3	6.7	1.0	.570
98-99	Philadelphia	50	40	1540	674	266	555	.479	1	5	.200	141	177	.797	137	225	362	58	157	2	39	40	101	30.8	13.5	7.2	1.2	.453
99-00	Philadelphia	65	20	1406	629	260	589	.441	0	4	.000	109	140	.779	154	233	387	39	194	1	29	22	91	21.6	9.7	6.0	0.6	.417
00-01	Philadelphia	35	4	542	213	88	224	.393	0	2	.000	37	54	.685	50	89	139	14	73	0	12	8	25	15.5	6.1	4.0	0.4	.344
01-02	Philadelphia	4	0	36	3	1	8	.125	0	0	.000	1	2	.500	3	3	6	0	2	0	0	2	2	9.0	0.8	1.5	0.0	.020
NBA Season Totals		552	214	12221	5059	2039	4083	.499	16	69	.232	965	1325	.728	1152	2006	3158	388	1629	29	306	347	743	22.1	9.2	5.7	0.7	....
93-94	Miami	2	0	11	1	0	2	.000	0	0	.000	1	2	.500	0	4	4	0	1	0	0	0	0	5.5	0.5	2.0	0.0	.174
96-97	Charlotte	3	0	31	6	2	3	.667	0	0	.000	2	2	1.000	4	4	8	2	5	0	2	1	2	10.3	2.0	2.7	0.7	.428
97-98	Charlotte	4	0	22	2	1	6	.167	0	0	.000	0	0	.000	3	2	5	1	2	0	0	0	1	5.5	0.5	1.3	0.3	.057
98-99	Philadelphia	8	8	239	108	42	96	.438	0	1	.000	24	29	.828	23	38	61	6	29	0	9	6	13	29.9	13.5	7.6	0.8	.450
99-00	Philadelphia	8	0	128	70	25	50	.500	0	0	.000	20	25	.800	17	23	40	2	23	0	5	2	5	16.0	8.8	5.0	0.3	.585
00-01	Philadelphia	12	0	100	38	17	29	.586	0	0	.000	4	4	1.000	10	8	18	7	30	2	2	0	5	8.3	3.2	1.5	0.6	.349
NBA Playoff Totals		37	8	531	225	87	186	.468	0	1	.000	51	62	.823	57	79	136	18	90	2	18	9	26	14.4	6.1	3.7	0.5	....

• GENSICHEN, Hal

Harold Gensichen

Born: 1921.　Height: 5'11".　Weight: 170 lbs.　Drafted: —　College: Western Michigan

YEAR	TEAM	GP	GS	MIN	PTS	FGM	FGA	FG%	3PM	3PA	3P%	FTM	FTA	FT%	ORB	DRB	TRB	AST	PF	DQ	STL	BLK	TO	MPG	PPG	RPG	APG	PCM
47-48	Flint-N	4	....	....	43	18	....	....	....	....	....	7	13	.538	....	....	....	....	....	....	....	....	....	....	10.8	....	....	....
47-48	Indianapolis-N	32	....	....	196	69	....	....	....	....	....	58	88	.659	....	....	....	....	....	....	....	....	....	....	6.1	....	....	....
NBL Season Totals		36	....	....	239	87	....	....	....	....	....	65	101	....	....	....	....	....	....	....	....	....	....	....	6.6	....	....	....

• GEORGE, Devean

Devean Jamar George

Born: Aug. 29, 1977. Minneapolis, MN, United States.　Height: 6'8".　Weight: 220 lbs.　Drafted: 1999　College: Augsburg (MN)

YEAR	TEAM	GP	GS	MIN	PTS	FGM	FGA	FG%	3PM	3PA	3P%	FTM	FTA	FT%	ORB	DRB	TRB	AST	PF	DQ	STL	BLK	TO	MPG	PPG	RPG	APG	PCM
99-00	LA Lakers	49	1	345	155	56	144	.389	16	47	.340	27	41	.659	29	46	75	12	54	0	10	4	21	7.0	3.2	1.5	0.2	.345
00-01	LA Lakers	59	1	593	182	64	207	.309	15	68	.221	39	55	.709	35	75	110	19	87	1	15	34	10.1	3.1	1.9	0.3	.208
01-02	LA Lakers	82	1	1759	581	215	523	.411	66	178	.371	85	126	.675	78	225	303	111	190	3	71	42	66	21.5	7.1	3.7	1.4	.361
02-03	LA Lakers	71	7	1613	492	180	461	.390	49	132	.371	83	105	.790	91	195	286	92	180	2	56	38	65	22.7	6.9	4.0	1.3	.330
NBA Season Totals		261	10	4310	1410	515	1335	.386	146	425	.344	234	327	.716	233	541	774	234	511	6	152	99	186	16.5	5.4	3.0	0.9	....
99-00	LA Lakers	9	0	45	22	7	19	.368	2	10	.200	6	11	.545	4	6	10	2	5	0	1	0	3	5.0	2.4	1.1	0.2	.356
00-01	LA Lakers	7	0	27	14	6	12	.500	1	2	.500	1	2	.500	3	2	5	1	6	0	0	0	3	3.9	2.0	0.7	0.1	.310
01-02	LA Lakers	19	0	327	95	38	104	.365	8	35	.229	11	15	.733	24	44	68	11	51	0	11	10	12	17.2	5.0	3.6	0.6	.282
02-03	LA Lakers	11	7	318	88	35	78	.449	10	30	.333	8	9	.889	11	38	49	24	29	0	11	4	12	28.9	8.0	4.5	2.2	.342
NBA Playoff Totals		46	7	717	219	86	213	.404	21	77	.273	26	37	.703	42	90	132	38	91	0	23	14	30	15.6	4.8	2.9	0.8	....

• GEORGE, Jack

John Edwin George Jr.

Born: Nov. 13, 1928. Swissvale, PA, United States. Died: Jan.30, 1989.　Height: 6'2".　Weight: 190 lbs.　Drafted: 1953　College: LaSalle

YEAR	TEAM	GP	GS	MIN	PTS	FGM	FGA	FG%	3PM	3PA	3P%	FTM	FTA	FT%	ORB	DRB	TRB	AST	PF	DQ	STL	BLK	TO	MPG	PPG	RPG	APG	PCM
53-54	Philadelphia	71	....	2648	675	259	736	.352	....	....	....	157	266	.590	....	....	386	312	210	4	....	....	....	37.3	9.5	5.4	4.4	.340
54-55	Philadelphia	68	....	2480	774	291	756	.385	....	....	....	192	291	.660	....	....	302	359	191	2	....	....	....	36.5	11.4	4.4	5.3	.399
55-56	Philadelphia	72	....	**2840**	1000	352	940	.374	....	....	....	296	391	.757	....	....	313	457	202	1	....	....	....	**39.4**	13.9	4.3	6.3	.438
56-57	Philadelphia	67	....	2229	706	253	750	.337	....	....	....	200	293	.683	....	....	318	307	165	3	....	....	....	33.3	10.5	4.7	4.6	.386

YEAR	TEAM	GP	GS	MIN	PTS	FGM	FGA	FG%	3PM	3PA	3P%	FTM	FTA	FT%	ORB	DRB	TRB	AST	PF	DQ	STL	BLK	TO	MPG	PPG	RPG	APG	PCM
57-58	Philadelphia	72	....	1910	642	232	627	.370	....	....	....	178	242	.736	....	....	288	234	140	1	....	....	....	26.5	8.9	4.0	3.3	.412
58-59	Philadelphia	46	....	1387	453	171	501	.341	....	....	....	111	152	.730	....	....	211	166	98	0	....	....	....	30.2	9.8	4.6	3.6	.374
58-59	New York	25	....	494	166	62	173	.358	....	....	....	42	51	.824	....	....	82	55	51	0	....	....	....	19.8	6.6	3.3	2.2	.385
59-60	New York	69	....	1604	655	250	650	.385	....	....	....	155	202	.767	....	....	197	240	148	1	....	....	....	23.2	9.5	2.9	3.5	.453
60-61	New York	16	....	268	82	31	93	.333	....	....	....	20	30	.667	....	....	32	39	37	0	....	....	....	16.8	5.1	2.0	2.4	.334
NBA Season Totals		506	....	15860	5153	1901	5226	.364	....	....	....	1351	1918	.704	....	....	2129	2169	1242	12	....	....	....	31.3	10.2	4.2	4.3	....
55-56	Philadelphia	10	....	405	136	46	118	.390	....	....	....	44	59	.746	....	....	47	52	37	2	....	....	....	40.5	13.6	4.7	5.2	.399
56-57	Philadelphia	2	....	63	18	7	15	.467	....	....	....	4	6	.667	....	....	7	6	5	0	....	....	....	31.5	9.0	3.5	3.0	.352
57-58	Philadelphia	8	....	277	76	30	81	.370	....	....	....	16	20	.800	....	....	38	31	14	0	....	....	....	34.6	9.5	4.8	3.9	.359
58-59	New York	2	....	31	8	4	12	.333	....	....	....	0	0	.000	....	....	4	3	4	0	....	....	....	15.5	4.0	2.0	1.5	.233
NBA Playoff Totals		22	....	776	238	87	226	.385	....	....	....	64	85	.753	....	....	96	92	60	2	....	....	....	35.3	10.8	4.4	4.2	....

• GEORGE, Tate

Tate Claude George

Born: May 29, 1968. Newark, NJ, United States. Height: 6'5". Weight: 190 lbs. Drafted: 1990 College: Connecticut

YEAR	TEAM	GP	GS	MIN	PTS	FGM	FGA	FG%	3PM	3PA	3P%	FTM	FTA	FT%	ORB	DRB	TRB	AST	PF	DQ	STL	BLK	TO	MPG	PPG	RPG	APG	PCM
90-91	New Jersey	56	11	594	192	80	193	.415	0	2	.000	32	40	.800	19	28	47	104	58	0	25	5	45	10.6	3.4	0.8	1.9	.331
91-92	New Jersey	70	2	1037	418	165	386	.427	1	6	.167	87	106	.821	36	69	105	162	98	0	41	3	84	14.8	6.0	1.5	2.3	.378
92-93	New Jersey	48	1	380	122	51	135	.378	0	5	.000	20	24	.833	9	18	27	59	25	0	10	3	29	7.9	2.5	0.6	1.2	.272
94-95	Milwaukee	3	0	8	4	1	3	.333	0	1	.000	2	2	1.000	1	0	1	0	1	0	0	0	2	2.7	1.3	0.3	0.0	.090
NBA Season Totals		177	14	2019	736	297	717	.414	1	14	.071	141	172	.820	65	115	180	325	182	0	76	11	160	11.4	4.2	1.0	1.8	....
91-92	New Jersey	4	0	44	15	7	23	.304	0	0	.000	1	3	.333	0	0	0	8	8	0	3	1	4	11.0	3.8	0.0	2.0	.092
92-93	New Jersey	2	0	22	4	2	7	.286	0	0	.000	0	0	.000	1	2	3	6	1	0	1	0	1	11.0	2.0	1.5	3.0	.367
NBA Playoff Totals		6	0	66	19	9	30	.300	0	0	.000	1	3	.333	1	2	3	14	9	0	4	1	5	11.0	3.2	0.5	2.3	....

• GERARD, Gus

Daniel James Gerard

Born: July 27, 1953. Uniontown, PA, United States. Height: 6'8". Weight: 200 lbs. Drafted: 1975 College: Virginia

YEAR	TEAM	GP	GS	MIN	PTS	FGM	FGA	FG%	3PM	3PA	3P%	FTM	FTA	FT%	ORB	DRB	TRB	AST	PF	DQ	STL	BLK	TO	MPG	PPG	RPG	APG	PCM
74-75	St. Louis-A	84	....	2702	1315	554	1220	.454	1	6	.167	206	279	.738	282	373	655	189	274	....	63	111	207	32.2	15.7	7.8	2.3	.504
75-76	Denver-A	60	....	1185	594	240	553	.434	3	7	.429	111	158	.703	94	207	301	122	169	....	51	54	141	19.8	9.9	5.0	2.0	.525
75-76	St. Louis-A	22	....	542	249	92	242	.380	1	2	.500	64	80	.800	47	89	136	25	69	....	18	18	45	24.6	11.3	6.2	1.1	.418
76-77	Denver	24	....	456	240	101	210	.481	....	....	....	38	56	.679	38	62	100	49	73	1	21	30	....	19.0	10.0	4.2	2.0	.545
76-77	Buffalo	41	....	592	240	100	244	.410	....	....	....	40	61	.656	51	66	117	43	91	0	23	32	....	14.4	5.9	2.9	1.0	.367
77-78	Buffalo	10	....	85	43	16	40	.400	....	....	....	11	15	.733	6	8	14	9	13	0	2	3	7	8.5	4.3	1.4	0.9	.414
77-78	Detroit	47	....	805	372	154	355	.434	....	....	....	64	93	.688	49	97	146	44	96	1	34	22	52	17.1	7.9	3.1	0.9	.400
78-79	Detroit	2	....	6	3	1	3	.333	....	....	....	1	2	.500	1	0	1	0	0	0	2	0	0	3.0	1.5	0.5	0.0	.575
78-79	Kansas City	56	....	459	215	83	191	.435	....	....	....	49	89	.551	39	58	97	21	74	1	18	13	34	8.2	3.8	1.7	0.4	.380
79-80	Kansas City	73	....	869	385	159	348	.457	1	3	.333	66	100	.660	77	100	177	43	96	1	41	26	51	11.9	5.3	2.4	0.6	.434
80-81	Kansas City	16	....	123	57	19	51	.373	0	3	.000	19	29	.655	13	16	29	6	24	0	3	6	6	7.7	3.6	1.8	0.4	.391
80-81	San Antonio	11	....	129	52	22	60	.367	0	1	.000	8	11	.727	17	21	38	9	17	0	7	3	8	11.7	4.7	3.5	0.8	.423
NBA Season Totals		280	....	3524	1607	655	1502	.436	1	7	.143	296	456	.649	291	428	719	224	484	4	151	135	158	12.6	5.7	2.6	0.8	....
ABA Season Totals		166	....	4429	2158	886	2015	.440	5	15	.333	381	517	.737	423	669	1092	336	512	....	132	183	393	26.7	13.0	6.6	2.0	....
Career Totals		446	....	7953	3765	1541	3517	.438	6	22	.273	677	973	.696	714	1097	1811	560	996	4	283	318	551	17.8	8.4	4.1	1.3	....
74-75	St. Louis-A	10	....	268	83	37	87	.425	0	0	.000	9	14	.643	17	33	50	16	32	....	6	7	28	26.8	8.3	5.0	1.6	.315
75-76	Denver-A	13	....	142	60	22	63	.349	0	1	.000	16	24	.667	13	20	33	12	26	....	8	7	19	10.9	4.6	2.5	0.9	.359
78-79	Kansas City	5	....	24	10	4	9	.444	....	....	....	2	4	.500	2	6	8	0	6	0	1	1	1	4.8	2.0	1.6	0.0	.417
79-80	Kansas City	3	....	26	10	4	10	.400	0	0	.000	2	4	.500	4	4	8	2	2	0	0	0	4	8.7	3.3	2.7	0.7	.330
NBA Playoff Totals		8	....	50	20	8	19	.421	0	0	.000	4	8	.500	6	10	16	2	8	0	1	1	5	6.3	2.5	2.0	0.3	....
ABA Playoff Totals		23	....	410	143	59	150	.393	0	1	.000	25	38	.658	30	53	83	28	58	....	14	14	47	17.8	6.2	3.6	1.2	....
Career Playoff Totals		31	....	460	163	67	169	.396	0	1	.000	29	46	.630	36	63	99	30	66	0	15	15	52	14.8	5.3	3.2	1.0	....

• GERBER, Bob

Robert Gerber

Born: 1916. Height: 6'5". Weight: 218 lbs. Drafted: — College: Toledo

YEAR	TEAM	GP	GS	MIN	PTS	FGM	FGA	FG%	3PM	3PA	3P%	FTM	FTA	FT%	ORB	DRB	TRB	AST	PF	DQ	STL	BLK	TO	MPG	PPG	RPG	APG	PCM
42-43	Toledo-N	1	....	....	22	9	....	....	....	....	....	4	....	....	....	....	....	....	....	....	....	....	....	....	22.0	....	....	....
45-46	Indianapolis-N	29	....	....	197	74	....	....	....	....	....	49	82	.598	....	....	....	....	....	....	....	....	....	....	6.8	....	....	....
46-47	Toledo-N	41	....	....	374	151	....	....	....	....	....	72	127	.567	....	....	....	....	54	....	....	....	....	....	9.1	....	....	....
47-48	Minneapolis-N	15	....	....	36	13	....	....	....	....	....	10	22	.455	....	....	....	....	....	....	....	....	....	....	2.4	....	....	....
47-48	Tri-Cities-N	7	....	....	6	3	....	....	....	....	....	0	5	.000	....	....	....	....	....	....	....	....	....	....	0.9	....	....	....
NBL Season Totals		93	....	....	635	250	....	....	....	....	....	135	236	....	....	....	....	....	54	....	....	....	....	....	6.8	....	....	....
46-47	Toledo-N	3	....	....	14	4	....	....	....	....	....	6	11	.545	....	....	....	....	....	....	....	....	....	....	4.7	....	....	....
NBL Playoff Totals		3	....	....	14	4	....	....	....	....	....	6	11	....	....	....	....	....	....	....	....	....	....	....	4.7	....	....	....

• GERVIN, Derrick

Derrick Eugene Gervin

Born: Mar. 28, 1963. Detroit, MI, United States. Height: 6'8". Weight: 200 lbs. Drafted: 1985 College: Texas (San Antonio)

YEAR	TEAM	GP	GS	MIN	PTS	FGM	FGA	FG%	3PM	3PA	3P%	FTM	FTA	FT%	ORB	DRB	TRB	AST	PF	DQ	STL	BLK	TO	MPG	PPG	RPG	APG	PCM
89-90	New Jersey	21	0	339	251	93	197	.472	0	3	.000	65	89	.730	29	36	65	8	47	0	20	7	13	16.1	12.0	3.1	0.4	.598
90-91	New Jersey	56	4	743	425	164	394	.416	7	28	.250	90	114	.789	40	70	110	30	88	0	19	19	45	13.3	7.6	2.0	0.5	.385
NBA Season Totals		77	4	1082	676	257	591	.435	7	31	.226	155	203	.764	69	106	175	38	135	0	39	26	58	14.1	8.8	2.3	0.5	....

• GERVIN, George

George (Iceman, Ice) Gervin

Born: Apr. 27, 1952. Detroit, MI, United States. Height: 6'7". Weight: 180 lbs. Drafted: 1974 College: Eastern Michigan HOF: 1996

YEAR	TEAM	GP	GS	MIN	PTS	FGM	FGA	FG%	3PM	3PA	3P%	FTM	FTA	FT%	ORB	DRB	TRB	AST	PF	DQ	STL	BLK	TO	MPG	PPG	RPG	APG	PCM
72-73	Virginia-A	30	....	689	424	161	341	.472	6	26	.231	96	118	.814	34	94	128	34	72	1	....	....	54	23.0	14.1	4.3	1.1	.541
73-74	San Antonio-A	25	....	783	486	185	395	.468	0	6	.000	116	136	.853	62	144	206	45	98	....	26	34	64	31.3	19.4	8.2	1.8	.617
73-74	Virginia-A	49	....	1728	1244	487	1031	.472	8	50	.160	262	328	.799	108	310	418	97	166	....	75	86	188	35.3	25.4	8.5	2.0	.664

YEAR	TEAM	GP	GS	MIN	PTS	FGM	FGA	FG%	3PM	3PA	3P%	FTM	FTA	FT%	ORB	DRB	TRB	AST	PF	DQ	STL	BLK	TO	MPG	PPG	RPG	APG	PCM
74-75	San Antonio-A	84	....	3113	1965	784	1655	.474	17	55	.309	380	458	.830	247	450	697	207	295	....	131	138	249	37.1	23.4	8.3	2.5	.602
75-76	San Antonio-A	81	....	2748	1768	706	1414	.499	14	55	.255	342	399	.857	179	367	546	201	288	....	110	119	217	33.9	21.8	6.7	2.5	.616
76-77	San Antonio	82	....	2705	1895	726	1335	.544	....	....	....	443	532	.833	134	320	454	238	286	12	105	104	....	33.0	23.1	5.5	2.9	.691
77-78	San Antonio	82	....	2857	**2232**	**864**	1611	.536	....	....	....	504	607	.830	118	302	420	302	255	3	136	110	303	34.8	**27.2**	5.1	3.7	.728
78-79	San Antonio	80	....	2888	**2365**	**947**	**1749**	.541	....	....	....	471	570	.826	142	258	400	219	275	5	137	91	288	36.1	**29.6**	5.0	2.7	.701
79-80	San Antonio	78	....	2934	**2585**	**1024**	**1940**	.528	32	102	.314	505	593	.852	154	249	403	202	208	0	110	79	257	37.6	**33.1**	5.2	2.6	.732
80-81	San Antonio	82	....	2765	2221	850	1729	.492	9	35	.257	512	620	.826	126	293	419	260	212	4	94	56	254	33.7	27.1	5.1	3.2	.667
81-82	San Antonio	79	79	2817	**2551**	**993**	**1987**	.500	10	36	.278	555	642	.864	138	254	392	187	215	2	77	45	213	35.7	**32.3**	5.0	2.4	.701
82-83	San Antonio	78	78	2830	2043	757	1553	.487	12	33	.364	517	606	.853	111	246	357	264	243	5	88	67	250	36.3	26.2	4.6	3.4	.601
83-84	San Antonio	76	76	2584	1967	765	1561	.490	10	24	.417	427	507	.842	106	207	313	220	219	3	79	47	220	34.0	25.9	4.1	2.9	.591
84-85	San Antonio	72	69	2091	1524	600	1182	.508	0	10	.000	324	384	.844	79	155	234	178	208	2	66	48	202	29.0	21.2	3.3	2.5	.566
85-86	Chicago	82	75	2065	1325	519	1100	.472	4	19	.211	283	322	.879	78	137	215	144	210	4	49	23	164	25.2	16.2	2.6	1.8	.454
NBA Season Totals		791	377	26536	20708	8045	15747	.511	77	259	.297	4541	5383	.844	1186	2421	3607	2214	2331	40	941	670	2151	33.5	26.2	4.6	2.8	....
ABA Season Totals		269	....	9061	5887	2323	4836	.480	45	192	.234	1196	1439	.831	630	1365	1995	584	919	1	342	377	772	33.7	21.9	7.4	2.2	....
Career Totals		1060	377	35597	26595	10368	20583	.504	122	451	.271	5737	6822	.841	1816	3786	5602	2798	3250	41	1283	1047	2923	33.6	25.1	5.3	2.6	....
72-73	Virginia-A	5	....	200	93	34	77	.442	1	5	.200	24	34	.706	16	22	38	8	15	0	....	....	18	40.0	18.6	7.6	1.6	.430
73-74	San Antonio-A	7	....	226	144	57	115	.496	1	1	1.000	29	31	.935	21	31	52	19	28	....	5	8	16	32.3	20.6	7.4	2.7	.653
74-75	San Antonio-A	6	....	276	204	79	171	.462	3	12	.250	43	52	.827	34	50	84	8	22	....	6	8	14	46.0	34.0	14.0	1.3	.696
75-76	San Antonio-A	7	....	288	190	67	128	.523	0	3	.000	56	69	.812	23	41	64	19	22	....	4	14	17	41.1	27.1	9.1	2.7	.688
76-77	San Antonio	2	....	62	50	19	44	.432	....	....	....	12	15	.800	5	6	11	3	9	1	1	2	....	31.0	25.0	5.5	1.5	.583
77-78	San Antonio	6	....	227	199	78	142	.549	....	....	....	43	56	.768	11	23	34	19	23	0	6	16	19	37.8	33.2	5.7	3.2	.797
78-79	San Antonio	14	....	513	400	158	295	.536	....	....	....	84	104	.808	33	49	82	35	51	1	27	15	40	36.6	28.6	5.9	2.5	.700
79-80	San Antonio	3	....	122	100	37	74	.500	0	2	.000	26	30	.867	9	11	20	12	8	0	5	3	9	40.7	33.3	6.7	4.0	.749
80-81	San Antonio	7	....	274	190	77	154	.500	0	3	.000	36	45	.800	9	26	35	24	19	1	5	5	20	39.1	27.1	5.0	3.4	.569
81-82	San Antonio	9	9	373	265	103	228	.452	0	3	.000	59	71	.831	19	47	66	41	36	1	10	4	31	41.4	29.4	7.3	4.6	.582
82-83	San Antonio	11	11	437	277	108	208	.519	0	2	.000	61	69	.884	21	53	74	37	39	1	12	4	46	39.7	25.2	6.7	3.4	.563
84-85	San Antonio	5	5	183	111	42	79	.532	0	3	.000	27	34	.794	3	15	18	14	19	0	3	3	20	36.6	22.2	3.6	2.8	.454
85-86	Chicago	2	0	11	0	0	1	.000	0	0	.000	0	0	.000	0	1	1	1	3	0	0	0	2	5.5	0.0	0.5	0.5	-.198
NBA Playoff Totals		59	25	2202	1592	622	1225	.508	0	13	.000	348	424	.821	110	231	341	186	207	5	69	52	187	37.3	27.0	5.8	3.2	....
ABA Playoff Totals		25	....	990	631	237	491	.483	5	21	.238	152	186	.817	94	144	238	54	87	0	15	30	65	39.6	25.2	9.5	2.2	....
Career Playoff Totals		84	25	3192	2223	859	1716	.501	5	34	.147	500	610	.820	204	375	579	240	294	5	84	82	252	38.0	26.5	6.9	2.9	....

• GETCHELL, Gorham

Charles Gorham Getchell

Born: Aug. 14, 1920. Abington, PA, United States. Died: July7, 1980. Height: 6'4". Weight: 205 lbs. Drafted: — College: Temple

YEAR	TEAM	GP	GS	MIN	PTS	FGM	FGA	FG%	3PM	3PA	3P%	FTM	FTA	FT%	ORB	DRB	TRB	AST	PF	DQ	STL	BLK	TO	MPG	PPG	RPG	APG	PCM
46-47	Pittsburgh	16	....	....	5	0	8	.000	....	....	....	5	5	1.000	....	....	....	0	5	....	....	....	....	....	0.3	....	0.0	....
NBA Season Totals		16	....	....	5	0	8	.000	....	....	....	5	5	1.000	....	....	....	0	5	....	....	....	....	....	0.3	....	0.0	....

• GIANELLI, John

John Arec Gianelli

Born: June 10, 1950. Stockton, CA, United States. Height: 6'10". Weight: 220 lbs. Drafted: 1972 College: Pacific

YEAR	TEAM	GP	GS	MIN	PTS	FGM	FGA	FG%	3PM	3PA	3P%	FTM	FTA	FT%	ORB	DRB	TRB	AST	PF	DQ	STL	BLK	TO	MPG	PPG	RPG	APG	PCM
72-73	New York	52	....	516	181	79	175	.451	....	....	....	23	33	.697	....	....	150	25	72	0	....	....	....	9.9	3.5	2.9	0.5	.428
73-74	New York	70	....	1423	508	208	434	.479	....	....	....	92	121	.760	110	233	343	77	159	1	23	42	....	20.3	7.3	4.9	1.1	.433
74-75	New York	80	....	2797	821	343	726	.472	....	....	....	135	195	.692	214	475	689	163	263	3	38	118	....	35.0	10.3	8.6	2.0	.404
75-76	New York	82	....	2332	764	325	687	.473	....	....	....	114	160	.713	187	365	552	115	194	1	25	62	....	28.4	9.3	6.7	1.4	.410
76-77	New York	19	....	630	207	86	182	.473	....	....	....	35	48	.729	60	118	178	26	54	0	14	28	....	33.2	10.9	9.4	1.4	.442
76-77	Buffalo	57	....	1283	397	171	397	.431	....	....	....	55	77	.714	94	203	297	57	117	0	21	70	....	22.5	7.0	5.2	1.0	.361
77-78	Milwaukee	82	....	2327	693	307	629	.488	....	....	....	79	123	.642	166	343	509	192	189	4	54	92	148	28.4	8.5	6.2	2.3	.416
78-79	Milwaukee	82	....	2057	584	256	527	.486	....	....	....	72	102	.706	122	286	408	160	196	4	44	67	107	25.1	7.1	5.0	2.0	.382
79-80	Utah	17	....	285	55	23	66	.348	0	0	.000	9	16	.563	14	48	62	17	26	0	6	7	22	16.8	3.2	3.6	1.0	.238
NBA Season Totals		541	....	13650	4210	1798	3823	.470	0	0	.000	614	875	.702	967	2071	3188	832	1270	13	225	486	277	25.2	7.8	5.9	1.5	....
72-73	New York	7	....	55	25	11	20	.550	....	....	....	3	7	.429	....	....	13	1	6	0	....	....	....	7.9	3.6	1.9	0.1	.460
73-74	New York	12	....	338	88	35	86	.407	....	....	....	18	25	.720	39	49	88	23	41	0	4	6	....	28.2	7.3	7.3	1.9	.371
74-75	New York	3	....	93	25	11	24	.458	....	....	....	3	3	1.000	5	9	14	2	10	0	0	4	....	31.0	8.3	4.7	0.7	.257
77-78	Milwaukee	9	....	290	70	25	59	.424	....	....	....	20	26	.769	16	42	58	14	24	0	8	11	13	32.2	7.8	6.4	1.6	.341
NBA Playoff Totals		31	....	776	208	82	189	.434	....	....	....	44	61	.721	60	100	173	40	81	0	12	21	13	25.0	6.7	5.6	1.3	....

• GIBBS, Dick

Dick Gibbs

Born: Dec. 20, 1948. Ames, IA, United States. Height: 6'5". Weight: 210 lbs. Drafted: 1971 College: Texas (El Paso)

YEAR	TEAM	GP	GS	MIN	PTS	FGM	FGA	FG%	3PM	3PA	3P%	FTM	FTA	FT%	ORB	DRB	TRB	AST	PF	DQ	STL	BLK	TO	MPG	PPG	RPG	APG	PCM
71-72	Houston	64	....	757	235	90	265	.340	....	....	....	55	66	.833	....	....	140	41	127	0	....	....	....	11.8	3.7	2.2	0.6	.253
72-73	Houston	1	....	2	0	0	1	.000	....	....	....	0	0	.000	....	....	0	1	1	0	....	....	....	2.0	0.0	0.0	1.0	-.073
72-73	Omaha	66	....	733	207	80	221	.362	....	....	....	47	63	.746	....	....	94	61	113	0	....	....	....	11.1	3.1	1.4	0.9	.247
73-74	Seattle	71	....	1528	766	302	700	.431	....	....	....	162	201	.806	91	132	223	79	195	1	39	18	....	21.5	10.8	3.1	1.1	.398
74-75	Washington	59	....	424	196	74	190	.389	....	....	....	48	64	.750	26	35	61	19	60	0	12	3	....	7.2	3.3	1.0	0.3	.327
75-76	Buffalo	72	....	866	335	129	301	.429	....	....	....	77	93	.828	42	64	106	49	133	2	16	14	....	12.0	4.7	1.5	0.7	.312
NBA Season Totals		333	....	4310	1739	675	1678	.402	....	....	....	389	487	.799	159	231	624	250	629	3	67	35	....	12.9	5.2	1.9	0.8	....
74-75	Washington	6	....	17	8	3	10	.300	....	....	....	2	2	1.000	0	1	1	2	2	0	3	0	....	2.8	1.3	0.2	0.3	.254
75-76	Buffalo	5	....	23	10	4	9	.444	....	....	....	2	2	1.000	0	1	1	2	8	0	0	0	....	4.6	2.0	0.2	0.4	.236
NBA Playoff Totals		11	....	40	18	7	19	.368	....	....	....	4	4	1.000	0	2	2	4	10	0	3	0	....	3.6	1.6	0.2	0.4	....

YEAR TEAM	GP	GS	MIN	PTS	FGM	FGA	FG%	3PM	3PA	3P%	FTM	FTA	FT%	ORB	DRB	TRB	AST	PF	DQ	STL	BLK	TO	MPG	PPG	RPG	APG	PCM

• GIBBS, Jim
Jim Gibbs

Born: 1919. Height: 6'5". Weight: 195 lbs. Drafted: — College: Central Missouri State

YEAR TEAM	GP	GS	MIN	PTS	FGM	FGA	FG%	3PM	3PA	3P%	FTM	FTA	FT%	ORB	DRB	TRB	AST	PF	DQ	STL	BLK	TO	MPG	PPG	RPG	APG	PCM
46-47 Toledo-N	1	....	....	0	0	....	....	....	....	....	0	0	.000	....	....	....	....	....	....	....	....	....	....	0.0	....	....	....
47-48 Flint-N	55	....	....	306	107	....	....	....	....	....	92	147	.626	....	....	....	....	156	....	....	....	....	....	5.6	....	....	....
NBL Season Totals	56	....	....	306	107	....	....	....	....	....	92	147		....	....	....	....	156	....	....	....	....	....	5.5	....	....	....

• GIBBS, John
John Gibbs

Born: 1915. Height: 6'6". Weight: 190 lbs. Drafted: — College: Central Missouri State

YEAR TEAM	GP	GS	MIN	PTS	FGM	FGA	FG%	3PM	3PA	3P%	FTM	FTA	FT%	ORB	DRB	TRB	AST	PF	DQ	STL	BLK	TO	MPG	PPG	RPG	APG	PCM
47-48 Flint-N	2	....	....	0	0	....	....	....	....	....	0	0	.000	....	....	....	....	2	....	....	....	....	....	0.0	....	....	....
NBL Season Totals	2	....	....	0	0	....	....	....	....	....	0	0		....	....	....	....	2	....	....	....	....	....	0.0	....	....	....

• GIBSON, Dee
Dee (Gibby) Gibson Jr.

Born: Aug. 25, 1923. Height: 5'11". Weight: 175 lbs. Drafted: 1948 College: Western Kentucky

YEAR TEAM	GP	GS	MIN	PTS	FGM	FGA	FG%	3PM	3PA	3P%	FTM	FTA	FT%	ORB	DRB	TRB	AST	PF	DQ	STL	BLK	TO	MPG	PPG	RPG	APG	PCM
48-49 Tri-Cities-N	64	....	....	301	94	....	....	....	....	....	113	177	.638	....	....	....	....	137	....	....	....	....	....	4.7	....	....	....
49-50 Tri-Cities	44	....	....	281	77	245	.314	....	....	....	127	177	.718	....	....	126	113	....	....	....	....	....	....	6.4	....	2.9	....
NBA Season Totals	44	....	....	281	77	245	.314	....	....	....	127	177	.718	....	....	126	113	....	....	....	....	....	....	6.4	....	2.9	....
NBL Season Totals	64	....	....	301	94	....	....	....	....	....	113	177		....	....	....	....	137	....	....	....	....	....	4.7	....	....	....
Career Totals	108	....	....	582	171	245	....	....	....	....	240	354		....	....	126	250	....	....	....	....	....	....	5.4	....	1.2	....
48-49 Tri-Cities-N	6	....	....	57	19	....	....	....	....	....	19	30	.633	....	....	....	....	....	....	....	....	....	....	9.5	....	....	....
49-50 Tri-Cities	3	....	....	11	4	11	.364	....	....	....	3	5	.600	....	....	2	11	....	....	....	....	....	....	3.7	....	0.7	....
NBA Playoff Totals	3	....	....	11	4	11	.364	....	....	....	3	5	.600	....	....	2	11	....	....	....	....	....	....	3.7	....	0.7	....
NBL Playoff Totals	6	....	....	57	19	....	....	....	....	....	19	30		....	....	....	....	....	....	....	....	....	....	9.5	....	....	....
Career Playoff Totals	9	....	....	68	23	11	....	....	....	....	22	35		....	....	2	11	....	....	....	....	....	....	7.6	....	0.2	....

• GIBSON, Hoot
Ward B. (Hoot) Gibson Jr.

Born: Dec. 5, 1921. Died: Feb.1, 1958. Height: 6'5". Weight: 198 lbs. Drafted: — College: Creighton

YEAR TEAM	GP	GS	MIN	PTS	FGM	FGA	FG%	3PM	3PA	3P%	FTM	FTA	FT%	ORB	DRB	TRB	AST	PF	DQ	STL	BLK	TO	MPG	PPG	RPG	APG	PCM
48-49 Denver-N	42	....	....	604	214	....	....	....	....	....	176	261	.674	....	....	....	....	....	....	....	....	....	....	14.4	....	....	....
48-49 Tri-Cities-N	20	....	....	201	77	....	....	....	....	....	47	73	.644	....	....	....	....	....	....	....	....	....	....	10.1	....	....	....
49-50 Boston	2	....	....	7	3	4	.750	....	....	....	1	4	.250	....	....	1	3	....	....	....	....	....	....	3.5	....	0.5	....
49-50 Waterloo	30	....	....	169	64	191	.335	....	....	....	41	60	.683	....	....	36	103	....	....	....	....	....	....	5.6	....	1.2	....
NBA Season Totals	32	....	....	176	67	195	.344	....	....	....	42	64	.656	....	....	37	106	....	....	....	....	....	....	5.5	....	1.2	....
NBL Season Totals	62	....	....	805	291	....	....	....	....	....	223	334		....	....	....	....	....	....	....	....	....	....	13.0	....	....	....
Career Totals	94	....	....	981	358	195	....	....	....	....	265	398		....	....	37	106	....	....	....	....	....	....	10.4	....	0.4	....
48-49 Tri-Cities-N	6	....	....	24	9	....	....	....	....	....	6	9	.667	....	....	....	....	....	....	....	....	....	....	4.0	....	....	....
NBL Playoff Totals	6	....	....	24	9	....	....	....	....	....	6	9		....	....	....	....	....	....	....	....	....	....	4.0	....	....	....

• GIBSON, Mel
Melvin L. Gibson

Born: Dec. 30, 1940. Height: 6'3". Weight: 180 lbs. Drafted: 1963 College: Western Carolina

YEAR TEAM	GP	GS	MIN	PTS	FGM	FGA	FG%	3PM	3PA	3P%	FTM	FTA	FT%	ORB	DRB	TRB	AST	PF	DQ	STL	BLK	TO	MPG	PPG	RPG	APG	PCM
63-64 LA Lakers	9	....	53	13	6	20	.300	....	....	....	1	2	.500	....	....	4	6	10	0	....	....	....	5.9	1.4	0.4	0.7	.156
NBA Season Totals	9	....	53	13	6	20	.300	....	....	....	1	2	.500	....	....	4	6	10	0	....	....	....	5.9	1.4	0.4	0.7	....

• GIBSON, Mike
Michael Jerome Gibson

Born: Oct. 27, 1960. Williamsburg Co., SC, United States. Height: 6'10". Weight: 205 lbs. Drafted: 1982 College: Spartanburg

YEAR TEAM	GP	GS	MIN	PTS	FGM	FGA	FG%	3PM	3PA	3P%	FTM	FTA	FT%	ORB	DRB	TRB	AST	PF	DQ	STL	BLK	TO	MPG	PPG	RPG	APG	PCM
83-84 Washington	32	0	229	53	21	55	.382	0	0	.000	11	17	.647	29	37	66	9	30	1	5	7	13	7.2	1.7	2.1	0.3	.326
85-86 Detroit	32	0	161	48	20	51	.392	0	0	.000	8	11	.727	15	25	40	5	35	0	8	4	6	5.0	1.5	1.3	0.2	.308
NBA Season Totals	64	0	390	101	41	106	.387	0	0	.000	19	28	.679	44	62	106	14	65	1	13	11	19	6.1	1.6	1.7	0.2	....

• GILBERTSON, Merlin
Merlin (Boody) Gilbertson

Born: 1922. Height: 6'3". Weight: 205 lbs. Drafted: — College: Washington

YEAR TEAM	GP	GS	MIN	PTS	FGM	FGA	FG%	3PM	3PA	3P%	FTM	FTA	FT%	ORB	DRB	TRB	AST	PF	DQ	STL	BLK	TO	MPG	PPG	RPG	APG	PCM
48-49 Sheboygan-N	64	....	....	248	87	....	....	....	....	....	74	115	.643	....	....	....	....	172	....	....	....	....	....	3.9	....	....	....
NBL Season Totals	64	....	....	248	87	....	....	....	....	....	74	115		....	....	....	....	172	....	....	....	....	....	3.9	....	....	....
48-49 Sheboygan-N	2	....	....	7	1	....	....	....	....	....	5	7	.714	....	....	....	....	....	....	....	....	....	....	3.5	....	....	....
NBL Playoff Totals	2	....	....	7	1	....	....	....	....	....	5	7		....	....	....	....	....	....	....	....	....	....	3.5	....	....	....

• GILHOOLEY, Frankie
Frank Gilhooley

Born: 1924. Height: 5'11". Weight: 180 lbs. Drafted: — College: Notre Dame

YEAR TEAM	GP	GS	MIN	PTS	FGM	FGA	FG%	3PM	3PA	3P%	FTM	FTA	FT%	ORB	DRB	TRB	AST	PF	DQ	STL	BLK	TO	MPG	PPG	RPG	APG	PCM
46-47 Toledo-N	8	....	....	7	3	....	....	....	....	....	1	6	.167	....	....	....	....	....	....	....	....	....	....	0.9	....	....	....
NBL Season Totals	8	....	....	7	3	....	....	....	....	....	1	6		....	....	....	....	....	....	....	....	....	....	0.9	....	....	....
46-47 Toledo-N	3	....	....	4	1	....	....	....	....	....	2	2	1.000	....	....	....	....	....	....	....	....	....	....	1.3	....	....	....
NBL Playoff Totals	3	....	....	4	1	....	....	....	....	....	2	2		....	....	....	....	....	....	....	....	....	....	1.3	....	....	....

Total Basketball

GILL, Eddie

Eddie Gill

Born: Aug. 16, 1978. Aurora, CO, United States. Height: 6' Weight: 190 lbs. Drafted: — College: Weber State

YEAR	TEAM	GP	GS	MIN	PTS	FGM	FGA	FG%	3PM	3PA	3P%	FTM	FTA	FT%	ORB	DRB	TRB	AST	PF	DQ	STL	BLK	TO	MPG	PPG	RPG	APG	PCM
00-01	New Jersey	8	0	152	39	16	41	.390	3	9	.333	4	5	.800	0	9	9	24	9	0	4	1	10	19.0	4.9	1.1	3.0	.277
01-02	Memphis	23	5	382	116	39	92	.424	7	22	.318	31	39	.795	7	21	28	49	38	0	11	3	34	16.6	5.0	1.2	2.1	.283
NBA Season Totals		31	5	534	155	55	133	.414	10	31	.323	35	44	.795	7	30	37	73	47	0	15	4	44	17.2	5.0	1.2	2.4	....

GILL, Kendall

Kendall Cedric Gill

Born: May 25, 1968. Chicago, IL, United States. Height: 6'5". Weight: 195 lbs. Drafted: 1990 College: Illinois

YEAR	TEAM	GP	GS	MIN	PTS	FGM	FGA	FG%	3PM	3PA	3P%	FTM	FTA	FT%	ORB	DRB	TRB	AST	PF	DQ	STL	BLK	TO	MPG	PPG	RPG	APG	PCM
90-91	Charlotte	82	36	1944	906	376	836	.450	2	14	.143	152	182	.835	105	158	263	303	186	0	104	39	164	23.7	11.0	3.2	3.7	.476
91-92	Charlotte	79	79	2906	1622	666	1427	.467	6	25	.240	284	381	.745	165	237	402	329	237	1	154	46	182	36.8	20.5	5.1	4.2	.517
92-93	Charlotte	69	42	2430	1167	463	1032	.449	17	62	.274	224	290	.772	120	220	340	268	191	2	98	36	173	35.2	16.9	4.9	3.9	.446
93-94	Seattle	79	77	2435	1111	429	969	.443	38	120	.317	215	275	.782	91	177	268	275	194	1	151	32	142	30.8	14.1	3.4	3.5	.444
94-95	Seattle	73	58	2125	1002	392	858	.457	63	171	.368	155	209	.742	99	191	290	192	186	0	117	28	139	29.1	13.7	4.0	2.6	.439
95-96	Charlotte	36	36	1265	464	179	372	.481	17	54	.315	89	117	.761	56	133	189	225	101	2	42	22	112	35.1	12.9	5.3	6.3	.469
95-96	New Jersey	11	10	418	192	67	152	.441	9	25	.360	49	59	.831	16	27	43	35	30	0	22	2	21	38.0	17.5	3.9	3.2	.415
96-97	New Jersey	82	81	3199	1789	644	1453	.443	74	220	.336	427	536	.797	183	316	499	326	225	2	154	46	221	39.0	21.8	6.1	4.0	.523
97-98	New Jersey	81	81	2733	1087	418	974	.429	26	101	.257	225	327	.688	112	279	391	200	268	4	156	64	122	33.7	13.4	4.8	2.5	.393
98-99	New Jersey	50	47	1606	588	236	593	.398	2	17	.118	114	167	.683	61	183	244	123	162	4	**134**	26	71	32.1	11.8	4.9	2.5	.378
99-00	New Jersey	76	75	2355	993	396	956	.414	20	78	.256	181	255	.710	82	201	283	210	211	3	139	41	89	31.0	13.1	3.7	2.8	.392
00-01	New Jersey	31	26	892	283	107	323	.331	4	14	.286	65	90	.722	32	99	131	87	64	0	47	7	48	28.8	9.1	4.2	2.8	.300
01-02	Miami	65	49	1410	372	162	422	.384	6	44	.136	42	62	.677	29	155	184	100	140	0	44	8	55	21.7	5.7	2.8	1.5	.239
02-03	Minnesota	82	34	2068	714	286	677	.422	19	59	.322	123	161	.764	51	197	248	156	176	2	78	15	108	25.2	8.7	3.0	1.9	.311
NBA Season Totals		896	756	27786	12290	4821	11044	.437	303	1004	.302	2345	3111	.754	1202	2573	3775	2829	2371	21	1440	412	1647	31.0	13.7	4.2	3.2	....
92-93	Charlotte	9	9	353	156	65	162	.401	1	6	.167	25	35	.714	26	20	46	26	29	0	21	6	19	39.2	17.3	5.1	2.9	.355
93-94	Seattle	5	5	153	67	26	60	.433	2	9	.222	13	21	.619	7	17	24	10	12	0	6	1	6	30.6	13.4	4.8	2.0	.395
94-95	Seattle	4	0	72	25	9	25	.360	2	8	.250	5	8	.625	1	3	4	10	6	0	4	1	4	18.0	6.3	1.0	2.5	.293
97-98	New Jersey	3	3	100	43	18	40	.450	0	0	.000	7	8	.875	3	10	13	3	15	1	4	1	4	33.3	14.3	4.3	1.0	.316
02-03	Minnesota	6	0	118	31	10	27	.370	2	4	.500	9	14	.643	6	7	13	7	12	0	4	1	4	19.7	5.2	2.2	1.2	.239
NBA Playoff Totals		27	17	796	322	128	314	.408	7	27	.259	59	86	.686	43	57	100	56	74	1	39	10	37	29.5	11.9	3.7	2.1	....

GILLERY, Ben

Benjamin Gillery

Born: Sept. 19, 1965. Detroit, MI, United States. Height: 7' Weight: 235 lbs. Drafted: — College: Georgetown

YEAR	TEAM	GP	GS	MIN	PTS	FGM	FGA	FG%	3PM	3PA	3P%	FTM	FTA	FT%	ORB	DRB	TRB	AST	PF	DQ	STL	BLK	TO	MPG	PPG	RPG	APG	PCM
88-89	Sacramento	24	0	84	25	6	19	.316	0	0	.000	13	23	.565	7	16	23	2	29	0	2	4	5	3.5	1.0	1.0	0.1	.229
NBA Season Totals		24	0	84	25	6	19	.316	0	0	.000	13	23	.565	7	16	23	2	29	0	2	4	5	3.5	1.0	1.0	0.1	....

GILLESPIE, Jack

Jack A. Gillespie

Born: Oct. 1, 1947. Height: 6'6". Weight: 215 lbs. Drafted: 1969 College: Montana State

YEAR	TEAM	GP	GS	MIN	PTS	FGM	FGA	FG%	3PM	3PA	3P%	FTM	FTA	FT%	ORB	DRB	TRB	AST	PF	DQ	STL	BLK	TO	MPG	PPG	RPG	APG	PCM
69-70	New York-A	2	....	27	2	0	5	.000	0	0	.000	2	2	1.000	2	5	7	0	3	0	....	....	0	13.5	1.0	3.5	0.0	.090
ABA Season Totals		2	....	27	2	0	5	.000	0	0	.000	2	2	1.000	2	5	7	0	3	0	....	....	0	13.5	1.0	3.5	0.0	....

GILLETTE, Gene

Gene Gillette

Born: 1921. Height: 6'2". Weight: 205 lbs. Drafted: — College: St. Mary's (CA)

YEAR	TEAM	GP	GS	MIN	PTS	FGM	FGA	FG%	3PM	3PA	3P%	FTM	FTA	FT%	ORB	DRB	TRB	AST	PF	DQ	STL	BLK	TO	MPG	PPG	RPG	APG	PCM
46-47	Washington	14	....	....	8	1	11	.091	....	....	....	6	9	.667	....	....	....	2	13	....	....	....	....	0.6	....	0.1		
NBA Season Totals		14	....	....	8	1	11	.091	....	....	....	6	9	.667	....	....	....	2	13	....	....	....	....	0.6	....	0.1		....

GILLIAM, Armon

Armen Louis (The Hammer) Gilliam   aka.: Armon Louis Gilliam

Born: May 28, 1964. Pittsburgh, PA, United States. Height: 6'9". Weight: 230 lbs. Drafted: 1987 College: UNLV

YEAR	TEAM	GP	GS	MIN	PTS	FGM	FGA	FG%	3PM	3PA	3P%	FTM	FTA	FT%	ORB	DRB	TRB	AST	PF	DQ	STL	BLK	TO	MPG	PPG	RPG	APG	PCM
87-88	Phoenix	55	53	1807	815	342	720	.475	0	0	.000	131	193	.679	134	300	434	72	143	1	58	29	121	32.9	14.8	7.9	1.3	.452
88-89	Phoenix	74	60	2120	1176	468	930	.503	0	0	.000	240	323	.743	165	376	541	52	176	2	54	27	141	28.6	15.9	7.3	0.7	.532
89-90	Phoenix	16	7	267	143	52	121	.430	0	0	.000	39	56	.696	26	44	70	8	28	0	6	5	18	16.7	8.9	4.4	0.5	.467
89-90	Charlotte	60	59	2159	1128	432	819	.527	0	2	.000	264	363	.727	185	344	529	91	184	4	63	46	168	36.0	18.8	8.8	1.5	.542
90-91	Charlotte	25	25	949	494	195	380	.513	0	0	.000	104	128	.813	86	148	234	27	65	1	34	21	65	38.0	19.8	9.4	1.1	.545
90-91	Philadelphia	50	50	1695	748	292	621	.470	0	2	.000	164	201	.816	134	230	364	78	120	1	35	32	110	33.9	15.0	7.3	1.6	.443
91-92	Philadelphia	81	81	2771	1367	512	1001	.511	0	2	.000	343	425	.807	234	426	660	118	176	1	51	56	162	34.2	16.9	8.1	1.5	.544
92-93	Philadelphia	80	26	1742	992	359	774	.464	0	1	.000	274	325	.843	136	336	472	116	123	0	37	54	160	21.8	12.4	5.9	1.5	.587
93-94	New Jersey	82	5	1969	970	348	682	.510	0	1	.000	274	361	.759	197	303	500	69	129	0	38	61	107	24.0	11.8	6.1	0.8	.554
94-95	New Jersey	82	30	2472	1212	455	905	.503	0	2	.000	302	392	.770	192	421	613	99	171	0	67	89	156	30.1	14.8	7.5	1.2	.545
95-96	New Jersey	78	76	2856	1429	576	1216	.474	0	1	.000	277	350	.791	241	472	713	140	180	1	73	53	179	36.6	18.3	9.1	1.8	.517
96-97	Milwaukee	80	25	2050	691	246	522	.471	0	0	.000	199	259	.768	136	361	497	53	206	0	61	40	104	25.6	8.6	6.2	0.7	.403
97-98	Milwaukee	82	25	2114	921	327	676	.484	0	4	.000	267	333	.802	146	293	439	104	177	1	65	37	148	25.8	11.2	5.4	1.3	.456
98-99	Milwaukee	34	0	668	281	101	223	.453	0	1	.000	79	101	.782	33	93	126	19	48	0	22	12	36	19.6	8.3	3.7	0.6	.408
99-00	Utah	50	0	782	333	133	305	.436	0	1	.000	67	86	.779	72	137	209	42	83	0	12	16	55	15.6	6.7	4.2	0.8	.437
NBA Season Totals		929	527	26421	12700	4838	9895	.489	0	17	.000	3024	3896	.776	2117	4284	6401	1088	2009	12	676	607	1730	28.4	13.7	6.9	1.2	....
88-89	Phoenix	9	0	126	73	27	51	.529	0	0	.000	19	22	.864	18	27	45	2	11	0	1	2	10	14.0	8.1	5.0	0.2	.648
90-91	Philadelphia	8	8	287	135	48	104	.462	0	0	.000	39	46	.848	14	38	52	10	16	0	5	6	15	35.9	16.9	6.5	1.3	.444
93-94	New Jersey	4	0	112	42	15	34	.441	0	1	.000	12	16	.750	1	24	25	1	7	0	2	7	3	28.0	10.5	6.3	0.3	.438
98-99	Milwaukee	3	0	35	17	6	15	.400	0	0	.000	5	5	1.000	0	5	5	1	4	0	2	1	1	11.7	5.7	1.7	0.3	.416
99-00	Utah	10	0	132	35	15	46	.326	0	0	.000	5	13	.385	6	23	29	4	15	0	4	4	11	13.2	3.5	2.9	0.4	.185
NBA Playoff Totals		34	8	692	302	111	250	.444	0	1	.000	80	102	.784	39	117	156	18	53	0	14	20	40	20.4	8.9	4.6	0.5	....

• GILLIAM, Herm

Herman L. Gilliam Jr.

Born: May 5, 1946. Winston-Salem, NC, United States. Height: 6'3". Weight: 190 lbs. Drafted: 1969 College: Purdue

YEAR	TEAM	GP	GS	MIN	PTS	FGM	FGA	FG%	3PM	3PA	3P%	FTM	FTA	FT%	ORB	DRB	TRB	AST	PF	DQ	STL	BLK	TO	MPG	PPG	RPG	APG	PCM
69-70	Cincinnati	57	....	1161	426	179	441	.406	....	....	....	68	91	.747	....	....	215	178	163	6	....	....	....	20.4	7.5	3.8	3.1	.433
70-71	Buffalo	80	....	2082	898	378	896	.422	....	....	....	142	189	.751	....	....	334	291	246	4	....	....	....	26.0	11.2	4.2	3.6	.454
71-72	Atlanta	82	....	2337	835	345	774	.446	....	....	....	145	173	.838	....	....	335	377	232	3	....	....	....	28.5	10.2	4.1	4.6	.458
72-73	Atlanta	76	....	2741	1065	471	1007	.468	....	....	....	123	150	.820	....	....	399	482	257	8	....	....	....	36.1	14.0	5.3	6.3	.502
73-74	Atlanta	62	....	2003	874	384	846	.454	....	....	....	106	134	.791	61	206	267	355	190	5	134	18	....	32.3	14.1	4.3	5.7	.511
74-75	Atlanta	60	....	1393	722	314	736	.427	....	....	....	94	113	.832	76	128	204	170	124	1	77	13	....	23.2	12.0	3.4	2.8	.481
75-76	Seattle	81	....	1644	688	299	676	.442	....	....	....	90	116	.776	56	164	220	202	139	0	82	12	....	20.3	8.5	2.7	2.5	.434
76-77	Portland	80	....	1665	744	326	744	.438	....	....	....	92	120	.767	64	137	201	170	168	1	76	6	....	20.8	9.3	2.5	2.1	.400
NBA Season Totals		**578**	**....**	**15026**	**6252**	**2696**	**6120**	**.441**	**....**	**....**	**....**	**860**	**1086**	**.792**	**257**	**635**	**2175**	**2225**	**1519**	**28**	**369**	**49**	**....**	**26.0**	**10.8**	**3.8**	**3.8**	**....**
71-72	Atlanta	6	....	173	66	28	71	.394	....	....	....	10	11	.909	....	....	30	33	15	0	....	....	....	28.8	11.0	5.0	5.5	.493
72-73	Atlanta	6	....	197	71	33	81	.407	....	....	....	5	5	1.000	....	....	32	31	19	1	....	....	....	32.8	11.8	5.3	5.2	.429
75-76	Seattle	6	....	86	17	6	27	.222	....	....	....	5	8	.625	3	8	11	12	10	0	6	0	....	14.3	2.8	1.8	2.0	.192
76-77	Portland	18	....	295	115	53	123	.431	....	....	....	9	12	.750	7	13	20	32	29	0	13	1	....	16.4	6.4	1.1	1.8	.320
NBA Playoff Totals		**36**	**....**	**751**	**269**	**120**	**302**	**.397**	**....**	**....**	**....**	**29**	**36**	**.806**	**10**	**21**	**93**	**108**	**73**	**1**	**19**	**1**	**....**	**20.9**	**7.5**	**2.6**	**3.0**	**....**

• GILMORE, Artis

Artis (The A-Train) Gilmore

Born: Sept. 21, 1948. Chipley, FL, United States. Height: 7'2". Weight: 240 lbs. Drafted: 1971 College: Jacksonville

YEAR	TEAM	GP	GS	MIN	PTS	FGM	FGA	FG%	3PM	3PA	3P%	FTM	FTA	FT%	ORB	DRB	TRB	AST	PF	DQ	STL	BLK	TO	MPG	PPG	RPG	APG	PCM
71-72	Kentucky-A	84	....	**3666**	2003	806	1348	**.598**	0	0	.000	391	605	.646	421	**1070**	**1491**	230	280	3	....	**422**	335	43.6	23.8	**17.8**	2.7	.785
72-73	Kentucky-A	84	....	3502	1743	687	1228	**.559**	1	2	.500	368	572	.643	**449**	**1027**	**1476**	295	302	9	....	**259**	286	41.7	20.8	**17.6**	3.5	.766
73-74	Kentucky-A	84	....	**3518**	1568	621	1260	.493	0	3	.000	326	489	.667	**478**	**1060**	**1538**	329	302	....	57	287	319	**41.9**	18.7	**18.3**	3.9	.715
74-75	Kentucky-A	84	....	**3493**	1981	784	1351	.580	1	2	.500	412	592	.696	427	**934**	**1361**	208	318	....	63	**258**	344	**41.6**	23.6	16.2	2.5	.772
75-76	Kentucky-A	84	....	3286	2067	773	1401	.552	0	0	.000	521	**764**	.682	**402**	**901**	**1303**	211	**341**	....	58	205	295	39.1	24.6	**15.5**	2.5	.804
76-77	Chicago	82	....	2877	1527	570	1091	.522	....	....	....	387	586	.660	313	757	1070	199	266	4	44	203	....	35.1	18.6	13.0	2.4	.704
77-78	Chicago	82	....	3067	1879	704	1260	.559	....	....	....	471	669	.704	318	753	1071	263	261	4	42	181	**369**	37.4	22.9	13.1	3.2	.749
78-79	Chicago	82	....	3265	1940	753	1310	.575	....	....	....	434	587	.739	293	750	1043	274	280	2	50	156	312	39.8	23.7	12.7	3.3	.732
79-80	Chicago	48	....	1568	855	305	513	.595	0	0	.000	245	344	.712	108	324	432	133	167	5	29	59	134	32.7	17.8	9.0	2.8	.664
80-81	Chicago	82	....	2832	1469	547	816	**.670**	0	0	.000	375	532	.705	220	608	828	172	295	2	47	198	238	34.5	17.9	10.1	2.1	.694
81-82	Chicago	82	82	2796	1517	546	837	**.652**	1	1	1.000	424	552	.768	224	611	835	136	287	4	49	221	230	34.1	18.5	10.2	1.7	.719
82-83	San Antonio	82	82	2797	1479	556	888	**.626**	0	6	.000	367	496	.740	299	685	984	126	273	4	40	192	254	34.1	18.0	12.0	1.5	.717
83-84	San Antonio	64	59	2034	982	351	556	**.631**	0	3	.000	280	390	.718	213	449	662	70	229	4	36	132	147	31.8	15.3	10.3	1.1	.661
84-85	San Antonio	81	81	2756	1548	532	854	.623	0	2	.000	484	646	.749	231	615	846	131	306	4	40	173	243	34.0	19.1	10.4	1.6	.700
85-86	San Antonio	71	71	2395	1184	423	684	.618	0	1	.000	338	482	.701	166	434	600	102	239	3	39	108	185	33.7	16.7	8.5	1.4	.582
86-87	San Antonio	82	74	2405	934	346	580	.597	0	0	.000	242	356	.680	185	394	579	150	235	2	39	95	180	29.3	11.4	7.1	1.8	.503
87-88	Chicago	24	23	372	101	41	80	.513	0	0	.000	19	37	.514	15	48	63	9	54	0	5	12	29	15.5	4.2	2.6	0.4	.237
87-88	Boston	47	4	521	164	58	101	.574	0	0	.000	48	91	.527	54	94	148	12	94	0	10	18	38	11.1	3.5	3.1	0.3	.387
NBA Season Totals		**909**	**476**	**29685**	**15579**	**5732**	**9570**	**.599**	**1**	**13**	**.077**	**4114**	**5768**	**.713**	**2639**	**6522**	**9161**	**1777**	**2986**	**38**	**470**	**1748**	**2359**	**32.7**	**17.1**	**10.1**	**2.0**	**....**
ABA Season Totals		**420**	**....**	**17465**	**9362**	**3671**	**6588**	**.557**	**2**	**7**	**.286**	**2018**	**3022**	**.668**	**2177**	**4992**	**7169**	**1273**	**1543**	**12**	**178**	**1431**	**1579**	**41.6**	**22.3**	**17.1**	**3.0**	**....**
Career Totals		**1329**	**476**	**47150**	**24941**	**9403**	**16158**	**.582**	**3**	**20**	**.150**	**6132**	**8790**	**.698**	**4816**	**11514**	**16330**	**3050**	**4529**	**50**	**648**	**3179**	**3938**	**35.5**	**18.8**	**12.3**	**2.3**	**....**
71-72	Kentucky-A	6	....	285	131	52	91	.571	0	1	.000	27	38	.711	28	78	106	25	17	....	....	....	29	47.5	21.8	17.7	4.2	.721
72-73	Kentucky-A	19	....	780	361	142	261	.544	0	0	.000	77	123	.626	84	176	260	75	68	1	....	....	63	41.1	19.0	13.7	3.9	.666
73-74	Kentucky-A	8	....	344	180	71	127	.559	0	0	.000	38	66	.576	47	102	149	28	20	....	7	30	29	43.0	22.5	18.6	3.5	.788
74-75	Kentucky-A	15	....	679	362	132	245	.539	0	0	.000	98	127	.772	75	189	264	38	59	....	15	31	59	45.3	24.1	17.6	2.5	.735
75-76	Kentucky-A	10	....	390	242	93	153	.608	0	0	.000	56	74	.757	50	102	152	19	49	....	11	36	44	39.0	24.2	15.2	1.9	.808
76-77	Chicago	3	....	126	56	19	40	.475	....	....	....	18	23	.783	15	24	39	6	9	0	3	8	....	42.0	18.7	13.0	2.0	.574
80-81	Chicago	6	....	247	108	35	60	.583	0	0	.000	38	55	.691	24	43	67	12	15	0	6	17	17	41.2	18.0	11.2	2.0	.608
82-83	San Antonio	11	11	401	184	76	132	.576	0	0	.000	32	46	.696	37	105	142	18	46	1	9	34	27	36.5	16.7	12.9	1.6	.670
84-85	San Antonio	5	5	185	89	29	52	.558	0	0	.000	31	45	.689	10	40	50	7	18	0	2	7	23	37.0	17.8	10.0	1.4	.506
85-86	San Antonio	3	3	107	40	16	24	.667	0	0	.000	8	14	.571	7	11	18	3	11	0	7	1	10	35.7	13.3	6.0	1.0	.400
87-88	Boston	14	0	86	15	4	8	.500	0	0	.000	7	14	.500	4	16	20	1	14	0	0	4	4	6.1	1.1	1.4	0.1	.246
NBA Playoff Totals		**42**	**19**	**1152**	**492**	**179**	**316**	**.566**	**0**	**0**	**.000**	**134**	**197**	**.680**	**97**	**239**	**336**	**47**	**113**	**1**	**27**	**71**	**81**	**27.4**	**11.7**	**8.0**	**1.1**	**....**
ABA Playoff Totals		**58**	**....**	**2478**	**1276**	**490**	**877**	**.559**	**0**	**1**	**.000**	**296**	**428**	**.692**	**284**	**647**	**931**	**185**	**213**	**1**	**33**	**97**	**224**	**42.7**	**22.0**	**16.1**	**3.2**	**....**
Career Playoff Totals		**100**	**19**	**3630**	**1768**	**669**	**1193**	**.561**	**0**	**1**	**.000**	**430**	**625**	**.688**	**381**	**886**	**1267**	**232**	**326**	**2**	**60**	**168**	**305**	**36.3**	**17.7**	**12.7**	**2.3**	**....**

• GILMORE, Walt

Walt Gilmore

Born: Feb. 27, 1947. Height: 6'6". Weight: 225 lbs. Drafted: 1970 College: Fort Valley State

YEAR	TEAM	GP	GS	MIN	PTS	FGM	FGA	FG%	3PM	3PA	3P%	FTM	FTA	FT%	ORB	DRB	TRB	AST	PF	DQ	STL	BLK	TO	MPG	PPG	RPG	APG	PCM
70-71	Portland	27	....	261	58	23	54	.426	....	....	....	12	26	.462	....	....	73	12	49	1	....	....	....	9.7	2.1	2.7	0.4	.309
NBA Season Totals		**27**	**....**	**261**	**58**	**23**	**54**	**.426**	**....**	**....**	**....**	**12**	**26**	**.462**	**....**	**....**	**73**	**12**	**49**	**1**	**....**	**....**	**....**	**9.7**	**2.1**	**2.7**	**0.4**	**....**

• GILMUR, Chuck

Charles E. Gilmur Jr.

Born: Aug. 13, 1922. Height: 6'4". Weight: 225 lbs. Drafted: — College: Washington

YEAR	TEAM	GP	GS	MIN	PTS	FGM	FGA	FG%	3PM	3PA	3P%	FTM	FTA	FT%	ORB	DRB	TRB	AST	PF	DQ	STL	BLK	TO	MPG	PPG	RPG	APG	PCM
46-47	Chicago	51	....	....	178	76	253	.300	....	....	....	26	66	.394	....	....	....	21	139	....	....	....	....	....	3.5	....	0.4	....
47-48	Chicago	48	....	....	459	181	597	.303	....	....	....	97	148	.655	....	....	....	77	**231**	....	....	....	....	....	9.6	....	1.6	....
48-49	Chicago	56	....	....	286	110	281	.391	....	....	....	66	121	.545	....	....	....	125	194	....	....	....	....	....	5.1	....	2.2	....
49-50	Washington	68	....	....	418	127	379	.335	....	....	....	164	241	.680	....	....	....	108	275	....	....	....	....	....	6.1	....	1.6	....
50-51	Washington	16	....	....	51	17	61	.279	....	....	....	17	32	.531	....	....	75	17	57	3	....	....	....	....	3.2	4.7	1.1	....
NBA Season Totals		**239**	**....**	**....**	**1392**	**511**	**1571**	**.325**	**....**	**....**	**....**	**370**	**608**	**.609**	**....**	**....**	**75**	**348**	**896**	**3**	**....**	**....**	**....**	**....**	**5.8**	**0.3**	**1.5**	**....**
46-47	Chicago	11	....	....	64	29	114	.254	....	....	....	6	13	.462	....	....	....	1	45	....	....	....	....	....	5.8	....	0.1	....
47-48	Chicago	5	....	....	44	13	65	.200	....	....	....	18	23	.783	....	....	....	10	27	....	....	....	....	....	8.8	....	2.0	....
48-49	Chicago	2	....	....	3	1	3	.333	....	....	....	1	3	.333	....	....	....	3	8	....	....	....	....	....	1.5	....	1.5	....
NBA Playoff Totals		**18**	**....**	**....**	**111**	**43**	**182**	**.236**	**....**	**....**	**....**	**25**	**39**	**.641**	**....**	**....**	**....**	**14**	**80**	**....**	**....**	**....**	**....**	**....**	**6.2**	**....**	**0.8**	**....**

YEAR	TEAM	GP	GS	MIN	PTS	FGM	FGA	FG%	3PM	3PA	3P%	FTM	FTA	FT%	ORB	DRB	TRB	AST	PF	DQ	STL	BLK	TO	MPG	PPG	RPG	APG	PCM

• GINOBILI, Emanuel
Emanuel Ginobili

Born: July 28, 1977. Bahia Blanca, Argentina.   Height: 6'6".   Weight: 210 lbs.   Drafted: 1999   College: none

YEAR	TEAM	GP	GS	MIN	PTS	FGM	FGA	FG%	3PM	3PA	3P%	FTM	FTA	FT%	ORB	DRB	TRB	AST	PF	DQ	STL	BLK	TO	MPG	PPG	RPG	APG	PCM
02-03	San Antonio	69	5	1432	525	174	397	.438	51	148	.345	126	171	.737	47	114	161	138	170	3	96	17	100	20.8	7.6	2.3	2.0	.373
NBA Season Totals		69	5	1432	525	174	397	.438	51	148	.345	126	171	.737	47	114	161	138	170	3	96	17	100	20.8	7.6	2.3	2.0	....
02-03	San Antonio	24	0	660	226	71	184	.386	28	73	.384	56	74	.757	29	63	92	70	62	1	41	9	36	27.5	9.4	3.8	2.9	.394
NBA Playoff Totals		24	0	660	226	71	184	.386	28	73	.384	56	74	.757	29	63	92	70	62	1	41	9	36	27.5	9.4	3.8	2.9	....

• GINSBURG, Hymie
Hymie Ginsburg

Born: 1914.   Height: 5'9".   Weight: 170 lbs.   Drafted: —   College: Geneva

YEAR	TEAM	GP	GS	MIN	PTS	FGM	FGA	FG%	3PM	3PA	3P%	FTM	FTA	FT%	ORB	DRB	TRB	AST	PF	DQ	STL	BLK	TO	MPG	PPG	RPG	APG	PCM
37-38	Pittsburgh-N	13	....	....	92	36	....	....	....	....	....	20	....												7.1	....	....	....
38-39	Pittsburgh-N	23	....	....	109	46	....	....	....	....	....	17	....												4.7	....	....	....
NBL Season Totals		36	....	....	201	82	....	....	....	....	....	37	....												5.6	....	....	....

• GIRICEK, Gordan
Gordan Giricek

Born: June 20, 1977. Zagreb, Croatia.   Height: 6'6".   Weight: 210 lbs.   Drafted: 1999   College: none

YEAR	TEAM	GP	GS	MIN	PTS	FGM	FGA	FG%	3PM	3PA	3P%	FTM	FTA	FT%	ORB	DRB	TRB	AST	PF	DQ	STL	BLK	TO	MPG	PPG	RPG	APG	PCM
02-03	Memphis	49	35	1187	548	207	478	.433	46	130	.354	88	107	.822	18	90	108	70	104	0	22	6	94	24.2	11.2	2.2	1.4	.304
02-03	Orlando	27	27	961	387	143	325	.440	39	119	.328	62	76	.816	18	112	130	67	55	0	30	2	51	35.6	14.3	4.8	2.5	.379
NBA Season Totals		76	62	2148	935	350	803	.436	85	249	.341	150	183	.820	36	202	238	137	159	0	52	8	145	28.3	12.3	3.1	1.8	....
02-03	Orlando	7	7	224	66	26	56	.464	5	15	.333	9	11	.818	4	18	22	7	27	0	2	1	13	32.0	9.4	3.1	1.0	.197
NBA Playoff Totals		7	7	224	66	26	56	.464	5	15	.333	9	11	.818	4	18	22	7	27	0	2	1	13	32.0	9.4	3.1	1.0	....

• GIVENS, Jack
Jack (Goose) Givens

Born: Sept. 21, 1956. Lexington, KY, United States.   Height: 6'5".   Weight: 205 lbs.   Drafted: 1978   College: Kentucky

YEAR	TEAM	GP	GS	MIN	PTS	FGM	FGA	FG%	3PM	3PA	3P%	FTM	FTA	FT%	ORB	DRB	TRB	AST	PF	DQ	STL	BLK	TO	MPG	PPG	RPG	APG	PCM
78-79	Atlanta	74	....	1347	570	234	564	.415	....	....	....	102	135	.756	98	116	214	83	121	0	72	17	74	18.2	7.7	2.9	1.1	.372
79-80	Atlanta	82	....	1254	470	182	473	.385	0	2	.000	106	128	.828	114	128	242	59	132	1	51	19	57	15.3	5.7	3.0	0.7	.345
NBA Season Totals		156	....	2601	1040	416	1037	.401	0	2	.000	208	263	.791	212	244	456	142	253	1	123	36	131	16.7	6.7	2.9	0.9	....
78-79	Atlanta	9	....	81	23	10	30	.333	....	....	....	3	3	1.000	7	14	21	3	9	0	1	2	5	9.0	2.6	2.3	0.3	.264
79-80	Atlanta	4	....	36	6	3	14	.214	0	0	.000	0	0	.000	1	4	5	3	7	0	2	0	3	9.0	1.5	1.3	0.8	-.006
NBA Playoff Totals		13	....	117	29	13	44	.295	0	0	.000	3	3	1.000	8	18	26	6	16	0	3	2	8	9.0	2.2	2.0	0.5	....

• GLAMACK, George
George Gregory (The Blind Bomber) Glamack

Born: June 7, 1919. Johnstown, PA, United States. Died: Mar.10, 1987.   Height: 6'6".   Weight: 225 lbs.   Drafted: —   College: North Carolina

YEAR	TEAM	GP	GS	MIN	PTS	FGM	FGA	FG%	3PM	3PA	3P%	FTM	FTA	FT%	ORB	DRB	TRB	AST	PF	DQ	STL	BLK	TO	MPG	PPG	RPG	APG	PCM
41-42	Wingfoots-N	24	....	....	256	87	....	....	....	....	....	82	....	....					....					10.7	....	....	....
45-46	Rochester-N	34	....	....	417	151	....	....	....	....	....	115	184	.625					....					12.3	....	....	....
46-47	Rochester-N	44	....	....	372	141	....	....	....	....	....	90	135	.667					139					8.5	....	....	....
47-48	Indianapolis-N	57	....	....	592	215	....	....	....	....	....	162	244	.664					151					10.4	....	....	....
48-49	Hammond-N	43	....	....	501	169	....	....	....	....	....	163	216	.755					120					11.7	....	....	....
48-49	Indianapolis	11	....	....	102	30	121	.248	....	....	....	42	55	.764					19	28				9.3	....	1.7	....
NBA Season Totals		11	....	....	102	30	121	.248				42	55	.764					19	28				9.3	....	1.7	....
NBL Season Totals		202	....	....	2138	763	....	....				612	779	....					410					10.6	....	....	....
Career Totals		213	....	....	2240	793	121					654	834	....					19	438				10.5	....	0.1	....
41-42	Wingfoots-N	3	....	....	37	11	....	....	....	....	....	15	....	....										12.3	....	....	....
45-46	Rochester-N	7	....	....	88	34	....	....	....	....	....	20	27	.741										12.6	....	....	....
46-47	Rochester-N	10	....	....	98	35	....	....	....	....	....	28	33	.848										9.8	....	....	....
47-48	Indianapolis-N	4	....	....	68	24	....	....	....	....	....	20	28	.714										17.0	....	....	....
48-49	Hammond-N	2	....	....	15	5	....	....	....	....	....	5	8	.625										7.5	....	....	....
NBL Playoff Totals		26	....	....	306	109	....	....				88	96	....										11.8	....	....	....

• GLANCY, Ed
Ed Glancy

Born: 1918.   Height: 6'3".   Weight: 180 lbs.   Drafted: —   College: Manhattan

YEAR	TEAM	GP	GS	MIN	PTS	FGM	FGA	FG%	3PM	3PA	3P%	FTM	FTA	FT%	ORB	DRB	TRB	AST	PF	DQ	STL	BLK	TO	MPG	PPG	RPG	APG	PCM
43-44	Oshkosh-N	5	....	....	9	3	....	....	....	....	....	3	....	....										1.8	....	....	....
NBL Season Totals		5	....	....	9	3	....	....				3	....	....										1.8	....	....	....

• GLASS, Gerald
Gerald Damon (World Class) Glass

Born: Nov. 12, 1967. Greenwood, MS, United States.   Height: 6'5".   Weight: 221 lbs.   Drafted: 1990   College: Mississippi

YEAR	TEAM	GP	GS	MIN	PTS	FGM	FGA	FG%	3PM	3PA	3P%	FTM	FTA	FT%	ORB	DRB	TRB	AST	PF	DQ	STL	BLK	TO	MPG	PPG	RPG	APG	PCM
90-91	Minnesota	51	3	606	352	149	340	.438	2	17	.118	52	76	.684	54	48	102	42	76	2	28	9	41	11.9	6.9	2.0	0.8	.435
91-92	Minnesota	75	41	1822	859	383	871	.440	16	54	.296	77	125	.616	107	153	260	175	171	0	66	30	105	24.3	11.5	3.5	2.3	.398
92-93	Minnesota	4	0	71	20	8	27	.296	0	2	.000	4	6	.667	1	2	3	9	6	0	3	0	5	17.8	5.0	0.8	2.3	.128
92-93	Detroit	56	5	777	296	134	312	.429	7	31	.226	21	33	.636	60	79	139	68	98	1	30	18	28	13.9	5.3	2.5	1.2	.385
95-96	New Jersey	10	0	56	21	10	28	.357	1	5	.200	0	0	.000	5	1	6	4	5	0	2	1	0	5.6	2.1	0.6	0.4	.258
95-96	Charlotte	5	0	15	5	2	5	.400	0	1	.000	1	1	1.000	1	1	2	0	5	0	1	0	0	3.0	1.0	0.4	0.0	.177
NBA Season Totals		201	49	3347	1553	686	1583	.433	26	110	.236	155	241	.643	228	284	512	298	361	3	130	58	179	16.7	7.7	2.5	1.5	....

• GLASS, Jim
James Glass

Born: 1921. Height: 6'8". Weight: 210 lbs. Drafted: — College: Toledo

YEAR TEAM	GP	GS	MIN	PTS	FGM	FGA	FG%	3PM	3PA	3P%	FTM	FTA	FT%	ORB	DRB	TRB	AST	PF	DQ	STL	BLK	TO	MPG	PPG	RPG	APG	PCM
44-45 Fort Wayne-N	14	....	....	7	2	....	....	....	....	....	3	....	....	....	....	....	....	....	....	....	....	....	....	0.5	....	....	....
NBL Season Totals	14	....	....	7	2	....	....	....	....	....	3	....	....	....	....	....	....	....	....	....	....	....	....	0.5	....	....	....
44-45 Fort Wayne-N	2	....	....	3	1	....	....	....	....	....	1	....	....	....	....	....	....	....	....	....	....	....	....	1.5	....	....	....
NBL Playoff Totals	2	....	....	3	1	....	....	....	....	....	1	....	....	....	....	....	....	....	....	....	....	....	....	1.5	....	....	....

• GLENN, Mike
Mike Theodore (Stinger) Glenn

Born: Sept. 10, 1955. Rome, GA, United States. Height: 6'2". Weight: 175 lbs. Drafted: 1977 College: Southern Illinois

YEAR TEAM	GP	GS	MIN	PTS	FGM	FGA	FG%	3PM	3PA	3P%	FTM	FTA	FT%	ORB	DRB	TRB	AST	PF	DQ	STL	BLK	TO	MPG	PPG	RPG	APG	PCM
77-78 Buffalo	56	....	947	441	195	370	.527	....	....	....	51	65	.785	14	65	79	78	98	0	35	5	50	16.9	7.9	1.4	1.4	.409
78-79 New York	75	....	1171	583	263	486	.541	....	....	....	57	63	.905	28	54	82	136	113	0	37	6	68	15.6	7.8	1.1	1.8	.453
79-80 New York	75	....	800	441	188	364	.516	2	10	.200	63	73	.863	21	45	66	85	79	0	35	7	38	10.7	5.9	0.9	1.1	.497
80-81 New York	82	....	1506	672	285	511	.558	4	11	.364	98	110	.891	27	61	88	108	126	0	72	5	66	18.4	8.2	1.1	1.3	.406
81-82 Atlanta	49	0	833	376	158	291	.543	1	2	.500	59	67	.881	5	56	61	87	80	0	26	3	29	17.0	7.7	1.2	1.8	.436
82-83 Atlanta	73	4	1124	534	230	444	.518	0	1	.000	74	89	.831	16	74	90	125	132	0	30	9	51	15.4	7.3	1.2	1.7	.429
83-84 Atlanta	81	0	1503	681	312	554	.563	1	2	.500	56	70	.800	17	87	104	171	146	1	46	5	65	18.6	8.4	1.3	2.1	.431
84-85 Milwaukee	60	5	1126	518	228	388	.588	0	2	.000	62	76	.816	20	61	81	122	74	0	27	0	54	18.8	8.6	1.4	2.0	.452
85-86 Milwaukee	38	1	573	235	94	190	.495	0	0	.000	47	49	.959	4	53	57	39	42	0	9	3	19	15.1	6.2	1.5	1.0	.373
86-87 Milwaukee	4	0	34	15	5	13	.385	0	0	.000	5	7	.714	0	2	2	1	3	0	1	0	0	8.5	3.8	0.5	0.3	.267
NBA Season Totals	593	10	9617	4496	1958	3611	.542	8	28	.286	572	669	.855	152	558	710	952	893	1	318	43	440	16.2	7.6	1.2	1.6	....
80-81 New York	2	....	26	11	4	7	.571	0	1	.000	3	3	1.000	1	3	4	1	0	0	1	0	2	13.0	5.5	2.0	0.5	.465
81-82 Atlanta	2	0	35	12	5	7	.714	0	0	.000	2	2	1.000	0	1	1	2	3	0	3	0	2	17.5	6.0	0.5	1.0	.365
82-83 Atlanta	3	0	67	28	12	22	.545	0	0	.000	4	4	1.000	0	5	5	3	10	0	2	0	5	22.3	9.3	1.7	1.0	.292
83-84 Atlanta	5	0	53	10	5	14	.357	0	0	.000	0	0	.000	1	4	5	5	9	0	2	0	2	10.6	2.0	1.0	1.0	.140
85-86 Milwaukee	10	0	114	36	13	36	.361	0	1	.000	10	12	.833	3	8	11	8	6	0	1	0	5	11.4	3.6	1.1	0.8	.228
NBA Playoff Totals	22	0	295	97	39	86	.453	0	2	.000	19	21	.905	5	21	26	19	28	0	9	0	16	13.4	4.4	1.2	0.9	....

• GLICK, Normie
Norman Stanley Glick

Born: Nov. 10, 1927. Height: 6'7". Weight: 190 lbs. Drafted: — College: Loyola (CA)

YEAR TEAM	GP	GS	MIN	PTS	FGM	FGA	FG%	3PM	3PA	3P%	FTM	FTA	FT%	ORB	DRB	TRB	AST	PF	DQ	STL	BLK	TO	MPG	PPG	RPG	APG	PCM
49-50 Minneapolis	1	....	....	2	1	1	1.000	....	....	....	0	0	.000	....	....	....	1	2	....	....	....	....	2.0	....	1.0	....
NBA Season Totals	1	....	....	2	1	1	1.000	....	....	....	0	0	.000	....	....	....	1	2	....	....	....	....	2.0	....	1.0	....

• GLOUCHKOV, Georgi
Georgi Nikolov Glouchkov

Born: Jan. 10, 1960. Triavna, Bulgaria. Height: 6'8". Weight: 235 lbs. Drafted: 1985 College: Akademik Varna (BUL)

YEAR TEAM	GP	GS	MIN	PTS	FGM	FGA	FG%	3PM	3PA	3P%	FTM	FTA	FT%	ORB	DRB	TRB	AST	PF	DQ	STL	BLK	TO	MPG	PPG	RPG	APG	PCM
85-86 Phoenix	49	16	772	239	84	209	.402	1	1	1.000	70	122	.574	31	132	163	32	124	0	26	25	78	15.8	4.9	3.3	0.7	.261
NBA Season Totals	49	16	772	239	84	209	.402	1	1	1.000	70	122	.574	31	132	163	32	124	0	26	25	78	15.8	4.9	3.3	0.7	....

• GLOVER, Clarence
Clarence Glover

Born: Nov. 1, 1947. Horse Caves, KY, United States. Height: 6'8". Weight: 210 lbs. Drafted: 1971 College: Western Kentucky

YEAR TEAM	GP	GS	MIN	PTS	FGM	FGA	FG%	3PM	3PA	3P%	FTM	FTA	FT%	ORB	DRB	TRB	AST	PF	DQ	STL	BLK	TO	MPG	PPG	RPG	APG	PCM
71-72 Boston	25	....	119	65	25	55	.455	....	....	....	15	32	.469	....	....	46	4	26	0	....	....	....	4.8	2.6	1.8	0.2	.544
NBA Season Totals	25	....	119	65	25	55	.455	....	....	....	15	32	.469	....	....	46	4	26	0	....	....	....	4.8	2.6	1.8	0.2	....
71-72 Boston	3	....	10	6	2	6	.333	....	....	....	2	2	1.000	....	....	3	0	1	0	....	....	....	3.3	2.0	1.0	0.0	.470
NBA Playoff Totals	3	....	10	6	2	6	.333	....	....	....	2	2	1.000	....	....	3	0	1	0	....	....	....	3.3	2.0	1.0	0.0	....

• GLOVER, Dion
Micaiah Diondae Glover

Born: Oct. 22, 1978. Marietta, GA, United States. Height: 6'5". Weight: 228 lbs. Drafted: 1999 College: Georgia Tech

YEAR TEAM	GP	GS	MIN	PTS	FGM	FGA	FG%	3PM	3PA	3P%	FTM	FTA	FT%	ORB	DRB	TRB	AST	PF	DQ	STL	BLK	TO	MPG	PPG	RPG	APG	PCM
99-00 Atlanta	30	1	446	195	66	171	.386	12	45	.267	51	70	.729	15	23	38	27	28	0	15	4	28	14.9	6.5	1.3	0.9	.301
00-01 Atlanta	57	7	929	338	141	336	.420	9	46	.196	47	69	.681	39	92	131	69	92	1	49	10	54	16.3	5.9	2.3	1.2	.334
01-02 Atlanta	55	25	1156	492	192	456	.421	30	91	.330	78	103	.757	36	133	169	84	89	1	45	14	76	21.0	8.9	3.1	1.5	.373
02-03 Atlanta	76	42	1889	737	277	648	.427	56	158	.354	127	162	.784	62	220	282	141	146	0	71	15	108	24.9	9.7	3.7	1.9	.375
NBA Season Totals	218	75	4420	1762	676	1611	.420	107	340	.315	303	404	.750	152	468	620	321	355	2	180	43	266	20.3	8.1	2.8	1.5	....

• GMINSKI, Mike
Michael Thomas (G-Man) Gminski

Born: Aug. 3, 1959. Monroe, CT, United States. Height: 6'11". Weight: 250 lbs. Drafted: 1980 College: Duke

YEAR TEAM	GP	GS	MIN	PTS	FGM	FGA	FG%	3PM	3PA	3P%	FTM	FTA	FT%	ORB	DRB	TRB	AST	PF	DQ	STL	BLK	TO	MPG	PPG	RPG	APG	PCM
80-81 New Jersey	56	....	1579	737	291	688	.423	0	1	.000	155	202	.767	137	282	419	72	127	1	54	100	129	28.2	13.2	7.5	1.3	.493
81-82 New Jersey	64	6	740	335	119	270	.441	0	0	.000	97	118	.822	70	116	186	41	69	0	17	48	58	11.6	5.2	2.9	0.6	.509
82-83 New Jersey	80	1	1255	601	213	426	.500	0	1	.000	175	225	.778	154	228	382	61	118	0	35	116	128	15.7	7.5	4.8	0.8	.610
83-84 New Jersey	82	2	1655	621	237	462	.513	0	3	.000	147	184	.799	161	272	433	92	162	0	37	70	123	20.2	7.6	5.3	1.1	.487
84-85 New Jersey	81	54	2418	1036	380	818	.465	0	1	.000	276	328	.841	229	404	633	158	135	0	38	92	138	29.9	12.8	7.8	2.0	.534
85-86 New Jersey	81	78	2525	1333	491	949	.517	0	1	.000	351	393	.893	206	462	668	133	163	0	56	71	138	31.2	16.5	8.2	1.6	.620
86-87 New Jersey	72	66	2272	1179	433	947	.457	0	0	.000	313	370	.846	192	438	630	99	159	0	52	69	130	31.6	16.4	8.8	1.4	.565
87-88 New Jersey	34	34	1194	573	215	474	.454	0	2	.000	143	166	.861	82	238	320	55	78	0	28	33	82	35.1	16.9	9.4	1.6	.521
87-88 Philadelphia	47	47	1767	792	290	652	.445	0	0	.000	212	226	.938	163	331	494	84	98	0	36	85	94	37.6	16.9	10.5	1.8	.553
88-89 Philadelphia	82	82	2739	1409	556	1166	.477	0	6	.000	297	341	.871	213	556	769	138	142	0	46	106	131	33.4	17.2	9.4	1.7	.598
89-90 Philadelphia	81	81	2659	1112	458	1002	.457	3	17	.176	193	235	.821	196	491	687	128	136	0	43	102	97	32.8	13.7	8.5	1.6	.505
90-91 Philadelphia	30	29	791	272	109	284	.384	1	8	.125	53	63	.841	71	130	201	33	41	0	16	34	30	26.4	9.1	6.7	1.1	.413
90-91 Charlotte	50	50	1405	572	248	524	.473	1	6	.167	75	95	.789	115	266	381	60	58	0	24	22	55	28.1	11.4	7.6	1.2	.491
91-92 Charlotte	35	10	499	202	90	199	.452	1	3	.333	21	28	.750	37	81	118	31	37	0	11	17	21	14.3	5.8	3.4	0.9	.460

YEAR	TEAM	GP	GS	MIN	PTS	FGM	FGA	FG%	3PM	3PA	3P%	FTM	FTA	FT%	ORB	DRB	TRB	AST	PF	DQ	STL	BLK	TO	MPG	PPG	RPG	APG	PCM
92-93	Charlotte	34	0	251	93	42	83	.506	0	0	.000	9	10	.900	34	51	85	7	28	0	1	9	10	7.4	2.7	2.5	0.2	.510
93-94	Charlotte	21	6	255	73	31	79	.392	0	0	.000	11	14	.786	19	40	59	11	20	0	13	13	11	12.1	3.5	2.8	0.5	.385
93-94	Milwaukee	8	1	54	13	5	24	.208	0	0	.000	3	4	.750	3	12	15	0	3	0	0	3	2	6.8	1.6	1.9	0.0	.156
NBA Season Totals		938	547	24058	10953	4208	9047	.465	6	49	.122	2531	3002	.843	2082	4398	6480	1203	1574	1	507	990	1377	25.6	11.7	6.9	1.3	....
81-82	New Jersey	1	0	10	5	2	3	.667	0	0	.000	1	2	.500	0	2	2	0	2	0	0	0	0	10.0	5.0	2.0	0.0	.454
82-83	New Jersey	2	0	29	15	6	9	.667	0	0	.000	3	4	.750	4	5	9	1	2	0	0	4	1	14.5	7.5	4.5	0.5	.788
83-84	New Jersey	11	0	223	94	29	50	.580	0	0	.000	36	52	.692	22	33	55	6	17	0	7	15	9	20.3	8.5	5.0	0.5	.578
84-85	New Jersey	3	0	81	42	18	33	.545	0	0	.000	6	6	1.000	4	15	19	4	5	0	3	5	10	27.0	14.0	6.3	1.3	.566
85-86	New Jersey	3	3	109	58	16	43	.372	0	0	.000	26	27	.963	11	19	30	5	11	0	4	2	9	36.3	19.3	10.0	1.7	.530
88-89	Philadelphia	3	3	118	49	19	48	.396	0	0	.000	11	16	.688	6	17	23	2	8	0	0	8	2	39.3	16.3	7.7	0.7	.382
89-90	Philadelphia	10	10	342	128	57	117	.487	0	5	.000	14	15	.933	8	46	54	11	27	0	8	23	17	34.2	12.8	5.4	1.1	.392
92-93	Charlotte	2	0	5	2	1	2	.500	0	0	.000	0	0	.000	0	1	1	0	0	0	0	0	0	2.5	1.0	0.5	0.0	.400
NBA Playoff Totals		35	16	917	393	148	305	.485	0	5	.000	97	122	.795	55	138	193	29	72	0	22	57	48	26.2	11.2	5.5	0.8	....

• GODFREAD, Dan

Daniel Joseph Godfread

Born: June 14, 1967. Fort Wayne, IN, United States. Height: 6'10". Weight: 250 lbs. Drafted: — College: Evansville

YEAR	TEAM	GP	GS	MIN	PTS	FGM	FGA	FG%	3PM	3PA	3P%	FTM	FTA	FT%	ORB	DRB	TRB	AST	PF	DQ	STL	BLK	TO	MPG	PPG	RPG	APG	PCM
90-91	Minnesota	10	0	20	13	5	12	.417	0	1	.000	3	4	.750	0	2	2	0	5	0	1	4	0	2.0	1.3	0.2	0.0	.510
91-92	Houston	1	0	2	0	0	0	.000	0	0	.000	0	0	.000	0	0	0	0	0	0	0	0	0	2.0	0.0	0.0	0.0	.000
NBA Season Totals		11	0	22	13	5	12	.417	0	1	.000	3	4	.750	0	2	2	0	5	0	1	4	0	2.0	1.2	0.2	0.0	....

• GOFF, Pim

Pim Goff

Born: 1913. Height: 6'4". Weight: 190 lbs. Drafted: — College: Illinois State

YEAR	TEAM	GP	GS	MIN	PTS	FGM	FGA	FG%	3PM	3PA	3P%	FTM	FTA	FT%	ORB	DRB	TRB	AST	PF	DQ	STL	BLK	TO	MPG	PPG	RPG	APG	PCM
39-40	Hammond-N	26	....	....	148	68	....	....	....	....	....	12	....	....	....	....	....	....	....	....	....	....	....	....	5.7	....	....	....
40-41	Hammond-N	12	....	....	40	18	....	....	....	....	....	4	....	....	....	....	....	....	....	....	....	....	....	....	3.3	....	....	....
NBL Season Totals		38	....	....	188	86	....	....	....	....	....	16	....	....	....	....	....	....	....	....	....	....	....	....	4.9	....	....	....

• GOLA, Tom

Thomas Joseph (Mt. All-Around) Gola

Born: Jan. 13, 1933. Philadelphia, PA, United States. Height: 6'6". Weight: 205 lbs. Drafted: 1955 College: LaSalle HOF: 1976

YEAR	TEAM	GP	GS	MIN	PTS	FGM	FGA	FG%	3PM	3PA	3P%	FTM	FTA	FT%	ORB	DRB	TRB	AST	PF	DQ	STL	BLK	TO	MPG	PPG	RPG	APG	PCM
55-56	Philadelphia	68	....	2346	732	244	592	.412	....	....	....	244	333	.733	....	....	616	404	272	11	....	....	....	34.5	10.8	9.1	5.9	.554
57-58	Philadelphia	59	....	2126	813	295	711	.415	....	....	....	223	299	.746	....	....	639	327	225	11	....	....	....	36.0	13.8	10.8	5.5	.603
58-59	Philadelphia	64	....	2333	901	310	773	.401	....	....	....	281	357	.787	....	....	710	269	243	7	....	....	....	36.5	14.1	11.1	4.2	.558
59-60	Philadelphia	75	....	2870	1122	426	983	.433	....	....	....	270	340	.794	....	....	779	409	**311**	9	....	....	....	38.3	15.0	10.4	5.5	.577
60-61	Philadelphia	74	....	2712	1050	420	940	.447	....	....	....	210	281	.747	....	....	692	292	321	13	....	....	....	36.6	14.2	9.4	3.9	.514
61-62	Philadelphia	60	....	2462	820	322	765	.421	....	....	....	176	230	.765	....	....	587	295	267	16	....	....	....	41.0	13.7	9.8	4.9	.474
62-63	San Francisco	21	....	822	272	111	243	.457	....	....	....	50	66	.758	....	....	58	73	93	4	....	....	....	39.1	13.0	2.8	3.5	.315
62-63	New York	52	....	1848	624	252	548	.460	....	....	....	120	153	.784	....	....	259	225	202	5	....	....	....	35.5	12.0	5.0	4.3	.419
63-64	New York	74	....	2156	670	258	602	.429	....	....	....	154	212	.726	....	....	469	257	278	7	....	....	....	29.1	9.1	6.3	3.5	.441
64-65	New York	77	....	1727	541	204	455	.448	....	....	....	133	180	.739	....	....	319	220	269	8	....	....	....	22.4	7.0	4.1	2.9	.430
65-66	New York	74	....	1127	326	122	271	.450	....	....	....	82	105	.781	....	....	289	191	207	3	....	....	....	15.2	4.4	3.9	2.6	.513
NBA Season Totals		698	....	22529	7871	2964	6883	.431	....	....	....	1943	2556	.760	....	....	5417	2962	2688	94	....	....	....	32.3	11.3	7.8	4.2	....
55-56	Philadelphia	10	....	360	123	38	107	.355	....	....	....	47	60	.783	....	....	101	58	47	2	....	....	....	36.0	12.3	10.1	5.8	.546
57-58	Philadelphia	8	....	327	110	36	109	.330	....	....	....	38	51	.745	....	....	84	32	24	0	....	....	....	40.9	13.8	10.5	4.0	.444
59-60	Philadelphia	9	....	340	113	42	102	.412	....	....	....	29	36	.806	....	....	95	50	41	3	....	....	....	37.8	12.6	10.6	5.6	.540
60-61	Philadelphia	3	....	127	29	7	34	.206	....	....	....	15	20	.750	....	....	37	15	14	1	....	....	....	42.3	9.7	12.3	5.0	.378
61-62	Philadelphia	9	....	316	57	19	70	.271	....	....	....	19	25	.760	....	....	74	24	38	2	....	....	....	35.1	6.3	8.2	2.7	.275
NBA Playoff Totals		39	....	1470	432	142	422	.336	....	....	....	148	192	.771	....	....	391	179	164	8	....	....	....	37.7	11.1	10.0	4.6	....

• GOLDFADEN, Ben

Benjamin Paul Goldfaden

Born: Sept. 6, 1913. Height: 6'1". Weight: 185 lbs. Drafted: — College: George Washington

YEAR	TEAM	GP	GS	MIN	PTS	FGM	FGA	FG%	3PM	3PA	3P%	FTM	FTA	FT%	ORB	DRB	TRB	AST	PF	DQ	STL	BLK	TO	MPG	PPG	RPG	APG	PCM
46-47	Washington	2	....	....	2	0	2	.000	....	....	....	2	4	.500	....	....	....	0	3	....	....	....	....	....	1.0	....	0.0	....
NBA Season Totals		2	....	....	2	0	2	.000	....	....	....	2	4	.500	....	....	....	0	3	....	....	....	....	....	1.0	....	0.0	....

• GOLDSMITH, Jack

Jack (Jackie) Goldsmith

Born: 1922. Height: 5'7". Weight: 150 lbs. Drafted: — College: Long Island University

YEAR	TEAM	GP	GS	MIN	PTS	FGM	FGA	FG%	3PM	3PA	3P%	FTM	FTA	FT%	ORB	DRB	TRB	AST	PF	DQ	STL	BLK	TO	MPG	PPG	RPG	APG	PCM
47-48	Toledo-N	12	....	....	46	20	....	....	....	....	....	6	9	.667	....	....	....	....	....	....	....	....	....	....	3.8	....	....	....
NBL Season Totals		12	....	....	46	20	....	....	....	....	....	6	9	....	....	....	....	....	....	....	....	....	....	....	3.8	....	....	....

• GOLDWIRE, Anthony

Anthony Goldwire

Born: Sept. 6, 1971. West Palm Beach, FL, United States. Height: 6'1". Weight: 182 lbs. Drafted: 1994 College: Houston

YEAR	TEAM	GP	GS	MIN	PTS	FGM	FGA	FG%	3PM	3PA	3P%	FTM	FTA	FT%	ORB	DRB	TRB	AST	PF	DQ	STL	BLK	TO	MPG	PPG	RPG	APG	PCM
95-96	Charlotte	42	8	621	231	76	189	.402	33	83	.398	46	60	.767	8	35	43	112	79	0	16	0	63	14.8	5.5	1.0	2.7	.316
96-97	Charlotte	33	9	576	190	62	154	.403	36	82	.439	30	40	.750	3	35	38	94	58	1	19	1	40	17.5	5.8	1.2	2.8	.329
96-97	Denver	27	21	612	197	69	176	.392	28	71	.394	31	38	.816	9	37	46	125	46	0	14	1	35	22.7	7.3	1.7	4.6	.376
97-98	Denver	82	32	2212	751	269	636	.423	63	164	.384	150	186	.806	40	107	147	277	149	0	86	7	82	27.0	9.2	1.8	3.4	.351
00-01	Denver	20	0	201	82	30	80	.375	9	34	.265	13	17	.765	1	11	12	34	13	0	9	0	15	10.1	4.1	0.6	1.7	.360
02-03	San Antonio	10	0	51	12	5	18	.278	2	8	.250	0	2	.000	0	3	3	3	5	0	3	0	2	5.1	1.2	0.3	0.3	.077
02-03	Washington	5	0	34	13	4	7	.571	1	1	1.000	4	5	.800	0	3	3	1	1	0	0	0	4	6.8	2.6	0.6	0.2	.281
NBA Season Totals		219	70	4307	1476	515	1260	.409	172	443	.388	274	348	.787	61	231	292	646	351	1	147	9	241	19.7	6.7	1.3	2.9	....

GONDREZICK, Glen

Glen Michael (Gondo) Gondrezick

Born: Aug. 30, 1955. Boulder, CO, United States.   Height: 6'6".   Weight: 218 lbs.   Drafted: 1977   College: UNLV

YEAR	TEAM	GP	GS	MIN	PTS	FGM	FGA	FG%	3PM	3PA	3P%	FTM	FTA	FT%	ORB	DRB	TRB	AST	PF	DQ	STL	BLK	TO	MPG	PPG	RPG	APG	PCM
77-78	New York	72	....	1017	345	131	339	.386	....	....	....	83	121	.686	92	158	250	83	181	0	56	18	79	14.1	4.8	3.5	1.2	.369
78-79	New York	75	....	1602	377	161	326	.494	....	....	....	55	97	.567	147	277	424	106	226	1	98	18	98	21.4	5.0	5.7	1.4	.388
79-80	Denver	59	....	1020	390	148	286	.517	2	6	.333	92	121	.760	107	152	259	81	119	0	68	16	59	17.3	6.6	4.4	1.4	.533
80-81	Denver	73	....	1077	422	155	329	.471	0	2	.000	112	137	.818	136	171	307	83	185	2	91	20	66	14.8	5.8	4.2	1.1	.538
81-82	Denver	80	0	1699	660	250	495	.505	0	3	.000	160	217	.737	140	283	423	152	229	0	92	36	104	21.2	8.3	5.3	1.9	.517
82-83	Denver	76	2	1130	350	134	294	.456	0	3	.000	82	114	.719	108	193	301	100	161	0	80	9	46	14.9	4.6	4.0	1.3	.477
NBA Season Totals		435	2	7545	2544	979	2069	.473	2	14	.143	584	807	.724	730	1234	1964	605	1101	3	485	117	452	17.3	5.8	4.5	1.4	....
77-78	New York	6	....	70	25	10	19	.526	....	....	....	5	8	.625	7	10	17	6	12	0	5	0	6	11.7	4.2	2.8	1.0	.447
81-82	Denver	3	0	51	18	8	20	.400	0	1	.000	2	3	.667	3	5	8	9	8	0	2	1	0	17.0	6.0	2.7	3.0	.444
82-83	Denver	6	0	66	15	7	19	.368	0	0	.000	1	2	.500	12	8	20	4	7	0	0	1	1	11.0	2.5	3.3	0.7	.348
NBA Playoff Totals		15	0	187	58	25	58	.431	0	1	.000	8	13	.615	22	23	45	19	27	0	7	2	7	12.5	3.9	3.0	1.3	....

GONDREZICK, Grant

Grant Gondrezick

Born: Jan. 19, 1963. Boulder, CO, United States.   Height: 6'5".   Weight: 205 lbs.   Drafted: 1986   College: Pepperdine

YEAR	TEAM	GP	GS	MIN	PTS	FGM	FGA	FG%	3PM	3PA	3P%	FTM	FTA	FT%	ORB	DRB	TRB	AST	PF	DQ	STL	BLK	TO	MPG	PPG	RPG	APG	PCM
86-87	Phoenix	64	1	836	349	135	300	.450	4	17	.235	75	107	.701	47	63	110	81	91	0	25	4	58	13.1	5.5	1.7	1.3	.359
88-89	LA Clippers	27	0	244	105	38	95	.400	3	11	.273	26	40	.650	15	21	36	34	36	0	13	1	16	9.0	3.9	1.3	1.3	.396
NBA Season Totals		91	1	1080	454	173	395	.438	7	28	.250	101	147	.687	62	84	146	115	127	0	38	5	74	11.9	5.0	1.6	1.3	....

GOODEN, Drew

Drew Gooden

Born: Sept. 24, 1981. Oakland, CA, United States.   Height: 6'10".   Weight: 230 lbs.   Drafted: 2002   College: Kansas

YEAR	TEAM	GP	GS	MIN	PTS	FGM	FGA	FG%	3PM	3PA	3P%	FTM	FTA	FT%	ORB	DRB	TRB	AST	PF	DQ	STL	BLK	TO	MPG	PPG	RPG	APG	PCM
02-03	Memphis	51	29	1329	616	255	576	.443	14	46	.304	92	132	.697	105	190	295	63	121	1	38	22	105	26.1	12.1	5.8	1.2	.412
02-03	Orlando	19	18	544	259	100	201	.498	0	2	.000	59	80	.738	58	102	160	20	51	1	15	13	45	28.6	13.6	8.4	1.1	.526
NBA Season Totals		70	47	1873	875	355	777	.457	14	48	.292	151	212	.712	163	292	455	83	172	2	53	35	150	26.8	12.5	6.5	1.2	....
02-03	Orlando	7	7	232	98	36	90	.400	0	3	.000	26	36	.722	28	61	89	4	23	1	3	6	12	33.1	14.0	12.7	0.6	.502
NBA Playoff Totals		7	7	232	98	36	90	.400	0	3	.000	26	36	.722	28	61	89	4	23	1	3	6	12	33.1	14.0	12.7	0.6	....

GOODRICH, Gail

Gail Charles (Stumpy) Goodrich Jr.

Born: Apr. 23, 1943. Los Angeles, CA, United States.   Height: 6'1".   Weight: 170 lbs.   Drafted: 1965   College: UCLA   HOF: 1996

YEAR	TEAM	GP	GS	MIN	PTS	FGM	FGA	FG%	3PM	3PA	3P%	FTM	FTA	FT%	ORB	DRB	TRB	AST	PF	DQ	STL	BLK	TO	MPG	PPG	RPG	APG	PCM
65-66	LA Lakers	65	....	1008	509	203	503	.404	....	....	....	103	149	.691	....	....	130	103	103	1	....	....	....	15.5	7.8	2.0	1.6	.439
66-67	LA Lakers	77	....	1780	957	352	776	.454	....	....	....	253	337	.751	....	....	251	210	294	3	....	....	....	23.1	12.4	3.3	2.7	.517
67-68	LA Lakers	79	....	2057	1092	395	812	.486	....	....	....	302	392	.770	....	....	199	205	228	2	....	....	....	26.0	13.8	2.5	2.6	.504
68-69	Phoenix	81	....	3236	1931	718	1746	.411	....	....	....	495	663	.747	....	....	437	518	253	3	....	....	....	40.0	23.8	5.4	6.4	.576
69-70	Phoenix	81	....	3234	1624	568	1251	.454	....	....	....	488	604	.808	....	....	340	605	251	3	....	....	....	39.9	20.0	4.2	7.5	.568
70-71	LA Lakers	79	....	2808	1380	558	1174	.475	....	....	....	264	343	.770	....	....	260	380	258	3	....	....	....	35.5	17.5	3.3	4.8	.485
71-72	LA Lakers	82	....	3040	2127	826	1695	.487	....	....	....	475	559	.850	....	....	295	365	210	0	....	....	....	37.1	25.9	3.6	4.5	.631
72-73	LA Lakers	76	....	2697	1814	750	1615	.464	....	....	....	314	374	.840	....	....	263	332	193	1	....	....	....	35.5	23.9	3.5	4.4	.581
73-74	LA Lakers	82	....	3061	2076	784	1773	.442	....	....	....	**508**	**588**	.864	95	155	250	427	227	3	126	12	....	37.3	25.3	3.0	5.2	.590
74-75	LA Lakers	72	....	2668	1630	656	1429	.459	....	....	....	318	378	.841	96	123	219	420	214	1	102	6	....	37.1	22.6	3.0	5.8	.571
75-76	LA Lakers	75	....	2646	1459	583	1321	.441	....	....	....	293	346	.847	94	120	214	421	238	3	123	17	....	35.3	19.5	2.9	5.6	.516
76-77	New Orleans	27	....	609	340	136	305	.446	....	....	....	68	85	.800	25	36	61	74	43	0	22	2	....	22.6	12.6	2.3	2.7	.501
77-78	New Orleans	81	....	2553	1304	520	1050	.495	....	....	....	264	332	.795	75	102	177	388	186	0	82	22	203	31.5	16.1	2.2	4.8	.483
78-79	New Orleans	74	....	2130	938	382	850	.449	....	....	....	174	204	.853	68	115	183	357	177	1	90	13	185	28.8	12.7	2.5	4.8	.427
NBA Season Totals		1031	....	33527	19181	7431	16300	.456	....	....	....	4319	5354	.807	453	651	3279	4805	2875	24	545	72	388	32.5	18.6	3.2	4.7	....
65-66	LA Lakers	11	....	290	115	43	92	.467	....	....	....	29	43	.674	....	....	42	33	35	0	....	....	....	26.4	10.5	3.8	3.0	.450
66-67	LA Lakers	3	....	81	33	11	31	.355	....	....	....	11	18	.611	....	....	9	10	5	0	....	....	....	27.0	11.0	3.0	3.3	.389
67-68	LA Lakers	10	....	100	60	23	47	.489	....	....	....	14	18	.778	....	....	14	14	10	0	....	....	....	10.0	6.0	1.4	1.4	.633
69-70	Phoenix	7	....	265	142	56	118	.475	....	....	....	30	35	.857	....	....	32	38	21	0	....	....	....	37.9	20.3	4.6	5.4	.554
70-71	LA Lakers	12	....	518	305	105	247	.425	....	....	....	95	113	.841	....	....	38	91	38	0	....	....	....	43.2	25.4	3.2	7.6	.570
71-72	LA Lakers	15	....	575	357	130	292	.445	....	....	....	97	108	.898	....	....	38	50	50	0	....	....	....	38.3	23.8	2.5	3.3	.487
72-73	LA Lakers	17	....	604	340	139	310	.448	....	....	....	62	79	.785	....	....	61	67	53	1	....	....	....	35.5	20.0	3.6	3.9	.484
73-74	LA Lakers	5	....	189	98	35	90	.389	....	....	....	28	33	.848	7	9	16	30	7	0	7	1	....	37.8	19.6	3.2	6.0	.498
NBA Playoff Totals		80	....	2622	1450	542	1227	.442	....	....	....	366	447	.819	7	9	250	333	219	1	7	1	....	32.8	18.1	3.1	4.2	....

GOODRICH, Steve

Steven Withington Goodrich

Born: Mar. 18, 1976. Philadelphia, PA, United States.   Height: 6'10".   Weight: 220 lbs.   Drafted: —   College: Princeton

YEAR	TEAM	GP	GS	MIN	PTS	FGM	FGA	FG%	3PM	3PA	3P%	FTM	FTA	FT%	ORB	DRB	TRB	AST	PF	DQ	STL	BLK	TO	MPG	PPG	RPG	APG	PCM
00-01	Chicago	12	0	133	19	7	18	.389	1	3	.333	4	7	.571	7	14	21	6	14	0	2	1	8	11.1	1.6	1.8	0.5	.169
01-02	New Jersey	9	0	50	5	2	10	.200	0	0	.000	1	2	.500	1	4	5	5	10	0	1	2	3	5.6	0.6	0.6	0.6	.055
NBA Season Totals		21	0	183	24	9	28	.321	1	3	.333	5	9	.556	8	18	26	11	24	0	3	3	11	8.7	1.1	1.2	0.5	....

GOODWIN, Pop

Wilfred R. (Pop) Goodwin

Born: Dec. 22, 1920.   Height: 6'2".   Weight: 203 lbs.   Drafted: —   College: none

YEAR	TEAM	GP	GS	MIN	PTS	FGM	FGA	FG%	3PM	3PA	3P%	FTM	FTA	FT%	ORB	DRB	TRB	AST	PF	DQ	STL	BLK	TO	MPG	PPG	RPG	APG	PCM
45-46	Sheboygan-N	2	....	....	3	1	....	....	....	....	....	1	....	....	....	....	....	....	....	....	....	....	....	1.5	....	....	....	....
46-47	Providence	55	....	....	256	98	348	.282	....	....	....	60	75	.800	....	....	15	94	....	....	....	....	....	....	4.7	....	0.3	....
47-48	Providence	24	....	....	91	36	155	.232	....	....	....	19	27	.704	....	....	7	36	....	....	....	....	....	....	3.8	....	0.3	....
NBA Season Totals		79	....	....	347	134	503	.266	....	....	....	79	102	.775	....	....	22	130	....	....	....	....	....	....	4.4	....	0.3	....
NBL Season Totals		2	....	....	3	1	....	....	....	....	....	1	....	....	....	....	....	....	....	....	....	....	....	....	1.5	....	....	....
Career Totals		81	....	....	350	135	503	....	....	....	....	80	102	....	....	....	22	130	....	....	....	....	....	....	4.3	....	0.3	....

• GORDON, Lancaster
Lancaster Gordon

Born: June 24, 1962. Jackson, MS, United States. Height: 6'3". Weight: 185 lbs. Drafted: 1984 College: Louisville

YEAR	TEAM	GP	GS	MIN	PTS	FGM	FGA	FG%	3PM	3PA	3P%	FTM	FTA	FT%	ORB	DRB	TRB	AST	PF	DQ	STL	BLK	TO	MPG	PPG	RPG	APG	PCM
84-85	LA Clippers	63	1	682	259	110	287	.383	2	9	.222	37	49	.755	26	35	61	88	61	0	33	6	69	10.8	4.1	1.0	1.4	.268
85-86	LA Clippers	60	1	704	312	130	345	.377	7	28	.250	45	56	.804	24	44	68	60	91	1	33	10	60	11.7	5.2	1.1	1.0	.251
86-87	LA Clippers	70	4	1130	526	221	545	.406	14	48	.292	70	95	.737	64	62	126	139	106	1	61	13	105	16.1	7.5	1.8	2.0	.354
87-88	LA Clippers	8	0	65	28	11	31	.355	0	0	.000	6	6	1.000	2	2	4	7	8	0	1	2	4	8.1	3.5	0.5	0.9	.245
NBA Season Totals		201	6	2581	1125	472	1208	.391	23	85	.271	158	206	.767	116	143	259	294	266	2	128	31	238	12.8	5.6	1.3	1.5	....

• GORDON, Paul
Paul C. Gordon Jr.

Born: Apr. 8, 1927. Height: 6'3". Weight: 185 lbs. Drafted: — College: Notre Dame

YEAR	TEAM	GP	GS	MIN	PTS	FGM	FGA	FG%	3PM	3PA	3P%	FTM	FTA	FT%	ORB	DRB	TRB	AST	PF	DQ	STL	BLK	TO	MPG	PPG	RPG	APG	PCM
49-50	Baltimore	4	....	....	3	0	6	.000	....	....	....	3	5	.600	....	....	....	3	3	....	....	....	....	....	0.8	....	0.8	....
NBA Season Totals		4	....	....	3	0	6	.000	....	....	....	3	5	.600	....	....	....	3	3	....	....	....	....	....	0.8	....	0.8	....

• GOTTLIEB, Leo
Leo (Ace) Gottlieb

Born: Nov. 28, 1920. New York, NY, United States. Died: Aug.1972. Height: 5'11". Weight: 180 lbs. Drafted: — College: none

YEAR	TEAM	GP	GS	MIN	PTS	FGM	FGA	FG%	3PM	3PA	3P%	FTM	FTA	FT%	ORB	DRB	TRB	AST	PF	DQ	STL	BLK	TO	MPG	PPG	RPG	APG	PCM
46-47	New York	57	....	....	334	149	494	.302	....	....	....	36	55	.655	....	....	....	24	71	....	....	....	....	....	5.9	....	0.4	....
47-48	New York	27	....	....	131	59	288	.205	....	....	....	13	21	.619	....	....	....	12	36	....	....	....	....	....	4.9	....	0.4	....
NBA Season Totals		84	....	....	465	208	782	.266	....	....	....	49	76	.645	....	....	....	36	107	....	....	....	....	....	5.5	....	0.4	....
46-47	New York	4	....	....	24	10	39	.256	....	....	....	4	6	.667	....	....	....	1	6	....	....	....	....	....	6.0	....	0.3	....
NBA Playoff Totals		4	....	....	24	10	39	.256	....	....	....	4	6	.667	....	....	....	1	6	....	....	....	....	....	6.0	....	0.3	....

• GOVAN, Gerald
Gerald Govan

Born: Jan. 2, 1942. Jersey City, NJ, United States. Height: 6'10". Weight: 220 lbs. Drafted: — College: St. Mary of the Plains

YEAR	TEAM	GP	GS	MIN	PTS	FGM	FGA	FG%	3PM	3PA	3P%	FTM	FTA	FT%	ORB	DRB	TRB	AST	PF	DQ	STL	BLK	TO	MPG	PPG	RPG	APG	PCM
67-68	New Orleans-A	78	....	1587	392	156	390	.400	1	1	1.000	79	131	.603	....	....	596	95	156	2	....	....	100	20.3	5.0	7.6	1.2	.452
68-69	New Orleans-A	77	....	1902	557	211	537	.393	1	4	.250	134	208	.644	210	491	701	150	238	4	....	....	162	24.7	7.2	9.1	1.9	.482
69-70	New Orleans-A	84	....	3701	1053	422	1044	.404	1	11	.091	208	285	.730	285	932	1217	385	273	5	....	....	272	44.1	12.5	14.5	4.6	.501
70-71	Memphis-A	84	....	**3698**	712	296	794	.373	1	4	.250	119	191	.623	277	861	1138	407	284	3	....	....	276	**44.0**	8.5	13.5	4.8	.425
71-72	Memphis-A	83	....	3414	716	277	719	.385	0	0	.000	162	230	.704	310	872	1182	348	260	5	....	....	241	41.1	8.6	14.2	4.2	.472
72-73	Utah-A	84	....	2408	539	229	530	.432	0	0	.000	81	135	.600	175	620	795	250	279	2	....	....	168	28.7	6.4	9.5	3.0	.460
73-74	Utah-A	83	....	2766	583	255	541	.471	0	2	.000	73	106	.689	142	586	728	245	260	....	60	50	156	33.3	7.0	8.8	3.0	.404
74-75	Utah-A	84	....	2791	562	239	602	.397	1	2	.500	83	105	.790	121	480	601	230	217	....	72	36	195	33.2	6.7	7.2	2.7	.331
75-76	Virginia-A	24	....	658	137	57	131	.435	0	0	.000	23	28	.821	44	117	161	54	65	....	7	11	47	27.4	5.7	6.7	2.3	.370
ABA Season Totals		681	....	22925	5251	2142	5288	.405	5	24	.208	962	1419	.678	1564	4959	7119	2164	2032	21	139	97	1617	33.7	7.7	10.5	3.2	....
67-68	New Orleans-A	17	....	290	68	24	77	.312	0	0	.000	20	32	.625	....	....	116	23	46	1	....	....	34	17.1	4.0	6.8	1.4	.425
68-69	New Orleans-A	11	....	317	123	51	114	.447	1	2	.500	20	27	.741	....	....	108	28	40	1	....	....	37	28.8	11.2	9.8	2.5	.547
70-71	Memphis-A	4	....	182	31	11	32	.344	0	0	.000	9	10	.900	27	34	61	22	18	0	....	....	13	45.5	7.8	15.3	5.5	.449
72-73	Utah-A	10	....	330	68	28	78	.359	0	0	.000	12	15	.800	19	93	112	36	37	1	....	....	26	33.0	6.8	11.2	3.6	.441
73-74	Utah-A	18	....	714	161	74	184	.402	0	0	.000	13	20	.650	49	197	246	73	65	....	18	22	34	39.7	8.9	13.7	4.1	.462
74-75	Utah-A	6	....	97	4	1	12	.083	0	0	.000	2	5	.400	3	11	14	8	17	....	1	4	7	16.2	0.7	2.3	1.3	.069
ABA Playoff Totals		66	....	1930	455	189	497	.380	1	2	.500	76	109	.697	98	335	657	190	223	3	19	26	151	29.2	6.9	10.0	2.9	....

• GOVEDARICA, Bato
Bato Zdravko Govedarica

Born: Apr. 17, 1928. Height: 5'11". Weight: 185 lbs. Drafted: 1951 College: DePaul

YEAR	TEAM	GP	GS	MIN	PTS	FGM	FGA	FG%	3PM	3PA	3P%	FTM	FTA	FT%	ORB	DRB	TRB	AST	PF	DQ	STL	BLK	TO	MPG	PPG	RPG	APG	PCM
53-54	Syracuse	23	....	258	75	25	79	.316	....	....	....	25	37	.676	....	....	18	24	44	1	....	....	....	11.2	3.3	0.8	1.0	.235
NBA Season Totals		23	....	258	75	25	79	.316	....	....	....	25	37	.676	....	....	18	24	44	1	....	....	....	11.2	3.3	0.8	1.0	....

• GRABOSKI, Joe
Joseph W. (Grabbo) Graboski

Born: Jan. 15, 1930. Died: July2, 1998. Height: 6'7". Weight: 195 lbs. Drafted: — College: none (HS: Tuley, IL)

YEAR	TEAM	GP	GS	MIN	PTS	FGM	FGA	FG%	3PM	3PA	3P%	FTM	FTA	FT%	ORB	DRB	TRB	AST	PF	DQ	STL	BLK	TO	MPG	PPG	RPG	APG	PCM
48-49	Chicago	45	....	....	125	54	157	.344	....	....	....	17	49	.347	....	....	....	18	86	....	....	....	....	....	2.8	....	0.4	....
49-50	Chicago	57	....	....	203	75	247	.304	....	....	....	53	89	.596	....	....	....	37	95	....	....	....	....	....	3.6	....	0.6	....
51-52	Indianapolis	66	....	2439	904	320	827	.387	....	....	....	264	396	.667	....	....	655	130	254	10	....	....	....	37.0	13.7	9.9	2.0	.426
52-53	Indianapolis	69	....	2769	894	272	799	.340	....	....	....	350	513	.682	....	....	687	156	303	18	....	....	....	40.1	13.0	10.0	2.3	.376
53-54	Philadelphia	71	....	2759	944	354	1000	.354	....	....	....	236	350	.674	....	....	670	163	223	4	....	....	....	38.9	13.3	9.4	2.3	.381
54-55	Philadelphia	70	....	2515	954	373	1096	.340	....	....	....	208	303	.686	....	....	636	182	259	8	....	....	....	35.9	13.6	9.1	2.6	.391
55-56	Philadelphia	72	....	2375	1034	397	1075	.369	....	....	....	240	340	.706	....	....	642	190	272	5	....	....	....	33.0	14.4	8.9	2.6	.463
56-57	Philadelphia	72	....	2501	1032	390	1118	.349	....	....	....	252	322	.783	....	....	614	140	244	5	....	....	....	34.7	14.3	8.5	1.9	.402
57-58	Philadelphia	72	....	2077	909	341	1017	.335	....	....	....	227	303	.749	....	....	570	125	249	3	....	....	....	28.8	12.6	7.9	1.7	.420
58-59	Philadelphia	72	....	2482	1058	394	1116	.353	....	....	....	270	360	.750	....	....	751	148	249	5	....	....	....	34.5	14.7	10.4	2.1	.458
59-60	Philadelphia	73	....	1269	565	217	583	.372	....	....	....	131	174	.753	....	....	358	111	147	1	....	....	....	17.4	7.7	4.9	1.5	.493
60-61	Philadelphia	68	....	1011	465	169	507	.333	....	....	....	127	183	.694	....	....	262	74	148	2	....	....	....	14.9	6.8	3.9	1.1	.417
61-62	StL/Chi	15	....	145	75	29	88	.330	....	....	....	17	27	.630	....	....	49	8	17	0	....	....	....	9.7	5.0	3.3	0.5	.458
61-62	Syracuse	23	....	323	118	48	133	.361	....	....	....	22	38	.579	....	....	105	20	45	0	....	....	....	14.0	5.1	4.6	0.9	.415
NBA Season Totals		845	....	22665	9280	3433	9763	.352	....	....	....	2414	3447	.700	....	....	5999	1502	2591	61	....	....	....	26.8	11.0	7.1	1.8	....
48-49	Chicago	1	....	....	0	0	6	.000	....	....	....	0	0	.000	....	....	....	0	1	....	....	....	....	....	0.0	....	0.0	....
49-50	Chicago	1	....	....	0	0	0	.000	....	....	....	0	0	.000	....	....	....	0	0	....	....	....	....	....	0.0	....	0.0	....
51-52	Indianapolis	2	....	96	46	19	48	.396	....	....	....	8	15	.533	....	....	23	3	7	0	....	....	....	48.0	23.0	11.5	1.5	.423
52-53	Indianapolis	2	....	76	34	14	28	.500	....	....	....	6	8	.750	....	....	16	0	5	0	....	....	....	38.0	17.0	8.0	0.0	.433
55-56	Philadelphia	10	....	313	132	53	154	.344	....	....	....	26	35	.743	....	....	94	27	37	2	....	....	....	31.3	13.2	9.4	2.7	.456
56-57	Philadelphia	2	....	91	35	13	40	.325	....	....	....	9	11	.818	....	....	22	4	7	0	....	....	....	45.5	17.5	11.0	2.0	.362
57-58	Philadelphia	8	....	252	98	40	138	.290	....	....	....	18	23	.783	....	....	82	30	21	0	....	....	....	31.5	12.3	10.3	3.8	.456
59-60	Philadelphia	9	....	129	41	17	58	.293	....	....	....	7	9	.778	....	....	30	9	23	0	....	....	....	14.3	4.6	3.3	1.0	.267

YEAR	TEAM	GP	GS	MIN	PTS	FGM	FGA	FG%	3PM	3PA	3P%	FTM	FTA	FT%	ORB	DRB	TRB	AST	PF	DQ	STL	BLK	TO	MPG	PPG	RPG	APG	PCM
60-61	Philadelphia	1	....	1	0	0	0	.000	....	....	....	0	0	.000	....	....	0	0	0	0	....	....	....	1.0	0.0	0.0	0.0	.000
61-62	Syracuse	4	....	24	3	1	7	.143	....	....	....	1	1	1.000	....	....	4	0	3	0	....	....	....	6.0	0.8	1.0	0.0	.011
NBA Playoff Totals		40	....	982	389	157	479	.328	....	....	....	75	102	.735	....	....	271	73	104	2	....	....	....	24.6	9.7	6.8	1.8	....

• GRACE, Ricky

Ricky Grace

Born: Aug. 20, 1967. Dallas, TX, United States.　　Height: 6'1".　　Weight: 180 lbs.　　Drafted: 1988　　College: Oklahoma

YEAR	TEAM	GP	GS	MIN	PTS	FGM	FGA	FG%	3PM	3PA	3P%	FTM	FTA	FT%	ORB	DRB	TRB	AST	PF	DQ	STL	BLK	TO	MPG	PPG	RPG	APG	PCM
93-94	Atlanta	3	0	8	4	2	3	.667	0	0	.000	0	2	.000	0	1	1	1	3	0	0	0	0	2.7	1.3	0.3	0.3	.349
NBA Season Totals		3	0	8	4	2	3	.667	0	0	.000	0	2	.000	0	1	1	1	3	0	0	0	0	2.7	1.3	0.3	0.3	....

• GRAF, Irwin

Irwin (Moose) Graf

Born: 1917.　　Height: 6'3".　　Weight: 200 lbs.　　Drafted: —　　College: Marquette

YEAR	TEAM	GP	GS	MIN	PTS	FGM	FGA	FG%	3PM	3PA	3P%	FTM	FTA	FT%	ORB	DRB	TRB	AST	PF	DQ	STL	BLK	TO	MPG	PPG	RPG	APG	PCM
38-39	Sheboygan-N	1	....	....	9	3	....	....	....	....	....	3	....	....	....	....	....	....	....	....	....	....	....	....	9.0	....	....	....
42-43	Sheboygan-N	5	....	....	4	2	....	....	....	....	....	0	....	....	....	....	....	....	....	....	....	....	....	....	0.8	....	....	....
NBL Season Totals		6	....	....	13	5	....	....	....	....	....	3	....	....	....	....	....	....	....	....	....	....	....	....	2.2	....	....	....

• GRAFFT, Fred

Fred Grafft

Born: 1915.　　Height: 5'9".　　Weight: —　　Drafted: —　　College: Gallagher Business School

YEAR	TEAM	GP	GS	MIN	PTS	FGM	FGA	FG%	3PM	3PA	3P%	FTM	FTA	FT%	ORB	DRB	TRB	AST	PF	DQ	STL	BLK	TO	MPG	PPG	RPG	APG	PCM
37-38	Kankakee-N	10	....	....	86	33	....	....	....	....	....	20	....	....	....	....	....	....	....	....	....	....	....	....	8.6	....	....	....
NBL Season Totals		10	....	....	86	33	....	....	....	....	....	20	....	....	....	....	....	....	....	....	....	....	....	....	8.6	....	....	....

• GRAHAM, Calvin

Calvin J. Graham

Born: June 7, 1944.　　Height: 6'2".　　Weight: 195 lbs.　　Drafted: —　　College: Gannon

YEAR	TEAM	GP	GS	MIN	PTS	FGM	FGA	FG%	3PM	3PA	3P%	FTM	FTA	FT%	ORB	DRB	TRB	AST	PF	DQ	STL	BLK	TO	MPG	PPG	RPG	APG	PCM
67-68	Pittsburgh-A	8	....	52	13	4	14	.286	0	0	.000	5	8	.625	....	....	10	0	12	0	....	....	1	6.5	1.6	1.3	0.0	.130
ABA Season Totals		8	....	52	13	4	14	.286	0	0	.000	5	8	.625	....	....	10	0	12	0	....	....	1	6.5	1.6	1.3	0.0	....

• GRAHAM, Greg

Gregory Lawrence Graham

Born: Nov. 26, 1970. Indianapolis, IN, United States.　　Height: 6'4".　　Weight: 174 lbs.　　Drafted: 1993　　College: Indiana

YEAR	TEAM	GP	GS	MIN	PTS	FGM	FGA	FG%	3PM	3PA	3P%	FTM	FTA	FT%	ORB	DRB	TRB	AST	PF	DQ	STL	BLK	TO	MPG	PPG	RPG	APG	PCM
93-94	Philadelphia	70	6	889	338	122	305	.400	2	25	.080	92	110	.836	21	65	86	66	54	0	61	4	63	12.7	4.8	1.2	0.9	.325
94-95	Philadelphia	50	7	775	251	95	223	.426	6	28	.214	55	73	.753	19	43	62	66	76	0	29	6	50	15.5	5.0	1.2	1.3	.259
95-96	Philadelphia	8	3	128	56	17	32	.531	7	14	.500	15	17	.882	5	10	15	11	16	0	5	0	17	16.0	7.0	1.9	1.4	.374
95-96	New Jersey	45	2	485	184	61	161	.379	25	68	.368	37	51	.725	12	30	42	41	48	0	20	1	27	10.8	4.1	0.9	0.9	.285
96-97	Seattle	28	0	197	93	29	80	.363	9	31	.290	26	40	.650	2	11	13	11	12	0	12	1	11	7.0	3.3	0.5	0.4	.300
97-98	Cleveland	6	0	56	16	7	12	.583	0	3	.000	2	2	1.000	0	1	1	6	7	0	1	0	10	9.3	2.7	0.2	1.0	.132
NBA Season Totals		207	18	2530	938	331	813	.407	49	169	.290	227	293	.775	59	160	219	201	213	0	128	12	178	12.2	4.5	1.1	1.0	....
96-97	Seattle	6	0	43	12	4	14	.286	1	4	.250	3	4	.750	0	5	5	6	5	0	2	0	1	7.2	2.0	0.8	1.0	.276
NBA Playoff Totals		6	0	43	12	4	14	.286	1	4	.250	3	4	.750	0	5	5	6	5	0	2	0	1	7.2	2.0	0.8	1.0	....

• GRAHAM, Mal

Robert Malcolm (Mal) Graham

Born: Feb. 23, 1945.　　Height: 6'1".　　Weight: 185 lbs.　　Drafted: 1967　　College: New York University

YEAR	TEAM	GP	GS	MIN	PTS	FGM	FGA	FG%	3PM	3PA	3P%	FTM	FTA	FT%	ORB	DRB	TRB	AST	PF	DQ	STL	BLK	TO	MPG	PPG	RPG	APG	PCM
67-68	Boston	48	....	786	290	117	272	.430	....	....	....	56	88	.636	....	....	94	61	123	0	....	....	....	16.4	6.0	2.0	1.3	.322
68-69	Boston	22	....	103	37	13	55	.236	....	....	....	11	14	.786	....	....	24	14	27	0	....	....	....	4.7	1.7	1.1	0.6	.250
NBA Season Totals		70	....	889	327	130	327	.398	....	....	....	67	102	.657	....	....	118	75	150	0	....	....	....	12.7	4.7	1.7	1.1	....
67-68	Boston	5	....	22	5	2	5	.400	....	....	....	1	3	.333	....	....	4	1	3	0	....	....	....	4.4	1.0	0.8	0.2	.228
68-69	Boston	2	....	3	0	0	2	.000	....	....	....	0	0	.000	....	....	0	1	0	0	....	....	....	1.5	0.0	0.0	0.5	-.169
NBA Playoff Totals		7	....	25	5	2	7	.286	....	....	....	1	3	.333	....	....	4	2	3	0	....	....	....	3.6	0.7	0.6	0.3	....

• GRAHAM, Orlando

Orlando Graham

Born: May 5, 1965. Montgomery, AL, United States.　　Height: 6'8".　　Weight: 220 lbs.　　Drafted: 1988　　College: Auburn-Montgomery

YEAR	TEAM	GP	GS	MIN	PTS	FGM	FGA	FG%	3PM	3PA	3P%	FTM	FTA	FT%	ORB	DRB	TRB	AST	PF	DQ	STL	BLK	TO	MPG	PPG	RPG	APG	PCM
88-89	Golden State	7	0	22	8	3	10	.300	0	0	.000	2	4	.500	8	3	11	0	6	0	0	0	2	3.1	1.1	1.6	0.0	.279
NBA Season Totals		7	0	22	8	3	10	.300	0	0	.000	2	4	.500	8	3	11	0	6	0	0	0	2	3.1	1.1	1.6	0.0	....
88-89	Golden State	2	0	8	3	1	2	.500	0	0	.000	1	2	.500	0	1	1	0	0	0	0	0	1	4.0	1.5	0.5	0.0	.201
NBA Playoff Totals		2	0	8	3	1	2	.500	0	0	.000	1	2	.500	0	1	1	0	0	0	0	0	1	4.0	1.5	0.5	0.0	....

• GRAHAM, Otto

Otto Everett Graham Jr.

Born: Dec. 6, 1921. Waukegan, IL, United States.　　Height: 6'1".　　Weight: 190 lbs.　　Drafted: —　　College: Northwestern

YEAR	TEAM	GP	GS	MIN	PTS	FGM	FGA	FG%	3PM	3PA	3P%	FTM	FTA	FT%	ORB	DRB	TRB	AST	PF	DQ	STL	BLK	TO	MPG	PPG	RPG	APG	PCM
45-46	Rochester-N	32	....	....	165	59	....	....	....	....	....	47	73	.644	....	....	....	....	....	....	....	....	....	....	5.2	....	....	....
NBL Season Totals		32	....	....	165	59	....	....	....	....	....	47	73		....	....	....	....	....	....	....	....	....	....	5.2	....	....	....
45-46	Rochester-N	5	....	....	6	3	....	....	....	....	....	0	0	.000	....	....	....	....	....	....	....	....	....	....	1.2	....	....	....
NBL Playoff Totals		5	....	....	6	3	....	....	....	....	....	0	0		....	....	....	....	....	....	....	....	....	....	1.2	....	....	....

YEAR	TEAM	GP	GS	MIN	PTS	FGM	FGA	FG%	3PM	3PA	3P%	FTM	FTA	FT%	ORB	DRB	TRB	AST	PF	DQ	STL	BLK	TO	MPG	PPG	RPG	APG	PCM

• GRAHAM, Paul

Paul (Snoop) Graham

Born: Nov. 28, 1967. Philadelphia, PA, United States.   Height: 6'6".   Weight: 200 lbs.   Drafted: —   College: Ohio University

YEAR	TEAM	GP	GS	MIN	PTS	FGM	FGA	FG%	3PM	3PA	3P%	FTM	FTA	FT%	ORB	DRB	TRB	AST	PF	DQ	STL	BLK	TO	MPG	PPG	RPG	APG	PCM
91-92	Atlanta	78	9	1718	791	305	682	.447	55	141	.390	126	170	.741	72	159	231	175	193	3	96	21	94	22.0	10.1	3.0	2.2	.439
92-93	Atlanta	80	11	1508	650	256	560	.457	42	141	.298	96	131	.733	61	129	190	164	185	0	86	6	120	18.9	8.1	2.4	2.1	.391
93-94	Atlanta	21	0	128	58	21	57	.368	3	13	.231	13	17	.765	4	8	12	13	11	0	4	5	4	6.1	2.8	0.6	0.6	.373
NBA Season Totals		179	20	3354	1499	582	1299	.448	100	295	.339	235	318	.739	137	296	433	352	389	3	186	32	218	18.7	8.4	2.4	2.0	....
92-93	Atlanta	2	0	27	4	2	8	.250	0	2	.000	0	0	.000	1	2	3	2	2	0	4	0	2	13.5	2.0	1.5	1.0	.158
93-94	Atlanta	1	0	2	2	1	2	.500	0	1	.000	0	0	.000	0	0	0	0	0	0	0	0	0	2.0	2.0	0.0	0.0	.542
NBA Playoff Totals		3	0	29	6	3	10	.300	0	3	.000	0	0	.000	1	2	3	2	2	0	4	0	2	9.7	2.0	1.0	0.7	....

• GRANDHOLM, Jim

James Thomas Grandholm

Born: Oct. 4, 1960. Elkhart, IN, United States.   Height: 7'   Weight: 235 lbs.   Drafted: 1984   College: South Florida

YEAR	TEAM	GP	GS	MIN	PTS	FGM	FGA	FG%	3PM	3PA	3P%	FTM	FTA	FT%	ORB	DRB	TRB	AST	PF	DQ	STL	BLK	TO	MPG	PPG	RPG	APG	PCM
90-91	Dallas	26	0	168	79	30	58	.517	9	17	.529	10	21	.476	20	30	50	8	33	0	2	8	10	6.5	3.0	1.9	0.3	.521
NBA Season Totals		26	0	168	79	30	58	.517	9	17	.529	10	21	.476	20	30	50	8	33	0	2	8	10	6.5	3.0	1.9	0.3	

• GRANDISON, Ron

Ron Calvin Grandison

Born: July 9, 1964. Los Angeles, CA, United States.   Height: 6'6".   Weight: 215 lbs.   Drafted: 1987   College: New Orleans

YEAR	TEAM	GP	GS	MIN	PTS	FGM	FGA	FG%	3PM	3PA	3P%	FTM	FTA	FT%	ORB	DRB	TRB	AST	PF	DQ	STL	BLK	TO	MPG	PPG	RPG	APG	PCM
88-89	Boston	72	0	528	177	59	142	.415	0	10	.000	59	80	.738	47	45	92	42	71	0	18	3	36	7.3	2.5	1.3	0.6	.329
91-92	Charlotte	3	0	25	10	2	4	.500	0	0	.000	6	10	.600	3	8	11	1	4	0	1	1	3	8.3	3.3	3.7	0.3	.591
94-95	New York	2	0	8	2	1	4	.250	0	0	.000	0	0	.000	3	2	5	2	2	0	0	0	0	4.0	1.0	2.5	1.0	.633
95-96	New York	18	3	235	43	13	39	.333	4	13	.308	13	19	.684	14	22	36	10	27	0	8	1	11	13.1	2.4	2.0	0.6	.194
95-96	Atlanta	4	0	19	4	2	4	.500	0	1	.000	0	0	.000	1	5	6	1	0	0	0	0	0	4.8	1.0	1.5	0.3	.464
95-96	New York	6	0	57	18	7	15	.467	0	0	.000	4	6	.667	5	8	13	2	4	0	4	1	1	9.5	3.0	2.2	0.3	.452
NBA Season Totals		105	3	872	254	84	208	.404	4	24	.167	82	115	.713	73	90	163	58	108	0	31	6	51	8.3	2.4	1.6	0.6	....
95-96	New York	2	0	3	0	0	1	.000	0	1	.000	0	0	.000	0	0	0	0	1	0	0	0	0	1.5	0.0	0.0	0.0	-.470
NBA Playoff Totals		2	0	3	0	0	1	.000	0	1	.000	0	0	.000	0	0	0	0	1	0	0	0	0	1.5	0.0	0.0	0.0	....

• GRANGER, Stewart

Stewart Francis Granger

Born: Oct. 27, 1961. Montreal, QU, Canada.   Height: 6'3".   Weight: 190 lbs.   Drafted: 1983   College: Villanova

YEAR	TEAM	GP	GS	MIN	PTS	FGM	FGA	FG%	3PM	3PA	3P%	FTM	FTA	FT%	ORB	DRB	TRB	AST	PF	DQ	STL	BLK	TO	MPG	PPG	RPG	APG	PCM
83-84	Cleveland	56	13	738	251	97	226	.429	4	13	.308	53	70	.757	8	47	55	134	97	0	24	0	56	13.2	4.5	1.0	2.4	.329
84-85	Atlanta	9	1	92	16	6	17	.353	0	1	.000	4	8	.500	1	5	6	12	13	0	2	0	12	10.2	1.8	0.7	1.3	.075
86-87	New York	15	0	166	49	20	54	.370	0	3	.000	9	11	.818	6	11	17	27	17	0	7	1	23	11.1	3.3	1.1	1.8	.236
NBA Season Totals		80	14	996	316	123	297	.414	4	17	.235	66	89	.742	15	63	78	173	127	0	33	1	91	12.5	4.0	1.0	2.2	

• GRANT, Brian

Brian Wade Grant

Born: Mar. 5, 1972. Columbus, OH, United States.   Height: 6'9".   Weight: 254 lbs.   Drafted: 1994   College: Xavier

YEAR	TEAM	GP	GS	MIN	PTS	FGM	FGA	FG%	3PM	3PA	3P%	FTM	FTA	FT%	ORB	DRB	TRB	AST	PF	DQ	STL	BLK	TO	MPG	PPG	RPG	APG	PCM
94-95	Sacramento	80	59	2289	1058	413	809	.511	1	4	.250	231	363	.636	207	391	598	99	276	4	49	116	160	28.6	13.2	7.5	1.2	.509
95-96	Sacramento	78	75	2398	1120	427	842	.507	4	17	.235	262	358	.732	175	370	545	127	269	9	40	103	187	30.7	14.4	7.0	1.6	.485
96-97	Sacramento	24	15	607	252	91	207	.440	0	0	.000	70	90	.778	49	93	142	28	75	0	19	25	43	25.3	10.5	5.9	1.2	.433
97-98	Portland	61	49	1921	737	283	557	.508	0	1	.000	171	228	.750	197	358	555	86	184	3	44	45	110	31.5	12.1	9.1	1.4	.499
98-99	Portland	48	46	1525	550	183	382	.479	0	0	.000	184	226	.814	173	297	470	67	136	1	21	34	96	31.8	11.5	9.8	1.4	.492
99-00	Portland	63	14	1322	459	173	352	.491	1	2	.500	112	166	.675	121	223	344	64	166	2	32	28	84	21.0	7.3	5.5	1.0	.421
00-01	Miami	82	79	2771	1250	484	1010	.479	0	1	.000	282	354	.797	217	501	718	101	293	5	60	71	170	33.8	15.2	8.8	1.2	.482
01-02	Miami	72	72	2256	673	286	610	.469	0	2	.000	101	119	.849	168	407	575	137	236	6	48	31	122	31.3	9.3	8.0	1.9	.397
02-03	Miami	82	82	2641	846	344	676	.509	0	0	.000	158	205	.771	241	596	837	104	300	4	63	47	129	32.2	10.3	10.2	1.3	.471
NBA Season Totals		590	491	17730	6945	2684	5445	.493	6	27	.222	1571	2109	.745	1548	3236	4784	813	1935	38	376	500	1101	30.1	11.8	8.1	1.4	....
95-96	Sacramento	4	4	124	39	16	42	.381	0	0	.000	7	14	.500	7	13	20	4	14	1	2	7	13	31.0	9.8	5.0	1.0	.193
97-98	Portland	4	4	135	53	19	36	.528	0	0	.000	15	18	.833	18	25	43	6	20	0	4	3	5	33.8	13.3	10.8	1.5	.553
98-99	Portland	13	13	482	171	63	119	.529	0	0	.000	45	72	.625	34	85	119	14	48	1	10	16	21	37.1	13.2	9.2	1.1	.443
99-00	Portland	16	0	320	87	29	65	.446	0	0	.000	29	39	.744	37	55	92	8	53	1	6	6	17	20.0	5.4	5.8	0.5	.355
00-01	Miami	3	0	84	30	10	24	.417	0	0	.000	10	14	.714	6	18	24	1	9	0	0	5	6	28.0	10.0	8.0	0.3	.397
NBA Playoff Totals		40	21	1145	380	137	286	.479	0	0	.000	106	157	.675	102	196	298	33	144	3	22	37	62	28.6	9.5	7.5	0.8	....

• GRANT, Bud

Harry Peter Grant

Born: May 20, 1927. Superior, WI, United States.   Height: 6'3".   Weight: 195 lbs.   Drafted: 1950   College: Minnesota

YEAR	TEAM	GP	GS	MIN	PTS	FGM	FGA	FG%	3PM	3PA	3P%	FTM	FTA	FT%	ORB	DRB	TRB	AST	PF	DQ	STL	BLK	TO	MPG	PPG	RPG	APG	PCM
49-50	Minneapolis	35	....	....	91	42	115	.365	....	....	....	7	17	.412	....	....	....	19	36	....	....	....	....	2.6	....	0.5	....
50-51	Minneapolis	61	....	....	158	53	184	.288	....	....	....	52	83	.627	....	....	115	71	106	0	....	....	....	2.6	1.9	1.2	
NBA Season Totals		96	....	....	249	95	299	.318	....	....	....	59	100	.590	....	....	115	90	142	0	....	....	....	2.6	1.2	0.9	....
49-50	Minneapolis	11	....	....	43	18	45	.400	....	....	....	7	14	.500	....	....	....	7	25	....	....	....	....	3.9	....	0.6	
50-51	Minneapolis	6	....	....	11	4	11	.364	....	....	....	3	3	1.000	....	....	5	0	12	0	....	....	....	1.8	0.8	0.0	
NBA Playoff Totals		17	....	....	54	22	56	.393	....	....	....	10	17	.588	....	....	5	7	37	0	....	....	....	3.2	0.3	0.4	....

• GRANT, Gary

Gary (The General) Grant

Born: Apr. 21, 1965. Canton, OH, United States.   Height: 6'3".   Weight: 185 lbs.   Drafted: 1988   College: Michigan

YEAR	TEAM	GP	GS	MIN	PTS	FGM	FGA	FG%	3PM	3PA	3P%	FTM	FTA	FT%	ORB	DRB	TRB	AST	PF	DQ	STL	BLK	TO	MPG	PPG	RPG	APG	PCM
88-89	LA Clippers	71	48	1924	846	361	830	.435	5	22	.227	119	162	.735	80	158	238	506	170	1	144	9	256	27.1	11.9	3.4	7.1	.508
89-90	LA Clippers	44	44	1529	575	241	517	.466	5	21	.238	88	113	.779	59	136	195	442	120	1	108	5	207	34.8	13.1	4.4	10.0	.532
90-91	LA Clippers	68	65	2105	590	265	587	.451	9	39	.231	51	74	.689	69	140	209	587	192	4	103	12	211	31.0	8.7	3.1	8.6	.438

YEAR	TEAM	GP	GS	MIN	PTS	FGM	FGA	FG%	3PM	3PA	3P%	FTM	FTA	FT%	ORB	DRB	TRB	AST	PF	DQ	STL	BLK	TO	MPG	PPG	RPG	APG	PCM
91-92	LA Clippers	78	53	2049	609	275	595	.462	15	51	.294	44	54	.815	34	150	184	538	181	4	138	14	187	26.3	7.8	2.4	6.9	.458
92-93	LA Clippers	74	8	1624	486	210	476	.441	11	42	.262	55	74	.743	27	112	139	353	168	2	106	9	126	21.9	6.6	1.9	4.8	.398
93-94	LA Clippers	78	8	1533	588	253	563	.449	17	62	.274	65	76	.855	42	100	142	291	139	1	119	12	133	19.7	7.5	1.8	3.7	.443
94-95	LA Clippers	33	2	470	205	78	166	.470	4	16	.250	45	55	.818	8	27	35	93	66	0	29	3	43	14.2	6.2	1.1	2.8	.443
95-96	New York	47	1	596	232	88	181	.486	8	24	.333	48	58	.828	12	40	52	69	91	0	39	3	47	12.7	4.9	1.1	1.5	.360
96-97	Miami	28	0	365	110	39	110	.355	14	46	.304	18	22	.818	8	30	38	45	39	0	16	0	28	13.0	3.9	1.4	1.6	.263
97-98	Portland	22	2	359	105	43	93	.462	7	19	.368	12	14	.857	8	40	48	84	30	0	17	2	24	16.3	4.8	2.2	3.8	.488
98-99	Portland	2	0	7	0	0	1	.000	0	0	.000	0	0	.000	0	0	0	3	0	0	1	0	0	3.5	0.0	0.0	1.5	.476
99-00	Portland	3	0	24	12	6	14	.429	0	0	.000	0	0	.000	0	3	3	1	3	0	1	0	2	8.0	4.0	1.0	0.3	.262
00-01	Portland	4	0	17	10	5	7	.714	0	0	.000	0	0	.000	0	0	0	1	1	0	0	0	0	4.3	2.5	0.0	0.3	.521
NBA Season Totals		552	231	12602	4368	1864	4140	.450	95	342	.278	545	702	.776	347	936	1283	3013	1200	13	821	69	1264	22.8	7.9	2.3	5.5	....
91-92	LA Clippers	5	1	77	22	10	21	.476	0	2	.000	2	2	1.000	0	4	4	18	10	0	3	2	8	15.4	4.4	0.8	3.6	.355
92-93	LA Clippers	5	0	101	21	10	31	.323	0	0	.000	1	2	.500	1	1	2	23	13	0	3	0	7	20.2	4.2	0.4	4.6	.174
95-96	New York	1	0	8	6	2	5	.400	2	3	.667	0	0	.000	2	1	3	0	0	0	1	0	1	8.0	6.0	3.0	0.0	.750
97-98	Portland	4	0	27	5	2	7	.286	1	4	.250	0	0	.000	2	3	5	7	2	0	1	1	2	6.8	1.3	1.3	1.8	.433
99-00	Portland	2	0	8	1	0	2	.000	0	0	.000	1	2	.500	0	0	0	1	0	0	0	0	0	4.0	0.5	0.0	0.5	-.022
NBA Playoff Totals		17	1	221	55	24	66	.364	3	9	.333	4	6	.667	5	9	14	49	25	0	8	3	18	13.0	3.2	0.8	2.9	....

• GRANT, Greg

Gregory Alan (Waterbug) Grant

Born: Aug. 29, 1966. Trenton, NJ, United States. Height: 5'7". Weight: 140 lbs. Drafted: 1989 College: Trenton State

YEAR	TEAM	GP	GS	MIN	PTS	FGM	FGA	FG%	3PM	3PA	3P%	FTM	FTA	FT%	ORB	DRB	TRB	AST	PF	DQ	STL	BLK	TO	MPG	PPG	RPG	APG	PCM
89-90	Phoenix	67	3	678	208	83	216	.384	3	16	.188	39	59	.661	16	43	59	168	58	0	36	1	74	10.1	3.1	0.9	2.5	.363
90-91	New York	22	0	107	26	10	27	.370	1	3	.333	5	6	.833	1	9	10	20	12	0	9	0	11	4.9	1.2	0.5	0.9	.307
91-92	Charlotte	13	0	57	1	0	8	.000	0	0	.000	1	2	.500	1	3	4	18	3	0	8	0	5	4.4	0.1	0.3	1.4	.307
91-92	Philadelphia	55	0	834	224	99	217	.456	7	18	.389	19	22	.864	13	52	65	199	73	0	37	2	39	15.2	4.1	1.2	3.6	.423
92-93	Philadelphia	72	0	996	194	77	220	.350	20	68	.294	20	31	.645	24	43	67	206	73	0	43	1	58	13.8	2.7	0.9	2.9	.292
94-95	Denver	14	0	151	31	10	33	.303	2	7	.286	9	12	.750	2	7	9	43	20	1	6	2	14	10.8	2.2	0.6	3.1	.312
95-96	Philadelphia	11	2	280	45	18	48	.375	4	18	.222	5	6	.833	3	18	21	60	28	0	12	2	15	25.5	4.1	1.9	5.5	.306
95-96	Washington	10	0	138	24	11	28	.393	2	10	.200	0	0	.000	1	5	6	23	8	0	8	0	10	13.8	2.4	0.6	2.3	.235
95-96	Denver	10	0	109	14	6	23	.261	2	6	.333	0	0	.000	3	4	7	14	7	0	2	0	5	10.9	1.4	0.7	1.4	.122
NBA Season Totals		274	5	3350	767	314	820	.383	41	146	.281	98	138	.710	64	184	248	751	282	1	161	8	231	12.2	2.8	0.9	2.7	....
89-90	Phoenix	7	0	47	19	9	20	.450	1	3	.333	0	0	.000	2	4	6	10	2	0	2	0	5	6.7	2.7	0.9	1.4	.451
94-95	Denver	3	0	20	2	0	6	.000	0	1	.000	2	2	1.000	3	0	3	5	5	0	1	0	0	6.7	0.7	1.0	1.7	.154
NBA Playoff Totals		10	0	67	21	9	26	.346	1	4	.250	2	2	1.000	5	4	9	15	7	0	3	0	5	6.7	2.1	0.9	1.5	....

• GRANT, Harvey

Harvey Grant

Born: July 4, 1965. Augusta, GA, United States. Height: 6'8". Weight: 195 lbs. Drafted: 1988 College: Oklahoma

YEAR	TEAM	GP	GS	MIN	PTS	FGM	FGA	FG%	3PM	3PA	3P%	FTM	FTA	FT%	ORB	DRB	TRB	AST	PF	DQ	STL	BLK	TO	MPG	PPG	RPG	APG	PCM
88-89	Washington	71	1	1193	396	181	390	.464	0	1	.000	34	57	.596	75	88	163	79	147	2	35	29	28	16.8	5.6	2.3	1.1	.329
89-90	Washington	81	15	1846	664	284	601	.473	0	8	.000	96	137	.701	138	204	342	131	194	1	52	43	81	22.8	8.2	4.2	1.6	.395
90-91	Washington	77	76	2842	1405	609	1224	.498	2	15	.133	185	249	.743	179	378	557	204	232	2	91	61	123	36.9	18.2	7.2	2.6	.513
91-92	Washington	64	60	2388	1155	489	1022	.478	1	8	.125	176	220	.800	157	275	432	170	178	1	74	27	109	37.3	18.0	6.8	2.7	.474
92-93	Washington	72	72	2667	1339	560	1149	.487	1	10	.100	218	300	.727	133	279	412	205	168	0	72	44	94	37.0	18.6	5.7	2.8	.486
93-94	Portland	77	73	2112	798	356	774	.460	2	7	.286	84	131	.641	109	242	351	107	179	1	70	49	54	27.4	10.4	4.6	1.4	.383
94-95	Portland	75	14	1771	683	286	621	.461	8	26	.308	103	146	.705	103	181	284	82	163	0	56	53	60	23.6	9.1	3.8	1.1	.379
95-96	Portland	76	75	2394	709	314	679	.462	21	67	.313	60	110	.545	117	244	361	111	173	1	60	43	84	31.5	9.3	4.8	1.5	.307
96-97	Washington	78	25	1604	316	129	314	.411	28	89	.315	30	39	.769	63	193	256	68	167	2	46	48	31	20.6	4.1	3.3	0.9	.269
97-98	Washington	65	8	895	170	75	196	.383	1	6	.167	19	30	.633	60	108	168	39	94	1	23	15	26	13.8	2.6	2.6	0.6	.244
98-99	Philadelphia	47	10	798	146	62	168	.369	1	6	.167	21	29	.724	36	74	110	23	73	1	20	16	21	17.0	3.1	2.3	0.5	.191
NBA Season Totals		783	429	20510	7781	3345	7138	.469	65	243	.267	1026	1448	.709	1170	2266	3436	1219	1768	12	599	428	711	26.2	9.9	4.4	1.6	....
93-94	Portland	4	1	76	34	17	33	.515	0	0	.000	0	0	.000	5	4	9	3	2	0	1	2	1	19.0	8.5	2.3	0.8	.418
94-95	Portland	3	3	115	43	14	28	.500	5	9	.556	10	16	.625	3	13	16	6	6	0	3	2	4	38.3	14.3	5.3	2.0	.405
95-96	Portland	5	5	164	27	13	38	.342	1	7	.143	0	4	.000	5	15	20	4	16	0	0	2	3	32.8	5.4	4.0	0.8	.099
96-97	Washington	3	0	29	0	0	3	.000	0	1	.000	0	0	.000	0	4	4	0	5	0	0	2	0	9.7	0.0	1.3	0.0	.016
98-99	Philadelphia	4	0	29	2	1	1	1.000	0	0	.000	0	0	.000	1	3	4	0	1	0	0	1	0	7.3	0.5	1.0	0.0	.207
NBA Playoff Totals		19	9	413	106	45	103	.437	6	17	.353	10	20	.500	14	39	53	13	30	0	4	9	8	21.7	5.6	2.8	0.7	....

• GRANT, Horace

Horace Junior (The General) Grant

Born: July 4, 1965. Augusta, GA, United States. Height: 6'10". Weight: 215 lbs. Drafted: 1987 College: Clemson

YEAR	TEAM	GP	GS	MIN	PTS	FGM	FGA	FG%	3PM	3PA	3P%	FTM	FTA	FT%	ORB	DRB	TRB	AST	PF	DQ	STL	BLK	TO	MPG	PPG	RPG	APG	PCM
87-88	Chicago	81	6	1827	622	254	507	.501	0	2	.000	114	182	.626	155	292	447	89	221	3	51	53	89	22.6	7.7	5.5	1.1	.425
88-89	Chicago	79	79	2809	950	405	781	.519	0	5	.000	140	199	.704	240	441	681	168	251	1	86	62	126	35.6	12.0	8.6	2.1	.459
89-90	Chicago	80	80	2753	1071	446	853	.523	0	0	.000	179	256	.699	236	393	629	227	230	1	92	84	112	34.4	13.4	7.9	2.8	.522
90-91	Chicago	78	76	2641	1000	401	733	.547	1	6	.167	197	277	.711	266	393	659	178	203	2	95	69	94	33.9	12.8	8.4	2.3	.541
91-92	Chicago	81	81	2859	1149	457	790	.578	0	2	.000	235	317	.741	344	463	807	217	196	0	100	131	97	35.3	14.2	10.0	2.7	.636
92-93	Chicago	77	77	2745	1017	421	829	.508	1	5	.200	174	281	.619	341	388	729	201	218	4	89	95	108	35.6	13.2	9.5	2.6	.528
93-94	Chicago	70	69	2570	1057	460	878	.524	0	6	.000	137	230	.596	306	463	769	236	164	0	74	84	112	36.7	15.1	11.0	3.4	.607
94-95	Orlando	74	74	2693	948	401	707	.567	0	8	.000	146	211	.692	223	492	715	173	203	2	76	88	81	36.4	12.8	9.7	2.3	.545
95-96	Orlando	63	62	2286	847	347	677	.513	1	6	.167	152	207	.734	178	402	580	170	144	1	62	74	63	36.3	13.4	9.2	2.7	.541
96-97	Orlando	67	67	2496	845	358	695	.515	1	6	.167	128	179	.715	206	394	600	163	157	1	101	65	101	37.3	12.6	9.0	2.4	.492
97-98	Orlando	76	76	2803	921	393	857	.459	0	7	.000	135	199	.678	228	390	618	172	180	0	81	79	91	36.9	12.1	8.1	2.3	.428
98-99	Orlando	50	50	1660	443	198	456	.434	0	2	.000	47	70	.671	117	234	351	90	99	0	46	60	44	33.2	8.9	7.0	1.8	.377
99-00	Seattle	76	76	2688	612	266	599	.444	0	4	.000	80	111	.721	167	424	591	188	192	0	55	60	61	35.4	8.1	7.8	2.5	.372
00-01	LA Lakers	77	77	2390	657	263	569	.462	0	3	.000	131	169	.775	220	325	545	121	181	2	51	61	48	31.0	8.5	7.1	1.6	.403
01-02	Orlando	76	76	2210	608	264	515	.513	0	0	.000	80	111	.721	159	322	481	104	118	0	57	49	51	29.1	8.0	6.3	1.4	.413
02-03	Orlando	5	1	85	26	13	25	.520	0	0	.000	0	0	.000	2	6	8	7	5	0	3	0	1	17.0	5.2	1.6	1.4	.348
NBA Season Totals		1110	1027	37515	12773	5347	10471	.511	4	62	.065	2075	2999	.692	3388	5822	9210	2504	2762	17	1119	1114	1279	33.8	11.5	8.3	2.3	....
87-88	Chicago	10	0	299	101	46	81	.568	0	1	.000	9	15	.600	25	45	70	16	35	2	14	2	7	29.9	10.1	7.0	1.6	.468
88-89	Chicago	17	17	625	184	72	139	.518	0	0	.000	40	50	.800	53	114	167	35	68	2	11	16	31	36.8	10.8	9.8	2.1	.439

YEAR	TEAM	GP	GS	MIN	PTS	FGM	FGA	FG%	3PM	3PA	3P%	FTM	FTA	FT%	ORB	DRB	TRB	AST	PF	DQ	STL	BLK	TO	MPG	PPG	RPG	APG	PCM
89-90	Chicago	16	16	616	195	81	159	.509	0	2	.000	33	53	.623	73	86	159	40	51	1	18	18	26	38.5	12.2	9.9	2.5	.470
90-91	Chicago	17	17	666	226	91	156	.583	0	0	.000	44	60	.733	56	82	138	38	45	0	15	6	20	39.2	13.3	8.1	2.2	.461
91-92	Chicago	22	22	856	249	99	183	.541	0	2	.000	51	76	.671	76	118	194	66	68	1	24	39	21	38.9	11.3	8.8	3.0	.488
92-93	Chicago	19	19	651	203	83	152	.546	0	0	.000	37	54	.685	61	95	156	44	60	1	23	23	17	34.3	10.7	8.2	2.3	.495
93-94	Chicago	10	10	393	162	65	120	.542	1	1	1.000	31	42	.738	30	44	74	26	23	0	10	18	10	39.3	16.2	7.4	2.6	.531
94-95	Orlando	21	21	869	287	121	224	.540	0	2	.000	45	59	.763	74	145	219	39	68	1	21	24	26	41.4	13.7	10.4	1.9	.479
95-96	Orlando	9	9	334	135	61	94	.649	0	0	.000	13	15	.867	31	63	94	13	23	0	7	6	6	37.1	15.0	10.4	1.4	.602
98-99	Orlando	4	4	128	27	11	30	.367	0	0	.000	5	8	.625	14	14	28	5	12	0	2	2	2	32.0	6.8	7.0	1.3	.279
99-00	Seattle	5	5	185	24	11	27	.407	0	0	.000	2	4	.500	8	23	31	10	12	0	8	5	1	37.0	4.8	6.2	2.0	.287
00-01	LA Lakers	16	16	423	96	37	96	.385	0	0	.000	22	30	.733	40	56	96	19	43	0	15	13	15	26.4	6.0	6.0	1.2	.328
01-02	Orlando	4	4	127	18	8	22	.364	0	0	.000	2	2	1.000	8	23	31	9	7	0	3	1	2	31.8	4.5	7.8	2.3	.330
NBA Playoff Totals		170	160	6172	1907	786	1483	.530	1	8	.125	334	468	.714	549	908	1457	360	515	8	171	173	184	36.3	11.2	8.6	2.1	....

• GRANT, Josh
Joshua David Grant

Born: Aug. 7, 1967. Salt Lake City, UT, United States.   Height: 6'9".   Weight: 223 lbs.   Drafted: 1993   College: Utah

YEAR	TEAM	GP	GS	MIN	PTS	FGM	FGA	FG%	3PM	3PA	3P%	FTM	FTA	FT%	ORB	DRB	TRB	AST	PF	DQ	STL	BLK	TO	MPG	PPG	RPG	APG	PCM
93-94	Golden State	53	0	382	157	59	146	.404	17	61	.279	22	29	.759	27	62	89	24	62	0	18	8	32	7.2	3.0	1.7	0.5	.387
NBA Season Totals		53	0	382	157	59	146	.404	17	61	.279	22	29	.759	27	62	89	24	62	0	18	8	32	7.2	3.0	1.7	0.5	
93-94	Golden State	1	0	1	0	0	0	.000	0	0	.000	0	0	.000	0	0	0	0	0	0	0	0	0	1.0	0.0	0.0	0.0	.000
NBA Playoff Totals		1	0	1	0	0	0	.000	0	0	.000	0	0	.000	0	0	0	0	0	0	0	0	0	1.0	0.0	0.0	0.0	....

• GRANT, Paul
Paul Edward Grant

Born: Jan. 6, 1974. Pittsburgh, PA, United States.   Height: 7'   Weight: 245 lbs.   Drafted: 1997   College: Wisconsin

YEAR	TEAM	GP	GS	MIN	PTS	FGM	FGA	FG%	3PM	3PA	3P%	FTM	FTA	FT%	ORB	DRB	TRB	AST	PF	DQ	STL	BLK	TO	MPG	PPG	RPG	APG	PCM
98-99	Minnesota	4	0	8	2	1	4	.250	0	0	.000	0	0	.000	1	0	1	0	4	0	0	0	1	2.0	0.5	0.3	0.0	-.306
98-99	Milwaukee	2	0	5	2	1	2	.500	0	0	.000	0	0	.000	0	0	0	0	0	0	1	0	1	2.5	1.0	0.0	0.0	.222
NBA Season Totals		6	0	13	4	2	6	.333	0	0	.000	0	0	.000	1	0	1	0	4	0	1	0	2	2.2	0.7	0.2	0.0	....

• GRANT, Travis
Travis (Machine Gun, The Machine) Grant

Born: Jan. 1, 1950. Clayton, AL, United States.   Height: 6'7".   Weight: 215 lbs.   Drafted: 1972   College: Kentucky State

YEAR	TEAM	GP	GS	MIN	PTS	FGM	FGA	FG%	3PM	3PA	3P%	FTM	FTA	FT%	ORB	DRB	TRB	AST	PF	DQ	STL	BLK	TO	MPG	PPG	RPG	APG	PCM
72-73	LA Lakers	33	....	153	125	51	116	.440	....	....	....	23	26	.885	....	....	52	7	19	0	....	....	....	4.6	3.8	1.6	0.2	.735
73-74	San Diego-A	56	....	1324	856	357	681	.524	1	4	.250	141	176	.801	106	192	298	63	118	....	46	12	88	23.6	15.3	5.3	1.1	.634
73-74	LA Lakers	3	....	6	3	1	4	.250	....	....	....	1	3	.333	0	1	1	0	1	0	0	0	....	2.0	1.0	0.3	0.0	.004
74-75	San Diego-A	53	....	1998	1335	576	1058	.544	1	2	.500	182	218	.835	117	211	328	98	160	....	44	21	118	37.7	25.2	6.2	1.8	.611
75-76	Indiana-A	34	....	567	326	146	275	.531	0	0	.000	34	46	.739	49	52	101	31	68	....	10	13	36	16.7	9.6	3.0	0.9	.529
75-76	Kentucky-A	22	....	261	122	52	123	.423	0	0	.000	18	23	.783	12	27	39	12	30	....	6	5	19	11.9	5.5	1.8	0.5	.349
NBA Season Totals		36	....	159	128	52	120	.433	....	....	....	24	29	.828	0	1	53	7	20	0	0	0	....	4.4	3.6	1.5	0.2	....
ABA Season Totals		165	....	4150	2639	1131	2137	.529	2	6	.333	375	463	.810	284	482	766	204	376	....	106	51	261	25.2	16.0	4.6	1.2	....
Career Totals		201	....	4309	2767	1183	2257	.524	2	6	.333	399	492	.811	284	483	819	211	396	0	106	51	261	21.4	13.8	4.1	1.0	....
72-73	LA Lakers	2	....	11	8	4	6	.667	....	....	....	0	0	.000	....	....	4	0	1	0	....	....	....	5.5	4.0	2.0	0.0	.844
75-76	Indiana-A	1	....	1	0	0	1	.000	0	0	.000	0	0	.000	0	0	0	0	0	....	0	0	0	1.0	0.0	0.0	0.0	-.891
NBA Playoff Totals		2	....	11	8	4	6	.667	....	....	....	0	0	.000	....	....	4	0	1	0	....	....	....	5.5	4.0	2.0	0.0	....
ABA Playoff Totals		1	....	1	0	0	1	.000	0	0	.000	0	0	.000	0	0	0	0	0	....	0	0	0	1.0	0.0	0.0	0.0	....
Career Playoff Totals		3	....	12	8	4	7	.571	0	0	.000	0	0	.000	0	0	4	0	1	0	0	0	0	4.0	2.7	1.3	0.0	....

• GRATE, Don
Donald (Buckeye) Grate

Born: Aug. 27, 1923. Greenfield, OH, United States.   Height: 6'2".   Weight: 185 lbs.   Drafted: —   College: Ohio State

YEAR	TEAM	GP	GS	MIN	PTS	FGM	FGA	FG%	3PM	3PA	3P%	FTM	FTA	FT%	ORB	DRB	TRB	AST	PF	DQ	STL	BLK	TO	MPG	PPG	RPG	APG	PCM
47-48	Indianapolis-N	11	....	....	31	14	....	....	....	....	....	3	6	.500	....	....	....	....	....	....	....	....	....	2.8	....	....	....	....
49-50	Sheboygan	2	....	....	4	1	6	.167	....	....	....	2	2	1.000	....	....	....	3	3	....	....	....	....	2.0	....	1.5	....	....
NBA Season Totals		2	....	....	4	1	6	.167	....	....	....	2	2	1.000	....	....	....	3	3	....	....	....	....	2.0	....	1.5	....	....
NBL Season Totals		11	....	....	31	14	....	....	....	....	....	3	6	....	....	....	....	....	....	....	....	....	....	2.8	....	....	....	....
Career Totals		13	....	....	35	15	6	....	....	....	....	5	8	....	....	....	....	3	3	....	....	....	....	2.7	....	0.2	....	....

• GRAUMAN, Walter
Walter (Boney) Grauman

Born: 1915.   Height: 6'2".   Weight: 200 lbs.   Drafted: —   College: none

YEAR	TEAM	GP	GS	MIN	PTS	FGM	FGA	FG%	3PM	3PA	3P%	FTM	FTA	FT%	ORB	DRB	TRB	AST	PF	DQ	STL	BLK	TO	MPG	PPG	RPG	APG	PCM
38-39	Sheboygan-N	1	....	....	0	0	....	....	....	....	....	0	....	....	....	....	....	....	....	....	....	....	....	0.0	....	....	....	....
NBL Season Totals		1	....	....	0	0	....	....	....	....	....	0	....	....	....	....	....	....	....	....	....	....	....	0.0	....	....	....	....

• GRAVES, Butch
Earl G. (Butch) Graves Jr.

Born: Jan. 5, 1962. Scarsdale, NY, United States.   Height: 6'3".   Weight: 200 lbs.   Drafted: 1984   College: Yale

YEAR	TEAM	GP	GS	MIN	PTS	FGM	FGA	FG%	3PM	3PA	3P%	FTM	FTA	FT%	ORB	DRB	TRB	AST	PF	DQ	STL	BLK	TO	MPG	PPG	RPG	APG	PCM
84-85	Cleveland	4	0	11	5	2	6	.333	0	1	.000	1	5	.200	0	2	2	1	4	0	1	0	1	2.8	1.3	0.5	0.3	.043
NBA Season Totals		4	0	11	5	2	6	.333	0	1	.000	1	5	.200	0	2	2	1	4	0	1	0	1	2.8	1.3	0.5	0.3	

• GRAY, Cortez
Cortez Gray

Born: Mar. 7, 1916. Died: July28, 1996.   Height: 6'5".   Weight: 185 lbs.   Drafted: —   College: Toledo

YEAR	TEAM	GP	GS	MIN	PTS	FGM	FGA	FG%	3PM	3PA	3P%	FTM	FTA	FT%	ORB	DRB	TRB	AST	PF	DQ	STL	BLK	TO	MPG	PPG	RPG	APG	PCM
42-43	Toledo-N	4	....	....	18	7	....	....	....	....	....	4	....	....	....	....	....	....	....	....	....	....	....	4.5	....	....	....	....
NBL Season Totals		4	....	....	18	7	....	....	....	....	....	4	....	....	....	....	....	....	....	....	....	....	....	4.5	....	....	....	....

YEAR	TEAM	GP	GS	MIN	PTS	FGM	FGA	FG%	3PM	3PA	3P%	FTM	FTA	FT%	ORB	DRB	TRB	AST	PF	DQ	STL	BLK	TO	MPG	PPG	RPG	APG	PCM

• GRAY, Devin
Devin Antione Gray

Born: May 31, 1972. Baltimore, MD, United States. Height: 6'7". Weight: 240 lbs. Drafted: — College: Clemson

YEAR	TEAM	GP	GS	MIN	PTS	FGM	FGA	FG%	3PM	3PA	3P%	FTM	FTA	FT%	ORB	DRB	TRB	AST	PF	DQ	STL	BLK	TO	MPG	PPG	RPG	APG	PCM
96-97	Sacramento	3	0	25	8	3	11	.273	0	0	.000	2	4	.500	3	6	9	2	3	0	3	0	0	8.3	2.7	3.0	0.7	.461
96-97	San Antonio	3	0	24	10	5	15	.333	0	0	.000	0	1	1.000	3	2	5	0	8	0	1	0	5	8.0	3.3	1.7	0.0	-.108
99-00	Houston	21	2	124	49	15	37	.405	0	0	.000	19	29	.655	11	14	25	5	22	0	5	3	4	5.9	2.3	1.2	0.2	.373
NBA Season Totals		27	2	173	67	23	63	.365	0	0	.000	21	34	.618	17	22	39	7	33	0	9	3	9	6.4	2.5	1.4	0.3	....

• GRAY, Ed
Edward Gray Jr.

Born: Sept. 27, 1975. Riverside, CA, United States. Height: 6'3". Weight: 210 lbs. Drafted: 1997 College: California

YEAR	TEAM	GP	GS	MIN	PTS	FGM	FGA	FG%	3PM	3PA	3P%	FTM	FTA	FT%	ORB	DRB	TRB	AST	PF	DQ	STL	BLK	TO	MPG	PPG	RPG	APG	PCM
97-98	Atlanta	30	3	472	227	77	202	.381	18	46	.391	55	65	.846	9	36	45	34	73	0	15	11	30	15.7	7.6	1.5	1.1	.316
98-99	Atlanta	30	3	337	146	53	182	.291	12	42	.286	28	37	.757	7	21	28	12	30	0	12	1	29	11.2	4.9	0.9	0.4	.113
NBA Season Totals		60	6	809	373	130	384	.339	30	88	.341	83	102	.814	16	57	73	46	103	0	27	12	59	13.5	6.2	1.2	0.8	....
98-99	Atlanta	8	0	71	44	15	41	.366	4	11	.364	10	11	.909	2	7	9	4	11	1	6	1	2	8.9	5.5	1.1	0.5	.457
NBA Playoff Totals		8	0	71	44	15	41	.366	4	11	.364	10	11	.909	2	7	9	4	11	1	6	1	2	8.9	5.5	1.1	0.5	....

• GRAY, Evric
Evric Gray

Born: Dec. 13, 1969. Bloomington, CA, United States. Height: 6'7". Weight: 235 lbs. Drafted: — College: UNLV

YEAR	TEAM	GP	GS	MIN	PTS	FGM	FGA	FG%	3PM	3PA	3P%	FTM	FTA	FT%	ORB	DRB	TRB	AST	PF	DQ	STL	BLK	TO	MPG	PPG	RPG	APG	PCM
96-97	New Jersey	5	0	42	13	4	15	.267	1	4	.250	4	4	1.000	1	2	3	2	5	0	1	0	3	8.4	2.6	0.6	0.4	.083
NBA Season Totals		5	0	42	13	4	15	.267	1	4	.250	4	4	1.000	1	2	3	2	5	0	1	0	3	8.4	2.6	0.6	0.4	....

• GRAY, Gary
Gary Michael Gray

Born: Feb. 23, 1945. Height: 6'1". Weight: 185 lbs. Drafted: 1967 College: Oklahoma City

YEAR	TEAM	GP	GS	MIN	PTS	FGM	FGA	FG%	3PM	3PA	3P%	FTM	FTA	FT%	ORB	DRB	TRB	AST	PF	DQ	STL	BLK	TO	MPG	PPG	RPG	APG	PCM
67-68	Cincinnati	44	....	276	105	49	134	.366	....	....	....	7	10	.700	....	....	23	26	48	0	....	....	....	6.3	2.4	0.5	0.6	.241
NBA Season Totals		44	....	276	105	49	134	.366	....	....	....	7	10	.700	....	....	23	26	48	0	....	....	....	6.3	2.4	0.5	0.6	....

• GRAY, Leonard
Leonard Earl Gray

Born: Dec. 19, 1951. Kansas City, KS, United States. Height: 6'8". Weight: 240 lbs. Drafted: 1974 College: Long Beach State

YEAR	TEAM	GP	GS	MIN	PTS	FGM	FGA	FG%	3PM	3PA	3P%	FTM	FTA	FT%	ORB	DRB	TRB	AST	PF	DQ	STL	BLK	TO	MPG	PPG	RPG	APG	PCM
74-75	Seattle	75	....	2280	860	378	773	.489	....	....	....	104	144	.722	133	345	478	163	292	9	63	24	....	30.4	11.5	6.4	2.2	.428
75-76	Seattle	66	....	2139	914	394	831	.474	....	....	....	126	169	.746	109	289	398	203	260	10	75	36	....	32.4	13.8	6.0	3.1	.459
76-77	Seattle	25	....	643	287	114	262	.435	....	....	....	59	78	.756	23	84	107	55	84	1	27	13	....	25.7	11.5	4.3	2.2	.419
76-77	Washington	58	....	996	347	144	330	.436	....	....	....	59	80	.738	61	125	186	69	189	8	31	18	....	17.2	6.0	3.2	1.2	.336
NBA Season Totals		224	....	6058	2408	1030	2196	.469	....	....	....	348	471	.739	326	843	1169	490	825	28	196	91	....	27.0	10.8	5.2	2.2	....
74-75	Seattle	9	....	263	89	39	80	.488	....	....	....	11	13	.846	11	34	45	20	41	0	12	5	....	29.2	9.9	5.0	2.2	.369
76-77	Washington	8	....	52	12	6	21	.286	....	....	....	0	0	.000	2	7	9	1	12	0	2	0	....	6.5	1.5	1.1	0.1	.053
NBA Playoff Totals		17	....	315	101	45	101	.446	....	....	....	11	13	.846	13	41	54	21	53	0	14	5	....	18.5	5.9	3.2	1.2	....

• GRAY, Stuart
Stuart Allan Gray

Born: May 27, 1963. Panama Canal Zone, Panama. Height: 7' Weight: 235 lbs. Drafted: 1984 College: UCLA

YEAR	TEAM	GP	GS	MIN	PTS	FGM	FGA	FG%	3PM	3PA	3P%	FTM	FTA	FT%	ORB	DRB	TRB	AST	PF	DQ	STL	BLK	TO	MPG	PPG	RPG	APG	PCM
84-85	Indiana	52	0	391	102	35	92	.380	0	0	.000	32	47	.681	29	94	123	15	82	1	9	14	52	7.5	2.0	2.4	0.3	.274
85-86	Indiana	67	3	423	155	54	108	.500	0	0	.000	47	74	.635	45	73	118	15	94	0	8	11	34	6.3	2.3	1.8	0.2	.379
86-87	Indiana	55	1	456	110	41	101	.406	0	0	.000	28	39	.718	39	90	129	26	93	0	10	28	39	8.3	2.0	2.3	0.5	.335
87-88	Indiana	74	0	807	224	90	193	.466	0	1	.000	44	73	.603	70	180	250	44	152	1	11	32	52	10.9	3.0	3.4	0.6	.391
88-89	Indiana	72	0	783	188	72	153	.471	0	1	.000	44	64	.688	84	161	245	29	128	0	11	21	50	10.9	2.6	3.4	0.4	.365
89-90	Charlotte	39	1	466	101	38	82	.463	0	2	.000	25	39	.641	38	93	131	17	64	0	12	24	20	11.9	2.6	3.4	0.4	.384
89-90	New York	19	0	94	15	4	17	.235	0	3	.000	7	8	.875	2	12	14	2	26	0	3	2	6	4.9	0.8	0.7	0.1	.048
90-91	New York	9	0	37	11	4	12	.333	0	0	.000	3	3	1.000	2	8	10	0	6	0	0	1	2	4.6	1.4	1.3	0.0	.247
NBA Season Totals		386	5	3457	906	338	758	.446	0	7	.000	230	347	.663	309	711	1020	148	645	2	64	133	255	9.0	2.3	2.6	0.4	....
86-87	Indiana	3	0	14	2	0	1	.000	0	0	.000	2	4	.500	2	5	7	0	3	0	0	0	0	4.7	0.7	2.3	0.0	.376
89-90	New York	4	0	12	4	2	5	.400	0	0	.000	0	0	.000	3	5	8	0	3	0	1	0	3	3.0	1.0	2.0	0.0	.450
NBA Playoff Totals		7	0	26	6	2	6	.333	0	0	.000	2	4	.500	5	10	15	0	6	0	1	0	3	3.7	0.9	2.1	0.0	....

• GRAY, Sylvester
Sylvester Gray

Born: July 8, 1967. Millington, TN, United States. Height: 6'6". Weight: 230 lbs. Drafted: 1988 College: Memphis State

YEAR	TEAM	GP	GS	MIN	PTS	FGM	FGA	FG%	3PM	3PA	3P%	FTM	FTA	FT%	ORB	DRB	TRB	AST	PF	DQ	STL	BLK	TO	MPG	PPG	RPG	APG	PCM
88-89	Miami	55	15	1220	440	167	398	.420	1	4	.250	105	156	.673	117	169	286	117	144	1	36	25	105	22.2	8.0	5.2	2.1	.397
NBA Season Totals		55	15	1220	440	167	398	.420	1	4	.250	105	156	.673	117	169	286	117	144	1	36	25	105	22.2	8.0	5.2	2.1	....

• GRAY, Wyndol

Wyndol Woodrow Gray

Born: Mar. 20, 1922. Died: Jan.30, 1994. Height: 6'1". Weight: 175 lbs. Drafted: — College: Bowling Green

YEAR	TEAM	GP	GS	MIN	PTS	FGM	FGA	FG%	3PM	3PA	3P%	FTM	FTA	FT%	ORB	DRB	TRB	AST	PF	DQ	STL	BLK	TO	MPG	PPG	RPG	APG	PCM
46-47	Boston	55	....	....	350	139	476	.292	....	....	....	72	124	.581	....	....	....	47	105	....	....	....	....	....	6.4	....	0.9	....
47-48	Toledo-N	2	....	....	6	2	....	....	....	....	....	2	4	.500	....	....	....	....	4	....	....	....	....	....	3.0	....	....	....
47-48	Providence	1	....	....	0	0	1	.000	....	....	....	0	1	.000	....	....	....	0	0	....	....	....	....	....	0.0	....	0.0	....
47-48	St. Louis	11	....	....	13	6	36	.167	....	....	....	1	3	.333	....	....	....	3	16	....	....	....	....	....	1.2	....	0.3	....
NBA Season Totals		67	....	....	363	145	513	.283	....	....	....	73	128	.570	....	....	....	50	121	....	....	....	....	....	5.4	....	0.7	....
NBL Season Totals		2	....	....	6	2	....	....	....	....	....	2	4	....	....	....	....	....	4	....	....	....	....	....	3.0	....	....	....
Career Totals		69	....	....	369	147	513	....	....	....	....	75	132	....	....	....	....	50	125	....	....	....	....	....	5.3	....	0.7	....

• GRAYER, Jeff

Jeffrey Grayer

Born: Dec. 17, 1965. Flint, MI, United States. Height: 6'5". Weight: 200 lbs. Drafted: 1988 College: Iowa State

YEAR	TEAM	GP	GS	MIN	PTS	FGM	FGA	FG%	3PM	3PA	3P%	FTM	FTA	FT%	ORB	DRB	TRB	AST	PF	DQ	STL	BLK	TO	MPG	PPG	RPG	APG	PCM
88-89	Milwaukee	11	2	200	81	32	73	.438	0	2	.000	17	20	.850	14	21	35	22	15	0	10	1	19	18.2	7.4	3.2	2.0	.416
89-90	Milwaukee	71	40	1427	548	224	487	.460	1	8	.125	99	152	.651	94	123	217	107	125	0	48	10	85	20.1	7.7	3.1	1.5	.357
90-91	Milwaukee	82	7	1422	521	210	485	.433	0	3	.000	101	147	.687	111	135	246	123	98	0	48	9	82	17.3	6.4	3.0	1.5	.376
91-92	Milwaukee	82	11	1659	739	309	689	.448	19	66	.288	102	153	.667	129	128	257	150	142	0	64	13	107	20.2	9.0	3.1	1.8	.403
92-93	Golden State	48	12	1025	423	165	353	.467	2	14	.143	91	136	.669	71	86	157	70	120	1	31	8	53	21.4	8.8	3.3	1.5	.369
93-94	Golden State	67	4	1096	455	191	363	.526	2	12	.167	71	118	.602	76	115	191	62	103	0	33	13	60	16.4	6.8	2.9	0.9	.418
94-95	Philadelphia	47	25	1098	389	163	381	.428	5	15	.333	58	83	.699	58	91	149	74	80	1	27	4	56	23.4	8.3	3.2	1.6	.301
96-97	Sacramento	25	0	316	91	38	83	.458	4	11	.364	11	20	.550	21	17	38	25	42	0	8	7	15	12.6	3.6	1.5	1.0	.277
97-98	Charlotte	1	0	11	0	0	4	.000	0	3	.000	0	0	.000	0	0	0	1	0	0	0	0	2	11.0	0.0	0.0	1.0	-.400
97-98	Golden State	4	0	23	10	4	7	.571	2	3	.667	0	0	.000	0	4	4	1	7	0	2	0	2	5.8	2.5	1.0	0.3	.383
NBA Season Totals		438	101	8277	3257	1336	2925	.457	35	137	.255	550	829	.663	574	720	1294	635	732	2	271	65	481	18.9	7.4	3.0	1.4	....
89-90	Milwaukee	4	0	12	0	0	0	.000	0	0	.000	0	0	.000	0	2	2	1	1	0	0	0	1	3.0	0.0	0.5	0.3	.128
90-91	Milwaukee	3	0	37	15	5	13	.385	0	0	.000	5	6	.833	3	3	6	6	2	0	1	0	3	12.3	5.0	2.0	2.0	.440
93-94	Golden State	3	0	46	24	11	20	.550	0	0	.000	2	3	.667	1	5	6	1	7	0	1	1	2	15.3	8.0	2.0	0.3	.406
NBA Playoff Totals		10	0	95	39	16	33	.485	0	0	.000	7	9	.778	4	10	14	8	10	0	2	1	6	9.5	3.9	1.4	0.8	....

• GREACEN, Bob

Robert Alexander Greacen

Born: Sept. 15, 1947. Height: 6'7". Weight: 206 lbs. Drafted: 1969 College: Rutgers

YEAR	TEAM	GP	GS	MIN	PTS	FGM	FGA	FG%	3PM	3PA	3P%	FTM	FTA	FT%	ORB	DRB	TRB	AST	PF	DQ	STL	BLK	TO	MPG	PPG	RPG	APG	PCM
69-70	Milwaukee	41	....	292	106	44	109	.404	....	....	....	18	28	.643	....	....	59	27	49	0	....	....	....	7.1	2.6	1.4	0.7	.360
70-71	Milwaukee	2	....	43	5	1	12	.083	....	....	....	3	7	.429	....	....	6	13	7	0	....	....	....	21.5	2.5	3.0	6.5	.251
71-72	New York-A	4	....	20	2	1	2	.500	0	0	.000	0	0	.000	1	1	2	1	1	0	....	....	2	5.0	0.5	0.5	0.3	.178
NBA Season Totals		43	....	335	111	45	121	.372	....	....	....	21	35	.600	....	....	65	40	56	0	....	....	....	7.8	2.6	1.5	0.9	....
ABA Season Totals		4	....	20	2	1	2	.500	0	0	.000	0	0	.000	1	1	2	1	1	0	....	....	2	5.0	0.5	0.5	0.3	....
Career Totals		47	....	355	113	46	123	.374	0	0	.000	21	35	.600	1	1	67	41	57	0	....	....	2	7.6	2.4	1.4	0.9	....
69-70	Milwaukee	1	....	8	2	1	4	.250	....	....	....	0	1	.000	....	....	2	3	0	0	....	....	....	8.0	2.0	2.0	3.0	.505
70-71	Milwaukee	7	....	16	12	4	11	.364	....	....	....	4	4	1.000	....	....	5	0	4	0	....	....	....	2.3	1.7	0.7	0.0	.535
NBA Playoff Totals		8	....	24	14	5	15	.333	....	....	....	4	5	.800	....	....	7	3	4	0	....	....	....	3.0	1.8	0.9	0.4	....

• GREEN, A.C.

A.C. Green Jr.

Born: Oct. 4, 1963. Portland, OR, United States. Height: 6'9". Weight: 220 lbs. Drafted: 1985 College: Oregon State

YEAR	TEAM	GP	GS	MIN	PTS	FGM	FGA	FG%	3PM	3PA	3P%	FTM	FTA	FT%	ORB	DRB	TRB	AST	PF	DQ	STL	BLK	TO	MPG	PPG	RPG	APG	PCM
85-86	LA Lakers	82	1	1542	521	209	388	.539	1	6	.167	102	167	.611	160	221	381	54	229	2	49	49	98	18.8	6.4	4.6	0.7	.409
86-87	LA Lakers	79	72	2240	852	316	587	.538	0	5	.000	220	282	.780	210	405	615	84	171	0	70	80	103	28.4	10.8	7.8	1.1	.535
87-88	LA Lakers	82	64	2636	937	322	640	.503	0	2	.000	293	379	.773	245	465	710	93	204	0	87	45	123	32.1	11.4	8.7	1.1	.484
88-89	LA Lakers	82	82	2510	1088	401	758	.529	4	17	.235	282	359	.786	258	481	739	103	172	0	94	55	123	30.6	13.3	9.0	1.3	.582
89-90	LA Lakers	82	82	2709	1061	385	806	.478	13	46	.283	278	370	.751	262	450	712	90	207	0	66	50	115	33.0	12.9	8.7	1.1	.476
90-91	LA Lakers	82	21	2164	750	258	542	.476	11	55	.200	223	302	.738	201	315	516	71	117	0	59	23	98	26.4	9.1	6.3	0.9	.432
91-92	LA Lakers	82	53	2902	1116	382	803	.476	12	56	.214	340	457	.744	306	456	762	117	141	0	91	36	115	35.4	13.6	9.3	1.4	.499
92-93	LA Lakers	82	55	2819	1051	379	706	.537	16	46	.348	277	375	.739	287	424	711	116	149	0	88	37	115	34.4	12.8	8.7	1.4	.506
93-94	Phoenix	82	55	2825	1204	465	926	.502	8	35	.229	266	362	.735	275	478	753	137	142	0	70	38	98	34.5	14.7	9.2	1.7	.538
94-95	Phoenix	82	52	2687	916	311	617	.504	43	127	.339	251	343	.732	194	475	669	127	146	0	55	31	115	32.8	11.2	8.2	1.5	.466
95-96	Phoenix	82	36	2113	612	215	444	.484	14	52	.269	168	237	.709	166	388	554	72	141	1	45	23	82	25.8	7.5	6.8	0.9	.417
96-97	Phoenix	27	19	548	153	61	128	.477	0	3	.000	31	48	.646	33	105	138	17	34	0	18	1	19	20.3	5.7	5.1	0.6	.390
96-97	Dallas	56	54	1944	444	173	356	.486	1	17	.059	97	149	.651	189	329	518	52	111	0	52	15	56	34.7	7.9	9.3	0.9	.384
97-98	Dallas	82	68	2649	600	242	534	.453	0	4	.000	116	162	.716	219	449	668	123	157	0	78	27	66	32.3	7.3	8.1	1.5	.385
98-99	Dallas	50	35	924	246	108	256	.422	0	8	.000	30	52	.577	82	146	228	25	69	0	28	8	19	18.5	4.9	4.6	0.5	.346
99-00	LA Lakers	82	82	1929	413	173	387	.447	1	4	.250	66	95	.695	160	326	486	80	127	0	53	18	53	23.5	5.0	5.9	1.0	.359
00-01	Miami	82	1	1411	367	144	324	.444	0	6	.000	79	111	.712	107	206	313	39	119	0	30	8	45	17.2	4.5	3.8	0.5	.323
NBA Season Totals		1278	832	36552	12331	4544	9202	.494	124	489	.254	3119	4250	.734	3354	6119	9473	1400	2436	3	1033	544	1443	28.6	9.6	7.4	1.1	....
85-86	LA Lakers	9	0	106	22	9	17	.529	0	0	.000	4	9	.444	3	13	16	0	13	0	1	3	4	11.8	2.4	1.8	0.0	.199
86-87	LA Lakers	18	18	505	207	71	130	.546	0	0	.000	65	87	.747	54	88	142	11	47	0	9	8	17	28.1	11.5	7.9	0.6	.523
87-88	LA Lakers	24	18	726	239	92	169	.544	0	0	.000	55	73	.753	57	118	175	20	61	0	11	12	26	30.3	10.0	7.3	0.8	.430
88-89	LA Lakers	15	15	502	152	47	114	.412	0	3	.000	58	76	.763	38	99	137	18	37	1	16	6	23	33.5	10.1	9.1	1.2	.418
89-90	LA Lakers	9	9	252	106	41	79	.519	0	0	.000	24	32	.750	34	47	81	9	22	0	5	4	14	28.0	11.8	9.0	1.0	.544
90-91	LA Lakers	19	1	400	124	41	97	.423	4	8	.500	38	54	.704	46	56	102	9	37	0	12	3	19	21.1	6.5	5.4	0.5	.370
91-92	LA Lakers	4	4	153	51	16	39	.410	0	0	.000	19	23	.826	15	21	36	7	10	0	7	0	5	38.3	12.8	9.0	1.8	.431
92-93	LA Lakers	5	5	220	49	18	42	.429	0	5	.000	13	21	.619	26	47	73	13	14	1	7	3	9	44.0	9.8	14.6	2.6	.451
93-94	Phoenix	10	2	350	125	40	83	.482	7	17	.412	38	62	.613	29	55	84	13	22	0	10	2	7	35.0	12.5	8.4	1.3	.458
94-95	Phoenix	10	10	368	128	36	78	.462	1	12	.083	55	63	.873	38	82	120	13	22	0	6	2	10	36.8	12.8	12.0	1.3	.541
95-96	Phoenix	4	4	87	19	6	17	.353	0	3	.000	7	8	.875	6	12	18	2	7	0	1	0	2	21.8	4.8	4.5	0.5	.264

YEAR	TEAM	GP	GS	MIN	PTS	FGM	FGA	FG%	3PM	3PA	3P%	FTM	FTA	FT%	ORB	DRB	TRB	AST	PF	DQ	STL	BLK	TO	MPG	PPG	RPG	APG	PCM
99-00	LA Lakers	23	23	429	90	37	90	.411	0	0	.000	16	23	.696	43	53	96	13	44	0	14	3	9	18.7	3.9	4.2	0.6	.297
00-01	Miami	3	0	21	3	1	3	.333	0	0	.000	1	1	1.000	1	3	4	2	4	0	1	0	1	7.0	1.0	1.3	0.7	.248
NBA Playoff Totals		153	109	4119	1315	455	958	.475	12	48	.250	393	532	.739	390	694	1084	130	340	2	100	46	146	26.9	8.6	7.1	0.8	....

• GREEN, Johnny

John M. (Jumpin' Johnny) Green

Born: Dec. 8, 1933. Dayton, OH, United States.   Height: 6'5".   Weight: 200 lbs.   Drafted: 1959   College: Michigan State

YEAR	TEAM	GP	GS	MIN	PTS	FGM	FGA	FG%	3PM	3PA	3P%	FTM	FTA	FT%	ORB	DRB	TRB	AST	PF	DQ	STL	BLK	TO	MPG	PPG	RPG	APG	PCM
59-60	New York	69	....	1232	481	209	468	.447	....	....	....	63	155	.406	....	....	539	52	195	3	....	....	....	17.9	7.0	7.8	0.8	.527
60-61	New York	78	....	1784	797	326	758	.430	....	....	....	145	278	.522	....	....	838	97	194	3	....	....	....	22.9	10.2	10.7	1.2	.618
61-62	New York	80	....	2789	1275	507	1164	.436	....	....	....	261	434	.601	....	....	1066	191	265	4	....	....	....	34.9	15.9	13.3	2.4	.594
62-63	New York	80	....	2553	1444	582	1261	.462	....	....	....	280	439	.638	....	....	964	152	243	5	....	....	....	31.9	18.1	12.1	1.9	.664
63-64	New York	80	....	2134	1159	482	1026	.470	....	....	....	195	392	.497	....	....	799	157	246	4	....	....	....	26.7	14.5	10.0	2.0	.645
64-65	New York	78	....	1720	857	346	737	.469	....	....	....	165	301	.548	....	....	545	129	194	3	....	....	....	22.1	11.0	7.0	1.7	.586
65-66	New York	7	....	208	101	43	79	.544	....	....	....	15	31	.484	....	....	74	11	21	0	....	....	....	29.7	14.4	10.6	1.6	.623
65-66	Baltimore	72	....	1437	817	315	589	.535	....	....	....	187	357	.524	....	....	571	96	162	3	....	....	....	20.0	11.3	7.9	1.3	.721
66-67	Baltimore	61	....	948	502	203	437	.465	....	....	....	96	207	.464	....	....	394	57	139	7	....	....	....	15.5	8.2	6.5	0.9	.631
67-68	San Diego	42	....	1073	582	241	526	.458	....	....	....	100	212	.472	....	....	423	59	112	3	....	....	....	25.5	13.9	10.1	1.4	.628
67-68	Philadelphia	35	....	367	177	69	150	.460	....	....	....	39	83	.470	....	....	122	21	51	0	....	....	....	10.5	5.1	3.5	0.6	.537
68-69	Philadelphia	74	....	795	349	146	282	.518	....	....	....	57	125	.456	....	....	330	47	110	1	....	....	....	10.7	4.7	4.5	0.6	.618
69-70	Cincinnati	78	....	2278	1216	481	860	**.559**	....	....	....	254	429	.592	....	....	841	112	268	6	....	....	....	29.2	15.6	10.8	1.4	.682
70-71	Cincinnati	75	....	2147	1252	502	855	**.587**	....	....	....	248	402	.617	....	....	656	89	233	7	....	....	....	28.6	16.7	8.7	1.2	.674
71-72	Cincinnati	82	....	1914	803	331	582	.569	....	....	....	141	250	.564	....	....	560	120	238	5	....	....	....	23.3	9.8	6.8	1.5	.552
72-73	Omaha	66	....	1245	469	190	317	.599	....	....	....	89	131	.679	....	....	361	59	185	7	....	....	....	18.9	7.1	5.5	0.9	.514
NBA Season Totals		1057	....	24624	12281	4973	10091	.493	....	....	....	2335	4226	.553	....	....	9083	1449	2856	61	....	....	....	23.3	11.6	8.6	1.4	....
65-66	Baltimore	3	....	96	41	20	34	.588	....	....	....	1	8	.125	....	....	27	4	9	0	....	....	....	32.0	13.7	9.0	1.3	.519
67-68	Philadelphia	12	....	219	96	38	65	.585	....	....	....	20	43	.465	....	....	66	8	19	0	....	....	....	18.3	8.0	5.5	0.7	.548
68-69	Philadelphia	5	....	44	23	9	16	.563	....	....	....	5	9	.556	....	....	14	1	12	1	....	....	....	8.8	4.6	2.8	0.2	.530
NBA Playoff Totals		20	....	359	160	67	115	.583	....	....	....	26	60	.433	....	....	107	13	40	1	....	....	....	18.0	8.0	5.4	0.7	....

• GREEN, Ken

Kenneth (Apple) Green

Born: Sept. 19, 1959. Newman, GA, United States.   Height: 6'8".   Weight: 215 lbs.   Drafted: 1981   College: Pan American

YEAR	TEAM	GP	GS	MIN	PTS	FGM	FGA	FG%	3PM	3PA	3P%	FTM	FTA	FT%	ORB	DRB	TRB	AST	PF	DQ	STL	BLK	TO	MPG	PPG	RPG	APG	PCM
85-86	New York	7	0	72	31	13	27	.481	0	0	.000	5	9	.556	12	15	27	2	8	0	4	0	1	10.3	4.4	3.9	0.3	.589
NBA Season Totals		7	0	72	31	13	27	.481	0	0	.000	5	9	.556	12	15	27	2	8	0	4	0	1	10.3	4.4	3.9	0.3	....

• GREEN, Kenny

Kenneth Leroy Green

Born: Oct. 11, 1964. Eustis, FL, United States.   Height: 6'6".   Weight: 210 lbs.   Drafted: 1985   College: Wake Forest

YEAR	TEAM	GP	GS	MIN	PTS	FGM	FGA	FG%	3PM	3PA	3P%	FTM	FTA	FT%	ORB	DRB	TRB	AST	PF	DQ	STL	BLK	TO	MPG	PPG	RPG	APG	PCM
85-86	Washington	20	0	221	109	44	101	.436	0	1	.000	21	26	.808	17	21	38	3	26	0	4	7	16	11.1	5.5	1.9	0.2	.342
85-86	Philadelphia	21	0	232	92	39	91	.429	0	0	.000	14	23	.609	10	25	35	6	27	0	1	2	19	11.0	4.4	1.7	0.3	.220
86-87	Philadelphia	19	0	172	64	25	70	.357	0	0	.000	14	19	.737	6	22	28	7	8	0	4	2	15	9.1	3.4	1.5	0.4	.240
NBA Season Totals		60	0	625	265	108	262	.412	0	1	.000	49	68	.721	33	68	101	16	61	0	9	11	50	10.4	4.4	1.7	0.3	....

• GREEN, Lamar

Lamar Anthony Green

Born: Mar. 22, 1947. Birmingham, AL, United States.   Height: 6'7".   Weight: 210 lbs.   Drafted: 1969   College: Morehead State

YEAR	TEAM	GP	GS	MIN	PTS	FGM	FGA	FG%	3PM	3PA	3P%	FTM	FTA	FT%	ORB	DRB	TRB	AST	PF	DQ	STL	BLK	TO	MPG	PPG	RPG	APG	PCM
69-70	Phoenix	58	....	700	243	101	234	.432	....	....	....	41	70	.586	....	....	276	17	115	2	....	....	....	12.1	4.2	4.8	0.3	.464
70-71	Phoenix	68	....	1326	398	167	369	.453	....	....	....	64	106	.604	....	....	466	53	202	5	....	....	....	19.5	5.9	6.9	0.8	.438
71-72	Phoenix	67	....	991	332	133	298	.446	....	....	....	66	90	.733	....	....	348	45	134	1	....	....	....	14.8	5.0	5.2	0.7	.477
72-73	Phoenix	80	....	2048	537	224	520	.431	....	....	....	89	118	.754	....	....	746	89	263	10	....	....	....	25.6	6.7	9.3	1.1	.439
73-74	Phoenix	72	....	1103	296	129	317	.407	....	....	....	38	68	.559	85	265	350	43	150	1	32	38	....	15.3	4.1	4.9	0.6	.369
74-75	Virginia-A	51	....	856	270	115	270	.426	0	0	.000	40	54	.741	86	169	255	47	139	....	13	25	60	16.8	5.3	5.0	0.9	.401
74-75	New Orleans	15	....	280	57	24	70	.343	....	....	....	9	20	.450	28	81	109	16	38	0	4	5	....	18.7	3.8	7.3	1.1	.386
NBA Season Totals		360	....	6448	1863	778	1808	.430	....	....	....	307	472	.650	113	346	2295	263	902	19	36	43	....	17.9	5.2	6.4	0.7	....
ABA Season Totals		51	....	856	270	115	270	.426	0	0	.000	40	54	.741	86	169	255	47	139	....	13	25	60	16.8	5.3	5.0	0.9	....
Career Totals		411	....	7304	2133	893	2078	.430	0	0	.000	347	526	.660	199	515	2550	310	1041	19	49	68	60	17.8	5.2	6.2	0.8	....
69-70	Phoenix	6	....	69	18	8	28	.286	....	....	....	2	5	.400	....	....	23	5	8	0	....	....	....	11.5	3.0	3.8	0.8	.310
NBA Playoff Totals		6	....	69	18	8	28	.286	....	....	....	2	5	.400	....	....	23	5	8	0	....	....	....	11.5	3.0	3.8	0.8	....

• GREEN, Litterial

Litterial Green

Born: Mar. 7, 1970. Pascagoula, MS, United States.   Height: 6'1".   Weight: 185 lbs.   Drafted: 1992   College: Georgia

YEAR	TEAM	GP	GS	MIN	PTS	FGM	FGA	FG%	3PM	3PA	3P%	FTM	FTA	FT%	ORB	DRB	TRB	AST	PF	DQ	STL	BLK	TO	MPG	PPG	RPG	APG	PCM
92-93	Orlando	52	4	626	235	87	198	.439	1	10	.100	60	96	.625	11	23	34	116	70	0	23	4	42	12.0	4.5	0.7	2.2	.357
93-94	Orlando	29	0	126	73	22	57	.386	1	4	.250	28	37	.757	6	6	12	9	16	0	6	1	12	4.3	2.5	0.4	0.3	.362
96-97	Detroit	45	0	311	90	30	64	.469	0	10	.000	30	47	.638	6	16	22	41	27	0	16	1	14	6.9	2.0	0.5	0.9	.337
97-98	Milwaukee	21	0	124	25	5	23	.217	0	2	.000	15	20	.750	1	6	7	16	11	0	4	0	8	5.9	1.2	0.3	0.8	.172
98-99	Cleveland	1	0	2	0	0	1	.000	0	0	.000	0	0	.000	0	0	0	0	0	0	0	0	0	2.0	0.0	0.0	0.0	-.445
NBA Season Totals		148	4	1189	423	144	343	.420	2	26	.077	133	200	.665	24	51	75	182	124	0	49	6	76	8.0	2.9	0.5	1.2	....

• GREEN, Luther
Luther Green

Born: Nov. 13, 1946. New York, NY, United States. Height: 6'7". Weight: 190 lbs. Drafted: 1969 College: Long Island University

YEAR TEAM	GP	GS	MIN	PTS	FGM	FGA	FG%	3PM	3PA	3P%	FTM	FTA	FT%	ORB	DRB	TRB	AST	PF	DQ	STL	BLK	TO	MPG	PPG	RPG	APG	PCM
69-70 New York-A	59	....	739	283	114	303	.376	0	3	.000	55	97	.567	96	167	263	27	117	2	....	....	54	12.5	4.8	4.5	0.5	.418
70-71 New York-A	26	....	164	98	40	88	.455	0	4	.000	18	44	.409	22	33	55	3	19	0	....	....	21	6.3	3.8	2.1	0.1	.544
72-73 Philadelphia	5	....	32	3	0	11	.000	....	....	....	3	9	.333	....	....	3	0	3	0	....	....	....	6.4	0.6	0.6	0.0	-.241
NBA Season Totals	5	....	32	3	0	11	.000	....	....	....	3	9	.333	....	....	3	0	3	0	....	....	....	6.4	0.6	0.6	0.0	....
ABA Season Totals	85	....	903	381	154	391	.394	0	7	.000	73	141	.518	118	200	318	30	136	2	....	....	75	10.6	4.5	3.7	0.4	....
Career Totals	90	....	935	384	154	402	.383	0	7	.000	76	150	.507	118	200	321	30	139	2	....	....	75	10.4	4.3	3.6	0.3	....
69-70 New York-A	7	....	82	33	11	29	.379	1	2	.500	10	15	.667	....	....	28	3	....	0	....	....	....	11.7	4.7	4.0	0.4	....
ABA Playoff Totals	7	....	82	33	11	29	.379	1	2	.500	10	15	.667	....	....	28	3	....	0	....	....	....	11.7	4.7	4.0	0.4	....

• GREEN, Mike
Michael Kenneth (Count) Green

Born: Aug. 6, 1951. McComb, MS, United States. Height: 6'10". Weight: 200 lbs. Drafted: 1973 College: Louisiana Tech

YEAR TEAM	GP	GS	MIN	PTS	FGM	FGA	FG%	3PM	3PA	3P%	FTM	FTA	FT%	ORB	DRB	TRB	AST	PF	DQ	STL	BLK	TO	MPG	PPG	RPG	APG	PCM
73-74 Denver-A	79	....	1648	904	367	799	.459	1	2	.500	169	226	.748	225	359	584	64	191	....	47	126	128	20.9	11.4	7.4	0.8	.607
74-75 Denver-A	81	....	2557	1411	593	1095	.542	0	4	.000	225	305	.738	282	467	749	101	271	....	85	174	203	31.6	17.4	9.2	1.2	.621
75-76 Virginia-A	54	....	1719	924	385	832	.463	0	4	.000	154	198	.778	196	323	519	82	187	....	68	80	136	31.8	17.1	9.6	1.5	.568
76-77 Seattle	76	....	1928	746	290	658	.441	....	....	....	166	235	.706	191	312	503	120	201	1	45	129	....	25.4	9.8	6.6	1.6	.458
77-78 Seattle	9	....	250	107	43	87	.494	....	....	....	21	31	.677	22	33	55	10	26	0	6	13	23	27.8	11.9	6.1	1.1	.435
77-78 San Antonio	63	....	1132	476	195	427	.457	....	....	....	86	111	.775	108	196	304	66	167	1	24	87	82	18.0	7.6	4.8	1.0	.490
78-79 San Antonio	76	....	1641	571	235	477	.493	....	....	....	101	144	.701	131	223	354	116	230	3	37	122	91	21.6	7.5	4.7	1.5	.450
79-80 Kansas City	21	....	459	162	69	159	.434	0	2	.000	24	42	.571	35	78	113	28	55	0	13	21	36	21.9	7.7	5.4	1.3	.389
NBA Season Totals	245	....	5410	2062	832	1808	.460	0	2	.000	398	563	.707	487	842	1329	340	679	5	125	372	232	22.1	8.4	5.4	1.4	....
ABA Season Totals	214	....	5924	3239	1345	2726	.493	1	10	.100	548	729	.752	703	1149	1852	247	649	....	200	380	467	27.7	15.1	8.7	1.2	....
Career Totals	459	....	11334	5301	2177	4534	.480	1	12	.083	946	1292	.732	1190	1991	3181	587	1328	5	325	752	699	24.7	11.5	6.9	1.3	....
74-75 Denver-A	13	....	487	277	112	226	.496	0	1	.000	53	60	.883	54	67	121	14	51	....	10	21	27	37.5	21.3	9.3	1.1	.561
77-78 San Antonio	6	....	174	65	28	58	.483	....	....	....	9	10	.900	17	27	44	11	21	0	5	16	8	29.0	10.8	7.3	1.8	.525
78-79 San Antonio	14	....	350	110	48	114	.421	....	....	....	14	21	.667	35	38	73	11	59	3	13	35	18	25.0	7.9	5.2	0.8	.359
NBA Playoff Totals	20	....	524	175	76	172	.442	....	....	....	23	31	.742	52	65	117	22	80	3	18	51	26	26.2	8.8	5.9	1.1	....
ABA Playoff Totals	13	....	487	277	112	226	.496	0	1	.000	53	60	.883	54	67	121	14	51	....	10	21	27	37.5	21.3	9.3	1.1	....
Career Playoff Totals	33	....	1011	452	188	398	.472	0	1	.000	76	91	.835	106	132	238	36	131	3	28	72	53	30.6	13.7	7.2	1.1	....

• GREEN, Rickey
Rickey Green

Born: Aug. 18, 1954. Chicago, IL, United States. Height: 6' Weight: 170 lbs. Drafted: 1977 College: Michigan

YEAR TEAM	GP	GS	MIN	PTS	FGM	FGA	FG%	3PM	3PA	3P%	FTM	FTA	FT%	ORB	DRB	TRB	AST	PF	DQ	STL	BLK	TO	MPG	PPG	RPG	APG	PCM
77-78 Golden State	76	....	1098	340	143	375	.381	....	....	....	54	90	.600	49	67	116	149	95	0	58	1	76	14.4	4.5	1.5	2.0	.304
78-79 Detroit	27	....	431	179	67	177	.379	....	....	....	45	67	.672	15	25	40	63	37	0	25	1	43	16.0	6.6	1.5	2.3	.334
80-81 Utah	47	....	1307	422	176	366	.481	0	1	.000	70	97	.722	30	86	116	235	123	2	75	1	85	27.8	9.0	2.5	5.0	.409
81-82 Utah	81	73	2822	1202	500	1015	.493	0	8	.000	202	264	.765	85	158	243	630	183	0	185	9	194	34.8	14.8	3.0	7.8	.538
82-83 Utah	78	78	2783	1115	464	942	.493	2	13	.154	185	232	.797	62	161	223	697	154	0	**220**	4	218	35.7	14.3	2.9	8.9	.562
83-84 Utah	81	81	2768	1072	439	904	.486	2	17	.118	192	234	.821	56	174	230	748	155	1	**215**	13	170	34.2	13.2	2.8	9.2	.584
84-85 Utah	77	77	2431	1000	381	798	.477	6	20	.300	232	267	.869	37	152	189	597	131	0	132	3	177	31.6	13.0	2.5	7.8	.538
85-86 Utah	80	44	2012	932	357	758	.471	5	29	.172	213	250	.852	32	103	135	411	130	0	106	6	128	25.2	11.7	1.7	5.1	.513
86-87 Utah	81	80	2090	781	301	644	.467	7	19	.368	172	208	.827	38	125	163	541	108	0	110	2	130	25.8	9.6	2.0	6.7	.530
87-88 Utah	81	3	1116	393	157	370	.424	4	19	.211	75	83	.904	14	66	80	300	83	0	57	1	97	13.8	4.9	1.0	3.7	.458
88-89 Charlotte	33	2	370	128	57	132	.432	1	5	.200	13	14	.929	4	19	23	82	16	0	18	0	26	11.2	3.9	0.7	2.5	.411
88-89 Milwaukee	30	0	501	163	72	132	.545	2	6	.333	17	19	.895	7	39	46	105	19	0	22	2	33	16.7	5.4	1.5	3.5	.487
89-90 Indiana	69	0	927	244	100	231	.433	1	11	.091	43	51	.843	9	45	54	182	60	0	51	1	62	13.4	3.5	0.8	2.6	.350
90-91 Philadelphia	79	75	2248	793	334	722	.463	8	36	.222	117	141	.830	33	104	137	413	130	0	57	6	111	28.5	10.0	1.7	5.2	.393
91-92 Boston	26	0	367	106	46	103	.447	1	4	.250	13	18	.722	3	21	24	68	28	0	17	1	18	14.1	4.1	0.9	2.6	.362
NBA Season Totals	946	513	23271	8870	3594	7669	.469	39	188	.207	1643	2035	.807	474	1345	1819	5221	1452	3	1348	51	1568	24.6	9.4	1.9	5.5	....
83-84 Utah	11	11	404	161	64	151	.424	1	4	.250	32	43	.744	9	25	34	104	17	0	19	4	29	36.7	14.6	3.1	9.5	.506
84-85 Utah	10	10	302	150	57	106	.538	1	7	.143	35	38	.921	10	20	30	75	23	0	12	0	20	30.2	15.0	3.0	7.5	.638
85-86 Utah	4	4	119	53	21	43	.488	1	2	.500	10	11	.909	0	9	9	38	1	0	2	0	5	29.8	13.3	2.3	9.5	.655
86-87 Utah	4	3	72	27	11	23	.478	0	1	.000	5	6	.833	1	7	8	25	5	0	2	0	7	18.0	6.8	2.0	6.3	.591
87-88 Utah	7	0	38	4	2	8	.250	0	0	.000	0	0	.000	0	1	1	9	2	0	2	0	3	5.4	0.6	0.1	1.3	.187
88-89 Milwaukee	8	0	110	29	12	29	.414	1	2	.500	4	4	1.000	3	10	13	18	9	0	5	0	4	13.8	3.6	1.6	2.3	.375
89-90 Indiana	3	0	31	2	1	7	.143	0	0	.000	0	0	.000	0	1	1	3	5	0	1	0	2	10.3	0.7	0.3	1.0	-.090
90-91 Philadelphia	8	8	199	59	24	55	.436	3	4	.750	8	9	.889	1	8	9	22	9	0	7	0	13	24.9	7.4	1.1	2.8	.260
NBA Playoff Totals	55	36	1275	485	192	422	.455	7	20	.350	94	111	.847	24	81	105	294	71	0	50	4	83	23.2	8.8	1.9	5.3	....

• GREEN, Sean
Sean Curtis Green

Born: Feb. 2, 1970. Santa Monica, CA, United States. Height: 6'5". Weight: 210 lbs. Drafted: 1991 College: Iona

YEAR TEAM	GP	GS	MIN	PTS	FGM	FGA	FG%	3PM	3PA	3P%	FTM	FTA	FT%	ORB	DRB	TRB	AST	PF	DQ	STL	BLK	TO	MPG	PPG	RPG	APG	PCM
91-92 Indiana	35	0	256	141	62	158	.392	2	10	.200	15	28	.536	22	20	42	22	31	0	13	6	28	7.3	4.0	1.2	0.6	.334
92-93 Indiana	13	0	81	62	28	55	.509	3	10	.300	3	4	.750	4	5	9	7	11	0	2	1	9	6.2	4.8	0.7	0.5	.512
93-94 Philadelphia	35	0	332	149	63	182	.346	10	41	.244	13	18	.722	10	24	34	16	21	0	18	6	28	9.5	4.3	1.0	0.5	.219
93-94 Utah	1	0	2	0	0	1	.000	0	0	.000	0	0	.000	0	0	0	0	0	0	0	0	0	2.0	0.0	0.0	0.0	-.459
NBA Season Totals	84	0	671	352	153	396	.386	15	61	.246	31	50	.620	36	49	85	45	63	0	33	13	65	8.0	4.2	1.0	0.5	....
91-92 Indiana	1	0	3	0	0	0	.000	0	0	.000	0	0	.000	0	0	0	0	0	0	0	0	0	3.0	0.0	0.0	0.0	.000
NBA Playoff Totals	1	0	3	0	0	0	.000	0	0	.000	0	0	.000	0	0	0	0	0	0	0	0	0	3.0	0.0	0.0	0.0	....

• GREEN, Si

Sihugo Green

Born: Aug. 20, 1933. New York, NY, United States. Died: Oct.4, 1980. Height: 6'2". Weight: 185 lbs. Drafted: 1956 College: Duquesne

YEAR	TEAM	GP	GS	MIN	PTS	FGM	FGA	FG%	3PM	3PA	3P%	FTM	FTA	FT%	ORB	DRB	TRB	AST	PF	DQ	STL	BLK	TO	MPG	PPG	RPG	APG	PCM
56-57	Rochester	13	....	423	149	50	143	.350	....	....	....	49	69	.710	....	....	67	47	36	1	....	....	....	32.5	11.5	5.2	3.6	.396
58-59	Cincinnati	20	....	666	250	100	268	.373	....	....	....	50	73	.685	....	....	140	85	65	0	....	....	....	33.3	12.5	7.0	4.3	.453
58-59	St. Louis	26	....	443	146	46	147	.313	....	....	....	54	87	.621	....	....	112	28	62	1	....	....	....	17.0	5.6	4.3	1.1	.346
59-60	St. Louis	70	....	1354	429	159	427	.372	....	....	....	111	175	.634	....	....	257	133	150	3	....	....	....	19.3	6.1	3.7	1.9	.373
60-61	St. Louis	76	....	1968	700	263	718	.366	....	....	....	174	247	.704	....	....	380	258	234	2	....	....	....	25.9	9.2	5.0	3.4	.430
61-62	StL/Chi	71	....	2388	900	341	905	.377	....	....	....	218	311	.701	....	....	399	318	226	3	....	....	....	33.6	12.7	5.6	4.5	.433
62-63	Chicago	73	....	2648	853	322	783	.411	....	....	....	209	306	.683	....	....	335	422	274	5	....	....	....	36.3	11.7	4.6	5.8	.422
63-64	Baltimore	75	....	2064	772	287	691	.415	....	....	....	198	290	.683	....	....	282	215	224	5	....	....	....	27.5	10.3	3.8	2.9	.396
64-65	Baltimore	70	....	1086	405	152	368	.413	....	....	....	101	161	.627	....	....	169	140	134	1	....	....	....	15.5	5.8	2.4	2.0	.430
65-66	Boston	10	....	92	32	12	31	.387	....	....	....	8	16	.500	....	....	11	9	16	0	....	....	....	9.2	3.2	1.1	0.9	.296
NBA Season Totals		504	....	13132	4636	1732	4481	.387	....	....	....	1172	1735	.676	....	....	2152	1655	1421	21	....	....	....	26.1	9.2	4.3	3.3	....
58-59	St. Louis	6	....	131	36	12	25	.480	....	....	....	12	24	.500	....	....	23	14	20	1	....	....	....	21.8	6.0	3.8	2.3	.374
59-60	St. Louis	14	....	565	197	81	171	.474	....	....	....	35	58	.603	....	....	121	88	50	1	....	....	....	40.4	14.1	8.6	6.3	.535
60-61	St. Louis	12	....	350	137	56	148	.378	....	....	....	25	37	.676	....	....	71	48	38	1	....	....	....	29.2	11.4	5.9	4.0	.461
64-65	Baltimore	9	....	65	18	7	16	.438	....	....	....	4	5	.800	....	....	7	15	13	0	....	....	....	7.2	2.0	0.8	1.7	.455
NBA Playoff Totals		41	....	1111	388	156	360	.433	....	....	....	76	124	.613	....	....	222	165	121	3	....	....	....	27.1	9.5	5.4	4.0	....

• GREEN, Sidney

Sidney Green

Born: Jan. 4, 1961. Brooklyn, NY, United States. Height: 6'9". Weight: 220 lbs. Drafted: 1983 College: UNLV

YEAR	TEAM	GP	GS	MIN	PTS	FGM	FGA	FG%	3PM	3PA	3P%	FTM	FTA	FT%	ORB	DRB	TRB	AST	PF	DQ	STL	BLK	TO	MPG	PPG	RPG	APG	PCM
83-84	Chicago	49	0	667	255	100	228	.439	0	0	.000	55	77	.714	58	116	174	25	128	1	18	17	59	13.6	5.2	3.6	0.5	.349
84-85	Chicago	48	1	740	295	108	250	.432	0	4	.000	79	98	.806	72	174	246	29	102	0	11	14	67	15.4	6.1	5.1	0.6	.442
85-86	Chicago	80	68	2307	1076	407	875	.465	0	8	.000	262	335	.782	208	450	658	139	292	5	70	37	224	28.8	13.5	8.2	1.7	.487
86-87	Detroit	80	69	1792	631	256	542	.472	0	2	.000	119	177	.672	196	457	653	62	197	0	41	50	128	22.4	7.9	8.2	0.8	.494
87-88	New York	82	65	2049	642	258	585	.441	0	2	.000	126	190	.663	221	421	642	93	318	9	65	32	148	25.0	7.8	7.8	1.1	.395
88-89	New York	82	0	1277	517	194	422	.460	0	3	.000	129	170	.759	157	237	394	76	172	0	47	18	123	15.6	6.3	4.8	0.9	.470
89-90	Orlando	73	31	1860	761	312	667	.468	1	3	.333	136	209	.651	166	422	588	99	231	4	50	26	117	25.5	10.4	8.1	1.4	.486
90-91	San Antonio	66	7	1099	443	177	384	.461	0	3	.000	89	105	.848	98	215	313	52	172	0	32	13	86	16.7	6.7	4.7	0.8	.429
91-92	San Antonio	80	1	1127	367	147	344	.427	0	0	.000	73	89	.820	92	250	342	36	148	0	29	11	64	14.1	4.6	4.3	0.5	.392
92-93	San Antonio	15	0	202	53	20	49	.408	0	0	.000	13	15	.867	18	53	71	19	21	1	5	3	12	13.5	3.5	4.7	1.3	.485
92-93	Charlotte	24	0	127	40	14	40	.350	0	2	.000	12	16	.750	14	33	47	5	16	0	1	2	7	5.3	1.7	2.0	0.2	.408
NBA Season Totals		679	242	13247	5080	1993	4386	.454	1	27	.037	1093	1481	.738	1300	2828	4128	635	1797	20	369	223	1035	19.5	7.5	6.1	0.9	....
84-85	Chicago	3	0	54	31	12	24	.500	0	0	.000	7	11	.636	10	5	15	2	8	0	0	1	1	18.0	10.3	5.0	0.7	.562
85-86	Chicago	3	0	53	18	6	20	.300	0	0	.000	6	12	.500	7	5	12	0	9	0	1	1	3	17.7	6.0	4.0	0.0	.156
86-87	Detroit	9	0	42	17	6	10	.600	0	0	.000	5	6	.833	3	6	9	1	2	0	1	2	3	4.7	1.9	1.0	0.1	.508
87-88	New York	4	4	93	16	8	17	.471	0	0	.000	0	0	.000	8	25	33	7	14	0	0	1	9	23.3	4.0	8.3	1.8	.343
88-89	New York	9	0	128	36	13	30	.433	0	0	.000	10	14	.714	14	22	36	5	23	0	2	1	7	14.2	4.0	4.0	0.6	.334
90-91	San Antonio	3	0	11	8	3	6	.500	0	0	.000	2	2	1.000	1	3	4	0	3	0	0	0	1	3.7	2.7	1.3	0.0	.600
91-92	San Antonio	3	0	47	9	3	10	.300	0	0	.000	3	4	.750	5	6	11	2	6	0	0	0	2	15.7	3.0	3.7	0.7	.207
92-93	Charlotte	9	0	78	15	7	18	.389	0	0	.000	1	3	.333	8	21	29	1	15	0	1	1	2	8.7	1.7	3.2	0.1	.320
NBA Playoff Totals		43	4	506	150	58	135	.430	0	0	.000	34	52	.654	56	93	149	18	80	0	5	7	28	11.8	3.5	3.5	0.4	....

• GREEN, Steve

Steven Michael Green

Born: Oct. 4, 1953. Madison, WI, United States. Height: 6'7". Weight: 220 lbs. Drafted: 1975 College: Indiana

YEAR	TEAM	GP	GS	MIN	PTS	FGM	FGA	FG%	3PM	3PA	3P%	FTM	FTA	FT%	ORB	DRB	TRB	AST	PF	DQ	STL	BLK	TO	MPG	PPG	RPG	APG	PCM
75-76	St. Louis-A	36	....	534	236	99	243	.407	0	5	.000	38	52	.731	38	44	82	35	79	....	19	7	32	14.8	6.6	2.3	1.0	.334
75-76	Utah-A	16	....	534	238	96	195	.492	0	0	.000	46	56	.821	46	66	112	29	71	....	12	3	40	33.4	14.9	7.0	1.8	.460
76-77	Indiana	70	....	918	450	183	424	.432	....	....	....	84	113	.743	79	98	177	46	157	2	46	12	....	13.1	6.4	2.5	0.7	.400
77-78	Indiana	44	....	449	151	56	128	.438	....	....	....	39	56	.696	31	40	71	30	67	0	14	2	22	10.2	3.4	1.6	0.7	.316
78-79	Indiana	39	....	265	104	42	89	.472	....	....	....	20	34	.588	22	30	52	21	39	0	11	3	16	6.8	2.7	1.3	0.5	.400
NBA Season Totals		153	....	1632	705	281	641	.438	....	....	....	143	203	.704	132	168	300	97	263	2	71	17	38	10.7	4.6	2.0	0.6	....
ABA Season Totals		52	....	1068	474	195	438	.445	0	5	.000	84	108	.778	84	110	194	64	150	....	31	10	72	20.5	9.1	3.7	1.2	....
Career Totals		205	....	2700	1179	476	1079	.441	0	5	.000	227	311	.730	216	278	494	161	413	2	102	27	110	13.2	5.8	2.4	0.8	....

• GREEN, Tommie

Tommie L. Green

Born: Apr. 8, 1956. Baton Rouge, LA, United States. Height: 6'2". Weight: 185 lbs. Drafted: 1978 College: Southern

YEAR	TEAM	GP	GS	MIN	PTS	FGM	FGA	FG%	3PM	3PA	3P%	FTM	FTA	FT%	ORB	DRB	TRB	AST	PF	DQ	STL	BLK	TO	MPG	PPG	RPG	APG	PCM
78-79	New Orleans	59	....	809	232	92	237	.388	....	....	....	48	63	.762	20	48	68	140	111	0	61	6	89	13.7	3.9	1.2	2.4	.298
NBA Season Totals		59	....	809	232	92	237	.388	....	....	....	48	63	.762	20	48	68	140	111	0	61	6	89	13.7	3.9	1.2	2.4	....

• GREENSPAN, Jerry

Gerald Greenspan

Born: Nov. 22, 1941. Height: 6'5". Weight: 195 lbs. Drafted: 1963 College: Maryland

YEAR	TEAM	GP	GS	MIN	PTS	FGM	FGA	FG%	3PM	3PA	3P%	FTM	FTA	FT%	ORB	DRB	TRB	AST	PF	DQ	STL	BLK	TO	MPG	PPG	RPG	APG	PCM
63-64	Philadelphia	20	....	280	98	32	90	.356	....	....	....	34	50	.680	....	....	72	11	54	0	....	....	....	14.0	4.9	3.6	0.6	.340
64-65	Philadelphia	5	....	49	24	8	13	.615	....	....	....	8	8	1.000	....	....	11	0	12	0	....	....	....	9.8	4.8	2.2	0.0	.490
NBA Season Totals		25	....	329	122	40	103	.388	....	....	....	42	58	.724	....	....	83	11	66	0	....	....	....	13.2	4.9	3.3	0.4	....

• GREENWOOD, Dave

David Kasim Greenwood

Born: May 27, 1957. Lynwood, CA, United States. Height: 6'9". Weight: 222 lbs. Drafted: 1979 College: UCLA

YEAR	TEAM	GP	GS	MIN	PTS	FGM	FGA	FG%	3PM	3PA	3P%	FTM	FTA	FT%	ORB	DRB	TRB	AST	PF	DQ	STL	BLK	TO	MPG	PPG	RPG	APG	PCM
79-80	Chicago	82	....	2791	1334	498	1051	.474	1	7	.143	337	416	.810	223	550	773	182	313	8	60	129	213	34.0	16.3	9.4	2.2	.549
80-81	Chicago	82	....	2710	1179	481	989	.486	0	2	.000	217	290	.748	243	481	724	218	282	5	77	124	189	33.0	14.4	8.8	2.7	.540
81-82	Chicago	82	82	2914	1200	480	1014	.473	0	3	.000	240	291	.825	192	594	786	262	292	1	70	92	180	35.5	14.6	9.6	3.2	.529
82-83	Chicago	79	61	2355	789	312	686	.455	0	4	.000	165	233	.708	217	548	765	151	261	5	54	90	150	29.8	10.0	9.7	1.9	.490

YEAR	TEAM	GP	GS	MIN	PTS	FGM	FGA	FG%	3PM	3PA	3P%	FTM	FTA	FT%	ORB	DRB	TRB	AST	PF	DQ	STL	BLK	TO	MPG	PPG	RPG	APG	PCM
83-84	Chicago	78	76	2718	951	369	753	.490	0	1	.000	213	289	.737	214	572	786	139	265	9	67	72	148	34.8	12.2	10.1	1.8	.481
84-85	Chicago	61	28	1523	371	152	332	.458	0	1	.000	67	94	.713	108	280	388	78	190	1	34	18	61	25.0	6.1	6.4	1.3	.354
85-86	San Antonio	68	24	1910	538	198	388	.510	0	1	.000	142	184	.772	151	380	531	90	207	3	37	52	116	28.1	7.9	7.8	1.3	.424
86-87	San Antonio	79	78	2587	916	336	655	.513	3	6	.500	241	307	.785	256	527	783	237	248	3	71	50	158	32.7	11.6	9.9	3.0	.549
87-88	San Antonio	45	40	1236	385	151	328	.460	0	2	.000	83	111	.748	92	208	300	97	134	2	33	22	72	27.5	8.6	6.7	2.2	.414
88-89	San Antonio	38	15	912	294	105	247	.425	0	0	.000	84	105	.800	92	146	238	55	123	2	30	24	53	24.0	7.7	6.3	1.4	.412
88-89	Denver	29	3	491	172	62	148	.419	0	0	.000	48	71	.676	48	116	164	41	78	3	17	28	35	16.9	5.9	5.7	1.4	.511
89-90	Detroit	37	0	205	60	22	52	.423	0	0	.000	16	29	.552	24	54	78	12	40	0	4	9	15	5.5	1.6	2.1	0.3	.444
90-91	San Antonio	63	11	1018	239	85	169	.503	0	2	.000	69	94	.734	61	160	221	52	172	3	29	25	69	16.2	3.8	3.5	0.8	.311
NBA Season Totals		823	418	23370	8428	3251	6812	.477	4	29	.138	1922	2514	.765	1921	4616	6537	1614	2605	45	583	735	1459	28.4	10.2	7.9	2.0	....
80-81	Chicago	6	....	212	107	51	87	.586	0	2	.000	5	12	.417	16	28	44	11	26	0	9	5	9	35.3	17.8	7.3	1.8	.546
84-85	Chicago	4	4	139	38	15	28	.536	0	0	.000	8	10	.800	10	21	31	5	14	0	6	4	7	34.8	9.5	7.8	1.3	.399
85-86	San Antonio	3	3	101	30	12	23	.522	0	0	.000	6	8	.750	1	17	18	3	12	0	3	1	1	33.7	10.0	6.0	1.0	.356
88-89	Denver	3	0	34	5	2	6	.333	0	0	.000	1	2	.500	2	9	11	1	7	0	1	1	6	11.3	1.7	3.7	0.3	.151
89-90	Detroit	5	0	47	5	2	4	.500	0	0	.000	1	4	.250	2	7	9	0	11	0	2	0	2	9.4	1.0	1.8	0.0	.106
90-91	San Antonio	1	0	5	2	1	1	1.000	0	0	.000	0	0	.000	1	1	2	2	0	0	0	0	1	5.0	2.0	2.0	2.0	1.013
NBA Playoff Totals		22	7	538	187	83	149	.557	0	2	.000	21	36	.583	32	83	115	22	70	0	21	11	26	24.5	8.5	5.2	1.0	....

• GREER, Hal

Harold Everett Greer

Born: June 26, 1936. Huntington, WV, United States. Height: 6'2". Weight: 175 lbs. Drafted: 1958 College: Marshall HOF: 1982

YEAR	TEAM	GP	GS	MIN	PTS	FGM	FGA	FG%	3PM	3PA	3P%	FTM	FTA	FT%	ORB	DRB	TRB	AST	PF	DQ	STL	BLK	TO	MPG	PPG	RPG	APG	PCM
58-59	Syracuse	68	....	1625	753	308	679	.454	....	....	....	137	176	.778	....	....	196	101	189	1	....	....	....	23.9	11.1	2.9	1.5	.407
59-60	Syracuse	70	....	1979	924	388	815	.476	....	....	....	148	189	.783	....	....	303	188	208	4	....	....	....	28.3	13.2	4.3	2.7	.490
60-61	Syracuse	79	....	2763	1551	623	1381	.451	....	....	....	305	394	.774	....	....	455	302	242	0	....	....	....	35.0	19.6	5.8	3.8	.568
61-62	Syracuse	71	....	2705	1619	644	1442	.447	....	....	....	331	404	.819	....	....	524	313	252	2	....	....	....	38.1	22.8	7.4	4.4	.614
62-63	Syracuse	80	....	2631	1562	600	1293	.464	....	....	....	362	434	.834	....	....	457	275	286	4	....	....	....	32.9	19.5	5.7	3.4	.595
63-64	Philadelphia	80	....	3157	1865	715	1611	.444	....	....	....	435	525	.829	....	....	484	374	291	6	....	....	....	39.5	23.3	6.1	4.7	.587
64-65	Philadelphia	70	....	2600	1413	539	1245	.433	....	....	....	335	413	.811	....	....	355	313	254	7	....	....	....	37.1	20.2	5.1	4.5	.539
65-66	Philadelphia	80	....	3326	1819	703	1580	.445	....	....	....	413	514	.804	....	....	473	384	315	6	....	....	....	41.6	22.7	5.9	4.8	.543
66-67	Philadelphia	80	....	3086	1765	699	1524	.459	....	....	....	367	466	.788	....	....	422	303	302	5	....	....	....	38.6	22.1	5.3	3.8	.534
67-68	Philadelphia	82	....	3263	1976	777	1626	.478	....	....	....	422	549	.769	....	....	444	372	289	6	....	....	....	39.8	24.1	5.4	4.5	.593
68-69	Philadelphia	82	....	3311	1896	732	1595	.459	....	....	....	432	543	.796	....	....	435	414	294	8	....	....	....	40.4	23.1	5.3	5.0	.559
69-70	Philadelphia	80	....	3024	1762	705	1551	.455	....	....	....	352	432	.815	....	....	376	405	300	8	....	....	....	37.8	22.0	4.7	5.1	.541
70-71	Philadelphia	81	....	3060	1508	591	1371	.431	....	....	....	326	405	.805	....	....	364	369	289	4	....	....	....	37.8	18.6	4.5	4.6	.462
71-72	Philadelphia	81	....	2410	959	389	866	.449	....	....	....	181	234	.774	....	....	271	316	268	10	....	....	....	29.8	11.8	3.3	3.9	.415
72-73	Philadelphia	38	....	848	214	91	232	.392	....	....	....	32	39	.821	....	....	106	111	76	1	....	....	....	22.3	5.6	2.8	2.9	.324
NBA Season Totals		1122	....	39788	21586	8504	18811	.452	....	....	....	4578	5717	.801	....	....	5665	4540	3855	72	....	....	....	35.5	19.2	5.0	4.0	....
58-59	Syracuse	9	....	278	104	39	93	.419	....	....	....	26	32	.813	....	....	47	20	35	2	....	....	....	30.9	11.6	5.2	2.2	.389
59-60	Syracuse	3	....	84	47	22	43	.512	....	....	....	3	4	.750	....	....	14	10	5	0	....	....	....	28.0	15.7	4.7	3.3	.618
60-61	Syracuse	8	....	232	115	41	106	.387	....	....	....	33	40	.825	....	....	33	19	32	1	....	....	....	29.0	14.4	4.1	2.4	.428
61-62	Syracuse	1	....	5	0	0	0	.000	....	....	....	0	0	.000	....	....	0	0	1	0	....	....	....	5.0	0.0	0.0	0.0	-.078
62-63	Syracuse	5	....	214	117	44	87	.506	....	....	....	29	35	.829	....	....	27	21	21	1	....	....	....	42.8	23.4	5.4	4.2	.556
63-64	Philadelphia	5	....	211	107	37	95	.389	....	....	....	33	39	.846	....	....	28	30	19	1	....	....	....	42.2	21.4	5.6	6.0	.524
64-65	Philadelphia	11	....	505	271	101	222	.455	....	....	....	69	87	.793	....	....	81	55	45	2	....	....	....	45.9	24.6	7.4	5.0	.562
65-66	Philadelphia	5	....	226	82	32	91	.352	....	....	....	18	23	.783	....	....	36	21	21	0	....	....	....	45.2	16.4	7.2	4.2	.351
66-67	Philadelphia	15	....	688	416	161	375	.429	....	....	....	94	118	.797	....	....	88	79	55	1	....	....	....	45.9	27.7	5.9	5.3	.551
67-68	Philadelphia	13	....	553	335	120	278	.432	....	....	....	95	111	.856	....	....	79	55	49	1	....	....	....	42.5	25.8	6.1	4.2	.564
68-69	Philadelphia	5	....	204	80	26	81	.321	....	....	....	28	36	.778	....	....	30	23	23	0	....	....	....	40.8	16.0	6.0	4.6	.357
69-70	Philadelphia	5	....	178	77	33	74	.446	....	....	....	11	13	.846	....	....	17	27	16	0	....	....	....	35.6	15.4	3.4	5.4	.439
70-71	Philadelphia	7	....	265	125	49	112	.438	....	....	....	27	36	.750	....	....	25	33	35	4	....	....	....	37.9	17.9	3.6	4.7	.419
NBA Playoff Totals		92	....	3643	1876	705	1657	.425	....	....	....	466	574	.812	....	....	505	393	357	13	....	....	....	39.6	20.4	5.5	4.3	....

• GREGOR, Gary

Gary W. Gregor

Born: Aug. 13, 1945. Charlestown, WV, United States. Height: 6'7". Weight: 225 lbs. Drafted: 1968 College: South Carolina

YEAR	TEAM	GP	GS	MIN	PTS	FGM	FGA	FG%	3PM	3PA	3P%	FTM	FTA	FT%	ORB	DRB	TRB	AST	PF	DQ	STL	BLK	TO	MPG	PPG	RPG	APG	PCM
68-69	Phoenix	80	....	2182	885	400	963	.415	....	....	....	85	131	.649	....	....	711	96	249	2	....	....	....	27.3	11.1	8.9	1.2	.457
69-70	Atlanta	81	....	1603	660	286	661	.433	....	....	....	88	113	.779	....	....	397	63	159	5	....	....	....	19.8	8.1	4.9	0.8	.417
70-71	Portland	44	....	1153	421	181	421	.430	....	....	....	59	89	.663	....	....	334	81	120	2	....	....	....	26.2	9.6	7.6	1.8	.459
71-72	Portland	82	....	2371	912	399	884	.451	....	....	....	114	151	.755	....	....	591	187	201	2	....	....	....	28.9	11.1	7.2	2.3	.470
72-73	New York-A	40	....	595	231	99	204	.485	1	1	1.000	32	39	.821	40	110	150	31	84	0	....	....	41	14.9	5.8	3.8	0.8	.445
72-73	Milwaukee	9	....	88	27	11	33	.333	....	....	....	5	7	.714	....	....	32	9	9	0	....	....	....	9.8	3.0	3.6	1.0	.467
73-74	New York-A	25	....	313	91	40	85	.471	2	3	.667	9	11	.818	22	49	71	15	48	....	4	1	10	12.5	3.6	2.8	0.6	.348
NBA Season Totals		296	....	7397	2905	1277	2962	.431	....	....	....	351	491	.715	....	....	2065	436	738	11	....	....	....	25.0	9.8	7.0	1.5	....
ABA Season Totals		65	....	908	322	139	289	.481	3	4	.750	41	50	.820	62	159	221	46	132	0	4	1	51	14.0	5.0	3.4	0.7	....
Career Totals		361	....	8305	3227	1416	3251	.436	3	4	.750	392	541	.725	62	159	2286	482	870	11	4	1	51	23.0	8.9	6.3	1.3	....
69-70	Atlanta	7	....	67	16	6	21	.286	....	....	....	4	6	.667	....	....	17	2	14	0	....	....	....	9.6	2.3	2.4	0.3	.193
72-73	New York-A	1	....	12	4	1	6	.167	0	0	.000	2	2	1.000	1	3	4	0	3	0	....	....	0	12.0	4.0	4.0	0.0	.146
NBA Playoff Totals		7	....	67	16	6	21	.286	....	....	....	4	6	.667	....	....	17	2	14	0	....	....	....	9.6	2.3	2.4	0.3	....
ABA Playoff Totals		1	....	12	4	1	6	.167	0	0	.000	2	2	1.000	1	3	4	0	3	0	....	....	0	12.0	4.0	4.0	0.0	....
Career Playoff Totals		8	....	79	20	7	27	.259	0	0	.000	6	8	.750	1	3	21	2	17	0	....	....	0	9.9	2.5	2.6	0.3	....

• GREGORY, Claude

Claude Andre Gregory

Born: Dec. 26, 1958. Washington, DC, United States. Height: 6'8". Weight: 205 lbs. Drafted: 1981 College: Wisconsin

YEAR	TEAM	GP	GS	MIN	PTS	FGM	FGA	FG%	3PM	3PA	3P%	FTM	FTA	FT%	ORB	DRB	TRB	AST	PF	DQ	STL	BLK	TO	MPG	PPG	RPG	APG	PCM
85-86	Washington	2	0	2	2	1	2	.500	0	0	.000	0	0	.000	2	0	2	0	1	0	1	0	2	1.0	1.0	1.0	0.0	.768
87-88	LA Clippers	23	2	313	134	61	134	.455	0	1	.000	12	36	.333	37	58	95	16	37	0	9	13	23	13.6	5.8	4.1	0.7	.454
NBA Season Totals		25	2	315	136	62	136	.456	0	1	.000	12	36	.333	39	58	97	16	38	0	10	13	25	12.6	5.4	3.9	0.6	....

YEAR	TEAM	GP	GS	MIN	PTS	FGM	FGA	FG%	3PM	3PA	3P%	FTM	FTA	FT%	ORB	DRB	TRB	AST	PF	DQ	STL	BLK	TO	MPG	PPG	RPG	APG	PCM

• GREIG, John
John W. Greig

Born: Apr. 28, 1961. Sacramento, CA, United States.   Height: 6'7".   Weight: 215 lbs.   Drafted: 1982   College: Oregon

YEAR	TEAM	GP	GS	MIN	PTS	FGM	FGA	FG%	3PM	3PA	3P%	FTM	FTA	FT%	ORB	DRB	TRB	AST	PF	DQ	STL	BLK	TO	MPG	PPG	RPG	APG	PCM
82-83	Seattle	9	0	26	19	7	13	.538	0	0	.000	5	6	.833	2	4	6	0	4	0	0	1	2	2.9	2.1	0.7	0.0	.609
NBA Season Totals		9	0	26	19	7	13	.538	0	0	.000	5	6	.833	2	4	6	0	4	0	0	1	2	2.9	2.1	0.7	0.0	....

• GREKIN, Norm
Norman Grekin

Born: June 22, 1930. Died: Sept.29, 1981.   Height: 6'5".   Weight: 180 lbs.   Drafted: 1953   College: LaSalle

YEAR	TEAM	GP	GS	MIN	PTS	FGM	FGA	FG%	3PM	3PA	3P%	FTM	FTA	FT%	ORB	DRB	TRB	AST	PF	DQ	STL	BLK	TO	MPG	PPG	RPG	APG	PCM
53-54	Philadelphia	1	....	1	0	0	0	.000	....	....	....	0	0	.000	....	....	0	0	1	0	....	....	....	1.0	0.0	0.0	0.0	-.355
NBA Season Totals		1	....	1	0	0	0	.000	....	....	....	0	0	.000	....	....	0	0	1	0	....	....	....	1.0	0.0	0.0	0.0	....

• GRENERT, Al
Al Grenert

Born: 1919.   Height: 6'   Weight: 190 lbs.   Drafted: —   College: New York University

YEAR	TEAM	GP	GS	MIN	PTS	FGM	FGA	FG%	3PM	3PA	3P%	FTM	FTA	FT%	ORB	DRB	TRB	AST	PF	DQ	STL	BLK	TO	MPG	PPG	RPG	APG	PCM
45-46	Sheboygan-N	31	....	....	174	64	....	....	....	....	....	46	66	.697	....	....	....	....	....		....	....		5.6		....	....	
46-47	Sheboygan-N	13	....	....	64	27	....	....	....	....	....	10	15	.667	....	....	....	....	....		....	....		4.9		....	....	
46-47	Tri-Cities-N	30	....	....	198	85	....	....	....	....	....	28	42	.667	....	....	....	....	....		....	....		6.6		....	....	
47-48	Tri-Cities-N	3	....	....	4	2	....	....	....	....	....	0	0	.000	....	....	....	....	....		....	....		1.3		....	....	
NBL Season Totals		77	....	....	440	178	....	....	....	....	....	84	123	....	....	....	....	....	....		....	....		5.7		....	....	
45-46	Sheboygan-N	4	....	....	14	6	....	....	....	....	....	2	4	.500	....	....	....	....	....		....	....		3.5		....	....	
47-48	Tri-Cities-N	6	....	....	3	1	....	....	....	....	....	1	2	.500	....	....	....	....	....		....	....		0.5		....	....	
NBL Playoff Totals		10	....	....	17	7	....	....	....	....	....	3	6	....	....	....	....	....	....		....	....		1.7		....	....	

• GREVEY, Kevin
Kevin Michael Grevey

Born: May 12, 1953. Hamilton, OH, United States.   Height: 6'5".   Weight: 210 lbs.   Drafted: 1975   College: Kentucky

YEAR	TEAM	GP	GS	MIN	PTS	FGM	FGA	FG%	3PM	3PA	3P%	FTM	FTA	FT%	ORB	DRB	TRB	AST	PF	DQ	STL	BLK	TO	MPG	PPG	RPG	APG	PCM
75-76	Washington	56	....	504	210	79	213	.371	....	....	....	52	58	.897	24	36	60	27	65	0	13	3	....	9.0	3.8	1.1	0.5	.291
76-77	Washington	76	....	1306	527	224	530	.423	....	....	....	79	119	.664	73	105	178	68	148	1	29	9	....	17.2	6.9	2.3	0.9	.316
77-78	Washington	81	....	2121	1253	505	1128	.448	....	....	....	243	308	.789	124	166	290	155	203	4	61	17	162	26.2	15.5	3.6	1.9	.446
78-79	Washington	65	....	1856	1009	418	922	.453	....	....	....	173	224	.772	90	142	232	153	159	1	46	14	117	28.6	15.5	3.6	2.4	.425
79-80	Washington	65	....	1818	912	331	804	.412	34	92	.370	216	249	.867	80	107	187	177	158	0	56	16	104	28.0	14.0	2.9	2.7	.402
80-81	Washington	75	....	2616	1289	500	1103	.453	45	136	.331	244	290	.841	67	152	219	300	161	1	68	17	143	34.9	17.2	2.9	4.0	.428
81-82	Washington	71	62	2164	945	376	857	.439	28	82	.341	165	193	.855	57	138	195	149	151	1	44	23	99	30.5	13.3	2.7	2.1	.338
82-83	Washington	41	11	756	297	114	294	.388	15	38	.395	54	69	.783	18	31	49	49	61	0	18	7	29	18.4	7.2	1.2	1.2	.258
83-84	Milwaukee	64	3	923	446	178	395	.451	15	53	.283	75	84	.893	30	51	81	75	95	0	27	4	45	14.4	7.0	1.3	1.2	.367
84-85	Milwaukee	78	6	1182	476	190	424	.448	8	33	.242	88	107	.822	27	76	103	94	85	1	30	2	55	15.2	6.1	1.3	1.2	.325
NBA Season Totals		672	82	15246	7364	2915	6670	.437	145	434	.334	1389	1701	.817	590	1004	1594	1247	1286	9	392	112	754	22.7	11.0	2.4	1.9	....
75-76	Washington	2	....	3	2	1	2	.500	....	....	....	0	0	.000	0	0	0	0	1	0	0	0	....	1.5	1.0	0.0	0.0	.238
76-77	Washington	9	....	225	87	36	88	.409	....	....	....	15	23	.652	10	6	16	8	20	0	2	5	....	25.0	9.7	1.8	0.9	.235
77-78	Washington	21	....	584	325	126	284	.444	....	....	....	73	90	.811	25	36	61	42	71	2	11	3	44	27.8	15.5	2.9	2.0	.381
78-79	Washington	19	....	527	244	102	256	.398	....	....	....	40	53	.755	26	22	48	30	62	1	15	7	40	27.7	12.8	2.5	1.6	.251
79-80	Washington	2	....	72	41	16	30	.533	5	10	.500	4	4	1.000	1	5	6	8	9	1	5	2	4	36.0	20.5	3.0	4.0	.572
81-82	Washington	7	1	159	66	23	56	.411	4	8	.500	16	19	.842	2	8	10	11	12	0	3	1	6	22.7	9.4	1.4	1.6	.301
83-84	Milwaukee	5	0	27	8	2	9	.222	0	0	.000	4	6	.667	0	2	2	1	1	0	0	1	1	5.4	1.6	0.4	0.2	.078
84-85	Milwaukee	5	0	28	12	4	13	.308	0	0	.000	4	4	1.000	1	1	2	2	5	0	2	0	1	5.6	2.4	0.4	0.4	.255
NBA Playoff Totals		70	1	1625	785	310	738	.420	9	18	.500	156	199	.784	65	80	145	102	181	4	38	18	95	23.2	11.2	2.1	1.5	....

• GREY, Dennis
Dennis Grey

Born: Aug. 26, 1947. San Diego, CA, United States.   Height: 6'8".   Weight: 215 lbs.   Drafted: —   College: California Western

YEAR	TEAM	GP	GS	MIN	PTS	FGM	FGA	FG%	3PM	3PA	3P%	FTM	FTA	FT%	ORB	DRB	TRB	AST	PF	DQ	STL	BLK	TO	MPG	PPG	RPG	APG	PCM
68-69	Los Angeles-A	58	....	1317	525	184	439	.419	0	1	.000	157	292	.538	111	209	320	52	196	11	....	....	129	22.7	9.1	5.5	0.9	.378
69-70	New York-A	4	....	74	18	6	24	.250	0	0	.000	6	12	.500	11	14	25	0	15	1	....	....	3	18.5	4.5	6.3	0.0	.203
ABA Season Totals		62	....	1391	543	190	463	.410	0	1	.000	163	304	.536	122	223	345	52	211	12	....	....	132	22.4	8.8	5.6	0.8	....

• GRIFFIN, Adrian
Adrian Griffin

Born: July 4, 1974. Wichita, KS, United States.   Height: 6'5".   Weight: 217 lbs.   Drafted: —   College: Seton Hall

YEAR	TEAM	GP	GS	MIN	PTS	FGM	FGA	FG%	3PM	3PA	3P%	FTM	FTA	FT%	ORB	DRB	TRB	AST	PF	DQ	STL	BLK	TO	MPG	PPG	RPG	APG	PCM
99-00	Boston	72	47	1927	485	175	413	.424	16	57	.281	119	158	.753	128	244	372	177	222	3	116	15	93	26.8	6.7	5.2	2.5	.372
00-01	Boston	44	0	377	93	33	97	.340	9	26	.346	18	24	.750	27	60	87	27	45	0	18	5	18	8.6	2.1	2.0	0.6	.332
01-02	Dallas	58	34	1383	415	179	359	.499	16	54	.296	41	49	.837	68	161	229	106	142	2	75	12	42	23.8	7.2	3.9	1.8	.396
02-03	Dallas	74	48	1373	325	146	337	.433	6	24	.250	27	32	.844	88	176	264	105	157	0	77	6	47	18.6	4.4	3.6	1.4	.339
NBA Season Totals		248	129	5060	1318	533	1206	.442	47	161	.292	205	263	.779	311	641	952	415	566	5	286	38	200	20.4	5.3	3.8	1.7	....
01-02	Dallas	4	1	57	20	10	17	.588	0	2	.000	0	2	.000	2	7	9	4	6	0	2	1	3	14.3	5.0	2.3	1.0	.396
02-03	Dallas	15	2	131	37	17	41	.415	1	3	.333	2	2	1.000	17	27	44	8	24	0	4	0	9	8.7	2.5	2.9	0.5	.370
NBA Playoff Totals		19	3	188	57	27	58	.466	1	5	.200	2	4	.500	19	34	53	12	30	0	6	1	12	9.9	3.0	2.8	0.6	....

• GRIFFIN, Eddie
Eddie J. Griffin

Born: May 30, 1982. Philadelpia, PA, United States.   Height: 6'10".   Weight: 220 lbs.   Drafted: 2001   College: Seton Hall

YEAR	TEAM	GP	GS	MIN	PTS	FGM	FGA	FG%	3PM	3PA	3P%	FTM	FTA	FT%	ORB	DRB	TRB	AST	PF	DQ	STL	BLK	TO	MPG	PPG	RPG	APG	PCM
01-02	Houston	73	24	1895	642	244	666	.366	90	273	.330	64	86	.744	117	299	416	53	117	1	17	134	47	26.0	8.8	5.7	0.7	.383
02-03	Houston	77	66	1884	664	271	678	.400	64	192	.333	58	94	.617	138	323	461	86	136	1	52	111	76	24.5	8.6	6.0	1.1	.429
NBA Season Totals		150	90	3779	1306	515	1344	.383	154	465	.331	122	180	.678	255	622	877	139	253	2	69	245	123	25.2	8.7	5.8	0.9	....

YEAR	TEAM	GP	GS	MIN	PTS	FGM	FGA	FG%	3PM	3PA	3P%	FTM	FTA	FT%	ORB	DRB	TRB	AST	PF	DQ	STL	BLK	TO	MPG	PPG	RPG	APG	PCM

• GRIFFIN, Greg
Greg Griffin

Born: Sept. 6, 1952. Cleveland, OH, United States.   Height: 6'7".   Weight: 190 lbs.   Drafted: 1977   College: Idaho State

YEAR	TEAM	GP	GS	MIN	PTS	FGM	FGA	FG%	3PM	3PA	3P%	FTM	FTA	FT%	ORB	DRB	TRB	AST	PF	DQ	STL	BLK	TO	MPG	PPG	RPG	APG	PCM
77-78	Phoenix	36	....	422	145	61	169	.361	....	....	....	23	36	.639	44	59	103	24	56	0	16	0	40	11.7	4.0	2.9	0.7	.276
NBA Season Totals		36		422	145	61	169	.361	....	....	....	23	36	.639	44	59	103	24	56	0	16	0	40	11.7	4.0	2.9	0.7	....
77-78	Phoenix	2	....	25	6	3	7	.429	....	....	....	0	0	.000	2	2	4	3	5	0	1	1	2	12.5	3.0	2.0	1.5	.288
NBA Playoff Totals		2		25	6	3	7	.429	....	....	....	0	0	.000	2	2	4	3	5	0	1	1	2	12.5	3.0	2.0	1.5	....

• GRIFFIN, Paul
Paul Arthur Griffin

Born: Jan. 20, 1954. Shelby, MI, United States.   Height: 6'9".   Weight: 205 lbs.   Drafted: 1976   College: Western Michigan

YEAR	TEAM	GP	GS	MIN	PTS	FGM	FGA	FG%	3PM	3PA	3P%	FTM	FTA	FT%	ORB	DRB	TRB	AST	PF	DQ	STL	BLK	TO	MPG	PPG	RPG	APG	PCM
76-77	New Orleans	81	....	1645	425	140	256	.547	....	....	....	145	201	.721	167	328	495	167	241	6	50	43	....	20.3	5.2	6.1	2.1	.495
77-78	New Orleans	82	....	1853	432	160	358	.447	....	....	....	112	157	.713	157	353	510	172	228	6	88	45	148	22.6	5.3	6.2	2.1	.413
78-79	New Orleans	77	....	1398	303	106	223	.475	....	....	....	91	147	.619	126	265	391	138	198	3	54	36	116	18.2	3.9	5.1	1.8	.403
79-80	San Antonio	82	....	1812	520	173	313	.553	0	0	.000	174	240	.725	154	284	438	250	306	9	81	53	131	22.1	6.3	5.3	3.0	.495
80-81	San Antonio	82	....	1930	502	166	325	.511	0	0	.000	170	253	.672	184	321	505	249	207	3	77	38	131	23.5	6.1	6.2	3.0	.488
81-82	San Antonio	23	0	459	88	32	66	.485	0	0	.000	24	37	.649	29	66	95	54	67	0	20	8	39	20.0	3.8	4.1	2.3	.339
82-83	San Antonio	53	0	956	173	60	116	.517	0	0	.000	53	76	.697	77	139	216	86	153	0	33	25	69	18.0	3.3	4.1	1.6	.337
NBA Season Totals		480	0	10053	2443	837	1657	.505	0	0	.000	769	1111	.692	894	1756	2650	1116	1400	27	403	248	634	20.9	5.1	5.5	2.3	....
79-80	San Antonio	3	....	69	20	7	14	.500	0	0	.000	6	6	1.000	3	12	15	6	9	0	0	1	7	23.0	6.7	5.0	2.0	.352
80-81	San Antonio	7	....	183	37	14	24	.583	0	0	.000	9	20	.450	16	24	40	29	28	2	6	5	9	26.1	5.3	5.7	4.1	.437
NBA Playoff Totals		10		252	57	21	38	.553	0	0	.000	15	26	.577	19	36	55	35	37	2	6	6	16	25.2	5.7	5.5	3.5	....

• GRIFFITH, Darrell
Darrell Steven (Dr. Dunkenstein) Griffith

Born: June 16, 1958. Louisville, KY, United States.   Height: 6'4".   Weight: 190 lbs.   Drafted: 1980   College: Louisville

YEAR	TEAM	GP	GS	MIN	PTS	FGM	FGA	FG%	3PM	3PA	3P%	FTM	FTA	FT%	ORB	DRB	TRB	AST	PF	DQ	STL	BLK	TO	MPG	PPG	RPG	APG	PCM
80-81	Utah	81	....	2867	1671	716	1544	.464	10	52	.192	229	320	.716	79	209	288	194	219	0	106	50	235	35.4	20.6	3.6	2.4	.411
81-82	Utah	80	79	2597	1582	689	1429	.482	15	52	.288	189	271	.697	128	177	305	187	213	0	95	34	192	32.5	19.8	3.8	2.3	.458
82-83	Utah	77	76	2787	1709	752	1554	.484	38	132	.288	167	246	.679	100	204	304	270	184	0	138	33	254	36.2	22.2	3.9	3.5	.489
83-84	Utah	82	82	2650	1636	697	1423	.490	91	252	.361	151	217	.696	95	243	338	283	202	1	114	23	246	32.3	20.0	4.1	3.5	.510
84-85	Utah	78	78	2776	1764	728	1593	.457	92	257	.358	216	298	.725	124	220	344	243	178	1	133	30	250	35.6	22.6	4.4	3.1	.481
86-87	Utah	76	10	1843	1142	463	1038	.446	67	200	.335	149	212	.703	81	146	227	129	167	0	97	29	137	24.3	15.0	3.0	1.7	.455
87-88	Utah	52	11	1052	589	251	585	.429	28	102	.275	59	92	.641	36	91	127	91	102	0	52	5	68	20.2	11.3	2.4	1.8	.399
88-89	Utah	82	73	2382	1135	466	1045	.446	61	196	.311	142	182	.780	77	253	330	130	175	0	86	22	139	29.0	13.8	4.0	1.6	.384
89-90	Utah	82	1	1444	733	301	649	.464	80	215	.372	51	78	.654	43	123	166	63	149	0	68	19	74	17.6	8.9	2.0	0.8	.387
90-91	Utah	75	2	1005	430	174	445	.391	48	138	.348	34	45	.756	17	73	90	37	100	1	42	7	45	13.4	5.7	1.2	0.5	.251
NBA Season Totals		765	412	21403	12391	5237	11305	.463	530	1596	.332	1387	1961	.707	780	1739	2519	1627	1689	3	931	252	1640	28.0	16.2	3.3	2.1	....
83-84	Utah	11	11	417	211	81	183	.443	16	45	.356	33	48	.688	16	49	65	41	24	0	19	2	31	37.9	19.2	5.9	3.7	.463
84-85	Utah	10	10	340	175	72	158	.456	13	36	.361	18	25	.720	6	23	29	25	21	0	12	5	25	34.0	17.5	2.9	2.5	.377
86-87	Utah	5	0	104	68	24	65	.369	6	15	.400	14	19	.737	5	7	12	8	5	0	6	2	12	20.8	13.6	2.4	1.6	.396
88-89	Utah	3	0	71	46	20	49	.408	6	19	.316	0	0	.000	3	9	12	0	7	0	4	1	5	23.7	15.3	4.0	0.0	.379
89-90	Utah	5	0	97	47	19	42	.452	5	9	.556	4	5	.800	6	15	21	3	3	0	6	1	3	19.4	9.4	4.2	0.6	.517
90-91	Utah	3	0	9	10	5	7	.714	0	0	.000	0	0	.000	1	1	2	0	0	0	0	0	1	3.0	3.3	0.7	0.0	1.007
NBA Playoff Totals		37	21	1038	557	221	504	.438	46	124	.371	69	97	.711	37	104	141	77	60	0	47	11	77	28.1	15.1	3.8	2.1	....

• GRIFFITH, Ken
Ken Griffith

Born: 1918.   Height: 6'2".   Weight: 195 lbs.   Drafted: —   College: Alderson-Broaddus

YEAR	TEAM	GP	GS	MIN	PTS	FGM	FGA	FG%	3PM	3PA	3P%	FTM	FTA	FT%	ORB	DRB	TRB	AST	PF	DQ	STL	BLK	TO	MPG	PPG	RPG	APG	PCM
41-42	Wingfoots-N	6	....	....	9	4	....	....	....	....	....	1	....	....	....	....	....	....	....	....	....	....	....	....	1.5	....	....	....
NBL Season Totals		6		....	9	4	....	....	....	....	....	1	....	....	....	....	....	....	....	....	....	....	....	....	1.5	....	....	....
41-42	Wingfoots-N	1	....	....	0	0	....	....	....	....	....	0	....	....	....	....	....	....	....	....	....	....	....	....	0.0	....	....	....
NBL Playoff Totals		1		....	0	0	....	....	....	....	....	0	....	....	....	....	....	....	....	....	....	....	....	....	0.0	....	....	....

• GRIGSBY, Chuck
Charles L. Grigsby

Born: Aug. 15, 1928. Dayton, OH, United States.   Height: 6'5".   Weight: 190 lbs.   Drafted: 1952   College: Dayton

YEAR	TEAM	GP	GS	MIN	PTS	FGM	FGA	FG%	3PM	3PA	3P%	FTM	FTA	FT%	ORB	DRB	TRB	AST	PF	DQ	STL	BLK	TO	MPG	PPG	RPG	APG	PCM
54-55	New York	7	....	45	16	7	19	.368	....	....	....	2	8	.250	....	....	11	7	9	0	....	....	....	6.4	2.3	1.6	1.0	.408
NBA Season Totals		7	....	45	16	7	19	.368	....	....	....	2	8	.250	....	....	11	7	9	0	....	....	....	6.4	2.3	1.6	1.0	....

• GRIMM, Derek
William Derek Grimm

Born: Aug. 3, 1974. Peoria, IL, United States.   Height: 6'9".   Weight: 230 lbs.   Drafted: —   College: Missouri

YEAR	TEAM	GP	GS	MIN	PTS	FGM	FGA	FG%	3PM	3PA	3P%	FTM	FTA	FT%	ORB	DRB	TRB	AST	PF	DQ	STL	BLK	TO	MPG	PPG	RPG	APG	PCM
97-98	Sacramento	9	0	34	14	4	14	.286	4	12	.333	2	2	1.000	0	4	4	0	6	0	3	1	3	3.8	1.6	0.4	0.0	.196
NBA Season Totals		9	0	34	14	4	14	.286	4	12	.333	2	2	1.000	0	4	4	0	6	0	3	1	3	3.8	1.6	0.4	0.0	....

• GRIMSHAW, Woody
George W. (Woody, Woodie) Grimshaw

Born: Sept. 24, 1919. Died: Oct.1974.   Height: 6'1".   Weight: 185 lbs.   Drafted: —   College: Brown

YEAR	TEAM	GP	GS	MIN	PTS	FGM	FGA	FG%	3PM	3PA	3P%	FTM	FTA	FT%	ORB	DRB	TRB	AST	PF	DQ	STL	BLK	TO	MPG	PPG	RPG	APG	PCM
46-47	Providence	21	....	....	61	20	56	.357	....	....	....	21	44	.477	....	....	....	1	25	....	....	....	....	....	2.9	....	0.0	....
NBA Season Totals		21	....	....	61	20	56	.357	....	....	....	21	44	.477	....	....	....	1	25	....	....	....	....	....	2.9	....	0.0	....

YEAR	TEAM	GP	GS	MIN	PTS	FGM	FGA	FG%	3PM	3PA	3P%	FTM	FTA	FT%	ORB	DRB	TRB	AST	PF	DQ	STL	BLK	TO	MPG	PPG	RPG	APG	PCM

• GROAT, Dick   Richard Morrow Groat

Born: Nov. 4, 1930. Wilkinsburg, PA, United States.   Height: 5'11".   Weight: 180 lbs.   Drafted: 1952   College: Duke

YEAR	TEAM	GP	GS	MIN	PTS	FGM	FGA	FG%	3PM	3PA	3P%	FTM	FTA	FT%	ORB	DRB	TRB	AST	PF	DQ	STL	BLK	TO	MPG	PPG	RPG	APG	PCM
52-53	Fort Wayne	26	....	663	309	100	272	.368	....	....	....	109	138	.790	....	....	86	69	90	7	....	....	....	25.5	11.9	3.3	2.7	.440
NBA Season Totals		26	....	663	309	100	272	.368	....	....	....	109	138	.790	....	....	86	69	90	7	....	....	....	25.5	11.9	3.3	2.7	....

• GROSS, Bob   Robert Edwin Gross

Born: Aug. 3, 1953. San Pedro, CA, United States.   Height: 6'6".   Weight: 200 lbs.   Drafted: 1975   College: Long Beach State

YEAR	TEAM	GP	GS	MIN	PTS	FGM	FGA	FG%	3PM	3PA	3P%	FTM	FTA	FT%	ORB	DRB	TRB	AST	PF	DQ	STL	BLK	TO	MPG	PPG	RPG	APG	PCM
75-76	Portland	76	....	1474	515	209	400	.523	....	....	....	97	142	.683	138	169	307	163	186	3	91	43	....	19.4	6.8	4.0	2.1	.476
76-77	Portland	82	....	2232	935	376	711	.529	....	....	....	183	215	.851	173	221	394	242	255	7	107	57	....	27.2	11.4	4.8	3.0	.510
77-78	Portland	72	....	2163	914	381	720	.529	....	....	....	152	190	.800	180	220	400	254	234	5	100	52	180	30.0	12.7	5.6	3.5	.513
78-79	Portland	53	....	1441	514	209	443	.472	....	....	....	96	119	.807	106	144	250	184	161	4	70	47	122	27.2	9.7	4.7	3.5	.447
79-80	Portland	62	....	1581	538	221	472	.468	1	10	.100	95	114	.833	84	165	249	228	179	3	60	47	167	25.5	8.7	4.0	3.7	.406
80-81	Portland	82	....	1934	641	253	479	.528	0	9	.000	135	159	.849	126	202	328	251	238	5	90	67	148	23.6	7.8	4.0	3.1	.463
81-82	Portland	59	24	1377	427	173	322	.537	3	6	.500	78	104	.750	101	158	259	125	162	2	75	41	89	23.3	7.2	4.4	2.1	.437
82-83	San Diego	27	3	373	83	35	82	.427	1	3	.333	12	19	.632	32	34	66	34	69	1	22	7	24	13.8	3.1	2.4	1.3	.289
NBA Season Totals		513	27	12575	4567	1857	3629	.512	5	28	.179	848	1062	.798	940	1313	2253	1481	1484	30	615	361	730	24.5	8.9	4.4	2.9	....
76-77	Portland	19	....	583	268	110	186	.591	....	....	....	48	54	.889	49	63	112	80	84	5	32	15	....	30.7	14.1	5.9	4.2	.602
79-80	Portland	3	....	51	12	3	9	.333	0	0	.000	6	6	1.000	1	3	4	4	8	0	1	0	3	17.0	4.0	1.3	1.3	.179
80-81	Portland	3	....	60	27	9	14	.643	0	0	.000	9	14	.643	5	3	8	5	9	0	2	2	5	20.0	9.0	2.7	1.7	.465
NBA Playoff Totals		25	....	694	307	122	209	.584	0	0	.000	63	74	.851	55	69	124	89	101	5	35	17	8	27.8	12.3	5.0	3.6	....

• GROSSO, Mike   Michael James Grosso

Born: Sept. 7, 1947. Raritan, NJ, United States.   Height: 6'9".   Weight: 230 lbs.   Drafted: 1970   College: Louisville

YEAR	TEAM	GP	GS	MIN	PTS	FGM	FGA	FG%	3PM	3PA	3P%	FTM	FTA	FT%	ORB	DRB	TRB	AST	PF	DQ	STL	BLK	TO	MPG	PPG	RPG	APG	PCM
71-72	Pittsburgh-A	25	....	335	103	45	102	.441	0	0	.000	13	23	.565	49	74	123	11	64	2	....	....	20	13.4	4.1	4.9	0.4	.420
ABA Season Totals		25	....	335	103	45	102	.441	0	0	.000	13	23	.565	49	74	123	11	64	2	....	....	20	13.4	4.1	4.9	0.4	....

• GROTE, Jerry   Jerry C. Grote

Born: Dec. 28, 1940.   Height: 6'4".   Weight: 215 lbs.   Drafted: 1962   College: Loyola (CA)

YEAR	TEAM	GP	GS	MIN	PTS	FGM	FGA	FG%	3PM	3PA	3P%	FTM	FTA	FT%	ORB	DRB	TRB	AST	PF	DQ	STL	BLK	TO	MPG	PPG	RPG	APG	PCM
64-65	LA Lakers	11	....	33	14	6	11	.545	....	....	....	2	2	1.000	....	....	4	4	5	0	....	....	....	3.0	1.3	0.4	0.4	.492
NBA Season Totals		11	....	33	14	6	11	.545	....	....	....	2	2	1.000	....	....	4	4	5	0	....	....	....	3.0	1.3	0.4	0.4	....

• GROVE, Al   Al Grove

Born: 1923.   Height: 6'1".   Weight: 185 lbs.   Drafted: —   College: Toledo

YEAR	TEAM	GP	GS	MIN	PTS	FGM	FGA	FG%	3PM	3PA	3P%	FTM	FTA	FT%	ORB	DRB	TRB	AST	PF	DQ	STL	BLK	TO	MPG	PPG	RPG	APG	PCM
48-49	Hammond-N	1	....	....	0	0	....	....	....	....	....	0	0	.000	....	....	....	0	....	....	....	....	....	....	0.0	....	....	....
NBL Season Totals		1	....	....	0	0	....	....	....	....	....	0	0	....	....	....	....	0	....	....	....	....	....	....	0.0	....	....	....

• GROZA, Alex   Alex John Groza

Born: Oct. 7, 1926. Martins Ferry, OH, United States. Died: Jan.21, 1995.   Height: 6'7".   Weight: 218 lbs.   Drafted: 1949   College: Kentucky

YEAR	TEAM	GP	GS	MIN	PTS	FGM	FGA	FG%	3PM	3PA	3P%	FTM	FTA	FT%	ORB	DRB	TRB	AST	PF	DQ	STL	BLK	TO	MPG	PPG	RPG	APG	PCM
49-50	Indianapolis	64	....	....	1496	521	1090	**.478**	....	....	....	454	623	.729	....	....	....	162	221	....	....	....	....	....	23.4	....	2.5	....
50-51	Indianapolis	66	....	....	1429	492	1046	**.470**	....	....	....	445	566	.786	....	....	709	156	237	8	....	....	....	....	21.7	10.7	2.4	....
NBA Season Totals		130	....	....	2925	1013	2136	.474	....	....	....	899	1189	.756	....	....	709	318	458	8	....	....	....	....	22.5	5.5	2.4	....
49-50	Indianapolis	6	....	....	137	44	74	.595	....	....	....	49	59	.831	....	....	....	12	21	....	....	....	....	....	22.8	....	2.0	....
50-51	Indianapolis	3	....	....	97	36	73	.493	....	....	....	25	33	.758	....	....	42	2	14	0	....	....	....	....	32.3	14.0	0.7	....
NBA Playoff Totals		9	....	....	234	80	147	.544	....	....	....	74	92	.804	....	....	42	14	35	0	....	....	....	....	26.0	4.7	1.6	....

• GRUBAR, Dick   Richard Arthur Grubar

Born: July 26, 1947. Schenectady, NY, United States.   Height: 6'4".   Weight: 184 lbs.   Drafted: 1969   College: North Carolina

YEAR	TEAM	GP	GS	MIN	PTS	FGM	FGA	FG%	3PM	3PA	3P%	FTM	FTA	FT%	ORB	DRB	TRB	AST	PF	DQ	STL	BLK	TO	MPG	PPG	RPG	APG	PCM
69-70	Indiana-A	2	....	8	4	2	3	.667	0	0	.000	0	0	.000	0	0	0	1	1	0	....	....	0	4.0	2.0	0.0	0.5	.482
ABA Season Totals		2	....	8	4	2	3	.667	0	0	.000	0	0	.000	0	0	0	1	1	0	....	....	0	4.0	2.0	0.0	0.5	....

• GRUENIG, Robert   Robert (Ace) Gruenig

Born: Mar. 12, 1913. Chicago, IL, United States. Died: Aug.11, 1958.   Height: 6'8".   Weight: 220 lbs.   Drafted: —   College: Northwestern (DNP)   HOF: 1963

YEAR	TEAM	GP	GS	MIN	PTS	FGM	FGA	FG%	3PM	3PA	3P%	FTM	FTA	FT%	ORB	DRB	TRB	AST	PF	DQ	STL	BLK	TO	MPG	PPG	RPG	APG	PCM
48-49	Denver-N	49	....	....	558	194	....	....	....	....	....	170	260	.654	....	....	....	91	....	....	....	....	....	....	11.4	....	....	....
NBL Season Totals		49	....	....	558	194	....	....	....	....	....	170	260	....	....	....	....	91	....	....	....	....	....	....	11.4	....	....	....

• GRUNFELD, Ernie   Ernest Grunfeld

Born: Apr. 24, 1955. Satu-Mare, Romania.   Height: 6'6".   Weight: 210 lbs.   Drafted: 1977   College: Tennessee

YEAR	TEAM	GP	GS	MIN	PTS	FGM	FGA	FG%	3PM	3PA	3P%	FTM	FTA	FT%	ORB	DRB	TRB	AST	PF	DQ	STL	BLK	TO	MPG	PPG	RPG	APG	PCM
77-78	Milwaukee	73	....	1261	502	204	461	.443	....	....	....	94	143	.657	70	124	194	145	150	1	54	19	95	17.3	6.9	2.7	2.0	.399
78-79	Milwaukee	82	....	1778	843	326	661	.493	....	....	....	191	251	.761	124	236	360	216	228	3	58	15	139	21.7	10.3	4.4	2.6	.517
79-80	Kansas City	80	....	1397	474	186	420	.443	1	2	.500	101	131	.771	87	145	232	109	151	1	56	9	80	17.5	5.9	2.9	1.4	.355
80-81	Kansas City	79	....	1584	595	260	486	.535	0	0	.000	75	101	.743	31	175	206	205	155	1	60	15	87	20.1	7.5	2.6	2.6	.446
81-82	Kansas City	81	11	1892	1030	420	822	.511	2	14	.143	188	229	.821	55	127	182	276	191	0	72	39	146	23.4	12.7	2.2	3.4	.521
82-83	New York	77	0	1422	415	167	377	.443	0	4	.000	81	98	.827	42	121	163	136	172	1	40	10	85	18.5	5.4	2.1	1.8	.285
83-84	New York	76	6	1119	398	166	362	.459	2	9	.222	64	83	.771	24	97	121	108	151	0	43	7	68	14.7	5.2	1.6	1.4	.311

YEAR	TEAM	GP	GS	MIN	PTS	FGM	FGA	FG%	3PM	3PA	3P%	FTM	FTA	FT%	ORB	DRB	TRB	AST	PF	DQ	STL	BLK	TO	MPG	PPG	RPG	APG	PCM
84-85	New York	69	0	1061	455	188	384	.490	2	8	.250	77	104	.740	41	110	151	105	129	2	50	7	41	15.4	6.6	2.2	1.5	.441
85-86	New York	76	0	1402	412	148	355	.417	26	61	.426	90	108	.833	42	164	206	119	192	2	39	13	53	18.4	5.4	2.7	1.6	.314
NBA Season Totals		693	17	12916	5124	2065	4328	.477	33	98	.337	961	1248	.770	516	1299	1815	1419	1511	11	472	134	794	18.6	7.4	2.6	2.0	....
77-78	Milwaukee	7	....	77	38	17	32	.531	....	....	....	4	5	.800	4	7	11	14	6	0	3	1	7	11.0	5.4	1.6	2.0	.579
79-80	Kansas City	3	....	32	11	5	9	.556	0	0	.000	1	3	.333	1	0	1	0	3	0	1	0	0	10.7	3.7	0.3	0.0	.216
80-81	Kansas City	15	....	633	252	98	201	.488	2	4	.500	54	67	.806	11	52	63	88	51	1	30	9	43	42.2	16.8	4.2	5.9	.440
82-83	New York	6	0	118	48	15	34	.441	0	0	.000	18	19	.947	2	6	8	10	17	0	7	2	9	19.7	8.0	1.3	1.7	.347
83-84	New York	11	0	84	26	11	23	.478	0	0	.000	4	4	1.000	1	8	9	6	12	0	2	0	4	7.6	2.4	0.8	0.5	.264
NBA Playoff Totals		42	0	944	375	146	299	.488	2	4	.500	81	98	.827	19	73	92	118	89	1	43	12	63	22.5	8.9	2.2	2.8	....

• GRUNZWEIG, Nick

Nick Grunzweig

Born: 1918. Height: 6'5". Weight: 215 lbs. Drafted: — College: Niagara

YEAR	TEAM	GP	GS	MIN	PTS	FGM	FGA	FG%	3PM	3PA	3P%	FTM	FTA	FT%	ORB	DRB	TRB	AST	PF	DQ	STL	BLK	TO	MPG	PPG	RPG	APG	PCM
46-47	Tri-Cities-N	43	....	....	120	39	....	....	....	....	....	42	70	.600	....	....	....	....	130	....	....	....	....	....	2.8	....	....	....
NBL Season Totals		43	....	....	120	39	....	....	....	....	....	42	70	....	....	....	....	....	130	....	....	....	....	....	2.8	....	....	....

• GUARILIA, Gene

Eugene Michael Guarilia

Born: Sept. 13, 1937. Duryea, PA, United States. Height: 6'5". Weight: 220 lbs. Drafted: 1959 College: George Washington

YEAR	TEAM	GP	GS	MIN	PTS	FGM	FGA	FG%	3PM	3PA	3P%	FTM	FTA	FT%	ORB	DRB	TRB	AST	PF	DQ	STL	BLK	TO	MPG	PPG	RPG	APG	PCM
59-60	Boston	48	....	423	145	58	154	.377	....	....	....	29	41	.707	....	....	85	18	57	1	....	....	....	8.8	3.0	1.8	0.4	.314
60-61	Boston	25	....	209	79	38	94	.404	....	....	....	3	10	.300	....	....	71	5	28	0	....	....	....	8.4	3.2	2.8	0.2	.399
61-62	Boston	45	....	367	163	61	161	.379	....	....	....	41	64	.641	....	....	124	11	56	0	....	....	....	8.2	3.6	2.8	0.2	.448
62-63	Boston	11	....	83	26	11	38	.289	....	....	....	4	11	.364	....	....	14	2	5	0	....	....	....	7.5	2.4	1.3	0.2	.161
NBA Season Totals		129	....	1082	413	168	447	.376	....	....	....	77	126	.611	....	....	294	36	146	1	....	....	....	8.4	3.2	2.3	0.3	....
59-60	Boston	7	....	41	14	4	18	.222	....	....	....	6	6	1.000	....	....	19	3	4	0	....	....	....	5.9	2.0	2.7	0.4	.488
61-62	Boston	5	....	26	6	2	8	.250	....	....	....	2	5	.400	....	....	4	1	6	0	....	....	....	5.2	1.2	0.8	0.2	.082
NBA Playoff Totals		12	....	67	20	6	26	.231	....	....	....	8	11	.727	....	....	23	4	10	0	....	....	....	5.6	1.7	1.9	0.3	....

• GUDMUNDSSON, Petur

Karl Petur Gudmundsson

Born: Oct. 30, 1958. Reykjavik, Iceland. Height: 7'2". Weight: 260 lbs. Drafted: 1981 College: Washington

YEAR	TEAM	GP	GS	MIN	PTS	FGM	FGA	FG%	3PM	3PA	3P%	FTM	FTA	FT%	ORB	DRB	TRB	AST	PF	DQ	STL	BLK	TO	MPG	PPG	RPG	APG	PCM
81-82	Portland	68	6	845	219	83	166	.500	1	1	1.000	52	76	.684	51	135	186	59	163	2	13	30	75	12.4	3.2	2.7	0.9	.310
85-86	LA Lakers	8	2	128	58	20	37	.541	0	0	.000	18	27	.667	17	21	38	3	25	1	3	4	11	16.0	7.3	4.8	0.4	.478
87-88	San Antonio	69	9	1017	395	139	280	.496	0	1	.000	117	145	.807	93	230	323	86	197	5	18	61	104	14.7	5.7	4.7	1.2	.519
88-89	San Antonio	5	3	70	21	9	25	.360	0	0	.000	3	4	.750	5	11	16	5	15	0	1	1	8	14.0	4.2	3.2	1.0	.190
NBA Season Totals		150	20	2060	693	251	508	.494	1	2	.500	190	252	.754	166	397	563	153	400	8	35	96	198	13.7	4.6	3.8	1.0	....
85-86	LA Lakers	12	0	111	42	16	27	.593	0	2	.000	10	15	.667	8	18	26	3	23	1	3	4	10	9.3	3.5	2.2	0.3	.391
87-88	San Antonio	2	0	6	0	0	2	.000	0	0	.000	0	0	.000	0	0	0	1	0	0	0	0	3	3.0	0.0	0.0	0.5	-.599
NBA Playoff Totals		14	0	117	42	16	29	.552	0	2	.000	10	15	.667	8	18	26	4	23	1	3	4	13	8.4	3.0	1.9	0.3	....

• GUERIN, Richie

Richard V. Guerin

Born: May 29, 1932. New York, NY, United States. Height: 6'4". Weight: 195 lbs. Drafted: 1954 College: Iona

YEAR	TEAM	GP	GS	MIN	PTS	FGM	FGA	FG%	3PM	3PA	3P%	FTM	FTA	FT%	ORB	DRB	TRB	AST	PF	DQ	STL	BLK	TO	MPG	PPG	RPG	APG	PCM
56-57	New York	72	....	1793	695	257	699	.368	....	....	....	181	292	.620	....	....	334	182	186	3	....	....	....	24.9	9.7	4.6	2.5	.408
57-58	New York	63	....	2368	1041	344	973	.354	....	....	....	353	511	.691	....	....	489	317	202	3	....	....	....	37.6	16.5	7.8	5.0	.511
58-59	New York	71	....	2558	1291	443	1046	.424	....	....	....	405	505	.802	....	....	518	364	255	1	....	....	....	36.0	18.2	7.3	5.1	.605
59-60	New York	74	....	2429	1615	579	1379	.420	....	....	....	457	591	.773	....	....	505	468	242	3	....	....	....	32.8	21.8	6.8	6.3	.754
60-61	New York	79	....	3023	1720	612	1545	.396	....	....	....	496	626	.792	....	....	628	503	310	3	....	....	....	38.3	21.8	7.9	6.4	.643
61-62	New York	78	....	3346	2303	839	1897	.442	....	....	....	625	762	.820	....	....	501	539	299	3	....	....	....	42.9	29.5	6.4	6.9	.704
62-63	New York	79	....	2712	1701	596	1380	.432	....	....	....	509	600	.848	....	....	331	348	228	2	....	....	....	34.3	21.5	4.2	4.4	.604
63-64	New York	2	....	26	26	11	16	.688	....	....	....	4	5	.800	....	....	3	4	5	0	....	....	....	13.0	13.0	1.5	2.0	1.038
63-64	St. Louis	78	....	2340	1023	340	830	.410	....	....	....	343	419	.819	....	....	253	371	271	4	....	....	....	30.0	13.1	3.2	4.8	.494
64-65	St. Louis	57	....	1678	821	295	662	.446	....	....	....	231	301	.767	....	....	149	271	193	1	....	....	....	29.4	14.4	2.6	4.8	.528
65-66	St. Louis	80	....	2363	1190	414	998	.415	....	....	....	362	446	.812	....	....	314	388	256	4	....	....	....	29.5	14.9	3.9	4.9	.557
66-67	St. Louis	79	....	2275	1092	394	904	.436	....	....	....	304	416	.731	....	....	192	345	247	2	....	....	....	28.8	13.8	2.4	4.4	.488
68-69	Atlanta	27	....	472	151	47	111	.423	....	....	....	57	74	.770	....	....	59	99	66	0	....	....	....	17.5	5.6	2.2	3.7	.482
69-70	Atlanta	8	....	64	7	3	11	.273	....	....	....	1	1	1.000	....	....	2	12	9	0	....	....	....	8.0	0.9	0.3	1.5	.175
NBA Season Totals		847	....	27447	14676	5174	12451	.416	....	....	....	4328	5549	.780	....	....	4278	4211	2769	29	....	....	....	32.4	17.3	5.1	5.0	....
58-59	New York	2	....	77	30	9	35	.257	....	....	....	12	14	.857	....	....	18	15	11	1	....	....	....	38.5	15.0	9.0	7.5	.491
63-64	St. Louis	12	....	428	217	75	169	.444	....	....	....	67	85	.788	....	....	50	49	54	1	....	....	....	35.7	18.1	4.2	4.1	.501
64-65	St. Louis	4	....	125	69	25	65	.385	....	....	....	19	25	.760	....	....	8	21	14	0	....	....	....	31.3	17.3	2.0	5.3	.501
65-66	St. Louis	10	....	399	206	72	159	.453	....	....	....	62	76	.816	....	....	37	79	41	0	....	....	....	39.9	20.6	3.7	7.9	.605
66-67	St. Louis	9	....	228	96	36	86	.419	....	....	....	24	30	.800	....	....	23	39	26	0	....	....	....	25.3	10.7	2.6	4.3	.477
68-69	Atlanta	3	....	32	3	1	4	.250	....	....	....	1	2	.500	....	....	5	7	8	0	....	....	....	10.7	1.0	1.7	2.3	.283
69-70	Atlanta	2	....	56	33	13	21	.619	....	....	....	7	7	1.000	....	....	8	4	6	0	....	....	....	28.0	16.5	4.0	2.0	.622
NBA Playoff Totals		42	....	1345	654	231	539	.429	....	....	....	192	239	.803	....	....	149	214	160	2	....	....	....	32.0	15.6	3.5	5.1	....

• GUGLIOTTA, Tom

Thomas James (Googs) Gugliotta

Born: Dec. 19, 1969. Huntington Station, NY, United States. Height: 6'10". Weight: 240 lbs. Drafted: 1992 College: North Carolina State

YEAR	TEAM	GP	GS	MIN	PTS	FGM	FGA	FG%	3PM	3PA	3P%	FTM	FTA	FT%	ORB	DRB	TRB	AST	PF	DQ	STL	BLK	TO	MPG	PPG	RPG	APG	PCM
92-93	Washington	81	81	2795	1187	484	1135	.426	38	135	.281	181	281	.644	219	562	781	306	195	0	134	35	227	34.5	14.7	9.6	3.8	.516
93-94	Washington	78	78	2795	1333	540	1159	.466	40	148	.270	213	311	.685	189	539	728	276	174	0	172	51	250	35.8	17.1	9.3	3.5	.566
94-95	Washington	6	6	226	96	33	83	.398	4	8	.500	26	33	.788	16	37	53	18	19	0	21	11	15	37.7	16.0	8.8	3.0	.538
94-95	Golden State	40	40	1324	435	176	397	.443	28	90	.311	55	97	.567	100	197	297	122	98	2	50	23	92	33.1	10.9	7.4	3.1	.417
94-95	Minnesota	31	17	1018	445	162	357	.454	28	88	.318	93	122	.762	49	173	222	139	86	0	61	28	81	32.8	14.4	7.2	4.5	.561
95-96	Minnesota	78	78	2835	1261	473	1004	.471	26	86	.302	289	374	.773	176	514	690	238	265	1	139	96	234	36.3	16.2	8.8	3.1	.529

YEAR	TEAM	GP	GS	MIN	PTS	FGM	FGA	FG%	3PM	3PA	3P%	FTM	FTA	FT%	ORB	DRB	TRB	AST	PF	DQ	STL	BLK	TO	MPG	PPG	RPG	APG	PCM
96-97	Minnesota	81	81	3131	1672	592	1339	.442	24	93	.258	464	566	.820	187	515	702	335	237	3	130	89	292	38.7	20.6	8.7	4.1	.563
97-98	Minnesota	41	41	1582	823	319	635	.502	2	17	.118	183	223	.821	106	250	356	167	102	0	61	22	111	38.6	20.1	8.7	4.1	.601
98-99	Phoenix	43	43	1563	729	277	573	.483	2	7	.286	173	218	.794	131	250	381	121	110	0	59	21	88	36.3	17.0	8.9	2.8	.552
99-00	Phoenix	54	54	1767	738	310	645	.481	1	8	.125	117	151	.775	141	284	425	124	152	2	80	31	106	32.7	13.7	7.9	2.3	.495
00-01	Phoenix	57	2	1159	362	149	380	.392	3	12	.250	61	77	.792	76	179	255	55	109	0	47	21	50	20.3	6.4	4.5	1.0	.349
01-02	Phoenix	44	40	1129	285	127	301	.422	3	9	.333	28	37	.757	59	162	221	77	116	1	39	30	61	25.7	6.5	5.0	1.8	.321
02-03	Phoenix	27	11	447	129	60	132	.455	0	1	.000	9	9	1.000	25	75	100	31	35	0	14	5	31	16.6	4.8	3.7	1.1	.361
NBA Season Totals		661	572	21771	9495	3702	8140	.455	199	702	.283	1892	2499	.757	1474	3737	5211	2009	1698	9	1007	463	1638	32.9	14.4	7.9	3.0	....
96-97	Minnesota	3	3	121	55	23	52	.442	3	4	.750	6	10	.600	2	14	16	13	13	0	7	2	6	40.3	18.3	5.3	4.3	.427
98-99	Phoenix	3	3	118	32	13	35	.371	0	0	.000	6	8	.750	6	19	25	10	10	0	4	3	8	39.3	10.7	8.3	3.3	.335
00-01	Phoenix	4	0	86	23	8	26	.308	0	0	.000	7	9	.778	4	11	15	3	9	0	8	1	5	21.5	5.8	3.8	0.8	.259
02-03	Phoenix	2	0	10	5	2	4	.500	0	0	.000	1	2	.500	0	2	2	0	2	0	0	0	0	5.0	2.5	1.0	0.0	.364
NBA Playoff Totals		12	6	335	115	46	117	.393	3	4	.750	20	29	.690	12	46	58	26	34	0	19	6	19	27.9	9.6	4.8	2.2	....

• GUIBERT, Andres

Andres Guibert

Born: Oct. 28, 1968. Havana, Cuba. Height: 6'10". Weight: 225 lbs. Drafted: — College: none (HS: Manuel Fajardo, CUBA)

YEAR	TEAM	GP	GS	MIN	PTS	FGM	FGA	FG%	3PM	3PA	3P%	FTM	FTA	FT%	ORB	DRB	TRB	AST	PF	DQ	STL	BLK	TO	MPG	PPG	RPG	APG	PCM
93-94	Minnesota	5	0	33	15	6	20	.300	0	0	.000	3	6	.500	10	6	16	2	6	0	0	1	6	6.6	3.0	3.2	0.4	.312
94-95	Minnesota	17	0	167	45	16	47	.340	0	4	.000	13	19	.684	16	29	45	10	29	0	8	1	12	9.8	2.6	2.6	0.6	.297
NBA Season Totals		22	0	200	60	22	67	.328	0	4	.000	16	25	.640	26	35	61	12	35	0	8	2	18	9.1	2.7	2.8	0.5	....

• GUIDINGER, Jay

Jay Patrick Guidinger

Born: Aug. 18, 1969. Milwaukee, WI, United States. Height: 6'10". Weight: 255 lbs. Drafted: — College: Minnesota (Duluth)

YEAR	TEAM	GP	GS	MIN	PTS	FGM	FGA	FG%	3PM	3PA	3P%	FTM	FTA	FT%	ORB	DRB	TRB	AST	PF	DQ	STL	BLK	TO	MPG	PPG	RPG	APG	PCM
92-93	Cleveland	32	5	215	51	19	55	.345	0	0	.000	13	25	.520	26	38	64	17	48	0	9	10	10	6.7	1.6	2.0	0.5	.352
93-94	Cleveland	32	0	131	47	16	32	.500	0	0	.000	15	21	.714	15	18	33	3	23	0	4	5	16	4.1	1.5	1.0	0.1	.352
NBA Season Totals		64	5	346	98	35	87	.402	0	0	.000	28	46	.609	41	56	97	20	71	0	13	15	26	5.4	1.5	1.5	0.3	....
92-93	Cleveland	4	0	15	2	1	3	.333	0	0	.000	0	2	.000	1	0	1	0	1	0	0	1	2	3.8	0.5	0.3	0.0	-.084
NBA Playoff Totals		4	0	15	2	1	3	.333	0	0	.000	0	2	.000	1	0	1	0	1	0	0	1	2	3.8	0.5	0.3	0.0	....

• GUNNING, Ken

Kenneth Gunning

Born: 1914. Height: — Weight: — Drafted: — College: Indiana

YEAR	TEAM	GP	GS	MIN	PTS	FGM	FGA	FG%	3PM	3PA	3P%	FTM	FTA	FT%	ORB	DRB	TRB	AST	PF	DQ	STL	BLK	TO	MPG	PPG	RPG	APG	PCM
37-38	Whiting-N	15	....	....	105	37	....	....	....	....	....	31	....	....	....	....	....	....	....	....	....	....	....	....	7.0	....	....	....
45-46	Indianapolis-N	1	....	....	0	0	....	....	....	....	....	0	0	.000	....	....	....	....	....	....	....	....	....	....	0.0	....	....	....
NBL Season Totals		16	....	....	105	37	....	....	....	....	....	31	0	....	....	....	....	....	....	....	....	....	....	....	6.6	....	....	....
37-38	Whiting-N	2	....	....	11	3	....	....	....	....	....	5	....	....	....	....	....	....	....	....	....	....	....	....	5.5	....	....	....
NBL Playoff Totals		2	....	....	11	3	....	....	....	....	....	5	....	....	....	....	....	....	....	....	....	....	....	....	5.5	....	....	....

• GUNTHER, Colby

Coulby Gunther

Born: Feb. 5, 1923. Height: 6'4". Weight: 190 lbs. Drafted: — College: Boston College

YEAR	TEAM	GP	GS	MIN	PTS	FGM	FGA	FG%	3PM	3PA	3P%	FTM	FTA	FT%	ORB	DRB	TRB	AST	PF	DQ	STL	BLK	TO	MPG	PPG	RPG	APG	PCM
46-47	Pittsburgh	52	....	....	734	254	756	.336	....	....	....	226	351	.644	....	....	....	32	117	....	....	....	....	....	14.1	....	0.6	....
48-49	St. Louis	32	....	....	159	57	181	.315	....	....	....	45	71	.634	....	....	....	33	64	....	....	....	....	....	5.0	....	1.0	....
NBA Season Totals		84	....	....	893	311	937	.332	....	....	....	271	422	.642	....	....	....	65	181	....	....	....	....	....	10.6	....	0.8	....
48-49	St. Louis	1	....	....	0	0	1	.000	....	....	....	0	0	.000	....	....	....	0	0	....	....	....	....	....	0.0	....	0.0	....
NBA Playoff Totals		1	....	....	0	0	1	.000	....	....	....	0	0	.000	....	....	....	0	0	....	....	....	....	....	0.0	....	0.0	....

• GUNTHER, Dave

David C. Gunther

Born: July 22, 1937. Height: 6'7". Weight: 190 lbs. Drafted: 1959 College: Iowa

YEAR	TEAM	GP	GS	MIN	PTS	FGM	FGA	FG%	3PM	3PA	3P%	FTM	FTA	FT%	ORB	DRB	TRB	AST	PF	DQ	STL	BLK	TO	MPG	PPG	RPG	APG	PCM
62-63	San Francisco	1	....	5	2	1	2	.500	....	....	....	0	0	.000	....	....	3	3	1	0	....	....	....	5.0	2.0	3.0	3.0	1.363
NBA Season Totals		1	....	5	2	1	2	.500	....	....	....	0	0	.000	....	....	3	3	1	0	....	....	....	5.0	2.0	3.0	3.0	....

• GUOKAS, Al

Albert G. (Gook) Guokas

Born: Aug. 7, 1925. Died: Aug.2, 1990. Height: 6'5". Weight: 200 lbs. Drafted: — College: St. Joseph's (PA)

YEAR	TEAM	GP	GS	MIN	PTS	FGM	FGA	FG%	3PM	3PA	3P%	FTM	FTA	FT%	ORB	DRB	TRB	AST	PF	DQ	STL	BLK	TO	MPG	PPG	RPG	APG	PCM
48-49	Denver-N	60	....	....	373	146	....	....	....	....	....	81	129	.628	....	....	....	....	182	....	....	....	....	6.2	....	....	....
49-50	Denver	41	....	....	197	86	271	.317	....	....	....	25	47	.532	....	....	....	85	116	....	....	....	....	....	4.8	....	2.1	....
49-50	Philadelphia	16	....	....	17	7	28	.250	....	....	....	3	3	1.000	....	....	....	10	27	....	....	....	....	....	1.1	....	0.6	....
NBA Season Totals		57	....	....	214	93	299	.311	....	....	....	28	50	.560	....	....	....	95	143	....	....	....	....	....	3.8	....	1.7	....
NBL Season Totals		60	....	....	373	146	....	....	....	....	....	81	129	....	....	....	....	....	182	....	....	....	....	....	6.2	....	....	....
Career Totals		117	....	....	587	239	299	....	....	....	....	109	179	....	....	....	....	95	325	....	....	....	....	....	5.0	....	0.8	....
49-50	Philadelphia	2	....	....	6	2	4	.500	....	....	....	2	6	.333	....	....	....	5	3	....	....	....	....	....	3.0	....	2.5	....
NBA Playoff Totals		2	....	....	6	2	4	.500	....	....	....	2	6	.333	....	....	....	5	3	....	....	....	....	....	3.0	....	2.5	....

• GUOKAS, Matt

Matthew George Guokas Jr.

Born: Feb. 25, 1944. Philadelphia, PA, United States. Height: 6'5". Weight: 175 lbs. Drafted: 1966 College: St. Joseph's (PA)

YEAR	TEAM	GP	GS	MIN	PTS	FGM	FGA	FG%	3PM	3PA	3P%	FTM	FTA	FT%	ORB	DRB	TRB	AST	PF	DQ	STL	BLK	TO	MPG	PPG	RPG	APG	PCM
66-67	Philadelphia	69	....	808	207	79	203	.389	....	....	....	49	81	.605	....	....	83	105	82	0	....	....	....	11.7	3.0	1.2	1.5	.316
67-68	Philadelphia	82	....	1612	498	190	393	.483	....	....	....	118	152	.776	....	....	185	191	172	0	....	....	....	19.7	6.1	2.3	2.3	.391

YEAR	TEAM	GP	GS	MIN	PTS	FGM	FGA	FG%	3PM	3PA	3P%	FTM	FTA	FT%	ORB	DRB	TRB	AST	PF	DQ	STL	BLK	TO	MPG	PPG	RPG	APG	PCM
68-69	Philadelphia	72	....	838	238	92	216	.426	....	....	....	54	81	.667	....	....	94	104	121	1	....	....	....	11.6	3.3	1.3	1.4	.325
69-70	Philadelphia	80	....	1558	484	189	416	.454	....	....	....	106	149	.711	....	....	216	222	201	0	....	....	....	19.5	6.1	2.7	2.8	.395
70-71	Philadelphia	1	....	5	0	0	0	.000	....	....	....	0	0	.000	....	....	1	0	0	0	....	....	....	5.0	0.0	1.0	0.0	.172
70-71	Chicago	78	....	2208	513	206	418	.493	....	....	....	101	138	.732	....	....	157	342	189	1	....	....	....	28.3	6.6	2.0	4.4	.343
71-72	Cincinnati	61	....	1975	446	191	385	.496	....	....	....	64	83	.771	....	....	142	321	150	0	....	....	....	32.4	7.3	2.3	5.3	.351
72-73	Omaha	79	....	2846	718	322	565	.570	....	....	....	74	90	.822	....	....	245	403	190	0	....	....	....	36.0	9.1	3.1	5.1	.384
73-74	Omaha	9	....	315	90	41	83	.494	2	....	....	8	12	.667	2	19	21	36	21	0	8	1	....	35.0	10.0	2.3	4.0	.327
73-74	Houston	·39	....	1007	207	93	203	.458	....	....	....	21	28	.750	17	43	60	133	73	0	27	14	....	25.8	5.3	1.5	3.4	.281
73-74	Buffalo	27	....	549	132	61	110	.555	....	....	....	10	20	.500	12	28	40	69	56	0	19	6	....	20.3	4.9	1.5	2.6	.320
74-75	Chicago	82	....	2089	588	255	500	.510	....	....	....	78	103	.757	24	115	139	178	154	1	45	17	....	25.5	7.2	1.7	2.2	.299
75-76	Chicago	18	....	278	81	36	74	.486	....	....	....	9	11	.818	4	12	16	28	23	0	5	1	....	15.4	4.5	0.9	1.6	.300
75-76	Kansas City	38	....	515	83	37	99	.374	....	....	....	9	16	.563	18	29	47	42	53	0	13	2	....	13.6	2.2	1.2	1.1	.179
NBA Season Totals		735	....	16603	4285	1792	3665	.489	....	....	....	701	964	.727	77	246	1446	2174	1485	3	117	41	....	22.6	5.8	2.0	3.0	....
66-67	Philadelphia	15	....	252	65	26	64	.406	....	....	....	13	17	.765	....	....	30	23	33	0	....	....	....	16.8	4.3	2.0	1.5	.284
67-68	Philadelphia	13	....	327	80	30	79	.380	....	....	....	20	27	.741	....	....	43	30	39	0	....	....	....	25.2	6.2	3.3	2.3	.284
68-69	Philadelphia	5	....	100	26	11	27	.407	....	....	....	4	5	.800	....	....	12	8	12	0	....	....	....	20.0	5.2	2.4	1.6	.265
69-70	Philadelphia	2	....	23	13	6	8	.750	....	....	....	1	1	1.000	....	....	3	1	1	0	....	....	....	11.5	6.5	1.5	0.5	.633
70-71	Chicago	6	....	83	20	8	14	.571	....	....	....	4	5	.800	....	....	8	12	8	0	....	....	....	13.8	3.3	1.3	2.0	.380
73-74	Buffalo	6	....	85	19	8	15	.533	3	....	....	3	4	.750	3	5	8	13	8	0	0	1	....	14.2	3.2	1.3	2.2	.364
74-75	Chicago	13	....	202	31	12	35	.343	....	....	....	7	8	.875	4	10	14	11	20	0	7	1	....	15.5	2.4	1.1	0.8	.134
NBA Playoff Totals		60	....	1072	254	101	242	.417	....	....	....	52	67	.776	7	15	118	98	121	0	7	2	....	17.9	4.2	2.0	1.6	....

• GUOKAS, Matthew

Matthew George Guokas Sr.

Born: Nov. 11, 1915. Died: Dec.9, 1993.   Height: 6'3".   Weight: 195 lbs.   Drafted: —   College: St. Joseph's (PA)

YEAR	TEAM	GP	GS	MIN	PTS	FGM	FGA	FG%	3PM	3PA	3P%	FTM	FTA	FT%	ORB	DRB	TRB	AST	PF	DQ	STL	BLK	TO	MPG	PPG	RPG	APG	PCM
46-47	Philadelphia	47	....	....	82	28	104	.269	....	....	....	26	47	.553	....	....	....	9	70	....	....	....	....	....	1.7	....	0.2	....
NBA Season Totals		47	....	....	82	28	104	.269	....	....	....	26	47	.553	....	....	....	9	70	....	....	....	....	....	1.7	....	0.2	....
46-47	Philadelphia	8	....	....	4	1	9	.111	....	....	....	2	5	.400	....	....	....	0	11	....	....	....	....	....	0.5	....	0.0	....
NBA Playoff Totals		8	....	....	4	1	9	.111	....	....	....	2	5	.400	....	....	....	0	11	....	....	....	....	....	0.5	....	0.0	....

• GUYTON, A.J.

Arthur James Guyton

Born: Feb. 12, 1978. Peoria, IL, United States.   Height: 6'1".   Weight: 180 lbs.   Drafted: 2000   College: Indiana

YEAR	TEAM	GP	GS	MIN	PTS	FGM	FGA	FG%	3PM	3PA	3P%	FTM	FTA	FT%	ORB	DRB	TRB	AST	PF	DQ	STL	BLK	TO	MPG	PPG	RPG	APG	PCM
00-01	Chicago	33	8	630	198	78	192	.406	27	69	.391	15	18	.833	10	26	36	64	35	0	9	5	24	19.1	6.0	1.1	1.9	.274
01-02	Chicago	45	6	607	244	88	244	.361	46	123	.374	22	27	.815	12	32	44	81	23	0	10	7	37	13.5	5.4	1.0	1.8	.330
02-03	Golden State	2	0	9	0	0	4	.000	0	1	.000	0	0	.000	0	0	0	2	0	0	1	0	1	4.5	0.0	0.0	1.0	-.161
NBA Season Totals		80	14	1246	442	166	440	.377	73	193	.378	37	45	.822	22	58	80	147	58	0	20	12	62	15.6	5.5	1.0	1.8	....

• HAARLOW, A.

A. William Haarlow

Born: May 5, 1913. Chicago, IL, United States.   Height: 6'1".   Weight: 170 lbs.   Drafted: —   College: Chicago

YEAR	TEAM	GP	GS	MIN	PTS	FGM	FGA	FG%	3PM	3PA	3P%	FTM	FTA	FT%	ORB	DRB	TRB	AST	PF	DQ	STL	BLK	TO	MPG	PPG	RPG	APG	PCM
37-38	Whiting-N	10	....	....	66	26	....	....	....	....	....	14	....	....	....	....	....	....	....	....	....	....	....	6.6	....	....	....	
NBL Season Totals		10	....	....	66	26	....	....	....	....	....	14	....	....	....	....	....	....	....	....	....	....	....	6.6	....	....	....	
37-38	Whiting-N	1	....	....	7	2	....	....	....	....	....	3	....	....	....	....	....	....	....	....	....	....	....	7.0	....	....	....	
NBL Playoff Totals		1	....	....	7	2	....	....	....	....	....	3	....	....	....	....	....	....	....	....	....	....	....	7.0	....	....	....	

• HACKETT, Rudy

Rudolph Hackett

Born: May 10, 1953. Mount Vernon, NY, United States.   Height: 6'9".   Weight: 210 lbs.   Drafted: 1975   College: Syracuse

YEAR	TEAM	GP	GS	MIN	PTS	FGM	FGA	FG%	3PM	3PA	3P%	FTM	FTA	FT%	ORB	DRB	TRB	AST	PF	DQ	STL	BLK	TO	MPG	PPG	RPG	APG	PCM
75-76	St. Louis-A	22	....	414	141	55	131	.420	0	0	.000	31	49	.633	20	58	78	28	48	....	15	8	24	18.8	6.4	3.5	1.3	.349
76-77	New York	1	....	8	2	0	2	.000	....	....	....	2	5	.400	1	2	3	0	1	0	0	0	....	8.0	2.0	3.0	0.0	.142
76-77	Indiana	5	....	38	12	3	8	.375	....	....	....	6	9	.667	3	7	10	3	7	0	0	1	....	7.6	2.4	2.0	0.6	.406
NBA Season Totals		6	....	46	14	3	10	.300	....	....	....	8	14	.571	4	9	13	3	8	0	0	1	....	7.7	2.3	2.2	0.5	....
ABA Season Totals		22	....	414	141	55	131	.420	0	0	.000	31	49	.633	20	58	78	28	48	....	15	8	24	18.8	6.4	3.5	1.3	....
Career Totals		28	....	460	155	58	141	.411	0	0	.000	39	63	.619	24	67	91	31	56	0	15	9	24	16.4	5.5	3.3	1.1	....

• HADNOT, Jim

James Weldon Hadnot

Born: Jan. 15, 1940. Jasper, TX, United States.   Height: 6'10".   Weight: 235 lbs.   Drafted: 1962   College: Providence

YEAR	TEAM	GP	GS	MIN	PTS	FGM	FGA	FG%	3PM	3PA	3P%	FTM	FTA	FT%	ORB	DRB	TRB	AST	PF	DQ	STL	BLK	TO	MPG	PPG	RPG	APG	PCM
67-68	Oakland-A	77	....	3004	1344	488	1045	.467	0	2	.000	368	551	.668	303	633	936	135	279	9	....	....	169	39.0	17.5	12.2	1.8	.541
ABA Season Totals		77	....	3004	1344	488	1045	.467	0	2	.000	368	551	.668	303	633	936	135	279	9	....	....	169	39.0	17.5	12.2	1.8	....

• HAFFNER, Scott

Scott Richard Haffner

Born: Feb. 2, 1966. Terre Haute, IN, United States.   Height: 6'3".   Weight: 180 lbs.   Drafted: 1989   College: Evansville

YEAR	TEAM	GP	GS	MIN	PTS	FGM	FGA	FG%	3PM	3PA	3P%	FTM	FTA	FT%	ORB	DRB	TRB	AST	PF	DQ	STL	BLK	TO	MPG	PPG	RPG	APG	PCM
89-90	Miami	43	6	559	196	88	217	.406	3	21	.143	17	25	.680	7	44	51	80	53	0	13	2	34	13.0	4.6	1.2	1.9	.289
90-91	Charlotte	7	0	50	17	8	21	.381	0	2	.000	1	2	.500	2	2	4	9	4	0	3	1	4	7.1	2.4	0.6	1.3	.317
NBA Season Totals		50	6	609	213	96	238	.403	3	23	.130	18	27	.667	9	46	55	89	57	0	16	3	38	12.2	4.3	1.1	1.8	....

• HAGAN, Cliff

Clifford Oldham (Li'l Abner) Hagan

HOF: 1978

Born: Dec. 9, 1931. Owensboro, KY, United States.   Height: 6'4".   Weight: 210 lbs.   Drafted: 1953   College: Kentucky

YEAR	TEAM	GP	GS	MIN	PTS	FGM	FGA	FG%	3PM	3PA	3P%	FTM	FTA	FT%	ORB	DRB	TRB	AST	PF	DQ	STL	BLK	TO	MPG	PPG	RPG	APG	PCM
56-57	St. Louis	67	....	971	368	134	371	.361	....	....	....	100	145	.690	....	....	247	86	165	3	....	....	....	14.5	5.5	3.7	1.3	.417
57-58	St. Louis	70	....	2190	1391	503	1135	.443	....	....	....	385	501	.768	....	....	707	175	267	9	....	....	....	31.3	19.9	10.1	2.5	.698

YEAR	TEAM	GP	GS	MIN	PTS	FGM	FGA	FG%	3PM	3PA	3P%	FTM	FTA	FT%	ORB	DRB	TRB	AST	PF	DQ	STL	BLK	TO	MPG	PPG	RPG	APG	PCM
58-59	St. Louis	72	....	2702	1707	646	1417	.456	....	....	....	415	536	.774	....	....	783	245	275	10	....	....	....	37.5	23.7	10.9	3.4	.693
59-60	St. Louis	75	....	2798	1859	719	1549	.464	....	....	....	421	524	.803	....	....	803	299	270	4	....	....	....	37.3	24.8	10.7	4.0	.740
60-61	St. Louis	77	....	2701	1705	661	1490	.444	....	....	....	383	467	.820	....	....	715	381	286	9	....	....	....	35.1	22.1	9.3	4.9	.722
61-62	St. Louis	77	....	2784	1764	701	1490	.470	....	....	....	362	439	.825	....	....	633	370	282	8	....	....	....	36.2	22.9	8.2	4.8	.702
62-63	St. Louis	79	....	1716	1226	491	1055	.465	....	....	....	244	305	.800	....	....	341	193	211	2	....	....	....	21.7	15.5	4.3	2.4	.685
63-64	St. Louis	77	....	2279	1413	572	1280	.447	....	....	....	269	331	.813	....	....	377	193	273	4	....	....	....	29.6	18.4	4.9	2.5	.553
64-65	St. Louis	77	....	1739	1000	393	901	.436	....	....	....	214	268	.799	....	....	276	136	182	0	....	....	....	22.6	13.0	3.6	1.8	.517
65-66	St. Louis	74	....	1851	1014	419	942	.445	....	....	....	176	206	.854	....	....	234	164	177	1	....	....	....	25.0	13.7	3.2	2.2	.489
67-68	Dallas-A	56	....	1737	1019	371	759	.489	0	3	.000	277	351	.789	....	....	334	276	202	6	....	....	216	31.0	18.2	6.0	4.9	.681
68-69	Dallas-A	35	....	579	387	132	259	.510	0	1	.000	123	144	.854	46	56	102	122	73	2	....	....	74	16.5	11.1	2.9	3.5	.802
69-70	Dallas-A	3	....	27	17	8	13	.615	0	1	.000	1	2	.500	1	2	3	6	2	0	....	....	4	9.0	5.7	1.0	2.0	.772
NBA Season Totals		745	....	21731	13447	5239	11630	.450	....	....	....	2969	3722	.798	....	....	5116	2242	2388	50	....	....	....	29.2	18.0	6.9	3.0	....
ABA Season Totals		94	....	2343	1423	511	1031	.496	0	5	.000	401	497	.807	47	58	439	404	277	8	....	....	294	24.9	15.1	4.7	4.3	....
Career Totals		839	....	24074	14870	5750	12661	.454	0	5	.000	3370	4219	.799	47	58	5555	2646	2665	58	....	....	294	28.7	17.7	6.6	3.2	....
56-57	St. Louis	10	....	319	170	62	143	.434	....	....	....	46	63	.730	....	....	112	28	47	3	....	....	....	31.9	17.0	11.2	2.8	.641
57-58	St. Louis	11	....	418	305	111	221	.502	....	....	....	83	99	.838	....	....	115	37	48	3	....	....	....	38.0	27.7	10.5	3.4	.795
58-59	St. Louis	6	....	259	171	63	123	.512	....	....	....	45	54	.833	....	....	72	16	21	0	....	....	....	43.2	28.5	12.0	2.7	.729
59-60	St. Louis	14	....	544	339	125	296	.422	....	....	....	89	109	.817	....	....	138	54	54	1	....	....	....	38.9	24.2	9.9	3.9	.649
60-61	St. Louis	12	....	455	264	104	235	.443	....	....	....	56	69	.812	....	....	118	54	45	1	....	....	....	37.9	22.0	9.8	4.5	.657
62-63	St. Louis	11	....	255	203	83	179	.464	....	....	....	37	53	.698	....	....	55	34	42	4	....	....	....	23.2	18.5	5.0	3.1	.740
63-64	St. Louis	12	....	392	195	75	175	.429	....	....	....	45	54	.833	....	....	74	57	34	0	....	....	....	32.7	16.3	6.2	4.8	.581
64-65	St. Louis	4	....	123	74	34	75	.453	....	....	....	6	12	.500	....	....	26	7	14	0	....	....	....	30.8	18.5	6.5	1.8	.516
65-66	St. Louis	10	....	200	113	44	97	.454	....	....	....	25	27	.926	....	....	34	18	15	0	....	....	....	20.0	11.3	3.4	1.8	.567
67-68	Dallas-A	3	....	70	37	14	37	.378	0	0	.000	9	13	.692	....	....	13	9	11	1	....	....	9	23.3	12.3	4.3	3.0	.472
68-69	Dallas-A	2	....	45	18	5	14	.357	0	0	.000	8	10	.800	1	5	6	14	5	0	....	....	3	22.5	9.0	3.0	7.0	.631
NBA Playoff Totals		90	....	2965	1834	701	1544	.454	....	....	....	432	540	.800	....	....	744	305	320	12	....	....	....	32.9	20.4	8.3	3.4	....
ABA Playoff Totals		5	....	115	55	19	51	.373	0	0	.000	17	23	.739	1	5	19	23	16	1	....	....	12	23.0	11.0	3.8	4.6	....
Career Playoff Totals		95	....	3080	1889	720	1595	.451	0	0	.000	449	563	.798	1	5	763	328	336	13	....	....	12	32.4	19.9	8.0	3.5	....

• HAGAN, Glenn

Glenn Kassabin Hagan

Born: June 25, 1955. Sanford, FL, United States.   Height: 6'   Weight: 170 lbs.   Drafted: 1978   College: St. Bonaventure

YEAR	TEAM	GP	GS	MIN	PTS	FGM	FGA	FG%	3PM	3PA	3P%	FTM	FTA	FT%	ORB	DRB	TRB	AST	PF	DQ	STL	BLK	TO	MPG	PPG	RPG	APG	PCM
81-82	Detroit	4	0	25	7	3	7	.429	0	0	.000	1	1	1.000	2	2	4	8	7	0	3	0	1	6.3	1.8	1.0	2.0	.570
NBA Season Totals		4	0	25	7	3	7	.429	0	0	.000	1	1	1.000	2	2	4	8	7	0	3	0	1	6.3	1.8	1.0	2.0	....

• HAGAN, Tom

Thomas Medard Hagan

Born: Jan. 29, 1947. Louisville, KY, United States.   Height: 6'3".   Weight: 185 lbs.   Drafted: 1969   College: Vanderbilt

YEAR	TEAM	GP	GS	MIN	PTS	FGM	FGA	FG%	3PM	3PA	3P%	FTM	FTA	FT%	ORB	DRB	TRB	AST	PF	DQ	STL	BLK	TO	MPG	PPG	RPG	APG	PCM
69-70	Dallas-A	24	....	226	103	37	81	.457	7	17	.412	22	29	.759	8	22	30	29	42	0	....	....	16	9.4	4.3	1.3	1.2	.456
70-71	Kentucky-A	4	....	34	4	2	10	.200	0	1	.000	0	2	.000	0	1	1	4	2	0	....	....	0	8.5	1.0	0.3	1.0	.047
70-71	Texas-A	45	....	656	251	98	236	.415	12	40	.300	43	61	.705	33	49	82	102	76	0	....	....	52	14.6	5.6	1.8	2.3	.443
ABA Season Totals		73	....	916	358	137	327	.419	19	58	.328	65	92	.707	41	72	113	135	120	0	....	....	68	12.5	4.9	1.5	1.8	....

• HAHN, Robert

Robert B. Hahn

Born: Aug. 25, 1925.   Height: 6'10".   Weight: 240 lbs.   Drafted: —   College: North Carolina State

YEAR	TEAM	GP	GS	MIN	PTS	FGM	FGA	FG%	3PM	3PA	3P%	FTM	FTA	FT%	ORB	DRB	TRB	AST	PF	DQ	STL	BLK	TO	MPG	PPG	RPG	APG	PCM
49-50	Chicago	10	....	....	10	4	13	.308	....	....	....	2	7	.286	....	....	1	17	....	....	....	....	....	1.0	....	0.1	....
NBA Season Totals		10	....	....	10	4	13	.308	....	....	....	2	7	.286	....	....	1	17	....	....	....	....	....	1.0	....	0.1	....

• HAINES, George

George Haines

Born: 1921.   Height: 5'10".   Weight: 160 lbs.   Drafted: —   College: Bucknell

YEAR	TEAM	GP	GS	MIN	PTS	FGM	FGA	FG%	3PM	3PA	3P%	FTM	FTA	FT%	ORB	DRB	TRB	AST	PF	DQ	STL	BLK	TO	MPG	PPG	RPG	APG	PCM
44-45	Pittsburgh-N	26	....	....	145	56	....	....	....	....	....	33	....	....	....	....	....	....	....	....	....	....	....	5.6	....	....	....
NBL Season Totals		26	....	....	145	56	....	....	....	....	....	33	....	....	....	....	....	....	....	....	....	....	....	5.6	....	....	....

• HAIR, Warren

Warren Hair

Born: —.   Height: —   Weight: —   Drafted: —   College: Gallagher Business School

YEAR	TEAM	GP	GS	MIN	PTS	FGM	FGA	FG%	3PM	3PA	3P%	FTM	FTA	FT%	ORB	DRB	TRB	AST	PF	DQ	STL	BLK	TO	MPG	PPG	RPG	APG	PCM
37-38	Kankakee-N	11	....	....	46	15	....	....	....	....	....	16	....	....	....	....	....	....	....	....	....	....	....	4.2	....	....	....
NBL Season Totals		11	....	....	46	15	....	....	....	....	....	16	....	....	....	....	....	....	....	....	....	....	....	4.2	....	....	....

• HAIRSTON, Al

Alan Leroy Hairston

Born: Dec. 11, 1945.   Height: 6'1".   Weight: 170 lbs.   Drafted: 1968   College: Bowling Green

YEAR	TEAM	GP	GS	MIN	PTS	FGM	FGA	FG%	3PM	3PA	3P%	FTM	FTA	FT%	ORB	DRB	TRB	AST	PF	DQ	STL	BLK	TO	MPG	PPG	RPG	APG	PCM
68-69	Seattle	39	....	274	84	38	114	.333	....	....	....	8	14	.571	....	....	36	38	35	0	....	....	....	7.0	2.2	0.9	1.0	.283
69-70	Seattle	3	....	20	7	3	8	.375	....	....	....	1	1	1.000	....	....	5	6	3	0	....	....	....	6.7	2.3	1.7	2.0	.620
NBA Season Totals		42	....	294	91	41	122	.336	....	....	....	9	15	.600	....	....	41	44	38	0	....	....	....	7.0	2.2	1.0	1.0	....

• HAIRSTON, Happy

Harold (Happy) Hairston

Born: May 31, 1942. Winston-Salem, NC, United States. Died: May 1, 2001.   Height: 6'7".   Weight: 225 lbs.   Drafted: 1964   College: New York University

YEAR	TEAM	GP	GS	MIN	PTS	FGM	FGA	FG%	3PM	3PA	3P%	FTM	FTA	FT%	ORB	DRB	TRB	AST	PF	DQ	STL	BLK	TO	MPG	PPG	RPG	APG	PCM
64-65	Cincinnati	61	....	736	372	131	351	.373	....	....	....	110	165	.667	....	....	293	27	95	0	....	....	....	12.1	6.1	4.8	0.4	.549
65-66	Cincinnati	72	....	1794	1016	398	814	.489	....	....	....	220	321	.685	....	....	546	44	216	3	....	....	....	24.9	14.1	7.6	0.6	.584
66-67	Cincinnati	79	....	2442	1174	461	962	.479	....	....	....	252	382	.660	....	....	631	62	273	5	....	....	....	30.9	14.9	8.0	0.8	.488
67-68	Cincinnati	48	....	1625	837	317	630	.503	....	....	....	203	296	.686	....	....	355	58	127	1	....	....	....	33.9	17.4	7.4	1.2	.525

YEAR	TEAM	GP	GS	MIN	PTS	FGM	FGA	FG%	3PM	3PA	3P%	FTM	FTA	FT%	ORB	DRB	TRB	AST	PF	DQ	STL	BLK	TO	MPG	PPG	RPG	APG	PCM
67-68	Detroit	26	....	892	490	164	357	.459	....	....	....	162	226	.717	....	....	262	37	72	0	....	....	....	34.3	18.8	10.1	1.4	.600
68-69	Detroit	81	....	2889	1464	530	1131	.469	....	....	....	404	553	.731	....	....	959	109	255	3	....	....	....	35.7	18.1	11.8	1.3	.596
69-70	Detroit	15	....	282	159	57	103	.553	....	....	....	45	63	.714	....	....	88	11	36	0	....	....	....	18.8	10.6	5.9	0.7	.654
69-70	LA Lakers	55	....	2145	1133	426	870	.490	....	....	....	281	350	.803	....	....	687	110	194	9	....	....	....	39.0	20.6	12.5	2.0	.631
70-71	LA Lakers	80	....	2921	1485	574	1233	.466	....	....	....	337	431	.782	....	....	797	168	256	2	....	....	....	36.5	18.6	10.0	2.1	.563
71-72	LA Lakers	80	....	2748	1047	368	798	.461	....	....	....	311	399	.779	....	....	1045	193	251	2	....	....	....	34.4	13.1	13.1	2.4	.601
72-73	LA Lakers	28	....	939	456	158	328	.482	....	....	....	140	178	.787	....	....	370	68	77	0	....	....	....	33.5	16.3	13.2	2.4	.699
73-74	LA Lakers	77	....	2634	1113	385	759	.507	....	....	....	343	445	.771	335	705	1040	208	264	2	64	17	....	34.2	14.5	13.5	2.7	.669
74-75	LA Lakers	74	....	2283	759	271	536	.506	....	....	....	217	271	.801	304	642	946	173	218	2	52	11	....	30.9	10.3	12.8	2.3	.623
NBA Season Totals		776	....	24330	11505	4240	8872	.478	....	....	....	3025	4080	.741	639	1347	8019	1268	2334	29	116	28	....	31.4	14.8	10.3	1.6	....
64-65	Cincinnati	3	....	39	12	5	18	.278	....	....	....	2	3	.667	....	....	20	3	2	0	....	....	....	13.0	4.0	6.7	1.0	.511
65-66	Cincinnati	5	....	150	77	25	62	.403	....	....	....	27	38	.711	....	....	37	0	20	1	....	....	....	30.0	15.4	7.4	0.0	.432
66-67	Cincinnati	4	....	140	64	28	54	.519	....	....	....	8	15	.533	....	....	27	6	15	0	....	....	....	35.0	16.0	6.8	1.5	.452
67-68	Detroit	6	....	149	70	29	71	.408	....	....	....	12	20	.600	....	....	37	7	22	1	....	....	....	24.8	11.7	6.2	1.2	.419
69-70	LA Lakers	16	....	296	118	47	108	.435	....	....	....	24	35	.686	....	....	76	20	31	0	....	....	....	18.5	7.4	4.8	1.3	.456
70-71	LA Lakers	12	....	471	204	83	164	.506	....	....	....	38	50	.760	....	....	109	34	41	1	....	....	....	39.3	17.0	9.1	2.8	.518
71-72	LA Lakers	15	....	577	202	74	168	.440	....	....	....	54	68	.794	....	....	197	31	44	1	....	....	....	38.5	13.5	13.1	2.1	.522
72-73	LA Lakers	3	....	26	8	1	9	.111	....	....	....	6	8	.750	....	....	4	1	2	0	....	....	....	8.7	2.7	1.3	0.3	.154
73-74	LA Lakers	5	....	172	46	15	36	.417	....	....	....	16	18	.889	15	37	52	19	8	0	5	1	....	34.4	9.2	10.4	3.8	.523
NBA Playoff Totals		69	....	2020	801	307	690	.445	....	....	....	187	255	.733	15	37	559	121	185	4	5	1	....	29.3	11.6	8.1	1.8	....

• HAIRSTON, Lindsay

Lindsay (Spider) Hairston

Born: Dec. 8, 1951. Detroit, MI, United States. Height: 6'7". Weight: 180 lbs. Drafted: 1975 College: Michigan State

YEAR	TEAM	GP	GS	MIN	PTS	FGM	FGA	FG%	3PM	3PA	3P%	FTM	FTA	FT%	ORB	DRB	TRB	AST	PF	DQ	STL	BLK	TO	MPG	PPG	RPG	APG	PCM
75-76	Detroit	47	....	651	273	104	228	.456	....	....	....	65	112	.580	65	114	179	21	84	2	21	32	....	13.9	5.8	3.8	0.4	.442
NBA Season Totals		47	....	651	273	104	228	.456	....	....	....	65	112	.580	65	114	179	21	84	2	21	32	....	13.9	5.8	3.8	0.4	....

• HAISLIP, Marcus

Marcus Deshon Haislip

Born: Dec. 22, 1980. Lewisburg, TN, United States. Height: 6'10". Weight: 230 lbs. Drafted: 2002 College: Tennessee

YEAR	TEAM	GP	GS	MIN	PTS	FGM	FGA	FG%	3PM	3PA	3P%	FTM	FTA	FT%	ORB	DRB	TRB	AST	PF	DQ	STL	BLK	TO	MPG	PPG	RPG	APG	PCM
02-03	Milwaukee	39	8	441	161	66	153	.431	3	12	.250	26	38	.684	21	32	53	9	55	1	7	18	21	11.3	4.1	1.4	0.2	.257
NBA Season Totals		39	8	441	161	66	153	.431	3	12	.250	26	38	.684	21	32	53	9	55	1	7	18	21	11.3	4.1	1.4	0.2	....
02-03	Milwaukee	2	1	24	10	4	6	.667	0	0	.000	2	4	.500	2	2	4	2	5	0	2	1	1	12.0	5.0	2.0	1.0	.527
NBA Playoff Totals		2	1	24	10	4	6	.667	0	0	.000	2	4	.500	2	2	4	2	5	0	2	1	1	12.0	5.0	2.0	1.0	....

• HALBERT, Chick

Charles P. (Chick) Halbert

Born: Feb. 27, 1919. Height: 6'9". Weight: 225 lbs. Drafted: — College: West Texas State

YEAR	TEAM	GP	GS	MIN	PTS	FGM	FGA	FG%	3PM	3PA	3P%	FTM	FTA	FT%	ORB	DRB	TRB	AST	PF	DQ	STL	BLK	TO	MPG	PPG	RPG	APG	PCM
46-47	Chicago	61	....	....	773	280	915	.306	....	....	....	213	356	.598	....	....	....	46	161	....	....	....	....	....	12.7	....	0.8	....
47-48	Chicago	6	....	....	31	12	55	.218	....	....	....	7	20	.350	....	....	....	2	14	....	....	....	....	....	5.2	....	0.3	....
47-48	Philadelphia	40	....	....	421	144	550	.262	....	....	....	133	200	.665	....	....	....	30	112	....	....	....	....	....	10.5	....	0.8	....
48-49	Boston	33	....	....	310	99	338	.293	....	....	....	112	188	.596	....	....	....	61	97	....	....	....	....	....	9.4	....	1.8	....
48-49	Providence	27	....	....	308	103	309	.333	....	....	....	102	157	.650	....	....	....	52	78	....	....	....	....	....	11.4	....	1.9	....
49-50	Washington	68	....	....	328	108	284	.380	....	....	....	112	175	.640	....	....	....	89	136	....	....	....	....	....	4.8	....	1.3	....
50-51	Was/Bal	68	....	....	500	164	449	.365	....	....	....	172	248	.694	....	....	539	158	216	7	....	....	....	....	7.4	7.9	2.3	....
NBA Season Totals		303	....	....	2671	910	2900	.314	....	....	....	851	1344	.633	....	....	539	438	814	7	....	....	....	....	8.8	1.8	1.4	....
46-47	Chicago	11	....	....	155	50	198	.253	....	....	....	55	91	.604	....	....	....	3	32	....	....	....	....	....	14.1	....	0.3	....
47-48	Philadelphia	13	....	....	149	49	185	.265	....	....	....	51	84	.607	....	....	....	4	45	....	....	....	....	....	11.5	....	0.3	....
49-50	Washington	2	....	....	19	7	16	.438	....	....	....	5	9	.556	....	....	....	3	7	....	....	....	....	....	9.5	....	1.5	....
NBA Playoff Totals		26	....	....	323	106	399	.266	....	....	....	111	184	.603	....	....	....	10	84	....	....	....	....	....	12.4	....	0.4	....

• HALBROOK, Swede

Harvey Wade (Swede) Halbrook

Born: Jan. 30, 1933. Died: Apr.5, 1988. Height: 7'3". Weight: 235 lbs. Drafted: 1956 College: Oregon State

YEAR	TEAM	GP	GS	MIN	PTS	FGM	FGA	FG%	3PM	3PA	3P%	FTM	FTA	FT%	ORB	DRB	TRB	AST	PF	DQ	STL	BLK	TO	MPG	PPG	RPG	APG	PCM
60-61	Syracuse	79	....	1131	386	155	463	.335	....	....	....	76	140	.543	....	....	550	31	262	9	....	....	....	14.3	4.9	7.0	0.4	.428
61-62	Syracuse	64	....	908	400	152	422	.360	....	....	....	96	151	.636	....	....	399	33	179	7	....	....	....	14.2	6.3	6.2	0.5	.495
NBA Season Totals		143	....	2039	786	307	885	.347	....	....	....	172	291	.591	....	....	949	64	441	16	....	....	....	14.3	5.5	6.6	0.4	....
60-61	Syracuse	8	....	172	62	24	72	.333	....	....	....	14	20	.700	....	....	83	12	21	0	....	....	....	21.5	7.8	10.4	1.5	.542
NBA Playoff Totals		8	....	172	62	24	72	.333	....	....	....	14	20	.700	....	....	83	12	21	0	....	....	....	21.5	7.8	10.4	1.5	....

• HALE, Bruce

William Bruce Hale

Born: Aug. 30, 1918. Medford, OR, United States. Died: Dec.30, 1980. Height: 6'1". Weight: 170 lbs. Drafted: — College: Santa Clara

YEAR	TEAM	GP	GS	MIN	PTS	FGM	FGA	FG%	3PM	3PA	3P%	FTM	FTA	FT%	ORB	DRB	TRB	AST	PF	DQ	STL	BLK	TO	MPG	PPG	RPG	APG	PCM
46-47	Chicago-N	41	....	....	428	156	....	....	....	....	....	116	141	.823	....	....	....	....	103	....	....	....	....	....	10.4	....	....	....
47-48	Indianapolis-N	48	....	....	547	196	....	....	....	....	....	155	215	.721	....	....	....	....	136	....	....	....	....	....	11.4	....	....	....
48-49	Indianapolis	18	....	....	226	78	237	.329	....	....	....	70	92	.761	....	....	....	69	40	....	....	....	....	....	12.6	....	3.8	....
48-49	Fort Wayne	34	....	....	320	109	348	.313	....	....	....	102	136	.750	....	....	....	87	72	....	....	....	....	....	9.4	....	2.6	....
49-50	Indianapolis	64	....	....	657	217	614	.353	....	....	....	223	285	.782	....	....	....	226	143	....	....	....	....	....	10.3	....	3.5	....
50-51	Indianapolis	26	....	....	94	40	135	.296	....	....	....	14	23	.609	....	....	49	42	30	0	....	....	....	....	3.6	1.9	1.6	....
NBA Season Totals		142	....	....	1297	444	1334	.333	....	....	....	409	536	.763	....	....	49	424	285	0	....	....	....	....	9.1	0.3	3.0	....
NBL Season Totals		89	....	....	975	352	....	....	....	....	....	271	356	....	....	....	....	....	239	....	....	....	....	....	11.0	....	....	....
Career Totals		231	....	....	2272	796	1334	....	....	....	....	680	892	....	....	....	49	424	524	0	....	....	....	....	9.8	0.2	1.8	....

YEAR TEAM	GP	GS	MIN	PTS	FGM	FGA	FG%	3PM	3PA	3P%	FTM	FTA	FT%	ORB	DRB	TRB	AST	PF	DQ	STL	BLK	TO	MPG	PPG	RPG	APG	PCM
46-47 Chicago-N	11	....	....	94	35	....	....	....	....	....	24	30	.800	....	....	....	....	....	....	....	....	....	....	8.5	....	....	....
47-48 Indianapolis-N	4	....	....	62	21	....	....	....	....	....	20	25	.800	....	....	....	....	....	....	....	....	....	....	15.5	....	....	....
49-50 Indianapolis	6	....	....	43	14	40	.350	....	....	....	15	17	.882	....	....	....	17	11	....	....	....	....	....	7.2	....	2.8	....
50-51 Indianapolis	1	....	....	0	0	0	.000	....	....	....	0	0	.000	....	....	0	0	0	0	....	....	....	....	0.0	0.0	0.0	....
NBA Playoff Totals	7	....	....	43	14	40	.350	....	....	....	15	17	.882	....	....	0	17	11	0	....	....	....	....	6.1	0.0	2.4	....
NBL Playoff Totals	15	....	....	156	56	....	....	....	....	....	44	55	....	....	....	....	....	....	....	....	....	....	....	10.4	....	....	....
Career Playoff Totals	22	....	....	199	70	40	....	....	....	....	59	72	....	....	....	0	17	11	0	....	....	....	....	9.0	0.0	0.8	....

• HALE, Hal

Hal Ries Hale

Born: Sept. 21, 1945. Height: 6'1". Weight: 180 lbs. Drafted: — College: Utah State

YEAR TEAM	GP	GS	MIN	PTS	FGM	FGA	FG%	3PM	3PA	3P%	FTM	FTA	FT%	ORB	DRB	TRB	AST	PF	DQ	STL	BLK	TO	MPG	PPG	RPG	APG	PCM
67-68 Houston-A	72	....	1706	361	133	408	.326	35	112	.313	60	89	.674	....	....	206	144	143	1	....	....	91	23.7	5.0	2.9	2.0	.235
ABA Season Totals	72	....	1706	361	133	408	.326	35	112	.313	60	89	.674	....	....	206	144	143	1	....	....	91	23.7	5.0	2.9	2.0	....
67-68 Houston-A	3	....	103	22	6	16	.375	3	3	1.000	7	7	1.000	....	....	8	3	10	0	....	....	0	34.3	7.3	2.7	1.0	.191
ABA Playoff Totals	3	....	103	22	6	16	.375	3	3	1.000	7	7	1.000	....	....	8	3	10	0	....	....	0	34.3	7.3	2.7	1.0	....

• HALEY, Jack

Jack Kevin Haley

Born: Jan. 27, 1964. Long Beach, CA, United States. Height: 6'10". Weight: 240 lbs. Drafted: 1987 College: UCLA

YEAR TEAM	GP	GS	MIN	PTS	FGM	FGA	FG%	3PM	3PA	3P%	FTM	FTA	FT%	ORB	DRB	TRB	AST	PF	DQ	STL	BLK	TO	MPG	PPG	RPG	APG	PCM
88-89 Chicago	51	1	289	110	37	78	.474	0	0	.000	36	46	.783	21	50	71	10	56	0	11	0	26	5.7	2.2	1.4	0.2	.360
89-90 Chicago	11	0	58	25	9	20	.450	0	0	.000	7	7	1.000	7	11	18	4	7	0	0	1	7	5.3	2.3	1.6	0.4	.464
89-90 New Jersey	56	26	1026	336	129	327	.394	0	1	.000	78	118	.661	108	174	282	22	163	1	18	11	67	18.3	6.0	5.0	0.4	.300
90-91 New Jersey	78	18	1178	434	161	343	.469	0	0	.000	112	181	.619	140	216	356	31	199	0	20	21	62	15.1	5.6	4.6	0.4	.412
91-92 LA Lakers	49	9	394	76	31	84	.369	0	0	.000	14	29	.483	31	64	95	7	75	0	7	8	25	8.0	1.6	1.9	0.1	.181
93-94 San Antonio	28	0	94	59	21	48	.438	0	0	.000	17	21	.810	6	18	24	1	18	0	0	0	11	3.4	2.1	0.9	0.0	.395
94-95 San Antonio	31	0	117	73	26	61	.426	0	1	.000	21	32	.656	8	19	27	2	31	0	3	5	12	3.8	2.4	0.9	0.1	.378
95-96 Chicago	1	0	7	5	2	6	.333	0	0	.000	1	2	.500	1	1	2	0	2	0	0	0	1	7.0	5.0	2.0	0.0	.110
96-97 New Jersey	20	0	74	40	13	37	.351	0	0	.000	14	19	.737	13	19	32	5	14	0	1	1	2	3.7	2.0	1.6	0.3	.594
97-98 New Jersey	16	0	51	22	5	18	.278	0	1	.000	12	21	.571	5	10	15	0	9	0	0	1	5	3.2	1.4	0.9	0.0	.234
NBA Season Totals	341	54	3288	1180	434	1022	.425	0	3	.000	312	476	.655	340	582	922	82	574	1	60	48	218	9.6	3.5	2.7	0.2	....
88-89 Chicago	5	0	7	5	2	3	.667	0	0	.000	1	2	.500	0	1	1	1	2	0	0	0	0	1.4	1.0	0.2	0.2	.668
91-92 LA Lakers	2	0	12	2	1	4	.250	0	0	.000	0	0	.000	1	0	1	1	3	0	0	0	0	6.0	1.0	0.5	0.5	-.015
93-94 San Antonio	3	0	11	13	4	8	.500	0	0	.000	5	6	.833	3	4	7	2	3	0	0	0	0	3.7	4.3	2.3	0.7	1.462
94-95 San Antonio	4	0	13	3	1	7	.143	0	0	.000	1	2	.500	2	4	6	0	2	0	0	1	1	3.3	0.8	1.5	0.0	.123
NBA Playoff Totals	14	0	43	23	8	22	.364	0	0	.000	7	10	.700	6	9	15	4	10	0	0	1	1	3.1	1.6	1.1	0.3	....

• HALIMON, Shaler

Shaler Halimon Jr.

Born: Mar. 30, 1945. Tampa, FL, United States. Height: 6'5". Weight: 199 lbs. Drafted: 1968 College: Utah State

YEAR TEAM	GP	GS	MIN	PTS	FGM	FGA	FG%	3PM	3PA	3P%	FTM	FTA	FT%	ORB	DRB	TRB	AST	PF	DQ	STL	BLK	TO	MPG	PPG	RPG	APG	PCM
68-69 Philadelphia	50	....	350	186	88	196	.449	....	....	....	10	32	.313	....	....	86	18	34	0	....	....	....	7.0	3.7	1.7	0.4	.472
69-70 Chicago	38	....	517	241	96	244	.393	....	....	....	49	73	.671	....	....	68	69	58	0	....	....	....	13.6	6.3	1.8	1.8	.410
70-71 Chicago	2	....	23	2	1	8	.125	....	....	....	0	1	.000	....	....	2	4	5	1	....	....	....	11.5	1.0	1.0	2.0	-.014
70-71 Portland	79	....	1629	707	300	775	.387	....	....	....	107	161	.665	....	....	415	211	178	1	....	....	....	20.6	8.9	5.3	2.7	.489
71-72 Dallas-A	55	....	770	308	123	294	.418	0	2	.000	62	86	.721	58	98	156	72	89	0	....	....	46	14.0	5.6	2.8	1.3	.423
71-72 Atlanta	1	....	4	0	0	0	.000	....	....	....	0	0	.000	....	....	0	0	1	0	....	....	....	4.0	0.0	0.0	0.0	-.108
72-73 Dallas-A	29	....	355	142	59	149	.396	1	7	.143	23	37	.622	16	38	54	49	53	1	....	....	43	12.2	4.9	1.9	1.7	.376
NBA Season Totals	170	....	2523	1136	485	1223	.397	....	....	....	166	267	.622	....	....	571	302	276	2	....	....	....	14.8	6.7	3.4	1.8	....
ABA Season Totals	84	....	1125	450	182	443	.411	1	9	.111	85	123	.691	74	136	210	121	142	1	....	....	89	13.4	5.4	2.5	1.4	....
Career Totals	254	....	3648	1586	667	1666	.400	1	9	.111	251	390	.644	74	136	781	423	418	3	....	....	89	14.4	6.2	3.1	1.7	....
68-69 Philadelphia	1	....	2	2	1	2	.500	....	....	....	0	0	.000	....	....	0	0	0	0	....	....	....	2.0	2.0	0.0	0.0	.582
69-70 Chicago	5	....	106	44	21	61	.344	....	....	....	2	3	.667	....	....	20	18	13	0	....	....	....	21.2	8.8	4.0	3.6	.381
71-72 Dallas-A	4	....	55	22	9	17	.529	0	0	.000	4	7	.571	3	10	13	7	4	0	....	....	5	13.8	5.5	3.3	1.8	.567
NBA Playoff Totals	6	....	108	46	22	63	.349	....	....	....	2	3	.667	....	....	20	18	13	0	....	....	....	18.0	7.7	3.3	3.0	....
ABA Playoff Totals	4	....	55	22	9	17	.529	0	0	.000	4	7	.571	3	10	13	7	4	0	....	....	5	13.8	5.5	3.3	1.8	....
Career Playoff Totals	10	....	163	68	31	80	.388	0	0	.000	6	10	.600	3	10	33	25	17	0	....	....	5	16.3	6.8	3.3	2.5	....

• HALLIBURTON, Jeff

Jeffrey Halliburton

Born: July 3, 1949. Height: 6'5". Weight: 193 lbs. Drafted: 1971 College: Drake

YEAR TEAM	GP	GS	MIN	PTS	FGM	FGA	FG%	3PM	3PA	3P%	FTM	FTA	FT%	ORB	DRB	TRB	AST	PF	DQ	STL	BLK	TO	MPG	PPG	RPG	APG	PCM
71-72 Atlanta	37	....	288	147	61	133	.459	....	....	....	25	30	.833	....	....	37	20	50	1	....	....	....	7.8	4.0	1.0	0.5	.402
72-73 Atlanta	24	....	238	121	50	116	.431	....	....	....	21	22	.955	....	....	26	28	29	0	....	....	....	9.9	5.0	1.1	1.2	.444
72-73 Philadelphia	31	....	549	294	122	280	.436	....	....	....	50	66	.758	....	....	82	68	78	0	....	....	....	17.7	9.5	2.6	2.2	.485
NBA Season Totals	92	....	1075	562	233	529	.440	....	....	....	96	118	.814	....	....	145	116	157	1	....	....	....	11.7	6.1	1.6	1.3	....
71-72 Atlanta	1	....	2	0	0	1	.000	....	....	....	0	0	.000	....	....	0	0	0	0	....	....	....	2.0	0.0	0.0	0.0	-.432
NBA Playoff Totals	1	....	2	0	0	1	.000	....	....	....	0	0	.000	....	....	0	0	0	0	....	....	....	2.0	0.0	0.0	0.0	....

• HAM, Darvin

Darvin Ham

Born: July 23, 1973. Saginaw, MI, United States. Height: 6'7". Weight: 220 lbs. Drafted: — College: Texas Tech

YEAR TEAM	GP	GS	MIN	PTS	FGM	FGA	FG%	3PM	3PA	3P%	FTM	FTA	FT%	ORB	DRB	TRB	AST	PF	DQ	STL	BLK	TO	MPG	PPG	RPG	APG	PCM
96-97 Denver	35	3	313	80	32	61	.525	0	0	.000	16	33	.485	29	27	56	14	57	3	8	8	21	8.9	2.3	1.6	0.4	.259
96-97 Indiana	1	0	5	3	1	1	1.000	0	0	.000	1	2	.500	0	0	0	0	0	0	1	0	1	5.0	3.0	0.0	0.0	.507
97-98 Washington	71	3	635	145	55	104	.529	0	0	.000	35	74	.473	72	59	131	16	118	1	21	25	36	8.9	2.0	1.8	0.2	.275
99-00 Milwaukee	35	21	792	177	71	128	.555	0	1	.000	35	78	.449	85	87	172	42	102	1	29	29	29	22.6	5.1	4.9	1.2	.363
00-01 Milwaukee	29	13	540	109	39	80	.488	2	3	.667	29	49	.592	56	65	121	25	85	0	17	21	33	18.6	3.8	4.2	0.9	.307

YEAR TEAM	GP	GS	MIN	PTS	FGM	FGA	FG%	3PM	3PA	3P%	FTM	FTA	FT%	ORB	DRB	TRB	AST	PF	DQ	STL	BLK	TO	MPG	PPG	RPG	APG	PCM
01-02 Milwaukee	70	2	1208	303	120	211	.569	1	7	.143	62	123	.504	91	111	202	73	175	0	25	37	83	17.3	4.3	2.9	1.0	.296
02-03 Atlanta	75	1	926	180	71	159	.447	0	3	.000	38	79	.481	73	80	153	38	127	0	16	19	65	12.3	2.4	2.0	0.5	.191
NBA Season Totals	316	43	4419	997	389	744	.523	3	14	.214	216	438	.493	406	429	835	208	664	5	117	139	268	14.0	3.2	2.6	0.7	....
99-00 Milwaukee	5	5	144	25	11	17	.647	0	1	.000	3	9	.333	17	12	29	7	22	0	1	8	7	28.8	5.0	5.8	1.4	.296
00-01 Milwaukee	14	6	132	29	9	15	.600	0	0	.000	11	20	.550	10	9	19	5	31	1	4	7	6	9.4	2.1	1.4	0.4	.248
NBA Playoff Totals	19	11	276	54	20	32	.625	0	1	.000	14	29	.483	27	21	48	12	53	1	5	15	13	14.5	2.8	2.5	0.6	....

• HAMANN, Ray

Ray Hamann

Born: 1911. Height: 6'4". Weight: 205 lbs. Drafted: — College: Wisconsin

37-38 Oshkosh-N	11	....	....	49	22	....	....	....	....	....	5	....	....	....	....	....	....	....	....	....	....	....	....	4.5	....	....	....
38-39 Oshkosh-N	18	....	....	60	27	....	....	....	....	....	6	....	....	....	....	....	....	....	....	....	....	....	....	3.3	....	....	....
NBL Season Totals	29	....	....	109	49	....	....	....	....	....	11	....	....	....	....	....	....	....	....	....	....	....	....	3.8	....	....	....
37-38 Oshkosh-N	3	....	....	12	6	....	....	....	....	....	0	....	....	....	....	....	....	....	....	....	....	....	....	4.0	....	....	....
38-39 Oshkosh-N	4	....	....	3	1	....	....	....	....	....	1	....	....	....	....	....	....	....	....	....	....	....	....	0.8	....	....	....
NBL Playoff Totals	7	....	....	15	7	....	....	....	....	....	1	....	....	....	....	....	....	....	....	....	....	....	....	2.1	....	....	....

• HAMER, Steve

Stevie Ray Hamer

Born: Nov. 13, 1973. Memphis, TN, United States. Height: 7' Weight: 245 lbs. Drafted: 1996 College: Tennessee

96-97 Boston	35	3	268	76	30	57	.526	0	2	.000	16	29	.552	17	43	60	7	39	0	2	4	14	7.7	2.2	1.7	0.2	.308
NBA Season Totals	35	3	268	76	30	57	.526	0	2	.000	16	29	.552	17	43	60	7	39	0	2	4	14	7.7	2.2	1.7	0.2	....

• HAMILTON, Dale

Dale B. (Ham) Hamilton

Born: Aug. 16, 1919. Height: 6' Weight: 180 lbs. Drafted: — College: Franklin (IN)

39-40 Hammond-N	7	....	....	11	5	....	....	....	....	....	1	....	....	....	....	....	....	....	....	....	....	....	....	1.6	....	....	....
41-42 Fort Wayne-N	16	....	....	36	10	....	....	....	....	....	16	....	....	....	....	....	....	....	....	....	....	....	....	2.3	....	....	....
42-43 Fort Wayne-N	18	....	....	17	8	....	....	....	....	....	1	....	....	....	....	....	....	....	....	....	....	....	....	0.9	....	....	....
43-44 Fort Wayne-N	11	....	....	4	2	....	....	....	....	....	0	....	....	....	....	....	....	....	....	....	....	....	....	0.4	....	....	....
44-45 Fort Wayne-N	2	....	....	0	0	....	....	....	....	....	0	....	....	....	....	....	....	....	....	....	....	....	....	0.0	....	....	....
46-47 Toledo-N	44	....	....	295	114	....	....	....	....	....	67	131	.511	....	....	....	....	94	....	....	....	....	....	6.7	....	....	....
47-48 Toledo-N	53	....	....	248	93	....	....	....	....	....	62	133	.466	....	....	....	....	130	....	....	....	....	....	4.7	....	....	....
48-49 Waterloo-N	62	....	....	250	78	....	....	....	....	....	94	179	.525	....	....	....	....	194	....	....	....	....	....	4.0	....	....	....
49-50 Waterloo	14	....	....	25	8	33	.242	....	....	....	9	19	.474	....	....	....	17	30	....	....	....	....	....	1.8	....	1.2	....
NBA Season Totals	14	....	....	25	8	33	.242	....	....	....	9	19	.474	....	....	....	17	30	....	....	....	....	....	1.8	....	1.2	....
NBL Season Totals	213	....	....	861	310	....	....	....	....	....	241	443	....	....	....	....	....	418	....	....	....	....	....	4.0	....	....	....
Career Totals	227	....	....	886	318	33	....	....	....	....	250	462	....	....	....	....	17	448	....	....	....	....	....	3.9	....	0.1	....
41-42 Fort Wayne-N	5	....	....	7	2	....	....	....	....	....	3	....	....	....	....	....	....	....	....	....	....	....	....	1.4	....	....	....
42-43 Fort Wayne-N	1	....	....	0	0	....	....	....	....	....	0	....	....	....	....	....	....	....	....	....	....	....	....	0.0	....	....	....
43-44 Fort Wayne-N	5	....	....	0	0	....	....	....	....	....	0	....	....	....	....	....	....	....	....	....	....	....	....	0.0	....	....	....
46-47 Toledo-N	4	....	....	19	6	....	....	....	....	....	7	20	.350	....	....	....	....	....	....	....	....	....	....	4.8	....	....	....
NBL Playoff Totals	15	....	....	26	8	....	....	....	....	....	10	20	....	....	....	....	....	....	....	....	....	....	....	1.7	....	....	....

• HAMILTON, Dennis

Dennis Eugene Hamilton

Born: May 8, 1944. Huntington Beach, CA, United States. Height: 6'8". Weight: 210 lbs. Drafted: — College: Arizona State

67-68 LA Lakers	44	....	378	121	54	108	.500	....	....	....	13	13	1.000	....	....	72	30	46	0	....	....	....	8.6	2.8	1.6	0.7	.405
68-69 Atlanta	25	....	141	76	37	67	.552	....	....	....	2	5	.400	....	....	29	8	19	0	....	....	....	5.6	3.0	1.2	0.3	.534
69-70 Pittsburgh-A	72	....	1331	456	190	375	.507	0	1	.000	76	100	.760	104	236	340	73	144	0	....	....	96	18.5	6.3	4.7	1.0	.451
70-71 Kentucky-A	3	....	11	3	1	2	.500	0	0	.000	1	1	1.000	0	1	1	1	1	0	....	....	3	3.7	1.0	0.3	0.3	.345
NBA Season Totals	69	....	519	197	91	175	.520	....	....	....	15	18	.833	....	....	101	38	65	0	....	....	....	7.5	2.9	1.5	0.6	....
ABA Season Totals	75	....	1342	459	191	377	.507	0	1	.000	77	101	.762	104	237	341	74	145	0	....	....	99	17.9	6.1	4.5	1.0	....
Career Totals	144	....	1861	656	282	552	.511	0	1	.000	92	119	.773	104	237	442	112	210	0	....	....	99	12.9	4.6	3.1	0.8	....
67-68 LA Lakers	2	....	11	2	1	3	.333	....	....	....	0	0	.000	....	....	2	1	0	0	....	....	....	5.5	1.0	1.0	0.5	.291
NBA Playoff Totals	2	....	11	2	1	3	.333	....	....	....	0	0	.000	....	....	2	1	0	0	....	....	....	5.5	1.0	1.0	0.5	....

• HAMILTON, Joe

James (Little Joe) Hamilton Jr.

Born: July 5, 1948. Lexington, KY, United States. Height: 5'10". Weight: 160 lbs. Drafted: 1970 College: North Texas State

70-71 Texas-A	84	....	2564	1318	500	1184	.422	85	285	.298	233	279	.835	96	189	285	365	279	6	....	....	138	30.5	15.7	3.4	4.3	.509
71-72 Dallas-A	82	....	1959	881	317	791	.401	46	132	.348	201	256	.785	41	153	194	240	202	1	....	....	110	23.9	10.7	2.4	2.9	.404
72-73 Dallas-A	83	....	2359	1015	370	902	.410	66	191	.346	209	262	.798	46	169	215	325	247	6	....	....	143	28.4	12.2	2.6	3.9	.404
73-74 Kentucky-A	30	....	546	249	103	250	.412	18	58	.310	25	33	.758	13	36	49	80	62	....	25	4	30	18.2	8.3	1.6	2.7	.414
73-74 San Antonio-A	43	....	1415	567	228	584	.390	19	86	.221	92	110	.836	27	89	116	162	92	....	51	1	82	32.9	13.2	2.7	3.8	.353
74-75 Kentucky-A	9	....	124	38	15	40	.375	3	5	.600	5	6	.833	2	9	11	21	13	....	4	0	9	13.8	4.2	1.2	2.3	.344
75-76 Utah-A	13	....	131	77	31	78	.397	6	21	.286	9	13	.692	5	9	14	15	12	....	8	0	6	10.1	5.9	1.1	1.2	.436
ABA Season Totals	344	....	9098	4145	1564	3829	.408	243	778	.312	774	959	.807	230	654	884	1208	907	13	88	5	518	26.4	12.0	2.6	3.5	....
70-71 Texas-A	4	....	101	44	17	52	.327	3	10	.300	7	7	1.000	8	12	20	15	10	0	....	....	4	25.3	11.0	5.0	3.8	.455
71-72 Dallas-A	4	....	89	40	15	46	.326	3	13	.231	7	9	.778	4	7	11	13	10	0	....	....	2	22.3	10.0	2.8	3.3	.356
73-74 Kentucky-A	7	....	129	51	16	47	.340	6	14	.429	13	17	.765	3	20	23	21	18	....	4	0	17	18.4	7.3	3.3	3.0	.455
ABA Playoff Totals	15	....	319	135	48	145	.331	12	37	.324	27	33	.818	15	39	54	49	38	0	4	0	23	21.3	9.0	3.6	3.3	....

YEAR	TEAM	GP	GS	MIN	PTS	FGM	FGA	FG%	3PM	3PA	3P%	FTM	FTA	FT%	ORB	DRB	TRB	AST	PF	DQ	STL	BLK	TO	MPG	PPG	RPG	APG	PCM

• HAMILTON, Ralph   Ralph Albert (Ham) Hamilton

Born: June 10, 1921. Died: June3, 1993.   Height: 6'1".   Weight: 188 lbs.   Drafted: —   College: Indiana

YEAR	TEAM	GP	GS	MIN	PTS	FGM	FGA	FG%	3PM	3PA	3P%	FTM	FTA	FT%	ORB	DRB	TRB	AST	PF	DQ	STL	BLK	TO	MPG	PPG	RPG	APG	PCM
47-48	Fort Wayne-N	49	....	....	387	143	....	....	....	....	....	101	135	.748	....	....	....	....	74	....	....	....	....	....	7.9	....	....	....
48-49	Fort Wayne	10	....	....	42	16	66	.242	....	....	....	10	13	.769	....	....	....	3	10	....	....	....	....	....	4.2	....	0.3	....
48-49	Indianapolis	38	....	....	247	98	381	.257	....	....	....	51	78	.654	....	....	....	80	57	....	....	....	....	....	6.5	....	2.1	....
NBA Season Totals		48	....	....	289	114	447	.255	....	....	....	61	91	.670	....	....	....	83	67	....	....	....	....	....	6.0	....	1.7	....
NBL Season Totals		49	....	....	387	143	....	....	....	....	....	101	135		....	....	....	....	74	....	....	....	....	....	7.9	....	....	....
Career Totals		97	....	....	676	257	447		....	....	....	162	226		....	....	....	83	141	....	....	....	....	....	7.0	....	0.9	....
47-48	Fort Wayne-N	2	....	....	4	1	....	....	....	....	....	2	4	.500	....	....	....	....	....	....	....	....	....	....	2.0	....	....	....
NBL Playoff Totals		2	....	....	4	1	....	....	....	....	....	2	4		....	....	....	....	....	....	....	....	....	....	2.0	....	....	....

• HAMILTON, Richard   Richard Clay Hamilton

Born: Feb. 14, 1978. Coatesville, PA, United States.   Height: 6'6".   Weight: 185 lbs.   Drafted: 1999   College: Connecticut

YEAR	TEAM	GP	GS	MIN	PTS	FGM	FGA	FG%	3PM	3PA	3P%	FTM	FTA	FT%	ORB	DRB	TRB	AST	PF	DQ	STL	BLK	TO	MPG	PPG	RPG	APG	PCM
99-00	Washington	71	12	1373	639	254	605	.420	28	77	.364	103	133	.774	38	91	129	108	142	0	28	6	84	19.3	9.0	1.8	1.5	.315
00-01	Washington	78	42	2519	1411	547	1249	.438	40	146	.274	277	319	.868	75	163	238	224	203	2	75	10	201	32.3	18.1	3.1	2.9	.408
01-02	Washington	63	57	2203	1260	472	1084	.435	16	42	.381	300	337	.890	73	143	216	171	136	0	38	14	132	35.0	20.0	3.4	2.7	.426
02-03	Detroit	82	82	2639	1612	570	1286	.443	32	119	.269	440	528	.833	88	230	318	208	249	2	64	13	200	32.2	19.7	3.9	2.5	.460
NBA Season Totals		294	193	8734	4922	1843	4224	.436	116	384	.302	1120	1317	.850	274	627	901	711	730	4	205	43	617	29.7	16.7	3.1	2.4	....
02-03	Detroit	17	17	659	383	134	303	.442	9	27	.333	106	117	.906	18	48	66	45	51	0	13	1	57	38.8	22.5	3.9	2.6	.412
NBA Playoff Totals		17	17	659	383	134	303	.442	9	27	.333	106	117	.906	18	48	66	45	51	0	13	1	57	38.8	22.5	3.9	2.6	....

• HAMILTON, Roy   Roy Lee Hamilton

Born: July 20, 1957. Los Angeles, CA, United States.   Height: 6'2".   Weight: 180 lbs.   Drafted: 1979   College: UCLA

YEAR	TEAM	GP	GS	MIN	PTS	FGM	FGA	FG%	3PM	3PA	3P%	FTM	FTA	FT%	ORB	DRB	TRB	AST	PF	DQ	STL	BLK	TO	MPG	PPG	RPG	APG	PCM
79-80	Detroit	72	....	1116	333	115	287	.401	0	2	.000	103	150	.687	45	62	107	192	82	0	48	5	115	15.5	4.6	1.5	2.7	.331
80-81	Portland	1	....	5	3	1	3	.333	0	0	.000	1	2	.500	2	1	3	0	1	0	0	0	1	5.0	3.0	3.0	0.0	.418
NBA Season Totals		73	....	1121	336	116	290	.400	0	2	.000	104	152	.684	47	63	110	192	83	0	48	5	116	15.4	4.6	1.5	2.6	....

• HAMILTON, Steve   Steve Absher Hamilton

Born: Nov. 30, 1935. Columbia, KY, United States. Died: Dec.2, 1997.   Height: 6'6".   Weight: 190 lbs.   Drafted: 1958   College: Morehead State

YEAR	TEAM	GP	GS	MIN	PTS	FGM	FGA	FG%	3PM	3PA	3P%	FTM	FTA	FT%	ORB	DRB	TRB	AST	PF	DQ	STL	BLK	TO	MPG	PPG	RPG	APG	PCM
58-59	Minneapolis	67	....	847	292	109	294	.371	....	....	....	74	109	.679	....	....	220	36	144	2	....	....	....	12.6	4.4	3.3	0.5	.349
59-60	Minneapolis	15	....	247	76	29	77	.377	....	....	....	18	23	.783	....	....	58	7	39	1	....	....	....	16.5	5.1	3.9	0.5	.306
NBA Season Totals		82	....	1094	368	138	371	.372	....	....	....	92	132	.697	....	....	278	43	183	3	....	....	....	13.3	4.5	3.4	0.5	....
58-59	Minneapolis	10	....	87	32	12	43	.279	....	....	....	8	10	.800	....	....	35	5	14	0	....	....	....	8.7	3.2	3.5	0.5	.405
NBA Playoff Totals		10	....	87	32	12	43	.279	....	....	....	8	10	.800	....	....	35	5	14	0	....	....	....	8.7	3.2	3.5	0.5	

• HAMILTON, Tang   Tephen Hamilton

Born: May 26, 1978. Jackson, MS, United States.   Height: 6'8".   Weight: 220 lbs.   Drafted: —   College: Mississippi State

YEAR	TEAM	GP	GS	MIN	PTS	FGM	FGA	FG%	3PM	3PA	3P%	FTM	FTA	FT%	ORB	DRB	TRB	AST	PF	DQ	STL	BLK	TO	MPG	PPG	RPG	APG	PCM
01-02	Miami	9	2	98	20	10	19	.526	0	1	.000	0	1	.000	6	12	18	5	10	0	4	0	2	10.9	2.2	2.0	0.6	.311
NBA Season Totals		9	2	98	20	10	19	.526	0	1	.000	0	1	.000	6	12	18	5	10	0	4	0	2	10.9	2.2	2.0	0.6	....

• HAMILTON, Thomas   Thomas Thaddeus Hamilton

Born: Apr. 3, 1975. Chicago, IL, United States.   Height: 7'2".   Weight: 330 lbs.   Drafted: —   College: Pittsburgh (DNP)

YEAR	TEAM	GP	GS	MIN	PTS	FGM	FGA	FG%	3PM	3PA	3P%	FTM	FTA	FT%	ORB	DRB	TRB	AST	PF	DQ	STL	BLK	TO	MPG	PPG	RPG	APG	PCM
95-96	Boston	11	0	70	25	9	31	.290	0	0	.000	7	18	.389	10	12	22	1	12	0	0	9	9	6.4	2.3	2.0	0.1	.218
99-00	Houston	22	7	273	82	35	79	.443	0	0	.000	12	23	.522	31	59	90	15	25	0	4	14	28	12.4	3.7	4.1	0.7	.420
NBA Season Totals		33	7	343	107	44	110	.400	0	0	.000	19	41	.463	41	71	112	16	37	0	4	23	37	10.4	3.2	3.4	0.5	....

• HAMILTON, Zendon   Zendon Hamilton

Born: Apr. 27, 1975. Floral Park, NY, United States.   Height: 6'11".   Weight: 250 lbs.   Drafted: —   College: St. John's (NY)

YEAR	TEAM	GP	GS	MIN	PTS	FGM	FGA	FG%	3PM	3PA	3P%	FTM	FTA	FT%	ORB	DRB	TRB	AST	PF	DQ	STL	BLK	TO	MPG	PPG	RPG	APG	PCM
00-01	LA Clippers	3	0	19	9	2	9	.222	0	0	.000	5	8	.625	3	5	8	0	4	0	0	0	2	6.3	3.0	2.7	0.0	.261
01-02	Denver	54	15	848	324	103	245	.420	0	0	.000	118	181	.652	110	143	253	14	104	0	21	18	60	15.7	6.0	4.7	0.3	.407
02-03	Toronto	3	0	12	6	2	5	.400	0	0	.000	2	2	1.000	1	3	4	0	2	0	1	0	1	4.0	2.0	1.3	0.0	.500
NBA Season Totals		60	15	879	339	107	259	.413	0	0	.000	125	191	.654	114	151	265	14	110	0	22	18	63	14.7	5.7	4.4	0.2	....

• HAMMINK, Geert   Geert Hendrik Hammink

Born: Apr. 12, 1969. Didam, Netherlands.   Height: 7'   Weight: 262 lbs.   Drafted: 1993   College: Louisiana State

YEAR	TEAM	GP	GS	MIN	PTS	FGM	FGA	FG%	3PM	3PA	3P%	FTM	FTA	FT%	ORB	DRB	TRB	AST	PF	DQ	STL	BLK	TO	MPG	PPG	RPG	APG	PCM
93-94	Orlando	1	0	3	2	1	3	.333	0	0	.000	0	0	.000	1	0	1	1	1	0	0	0	0	3.0	2.0	1.0	1.0	.569
94-95	Orlando	1	0	7	4	1	3	.333	0	0	.000	2	2	1.000	0	2	2	1	1	0	0	0	0	7.0	4.0	2.0	1.0	.656
95-96	Orlando	3	0	7	4	1	2	.500	0	0	.000	2	4	.500	2	1	3	0	1	0	0	0	2	2.3	1.3	1.0	0.0	.370
95-96	Golden State	3	0	10	4	1	2	.500	0	0	.000	2	3	.667	0	1	1	0	1	0	0	0	0	3.3	1.3	0.3	0.0	.306
NBA Season Totals		8	0	27	14	4	10	.400	0	0	.000	6	9	.667	3	4	7	2	4	0	0	0	2	3.4	1.8	0.9	0.3	....

Total Basketball

YEAR	TEAM	GP	GS	MIN	PTS	FGM	FGA	FG%	3PM	3PA	3P%	FTM	FTA	FT%	ORB	DRB	TRB	AST	PF	DQ	STL	BLK	TO	MPG	PPG	RPG	APG	PCM

• HAMMOND, Julian

Julian Hammond

Born: May 27, 1943. Chicago, IL, United States.   Height: 6'5".   Weight: 205 lbs.   Drafted: 1966   College: Tulsa

YEAR	TEAM	GP	GS	MIN	PTS	FGM	FGA	FG%	3PM	3PA	3P%	FTM	FTA	FT%	ORB	DRB	TRB	AST	PF	DQ	STL	BLK	TO	MPG	PPG	RPG	APG	PCM
67-68	Denver-A	74	....	1364	591	224	458	.489	0	0	.000	143	209	.684	....	....	327	62	112	0		....	98	18.4	8.0	4.4	0.8	.489
68-69	Denver-A	78	....	2335	823	329	601	.547	0	0	.000	165	253	.652	266	334	600	124	213	3		....	152	29.9	10.6	7.7	1.6	.478
69-70	Denver-A	69	....	1847	827	329	660	.498	0	1	.000	169	243	.695	204	267	471	109	183	2		....	158	26.8	12.0	6.8	1.6	.520
70-71	Denver-A	83	....	2082	1143	435	834	.522	0	0	.000	273	375	.728	238	285	523	97	189	0		....	180	25.1	13.8	6.3	1.2	.597
71-72	Denver-A	25	....	411	163	66	140	.471	0	0	.000	31	50	.620	48	67	115	29	47	0		....	30	16.4	6.5	4.6	1.2	.493
ABA Season Totals		329	....	8039	3547	1383	2693	.514	0	1	.000	781	1130	.691	756	953	2036	421	744	5		....	618	24.4	10.8	6.2	1.3	....
67-68	Denver-A	5	....	153	60	22	38	.579	0	0	.000	16	24	.667	....	....	28	8	17	1		....	11	30.6	12.0	5.6	1.6	.451
68-69	Denver-A	7	....	191	91	33	64	.516	0	0	.000	25	33	.758	....	....	50	4	26	1		....	14	27.3	13.0	7.1	0.6	.509
69-70	Denver-A	12	....	395	192	85	170	.500	0	0	.000	22	36	.611	45	34	79	34	49	1		....	27	32.9	16.0	6.6	2.8	.503
ABA Playoff Totals		24	....	739	343	140	272	.515	0	0	.000	63	93	.677	45	34	157	46	92	3		....	52	30.8	14.3	6.5	1.9	....

• HAMMONDS, Tom

Tom Edward (The Terminator) Hammonds

Born: Mar. 27, 1967. Fort Walton, FL, United States.   Height: 6'9".   Weight: 215 lbs.   Drafted: 1989   College: Georgia Tech

YEAR	TEAM	GP	GS	MIN	PTS	FGM	FGA	FG%	3PM	3PA	3P%	FTM	FTA	FT%	ORB	DRB	TRB	AST	PF	DQ	STL	BLK	TO	MPG	PPG	RPG	APG	PCM
89-90	Washington	61	8	805	321	129	295	.437	0	1	.000	63	98	.643	61	107	168	51	98	0	11	14	49	13.2	5.3	2.8	0.8	.363
90-91	Washington	70	7	1023	367	155	336	.461	0	4	.000	57	79	.722	58	148	206	43	108	0	15	7	56	14.6	5.2	2.9	0.6	.336
91-92	Washington	37	19	984	440	195	400	.488	0	1	.000	50	82	.610	49	136	185	36	118	1	22	13	59	26.6	11.9	5.0	1.0	.374
92-93	Charlotte	19	5	142	43	19	45	.422	0	0	.000	5	8	.625	5	26	31	8	20	0	0	4	4	7.5	2.3	1.6	0.4	.320
92-93	Denver	35	0	571	205	86	176	.489	0	1	.000	33	54	.611	33	63	96	16	57	0	18	8	32	16.3	5.9	2.7	0.5	.325
93-94	Denver	74	2	877	301	115	230	.500	0	0	.000	71	104	.683	62	137	199	34	91	0	20	12	44	11.9	4.1	2.7	0.5	.396
94-95	Denver	70	5	956	410	139	260	.535	0	1	.000	132	177	.746	55	167	222	36	132	1	11	14	56	13.7	5.9	3.2	0.5	.451
95-96	Denver	71	4	1045	342	127	268	.474	0	0	.000	88	115	.765	85	138	223	23	137	0	23	13	50	14.7	4.8	3.1	0.3	.338
96-97	Denver	81	8	1758	506	191	398	.480	0	2	.000	124	172	.721	135	266	401	64	205	0	16	24	89	21.7	6.2	5.0	0.8	.337
97-98	Minnesota	57	2	1140	346	127	246	.516	0	1	.000	92	132	.697	100	171	271	36	127	1	15	17	46	20.0	6.1	4.8	0.6	.382
98-99	Minnesota	49	0	716	212	82	179	.458	0	0	.000	48	75	.640	54	82	136	20	88	1	8	7	32	14.6	4.3	2.8	0.4	.283
99-00	Minnesota	56	0	372	117	42	97	.433	0	0	.000	33	56	.589	34	67	101	10	55	0	8	3	21	6.6	2.1	1.8	0.2	.337
00-01	Minnesota	7	0	30	7	3	10	.300	0	0	.000	1	2	.500	2	2	4	1	8	1	0	0	3	4.3	1.0	0.6	0.1	-.044
NBA Season Totals		687	60	10419	3617	1410	2940	.480	0	11	.000	797	1154	.691	733	1510	2243	378	1244	5	167	136	541	15.2	5.3	3.3	0.6	....
93-94	Denver	8	0	49	9	2	9	.222	0	0	.000	5	6	.833	5	8	13	2	6	0	0	0	1	6.1	1.1	1.6	0.3	.256
94-95	Denver	3	0	44	20	9	14	.643	0	0	.000	2	6	.333	3	4	7	1	12	0	0	2	4	14.7	6.7	2.3	0.3	.308
97-98	Minnesota	5	1	113	36	12	28	.429	0	0	.000	12	16	.750	10	12	22	2	18	0	0	1	4	22.6	7.2	4.4	0.4	.273
98-99	Minnesota	4	0	18	4	0	0	.000	0	0	.000	4	4	1.000	0	2	2	0	4	0	0	0	1	4.5	1.0	0.5	0.0	.173
99-00	Minnesota	1	0	2	0	0	0	.000	0	0	.000	0	0	.000	0	0	0	0	0	0	0	0	0	2.0	0.0	0.0	0.0	.000
NBA Playoff Totals		21	1	226	69	23	51	.451	0	0	.000	23	32	.719	18	26	44	5	40	0	0	3	10	10.8	3.3	2.1	0.2	....

• HAMOOD, Joe

Joseph Hamood

Born: Sept. 7, 1943. Died: Aug.19, 1970.   Height: 6'   Weight: 180 lbs.   Drafted: —   College: Houston

YEAR	TEAM	GP	GS	MIN	PTS	FGM	FGA	FG%	3PM	3PA	3P%	FTM	FTA	FT%	ORB	DRB	TRB	AST	PF	DQ	STL	BLK	TO	MPG	PPG	RPG	APG	PCM
67-68	Houston-A	76	....	1839	750	274	819	.335	16	78	.205	186	252	.738	....	....	217	227	200	2		....	126	24.2	9.9	2.9	3.0	.344
ABA Season Totals		76	....	1839	750	274	819	.335	16	78	.205	186	252	.738	....	....	217	227	200	2		....	126	24.2	9.9	2.9	3.0	....
67-68	Houston-A	3	....	42	7	3	17	.176	0	3	.000	1	2	.500	....	....	5	2	8	0		....	1	14.0	2.3	1.7	0.7	-.044
ABA Playoff Totals		3	....	42	7	3	17	.176	0	3	.000	1	2	.500	....	....	5	2	8	0		....	1	14.0	2.3	1.7	0.7	....

• HANCOCK, Darrin

Darrin Hancock

Born: Nov. 3, 1971. Birmingham, AL, United States.   Height: 6'7".   Weight: 205 lbs.   Drafted: 1994   College: Kansas

YEAR	TEAM	GP	GS	MIN	PTS	FGM	FGA	FG%	3PM	3PA	3P%	FTM	FTA	FT%	ORB	DRB	TRB	AST	PF	DQ	STL	BLK	TO	MPG	PPG	RPG	APG	PCM
94-95	Charlotte	46	7	424	153	68	121	.562	1	3	.333	16	39	.410	14	39	53	30	48	0	19	4	32	9.2	3.3	1.2	0.7	.338
95-96	Charlotte	63	7	838	272	112	214	.523	1	3	.333	47	73	.644	40	58	98	47	94	2	28	5	57	13.3	4.3	1.6	0.7	.285
96-97	Milwaukee	9	0	39	4	2	6	.333	0	0	.000	0	0	.000	1	4	5	4	7	0	2	0	4	4.3	0.4	0.6	0.4	.105
96-97	San Antonio	1	0	8	4	1	2	.500	0	0	.000	2	2	1.000	0	0	0	1	2	0	0	0	0	8.0	4.0	0.0	1.0	.401
96-97	Atlanta	14	0	86	34	13	27	.481	0	0	.000	8	12	.667	3	10	13	7	6	0	7	1	7	6.1	2.4	0.9	0.5	.428
NBA Season Totals		133	14	1395	467	196	370	.530	2	6	.333	73	126	.579	58	111	169	89	157	2	56	10	100	10.5	3.5	1.3	0.7	....
94-95	Charlotte	3	0	18	4	2	6	.333	0	0	.000	0	0	.000	2	2	4	1	5	0	1	0	3	6.0	1.3	1.3	0.3	.047
96-97	Atlanta	6	0	33	4	2	5	.400	0	1	.000	0	3	.000	2	3	5	1	5	0	1	1	1	5.5	0.7	0.8	0.2	.125
NBA Playoff Totals		9	0	51	8	4	11	.364	0	1	.000	0	3	.000	4	5	9	2	10	0	2	1	4	5.7	0.9	1.0	0.2	....

• HANKINS, Cecil

Cecil O. Hankins

Born: Jan. 6, 1922.   Height: 6'1".   Weight: 175 lbs.   Drafted: —   College: Oklahoma A&M

YEAR	TEAM	GP	GS	MIN	PTS	FGM	FGA	FG%	3PM	3PA	3P%	FTM	FTA	FT%	ORB	DRB	TRB	AST	PF	DQ	STL	BLK	TO	MPG	PPG	RPG	APG	PCM
46-47	St. Louis	55	....	....	324	117	391	.299	....	....	....	90	150	.600	....	....	....	14	49	....	....	....	....		5.9	....	0.3	....
47-48	Sheboygan-N	1	....	....	1	0		....	....	....	....	1	1	1.000	....	....	....		2	....	....	....	....		1.0	....		....
47-48	Boston	25	....	70	23		116	.198	....	....	....	24	35	.686	....	....	8		28	....	....	....	....		2.8	....	0.3	....
NBA Season Totals		80	....	....	394	140	507	.276	....	....	....	114	185	.616	....	....	22		77	....	....	....	....		4.9	....	0.3	....
NBL Season Totals		1	....	....	1	0		....	....	....	....	1	1		....	....	....		2	....	....	....	....		1.0	....		....
Career Totals		81	....	....	395	140	507		....	....	....	115	186		....	....	22		79	....	....	....	....		4.9	....	0.3	....
46-47	St. Louis	2	....	....	5	2	7	.286	....	....	....	1	2	.500	....	....	0		1	....	....	....	....		2.5	....	0.0	....
NBA Playoff Totals		2	....	....	5	2	7	.286	....	....	....	1	2	.500	....	....	0		1	....	....	....	....		2.5	....	0.0	....

• HANKINSON, Phil

Phil Hankinson

Born: July 26, 1951. Augusta, GA, United States. Died: Nov.19, 1996. Height: 6'8". Weight: 195 lbs. Drafted: 1973 College: Pennsylvania

YEAR TEAM	GP	GS	MIN	PTS	FGM	FGA	FG%	3PM	3PA	3P%	FTM	FTA	FT%	ORB	DRB	TRB	AST	PF	DQ	STL	BLK	TO	MPG	PPG	RPG	APG	PCM
73-74 Boston	28	....	163	110	50	103	.485	....	....	....	10	13	.769	22	28	50	4	18	0	3	1	....	5.8	3.9	1.8	0.1	.633
74-75 Boston	3	....	24	12	6	11	.545	....	....	....	0	0	.000	1	6	7	2	3	0	1	0	....	8.0	4.0	2.3	0.7	.613
NBA Season Totals	31	....	187	122	56	114	.491	....	....	....	10	13	.769	23	34	57	6	21	0	4	1	....	6.0	3.9	1.8	0.2	....
73-74 Boston	2	....	5	6	2	4	.500	....	....	....	2	2	1.000	0	1	1	0	0	0	0	1	....	2.5	3.0	0.5	0.0	1.030
74-75 Boston	2	....	3	2	1	3	.333	....	....	....	0	0	.000	2	0	2	0	0	0	0	0	....	1.5	1.0	1.0	0.0	.667
NBA Playoff Totals	4	....	8	8	3	7	.429	....	....	....	2	2	1.000	2	1	3	0	0	0	0	1	....	2.0	2.0	0.8	0.0	....

• HANNUM, Alex

Alexander Murray Hannum

Born: July 19, 1923. Los Angeles, CA, United States. Died: Jan.18, 2002. Height: 6'7". Weight: 210 lbs. Drafted: 1948 College: USC

YEAR TEAM	GP	GS	MIN	PTS	FGM	FGA	FG%	3PM	3PA	3P%	FTM	FTA	FT%	ORB	DRB	TRB	AST	PF	DQ	STL	BLK	TO	MPG	PPG	RPG	APG	PCM
48-49 Oshkosh-N	64	....	....	365	126	....	....	....	....	....	113	191	.592	....	....	....	....	188	....	....	....	....	....	5.7	....	....	....
49-50 Syracuse	64	....	....	482	177	488	.363	....	....	....	128	186	.688	....	....	....	129	264	....	....	....	....	....	7.5	....	2.0	....
50-51 Syracuse	63	....	....	471	182	494	.368	....	....	....	107	197	.543	....	....	301	119	271	16	....	....	....	....	7.5	4.8	1.9	....
51-52 Bal/Roc	66	....	1508	438	170	462	.368	....	....	....	98	138	.710	....	....	336	133	271	16	....	....	....	22.8	6.6	5.1	2.0	.352
52-53 Rochester	68	....	1288	346	129	360	.358	....	....	....	88	133	.662	....	....	279	81	258	18	....	....	....	18.9	5.1	4.1	1.2	.291
53-54 Rochester	72	....	1707	452	175	503	.348	....	....	....	102	164	.622	....	....	350	105	279	11	....	....	....	23.7	6.3	4.9	1.5	.282
54-55 Milwaukee	53	....	1088	313	126	358	.352	....	....	....	61	107	.570	....	....	245	105	206	9	....	....	....	20.5	5.9	4.6	2.0	.330
55-56 St. Louis	71	....	1480	385	146	453	.322	....	....	....	93	154	.604	....	....	344	157	271	10	....	....	....	20.8	5.4	4.8	2.2	.325
56-57 FtW/StL	59	....	642	191	77	223	.345	....	....	....	37	56	.661	....	....	158	28	135	2	....	....	....	10.9	3.2	2.7	0.5	.277
NBA Season Totals	516	....	7713	3078	1182	3341	.354	....	....	....	714	1135	.629	....	....	2013	857	1955	82	....	....	....	14.9	6.0	3.9	1.7	....
NBL Season Totals	64	....	....	365	126	....	....	....	....	....	113	191	....	....	....	....	....	188	....	....	....	....	....	5.7	....	....	....
Career Totals	580	....	7713	3443	1308	3341	....	....	....	....	827	1326	....	....	....	2013	857	2143	82	....	....	....	13.3	5.9	3.5	1.5	....
48-49 Oshkosh-N	7	....	....	40	12	....	....	....	....	....	16	26	.615	....	....	....	....	....	....	....	....	....	....	5.7	....	....	....
49-50 Syracuse	11	....	....	93	38	86	.442	....	....	....	17	34	.500	....	....	....	10	50	....	....	....	....	....	8.5	....	0.9	....
50-51 Syracuse	7	....	....	42	17	39	.436	....	....	....	8	10	.800	....	....	47	17	37	3	....	....	....	....	6.0	6.7	2.4	....
51-52 Rochester	6	....	146	40	16	42	.381	....	....	....	8	13	.615	....	....	26	8	30	3	....	....	....	24.3	6.7	4.3	1.3	.259
52-53 Rochester	3	....	52	11	4	10	.400	....	....	....	3	8	.375	....	....	4	2	16	1	....	....	....	17.3	3.7	1.3	0.7	.087
53-54 Rochester	6	....	107	39	12	29	.414	....	....	....	15	24	.625	....	....	22	5	28	3	....	....	....	17.8	6.5	3.7	0.8	.335
55-56 St. Louis	8	....	159	61	21	66	.318	....	....	....	19	35	.543	....	....	29	10	36	3	....	....	....	19.9	7.6	3.6	1.3	.261
56-57 St. Louis	2	....	6	0	0	2	.000	....	....	....	0	0	.000	....	....	0	0	2	0	....	....	....	3.0	0.0	0.0	0.0	-.373
NBA Playoff Totals	43	....	470	286	108	274	.394	....	....	....	70	124	.565	....	....	128	52	199	13	....	....	....	10.9	6.7	3.0	1.2	....
NBL Playoff Totals	7	....	....	40	12	....	....	....	....	....	16	26	....	....	....	....	....	....	....	....	....	....	....	5.7	....	....	....
Career Playoff Totals	50	....	470	326	120	274	....	....	....	....	86	150	....	....	....	128	52	199	13	....	....	....	9.4	6.5	2.6	1.0	....

• HANRAHAN, Don

Donald Hanrahan

Born: Feb. 6, 1929. Height: 6'7". Weight: 200 lbs. Drafted: — College: Loyola (IL)

YEAR TEAM	GP	GS	MIN	PTS	FGM	FGA	FG%	3PM	3PA	3P%	FTM	FTA	FT%	ORB	DRB	TRB	AST	PF	DQ	STL	BLK	TO	MPG	PPG	RPG	APG	PCM
52-53 Indianapolis	18	....	121	33	11	32	.344	....	....	....	11	15	.733	....	....	30	11	24	1	....	....	....	6.7	1.8	1.7	0.6	.359
NBA Season Totals	18	....	121	33	11	32	.344	....	....	....	11	15	.733	....	....	30	11	24	1	....	....	....	6.7	1.8	1.7	0.6	....

• HANS, Rollen

Rollen F. Hans

Born: Apr. 13, 1931. Height: 6'2". Weight: 210 lbs. Drafted: — College: Long Island University

YEAR TEAM	GP	GS	MIN	PTS	FGM	FGA	FG%	3PM	3PA	3P%	FTM	FTA	FT%	ORB	DRB	TRB	AST	PF	DQ	STL	BLK	TO	MPG	PPG	RPG	APG	PCM
53-54 Baltimore	67	....	1556	483	191	515	.371	....	....	....	101	180	.561	....	....	160	181	172	1	....	....	....	23.2	7.2	2.4	2.7	.328
54-55 Baltimore	13	....	178	73	30	67	.448	....	....	....	13	25	.520	....	....	16	26	20	0	....	....	....	13.7	5.6	1.2	2.0	.436
NBA Season Totals	80	....	1734	556	221	582	.380	....	....	....	114	205	.556	....	....	176	207	192	1	....	....	....	21.7	7.0	2.2	2.6	....

• HANSEN, Bob

Robert Louis Hansen II

Born: Jan. 18, 1961. Des Moines, IA, United States. Height: 6'6". Weight: 190 lbs. Drafted: 1983 College: Iowa

YEAR TEAM	GP	GS	MIN	PTS	FGM	FGA	FG%	3PM	3PA	3P%	FTM	FTA	FT%	ORB	DRB	TRB	AST	PF	DQ	STL	BLK	TO	MPG	PPG	RPG	APG	PCM
83-84 Utah	55	0	419	148	65	145	.448	0	8	.000	18	28	.643	13	35	48	44	62	0	15	4	33	7.6	2.7	0.9	0.8	.284
84-85 Utah	54	4	646	261	110	225	.489	1	7	.143	40	72	.556	20	50	70	75	88	0	25	1	49	12.0	4.8	1.3	1.4	.343
85-86 Utah	82	82	2032	710	299	628	.476	17	50	.340	95	132	.720	82	162	244	193	205	1	74	9	123	24.8	8.7	3.0	2.4	.339
86-87 Utah	72	72	1453	696	272	601	.453	16	45	.356	136	179	.760	84	119	203	102	146	0	44	6	79	20.2	9.7	2.8	1.4	.394
87-88 Utah	81	51	1796	777	316	611	.517	32	97	.330	113	152	.743	64	123	187	175	193	2	65	5	89	22.2	9.6	2.3	2.2	.411
88-89 Utah	46	9	964	341	140	300	.467	19	54	.352	42	75	.560	29	99	128	50	105	0	37	6	41	21.0	7.4	2.8	1.1	.314
89-90 Utah	81	81	2174	617	265	568	.467	54	154	.351	33	64	.516	66	163	229	149	194	2	52	11	81	26.8	7.6	2.8	1.8	.269
90-91 Sacramento	36	24	811	229	96	256	.375	19	69	.275	18	36	.500	33	63	96	90	72	1	20	5	32	22.5	6.4	2.7	2.5	.267
91-92 Sacramento	2	2	40	8	4	9	.444	0	2	.000	0	0	.000	2	2	4	1	6	0	1	0	0	20.0	4.0	2.0	0.5	.157
91-92 Chicago	66	0	769	165	75	169	.444	7	25	.280	8	22	.364	15	58	73	68	128	0	26	3	26	11.7	2.5	1.1	1.0	.202
NBA Season Totals	575	325	11104	3952	1642	3512	.468	165	511	.323	503	760	.662	408	874	1282	947	1199	6	359	50	553	19.3	6.9	2.2	1.6	....
83-84 Utah	4	0	18	7	2	7	.286	2	3	.667	1	2	.500	2	5	7	2	4	0	0	0	2	4.5	1.8	1.8	0.5	.379
84-85 Utah	8	0	34	9	2	8	.250	0	0	.000	5	8	.625	1	3	4	6	6	0	3	0	3	4.3	1.1	0.5	0.8	.275
85-86 Utah	4	4	140	64	27	37	.730	2	3	.667	8	9	.889	10	8	18	11	16	0	3	1	7	35.0	16.0	4.5	2.8	.518
86-87 Utah	5	5	142	61	21	49	.429	2	5	.400	17	20	.850	3	12	15	11	14	0	1	1	7	28.4	12.2	3.0	2.2	.339
87-88 Utah	11	11	408	169	67	135	.496	19	36	.528	16	22	.727	8	31	39	32	42	1	7	0	27	37.1	15.4	3.5	2.9	.331
88-89 Utah	3	3	123	33	11	35	.314	3	9	.333	8	10	.800	5	12	17	4	15	0	1	2	6	41.0	11.0	5.7	1.3	.163
89-90 Utah	5	5	145	50	21	43	.488	7	14	.500	1	4	.250	7	7	14	5	14	0	3	0	4	29.0	10.0	2.8	1.0	.268
91-92 Chicago	9	0	69	22	9	22	.409	3	6	.500	1	3	.333	4	5	9	10	10	0	1	0	2	7.7	2.4	1.0	1.1	.326
NBA Playoff Totals	49	28	1079	415	160	336	.476	38	76	.500	57	78	.731	40	83	123	81	121	1	19	4	58	22.0	8.5	2.5	1.7	....

YEAR	TEAM	GP	GS	MIN	PTS	FGM	FGA	FG%	3PM	3PA	3P%	FTM	FTA	FT%	ORB	DRB	TRB	AST	PF	DQ	STL	BLK	TO	MPG	PPG	RPG	APG	PCM

• HANSEN, Glenn   Glenn R. Hansen

Born: Apr. 21, 1952. Devils Lake, ND, United States.   Height: 6'4".   Weight: 205 lbs.   Drafted: 1975   College: Louisiana State

YEAR	TEAM	GP	GS	MIN	PTS	FGM	FGA	FG%	3PM	3PA	3P%	FTM	FTA	FT%	ORB	DRB	TRB	AST	PF	DQ	STL	BLK	TO	MPG	PPG	RPG	APG	PCM
75-76	Kansas City	66	....	1145	431	173	420	.412	....	....	....	85	117	.726	77	110	187	67	144	1	47	13	....	17.3	6.5	2.8	1.0	.332
76-77	Kansas City	41	....	289	157	67	155	.432	....	....	....	23	32	.719	28	31	59	25	44	0	13	3	....	7.0	3.8	1.4	0.6	.476
77-78	Chicago	2	....	4	0	0	2	.000	....	....	....	0	0	.000	0	0	0	0	0	0	0	0	1	2.0	0.0	0.0	0.0	-.656
77-78	Kansas City	3	....	9	0	0	5	.000	....	....	....	0	0	.000	1	0	1	1	3	0	1	0	0	3.0	0.0	0.3	0.3	-.313
NBA Season Totals		112	....	1447	588	240	582	.412	....	....	....	108	149	.725	106	141	247	93	191	1	61	16	1	12.9	5.3	2.2	0.8	....

• HANSEN, Lars   Lars Hansen

Born: Sept. 14, 1954. Copenhagen, Denmark.   Height: 6'10".   Weight: 225 lbs.   Drafted: 1977   College: Washington

YEAR	TEAM	GP	GS	MIN	PTS	FGM	FGA	FG%	3PM	3PA	3P%	FTM	FTA	FT%	ORB	DRB	TRB	AST	PF	DQ	STL	BLK	TO	MPG	PPG	RPG	APG	PCM
78-79	Seattle	15	....	205	76	29	57	.509	....	....	....	18	31	.581	22	37	59	14	28	0	1	1	9	13.7	5.1	3.9	0.9	.461
NBA Season Totals		15	....	205	76	29	57	.509	....	....	....	18	31	.581	22	37	59	14	28	0	1	1	9	13.7	5.1	3.9	0.9	....

• HANSHAW, Bob   Bob Hanshaw

Born: 1919.   Height: 6'   Weight: 180 lbs.   Drafted: —   College: none

YEAR	TEAM	GP	GS	MIN	PTS	FGM	FGA	FG%	3PM	3PA	3P%	FTM	FTA	FT%	ORB	DRB	TRB	AST	PF	DQ	STL	BLK	TO	MPG	PPG	RPG	APG	PCM
45-46	Youngstown-N	3	....	....	3	1	....	....	....	....	....	1	....	....	....	....	....	....	....	....	....	....	....	1.0	....	....	....	....
NBL Season Totals		3	....	....	3	1	....	....	....	....	....	1	....	....	....	....	....	....	....	....	....	....	....	1.0	....	....	....	....

• HANSON, Reggie   Reginald Leonard Hanson

Born: Oct. 6, 1968. Charlotte, NC, United States.   Height: 6'8".   Weight: 195 lbs.   Drafted: —   College: Kentucky

YEAR	TEAM	GP	GS	MIN	PTS	FGM	FGA	FG%	3PM	3PA	3P%	FTM	FTA	FT%	ORB	DRB	TRB	AST	PF	DQ	STL	BLK	TO	MPG	PPG	RPG	APG	PCM
97-98	Boston	8	0	26	6	3	6	.500	0	0	.000	0	0	.000	3	3	6	1	8	0	2	1	3	3.3	0.8	0.8	0.1	.237
NBA Season Totals		8	0	26	6	3	6	.500	0	0	.000	0	0	.000	3	3	6	1	8	0	2	1	3	3.3	0.8	0.8	0.1	....

• HANZLIK, Bill   William Henry Hanzlik

Born: Dec. 6, 1957. Middletown, OH, United States.   Height: 6'7".   Weight: 185 lbs.   Drafted: 1980   College: Notre Dame

YEAR	TEAM	GP	GS	MIN	PTS	FGM	FGA	FG%	3PM	3PA	3P%	FTM	FTA	FT%	ORB	DRB	TRB	AST	PF	DQ	STL	BLK	TO	MPG	PPG	RPG	APG	PCM
80-81	Seattle	74	....	1259	396	138	289	.478	1	5	.200	119	150	.793	67	86	153	111	168	1	58	20	81	17.0	5.4	2.1	1.5	.338
81-82	Seattle	81	76	1974	472	167	357	.468	0	4	.000	138	176	.784	99	167	266	183	250	3	81	30	105	24.4	5.8	3.3	2.3	.310
82-83	Denver	82	8	1547	500	187	437	.428	1	7	.143	125	160	.781	80	156	236	268	220	0	75	15	148	18.9	6.1	2.9	3.3	.397
83-84	Denver	80	14	1469	434	132	306	.431	3	12	.250	167	207	.807	66	139	205	252	255	6	68	19	112	18.4	5.4	2.6	3.2	.389
84-85	Denver	80	1	1673	621	220	522	.421	1	15	.067	180	238	.756	88	119	207	210	291	5	84	26	112	20.9	7.8	2.6	2.6	.354
85-86	Denver	79	0	1982	988	331	741	.447	8	41	.195	318	405	.785	88	176	264	316	277	2	107	16	166	25.1	12.5	3.3	4.0	.495
86-87	Denver	73	10	1990	952	307	746	.412	22	80	.275	316	402	.786	79	177	256	280	245	3	87	28	131	27.3	13.0	3.5	3.8	.458
87-88	Denver	77	0	1334	350	109	287	.380	3	16	.188	129	163	.791	39	132	171	166	185	1	64	17	92	17.3	4.5	2.2	2.2	.306
88-89	Denver	41	0	701	201	66	151	.437	1	5	.200	68	87	.782	18	75	93	86	82	1	25	5	53	17.1	4.9	2.3	2.1	.331
89-90	Denver	81	0	1605	500	179	396	.452	6	31	.194	136	183	.743	67	140	207	186	249	7	78	29	89	19.8	6.2	2.6	2.3	.353
NBA Season Totals		748	109	15534	5414	1836	4232	.434	46	216	.213	1696	2171	.781	691	1367	2058	2058	2222	29	727	205	1089	20.8	7.2	2.8	2.8	....
81-82	Seattle	8	8	203	52	16	34	.471	0	1	.000	20	22	.909	10	22	32	20	26	1	6	5	13	25.4	6.5	4.0	2.5	.353
82-83	Denver	8	1	157	54	20	50	.400	0	2	.000	14	17	.824	3	22	25	21	26	0	6	5	11	19.6	6.8	3.1	2.6	.379
83-84	Denver	5	1	82	28	11	19	.579	0	2	.000	6	6	1.000	3	5	8	21	16	0	3	0	6	16.4	5.6	1.6	4.2	.491
84-85	Denver	15	0	310	120	45	92	.489	0	1	.000	30	41	.732	24	22	46	33	57	2	14	6	22	20.7	8.0	3.1	2.2	.390
85-86	Denver	6	0	102	44	15	28	.536	1	1	1.000	13	16	.813	2	4	6	19	12	0	1	1	7	17.0	7.3	1.0	3.2	.453
86-87	Denver	3	2	76	25	8	25	.320	0	2	.000	9	15	.600	0	6	6	7	6	0	4	0	3	25.3	8.3	2.0	2.3	.231
87-88	Denver	11	0	212	58	20	56	.357	0	8	.000	18	26	.692	11	18	29	26	40	1	5	9	14	19.3	5.3	2.6	2.4	.268
88-89	Denver	3	3	106	38	14	33	.424	3	6	.500	7	12	.583	6	14	20	9	13	0	5	1	2	35.3	12.7	6.7	3.0	.414
89-90	Denver	3	0	79	21	5	17	.294	1	3	.333	10	10	1.000	5	5	10	11	13	1	5	2	• 2	26.3	7.0	3.3	3.7	.372
NBA Playoff Totals		62	15	1327	440	154	354	.435	5	26	.192	127	165	.770	64	118	182	167	209	5	49	29	80	21.4	7.1	2.9	2.7	....

• HAPAC, Bill   William Hapac

Born: Jan. 26, 1918. Cicero, IL, United States. Died: Mar.9, 1967.   Height: 6'2".   Weight: 188 lbs.   Drafted: —   College: Illinois

YEAR	TEAM	GP	GS	MIN	PTS	FGM	FGA	FG%	3PM	3PA	3P%	FTM	FTA	FT%	ORB	DRB	TRB	AST	PF	DQ	STL	BLK	TO	MPG	PPG	RPG	APG	PCM
40-41	Chicago-N	24	....	....	227	80	....	....	....	....	....	67	....	....	....	....	....	....	....	....	....	....	....	9.5	....	....	....	....
45-46	Chicago-N	19	....	....	105	35	....	....	....	....	....	35	61	.574	....	....	....	....	....	....	....	....	....	5.5	....	....	....	....
46-47	Anderson-N	41	....	....	277	93	....	....	....	....	....	91	134	.679	....	....	....	....	125	....	....	....	....	6.8	....	....	....	....
47-48	Oshkosh-N	47	....	....	230	78	....	....	....	....	....	74	119	.622	....	....	....	....	127	....	....	....	....	4.9	....	....	....	....
NBL Season Totals		131	....	....	839	286	....	....	....	....	....	267	314	....	....	....	....	....	252	....	....	....	....	6.4	....	....	....	....
47-48	Oshkosh-N	4	....	....	23	6	....	....	....	....	....	11	16	.688	....	....	....	....	....	....	....	....	....	5.8	....	....	....	....
NBL Playoff Totals		4	....	....	23	6	....	....	....	....	....	11	16		....	....	....	....	....	....	....	....	....	5.8	....	....	....	....

• HARDAWAY, Penny   Anfernee Deon (Penny) Hardaway

Born: July 18, 1971. Memphis, TN, United States.   Height: 6'7".   Weight: 195 lbs.   Drafted: 1993   College: Memphis State

YEAR	TEAM	GP	GS	MIN	PTS	FGM	FGA	FG%	3PM	3PA	3P%	FTM	FTA	FT%	ORB	DRB	TRB	AST	PF	DQ	STL	BLK	TO	MPG	PPG	RPG	APG	PCM
93-94	Orlando	82	82	3015	1313	509	1092	.466	50	187	.267	245	330	.742	192	247	439	544	205	2	190	51	295	36.8	16.0	5.4	6.6	.527
94-95	Orlando	77	77	2901	1613	585	1142	.512	87	249	.349	356	463	.769	139	197	336	551	158	1	130	26	262	37.7	20.9	4.4	7.2	.609
95-96	Orlando	82	82	3015	1780	623	1215	.513	89	283	.314	445	580	.767	129	225	354	582	160	0	166	41	230	36.8	21.7	4.3	7.1	.668
96-97	Orlando	59	59	2221	1210	421	941	.447	85	267	.318	283	345	.820	82	181	263	332	123	1	93	35	148	37.6	20.5	4.5	5.6	.549
97-98	Orlando	19	15	625	311	103	273	.377	15	50	.300	90	118	.763	8	68	76	68	45	0	28	15	46	32.9	16.4	4.0	3.6	.420
98-99	Orlando	50	50	1944	791	301	717	.420	40	140	.286	149	211	.706	74	210	284	266	111	0	111	23	150	38.9	15.8	5.7	5.3	.452
99-00	Phoenix	60	60	2253	1015	378	798	.474	33	102	.324	226	286	.790	91	256	347	315	164	1	94	38	153	37.6	16.9	5.8	5.3	.520

YEAR	TEAM	GP	GS	MIN	PTS	FGM	FGA	FG%	3PM	3PA	3P%	FTM	FTA	FT%	ORB	DRB	TRB	AST	PF	DQ	STL	BLK	TO	MPG	PPG	RPG	APG	PCM
00-01	Phoenix	4	4	112	39	15	36	.417	2	8	.250	7	11	.636	5	13	18	15	6	0	6	1	3	28.0	9.8	4.5	3.8	.464
01-02	Phoenix	80	55	2462	959	389	931	.418	23	83	.277	158	195	.810	98	252	350	324	184	0	122	32	189	30.8	12.0	4.4	4.1	.409
02-03	Phoenix	58	51	1779	615	256	573	.447	26	73	.356	77	97	.794	66	192	258	235	150	1	66	26	145	30.7	10.6	4.4	4.1	.389
NBA Season Totals		571	535	20327	9646	3580	7718	.464	450	1442	.312	2036	2636	.772	884	1841	2725	3232	1306	6	1006	288	1621	35.6	16.9	4.8	5.7	....
93-94	Orlando	3	3	133	56	22	50	.440	5	11	.455	7	10	.700	8	12	20	21	10	0	5	6	20	44.3	18.7	6.7	7.0	.430
94-95	Orlando	21	21	849	412	144	305	.472	40	99	.404	84	111	.757	30	49	79	162	70	0	40	15	73	40.4	19.6	3.8	7.7	.524
95-96	Orlando	12	12	473	280	101	217	.465	20	55	.364	58	78	.744	20	36	56	72	27	1	20	4	26	39.4	23.3	4.7	6.0	.583
96-97	Orlando	5	5	220	155	52	111	.468	11	30	.367	40	54	.741	7	23	30	17	14	0	12	7	9	44.0	31.0	6.0	3.4	.647
98-99	Orlando	4	4	167	76	20	57	.351	6	13	.462	30	39	.769	9	11	20	22	13	0	9	1	12	41.8	19.0	5.0	5.5	.442
99-00	Phoenix	9	9	386	183	67	145	.462	5	19	.263	44	62	.710	14	30	44	51	29	0	14	9	25	42.9	20.3	4.9	5.7	.478
02-03	Phoenix	6	6	244	76	27	70	.386	9	25	.360	13	18	.722	9	27	36	26	26	2	13	5	13	40.7	12.7	6.0	4.3	.363
NBA Playoff Totals		60	60	2472	1238	433	955	.453	96	252	.381	276	372	.742	97	188	285	371	189	3	113	47	178	41.2	20.6	4.8	6.2	....

• HARDAWAY, Tim

Timothy Duane Hardaway

Born: Sept. 1, 1966. Chicago, IL, United States. Height: 6' Weight: 175 lbs. Drafted: 1989 College: Texas (El Paso)

YEAR	TEAM	GP	GS	MIN	PTS	FGM	FGA	FG%	3PM	3PA	3P%	FTM	FTA	FT%	ORB	DRB	TRB	AST	PF	DQ	STL	BLK	TO	MPG	PPG	RPG	APG	PCM
89-90	Golden State	79	78	2663	1162	464	985	.471	23	84	.274	211	276	.764	57	253	310	689	232	6	165	12	261	33.7	14.7	3.9	8.7	.555
90-91	Golden State	82	82	3215	1881	739	1551	.476	97	252	.385	306	381	.803	87	245	332	793	228	7	214	12	271	39.2	22.9	4.0	9.7	.652
91-92	Golden State	81	81	3332	1893	734	1592	.461	127	376	.338	298	389	.766	81	229	310	807	208	1	164	13	267	41.1	23.4	3.8	10.0	.608
92-93	Golden State	66	66	2609	1419	522	1168	.447	102	309	.330	273	367	.744	60	203	263	699	152	0	116	12	218	39.5	21.5	4.0	10.6	.617
94-95	Golden State	62	62	2321	1247	430	1007	.427	168	444	.378	219	288	.760	46	144	190	578	155	1	88	12	217	37.4	20.1	3.1	9.3	.553
95-96	Golden State	52	18	1487	735	255	606	.421	85	232	.366	140	182	.769	22	109	131	360	131	3	74	11	125	28.6	14.1	2.5	6.9	.532
95-96	Miami	28	28	1047	482	164	386	.425	53	147	.361	101	123	.821	13	85	98	280	70	0	58	6	109	37.4	17.2	3.5	10.0	.551
96-97	Miami	81	81	3136	1644	575	1384	.415	203	590	.344	291	364	.799	49	228	277	695	165	2	151	9	227	38.7	20.3	3.4	8.6	.548
97-98	Miami	81	81	3031	1528	558	1296	.431	155	442	.351	257	329	.781	48	251	299	672	200	2	136	16	227	37.4	18.9	3.7	8.3	.548
98-99	Miami	48	48	1772	835	301	752	.400	112	311	.360	121	149	.812	15	137	152	352	102	1	57	6	131	36.9	17.4	3.2	7.3	.475
99-00	Miami	52	52	1672	696	246	638	.386	94	256	.367	110	133	.827	25	125	150	385	112	0	49	4	119	32.2	13.4	2.9	7.4	.464
00-01	Miami	77	77	2613	1150	408	1042	.392	189	517	.366	145	181	.801	26	178	204	483	155	1	90	6	189	33.9	14.9	2.6	6.3	.431
01-02	Dallas	54	2	1276	518	179	494	.362	95	279	.341	65	78	.833	13	84	97	201	84	0	40	8	73	23.6	9.6	1.8	3.7	.371
01-02	Denver	14	14	325	134	47	126	.373	28	75	.373	12	19	.632	1	26	27	77	25	0	17	2	38	23.2	9.6	1.9	5.5	.429
02-03	Indiana	10	0	127	49	18	49	.367	11	31	.355	2	4	.500	1	14	15	24	8	0	9	0	11	12.7	4.9	1.5	2.4	.428
NBA Season Totals		867	770	30626	15373	5640	13076	.431	1542	4345	.355	2551	3263	.782	544	2311	2855	7095	2027	24	1428	129	2483	35.3	17.7	3.3	8.2	....
90-91	Golden State	9	9	396	227	90	185	.486	17	48	.354	30	38	.789	5	28	33	101	22	0	28	7	25	44.0	25.2	3.7	11.2	.688
91-92	Golden State	4	4	176	98	32	80	.400	10	29	.345	24	37	.649	6	9	15	29	14	0	13	0	14	44.0	24.5	3.8	7.3	.483
95-96	Miami	3	3	110	53	20	43	.465	8	22	.364	5	7	.714	1	4	5	17	10	0	3	0	15	36.7	17.7	1.7	5.7	.338
96-97	Miami	17	17	701	318	103	287	.359	42	134	.313	70	88	.795	13	56	69	119	37	0	27	1	53	41.2	18.7	4.1	7.0	.412
97-98	Miami	5	5	222	130	42	94	.447	17	39	.436	29	37	.784	3	14	17	33	9	0	6	0	18	44.4	26.0	3.4	6.6	.518
98-99	Miami	5	5	182	45	15	56	.268	5	25	.200	10	16	.625	3	11	14	32	14	0	5	1	18	36.4	9.0	2.8	6.4	.203
99-00	Miami	7	7	182	54	20	68	.294	7	34	.206	7	10	.700	1	14	15	33	10	0	5	0	11	26.0	7.7	2.1	4.7	.268
00-01	Miami	2	2	36	5	2	9	.222	1	3	.333	0	0	.000	1	1	2	9	4	0	0	0	8	18.0	2.5	1.0	4.5	.040
02-03	Indiana	4	0	47	13	5	15	.333	3	10	.300	0	0	.000	0	2	2	9	2	0	1	0	3	11.8	3.3	0.5	2.3	.273
NBA Playoff Totals		56	52	2052	943	329	837	.393	110	344	.320	175	233	.751	33	139	172	382	122	0	88	9	165	36.6	16.8	3.1	6.8	....

• HARDING, Reggie

Reginald Harding

Born: May 4, 1942. Died: Sept.2, 1972. Height: 7' Weight: 249 lbs. Drafted: 1963 College: none

YEAR	TEAM	GP	GS	MIN	PTS	FGM	FGA	FG%	3PM	3PA	3P%	FTM	FTA	FT%	ORB	DRB	TRB	AST	PF	DQ	STL	BLK	TO	MPG	PPG	RPG	APG	PCM
63-64	Detroit	39	....	1158	429	184	460	.400	....	....	....	61	98	.622	....	....	410	52	119	1	....	....	....	29.7	11.0	10.5	1.3	.463
64-65	Detroit	78	....	2699	938	405	987	.410	....	....	....	128	209	.612	....	....	906	179	258	5	....	....	....	34.6	12.0	11.6	2.3	.473
66-67	Detroit	74	....	1367	407	172	383	.449	....	....	....	63	103	.612	....	....	455	94	164	2	....	....	....	18.5	5.5	6.1	1.3	.463
67-68	Indiana-A	25	....	840	336	142	314	.452	0	1	.000	52	90	.578	....	....	334	53	59	0	....	....	77	33.6	13.4	13.4	2.1	.586
67-68	Chicago	14	....	305	65	24	71	.338	....	....	....	17	33	.515	....	....	94	18	35	0	....	....	....	21.8	4.6	6.7	1.3	.340
NBA Season Totals		205	....	5529	1839	785	1901	.413	....	....	....	269	443	.607	....	....	1865	343	576	8	....	....	....	27.0	9.0	9.1	1.7	....
ABA Season Totals		25	....	840	336	142	314	.452	0	1	.000	52	90	.578	....	....	334	53	59	0	....	....	77	33.6	13.4	13.4	2.1	....
Career Totals		230	....	6369	2175	927	2215	.419	0	1	.000	321	533	.602	....	....	2199	396	635	8	....	....	77	27.7	9.5	9.6	1.7	....

• HARDNETT, Charlie

Charles Hardnett

Born: Sept. 13, 1938. Atlanta, GA, United States. Height: 6'8". Weight: 225 lbs. Drafted: 1962 College: Grambling

YEAR	TEAM	GP	GS	MIN	PTS	FGM	FGA	FG%	3PM	3PA	3P%	FTM	FTA	FT%	ORB	DRB	TRB	AST	PF	DQ	STL	BLK	TO	MPG	PPG	RPG	APG	PCM
62-63	Chicago	78	....	1657	827	301	683	.441	....	....	....	225	349	.645	....	....	602	74	225	4	....	....	....	21.2	10.6	7.7	0.9	.575
63-64	Baltimore	66	....	617	298	107	260	.412	....	....	....	84	125	.672	....	....	251	27	114	1	....	....	....	9.3	4.5	3.8	0.4	.562
64-65	Baltimore	20	....	200	73	25	80	.313	....	....	....	23	39	.590	....	....	77	2	37	0	....	....	....	10.0	3.7	3.9	0.1	.360
NBA Season Totals		164	....	2474	1198	433	1023	.423	....	....	....	332	513	.647	....	....	930	103	376	5	....	....	....	15.1	7.3	5.7	0.6	....
64-65	Baltimore	5	....	22	10	4	10	.400	....	....	....	2	5	.400	....	....	6	2	2	0	....	....	....	4.4	2.0	1.2	0.4	.479
NBA Playoff Totals		5	....	22	10	4	10	.400	....	....	....	2	5	.400	....	....	6	2	2	0	....	....	....	4.4	2.0	1.2	0.4	....

• HARDY, Alan

Alan Timothy Hardy

Born: May 25, 1957. Detroit, MI, United States. Height: 6'7". Weight: 195 lbs. Drafted: — College: Michigan

YEAR	TEAM	GP	GS	MIN	PTS	FGM	FGA	FG%	3PM	3PA	3P%	FTM	FTA	FT%	ORB	DRB	TRB	AST	PF	DQ	STL	BLK	TO	MPG	PPG	RPG	APG	PCM
80-81	LA Lakers	22	....	111	51	22	59	.373	0	0	.000	7	10	.700	8	11	19	3	13	0	1	9	11	5.0	2.3	0.9	0.1	.267
81-82	Detroit	38	0	310	142	62	136	.456	0	5	.000	18	29	.621	14	20	34	20	32	0	9	4	19	8.2	3.7	0.9	0.5	.327
NBA Season Totals		60	0	421	193	84	195	.431	0	5	.000	25	39	.641	22	31	53	23	45	0	10	13	30	7.0	3.2	0.9	0.4	....

• HARDY, Darrell
Darrell Gene Hardy

Born: 1944. Height: 6'7". Weight: 220 lbs. Drafted: 1967 College: Baylor

YEAR	TEAM	GP	GS	MIN	PTS	FGM	FGA	FG%	3PM	3PA	3P%	FTM	FTA	FT%	ORB	DRB	TRB	AST	PF	DQ	STL	BLK	TO	MPG	PPG	RPG	APG	PCM
67-68	Houston-A	17	....	172	89	32	74	.432	0	1	.000	25	35	.714	....	....	56	8	23	0	....	....	12	10.1	5.2	3.3	0.5	.560
ABA Season Totals		17	....	172	89	32	74	.432	0	1	.000	25	35	.714	....	....	56	8	23	0	....	....	12	10.1	5.2	3.3	0.5	....

• HARDY, James
James Percival Hardy

Born: Dec. 1, 1956. Knoxville, AL, United States. Height: 6'8". Weight: 220 lbs. Drafted: 1978 College: San Francisco

YEAR	TEAM	GP	GS	MIN	PTS	FGM	FGA	FG%	3PM	3PA	3P%	FTM	FTA	FT%	ORB	DRB	TRB	AST	PF	DQ	STL	BLK	TO	MPG	PPG	RPG	APG	PCM
78-79	New Orleans	68	....	1456	453	196	426	.460	....	....	....	61	88	.693	121	189	310	65	133	1	52	61	95	21.4	6.7	4.6	1.0	.371
79-80	Utah	76	....	1600	420	184	363	.507	1	2	.500	51	66	.773	124	275	399	104	207	4	47	87	106	21.1	5.5	5.3	1.4	.411
80-81	Utah	23	....	509	115	52	111	.468	0	0	.000	11	20	.550	39	94	133	36	58	2	21	20	23	22.1	5.0	5.8	1.6	.408
81-82	Utah	82	17	1814	422	179	369	.485	0	1	.000	64	93	.688	153	317	470	110	192	2	58	67	82	22.1	5.1	5.7	1.3	.406
NBA Season Totals		249	17	5379	1410	611	1269	.481	1	3	.333	187	267	.700	437	875	1312	315	590	9	178	235	306	21.6	5.7	5.3	1.3	....

• HARGE, Ira
Ira Lee Harge

Born: Mar. 14, 1941. Anguila, MS, United States. Height: 6'9". Weight: 225 lbs. Drafted: 1964 College: New Mexico

YEAR	TEAM	GP	GS	MIN	PTS	FGM	FGA	FG%	3PM	3PA	3P%	FTM	FTA	FT%	ORB	DRB	TRB	AST	PF	DQ	STL	BLK	TO	MPG	PPG	RPG	APG	PCM
67-68	Oakland-A	30	....	1047	353	135	340	.397	0	0	.000	83	114	.728	....	....	445	61	100	1	....	....	71	34.9	11.8	14.8	2.0	.544
67-68	Pittsburgh-A	52	....	1652	471	176	441	.399	0	0	.000	119	184	.647	....	....	593	38	194	6	....	....	111	31.8	9.1	11.4	0.7	.412
68-69	Oakland-A	78	....	2095	661	269	578	.465	0	0	.000	123	200	.615	269	547	816	96	245	1	....	....	222	26.9	8.5	10.5	1.2	.510
69-70	Washington-A	84	....	2991	1026	415	886	.468	0	0	.000	196	289	.678	334	843	1177	200	328	8	....	....	273	35.6	12.2	14.0	2.4	.562
70-71	Carolina-A	29	....	892	304	131	289	.453	0	1	.000	42	82	.512	120	219	339	57	104	3	....	....	92	30.8	10.5	11.7	2.0	.515
70-71	Florida-A	53	....	2042	815	329	710	.463	2	4	.500	155	224	.692	208	538	746	145	187	0	....	....	140	38.5	15.4	14.1	2.7	.577
71-72	Florida-A	53	....	1809	596	256	561	.456	0	1	.000	84	123	.683	190	436	626	99	191	2	....	....	128	34.1	11.2	11.8	1.9	.491
71-72	Utah-A	31	....	455	136	58	118	.492	0	0	.000	20	27	.741	48	106	154	31	76	0	....	....	35	14.7	4.4	5.0	1.0	.477
72-73	Carolina-A	4	....	77	12	5	18	.278	0	0	.000	2	4	.500	7	16	23	3	16	0	....	....	11	19.3	3.0	5.8	0.8	.210
72-73	Utah-A	13	....	100	22	9	22	.409	0	0	.000	4	6	.667	8	28	36	6	27	0	....	....	6	7.7	1.7	2.8	0.5	.362
ABA Season Totals		427	....	13160	4396	1783	3963	.450	2	6	.333	828	1253	.661	1184	2733	4955	736	1468	21	....	....	1089	30.8	10.3	11.6	1.7	....
68-69	Oakland-A	16	....	445	114	45	108	.417	0	0	.000	24	39	.615	68	124	192	20	50	1	....	....	31	27.8	7.1	12.0	1.3	.494
69-70	Washington-A	7	....	267	71	30	67	.448	0	2	.000	11	18	.611	19	76	95	19	....	0	....	....	19	38.1	10.1	13.6	2.7	....
70-71	Florida-A	6	....	233	103	46	82	.561	0	1	.000	11	19	.579	25	73	98	14	17	0	....	....	12	38.8	17.2	16.3	2.3	.684
71-72	Utah-A	10	....	106	27	11	25	.440	0	0	.000	5	7	.714	15	25	40	8	23	0	....	....	8	10.6	2.7	4.0	0.8	.451
ABA Playoff Totals		39	....	1051	315	132	282	.468	0	3	.000	51	83	.614	127	298	425	61	90	1	....	....	70	26.9	8.1	10.9	1.6	....

• HARGIS, John
John Arlington (Shotgun) Hargis

Born: Aug. 20, 1920. Nacogdoches, TX, United States. Died: Jan.2, 1986. Height: 6'2". Weight: 180 lbs. Drafted: — College: Texas

YEAR	TEAM	GP	GS	MIN	PTS	FGM	FGA	FG%	3PM	3PA	3P%	FTM	FTA	FT%	ORB	DRB	TRB	AST	PF	DQ	STL	BLK	TO	MPG	PPG	RPG	APG	PCM
47-48	Anderson-N	59	....	....	642	235	....	....	....	....	....	172	329	.523	....	....	....	....	149	....	....	....	....	....	10.9	....	....	....
48-49	Anderson-N	57	....	....	444	169	....	....	....	....	....	106	173	.613	....	....	....	....	129	....	....	....	....	....	7.8	....	....	....
49-50	Anderson	60	....	....	643	223	550	.405	....	....	....	197	277	.711	....	....	....	102	170	....	....	....	....	....	10.7	....	1.7	....
50-51	Fort Wayne	14	....	....	67	25	66	.379	....	....	....	17	24	.708	....	....	30	9	26	0	....	....	....	....	4.8	2.1	0.6	....
50-51	Tri-Cities	14	....	....	55	23	66	.348	....	....	....	9	15	.600	....	....	30	9	27	0	....	....	....	....	3.9	2.1	0.6	....
NBA Season Totals		88	....	....	765	271	682	.397	....	....	....	223	316	.706	....	....	60	120	223	0	....	....	....	....	8.7	0.7	1.4	....
NBL Season Totals		116	....	....	1086	404	....	....	....	....	....	278	502	....	....	....	....	....	278	....	....	....	....	....	9.4	....	....	....
Career Totals		204	....	....	1851	675	682	....	....	....	....	501	818	....	....	....	60	120	501	0	....	....	....	....	9.1	0.3	0.6	....
47-48	Anderson-N	6	....	....	85	30	....	....	....	....	....	25	38	.658	....	....	....	....	....	....	....	....	....	....	14.2	....	....	....
48-49	Anderson-N	7	....	....	72	22	....	....	....	....	....	28	43	.651	....	....	....	....	....	....	....	....	....	....	10.3	....	....	....
49-50	Anderson	8	....	....	101	32	89	.360	....	....	....	37	45	.822	....	....	....	13	26	....	....	....	....	....	12.6	....	1.6	....
NBA Playoff Totals		8	....	....	101	32	89	.360	....	....	....	37	45	.822	....	....	....	13	26	....	....	....	....	....	12.6	....	1.6	....
NBL Playoff Totals		13	....	....	157	52	....	....	....	....	....	53	81	....	....	....	....	....	....	....	....	....	....	....	12.1	....	....	....
Career Playoff Totals		21	....	....	258	84	89	....	....	....	....	90	126	....	....	....	....	13	26	....	....	....	....	....	12.3	....	0.6	....

• HARKNESS, Jerry
Jerald B. Harkness

Born: May 7, 1940. New York, NY, United States. Height: 6'2". Weight: 175 lbs. Drafted: 1963 College: Loyola (IL)

YEAR	TEAM	GP	GS	MIN	PTS	FGM	FGA	FG%	3PM	3PA	3P%	FTM	FTA	FT%	ORB	DRB	TRB	AST	PF	DQ	STL	BLK	TO	MPG	PPG	RPG	APG	PCM
63-64	New York	5	....	59	29	13	30	.433	....	....	....	3	8	.375	....	....	6	6	4	0	....	....	....	11.8	5.8	1.2	1.2	.411
67-68	Indiana-A	71	....	1241	497	172	394	.437	1	5	.200	152	223	.682	....	....	193	129	109	1	....	....	77	17.5	7.0	2.7	1.8	.443
68-69	Indiana-A	10	....	272	92	31	67	.463	0	0	.000	30	47	.638	10	24	34	21	17	0	....	....	20	27.2	9.2	3.4	2.1	.366
NBA Season Totals		5	....	59	29	13	30	.433	....	....	....	3	8	.375	....	....	6	6	4	0	....	....	....	11.8	5.8	1.2	1.2	....
ABA Season Totals		81	....	1513	589	203	461	.440	1	5	.200	182	270	.674	10	24	227	150	126	1	....	....	97	18.7	7.3	2.8	1.9	....
Career Totals		86	....	1572	618	216	491	.440	1	5	.200	185	278	.665	10	24	233	156	130	1	....	....	97	18.3	7.2	2.7	1.8	....
67-68	Indiana-A	3	....	32	10	4	12	.333	0	0	.000	2	2	1.000	....	....	5	5	6	0	....	....	3	10.7	3.3	1.7	1.7	.340
ABA Playoff Totals		3	....	32	10	4	12	.333	0	0	.000	2	2	1.000	....	....	5	5	6	0	....	....	3	10.7	3.3	1.7	1.7	....

• HARLICKA, Skip
Jules Peter (Skip) Harlicka

Born: Oct. 14, 1946. Height: 6'1". Weight: 185 lbs. Drafted: 1968 College: South Carolina

YEAR	TEAM	GP	GS	MIN	PTS	FGM	FGA	FG%	3PM	3PA	3P%	FTM	FTA	FT%	ORB	DRB	TRB	AST	PF	DQ	STL	BLK	TO	MPG	PPG	RPG	APG	PCM
68-69	Atlanta	26	....	218	106	41	90	.456	....	....	....	24	31	.774	....	....	16	37	29	0	....	....	....	8.4	4.1	0.6	1.4	.488
NBA Season Totals		26	....	218	106	41	90	.456	....	....	....	24	31	.774	....	....	16	37	29	0	....	....	....	8.4	4.1	0.6	1.4	....
68-69	Atlanta	1	....	1	0	0	0	.000	....	....	....	0	0	.000	....	....	0	0	1	0	....	....	....	1.0	0.0	0.0	0.0	-.418
NBA Playoff Totals		1	....	1	0	0	0	.000	....	....	....	0	0	.000	....	....	0	0	1	0	....	....	....	1.0	0.0	0.0	0.0	....

• HARMON, Jerome

Jerome Harmon

Born: Feb. 6, 1969. Gary, IN, United States. Height: 6'4". Weight: 190 lbs. Drafted: — College: Louisville

YEAR TEAM	GP	GS	MIN	PTS	FGM	FGA	FG%	3PM	3PA	3P%	FTM	FTA	FT%	ORB	DRB	TRB	AST	PF	DQ	STL	BLK	TO	MPG	PPG	RPG	APG	PCM
94-95 Philadelphia	10	0	158	46	21	53	.396	1	1	1.000	3	6	.500	9	14	23	12	12	0	9	0	7	15.8	4.6	2.3	1.2	.286
NBA Season Totals	10	0	158	46	21	53	.396	1	1	1.000	3	6	.500	9	14	23	12	12	0	9	0	7	15.8	4.6	2.3	1.2	....

• HARPER, Derek

Derek Ricardo Harper

Born: Oct. 13, 1961. Elberton, GA, United States. Height: 6'4". Weight: 185 lbs. Drafted: 1983 College: Illinois

YEAR TEAM	GP	GS	MIN	PTS	FGM	FGA	FG%	3PM	3PA	3P%	FTM	FTA	FT%	ORB	DRB	TRB	AST	PF	DQ	STL	BLK	TO	MPG	PPG	RPG	APG	PCM
83-84 Dallas	82	1	1712	469	200	451	.443	3	26	.115	66	98	.673	53	119	172	239	143	0	95	21	115	20.9	5.7	2.1	2.9	.333
84-85 Dallas	82	1	2218	790	329	633	.520	21	61	.344	111	154	.721	47	152	199	360	194	1	144	37	123	27.0	9.6	2.4	4.4	.460
85-86 Dallas	79	39	2150	963	390	730	.534	12	51	.235	171	229	.747	75	151	226	416	166	1	153	23	142	27.2	12.2	2.9	5.3	.572
86-87 Dallas	77	76	2556	1230	497	993	.501	76	212	.358	160	234	.684	51	148	199	609	195	0	167	25	139	33.2	16.0	2.6	7.9	.598
87-88 Dallas	82	82	3032	1393	536	1167	.459	60	192	.313	261	344	.759	71	175	246	634	164	0	168	35	189	37.0	17.0	3.0	7.7	.531
88-89 Dallas	81	81	2968	1404	538	1127	.477	99	278	.356	229	284	.806	46	182	228	570	219	3	172	41	203	36.6	17.3	2.8	7.0	.526
89-90 Dallas	82	82	3007	1473	567	1161	.488	89	240	.371	250	315	.794	54	190	244	609	224	1	187	26	205	36.7	18.0	3.0	7.4	.554
90-91 Dallas	77	77	2879	1519	572	1226	.467	89	246	.362	286	391	.731	59	174	233	548	222	1	147	14	177	37.4	19.7	3.0	7.1	.536
91-92 Dallas	65	64	2252	1152	448	1011	.443	58	186	.312	198	261	.759	49	121	170	373	150	0	101	17	156	34.6	17.7	2.6	5.7	.467
92-93 Dallas	62	60	2108	1126	393	939	.419	101	257	.393	239	316	.756	42	81	123	334	145	1	80	16	136	34.0	18.2	2.0	5.4	.449
93-94 Dallas	28	28	893	325	130	342	.380	37	105	.352	28	50	.560	10	45	55	98	46	0	45	4	53	31.9	11.6	2.0	3.5	.283
93-94 New York	54	27	1311	466	173	402	.430	36	98	.367	84	113	.743	10	76	86	236	117	0	80	4	81	24.3	8.6	1.6	4.4	.401
94-95 New York	80	80	2716	919	337	756	.446	106	292	.363	139	192	.724	31	163	194	458	219	0	79	10	152	34.0	11.5	2.4	5.7	.371
95-96 New York	82	82	2893	1149	436	939	.464	121	325	.372	156	206	.757	32	170	202	352	201	0	131	5	180	35.3	14.0	2.5	4.3	.373
96-97 Dallas	75	29	2210	753	299	674	.444	60	176	.341	95	128	.742	30	107	137	321	144	0	92	12	135	29.5	10.0	1.8	4.3	.345
97-98 Orlando	66	45	1761	566	226	542	.417	59	164	.360	55	79	.696	23	80	103	233	140	0	72	10	99	26.7	8.6	1.6	3.5	.303
98-99 LA Lakers	45	29	1120	309	120	291	.412	43	117	.368	26	32	.813	13	54	67	187	66	0	44	4	52	24.9	6.9	1.5	4.2	.347
NBA Season Totals	1199	883	37786	16006	6191	13384	.463	1070	3026	.354	2554	3426	.745	696	2188	2884	6577	2755	8	1957	304	2337	31.5	13.3	2.4	5.5	....
83-84 Dallas	10	0	226	50	21	54	.389	3	8	.375	5	7	.714	8	12	20	28	16	0	11	2	6	22.6	5.0	2.0	2.8	.292
84-85 Dallas	4	0	132	26	10	21	.476	1	3	.333	5	7	.714	1	11	12	20	12	0	6	1	4	33.0	6.5	3.0	5.0	.338
85-86 Dallas	10	10	348	134	57	107	.533	8	14	.571	12	16	.750	13	6	19	76	27	0	23	0	23	34.8	13.4	1.9	7.6	.495
86-87 Dallas	4	4	123	66	20	40	.500	2	9	.222	24	30	.800	2	10	12	27	7	0	7	0	5	30.8	16.5	3.0	6.8	.677
87-88 Dallas	17	17	602	230	89	202	.441	9	36	.250	43	59	.729	11	32	43	121	44	0	32	5	32	35.4	13.5	2.5	7.1	.450
89-90 Dallas	3	3	119	58	21	48	.438	5	16	.313	11	16	.688	2	6	8	23	13	0	4	0	12	39.7	19.3	2.7	7.7	.409
93-94 New York	23	22	750	263	99	231	.429	29	85	.341	36	56	.643	13	41	54	103	63	1	42	1	41	32.6	11.4	2.3	4.5	.356
94-95 New York	11	11	388	157	56	109	.514	27	47	.574	18	24	.750	5	33	38	62	29	0	11	1	26	35.3	14.3	3.5	5.6	.462
95-96 New York	8	8	293	80	29	82	.354	11	35	.314	11	15	.733	0	17	17	38	24	0	10	1	14	36.6	10.0	2.1	4.8	.240
98-99 LA Lakers	7	0	113	30	13	31	.419	1	10	.100	3	6	.500	1	9	10	15	2	0	2	0	4	16.1	4.3	1.4	2.1	.315
NBA Playoff Totals	97	75	3094	1094	415	925	.449	96	263	.365	168	236	.712	56	177	233	513	237	1	148	11	167	31.9	11.3	2.4	5.3	....

• HARPER, Mike

Michael Edward Harper

Born: Dec. 9, 1957. Chicago, IL, United States. Height: 6'10". Weight: 195 lbs. Drafted: 1980 College: North Park

YEAR TEAM	GP	GS	MIN	PTS	FGM	FGA	FG%	3PM	3PA	3P%	FTM	FTA	FT%	ORB	DRB	TRB	AST	PF	DQ	STL	BLK	TO	MPG	PPG	RPG	APG	PCM
80-81 Portland	55	....	461	149	56	136	.412	0	3	.000	37	85	.435	28	65	93	17	73	0	23	20	33	8.4	2.7	1.7	0.3	.289
81-82 Portland	68	38	1433	464	184	370	.497	0	1	.000	96	153	.627	127	212	339	54	229	7	55	82	95	21.1	6.8	5.0	0.8	.398
NBA Season Totals	123	38	1894	613	240	506	.474	0	4	.000	133	238	.559	155	277	432	71	302	7	78	102	128	15.4	5.0	3.5	0.6	....
80-81 Portland	1	....	6	3	1	1	1.000	0	0	.000	1	1	1.000	0	1	1	0	0	0	0	0	0	6.0	3.0	1.0	0.0	.652
NBA Playoff Totals	1	....	6	3	1	1	1.000	0	0	.000	1	1	1.000	0	1	1	0	0	0	0	0	0	6.0	3.0	1.0	0.0	....

• HARPER, Ron

Ronald (Hollywood) Harper

Born: Jan. 20, 1964. Dayton, OH, United States. Height: 6'6". Weight: 185 lbs. Drafted: 1986 College: Miami (OH)

YEAR TEAM	GP	GS	MIN	PTS	FGM	FGA	FG%	3PM	3PA	3P%	FTM	FTA	FT%	ORB	DRB	TRB	AST	PF	DQ	STL	BLK	TO	MPG	PPG	RPG	APG	PCM
86-87 Cleveland	82	82	3064	1874	734	1614	.455	20	94	.213	386	564	.684	169	223	392	394	247	3	209	84	**344**	37.4	22.9	4.8	4.8	.521
87-88 Cleveland	57	52	1830	879	340	732	.464	3	20	.150	196	278	.705	64	159	223	281	157	3	122	52	160	32.1	15.4	3.9	4.9	.505
88-89 Cleveland	82	82	2851	1526	587	1149	.511	29	116	.250	323	430	.751	122	287	409	434	224	1	185	74	230	34.8	18.6	5.0	5.3	.604
89-90 Cleveland	7	7	262	154	61	138	.442	1	5	.200	31	41	.756	19	29	48	49	25	1	14	9	18	37.4	22.0	6.9	7.0	.638
89-90 LA Clippers	28	28	1105	644	240	499	.481	13	46	.283	151	190	.795	55	103	158	133	80	0	67	32	81	39.5	23.0	5.6	4.8	.590
90-91 LA Clippers	39	34	1383	763	285	729	.391	48	148	.324	145	217	.668	58	130	188	209	111	0	66	35	129	35.5	19.6	4.8	5.4	.460
91-92 LA Clippers	82	82	3144	1495	569	1292	.440	64	211	.303	293	398	.736	120	327	447	417	199	0	152	72	254	38.3	18.2	5.5	5.1	.482
92-93 LA Clippers	80	77	2970	1443	542	1203	.451	52	186	.280	307	399	.769	117	308	425	360	212	1	177	70	224	37.1	18.0	5.3	4.5	.501
93-94 LA Clippers	75	75	2856	1508	569	1335	.426	71	236	.301	299	418	.715	129	331	460	344	167	0	144	54	240	38.1	20.1	6.1	4.6	.501
94-95 Chicago	77	53	1536	530	209	491	.426	31	110	.282	81	131	.618	51	129	180	157	132	1	97	27	100	19.9	6.9	2.3	2.0	.350
95-96 Chicago	80	80	1886	594	234	501	.467	28	104	.269	98	139	.705	74	139	213	208	137	0	105	32	72	23.6	7.4	2.7	2.6	.393
96-97 Chicago	76	74	1740	480	177	406	.436	68	188	.362	58	82	.707	46	147	193	191	138	0	86	38	53	22.9	6.3	2.5	2.5	.368
97-98 Chicago	82	82	2284	764	293	665	.441	16	84	.190	162	216	.750	107	183	290	241	181	0	108	48	90	27.9	9.3	3.5	2.9	.396
98-99 Chicago	35	35	1107	392	147	390	.377	27	85	.318	71	101	.703	49	131	180	115	80	0	60	35	65	31.6	11.2	5.1	3.3	.399
99-00 LA Lakers	80	78	2042	557	212	531	.399	33	106	.311	100	147	.680	96	241	337	270	164	0	85	39	132	25.5	7.0	4.2	3.4	.375
00-01 LA Lakers	47	46	1139	307	127	271	.469	19	72	.264	34	48	.708	46	120	166	113	70	0	39	25	62	24.2	6.5	3.5	2.4	.365
NBA Season Totals	1009	967	31199	13910	5326	11946	.446	523	1811	.289	2735	3799	.720	1322	2987	4309	3916	2324	10	1716	726	2254	30.9	13.8	4.3	3.9	....
87-88 Cleveland	4	4	134	71	30	63	.476	0	2	.000	11	16	.688	4	16	20	15	9	0	11	4	11	33.5	17.8	5.0	3.8	.538
88-89 Cleveland	5	5	189	98	39	69	.565	0	2	.000	20	26	.769	7	14	21	20	20	1	11	4	7	37.8	19.6	4.2	4.0	.563
91-92 LA Clippers	5	5	206	90	39	87	.448	1	9	.111	11	14	.786	10	22	32	23	13	0	5	4	15	41.2	18.0	6.4	4.6	.421
92-93 LA Clippers	5	5	174	90	37	78	.474	5	10	.500	11	17	.647	4	16	20	16	7	0	15	10	11	34.8	18.0	4.0	3.2	.543
94-95 Chicago	6	0	40	12	6	14	.429	0	2	.000	0	0	.000	2	4	6	4	6	0	3	1	1	6.7	2.0	1.0	0.7	.359
95-96 Chicago	18	16	494	158	57	134	.425	15	47	.319	29	42	.690	26	41	67	45	38	0	25	7	18	27.4	8.8	3.7	2.5	.375
96-97 Chicago	19	19	515	142	50	125	.400	21	61	.344	21	28	.750	20	61	81	57	43	1	24	14	11	27.1	7.5	4.3	3.0	.408
97-98 Chicago	21	21	563	141	56	122	.459	5	19	.263	24	39	.615	22	55	77	48	42	0	20	18	18	26.8	6.7	3.7	2.3	.347
99-00 LA Lakers	23	23	643	198	78	181	.431	9	39	.231	33	47	.702	30	55	85	73	63	0	23	13	28	28.0	8.6	3.7	3.2	.363
00-01 LA Lakers	6	0	42	13	5	10	.500	1	4	.250	2	3	.667	1	7	8	4	4	0	4	1	1	7.0	2.2	1.3	0.7	.511
NBA Playoff Totals	112	98	3000	1013	397	883	.450	57	195	.292	162	232	.698	126	291	417	305	245	2	141	76	121	26.8	9.0	3.7	2.7	....

• HARPRING, Matthew

Matthew Joseph Harpring

Born: May 31, 1976. Cincinnati, OH, United States.   Height: 6'7".   Weight: 231 lbs.   Drafted: 1998   College: Georgia Tech

YEAR	TEAM	GP	GS	MIN	PTS	FGM	FGA	FG%	3PM	3PA	3P%	FTM	FTA	FT%	ORB	DRB	TRB	AST	PF	DQ	STL	BLK	TO	MPG	PPG	RPG	APG	PCM
98-99	Orlando	50	22	1114	408	148	320	.463	10	25	.400	102	143	.713	88	126	214	45	112	0	30	6	73	22.3	8.2	4.3	0.9	.354
99-00	Orlando	4	0	63	16	4	17	.235	2	2	1.000	6	7	.857	5	7	12	8	7	0	5	1	1	15.8	4.0	3.0	2.0	.393
00-01	Cleveland	56	55	1615	623	238	524	.454	13	52	.250	134	165	.812	90	152	242	102	161	1	42	17	90	28.8	11.1	4.3	1.8	.360
01-02	Philadelphia	81	81	2540	958	386	838	.461	21	69	.304	165	222	.743	203	370	573	107	201	1	70	5	127	31.4	11.8	7.1	1.3	.402
02-03	Utah	78	69	2557	1370	521	1020	.511	66	160	.413	262	331	.792	190	324	514	133	217	4	73	17	160	32.8	17.6	6.6	1.7	.522
NBA Season Totals		269	227	7889	3375	1297	2719	.477	112	308	.364	669	868	.771	576	979	1555	395	698	6	220	46	451	29.3	12.5	5.8	1.5	....
98-99	Orlando	4	0	82	33	12	26	.462	1	5	.200	8	11	.727	7	13	20	7	9	0	1	0	5	20.5	8.3	5.0	1.8	.454
01-02	Philadelphia	5	5	119	51	22	44	.500	0	0	.000	7	9	.778	13	13	26	7	12	0	5	0	5	23.8	10.2	5.2	1.4	.470
02-03	Utah	5	5	156	74	30	62	.484	1	7	.143	13	16	.813	9	18	27	5	23	1	5	1	8	31.2	14.8	5.4	1.0	.393
NBA Playoff Totals		14	10	357	158	64	132	.485	2	12	.167	28	36	.778	29	44	73	19	44	1	11	1	18	25.5	11.3	5.2	1.4	....

• HARRINGTON, Adam

Adam Philip Harrington

Born: July 5, 1980. Bernardston, MA, United States.   Height: 6'5".   Weight: 200 lbs.   Drafted: —   College: Auburn

YEAR	TEAM	GP	GS	MIN	PTS	FGM	FGA	FG%	3PM	3PA	3P%	FTM	FTA	FT%	ORB	DRB	TRB	AST	PF	DQ	STL	BLK	TO	MPG	PPG	RPG	APG	PCM
02-03	Dallas	13	0	37	11	4	17	.235	1	3	.333	2	2	1.000	0	2	2	2	2	0	1	1	2	2.8	0.8	0.2	0.2	.062
02-03	Denver	6	0	74	19	7	20	.350	4	11	.364	1	2	.500	1	5	6	10	6	0	1	0	0	12.3	3.2	1.0	1.7	.288
NBA Season Totals		19	0	111	30	11	37	.297	5	14	.357	3	4	.750	1	7	8	12	8	0	2	1	2	5.8	1.6	0.4	0.6	....

• HARRINGTON, Al

Albert Harrington

Born: Feb. 17, 1980.   Height: 6'9".   Weight: 230 lbs.   Drafted: 1998   College: none (HS: Roselle/St. Patrick's, NJ)

YEAR	TEAM	GP	GS	MIN	PTS	FGM	FGA	FG%	3PM	3PA	3P%	FTM	FTA	FT%	ORB	DRB	TRB	AST	PF	DQ	STL	BLK	TO	MPG	PPG	RPG	APG	PCM
98-99	Indiana	21	0	160	45	18	56	.321	0	5	.000	9	15	.600	20	19	39	5	26	0	4	2	11	7.6	2.1	1.9	0.2	.205
99-00	Indiana	50	0	854	328	121	264	.458	8	34	.235	78	111	.703	47	112	159	38	130	0	25	9	65	17.1	6.6	3.2	0.8	.330
00-01	Indiana	78	38	1892	586	241	543	.444	1	7	.143	103	157	.656	119	262	381	130	223	2	63	18	148	24.3	7.5	4.9	1.7	.325
01-02	Indiana	44	1	1313	576	230	484	.475	1	3	.333	115	144	.799	96	180	276	54	166	4	41	21	78	29.8	13.1	6.3	1.2	.421
02-03	Indiana	82	37	2467	1002	389	896	.434	13	46	.283	211	274	.770	159	352	511	125	280	3	71	33	163	30.1	12.2	6.2	1.5	.378
NBA Season Totals		275	76	6686	2537	999	2243	.445	23	95	.242	516	701	.736	441	925	1366	352	825	9	204	83	465	24.3	9.2	5.0	1.3	....
00-01	Indiana	3	0	40	5	2	13	.154	0	2	.000	1	2	.500	3	1	4	3	8	0	0	0	1	13.3	1.7	1.3	1.0	-.073
02-03	Indiana	6	0	103	18	7	33	.212	0	4	.000	4	6	.667	7	15	22	5	21	0	6	3	10	17.2	3.0	3.7	0.8	.082
NBA Playoff Totals		9	0	143	23	9	46	.196	0	6	.000	5	8	.625	10	16	26	8	29	0	6	3	11	15.9	2.6	2.9	0.9	....

• HARRINGTON, Junior

Lorinza Harrington Jr.

Born: Oct. 2, 1980. Wagram, NC, United States.   Height: 6'4".   Weight: 180 lbs.   Drafted: —   College: Wingate

YEAR	TEAM	GP	GS	MIN	PTS	FGM	FGA	FG%	3PM	3PA	3P%	FTM	FTA	FT%	ORB	DRB	TRB	AST	PF	DQ	STL	BLK	TO	MPG	PPG	RPG	APG	PCM
02-03	Denver	82	51	2003	418	169	467	.362	7	28	.250	73	112	.652	44	206	250	277	250	6	80	15	157	24.4	5.1	3.0	3.4	.244
NBA Season Totals		82	51	2003	418	169	467	.362	7	28	.250	73	112	.652	44	206	250	277	250	6	80	15	157	24.4	5.1	3.0	3.4	....

• HARRINGTON, Othella

Othella Harrington

Born: Jan. 31, 1974. Jackson, MS, United States.   Height: 6'9".   Weight: 235 lbs.   Drafted: 1996   College: Georgetown

YEAR	TEAM	GP	GS	MIN	PTS	FGM	FGA	FG%	3PM	3PA	3P%	FTM	FTA	FT%	ORB	DRB	TRB	AST	PF	DQ	STL	BLK	TO	MPG	PPG	RPG	APG	PCM
96-97	Houston	57	1	860	273	112	204	.549	0	3	.000	49	81	.605	75	123	198	18	112	2	12	22	57	15.1	4.8	3.5	0.3	.352
97-98	Houston	58	3	903	350	129	266	.485	0	1	.000	92	122	.754	73	134	207	24	112	1	10	27	46	15.6	6.0	3.6	0.4	.406
98-99	Houston	41	10	903	400	156	304	.513	0	0	.000	88	122	.721	72	174	246	15	103	0	6	25	61	22.0	9.8	6.0	0.4	.461
99-00	Vancouver	82	82	2677	1076	420	830	.506	0	2	.000	236	298	.792	196	367	563	97	287	1	36	58	217	32.6	13.1	6.9	1.2	.392
00-01	Vancouver	44	40	1267	480	180	386	.466	0	3	.000	120	154	.779	102	187	289	36	136	3	19	26	104	28.8	10.9	6.6	0.8	.367
00-01	New York	30	5	548	185	67	121	.554	0	0	.000	51	70	.729	37	62	99	20	101	1	15	19	41	18.3	6.2	3.3	0.7	.342
01-02	New York	77	4	1564	596	237	450	.527	0	2	.000	122	172	.709	125	224	349	37	250	5	30	36	95	20.3	7.7	4.5	0.5	.382
02-03	New York	74	64	1851	573	225	443	.508	0	0	.000	123	150	.820	165	311	476	62	231	2	12	23	90	25.0	7.7	6.4	0.8	.382
NBA Season Totals		463	209	10573	3933	1526	3004	.508	0	11	.000	881	1169	.754	845	1582	2427	309	1332	15	140	236	711	22.8	8.5	5.2	0.7	....
96-97	Houston	7	0	15	9	1	2	.500	0	0	.000	7	10	.700	1	3	4	0	1	0	0	0	2	2.1	1.3	0.6	0.0	.538
97-98	Houston	3	0	23	16	6	12	.500	0	1	.000	4	5	.800	3	4	7	0	1	0	0	1	0	7.7	5.3	2.3	0.0	.735
98-99	Houston	4	0	42	22	9	14	.643	0	0	.000	4	6	.667	5	9	14	1	2	0	0	1	3	10.5	5.5	3.5	0.3	.656
00-01	New York	5	1	77	18	7	14	.500	0	0	.000	4	5	.800	7	8	15	2	16	1	4	2	3	15.4	3.6	3.0	0.4	.292
NBA Playoff Totals		19	1	157	65	23	42	.548	0	1	.000	19	26	.731	16	24	40	3	20	1	4	4	8	8.3	3.4	2.1	0.2	....

• HARRIS, Art

Arthur Carlos Harris Jr.

Born: Jan. 13, 1947.   Height: 6'4".   Weight: 185 lbs.   Drafted: 1968   College: Stanford

YEAR	TEAM	GP	GS	MIN	PTS	FGM	FGA	FG%	3PM	3PA	3P%	FTM	FTA	FT%	ORB	DRB	TRB	AST	PF	DQ	STL	BLK	TO	MPG	PPG	RPG	APG	PCM
68-69	Seattle	80	....	2556	993	416	1054	.395	....	....	....	161	251	.641	....	....	301	258	326	14	....	....	....	32.0	12.4	3.8	3.2	.328
69-70	Seattle	5	....	178	60	28	73	.384	....	....	....	4	9	.444	....	....	19	20	11	0	....	....	....	35.6	12.0	3.8	4.0	.295
69-70	Phoenix	76	....	1375	596	257	650	.395	....	....	....	82	125	.656	....	....	142	211	209	0	....	....	....	18.1	7.8	1.9	2.8	.364
70-71	Phoenix	56	....	952	467	199	484	.411	....	....	....	69	113	.611	....	....	100	132	137	0	....	....	....	17.0	8.3	1.8	2.4	.400
71-72	Phoenix	21	....	145	55	23	70	.329	....	....	....	9	21	.429	....	....	13	18	26	0	....	....	....	6.9	2.6	0.6	0.9	.205
NBA Season Totals		238	....	5206	2171	923	2331	.396	....	....	....	325	519	.626	....	....	575	639	709	14	....	....	....	21.9	9.1	2.4	2.7	....
69-70	Phoenix	7	....	89	30	15	42	.357	....	....	....	0	2	.000	....	....	13	12	13	0	....	....	....	12.7	4.3	1.9	1.7	.276
NBA Playoff Totals		7	....	89	30	15	42	.357	....	....	....	0	2	.000	....	....	13	12	13	0	....	....	....	12.7	4.3	1.9	1.7	....

• HARRIS, Bernie

C. Bernard Harris

Born: Nov. 26, 1950. Roanoke, VA, United States. Height: 6'10". Weight: 200 lbs. Drafted: 1974 College: Virginia Commonwealth

YEAR	TEAM	GP	GS	MIN	PTS	FGM	FGA	FG%	3PM	3PA	3P%	FTM	FTA	FT%	ORB	DRB	TRB	AST	PF	DQ	STL	BLK	TO	MPG	PPG	RPG	APG	PCM
74-75	Buffalo	11	....	25	5	2	11	.182	....	....	....	1	2	.500	2	6	8	1	0	0	0	1	....	2.3	0.5	0.7	0.1	.195
NBA Season Totals		11	....	25	5	2	11	.182	....	....	....	1	2	.500	2	6	8	1	0	0	0	1	....	2.3	0.5	0.7	0.1	....

• HARRIS, Billy

Billy Harris

Born: Nov. 12, 1951. Chicago, IL, United States. Height: 6'2". Weight: 185 lbs. Drafted: 1973 College: Northern Illinois

YEAR	TEAM	GP	GS	MIN	PTS	FGM	FGA	FG%	3PM	3PA	3P%	FTM	FTA	FT%	ORB	DRB	TRB	AST	PF	DQ	STL	BLK	TO	MPG	PPG	RPG	APG	PCM
74-75	San Diego-A	76	....	1221	609	264	664	.398	16	73	.219	65	96	.677	58	64	122	111	166	....	55	6	79	16.1	8.0	1.6	1.5	.326
ABA Season Totals		76	....	1221	609	264	664	.398	16	73	.219	65	96	.677	58	64	122	111	166	....	55	6	79	16.1	8.0	1.6	1.5	....

• HARRIS, Bob

Robert Azzel (Gabby) Harris

Born: Mar. 16, 1927. Linden, TN, United States. Height: 6'7". Weight: 195 lbs. Drafted: 1949 College: Oklahoma A&M

YEAR	TEAM	GP	GS	MIN	PTS	FGM	FGA	FG%	3PM	3PA	3P%	FTM	FTA	FT%	ORB	DRB	TRB	AST	PF	DQ	STL	BLK	TO	MPG	PPG	RPG	APG	PCM
49-50	Fort Wayne	62	....	....	476	168	465	.361	....	....	....	140	223	.628	....	....	....	129	190	....	....	....	....	....	7.7	....	2.1	....
50-51	FtW/Bos	56	....	....	282	98	295	.332	....	....	....	86	127	.677	....	....	291	64	157	4	....	....	....	....	5.0	5.2	1.1	....
51-52	Boston	66	....	1899	514	190	463	.410	....	....	....	134	209	.641	....	....	531	120	194	5	....	....	....	28.8	7.8	8.0	1.8	.398
52-53	Boston	70	....	1971	517	192	459	.418	....	....	....	133	226	.588	....	....	485	95	238	6	....	....	....	28.2	7.4	6.9	1.4	.343
53-54	Boston	71	....	1898	420	156	409	.381	....	....	....	108	172	.628	....	....	517	94	224	8	....	....	....	26.7	5.9	7.3	1.3	.330
NBA Season Totals		325	....	5768	2209	804	2091	.385	....	....	....	601	957	.628	....	....	1824	502	1003	23	....	....	....	17.7	6.8	5.6	1.5	....
49-50	Fort Wayne	4	....	....	30	9	32	.281	....	....	....	12	20	.600	....	....	....	11	15	....	....	....	....	....	7.5	....	2.8	....
50-51	Boston	2	....	....	7	1	10	.100	....	....	....	5	7	.714	....	....	4	2	4	0	....	....	....	....	3.5	2.0	1.0	....
51-52	Boston	3	....	87	23	9	21	.429	....	....	....	5	5	1.000	....	....	25	4	16	1	....	....	....	29.0	7.7	8.3	1.3	.364
52-53	Boston	6	....	193	50	16	35	.457	....	....	....	18	24	.750	....	....	56	12	28	3	....	....	....	32.2	8.3	9.3	2.0	.413
53-54	Boston	6	....	150	48	16	25	.640	....	....	....	16	23	.696	....	....	35	3	25	1	....	....	....	25.0	8.0	5.8	0.5	.393
NBA Playoff Totals		21	....	430	158	51	123	.415	....	....	....	56	79	.709	....	....	120	32	88	5	....	....	....	20.5	7.5	5.7	1.5	....

• HARRIS, Chris

Christopher R. Harris

Born: Aug. 11, 1933. Great Britain. Height: 6'3". Weight: 190 lbs. Drafted: — College: Dayton

YEAR	TEAM	GP	GS	MIN	PTS	FGM	FGA	FG%	3PM	3PA	3P%	FTM	FTA	FT%	ORB	DRB	TRB	AST	PF	DQ	STL	BLK	TO	MPG	PPG	RPG	APG	PCM
55-56	St. Louis	15	....	168	41	15	60	.250	....	....	....	11	18	.611	....	....	18	18	17	0	....	....	....	11.2	2.7	1.2	1.2	.200
55-56	Rochester	26	....	252	60	22	89	.247	....	....	....	16	27	.593	....	....	26	26	26	0	....	....	....	9.7	2.3	1.0	1.0	.186
NBA Season Totals		41	....	420	101	37	149	.248	....	....	....	27	45	.600	....	....	44	44	43	0	....	....	....	10.2	2.5	1.1	1.1	....

• HARRIS, Lucious

Lucious H. Harris Jr.

Born: Dec. 18, 1970. Los Angeles, CA, United States. Height: 6'5". Weight: 190 lbs. Drafted: 1993 College: Long Beach State

YEAR	TEAM	GP	GS	MIN	PTS	FGM	FGA	FG%	3PM	3PA	3P%	FTM	FTA	FT%	ORB	DRB	TRB	AST	PF	DQ	STL	BLK	TO	MPG	PPG	RPG	APG	PCM
93-94	Dallas	77	0	1165	418	162	385	.421	7	33	.212	87	119	.731	45	112	157	106	117	0	49	10	77	15.1	5.4	2.0	1.4	.333
94-95	Dallas	79	31	1695	751	280	610	.459	55	142	.387	136	170	.800	85	135	220	132	105	0	58	14	79	21.5	9.5	2.8	1.7	.423
95-96	Dallas	61	1	1016	481	183	397	.461	47	125	.376	68	87	.782	41	81	122	79	56	0	35	3	49	16.7	7.9	2.0	1.3	.426
96-97	Philadelphia	54	3	813	293	112	294	.381	36	99	.364	33	47	.702	27	44	71	50	45	0	41	3	32	15.1	5.4	1.3	0.9	.279
97-98	New Jersey	50	0	671	191	69	177	.390	12	39	.308	41	55	.745	21	31	52	42	77	0	42	5	20	13.4	3.8	1.0	0.8	.251
98-99	New Jersey	36	5	602	193	73	181	.403	11	50	.220	36	48	.750	21	46	67	31	52	1	18	7	18	16.7	5.4	1.9	0.9	.280
99-00	New Jersey	77	11	1510	513	198	463	.428	38	115	.330	79	99	.798	53	134	187	100	98	0	65	6	42	19.6	6.7	2.4	1.3	.347
00-01	New Jersey	73	50	2071	683	265	624	.425	46	132	.348	107	139	.770	71	217	288	135	127	1	74	16	64	28.4	9.4	3.9	1.8	.348
01-02	New Jersey	74	0	1553	675	249	537	.464	44	118	.373	133	158	.842	49	158	207	116	99	1	53	6	61	21.0	9.1	2.8	1.6	.432
02-03	New Jersey	77	25	1973	795	298	721	.413	47	136	.346	152	189	.804	63	169	232	155	95	0	53	8	71	25.6	10.3	3.0	2.0	.366
NBA Season Totals		658	126	13069	4993	1889	4389	.430	343	989	.347	872	1111	.785	476	1127	1603	946	871	3	488	78	513	19.9	7.6	2.4	1.4	....
97-98	New Jersey	3	0	52	9	2	6	.333	0	2	.000	5	6	.833	1	7	8	1	11	0	2	0	2	17.3	3.0	2.7	0.3	.159
01-02	New Jersey	20	0	418	177	65	133	.489	8	22	.364	39	47	.830	13	41	54	18	29	0	13	0	16	20.9	8.9	2.7	0.9	.394
02-03	New Jersey	20	0	435	155	54	138	.391	11	33	.333	36	46	.783	19	33	52	32	39	0	9	0	22	21.8	7.8	2.6	1.6	.292
NBA Playoff Totals		43	0	905	341	121	277	.437	19	57	.333	80	99	.808	33	81	114	51	79	0	24	0	40	21.0	7.9	2.7	1.2	....

• HARRIS, Luther

Luther Harris

Born: 1923. Wood River, IL, United States. Height: 6'3". Weight: 195 lbs. Drafted: — College: —

YEAR	TEAM	GP	GS	MIN	PTS	FGM	FGA	FG%	3PM	3PA	3P%	FTM	FTA	FT%	ORB	DRB	TRB	AST	PF	DQ	STL	BLK	TO	MPG	PPG	RPG	APG	PCM
46-47	Sheboygan-N	44	....	....	467	170	....	....	....	....	....	127	179	.709	....	....	....	....	137	....	....	....	....	....	10.6	....	....	....
47-48	Sheboygan-N	24	....	....	137	50	....	....	....	....	....	37	61	.607	....	....	....	....	....	....	....	....	....	....	5.7	....	....	....
47-48	Tri-Cities-N	23	....	....	85	26	....	....	....	....	....	33	55	.600	....	....	....	....	....	....	....	....	....	....	3.7	....	....	....
48-49	Tri-Cities-N	63	....	....	338	118	....	....	....	....	....	102	152	.671	....	....	....	....	155	....	....	....	....	....	5.4	....	....	....
NBL Season Totals		154	....	....	1027	364	....	....	....	....	....	299	447	....	....	....	....	....	292	....	....	....	....	....	6.7	....	....	....
46-47	Sheboygan-N	5	....	....	27	11	....	....	....	....	....	5	14	.357	....	....	....	....	....	....	....	....	....	....	5.4	....	....	....
47-48	Tri-Cities-N	6	....	....	23	7	....	....	....	....	....	9	14	.643	....	....	....	....	....	....	....	....	....	....	3.8	....	....	....
48-49	Tri-Cities-N	6	....	....	8	3	....	....	....	....	....	2	5	.400	....	....	....	....	....	....	....	....	....	....	1.3	....	....	....
NBL Playoff Totals		17	....	....	58	21	....	....	....	....	....	16	33	....	....	....	....	....	....	....	....	....	....	....	3.4	....	....	....

• HARRIS, Steve

Steven Dwayne Harris

Born: Oct. 15, 1963. Kansas City, MO, United States. Height: 6'5". Weight: 195 lbs. Drafted: 1985 College: Tulsa

YEAR	TEAM	GP	GS	MIN	PTS	FGM	FGA	FG%	3PM	3PA	3P%	FTM	FTA	FT%	ORB	DRB	TRB	AST	PF	DQ	STL	BLK	TO	MPG	PPG	RPG	APG	PCM
85-86	Houston	57	0	482	257	103	233	.442	1	5	.200	50	54	.926	25	32	57	50	55	0	21	4	34	8.5	4.5	1.0	0.9	.429
86-87	Houston	74	3	1174	613	251	599	.419	0	8	.000	111	130	.854	71	99	170	100	111	1	37	16	74	15.9	8.3	2.3	1.4	.404
87-88	Houston	14	10	199	83	34	86	.395	0	1	.000	15	16	.938	12	9	21	17	15	0	8	2	6	14.2	5.9	1.5	1.2	.344

YEAR	TEAM	GP	GS	MIN	PTS	FGM	FGA	FG%	3PM	3PA	3P%	FTM	FTA	FT%	ORB	DRB	TRB	AST	PF	DQ	STL	BLK	TO	MPG	PPG	RPG	APG	PCM
87-88	Golden State	44	16	885	452	189	401	.471	0	6	.000	74	97	.763	41	64	105	70	74	0	42	6	48	20.1	10.3	2.4	1.6	.431
88-89	Detroit	3	0	7	4	1	4	.250	0	0	.000	2	2	1.000	0	2	2	0	1	0	1	0	0	2.3	1.3	0.7	0.0	.505
89-90	LA Clippers	15	0	93	31	14	40	.350	0	0	.000	3	4	.750	5	5	10	1	9	0	7	1	5	6.2	2.1	0.7	0.1	.163
NBA Season Totals		207	29	2840	1440	592	1363	.434	1	20	.050	255	303	.842	154	211	365	238	265	1	116	29	167	13.7	7.0	1.8	1.1	....
85-86	Houston	15	0	83	30	14	29	.483	0	0	.000	2	5	.400	5	5	10	2	3	0	4	3	2	5.5	2.0	0.7	0.1	.354
86-87	Houston	9	0	91	37	16	43	.372	0	1	.000	5	6	.833	3	4	7	5	15	0	3	0	3	10.1	4.1	0.8	0.6	.179
NBA Playoff Totals		24	0	174	67	30	72	.417	0	1	.000	7	11	.636	8	9	17	7	18	0	7	3	5	7.3	2.8	0.7	0.3	....

• HARRIS, Tony

Tony Dwayne Harris

Born: May 13, 1967. Monroe, LA, United States. Height: 6'3". Weight: 190 lbs. Drafted: — College: New Orleans

YEAR	TEAM	GP	GS	MIN	PTS	FGM	FGA	FG%	3PM	3PA	3P%	FTM	FTA	FT%	ORB	DRB	TRB	AST	PF	DQ	STL	BLK	TO	MPG	PPG	RPG	APG	PCM
90-91	Philadelphia	6	0	41	10	4	16	.250	0	2	.000	2	4	.500	0	1	1	0	5	0	1	0	3	6.8	1.7	0.2	0.0	-.132
93-94	Boston	5	0	88	44	9	31	.290	3	9	.333	23	25	.920	3	7	10	8	8	0	4	0	6	17.6	8.8	2.0	1.6	.400
94-95	Boston	3	0	18	14	3	8	.375	0	1	.000	8	9	.889	0	0	0	0	2	0	0	0	1	6.0	4.7	0.0	0.0	.387
NBA Season Totals		14	0	147	68	16	55	.291	3	12	.250	33	38	.868	3	8	11	8	15	0	5	0	10	10.5	4.9	0.8	0.6	....

• HARRISON, Bob

Robert William (Tiger) Harrison

Born: Aug. 12, 1927. Height: 6'1". Weight: 190 lbs. Drafted: 1949 College: Michigan

YEAR	TEAM	GP	GS	MIN	PTS	FGM	FGA	FG%	3PM	3PA	3P%	FTM	FTA	FT%	ORB	DRB	TRB	AST	PF	DQ	STL	BLK	TO	MPG	PPG	RPG	APG	PCM
49-50	Minneapolis	66	....	....	300	125	348	.359	....	....	....	50	74	.676	....	....	....	131	175	....	....	....	....	....	4.5	....	2.0	....
50-51	Minneapolis	68	....	....	401	150	432	.347	....	....	....	101	128	.789	....	....	172	195	218	5	....	....	....	....	5.9	2.5	2.9	....
51-52	Minneapolis	65	....	1712	401	156	487	.320	....	....	....	89	124	.718	....	....	160	188	203	9	....	....	....	26.3	6.2	2.5	2.9	.255
52-53	Minneapolis	70	....	1643	497	195	518	.376	....	....	....	107	165	.648	....	....	153	160	264	16	....	....	....	23.5	7.1	2.2	2.3	.281
53-54	Min/Mil	64	....	1443	382	144	449	.321	....	....	....	94	158	.595	....	....	130	139	218	9	....	....	....	22.5	6.0	2.0	2.2	.234
54-55	Milwaukee	72	....	2300	724	299	875	.342	....	....	....	126	185	.681	....	....	226	252	291	14	....	....	....	31.9	10.1	3.1	3.5	.280
55-56	St. Louis	72	....	2219	617	260	725	.359	....	....	....	97	146	.664	....	....	195	277	246	6	....	....	....	30.8	8.6	2.7	3.8	.290
56-57	St. Louis	10	....	85	33	14	41	.341	....	....	....	5	10	.500	....	....	10	12	20	0	....	....	....	8.5	3.3	1.0	1.2	.306
56-57	Syracuse	56	....	1725	546	229	588	.389	....	....	....	88	120	.733	....	....	146	148	200	5	....	....	....	30.8	9.8	2.6	2.6	.282
57-58	Syracuse	72	....	1799	517	210	604	.348	....	....	....	97	122	.795	....	....	166	169	200	1	....	....	....	25.0	7.2	2.3	2.3	.269
NBA Season Totals		615	....	12926	4418	1782	5067	.352	....	....	....	854	1232	.693	....	....	1358	1671	2035	65	....	....	....	21.0	7.2	2.2	2.7	....
49-50	Minneapolis	12	....	....	42	16	37	.432	....	....	....	10	14	.714	....	....	....	12	34	....	....	....	....	....	3.5	....	1.0	....
50-51	Minneapolis	7	....	....	54	24	52	.462	....	....	....	6	8	.750	....	....	27	19	30	3	....	....	....	....	7.7	3.9	2.7	....
51-52	Minneapolis	12	....	235	74	30	68	.441	....	....	....	14	17	.824	....	....	20	24	39	2	....	....	....	19.6	6.2	1.7	2.0	.329
52-53	Minneapolis	12	....	204	60	25	65	.385	....	....	....	10	20	.500	....	....	22	14	32	1	....	....	....	17.0	5.0	1.8	1.2	.243
55-56	St. Louis	8	....	256	66	27	75	.360	....	....	....	12	19	.632	....	....	24	29	27	1	....	....	....	32.0	8.3	3.0	3.6	.276
56-57	Syracuse	5	....	133	32	12	45	.267	....	....	....	8	9	.889	....	....	13	15	21	1	....	....	....	26.6	6.4	2.6	3.0	.208
57-58	Syracuse	3	....	43	10	4	16	.250	....	....	....	2	3	.667	....	....	7	5	6	0	....	....	....	14.3	3.3	2.3	1.7	.236
NBA Playoff Totals		59	....	871	338	138	358	.385	....	....	....	62	90	.689	....	....	113	118	189	8	....	....	....	14.8	5.7	1.9	2.0	....

• HART, Jason

Jason Keema Hart

Born: Apr. 29, 1978. Los Angeles, CA, United States. Height: 6'3". Weight: 185 lbs. Drafted: 2000 College: Syracuse

YEAR	TEAM	GP	GS	MIN	PTS	FGM	FGA	FG%	3PM	3PA	3P%	FTM	FTA	FT%	ORB	DRB	TRB	AST	PF	DQ	STL	BLK	TO	MPG	PPG	RPG	APG	PCM
00-01	Milwaukee	1	0	10	2	1	1	1.000	0	0	.000	0	0	.000	0	0	0	1	0	0	0	0	2	10.0	2.0	0.0	1.0	.131
01-02	San Antonio	10	0	92	26	10	19	.526	0	2	.000	6	6	1.000	4	9	13	12	16	0	7	1	8	9.2	2.6	1.3	1.2	.386
NBA Season Totals		11	0	102	28	11	20	.550	0	2	.000	6	6	1.000	4	9	13	13	16	0	7	1	10	9.3	2.5	1.2	1.2	....

• HARTMAN, Huck

Huck Hartman

Born: 1921. Height: 6'7". Weight: 210 lbs. Drafted: — College: Washington & Jefferson

YEAR	TEAM	GP	GS	MIN	PTS	FGM	FGA	FG%	3PM	3PA	3P%	FTM	FTA	FT%	ORB	DRB	TRB	AST	PF	DQ	STL	BLK	TO	MPG	PPG	RPG	APG	PCM
44-45	Pittsburgh-N	30	....	....	327	127	....	....	....	....	....	73	....	....	....	....	....	....	....	....	....	....	....	....	10.9	....	....	....
45-46	Youngstown-N	26	....	....	197	63	....	....	....	....	....	71	91	.780	....	....	....	....	....	....	....	....	....	....	7.6	....	....	....
NBL Season Totals		56	....	....	524	190	....	....	....	....	....	144	91	....	....	....	....	....	....	....	....	....	....	....	9.4	....	....	....

• HARVEY, Antonio

Antonio Harvey

Born: July 6, 1970. Pascagoula, MS, United States. Height: 6'11". Weight: 225 lbs. Drafted: — College: Pfeiffer

YEAR	TEAM	GP	GS	MIN	PTS	FGM	FGA	FG%	3PM	3PA	3P%	FTM	FTA	FT%	ORB	DRB	TRB	AST	PF	DQ	STL	BLK	TO	MPG	PPG	RPG	APG	PCM
93-94	LA Lakers	27	6	247	70	29	79	.367	0	0	.000	12	26	.462	26	33	59	5	39	0	8	19	16	9.1	2.6	2.2	0.2	.281
94-95	LA Lakers	59	8	572	179	77	176	.438	1	1	1.000	24	45	.533	39	63	102	23	87	0	15	41	24	9.7	3.0	1.7	0.4	.324
95-96	Vancouver	18	6	410	98	39	95	.411	0	2	.000	20	43	.465	27	67	94	9	38	0	14	21	18	22.8	5.4	5.2	0.5	.318
95-96	LA Clippers	37	9	411	106	44	129	.341	0	0	.000	18	40	.450	42	64	106	6	38	0	13	26	26	11.1	2.9	2.9	0.2	.283
96-97	Seattle	6	0	26	15	5	11	.455	0	0	.000	5	6	.833	2	8	10	1	8	0	0	4	1	4.3	2.5	1.7	0.2	.708
99-00	Portland	19	0	137	41	17	30	.567	0	0	.000	7	12	.583	8	25	33	5	20	0	1	6	12	7.2	2.2	1.7	0.3	.356
00-01	Portland	12	0	72	31	13	28	.464	0	0	.000	5	6	.833	5	9	14	4	10	0	1	6	3	6.0	2.6	1.2	0.3	.461
01-02	Seattle	5	3	47	9	4	12	.333	0	0	.000	1	2	.500	5	4	9	5	8	0	1	3	3	9.4	1.8	1.8	1.0	.260
02-03	Atlanta	4	0	32	4	2	5	.400	0	0	.000	0	0	.000	1	5	6	0	7	0	1	4	3	8.0	1.0	1.5	0.0	.168
NBA Season Totals		187	32	1954	553	230	565	.407	1	3	.333	92	180	.511	155	278	433	58	255	0	54	130	106	10.4	3.0	2.3	0.3	....
94-95	LA Lakers	3	0	4	0	0	0	.000	0	0	.000	0	0	.000	0	1	1	0	0	0	0	0	1	1.3	0.0	0.3	0.0	.235
00-01	Portland	2	0	14	0	0	1	.000	0	0	.000	0	0	.000	1	5	6	0	4	0	0	0	1	7.0	0.0	3.0	0.0	.128
NBA Playoff Totals		5	0	18	0	0	1	.000	0	0	.000	0	0	.000	1	6	7	0	4	0	0	0	1	3.6	0.0	1.4	0.0	....

YEAR	TEAM	GP	GS	MIN	PTS	FGM	FGA	FG%	3PM	3PA	3P%	FTM	FTA	FT%	ORB	DRB	TRB	AST	PF	DQ	STL	BLK	TO	MPG	PPG	RPG	APG	PCM

• HARVEY, Don
Don Harvey

Born: 1920. Height: 5'11". Weight: 180 lbs. Drafted: — College: Missouri

YEAR	TEAM	GP	GS	MIN	PTS	FGM	FGA	FG%	3PM	3PA	3P%	FTM	FTA	FT%	ORB	DRB	TRB	AST	PF	DQ	STL	BLK	TO	MPG	PPG	RPG	APG	PCM
45-46	Sheboygan-N	1	....	....	0	0	....	....	....	....	....	0	0	.000	....	....	....	....	....	....	....	....	....	0.0	....	....	....	....
NBL Season Totals		1	....	....	0	0	....	....	....	....	....	0	0	....	....	....	....	....	....	....	....	....	....	0.0	....	....	....	....
45-46	Sheboygan-N	1	....	....	2	1	....	....	....	....	....	0	....	....	....	....	....	....	....	....	....	....	....	2.0	....	....	....	....
NBL Playoff Totals		1	....	....	2	1	....	....	....	....	....	0	....	....	....	....	....	....	....	....	....	....	....	2.0	....	....	....	....

• HARVEY, Donnell
Donnell Eugene Harvey

Born: Aug. 26, 1980. Shellman, GA, United States. Height: 6'8". Weight: 220 lbs. Drafted: 2000 College: Florida

YEAR	TEAM	GP	GS	MIN	PTS	FGM	FGA	FG%	3PM	3PA	3P%	FTM	FTA	FT%	ORB	DRB	TRB	AST	PF	DQ	STL	BLK	TO	MPG	PPG	RPG	APG	PCM
00-01	Dallas	18	0	65	22	8	14	.571	0	0	.000	6	16	.375	6	14	20	2	15	0	3	1	7	3.6	1.2	1.1	0.1	.352
01-02	Dallas	18	0	162	38	14	26	.538	0	0	.000	10	22	.455	12	34	46	5	27	0	4	5	8	9.0	2.1	2.6	0.3	.355
01-02	Denver	29	4	679	232	94	191	.492	0	0	.000	44	68	.647	68	113	181	32	88	1	17	19	25	23.4	8.0	6.2	1.1	.445
02-03	Denver	77	27	1613	611	246	551	.446	1	7	.143	118	176	.670	125	284	409	100	203	2	48	27	123	20.9	7.9	5.3	1.3	.405
NBA Season Totals		142	31	2519	903	362	782	.463	1	7	.143	178	282	.631	211	445	656	139	333	3	72	52	163	17.7	6.4	4.6	1.0	....

• HASHU, Nick
Nick Hashu

Born: 1917. Height: 6'1". Weight: 195 lbs. Drafted: — College: Valparaiso

YEAR	TEAM	GP	GS	MIN	PTS	FGM	FGA	FG%	3PM	3PA	3P%	FTM	FTA	FT%	ORB	DRB	TRB	AST	PF	DQ	STL	BLK	TO	MPG	PPG	RPG	APG	PCM
38-39	Hammond-N	15	....	....	28	10	....	....	....	....	....	8	....	....	....	....	....	....	....	....	....	....	....	1.9	....	....	....	....
44-45	Chicago-N	2	....	....	10	4	....	....	....	....	....	2	....	....	....	....	....	....	....	....	....	....	....	5.0	....	....	....	....
45-46	Chicago-N	6	....	....	18	8	....	....	....	....	....	2	....	....	....	....	....	....	....	....	....	....	....	3.0	....	....	....	....
NBL Season Totals		23	....	....	56	22	....	....	....	....	....	12	....	....	....	....	....	....	....	....	....	....	....	2.4	....	....	....	....
44-45	Chicago-N	3	....	....	8	4	....	....	....	....	....	0	....	....	....	....	....	....	....	....	....	....	....	2.7	....	....	....	....
NBL Playoff Totals		3	....	....	8	4	....	....	....	....	....	0	....	....	....	....	....	....	....	....	....	....	....	2.7	....	....	....	....

• HASKIN, Scott
Scott Russell Haskin

Born: Sept. 19, 1970. Riverside, CA, United States. Height: 6'11". Weight: 250 lbs. Drafted: 1993 College: Oregon State

YEAR	TEAM	GP	GS	MIN	PTS	FGM	FGA	FG%	3PM	3PA	3P%	FTM	FTA	FT%	ORB	DRB	TRB	AST	PF	DQ	STL	BLK	TO	MPG	PPG	RPG	APG	PCM
93-94	Indiana	27	2	186	55	21	45	.467	0	0	.000	13	19	.684	17	38	55	6	33	0	2	15	14	6.9	2.0	2.0	0.2	.402
NBA Season Totals		27	2	186	55	21	45	.467	0	0	.000	13	19	.684	17	38	55	6	33	0	2	15	14	6.9	2.0	2.0	0.2	....

• HASKINS, Clem
Clem Smith (The Gem) Haskins

Born: July 11, 1943. Campbellsville, KY, United States. Height: 6'3". Weight: 195 lbs. Drafted: 1967 College: Western Kentucky

YEAR	TEAM	GP	GS	MIN	PTS	FGM	FGA	FG%	3PM	3PA	3P%	FTM	FTA	FT%	ORB	DRB	TRB	AST	PF	DQ	STL	BLK	TO	MPG	PPG	RPG	APG	PCM
67-68	Chicago	76	....	1477	679	273	650	.420	....	....	....	133	202	.658	....	....	227	165	175	1	....	....	....	19.4	8.9	3.0	2.2	.447
68-69	Chicago	79	....	2874	1356	537	1275	.421	....	....	....	282	361	.781	....	....	359	306	230	0	....	....	....	36.4	17.2	4.5	3.9	.441
69-70	Chicago	82	....	3214	1668	668	1486	.450	....	....	....	332	424	.783	....	....	378	624	237	0	....	....	....	39.2	20.3	4.6	7.6	.571
70-71	Phoenix	82	....	2764	1462	562	1277	.440	....	....	....	338	431	.784	....	....	324	383	207	2	....	....	....	33.7	17.8	4.0	4.7	.519
71-72	Phoenix	79	....	2453	1238	509	1054	.483	....	....	....	220	258	.853	....	....	270	290	194	1	....	....	....	31.1	15.7	3.4	3.7	.501
72-73	Phoenix	77	....	1581	808	339	731	.464	....	....	....	130	156	.833	....	....	173	203	143	2	....	....	....	20.5	10.5	2.2	2.6	.493
73-74	Phoenix	81	....	1822	899	364	792	.460	....	....	....	171	203	.842	78	144	222	259	166	1	81	16	....	22.5	11.1	2.7	3.2	.514
74-75	Washington	70	....	702	283	115	290	.397	....	....	....	53	63	.841	29	51	80	79	73	0	23	6	....	10.0	4.0	1.1	1.1	.366
75-76	Washington	55	....	737	350	148	269	.550	....	....	....	54	65	.831	12	42	54	73	79	0	23	8	....	13.4	6.4	1.0	1.3	.458
NBA Season Totals		681	....	17624	8743	3515	7824	.449	....	....	....	1713	2163	.792	119	237	2087	2382	1504	7	127	30	....	25.9	12.8	3.1	3.5	....
67-68	Chicago	5	....	53	26	11	28	.393	....	....	....	4	6	.667	....	....	9	7	5	0	....	....	....	10.6	5.2	1.8	1.4	.476
69-70	Chicago	5	....	154	81	32	68	.471	....	....	....	17	19	.895	....	....	16	25	13	0	....	....	....	30.8	16.2	3.2	5.0	.551
74-75	Washington	13	....	75	35	15	28	.536	....	....	....	5	8	.625	5	2	7	4	17	0	2	1	....	5.8	2.7	0.5	0.3	.346
75-76	Washington	5	....	40	22	10	21	.476	....	....	....	2	5	.400	1	4	5	2	6	0	0	0	....	8.0	4.4	1.0	0.4	.382
NBA Playoff Totals		28	....	322	164	68	145	.469	....	....	....	28	38	.737	6	6	37	38	41	0	2	1	....	11.5	5.9	1.3	1.4	....

• HASSELL, Trenton
Trenton Lavar Hassell

Born: Mar. 4, 1979. Clarksville, TN, United States. Height: 6'5". Weight: 200 lbs. Drafted: 2001 College: Austin Peay

YEAR	TEAM	GP	GS	MIN	PTS	FGM	FGA	FG%	3PM	3PA	3P%	FTM	FTA	FT%	ORB	DRB	TRB	AST	PF	DQ	STL	BLK	TO	MPG	PPG	RPG	APG	PCM
01-02	Chicago	78	47	2237	681	267	628	.425	60	165	.364	87	114	.763	65	190	255	172	184	2	55	44	101	28.7	8.7	3.3	2.2	.302
02-03	Chicago	82	53	2000	342	144	392	.367	13	40	.325	41	55	.745	37	218	255	151	197	2	45	61	83	24.4	4.2	3.1	1.8	.219
NBA Season Totals		160	100	4237	1023	411	1020	.403	73	205	.356	128	169	.757	102	408	510	323	381	4	100	105	184	26.5	6.4	3.2	2.0	....

• HASSETT, Billy
William Joseph Hassett

Born: Oct. 21, 1921. Died: Nov.15, 1992. Height: 5'11". Weight: 180 lbs. Drafted: — College: Notre Dame

YEAR	TEAM	GP	GS	MIN	PTS	FGM	FGA	FG%	3PM	3PA	3P%	FTM	FTA	FT%	ORB	DRB	TRB	AST	PF	DQ	STL	BLK	TO	MPG	PPG	RPG	APG	PCM
46-47	Tri-Cities-N	27	....	....	212	73	....	....	....	....	....	66	101	.653	....	....	....	58	....	....	....	....	....	7.9	....	....	....	....
47-48	Tri-Cities-N	56	....	....	601	199	....	....	....	....	....	203	269	.755	....	....	....	145	....	....	....	....	....	10.7	....	....	....	....
48-49	Tri-Cities-N	64	....	....	356	125	....	....	....	....	....	106	156	.679	....	....	....	152	....	....	....	....	....	5.6	....	....	....	....
49-50	Tri-Cities	18	....	....	161	46	157	.293	....	....	....	69	94	.734	....	....	68	54	....	....	....	....	....	8.9	....	3.8	....	....
49-50	Minneapolis	42	....	....	111	38	145	.262	....	....	....	35	67	.522	....	....	69	82	....	....	....	....	....	2.6	....	1.6	....	....
50-51	Baltimore	31	....	....	133	45	160	.281	....	....	....	43	63	.683	....	....	34	47	72	1	....	....	....	4.3	1.1	1.5	....	....
NBA Season Totals		91	....	....	405	129	462	.279	....	....	....	147	224	.656	....	....	34	184	208	1	....	....	....	4.5	0.4	2.0	....	....
NBL Season Totals		147	....	....	1169	397	....	....	....	....	....	375	526	....	....	....	....	355	....	....	....	....	....	8.0	....	....	....	....
Career Totals		238	....	....	1574	526	462	....	....	....	....	522	750	....	....	....	34	184	563	1	....	....	....	6.6	0.1	0.8	....	....

YEAR TEAM	GP	GS	MIN	PTS	FGM	FGA	FG%	3PM	3PA	3P%	FTM	FTA	FT%	ORB	DRB	TRB	AST	PF	DQ	STL	BLK	TO	MPG	PPG	RPG	APG	PCM
47-48 Tri-Cities-N	6	....	....	53	18	....	....	....	....	....	17	26	.654	....	....	....	....	....	....	....	....	....	....	8.8	....	....	....
48-49 Tri-Cities-N	5	....	....	39	11	....	....	....	....	....	17	21	.810	....	....	....	....	....	....	....	....	....	....	7.8	....	....	....
49-50 Minneapolis	7	....	....	9	3	12	.250	....	....	....	3	10	.300	....	....	....	4	8	....	....	....	....	....	1.3	....	0.6	....
NBA Playoff Totals	7	....	....	9	3	12	.250	....	....	....	3	10	.300	....	....	....	4	8	....	....	....	....	....	1.3	....	0.6	....
NBL Playoff Totals	11	....	....	92	29	....	....	....	....	....	34	47	....	....	....	....	....	....	....	....	....	....	....	8.4	....	....	....
Career Playoff Totals	18	....	....	101	32	12	....	....	....	....	37	57	....	....	....	....	4	8	....	....	....	....	....	5.6	....	0.2	....

• HASSETT, Joe

Joseph Patrick Hassett Jr.

Born: Sept. 11, 1955. Providence, RI, United States.   Height: 6'5".   Weight: 180 lbs.   Drafted: 1977   College: Providence

YEAR TEAM	GP	GS	MIN	PTS	FGM	FGA	FG%	3PM	3PA	3P%	FTM	FTA	FT%	ORB	DRB	TRB	AST	PF	DQ	STL	BLK	TO	MPG	PPG	RPG	APG	PCM
77-78 Seattle	48	....	404	192	91	205	.444	....	....	....	10	12	.833	14	22	36	41	45	0	21	0	34	8.4	4.0	0.8	0.9	.341
78-79 Seattle	55	....	463	223	100	211	.474	....	....	....	23	23	1.000	13	32	45	42	58	0	14	4	33	8.4	4.1	0.8	0.8	.368
79-80 Indiana	74	....	1135	523	215	509	.422	69	198	.348	24	29	.828	35	59	94	104	85	0	46	8	44	15.3	7.1	1.3	1.4	.374
80-81 Dallas	17	....	280	138	59	142	.415	10	40	.250	10	13	.769	11	14	25	18	21	0	5	0	10	16.5	8.1	1.5	1.1	.319
80-81 Golden State	24	....	434	218	84	198	.424	43	116	.371	7	8	.875	13	30	43	56	44	0	8	2	12	18.1	9.1	1.8	2.3	.442
81-82 Golden State	68	2	787	390	144	382	.377	71	**214**	.332	31	37	.838	13	40	53	104	94	1	30	3	34	11.6	5.7	0.8	1.5	.362
82-83 Golden State	6	2	139	39	19	44	.432	1	9	.111	0	0	.000	3	8	11	21	14	0	2	0	9	23.2	6.5	1.8	3.5	.265
NBA Season Totals	292	4	3642	1723	712	1691	.421	194	577	.336	105	122	.861	102	205	307	386	361	1	126	17	176	12.5	5.9	1.1	1.3	....
77-78 Seattle	8	....	22	14	7	13	.538	....	....	....	0	0	.000	0	2	2	0	1	0	1	0	1	2.8	1.8	0.3	0.0	.457
78-79 Seattle	8	....	15	6	3	7	.429	....	....	....	0	0	.000	0	1	1	1	0	0	0	0	2	1.9	0.8	0.1	0.1	.174
NBA Playoff Totals	16	....	37	20	10	20	.500	....	....	....	0	0	.000	0	3	3	1	1	0	1	0	3	2.3	1.3	0.2	0.1	....

• HASSMILLER, Bob

Robert Hassmiller

Born: Dec. 17, 1916.   Died: Sept.1980.   Height: 6'1".   Weight: 185 lbs.   Drafted: —   College: Fordham

YEAR TEAM	GP	GS	MIN	PTS	FGM	FGA	FG%	3PM	3PA	3P%	FTM	FTA	FT%	ORB	DRB	TRB	AST	PF	DQ	STL	BLK	TO	MPG	PPG	RPG	APG	PCM
39-40 Non-Skids-N	23	....	....	72	32	....	....	....	....	....	8	....	....	....	....	....	....	....	....	....	....	....	3.1	....	....	....	....
40-41 Non-Skids-N	24	....	....	114	52	....	....	....	....	....	10	....	....	....	....	....	....	....	....	....	....	....	4.8	....	....	....	....
41-42 Toledo-N	2	....	....	5	2	....	....	....	....	....	1	....	....	....	....	....	....	....	....	....	....	....	2.5	....	....	....	....
NBL Season Totals	49	....	....	191	86	....	....	....	....	....	19	....	....	....	....	....	....	....	....	....	....	....	3.9	....	....	....	....
39-40 Non-Skids-N	4	....	....	19	9	....	....	....	....	....	1	....	....	....	....	....	....	....	....	....	....	....	4.8	....	....	....	....
40-41 Non-Skids-N	2	....	....	2	1	....	....	....	....	....	0	....	....	....	....	....	....	....	....	....	....	....	1.0	....	....	....	....
NBL Playoff Totals	6	....	....	21	10	....	....	....	....	....	1	....	....	....	....	....	....	....	....	....	....	....	3.5	....	....	....	....

• HASTINGS, Scott

Scott Alan Hastings

Born: June 3, 1960. Independence, KS, United States.   Height: 6'10".   Weight: 235 lbs.   Drafted: 1982   College: Arkansas

YEAR TEAM	GP	GS	MIN	PTS	FGM	FGA	FG%	3PM	3PA	3P%	FTM	FTA	FT%	ORB	DRB	TRB	AST	PF	DQ	STL	BLK	TO	MPG	PPG	RPG	APG	PCM
82-83 New York	21	0	98	23	8	22	.364	0	1	.000	7	14	.500	10	21	31	1	31	0	5	0	6	4.7	1.1	1.5	0.0	.218
82-83 Atlanta	10	0	42	14	5	16	.313	0	2	.000	4	6	.667	5	5	10	2	3	0	1	1	3	4.2	1.4	1.0	0.2	.289
83-84 Atlanta	68	8	1135	305	111	237	.468	1	4	.250	82	104	.788	96	174	270	46	220	7	40	36	68	16.7	4.5	4.0	0.7	.337
84-85 Atlanta	64	1	825	241	89	188	.473	0	0	.000	63	81	.778	59	100	159	46	135	1	24	23	51	12.9	3.8	2.5	0.7	.329
85-86 Atlanta	62	0	650	193	65	159	.409	3	4	.750	60	70	.857	44	80	124	26	118	2	14	9	37	10.5	3.1	2.0	0.4	.270
86-87 Atlanta	40	0	256	71	23	68	.338	2	12	.167	23	29	.793	16	54	70	13	35	0	10	7	12	6.4	1.8	1.8	0.3	.366
87-88 Atlanta	55	0	403	110	40	82	.488	5	12	.417	25	27	.926	27	70	97	16	67	1	8	10	17	7.3	2.0	1.8	0.3	.365
88-89 Miami	75	6	1206	386	143	328	.436	9	28	.321	91	107	.850	72	159	231	59	203	5	32	42	68	16.1	5.1	3.1	0.8	.328
89-90 Detroit	40	0	166	42	10	33	.303	3	12	.250	19	22	.864	7	25	32	8	31	0	3	3	8	4.2	1.1	0.8	0.2	.248
90-91 Detroit	27	0	113	48	16	28	.571	3	4	.750	13	13	1.000	14	14	28	7	23	0	0	0	8	4.2	1.8	1.0	0.3	.462
91-92 Denver	40	4	421	58	17	50	.340	0	9	.000	24	28	.857	30	68	98	26	56	0	10	15	24	10.5	1.5	2.5	0.7	.283
92-93 Denver	76	0	670	156	57	112	.509	2	8	.250	40	55	.727	44	93	137	34	115	1	12	8	30	8.8	2.1	1.8	0.4	.297
NBA Season Totals	578	19	5985	1647	584	1323	.441	28	96	.292	451	556	.811	424	863	1287	284	1037	17	159	153	332	10.4	2.8	2.2	0.5	....
83-84 Atlanta	5	0	32	7	2	9	.222	0	0	.000	3	4	.750	2	6	8	1	4	0	1	0	2	6.4	1.4	1.6	0.2	.180
85-86 Atlanta	9	0	49	28	11	14	.786	1	4	.250	5	11	.455	3	7	10	2	11	0	2	0	5	5.4	3.1	1.1	0.2	.530
86-87 Atlanta	4	0	21	6	2	3	.667	0	0	.000	2	2	1.000	1	5	6	0	5	0	1	1	0	5.3	1.5	1.5	0.0	.485
87-88 Atlanta	11	0	103	26	9	14	.643	0	1	.000	8	8	1.000	7	10	17	3	21	1	3	1	5	9.4	2.4	1.5	0.3	.288
89-90 Detroit	5	0	16	2	1	4	.250	0	3	.000	0	0	.000	0	0	0	0	4	0	1	0	0	3.2	0.4	0.0	0.0	-.109
90-91 Detroit	10	0	35	8	3	6	.500	2	4	.500	0	0	.000	2	4	6	3	6	0	0	1	1	3.5	0.8	0.6	0.3	.320
NBA Playoff Totals	44	0	256	77	28	50	.560	3	12	.250	18	25	.720	15	32	47	9	51	1	8	3	13	5.8	1.8	1.1	0.2	....

• HASTON, Kirk

Kirk Haston

Born: Mar. 10, 1979. Loblesville, TN, United States.   Height: 6'9".   Weight: 242 lbs.   Drafted: 2001   College: Indiana

YEAR TEAM	GP	GS	MIN	PTS	FGM	FGA	FG%	3PM	3PA	3P%	FTM	FTA	FT%	ORB	DRB	TRB	AST	PF	DQ	STL	BLK	TO	MPG	PPG	RPG	APG	PCM
01-02 Charlotte	15	0	77	26	11	39	.282	0	3	.000	4	8	.500	5	15	20	5	9	0	0	1	3	5.1	1.7	1.3	0.3	.215
02-03 New Orleans	12	0	57	6	2	17	.118	0	3	.000	2	4	.500	0	7	7	3	10	0	0	5	7	4.8	0.5	0.6	0.3	-.092
NBA Season Totals	27	0	134	32	13	56	.232	0	6	.000	6	12	.500	5	22	27	8	19	0	0	6	10	5.0	1.2	1.0	0.3	....
01-02 Charlotte	2	0	4	2	1	1	1.000	0	0	.000	0	0	.000	0	1	1	0	1	0	1	0	0	2.0	1.0	0.5	0.0	.840
NBA Playoff Totals	2	0	4	2	1	1	1.000	0	0	.000	0	0	.000	0	1	1	0	1	0	1	0	0	2.0	1.0	0.5	0.0	....

• HATTON, Vern

Walter Vernon Hatton

Born: Jan. 13, 1936. Owingsville, KY, United States.   Height: 6'3".   Weight: 195 lbs.   Drafted: 1958   College: Kentucky

YEAR TEAM	GP	GS	MIN	PTS	FGM	FGA	FG%	3PM	3PA	3P%	FTM	FTA	FT%	ORB	DRB	TRB	AST	PF	DQ	STL	BLK	TO	MPG	PPG	RPG	APG	PCM
58-59 Cincinnati	24	....	657	166	66	207	.319	....	....	....	34	51	.667	....	....	81	30	55	0	....	....	....	27.4	6.9	3.4	1.3	.200
58-59 Philadelphia	40	....	452	209	83	211	.393	....	....	....	43	65	.662	....	....	97	48	56	0	....	....	....	11.3	5.2	2.4	1.2	.478
59-60 Philadelphia	67	....	1049	307	127	356	.357	....	....	....	53	87	.609	....	....	159	82	61	0	....	....	....	15.7	4.6	2.4	1.2	.305

YEAR	TEAM	GP	GS	MIN	PTS	FGM	FGA	FG%	3PM	3PA	3P%	FTM	FTA	FT%	ORB	DRB	TRB	AST	PF	DQ	STL	BLK	TO	MPG	PPG	RPG	APG	PCM
60-61	Philadelphia	54	....	610	240	97	304	.319	....	....	....	46	56	.821	....	....	92	59	59	0	....	....	....	11.3	4.4	1.7	1.1	.327
61-62	Chi/StL	40	....	898	322	112	331	.338	....	....	....	98	125	.784	....	....	102	99	63	0	....	....	....	22.5	8.1	2.6	2.5	.352
NBA Season Totals		225	....	3666	1244	485	1409	.344	....	....	....	274	384	.714	....	....	531	318	294	0	....	....	....	16.3	5.5	2.4	1.4	....
59-60	Philadelphia	6	....	17	9	4	13	.308	....	....	....	1	3	.333	....	....	3	1	3	0	....	....	....	2.8	1.5	0.5	0.2	.225
NBA Playoff Totals		6	....	17	9	4	13	.308	....	....	....	1	3	.333	....	....	3	1	3	0	....	....	....	2.8	1.5	0.5	0.2	....

• HAVLICEK, John

John J. (Hondo) Havlicek

Born: Apr. 8, 1940. Martins Ferry, OH, United States. Height: 6'5". Weight: 203 lbs. Drafted: 1962 College: Ohio State HOF: 1984

YEAR	TEAM	GP	GS	MIN	PTS	FGM	FGA	FG%	3PM	3PA	3P%	FTM	FTA	FT%	ORB	DRB	TRB	AST	PF	DQ	STL	BLK	TO	MPG	PPG	RPG	APG	PCM
62-63	Boston	80	....	2200	1140	483	1085	.445	....	....	....	174	239	.728	....	....	534	179	189	2	....	....	....	27.5	14.3	6.7	2.2	.546
63-64	Boston	80	....	2587	1595	640	1535	.417	....	....	....	315	422	.746	....	....	428	238	227	1	....	....	....	32.3	19.9	5.4	3.0	.538
64-65	Boston	75	....	2169	1375	570	1420	.401	....	....	....	235	316	.744	....	....	371	199	200	2	....	....	....	28.9	18.3	4.9	2.7	.528
65-66	Boston	71	....	2175	1334	530	1328	.399	....	....	....	274	349	.785	....	....	423	210	158	1	....	....	....	30.6	18.8	6.0	3.0	.554
66-67	Boston	81	....	2602	1733	684	1540	.444	....	....	....	365	441	.828	....	....	532	278	210	0	....	....	....	32.1	21.4	6.6	3.4	.652
67-68	Boston	82	....	2921	1700	666	1551	.429	....	....	....	368	453	.812	....	....	546	384	237	2	....	....	....	35.6	20.7	6.7	4.7	.603
68-69	Boston	82	....	3174	1771	692	1709	.405	....	....	....	387	496	.780	....	....	570	441	247	0	....	....	....	38.7	21.6	7.0	5.4	.555
69-70	Boston	81	....	3369	1960	736	1585	.464	....	....	....	488	578	.844	....	....	635	550	211	1	....	....	....	41.6	24.2	7.8	6.8	.669
70-71	Boston	81	....	**3678**	2338	892	1982	.450	....	....	....	554	677	.818	....	....	730	607	200	0	....	....	....	**45.4**	28.9	9.0	7.5	.702
71-72	Boston	82	....	**3698**	2252	897	1957	.458	....	....	....	458	549	.834	....	....	672	614	183	1	....	....	....	**45.1**	27.5	8.2	7.5	.675
72-73	Boston	80	....	3367	1902	766	1704	.450	....	....	....	370	431	.858	....	....	567	529	195	1	....	....	....	42.1	23.8	7.1	6.6	.617
73-74	Boston	76	....	3091	1716	685	1502	.456	....	....	....	346	416	.832	138	349	487	447	196	1	95	32	....	40.7	22.6	6.4	5.9	.594
74-75	Boston	82	....	3132	1573	642	1411	.455	....	....	....	289	332	.870	154	330	484	432	231	2	110	16	....	38.2	19.2	5.9	5.3	.546
75-76	Boston	76	....	2598	1289	504	1121	.450	....	....	....	281	333	.844	116	198	314	278	204	1	97	29	....	34.2	17.0	4.1	3.7	.476
76-77	Boston	79	....	2913	1395	580	1283	.452	....	....	....	235	288	.816	109	273	382	400	208	4	84	18	....	36.9	17.7	4.8	5.1	.501
77-78	Boston	82	....	2797	1322	546	1217	.449	....	....	....	230	269	.855	93	239	332	328	185	2	90	22	205	34.1	16.1	4.0	4.0	.434
NBA Season Totals		1270	....	46471	26395	10513	23930	.439	....	....	....	5369	6589	.815	610	1389	8007	6114	3281	21	476	117	205	36.6	20.8	6.3	4.8	....
62-63	Boston	11	....	254	130	56	125	.448	....	....	....	18	27	.667	....	....	53	17	28	1	....	....	....	23.1	11.8	4.8	1.5	.485
63-64	Boston	10	....	289	157	61	159	.384	....	....	....	35	44	.795	....	....	43	32	26	0	....	....	....	28.9	15.7	4.3	3.2	.483
64-65	Boston	12	....	405	222	88	250	.352	....	....	....	46	55	.836	....	....	88	29	44	1	....	....	....	33.8	18.5	7.3	2.4	.446
65-66	Boston	17	....	719	401	153	374	.409	....	....	....	95	113	.841	....	....	154	70	69	2	....	....	....	42.3	23.6	9.1	4.1	.556
66-67	Boston	9	....	330	247	95	212	.448	....	....	....	57	71	.803	....	....	73	28	30	0	....	....	....	36.7	27.4	8.1	3.1	.691
67-68	Boston	19	....	862	493	184	407	.452	....	....	....	125	151	.828	....	....	164	142	67	1	....	....	....	45.4	25.9	8.6	7.5	.672
68-69	Boston	18	....	850	458	170	382	.445	....	....	....	118	138	.855	....	....	179	100	58	2	....	....	....	47.2	25.4	9.9	5.6	.605
71-72	Boston	11	....	517	301	108	235	.460	....	....	....	85	99	.859	....	....	92	70	35	1	....	....	....	47.0	27.4	8.4	6.4	.637
72-73	Boston	12	....	479	285	112	235	.477	....	....	....	61	74	.824	....	....	62	65	24	0	....	....	....	39.9	23.8	5.2	5.4	.608
73-74	Boston	18	....	811	487	199	411	.484	....	....	....	89	101	.881	28	88	116	108	43	0	24	6	....	45.1	27.1	6.4	6.0	.624
74-75	Boston	11	....	464	232	83	192	.432	....	....	....	66	76	.868	18	39	57	51	38	1	16	1	....	42.2	21.1	5.2	4.6	.486
75-76	Boston	15	....	505	198	80	180	.444	....	....	....	38	47	.809	18	38	56	51	32	0	12	5	....	33.7	13.2	3.7	3.4	.398
76-77	Boston	9	....	375	165	62	167	.371	....	....	....	41	50	.820	15	34	49	62	33	0	8	4	....	41.7	18.3	5.4	6.9	.451
NBA Playoff Totals		172	....	6860	3776	1451	3329	.436	....	....	....	874	1046	.836	79	199	1186	825	527	9	60	16	....	39.9	22.0	6.9	4.8	....

• HAWES, Steve

Steven Sherburne Hawes

Born: May 26, 1950. Seattle, WA, United States. Height: 6'9". Weight: 220 lbs. Drafted: 1972 College: Washington

YEAR	TEAM	GP	GS	MIN	PTS	FGM	FGA	FG%	3PM	3PA	3P%	FTM	FTA	FT%	ORB	DRB	TRB	AST	PF	DQ	STL	BLK	TO	MPG	PPG	RPG	APG	PCM
74-75	Houston	55	....	897	325	140	279	.502	....	....	....	45	55	.818	80	195	275	88	99	1	36	36	....	16.3	5.9	5.0	1.6	.552
75-76	Houston	6	....	51	10	5	13	.385	....	....	....	0	0	.000	5	13	18	10	6	0	0	0	....	8.5	1.7	3.0	1.7	.538
75-76	Portland	66	....	1360	475	194	390	.497	....	....	....	87	120	.725	166	313	479	105	163	5	44	25	....	20.6	7.2	7.3	1.6	.554
76-77	Atlanta	44	....	945	361	147	305	.482	....	....	....	67	88	.761	78	183	261	63	141	4	36	24	....	21.5	8.2	5.9	1.4	.478
77-78	Atlanta	75	....	2325	949	387	854	.453	....	....	....	175	214	.818	180	510	690	190	230	4	78	57	150	31.0	12.7	9.2	2.5	.528
78-79	Atlanta	81	....	2205	852	372	756	.492	....	....	....	108	132	.818	190	401	591	184	264	1	79	47	146	27.2	10.5	7.3	2.3	.496
79-80	Atlanta	82	....	1853	761	304	605	.502	3	8	.375	150	182	.824	148	348	496	144	205	4	74	29	123	22.6	9.3	6.0	1.8	.523
80-81	Atlanta	74	....	2309	889	333	637	.523	1	4	.250	222	278	.799	165	396	561	168	289	13	73	32	163	31.2	12.0	7.6	2.3	.475
81-82	Atlanta	49	42	1317	456	178	370	.481	4	10	.400	96	126	.762	89	231	320	142	156	4	36	34	88	26.9	9.3	6.5	2.9	.474
82-83	Atlanta	46	3	860	230	91	244	.373	2	14	.143	46	62	.742	53	175	228	59	110	2	29	8	74	18.7	5.0	5.0	1.3	.317
82-83	Seattle	31	1	556	170	72	146	.493	3	7	.429	23	32	.719	28	105	133	36	79	0	9	6	34	17.9	5.5	4.3	1.2	.370
83-84	Seattle	79	0	1153	290	114	237	.481	1	4	.250	61	78	.782	50	170	220	99	144	2	24	16	55	14.6	3.7	2.8	1.3	.345
NBA Season Totals		688	46	15831	5768	2337	4836	.483	14	47	.298	1080	1367	.790	1232	3040	4272	1288	1886	40	518	314	833	23.0	8.4	6.2	1.9	....
74-75	Houston	8	....	128	44	18	38	.474	....	....	....	8	9	.889	3	26	29	13	11	0	3	3	....	16.0	5.5	3.6	1.6	.480
77-78	Atlanta	2	....	71	16	7	18	.389	....	....	....	2	3	.667	3	14	17	8	5	0	1	2	6	35.5	8.0	8.5	4.0	.352
78-79	Atlanta	9	....	243	89	40	81	.494	....	....	....	9	12	.750	27	36	63	29	33	2	8	3	5	27.0	9.9	7.0	3.2	.535
79-80	Atlanta	5	....	149	52	18	41	.439	0	0	.000	16	18	.889	13	22	35	12	22	1	9	1	8	29.8	10.4	7.0	2.4	.449
81-82	Atlanta	1	0	12	7	2	5	.400	0	0	.000	3	4	.750	3	2	5	0	1	0	0	0	0	12.0	7.0	5.0	0.0	.660
82-83	Seattle	2	0	35	12	5	10	.500	0	0	.000	2	3	.667	1	5	6	2	8	0	0	0	3	17.5	6.0	3.0	1.0	.238
83-84	Seattle	5	0	74	15	6	14	.429	1	2	.500	2	2	1.000	8	12	20	7	6	0	2	0	2	14.8	3.0	4.0	1.4	.417
NBA Playoff Totals		32	0	712	235	96	207	.464	1	2	.500	42	51	.824	58	117	175	71	86	3	23	9	24	22.3	7.3	5.5	2.2	....

• HAWKINS, Connie

Cornelius L. (Hawk) Hawkins

Born: July 17, 1942. Brooklyn, NY, United States. Height: 6'8". Weight: 210 lbs. Drafted: — College: Iowa HOF: 1992

YEAR	TEAM	GP	GS	MIN	PTS	FGM	FGA	FG%	3PM	3PA	3P%	FTM	FTA	FT%	ORB	DRB	TRB	AST	PF	DQ	STL	BLK	TO	MPG	PPG	RPG	APG	PCM
67-68	Pittsburgh-A	70	....	3146	1875	635	1223	.519	2	9	.222	**603**	**789**	.764	368	577	945	320	248	2	....	....	200	**44.9**	**26.8**	13.5	4.6	.752
68-69	Minnesota-A	47	....	1852	1420	496	971	.511	3	22	.136	425	554	.767	167	367	534	184	166	3	....	....	155	39.4	30.2	11.4	3.9	.839
69-70	Phoenix	81	....	3312	1995	709	1447	.490	....	....	....	577	741	.779	....	....	846	391	287	4	....	....	....	40.9	24.6	10.4	4.8	.703
70-71	Phoenix	71	....	2662	1481	512	1181	.434	....	....	....	457	560	.816	....	....	643	322	197	2	....	....	....	37.5	20.9	9.1	4.5	.637
71-72	Phoenix	76	....	2798	1598	571	1244	.459	....	....	....	456	565	.807	....	....	633	296	235	2	....	....	....	36.8	21.0	8.3	3.9	.626
72-73	Phoenix	75	....	2768	1204	441	920	.479	....	....	....	322	404	.797	....	....	641	304	229	5	....	....	....	36.9	16.1	8.5	4.1	.562
73-74	Phoenix	8	....	223	90	36	74	.486	....	....	....	18	27	.667	14	29	43	28	20	0	8	3	....	27.9	11.3	5.4	3.5	.512
73-74	LA Lakers	71	....	2538	909	368	733	.502	....	....	....	173	224	.772	162	360	522	379	203	0	105	78	....	35.7	12.8	7.4	5.3	.540

YEAR	TEAM	GP	GS	MIN	PTS	FGM	FGA	FG%	3PM	3PA	3P%	FTM	FTA	FT%	ORB	DRB	TRB	AST	PF	DQ	STL	BLK	TO	MPG	PPG	RPG	APG	PCM
74-75	LA Lakers	43	....	1026	346	139	324	.429	....	....	....	68	99	.687	54	144	198	120	116	1	51	23	....	23.9	8.0	4.6	2.8	.421
75-76	Atlanta	74	....	1907	610	237	530	.447	....	....	....	136	191	.712	102	343	445	212	172	2	80	46	....	25.8	8.2	6.0	2.9	.464
NBA Season Totals		499	....	17234	8233	3013	6453	.467	....	....	....	2207	2811	.785	332	876	3971	2052	1459	16	244	150	....	34.5	16.5	8.0	4.1	....
ABA Season Totals		117	....	4998	3295	1131	2194	.515	5	31	.161	1028	1343	.765	535	944	1479	504	414	5	....	....	355	42.7	28.2	12.6	4.3	....
Career Totals		616	....	22232	11528	4144	8647	.479	5	31	.161	3235	4154	.779	867	1820	5450	2556	1873	21	244	150	355	36.1	18.7	8.8	4.1	....
67-68	Pittsburgh-A	14	....	616	419	145	244	.594	0	0	.000	129	177	.729	55	117	172	64	58	4	....	....	48	44.0	29.9	12.3	4.6	.829
68-69	Minnesota-A	7	....	320	174	65	172	.378	4	8	.500	40	62	.645	39	47	86	27	25	0	....	....	19	45.7	24.9	12.3	3.9	.521
69-70	Phoenix	7	....	328	178	62	150	.413	....	....	....	54	66	.818	....	....	97	41	22	0	....	....	....	46.9	25.4	13.9	5.9	.661
73-74	LA Lakers	5	....	172	54	21	60	.350	....	....	....	12	15	.800	14	26	40	16	13	0	7	1	....	34.4	10.8	8.0	3.2	.386
NBA Playoff Totals		12	....	500	232	83	210	.395	....	....	....	66	81	.815	14	26	137	57	35	0	7	1	....	41.7	19.3	11.4	4.8	....
ABA Playoff Totals		21	....	936	593	210	416	.505	4	8	.500	169	239	.707	94	164	258	91	83	4	....	....	67	44.6	28.2	12.3	4.3	....
Career Playoff Totals		33	....	1436	825	293	626	.468	4	8	.500	235	320	.734	108	190	395	148	118	4	7	1	67	43.5	25.0	12.0	4.5	....

• HAWKINS, Earle

Earle Hawkins

Born: 1921. Height: 6'4". Weight: 225 lbs. Drafted: — College: Auburn

YEAR	TEAM	GP	GS	MIN	PTS	FGM	FGA	FG%	3PM	3PA	3P%	FTM	FTA	FT%	ORB	DRB	TRB	AST	PF	DQ	STL	BLK	TO	MPG	PPG	RPG	APG	PCM
48-49	Tri-Cities-N	2	....	....	5	2	....	....	....	....	....	1	1	1.000	....	....	....	....	....	....	....	....	....	....	2.5	....	....	....
NBL Season Totals		2	....	....	5	2	....	....	....	....	....	1	1	....	....	....	....	....	....	....	....	....	....	....	2.5	....	....	....

• HAWKINS, Hersey

Hersey R. Hawkins Jr.

Born: Sept. 29, 1966. Chicago, IL, United States. Height: 6'3". Weight: 190 lbs. Drafted: 1988 College: Bradley

YEAR	TEAM	GP	GS	MIN	PTS	FGM	FGA	FG%	3PM	3PA	3P%	FTM	FTA	FT%	ORB	DRB	TRB	AST	PF	DQ	STL	BLK	TO	MPG	PPG	RPG	APG	PCM
88-89	Philadelphia	79	79	2577	1196	442	971	.455	71	166	.428	241	290	.831	51	174	225	239	184	0	120	37	158	32.6	15.1	2.8	3.0	.411
89-90	Philadelphia	82	82	2856	1515	522	1136	.460	84	200	.420	387	436	.888	85	219	304	261	217	2	130	28	189	34.8	18.5	3.7	3.2	.472
90-91	Philadelphia	80	80	3110	1767	590	1251	.472	108	270	.400	479	550	.871	48	262	310	299	182	0	178	39	216	38.9	22.1	3.9	3.7	.528
91-92	Philadelphia	81	81	3013	1536	521	1127	.462	91	229	.397	403	461	.874	53	218	271	248	174	0	157	43	186	37.2	19.0	3.3	3.1	.463
92-93	Philadelphia	81	81	2977	1643	551	1172	.470	122	307	.397	419	487	.860	91	255	346	317	189	0	137	30	178	36.8	20.3	4.3	3.9	.536
93-94	Charlotte	82	82	2648	1180	395	859	.460	78	235	.332	312	362	.862	89	288	377	216	167	2	135	22	156	32.3	14.4	4.6	2.6	.467
94-95	Charlotte	82	82	2731	1172	390	809	.482	131	298	.440	261	301	.867	60	254	314	262	178	1	122	18	148	33.3	14.3	3.8	3.2	.455
95-96	Seattle	82	82	2823	1279	443	936	.473	146	380	.384	247	283	.873	86	211	297	218	172	0	149	14	164	34.4	15.6	3.6	2.7	.435
96-97	Seattle	82	82	2755	1139	369	795	.464	143	355	.403	258	295	.875	92	228	320	250	146	1	159	12	131	33.6	13.9	3.9	3.0	.457
97-98	Seattle	82	82	2597	862	280	636	.440	125	301	.415	177	204	.868	71	263	334	221	153	0	148	17	98	31.7	10.5	4.1	2.7	.408
98-99	Seattle	50	34	1644	516	171	408	.419	55	180	.306	119	132	.902	51	150	201	123	90	1	80	18	80	32.9	10.3	4.0	2.5	.359
99-00	Chicago	61	49	1622	480	159	375	.424	55	141	.390	107	119	.899	31	144	175	134	146	1	74	15	100	26.6	7.9	2.9	2.2	.313
00-01	Charlotte	59	0	681	183	56	137	.409	17	46	.370	54	63	.857	17	63	80	72	45	0	33	9	19	11.5	3.1	1.4	1.2	.379
NBA Season Totals		983	896	32034	14468	4889	10612	.461	1226	3108	.394	3464	3983	.870	825	2729	3554	2860	2043	8	1622	302	1823	32.6	14.7	3.6	2.9	....
88-89	Philadelphia	3	3	72	8	3	24	.125	0	5	.000	2	2	1.000	1	4	5	4	6	0	3	1	3	24.0	2.7	1.7	1.3	-.062
89-90	Philadelphia	10	10	415	235	81	163	.497	14	36	.389	59	63	.937	8	23	31	36	25	0	12	7	31	41.5	23.5	3.1	3.6	.483
90-91	Philadelphia	8	8	329	167	47	101	.465	14	26	.538	59	63	.937	8	38	46	27	29	1	20	10	16	41.1	20.9	5.8	3.4	.565
94-95	Charlotte	4	4	130	45	13	32	.406	4	13	.308	15	17	.882	5	16	21	8	13	1	6	2	9	32.5	11.3	5.3	2.0	.365
95-96	Seattle	21	21	713	259	76	168	.452	22	64	.344	85	95	.895	17	46	63	46	55	0	27	4	33	34.0	12.3	3.0	2.2	.348
96-97	Seattle	12	12	483	183	62	132	.470	27	59	.458	32	35	.914	17	37	54	34	32	0	30	4	21	40.3	15.3	4.5	2.8	.415
97-98	Seattle	10	10	337	134	41	88	.466	17	43	.395	35	40	.875	17	40	57	36	24	0	18	1	9	33.7	13.4	5.7	3.6	.528
00-01	Charlotte	6	0	50	12	3	8	.375	1	4	.250	5	7	.714	1	8	9	4	4	0	3	0	0	8.3	2.0	1.5	0.7	.400
NBA Playoff Totals		74	68	2529	1043	326	716	.455	99	250	.396	292	322	.907	74	212	286	195	188	2	119	29	122	34.2	14.1	3.9	2.6	....

• HAWKINS, Juaquin

Juaguin Juan Hawkins

Born: July 2, 1973. Gardena, CA, United States. Height: 6'7". Weight: 220 lbs. Drafted: — College: Long Beach State

YEAR	TEAM	GP	GS	MIN	PTS	FGM	FGA	FG%	3PM	3PA	3P%	FTM	FTA	FT%	ORB	DRB	TRB	AST	PF	DQ	STL	BLK	TO	MPG	PPG	RPG	APG	PCM
02-03	Houston	58	10	685	134	57	148	.385	10	24	.417	10	20	.500	16	62	78	47	57	0	29	6	29	11.8	2.3	1.3	0.8	.217
NBA Season Totals		58	10	685	134	57	148	.385	10	24	.417	10	20	.500	16	62	78	47	57	0	29	6	29	11.8	2.3	1.3	0.8	....

• HAWKINS, Marshall

James Marshall Hawkins

Born: Aug. 3, 1924. Huntington, WV, United States. Height: 6'3". Weight: 205 lbs. Drafted: 1948 College: Tennessee

YEAR	TEAM	GP	GS	MIN	PTS	FGM	FGA	FG%	3PM	3PA	3P%	FTM	FTA	FT%	ORB	DRB	TRB	AST	PF	DQ	STL	BLK	TO	MPG	PPG	RPG	APG	PCM
48-49	Oshkosh-N	64	....	....	516	200	....	....	....	....	....	116	160	.725	....	....	....	....	149	....	....	....	....	....	8.1	....	....	....
49-50	Indianapolis	39	....	....	152	55	195	.282	....	....	....	42	61	.689	....	....	....	51	87	....	....	....	....	....	3.9	....	1.3	....
NBA Season Totals		39	....	....	152	55	195	.282	....	....	....	42	61	.689	....	....	....	51	87	....	....	....	....	....	3.9	....	1.3	....
NBL Season Totals		64	....	....	516	200	....	....	....	....	....	116	160	....	....	....	....	....	149	....	....	....	....	....	8.1	....	....	....
Career Totals		103	....	....	668	255	195	....	....	....	....	158	221	....	....	....	....	51	236	....	....	....	....	....	6.5	....	0.5	....
48-49	Oshkosh-N	7	....	....	70	25	....	....	....	....	....	20	26	.769	....	....	....	....	....	....	....	....	....	....	10.0	....	....	....
49-50	Indianapolis	2	....	....	0	0	1	.000	....	....	....	0	0	.000	....	....	....	0	1	....	....	....	....	....	0.0	....	0.0	....
NBA Playoff Totals		2	....	....	0	0	1	.000	....	....	....	0	0	.000	....	....	....	0	1	....	....	....	....	....	0.0	....	0.0	....
NBL Playoff Totals		7	....	....	70	25	....	....	....	....	....	20	26	....	....	....	....	....	....	....	....	....	....	....	10.0	....	....	....
Career Playoff Totals		9	....	....	70	25	1	....	....	....	....	20	26	....	....	....	....	0	1	....	....	....	....	....	7.8	....	0.0	....

• HAWKINS, Michael

Steve Michael Hawkins

Born: Oct. 28, 1972. Canton, OH, United States. Height: 6' Weight: 178 lbs. Drafted: — College: Xavier (OH)

YEAR	TEAM	GP	GS	MIN	PTS	FGM	FGA	FG%	3PM	3PA	3P%	FTM	FTA	FT%	ORB	DRB	TRB	AST	PF	DQ	STL	BLK	TO	MPG	PPG	RPG	APG	PCM
96-97	Boston	29	0	326	80	29	68	.426	10	31	.323	12	15	.800	9	22	31	64	40	0	16	1	29	11.2	2.8	1.1	2.2	.336
98-99	Sacramento	24	0	203	36	14	40	.350	5	19	.263	3	3	1.000	10	15	25	27	14	0	3	1	13	8.5	1.5	1.0	1.1	.251
99-00	Charlotte	12	0	36	8	3	13	.231	1	5	.200	1	2	.500	0	7	7	13	2	0	0	0	3	3.0	0.7	0.6	1.1	.427
00-01	Cleveland	10	0	76	8	3	9	.333	2	4	.500	0	0	.000	2	3	5	13	13	0	2	0	6	7.6	0.8	0.5	1.3	.158
NBA Season Totals		75	0	641	132	49	130	.377	18	59	.305	16	20	.800	21	47	68	117	69	0	21	2	51	8.5	1.8	0.9	1.6	....

YEAR	TEAM	GP	GS	MIN	PTS	FGM	FGA	FG%	3PM	3PA	3P%	FTM	FTA	FT%	ORB	DRB	TRB	AST	PF	DQ	STL	BLK	TO	MPG	PPG	RPG	APG	PCM
98-99	Sacramento	2	0	10	2	0	1	.000	0	1	.000	2	2	1.000	0	0	0	0	1	0	0	0	0	5.0	1.0	0.0	0.0	.067
NBA Playoff Totals		2	0	10	2	0	1	.000	0	1	.000	2	2	1.000	0	0	0	0	1	0	0	0	0	5.0	1.0	0.0	0.0	....

• HAWKINS, Robert

Robert (Bubbles) Hawkins

Born: June 30, 1954. Detroit, MI, United States. Died: Nov.28, 1993. Height: 6'4". Weight: 190 lbs. Drafted: 1975 College: Illinois State

YEAR	TEAM	GP	GS	MIN	PTS	FGM	FGA	FG%	3PM	3PA	3P%	FTM	FTA	FT%	ORB	DRB	TRB	AST	PF	DQ	STL	BLK	TO	MPG	PPG	RPG	APG	PCM
75-76	Golden State	32	....	153	126	53	104	.510	....	....	....	20	31	.645	16	14	30	16	31	0	10	8	....	4.8	3.9	0.9	0.5	.707
76-77	New York	52	....	1481	1006	406	909	.447	....	....	....	194	282	.688	67	87	154	93	163	2	77	26	....	28.5	19.3	3.0	1.8	.474
77-78	New Jersey	15	....	343	163	69	150	.460	....	....	....	25	29	.862	21	29	50	37	51	1	22	13	44	22.9	10.9	3.3	2.5	.424
78-79	Detroit	4	....	28	18	6	16	.375	....	....	....	6	6	1.000	3	3	6	4	7	0	5	0	2	7.0	4.5	1.5	1.0	.656
NBA Season Totals		103	....	2005	1313	534	1179	.453	....	....	....	245	348	.704	107	133	240	150	252	3	114	47	46	19.5	12.7	2.3	1.5	....
75-76	Golden State	5	....	12	10	4	5	.800	....	....	....	2	2	1.000	0	0	0	2	6	0	1	0	....	2.4	2.0	0.0	0.4	.738
NBA Playoff Totals		5	....	12	10	4	5	.800	....	....	....	2	2	1.000	0	0	0	2	6	0	1	0	....	2.4	2.0	0.0	0.4	....

• HAWKINS, Tom

Thomas Jerome (Hawk) Hawkins

Born: Dec. 22, 1936. Chicago, IL, United States. Height: 6'5". Weight: 210 lbs. Drafted: 1959 College: Notre Dame

YEAR	TEAM	GP	GS	MIN	PTS	FGM	FGA	FG%	3PM	3PA	3P%	FTM	FTA	FT%	ORB	DRB	TRB	AST	PF	DQ	STL	BLK	TO	MPG	PPG	RPG	APG	PCM
59-60	Minneapolis	69	....	1467	546	220	579	.380	....	....	....	106	164	.646	....	....	428	54	188	3	....	....	....	21.3	7.9	6.2	0.8	.390
60-61	LA Lakers	78	....	1846	760	310	719	.431	....	....	....	140	235	.596	....	....	479	88	209	2	....	....	....	23.7	9.7	6.1	1.1	.437
61-62	LA Lakers	79	....	1903	721	289	704	.411	....	....	....	143	222	.644	....	....	514	95	244	7	....	....	....	24.1	9.1	6.5	1.2	.414
62-63	Cincinnati	79	....	1721	745	299	635	.471	....	....	....	147	241	.610	....	....	543	100	197	2	....	....	....	21.8	9.4	6.9	1.3	.531
63-64	Cincinnati	73	....	1770	625	256	580	.441	....	....	....	113	188	.601	....	....	435	74	198	4	....	....	....	24.2	8.6	6.0	1.0	.393
64-65	Cincinnati	79	....	1864	556	220	538	.409	....	....	....	116	204	.569	....	....	475	80	240	4	....	....	....	23.6	7.0	6.0	1.0	.348
65-66	Cincinnati	79	....	2126	662	273	604	.452	....	....	....	116	209	.555	....	....	575	99	274	4	....	....	....	26.9	8.4	7.3	1.3	.390
66-67	LA Lakers	76	....	1798	632	275	572	.481	....	....	....	82	173	.474	....	....	434	83	207	1	....	....	....	23.7	8.3	5.7	1.1	.402
67-68	LA Lakers	78	....	2463	903	389	779	.499	....	....	....	125	229	.546	....	....	458	117	289	7	....	....	....	31.6	11.6	5.9	1.5	.382
68-69	LA Lakers	74	....	1507	522	230	461	.499	....	....	....	62	151	.411	....	....	266	81	168	1	....	....	....	20.4	7.1	3.6	1.1	.357
NBA Season Totals		764	....	18465	6672	2761	6171	.447	....	....	....	1150	2016	.570	....	....	4607	871	2214	35	....	....	....	24.2	8.7	6.0	1.1	....
59-60	Minneapolis	8	....	119	59	22	45	.489	....	....	....	15	18	.833	....	....	21	3	24	0	....	....	....	14.9	7.4	2.6	0.4	.429
60-61	LA Lakers	12	....	283	139	54	116	.466	....	....	....	31	47	.660	....	....	76	13	43	0	....	....	....	23.6	11.6	6.3	1.1	.506
61-62	LA Lakers	13	....	203	54	22	61	.361	....	....	....	10	24	.417	....	....	66	19	34	0	....	....	....	15.6	4.2	5.1	1.5	.392
62-63	Cincinnati	12	....	261	126	46	91	.505	....	....	....	34	47	.723	....	....	81	23	45	2	....	....	....	21.8	10.5	6.8	1.9	.611
63-64	Cincinnati	10	....	273	101	43	97	.443	....	....	....	15	22	.682	....	....	93	11	38	2	....	....	....	27.3	10.1	9.3	1.1	.466
64-65	Cincinnati	4	....	95	38	17	33	.515	....	....	....	4	5	.800	....	....	28	1	13	0	....	....	....	23.8	9.5	7.0	0.3	.453
65-66	Cincinnati	5	....	109	23	11	24	.458	....	....	....	1	6	.167	....	....	22	1	16	0	....	....	....	21.8	4.6	4.4	0.2	.211
66-67	LA Lakers	3	....	95	30	13	31	.419	....	....	....	4	8	.500	....	....	20	10	12	1	....	....	....	31.7	10.0	6.7	3.3	.392
67-68	LA Lakers	15	....	478	142	59	129	.457	....	....	....	24	40	.600	....	....	90	18	53	2	....	....	....	31.9	9.5	6.0	1.2	.318
68-69	LA Lakers	14	....	180	55	24	50	.480	....	....	....	7	18	.389	....	....	40	7	32	0	....	....	....	12.9	3.9	2.9	0.5	.316
NBA Playoff Totals		96	....	2096	767	311	677	.459	....	....	....	145	235	.617	....	....	537	106	310	7	....	....	....	21.8	8.0	5.6	1.1	....

• HAWLEY, Chuck

Chuck Hawley

Born: 1915. Height: 6'3". Weight: 195 lbs. Drafted: — College: none

YEAR	TEAM	GP	GS	MIN	PTS	FGM	FGA	FG%	3PM	3PA	3P%	FTM	FTA	FT%	ORB	DRB	TRB	AST	PF	DQ	STL	BLK	TO	MPG	PPG	RPG	APG	PCM
46-47	Detroit-N	12	....	....	17	6	....	....	....	....	....	5	6	.833	....	....	....	....	....	....	....	....	....	....	1.4	....	....	....
NBL Season Totals		12	....	....	17	6	....	....	....	....	....	5	6	....	....	....	....	....	....	....	....	....	....	....	1.4	....	....	....

• HAWTHORNE, Nate

Nate Hawthorne

Born: Jan. 15, 1950. Mt. Vernon, IL, United States. Height: 6'4". Weight: 190 lbs. Drafted: 1973 College: Southern Illinois

YEAR	TEAM	GP	GS	MIN	PTS	FGM	FGA	FG%	3PM	3PA	3P%	FTM	FTA	FT%	ORB	DRB	TRB	AST	PF	DQ	STL	BLK	TO	MPG	PPG	RPG	APG	PCM
73-74	LA Lakers	33	....	229	106	38	93	.409	....	....	....	30	48	.625	16	16	32	23	33	1	9	6	....	6.9	3.2	1.0	0.7	.398
74-75	Phoenix	50	....	618	297	118	287	.411	....	....	....	61	94	.649	34	58	92	39	94	0	30	21	....	12.4	5.9	1.8	0.8	.359
75-76	Phoenix	79	....	1144	479	182	423	.430	....	....	....	115	170	.676	86	123	209	46	147	0	33	15	....	14.5	6.1	2.6	0.6	.365
NBA Season Totals		162	....	1991	882	338	803	.421	....	....	....	206	312	.660	136	197	333	108	274	1	72	42	....	12.3	5.4	2.1	0.7	....
73-74	LA Lakers	3	....	14	6	1	7	.143	....	....	....	4	5	.800	2	0	2	2	0	0	1	1	....	4.7	2.0	0.7	0.7	.319
75-76	Phoenix	15	....	81	26	9	26	.346	....	....	....	8	11	.727	5	11	16	4	20	0	5	1	....	5.4	1.7	1.1	0.3	.245
NBA Playoff Totals		18	....	95	32	10	33	.303	....	....	....	12	16	.750	7	11	18	6	20	0	6	2	....	5.3	1.8	1.0	0.3	....

• HAYES, Elvin

Elvin Ernest (The Big E) Hayes

Born: Nov. 17, 1945. Rayville, LA, United States. Height: 6'9". Weight: 235 lbs. Drafted: 1968 College: Houston HOF: 1990

YEAR	TEAM	GP	GS	MIN	PTS	FGM	FGA	FG%	3PM	3PA	3P%	FTM	FTA	FT%	ORB	DRB	TRB	AST	PF	DQ	STL	BLK	TO	MPG	PPG	RPG	APG	PCM
68-69	San Diego	82	....	**3695**	**2327**	**930**	**2082**	.447	....	....	....	467	746	.626	....	....	1406	113	266	2	....	....	....	45.1	**28.4**	17.1	1.4	.661
69-70	San Diego	82	....	**3665**	2256	914	**2020**	.452	....	....	....	428	622	.688	....	....	**1386**	162	270	5	....	....	....	**44.7**	27.5	16.9	2.0	.677
70-71	San Diego	82	....	3633	2350	948	**2215**	.428	....	....	....	454	676	.672	....	....	1362	186	225	1	....	....	....	44.3	28.7	16.6	2.3	.675
71-72	Houston	82	....	3461	2063	832	1918	.434	....	....	....	399	615	.649	....	....	1197	270	233	1	....	....	....	42.2	25.2	14.6	3.3	.656
72-73	Baltimore	81	....	3347	1717	713	1607	.444	....	....	....	291	434	.671	....	....	1177	127	232	3	....	....	....	41.3	21.2	14.5	1.6	.581
73-74	Washington	81	....	**3602**	1735	689	1627	.423	....	....	....	357	495	.721	**354**	**1109**	**1463**	163	252	1	86	240	....	**44.5**	21.4	**18.1**	2.0	.612
74-75	Washington	82	....	3465	1887	739	1668	.443	....	....	....	409	534	.766	221	783	1004	206	238	0	158	187	....	42.3	23.0	12.2	2.5	.587
75-76	Washington	80	....	2975	1585	649	1381	.470	....	....	....	287	457	.628	210	668	878	121	293	5	104	202	....	37.2	19.8	11.0	1.5	.555
76-77	Washington	82	....	**3364**	1942	760	1516	.501	....	....	....	422	614	.687	289	740	1029	158	312	1	87	220	....	41.0	23.7	12.5	1.9	.636
77-78	Washington	81	....	3246	1598	636	1409	.451	....	....	....	326	514	.634	335	740	1075	149	313	7	96	159	227	40.1	19.7	13.3	1.8	.565
78-79	Washington	82	....	3105	1789	720	1477	.487	....	....	....	349	534	.654	312	682	994	143	308	5	75	190	238	37.9	21.8	12.1	1.7	.632
79-80	Washington	81	....	3183	1859	761	1677	.454	3	13	.231	334	478	.699	269	627	896	129	309	9	62	189	219	39.3	23.0	11.1	1.6	.567
80-81	Washington	81	....	2931	1439	584	1296	.451	0	10	.000	271	439	.617	235	554	789	98	300	6	68	171	186	36.2	17.8	9.7	1.2	.495
81-82	Houston	82	82	3032	1318	519	1100	.472	0	5	.000	280	422	.664	267	480	747	144	287	4	62	104	205	37.0	16.1	9.1	1.8	.459

YEAR TEAM	GP	GS	MIN	PTS	FGM	FGA	FG%	3PM	3PA	3P%	FTM	FTA	FT%	ORB	DRB	TRB	AST	PF	DQ	STL	BLK	TO	MPG	PPG	RPG	APG	PCM
82-83 Houston	81	43	2302	1046	424	890	.476	2	4	.500	196	287	.683	199	417	616	158	232	2	50	81	203	28.4	12.9	7.6	2.0	.497
83-84 Houston	81	4	994	402	158	389	.406	0	2	.000	86	132	.652	87	173	260	71	123	1	16	28	81	12.3	5.0	3.2	0.9	.394
NBA Season Totals	1303	129	50000	27313	10976	24272	.452	5	34	.147	5356	7999	.670	2778	6973	16279	2398	4193	53	864	1771	1359	38.4	21.0	12.5	1.8	....
68-69 San Diego	6	....	278	155	60	114	.526	....	....	....	35	53	.660	....	....	83	5	21	0	....	....	....	46.3	25.8	13.8	0.8	.607
72-73 Baltimore	5	....	228	129	53	105	.505	....	....	....	23	33	.697	....	....	57	5	16	0	....	....	....	45.6	25.8	11.4	1.0	.561
73-74 Washington	7	....	323	181	76	143	.531	....	....	....	29	41	.707	31	80	111	21	23	0	5	15	....	46.1	25.9	15.9	3.0	.705
74-75 Washington	17	....	751	434	174	372	.468	....	....	....	86	127	.677	46	140	186	37	70	3	26	39	....	44.2	25.5	10.9	2.2	.558
75-76 Washington	7	....	305	140	54	122	.443	....	....	....	32	55	.582	16	72	88	10	24	0	5	28	....	43.6	20.0	12.6	1.4	.487
76-77 Washington	9	....	405	189	74	173	.428	....	....	....	41	59	.695	29	93	122	17	39	0	10	22	....	45.0	21.0	13.6	1.9	.503
77-78 Washington	21	....	868	457	189	385	.491	....	....	....	79	133	.594	103	176	279	43	86	2	32	52	58	41.3	21.8	13.3	2.0	.622
78-79 Washington	19	....	786	427	170	396	.429	....	....	....	87	130	.669	94	172	266	38	79	3	17	52	56	41.4	22.5	14.0	2.0	.587
79-80 Washington	2	....	92	40	16	41	.390	0	0	.000	8	10	.800	10	12	22	6	8	0	0	4	4	46.0	20.0	11.0	3.0	.428
81-82 Houston	3	3	124	42	17	50	.340	0	0	.000	8	15	.533	7	23	30	3	12	0	2	10	6	41.3	14.0	10.0	1.0	.317
NBA Playoff Totals	96	3	4160	2194	883	1901	.464	0	0	.000	428	656	.652	336	768	1244	185	378	8	97	222	124	43.3	22.9	13.0	1.9	....

• HAYES, Jim

Jim Hayes

Born: Feb. 18, 1948. Rockville Centre, NY, United States. Height: 6'3". Weight: 200 lbs. Drafted: 1970 College: Boston University

YEAR TEAM	GP	GS	MIN	PTS	FGM	FGA	FG%	3PM	3PA	3P%	FTM	FTA	FT%	ORB	DRB	TRB	AST	PF	DQ	STL	BLK	TO	MPG	PPG	RPG	APG	PCM
70-71 New York-A	47	....	494	144	46	109	.422	0	0	.000	52	67	.776	20	25	45	47	73	1	....	....	45	10.5	3.1	1.0	1.0	.305
ABA Season Totals	47	....	494	144	46	109	.422	0	0	.000	52	67	.776	20	25	45	47	73	1	....	....	45	10.5	3.1	1.0	1.0	....

• HAYES, Ray

Ray Hayes

Born: 1906. Height: 6' Weight: 180 lbs. Drafted: — College: Chicago

YEAR TEAM	GP	GS	MIN	PTS	FGM	FGA	FG%	3PM	3PA	3P%	FTM	FTA	FT%	ORB	DRB	TRB	AST	PF	DQ	STL	BLK	TO	MPG	PPG	RPG	APG	PCM
39-40 Chicago-N	4	....	....	3	1	....	....	....	....	....	1	....	....	....	....	....	....	....	....	....	....	....	....	0.8	....	....	....
NBL Season Totals	4	....	....	3	1	....	....	....	....	....	1	....	....	....	....	....	....	....	....	....	....	....	....	0.8	....	....	....

• HAYES, Steve

Steven Leonard Hayes

Born: Aug. 2, 1955. American Falls, ID, United States. Height: 7' Weight: 205 lbs. Drafted: 1977 College: Idaho State

YEAR TEAM	GP	GS	MIN	PTS	FGM	FGA	FG%	3PM	3PA	3P%	FTM	FTA	FT%	ORB	DRB	TRB	AST	PF	DQ	STL	BLK	TO	MPG	PPG	RPG	APG	PCM
81-82 San Antonio	9	0	75	23	8	18	.444	0	0	.000	7	12	.583	7	10	17	4	17	0	1	2	2	8.3	2.6	1.9	0.4	.327
81-82 Detroit	26	0	412	117	46	93	.495	0	0	.000	25	41	.610	32	68	100	24	54	0	3	18	18	15.8	4.5	3.8	0.9	.394
82-83 Cleveland	65	3	1058	237	104	217	.479	0	1	.000	29	51	.569	102	134	236	36	215	9	17	41	52	16.3	3.6	3.6	0.6	.270
83-84 Seattle	43	0	253	57	26	50	.520	0	0	.000	5	14	.357	19	43	62	13	52	0	5	18	13	5.9	1.3	1.4	0.3	.345
84-85 Philadelphia	11	0	101	22	10	18	.556	0	0	.000	2	4	.500	11	23	34	1	19	0	1	4	2	9.2	2.0	3.1	0.1	.399
85-86 Utah	58	0	397	89	39	87	.448	0	0	.000	11	36	.306	32	45	77	7	81	0	5	19	17	6.8	1.5	1.3	0.1	.203
NBA Season Totals	212	3	2296	545	233	483	.482	0	1	.000	79	158	.500	203	323	526	85	438	9	32	102	104	10.8	2.6	2.5	0.4	....
85-86 Utah	1	0	1	2	1	1	1.000	0	0	.000	0	0	.000	0	1	1	0	0	0	0	0	0	1.0	2.0	1.0	0.0	2.929
NBA Playoff Totals	1	0	1	2	1	1	1.000	0	0	.000	0	0	.000	0	1	1	0	0	0	0	0	0	1.0	2.0	1.0	0.0	....

• HAYWOOD, Brendan

Brendan Todd Haywood

Born: Nov. 11, 1979. New York, NY, United States. Height: 7' Weight: 268 lbs. Drafted: 2001 College: North Carolina

YEAR TEAM	GP	GS	MIN	PTS	FGM	FGA	FG%	3PM	3PA	3P%	FTM	FTA	FT%	ORB	DRB	TRB	AST	PF	DQ	STL	BLK	TO	MPG	PPG	RPG	APG	PCM
01-02 Washington	62	2	1266	315	109	221	.493	0	0	.000	97	160	.606	143	179	322	29	158	1	21	91	50	20.4	5.1	5.2	0.5	.389
02-03 Washington	81	69	1925	501	173	339	.510	0	0	.000	155	245	.633	192	212	404	29	225	3	32	119	65	23.8	6.2	5.0	0.4	.355
NBA Season Totals	143	71	3191	816	282	560	.504	0	0	.000	252	405	.622	335	391	726	58	383	4	53	210	115	22.3	5.7	5.1	0.4	....

• HAYWOOD, Spencer

Spencer Haywood

Born: Apr. 22, 1949. Silver City, MS, United States. Height: 6'8". Weight: 225 lbs. Drafted: 1971 College: Detroit

YEAR TEAM	GP	GS	MIN	PTS	FGM	FGA	FG%	3PM	3PA	3P%	FTM	FTA	FT%	ORB	DRB	TRB	AST	PF	DQ	STL	BLK	TO	MPG	PPG	RPG	APG	PCM
69-70 Denver-A	84	....	**3808**	**2519**	**986**	**1998**	.493	0	11	.000	547	705	.776	**533**	**1104**	**1637**	190	221	1	....	....	253	**45.3**	**30.0**	**19.5**	2.3	.817
70-71 Seattle	33	....	1162	680	260	579	.449	....	....	....	160	218	.734	....	....	396	48	84	1	....	....	....	35.2	20.6	12.0	1.5	.637
71-72 Seattle	73	....	3167	1914	717	1557	.461	....	....	....	480	586	.819	....	....	926	148	208	0	....	....	....	43.4	26.2	12.7	2.0	.638
72-73 Seattle	77	....	3259	2251	889	1868	.476	....	....	....	473	564	.839	....	....	995	196	213	2	....	....	....	42.3	29.2	12.9	2.5	.724
73-74 Seattle	75	....	3039	1761	694	1520	.457	....	....	....	373	458	.814	318	689	1007	240	198	2	65	106	....	40.5	23.5	13.4	3.2	.681
74-75 Seattle	68	....	2529	1525	608	1325	.459	....	....	....	309	381	.811	198	432	630	137	173	1	54	108	....	37.2	22.4	9.3	2.0	.594
75-76 New York	78	....	2892	1549	605	1360	.445	....	....	....	339	448	.757	234	644	878	92	255	1	53	80	....	37.1	19.9	11.3	1.2	.554
76-77 New York	31	....	1021	513	202	449	.450	....	....	....	109	131	.832	77	203	280	50	72	0	14	29	....	32.9	16.5	9.0	1.6	.546
77-78 New York	67	....	1765	920	412	852	.484	....	....	....	96	135	.711	141	301	442	126	188	1	37	72	141	26.3	13.7	6.6	1.9	.530
78-79 New York	34	....	1023	605	249	509	.489	....	....	....	107	146	.733	66	140	206	56	108	2	10	29	88	30.1	17.8	6.1	1.6	.497
78-79 New Orleans	34	....	1338	816	346	696	.497	....	....	....	124	146	.849	106	221	327	71	128	6	30	53	112	39.4	24.0	9.6	2.1	.583
79-80 LA Lakers	76	....	1544	736	288	591	.487	1	4	.250	159	206	.772	132	214	346	93	197	2	35	57	137	20.3	9.7	4.6	1.2	.470
81-82 Washington	76	63	2086	1009	395	829	.476	0	3	.000	219	260	.842	144	278	422	64	249	6	45	68	175	27.4	13.3	5.6	0.8	.420
82-83 Washington	38	25	775	313	125	312	.401	0	1	.000	63	87	.724	77	106	183	30	94	2	12	27	68	20.4	8.2	4.8	0.8	.339
NBA Season Totals	760	88	25600	14592	5790	12447	.465	1	8	.125	3011	3766	.800	1493	3228	7038	1351	2167	26	355	629	721	33.7	19.2	9.3	1.8	....
ABA Season Totals	84	....	3808	2519	986	1998	.493	0	11	.000	547	705	.776	533	1104	1637	190	221	1	....	....	253	45.3	30.0	19.5	2.3	....
Career Totals	844	88	29408	17111	6776	14445	.469	1	19	.053	3558	4471	.796	2026	4332	8675	1541	2388	27	355	629	974	34.8	20.3	10.3	1.8	....
69-70 Denver-A	12	....	568	440	185	362	.511	1	5	.200	69	83	.831	79	158	237	39	31	0	....	....	41	47.3	36.7	19.8	3.3	.910
74-75 Seattle	9	....	337	141	47	131	.359	....	....	....	47	61	.770	20	61	81	18	29	0	7	11	....	37.4	15.7	9.0	2.0	.418
77-78 New York	6	....	177	97	43	85	.506	....	....	....	11	11	1.000	19	23	42	12	24	1	2	5	10	29.5	16.2	7.0	2.0	.550
79-80 LA Lakers	11	....	145	63	25	53	.472	0	1	.000	13	16	.813	14	12	26	4	17	0	0	6	20	13.2	5.7	2.4	0.4	.302
81-82 Washington	7	7	231	140	57	115	.496	0	0	.000	26	35	.743	16	23	39	7	28	0	4	14	15	33.0	20.0	5.6	1.0	.501
NBA Playoff Totals	33	7	890	441	172	384	.448	0	1	.000	97	123	.789	69	119	188	41	98	1	13	36	45	27.0	13.4	5.7	1.2	....
ABA Playoff Totals	12	....	568	440	185	362	.511	1	5	.200	69	83	.831	79	158	237	39	31	0	....	....	41	**47.3**	**36.7**	**19.8**	3.3	....
Career Playoff Totals	45	7	1458	881	357	746	.479	1	6	.167	166	206	.806	148	277	425	80	129	1	13	36	86	32.4	19.6	9.4	1.8	....

YEAR TEAM	GP	GS	MIN	PTS	FGM	FGA	FG%	3PM	3PA	3P%	FTM	FTA	FT%	ORB	DRB	TRB	AST	PF	DQ	STL	BLK	TO	MPG	PPG	RPG	APG	PCM

• HAZEN, John — John W. Hazen

Born: Feb. 2, 1927.　Height: 6'2".　Weight: 172 lbs.　Drafted: —　College: Indiana State

YEAR TEAM	GP	GS	MIN	PTS	FGM	FGA	FG%	3PM	3PA	3P%	FTM	FTA	FT%	ORB	DRB	TRB	AST	PF	DQ	STL	BLK	TO	MPG	PPG	RPG	APG	PCM
48-49 Boston	6	....	....	18	6	17	.353	....	....	....	6	7	.857	....	....	....	3	10	....	....	....	....	....	3.0	....	0.5	....
NBA Season Totals	6	....	....	18	6	17	.353	....	....	....	6	7	.857	....	....	....	3	10	....	....	....	....	....	3.0	....	0.5	....

• HEAL, Shane — Shane Heal

Born: Sept. 6, 1971. Melbourne, Australia.　Height: 6'　Weight: 180 lbs.　Drafted: —　College: none (HS: Upper Yarra Tech, AUS)

YEAR TEAM	GP	GS	MIN	PTS	FGM	FGA	FG%	3PM	3PA	3P%	FTM	FTA	FT%	ORB	DRB	TRB	AST	PF	DQ	STL	BLK	TO	MPG	PPG	RPG	APG	PCM
96-97 Minnesota	43	0	236	75	26	97	.268	20	65	.308	3	5	.600	2	16	18	33	20	0	3	3	17	5.5	1.7	0.4	0.8	.171
NBA Season Totals	43	0	236	75	26	97	.268	20	65	.308	3	5	.600	2	16	18	33	20	0	3	3	17	5.5	1.7	0.4	0.8	....
96-97 Minnesota	2	0	3	6	2	2	1.000	2	2	1.000	0	0	.000	0	0	0	1	0	0	0	0	0	1.5	3.0	0.0	0.5	2.356
NBA Playoff Totals	2	0	3	6	2	2	1.000	2	2	1.000	0	0	.000	0	0	0	1	0	0	0	0	0	1.5	3.0	0.0	0.5	....

• HEANEY, Brian — Brian Patrick Heaney

Born: Sept. 3, 1946.　Height: 6'2".　Weight: 180 lbs.　Drafted: 1969　College: Acadia

YEAR TEAM	GP	GS	MIN	PTS	FGM	FGA	FG%	3PM	3PA	3P%	FTM	FTA	FT%	ORB	DRB	TRB	AST	PF	DQ	STL	BLK	TO	MPG	PPG	RPG	APG	PCM
69-70 Baltimore	14	....	70	28	13	24	.542	....	....	....	2	4	.500	....	....	4	6	17	0	....	....	....	5.0	2.0	0.3	0.4	.289
NBA Season Totals	14	....	70	28	13	24	.542	....	....	....	2	4	.500	....	....	4	6	17	0	....	....	....	5.0	2.0	0.3	0.4	....
69-70 Baltimore	6	....	7	0	0	2	.000	....	....	....	0	0	.000	....	....	1	1	0	0	....	....	....	1.2	0.0	0.2	0.2	.034
NBA Playoff Totals	6	....	7	0	0	2	.000	....	....	....	0	0	.000	....	....	1	1	0	0	....	....	....	1.2	0.0	0.2	0.2	....

• HEARD, Gar — Garfield Heard

Born: May 3, 1948. Hogansville, GA, United States.　Height: 6'6".　Weight: 219 lbs.　Drafted: 1970　College: Oklahoma

YEAR TEAM	GP	GS	MIN	PTS	FGM	FGA	FG%	3PM	3PA	3P%	FTM	FTA	FT%	ORB	DRB	TRB	AST	PF	DQ	STL	BLK	TO	MPG	PPG	RPG	APG	PCM
70-71 Seattle	65	....	1027	386	152	399	.381	....	....	....	82	125	.656	....	....	328	45	126	0	....	....	....	15.8	5.9	5.0	0.7	.423
71-72 Seattle	58	....	1499	459	190	474	.401	....	....	....	79	128	.617	....	....	442	55	126	2	....	....	....	25.8	7.9	7.6	0.9	.389
72-73 Seattle	3	....	17	9	4	9	.444	....	....	....	1	1	1.000	....	....	6	2	4	0	....	....	....	5.7	3.0	2.0	0.7	.613
72-73 Chicago	78	....	1535	807	346	815	.425	....	....	....	115	177	.650	....	....	447	58	167	0	....	....	....	19.7	10.3	5.7	0.7	.493
73-74 Buffalo	81	....	2889	1239	524	1205	.435	....	....	....	191	294	.650	270	677	947	180	300	3	136	230	....	35.7	15.3	11.7	2.2	.519
74-75 Buffalo	67	....	2148	742	318	819	.388	....	....	....	106	188	.564	185	481	666	190	242	2	106	120	....	32.1	11.1	9.9	2.8	.448
75-76 Buffalo	50	....	1527	496	207	492	.421	....	....	....	82	135	.607	138	373	511	126	183	0	66	55	....	30.5	9.9	10.2	2.5	.480
75-76 Phoenix	36	....	1220	446	185	409	.452	....	....	....	76	113	.673	109	249	358	64	120	2	51	41	....	33.9	12.4	9.9	1.8	.465
76-77 Phoenix	46	....	1363	446	173	457	.379	....	....	....	100	138	.725	120	320	440	89	139	2	55	55	....	29.6	9.7	9.6	1.9	.444
77-78 Phoenix	80	....	2099	620	265	625	.424	....	....	....	90	147	.612	166	486	652	132	213	0	129	101	120	26.2	7.8	8.2	1.7	.477
78-79 Phoenix	63	....	1213	395	162	367	.441	....	....	....	71	103	.689	98	253	351	60	141	1	53	57	63	19.3	6.3	5.6	1.0	.459
79-80 Phoenix	82	....	1403	406	171	410	.417	0	2	.000	64	86	.744	118	262	380	97	177	0	84	49	90	17.1	5.0	4.6	1.2	.420
80-81 San Diego	78	....	1631	377	149	396	.376	0	7	.000	79	101	.782	120	228	348	122	196	0	104	72	78	20.9	4.8	4.5	1.6	.363
NBA Season Totals	787	....	19571	6828	2846	6877	.414	0	9	.000	1136	1736	.654	1324	3329	5876	1220	2134	12	784	780	351	24.9	8.7	7.5	1.6	....
72-73 Chicago	2	....	9	4	2	4	.500	....	....	....	0	0	.000	....	....	3	0	4	0	....	....	....	4.5	2.0	1.5	0.0	.349
73-74 Buffalo	6	....	240	101	42	92	.457	....	....	....	17	24	.708	22	66	88	15	20	0	9	12	....	40.0	16.8	14.7	2.5	.580
74-75 Buffalo	7	....	250	82	38	96	.396	....	....	....	6	14	.429	24	52	76	18	28	0	9	8	....	35.7	11.7	10.9	2.6	.411
75-76 Phoenix	19	....	721	265	105	238	.441	....	....	....	55	81	.679	53	144	197	33	56	0	39	37	....	37.9	13.9	10.4	1.7	.447
77-78 Phoenix	2	....	62	13	6	17	.353	....	....	....	1	2	.500	4	12	16	5	4	0	2	4	2	31.0	6.5	8.0	2.5	.392
78-79 Phoenix	15	....	320	82	32	86	.372	....	....	....	18	30	.600	24	82	106	13	39	0	12	26	21	21.3	5.5	7.1	0.9	.423
79-80 Phoenix	8	....	223	55	22	56	.393	0	0	.000	11	15	.733	19	32	51	12	23	0	9	11	8	27.9	6.9	6.4	1.5	.368
NBA Playoff Totals	59	....	1825	602	247	589	.419	0	0	.000	108	166	.651	146	388	537	96	174	0	80	98	31	30.9	10.2	9.1	1.6	....

• HECOMOVICH, Pete — Peter Hecomovich

Born: June 13, 1918. Died: May 21, 1993.　Height: 6'4".　Weight: 205 lbs.　Drafted: —　College: —

YEAR TEAM	GP	GS	MIN	PTS	FGM	FGA	FG%	3PM	3PA	3P%	FTM	FTA	FT%	ORB	DRB	TRB	AST	PF	DQ	STL	BLK	TO	MPG	PPG	RPG	APG	PCM
40-41 Oshkosh-N	1	....	....	0	0	....	....	....	....	....	0	....	....	....	....	....	....	....	....	....	....	....	....	0.0	....	....	....
NBL Season Totals	1	....	....	0	0	....	....	....	....	....	0	....	....	....	....	....	....	....	....	....	....	....	....	0.0	....	....	....

• HEDDERICK, Herm — Herman Arthur Hedderick

Born: Jan. 1, 1930.　Height: 6'5".　Weight: 170 lbs.　Drafted: 1952　College: Canisius

YEAR TEAM	GP	GS	MIN	PTS	FGM	FGA	FG%	3PM	3PA	3P%	FTM	FTA	FT%	ORB	DRB	TRB	AST	PF	DQ	STL	BLK	TO	MPG	PPG	RPG	APG	PCM
54-55 New York	5	....	23	4	2	9	.222	....	....	....	0	1	.000	....	....	4	2	3	0	....	....	....	4.6	0.8	0.8	0.4	.119
NBA Season Totals	5	....	23	4	2	9	.222	....	....	....	0	1	.000	....	....	4	2	3	0	....	....	....	4.6	0.8	0.8	0.4	....

• HEGGS, Alvin — Alvin Heggs

Born: Dec. 12, 1967. Jacksonville, FL, United States.　Height: 6'8".　Weight: 225 lbs.　Drafted: —　College: Texas

YEAR TEAM	GP	GS	MIN	PTS	FGM	FGA	FG%	3PM	3PA	3P%	FTM	FTA	FT%	ORB	DRB	TRB	AST	PF	DQ	STL	BLK	TO	MPG	PPG	RPG	APG	PCM
95-96 Houston	4	0	14	8	3	5	.600	0	0	.000	2	3	.667	1	1	2	0	0	0	0	0	0	3.5	2.0	0.5	0.0	.538
NBA Season Totals	4	0	14	8	3	5	.600	0	0	.000	2	3	.667	1	1	2	0	0	0	0	0	0	3.5	2.0	0.5	0.0	....

• HEINSOHN, Tom — Thomas William (Ack-Ack) Heinsohn

Born: Aug. 26, 1934. Union City, NJ, United States.　Height: 6'7".　Weight: 218 lbs.　Drafted: 1956　College: Holy Cross　HOF: 1986

YEAR TEAM	GP	GS	MIN	PTS	FGM	FGA	FG%	3PM	3PA	3P%	FTM	FTA	FT%	ORB	DRB	TRB	AST	PF	DQ	STL	BLK	TO	MPG	PPG	RPG	APG	PCM
56-57 Boston	72	....	2150	1163	446	1123	.397	....	....	....	271	343	.790	....	....	705	117	304	12	....	....	....	29.9	16.2	9.8	1.6	.554
57-58 Boston	69	....	2206	1230	468	1226	.382	....	....	....	294	394	.746	....	....	705	125	274	6	....	....	....	32.0	17.8	10.2	1.8	.550
58-59 Boston	66	....	2089	1242	465	1192	.390	....	....	....	312	391	.798	....	....	638	164	271	11	....	....	....	31.7	18.8	9.7	2.5	.597
59-60 Boston	75	....	2420	1629	673	1590	.423	....	....	....	283	386	.733	....	....	794	171	275	8	....	....	....	32.3	21.7	10.6	2.3	.664
60-61 Boston	74	....	2256	1579	627	1566	.400	....	....	....	325	424	.767	....	....	732	141	260	7	....	....	....	30.5	21.3	9.9	1.9	.647

YEAR	TEAM	GP	GS	MIN	PTS	FGM	FGA	FG%	3PM	3PA	3P%	FTM	FTA	FT%	ORB	DRB	TRB	AST	PF	DQ	STL	BLK	TO	MPG	PPG	RPG	APG	PCM
61-62	Boston	79	....	2383	1742	692	1613	.429	....	....	....	358	437	.819	....	....	747	165	280	2	....	....	....	30.2	22.1	9.5	2.1	.700
62-63	Boston	76	....	2004	1440	550	1300	.423	....	....	....	340	407	.835	....	....	569	95	270	4	....	....	....	26.4	18.9	7.5	1.3	.638
63-64	Boston	76	....	2040	1257	487	1223	.398	....	....	....	283	342	.827	....	....	460	183	268	3	....	....	....	26.8	16.5	6.1	2.4	.558
64-65	Boston	67	....	1706	912	365	954	.383	....	....	....	182	229	.795	....	....	399	157	252	5	....	....	....	25.5	13.6	6.0	2.3	.495
NBA Season Totals		654	....	19254	12194	4773	11787	.405	....	....	....	2648	3353	.790	....	....	5749	1318	2454	58	....	....	....	29.4	18.6	8.8	2.0	....
56-57	Boston	10	....	370	226	90	231	.390	....	....	....	46	69	.667	....	....	117	20	40	1	....	....	....	37.0	22.6	11.7	2.0	.567
57-58	Boston	11	....	349	192	68	194	.351	....	....	....	56	72	.778	....	....	119	18	52	3	....	....	....	31.7	17.5	10.8	1.6	.530
58-59	Boston	11	....	348	219	91	220	.414	....	....	....	37	56	.661	....	....	98	32	41	0	....	....	....	31.6	19.9	8.9	2.9	.612
59-60	Boston	13	....	423	284	112	267	.419	....	....	....	60	80	.750	....	....	126	27	53	2	....	....	....	32.5	21.8	9.7	2.1	.634
60-61	Boston	10	....	291	197	82	201	.408	....	....	....	33	43	.767	....	....	99	20	36	1	....	....	....	29.1	19.7	9.9	2.0	.650
61-62	Boston	14	....	445	290	116	291	.399	....	....	....	58	76	.763	....	....	115	34	58	4	....	....	....	31.8	20.7	8.2	2.4	.573
62-63	Boston	13	....	413	321	123	270	.456	....	....	....	75	98	.765	....	....	116	15	55	2	....	....	....	31.8	24.7	8.9	1.2	.687
63-64	Boston	10	....	308	174	70	170	.412	....	....	....	34	42	.810	....	....	80	26	36	0	....	....	....	30.8	17.4	8.0	2.6	.562
64-65	Boston	12	....	276	152	66	181	.365	....	....	....	20	32	.625	....	....	84	23	46	1	....	....	....	23.0	12.7	7.0	1.9	.486
NBA Playoff Totals		104	....	3223	2055	818	2025	.404	....	....	....	419	568	.738	....	....	954	215	417	14	....	....	....	31.0	19.8	9.2	2.1	....

• HEMRIC, Dick

Ned Dixon (Dick) Hemric

Born: Aug. 29, 1933. Jonesville, NC, United States. Height: 6'6". Weight: 220 lbs. Drafted: 1955 College: Wake Forest

YEAR	TEAM	GP	GS	MIN	PTS	FGM	FGA	FG%	3PM	3PA	3P%	FTM	FTA	FT%	ORB	DRB	TRB	AST	PF	DQ	STL	BLK	TO	MPG	PPG	RPG	APG	PCM
55-56	Boston	71	....	1329	499	161	400	.403	....	....	....	177	273	.648	....	....	399	60	142	2	....	....	....	18.7	7.0	5.6	0.8	.455
56-57	Boston	67	....	1055	364	109	317	.344	....	....	....	146	210	.695	....	....	304	42	98	0	....	....	....	15.7	5.4	4.5	0.6	.406
NBA Season Totals		138	....	2384	863	270	717	.377	....	....	....	323	483	.669	....	....	703	102	240	2	....	....	....	17.3	6.3	5.1	0.7	....
55-56	Boston	3	....	54	19	5	24	.208	....	....	....	9	16	.563	....	....	22	1	7	0	....	....	....	18.0	6.3	7.3	0.3	.318
56-57	Boston	2	....	19	2	1	7	.143	....	....	....	0	0	.000	....	....	9	1	1	0	....	....	....	9.5	1.0	4.5	0.5	.269
NBA Playoff Totals		5	....	73	21	6	31	.194	....	....	....	9	16	.563	....	....	31	2	8	0	....	....	....	14.6	4.2	6.2	0.4	....

• HENDERSON, Alan

Alan Lybrooks Henderson

Born: Dec. 2, 1972. Indianapolis, IN, United States. Height: 6'9". Weight: 235 lbs. Drafted: 1995 College: Indiana

YEAR	TEAM	GP	GS	MIN	PTS	FGM	FGA	FG%	3PM	3PA	3P%	FTM	FTA	FT%	ORB	DRB	TRB	AST	PF	DQ	STL	BLK	TO	MPG	PPG	RPG	APG	PCM
95-96	Atlanta	79	4	1416	503	192	434	.442	0	3	.000	119	200	.595	164	192	356	51	217	5	44	43	87	17.9	6.4	4.5	0.6	.370
96-97	Atlanta	30	0	501	199	77	162	.475	0	0	.000	45	75	.600	47	69	116	23	73	1	21	6	30	16.7	6.6	3.9	0.8	.403
97-98	Atlanta	69	33	2000	986	365	753	.485	3	6	.500	253	388	.652	199	243	442	73	175	1	42	36	110	29.0	14.3	6.4	1.1	.472
98-99	Atlanta	38	37	1142	474	187	423	.442	0	1	.000	100	149	.671	100	150	250	28	96	1	33	19	58	30.1	12.5	6.6	0.7	.392
99-00	Atlanta	82	82	2775	1083	429	930	.461	1	10	.100	224	334	.671	265	306	571	77	233	3	81	54	139	33.8	13.2	7.0	0.9	.384
00-01	Atlanta	73	42	1810	769	298	671	.444	0	1	.000	173	271	.638	180	226	406	50	164	2	51	29	126	24.8	10.5	5.6	0.7	.384
01-02	Atlanta	26	1	422	143	59	116	.509	1	1	1.000	24	45	.533	31	66	97	11	40	0	11	15	21	16.2	5.5	3.7	0.4	.399
02-03	Atlanta	82	3	1494	394	153	327	.468	0	2	.000	88	138	.638	156	242	398	41	168	1	33	32	61	18.2	4.8	4.9	0.5	.366
NBA Season Totals		479	202	11560	4551	1760	3816	.461	5	24	.208	1026	1600	.641	1142	1494	2636	354	1166	14	316	234	632	24.1	9.5	5.5	0.7	....
95-96	Atlanta	10	0	145	53	23	40	.575	0	0	.000	7	10	.700	17	10	27	7	20	0	1	4	9	14.5	5.3	2.7	0.7	.381
96-97	Atlanta	10	0	136	58	19	34	.559	0	0	.000	20	26	.769	11	22	33	0	26	0	1	3	7	13.6	5.8	3.3	0.0	.420
97-98	Atlanta	4	4	126	51	20	38	.526	0	1	.000	11	18	.611	10	12	22	4	13	0	3	1	6	31.5	12.8	5.5	1.0	.381
98-99	Atlanta	1	0	4	0	0	0	.000	0	0	.000	0	0	.000	0	0	0	0	1	0	0	0	0	4.0	0.0	0.0	0.0	-.111
NBA Playoff Totals		25	4	411	162	62	112	.554	0	1	.000	38	54	.704	38	44	82	11	60	0	5	8	22	16.4	6.5	3.3	0.4	....

• HENDERSON, Cedric

Cedric Earl Henderson

Born: Mar. 11, 1975. Memphis, TN, United States. Height: 6'7". Weight: 215 lbs. Drafted: 1997 College: Memphis

YEAR	TEAM	GP	GS	MIN	PTS	FGM	FGA	FG%	3PM	3PA	3P%	FTM	FTA	FT%	ORB	DRB	TRB	AST	PF	DQ	STL	BLK	TO	MPG	PPG	RPG	APG	PCM
97-98	Cleveland	82	71	2527	832	348	725	.480	0	4	.000	136	190	.716	71	254	325	168	238	3	96	45	164	30.8	10.1	4.0	2.0	.321
98-99	Cleveland	50	48	1517	454	189	453	.417	2	12	.167	74	91	.813	45	152	197	113	136	2	58	24	97	30.3	9.1	3.9	2.3	.289
99-00	Cleveland	61	7	1107	328	129	326	.396	1	15	.067	69	104	.663	34	106	140	55	99	0	39	17	68	18.1	5.4	2.3	0.9	.239
00-01	Cleveland	55	10	961	235	102	262	.389	1	8	.125	30	46	.652	19	71	90	79	101	0	29	23	63	17.5	4.3	1.6	1.4	.205
01-02	Golden State	12	0	70	36	15	31	.484	2	4	.500	4	7	.571	1	2	3	4	4	0	6	2	8	5.8	3.0	0.3	0.3	.363
NBA Season Totals		260	136	6182	1885	783	1797	.436	6	43	.140	313	438	.715	170	585	755	419	578	5	228	111	400	23.8	7.3	2.9	1.6	....
97-98	Cleveland	4	4	157	30	11	28	.393	0	1	.000	8	13	.615	4	13	17	11	14	0	6	0	13	39.3	7.5	4.3	2.8	.171
NBA Playoff Totals		4	4	157	30	11	28	.393	0	1	.000	8	13	.615	4	13	17	11	14	0	6	0	13	39.3	7.5	4.3	2.8	....

• HENDERSON, Cedric

Cedric Henderson

Born: Oct. 3, 1965. Marietta, GA, United States. Height: 6'8". Weight: 210 lbs. Drafted: 1986 College: Georgia

YEAR	TEAM	GP	GS	MIN	PTS	FGM	FGA	FG%	3PM	3PA	3P%	FTM	FTA	FT%	ORB	DRB	TRB	AST	PF	DQ	STL	BLK	TO	MPG	PPG	RPG	APG	PCM
86-87	Atlanta	6	0	10	5	2	5	.400	0	0	.000	1	1	1.000	2	1	3	0	1	0	0	0	1	1.7	0.8	0.5	0.0	.360
86-87	Milwaukee	2	0	6	6	2	3	.667	0	0	.000	2	2	1.000	1	4	5	0	1	0	0	0	3	3.0	3.0	2.5	0.0	1.078
NBA Season Totals		8	0	16	11	4	8	.500	0	0	.000	3	3	1.000	3	5	8	0	2	0	0	0	4	2.0	1.4	1.0	0.0	....

• HENDERSON, Curt

Curt Henderson

Born: 1917. Height: 5'8". Weight: 150 lbs. Drafted: — College: Southern Illinois

YEAR	TEAM	GP	GS	MIN	PTS	FGM	FGA	FG%	3PM	3PA	3P%	FTM	FTA	FT%	ORB	DRB	TRB	AST	PF	DQ	STL	BLK	TO	MPG	PPG	RPG	APG	PCM
46-47	Detroit-N	4	....	....	4	1	....	....	....	....	....	2	3	.667	....	....	....	....	....	....	....	....	....	1.0	....	....	....
NBL Season Totals		4	....	....	4	1	....	....	....	....	....	2	3		....	....	....	....	....	....	....	....	....	1.0	....	....	....

• HENDERSON, Dave
David McKinley Henderson

Born: July 21, 1964. Henderson, NC, United States. Height: 6'5". Weight: 195 lbs. Drafted: 1986 College: Duke

YEAR	TEAM	GP	GS	MIN	PTS	FGM	FGA	FG%	3PM	3PA	3P%	FTM	FTA	FT%	ORB	DRB	TRB	AST	PF	DQ	STL	BLK	TO	MPG	PPG	RPG	APG	PCM
87-88	Philadelphia	22	1	351	126	47	116	.405	0	1	.000	32	47	.681	11	24	35	34	41	0	12	5	40	16.0	5.7	1.6	1.5	.237
NBA Season Totals		22	1	351	126	47	116	.405	0	1	.000	32	47	.681	11	24	35	34	41	0	12	5	40	16.0	5.7	1.6	1.5	....

• HENDERSON, Gerald
Jerome McKinley Henderson

Born: Jan. 16, 1956. Richmond, VA, United States. Height: 6'2". Weight: 175 lbs. Drafted: 1978 College: Virginia Commonwealth

YEAR	TEAM	GP	GS	MIN	PTS	FGM	FGA	FG%	3PM	3PA	3P%	FTM	FTA	FT%	ORB	DRB	TRB	AST	PF	DQ	STL	BLK	TO	MPG	PPG	RPG	APG	PCM
79-80	Boston	76	....	1061	473	191	382	.500	2	6	.333	89	129	.690	37	46	83	147	96	0	45	15	106	14.0	6.2	1.1	1.9	.408
80-81	Boston	82	....	1608	636	261	579	.451	1	16	.063	113	157	.720	43	89	132	213	177	0	79	12	164	19.6	7.8	1.6	2.6	.330
81-82	Boston	82	31	1844	833	353	705	.501	2	12	.167	125	172	.727	47	105	152	252	199	3	82	11	148	22.5	10.2	1.9	3.1	.410
82-83	Boston	82	9	1551	671	286	618	.463	3	16	.188	96	133	.722	57	67	124	195	190	6	95	3	131	18.9	8.2	1.5	2.4	.365
83-84	Boston	78	78	2088	908	376	718	.524	20	57	.351	136	177	.768	68	79	147	300	209	1	117	14	164	26.8	11.6	1.9	3.8	.431
84-85	Seattle	79	78	2648	1062	427	891	.479	9	38	.237	199	255	.780	71	119	190	559	196	1	140	9	229	33.5	13.4	2.4	7.1	.458
85-86	Seattle	82	82	2568	1071	434	900	.482	18	52	.346	185	223	.830	89	98	187	487	230	2	138	11	180	31.3	13.1	2.3	5.9	.460
86-87	Seattle	6	6	155	67	25	50	.500	0	3	.000	17	18	.944	6	3	9	32	17	0	6	0	15	25.8	11.2	1.5	5.3	.449
86-87	New York	68	53	1890	738	273	624	.438	19	74	.257	173	212	.816	44	122	166	439	191	1	95	11	156	27.8	10.9	2.4	6.5	.466
87-88	New York	6	2	69	14	5	14	.357	2	4	.500	2	2	1.000	1	9	10	13	14	0	2	0	8	11.5	2.3	1.7	2.2	.242
87-88	Philadelphia	69	3	1436	581	189	439	.431	67	159	.421	136	168	.810	26	71	97	218	173	0	67	5	124	20.8	8.4	1.4	3.2	.367
88-89	Philadelphia	65	0	986	425	144	348	.414	33	107	.308	104	127	.819	17	51	68	140	121	1	42	3	72	15.2	6.5	1.0	2.2	.361
89-90	Milwaukee	11	0	129	27	11	26	.423	3	7	.429	2	2	1.000	3	9	12	13	14	0	8	0	8	11.7	2.5	1.1	1.2	.244
89-90	Detroit	46	0	335	108	42	83	.506	14	31	.452	10	13	.769	8	23	31	61	36	0	8	2	14	7.3	2.3	0.7	1.3	.422
90-91	Detroit	23	10	392	123	50	117	.427	7	21	.333	16	21	.762	8	29	37	62	43	0	12	2	28	17.0	5.3	1.6	2.7	.321
91-92	Houston	8	0	34	12	4	11	.364	0	3	.000	4	6	.667	1	1	2	5	4	0	0	0	4	4.3	1.5	0.3	0.6	.183
91-92	Detroit	8	0	62	24	8	21	.381	3	5	.600	5	5	1.000	0	6	6	5	8	0	3	0	4	7.8	3.0	0.8	0.6	.294
NBA Season Totals		871	352	18856	7773	3079	6526	.472	203	611	.332	1412	1820	.776	526	927	1453	3141	1918	15	939	98	1555	21.6	8.9	1.7	3.6	....
79-80	Boston	9	....	101	42	15	37	.405	0	2	.000	12	20	.600	4	6	10	12	8	0	4	0	7	11.2	4.7	1.1	1.3	.340
80-81	Boston	16	....	228	92	41	86	.477	0	1	.000	10	12	.833	10	15	25	26	24	0	10	3	12	14.3	5.8	1.6	1.6	.400
81-82	Boston	12	4	310	100	38	93	.409	0	2	.000	24	35	.686	12	13	25	48	30	0	14	2	25	25.8	8.3	2.1	4.0	.313
82-83	Boston	7	7	187	76	35	85	.412	0	3	.000	6	7	.857	8	6	14	31	25	1	11	1	14	26.7	10.9	2.0	4.4	.342
83-84	Boston	23	23	616	287	115	237	.485	3	11	.273	54	75	.720	23	29	52	97	78	0	34	1	41	26.8	12.5	2.3	4.2	.445
88-89	Philadelphia	3	0	69	24	10	25	.400	2	7	.286	2	6	.333	3	4	7	5	10	0	2	0	5	23.0	8.0	2.3	1.7	.183
89-90	Detroit	8	0	19	2	1	5	.200	0	3	.000	0	0	.000	2	1	3	4	3	0	2	0	1	2.4	0.3	0.4	0.5	.255
90-91	Detroit	10	1	40	8	4	16	.250	0	3	.000	0	0	.000	1	0	1	6	4	0	1	0	0	4.0	0.8	0.1	0.6	.080
NBA Playoff Totals		88	35	1570	631	259	584	.443	5	32	.156	108	155	.697	63	74	137	229	182	1	78	7	105	17.8	7.2	1.6	2.6	....

• HENDERSON, Jerome
Jerome D. Henderson

Born: Oct. 5, 1959. Los Angeles, CA, United States. Height: 6'11". Weight: 230 lbs. Drafted: — College: New Mexico

YEAR	TEAM	GP	GS	MIN	PTS	FGM	FGA	FG%	3PM	3PA	3P%	FTM	FTA	FT%	ORB	DRB	TRB	AST	PF	DQ	STL	BLK	TO	MPG	PPG	RPG	APG	PCM
85-86	LA Lakers	1	0	3	4	2	3	.667	0	0	.000	0	0	.000	0	1	1	0	1	0	0	0	0	3.0	4.0	1.0	0.0	1.179
86-87	Milwaukee	6	0	36	12	4	13	.308	0	0	.000	4	4	1.000	2	5	7	0	12	0	1	1	6	6.0	2.0	1.2	0.0	.023
NBA Season Totals		7	0	39	16	6	16	.375	0	0	.000	4	4	1.000	2	6	8	0	13	0	1	1	6	5.6	2.3	1.1	0.0	....
86-87	Milwaukee	1	0	1	0	0	0	.000	0	0	.000	0	0	.000	0	0	0	0	1	0	0	0	0	1.0	0.0	0.0	0.0	-.466
NBA Playoff Totals		1	0	1	0	0	0	.000	0	0	.000	0	0	.000	0	0	0	0	1	0	0	0	0	1.0	0.0	0.0	0.0	....

• HENDERSON, Kevin
Kevin Dwayne Henderson

Born: Mar. 22, 1964. Baltimore, MD, United States. Height: 6'4". Weight: 195 lbs. Drafted: 1986 College: Cal State Fullerton

YEAR	TEAM	GP	GS	MIN	PTS	FGM	FGA	FG%	3PM	3PA	3P%	FTM	FTA	FT%	ORB	DRB	TRB	AST	PF	DQ	STL	BLK	TO	MPG	PPG	RPG	APG	PCM
86-87	Golden State	5	0	45	8	3	8	.375	0	0	.000	2	2	1.000	1	2	3	11	9	0	1	0	4	9.0	1.6	0.6	2.2	.243
87-88	Golden State	12	2	170	48	19	48	.396	0	1	.000	10	14	.714	6	11	17	21	24	0	8	0	16	14.2	4.0	1.4	1.8	.228
87-88	Cleveland	5	0	20	9	2	5	.400	0	0	.000	5	12	.417	3	1	4	2	2	0	0	0	2	4.0	1.8	0.8	0.4	.301
NBA Season Totals		22	2	235	65	24	61	.393	0	1	.000	17	28	.607	10	14	24	34	35	0	9	0	22	10.7	3.0	1.1	1.5	....

• HENDERSON, Milton
Milton Henderson Jr.

Born: Oct. 30, 1976. Bakersfield, CA, United States. Height: 6'8". Weight: 226 lbs. Drafted: 1998 College: UCLA

YEAR	TEAM	GP	GS	MIN	PTS	FGM	FGA	FG%	3PM	3PA	3P%	FTM	FTA	FT%	ORB	DRB	TRB	AST	PF	DQ	STL	BLK	TO	MPG	PPG	RPG	APG	PCM
98-99	Vancouver	30	0	331	97	35	96	.365	2	5	.400	25	45	.556	20	27	47	22	29	1	9	4	18	11.0	3.2	1.6	0.7	.250
NBA Season Totals		30	0	331	97	35	96	.365	2	5	.400	25	45	.556	20	27	47	22	29	1	9	4	18	11.0	3.2	1.6	0.7	....

• HENDERSON, Tom
Thomas Edward Henderson

Born: Jan. 26, 1952. Newberry, SC, United States. Height: 6'3". Weight: 190 lbs. Drafted: 1974 College: Hawaii

YEAR	TEAM	GP	GS	MIN	PTS	FGM	FGA	FG%	3PM	3PA	3P%	FTM	FTA	FT%	ORB	DRB	TRB	AST	PF	DQ	STL	BLK	TO	MPG	PPG	RPG	APG	PCM
74-75	Atlanta	79	....	2131	902	367	893	.411	....	....	....	168	241	.697	51	161	212	314	149	0	105	7	....	27.0	11.4	2.7	4.0	.422
75-76	Atlanta	81	....	2900	1154	469	1136	.413	....	....	....	216	305	.708	58	207	265	374	195	1	137	10	....	35.8	14.2	3.3	4.6	.384
76-77	Atlanta	46	....	1568	518	196	453	.433	....	....	....	126	168	.750	18	106	124	386	74	0	79	8	....	34.1	11.3	2.7	8.4	.505
76-77	Washington	41	....	1223	457	175	373	.469	....	....	....	107	145	.738	25	90	115	212	74	0	59	9	....	29.8	11.1	2.8	5.2	.473
77-78	Washington	75	....	2315	857	339	784	.432	....	....	....	179	240	.746	66	127	193	406	131	0	93	15	195	30.9	11.4	2.6	5.4	.403
78-79	Washington	70	....	2081	754	299	641	.466	....	....	....	156	195	.800	51	112	163	419	123	0	87	10	147	29.7	10.8	2.3	6.0	.450
79-80	Houston	66	....	1551	364	154	323	.477	0	2	.000	56	77	.727	34	77	111	274	107	1	55	4	99	23.5	5.5	1.7	4.2	.334
80-81	Houston	66	....	1411	352	137	332	.413	0	3	.000	78	95	.821	30	74	104	307	111	1	53	4	92	21.4	5.3	1.6	4.7	.364
81-82	Houston	75	23	1721	471	183	403	.454	0	2	.000	105	150	.700	33	105	138	306	120	0	55	7	105	22.9	6.3	1.8	4.1	.354
82-83	Houston	51	2	789	259	107	263	.407	0	2	.000	45	57	.789	18	51	69	138	57	0	37	2	51	15.5	5.1	1.4	2.7	.368
NBA Season Totals		650	25	17690	6088	2426	5601	.433	0	9	.000	1236	1673	.739	384	1110	1494	3136	1141	3	760	76	689	27.2	9.4	2.3	4.8	....
76-77	Washington	9	....	322	122	48	108	.444	....	....	....	26	36	.722	8	12	20	63	24	1	11	2	....	35.8	13.6	2.2	7.0	.449
77-78	Washington	21	....	597	202	72	173	.416	....	....	....	58	79	.734	17	30	47	106	36	0	27	5	31	28.4	9.6	2.2	5.0	.419
78-79	Washington	19	....	559	166	64	175	.366	....	....	....	38	52	.731	15	20	35	107	45	1	17	6	40	29.4	8.7	1.8	5.6	.311

YEAR	TEAM	GP	GS	MIN	PTS	FGM	FGA	FG%	3PM	3PA	3P%	FTM	FTA	FT%	ORB	DRB	TRB	AST	PF	DQ	STL	BLK	TO	MPG	PPG	RPG	APG	PCM
79-80	Houston	7	....	203	56	22	46	.478	0	1	.000	12	15	.800	5	11	16	42	19	0	7	4	11	29.0	8.0	2.3	6.0	.418
80-81	Houston	21	....	615	141	59	132	.447	0	1	.000	23	28	.821	14	41	55	104	39	0	17	1	34	29.3	6.7	2.6	5.0	.330
81-82	Houston	3	3	68	14	5	16	.313	0	0	.000	4	4	1.000	5	3	8	9	5	0	0	0	4	22.7	4.7	2.7	3.0	.220
NBA Playoff Totals		80	3	2364	701	270	650	.415	0	2	.000	161	214	.752	64	117	181	431	168	2	79	18	120	29.6	8.8	2.3	5.4	....

• HENDRICKSON, Mark

Mark Allan Hendrickson

Born: June 23, 1974. Mount Vernon, WA, United States.   Height: 6'9".   Weight: 220 lbs.   Drafted: 1996   College: Washington State

YEAR	TEAM	GP	GS	MIN	PTS	FGM	FGA	FG%	3PM	3PA	3P%	FTM	FTA	FT%	ORB	DRB	TRB	AST	PF	DQ	STL	BLK	TO	MPG	PPG	RPG	APG	PCM
96-97	Philadelphia	29	1	301	85	32	77	.416	3	12	.250	18	26	.692	35	57	92	3	32	1	10	4	15	10.4	2.9	3.2	0.1	.374
97-98	Sacramento	48	1	737	163	58	149	.389	0	5	.000	47	57	.825	33	110	143	41	60	0	26	9	29	15.4	3.4	3.0	0.9	.310
98-99	New Jersey	22	6	399	120	39	88	.443	0	1	.000	42	50	.840	27	41	68	13	39	0	12	1	15	18.1	5.5	3.1	0.6	.322
99-00	Cleveland	10	0	47	12	5	7	.714	0	0	.000	2	2	1.000	2	9	11	3	7	0	2	1	3	4.7	1.2	1.1	0.3	.431
99-00	New Jersey	5	0	24	1	0	1	.000	0	0	.000	1	2	.500	1	1	2	3	1	0	0	0	0	4.8	0.2	0.4	0.6	.178
NBA Season Totals		114	8	1508	381	134	322	.416	3	18	.167	110	137	.803	98	218	316	63	139	1	50	15	62	13.2	3.3	2.8	0.6	....

• HENNESSY, Larry

Lawrence E. Hennessy

Born: May 20, 1929.   Height: 6'3".   Weight: 185 lbs.   Drafted: 1953   College: Villanova

YEAR	TEAM	GP	GS	MIN	PTS	FGM	FGA	FG%	3PM	3PA	3P%	FTM	FTA	FT%	ORB	DRB	TRB	AST	PF	DQ	STL	BLK	TO	MPG	PPG	RPG	APG	PCM
55-56	Philadelphia	53	....	444	196	85	247	.344	....	....	....	26	32	.813	....	....	49	46	37	0	....	....	....	8.4	3.7	0.9	0.9	.339
56-57	Syracuse	21	....	373	135	56	175	.320	....	....	....	23	32	.719	....	....	45	27	28	0	....	....	....	17.8	6.4	2.1	1.3	.268
NBA Season Totals		74	....	817	331	141	422	.334	....	....	....	49	64	.766	....	....	94	73	65	0	....	....	....	11.0	4.5	1.3	1.0	....
55-56	Philadelphia	3	....	11	0	0	9	.000	....	....	....	0	0	.000	....	....	1	2	1	0	....	....	....	3.7	0.0	0.3	0.7	-.363
NBA Playoff Totals		3	....	11	0	0	9	.000	....	....	....	0	0	.000	....	....	1	2	1	0	....	....	....	3.7	0.0	0.3	0.7	....

• HENRIKSEN, Don

Donald Anton Henriksen

Born: Oct. 10, 1929.   Height: 6'7".   Weight: 225 lbs.   Drafted: —   College: California

YEAR	TEAM	GP	GS	MIN	PTS	FGM	FGA	FG%	3PM	3PA	3P%	FTM	FTA	FT%	ORB	DRB	TRB	AST	PF	DQ	STL	BLK	TO	MPG	PPG	RPG	APG	PCM
52-53	Baltimore	68	....	2263	574	199	475	.419	....	....	....	176	281	.626	....	....	506	129	242	12	....	....	....	33.3	8.4	7.4	1.9	.344
54-55	Baltimore	14	....	429	107	28	91	.308	....	....	....	51	65	.785	....	....	49	32	42	2	....	....	....	30.6	7.6	3.5	2.3	.269
54-55	Rochester	56	....	1235	308	111	315	.352	....	....	....	86	130	.662	....	....	435	79	148	0	....	....	....	22.1	5.5	7.8	1.4	.411
NBA Season Totals		138	....	3927	989	338	881	.384	....	....	....	313	476	.658	....	....	990	240	432	14	....	....	....	28.5	7.2	7.2	1.7	....
52-53	Baltimore	2	....	94	25	10	15	.667	....	....	....	5	9	.556	....	....	24	8	11	1	....	....	....	47.0	12.5	12.0	4.0	.463
54-55	Rochester	3	....	70	13	3	12	.250	....	....	....	7	10	.700	....	....	16	3	5	0	....	....	....	23.3	4.3	5.3	1.0	.271
NBA Playoff Totals		5	....	164	38	13	27	.481	....	....	....	12	19	.632	....	....	40	11	16	1	....	....	....	32.8	7.6	8.0	2.2	....

• HENRY, Al

Albert J. (The Tree) Henry Jr.

Born: Feb. 9, 1949.   Height: 6'9".   Weight: 190 lbs.   Drafted: 1970   College: Wisconsin

YEAR	TEAM	GP	GS	MIN	PTS	FGM	FGA	FG%	3PM	3PA	3P%	FTM	FTA	FT%	ORB	DRB	TRB	AST	PF	DQ	STL	BLK	TO	MPG	PPG	RPG	APG	PCM
70-71	Philadelphia	6	....	26	7	1	6	.167	....	....	....	5	7	.714	....	....	11	0	1	0	....	....	....	4.3	1.2	1.8	0.0	.418
71-72	Philadelphia	43	....	421	187	68	156	.436	....	....	....	51	73	.699	....	....	137	8	42	0	....	....	....	9.8	4.3	3.2	0.2	.501
NBA Season Totals		49	....	447	194	69	162	.426	....	....	....	56	80	.700	....	....	148	8	43	0	....	....	....	9.1	4.0	3.0	0.2	....

• HENRY, Bill

William Gambrell (Big Bill) Henry

Born: Dec. 27, 1924. Dallas, TX, United States. Died: Dec.1985.   Height: 6'9".   Weight: 215 lbs.   Drafted: —   College: Rice

YEAR	TEAM	GP	GS	MIN	PTS	FGM	FGA	FG%	3PM	3PA	3P%	FTM	FTA	FT%	ORB	DRB	TRB	AST	PF	DQ	STL	BLK	TO	MPG	PPG	RPG	APG	PCM
48-49	Fort Wayne	32	....	....	317	96	300	.320	....	....	....	125	203	.616	....	....	....	55	110	....	....	....	....	9.9	....	1.7	....	
49-50	Fort Wayne	44	....	....	214	65	209	.311	....	....	....	84	125	.672	....	....	....	39	99	....	....	....	....	4.9	....	0.9	....	
49-50	Tri-Cities	19	....	....	82	24	69	.348	....	....	....	34	51	.667	....	....	....	9	23	....	....	....	....	4.3	....	0.5	....	
NBA Season Totals		95	....	....	613	185	578	.320	....	....	....	243	379	.641	....	....	....	103	232	....	....	....	....	6.5	....	1.1	....	
49-50	Tri-Cities	3	....	....	9	2	17	.118	....	....	....	5	9	.556	....	....	....	5	14	....	....	....	....	3.0	....	1.7	....	
NBA Playoff Totals		3	....	....	9	2	17	.118	....	....	....	5	9	.556	....	....	....	5	14	....	....	....	....	3.0	....	1.7	....	

• HENRY, Carl

Carl J. Henry

Born: Aug. 16, 1960. Hollis, OK, United States.   Height: 6'6".   Weight: 205 lbs.   Drafted: 1984   College: Kansas

YEAR	TEAM	GP	GS	MIN	PTS	FGM	FGA	FG%	3PM	3PA	3P%	FTM	FTA	FT%	ORB	DRB	TRB	AST	PF	DQ	STL	BLK	TO	MPG	PPG	RPG	APG	PCM
85-86	Sacramento	28	0	149	78	31	67	.463	4	10	.400	12	17	.706	8	11	19	4	11	0	5	0	8	5.3	2.8	0.7	0.1	.378
NBA Season Totals		28	0	149	78	31	67	.463	4	10	.400	12	17	.706	8	11	19	4	11	0	5	0	8	5.3	2.8	0.7	0.1	....
85-86	Sacramento	1	0	2	3	1	1	1.000	1	1	1.000	0	0	.000	0	0	0	0	0	0	0	0	0	2.0	3.0	0.0	0.0	1.500
NBA Playoff Totals		1	0	2	3	1	1	1.000	1	1	1.000	0	0	.000	0	0	0	0	0	0	0	0	0	2.0	3.0	0.0	0.0	....

• HENRY, Connor

Conner Henry

Born: July 21, 1963. Claremont, CA, United States.   Height: 6'7".   Weight: 195 lbs.   Drafted: 1986   College: Cal State Santa Barbara

YEAR	TEAM	GP	GS	MIN	PTS	FGM	FGA	FG%	3PM	3PA	3P%	FTM	FTA	FT%	ORB	DRB	TRB	AST	PF	DQ	STL	BLK	TO	MPG	PPG	RPG	APG	PCM
86-87	Houston	18	0	92	24	8	33	.242	1	11	.091	7	10	.700	0	7	7	8	7	0	3	0	9	5.1	1.3	0.4	0.4	.060
86-87	Boston	36	0	231	98	38	103	.369	12	31	.387	10	17	.588	7	20	27	27	27	0	6	1	18	6.4	2.7	0.8	0.8	.283
87-88	Boston	10	0	81	34	11	28	.393	3	8	.375	9	10	.900	2	8	10	12	11	0	1	1	9	8.1	3.4	1.0	1.2	.348
87-88	Milwaukee	14	2	145	32	13	41	.317	2	6	.333	4	7	.571	5	14	19	29	11	0	4	1	14	10.4	2.3	1.4	2.1	.274
87-88	Sacramento	15	0	207	117	38	81	.469	15	31	.484	26	30	.867	6	14	20	26	15	0	7	3	17	13.8	7.8	1.3	1.7	.522
NBA Season Totals		93	2	756	305	108	286	.378	33	87	.379	56	74	.757	20	63	83	102	71	0	21	6	67	8.1	3.3	0.9	1.1	....
86-87	Boston	11	0	35	22	8	16	.500	1	5	.200	5	10	.500	3	3	6	0	3	0	0	0	4	3.2	2.0	0.5	0.0	.363
NBA Playoff Totals		11	0	35	22	8	16	.500	1	5	.200	5	10	.500	3	3	6	0	3	0	0	0	4	3.2	2.0	0.5	0.0	....

YEAR	TEAM	GP	GS	MIN	PTS	FGM	FGA	FG%	3PM	3PA	3P%	FTM	FTA	FT%	ORB	DRB	TRB	AST	PF	DQ	STL	BLK	TO	MPG	PPG	RPG	APG	PCM

• HENRY, Skeeter
Herman (Skeeter) Henry

Born: Dec. 8, 1967. Dallas, TX, United States.   Height: 6'7".   Weight: 190 lbs.   Drafted: —   College: Oklahoma

YEAR	TEAM	GP	GS	MIN	PTS	FGM	FGA	FG%	3PM	3PA	3P%	FTM	FTA	FT%	ORB	DRB	TRB	AST	PF	DQ	STL	BLK	TO	MPG	PPG	RPG	APG	PCM
93-94	Phoenix	4	0	15	4	1	5	.200	0	2	.000	2	4	.500	0	2	2	4	1	0	0	0	1	3.8	1.0	0.5	1.0	.280
NBA Season Totals		4	0	15	4	1	5	.200	0	2	.000	2	4	.500	0	2	2	4	1	0	0	0	1	3.8	1.0	0.5	1.0	....
93-94	Phoenix	3	0	16	2	1	6	.167	0	2	.000	0	0	.000	1	2	3	3	1	0	0	0	1	5.3	0.7	1.0	1.0	.127
NBA Playoff Totals		3	0	16	2	1	6	.167	0	2	.000	0	0	.000	1	2	3	3	1	0	0	0	1	5.3	0.7	1.0	1.0	

• HENSON, Steve
Steven Michael Henson

Born: Feb. 2, 1968. Junction City, KS, United States.   Height: 5'11".   Weight: 177 lbs.   Drafted: 1990   College: Kansas State

YEAR	TEAM	GP	GS	MIN	PTS	FGM	FGA	FG%	3PM	3PA	3P%	FTM	FTA	FT%	ORB	DRB	TRB	AST	PF	DQ	STL	BLK	TO	MPG	PPG	RPG	APG	PCM
90-91	Milwaukee	68	0	690	214	79	189	.418	18	54	.333	38	42	.905	14	37	51	131	83	0	32	0	41	10.1	3.1	0.8	1.9	.362
91-92	Milwaukee	50	1	386	150	52	144	.361	23	48	.479	23	29	.793	17	24	41	82	50	0	15	1	40	7.7	3.0	0.8	1.6	.368
92-93	Atlanta	53	2	719	213	71	182	.390	37	80	.463	34	40	.850	12	43	55	155	85	0	30	1	53	13.6	4.0	1.0	2.9	.366
93-94	Charlotte	3	0	17	3	1	2	.500	1	1	1.000	0	0	.000	0	1	1	5	3	0	0	0	1	5.7	1.0	0.3	1.7	.360
94-95	Portland	37	0	380	119	37	86	.430	23	52	.442	22	25	.880	3	23	26	85	52	1	9	0	30	10.3	3.2	0.7	2.3	.374
97-98	Detroit	23	0	65	36	13	26	.500	3	8	.375	7	7	1.000	0	2	2	4	9	0	1	0	7	2.8	1.6	0.1	0.2	.318
98-99	Detroit	4	0	25	4	1	2	.500	0	0	.000	2	2	1.000	0	0	0	3	1	0	1	0	3	6.3	1.0	0.0	0.8	.169
NBA Season Totals		238	3	2282	739	254	631	.403	105	243	.432	126	145	.869	46	130	176	465	283	1	88	2	175	9.6	3.1	0.7	2.0	....
90-91	Milwaukee	3	0	40	17	6	12	.500	2	3	.667	3	4	.750	0	3	3	3	3	0	1	0	6	13.3	5.7	1.0	1.0	.272
92-93	Atlanta	3	0	47	8	3	9	.333	2	5	.400	0	0	.000	1	3	4	5	4	0	4	0	2	15.7	2.7	1.3	1.7	.244
NBA Playoff Totals		6	0	87	25	9	21	.429	4	8	.500	3	4	.750	1	6	7	8	7	0	5	0	8	14.5	4.2	1.2	1.3	

• HENTZ, Charles
Charles (Helicopter) Hentz

Born: Sept. 13, 1947.   Height: 6'5".   Weight: 210 lbs.   Drafted: 1969   College: Arkansas AM&N

YEAR	TEAM	GP	GS	MIN	PTS	FGM	FGA	FG%	3PM	3PA	3P%	FTM	FTA	FT%	ORB	DRB	TRB	AST	PF	DQ	STL	BLK	TO	MPG	PPG	RPG	APG	PCM
70-71	Pittsburgh-A	57	....	1075	341	142	303	.469	0	4	.000	57	98	.582	148	238	386	31	114	1	....	....		82	18.9	6.0	6.8	0.5	.462
ABA Season Totals		57	....	1075	341	142	303	.469	0	4	.000	57	98	.582	148	238	386	31	114	1	....	....		82	18.9	6.0	6.8	0.5	....

• HERMAN, Bill
William R. Herman

Born: May 17, 1924.   Height: 6'3".   Weight: 170 lbs.   Drafted: —   College: Mount Union

YEAR	TEAM	GP	GS	MIN	PTS	FGM	FGA	FG%	3PM	3PA	3P%	FTM	FTA	FT%	ORB	DRB	TRB	AST	PF	DQ	STL	BLK	TO	MPG	PPG	RPG	APG	PCM
49-50	Denver	13	....	....	56	25	65	.385	....	....	....	6	11	.545	....	....	15	13	....	....	....	....		4.3	....	1.2	....	
NBA Season Totals		13	....	....	56	25	65	.385	....	....	....	6	11	.545	....	....	15	13	....	....	....	....		4.3	....	1.2	....	

• HERMAN, Paul
Paul Herman

Born: 1921.   Height: 6'1".   Weight: 175 lbs.   Drafted: —   College: Tennessee

YEAR	TEAM	GP	GS	MIN	PTS	FGM	FGA	FG%	3PM	3PA	3P%	FTM	FTA	FT%	ORB	DRB	TRB	AST	PF	DQ	STL	BLK	TO	MPG	PPG	RPG	APG	PCM
46-47	Youngstown-N	44	....	....	263	109	....	....	....	....	....	45	77	.584	....	....	....	69	....	....	....	....		6.0	....	....	....	
47-48	Flint-N	2	....	....	3	1	....	....	....	....	....	1	3	.333	....	....	....	1	....	....	....	....		1.5	....	....	....	
NBL Season Totals		46	....	....	266	110	....	....	....	....	....	46	80	....	....	....	....	70	....	....	....	....		5.8	....	....	....	

• HERMSEN, Kleggie
Clarence Henry (Kleggie) Hermsen

Born: Mar. 12, 1923. Hill City, MN, United States. Died: Mar.2, 1994.   Height: 6'9".   Weight: 225 lbs.   Drafted: —   College: Minnesota

YEAR	TEAM	GP	GS	MIN	PTS	FGM	FGA	FG%	3PM	3PA	3P%	FTM	FTA	FT%	ORB	DRB	TRB	AST	PF	DQ	STL	BLK	TO	MPG	PPG	RPG	APG	PCM
43-44	Sheboygan-N	12	....	....	11	3	....	....	....	....	....	5	....	....	....	....	....	....	....	....	....	....		0.9	....	....	....	
45-46	Sheboygan-N	21	....	....	55	19	....	....	....	....	....	17	....	....	....	....	....	....	....	....	....	....		2.6	....	....	....	
46-47	Cleveland	11	....	....	43	18	67	.269	....	....	....	7	15	.467	....	....	....	10	32	....	....	....		3.9	....	0.9	....	
46-47	Toronto	21	....	....	254	95	327	.291	....	....	....	64	97	.660	....	....	....	15	54	....	....	....		12.1	....	0.7	....	
47-48	Baltimore	48	....	....	575	212	765	.277	....	....	....	151	227	.665	....	....	....	48	154	....	....	....		12.0	....	1.0	....	
48-49	Washington	60	....	....	708	248	794	.312	....	....	....	212	311	.682	....	....	....	99	257	....	....	....		11.8	....	1.7	....	
49-50	Chicago	67	....	....	545	196	615	.319	....	....	....	153	247	.619	....	....	....	98	267	....	....	....		8.1	....	1.5	....	
50-51	Tri/Bos	71	....	....	533	189	644	.293	....	....	....	155	237	.654	....	....	448	92	261	8	....	....		7.5	6.3	1.3	....	
52-53	Bos/Ind	10	....	62	11	4	31	.129	....	....	....	3	5	.600	....	....	19	4	18	0	....	....		6.2	1.1	1.9	0.4	.050
NBA Season Totals		288	....	62	2669	962	3243	.297	....	....	....	745	1139	.654	....	....	467	366	1043	8	....	....		0.2	9.3	1.6	1.3	
NBL Season Totals		33	....	....	66	22	....	....	....	....	....	22	....	....	....	....	....	....	....	....	....	....		2.0	....	....	....	
Career Totals		321	....	62	2735	984	3243	....	....	....	....	767	1139	....	....	....	467	366	1043	8	....	....		0.2	8.5	1.5	1.1	
45-46	Sheboygan-N	5	....	....	13	4	....	....	....	....	....	5	8	.625	....	....	....	....	....	....	....	....		2.6	....	....	....	
47-48	Baltimore	11	....	....	121	38	151	.252	....	....	....	45	63	.714	....	....	....	12	45	....	....	....		11.0	....	1.1	....	
48-49	Washington	11	....	....	135	40	149	.268	....	....	....	55	83	.663	....	....	....	12	53	....	....	....		12.3	....	1.1	....	
49-50	Chicago	2	....	....	18	7	24	.292	....	....	....	4	5	.800	....	....	....	5	12	....	....	....		9.0	....	2.5	....	
50-51	Boston	2	....	....	2	1	6	.167	....	....	....	0	0	.000	....	....	3	0	6	0	....	....		1.0	1.5	0.0	....	
NBA Playoff Totals		26	....	....	276	86	330	.261	....	....	....	104	151	.689	....	....	3	29	116	0	....	....		10.6	0.1	1.1	....	
NBL Playoff Totals		5	....	....	13	4	....	....	....	....	....	5	8	....	....	....	....	....	....	....	....	....		2.6	....	....	....	
Career Playoff Totals		31	....	....	289	90	330	....	....	....	....	109	159	....	....	....	3	29	116	0	....	....		9.3	0.1	0.9	....	

• HERREN, Chris
Chris Albert Herren

Born: Sept. 27, 1975. Fall River, MA, United States.   Height: 6'2".   Weight: 197 lbs.   Drafted: 1999   College: Fresno State

YEAR	TEAM	GP	GS	MIN	PTS	FGM	FGA	FG%	3PM	3PA	3P%	FTM	FTA	FT%	ORB	DRB	TRB	AST	PF	DQ	STL	BLK	TO	MPG	PPG	RPG	APG	PCM
99-00	Denver	45	1	597	141	45	124	.363	24	67	.358	27	40	.675	12	40	52	111	74	0	15	2	42	13.3	3.1	1.2	2.5	.294
00-01	Boston	25	7	408	83	29	96	.302	16	55	.291	9	12	.750	4	17	21	56	43	0	14	0	20	16.3	3.3	0.8	2.2	.190
NBA Season Totals		70	8	1005	224	74	220	.336	40	122	.328	36	52	.692	16	57	73	167	117	0	29	2	62	14.4	3.2	1.0	2.4	....

YEAR	TEAM	GP	GS	MIN	PTS	FGM	FGA	FG%	3PM	3PA	3P%	FTM	FTA	FT%	ORB	DRB	TRB	AST	PF	DQ	STL	BLK	TO	MPG	PPG	RPG	APG	PCM

• HERRERA, Carl
Carl Victor Herrera

Born: Dec. 14, 1966. Trinidad, Trinidad.   Height: 6'9".   Weight: 215 lbs.   Drafted: 1990   College: Houston

YEAR	TEAM	GP	GS	MIN	PTS	FGM	FGA	FG%	3PM	3PA	3P%	FTM	FTA	FT%	ORB	DRB	TRB	AST	PF	DQ	STL	BLK	TO	MPG	PPG	RPG	APG	PCM
91-92	Houston	43	7	566	191	83	161	.516	0	1	.000	25	44	.568	33	66	99	27	60	0	16	25	39	13.2	4.4	2.3	0.6	.361
92-93	Houston	81	12	1800	605	240	444	.541	0	2	.000	125	176	.710	148	306	454	61	190	1	47	34	89	22.2	7.5	5.6	0.8	.435
93-94	Houston	75	0	1292	353	142	310	.458	0	0	.000	69	97	.711	101	184	285	37	159	0	32	26	68	17.2	4.7	3.8	0.5	.314
94-95	Houston	61	26	1331	415	171	327	.523	0	2	.000	73	117	.624	98	180	278	44	136	0	40	38	73	21.8	6.8	4.6	0.7	.373
95-96	San Antonio	44	6	393	85	40	97	.412	0	1	.000	5	17	.294	30	51	81	16	61	0	9	8	31	8.9	1.9	1.8	0.4	.196
96-97	San Antonio	75	58	1837	597	257	593	.433	2	6	.333	81	118	.686	118	222	340	50	217	3	62	53	98	24.5	8.0	4.5	0.7	.300
97-98	San Antonio	58	1	516	170	76	175	.434	0	1	.000	18	44	.409	24	67	91	22	71	1	19	12	41	8.9	2.9	1.6	0.4	.258
98-99	Vancouver	4	0	42	6	3	13	.231	0	0	.000	0	2	.000	5	3	8	3	3	0	0	0	4	10.5	1.5	2.0	0.8	.042
98-99	Denver	24	0	265	59	27	63	.429	0	1	.000	5	9	.556	20	34	54	1	37	0	12	7	12	11.0	2.5	2.3	0.0	.242
NBA Season Totals		465	110	8042	2481	1039	2183	.476	2	14	.143	401	624	.643	577	1113	1690	261	934	5	237	203	455	17.3	5.3	3.6	0.6	....
92-93	Houston	12	0	195	56	22	57	.386	0	2	.000	12	20	.600	16	29	45	7	36	1	3	2	11	16.3	4.7	3.8	0.6	.239
93-94	Houston	16	0	248	75	31	58	.534	0	0	.000	13	16	.813	14	31	45	3	37	1	5	3	7	15.5	4.7	2.8	0.2	.312
94-95	Houston	1	0	6	2	1	1	1.000	0	0	.000	0	0	.000	0	0	0	1	0	0	0	0	0	6.0	2.0	0.0	1.0	.510
95-96	San Antonio	7	0	28	2	0	3	.000	0	0	.000	2	2	1.000	2	2	4	1	7	0	2	1	3	4.0	0.3	0.6	0.1	.025
97-98	San Antonio	5	0	25	2	1	3	.333	0	0	.000	0	0	.000	0	4	4	1	4	0	0	0	1	5.0	0.4	0.8	0.2	.087
NBA Playoff Totals		41	0	502	137	55	122	.451	0	2	.000	27	38	.711	32	66	98	13	84	2	10	6	22	12.2	3.3	2.4	0.3	....

• HERRON, Keith
Keith Orlando Herron

Born: June 14, 1956. Memphis, TN, United States.   Height: 6'6".   Weight: 195 lbs.   Drafted: 1978   College: Villanova

YEAR	TEAM	GP	GS	MIN	PTS	FGM	FGA	FG%	3PM	3PA	3P%	FTM	FTA	FT%	ORB	DRB	TRB	AST	PF	DQ	STL	BLK	TO	MPG	PPG	RPG	APG	PCM
78-79	Atlanta	14	....	81	40	14	48	.292	....	....	....	12	13	.923	4	6	10	3	11	0	6	2	6	5.8	2.9	0.7	0.2	.224
80-81	Detroit	80	....	2270	1094	432	954	.453	2	11	.182	228	267	.854	98	113	211	148	154	1	91	26	152	28.4	13.7	2.6	1.9	.375
81-82	Cleveland	30	0	269	85	39	106	.368	0	1	.000	7	8	.875	10	11	21	23	25	0	8	2	12	9.0	2.8	0.7	0.8	.199
NBA Season Totals		124	0	2620	1219	485	1108	.438	2	12	.167	247	288	.858	112	130	242	174	190	1	105	30	170	21.1	9.8	2.0	1.4	....

• HERTZBERG, Sonny
Sidney Hertzberg

Born: July 29, 1922. Brooklyn, NY, United States.   Height: 5'10".   Weight: 175 lbs.   Drafted: —   College: CCNY

YEAR	TEAM	GP	GS	MIN	PTS	FGM	FGA	FG%	3PM	3PA	3P%	FTM	FTA	FT%	ORB	DRB	TRB	AST	PF	DQ	STL	BLK	TO	MPG	PPG	RPG	APG	PCM
46-47	New York	59	....	....	515	201	695	.289	....	....	....	113	149	.758	....	....	....	37	109	....	....	....	....	8.7		0.6		
47-48	New York	4	....	....	5	1	14	.071	....	....	....	3	4	.750	....	....	....	1	3	....	....	....	....	1.3		0.3		
47-48	Washington	37	....	....	273	109	400	.273	....	....	....	55	69	.797	....	....	....	22	58	....	....	....	....	7.4		0.6		
48-49	Washington	60	....	....	442	154	541	.285	....	....	....	134	164	.817	....	....	....	114	140	....	....	....	....	7.4		1.9		
49-50	Boston	68	....	....	693	275	865	.318	....	....	....	143	191	.749	....	....	....	200	153	....	....	....	....	10.2		2.9		
50-51	Boston	65	....	....	635	206	651	.316	....	....	....	223	270	.826	....	....	260	244	156	4	....	....	....	9.8	4.0	3.8		
NBA Season Totals		293	....	....	2563	946	3166	.299	....	....	....	671	847	.792	....	....	260	618	619	4	....	....	....	8.7	0.9	2.1		
46-47	New York	5	....	....	36	15	69	.217	....	....	....	6	8	.750	....	....	....	5	14	....	....	....	....	7.2		1.0		
48-49	Washington	11	....	....	118	39	112	.348	....	....	....	40	47	.851	....	....	....	27	33	....	....	....	....	10.7		2.5		
50-51	Boston	2	....	....	10	3	13	.231	....	....	....	4	5	.800	....	....	2	3	8	0	....	....	....	5.0	1.0	1.5		
NBA Playoff Totals		18	....	....	164	57	194	.294	....	....	....	50	60	.833	....	....	2	35	55	0	....	....	....	9.1	0.1	1.9		

• HESIK, George
George Hesik

Born: June 15, 1913. Died: Apr.18, 1994.   Height: 6'2".   Weight: 195 lbs.   Drafted: —   College: Marquette

YEAR	TEAM	GP	GS	MIN	PTS	FGM	FGA	FG%	3PM	3PA	3P%	FTM	FTA	FT%	ORB	DRB	TRB	AST	PF	DQ	STL	BLK	TO	MPG	PPG	RPG	APG	PCM
38-39	Wingfoots-N	23	....	....	69	24	....	....	....	....	....	21	....	....	....	....	....	....	....	....	....	....	....	3.0		....	....
39-40	Sheboygan-N	26	....	....	111	31	....	....	....	....	....	49	....	....	....	....	....	....	....	....	....	....	....	4.3		....	....
40-41	Sheboygan-N	23	....	....	80	24	....	....	....	....	....	32	....	....	....	....	....	....	....	....	....	....	....	3.5		....	....
41-42	Sheboygan-N	18	....	....	58	20	....	....	....	....	....	18	....	....	....	....	....	....	....	....	....	....	....	3.2		....	....
NBL Season Totals		90	....	....	318	99	....	....	....	....	....	120	....	....	....	....	....	....	....	....	....	....	....	3.5		....	....
39-40	Sheboygan-N	3	....	....	9	2	....	....	....	....	....	5	....	....	....	....	....	....	....	....	....	....	....	3.0		....	....
40-41	Sheboygan-N	6	....	....	28	9	....	....	....	....	....	10	....	....	....	....	....	....	....	....	....	....	....	4.7		....	....
NBL Playoff Totals		9	....	....	37	11	....	....	....	....	....	15	....	....	....	....	....	....	....	....	....	....	....	4.1		....	....

• HESTER, Dan
Dan W. Hester

Born: Nov. 8, 1948.   Height: 6'8".   Weight: 210 lbs.   Drafted: 1970   College: Louisiana State

YEAR	TEAM	GP	GS	MIN	PTS	FGM	FGA	FG%	3PM	3PA	3P%	FTM	FTA	FT%	ORB	DRB	TRB	AST	PF	DQ	STL	BLK	TO	MPG	PPG	RPG	APG	PCM
70-71	Denver-A	35	....	462	205	79	207	.382	5	11	.455	42	51	.824	75	123	198	30	66	1	....	....	32	13.2	5.9	5.7	0.9	.578
70-71	Kentucky-A	7	....	93	43	18	38	.474	0	1	.000	7	9	.778	8	28	36	5	16	1	....	....	12	13.3	6.1	5.1	0.7	.587
ABA Season Totals		42	....	555	248	97	245	.396	5	12	.417	49	60	.817	83	151	234	35	82	2	....	....	44	13.2	5.9	5.6	0.8	....
70-71	Kentucky-A	7	....	42	16	4	14	.286	0	0	.000	8	9	.889	3	10	13	1	9	0	....	....	2	6.0	2.3	1.9	0.1	.371
ABA Playoff Totals		7	....	42	16	4	14	.286	0	0	.000	8	9	.889	3	10	13	1	9	0	....	....	2	6.0	2.3	1.9	0.1	....

• HETZEL, Fred
Fred W. Hetzel

Born: July 21, 1942. Washington, DC, United States.   Height: 6'8".   Weight: 220 lbs.   Drafted: 1965   College: Davidson

YEAR	TEAM	GP	GS	MIN	PTS	FGM	FGA	FG%	3PM	3PA	3P%	FTM	FTA	FT%	ORB	DRB	TRB	AST	PF	DQ	STL	BLK	TO	MPG	PPG	RPG	APG	PCM
65-66	San Francisco	56	....	722	383	160	401	.399	....	....	....	63	92	.685	....	....	290	27	121	2	....	....	....	12.9	6.8	5.2	0.5	.548
66-67	San Francisco	77	....	2123	938	373	932	.400	....	....	....	192	237	.810	....	....	639	111	228	3	....	....	....	27.6	12.2	8.3	1.4	.484
67-68	San Francisco	77	....	2394	1461	533	1287	.414	....	....	....	395	474	.833	....	....	546	131	262	7	....	....	....	31.1	19.0	7.1	1.7	.550
68-69	Milwaukee	53	....	1591	843	316	760	.416	....	....	....	211	252	.837	....	....	473	83	193	6	....	....	....	30.0	15.9	8.9	1.6	.544
68-69	Cincinnati	31	....	685	368	140	287	.488	....	....	....	88	105	.838	....	....	140	29	94	3	....	....	....	22.1	11.9	4.5	0.9	.510

YEAR	TEAM	GP	GS	MIN	PTS	FGM	FGA	FG%	3PM	3PA	3P%	FTM	FTA	FT%	ORB	DRB	TRB	AST	PF	DQ	STL	BLK	TO	MPG	PPG	RPG	APG	PCM
69-70	Philadelphia	63	....	757	383	156	323	.483	....	....	....	71	85	.835	....	....	207	44	110	3	....	....	....	12.0	6.1	3.3	0.7	.545
70-71	LA Lakers	59	....	613	282	111	256	.434	....	....	....	60	77	.779	....	....	149	37	99	3	....	....	....	10.4	4.8	2.5	0.6	.453
NBA Season Totals		416	....	8885	4658	1789	4246	.421	....	....	....	1080	1322	.817	....	....	2444	462	1107	27	....	....	....	21.4	11.2	5.9	1.1	....
66-67	San Francisco	13	....	308	124	51	133	.383	....	....	....	22	28	.786	....	....	93	23	36	1	....	....	....	23.7	9.5	7.2	1.8	.467
67-68	San Francisco	10	....	321	188	69	150	.460	....	....	....	50	61	.820	....	....	66	16	44	2	....	....	....	32.1	18.8	6.6	1.6	.540
69-70	Philadelphia	5	....	75	35	13	25	.520	....	....	....	9	11	.818	....	....	18	3	10	0	....	....	....	15.0	7.0	3.6	0.6	.511
70-71	LA Lakers	7	....	38	12	5	15	.333	....	....	....	2	2	1.000	....	....	7	2	5	0	....	....	....	5.4	1.7	1.0	0.3	.251
NBA Playoff Totals		35	....	742	359	138	323	.427	....	....	....	83	102	.814	....	....	184	44	95	3	....	....	....	21.2	10.3	5.3	1.3	

• HEWITT, Bill

William Severlyn Hewitt

Born: Aug. 8, 1944. Cambridge, MA, United States.   Height: 6'7".   Weight: 210 lbs.   Drafted: 1968   College: USC

YEAR	TEAM	GP	GS	MIN	PTS	FGM	FGA	FG%	3PM	3PA	3P%	FTM	FTA	FT%	ORB	DRB	TRB	AST	PF	DQ	STL	BLK	TO	MPG	PPG	RPG	APG	PCM
68-69	LA Lakers	75	....	1455	539	239	528	.453	....	....	....	61	106	.575	....	....	332	76	139	1	....	....	....	19.4	7.2	4.4	1.0	.403
69-70	LA Lakers	20	....	478	66	25	88	.284	....	....	....	16	31	.516	....	....	141	28	39	0	....	....	....	23.9	3.3	7.1	1.4	.298
69-70	Detroit	45	....	801	208	85	210	.405	....	....	....	38	63	.603	....	....	213	36	91	1	....	....	....	17.8	4.6	4.7	0.8	.343
70-71	Detroit	62	....	1725	475	203	435	.467	....	....	....	69	120	.575	....	....	454	124	189	5	....	....	....	27.8	7.7	7.3	2.0	.408
71-72	Detroit	68	....	1203	303	131	277	.473	....	....	....	41	82	.500	....	....	370	71	134	1	....	....	....	17.7	4.5	5.4	1.0	.417
72-73	Buffalo	73	....	1332	345	152	364	.418	....	....	....	41	74	.554	....	....	368	110	154	3	....	....	....	18.2	4.7	5.0	1.5	.394
74-75	Chicago	18	....	467	126	56	129	.434	....	....	....	14	23	.609	30	86	116	24	46	1	9	10	....	25.9	7.0	6.4	1.3	.357
NBA Season Totals		361	....	7461	2062	891	2031	.439	....	....	....	280	499	.561	30	86	1994	469	792	12	9	10	....	20.7	5.7	5.5	1.3	
68-69	LA Lakers	15	....	412	140	61	151	.404	....	....	....	18	29	.621	....	....	78	17	40	0	....	....	....	27.5	9.3	5.2	1.1	.312
NBA Playoff Totals		15	....	412	140	61	151	.404	....	....	....	18	29	.621	....	....	78	17	40	0	....	....	....	27.5	9.3	5.2	1.1	

• HEWSON, Jack

John G. Hewson

Born: Sept. 7, 1924.   Height: 6'6".   Weight: 195 lbs.   Drafted: 1947   College: Temple

YEAR	TEAM	GP	GS	MIN	PTS	FGM	FGA	FG%	3PM	3PA	3P%	FTM	FTA	FT%	ORB	DRB	TRB	AST	PF	DQ	STL	BLK	TO	MPG	PPG	RPG	APG	PCM
47-48	Boston	24	....	....	65	22	89	.247	....	....	....	21	30	.700	....	....	....	1	9	....	....	....	....	2.7	....	0.0		
NBA Season Totals		24	....	....	65	22	89	.247	....	....	....	21	30	.700	....	....	....	1	9	....	....	....	....	2.7	....	0.0		

• HEYMAN, Art

Arthur Bruce Heyman

Born: June 24, 1941. New York, NY, United States.   Height: 6'5".   Weight: 205 lbs.   Drafted: 1963   College: Duke

YEAR	TEAM	GP	GS	MIN	PTS	FGM	FGA	FG%	3PM	3PA	3P%	FTM	FTA	FT%	ORB	DRB	TRB	AST	PF	DQ	STL	BLK	TO	MPG	PPG	RPG	APG	PCM
63-64	New York	75	....	2236	1153	432	1003	.431	....	....	....	289	422	.685	....	....	298	256	229	2	....	....	....	29.8	15.4	4.0	3.4	.498
64-65	New York	55	....	663	316	114	267	.427	....	....	....	88	132	.667	....	....	99	79	96	0	....	....	....	12.1	5.7	1.8	1.4	.480
65-66	Cincinnati	11	....	100	40	15	43	.349	....	....	....	10	17	.588	....	....	13	7	19	0	....	....	....	9.1	3.6	1.2	0.6	.266
65-66	Philadelphia	6	....	20	10	3	9	.333	....	....	....	4	5	.800	....	....	4	4	4	0	....	....	....	3.3	1.7	0.7	0.7	.567
67-68	New Jersey-A	19	....	439	262	97	252	.385	3	17	.176	65	101	.644	....	....	70	37	35	0	....	....	54	23.1	13.8	3.7	1.9	.468
67-68	Pittsburgh-A	54	....	2116	1087	360	806	.447	32	117	.274	335	446	.751	....	....	426	239	153	0	....	....	185	39.2	20.1	7.9	4.4	.586
68-69	Minnesota-A	71	....	2362	1022	350	832	.421	37	118	.314	285	409	.697	223	271	494	217	195	2	....	....	163	33.3	14.4	7.0	3.1	.484
69-70	Miami-A	18	....	300	140	47	105	.448	0	4	.000	46	65	.708	33	24	57	20	31	1	....	....	38	16.7	7.8	3.2	1.1	.468
69-70	Pittsburgh-A	1	....	4	0	0	1	.000	0	0	.000	0	0	.000	0	0	0	0	1	0	....	....	1	4.0	0.0	0.0	0.0	-.322
NBA Season Totals		147	....	3019	1519	564	1322	.427	....	....	....	391	576	.679	....	....	414	346	348	2	....	....	....	20.5	10.3	2.8	2.4	
ABA Season Totals		163	....	5221	2511	854	1996	.428	72	256	.281	731	1021	.716	256	295	1047	513	415	3	....	....	441	32.0	15.4	6.4	3.1	
Career Totals		310	....	8240	4030	1418	3318	.427	72	256	.281	1122	1597	.703	256	295	1461	859	763	5	....	....	441	26.6	13.0	4.7	2.8	
67-68	Pittsburgh-A	15	....	564	296	94	194	.485	14	37	.378	94	139	.676	....	....	107	58	44	0	....	....	53	37.6	19.7	7.1	3.9	.590
68-69	Minnesota-A	7	....	264	121	41	92	.446	7	18	.389	32	41	.780	....	....	51	20	24	1	....	....	18	37.7	17.3	7.3	2.9	.491
ABA Playoff Totals		22	....	828	417	135	286	.472	21	55	.382	126	180	.700	....	....	158	78	68	1	....	....	71	37.6	19.0	7.2	3.5	

• HICKEY, Nat

Matthew Hickey

Born: Jan. 30, 1902. Died: Sept.1979.   Height: 5'11".   Weight: 180 lbs.   Drafted: —   College: none

YEAR	TEAM	GP	GS	MIN	PTS	FGM	FGA	FG%	3PM	3PA	3P%	FTM	FTA	FT%	ORB	DRB	TRB	AST	PF	DQ	STL	BLK	TO	MPG	PPG	RPG	APG	PCM
44-45	Pittsburgh-N	2	....	....	8	3	....	....	....	....	....	2	....	....	....	....	....	....	....	....	....	....	....	4.0	....	....		
45-46	Indianapolis-N	13	....	....	73	30	....	....	....	....	....	13	....	....	....	....	....	....	....	....	....	....	....	5.6	....	....		
46-47	Tri-Cities-N	8	....	....	24	9	....	....	....	....	....	6	12	.500	....	....	....	....	....	....	....	....	....	3.0	....	....		
47-48	Tri-Cities-N	3	....	....	3	1	....	....	....	....	....	1	1	1.000	....	....	....	....	....	....	....	....	....	1.0	....	....		
47-48	Providence	2	....	....	2	0	6	.000	....	....	....	2	3	.667	....	....	....	0	5	....	....	....	....	1.0	....	0.0		
NBA Season Totals		2	....	....	2	0	6	.000	....	....	....	2	3	.667	....	....	....	0	5	....	....	....	....	1.0	....	0.0		
NBL Season Totals		26	....	....	108	43	....	....	....	....	....	22	13	....	....	....	....	....	....	....	....	....	....	4.2	....	....		
Career Totals		28	....	....	110	43	6	....	....	....	....	24	16	....	....	....	....	0	5	....	....	....	....	3.9	....	0.0		

• HICKS, Phil

Phillip James Hicks

Born: Jan. 31, 1953. Chicago, IL, United States.   Height: 6'7".   Weight: 205 lbs.   Drafted: 1976   College: Tulane

YEAR	TEAM	GP	GS	MIN	PTS	FGM	FGA	FG%	3PM	3PA	3P%	FTM	FTA	FT%	ORB	DRB	TRB	AST	PF	DQ	STL	BLK	TO	MPG	PPG	RPG	APG	PCM
76-77	Houston	2	....	7	0	0	2	.000	....	....	....	0	0	.000	1	0	1	1	1	0	1	0	....	3.5	0.0	0.5	0.5	-.023
76-77	Chicago	35	....	255	93	41	87	.471	....	....	....	11	13	.846	25	40	65	23	36	0	7	0	....	7.3	2.7	1.9	0.7	.467
78-79	Denver	20	....	128	39	18	43	.419	....	....	....	3	5	.600	13	15	28	8	20	0	5	0	14	6.4	2.0	1.4	0.4	.254
NBA Season Totals		57	....	390	132	59	132	.447	....	....	....	14	18	.778	39	55	94	32	57	0	13	0	14	6.8	2.3	1.6	0.6	
76-77	Chicago	1	....	4	0	0	2	.000	....	....	....	0	0	.000	1	2	3	0	1	0	0	0	....	4.0	0.0	3.0	0.0	.108
NBA Playoff Totals		1	....	4	0	0	2	.000	....	....	....	0	0	.000	1	2	3	0	1	0	0	0	....	4.0	0.0	3.0	0.0	

YEAR	TEAM	GP	GS	MIN	PTS	FGM	FGA	FG%	3PM	3PA	3P%	FTM	FTA	FT%	ORB	DRB	TRB	AST	PF	DQ	STL	BLK	TO	MPG	PPG	RPG	APG	PCM

• HIGGINS, Bill
William (Bill) Higgins

Born: Dec. 15, 1952. Toledo, OH, United States.   Height: 6'2".   Weight: 180 lbs.   Drafted: 1975   College: Ashland

YEAR	TEAM	GP	GS	MIN	PTS	FGM	FGA	FG%	3PM	3PA	3P%	FTM	FTA	FT%	ORB	DRB	TRB	AST	PF	DQ	STL	BLK	TO	MPG	PPG	RPG	APG	PCM
74-75	Virginia-A	15	....	348	138	61	139	.439	1	5	.200	15	23	.652	5	16	21	32	41	....	8	1	40	23.2	9.2	1.4	2.1	.291
ABA Season Totals		15	....	348	138	61	139	.439	1	5	.200	15	23	.652	5	16	21	32	41	....	8	1	40	23.2	9.2	1.4	2.1	....

• HIGGINS, Earle
Earle Brent (Sticks) Higgins

Born: Dec. 30, 1946.   Height: 6'8".   Weight: 195 lbs.   Drafted: 1970   College: Eastern Michigan

YEAR	TEAM	GP	GS	MIN	PTS	FGM	FGA	FG%	3PM	3PA	3P%	FTM	FTA	FT%	ORB	DRB	TRB	AST	PF	DQ	STL	BLK	TO	MPG	PPG	RPG	APG	PCM
70-71	Indiana-A	53	....	467	231	104	223	.466	3	17	.176	20	30	.667	48	80	128	35	109	4	....	....	26	8.8	4.4	2.4	0.7	.498
ABA Season Totals		53	....	467	231	104	223	.466	3	17	.176	20	30	.667	48	80	128	35	109	4	....	....	26	8.8	4.4	2.4	0.7	....
70-71	Indiana-A	5	....	31	18	6	20	.300	0	2	.000	6	7	.857	10	3	13	1	5	0	....	....	1	6.2	3.6	2.6	0.2	.516
ABA Playoff Totals		5	....	31	18	6	20	.300	0	2	.000	6	7	.857	10	3	13	1	5	0	....	....	1	6.2	3.6	2.6	0.2	....

• HIGGINS, Jim
Jim Higgins

Born: —.   Height: 6'8".   Weight: —   Drafted: —   College: none

YEAR	TEAM	GP	GS	MIN	PTS	FGM	FGA	FG%	3PM	3PA	3P%	FTM	FTA	FT%	ORB	DRB	TRB	AST	PF	DQ	STL	BLK	TO	MPG	PPG	RPG	APG	PCM
40-41	Hammond-N	1	....	....	1	0	....	....	....	....	....	1	....	....	....	....	....	....	....	....	....	....	....	....	1.0	....	....	.097
NBL Season Totals		1	....	....	1	0	....	....	....	....	....	1	....	....	....	....	....	....	....	....	....	....	....	....	1.0	....	....	....

• HIGGINS, Mike
Michael S. (Mike) Higgins

Born: Feb. 17, 1967. Grand Island, NE, United States.   Height: 6'9".   Weight: 220 lbs.   Drafted: —   College: Northern Colorado

YEAR	TEAM	GP	GS	MIN	PTS	FGM	FGA	FG%	3PM	3PA	3P%	FTM	FTA	FT%	ORB	DRB	TRB	AST	PF	DQ	STL	BLK	TO	MPG	PPG	RPG	APG	PCM
89-90	LA Lakers	6	0	18	1	0	0	.000	0	0	.000	1	2	.500	1	0	1	1	4	0	1	2	0	3.0	0.2	0.2	0.2	.193
89-90	Denver	5	0	32	13	3	8	.375	0	0	.000	7	8	.875	1	2	3	2	1	0	1	0	1	6.4	2.6	0.6	0.4	.385
90-91	Sacramento	7	0	61	16	6	10	.600	0	0	.000	4	7	.571	4	1	5	2	16	1	0	2	4	8.7	2.3	0.7	0.3	.137
NBA Season Totals		18	0	111	30	9	18	.500	0	0	.000	12	17	.706	6	3	9	5	21	1	2	4	5	6.2	1.7	0.5	0.3	....

• HIGGINS, Rod
Roderick Dwayne (Rod) Higgins

Born: Jan. 31, 1960. Monroe, LA, United States.   Height: 6'7".   Weight: 200 lbs.   Drafted: 1982   College: Fresno State

YEAR	TEAM	GP	GS	MIN	PTS	FGM	FGA	FG%	3PM	3PA	3P%	FTM	FTA	FT%	ORB	DRB	TRB	AST	PF	DQ	STL	BLK	TO	MPG	PPG	RPG	APG	PCM
82-83	Chicago	82	42	2196	848	313	698	.448	13	41	.317	209	264	.792	159	207	366	175	248	3	66	65	123	26.8	10.3	4.5	2.1	.407
83-84	Chicago	78	6	1577	500	193	432	.447	1	22	.045	113	156	.724	87	119	206	116	161	0	49	29	78	20.2	6.4	2.6	1.5	.316
84-85	Chicago	68	5	942	308	119	270	.441	10	37	.270	60	90	.667	55	92	147	73	91	0	21	13	48	13.9	4.5	2.2	1.1	.332
85-86	Seattle	12	0	94	22	9	27	.333	1	4	.250	3	5	.600	3	9	12	6	11	0	2	1	4	7.8	1.8	1.0	0.5	.169
85-86	San Antonio	11	0	128	47	18	40	.450	0	2	.000	11	16	.688	5	19	24	12	21	0	2	3	6	11.6	4.3	2.2	1.1	.381
85-86	New Jersey	2	0	29	6	3	16	.188	0	2	.000	0	0	.000	3	5	8	1	6	0	1	4	2	14.5	3.0	4.0	0.5	.084
85-86	Chicago	5	0	81	23	9	23	.391	0	1	.000	5	6	.833	3	4	7	5	11	0	4	3	2	16.2	4.6	1.4	1.0	.258
86-87	Golden State	73	28	1497	631	214	412	.519	3	17	.176	200	240	.833	72	165	237	96	145	0	40	21	73	20.5	8.6	3.2	1.3	.449
87-88	Golden State	68	67	2188	1054	381	725	.526	19	39	.487	273	322	.848	94	199	293	188	188	2	70	31	109	32.2	15.5	4.3	2.8	.498
88-89	Golden State	81	1	1887	856	301	633	.476	66	168	.393	188	229	.821	111	265	376	160	172	2	39	42	73	23.3	10.6	4.6	2.0	.517
89-90	Golden State	82	2	1993	909	304	632	.481	67	193	.347	234	285	.821	120	302	422	129	184	0	47	53	90	24.3	11.1	5.1	1.6	.519
90-91	Golden State	82	9	2024	776	259	559	.463	73	220	.332	185	226	.819	109	245	354	113	198	2	52	37	66	24.7	9.5	4.3	1.4	.423
91-92	Golden State	25	6	535	255	87	211	.412	33	95	.347	48	59	.814	30	55	85	22	75	2	15	13	15	21.4	10.2	3.4	0.9	.401
92-93	Sacramento	69	4	1425	571	199	483	.412	43	133	.323	130	151	.861	66	127	193	119	141	0	51	29	62	20.7	8.3	2.8	1.7	.389
93-94	Cleveland	36	11	547	195	71	163	.436	22	50	.440	31	42	.738	25	57	82	36	53	1	25	14	22	15.2	5.4	2.3	1.0	.386
94-95	Golden State	5	2	46	10	3	12	.250	1	6	.167	3	4	.750	4	3	7	3	7	0	1	1	1	9.2	2.0	1.4	0.6	.185
NBA Season Totals		779	203	17189	7011	2483	5336	.465	352	1030	.342	1693	2095	.808	946	1873	2819	1254	1712	12	485	359	774	22.1	9.0	3.6	1.6	....
84-85	Chicago	1	0	1	0	0	0	.000	0	0	.000	0	0	.000	0	0	0	0	0	0	0	0	0	1.0	0.0	0.0	0.0	.000
86-87	Golden State	10	8	177	43	18	46	.391	1	1	1.000	6	9	.667	5	16	21	12	20	0	11	6	2	17.7	4.3	2.1	1.2	.297
88-89	Golden State	8	7	267	119	40	82	.488	10	35	.286	29	34	.853	23	36	59	20	19	0	13	7	11	33.4	14.9	7.4	2.5	.575
90-91	Golden State	9	3	214	83	26	61	.426	8	26	.308	23	28	.821	9	20	29	18	28	0	2	8	7	23.8	9.2	3.2	2.0	.393
91-92	Golden State	2	2	17	6	2	5	.400	0	2	.000	2	2	1.000	0	0	0	1	1	0	1	0	0	8.5	3.0	0.0	0.5	.279
93-94	Cleveland	3	2	57	11	4	11	.364	2	7	.286	1	2	.500	2	2	4	4	10	0	1	1	3	19.0	3.7	1.3	1.3	.116
NBA Playoff Totals		33	22	733	262	90	205	.439	21	71	.296	61	75	.813	39	74	113	55	78	0	28	22	23	22.2	7.9	3.4	1.7	....

• HIGGINS, Sean
Sean Marielle (The Dean) Higgins

Born: Dec. 30, 1968. Los Angeles, CA, United States.   Height: 6'9".   Weight: 205 lbs.   Drafted: 1990   College: Michigan

YEAR	TEAM	GP	GS	MIN	PTS	FGM	FGA	FG%	3PM	3PA	3P%	FTM	FTA	FT%	ORB	DRB	TRB	AST	PF	DQ	STL	BLK	TO	MPG	PPG	RPG	APG	PCM
90-91	San Antonio	50	0	464	225	97	212	.458	3	19	.158	28	33	.848	18	45	63	35	53	0	8	1	50	9.3	4.5	1.3	0.7	.320
91-92	San Antonio	6	0	36	15	4	15	.267	0	1	.000	7	7	1.000	2	6	8	4	6	0	2	0	4	6.0	2.5	1.3	0.7	.329
91-92	Orlando	32	12	580	276	123	262	.469	6	24	.250	24	29	.828	27	67	94	37	52	0	14	6	38	18.1	8.6	2.9	1.2	.398
92-93	Golden State	29	4	591	240	96	215	.447	13	37	.351	35	47	.745	23	45	68	66	54	0	13	5	64	20.4	8.3	2.3	2.3	.320
94-95	New Jersey	57	7	735	268	105	273	.385	23	78	.295	35	40	.875	25	52	77	29	93	1	10	9	34	12.9	4.7	1.4	0.5	.209
95-96	Philadelphia	44	4	916	351	134	323	.415	48	129	.372	35	37	.946	20	72	92	55	90	1	24	11	48	20.8	8.0	2.1	1.3	.287
97-98	Portland	2	0	12	0	0	5	.000	0	2	.000	0	0	.000	0	0	0	3	0	2	0	1	6.0	0.0	0.0	0.0	-.419
NBA Season Totals		220	27	3334	1375	559	1305	.428	93	290	.321	164	193	.850	115	287	402	226	351	2	73	32	239	15.2	6.3	1.8	1.0	....
90-91	San Antonio	3	0	13	0	0	2	.000	0	0	.000	0	0	.000	0	0	0	1	1	0	0	0	0	4.3	0.0	0.0	0.3	-.097
NBA Playoff Totals		3	0	13	0	0	2	.000	0	0	.000	0	0	.000	0	0	0	1	1	0	0	0	0	4.3	0.0	0.0	0.3	....

• HIGGS, Kenny
Kenneth Lee (Kenny) Higgs Jr.

Born: Jan. 31, 1955. Owensboro, KY, United States. Height: 6' Weight: 180 lbs. Drafted: 1978 College: Louisiana State

YEAR TEAM	GP	GS	MIN	PTS	FGM	FGA	FG%	3PM	3PA	3P%	FTM	FTA	FT%	ORB	DRB	TRB	AST	PF	DQ	STL	BLK	TO	MPG	PPG	RPG	APG	PCM
78-79 Cleveland	68	....	1050	339	127	279	.455	....	....	....	85	111	.766	18	84	102	141	176	2	66	11	48	15.4	5.0	1.5	2.1	.367
80-81 Denver	72	....	1689	562	209	474	.441	4	34	.118	140	172	.814	24	121	145	408	243	5	101	6	166	23.5	7.8	2.0	5.7	.425
81-82 Denver	76	49	1696	569	202	468	.432	4	21	.190	161	197	.817	23	121	144	395	263	8	72	6	160	22.3	7.5	1.9	5.2	.395
NBA Season Totals	216	49	4435	1470	538	1221	.441	8	55	.145	386	480	.804	65	326	391	944	682	15	239	23	374	20.5	6.8	1.8	4.4	....
81-82 Denver	3	0	54	23	8	21	.381	0	2	.000	7	12	.583	1	2	3	6	12	0	3	0	5	18.0	7.7	1.0	2.0	.196
NBA Playoff Totals	3	0	54	23	8	21	.381	0	2	.000	7	12	.583	1	2	3	6	12	0	3	0	5	18.0	7.7	1.0	2.0	....

• HIGH, Johnny
Johnny Harold (Sky) High

Born: Apr. 25, 1957. Birmingham, AL, United States. Died: June13, 1987. Height: 6'3". Weight: 185 lbs. Drafted: 1979 College: Nevada-Reno

YEAR TEAM	GP	GS	MIN	PTS	FGM	FGA	FG%	3PM	3PA	3P%	FTM	FTA	FT%	ORB	DRB	TRB	AST	PF	DQ	STL	BLK	TO	MPG	PPG	RPG	APG	PCM
79-80 Phoenix	82	....	1121	409	144	323	.446	1	7	.143	120	178	.674	69	104	173	119	172	1	71	15	123	13.7	5.0	2.1	1.5	.354
80-81 Phoenix	81	....	1750	677	246	576	.427	2	24	.083	183	264	.693	89	139	228	202	251	2	129	26	186	21.6	8.4	2.8	2.5	.357
82-83 Phoenix	82	2	1155	264	100	217	.461	1	5	.200	63	136	.463	45	105	150	153	205	0	85	34	107	14.1	3.2	1.8	1.9	.301
83-84 Phoenix	29	9	512	46	18	52	.346	0	2	.000	10	29	.345	16	50	66	51	84	1	40	11	38	17.7	1.6	2.3	1.8	.185
NBA Season Totals	274	11	4538	1396	508	1168	.435	4	38	.105	376	607	.619	219	398	617	525	712	4	325	86	454	16.6	5.1	2.3	1.9	....
79-80 Phoenix	8	....	120	32	12	31	.387	0	2	.000	8	16	.500	10	15	25	20	20	0	6	2	7	15.0	4.0	3.1	2.5	.396
80-81 Phoenix	7	....	117	37	14	33	.424	0	0	.000	9	14	.643	9	10	19	6	24	0	6	2	6	16.7	5.3	2.7	0.9	.275
82-83 Phoenix	3	0	45	10	5	11	.455	0	1	.000	0	2	.000	7	3	10	6	7	0	3	1	1	15.0	3.3	3.3	2.0	.419
NBA Playoff Totals	18	0	282	79	31	75	.413	0	3	.000	17	32	.531	26	28	54	32	51	0	15	5	14	15.7	4.4	3.0	1.8	....

• HIGHTOWER, Wayne
Wayne A. (Spain) Hightower

Born: Jan. 14, 1940. Philadelphia, PA, United States. Died: Apr.18, 2002. Height: 6'8". Weight: 192 lbs. Drafted: 1962 College: Kansas

YEAR TEAM	GP	GS	MIN	PTS	FGM	FGA	FG%	3PM	3PA	3P%	FTM	FTA	FT%	ORB	DRB	TRB	AST	PF	DQ	STL	BLK	TO	MPG	PPG	RPG	APG	PCM
62-63 San Francisco	66	....	1387	489	192	548	.350	....	....	....	105	157	.669	....	....	354	51	181	5	....	....	....	21.0	7.4	5.4	0.8	.329
63-64 San Francisco	79	....	2536	1046	393	1022	.385	....	....	....	260	329	.790	....	....	566	133	269	7	....	....	....	32.1	13.2	7.2	1.7	.405
64-65 San Francisco	48	....	1037	405	136	396	.343	....	....	....	133	173	.769	....	....	247	38	143	1	....	....	....	21.6	8.4	5.1	0.8	.358
64-65 Baltimore	27	....	510	182	60	174	.345	....	....	....	62	81	.765	....	....	173	16	61	1	....	....	....	18.9	6.7	6.4	0.6	.424
65-66 Baltimore	24	....	460	183	63	186	.339	....	....	....	57	78	.731	....	....	131	35	61	2	....	....	....	19.2	7.6	5.5	1.5	.434
66-67 Baltimore	43	....	746	295	103	308	.334	....	....	....	89	124	.718	....	....	241	36	110	5	....	....	....	17.3	6.9	5.6	0.8	.415
66-67 Detroit	29	....	564	248	92	259	.355	....	....	....	64	86	.744	....	....	164	28	80	1	....	....	....	19.4	8.6	5.7	1.0	.423
67-68 Denver-A	74	....	2459	1282	431	1126	.383	0	6	.000	420	543	.773	....	....	536	143	237	5	....	....	165	33.2	17.3	7.2	1.9	.475
68-69 Denver-A	67	....	2318	933	311	762	.408	0	2	.000	311	426	.730	155	486	641	203	241	5	....	....	176	34.6	13.9	9.6	3.0	.507
69-70 Los Angeles-A	27	....	961	489	180	403	.447	0	2	.000	129	170	.759	78	177	255	71	101	4	....	....	74	35.6	18.1	9.4	2.6	.558
70-71 Texas-A	33	....	1220	478	172	421	.409	0	2	.000	134	182	.736	116	212	328	90	97	1	....	....	61	37.0	14.5	9.9	2.7	.485
70-71 Utah-A	35	....	1135	468	167	427	.391	0	1	.000	134	179	.749	103	184	287	104	107	1	....	....	84	32.4	13.4	8.2	3.0	.488
71-72 Carolina-A	13	....	141	70	20	64	.313	0	2	.000	30	36	.833	17	26	43	11	19	0	....	....	12	10.8	5.4	3.3	0.8	.500
NBA Season Totals	316	....	7240	2848	1039	2893	.359	....	....	....	770	1028	.749	....	....	1876	337	905	22	....	....	....	22.9	9.0	5.9	1.1	....
ABA Season Totals	249	....	8234	3720	1281	3203	.400	0	15	.000	1158	1536	.754	469	1085	2090	622	802	16	....	....	572	33.1	14.9	8.4	2.5	....
Career Totals	565	....	15474	6568	2320	6096	.381	0	15	.000	1928	2564	.752	469	1085	3966	959	1707	38	....	....	572	27.4	11.6	7.0	1.7	....
63-64 San Francisco	12	....	286	81	29	112	.259	....	....	....	23	33	.697	....	....	50	18	42	1	....	....	....	23.8	6.8	4.2	1.5	.200
64-65 Baltimore	10	....	196	68	27	64	.422	....	....	....	14	22	.636	....	....	57	8	25	0	....	....	....	19.6	6.8	5.7	0.8	.411
67-68 Denver-A	5	....	209	113	35	100	.350	0	1	.000	43	54	.796	....	....	44	11	25	2	....	....	22	41.8	22.6	8.8	2.2	.447
68-69 Denver-A	7	....	187	84	25	63	.397	0	0	.000	34	45	.756	....	....	47	12	22	1	....	....	18	26.7	12.0	6.7	1.7	.488
70-71 Texas-A	4	....	126	35	11	34	.324	0	0	.000	13	17	.765	16	16	32	11	12	0	....	....	9	31.5	8.8	8.0	2.8	.389
NBA Playoff Totals	22	....	482	149	56	176	.318	....	....	....	37	55	.673	....	....	107	26	67	1	....	....	....	21.9	6.8	4.9	1.2	....
ABA Playoff Totals	16	....	522	232	71	197	.360	0	1	.000	90	116	.776	16	16	123	34	59	3	....	....	49	32.6	14.5	7.7	2.1	....
Career Playoff Totals	38	....	1004	381	127	373	.340	0	1	.000	127	171	.743	16	16	230	60	126	4	....	....	49	26.4	10.0	6.1	1.6	....

• HILARIO, Nene
Maybyner Rodney Hilario

Born: Sept. 13, 1982. Sao Carlos, Brazil. Height: 6'11". Weight: 260 lbs. Drafted: 2002 College: none (HS: Instituto Alvara Guiao, BRA)

YEAR TEAM	GP	GS	MIN	PTS	FGM	FGA	FG%	3PM	3PA	3P%	FTM	FTA	FT%	ORB	DRB	TRB	AST	PF	DQ	STL	BLK	TO	MPG	PPG	RPG	APG	PCM
02-03 Denver	80	53	2251	839	321	619	.519	0	3	.000	197	341	.578	208	283	491	149	295	4	127	65	181	28.1	10.5	6.1	1.9	.439
NBA Season Totals	80	53	2251	839	321	619	.519	0	3	.000	197	341	.578	208	283	491	149	295	4	127	65	181	28.1	10.5	6.1	1.9	....

• HILGEMAN, Jim
Jim (Wiggles) Hilgeman

Born: 1916. Height: 6' Weight: 170 lbs. Drafted: — College: Toledo

YEAR TEAM	GP	GS	MIN	PTS	FGM	FGA	FG%	3PM	3PA	3P%	FTM	FTA	FT%	ORB	DRB	TRB	AST	PF	DQ	STL	BLK	TO	MPG	PPG	RPG	APG	PCM
37-38 Fort Wayne-N	17	....	....	130	50	....	....	....	....	....	30	....	....	....	....	....	....	....	....	....	....	....	....	7.6	....	....	....
41-42 Fort Wayne-N	4	....	....	2	1	....	....	....	....	....	0	....	....	....	....	....	....	....	....	....	....	....	....	0.5	....	....	....
NBL Season Totals	21	....	....	132	51	....	....	....	....	....	30	....	....	....	....	....	....	....	....	....	....	....	....	6.3	....	....	....

• HILL, Armond
Armond G. Hill

Born: Mar. 31, 1953. Brooklyn, NY, United States. Height: 6'4". Weight: 190 lbs. Drafted: 1976 College: Princeton

YEAR TEAM	GP	GS	MIN	PTS	FGM	FGA	FG%	3PM	3PA	3P%	FTM	FTA	FT%	ORB	DRB	TRB	AST	PF	DQ	STL	BLK	TO	MPG	PPG	RPG	APG	PCM
76-77 Atlanta	81	....	1825	489	175	439	.399	....	....	....	139	174	.799	39	104	143	403	245	8	85	6	....	22.5	6.0	1.8	5.0	.396
77-78 Atlanta	82	....	2530	797	304	732	.415	....	....	....	189	223	.848	59	172	231	427	302	15	151	15	238	30.9	9.7	2.8	5.2	.354
78-79 Atlanta	82	....	2527	838	296	682	.434	....	....	....	246	288	.854	41	123	164	480	292	8	102	16	205	30.8	10.2	2.0	5.9	.372
79-80 Atlanta	79	....	2092	479	177	431	.411	1	4	.250	124	146	.849	31	107	138	424	261	7	107	8	174	26.5	6.1	1.7	5.4	.314
80-81 Atlanta	24	....	624	120	39	116	.336	0	1	.000	42	50	.840	10	41	51	118	60	0	26	3	58	26.0	5.0	2.1	4.9	.268
80-81 Seattle	51	....	1114	255	78	219	.356	0	6	.000	99	122	.811	31	77	108	174	147	3	40	8	71	21.8	5.0	2.1	3.4	.284
81-82 Seattle	21	4	243	55	19	37	.514	0	0	.000	17	23	.739	6	19	25	25	37	0	5	2	15	11.6	2.6	1.2	1.2	.252
81-82 San Diego	19	14	480	90	34	89	.382	0	2	.000	22	32	.688	6	21	27	81	51	0	16	3	51	25.3	4.7	1.4	4.3	.196

YEAR	TEAM	GP	GS	MIN	PTS	FGM	FGA	FG%	3PM	3PA	3P%	FTM	FTA	FT%	ORB	DRB	TRB	AST	PF	DQ	STL	BLK	TO	MPG	PPG	RPG	APG	PCM
82-83	Milwaukee	14	3	169	46	14	26	.538	0	0	.000	18	22	.818	5	15	20	27	20	0	9	0	13	12.1	3.3	1.4	1.9	.405
83-84	Atlanta	15	2	181	45	14	46	.304	0	0	.000	17	21	.810	2	8	10	35	30	1	7	0	14	12.1	3.0	0.7	2.3	.219
NBA Season Totals		468	23	11785	3214	1150	2817	.408	1	13	.077	913	1101	.829	230	687	917	2194	1445	42	548	61	839	25.2	6.9	2.0	4.7	....
77-78	Atlanta	2	....	61	16	6	15	.400	....	....	....	4	4	1.000	0	3	3	7	7	0	2	0	5	30.5	8.0	1.5	3.5	.212
78-79	Atlanta	9	....	267	66	29	71	.408	....	....	....	8	12	.667	2	15	17	50	33	1	12	1	23	29.7	7.3	1.9	5.6	.274
79-80	Atlanta	5	....	109	35	12	30	.400	0	1	.000	11	12	.917	2	4	6	15	14	0	4	1	11	21.8	7.0	1.2	3.0	.260
NBA Playoff Totals		16	....	437	117	47	116	.405	0	1	.000	23	28	.821	4	22	26	72	54	1	18	2	39	27.3	7.3	1.6	4.5	....

• HILL, Cleo

Cleo Hill

Born: May 24, 1938. Newark, NJ, United States.　Height: 6'1".　Weight: 185 lbs.　Drafted: 1961　College: Winston-Salem State

YEAR	TEAM	GP	GS	MIN	PTS	FGM	FGA	FG%	3PM	3PA	3P%	FTM	FTA	FT%	ORB	DRB	TRB	AST	PF	DQ	STL	BLK	TO	MPG	PPG	RPG	APG	PCM
61-62	St. Louis	58	....	1050	320	107	309	.346	....	....		106	137	.774	....	....	178	114	98	1	....	....	....	18.1	5.5	3.1	2.0	.371
NBA Season Totals		58	....	1050	320	107	309	.346	....	....		106	137	.774	....	....	178	114	98	1	....	....	....	18.1	5.5	3.1	2.0	

• HILL, Gary

Gary W. Hill

Born: Oct. 7, 1941.　Height: 6'4".　Weight: 185 lbs.　Drafted: 1963　College: Oklahoma City

YEAR	TEAM	GP	GS	MIN	PTS	FGM	FGA	FG%	3PM	3PA	3P%	FTM	FTA	FT%	ORB	DRB	TRB	AST	PF	DQ	STL	BLK	TO	MPG	PPG	RPG	APG	PCM
63-64	San Francisco	67	....	1015	343	146	384	.380	....	....		51	77	.662	....	....	114	103	165	2	....	....	....	15.1	5.1	1.7	1.5	.294
64-65	San Francisco	9	....	88	27	10	35	.286	....	....		7	14	.500	....	....	15	6	10	0	....	....	....	9.8	3.0	1.7	0.7	.229
64-65	Baltimore	3	....	15	0	0	1	.000	....	....		0	0	.000	....	....	1	1	1	0	....	....	....	5.0	0.0	0.3	0.3	.057
NBA Season Totals		79	....	1118	370	156	420	.371	....	....		58	91	.637	....	....	130	110	176	2	....	....	....	14.2	4.7	1.6	1.4	
63-64	San Francisco	9	....	69	28	12	24	.500	....	....		4	13	.308	....	....	6	8	13	0	....	....	....	7.7	3.1	0.7	0.9	.356
NBA Playoff Totals		9	....	69	28	12	24	.500	....	....		4	13	.308	....	....	6	8	13	0	....	....	....	7.7	3.1	0.7	0.9	

• HILL, Grant

Grant Henry Hill

Born: Oct. 5, 1972. Dallas, TX, United States.　Height: 6'8".　Weight: 225 lbs.　Drafted: 1994　College: Duke

YEAR	TEAM	GP	GS	MIN	PTS	FGM	FGA	FG%	3PM	3PA	3P%	FTM	FTA	FT%	ORB	DRB	TRB	AST	PF	DQ	STL	BLK	TO	MPG	PPG	RPG	APG	PCM
94-95	Detroit	70	69	2678	1394	508	1064	.477	4	27	.148	374	511	.732	125	320	445	353	203	1	124	62	203	38.3	19.9	6.4	5.0	.556
95-96	Detroit	80	80	3260	1618	564	1221	.462	5	26	.192	485	646	.751	127	656	783	548	242	1	100	48	264	40.8	20.2	9.8	6.9	.619
96-97	Detroit	80	80	3147	1710	625	1259	.496	10	33	.303	450	633	.711	123	598	721	583	186	0	144	48	256	39.3	21.4	9.0	7.3	.693
97-98	Detroit	81	81	3294	1712	615	1361	.452	3	21	.143	479	647	.740	93	530	623	551	196	1	143	53	284	40.7	21.1	7.7	6.8	.592
98-99	Detroit	50	50	1852	1053	384	802	.479	0	14	.000	285	379	.752	65	290	355	300	114	0	80	27	184	37.0	21.1	7.1	6.0	.631
99-00	Detroit	74	74	2776	1906	696	1422	.489	34	98	.347	480	604	.795	97	393	490	385	190	0	103	43	240	37.5	25.8	6.6	5.2	.679
00-01	Orlando	4	4	133	55	19	43	.442	1	1	1.000	16	26	.615	8	17	25	25	9	0	5	2	11	33.3	13.8	6.3	6.3	.536
01-02	Orlando	14	14	512	235	83	195	.426	0	2	.000	69	80	.863	29	96	125	64	40	2	8	4	37	36.6	16.8	8.9	4.6	.529
02-03	Orlando	29	29	843	421	151	307	.492	1	4	.250	118	144	.819	40	166	206	122	46	0	28	13	84	29.1	14.5	7.1	4.2	.626
NBA Season Totals		482	481	18495	10104	3645	7674	.475	58	226	.257	2756	3670	.751	707	3066	3773	2931	1226	5	735	300	1563	38.4	21.0	7.8	6.1	....
95-96	Detroit	3	3	115	57	22	39	.564	1	2	.500	12	14	.857	4	18	22	11	13	0	3	0	8	38.3	19.0	7.3	3.7	.536
96-97	Detroit	5	5	203	118	45	103	.437	0	0	.000	28	39	.718	13	21	34	27	14	0	4	5	19	40.6	23.6	6.8	5.4	.510
98-99	Detroit	5	5	176	97	42	92	.457	0	1	.000	13	16	.813	7	29	36	37	12	0	10	2	12	35.2	19.4	7.2	7.4	.676
99-00	Detroit	2	2	55	22	6	16	.375	1	2	.500	9	10	.900	0	11	11	9	7	0	1	0	10	27.5	11.0	5.5	4.5	.381
NBA Playoff Totals		15	15	549	294	115	250	.460	2	5	.400	62	79	.785	24	79	103	84	46	0	18	7	49	36.6	19.6	6.9	5.6	....

• HILL, Mort

Mort Hill

Born: 1921.　Height: 6'1".　Weight: 175 lbs.　Drafted: —　College: Cal State Santa Barbara

YEAR	TEAM	GP	GS	MIN	PTS	FGM	FGA	FG%	3PM	3PA	3P%	FTM	FTA	FT%	ORB	DRB	TRB	AST	PF	DQ	STL	BLK	TO	MPG	PPG	RPG	APG	PCM
46-47	Syracuse-N	3	....	....	2	1	....	....	....	....	....	0	0	.000	....	....	....	....	....	....	....	....	....	0.7	....	....	....	
NBL Season Totals		3	....	....	2	1	....	....	....	....	....	0	0		....	....	....	....	....	....	....	....	....	0.7	....	....	....	

• HILL, Simmie

Simmie Hill Jr.

Born: Nov. 14, 1946. Midland, PA, United States.　Height: 6'7".　Weight: 233 lbs.　Drafted: 1969　College: Texas Baptist

YEAR	TEAM	GP	GS	MIN	PTS	FGM	FGA	FG%	3PM	3PA	3P%	FTM	FTA	FT%	ORB	DRB	TRB	AST	PF	DQ	STL	BLK	TO	MPG	PPG	RPG	APG	PCM
69-70	Los Angeles-A	6	....	41	19	8	25	.320	0	1	.000	3	3	1.000	4	8	12	1	7	0	....	....	7	6.8	3.2	2.0	0.2	.313
69-70	Miami-A	47	....	1458	706	289	684	.423	5	29	.172	123	164	.750	166	223	389	46	194	10	....	....	140	31.0	15.0	8.3	1.0	.448
71-72	Dallas-A	70	....	1845	695	281	629	.447	4	13	.308	129	164	.787	127	279	406	94	234	8	....	....	125	26.4	9.9	5.8	1.3	.397
72-73	San Diego-A	69	....	1658	760	315	743	.424	27	69	.391	103	135	.763	126	225	351	131	221	4	....	....	150	24.0	11.0	5.1	1.9	.435
73-74	San Antonio-A	60	....	837	269	112	244	.459	0	11	.000	45	62	.726	59	113	172	62	145	....	13	16	63	14.0	4.5	2.9	1.0	.364
ABA Season Totals		252	....	5839	2449	1005	2325	.432	36	123	.293	403	528	.763	482	848	1330	334	801	22	13	16	485	23.2	9.7	5.3	1.3	....
71-72	Dallas-A	4	....	121	41	18	40	.450	0	0	.000	5	7	.714	10	12	22	11	15	0	....	....	6	30.3	10.3	5.5	2.8	.379
72-73	San Diego-A	4	....	85	29	13	36	.361	0	3	.000	3	5	.600	7	10	17	3	11	1	....	....	8	21.3	7.3	4.3	0.8	.248
73-74	San Antonio-A	4	....	20	2	1	3	.333	0	1	.000	0	0	.000	0	0	0	2	2	....	0	0	3	5.0	0.5	0.0	0.5	.086
ABA Playoff Totals		12	....	226	72	32	79	.405	0	4	.000	8	12	.667	17	22	39	16	28	1	0	0	17	18.8	6.0	3.3	1.3	....

• HILL, Tyrone

Tyrone Hill

Born: Mar. 19, 1968. Cincinnati, OH, United States.　Height: 6'9".　Weight: 240 lbs.　Drafted: 1990　College: Xavier (OH)

YEAR	TEAM	GP	GS	MIN	PTS	FGM	FGA	FG%	3PM	3PA	3P%	FTM	FTA	FT%	ORB	DRB	TRB	AST	PF	DQ	STL	BLK	TO	MPG	PPG	RPG	APG	PCM
90-91	Golden State	74	22	1192	390	147	299	.492	0	0	.000	96	152	.632	157	226	383	19	264	8	33	30	74	16.1	5.3	5.2	0.3	.391
91-92	Golden State	82	75	1886	671	254	487	.522	0	1	.000	163	235	.694	182	411	593	47	**315**	7	73	43	107	23.0	8.2	7.2	0.6	.469
92-93	Golden State	74	66	2070	640	251	494	.508	0	4	.000	138	221	.624	255	499	754	68	320	8	41	40	89	28.0	8.6	10.2	0.9	.480
93-94	Cleveland	57	20	1447	603	216	398	.543	0	2	.000	171	256	.668	184	315	499	46	193	5	53	35	80	25.4	10.6	8.8	0.8	.569
94-95	Cleveland	70	67	2397	963	350	694	.504	0	1	.000	263	397	.662	269	496	765	55	245	4	55	41	154	34.2	13.8	10.9	0.8	.494
95-96	Cleveland	44	2	929	341	130	254	.512	0	0	.000	81	135	.600	94	150	244	33	144	3	31	20	66	21.1	7.8	5.5	0.8	.411
96-97	Cleveland	74	70	2582	955	357	595	.600	0	1	.000	241	381	.633	259	477	736	92	268	6	63	30	148	34.9	12.9	9.9	1.2	.494
97-98	Milwaukee	57	56	2064	571	208	418	.498	0	1	.000	155	255	.608	212	396	608	88	230	8	67	30	108	36.2	10.0	10.7	1.5	.421
98-99	Milwaukee	17	17	517	146	50	118	.424	0	0	.000	46	81	.568	51	83	134	17	68	0	18	8	24	30.4	8.6	7.9	1.0	.347

YEAR TEAM	GP	GS	MIN	PTS	FGM	FGA	FG%	3PM	3PA	3P%	FTM	FTA	FT%	ORB	DRB	TRB	AST	PF	DQ	STL	BLK	TO	MPG	PPG	RPG	APG	PCM
98-99 Philadelphia	21	6	587	179	72	150	.480	0	0	.000	35	69	.507	64	89	153	18	77	2	16	8	35	28.0	8.5	7.3	0.9	.352
99-00 Philadelphia	68	65	2155	815	318	656	.485	0	1	.000	179	259	.691	220	405	625	52	243	3	64	27	124	31.7	12.0	9.2	0.8	.444
00-01 Philadelphia	76	75	2363	728	278	587	.474	0	1	.000	172	273	.630	239	448	687	48	242	2	37	27	127	31.1	9.6	9.0	0.6	.385
01-02 Cleveland	26	26	810	209	71	182	.390	0	1	.000	67	103	.650	79	195	274	23	102	3	17	13	48	31.2	8.0	10.5	0.9	.374
02-03 Cleveland	32	25	855	203	85	197	.431	0	0	.000	33	45	.733	70	197	267	32	104	4	31	19	52	26.7	6.3	8.3	1.0	.379
02-03 Philadelphia	24	18	496	109	44	109	.404	0	0	.000	21	35	.600	56	68	124	9	68	0	15	7	16	20.7	4.5	5.2	0.4	.284
NBA Season Totals	796	610	22350	7523	2831	5638	.502	0	13	.000	1861	2897	.642	2391	4455	6846	647	2883	63	614	378	1252	28.1	9.5	8.6	0.8	....
90-91 Golden State	9	0	80	22	9	14	.643	0	1	.000	4	6	.667	7	16	23	2	25	2	3	4	2	8.9	2.4	2.6	0.2	.412
91-92 Golden State	4	1	47	6	3	7	.429	0	0	.000	0	2	.000	3	5	8	1	12	0	2	0	3	11.8	1.5	2.0	0.3	.071
93-94 Cleveland	3	3	123	42	11	27	.407	0	0	.000	20	37	.541	14	17	31	4	14	1	1	1	8	41.0	14.0	10.3	1.3	.328
94-95 Cleveland	4	4	139	34	9	29	.310	0	1	.000	16	25	.640	8	15	23	3	18	1	7	1	10	34.8	8.5	5.8	0.8	.183
95-96 Cleveland	3	0	53	25	9	12	.750	0	0	.000	7	9	.778	7	8	15	0	11	1	0	0	3	17.7	8.3	5.0	0.0	.516
98-99 Philadelphia	8	1	196	45	19	39	.487	0	0	.000	7	19	.368	19	40	59	0	33	1	3	2	6	24.5	5.6	7.4	0.0	.300
99-00 Philadelphia	10	10	352	123	46	100	.460	0	1	.000	31	44	.705	36	61	97	9	38	0	9	1	12	35.2	12.3	9.7	0.9	.417
00-01 Philadelphia	23	23	742	166	65	159	.409	0	1	.000	36	53	.679	54	114	168	10	80	0	13	12	26	32.3	7.2	7.3	0.4	.268
02-03 Philadelphia	10	0	141	28	12	19	.632	0	0	.000	4	4	1.000	12	16	28	2	29	0	1	1	6	14.1	2.8	2.8	0.2	.230
NBA Playoff Totals	74	42	1873	491	183	406	.451	0	4	.000	125	199	.628	160	292	452	31	260	6	39	22	76	25.3	6.6	6.1	0.4	....

• HILLHOUSE, Art

Arthur Sherwood (Art) Hillhouse

Born: June 12, 1916. Died: Oct.1980. Height: 6'7". Weight: 220 lbs. Drafted: — College: Long Island University

YEAR TEAM	GP	GS	MIN	PTS	FGM	FGA	FG%	3PM	3PA	3P%	FTM	FTA	FT%	ORB	DRB	TRB	AST	PF	DQ	STL	BLK	TO	MPG	PPG	RPG	APG	PCM
46-47 Philadelphia	60	....	....	360	120	412	.291	....	....	....	120	166	.723	....	....	....	41	139	....	....	....	....	....	6.0	....	0.7	....
47-48 Philadelphia	11	....	....	58	14	71	.197	....	....	....	30	37	.811	....	....	....	3	30	....	....	....	....	....	5.3	....	0.3	....
NBA Season Totals	71	....	....	418	134	483	.277	....	....	....	150	203	.739	....	....	....	44	169	....	....	....	....	....	5.9	....	0.6	....
46-47 Philadelphia	10	....	....	87	24	91	.264	....	....	....	39	46	.848	....	....	....	8	41	....	....	....	....	....	8.7	....	0.8	....
NBA Playoff Totals	10	....	....	87	24	91	.264	....	....	....	39	46	.848	....	....	....	8	41	....	....	....	....	....	8.7	....	0.8	....

• HILLMAN, Darnell

Darnell (Dr. Dunk) Hillman

Born: Aug. 29, 1949. Sacramento, CA, United States. Height: 6'9". Weight: 215 lbs. Drafted: 1971 College: San Jose State

YEAR TEAM	GP	GS	MIN	PTS	FGM	FGA	FG%	3PM	3PA	3P%	FTM	FTA	FT%	ORB	DRB	TRB	AST	PF	DQ	STL	BLK	TO	MPG	PPG	RPG	APG	PCM
71-72 Indiana-A	73	....	1386	515	200	410	.488	1	5	.200	114	177	.644	152	326	478	49	210	4	....	....	84	19.0	7.1	6.5	0.7	.495
72-73 Indiana-A	84	....	2541	804	328	735	.446	0	9	.000	148	252	.587	218	517	735	128	291	3	....	116	154	30.3	9.6	8.8	1.5	.418
73-74 Indiana-A	83	....	2319	758	328	658	.498	3	8	.375	99	191	.518	198	478	676	96	295	....	70	177	177	27.9	9.1	8.1	1.2	.431
74-75 Indiana-A	81	....	2603	1124	486	923	.527	0	4	.000	152	202	.752	296	451	747	131	330	....	73	132	209	32.1	13.9	9.2	1.6	.529
75-76 Indiana-A	74	....	2166	994	375	828	.453	1	4	.250	243	336	.723	248	422	670	147	306	....	80	80	196	29.3	13.4	9.1	2.0	.541
76-77 Indiana	82	....	2302	879	359	811	.443	....	....	....	161	244	.660	228	465	693	166	353	15	95	106	....	28.1	10.7	8.5	2.0	.472
77-78 New Jersey	45	....	1220	590	236	501	.471	....	....	....	118	205	.576	126	212	338	49	160	7	49	44	108	27.1	13.1	7.5	1.1	.482
77-78 Denver	33	....	746	257	104	209	.498	....	....	....	49	81	.605	73	166	239	53	130	4	14	37	66	22.6	7.8	7.2	1.6	.469
78-79 Kansas City	78	....	1618	547	211	428	.493	....	....	....	125	224	.558	138	293	431	91	288	11	50	66	133	20.7	7.0	5.5	1.2	.402
79-80 Golden State	49	....	708	198	82	179	.458	0	0	.000	34	68	.500	59	121	180	47	128	2	21	24	59	14.4	4.0	3.7	1.0	.337
NBA Season Totals	287	....	6594	2471	992	2128	.466	0	0	.000	487	822	.592	624	1257	1881	406	1059	39	229	277	366	23.0	8.6	6.6	1.4	....
ABA Season Totals	395	....	11015	4195	1717	3554	.483	5	30	.167	756	1158	.653	1112	2194	3306	551	1432	7	223	505	820	27.9	10.6	8.4	1.4	....
Career Totals	682	....	17609	6666	2709	5682	.477	5	30	.167	1243	1980	.628	1736	3451	5187	957	2491	46	452	782	1186	25.8	9.8	7.6	1.4	....
71-72 Indiana-A	20	....	327	124	53	95	.558	0	2	.000	18	33	.545	45	65	110	9	52	....	....	....	20	16.4	6.2	5.5	0.5	.503
72-73 Indiana-A	18	....	485	106	43	101	.426	0	0	.000	20	35	.571	39	96	135	17	44	0	....	....	29	26.9	5.9	7.5	0.9	.345
73-74 Indiana-A	14	....	352	117	47	85	.553	0	1	.000	23	46	.500	37	63	100	12	44	....	6	16	20	25.1	8.4	7.1	0.9	.441
74-75 Indiana-A	17	....	482	181	73	146	.500	0	0	.000	35	51	.686	40	93	133	14	68	....	10	30	24	28.4	10.6	7.8	0.8	.441
75-76 Indiana-A	3	....	111	43	16	39	.410	0	0	.000	11	14	.786	13	18	31	10	14	....	6	5	10	37.0	14.3	10.3	3.3	.483
77-78 Denver	13	....	260	73	31	79	.392	....	....	....	11	15	.733	25	55	80	18	49	1	6	7	24	20.0	5.6	6.2	1.4	.340
78-79 Kansas City	5	....	112	29	10	32	.313	....	....	....	9	17	.529	19	14	33	8	17	0	4	3	10	22.4	5.8	6.6	1.6	.302
NBA Playoff Totals	18	....	372	102	41	111	.369	....	....	....	20	32	.625	44	69	113	26	66	1	10	10	34	20.7	5.7	6.3	1.4	....
ABA Playoff Totals	72	....	1757	571	232	466	.498	0	3	.000	107	179	.598	174	335	509	62	222	0	22	51	103	24.4	7.9	7.1	0.9	....
Career Playoff Totals	90	....	2129	673	273	577	.473	0	3	.000	127	211	.602	218	404	622	88	288	1	32	61	137	23.7	7.5	6.9	1.0	....

• HILTON, Fred

Fred Hilton

Born: Jan. 15, 1948. Height: 6'3". Weight: 185 lbs. Drafted: 1971 College: Grambling

YEAR TEAM	GP	GS	MIN	PTS	FGM	FGA	FG%	3PM	3PA	3P%	FTM	FTA	FT%	ORB	DRB	TRB	AST	PF	DQ	STL	BLK	TO	MPG	PPG	RPG	APG	PCM
71-72 Buffalo	61	....	1349	708	309	795	.389	....	....	....	90	122	.738	....	....	156	116	145	0	....	....	....	22.1	11.6	2.6	1.9	.354
72-73 Buffalo	59	....	731	423	191	494	.387	....	....	....	41	53	.774	....	....	98	74	100	0	....	....	....	12.4	7.2	1.7	1.3	.388
NBA Season Totals	120	....	2080	1131	500	1289	.388	....	....	....	131	175	.749	....	....	254	190	245	0	....	....	....	17.3	9.4	2.1	1.6	....

• HINSON, Roy

Roy Manus Hinson Jr.

Born: May 2, 1961. Trenton, NJ, United States. Height: 6'9". Weight: 210 lbs. Drafted: 1983 College: Rutgers

YEAR TEAM	GP	GS	MIN	PTS	FGM	FGA	FG%	3PM	3PA	3P%	FTM	FTA	FT%	ORB	DRB	TRB	AST	PF	DQ	STL	BLK	TO	MPG	PPG	RPG	APG	PCM
83-84 Cleveland	80	61	1858	437	184	371	.496	0	0	.000	69	117	.590	175	324	499	69	306	11	31	145	112	23.2	5.5	6.2	0.9	.375
84-85 Cleveland	76	75	2344	1201	465	925	.503	0	3	.000	271	376	.721	186	410	596	68	311	13	51	173	175	30.8	15.8	7.8	0.9	.534
85-86 Cleveland	82	82	2834	1606	621	1167	.532	0	4	.000	364	506	.719	167	472	639	102	316	7	62	112	189	34.6	19.6	7.8	1.2	.556
86-87 Philadelphia	76	58	2489	1059	393	823	.478	0	1	.000	273	360	.758	150	338	488	60	281	4	45	161	152	32.8	13.9	6.4	0.8	.424
87-88 Philadelphia	29	10	845	335	123	272	.452	0	1	.000	89	124	.718	53	116	169	27	90	3	24	68	64	29.1	11.6	5.8	0.9	.415
87-88 New Jersey	48	47	1747	843	330	658	.502	0	1	.000	183	227	.806	106	242	348	72	185	3	45	72	106	36.4	17.6	7.3	1.5	.482
88-89 New Jersey	82	39	2542	1308	495	1027	.482	0	2	.000	318	420	.757	152	370	522	71	298	3	34	121	164	31.0	16.0	6.4	0.9	.464
89-90 New Jersey	25	19	793	376	145	286	.507	0	0	.000	86	99	.869	61	111	172	22	87	0	14	27	53	31.7	15.0	6.9	0.9	.467
90-91 New Jersey	9	0	91	41	20	39	.513	0	0	.000	1	3	.333	6	13	19	4	14	0	0	3	6	10.1	4.6	2.1	0.4	.385
NBA Season Totals	507	391	15543	7206	2776	5568	.499	0	12	.000	1654	2232	.741	1056	2396	3452	495	1888	44	306	882	1021	30.7	14.2	6.8	1.0	....

YEAR	TEAM	GP	GS	MIN	PTS	FGM	FGA	FG%	3PM	3PA	3P%	FTM	FTA	FT%	ORB	DRB	TRB	AST	PF	DQ	STL	BLK	TO	MPG	PPG	RPG	APG	PCM
84-85	Cleveland	4	4	120	67	26	48	.542	0	0	.000	15	23	.652	10	20	30	3	18	1	3	9	8	30.0	16.8	7.5	0.8	.577
86-87	Philadelphia	5	0	159	86	31	52	.596	0	0	.000	24	38	.632	6	17	23	3	18	0	4	10	2	31.8	17.2	4.6	0.6	.549
NBA Playoff Totals		9	4	279	153	57	100	.570	0	0	.000	39	61	.639	16	37	53	6	36	1	7	19	10	31.0	17.0	5.9	0.7	....

• HINTZ, Pat

Pat Hintz

Born: 1914. Height: 6' Weight: 175 lbs. Drafted: — College: Toledo

YEAR	TEAM	GP	GS	MIN	PTS	FGM	FGA	FG%	3PM	3PA	3P%	FTM	FTA	FT%	ORB	DRB	TRB	AST	PF	DQ	STL	BLK	TO	MPG	PPG	RPG	APG	PCM
41-42	Toledo-N	1	....	....	0	0	....	....	....	....	....	0	....	....	....	....	....	....	....	....	....	....	....	....	0.0	....	....	....
42-43	Toledo-N	4	....	....	40	18	....	....	....	....	....	4	....	....	....	....	....	....	....	....	....	....	....	....	10.0	....	....	....
NBL Season Totals		5	....	....	40	18	....	....	....	....	....	4	....	....	....	....	....	....	....	....	....	....	....	....	8.0	....	....	....

• HIRSCH, Mel

Melvin M. Hirsch

Born: July 31, 1921. Died: Dec.1968. Height: 5'6". Weight: 165 lbs. Drafted: — College: Brooklyn

YEAR	TEAM	GP	GS	MIN	PTS	FGM	FGA	FG%	3PM	3PA	3P%	FTM	FTA	FT%	ORB	DRB	TRB	AST	PF	DQ	STL	BLK	TO	MPG	PPG	RPG	APG	PCM
46-47	Boston	13	....	....	19	9	45	.200	....	....	....	1	2	.500	....	....	....	10	18	....	....	....	....	....	1.5	....	0.8	....
NBA Season Totals		13	....	....	19	9	45	.200	....	....	....	1	2	.500	....	....	....	10	18	....	....	....	....	....	1.5	....	0.8	....

• HITCH, Lew

Lewis Rufus Hitch

Born: July 16, 1929. Griggsville, IL, United States. Height: 6'8". Weight: 200 lbs. Drafted: 1951 College: Kansas State

YEAR	TEAM	GP	GS	MIN	PTS	FGM	FGA	FG%	3PM	3PA	3P%	FTM	FTA	FT%	ORB	DRB	TRB	AST	PF	DQ	STL	BLK	TO	MPG	PPG	RPG	APG	PCM
51-52	Minneapolis	61	....	849	217	77	215	.358	....	....	....	63	94	.670	....	....	243	50	89	3	....	....	....	13.9	3.6	4.0	0.8	.369
52-53	Minneapolis	70	....	1027	261	89	255	.349	....	....	....	83	136	.610	....	....	275	66	122	2	....	....	....	14.7	3.7	3.9	0.9	.351
53-54	Milwaukee	72	....	2452	575	221	603	.367	....	....	....	133	208	.639	....	....	691	141	176	3	....	....	....	34.1	8.0	9.6	2.0	.362
54-55	Mil/Min	74	....	1774	449	167	417	.400	....	....	....	115	169	.680	....	....	438	125	110	0	....	....	....	24.0	6.1	5.9	1.7	.386
55-56	Minneapolis	69	....	1129	288	94	235	.400	....	....	....	100	132	.758	....	....	283	77	85	0	....	....	....	16.4	4.2	4.1	1.1	.396
56-57	Rochester	30	....	531	141	52	138	.377	....	....	....	37	51	.725	....	....	116	12	55	0	....	....	....	17.7	4.7	3.9	0.4	.288
56-57	Philadelphia	38	....	602	144	59	158	.373	....	....	....	26	37	.703	....	....	137	28	48	0	....	....	....	15.8	3.8	3.6	0.7	.308
NBA Season Totals		414	....	8364	2075	759	2021	.376	....	....	....	557	827	.674	....	....	2183	499	685	8	....	....	....	20.2	5.0	5.3	1.2	....
51-52	Minneapolis	13	....	152	24	9	25	.360	....	....	....	6	21	.286	....	....	44	9	16	0	....	....	....	11.7	1.8	3.4	0.7	.293
52-53	Minneapolis	12	....	189	49	16	46	.348	....	....	....	17	32	.531	....	....	64	11	32	1	....	....	....	15.8	4.1	5.3	0.9	.374
54-55	Minneapolis	7	....	137	55	16	40	.400	....	....	....	23	29	.793	....	....	42	10	9	0	....	....	....	19.6	7.9	6.0	1.4	.550
55-56	Minneapolis	3	....	54	15	4	13	.308	....	....	....	7	10	.700	....	....	15	2	7	0	....	....	....	18.0	5.0	5.0	0.7	.338
56-57	Philadelphia	2	....	3	2	0	1	.000	....	....	....	2	2	1.000	....	....	2	0	0	0	....	....	....	1.5	1.0	1.0	0.0	.915
NBA Playoff Totals		37	....	535	145	45	125	.360	....	....	....	55	94	.585	....	....	167	32	64	1	....	....	....	14.5	3.9	4.5	0.9	....

• HITT, Joel

Joel R. Hitt Jr.

Born: Dec. 30, 1916. Goss, MS, United States. Height: 6'2". Weight: 180 lbs. Drafted: — College: Mississippi College

YEAR	TEAM	GP	GS	MIN	PTS	FGM	FGA	FG%	3PM	3PA	3P%	FTM	FTA	FT%	ORB	DRB	TRB	AST	PF	DQ	STL	BLK	TO	MPG	PPG	RPG	APG	PCM
39-40	Wingfoots-N	13	....	....	9	3	....	....	....	....	....	3	....	....	....	....	....	....	....	....	....	....	....	....	0.7	....	....	....
NBL Season Totals		13	....	....	9	3	....	....	....	....	....	3	....	....	....	....	....	....	....	....	....	....	....	....	0.7	....	....	....

• HODGE, Donald

Donald Jerome Hodge

Born: Feb. 25, 1969. Washington, DC, United States. Height: 7' Weight: 230 lbs. Drafted: 1991 College: Temple

YEAR	TEAM	GP	GS	MIN	PTS	FGM	FGA	FG%	3PM	3PA	3P%	FTM	FTA	FT%	ORB	DRB	TRB	AST	PF	DQ	STL	BLK	TO	MPG	PPG	RPG	APG	PCM
91-92	Dallas	51	27	1058	426	163	328	.497	0	0	.000	100	150	.667	118	157	275	39	128	2	25	23	77	20.7	8.4	5.4	0.8	.435
92-93	Dallas	79	8	1267	393	161	400	.403	0	0	.000	71	104	.683	93	201	294	75	204	2	33	37	87	16.0	5.0	3.7	0.9	.314
93-94	Dallas	50	0	428	136	46	101	.455	0	0	.000	44	52	.846	46	49	95	32	66	1	15	13	30	8.6	2.7	1.9	0.6	.401
94-95	Dallas	54	0	633	209	83	204	.407	4	14	.286	39	51	.765	40	82	122	41	107	1	10	14	38	11.7	3.9	2.3	0.8	.292
95-96	Dallas	13	0	113	18	9	24	.375	0	0	.000	0	0	.000	9	13	22	4	26	0	1	8	3	8.7	1.4	1.7	0.3	.197
95-96	Charlotte	2	0	2	0	0	0	.000	0	0	.000	0	0	.000	0	1	1	0	0	0	0	0	0	1.0	0.0	0.5	0.0	.470
NBA Season Totals		249	35	3501	1182	462	1057	.437	4	14	.286	254	357	.711	306	503	809	191	531	6	84	95	235	14.1	4.7	3.2	0.8	....

• HODGES, Craig

Craig Anthony Hodges

Born: June 27, 1960. Park Forest, IL, United States. Height: 6'2". Weight: 190 lbs. Drafted: 1982 College: Long Beach State

YEAR	TEAM	GP	GS	MIN	PTS	FGM	FGA	FG%	3PM	3PA	3P%	FTM	FTA	FT%	ORB	DRB	TRB	AST	PF	DQ	STL	BLK	TO	MPG	PPG	RPG	APG	PCM
82-83	San Diego	76	48	2022	750	318	704	.452	20	90	.222	94	130	.723	53	69	122	275	192	3	82	4	160	26.6	9.9	1.6	3.6	.319
83-84	San Diego	76	28	1571	592	258	573	.450	10	46	.217	66	88	.750	22	64	86	116	166	2	58	1	84	20.7	7.8	1.1	1.5	.250
84-85	Milwaukee	82	63	2496	871	359	732	.490	47	135	.348	106	130	.815	74	112	186	349	262	8	96	1	131	30.4	10.6	2.3	4.3	.362
85-86	Milwaukee	66	66	1739	716	284	568	.500	73	162	**.451**	75	86	.872	39	78	117	229	157	3	74	2	86	26.3	10.8	1.8	3.5	.413
86-87	Milwaukee	78	43	2147	846	315	682	.462	85	228	.373	131	147	.891	48	92	140	240	189	3	76	7	125	27.5	10.8	1.8	3.1	.352
87-88	Milwaukee	43	0	983	397	155	345	.449	55	118	**.466**	32	39	.821	12	34	46	109	80	1	30	0	47	22.9	9.2	1.1	2.5	.328
87-88	Phoenix	23	0	462	232	87	178	.489	31	57	**.544**	27	32	.844	7	25	32	44	38	0	16	2	28	20.1	10.1	1.4	1.9	.421
88-89	Phoenix	10	0	92	39	16	36	.444	4	12	.333	3	4	.750	2	3	5	8	8	0	2	0	5	9.2	3.9	0.5	0.8	.290
88-89	Chicago	49	6	1112	490	187	394	.475	71	168	.423	45	53	.849	21	63	84	138	82	0	41	4	54	22.7	10.0	1.7	2.8	.425
89-90	Chicago	63	0	1055	407	145	331	.438	87	181	.481	30	33	.909	11	42	53	110	87	1	30	2	32	16.7	6.5	0.8	1.7	.339
90-91	Chicago	73	0	843	362	146	344	.424	44	115	.383	26	27	.963	10	32	42	97	74	0	34	2	37	11.5	5.0	0.6	1.3	.337
91-92	Chicago	56	2	555	238	93	242	.384	36	96	.375	16	17	.941	7	17	24	54	33	0	14	1	22	9.9	4.3	0.4	1.0	.284
NBA Season Totals		695	256	15077	5940	2363	5129	.461	563	1408	.400	651	786	.828	306	631	937	1769	1368	21	553	26	811	21.7	8.5	1.3	2.5	....
84-85	Milwaukee	8	8	216	64	28	77	.364	4	23	.174	4	5	.800	2	11	13	26	29	2	12	1	18	27.0	8.0	1.6	3.3	.183
85-86	Milwaukee	14	14	460	189	74	145	.510	14	31	.452	27	34	.794	9	16	25	63	44	1	32	2	24	32.9	13.5	1.8	4.5	.433
86-87	Milwaukee	12	0	226	95	40	77	.519	5	17	.294	10	11	.909	11	11	22	20	16	0	9	2	3	18.8	7.9	1.8	1.7	.451
88-89	Chicago	17	17	554	191	73	177	.412	35	88	.398	10	14	.714	8	17	25	62	55	1	22	3	24	32.6	11.2	1.5	3.6	.284
89-90	Chicago	16	1	254	71	28	74	.378	12	41	.293	3	4	.750	6	12	18	17	31	1	4	0	14	15.9	4.4	1.1	1.1	.151
90-91	Chicago	17	0	209	80	33	78	.423	11	28	.393	3	4	.750	0	4	4	10	21	0	11	0	11	12.3	4.7	0.2	0.6	.202
91-92	Chicago	17	0	137	42	16	41	.390	9	20	.450	1	2	.500	3	1	4	5	10	0	5	0	8	8.1	2.5	0.2	0.3	.146
NBA Playoff Totals		101	40	2056	732	292	669	.436	90	248	.363	58	74	.784	39	72	111	203	206	5	95	8	102	20.4	7.2	1.1	2.0	....

• HOEFER, Charlie

Adolph Charles (Dutch) Hoefer

Born: July 12, 1917. Height: 5'9". Weight: 158 lbs. Drafted: — College: Queens

YEAR TEAM	GP	GS	MIN	PTS	FGM	FGA	FG%	3PM	3PA	3P%	FTM	FTA	FT%	ORB	DRB	TRB	AST	PF	DQ	STL	BLK	TO	MPG	PPG	RPG	APG	PCM
46-47 Toronto	23	....	....	140	54	198	.273	....	....	....	32	46	.696	....	....	....	9	61	....	....	....	....	....	6.1	....	0.4	....
46-47 Boston	35	....	....	211	76	316	.241	....	....	....	59	93	.634	....	....	....	24	81	....	....	....	....	....	6.0	....	0.7	....
47-48 Boston	7	....	....	10	3	19	.158	....	....	....	4	8	.500	....	....	....	3	17	....	....	....	....	....	1.4	....	0.4	....
NBA Season Totals	65	....	....	361	133	533	.250	....	....	....	95	147	.646	....	....	....	36	159	....	....	....	....	....	5.6	....	0.6	....

• HOEKSTRA, Johnny

Johnny Hoekstra

Born: 1917. Height: 6'5". Weight: 225 lbs. Drafted: — College: Gallagher Business School

YEAR TEAM	GP	GS	MIN	PTS	FGM	FGA	FG%	3PM	3PA	3P%	FTM	FTA	FT%	ORB	DRB	TRB	AST	PF	DQ	STL	BLK	TO	MPG	PPG	RPG	APG	PCM
37-38 Kankakee-N	12	....	....	70	27	....	....	....	....	....	16	....	....	....	....	....	....	....	....	....	....	....	....	5.8	....	....	....
NBL Season Totals	12	....	....	70	27	....	....	....	....	....	16	....	....	....	....	....	....	....	....	....	....	....	....	5.8	....	....	....

• HOFFMAN, Howie

Howard Hoffman

Born: 1920. Height: 6'4". Weight: 195 lbs. Drafted: — College: Purdue

YEAR TEAM	GP	GS	MIN	PTS	FGM	FGA	FG%	3PM	3PA	3P%	FTM	FTA	FT%	ORB	DRB	TRB	AST	PF	DQ	STL	BLK	TO	MPG	PPG	RPG	APG	PCM
44-45 Oshkosh-N	18	....	....	105	44	....	....	....	....	....	17	....	....	....	....	....	....	....	....	....	....	....	....	5.8	....	....	....
46-47 Anderson-N	5	....	....	13	5	....	....	....	....	....	3	6	.500	....	....	....	....	....	....	....	....	....	....	2.6	....	....	....
NBL Season Totals	23	....	....	118	49	....	....	....	....	....	20	6	....	....	....	....	....	....	....	....	....	....	....	5.1	....	....	....

• HOFFMAN, Paul

Paul James (Bear, The Body) Hoffman

Born: Apr. 12, 1922. Died: Nov.12, 1998. Height: 6'2". Weight: 195 lbs. Drafted: 1947 College: Purdue

YEAR TEAM	GP	GS	MIN	PTS	FGM	FGA	FG%	3PM	3PA	3P%	FTM	FTA	FT%	ORB	DRB	TRB	AST	PF	DQ	STL	BLK	TO	MPG	PPG	RPG	APG	PCM
47-48 Baltimore	37	....	....	388	142	408	.348	....	....	....	104	157	.662	....	....	....	23	123	....	....	....	....	....	10.5	....	0.6	....
49-50 Baltimore	60	....	....	866	312	914	.341	....	....	....	242	364	.665	....	....	....	161	234	....	....	....	....	....	14.4	....	2.7	....
50-51 Baltimore	41	....	....	359	127	399	.318	....	....	....	105	156	.673	....	....	202	111	135	2	....	....	....	....	8.8	4.9	2.7	....
52-53 Baltimore	69	....	1955	704	240	656	.366	....	....	....	224	342	.655	....	....	317	237	282	13	....	....	....	28.3	10.2	4.6	3.4	.404
53-54 Baltimore	72	....	2505	723	253	761	.332	....	....	....	217	303	.716	....	....	486	285	271	10	....	....	....	34.8	10.0	6.8	4.0	.379
54-55 Bal/NY/Phi	38	....	670	194	65	216	.301	....	....	....	64	93	.688	....	....	124	94	93	0	....	....	....	17.6	5.1	3.3	2.5	.366
NBA Season Totals	317	....	5130	3234	1139	3354	.340	....	....	....	956	1415	.676	....	....	1129	911	1138	25	....	....	....	16.2	10.2	3.6	2.9	....
47-48 Baltimore	11	....	....	129	44	141	.312	....	....	....	41	62	.661	....	....	....	7	39	....	....	....	....	....	11.7	....	0.6	....
52-53 Baltimore	2	....	81	17	5	28	.179	....	....	....	7	12	.583	....	....	7	11	10	1	....	....	....	40.5	8.5	3.5	5.5	.173
NBA Playoff Totals	13	....	81	146	49	169	.290	....	....	....	48	74	.649	....	....	7	18	49	1	....	....	....	6.2	11.2	0.5	1.4	....

• HOGAN, George

George Hogan

Born: 1917. Height: 6'1". Weight: 171 lbs. Drafted: — College: Loyola (IL)

YEAR TEAM	GP	GS	MIN	PTS	FGM	FGA	FG%	3PM	3PA	3P%	FTM	FTA	FT%	ORB	DRB	TRB	AST	PF	DQ	STL	BLK	TO	MPG	PPG	RPG	APG	PCM
39-40 Chicago-N	13	....	....	20	7	....	....	....	....	....	6	....	....	....	....	....	....	....	....	....	....	....	....	1.5	....	....	....
39-40 Hammond-N	13	....	....	41	17	....	....	....	....	....	7	....	....	....	....	....	....	....	....	....	....	....	....	3.2	....	....	....
40-41 Chicago-N	22	....	....	49	19	....	....	....	....	....	11	....	....	....	....	....	....	....	....	....	....	....	....	2.2	....	....	....
41-42 Chicago-N	20	....	....	104	43	....	....	....	....	....	18	....	....	....	....	....	....	....	....	....	....	....	....	5.2	....	....	....
45-46 Chicago-N	3	....	....	4	2	....	....	....	....	....	0	0	.000	....	....	....	....	....	....	....	....	....	....	1.3	....	....	....
NBL Season Totals	71	....	....	218	88	....	....	....	....	....	42	0	....	....	....	....	....	....	....	....	....	....	....	3.1	....	....	....

• HOGSETT, Bob

Robert L. Hogsett

Born: Jan. 29, 1941. Died: Dec.5, 1984. Height: 6'7". Weight: 230 lbs. Drafted: — College: Tennessee

YEAR TEAM	GP	GS	MIN	PTS	FGM	FGA	FG%	3PM	3PA	3P%	FTM	FTA	FT%	ORB	DRB	TRB	AST	PF	DQ	STL	BLK	TO	MPG	PPG	RPG	APG	PCM
66-67 Detroit	7	....	22	16	5	16	.313	....	....	....	6	6	1.000	....	....	3	1	5	0	....	....	....	3.1	2.3	0.4	0.1	.402
67-68 Pittsburgh-A	13	....	119	21	7	20	.350	0	0	.000	7	17	.412	....	....	23	1	11	0	....	....	4	9.2	1.6	1.8	0.1	.183
NBA Season Totals	7	....	22	16	5	16	.313	....	....	....	6	6	1.000	....	....	3	1	5	0	....	....	....	3.1	2.3	0.4	0.1	....
ABA Season Totals	13	....	119	21	7	20	.350	0	0	.000	7	17	.412	....	....	23	1	11	0	....	....	4	9.2	1.6	1.8	0.1	....
Career Totals	20	....	141	37	12	36	.333	0	0	.000	13	23	.565	....	....	26	2	16	0	....	....	4	7.1	1.9	1.3	0.1	....

• HOGUE, Duke

Paul H. (Duke) Hogue

Born: Apr. 28, 1940. Knoxville, TN, United States. Height: 6'9". Weight: 240 lbs. Drafted: 1962 College: Cincinnati

YEAR TEAM	GP	GS	MIN	PTS	FGM	FGA	FG%	3PM	3PA	3P%	FTM	FTA	FT%	ORB	DRB	TRB	AST	PF	DQ	STL	BLK	TO	MPG	PPG	RPG	APG	PCM
62-63 New York	50	....	1340	383	152	419	.363	....	....	....	79	174	.454	....	....	430	42	220	12	....	....	....	26.8	7.7	8.6	0.8	.327
63-64 New York	6	....	89	19	9	16	.563	....	....	....	1	5	.200	....	....	15	5	15	0	....	....	....	14.8	3.2	2.5	0.8	.269
63-64 Baltimore	9	....	58	7	3	14	.214	....	....	....	1	2	.500	....	....	16	1	20	1	....	....	....	6.4	0.8	1.8	0.1	.068
NBA Season Totals	65	....	1487	409	164	449	.365	....	....	....	81	181	.448	....	....	461	48	255	13	....	....	....	22.9	6.3	7.1	0.7	....

• HOIBERG, Fred

Fredrick Kristian (The Mayor) Hoiberg

Born: Oct. 15, 1972. Lincoln, NE, United States. Height: 6'4". Weight: 203 lbs. Drafted: 1995 College: Iowa State

YEAR TEAM	GP	GS	MIN	PTS	FGM	FGA	FG%	3PM	3PA	3P%	FTM	FTA	FT%	ORB	DRB	TRB	AST	PF	DQ	STL	BLK	TO	MPG	PPG	RPG	APG	PCM
95-96 Indiana	15	1	85	32	8	19	.421	1	3	.333	15	18	.833	4	5	9	8	12	0	6	1	8	5.7	2.1	0.6	0.5	.360
96-97 Indiana	47	0	572	224	67	156	.429	29	70	.414	61	77	.792	13	68	81	41	51	0	27	6	24	12.2	4.8	1.7	0.9	.415
97-98 Indiana	65	1	874	261	85	222	.383	32	85	.376	59	69	.855	14	109	123	45	101	0	40	3	20	13.4	4.0	1.9	0.7	.306
98-99 Indiana	12	0	87	19	6	21	.286	1	9	.111	6	6	1.000	2	9	11	4	11	0	0	0	3	7.3	1.6	0.9	0.3	.142
99-00 Chicago	31	11	845	279	89	230	.387	32	94	.340	69	76	.908	7	103	110	85	66	0	40	2	43	27.3	9.0	3.5	2.7	.366
00-01 Chicago	74	37	2247	673	217	495	.438	103	250	.412	136	157	.866	21	287	308	263	155	0	98	12	74	30.4	9.1	4.2	3.6	.420
01-02 Chicago	79	8	1409	345	121	291	.416	24	92	.261	79	94	.840	18	192	210	136	87	2	61	5	32	17.8	4.4	2.7	1.7	.365
02-03 Chicago	63	0	783	144	49	126	.389	5	21	.238	41	50	.820	11	126	137	70	59	0	40	5	25	12.4	2.3	2.2	1.1	.335
NBA Season Totals	386	58	6902	1977	642	1560	.412	227	624	.364	466	547	.852	90	899	989	652	542	2	312	34	229	17.9	5.1	2.6	1.7	....

YEAR	TEAM	GP	GS	MIN	PTS	FGM	FGA	FG%	3PM	3PA	3P%	FTM	FTA	FT%	ORB	DRB	TRB	AST	PF	DQ	STL	BLK	TO	MPG	PPG	RPG	APG	PCM
97-98	Indiana	2	0	20	9	3	8	.375	1	2	.500	2	2	1.000	1	3	4	1	2	0	1	0	0	10.0	4.5	2.0	0.5	.459
98-99	Indiana	4	0	20	4	2	4	.500	0	0	.000	0	0	.000	0	3	3	2	1	0	3	0	0	5.0	1.0	0.8	0.5	.467
NBA Playoff Totals		6	0	40	13	5	12	.417	1	2	.500	2	2	1.000	1	6	7	3	3	0	4	0	0	6.7	2.2	1.2	0.5	....

• HOLCOMB, Doug
Douglas M. Holcomb

Born: Feb. 9, 1925. Height: 6'4". Weight: 200 lbs. Drafted: — College: Wisconsin

YEAR	TEAM	GP	GS	MIN	PTS	FGM	FGA	FG%	3PM	3PA	3P%	FTM	FTA	FT%	ORB	DRB	TRB	AST	PF	DQ	STL	BLK	TO	MPG	PPG	RPG	APG	PCM
48-49	Baltimore	3	....	....	15	3	12	.250	....	....	....	9	14	.643	....	....	....	5	5	....	....	....	....	5.0	....	1.7	....	
NBA Season Totals		3	....	....	15	3	12	.250	....	....	....	9	14	.643	....	....	....	5	5	....	....	....	....	5.0	....	1.7	....	

• HOLLAND, Bill
Bill Holland

Born: 1914. Height: 6'5". Weight: 210 lbs. Drafted: — College: Edinboro

YEAR	TEAM	GP	GS	MIN	PTS	FGM	FGA	FG%	3PM	3PA	3P%	FTM	FTA	FT%	ORB	DRB	TRB	AST	PF	DQ	STL	BLK	TO	MPG	PPG	RPG	APG	PCM
37-38	Warren-N	2	....	....	7	3	....	....	....	....	....	1	....	....	....	....	....	....	....	....	....	....	....		3.5	....	....	
38-39	Cleveland-N	27	....	....	180	73	....	....	....	....	....	34	....	....	....	....	....	....	....	....	....	....	....		6.7	....	....	
39-40	Detroit-N	27	....	....	107	36	....	....	....	....	....	35	....	....	....	....	....	....	....	....	....	....	....		4.0	....	....	
NBL Season Totals		56	....	....	294	112	....	....	....	....	....	70	....	....	....	....	....	....	....	....	....	....	....		5.3	....	....	
39-40	Detroit-N	3	....	....	3	1	....	....	....	....	....	1	....	....	....	....	....	....	....	....	....	....	....		1.0	....	....	
NBL Playoff Totals		3	....	....	3	1	....	....	....	....	....	1	....	....	....	....	....	....	....	....	....	....	....		1.0	....	....	

• HOLLAND, Brad
John Bradley Holland

Born: Dec. 6, 1956. Billings, MT, United States. Height: 6'3". Weight: 180 lbs. Drafted: 1979 College: UCLA

YEAR	TEAM	GP	GS	MIN	PTS	FGM	FGA	FG%	3PM	3PA	3P%	FTM	FTA	FT%	ORB	DRB	TRB	AST	PF	DQ	STL	BLK	TO	MPG	PPG	RPG	APG	PCM
79-80	LA Lakers	38	....	197	106	44	104	.423	3	15	.200	15	16	.938	4	13	17	22	24	0	15	1	11	5.2	2.8	0.4	0.6	.428
80-81	LA Lakers	41	....	295	130	47	111	.423	1	3	.333	35	49	.714	9	20	29	23	44	0	21	1	33	7.2	3.2	0.7	0.6	.294
81-82	Washington	13	3	185	57	27	73	.370	0	3	.000	3	4	.750	6	7	13	16	12	0	11	1	7	14.2	4.4	1.0	1.2	.230
81-82	Milwaukee	1	0	9	0	0	5	.000	0	0	.000	0	2	.000	0	0	0	2	1	0	0	0	1	9.0	0.0	0.0	2.0	-.528
NBA Season Totals		93	3	686	293	118	293	.403	4	21	.190	53	71	.746	19	40	59	63	81	0	47	3	52	7.4	3.2	0.6	0.7	....
79-80	LA Lakers	9	....	32	14	5	10	.500	0	0	.000	4	4	1.000	2	3	5	3	8	0	5	0	3	3.6	1.6	0.6	0.3	.484
80-81	LA Lakers	1	....	1	0	0	0	.000	0	0	.000	0	0	.000	0	0	0	0	0	0	0	0	1	1.0	0.0	0.0	0.0	-.911
81-82	Milwaukee	1	0	3	2	1	1	1.000	0	0	.000	0	0	.000	0	0	0	1	0	0	0	0	0	3.0	2.0	0.0	1.0	1.026
NBA Playoff Totals		11	0	36	16	6	11	.545	0	0	.000	4	4	1.000	2	3	5	4	8	0	5	0	4	3.3	1.5	0.5	0.4	....

• HOLLAND, Joe
Joseph Burnett Holland Sr.

Born: Sept. 26, 1925. Benton, KY, United States. Height: 6'4". Weight: 185 lbs. Drafted: 1948 College: Kentucky

YEAR	TEAM	GP	GS	MIN	PTS	FGM	FGA	FG%	3PM	3PA	3P%	FTM	FTA	FT%	ORB	DRB	TRB	AST	PF	DQ	STL	BLK	TO	MPG	PPG	RPG	APG	PCM
49-50	Indianapolis	64	....	....	388	145	453	.320	....	....	....	98	142	.690	....	....	....	130	220	....	....	....	....	6.1	....	2.0	....	
50-51	Indianapolis	67	....	....	470	196	594	.330	....	....	....	78	137	.569	....	....	344	150	228	8	....	....	....	7.0	5.1	2.2	....	
51-52	Indianapolis	55	....	737	226	93	265	.351	....	....	....	40	69	.580	....	....	166	47	90	0	....	....	....	13.4	4.1	3.0	0.9	.326
NBA Season Totals		186	....	737	1084	434	1312	.331	....	....	....	216	348	.621	....	....	510	327	538	8	....	....	....	4.0	5.8	2.7	1.8	....
49-50	Indianapolis	6	....	....	48	21	61	.344	....	....	....	6	15	.400	....	....	15	29	....	....	....	....		8.0	....	2.5	....	
50-51	Indianapolis	3	....	....	35	17	36	.472	....	....	....	1	4	.250	....	....	12	11	10	0	....	....	....	11.7	4.0	3.7	....	
51-52	Indianapolis	1	....	1	0	0	0	.000	....	....	....	0	0	.000	....	....	0	0	0	0	....	....	....	1.0	0.0	0.0	0.0	.000
NBA Playoff Totals		10	....	1	83	38	97	.392	....	....	....	7	19	.368	....	....	12	26	39	0	....	....	....	0.1	8.3	1.2	2.6	....

• HOLLAND, Wilbur
Wilbur Holland

Born: Nov. 8, 1951. Columbus, GA, United States. Height: 6' Weight: 175 lbs. Drafted: 1975 College: New Orleans

YEAR	TEAM	GP	GS	MIN	PTS	FGM	FGA	FG%	3PM	3PA	3P%	FTM	FTA	FT%	ORB	DRB	TRB	AST	PF	DQ	STL	BLK	TO	MPG	PPG	RPG	APG	PCM
75-76	Atlanta	33	....	351	192	85	213	.399	....	....	....	22	34	.647	15	26	41	26	48	0	20	2	....	10.6	5.8	1.2	0.8	.346
76-77	Chicago	79	....	2453	1176	509	1120	.454	....	....	....	158	192	.823	78	175	253	253	201	3	169	16	....	31.1	14.9	3.2	3.2	.429
77-78	Chicago	82	....	2884	1361	569	1285	.443	....	....	....	223	279	.799	105	189	294	313	258	4	164	14	221	35.2	16.6	3.6	3.8	.405
78-79	Chicago	82	....	2483	1031	445	940	.473	....	....	....	141	176	.801	78	176	254	330	240	9	122	12	189	30.3	12.6	3.1	4.0	.405
NBA Season Totals		276	....	8171	3760	1608	3558	.452	....	....	....	544	681	.799	276	566	842	922	747	16	475	44	410	29.6	13.6	3.1	3.3	....
76-77	Chicago	3	....	84	44	17	34	.500	....	....	....	10	10	1.000	5	4	9	3	8	0	1	0	....	28.0	14.7	3.0	1.0	.441
NBA Playoff Totals		3	....	84	44	17	34	.500	....	....	....	10	10	1.000	5	4	9	3	8	0	1	0	....	28.0	14.7	3.0	1.0	....

• HOLLINS, Lionel
Lionel Eugene Hollins

Born: Oct. 19, 1953. Ark City, KS, United States. Height: 6'3". Weight: 185 lbs. Drafted: 1975 College: Arizona State

YEAR	TEAM	GP	GS	MIN	PTS	FGM	FGA	FG%	3PM	3PA	3P%	FTM	FTA	FT%	ORB	DRB	TRB	AST	PF	DQ	STL	BLK	TO	MPG	PPG	RPG	APG	PCM
75-76	Portland	74	....	1891	800	311	738	.421	....	....	....	178	247	.721	39	136	175	306	235	5	131	28	....	25.6	10.8	2.4	4.1	.425
76-77	Portland	76	....	2224	1119	452	1046	.432	....	....	....	215	287	.749	52	158	210	313	265	5	166	38	....	29.3	14.7	2.8	4.1	.449
77-78	Portland	81	....	2741	1285	531	1202	.442	....	....	....	223	300	.743	81	196	277	380	268	4	157	29	243	33.8	15.9	3.4	4.7	.426
78-79	Portland	64	....	1967	976	402	886	.454	....	....	....	172	221	.778	32	117	149	325	199	3	114	24	224	30.7	15.3	2.3	5.1	.429
79-80	Portland	20	....	413	199	82	213	.385	1	10	.100	34	53	.642	5	15	20	50	35	0	30	1	60	20.7	10.0	1.0	2.5	.248
79-80	Philadelphia	27	....	796	329	130	313	.415	2	10	.200	67	87	.770	24	45	69	112	68	0	46	9	68	29.5	12.2	2.6	4.1	.373
80-81	Philadelphia	82	....	2154	781	327	696	.470	2	15	.133	125	171	.731	47	144	191	352	205	2	104	18	205	26.3	9.5	2.3	4.3	.377
81-82	Philadelphia	81	81	2257	894	380	797	.477	2	16	.125	132	188	.702	35	152	187	316	198	1	103	20	146	27.9	11.0	2.3	3.9	.392
82-83	San Diego	56	54	1844	758	313	717	.437	3	21	.143	129	179	.721	30	98	128	373	155	2	111	14	196	32.9	13.5	2.3	6.7	.413
83-84	Detroit	32	0	216	59	24	63	.381	0	2	.000	11	13	.846	4	18	22	62	26	0	13	1	26	6.8	1.8	0.7	1.9	.395
84-85	Houston	80	60	1950	609	249	540	.461	3	13	.231	108	136	.794	33	140	173	417	187	1	78	10	168	24.4	7.6	2.2	5.2	.395
NBA Season Totals		673	195	18453	7809	3201	7211	.444	13	87	.149	1394	1882	.741	382	1219	1601	3006	1841	23	1053	192	1336	27.4	11.6	2.4	4.5	....

YEAR	TEAM	GP	GS	MIN	PTS	FGM	FGA	FG%	3PM	3PA	3P%	FTM	FTA	FT%	ORB	DRB	TRB	AST	PF	DQ	STL	BLK	TO	MPG	PPG	RPG	APG	PCM
76-77	Portland	19	....	682	328	134	321	.417	....	....	....	60	88	.682	13	39	52	85	74	2	47	5	....	35.9	17.3	2.7	4.5	.387
77-78	Portland	6	....	223	100	40	89	.449	....	....	....	20	29	.690	5	24	29	33	21	1	7	0	19	37.2	16.7	4.8	5.5	.430
78-79	Portland	3	....	66	21	8	26	.308	....	....	....	5	7	.714	1	2	3	5	8	0	3	0	7	22.0	7.0	1.0	1.7	.075
79-80	Philadelphia	18	....	618	248	97	233	.416	0	10	.000	54	68	.794	17	54	71	113	49	0	27	3	46	34.3	13.8	3.9	6.3	.437
80-81	Philadelphia	16	....	490	163	67	152	.441	0	1	.000	29	37	.784	8	26	34	65	42	0	17	1	19	30.6	10.2	2.1	4.1	.334
81-82	Philadelphia	8	2	114	34	15	49	.306	0	1	.000	4	6	.667	1	8	9	25	11	0	9	1	13	14.3	4.3	1.1	3.1	.256
83-84	Detroit	2	0	6	0	0	1	.000	0	0	.000	0	0	.000	0	0	0	0	0	0	1	2	3.0	0.0	0.0	0.0	-.310
84-85	Houston	5	1	94	17	8	26	.308	0	0	.000	1	1	1.000	1	8	9	18	16	1	4	0	7	18.8	3.4	1.8	3.6	.187
NBA Playoff Totals		77	3	2293	911	369	897	.411	0	12	.000	173	236	.733	46	161	207	344	221	4	114	11	113	29.8	11.8	2.7	4.5	....

• HOLLIS, Essie

Essie B. Hollis

Born: May 16, 1955. Erie, PA, United States.   Height: 6'6".   Weight: 195 lbs.   Drafted: 1977   College: St. Bonaventure

YEAR	TEAM	GP	GS	MIN	PTS	FGM	FGA	FG%	3PM	3PA	3P%	FTM	FTA	FT%	ORB	DRB	TRB	AST	PF	DQ	STL	BLK	TO	MPG	PPG	RPG	APG	PCM
78-79	Detroit	25	....	154	69	30	75	.400	....	....	....	9	12	.750	21	24	45	6	28	0	11	1	15	6.2	2.8	1.8	0.2	.383
NBA Season Totals		25	....	154	69	30	75	.400	....	....	....	9	12	.750	21	24	45	6	28	0	11	1	15	6.2	2.8	1.8	0.2	....

• HOLM, Bobby

Robert Holm

Born: 1919.   Height: 6'   Weight: 200 lbs.   Drafted: —   College: Seton Hall

YEAR	TEAM	GP	GS	MIN	PTS	FGM	FGA	FG%	3PM	3PA	3P%	FTM	FTA	FT%	ORB	DRB	TRB	AST	PF	DQ	STL	BLK	TO	MPG	PPG	RPG	APG	PCM
44-45	Sheboygan-N	30	....	....	164	57	....	....	....	....	....	50	....	....	....	....	....	....	....	....	....	....	....	....	5.5	....	....	....
45-46	Sheboygan-N	33	....	....	182	70	....	....	....	....	....	42	55	.764	....	....	....	....	....	....	....	....	....	....	5.5	....	....	....
46-47	Sheboygan-N	44	....	....	204	63	....	....	....	....	....	78	101	.772	....	....	....	101	....	....	....	....	....	....	4.6	....	....	....
NBL Season Totals		107	....	....	550	190	....	....	....	....	....	170	156	....	....	....	....	101	....	....	....	....	....	....	5.1	....	....	....
44-45	Sheboygan-N	8	....	....	45	16	....	....	....	....	....	13	....	....	....	....	....	....	....	....	....	....	....	....	5.6	....	....	....
45-46	Sheboygan-N	8	....	....	49	21	....	....	....	....	....	7	13	.538	....	....	....	....	....	....	....	....	....	....	6.1	....	....	....
46-47	Sheboygan-N	5	....	....	22	10	....	....	....	....	....	2	2	1.000	....	....	....	....	....	....	....	....	....	....	4.4	....	....	....
NBL Playoff Totals		21	....	....	116	47	....	....	....	....	....	22	15	....	....	....	....	....	....	....	....	....	....	....	5.5	....	....	....

• HOLMAN, Dennis

Dennis R. (Denny) Holman

Born: Oct. 8, 1945.   Height: 6'3".   Weight: 175 lbs.   Drafted: —   College: Southern Methodist

YEAR	TEAM	GP	GS	MIN	PTS	FGM	FGA	FG%	3PM	3PA	3P%	FTM	FTA	FT%	ORB	DRB	TRB	AST	PF	DQ	STL	BLK	TO	MPG	PPG	RPG	APG	PCM
67-68	Dallas-A	46	....	554	176	55	153	.359	4	9	.444	62	103	.602	....	....	78	73	85	1	....	....	40	12.0	3.8	1.7	1.6	.348
ABA Season Totals		46	....	554	176	55	153	.359	4	9	.444	62	103	.602	....	....	78	73	85	1	....	....	40	12.0	3.8	1.7	1.6	....
67-68	Dallas-A	8	....	128	31	9	31	.290	1	2	.500	12	12	1.000	....	....	16	15	19	0	....	....	9	16.0	3.9	2.0	1.9	.279
ABA Playoff Totals		8	....	128	31	9	31	.290	1	2	.500	12	12	1.000	....	....	16	15	19	0	....	....	9	16.0	3.9	2.0	1.9	....

• HOLMES, Ife

Ife Holmes

Born: 1907.   Height: 5'6".   Weight: 150 lbs.   Drafted: —   College: DePauw

YEAR	TEAM	GP	GS	MIN	PTS	FGM	FGA	FG%	3PM	3PA	3P%	FTM	FTA	FT%	ORB	DRB	TRB	AST	PF	DQ	STL	BLK	TO	MPG	PPG	RPG	APG	PCM
37-38	Fort Wayne-N	15	....	....	41	17	....	....	....	....	....	7	....	....	....	....	....	....	....	....	....	....	....	....	2.7	....	....	....
NBL Season Totals		15	....	....	41	17	....	....	....	....	....	7	....	....	....	....	....	....	....	....	....	....	....	....	2.7	....	....	....

• HOLSTEIN, Jim

James H. Holstein

Born: Sept. 24, 1930.   Height: 6'3".   Weight: 180 lbs.   Drafted: 1952   College: Cincinnati

YEAR	TEAM	GP	GS	MIN	PTS	FGM	FGA	FG%	3PM	3PA	3P%	FTM	FTA	FT%	ORB	DRB	TRB	AST	PF	DQ	STL	BLK	TO	MPG	PPG	RPG	APG	PCM
52-53	Minneapolis	66	....	989	266	98	274	.358	....	....	....	70	105	.667	....	....	173	74	128	1	....	....	....	15.0	4.0	2.6	1.1	.303
53-54	Minneapolis	70	....	1155	240	88	288	.306	....	....	....	64	112	.571	....	....	204	79	140	0	....	....	....	16.5	3.4	2.9	1.1	.241
54-55	Minneapolis	62	....	980	281	107	330	.324	....	....	....	67	94	.713	....	....	206	58	107	0	....	....	....	15.8	4.5	3.3	0.9	.296
55-56	Fort Wayne	27	....	352	72	24	89	.270	....	....	....	24	37	.649	....	....	76	38	51	1	....	....	....	13.0	2.7	2.8	1.4	.293
NBA Season Totals		225	....	3476	859	317	981	.323	....	....	....	225	348	.647	....	....	659	249	426	2	....	....	....	15.4	3.8	2.9	1.1	....
52-53	Minneapolis	12	....	192	52	20	42	.476	....	....	....	12	23	.522	....	....	30	11	30	0	....	....	....	16.0	4.3	2.5	0.9	.297
53-54	Minneapolis	13	....	188	46	15	49	.306	....	....	....	16	23	.696	....	....	35	11	28	0	....	....	....	14.5	3.5	2.7	0.8	.258
54-55	Minneapolis	7	....	117	40	16	38	.421	....	....	....	8	9	.889	....	....	30	6	8	0	....	....	....	16.7	5.7	4.3	0.9	.428
NBA Playoff Totals		32	....	497	138	51	129	.395	....	....	....	36	55	.655	....	....	95	28	66	0	....	....	....	15.5	4.3	3.0	0.9	....

• HOLT, A.W.

Alvin William Holt

Born: Aug. 26, 1946.   Height: 6'7".   Weight: 210 lbs.   Drafted: —   College: Jackson State

YEAR	TEAM	GP	GS	MIN	PTS	FGM	FGA	FG%	3PM	3PA	3P%	FTM	FTA	FT%	ORB	DRB	TRB	AST	PF	DQ	STL	BLK	TO	MPG	PPG	RPG	APG	PCM
70-71	Chicago	6	....	14	4	1	8	.125	....	....	....	2	3	.667	....	....	4	0	1	0	....	....	....	2.3	0.7	0.7	0.0	.040
NBA Season Totals		6	....	14	4	1	8	.125	....	....	....	2	3	.667	....	....	4	0	1	0	....	....	....	2.3	0.7	0.7	0.0	....

• HOLTON, Mike

Michael David Holton

Born: Aug. 4, 1961. Seattle, WA, United States.   Height: 6'4".   Weight: 185 lbs.   Drafted: 1983   College: UCLA

YEAR	TEAM	GP	GS	MIN	PTS	FGM	FGA	FG%	3PM	3PA	3P%	FTM	FTA	FT%	ORB	DRB	TRB	AST	PF	DQ	STL	BLK	TO	MPG	PPG	RPG	APG	PCM
84-85	Phoenix	74	59	1761	624	257	576	.446	14	45	.311	96	118	.814	30	102	132	198	141	0	59	6	126	23.8	8.4	1.8	2.7	.300
85-86	Phoenix	4	0	65	12	4	20	.200	0	2	.000	4	6	.667	1	2	3	7	7	0	2	0	4	16.3	3.0	0.8	1.8	.021
85-86	Chicago	24	0	447	171	73	155	.471	1	10	.100	24	38	.632	10	20	30	48	40	1	23	0	24	18.6	7.1	1.3	2.0	.331
86-87	Portland	58	1	479	191	70	171	.409	7	23	.304	44	55	.800	9	29	38	73	51	0	16	2	41	8.3	3.3	0.7	1.3	.334
87-88	Portland	82	2	1279	436	163	353	.462	3	15	.200	107	129	.829	50	99	149	211	154	0	41	10	82	15.6	5.3	1.8	2.6	.400
88-89	Charlotte	67	60	1696	553	215	504	.427	3	14	.214	120	143	.839	30	75	105	424	165	0	66	12	121	25.3	8.3	1.6	6.3	.418
89-90	Charlotte	16	0	109	29	14	26	.538	0	0	.000	1	2	.500	1	1	2	16	19	0	1	0	13	6.8	1.8	0.1	1.0	.147
NBA Season Totals		325	122	5836	2016	796	1805	.441	28	109	.257	396	491	.807	131	328	459	977	577	1	208	30	411	18.0	6.2	1.4	3.0	....

YEAR TEAM	GP	GS	MIN	PTS	FGM	FGA	FG%	3PM	3PA	3P%	FTM	FTA	FT%	ORB	DRB	TRB	AST	PF	DQ	STL	BLK	TO	MPG	PPG	RPG	APG	PCM
84-85 Phoenix	3	0	55	22	9	19	.474	0	4	.000	4	4	1.000	0	2	2	9	8	0	0	0	3	18.3	7.3	0.7	3.0	.321
86-87 Portland	2	0	9	2	1	2	.500	0	0	.000	0	0	.000	0	1	1	0	1	0	0	0	0	4.5	1.0	0.5	0.0	.171
87-88 Portland	4	0	34	6	3	13	.231	0	1	.000	0	0	.000	1	4	5	6	6	0	2	0	1	8.5	1.5	1.3	1.5	.173
NBA Playoff Totals	9	0	98	30	13	34	.382	0	5	.000	4	4	1.000	1	7	8	15	15	0	2	0	4	10.9	3.3	0.9	1.7	....

• HOLUB, Dick

Richard W. Holub

Born: Oct. 29, 1921. Height: 6'6". Weight: 205 lbs. Drafted: 1947 College: Long Island University

47-48 New York	48	....	....	504	195	662	.295	....	....	....	114	180	.633	....	....	....	37	159	....	....	....	....	....	10.5	....	0.8	....
NBA Season Totals	48	....	....	504	195	662	.295	....	....	....	114	180	.633	....	....	....	37	159	....	....	....	....	....	10.5	....	0.8	....
47-48 New York	3	....	....	26	9	36	.250	....	....	....	8	14	.571	....	....	....	0	12	....	....	....	....	....	8.7	....	0.0	....
NBA Playoff Totals	3	....	....	26	9	36	.250	....	....	....	8	14	.571	....	....	....	0	12	....	....	....	....	....	8.7	....	0.0	....

• HOLUP, Joe

Joseph J. Holup

Born: Feb. 26, 1934. Height: 6'6". Weight: 215 lbs. Drafted: 1956 College: George Washington

56-57 Syracuse	71	....	1284	524	160	487	.329	....	....	....	204	253	.806	....	....	279	84	177	5	....	....	....	18.1	7.4	3.9	1.2	.397
57-58 Syracuse	16	....	133	44	14	57	.246	....	....	....	16	23	.696	....	....	23	13	23	0	....	....	....	8.3	2.8	1.4	0.8	.263
57-58 Detroit	37	....	607	209	77	221	.348	....	....	....	55	71	.775	....	....	198	23	76	2	....	....	....	16.4	5.6	5.4	0.6	.402
58-59 Detroit	68	....	1502	570	209	580	.360	....	....	....	152	200	.760	....	....	352	73	239	12	....	....	....	22.1	8.4	5.2	1.1	.359
NBA Season Totals	192	....	3526	1347	460	1345	.342	....	....	....	427	547	.781	....	....	852	193	515	19	....	....	....	18.4	7.0	4.4	1.0	....
56-57 Syracuse	5	....	88	20	6	28	.214	....	....	....	8	12	.667	....	....	20	1	3	0	....	....	....	17.6	4.0	4.0	0.2	.195
57-58 Detroit	7	....	134	42	15	43	.349	....	....	....	12	16	.750	....	....	36	3	20	0	....	....	....	19.1	6.0	5.1	0.4	.320
58-59 Detroit	3	....	36	12	3	14	.214	....	....	....	6	7	.857	....	....	8	3	7	0	....	....	....	12.0	4.0	2.7	1.0	.291
NBA Playoff Totals	15	....	258	74	24	85	.282	....	....	....	26	35	.743	....	....	64	7	30	0	....	....	....	17.2	4.9	4.3	0.5	....

• HOLZMAN, Red

William Holzman

Born: Aug. 10, 1920. Brooklyn, NY, United States. Died: Nov.13, 1998. Height: 5'10". Weight: 175 lbs. Drafted: — College: CCNY

45-46 Rochester-N	34	....	....	363	143	....	....	....	....	....	77	115	.670	....	....	....	....	....	....	....	....	....	....	10.7	....	....	....
46-47 Rochester-N	44	....	....	528	227	....	....	....	....	....	74	139	.532	....	....	....	....	68	....	....	....	....	....	12.0	....	....	....
47-48 Rochester-N	60	....	....	609	246	....	....	....	....	....	117	182	.643	....	....	....	....	58	....	....	....	....	....	10.2	....	....	....
48-49 Rochester	60	....	....	546	225	691	.326	....	....	....	96	157	.611	....	....	....	149	93	....	....	....	....	....	9.1	....	2.5	....
49-50 Rochester	68	....	....	556	206	625	.330	....	....	....	144	210	.686	....	....	....	200	67	....	....	....	....	....	8.2	....	2.9	....
50-51 Rochester	68	....	....	496	183	561	.326	....	....	....	130	179	.726	....	....	152	147	94	0	....	....	....	....	7.3	2.2	2.2	....
51-52 Rochester	65	....	1065	269	104	372	.280	....	....	....	61	85	.718	....	....	106	115	95	1	....	....	....	16.4	4.1	1.6	1.8	.244
52-53 Rochester	46	....	392	103	38	149	.255	....	....	....	27	38	.711	....	....	40	35	56	2	....	....	....	8.5	2.2	0.9	0.8	.184
53-54 Milwaukee	51	....	649	196	74	224	.330	....	....	....	48	73	.658	....	....	46	75	73	1	....	....	....	12.7	3.8	0.9	1.5	.284
NBA Season Totals	358	....	2106	2166	830	2622	.317	....	....	....	506	742	.682	....	....	344	721	478	4	....	....	....	5.9	6.1	1.0	2.0	....
NBL Season Totals	138	....	....	1500	616	....	....	....	....	....	268	436	....	....	....	....	....	126	....	....	....	....	....	10.9	....	....	....
Career Totals	496	....	2106	3666	1446	2622	....	....	....	....	774	1178	....	....	....	344	721	604	4	....	....	....	4.2	7.4	0.7	1.5	....
45-46 Rochester-N	7	....	....	81	30	....	....	....	....	....	21	31	.677	....	....	....	....	....	....	....	....	....	....	11.6	....	....	....
46-47 Rochester-N	11	....	....	106	42	....	....	....	....	....	22	29	.759	....	....	....	....	....	....	....	....	....	....	9.6	....	....	....
47-48 Rochester-N	10	....	....	80	35	....	....	....	....	....	10	15	.667	....	....	....	....	....	....	....	....	....	....	8.0	....	....	....
48-49 Rochester	4	....	....	41	18	40	.450	....	....	....	5	6	.833	....	....	....	13	3	....	....	....	....	....	10.3	....	3.3	....
49-50 Rochester	2	....	....	7	3	9	.333	....	....	....	1	2	.500	....	....	....	0	3	....	....	....	....	....	3.5	....	0.0	....
50-51 Rochester	14	....	....	85	31	76	.408	....	....	....	23	34	.676	....	....	19	20	14	0	....	....	....	....	6.1	1.4	1.4	....
51-52 Rochester	6	....	65	7	3	15	.200	....	....	....	1	6	.167	....	....	6	2	3	0	....	....	....	10.8	1.2	1.0	0.3	.038
52-53 Rochester	2	....	14	3	1	5	.200	....	....	....	1	4	.250	....	....	1	1	4	0	....	....	....	7.0	1.5	0.5	0.5	-.031
NBA Playoff Totals	28	....	79	143	56	145	.386	....	....	....	31	52	.596	....	....	26	36	27	0	....	....	....	2.8	5.1	0.9	1.3	....
NBL Playoff Totals	28	....	....	267	107	....	....	....	....	....	53	75	....	....	....	....	....	....	....	....	....	....	....	9.5	....	....	....
Career Playoff Totals	56	....	79	410	163	145	....	....	....	....	84	127	....	....	....	26	36	27	0	....	....	....	1.4	7.3	0.5	0.6	....

• HOMER, Jim

James Homer

Born: 1923. Height: 6'5". Weight: 220 lbs. Drafted: — College: Alabama

47-48 Syracuse-N	56	....	....	698	250	....	....	....	....	....	198	324	.611	....	....	....	....	189	....	....	....	....	....	12.5	....	....	....
48-49 Syracuse-N	59	....	....	386	141	....	....	....	....	....	104	164	.634	....	....	....	....	181	....	....	....	....	....	6.5	....	....	....
NBL Season Totals	115	....	....	1084	391	....	....	....	....	....	302	488	....	....	....	....	....	370	....	....	....	....	....	9.4	....	....	....
47-48 Syracuse-N	3	....	....	36	11	....	....	....	....	....	14	18	.778	....	....	....	....	....	....	....	....	....	....	12.0	....	....	....
48-49 Syracuse-N	6	....	....	32	13	....	....	....	....	....	6	14	.429	....	....	....	....	....	....	....	....	....	....	5.3	....	....	....
NBL Playoff Totals	9	....	....	68	24	....	....	....	....	....	20	32	....	....	....	....	....	....	....	....	....	....	....	7.6	....	....	....

• HONEYCUTT, Jerald

Jerald DeWayne Honeycutt

Born: Oct. 20, 1974. Shreveport, LA, United States. Height: 6'9". Weight: 245 lbs. Drafted: 1997 College: Tulane

97-98 Milwaukee	38	0	530	245	90	221	.407	29	77	.377	36	58	.621	27	66	93	33	83	0	20	6	49	13.9	6.4	2.4	0.9	.334
98-99 Milwaukee	3	0	12	5	2	5	.400	0	3	.000	1	2	.500	0	1	1	0	6	0	1	0	1	4.0	1.7	0.3	0.0	.009
98-99 Philadelphia	13	0	90	25	7	27	.259	5	14	.357	6	8	.750	3	8	11	3	10	0	4	2	8	6.9	1.9	0.8	0.2	.147
NBA Season Totals	54	0	632	275	99	253	.391	34	94	.362	43	68	.632	30	75	105	36	99	0	25	8	58	11.7	5.1	1.9	0.7	....
98-99 Philadelphia	6	0	12	2	1	5	.200	0	3	.000	0	0	.000	1	0	1	0	3	0	0	0	1	2.0	0.3	0.2	0.0	-.241
NBA Playoff Totals	6	0	12	2	1	5	.200	0	3	.000	0	0	.000	1	0	1	0	3	0	0	0	1	2.0	0.3	0.2	0.0	....

HOOD, Derek
Derek Hood

Born: Dec. 22, 1976. Kansas City, MO, United States.   Height: 6'8".   Weight: 222 lbs.   Drafted: —   College: Arkansas

YEAR	TEAM	GP	GS	MIN	PTS	FGM	FGA	FG%	3PM	3PA	3P%	FTM	FTA	FT%	ORB	DRB	TRB	AST	PF	DQ	STL	BLK	TO	MPG	PPG	RPG	APG	PCM
99-00	Charlotte	2	0	4	0	0	3	.000	0	0	.000	0	0	.000	0	1	1	0	0	0	0	0	0	2.0	0.0	0.5	0.0	-.454
NBA Season Totals		2	0	4	0	0	3	.000	0	0	.000	0	0	.000	0	1	1	0	0	0	0	0	0	2.0	0.0	0.5	0.0	....

HOOPER, Bobby
Bobby Joe (Bobby Joe) Hooper

Born: Dec. 22, 1946. Lee's Creek, OH, United States.   Height: 6'   Weight: 180 lbs.   Drafted: 1968   College: Dayton

YEAR	TEAM	GP	GS	MIN	PTS	FGM	FGA	FG%	3PM	3PA	3P%	FTM	FTA	FT%	ORB	DRB	TRB	AST	PF	DQ	STL	BLK	TO	MPG	PPG	RPG	APG	PCM
68-69	Indiana-A	54	....	955	271	112	271	.413	4	32	.125	43	59	.729	35	74	109	142	91	0	....	....	52	17.7	5.0	2.0	2.6	.361
ABA Season Totals		54	....	955	271	112	271	.413	4	32	.125	43	59	.729	35	74	109	142	91	0	....	....	52	17.7	5.0	2.0	2.6	
68-69	Indiana-A	16	....	288	76	25	74	.338	4	16	.250	22	26	.846	....	....	38	45	41	0	....	....	13	18.0	4.8	2.4	2.8	.343
ABA Playoff Totals		16	....	288	76	25	74	.338	4	16	.250	22	26	.846	....	....	38	45	41	0	....	....	13	18.0	4.8	2.4	2.8	

HOOSER, Carroll
Carroll L. Hooser

Born: Mar. 5, 1944. Dallas, TX, United States.   Height: 6'7".   Weight: 230 lbs.   Drafted: 1966   College: Southern Methodist

YEAR	TEAM	GP	GS	MIN	PTS	FGM	FGA	FG%	3PM	3PA	3P%	FTM	FTA	FT%	ORB	DRB	TRB	AST	PF	DQ	STL	BLK	TO	MPG	PPG	RPG	APG	PCM
67-68	Dallas-A	56	....	720	316	128	297	.431	1	1	1.000	59	83	.711	....	....	216	29	139	6	....	....	49	12.9	5.6	3.9	0.5	.446
ABA Season Totals		56	....	720	316	128	297	.431	1	1	1.000	59	83	.711	....	....	216	29	139	6	....	....	49	12.9	5.6	3.9	0.5	
67-68	Dallas-A	3	....	6	2	1	2	.500	0	0	.000	0	0	.000	....	....	2	0	3	0	....	....	2	2.0	0.7	0.7	0.0	.264
ABA Playoff Totals		3	....	6	2	1	2	.500	0	0	.000	0	0	.000	....	....	2	0	3	0	....	....	2	2.0	0.7	0.7	0.0	

HOOVER, Tom
Thomas Lee Hoover Jr.

Born: Jan. 23, 1941. Washington, DC, United States.   Height: 6'9".   Weight: 230 lbs.   Drafted: 1963   College: Villanova

YEAR	TEAM	GP	GS	MIN	PTS	FGM	FGA	FG%	3PM	3PA	3P%	FTM	FTA	FT%	ORB	DRB	TRB	AST	PF	DQ	STL	BLK	TO	MPG	PPG	RPG	APG	PCM
63-64	New York	59	....	988	285	102	247	.413	....	....	....	81	132	.614	....	....	331	36	185	4	....	....	....	16.7	4.8	5.6	0.6	.387
64-65	New York	24	....	153	34	13	32	.406	....	....	....	8	14	.571	....	....	58	12	37	0	....	....	....	6.4	1.4	2.4	0.5	.407
66-67	St. Louis	17	....	129	31	13	31	.419	....	....	....	5	13	.385	....	....	36	8	35	1	....	....	....	7.6	1.8	2.1	0.5	.293
67-68	Denver-A	70	....	1588	454	161	357	.451	4	10	.400	128	206	.621	....	....	491	64	268	8	....	....	139	22.7	6.5	7.0	0.9	.397
68-69	Houston-A	4	....	80	33	14	28	.500	0	0	.000	5	6	.833	8	22	30	5	15	1	....	....	8	20.0	8.3	7.5	1.3	.570
68-69	Minnesota-A	9	....	83	34	12	26	.462	0	0	.000	10	21	.476	16	15	31	6	21	1	....	....	8	9.2	3.8	3.4	0.7	.503
68-69	New York-A	40	....	1256	440	165	354	.466	0	2	.000	110	162	.679	121	290	411	106	187	11	....	....	156	31.4	11.0	10.3	2.7	.517
NBA Season Totals		100	....	1270	350	128	310	.413	....	....	....	94	159	.591	....	....	425	56	257	5	....	....	....	12.7	3.5	4.3	0.6	....
ABA Season Totals		123	....	3007	961	352	765	.460	4	12	.333	253	395	.641	145	327	963	181	491	21	....	....	311	24.4	7.8	7.8	1.5	....
Career Totals		223	....	4277	1311	480	1075	.447	4	12	.333	347	554	.626	145	327	1388	237	748	26	....	....	311	19.2	5.9	6.2	1.1	....
65-66	LA Lakers	4	....	11	4	2	3	.667	....	....	....	0	0	.000	....	....	3	1	3	0	....	....	....	2.8	1.0	0.8	0.3	.510
67-68	Denver-A	2	....	16	13	4	7	.571	0	0	.000	5	7	.714	....	....	4	1	6	0	....	....	2	8.0	6.5	2.0	0.5	.730
NBA Playoff Totals		4	....	11	4	2	3	.667	....	....	....	0	0	.000	....	....	3	1	3	0	....	....	....	2.8	1.0	0.8	0.3	....
ABA Playoff Totals		2	....	16	13	4	7	.571	0	0	.000	5	7	.714	....	....	4	1	6	0	....	....	2	8.0	6.5	2.0	0.5	....
Career Playoff Totals		6	....	27	17	6	10	.600	0	0	.000	5	7	.714	....	....	7	2	9	0	....	....	2	4.5	2.8	1.2	0.3	....

HOPKINS, Bob
Robert M. Hopkins

Born: Nov. 3, 1934. Jonesboro, LA, United States.   Height: 6'8".   Weight: 205 lbs.   Drafted: 1956   College: Grambling

YEAR	TEAM	GP	GS	MIN	PTS	FGM	FGA	FG%	3PM	3PA	3P%	FTM	FTA	FT%	ORB	DRB	TRB	AST	PF	DQ	STL	BLK	TO	MPG	PPG	RPG	APG	PCM
56-57	Syracuse	62	....	764	354	130	343	.379	....	....	....	94	126	.746	....	....	233	22	106	0	....	....	....	12.3	5.7	3.8	0.4	.452
57-58	Syracuse	69	....	1224	565	221	554	.399	....	....	....	123	161	.764	....	....	392	45	162	5	....	....	....	17.7	8.2	5.7	0.7	.484
58-59	Syracuse	67	....	1518	668	246	611	.403	....	....	....	176	234	.752	....	....	436	67	181	5	....	....	....	22.7	10.0	6.5	1.0	.471
59-60	Syracuse	75	....	1616	650	257	660	.389	....	....	....	136	174	.782	....	....	465	55	193	4	....	....	....	21.5	8.7	6.2	0.7	.420
NBA Season Totals		273	....	5122	2237	854	2168	.394	....	....	....	529	695	.761	....	....	1526	189	642	14	....	....	....	18.8	8.2	5.6	0.7	....
56-57	Syracuse	5	....	73	28	9	25	.360	....	....	....	10	15	.667	....	....	19	2	4	1	....	....	....	14.6	5.6	3.8	0.4	.403
57-58	Syracuse	3	....	39	12	4	16	.250	....	....	....	4	6	.667	....	....	14	0	7	0	....	....	....	13.0	4.0	4.7	0.0	.261
58-59	Syracuse	9	....	203	74	23	68	.338	....	....	....	28	34	.824	....	....	60	9	33	1	....	....	....	22.6	8.2	6.7	1.0	.403
59-60	Syracuse	1	....	19	7	2	8	.250	....	....	....	3	3	1.000	....	....	6	0	3	0	....	....	....	19.0	7.0	6.0	0.0	.309
NBA Playoff Totals		18	....	334	121	38	117	.325	....	....	....	45	58	.776	....	....	99	11	47	2	....	....	....	18.6	6.7	5.5	0.6	....

HOPPEN, Dave
David Dirk Hoppen

Born: Mar. 13, 1964. Omaha, NE, United States.   Height: 6'11".   Weight: 235 lbs.   Drafted: 1986   College: Nebraska

YEAR	TEAM	GP	GS	MIN	PTS	FGM	FGA	FG%	3PM	3PA	3P%	FTM	FTA	FT%	ORB	DRB	TRB	AST	PF	DQ	STL	BLK	TO	MPG	PPG	RPG	APG	PCM
87-88	Milwaukee	3	0	35	11	4	11	.364	0	0	.000	3	3	1.000	4	3	7	2	3	0	0	0	2	11.7	3.7	2.3	0.7	.282
87-88	Golden State	36	8	607	211	80	172	.465	0	1	.000	51	59	.864	54	113	167	30	84	1	13	6	36	16.9	5.9	4.6	0.8	.419
88-89	Charlotte	77	36	1419	500	199	353	.564	1	2	.500	101	139	.727	123	261	384	57	239	4	25	21	77	18.4	6.5	5.0	0.7	.435
89-90	Charlotte	10	2	135	40	16	41	.390	0	0	.000	8	10	.800	19	17	36	6	26	0	2	1	8	13.5	4.0	3.6	0.6	.288
90-91	Charlotte	19	0	112	44	18	32	.563	0	1	.000	8	10	.800	14	16	30	3	18	0	2	1	11	5.9	2.3	1.6	0.2	.405
90-91	Philadelphia	11	0	43	20	6	12	.500	0	1	.000	8	12	.667	4	5	9	0	11	0	1	0	1	3.9	1.8	0.8	0.0	.367
91-92	Philadelphia	11	0	40	9	2	7	.286	0	0	.000	5	10	.500	1	9	10	2	6	0	0	0	3	3.6	0.8	0.9	0.2	.197
92-93	New Jersey	2	0	10	2	1	1	1.000	0	0	.000	0	2	.000	1	3	4	0	2	0	0	0	0	5.0	1.0	2.0	0.0	.387
NBA Season Totals		169	46	2401	837	326	629	.518	1	5	.200	184	245	.751	220	427	647	100	389	5	43	29	138	14.2	5.0	3.8	0.6	....
90-91	Philadelphia	3	0	9	6	3	3	1.000	0	0	.000	0	2	.000	0	3	3	0	1	0	0	0	0	3.0	2.0	1.0	0.0	.822
NBA Playoff Totals		3	0	9	6	3	3	1.000	0	0	.000	0	2	.000	0	3	3	0	1	0	0	0	0	3.0	2.0	1.0	0.0	....

• HOPSON, Dennis

Dennis Hopson

Born: Apr. 22, 1965. Toledo, OH, United States. Height: 6'5". Weight: 200 lbs. Drafted: 1987 College: Ohio State

YEAR	TEAM	GP	GS	MIN	PTS	FGM	FGA	FG%	3PM	3PA	3P%	FTM	FTA	FT%	ORB	DRB	TRB	AST	PF	DQ	STL	BLK	TO	MPG	PPG	RPG	APG	PCM
87-88	New Jersey	61	19	1365	587	222	549	.404	12	45	.267	131	177	.740	63	80	143	118	145	0	57	25	122	22.4	9.6	2.3	1.9	.304
88-89	New Jersey	62	36	1551	788	299	714	.419	4	27	.148	186	219	.849	91	111	202	103	150	0	70	30	99	25.0	12.7	3.3	1.7	.397
89-90	New Jersey	79	64	2551	1251	474	1093	.434	32	101	.317	271	342	.792	113	166	279	151	183	1	100	51	166	32.3	15.8	3.5	1.9	.376
90-91	Chicago	61	0	728	264	104	244	.426	1	5	.200	55	83	.663	49	60	109	65	79	0	25	14	61	11.9	4.3	1.8	1.1	.321
91-92	Chicago	2	0	10	2	1	2	.500	0	0	.000	0	0	.000	0	0	0	0	2	0	1	0	0	5.0	1.0	0.0	0.0	.107
91-92	Sacramento	69	0	1304	741	275	591	.465	12	47	.255	179	253	.708	105	101	206	102	113	0	66	39	97	18.9	10.7	3.0	1.5	.513
NBA Season Totals		334	119	7509	3633	1375	3193	.431	61	225	.271	822	1074	.765	421	518	939	539	672	1	319	159	545	22.5	10.9	2.8	1.6	....
90-91	Chicago	5	0	18	8	2	6	.333	0	0	.000	4	9	.444	2	2	4	1	2	0	0	1	1	3.6	1.6	0.8	0.2	.322
NBA Playoff Totals		5	0	18	8	2	6	.333	0	0	.000	4	9	.444	2	2	4	1	2	0	0	1	1	3.6	1.6	0.8	0.2	....

• HORAN, Johnny

John F. (The Vertical Hyphen) Horan

Born: Nov. 24, 1932. Died: Nov.14, 1980. Height: 6'8". Weight: 190 lbs. Drafted: 1955 College: Dayton

YEAR	TEAM	GP	GS	MIN	PTS	FGM	FGA	FG%	3PM	3PA	3P%	FTM	FTA	FT%	ORB	DRB	TRB	AST	PF	DQ	STL	BLK	TO	MPG	PPG	RPG	APG	PCM
55-56	Fort Wayne	7	....	43	22	8	26	.308	....	....	....	6	6	1.000	....	....	4	1	14	0	....	....	....	6.1	3.1	0.6	0.1	.169
55-56	Minneapolis	12	....	50	12	4	16	.250	....	....	....	4	5	.800	....	....	6	1	7	0	....	....	....	4.2	1.0	0.5	0.1	.113
NBA Season Totals		19	....	93	34	12	42	.286	....	....	....	10	11	.909	....	....	10	2	21	0	....	....	....	4.9	1.8	0.5	0.1	....

• HORDGES, Cedrick

Cedrick Tyrone Hordges

Born: Jan. 8, 1957. Montgomery, AL, United States. Height: 6'8". Weight: 220 lbs. Drafted: 1979 College: South Carolina

YEAR	TEAM	GP	GS	MIN	PTS	FGM	FGA	FG%	3PM	3PA	3P%	FTM	FTA	FT%	ORB	DRB	TRB	AST	PF	DQ	STL	BLK	TO	MPG	PPG	RPG	APG	PCM
80-81	Denver	68	....	1599	572	221	480	.460	0	3	.000	130	186	.699	120	338	458	104	226	4	33	19	122	23.5	8.4	6.7	1.5	.422
81-82	Denver	77	1	1372	527	204	414	.493	3	13	.231	116	199	.583	119	276	395	65	230	1	26	19	108	17.8	6.8	5.1	0.8	.412
NBA Season Totals		145	1	2971	1099	425	894	.475	3	16	.188	246	385	.639	239	614	853	169	456	5	59	38	230	20.5	7.6	5.9	1.2	....
81-82	Denver	3	0	45	19	8	19	.421	0	1	.000	3	4	.750	2	11	13	2	4	0	1	0	4	15.0	6.3	4.3	0.7	.399
NBA Playoff Totals		3	0	45	19	8	19	.421	0	1	.000	3	4	.750	2	11	13	2	4	0	1	0	4	15.0	6.3	4.3	0.7	....

• HORFORD, Tito

Alfredo William (Tito) Horford

Born: Jan. 19, 1966. LaRomana, Dominican Rep.. Height: 7'1". Weight: 245 lbs. Drafted: 1988 College: Miami (FL)

YEAR	TEAM	GP	GS	MIN	PTS	FGM	FGA	FG%	3PM	3PA	3P%	FTM	FTA	FT%	ORB	DRB	TRB	AST	PF	DQ	STL	BLK	TO	MPG	PPG	RPG	APG	PCM
88-89	Milwaukee	25	0	112	42	15	46	.326	0	0	.000	12	19	.632	9	13	22	3	14	0	1	7	15	4.5	1.7	0.9	0.1	.184
89-90	Milwaukee	35	0	236	51	18	62	.290	0	0	.000	15	24	.625	19	40	59	2	33	0	5	16	14	6.7	1.5	1.7	0.1	.229
93-94	Washington	3	0	28	0	0	2	.000	0	0	.000	0	0	.000	1	2	3	0	3	0	1	3	1	9.3	0.0	1.0	0.0	.082
NBA Season Totals		63	0	376	93	33	110	.300	0	0	.000	27	43	.628	29	55	84	5	50	0	7	26	30	6.0	1.5	1.3	0.1	....
89-90	Milwaukee	2	0	2	2	1	1	1.000	0	0	.000	0	0	.000	0	0	0	0	0	0	0	0	0	1.0	1.0	0.0	0.0	1.000
NBA Playoff Totals		2	0	2	2	1	1	1.000	0	0	.000	0	0	.000	0	0	0	0	0	0	0	0	0	1.0	1.0	0.0	0.0	....

• HORN, Ron

Ronald Leroy Horn

Born: May 24, 1938. Marion, IN, United States. Height: 6'7". Weight: 220 lbs. Drafted: 1961 College: Indiana

YEAR	TEAM	GP	GS	MIN	PTS	FGM	FGA	FG%	3PM	3PA	3P%	FTM	FTA	FT%	ORB	DRB	TRB	AST	PF	DQ	STL	BLK	TO	MPG	PPG	RPG	APG	PCM
61-62	St. Louis	3	....	25	3	1	12	.083	....	....	....	1	2	.500	....	....	6	1	4	0	....	....	....	8.3	1.0	2.0	0.3	-.066
62-63	LA Lakers	28	....	289	74	27	82	.329	....	....	....	20	29	.690	....	....	71	10	46	0	....	....	....	10.3	2.6	2.5	0.4	.266
67-68	Denver-A	1	....	6	2	0	2	.000	0	0	.000	2	2	1.000	....	....	1	0	0	0	....	....	1	6.0	2.0	1.0	0.0	.195
NBA Season Totals		31	....	314	77	28	94	.298	....	....	....	21	31	.677	....	....	77	11	50	0	....	....	....	10.1	2.5	2.5	0.4	....
ABA Season Totals		1	....	6	2	0	2	.000	0	0	.000	2	2	1.000	....	....	1	0	0	0	....	....	1	6.0	2.0	1.0	0.0	....
Career Totals		32	....	320	79	28	96	.292	0	0	.000	23	33	.697	....	....	78	11	50	0	....	....	1	10.0	2.5	2.4	0.3	....
62-63	LA Lakers	7	....	55	12	4	12	.333	....	....	....	4	5	.800	....	....	11	2	13	0	....	....	....	7.9	1.7	1.6	0.3	.205
NBA Playoff Totals		7	....	55	12	4	12	.333	....	....	....	4	5	.800	....	....	11	2	13	0	....	....	....	7.9	1.7	1.6	0.3	....

• HORNACEK, Jeff

Jeffrey John Hornacek

Born: May 3, 1963. Elmhurst, IL, United States. Height: 6'3". Weight: 190 lbs. Drafted: 1986 College: Iowa State

YEAR	TEAM	GP	GS	MIN	PTS	FGM	FGA	FG%	3PM	3PA	3P%	FTM	FTA	FT%	ORB	DRB	TRB	AST	PF	DQ	STL	BLK	TO	MPG	PPG	RPG	APG	PCM
86-87	Phoenix	80	3	1561	424	159	350	.454	12	43	.279	94	121	.777	41	143	184	361	130	0	70	5	152	19.5	5.3	2.3	4.5	.422
87-88	Phoenix	82	49	2243	781	306	605	.506	17	58	.293	152	185	.822	71	191	262	540	151	0	107	10	156	27.4	9.5	3.2	6.6	.536
88-89	Phoenix	78	73	2487	1054	440	889	.495	27	81	.333	147	178	.826	75	191	266	465	188	0	129	8	109	31.9	13.5	3.4	6.0	.525
89-90	Phoenix	67	60	2278	1179	483	901	.536	40	98	.408	173	202	.856	86	227	313	337	144	2	117	14	127	34.0	17.6	4.7	5.0	.598
90-91	Phoenix	80	77	2733	1350	544	1051	.518	61	146	.418	201	224	.897	74	247	321	409	185	1	111	16	128	34.2	16.9	4.0	5.1	.554
91-92	Phoenix	81	81	3073	1632	635	1240	.512	83	189	.439	279	315	.886	106	301	407	411	218	1	158	31	170	37.9	20.1	5.0	5.1	.582
92-93	Philadelphia	79	78	2860	1511	582	1239	.470	97	249	.390	250	289	.865	84	258	342	548	203	2	131	21	221	36.2	19.1	4.3	6.9	.568
93-94	Philadelphia	53	53	1994	880	325	715	.455	52	166	.313	178	204	.873	41	171	212	315	115	0	95	10	138	37.6	16.6	4.0	5.9	.483
93-94	Utah	27	9	826	394	147	289	.509	18	42	.429	82	92	.891	19	48	67	104	71	0	32	3	32	30.6	14.6	2.5	3.9	.488
94-95	Utah	81	81	2696	1337	482	937	.514	89	219	.406	284	322	.882	53	157	210	347	181	1	129	17	146	33.3	16.5	2.6	4.3	.509
95-96	Utah	82	59	2588	1247	442	880	.502	104	223	.466	259	290	.893	62	147	209	340	171	1	106	20	123	31.6	15.2	2.5	4.1	.502
96-97	Utah	82	82	2592	1191	413	856	.482	72	195	.369	293	326	.899	60	181	241	361	188	1	124	26	131	31.6	14.5	2.9	4.4	.503
97-98	Utah	80	80	2460	1139	399	828	.482	56	127	.441	285	322	.885	65	205	270	349	175	1	109	15	128	30.8	14.2	3.4	4.4	.517
98-99	Utah	48	48	1435	587	214	449	.477	34	81	.420	125	140	.893	33	127	160	192	95	0	52	14	82	29.9	12.2	3.3	4.0	.467
99-00	Utah	77	77	2133	953	358	728	.492	66	138	.478	171	180	**.950**	49	133	182	202	149	1	66	16	113	27.7	12.4	2.4	2.6	.423
NBA Season Totals		1077	910	33959	15659	5929	11957	.496	828	2055	.403	2973	3390	.877	919	2727	3646	5281	2364	11	1536	226	1956	31.5	14.5	3.4	4.9	....
88-89	Phoenix	12	12	374	169	74	149	.497	0	7	.000	21	25	.840	25	44	69	62	34	0	16	3	18	31.2	14.1	5.8	5.2	.570
89-90	Phoenix	16	16	583	298	112	219	.511	6	24	.250	68	73	.932	13	49	62	73	43	1	24	0	34	36.4	18.6	3.9	4.6	.517
90-91	Phoenix	4	4	145	73	22	51	.431	3	6	.500	26	28	.929	3	22	25	8	13	0	3	2	3	36.3	18.3	6.3	2.0	.501
91-92	Phoenix	8	8	343	163	62	128	.484	8	17	.471	31	34	.912	12	39	51	42	23	0	14	2	19	42.9	20.4	6.4	5.3	.522

YEAR	TEAM	GP	GS	MIN	PTS	FGM	FGA	FG%	3PM	3PA	3P%	FTM	FTA	FT%	ORB	DRB	TRB	AST	PF	DQ	STL	BLK	TO	MPG	PPG	RPG	APG	PCM
93-94	Utah	16	16	558	247	85	179	.475	15	34	.441	62	68	.912	11	28	39	64	45	0	24	6	28	34.9	15.4	2.4	4.0	.438
94-95	Utah	5	5	178	70	26	51	.510	7	13	.538	11	14	.786	3	3	6	20	19	1	8	1	7	35.6	14.0	1.2	4.0	.365
95-96	Utah	18	18	644	315	104	207	.502	34	58	.586	73	82	.890	22	43	65	60	42	1	19	3	27	35.8	17.5	3.6	3.3	.488
96-97	Utah	20	20	704	291	90	208	.433	19	53	.358	92	105	.876	22	67	89	73	53	1	21	4	36	35.2	14.6	4.5	3.7	.427
97-98	Utah	20	20	636	217	74	178	.416	14	30	.467	55	65	.846	7	43	50	64	51	1	20	4	32	31.8	10.9	2.5	3.2	.317
98-99	Utah	11	11	304	134	49	106	.462	7	18	.389	29	33	.879	9	32	41	26	34	1	11	0	12	27.6	12.2	3.7	2.4	.431
99-00	Utah	10	10	297	115	43	102	.422	9	22	.409	20	24	.833	9	21	30	33	28	0	10	0	15	29.7	11.5	3.0	3.3	.356
NBA Playoff Totals		140	140	4766	2092	741	1578	.470	122	282	.433	488	551	.886	136	391	527	525	385	6	170	25	231	34.0	14.9	3.8	3.8	....

• HORRY, Robert

Robert Keith Horry

Born: Aug. 25, 1970. Andalusia, AL, United States. Height: 6'9". Weight: 220 lbs. Drafted: 1992 College: Alabama

YEAR	TEAM	GP	GS	MIN	PTS	FGM	FGA	FG%	3PM	3PA	3P%	FTM	FTA	FT%	ORB	DRB	TRB	AST	PF	DQ	STL	BLK	TO	MPG	PPG	RPG	APG	PCM
92-93	Houston	79	79	2330	801	323	682	.474	12	47	.255	143	200	.715	113	279	392	191	210	1	80	81	158	29.5	10.1	5.0	2.4	.392
93-94	Houston	81	81	2370	803	322	702	.459	44	136	.324	115	157	.732	128	312	440	231	186	0	119	75	138	29.3	9.9	5.4	2.9	.445
94-95	Houston	64	61	2074	652	240	537	.447	86	227	.379	86	113	.761	81	243	324	216	161	0	94	76	122	32.4	10.2	5.1	3.4	.416
95-96	Houston	71	71	2634	853	300	732	.410	142	388	.366	111	143	.776	97	315	412	281	197	3	116	109	163	37.1	12.0	5.8	4.0	.411
96-97	Phoenix	32	15	719	220	82	195	.421	24	78	.308	32	50	.640	40	79	119	54	81	1	28	26	45	22.5	6.9	3.7	1.7	.341
96-97	LA Lakers	22	14	676	203	75	165	.455	25	76	.329	28	40	.700	28	90	118	56	72	1	38	29	26	30.7	9.2	5.4	2.5	.426
97-98	LA Lakers	72	71	2192	536	200	420	.476	19	93	.204	117	169	.692	186	356	542	163	238	5	112	94	101	30.4	7.4	7.5	2.3	.443
98-99	LA Lakers	38	5	744	188	67	146	.459	20	45	.444	34	46	.739	56	96	152	56	103	2	36	39	49	19.6	4.9	4.0	1.5	.386
99-00	LA Lakers	76	0	1685	436	159	363	.438	29	94	.309	89	113	.788	133	228	361	118	189	0	84	80	73	22.2	5.7	4.8	1.6	.411
00-01	LA Lakers	79	1	1587	407	147	380	.387	54	156	.346	59	83	.711	93	203	296	128	210	3	54	54	79	20.1	5.2	3.7	1.6	.331
01-02	LA Lakers	81	23	2140	550	183	460	.398	76	203	.374	108	138	.783	130	349	479	232	208	1	77	89	88	26.4	6.8	5.9	2.9	.444
02-03	LA Lakers	80	26	2343	522	184	476	.387	51	177	.288	103	134	.769	181	333	514	233	247	2	96	61	112	29.3	6.5	6.4	2.9	.381
NBA Season Totals		775	447	21494	6171	2282	5258	.434	582	1720	.338	1025	1386	.740	1266	2883	4149	1959	2102	19	934	813	1154	27.7	8.0	5.4	2.5	....
92-93	Houston	12	12	374	123	47	101	.465	9	30	.300	20	27	.741	14	48	62	38	30	1	18	16	28	31.2	10.3	5.2	3.2	.426
93-94	Houston	23	23	778	269	98	226	.434	34	89	.382	39	51	.765	40	101	141	82	68	0	35	20	27	33.8	11.7	6.1	3.6	.461
94-95	Houston	22	22	841	288	93	209	.445	44	110	.400	58	78	.744	40	115	155	76	69	2	32	26	25	38.2	13.1	7.0	3.5	.469
95-96	Houston	8	8	308	105	37	91	.407	21	53	.396	10	23	.435	15	42	57	24	29	1	21	13	15	38.5	13.1	7.1	3.0	.427
96-97	LA Lakers	9	9	279	60	17	38	.447	12	28	.429	14	18	.778	12	36	48	13	27	0	10	7	11	31.0	6.7	5.3	1.4	.323
97-98	LA Lakers	13	13	422	112	39	70	.557	6	17	.353	28	41	.683	34	50	84	40	45	0	14	14	18	32.5	8.6	6.5	3.1	.442
98-99	LA Lakers	8	0	177	40	12	26	.462	5	12	.417	11	14	.786	10	26	36	11	29	1	6	6	7	22.1	5.0	4.5	1.4	.350
99-00	LA Lakers	23	0	618	175	59	145	.407	17	59	.288	40	57	.702	38	85	123	58	88	3	20	19	30	26.9	7.6	5.3	2.5	.376
00-01	LA Lakers	16	0	382	94	32	87	.368	17	47	.362	13	22	.591	30	53	83	31	50	0	22	16	18	23.9	5.9	5.2	1.9	.379
01-02	LA Lakers	19	14	703	176	61	136	.449	24	62	.387	30	38	.789	36	118	154	61	65	1	33	16	30	37.0	9.3	8.1	3.2	.425
02-03	LA Lakers	12	10	373	67	30	94	.319	2	38	.053	5	9	.556	23	57	80	37	37	0	15	12	17	31.1	5.6	6.7	3.1	.301
NBA Playoff Totals		165	111	5255	1509	525	1223	.429	191	545	.350	268	378	.709	292	731	1023	471	537	9	226	165	226	31.8	9.1	6.2	2.9	....

• HORTON, Ed

Edward C. Horton

Born: Dec. 17, 1967. Springfield, IL, United States. Height: 6'8". Weight: 230 lbs. Drafted: 1989 College: Iowa

YEAR	TEAM	GP	GS	MIN	PTS	FGM	FGA	FG%	3PM	3PA	3P%	FTM	FTA	FT%	ORB	DRB	TRB	AST	PF	DQ	STL	BLK	TO	MPG	PPG	RPG	APG	PCM
89-90	Washington	45	10	374	202	80	162	.494	0	4	.000	42	69	.609	59	49	108	19	63	1	9	5	41	8.3	4.5	2.4	0.4	.479
NBA Season Totals		45	10	374	202	80	162	.494	0	4	.000	42	69	.609	59	49	108	19	63	1	9	5	41	8.3	4.5	2.4	0.4	....

• HOSKET, Bill

Wilmer Frederick Hosket

Born: Dec. 20, 1946. Dayton, OH, United States. Height: 6'8". Weight: 225 lbs. Drafted: 1968 College: Ohio State

YEAR	TEAM	GP	GS	MIN	PTS	FGM	FGA	FG%	3PM	3PA	3P%	FTM	FTA	FT%	ORB	DRB	TRB	AST	PF	DQ	STL	BLK	TO	MPG	PPG	RPG	APG	PCM
68-69	New York	50	....	351	130	53	123	.431	....	....	....	24	42	.571	....	....	94	19	77	0	....	....	....	7.0	2.6	1.9	0.4	.377
69-70	New York	36	....	235	118	46	91	.505	....	....	....	26	33	.788	....	....	63	17	36	0	....	....	....	6.5	3.3	1.8	0.5	.570
70-71	Buffalo	13	....	217	105	47	90	.522	....	....	....	11	17	.647	....	....	75	20	27	1	....	....	....	16.7	8.1	5.8	1.5	.650
71-72	Buffalo	44	....	592	220	89	181	.492	....	....	....	42	52	.808	....	....	123	38	79	0	....	....	....	13.5	5.0	2.8	0.9	.425
NBA Season Totals		143	....	1395	573	235	485	.485	....	....	....	103	144	.715	....	....	355	94	219	1	....	....	....	9.8	4.0	2.5	0.7	....
68-69	New York	4	....	22	6	3	6	.500	....	....	....	0	1	.000	....	....	7	2	3	0	....	....	....	5.5	1.5	1.8	0.5	.455
69-70	New York	5	....	29	11	4	10	.400	....	....	....	3	4	.750	....	....	5	2	6	0	....	....	....	5.8	2.2	1.0	0.4	.320
NBA Playoff Totals		9	....	51	17	7	16	.438	....	....	....	3	5	.600	....	....	12	4	9	0	....	....	....	5.7	1.9	1.3	0.4	....

• HOSKET, Bill

William Hosket

Born: 1911. Height: 6'5". Weight: — Drafted: — College: Ohio State

YEAR	TEAM	GP	GS	MIN	PTS	FGM	FGA	FG%	3PM	3PA	3P%	FTM	FTA	FT%	ORB	DRB	TRB	AST	PF	DQ	STL	BLK	TO	MPG	PPG	RPG	APG	PCM
37-38	Dayton-N	10	....	....	34	11	....	....	....	....	....	12	....	....	....	....	....	....	....	....	....	....	....	....	3.4	....	....	....
NBL Season Totals		10	....	....	34	11	....	....	....	....	....	12	....	....	....	....	....	....	....	....	....	....	....	....	3.4	....	....	....

• HOUBREGS, Bob

Robert J. (Houby) Houbregs

Born: Mar. 12, 1932. Vancouver, BC, Canada. Height: 6'7". Weight: 210 lbs. Drafted: 1953 College: Washington

HOF: 1987

YEAR	TEAM	GP	GS	MIN	PTS	FGM	FGA	FG%	3PM	3PA	3P%	FTM	FTA	FT%	ORB	DRB	TRB	AST	PF	DQ	STL	BLK	TO	MPG	PPG	RPG	APG	PCM
53-54	Mil/Bal	70	....	1970	608	209	562	.372	....	....	....	190	266	.714	....	....	375	123	209	2	....	....	....	28.1	8.7	5.4	1.8	.346
54-55	Bal/Bos/FtW	64	....	1326	425	148	386	.383	....	....	....	129	182	.709	....	....	297	86	180	5	....	....	....	20.7	6.6	4.6	1.3	.369
55-56	Fort Wayne	70	....	1535	777	247	575	.430	....	....	....	283	383	.739	....	....	414	159	147	0	....	....	....	21.9	11.1	5.9	2.3	.616
56-57	Fort Wayne	60	....	1592	673	253	585	.432	....	....	....	167	234	.714	....	....	401	113	118	2	....	....	....	26.5	11.2	6.7	1.9	.501
57-58	Detroit	17	....	302	128	49	137	.358	....	....	....	30	43	.698	....	....	65	19	36	0	....	....	....	17.8	7.5	3.8	1.1	.389
NBA Season Totals		281	....	6725	2611	906	2245	.404	....	....	....	799	1108	.721	....	....	1552	500	690	9	....	....	....	23.9	9.3	5.5	1.8	....
54-55	Fort Wayne	11	....	213	77	24	63	.381	....	....	....	29	37	.784	....	....	62	19	31	0	....	....	....	19.4	7.0	5.6	1.7	.485
55-56	Fort Wayne	10	....	217	103	36	78	.462	....	....	....	31	44	.705	....	....	67	14	21	1	....	....	....	21.7	10.3	6.7	1.4	.583
56-57	Fort Wayne	2	....	38	22	7	17	.412	....	....	....	8	11	.727	....	....	6	3	3	0	....	....	....	19.0	11.0	3.0	1.5	.541
NBA Playoff Totals		23	....	468	202	67	158	.424	....	....	....	68	92	.739	....	....	135	36	55	1	....	....	....	20.3	8.8	5.9	1.6	....

• HOUSE, Eddie

Edward L. House II

Born: May 14, 1978. Berkeley, CA, United States. Height: 6'1". Weight: 180 lbs. Drafted: 2000 College: Arizona State

YEAR	TEAM	GP	GS	MIN	PTS	FGM	FGA	FG%	3PM	3PA	3P%	FTM	FTA	FT%	ORB	DRB	TRB	AST	PF	DQ	STL	BLK	TO	MPG	PPG	RPG	APG	PCM
00-01	Miami	50	0	550	251	104	247	.421	19	55	.345	24	35	.686	5	37	42	52	58	0	13	0	35	11.0	5.0	0.8	1.0	.303
01-02	Miami	64	3	1230	514	209	524	.399	54	157	.344	42	49	.857	17	93	110	123	98	1	43	5	80	19.2	8.0	1.7	1.9	.314
02-03	Miami	55	7	1025	411	172	444	.387	36	120	.300	31	36	.861	17	84	101	87	73	0	44	1	46	18.6	7.5	1.8	1.6	.307
NBA Season Totals		169	10	2805	1176	485	1215	.399	109	332	.328	97	120	.808	39	214	253	262	229	1	100	6	161	16.6	7.0	1.5	1.6	....
00-01	Miami	3	0	64	38	16	40	.400	2	7	.286	4	5	.800	1	4	5	5	7	0	3	1	5	21.3	12.7	1.7	1.7	.343
NBA Playoff Totals		3	0	64	38	16	40	.400	2	7	.286	4	5	.800	1	4	5	5	7	0	3	1	5	21.3	12.7	1.7	1.7	....

• HOUSTON, Allan

Allan Wade Houston

Born: Apr. 20, 1971. Louisville, KY, United States. Height: 6'6". Weight: 200 lbs. Drafted: 1993 College: Tennessee

YEAR	TEAM	GP	GS	MIN	PTS	FGM	FGA	FG%	3PM	3PA	3P%	FTM	FTA	FT%	ORB	DRB	TRB	AST	PF	DQ	STL	BLK	TO	MPG	PPG	RPG	APG	PCM
93-94	Detroit	79	20	1519	668	272	671	.405	35	117	.299	89	108	.824	19	101	120	100	165	2	34	13	103	19.2	8.5	1.5	1.3	.253
94-95	Detroit	76	39	1996	1101	398	859	.463	158	373	.424	147	171	.860	29	138	167	164	182	0	61	14	114	26.3	14.5	2.2	2.2	.434
95-96	Detroit	82	75	3072	1617	564	1244	.453	191	447	.427	298	362	.823	54	246	300	250	233	1	61	16	230	37.5	19.7	3.7	3.0	.404
96-97	New York	81	81	2681	1197	437	1032	.423	148	384	.385	175	218	.803	43	197	240	179	233	6	41	18	170	33.1	14.8	3.0	2.2	.308
97-98	New York	82	82	2848	1509	571	1277	.447	82	213	.385	285	335	.851	43	231	274	212	207	2	63	24	197	34.7	18.4	3.3	2.6	.395
98-99	New York	50	50	1815	813	294	703	.418	57	140	.407	168	195	.862	20	132	152	137	115	1	35	9	130	36.3	16.3	3.0	2.7	.329
99-00	New York	82	82	3169	1614	614	1271	.483	106	243	.436	280	334	.838	38	233	271	224	219	1	65	14	186	38.6	19.7	3.3	2.7	.406
00-01	New York	78	78	2858	1459	542	1208	.449	96	252	.381	279	307	.909	20	263	283	173	190	5	52	10	161	36.6	18.7	3.6	2.2	.392
01-02	New York	77	77	2914	1567	568	1301	.437	136	346	.393	295	339	.870	37	215	252	190	182	0	54	10	170	37.8	20.4	3.3	2.5	.391
02-03	New York	82	82	3108	1845	652	1465	.445	178	450	.396	363	395	**.919**	26	205	231	220	191	2	54	7	178	37.9	22.5	2.8	2.7	.434
NBA Season Totals		769	666	25980	13390	4912	11031	.445	1187	2965	.400	2379	2764	.861	329	1961	2290	1849	1917	20	520	135	1639	33.8	17.4	3.0	2.4	....
95-96	Detroit	3	3	136	75	25	58	.431	7	21	.333	18	20	.900	1	7	8	6	11	0	0	1	11	45.3	25.0	2.7	2.0	.311
96-97	New York	9	9	360	173	58	133	.436	26	52	.500	31	35	.886	3	20	23	21	14	0	6	3	24	40.0	19.2	2.6	2.3	.346
97-98	New York	10	10	403	211	76	175	.434	9	23	.391	50	58	.862	6	32	38	28	27	0	5	1	32	40.3	21.1	3.8	2.8	.362
98-99	New York	20	20	783	370	135	305	.443	9	36	.250	91	103	.883	6	48	54	51	40	0	8	1	50	39.2	18.5	2.7	2.6	.337
99-00	New York	16	16	654	281	103	235	.438	19	38	.500	56	65	.862	3	49	52	26	42	0	19	3	36	40.9	17.6	3.3	1.6	.307
00-01	New York	5	5	189	104	38	64	.594	6	11	.545	22	22	1.000	0	9	9	7	17	0	5	1	10	37.8	20.8	1.8	1.4	.451
NBA Playoff Totals		63	63	2525	1214	435	970	.448	76	181	.420	268	303	.884	19	165	184	139	151	0	43	10	163	40.1	19.3	2.9	2.2	....

• HOUSTON, Byron

Byron Dwight Houston

Born: Nov. 22, 1969. Watonga, KS, United States. Height: 6'5". Weight: 250 lbs. Drafted: 1992 College: Oklahoma State

YEAR	TEAM	GP	GS	MIN	PTS	FGM	FGA	FG%	3PM	3PA	3P%	FTM	FTA	FT%	ORB	DRB	TRB	AST	PF	DQ	STL	BLK	TO	MPG	PPG	RPG	APG	PCM
92-93	Golden State	79	8	1274	421	145	325	.446	2	7	.286	129	194	.665	119	196	315	69	253	12	44	43	87	16.1	5.3	4.0	0.9	.371
93-94	Golden State	71	2	866	196	81	177	.458	1	7	.143	33	54	.611	67	127	194	32	181	4	33	31	50	12.2	2.8	2.7	0.5	.278
94-95	Seattle	39	0	258	132	49	107	.458	6	22	.273	28	38	.737	20	35	55	6	50	0	13	5	20	6.6	3.4	1.4	0.2	.409
95-96	Sacramento	25	0	276	86	32	64	.500	1	3	.333	21	26	.808	31	53	84	7	59	2	13	7	18	11.0	3.4	3.4	0.3	.413
NBA Season Totals		214	10	2674	835	307	673	.456	10	39	.256	211	312	.676	237	411	648	114	543	18	103	86	175	12.5	3.9	3.0	0.5	....
93-94	Golden State	3	2	46	15	6	8	.750	0	0	.000	3	5	.600	2	3	5	3	9	0	1	2	0	15.3	5.0	1.7	1.0	.407
94-95	Seattle	1	0	1	0	0	1	.000	0	0	.000	0	0	.000	0	0	0	0	0	0	0	0	0	1.0	0.0	0.0	0.0	-.938
NBA Playoff Totals		4	2	47	15	6	9	.667	0	0	.000	3	5	.600	2	3	5	3	9	0	1	2	0	11.8	3.8	1.3	0.8	....

• HOVASSE, Tom

Tom Wayne Hovasse

Born: Jan. 31, 1967. Durango, CO, United States. Height: 6'8". Weight: 205 lbs. Drafted: — College: Penn State

YEAR	TEAM	GP	GS	MIN	PTS	FGM	FGA	FG%	3PM	3PA	3P%	FTM	FTA	FT%	ORB	DRB	TRB	AST	PF	DQ	STL	BLK	TO	MPG	PPG	RPG	APG	PCM
94-95	Atlanta	2	0	4	0	0	1	.000	0	1	.000	0	0	.000	0	0	0	0	1	0	1	0	0	2.0	0.0	0.0	0.0	-.117
NBA Season Totals		2	0	4	0	0	1	.000	0	1	.000	0	0	.000	0	0	0	0	1	0	1	0	0	2.0	0.0	0.0	0.0	....

• HOWARD, Brian

Brian Eugene Howard

Born: Oct. 19, 1967. Winston-Salem, NC, United States. Height: 6'6". Weight: 204 lbs. Drafted: — College: North Carolina State

YEAR	TEAM	GP	GS	MIN	PTS	FGM	FGA	FG%	3PM	3PA	3P%	FTM	FTA	FT%	ORB	DRB	TRB	AST	PF	DQ	STL	BLK	TO	MPG	PPG	RPG	APG	PCM
91-92	Dallas	27	0	318	131	54	104	.519	1	2	.500	22	31	.710	17	34	51	14	55	2	11	8	16	11.8	4.9	1.9	0.5	.377
92-93	Dallas	68	22	1295	439	183	414	.442	1	7	.143	72	94	.766	66	146	212	67	217	8	55	34	68	19.0	6.5	3.1	1.0	.310
NBA Season Totals		95	22	1613	570	237	518	.458	2	9	.222	94	125	.752	83	180	263	81	272	10	66	42	84	17.0	6.0	2.8	0.9	....

• HOWARD, Greg

Gregory Darryle (Stretch) Howard

Born: Jan. 8, 1948. Pittsburgh, PA, United States. Height: 6'9". Weight: 215 lbs. Drafted: 1970 College: New Mexico

YEAR	TEAM	GP	GS	MIN	PTS	FGM	FGA	FG%	3PM	3PA	3P%	FTM	FTA	FT%	ORB	DRB	TRB	AST	PF	DQ	STL	BLK	TO	MPG	PPG	RPG	APG	PCM
70-71	Phoenix	44	....	426	173	68	173	.393	....	....	....	37	58	.638	....	....	119	26	67	0	....	....	....	9.7	3.9	2.7	0.6	.415
71-72	Cleveland	48	....	426	139	50	131	.382	....	....	....	39	51	.765	....	....	108	27	50	0	....	....	....	8.9	2.9	2.3	0.6	.390
NBA Season Totals		92	....	852	312	118	304	.388	....	....	....	76	109	.697	....	....	227	53	117	0	....	....	....	9.3	3.4	2.5	0.6	....

• HOWARD, Juwan

Juwan Antonio Howard

Born: Feb. 7, 1973. Chicago, IL, United States. Height: 6'9". Weight: 240 lbs. Drafted: 1994 College: Michigan

YEAR	TEAM	GP	GS	MIN	PTS	FGM	FGA	FG%	3PM	3PA	3P%	FTM	FTA	FT%	ORB	DRB	TRB	AST	PF	DQ	STL	BLK	TO	MPG	PPG	RPG	APG	PCM
94-95	Washington	65	52	2348	1104	455	931	.489	0	7	.000	194	292	.664	184	361	545	165	236	2	52	15	169	36.1	17.0	8.4	2.5	.465
95-96	Washington	81	81	3294	1789	733	1500	.489	4	13	.308	319	426	.749	188	472	660	360	269	3	67	39	300	40.7	22.1	8.1	4.4	.519
96-97	Washington	82	82	3324	1570	638	1313	.486	0	2	.000	294	389	.756	202	450	652	311	259	3	93	23	246	40.5	19.1	8.0	3.8	.480
97-98	Washington	64	64	2559	1184	463	991	.467	0	2	.000	258	358	.721	161	288	449	208	225	3	82	23	186	40.0	18.5	7.0	3.3	.436
98-99	Washington	36	36	1430	682	286	604	.474	0	3	.000	110	146	.753	90	203	293	107	130	1	42	14	95	39.7	18.9	8.1	3.0	.469
99-00	Washington	82	82	2909	1220	509	1108	.459	0	7	.000	202	275	.735	132	338	470	247	299	0	67	21	225	35.5	14.9	5.7	3.0	.371
00-01	Washington	54	54	1981	981	392	827	.474	0	0	.000	197	256	.770	121	258	379	154	186	1	46	21	169	36.7	18.2	7.0	2.9	.454
00-01	Dallas	27	27	993	481	191	391	.488	0	3	.000	99	127	.780	50	143	193	70	106	1	29	16	73	36.8	17.8	7.1	2.6	.470

YEAR	TEAM	GP	GS	MIN	PTS	FGM	FGA	FG%	3PM	3PA	3P%	FTM	FTA	FT%	ORB	DRB	TRB	AST	PF	DQ	STL	BLK	TO	MPG	PPG	RPG	APG	PCM
01-02	Dallas	53	44	1659	684	270	585	.462	0	1	.000	144	191	.754	138	252	390	93	170	1	28	30	78	31.3	12.9	7.4	1.8	.444
01-02	Denver	28	28	976	501	192	420	.457	0	1	.000	117	152	.770	85	137	222	76	95	3	18	17	74	34.9	17.9	7.9	2.7	.496
02-03	Denver	77	77	2729	1418	567	1261	.450	2	4	.500	282	351	.803	181	404	585	234	239	2	77	27	189	35.4	18.4	7.6	3.0	.497
NBA Season Totals		649	627	24202	11614	4696	9931	.473	6	43	.140	2216	2963	.748	1532	3306	4838	2025	2214	20	601	246	1804	37.3	17.9	7.5	3.1	....
96-97	Washington	3	3	129	56	20	43	.465	0	0	.000	16	18	.889	10	8	18	5	9	0	2	2	3	43.0	18.7	6.0	1.7	.407
00-01	Dallas	10	10	391	134	49	136	.360	0	0	.000	36	45	.800	29	54	83	14	38	0	6	5	14	39.1	13.4	8.3	1.4	.312
NBA Playoff Totals		13	13	520	190	69	179	.385	0	0	.000	52	63	.825	39	62	101	19	47	0	8	7	17	40.0	14.6	7.8	1.5	....

• HOWARD, Mo

Maurice Howard

Born: Aug. 25, 1954. Philadelphia, PA, United States.　Height: 6'2".　Weight: 170 lbs.　Drafted: 1976　College: Maryland

YEAR	TEAM	GP	GS	MIN	PTS	FGM	FGA	FG%	3PM	3PA	3P%	FTM	FTA	FT%	ORB	DRB	TRB	AST	PF	DQ	STL	BLK	TO	MPG	PPG	RPG	APG	PCM
76-77	Cleveland	9	....	28	21	8	15	.533	....	....	....	5	6	.833	2	3	5	5	7	0	1	2	....	3.1	2.3	0.6	0.6	.768
76-77	New Orleans	23	....	317	131	56	117	.479	....	....	....	19	29	.655	15	19	34	37	44	0	16	6	....	13.8	5.7	1.5	1.6	.399
NBA Season Totals		32	....	345	152	64	132	.485	....	....	....	24	35	.686	17	22	39	42	51	0	17	8	....	10.8	4.8	1.2	1.3	....

• HOWARD, Otis

Willie Otis Howard

Born: Nov. 5, 1956. Oak Ridge, TN, United States.　Height: 6'7".　Weight: 220 lbs.　Drafted: 1978　College: Austin Peay

YEAR	TEAM	GP	GS	MIN	PTS	FGM	FGA	FG%	3PM	3PA	3P%	FTM	FTA	FT%	ORB	DRB	TRB	AST	PF	DQ	STL	BLK	TO	MPG	PPG	RPG	APG	PCM
78-79	Milwaukee	3	....	22	10	5	11	.455	....	....	....	0	0	.000	5	2	7	1	8	0	0	0	2	7.3	3.3	2.3	0.3	.301
78-79	Detroit	11	....	91	49	19	45	.422	....	....	....	11	23	.478	13	21	34	4	16	0	2	2	6	8.3	4.5	3.1	0.4	.508
NBA Season Totals		14	....	113	59	24	56	.429	....	....	....	11	23	.478	18	23	41	5	24	0	2	2	8	8.1	4.2	2.9	0.4	....

• HOWARD, Stephen

Stephen Christopher Howard

Born: July 15, 1970. Dallas, TX, United States.　Height: 6'9".　Weight: 225 lbs.　Drafted: —　College: DePaul

YEAR	TEAM	GP	GS	MIN	PTS	FGM	FGA	FG%	3PM	3PA	3P%	FTM	FTA	FT%	ORB	DRB	TRB	AST	PF	DQ	STL	BLK	TO	MPG	PPG	RPG	APG	PCM
92-93	Utah	49	0	260	104	35	93	.376	0	0	.000	34	53	.642	26	34	60	10	58	0	15	12	25	5.3	2.1	1.2	0.2	.317
93-94	Utah	9	0	53	31	10	17	.588	0	0	.000	11	16	.688	10	6	16	1	13	0	1	3	6	5.9	3.4	1.8	0.1	.571
96-97	San Antonio	7	0	69	26	7	12	.583	0	0	.000	12	14	.857	4	5	9	1	7	0	8	2	5	9.9	3.7	1.3	0.1	.453
96-97	Seattle	42	0	349	150	55	96	.573	0	0	.000	40	67	.597	25	51	76	10	55	0	11	10	21	8.3	3.6	1.8	0.2	.444
97-98	Seattle	13	0	53	25	8	21	.381	0	0	.000	9	18	.500	6	6	12	3	13	0	3	1	7	4.1	1.9	0.9	0.2	.274
NBA Season Totals		120	0	784	336	115	239	.481	0	0	.000	106	168	.631	71	102	173	25	146	0	38	28	64	6.5	2.8	1.4	0.2	....
93-94	Utah	10	0	27	14	3	11	.273	0	0	.000	8	11	.727	3	7	10	0	11	0	0	0	2	2.7	1.4	1.0	0.0	.281
96-97	Utah	5	0	13	9	3	6	.500	0	0	.000	3	4	.750	0	1	1	0	2	0	1	0	0	2.6	1.8	0.2	0.0	.513
NBA Playoff Totals		15	0	40	23	6	17	.353	0	0	.000	11	15	.733	3	8	11	0	13	0	1	0	2	2.7	1.5	0.7	0.0	....

• HOWELL, Bailey

Bailey E. Howell

Born: Jan. 20, 1937. Middleton, TN, United States.　Height: 6'7".　Weight: 210 lbs.　Drafted: 1959　College: Mississippi State

HOF: 1997

YEAR	TEAM	GP	GS	MIN	PTS	FGM	FGA	FG%	3PM	3PA	3P%	FTM	FTA	FT%	ORB	DRB	TRB	AST	PF	DQ	STL	BLK	TO	MPG	PPG	RPG	APG	PCM
59-60	Detroit	75	....	2346	1332	510	1119	.456	....	....	....	312	422	.739			790	63	282	13	....	....	....	31.3	17.8	10.5	0.8	.596
60-61	Detroit	77	....	2952	1815	607	1293	.469	....	....	....	601	798	.753			1111	196	297	10	....	....	....	38.3	23.6	14.4	2.5	.743
61-62	Detroit	79	....	2857	1576	553	1193	.464	....	....	....	470	612	.768			996	186	317	10	....	....	....	36.2	19.9	12.6	2.4	.666
62-63	Detroit	79	....	2971	1793	637	1235	.516	....	....	....	519	650	.798			910	232	300	9	....	....	....	37.6	22.7	11.5	2.9	.724
63-64	Detroit	77	....	2700	1666	598	1267	.472	....	....	....	470	581	.809			776	205	290	9	....	....	....	35.1	21.6	10.1	2.7	.683
64-65	Baltimore	80	....	2975	1534	515	1040	.495	....	....	....	504	629	.801			869	208	**345**	10	....	....	....	37.2	19.2	10.9	2.6	.630
65-66	Baltimore	79	....	2328	1364	481	986	.488	....	....	....	402	551	.730			773	155	306	12	....	....	....	29.5	17.3	9.8	2.0	.681
66-67	Boston	81	....	2503	1621	636	1242	.512	....	....	....	349	471	.741			677	103	296	4	....	....	....	30.9	20.0	8.4	1.3	.653
67-68	Boston	82	....	2801	1621	643	1336	.481	....	....	....	335	461	.727			805	133	285	4	....	....	....	34.2	19.8	9.8	1.6	.609
68-69	Boston	78	....	2527	1537	612	1257	.487	....	....	....	313	426	.735			685	137	285	3	....	....	....	32.4	19.7	8.8	1.8	.619
69-70	Boston	82	....	2078	1033	399	931	.429	....	....	....	235	308	.763			550	120	261	4	....	....	....	25.3	12.6	6.7	1.5	.499
70-71	Philadelphia	82	....	1589	878	324	686	.472	....	....	....	230	315	.730			441	115	234	2	....	....	....	19.4	10.7	5.4	1.4	.591
NBA Season Totals		951	....	30627	17770	6515	13585	.480	....	....	....	4740	6224	.762			9383	1853	3498	90	....	....	....	32.2	18.7	9.9	1.9	....
59-60	Detroit	2	....	72	34	14	41	.341	....	....	....	6	8	.750			17	3	8	0	....	....	....	36.0	17.0	8.5	1.5	.367
60-61	Detroit	5	....	154	56	20	57	.351	....	....	....	16	23	.696			46	22	22	1	....	....	....	30.8	11.2	9.2	4.4	.513
61-62	Detroit	10	....	378	200	69	163	.423	....	....	....	62	75	.827			96	23	48	3	....	....	....	37.8	20.0	9.6	2.3	.544
62-63	Detroit	4	....	163	71	24	64	.375	....	....	....	23	27	.852			42	11	19	1	....	....	....	40.8	17.8	10.5	2.8	.471
64-65	Baltimore	9	....	350	187	67	130	.515	....	....	....	53	70	.757			105	19	38	3	....	....	....	38.9	20.8	11.7	2.1	.633
65-66	Baltimore	3	....	94	54	23	50	.460	....	....	....	8	11	.727			30	2	13	1	....	....	....	31.3	18.0	10.0	0.7	.559
66-67	Boston	9	....	241	138	59	122	.484	....	....	....	20	30	.667			66	5	35	2	....	....	....	26.8	15.3	7.3	0.6	.533
67-68	Boston	19	....	597	344	135	264	.511	....	....	....	74	107	.692			146	22	84	6	....	....	....	31.4	18.1	7.7	1.2	.565
68-69	Boston	18	....	551	270	112	229	.489	....	....	....	46	64	.719			118	19	84	3	....	....	....	30.6	15.0	6.6	1.1	.454
70-71	Philadelphia	7	....	122	47	19	45	.422	....	....	....	9	18	.500			31	4	25	1	....	....	....	17.4	6.7	4.4	0.6	.338
NBA Playoff Totals		86	....	2722	1401	542	1165	.465	....	....	....	317	433	.732			697	130	376	21	....	....	....	31.7	16.3	8.1	1.5	....

• HUBBARD, Bob

Robert Cecil Hubbard

Born: Dec. 27, 1922.　Height: 6'6".　Weight: 215 lbs.　Drafted: 1947　College: Springfield

YEAR	TEAM	GP	GS	MIN	PTS	FGM	FGA	FG%	3PM	3PA	3P%	FTM	FTA	FT%	ORB	DRB	TRB	AST	PF	DQ	STL	BLK	TO	MPG	PPG	RPG	APG	PCM
47-48	Tri-Cities-N	20	....		76	27	....	....	....	....	....	22	26	.846											3.8			....
47-48	Providence	28	....		152	58	199	.291	....	....	....	36	52	.692				11	34						5.4		0.4	....
48-49	Providence	34	....		72	25	135	.185	....	....	....	22	34	.647				18	39						2.1		0.5	....
NBA Season Totals		62	....		224	83	334	.249	....	....	....	58	86	.674	....	....		29	73	....	....	....			3.6		0.5	....
NBL Season Totals		20	....		76	27	....	....	....	....	....	22	26	....											3.8			....
Career Totals		82	....		300	110	334	....	....	....	....	80	112	....	....	....		29	73	....	....	....			3.7		0.4	....

• HUBBARD, Phil
Philip Gregory Hubbard

Born: Dec. 13, 1956. Canton, OH, United States. Height: 6'8". Weight: 215 lbs. Drafted: 1979 College: Michigan

YEAR	TEAM	GP	GS	MIN	PTS	FGM	FGA	FG%	3PM	3PA	3P%	FTM	FTA	FT%	ORB	DRB	TRB	AST	PF	DQ	STL	BLK	TO	MPG	PPG	RPG	APG	PCM
79-80	Detroit	64	....	1189	585	210	451	.466	0	2	.000	165	220	.750	114	206	320	70	202	9	48	10	122	18.6	9.1	5.0	1.1	.470
80-81	Detroit	80	....	2289	1161	433	880	.492	1	3	.333	294	426	.690	236	350	586	150	317	14	80	20	232	28.6	14.5	7.3	1.9	.492
81-82	Detroit	52	38	1104	520	207	410	.505	0	3	.000	106	163	.650	101	171	272	67	176	1	38	16	99	21.2	10.0	5.2	1.3	.459
81-82	Cleveland	31	2	735	323	119	255	.467	0	1	.000	85	117	.726	86	115	201	24	116	2	27	3	62	23.7	10.4	6.5	0.8	.423
82-83	Cleveland	82	38	1953	780	288	597	.482	0	2	.000	204	296	.689	222	249	471	89	271	11	87	8	156	23.8	9.5	5.7	1.1	.412
83-84	Cleveland	80	6	1799	863	321	628	.511	0	1	.000	221	299	.739	172	208	380	86	244	3	71	6	112	22.5	10.8	4.8	1.1	.467
84-85	Cleveland	76	55	2249	1201	415	822	.505	0	4	.000	371	494	.751	214	265	479	114	258	8	81	9	175	29.6	15.8	6.3	1.5	.504
85-86	Cleveland	23	21	640	262	93	198	.470	0	1	.000	76	112	.679	48	72	120	29	78	2	20	3	67	27.8	11.4	5.2	1.3	.333
86-87	Cleveland	68	68	2083	804	321	605	.531	0	4	.000	162	272	.596	178	210	388	136	224	6	66	7	156	30.6	11.8	5.7	2.0	.391
87-88	Cleveland	78	59	1631	656	237	485	.489	0	5	.000	182	243	.749	117	164	281	81	167	1	50	7	117	20.9	8.4	3.6	1.0	.375
88-89	Cleveland	31	0	191	73	28	63	.444	0	0	.000	17	25	.680	14	26	40	11	20	0	6	0	9	6.2	2.4	1.3	0.4	.385
NBA Season Totals		665	287	15863	7228	2672	5394	.495	1	26	.038	1883	2667	.706	1502	2036	3538	857	2073	57	574	89	1307	23.9	10.9	5.3	1.3	....
84-85	Cleveland	4	4	101	62	24	45	.533	1	1	1.000	13	17	.765	11	9	20	3	16	0	3	0	7	25.3	15.5	5.0	0.8	.507
87-88	Cleveland	3	0	21	2	1	6	.167	0	0	.000	0	1	.000	1	2	3	0	1	0	0	0	1	7.0	0.7	1.0	0.0	-.082
88-89	Cleveland	1	0	1	0	0	0	.000	0	0	.000	0	0	.000	0	0	0	0	0	0	0	0	0	1.0	0.0	0.0	0.0	.000
NBA Playoff Totals		8	4	123	64	25	51	.490	1	1	1.000	13	18	.722	12	11	23	3	17	0	3	0	8	15.4	8.0	2.9	0.4	....

• HUBER, Lee
Lee Huber

Born: July 20, 1919. Louisville, KY, United States. Died: Nov.9, 1995. Height: 6'1". Weight: — Drafted: — College: Kentucky

YEAR	TEAM	GP	GS	MIN	PTS	FGM	FGA	FG%	3PM	3PA	3P%	FTM	FTA	FT%	ORB	DRB	TRB	AST	PF	DQ	STL	BLK	TO	MPG	PPG	RPG	APG	PCM
41-42	Wingfoots-N	11	....	....	70	32	....	....				6												6.4			
NBL Season Totals		11	....		70	32	....	....				6												6.4			

• HUDSON, Lou
Louis Clyde (Sweet Lou, Super Lou) Hudson

Born: July 11, 1944. Greensboro, NC, United States. Height: 6'5". Weight: 210 lbs. Drafted: 1966 College: Minnesota

YEAR	TEAM	GP	GS	MIN	PTS	FGM	FGA	FG%	3PM	3PA	3P%	FTM	FTA	FT%	ORB	DRB	TRB	AST	PF	DQ	STL	BLK	TO	MPG	PPG	RPG	APG	PCM
66-67	St. Louis	80	....	2446	1471	620	1328	.467				231	327	.706	....	....	435	95	277	3				30.6	18.4	5.4	1.2	.498
67-68	St. Louis	46	....	966	574	227	500	.454				120	164	.732	....	....	193	65	113	2				21.0	12.5	4.2	1.4	.544
68-69	Atlanta	81	....	2869	1770	716	1455	.492				338	435	.777	....	....	533	216	248	0				35.4	21.9	6.6	2.7	.594
69-70	Atlanta	80	....	3091	2031	830	1564	.531				371	450	.824	....	....	373	276	225	1				38.6	25.4	4.7	3.5	.611
70-71	Atlanta	76	....	3113	2039	829	1713	.484				381	502	.759	....	....	386	257	186	0				41.0	26.8	5.1	3.4	.569
71-72	Atlanta	77	....	3042	1899	775	1540	.503				349	430	.812	....	....	385	309	225	0				39.5	24.7	5.0	4.0	.588
72-73	Atlanta	75	....	3027	2029	816	1710	.477				397	481	.825	....	....	467	258	197	1				40.4	27.1	6.2	3.4	.607
73-74	Atlanta	65	....	2588	1651	678	1356	.500				295	353	.836	126	224	350	213	205	3	160	29		39.8	25.4	5.4	3.3	.581
74-75	Atlanta	11	....	380	242	97	225	.431				48	57	.842	14	33	47	40	33	1	13	2		34.5	22.0	4.3	3.6	.529
75-76	Atlanta	81	....	2558	1375	569	1205	.472				237	291	.814	104	196	300	214	241	3	124	17		31.6	17.0	3.7	2.6	.471
76-77	Atlanta	58	....	1745	968	413	905	.456				142	169	.840	48	81	129	155	160	2	67	19		30.1	16.7	2.2	2.7	.430
77-78	LA Lakers	82	....	2283	1123	493	992	.497				137	177	.774	80	108	188	193	196	0	94	14	148	27.8	13.7	2.3	2.4	.407
78-79	LA Lakers	78	....	1686	768	329	636	.517				110	124	.887	64	76	140	141	133	1	58	17	101	21.6	9.8	1.8	1.8	.406
NBA Season Totals		890	....	29794	17940	7392	15129	.489				3156	3960	.797	436	718	3926	2432	2439	17	516	98	249	33.5	20.2	4.4	2.7	....
66-67	St. Louis	9	....	317	203	77	179	.430				49	68	.721	....	....	48	15	35	1				35.2	22.6	5.3	1.7	.494
67-68	St. Louis	6	....	181	130	44	99	.444				42	47	.894	....	....	43	14	21	0				30.2	21.7	7.2	2.3	.701
68-69	Atlanta	11	....	424	242	101	216	.468				40	52	.769	....	....	59	32	43	1				38.5	22.0	5.4	2.9	.494
69-70	Atlanta	9	....	360	197	78	187	.417				41	50	.820	....	....	40	33	34	2				40.0	21.9	4.4	3.7	.429
70-71	Atlanta	5	....	213	127	49	108	.454				29	39	.744	....	....	35	15	19	0				42.6	25.4	7.0	3.0	.521
71-72	Atlanta	6	....	266	150	63	139	.453				24	29	.828	....	....	33	21	13	0				44.3	25.0	5.5	3.5	.485
72-73	Atlanta	6	....	255	178	76	166	.458				26	29	.897	....	....	47	17	16	0				42.5	29.7	7.8	2.8	.598
77-78	LA Lakers	3	....	93	35	14	38	.368				7	8	.875	7	2	9	9	9	0	5	0	5	31.0	11.7	3.0	3.0	.297
78-79	LA Lakers	6	....	90	38	17	32	.531				4	4	1.000	1	3	4	8	6	0	1	0	5	15.0	6.3	0.7	1.3	.341
NBA Playoff Totals		61	....	2199	1300	519	1164	.446				262	326	.804	8	5	318	164	196	4	6	0	10	36.0	21.3	5.2	2.7	....

• HUDSON, Roosie
Roosevelt Hudson

Born: July 15, 1915. Died: Feb.1985. Height: 6' Weight: 160 lbs. Drafted: — College: Morris Brown

YEAR	TEAM	GP	GS	MIN	PTS	FGM	FGA	FG%	3PM	3PA	3P%	FTM	FTA	FT%	ORB	DRB	TRB	AST	PF	DQ	STL	BLK	TO	MPG	PPG	RPG	APG	PCM
42-43	Chicago-N	21	....	....	127	50	....	....				27												6.0			
NBL Season Totals		21	....		127	50						27												6.0			
42-43	Chicago-N	2	....	....	3	0						3												1.5			
NBL Playoff Totals		2	....		3	0						3												1.5			

• HUDSON, Troy
Troy Hudson

Born: Mar. 13, 1976. Carbondale, IL, United States. Height: 6'1". Weight: 170 lbs. Drafted: — College: Southern Illinois

YEAR	TEAM	GP	GS	MIN	PTS	FGM	FGA	FG%	3PM	3PA	3P%	FTM	FTA	FT%	ORB	DRB	TRB	AST	PF	DQ	STL	BLK	TO	MPG	PPG	RPG	APG	PCM
97-98	Utah	8	0	23	12	6	14	.429	0	3	.000	0	0	.000	1	1	2	4	1	0	2	0	1	2.9	1.5	0.3	0.5	.492
98-99	LA Clippers	25	6	524	169	60	150	.400	15	47	.319	34	38	.895	15	40	55	92	28	1	11	2	38	21.0	6.8	2.2	3.7	.389
99-00	LA Clippers	62	38	1592	545	204	541	.377	60	193	.311	77	95	.811	28	120	148	242	65	0	43	0	108	25.7	8.8	2.4	3.9	.340
00-01	Orlando	75	7	1008	357	125	372	.336	22	109	.202	85	104	.817	38	67	105	162	82	0	37	3	92	13.4	4.8	1.4	2.2	.313
01-02	Orlando	81	4	1854	950	354	815	.434	66	187	.353	176	201	.876	30	115	145	255	119	0	57	6	163	22.9	11.7	1.8	3.1	.424
02-03	Minnesota	79	74	2601	1123	409	956	.428	97	266	.365	208	231	.900	42	141	183	452	160	1	60	7	182	32.9	14.2	2.3	5.7	.422
NBA Season Totals		330	129	7602	3156	1158	2848	.407	260	805	.323	580	669	.867	154	484	638	1207	455	2	210	18	584	23.0	9.6	1.9	3.7	....
00-01	Orlando	4	0	56	17	6	21	.286	0	3	.000	5	6	.833	5	4	9	9	3	0	1	0	3	14.0	4.3	2.3	2.3	.320
01-02	Orlando	4	0	105	51	18	48	.375	0	5	.000	15	16	.938	0	4	4	6	4	0	0	0	8	26.3	12.8	1.0	1.5	.233
02-03	Minnesota	6	6	221	141	44	106	.415	17	39	.436	36	38	.947	1	11	12	33	5	0	8	0	16	36.8	23.5	2.0	5.5	.548
NBA Playoff Totals		14	6	382	209	68	175	.389	17	47	.362	56	60	.933	6	19	25	48	12	0	9	0	27	27.3	14.9	1.8	3.4	....

YEAR	TEAM	GP	GS	MIN	PTS	FGM	FGA	FG%	3PM	3PA	3P%	FTM	FTA	FT%	ORB	DRB	TRB	AST	PF	DQ	STL	BLK	TO	MPG	PPG	RPG	APG	PCM

• HUFFMAN, Marv — Marvin Huffman

Born: Mar. 14, 1917. Died: May 1983.   Height: 6'2".   Weight: 185 lbs.   Drafted: —   College: Indiana

YEAR	TEAM	GP	GS	MIN	PTS	FGM	FGA	FG%	3PM	3PA	3P%	FTM	FTA	FT%	ORB	DRB	TRB	AST	PF	DQ	STL	BLK	TO	MPG	PPG	RPG	APG	PCM
40-41	Wingfoots-N	22	....	....	113	47	....	....	....	....	....	....	19	....	....	....	....	....	....	....	....	....	....	....	5.1	....	....	....
NBL Season Totals		22	....	....	113	47	....	....	....	....	....	....	19	....	....	....	....	....	....	....	....	....	....	....	5.1	....	....	....

• HUFFMAN, Nate — Nate Thomas Huffman

Born: Apr. 2, 1975. Battle Creek, MI, United States.   Height: 7'1".   Weight: 245 lbs.   Drafted: —   College: Central Michigan

YEAR	TEAM	GP	GS	MIN	PTS	FGM	FGA	FG%	3PM	3PA	3P%	FTM	FTA	FT%	ORB	DRB	TRB	AST	PF	DQ	STL	BLK	TO	MPG	PPG	RPG	APG	PCM
02-03	Toronto	7	0	76	23	9	25	.360	0	0	.000	5	8	.625	9	14	23	5	13	0	1	3	3	10.9	3.3	3.3	0.7	.374
NBA Season Totals		7	0	76	23	9	25	.360	0	0	.000	5	8	.625	9	14	23	5	13	0	1	3	3	10.9	3.3	3.3	0.7	....

• HUFFMAN, Vernon — Vernon R. Huffman

Born: Dec. 18, 1914. Moreland, IN, United States. Died: Mar.18, 1995.   Height: 6'2".   Weight: 215 lbs.   Drafted: —   College: Indiana

YEAR	TEAM	GP	GS	MIN	PTS	FGM	FGA	FG%	3PM	3PA	3P%	FTM	FTA	FT%	ORB	DRB	TRB	AST	PF	DQ	STL	BLK	TO	MPG	PPG	RPG	APG	PCM
38-39	Indianapolis-N	3	....	....	20	7	....	....	....	....	....	....	6	....	....	....	....	....	....	....	....	....	....	....	6.7	....	....	....
NBL Season Totals		3	....	....	20	7	....	....	....	....	....	....	6	....	....	....	....	....	....	....	....	....	....	....	6.7	....	....	....

• HUGHES, Eddie — Eddie Hughes

Born: May 26, 1960. Greenville, MS, United States.   Height: 5'10".   Weight: —   Drafted: 1982   College: Colorado State

YEAR	TEAM	GP	GS	MIN	PTS	FGM	FGA	FG%	3PM	3PA	3P%	FTM	FTA	FT%	ORB	DRB	TRB	AST	PF	DQ	STL	BLK	TO	MPG	PPG	RPG	APG	PCM
87-88	Utah	11	0	42	17	5	13	.385	1	6	.167	6	6	1.000	3	1	4	8	5	0	0	0	6	3.8	1.5	0.4	0.7	.331
88-89	Denver	26	1	224	70	28	64	.438	7	22	.318	7	12	.583	6	13	19	35	30	0	17	2	10	8.6	2.7	0.7	1.3	.374
89-90	Denver	60	7	892	209	83	202	.411	20	49	.408	23	34	.676	15	55	70	116	87	0	48	1	42	14.9	3.5	1.2	1.9	.277
NBA Season Totals		97	8	1158	296	116	279	.416	28	77	.364	36	52	.692	24	69	93	159	122	0	65	3	58	11.9	3.1	1.0	1.6	....
87-88	Utah	7	0	16	5	2	7	.286	1	3	.333	0	0	.000	0	0	0	1	1	0	1	0	1	2.3	0.7	0.0	0.1	.059
NBA Playoff Totals		7	0	16	5	2	7	.286	1	3	.333	0	0	.000	0	0	0	1	1	0	1	0	1	2.3	0.7	0.0	0.1	....

• HUGHES, Kim — Kim Galen Hughes

Born: June 4, 1952. Freeport, IL, United States.   Height: 6'11".   Weight: 220 lbs.   Drafted: 1974   College: Wisconsin

YEAR	TEAM	GP	GS	MIN	PTS	FGM	FGA	FG%	3PM	3PA	3P%	FTM	FTA	FT%	ORB	DRB	TRB	AST	PF	DQ	STL	BLK	TO	MPG	PPG	RPG	APG	PCM
75-76	New York-A	84	....	2162	692	300	566	.530	0	0	.000	92	202	.455	341	434	775	18	71	....	98	120	102	25.7	8.2	9.2	0.2	.502
76-77	New York	81	....	2081	321	151	354	.427	....	....	....	19	69	.275	189	375	564	98	308	9	122	119	....	25.7	4.0	7.0	1.2	.283
77-78	New Jersey	56	....	854	123	57	160	.356	....	....	....	9	29	.310	95	145	240	38	163	9	49	49	56	15.3	2.2	4.3	0.7	.284
78-79	Denver	81	....	1086	214	98	182	.538	....	....	....	18	45	.400	112	223	335	74	215	2	56	102	81	13.4	2.6	4.1	0.9	.443
79-80	Denver	70	....	1208	219	102	202	.505	0	0	.000	15	41	.366	125	201	326	74	184	3	66	77	49	17.3	3.1	4.7	1.1	.409
80-81	Denver	8	....	159	23	11	25	.440	0	0	.000	1	2	.500	19	31	50	11	33	2	11	14	11	19.9	2.9	6.3	1.4	.409
80-81	Cleveland	45	....	331	32	16	45	.356	0	0	.000	0	0	.000	29	48	77	24	73	0	17	21	32	7.4	0.7	1.7	0.5	.224
NBA Season Totals		341	....	5719	932	435	968	.449	0	0	.000	62	186	.333	569	1023	1592	319	976	25	321	382	229	16.8	2.7	4.7	0.9	....
ABA Season Totals		84	....	2162	692	300	566	.530	0	0	.000	92	202	.455	341	434	775	18	71	....	98	120	102	25.7	8.2	9.2	0.2	....
Career Totals		425	....	7881	1624	735	1534	.479	0	0	.000	154	388	.397	910	1457	2367	337	1047	25	419	502	331	18.5	3.8	5.6	0.8	....
75-76	New York-A	12	....	266	60	29	57	.509	0	0	.000	2	5	.400	34	38	72	9	53	....	10	13	9	22.2	5.0	6.0	0.8	.317
78-79	Denver	3	....	35	3	1	2	.500	....	....	....	1	2	.500	3	8	11	0	8	0	2	0	3	11.7	1.0	3.7	0.0	.201
NBA Playoff Totals		3	....	35	3	1	2	.500	....	....	....	1	2	.500	3	8	11	0	8	0	2	0	3	11.7	1.0	3.7	0.0	....
ABA Playoff Totals		12	....	266	60	29	57	.509	0	0	.000	2	5	.400	34	38	72	9	53	....	10	13	9	22.2	5.0	6.0	0.8	....
Career Playoff Totals		15	....	301	63	30	59	.508	0	0	.000	3	7	.429	37	46	83	9	61	0	12	13	12	20.1	4.2	5.5	0.6	....

• HUGHES, Larry — Larry Darnell Hughes

Born: Jan. 23, 1979. St. Louis, MO, United States.   Height: 6'5".   Weight: 184 lbs.   Drafted: 1998   College: Saint Louis

YEAR	TEAM	GP	GS	MIN	PTS	FGM	FGA	FG%	3PM	3PA	3P%	FTM	FTA	FT%	ORB	DRB	TRB	AST	PF	DQ	STL	BLK	TO	MPG	PPG	RPG	APG	PCM
98-99	Philadelphia	50	1	988	455	170	414	.411	8	52	.154	107	151	.709	83	106	189	77	97	0	44	14	68	19.8	9.1	3.8	1.5	.425
99-00	Philadelphia	50	5	1018	501	192	461	.416	11	51	.216	106	142	.746	52	107	159	75	94	0	54	12	95	20.4	10.0	3.2	1.5	.391
99-00	Golden State	32	32	1306	725	267	686	.389	18	74	.243	173	235	.736	61	129	190	130	97	2	61	16	100	40.8	22.7	5.9	4.1	.433
00-01	Golden State	50	45	1846	823	308	805	.383	14	75	.187	193	252	.766	76	200	276	223	147	2	96	29	152	36.9	16.5	5.5	4.5	.408
01-02	Golden State	73	56	2050	895	343	810	.423	18	93	.194	191	259	.737	83	162	245	316	150	0	113	23	171	28.1	12.3	3.4	4.3	.443
02-03	Washington	67	56	2136	857	346	741	.467	29	79	.367	136	186	.731	67	241	308	205	149	1	86	24	136	31.9	12.8	4.6	3.1	.416
NBA Season Totals		322	195	9344	4256	1626	3917	.415	98	424	.231	906	1225	.740	422	945	1367	1026	734	5	454	118	722	29.0	13.2	4.2	3.2	....
98-99	Philadelphia	8	2	198	82	31	77	.403	0	7	.000	20	24	.833	17	20	37	16	21	0	15	9	12	24.8	10.3	4.6	2.0	.461
NBA Playoff Totals		8	2	198	82	31	77	.403	0	7	.000	20	24	.833	17	20	37	16	21	0	15	9	12	24.8	10.3	4.6	2.0	....

• HUGHES, Rick — Rick Hughes

Born: Aug. 22, 1973. Cincinnati, OH, United States.   Height: 6'9".   Weight: 235 lbs.   Drafted: —   College: Thomas More

YEAR	TEAM	GP	GS	MIN	PTS	FGM	FGA	FG%	3PM	3PA	3P%	FTM	FTA	FT%	ORB	DRB	TRB	AST	PF	DQ	STL	BLK	TO	MPG	PPG	RPG	APG	PCM
99-00	Dallas	21	0	224	82	35	72	.486	0	1	.000	12	26	.462	24	25	49	9	30	0	3	1	14	10.7	3.9	2.3	0.4	.329
NBA Season Totals		21	0	224	82	35	72	.486	0	1	.000	12	26	.462	24	25	49	9	30	0	3	1	14	10.7	3.9	2.3	0.4	....

YEAR TEAM	GP	GS	MIN	PTS	FGM	FGA	FG%	3PM	3PA	3P%	FTM	FTA	FT%	ORB	DRB	TRB	AST	PF	DQ	STL	BLK	TO	MPG	PPG	RPG	APG	PCM

• HUGHES, Rick

Alfredrick Hughes

Born: July 19, 1962. Chicago, IL, United States. Height: 6'5". Weight: 215 lbs. Drafted: 1985 College: Loyola (IL)

YEAR TEAM	GP	GS	MIN	PTS	FGM	FGA	FG%	3PM	3PA	3P%	FTM	FTA	FT%	ORB	DRB	TRB	AST	PF	DQ	STL	BLK	TO	MPG	PPG	RPG	APG	PCM
85-86 San Antonio	68	0	866	356	152	372	.409	3	17	.176	49	84	.583	49	64	113	61	79	0	26	5	61	12.7	5.2	1.7	0.9	.278
NBA Season Totals	68	0	866	356	152	372	.409	3	17	.176	49	84	.583	49	64	113	61	79	0	26	5	61	12.7	5.2	1.7	0.9	....
85-86 San Antonio	3	0	18	8	4	9	.444	0	0	.000	0	0	.000	0	0	0	1	3	0	1	0	1	6.0	2.7	0.0	0.3	.168
NBA Playoff Totals	3	0	18	8	4	9	.444	0	0	.000	0	0	.000	0	0	0	1	3	0	1	0	1	6.0	2.7	0.0	0.3	....

• HULL, Harold

Harold Hull

Born: 1920. Height: 6'4". Weight: 190 lbs. Drafted: — College: Northwest Missouri State

YEAR TEAM	GP	GS	MIN	PTS	FGM	FGA	FG%	3PM	3PA	3P%	FTM	FTA	FT%	ORB	DRB	TRB	AST	PF	DQ	STL	BLK	TO	MPG	PPG	RPG	APG	PCM
41-42 Wingfoots-N	12	....	....	14	3	....	....	....	....	....	8	....	....	....	....	....	....	....	....	....	....	....	....	1.2	....	....	....
NBL Season Totals	12	....	....	14	3	....	....	....	....	....	8	....	....	....	....	....	....	....	....	....	....	....	....	1.2	....	....	....
41-42 Wingfoots-N	2	....	....	4	0	....	....	....	....	....	4	....	....	....	....	....	....	....	....	....	....	....	....	2.0	....	....	....
NBL Playoff Totals	2	....	....	4	0	....	....	....	....	....	4	....	....	....	....	....	....	....	....	....	....	....	....	2.0	....	....	....

• HUMMER, John

John R. Hummer

Born: May 4, 1948. Washington, DC, United States. Height: 6'9". Weight: 230 lbs. Drafted: 1970 College: Princeton

YEAR TEAM	GP	GS	MIN	PTS	FGM	FGA	FG%	3PM	3PA	3P%	FTM	FTA	FT%	ORB	DRB	TRB	AST	PF	DQ	STL	BLK	TO	MPG	PPG	RPG	APG	PCM
70-71 Buffalo	81	....	2637	913	339	764	.444	....	....	....	235	405	.580	....	....	717	163	284	10	....	....	....	32.6	11.3	8.9	2.0	.438
71-72 Buffalo	55	....	1186	284	113	290	.390	....	....	....	58	124	.468	....	....	229	72	178	4	....	....	....	21.6	5.2	4.2	1.3	.257
72-73 Buffalo	66	....	1546	527	206	464	.444	....	....	....	115	205	.561	....	....	323	138	185	5	....	....	....	23.4	8.0	4.9	2.1	.403
73-74 Chicago	18	....	186	60	23	46	.500	....	....	....	14	28	.500	13	24	37	13	30	0	3	1	....	10.3	3.3	2.1	0.7	.366
73-74 Seattle	35	....	933	287	121	259	.467	....	....	....	45	96	.469	71	175	246	94	89	0	25	21	....	26.7	8.2	7.0	2.7	.458
74-75 Seattle	43	....	568	96	41	108	.380	....	....	....	14	51	.275	28	76	104	38	63	0	8	7	....	13.2	2.2	2.4	0.9	.226
75-76 Seattle	29	....	364	81	32	67	.478	....	....	....	17	41	.415	21	56	77	25	71	5	6	9	....	12.6	2.8	2.7	0.9	.288
NBA Season Totals	327	....	7420	2248	875	1998	.438	....	....	....	498	950	.524	133	331	1733	543	900	24	42	38	....	22.7	6.9	5.3	1.7	....
74-75 Seattle	6	....	68	0	0	7	.000	....	....	....	0	0	.000	1	8	9	4	7	0	2	0	....	11.3	0.0	1.5	0.7	.049
75-76 Seattle	3	....	16	4	2	3	.667	....	....	....	0	0	.000	1	0	1	0	3	0	0	0	....	5.3	1.3	0.3	0.0	.170
NBA Playoff Totals	9	....	84	4	2	10	.200	....	....	....	0	0	.000	2	8	10	4	10	0	2	0	....	9.3	0.4	1.1	0.4	....

• HUMPHREY, Ryan

Ryan Ashley Humphrey

Born: July 24, 1979. Tulsa, OK, United States. Height: 6'8". Weight: 235 lbs. Drafted: 2002 College: Notre Dame

YEAR TEAM	GP	GS	MIN	PTS	FGM	FGA	FG%	3PM	3PA	3P%	FTM	FTA	FT%	ORB	DRB	TRB	AST	PF	DQ	STL	BLK	TO	MPG	PPG	RPG	APG	PCM
02-03 Orlando	35	1	322	64	23	85	.271	0	0	.000	18	28	.643	30	39	69	7	57	1	4	16	21	9.2	1.8	2.0	0.2	.145
02-03 Memphis	13	0	122	29	12	35	.343	0	0	.000	5	11	.455	4	26	30	4	18	0	5	2	2	9.4	2.2	2.3	0.3	.274
NBA Season Totals	48	1	444	93	35	120	.292	0	0	.000	23	39	.590	34	65	99	11	75	1	9	18	23	9.3	1.9	2.1	0.2	....

• HUMPHRIES, Jay

John Jay Humphries

Born: Oct. 17, 1962. Los Angeles, CA, United States. Height: 6'3". Weight: 185 lbs. Drafted: 1984 College: Colorado

YEAR TEAM	GP	GS	MIN	PTS	FGM	FGA	FG%	3PM	3PA	3P%	FTM	FTA	FT%	ORB	DRB	TRB	AST	PF	DQ	STL	BLK	TO	MPG	PPG	RPG	APG	PCM
84-85 Phoenix	80	39	2062	703	279	626	.446	4	20	.200	141	170	.829	32	132	164	350	209	2	107	8	168	25.8	8.8	2.1	4.4	.362
85-86 Phoenix	82	82	2733	905	352	735	.479	4	29	.138	197	257	.767	56	204	260	526	222	1	132	9	189	33.3	11.0	3.2	6.4	.431
86-87 Phoenix	82	82	2579	923	359	753	.477	5	27	.185	200	260	.769	62	198	260	632	239	1	112	9	197	31.5	11.3	3.2	7.7	.490
87-88 Phoenix	50	33	1557	634	264	484	.545	3	16	.188	103	139	.741	44	107	151	354	154	1	61	4	110	31.1	12.7	3.0	7.1	.525
87-88 Milwaukee	18	0	252	49	20	54	.370	0	2	.000	9	14	.643	5	18	23	41	23	0	20	1	20	14.0	2.7	1.3	2.3	.279
88-89 Milwaukee	73	50	2220	844	345	714	.483	25	94	.266	129	158	.816	70	119	189	405	187	1	142	5	161	30.4	11.6	2.6	5.5	.449
89-90 Milwaukee	81	81	2818	1237	496	1005	.494	21	70	.300	224	285	.786	80	189	269	472	253	2	156	11	154	34.8	15.3	3.3	5.8	.489
90-91 Milwaukee	80	80	2726	1215	482	960	.502	60	161	.373	191	239	.799	57	163	220	538	237	2	129	7	152	34.1	15.2	2.8	6.7	.514
91-92 Milwaukee	71	71	2261	991	377	803	.469	42	144	.292	195	249	.783	44	140	184	466	210	2	119	13	149	31.8	14.0	2.6	6.6	.498
92-93 Utah	78	20	2034	690	287	659	.436	15	75	.200	101	130	.777	40	103	143	317	236	3	101	11	133	26.1	8.8	1.8	4.1	.330
93-94 Utah	75	19	1619	561	233	535	.436	38	96	.396	57	76	.750	35	92	127	219	168	0	65	11	98	21.6	7.5	1.7	2.9	.328
94-95 Utah	12	0	149	10	4	25	.160	2	3	.667	0	0	.000	2	8	10	9	25	0	7	0	12	12.4	0.8	0.8	0.8	-.048
94-95 Boston	6	0	52	10	4	9	.444	0	1	.000	2	4	.500	2	1	3	10	10	0	2	0	5	8.7	1.7	0.5	1.7	.198
NBA Season Totals	788	557	23062	8772	3502	7362	.476	219	738	.297	1549	1981	.782	529	1474	2003	4339	2173	15	1153	89	1548	29.3	11.1	2.5	5.5	....
84-85 Phoenix	3	3	90	49	20	31	.645	0	0	.000	9	12	.750	1	4	5	16	12	0	2	0	8	30.0	16.3	1.7	5.3	.532
87-88 Milwaukee	2	0	18	0	0	5	.000	0	0	.000	0	0	.000	1	2	3	1	6	0	1	0	1	9.0	0.0	1.5	0.5	-.200
88-89 Milwaukee	9	9	323	131	49	99	.495	3	18	.167	30	34	.882	8	19	27	70	29	0	8	0	12	35.9	14.6	3.0	7.8	.512
89-90 Milwaukee	3	2	79	27	8	15	.533	1	3	.333	10	13	.769	1	4	5	19	6	0	3	0	8	26.3	9.0	1.7	6.3	.461
90-91 Milwaukee	3	3	123	45	17	32	.531	2	5	.400	9	10	.900	2	4	6	25	17	2	2	0	6	41.0	15.0	2.0	8.3	.416
92-93 Utah	5	0	115	26	11	33	.333	2	8	.250	2	4	.500	5	5	10	17	8	0	3	3	6	23.0	5.2	2.0	3.4	.246
93-94 Utah	16	0	356	118	46	108	.426	7	22	.318	19	28	.679	8	29	37	39	45	0	13	2	16	22.3	7.4	2.3	2.4	.314
NBA Playoff Totals	41	17	1104	396	151	323	.467	15	56	.268	79	101	.782	26	67	93	187	123	2	32	5	57	26.9	9.7	2.3	4.6	....

• HUNDLEY, Hot Rod

Rodney Clark (Hot Rod) Hundley

Born: Oct. 26, 1934. Charleston, WV, United States. Height: 6'4". Weight: 185 lbs. Drafted: 1957 College: West Virginia

YEAR TEAM	GP	GS	MIN	PTS	FGM	FGA	FG%	3PM	3PA	3P%	FTM	FTA	FT%	ORB	DRB	TRB	AST	PF	DQ	STL	BLK	TO	MPG	PPG	RPG	APG	PCM
57-58 Minneapolis	65	....	1154	452	174	548	.318	....	....	....	104	162	.642	....	....	186	121	99	0	....	....	....	17.8	7.0	2.9	1.9	.357
58-59 Minneapolis	71	....	1664	682	259	719	.360	....	....	....	164	218	.752	....	....	250	205	139	0	....	....	....	23.4	9.6	3.5	2.9	.425
59-60 Minneapolis	73	....	2279	933	365	1019	.358	....	....	....	203	273	.744	....	....	390	338	194	0	....	....	....	31.2	12.8	5.3	4.6	.463
60-61 LA Lakers	79	....	2172	869	323	921	.351	....	....	....	223	296	.753	....	....	289	350	144	0	....	....	....	27.5	11.0	3.7	4.4	.453
61-62 LA Lakers	78	....	1492	429	173	509	.340	....	....	....	83	127	.654	....	....	199	290	129	1	....	....	....	19.1	5.5	2.6	3.7	.407
62-63 LA Lakers	65	....	785	260	88	262	.336	....	....	....	84	119	.706	....	....	106	151	81	0	....	....	....	12.1	4.0	1.6	2.3	.437
NBA Season Totals	431	....	9546	3625	1382	3978	.347	....	....	....	861	1195	.721	....	....	1420	1455	786	1	....	....	....	22.1	8.4	3.3	3.4	....

YEAR	TEAM	GP	GS	MIN	PTS	FGM	FGA	FG%	3PM	3PA	3P%	FTM	FTA	FT%	ORB	DRB	TRB	AST	PF	DQ	STL	BLK	TO	MPG	PPG	RPG	APG	PCM
58-59	Minneapolis	13	....	175	52	20	58	.345	....	....	....	12	14	.857	....	....	23	20	15	0	....	....	....	13.5	4.0	1.8	1.5	.339
59-60	Minneapolis	9	....	337	106	41	122	.336	....	....	....	24	37	.649	....	....	61	55	18	0	....	....	....	37.4	11.8	6.8	6.1	.438
60-61	LA Lakers	12	....	287	80	30	101	.297	....	....	....	20	29	.690	....	....	41	45	19	0	....	....	....	23.9	6.7	3.4	3.8	.356
61-62	LA Lakers	12	....	187	23	7	25	.280	....	....	....	9	12	.750	....	....	18	32	27	0	....	....	....	15.6	1.9	1.5	2.7	.269
62-63	LA Lakers	7	....	34	9	3	10	.300	....	....	....	3	3	1.000	....	....	6	5	1	0	....	....	....	4.9	1.3	0.9	0.7	.408
NBA Playoff Totals		53	....	1020	270	101	316	.320	....	....	....	68	95	.716	....	....	149	157	80	0	....	....	....	19.2	5.1	2.8	3.0	....

• HUNTER, Cedric

Cedric R. Hunter

Born: Jan. 16, 1965. Omaha, NE, United States.   Height: 6'.   Weight: 180 lbs.   Drafted: —   College: Kansas

YEAR	TEAM	GP	GS	MIN	PTS	FGM	FGA	FG%	3PM	3PA	3P%	FTM	FTA	FT%	ORB	DRB	TRB	AST	PF	DQ	STL	BLK	TO	MPG	PPG	RPG	APG	PCM
91-92	Charlotte	1	0	1	0	0	0	.000	0	0	.000	0	0	.000	0	0	0	0	0	0	0	0	0	1.0	0.0	0.0	0.0	.000
NBA Season Totals		1	0	1	0	0	0	.000	0	0	.000	0	0	.000	0	0	0	0	0	0	0	0	0	1.0	0.0	0.0	0.0	....

• HUNTER, Les

Leslie (Big Game) Hunter

Born: Aug. 16, 1942. Nashville, TN, United States.   Height: 6'7".   Weight: 210 lbs.   Drafted: 1964   College: Loyola (IL)

YEAR	TEAM	GP	GS	MIN	PTS	FGM	FGA	FG%	3PM	3PA	3P%	FTM	FTA	FT%	ORB	DRB	TRB	AST	PF	DQ	STL	BLK	TO	MPG	PPG	RPG	APG	PCM
64-65	Baltimore	24	....	114	42	18	64	.281	....	....	....	6	14	.429	....	....	50	11	16	0	....	....	....	4.8	1.8	2.1	0.5	.433
67-68	Minnesota-A	75	....	2552	1318	513	1207	.425	2	17	.118	290	468	.620	332	406	738	116	297	7	....	....	204	34.0	17.6	9.8	1.5	.507
68-69	Miami-A	77	....	2537	1287	476	1073	.444	0	5	.000	335	448	.748	267	476	743	127	311	14	....	....	220	32.9	16.7	9.6	1.6	.542
69-70	New York-A	79	....	2859	1295	486	1122	.433	6	41	.146	317	432	.734	234	439	673	215	335	15	....	....	297	36.2	16.4	8.5	2.7	.482
70-71	Kentucky-A	75	....	1415	713	274	606	.452	10	49	.204	155	215	.721	153	319	472	93	242	3	....	....	135	18.9	9.5	6.3	1.2	.576
70-71	New York-A	5	....	110	32	14	39	.359	0	0	.000	4	8	.500	6	15	21	2	11	0	....	....	17	22.0	6.4	4.2	0.4	.229
71-72	Kentucky-A	70	....	967	472	183	383	.478	5	16	.313	101	144	.701	65	160	225	93	154	0	....	....	93	13.8	6.7	3.2	1.3	.529
72-73	Memphis-A	63	....	1333	576	236	474	.498	9	33	.273	95	135	.704	94	208	302	95	183	4	....	....	95	21.2	9.1	4.8	1.5	.479
NBA Season Totals		24	....	114	42	18	64	.281	....	....	....	6	14	.429	....	....	50	11	16	0	....	....	....	4.8	1.8	2.1	0.5	....
ABA Season Totals		444	....	11773	5693	2182	4904	.445	32	161	.199	1297	1850	.701	1151	2023	3174	741	1533	43	....	....	1061	26.5	12.8	7.1	1.7	....
Career Totals		468	....	11887	5735	2200	4968	.443	32	161	.199	1303	1864	.699	1151	2023	3224	752	1549	43	....	....	1061	25.4	12.3	6.9	1.6	....
67-68	Minnesota-A	10	....	388	214	76	188	.404	0	4	.000	62	98	.633	50	60	110	24	48	3	....	....	27	38.8	21.4	11.0	2.4	.530
68-69	Miami-A	10	....	209	117	42	116	.362	2	3	.667	31	42	.738	....	....	88	13	39	2	....	....	18	20.9	11.7	8.8	1.3	.586
69-70	New York-A	7	....	233	113	45	100	.450	3	10	.300	20	29	.690	....	....	42	11	....	0	....	....	....	33.3	16.1	6.0	1.6	....
70-71	Kentucky-A	19	....	352	176	65	168	.387	1	5	.200	45	73	.616	25	63	88	33	76	3	....	....	38	18.5	9.3	4.6	1.7	.460
71-72	Kentucky-A	6	....	123	55	22	41	.537	2	6	.333	9	11	.818	....	....	21	8	14	....	....	....	10	20.5	9.2	3.5	1.3	.477
ABA Playoff Totals		52	....	1305	675	250	613	.408	8	28	.286	167	253	.660	75	123	349	89	177	8	....	....	93	25.1	13.0	6.7	1.7	....

• HUNTER, Lindsey

Lindsey Benson Hunter Jr.

Born: Dec. 3, 1970. Utica, MS, United States.   Height: 6'2".   Weight: 170 lbs.   Drafted: 1993   College: Jackson State

YEAR	TEAM	GP	GS	MIN	PTS	FGM	FGA	FG%	3PM	3PA	3P%	FTM	FTA	FT%	ORB	DRB	TRB	AST	PF	DQ	STL	BLK	TO	MPG	PPG	RPG	APG	PCM
93-94	Detroit	82	26	2172	843	335	893	.375	69	207	.333	104	142	.732	47	142	189	390	174	1	121	10	180	26.5	10.3	2.3	4.8	.361
94-95	Detroit	42	26	944	314	119	318	.374	36	108	.333	40	55	.727	24	51	75	159	94	1	51	7	80	22.5	7.5	1.8	3.8	.312
95-96	Detroit	80	48	2138	679	239	628	.381	117	289	.405	84	120	.700	44	150	194	188	185	0	84	18	80	26.7	8.5	2.4	2.4	.286
96-97	Detroit	82	76	3023	1166	421	1042	.404	166	468	.355	158	203	.778	59	174	233	154	206	1	129	24	98	36.9	14.2	2.8	1.9	.299
97-98	Detroit	71	67	2505	862	316	826	.383	85	265	.321	145	196	.740	61	186	247	224	174	3	123	10	107	35.3	12.1	3.5	3.2	.313
98-99	Detroit	49	49	1755	582	228	524	.435	59	153	.386	67	89	.753	26	142	168	193	126	2	86	8	92	35.8	11.9	3.4	3.9	.352
99-00	Detroit	82	82	2919	1043	379	892	.425	168	389	.432	117	154	.760	35	215	250	327	216	2	129	22	145	35.6	12.7	3.0	4.0	.360
00-01	Milwaukee	82	5	2002	825	298	783	.381	152	407	.373	77	96	.802	32	137	169	222	172	1	102	12	68	24.4	10.1	2.1	2.7	.370
01-02	LA Lakers	82	47	1616	473	187	490	.382	79	208	.380	20	40	.500	18	103	121	129	120	0	66	19	55	19.7	5.8	1.5	1.6	.256
02-03	Toronto	29	0	672	280	106	302	.351	34	107	.318	34	47	.723	15	44	59	71	50	1	35	5	57	23.2	9.7	2.0	2.4	.281
NBA Season Totals		681	426	19746	7067	2628	6698	.392	965	2601	.371	846	1142	.741	361	1344	1705	2057	1517	12	926	135	962	29.0	10.4	2.5	3.0	....
95-96	Detroit	2	0	36	6	2	8	.250	1	4	.250	1	2	.500	1	1	2	1	2	0	1	0	0	18.0	3.0	1.0	0.5	.079
96-97	Detroit	5	5	201	75	29	66	.439	12	29	.414	5	7	.714	4	14	18	6	9	0	6	1	1	40.2	15.0	3.6	1.2	.319
98-99	Detroit	5	5	180	36	14	53	.264	3	11	.273	5	5	1.000	5	10	15	12	11	0	7	0	7	36.0	7.2	3.0	2.4	.128
99-00	Detroit	3	3	93	25	10	32	.313	1	9	.111	4	6	.667	0	7	7	5	4	0	5	1	5	31.0	8.3	2.3	1.7	.162
00-01	Milwaukee	18	0	289	64	24	99	.242	8	53	.151	8	11	.727	2	29	31	34	24	0	14	3	13	16.1	3.6	1.7	1.9	.185
01-02	LA Lakers	18	0	132	36	14	45	.311	8	29	.276	0	0	.000	2	5	7	10	19	0	2	0	5	7.3	2.0	0.4	0.6	.105
NBA Playoff Totals		51	13	931	242	93	303	.307	33	135	.244	23	31	.742	14	66	80	68	69	0	35	5	31	18.3	4.7	1.6	1.3	....

• HUNTER, Steven

Steven D. Hunter

Born: Oct. 31, 1981. Chicago, IL, United States.   Height: 7'.   Weight: 220 lbs.   Drafted: 2001   College: DePaul

YEAR	TEAM	GP	GS	MIN	PTS	FGM	FGA	FG%	3PM	3PA	3P%	FTM	FTA	FT%	ORB	DRB	TRB	AST	PF	DQ	STL	BLK	TO	MPG	PPG	RPG	APG	PCM
01-02	Orlando	53	21	516	189	67	147	.456	0	0	.000	55	94	.585	40	57	97	5	81	0	5	43	16	9.7	3.6	1.8	0.1	.358
02-03	Orlando	33	5	447	130	56	103	.544	0	0	.000	18	44	.409	38	55	93	6	56	0	9	36	15	13.5	3.9	2.8	0.2	.377
NBA Season Totals		86	26	963	319	123	250	.492	0	0	.000	73	138	.529	78	112	190	11	137	0	14	79	31	11.2	3.7	2.2	0.1	....
02-03	Orlando	7	0	41	6	3	10	.300	0	0	.000	0	3	.000	1	2	3	1	10	0	0	3	1	5.9	0.9	0.4	0.1	-.015
NBA Playoff Totals		7	0	41	6	3	10	.300	0	0	.000	0	3	.000	1	2	3	1	10	0	0	3	1	5.9	0.9	0.4	0.1	....

• HURLEY, Bobby

Robert Matthew Hurley

Born: June 28, 1971. Jersey City, NJ, United States.   Height: 6'.   Weight: 165 lbs.   Drafted: 1993   College: Duke

YEAR	TEAM	GP	GS	MIN	PTS	FGM	FGA	FG%	3PM	3PA	3P%	FTM	FTA	FT%	ORB	DRB	TRB	AST	PF	DQ	STL	BLK	TO	MPG	PPG	RPG	APG	PCM
93-94	Sacramento	19	19	499	134	54	146	.370	2	16	.125	24	30	.800	6	28	34	115	28	0	13	1	48	26.3	7.1	1.8	6.1	.318
94-95	Sacramento	68	6	1105	285	103	284	.363	21	76	.276	58	76	.763	14	56	70	226	79	0	29	0	109	16.3	4.2	1.0	3.3	.272
95-96	Sacramento	72	22	1059	220	65	230	.283	22	76	.289	68	85	.800	12	63	75	216	121	0	28	3	86	14.7	3.1	1.0	3.0	.234
96-97	Sacramento	49	12	632	143	46	125	.368	14	45	.311	37	53	.698	9	29	38	146	53	0	27	3	54	12.9	2.9	0.8	3.0	.326
97-98	Sacramento	34	3	417	128	47	115	.409	4	15	.267	30	37	.811	7	29	36	80	36	0	13	0	41	12.3	3.8	1.1	2.4	.336
97-98	Vancouver	27	0	458	122	46	123	.374	1	7	.143	29	39	.744	5	25	30	97	43	0	10	0	43	17.0	4.5	1.1	3.6	.283
NBA Season Totals		269	62	4170	1032	361	1023	.353	64	235	.272	246	320	.769	53	230	283	880	360	0	120	7	381	15.5	3.8	1.1	3.3	....

YEAR TEAM	GP	GS	MIN	PTS	FGM	FGA	FG%	3PM	3PA	3P%	FTM	FTA	FT%	ORB	DRB	TRB	AST	PF	DQ	STL	BLK	TO	MPG	PPG	RPG	APG	PCM
95-96 Sacramento	1	0	2	0	0	0	.000	0	0	.000	0	0	.000	0	0	0	0	0	0	0	0	0	2.0	0.0	0.0	0.0	.000
NBA Playoff Totals	1	0	2	0	0	0	.000	0	0	.000	0	0	.000	0	0	0	0	0	0	0	0	0	2.0	0.0	0.0	0.0	....

• HURLEY, Roy
Roy Leonard Hurley

Born: Aug. 12, 1922. Arcadia, CA, United States. Died: Oct.14, 1993.   Height: 6'2".   Weight: 170 lbs.   Drafted: —   College: Murray State

YEAR TEAM	GP	GS	MIN	PTS	FGM	FGA	FG%	3PM	3PA	3P%	FTM	FTA	FT%	ORB	DRB	TRB	AST	PF	DQ	STL	BLK	TO	MPG	PPG	RPG	APG	PCM
45-46 Indianapolis-N	30	....	....	176	76	....	....	....	....	....	24	38	.632	....	....	....								5.9	....	....	....
46-47 Toronto	46	....	....	239	100	447	.224	....	....	....	39	64	.609	....	....	....	34	85						5.2	....	0.7	....
47-48 Syracuse-N	4	....	....	6	1	....	....	....	....	....	4	5	.800	....	....	....								1.5	....	....	....
47-48 Tri-Cities-N	12	....	....	45	18	....	....	....	....	....	9	16	.563	....	....	....								3.8	....	....	....
NBA Season Totals	46	....	....	239	100	447	.224	....	....	....	39	64	.609	....	....	....	34	85						5.2	....	0.7	....
NBL Season Totals	46	....	....	227	95	....	....	....	....	....	37	59	....	....	....	....								4.9	....	....	....
Career Totals	92	....	....	466	195	447	....	....	....	....	76	123	....	....	....	....	34	85						5.1	....	0.4	....

• HUSTON, Geoff
Geoffrey Angier Huston

Born: Nov. 8, 1957. Brooklyn, NY, United States.   Height: 6'2".   Weight: 175 lbs.   Drafted: 1979   College: Texas Tech

YEAR TEAM	GP	GS	MIN	PTS	FGM	FGA	FG%	3PM	3PA	3P%	FTM	FTA	FT%	ORB	DRB	TRB	AST	PF	DQ	STL	BLK	TO	MPG	PPG	RPG	APG	PCM
79-80 New York	71	....	923	219	94	241	.390	3	17	.176	28	38	.737	14	44	58	159	83	0	39	5	71	13.0	3.1	0.8	2.2	.267
80-81 Dallas	56	....	1892	899	385	789	.488	1	4	.250	128	185	.692	33	66	99	277	113	1	45	6	146	33.8	16.1	1.8	4.9	.401
80-81 Cleveland	25	....	542	174	76	153	.497	0	1	.000	22	27	.815	12	27	39	117	35	0	13	1	30	21.7	7.0	1.6	4.7	.432
81-82 Cleveland	78	43	2409	806	325	672	.484	3	10	.300	153	200	.765	53	97	150	590	169	1	70	11	172	30.9	10.3	1.9	7.6	.447
82-83 Cleveland	80	79	2716	974	401	832	.482	4	12	.333	168	245	.686	41	118	159	487	215	1	74	4	192	34.0	12.2	2.0	6.1	.379
83-84 Cleveland	77	56	2041	808	348	699	.498	2	11	.182	110	154	.714	32	64	96	413	126	0	38	1	146	26.5	10.5	1.2	5.4	.409
84-85 Cleveland	8	0	93	26	12	25	.480	0	0	.000	2	3	.667	0	1	1	23	8	0	0	0	8	11.6	3.3	0.1	2.9	.298
85-86 Golden State	82	0	1208	345	140	273	.513	2	6	.333	63	92	.685	10	55	65	342	67	0	38	4	82	14.7	4.2	0.8	4.2	.469
86-87 LA Clippers	19	8	428	129	55	121	.455	1	2	.500	18	34	.529	6	11	17	101	28	0	14	0	46	22.5	6.8	0.9	5.3	.330
NBA Season Totals	496	186	12252	4380	1836	3805	.483	16	63	.254	692	978	.708	201	483	684	2509	844	3	331	32	893	24.7	8.8	1.4	5.1	....

• HUSTON, Paul
Paul F. (Shad) Huston

Born: June 2, 1925.   Height: 6'3".   Weight: 175 lbs.   Drafted: 1947   College: Ohio State

YEAR TEAM	GP	GS	MIN	PTS	FGM	FGA	FG%	3PM	3PA	3P%	FTM	FTA	FT%	ORB	DRB	TRB	AST	PF	DQ	STL	BLK	TO	MPG	PPG	RPG	APG	PCM
47-48 Chicago	46	....	....	164	51	215	.237	....	....	....	62	89	.697	....	....	....	27	82	....	....	....	....		3.6	....	0.6	....
NBA Season Totals	46	....	....	164	51	215	.237	....	....	....	62	89	.697	....	....	....	27	82	....	....	....	....		3.6	....	0.6	....
47-48 Chicago	5	....	....	13	3	19	.158	....	....	....	7	13	.538	....	....	....	2	14	....	....	....	....		2.6	....	0.4	....
NBA Playoff Totals	5	....	....	13	3	19	.158	....	....	....	7	13	.538	....	....	....	2	14	....	....	....	....		2.6	....	0.4	....

• HUTCHESON, Harold
Harold Hutcheson

Born: 1920.   Height: 6'5".   Weight: 190 lbs.   Drafted: —   College: Maryville Teachers

YEAR TEAM	GP	GS	MIN	PTS	FGM	FGA	FG%	3PM	3PA	3P%	FTM	FTA	FT%	ORB	DRB	TRB	AST	PF	DQ	STL	BLK	TO	MPG	PPG	RPG	APG	PCM
48-49 Denver-N	59	....	....	265	106	....	....	....	....	....	53	78	.679	....	....	....								4.5	....	....	....
NBL Season Totals	59	....	....	265	106	....	....	....	....	....	53	78	....	....	....	....								4.5	....	....	....

• HUTCHINS, Dar
Darwin Hutchins

Born: 1915.   Height: 6'6".   Weight: 195 lbs.   Drafted: —   College: Bradley

YEAR TEAM	GP	GS	MIN	PTS	FGM	FGA	FG%	3PM	3PA	3P%	FTM	FTA	FT%	ORB	DRB	TRB	AST	PF	DQ	STL	BLK	TO	MPG	PPG	RPG	APG	PCM
39-40 Hammond-N	24	....	....	156	59	....	....	....	....	....	38	....	....	....	....	....								6.5	....	....	....
40-41 Hammond-N	24	....	....	168	70	....	....	....	....	....	28	....	....	....	....	....								7.0	....	....	....
NBL Season Totals	48	....	....	324	129	....	....	....	....	....	66	....	....	....	....	....								6.8	....	....	....

• HUTCHINS, Mel
Melvin R. (Hutch) Hutchins

Born: Nov. 22, 1928. Sacramento, CA, United States.   Height: 6'6".   Weight: 200 lbs.   Drafted: 1951   College: Brigham Young

YEAR TEAM	GP	GS	MIN	PTS	FGM	FGA	FG%	3PM	3PA	3P%	FTM	FTA	FT%	ORB	DRB	TRB	AST	PF	DQ	STL	BLK	TO	MPG	PPG	RPG	APG	PCM
51-52 Milwaukee	66	....	2618	607	231	633	.365	....	....	....	145	225	.644	....	**880**		190	192	5	....		....	39.7	9.2	13.3	2.9	.418
52-53 Milwaukee	71	....	2891	831	319	842	.379	....	....	....	193	295	.654	....	793		227	214	5	....		....	40.7	11.7	11.2	3.2	.416
53-54 Fort Wayne	72	....	2934	741	295	736	.401	....	....	....	151	223	.677	....	695		210	229	4	....		....	40.8	10.3	9.7	2.9	.370
54-55 Fort Wayne	72	....	2860	864	341	903	.378	....	....	....	182	257	.708	....	665		247	232	0	....		....	39.7	12.0	9.2	3.4	.399
55-56 Fort Wayne	66	....	2240	792	325	764	.425	....	....	....	142	221	.643	....	496		180	166	1	....		....	33.9	12.0	7.5	2.7	.431
56-57 Fort Wayne	72	....	2647	890	369	953	.387	....	....	....	152	206	.738	....	571		210	182	0	....		....	36.8	12.4	7.9	2.9	.399
57-58 New York	18	....	384	126	51	131	.389	....	....	....	24	43	.558	....	86		34	31	0	....		....	21.3	7.0	4.8	1.9	.405
NBA Season Totals	437	....	16574	4851	1931	4962	.389	....	....	....	989	1470	.673	....	4186		1298	1246	15	....		....	37.9	11.1	9.6	3.0	....
53-54 Fort Wayne	4	....	162	42	15	46	.326	....	....	....	12	17	.706	....	37		6	18	1	....		....	40.5	10.5	9.3	1.5	.283
54-55 Fort Wayne	11	....	417	158	60	144	.417	....	....	....	38	56	.679	....	89		31	47	3	....		....	37.9	14.4	8.1	2.8	.422
55-56 Fort Wayne	10	....	377	93	34	112	.304	....	....	....	25	41	.610	....	88		23	27	1	....		....	37.7	9.3	8.8	2.3	.299
56-57 Fort Wayne	2	....	68	23	9	30	.300	....	....	....	5	7	.714	....	23		10	8	0	....		....	34.0	11.5	11.5	5.0	.490
NBA Playoff Totals	27	....	1024	316	118	332	.355	....	....	....	80	121	.661	....	237		70	100	5	....		....	37.9	11.7	8.8	2.6	....

• HUTCHINSON, Herbie
Herb (Reindeer) Hutchinson

Born: —.   Height: —   Weight: —   Drafted: —   College: —

YEAR TEAM	GP	GS	MIN	PTS	FGM	FGA	FG%	3PM	3PA	3P%	FTM	FTA	FT%	ORB	DRB	TRB	AST	PF	DQ	STL	BLK	TO	MPG	PPG	RPG	APG	PCM
37-38 Columbus-N	7	....	....	56	25	....	....	....	....	....	6	....	....	....	....	....								8.0	....	....	....
NBL Season Totals	7	....	....	56	25	....	....	....	....	....	6	....	....	....	....	....								8.0	....	....	....

YEAR	TEAM	GP	GS	MIN	PTS	FGM	FGA	FG%	3PM	3PA	3P%	FTM	FTA	FT%	ORB	DRB	TRB	AST	PF	DQ	STL	BLK	TO	MPG	PPG	RPG	APG	PCM

• HUTTON, Joe
Joseph W. Hutton Jr.

Born: Oct. 6, 1928.　Height: 6'1".　Weight: 170 lbs.　Drafted: 1950　College: Hamline

50-51	Minneapolis	60	....	....	147	59	180	.328	....	....	....	29	43	.674	....	....	102	53	89	1	....	....	....	....	2.5	1.7	0.9	....
51-52	Minneapolis	60	....	723	155	53	158	.335	....	....	....	49	70	.700	....	....	85	62	110	1	....	....	....	12.1	2.6	1.4	1.0	.241
NBA Season Totals		120	....	723	302	112	338	.331	....	....	....	78	113	.690	....	....	187	115	199	2	....	....	....	6.0	2.5	1.6	1.0	
50-51	Minneapolis	7	....	....	2	0	3	.000	....	....	....	2	4	.500	....	....	3	1	5	0	....	....	....	....	0.3	0.4	0.1	....
51-52	Minneapolis	12	....	139	33	12	29	.414	....	....	....	9	14	.643	....	....	13	12	17	0	....	....	....	11.6	2.8	1.1	1.0	.272
NBA Playoff Totals		19	....	139	35	12	32	.375	....	....	....	11	18	.611	....	....	16	13	22	0	....	....	....	7.3	1.8	0.8	0.7	

• HYATT, Art
Art Hyatt

Born: 1913.　Height: 6'2".　Weight: 190 lbs.　Drafted: —　College: none

38-39	Cleveland-N	7	....	....	37	14	....	....	....	....	....	9	....	....	....	....	....	....	....	....	....	....	....	....	5.3	....	....	....
39-40	Detroit-N	16	....	....	32	13	....	....	....	....	....	6	....	....	....	....	....	....	....	....	....	....	....	....	2.0	....	....	....
NBL Season Totals		23	....	....	69	27	....	....	....	....	....	15	....	....	....	....	....	....	....	....	....	....	....	....	3.0	....	....	....

• HYDER, Greg
Gregory Peck Hyder

Born: June 21, 1948.　Height: 6'6".　Weight: 215 lbs.　Drafted: 1970　College: Eastern New Mexico

| 70-71 | Cincinnati | 77 | .... | 1359 | 417 | 183 | 409 | .447 | .... | .... | .... | 51 | 71 | .718 | .... | .... | 332 | 48 | 187 | 2 | .... | .... | .... | 17.6 | 5.4 | 4.3 | 0.6 | .349 |
| **NBA Season Totals** | | 77 | .... | 1359 | 417 | 183 | 409 | .447 | .... | .... | .... | 51 | 71 | .718 | .... | .... | 332 | 48 | 187 | 2 | .... | .... | .... | 17.6 | 5.4 | 4.3 | 0.6 | |

• IAVARONI, Marc
Marcus John Iavaroni

Born: Sept. 15, 1956. Jamaica, NY, United States.　Height: 6'8".　Weight: 210 lbs.　Drafted: 1978　College: Virginia

82-83	Philadelphia	80	77	1612	404	163	353	.462	0	2	.000	78	113	.690	117	212	329	83	238	0	32	44	136	20.2	5.1	4.1	1.0	.275
83-84	Philadelphia	78	71	1532	395	149	322	.463	0	2	.000	97	131	.740	91	219	310	95	222	1	36	55	125	19.6	5.1	4.0	1.2	.309
84-85	Philadelphia	12	10	156	30	12	31	.387	0	0	.000	6	6	1.000	11	18	29	6	24	0	4	3	16	13.0	2.5	2.4	0.5	.168
84-85	San Antonio	57	33	1178	381	150	323	.464	0	4	.000	81	122	.664	84	191	275	113	193	5	31	32	103	20.7	6.7	4.8	2.0	.382
85-86	San Antonio	42	7	669	191	74	163	.454	0	2	.000	43	67	.642	42	90	132	53	109	0	22	14	50	15.9	4.5	3.1	1.3	.318
85-86	Utah	26	2	345	105	36	81	.444	0	0	.000	33	48	.688	21	56	77	29	54	0	10	3	21	13.3	4.0	3.0	1.1	.366
86-87	Utah	78	0	845	278	100	215	.465	0	4	.000	78	116	.672	64	109	173	36	154	0	16	11	55	10.8	3.6	2.2	0.5	.302
87-88	Utah	81	71	1238	364	143	308	.464	0	2	.000	78	99	.788	94	174	268	67	162	1	23	25	81	15.3	4.5	3.3	0.8	.336
88-89	Utah	77	50	796	180	72	163	.442	0	1	.000	36	44	.818	41	91	132	32	99	0	11	13	54	10.3	2.3	1.7	0.4	.219
NBA Season Totals		531	321	8371	2328	899	1959	.459	0	17	.000	530	746	.710	565	1160	1725	514	1255	7	185	200	641	15.8	4.4	3.2	1.0	....
82-83	Philadelphia	13	13	283	67	29	52	.558	0	0	.000	9	18	.500	22	35	57	19	42	1	8	7	13	21.8	5.2	4.4	1.5	.344
83-84	Philadelphia	4	2	64	22	7	15	.467	1	2	.500	7	8	.875	3	5	8	3	18	1	1	1	5	16.0	5.5	2.0	0.8	.212
84-85	San Antonio	5	5	116	45	15	28	.536	0	1	.000	15	20	.750	8	18	26	13	23	1	5	2	15	23.2	9.0	5.2	2.6	.435
85-86	Utah	4	0	73	13	5	16	.313	0	0	.000	3	4	.750	4	5	9	6	9	0	1	0	4	18.3	3.3	2.3	1.5	.139
86-87	Utah	5	0	47	10	4	10	.400	0	0	.000	2	3	.667	8	5	13	4	7	0	0	3	6	9.4	2.0	2.6	0.8	.304
87-88	Utah	11	11	137	44	16	29	.552	0	0	.000	12	14	.857	5	14	19	14	26	0	2	2	6	12.5	4.0	1.7	1.3	.362
88-89	Utah	1	0	1	0	0	1	.000	0	1	.000	0	0	.000	0	0	0	0	1	0	0	0	0	1.0	0.0	0.0	0.0	-1.40
NBA Playoff Totals		43	31	721	201	76	151	.503	1	4	.250	48	67	.716	50	82	132	59	126	3	17	15	49	16.8	4.7	3.1	1.4	....

• ILGAUSKAS, Zydrunas
Zydrunas Ilgauskas

Born: June 5, 1975. Kaunas, Lithuania.　Height: 7'3".　Weight: 238 lbs.　Drafted: 1996　College: none

97-98	Cleveland	82	81	2379	1139	454	876	.518	1	4	.250	230	302	.762	279	444	723	71	288	4	52	135	148	29.0	13.9	8.8	0.9	.573
98-99	Cleveland	5	5	171	76	29	57	.509	0	0	.000	18	30	.600	17	27	44	4	24	1	4	7	9	34.2	15.2	8.8	0.8	.470
00-01	Cleveland	24	24	616	281	114	234	.487	0	2	.000	53	78	.679	65	95	160	18	78	0	15	37	60	25.7	11.7	6.7	0.8	.460
01-02	Cleveland	62	23	1329	690	241	567	.425	0	5	.000	208	276	.754	136	198	334	70	187	4	17	84	94	21.4	11.1	5.4	1.1	.500
02-03	Cleveland	81	81	2434	1390	495	1122	.441	0	5	.000	400	512	.781	240	371	611	127	274	4	56	152	210	30.0	17.2	7.5	1.6	.549
NBA Season Totals		254	214	6929	3576	1333	2856	.467	1	16	.063	909	1198	.759	737	1135	1872	290	851	13	144	415	521	27.3	14.1	7.4	1.1	
97-98	Cleveland	4	4	147	69	28	49	.571	0	0	.000	13	25	.520	14	16	30	2	22	2	2	5	10	36.8	17.3	7.5	0.5	.416
NBA Playoff Totals		4	4	147	69	28	49	.571	0	0	.000	13	25	.520	14	16	30	2	22	2	2	5	10	36.8	17.3	7.5	0.5	....

• IMHOFF, Darrall
Darrall Tucker (Big D) Imhoff

Born: Oct. 11, 1938. San Gabriel, CA, United States.　Height: 6'10".　Weight: 220 lbs.　Drafted: 1960　College: California

60-61	New York	62	....	994	293	122	310	.394	....	....	....	49	96	.510	....	....	296	51	143	2	....	....	....	16.0	4.7	4.8	0.8	.368
61-62	New York	76	....	1501	452	186	482	.386	....	....	....	80	139	.576	....	....	470	82	230	10	....	....	....	19.8	5.9	6.2	1.1	.383
62-63	Detroit	45	....	458	120	48	153	.314	....	....	....	24	50	.480	....	....	155	28	66	1	....	....	....	10.2	2.7	3.4	0.6	.343
63-64	Detroit	58	....	871	277	104	251	.414	....	....	....	69	114	.605	....	....	283	56	167	5	....	....	....	15.0	4.8	4.9	1.0	.423
64-65	LA Lakers	76	....	1521	378	145	311	.466	....	....	....	88	154	.571	....	....	500	87	238	7	....	....	....	20.0	5.0	6.6	1.1	.411
65-66	LA Lakers	77	....	1413	379	151	337	.448	....	....	....	77	136	.566	....	....	509	113	234	7	....	....	....	18.4	4.9	6.6	1.5	.463
66-67	LA Lakers	81	....	2725	867	370	780	.474	....	....	....	127	207	.614	....	....	1080	222	281	7	....	....	....	33.6	10.7	13.3	2.7	.559
67-68	LA Lakers	82	....	2271	763	293	613	.478	....	....	....	177	286	.619	....	....	893	206	264	3	....	....	....	27.7	9.3	10.9	2.5	.581
68-69	Philadelphia	82	....	2360	752	279	593	.470	....	....	....	194	325	.597	....	....	792	218	310	12	....	....	....	28.8	9.2	9.7	2.7	.517
69-70	Philadelphia	79	....	2474	1075	430	796	.540	....	....	....	215	331	.650	....	....	754	211	294	7	....	....	....	31.3	13.6	9.5	2.7	.595
70-71	Cincinnati	34	....	826	275	119	258	.461	....	....	....	37	73	.507	....	....	233	79	120	5	....	....	....	24.3	8.1	6.9	2.3	.459
71-72	Cincinnati	9	....	76	23	10	29	.345	....	....	....	3	8	.375	....	....	27	2	22	1	....	....	....	8.4	2.6	3.0	0.2	.270
71-72	Portland	40	....	404	105	42	103	.408	....	....	....	21	35	.600	....	....	107	50	76	1	....	....	....	10.1	2.6	2.7	1.3	.403
NBA Season Totals		801	....	17894	5759	2299	5016	.458	....	....	....	1161	1954	.594	....	....	6099	1405	2445	68	....	....	....	22.3	7.2	7.6	1.8	....

YEAR	TEAM	GP	GS	MIN	PTS	FGM	FGA	FG%	3PM	3PA	3P%	FTM	FTA	FT%	ORB	DRB	TRB	AST	PF	DQ	STL	BLK	TO	MPG	PPG	RPG	APG	PCM
62-63	Detroit	1	....	2	0	0	0	.000	....	....	....	0	0	.000	....	....	1	0	0	0	....	....	....	2.0	0.0	1.0	0.0	.396
64-65	LA Lakers	11	....	151	33	13	24	.542	....	....	....	7	12	.583	....	....	43	13	26	0	....	....	....	13.7	3.0	3.9	1.2	.409
65-66	LA Lakers	14	....	243	41	14	40	.350	....	....	....	13	18	.722	....	....	81	30	42	1	....	....	....	17.4	2.9	5.8	2.1	.420
66-67	LA Lakers	3	....	86	30	13	24	.542	....	....	....	4	5	.800	....	....	37	5	8	0	....	....	....	28.7	10.0	12.3	1.7	.618
67-68	LA Lakers	15	....	440	114	44	89	.494	....	....	....	26	51	.510	....	....	163	30	56	0	....	....	....	29.3	7.6	10.9	2.0	.482
68-69	Philadelphia	5	....	191	91	33	66	.500	....	....	....	25	38	.658	....	....	82	12	24	1	....	....	....	38.2	18.2	16.4	2.4	.683
69-70	Philadelphia	5	....	138	45	22	48	.458	....	....	....	1	7	.143	....	....	35	11	23	0	....	....	....	27.6	9.0	7.0	2.2	.380
NBA Playoff Totals		54	....	1251	354	139	291	.478	....	....	....	76	131	.580	....	....	442	101	179	2	....	....	....	23.2	6.6	8.2	1.9	....

• INGELSBY, Tom

Tom Ingelsby

Born: Feb. 12, 1951. Philadelphia, PA, United States. Height: 6'3". Weight: 180 lbs. Drafted: 1973 College: Villanova

YEAR	TEAM	GP	GS	MIN	PTS	FGM	FGA	FG%	3PM	3PA	3P%	FTM	FTA	FT%	ORB	DRB	TRB	AST	PF	DQ	STL	BLK	TO	MPG	PPG	RPG	APG	PCM
73-74	Atlanta	48	....	398	129	50	131	.382	....	....	....	29	37	.784	10	34	44	37	43	0	19	4	....	8.3	2.7	0.9	0.8	.297
74-75	St. Louis-A	22	....	344	109	44	90	.489	1	5	.200	20	27	.741	22	28	50	38	19	....	14	1	17	15.6	5.0	2.3	1.7	.416
75-76	San Diego-A	5	....	14	4	1	3	.333	0	0	.000	2	2	1.000	1	2	3	0	1	....	0	0	0	2.8	0.8	0.6	0.0	.318
NBA Season Totals		48	....	398	129	50	131	.382	....	....	....	29	37	.784	10	34	44	37	43	0	19	4	....	8.3	2.7	0.9	0.8	....
ABA Season Totals		27	....	358	113	45	93	.484	1	5	.200	22	29	.759	23	30	53	38	20	....	14	1	17	13.3	4.2	2.0	1.4	....
Career Totals		75	....	756	242	95	224	.424	1	5	.200	51	66	.773	33	64	97	75	63	0	33	5	17	10.1	3.2	1.3	1.0	....

• INGRAM, McCoy

Joel McCoy Ingram

Born: Aug. 31, 1931. Height: 6' Weight: 210 lbs. Drafted: — College: Jackson State

YEAR	TEAM	GP	GS	MIN	PTS	FGM	FGA	FG%	3PM	3PA	3P%	FTM	FTA	FT%	ORB	DRB	TRB	AST	PF	DQ	STL	BLK	TO	MPG	PPG	RPG	APG	PCM
57-58	Minneapolis	24	....	267	67	27	103	.262	....	....	....	13	28	.464	....	....	116	20	44	1	....	....	....	11.1	2.8	4.8	0.8	.375
NBA Season Totals		24	....	267	67	27	103	.262	....	....	....	13	28	.464	....	....	116	20	44	1	....	....	....	11.1	2.8	4.8	0.8	....

• INNIGER, Ervin

Ervin Lee (Erv, Irv) Inniger Jr.

Born: Jan. 16, 1945. Berne, IN, United States. Height: 6'4". Weight: 190 lbs. Drafted: — College: Indiana

YEAR	TEAM	GP	GS	MIN	PTS	FGM	FGA	FG%	3PM	3PA	3P%	FTM	FTA	FT%	ORB	DRB	TRB	AST	PF	DQ	STL	BLK	TO	MPG	PPG	RPG	APG	PCM
67-68	Minnesota-A	75	....	1993	794	345	790	.437	5	35	.143	99	137	.723	....	....	325	115	201	2	....	....	94	26.6	10.6	4.3	1.5	.366
68-69	Miami-A	34	....	484	170	73	182	.401	3	13	.231	21	25	.840	19	41	60	41	59	0	....	....	30	14.2	5.0	1.8	1.2	.305
ABA Season Totals		109	....	2477	964	418	972	.430	8	48	.167	120	162	.741	19	41	385	156	260	2	....	....	124	22.7	8.8	3.5	1.4	....
67-68	Minnesota-A	10	....	364	138	55	140	.393	2	11	.182	26	32	.813	....	....	57	35	36	0	....	....	15	36.4	13.8	5.7	3.5	.380
ABA Playoff Totals		10	....	364	138	55	140	.393	2	11	.182	26	32	.813	....	....	57	35	36	0	....	....	15	36.4	13.8	5.7	3.5	....

• IRVIN, Byron

Byron Edward Irvin

Born: Dec. 2, 1966. LaGrange, IL, United States. Height: 6'5". Weight: 190 lbs. Drafted: 1989 College: Missouri

YEAR	TEAM	GP	GS	MIN	PTS	FGM	FGA	FG%	3PM	3PA	3P%	FTM	FTA	FT%	ORB	DRB	TRB	AST	PF	DQ	STL	BLK	TO	MPG	PPG	RPG	APG	PCM
89-90	Portland	50	2	488	258	96	203	.473	5	14	.357	61	91	.670	30	44	74	47	40	0	28	1	40	9.8	5.2	1.5	0.9	.479
90-91	Washington	33	4	316	171	60	129	.465	1	5	.200	50	61	.820	24	21	45	24	32	0	15	2	17	9.6	5.2	1.4	0.7	.488
92-93	Washington	4	2	45	22	9	18	.500	1	1	1.000	3	6	.500	2	2	4	2	5	0	1	0	4	11.3	5.5	1.0	0.5	.288
NBA Season Totals		87	8	849	451	165	350	.471	7	20	.350	114	158	.722	56	67	123	73	77	0	44	3	61	9.8	5.2	1.4	0.8	....
89-90	Portland	4	0	47	15	5	22	.227	0	0	.000	5	6	.833	4	4	8	5	7	0	2	0	3	11.8	3.8	2.0	1.3	.153
NBA Playoff Totals		4	0	47	15	5	22	.227	0	0	.000	5	6	.833	4	4	8	5	7	0	2	0	3	11.8	3.8	2.0	1.3	....

• IRVINE, George

George R. (Hawkeye) Irvine

Born: Feb. 1, 1948. Seattle, WA, United States. Height: 6'6". Weight: 200 lbs. Drafted: 1970 College: Washington

YEAR	TEAM	GP	GS	MIN	PTS	FGM	FGA	FG%	3PM	3PA	3P%	FTM	FTA	FT%	ORB	DRB	TRB	AST	PF	DQ	STL	BLK	TO	MPG	PPG	RPG	APG	PCM
70-71	Virginia-A	34	....	338	194	83	149	.557	2	8	.250	26	35	.743	21	44	65	25	67	0	....	....	25	9.9	5.7	1.9	0.7	.570
71-72	Virginia-A	75	....	1362	457	200	397	.504	3	10	.300	54	75	.720	82	135	217	70	202	2	....	....	74	18.2	6.1	2.9	0.9	.334
72-73	Virginia-A	79	....	2075	1024	424	805	.527	7	33	.212	169	203	.833	108	188	296	149	267	2	....	....	138	26.3	13.0	3.7	1.9	.471
73-74	Virginia-A	75	....	1140	640	254	516	.492	12	46	.261	120	138	.870	56	121	177	76	134	....	28	16	67	15.2	8.5	2.4	1.0	.516
74-75	Virginia-A	59	....	1522	774	311	589	.528	13	37	.351	139	164	.848	73	130	203	108	171	....	32	12	94	25.8	13.1	3.4	1.8	.487
75-76	Denver-A	3	....	14	4	2	6	.333	0	1	.000	0	0	.000	1	0	1	0	1	....	0	0	1	4.7	1.3	0.3	0.0	.063
ABA Season Totals		325	....	6451	3093	1274	2462	.517	37	135	.274	508	615	.826	341	618	959	428	842	4	60	28	399	19.8	9.5	3.0	1.3	....
70-71	Virginia-A	7	....	25	7	3	6	.500	0	2	.000	1	1	1.000	2	3	5	2	7	0	....	....	1	3.6	1.0	0.7	0.3	.328
71-72	Virginia-A	11	....	285	137	56	86	.651	0	1	.000	25	31	.806	8	19	27	10	45	2	....	....	15	25.9	12.5	2.5	0.9	.432
72-73	Virginia-A	5	....	53	17	6	15	.400	0	0	.000	5	5	1.000	2	3	5	5	8	0	....	....	8	10.6	3.4	1.0	1.0	.289
73-74	Virginia-A	5	....	109	59	24	55	.436	1	7	.143	10	10	1.000	3	8	11	10	13	....	3	1	6	21.8	11.8	2.2	2.0	.437
ABA Playoff Totals		28	....	472	220	89	162	.549	1	10	.100	41	47	.872	15	33	48	27	73	2	3	1	30	16.9	7.9	1.7	1.0	....

• ISAACS, Johnny

John Isaacs

Born: 1915. Height: 6'3". Weight: 190 lbs. Drafted: — College: none

YEAR	TEAM	GP	GS	MIN	PTS	FGM	FGA	FG%	3PM	3PA	3P%	FTM	FTA	FT%	ORB	DRB	TRB	AST	PF	DQ	STL	BLK	TO	MPG	PPG	RPG	APG	PCM
48-49	Dayton-N	8	....	....	58	18	....	....	....	....	....	22	34	.647	....	....	....	....	....	....	....	....	....	....	7.3	....	....	....
NBL Season Totals		8	....	....	58	18	....	....	....	....	....	22	34	....	....	....	....	....	....	....	....	....	....	....	7.3	....	....	....

• ISSEL, Dan

Daniel Paul (Horse) Issel

Born: Oct. 25, 1948. Batavia, IL, United States. Height: 6'9". Weight: 235 lbs. Drafted: 1970 College: Kentucky HOF: 1993

YEAR	TEAM	GP	GS	MIN	PTS	FGM	FGA	FG%	3PM	3PA	3P%	FTM	FTA	FT%	ORB	DRB	TRB	AST	PF	DQ	STL	BLK	TO	MPG	PPG	RPG	APG	PCM
70-71	Kentucky-A	83	....	3274	**2480**	**938**	1934	.485	0	15	.000	604	748	.807	421	672	1093	162	323	9	....	....	221	39.4	**29.9**	13.2	2.0	.783
71-72	Kentucky-A	83	....	3570	**2538**	972	2001	.486	3	11	.273	591	**753**	.785	353	578	931	195	242	3	....	....	244	43.0	30.6	11.2	2.3	.698
72-73	Kentucky-A	84	....	**3531**	**2292**	**902**	1757	.513	3	15	.200	485	635	.764	329	593	922	220	255	2	....	....	216	42.0	27.3	11.0	2.6	.683
73-74	Kentucky-A	83	....	3347	2118	829	1726	.480	3	17	.176	457	581	.787	346	501	847	137	199	....	69	32	171	40.3	25.5	10.2	1.7	.625

YEAR	TEAM	GP	GS	MIN	PTS	FGM	FGA	FG%	3PM	3PA	3P%	FTM	FTA	FT%	ORB	DRB	TRB	AST	PF	DQ	STL	BLK	TO	MPG	PPG	RPG	APG	PCM
74-75	Kentucky-A	83	....	2864	1465	614	1303	.471	0	5	.000	237	321	.738	258	452	710	188	197	....	76	48	157	34.5	17.7	8.6	2.3	.547
75-76	Denver-A	84	....	2856	1930	752	1472	.511	1	4	.250	425	521	.816	303	620	923	201	266	....	100	56	200	34.0	23.0	11.0	2.4	.761
76-77	Denver	79	....	2507	1765	660	1282	.515	....	....	....	445	558	.797	211	485	696	177	246	7	91	29	....	31.7	22.3	8.8	2.2	.748
77-78	Denver	82	....	2851	1746	659	1287	.512	....	....	....	428	547	.782	253	577	830	304	279	5	100	41	262	34.8	21.3	10.1	3.7	.696
78-79	Denver	81	....	2742	1380	532	1030	.517	....	....	....	316	419	.754	240	498	738	255	233	6	61	46	170	33.9	17.0	9.1	3.1	.609
79-80	Denver	82	....	2938	1951	715	1416	.505	4	12	.333	517	667	.775	236	483	719	198	190	1	88	54	164	35.8	23.8	8.8	2.4	.684
80-81	Denver	80	....	2641	1749	614	1220	.503	2	12	.167	519	684	.759	229	447	676	158	249	6	83	53	128	33.0	21.9	8.5	2.0	.683
81-82	Denver	81	81	2472	1852	651	1236	.527	4	6	.667	546	655	.834	174	434	608	179	245	4	67	55	170	30.5	22.9	7.5	2.2	.752
82-83	Denver	80	80	2431	1726	661	1296	.510	4	19	.211	400	479	.835	151	445	596	223	227	0	83	43	176	30.4	21.6	7.5	2.8	.721
83-84	Denver	76	66	2076	1506	569	1153	.493	4	19	.211	364	428	.850	112	401	513	173	182	2	60	44	122	27.3	19.8	6.8	2.3	.720
84-85	Denver	77	9	1684	984	363	791	.459	1	7	.143	257	319	.806	80	251	331	137	171	1	65	31	92	21.9	12.8	4.3	1.8	.555
NBA Season Totals		718	236	22342	14659	5424	10711	.506	19	75	.253	3792	4756	.797	1686	4021	5707	1804	2022	32	698	396	1284	31.1	20.4	7.9	2.5	....
ABA Season Totals		500	....	19442	12823	5007	10193	.491	10	67	.149	2799	3559	.786	2010	3416	5426	1103	1482	14	245	136	1209	38.9	25.6	10.9	2.2	....
Career Totals		1218	236	41784	27482	10431	20904	.499	29	142	.204	6591	8315	.793	3696	7437	11133	2907	3504	46	943	532	2493	34.3	22.6	9.1	2.4	....
70-71	Kentucky-A	19	....	670	534	206	408	.505	0	0	.000	122	139	.878	79	142	221	28	78	5	....	....	56	35.3	28.1	11.6	1.5	.813
71-72	Kentucky-A	6	....	269	132	47	114	.412	0	1	.000	38	50	.760	22	32	54	5	23	....	....	....	31	44.8	22.0	9.0	0.8	.412
72-73	Kentucky-A	19	....	825	521	198	398	.497	1	6	.167	124	156	.795	60	165	225	28	71	1	....	....	47	43.4	27.4	11.8	1.5	.640
73-74	Kentucky-A	8	....	311	148	60	135	.444	0	0	.000	28	33	.848	33	54	87	14	23	....	4	6	16	38.9	18.5	10.9	1.8	.522
74-75	Kentucky-A	15	....	578	304	122	261	.467	0	0	.000	60	74	.811	36	83	119	29	51	....	16	12	33	38.5	20.3	7.9	1.9	.501
75-76	Denver-A	13	....	470	266	111	227	.489	0	1	.000	44	56	.786	48	108	156	32	62	....	13	8	21	36.2	20.5	12.0	2.5	.647
76-77	Denver	6	....	222	132	49	96	.510	....	....	....	34	45	.756	18	40	58	17	20	0	5	4	....	37.0	22.0	9.7	2.8	.664
77-78	Denver	13	....	460	262	103	212	.486	....	....	....	56	65	.862	41	93	134	53	43	1	7	3	39	35.4	20.2	10.3	4.1	.642
78-79	Denver	3	....	109	73	24	45	.533	....	....	....	25	31	.806	7	21	28	10	15	0	0	0	9	36.3	24.3	9.3	3.3	.668
81-82	Denver	3	3	103	76	32	60	.533	0	0	.000	12	12	1.000	8	13	21	5	10	0	3	1	7	34.3	25.3	7.0	1.7	.656
82-83	Denver	8	8	227	163	69	136	.507	0	1	.000	25	29	.862	13	45	58	25	18	0	9	5	10	28.4	20.4	7.3	3.1	.775
83-84	Denver	5	5	153	137	52	102	.510	1	2	.500	32	39	.821	10	30	40	8	15	0	6	6	15	30.6	27.4	8.0	1.6	.805
84-85	Denver	15	4	325	186	73	159	.459	1	1	1.000	39	48	.813	14	40	54	27	36	0	12	5	13	21.7	12.4	3.6	1.8	.516
NBA Playoff Totals		53	20	1599	1029	402	810	.496	2	4	.500	223	269	.829	111	282	393	145	157	1	42	24	93	30.2	19.4	7.4	2.7	....
ABA Playoff Totals		80	....	3123	1905	744	1543	.482	1	8	.125	416	508	.819	278	584	862	136	308	6	33	26	204	39.0	23.8	10.8	1.7	....
Career Playoff Totals		133	20	4722	2934	1146	2353	.487	3	12	.250	639	777	.822	389	866	1255	281	465	7	75	50	297	35.5	22.1	9.4	2.1	....

• IUZZOLINO, Mike

Michael Alan Iuzzolino

Born: Jan. 22, 1968. Altoona, PA, United States. Height: 5'10". Weight: 175 lbs. Drafted: 1991 College: St. Francis (PA)

YEAR	TEAM	GP	GS	MIN	PTS	FGM	FGA	FG%	3PM	3PA	3P%	FTM	FTA	FT%	ORB	DRB	TRB	AST	PF	DQ	STL	BLK	TO	MPG	PPG	RPG	APG	PCM
91-92	Dallas	52	21	1280	486	160	355	.451	59	136	.434	107	128	.836	27	71	98	194	79	0	33	1	94	24.6	9.3	1.9	3.7	.392
92-93	Dallas	70	23	1769	610	221	478	.462	54	144	.375	114	149	.765	31	109	140	328	101	0	49	6	126	25.3	8.7	2.0	4.7	.408
NBA Season Totals		122	44	3049	1096	381	833	.457	113	280	.404	221	277	.798	58	180	238	522	180	0	82	7	220	25.0	9.0	2.0	4.3	....

• IVERSON, Allen

Allen Iverson

Born: June 7, 1975. Hampton, VA, United States. Height: 6' Weight: 165 lbs. Drafted: 1996 College: Georgetown

YEAR	TEAM	GP	GS	MIN	PTS	FGM	FGA	FG%	3PM	3PA	3P%	FTM	FTA	FT%	ORB	DRB	TRB	AST	PF	DQ	STL	BLK	TO	MPG	PPG	RPG	APG	PCM
96-97	Philadelphia	76	74	3045	1787	625	1504	.416	155	455	.341	382	544	.702	115	197	312	567	233	5	157	24	**334**	40.1	23.5	4.1	7.5	.505
97-98	Philadelphia	80	80	3150	1758	649	1407	.461	70	235	.298	390	535	.729	86	210	296	494	200	2	176	25	240	39.4	22.0	3.7	6.2	.533
98-99	Philadelphia	48	48	1990	1284	435	**1056**	.412	58	199	.291	356	474	.751	66	170	236	223	98	0	110	7	167	**41.5**	**26.8**	4.9	4.6	.527
99-00	Philadelphia	70	70	2853	1989	729	**1733**	.421	89	261	.341	442	620	.713	71	196	267	328	162	1	144	5	230	40.8	28.4	3.8	4.7	.508
00-01	Philadelphia	71	71	2979	2207	762	1813	.420	98	306	.320	585	719	.814	50	223	273	325	147	0	178	20	237	42.0	**31.1**	3.8	4.6	.572
01-02	Philadelphia	60	59	2622	1883	665	1669	.398	78	268	.291	475	585	.812	44	225	269	331	102	0	168	13	237	43.7	**31.4**	4.5	5.5	.546
02-03	Philadelphia	82	82	**3485**	2262	804	**1940**	.414	84	303	.277	570	736	.774	68	276	344	454	149	2	**225**	13	286	**42.5**	27.6	4.2	5.5	.531
NBA Season Totals		487	484	20124	13170	4669	11122	.420	632	2027	.312	3200	4213	.760	500	1497	1997	2722	1091	10	1158	107	1731	41.3	27.0	4.1	5.6	....
98-99	Philadelphia	8	8	358	228	88	214	.411	15	53	.283	37	52	.712	14	19	33	39	19	0	20	2	24	44.8	28.5	4.1	4.9	.480
99-00	Philadelphia	10	10	444	262	91	237	.384	12	39	.308	68	92	.739	14	26	40	45	24	0	12	1	32	44.4	26.2	4.0	4.5	.396
00-01	Philadelphia	22	22	1016	723	257	661	.389	48	142	.338	161	208	.774	15	89	104	134	55	0	52	7	63	46.2	32.9	4.7	6.1	.543
01-02	Philadelphia	5	5	209	150	45	118	.381	9	27	.333	51	63	.810	1	17	18	21	8	0	13	0	12	41.8	30.0	3.6	4.2	.550
02-03	Philadelphia	12	12	558	380	137	329	.416	19	55	.345	87	118	.737	11	41	52	89	25	0	29	1	47	46.5	31.7	4.3	7.4	.554
NBA Playoff Totals		57	57	2585	1743	618	1559	.396	103	316	.326	404	533	.758	55	192	247	328	131	0	126	11	178	45.4	30.6	4.3	5.8	....

• IVERSON, Willie

Willie Iverson

Born: Oct. 8, 1945. Detroit, MI, United States. Height: 6' Weight: 180 lbs. Drafted: — College: Central Michigan

YEAR	TEAM	GP	GS	MIN	PTS	FGM	FGA	FG%	3PM	3PA	3P%	FTM	FTA	FT%	ORB	DRB	TRB	AST	PF	DQ	STL	BLK	TO	MPG	PPG	RPG	APG	PCM
68-69	Miami-A	28	....	531	136	50	146	.342	0	2	.000	36	60	.600	12	34	46	80	47	0	....	....	55	19.0	4.9	1.6	2.9	.290
ABA Season Totals		28	....	531	136	50	146	.342	0	2	.000	36	60	.600	12	34	46	80	47	0	....	....	55	19.0	4.9	1.6	2.9	....

• IVORY, Elvin

Elvin Dennis (Little E) Ivory

Born: July 2, 1948. Birmingham, AL, United States. Height: 6'8". Weight: 210 lbs. Drafted: — College: Southwestern Louisiana

YEAR	TEAM	GP	GS	MIN	PTS	FGM	FGA	FG%	3PM	3PA	3P%	FTM	FTA	FT%	ORB	DRB	TRB	AST	PF	DQ	STL	BLK	TO	MPG	PPG	RPG	APG	PCM
68-69	Los Angeles-A	20	....	188	88	38	87	.437	1	4	.250	11	17	.647	34	132	166	9	38	0	....	....	14	9.4	4.4	8.3	0.5	.956
ABA Season Totals		20	....	188	88	38	87	.437	1	4	.250	11	17	.647	34	132	166	9	38	0	....	....	14	9.4	4.4	8.3	0.5	....

• JABALI, Warren

Warren Jabali aka.: Warren Edward Armstrong

Born: Aug. 29, 1946. Kansas City, KS, United States. Height: 6'2". Weight: 200 lbs. Drafted: 1968 College: Wichita State

YEAR	TEAM	GP	GS	MIN	PTS	FGM	FGA	FG%	3PM	3PA	3P%	FTM	FTA	FT%	ORB	DRB	TRB	AST	PF	DQ	STL	BLK	TO	MPG	PPG	RPG	APG	PCM
68-69	Oakland-A	71	....	2545	1530	573	1276	.449	11	44	.250	373	545	.684	255	433	688	252	263	4	....	....	307	35.8	21.5	9.7	3.5	.636
69-70	Washington-A	40	....	1510	913	342	768	.445	19	62	.306	210	293	.717	114	302	416	173	143	5	....	....	205	37.8	22.8	10.4	4.3	.666
70-71	Indiana-A	62	....	1586	682	227	554	.410	47	163	.288	181	238	.761	64	234	298	214	205	4	....	....	190	25.6	11.0	4.8	3.5	.511
71-72	Florida-A	81	....	3313	1615	569	1304	.436	102	**285**	.358	375	496	.756	167	489	656	495	298	8	....	....	332	40.9	19.9	8.1	6.1	.578

YEAR	TEAM	GP	GS	MIN	PTS	FGM	FGA	FG%	3PM	3PA	3P%	FTM	FTA	FT%	ORB	DRB	TRB	AST	PF	DQ	STL	BLK	TO	MPG	PPG	RPG	APG	PCM
72-73	Denver-A	82	....	2738	1398	441	974	.453	36	140	.257	480	596	.805	129	295	424	539	280	8	175	....	302	33.4	17.0	5.2	6.6	.627
73-74	Denver-A	49	....	1711	779	257	657	.391	45	123	.366	220	274	.803	82	164	246	358	167	....	97	10	195	34.9	15.9	5.0	7.3	.562
74-75	San Diego-A	62	....	1861	749	254	648	.392	62	193	.321	179	227	.789	72	185	257	358	188	....	112	19	184	30.0	12.1	4.1	5.8	.495
ABA Season Totals		447	....	15264	7666	2663	6181	.431	322	1010	.319	2018	2669	.756	883	2102	2985	2389	1544	29	384		29	1715	34.1	17.1	6.7	5.3	....
68-69	Oakland-A	16	....	662	460	161	350	.460	3	17	.176	135	202	.668	68	139	207	46	56	1	....	....	79	41.4	28.8	12.9	2.9	.718
70-71	Indiana-A	11	....	250	86	29	96	.302	3	28	.107	25	31	.806	12	28	40	33	27	0	....	....	21	22.7	7.8	3.6	3.0	.363
71-72	Florida-A	4	....	171	75	22	59	.373	5	15	.333	26	33	.788	13	39	52	22	17	....	....	....	19	42.8	18.8	13.0	5.5	.598
72-73	Denver-A	5	....	126	30	9	27	.333	0	6	.000	12	16	.750	2	5	7	14	11	0	....	....	11	25.2	6.0	1.4	2.8	.228
ABA Playoff Totals		36	....	1209	651	221	532	.415	11	66	.167	198	282	.702	95	211	306	115	111	1	....	....	130	33.6	18.1	8.5	3.2	....

• JABLONSKI, George

George (Jabbo) Jablonski

Born: 1919.   Height: 6'7".   Weight: 215 lbs.   Drafted: —   College: Wisconsin (Milwaukee)

YEAR	TEAM	GP	GS	MIN	PTS	FGM	FGA	FG%	3PM	3PA	3P%	FTM	FTA	FT%	ORB	DRB	TRB	AST	PF	DQ	STL	BLK	TO	MPG	PPG	RPG	APG	PCM
42-43	Sheboygan-N	11	....	....	19	7	....	....	....	....	....	5	....	....	....	....	....	....	....	....	....	....	....	....	1.7	....	....	....
NBL Season Totals		11	....	....	19	7	....	....	....	....	....	5	....	....	....	....	....	....	....	....	....	....	....	....	1.7	....	....	....
42-43	Sheboygan-N	5	....	....	13	3	....	....	....	....	....	7	....	....	....	....	....	....	....	....	....	....	....	....	2.6	....	....	....
43-44	Sheboygan-N	2	....	....	5	1	....	....	....	....	....	3	....	....	....	....	....	....	....	....	....	....	....	....	2.5	....	....	....
NBL Playoff Totals		7	....	....	18	4	....	....	....	....	....	10	....	....	....	....	....	....	....	....	....	....	....	....	2.6	....	....	....

• JACKSON, Al

Alvin Jackson

Born: July 29, 1943. Cleveland, OH, United States.   Height: 6'1".   Weight: 185 lbs.   Drafted: —   College: Wilberforce

YEAR	TEAM	GP	GS	MIN	PTS	FGM	FGA	FG%	3PM	3PA	3P%	FTM	FTA	FT%	ORB	DRB	TRB	AST	PF	DQ	STL	BLK	TO	MPG	PPG	RPG	APG	PCM
67-68	Cincinnati	2	....	17	0	0	3	.000	....	....	....	0	0	.000	....	0	1	6	0	....	....	....	....	8.5	0.0	0.0	0.5	-.211
NBA Season Totals		2	....	17	0	0	3	.000	....	....	....	0	0	.000	....	0	1	6	0	....	....	....	....	8.5	0.0	0.0	0.5	....

• JACKSON, Bobby

Bobby Jackson

Born: Mar. 13, 1973. East Spencer, NC, United States.   Height: 6'1".   Weight: 185 lbs.   Drafted: 1997   College: Minnesota

YEAR	TEAM	GP	GS	MIN	PTS	FGM	FGA	FG%	3PM	3PA	3P%	FTM	FTA	FT%	ORB	DRB	TRB	AST	PF	DQ	STL	BLK	TO	MPG	PPG	RPG	APG	PCM
97-98	Denver	68	53	2042	790	310	791	.392	21	81	.259	149	183	.814	78	224	302	317	160	0	105	11	184	30.0	11.6	4.4	4.7	.401
98-99	Minnesota	50	12	941	353	141	348	.405	10	27	.370	61	79	.772	43	92	135	167	75	1	39	3	75	18.8	7.1	2.7	3.3	.429
99-00	Minnesota	73	10	1034	369	140	346	.405	13	46	.283	76	98	.776	50	103	153	172	114	0	48	7	58	14.2	5.1	2.1	2.4	.430
00-01	Sacramento	79	7	1648	566	231	526	.439	39	104	.375	65	88	.739	74	172	246	161	139	0	87	7	103	20.9	7.2	3.1	2.0	.375
01-02	Sacramento	81	3	1750	896	334	754	.443	79	219	.361	149	184	.810	82	169	251	164	145	1	73	10	93	21.6	11.1	3.1	2.0	.476
02-03	Sacramento	59	26	1676	895	340	732	.464	89	235	.379	126	149	.846	57	162	219	182	126	0	71	3	106	28.4	15.2	3.7	3.1	.501
NBA Season Totals		410	111	9091	3869	1496	3497	.428	251	712	.353	626	781	.802	384	922	1306	1163	759	2	423	42	619	22.2	9.4	3.2	2.8	....
98-99	Minnesota	4	0	27	4	2	10	.200	0	3	.000	0	0	.000	1	3	4	2	3	0	0	0	1	6.8	1.0	1.0	0.5	.016
99-00	Minnesota	3	0	30	15	4	8	.500	1	3	.333	6	6	1.000	0	5	5	4	4	0	2	1	2	10.0	5.0	1.7	1.3	.646
00-01	Sacramento	8	0	182	56	21	48	.438	4	14	.286	10	14	.714	6	20	26	18	18	0	8	0	7	22.8	7.0	3.3	2.3	.362
01-02	Sacramento	16	1	374	175	65	146	.445	11	43	.256	34	43	.791	15	37	52	32	31	0	14	3	18	23.4	10.9	3.3	2.0	.440
02-03	Sacramento	12	0	331	172	63	138	.457	15	43	.349	31	35	.886	11	43	54	40	22	1	12	1	17	27.6	14.3	4.5	3.3	.547
NBA Playoff Totals		43	1	944	422	155	350	.443	31	106	.292	81	98	.827	33	108	141	96	78	1	36	5	45	22.0	9.8	3.3	2.2	....

• JACKSON, Greg

Gregory Jackson

Born: Aug. 2, 1952. Brooklyn, NY, United States.   Height: 6'   Weight: 180 lbs.   Drafted: 1974   College: Guilford

YEAR	TEAM	GP	GS	MIN	PTS	FGM	FGA	FG%	3PM	3PA	3P%	FTM	FTA	FT%	ORB	DRB	TRB	AST	PF	DQ	STL	BLK	TO	MPG	PPG	RPG	APG	PCM
74-75	New York	5	....	27	8	4	10	.400	....	....	....	0	0	.000	2	0	2	3	5	0	0	0	....	5.4	1.6	0.4	0.6	.218
74-75	Phoenix	44	....	775	174	69	166	.416	....	....	....	36	62	.581	17	50	67	93	125	5	23	9	....	17.6	4.0	1.5	2.1	.246
NBA Season Totals		49	....	802	182	73	176	.415	....	....	....	36	62	.581	19	50	69	96	130	5	23	9	....	16.4	3.7	1.4	2.0	....

• JACKSON, Jaren

Jaren Jackson

Born: Oct. 27, 1967. New Orleans, LA, United States.   Height: 6'4".   Weight: 190 lbs.   Drafted: —   College: Georgetown

YEAR	TEAM	GP	GS	MIN	PTS	FGM	FGA	FG%	3PM	3PA	3P%	FTM	FTA	FT%	ORB	DRB	TRB	AST	PF	DQ	STL	BLK	TO	MPG	PPG	RPG	APG	PCM
89-90	New Jersey	28	0	160	67	25	69	.362	0	3	.000	17	21	.810	16	8	24	13	16	0	13	1	17	5.7	2.4	0.9	0.5	.312
91-92	Golden State	5	0	54	26	11	23	.478	0	0	.000	4	6	.667	5	5	10	3	7	1	2	0	4	10.8	5.2	2.0	0.6	.395
92-93	LA Clippers	34	0	350	131	53	128	.414	2	5	.400	23	27	.852	19	20	39	35	45	1	19	5	17	10.3	3.9	1.1	1.0	.338
93-94	Portland	29	0	187	80	34	87	.391	0	6	.000	12	14	.857	6	11	17	27	20	0	4	2	15	6.4	2.8	0.6	0.9	.310
94-95	Philadelphia	21	1	257	70	25	68	.368	4	15	.267	16	24	.667	18	24	42	19	33	0	9	5	17	12.2	3.3	2.0	0.9	.261
95-96	Houston	4	0	33	8	0	8	.000	0	5	.000	8	10	.800	0	3	3	0	5	0	1	0	8	8.2	2.0	0.8	0.0	.029
96-97	Washington	75	0	1133	374	134	329	.407	53	158	.335	53	69	.768	31	101	132	65	131	0	45	16	60	15.1	5.0	1.8	0.9	.280
97-98	San Antonio	82	45	2226	722	258	654	.394	112	297	.377	94	118	.797	55	155	210	156	222	3	60	8	107	27.1	8.8	2.6	1.9	.257
98-99	San Antonio	47	13	861	301	108	284	.380	53	147	.361	32	39	.821	21	78	99	49	63	0	41	9	37	18.3	6.4	2.1	1.0	.311
99-00	San Antonio	81	12	1691	513	186	488	.381	108	306	.353	33	51	.647	34	147	181	118	157	0	54	7	66	20.9	6.3	2.2	1.5	.265
00-01	San Antonio	16	0	114	39	16	40	.400	7	18	.389	0	2	.000	1	11	12	7	13	0	5	0	3	7.1	2.4	0.8	0.4	.272
01-02	Orlando	9	0	144	39	15	37	.405	7	20	.350	2	4	.500	1	16	17	8	13	0	5	0	8	16.0	4.3	1.9	0.9	.234
NBA Season Totals		431	71	7210	2370	865	2215	.391	346	980	.353	294	385	.764	207	579	786	500	725	5	258	53	351	16.7	5.5	1.8	1.2	....
92-93	LA Clippers	4	0	28	10	5	13	.385	0	1	.000	0	0	.000	4	1	5	2	6	0	2	0	3	7.0	2.5	1.3	0.5	.200
93-94	Portland	1	0	1	0	0	0	.000	0	0	.000	0	0	.000	0	0	0	0	0	0	0	0	0	1.0	0.0	0.0	0.0	....
96-97	Washington	3	0	11	0	0	0	.000	0	0	.000	0	2	.000	1	1	2	1	7	0	0	0	2	3.7	0.0	0.7	0.3	-.284
97-98	San Antonio	9	8	319	92	30	88	.341	18	59	.305	14	19	.737	4	35	39	14	31	1	5	1	12	35.4	10.2	4.3	1.6	.213
98-99	San Antonio	17	0	345	140	50	131	.382	31	86	.360	9	13	.692	6	35	41	18	33	0	13	0	20	20.3	8.2	2.4	1.1	.295
99-00	San Antonio	2	0	19	2	0	3	.000	0	1	.000	2	4	.500	0	1	1	2	1	0	1	0	0	9.5	1.0	0.5	1.0	.101
01-02	Orlando	3	0	5	0	0	0	.000	0	0	.000	0	0	.000	0	1	1	0	3	0	0	0	1	1.7	0.0	0.3	0.0	-.272
NBA Playoff Totals		39	8	728	244	85	235	.362	49	147	.333	25	38	.658	15	74	89	37	81	1	21	1	38	18.7	6.3	2.3	0.9	....

• JACKSON, Jermaine

Jermaine Jackson

Born: June 7, 1976. Detroit, MI, United States. Height: 6'4". Weight: 204 lbs. Drafted: — College: Detroit Mercy

YEAR TEAM	GP	GS	MIN	PTS	FGM	FGA	FG%	3PM	3PA	3P%	FTM	FTA	FT%	ORB	DRB	TRB	AST	PF	DQ	STL	BLK	TO	MPG	PPG	RPG	APG	PCM
99-00 Detroit	7	0	73	7	1	11	.091	0	1	.000	5	8	.625	1	10	11	4	7	0	3	0	7	10.4	1.0	1.6	0.6	.056
01-02 Toronto	24	0	280	57	20	42	.476	1	2	.500	16	24	.667	3	24	27	57	24	0	9	1	14	11.7	2.4	1.1	2.4	.378
02-03 Toronto	24	1	286	66	21	68	.309	1	9	.111	23	27	.852	10	15	25	39	24	0	9	3	19	11.9	2.8	1.0	1.6	.243
02-03 Atlanta	29	0	273	55	19	42	.452	0	1	.000	17	28	.607	9	23	32	35	27	0	10	3	15	9.4	1.9	1.1	1.2	.302
NBA Season Totals	84	1	912	185	61	163	.374	2	13	.154	61	87	.701	23	72	95	135	82	0	31	7	55	10.9	2.2	1.1	1.6	....
01-02 Toronto	4	0	12	6	2	3	.667	0	0	.000	2	6	.333	0	1	1	0	2	0	0	0	3	3.0	1.5	0.3	0.0	.047
NBA Playoff Totals	4	0	12	6	2	3	.667	0	0	.000	2	6	.333	0	1	1	0	2	0	0	0	3	3.0	1.5	0.3	0.0	....

• JACKSON, Jim

James Arthur Jackson

Born: Oct. 14, 1970. Toledo, OH, United States. Height: 6'6". Weight: 220 lbs. Drafted: 1992 College: Ohio State

YEAR TEAM	GP	GS	MIN	PTS	FGM	FGA	FG%	3PM	3PA	3P%	FTM	FTA	FT%	ORB	DRB	TRB	AST	PF	DQ	STL	BLK	TO	MPG	PPG	RPG	APG	PCM
92-93 Dallas	28	28	938	457	184	466	.395	21	73	.288	68	92	.739	42	80	122	131	80	0	40	11	115	33.5	16.3	4.4	4.7	.362
93-94 Dallas	82	82	3066	1576	637	1432	.445	17	60	.283	285	347	.821	169	219	388	374	161	0	87	25	**336**	37.4	19.2	4.7	4.6	.424
94-95 Dallas	51	51	1982	1309	484	1026	.472	35	110	.318	306	380	.805	120	140	260	191	92	0	28	12	158	38.9	25.7	5.1	3.7	.534
95-96 Dallas	82	82	2820	1604	569	1308	.435	121	333	.363	345	418	.825	173	237	410	235	165	0	47	22	189	34.4	19.6	5.0	2.9	.468
96-97 Dallas	46	46	1676	714	260	588	.442	46	139	.331	148	188	.787	81	146	227	156	113	0	57	15	106	36.4	15.5	4.9	3.4	.408
96-97 New Jersey	31	31	1155	512	184	441	.417	40	108	.370	104	122	.852	51	133	184	160	81	0	29	17	102	37.3	16.5	5.9	5.2	.447
97-98 Philadelphia	48	47	1788	657	246	535	.460	39	112	.348	126	154	.818	69	158	227	223	112	0	41	6	144	37.3	13.7	4.7	4.6	.386
97-98 Golden State	31	31	1258	585	230	572	.402	22	79	.278	103	128	.805	61	112	173	158	74	0	38	2	118	40.6	18.9	5.6	5.1	.386
98-99 Portland	49	9	1175	414	152	370	.411	25	90	.278	85	101	.842	36	123	159	128	80	0	43	6	82	24.0	8.4	3.2	2.6	.367
99-00 Atlanta	79	76	2767	1317	507	1235	.411	117	303	.386	186	212	.877	101	293	394	230	167	0	57	10	185	35.0	16.7	5.0	2.9	.387
00-01 Atlanta	17	14	550	243	77	217	.355	16	38	.421	73	85	.859	17	62	79	50	42	0	19	4	48	32.4	14.3	4.6	2.9	.358
00-01 Cleveland	39	26	1140	400	162	415	.390	10	42	.238	66	84	.786	36	109	145	113	97	0	34	6	82	29.2	10.3	3.7	2.9	.297
01-02 Miami	55	19	1825	589	238	538	.442	38	81	.469	75	87	.862	54	236	290	140	145	0	42	14	106	33.2	10.7	5.3	2.5	.338
02-03 Sacramento	63	0	1309	487	204	462	.442	32	71	.451	47	55	.855	84	178	262	118	132	0	31	4	80	20.8	7.7	4.2	1.9	.393
NBA Season Totals	701	542	23449	10864	4134	9605	.430	579	1639	.353	2017	2453	.822	1094	2226	3320	2407	1541	0	593	154	1851	33.5	15.5	4.7	3.4	....
98-99 Portland	13	0	265	95	26	72	.361	5	18	.278	38	42	.905	8	22	30	19	26	0	7	1	18	20.4	7.3	2.3	1.5	.301
02-03 Sacramento	12	0	296	135	49	98	.500	13	28	.464	24	31	.774	16	31	47	14	34	1	8	3	17	24.7	11.3	3.9	1.2	.420
NBA Playoff Totals	25	0	561	230	75	170	.441	18	46	.391	62	73	.849	24	53	77	33	60	1	15	4	35	22.4	9.2	3.1	1.3	....

• JACKSON, Luke

Lucious Brown Jackson

Born: Oct. 31, 1941. San Marcos, TX, United States. Height: 6'9". Weight: 240 lbs. Drafted: 1964 College: Pan American

YEAR TEAM	GP	GS	MIN	PTS	FGM	FGA	FG%	3PM	3PA	3P%	FTM	FTA	FT%	ORB	DRB	TRB	AST	PF	DQ	STL	BLK	TO	MPG	PPG	RPG	APG	PCM
64-65 Philadelphia	76	....	2590	1126	419	1013	.414	....	....	....	288	404	.713	....	....	980	93	251	4	....	....	....	34.1	14.8	12.9	1.2	.539
65-66 Philadelphia	79	....	1966	650	246	614	.401	....	....	....	158	214	.738	....	....	676	132	216	2	....	....	....	24.9	8.2	8.6	1.7	.481
66-67 Philadelphia	81	....	2377	970	386	882	.438	....	....	....	198	261	.759	....	....	724	114	276	6	....	....	....	29.3	12.0	8.9	1.4	.485
67-68 Philadelphia	82	....	2570	968	401	927	.433	....	....	....	166	231	.719	....	....	872	139	287	6	....	....	....	31.3	11.8	10.6	1.7	.494
68-69 Philadelphia	25	....	840	359	145	332	.437	....	....	....	69	97	.711	....	....	286	54	102	3	....	....	....	33.6	14.4	11.4	2.2	.536
69-70 Philadelphia	37	....	583	202	71	181	.392	....	....	....	60	81	.741	....	....	198	50	80	0	....	....	....	15.8	5.5	5.4	1.4	.499
70-71 Philadelphia	79	....	1774	529	199	529	.376	....	....	....	131	189	.693	....	....	568	148	211	3	....	....	....	22.5	6.7	7.2	1.9	.443
71-72 Philadelphia	63	....	1083	366	137	346	.396	....	....	....	92	133	.692	....	....	309	88	141	1	....	....	....	17.2	5.8	4.9	1.4	.437
NBA Season Totals	522	....	13783	5170	2004	4824	.415	....	....	....	1162	1610	.722	....	....	4613	818	1564	25	....	....	....	26.4	9.9	8.8	1.6	....
64-65 Philadelphia	11	....	321	113	44	130	.338	....	....	....	25	32	.781	....	....	79	24	31	0	....	....	....	29.2	10.3	7.2	2.2	.382
65-66 Philadelphia	5	....	163	60	21	49	.429	....	....	....	18	22	.818	....	....	44	8	21	2	....	....	....	32.6	12.0	8.8	1.6	.445
66-67 Philadelphia	15	....	543	165	64	161	.398	....	....	....	37	51	.725	....	....	176	30	47	1	....	....	....	36.2	11.0	11.7	2.0	.442
67-68 Philadelphia	13	....	432	148	62	158	.392	....	....	....	24	35	.686	....	....	115	16	59	3	....	....	....	33.2	11.4	8.8	1.2	.358
69-70 Philadelphia	5	....	73	20	9	19	.474	....	....	....	2	2	1.000	....	....	33	3	11	1	....	....	....	14.6	4.0	6.6	0.6	.531
70-71 Philadelphia	7	....	160	39	16	38	.421	....	....	....	7	10	.700	....	....	61	11	17	0	....	....	....	22.9	5.6	8.7	1.6	.478
NBA Playoff Totals	56	....	1692	545	216	555	.389	....	....	....	113	152	.743	....	....	508	92	186	7	....	....	....	30.2	9.7	9.1	1.6	....

• JACKSON, Marc

Marc Anthony Jackson

Born: Jan. 16, 1975. Philadelphia, PA, United States. Height: 6'10". Weight: 270 lbs. Drafted: 1997 College: Temple

YEAR TEAM	GP	GS	MIN	PTS	FGM	FGA	FG%	3PM	3PA	3P%	FTM	FTA	FT%	ORB	DRB	TRB	AST	PF	DQ	STL	BLK	TO	MPG	PPG	RPG	APG	PCM
00-01 Golden State	48	35	1410	633	237	508	.467	5	23	.217	154	192	.802	119	242	361	59	138	1	34	27	93	29.4	13.2	7.5	1.2	.476
01-02 Golden State	17	0	169	84	22	65	.338	0	0	.000	40	48	.833	17	26	43	7	25	0	5	3	12	9.9	4.9	2.5	0.4	.432
01-02 Minnesota	22	0	326	102	38	99	.384	0	1	.000	26	32	.813	31	54	85	7	44	0	6	3	18	14.8	4.6	3.9	0.3	.309
02-03 Minnesota	77	0	1040	421	153	349	.438	1	1	1.000	114	149	.765	86	139	225	37	137	0	24	30	59	13.5	5.5	2.9	0.5	.390
NBA Season Totals	164	35	2945	1240	450	1021	.441	6	25	.240	334	421	.793	253	461	714	110	344	1	69	63	182	18.0	7.6	4.4	0.7	....
01-02 Minnesota	1	0	1	0	0	0	.000	0	0	.000	0	0	.000	0	0	0	0	1	0	0	0	0	1.0	0.0	0.0	0.0	-.453
02-03 Minnesota	6	0	110	50	17	32	.531	0	1	.000	16	19	.842	10	23	33	8	19	0	2	1	9	18.3	8.3	5.5	1.3	.542
NBA Playoff Totals	7	0	111	50	17	32	.531	0	1	.000	16	19	.842	10	23	33	8	20	0	2	1	9	15.9	7.1	4.7	1.1	....

• JACKSON, Mark

Mark A. (Action) Jackson

Born: Apr. 1, 1965. Brooklyn, NY, United States. Height: 6'1". Weight: 180 lbs. Drafted: 1987 College: St. John's (NY)

YEAR TEAM	GP	GS	MIN	PTS	FGM	FGA	FG%	3PM	3PA	3P%	FTM	FTA	FT%	ORB	DRB	TRB	AST	PF	DQ	STL	BLK	TO	MPG	PPG	RPG	APG	PCM
87-88 New York	82	80	3249	1114	438	1013	.432	32	126	.254	206	266	.774	120	276	396	868	244	2	205	6	254	39.6	13.6	4.8	10.6	.521
88-89 New York	72	72	2477	1219	479	1025	.467	81	240	.338	180	258	.698	106	235	341	619	163	1	139	7	223	34.4	16.9	4.7	8.6	.608
89-90 New York	82	69	2428	809	327	749	.437	35	131	.267	120	165	.727	106	212	318	604	121	0	109	4	213	29.6	9.9	3.9	7.4	.487
90-91 New York	72	21	1595	630	250	508	.492	13	51	.255	117	160	.731	62	135	197	452	81	0	60	9	137	22.2	8.8	2.7	6.3	.586
91-92 New York	81	81	2461	916	367	747	.491	11	43	.256	171	222	.770	95	210	305	694	153	0	112	13	211	30.4	11.3	3.8	8.6	.575
92-93 LA Clippers	82	81	3117	1181	459	945	.486	22	82	.268	241	300	.803	129	259	388	724	158	0	136	12	221	38.0	14.4	4.7	8.8	.543
93-94 LA Clippers	79	79	2711	865	331	732	.452	36	127	.283	167	211	.791	107	241	348	678	115	0	120	6	229	34.3	10.9	4.4	8.6	.510
94-95 Indiana	82	67	2402	624	239	566	.422	27	87	.310	119	153	.778	73	233	306	616	148	0	105	16	213	29.3	7.6	3.7	7.5	.452
95-96 Indiana	81	81	2643	806	296	626	.473	64	149	.430	150	191	.785	66	241	307	635	153	0	100	5	203	32.6	10.0	3.8	7.8	.482

YEAR	TEAM	GP	GS	MIN	PTS	FGM	FGA	FG%	3PM	3PA	3P%	FTM	FTA	FT%	ORB	DRB	TRB	AST	PF	DQ	STL	BLK	TO	MPG	PPG	RPG	APG	PCM
96-97	Denver	52	52	2001	541	192	452	.425	48	121	.397	109	136	.801	71	200	271	**641**	104	0	51	9	172	38.5	10.4	5.2	**12.3**	**.535**
96-97	Indiana	30	30	1053	271	97	227	.427	18	57	.316	59	77	.766	20	104	124	**294**	57	0	46	3	102	35.1	9.0	4.1	**9.8**	**.470**
97-98	Indiana	82	82	2413	678	249	598	.416	43	137	.314	137	180	.761	67	255	322	713	132	0	84	2	172	29.4	8.3	3.9	8.7	.526
98-99	Indiana	49	49	1382	373	138	329	.419	32	103	.311	65	79	.823	33	151	184	386	58	0	42	3	99	28.2	7.6	3.8	7.9	.518
99-00	Indiana	81	81	2190	660	246	570	.432	89	221	.403	79	98	.806	63	233	296	650	111	0	76	10	174	27.0	8.1	3.7	8.0	.550
00-01	Toronto	54	54	1802	461	170	403	.422	57	165	.345	64	76	.842	42	143	185	498	83	0	63	7	117	33.4	8.5	3.4	9.2	.489
00-01	New York	29	28	786	170	74	180	.411	13	42	.310	9	17	.529	21	99	120	163	56	0	21	0	58	27.1	5.9	4.1	5.6	.382
01-02	New York	82	82	2367	686	260	592	.439	79	195	.405	87	110	.791	56	253	309	605	162	0	74	1	150	28.9	8.4	3.8	7.4	.497
02-03	Utah	82	0	1467	382	147	369	.398	27	95	.284	61	80	.763	34	142	176	375	90	0	48	3	152	17.9	4.7	2.1	4.6	.415
NBA Season Totals		1254	1089	38544	12386	4759	10631	.448	727	2172	.335	2141	2779	.770	1271	3622	4893	10215	2189	3	1591	116	3100	30.7	9.9	3.9	8.1	....
87-88	New York	4	4	171	57	22	60	.367	5	12	.417	8	11	.727	6	13	19	39	13	0	10	0	14	42.8	14.3	4.8	9.8	.408
88-89	New York	9	9	336	132	51	100	.510	11	28	.393	19	28	.679	7	24	31	91	9	0	10	3	28	37.3	14.7	3.4	10.1	.566
89-90	New York	9	0	81	34	13	31	.419	0	2	.000	8	11	.727	1	4	5	21	5	0	2	0	7	9.0	3.8	0.6	2.3	.441
90-91	New York	3	0	36	2	1	3	.333	0	0	.000	0	0	.000	0	0	0	8	1	0	1	1	5	12.0	0.7	0.0	2.7	.150
91-92	New York	12	12	368	100	37	92	.402	4	21	.190	22	27	.815	12	15	27	86	26	0	10	0	30	30.7	8.3	2.3	7.2	.362
92-93	LA Clippers	5	5	188	76	28	64	.438	1	2	.500	19	22	.864	8	21	29	38	8	0	8	1	13	37.6	15.2	5.8	7.6	.538
94-95	Indiana	17	17	553	168	59	130	.454	16	40	.400	34	46	.739	27	62	89	121	34	0	15	0	41	32.5	9.9	5.2	7.1	.484
95-96	Indiana	5	5	186	53	18	51	.353	4	18	.222	13	17	.765	3	22	25	30	9	0	6	0	13	37.2	10.6	5.0	6.0	.347
97-98	Indiana	16	16	494	147	53	127	.417	14	37	.378	27	34	.794	18	55	73	133	28	0	23	0	47	30.9	9.2	4.6	8.3	.511
98-99	Indiana	13	13	451	146	51	103	.495	14	34	.412	30	42	.714	14	45	59	112	32	0	14	1	35	34.7	11.2	4.5	8.6	.531
99-00	Indiana	23	23	634	187	69	176	.392	21	67	.313	28	31	.903	12	74	86	178	42	0	19	2	43	27.6	8.1	3.7	7.7	.508
00-01	New York	5	5	156	45	20	40	.500	2	8	.250	3	3	1.000	3	23	26	26	6	0	8	0	10	31.2	9.0	5.2	5.2	.478
02-03	Utah	5	0	83	36	15	30	.500	5	9	.556	1	1	1.000	2	3	5	16	11	0	3	0	4	16.6	7.2	1.0	3.2	.464
NBA Playoff Totals		126	109	3737	1183	437	1007	.434	97	278	.349	212	273	.777	113	361	474	899	224	0	129	8	290	29.7	9.4	3.8	7.1	....

• JACKSON, Mervin

Mervin P. (The Magician) Jackson Jr.

Born: Aug. 15, 1946. Savannah, GA, United States. Height: 6'3". Weight: 175 lbs. Drafted: 1968 College: Utah

YEAR	TEAM	GP	GS	MIN	PTS	FGM	FGA	FG%	3PM	3PA	3P%	FTM	FTA	FT%	ORB	DRB	TRB	AST	PF	DQ	STL	BLK	TO	MPG	PPG	RPG	APG	PCM
68-69	Los Angeles-A	71	....	2314	1114	423	1000	.423	19	62	.306	249	302	.825	142	157	299	237	262	9	....	....	191	32.6	15.7	4.2	3.3	.437
69-70	Los Angeles-A	52	....	1118	446	169	475	.356	16	44	.364	92	114	.807	39	99	138	114	145	4	....	....	84	21.5	8.6	2.7	2.2	.322
70-71	Utah-A	65	....	1902	905	351	836	.420	7	20	.350	196	244	.803	92	170	262	225	207	5	....	....	140	29.3	13.9	4.0	3.5	.470
71-72	Utah-A	52	....	1136	467	185	412	.449	5	15	.333	92	109	.844	48	75	123	155	150	1	....	....	88	21.8	9.0	2.4	3.0	.419
72-73	Memphis-A	22	....	420	100	34	103	.330	4	11	.364	28	35	.800	9	29	38	82	61	1	....	....	35	19.1	4.5	1.7	3.7	.314
ABA Season Totals		262	....	6890	3032	1162	2826	.411	51	152	.336	657	804	.817	330	530	860	813	825	20	....	....	538	26.3	11.6	3.3	3.1	....
69-70	Los Angeles-A	17	....	526	252	102	229	.445	9	22	.409	39	48	.813	....	....	74	53	....	0	....	....	26	30.9	14.8	4.4	3.1	....
70-71	Utah-A	18	....	598	274	114	237	.481	3	8	.375	43	54	.796	26	53	79	109	47	0	....	....	42	33.2	15.2	4.4	6.1	.579
71-72	Utah-A	11	....	267	83	34	77	.442	0	0	.000	15	18	.833	9	17	26	26	40	1	....	....	16	24.3	7.5	2.4	2.4	.293
ABA Playoff Totals		46	....	1391	609	250	543	.460	12	30	.400	97	120	.808	35	70	179	188	87	1	....	....	84	30.2	13.2	3.9	4.1	....

• JACKSON, Michael

Michael Jackson

Born: July 13, 1964. Fairfax, VA, United States. Height: 6'2". Weight: 183 lbs. Drafted: 1986 College: Georgetown

YEAR	TEAM	GP	GS	MIN	PTS	FGM	FGA	FG%	3PM	3PA	3P%	FTM	FTA	FT%	ORB	DRB	TRB	AST	PF	DQ	STL	BLK	TO	MPG	PPG	RPG	APG	PCM
87-88	Sacramento	58	0	760	157	64	171	.374	6	25	.240	23	32	.719	17	42	59	179	81	0	20	5	58	13.1	2.7	1.0	3.1	.304
88-89	Sacramento	14	0	70	21	9	24	.375	2	6	.333	1	2	.500	1	3	4	11	12	0	3	0	4	5.0	1.5	0.3	0.8	.222
89-90	Sacramento	17	0	58	10	3	11	.273	1	2	.500	3	6	.500	2	5	7	8	3	0	5	0	3	3.4	0.6	0.4	0.5	.287
NBA Season Totals		89	0	888	188	76	206	.369	9	33	.273	27	40	.675	20	50	70	198	96	0	28	5	65	10.0	2.1	0.8	**2.2**	....

• JACKSON, Mike

Michael Jackson

Born: July 31, 1949. Washington, DC, United States. Height: 6'7". Weight: 215 lbs. Drafted: 1972 College: Los Angeles State

YEAR	TEAM	GP	GS	MIN	PTS	FGM	FGA	FG%	3PM	3PA	3P%	FTM	FTA	FT%	ORB	DRB	TRB	AST	PF	DQ	STL	BLK	TO	MPG	PPG	RPG	APG	PCM
72-73	Utah-A	30	....	191	100	36	83	.434	0	0	.000	28	46	.609	24	38	62	2	46	0	....	....	27	6.4	3.3	2.1	0.1	.455
73-74	Memphis-A	39	....	797	339	140	252	.556	3	7	.429	56	84	.667	78	135	213	34	119	....	12	5	57	20.4	8.7	5.5	0.9	.504
73-74	Utah-A	33	....	677	268	107	237	.451	0	0	.000	54	68	.794	62	105	167	23	103	....	13	10	52	20.5	8.1	5.1	0.7	.407
74-75	Virginia-A	82	....	2023	997	382	724	.528	1	3	.333	232	295	.786	183	274	457	82	308	....	47	19	212	24.7	12.2	5.6	1.0	.507
75-76	Virginia-A	80	....	2230	979	390	781	.499	0	5	.000	199	250	.796	209	398	607	113	306	....	45	29	190	27.9	12.2	7.6	1.4	.510
ABA Season Totals		264	....	5918	2683	1055	2077	.508	4	15	.267	569	743	.766	556	950	1506	254	882	0	117	63	538	22.4	10.2	5.7	1.0	....
72-73	Utah-A	1	....	2	0	0	0	.000	0	0	.000	0	0	.000	0	0	0	0	2	0	....	....	0	2.0	0.0	0.0	0.0	-.450
ABA Playoff Totals		1	....	2	0	0	0	.000	0	0	.000	0	0	.000	0	0	0	0	2	0	....	....	0	2.0	0.0	0.0	0.0	....

• JACKSON, Myron

Myron Jackson

Born: May 6, 1964. Hamburg, AR, United States. Height: 6'3". Weight: 185 lbs. Drafted: 1986 College: Arkansas-Little Rock

YEAR	TEAM	GP	GS	MIN	PTS	FGM	FGA	FG%	3PM	3PA	3P%	FTM	FTA	FT%	ORB	DRB	TRB	AST	PF	DQ	STL	BLK	TO	MPG	PPG	RPG	APG	PCM
86-87	Dallas	8	0	22	11	2	9	.222	0	0	.000	7	8	.875	1	2	3	6	1	0	1	0	5	2.8	1.4	0.4	0.8	.411
NBA Season Totals		8	0	22	11	2	9	.222	0	0	.000	7	8	.875	1	2	3	6	1	0	1	0	5	2.8	1.4	0.4	0.8	....

• JACKSON, Phil

Philip D. (Action) Jackson

Born: Sept. 17, 1945. Deer Lodge, MT, United States. Height: 6'8". Weight: 220 lbs. Drafted: 1967 College: North Dakota

YEAR	TEAM	GP	GS	MIN	PTS	FGM	FGA	FG%	3PM	3PA	3P%	FTM	FTA	FT%	ORB	DRB	TRB	AST	PF	DQ	STL	BLK	TO	MPG	PPG	RPG	APG	PCM
67-68	New York	75	....	1093	463	182	455	.400	....	....	....	99	168	.589	....	....	338	55	212	3	....	....	....	14.6	6.2	4.5	0.7	.429
68-69	New York	47	....	924	332	126	294	.429	....	....	....	80	119	.672	....	....	246	43	168	6	....	....	....	19.7	7.1	5.2	0.9	.390
70-71	New York	71	....	771	331	118	263	.449	....	....	....	95	133	.714	....	....	238	31	169	4	....	....	....	10.9	4.7	3.4	0.4	.463
71-72	New York	80	....	1273	577	205	466	.440	....	....	....	167	228	.732	....	....	326	72	224	4	....	....	....	15.9	7.2	4.1	0.9	.465
72-73	New York	80	....	1393	644	245	553	.443	....	....	....	154	195	.790	....	....	344	94	218	2	....	....	....	17.4	8.1	4.3	1.2	.482
73-74	New York	82	....	2050	913	361	757	.477	....	....	....	191	246	.776	123	355	478	134	277	7	42	67	....	25.0	11.1	5.8	1.6	.486
74-75	New York	78	....	2285	841	324	712	.455	....	....	....	193	253	.763	137	463	600	136	**330**	10	84	53	....	29.3	10.8	7.7	1.7	.443
75-76	New York	80	....	1461	480	185	387	.478	....	....	....	110	150	.733	80	263	343	105	275	3	41	20	....	18.3	6.0	4.3	1.3	.401
76-77	New York	76	....	1033	255	102	232	.440	....	....	....	51	71	.718	75	154	229	85	184	4	33	18	....	13.6	3.4	3.0	1.1	.338

YEAR	TEAM	GP	GS	MIN	PTS	FGM	FGA	FG%	3PM	3PA	3P%	FTM	FTA	FT%	ORB	DRB	TRB	AST	PF	DQ	STL	BLK	TO	MPG	PPG	RPG	APG	PCM
77-78	New York	63	....	654	153	55	115	.478	....	....	....	43	56	.768	29	81	110	46	106	0	31	15	44	10.4	2.4	1.7	0.7	.303
78-79	New Jersey	59	....	1070	374	144	303	.475	....	....	....	86	105	.819	59	119	178	85	168	7	45	22	77	18.1	6.3	3.0	1.4	.366
79-80	New Jersey	16	....	194	65	29	46	.630	0	2	.000	7	10	.700	12	12	24	12	35	1	5	4	10	12.1	4.1	1.5	0.8	.342
NBA Season Totals		807	....	14201	5428	2076	4583	.453	0	2	.000	1276	1734	.736	515	1447	3454	898	2366	51	281	199	131	17.6	6.7	4.3	1.1	....
67-68	New York	6	....	90	24	10	35	.286	....	....	....	4	5	.800	....	....	25	2	23	0	....	....	....	15.0	4.0	4.2	0.3	.187
70-71	New York	5	....	30	9	4	14	.286	....	....	....	1	1	1.000	....	....	10	2	8	0	....	....	....	6.0	1.8	2.0	0.4	.261
71-72	New York	16	....	320	156	57	120	.475	....	....	....	42	57	.737	....	....	82	15	51	1	....	....	....	20.0	9.8	5.1	0.9	.503
72-73	New York	17	....	338	148	60	120	.500	....	....	....	28	38	.737	....	....	72	24	59	3	....	....	....	19.9	8.7	4.2	1.4	.462
73-74	New York	12	....	297	135	54	116	.466	....	....	....	27	30	.900	15	42	57	15	40	0	10	5	....	24.8	11.3	4.8	1.3	.437
74-75	New York	3	....	78	27	10	21	.476	....	....	....	7	8	.875	5	20	25	2	15	0	4	3	....	26.0	9.0	8.3	0.7	.441
77-78	New York	6	....	50	12	4	8	.500	....	....	....	4	6	.667	4	6	10	3	11	0	3	0	....	8.3	2.0	1.7	0.5	.281
78-79	New Jersey	2	....	20	4	1	3	.333	....	....	....	2	2	1.000	2	1	3	0	1	0	1	0	0	10.0	2.0	1.5	0.0	.267
NBA Playoff Totals		67	....	1223	515	200	437	.458	....	....	....	115	147	.782	26	69	284	63	208	4	18	8	4	18.3	7.7	4.2	0.9	....

• JACKSON, Ralph
Ralph A. Jackson III

Born: Oct. 26, 1962. Los Angeles, CA, United States. Height: 6'2". Weight: 190 lbs. Drafted: 1984 College: UCLA

YEAR	TEAM	GP	GS	MIN	PTS	FGM	FGA	FG%	3PM	3PA	3P%	FTM	FTA	FT%	ORB	DRB	TRB	AST	PF	DQ	STL	BLK	TO	MPG	PPG	RPG	APG	PCM
84-85	Indiana	1	0	12	2	1	3	.333	0	0	.000	0	0	.000	1	0	1	4	1	0	2	0	1	12.0	2.0	1.0	4.0	.484
NBA Season Totals		1	0	12	2	1	3	.333	0	0	.000	0	0	.000	1	0	1	4	1	0	2	0	1	12.0	2.0	1.0	4.0	....

• JACKSON, Randell
Randell Jackson

Born: Jan. 16, 1976. Boston, MA, United States. Height: 6'11". Weight: 215 lbs. Drafted: — College: Florida State

YEAR	TEAM	GP	GS	MIN	PTS	FGM	FGA	FG%	3PM	3PA	3P%	FTM	FTA	FT%	ORB	DRB	TRB	AST	PF	DQ	STL	BLK	TO	MPG	PPG	RPG	APG	PCM
98-99	Washington	27	8	271	114	46	108	.426	1	7	.143	21	32	.656	30	24	54	8	29	0	3	11	26	10.0	4.2	2.0	0.3	.322
99-00	Dallas	1	0	1	0	0	0	.000	0	0	.000	0	0	.000	0	0	0	0	0	0	0	0	0	1.0	0.0	0.0	0.0	.000
NBA Season Totals		28	8	272	114	46	108	.426	1	7	.143	21	32	.656	30	24	54	8	29	0	3	11	26	9.7	4.1	1.9	0.3	....

• JACKSON, Stan
Stan Jackson

Born: —. Height: — Weight: — Drafted: — College: Syracuse

YEAR	TEAM	GP	GS	MIN	PTS	FGM	FGA	FG%	3PM	3PA	3P%	FTM	FTA	FT%	ORB	DRB	TRB	AST	PF	DQ	STL	BLK	TO	MPG	PPG	RPG	APG	PCM
37-38	Buffalo-N	7	....	....	18	8	....	....	....	....	....	2	....	....	....	....	....	....	....	....	....	....	....	2.6	....	....	....	....
NBL Season Totals		7	....	....	18	8	....	....	....	....	....	2	....	....	....	....	....	....	....	....	....	....	....	2.6	....	....	....	....

• JACKSON, Stanley
Stanley Leon Jackson

Born: Oct. 10, 1970. Tuskegee, AL, United States. Height: 6'3". Weight: 185 lbs. Drafted: — College: Alabama-Birmingham

YEAR	TEAM	GP	GS	MIN	PTS	FGM	FGA	FG%	3PM	3PA	3P%	FTM	FTA	FT%	ORB	DRB	TRB	AST	PF	DQ	STL	BLK	TO	MPG	PPG	RPG	APG	PCM
93-94	Minnesota	17	0	92	38	17	33	.515	1	5	.200	3	3	1.000	12	15	27	16	13	0	5	0	10	5.4	2.2	1.6	0.9	.596
NBA Season Totals		17	0	92	38	17	33	.515	1	5	.200	3	3	1.000	12	15	27	16	13	0	5	0	10	5.4	2.2	1.6	0.9	....

• JACKSON, Stephen
Stephen Jesse Jackson

Born: Apr. 5, 1978. Houston, TX, United States. Height: 6'8". Weight: 218 lbs. Drafted: 1997 College: none

YEAR	TEAM	GP	GS	MIN	PTS	FGM	FGA	FG%	3PM	3PA	3P%	FTM	FTA	FT%	ORB	DRB	TRB	AST	PF	DQ	STL	BLK	TO	MPG	PPG	RPG	APG	PCM
00-01	New Jersey	77	40	1660	635	243	572	.425	52	155	.335	97	135	.719	41	167	208	140	166	2	86	14	130	21.6	8.2	2.7	1.8	.339
01-02	San Antonio	23	1	227	89	34	91	.374	9	36	.250	12	17	.706	3	23	26	11	29	0	15	3	23	9.9	3.9	1.1	0.5	.234
02-03	San Antonio	80	58	2252	946	356	818	.435	95	297	.320	139	183	.760	66	220	286	183	202	1	125	30	176	28.2	11.8	3.6	2.3	.380
NBA Season Totals		180	99	4139	1670	633	1481	.427	156	488	.320	248	335	.740	110	410	520	334	397	3	226	47	329	23.0	9.3	2.9	1.9	....
02-03	San Antonio	24	24	811	307	108	261	.414	38	113	.336	53	66	.803	19	79	98	65	53	0	33	9	68	33.8	12.8	4.1	2.7	.338
NBA Playoff Totals		24	24	811	307	108	261	.414	38	113	.336	53	66	.803	19	79	98	65	53	0	33	9	68	33.8	12.8	4.1	2.7	....

• JACKSON, Tony
Tony B. Jackson

Born: Nov. 7, 1942. Brooklyn, NY, United States. Height: 6'4". Weight: 200 lbs. Drafted: 1961 College: St. John's (NY)

YEAR	TEAM	GP	GS	MIN	PTS	FGM	FGA	FG%	3PM	3PA	3P%	FTM	FTA	FT%	ORB	DRB	TRB	AST	PF	DQ	STL	BLK	TO	MPG	PPG	RPG	APG	PCM
67-68	New Jersey-A	74	....	2638	1439	449	1171	.383	91	302	.301	450	543	.829	....	....	500	140	184	1	....	....	144	35.6	19.4	6.8	1.9	.494
68-69	Houston-A	60	....	1423	750	210	583	.360	32	145	.221	298	336	.887	99	138	237	138	143	2	....	....	151	23.7	12.5	4.0	2.3	.501
68-69	Minnesota-A	1	....	10	0	0	2	.000	0	0	.000	0	0	.000	1	0	1	1	2	0	....	....	0	10.0	0.0	1.0	1.0	-.057
68-69	New York-A	3	....	20	1	0	3	.000	0	0	.000	1	1	1.000	0	3	3	0	2	0	....	....	0	6.7	0.3	1.0	0.0	.007
ABA Season Totals		138	....	4091	2190	659	1759	.375	123	447	.275	749	880	.851	100	141	741	279	331	3	....	....	295	29.6	15.9	5.4	2.0	....

• JACKSON, Tony
Anthony Eugene Jackson

Born: Jan. 17, 1958. Lexington, KY, United States. Height: 6' Weight: 170 lbs. Drafted: 1980 College: Florida State

YEAR	TEAM	GP	GS	MIN	PTS	FGM	FGA	FG%	3PM	3PA	3P%	FTM	FTA	FT%	ORB	DRB	TRB	AST	PF	DQ	STL	BLK	TO	MPG	PPG	RPG	APG	PCM
80-81	LA Lakers	2	....	14	2	1	3	.333	0	0	.000	0	0	.000	0	2	2	2	1	0	2	0	0	7.0	1.0	1.0	1.0	.396
NBA Season Totals		2	....	14	2	1	3	.333	0	0	.000	0	0	.000	0	2	2	2	1	0	2	0	0	7.0	1.0	1.0	1.0	....

• JACKSON, Tracy
Tracy Cordell Jackson

Born: Apr. 21, 1959. Rockville, MD, United States. Height: 6'6". Weight: 205 lbs. Drafted: 1981 College: Notre Dame

YEAR	TEAM	GP	GS	MIN	PTS	FGM	FGA	FG%	3PM	3PA	3P%	FTM	FTA	FT%	ORB	DRB	TRB	AST	PF	DQ	STL	BLK	TO	MPG	PPG	RPG	APG	PCM
81-82	Boston	11	0	66	26	10	26	.385	0	0	.000	6	10	.600	7	5	12	5	5	0	3	0	6	6.0	2.4	1.1	0.5	.315
81-82	Chicago	38	0	412	170	69	146	.473	0	0	.000	32	39	.821	28	23	51	22	43	0	11	3	19	10.8	4.5	1.3	0.6	.345
82-83	Chicago	78	3	1309	492	199	426	.467	2	13	.154	92	126	.730	87	92	179	105	132	0	64	11	86	16.8	6.3	2.3	1.3	.366
83-84	Indiana	2	0	10	6	1	4	.250	0	0	.000	4	4	1.000	1	0	1	0	3	0	0	0	1	5.0	3.0	0.5	0.0	.182
NBA Season Totals		129	3	1797	694	279	602	.463	2	13	.154	134	179	.749	123	120	243	132	183	0	78	14	112	13.9	5.4	1.9	1.0	....

YEAR	TEAM	GP	GS	MIN	PTS	FGM	FGA	FG%	3PM	3PA	3P%	FTM	FTA	FT%	ORB	DRB	TRB	AST	PF	DQ	STL	BLK	TO	MPG	PPG	RPG	APG	PCM

• JACKSON, Wardell
Wardell Jackson

Born: July 18, 1951. Yazoo City, MI, United States.   Height: 6'7".   Weight: 200 lbs.   Drafted: 1974   College: Ohio State

YEAR	TEAM	GP	GS	MIN	PTS	FGM	FGA	FG%	3PM	3PA	3P%	FTM	FTA	FT%	ORB	DRB	TRB	AST	PF	DQ	STL	BLK	TO	MPG	PPG	RPG	APG	PCM
74-75	Seattle	56	....	939	243	96	242	.397	....	....	....	51	71	.718	53	80	133	30	126	2	26	5	....	16.8	4.3	2.4	0.5	.217
NBA Season Totals		56	....	939	243	96	242	.397	....	....	....	51	71	.718	53	80	133	30	126	2	26	5	....	16.8	4.3	2.4	0.5	....

• JACOBS, Fred
Winfred O. Jacobs

Born: Dec. 2, 1922.   Height: 6'3".   Weight: 175 lbs.   Drafted: —   College: Denver

YEAR	TEAM	GP	GS	MIN	PTS	FGM	FGA	FG%	3PM	3PA	3P%	FTM	FTA	FT%	ORB	DRB	TRB	AST	PF	DQ	STL	BLK	TO	MPG	PPG	RPG	APG	PCM
46-47	St. Louis	18	....	....	50	19	69	.275	....	....	....	12	25	.480	....	....	....	5	25	....	....	....	....	....	2.8	....	0.3	....
NBA Season Totals		18	....	....	50	19	69	.275	....	....	....	12	25	.480	....	....	....	5	25	....	....	....	....	....	2.8	....	0.3	....

• JACOBSEN, Casey
Casey Garder Jacobsen

Born: Mar. 19, 1981. Glendora, CA, United States.   Height: 6'6".   Weight: 215 lbs.   Drafted: 2002   College: Stanford

YEAR	TEAM	GP	GS	MIN	PTS	FGM	FGA	FG%	3PM	3PA	3P%	FTM	FTA	FT%	ORB	DRB	TRB	AST	PF	DQ	STL	BLK	TO	MPG	PPG	RPG	APG	PCM
02-03	Phoenix	72	0	1145	368	122	327	.373	52	165	.315	72	105	.686	29	54	83	73	90	0	35	6	55	15.9	5.1	1.2	1.0	.234
NBA Season Totals		72	0	1145	368	122	327	.373	52	165	.315	72	105	.686	29	54	83	73	90	0	35	6	55	15.9	5.1	1.2	1.0	....
02-03	Phoenix	6	0	39	6	2	10	.200	2	5	.400	0	2	.000	1	2	3	2	4	0	3	0	1	6.5	1.0	0.5	0.3	.070
NBA Playoff Totals		6	0	39	6	2	10	.200	2	5	.400	0	2	.000	1	2	3	2	4	0	3	0	1	6.5	1.0	0.5	0.3	....

• JACOBSON, Samuel
Samuel Ryan Jacobson

Born: July 22, 1975. Cottage Grove, MN, United States.   Height: 6'4".   Weight: 215 lbs.   Drafted: 1998   College: Minnesota

YEAR	TEAM	GP	GS	MIN	PTS	FGM	FGA	FG%	3PM	3PA	3P%	FTM	FTA	FT%	ORB	DRB	TRB	AST	PF	DQ	STL	BLK	TO	MPG	PPG	RPG	APG	PCM
98-99	LA Lakers	2	0	12	8	3	5	.600	0	1	.000	2	2	1.000	0	3	3	0	2	0	0	0	1	6.0	4.0	1.5	0.0	.593
99-00	LA Lakers	3	0	18	10	5	9	.556	0	0	.000	0	2	.000	0	1	1	2	1	0	1	0	2	6.0	3.3	0.3	0.7	.399
99-00	Golden State	49	5	663	245	103	203	.507	9	24	.375	30	39	.769	25	45	70	30	112	3	29	3	31	13.5	5.0	1.4	0.6	.296
00-01	Minnesota	14	0	59	20	9	18	.500	0	0	.000	2	3	.667	3	3	6	4	19	0	3	0	0	4.2	1.4	0.4	0.3	.261
NBA Season Totals		68	5	752	283	120	235	.511	9	25	.360	34	46	.739	28	52	80	36	134	3	33	3	34	11.1	4.2	1.2	0.5	....

• JACOBSON, Stub
Stub Jacobson

Born: —.   Height: 6'6".   Weight: —   Drafted: —   College: —

YEAR	TEAM	GP	GS	MIN	PTS	FGM	FGA	FG%	3PM	3PA	3P%	FTM	FTA	FT%	ORB	DRB	TRB	AST	PF	DQ	STL	BLK	TO	MPG	PPG	RPG	APG	PCM
37-38	Warren-N	4	....	....	6	2	....	....	....	....	....	2	....	....	....	....	....	....	....	....	....	....	....	1.5	....	....	....
NBL Season Totals		4	....	....	6	2	....	....	....	....	....	2	....	....	....	....	....	....	....	....	....	....	....	1.5	....	....	....

• JAGNOW, Lou
Lou Jagnow

Born: 1910.   Height: 6'1".   Weight: 180 lbs.   Drafted: —   College: Carnegie-Mellon

YEAR	TEAM	GP	GS	MIN	PTS	FGM	FGA	FG%	3PM	3PA	3P%	FTM	FTA	FT%	ORB	DRB	TRB	AST	PF	DQ	STL	BLK	TO	MPG	PPG	RPG	APG	PCM
39-40	Detroit-N	1	....	....	1	0	....	....	....	....	....	1	....	....	....	....	....	....	....	....	....	....	....	1.0	....	....	....
NBL Season Totals		1	....	....	1	0	....	....	....	....	....	1	....	....	....	....	....	....	....	....	....	....	....	1.0	....	....	....
39-40	Detroit-N	1	....	....	0	0	....	....	....	....	....	0	....	....	....	....	....	....	....	....	....	....	....	0.0	....	....	....
NBL Playoff Totals		1	....	....	0	0	....	....	....	....	....	0	....	....	....	....	....	....	....	....	....	....	....	0.0	....	....	....

• JAMERSON, Dave
John David Jamerson

Born: Aug. 13, 1967. Clarksburg, WV, United States.   Height: 6'5".   Weight: 190 lbs.   Drafted: 1990   College: Ohio University

YEAR	TEAM	GP	GS	MIN	PTS	FGM	FGA	FG%	3PM	3PA	3P%	FTM	FTA	FT%	ORB	DRB	TRB	AST	PF	DQ	STL	BLK	TO	MPG	PPG	RPG	APG	PCM
90-91	Houston	37	0	202	113	43	113	.381	5	19	.263	22	27	.815	9	21	30	27	24	0	6	1	19	5.5	3.1	0.8	0.7	.395
91-92	Houston	48	0	378	191	79	191	.414	8	28	.286	25	27	.926	22	21	43	33	39	0	17	0	24	7.9	4.0	0.9	0.7	.362
93-94	Utah	1	0	4	1	0	2	.000	0	0	.000	1	1	1.000	0	1	1	0	0	0	0	0	0	4.0	1.0	1.0	0.0	.021
93-94	New Jersey	4	0	10	1	0	5	.000	0	0	.000	1	2	.500	0	3	3	1	0	0	0	0	1	2.5	0.3	0.8	0.3	-.113
NBA Season Totals		90	0	594	306	122	311	.392	13	47	.277	49	57	.860	31	46	77	61	63	0	23	1	44	6.6	3.4	0.9	0.7	....
90-91	Houston	2	0	21	16	5	13	.385	0	1	.000	6	6	1.000	1	2	3	4	4	0	1	0	1	10.5	8.0	1.5	2.0	.654
NBA Playoff Totals		2	0	21	16	5	13	.385	0	1	.000	6	6	1.000	1	2	3	4	4	0	1	0	1	10.5	8.0	1.5	2.0	....

• JAMES, —
James

Born: —.   Height: —   Weight: —   Drafted: —   College: —

YEAR	TEAM	GP	GS	MIN	PTS	FGM	FGA	FG%	3PM	3PA	3P%	FTM	FTA	FT%	ORB	DRB	TRB	AST	PF	DQ	STL	BLK	TO	MPG	PPG	RPG	APG	PCM
38-39	Hammond-N	4	....	....	21	6	....	....	....	....	....	9	....	....	....	....	....	....	....	....	....	....	....	5.3	....	....	....
NBL Season Totals		4	....	....	21	6	....	....	....	....	....	9	....	....	....	....	....	....	....	....	....	....	....	5.3	....	....	....

• JAMES, Aaron
Aaron James

Born: Oct. 5, 1952. New Orleans, LA, United States.   Height: 6'8".   Weight: 210 lbs.   Drafted: 1974   College: Grambling

YEAR	TEAM	GP	GS	MIN	PTS	FGM	FGA	FG%	3PM	3PA	3P%	FTM	FTA	FT%	ORB	DRB	TRB	AST	PF	DQ	STL	BLK	TO	MPG	PPG	RPG	APG	PCM
74-75	New Orleans	76	....	1731	887	370	776	.477	....	....	....	147	189	.778	140	226	366	66	217	4	41	15	....	22.8	11.7	4.8	0.9	.473
75-76	New Orleans	75	....	1346	677	262	594	.441	....	....	....	153	204	.750	93	156	249	59	172	1	33	6	....	17.9	9.0	3.3	0.8	.429
76-77	New Orleans	52	....	1059	565	238	486	.490	....	....	....	89	114	.781	56	130	186	55	127	1	20	5	....	20.4	10.9	3.6	1.1	.480
77-78	New Orleans	80	....	2118	973	428	861	.497	....	....	....	117	157	.745	163	258	421	112	254	5	36	22	128	26.5	12.2	5.3	1.4	.424
78-79	New Orleans	73	....	1417	727	311	630	.494	....	....	....	105	140	.750	97	151	248	78	202	1	28	21	110	19.4	10.0	3.4	1.1	.415
NBA Season Totals		356	....	7671	3829	1609	3347	.481	....	....	....	611	804	.760	549	921	1470	370	972	12	158	69	238	21.5	10.8	4.1	1.0	....

JAMES, Billy

Mack William James

Born: Feb. 11, 1950.   Height: 6'3".   Weight: 185 lbs.   Drafted: —   College: Marshall

YEAR TEAM	GP	GS	MIN	PTS	FGM	FGA	FG%	3PM	3PA	3P%	FTM	FTA	FT%	ORB	DRB	TRB	AST	PF	DQ	STL	BLK	TO	MPG	PPG	RPG	APG	PCM
73-74 Kentucky-A	1	....	10	2	1	3	.333	0	0	.000	0	0	.000	0	0	0	1	3	....	0	0	1	10.0	2.0	0.0	1.0	.014
ABA Season Totals	1	....	10	2	1	3	.333	0	0	.000	0	0	.000	0	0	0	1	3	....	0	0	1	10.0	2.0	0.0	1.0	....

JAMES, Gene

Harold Gene (Goose) James

Born: Feb. 15, 1925. Ironton, OH, United States. Died: July6, 1997.   Height: 6'4".   Weight: 180 lbs.   Drafted: —   College: Marshall

YEAR TEAM	GP	GS	MIN	PTS	FGM	FGA	FG%	3PM	3PA	3P%	FTM	FTA	FT%	ORB	DRB	TRB	AST	PF	DQ	STL	BLK	TO	MPG	PPG	RPG	APG	PCM
48-49 New York	11	....	....	42	18	48	.375	....	....	....	6	12	.500	....	....	....	5	20	....	....	....	....	....	3.8	....	0.5	
49-50 New York	29	....	....	52	19	64	.297	....	....	....	14	31	.452	....	....	....	20	53	....	....	....	....	....	1.8	....	0.7	
50-51 New York	6	....	....	3	1	3	.333	....	....	....	1	1	1.000	....	....	4	4	11	1	....	....	....	....	0.5	0.7	0.7	
50-51 Baltimore	42	....	....	199	78	232	.336	....	....	....	43	70	.614	....	....	137	66	107	1	....	....	....	....	4.7	3.3	1.6	
NBA Season Totals	88	....	....	296	116	347	.334	....	....	....	64	114	.561	....	....	141	95	191	2	....	....	....	....	3.4	1.6	1.1	
48-49 New York	3	....	....	2	0	6	.000	....	....	....	2	4	.500	....	....	....	2	6	....	....	....	....	....	0.7	....	0.7	
49-50 New York	1	....	....	2	1	3	.333	....	....	....	0	0	.000	....	....	....	0	0	....	....	....	....	....	2.0	....	0.0	
NBA Playoff Totals	4	....	....	4	1	9	.111	....	....	....	2	4	.500	....	....	....	2	6	....	....	....	....	....	1.0	....	0.5	

JAMES, Henry

Henry Charles James

Born: July 29, 1965. Centreville, AL, United States.   Height: 6'8".   Weight: 220 lbs.   Drafted: —   College: St. Mary's (TX)

YEAR TEAM	GP	GS	MIN	PTS	FGM	FGA	FG%	3PM	3PA	3P%	FTM	FTA	FT%	ORB	DRB	TRB	AST	PF	DQ	STL	BLK	TO	MPG	PPG	RPG	APG	PCM
90-91 Cleveland	37	4	505	300	112	254	.441	24	60	.400	52	72	.722	26	53	79	32	59	1	15	5	37	13.6	8.1	2.1	0.9	.441
91-92 Cleveland	65	5	866	418	164	403	.407	29	90	.322	61	76	.803	35	77	112	25	94	1	16	11	46	13.3	6.4	1.7	0.4	.299
92-93 Sacramento	8	0	79	60	20	45	.444	3	10	.300	17	20	.850	6	4	10	1	9	0	3	0	7	9.9	7.5	1.3	0.1	.478
92-93 Utah	2	0	9	7	1	6	.167	0	3	.000	5	6	.833	1	0	1	0	0	0	0	0	0	4.5	3.5	0.5	0.0	.311
93-94 LA Clippers	12	0	75	41	16	42	.381	4	18	.222	5	5	1.000	6	8	14	1	9	0	2	0	2	6.3	3.4	1.2	0.1	.359
95-96 Houston	7	0	58	30	10	24	.417	5	15	.333	5	5	1.000	3	3	6	2	13	0	0	0	4	8.3	4.3	0.9	0.3	.254
96-97 Atlanta	53	15	945	356	125	306	.408	76	181	.420	30	36	.833	27	54	81	21	98	1	11	1	27	17.8	6.7	1.5	0.4	.236
97-98 Cleveland	28	0	166	80	24	59	.407	11	25	.440	21	22	.955	2	13	15	5	24	0	1	1	11	5.9	2.9	0.5	0.2	.286
NBA Season Totals	212	24	2703	1292	472	1139	.414	152	402	.378	196	242	.810	106	212	318	87	306	3	48	18	134	12.8	6.1	1.5	0.4	....
91-92 Cleveland	8	0	22	4	1	10	.100	0	3	.000	2	4	.500	1	1	2	2	2	0	1	0	1	2.8	0.5	0.3	0.3	-.101
96-97 Atlanta	8	0	45	8	3	13	.231	2	6	.333	0	0	.000	1	0	1	2	12	0	1	0	4	5.6	1.0	0.1	0.3	-.148
NBA Playoff Totals	16	0	67	12	4	23	.174	2	9	.222	2	4	.500	2	1	3	4	14	0	2	0	5	4.2	0.8	0.2	0.3	....

JAMES, Jerome

Jerome Keith James

Born: Nov. 17, 1975. Tampa, FL, United States.   Height: 7'   Weight: 300 lbs.   Drafted: 1998   College: Florida A&M

YEAR TEAM	GP	GS	MIN	PTS	FGM	FGA	FG%	3PM	3PA	3P%	FTM	FTA	FT%	ORB	DRB	TRB	AST	PF	DQ	STL	BLK	TO	MPG	PPG	RPG	APG	PCM
98-99 Sacramento	16	0	42	24	9	24	.375	0	0	.000	6	12	.500	6	11	17	1	11	0	2	6	9	2.6	1.5	1.1	0.1	.439
01-02 Seattle	56	40	949	298	134	273	.491	0	0	.000	30	60	.500	89	143	232	24	174	0	25	86	74	16.9	5.3	4.1	0.4	.368
02-03 Seattle	51	16	766	276	111	232	.478	0	0	.000	54	92	.587	78	138	216	27	166	3	12	82	75	15.0	5.4	4.2	0.5	.413
NBA Season Totals	123	56	1757	598	254	529	.480	0	0	.000	90	164	.549	173	292	465	52	351	3	39	174	158	14.3	4.9	3.8	0.4	....
98-99 Sacramento	1	0	4	5	1	2	.500	0	0	.000	3	4	.750	1	1	2	0	1	0	0	0	1	4.0	5.0	2.0	0.0	1.028
01-02 Seattle	5	1	70	18	9	23	.391	0	0	.000	0	2	.000	4	8	12	4	18	1	0	5	4	14.0	3.6	2.4	0.8	.177
NBA Playoff Totals	6	1	74	23	10	25	.400	0	0	.000	3	6	.500	5	9	14	4	19	1	0	5	5	12.3	3.8	2.3	0.7	....

JAMES, Mike

Michael Lamont James

Born: June 23, 1975. Copaigue, NY, United States.   Height: 6'2".   Weight: 188 lbs.   Drafted: —   College: Duquesne

YEAR TEAM	GP	GS	MIN	PTS	FGM	FGA	FG%	3PM	3PA	3P%	FTM	FTA	FT%	ORB	DRB	TRB	AST	PF	DQ	STL	BLK	TO	MPG	PPG	RPG	APG	PCM
01-02 Miami	15	0	119	42	15	43	.349	8	21	.381	4	7	.571	2	12	14	19	17	0	6	1	13	7.9	2.8	0.9	1.3	.299
02-03 Miami	78	8	1722	607	218	585	.373	67	228	.294	104	142	.732	26	123	149	246	176	1	64	5	108	22.1	7.8	1.9	3.2	.317
NBA Season Totals	93	8	1841	649	233	628	.371	75	249	.301	108	149	.725	28	135	163	265	193	1	70	6	121	19.8	7.0	1.8	2.8	....

JAMES, Tim

Tim O'Connor James

Born: Dec. 26, 1976. Miami, FL, United States.   Height: 6'7".   Weight: 212 lbs.   Drafted: 1999   College: Miami (FL)

YEAR TEAM	GP	GS	MIN	PTS	FGM	FGA	FG%	3PM	3PA	3P%	FTM	FTA	FT%	ORB	DRB	TRB	AST	PF	DQ	STL	BLK	TO	MPG	PPG	RPG	APG	PCM
99-00 Miami	4	0	23	11	5	14	.357	0	0	.000	1	3	.333	3	1	4	2	1	0	0	3	2	5.8	2.8	1.0	0.5	.356
00-01 Charlotte	30	0	197	45	16	52	.308	1	3	.333	12	14	.857	15	20	35	8	27	0	2	5	8	6.6	1.5	1.2	0.3	.198
01-02 Philadelphia	9	0	41	12	5	13	.385	0	0	.000	2	6	.333	5	2	7	1	5	0	0	1	3	4.6	1.3	0.8	0.1	.154
NBA Season Totals	43	0	261	68	26	79	.329	1	3	.333	15	23	.652	23	23	46	11	33	0	2	9	13	6.1	1.6	1.1	0.3	....

JAMISON, Antawn

Antawn Cortez Jamison

Born: June 12, 1976. Shreveport, LA, United States.   Height: 6'8".   Weight: 223 lbs.   Drafted: 1998   College: North Carolina

YEAR TEAM	GP	GS	MIN	PTS	FGM	FGA	FG%	3PM	3PA	3P%	FTM	FTA	FT%	ORB	DRB	TRB	AST	PF	DQ	STL	BLK	TO	MPG	PPG	RPG	APG	PCM
98-99 Golden State	47	24	1058	449	178	394	.452	3	10	.300	90	153	.588	131	170	301	34	102	1	38	16	68	22.5	9.6	6.4	0.7	.450
99-00 Golden State	43	41	1556	841	356	756	.471	2	7	.286	127	208	.611	172	187	359	90	115	0	30	15	113	36.2	19.6	8.3	2.1	.483
00-01 Golden State	82	82	3394	2044	800	1812	.442	62	205	.302	382	534	.715	280	435	715	164	225	2	114	28	199	41.4	24.9	8.7	2.0	.512
01-02 Golden State	82	82	3033	1619	614	1375	.447	68	210	.324	323	440	.734	211	345	556	161	187	0	70	45	161	37.0	19.7	6.8	2.0	.471
02-03 Golden State	82	82	3226	1822	691	1471	.470	65	209	.311	375	475	.789	195	383	578	156	197	1	76	45	177	39.3	22.2	7.0	1.9	.503
NBA Season Totals	336	311	12267	6775	2639	5808	.454	200	641	.312	1297	1810	.717	989	1520	2509	605	826	4	328	149	718	36.5	20.2	7.5	1.8	....

JAMISON, Harold
Harold Sherill Jamison

Born: Nov. 20, 1976. Orangeburg, SC, United States. Height: 6'8". Weight: 260 lbs. Drafted: — College: Clemson

YEAR	TEAM	GP	GS	MIN	PTS	FGM	FGA	FG%	3PM	3PA	3P%	FTM	FTA	FT%	ORB	DRB	TRB	AST	PF	DQ	STL	BLK	TO	MPG	PPG	RPG	APG	PCM
99-00	Miami	12	0	74	18	7	20	.350	0	0	.000	4	18	.222	16	5	21	4	17	0	2	1	4	6.2	1.5	1.8	0.3	.198
01-02	LA Clippers	25	2	176	54	22	43	.512	0	0	.000	10	15	.667	24	15	39	6	23	0	5	1	6	7.0	2.2	1.6	0.2	.365
NBA Season Totals		37	2	250	72	29	63	.460	0	0	.000	14	33	.424	40	20	60	10	40	0	7	2	10	6.8	1.9	1.6	0.3	....

JANISCH, John
John Albert Janisch

Born: Mar. 15, 1920. Died: Aug.25, 1992. Height: 6'3". Weight: 200 lbs. Drafted: — College: Valparaiso

YEAR	TEAM	GP	GS	MIN	PTS	FGM	FGA	FG%	3PM	3PA	3P%	FTM	FTA	FT%	ORB	DRB	TRB	AST	PF	DQ	STL	BLK	TO	MPG	PPG	RPG	APG	PCM
46-47	Detroit	60	....	....	697	283	983	.288	....	....	....	131	198	.662	....	....	....	49	132	....	....	....	....	....	11.6	....	0.8	....
47-48	Flint-N	36	....	....	93	36	....	....	....	....	....	21	28	.750	....	....	....	....	38	....	....	....	....	....	2.6	....	....	....
47-48	Boston	3	....	....	3	1	7	.143	....	....	....	1	2	.500	....	....	....	0	3	....	....	....	....	....	1.0	....	0.0	....
47-48	Providence	7	....	....	34	13	43	.302	....	....	....	8	14	.571	....	....	....	2	2	....	....	....	....	....	4.9	....	0.3	....
NBA Season Totals		70	....	....	734	297	1033	.288	....	....	....	140	214	.654	....	....	....	51	137	....	....	....	....	....	10.5	....	0.7	....
NBL Season Totals		36	....	....	93	36	....	....	....	....	....	21	28	....	....	....	....	....	38	....	....	....	....	....	2.6	....	....	....
Career Totals		106	....	....	827	333	1033	....	....	....	....	161	242	....	....	....	....	51	175	....	....	....	....	....	7.8	....	0.5	....

JANOTTA, Howie
Howard Janotta

Born: Oct. 19, 1924. Height: 6'3". Weight: 185 lbs. Drafted: — College: Seton Hall

YEAR	TEAM	GP	GS	MIN	PTS	FGM	FGA	FG%	3PM	3PA	3P%	FTM	FTA	FT%	ORB	DRB	TRB	AST	PF	DQ	STL	BLK	TO	MPG	PPG	RPG	APG	PCM
49-50	Baltimore	9	....	....	31	9	30	.300	....	....	....	13	16	.813	....	....	....	4	10	....	....	....	....	....	3.4	....	0.4	....
NBA Season Totals		9	....	....	31	9	30	.300	....	....	....	13	16	.813	....	....	....	4	10	....	....	....	....	....	3.4	....	0.4	....

JARIC, Marko
Jaric Jaric

Born: Oct. 12, 1978. Belgrade, Yugoslavia. Height: 6'7". Weight: 198 lbs. Drafted: 2000 College: none

YEAR	TEAM	GP	GS	MIN	PTS	FGM	FGA	FG%	3PM	3PA	3P%	FTM	FTA	FT%	ORB	DRB	TRB	AST	PF	DQ	STL	BLK	TO	MPG	PPG	RPG	APG	PCM
02-03	LA Clippers	66	12	1379	490	179	446	.401	53	166	.319	79	105	.752	35	125	160	193	125	0	97	11	103	20.9	7.4	2.4	2.9	.391
NBA Season Totals		66	12	1379	490	179	446	.401	53	166	.319	79	105	.752	35	125	160	193	125	0	97	11	103	20.9	7.4	2.4	2.9	....

JAROS, Tony
Anthony Joseph Jaros

Born: Feb. 22, 1920. Died: Apr.22, 1995. Height: 6'3". Weight: 185 lbs. Drafted: — College: Minnesota

YEAR	TEAM	GP	GS	MIN	PTS	FGM	FGA	FG%	3PM	3PA	3P%	FTM	FTA	FT%	ORB	DRB	TRB	AST	PF	DQ	STL	BLK	TO	MPG	PPG	RPG	APG	PCM
46-47	Chicago	59	....	....	482	177	613	.289	....	....	....	128	181	.707	....	....	....	28	156	....	....	....	....	....	8.2	....	0.5	....
47-48	Minneapolis-N	58	....	....	273	95	....	....	....	....	....	83	114	.728	....	....	....	....	90	....	....	....	....	....	4.7	....	....	....
48-49	Minneapolis	59	....	....	343	132	385	.343	....	....	....	79	110	.718	....	....	....	58	114	....	....	....	....	....	5.8	....	1.0	....
49-50	Minneapolis	61	....	....	240	84	289	.291	....	....	....	72	96	.750	....	....	....	60	106	....	....	....	....	....	3.9	....	1.0	....
50-51	Minneapolis	63	....	....	241	88	287	.307	....	....	....	65	103	.631	....	....	131	72	131	0	....	....	....	....	3.8	2.1	1.1	....
NBA Season Totals		242	....	....	1306	481	1574	.306	....	....	....	344	490	.702	....	....	131	218	507	0	....	....	....	....	5.4	0.5	0.9	....
NBL Season Totals		58	....	....	273	95	....	....	....	....	....	83	114	....	....	....	....	....	90	....	....	....	....	....	4.7	....	....	....
Career Totals		300	....	....	1579	576	1574	....	....	....	....	427	604	....	....	....	131	218	597	0	....	....	....	....	5.3	0.4	0.7	....
46-47	Chicago	11	....	....	102	40	151	.265	....	....	....	22	31	.710	....	....	....	4	32	....	....	....	....	....	9.3	....	0.4	....
47-48	Minneapolis-N	10	....	....	80	29	....	....	....	....	....	22	33	.667	....	....	....	....	....	....	....	....	....	....	8.0	....	....	....
48-49	Minneapolis	10	....	....	58	20	56	.357	....	....	....	18	23	.783	....	....	....	11	28	....	....	....	....	....	5.8	....	1.1	....
49-50	Minneapolis	2	....	....	1	0	3	.000	....	....	....	1	2	.500	....	....	....	0	2	....	....	....	....	....	0.5	....	0.0	....
50-51	Minneapolis	7	....	....	20	6	20	.300	....	....	....	8	11	.727	....	....	7	6	11	0	....	....	....	....	2.9	1.0	0.9	....
NBA Playoff Totals		30	....	....	181	66	230	.287	....	....	....	49	67	.731	....	....	7	21	73	0	....	....	....	....	6.0	0.2	0.7	....
NBL Playoff Totals		10	....	....	80	29	....	....	....	....	....	22	33	....	....	....	....	....	....	....	....	....	....	....	8.0	....	....	....
Career Playoff Totals		40	....	....	261	95	230	....	....	....	....	71	100	....	....	....	7	21	73	0	....	....	....	....	6.5	0.2	0.5	....

JARVIS, Jim
James C. Jarvis

Born: Mar. 3, 1943. Roseburg, OR, United States. Height: 6'1". Weight: 175 lbs. Drafted: 1965 College: Oregon State

YEAR	TEAM	GP	GS	MIN	PTS	FGM	FGA	FG%	3PM	3PA	3P%	FTM	FTA	FT%	ORB	DRB	TRB	AST	PF	DQ	STL	BLK	TO	MPG	PPG	RPG	APG	PCM
67-68	Pittsburgh-A	63	....	818	329	132	343	.385	12	48	.250	53	64	.828	....	....	106	72	103	0	....	....	48	13.0	5.2	1.7	1.1	.341
68-69	Los Angeles-A	51	....	777	359	133	357	.373	17	42	.405	76	97	.784	57	58	115	65	113	1	....	....	62	15.2	7.0	2.3	1.3	.363
68-69	Minnesota-A	11	....	134	40	14	45	.311	2	5	.400	10	12	.833	3	11	14	15	24	0	....	....	9	12.2	3.6	1.3	1.4	.234
ABA Season Totals		125	....	1729	728	279	745	.374	31	95	.326	139	173	.803	60	69	235	152	240	1	....	....	119	13.8	5.8	1.9	1.2	....
67-68	Pittsburgh-A	15	....	211	94	39	89	.438	0	2	.000	16	20	.800	....	....	21	15	29	0	....	....	11	14.1	6.3	1.4	1.0	.350
ABA Playoff Totals		15	....	211	94	39	89	.438	0	2	.000	16	20	.800	....	....	21	15	29	0	....	....	11	14.1	6.3	1.4	1.0	....

JEANNETTE, Buddy
Harry Edward Jeannette

Born: Sept. 15, 1917. New Kensington, PA, United States. Died: Mar.11, 1998. Height: 5'11". Weight: 175 lbs. Drafted: — College: Washington & Jefferson
HOF: 1994

YEAR	TEAM	GP	GS	MIN	PTS	FGM	FGA	FG%	3PM	3PA	3P%	FTM	FTA	FT%	ORB	DRB	TRB	AST	PF	DQ	STL	BLK	TO	MPG	PPG	RPG	APG	PCM
38-39	Cleveland-N	26	....	....	173	54	....	....	....	....	....	65	....	....	....	....	....	....	....	....	....	....	....	....	6.7	....	....	....
39-40	Detroit-N	25	....	....	142	45	....	....	....	....	....	52	....	....	....	....	....	....	....	....	....	....	....	....	5.7	....	....	....
40-41	Detroit-N	23	....	....	204	75	....	....	....	....	....	54	....	....	....	....	....	....	....	....	....	....	....	....	8.9	....	....	....
42-43	Sheboygan-N	4	....	....	62	24	....	....	....	....	....	14	....	....	....	....	....	....	....	....	....	....	....	....	15.5	....	....	....
43-44	Fort Wayne-N	22	....	....	184	68	....	....	....	....	....	48	....	....	....	....	....	....	....	....	....	....	....	....	8.4	....	....	....
44-45	Fort Wayne-N	27	....	....	252	85	....	....	....	....	....	82	....	....	....	....	....	....	....	....	....	....	....	....	9.3	....	....	....
45-46	Fort Wayne-N	34	....	....	303	99	....	....	....	....	....	105	136	.772	....	....	....	....	....	....	....	....	....	....	8.9	....	....	....
47-48	Baltimore	46	....	....	491	150	430	.349	....	....	....	191	252	.758	....	....	....	70	147	....	....	....	....	....	10.7	....	1.5	....

YEAR	TEAM	GP	GS	MIN	PTS	FGM	FGA	FG%	3PM	3PA	3P%	FTM	FTA	FT%	ORB	DRB	TRB	AST	PF	DQ	STL	BLK	TO	MPG	PPG	RPG	APG	PCM
48-49	Baltimore	56	....	....	313	73	199	.367	....	....	....	167	213	.784	....	....	....	124	157	....	....	....	....		5.6	....	2.2	
49-50	Baltimore	37	....	....	193	42	148	.284	....	....	....	109	133	.820	....	....	....	93	82	....	....	....	....		5.2	....	2.5	
NBA Season Totals		139	....	....	997	265	777	.341	....	....	....	467	598	.781	....	....	....	287	386	....	....	....	....		7.2	....	2.1	
NBL Season Totals		161	....	....	1320	450	....	....	....	....	....	420	136	....	....	....	....	....	....	....	....	....	....		8.2	....	....	....
Career Totals		300	....	....	2317	715	777	....	....	....	....	887	734	....	....	....	....	287	386	....	....	....	....		7.7	....	1.0	....
39-40	Detroit-N	3	....	....	20	6	....	....	....	....	....	8													6.7			
40-41	Detroit-N	3	....	....	21	8	....	....	....	....	....	5													7.0			
42-43	Sheboygan-N	5	....	....	49	16	....	....	....	....	....	17													9.8			
43-44	Fort Wayne-N	5	....	....	34	12	....	....	....	....	....	10													6.8			
44-45	Fort Wayne-N	7	....	....	67	22	....	....	....	....	....	23													9.6			
45-46	Fort Wayne-N	4	....	....	19	7	....	....	....	....	....	5	6	.833											4.8			
47-48	Baltimore	11	....	....	97	30	61	.492	....	....	....	37	42	.881				12	45						8.8		1.1	
48-49	Baltimore	3	....	....	8	2	13	.154	....	....	....	4	4	1.000				5	11						2.7		1.7	
NBA Playoff Totals		14	....	....	105	32	74	.432	....	....	....	41	46	.891				17	56						7.5	....	1.2	
NBL Playoff Totals		27	....	....	210	71	....	....	....	....	....	68	6	....											7.8			
Career Playoff Totals		41	....	....	315	103	74	....	....	....	....	109	52	....				17	56						7.7	....	0.4	....

• JEELANI, Abdul

Abdul Qadir Jeelani   aka.: Gary Cole

Born: Feb. 10, 1954. Bells, TN, United States.   Height: 6'8".   Weight: 210 lbs.   Drafted: —   College: Wisconsin (Parkside)

YEAR	TEAM	GP	GS	MIN	PTS	FGM	FGA	FG%	3PM	3PA	3P%	FTM	FTA	FT%	ORB	DRB	TRB	AST	PF	DQ	STL	BLK	TO	MPG	PPG	RPG	APG	PCM
79-80	Portland	77	....	1286	737	288	565	.510	0	6	.000	161	204	.789	114	156	270	95	155	0	40	40	116	16.7	9.6	3.5	1.2	.554
80-81	Dallas	66	....	1108	553	187	440	.425	0	1	.000	179	220	.814	83	147	230	65	123	2	44	31	86	16.8	8.4	3.5	1.0	.468
NBA Season Totals		143	....	2394	1290	475	1005	.473	0	7	.000	340	424	.802	197	303	500	160	278	2	84	71	202	16.7	9.0	3.5	1.1	....

• JEFFERIES, Chris

Christopher Allen Jefferies

Born: Feb. 13, 1980. Fresno, CA, United States.   Height: 6'8".   Weight: 225 lbs.   Drafted: 2002   College: Fresno State

YEAR	TEAM	GP	GS	MIN	PTS	FGM	FGA	FG%	3PM	3PA	3P%	FTM	FTA	FT%	ORB	DRB	TRB	AST	PF	DQ	STL	BLK	TO	MPG	PPG	RPG	APG	PCM
02-03	Toronto	51	10	665	197	75	194	.387	18	54	.333	29	43	.674	16	43	59	22	56	0	19	16	45	13.0	3.9	1.2	0.4	.189
NBA Season Totals		51	10	665	197	75	194	.387	18	54	.333	29	43	.674	16	43	59	22	56	0	19	16	45	13.0	3.9	1.2	0.4	....

• JEFFERSON, Richard

Richard Allen Jefferson

Born: June 21, 1980. Los Angeles, CA, United States.   Height: 6'7".   Weight: 222 lbs.   Drafted: 2001   College: Arizona

YEAR	TEAM	GP	GS	MIN	PTS	FGM	FGA	FG%	3PM	3PA	3P%	FTM	FTA	FT%	ORB	DRB	TRB	AST	PF	DQ	STL	BLK	TO	MPG	PPG	RPG	APG	PCM
01-02	New Jersey	79	9	1917	742	270	591	.457	13	56	.232	189	265	.713	85	208	293	140	211	5	64	48	107	24.3	9.4	3.7	1.8	.388
02-03	New Jersey	80	80	2878	1242	456	911	.501	6	24	.250	324	436	.743	150	364	514	201	216	1	80	44	156	36.0	15.5	6.4	2.5	.465
NBA Season Totals		159	89	4795	1984	726	1502	.483	19	80	.238	513	701	.732	235	572	807	341	427	6	144	92	263	30.2	12.5	5.1	2.1	....
01-02	New Jersey	20	0	441	139	53	114	.465	0	2	.000	33	60	.550	16	76	92	25	40	0	11	9	26	22.1	7.0	4.6	1.3	.360
02-03	New Jersey	20	20	711	281	110	231	.476	0	3	.000	61	85	.718	29	98	127	47	67	0	16	4	46	35.6	14.1	6.4	2.4	.384
NBA Playoff Totals		40	20	1152	420	163	345	.472	0	5	.000	94	145	.648	45	174	219	72	107	0	27	13	72	28.8	10.5	5.5	1.8	....

• JEFFRIES, Jared

Jared Scott Carter Jeffries

Born: Nov. 25, 1981. Bloomington, IN, United States.   Height: 6'11".   Weight: 230 lbs.   Drafted: 2002   College: Indiana

YEAR	TEAM	GP	GS	MIN	PTS	FGM	FGA	FG%	3PM	3PA	3P%	FTM	FTA	FT%	ORB	DRB	TRB	AST	PF	DQ	STL	BLK	TO	MPG	PPG	RPG	APG	PCM
02-03	Washington	20	1	291	79	30	63	.476	3	6	.500	16	29	.552	26	32	58	16	28	0	8	5	21	14.6	4.0	2.9	0.8	.321
NBA Season Totals		20	1	291	79	30	63	.476	3	6	.500	16	29	.552	26	32	58	16	28	0	8	5	21	14.6	4.0	2.9	0.8	....

• JENNINGS, Jack

Jack Jennings

Born: 1918.   Height: 6'6".   Weight: 195 lbs.   Drafted: —   College: Washington State

YEAR	TEAM	GP	GS	MIN	PTS	FGM	FGA	FG%	3PM	3PA	3P%	FTM	FTA	FT%	ORB	DRB	TRB	AST	PF	DQ	STL	BLK	TO	MPG	PPG	RPG	APG	PCM
40-41	Non-Skids-N	19	....	....	94	41	....	....	....	....	....	12													4.9			
NBL Season Totals		19	....	....	94	41	....	....	....	....	....	12													4.9			
40-41	Non-Skids-N	2	....	....	4	2	....	....	....	....	....	0													2.0			
NBL Playoff Totals		2	....	....	4	2	....	....	....	....	....	0													2.0			

• JENNINGS, Keith

Keith Russell (Mister) Jennings

Born: Nov. 2, 1968. Culpepper, VA, United States.   Height: 5'7".   Weight: 160 lbs.   Drafted: —   College: East Tennessee State

YEAR	TEAM	GP	GS	MIN	PTS	FGM	FGA	FG%	3PM	3PA	3P%	FTM	FTA	FT%	ORB	DRB	TRB	AST	PF	DQ	STL	BLK	TO	MPG	PPG	RPG	APG	PCM
92-93	Golden State	8	0	136	69	25	42	.595	5	9	.556	14	18	.778	2	9	11	23	18	0	4	0	7	17.0	8.6	1.4	2.9	.551
93-94	Golden State	76	2	1097	432	138	342	.404	56	151	.371	100	120	.833	16	73	89	218	62	0	65	0	76	14.4	5.7	1.2	2.9	.469
94-95	Golden State	80	24	1722	589	190	425	.447	75	204	.368	134	153	.876	26	122	148	373	133	0	95	2	120	21.5	7.4	1.9	4.7	.471
NBA Season Totals		164	26	2955	1090	353	809	.436	136	364	.374	248	291	.852	44	204	248	614	213	0	164	2	203	18.0	6.6	1.5	3.7	....
93-94	Golden State	3	0	39	15	4	13	.308	1	5	.200	6	7	.857	1	4	5	4	11	0	1	0	4	13.0	5.0	1.7	1.3	.190
NBA Playoff Totals		3	0	39	15	4	13	.308	1	5	.200	6	7	.857	1	4	5	4	11	0	1	0	4	13.0	5.0	1.7	1.3	....

• JENT, Chris

Chris Jent

Born: Jan. 11, 1970. Orange, CA, United States.   Height: 6'7".   Weight: 220 lbs.   Drafted: —   College: Ohio State

YEAR	TEAM	GP	GS	MIN	PTS	FGM	FGA	FG%	3PM	3PA	3P%	FTM	FTA	FT%	ORB	DRB	TRB	AST	PF	DQ	STL	BLK	TO	MPG	PPG	RPG	APG	PCM
93-94	Houston	3	0	78	31	13	26	.500	4	11	.364	1	2	.500	4	11	15	7	13	1	0	0	5	26.0	10.3	5.0	2.3	.377

YEAR	TEAM	GP	GS	MIN	PTS	FGM	FGA	FG%	3PM	3PA	3P%	FTM	FTA	FT%	ORB	DRB	TRB	AST	PF	DQ	STL	BLK	TO	MPG	PPG	RPG	APG	PCM
96-97	New York	3	0	10	6	2	6	.333	2	3	.667	0	0	.000	1	0	1	1	2	0	0	0	0	3.3	2.0	0.3	0.3	.334
NBA Season Totals		6	0	88	37	15	32	.469	6	14	.429	1	2	.500	5	11	16	8	15	1	0	0	5	14.7	6.2	2.7	1.3	....
93-94	Houston	11	0	62	13	5	20	.250	3	13	.231	0	0	.000	1	8	9	7	7	0	2	0	3	5.6	1.2	0.8	0.6	.177
NBA Playoff Totals		11	0	62	13	5	20	.250	3	13	.231	0	0	.000	1	8	9	7	7	0	2	0	3	5.6	1.2	0.8	0.6	....

• JEPSEN, Les
Leslie Burnell (Big Boy) Jepsen

Born: June 24, 1967. Bowbells, ND, United States.   Height: 7'   Weight: 237 lbs.   Drafted: 1990   College: Iowa

YEAR	TEAM	GP	GS	MIN	PTS	FGM	FGA	FG%	3PM	3PA	3P%	FTM	FTA	FT%	ORB	DRB	TRB	AST	PF	DQ	STL	BLK	TO	MPG	PPG	RPG	APG	PCM
90-91	Golden State	21	0	105	28	11	36	.306	0	1	.000	6	9	.667	17	20	37	1	16	0	1	3	2	5.0	1.3	1.8	0.0	.317
91-92	Sacramento	31	0	87	25	9	24	.375	0	1	.000	7	11	.636	12	18	30	1	17	0	1	5	3	2.8	0.8	1.0	0.0	.380
NBA Season Totals		52	0	192	53	20	60	.333	0	2	.000	13	20	.650	29	38	67	2	33	0	2	8	5	3.7	1.0	1.3	0.0	....

• JESKO, Bill
Bill Jesko

Born: 1915.   Height: 5'10".   Weight: 170 lbs.   Drafted: —   College: Pittsburgh

YEAR	TEAM	GP	GS	MIN	PTS	FGM	FGA	FG%	3PM	3PA	3P%	FTM	FTA	FT%	ORB	DRB	TRB	AST	PF	DQ	STL	BLK	TO	MPG	PPG	RPG	APG	PCM
37-38	Pittsburgh-N	10	....	....	42	14	....	....	....	....	....	14	....	....	....	....	....	....	....	....	....	....	....	4.2	....	....	....
38-39	Pittsburgh-N	24	....	....	151	66	....	....	....	....	....	19	....	....	....	....	....	....	....	....	....	....	....	6.3	....	....	....
NBL Season Totals		34	....	....	193	80	....	....	....	....	....	33	....	....	....	....	....	....	....	....	....	....	....	5.7	....	....	....

• JETER, Hal
Harold Jeter

Born: May 17, 1945.   Height: 6'3".   Weight: 190 lbs.   Drafted: —   College: Drake

YEAR	TEAM	GP	GS	MIN	PTS	FGM	FGA	FG%	3PM	3PA	3P%	FTM	FTA	FT%	ORB	DRB	TRB	AST	PF	DQ	STL	BLK	TO	MPG	PPG	RPG	APG	PCM
69-70	Washington-A	5	....	19	2	1	4	.250	0	0	.000	0	0	.000	1	0	1	0	8	0	....	....	3	3.8	0.4	0.2	0.0	-.166
ABA Season Totals		5	....	19	2	1	4	.250	0	0	.000	0	0	.000	1	0	1	0	8	0	....	....	3	3.8	0.4	0.2	0.0	....

• JOACHIM, Charlie
Charlie (Pappy) Joachim

Born: 1920.   Height: 6'2".   Weight: 184 lbs.   Drafted: —   College: Mt. Union

YEAR	TEAM	GP	GS	MIN	PTS	FGM	FGA	FG%	3PM	3PA	3P%	FTM	FTA	FT%	ORB	DRB	TRB	AST	PF	DQ	STL	BLK	TO	MPG	PPG	RPG	APG	PCM
46-47	Youngstown-N	33	....	....	352	125	....	....	....	....	....	102	143	.713	....	....	....	120	....	....	....	....	....	10.7	....	....	....
47-48	Flint-N	15	....	....	65	19	....	....	....	....	....	27	37	.730	....	....	....	....	....	....	....	....	....	4.3	....	....	....
NBL Season Totals		48	....	....	417	144	....	....	....	....	....	129	180	....	....	....	....	120	....	....	....	....	....	8.7	....	....	....

• JOHNSON, Al
Al (Big Train) Johnson

Born: 1913.   Height: 6'3".   Weight: 210 lbs.   Drafted: —   College: Illinois

YEAR	TEAM	GP	GS	MIN	PTS	FGM	FGA	FG%	3PM	3PA	3P%	FTM	FTA	FT%	ORB	DRB	TRB	AST	PF	DQ	STL	BLK	TO	MPG	PPG	RPG	APG	PCM
42-43	Chicago-N	1	....	....	2	1	....	....	....	....	....	0	....	....	....	....	....	....	....	....	....	....	....	2.0	....	....	....
NBL Season Totals		1	....	....	2	1	....	....	....	....	....	0	....	....	....	....	....	....	....	....	....	....	....	2.0	....	....	....
42-43	Chicago-N	2	....	....	0	0	....	....	....	....	....	0	....	....	....	....	....	....	....	....	....	....	....	0.0	....	....	....
NBL Playoff Totals		2	....	....	0	0	....	....	....	....	....	0	....	....	....	....	....	....	....	....	....	....	....	0.0	....	....	....

• JOHNSON, Andy
Andrew Johnson Jr.

Born: Nov. 8, 1932. Kalamazoo, MI, United States.   Height: 6'5".   Weight: 215 lbs.   Drafted: —   College: Portland

YEAR	TEAM	GP	GS	MIN	PTS	FGM	FGA	FG%	3PM	3PA	3P%	FTM	FTA	FT%	ORB	DRB	TRB	AST	PF	DQ	STL	BLK	TO	MPG	PPG	RPG	APG	PCM
58-59	Philadelphia	67	....	1158	463	174	466	.373	....	....	....	115	191	.602	....	....	212	90	176	4	....	....	....	17.3	6.9	3.2	1.3	.363
59-60	Philadelphia	75	....	1421	615	245	648	.378	....	....	....	125	208	.601	....	....	282	152	196	5	....	....	....	18.9	8.2	3.8	2.0	.427
60-61	Philadelphia	79	....	2000	755	299	834	.359	....	....	....	157	275	.571	....	....	345	205	196	3	....	....	....	25.3	9.6	4.4	2.6	.362
61-62	Chicago	71	....	2193	1014	365	814	.448	....	....	....	284	452	.628	....	....	351	228	247	5	....	....	....	30.9	14.3	4.9	3.2	.480
NBA Season Totals		292	....	6772	2847	1083	2762	.392	....	....	....	681	1126	.605	....	....	1190	675	868	17	....	....	....	23.2	9.8	4.1	2.3	....
59-60	Philadelphia	9	....	183	80	28	67	.418	....	....	....	24	47	.511	....	....	45	21	26	1	....	....	....	20.3	8.9	5.0	2.3	.503
60-61	Philadelphia	3	....	50	20	7	22	.318	....	....	....	6	9	.667	....	....	10	1	11	0	....	....	....	16.7	6.7	3.3	0.3	.242
NBA Playoff Totals		12	....	233	100	35	89	.393	....	....	....	30	56	.536	....	....	55	22	37	1	....	....	....	19.4	8.3	4.6	1.8	....

• JOHNSON, Anthony
Anthony Mark Johnson

Born: Oct. 10, 1974. Charleston, SC, United States.   Height: 6'3".   Weight: 190 lbs.   Drafted: 1997   College: College of Charleston

YEAR	TEAM	GP	GS	MIN	PTS	FGM	FGA	FG%	3PM	3PA	3P%	FTM	FTA	FT%	ORB	DRB	TRB	AST	PF	DQ	STL	BLK	TO	MPG	PPG	RPG	APG	PCM
97-98	Sacramento	77	62	2266	574	226	609	.371	42	128	.328	80	110	.727	51	120	171	329	188	1	64	6	123	29.4	7.5	2.2	4.3	.260
98-99	Atlanta	49	2	885	244	91	225	.404	5	19	.263	57	82	.695	16	59	75	107	67	0	35	7	65	18.1	5.0	1.5	2.2	.281
99-00	Atlanta	38	2	423	92	36	103	.350	1	6	.167	19	24	.792	15	24	39	59	41	0	23	2	24	11.1	2.4	1.0	1.6	.262
99-00	Orlando	18	4	214	62	26	61	.426	1	5	.200	9	15	.600	6	6	12	13	17	0	10	2	8	11.9	3.4	0.7	0.7	.227
00-01	Atlanta	25	0	279	64	26	71	.366	0	3	.000	12	17	.706	3	20	23	34	41	0	17	5	20	11.2	2.6	0.9	1.4	.225
00-01	Cleveland	28	0	232	66	27	81	.333	1	2	.500	11	16	.688	7	14	21	44	21	0	6	1	14	8.3	2.4	0.8	1.6	.288
01-02	New Jersey	34	0	366	94	37	90	.411	4	12	.333	16	25	.640	10	19	29	48	30	0	31	1	20	10.8	2.8	0.9	1.4	.322
02-03	New Jersey	66	2	842	270	103	231	.446	13	35	.371	51	74	.689	13	65	78	86	93	1	37	5	41	12.8	4.1	1.2	1.3	.317
NBA Season Totals		335	72	5507	1466	572	1471	.389	67	210	.319	255	363	.702	121	327	448	720	498	2	223	29	315	16.4	4.4	1.3	2.1	....
98-99	Atlanta	9	0	111	24	8	29	.276	1	2	.500	7	10	.700	3	6	9	10	9	0	1	1	5	12.3	2.7	1.0	1.1	.148
01-02	New Jersey	19	0	161	50	20	53	.377	1	10	.100	9	11	.818	2	12	14	21	24	0	6	0	8	8.5	2.6	0.7	1.1	.262
02-03	New Jersey	17	0	122	42	17	31	.548	3	6	.500	5	6	.833	3	9	12	19	15	0	2	0	8	7.2	2.5	0.7	1.1	.395
NBA Playoff Totals		45	0	394	116	45	113	.398	5	18	.278	21	27	.778	8	27	35	50	48	0	9	1	21	8.8	2.6	0.8	1.1	....

• JOHNSON, Arnie

Arnitz L. Johnson

Born: May 17, 1920. Gonvick, MN, United States. Height: 6'5". Weight: 236 lbs. Drafted: — College: Bemidji State

YEAR	TEAM	GP	GS	MIN	PTS	FGM	FGA	FG%	3PM	3PA	3P%	FTM	FTA	FT%	ORB	DRB	TRB	AST	PF	DQ	STL	BLK	TO	MPG	PPG	RPG	APG	PCM
46-47	Rochester-N	32	....	....	204	68	....	....	....	....	....	68	98	.694	....	....	....	....	74	....	....	....	....	....	6.4	....	....	....
47-48	Rochester-N	57	....	....	299	101	....	....	....	....	....	97	147	.660	....	....	....	....	153	....	....	....	....	....	5.2	....	....	....
48-49	Rochester	60	....	....	511	156	375	.416	....	....	....	199	284	.701	....	....	....	80	247	....	....	....	....	....	8.5	....	1.3	....
49-50	Rochester	68	....	....	498	149	376	.396	....	....	....	200	294	.680	....	....	....	141	260	....	....	....	....	....	7.3	....	2.1	....
50-51	Rochester	68	....	....	639	185	403	.459	....	....	....	269	371	.725	....	....	449	175	290	11	....	....	....	....	9.4	6.6	2.6	....
51-52	Rochester	66	....	2158	657	178	411	.433	....	....	....	301	387	.778	....	....	404	182	259	9	....	....	....	32.7	10.0	6.1	2.8	.413
52-53	Rochester	70	....	1984	583	140	369	.379	....	....	....	303	405	.748	....	....	419	153	282	14	....	....	....	28.3	8.3	6.0	2.2	.392
NBA Season Totals		332	....	4142	2888	808	1934	.418	....	....	....	1272	1741	.731	....	....	1272	731	1338	34	....	....	....	12.5	8.7	3.8	2.2	....
NBL Season Totals		89	....	....	503	169	....	....	....	....	....	165	245	....	....	....	....	....	227	....	....	....	....	....	5.7	....	....	....
Career Totals		421	....	4142	3391	977	1934	....	....	....	....	1437	1986	....	....	....	1272	731	1565	34	....	....	....	9.8	8.1	3.0	1.7	....
47-48	Rochester-N	11	....	....	66	23	....	....	....	....	....	20	24	.833	....	....	....	....	....	....	....	....	....	....	6.0	....	....	....
48-49	Rochester	4	....	....	38	11	41	.268	....	....	....	16	22	.727	....	....	....	7	16	....	....	....	....	....	9.5	....	1.8	....
49-50	Rochester	2	....	....	20	6	12	.500	....	....	....	8	12	.667	....	....	....	5	11	....	....	....	....	....	10.0	....	2.5	....
50-51	Rochester	14	....	....	157	48	107	.449	....	....	....	61	78	.782	....	....	126	40	68	2	....	....	....	....	11.2	9.0	2.9	....
51-52	Rochester	6	....	166	39	8	27	.296	....	....	....	23	32	.719	....	....	31	24	27	0	....	....	....	27.7	6.5	5.2	4.0	.396
52-53	Rochester	3	....	87	24	4	14	.286	....	....	....	16	21	.762	....	....	18	6	15	1	....	....	....	29.0	8.0	6.0	2.0	.347
NBA Playoff Totals		29	....	253	278	77	201	.383	....	....	....	124	165	.752	....	....	175	82	137	3	....	....	....	8.7	9.6	6.0	2.8	....
NBL Playoff Totals		11	....	....	66	23	....	....	....	....	....	20	24	....	....	....	....	....	....	....	....	....	....	....	6.0	....	....	....
Career Playoff Totals		40	....	253	344	100	201	....	....	....	....	144	189	....	....	....	175	82	137	3	....	....	....	6.3	8.6	4.4	2.1	....

• JOHNSON, Avery

Avery (Taz) Johnson

Born: Mar. 25, 1965. New Orleans, LA, United States. Height: 5'10". Weight: 175 lbs. Drafted: — College: Southern

YEAR	TEAM	GP	GS	MIN	PTS	FGM	FGA	FG%	3PM	3PA	3P%	FTM	FTA	FT%	ORB	DRB	TRB	AST	PF	DQ	STL	BLK	TO	MPG	PPG	RPG	APG	PCM
88-89	Seattle	43	0	291	68	29	83	.349	1	9	.111	9	16	.563	11	13	24	73	34	0	21	3	17	6.8	1.6	0.6	1.7	.363
89-90	Seattle	53	10	575	140	55	142	.387	1	4	.250	29	40	.725	21	22	43	162	55	0	26	1	48	10.8	2.6	0.8	3.1	.383
90-91	Denver	21	4	217	79	29	68	.426	0	4	.000	21	32	.656	9	12	21	77	22	0	14	2	27	10.3	3.8	1.0	3.7	.547
90-91	San Antonio	47	10	742	241	101	209	.483	1	5	.200	38	55	.691	13	43	56	153	40	0	33	2	47	15.8	5.1	1.2	3.3	.429
91-92	San Antonio	20	14	463	135	55	108	.509	1	5	.200	24	32	.750	5	30	35	100	43	1	21	3	46	23.2	6.8	1.8	5.0	.391
91-92	Houston	49	1	772	251	103	222	.464	3	10	.300	42	69	.609	8	37	45	166	46	0	40	6	64	15.8	5.1	0.9	3.4	.401
92-93	San Antonio	75	49	2030	656	256	510	.502	0	8	.000	144	182	.791	20	126	146	561	141	0	85	16	143	27.1	8.7	1.9	7.5	.508
93-94	Golden State	82	70	2332	890	356	724	.492	0	12	.000	178	253	.704	41	135	176	433	160	0	113	8	172	28.4	10.9	2.1	5.3	.441
94-95	San Antonio	82	82	3011	1101	448	863	.519	3	22	.136	202	295	.685	49	159	208	670	154	0	114	13	205	36.7	13.4	2.5	8.2	.475
95-96	San Antonio	82	82	3084	1071	438	887	.494	6	31	.194	189	262	.721	37	169	206	789	179	1	119	21	197	37.6	13.1	2.5	9.6	.489
96-97	San Antonio	76	76	2472	800	327	685	.477	6	26	.231	140	203	.690	32	115	147	513	158	1	96	15	144	32.5	10.5	1.9	6.8	.412
97-98	San Antonio	75	73	2674	766	321	671	.478	2	13	.154	122	168	.726	30	120	150	591	140	0	84	18	165	35.7	10.2	2.0	7.9	.404
98-99	San Antonio	50	50	1672	487	218	461	.473	1	12	.083	50	88	.568	22	96	118	369	101	0	51	11	112	33.4	9.7	2.4	7.4	.406
99-00	San Antonio	82	82	2571	919	402	850	.473	1	9	.111	114	155	.735	33	125	158	491	150	0	76	18	140	31.4	11.2	1.9	6.0	.414
00-01	San Antonio	55	20	1290	310	134	300	.447	1	6	.167	41	60	.683	21	64	85	237	90	0	33	4	60	23.5	5.6	1.5	4.3	.332
01-02	Denver	51	13	1200	481	186	383	.486	0	5	.000	109	146	.747	14	50	64	258	69	0	35	8	67	23.5	9.4	1.3	5.1	.477
01-02	Dallas	17	0	152	54	21	49	.429	0	0	.000	12	17	.706	0	5	5	28	17	0	5	1	9	8.9	3.2	0.3	1.6	.336
02-03	Dallas	48	0	430	156	63	150	.420	0	2	.000	30	39	.769	10	21	31	64	26	0	15	1	29	9.0	3.3	0.6	1.3	.343
NBA Season Totals		1008	636	25978	8605	3542	7365	.481	27	183	.148	1494	2112	.707	376	1342	1718	5735	1625	3	981	151	1692	25.8	8.5	1.7	5.7	....
88-89	Seattle	6	0	31	11	5	12	.417	0	4	.000	1	2	.500	2	2	4	5	1	0	4	0	0	5.2	1.8	0.7	0.8	.527
90-91	San Antonio	3	0	19	2	0	5	.000	0	1	.000	2	2	1.000	0	0	0	4	3	0	1	0	0	6.3	0.7	0.0	1.3	.060
92-93	San Antonio	10	10	314	82	36	70	.514	0	1	.000	10	14	.714	8	23	31	81	27	0	10	1	23	31.4	8.2	3.1	8.1	.446
93-94	Golden State	3	0	41	18	9	17	.529	0	1	.000	0	0	.000	0	3	3	10	2	0	4	1	3	13.7	6.0	1.0	3.3	.614
94-95	San Antonio	15	15	575	218	91	176	.517	0	1	.000	36	58	.621	9	23	32	125	29	0	20	6	30	38.3	14.5	2.1	8.3	.475
95-96	San Antonio	10	10	407	123	52	121	.430	0	2	.000	19	27	.704	6	30	36	94	21	0	20	1	24	40.7	12.3	3.6	9.4	.430
97-98	San Antonio	9	9	342	156	61	101	.604	0	2	.000	34	51	.667	3	10	13	55	27	0	9	0	21	38.0	17.3	1.4	6.1	.467
98-99	San Antonio	17	17	653	215	91	187	.487	1	3	.333	32	47	.681	9	33	42	126	30	0	20	1	50	38.4	12.6	2.5	7.4	.400
99-00	San Antonio	4	4	144	48	19	42	.452	0	0	.000	10	14	.714	2	7	9	21	10	0	4	0	10	36.0	12.0	2.3	5.3	.322
00-01	San Antonio	13	0	281	76	34	88	.386	0	1	.000	8	15	.533	3	13	16	41	24	1	10	1	10	21.6	5.8	1.2	3.2	.263
NBA Playoff Totals		90	65	2807	949	398	819	.486	1	16	.063	152	230	.661	42	144	186	562	174	1	102	11	171	31.2	10.5	2.1	6.2	....

• JOHNSON, Bob

Bob Johnson

Born: 1917. Height: 6'2". Weight: 170 lbs. Drafted: — College: Pittsburgh

YEAR	TEAM	GP	GS	MIN	PTS	FGM	FGA	FG%	3PM	3PA	3P%	FTM	FTA	FT%	ORB	DRB	TRB	AST	PF	DQ	STL	BLK	TO	MPG	PPG	RPG	APG	PCM
38-39	Wingfoots-N	4	....	....	15	6	....	....	....	....	....	3	....	....	....	....	....	....	....	....	....	....	....	....	3.8	....	....	....
NBL Season Totals		4	....	....	15	6	....	....	....	....	....	3	....	....	....	....	....	....	....	....	....	....	....	....	3.8	....	....	....

• JOHNSON, Buck

Alfonso (Buck) Johnson Jr.

Born: Jan. 3, 1964. Birmingham, AL, United States. Height: 6'7". Weight: 190 lbs. Drafted: 1986 College: Alabama

YEAR	TEAM	GP	GS	MIN	PTS	FGM	FGA	FG%	3PM	3PA	3P%	FTM	FTA	FT%	ORB	DRB	TRB	AST	PF	DQ	STL	BLK	TO	MPG	PPG	RPG	APG	PCM
86-87	Houston	60	3	520	228	94	201	.468	0	1	.000	40	58	.690	38	50	88	40	81	0	17	15	36	8.7	3.8	1.5	0.7	.391
87-88	Houston	70	2	879	378	155	298	.520	1	8	.125	67	91	.736	77	91	168	49	127	0	30	26	56	12.6	5.4	2.4	0.7	.436
88-89	Houston	67	51	1850	642	270	515	.524	1	9	.111	101	134	.754	114	172	286	126	213	4	64	35	107	27.6	9.6	4.3	1.9	.375
89-90	Houston	82	82	2832	1215	504	1019	.495	2	17	.118	205	270	.759	113	268	381	252	321	8	104	62	164	34.5	14.8	4.6	3.1	.416
90-91	Houston	73	70	2279	991	416	873	.477	2	15	.133	157	216	.727	108	222	330	142	240	5	81	47	124	31.2	13.6	4.5	1.9	.350
91-92	Houston	80	69	2202	685	290	633	.458	1	9	.111	104	143	.727	95	217	312	158	234	2	72	49	104	27.5	8.6	3.9	2.0	.324
92-93	Washington	73	19	1287	478	193	403	.479	0	3	.000	92	126	.730	78	117	195	89	187	2	36	18	73	17.6	6.5	2.7	1.2	.340
NBA Season Totals		505	296	11849	4617	1922	3942	.488	7	62	.113	766	1038	.738	623	1137	1760	856	1403	21	404	252	664	23.5	9.1	3.5	1.7	....
86-87	Houston	5	0	10	4	2	6	.333	0	0	.000	0	0	.000	0	0	0	0	1	0	0	0	2	2.0	0.8	0.0	0.0	-.205

YEAR	TEAM	GP	GS	MIN	PTS	FGM	FGA	FG%	3PM	3PA	3P%	FTM	FTA	FT%	ORB	DRB	TRB	AST	PF	DQ	STL	BLK	TO	MPG	PPG	RPG	APG	PCM
87-88	Houston	4	0	20	5	2	3	.667	0	0	.000	1	2	.500	2	2	4	0	1	0	1	0	4	5.0	1.3	1.0	0.0	.203
88-89	Houston	4	4	118	46	19	40	.475	0	1	.000	8	14	.571	7	8	15	13	15	0	3	2	6	29.5	11.5	3.8	3.3	.370
89-90	Houston	4	4	148	51	20	48	.417	0	1	.000	11	13	.846	8	8	16	9	16	0	6	2	4	37.0	12.8	4.0	2.3	.302
90-91	Houston	3	3	86	24	10	28	.357	0	0	.000	4	4	1.000	4	10	14	8	13	0	2	1	5	28.7	8.0	4.7	2.7	.243
NBA Playoff Totals		20	11	382	130	53	125	.424	0	2	.000	24	33	.727	21	28	49	30	46	0	12	5	21	19.1	6.5	2.5	1.5	....

• JOHNSON, Charles

Charles (C.J.) Johnson

Born: Mar. 31, 1949. Corpus Christi, TX, United States.   Height: 6'   Weight: 170 lbs.   Drafted: 1971   College: California

YEAR	TEAM	GP	GS	MIN	PTS	FGM	FGA	FG%	3PM	3PA	3P%	FTM	FTA	FT%	ORB	DRB	TRB	AST	PF	DQ	STL	BLK	TO	MPG	PPG	RPG	APG	PCM
72-73	Golden State	70	....	887	375	171	400	.428	....	....	....	33	46	.717	....	....	132	118	105	0	....	....	....	12.7	5.4	1.9	1.7	.424
73-74	Golden State	59	....	1051	426	194	468	.415	....	....	....	38	55	.691	49	126	175	102	111	1	62	7	....	17.8	7.2	3.0	1.7	.385
74-75	Golden State	79	....	2171	863	394	957	.412	....	....	....	75	102	.735	134	177	311	233	204	2	138	8	....	27.5	10.9	3.9	2.9	.376
75-76	Golden State	81	....	1549	744	342	732	.467	....	....	....	60	79	.759	77	125	202	122	178	1	100	7	....	19.1	9.2	2.5	1.5	.412
76-77	Golden State	79	....	1196	559	255	583	.437	....	....	....	49	69	.710	50	91	141	91	134	1	77	7	....	15.1	7.1	1.8	1.2	.363
77-78	Golden State	32	....	492	199	96	235	.409	....	....	....	7	10	.700	23	39	62	48	53	0	31	4	22	15.4	6.2	1.9	1.5	.351
77-78	Washington	39	....	807	324	141	346	.408	....	....	....	42	51	.824	20	73	93	82	76	0	31	1	51	20.7	8.3	2.4	2.1	.328
78-79	Washington	82	....	1819	751	342	786	.435	....	....	....	67	79	.848	70	132	202	177	161	0	95	6	90	22.2	9.2	2.5	2.2	.363
NBA Season Totals		521		9972	4241	1935	4507	.429	....	....	....	371	491	.756	423	763	1318	973	1022	5	534	40	163	19.1	8.1	2.5	1.9	....
72-73	Golden State	6	....	70	23	10	26	.385	....	....	....	3	6	.500	....	....	10	11	4	0	....	....	....	11.7	3.8	1.7	1.8	.392
74-75	Golden State	17	....	508	212	97	231	.420	....	....	....	18	24	.750	19	41	60	35	54	1	25	6	....	29.9	12.5	3.5	2.1	.322
75-76	Golden State	13	....	284	120	52	127	.409	....	....	....	16	19	.842	14	21	35	20	39	0	22	0	....	21.8	9.2	2.7	1.5	.319
76-77	Golden State	10	....	161	65	29	74	.392	....	....	....	7	8	.875	5	10	15	7	16	0	8	1	....	16.1	6.5	1.5	0.7	.247
77-78	Washington	21	....	425	215	93	229	.406	....	....	....	29	37	.784	20	33	53	48	51	0	30	0	26	20.2	10.2	2.5	2.3	.410
78-79	Washington	18	....	275	87	40	119	.336	....	....	....	7	13	.538	13	21	34	21	37	0	3	3	11	15.3	4.8	1.9	1.2	.167
NBA Playoff Totals		85		1723	722	321	806	.398	....	....	....	80	107	.748	71	126	207	142	201	1	88	10	37	20.3	8.5	2.4	1.7	....

• JOHNSON, Cheese

Lynbert R. (Cheese) Johnson

Born: Sept. 7, 1957. New York, NY, United States.   Height: 6'6".   Weight: 195 lbs.   Drafted: 1979   College: Wichita State

YEAR	TEAM	GP	GS	MIN	PTS	FGM	FGA	FG%	3PM	3PA	3P%	FTM	FTA	FT%	ORB	DRB	TRB	AST	PF	DQ	STL	BLK	TO	MPG	PPG	RPG	APG	PCM
79-80	Golden State	9	....	53	27	12	30	.400	0	0	.000	3	5	.600	6	8	14	2	11	0	1	0	4	5.9	3.0	1.6	0.2	.320
NBA Season Totals		9	....	53	27	12	30	.400	0	0	.000	3	5	.600	6	8	14	2	11	0	1	0	4	5.9	3.0	1.6	0.2	....

• JOHNSON, Clay

Clayton H. Johnson

Born: July 18, 1956. Yazoo City, MS, United States.   Height: 6'4".   Weight: 175 lbs.   Drafted: 1978   College: Missouri

YEAR	TEAM	GP	GS	MIN	PTS	FGM	FGA	FG%	3PM	3PA	3P%	FTM	FTA	FT%	ORB	DRB	TRB	AST	PF	DQ	STL	BLK	TO	MPG	PPG	RPG	APG	PCM
81-82	LA Lakers	7	0	65	25	11	20	.550	0	0	.000	3	6	.500	8	4	12	7	13	0	3	3	7	9.3	3.6	1.7	1.0	.416
82-83	LA Lakers	48	0	447	144	53	135	.393	0	2	.000	38	48	.792	40	29	69	24	62	0	22	4	24	9.3	3.0	1.4	0.5	.286
83-84	Seattle	25	0	176	55	20	50	.400	1	1	1.000	14	22	.636	6	6	12	14	24	0	8	2	13	7.0	2.2	0.5	0.6	.202
NBA Season Totals		80	0	688	224	84	205	.410	1	3	.333	55	76	.724	54	39	93	45	99	0	33	9	44	8.6	2.8	1.2	0.6	....
81-82	LA Lakers	7	0	38	12	5	9	.556	0	0	.000	2	2	1.000	1	2	3	1	6	0	1	0	1	5.4	1.7	0.4	0.1	.247
82-83	LA Lakers	7	0	20	8	4	7	.571	0	1	.000	0	0	.000	2	2	4	1	3	0	1	0	1	2.9	1.1	0.6	0.1	.432
83-84	Seattle	3	0	9	4	2	4	.500	0	1	.000	0	0	.000	1	0	1	1	3	0	1	0	0	3.0	1.3	0.3	0.3	.408
NBA Playoff Totals		17	0	67	24	11	20	.550	0	2	.000	2	2	1.000	4	4	8	3	12	0	3	0	2	3.9	1.4	0.5	0.2	....

• JOHNSON, Clemon

Clemon Johnson

Born: Sept. 12, 1956. Monticello, FL, United States.   Height: 6'10".   Weight: 240 lbs.   Drafted: 1978   College: Florida A&M

YEAR	TEAM	GP	GS	MIN	PTS	FGM	FGA	FG%	3PM	3PA	3P%	FTM	FTA	FT%	ORB	DRB	TRB	AST	PF	DQ	STL	BLK	TO	MPG	PPG	RPG	APG	PCM
78-79	Portland	74	....	794	240	102	217	.470	....	....	....	36	74	.486	83	143	226	78	121	1	23	36	67	10.7	3.2	3.1	1.1	.437
79-80	Indiana	79	....	1541	472	199	396	.503	0	0	.000	74	117	.632	145	249	394	115	211	2	48	121	79	19.5	6.0	5.0	1.5	.482
80-81	Indiana	81	....	1643	582	235	466	.504	0	1	.000	112	189	.593	173	295	468	144	185	1	44	119	122	20.3	7.2	5.8	1.8	.531
81-82	Indiana	79	42	1979	747	312	641	.487	0	0	.000	123	189	.651	184	387	571	127	241	3	60	112	134	25.1	9.5	7.2	1.6	.506
82-83	Indiana	51	7	1216	493	208	399	.521	0	1	.000	77	122	.631	115	204	319	115	137	2	51	63	87	23.8	9.7	6.3	2.3	.557
82-83	Philadelphia	32	4	698	216	91	182	.500	0	0	.000	34	58	.586	75	130	205	24	84	1	16	29	35	21.8	6.8	6.4	0.8	.438
83-84	Philadelphia	80	10	1721	455	193	412	.468	0	0	.000	69	113	.611	131	267	398	55	205	1	35	65	96	21.5	5.7	5.0	0.7	.330
84-85	Philadelphia	58	0	875	270	117	235	.498	0	1	.000	36	49	.735	92	129	221	33	112	0	15	44	41	15.1	4.7	3.8	0.6	.411
85-86	Philadelphia	75	2	1069	261	105	223	.471	0	0	.000	51	81	.630	106	149	255	15	129	0	23	62	38	14.3	3.5	3.4	0.2	.350
86-87	Seattle	78	7	1051	246	88	178	.494	0	2	.000	70	110	.636	106	171	277	21	137	0	21	42	39	13.5	3.2	3.6	0.3	.364
87-88	Seattle	74	26	723	120	49	105	.467	0	0	.000	22	32	.688	66	108	174	17	104	0	13	24	30	9.8	1.6	2.4	0.2	.279
NBA Season Totals		761	98	13310	4102	1699	3454	.492	0	5	.000	704	1134	.621	1276	2232	3508	744	1666	11	349	717	768	17.5	5.4	4.6	1.0	....
78-79	Portland	3	....	47	14	4	11	.364	....	....	....	6	11	.545	5	12	17	2	5	0	2	4	7	15.7	4.7	5.7	0.7	.421
80-81	Indiana	2	....	55	15	5	12	.417	0	0	.000	5	10	.500	10	10	20	3	3	0	4	2	3	27.5	7.5	10.0	1.5	.531
82-83	Philadelphia	12	0	202	50	25	49	.510	0	0	.000	0	4	.000	21	22	43	7	28	0	4	5	12	16.8	4.2	3.6	0.6	.286
83-84	Philadelphia	5	0	45	8	4	12	.333	0	0	.000	0	0	.000	3	3	6	0	8	0	1	4	3	9.0	1.6	1.2	0.0	.095
84-85	Philadelphia	13	0	165	42	13	33	.394	0	1	.000	16	21	.762	17	19	36	2	32	0	3	6	13	12.7	3.2	2.8	0.2	.231
85-86	Philadelphia	12	2	303	74	29	53	.547	0	0	.000	16	25	.640	23	37	60	8	35	0	11	15	10	25.3	6.2	5.0	0.7	.364
86-87	Seattle	14	7	262	60	24	53	.453	0	1	.000	12	19	.632	25	24	49	4	18	0	7	15	2	18.7	4.3	3.5	0.3	.343
87-88	Seattle	5	....	39	7	3	7	.429	0	0	.000	1	2	.500	0	7	7	0	10	0	1	1	2	7.8	1.4	1.4	0.0	.120
NBA Playoff Totals		66	9	1118	270	107	230	.465	0	2	.000	56	92	.609	104	134	238	26	139	0	33	52	52	16.9	4.1	3.6	0.4	....

• JOHNSON, Darryl

Darryl Damone Johnson

Born: Oct. 26, 1965. Flint, MI, United States.   Height: 6'1".   Weight: 170 lbs.   Drafted: 1987   College: Michigan State

YEAR	TEAM	GP	GS	MIN	PTS	FGM	FGA	FG%	3PM	3PA	3P%	FTM	FTA	FT%	ORB	DRB	TRB	AST	PF	DQ	STL	BLK	TO	MPG	PPG	RPG	APG	PCM
95-96	Cleveland	11	0	28	12	5	12	.417	0	1	.000	2	2	1.000	2	0	2	1	3	0	0	0	1	2.5	1.1	0.2	0.1	.215
NBA Season Totals		11	0	28	12	5	12	.417	0	1	.000	2	2	1.000	2	0	2	1	3	0	0	0	1	2.5	1.1	0.2	0.1	....

• JOHNSON, Dave

Dave M. Johnson

Born: Nov. 16, 1970. Morgan City, LA, United States. Height: 6'7". Weight: 210 lbs. Drafted: 1992 College: Syracuse

YEAR TEAM	GP	GS	MIN	PTS	FGM	FGA	FG%	3PM	3PA	3P%	FTM	FTA	FT%	ORB	DRB	TRB	AST	PF	DQ	STL	BLK	TO	MPG	PPG	RPG	APG	PCM
92-93 Portland	42	0	356	157	57	149	.383	3	14	.214	40	59	.678	18	30	48	13	23	0	8	1	29	8.5	3.7	1.1	0.3	.257
93-94 Chicago	17	0	119	47	17	54	.315	0	1	.000	13	21	.619	9	7	16	4	7	0	4	0	9	7.0	2.8	0.9	0.2	.173
NBA Season Totals	59	0	475	204	74	203	.365	3	15	.200	53	80	.663	27	37	64	17	30	0	12	1	38	8.1	3.5	1.1	0.3	....

• JOHNSON, DeMarco

DeMarco Antonio Johnson

Born: Oct. 6, 1975. Charlotte, NC, United States. Height: 6'9". Weight: 245 lbs. Drafted: 1998 College: North Carolina (Charlotte)

YEAR TEAM	GP	GS	MIN	PTS	FGM	FGA	FG%	3PM	3PA	3P%	FTM	FTA	FT%	ORB	DRB	TRB	AST	PF	DQ	STL	BLK	TO	MPG	PPG	RPG	APG	PCM
99-00 New York	5	0	37	6	3	9	.333	0	0	.000	0	0	.000	3	4	7	0	5	0	1	0	3	7.4	1.2	1.4	0.0	.076
NBA Season Totals	5	0	37	6	3	9	.333	0	0	.000	0	0	.000	3	4	7	0	5	0	1	0	3	7.4	1.2	1.4	0.0	....

• JOHNSON, Dennis

Dennis Wayne (D.J.) Johnson

Born: Sept. 18, 1954. San Pedro, CA, United States. Height: 6'4". Weight: 185 lbs. Drafted: 1976 College: Pepperdine

YEAR TEAM	GP	GS	MIN	PTS	FGM	FGA	FG%	3PM	3PA	3P%	FTM	FTA	FT%	ORB	DRB	TRB	AST	PF	DQ	STL	BLK	TO	MPG	PPG	RPG	APG	PCM
76-77 Seattle	81	....	1667	749	285	566	.504	....	....	....	179	287	.624	161	141	302	123	221	3	123	57	....	20.6	9.2	3.7	1.5	.459
77-78 Seattle	81	....	2209	1031	367	881	.417	....	....	....	297	406	.732	152	142	294	230	213	2	118	51	162	27.3	12.7	3.6	2.8	.436
78-79 Seattle	80	....	2717	1270	482	1110	.434	....	....	....	306	392	.781	146	228	374	280	209	2	100	97	192	34.0	15.9	4.7	3.5	.450
79-80 Seattle	81	....	2937	1540	574	1361	.422	12	58	.207	380	487	.780	173	241	414	332	267	6	144	82	227	36.3	19.0	5.1	4.1	.475
80-81 Phoenix	79	....	2615	1486	532	1220	.436	11	51	.216	411	501	.820	160	203	363	291	244	2	136	61	205	33.1	18.8	4.6	3.7	.515
81-82 Phoenix	80	77	2937	1561	577	1228	.470	8	42	.190	399	495	.806	142	268	410	369	253	6	105	55	232	36.7	19.5	5.1	4.6	.514
82-83 Phoenix	77	74	2551	1093	398	861	.462	5	31	.161	292	369	.791	92	243	335	388	204	1	97	39	200	33.1	14.2	4.4	5.0	.478
83-84 Boston	80	78	2665	1053	384	878	.437	4	32	.125	281	330	.852	87	193	280	338	251	6	93	57	168	33.3	13.2	3.5	4.2	.398
84-85 Boston	80	77	2976	1254	493	1066	.462	7	26	.269	261	306	.853	91	226	317	543	224	2	96	39	208	37.2	15.7	4.0	6.8	.471
85-86 Boston	78	78	2732	1213	482	1060	.455	6	42	.143	243	297	.818	69	199	268	456	206	3	110	35	172	35.0	15.6	3.4	5.8	.464
86-87 Boston	79	78	2933	1062	423	953	.444	7	62	.113	209	251	.833	45	216	261	594	201	0	87	38	174	37.1	13.4	3.3	7.5	.439
87-88 Boston	77	74	2670	971	352	803	.438	12	46	.261	255	298	.856	62	178	240	598	204	0	93	29	193	34.7	12.6	3.1	7.8	.461
88-89 Boston	72	72	2309	721	277	638	.434	7	50	.140	160	195	.821	31	159	190	472	211	3	94	21	173	32.1	10.0	2.6	6.6	.389
89-90 Boston	75	65	2036	531	206	475	.434	1	24	.042	118	140	.843	48	153	201	485	179	2	81	14	120	27.1	7.1	2.7	6.5	.425
NBA Season Totals	1100	673	35954	15535	5832	13100	.445	80	464	.172	3791	4754	.797	1459	2790	4249	5499	3087	38	1477	675	2426	32.7	14.1	3.9	5.0	....
77-78 Seattle	22	....	827	354	121	294	.412	....	....	....	112	159	.704	47	54	101	72	63	0	23	23	56	37.6	16.1	4.6	3.3	.381
78-79 Seattle	17	....	691	356	136	302	.450	....	....	....	84	109	.771	44	60	104	69	63	0	28	26	51	40.6	20.9	6.1	4.1	.491
79-80 Seattle	15	....	582	257	100	244	.410	5	15	.333	52	62	.839	25	39	64	57	48	2	27	10	43	38.8	17.1	4.3	3.8	.370
80-81 Phoenix	7	....	267	137	52	110	.473	1	5	.200	32	42	.762	7	26	33	20	18	0	9	9	19	38.1	19.6	4.7	2.9	.458
81-82 Phoenix	7	7	271	156	63	132	.477	0	3	.000	30	39	.769	13	18	31	32	28	2	15	4	25	38.7	22.3	4.4	4.6	.491
82-83 Phoenix	3	3	108	54	22	48	.458	0	1	.000	10	12	.833	6	17	23	17	9	0	5	2	8	36.0	18.0	7.7	5.7	.593
83-84 Boston	22	22	808	365	129	319	.404	3	7	.429	104	120	.867	30	49	79	97	75	1	25	7	53	36.7	16.6	3.6	4.4	.376
84-85 Boston	21	21	848	364	142	319	.445	0	14	.000	80	93	.860	24	60	84	154	66	0	31	9	72	40.4	17.3	4.0	7.3	.442
85-86 Boston	18	18	715	291	109	245	.445	6	16	.375	67	84	.798	23	53	76	107	58	2	39	5	51	39.7	16.2	4.2	5.9	.431
86-87 Boston	23	23	964	435	168	361	.465	3	26	.115	96	113	.850	24	67	91	205	71	0	16	8	44	41.9	18.9	4.0	8.9	.518
87-88 Boston	17	17	702	270	91	210	.433	6	16	.375	82	103	.796	15	62	77	139	51	0	24	8	45	41.3	15.9	4.5	8.2	.475
88-89 Boston	3	1	59	8	4	15	.267	0	0	.000	0	0	.000	2	2	4	9	8	0	3	0	3	19.7	2.7	1.3	3.0	.125
89-90 Boston	5	5	162	69	30	62	.484	2	6	.333	7	7	1.000	2	12	14	28	17	1	2	2	10	32.4	13.8	2.8	5.6	.422
NBA Playoff Totals	180	117	7004	3116	1167	2661	.439	26	109	.239	756	943	.802	262	519	781	1006	575	8	247	113	480	38.9	17.3	4.3	5.6	....

• JOHNSON, DerMarr

DerMarr Miles Johnson

Born: May 5, 1980. Washington, DC, United States. Height: 6'9". Weight: 201 lbs. Drafted: 2000 College: Cincinnati

YEAR TEAM	GP	GS	MIN	PTS	FGM	FGA	FG%	3PM	3PA	3P%	FTM	FTA	FT%	ORB	DRB	TRB	AST	PF	DQ	STL	BLK	TO	MPG	PPG	RPG	APG	PCM
00-01 Atlanta	78	21	1313	397	146	390	.374	41	127	.323	64	87	.736	56	122	178	64	134	0	43	30	93	16.8	5.1	2.3	0.8	.244
01-02 Atlanta	72	46	1727	602	214	540	.396	89	247	.360	85	105	.810	59	188	247	81	163	1	62	56	102	24.0	8.4	3.4	1.1	.319
NBA Season Totals	150	67	3040	999	360	930	.387	130	374	.348	149	192	.776	115	310	425	145	297	1	105	86	195	20.3	6.7	2.8	1.0	....

• JOHNSON, Ed

Ed L. Johnson

Born: June 17, 1944. Atlanta, GA, United States. Height: 6'8". Weight: 205 lbs. Drafted: 1968 College: Tennessee State

YEAR TEAM	GP	GS	MIN	PTS	FGM	FGA	FG%	3PM	3PA	3P%	FTM	FTA	FT%	ORB	DRB	TRB	AST	PF	DQ	STL	BLK	TO	MPG	PPG	RPG	APG	PCM
68-69 Los Angeles-A	58	....	1662	682	263	548	.480	0	1	.000	156	303	.515	198	341	539	58	281	18	....	....	127	28.7	11.8	9.3	1.0	.471
69-70 New York-A	74	....	2486	1037	405	848	.478	1	2	.500	226	404	.559	328	551	879	88	305	18	....	....	218	33.6	14.0	11.9	1.2	.525
70-71 New York-A	26	....	592	268	97	218	.445	0	0	.000	74	110	.673	83	139	222	26	80	3	....	....	66	22.8	10.3	8.5	1.0	.564
70-71 Texas-A	8	....	159	52	22	47	.468	0	0	.000	8	20	.400	17	31	48	8	21	1	....	....	10	19.9	6.5	6.0	1.0	.420
ABA Season Totals	166	....	4899	2039	787	1661	.474	1	3	.333	464	837	.554	626	1062	1688	180	687	40	....	....	421	29.5	12.3	10.2	1.1	....
69-70 New York-A	7	....	216	94	32	69	.464	0	0	.000	30	52	.577	....	....	67	5	....	4	....	....	....	30.9	13.4	9.6	0.7	....
ABA Playoff Totals	7	....	216	94	32	69	.464	0	0	.000	30	52	.577	....	....	67	5	....	4	....	....	....	30.9	13.4	9.6	0.7	....

• JOHNSON, Eddie

Edward (Fast Eddie) Johnson Jr.

Born: Feb. 24, 1955. Ocala, FL, United States. Height: 6'2". Weight: 180 lbs. Drafted: 1977 College: Auburn

YEAR TEAM	GP	GS	MIN	PTS	FGM	FGA	FG%	3PM	3PA	3P%	FTM	FTA	FT%	ORB	DRB	TRB	AST	PF	DQ	STL	BLK	TO	MPG	PPG	RPG	APG	PCM
77-78 Atlanta	79	....	1875	828	332	686	.484	....	....	....	164	201	.816	51	102	153	235	232	4	100	4	166	23.7	10.5	1.9	3.0	.397
78-79 Atlanta	78	....	2413	1245	501	982	.510	....	....	....	243	292	.832	65	105	170	360	241	6	121	11	211	30.9	16.0	2.2	4.6	.481
79-80 Atlanta	79	....	2622	1465	590	1212	.487	5	13	.385	280	338	.828	95	105	200	370	216	2	120	24	190	33.2	18.5	2.5	4.7	.504
80-81 Atlanta	75	....	2693	1431	573	1136	.504	6	20	.300	279	356	.784	60	119	179	407	188	2	126	11	195	35.9	19.1	2.4	5.4	.502
81-82 Atlanta	68	57	2314	1211	455	1011	.450	7	30	.233	294	385	.764	63	128	191	358	188	1	102	16	184	34.0	17.8	2.8	5.3	.463
82-83 Atlanta	61	57	1813	978	389	858	.453	14	41	.341	186	237	.785	26	98	124	318	138	2	61	6	159	29.7	16.0	2.0	5.2	.468
83-84 Atlanta	67	43	1893	886	353	798	.442	16	43	.372	164	213	.770	31	115	146	374	155	2	58	7	174	28.3	13.2	2.2	5.6	.429
84-85 Atlanta	73	66	2367	1193	453	946	.479	22	72	.306	265	332	.798	38	154	192	566	184	1	43	7	241	32.4	16.3	2.6	7.8	.516
85-86 Atlanta	39	5	862	394	155	328	.473	5	20	.250	79	110	.718	17	58	75	219	72	1	10	1	90	22.1	10.1	1.9	5.6	.483
85-86 Cleveland	32	4	615	315	129	293	.440	24	65	.369	33	45	.733	13	33	46	114	56	0	8	1	61	19.2	9.8	1.4	3.6	.403

YEAR	TEAM	GP	GS	MIN	PTS	FGM	FGA	FG%	3PM	3PA	3P%	FTM	FTA	FT%	ORB	DRB	TRB	AST	PF	DQ	STL	BLK	TO	MPG	PPG	RPG	APG	PCM
86-87	Seattle	24	0	508	217	85	186	.457	5	15	.333	42	55	.764	11	35	46	115	36	0	12	1	41	21.2	9.0	1.9	4.8	.472
NBA Season Totals		675	232	19975	10163	4015	8436	.476	104	319	.326	2029	2564	.791	470	1052	1522	3436	1706	21	761	89	1712	29.6	15.1	2.3	5.1	....
77-78	Atlanta	2	....	64	31	12	19	.632	....	....	....	7	8	.875	2	4	6	6	10	1	8	1	5	32.0	15.5	3.0	3.0	.556
78-79	Atlanta	9	....	262	148	65	128	.508	....	....	....	18	25	.720	8	15	23	45	22	0	4	2	19	29.1	16.4	2.6	5.0	.523
79-80	Atlanta	5	....	188	97	38	74	.514	0	0	.000	21	28	.750	3	15	18	21	12	0	8	2	11	37.6	19.4	3.6	4.2	.501
81-82	Atlanta	2	2	67	22	9	26	.346	0	0	.000	4	4	1.000	0	6	6	9	8	0	0	1	7	33.5	11.0	3.0	4.5	.185
83-84	Atlanta	5	1	123	54	19	54	.352	1	6	.167	15	22	.682	2	7	9	24	11	0	6	0	7	24.6	10.8	1.8	4.8	.376
86-87	Seattle	14	0	181	90	31	58	.534	2	5	.400	26	30	.867	5	9	14	45	16	0	5	0	9	12.9	6.4	1.0	3.2	.624
NBA Playoff Totals		37	3	885	442	174	359	.485	3	11	.273	91	117	.778	20	56	76	150	79	1	31	6	58	23.9	11.9	2.1	4.1	....

• JOHNSON, Eddie

Edward Arnet Johnson

Born: May 1, 1959. Chicago, IL, United States. Height: 6'7". Weight: 215 lbs. Drafted: 1981 College: Illinois

YEAR	TEAM	GP	GS	MIN	PTS	FGM	FGA	FG%	3PM	3PA	3P%	FTM	FTA	FT%	ORB	DRB	TRB	AST	PF	DQ	STL	BLK	TO	MPG	PPG	RPG	APG	PCM
81-82	Kansas City	74	27	1517	690	295	643	.459	1	11	.091	99	149	.664	128	194	322	109	210	6	50	14	96	20.5	9.3	4.4	1.5	.418
82-83	Kansas City	82	82	2933	1621	677	1370	.494	20	71	.282	247	317	.779	191	310	501	216	259	3	70	20	180	35.8	19.8	6.1	2.6	.496
83-84	Kansas City	82	82	2920	1794	753	1552	.485	20	64	.313	268	331	.810	165	290	455	296	266	4	76	21	213	35.6	21.9	5.5	3.6	.524
84-85	Kansas City	82	81	3029	1876	769	1565	.491	13	54	.241	325	373	.871	151	256	407	273	237	2	83	22	221	36.9	22.9	5.0	3.3	.516
85-86	Sacramento	82	30	2514	1530	623	1311	.475	4	20	.200	280	343	.816	173	246	419	214	237	0	54	17	189	30.7	18.7	5.1	2.6	.501
86-87	Sacramento	81	30	2457	1516	606	1309	.463	37	118	.314	267	322	.829	146	207	353	251	218	4	42	19	162	30.3	18.7	4.4	3.1	.504
87-88	Phoenix	73	59	2177	1294	533	1110	.480	24	94	.255	204	240	.850	121	197	318	180	190	0	33	9	139	29.8	17.7	4.4	2.5	.482
88-89	Phoenix	70	7	2043	1504	608	1224	.497	71	172	.413	217	250	.868	91	215	306	162	198	0	47	7	119	29.2	21.5	4.4	2.3	.598
89-90	Phoenix	64	4	1811	1080	411	907	.453	70	184	.380	188	205	.917	69	177	246	107	174	4	32	10	109	28.3	16.9	3.8	1.7	.446
90-91	Phoenix	15	0	312	203	88	186	.473	6	21	.286	21	29	.724	16	30	46	17	37	0	9	2	24	20.8	13.5	3.1	1.1	.447
90-91	Seattle	66	27	1773	1151	455	936	.486	33	99	.333	208	228	.912	91	134	225	94	144	0	49	7	99	26.9	17.4	3.4	1.4	.505
91-92	Seattle	81	19	2366	1386	534	1164	.459	27	107	.252	291	338	.861	118	174	292	161	199	0	55	11	130	29.2	17.1	3.6	2.0	.453
92-93	Seattle	82	0	1869	1177	463	991	.467	17	56	.304	234	257	.911	124	148	272	135	173	0	36	4	131	22.8	14.4	3.3	1.6	.485
93-94	Charlotte	73	27	1460	836	339	738	.459	59	150	.393	99	127	.780	80	144	224	125	143	2	36	8	88	20.0	11.5	3.1	1.7	.474
95-96	Indiana	62	1	1002	475	180	436	.413	45	128	.352	70	79	.886	45	108	153	69	104	1	20	4	56	16.2	7.7	2.5	1.1	.367
96-97	Indiana	28	0	306	147	59	136	.434	9	28	.321	20	27	.741	3	37	40	17	33	0	5	1	17	10.9	5.3	1.4	0.6	.333
96-97	Houston	24	2	607	277	101	226	.447	40	103	.388	35	41	.854	24	74	98	35	48	0	10	1	31	25.3	11.5	4.1	1.5	.404
97-98	Houston	75	1	1490	633	227	544	.417	66	198	.333	113	136	.831	50	103	153	88	89	0	32	3	60	19.9	8.4	2.0	1.2	.338
98-99	Houston	3	0	18	12	6	13	.462	0	1	.000	0	0	.000	0	2	2	1	3	0	0	0	2	6.0	4.0	0.7	0.3	.309
NBA Season Totals		1199	479	32604	19202	7727	16361	.472	562	1679	.335	3186	3792	.840	1786	3046	4832	2550	2962	26	739	180	2066	27.2	16.0	4.0	2.1	....
83-84	Kansas City	3	3	107	51	21	48	.438	2	5	.400	7	7	1.000	4	6	10	12	8	0	3	1	2	35.7	17.0	3.3	4.0	.431
85-86	Sacramento	3	1	96	56	24	55	.436	0	3	.000	8	9	.889	10	11	21	4	7	0	3	1	6	32.0	18.7	7.0	1.3	.473
88-89	Phoenix	12	0	392	213	85	206	.413	13	38	.342	30	39	.769	28	59	87	25	41	1	12	2	18	32.7	17.8	7.3	2.1	.462
89-90	Phoenix	16	0	337	196	72	160	.450	15	38	.395	37	47	.787	15	42	57	17	40	0	10	4	20	21.1	12.3	3.6	1.1	.463
90-91	Seattle	5	5	171	120	46	89	.517	4	15	.267	24	29	.828	12	9	21	7	13	0	7	1	8	34.2	24.0	4.2	1.4	.576
91-92	Seattle	9	0	247	166	65	137	.474	4	22	.182	32	34	.941	8	19	27	8	19	0	3	3	15	27.4	18.4	3.0	0.9	.464
92-93	Seattle	19	0	382	205	82	210	.390	12	36	.333	29	31	.935	17	28	45	17	44	2	3	1	19	20.1	10.8	2.4	0.9	.289
95-96	Indiana	1	0	9	0	0	5	.000	0	2	.000	0	0	.000	0	0	0	1	0	0	0	0	0	9.0	0.0	0.0	1.0	-.404
96-97	Houston	16	0	284	133	48	117	.410	14	47	.298	23	24	.958	15	21	36	10	17	0	5	0	7	17.8	8.3	2.3	0.6	.362
97-98	Houston	5	0	89	28	9	27	.333	3	10	.300	7	8	.875	4	4	8	1	10	0	0	0	3	17.8	5.6	1.6	0.2	.137
NBA Playoff Totals		89	9	2114	1168	452	1054	.429	67	216	.310	197	228	.864	113	199	312	102	199	3	46	13	98	23.8	13.1	3.5	1.1	....

• JOHNSON, Elmer

Elmer Johnson

Born: 1910. Height: 6'4". Weight: 190 lbs. Drafted: — College: Northwestern

YEAR	TEAM	GP	GS	MIN	PTS	FGM	FGA	FG%	3PM	3PA	3P%	FTM	FTA	FT%	ORB	DRB	TRB	AST	PF	DQ	STL	BLK	TO	MPG	PPG	RPG	APG	PCM
39-40	Chicago-N	28	....	....	103	32	....	....	....	....	....	39	....	....	....	....	....	....	....	....	....	....	....	....	3.7	....	....	....
40-41	Chicago-N	13	....	....	12	4	....	....	....	....	....	4	....	....	....	....	....	....	....	....	....	....	....	....	0.9	....	....	....
NBL Season Totals		41	....	....	115	36	....	....	....	....	....	43	....	....	....	....	....	....	....	....	....	....	....	....	2.8	....	....	....

• JOHNSON, Eric

Eric Johnson

Born: Feb. 7, 1966. Brooklyn, NY, United States. Height: 6'2". Weight: 205 lbs. Drafted: — College: Nebraska

YEAR	TEAM	GP	GS	MIN	PTS	FGM	FGA	FG%	3PM	3PA	3P%	FTM	FTA	FT%	ORB	DRB	TRB	AST	PF	DQ	STL	BLK	TO	MPG	PPG	RPG	APG	PCM
89-90	Utah	48	2	272	54	20	84	.238	1	6	.167	13	17	.765	8	20	28	64	49	1	17	2	24	5.7	1.1	0.6	1.3	.216
NBA Season Totals		48	2	272	54	20	84	.238	1	6	.167	13	17	.765	8	20	28	64	49	1	17	2	24	5.7	1.1	0.6	1.3	....
89-90	Utah	1	0	3	0	0	0	.000	0	0	.000	0	0	.000	0	0	0	0	0	0	0	0	0	3.0	0.0	0.0	0.0	.000
NBA Playoff Totals		1	0	3	0	0	0	.000	0	0	.000	0	0	.000	0	0	0	0	0	0	0	0	0	3.0	0.0	0.0	0.0	....

• JOHNSON, Ervin

Ervin Johnson Jr.

Born: Dec. 21, 1967. New Orleans, LA, United States. Height: 6'11". Weight: 245 lbs. Drafted: 1993 College: New Orleans

YEAR	TEAM	GP	GS	MIN	PTS	FGM	FGA	FG%	3PM	3PA	3P%	FTM	FTA	FT%	ORB	DRB	TRB	AST	PF	DQ	STL	BLK	TO	MPG	PPG	RPG	APG	PCM
93-94	Seattle	45	3	280	117	44	106	.415	0	0	.000	29	46	.630	48	70	118	7	45	0	10	22	23	6.2	2.6	2.6	0.2	.556
94-95	Seattle	64	30	907	199	85	192	.443	0	1	.000	29	46	.630	101	188	289	16	163	1	17	67	51	14.2	3.1	4.5	0.3	.367
95-96	Seattle	81	60	1519	446	180	352	.511	1	3	.333	85	127	.669	129	304	433	48	245	3	40	129	97	18.8	5.5	5.3	0.6	.444
96-97	Denver	82	82	2599	582	243	467	.520	0	2	.000	96	156	.615	231	**682**	913	71	288	5	65	227	115	31.7	7.1	11.1	0.9	.501
97-98	Milwaukee	81	81	2261	649	253	471	.537	0	0	.000	143	238	.601	242	443	685	59	**321**	7	79	158	113	27.9	8.0	8.5	0.7	.470
98-99	Milwaukee	50	7	1027	256	96	189	.508	0	0	.000	64	105	.610	120	200	320	19	151	1	29	57	47	20.5	5.1	6.4	0.4	.417
99-00	Milwaukee	80	74	2129	383	144	279	.516	0	1	.000	95	157	.605	233	415	648	44	298	6	81	127	80	26.6	4.8	8.1	0.6	.399
00-01	Milwaukee	82	19	1981	266	108	198	.545	0	0	.000	50	93	.538	205	408	613	40	257	4	44	97	47	24.2	3.2	7.5	0.5	.368
01-02	Milwaukee	81	9	1659	208	89	193	.461	0	1	.000	30	66	.455	142	324	466	27	219	4	37	82	52	20.5	2.6	5.8	0.3	.308
02-03	Milwaukee	69	17	1170	152	61	135	.452	0	0	.000	30	44	.682	117	177	294	24	178	3	34	63	34	17.0	2.2	4.3	0.3	.297
NBA Season Totals		715	382	15532	3258	1303	2582	.505	1	8	.125	651	1078	.604	1568	3211	4779	355	2165	34	436	1029	659	21.7	4.6	6.7	0.5	....
93-94	Seattle	2	0	8	0	0	1	.000	0	0	.000	0	0	.000	0	4	4	0	1	0	0	0	1	4.0	0.0	2.0	0.0	.172
94-95	Seattle	4	2	54	14	4	14	.286	0	0	.000	6	6	1.000	8	13	21	0	16	0	1	4	1	13.5	3.5	5.3	0.0	.381

YEAR	TEAM	GP	GS	MIN	PTS	FGM	FGA	FG%	3PM	3PA	3P%	FTM	FTA	FT%	ORB	DRB	TRB	AST	PF	DQ	STL	BLK	TO	MPG	PPG	RPG	APG	PCM
95-96	Seattle	18	18	253	55	23	62	.371	0	0	.000	9	11	.818	28	42	70	7	45	0	6	15	14	14.1	3.1	3.9	0.4	.301
98-99	Milwaukee	3	2	92	13	6	13	.462	0	0	.000	1	2	.500	8	10	18	1	9	0	2	5	0	30.7	4.3	6.0	0.3	.279
99-00	Milwaukee	5	5	155	31	10	20	.500	0	0	.000	11	18	.611	14	35	49	2	19	0	6	6	3	31.0	6.2	9.8	0.4	.419
00-01	Milwaukee	18	10	577	98	39	68	.574	0	0	.000	20	32	.625	59	135	194	10	52	1	9	37	12	32.1	5.4	10.8	0.6	.449
02-03	Milwaukee	6	3	76	6	3	8	.375	0	0	.000	0	0	.000	6	18	24	3	20	0	3	5	3	12.7	1.0	4.0	0.5	.289
NBA Playoff Totals		56	40	1215	217	85	186	.457	0	0	.000	47	69	.681	123	257	380	23	162	1	27	72	34	21.7	3.9	6.8	0.4	....

• JOHNSON, Frank

Franklin Lenard Johnson

Born: Nov. 23, 1958. Weirsdale, FL, United States. Height: 6'1". Weight: 185 lbs. Drafted: 1981 College: Wake Forest

YEAR	TEAM	GP	GS	MIN	PTS	FGM	FGA	FG%	3PM	3PA	3P%	FTM	FTA	FT%	ORB	DRB	TRB	AST	PF	DQ	STL	BLK	TO	MPG	PPG	RPG	APG	PCM
81-82	Washington	79	29	2027	842	336	812	.414	17	79	.215	153	204	.750	34	113	147	380	196	1	76	7	158	25.7	10.7	1.9	4.8	.378
82-83	Washington	68	65	2324	852	321	786	.408	14	61	.230	196	261	.751	46	132	178	549	170	1	110	6	238	34.2	12.5	2.6	8.1	.422
83-84	Washington	82	81	2686	982	392	840	.467	11	43	.256	187	252	.742	58	126	184	567	174	1	96	6	189	32.8	12.0	2.2	6.9	.429
84-85	Washington	46	1	925	428	175	358	.489	6	17	.353	72	96	.750	23	40	63	143	72	0	43	3	60	20.1	9.3	1.4	3.1	.444
85-86	Washington	14	9	402	176	69	154	.448	0	3	.000	38	54	.704	7	21	28	76	30	0	11	1	29	28.7	12.6	2.0	5.4	.416
86-87	Washington	18	10	399	153	59	128	.461	0	1	.000	35	49	.714	10	20	30	58	31	0	21	0	31	22.2	8.5	1.7	3.2	.372
87-88	Washington	75	17	1258	554	216	498	.434	1	9	.111	121	149	.812	39	82	121	188	120	0	70	4	98	16.8	7.4	1.6	2.5	.408
88-89	Houston	67	0	879	294	109	246	.443	1	6	.167	75	93	.806	22	57	79	181	91	0	42	0	101	13.1	4.4	1.2	2.7	.373
92-93	Phoenix	77	0	1122	332	136	312	.436	1	12	.083	59	76	.776	41	72	113	186	111	0	60	8	77	14.6	4.3	1.5	2.4	.360
93-94	Phoenix	70	5	875	324	134	299	.448	2	12	.167	54	69	.783	29	53	82	148	120	0	41	1	63	12.5	4.6	1.2	2.1	.374
NBA Season Totals		596	217	12897	4937	1947	4433	.439	53	243	.218	990	1303	.760	309	716	1025	2476	1115	3	570	36	1044	21.6	8.3	1.7	4.2	....
81-82	Washington	7	7	280	109	40	104	.385	5	12	.417	24	28	.857	7	15	22	59	24	0	10	0	29	40.0	15.6	3.1	8.4	.370
83-84	Washington	4	4	156	57	24	42	.571	1	3	.333	8	8	1.000	4	9	13	25	16	0	5	0	9	39.0	14.3	3.3	6.3	.436
84-85	Washington	2	0	39	15	4	14	.286	1	6	.167	6	6	1.000	1	3	4	7	5	0	2	0	2	19.5	7.5	2.0	3.5	.373
86-87	Washington	3	0	28	8	2	7	.286	0	0	.000	4	4	1.000	2	0	2	5	3	0	1	0	4	9.3	2.7	0.7	1.7	.227
87-88	Washington	5	0	44	18	7	22	.318	0	2	.000	4	4	1.000	0	2	2	1	4	0	4	0	2	8.8	3.6	0.4	0.2	.158
88-89	Houston	4	0	36	10	2	6	.333	0	1	.000	6	10	.600	1	4	5	7	3	0	1	0	4	9.0	2.5	1.3	1.8	.344
92-93	Phoenix	22	0	172	70	22	50	.440	1	3	.333	25	29	.862	3	8	11	17	26	0	6	0	7	7.8	3.2	0.5	0.8	.333
93-94	Phoenix	7	0	46	3	1	12	.083	0	2	.000	1	2	.500	2	2	4	5	6	0	2	0	3	6.6	0.4	0.6	0.7	-.046
NBA Playoff Totals		54	11	801	290	102	257	.397	8	29	.276	78	91	.857	20	43	63	126	87	0	31	0	60	14.8	5.4	1.2	2.3	....

• JOHNSON, George

George E. Johnson

Born: June 19, 1947. Herleton, TX, United States. Height: 6'11". Weight: 245 lbs. Drafted: 1970 College: Stephen F. Austin State

YEAR	TEAM	GP	GS	MIN	PTS	FGM	FGA	FG%	3PM	3PA	3P%	FTM	FTA	FT%	ORB	DRB	TRB	AST	PF	DQ	STL	BLK	TO	MPG	PPG	RPG	APG	PCM
70-71	Baltimore	24	....	337	93	41	100	.410	....	....	....	11	30	.367	....	....	114	10	63	1	....	....	....	14.0	3.9	4.8	0.4	.346
71-72	Dallas-A	67	....	1477	317	128	282	.454	0	0	.000	61	103	.592	126	338	464	59	209	5	....	....	84	22.0	4.7	6.9	0.9	.369
72-73	Houston	19	....	169	43	20	39	.513	....	....	....	3	4	.750	....	....	45	3	33	0	....	....	....	8.9	2.3	2.4	0.2	.320
73-74	Houston	26	....	238	54	23	51	.451	....	....	....	8	17	.471	20	41	61	9	46	1	8	8	....	9.2	2.1	2.3	0.3	.290
NBA Season Totals		69	....	744	190	84	190	.442	....	....	....	22	51	.431	20	41	220	22	142	2	8	8	....	10.8	2.8	3.2	0.3	....
ABA Season Totals		67	....	1477	317	128	282	.454	0	0	.000	61	103	.592	126	338	464	59	209	5	....	....	84	22.0	4.7	6.9	0.9	....
Career Totals		136	....	2221	507	212	472	.449	0	0	.000	83	154	.539	146	379	684	81	351	7	8	8	84	16.3	3.7	5.0	0.6	....
70-71	Baltimore	11	....	35	15	7	13	.538	....	....	....	1	2	.500	....	....	11	2	9	0	....	....	....	3.2	1.4	1.0	0.2	.494
71-72	Dallas-A	4	....	96	6	3	9	.333	0	0	.000	0	0	.000	6	18	24	9	16	1	....	....	6	24.0	1.5	6.0	2.3	.259
NBA Playoff Totals		11	....	35	15	7	13	.538	....	....	....	1	2	.500	....	....	11	2	9	0	....	....	....	3.2	1.4	1.0	0.2	....
ABA Playoff Totals		4	....	96	6	3	9	.333	0	0	.000	0	0	.000	6	18	24	9	16	1	....	....	6	24.0	1.5	6.0	2.3	....
Career Playoff Totals		15	....	131	21	10	22	.455	0	0	.000	1	2	.500	6	18	35	11	25	1	....	....	6	8.7	1.4	2.3	0.7	....

• JOHNSON, George

George Thomas Johnson

Born: Dec. 18, 1948. Tylertown, MS, United States. Height: 6'11". Weight: 205 lbs. Drafted: 1970 College: Dillard

YEAR	TEAM	GP	GS	MIN	PTS	FGM	FGA	FG%	3PM	3PA	3P%	FTM	FTA	FT%	ORB	DRB	TRB	AST	PF	DQ	STL	BLK	TO	MPG	PPG	RPG	APG	PCM
72-73	Golden State	56	....	349	89	41	100	.410	....	....	....	7	17	.412	....	....	138	8	40	0	....	....	....	6.2	1.6	2.5	0.1	.414
73-74	Golden State	66	....	1291	405	173	358	.483	....	....	....	59	107	.551	190	332	522	73	176	3	35	124	....	19.6	6.1	7.9	1.1	.527
74-75	Golden State	82	....	1439	364	152	319	.476	....	....	....	60	91	.659	217	357	574	67	206	1	32	136	....	17.5	4.4	7.0	0.8	.477
75-76	Golden State	82	....	1745	400	165	341	.484	....	....	....	70	104	.673	200	427	627	82	275	6	51	174	....	21.3	4.9	7.6	1.0	.429
76-77	Golden State	39	....	597	171	73	150	.487	....	....	....	25	31	.806	87	124	211	26	105	2	15	73	....	15.3	4.4	5.4	0.7	.449
76-77	Buffalo	39	....	1055	296	125	279	.448	....	....	....	46	67	.687	117	283	400	78	141	6	22	104	....	27.1	7.6	10.3	2.0	.500
77-78	New Jersey	81	....	2411	703	285	721	.395	....	....	....	133	185	.719	245	534	779	111	339	**20**	78	**274**	219	29.8	8.7	9.6	1.4	.445
78-79	New Jersey	78	....	2058	517	206	483	.427	....	....	....	105	138	.761	201	415	616	88	315	8	68	253	179	26.4	6.6	7.9	1.1	.432
79-80	New Jersey	81	....	2119	585	248	543	.457	0	1	.000	89	126	.706	192	410	602	173	312	7	53	258	203	26.2	7.2	7.4	2.1	.468
80-81	San Antonio	82	....	1935	408	164	347	.473	0	0	.000	80	109	.734	215	387	602	92	273	3	47	**278**	107	23.6	5.0	7.3	1.1	.491
81-82	San Antonio	75	62	1578	225	91	195	.467	0	0	.000	43	64	.672	152	302	454	79	259	6	20	**234**	90	21.0	3.0	6.1	1.1	.415
82-83	Atlanta	37	0	461	64	25	57	.439	0	0	.000	14	19	.737	44	73	117	17	69	0	10	59	19	12.5	1.7	3.2	0.5	.371
84-85	New Jersey	65	0	800	107	42	79	.532	1	1	1.000	22	27	.815	74	111	185	22	151	2	19	78	39	12.3	1.6	2.8	0.3	.312
85-86	Seattle	41	0	264	35	12	23	.522	0	0	.000	11	16	.688	26	34	60	13	46	0	6	37	12	6.4	0.9	1.5	0.3	.377
NBA Season Totals		904	62	18102	4369	1802	3995	.451	1	2	.500	764	1101	.694	1960	3789	5887	929	2707	64	456	2082	868	20.0	4.8	6.5	1.0	....
72-73	Golden State	9	....	45	13	6	15	.400	....	....	....	1	4	.250	....	....	14	3	7	0	....	....	....	5.0	1.4	1.6	0.3	.365
74-75	Golden State	17	....	321	88	36	63	.571	....	....	....	16	27	.593	54	72	126	15	50	1	9	40	....	18.9	5.2	7.4	0.9	.510
75-76	Golden State	13	....	261	76	31	54	.574	....	....	....	14	19	.737	38	49	87	17	46	0	14	23	....	20.1	5.8	6.7	1.3	.492
78-79	New Jersey	2	....	70	29	14	21	.667	....	....	....	1	3	.333	8	17	25	2	8	1	2	7	4	35.0	14.5	12.5	1.0	.677
80-81	San Antonio	7	....	171	31	12	26	.462	0	0	.000	7	10	.700	24	39	63	6	20	0	3	16	3	24.4	4.4	9.0	0.9	.505
81-82	San Antonio	9	9	175	11	4	8	.500	0	0	.000	3	5	.600	12	34	46	12	34	0	6	15	4	19.4	1.2	5.1	1.3	.353
82-83	Atlanta	1	0	2	0	0	0	.000	0	0	.000	0	0	.000	0	0	0	0	0	0	0	0	0	2.0	0.0	0.0	0.0	.000
84-85	New Jersey	1	0	4	0	0	0	.000	0	0	.000	0	0	.000	0	0	0	0	0	0	0	0	0	4.0	0.0	0.0	0.0	.000
NBA Playoff Totals		59	9	1049	248	103	187	.551	0	0	.000	42	68	.618	136	211	361	55	165	2	34	101	11	17.8	4.2	6.1	0.9	....

• JOHNSON, George

George L. Johnson

Born: Dec. 8, 1956. Brooklyn, NY, United States. Height: 6'7". Weight: 210 lbs. Drafted: 1978 College: St. John's (NY)

YEAR	TEAM	GP	GS	MIN	PTS	FGM	FGA	FG%	3PM	3PA	3P%	FTM	FTA	FT%	ORB	DRB	TRB	AST	PF	DQ	STL	BLK	TO	MPG	PPG	RPG	APG	PCM
78-79	Milwaukee	67	....	1157	414	165	342	.482	....	....	....	84	117	.718	106	254	360	81	187	5	75	49	101	17.3	6.2	5.4	1.2	.509
79-80	Denver	75	....	1938	768	309	649	.476	2	9	.222	148	189	.783	190	394	584	157	260	4	84	67	150	25.8	10.2	7.8	2.1	.529
80-81	Indiana	43	....	930	457	182	394	.462	0	5	.000	93	122	.762	99	179	278	86	120	1	47	23	86	21.6	10.6	6.5	2.0	.568
81-82	Indiana	59	4	720	300	120	291	.412	0	2	.000	60	80	.750	72	145	217	40	147	2	36	25	71	12.2	5.1	3.7	0.7	.416
82-83	Indiana	82	64	2297	951	409	858	.477	7	38	.184	126	172	.733	176	369	545	220	279	6	77	53	246	28.0	11.6	6.6	2.7	.448
83-84	Indiana	81	20	2073	1056	411	884	.465	11	47	.234	223	270	.826	139	321	460	195	256	3	82	49	186	25.6	13.0	5.7	2.4	.512
84-85	Philadelphia	55	3	756	264	107	263	.407	1	10	.100	49	56	.875	48	116	164	38	99	0	31	16	50	13.7	4.8	3.0	0.7	.344
85-86	Washington	2	0	7	4	1	3	.333	0	0	.000	2	2	1.000	1	1	2	0	1	0	0	0	1	3.5	2.0	1.0	0.0	.372
NBA Season Totals		464	91	9878	4214	1704	3684	.463	21	111	.189	785	1008	.779	831	1779	2610	817	1349	21	432	282	891	21.3	9.1	5.6	1.8	....
80-81	Indiana	2	....	23	10	5	8	.625	0	0	.000	0	0	.000	1	3	4	1	1	0	0	0	2	11.5	5.0	2.0	0.5	.423
84-85	Philadelphia	5	0	24	11	5	8	.625	1	1	1.000	0	0	.000	3	4	7	0	2	0	0	0	1	4.8	2.2	1.4	0.0	.536
NBA Playoff Totals		7	0	47	21	10	16	.625	1	1	1.000	0	0	.000	4	7	11	1	3	0	0	0	3	6.7	3.0	1.6	0.1	....

• JOHNSON, Gus

Gus (Honeycomb) Johnson Jr.

Born: Dec. 13, 1935. Akron, OH, United States. Died: Apr.29, 1987. Height: 6'6". Weight: 230 lbs. Drafted: 1963 College: Idaho

YEAR	TEAM	GP	GS	MIN	PTS	FGM	FGA	FG%	3PM	3PA	3P%	FTM	FTA	FT%	ORB	DRB	TRB	AST	PF	DQ	STL	BLK	TO	MPG	PPG	RPG	APG	PCM
63-64	Baltimore	78	....	2847	1352	571	1329	.430	....	....	....	210	319	.658	....	....	1064	169	321	**11**	....	....	....	36.5	17.3	13.6	2.2	.572
64-65	Baltimore	76	....	2899	1415	577	1379	.418	....	....	....	261	386	.676	....	....	988	270	258	4	....	....	....	38.1	18.6	13.0	3.6	.601
65-66	Baltimore	42	....	1284	677	273	661	.413	....	....	....	131	178	.736	....	....	546	114	136	3	....	....	....	30.6	16.1	13.0	2.7	.676
66-67	Baltimore	73	....	2626	1511	620	1377	.450	....	....	....	271	383	.708	....	....	855	194	281	7	....	....	....	36.0	20.7	11.7	2.7	.634
67-68	Baltimore	60	....	2271	1144	482	1033	.467	....	....	....	180	270	.667	....	....	782	159	223	7	....	....	....	37.9	19.1	13.0	2.7	.614
68-69	Baltimore	49	....	1671	878	359	782	.459	....	....	....	160	223	.717	....	....	568	97	176	1	....	....	....	34.1	17.9	11.6	2.0	.606
69-70	Baltimore	78	....	2919	1353	578	1282	.451	....	....	....	197	272	.724	....	....	1086	264	269	6	....	....	....	37.4	17.3	13.9	3.4	.628
70-71	Baltimore	66	....	2538	1202	494	1090	.453	....	....	....	214	290	.738	....	....	1128	192	227	4	....	....	....	38.5	18.2	17.1	2.9	.689
71-72	Baltimore	39	....	668	249	103	269	.383	....	....	....	43	63	.683	....	....	226	51	91	0	....	....	....	17.1	6.4	5.8	1.3	.465
72-73	Indiana-A	50	....	753	299	132	299	.441	4	21	.190	31	42	.738	85	160	245	62	113	1	....	....	70	15.1	6.0	4.9	1.2	.507
72-73	Phoenix	21	....	417	163	69	181	.381	....	....	....	25	36	.694	....	....	136	31	55	0	....	....	....	19.9	7.8	6.5	1.5	.457
NBA Season Totals		582	....	20140	9944	4126	9383	.440	....	....	....	1692	2420	.699	....	....	7379	1541	2037	43	....	....	....	34.6	17.1	12.7	2.6	....
ABA Season Totals		50	....	753	299	132	299	.441	4	21	.190	31	42	.738	85	160	245	62	113	1	....	....	70	15.1	6.0	4.9	1.2	....
Career Totals		632	....	20893	10243	4258	9682	.440	4	21	.190	1723	2462	.700	85	160	7624	1603	2150	44	....	....	70	33.1	16.2	12.1	2.5	....
64-65	Baltimore	10	....	377	158	62	173	.358	....	....	....	34	46	.739	....	....	111	34	38	1	....	....	....	37.7	15.8	11.1	3.4	.479
65-66	Baltimore	1	....	8	2	1	4	.250	....	....	....	0	0	.000	....	....	0	0	1	0	....	....	....	8.0	2.0	0.0	0.0	-.093
69-70	Baltimore	7	....	298	129	51	111	.459	....	....	....	27	34	.794	....	....	80	9	20	0	....	....	....	42.6	18.4	11.4	1.3	.486
70-71	Baltimore	11	....	365	143	54	128	.422	....	....	....	35	47	.745	....	....	114	30	34	0	....	....	....	33.2	13.0	10.4	2.7	.526
71-72	Baltimore	5	....	77	20	9	30	.300	....	....	....	2	2	1.000	....	....	25	3	17	0	....	....	....	15.4	4.0	5.0	0.6	.254
72-73	Indiana-A	17	....	184	42	15	59	.254	0	3	.000	12	16	.750	23	46	69	15	27	0	....	....	18	10.8	2.5	4.1	0.9	.364
NBA Playoff Totals		34	....	1125	452	177	446	.397	....	....	....	98	129	.760	....	....	330	76	110	1	....	....	....	33.1	13.3	9.7	2.2	....
ABA Playoff Totals		17	....	184	42	15	59	.254	0	3	.000	12	16	.750	23	46	69	15	27	0	....	....	18	10.8	2.5	4.1	0.9	....
Career Playoff Totals		51	....	1309	494	192	505	.380	0	3	.000	110	145	.759	23	46	399	91	137	1	....	....	18	25.7	9.7	7.8	1.8	....

• JOHNSON, Harold

Harold H. Johnson

Born: Jan. 20, 1920. Height: 6'6". Weight: 240 lbs. Drafted: — College: Indiana State

YEAR	TEAM	GP	GS	MIN	PTS	FGM	FGA	FG%	3PM	3PA	3P%	FTM	FTA	FT%	ORB	DRB	TRB	AST	PF	DQ	STL	BLK	TO	MPG	PPG	RPG	APG	PCM
46-47	Detroit	27	....	....	15	4	20	.200	....	....	....	7	14	.500	....	....	....	11	13	....	....	....	....	....	0.6	....	0.4	....
NBA Season Totals		27	....	....	15	4	20	.200	....	....	....	7	14	.500	....	....	....	11	13	....	....	....	....	....	0.6	....	0.4	....

• JOHNSON, Joe

Joe Marcu Johnson

Born: June 29, 1981. Little Rock, AR, United States. Height: 6'8". Weight: 225 lbs. Drafted: 2001 College: Arkansas

YEAR	TEAM	GP	GS	MIN	PTS	FGM	FGA	FG%	3PM	3PA	3P%	FTM	FTA	FT%	ORB	DRB	TRB	AST	PF	DQ	STL	BLK	TO	MPG	PPG	RPG	APG	PCM
01-02	Boston	48	33	1003	304	130	296	.439	24	88	.273	20	26	.769	40	99	139	74	59	0	33	9	28	20.9	6.3	2.9	1.5	.343
01-02	Phoenix	29	27	913	277	121	288	.420	14	42	.333	21	27	.778	35	83	118	105	55	0	26	11	43	31.5	9.6	4.1	3.6	.344
02-03	Phoenix	82	34	2255	803	316	796	.397	75	205	.366	96	124	.774	57	207	264	210	143	0	62	19	108	27.5	9.8	3.2	2.6	.326
NBA Season Totals		159	94	4171	1384	567	1380	.411	113	335	.337	137	177	.774	132	389	521	389	257	0	121	39	179	26.2	8.7	3.3	2.4	....
02-03	Phoenix	6	0	164	32	14	51	.275	2	13	.154	2	5	.400	6	20	26	8	15	0	4	2	12	27.3	5.3	4.3	1.3	.104
NBA Playoff Totals		6	0	164	32	14	51	.275	2	13	.154	2	5	.400	6	20	26	8	15	0	4	2	12	27.3	5.3	4.3	1.3	....

• JOHNSON, John

John Howard Getty (J.J.) Johnson

Born: Oct. 18, 1947. Carthage, MS, United States. Height: 6'7". Weight: 200 lbs. Drafted: 1970 College: Iowa

YEAR	TEAM	GP	GS	MIN	PTS	FGM	FGA	FG%	3PM	3PA	3P%	FTM	FTA	FT%	ORB	DRB	TRB	AST	PF	DQ	STL	BLK	TO	MPG	PPG	RPG	APG	PCM
70-71	Cleveland	67	....	2310	1110	435	1032	.422	....	....	....	240	298	.805	....	....	453	323	251	3	....	....	....	34.5	16.6	6.8	4.8	.529
71-72	Cleveland	82	....	3041	1391	557	1286	.433	....	....	....	277	353	.785	....	....	631	415	268	2	....	....	....	37.1	17.0	7.7	5.1	.536
72-73	Cleveland	82	....	2815	1183	492	1143	.430	....	....	....	199	271	.734	....	....	552	309	246	3	....	....	....	34.3	14.4	6.7	3.8	.467
73-74	Portland	69	....	2287	1130	459	990	.464	....	....	....	212	261	.812	160	355	515	284	221	1	69	29	....	33.1	16.4	7.5	4.1	.581
74-75	Portland	80	....	2540	1290	527	1082	.487	....	....	....	236	301	.784	162	339	501	240	249	3	75	39	....	31.8	16.1	6.3	3.0	.545
75-76	Portland	9	....	212	105	41	88	.466	....	....	....	23	27	.852	13	27	40	20	31	1	7	8	....	23.6	11.7	4.4	2.2	.504
75-76	Houston	67	....	1485	647	275	609	.452	....	....	....	97	128	.758	81	211	292	197	163	0	50	28	....	22.2	9.7	4.4	2.9	.507
76-77	Houston	79	....	1738	732	319	696	.458	....	....	....	94	132	.712	75	191	266	163	199	1	47	24	....	22.0	9.3	3.4	2.1	.414
77-78	Houston	1	....	11	4	1	4	.250	....	....	....	2	3	.667	2	1	3	1	3	0	0	0	3	11.0	4.0	3.0	1.0	.068
77-78	Seattle	76	....	1812	813	341	820	.416	....	....	....	131	174	.753	100	207	307	210	194	0	43	19	167	23.8	10.7	4.0	2.8	.388
78-79	Seattle	82	....	2386	902	356	821	.434	....	....	....	190	250	.760	127	285	412	358	245	2	59	25	254	29.1	11.0	5.0	4.4	.402
79-80	Seattle	81	....	2533	915	377	772	.488	0	0	.000	161	201	.801	163	263	426	424	213	1	76	35	243	31.3	11.3	5.3	5.2	.463
80-81	Seattle	80	....	2324	919	373	866	.431	0	1	.000	173	214	.808	135	227	362	312	202	2	57	25	232	29.1	11.5	4.5	3.9	.384

YEAR	TEAM	GP	GS	MIN	PTS	FGM	FGA	FG%	3PM	3PA	3P%	FTM	FTA	FT%	ORB	DRB	TRB	AST	PF	DQ	STL	BLK	TO	MPG	PPG	RPG	APG	PCM
81-82	Seattle	14	1	187	59	22	45	.489	0	0	.000	15	20	.750	3	15	18	29	20	0	4	3	17	13.4	4.2	1.3	2.1	.347
NBA Season Totals		869	1	25681	11200	4575	10254	.446	0	1	.000	2050	2633	.779	1021	2121	4778	3285	2505	19	487	235	916	29.6	12.9	5.5	3.8	....
76-77	Houston	12	....	146	58	24	61	.393	....	....	....	10	15	.667	7	22	29	9	20	0	4	0	....	12.2	4.8	2.4	0.8	.346
77-78	Seattle	22	....	596	222	95	224	.424	....	....	....	32	46	.696	35	64	99	56	64	1	8	6	52	27.1	10.1	4.5	2.5	.321
78-79	Seattle	17	....	615	207	83	175	.474	....	....	....	41	64	.641	40	75	115	91	49	0	17	3	65	36.2	12.2	6.8	5.4	.415
79-80	Seattle	15	....	486	186	78	158	.494	0	1	.000	30	37	.811	44	58	102	85	45	0	8	3	56	32.4	12.4	6.8	5.7	.483
81-82	Seattle	7	0	159	38	15	38	.395	0	0	.000	8	11	.727	7	7	14	34	17	0	6	0	11	22.7	5.4	2.0	4.9	.331
NBA Playoff Totals		73	0	2002	711	295	656	.450	0	1	.000	121	173	.699	133	226	359	275	195	1	43	12	184	27.4	9.7	4.9	3.8	....

• JOHNSON, Kannard

Kannard Johnson

Born: June 24, 1965. Cincinnati, OH, United States. Height: 6'9". Weight: 220 lbs. Drafted: 1987 College: Western Kentucky

YEAR	TEAM	GP	GS	MIN	PTS	FGM	FGA	FG%	3PM	3PA	3P%	FTM	FTA	FT%	ORB	DRB	TRB	AST	PF	DQ	STL	BLK	TO	MPG	PPG	RPG	APG	PCM
87-88	Cleveland	4	0	12	2	1	3	.333	0	0	.000	0	0	.000	0	0	0	0	1	0	1	0	2	3.0	0.5	0.0	0.0	-.105
NBA Season Totals		4	0	12	2	1	3	.333	0	0	.000	0	0	.000	0	0	0	0	1	0	1	0	2	3.0	0.5	0.0	0.0	....

• JOHNSON, Ken

Kenyata Allen Johnson

Born: Feb. 1, 1978. Detroit, MI, United States. Height: 6'11". Weight: 240 lbs. Drafted: — College: Ohio State

YEAR	TEAM	GP	GS	MIN	PTS	FGM	FGA	FG%	3PM	3PA	3P%	FTM	FTA	FT%	ORB	DRB	TRB	AST	PF	DQ	STL	BLK	TO	MPG	PPG	RPG	APG	PCM
02-03	Miami	16	0	156	32	15	37	.405	0	0	.000	2	6	.333	4	28	32	0	20	0	1	12	6	9.8	2.0	2.0	0.0	.234
NBA Season Totals		16	0	156	32	15	37	.405	0	0	.000	2	6	.333	4	28	32	0	20	0	1	12	6	9.8	2.0	2.0	0.0	....

• JOHNSON, Ken

Kenneth H. Johnson

Born: Nov. 7, 1962. Tuskegee, AL, United States. Height: 6'8". Weight: 240 lbs. Drafted: 1985 College: Michigan State

YEAR	TEAM	GP	GS	MIN	PTS	FGM	FGA	FG%	3PM	3PA	3P%	FTM	FTA	FT%	ORB	DRB	TRB	AST	PF	DQ	STL	BLK	TO	MPG	PPG	RPG	APG	PCM
85-86	Portland	64	0	815	263	113	214	.528	0	0	.000	37	85	.435	90	153	243	19	147	1	13	22	58	12.7	4.1	3.8	0.3	.372
NBA Season Totals		64	0	815	263	113	214	.528	0	0	.000	37	85	.435	90	153	243	19	147	1	13	22	58	12.7	4.1	3.8	0.3	....
85-86	Portland	2	0	11	0	0	0	.000	0	0	.000	0	0	.000	0	2	2	0	1	0	2	0	1	5.5	0.0	1.0	0.0	.211
NBA Playoff Totals		2	0	11	0	0	0	.000	0	0	.000	0	0	.000	0	2	2	0	1	0	2	0	1	5.5	0.0	1.0	0.0	....

• JOHNSON, Kevin

Kevin Maurice (K.J.) Johnson

Born: Mar. 4, 1966. Sacramento, CA, United States. Height: 6'1". Weight: 180 lbs. Drafted: 1987 College: California

YEAR	TEAM	GP	GS	MIN	PTS	FGM	FGA	FG%	3PM	3PA	3P%	FTM	FTA	FT%	ORB	DRB	TRB	AST	PF	DQ	STL	BLK	TO	MPG	PPG	RPG	APG	PCM
87-88	Cleveland	52	3	1043	380	143	311	.460	2	9	.222	92	112	.821	10	62	72	193	96	1	60	17	83	20.1	7.3	1.4	3.7	.419
87-88	Phoenix	28	25	874	352	132	285	.463	3	15	.200	85	99	.859	26	93	119	244	59	0	43	7	64	31.2	12.6	4.3	8.7	.611
88-89	Phoenix	81	81	3179	1650	570	1128	.505	2	22	.091	508	576	.882	46	294	340	991	226	1	135	24	**324**	39.2	20.4	4.2	12.2	.698
89-90	Phoenix	74	74	2782	1665	578	1159	.499	8	41	.195	501	598	.838	42	228	270	846	143	0	95	14	266	37.6	22.5	3.6	11.4	.724
90-91	Phoenix	77	76	2772	1710	591	1145	.516	9	44	.205	519	616	.843	54	217	271	781	174	0	163	11	270	36.0	22.2	3.5	10.1	.744
91-92	Phoenix	78	78	2894	1536	539	1125	.479	10	46	.217	448	555	.807	61	231	292	836	180	0	116	23	273	37.1	19.7	3.7	10.7	.657
92-93	Phoenix	49	47	1643	791	282	565	.499	1	8	.125	226	276	.819	30	74	104	384	100	0	85	19	152	33.5	16.1	2.1	7.8	.559
93-94	Phoenix	67	67	2449	1340	477	980	.487	6	27	.222	380	464	.819	55	112	167	637	127	1	125	10	235	36.6	20.0	2.5	9.5	.626
94-95	Phoenix	47	35	1352	730	246	523	.470	4	26	.154	234	289	.810	32	83	115	360	88	0	47	18	103	28.8	15.5	2.4	7.7	.634
95-96	Phoenix	56	55	2007	1047	342	674	.507	21	57	.368	342	398	.859	42	179	221	517	144	0	82	13	168	35.8	18.7	3.9	9.2	.662
96-97	Phoenix	70	70	2658	1410	441	890	.496	89	202	.441	439	515	.852	54	199	253	653	141	0	102	12	217	38.0	20.1	3.6	9.3	.650
97-98	Phoenix	50	12	1290	476	155	347	.447	4	26	.154	162	186	.871	35	129	164	245	57	0	27	8	100	25.8	9.5	3.3	4.9	.480
99-00	Phoenix	6	0	113	40	16	28	.571	1	1	1.000	7	7	1.000	0	16	16	24	6	0	2	0	7	18.8	6.7	2.7	4.0	.554
NBA Season Totals		735	623	25056	13127	4512	9160	.493	160	524	.305	3943	4691	.841	487	1917	2404	6711	1541	3	1082	176	2262	34.1	17.9	3.3	9.1	....
88-89	Phoenix	12	12	494	285	90	182	.495	3	10	.300	102	110	.927	12	39	51	147	28	0	19	5	55	41.2	23.8	4.3	12.3	.726
89-90	Phoenix	16	16	582	340	123	257	.479	2	11	.182	92	112	.821	9	44	53	170	28	0	25	0	62	36.4	21.3	3.3	10.6	.666
90-91	Phoenix	4	4	146	51	16	53	.302	1	7	.143	18	30	.600	2	11	13	39	9	0	2	1	12	36.5	12.8	3.3	9.8	.356
91-92	Phoenix	8	8	335	189	62	128	.484	3	6	.500	62	72	.861	8	25	33	93	24	1	12	2	25	41.9	23.6	4.1	11.6	.692
92-93	Phoenix	23	23	914	410	143	298	.480	0	3	.000	124	156	.795	10	52	62	182	57	1	35	13	84	39.7	17.8	2.7	7.9	.484
93-94	Phoenix	10	10	427	266	97	212	.458	3	10	.300	69	81	.852	10	25	35	96	23	0	10	1	34	42.7	26.6	3.5	9.6	.608
94-95	Phoenix	10	10	371	248	86	150	.573	5	10	.500	71	84	.845	7	34	41	93	25	0	9	4	34	37.1	24.8	4.1	9.3	.775
95-96	Phoenix	4	4	151	69	27	57	.474	1	4	.250	14	17	.824	2	15	17	43	8	0	2	2	11	37.8	17.3	4.3	10.8	.600
96-97	Phoenix	5	5	208	84	26	88	.295	3	22	.136	29	33	.879	8	14	22	30	15	1	13	0	18	41.6	16.8	4.4	6.0	.314
97-98	Phoenix	4	1	122	55	23	42	.548	1	4	.250	8	12	.667	2	7	9	19	6	0	2	1	6	30.5	13.8	2.3	4.8	.485
99-00	Phoenix	9	0	129	29	12	37	.324	0	3	.000	5	6	.833	0	13	13	23	10	0	3	1	13	14.3	3.2	1.4	2.6	.233
NBA Playoff Totals		105	93	3879	2026	705	1504	.469	22	90	.244	594	713	.833	70	279	349	935	233	3	132	30	354	36.9	19.3	3.3	8.9	....

• JOHNSON, Larry

Larry Johnson

Born: Nov. 28, 1954. Morganfield, KY, United States. Height: 6'3". Weight: 205 lbs. Drafted: 1977 College: Kentucky

YEAR	TEAM	GP	GS	MIN	PTS	FGM	FGA	FG%	3PM	3PA	3P%	FTM	FTA	FT%	ORB	DRB	TRB	AST	PF	DQ	STL	BLK	TO	MPG	PPG	RPG	APG	PCM
77-78	Buffalo	4	....	38	6	3	13	.231	....	....	....	0	2	.000	1	4	5	7	3	0	5	2	3	9.5	1.5	1.3	1.8	.285
NBA Season Totals		4	....	38	6	3	13	.231	....	....	....	0	2	.000	1	4	5	7	3	0	5	2	3	9.5	1.5	1.3	1.8	....

• JOHNSON, Larry

Larry Demetric (Grandmama) Johnson

Born: Mar. 14, 1969. Tyler, TX, United States. Height: 6'6". Weight: 250 lbs. Drafted: 1991 College: UNLV

YEAR	TEAM	GP	GS	MIN	PTS	FGM	FGA	FG%	3PM	3PA	3P%	FTM	FTA	FT%	ORB	DRB	TRB	AST	PF	DQ	STL	BLK	TO	MPG	PPG	RPG	APG	PCM
91-92	Charlotte	82	77	3047	1576	616	1258	.490	5	22	.227	339	409	.829	323	576	899	292	225	3	81	51	164	37.2	19.2	11.0	3.6	.643
92-93	Charlotte	82	82	**3323**	1810	728	1385	.526	18	71	.254	336	438	.767	281	583	864	353	187	0	53	27	230	**40.5**	22.1	10.5	4.3	.633
93-94	Charlotte	51	51	1757	834	346	672	.515	5	21	.238	137	197	.695	143	305	448	184	131	0	29	14	117	34.5	16.4	8.8	3.6	.563
94-95	Charlotte	81	81	3234	1525	585	1219	.480	81	210	.386	274	354	.774	190	395	585	369	174	2	78	28	211	39.9	18.8	7.2	4.6	.511
95-96	Charlotte	81	81	3274	1660	583	1225	.476	67	183	.366	427	564	.757	249	434	683	355	173	0	55	43	178	40.4	20.5	8.4	4.4	.566
96-97	New York	76	76	2613	976	376	735	.512	34	105	.324	190	274	.693	165	228	393	174	249	3	64	36	137	34.4	12.8	5.2	2.3	.384
97-98	New York	70	70	2412	1087	429	884	.485	15	63	.238	214	283	.756	175	226	401	150	193	2	40	13	126	34.5	15.5	5.7	2.1	.420
98-99	New York	49	48	1639	587	210	458	.459	33	92	.359	134	164	.817	91	193	284	119	147	1	34	10	89	33.4	12.0	5.8	2.4	.386

YEAR	TEAM	GP	GS	MIN	PTS	FGM	FGA	FG%	3PM	3PA	3P%	FTM	FTA	FT%	ORB	DRB	TRB	AST	PF	DQ	STL	BLK	TO	MPG	PPG	RPG	APG	PCM
99-00	New York	70	68	2281	750	282	652	.433	58	174	.333	128	167	.766	87	293	380	175	205	1	42	7	94	32.6	10.7	5.4	2.5	.350
00-01	New York	65	65	2105	645	246	598	.411	51	163	.313	102	128	.797	90	273	363	127	209	2	39	29	97	32.4	9.9	5.6	2.0	.315
NBA Season Totals		707	699	25685	11450	4401	9086	.484	367	1104	.332	2281	2978	.766	1794	3506	5300	2298	1893	14	515	258	1443	36.3	16.2	7.5	3.3	....
92-93	Charlotte	9	9	348	178	68	122	.557	1	4	.250	41	52	.788	19	43	62	30	27	0	5	2	19	38.7	19.8	6.9	3.3	.542
94-95	Charlotte	4	4	172	83	31	65	.477	1	9	.111	20	25	.800	10	13	23	11	7	0	4	2	6	43.0	20.8	5.8	2.8	.458
96-97	New York	9	9	295	124	43	77	.558	6	17	.353	32	38	.842	11	25	36	23	27	0	7	1	15	32.8	13.8	4.0	2.6	.436
97-98	New York	8	8	310	143	52	107	.486	2	10	.200	37	50	.740	25	28	53	13	30	0	10	3	25	38.8	17.9	6.6	1.6	.402
98-99	New York	20	20	683	229	87	204	.426	24	82	.293	31	46	.674	22	75	97	31	64	2	21	1	33	34.2	11.5	4.9	1.6	.294
99-00	New York	16	16	589	180	70	152	.461	13	33	.394	27	34	.794	15	65	80	26	47	1	8	2	23	36.8	11.3	5.0	1.6	.289
NBA Playoff Totals		66	66	2397	937	351	727	.483	47	155	.303	188	245	.767	102	249	351	134	202	3	55	11	121	36.3	14.2	5.3	2.0	....

• JOHNSON, Lee

Lee Johnson

Born: June 16, 1957. Plummerville, AR, United States. Height: 6'11". Weight: 205 lbs. Drafted: 1979 College: East Texas State

YEAR	TEAM	GP	GS	MIN	PTS	FGM	FGA	FG%	3PM	3PA	3P%	FTM	FTA	FT%	ORB	DRB	TRB	AST	PF	DQ	STL	BLK	TO	MPG	PPG	RPG	APG	PCM
80-81	Houston	10	....	80	17	7	23	.304	0	0	.000	3	5	.600	6	14	20	1	17	0	0	5	4	8.0	1.7	2.0	0.1	.175
80-81	Detroit	2	....	10	0	0	2	.000	0	0	.000	0	0	.000	0	2	2	0	1	0	0	0	3	5.0	0.0	1.0	0.0	-.319
NBA Season Totals		12	....	90	17	7	25	.280	0	0	.000	3	5	.600	6	16	22	1	18	0	0	5	7	7.5	1.4	1.8	0.1	....

• JOHNSON, Magic

Earvin (Magic) Johnson Jr.

Born: Aug. 14, 1959. Lansing, MI, United States. Height: 6'8". Weight: 215 lbs. Drafted: 1979 College: Michigan State HOF: 2002

YEAR	TEAM	GP	GS	MIN	PTS	FGM	FGA	FG%	3PM	3PA	3P%	FTM	FTA	FT%	ORB	DRB	TRB	AST	PF	DQ	STL	BLK	TO	MPG	PPG	RPG	APG	PCM
79-80	LA Lakers	77	....	2795	1387	503	949	.530	7	31	.226	374	462	.810	166	430	596	563	218	1	187	41	308	36.3	18.0	7.7	7.3	.690
80-81	LA Lakers	37	....	1371	798	312	587	.532	3	17	.176	171	225	.760	101	219	320	317	100	0	127	27	144	37.1	21.6	8.6	8.6	.819
81-82	LA Lakers	78	77	2991	1447	556	1036	.537	6	29	.207	329	433	.760	252	499	751	743	223	1	208	34	289	38.3	18.6	9.6	9.5	.770
82-83	LA Lakers	79	79	2907	1326	511	933	.548	0	21	.000	304	380	.800	214	469	683	**829**	200	1	176	47	300	36.8	16.8	8.6	**10.5**	**.784**
83-84	LA Lakers	67	66	2567	1178	441	780	.565	6	29	.207	290	358	.810	99	392	491	875	169	1	150	49	308	38.3	17.6	7.3	**13.1**	.796
84-85	LA Lakers	77	77	2781	1406	504	899	.561	7	37	.189	391	464	.843	90	386	476	968	155	0	113	25	308	36.1	18.3	6.2	12.6	.809
85-86	LA Lakers	72	70	2578	1354	483	918	.526	10	43	.233	378	434	.871	85	341	426	**907**	133	0	113	16	274	35.8	18.8	5.9	**12.6**	**.812**
86-87	LA Lakers	80	80	2904	1909	683	1308	.522	8	39	.205	535	631	.848	122	382	504	**977**	168	0	138	36	304	36.3	23.9	6.3	**12.2**	**.894**
87-88	LA Lakers	72	70	2637	1408	490	996	.492	11	56	.196	417	489	.853	88	361	449	858	147	0	114	13	266	36.6	19.6	6.2	11.9	.773
88-89	LA Lakers	77	77	2886	1730	579	1137	.509	59	188	.314	513	563	**.911**	111	496	607	988	172	0	138	22	316	37.5	22.5	7.9	12.8	.896
89-90	LA Lakers	79	79	2937	1765	546	1138	.480	106	276	.384	567	637	.890	128	394	522	907	167	1	132	34	292	37.2	22.3	6.6	11.5	.829
90-91	LA Lakers	79	79	2933	1531	466	976	.477	80	250	.320	519	573	.906	105	446	551	989	150	0	102	17	**316**	37.1	19.4	7.0	12.5	.800
95-96	LA Lakers	32	9	958	468	137	294	.466	22	58	.379	172	201	.856	40	143	183	220	48	0	26	13	102	29.9	14.6	5.7	6.9	.658
NBA Season Totals		906	763	33245	17707	6211	11951	.520	325	1074	.303	4960	5850	.848	1601	4958	6559	10141	2050	5	1724	374	3527	36.7	19.5	7.2	**11.2**	....
79-80	LA Lakers	16	....	658	293	103	199	.518	2	8	.250	85	106	.802	52	116	168	151	47	1	49	6	65	41.1	18.3	10.5	9.4	.735
80-81	LA Lakers	3	....	127	51	19	49	.388	0	0	.000	13	20	.650	8	33	41	21	14	1	8	3	11	42.3	17.0	13.7	7.0	.585
81-82	LA Lakers	14	14	562	243	83	157	.529	0	4	.000	77	93	.828	54	104	158	130	50	0	40	3	44	40.1	17.4	11.3	9.3	.764
82-83	LA Lakers	15	15	643	268	100	206	.485	0	11	.000	68	81	.840	51	77	128	192	49	0	34	12	64	42.9	17.9	8.5	12.8	.707
83-84	LA Lakers	21	21	837	382	151	274	.551	0	7	.000	80	100	.800	26	113	139	284	71	0	42	20	79	39.9	18.2	6.6	13.5	.768
84-85	LA Lakers	19	19	687	333	116	226	.513	1	7	.143	100	118	.847	19	115	134	289	48	0	32	4	76	36.2	17.5	7.1	15.2	.868
85-86	LA Lakers	14	14	541	302	110	205	.537	0	11	.000	82	107	.766	21	79	100	211	43	0	27	1	45	38.6	21.6	7.1	15.1	.897
86-87	LA Lakers	18	18	666	392	146	271	.539	2	10	.200	98	118	.831	28	111	139	219	37	0	31	7	51	37.0	21.8	7.7	12.2	.902
87-88	LA Lakers	24	24	965	477	169	329	.514	7	14	.500	132	155	.852	32	98	130	303	61	0	34	4	83	40.2	19.9	5.4	12.6	.717
88-89	LA Lakers	14	14	518	258	85	174	.489	10	35	.286	78	86	.907	15	68	83	165	30	1	27	3	53	37.0	18.4	5.9	11.8	.753
89-90	LA Lakers	9	9	376	227	76	155	.490	5	25	.200	70	79	.886	12	45	57	115	28	0	11	1	36	41.8	25.2	6.3	12.8	.768
90-91	LA Lakers	19	19	823	414	118	268	.440	21	71	.296	157	178	.882	23	131	154	240	43	0	23	0	77	43.3	21.8	8.1	12.6	.721
95-96	LA Lakers	4	0	135	61	15	39	.385	3	9	.333	28	33	.848	8	26	34	26	3	0	0	0	12	33.8	15.3	8.5	6.5	.614
NBA Playoff Totals		190	167	7538	3701	1291	2552	.506	51	212	.241	1068	1274	.838	349	1116	1465	**2346**	524	3	358	64	**696**	39.7	19.5	7.7	**12.3**	....

• JOHNSON, Marques

Marques Kevin Johnson

Born: Feb. 8, 1956. Nachitoches, LA, United States. Height: 6'7". Weight: 218 lbs. Drafted: 1977 College: UCLA

YEAR	TEAM	GP	GS	MIN	PTS	FGM	FGA	FG%	3PM	3PA	3P%	FTM	FTA	FT%	ORB	DRB	TRB	AST	PF	DQ	STL	BLK	TO	MPG	PPG	RPG	APG	PCM
77-78	Milwaukee	80	....	2765	1557	628	1204	.522	....	....	....	301	409	.736	292	555	847	190	221	3	92	103	176	34.6	19.5	10.6	2.4	.680
78-79	Milwaukee	77	....	2779	1972	820	1491	.550	....	....	....	332	437	.760	212	374	586	234	186	1	116	89	169	36.1	25.6	7.6	3.0	.740
79-80	Milwaukee	77	....	2686	1671	689	1267	.544	2	9	.222	291	368	.791	217	349	566	273	173	0	100	70	185	34.9	21.7	7.4	3.5	.682
80-81	Milwaukee	76	....	2542	1541	636	1153	.552	0	9	.000	269	381	.706	225	293	518	346	196	1	115	41	190	33.4	20.3	6.8	4.6	.687
81-82	Milwaukee	60	52	1900	990	404	760	.532	0	4	.000	182	260	.700	153	211	364	213	142	1	59	35	144	31.7	16.5	6.1	3.6	.568
82-83	Milwaukee	80	80	2853	1714	723	1420	.509	4	20	.200	264	359	.735	196	366	562	363	211	0	100	56	200	35.7	21.4	7.0	4.5	.636
83-84	Milwaukee	74	74	2715	1535	646	1288	.502	2	13	.154	241	340	.709	173	307	480	315	194	1	115	45	178	36.7	20.7	6.5	4.3	.578
84-85	LA Clippers	72	68	2448	1181	494	1094	.452	3	13	.231	190	260	.731	188	240	428	248	193	2	72	30	173	34.0	16.4	5.9	3.4	.448
85-86	LA Clippers	75	75	2605	1525	613	1201	.510	1	15	.067	298	392	.760	156	260	416	283	214	2	107	50	180	34.7	20.3	5.5	3.8	.577
86-87	LA Clippers	10	10	302	166	68	155	.439	0	6	.000	30	42	.714	9	24	33	28	24	0	12	5	17	30.2	16.6	3.3	2.8	.427
89-90	Golden State	10	0	99	40	12	32	.375	2	3	.667	14	17	.824	8	9	17	9	12	0	0	1	10	9.9	4.0	1.7	0.9	.316
NBA Season Totals		691	359	23694	13892	5733	11065	.518	14	92	.152	2412	3265	.739	1829	2988	4817	2502	1766	11	888	525	1622	34.3	20.1	7.0	3.6	....
77-78	Milwaukee	9	....	321	216	84	153	.549	....	....	....	48	64	.750	35	77	112	31	25	0	10	17	14	35.7	24.0	12.4	3.4	.878
79-80	Milwaukee	7	....	303	139	54	128	.422	1	3	.333	30	40	.750	17	31	48	20	20	0	5	6	8	43.3	19.9	6.9	2.9	.418
80-81	Milwaukee	7	....	266	173	75	135	.556	0	1	.000	23	32	.719	41	25	66	34	14	0	10	7	13	38.0	24.7	9.4	4.9	.784
81-82	Milwaukee	6	1	235	113	44	100	.440	1	4	.250	24	42	.571	23	21	44	20	25	1	6	2	12	39.2	18.8	7.3	3.3	.426
82-83	Milwaukee	9	9	382	198	85	175	.486	0	1	.000	28	43	.651	28	44	72	38	22	0	8	7	21	42.4	22.0	8.0	4.2	.527
83-84	Milwaukee	16	16	605	324	129	273	.473	1	4	.250	65	90	.722	29	56	85	55	50	0	17	6	43	37.8	20.3	5.3	3.4	.454
NBA Playoff Totals		54	26	2112	1163	471	964	.489	3	13	.231	218	311	.701	173	254	427	198	156	1	56	45	111	39.1	21.5	7.9	3.7	....

• JOHNSON, Mickey

Wallace Edgar (Mickey) Johnson

Born: Aug. 31, 1952. Chicago, IL, United States. Height: 6'10". Weight: 190 lbs. Drafted: 1974 College: Aurora

YEAR	TEAM	GP	GS	MIN	PTS	FGM	FGA	FG%	3PM	3PA	3P%	FTM	FTA	FT%	ORB	DRB	TRB	AST	PF	DQ	STL	BLK	TO	MPG	PPG	RPG	APG	PCM
74-75	Chicago	38	....	291	143	53	118	.449	....	....	....	37	58	.638	32	62	94	20	57	1	10	11	....	7.7	3.8	2.5	0.5	.541
75-76	Chicago	81	....	2390	1239	478	1033	.463	....	....	....	283	360	.786	279	479	758	130	292	8	93	66	....	29.5	15.3	9.4	1.6	.587
76-77	Chicago	81	....	2847	1400	538	1205	.446	....	....	....	324	407	.796	297	531	828	195	315	10	103	64	....	35.1	17.3	10.2	2.4	.558

YEAR	TEAM	GP	GS	MIN	PTS	FGM	FGA	FG%	3PM	3PA	3P%	FTM	FTA	FT%	ORB	DRB	TRB	AST	PF	DQ	STL	BLK	TO	MPG	PPG	RPG	APG	PCM
77-78	Chicago	81	....	2870	1484	561	1215	.462	....	....	....	362	446	.812	218	520	738	267	317	8	92	68	267	35.4	18.3	9.1	3.3	.554
78-79	Chicago	82	....	2594	1265	496	1105	.449	....	....	....	273	329	.830	193	434	627	380	286	9	88	59	312	31.6	15.4	7.6	4.6	.539
79-80	Indiana	82	....	2647	1566	588	1271	.463	5	32	.156	385	482	.799	258	423	681	344	291	11	153	112	287	32.3	19.1	8.3	4.2	.659
80-81	Milwaukee	82	....	2118	1023	379	846	.448	3	18	.167	262	332	.789	183	362	545	286	256	4	94	71	230	25.8	12.5	6.6	3.5	.566
81-82	Milwaukee	76	71	1934	978	372	757	.491	1	7	.143	233	291	.801	133	321	454	215	240	4	72	45	190	25.4	12.9	6.0	2.8	.553
82-83	Milwaukee	6	0	153	67	30	66	.455	0	2	.000	7	9	.778	9	16	25	11	22	0	1	2	12	25.5	11.2	4.2	1.8	.328
82-83	New Jersey	42	7	1001	564	199	496	.401	2	17	.118	164	201	.816	66	158	224	144	135	4	56	21	122	23.8	13.4	5.3	3.4	.538
82-83	Golden State	30	9	899	466	162	359	.451	1	17	.059	141	170	.829	88	157	245	100	131	6	25	23	105	30.0	15.5	8.2	3.3	.551
83-84	Golden State	78	25	2122	1062	359	852	.421	5	29	.172	339	432	.785	198	320	518	219	290	3	101	30	218	27.2	13.6	6.6	2.8	.500
84-85	Golden State	66	9	1565	875	304	714	.426	7	30	.233	260	316	.823	149	247	396	149	221	5	70	35	145	23.7	13.3	6.0	2.3	.546
85-86	New Jersey	79	4	1574	616	214	507	.422	5	24	.208	183	233	.785	98	234	332	217	248	1	67	25	166	19.9	7.8	4.2	2.7	.430
NBA Season Totals		904	125	25005	12748	4733	10544	.449	29	176	.165	3253	4066	.800	2201	4264	6465	2677	3101	74	1025	632	2054	27.7	14.1	7.2	3.0	....
74-75	Chicago	3	....	5	2	1	3	.333	....	....	....	0	0	.000	0	0	0	0	2	0	0	1	....	1.7	0.7	0.0	0.0	-.112
76-77	Chicago	3	....	124	82	34	72	.472	....	....	....	14	16	.875	14	25	39	7	13	0	5	2	....	41.3	27.3	13.0	2.3	.680
80-81	Milwaukee	7	....	170	82	26	65	.400	0	1	.000	30	35	.857	24	23	47	13	25	0	9	6	21	24.3	11.7	6.7	1.9	.496
81-82	Milwaukee	6	6	206	119	43	75	.573	0	1	.000	33	39	.846	15	17	32	18	27	0	8	4	13	34.3	19.8	5.3	3.0	.594
85-86	New Jersey	3	0	54	17	5	19	.263	0	2	.000	7	11	.636	2	9	11	2	7	0	2	0	3	18.0	5.7	3.7	0.7	.191
NBA Playoff Totals		22	6	559	302	109	234	.466	0	4	.000	84	101	.832	55	74	129	40	74	0	24	13	37	25.4	13.7	5.9	1.8	....

• JOHNSON, Morris

Morris (Swede, Mally) Johnson

Born: 1909. Height: 5'9". Weight: — Drafted: — College: North Carolina State

YEAR	TEAM	GP	GS	MIN	PTS	FGM	FGA	FG%	3PM	3PA	3P%	FTM	FTA	FT%	ORB	DRB	TRB	AST	PF	DQ	STL	BLK	TO	MPG	PPG	RPG	APG	PCM
37-38	Non-Skids-N	11	....	....	36	15	....	....	....	....	....	6	....	....	....	....	....	....	....	....	....	....	....	....	3.3	....	....	....
38-39	Non-Skids-N	12	....	....	12	5	....	....	....	....	....	2	....	....	....	....	....	....	....	....	....	....	....	....	1.0	....	....	....
NBL Season Totals		23	....	....	48	20	....	....	....	....	....	8	....	....	....	....	....	....	....	....	....	....	....	....	2.1	....	....	....
37-38	Non-Skids-N	2	....	....	1	0	....	....	....	....	....	1	....	....	....	....	....	....	....	....	....	....	....	....	0.5	....	....	....
38-39	Non-Skids-N	1	....	....	0	0	....	....	....	....	....	0	....	....	....	....	....	....	....	....	....	....	....	....	0.0	....	....	....
NBL Playoff Totals		3	....	....	1	0	....	....	....	....	....	1	....	....	....	....	....	....	....	....	....	....	....	....	0.3	....	....	....

• JOHNSON, Neil

Neil A. Johnson

Born: Apr. 17, 1943. Jackson, MI, United States. Height: 6'7". Weight: 220 lbs. Drafted: 1966 College: Creighton

YEAR	TEAM	GP	GS	MIN	PTS	FGM	FGA	FG%	3PM	3PA	3P%	FTM	FTA	FT%	ORB	DRB	TRB	AST	PF	DQ	STL	BLK	TO	MPG	PPG	RPG	APG	PCM
66-67	New York	51	....	522	175	59	171	.345	....	....	....	57	86	.663	....	....	167	38	102	0	....	....	....	10.2	3.4	3.3	0.7	.407
67-68	New York	43	....	286	111	44	106	.415	....	....	....	23	48	.479	....	....	75	33	63	0	....	....	....	6.7	2.6	1.7	0.8	.440
68-69	Phoenix	80	....	1319	464	177	368	.481	....	....	....	110	177	.621	....	....	396	134	214	3	....	....	....	16.5	5.8	5.0	1.7	.511
69-70	Phoenix	28	....	136	48	20	60	.333	....	....	....	8	12	.667	....	....	47	12	38	0	....	....	....	4.9	1.7	1.7	0.4	.361
70-71	Virginia-A	78	....	1838	990	398	758	.525	0	2	.000	194	259	.749	268	400	668	179	295	**13**	....	....	163	23.6	12.7	8.6	2.3	.711
71-72	Virginia-A	31	....	874	322	128	273	.469	1	3	.333	65	94	.691	109	177	286	78	123	5	....	....	67	28.2	10.4	9.2	2.5	.534
72-73	Virginia-A	69	....	1442	523	210	429	.490	0	1	.000	103	156	.660	156	208	364	158	232	5	....	....	131	20.9	7.6	5.3	2.3	.485
NBA Season Totals		202	....	2263	798	300	705	.426	....	....	....	198	323	.613	....	....	685	217	417	3	....	....	....	11.2	4.0	3.4	1.1	....
ABA Season Totals		178	....	4154	1835	736	1460	.504	1	6	.167	362	509	.711	533	785	1318	415	650	23	....	....	361	23.3	10.3	7.4	2.3	....
Career Totals		380	....	6417	2633	1036	2165	.479	1	6	.167	560	832	.673	533	785	2003	632	1067	26	....	....	361	16.9	6.9	5.3	1.7	....
66-67	New York	4	....	64	23	8	27	.296	....	....	....	7	8	.875	....	....	23	5	8	0	....	....	....	16.0	5.8	5.8	1.3	.447
67-68	New York	2	....	6	4	2	4	.500	....	....	....	0	0	.000	....	....	3	0	1	0	....	....	....	3.0	2.0	1.5	0.0	.733
69-70	Phoenix	2	....	7	2	1	3	.333	....	....	....	0	0	.000	....	....	4	0	4	0	....	....	....	3.5	1.0	2.0	0.0	.286
70-71	Virginia-A	12	....	253	112	41	92	.446	1	1	1.000	29	44	.659	40	60	100	32	54	2	....	....	17	21.1	9.3	8.3	2.7	.640
72-73	Virginia-A	5	....	98	32	13	26	.500	0	0	.000	6	8	.750	7	14	21	5	16	0	....	....	7	19.6	6.4	4.2	1.0	.374
NBA Playoff Totals		8	....	77	29	11	34	.324	....	....	....	7	8	.875	....	....	30	5	13	0	....	....	....	9.6	3.6	3.8	0.6	....
ABA Playoff Totals		17	....	351	144	54	118	.458	1	1	1.000	35	52	.673	47	74	121	37	70	2	....	....	24	20.6	8.5	7.1	2.2	....
Career Playoff Totals		25	....	428	173	65	152	.428	1	1	1.000	42	60	.700	47	74	151	42	83	2	....	....	24	17.1	6.9	6.0	1.7	....

• JOHNSON, Ollie

Ollie Johnson

Born: May 11, 1949. Philadelphia, PA, United States. Height: 6'6". Weight: 200 lbs. Drafted: 1972 College: Temple

YEAR	TEAM	GP	GS	MIN	PTS	FGM	FGA	FG%	3PM	3PA	3P%	FTM	FTA	FT%	ORB	DRB	TRB	AST	PF	DQ	STL	BLK	TO	MPG	PPG	RPG	APG	PCM
72-73	Portland	78	....	2138	772	308	620	.497	....	....	....	156	206	.757	....	....	417	200	166	0	....	....	....	27.4	9.9	5.3	2.6	.467
73-74	Portland	79	....	1718	495	209	434	.482	....	....	....	77	94	.819	116	208	324	167	179	2	60	30	....	21.7	6.3	4.1	2.1	.400
74-75	New Orleans	43	....	1159	340	139	299	.465	....	....	....	62	77	.805	60	117	177	80	103	1	42	20	....	27.0	7.9	4.1	1.9	.342
74-75	Omaha	30	....	508	161	64	130	.492	....	....	....	33	37	.892	27	39	66	30	69	0	17	13	....	16.9	5.4	2.2	1.0	.323
75-76	Kansas City	81	....	2150	821	348	678	.513	....	....	....	125	149	.839	116	241	357	146	217	4	67	42	....	26.5	10.1	4.4	1.8	.422
76-77	Kansas City	81	....	1386	537	218	446	.489	....	....	....	101	115	.878	68	144	212	105	169	1	43	21	....	17.1	6.6	2.6	1.3	.407
77-78	Atlanta	82	....	1704	695	292	619	.472	....	....	....	111	130	.854	89	171	260	120	180	2	80	36	107	20.8	8.5	3.2	1.5	.406
78-79	Chicago	71	....	1734	650	281	540	.520	....	....	....	88	110	.800	58	169	227	163	182	2	54	33	114	24.4	9.2	3.2	2.3	.395
79-80	Chicago	79	....	1535	607	262	527	.497	1	11	.091	82	93	.882	50	113	163	161	165	0	59	24	95	19.4	7.7	2.1	2.0	.391
80-81	Philadelphia	40	....	372	202	87	158	.551	1	6	.167	27	31	.871	8	47	55	30	45	0	20	2	24	9.3	5.1	1.4	0.8	.527
81-82	Philadelphia	26	0	150	61	27	54	.500	1	3	.333	6	7	.857	7	15	22	10	28	0	13	3	13	5.8	2.3	0.8	0.4	.377
NBA Season Totals		690	0	14554	5341	2235	4505	.496	3	20	.150	868	1049	.827	599	1264	2280	1212	1503	12	455	224	353	21.1	7.7	3.3	1.8	....
74-75	Omaha	6	....	166	64	26	56	.464	....	....	....	12	12	1.000	10	13	23	6	16	0	7	4	....	27.7	10.7	3.8	1.0	.350
77-78	Atlanta	2	....	21	8	4	11	.364	....	....	....	0	0	.000	1	2	3	2	4	0	1	1	0	10.5	4.0	1.5	1.0	.321
80-81	Philadelphia	8	....	22	6	3	10	.300	0	1	.000	0	0	.000	2	3	5	2	1	0	2	1	2	2.8	0.8	0.6	0.3	.310
NBA Playoff Totals		16	....	209	78	33	77	.429	0	1	.000	12	12	1.000	13	18	31	10	21	0	10	6	2	13.1	4.9	1.9	0.6	....

• JOHNSON, Ralph

David Ralph (Boag) Johnson

Born: Dec. 6, 1921. Height: 5'11". Weight: 170 lbs. Drafted: — College: Huntington

YEAR	TEAM	GP	GS	MIN	PTS	FGM	FGA	FG%	3PM	3PA	3P%	FTM	FTA	FT%	ORB	DRB	TRB	AST	PF	DQ	STL	BLK	TO	MPG	PPG	RPG	APG	PCM
47-48	Anderson-N	57	....	....	199	84	....	....	....	....	....	31	53	.585	....	....	....	....	99	....	....	....	....	....	3.5	....	....	....
48-49	Anderson-N	64	....	....	521	218	....	....	....	....	....	85	127	.669	....	....	....	....	178	....	....	....	....	....	8.1	....	....	....

YEAR	TEAM	GP	GS	MIN	PTS	FGM	FGA	FG%	3PM	3PA	3P%	FTM	FTA	FT%	ORB	DRB	TRB	AST	PF	DQ	STL	BLK	TO	MPG	PPG	RPG	APG	PCM
49-50	Anderson	35	....	....	337	133	426	.312	....	....	....	71	83	.855	....	....	....	....	104	112	....	....	....	....	....	9.6	....	3.0	....
49-50	Fort Wayne	32	....	....	253	110	353	.312	....	....	....	33	46	.717	....	....	....	....	67	95	....	....	....	....	....	7.9	....	2.1	....
50-51	Fort Wayne	68	....	....	584	235	737	.319	....	....	....	114	162	.704	....	....	275	....	183	247	11	....	....	....	....	8.6	4.0	2.7	....
51-52	Fort Wayne	66	....	2265	523	211	592	.356	....	....	....	101	140	.721	....	....	222	....	210	243	6	....	....	....	34.3	7.9	3.4	3.2	.256
52-53	Fort Wayne	3	....	30	8	3	9	.333	....	....	....	2	3	.667	....	....	1	....	5	6	0	....	....	....	10.0	2.7	0.3	1.7	.274
NBA Season Totals		204	....	2295	1705	692	2117	.327	....	....	....	321	434	.740	....	....	498	....	569	703	17	....	....	....	11.3	8.4	2.4	2.8	....
NBL Season Totals		121	....	....	720	302	....	....	....	....	....	116	180	....	....	....	....	....	277	....	....	....	....	....	....	6.0	....	....	....
Career Totals		325	....	2295	2425	994	2117	....	....	....	....	437	614	....	....	....	498	....	569	980	17	....	....	....	7.1	7.5	1.5	1.8	....
47-48	Anderson-N	6	....	....	33	15	....	....	....	....	....	3	5	.600	....	....	....	....	....	....	....	....	....	....	....	5.5	....	....	....
48-49	Anderson-N	7	....	....	86	34	....	....	....	....	....	18	23	.783	....	....	....	....	....	....	....	....	....	....	....	12.3	....	....	....
49-50	Fort Wayne	4	....	....	28	8	32	.250	....	....	....	12	16	.750	....	....	....	....	8	13	....	....	....	....	....	7.0	....	2.0	....
50-51	Fort Wayne	3	....	....	25	12	32	.375	....	....	....	1	2	.500	....	....	7	....	7	17	2	....	....	....	....	8.3	2.3	2.3	....
51-52	Fort Wayne	2	....	70	17	8	23	.348	....	....	....	1	1	1.000	....	....	6	....	7	11	1	....	....	....	35.0	8.5	3.0	3.5	.224
NBA Playoff Totals		9	....	70	70	28	87	.322	....	....	....	14	19	.737	....	....	13	....	22	41	3	....	....	....	7.8	7.8	1.4	2.4	....
NBL Playoff Totals		13	....	....	119	49	....	....	....	....	....	21	28	....	....	....	....	....	....	....	....	....	....	....	....	9.2	....	....	....
Career Playoff Totals		22	....	70	189	77	87	....	....	....	....	35	47	....	....	....	13	....	22	41	3	....	....	....	3.2	8.6	0.6	1.0	....

• JOHNSON, Reggie

Reginald Johnson

Born: June 25, 1957. Atlanta, GA, United States.   Height: 6'9".   Weight: 205 lbs.   Drafted: 1980   College: Tennessee

YEAR	TEAM	GP	GS	MIN	PTS	FGM	FGA	FG%	3PM	3PA	3P%	FTM	FTA	FT%	ORB	DRB	TRB	AST	PF	DQ	STL	BLK	TO	MPG	PPG	RPG	APG	PCM
80-81	San Antonio	79	....	1716	808	340	682	.499	0	1	.000	128	193	.663	132	226	358	78	283	8	45	48	126	21.7	10.2	4.5	1.0	.419
81-82	San Antonio	21	0	504	220	94	194	.485	0	0	.000	32	40	.800	43	94	137	20	67	0	7	16	25	24.0	10.5	6.5	1.0	.475
81-82	Cleveland	23	0	617	223	94	175	.537	0	0	.000	35	44	.795	43	82	125	22	73	1	6	17	23	26.8	9.7	5.4	1.0	.404
81-82	Kansas City	31	9	783	377	163	293	.556	0	1	.000	51	72	.708	54	135	189	31	117	4	20	27	50	25.3	12.2	6.1	1.0	.509
82-83	Kansas City	50	0	992	430	178	355	.501	1	4	.250	73	100	.730	75	126	201	48	150	2	18	26	70	19.8	8.6	4.0	1.0	.404
82-83	Philadelphia	29	8	549	160	69	154	.448	0	0	.000	22	30	.733	32	58	90	23	82	1	8	17	35	18.9	5.5	3.1	0.8	.255
83-84	New Jersey	72	4	818	346	127	256	.496	0	1	.000	92	126	.730	53	85	138	40	141	1	24	18	58	11.4	4.8	1.9	0.6	.368
NBA Season Totals		305	21	5979	2564	1065	2109	.505	1	7	.143	433	605	.716	432	806	1238	262	913	17	128	169	387	19.6	8.4	4.1	0.9	....
80-81	San Antonio	7	....	224	89	35	73	.479	0	0	.000	19	25	.760	15	19	34	16	27	2	4	5	10	32.0	12.7	4.9	2.3	.388
82-83	Philadelphia	5	0	32	6	2	4	.500	0	0	.000	2	2	1.000	0	0	0	3	5	0	1	0	3	6.4	1.2	0.0	0.6	.107
83-84	New Jersey	7	0	17	5	0	4	.000	0	0	.000	5	6	.833	1	4	5	0	2	0	0	1	4	2.4	0.7	0.7	0.0	.103
NBA Playoff Totals		19	0	273	100	37	81	.457	0	0	.000	26	33	.788	16	23	39	19	34	2	5	6	17	14.4	5.3	2.1	1.0	....

• JOHNSON, Rich

Richard Lewis Johnson

Born: Dec. 18, 1946.   Height: 6'7".   Weight: 210 lbs.   Drafted: 1968   College: Grambling

YEAR	TEAM	GP	GS	MIN	PTS	FGM	FGA	FG%	3PM	3PA	3P%	FTM	FTA	FT%	ORB	DRB	TRB	AST	PF	DQ	STL	BLK	TO	MPG	PPG	RPG	APG	PCM
68-69	Boston	31	....	163	69	29	76	.382	....	....	....	11	23	.478	....	....	52	7	40	0	....	....	....	5.3	2.2	1.7	0.2	.366
69-70	Boston	65	....	898	380	167	361	.463	....	....	....	46	70	.657	....	....	208	32	155	3	....	....	....	13.8	5.8	3.2	0.5	.389
70-71	Carolina-A	25	....	395	169	70	151	.464	0	0	.000	29	41	.707	27	83	110	11	65	1	....	....	12	15.8	6.8	4.4	0.4	.442
70-71	Florida-A	7	....	117	36	16	28	.571	0	0	.000	4	7	.571	13	18	31	5	15	0	....	....	13	16.7	5.1	4.4	0.7	.427
70-71	Pittsburgh-A	6	....	30	15	6	12	.500	0	0	.000	3	6	.500	6	5	11	3	3	0	....	....	2	5.0	2.5	1.8	0.5	.673
70-71	Boston	1	....	13	8	4	5	.800	....	....	....	0	0	.000	....	....	5	0	3	0	....	....	....	13.0	8.0	5.0	0.0	.781
NBA Season Totals		97	....	1074	457	200	442	.452	....	....	....	57	93	.613	....	....	265	39	198	3	....	....	....	11.1	4.7	2.7	0.4	....
ABA Season Totals		38	....	542	220	92	191	.482	0	0	.000	36	54	.667	46	106	152	19	83	1	....	....	27	14.3	5.8	4.0	0.5	....
Career Totals		135	....	1616	677	292	633	.461	0	0	.000	93	147	.633	46	106	417	58	281	4	....	....	27	12.0	5.0	3.1	0.4	....
68-69	Boston	2	....	4	2	1	1	1.000	....	....	....	0	0	.000	....	....	2	0	0	0	....	....	....	2.0	1.0	1.0	0.0	.918
NBA Playoff Totals		2	....	4	2	1	1	1.000	....	....	....	0	0	.000	....	....	2	0	0	0	....	....	....	2.0	1.0	1.0	0.0	....

• JOHNSON, Ron

Ronald F. Johnson

Born: July 20, 1938.   Height: 6'8".   Weight: 215 lbs.   Drafted: 1960   College: Minnesota

YEAR	TEAM	GP	GS	MIN	PTS	FGM	FGA	FG%	3PM	3PA	3P%	FTM	FTA	FT%	ORB	DRB	TRB	AST	PF	DQ	STL	BLK	TO	MPG	PPG	RPG	APG	PCM
60-61	Detroit	6	....	49	31	11	30	.367	....	....	....	9	14	.643	....	....	14	1	6	0	....	....	....	8.2	5.2	2.3	0.2	.495
60-61	LA Lakers	8	....	43	6	2	13	.154	....	....	....	2	3	.667	....	....	15	1	4	0	....	....	....	5.4	0.8	1.9	0.1	.195
NBA Season Totals		14	....	92	37	13	43	.302	....	....	....	11	17	.647	....	....	29	2	10	0	....	....	....	6.6	2.6	2.1	0.1	....

• JOHNSON, Splinter

Splinter Johnson

Born: 1920.   Height: 6'3".   Weight: 190 lbs.   Drafted: —   College: Purdue

YEAR	TEAM	GP	GS	MIN	PTS	FGM	FGA	FG%	3PM	3PA	3P%	FTM	FTA	FT%	ORB	DRB	TRB	AST	PF	DQ	STL	BLK	TO	MPG	PPG	RPG	APG	PCM
40-41	Hammond-N	23	....	....	93	35	....	....	....	....	....	23	....	....	....	....	....	....	....	....	....	....	....	....	....	4.0	....	....	....
NBL Season Totals		23	....	....	93	35	....	....	....	....	....	23	....	....	....	....	....	....	....	....	....	....	....	....	....	4.0	....	....	....

• JOHNSON, Steffond

Steffond O'Shea Johnson

Born: Nov. 4, 1962. Longview, TX, United States.   Height: 6'8".   Weight: 240 lbs.   Drafted: 1986   College: San Diego State

YEAR	TEAM	GP	GS	MIN	PTS	FGM	FGA	FG%	3PM	3PA	3P%	FTM	FTA	FT%	ORB	DRB	TRB	AST	PF	DQ	STL	BLK	TO	MPG	PPG	RPG	APG	PCM
86-87	LA Clippers	29	0	234	74	27	64	.422	0	3	.000	20	38	.526	15	28	43	5	55	2	9	2	17	8.1	2.6	1.5	0.2	.194
NBA Season Totals		29	0	234	74	27	64	.422	0	3	.000	20	38	.526	15	28	43	5	55	2	9	2	17	8.1	2.6	1.5	0.2	....

• JOHNSON, Steve

Clarence Stephen Johnson

Born: Nov. 3, 1957. Akron, OH, United States.   Height: 6'10".   Weight: 235 lbs.   Drafted: 1981   College: Oregon State

YEAR	TEAM	GP	GS	MIN	PTS	FGM	FGA	FG%	3PM	3PA	3P%	FTM	FTA	FT%	ORB	DRB	TRB	AST	PF	DQ	STL	BLK	TO	MPG	PPG	RPG	APG	PCM
81-82	Kansas City	78	50	1741	1002	395	644	.613	0	0	.000	212	330	.642	152	307	459	91	**372**	**25**	39	89	195	22.3	12.8	5.9	1.2	.578
82-83	Kansas City	79	21	1544	928	371	595	.624	0	0	.000	186	324	.574	140	258	398	95	323	9	40	83	182	19.5	11.7	5.0	1.2	.601
83-84	Kansas City	50	13	893	479	189	342	.553	0	0	.000	101	177	.571	94	158	252	63	188	7	22	48	105	17.9	9.6	5.0	1.3	.541
83-84	Chicago	31	8	594	290	113	198	.571	0	0	.000	64	110	.582	68	98	166	18	119	8	15	21	59	19.2	9.4	5.4	0.6	.482

YEAR	TEAM	GP	GS	MIN	PTS	FGM	FGA	FG%	3PM	3PA	3P%	FTM	FTA	FT%	ORB	DRB	TRB	AST	PF	DQ	STL	BLK	TO	MPG	PPG	RPG	APG	PCM
84-85	Chicago	74	54	1659	743	281	516	.545	0	3	.000	181	252	.718	146	291	437	64	265	7	37	62	148	22.4	10.0	5.9	0.9	.481
85-86	San Antonio	71	55	1828	983	362	573	**.632**	0	0	.000	259	373	.694	143	319	462	95	291	**13**	44	66	192	25.7	13.8	6.5	1.3	.576
86-87	Portland	79	74	2345	1330	494	889	.556	0	0	.000	342	490	.698	194	372	566	155	**340**	**16**	49	76	277	29.7	16.8	7.2	2.0	.548
87-88	Portland	43	33	1050	662	258	488	.529	0	1	.000	146	249	.586	84	158	242	57	151	4	17	32	120	24.4	15.4	5.6	1.3	.523
88-89	Portland	72	11	1477	721	296	565	.524	0	0	.000	129	245	.527	135	223	358	105	254	3	20	44	137	20.5	10.0	5.0	1.5	.458
89-90	Minnesota	4	0	17	0	0	2	.000	0	0	.000	0	0	.000	0	3	3	1	4	0	0	0	6	4.3	0.0	0.8	0.3	-.323
89-90	Seattle	21	0	242	117	48	90	.533	0	0	.000	21	35	.600	19	31	50	16	52	0	3	5	25	11.5	5.6	2.4	0.8	.391
90-91	Golden State	24	8	228	90	34	63	.540	0	0	.000	22	37	.595	18	39	57	17	50	1	4	4	24	9.5	3.8	2.4	0.7	.390
NBA Season Totals		626	327	13618	7345	2841	4965	.572	0	4	.000	1663	2622	.634	1193	2257	3450	777	2409	93	290	530	1470	21.8	11.7	5.5	1.2	....
84-85	Chicago	3	0	22	6	2	7	.286	0	0	.000	2	2	1.000	3	2	5	2	4	0	0	0	2	7.3	2.0	1.7	0.7	.200
85-86	San Antonio	3	0	53	15	5	15	.333	0	0	.000	5	11	.455	2	4	6	2	14	1	0	1	6	17.7	5.0	2.0	0.7	-.010
86-87	Portland	4	4	137	83	28	61	.459	0	0	.000	27	43	.628	17	23	40	2	15	0	2	1	9	34.3	20.8	10.0	0.5	.523
88-89	Portland	3	0	34	7	2	8	.250	0	0	.000	3	3	1.000	1	3	4	0	7	0	2	0	3	11.3	2.3	1.3	0.0	.028
NBA Playoff Totals		13	4	246	111	37	91	.407	0	0	.000	37	59	.627	23	32	55	6	40	1	4	2	20	18.9	8.5	4.2	0.5	....

• JOHNSON, Stew

Stewart Johnson

Born: Aug. 19, 1944. Clairton, PA, United States. Height: 6'8". Weight: 220 lbs. Drafted: — College: Murray State

YEAR	TEAM	GP	GS	MIN	PTS	FGM	FGA	FG%	3PM	3PA	3P%	FTM	FTA	FT%	ORB	DRB	TRB	AST	PF	DQ	STL	BLK	TO	MPG	PPG	RPG	APG	PCM
67-68	Kentucky-A	17	....	279	133	55	162	.340	9	26	.346	14	25	.560	....	....	88	5	19	0	....	....	19	16.4	7.8	5.2	0.3	.397
67-68	New Jersey-A	55	....	1196	471	200	581	.344	16	53	.302	55	88	.625	....	....	327	44	128	2	....	....	70	21.7	8.6	5.9	0.8	.344
68-69	Houston-A	69	....	2279	1421	588	1372	.429	62	175	.354	183	236	.775	186	374	560	133	154	0	....	....	163	33.0	20.6	8.1	1.9	.567
68-69	New York-A	9	....	205	74	28	72	.389	2	8	.250	16	17	.941	12	32	44	9	24	1	....	....	9	22.8	8.2	4.9	1.0	.359
69-70	Pittsburgh-A	81	....	2347	1240	544	1337	.407	15	55	.273	137	176	.778	184	363	547	120	210	2	....	....	150	29.0	15.3	6.8	1.5	.451
70-71	Pittsburgh-A	84	....	2595	1342	593	1350	.439	12	40	.300	144	171	.842	194	452	646	123	221	1	....	....	160	30.9	16.0	7.7	1.5	.501
71-72	Carolina-A	50	....	1125	632	283	658	.430	13	40	.325	53	73	.726	90	182	272	73	116	1	....	....	67	22.5	12.6	5.4	1.5	.501
71-72	Pittsburgh-A	17	....	409	193	85	216	.394	3	7	.429	20	26	.769	26	84	110	15	43	0	....	....	24	24.1	11.4	6.5	0.9	.415
72-73	San Diego-A	80	....	2952	1770	769	1748	.440	37	133	.278	195	238	.819	178	419	597	174	258	6	....	....	161	36.9	22.1	7.5	2.2	.502
73-74	San Diego-A	84	....	2652	1690	716	1668	.429	59	190	.311	199	235	.847	181	350	531	127	162	....	72	13	136	31.6	20.1	6.3	1.5	.524
74-75	Memphis-A	72	....	2559	1280	592	1323	.447	37	120	.308	59	81	.728	127	315	442	120	199	....	90	21	101	35.5	17.8	6.1	1.7	.414
74-75	San Diego-A	9	....	253	151	72	170	.424	3	12	.250	4	5	.800	11	40	51	18	29	....	6	5	17	28.1	16.8	5.7	2.0	.458
75-76	San Antonio-A	10	....	123	45	21	78	.269	1	8	.125	2	4	.500	10	9	19	15	16	....	2	0	2	12.3	4.5	1.9	1.5	.161
75-76	San Diego-A	10	....	227	96	40	119	.336	0	5	.000	16	18	.889	12	17	29	8	19	....	6	1	11	22.7	9.6	2.9	0.8	.225
ABA Season Totals		647	....	19201	10538	4586	10854	.423	269	872	.308	1097	1393	.788	1211	2637	4263	984	1598	13	176	40	1090	29.7	16.3	6.6	1.5	....
72-73	San Diego-A	4	....	151	73	32	82	.390	4	13	.308	5	7	.714	6	19	25	8	10	0	....		6	37.8	18.3	6.3	2.0	.357
73-74	San Diego-A	6	....	213	93	42	114	.368	5	12	.417	4	6	.667	15	27	42	13	14	....	5	2	8	35.5	15.5	7.0	2.2	.353
74-75	Memphis-A	5	....	205	72	29	68	.426	3	5	.600	11	12	.917	5	21	26	12	8	....	11	5	9	41.0	14.4	5.2	2.4	.341
ABA Playoff Totals		15	....	569	238	103	264	.390	12	30	.400	20	25	.800	26	67	93	33	32	0	16	7	23	37.9	15.9	6.2	2.2	....

• JOHNSON, Vinnie

Vincent (Microwave) Johnson

Born: Sept. 1, 1956. Brooklyn, NY, United States. Height: 6'2". Weight: 200 lbs. Drafted: 1979 College: Baylor

YEAR	TEAM	GP	GS	MIN	PTS	FGM	FGA	FG%	3PM	3PA	3P%	FTM	FTA	FT%	ORB	DRB	TRB	AST	PF	DQ	STL	BLK	TO	MPG	PPG	RPG	APG	PCM
79-80	Seattle	38	....	325	121	45	115	.391	0	1	.000	31	39	.795	19	36	55	54	40	0	19	4	42	8.6	3.2	1.4	1.4	.393
80-81	Seattle	81	....	2311	1053	419	785	.534	1	5	.200	214	270	.793	193	173	366	341	198	0	78	20	219	28.5	13.0	4.5	4.2	.519
81-82	Seattle	7	0	104	27	9	22	.409	0	1	.000	9	12	.750	7	8	15	11	8	0	6	2	5	14.9	3.9	2.1	1.6	.369
81-82	Detroit	67	15	1191	517	208	422	.493	3	11	.273	98	130	.754	75	69	144	160	93	0	50	23	94	17.8	7.7	2.1	2.4	.460
82-83	Detroit	82	51	2511	1296	520	1013	.513	11	40	.275	245	315	.778	167	186	353	301	263	2	93	49	156	30.6	15.8	4.3	3.7	.533
83-84	Detroit	82	0	1909	1063	426	901	.473	4	19	.211	207	275	.753	130	107	237	271	196	1	44	19	131	23.3	13.0	2.9	3.3	.495
84-85	Detroit	82	16	2093	1051	428	942	.454	5	27	.185	190	247	.769	134	118	252	325	205	2	71	20	131	25.5	12.8	3.1	4.0	.475
85-86	Detroit	79	12	1978	1097	465	996	.467	2	13	.154	165	214	.771	119	107	226	269	180	2	80	23	87	25.0	13.9	2.9	3.4	.511
86-87	Detroit	78	8	2166	1228	533	1154	.462	4	14	.286	158	201	.786	123	134	257	300	159	0	92	16	133	27.8	15.7	3.3	3.8	.504
87-88	Detroit	82	1	1935	1002	425	959	.443	5	24	.208	147	217	.677	90	141	231	267	164	0	58	18	156	23.6	12.2	2.8	3.3	.424
88-89	Detroit	82	21	2073	1130	462	996	.464	13	44	.295	193	263	.734	109	146	255	242	155	0	74	17	107	25.3	13.8	3.1	3.0	.487
89-90	Detroit	82	12	1972	804	334	775	.431	5	34	.147	131	196	.668	108	148	256	255	143	0	71	13	123	24.0	9.8	3.1	3.1	.389
90-91	Detroit	82	28	2390	958	406	936	.434	11	34	.324	135	209	.646	110	170	280	271	166	0	75	15	115	29.1	11.7	3.4	3.3	.368
91-92	San Antonio	60	23	1350	478	202	499	.405	19	60	.317	55	85	.647	67	115	182	145	93	0	41	14	72	22.5	8.0	3.0	2.4	.336
NBA Season Totals		984	187	24308	11825	4882	10515	.464	83	327	.254	1978	2673	.740	1451	1658	3109	3212	2063	7	852	253	1571	24.7	12.0	3.2	3.3	....
79-80	Seattle	5	....	12	2	1	3	.333	0	0	.000	0	0	.000	0	2	2	2	1	0	1	0	0	2.4	0.4	0.4	0.4	.387
83-84	Detroit	5	0	132	51	17	46	.370	0	1	.000	17	19	.895	5	9	14	12	9	0	1	1	4	26.4	10.2	2.8	2.4	.325
84-85	Detroit	9	0	235	128	53	103	.515	0	3	.000	22	28	.786	15	12	27	29	24	0	6	1	15	26.1	14.2	3.0	3.2	.494
85-86	Detroit	4	0	85	51	22	49	.449	0	1	.000	7	13	.538	8	9	17	11	9	0	3	0	5	21.3	12.8	4.3	2.8	.525
86-87	Detroit	15	0	388	221	95	207	.459	0	2	.000	31	36	.861	20	24	44	62	33	0	9	4	23	25.9	14.7	2.9	4.1	.508
87-88	Detroit	23	0	477	236	101	239	.423	0	7	.143	33	50	.660	35	40	75	43	48	0	17	4	21	20.7	10.3	3.3	1.9	.404
88-89	Detroit	17	0	372	239	91	200	.455	10	24	.417	47	62	.758	16	29	45	43	32	0	4	3	21	21.9	14.1	2.6	2.5	.512
89-90	Detroit	20	0	463	206	85	184	.462	2	7	.286	34	43	.791	28	28	56	54	38	0	8	4	31	23.2	10.3	2.8	2.7	.396
90-91	Detroit	15	3	438	228	102	220	.464	2	13	.154	22	31	.710	37	39	76	43	33	0	11	4	17	29.2	15.2	5.1	2.9	.487
91-92	San Antonio	3	0	69	25	11	24	.458	2	4	.500	1	2	.500	3	5	8	7	7	0	5	1	5	23.0	8.3	2.7	2.3	.363
NBA Playoff Totals		116	3	2671	1387	578	1275	.453	17	62	.274	214	284	.754	167	197	364	306	234	0	65	22	142	23.0	12.0	3.1	2.6	....

• JOHNSTON, Nate

Nate Johnston

Born: Dec. 18, 1966. Birmingham, AL, United States. Height: 6'8". Weight: 210 lbs. Drafted: 1988 College: Tampa

YEAR	TEAM	GP	GS	MIN	PTS	FGM	FGA	FG%	3PM	3PA	3P%	FTM	FTA	FT%	ORB	DRB	TRB	AST	PF	DQ	STL	BLK	TO	MPG	PPG	RPG	APG	PCM
89-90	Utah	6	0	13	11	4	11	.364	1	1	1.000	2	2	1.000	2	0	2	0	0	0	0	1	1	2.2	1.8	0.3	0.0	.486
89-90	Portland	15	0	74	35	14	37	.378	0	3	.000	7	11	.636	11	10	21	1	11	1	3	7	5	4.9	2.3	1.4	0.1	.430
NBA Season Totals		21	0	87	46	18	48	.375	1	4	.250	9	13	.692	13	10	23	1	11	1	3	8	6	4.1	2.2	1.1	0.0	....
89-90	Portland	3	0	19	13	6	11	.545	0	0	.000	1	1	1.000	2	4	6	1	5	0	1	1	0	6.3	4.3	2.0	0.3	.765
NBA Playoff Totals		3	0	19	13	6	11	.545	0	0	.000	1	1	1.000	2	4	6	1	5	0	1	1	0	6.3	4.3	2.0	0.3	....

YEAR	TEAM	GP	GS	MIN	PTS	FGM	FGA	FG%	3PM	3PA	3P%	FTM	FTA	FT%	ORB	DRB	TRB	AST	PF	DQ	STL	BLK	TO	MPG	PPG	RPG	APG	PCM

• JOHNSTON, Neil

Donald Neil (Gabby) Johnston

Born: Feb. 4, 1929. Chillicothe, OH, United States. Died: Sept.28, 1978.   Height: 6'8".   Weight: 210 lbs.   Drafted: —   College: Ohio State   HOF: 1990

YEAR	TEAM	GP	GS	MIN	PTS	FGM	FGA	FG%	3PM	3PA	3P%	FTM	FTA	FT%	ORB	DRB	TRB	AST	PF	DQ	STL	BLK	TO	MPG	PPG	RPG	APG	PCM
51-52	Philadelphia	64	....	993	382	141	299	.472	....	....	....	100	151	.662	....	....	342	39	154	5	....	....	....	15.5	6.0	5.3	0.6	.494
52-53	Philadelphia	70	....	3166	1564	504	1114	.452	....	....	....	556	794	.700	....	....	976	197	248	6	....	....	....	45.2	22.3	13.9	2.8	.602
53-54	Philadelphia	72	....	3296	1759	591	1317	.449	....	....	....	577	772	.747	....	....	797	203	259	7	....	....	....	45.8	24.4	11.1	2.8	.580
54-55	Philadelphia	72	....	2917	1631	521	1184	.440	....	....	....	589	769	.766	....	....	1085	215	255	4	....	....	....	40.5	22.7	15.1	3.0	.704
55-56	Philadelphia	70	....	2594	1547	499	1092	.457	....	....	....	549	685	.801	....	....	872	225	251	8	....	....	....	37.1	22.1	12.5	3.2	.729
56-57	Philadelphia	69	....	2531	1575	520	1163	.447	....	....	....	535	648	.825	....	....	855	203	231	2	....	....	....	36.7	22.8	12.4	2.9	.735
57-58	Philadelphia	71	....	2408	1388	473	1102	.429	....	....	....	442	540	.819	....	....	790	166	233	4	....	....	....	33.9	19.5	11.1	2.3	.663
58-59	Philadelphia	28	....	393	177	54	164	.329	....	....	....	69	88	.784	....	....	139	21	50	0	....	....	....	14.0	6.3	5.0	0.8	.507
NBA Season Totals		516	....	18298	10023	3303	7435	.444	....	....	....	3417	4447	.768	....	....	5856	1269	1681	36	....	....	....	35.5	19.4	11.3	2.5	....
51-52	Philadelphia	3	....	32	16	5	10	.500	....	....	....	6	8	.750	....	....	10	1	8	0	....	....	....	10.7	5.3	3.3	0.3	.540
55-56	Philadelphia	10	....	397	203	69	169	.408	....	....	....	65	92	.707	....	....	143	51	41	0	....	....	....	39.7	20.3	14.3	5.1	.688
56-57	Philadelphia	2	....	84	38	17	53	.321	....	....	....	4	6	.667	....	....	35	9	9	0	....	....	....	42.0	19.0	17.5	4.5	.529
57-58	Philadelphia	8	....	189	87	30	78	.385	....	....	....	27	33	.818	....	....	69	14	18	0	....	....	....	23.6	10.9	8.6	1.8	.589
NBA Playoff Totals		23	....	702	344	121	310	.390	....	....	....	102	139	.734	....	....	257	75	76	0	....	....	....	30.5	15.0	11.2	3.3	....

• JOHNSTONE, Jim

James Robert Johnstone

Born: Sept. 20, 1960. New Canaan, CT, United States.   Height: 6'11".   Weight: 245 lbs.   Drafted: 1982   College: Wake Forest

YEAR	TEAM	GP	GS	MIN	PTS	FGM	FGA	FG%	3PM	3PA	3P%	FTM	FTA	FT%	ORB	DRB	TRB	AST	PF	DQ	STL	BLK	TO	MPG	PPG	RPG	APG	PCM
82-83	San Antonio	7	0	54	7	2	10	.200	0	0	.000	3	5	.600	4	12	16	1	9	0	1	1	4	7.7	1.0	2.3	0.1	.158
82-83	Detroit	16	0	137	24	9	20	.450	0	0	.000	6	15	.400	11	19	30	10	24	0	2	6	11	8.6	1.5	1.9	0.6	.252
NBA Season Totals		23	0	191	31	11	30	.367	0	0	.000	9	20	.450	15	31	46	11	33	0	3	7	15	8.3	1.3	2.0	0.5	....

• JOLLIFF, Howie

Howard Jolliff

Born: July 20, 1938.   Height: 6'7".   Weight: 218 lbs.   Drafted: 1960   College: Ohio University

YEAR	TEAM	GP	GS	MIN	PTS	FGM	FGA	FG%	3PM	3PA	3P%	FTM	FTA	FT%	ORB	DRB	TRB	AST	PF	DQ	STL	BLK	TO	MPG	PPG	RPG	APG	PCM
60-61	LA Lakers	46	....	352	103	46	141	.326	....	....	....	11	23	.478	....	....	141	16	53	0	....	....	....	7.7	2.2	3.1	0.3	.378
61-62	LA Lakers	64	....	1094	249	104	253	.411	....	....	....	41	78	.526	....	....	383	76	175	4	....	....	....	17.1	3.9	6.0	1.2	.404
62-63	LA Lakers	28	....	293	36	15	55	.273	....	....	....	6	9	.667	....	....	62	20	49	1	....	....	....	10.5	1.3	2.2	0.7	.195
NBA Season Totals		138	....	1739	388	165	449	.367	....	....	....	58	110	.527	....	....	586	112	277	5	....	....	....	12.6	2.8	4.2	0.8	....
60-61	LA Lakers	4	....	35	12	6	13	.462	....	....	....	0	0	.000	....	....	25	8	4	0	....	....	....	8.8	3.0	6.3	2.0	.974
61-62	LA Lakers	9	....	77	12	2	9	.222	....	....	....	8	8	1.000	....	....	28	7	17	1	....	....	....	8.6	1.3	3.1	0.8	.393
NBA Playoff Totals		13	....	112	24	8	22	.364	....	....	....	8	8	1.000	....	....	53	15	21	1	....	....	....	8.6	1.8	4.1	1.2	....

• JONES, Alvin

Alvin Robert Jones III

Born: Sept. 9, 1978. Luxembourg, Luxembourg.   Height: 6'11".   Weight: 265 lbs.   Drafted: —   College: Georgia Tech

YEAR	TEAM	GP	GS	MIN	PTS	FGM	FGA	FG%	3PM	3PA	3P%	FTM	FTA	FT%	ORB	DRB	TRB	AST	PF	DQ	STL	BLK	TO	MPG	PPG	RPG	APG	PCM
01-02	Philadelphia	23	2	126	26	8	20	.400	0	0	.000	10	20	.500	13	23	36	3	35	0	3	9	11	5.5	1.1	1.6	0.1	.250
NBA Season Totals		23	2	126	26	8	20	.400	0	0	.000	10	20	.500	13	23	36	3	35	0	3	9	11	5.5	1.1	1.6	0.1	....
01-02	Philadelphia	2	0	5	0	0	0	.000	0	0	.000	0	0	.000	0	1	1	0	0	0	0	0	1	2.5	0.0	0.5	0.0	.000
NBA Playoff Totals		2	0	5	0	0	0	.000	0	0	.000	0	0	.000	0	1	1	0	0	0	0	0	1	2.5	0.0	0.5	0.0	....

• JONES, Anthony

Anthony Hamilton Jones

Born: Sept. 13, 1962. Washington, DC, United States.   Height: 6'6".   Weight: 195 lbs.   Drafted: 1986   College: UNLV

YEAR	TEAM	GP	GS	MIN	PTS	FGM	FGA	FG%	3PM	3PA	3P%	FTM	FTA	FT%	ORB	DRB	TRB	AST	PF	DQ	STL	BLK	TO	MPG	PPG	RPG	APG	PCM
86-87	Washington	16	1	114	37	14	33	.424	0	1	.000	9	13	.692	1	8	9	7	11	0	10	1	11	7.1	2.3	0.6	0.4	.247
86-87	San Antonio	49	3	744	286	119	289	.412	7	19	.368	41	52	.788	39	56	95	66	68	0	32	18	39	15.2	5.8	1.9	1.3	.350
88-89	Chicago	8	0	65	12	5	15	.333	0	1	.000	2	2	1.000	4	4	8	4	7	0	2	1	1	8.1	1.5	1.0	0.5	.200
88-89	Dallas	25	0	131	64	24	64	.375	4	15	.267	12	14	.857	10	10	20	13	13	0	9	2	5	5.2	2.6	0.8	0.5	.442
89-90	Dallas	66	0	650	195	72	194	.371	4	13	.308	47	69	.681	33	49	82	29	77	0	32	16	40	9.8	3.0	1.2	0.4	.230
NBA Season Totals		164	4	1704	594	234	595	.393	15	49	.306	111	150	.740	87	127	214	119	176	0	85	38	96	10.4	3.6	1.3	0.7	....
89-90	Dallas	1	0	3	0	0	0	.000	0	0	.000	0	0	.000	0	0	0	0	0	0	0	0	0	3.0	0.0	0.0	0.0	.000
NBA Playoff Totals		1	0	3	0	0	0	.000	0	0	.000	0	0	.000	0	0	0	0	0	0	0	0	0	3.0	0.0	0.0	0.0	....

• JONES, Askia

Askia Jones

Born: Dec. 3, 1971. Philadelphia, PA, United States.   Height: 6'5".   Weight: 200 lbs.   Drafted: —   College: Kansas State

YEAR	TEAM	GP	GS	MIN	PTS	FGM	FGA	FG%	3PM	3PA	3P%	FTM	FTA	FT%	ORB	DRB	TRB	AST	PF	DQ	STL	BLK	TO	MPG	PPG	RPG	APG	PCM
94-95	Minnesota	11	0	139	45	15	44	.341	2	12	.167	13	16	.813	6	5	11	16	19	0	6	0	9	12.6	4.1	1.0	1.5	.230
NBA Season Totals		11	0	139	45	15	44	.341	2	12	.167	13	16	.813	6	5	11	16	19	0	6	0	9	12.6	4.1	1.0	1.5	....

• JONES, Bill

Clarence William (Bill) Jones

Born: Mar. 18, 1966. Detroit, MI, United States.   Height: 6'7".   Weight: 175 lbs.   Drafted: —   College: Iowa

YEAR	TEAM	GP	GS	MIN	PTS	FGM	FGA	FG%	3PM	3PA	3P%	FTM	FTA	FT%	ORB	DRB	TRB	AST	PF	DQ	STL	BLK	TO	MPG	PPG	RPG	APG	PCM
88-89	New Jersey	37	0	307	129	50	102	.490	0	1	.000	29	43	.674	20	27	47	20	38	0	17	6	19	8.3	3.5	1.3	0.5	.408
NBA Season Totals		37	0	307	129	50	102	.490	0	1	.000	29	43	.674	20	27	47	20	38	0	17	6	19	8.3	3.5	1.3	0.5	....

• JONES, Billy

Billy Jones

Born: 1914. Height: 6' Weight: 185 lbs. Drafted: — College: Toledo

YEAR	TEAM	GP	GS	MIN	PTS	FGM	FGA	FG%	3PM	3PA	3P%	FTM	FTA	FT%	ORB	DRB	TRB	AST	PF	DQ	STL	BLK	TO	MPG	PPG	RPG	APG	PCM
42-43	Toledo-N	4	....	....	22	11	....	....	....	....	....	0	....	....	....	....	....	....	....	....	....	....	....	....	5.5	....	....	....
NBL Season Totals		4	....	....	22	11	....	....	....	....	....	0	....	....	....	....	....	....	....	....	....	....	....	....	5.5	....	....	....

• JONES, Bobby

Robert Clyde Jones

Born: Dec. 18, 1951. Charlotte, NC, United States. Height: 6'9". Weight: 210 lbs. Drafted: 1974 College: North Carolina

YEAR	TEAM	GP	GS	MIN	PTS	FGM	FGA	FG%	3PM	3PA	3P%	FTM	FTA	FT%	ORB	DRB	TRB	AST	PF	DQ	STL	BLK	TO	MPG	PPG	RPG	APG	PCM
74-75	Denver-A	84	....	2706	1245	529	876	**.604**	0	1	.000	187	269	.695	230	462	692	303	263	....	167	153	234	32.2	14.8	8.2	3.6	.641
75-76	Denver-A	83	....	2845	1235	510	898	**.568**	0	0	.000	215	308	.698	241	550	791	331	253	....	170	184	232	34.3	14.9	9.5	4.0	.635
76-77	Denver	82	....	2419	1238	501	879	.570	....	....	....	236	329	.717	174	504	678	264	238	3	186	162	....	29.5	15.1	8.3	3.2	.684
77-78	Denver	75	....	2440	1088	440	761	**.578**	....	....	....	208	277	.751	164	472	636	252	221	2	137	126	195	32.5	14.5	8.5	3.4	.647
78-79	Philadelphia	80	....	2304	965	378	704	.537	....	....	....	209	277	.755	199	332	531	201	245	2	107	96	168	28.8	12.1	6.6	2.5	.548
79-80	Philadelphia	81	....	2125	1053	398	748	.532	0	3	.000	257	329	.781	152	298	450	146	223	3	102	118	146	26.2	13.0	5.6	1.8	.582
80-81	Philadelphia	81	....	2046	1096	407	755	.539	0	3	.000	282	347	.813	142	293	435	226	226	2	95	74	146	25.3	13.5	5.4	2.8	.640
81-82	Philadelphia	76	73	2181	1095	416	737	.564	0	3	.000	263	333	.790	109	284	393	189	211	3	99	112	144	28.7	14.4	5.2	2.5	.595
82-83	Philadelphia	74	0	1749	665	250	460	.543	0	1	.000	165	208	.793	102	242	344	142	199	4	85	91	111	23.6	9.0	4.6	1.9	.510
83-84	Philadelphia	75	0	1761	619	226	432	.523	0	1	.000	167	213	.784	92	231	323	187	199	1	107	103	98	23.5	8.3	4.3	2.5	.521
84-85	Philadelphia	80	8	1633	600	207	385	.538	0	4	.000	186	216	.861	105	192	297	155	183	2	84	50	120	20.4	7.5	3.7	1.9	.484
85-86	Philadelphia	70	42	1519	492	189	338	.559	0	1	.000	114	145	.786	49	120	169	126	159	0	48	49	91	21.7	7.0	2.4	1.8	.371
NBA Season Totals		774	123	20177	8911	3412	6199	.550	0	16	.000	2087	2674	.780	1288	2968	4256	1888	2104	22	1050	981	1219	26.1	11.5	5.5	2.4	....
ABA Season Totals		167	....	5551	2480	1039	1774	.586	0	1	.000	402	577	.697	471	1012	1483	634	516	....	337	337	466	33.2	14.9	8.9	3.8	....
Career Totals		941	123	25728	11391	4451	7973	.558	0	17	.000	2489	3251	.766	1759	3980	5739	2522	2620	22	1387	1318	1685	27.3	12.1	6.1	2.7	....
74-75	Denver-A	13	....	428	169	69	129	.535	0	1	.000	31	40	.775	35	76	111	38	49	....	12	12	31	32.9	13.0	8.5	2.9	.539
75-76	Denver-A	13	....	431	178	74	127	.583	0	0	.000	30	41	.732	41	71	112	59	53	....	16	20	34	33.2	13.7	8.6	4.5	.621
76-77	Denver	6	....	187	72	31	64	.484	....	....	....	10	17	.588	11	24	35	21	25	1	17	14	....	31.2	12.0	5.8	3.5	.448
77-78	Denver	13	....	390	166	66	116	.569	....	....	....	34	46	.739	36	66	102	35	42	1	16	9	24	30.0	12.8	7.8	2.7	.585
78-79	Philadelphia	9	....	260	118	48	87	.552	....	....	....	22	26	.846	12	31	43	19	30	0	5	4	15	28.9	13.1	4.8	2.1	.469
79-80	Philadelphia	18	....	470	233	90	172	.523	0	1	.000	53	62	.855	29	57	86	31	56	1	21	32	23	26.1	12.9	4.8	1.7	.571
80-81	Philadelphia	16	....	443	235	81	160	.506	0	0	.000	73	88	.830	35	53	88	33	60	1	18	21	32	27.7	14.7	5.5	2.1	.567
81-82	Philadelphia	21	12	589	256	94	174	.540	0	0	.000	68	81	.840	37	62	99	52	69	0	15	22	33	28.0	12.2	4.7	2.5	.502
82-83	Philadelphia	12	0	324	103	43	78	.551	0	1	.000	17	20	.850	19	39	58	34	29	0	15	18	18	27.0	8.6	4.8	2.8	.494
83-84	Philadelphia	5	3	130	48	15	31	.484	0	0	.000	18	19	.947	9	14	23	9	12	0	3	7	8	26.0	9.6	4.6	1.8	.461
84-85	Philadelphia	13	11	309	106	46	78	.590	0	0	.000	14	20	.700	22	26	48	16	38	0	12	15	19	23.8	8.2	3.7	1.2	.404
85-86	Philadelphia	12	5	329	116	39	74	.527	0	1	.000	38	50	.760	9	23	32	34	39	0	10	14	15	27.4	9.7	2.7	2.8	.408
NBA Playoff Totals		125	31	3431	1453	553	1034	.535	0	3	.000	347	429	.809	219	395	614	284	400	4	132	156	187	27.4	11.6	4.9	2.3	....
ABA Playoff Totals		26	....	859	347	143	256	.559	0	1	.000	61	81	.753	76	147	223	97	102	....	28	32	65	33.0	13.3	8.6	3.7	....
Career Playoff Totals		151	31	4290	1800	696	1290	.540	0	4	.000	408	510	.800	295	542	837	381	502	4	160	188	252	28.4	11.9	5.5	2.5	....

• JONES, Caldwell

Caldwell (Pops) Jones

Born: Aug. 4, 1950. McGehee, AR, United States. Height: 6'11". Weight: 217 lbs. Drafted: 1973 College: Albany State (GA)

YEAR	TEAM	GP	GS	MIN	PTS	FGM	FGA	FG%	3PM	3PA	3P%	FTM	FTA	FT%	ORB	DRB	TRB	AST	PF	DQ	STL	BLK	TO	MPG	PPG	RPG	APG	PCM
73-74	San Diego-A	79	....	2929	1187	507	1091	.465	2	8	.250	171	230	.743	322	773	1095	144	319	....	64	**316**	155	37.1	15.0	13.9	1.8	.556
74-75	San Diego-A	76	....	3004	1479	606	1240	.489	3	11	.273	264	335	.788	311	763	1074	162	269	....	60	246	192	39.5	19.5	14.1	2.1	.632
75-76	Kentucky-A	15	....	457	186	80	171	.468	0	0	.000	26	37	.703	59	99	158	13	73	....	17	16	36	30.5	12.4	10.5	0.9	.487
75-76	San Diego-A	10	....	407	159	69	160	.431	0	0	.000	21	33	.636	42	94	136	22	42	....	13	37	23	40.7	15.9	13.6	2.2	.490
75-76	St. Louis-A	51	....	1810	641	274	569	.482	0	7	.000	93	116	.802	145	414	559	112	206	....	51	165	107	35.5	12.6	11.0	2.2	.496
76-77	Philadelphia	82	....	2023	494	215	424	.507	....	....	....	64	116	.552	190	476	666	92	301	3	43	200	....	24.7	6.0	8.1	1.1	.416
77-78	Philadelphia	80	....	1636	434	169	359	.471	....	....	....	96	153	.627	165	405	570	92	281	4	26	127	128	20.5	5.4	7.1	1.2	.455
78-79	Philadelphia	78	....	2171	725	302	637	.474	....	....	....	121	162	.747	177	570	747	151	303	10	39	157	156	27.8	9.3	9.6	1.9	.526
79-80	Philadelphia	80	....	2771	588	232	532	.436	0	2	.000	124	178	.697	219	731	950	164	298	5	43	162	216	34.6	7.4	11.9	2.1	.428
80-81	Philadelphia	81	....	2639	584	218	485	.449	0	0	.000	148	193	.767	200	613	813	122	271	2	53	134	170	32.6	7.2	10.0	1.5	.411
81-82	Philadelphia	81	47	2446	641	231	465	.497	0	3	.000	179	219	.817	164	544	708	100	301	3	38	146	154	30.2	7.9	8.7	1.2	.432
82-83	Houston	82	82	2440	776	307	677	.453	0	2	.000	162	206	.786	222	446	668	138	278	2	46	131	172	29.8	9.5	8.1	1.7	.433
83-84	Houston	81	73	2506	801	318	633	.502	1	3	.333	164	196	.837	168	414	582	156	335	7	46	80	162	30.9	9.9	7.2	1.9	.404
84-85	Chicago	42	32	885	142	53	115	.461	0	2	.000	36	47	.766	49	162	211	34	125	3	12	31	42	21.1	3.4	5.0	0.8	.288
85-86	Portland	80	19	1437	376	126	254	.496	0	7	.000	124	150	.827	105	250	355	74	244	2	38	61	104	18.0	4.7	4.4	0.9	.373
86-87	Portland	78	37	1578	319	111	224	.496	0	2	.000	97	124	.782	114	341	455	64	227	5	23	77	86	20.2	4.1	5.8	0.8	.381
87-88	Portland	79	77	1778	334	128	263	.487	0	4	.000	78	106	.736	105	303	408	81	251	0	29	99	79	22.5	4.2	5.2	1.0	.332
88-89	Portland	72	40	1279	202	77	183	.421	0	1	.000	48	61	.787	88	212	300	59	166	0	24	85	86	17.8	2.8	4.2	0.8	.300
89-90	San Antonio	72	2	885	173	67	144	.465	1	5	.200	38	54	.704	76	154	230	20	146	2	20	27	50	12.3	2.4	3.2	0.3	.293
NBA Season Totals		1068	409	26474	6589	2554	5395	.473	2	31	.065	1479	1965	.753	2042	5621	7663	1347	3527	48	480	1517	1605	24.8	6.2	7.2	1.3	....
ABA Season Totals		231	....	8607	3652	1536	3231	.475	5	26	.192	575	751	.766	879	2143	3022	453	909	....	205	780	513	37.3	15.8	13.1	2.0	....
Career Totals		1299	409	35081	10241	4090	8626	.474	7	57	.123	2054	2716	.756	2921	7764	10685	1800	4436	48	685	2297	2118	27.0	7.9	8.2	1.4	....
73-74	San Diego-A	6	....	277	83	36	88	.409	0	0	.000	11	16	.688	21	73	94	15	19	....	6	14	9	46.2	13.8	15.7	2.5	.454
76-77	Philadelphia	19	....	513	92	37	73	.507	....	....	....	18	30	.600	38	112	150	20	81	4	9	40	....	27.0	4.8	7.9	1.1	.337
77-78	Philadelphia	10	....	301	64	28	56	.500	....	....	....	8	10	.800	22	84	106	14	36	2	5	30	19	30.1	6.4	10.6	1.4	.483
78-79	Philadelphia	9	....	320	114	43	89	.483	....	....	....	28	36	.778	37	84	121	21	36	0	4	22	21	35.6	12.7	13.4	2.3	.591
79-80	Philadelphia	18	....	639	158	58	129	.450	0	3	.000	42	52	.808	50	135	185	34	75	1	13	37	37	35.5	8.8	10.3	1.9	.425
80-81	Philadelphia	16	....	580	139	54	95	.568	0	0	.000	31	42	.738	37	118	155	27	53	0	7	31	33	36.3	8.7	9.7	1.7	.427
81-82	Philadelphia	21	21	679	183	74	160	.463	0	0	.000	35	41	.854	52	137	189	19	77	1	11	40	29	32.3	8.7	9.0	0.9	.413
84-85	Chicago	2	0	18	10	5	6	.833	0	1	.000	0	0	.000	1	4	5	0	7	1	0	1	1	9.0	5.0	2.5	0.0	.581
85-86	Portland	4	0	73	14	6	17	.353	0	0	.000	2	4	.500	9	10	19	3	13	0	0	2	4	18.3	3.5	4.8	0.8	.217
86-87	Portland	4	4	129	15	5	12	.417	0	0	.000	5	6	.833	9	22	31	6	15	0	0	6	5	32.3	3.8	7.8	1.5	.289
87-88	Portland	4	4	98	13	6	16	.375	0	0	.000	1	2	.500	4	13	17	1	17	0	2	8	2	24.5	3.3	4.3	0.3	.201
88-89	Portland	3	1	50	4	2	3	.667	0	0	.000	0	0	.000	2	0	2	0	6	0	0	3	3	16.7	1.3	0.7	0.0	.043

YEAR	TEAM	GP	GS	MIN	PTS	FGM	FGA	FG%	3PM	3PA	3P%	FTM	FTA	FT%	ORB	DRB	TRB	AST	PF	DQ	STL	BLK	TO	MPG	PPG	RPG	APG	PCM
89-90	San Antonio	9	0	66	8	4	9	.444	0	0	.000	0	1	.000	6	7	13	2	10	0	0	3	3	7.3	0.9	1.4	0.2	.189
NBA Playoff Totals		119	30	3466	814	322	665	.484	0	4	.000	170	224	.759	267	726	993	147	426	9	51	223	157	29.1	6.8	8.3	1.2	
ABA Playoff Totals		6	....	277	83	36	88	.409	0	0	.000	11	16	.688	21	73	94	15	19	....	6	14	9	46.2	13.8	15.7	2.5	
Career Playoff Totals		125	30	3743	897	358	753	.475	0	4	.000	181	240	.754	288	799	1087	162	445	9	57	237	166	29.9	7.2	8.7	1.3	

• JONES, Casey

Casey Jones

Born: 1915.   Height: 6'2".   Weight: 175 lbs.   Drafted: —   College: none

YEAR	TEAM	GP	GS	MIN	PTS	FGM	FGA	FG%	3PM	3PA	3P%	FTM	FTA	FT%	ORB	DRB	TRB	AST	PF	DQ	STL	BLK	TO	MPG	PPG	RPG	APG	PCM
42-43	Toledo-N	3	....	....	7	3	....	....	....	....	....	1	....	....	....	....	....	....	....	....	....	....	....	2.3	....	....	....	
NBL Season Totals		3	....	....	7	3	....	....	....	....	....	1	....	....	....	....	....	....	....	....	....	....	....	2.3	....	....	....	

• JONES, Charles

Charles (C.J., Gadget) Jones

Born: Apr. 3, 1957. McGehee, AR, United States.   Height: 6'9".   Weight: 215 lbs.   Drafted: 1979   College: Albany State (GA)

YEAR	TEAM	GP	GS	MIN	PTS	FGM	FGA	FG%	3PM	3PA	3P%	FTM	FTA	FT%	ORB	DRB	TRB	AST	PF	DQ	STL	BLK	TO	MPG	PPG	RPG	APG	PCM
83-84	Philadelphia	1	0	3	1	0	1	.000	0	0	.000	1	4	.250	0	0	0	0	1	0	0	0	0	3.0	1.0	0.0	0.0	-.597
84-85	Chicago	3	0	29	8	2	4	.500	0	0	.000	4	6	.667	2	4	6	1	6	0	0	5	4	9.7	2.7	2.0	0.3	.345
84-85	Washington	28	4	638	166	65	123	.528	0	0	.000	36	52	.692	69	109	178	25	101	3	22	74	22	22.8	5.9	6.4	0.9	.500
85-86	Washington	81	58	1609	312	129	254	.508	0	2	.000	54	86	.628	122	199	321	76	235	2	57	133	73	19.9	3.9	4.0	0.9	.348
86-87	Washington	79	64	1609	284	118	249	.474	0	1	.000	48	76	.632	144	212	356	80	252	2	67	165	79	20.4	3.6	4.5	1.0	.367
87-88	Washington	69	49	1313	197	72	177	.407	0	1	.000	53	75	.707	106	219	325	59	226	5	53	113	55	19.0	2.9	4.7	0.9	.345
88-89	Washington	53	45	1154	136	60	125	.480	0	1	.000	16	25	.640	77	180	257	42	187	4	39	76	37	21.8	2.6	4.8	0.8	.295
89-90	Washington	81	81	2240	256	94	185	.508	0	0	.000	68	105	.648	145	359	504	139	296	10	50	197	73	27.7	3.2	6.2	1.7	.356
90-91	Washington	62	54	1499	163	67	124	.540	0	0	.000	29	50	.580	119	240	359	48	199	2	51	124	43	24.2	2.6	5.8	0.8	.345
91-92	Washington	75	32	1365	86	33	90	.367	0	0	.000	20	40	.500	105	212	317	62	214	0	43	92	38	18.2	1.1	4.2	0.8	.275
92-93	Washington	67	21	1206	88	33	63	.524	0	1	.000	22	38	.579	87	190	277	42	144	1	38	77	40	18.0	1.3	4.1	0.6	.297
93-94	Detroit	42	0	877	91	36	78	.462	0	1	.000	19	34	.559	89	146	235	29	136	0	14	43	13	20.9	2.2	5.6	0.7	.308
94-95	Houston	3	0	36	3	1	3	.333	0	0	.000	1	2	.500	2	5	7	0	8	0	0	1	0	12.0	1.0	2.3	0.0	.122
95-96	Houston	46	0	297	16	6	19	.316	0	0	.000	4	13	.308	28	46	74	12	44	0	5	24	5	6.5	0.3	1.6	0.3	.282
96-97	Houston	12	0	93	4	2	5	.400	0	0	.000	0	0	.000	5	8	13	3	8	0	2	4	0	7.8	0.3	1.1	0.3	.198
97-98	Houston	24	0	127	15	7	10	.700	0	0	.000	1	2	.500	12	12	24	5	22	0	1	6	5	5.3	0.6	1.0	0.2	.244
NBA Season Totals		726	408	14095	1826	725	1510	.480	0	7	.000	376	608	.618	1112	2141	3253	623	2079	29	442	1134	487	19.4	2.5	4.5	0.9	
84-85	Washington	4	0	110	29	10	19	.526	0	0	.000	9	16	.563	11	15	26	3	16	0	3	10	6	27.5	7.3	6.5	0.8	.399
85-86	Washington	5	5	72	12	4	11	.364	0	0	.000	4	4	1.000	6	3	9	3	13	0	2	2	5	14.4	2.4	1.8	0.6	.140
86-87	Washington	3	3	56	6	3	5	.600	0	0	.000	0	0	.000	1	7	8	3	9	0	2	5	1	18.7	2.0	2.7	1.0	.289
87-88	Washington	5	1	95	3	1	5	.200	0	0	.000	1	2	.500	5	12	17	2	18	0	2	4	0	19.0	0.6	3.4	0.4	.147
94-95	Houston	19	0	237	14	5	13	.385	0	1	.000	4	12	.333	12	32	44	0	55	0	4	10	5	12.5	0.7	2.3	0.0	.113
95-96	Houston	3	0	8	0	0	1	.000	0	0	.000	0	0	.000	0	1	1	0	0	0	0	0	0	2.7	0.0	0.3	0.0	.000
96-97	Houston	1	0	2	0	0	0	.000	0	0	.000	0	0	.000	0	0	0	1	0	0	0	0	0	2.0	0.0	0.0	1.0	.534
97-98	Houston	4	0	11	2	0	0	.000	0	0	.000	2	2	1.000	1	2	3	1	4	0	0	0	0	2.8	0.5	0.8	0.3	.364
NBA Playoff Totals		44	9	591	66	23	54	.426	0	1	.000	20	36	.556	36	72	108	13	115	0	13	31	17	13.4	1.5	2.5	0.3	

• JONES, Charles

Charles Rahmel Jones

Born: July 17, 1975. Brooklyn, NY, United States.   Height: 6'3".   Weight: 180 lbs.   Drafted: —   College: Long Island University

YEAR	TEAM	GP	GS	MIN	PTS	FGM	FGA	FG%	3PM	3PA	3P%	FTM	FTA	FT%	ORB	DRB	TRB	AST	PF	DQ	STL	BLK	TO	MPG	PPG	RPG	APG	PCM
98-99	Chicago	29	5	476	108	39	123	.317	19	61	.311	11	22	.500	9	33	42	41	30	0	18	5	29	16.4	3.7	1.4	1.4	.195
99-00	LA Clippers	56	0	662	188	66	201	.328	39	118	.331	17	23	.739	17	45	62	94	46	0	30	5	28	11.8	3.4	1.1	1.7	.313
NBA Season Totals		85	5	1138	296	105	324	.324	58	179	.324	28	45	.622	26	78	104	135	76	0	48	10	57	13.4	3.5	1.2	1.6	

• JONES, Charles

Charles Alexander (Charles A.) Jones

Born: Jan. 12, 1962. Scooba, MS, United States.   Height: 6'8".   Weight: 215 lbs.   Drafted: 1984   College: Louisville

YEAR	TEAM	GP	GS	MIN	PTS	FGM	FGA	FG%	3PM	3PA	3P%	FTM	FTA	FT%	ORB	DRB	TRB	AST	PF	DQ	STL	BLK	TO	MPG	PPG	RPG	APG	PCM
84-85	Phoenix	78	14	1565	654	236	454	.520	0	4	.000	182	281	.648	139	255	394	128	149	0	45	61	140	20.1	8.4	5.1	1.6	.516
85-86	Phoenix	43	18	742	200	75	164	.457	0	1	.000	50	98	.510	65	128	193	52	87	0	32	25	56	17.3	4.7	4.5	1.2	.392
87-88	Portland	37	0	186	51	16	40	.400	0	1	.000	19	33	.576	11	20	31	8	28	0	3	6	11	5.0	1.4	0.8	0.2	.240
88-89	Washington	43	0	516	110	38	82	.463	1	3	.333	33	53	.623	54	86	140	18	49	0	18	16	22	12.0	2.6	3.3	0.4	.383
NBA Season Totals		201	32	3009	1015	365	740	.493	1	9	.111	284	465	.611	269	489	758	206	313	0	98	108	229	15.0	5.0	3.8	1.0	
84-85	Phoenix	2	0	34	12	3	5	.600	0	0	.000	6	6	1.000	1	2	3	3	4	0	0	3	3	17.0	6.0	1.5	1.5	.420
87-88	Portland	2	0	2	0	0	1	.000	0	0	.000	0	0	.000	0	1	1	0	0	0	0	0	0	1.0	0.0	0.5	0.0	.000
NBA Playoff Totals		4	0	36	12	3	6	.500	0	0	.000	6	6	1.000	1	3	4	3	4	0	0	3	3	9.0	3.0	1.0	0.8	

• JONES, Collis

J. Collis Jones

Born: July 3, 1949. Washington, DC, United States.   Height: 6'7".   Weight: 203 lbs.   Drafted: 1971   College: Notre Dame

YEAR	TEAM	GP	GS	MIN	PTS	FGM	FGA	FG%	3PM	3PA	3P%	FTM	FTA	FT%	ORB	DRB	TRB	AST	PF	DQ	STL	BLK	TO	MPG	PPG	RPG	APG	PCM
71-72	Dallas-A	78	....	1428	425	163	372	.438	1	4	.250	98	154	.636	154	180	334	78	200	6	....	....	83	18.3	5.4	4.3	1.0	.357
72-73	Dallas-A	81	....	2204	941	357	768	.465	0	6	.000	227	318	.714	262	260	522	143	230	3	....	....	145	27.2	11.6	6.4	1.8	.478
73-74	Kentucky-A	58	....	719	255	102	263	.388	0	3	.000	51	78	.654	94	90	184	36	91	....	21	13	38	12.4	4.4	3.2	0.6	.369
74-75	Memphis-A	81	....	1880	805	333	702	.474	5	15	.333	134	177	.757	150	219	369	81	186	....	105	33	69	23.2	9.9	4.6	1.0	.422
ABA Season Totals		298	....	6231	2426	955	2105	.454	6	28	.214	510	727	.702	660	749	1409	338	707	9	126	46	335	20.9	8.1	4.7	1.1	
71-72	Dallas-A	3	....	35	12	4	10	.400	0	0	.000	4	8	.500	10	4	14	1	7	1	....	....	1	11.7	4.0	4.7	0.3	.438
73-74	Kentucky-A	4	....	28	13	4	12	.333	0	1	.000	5	8	.625	2	0	2	0	3	....	0	0	0	7.0	3.3	0.5	0.0	.189
74-75	Memphis-A	5	....	193	46	20	51	.392	0	0	.000	6	10	.600	13	20	33	3	18	....	9	1	10	38.6	9.2	6.6	0.6	.214
ABA Playoff Totals		12	....	256	71	28	73	.384	0	1	.000	15	26	.577	25	24	49	4	28	1	9	1	11	21.3	5.9	4.1	0.3	

• JONES, Damon

Damon Jones

Born: Aug. 25, 1976. Galveston, TX, United States. Height: 6'3". Weight: 185 lbs. Drafted: — College: Houston

YEAR	TEAM	GP	GS	MIN	PTS	FGM	FGA	FG%	3PM	3PA	3P%	FTM	FTA	FT%	ORB	DRB	TRB	AST	PF	DQ	STL	BLK	TO	MPG	PPG	RPG	APG	PCM
98-99	New Jersey	11	0	131	49	14	44	.318	10	29	.345	11	13	.846	2	11	13	13	7	0	7	0	5	11.9	4.5	1.2	1.2	.352
98-99	Boston	13	0	213	76	29	75	.387	15	33	.455	3,	4	.750	4	27	31	29	16	0	6	0	12	16.4	5.8	2.4	2.2	.385
99-00	Golden State	13	1	196	68	25	54	.463	11	23	.478	7	9	.778	0	16	16	39	13	0	6	0	15	15.1	5.2	1.2	3.0	.428
99-00	Dallas	42	0	416	165	55	154	.357	30	91	.330	25	39	.641	12	27	39	57	21	0	12	1	25	9.9	3.9	0.9	1.4	.351
00-01	Vancouver	71	10	1415	461	170	416	.409	84	231	.364	37	52	.712	16	108	124	224	58	0	36	1	76	19.9	6.5	1.7	3.2	.375
01-02	Detroit	67	0	1084	340	114	284	.401	69	186	.371	43	59	.729	13	90	103	140	83	0	23	1	61	16.2	5.1	1.5	2.1	.327
02-03	Sacramento	49	1	709	224	80	210	.381	44	121	.364	20	27	.741	11	59	70	80	42	0	18	4	23	14.5	4.6	1.4	1.6	.330
NBA Season Totals		266	12	4164	1383	487	1237	.394	263	714	.368	146	203	.719	58	338	396	582	240	0	108	7	217	15.7	5.2	1.5	2.2	....
01-02	Detroit	10	0	181	43	16	42	.381	8	27	.296	3	4	.750	1	20	21	25	14	0	5	0	6	18.1	4.3	2.1	2.5	.321
NBA Playoff Totals		10	0	181	43	16	42	.381	8	27	.296	3	4	.750	1	20	21	25	14	0	5	0	6	18.1	4.3	2.1	2.5	....

• JONES, Dontae'

Dontae' Antijuaine Jones

Born: June 2, 1975. Nashville, TN, United States. Height: 6'8". Weight: 220 lbs. Drafted: 1996 College: Mississippi State

YEAR	TEAM	GP	GS	MIN	PTS	FGM	FGA	FG%	3PM	3PA	3P%	FTM	FTA	FT%	ORB	DRB	TRB	AST	PF	DQ	STL	BLK	TO	MPG	PPG	RPG	APG	PCM
97-98	Boston	15	0	91	44	19	57	.333	6	23	.261	0	0	.000	3	6	9	5	12	0	2	3	11	6.1	2.9	0.6	0.3	.131
NBA Season Totals		15	0	91	44	19	57	.333	6	23	.261	0	0	.000	3	6	9	5	12	0	2	3	11	6.1	2.9	0.6	0.3	....

• JONES, Dwight

Dwight E. Jones

Born: Feb. 27, 1952. Houston, TX, United States. Height: 6'10". Weight: 210 lbs. Drafted: 1973 College: Houston

YEAR	TEAM	GP	GS	MIN	PTS	FGM	FGA	FG%	3PM	3PA	3P%	FTM	FTA	FT%	ORB	DRB	TRB	AST	PF	DQ	STL	BLK	TO	MPG	PPG	RPG	APG	PCM
73-74	Atlanta	74	....	1448	592	238	502	.474	....	....	....	116	156	.744	145	309	454	86	197	3	29	64	....	19.6	8.0	6.1	1.2	.519
74-75	Atlanta	75	....	2086	778	323	752	.430	....	....	....	132	183	.721	236	461	697	152	226	1	51	51	....	27.8	10.4	9.3	2.0	.509
75-76	Atlanta	66	....	1762	665	251	542	.463	....	....	....	163	219	.744	171	353	524	83	214	8	52	61	....	26.7	10.1	7.9	1.3	.479
76-77	Houston	74	....	1239	435	167	338	.494	....	....	....	101	126	.802	98	186	284	48	175	1	38	19	....	16.7	5.9	3.8	0.6	.404
77-78	Houston	82	....	2476	873	346	777	.445	....	....	....	181	233	.777	215	426	641	109	265	2	77	39	164	30.2	10.6	7.8	1.3	.403
78-79	Houston	81	....	1215	458	181	395	.458	....	....	....	96	132	.727	110	218	328	57	204	1	34	26	105	15.0	5.7	4.0	0.7	.391
79-80	Houston	21	....	278	127	50	119	.420	0	0	.000	27	36	.750	31	41	72	11	48	0	4	5	21	13.2	6.0	3.4	0.5	.378
79-80	Chicago	53	....	1170	533	207	387	.535	0	0	.000	119	165	.721	83	213	296	90	159	0	24	37	101	22.1	10.1	5.6	1.7	.519
80-81	Chicago	81	....	1574	615	245	507	.483	0	0	.000	125	161	.776	127	274	401	99	200	1	40	36	130	19.4	7.6	5.0	1.2	.440
81-82	Chicago	78	18	2040	779	303	572	.530	1	1	1.000	172	238	.723	156	351	507	114	217	0	49	36	156	26.2	10.0	6.5	1.5	.454
82-83	Chicago	49	2	673	219	86	193	.446	0	0	.000	47	75	.627	56	139	195	40	90	0	18	14	64	13.7	4.5	4.0	0.8	.387
82-83	LA Lakers	32	0	491	156	62	132	.470	0	1	.000	32	48	.667	28	86	114	22	82	0	13	9	35	15.3	4.9	3.6	0.7	.334
NBA Season Totals		766	20	16452	6230	2459	5216	.471	1	2	.500	1311	1772	.740	1456	3057	4513	911	2077	17	429	397	776	21.5	8.1	5.9	1.2	....
76-77	Houston	12	....	246	74	28	63	.444	....	....	....	18	23	.783	13	38	51	15	32	2	8	3	....	20.5	6.2	4.3	1.3	.361
78-79	Houston	2	....	33	20	7	13	.538	....	....	....	6	6	1.000	4	8	12	3	3	0	1	4	6	16.5	10.0	6.0	1.5	.801
79-80	Houston	6	....	70	28	11	18	.611	0	0	.000	6	9	.667	8	14	22	4	8	0	0	2	4	11.7	4.7	3.7	0.7	.560
80-81	Chicago	6	....	217	75	29	61	.475	0	0	.000	17	17	1.000	18	41	59	11	21	0	5	3	16	36.2	12.5	9.8	1.8	.437
82-83	LA Lakers	7	0	59	12	5	16	.313	0	0	.000	2	5	.400	4	8	12	0	11	0	1	0	5	8.4	1.7	1.7	0.0	.051
NBA Playoff Totals		33	0	625	209	80	171	.468	0	0	.000	49	60	.817	47	109	156	33	75	2	15	12	31	18.9	6.3	4.7	1.0	....

• JONES, Earl

Earl Jones

Born: Jan. 13, 1961. Oak Hill, WV, United States. Height: 7' Weight: 210 lbs. Drafted: 1984 College: District of Columbia

YEAR	TEAM	GP	GS	MIN	PTS	FGM	FGA	FG%	3PM	3PA	3P%	FTM	FTA	FT%	ORB	DRB	TRB	AST	PF	DQ	STL	BLK	TO	MPG	PPG	RPG	APG	PCM
84-85	LA Lakers	2	0	7	0	0	1	.000	0	0	.000	0	0	.000	0	0	0	0	0	0	0	0	1	3.5	0.0	0.0	0.0	-.266
85-86	Milwaukee	12	0	43	13	5	12	.417	0	0	.000	3	4	.750	4	6	10	4	13	0	0	1	7	3.6	1.1	0.8	0.3	.186
NBA Season Totals		14	0	50	13	5	13	.385	0	0	.000	3	4	.750	4	6	10	4	13	0	0	1	8	3.6	0.9	0.7	0.3	....

• JONES, Eddie

Eddie Charles Jones

Born: Oct. 20, 1971. Pompano Beach, FL, United States. Height: 6'6". Weight: 190 lbs. Drafted: 1994 College: Temple

YEAR	TEAM	GP	GS	MIN	PTS	FGM	FGA	FG%	3PM	3PA	3P%	FTM	FTA	FT%	ORB	DRB	TRB	AST	PF	DQ	STL	BLK	TO	MPG	PPG	RPG	APG	PCM
94-95	LA Lakers	64	58	1981	897	342	744	.460	91	246	.370	122	169	.722	79	170	249	128	175	1	131	41	77	31.0	14.0	3.9	2.0	.441
95-96	LA Lakers	70	66	2184	893	337	685	.492	83	227	.366	136	184	.739	45	188	233	246	162	0	129	45	98	31.2	12.8	3.3	3.5	.466
96-97	LA Lakers	80	80	2998	1374	473	1081	.438	152	389	.391	276	337	.819	90	236	326	270	226	3	189	49	168	37.5	17.2	4.1	3.4	.444
97-98	LA Lakers	80	80	2910	1349	486	1005	.484	143	368	.389	234	306	.765	85	217	302	246	164	0	160	55	144	36.4	16.9	3.8	3.1	.472
98-99	LA Lakers	20	20	724	271	96	227	.423	20	64	.313	59	80	.738	20	56	76	61	42	0	35	24	21	36.2	13.6	3.8	3.1	.408
98-99	Charlotte	30	30	1157	509	164	368	.446	28	78	.359	153	191	.801	30	88	118	125	86	1	90	34	72	38.6	17.0	3.9	4.2	.486
99-00	Charlotte	72	72	2807	1446	478	1119	.427	128	341	.375	362	419	.864	81	262	343	305	176	1	**192**	49	160	39.0	20.1	4.8	4.2	.526
00-01	Miami	63	58	2282	1094	388	871	.445	90	238	.378	228	270	.844	75	217	292	171	183	5	110	58	135	36.2	17.4	4.6	2.7	.456
01-02	Miami	81	81	3156	1480	517	1198	.432	149	382	.390	297	355	.837	61	317	378	262	258	2	117	77	148	39.0	18.3	4.7	3.2	.441
02-03	Miami	47	47	1789	869	291	688	.423	98	241	.407	189	230	.822	35	191	226	173	137	1	64	31	85	38.1	18.5	4.8	3.7	.464
NBA Season Totals		607	592	21988	10182	3572	7986	.447	982	2574	.382	2056	2541	.809	601	1942	2543	1987	1609	14	1217	463	1108	36.2	16.8	4.2	3.3	....
94-95	LA Lakers	10	0	286	87	30	80	.375	12	27	.444	15	21	.714	7	25	32	20	27	0	8	9	17	28.6	8.7	3.2	2.0	.265
95-96	LA Lakers	4	4	155	69	27	49	.551	10	19	.526	5	8	.625	7	14	21	6	16	0	8	1	4	38.8	17.3	5.3	1.5	.453
96-97	LA Lakers	9	9	283	101	33	72	.458	9	24	.375	26	35	.743	8	23	31	29	24	0	9	4	13	31.4	11.2	3.4	3.2	.386
97-98	LA Lakers	13	13	476	221	69	148	.466	20	48	.417	63	76	.829	12	39	51	32	37	0	26	21	17	36.6	17.0	3.9	2.5	.493
99-00	Charlotte	4	4	171	68	22	58	.379	9	26	.346	15	16	.938	4	16	20	19	12	0	10	3	5	42.8	17.0	5.0	4.8	.442
00-01	Miami	3	3	108	57	22	44	.500	7	16	.438	6	7	.857	2	16	18	7	9	0	3	1	7	36.0	19.0	6.0	2.3	.499
NBA Playoff Totals		43	33	1479	603	203	451	.450	67	160	.419	130	163	.798	40	133	173	113	125	0	64	39	63	34.4	14.0	4.0	2.6	....

• JONES, Edgar

Edgar (E.J.) Jones Jr.

Born: June 17, 1956. Fort Rucker, AL, United States. Height: 6'10". Weight: 225 lbs. Drafted: 1979 College: Nevada-Reno

YEAR	TEAM	GP	GS	MIN	PTS	FGM	FGA	FG%	3PM	3PA	3P%	FTM	FTA	FT%	ORB	DRB	TRB	AST	PF	DQ	STL	BLK	TO	MPG	PPG	RPG	APG	PCM
80-81	New Jersey	60	....	950	524	189	357	.529	0	4	.000	146	218	.670	92	171	263	43	185	4	36	81	102	15.8	8.7	4.4	0.7	.583
81-82	Detroit	48	19	802	375	142	259	.548	1	2	.500	90	129	.698	70	137	207	40	149	3	28	92	67	16.7	7.8	4.3	0.8	.578

YEAR	TEAM	GP	GS	MIN	PTS	FGM	FGA	FG%	3PM	3PA	3P%	FTM	FTA	FT%	ORB	DRB	TRB	AST	PF	DQ	STL	BLK	TO	MPG	PPG	RPG	APG	PCM
82-83	Detroit	49	25	1036	409	145	294	.493	2	6	.333	117	172	.680	80	191	271	69	160	5	28	77	103	21.1	8.3	5.5	1.4	.482
82-83	San Antonio	28	3	622	268	92	185	.497	0	3	.000	84	114	.737	56	121	177	20	107	5	14	31	42	22.2	9.6	6.3	0.7	.493
83-84	San Antonio	81	33	1770	826	322	644	.500	6	19	.316	176	242	.727	143	306	449	85	298	7	64	107	122	21.9	10.2	5.5	1.0	.515
84-85	San Antonio	18	2	322	129	44	91	.484	0	1	.000	41	51	.804	16	46	62	18	52	1	9	18	27	17.9	7.2	3.4	1.0	.454
84-85	Cleveland	26	3	447	213	86	184	.467	0	3	.000	41	60	.683	34	75	109	11	71	1	11	11	34	17.2	8.2	4.2	0.4	.407
85-86	Cleveland	53	6	1011	513	187	370	.505	7	23	.304	132	178	.742	71	136	207	45	142	0	30	38	64	19.1	9.7	3.9	0.8	.494
NBA Season Totals		363	91	6960	3257	1207	2384	.506	16	61	.262	827	1164	.710	562	1183	1745	331	1164	26	220	455	561	19.2	9.0	4.8	0.9	....
82-83	San Antonio	11	0	193	75	28	62	.452	0	2	.000	19	33	.576	23	30	53	17	44	1	6	14	18	17.5	6.8	4.8	1.5	.448
84-85	Cleveland	4	0	45	25	9	18	.500	0	1	.000	7	8	.875	2	6	8	3	6	0	2	0	2	11.3	6.3	2.0	0.8	.534
NBA Playoff Totals		15	0	238	100	37	80	.463	0	3	.000	26	41	.634	25	36	61	20	50	1	8	14	20	15.9	6.7	4.1	1.3	....

• JONES, Fred

Frederick Terrell Jones

Born: Mar. 11, 1979. Malvern, AR, United States.   Height: 6'4".   Weight: 210 lbs.   Drafted: 2002   College: Oregon

YEAR	TEAM	GP	GS	MIN	PTS	FGM	FGA	FG%	3PM	3PA	3P%	FTM	FTA	FT%	ORB	DRB	TRB	AST	PF	DQ	STL	BLK	TO	MPG	PPG	RPG	APG	PCM
02-03	Indiana	19	1	115	23	9	24	.375	2	7	.286	3	4	.750	4	5	9	5	13	0	6	1	6	6.1	1.2	0.5	0.3	.153
NBA Season Totals		19	1	115	23	9	24	.375	2	7	.286	3	4	.750	4	5	9	5	13	0	6	1	6	6.1	1.2	0.5	0.3	....

• JONES, Hutch

Willie D. (Hutch) Jones

Born: Sept. 1, 1959. Buffalo, NY, United States.   Height: 6'8".   Weight: 190 lbs.   Drafted: 1982   College: Vanderbilt

YEAR	TEAM	GP	GS	MIN	PTS	FGM	FGA	FG%	3PM	3PA	3P%	FTM	FTA	FT%	ORB	DRB	TRB	AST	PF	DQ	STL	BLK	TO	MPG	PPG	RPG	APG	PCM
82-83	San Diego	9	0	85	40	17	37	.459	0	0	.000	6	6	1.000	10	7	17	4	14	0	3	0	6	9.4	4.4	1.9	0.4	.384
83-84	San Diego	4	0	18	1	0	3	.000	0	0	.000	1	4	.250	0	0	0	0	0	0	1	0	2	4.5	0.3	0.0	0.0	-.229
NBA Season Totals		13	0	103	41	17	40	.425	0	0	.000	7	10	.700	10	7	17	4	14	0	4	0	8	7.9	3.2	1.3	0.3	....

• JONES, Jake

Jacob Jones

Born: May 9, 1949.   Height: 6'3".   Weight: 180 lbs.   Drafted: 1971   College: Assumption

YEAR	TEAM	GP	GS	MIN	PTS	FGM	FGA	FG%	3PM	3PA	3P%	FTM	FTA	FT%	ORB	DRB	TRB	AST	PF	DQ	STL	BLK	TO	MPG	PPG	RPG	APG	PCM
71-72	Philadelphia	6	....	41	19	6	18	.333	....	....	....	7	10	.700	....	....	6	2	3	0	....	....	....	6.8	3.2	1.0	0.3	.329
71-72	Cincinnati	11	....	161	57	22	54	.407	....	....	....	13	21	.619	....	....	20	10	19	0	....	....	....	14.6	5.2	1.8	0.9	.288
NBA Season Totals		17	....	202	76	28	72	.389	....	....	....	20	31	.645	....	....	26	12	22	0	....	....	....	11.9	4.5	1.5	0.7	....

• JONES, Jimmy

James Jones

Born: Jan. 1, 1945. Tallulah, LA, United States.   Height: 6'4".   Weight: 188 lbs.   Drafted: 1967   College: Grambling

YEAR	TEAM	GP	GS	MIN	PTS	FGM	FGA	FG%	3PM	3PA	3P%	FTM	FTA	FT%	ORB	DRB	TRB	AST	PF	DQ	STL	BLK	TO	MPG	PPG	RPG	APG	PCM
67-68	New Orleans-A	78	....	**3255**	1464	551	1181	.467	2	9	.222	360	508	.709	....	....	443	179	243	6	....	....	241	41.7	18.8	5.7	2.3	.417
68-69	New Orleans-A	77	....	3188	2050	**764**	1429	.535	1	7	.143	521	647	.805	141	300	441	437	225	4	....	....	198	41.4	26.6	5.7	5.7	.692
69-70	New Orleans-A	70	....	2513	1448	533	1072	.497	2	9	.222	380	469	.810	85	230	315	340	238	5	....	....	275	35.9	20.7	4.5	4.9	.598
70-71	Memphis-A	80	....	3004	1564	593	1220	.486	4	7	.571	374	481	.778	121	265	386	468	240	3	....	....	294	37.6	19.6	4.8	5.9	.597
71-72	Utah-A	78	....	2903	1207	462	903	.512	1	6	.167	282	362	.779	92	285	377	485	252	1	....	....	270	37.2	15.5	4.8	6.2	.533
72-73	Utah-A	80	....	2848	1337	496	948	.523	0	1	.000	345	432	.799	72	263	335	448	271	5	....	....	267	35.6	16.7	4.2	5.6	.549
73-74	Utah-A	83	....	3162	1395	583	1060	.550	0	1	.000	229	259	**.884**	103	258	361	429	205	....	154	32	238	38.1	16.8	4.3	5.2	.533
74-75	Washington	73	....	1424	517	207	400	.518	....	....	....	103	142	.725	36	101	137	162	190	0	76	10	....	19.5	7.1	1.9	2.2	.391
75-76	Washington	64	....	1133	378	153	308	.497	....	....	....	72	94	.766	32	99	131	120	127	1	33	5	....	17.7	5.9	2.0	1.9	.380
76-77	Washington	3	....	33	6	2	9	.222	....	....	....	2	4	.500	1	3	4	1	4	0	2	0	....	11.0	2.0	1.3	0.3	.059
NBA Season Totals		140	....	2590	901	362	717	.505	....	....	....	177	240	.738	69	203	272	283	321	1	111	15	....	18.5	6.4	1.9	2.0	....
ABA Season Totals		546	....	20873	10465	3982	7813	.510	10	40	.250	2491	3158	.789	614	1601	2658	2786	1674	24	154	32	1783	38.2	19.2	4.9	5.1	....
Career Totals		686	....	23463	11366	4344	8530	.509	10	40	.250	2668	3398	.785	683	1804	2930	3069	1995	25	265	47	1783	34.2	16.6	4.3	4.5	....
67-68	New Orleans-A	17	....	785	375	144	315	.457	0	1	.000	87	118	.737	....	....	117	56	56	2	....	....	41	46.2	22.1	6.9	3.3	.458
68-69	New Orleans-A	11	....	445	332	123	223	.552	0	4	.000	86	113	.761	....	....	58	59	35	0	....	....	35	40.5	30.2	5.3	5.4	.757
70-71	Memphis-A	4	....	130	65	24	48	.500	0	0	.000	17	25	.680	5	19	24	15	16	0	....	....	17	32.5	16.3	6.0	3.8	.564
71-72	Utah-A	11	....	435	231	93	172	.541	0	0	.000	45	63	.714	9	35	44	69	40	0	....	....	37	39.5	21.0	4.0	6.3	.580
72-73	Utah-A	10	....	316	163	64	130	.492	0	0	.000	35	44	.795	16	25	41	43	37	0	....	....	26	31.6	16.3	4.1	4.3	.529
73-74	Utah-A	18	....	742	374	154	267	.577	0	2	.000	66	85	.776	30	57	87	98	60	....	27	5	49	41.2	20.8	4.8	5.4	.579
74-75	Washington	11	....	206	68	29	64	.453	....	....	....	10	11	.909	5	17	22	21	21	0	16	1	....	18.7	6.2	2.0	1.9	.348
75-76	Washington	7	....	165	62	22	45	.489	....	....	....	18	21	.857	2	15	17	10	15	0	10	0	....	23.6	8.9	2.4	1.4	.367
NBA Playoff Totals		18	....	371	130	51	109	.468	....	....	....	28	32	.875	7	32	39	31	36	0	26	1	....	20.6	7.2	2.2	1.7	....
ABA Playoff Totals		71	....	2853	1540	602	1155	.521	0	7	.000	336	448	.750	60	136	371	340	244	2	27	5	205	40.2	21.7	5.2	4.8	....
Career Playoff Totals		89	....	3224	1670	653	1264	.517	0	7	.000	364	480	.758	67	168	410	371	280	2	53	6	205	36.2	18.8	4.6	4.2	....

• JONES, Johnny

John Jones

Born: Mar. 12, 1943. Washington, DC, United States.   Height: 6'7".   Weight: 205 lbs.   Drafted: —   College: Los Angeles State

YEAR	TEAM	GP	GS	MIN	PTS	FGM	FGA	FG%	3PM	3PA	3P%	FTM	FTA	FT%	ORB	DRB	TRB	AST	PF	DQ	STL	BLK	TO	MPG	PPG	RPG	APG	PCM
67-68	Boston	51	....	475	214	86	253	.340	....	....	....	42	68	.618	....	....	114	26	60	0	....	....	....	9.3	4.2	2.2	0.5	.355
68-69	Kentucky-A	29	....	449	203	81	213	.380	0	3	.000	41	71	.577	54	63	117	34	53	0	....	....	39	15.5	7.0	4.0	1.2	.431
NBA Season Totals		51	....	475	214	86	253	.340	....	....	....	42	68	.618	....	....	114	26	60	0	....	....	....	9.3	4.2	2.2	0.5	....
ABA Season Totals		29	....	449	203	81	213	.380	0	3	.000	41	71	.577	54	63	117	34	53	0	....	....	39	15.5	7.0	4.0	1.2	....
Career Totals		80	....	924	417	167	466	.358	0	3	.000	83	139	.597	54	63	231	60	113	0	....	....	39	11.6	5.2	2.9	0.8	....
67-68	Boston	5	....	10	6	3	6	.500	....	....	....	0	0	.000	....	....	4	0	2	0	....	....	....	2.0	1.2	0.8	0.0	.600
NBA Playoff Totals		5	....	10	6	3	6	.500	....	....	....	0	0	.000	....	....	4	0	2	0	....	....	....	2.0	1.2	0.8	0.0	....

• JONES, Jumaine
Jumaine Lanard Jones

Born: Feb. 10, 1979. Cocoa, FL, United States. Height: 6'8". Weight: 218 lbs. Drafted: 1999 College: Georgia

YEAR	TEAM	GP	GS	MIN	PTS	FGM	FGA	FG%	3PM	3PA	3P%	FTM	FTA	FT%	ORB	DRB	TRB	AST	PF	DQ	STL	BLK	TO	MPG	PPG	RPG	APG	PCM
99-00	Philadelphia	33	0	138	57	22	58	.379	2	4	.500	11	18	.611	16	22	38	5	10	0	6	5	14	4.2	1.7	1.2	0.2	.390
00-01	Philadelphia	65	0	866	304	122	275	.444	20	60	.333	40	53	.755	63	126	189	32	68	0	30	15	39	13.3	4.7	2.9	0.5	.393
01-02	Cleveland	81	36	2142	671	287	640	.448	52	168	.310	45	68	.662	125	365	490	116	184	3	75	46	79	26.4	8.3	6.0	1.4	.404
02-03	Cleveland	80	12	2204	784	308	710	.434	111	314	.354	57	83	.687	106	299	405	112	176	1	67	22	107	27.6	9.8	5.1	1.4	.363
NBA Season Totals		259	48	5350	1816	739	1683	.439	185	546	.339	153	222	.689	310	812	1122	265	438	4	178	88	239	20.7	7.0	4.3	1.0	....
99-00	Philadelphia	4	0	8	2	1	3	.333	0	2	.000	0	0	.000	0	0	0	0	0	0	0	0	0	2.0	0.5	0.0	0.0	.023
00-01	Philadelphia	23	14	447	127	52	125	.416	8	32	.250	15	21	.714	35	49	84	17	33	0	10	11	14	19.4	5.5	3.7	0.7	.323
NBA Playoff Totals		27	14	455	129	53	128	.414	8	34	.235	15	21	.714	35	49	84	17	33	0	10	11	14	16.9	4.8	3.1	0.6	....

• JONES, K.C.
K.C. Jones

Born: May 25, 1932. Taylor, TX, United States. Height: 6'1". Weight: 200 lbs. Drafted: 1956 College: San Francisco HOF: 1989

YEAR	TEAM	GP	GS	MIN	PTS	FGM	FGA	FG%	3PM	3PA	3P%	FTM	FTA	FT%	ORB	DRB	TRB	AST	PF	DQ	STL	BLK	TO	MPG	PPG	RPG	APG	PCM
58-59	Boston	49	....	609	171	65	192	.339	....	....	....	41	68	.603	....	....	127	70	58	0	....	....	....	12.4	3.5	2.6	1.4	.372
59-60	Boston	74	....	1274	466	169	414	.408	....	....	....	128	170	.753	....	....	199	189	109	1	....	....	....	17.2	6.3	2.7	2.6	.478
60-61	Boston	78	....	1605	592	203	601	.338	....	....	....	186	280	.664	....	....	279	253	190	3	....	....	....	20.6	7.6	3.6	3.2	.440
61-62	Boston	80	....	2054	735	294	724	.406	....	....	....	147	232	.634	....	....	298	343	206	1	....	....	....	25.7	9.2	3.7	4.3	.456
62-63	Boston	79	....	1945	572	230	591	.389	....	....	....	112	177	.633	....	....	263	317	221	3	....	....	....	24.6	7.2	3.3	4.0	.393
63-64	Boston	80	....	2424	654	283	722	.392	....	....	....	88	168	.524	....	....	372	407	253	0	....	....	....	30.3	8.2	4.7	5.1	.400
64-65	Boston	78	....	2434	649	253	639	.396	....	....	....	143	227	.630	....	....	318	437	263	5	....	....	....	31.2	8.3	4.1	5.6	.412
65-66	Boston	80	....	2710	689	240	619	.388	....	....	....	209	303	.690	....	....	304	503	243	4	....	....	....	33.9	8.6	3.8	6.3	.409
66-67	Boston	78	....	2446	483	182	459	.397	....	....	....	119	189	.630	....	....	239	389	273	7	....	....	....	31.4	6.2	3.1	5.0	.321
NBA Season Totals		676	....	17501	5011	1919	4961	.387	....	....	....	1173	1814	.647	....	....	2399	2908	1816	24	....	....	....	25.9	7.4	3.5	4.3	....
58-59	Boston	8	....	75	15	5	20	.250	....	....	....	5	5	1.000	....	....	12	10	8	0	....	....	....	9.4	1.9	1.5	1.3	.296
59-60	Boston	13	....	232	71	27	80	.338	....	....	....	17	22	.773	....	....	45	14	28	0	....	....	....	17.8	5.5	3.5	1.1	.301
60-61	Boston	9	....	103	25	9	30	.300	....	....	....	7	14	.500	....	....	19	15	17	0	....	....	....	11.4	2.8	2.1	1.7	.320
61-62	Boston	14	....	329	126	44	102	.431	....	....	....	38	53	.717	....	....	56	55	50	1	....	....	....	23.5	9.0	4.0	3.9	.505
62-63	Boston	13	....	250	59	19	64	.297	....	....	....	21	30	.700	....	....	36	37	42	1	....	....	....	19.2	4.5	2.8	2.8	.306
63-64	Boston	10	....	312	63	25	72	.347	....	....	....	13	25	.520	....	....	37	68	40	0	....	....	....	31.2	6.3	3.7	6.8	.378
64-65	Boston	12	....	396	121	43	104	.413	....	....	....	35	45	.778	....	....	39	74	49	1	....	....	....	33.0	10.1	3.3	6.2	.436
65-66	Boston	17	....	543	129	45	109	.413	....	....	....	39	57	.684	....	....	52	75	65	0	....	....	....	31.9	7.6	3.1	4.4	.328
66-67	Boston	9	....	254	59	24	75	.320	....	....	....	11	18	.611	....	....	24	48	36	1	....	....	....	28.2	6.6	2.7	5.3	.307
NBA Playoff Totals		105	....	2494	668	241	656	.367	....	....	....	186	269	.691	....	....	320	396	335	4	....	....	....	23.8	6.4	3.0	3.8	....

• JONES, Larry
Walter Jones

Born: Sept. 22, 1942. Columbus, OH, United States. Height: 6'2". Weight: 180 lbs. Drafted: 1964 College: Toledo

YEAR	TEAM	GP	GS	MIN	PTS	FGM	FGA	FG%	3PM	3PA	3P%	FTM	FTA	FT%	ORB	DRB	TRB	AST	PF	DQ	STL	BLK	TO	MPG	PPG	RPG	APG	PCM
64-65	Philadelphia	23	....	359	131	47	153	.307	....	....	....	37	52	.712	....	....	57	40	46	2	....	....	....	15.6	5.7	2.5	1.7	.332
67-68	Denver-A	76	....	3085	1742	602	1409	.427	8	42	.190	530	683	.776	....	....	599	270	268	4	....	....	232	40.6	22.9	7.9	3.6	.554
68-69	Denver-A	75	....	3042	**2133**	759	1631	.465	24	100	.240	**591**	**760**	.778	165	328	493	258	273	3	....	....	218	40.6	28.4	6.6	3.4	.629
69-70	Denver-A	75	....	3027	1870	625	1441	.434	41	165	.248	579	732	.791	143	248	391	426	228	1	....	....	237	40.4	24.9	5.2	5.7	.604
70-71	Florida-A	84	....	3611	2044	764	1636	.467	45	124	.363	471	587	.802	177	276	453	390	269	3	....	....	247	43.0	24.3	5.4	4.6	.560
71-72	Florida-A	66	....	2255	1164	423	797	.531	18	60	.300	300	373	.804	133	176	309	210	203	0	....	....	135	34.2	17.6	4.7	3.2	.541
72-73	Dallas-A	53	....	1254	530	187	400	.468	12	46	.261	144	173	.832	63	115	178	163	141	2	....	....	83	23.7	10.0	3.4	3.1	.480
72-73	Utah-A	27	....	447	168	53	121	.438	4	11	.364	58	71	.817	25	36	61	43	43	0	....	....	21	16.6	6.2	2.3	1.6	.411
73-74	Philadelphia	72	....	1876	723	263	622	.423	....	....	....	197	235	.838	71	113	184	230	116	0	85	18	....	26.1	10.0	2.6	3.2	.412
NBA Season Totals		95	....	2235	854	310	775	.400	....	....	....	234	287	.815	71	113	241	270	162	2	85	18	....	23.5	9.0	2.5	2.8	....
ABA Season Totals		456	....	16721	9651	3413	7435	.459	152	548	.277	2673	3379	.791	706	1179	2484	1760	1425	13	....	....	1173	36.7	21.2	5.4	3.9	....
Career Totals		551	....	18956	10505	3723	8210	.453	152	548	.277	2907	3666	.793	777	1292	2725	2030	1587	15	85	18	1173	34.4	19.1	4.9	3.7	....
64-65	Philadelphia	5	....	25	17	5	12	.417	....	....	....	7	11	.636	....	....	4	2	5	0	....	....	....	5.0	3.4	0.8	0.4	.548
67-68	Denver-A	1	....	41	29	12	20	.600	0	0	.000	5	8	.625	....	....	4	4	5	0	....	....	4	41.0	29.0	4.0	4.0	.660
68-69	Denver-A	7	....	282	154	48	134	.358	3	8	.375	55	76	.724	....	....	54	32	21	0	....	....	17	40.3	22.0	7.7	4.6	.514
69-70	Denver-A	12	....	535	319	113	207	.546	5	20	.250	88	101	.871	23	41	64	76	41	0	....	....	29	44.6	26.6	5.3	6.3	.667
70-71	Florida-A	6	....	216	103	34	86	.395	2	8	.250	33	36	.917	7	18	25	37	20	1	....	....	20	36.0	17.2	4.2	6.2	.539
71-72	Florida-A	4	....	115	40	13	38	.342	0	1	.000	14	17	.824	....	....	13	9	12	....	....	....	5	28.8	10.0	3.3	2.3	.287
NBA Playoff Totals		5	....	25	17	5	12	.417	....	....	....	7	11	.636	....	....	4	2	5	0	....	....	....	5.0	3.4	0.8	0.4	....
ABA Playoff Totals		30	....	1189	645	220	485	.454	10	37	.270	195	238	.819	30	59	160	158	99	1	....	....	75	39.6	21.5	5.3	5.3	....
Career Playoff Totals		35	....	1214	662	225	497	.453	10	37	.270	202	249	.811	30	59	164	160	104	1	....	....	75	34.7	18.9	4.7	4.6	....

• JONES, Major
Major James Brooks Jones

Born: July 9, 1953. McGhee, AR, United States. Height: 6'9". Weight: 225 lbs. Drafted: 1976 College: Albany State (GA)

YEAR	TEAM	GP	GS	MIN	PTS	FGM	FGA	FG%	3PM	3PA	3P%	FTM	FTA	FT%	ORB	DRB	TRB	AST	PF	DQ	STL	BLK	TO	MPG	PPG	RPG	APG	PCM
79-80	Houston	82	....	1545	438	188	392	.480	1	3	.333	61	108	.565	147	234	381	67	186	0	50	67	115	18.8	5.3	4.6	0.8	.368
80-81	Houston	68	....	1003	298	117	252	.464	0	1	.000	64	101	.634	96	138	234	41	112	0	18	23	54	14.8	4.4	3.4	0.6	.352
81-82	Houston	60	6	746	268	113	213	.531	0	3	.000	42	77	.545	80	122	202	25	100	0	20	29	48	12.4	4.5	3.4	0.4	.439
82-83	Houston	60	4	878	340	142	311	.457	0	2	.000	56	102	.549	114	149	263	39	104	0	22	22	84	14.6	5.7	4.4	0.7	.414
83-84	Houston	57	5	473	170	70	130	.538	0	0	.000	30	49	.612	33	82	115	28	63	0	14	14	29	8.3	3.0	2.0	0.5	.448
84-85	Detroit	47	0	418	129	48	87	.552	0	0	.000	33	51	.647	48	80	128	15	58	0	9	14	33	8.9	2.7	2.7	0.3	.438
NBA Season Totals		374	15	5063	1643	678	1385	.490	1	9	.111	286	488	.586	518	805	1323	215	623	0	133	169	363	13.5	4.4	3.5	0.6	....
80-81	Houston	12	....	88	22	10	21	.476	0	0	.000	2	5	.400	7	11	18	5	15	0	3	2	2	7.3	1.8	1.5	0.4	.322
81-82	Houston	6	....	70	28	11	18	.611	0	0	.000	6	9	.667	8	14	22	4	8	0	0	2	4	11.7	4.7	3.7	0.7	.560
84-85	Detroit	1	0	4	2	1	1	1.000	0	0	.000	0	0	.000	0	0	0	0	0	0	0	0	0	4.0	2.0	0.0	0.0	.500
NBA Playoff Totals		19	0	162	52	22	40	.550	0	0	.000	8	14	.571	15	25	40	9	23	0	3	4	6	8.5	2.7	2.1	0.5	....

YEAR	TEAM	GP	GS	MIN	PTS	FGM	FGA	FG%	3PM	3PA	3P%	FTM	FTA	FT%	ORB	DRB	TRB	AST	PF	DQ	STL	BLK	TO	MPG	PPG	RPG	APG	PCM

• JONES, Mark

Mark Anthony Jones

Born: Apr. 10, 1961. Rochester, NY, United States.　　Height: 6'1".　　Weight: 175 lbs.　　Drafted: 1983　　College: St. Bonaventure

YEAR	TEAM	GP	GS	MIN	PTS	FGM	FGA	FG%	3PM	3PA	3P%	FTM	FTA	FT%	ORB	DRB	TRB	AST	PF	DQ	STL	BLK	TO	MPG	PPG	RPG	APG	PCM
83-84	New Jersey	6	0	16	7	3	6	.500	0	1	.000	1	2	.500	2	0	2	5	2	0	0	0	2	2.7	1.2	0.3	0.8	.510
NBA Season Totals		6	0	16	7	3	6	.500	0	1	.000	1	2	.500	2	0	2	5	2	0	0	0	2	2.7	1.2	0.3	0.8	....

• JONES, Nick

Ryan Nicholas Jones

Born: Mar. 28, 1945.　　Height: 6'2".　　Weight: 190 lbs.　　Drafted: 1967　　College: Oregon

YEAR	TEAM	GP	GS	MIN	PTS	FGM	FGA	FG%	3PM	3PA	3P%	FTM	FTA	FT%	ORB	DRB	TRB	AST	PF	DQ	STL	BLK	TO	MPG	PPG	RPG	APG	PCM
67-68	San Diego	42	....	603	227	86	232	.371	....	....	....	55	69	.797	....	....	67	89	84	0	....	....	....	14.4	5.4	1.6	2.1	.384
68-69	Dallas-A	4	....	60	14	6	20	.300	0	2	.000	2	6	.333	4	1	5	5	10	0	....	....	6	15.0	3.5	1.3	1.3	.100
68-69	Miami-A	3	....	21	6	3	8	.375	0	0	.000	0	0	.000	1	2	3	1	4	0	....	....	0	7.0	2.0	1.0	0.3	.177
70-71	San Francisco	81	....	1183	561	225	523	.430	....	....	....	111	151	.735	....	....	110	113	192	2	....	....	....	14.6	6.9	1.4	1.4	.362
71-72	Golden State	65	....	478	215	82	196	.418	....	....	....	51	61	.836	....	....	39	45	109	0	....	....	....	7.4	3.3	0.6	0.7	.314
72-73	Dallas-A	3	....	16	8	3	8	.375	0	0	.000	2	3	.667	1	0	1	1	4	0	....	....	2	5.3	2.7	0.3	0.3	.204
NBA Season Totals		188	....	2264	1003	393	951	.413	....	....	....	217	281	.772	....	....	216	247	385	2	....	....	....	12.0	5.3	1.1	1.3	....
ABA Season Totals		10	....	97	28	12	36	.333	0	2	.000	4	9	.444	6	3	9	7	18	0	....	....	8	9.7	2.8	0.9	0.7	....
Career Totals		198	....	2361	1031	405	987	.410	0	2	.000	221	290	.762	6	3	225	254	403	2	....	....	8	11.9	5.2	1.1	1.3	....
70-71	San Francisco	5	....	77	29	7	26	.269	....	....	....	15	18	.833	....	....	5	5	9	0	....	....	....	15.4	5.8	1.0	1.0	.227
71-72	Golden State	2	....	7	4	1	2	.500	....	....	....	2	2	1.000	....	....	0	2	0	0	....	....	....	3.5	2.0	0.0	1.0	.773
NBA Playoff Totals		7	....	84	33	8	28	.286	....	....	....	17	20	.850	....	....	5	7	9	0	....	....	....	12.0	4.7	0.7	1.0	....

• JONES, Ozell

Ozell Jones

Born: Nov. 20, 1960. Long Beach, CA, United States.　　Height: 6'11".　　Weight: 235 lbs.　　Drafted: 1984　　College: Cal State Fullerton

YEAR	TEAM	GP	GS	MIN	PTS	FGM	FGA	FG%	3PM	3PA	3P%	FTM	FTA	FT%	ORB	DRB	TRB	AST	PF	DQ	STL	BLK	TO	MPG	PPG	RPG	APG	PCM
84-85	San Antonio	67	6	888	245	106	180	.589	0	1	.000	33	83	.398	65	173	238	56	139	1	30	57	60	13.3	3.7	3.6	0.8	.445
85-86	LA Clippers	3	0	18	0	0	2	.000	0	0	.000	0	0	.000	0	2	2	0	5	0	2	1	3	6.0	0.0	0.7	0.0	-.129
NBA Season Totals		70	6	906	245	106	182	.582	0	1	.000	33	83	.398	65	175	240	56	144	1	32	58	63	12.9	3.5	3.4	0.8	....
84-85	San Antonio	5	0	73	17	8	11	.727	0	0	.000	1	6	.167	5	12	17	4	18	1	1	4	7	14.6	3.4	3.4	0.8	.298
NBA Playoff Totals		5	0	73	17	8	11	.727	0	0	.000	1	6	.167	5	12	17	4	18	1	1	4	7	14.6	3.4	3.4	0.8	....

• JONES, Popeye

Ronald Jerome (Popeye) Jones

Born: June 17, 1970. Dresden, TN, United States.　　Height: 6'8".　　Weight: 250 lbs.　　Drafted: 1992　　College: Murray State

YEAR	TEAM	GP	GS	MIN	PTS	FGM	FGA	FG%	3PM	3PA	3P%	FTM	FTA	FT%	ORB	DRB	TRB	AST	PF	DQ	STL	BLK	TO	MPG	PPG	RPG	APG	PCM
93-94	Dallas	81	47	1773	468	195	407	.479	0	1	.000	78	107	.729	299	306	605	99	246	2	61	31	97	21.9	5.8	7.5	1.2	.454
94-95	Dallas	80	80	2385	825	372	839	.443	1	12	.083	80	124	.645	**329**	515	844	163	267	5	35	27	128	29.8	10.3	10.6	2.0	.480
95-96	Dallas	68	68	2322	770	327	733	.446	14	39	.359	102	133	.767	260	477	737	132	262	8	54	27	109	34.1	11.3	10.8	1.9	.455
96-97	Toronto	79	61	2421	616	258	537	.480	1	13	.077	99	121	.818	270	410	680	84	269	3	58	39	119	30.6	7.8	8.6	1.1	.381
97-98	Toronto	14	4	352	120	52	127	.409	2	3	.667	14	19	.737	50	52	102	18	39	0	10	3	15	25.1	8.6	7.3	1.3	.404
98-99	Boston	18	2	206	54	20	51	.392	0	1	.000	14	17	.824	28	24	52	15	31	0	5	0	7	11.4	3.0	2.9	0.8	.352
99-00	Denver	40	1	330	104	44	104	.423	2	3	.667	14	19	.737	41	62	103	19	50	1	3	6	13	8.3	2.6	2.6	0.5	.410
00-01	Washington	45	1	638	162	60	153	.392	1	6	.167	41	55	.745	83	137	220	31	95	0	19	8	21	14.2	3.6	4.9	0.7	.418
01-02	Washington	79	40	1920	554	222	508	.437	4	11	.364	106	130	.815	233	345	578	127	209	4	50	19	88	24.3	7.0	7.3	1.6	.435
02-03	Dallas	26	0	222	53	24	62	.387	0	0	.000	5	11	.455	29	30	59	8	31	0	5	1	15	8.5	2.0	2.3	0.3	.252
NBA Season Totals		530	304	12569	3726	1574	3521	.447	25	89	.281	553	736	.751	1622	2358	3980	696	1499	23	300	161	612	23.7	7.0	7.5	1.3	....

• JONES, Rich

Richard Wesley (House) Jones

Born: Dec. 27, 1946. Memphis, TN, United States.　　Height: 6'6".　　Weight: 220 lbs.　　Drafted: 1969　　College: Memphis State

YEAR	TEAM	GP	GS	MIN	PTS	FGM	FGA	FG%	3PM	3PA	3P%	FTM	FTA	FT%	ORB	DRB	TRB	AST	PF	DQ	STL	BLK	TO	MPG	PPG	RPG	APG	PCM
69-70	Dallas-A	2	....	50	28	9	20	.450	0	0	.000	10	11	.909	7	16	23	1	11	1	....	....	6	25.0	14.0	11.5	0.5	.686
70-71	Texas-A	79	....	2074	950	371	910	.408	33	95	.347	175	230	.761	172	353	525	182	246	3	....	....	174	26.3	12.0	6.6	2.3	.500
71-72	Dallas-A	82	....	2932	1176	475	1053	.451	14	47	.298	212	279	.760	199	497	696	222	298	5	....	....	152	35.8	14.3	8.5	2.7	.467
72-73	Dallas-A	67	61	2691	1495	564	1364	.413	43	127	.339	324	414	.783	174	493	667	274	240	5	....	....	225	40.2	22.3	10.0	4.1	.568
73-74	San Antonio-A	78	....	2843	1219	510	1175	.434	13	46	.283	186	241	.772	170	411	581	268	273	....	70	13	145	36.4	15.6	7.4	3.4	.462
74-75	San Antonio-A	83	....	3097	1598	649	1480	.439	13	50	.260	287	374	.767	247	398	645	270	297	....	88	32	210	37.3	19.3	7.8	3.3	.505
75-76	New York-A	83	....	2427	1096	441	1153	.382	15	67	.224	199	261	.762	103	325	428	131	294	....	81	21	159	29.2	13.2	5.2	1.6	.342
76-77	New York	34	....	877	360	134	348	.385	....	....	....	92	121	.760	48	146	194	46	109	2	38	11	....	25.8	10.6	5.7	1.4	.383
NBA Season Totals		34	....	877	360	134	348	.385	....	....	....	92	121	.760	48	146	194	46	109	2	38	11	....	25.8	10.6	5.7	1.4	....
ABA Season Totals		474	....	16114	7562	3019	7155	.422	131	432	.303	1393	1810	.770	1072	2493	3565	1348	1659	14	239	66	1071	34.0	16.0	7.5	2.8	....
Career Totals		508	....	16991	7922	3153	7503	.420	131	432	.303	1485	1931	.769	1120	2639	3759	1394	1768	16	277	77	1071	33.4	15.6	7.4	2.7	....
68-69	Dallas-A	6	....	91	36	16	40	.400	0	1	.000	4	8	.500	5	18	23	5	....	0	....	....	9	15.2	6.0	3.8	0.8	....
70-71	Texas-A	4	....	103	37	12	40	.300	2	8	.250	11	15	.733	11	11	22	10	10	0	....	....	6	25.8	9.3	5.5	2.5	.375
71-72	Dallas-A	4	....	145	38	17	43	.395	1	4	.250	3	6	.500	10	22	32	14	20	1	....	....	7	36.3	9.5	8.0	3.5	.337
73-74	San Antonio-A	7	....	239	121	48	93	.516	1	3	.333	24	29	.828	12	34	46	18	28	....	5	2	15	34.1	17.3	6.6	2.6	.537
74-75	San Antonio-A	6	....	178	63	30	87	.345	1	7	.143	2	7	.286	21	24	45	15	25	....	7	4	11	29.7	10.5	7.5	2.5	.313
75-76	New York-A	12	....	421	164	72	193	.373	2	15	.133	18	27	.667	15	72	87	27	43	....	21	8	29	35.1	13.7	7.3	2.3	.334
ABA Playoff Totals		39	....	1177	459	195	496	.393	7	38	.184	62	92	.674	74	181	255	89	126	1	33	14	77	30.2	11.8	6.5	2.3	....

• JONES, Robin

Robin Dale Jones

Born: Feb. 2, 1954. St. Louis, MO, United States. Height: 6'9". Weight: 225 lbs. Drafted: — College: St. Louis

YEAR TEAM	GP	GS	MIN	PTS	FGM	FGA	FG%	3PM	3PA	3P%	FTM	FTA	FT%	ORB	DRB	TRB	AST	PF	DQ	STL	BLK	TO	MPG	PPG	RPG	APG	PCM
76-77 Portland	63	....	1065	344	139	299	.465	....	....	....	66	109	.606	103	193	296	80	124	3	37	38	....	16.9	5.5	4.7	1.3	.451
77-78 Houston	12	....	66	26	11	20	.550	....	....	....	4	10	.400	5	9	14	2	16	0	1	1	7	5.5	2.2	1.2	0.2	.282
NBA Season Totals	75	....	1131	370	150	319	.470	....	....	....	70	119	.588	108	202	310	82	140	3	38	39	7	15.1	4.9	4.1	1.1	....
76-77 Portland	19	....	105	36	15	32	.469	....	....	....	6	9	.667	8	15	23	9	24	0	4	4	....	5.5	1.9	1.2	0.5	.379
NBA Playoff Totals	19	....	105	36	15	32	.469	....	....	....	6	9	.667	8	15	23	9	24	0	4	4	....	5.5	1.9	1.2	0.5	....

• JONES, Sam

Samuel Jones

Born: June 24, 1933. Wilmington, NC, United States. Height: 6'4". Weight: 198 lbs. Drafted: 1957 College: North Carolina College HOF: 1984

YEAR TEAM	GP	GS	MIN	PTS	FGM	FGA	FG%	3PM	3PA	3P%	FTM	FTA	FT%	ORB	DRB	TRB	AST	PF	DQ	STL	BLK	TO	MPG	PPG	RPG	APG	PCM
57-58 Boston	56	....	594	260	100	233	.429	....	....	....	60	84	.714	....	....	160	37	42	0	....	....	....	10.6	4.6	2.9	0.7	.510
58-59 Boston	71	....	1466	761	305	703	.434	....	....	....	151	196	.770	....	....	428	101	102	0	....	....	....	20.6	10.7	6.0	1.4	.583
59-60 Boston	74	....	1512	878	355	782	.454	....	....	....	168	220	.764	....	....	375	125	101	1	....	....	....	20.4	11.9	5.1	1.7	.619
60-61 Boston	78	....	2028	1171	480	1069	.449	....	....	....	211	268	.787	....	....	421	217	148	1	....	....	....	26.0	15.0	5.4	2.8	.608
61-62 Boston	78	....	2388	1435	596	1284	.464	....	....	....	243	297	.818	....	....	458	232	149	0	....	....	....	30.6	18.4	5.9	3.0	.611
62-63 Boston	76	....	2323	1499	621	1305	.476	....	....	....	257	324	.793	....	....	396	241	162	1	....	....	....	30.6	19.7	5.2	3.2	.634
63-64 Boston	76	....	2381	1473	612	1359	.450	....	....	....	249	318	.783	....	....	349	202	192	1	....	....	....	31.3	19.4	4.6	2.7	.550
64-65 Boston	80	....	2885	2070	821	1818	.452	....	....	....	428	522	.820	....	....	411	223	176	0	....	....	....	36.1	25.9	5.1	2.8	.621
65-66 Boston	67	....	2155	1577	626	1335	.469	....	....	....	325	407	.799	....	....	347	216	170	0	....	....	....	32.2	23.5	5.2	3.2	.676
66-67 Boston	72	....	2325	1594	638	1406	.454	....	....	....	318	371	.857	....	....	338	217	191	1	....	....	....	32.3	22.1	4.7	3.0	.609
67-68 Boston	73	....	2408	1553	621	1348	.461	....	....	....	311	376	.827	....	....	357	216	181	0	....	....	....	33.0	21.3	4.9	3.0	.589
68-69 Boston	70	....	1820	1140	496	1103	.450	....	....	....	148	189	.783	....	....	265	182	121	0	....	....	....	26.0	16.3	3.8	2.6	.548
NBA Season Totals	871	....	24285	15411	6271	13745	.456	....	....	....	2869	3572	.803	....	....	4305	2209	1735	5	....	....	....	27.9	17.7	4.9	2.5	....
57-58 Boston	8	....	75	31	10	22	.455	....	....	....	11	16	.688	....	....	24	4	7	0	....	....	....	9.4	3.9	3.0	0.5	.539
58-59 Boston	11	....	192	113	40	108	.370	....	....	....	33	39	.846	....	....	63	17	14	0	....	....	....	17.5	10.3	5.7	1.5	.640
59-60 Boston	13	....	197	107	45	117	.385	....	....	....	17	21	.810	....	....	41	18	17	0	....	....	....	15.2	8.2	3.2	1.4	.498
60-61 Boston	10	....	258	131	50	112	.446	....	....	....	31	35	.886	....	....	54	22	24	0	....	....	....	25.8	13.1	5.4	2.2	.549
61-62 Boston	14	....	504	288	123	277	.444	....	....	....	42	60	.700	....	....	101	44	30	0	....	....	....	36.0	20.6	7.2	3.1	.559
62-63 Boston	13	....	450	309	120	248	.484	....	....	....	69	83	.831	....	....	81	32	42	1	....	....	....	34.6	23.8	6.2	2.5	.641
63-64 Boston	10	....	356	232	91	181	.503	....	....	....	50	68	.735	....	....	47	23	24	0	....	....	....	35.6	23.2	4.7	2.3	.591
64-65 Boston	12	....	495	343	135	294	.459	....	....	....	73	84	.869	....	....	55	30	39	1	....	....	....	41.3	28.6	4.6	2.5	.567
65-66 Boston	17	....	602	422	154	343	.449	....	....	....	114	136	.838	....	....	86	53	65	1	....	....	....	35.4	24.8	5.1	3.1	.617
66-67 Boston	9	....	326	240	95	207	.459	....	....	....	50	58	.862	....	....	46	28	30	1	....	....	....	36.2	26.7	5.1	3.1	.632
67-68 Boston	19	....	685	390	162	367	.441	....	....	....	66	84	.786	....	....	64	50	58	0	....	....	....	36.1	20.5	3.4	2.6	.449
68-69 Boston	18	....	514	303	124	296	.419	....	....	....	55	69	.797	....	....	58	37	45	1	....	....	....	28.6	16.8	3.2	2.1	.440
NBA Playoff Totals	154	....	4654	2909	1149	2572	.447	....	....	....	611	753	.811	....	....	720	358	395	5	....	....	....	30.2	18.9	4.7	2.3	....

• JONES, Shelton

Shelton Jones

Born: Apr. 6, 1966. Copaigue, NY, United States. Height: 6'9". Weight: 210 lbs. Drafted: 1988 College: St. John's (NY)

YEAR TEAM	GP	GS	MIN	PTS	FGM	FGA	FG%	3PM	3PA	3P%	FTM	FTA	FT%	ORB	DRB	TRB	AST	PF	DQ	STL	BLK	TO	MPG	PPG	RPG	APG	PCM
88-89 San Antonio	7	0	92	26	9	25	.360	0	0	.000	8	13	.615	6	10	16	7	8	0	2	2	7	13.1	3.7	2.3	1.0	.268
88-89 Golden State	2	0	13	6	3	5	.600	0	0	.000	0	0	.000	2	0	2	2	0	0	3	0	1	6.5	3.0	1.0	1.0	.769
88-89 Philadelphia	42	34	577	212	81	179	.453	0	1	.000	50	67	.746	24	71	95	33	50	0	16	13	34	13.7	5.0	2.3	0.8	.362
NBA Season Totals	51	34	682	244	93	209	.445	0	1	.000	58	80	.725	32	81	113	42	58	0	21	15	42	13.4	4.8	2.2	0.8	....

• JONES, Steve

Stephen Howard (Snapper) Jones

Born: Oct. 17, 1942. Alexandria, LA, United States. Height: 6'5". Weight: 205 lbs. Drafted: — College: Oregon

YEAR TEAM	GP	GS	MIN	PTS	FGM	FGA	FG%	3PM	3PA	3P%	FTM	FTA	FT%	ORB	DRB	TRB	AST	PF	DQ	STL	BLK	TO	MPG	PPG	RPG	APG	PCM
67-68 Oakland-A	76	....	1950	765	278	665	.418	23	54	.426	186	233	.798	....	....	343	111	239	7	....	....	135	25.7	10.1	4.5	1.5	.379
68-69 New Orleans-A	78	....	3024	1552	576	1372	.420	52	151	.344	348	437	.796	149	244	393	226	280	4	....	....	192	38.8	19.9	5.0	2.9	.432
69-70 New Orleans-A	84	....	3116	1805	689	1558	.442	15	66	.227	412	495	.832	142	246	388	195	290	3	....	....	251	37.1	21.5	4.6	2.3	.467
70-71 Memphis-A	83	....	2923	1836	732	1556	.470	40	108	.370	332	400	.830	113	186	299	182	234	2	....	....	180	35.2	22.1	3.6	2.2	.518
71-72 Dallas-A	84	....	3091	1537	572	1343	.426	26	78	.333	367	422	.870	74	243	317	237	268	3	....	....	205	36.8	18.3	3.8	2.8	.408
72-73 Carolina-A	67	....	1670	852	348	696	.500	11	28	.393	145	178	.815	50	128	178	84	177	1	....	....	110	24.9	12.7	2.7	1.3	.418
72-73 Dallas-A	13	....	459	221	82	187	.439	2	3	.667	55	69	.797	6	40	46	35	43	2	....	....	40	35.3	17.0	3.5	2.7	.394
73-74 Carolina-A	44	....	935	366	161	365	.441	0	7	.000	44	59	.746	30	65	95	57	96	....	13	9	66	21.3	8.3	2.2	1.3	.310
73-74 Denver-A	42	....	1157	575	239	534	.448	13	36	.361	84	109	.771	32	107	139	128	127	....	13	6	109	27.5	13.7	3.3	3.0	.451
74-75 St. Louis-A	69	....	1884	749	287	654	.439	4	19	.211	171	206	.830	43	151	194	197	131	....	53	7	147	27.3	10.9	2.8	2.9	.393
75-76 Portland	64	....	819	414	168	380	.442	....	....	....	78	94	.830	13	62	75	63	96	0	17	6	....	12.8	6.5	1.2	1.0	.391
NBA Season Totals	64	....	819	414	168	380	.442	....	....	....	78	94	.830	13	62	75	63	96	0	17	6	....	12.8	6.5	1.2	1.0	....
ABA Season Totals	640	....	20209	10258	3964	8930	.444	186	550	.338	2144	2608	.822	639	1410	2392	1452	1885	22	79	22	1435	31.6	16.0	3.7	2.3	....
Career Totals	704	....	21028	10672	4132	9310	.444	186	550	.338	2222	2702	.822	652	1472	2467	1515	1981	22	96	28	1435	29.9	15.2	3.5	2.2	....
68-69 New Orleans-A	11	....	428	185	72	174	.414	4	15	.267	37	50	.740	....	....	54	18	44	0	....	....	36	38.9	16.8	4.9	1.6	.327
70-71 Memphis-A	4	....	163	91	39	88	.443	2	7	.286	11	11	1.000	8	13	21	9	14	0	....	....	12	40.8	22.8	5.3	2.3	.452
71-72 Dallas-A	4	....	137	78	30	63	.476	0	3	.000	18	21	.857	7	12	19	11	19	1	....	....	6	34.3	19.5	4.8	2.8	.499
72-73 Carolina-A	12	....	368	158	61	135	.452	2	4	.500	34	42	.810	8	28	36	9	40	2	....	....	28	30.7	13.2	3.0	0.8	.305
74-75 St. Louis-A	6	....	128	55	22	45	.489	0	1	.000	11	17	.647	1	13	14	14	15	....	2	3	8	21.3	9.2	2.3	2.3	.416
ABA Playoff Totals	37	....	1224	567	224	505	.444	8	30	.267	111	141	.787	24	66	144	61	132	3	2	3	90	33.1	15.3	3.9	1.6	....

• JONES, Wah Wah

Wallace Clayton (Wah Wah) Jones

Born: July 14, 1926. Harlan, KY, United States. Height: 6'4". Weight: 225 lbs. Drafted: 1949 College: Kentucky

YEAR	TEAM	GP	GS	MIN	PTS	FGM	FGA	FG%	3PM	3PA	3P%	FTM	FTA	FT%	ORB	DRB	TRB	AST	PF	DQ	STL	BLK	TO	MPG	PPG	RPG	APG	PCM
49-50	Indianapolis	60	....	....	751	264	706	.374	....	....	....	223	297	.751	....	....	....	194	241	....	....	....	....	....	12.5	....	3.2	....
50-51	Indianapolis	22	....	....	247	93	237	.392	....	....	....	61	77	.792	....	....	125	85	74	4	....	....	....	....	11.2	5.7	3.9	....
51-52	Indianapolis	58	....	1320	430	164	524	.313	....	....	....	102	136	.750	....	....	283	150	137	3	....	....	....	22.8	7.4	4.9	2.6	.385
NBA Season Totals		140	....	1320	1428	521	1467	.355	....	....	....	386	510	.757	....	....	408	429	452	7	....	....	....	9.4	10.2	2.9	3.1	....
49-50	Indianapolis	5	....	....	73	22	73	.301	....	....	....	29	34	.853	....	....	....	22	26	....	....	....	....	....	14.6	....	4.4	....
51-52	Indianapolis	1	....	8	2	1	3	.333	....	....	....	0	0	.000	....	....	0	0	2	0	....	....	....	8.0	2.0	0.0	0.0	-.017
NBA Playoff Totals		6	....	8	75	23	76	.303	....	....	....	29	34	.853	....	....	0	22	28	0	....	....	....	1.3	12.5	0.0	3.7	....

• JONES, Wali

Wali Jones aka.: Walter Jones

Born: Feb. 14, 1942. Philadelphia, PA, United States. Height: 6'2". Weight: 180 lbs. Drafted: 1964 College: Villanova

YEAR	TEAM	GP	GS	MIN	PTS	FGM	FGA	FG%	3PM	3PA	3P%	FTM	FTA	FT%	ORB	DRB	TRB	AST	PF	DQ	STL	BLK	TO	MPG	PPG	RPG	APG	PCM
64-65	Baltimore	77	....	1250	407	154	411	.375	....	....	....	99	136	.728	....	....	140	200	196	1	....	....	....	16.2	5.3	1.8	2.6	.379
65-66	Philadelphia	80	....	2196	720	296	799	.370	....	....	....	128	172	.744	....	....	169	273	250	6	....	....	....	27.5	9.0	2.1	3.4	.307
66-67	Philadelphia	81	....	2249	1069	423	982	.431	....	....	....	223	266	.838	....	....	265	303	246	6	....	....	....	27.8	13.2	3.3	3.7	.482
67-68	Philadelphia	77	....	2058	985	413	1040	.397	....	....	....	159	202	.787	....	....	219	245	225	5	....	....	....	26.7	12.8	2.8	3.2	.412
68-69	Philadelphia	81	....	2340	1071	432	1005	.430	....	....	....	207	256	.809	....	....	251	292	280	5	....	....	....	28.9	13.2	3.1	3.6	.429
69-70	Philadelphia	78	....	1740	922	366	851	.430	....	....	....	190	226	.841	....	....	173	276	210	2	....	....	....	22.3	11.8	2.2	3.5	.488
70-71	Philadelphia	41	....	962	415	168	418	.402	....	....	....	79	101	.782	....	....	64	128	110	1	....	....	....	23.5	10.1	1.6	3.1	.358
71-72	Milwaukee	48	....	1030	362	144	354	.407	....	....	....	74	90	.822	....	....	75	141	112	0	....	....	....	21.5	7.5	1.6	2.9	.340
72-73	Milwaukee	27	....	419	134	59	145	.407	....	....	....	16	18	.889	....	....	29	56	39	0	....	....	....	15.5	5.0	1.1	2.1	.314
74-75	Utah-A	71	....	1339	532	212	524	.405	6	25	.240	102	124	.823	15	62	77	152	147	....	42	3	76	18.9	7.5	1.1	2.1	.312
75-76	Detroit	1	....	19	8	4	11	.364	....	....	....	0	0	.000	0	0	0	2	2	0	2	0	....	19.0	8.0	0.0	2.0	.180
75-76	Philadelphia	16	....	157	47	19	38	.500	....	....	....	9	13	.692	0	9	9	31	25	0	4	0	....	9.8	2.9	0.6	1.9	.391
NBA Season Totals		607	....	14420	6140	2478	6054	.409	....	....	....	1184	1480	.800	0	9	1394	1947	1695	26	6	0	....	23.8	10.1	2.3	3.2	....
ABA Season Totals		71	....	1339	532	212	524	.405	6	25	.240	102	124	.823	15	62	77	152	147	....	42	3	76	18.9	7.5	1.1	2.1	....
Career Totals		678	....	15759	6672	2690	6578	.409	6	25	.240	1286	1604	.802	15	71	1471	2099	1842	26	48	3	76	23.2	9.8	2.2	3.1	....
64-65	Baltimore	10	....	162	73	29	63	.460	....	....	....	15	20	.750	....	....	20	18	28	1	....	....	....	16.2	7.3	2.0	1.8	.443
65-66	Philadelphia	5	....	156	65	25	77	.325	....	....	....	15	22	.682	....	....	15	18	18	0	....	....	....	31.2	13.0	3.0	3.6	.308
66-67	Philadelphia	15	....	476	263	109	244	.447	....	....	....	45	58	.776	....	....	42	61	58	0	....	....	....	31.7	17.5	2.8	4.1	.492
67-68	Philadelphia	13	....	387	183	69	193	.358	....	....	....	45	57	.789	....	....	31	39	48	2	....	....	....	29.8	14.1	2.4	3.0	.340
68-69	Philadelphia	5	....	103	32	12	45	.267	....	....	....	8	10	.800	....	....	16	9	17	1	....	....	....	20.6	6.4	3.2	1.8	.197
69-70	Philadelphia	5	....	160	79	34	65	.523	....	....	....	11	14	.786	....	....	11	24	16	0	....	....	....	32.0	15.8	2.2	4.8	.500
70-71	Philadelphia	7	....	115	48	19	52	.365	....	....	....	10	13	.769	....	....	12	11	22	0	....	....	....	16.4	6.9	1.7	1.6	.276
71-72	Milwaukee	9	....	200	90	36	82	.439	....	....	....	18	21	.857	....	....	18	20	27	1	....	....	....	22.2	10.0	2.0	2.2	.378
74-75	Utah-A	5	....	46	22	8	21	.381	0	0	.000	6	6	1.000	1	1	2	4	6	....	4	0	7	9.2	4.4	0.4	0.8	.305
75-76	Philadelphia	1	....	2	0	0	0	.000	....	....	....	0	0	.000	0	1	1	2	0	0	0	0	....	2.0	0.0	1.0	2.0	1.571
NBA Playoff Totals		70	....	1761	833	333	821	.406	....	....	....	167	215	.777	0	1	166	202	234	5	0	0	....	25.2	11.9	2.4	2.9	....
ABA Playoff Totals		5	....	46	22	8	21	.381	0	0	.000	6	6	1.000	1	1	2	4	6	....	4	0	7	9.2	4.4	0.4	0.8	....
Career Playoff Totals		75	....	1807	855	341	842	.405	0	0	.000	173	221	.783	1	2	168	206	240	5	4	0	7	24.1	11.4	2.2	2.7	....

• JONES, Wil

Wilbert Jones

Born: Feb. 27, 1947. McGehee, AR, United States. Height: 6'8". Weight: 205 lbs. Drafted: 1969 College: Albany State (GA)

YEAR	TEAM	GP	GS	MIN	PTS	FGM	FGA	FG%	3PM	3PA	3P%	FTM	FTA	FT%	ORB	DRB	TRB	AST	PF	DQ	STL	BLK	TO	MPG	PPG	RPG	APG	PCM
69-70	Miami-A	74	....	1697	606	243	616	.394	2	11	.182	118	162	.728	223	342	565	48	207	5	....	....	102	22.9	8.2	7.6	0.6	.423
70-71	Memphis-A	84	....	2234	955	390	811	.481	1	13	.077	174	258	.674	309	371	680	152	249	5	....	....	135	26.6	11.4	8.1	1.8	.542
71-72	Memphis-A	84	....	3098	1254	506	1078	.469	2	16	.125	240	320	.750	371	505	876	154	322	4	....	....	160	36.9	14.9	10.4	1.8	.490
72-73	Memphis-A	76	....	2316	835	344	722	.476	1	7	.143	146	198	.737	245	359	604	117	281	9	....	....	130	30.5	11.0	7.9	1.5	.439
73-74	Memphis-A	81	....	2842	1072	453	997	.454	3	26	.115	163	220	.741	205	460	665	205	276	....	105	82	184	35.1	13.2	8.2	2.5	.446
74-75	Kentucky-A	84	....	2689	1055	458	948	.483	0	5	.000	139	189	.735	198	409	607	256	**353**	....	108	70	199	32.0	12.6	7.2	3.0	.470
75-76	Kentucky-A	83	....	2635	1127	483	1015	.476	3	6	.500	158	204	.775	243	382	625	209	326	....	84	54	200	31.7	13.6	7.5	2.5	.484
76-77	Indiana	80	....	2709	1042	438	1019	.430	....	....	....	166	223	.744	218	386	604	189	305	10	102	80	....	33.9	13.0	7.6	2.4	.414
77-78	Buffalo	79	....	1711	536	226	514	.440	....	....	....	84	119	.706	106	228	334	116	255	7	70	43	134	21.7	6.8	4.2	1.5	.328
NBA Season Totals		159	....	4420	1578	664	1533	.433	....	....	....	250	342	.731	324	614	938	305	560	17	172	123	134	27.8	9.9	5.9	1.9	....
ABA Season Totals		566	....	17511	6904	2877	6187	.465	12	84	.143	1138	1551	.734	1794	2828	4622	1141	2014	23	297	206	1110	30.9	12.2	8.2	2.0	....
Career Totals		725	....	21931	8482	3541	7720	.459	12	84	.143	1388	1893	.733	2118	3442	5560	1446	2574	40	469	329	1244	30.2	11.7	7.7	2.0	....
70-71	Memphis-A	4	....	158	60	28	56	.500	0	0	.000	4	6	.667	21	28	49	13	17	1	....	....	7	39.5	15.0	12.3	3.3	.537
74-75	Kentucky-A	15	....	454	143	62	142	.437	0	1	.000	19	24	.792	48	52	100	48	60	....	17	12	30	30.3	9.5	6.7	3.2	.408
75-76	Kentucky-A	10	....	324	120	52	108	.481	0	1	.000	16	17	.941	26	41	67	20	41	....	11	0	21	32.4	12.0	6.7	2.0	.411
ABA Playoff Totals		29	....	936	323	142	306	.464	0	2	.000	39	47	.830	95	121	216	81	118	1	28	12	58	32.3	11.1	7.4	2.8	....

• JONES, Willie

William A. Jones

Born: June 29, 1936. Height: 6'3". Weight: 185 lbs. Drafted: 1960 College: Northwestern

YEAR	TEAM	GP	GS	MIN	PTS	FGM	FGA	FG%	3PM	3PA	3P%	FTM	FTA	FT%	ORB	DRB	TRB	AST	PF	DQ	STL	BLK	TO	MPG	PPG	RPG	APG	PCM
60-61	Detroit	35	....	452	196	78	216	.361	....	....	....	40	63	.635	....	....	94	63	90	2	....	....	....	12.9	5.6	2.7	1.8	.437
61-62	Detroit	69	....	1006	418	177	475	.373	....	....	....	64	101	.634	....	....	177	115	137	1	....	....	....	14.6	6.1	2.6	1.7	.393
62-63	Detroit	79	....	1470	728	305	730	.418	....	....	....	118	164	.720	....	....	233	188	207	4	....	....	....	18.6	9.2	2.9	2.4	.478
63-64	Detroit	77	....	1539	630	265	680	.390	....	....	....	100	141	.709	....	....	253	172	211	5	....	....	....	20.0	8.2	3.3	2.2	.400
64-65	Detroit	12	....	101	44	21	52	.404	....	....	....	2	6	.333	....	....	10	7	13	0	....	....	....	8.4	3.7	0.8	0.6	.297
NBA Season Totals		272	....	4568	2016	846	2153	.393	....	....	....	324	475	.682	....	....	767	545	658	12	....	....	....	16.8	7.4	2.8	2.0	....
60-61	Detroit	3	....	40	30	12	29	.414	....	....	....	6	7	.857	....	....	7	6	6	0	....	....	....	13.3	10.0	2.3	2.0	.679
61-62	Detroit	9	....	180	99	43	101	.426	....	....	....	13	14	.929	....	....	23	31	27	2	....	....	....	20.0	11.0	2.6	3.4	.547
62-63	Detroit	4	....	67	28	11	28	.393	....	....	....	6	8	.750	....	....	7	6	10	0	....	....	....	16.8	7.0	1.8	1.5	.337
NBA Playoff Totals		16	....	287	157	66	158	.418	....	....	....	25	29	.862	....	....	37	43	43	2	....	....	....	17.9	9.8	2.3	2.7	....

• JORDAN, Adonis

Adonis Adelecino Jordan

Born: Aug. 21, 1970. Brooklyn, NY, United States. Height: 5'11". Weight: 170 lbs. Drafted: 1993 College: Kansas

YEAR TEAM	GP	GS	MIN	PTS	FGM	FGA	FG%	3PM	3PA	3P%	FTM	FTA	FT%	ORB	DRB	TRB	AST	PF	DQ	STL	BLK	TO	MPG	PPG	RPG	APG	PCM
93-94 Denver	6	0	79	15	6	23	.261	3	10	.300	0	0	.000	3	3	6	19	6	0	0	1	6	13.2	2.5	1.0	3.2	.230
98-99 Milwaukee	4	0	18	6	2	4	.500	0	2	.000	2	4	.500	0	0	0	3	0	0	3	0	2	4.5	1.5	0.0	0.8	.420
NBA Season Totals	10	0	97	21	8	27	.296	3	12	.250	2	4	.500	3	3	6	22	6	0	3	1	8	9.7	2.1	0.6	2.2	....

• JORDAN, Charles

Charles C. Jordan

Born: Jan. 31, 1954. Indianapolis, IN, United States. Height: 6'8". Weight: 220 lbs. Drafted: — College: Canisius

YEAR TEAM	GP	GS	MIN	PTS	FGM	FGA	FG%	3PM	3PA	3P%	FTM	FTA	FT%	ORB	DRB	TRB	AST	PF	DQ	STL	BLK	TO	MPG	PPG	RPG	APG	PCM
75-76 Indiana-A	71	....	855	369	162	373	.434	2	10	.200	43	72	.597	94	122	216	53	184	....	33	13	84	12.0	5.2	3.0	0.7	.395
ABA Season Totals	71	....	855	369	162	373	.434	2	10	.200	43	72	.597	94	122	216	53	184	....	33	13	84	12.0	5.2	3.0	0.7	....
75-76 Indiana-A	2	....	18	2	1	6	.167	0	0	.000	0	0	.000	0	5	5	2	9	....	2	0	1	9.0	1.0	2.5	1.0	.012
ABA Playoff Totals	2	....	18	2	1	6	.167	0	0	.000	0	0	.000	0	5	5	2	9	....	2	0	1	9.0	1.0	2.5	1.0	....

• JORDAN, Eddie

Edward Montgomery (Fast Eddie) Jordan

Born: Jan. 29, 1955. Washington, DC, United States. Height: 6'1". Weight: 170 lbs. Drafted: 1977 College: Rutgers

YEAR TEAM	GP	GS	MIN	PTS	FGM	FGA	FG%	3PM	3PA	3P%	FTM	FTA	FT%	ORB	DRB	TRB	AST	PF	DQ	STL	BLK	TO	MPG	PPG	RPG	APG	PCM
77-78 Cleveland	22	....	171	50	19	56	.339	....	....	....	12	16	.750	2	9	11	32	10	0	12	1	13	7.8	2.3	0.5	1.5	.334
77-78 New Jersey	51	....	1042	511	196	482	.407	....	....	....	119	151	.788	33	75	108	145	84	0	114	18	92	20.4	10.0	2.1	2.8	.482
78-79 New Jersey	82	....	2260	1015	401	960	.418	....	....	....	213	274	.777	74	141	215	365	209	0	**201**	40	246	27.6	12.4	2.6	4.5	.435
79-80 New Jersey	82	....	2657	1087	437	1017	.430	12	48	.250	201	258	.779	62	208	270	557	238	7	223	27	254	32.4	13.3	3.3	6.8	.481
80-81 New Jersey	14	....	239	87	30	73	.411	3	10	.300	24	32	.750	5	13	18	46	29	0	24	1	22	17.1	6.2	1.3	3.3	.419
80-81 LA Lakers	60	....	987	306	120	279	.430	3	12	.250	63	95	.663	25	55	80	195	136	0	74	7	120	16.5	5.1	1.3	3.3	.339
81-82 LA Lakers	58	0	608	222	89	208	.428	1	9	.111	43	54	.796	4	39	43	131	98	0	62	1	64	10.5	3.8	0.7	2.3	.398
82-83 LA Lakers	35	0	333	94	40	132	.303	3	16	.188	11	17	.647	8	18	26	80	52	0	31	1	53	9.5	2.7	0.7	2.3	.232
83-84 Portland	13	0	183	33	13	41	.317	0	3	.000	7	10	.700	3	10	13	39	32	0	21	0	18	14.1	2.5	1.0	3.0	.258
83-84 LA Lakers	3	0	27	9	4	8	.500	0	0	.000	1	2	.500	0	4	4	5	5	0	4	0	8	9.0	3.0	1.3	1.7	.290
NBA Season Totals	420	0	8507	3414	1349	3256	.414	22	98	.224	694	909	.763	216	572	788	1595	893	7	766	96	890	20.3	8.1	1.9	3.8	....
78-79 New Jersey	2	....	83	38	15	38	.395	....	....	....	8	9	.889	6	9	15	17	6	0	8	3	6	41.5	19.0	7.5	8.5	.613
80-81 LA Lakers	2	....	4	0	0	0	.000	0	0	.000	0	0	.000	0	0	0	1	0	0	0	0	0	2.0	0.0	0.0	0.5	.272
81-82 LA Lakers	3	0	6	0	0	2	.000	0	1	.000	0	0	.000	0	0	0	5	0	0	2	0	1	2.0	0.0	0.0	1.7	.746
NBA Playoff Totals	7	0	93	38	15	40	.375	0	1	.000	8	9	.889	6	9	15	23	6	0	10	3	7	13.3	5.4	2.1	3.3	....

• JORDAN, Ken

Ken Jordan

Born: 1912. Height: 6'2". Weight: 180 lbs. Drafted: — College: Xavier (OH)

YEAR TEAM	GP	GS	MIN	PTS	FGM	FGA	FG%	3PM	3PA	3P%	FTM	FTA	FT%	ORB	DRB	TRB	AST	PF	DQ	STL	BLK	TO	MPG	PPG	RPG	APG	PCM
37-38 Cincinnati-N	8	....	....	38	14	....	....	....	....	....	10	....	....	....	....	....	....	....	....	....	....	....	....	4.8	....	....	....
NBL Season Totals	8	....	....	38	14	....	....	....	....	....	10	....	....	....	....	....	....	....	....	....	....	....	....	4.8	....	....	....

• JORDAN, Michael

Michael Jeffrey (Air) Jordan

Born: Feb. 17, 1963. Brooklyn, NY, United States. Height: 6'6". Weight: 195 lbs. Drafted: 1984 College: North Carolina

YEAR TEAM	GP	GS	MIN	PTS	FGM	FGA	FG%	3PM	3PA	3P%	FTM	FTA	FT%	ORB	DRB	TRB	AST	PF	DQ	STL	BLK	TO	MPG	PPG	RPG	APG	PCM
84-85 Chicago	82	82	3144	**2313**	837	1625	.515	9	52	.173	630	746	.845	167	367	534	481	285	4	196	69	287	38.3	28.2	6.5	5.9	.758
85-86 Chicago	18	7	451	408	150	328	.457	3	18	.167	105	125	.840	23	41	64	53	46	0	37	21	45	25.1	22.7	3.6	2.9	.754
86-87 Chicago	82	82	**3281**	**3041**	**1098**	**2279**	.482	12	66	.182	**833**	**972**	.857	166	264	430	377	237	0	236	125	271	40.0	**37.1**	5.2	4.6	.809
87-88 Chicago	82	82	**3311**	**2868**	**1069**	**1998**	.535	7	53	.132	**723**	860	.841	139	310	449	485	270	2	**259**	131	254	**40.4**	**35.0**	5.5	5.9	.869
88-89 Chicago	81	81	**3255**	**2633**	**966**	1795	.538	27	98	.276	674	793	.850	149	503	652	650	247	2	234	65	292	**40.2**	**32.5**	8.0	8.0	.922
89-90 Chicago	82	82	3197	**2753**	**1034**	**1964**	.526	92	245	.376	593	699	.848	143	422	565	519	241	0	**227**	54	246	39.0	**33.6**	6.9	6.3	.886
90-91 Chicago	82	82	3034	**2580**	**990**	**1837**	.539	29	93	.312	571	671	.851	118	374	492	453	229	1	223	83	205	37.0	**31.5**	6.0	5.5	.881
91-92 Chicago	80	80	3102	**2404**	**943**	**1818**	.519	27	100	.270	491	590	.832	91	420	511	489	201	1	182	75	200	38.8	**30.1**	6.4	6.1	.807
92-93 Chicago	78	78	3067	**2541**	**992**	**2003**	.495	81	230	.352	476	569	.837	135	387	522	428	188	0	**221**	61	211	39.3	**32.6**	6.7	5.5	.807
94-95 Chicago	17	17	668	457	166	404	.411	16	32	.500	109	136	.801	25	92	117	90	47	0	30	13	36	39.3	26.9	6.9	5.3	.615
95-96 Chicago	82	82	3090	**2491**	**916**	**1850**	.495	111	260	.427	548	657	.834	148	395	543	352	195	0	180	42	197	37.7	**30.4**	6.6	4.3	.769
96-97 Chicago	82	82	3106	**2431**	**920**	**1892**	.486	111	297	.374	480	576	.833	113	369	482	352	156	0	140	44	164	37.9	**29.6**	5.9	4.3	.725
97-98 Chicago	82	82	3181	**2357**	**881**	**1893**	.465	30	126	.238	565	721	.784	130	345	475	283	151	0	141	45	189	38.8	**28.7**	5.8	3.5	.638
01-02 Washington	60	53	2092	1375	551	1324	.416	10	53	.189	263	333	.790	50	289	339	310	119	0	85	26	162	34.9	22.9	5.7	5.2	.568
02-03 Washington	82	67	3034	1640	679	1527	.445	16	55	.291	266	324	.821	71	426	497	311	171	1	123	39	173	37.0	20.0	6.1	3.8	.510
NBA Season Totals	1072	1039	41013	32292	12192	24537	.497	581	1778	.327	7327	8772	.835	1668	5004	6672	5633	2783	11	2514	893	2932	38.3	**30.1**	6.2	5.3	....
84-85 Chicago	4	4	171	117	34	78	.436	1	8	.125	48	58	.828	7	16	23	34	15	0	11	4	15	42.8	29.3	5.8	8.5	.714
85-86 Chicago	3	3	135	131	48	95	.505	1	1	1.000	34	39	.872	5	14	19	17	13	1	7	4	14	45.0	43.7	6.3	5.7	.830
86-87 Chicago	3	3	128	107	35	84	.417	2	5	.400	35	39	.897	7	14	21	18	11	0	6	7	8	42.7	35.7	7.0	6.0	.764
87-88 Chicago	10	10	427	363	138	260	.531	1	3	.333	86	99	.869	23	48	71	47	38	1	24	11	39	42.7	36.3	7.1	4.7	.792
88-89 Chicago	17	17	718	591	199	390	.510	10	35	.286	183	229	.799	26	93	119	130	65	1	42	13	68	42.2	34.8	7.0	7.6	.835
89-90 Chicago	16	16	674	587	219	426	.514	16	50	.320	133	159	.836	24	91	115	109	54	0	45	14	56	42.1	36.7	7.2	6.8	.863
90-91 Chicago	17	17	689	529	197	376	.524	10	26	.385	125	148	.845	18	90	108	142	53	0	40	23	43	40.5	31.1	6.4	8.4	.867
91-92 Chicago	22	22	920	759	290	581	.499	17	44	.386	162	189	.857	37	100	137	127	62	0	44	16	81	41.8	34.5	6.2	5.8	.751
92-93 Chicago	19	19	783	666	251	528	.475	28	72	.389	136	169	.805	32	96	128	114	58	0	39	17	45	41.2	35.1	6.7	6.0	.787
94-95 Chicago	10	10	420	315	120	248	.484	11	30	.367	64	79	.810	20	45	65	45	30	0	23	14	41	42.0	31.5	6.5	4.5	.664
95-96 Chicago	18	18	733	552	187	407	.459	25	62	.403	153	187	.818	31	58	89	74	49	0	33	6	42	40.7	30.7	4.9	4.1	.635
96-97 Chicago	19	19	804	590	227	498	.456	13	67	.194	123	148	.831	42	108	150	91	46	0	30	17	49	42.3	31.1	7.9	4.8	.671
97-98 Chicago	21	21	872	680	243	526	.462	13	43	.302	181	223	.812	33	74	107	74	47	0	32	12	45	41.5	32.4	5.1	3.5	.639
NBA Playoff Totals	179	179	7474	**5987**	2188	**4497**	.487	148	446	.332	**1463**	**1766**	.828	305	847	1152	1022	541	3	376	158	546	41.8	**33.4**	6.4	5.7	....

• JORDAN, Reggie

Reginald Jordan

Born: Jan. 26, 1968. Chicago, IL, United States.   Height: 6'4".   Weight: 195 lbs.   Drafted: —   College: New Mexico State

YEAR TEAM	GP	GS	MIN	PTS	FGM	FGA	FG%	3PM	3PA	3P%	FTM	FTA	FT%	ORB	DRB	TRB	AST	PF	DQ	STL	BLK	TO	MPG	PPG	RPG	APG	PCM
93-94 LA Lakers	23	0	259	125	44	103	.427	2	4	.500	35	51	.686	46	21	67	26	26	0	14	5	14	11.3	5.4	2.9	1.1	.563
95-96 Atlanta	24	0	247	94	36	71	.507	0	0	.000	22	38	.579	23	29	52	29	30	0	12	7	19	10.3	3.9	2.2	1.2	.482
96-97 Portland	9	0	99	20	8	16	.500	0	0	.000	4	10	.400	11	12	23	11	13	0	5	3	6	11.0	2.2	2.6	1.2	.391
96-97 Minnesota	10	0	31	20	8	10	.800	0	0	.000	4	7	.571	0	4	4	1	2	0	2	0	2	3.1	2.0	0.4	0.1	.665
97-98 Minnesota	57	1	487	149	54	113	.478	0	1	.000	41	72	.569	57	40	97	50	63	0	35	9	29	8.5	2.6	1.7	0.9	.429
98-99 Minnesota	27	1	296	51	15	54	.278	0	0	.000	21	38	.553	27	32	59	41	38	0	12	5	14	11.0	1.9	2.2	1.5	.313
99-00 Washington	36	0	243	41	17	53	.321	0	1	.000	7	13	.538	16	25	41	32	29	0	12	2	19	6.8	1.1	1.1	0.9	.247
NBA Season Totals	186	2	1662	500	182	420	.433	2	6	.333	134	229	.585	180	163	343	190	201	0	92	31	103	8.9	2.7	1.8	1.0	....
95-96 Atlanta	10	0	59	17	7	13	.538	0	0	.000	3	7	.429	1	5	6	9	7	0	5	1	3	5.9	1.7	0.6	0.9	.410
97-98 Minnesota	2	0	29	12	5	8	.625	1	1	1.000	1	2	.500	3	6	9	3	5	0	1	0	0	14.5	6.0	4.5	1.5	.652
NBA Playoff Totals	12	0	88	29	12	21	.571	1	1	1.000	4	9	.444	4	11	15	12	12	0	6	1	3	7.3	2.4	1.3	1.0	....

• JORDAN, Thomas

Thomas Jordan

Born: May 23, 1968. Baltimore, MD, United States.   Height: 6'10".   Weight: 220 lbs.   Drafted: —   College: Oklahoma State

YEAR TEAM	GP	GS	MIN	PTS	FGM	FGA	FG%	3PM	3PA	3P%	FTM	FTA	FT%	ORB	DRB	TRB	AST	PF	DQ	STL	BLK	TO	MPG	PPG	RPG	APG	PCM
92-93 Philadelphia	4	0	106	44	18	41	.439	0	0	.000	8	17	.471	5	14	19	3	14	0	3	5	12	26.5	11.0	4.8	0.8	.274
NBA Season Totals	4	0	106	44	18	41	.439	0	0	.000	8	17	.471	5	14	19	3	14	0	3	5	12	26.5	11.0	4.8	0.8	....

• JORDAN, Walter

Walter Lee Jordan

Born: Feb. 19, 1956. Perry, AL, United States.   Height: 6'7".   Weight: 198 lbs.   Drafted: 1978   College: Purdue

YEAR TEAM	GP	GS	MIN	PTS	FGM	FGA	FG%	3PM	3PA	3P%	FTM	FTA	FT%	ORB	DRB	TRB	AST	PF	DQ	STL	BLK	TO	MPG	PPG	RPG	APG	PCM
80-81 Cleveland	30	....	207	68	29	75	.387	0	0	.000	10	17	.588	23	19	42	11	35	0	11	5	18	6.9	2.3	1.4	0.4	.268
NBA Season Totals	30	....	207	68	29	75	.387	0	0	.000	10	17	.588	23	19	42	11	35	0	11	5	18	6.9	2.3	1.4	0.4	....

• JORDON, Phil

Philip Jordon

Born: Sept. 12, 1933. Lakeport, CA, United States. Died: June 7, 1965.   Height: 6'10".   Weight: 205 lbs.   Drafted: 1956   College: Whitworth

YEAR TEAM	GP	GS	MIN	PTS	FGM	FGA	FG%	3PM	3PA	3P%	FTM	FTA	FT%	ORB	DRB	TRB	AST	PF	DQ	STL	BLK	TO	MPG	PPG	RPG	APG	PCM
56-57 New York	9		91	44	18	49	.367	....	....	....	8	12	.667			34	2	15	0	....	....		10.1	4.9	3.8	0.2	.458
57-58 New York	12		75	37	16	34	.471	....	....	....	5	6	.833			24	5	11	0	....	....		6.3	3.1	2.0	0.4	.578
57-58 Detroit	46		823	413	177	433	.409	....	....	....	59	87	.678			277	32	97	1	....	....		17.9	9.0	6.0	0.7	.514
58-59 Detroit	72		2058	1029	399	967	.413	....	....	....	231	303	.762			594	83	193	1	....	....		28.6	14.3	8.3	1.2	.511
59-60 Cincinnati	75		2066	1004	381	970	.393	....	....	....	242	338	.716			624	207	227	7	....	....		27.5	13.4	8.3	2.8	.564
60-61 Cincinnati	48		1140	521	202	511	.395	....	....	....	117	170	.688			424	107	150	1	....	....		23.8	10.9	8.8	2.2	.582
60-61 New York	31		924	405	158	429	.368	....	....	....	89	127	.701			250	74	123	4	....	....		29.8	13.1	8.1	2.4	.454
61-62 New York	76		2195	902	403	1028	.392	....	....	....	96	168	.571			482	156	258	7	....	....		28.9	11.9	6.3	2.1	.388
62-63 St. Louis	73		1420	478	211	527	.400	....	....	....	56	101	.554			319	103	172	3	....	....		19.5	6.5	4.4	1.4	.366
NBA Season Totals	442	....	10792	4833	1965	4948	.397	....	....	....	903	1312	.688			3028	769	1246	24	....	....		24.4	10.9	6.9	1.7	....
57-58 Detroit	6		62	39	12	30	.400	....	....	....	15	20	.750			12	2	15	0	....	....		10.3	6.5	2.0	0.3	.482
58-59 Detroit	3		99	45	15	45	.333	....	....	....	15	18	.833			24	5	9	0	....	....		33.0	15.0	8.0	1.7	.426
62-63 St. Louis	7		82	21	9	24	.375	....	....	....	3	4	.750			15	7	10	0	....	....		11.7	3.0	2.1	1.0	.306
NBA Playoff Totals	16	....	243	105	36	99	.364	....	....	....	33	42	.786			51	14	34	0	....	....		15.2	6.6	3.2	0.9	....

• JORGENSEN, Johnny

John J. Jorgensen

Born: Dec. 28, 1921. Died: Jan. 19, 1973.   Height: 6'2".   Weight: 185 lbs.   Drafted: —   College: DePaul

YEAR TEAM	GP	GS	MIN	PTS	FGM	FGA	FG%	3PM	3PA	3P%	FTM	FTA	FT%	ORB	DRB	TRB	AST	PF	DQ	STL	BLK	TO	MPG	PPG	RPG	APG	PCM
47-48 Minneapolis-N	38	....	....	101	37	....	....				27	49	.551				....	52				....		2.7		....	
47-48 Chicago	1		....	4	2	2	1.000				0	0	.000				0	1						4.0		0.0	
47-48 Baltimore	2		....	5	2	7	.286				1	1	1.000				0	1						2.5		0.0	
48-49 Minneapolis	48		....	106	41	114	.360				24	33	.727				33	68				....		2.2		0.7	
NBA Season Totals	51		....	115	45	123	.366				25	34	.735				33	70				....		2.3		0.6	
NBL Season Totals	38		....	101	37	....					27	49	....				....	52				....		2.7			
Career Totals	89		....	216	82	123					52	83					33	122				....		2.4		0.4	
47-48 Minneapolis-N	10		....	26	11	....					4	8	.500				....					....		2.6			
48-49 Minneapolis	6		....	7	3	7	.429				1	1	1.000				0	4						1.2		0.0	
NBA Playoff Totals	6		....	7	3	7	.429				1	1	1.000				0	4				....		1.2		0.0	
NBL Playoff Totals	10		....	26	11	....					4	8					....					....		2.6			
Career Playoff Totals	16		....	33	14	7					5	9					0	4				....		2.1		0.0	

• JORGENSEN, Noble

Noble Gordon (Jorgy) Jorgensen

Born: May 18, 1925. Died: Nov. 1982.   Height: 6'9".   Weight: 228 lbs.   Drafted: —   College: Iowa

YEAR TEAM	GP	GS	MIN	PTS	FGM	FGA	FG%	3PM	3PA	3P%	FTM	FTA	FT%	ORB	DRB	TRB	AST	PF	DQ	STL	BLK	TO	MPG	PPG	RPG	APG	PCM
46-47 Pittsburgh	15		....	66	25	112	.223				16	25	.640				4	40				....		4.4		0.3	
48-49 Sheboygan-N	63		....	630	218	....					194	255	.761				....	189				....		10.0			
49-50 Sheboygan	54		....	704	218	618	.353				268	350	.766				90	201				....		13.0		1.7	
50-51 Tri/Syr	63		....	628	223	600	.372				182	265	.687			338	91	237	8			....		10.0	5.4	1.4	
51-52 Syracuse	66		1318	529	190	460	.413				149	187	.797			288	63	190	2			....	20.0	8.0	4.4	1.0	.411
52-53 Syracuse	70		1355	436	145	436	.333				146	199	.734			236	76	247	7			....	19.4	6.2	3.4	1.1	.284
NBA Season Totals	268		....	2673	2363	801	2226	.360				761	1026	.742			862	324	915	17			....		10.0	8.8	3.2	1.2
NBL Season Totals	63		....	630	218	....					194	255					....	189				....		10.0			
Career Totals	331		....	2673	2993	1019	2226	....				955	1281				862	324	1104	17			....		8.1	9.0	2.6	1.0

YEAR	TEAM	GP	GS	MIN	PTS	FGM	FGA	FG%	3PM	3PA	3P%	FTM	FTA	FT%	ORB	DRB	TRB	AST	PF	DQ	STL	BLK	TO	MPG	PPG	RPG	APG	PCM
48-49	Sheboygan-N	2	....	....	29	11			....	....	....	7	8	.875	....	....	....	....	....	....	....	....	....	....	14.5			....
49-50	Sheboygan	3	....	....	52	17	44	.386	....	....	....	18	30	.600	....	....	....	8	15		....	....	....	....	17.3		2.7	....
50-51	Syracuse	7	....	....	50	18	43	.419	....	....	....	14	22	.636	....	....	21	7	19	0	....	....	....	....	7.1	3.0	1.0	....
51-52	Syracuse	7	....	150	61	19	52	.365	....	....	....	23	31	.742	....	....	27	5	30	2	....	....	....	21.4	8.7	3.9	0.7	.331
52-53	Syracuse	2	....	44	14	5	9	.556	....	....	....	4	6	.667	....	....	10	3	11	1	....	....	....	22.0	7.0	5.0	1.5	.397
NBA Playoff Totals		19	....	194	177	59	148	.399				59	89	.663	....	....	58	23	75	3	....	....	....	10.2	9.3	3.1	1.2	....
NBL Playoff Totals		2	....	....	29	11						7	8		....	....	....	....	....	....	....	....	....	....	14.5			....
Career Playoff Totals		21	....	194	206	70	148					66	97		....	....	58	23	75	3	....	....	....	9.2	9.8	2.8	1.1	....

• JORGENSEN, Roger

Roger Kennedy Jorgensen

Born: Sept. 2, 1920.   Height: 6'5".   Weight: 200 lbs.   Drafted: —   College: Ohio State

YEAR	TEAM	GP	GS	MIN	PTS	FGM	FGA	FG%	3PM	3PA	3P%	FTM	FTA	FT%	ORB	DRB	TRB	AST	PF	DQ	STL	BLK	TO	MPG	PPG	RPG	APG	PCM
46-47	Pittsburgh	28	....	....	41	14	54	.259	....	....	....	13	19	.684	....	....	....	1	36	....	....	....	....	....	1.5	....	0.0	....
NBA Season Totals		28	....	....	41	14	54	.259	....	....	....	13	19	.684	....	....	....	1	36	....	....	....	....	....	1.5	....	0.0	....

• JOSEPH, Garth

Garth Joseph

Born: Aug. 8, 1973. Roseau, Dominican Rep..   Height: 7'2".   Weight: 315 lbs.   Drafted: —   College: St. Rose

YEAR	TEAM	GP	GS	MIN	PTS	FGM	FGA	FG%	3PM	3PA	3P%	FTM	FTA	FT%	ORB	DRB	TRB	AST	PF	DQ	STL	BLK	TO	MPG	PPG	RPG	APG	PCM
00-01	Toronto	2	0	8	2	1	2	.500	0	0	.000	0	0	.000	2	0	2	1	1	0	0	0	1	4.0	1.0	1.0	0.5	.332
00-01	Denver	2	0	8	0	0	3	.000	0	0	.000	0	2	.000	0	0	0	0	0	0	0	1	1	4.0	0.0	0.0	0.0	-.449
NBA Season Totals		4	0	16	2	1	5	.200	0	0	.000	0	2	.000	2	0	2	1	1	0	0	1	2	4.0	0.5	0.5	0.3	....

• JOSEPH, Yvon

Yvon Joseph

Born: Oct. 31, 1957. Cap-Haitian, Haiti.   Height: 6'11".   Weight: 245 lbs.   Drafted: 1985   College: Georgia Tech

YEAR	TEAM	GP	GS	MIN	PTS	FGM	FGA	FG%	3PM	3PA	3P%	FTM	FTA	FT%	ORB	DRB	TRB	AST	PF	DQ	STL	BLK	TO	MPG	PPG	RPG	APG	PCM
85-86	New Jersey	1	0	5	2	0	0	.000	0	0	.000	2	2	1.000	0	0	0	0	1	0	0	0	0	5.0	2.0	0.0	0.0	.307
NBA Season Totals		1	0	5	2	0	0	.000	0	0	.000	2	2	1.000	0	0	0	0	1	0	0	0	0	5.0	2.0	0.0	0.0	....

• JOYCE, Jimmy

Jimmy Joyce

Born: 1924.   Height: 6'5".   Weight: 195 lbs.   Drafted: —   College: Temple

YEAR	TEAM	GP	GS	MIN	PTS	FGM	FGA	FG%	3PM	3PA	3P%	FTM	FTA	FT%	ORB	DRB	TRB	AST	PF	DQ	STL	BLK	TO	MPG	PPG	RPG	APG	PCM
47-48	Tri-Cities-N	4	....	....	1	0			....	....	....	1	1	1.000	....	....	....	....	....	....	....	....	....	....	0.3	....	....	....
NBL Season Totals		4	....	....	1	0			....	....	....	1	1	....	....	....	....	....	....	....	....	....	....	....	0.3	....	....	....

• JOYCE, Kevin

Kevin Francis Joyce

Born: June 27, 1951. Bayside, NY, United States.   Height: 6'3".   Weight: 190 lbs.   Drafted: 1973   College: South Carolina

YEAR	TEAM	GP	GS	MIN	PTS	FGM	FGA	FG%	3PM	3PA	3P%	FTM	FTA	FT%	ORB	DRB	TRB	AST	PF	DQ	STL	BLK	TO	MPG	PPG	RPG	APG	PCM
73-74	Indiana-A	56	....	987	411	171	432	.396	5	27	.185	64	78	.821	33	59	92	128	86	....	32	8	80	17.6	7.3	1.6	2.3	.374
74-75	Indiana-A	81	....	2828	1210	530	1245	.426	8	42	.190	142	180	.789	60	103	163	322	259	....	107	23	151	34.9	14.9	2.0	4.0	.335
75-76	Kentucky-A	34	....	650	190	78	203	.384	1	7	.143	33	42	.786	6	36	42	83	75	....	19	3	57	19.1	5.6	1.2	2.4	.263
75-76	San Diego-A	9	....	266	95	36	108	.333	1	5	.200	22	32	.688	1	6	7	47	21	....	12	0	34	29.6	10.6	0.8	5.2	.283
ABA Season Totals		180	....	4731	1906	815	1988	.410	15	81	.185	261	332	.786	100	204	304	580	441	....	170	34	322	26.3	10.6	1.7	3.2	....
73-74	Indiana-A	10	....	136	44	17	53	.321	2	7	.286	8	10	.800	3	6	9	12	20	....	4	2	10	13.6	4.4	0.9	1.2	.185
74-75	Indiana-A	18	....	593	213	88	211	.417	5	13	.385	32	41	.780	3	28	31	45	55	....	17	9	31	32.9	11.8	1.7	2.5	.258
75-76	Kentucky-A	9	....	117	30	10	36	.278	0	0	.000	10	12	.833	1	2	3	30	14	....	3	0	17	13.0	3.3	0.3	3.3	.305
ABA Playoff Totals		37	....	846	287	115	300	.383	7	20	.350	50	63	.794	7	36	43	87	89	....	24	11	58	22.9	7.8	1.2	2.4	....

• JOYNER, Butch

Harry C. (Butch) Joyner

Born: Apr. 26, 1945.   Height: 6'5".   Weight: 200 lbs.   Drafted: 1968   College: Indiana

YEAR	TEAM	GP	GS	MIN	PTS	FGM	FGA	FG%	3PM	3PA	3P%	FTM	FTA	FT%	ORB	DRB	TRB	AST	PF	DQ	STL	BLK	TO	MPG	PPG	RPG	APG	PCM
68-69	Indiana-A	2	....	5	0	0	0	.000	0	0	.000	0	0	.000	0	1	1	0	1	0	....	....	0	2.5	0.0	0.5	0.0	.086
ABA Season Totals		2	....	5	0	0	0	.000	0	0	.000	0	0	.000	0	1	1	0	1	0	....	....	0	2.5	0.0	0.5	0.0	....

• JUDKINS, Jeff

Jeffrey Reed Judkins

Born: Mar. 23, 1956. Salt Lake City, UT, United States.   Height: 6'6".   Weight: 185 lbs.   Drafted: 1978   College: Utah

YEAR	TEAM	GP	GS	MIN	PTS	FGM	FGA	FG%	3PM	3PA	3P%	FTM	FTA	FT%	ORB	DRB	TRB	AST	PF	DQ	STL	BLK	TO	MPG	PPG	RPG	APG	PCM
78-79	Boston	81	....	1521	709	295	587	.503	....	....	....	119	146	.815	70	121	191	145	184	1	81	12	105	18.8	8.8	2.4	1.8	.442
79-80	Boston	65	....	674	351	139	276	.504	11	27	.407	62	76	.816	32	34	66	47	91	0	29	5	52	10.4	5.4	1.0	0.7	.407
80-81	Utah	62	....	666	238	92	216	.426	9	28	.321	45	51	.882	29	64	93	59	84	0	16	2	31	10.7	3.8	1.5	1.0	.332
81-82	Detroit	30	0	251	79	31	81	.383	1	10	.100	16	26	.615	14	20	34	14	33	0	6	5	9	8.4	2.6	1.1	0.5	.245
82-83	Portland	34	....	309	105	39	88	.443	2	8	.250	25	30	.833	18	25	43	17	39	0	15	2	17	9.1	3.1	1.3	0.5	.318
NBA Season Totals		272	0	3421	1482	596	1248	.478	23	73	.315	267	329	.812	163	264	427	282	431	1	147	26	214	12.6	5.4	1.6	1.0	....
79-80	Boston	7	....	10	9	4	8	.500	1	3	.333	0	0	.000	3	1	4	0	0	0	1	0	0	1.4	1.3	0.6	0.0	.991
NBA Playoff Totals		7	....	10	9	4	8	.500	1	3	.333	0	0	.000	3	1	4	0	0	0	1	0	0	1.4	1.3	0.6	0.0	....

• JUNTUNEN, Paul

Paul Juntunen

Born: 1921.   Height: 6'1".   Weight: 180 lbs.   Drafted: —   College: Wayne State (MI)

YEAR	TEAM	GP	GS	MIN	PTS	FGM	FGA	FG%	3PM	3PA	3P%	FTM	FTA	FT%	ORB	DRB	TRB	AST	PF	DQ	STL	BLK	TO	MPG	PPG	RPG	APG	PCM
46-47	Detroit-N	43	....	....	178	76	....	....	....	....	....	26	38	.684	....	....	....	....	97	....	....	....	....	....	4.1	....	....	....
48-49	Detroit-N	4	....	....	8	4	....	....	....	....	....	0	1	.000	....	....	....	....	....	....	....	....	....	....	2.0	....	....	....
NBL Season Totals		47	....	....	186	80	....	....	....	....	....	26	39	....	....	....	....	....	97	....	....	....	....	....	4.0	....	....	....

YEAR TEAM	GP	GS	MIN	PTS	FGM	FGA	FG%	3PM	3PA	3P%	FTM	FTA	FT%	ORB	DRB	TRB	AST	PF	DQ	STL	BLK	TO	MPG	PPG	RPG	APG	PCM

• KACHAN, Whitey
Edwin John (Whitey) Kachan

Born: Sept. 15, 1925.   Height: 6'2".   Weight: 175 lbs.   Drafted: 1948   College: DePaul

YEAR TEAM	GP	GS	MIN	PTS	FGM	FGA	FG%	3PM	3PA	3P%	FTM	FTA	FT%	ORB	DRB	TRB	AST	PF	DQ	STL	BLK	TO	MPG	PPG	RPG	APG	PCM
48-49 Chicago	33	....	....	65	22	100	.220	....	....	....	21	34	.618	....	....	....	25	57	....	....	....	....	....	2.0	....	0.8	....
48-49 Minneapolis	19	....	....	47	16	42	.381	....	....	....	15	22	.682	....	....	....	12	24	....	....	....	....	....	2.5	....	0.6	....
NBA Season Totals	52	....	....	112	38	142	.268	....	....	....	36	56	.643	....	....	....	37	81	....	....	....	....	....	2.2	....	0.7	....
48-49 Minneapolis	8	....	....	4	2	5	.400	....	....	....	0	0	.000	....	....	....	2	3	....	....	....	....	....	0.5	....	0.3	....
NBA Playoff Totals	8	....	....	4	2	5	.400	....	....	....	0	0	.000	....	....	....	2	3	....	....	....	....	....	0.5	....	0.3	....

• KAFTAN, George
George A. (The Golden Greek) Kaftan

Born: Feb. 22, 1928. New York, NY, United States.   Height: 6'3".   Weight: 190 lbs.   Drafted: —   College: Holy Cross

YEAR TEAM	GP	GS	MIN	PTS	FGM	FGA	FG%	3PM	3PA	3P%	FTM	FTA	FT%	ORB	DRB	TRB	AST	PF	DQ	STL	BLK	TO	MPG	PPG	RPG	APG	PCM
48-49 Boston	21	....	....	304	116	315	.368	....	....	....	72	115	.626	....	....	....	61	28	....	....	....	....	....	14.5	....	2.9	....
49-50 Boston	55	....	....	534	199	535	.372	....	....	....	136	208	.654	....	....	....	145	92	....	....	....	....	....	9.7	....	2.6	....
50-51 New York	61	....	....	300	111	286	.388	....	....	....	78	125	.624	....	....	153	74	102	1	....	....	....	....	4.9	2.5	1.2	....
51-52 New York	52	....	955	322	115	307	.375	....	....	....	92	134	.687	....	....	196	88	107	0	....	....	....	18.4	6.2	3.8	1.7	.403
52-53 Baltimore	23	....	380	134	45	142	.317	....	....	....	44	67	.657	....	....	75	31	59	2	....	....	....	16.5	5.8	3.3	1.3	.337
NBA Season Totals	212	....	1335	1594	586	1585	.370	....	....	....	422	649	.650	....	....	424	399	388	3	....	....	....	6.3	7.5	2.0	1.9	
50-51 New York	8	....	....	13	6	18	.333	....	....	....	1	3	.333	....	....	6	2	7	0	....	....	....	....	1.6	0.8	0.3	
51-52 New York	13	....	232	80	26	66	.394	....	....	....	28	42	.667	....	....	30	22	41	3	....	....	....	17.8	6.2	2.3	1.7	.352
NBA Playoff Totals	21	....	232	93	32	84	.381	....	....	....	29	45	.644	....	....	36	24	48	3	....	....	....	11.0	4.4	1.7	1.1	

• KALAFAT, Ed
Edward L. Kalafat

Born: Oct. 13, 1932.   Height: 6'6".   Weight: 245 lbs.   Drafted: 1954   College: Minnesota

YEAR TEAM	GP	GS	MIN	PTS	FGM	FGA	FG%	3PM	3PA	3P%	FTM	FTA	FT%	ORB	DRB	TRB	AST	PF	DQ	STL	BLK	TO	MPG	PPG	RPG	APG	PCM
54-55 Minneapolis	72	....	1102	347	118	375	.315	....	....	....	111	168	.661	....	....	317	75	205	9	....	....	....	15.3	4.8	4.4	1.0	.351
55-56 Minneapolis	72	....	1639	574	194	540	.359	....	....	....	186	252	.738	....	....	440	130	236	2	....	....	....	22.8	8.0	6.1	1.8	.422
56-57 Minneapolis	65	....	1617	553	178	507	.351	....	....	....	197	298	.661	....	....	425	105	243	9	....	....	....	24.9	8.5	6.5	1.6	.388
NBA Season Totals	209	....	4358	1474	490	1422	.345	....	....	....	494	718	.688	....	....	1182	310	684	20	....	....	....	20.9	7.1	5.7	1.5	
54-55 Minneapolis	7	....	76	7	2	22	.091	....	....	....	3	10	.300	....	....	18	0	16	1	....	....	....	10.9	1.0	2.6	0.0	-.041
55-56 Minneapolis	3	....	55	33	9	21	.429	....	....	....	15	19	.789	....	....	21	2	13	1	....	....	....	18.3	11.0	7.0	0.7	.652
56-57 Minneapolis	5	....	104	63	21	36	.583	....	....	....	21	31	.677	....	....	24	9	20	1	....	....	....	20.8	12.6	4.8	1.8	.671
NBA Playoff Totals	15	....	235	103	32	79	.405	....	....	....	39	60	.650	....	....	63	11	49	3	....	....	....	15.7	6.9	4.2	0.7	

• KAPLOWITZ, Ralph
Ralph (Kappy) Kaplowitz

Born: May 18, 1919.   Height: 6'2".   Weight: 170 lbs.   Drafted: —   College: New York University

YEAR TEAM	GP	GS	MIN	PTS	FGM	FGA	FG%	3PM	3PA	3P%	FTM	FTA	FT%	ORB	DRB	TRB	AST	PF	DQ	STL	BLK	TO	MPG	PPG	RPG	APG	PCM
46-47 New York	27	....	....	194	71	274	.259	....	....	....	52	71	.732	....	....	....	25	57	....	....	....	....	....	7.2	....	0.9	....
46-47 Philadelphia	30	....	....	209	75	258	.291	....	....	....	59	80	.738	....	....	....	13	65	....	....	....	....	....	7.0	....	0.4	....
47-48 Philadelphia	48	....	....	189	71	292	.243	....	....	....	47	60	.783	....	....	....	19	100	....	....	....	....	....	3.9	....	0.4	....
NBA Season Totals	105	....	....	592	217	824	.263	....	....	....	158	211	.749	....	....	....	57	222	....	....	....	....	....	5.6	....	0.5	....
46-47 Philadelphia	10	....	....	66	22	98	.224	....	....	....	22	27	.815	....	....	....	6	25	....	....	....	....	....	6.6	....	0.6	....
47-48 Philadelphia	13	....	....	86	32	93	.344	....	....	....	22	29	.759	....	....	....	7	22	....	....	....	....	....	6.6	....	0.5	....
NBA Playoff Totals	23	....	....	152	54	191	.283	....	....	....	44	56	.786	....	....	....	13	47	....	....	....	....	....	6.6	....	0.6	....

• KAPPEN, Tony
Anthony George Kappen

Born: Apr. 13, 1919. Died: Dec.18, 1993.   Height: 5'10".   Weight: 165 lbs.   Drafted: —   College: none

YEAR TEAM	GP	GS	MIN	PTS	FGM	FGA	FG%	3PM	3PA	3P%	FTM	FTA	FT%	ORB	DRB	TRB	AST	PF	DQ	STL	BLK	TO	MPG	PPG	RPG	APG	PCM
46-47 Boston	18	....	....	74	25	91	.275	....	....	....	24	38	.632	....	....	....	6	17	....	....	....	....	....	4.1	....	0.3	....
46-47 Pittsburgh	41	....	....	310	103	446	.231	....	....	....	104	123	.846	....	....	....	22	61	....	....	....	....	....	7.6	....	0.5	....
NBA Season Totals	59	....	....	384	128	537	.238	....	....	....	128	161	.795	....	....	....	28	78	....	....	....	....	....	6.5	....	0.5	....

• KARL, George
George Matthew Karl

Born: May 12, 1951. Penn Hills, PA, United States.   Height: 6'2".   Weight: 185 lbs.   Drafted: 1973   College: North Carolina

YEAR TEAM	GP	GS	MIN	PTS	FGM	FGA	FG%	3PM	3PA	3P%	FTM	FTA	FT%	ORB	DRB	TRB	AST	PF	DQ	STL	BLK	TO	MPG	PPG	RPG	APG	PCM
73-74 San Antonio-A	74	....	1339	574	236	502	.470	8	22	.364	94	113	.832	41	85	126	160	161	....	65	10	92	18.1	7.8	1.7	2.2	.418
74-75 San Antonio-A	82	....	1629	663	261	534	.489	4	23	.174	137	177	.774	47	108	155	334	207	....	96	7	158	19.9	8.1	1.9	4.1	.503
75-76 San Antonio-A	75	....	1200	381	150	334	.449	0	9	.000	81	106	.764	13	53	66	250	149	....	60	3	108	16.0	5.1	0.9	3.3	.396
76-77 San Antonio	29	....	251	79	25	73	.342	....	....	....	29	42	.690	4	13	17	46	36	0	10	0	....	8.7	2.7	0.6	1.6	.332
77-78 San Antonio	4	....	30	6	2	6	.333	....	....	....	2	2	1.000	0	5	5	5	6	0	1	0	4	7.5	1.5	1.3	1.3	.242
NBA Season Totals	33	....	281	85	27	79	.342	....	....	....	31	44	.705	4	18	22	51	42	0	11	0	4	8.5	2.6	0.7	1.5	
ABA Season Totals	231	....	4168	1618	647	1370	.472	12	54	.222	312	396	.788	101	246	347	744	517	....	221	20	358	18.0	7.0	1.5	3.2	
Career Totals	264	....	4449	1703	674	1449	.465	12	54	.222	343	440	.780	105	264	369	795	559	0	232	20	362	16.9	6.5	1.4	3.0	
73-74 San Antonio-A	7	....	141	28	13	28	.464	0	1	.000	2	5	.400	3	12	15	23	19	....	10	0	12	20.1	4.0	2.1	3.3	.318
74-75 San Antonio-A	4	....	40	5	1	8	.125	0	1	.000	3	4	.750	0	3	3	5	5	....	1	0	2	10.0	1.3	0.8	1.3	.109
75-76 San Antonio-A	6	....	64	26	10	22	.455	0	1	.000	6	9	.667	1	3	4	17	12	....	5	0	5	10.7	4.3	0.7	2.8	.485
76-77 San Antonio	1	....	1	0	0	0	.000	....	....	....	0	0	.000	0	0	0	0	0	0	0	0	0	1.0	0.0	0.0	0.0	.000
NBA Playoff Totals	1	....	1	0	0	0	.000	....	....	....	0	0	.000	0	0	0	0	0	0	0	0	0	1.0	0.0	0.0	0.0	
ABA Playoff Totals	17	....	245	59	24	58	.414	0	3	.000	11	18	.611	4	18	22	45	36	....	16	0	19	14.4	3.5	1.3	2.6	
Career Playoff Totals	18	....	246	59	24	58	.414	0	3	.000	11	18	.611	4	18	22	45	36	0	16	0	19	13.7	3.3	1.2	2.5	

YEAR	TEAM	GP	GS	MIN	PTS	FGM	FGA	FG%	3PM	3PA	3P%	FTM	FTA	FT%	ORB	DRB	TRB	AST	PF	DQ	STL	BLK	TO	MPG	PPG	RPG	APG	PCM

• KASETA, Tony
Tony Kaseta

Born: 1923.   Height: 6'8".   Weight: 220 lbs.   Drafted: —   College: none

YEAR	TEAM	GP	GS	MIN	PTS	FGM	FGA	FG%	3PM	3PA	3P%	FTM	FTA	FT%	ORB	DRB	TRB	AST	PF	DQ	STL	BLK	TO	MPG	PPG	RPG	APG	PCM
48-49	Detroit-N	17	....	....	52	16	....	....	....	....	....	20	32	.625	....	....	....	....	....	....	....	....	....	....	3.1	....	....	....
NBL Season Totals		17	....	....	52	16	....	....	....	....	....	20	32		....	....	....	....	....	....	....	....	....	....	3.1	....	....	....

• KASID, Ed
Edward Kasid

Born: Aug. 13, 1923.   Height: 5'11".   Weight: 185 lbs.   Drafted: —   College: none

YEAR	TEAM	GP	GS	MIN	PTS	FGM	FGA	FG%	3PM	3PA	3P%	FTM	FTA	FT%	ORB	DRB	TRB	AST	PF	DQ	STL	BLK	TO	MPG	PPG	RPG	APG	PCM
46-47	Toronto	8	....	....	12	6	21	.286	....	....	....	0	6	.000	....	....	....	6	8	....	....	....	....	....	1.5	....	0.8	....
NBA Season Totals		8	....	....	12	6	21	.286	....	....	....	0	6	.000	....	....	....	6	8	....	....	....	....	....	1.5	....	0.8	....

• KATKAVECK, Leo
Leo Frank Katkaveck

Born: Apr. 17, 1923.   Height: 6'   Weight: 185 lbs.   Drafted: 1948   College: North Carolina State

YEAR	TEAM	GP	GS	MIN	PTS	FGM	FGA	FG%	3PM	3PA	3P%	FTM	FTA	FT%	ORB	DRB	TRB	AST	PF	DQ	STL	BLK	TO	MPG	PPG	RPG	APG	PCM
48-49	Washington	53	....	....	221	84	253	.332	....	....	....	53	71	.746	....	....	....	68	110	....	....	....	....	....	4.2	....	1.3	....
49-50	Washington	54	....	....	236	101	330	.306	....	....	....	34	56	.607	....	....	....	68	102	....	....	....	....	....	4.4	....	1.3	....
NBA Season Totals		107	....	....	457	185	583	.317	....	....	....	87	127	.685	....	....	....	136	212	....	....	....	....	....	4.3	....	1.3	....
48-49	Washington	9	....	....	20	7	29	.241	....	....	....	6	8	.750	....	....	....	10	13	....	....	....	....	....	2.2	....	1.1	....
49-50	Washington	2	....	....	6	2	13	.154	....	....	....	2	3	.667	....	....	....	3	7	....	....	....	....	....	3.0	....	1.5	....
NBA Playoff Totals		11	....	....	26	9	42	.214	....	....	....	8	11	.727	....	....	....	13	20	....	....	....	....	....	2.4	....	1.2	....

• KAUFFMAN, Bob
Robert (Horse, Ajax) Kauffman

Born: July 13, 1946. Brooklyn, NY, United States.   Height: 6'8".   Weight: 240 lbs.   Drafted: 1968   College: Guilford

YEAR	TEAM	GP	GS	MIN	PTS	FGM	FGA	FG%	3PM	3PA	3P%	FTM	FTA	FT%	ORB	DRB	TRB	AST	PF	DQ	STL	BLK	TO	MPG	PPG	RPG	APG	PCM
68-69	Seattle	82	....	1660	641	219	496	.442	....	....	....	203	289	.702	....	....	484	83	252	8	....	....	....	....	20.2	7.8	5.9	1.0	.463
69-70	Chicago	64	....	775	276	94	221	.425	....	....	....	88	123	.715	....	....	211	76	117	1	....	....	....	....	12.1	4.3	3.3	1.2	.475
70-71	Buffalo	78	....	2778	1591	616	1309	.471	....	....	....	359	485	.740	....	....	837	354	263	8	....	....	....	....	35.6	20.4	10.7	4.5	.702
71-72	Buffalo	77	....	3205	1457	558	1123	.497	....	....	....	341	429	.795	....	....	787	297	273	7	....	....	....	....	41.6	18.9	10.2	3.9	.571
72-73	Buffalo	77	....	3049	1350	535	1059	.505	....	....	....	280	359	.780	....	....	855	396	211	1	....	....	....	....	39.6	17.5	11.1	5.1	.643
73-74	Buffalo	74	....	1304	449	171	366	.467	....	....	....	107	150	.713	97	229	326	142	155	0	37	18	....	....	17.6	6.1	4.4	1.9	.490
74-75	Atlanta	73	....	797	285	113	261	.433	....	....	....	59	84	.702	67	115	182	81	103	1	19	4	....	....	10.9	3.9	2.5	1.1	.442
NBA Season Totals		525	....	13568	6049	2306	4835	.477	....	....	....	1437	1919	.749	164	344	3682	1429	1374	26	56	22	....	....	25.8	11.5	7.0	2.7	....
69-70	Chicago	3	....	14	4	1	3	.333	....	....	....	2	3	.667	....	....	6	4	2	0	....	....	....	....	4.7	1.3	2.0	1.3	.763
73-74	Buffalo	2	....	10	2	1	3	.333	....	....	....	0	2	.000	1	0	1	2	3	0	0	0	....	....	5.0	1.0	0.5	1.0	.132
NBA Playoff Totals		5	....	24	6	2	6	.333	....	....	....	2	5	.400	1	0	7	6	5	0	0	0	....	....	4.8	1.2	1.4	1.2	....

• KAUTZ, Wilbert
Wilbert (Wibs) Kautz

Born: Sept. 7, 1915. Chicago, IL, United States. Died: May1979.   Height: 5'12".   Weight: 180 lbs.   Drafted: —   College: Loyola (IL)

YEAR	TEAM	GP	GS	MIN	PTS	FGM	FGA	FG%	3PM	3PA	3P%	FTM	FTA	FT%	ORB	DRB	TRB	AST	PF	DQ	STL	BLK	TO	MPG	PPG	RPG	APG	PCM
39-40	Chicago-N	28	....	....	273	105	....	....	....	....	....	63	....	....	....	....	....	....	....	....	....	....	....	....	9.8	....	....	....
40-41	Chicago-N	21	....	....	227	94	....	....	....	....	....	39	....	....	....	....	....	....	....	....	....	....	....	....	10.8	....	....	....
41-42	Chicago-N	20	....	....	210	85	....	....	....	....	....	40	....	....	....	....	....	....	....	....	....	....	....	....	10.5	....	....	....
46-47	Chicago	50	....	....	253	107	420	.255	....	....	....	39	73	.534	....	....	....	37	114	....	....	....	....	....	5.1	....	0.7	....
NBA Season Totals		50	....	....	253	107	420	.255	....	....	....	39	73	.534	....	....	....	37	114	....	....	....	....	....	5.1	....	0.7	....
NBL Season Totals		69	....	....	710	284	....	....	....	....	....	142	....	....	....	....	....	....	....	....	....	....	....	....	10.3	....	....	....
Career Totals		119	....	....	963	391	420		....	....	....	181	73		....	....	....	37	114	....	....	....	....	....	8.1	....	0.3	....
46-47	Chicago	9	....	....	22	10	45	.222	....	....	....	2	6	.333	....	....	....	0	14	....	....	....	....	....	2.4	....	0.0	....
NBA Playoff Totals		9	....	....	22	10	45	.222	....	....	....	2	6	.333	....	....	....	0	14	....	....	....	....	....	2.4	....	0.0	....

• KEA, Clarence
Clarence Leroy Kea

Born: Feb. 2, 1959. Wilmington, NC, United States.   Height: 6'6".   Weight: 218 lbs.   Drafted: 1980   College: Lamar

YEAR	TEAM	GP	GS	MIN	PTS	FGM	FGA	FG%	3PM	3PA	3P%	FTM	FTA	FT%	ORB	DRB	TRB	AST	PF	DQ	STL	BLK	TO	MPG	PPG	RPG	APG	PCM
80-81	Dallas	16	....	199	117	37	81	.457	0	1	.000	43	62	.694	28	39	67	5	44	2	6	1	16	12.4	7.3	4.2	0.3	.535
81-82	Dallas	35	0	248	81	26	49	.531	0	0	.000	29	42	.690	26	35	61	14	55	0	4	3	18	7.1	2.3	1.7	0.4	.362
NBA Season Totals		51	0	447	198	63	130	.485	0	1	.000	72	104	.692	54	74	128	19	99	2	10	4	34	8.8	3.9	2.5	0.4	

• KEARNS, Mike
Michael Joseph Kearns

Born: June 18, 1929.   Height: 6'2".   Weight: 178 lbs.   Drafted: 1951   College: Princeton

YEAR	TEAM	GP	GS	MIN	PTS	FGM	FGA	FG%	3PM	3PA	3P%	FTM	FTA	FT%	ORB	DRB	TRB	AST	PF	DQ	STL	BLK	TO	MPG	PPG	RPG	APG	PCM
54-55	Philadelphia	6	....	25	1	0	5	.000	....	....	....	1	4	.250	....	....	3	5	1	0	....	....	....	4.2	0.2	0.5	0.8	.169
NBA Season Totals		6	....	25	1	0	5	.000	....	....	....	1	4	.250	....	....	3	5	1	0	....	....	....	4.2	0.2	0.5	0.8	....

• KEARNS, Tommy
Thomas Francis Kearns Jr.

Born: Oct. 6, 1936. New York, NY, United States.   Height: 5'11".   Weight: 185 lbs.   Drafted: 1958   College: North Carolina

YEAR	TEAM	GP	GS	MIN	PTS	FGM	FGA	FG%	3PM	3PA	3P%	FTM	FTA	FT%	ORB	DRB	TRB	AST	PF	DQ	STL	BLK	TO	MPG	PPG	RPG	APG	PCM
58-59	Syracuse	1	....	7	2	1	1	1.000	....	....	....	0	0	.000	....	....	0	0	1	0	....	....	....	7.0	2.0	0.0	0.0	.232
NBA Season Totals		1	....	7	2	1	1	1.000	....	....	....	0	0	.000	....	....	0	0	1	0	....	....	....	7.0	2.0	0.0	0.0	....

• KEEFE, Adam

Adam Thomas Keefe

Born: Feb. 22, 1970. Irvine, CA, United States. Height: 6'9". Weight: 230 lbs. Drafted: 1992 College: Stanford

YEAR TEAM	GP	GS	MIN	PTS	FGM	FGA	FG%	3PM	3PA	3P%	FTM	FTA	FT%	ORB	DRB	TRB	AST	PF	DQ	STL	BLK	TO	MPG	PPG	RPG	APG	PCM
92-93 Atlanta	82	6	1549	542	188	376	.500	0	1	.000	166	237	.700	171	261	432	80	195	1	57	16	98	18.9	6.6	5.3	1.0	.457
93-94 Atlanta	63	1	763	273	96	213	.451	0	0	.000	81	111	.730	77	124	201	34	80	0	20	9	63	12.1	4.3	3.2	0.5	.400
94-95 Utah	75	0	1270	461	172	298	.577	0	0	.000	117	173	.676	135	192	327	30	141	0	36	25	60	16.9	6.1	4.4	0.4	.465
95-96 Utah	82	0	1708	499	180	346	.520	0	4	.000	139	201	.692	176	279	455	64	174	0	51	41	90	20.8	6.1	5.5	0.8	.427
96-97 Utah	62	0	915	235	82	160	.513	0	1	.000	71	103	.689	75	141	216	32	97	0	30	13	43	14.8	3.8	3.5	0.5	.369
97-98 Utah	80	75	2047	620	229	424	.540	0	0	.000	162	200	.810	179	259	438	89	172	0	52	24	72	25.6	7.8	5.5	1.1	.414
98-99 Utah	44	0	642	174	56	124	.452	0	4	.000	62	89	.697	51	91	142	28	63	0	16	12	33	14.6	4.0	3.2	0.6	.353
99-00 Utah	62	3	604	135	53	130	.408	0	1	.000	29	36	.806	45	91	136	34	90	0	17	13	46	9.7	2.2	2.2	0.5	.277
00-01 Golden State	67	13	836	168	64	159	.403	1	3	.333	39	63	.619	90	119	209	36	102	0	28	20	40	12.5	2.5	3.1	0.5	.312
NBA Season Totals	617	98	10334	3107	1120	2230	.502	1	14	.071	866	1213	.714	999	1557	2556	427	1114	1	307	173	545	16.7	5.0	4.1	0.7	....
92-93 Atlanta	3	0	53	18	7	13	.538	0	0	.000	4	6	.667	4	9	13	6	7	0	1	0	3	17.7	6.0	4.3	2.0	.469
93-94 Atlanta	7	0	62	16	6	10	.600	0	0	.000	4	9	.444	3	10	13	2	9	0	1	1	4	8.9	2.3	1.9	0.3	.293
94-95 Utah	4	0	69	18	7	12	.583	0	0	.000	4	6	.667	8	9	17	2	4	0	5	1	0	17.3	4.5	4.3	0.5	.496
95-96 Utah	17	0	178	58	23	34	.676	1	2	.500	11	17	.647	9	24	33	2	23	0	3	1	8	10.5	3.4	1.9	0.1	.356
96-97 Utah	8	0	59	8	2	6	.333	0	0	.000	4	6	.667	3	13	16	2	5	0	2	1	2	7.4	1.0	2.0	0.3	.322
97-98 Utah	15	10	154	31	10	29	.345	0	0	.000	11	17	.647	13	21	34	2	18	0	4	2	3	10.3	2.1	2.3	0.1	.251
98-99 Utah	10	0	101	41	18	30	.600	0	0	.000	5	5	1.000	7	17	24	3	17	0	4	3	8	10.1	4.1	2.4	0.3	.461
NBA Playoff Totals	64	10	676	190	73	134	.545	1	2	.500	43	66	.652	47	103	150	19	83	0	20	9	28	10.6	3.0	2.3	0.3	....

• KEELING, Harold

Harold A. Keeling

Born: Sept. 18, 1963. New Orleans, LA, United States. Height: 6'4". Weight: 185 lbs. Drafted: 1985 College: Santa Clara

YEAR TEAM	GP	GS	MIN	PTS	FGM	FGA	FG%	3PM	3PA	3P%	FTM	FTA	FT%	ORB	DRB	TRB	AST	PF	DQ	STL	BLK	TO	MPG	PPG	RPG	APG	PCM
85-86 Dallas	20	0	75	44	17	39	.436	0	0	.000	10	14	.714	3	3	6	10	9	0	7	0	6	3.8	2.2	0.3	0.5	.463
NBA Season Totals	20	0	75	44	17	39	.436	0	0	.000	10	14	.714	3	3	6	10	9	0	7	0	6	3.8	2.2	0.3	0.5	....
85-86 Dallas	1	0	1	0	0	0	.000	0	0	.000	0	0	.000	0	0	0	0	0	0	0	0	0	1.0	0.0	0.0	0.0	.000
NBA Playoff Totals	1	0	1	0	0	0	.000	0	0	.000	0	0	.000	0	0	0	0	0	0	0	0	0	1.0	0.0	0.0	0.0	....

• KELLER, Bill

William Curry Keller

Born: Aug. 30, 1947. Indianapolis, IN, United States. Height: 5'10". Weight: 177 lbs. Drafted: 1969 College: Purdue

YEAR TEAM	GP	GS	MIN	PTS	FGM	FGA	FG%	3PM	3PA	3P%	FTM	FTA	FT%	ORB	DRB	TRB	AST	PF	DQ	STL	BLK	TO	MPG	PPG	RPG	APG	PCM
69-70 Indiana-A	82	....	1482	710	252	634	.397	42	154	.273	164	193	.850	75	99	174	235	153	0	....	....	115	18.1	8.7	2.1	2.9	.487
70-71 Indiana-A	83	....	2490	1185	417	980	.426	84	230	.365	267	308	.867	81	159	240	437	170	1	....	....	196	30.0	14.3	2.9	5.3	.548
71-72 Indiana-A	76	....	1729	737	264	619	.426	56	169	.331	153	174	.879	62	102	164	264	118	1	....	....	131	22.8	9.7	2.2	3.5	.465
72-73 Indiana-A	83	....	2251	1147	421	973	.433	**71**	**222**	.320	234	269	**.870**	82	122	204	361	162	1	....	....	171	27.1	13.8	2.5	4.3	.508
73-74 Indiana-A	75	....	1428	715	279	615	.454	50	131	.382	107	123	.870	44	84	128	172	83	....	37	3	100	19.0	9.5	1.7	2.3	.484
74-75 Indiana-A	79	....	1918	987	397	908	.437	**80**	**240**	.333	113	128	.883	90	121	211	204	101	....	59	3	109	24.3	12.5	2.7	2.6	.467
75-76 Indiana-A	78	....	2311	1107	410	1011	.406	**123**	**349**	.352	164	183	**.896**	81	147	228	307	116	....	59	5	148	29.6	14.2	2.9	3.9	.457
ABA Season Totals	556	....	13609	6588	2440	5740	.425	506	1495	.338	1202	1378	.872	515	834	1349	1980	903	3	155	11	970	24.5	11.8	2.4	3.6	....
69-70 Indiana-A	15	....	527	195	75	177	.424	3	23	.130	42	46	.913	19	32	51	68	41	0	....	....	29	35.1	13.0	3.4	4.5	.398
70-71 Indiana-A	11	....	448	237	82	190	.432	23	58	.397	50	58	.862	15	27	42	59	23	0	....	....	45	40.7	21.5	3.8	5.4	.541
71-72 Indiana-A	20	....	532	240	84	188	.447	19	48	.396	53	63	.841	15	20	35	84	47	....	....	....	26	26.6	12.0	1.8	4.2	.467
72-73 Indiana-A	17	....	348	153	57	149	.383	8	36	.222	31	38	.816	18	34	52	63	35	0	....	....	16	20.5	9.0	3.1	3.7	.481
73-74 Indiana-A	12	....	194	113	41	93	.441	15	40	.375	16	19	.842	9	9	18	25	12	....	5	0	16	16.2	9.4	1.5	2.1	.546
74-75 Indiana-A	17	....	405	183	68	162	.420	17	43	.395	30	30	1.000	8	16	24	29	24	....	7	0	22	23.8	10.8	1.4	1.7	.352
75-76 Indiana-A	3	....	50	18	8	16	.500	2	7	.286	0	1	.000	0	3	3	6	2	....	1	0	2	16.7	6.0	1.0	2.0	.377
ABA Playoff Totals	95	....	2504	1139	415	975	.426	87	255	.341	222	255	.871	84	141	225	334	184	0	13	0	156	26.4	12.0	2.4	3.5	....

• KELLER, Gary

Gary J. Keller

Born: June 13, 1944. Elizabeth, NJ, United States. Height: 6'9". Weight: 220 lbs. Drafted: 1967 College: Florida

YEAR TEAM	GP	GS	MIN	PTS	FGM	FGA	FG%	3PM	3PA	3P%	FTM	FTA	FT%	ORB	DRB	TRB	AST	PF	DQ	STL	BLK	TO	MPG	PPG	RPG	APG	PCM
67-68 Minnesota-A	69	....	1211	507	184	483	.381	0	2	.000	139	214	.650	....	....	383	39	168	7	....	....	87	17.6	7.3	5.6	0.6	.431
68-69 Miami-A	53	....	503	228	78	192	.406	0	3	.000	72	120	.600	74	93	167	8	102	2	....	....	41	9.5	4.3	3.2	0.2	.434
ABA Season Totals	122	....	1714	735	262	675	.388	0	5	.000	211	334	.632	74	93	550	47	270	9	....	....	128	14.0	6.0	4.5	0.4	....
67-68 Minnesota-A	10	....	142	63	25	67	.373	0	0	.000	13	23	.565	....	....	50	8	27	0	....	....	15	14.2	6.3	5.0	0.8	.448
68-69 Miami-A	6	....	57	30	12	21	.571	0	0	.000	6	10	.600	....	....	23	3	12	0	....	....	2	9.5	5.0	3.8	0.5	.677
ABA Playoff Totals	16	....	199	93	37	88	.420	0	0	.000	19	33	.576	....	....	73	11	39	0	....	....	17	12.4	5.8	4.6	0.7	....

• KELLER, Jack

Jack Keller

Born: 1920. Height: 6'2". Weight: 185 lbs. Drafted: — College: none

YEAR TEAM	GP	GS	MIN	PTS	FGM	FGA	FG%	3PM	3PA	3P%	FTM	FTA	FT%	ORB	DRB	TRB	AST	PF	DQ	STL	BLK	TO	MPG	PPG	RPG	APG	PCM
41-42 Fort Wayne-N	18	....	....	52	18	....	....	....	....	....	16	....	....	....	....	....	....	....	....	....	....	....	....	2.9	....	....	....
42-43 Fort Wayne-N	9	....	....	3	1	....	....	....	....	....	1	....	....	....	....	....	....	....	....	....	....	....	....	0.3	....	....	....
NBL Season Totals	27	....	....	55	19	....	....	....	....	....	17	....	....	....	....	....	....	....	....	....	....	....	....	2.0	....	....	....
41-42 Fort Wayne-N	4	....	....	6	1	....	....	....	....	....	4	....	....	....	....	....	....	....	....	....	....	....	....	1.5	....	....	....
42-43 Fort Wayne-N	1	....	....	0	0	....	....	....	....	....	0	....	....	....	....	....	....	....	....	....	....	....	....	0.0	....	....	....
NBL Playoff Totals	5	....	....	6	1	....	....	....	....	....	4	....	....	....	....	....	....	....	....	....	....	....	....	1.2	....	....	....

• KELLER, Ken

Kenneth W. Keller

Born: 1922. Died: Feb.24, 1983. Height: 6'1". Weight: 180 lbs. Drafted: — College: St. John's (NY)

YEAR TEAM	GP	GS	MIN	PTS	FGM	FGA	FG%	3PM	3PA	3P%	FTM	FTA	FT%	ORB	DRB	TRB	AST	PF	DQ	STL	BLK	TO	MPG	PPG	RPG	APG	PCM
46-47 Washington	25	....	....	22	10	30	.333	....	....	....	2	4	.500	....	....	....	1	14	....	....	....	....	....	0.9	....	0.0	....

YEAR	TEAM	GP	GS	MIN	PTS	FGM	FGA	FG%	3PM	3PA	3P%	FTM	FTA	FT%	ORB	DRB	TRB	AST	PF	DQ	STL	BLK	TO	MPG	PPG	RPG	APG	PCM
46-47	Providence	3	....	....	0	0	0	.000	....	....	....	0	1	.000	....	....	....	....	0	1	....	....	....	....	0.0	....	0.0	....
NBA Season Totals		28	....	....	22	10	30	.333	....	....	....	2	5	.400	....	....	....	....	1	15	....	....	....	....	0.8	....	0.0	....

• KELLEY, Rich
Richard Ryland Kelley

Born: Mar. 23, 1953. San Mateo, CA, United States. Height: 7' Weight: 235 lbs. Drafted: 1975 College: Stanford

YEAR	TEAM	GP	GS	MIN	PTS	FGM	FGA	FG%	3PM	3PA	3P%	FTM	FTA	FT%	ORB	DRB	TRB	AST	PF	DQ	STL	BLK	TO	MPG	PPG	RPG	APG	PCM
75-76	New Orleans	75	....	1346	527	184	379	.485	....	....	....	159	205	.776	193	335	528	155	209	5	52	60	....	17.9	7.0	7.0	2.1	.654
76-77	New Orleans	76	....	1505	524	184	386	.477	....	....	....	156	197	.792	210	377	587	208	244	7	45	63	....	19.8	6.9	7.7	2.7	.644
77-78	New Orleans	82	....	2119	833	304	602	.505	....	....	....	225	289	.779	249	510	759	233	293	6	89	129	221	25.8	10.2	9.3	2.8	.632
78-79	New Orleans	80	....	2705	1253	440	870	.506	....	....	....	373	458	.814	303	723	1026	285	309	8	126	166	288	33.8	15.7	12.8	3.6	.713
79-80	New Jersey	57	....	1466	569	186	399	.466	0	3	.000	197	250	.788	156	241	397	128	215	5	50	79	154	25.7	10.0	7.0	2.2	.499
79-80	Phoenix	23	....	373	133	43	85	.506	0	0	.000	47	60	.783	44	74	118	50	58	0	28	17	46	16.2	5.8	5.1	2.2	.599
80-81	Phoenix	81	....	1686	567	196	387	.506	0	2	.000	175	231	.758	131	310	441	282	210	0	79	63	211	20.8	7.0	5.4	3.5	.544
81-82	Phoenix	81	39	1892	639	236	505	.467	0	1	.000	167	223	.749	168	329	497	293	292	14	64	71	243	23.4	7.9	6.1	3.6	.479
82-83	Denver	38	0	565	173	59	141	.418	0	0	.000	55	70	.786	61	111	172	59	115	3	21	18	53	14.9	4.6	4.5	1.6	.438
82-83	Utah	32	23	780	229	71	152	.467	0	0	.000	87	105	.829	70	162	232	79	106	1	33	21	64	24.4	7.2	7.3	2.5	.496
83-84	Utah	75	30	1674	388	132	264	.500	0	0	.000	124	162	.765	140	350	490	157	273	6	55	29	150	22.3	5.2	6.5	2.1	.408
84-85	Utah	77	34	1276	290	103	216	.477	0	2	.000	84	112	.750	118	232	350	120	227	5	42	30	123	16.6	3.8	4.5	1.6	.370
85-86	Sacramento	37	0	324	74	28	49	.571	0	2	.000	18	22	.818	29	52	81	43	62	0	10	3	22	8.8	2.0	2.2	1.2	.422
NBA Season Totals		814	126	17711	6199	2166	4435	.488	0	10	.000	1867	2384	.783	1872	3806	5678	2092	2613	60	694	749	1575	21.8	7.6	7.0	2.6	....
79-80	Phoenix	8	....	146	47	19	44	.432	0	1	.000	9	10	.900	14	22	36	22	17	0	9	7	10	18.3	5.9	4.5	2.8	.537
80-81	Phoenix	7	....	113	29	10	25	.400	0	1	.000	9	14	.643	13	22	35	13	12	0	6	3	14	16.1	4.1	5.0	1.9	.434
81-82	Phoenix	7	7	191	68	27	54	.500	0	0	.000	14	20	.700	18	30	48	30	25	0	6	3	12	27.3	9.7	6.9	4.3	.538
83-84	Utah	11	0	201	55	15	27	.556	0	0	.000	25	29	.862	19	39	58	22	42	1	9	6	17	18.3	5.0	5.3	2.0	.488
84-85	Utah	9	5	174	49	18	38	.474	0	0	.000	13	15	.867	25	32	57	14	32	1	7	5	14	19.3	5.4	6.3	1.6	.464
85-86	Sacramento	3	0	35	11	3	9	.333	0	0	.000	5	6	.833	6	6	12	4	5	0	2	0	2	11.7	3.7	4.0	1.3	.516
NBA Playoff Totals		45	12	860	259	92	197	.467	0	2	.000	75	94	.798	95	151	246	105	133	2	39	24	69	19.1	5.8	5.5	2.3	....

• KELLOGG, Clark
Clark Clifton Kellogg Jr.

Born: July 2, 1961. Cleveland, OH, United States. Height: 6'7". Weight: 225 lbs. Drafted: 1982 College: Ohio State

YEAR	TEAM	GP	GS	MIN	PTS	FGM	FGA	FG%	3PM	3PA	3P%	FTM	FTA	FT%	ORB	DRB	TRB	AST	PF	DQ	STL	BLK	TO	MPG	PPG	RPG	APG	PCM
82-83	Indiana	81	81	2761	1625	680	1420	.479	4	18	.222	261	352	.741	340	520	860	223	298	6	141	43	219	34.1	20.1	10.6	2.8	.641
83-84	Indiana	79	79	2676	1506	619	1193	.519	7	21	.333	261	340	.768	230	489	719	234	242	2	121	28	221	33.9	19.1	9.1	3.0	.626
84-85	Indiana	77	65	2449	1432	562	1112	.505	7	14	.500	301	396	.760	224	500	724	244	247	2	86	26	231	31.8	18.6	9.4	3.2	.647
85-86	Indiana	19	12	568	335	139	294	.473	4	13	.308	53	69	.768	51	117	168	57	59	2	28	8	61	29.9	17.6	8.8	3.0	.616
86-87	Indiana	4	4	60	20	8	22	.364	1	2	.500	3	4	.750	7	4	11	6	12	0	5	0	4	15.0	5.0	2.8	1.5	.308
NBA Season Totals		260	241	8514	4918	2008	4041	.497	23	68	.338	879	1161	.757	852	1630	2482	764	858	12	381	105	736	32.7	18.9	9.5	2.9	....

• KELLY, Arvesta
Arvesta Kelly

Born: Nov. 20, 1945. Jackson, MS, United States. Height: 6'2". Weight: 175 lbs. Drafted: 1967 College: Lincoln (MO)

YEAR	TEAM	GP	GS	MIN	PTS	FGM	FGA	FG%	3PM	3PA	3P%	FTM	FTA	FT%	ORB	DRB	TRB	AST	PF	DQ	STL	BLK	TO	MPG	PPG	RPG	APG	PCM
67-68	Pittsburgh-A	16	....	146	63	26	76	.342	3	13	.231	8	13	.615	....	....	33	13	34	0	....	....	10	9.1	3.9	2.1	0.8	.328
68-69	Minnesota-A	68	....	1066	398	155	425	.365	25	105	.238	63	103	.612	54	103	157	61	141	0	....	....	89	15.7	5.9	2.3	0.9	.275
69-70	Pittsburgh-A	70	....	2391	957	384	778	.494	21	74	.284	168	257	.654	122	145	267	226	195	4	....	....	209	34.2	13.7	3.8	3.2	.412
70-71	Carolina-A	5	....	45	14	4	8	.500	0	0	.000	6	8	.750	1	0	1	0	8	0	....	....	8	9.0	2.8	0.2	0.0	.169
70-71	Pittsburgh-A	17	....	135	44	16	27	.593	0	3	.000	12	23	.522	8	16	24	17	26	0	....	....	13	7.9	2.6	1.4	1.0	.444
71-72	Indiana-A	4	....	41	6	3	9	.333	0	0	.000	0	0	.000	1	6	7	2	10	0	....	....	2	10.3	1.5	1.8	0.5	.115
71-72	Pittsburgh-A	8	....	71	24	10	20	.500	1	3	.333	3	4	.750	4	4	8	12	10	1	....	....	6	8.9	3.0	1.0	1.5	.435
ABA Season Totals		188	....	3895	1506	598	1343	.445	50	198	.253	260	408	.637	190	274	497	331	424	5	....	....	337	20.7	8.0	2.6	1.8	....
67-68	Pittsburgh-A	8	....	27	16	5	14	.357	2	4	.500	4	5	.800	....	....	5	0	8	0	....	....	2	3.4	2.0	0.6	0.0	.331
68-69	Minnesota-A	5	....	50	24	8	22	.364	5	14	.357	3	3	1.000	....	....	11	5	14	0	....	....	4	10.0	4.8	2.2	1.0	.423
ABA Playoff Totals		13	....	77	40	13	36	.361	7	18	.389	7	8	.875	....	....	16	5	22	0	....	....	6	5.9	3.1	1.2	0.4	....

• KELLY, Jerry
Gerard Allan Kelly

Born: June 14, 1918. Height: 6'2". Weight: 172 lbs. Drafted: — College: John Marshall

YEAR	TEAM	GP	GS	MIN	PTS	FGM	FGA	FG%	3PM	3PA	3P%	FTM	FTA	FT%	ORB	DRB	TRB	AST	PF	DQ	STL	BLK	TO	MPG	PPG	RPG	APG	PCM
46-47	Boston	43	....	....	256	91	313	.291	....	....	....	74	111	.667	....	....	....	21	128	....	....	....	....	....	6.0	....	0.5	....
47-48	Providence	3	....	....	6	3	10	.300	....	....	....	0	1	.000	....	....	....	0	3	....	....	....	....	....	2.0	....	0.0	....
NBA Season Totals		46	....	....	262	94	323	.291	....	....	....	74	112	.661	....	....	....	21	131	....	....	....	....	....	5.7	....	0.5	....

• KELLY, Tom
Thomas Edward Kelly

Born: Mar. 5, 1924. Height: 6' Weight: 170 lbs. Drafted: 1948 College: New York University

YEAR	TEAM	GP	GS	MIN	PTS	FGM	FGA	FG%	3PM	3PA	3P%	FTM	FTA	FT%	ORB	DRB	TRB	AST	PF	DQ	STL	BLK	TO	MPG	PPG	RPG	APG	PCM
48-49	Boston	27	....	....	191	73	218	.335	....	....	....	45	73	.616	....	....	....	38	73	....	....	....	....	....	7.1	....	1.4	....
NBA Season Totals		27	....	....	191	73	218	.335	....	....	....	45	73	.616	....	....	....	38	73	....	....	....	....	....	7.1	....	1.4	....

• KELLY, Tony
Tony Kelly

Born: 1920. Height: 6'1". Weight: 165 lbs. Drafted: — College: DePaul

YEAR	TEAM	GP	GS	MIN	PTS	FGM	FGA	FG%	3PM	3PA	3P%	FTM	FTA	FT%	ORB	DRB	TRB	AST	PF	DQ	STL	BLK	TO	MPG	PPG	RPG	APG	PCM
43-44	Sheboygan-N	19	....	....	110	40	....	....	....	....	....	30	....	....	....	....	....	....	....	....	....	....	....	5.8	....	....	....
44-45	Sheboygan-N	28	....	....	105	35	....	....	....	....	....	35	....	....	....	....	....	....	....	....	....	....	....	3.8	....	....	....
45-46	Sheboygan-N	29	....	....	81	26	....	....	....	....	....	29	....	....	....	....	....	....	....	....	....	....	....	2.8	....	....	....
NBL Season Totals		76	....	....	296	101	....	....	....	....	....	94	....	....	....	....	....	....	....	....	....	....	....	3.9	....	....	....

YEAR	TEAM	GP	GS	MIN	PTS	FGM	FGA	FG%	3PM	3PA	3P%	FTM	FTA	FT%	ORB	DRB	TRB	AST	PF	DQ	STL	BLK	TO	MPG	PPG	RPG	APG	PCM
43-44	Sheboygan-N	6	....	....	34	13	....	....	....	....	....	8	....	....	....	....	....	....	....	....	....	....	....	....	5.7	....	....	....
44-45	Sheboygan-N	8	....	....	29	10	....	....	....	....	....	9	....	....	....	....	....	....	....	....	....	....	....	....	3.6	....	....	....
45-46	Sheboygan-N	8	....	....	29	11	....	....	....	....	....	7	9	.778	....	....	....	....	....	....	....	....	....	....	3.6	....	....	....
NBL Playoff Totals		22	....	....	92	34	....	....	....	....	....	24	9	....	....	....	....	....	....	....	....	....	....	....	4.2	....	....	....

• KELSER, Greg

Gregory (Special K) Kelser

Born: Sept. 17, 1957. Panama City, FL, United States. Height: 6'7". Weight: 190 lbs. Drafted: 1979 College: Michigan State

YEAR	TEAM	GP	GS	MIN	PTS	FGM	FGA	FG%	3PM	3PA	3P%	FTM	FTA	FT%	ORB	DRB	TRB	AST	PF	DQ	STL	BLK	TO	MPG	PPG	RPG	APG	PCM
79-80	Detroit	50	....	1233	709	280	593	.472	3	15	.200	146	203	.719	124	152	276	108	176	5	60	34	140	24.7	14.2	5.5	2.2	.525
80-81	Detroit	25	....	654	308	120	285	.421	0	2	.000	68	106	.642	53	67	120	45	89	0	34	29	78	26.2	12.3	4.8	1.8	.374
81-82	Detroit	11	0	183	97	35	86	.407	0	3	.000	27	41	.659	13	26	39	12	32	0	5	7	22	16.6	8.8	3.5	1.1	.374
81-82	Seattle	49	10	558	240	81	185	.438	0	0	.000	78	119	.655	67	87	154	45	99	0	13	14	64	11.4	4.9	3.1	0.9	.423
82-83	Seattle	80	9	1507	667	247	450	.549	0	3	.000	173	257	.673	158	245	403	97	243	5	52	35	152	18.8	8.3	5.0	1.2	.496
83-84	San Diego	80	21	1783	878	313	603	.519	2	6	.333	250	356	.702	188	203	391	91	249	3	68	31	192	22.3	11.0	4.9	1.1	.459
84-85	Indiana	10	0	114	62	21	53	.396	0	1	.000	20	28	.714	6	13	19	13	16	0	7	0	12	11.4	6.2	1.9	1.3	.420
NBA Season Totals		305	40	6032	2961	1097	2255	.486	5	30	.167	762	1110	.686	609	793	1402	411	904	13	239	150	660	19.8	9.7	4.6	1.3	....
81-82	Seattle	3	0	6	4	0	2	.000	0	0	.000	4	4	1.000	1	2	3	1	2	0	0	0	2	2.0	1.3	1.0	0.3	.540
82-83	Seattle	2	0	19	4	2	5	.400	0	0	.000	0	0	.000	3	3	6	1	4	0	1	0	0	9.5	2.0	3.0	0.5	.363
NBA Playoff Totals		5	0	25	8	2	7	.286	0	0	.000	4	4	1.000	4	5	9	2	6	0	1	0	2	5.0	1.6	1.8	0.4	....

• KELSO, Ben

Ben Kelso

Born: Apr. 11, 1949. Height: 6'3". Weight: 195 lbs. Drafted: 1973 College: Central Michigan

YEAR	TEAM	GP	GS	MIN	PTS	FGM	FGA	FG%	3PM	3PA	3P%	FTM	FTA	FT%	ORB	DRB	TRB	AST	PF	DQ	STL	BLK	TO	MPG	PPG	RPG	APG	PCM
73-74	Detroit	46	....	298	85	35	96	.365	....	....	....	15	22	.682	15	16	31	18	45	0	12	1	....	6.5	1.8	0.7	0.4	.195
NBA Season Totals		46	....	298	85	35	96	.365	....	....	....	15	22	.682	15	16	31	18	45	0	12	1	....	6.5	1.8	0.7	0.4	....
73-74	Detroit	1	....	1	0	0	2	.000	....	....	....	0	0	.000	0	1	1	1	0	0	0	0	....	1.0	0.0	1.0	1.0	.298
NBA Playoff Totals		1	....	1	0	0	2	.000	....	....	....	0	0	.000	0	1	1	1	0	0	0	0	....	1.0	0.0	1.0	1.0	....

• KEMP, Shawn

Shawn T. (Rain Man) Kemp

Born: Nov. 26, 1969. Elkhart, IN, United States. Height: 6'10". Weight: 230 lbs. Drafted: 1989 College: Trinity Valley CC (DNP)

YEAR	TEAM	GP	GS	MIN	PTS	FGM	FGA	FG%	3PM	3PA	3P%	FTM	FTA	FT%	ORB	DRB	TRB	AST	PF	DQ	STL	BLK	TO	MPG	PPG	RPG	APG	PCM
89-90	Seattle	81	1	1120	525	203	424	.479	2	12	.167	117	159	.736	146	200	346	26	204	5	47	70	105	13.8	6.5	4.3	0.3	.505
90-91	Seattle	81	66	2442	1214	462	909	.508	2	12	.167	288	436	.661	267	412	679	144	319	11	77	123	203	30.1	15.0	8.4	1.8	.558
91-92	Seattle	64	23	1808	994	362	718	.504	0	3	.000	270	361	.748	264	401	665	86	261	**13**	70	124	154	28.3	15.5	10.4	1.3	.690
92-93	Seattle	78	68	2582	1388	515	1047	.492	0	4	.000	358	503	.712	287	546	833	155	327	13	119	146	218	33.1	17.8	10.7	2.0	.642
93-94	Seattle	79	73	2597	1431	533	990	.538	1	4	.250	364	491	.741	312	539	851	207	**312**	**11**	142	166	261	32.9	18.1	10.8	2.6	.716
94-95	Seattle	82	79	2679	1530	545	997	.547	2	7	.286	438	585	.749	318	575	893	149	337	9	102	122	262	32.7	18.7	10.9	1.8	.687
95-96	Seattle	79	76	2631	1550	526	937	.561	5	12	.417	493	664	.742	276	628	904	173	299	6	93	127	316	33.3	19.6	11.4	2.2	.717
96-97	Seattle	81	75	2750	1516	526	1032	.510	12	33	.364	452	609	.742	275	532	807	156	**320**	**11**	125	81	284	34.0	18.7	10.0	1.9	.607
97-98	Cleveland	80	80	2769	1442	518	1164	.445	2	8	.250	404	556	.727	219	526	745	197	310	**15**	108	90	272	34.6	18.0	9.3	2.5	.530
98-99	Cleveland	42	42	1475	862	277	575	.482	1	2	.500	307	389	.789	131	257	388	101	159	2	48	45	127	35.1	20.5	9.2	2.4	.622
99-00	Cleveland	82	82	2492	1463	484	1160	.417	2	6	.333	493	635	.776	231	494	725	138	**371**	**13**	100	96	291	30.4	17.8	8.8	1.7	.537
00-01	Portland	68	3	1083	441	168	413	.407	4	11	.364	101	131	.771	63	196	259	65	184	3	45	23	99	15.9	6.5	3.8	1.0	.371
01-02	Portland	75	5	1233	454	175	407	.430	0	4	.000	104	131	.794	90	198	288	52	184	1	43	33	81	16.4	6.1	3.8	0.7	.374
02-03	Orlando	79	55	1634	537	211	505	.418	0	1	.000	115	155	.742	147	304	451	55	239	2	66	33	102	20.7	6.8	5.7	0.7	.373
NBA Season Totals		1051	728	29295	15347	5505	11278	.488	33	119	.277	4304	5805	.741	3026	5808	8834	1704	3826	115	1185	1279	2775	27.9	14.6	8.4	1.6	....
90-91	Seattle	5	5	149	66	22	57	.386	0	1	.000	22	27	.815	13	23	36	6	20	1	3	4	16	29.8	13.2	7.2	1.2	.358
91-92	Seattle	9	9	338	157	48	101	.475	0	0	.000	61	80	.763	47	63	110	4	41	0	5	14	27	37.6	17.4	12.2	0.4	.529
92-93	Seattle	19	19	663	313	110	215	.512	0	0	.000	93	115	.809	80	110	190	49	78	2	29	40	54	34.9	16.5	10.0	2.6	.621
93-94	Seattle	5	5	206	74	26	70	.371	0	0	.000	22	33	.667	20	29	49	17	18	0	10	12	14	41.2	14.8	9.8	3.4	.442
94-95	Seattle	4	4	160	99	33	57	.579	1	1	1.000	32	39	.821	17	31	48	11	17	0	8	7	15	40.0	24.8	12.0	2.8	.762
95-96	Seattle	20	20	720	418	147	258	.570	0	3	.000	124	156	.795	66	142	208	30	84	3	24	40	80	36.0	20.9	10.4	1.5	.655
96-97	Seattle	12	12	442	259	85	175	.486	2	10	.200	87	105	.829	52	96	148	36	55	2	14	16	47	36.8	21.6	12.3	3.0	.682
97-98	Cleveland	4	4	152	104	33	71	.465	0	0	.000	38	45	.844	16	25	41	8	12	0	5	4	16	38.0	26.0	10.3	2.0	.660
01-02	Portland	3	0	35	11	2	7	.286	0	0	.000	7	10	.700	2	6	8	0	8	0	1	0	2	11.7	3.7	2.7	0.0	.224
02-03	Orlando	7	0	72	21	8	21	.381	0	0	.000	5	6	.833	1	14	15	0	13	0	0	0	4	10.3	3.0	2.1	0.0	.178
NBA Playoff Totals		88	78	2937	1522	514	1032	.498	3	15	.200	491	616	.797	314	539	853	161	346	8	99	137	275	33.4	17.3	9.7	1.8	....

• KEMPTON, Tim

Timothy Joseph Kempton

Born: Jan. 25, 1964. Jamaica, NY, United States. Height: 6'10". Weight: 245 lbs. Drafted: 1986 College: Notre Dame

YEAR	TEAM	GP	GS	MIN	PTS	FGM	FGA	FG%	3PM	3PA	3P%	FTM	FTA	FT%	ORB	DRB	TRB	AST	PF	DQ	STL	BLK	TO	MPG	PPG	RPG	APG	PCM
86-87	LA Clippers	66	6	936	289	97	206	.471	0	1	.000	95	137	.693	70	124	194	53	162	6	38	12	46	14.2	4.4	2.9	0.8	.356
88-89	Charlotte	79	0	1341	484	171	335	.510	0	1	.000	142	207	.686	91	213	304	102	215	3	41	14	119	17.0	6.1	3.8	1.3	.398
89-90	Denver	71	14	1061	383	153	312	.490	0	1	.000	77	114	.675	51	167	218	118	144	2	30	9	78	14.9	5.4	3.1	1.7	.417
92-93	Phoenix	30	0	167	56	19	48	.396	0	0	.000	18	31	.581	12	27	39	19	30	0	4	4	15	5.6	1.9	1.3	0.6	.353
93-94	Charlotte	9	0	103	25	9	26	.346	0	0	.000	7	10	.700	6	8	14	6	25	0	4	1	4	11.4	2.8	1.6	0.7	.163
93-94	Cleveland	4	0	33	14	6	12	.500	0	0	.000	2	6	.333	4	6	10	3	8	0	2	1	7	8.3	3.5	2.5	0.8	.356
95-96	Atlanta	3	0	11	0	0	0	.000	0	0	.000	0	0	.000	0	2	2	1	5	0	0	0	1	3.7	0.0	0.7	0.3	-.032
96-97	San Antonio	10	0	59	4	1	5	.200	0	0	.000	2	2	1.000	3	5	8	2	4	0	1	1	7	5.9	0.4	0.8	0.2	.057
97-98	Orlando	3	0	15	0	0	2	.000	0	0	.000	0	0	.000	0	1	1	1	3	0	0	0	0	5.0	0.0	0.3	0.3	-.080
97-98	Toronto	5	0	32	4	2	7	.286	0	0	.000	0	0	.000	4	1	5	2	7	0	1	2	4	6.4	0.8	1.0	0.4	.064
NBA Season Totals		280	20	3758	1259	458	953	.481	0	3	.000	343	507	.677	241	554	795	307	603	11	121	44	281	13.4	4.5	2.8	1.1	....
89-90	Denver	3	1	32	18	7	9	.778	0	0	.000	4	4	1.000	1	4	5	4	8	0	0	0	2	10.7	6.0	1.7	1.3	.608
93-94	Cleveland	3	1	89	26	10	25	.400	0	0	.000	6	6	1.000	10	6	16	8	9	0	3	0	4	29.7	8.7	5.3	2.7	.343
NBA Playoff Totals		6	2	121	44	17	34	.500	0	0	.000	10	10	1.000	11	10	21	12	17	0	3	0	6	20.2	7.3	3.5	2.0	....

YEAR	TEAM	GP	GS	MIN	PTS	FGM	FGA	FG%	3PM	3PA	3P%	FTM	FTA	FT%	ORB	DRB	TRB	AST	PF	DQ	STL	BLK	TO	MPG	PPG	RPG	APG	PCM

• KENDRICK, Frank
Frank Edward Kendrick

Born: Sept. 11, 1950. Indianapolis, IN, United States. Height: 6'6". Weight: 198 lbs. Drafted: 1974 College: Purdue

YEAR	TEAM	GP	GS	MIN	PTS	FGM	FGA	FG%	3PM	3PA	3P%	FTM	FTA	FT%	ORB	DRB	TRB	AST	PF	DQ	STL	BLK	TO	MPG	PPG	RPG	APG	PCM
74-75	Golden State	24	....	121	80	31	77	.403	....	....	....	18	22	.818	19	17	36	6	22	0	11	3	....	5.0	3.3	1.5	0.3	.556
NBA Season Totals		24	....	121	80	31	77	.403	....	....	....	18	22	.818	19	17	36	6	22	0	11	3	....	5.0	3.3	1.5	0.3	....

• KENNEDY, Goo
Eugene (Goo) Kennedy

Born: Aug. 23, 1949. Charlotte, SC, United States. Height: 6'5". Weight: 205 lbs. Drafted: 1971 College: Texas Christian

YEAR	TEAM	GP	GS	MIN	PTS	FGM	FGA	FG%	3PM	3PA	3P%	FTM	FTA	FT%	ORB	DRB	TRB	AST	PF	DQ	STL	BLK	TO	MPG	PPG	RPG	APG	PCM
71-72	Dallas-A	65	....	1453	556	234	406	.576	0	0	.000	88	133	.662	167	318	485	65	262	**19**	....	....	75	22.4	8.6	7.5	1.0	.529
72-73	Dallas-A	70	....	1809	878	365	664	.550	0	0	.000	148	232	.638	167	323	490	75	275	8	....	....	113	25.8	12.5	7.0	1.1	.537
73-74	San Antonio-A	76	....	1440	448	194	352	.551	0	0	.000	60	87	.690	121	266	387	83	240	....	59	15	79	18.9	5.9	5.1	1.1	.434
74-75	St. Louis-A	74	....	1532	692	281	536	.524	1	1	1.000	129	178	.725	171	202	373	59	190	....	64	10	92	20.7	9.4	5.0	0.8	.494
75-76	Utah-A	16	....	271	100	38	69	.551	0	0	.000	24	37	.649	30	50	80	11	43	....	10	2	12	16.9	6.3	5.0	0.7	.483
76-77	Houston	32	....	277	65	31	58	.534	....	....	....	3	8	.375	14	37	51	6	45	1	7	5	....	8.7	2.0	1.6	0.2	.256
NBA Season Totals		32	....	277	65	31	58	.534	....	....	....	3	8	.375	14	37	51	6	45	1	7	5	....	8.7	2.0	1.6	0.2	....
ABA Season Totals		301	....	6505	2674	1112	2027	.549	1	1	1.000	449	667	.673	656	1159	1815	293	1010	27	133	27	371	21.6	8.9	6.0	1.0	....
Career Totals		333	....	6782	2739	1143	2085	.548	1	1	1.000	452	675	.670	670	1196	1866	299	1055	28	140	32	371	20.4	8.2	5.6	0.9	....
71-72	Dallas-A	2	....	47	18	8	12	.667	0	0	.000	2	2	1.000	2	4	6	4	8	1	....	....	3	23.5	9.0	3.0	2.0	.441
73-74	San Antonio-A	6	....	71	27	12	28	.429	0	1	.000	3	4	.750	9	9	18	1	15	....	0	1	3	11.8	4.5	3.0	0.2	.324
74-75	St. Louis-A	8	....	47	28	9	22	.409	0	0	.000	10	14	.714	6	12	18	1	8	....	1	0	3	5.9	3.5	2.3	0.1	.601
76-77	Houston	6	....	35	12	5	10	.500	....	....	....	2	2	1.000	4	8	12	0	6	0	0	0	....	5.8	2.0	2.0	0.0	.441
NBA Playoff Totals		6	....	35	12	5	10	.500	....	....	....	2	2	1.000	4	8	12	0	6	0	0	0	....	5.8	2.0	2.0	0.00	....
ABA Playoff Totals		16	....	165	73	29	62	.468	0	1	.000	15	20	.750	17	25	42	6	31	1	1	1	9	10.3	4.6	2.6	0.4	....
Career Playoff Totals		22	....	200	85	34	72	.472	0	1	.000	17	22	.773	21	33	54	6	37	1	1	1	9	9.1	3.9	2.5	0.3	....

• KENNEDY, Joe
Joseph A. Kennedy

Born: Jan. 12, 1947. Height: 6'6". Weight: 210 lbs. Drafted: 1968 College: Duke

YEAR	TEAM	GP	GS	MIN	PTS	FGM	FGA	FG%	3PM	3PA	3P%	FTM	FTA	FT%	ORB	DRB	TRB	AST	PF	DQ	STL	BLK	TO	MPG	PPG	RPG	APG	PCM
68-69	Seattle	72	....	1241	446	174	441	.395	....	....	....	98	124	.790	....	....	241	60	158	2	....	....	....	17.2	6.2	3.3	0.8	.336
69-70	Seattle	14	....	82	8	3	34	.088	....	....	....	2	2	1.000	....	....	20	7	7	0	....	....	....	5.9	0.6	1.4	0.5	.038
70-71	Pittsburgh-A	82	....	1382	508	189	498	.380	0	2	.000	130	160	.813	148	193	341	73	156	0	....	....	97	16.9	6.2	4.2	0.9	.396
NBA Season Totals		86	....	1323	454	177	475	.373	....	....	....	100	126	.794	....	....	261	67	165	2	....	....	....	15.4	5.3	3.0	0.8	....
ABA Season Totals		82	....	1382	508	189	498	.380	0	2	.000	130	160	.813	148	193	341	73	156	0	....	....	97	16.9	6.2	4.2	0.9	....
Career Totals		168	....	2705	962	366	973	.376	0	2	.000	230	286	.804	148	193	602	140	321	2	....	....	97	16.1	5.7	3.6	0.8	....

• KENNEDY, Pickles
William R. (Pickles) Kennedy

Born: May 17, 1938. Philadelphia, PA, United States. Height: 5'11". Weight: 180 lbs. Drafted: 1960 College: Temple

YEAR	TEAM	GP	GS	MIN	PTS	FGM	FGA	FG%	3PM	3PA	3P%	FTM	FTA	FT%	ORB	DRB	TRB	AST	PF	DQ	STL	BLK	TO	MPG	PPG	RPG	APG	PCM
60-61	Philadelphia	7	....	52	12	4	21	.190	....	....	....	4	6	.667	....	....	8	9	6	0	....	....	....	7.4	1.7	1.1	1.3	.255
NBA Season Totals		7	....	52	12	4	21	.190	....	....	....	4	6	.667	....	....	8	9	6	0	....	....	....	7.4	1.7	1.1	1.3	....

• KENNEY, Larry
Larry Kenney

Born: —. Height: — Weight: — Drafted: — College: St. Joseph's (PA)

YEAR	TEAM	GP	GS	MIN	PTS	FGM	FGA	FG%	3PM	3PA	3P%	FTM	FTA	FT%	ORB	DRB	TRB	AST	PF	DQ	STL	BLK	TO	MPG	PPG	RPG	APG	PCM
45-46	Youngstown-N	1	....	....	0	0	....	....	....	....	....	0	0	.000	....	....	....	....	....	....	....	....	....	0.0	....	....	....	....
NBL Season Totals		1	....	....	0	0	....	....	....	....	....	0	0	....	....	....	....	....	....	....	....	....	....	0.0	....	....	....	....

• KENON, Larry
Larry Joe (K, Special K, Dr. K) Kenon

Born: Dec. 13, 1952. Birmingham, AL, United States. Height: 6'9". Weight: 205 lbs. Drafted: 1973 College: Memphis State

YEAR	TEAM	GP	GS	MIN	PTS	FGM	FGA	FG%	3PM	3PA	3P%	FTM	FTA	FT%	ORB	DRB	TRB	AST	PF	DQ	STL	BLK	TO	MPG	PPG	RPG	APG	PCM
73-74	New York-A	84	....	2908	1334	589	1274	.462	0	1	.000	156	222	.703	375	587	962	112	251	....	79	19	250	34.6	15.9	11.5	1.3	.538
74-75	New York-A	84	....	3165	1570	676	1327	.509	1	2	.500	217	282	.770	279	621	900	122	229	....	107	30	206	37.7	18.7	10.7	1.5	.568
75-76	San Antonio-A	81	....	2920	1515	647	1344	.481	0	1	.000	221	283	.781	287	610	897	151	165	....	91	43	243	36.0	18.7	11.1	1.9	.603
76-77	San Antonio	78	....	2936	1705	706	1435	.492	....	....	....	293	356	.823	282	597	879	229	190	0	167	60	....	37.6	21.9	11.3	2.9	.676
77-78	San Antonio	81	....	2869	1672	698	1426	.489	....	....	....	276	323	.854	245	528	773	268	209	2	115	24	275	35.4	20.6	9.5	3.3	.621
78-79	San Antonio	81	....	2947	1791	748	1484	.504	....	....	....	295	349	.845	260	530	790	335	192	1	154	19	300	36.4	22.1	9.8	4.1	.673
79-80	San Antonio	78	....	2798	1565	647	1333	.485	1	9	.111	270	345	.783	258	517	775	231	192	0	111	18	234	35.9	20.1	9.9	3.0	.601
80-81	Chicago	77	....	2161	1088	454	946	.480	0	0	.000	180	245	.735	179	219	398	120	160	2	75	18	162	28.1	14.1	5.2	1.6	.448
81-82	Chicago	60	30	1036	434	192	412	.466	0	0	.000	50	88	.568	72	108	180	65	71	0	30	7	84	17.3	7.2	3.0	1.1	.361
82-83	Chicago	2	0	25	4	2	6	.333	0	0	.000	0	0	.000	1	3	4	0	2	0	1	0	2	5.0	0.8	0.8	0.0	.088
82-83	Golden State	11	0	121	41	17	39	.436	0	0	.000	7	11	.636	13	13	26	5	13	0	1	0	6	11.0	3.7	2.4	0.5	.313
82-83	Cleveland	32	7	624	235	100	212	.472	0	1	.000	35	46	.761	52	65	117	34	49	0	21	9	38	19.5	7.3	3.7	1.1	.389
NBA Season Totals		503	37	15517	8535	3564	7293	.489	1	10	.100	1406	1763	.798	1362	2580	3942	1287	1078	5	675	155	1101	30.8	17.0	7.8	2.6	....
ABA Season Totals		249	....	8993	4419	1912	3945	.485	1	4	.250	594	787	.755	941	1818	2759	385	645	....	277	92	699	36.1	17.7	11.1	1.5	....
Career Totals		752	37	24510	12954	5476	11238	.487	2	14	.143	2000	2550	.784	2303	4398	6701	1672	1723	5	952	247	1800	32.6	17.2	8.9	2.2	....
73-74	New York-A	14	....	470	221	101	204	.495	0	0	.000	19	31	.613	67	96	163	25	33	....	15	2	38	33.6	15.8	11.6	1.8	.599
74-75	New York-A	5	....	199	107	47	88	.534	0	0	.000	13	17	.765	21	43	64	5	17	....	10	0	19	39.8	21.4	12.8	1.0	.621
75-76	San Antonio-A	7	....	277	150	61	131	.466	1	3	.333	27	30	.900	30	50	80	16	16	....	5	4	33	39.6	21.4	11.4	2.3	.607
76-77	San Antonio	2	....	79	34	16	33	.485	....	....	....	2	2	1.000	3	12	15	6	9	1	5	1	....	39.5	17.0	7.5	3.0	.446
77-78	San Antonio	6	....	200	106	46	103	.447	....	....	....	14	19	.737	16	39	55	22	23	0	5	2	19	33.3	17.7	9.2	3.7	.531
78-79	San Antonio	14	....	557	295	128	292	.438	....	....	....	39	53	.736	57	103	160	42	42	0	20	1	33	39.8	21.1	11.4	3.0	.542

YEAR	TEAM	GP	GS	MIN	PTS	FGM	FGA	FG%	3PM	3PA	3P%	FTM	FTA	FT%	ORB	DRB	TRB	AST	PF	DQ	STL	BLK	TO	MPG	PPG	RPG	APG	PCM
79-80	San Antonio	3	....	81	26	10	34	.294	0	0	.000	6	11	.545	6	7	13	4	6	0	0	0	5	27.0	8.7	4.3	1.3	.135
80-81	Chicago	6	....	114	40	18	46	.391	0	1	.000	4	8	.500	17	10	27	8	4	0	4	1	1	19.0	6.7	4.5	1.3	.419
NBA Playoff Totals		31	....	1031	501	218	508	.429	0	1	.000	65	93	.699	99	171	270	82	84	1	34	5	58	33.3	16.2	8.7	2.6	....
ABA Playoff Totals		26	....	946	478	209	423	.494	1	3	.333	59	78	.756	118	189	307	46	66	....	30	6	90	36.4	18.4	11.8	1.8	....
Career Playoff Totals		57	....	1977	979	427	931	.459	1	4	.250	124	171	.725	217	360	577	128	150	1	64	11	148	34.7	17.2	10.1	2.2	....

• KENVILLE, Billy

William McGill (The Kid) Kenville

Born: Dec. 1, 1930. Elmhurst, NY, United States. Height: 6'2". Weight: 187 lbs. Drafted: — College: St. Bonaventure

53-54	Syracuse	72	....	1405	434	149	388	.384	....	....	....	136	182	.747	....	....	247	122	138	0	....	....	....	19.5	6.0	3.4	1.7	.378
54-55	Syracuse	70	....	1380	498	172	482	.357	....	....	....	154	201	.766	....	....	247	150	132	1	....	....	....	19.7	7.1	3.5	2.1	.413
55-56	Syracuse	72	....	1278	535	170	448	.379	....	....	....	195	257	.759	....	....	215	159	132	0	....	....	....	17.8	7.4	3.0	2.2	.477
56-57	Fort Wayne	71	....	1701	582	204	608	.336	....	....	....	174	218	.798	....	....	324	172	169	3	....	....	....	24.0	8.2	4.6	2.4	.387
57-58	Detroit	35	....	649	258	106	280	.379	....	....	....	46	75	.613	....	....	102	66	68	0	....	....	....	18.5	7.4	2.9	1.9	.391
59-60	Detroit	25	....	365	127	47	131	.359	....	....	....	33	41	.805	....	....	71	46	31	0	....	....	....	14.6	5.1	2.8	1.8	.437
NBA Season Totals		345	....	6778	2434	848	2337	.363	....	....	....	738	974	.758	....	....	1206	715	670	4	....	....	....	19.6	7.1	3.5	2.1	....
53-54	Syracuse	13	....	374	116	36	74	.486	....	....	....	44	62	.710	....	....	48	25	46	1	....	....	....	28.8	8.9	3.7	1.9	.355
54-55	Syracuse	11	....	130	70	17	48	.354	....	....	....	36	49	.735	....	....	31	11	23	1	....	....	....	11.8	6.4	2.8	1.0	.540
55-56	Syracuse	8	....	128	48	16	45	.356	....	....	....	16	23	.696	....	....	17	14	21	0	....	....	....	16.0	6.0	2.1	1.8	.356
56-57	Fort Wayne	2	....	30	4	2	13	.154	....	....	....	0	1	.000	....	....	1	5	1	0	....	....	....	15.0	2.0	0.5	2.5	.069
57-58	Detroit	7	....	99	46	18	44	.409	....	....	....	10	18	.556	....	....	19	5	12	0	....	....	....	14.1	6.6	2.7	0.7	.404
NBA Playoff Totals		41	....	761	284	89	224	.397	....	....	....	106	153	.693	....	....	116	60	103	2	....	....	....	18.6	6.9	2.8	1.5	....

• KERNER, Jonathan

Jonathan Kerner

Born: June 6, 1974. Atlanta, GA, United States. Height: 6'11". Weight: 245 lbs. Drafted: — College: East Carolina

98-99	Orlando	1	0	5	0	0	1	.000	0	0	.000	0	0	.000	0	0	0	0	2	0	0	0	0	5.0	0.0	0.0	0.0	-.356
NBA Season Totals		1	0	5	0	0	1	.000	0	0	.000	0	0	.000	0	0	0	0	2	0	0	0	0	5.0	0.0	0.0	0.0	....

• KERR, Red

John G. (Red) Kerr

Born: Aug. 17, 1932. Chicago, IL, United States. Height: 6'9". Weight: 230 lbs. Drafted: 1954 College: Illinois

54-55	Syracuse	72	....	1529	754	301	718	.419	....	....	....	152	223	.682	....	....	474	80	165	2	....	....	....	21.2	10.5	6.6	1.1	.528
55-56	Syracuse	72	....	2114	961	377	935	.403	....	....	....	207	316	.655	....	....	607	84	168	3	....	....	....	29.4	13.3	8.4	1.2	.472
56-57	Syracuse	72	....	2191	891	333	827	.403	....	....	....	225	313	.719	....	....	807	90	190	3	....	....	....	30.4	12.4	11.2	1.3	.517
57-58	Syracuse	72	....	2384	1094	407	1020	.399	....	....	....	280	422	.664	....	....	963	88	197	4	....	....	....	33.1	15.2	13.4	1.2	.561
58-59	Syracuse	72	....	2671	1285	502	1139	.441	....	....	....	281	367	.766	....	....	1008	142	183	1	....	....	....	37.1	17.8	14.0	2.0	.614
59-60	Syracuse	75	....	2372	1105	436	1111	.392	....	....	....	233	310	.752	....	....	913	167	207	4	....	....	....	31.6	14.7	12.2	2.2	.584
60-61	Syracuse	79	....	2676	1056	419	1056	.397	....	....	....	218	299	.729	....	....	951	199	230	4	....	....	....	33.9	13.4	12.0	2.5	.532
61-62	Syracuse	80	....	2767	1304	541	1220	.443	....	....	....	222	302	.735	....	....	1176	243	272	7	....	....	....	34.6	16.3	14.7	3.0	.669
62-63	Syracuse	80	....	2561	1255	507	1069	.474	....	....	....	241	320	.753	....	....	1039	214	208	3	....	....	....	32.0	15.7	13.0	2.7	.694
63-64	Philadelphia	80	....	2938	1340	536	1250	.429	....	....	....	268	357	.751	....	....	1017	275	187	2	....	....	....	36.7	16.8	12.7	3.4	.614
64-65	Philadelphia	80	....	1810	654	264	714	.370	....	....	....	126	181	.696	....	....	551	197	132	1	....	....	....	22.6	8.2	6.9	2.5	.499
65-66	Baltimore	71	....	1770	781	286	692	.413	....	....	....	209	272	.768	....	....	586	225	148	0	....	....	....	24.9	11.0	8.3	3.2	.629
NBA Season Totals		905	....	27783	12480	4909	11751	.418	....	....	....	2662	3682	.723	....	....	10092	2004	2287	34	....	....	....	30.7	13.8	11.2	2.2	....
54-55	Syracuse	11	....	363	152	59	151	.391	....	....	....	34	61	.557	....	....	118	13	27	0	....	....	....	33.0	13.8	10.7	1.2	.461
55-56	Syracuse	8	....	213	89	37	77	.481	....	....	....	15	33	.455	....	....	68	10	23	0	....	....	....	26.6	11.1	8.5	1.3	.503
56-57	Syracuse	5	....	162	76	28	65	.431	....	....	....	20	29	.690	....	....	69	6	7	0	....	....	....	32.4	15.2	13.8	1.2	.626
57-58	Syracuse	3	....	116	50	18	55	.327	....	....	....	14	18	.778	....	....	61	3	5	0	....	....	....	38.7	16.7	20.3	1.0	.586
58-59	Syracuse	9	....	312	130	50	142	.352	....	....	....	30	33	.909	....	....	108	24	20	0	....	....	....	34.7	14.4	12.0	2.7	.524
59-60	Syracuse	3	....	104	41	15	51	.294	....	....	....	11	12	.917	....	....	25	9	9	0	....	....	....	34.7	13.7	8.3	3.0	.386
60-61	Syracuse	8	....	210	76	30	88	.341	....	....	....	16	23	.696	....	....	99	20	18	0	....	....	....	26.3	9.5	12.4	2.5	.583
61-62	Syracuse	5	....	193	88	41	109	.376	....	....	....	6	8	.750	....	....	80	10	15	0	....	....	....	38.6	17.6	16.0	2.0	.533
62-63	Syracuse	5	....	187	68	26	60	.433	....	....	....	16	21	.762	....	....	75	9	12	0	....	....	....	37.4	13.6	15.0	1.8	.559
63-64	Philadelphia	5	....	185	95	40	83	.482	....	....	....	15	20	.750	....	....	69	16	12	0	....	....	....	37.0	19.0	13.8	3.2	.693
64-65	Philadelphia	11	....	181	63	24	67	.358	....	....	....	15	21	.714	....	....	38	28	20	0	....	....	....	16.5	5.7	3.5	2.5	.462
65-66	Baltimore	3	....	49	5	2	11	.182	....	....	....	1	2	.500	....	....	17	4	5	0	....	....	....	16.3	1.7	5.7	1.3	.281
NBA Playoff Totals		76	....	2275	933	370	959	.386	....	....	....	193	281	.687	....	....	827	152	173	0	....	....	....	29.9	12.3	10.9	2.0	....

• KERR, Steve

Stephen Douglas Kerr

Born: Sept. 27, 1965. Beirut, Lebanon. Height: 6'3". Weight: 175 lbs. Drafted: 1988 College: Arizona

88-89	Phoenix	26	0	157	54	20	46	.435	8	17	.471	6	9	.667	3	14	17	24	12	0	7	0	5	6.0	2.1	0.7	0.9	.422
89-90	Cleveland	78	5	1664	520	192	432	.444	73	144	**.507**	63	73	.863	12	86	98	248	59	0	45	7	70	21.3	6.7	1.3	3.2	.361
90-91	Cleveland	57	4	905	271	99	223	.444	28	62	.452	45	53	.849	5	32	37	131	52	0	29	4	40	15.9	4.8	0.6	2.3	.326
91-92	Cleveland	48	20	847	319	121	237	.511	32	74	.432	45	54	.833	14	64	78	110	29	0	27	10	29	17.6	6.6	1.6	2.3	.462
92-93	Cleveland	5	0	41	12	5	10	.500	0	2	.000	2	2	1.000	0	7	7	11	2	0	2	0	2	8.2	2.4	1.4	2.2	.602
92-93	Orlando	47	0	440	122	48	112	.429	6	24	.250	20	22	.909	5	33	38	59	34	0	8	1	24	9.4	2.6	0.8	1.3	.295
93-94	Chicago	82	0	2036	709	287	577	.497	52	124	.419	83	97	.856	26	105	131	210	97	0	75	3	57	24.8	8.6	1.6	2.6	.373
94-95	Chicago	82	0	1839	674	261	495	.527	89	170	**.524**	63	81	.778	20	99	119	151	114	0	44	3	49	22.4	8.2	1.5	1.8	.360
95-96	Chicago	82	0	1919	688	244	482	.506	122	237	.515	78	84	.929	25	85	110	192	109	0	63	2	41	23.4	8.4	1.3	2.3	.385
96-97	Chicago	82	0	1861	662	249	467	.533	110	237	.464	54	67	.806	29	101	130	175	98	0	67	3	41	22.7	8.1	1.6	2.1	.399
97-98	Chicago	50	0	1119	376	137	302	.454	57	130	.438	45	49	.918	14	63	77	96	71	0	26	5	25	22.4	7.5	1.5	1.9	.331
98-99	San Antonio	44	0	734	192	68	174	.391	25	80	.313	31	35	.886	6	38	44	49	28	0	23	3	22	16.7	4.4	1.0	1.1	.246
99-00	San Antonio	32	0	268	89	32	74	.432	16	31	.516	9	11	.818	3	16	19	12	14	0	4	0	7	8.4	2.8	0.6	0.4	.266
00-01	San Antonio	55	1	650	181	67	159	.421	33	77	.429	14	15	.933	6	29	35	57	30	0	16	1	21	11.8	3.3	0.6	1.0	.269

YEAR	TEAM	GP	GS	MIN	PTS	FGM	FGA	FG%	3PM	3PA	3P%	FTM	FTA	FT%	ORB	DRB	TRB	AST	PF	DQ	STL	BLK	TO	MPG	PPG	RPG	APG	PCM
01-02	Portland	65	0	775	269	102	217	.470	26	66	.394	39	40	.975	6	54	60	63	49	0	13	1	24	11.9	4.1	0.9	1.0	.331
02-03	San Antonio	75	0	951	299	110	256	.430	49	124	.395	30	34	.882	12	48	60	70	49	0	27	3	35	12.7	4.0	0.8	0.9	.283
NBA Season Totals		910	30	16206	5437	2042	4263	.479	726	1599	**.454**	627	726	.864	186	874	1060	1658	847	0	476	46	492	17.8	6.0	1.2	1.8	....
89-90	Cleveland	5	0	73	8	4	14	.286	0	3	.000	0	0	.000	1	5	6	10	6	0	4	0	2	14.6	1.6	1.2	2.0	.191
91-92	Cleveland	12	3	149	44	18	41	.439	3	11	.273	5	5	1.000	1	5	6	10	12	0	5	0	4	12.4	3.7	0.5	0.8	.230
93-94	Chicago	10	0	186	35	13	36	.361	6	16	.375	3	3	1.000	2	12	14	10	13	0	7	0	1	18.6	3.5	1.4	1.0	.200
94-95	Chicago	10	0	193	51	19	40	.475	8	19	.421	5	5	1.000	1	5	6	15	14	0	1	0	0	19.3	5.1	0.6	1.5	.245
95-96	Chicago	18	0	357	122	39	87	.448	17	53	.321	27	31	.871	3	15	18	31	21	0	14	0	13	19.8	6.8	1.0	1.7	.325
96-97	Chicago	19	0	341	95	33	77	.429	16	42	.381	13	14	.929	4	14	18	20	25	0	17	2	8	17.9	5.0	0.9	1.1	.265
97-98	Chicago	21	0	415	103	33	76	.434	19	41	.463	18	22	.818	8	9	17	35	26	0	7	0	5	19.8	4.9	0.8	1.7	.254
98-99	San Antonio	11	0	97	24	8	30	.267	3	13	.231	5	6	.833	3	6	9	8	5	0	2	0	4	8.8	2.2	0.8	0.7	.174
00-01	San Antonio	9	0	101	30	12	25	.480	5	15	.333	1	2	.500	3	6	9	6	8	0	4	1	2	11.2	3.3	1.0	0.7	.314
01-02	Portland	3	0	39	19	6	14	.429	2	8	.250	5	5	1.000	0	4	4	5	6	0	1	0	1	13.0	6.3	1.3	1.7	.465
02-03	San Antonio	10	0	46	22	7	11	.636	5	6	.833	3	4	.750	1	2	3	6	6	0	1	0	1	4.6	2.2	0.3	0.6	.532
NBA Playoff Totals		128	3	1997	553	192	451	.426	84	227	.370	85	97	.876	27	83	110	156	142	0	63	3	41	15.6	4.3	0.9	1.2	....

• KERRIS, Jack

John E. Kerris

Born: Jan. 30, 1925. Height: 6'6". Weight: 215 lbs. Drafted: 1949 College: Loyola (IL)

YEAR	TEAM	GP	GS	MIN	PTS	FGM	FGA	FG%	3PM	3PA	3P%	FTM	FTA	FT%	ORB	DRB	TRB	AST	PF	DQ	STL	BLK	TO	MPG	PPG	RPG	APG	PCM
49-50	Tri-Cities	4	....	....	26	8	26	.308	....	....	....	10	12	.833	....	....	....	8	13	....	....	....	....	....	6.5	....	2.0	....
49-50	Fort Wayne	64	....	....	457	149	455	.327	....	....	....	159	248	.641	....	....	....	110	162	....	....	....	....	....	7.1	....	1.7	....
50-51	Fort Wayne	68	....	....	711	255	689	.370	....	....	....	201	295	.681	....	....	477	181	253	12	....	....	....	....	10.5	7.0	2.7	....
51-52	Fort Wayne	66	....	2148	589	186	480	.388	....	....	....	217	325	.668	....	....	514	212	265	16	....	....	....	32.5	8.9	7.8	3.2	.413
52-53	FtW/Bal	69	....	1424	274	93	256	.363	....	....	....	88	140	.629	....	....	295	156	165	7	....	....	....	20.6	4.0	4.3	2.3	.344
NBA Season Totals		271	....	3572	2057	691	1906	.363	....	....	....	675	1020	.662	....	....	1286	667	858	35	....	....	....	13.2	7.6	4.7	2.5	....
49-50	Fort Wayne	4	....	....	37	12	30	.400	....	....	....	13	22	.591	....	....	....	5	17	....	....	....	....	....	9.3	....	1.3	....
50-51	Fort Wayne	3	....	....	23	9	26	.346	....	....	....	5	10	.500	....	....	20	10	15	1	....	....	....	....	7.7	6.7	3.3	....
51-52	Fort Wayne	2	....	63	25	7	20	.350	....	....	....	11	20	.550	....	....	18	9	11	1	....	....	....	31.5	12.5	9.0	4.5	.525
52-53	Baltimore	2	....	31	7	2	10	.200	....	....	....	3	3	1.000	....	....	2	0	4	0	....	....	....	15.5	3.5	1.0	0.0	.039
NBA Playoff Totals		11	....	94	92	30	86	.349	....	....	....	32	55	.582	....	....	40	24	47	2	....	....	....	8.5	8.4	3.6	2.2	....

• KERSEY, Jerome

Jerome Kersey

Born: June 26, 1962. Clarksville, VA, United States. Height: 6'7". Weight: 215 lbs. Drafted: 1984 College: Longwood

YEAR	TEAM	GP	GS	MIN	PTS	FGM	FGA	FG%	3PM	3PA	3P%	FTM	FTA	FT%	ORB	DRB	TRB	AST	PF	DQ	STL	BLK	TO	MPG	PPG	RPG	APG	PCM
84-85	Portland	77	0	958	473	178	372	.478	0	3	.000	117	181	.646	95	111	206	63	147	1	49	29	69	12.4	6.1	2.7	0.8	.482
85-86	Portland	79	2	1217	672	258	470	.549	0	6	.000	156	229	.681	137	156	293	83	208	2	85	32	111	15.4	8.5	3.7	1.1	.584
86-87	Portland	82	8	2088	1009	373	733	.509	1	23	.043	262	364	.720	201	295	496	194	328	5	122	77	148	25.5	12.3	6.0	2.4	.570
87-88	Portland	79	75	2888	1516	611	1225	.499	3	15	.200	291	396	.735	211	446	657	243	302	8	127	65	158	36.6	19.2	8.3	3.1	.574
88-89	Portland	76	76	2716	1330	533	1137	.469	6	21	.286	258	372	.694	246	383	629	243	277	6	137	84	167	35.7	17.5	8.3	3.2	.546
89-90	Portland	82	82	2843	1310	519	1085	.478	3	20	.150	269	390	.690	251	439	690	188	304	7	121	63	148	34.7	16.0	8.4	2.3	.514
90-91	Portland	73	72	2359	1084	424	887	.478	4	13	.308	232	327	.709	169	312	481	227	251	4	101	76	146	32.3	14.8	6.6	3.1	.513
91-92	Portland	77	76	2553	971	398	852	.467	1	8	.125	174	262	.664	241	392	633	243	254	1	114	71	146	33.2	12.6	8.2	3.2	.499
92-93	Portland	65	50	1719	686	281	642	.438	8	28	.286	116	183	.634	126	280	406	121	181	2	80	41	85	26.4	10.6	6.2	1.9	.451
93-94	Portland	78	6	1276	508	203	469	.433	1	8	.125	101	135	.748	130	201	331	75	213	1	71	49	62	16.4	6.5	4.2	1.0	.461
94-95	Portland	63	0	1143	508	203	489	.415	7	27	.259	95	124	.766	93	163	256	82	173	1	52	35	63	18.1	8.1	4.1	1.3	.433
95-96	Golden State	76	58	1620	510	205	500	.410	3	17	.176	97	147	.660	154	209	363	114	205	2	91	45	76	21.3	6.7	4.8	1.5	.390
96-97	LA Lakers	70	44	1766	476	194	449	.432	17	65	.262	71	118	.602	112	251	363	89	219	0	119	49	77	25.2	6.8	5.2	1.3	.358
97-98	Seattle	37	2	717	234	97	233	.416	1	10	.100	39	65	.600	56	79	135	44	104	1	52	14	37	19.4	6.3	3.6	1.2	.346
98-99	San Antonio	45	0	699	145	68	200	.340	3	14	.214	6	14	.429	42	88	130	41	92	1	37	14	30	15.5	3.2	2.9	0.9	.233
99-00	San Antonio	72	18	1310	321	146	354	.412	0	9	.000	29	41	.707	58	167	225	69	161	0	67	47	51	18.2	4.5	3.1	1.0	.298
00-01	Milwaukee	22	2	243	72	32	69	.464	0	1	.000	8	16	.500	8	37	45	15	36	1	14	8	6	11.0	3.3	2.0	0.7	.372
NBA Season Totals		1153	571	28115	11825	4723	10166	.465	58	288	.201	2321	3364	.690	2330	4009	6339	2134	3455	43	1439	799	1580	24.4	10.3	5.5	1.9	....
84-85	Portland	8	0	60	38	16	31	.516	0	0	.000	6	8	.750	5	4	9	6	11	0	7	2	2	7.5	4.8	1.1	0.8	.655
85-86	Portland	4	0	56	22	9	22	.409	0	1	.000	4	4	1.000	7	8	15	4	13	0	1	4	6	14.0	5.5	3.8	1.0	.378
86-87	Portland	4	0	60	24	10	25	.400	0	0	.000	4	4	1.000	6	13	19	3	13	0	5	1	6	15.0	6.0	4.8	0.8	.415
87-88	Portland	4	4	127	79	32	65	.492	0	1	.000	15	21	.714	17	13	30	9	17	1	7	4	5	31.8	19.8	7.5	2.3	.635
88-89	Portland	3	3	117	61	23	47	.489	0	2	.000	15	19	.789	11	19	30	7	12	0	10	1	4	39.0	20.3	10.0	2.3	.625
89-90	Portland	21	21	831	435	166	361	.460	0	3	.000	103	144	.715	66	108	174	45	87	2	34	20	45	39.6	20.7	8.3	2.1	.495
90-91	Portland	16	16	588	286	105	226	.465	0	0	.000	76	101	.752	52	59	111	49	68	2	28	7	17	36.8	17.9	6.9	3.1	.514
91-92	Portland	21	21	756	341	131	257	.510	0	3	.000	79	114	.693	59	103	162	75	85	2	41	19	53	36.0	16.2	7.7	3.6	.536
92-93	Portland	4	1	98	57	22	42	.524	1	1	1.000	12	17	.706	10	24	34	4	15	0	4	2	2	24.5	14.3	8.5	1.0	.701
93-94	Portland	3	0	38	11	5	16	.313	0	0	.000	1	5	.200	5	4	9	0	5	0	1	1	0	12.7	3.7	3.0	0.0	.181
94-95	Portland	3	0	63	38	16	28	.571	0	2	.000	6	9	.667	2	6	8	3	11	1	3	1	0	21.0	12.7	2.7	1.0	.550
96-97	LA Lakers	9	0	210	49	17	35	.486	0	1	.000	15	19	.789	14	34	48	14	34	2	9	6	3	23.3	5.4	5.3	1.6	.407
97-98	Seattle	10	5	213	78	31	72	.431	0	3	.000	16	19	.842	17	23	40	9	32	0	10	10	13	21.3	7.8	4.0	0.9	.363
98-99	San Antonio	14	0	152	36	15	43	.349	1	4	.250	5	7	.714	10	20	30	4	19	0	6	1	6	10.9	2.6	2.1	0.3	.222
99-00	San Antonio	2	0	25	2	1	7	.143	0	0	.000	0	0	.000	2	2	4	1	5	0	2	1	1	12.5	1.0	2.0	0.5	.033
NBA Playoff Totals		126	71	3394	1557	599	1277	.469	2	21	.095	357	491	.727	283	440	723	233	427	10	168	80	163	26.9	12.4	5.7	1.8	....

• KERWIN, Tom

Thomas Vincent Kerwin

Born: July 7, 1944. Height: 6'7". Weight: 210 lbs. Drafted: 1966 College: Centenary

YEAR	TEAM	GP	GS	MIN	PTS	FGM	FGA	FG%	3PM	3PA	3P%	FTM	FTA	FT%	ORB	DRB	TRB	AST	PF	DQ	STL	BLK	TO	MPG	PPG	RPG	APG	PCM
67-68	Pittsburgh-A	13	....	68	14	7	22	.318	0	0	.000	0	2	.000	....	....	20	1	5	0	....	....	2	5.2	1.1	1.5	0.1	.241
ABA Season Totals		13	....	68	14	7	22	.318	0	0	.000	0	2	.000	....	....	20	1	5	0	....	....	2	5.2	1.1	1.5	0.1	....

YEAR	TEAM	GP	GS	MIN	PTS	FGM	FGA	FG%	3PM	3PA	3P%	FTM	FTA	FT%	ORB	DRB	TRB	AST	PF	DQ	STL	BLK	TO	MPG	PPG	RPG	APG	PCM

• KESSLER, Alec

Alec Christopher Kessler

Born: Jan. 13, 1967. Minneapolis, MN, United States.   Height: 6'11".   Weight: 230 lbs.   Drafted: 1990   College: Georgia

YEAR	TEAM	GP	GS	MIN	PTS	FGM	FGA	FG%	3PM	3PA	3P%	FTM	FTA	FT%	ORB	DRB	TRB	AST	PF	DQ	STL	BLK	TO	MPG	PPG	RPG	APG	PCM
90-91	Miami	78	18	1259	486	199	468	.425	0	4	.000	88	131	.672	115	221	336	31	189	1	17	26	109	16.1	6.2	4.3	0.4	.327
91-92	Miami	77	4	1197	410	158	383	.413	0	0	.000	94	115	.817	114	200	314	34	185	3	17	32	62	15.5	5.3	4.1	0.4	.352
92-93	Miami	40	2	415	155	57	122	.467	5	11	.455	36	47	.766	25	66	91	14	63	0	4	12	20	10.4	3.9	2.3	0.4	.376
93-94	Miami	15	0	66	33	11	25	.440	5	9	.556	6	8	.750	4	6	10	2	14	0	1	1	5	4.4	2.2	0.7	0.1	.324
NBA Season Totals		210	24	2937	1084	425	998	.426	10	24	.417	224	301	.744	258	493	751	81	451	4	39	71	196	14.0	5.2	3.6	0.4	....
91-92	Miami	2	0	12	2	0	2	.000	0	0	.000	2	2	1.000	0	1	1	0	1	0	0	0	1	6.0	1.0	0.5	0.0	-.027
NBA Playoff Totals		2	0	12	2	0	2	.000	0	0	.000	2	2	1.000	0	1	1	0	1	0	0	0	1	6.0	1.0	0.5	0.0	....

• KESSLER, Robert

Robert Kessler

Born: Nov. 25, 1914. Indianapolis, IN, United States.   Height: 6'   Weight: 165 lbs.   Drafted: —   College: Purdue

YEAR	TEAM	GP	GS	MIN	PTS	FGM	FGA	FG%	3PM	3PA	3P%	FTM	FTA	FT%	ORB	DRB	TRB	AST	PF	DQ	STL	BLK	TO	MPG	PPG	RPG	APG	PCM
37-38	Indianapolis-N	10	....	....	103	36	....	....	....	....	....	31	....	....	....	....	....	....	....	....	....	....	....	....	10.3	....	....	....
38-39	Hammond-N	4	....	....	22	9	....	....	....	....	....	4	....	....	....	....	....	....	....	....	....	....	....	....	5.5	....	....	....
NBL Season Totals		14	....	....	125	45	....	....	....	....	....	35	....	....	....	....	....	....	....	....	....	....	....	....	8.9	....	....	....

• KESSY, Paul

Paul Kessy

Born: 1917.   Height: 6'3".   Weight: 170 lbs.   Drafted: —   College: Wisconsin (Milwaukee)

YEAR	TEAM	GP	GS	MIN	PTS	FGM	FGA	FG%	3PM	3PA	3P%	FTM	FTA	FT%	ORB	DRB	TRB	AST	PF	DQ	STL	BLK	TO	MPG	PPG	RPG	APG	PCM
44-45	Cleveland-N	4	....	....	0	0	....	....	....	....	....	0	....	....	....	....	....	....	....	....	....	....	....	....	0.0	....	....	....
44-45	Pittsburgh-N	2	....	....	3	1	....	....	....	....	....	1	....	....	....	....	....	....	....	....	....	....	....	....	1.5	....	....	....
NBL Season Totals		6	....	....	3	1	....	....	....	....	....	1	....	....	....	....	....	....	....	....	....	....	....	....	0.5	....	....	....

• KETNER, Lari

Lari Arthur Ketner

Born: Feb. 1, 1977. Philadelphia, PA, United States.   Height: 6'9".   Weight: 277 lbs.   Drafted: 1999   College: Massachusetts

YEAR	TEAM	GP	GS	MIN	PTS	FGM	FGA	FG%	3PM	3PA	3P%	FTM	FTA	FT%	ORB	DRB	TRB	AST	PF	DQ	STL	BLK	TO	MPG	PPG	RPG	APG	PCM
99-00	Chicago	6	0	41	10	4	10	.400	0	0	.000	2	2	1.000	0	7	7	1	8	1	1	1	3	6.8	1.7	1.2	0.2	.182
99-00	Cleveland	16	0	91	24	9	22	.409	0	0	.000	6	10	.600	12	15	27	0	12	0	3	2	7	5.7	1.5	1.7	0.0	.304
00-01	Indiana	3	0	7	0	0	0	.000	0	0	.000	0	0	.000	0	0	0	1	0	0	0	0	2	2.3	0.0	0.0	0.3	-.099
NBA Season Totals		25	0	139	34	13	32	.406	0	0	.000	8	12	.667	12	22	34	2	20	1	4	3	12	5.6	1.4	1.4	0.1	....

• KEYE, Julius

Julius Keye

Born: Sept. 5, 1946. Toccoa, GA, United States. Died: Sept.13, 1984.   Height: 6'10".   Weight: 200 lbs.   Drafted: 1969   College: Alcorn A&M

YEAR	TEAM	GP	GS	MIN	PTS	FGM	FGA	FG%	3PM	3PA	3P%	FTM	FTA	FT%	ORB	DRB	TRB	AST	PF	DQ	STL	BLK	TO	MPG	PPG	RPG	APG	PCM
69-70	Denver-A	77	....	1641	606	245	618	.396	0	7	.000	116	193	.601	188	342	530	47	209	2	....	....	99	21.3	7.9	6.9	0.6	.409
70-71	Denver-A	83	....	3634	1222	505	1177	.429	0	0	.000	212	317	.669	370	**1084**	1454	140	317	.5	....	....	215	43.8	14.7	17.5	1.7	.508
71-72	Denver-A	84	....	2557	492	192	476	.403	0	2	.000	108	174	.621	315	667	982	153	346	13	....	....	139	30.4	5.9	11.7	1.8	.429
72-73	Denver-A	83	....	3016	459	163	375	.435	3	8	.375	130	233	.558	275	617	892	180	269	3	....	226	134	36.3	5.5	10.7	2.2	.365
73-74	Denver-A	79	....	2595	352	147	329	.447	1	5	.200	57	84	.679	225	464	689	135	240	....	40	149	87	32.8	4.5	8.7	1.7	.319
74-75	Memphis-A	12	....	233	30	12	47	.255	0	0	.000	6	8	.750	16	39	55	2	26	....	4	5	8	19.4	2.5	4.6	0.2	.161
ABA Season Totals		418	....	13676	3161	1264	3022	.418	4	22	.182	629	1009	.623	1389	3213	4602	657	1407	23	44	380	682	32.7	7.6	11.0	1.6	....
69-70	Denver-A	7	....	138	23	10	42	.238	0	1	.000	3	6	.500	10	19	29	6	16	0	....	....	10	19.7	3.3	4.1	0.9	.139
71-72	Denver-A	7	....	302	57	27	59	.458	0	0	.000	3	8	.375	45	68	113	20	30	1	....	....	10	43.1	8.1	16.1	2.9	.448
72-73	Denver-A	5	....	203	49	20	34	.588	0	1	.000	9	17	.529	28	40	68	16	16	0	....	....	11	40.6	9.8	13.6	3.2	.514
ABA Playoff Totals		19	....	643	129	57	135	.422	0	2	.000	15	31	.484	83	127	210	42	62	1	....	....	31	33.8	6.8	11.1	2.2	....

• KEYS, Randolph

Randolph Keys

Born: Apr. 19, 1966. Collins, MS, United States.   Height: 6'7".   Weight: 195 lbs.   Drafted: 1988   College: Southern Mississippi

YEAR	TEAM	GP	GS	MIN	PTS	FGM	FGA	FG%	3PM	3PA	3P%	FTM	FTA	FT%	ORB	DRB	TRB	AST	PF	DQ	STL	BLK	TO	MPG	PPG	RPG	APG	PCM
88-89	Cleveland	42	0	331	169	74	172	.430	1	10	.100	20	29	.690	23	33	56	19	51	0	12	6	21	7.9	4.0	1.3	0.5	.361
89-90	Cleveland	48	13	892	365	151	359	.421	2	10	.200	61	82	.744	52	85	137	39	117	0	38	2	48	18.6	7.6	2.9	0.8	.300
89-90	Charlotte	32	5	723	336	142	319	.445	12	33	.364	40	58	.690	48	68	116	49	107	1	30	6	38	22.6	10.5	3.6	1.5	.374
90-91	Charlotte	44	0	473	140	59	145	.407	3	14	.214	19	33	.576	40	60	100	18	93	0	22	15	35	10.8	3.2	2.3	0.4	.263
94-95	LA Lakers	6	0	83	20	9	26	.346	0	9	.000	2	2	1.000	6	11	17	2	16	0	1	2	2	13.8	3.3	2.8	0.3	.187
95-96	Milwaukee	69	1	816	232	87	208	.418	22	71	.310	36	43	.837	41	84	125	65	139	2	32	13	35	11.8	3.4	1.8	0.9	.301
NBA Season Totals		241	19	3318	1262	522	1229	.425	40	147	.272	178	247	.721	210	341	551	192	523	3	135	44	179	13.8	5.2	2.3	0.8	....
88-89	Cleveland	1	0	12	0	0	3	.000	0	1	.000	0	0	.000	0	3	3	1	1	0	0	0	2	12.0	0.0	3.0	1.0	-.105
NBA Playoff Totals		1	0	12	0	0	3	.000	0	1	.000	0	0	.000	0	3	3	1	1	0	0	0	2	12.0	0.0	3.0	1.0	....

• KIDD, Jason

Jason Frederick Kidd

Born: Mar. 23, 1973. San Francisco, CA, United States.   Height: 6'4".   Weight: 205 lbs.   Drafted: 1994   College: California

YEAR	TEAM	GP	GS	MIN	PTS	FGM	FGA	FG%	3PM	3PA	3P%	FTM	FTA	FT%	ORB	DRB	TRB	AST	PF	DQ	STL	BLK	TO	MPG	PPG	RPG	APG	PCM
94-95	Dallas	79	79	2668	922	330	857	.385	70	257	.272	192	275	.698	152	278	430	607	146	0	151	24	253	33.8	11.7	5.4	7.7	.485
95-96	Dallas	81	81	3034	1348	493	1293	.381	133	396	.336	229	331	.692	203	350	553	783	155	0	175	26	**324**	37.5	16.6	6.8	9.7	.563
96-97	Dallas	22	22	791	217	75	203	.369	21	65	.323	46	69	.667	30	60	90	200	42	0	45	8	66	36.0	9.9	4.1	9.1	.446
96-97	Phoenix	33	23	1173	382	138	326	.423	40	100	.400	66	96	.688	34	125	159	296	72	0	79	12	76	35.5	11.6	4.8	9.0	.544
97-98	Phoenix	82	82	3118	954	357	859	.416	73	233	.313	167	209	.799	108	402	510	745	142	0	162	26	262	38.0	11.6	6.2	9.1	.519
98-99	Phoenix	50	50	**2060**	846	310	698	.444	45	123	.366	181	239	.757	87	252	339	**539**	108	1	114	19	150	41.2	16.9	6.8	**10.8**	**.637**
99-00	Phoenix	67	67	2616	959	350	855	.409	56	166	.337	203	245	.829	96	387	483	678	148	2	134	28	226	39.0	14.3	7.2	**10.1**	.587
00-01	Phoenix	77	76	3065	1299	451	1097	.411	69	232	.297	328	403	.814	91	403	494	**753**	171	1	166	23	286	39.8	16.9	6.4	**9.8**	.586

YEAR	TEAM	GP	GS	MIN	PTS	FGM	FGA	FG%	3PM	3PA	3P%	FTM	FTA	FT%	ORB	DRB	TRB	AST	PF	DQ	STL	BLK	TO	MPG	PPG	RPG	APG	PCM
01-02	New Jersey	82	82	3056	1208	445	1138	.391	117	364	.321	201	247	.814	130	465	595	808	136	0	**175**	20	**286**	37.3	14.7	7.3	9.9	.602
02-03	New Jersey	80	80	2989	1495	515	1244	.414	126	370	.341	339	403	.841	110	394	504	**711**	127	0	179	25	296	37.4	18.7	6.3	**8.9**	**.635**
NBA Season Totals		653	642	24570	9630	3464	8570	.404	750	2306	.325	1952	2517	.776	1041	3116	4157	6120	1247	4	1380	211	2225	37.6	14.7	6.4	9.4	....
96-97	Phoenix	5	5	207	60	21	53	.396	8	22	.364	10	19	.526	4	26	30	49	11	0	11	2	13	41.4	12.0	6.0	9.8	.489
97-98	Phoenix	4	4	171	57	22	58	.379	0	7	.000	13	16	.813	5	18	23	31	13	0	16	2	12	42.8	14.3	5.8	7.8	.450
98-99	Phoenix	3	3	126	45	18	43	.419	4	16	.250	5	7	.714	1	6	7	31	12	0	5	1	9	42.0	15.0	2.3	10.3	.433
99-00	Phoenix	6	6	229	59	22	55	.400	8	22	.364	7	9	.778	8	32	40	53	14	0	11	1	23	38.2	9.8	6.7	8.8	.463
00-01	Phoenix	4	4	166	57	22	69	.319	4	17	.235	9	12	.750	9	15	24	53	13	0	8	0	12	41.5	14.3	6.0	13.3	.506
01-02	New Jersey	20	20	803	391	147	354	.415	17	90	.189	80	99	.808	42	122	164	182	40	0	34	8	67	40.2	19.6	8.2	9.1	.625
02-03	New Jersey	20	20	852	402	137	341	.402	34	104	.327	94	114	.825	36	118	154	163	46	0	36	4	79	42.6	20.1	7.7	8.2	.551
NBA Playoff Totals		62	62	2554	1071	389	973	.400	75	278	.270	218	276	.790	105	337	442	562	149	0	121	18	215	41.2	17.3	7.1	9.1	....

• KIDD, Warren
Warren Lynn Kidd

Born: Sept. 9, 1970. Harpersville, AL, United States.   Height: 6'9".   Weight: 235 lbs.   Drafted: —   College: Middle Tennessee State

YEAR	TEAM	GP	GS	MIN	PTS	FGM	FGA	FG%	3PM	3PA	3P%	FTM	FTA	FT%	ORB	DRB	TRB	AST	PF	DQ	STL	BLK	TO	MPG	PPG	RPG	APG	PCM
93-94	Philadelphia	68	14	884	247	100	169	.592	0	0	.000	47	86	.547	76	157	233	19	129	0	19	23	41	13.0	3.6	3.4	0.3	.387
NBA Season Totals		68	14	884	247	100	169	.592	0	0	.000	47	86	.547	76	157	233	19	129	0	19	23	41	13.0	3.6	3.4	0.3	....

• KIFFIN, Irv
Irvin A. Kiffin Jr.

Born: Aug. 8, 1951. New York, NY, United States.   Height: 6'9".   Weight: 225 lbs.   Drafted: —   College: Oklahoma Baptist

YEAR	TEAM	GP	GS	MIN	PTS	FGM	FGA	FG%	3PM	3PA	3P%	FTM	FTA	FT%	ORB	DRB	TRB	AST	PF	DQ	STL	BLK	TO	MPG	PPG	RPG	APG	PCM
79-80	San Antonio	26	....	212	82	32	96	.333	0	0	.000	18	25	.720	12	28	40	19	43	0	10	2	31	8.2	3.2	1.5	0.7	.195
NBA Season Totals		26	....	212	82	32	96	.333	0	0	.000	18	25	.720	12	28	40	19	43	0	10	2	31	8.2	3.2	1.5	0.7	....

• KILEY, Jack
John F. Kiley

Born: Jan. 5, 1929. Died: Feb.16, 1982.   Height: 6'1".   Weight: 170 lbs.   Drafted: 1951   College: Syracuse

YEAR	TEAM	GP	GS	MIN	PTS	FGM	FGA	FG%	3PM	3PA	3P%	FTM	FTA	FT%	ORB	DRB	TRB	AST	PF	DQ	STL	BLK	TO	MPG	PPG	RPG	APG	PCM
51-52	Fort Wayne	47	....	477	118	44	193	.228	....	....	....	30	54	.556	....	....	49	62	54	2	....	....	....	10.1	2.5	1.0	1.3	.208
52-53	Fort Wayne	6	....	27	6	2	10	.200	....	....	....	2	2	1.000	....	....	2	3	7	0	....	....	....	4.5	1.0	0.3	0.5	.109
NBA Season Totals		53	....	504	124	46	203	.227	....	....	....	32	56	.571	....	....	51	65	61	2	....	....	....	9.5	2.3	1.0	1.2	....
51-52	Fort Wayne	1	....	2	2	1	3	.333	....	....	....	0	0	.000	....	....	0	1	0	0	....	....	....	2.0	2.0	0.0	1.0	.934
NBA Playoff Totals		1	....	2	2	1	3	.333	....	....	....	0	0	.000	....	....	0	1	0	0	....	....	....	2.0	2.0	0.0	1.0	....

• KILLUM, Earnie
Earnest Killum

Born: June 11, 1948.   Height: 6'3".   Weight: 180 lbs.   Drafted: 1970   College: Stetson

YEAR	TEAM	GP	GS	MIN	PTS	FGM	FGA	FG%	3PM	3PA	3P%	FTM	FTA	FT%	ORB	DRB	TRB	AST	PF	DQ	STL	BLK	TO	MPG	PPG	RPG	APG	PCM
70-71	LA Lakers	4	....	12	1	0	4	.000	....	....	....	1	1	1.000	....	....	2	0	1	0	....	....	....	3.0	0.3	0.5	0.0	-.096
NBA Season Totals		4	....	12	1	0	4	.000	....	....	....	1	1	1.000	....	....	2	0	1	0	....	....	....	3.0	0.3	0.5	0.0	....
70-71	LA Lakers	2	....	4	4	1	1	1.000	....	....	....	2	3	.667	....	....	0	0	1	0	....	....	....	2.0	2.0	0.0	0.0	.785
NBA Playoff Totals		2	....	4	4	1	1	1.000	....	....	....	2	3	.667	....	....	0	0	1	0	....	....	....	2.0	2.0	0.0	0.0	....

• KILPATRICK, Carl
Carl Kilpatrick

Born: May 16, 1956. Bastrop, LA, United States.   Height: 6'10".   Weight: 230 lbs.   Drafted: 1978   College: Northeast Louisiana

YEAR	TEAM	GP	GS	MIN	PTS	FGM	FGA	FG%	3PM	3PA	3P%	FTM	FTA	FT%	ORB	DRB	TRB	AST	PF	DQ	STL	BLK	TO	MPG	PPG	RPG	APG	PCM
79-80	Utah	2	....	6	3	1	2	.500	0	0	.000	1	2	.500	1	3	4	0	1	0	0	0	0	3.0	1.5	2.0	0.0	.802
NBA Season Totals		2	....	6	3	1	2	.500	0	0	.000	1	2	.500	1	3	4	0	1	0	0	0	0	3.0	1.5	2.0	0.0	....

• KIMBALL, Toby
Thomas Kimball

Born: Sept. 7, 1942. Framingham, MA, United States.   Height: 6'6".   Weight: 220 lbs.   Drafted: 1965   College: Connecticut

YEAR	TEAM	GP	GS	MIN	PTS	FGM	FGA	FG%	3PM	3PA	3P%	FTM	FTA	FT%	ORB	DRB	TRB	AST	PF	DQ	STL	BLK	TO	MPG	PPG	RPG	APG	PCM
66-67	Boston	38	....	222	97	35	97	.361	....	....	....	27	40	.675	....	....	146	13	42	0	....	....	....	5.8	2.6	3.8	0.3	.710
67-68	San Diego	81	....	2519	889	354	894	.396	....	....	....	181	306	.592	....	....	947	147	273	3	....	....	....	31.1	11.0	11.7	1.8	.489
68-69	San Diego	76	....	1680	595	239	537	.445	....	....	....	117	250	.468	....	....	669	90	216	6	....	....	....	22.1	7.8	8.8	1.2	.514
69-70	San Diego	77	....	1622	543	218	508	.429	....	....	....	107	185	.578	....	....	621	95	187	1	....	....	....	21.1	7.1	8.1	1.2	.508
70-71	San Diego	80	....	1100	273	111	287	.387	....	....	....	51	108	.472	....	....	406	62	128	1	....	....	....	13.8	3.4	5.1	0.8	.420
71-72	Milwaukee	74	....	971	258	107	229	.467	....	....	....	44	81	.543	....	....	312	60	137	0	....	....	....	13.1	3.5	4.2	0.8	.428
72-73	Omaha	67	....	743	236	96	220	.436	....	....	....	44	67	.657	....	....	191	27	86	2	....	....	....	11.1	3.5	2.9	0.4	.374
73-74	Philadelphia	75	....	1592	559	216	456	.474	....	....	....	127	185	.686	185	367	552	73	199	1	49	23	....	21.2	7.5	7.4	1.0	.502
74-75	New Orleans	3	....	90	20	7	23	.304	....	....	....	6	7	.857	8	18	26	4	12	0	2	0	....	30.0	6.7	8.7	1.3	.306
NBA Season Totals		571	....	10539	3470	1383	3251	.425	....	....	....	704	1229	.573	193	385	3870	571	1280	14	51	23	....	18.5	6.1	6.8	1.0	....
66-67	Boston	1	....	4	0	0	2	.000	....	....	....	0	0	.000	....	....	3	0	1	0	....	....	....	4.0	0.0	3.0	0.0	.100
68-69	San Diego	6	....	197	59	23	53	.434	....	....	....	13	25	.520	....	....	74	4	17	0	....	....	....	32.8	9.8	12.3	0.7	.448
71-72	Milwaukee	7	....	36	12	5	12	.417	....	....	....	2	2	1.000	....	....	6	2	3	0	....	....	....	5.1	1.7	0.9	0.3	.336
NBA Playoff Totals		14	....	237	71	28	67	.418	....	....	....	15	27	.556	....	....	83	6	21	0	....	....	....	16.9	5.1	5.9	0.4	....

• KIMBLE, Bo
Gregory Kevin (Bo) Kimble

Born: Apr. 9, 1966. Philadelphia, PA, United States.   Height: 6'4".   Weight: 190 lbs.   Drafted: 1990   College: Loyola Marymount

YEAR	TEAM	GP	GS	MIN	PTS	FGM	FGA	FG%	3PM	3PA	3P%	FTM	FTA	FT%	ORB	DRB	TRB	AST	PF	DQ	STL	BLK	TO	MPG	PPG	RPG	APG	PCM
90-91	LA Clippers	62	22	1004	429	159	418	.380	19	65	.292	92	119	.773	42	77	119	76	158	2	30	8	74	16.2	6.9	1.9	1.2	.259
91-92	LA Clippers	34	0	277	112	44	111	.396	4	13	.308	20	31	.645	13	19	32	17	37	0	10	6	14	8.1	3.3	0.9	0.5	.279
92-93	New York	9	0	55	33	14	33	.424	2	8	.250	3	8	.375	3	8	11	5	10	0	1	0	6	6.1	3.7	1.2	0.6	.349
NBA Season Totals		105	22	1336	574	217	562	.386	25	86	.291	115	158	.728	58	104	162	98	205	2	41	14	94	12.7	5.5	1.5	0.9	....

YEAR	TEAM	GP	GS	MIN	PTS	FGM	FGA	FG%	3PM	3PA	3P%	FTM	FTA	FT%	ORB	DRB	TRB	AST	PF	DQ	STL	BLK	TO	MPG	PPG	RPG	APG	PCM
91-92	LA Clippers	3	0	5	0	0	1	.000	0	0	.000	0	0	.000	0	0	0	1	2	0	0	0	1	1.7	0.0	0.0	0.3	-.343
NBA Playoff Totals		3	0	5	0	0	1	.000	0	0	.000	0	0	.000	0	0	0	1	2	0	0	0	1	1.7	0.0	0.0	0.3	....

• KIMBROUGH, Stan
Stan Kimbrough

Born: Apr. 24, 1966. Tuscaloosa, AL, United States.   Height: 5'11".   Weight: 153 lbs.   Drafted: —   College: Xavier (OH)

YEAR	TEAM	GP	GS	MIN	PTS	FGM	FGA	FG%	3PM	3PA	3P%	FTM	FTA	FT%	ORB	DRB	TRB	AST	PF	DQ	STL	BLK	TO	MPG	PPG	RPG	APG	PCM
89-90	Detroit	10	0	50	16	7	16	.438	0	0	.000	2	2	1.000	4	3	7	5	4	0	4	0	4	5.0	1.6	0.7	0.5	.351
92-93	Sacramento	3	0	15	5	2	6	.333	1	2	.500	0	0	.000	0	0	0	1	1	0	1	0	0	5.0	1.7	0.0	0.3	.187
NBA Season Totals		13	0	65	21	9	22	.409	1	2	.500	2	2	1.000	4	3	7	6	5	0	5	0	4	5.0	1.6	0.5	0.5	....

• KINCH, Chad
Chadwick Oliver Kinch

Born: May 22, 1958. Perth Amboy, NJ, United States. Died: Apr.3, 1994.   Height: 6'4".   Weight: 190 lbs.   Drafted: 1980   College: North Carolina (Charlotte)

YEAR	TEAM	GP	GS	MIN	PTS	FGM	FGA	FG%	3PM	3PA	3P%	FTM	FTA	FT%	ORB	DRB	TRB	AST	PF	DQ	STL	BLK	TO	MPG	PPG	RPG	APG	PCM
80-81	Cleveland	29	....	247	80	38	96	.396	0	0	.000	4	5	.800	7	17	24	35	24	0	9	5	23	8.5	2.8	0.8	1.2	.274
80-81	Dallas	12	....	106	38	14	45	.311	0	0	.000	10	13	.769	0	9	9	10	9	0	2	1	8	8.8	3.2	0.8	0.8	.178
NBA Season Totals		41	....	353	118	52	141	.369	0	0	.000	14	18	.778	7	26	33	45	33	0	11	6	31	8.6	2.9	0.8	1.1	....

• KING, Albert
Albert King

Born: Dec. 17, 1959. Brooklyn, NY, United States.   Height: 6'6".   Weight: 190 lbs.   Drafted: 1981   College: Maryland

YEAR	TEAM	GP	GS	MIN	PTS	FGM	FGA	FG%	3PM	3PA	3P%	FTM	FTA	FT%	ORB	DRB	TRB	AST	PF	DQ	STL	BLK	TO	MPG	PPG	RPG	APG	PCM
81-82	New Jersey	76	52	1694	918	391	812	.482	3	13	.231	133	171	.778	105	207	312	142	261	4	64	36	182	22.3	12.1	4.1	1.9	.447
82-83	New Jersey	79	75	2447	1346	582	1226	.475	6	23	.261	176	227	.775	157	299	456	291	278	5	95	41	245	31.0	17.0	5.8	3.7	.511
83-84	New Jersey	79	53	2103	1165	465	946	.492	3	22	.136	232	295	.786	125	263	388	203	258	6	91	33	205	26.6	14.7	4.9	2.6	.509
84-85	New Jersey	42	7	860	537	226	460	.491	0	8	.000	85	104	.817	70	89	159	58	110	0	41	9	63	20.5	12.8	3.8	1.4	.531
85-86	New Jersey	73	69	1998	1047	438	961	.456	4	23	.174	167	203	.823	116	250	366	181	205	4	58	24	183	27.4	14.3	5.0	2.5	.445
86-87	New Jersey	61	15	1291	582	244	573	.426	13	32	.406	81	100	.810	82	132	214	103	177	5	34	28	104	21.2	9.5	3.5	1.7	.352
87-88	Philadelphia	72	44	1593	517	211	540	.391	17	49	.347	78	103	.757	71	145	216	109	219	4	39	18	94	22.1	7.2	3.0	1.5	.356
88-89	San Antonio	46	11	791	327	141	327	.431	8	32	.250	37	48	.771	33	107	140	79	97	2	27	7	74	17.2	7.1	3.0	1.7	.356
91-92	Washington	6	0	59	31	11	30	.367	2	7	.286	7	8	.875	1	10	11	5	7	0	3	0	2	9.8	5.2	1.8	0.8	.443
NBA Season Totals		534	326	12836	6470	2709	5875	.461	56	209	.268	996	1259	.791	760	1502	2262	1171	1612	30	452	196	1152	24.0	12.1	4.2	2.2	....
81-82	New Jersey	2	2	58	40	18	33	.545	0	0	.000	4	5	.800	3	5	8	6	8	0	5	1	5	29.0	20.0	4.0	3.0	.635
82-83	New Jersey	2	2	68	42	18	38	.474	1	2	.500	5	6	.833	4	4	8	3	12	2	2	0	4	34.0	21.0	4.0	1.5	.394
83-84	New Jersey	11	0	295	138	53	128	.414	0	2	.000	32	46	.696	25	33	58	25	32	0	10	4	23	26.8	12.5	5.3	2.3	.404
84-85	New Jersey	3	3	105	66	28	57	.491	1	1	1.000	9	13	.692	4	19	23	5	14	0	7	2	10	35.0	22.0	7.7	1.7	.537
85-86	New Jersey	3	3	98	41	18	42	.429	1	4	.250	4	4	1.000	8	5	13	10	15	1	2	1	5	32.7	13.7	4.3	3.3	.333
NBA Playoff Totals		21	10	624	327	135	298	.453	3	9	.333	54	74	.730	44	66	110	49	81	3	26	8	47	29.7	15.6	5.2	2.3	....

• KING, Bernard
Bernard (B) King

Born: Dec. 4, 1956. Brooklyn, NY, United States.   Height: 6'7".   Weight: 205 lbs.   Drafted: 1977   College: Tennessee

YEAR	TEAM	GP	GS	MIN	PTS	FGM	FGA	FG%	3PM	3PA	3P%	FTM	FTA	FT%	ORB	DRB	TRB	AST	PF	DQ	STL	BLK	TO	MPG	PPG	RPG	APG	PCM
77-78	New Jersey	79	....	3092	1909	798	1665	.479	....	....	....	313	462	.677	265	486	751	193	302	5	122	36	308	39.1	24.2	9.5	2.4	.549
78-79	New Jersey	82	....	2859	1769	710	1359	.522	....	....	....	349	619	.564	251	418	669	295	326	10	118	39	320	34.9	21.6	8.2	3.6	.594
79-80	Utah	19	....	419	176	71	137	.518	0	0	.000	34	63	.540	24	64	88	52	66	3	7	4	49	22.1	9.3	4.6	2.7	.419
80-81	Golden State	81	....	2914	1771	731	1244	.588	2	6	.333	307	437	.703	178	373	551	287	304	5	72	34	267	36.0	21.9	6.8	3.5	.609
81-82	Golden State	79	77	2861	1833	740	1307	.566	1	5	.200	352	499	.705	140	329	469	282	285	6	78	23	269	36.2	23.2	5.9	3.6	.592
82-83	New York	68	68	2207	1486	603	1142	.528	0	6	.000	280	388	.722	99	227	326	195	233	5	90	13	197	32.5	21.9	4.8	2.9	.575
83-84	New York	77	76	2667	2027	795	1391	.572	0	4	.000	437	552	.779	123	271	394	164	273	2	75	17	200	34.6	26.3	5.1	2.1	.649
84-85	New York	55	55	2063	1809	691	1303	.530	1	10	.100	426	552	.772	114	203	317	204	191	3	71	15	204	37.5	**32.9**	5.8	3.7	.724
86-87	New York	6	4	214	136	52	105	.495	0	0	.000	32	43	.744	13	19	32	19	14	0	2	0	15	35.7	22.7	5.3	3.2	.528
87-88	Washington	69	38	2044	1188	470	938	.501	1	6	.167	247	324	.762	86	194	280	192	202	3	49	10	214	29.6	17.2	4.1	2.8	.462
88-89	Washington	81	....	2559	1674	654	1371	.477	5	30	.167	361	441	.819	133	251	384	294	219	1	64	18	227	31.6	20.7	4.7	3.6	.547
89-90	Washington	82	82	2687	1837	711	1459	.487	3	23	.130	412	513	.803	129	275	404	376	230	1	51	7	246	32.8	22.4	4.9	4.6	.589
90-91	Washington	64	64	2401	1817	713	1511	.472	8	37	.216	383	485	.790	114	205	319	292	187	1	56	16	256	37.5	28.4	5.0	4.6	.573
92-93	New Jersey	32	2	430	223	91	177	.514	2	7	.286	39	57	.684	35	41	76	18	53	0	11	3	22	13.4	7.0	2.4	0.6	.447
NBA Season Totals		874	547	29417	19655	7830	15109	.518	23	134	.172	3972	5444	.730	1704	3356	5060	2863	2885	45	866	230	2794	33.7	22.5	5.8	3.3	....
78-79	New Jersey	2	....	81	52	21	42	.500	....	....	....	10	24	.417	5	6	11	7	10	0	4	0	6	40.5	26.0	5.5	3.5	.471
82-83	New York	6	6	184	141	56	97	.577	1	3	.333	28	35	.800	8	16	24	13	16	0	2	0	10	30.7	23.5	4.0	2.2	.665
83-84	New York	12	12	477	417	162	282	.574	0	1	.000	93	123	.756	28	46	74	36	48	0	14	6	31	39.8	34.8	6.2	3.0	.768
87-88	Washington	5	4	168	69	26	53	.491	0	0	.000	17	21	.810	3	8	11	9	17	0	3	0	14	33.6	13.8	2.2	1.8	.260
92-93	New Jersey	3	1	24	8	4	7	.571	0	0	.000	0	0	.000	1	0	1	0	3	0	1	0	1	8.0	2.7	0.3	0.0	.197
NBA Playoff Totals		28	23	934	687	269	481	.559	1	4	.250	148	203	.729	45	76	121	65	94	0	24	6	62	33.4	24.5	4.3	2.3	....

• KING, Chris
Christopher Donnell King

Born: July 24, 1969. Newton Grove, NC, United States.   Height: 6'8".   Weight: 215 lbs.   Drafted: 1992   College: Wake Forest

YEAR	TEAM	GP	GS	MIN	PTS	FGM	FGA	FG%	3PM	3PA	3P%	FTM	FTA	FT%	ORB	DRB	TRB	AST	PF	DQ	STL	BLK	TO	MPG	PPG	RPG	APG	PCM
93-94	Seattle	15	0	86	55	19	48	.396	2	7	.286	15	26	.577	5	10	15	11	12	0	4	0	12	5.7	3.7	1.0	0.7	.421
95-96	Vancouver	80	66	1930	634	250	585	.427	44	113	.389	90	136	.662	102	183	285	104	163	0	68	33	104	24.1	7.9	3.6	1.3	.309
98-99	Utah	8	0	42	4	2	7	.286	0	0	.000	0	4	.000	1	10	11	1	8	0	2	1	4	5.3	0.5	1.4	0.1	.101
NBA Season Totals		103	66	2058	693	271	640	.423	46	120	.383	105	166	.633	108	203	311	116	183	0	74	34	120	20.0	6.7	3.0	1.1	....
93-94	Seattle	2	0	7	0	0	1	.000	0	0	.000	0	2	.000	0	0	0	0	1	0	1	0	0	3.5	0.0	0.0	0.0	-.197
NBA Playoff Totals		2	0	7	0	0	1	.000	0	0	.000	0	2	.000	0	0	0	0	1	0	1	0	0	3.5	0.0	0.0	0.0	....

• KING, Dan
Daniel King

Born: Jan. 7, 1931. Height: 6'6". Weight: 220 lbs. Drafted: — College: Western Kentucky

YEAR	TEAM	GP	GS	MIN	PTS	FGM	FGA	FG%	3PM	3PA	3P%	FTM	FTA	FT%	ORB	DRB	TRB	AST	PF	DQ	STL	BLK	TO	MPG	PPG	RPG	APG	PCM
54-55	Baltimore	12	....	103	19	7	22	.318	....	....	....	5	10	.500	....	....	25	3	5	0	....	....	....	8.6	1.6	2.1	0.3	.257
NBA Season Totals		12	....	103	19	7	22	.318	....	....	....	5	10	.500	....	....	25	3	5	0	....	....	....	8.6	1.6	2.1	0.3	....

• KING, Dolly
William (Dolly) King

Born: Nov. 15, 1916. Died: Jan.29, 1969. Height: 6'4". Weight: 217 lbs. Drafted: — College: Long Island University

YEAR	TEAM	GP	GS	MIN	PTS	FGM	FGA	FG%	3PM	3PA	3P%	FTM	FTA	FT%	ORB	DRB	TRB	AST	PF	DQ	STL	BLK	TO	MPG	PPG	RPG	APG	PCM
46-47	Rochester-N	41	....	....	164	52	....	....	....	....	....	60	97	.619	....	....	....	....	85	....	....	....	....	....	4.0	....	....	....
48-49	Dayton-N	1	....	....	11	3	....	....	....	....	....	5	7	.714	....	....	....	....	....	....	....	....	....	....	11.0	....	....	....
NBL Season Totals		42	....	....	175	55	....	....	....	....	....	65	104	....	....	....	....	....	85	....	....	....	....	....	4.2	....	....	....
46-47	Rochester-N	11	....	....	91	30	....	....	....	....	....	31	43	.721	....	....	....	....	....	....	....	....	....	....	8.3	....	....	....
NBL Playoff Totals		11	....	....	91	30	....	....	....	....	....	31	43	....	....	....	....	....	....	....	....	....	....	....	8.3	....	....	....

• KING, Frankie
Frankie Alexander King

Born: June 6, 1972. Baxley, GA, United States. Height: 6'1". Weight: 185 lbs. Drafted: 1995 College: Western Carolina

YEAR	TEAM	GP	GS	MIN	PTS	FGM	FGA	FG%	3PM	3PA	3P%	FTM	FTA	FT%	ORB	DRB	TRB	AST	PF	DQ	STL	BLK	TO	MPG	PPG	RPG	APG	PCM
95-96	LA Lakers	6	0	20	7	3	11	.273	0	1	.000	1	3	.333	1	1	2	2	4	0	2	0	2	3.3	1.2	0.3	0.3	.033
96-97	Philadelphia	7	0	59	20	7	17	.412	1	2	.500	5	5	1.000	4	10	14	5	7	0	4	0	3	8.4	2.9	2.0	0.7	.453
NBA Season Totals		13	0	79	27	10	28	.357	1	3	.333	6	8	.750	5	11	16	7	11	0	6	0	5	6.1	2.1	1.2	0.5	....

• KING, George
George Smith (USA) King Jr.

Born: Aug. 16, 1928. Charleston, WV, United States. Height: 6' Weight: 175 lbs. Drafted: 1950 College: Morris-Harvey

YEAR	TEAM	GP	GS	MIN	PTS	FGM	FGA	FG%	3PM	3PA	3P%	FTM	FTA	FT%	ORB	DRB	TRB	AST	PF	DQ	STL	BLK	TO	MPG	PPG	RPG	APG	PCM
51-52	Syracuse	66	....	1889	658	235	579	.406	....	....	....	188	264	.712	....	....	274	244	199	6	....	....	....	28.6	10.0	4.2	3.7	.437
52-53	Syracuse	71	....	2519	794	255	635	.402	....	....	....	284	442	.643	....	....	281	364	244	2	....	....	....	35.5	11.2	4.0	5.1	.413
53-54	Syracuse	72	....	2370	817	280	744	.376	....	....	....	257	410	.627	....	....	268	272	179	2	....	....	....	32.9	11.3	3.7	3.8	.384
54-55	Syracuse	67	....	2015	596	228	605	.377	....	....	....	140	229	.611	....	....	227	331	148	0	....	....	....	30.1	8.9	3.4	4.9	.401
55-56	Syracuse	72	....	2343	744	284	763	.372	....	....	....	176	275	.640	....	....	250	410	150	2	....	....	....	32.5	10.3	3.5	5.7	.420
57-58	Cincinnati	63	....	2272	610	235	645	.364	....	....	....	140	227	.617	....	....	306	337	124	0	....	....	....	36.1	9.7	4.9	5.3	.390
NBA Season Totals		411	....	13408	4219	1517	3971	.382	....	....	....	1185	1847	.642	....	....	1606	1958	1044	12	....	....	....	32.6	10.3	3.9	4.8	....
51-52	Syracuse	6	....	207	57	19	54	.352	....	....	....	19	28	.679	....	....	29	21	17	0	....	....	....	34.5	9.5	4.8	3.5	.341
52-53	Syracuse	2	....	67	22	6	13	.462	....	....	....	10	12	.833	....	....	5	9	12	2	....	....	....	33.5	11.0	2.5	4.5	.403
53-54	Syracuse	10	....	286	88	25	62	.403	....	....	....	38	63	.603	....	....	22	21	30	1	....	....	....	28.6	8.8	2.2	2.1	.297
54-55	Syracuse	11	....	371	127	46	117	.393	....	....	....	35	55	.636	....	....	41	62	33	0	....	....	....	33.7	11.5	3.7	5.6	.436
55-56	Syracuse	8	....	317	116	39	108	.361	....	....	....	38	48	.792	....	....	47	60	16	0	....	....	....	39.6	14.5	5.9	7.5	.516
57-58	Cincinnati	2	....	79	18	7	28	.250	....	....	....	4	6	.667	....	....	5	7	5	0	....	....	....	39.5	9.0	2.5	3.5	.161
NBA Playoff Totals		39	....	1327	428	142	382	.372	....	....	....	144	212	.679	....	....	149	180	113	3	....	....	....	34.0	11.0	3.8	4.6	....

• KING, Gerard
Gerard King

Born: Nov. 25, 1972. Height: 6'9". Weight: 230 lbs. Drafted: — College: Nicholls State

YEAR	TEAM	GP	GS	MIN	PTS	FGM	FGA	FG%	3PM	3PA	3P%	FTM	FTA	FT%	ORB	DRB	TRB	AST	PF	DQ	STL	BLK	TO	MPG	PPG	RPG	APG	PCM
98-99	San Antonio	19	0	63	23	6	14	.429	0	0	.000	11	18	.611	6	8	14	4	12	0	2	1	4	3.3	1.2	0.7	0.2	.372
99-00	Washington	62	28	1060	327	139	277	.502	0	0	.000	49	66	.742	84	166	250	49	132	0	34	15	41	17.1	5.3	4.0	0.8	.398
00-01	Washington	45	3	706	216	90	176	.511	0	0	.000	36	45	.800	39	90	129	31	94	2	14	11	47	15.7	4.8	2.9	0.7	.316
NBA Season Totals		126	31	1829	566	235	467	.503	0	0	.000	96	129	.744	129	264	393	84	238	2	50	27	92	14.5	4.5	3.1	0.7	....
98-99	San Antonio	8	0	14	4	2	4	.500	0	0	.000	0	0	.000	0	4	4	1	2	0	0	1	1	1.8	0.5	0.5	0.1	.429
NBA Playoff Totals		8	0	14	4	2	4	.500	0	0	.000	0	0	.000	0	4	4	1	2	0	0	1	1	1.8	0.5	0.5	0.1	....

• KING, Jim
James Leonard (Country) King

Born: Feb. 7, 1941. Tulsa, OK, United States. Height: 6'2". Weight: 175 lbs. Drafted: 1963 College: Tulsa

YEAR	TEAM	GP	GS	MIN	PTS	FGM	FGA	FG%	3PM	3PA	3P%	FTM	FTA	FT%	ORB	DRB	TRB	AST	PF	DQ	STL	BLK	TO	MPG	PPG	RPG	APG	PCM
63-64	LA Lakers	60	....	762	234	84	198	.424	....	....	....	66	101	.653	....	....	113	110	99	0	....	....	....	12.7	3.9	1.9	1.8	.414
64-65	LA Lakers	77	....	1671	486	184	469	.392	....	....	....	118	151	.781	....	....	214	178	193	2	....	....	....	21.7	6.3	2.8	2.3	.338
65-66	LA Lakers	76	....	1499	570	238	545	.437	....	....	....	94	115	.817	....	....	204	223	181	1	....	....	....	19.7	7.5	2.7	2.9	.454
66-67	San Francisco	67	....	1667	746	286	685	.418	....	....	....	174	221	.787	....	....	319	240	193	5	....	....	....	24.9	11.1	4.8	3.6	.525
67-68	San Francisco	54	....	1743	897	340	800	.425	....	....	....	217	268	.810	....	....	243	226	172	1	....	....	....	32.3	16.6	4.5	4.2	.520
68-69	San Francisco	46	....	1010	352	137	394	.348	....	....	....	78	108	.722	....	....	120	123	99	1	....	....	....	22.0	7.7	2.6	2.7	.323
69-70	San Francisco	3	....	105	49	19	46	.413	....	....	....	11	14	.786	....	....	16	10	8	0	....	....	....	35.0	16.3	5.3	3.3	.435
69-70	Cincinnati	31	....	286	90	34	83	.410	....	....	....	22	27	.815	....	....	46	42	39	0	....	....	....	9.2	2.9	1.5	1.4	.402
70-71	Chicago	55	....	645	264	100	228	.439	....	....	....	64	79	.810	....	....	68	78	55	0	....	....	....	11.7	4.8	1.2	1.4	.420
71-72	Chicago	73	....	1017	413	162	356	.455	....	....	....	89	113	.788	....	....	81	101	103	0	....	....	....	13.9	5.7	1.1	1.4	.369
72-73	Chicago	65	....	785	276	116	263	.441	....	....	....	44	52	.846	....	....	76	81	76	0	....	....	....	12.1	4.2	1.2	1.2	.346
NBA Season Totals		607	....	11190	4377	1700	4067	.418	....	....	....	977	1249	.782	....	....	1500	1412	1218	10	....	....	....	18.4	7.2	2.5	2.3	....
63-64	LA Lakers	4	....	51	12	4	10	.400	....	....	....	4	4	1.000	....	....	4	6	2	0	....	....	....	12.8	3.0	1.0	1.5	.333
64-65	LA Lakers	11	....	184	71	28	63	.444	....	....	....	15	17	.882	....	....	36	24	29	1	....	....	....	16.7	6.5	3.3	2.2	.486
65-66	LA Lakers	13	....	287	82	35	84	.417	....	....	....	12	17	.706	....	....	33	31	40	1	....	....	....	22.1	6.3	2.5	2.4	.312
66-67	San Francisco	15	....	458	244	102	216	.472	....	....	....	40	58	.690	....	....	101	50	59	2	....	....	....	30.5	16.3	6.7	3.3	.574
67-68	San Francisco	9	....	113	44	16	38	.421	....	....	....	12	19	.632	....	....	19	20	15	0	....	....	....	12.6	4.9	2.1	2.2	.503
68-69	San Francisco	6	....	142	72	29	78	.372	....	....	....	14	18	.778	....	....	25	17	10	0	....	....	....	23.7	12.0	4.2	2.8	.464
70-71	Chicago	7	....	147	46	19	45	.422	....	....	....	8	12	.667	....	....	21	27	25	0	....	....	....	21.0	6.6	3.0	3.9	.408

YEAR	TEAM	GP	GS	MIN	PTS	FGM	FGA	FG%	3PM	3PA	3P%	FTM	FTA	FT%	ORB	DRB	TRB	AST	PF	DQ	STL	BLK	TO	MPG	PPG	RPG	APG	PCM
71-72	Chicago	4	....	56	26	11	24	.458	....	....	....	4	4	1.000	....	....	6	5	11	0	....	....	....	14.0	6.5	1.5	1.3	.373
72-73	Chicago	4	....	14	5	2	6	.333	....	....	....	1	2	.500	....	....	1	2	3	0	....	....	....	3.5	1.3	0.3	0.5	.214
NBA Playoff Totals		73	....	1452	602	246	564	.436	....	....	....	110	151	.728	....	....	246	182	194	4	....	....	....	19.9	8.2	3.4	2.5	

• KING, Jimmy

Jimmy Hal King

Born: Aug. 9, 1973. South Bend, IN, United States.   Height: 6'5".   Weight: 210 lbs.   Drafted: 1995   College: Michigan

YEAR	TEAM	GP	GS	MIN	PTS	FGM	FGA	FG%	3PM	3PA	3P%	FTM	FTA	FT%	ORB	DRB	TRB	AST	PF	DQ	STL	BLK	TO	MPG	PPG	RPG	APG	PCM
95-96	Toronto	62	1	868	279	110	255	.431	5	34	.147	54	77	.701	43	67	110	88	76	0	21	13	62	14.0	4.5	1.8	1.4	.307
96-97	Denver	2	0	22	6	2	6	.333	0	0	.000	2	4	.500	2	0	2	2	2	0	3	0	1	11.0	3.0	1.0	1.0	.285
NBA Season Totals		64	1	890	285	112	261	.429	5	34	.147	56	81	.691	45	67	112	90	78	0	24	13	63	13.9	4.5	1.8	1.4	

• KING, LeRoy

LeRoy King

Born: 1921.   Height: 6'7".   Weight: 200 lbs.   Drafted: —   College: Monmouth

YEAR	TEAM	GP	GS	MIN	PTS	FGM	FGA	FG%	3PM	3PA	3P%	FTM	FTA	FT%	ORB	DRB	TRB	AST	PF	DQ	STL	BLK	TO	MPG	PPG	RPG	APG	PCM
47-48	Rochester-N	12	....	....	12	3	....	....	....	....	....	6	8	.750	....	....	....	....	....	....	....	....	....	....	1.0	....	....	....
NBL Season Totals		12	....	....	12	3	....	....	....	....	....	6	8	....	....	....	....	....	....	....	....	....	....	....	1.0	....	....	....

• KING, Loyd

Loyd Harold King

Born: May 29, 1949. Asheville, NC, United States.   Height: 6'2".   Weight: 180 lbs.   Drafted: 1971   College: Virginia Tech

YEAR	TEAM	GP	GS	MIN	PTS	FGM	FGA	FG%	3PM	3PA	3P%	FTM	FTA	FT%	ORB	DRB	TRB	AST	PF	DQ	STL	BLK	TO	MPG	PPG	RPG	APG	PCM
71-72	Memphis-A	74	....	1153	487	185	494	.374	21	87	.241	96	119	.807	36	77	113	103	76	2	....	....	76	15.6	6.6	1.5	1.4	.335
72-73	Memphis-A	10	....	102	19	6	29	.207	0	3	.000	7	8	.875	2	10	12	14	20	0	....	....	4	10.2	1.9	1.2	1.4	.148
ABA Season Totals		84	....	1255	506	191	523	.365	21	90	.233	103	127	.811	38	87	125	117	96	2	....	....	80	14.9	6.0	1.5	1.4	

• KING, Maury

Maurice E. King

Born: Mar. 12, 1935.   Height: 6'2".   Weight: 195 lbs.   Drafted: 1957   College: Kansas

YEAR	TEAM	GP	GS	MIN	PTS	FGM	FGA	FG%	3PM	3PA	3P%	FTM	FTA	FT%	ORB	DRB	TRB	AST	PF	DQ	STL	BLK	TO	MPG	PPG	RPG	APG	PCM
59-60	Boston	1	....	19	10	5	8	.625	....	....	....	0	1	.000	....	....	4	2	3	0	....	....	....	19.0	10.0	4.0	2.0	.617
62-63	Chicago	37	....	954	216	94	241	.390	....	....	....	28	34	.824	....	....	102	142	87	0	....	....	....	25.8	5.8	2.8	3.8	.331
NBA Season Totals		38	....	973	226	99	249	.398	....	....	....	28	35	.800	....	....	106	144	90	0	....	....	....	25.6	5.9	2.8	3.8	

• KING, Reggie

Reginald Biddings (Reggie) King

Born: Feb. 14, 1957. Birmingham, AL, United States.   Height: 6'6".   Weight: 225 lbs.   Drafted: 1979   College: Alabama

YEAR	TEAM	GP	GS	MIN	PTS	FGM	FGA	FG%	3PM	3PA	3P%	FTM	FTA	FT%	ORB	DRB	TRB	AST	PF	DQ	STL	BLK	TO	MPG	PPG	RPG	APG	PCM
79-80	Kansas City	82	....	2052	673	257	499	.515	0	1	.000	159	219	.726	184	382	566	106	230	2	69	31	98	25.0	8.2	6.9	1.3	.464
80-81	Kansas City	81	....	2743	1208	472	867	.544	0	0	.000	264	386	.684	235	551	786	122	227	2	102	41	162	33.9	14.9	9.7	1.5	.554
81-82	Kansas City	80	76	2609	967	383	752	.509	0	0	.000	201	285	.705	162	361	523	173	221	6	84	29	152	32.6	12.1	6.5	2.2	.429
82-83	Kansas City	58	5	995	284	104	225	.462	0	0	.000	73	96	.760	91	149	240	58	94	1	28	11	64	17.2	4.8	4.1	1.0	.379
83-84	Seattle	77	42	2086	602	233	448	.520	0	2	.000	136	206	.660	134	336	470	179	159	2	54	24	123	27.1	7.8	6.1	2.3	.423
84-85	Seattle	60	5	860	167	63	149	.423	0	0	.000	41	59	.695	44	78	122	53	74	1	28	11	42	14.3	2.8	2.0	0.9	.246
NBA Season Totals		438	128	11345	3898	1512	2940	.514	0	3	.000	874	1251	.699	850	1857	2707	691	1005	14	365	147	641	25.9	8.9	6.2	1.6	
79-80	Kansas City	3	....	77	25	10	21	.476	0	0	.000	5	9	.556	7	18	25	4	10	0	1	0	2	25.7	8.3	8.3	1.3	.452
80-81	Kansas City	15	....	620	319	122	248	.492	0	1	.000	75	102	.735	56	93	149	25	49	0	18	10	35	41.3	21.3	9.9	1.7	.526
83-84	Seattle	5	0	91	10	5	12	.417	0	0	.000	0	0	.000	6	11	17	6	14	0	2	3	7	18.2	2.0	3.4	1.2	.191
NBA Playoff Totals		23	0	788	354	137	281	.488	0	1	.000	80	111	.721	69	122	191	35	73	0	21	13	44	34.3	15.4	8.3	1.5	

• KING, Rich

Richard Thomas (Rich) King

Born: Apr. 4, 1969. Lincoln, NE, United States.   Height: 7'2".   Weight: 260 lbs.   Drafted: 1991   College: Nebraska

YEAR	TEAM	GP	GS	MIN	PTS	FGM	FGA	FG%	3PM	3PA	3P%	FTM	FTA	FT%	ORB	DRB	TRB	AST	PF	DQ	STL	BLK	TO	MPG	PPG	RPG	APG	PCM
91-92	Seattle	40	2	213	88	27	71	.380	0	1	.000	34	45	.756	20	29	49	12	42	0	4	5	20	5.3	2.2	1.2	0.3	.332
92-93	Seattle	3	0	12	6	2	5	.400	0	0	.000	2	2	1.000	1	4	5	1	1	0	0	0	3	4.0	2.0	1.7	0.3	.472
93-94	Seattle	27	0	78	41	15	34	.441	0	1	.000	11	22	.500	9	11	20	8	18	0	1	2	8	2.9	1.5	0.7	0.3	.419
94-95	Seattle	2	0	6	0	0	2	.000	0	0	.000	0	2	.000	0	0	0	0	1	0	0	0	0	3.0	0.0	0.0	0.0	-.547
NBA Season Totals		72	2	309	135	44	112	.393	0	2	.000	47	71	.662	30	44	74	21	62	0	5	7	31	4.3	1.9	1.0	0.3	

• KING, Ron

Ron King

Born: July 11, 1951. Louisville, KY, United States.   Height: 6'4".   Weight: 185 lbs.   Drafted: 1973   College: Florida State

YEAR	TEAM	GP	GS	MIN	PTS	FGM	FGA	FG%	3PM	3PA	3P%	FTM	FTA	FT%	ORB	DRB	TRB	AST	PF	DQ	STL	BLK	TO	MPG	PPG	RPG	APG	PCM
73-74	Kentucky-A	9	....	126	64	24	70	.343	2	6	.333	14	17	.824	8	11	19	14	14	....	5	2	7	14.0	7.1	2.1	1.6	.393
ABA Season Totals		9	....	126	64	24	70	.343	2	6	.333	14	17	.824	8	11	19	14	14	....	5	2	7	14.0	7.1	2.1	1.6	

• KING, Stacey

Ronald Stacey King

Born: Jan. 29, 1967. Lawton, OK, United States.   Height: 6'11".   Weight: 230 lbs.   Drafted: 1989   College: Oklahoma

YEAR	TEAM	GP	GS	MIN	PTS	FGM	FGA	FG%	3PM	3PA	3P%	FTM	FTA	FT%	ORB	DRB	TRB	AST	PF	DQ	STL	BLK	TO	MPG	PPG	RPG	APG	PCM
89-90	Chicago	82	2	1777	728	267	530	.504	0	1	.000	194	267	.727	169	215	384	87	215	0	38	58	123	21.7	8.9	4.7	1.1	.435
90-91	Chicago	76	6	1198	419	156	334	.467	0	2	.000	107	152	.704	72	136	208	65	134	0	24	42	91	15.8	5.5	2.7	0.9	.342
91-92	Chicago	79	12	1268	551	215	425	.506	2	5	.400	119	158	.753	87	118	205	77	129	0	21	25	79	16.1	7.0	2.6	1.0	.410
92-93	Chicago	76	3	1059	408	160	340	.471	2	6	.333	86	122	.705	105	102	207	71	128	0	26	20	68	13.9	5.4	2.7	0.9	.389
93-94	Chicago	31	15	537	172	68	171	.398	0	2	.000	36	53	.679	50	82	132	39	64	1	18	12	43	17.3	5.5	4.3	1.3	.357
93-94	Minnesota	18	15	516	213	78	170	.459	0	0	.000	57	83	.687	40	69	109	19	57	0	13	30	40	28.7	11.8	6.1	1.1	.414
94-95	Minnesota	50	10	792	266	99	212	.467	0	1	.000	68	102	.667	54	111	165	26	126	1	24	20	65	15.8	5.3	3.3	0.5	.313

YEAR	TEAM	GP	GS	MIN	PTS	FGM	FGA	FG%	3PM	3PA	3P%	FTM	FTA	FT%	ORB	DRB	TRB	AST	PF	DQ	STL	BLK	TO	MPG	PPG	RPG	APG	PCM
95-96	Miami	15	0	156	38	17	36	.472	0	0	.000	4	8	.500	9	14	23	2	39	2	7	2	18	10.4	2.5	1.5	0.1	.098
96-97	Boston	5	0	33	12	5	7	.714	0	0	.000	2	3	.667	1	8	9	1	3	0	1	1	6.6	2.4	1.8	0.2	.537
96-97	Dallas	6	0	70	12	6	15	.400	0	0	.000	0	4	.000	10	8	18	0	11	0	2	0	5	11.7	2.0	3.0	0.0	.151
NBA Season Totals		438	63	7406	2819	1071	2240	.478	4	17	.235	673	952	.707	597	863	1460	387	906	4	173	210	533	16.9	6.4	3.3	0.9	....
89-90	Chicago	16	2	281	110	37	91	.407	0	1	.000	36	47	.766	17	34	51	9	32	0	6	8	17	17.6	6.9	3.2	0.6	.334
90-91	Chicago	11	0	86	23	8	27	.296	0	1	.000	7	11	.636	9	13	22	2	15	0	1	1	9	7.8	2.1	2.0	0.2	.146
91-92	Chicago	14	0	111	53	18	40	.450	2	2	1.000	15	23	.652	7	13	20	5	12	0	5	2	10	7.9	3.8	1.4	0.4	.400
92-93	Chicago	19	0	229	77	26	66	.394	0	0	.000	25	31	.806	20	20	40	14	38	0	9	4	14	12.1	4.1	2.1	0.7	.308
95-96	Miami	1	0	12	1	0	3	.000	0	0	.000	1	2	.500	0	3	3	1	1	0	0	0	0	12.0	1.0	3.0	1.0	.093
NBA Playoff Totals		61	2	719	264	89	227	.392	2	4	.500	84	114	.737	53	83	136	31	98	0	21	15	50	11.8	4.3	2.2	0.5	....

• KING, Tom

Thomas Van Dyke King

Born: Mar. 9, 1924.   Height: 6'   Weight: 165 lbs.   Drafted: —   College: Michigan

YEAR	TEAM	GP	GS	MIN	PTS	FGM	FGA	FG%	3PM	3PA	3P%	FTM	FTA	FT%	ORB	DRB	TRB	AST	PF	DQ	STL	BLK	TO	MPG	PPG	RPG	APG	PCM
46-47	Detroit	58	....	....	295	97	410	.237	....	....	....	101	160	.631				32	102						5.1	....	0.6	....
NBA Season Totals		58	....	....	295	97	410	.237	....	....	....	101	160	.631				32	102						5.1	....	0.6	....

• KING, Willie

Willie King

Born: —.   Height: 5'7".   Weight: —   Drafted: —   College: none

YEAR	TEAM	GP	GS	MIN	PTS	FGM	FGA	FG%	3PM	3PA	3P%	FTM	FTA	FT%	ORB	DRB	TRB	AST	PF	DQ	STL	BLK	TO	MPG	PPG	RPG	APG	PCM
46-47	Detroit-N	14	....	....	115	42						31	49	.633					31						8.2	....	....
NBL Season Totals		14	....	....	115	42						31	49						31						8.2	....	....

• KINNEY, Bob

Robert Paul (Hi-Pocket, Bat-em Bob) Kinney

Born: Sept. 16, 1920. Fort Scott, KS, United States. Died: Sept.2, 1985.   Height: 6'6".   Weight: 215 lbs.   Drafted: —   College: Rice

YEAR	TEAM	GP	GS	MIN	PTS	FGM	FGA	FG%	3PM	3PA	3P%	FTM	FTA	FT%	ORB	DRB	TRB	AST	PF	DQ	STL	BLK	TO	MPG	PPG	RPG	APG	PCM
45-46	Fort Wayne-N	13	....	....	34	16						2													2.6	....	....
46-47	Fort Wayne-N	44	....	....	246	102						42	84	.500				....	129						5.6	....	....
47-48	Fort Wayne-N	58	....	....	390	149						92	147	.626				....	192						6.7	....	....
48-49	Fort Wayne	37	....	....	254	86	271	.317				82	143	.573				51	135						6.9	....	1.4	....
48-49	Boston	21	....	....	204	75	224	.335				54	91	.593				26	89						9.7	....	1.2	....
49-50	Boston	60	....	....	667	233	621	.375				201	320	.628				100	251						11.1	....	1.7	....
NBA Season Totals		118	....	....	1125	394	1116	.353				337	554	.608				177	475						9.5	....	1.5	....
NBL Season Totals		115	....	....	670	267						136	231					....	321						5.8	....	....
Career Totals		233	....	....	1795	661	1116					473	785					177	796						7.7	....	0.8	....
45-46	Fort Wayne-N	3	....	....	11	5						1	2	.500											3.7	....	....
46-47	Fort Wayne-N	8	....	....	53	18						17	22	.773											6.6	....	....
47-48	Fort Wayne-N	4	....	....	43	20						3	8	.375											10.8	....	....
NBL Playoff Totals		15	....	....	107	43						21	32												7.1	....	....

• KINNEY, Joe

Joe Kinney

Born: —.   Height: 6'6".   Weight: —   Drafted: —   College: West Virginia Wesleyan

YEAR	TEAM	GP	GS	MIN	PTS	FGM	FGA	FG%	3PM	3PA	3P%	FTM	FTA	FT%	ORB	DRB	TRB	AST	PF	DQ	STL	BLK	TO	MPG	PPG	RPG	APG	PCM
38-39	Pittsburgh-N	2	....	....	3	1						1													1.5	....	....
NBL Season Totals		2	....	....	3	1						1													1.5	....	....

• KIRILENKO, Andrei

Andrei Kirilenko

Born: Feb. 18, 1981. Moscow, Russia.   Height: 6'9".   Weight: 220 lbs.   Drafted: 1999   College: none

YEAR	TEAM	GP	GS	MIN	PTS	FGM	FGA	FG%	3PM	3PA	3P%	FTM	FTA	FT%	ORB	DRB	TRB	AST	PF	DQ	STL	BLK	TO	MPG	PPG	RPG	APG	PCM
01-02	Utah	82	40	2151	880	285	633	.450	25	100	.250	285	371	.768	149	253	402	94	156	2	116	159	108	26.2	10.7	4.9	1.1	.499
02-03	Utah	80	11	2213	963	315	642	.491	37	114	.325	296	370	.800	147	273	420	138	185	0	118	175	136	27.7	12.0	5.3	1.7	.553
NBA Season Totals		162	51	4364	1843	600	1275	.471	62	214	.290	581	741	.784	296	526	822	232	341	2	234	334	244	26.9	11.4	5.1	1.4	....
01-02	Utah	4	4	122	35	11	28	.393	0	4	.000	13	16	.813	4	11	15	4	10	0	7	10	6	30.5	8.8	3.8	1.0	.341
02-03	Utah	5	0	145	58	18	43	.419	1	7	.143	21	24	.875	8	16	24	7	6	0	3	10	6	29.0	11.6	4.8	1.4	.462
NBA Playoff Totals		9	4	267	93	29	71	.408	1	11	.091	34	40	.850	12	27	39	11	16	0	10	20	12	29.7	10.3	4.3	1.2	....

• KIRK, Walt

Walton (Junior) Kirk Jr.

Born: Sept. 3, 1924. Mount Vernon, IL, United States.   Height: 6'3".   Weight: 173 lbs.   Drafted: —   College: Illinois

YEAR	TEAM	GP	GS	MIN	PTS	FGM	FGA	FG%	3PM	3PA	3P%	FTM	FTA	FT%	ORB	DRB	TRB	AST	PF	DQ	STL	BLK	TO	MPG	PPG	RPG	APG	PCM
47-48	Fort Wayne-N	45	....	....	168	62						44	90	.489				....	84						3.7	....	....
48-49	Fort Wayne	14	....	....	69	22	61	.361				25	33	.758				12	24						4.9	....	0.9	....
48-49	Indianapolis	35	....	....	378	118	345	.342				142	198	.717				106	103						10.8	....	3.0	....
49-50	Anderson	26	....	....	119	31	125	.248				57	83	.687				43	63						4.6	....	1.7	....
49-50	Tri-Cities	32	....	....	230	66	236	.280				98	133	.737				60	92						7.2	....	1.9	....
51-52	Milwaukee	11	....	396	111	28	101	.277				55	78	.705			44	28	47	3				36.0	10.1	4.0	2.5	.257
NBA Season Totals		118	....	396	907	265	868	.305				377	525	.718			44	249	329	3				3.4	7.7	0.4	2.1	....
NBL Season Totals		45	....	....	168	62						44	90					....	84						3.7	....	....
Career Totals		163	....	396	1075	327	868					421	615				44	249	413	3				2.4	6.6	0.3	1.5	....

YEAR	TEAM	GP	GS	MIN	PTS	FGM	FGA	FG%	3PM	3PA	3P%	FTM	FTA	FT%	ORB	DRB	TRB	AST	PF	DQ	STL	BLK	TO	MPG	PPG	RPG	APG	PCM
47-48	Fort Wayne-N	3	....	....	7	3	....	....	....	....	....	1	6	.167	....	....	....	....	....	....	....	....	....	....	2.3	....	....	....
49-50	Tri-Cities	3	....	....	5	2	7	.286	....	....	....	1	6	.167	....	....	....	1	8	....	....	....	....	....	1.7	....	0.3	....
NBA Playoff Totals		3	....	....	5	2	7	.286	....	....	....	1	6	.167	....	....	....	1	8	....	....	....	....	....	1.7	....	0.3	....
NBL Playoff Totals		3	....	....	7	3	....	....	....	....	....	1	6		....	....	....	....	....	....	....	....	....	....	2.3	....	....	....
Career Playoff Totals		6	....	....	12	5	7	....	....	....	....	2	12		....	....	....	1	8	....	....	....	....	....	2.0	....	0.2	....

• KIRKLAND, Wilber

Wilber Kirkland

Born: 1947.　　Height: 6'7".　　Weight: 190 lbs.　　Drafted: —　　College: Cheyney State

YEAR	TEAM	GP	GS	MIN	PTS	FGM	FGA	FG%	3PM	3PA	3P%	FTM	FTA	FT%	ORB	DRB	TRB	AST	PF	DQ	STL	BLK	TO	MPG	PPG	RPG	APG	PCM
69-70	Pittsburgh-A	2	....	27	6	3	7	.429	0	0	.000	0	0	.000	1	10	11	1	5	0	....	....	2	13.5	3.0	5.5	0.5	.408
ABA Season Totals		2	....	27	6	3	7	.429	0	0	.000	0	0	.000	1	10	11	1	5	0	....	....	2	13.5	3.0	5.5	0.5	....

• KISSANE, Jim

James J. Kissane Jr.

Born: Aug. 17, 1946. New Hyde Park, NY, United States.　　Height: 6'7".　　Weight: 210 lbs.　　Drafted: 1968　　College: Boston College

YEAR	TEAM	GP	GS	MIN	PTS	FGM	FGA	FG%	3PM	3PA	3P%	FTM	FTA	FT%	ORB	DRB	TRB	AST	PF	DQ	STL	BLK	TO	MPG	PPG	RPG	APG	PCM
68-69	Minnesota-A	2	....	15	6	2	6	.333	0	0	.000	2	2	1.000	0	3	3	0	3	0	....	....	1	7.5	3.0	1.5	0.0	.257
ABA Season Totals		2	....	15	6	2	6	.333	0	0	.000	2	2	1.000	0	3	3	0	3	0	....	....	1	7.5	3.0	1.5	0.0	....

• KISTLER, Doug

Douglas C. Kistler

Born: Mar. 21, 1938. Died: Feb.29, 1980.　　Height: 6'9".　　Weight: 210 lbs.　　Drafted: 1961　　College: Duke

YEAR	TEAM	GP	GS	MIN	PTS	FGM	FGA	FG%	3PM	3PA	3P%	FTM	FTA	FT%	ORB	DRB	TRB	AST	PF	DQ	STL	BLK	TO	MPG	PPG	RPG	APG	PCM
61-62	New York	5	....	13	8	3	6	.500	....	....	....	2	4	.500	....	....	1	0	2	0	....	....	....	2.6	1.6	0.2	0.0	.375
NBA Season Totals		5	....	13	8	3	6	.500	....	....	....	2	4	.500	....	....	1	0	2	0	....	....	....	2.6	1.6	0.2	0.0	....

• KITCHEN, Curtis

Curtis Kitchen

Born: Jan. 30, 1964. Cape Coral, FL, United States.　　Height: 6'9".　　Weight: 235 lbs.　　Drafted: 1986　　College: South Florida

YEAR	TEAM	GP	GS	MIN	PTS	FGM	FGA	FG%	3PM	3PA	3P%	FTM	FTA	FT%	ORB	DRB	TRB	AST	PF	DQ	STL	BLK	TO	MPG	PPG	RPG	APG	PCM
86-87	Seattle	6	0	31	9	3	6	.500	0	1	.000	3	4	.750	4	5	9	1	4	0	2	3	0	5.2	1.5	1.5	0.2	.580
NBA Season Totals		6	0	31	9	3	6	.500	0	1	.000	3	4	.750	4	5	9	1	4	0	2	3	0	5.2	1.5	1.5	0.2	....
86-87	Seattle	8	0	23	2	1	2	.500	0	0	.000	0	4	.000	2	4	6	0	7	0	0	2	0	2.9	0.3	0.8	0.0	.148
NBA Playoff Totals		8	0	23	2	1	2	.500	0	0	.000	0	4	.000	2	4	6	0	7	0	0	2	0	2.9	0.3	0.8	0.0	....

• KITE, Greg

Gregory Fuller Kite

Born: Aug. 5, 1961. Houston, TX, United States.　　Height: 6'11".　　Weight: 250 lbs.　　Drafted: 1983　　College: Brigham Young

YEAR	TEAM	GP	GS	MIN	PTS	FGM	FGA	FG%	3PM	3PA	3P%	FTM	FTA	FT%	ORB	DRB	TRB	AST	PF	DQ	STL	BLK	TO	MPG	PPG	RPG	APG	PCM
83-84	Boston	35	0	197	65	30	66	.455	0	0	.000	5	16	.313	27	35	62	7	42	0	1	5	21	5.6	1.9	1.8	0.2	.295
84-85	Boston	55	4	424	88	33	88	.375	0	0	.000	22	32	.688	38	51	89	17	84	3	3	10	28	7.7	1.6	1.6	0.3	.189
85-86	Boston	64	2	464	83	34	91	.374	0	1	.000	15	39	.385	35	93	128	17	81	1	3	28	32	7.3	1.3	2.0	0.3	.253
86-87	Boston	74	1	745	123	47	110	.427	0	1	.000	29	76	.382	61	108	169	27	148	2	17	46	37	10.1	1.7	2.3	0.4	.247
87-88	Boston	13	0	86	19	9	23	.391	0	0	.000	1	6	.167	10	14	24	2	16	0	3	8	9	6.6	1.5	1.8	0.2	.262
87-88	LA Clippers	40	19	977	205	83	182	.456	0	1	.000	39	73	.534	75	165	240	45	137	1	16	50	64	24.4	5.1	6.0	1.1	.314
88-89	LA Clippers	58	12	729	112	49	121	.405	0	0	.000	14	31	.452	66	124	190	29	118	0	23	46	46	12.6	1.9	3.3	0.5	.290
88-89	Charlotte	12	12	213	38	16	30	.533	0	0	.000	6	10	.600	15	38	53	7	43	1	4	8	12	17.8	3.2	4.4	0.6	.281
89-90	Sacramento	71	47	1515	230	101	234	.432	1	1	1.000	27	54	.500	131	246	377	76	201	2	31	51	78	21.3	3.2	5.3	1.1	.288
90-91	Orlando	82	82	2225	395	166	338	.491	0	0	.000	63	123	.512	189	399	588	59	298	4	25	81	98	27.1	4.8	7.2	0.7	.309
91-92	Orlando	72	44	1479	228	94	215	.437	0	1	.000	40	68	.588	156	246	402	44	212	2	30	57	58	20.5	3.2	5.6	0.6	.305
92-93	Orlando	64	1	640	89	38	84	.452	0	1	.000	13	24	.542	66	127	193	10	133	1	13	12	32	10.0	1.4	3.0	0.2	.255
93-94	Orlando	29	0	309	34	13	35	.371	0	0	.000	8	22	.364	22	48	70	4	61	0	2	12	17	10.7	1.2	2.4	0.1	.146
94-95	New York	2	0	16	0	0	3	.000	0	0	.000	0	0	.000	2	2	4	0	2	0	0	0	1	8.0	0.0	2.0	0.0	-.059
94-95	Indiana	9	0	61	8	3	14	.214	0	0	.000	2	10	.200	10	8	18	1	13	0	0	0	5	6.8	0.9	2.0	0.1	.018
NBA Season Totals		680	225	10080	1717	716	1634	.438	1	6	.167	284	584	.486	903	1704	2607	345	1589	17	171	414	538	14.8	2.5	3.8	0.5	....
83-84	Boston	11	0	38	7	1	8	.125	0	0	.000	5	6	.833	5	4	9	3	9	0	0	1	3	3.5	0.6	0.8	0.3	.146
84-85	Boston	9	0	63	11	5	12	.417	0	0	.000	1	2	.500	5	11	16	3	13	0	1	0	2	7.0	1.2	1.8	0.3	.240
85-86	Boston	13	0	78	18	7	10	.700	0	0	.000	4	7	.571	5	14	19	3	20	0	2	4	3	6.0	1.4	1.5	0.2	.361
86-87	Boston	20	1	172	17	7	20	.350	0	0	.000	3	7	.429	15	31	46	8	43	1	2	8	7	8.6	0.9	2.3	0.4	.216
94-95	Indiana	8	0	27	4	1	3	.333	0	0	.000	2	2	1.000	3	4	7	0	9	0	1	0	2	3.4	0.5	0.9	0.0	.131
NBA Playoff Totals		61	1	378	57	21	53	.396	0	0	.000	15	24	.625	33	64	97	17	94	1	6	13	17	6.2	0.9	1.6	0.3	....

• KITTERMAN, Bob

Bob Kitterman

Born: 1925.　　Height: 6'　　Weight: 180 lbs.　　Drafted: —　　College: —

YEAR	TEAM	GP	GS	MIN	PTS	FGM	FGA	FG%	3PM	3PA	3P%	FTM	FTA	FT%	ORB	DRB	TRB	AST	PF	DQ	STL	BLK	TO	MPG	PPG	RPG	APG	PCM
47-48	Syracuse-N	54	....	....	272	117	....	....	....	....	....	38	53	.717	....	....	....	58	....	....	....	....	....	5.0	....	....	....
NBL Season Totals		54	....	....	272	117	....	....	....	....	....	38	53		....	....	....	58	....	....	....	....	....	5.0	....	....	....
47-48	Syracuse-N	3	....	....	12	5	....	....	....	....	....	2	2	1.000	....	....	....	....	....	....	....	....	....	4.0	....	....	....
NBL Playoff Totals		3	....	....	12	5	....	....	....	....	....	2	2		....	....	....	....	....	....	....	....	....	4.0	....	....	....

• KITTLES, Kerry

Kerry Kittles

Born: June 12, 1974. Dayton, OH, United States.　　Height: 6'5".　　Weight: 179 lbs.　　Drafted: 1996　　College: Villanova

YEAR	TEAM	GP	GS	MIN	PTS	FGM	FGA	FG%	3PM	3PA	3P%	FTM	FTA	FT%	ORB	DRB	TRB	AST	PF	DQ	STL	BLK	TO	MPG	PPG	RPG	APG	PCM
96-97	New Jersey	82	57	3012	1347	507	1189	.426	158	419	.377	175	227	.771	106	213	319	249	165	1	157	35	123	36.7	16.4	3.9	3.0	.411
97-98	New Jersey	77	76	2814	1328	508	1154	.440	110	263	.418	202	250	.808	132	230	362	176	152	0	132	37	108	36.5	17.2	4.7	2.3	.435
98-99	New Jersey	46	40	1570	592	227	613	.370	50	158	.316	88	114	.772	52	139	191	116	82	0	79	26	66	34.1	12.9	4.2	2.5	.340

YEAR	TEAM	GP	GS	MIN	PTS	FGM	FGA	FG%	3PM	3PA	3P%	FTM	FTA	FT%	ORB	DRB	TRB	AST	PF	DQ	STL	BLK	TO	MPG	PPG	RPG	APG	PCM
99-00	New Jersey	62	61	1896	807	305	698	.437	96	240	.400	101	127	.795	46	179	225	142	120	0	79	19	56	30.6	13.0	3.6	2.3	.412
01-02	New Jersey	82	82	2601	1102	438	940	.466	98	242	.405	128	172	.744	68	207	275	216	108	0	130	31	109	31.7	13.4	3.4	2.6	.427
02-03	New Jersey	65	57	1951	848	332	711	.467	78	219	.356	106	135	.785	52	200	252	170	110	1	101	30	55	30.0	13.0	3.9	2.6	.474
NBA Season Totals		414	373	13844	6024	2317	5305	.437	590	1541	.383	800	1025	.780	456	1168	1624	1069	737	2	678	178	517	33.4	14.6	3.9	2.6	....
97-98	New Jersey	3	3	126	49	17	40	.425	5	13	.385	10	11	.909	0	15	15	8	12	1	4	2	7	42.0	16.3	5.0	2.7	.345
01-02	New Jersey	20	20	580	241	94	216	.435	18	68	.265	35	45	.778	19	44	63	45	37	0	32	9	17	29.0	12.1	3.2	2.3	.409
02-03	New Jersey	20	20	613	216	79	200	.395	26	63	.413	32	42	.762	19	51	70	40	39	0	29	5	17	30.7	10.8	3.5	2.0	.337
NBA Playoff Totals		43	43	1319	506	190	456	.417	49	144	.340	77	98	.786	38	110	148	93	88	1	65	16	41	30.7	11.8	3.4	2.2	....

• KLEIN, Dick

Dick Klein

Born: 1920. Died: Oct.12, 2000. Height: 6'3". Weight: 215 lbs. Drafted: — College: Northwestern

YEAR	TEAM	GP	GS	MIN	PTS	FGM	FGA	FG%	3PM	3PA	3P%	FTM	FTA	FT%	ORB	DRB	TRB	AST	PF	DQ	STL	BLK	TO	MPG	PPG	RPG	APG	PCM
45-46	Chicago-N	15	....	....	73	30	....	....	....	....	....	13	....	....	....	....	....	....	....	....	....	....	....	....	4.9	....	....	....
NBL Season Totals		15	....	....	73	30	....	....	....	....	....	13	....	....	....	....	....	....	....	....	....	....	....	....	4.9	....	....	....

• KLEINE, Joe

Joseph William Kleine

Born: Jan. 4, 1962. Colorado Springs, CO, United States. Height: 6'11". Weight: 255 lbs. Drafted: 1985 College: Arkansas

YEAR	TEAM	GP	GS	MIN	PTS	FGM	FGA	FG%	3PM	3PA	3P%	FTM	FTA	FT%	ORB	DRB	TRB	AST	PF	DQ	STL	BLK	TO	MPG	PPG	RPG	APG	PCM
85-86	Sacramento	80	18	1180	414	160	344	.465	0	0	.000	94	130	.723	113	260	373	46	224	1	24	34	104	14.8	5.2	4.7	0.6	.403
86-87	Sacramento	79	31	1658	622	256	543	.471	0	1	.000	110	140	.786	173	310	483	71	213	2	35	30	87	21.0	7.9	6.1	0.9	.450
87-88	Sacramento	82	60	1999	801	324	686	.472	0	0	.000	153	188	.814	179	400	579	93	228	1	28	59	107	24.4	9.8	7.1	1.1	.481
88-89	Sacramento	47	11	913	313	116	303	.383	0	1	.000	81	88	.920	75	166	241	35	126	2	18	18	66	19.4	6.7	5.1	0.7	.341
88-89	Boston	28	2	498	171	59	129	.457	0	1	.000	53	64	.828	49	88	137	32	66	0	15	5	36	17.8	6.1	4.9	1.1	.435
89-90	Boston	81	4	1365	435	176	367	.480	0	4	.000	83	100	.830	117	238	355	46	170	0	15	27	65	16.9	5.4	4.4	0.6	.387
90-91	Boston	72	1	850	258	102	218	.468	0	2	.000	54	69	.783	71	173	244	21	108	0	15	14	50	11.8	3.6	3.4	0.3	.380
91-92	Boston	70	3	991	326	144	293	.491	4	8	.500	34	48	.708	94	202	296	32	99	0	23	14	28	14.2	4.7	4.2	0.5	.457
92-93	Boston	78	3	1129	257	108	267	.404	0	6	.000	41	58	.707	113	233	346	39	123	0	17	16	39	14.5	3.3	4.4	0.5	.356
93-94	Phoenix	74	4	848	285	125	256	.488	5	11	.455	30	39	.769	50	143	193	45	118	1	14	19	37	11.5	3.9	2.6	0.6	.388
94-95	Phoenix	75	42	968	280	119	265	.449	0	2	.000	42	49	.857	82	177	259	39	174	2	14	18	38	12.9	3.7	3.5	0.5	.348
95-96	Phoenix	56	9	663	164	71	169	.420	2	7	.286	20	25	.800	36	96	132	44	113	0	13	6	39	11.8	2.9	2.4	0.8	.254
96-97	Phoenix	23	10	365	78	32	80	.400	1	1	1.000	13	18	.722	21	59	80	12	47	0	9	6	21	15.9	3.4	3.5	0.5	.249
96-97	LA Lakers	8	0	30	6	2	8	.250	0	0	.000	2	2	1.000	2	7	9	0	6	0	0	0	0	3.8	0.8	1.1	0.0	.200
96-97	New Jersey	28	0	453	84	35	82	.427	1	2	.500	13	18	.722	39	75	114	23	57	0	8	12	22	16.2	3.0	4.1	0.8	.310
97-98	Chicago	46	1	397	93	39	106	.368	0	0	.000	15	18	.833	27	50	77	30	63	0	4	5	28	8.6	2.0	1.7	0.7	.219
98-99	Phoenix	31	5	374	68	30	74	.405	0	2	.000	8	12	.667	27	40	67	12	46	0	8	1	10	12.1	2.2	2.2	0.4	.210
99-00	Portland	7	0	31	11	4	11	.364	0	0	.000	3	3	1.000	0	6	6	2	7	0	1	0	2	4.4	1.6	0.9	0.3	.264
NBA Season Totals		965	204	14712	4666	1902	4201	.453	13	48	.271	849	1069	.794	1268	2723	3991	622	1988	9	261	284	779	15.2	4.8	4.1	0.6	....
85-86	Sacramento	3	0	45	15	5	13	.385	0	0	.000	5	6	.833	8	6	14	1	8	0	1	1	2	15.0	5.0	4.7	0.3	.388
88-89	Boston	3	0	65	19	6	11	.545	0	1	.000	7	9	.778	4	13	17	2	9	0	0	1	6	21.7	6.3	5.7	0.7	.347
89-90	Boston	5	0	79	31	13	17	.765	0	1	.000	5	6	.833	3	11	14	2	12	0	2	3	4	15.8	6.2	2.8	0.4	.473
90-91	Boston	5	1	31	8	4	9	.444	0	0	.000	0	0	.000	5	6	11	1	7	0	0	0	2	6.2	1.6	2.2	0.2	.308
91-92	Boston	9	0	82	20	9	22	.409	0	1	.000	2	2	1.000	6	16	22	1	11	0	0	1	3	9.1	2.2	2.4	0.1	.274
92-93	Boston	4	0	29	6	3	5	.600	0	0	.000	0	0	.000	0	5	5	0	4	0	0	1	0	7.3	1.5	1.3	0.0	.271
93-94	Phoenix	8	0	81	28	12	28	.429	0	0	.000	4	6	.667	5	12	17	3	15	0	1	4	2	10.1	3.5	2.1	0.4	.335
94-95	Phoenix	10	10	167	63	31	54	.574	1	2	.500	0	0	.000	8	23	31	8	35	0	5	3	6	16.7	6.3	3.1	0.8	.386
95-96	Phoenix	2	0	8	0	0	2	.000	0	0	.000	0	0	.000	1	0	1	0	1	0	1	0	1	4.0	0.0	0.5	0.0	-.176
98-99	Phoenix	1	0	5	2	1	2	.500	0	0	.000	0	0	.000	0	1	1	0	1	0	1	1	0	5.0	2.0	1.0	0.0	.667
NBA Playoff Totals		50	11	592	192	84	163	.515	1	5	.200	23	29	.793	40	93	133	18	103	0	11	15	26	11.8	3.8	2.7	0.4	....

• KLIER, Leo

Leo Anthony (Crystal) Klier

Born: May 21, 1923. Washington, IN, United States. Height: 6'2". Weight: 170 lbs. Drafted: — College: Notre Dame

YEAR	TEAM	GP	GS	MIN	PTS	FGM	FGA	FG%	3PM	3PA	3P%	FTM	FTA	FT%	ORB	DRB	TRB	AST	PF	DQ	STL	BLK	TO	MPG	PPG	RPG	APG	PCM
46-47	Indianapolis-N	44	....	....	417	162	....	....	....	....	....	93	128	.727	....	....	....	....	97	....	....	....	....	....	9.5	....	....	....
47-48	Indianapolis-N	56	....	....	606	227	....	....	....	....	....	152	223	.682	....	....	....	....	159	....	....	....	....	....	10.8	....	....	....
48-49	Fort Wayne	47	....	....	347	125	492	.254	....	....	....	97	137	.708	....	....	....	56	124	....	....	....	....	....	7.4	....	1.2	....
49-50	Fort Wayne	66	....	....	455	157	516	.304	....	....	....	141	190	.742	....	....	....	121	177	....	....	....	....	....	6.9	....	1.8	....
NBA Season Totals		113	....	....	802	282	1008	.280	....	....	....	238	327	.728	....	....	....	177	301	....	....	....	....	....	7.1	....	1.6	....
NBL Season Totals		100	....	....	1023	389	....	....	....	....	....	245	351	....	....	....	....	....	256	....	....	....	....	....	10.2	....	....	....
Career Totals		213	....	....	1825	671	1008	....	....	....	....	483	678	....	....	....	....	177	557	....	....	....	....	....	8.6	....	0.8	....
46-47	Indianapolis-N	5	....	....	41	16	....	....	....	....	....	9	12	.750	....	....	....	....	....	....	....	....	....	....	8.2	....	....	....
47-48	Indianapolis-N	4	....	....	49	16	....	....	....	....	....	17	23	.739	....	....	....	....	....	....	....	....	....	....	12.3	....	....	....
49-50	Fort Wayne	2	....	....	1	0	3	.000	....	....	....	1	1	1.000	....	....	....	3	1	....	....	....	....	....	0.5	....	1.5	....
NBA Playoff Totals		2	....	....	1	0	3	.000	....	....	....	1	1	1.000	....	....	....	3	1	....	....	....	....	....	0.5	....	1.5	....
NBL Playoff Totals		9	....	....	90	32	....	....	....	....	....	26	35	....	....	....	....	....	....	....	....	....	....	....	10.0	....	....	....
Career Playoff Totals		11	....	....	91	32	3	....	....	....	....	27	36	....	....	....	....	3	1	....	....	....	....	....	8.3	....	0.3	....

• KLOTZ, Herm

Louis Herman (Red) Klotz

Born: Oct. 21, 1921. Philadelphia, PA, United States. Height: 5'7". Weight: 150 lbs. Drafted: — College: Villanova

YEAR	TEAM	GP	GS	MIN	PTS	FGM	FGA	FG%	3PM	3PA	3P%	FTM	FTA	FT%	ORB	DRB	TRB	AST	PF	DQ	STL	BLK	TO	MPG	PPG	RPG	APG	PCM
47-48	Baltimore	11	....	....	15	7	31	.226	....	....	....	1	3	.333	....	....	....	7	3	....	....	....	....	....	1.4	....	0.6	....
NBA Season Totals		11	....	....	15	7	31	.226	....	....	....	1	3	.333	....	....	....	7	3	....	....	....	....	....	1.4	....	0.6	....
47-48	Baltimore	6	....	....	6	2	9	.222	....	....	....	2	3	.667	....	....	....	1	3	....	....	....	....	....	1.0	....	0.2	....
NBA Playoff Totals		6	....	....	6	2	9	.222	....	....	....	2	3	.667	....	....	....	1	3	....	....	....	....	....	1.0	....	0.2	....

• KLUEH, Duane

Duane M. Klueh

Born: Jan. 6, 1926. Bottineau, ND, United States. Height: 6'3". Weight: 175 lbs. Drafted: 1949 College: Indiana State

YEAR	TEAM	GP	GS	MIN	PTS	FGM	FGA	FG%	3PM	3PA	3P%	FTM	FTA	FT%	ORB	DRB	TRB	AST	PF	DQ	STL	BLK	TO	MPG	PPG	RPG	APG	PCM
49-50	Denver	33	....	....	331	110	302	.364	....	....	....	111	153	.725	....	....	....	63	73	....	....	....	....	....	10.0	....	1.9	....
49-50	Fort Wayne	19	....	....	144	49	112	.438	....	....	....	46	69	.667	....	....	....	28	38	....	....	....	....	....	7.6	....	1.5	....
50-51	Fort Wayne	61	....	....	449	157	458	.343	....	....	....	135	184	.734	....	....	183	82	143	5	....	....	....	....	7.4	3.0	1.3	....
NBA Season Totals		113	....	....	924	316	872	.362	....	....	....	292	406	.719	....	....	183	173	254	5	....	....	....	....	8.2	1.6	1.5	....
49-50	Fort Wayne	2	....	....	9	2	10	.200	....	....	....	5	5	1.000	....	....	....	3	8	....	....	....	....	....	4.5	....	1.5	....
50-51	Fort Wayne	2	....	....	2	1	6	.167	....	....	....	0	0	.000	....	....	3	3	3	0	....	....	....	....	1.0	1.5	1.5	....
NBA Playoff Totals		4	....	....	11	3	16	.188	....	....	....	5	5	1.000	....	....	3	6	11	0	....	....	....	....	2.8	0.8	1.5	....

• KLUTTZ, Lonnie

Lonnie Gene Kluttz

Born: Sept. 17, 1945. Height: 6'7". Weight: 220 lbs. Drafted: 1970 College: North Carolina A&T

YEAR	TEAM	GP	GS	MIN	PTS	FGM	FGA	FG%	3PM	3PA	3P%	FTM	FTA	FT%	ORB	DRB	TRB	AST	PF	DQ	STL	BLK	TO	MPG	PPG	RPG	APG	PCM
70-71	Carolina-A	3	....	8	0	0	4	.000	0	0	.000	0	0	.000	2	3	5	0	3	0	....	....	0	2.7	0.0	1.7	0.0	-.050
ABA Season Totals		3	....	8	0	0	4	.000	0	0	.000	0	0	.000	2	3	5	0	3	0	....	....	0	2.7	0.0	1.7	0.0	....

• KNIGHT, Billy

William R. (Mooney) Knight

Born: June 9, 1952. Braddock, PA, United States. Height: 6'6". Weight: 195 lbs. Drafted: 1974 College: Pittsburgh

YEAR	TEAM	GP	GS	MIN	PTS	FGM	FGA	FG%	3PM	3PA	3P%	FTM	FTA	FT%	ORB	DRB	TRB	AST	PF	DQ	STL	BLK	TO	MPG	PPG	RPG	APG	PCM
74-75	Indiana-A	80	....	2559	1371	580	1087	.534	4	16	.250	207	259	.799	284	348	632	168	194	....	115	29	236	32.0	17.1	7.9	2.1	.609
75-76	Indiana-A	70	....	2775	1969	774	1567	.494	6	15	.400	415	501	.828	294	414	708	259	206	....	92	23	299	39.6	28.1	10.1	3.7	.739
76-77	Indiana	78	....	3117	2075	831	1687	.493	....	....	....	413	506	.816	223	359	582	260	197	0	117	19	....	40.0	26.6	7.5	3.3	.645
77-78	Buffalo	53	....	2155	1215	457	926	.494	....	....	....	301	372	.809	126	257	383	161	137	0	82	13	170	40.7	22.9	7.2	3.0	.540
78-79	Boston	40	....	1119	556	219	436	.502	....	....	....	118	146	.808	41	132	173	66	86	1	31	3	128	28.0	13.9	4.3	1.7	.405
78-79	Indiana	39	....	976	575	222	399	.556	....	....	....	131	150	.873	53	121	174	86	74	0	32	5	98	25.0	14.7	4.5	2.2	.585
79-80	Indiana	75	....	1910	986	385	722	.533	4	15	.267	212	262	.809	136	225	361	155	96	0	82	9	135	25.5	13.1	4.8	2.1	.561
80-81	Indiana	82	....	2385	1436	546	1025	.533	3	19	.158	341	410	.832	191	219	410	157	155	1	84	12	180	29.1	17.5	5.0	1.9	.573
81-82	Indiana	81	19	1803	998	378	764	.495	9	32	.281	233	282	.826	97	160	257	118	132	0	63	14	138	22.3	12.3	3.2	1.5	.481
82-83	Indiana	80	54	2262	1370	512	984	.520	3	19	.158	343	408	.841	152	172	324	192	143	0	66	8	192	28.3	17.1	4.1	2.4	.551
83-84	Kansas City	75	39	1885	963	358	729	.491	4	14	.286	243	283	.859	89	166	255	160	122	0	54	6	158	25.1	12.8	3.4	2.1	.456
84-85	Kansas City	16	0	189	76	31	69	.449	1	1	1.000	13	16	.813	10	12	22	21	14	0	2	1	13	11.8	4.8	1.4	1.3	.351
84-85	San Antonio	52	1	611	311	125	285	.439	10	24	.417	51	57	.895	40	56	96	59	48	0	14	1	57	11.8	6.0	1.8	1.1	.409
NBA Season Totals		671	113	18412	10561	4064	8026	.506	34	124	.274	2399	2892	.830	1158	1879	3037	1435	1204	2	627	91	1269	27.4	15.7	4.5	2.1	....
ABA Season Totals		150	....	5334	3340	1354	2654	.510	10	31	.323	622	760	.818	578	762	1340	427	400	....	207	52	535	35.6	22.3	8.9	2.8	....
Career Totals		821	113	23746	13901	5418	10680	.507	44	155	.284	3021	3652	.827	1736	2641	4377	1862	1604	2	834	143	1804	28.9	16.9	5.3	2.3	....
74-75	Indiana-A	18	....	763	434	176	310	.568	0	2	.000	82	97	.845	64	96	160	43	45	....	17	1	55	42.4	24.1	8.9	2.4	.627
75-76	Indiana-A	3	....	143	101	41	74	.554	0	1	.000	19	22	.864	10	22	32	12	9	....	2	0	20	47.7	33.7	10.7	4.0	.756
80-81	Indiana	2	....	71	37	16	30	.533	0	0	.000	5	8	.625	6	6	12	5	5	0	1	0	5	35.5	18.5	6.0	2.5	.470
83-84	Kansas City	3	0	37	18	8	24	.333	0	0	.000	2	2	1.000	2	1	3	2	2	0	0	0	2	12.3	6.0	1.0	0.7	.142
84-85	San Antonio	5	0	45	16	8	15	.533	0	4	.000	0	0	.000	3	3	6	3	2	0	2	0	2	9.0	3.2	1.2	0.6	.385
NBA Playoff Totals		10	0	153	71	32	69	.464	0	4	.000	7	10	.700	11	10	21	10	9	0	3	0	9	15.3	7.1	2.1	1.0	....
ABA Playoff Totals		21	....	906	535	217	384	.565	0	3	.000	101	119	.849	74	118	192	55	54	....	19	1	75	43.1	25.5	9.1	2.6	....
Career Playoff Totals		31	0	1059	606	249	453	.550	0	7	.000	108	129	.837	85	128	213	65	63	0	22	1	84	34.2	19.5	6.9	2.1	....

• KNIGHT, Bob

Robert Knight

Born: 1931. Height: 6'2". Weight: 185 lbs. Drafted: — College: none

YEAR	TEAM	GP	GS	MIN	PTS	FGM	FGA	FG%	3PM	3PA	3P%	FTM	FTA	FT%	ORB	DRB	TRB	AST	PF	DQ	STL	BLK	TO	MPG	PPG	RPG	APG	PCM
54-55	New York	2	....	29	7	3	7	.429	....	....	....	1	1	1.000	....	....	1	8	6	0	....	....	....	14.5	3.5	0.5	4.0	.430
NBA Season Totals		2	....	29	7	3	7	.429	....	....	....	1	1	1.000	....	....	1	8	6	0	....	....	....	14.5	3.5	0.5	4.0	....

• KNIGHT, Brevin

Brevin Knight

Born: Nov. 8, 1975. Livingston, NJ, United States. Height: 5'10". Weight: 173 lbs. Drafted: 1997 College: Stanford

YEAR	TEAM	GP	GS	MIN	PTS	FGM	FGA	FG%	3PM	3PA	3P%	FTM	FTA	FT%	ORB	DRB	TRB	AST	PF	DQ	STL	BLK	TO	MPG	PPG	RPG	APG	PCM
97-98	Cleveland	80	76	2483	723	261	592	.441	0	7	.000	201	251	.801	67	186	253	656	271	5	**196**	18	192	31.0	9.0	3.2	8.2	.498
98-99	Cleveland	39	38	1186	373	134	315	.425	0	5	.000	105	141	.745	16	115	131	302	115	1	70	7	105	30.4	9.6	3.4	7.7	.482
99-00	Cleveland	65	46	1754	602	230	558	.412	2	10	.200	140	184	.761	38	155	193	458	185	2	107	21	157	27.0	9.3	3.0	7.0	.484
00-01	Cleveland	6	0	93	9	2	15	.133	0	0	.000	5	6	.833	1	6	7	25	17	0	6	1	7	15.5	1.5	1.2	4.2	.248
00-01	Atlanta	47	43	1364	324	137	356	.385	1	10	.100	49	60	.817	22	139	161	286	138	2	95	3	84	29.0	6.9	3.4	6.1	.391
01-02	Memphis	53	11	1151	371	141	334	.422	2	8	.250	87	115	.757	11	98	109	302	135	1	79	7	111	21.7	7.0	2.1	5.7	.459
02-03	Memphis	55	4	928	216	97	228	.425	2	8	.250	20	37	.541	15	66	81	233	123	0	69	2	94	16.9	3.9	1.5	4.2	.367
NBA Season Totals		345	218	8959	2618	1002	2398	.418	7	48	.146	607	794	.764	170	765	935	2262	984	11	622	59	750	26.0	7.6	2.7	6.6	....
97-98	Cleveland	4	4	132	18	6	21	.286	0	0	.000	6	10	.600	0	16	16	23	16	1	10	1	8	33.0	4.5	4.0	5.8	.284
NBA Playoff Totals		4	4	132	18	6	21	.286	0	0	.000	6	10	.600	0	16	16	23	16	1	10	1	8	33.0	4.5	4.0	5.8	....

• KNIGHT, Negele

Negele Oscar Knight

Born: Mar. 6, 1967. Detroit, MI, United States. Height: 6'1". Weight: 175 lbs. Drafted: 1990 College: Dayton

YEAR	TEAM	GP	GS	MIN	PTS	FGM	FGA	FG%	3PM	3PA	3P%	FTM	FTA	FT%	ORB	DRB	TRB	AST	PF	DQ	STL	BLK	TO	MPG	PPG	RPG	APG	PCM
90-91	Phoenix	64	6	792	339	131	308	.425	6	25	.240	71	118	.602	20	51	71	191	83	0	20	7	77	12.4	5.3	1.1	3.0	.425
91-92	Phoenix	42	1	631	243	103	217	.475	4	13	.308	33	48	.688	16	30	46	112	58	0	24	3	59	15.0	5.8	1.1	2.7	.374
92-93	Phoenix	52	35	888	315	124	317	.391	0	7	.000	67	86	.779	28	36	64	145	66	1	23	4	73	17.1	6.1	1.2	2.8	.300
93-94	Phoenix	1	0	8	2	1	4	.250	0	0	.000	0	0	.000	0	0	0	0	1	0	0	1	0	8.0	2.0	0.0	0.0	-.037
93-94	San Antonio	64	18	1430	593	224	471	.476	4	21	.190	141	174	.810	28	75	103	197	120	0	34	10	96	22.3	9.3	1.6	3.1	.389

YEAR	TEAM	GP	GS	MIN	PTS	FGM	FGA	FG%	3PM	3PA	3P%	FTM	FTA	FT%	ORB	DRB	TRB	AST	PF	DQ	STL	BLK	TO	MPG	PPG	RPG	APG	PCM
94-95	Portland	3	0	43	18	7	15	.467	0	0	.000	4	4	1.000	1	2	3	11	5	0	1	0	4	14.3	6.0	1.0	3.7	.461
94-95	Detroit	44	17	665	181	78	199	.392	11	28	.393	14	21	.667	20	38	58	116	65	0	20	5	44	15.1	4.1	1.3	2.6	.291
98-99	Toronto	6	0	56	8	3	8	.375	0	1	.000	2	4	.500	1	5	6	8	5	0	1	0	7	9.3	1.3	1.0	1.3	.167
NBA Season Totals		276	77	4513	1699	671	1539	.436	25	95	.263	332	455	.730	114	237	351	780	403	1	123	30	360	16.4	6.2	1.3	2.8	....
90-91	Phoenix	4	0	56	32	13	26	.500	1	3	.333	5	7	.714	1	3	4	9	7	0	1	0	4	14.0	8.0	1.0	2.3	.468
92-93	Phoenix	9	1	34	18	9	16	.563	0	0	.000	0	0	.000	1	2	3	7	1	0	0	1	3	3.8	2.0	0.3	0.8	.571
93-94	San Antonio	4	0	108	37	13	41	.317	0	3	.000	11	12	.917	3	3	6	12	9	0	3	0	7	27.0	9.3	1.5	3.0	.200
NBA Playoff Totals		17	1	198	87	35	83	.422	1	6	.167	16	19	.842	5	8	13	28	17	0	4	1	14	11.6	5.1	0.8	1.6	....

• KNIGHT, Ron
Ronald Eugene Knight

Born: Aug. 4, 1947. Height: 6'7". Weight: 215 lbs. Drafted: 1970 College: Los Angeles State

YEAR	TEAM	GP	GS	MIN	PTS	FGM	FGA	FG%	3PM	3PA	3P%	FTM	FTA	FT%	ORB	DRB	TRB	AST	PF	DQ	STL	BLK	TO	MPG	PPG	RPG	APG	PCM
70-71	Portland	52	....	662	217	99	230	.430	....	....	....	19	38	.500	....	....	167	50	99	1	....	....	....	12.7	4.2	3.2	1.0	.384
71-72	Portland	49	....	483	255	112	257	.436	....	....	....	31	62	.500	....	....	116	33	52	0	....	....	....	9.9	5.2	2.4	0.7	.479
NBA Season Totals		101	....	1145	472	211	487	.433	....	....	....	50	100	.500	....	....	283	83	151	1	....	....	....	11.3	4.7	2.8	0.8	....

• KNIGHT, Toby
Toby Thomas Knight

Born: May 3, 1955. Bronx, NY, United States. Height: 6'9". Weight: 210 lbs. Drafted: 1977 College: Notre Dame

YEAR	TEAM	GP	GS	MIN	PTS	FGM	FGA	FG%	3PM	3PA	3P%	FTM	FTA	FT%	ORB	DRB	TRB	AST	PF	DQ	STL	BLK	TO	MPG	PPG	RPG	APG	PCM
77-78	New York	80	....	1169	507	222	465	.477	....	....	....	63	97	.649	121	200	321	38	211	1	50	28	96	14.6	6.3	4.0	0.5	.423
78-79	New York	82	....	2667	1363	609	1174	.519	....	....	....	145	206	.704	201	347	548	124	309	7	61	60	164	32.5	16.6	6.7	1.5	.480
79-80	New York	81	....	2945	1549	669	1265	.529	0	2	.000	211	261	.808	201	292	493	150	302	4	117	86	162	36.4	19.1	6.1	1.9	.509
81-82	New York	40	0	550	221	102	183	.557	0	0	.000	17	25	.680	33	49	82	23	74	0	14	11	20	13.8	5.5	2.1	0.6	.388
NBA Season Totals		283	0	7331	3640	1602	3087	.519	0	2	.000	436	589	.740	556	888	1444	335	896	12	242	185	442	25.9	12.9	5.1	1.2	....
77-78	New York	6	....	48	16	6	20	.300	....	....	....	4	8	.500	9	10	19	1	9	0	1	4	3	8.0	2.7	3.2	0.2	.366
NBA Playoff Totals		6	....	48	16	6	20	.300	....	....	....	4	8	.500	9	10	19	1	9	0	1	4	3	8.0	2.7	3.2	0.2	....

• KNIGHT, Travis
Travis James Knight

Born: Sept. 13, 1974. Salt Lake City, UT, United States. Height: 7' Weight: 235 lbs. Drafted: 1996 College: Connecticut

YEAR	TEAM	GP	GS	MIN	PTS	FGM	FGA	FG%	3PM	3PA	3P%	FTM	FTA	FT%	ORB	DRB	TRB	AST	PF	DQ	STL	BLK	TO	MPG	PPG	RPG	APG	PCM
96-97	LA Lakers	71	14	1156	342	140	275	.509	0	0	.000	62	100	.620	130	189	319	39	170	2	31	59	50	16.3	4.8	4.5	0.5	.429
97-98	Boston	74	21	1503	482	193	438	.441	15	55	.273	81	103	.786	146	219	365	104	253	3	54	82	89	20.3	6.5	4.9	1.4	.414
98-99	LA Lakers	37	23	525	156	67	130	.515	0	1	.000	22	29	.759	34	94	128	31	108	2	21	27	35	14.2	4.2	3.5	0.8	.397
99-00	LA Lakers	63	0	410	109	46	118	.390	0	0	.000	17	28	.607	46	83	129	23	88	1	6	23	26	6.5	1.7	2.0	0.4	.350
00-01	New York	45	0	256	29	10	53	.189	0	1	.000	9	18	.500	19	34	53	5	47	0	5	11	10	5.7	0.6	1.2	0.1	.093
01-02	New York	49	0	429	98	41	113	.363	0	0	.000	16	21	.762	48	56	104	8	95	0	11	10	27	8.8	2.0	2.1	0.2	.198
02-03	New York	32	0	287	60	25	65	.385	0	1	.000	10	13	.769	18	44	62	14	44	0	8	9	10	9.0	1.9	1.9	0.4	.280
NBA Season Totals		371	58	4566	1276	522	1192	.438	15	58	.259	217	312	.696	441	719	1160	224	805	8	136	221	247	12.3	3.4	3.1	0.6	....
96-97	LA Lakers	9	0	93	19	8	10	.800	0	0	.000	3	4	.750	3	15	18	3	16	0	3	3	2	10.3	2.1	2.0	0.3	.354
98-99	LA Lakers	3	0	10	3	1	3	.333	0	0	.000	1	2	.500	0	5	5	1	7	1	0	0	3	3.3	1.0	1.7	0.3	.056
99-00	LA Lakers	14	0	48	18	8	15	.533	0	0	.000	2	6	.333	3	2	5	0	16	0	1	3	6	3.4	1.3	0.4	0.0	.110
00-01	New York	1	0	1	0	0	0	.000	0	0	.000	0	0	.000	0	0	0	0	1	0	0	0	0	1.0	0.0	0.0	0.0	-.449
NBA Playoff Totals		27	0	152	40	17	28	.607	0	0	.000	6	12	.500	6	22	28	4	40	1	4	6	11	5.6	1.5	1.0	0.1	....

• KNOBLAUCH, Buzz
Buzz Knoblauch

Born: 1916. Height: 6'1". Weight: 170 lbs. Drafted: — College: Carroll (WI)

YEAR	TEAM	GP	GS	MIN	PTS	FGM	FGA	FG%	3PM	3PA	3P%	FTM	FTA	FT%	ORB	DRB	TRB	AST	PF	DQ	STL	BLK	TO	MPG	PPG	RPG	APG	PCM
39-40	Oshkosh-N	3	....	....	2	1	....	....	....	....	....	0	....	....	....	....	....	....	....	....	....	....	....	....	0.7	....	....	....
NBL Season Totals		3	....	....	2	1	....	....	....	....	....	0	....	....	....	....	....	....	....	....	....	....	....	....	0.7	....	....	....

• KNOREK, Lee
Lee J. Knorek

Born: July 15, 1921. Warsaw, Poland. Height: 6'7". Weight: 215 lbs. Drafted: — College: Detroit

YEAR	TEAM	GP	GS	MIN	PTS	FGM	FGA	FG%	3PM	3PA	3P%	FTM	FTA	FT%	ORB	DRB	TRB	AST	PF	DQ	STL	BLK	TO	MPG	PPG	RPG	APG	PCM
46-47	New York	22	....	....	171	62	219	.283	....	....	....	47	72	.653	....	....	....	21	64	....	....	....	....	....	7.8	....	1.0	....
47-48	New York	48	....	....	259	99	369	.268	....	....	....	61	120	.508	....	....	....	50	171	....	....	....	....	....	5.4	....	1.0	....
48-49	New York	60	....	....	443	156	457	.341	....	....	....	131	183	.716	....	....	....	135	258	....	....	....	....	....	7.4	....	2.3	....
49-50	Baltimore	1	....	....	0	0	2	.000	....	....	....	0	0	....	....	....	....	0	4	....	....	....	....	....	0.0	....	0.0	....
NBA Season Totals		131	....	....	873	317	1047	.303	....	....	....	239	375	.637	....	....	....	206	497	....	....	....	....	....	6.7	....	1.6	....
46-47	New York	5	....	....	53	21	58	.362	....	....	....	11	19	.579	....	....	....	8	22	....	....	....	....	....	10.6	....	1.6	....
47-48	New York	3	....	....	38	14	34	.412	....	....	....	10	13	.769	....	....	....	5	10	....	....	....	....	....	12.7	....	1.7	....
48-49	New York	6	....	....	39	15	37	.405	....	....	....	9	16	.563	....	....	....	10	25	....	....	....	....	....	6.5	....	1.7	....
NBA Playoff Totals		14	....	....	130	50	129	.388	....	....	....	30	48	.625	....	....	....	23	57	....	....	....	....	....	9.3	....	1.6	....

• KNOSTMAN, Dick
Richard W. Knostman

Born: Aug. 9, 1931. Wamego, KS, United States. Height: 6'6". Weight: 215 lbs. Drafted: 1953 College: Kansas State

YEAR	TEAM	GP	GS	MIN	PTS	FGM	FGA	FG%	3PM	3PA	3P%	FTM	FTA	FT%	ORB	DRB	TRB	AST	PF	DQ	STL	BLK	TO	MPG	PPG	RPG	APG	PCM
53-54	Syracuse	5	....	47	13	3	10	.300	....	....	....	7	11	.636	....	....	17	6	9	0	....	....	....	9.4	2.6	3.4	1.2	.494
NBA Season Totals		5	....	47	13	3	10	.300	....	....	....	7	11	.636	....	....	17	6	9	0	....	....	....	9.4	2.6	3.4	1.2	....

KNOWLES, Rod
W. Rodney Knowles

Born: Feb. 27, 1946.   Height: 6'9".   Weight: 215 lbs.   Drafted: 1968   College: Davidson

YEAR	TEAM	GP	GS	MIN	PTS	FGM	FGA	FG%	3PM	3PA	3P%	FTM	FTA	FT%	ORB	DRB	TRB	AST	PF	DQ	STL	BLK	TO	MPG	PPG	RPG	APG	PCM
68-69	New York-A	1	....	3	0	0	0	.000	0	0	.000	0	0	.000	0	0	0	0	1	0	....	....	0	3.0	0.0	0.0	0.0	-.143
68-69	Phoenix	8	....	40	9	4	14	.286	....	....	....	1	3	.333	....	....	9	0	10	0	....	....	0	5.0	1.1	1.1	0.0	.079
NBA Season Totals		8	....	40	9	4	14	.286	....	....	....	1	3	.333	....	....	9	0	10	0	....	....	0	5.0	1.1	1.1	0.0	....
ABA Season Totals		1	....	3	0	0	0	.000	0	0	.000	0	0	.000	0	0	0	0	1	0	....	....	0	3.0	0.0	0.0	0.0	....
Career Totals		9	....	43	9	4	14	.286	0	0	.000	1	3	.333	0	0	9	0	11	0	....	....	0	4.8	1.0	1.0	0.0	....

KOFOED, Bart
Bart Kofoed

Born: Mar. 24, 1964. Omaha, NE, United States.   Height: 6'4".   Weight: 210 lbs.   Drafted: 1987   College: Kearney State

YEAR	TEAM	GP	GS	MIN	PTS	FGM	FGA	FG%	3PM	3PA	3P%	FTM	FTA	FT%	ORB	DRB	TRB	AST	PF	DQ	STL	BLK	TO	MPG	PPG	RPG	APG	PCM
87-88	Utah	36	0	225	46	18	48	.375	2	7	.286	8	13	.615	4	11	15	23	42	0	6	1	18	6.3	1.3	0.4	0.6	.109
88-89	Utah	19	0	176	30	12	33	.364	0	1	.000	6	11	.545	4	7	11	20	22	0	9	0	13	9.3	1.6	0.6	1.1	.147
90-91	Golden State	5	0	21	3	0	3	.000	0	0	.000	3	6	.500	2	1	3	4	4	0	0	0	2	4.2	0.6	0.6	0.8	.102
91-92	Seattle	44	0	239	66	25	53	.472	1	7	.143	15	26	.577	6	20	26	51	26	0	2	2	22	5.4	1.5	0.6	1.2	.355
92-93	Boston	7	0	41	17	3	13	.231	0	1	.000	11	14	.786	0	1	1	10	1	0	2	1	3	5.9	2.4	0.1	1.4	.425
NBA Season Totals		111	0	702	162	58	150	.387	3	16	.188	43	70	.614	16	40	56	108	95	0	19	4	58	6.3	1.5	0.5	1.0	....
87-88	Utah	10	0	109	21	9	23	.391	1	5	.200	2	2	1.000	3	11	14	11	18	0	1	0	9	10.9	2.1	1.4	1.1	.155
NBA Playoff Totals		10	0	109	21	9	23	.391	1	5	.200	2	2	1.000	3	11	14	11	18	0	1	0	9	10.9	2.1	1.4	1.1	....

KOJIS, Don
Donald R. Kojis

Born: Jan. 15, 1939. Milwaukee, WI, United States.   Height: 6'3".   Weight: 202 lbs.   Drafted: 1961   College: Marquette

YEAR	TEAM	GP	GS	MIN	PTS	FGM	FGA	FG%	3PM	3PA	3P%	FTM	FTA	FT%	ORB	DRB	TRB	AST	PF	DQ	STL	BLK	TO	MPG	PPG	RPG	APG	PCM
63-64	Baltimore	78	....	1148	488	203	484	.419	....	....	....	82	146	.562	....	....	309	57	123	0	....	....	....	14.7	6.3	4.0	0.7	.441
64-65	Detroit	65	....	836	422	180	416	.433	....	....	....	62	98	.633	....	....	243	63	115	1	....	....	....	12.9	6.5	3.7	1.0	.535
65-66	Detroit	60	....	783	440	182	439	.415	....	....	....	76	141	.539	....	....	260	42	94	0	....	....	....	13.1	7.3	4.3	0.7	.551
66-67	Chicago	78	....	1655	792	329	773	.426	....	....	....	134	222	.604	....	....	479	70	204	3	....	....	....	21.2	10.2	6.1	0.9	.476
67-68	San Diego	69	....	2548	1360	530	1189	.446	....	....	....	300	413	.726	....	....	710	176	259	5	....	....	....	36.9	19.7	10.3	2.6	.574
68-69	San Diego	81	....	3130	1820	687	1582	.434	....	....	....	446	596	.748	....	....	776	214	303	6	....	....	....	38.6	22.5	9.6	2.6	.569
69-70	San Diego	56	....	1578	857	338	756	.447	....	....	....	181	241	.751	....	....	388	78	135	1	....	....	....	28.2	15.3	6.9	1.4	.527
70-71	Seattle	79	....	2143	1157	454	1018	.446	....	....	....	249	320	.778	....	....	435	130	220	3	....	....	....	27.1	14.6	5.5	1.6	.499
71-72	Seattle	73	....	1857	832	322	687	.469	....	....	....	188	237	.793	....	....	335	82	168	1	....	....	....	25.4	11.4	4.6	1.1	.434
72-73	Omaha	77	....	1240	658	276	575	.480	....	....	....	106	137	.774	....	....	198	80	128	0	....	....	....	16.1	8.5	2.6	1.0	.479
73-74	Omaha	77	....	2091	1010	400	836	.478	....	....	....	210	272	.772	126	257	383	110	157	2	77	15	....	27.2	13.1	5.0	1.4	.477
74-75	Omaha	21	....	232	112	46	98	.469	....	....	....	20	30	.667	14	25	39	10	31	0	12	1	....	11.0	5.3	1.9	0.5	.409
NBA Season Totals		814	....	19241	9948	3947	8853	.446	....	....	....	2054	2853	.720	140	282	4555	1112	1937	22	89	16	....	23.6	12.2	5.6	1.4	....
66-67	Chicago	3	....	104	51	23	48	.479	....	....	....	5	8	.625	....	....	30	4	10	0	....	....	....	34.7	17.0	10.0	1.3	.525
68-69	San Diego	6	....	232	121	48	109	.440	....	....	....	25	31	.806	....	....	51	21	22	1	....	....	....	38.7	20.2	8.5	3.5	.540
74-75	Omaha	4	....	22	7	1	6	.167	....	....	....	5	6	.833	1	3	4	1	3	0	1	0	....	5.5	1.8	1.0	0.3	.254
NBA Playoff Totals		13	....	358	179	72	163	.442	....	....	....	35	45	.778	1	3	85	26	35	1	1	0	....	27.5	13.8	6.5	2.0	....

KOLAR, Eddie
Eddie Kolar

Born: 1909.   Height: 5'10".   Weight: 170 lbs.   Drafted: —   College: none

YEAR	TEAM	GP	GS	MIN	PTS	FGM	FGA	FG%	3PM	3PA	3P%	FTM	FTA	FT%	ORB	DRB	TRB	AST	PF	DQ	STL	BLK	TO	MPG	PPG	RPG	APG	PCM
38-39	Sheboygan-N	1	....	....	4	1	....	....	....	....	....	2	....	....	....	....	....	....	....	....	....	....	....	4.0	....	....	....
NBL Season Totals		1	....	....	4	1	....	....	....	....	....	2	....	....	....	....	....	....	....	....	....	....	....	4.0	....	....	....

KOLAR, Otto
Otto Kolar

Born: Dec. 7, 1911. Died: Apr.10, 1995.   Height: 6'3".   Weight: 180 lbs.   Drafted: —   College: Wisconsin (Oshkosh)

YEAR	TEAM	GP	GS	MIN	PTS	FGM	FGA	FG%	3PM	3PA	3P%	FTM	FTA	FT%	ORB	DRB	TRB	AST	PF	DQ	STL	BLK	TO	MPG	PPG	RPG	APG	PCM
38-39	Sheboygan-N	26	....	....	136	57	....	....	....	....	....	22	....	....	....	....	....	....	....	....	....	....	....	5.2	....	....	....
39-40	Sheboygan-N	27	....	....	146	55	....	....	....	....	....	36	....	....	....	....	....	....	....	....	....	....	....	5.4	....	....	....
40-41	Sheboygan-N	24	....	....	138	53	....	....	....	....	....	32	....	....	....	....	....	....	....	....	....	....	....	5.8	....	....	....
41-42	Chicago-N	18	....	....	68	27	....	....	....	....	....	14	....	....	....	....	....	....	....	....	....	....	....	3.8	....	....	....
NBL Season Totals		95	....	....	488	192	....	....	....	....	....	104	....	....	....	....	....	....	....	....	....	....	....	5.1	....	....	....
39-40	Sheboygan-N	3	....	....	9	4	....	....	....	....	....	1	....	....	....	....	....	....	....	....	....	....	....	3.0	....	....	....
40-41	Sheboygan-N	6	....	....	41	17	....	....	....	....	....	7	....	....	....	....	....	....	....	....	....	....	....	6.8	....	....	....
NBL Playoff Totals		9	....	....	50	21	....	....	....	....	....	8	....	....	....	....	....	....	....	....	....	....	....	5.6	....	....	....

KOMENICH, Bill
Bill Komenich

Born: 1918.   Height: 6'3".   Weight: 210 lbs.   Drafted: —   College: Marquette

YEAR	TEAM	GP	GS	MIN	PTS	FGM	FGA	FG%	3PM	3PA	3P%	FTM	FTA	FT%	ORB	DRB	TRB	AST	PF	DQ	STL	BLK	TO	MPG	PPG	RPG	APG	PCM
41-42	Oshkosh-N	24	....	....	80	31	....	....	....	....	....	18	....	....	....	....	....	....	....	....	....	....	....	3.3	....	....	....
42-43	Oshkosh-N	17	....	....	64	23	....	....	....	....	....	18	....	....	....	....	....	....	....	....	....	....	....	3.8	....	....	....
44-45	Oshkosh-N	24	....	....	45	16	....	....	....	....	....	13	....	....	....	....	....	....	....	....	....	....	....	1.9	....	....	....
NBL Season Totals		65	....	....	189	70	....	....	....	....	....	49	....	....	....	....	....	....	....	....	....	....	....	2.9	....	....	....
41-42	Oshkosh-N	5	....	....	25	7	....	....	....	....	....	11	....	....	....	....	....	....	....	....	....	....	....	5.0	....	....	....
NBL Playoff Totals		5	....	....	25	7	....	....	....	....	....	11	....	....	....	....	....	....	....	....	....	....	....	5.0	....	....	....

• KOMENICH, Milo

Milan Komenich

Born: June 22, 1920. Died: May25, 1977. Height: 6'7". Weight: 212 lbs. Drafted: — College: Wyoming

YEAR	TEAM	GP	GS	MIN	PTS	FGM	FGA	FG%	3PM	3PA	3P%	FTM	FTA	FT%	ORB	DRB	TRB	AST	PF	DQ	STL	BLK	TO	MPG	PPG	RPG	APG	PCM
46-47	Fort Wayne-N	36	....	....	123	50	....	....	....	....	....	23	50	.460	....	....	....	....	59	....	....	....	....	....	3.4	....	....	....
47-48	Anderson-N	43	....	....	283	120	....	....	....	....	....	43	88	.489	....	....	....	....	....	....	....	....	....	....	6.6	....	....	....
47-48	Fort Wayne-N	7	....	....	15	7	....	....	....	....	....	1	7	.143	....	....	....	....	....	....	....	....	....	....	2.1	....	....	....
48-49	Anderson-N	64	....	....	610	243	....	....	....	....	....	124	217	.571	....	....	....	....	209	....	....	....	....	....	9.5	....	....	....
49-50	Anderson	64	....	....	634	244	861	.283	....	....	....	146	250	.584	....	....	....	124	246	....	....	....	....	....	9.9	....	1.9	....
NBA Season Totals		64	....	....	634	244	861	.283	....	....	....	146	250	.584	....	....	....	124	246	....	....	....	....	....	9.9	....	1.9	....
NBL Season Totals		150	....	....	1031	420	....	....	....	....	....	191	362	....	....	....	....	....	268	....	....	....	....	....	6.9	....	....	....
Career Totals		214	....	....	1665	664	861	....	....	....	....	337	612	....	....	....	....	124	514	....	....	....	....	....	7.8	....	0.6	....
46-47	Fort Wayne-N	8	....	....	36	15	....	....	....	....	....	6	14	.429	....	....	....	....	....	....	....	....	....	....	4.5	....	....	....
47-48	Anderson-N	6	....	....	27	10	....	....	....	....	....	7	14	.500	....	....	....	....	....	....	....	....	....	....	4.5	....	....	....
48-49	Anderson-N	7	....	....	76	25	....	....	....	....	....	26	41	.634	....	....	....	....	0	....	....	....	....	....	10.9	....	....	....
49-50	Anderson	8	....	....	68	26	107	.243	....	....	....	16	28	.571	....	....	....	14	36	....	....	....	....	....	8.5	....	1.8	....
NBA Playoff Totals		8	....	....	68	26	107	.243	....	....	....	16	28	.571	....	....	....	14	36	....	....	....	....	....	8.5	....	1.8	....
NBL Playoff Totals		21	....	....	139	50	....	....	....	....	....	39	69	....	....	....	....	....	0	....	....	....	....	....	6.6	....	....	....
Career Playoff Totals		29	....	....	207	76	107	....	....	....	....	55	97	....	....	....	....	14	36	....	....	....	....	....	7.1	....	0.5	....

• KOMIVES, Howard

Howard K. (Butch) Komives

Born: May 9, 1941. Toledo, OH, United States. Height: 6'1". Weight: 185 lbs. Drafted: 1964 College: Bowling Green

YEAR	TEAM	GP	GS	MIN	PTS	FGM	FGA	FG%	3PM	3PA	3P%	FTM	FTA	FT%	ORB	DRB	TRB	AST	PF	DQ	STL	BLK	TO	MPG	PPG	RPG	APG	PCM
64-65	New York	80	....	2376	974	381	1020	.374	....	....	....	212	254	.835	....	....	195	265	246	2	....	....	....	29.7	12.2	2.4	3.3	.357
65-66	New York	80	....	2612	1113	436	1116	.391	....	....	....	241	280	.861	....	....	281	425	278	5	....	....	....	32.7	13.9	3.5	5.3	.457
66-67	New York	65	....	2282	1021	402	995	.404	....	....	....	217	253	.858	....	....	183	401	213	1	....	....	....	35.1	15.7	2.8	6.2	.472
67-68	New York	78	....	1660	598	233	631	.369	....	....	....	132	161	.820	....	....	168	246	170	1	....	....	....	21.3	7.7	2.2	3.2	.380
68-69	New York	32	....	836	287	107	309	.346	....	....	....	73	86	.849	....	....	95	137	96	0	....	....	....	26.1	9.0	3.0	4.3	.373
68-69	Detroit	53	....	1726	682	272	665	.409	....	....	....	138	178	.775	....	....	204	266	178	1	....	....	....	32.6	12.9	3.8	5.0	.430
69-70	Detroit	82	....	2418	916	363	878	.413	....	....	....	190	234	.812	....	....	193	312	247	2	....	....	....	29.5	11.2	2.4	3.8	.353
70-71	Detroit	82	....	1932	671	275	715	.385	....	....	....	121	151	.801	....	....	152	262	184	0	....	....	....	23.6	8.2	1.9	3.2	.326
71-72	Detroit	79	....	2071	688	262	702	.373	....	....	....	164	203	.808	....	....	172	291	196	0	....	....	....	26.2	8.7	2.2	3.7	.331
72-73	Buffalo	67	....	1468	411	163	429	.380	....	....	....	85	98	.867	....	....	118	239	155	1	....	....	....	21.9	6.1	1.8	3.6	.330
73-74	Omaha	44	....	830	189	78	192	.406	....	....	....	33	38	.868	10	33	43	97	83	0	32	3	....	18.9	4.3	1.0	2.2	.244
NBA Season Totals		742	....	20211	7550	2972	7652	.388	....	....	....	1606	1936	.830	10	33	1804	2941	2046	13	32	3	....	27.2	10.2	2.4	4.0	....
66-67	New York	4	....	128	42	16	59	.271	....	....	....	10	13	.769	....	....	11	15	13	0	....	....	....	32.0	10.5	2.8	3.8	.220
67-68	New York	6	....	135	34	15	44	.341	....	....	....	4	6	.667	....	....	14	23	22	1	....	....	....	22.5	5.7	2.3	3.8	.297
NBA Playoff Totals		10	....	263	76	31	103	.301	....	....	....	14	19	.737	....	....	25	38	35	1	....	....	....	26.3	7.6	2.5	3.8	....

• KONCAK, Jon

Jon Francis (Kak) Koncak

Born: May 17, 1963. Cedar Rapids, IA, United States. Height: 7' Weight: 250 lbs. Drafted: 1985 College: Southern Methodist

YEAR	TEAM	GP	GS	MIN	PTS	FGM	FGA	FG%	3PM	3PA	3P%	FTM	FTA	FT%	ORB	DRB	TRB	AST	PF	DQ	STL	BLK	TO	MPG	PPG	RPG	APG	PCM
85-86	Atlanta	82	15	1695	682	263	519	.507	0	1	.000	156	257	.607	171	296	467	55	296	10	37	69	115	20.7	8.3	5.7	0.7	.439
86-87	Atlanta	82	19	1684	463	169	352	.480	0	1	.000	125	191	.654	153	340	493	31	262	2	52	76	90	20.5	5.6	6.0	0.4	.396
87-88	Atlanta	49	22	1073	279	98	203	.483	0	2	.000	83	136	.610	103	230	333	19	161	1	36	56	54	21.9	5.7	6.8	0.4	.417
88-89	Atlanta	74	22	1531	345	141	269	.524	0	3	.000	63	114	.553	147	306	453	56	238	4	54	98	59	20.7	4.7	6.1	0.8	.431
89-90	Atlanta	54	28	977	198	78	127	.614	0	1	.000	42	79	.532	58	168	226	23	182	4	38	34	49	18.1	3.7	4.2	0.4	.314
90-91	Atlanta	77	61	1931	313	140	321	.436	1	8	.125	32	54	.593	101	274	375	124	265	6	74	76	46	25.1	4.1	4.9	1.6	.305
91-92	Atlanta	77	14	1489	241	111	284	.391	0	12	.000	19	29	.655	62	199	261	132	207	2	50	67	54	19.3	3.1	3.4	1.7	.283
92-93	Atlanta	78	65	1975	275	124	267	.464	3	8	.375	24	50	.480	100	327	427	140	264	6	75	100	55	25.3	3.5	5.5	1.8	.337
93-94	Atlanta	82	78	1823	342	159	369	.431	0	3	.000	24	36	.667	83	282	365	102	236	1	63	125	41	22.2	4.2	4.5	1.2	.338
94-95	Atlanta	62	20	943	179	77	187	.412	12	36	.333	13	24	.542	23	161	184	52	137	1	36	46	19	15.2	2.9	3.0	0.8	.311
95-96	Orlando	67	35	1288	203	84	175	.480	3	9	.333	32	57	.561	63	209	272	51	226	7	27	44	40	19.2	3.0	4.1	0.8	.263
NBA Season Totals		784	379	16409	3520	1444	3073	.470	19	84	.226	613	1027	.597	1064	2792	3856	785	2474	44	542	791	622	20.9	4.5	4.9	1.0	....
85-86	Atlanta	9	0	193	54	14	29	.483	0	0	.000	26	46	.565	11	23	34	5	27	2	6	10	7	21.4	6.0	3.8	0.6	.329
86-87	Atlanta	8	0	86	20	7	13	.538	0	0	.000	6	8	.750	5	20	25	3	24	0	3	4	0	10.8	2.5	3.1	0.4	.411
88-89	Atlanta	5	5	192	64	18	29	.621	0	0	.000	28	33	.848	16	32	48	4	23	1	2	8	8	38.4	12.8	9.6	0.8	.477
90-91	Atlanta	5	5	133	10	4	14	.286	0	0	.000	2	2	1.000	4	19	23	7	17	0	2	4	3	26.6	2.0	4.6	1.4	.184
92-93	Atlanta	3	3	89	3	1	10	.100	0	0	.000	1	2	.500	8	16	24	4	9	0	3	5	2	29.7	1.0	8.0	1.3	.249
93-94	Atlanta	11	11	195	58	27	66	.409	0	0	.000	4	10	.400	5	25	30	13	32	0	6	12	6	17.7	5.3	2.7	1.2	.294
95-96	Orlando	12	3	140	11	4	7	.571	0	0	.000	3	7	.429	8	15	23	3	39	1	5	4	3	11.7	0.9	1.9	0.3	.132
NBA Playoff Totals		53	27	1028	220	75	168	.446	0	0	.000	70	108	.648	57	150	207	39	171	4	27	47	29	19.4	4.2	3.9	0.7	....

• KONDLA, Tom

Thomas A. Kondla

Born: Nov. 30, 1946. Brookfield, IL, United States. Height: 6'8". Weight: 225 lbs. Drafted: 1968 College: Minnesota

YEAR	TEAM	GP	GS	MIN	PTS	FGM	FGA	FG%	3PM	3PA	3P%	FTM	FTA	FT%	ORB	DRB	TRB	AST	PF	DQ	STL	BLK	TO	MPG	PPG	RPG	APG	PCM
68-69	Houston-A	40	....	342	134	57	143	.399	0	1	.000	20	43	.465	45	79	124	13	53	0	....	....	23	8.6	3.4	3.1	0.3	.435
68-69	Minnesota-A	2	....	11	4	1	2	.500	0	0	.000	2	3	.667	0	1	1	0	3	0	....	....	0	5.5	2.0	0.5	0.0	.208
ABA Season Totals		42	....	353	138	58	145	.400	0	1	.000	22	46	.478	45	80	125	13	56	0	....	....	23	8.4	3.3	3.0	0.3	....

• KOPER, Bud

Herbert L. (Bud) Koper

Born: Aug. 9, 1942. Rocky, OK, United States. Height: 6'6". Weight: 210 lbs. Drafted: 1964 College: Oklahoma City

YEAR	TEAM	GP	GS	MIN	PTS	FGM	FGA	FG%	3PM	3PA	3P%	FTM	FTA	FT%	ORB	DRB	TRB	AST	PF	DQ	STL	BLK	TO	MPG	PPG	RPG	APG	PCM
64-65	San Francisco	54	....	631	247	106	241	.440	....	....	....	35	42	.833	....	....	61	43	59	1	....	....	....	11.7	4.6	1.1	0.8	.345
NBA Season Totals		54	....	631	247	106	241	.440	....	....	....	35	42	.833	....	....	61	43	59	1	....	....	....	11.7	4.6	1.1	0.8	....

YEAR	TEAM	GP	GS	MIN	PTS	FGM	FGA	FG%	3PM	3PA	3P%	FTM	FTA	FT%	ORB	DRB	TRB	AST	PF	DQ	STL	BLK	TO	MPG	PPG	RPG	APG	PCM

• KOPICKI, Joe   Joseph Gerard Kopicki

Born: June 12, 1960. Warren, MI, United States.   Height: 6'9".   Weight: 240 lbs.   Drafted: 1982   College: Detroit

YEAR	TEAM	GP	GS	MIN	PTS	FGM	FGA	FG%	3PM	3PA	3P%	FTM	FTA	FT%	ORB	DRB	TRB	AST	PF	DQ	STL	BLK	TO	MPG	PPG	RPG	APG	PCM
82-83	Washington	17	1	201	67	23	51	.451	0	1	.000	21	25	.840	18	44	62	9	21	0	9	2	9	11.8	3.9	3.6	0.5	.488
83-84	Washington	59	2	678	220	64	132	.485	1	7	.143	91	112	.813	64	102	166	46	71	0	15	5	41	11.5	3.7	2.8	0.8	.440
84-85	Denver	42	0	308	145	50	95	.526	2	3	.667	43	54	.796	29	57	86	29	58	0	13	1	29	7.3	3.5	2.0	0.7	.546
NBA Season Totals		118	3	1187	432	137	278	.493	3	11	.273	155	191	.812	111	203	314	84	150	0	37	8	79	10.1	3.7	2.7	0.7	....
83-84	Washington	3	0	25	6	3	6	.500	0	0	.000	0	0	.000	0	5	5	1	6	0	0	0	2	8.3	2.0	1.7	0.3	.171
84-85	Denver	7	0	32	21	6	16	.375	0	0	.000	9	17	.529	2	11	13	3	5	0	1	1	1	4.6	3.0	1.9	0.4	.684
NBA Playoff Totals		10	0	57	27	9	22	.409	0	0	.000	9	17	.529	2	16	18	4	11	0	1	1	3	5.7	2.7	1.8	0.4	....

• KORNET, Frank   Francis Milton Kornet

Born: Jan. 27, 1967. Lexington, KY, United States.   Height: 6'9".   Weight: 225 lbs.   Drafted: 1989   College: Vanderbilt

89-90	Milwaukee	57	0	438	113	42	114	.368	5	20	.250	24	39	.615	25	46	71	21	54	0	14	3	23	7.7	2.0	1.2	0.4	.220
90-91	Milwaukee	32	0	157	58	23	62	.371	5	18	.278	7	13	.538	10	14	24	9	28	0	5	1	10	4.9	1.8	0.8	0.3	.217
NBA Season Totals		89	0	595	171	65	176	.369	10	38	.263	31	52	.596	35	60	95	30	82	0	19	4	33	6.7	1.9	1.1	0.3	....
89-90	Milwaukee	2	0	4	0	0	1	.000	0	1	.000	0	0	.000	0	1	1	0	1	0	0	0	1	2.0	0.0	0.5	0.0	-.351
NBA Playoff Totals		2	0	4	0	0	1	.000	0	1	.000	0	0	.000	0	1	1	0	1	0	0	0	1	2.0	0.0	0.5	0.0	....

• KOROVIN, Hal   Harold Korovin

Born: 1925.   Height: 6'5".   Weight: 205 lbs.   Drafted: —   College: CCNY

47-48	Flint-N	3	....	....	11	4	....	....				3	5	.600	....	....	....	10	....	....	....	....		3.7			....
NBL Season Totals		3	....	....	11	4	....	....				3	5		....	....	....	10	....	....	....	....		3.7			....

• KOSKI, Tony   Anthony P. Koski

Born: June 26, 1946.   Height: 6'8".   Weight: 215 lbs.   Drafted: —   College: Providence

68-69	New York-A	5	....	30	6	2	7	.286	0	0	.000	2	2	1.000	4	3	7	4	9	0	....	....	2	6.0	1.2	1.4	0.8	.281
ABA Season Totals		5	....	30	6	2	7	.286	0	0	.000	2	2	1.000	4	3	7	4	9	0	....	....	2	6.0	1.2	1.4	0.8	....

• KOSMALSKI, Len   Leonard J. Kosmalski

Born: Nov. 29, 1951. Cleveland, OH, United States.   Height: 6'12".   Weight: 245 lbs.   Drafted: 1974   College: Tennessee

74-75	Omaha	67	....	413	90	33	83	.398	....	....	....	24	29	.828	31	88	119	41	64	0	6	6	....	6.2	1.3	1.8	0.6	.403
75-76	Kansas City	9	....	93	20	8	20	.400	....	....	....	4	7	.571	9	16	25	12	11	0	3	4	....	10.3	2.2	2.8	1.3	.418
NBA Season Totals		76	....	506	110	41	103	.398	....	....	....	28	36	.778	40	104	144	53	75	0	9	10	....	6.7	1.4	1.9	0.7	....
74-75	Omaha	6	....	29	6	2	3	.667	....	..→	....	2	3	.667	1	9	10	5	4	0	1	0	....	4.8	1.0	1.7	0.8	.596
NBA Playoff Totals		6	....	29	6	2	3	.667	....	....	....	2	3	.667	1	9	10	5	4	0	1	0	....	4.8	1.0	1.7	0.8	....

• KOSTECKA, Andy   Andrew Kostecka

Born: Feb. 10, 1921.   Height: 6'3".   Weight: 203 lbs.   Drafted: 1948   College: Georgetown

48-49	Indianapolis	21	....	....	135	46	110	.418	....	....	....	43	70	.614	....	....	....	14	48	....	....	....	....	6.4	....	0.7	....
NBA Season Totals		21	....	....	135	46	110	.418	....	....	....	43	70	.614	....	....	....	14	48	....	....	....	....	6.4	....	0.7	....

• KOTTMAN, Harold   Harold M. Kottman

Born: Aug. 22, 1922.   Height: 6'8".   Weight: 220 lbs.   Drafted: —   College: Culver Stockton

46-47	Boston	53	....	....	165	59	188	.314	....	....	....	47	101	.465	....	....	....	17	58	....	....	....	....	3.1	....	0.3	....
NBA Season Totals		53	....	....	165	59	188	.314	....	....	....	47	101	.465	....	....	....	17	58	....	....	....	....	3.1	....	0.3	....

• KOTZ, John   John Kotz

Born: Mar. 27, 1919. Rhinelander, WI, United States. Died: May 8, 1999.   Height: 6'3".   Weight: 200 lbs.   Drafted: —   College: Wisconsin

45-46	Sheboygan-N	11	....	....	74	26	....	....	....	....	....	22	....	....	....	....	....	....	....	....	....	....	....	6.7	....	....	....
NBL Season Totals		11	....	....	74	26	....	....	....	....	....	22	....	....	....	....	....	....	....	....	....	....	....	6.7	....	....	....
45-46	Sheboygan-N	3	....	....	7	3	....	....	....	....	....	1	1	1.000	....	....	....	....	....	....	....	....	....	2.3	....	....	....
NBL Playoff Totals		3	....	....	7	3	....	....	....	....	....	1	1	....	....	....	....	....	....	....	....	....	....	2.3	....	....	....

• KOZELKO, Tom   Thomas William Kozelko

Born: July 1, 1951. Traverse City, MI, United States.   Height: 6'8".   Weight: 220 lbs.   Drafted: 1973   College: Toledo

73-74	Washington	49	....	573	141	59	133	.444	....	....	....	23	32	.719	52	72	124	25	82	3	21	7	....	11.7	2.9	2.5	0.5	.303
74-75	Washington	73	....	754	151	60	167	.359	....	....	....	31	36	.861	50	90	140	41	125	4	28	5	....	10.3	2.1	1.9	0.6	.226
75-76	Washington	67	....	584	115	48	99	.485	....	....	....	19	30	.633	19	63	82	33	74	0	19	4	....	8.7	1.7	1.2	0.5	.245
NBA Season Totals		189	....	1911	407	167	399	.419	....	....	....	73	98	.745	121	225	346	99	281	7	68	16	....	10.1	2.2	1.8	0.5	....

YEAR	TEAM	GP	GS	MIN	PTS	FGM	FGA	FG%	3PM	3PA	3P%	FTM	FTA	FT%	ORB	DRB	TRB	AST	PF	DQ	STL	BLK	TO	MPG	PPG	RPG	APG	PCM
73-74	Washington	7	....	58	23	10	13	.769	....	....	....	3	4	.750	4	4	8	1	10	1	0	0	....	8.3	3.3	1.1	0.1	.409
74-75	Washington	13	....	54	14	5	11	.455	....	....	....	4	5	.800	4	3	7	1	8	0	0	0	....	4.2	1.1	0.5	0.1	.225
75-76	Washington	5	....	14	2	0	1	.000	....	....	....	2	2	1.000	1	1	2	0	0	0	0	1	....	2.8	0.4	0.4	0.0	.204
NBA Playoff Totals		25	....	126	39	15	25	.600	....	....	....	9	11	.818	9	8	17	2	18	1	0	1	....	5.0	1.6	0.7	0.1	....

• KOZLICKI, Ronald

Ronald F. (Koz) Kozlicki

Born: Dec. 12, 1944. Chicago, IL, United States.　　Height: 6'7".　　Weight: 215 lbs.　　Drafted: 1967　　College: Northwestern

YEAR	TEAM	GP	GS	MIN	PTS	FGM	FGA	FG%	3PM	3PA	3P%	FTM	FTA	FT%	ORB	DRB	TRB	AST	PF	DQ	STL	BLK	TO	MPG	PPG	RPG	APG	PCM
67-68	Indiana-A	37	....	354	109	41	121	.339	6	29	.207	21	34	.618	....	....	69	14	31	0	....	....	19	9.6	2.9	1.9	0.4	.277
ABA Season Totals		37	....	354	109	41	121	.339	6	29	.207	21	34	.618	....	....	69	14	31	0	....	....	19	9.6	2.9	1.9	0.4	
67-68	Indiana-A	2	....	5	0	0	2	.000	0	1	.000	0	0	.000	....	....	1	0	1	0	....	....	1	2.5	0.0	0.5	0.0	-.249
ABA Playoff Totals		2	....	5	0	0	2	.000	0	1	.000	0	0	.000	....	....	1	0	1	0	....	....	1	2.5	0.0	0.5	0.0	....

• KRAFFT, Vic

Victor Krafft

Born: 1919.　　Height: 6'3".　　Weight: 195 lbs.　　Drafted: —　　College: none

YEAR	TEAM	GP	GS	MIN	PTS	FGM	FGA	FG%	3PM	3PA	3P%	FTM	FTA	FT%	ORB	DRB	TRB	AST	PF	DQ	STL	BLK	TO	MPG	PPG	RPG	APG	PCM
48-49	Dayton-N	3	....	....	6	3	....	....	....	....	....	0	1	.000	....	....	....	....	....	....	....	....	....	2.0	....	....	....	
NBL Season Totals		3	....	....	6	3	....	....	....	....	....	0	1		....	....	....	....	....	....	....	....	....	2.0	....	....	....	

• KRAMER, Arvid

Arvid Kramer

Born: Oct. 2, 1956. Fulda, MN, United States.　　Height: 6'9".　　Weight: 220 lbs.　　Drafted: 1979　　College: Augustana (SD)

YEAR	TEAM	GP	GS	MIN	PTS	FGM	FGA	FG%	3PM	3PA	3P%	FTM	FTA	FT%	ORB	DRB	TRB	AST	PF	DQ	STL	BLK	TO	MPG	PPG	RPG	APG	PCM
79-80	Denver	8	....	45	16	7	22	.318	0	0	.000	2	2	1.000	6	6	12	3	8	0	0	5	5	5.6	2.0	1.5	0.4	.288
NBA Season Totals		8	....	45	16	7	22	.318	0	0	.000	2	2	1.000	6	6	12	3	8	0	0	5	5	5.6	2.0	1.5	0.4	

• KRAMER, Barry

Barry D. Kramer

Born: Nov. 10, 1942. Schenectady, NY, United States.　　Height: 6'4".　　Weight: 200 lbs.　　Drafted: 1964　　College: New York University

YEAR	TEAM	GP	GS	MIN	PTS	FGM	FGA	FG%	3PM	3PA	3P%	FTM	FTA	FT%	ORB	DRB	TRB	AST	PF	DQ	STL	BLK	TO	MPG	PPG	RPG	APG	PCM
64-65	San Francisco	33	....	276	102	36	100	.360	....	....	....	30	44	.682	....	....	59	26	36	0	....	....	....	8.4	3.1	1.8	0.8	.402
64-65	New York	19	....	231	84	27	86	.314	....	....	....	30	40	.750	....	....	41	15	31	1	....	....	....	12.2	4.4	2.2	0.8	.316
69-70	New York-A	7	....	56	27	10	31	.323	0	1	.000	7	8	.875	7	6	13	3	10	0	....	....	11	8.0	3.9	1.9	0.4	.336
NBA Season Totals		52	....	507	186	63	186	.339	....	....	....	60	84	.714	....	....	100	41	67	1	....	....	....	9.8	3.6	1.9	0.8	
ABA Season Totals		7	....	56	27	10	31	.323	0	1	.000	7	8	.875	7	6	13	3	10	0	....	....	11	8.0	3.9	1.9	0.4	....
Career Totals		59	....	563	213	73	217	.336	0	1	.000	67	92	.728	7	6	113	44	77	1	....	....	11	9.5	3.6	1.9	0.7	

• KRAMER, Bob

Bob Kramer

Born: 1921.　　Height: 6'3".　　Weight: —　　Drafted: —　　College: North Carolina

YEAR	TEAM	GP	GS	MIN	PTS	FGM	FGA	FG%	3PM	3PA	3P%	FTM	FTA	FT%	ORB	DRB	TRB	AST	PF	DQ	STL	BLK	TO	MPG	PPG	RPG	APG	PCM
42-43	Oshkosh-N	5	....	....	12	6	....	....	....	....	....	0	....	....	....	....	....	....	....	....	....	....	....	2.4	....	....	....	
46-47	Oshkosh-N	1	....	....	0	0	....	....	....	....	....	0	0	.000	....	....	....	....	0	0	....	....	....	0.0	....	....	....	
46-47	Youngstown-N	2	....	....	6	2	....	....	....	....	....	2	3	.667	....	....	....	....	....	....	....	....	....	3.0	....	....	....	
NBL Season Totals		8	....	....	18	8	....	....	....	....	....	2	3		....	....	....	....	0	0	....	....	....	2.3	....	....	....	
42-43	Oshkosh-N	2	....	....	0	0	....	....	....	....	....	0	....	....	....	....	....	....	....	....	....	....	....	0.0	....	....	....	
NBL Playoff Totals		2	....	....	0	0	....	....	....	....	....	0	....	....	....	....	....	....	....	....	....	....	....	0.0	....	....	....	

• KRAMER, Joel

Joel Bruce Kramer

Born: Nov. 30, 1955. San Diego, CA, United States.　　Height: 6'7".　　Weight: 203 lbs.　　Drafted: 1978　　College: San Diego State

YEAR	TEAM	GP	GS	MIN	PTS	FGM	FGA	FG%	3PM	3PA	3P%	FTM	FTA	FT%	ORB	DRB	TRB	AST	PF	DQ	STL	BLK	TO	MPG	PPG	RPG	APG	PCM
78-79	Phoenix	82	....	1401	487	181	370	.489	....	....	....	125	176	.710	134	203	337	92	224	2	45	23	98	17.1	5.9	4.1	1.1	.407
79-80	Phoenix	54	....	711	190	67	143	.469	0	1	.000	56	70	.800	49	102	151	75	104	0	26	5	49	13.2	3.5	2.8	1.4	.380
80-81	Phoenix	82	....	1065	335	136	258	.527	0	1	.000	63	91	.692	77	155	232	88	132	0	35	17	66	13.0	4.1	2.8	1.1	.418
81-82	Phoenix	56	0	549	143	55	133	.414	0	0	.000	33	42	.786	36	72	108	51	62	0	19	11	28	9.8	2.6	1.9	0.9	.355
82-83	Phoenix	54	4	458	102	44	104	.423	0	1	.000	14	16	.875	41	47	88	37	63	0	15	6	22	8.5	1.9	1.6	0.7	.301
NBA Season Totals		328	4	4184	1257	483	1008	.479	0	3	.000	291	395	.737	337	579	916	343	585	2	140	62	263	12.8	3.8	2.8	1.0	
78-79	Phoenix	15	....	257	90	32	59	.542	....	....	....	26	36	.722	21	36	57	19	44	2	9	7	16	17.1	6.0	3.8	1.3	.442
80-81	Phoenix	7	....	101	27	13	25	.520	0	0	.000	1	2	.500	2	14	16	4	18	0	2	2	1	14.4	3.9	2.3	0.6	.288
81-82	Phoenix	4	0	20	12	5	7	.714	0	0	.000	2	3	.667	2	3	5	1	2	0	1	0	1	5.0	3.0	1.3	0.3	.723
82-83	Phoenix	2	0	6	0	0	2	.000	0	0	.000	0	0	.000	0	0	0	0	0	0	0	0	0	3.0	0.0	0.0	0.0	-.301
NBA Playoff Totals		28	0	384	129	50	93	.538	0	0	.000	29	41	.707	25	53	78	24	64	2	12	9	18	13.7	4.6	2.8	0.9	....

• KRAMER, Steven

Steven P. Kramer

Born: Jan. 1, 1945. Sandy, UT, United States.　　Height: 6'5".　　Weight: 200 lbs.　　Drafted: —　　College: Brigham Young

YEAR	TEAM	GP	GS	MIN	PTS	FGM	FGA	FG%	3PM	3PA	3P%	FTM	FTA	FT%	ORB	DRB	TRB	AST	PF	DQ	STL	BLK	TO	MPG	PPG	RPG	APG	PCM
67-68	Anaheim-A	50	....	1140	566	218	497	.439	1	5	.200	129	165	.782	....	....	173	85	149	3	....	....	96	22.8	11.3	3.5	1.7	.439
68-69	Houston-A	23	....	701	321	113	281	.402	0	1	.000	95	117	.812	47	38	85	112	96	4	....	....	69	30.5	14.0	3.7	4.9	.467
69-70	Carolina-A	51	....	447	161	49	107	.458	0	2	.000	63	86	.733	18	34	52	39	70	0	....	....	42	8.8	3.2	1.0	0.8	.359
ABA Season Totals		124	....	2288	1048	380	885	.429	1	8	.125	287	368	.780	65	72	310	236	315	7	....	....	207	18.5	8.5	2.5	1.9	
69-70	Carolina-A	2	....	20	7	2	5	.400	0	0	.000	3	3	1.000	....	....	4	0	....	....	....	....	....	10.0	3.5	2.0	0.0	....
ABA Playoff Totals		2	....	20	7	2	5	.400	0	0	.000	3	3	1.000	....	....	4	0	....	....	....	....	....	10.0	3.5	2.0	0.0	....

YEAR	TEAM	GP	GS	MIN	PTS	FGM	FGA	FG%	3PM	3PA	3P%	FTM	FTA	FT%	ORB	DRB	TRB	AST	PF	DQ	STL	BLK	TO	MPG	PPG	RPG	APG	PCM

• KRAUS, Dan
Daniel Joseph Kraus

Born: Feb. 13, 1923.   Height: 6'   Weight: 195 lbs.   Drafted: 1948   College: Georgetown

YEAR	TEAM	GP	GS	MIN	PTS	FGM	FGA	FG%	3PM	3PA	3P%	FTM	FTA	FT%	ORB	DRB	TRB	AST	PF	DQ	STL	BLK	TO	MPG	PPG	RPG	APG	PCM
48-49	Baltimore	13	....	....	21	5	35	.143	....	....	....	11	24	.458	....	....		7	24	....	....	....			1.6	....	0.5	....
NBA Season Totals		13	....	....	21	5	35	.143	....	....	....	11	24	.458	....	....		7	24	....	....	....			1.6	....	0.5	....

• KRAUTBLATT, Herb
Herbert Krautblatt

Born: Nov. 19, 1926.   Height: 6'1".   Weight: 190 lbs.   Drafted: 1948   College: Rider

YEAR	TEAM	GP	GS	MIN	PTS	FGM	FGA	FG%	3PM	3PA	3P%	FTM	FTA	FT%	ORB	DRB	TRB	AST	PF	DQ	STL	BLK	TO	MPG	PPG	RPG	APG	PCM
48-49	Baltimore	10	....	....	13	4	18	.222	....	....	....	5	11	.455	....	....		4	14	....	....	....			1.3	....	0.4	....
NBA Season Totals		10	....	....	13	4	18	.222	....	....	....	5	11	.455	....	....		4	14	....	....	....			1.3	....	0.4	....

• KREBS, Jim
James (Red) Krebs

Born: Sept. 8, 1935. Webster Groves, MO, United States. Died: May 6, 1965.   Height: 6'8".   Weight: 230 lbs.   Drafted: 1957   College: Southern Methodist

YEAR	TEAM	GP	GS	MIN	PTS	FGM	FGA	FG%	3PM	3PA	3P%	FTM	FTA	FT%	ORB	DRB	TRB	AST	PF	DQ	STL	BLK	TO	MPG	PPG	RPG	APG	PCM
57-58	Minneapolis	68	....	1259	533	199	527	.378	....	....	....	135	176	.767	....	....	502	27	182	4	....	....		18.5	7.8	7.4	0.4	.487
58-59	Minneapolis	72	....	1578	634	271	679	.399	....	....	....	92	123	.748	....	....	491	50	212	4	....	....		21.9	8.8	6.8	0.7	.423
59-60	Minneapolis	75	....	1269	572	237	605	.392	....	....	....	98	136	.721	....	....	327	38	210	2	....	....		16.9	7.6	4.4	0.5	.390
60-61	LA Lakers	75	....	1655	617	271	692	.392	....	....	....	75	93	.806	....	....	456	68	223	2	....	....		22.1	8.2	6.1	0.9	.384
61-62	LA Lakers	78	....	2012	780	312	701	.445	....	....	....	156	208	.750	....	....	616	110	290	9	....	....		25.8	10.0	7.9	1.4	.476
62-63	LA Lakers	79	....	1913	659	272	627	.434	....	....	....	115	154	.747	....	....	502	87	256	2	....	....		24.2	8.3	6.4	1.1	.399
63-64	LA Lakers	68	....	975	333	134	357	.375	....	....	....	65	85	.765	....	....	283	49	166	6	....	....		14.3	4.9	4.2	0.7	.377
NBA Season Totals		515	....	10661	4128	1696	4188	.405	....	....	....	736	975	.755	....	....	3177	429	1539	29	....	....		20.7	8.0	6.2	0.8	
58-59	Minneapolis	13	....	213	94	36	103	.350	....	....	....	22	23	.957	....	....	77	5	36	1	....	....		16.4	7.2	5.9	0.4	.441
59-60	Minneapolis	9	....	157	51	23	55	.418	....	....	....	5	10	.500	....	....	47	8	31	0	....	....		17.4	5.7	5.2	0.9	.374
60-61	LA Lakers	12	....	183	46	16	47	.340	....	....	....	14	18	.778	....	....	60	9	37	3	....	....		15.3	3.8	5.0	0.8	.348
61-62	LA Lakers	11	....	327	82	30	90	.333	....	....	....	22	26	.846	....	....	102	21	50	4	....	....		29.7	7.5	9.3	1.9	.365
62-63	LA Lakers	13	....	199	42	16	47	.340	....	....	....	10	15	.667	....	....	40	4	49	4	....	....		15.3	3.2	3.1	0.3	.164
63-64	LA Lakers	4	....	50	14	6	9	.667	....	....	....	2	4	.500	....	....	22	6	8	0	....	....		12.5	3.5	5.5	1.5	.644
NBA Playoff Totals		62	....	1129	329	127	351	.362	....	....	....	75	96	.781	....	....	348	53	211	12	....	....		18.2	5.3	5.6	0.9	

• KREKLOW, Wayne
Wayne R. Kreklow

Born: Jan. 4, 1957. Neenah, WI, United States.   Height: 6'4".   Weight: 175 lbs.   Drafted: 1979   College: Drake

YEAR	TEAM	GP	GS	MIN	PTS	FGM	FGA	FG%	3PM	3PA	3P%	FTM	FTA	FT%	ORB	DRB	TRB	AST	PF	DQ	STL	BLK	TO	MPG	PPG	RPG	APG	PCM
80-81	Boston	25	....	100	30	11	47	.234	1	4	.250	7	10	.700	2	10	12	9	20	0	2	1	10	4.0	1.2	0.5	0.4	.011
NBA Season Totals		25	....	100	30	11	47	.234	1	4	.250	7	10	.700	2	10	12	9	20	0	2	1	10	4.0	1.2	0.5	0.4	....

• KRON, Tommy
Thomas M. Kron

Born: Feb. 28, 1943. Tell City, IN, United States.   Height: 6'5".   Weight: 200 lbs.   Drafted: 1966   College: Kentucky

YEAR	TEAM	GP	GS	MIN	PTS	FGM	FGA	FG%	3PM	3PA	3P%	FTM	FTA	FT%	ORB	DRB	TRB	AST	PF	DQ	STL	BLK	TO	MPG	PPG	RPG	APG	PCM
66-67	St. Louis	32	....	221	67	27	87	.310	....	....	....	13	19	.684	....	....	36	46	35	0	....	....		6.9	2.1	1.1	1.4	.393
67-68	Seattle	76	....	1794	738	277	699	.396	....	....	....	184	233	.790	....	....	355	281	231	4	....	....		23.6	9.7	4.7	3.7	.508
68-69	Seattle	76	....	1124	388	146	372	.392	....	....	....	96	137	.701	....	....	212	191	179	2	....	....		14.8	5.1	2.8	2.5	.451
69-70	Kentucky-A	40	....	493	158	55	147	.374	7	19	.368	41	46	.891	24	45	69	87	80	1	....	....	59	12.3	4.0	1.7	2.2	.408
NBA Season Totals		184	....	3139	1193	450	1158	.389	....	....	....	293	389	.753	....	....	603	518	445	6	....	....		17.1	6.5	3.3	2.8	
ABA Season Totals		40	....	493	158	55	147	.374	7	19	.368	41	46	.891	24	45	69	87	80	1	....	....	59	12.3	4.0	1.7	2.2	
Career Totals		224	....	3632	1351	505	1305	.387	7	19	.368	334	435	.768	24	45	672	605	525	7	....	....	59	16.2	6.0	3.0	2.7	
66-67	St. Louis	1	....	1	0	0	1	.000	....	....	....	0	0	.000	....	....	0	0	1	0	....	....		1.0	0.0	0.0	0.0	-1.20
NBA Playoff Totals		1	....	1	0	0	1	.000	....	....	....	0	0	.000	....	....	0	0	1	0	....	....		1.0	0.0	0.0	0.0	

• KROPP, Tom
Thomas Carl (Tom) Kropp

Born: Feb. 12, 1953. Grand Island, NE, United States.   Height: 6'3".   Weight: 205 lbs.   Drafted: 1975   College: Kearney State

YEAR	TEAM	GP	GS	MIN	PTS	FGM	FGA	FG%	3PM	3PA	3P%	FTM	FTA	FT%	ORB	DRB	TRB	AST	PF	DQ	STL	BLK	TO	MPG	PPG	RPG	APG	PCM
75-76	Washington	25	....	72	19	7	30	.233	....	....	....	5	6	.833	5	10	15	8	20	0	2	0	....	2.9	0.8	0.6	0.3	.170
76-77	Chicago	53	....	480	174	73	152	.480	....	....	....	28	41	.683	21	26	47	39	77	1	18	1	....	9.1	3.3	0.9	0.7	.316
NBA Season Totals		78	....	552	193	80	182	.440	....	....	....	33	47	.702	26	36	62	47	97	1	20	1	....	7.1	2.5	0.8	0.6	....
75-76	Washington	1	....	2	2	1	1	1.000	....	....	....	0	0	.000	0	0	0	1	0	0	0	0	....	2.0	2.0	0.0	0.0	.786
76-77	Chicago	1	....	2	0	0	1	.000	....	....	....	0	0	.000	0	0	0	2	0	0	0	0	....	2.0	0.0	0.0	0.0	-.432
NBA Playoff Totals		2	....	4	2	1	1	1.000	....	....	....	0	0	.000	0	0	0	3	0	0	0	0	....	2.0	1.0	0.0	0.0	....

• KRUSE, Joe
Joe Kruse

Born: 1914.   Height: 6'2".   Weight: 200 lbs.   Drafted: —   College: Xavier (OH)

YEAR	TEAM	GP	GS	MIN	PTS	FGM	FGA	FG%	3PM	3PA	3P%	FTM	FTA	FT%	ORB	DRB	TRB	AST	PF	DQ	STL	BLK	TO	MPG	PPG	RPG	APG	PCM
37-38	Cincinnati-N	6	....	....	20	8	....	....	....	....	....	4	....	....	....	....	....	....	....	....	....	....		3.3	....	....	....	
NBL Season Totals		6	....	....	20	8	....	....	....	....	....	4	....	....	....	....	....	....	....	....	....	....		3.3	....	....	....	

• KRYSTKOWIAK, Larry
Larry Brett (Special K) Krystkowiak

Born: Sept. 23, 1964. Missoula, MT, United States.   Height: 6'9".   Weight: 220 lbs.   Drafted: 1986   College: Montana

YEAR	TEAM	GP	GS	MIN	PTS	FGM	FGA	FG%	3PM	3PA	3P%	FTM	FTA	FT%	ORB	DRB	TRB	AST	PF	DQ	STL	BLK	TO	MPG	PPG	RPG	APG	PCM
86-87	San Antonio	68	2	1004	451	170	373	.456	1	12	.083	110	148	.743	77	162	239	85	141	1	22	12	68	14.8	6.6	3.5	1.3	.459
87-88	Milwaukee	50	7	1050	359	128	266	.481	0	3	.000	103	127	.811	88	143	231	50	137	0	18	8	55	21.0	7.2	4.6	1.0	.378
88-89	Milwaukee	80	77	2472	1017	362	766	.473	4	12	.333	289	351	.823	198	412	610	107	219	0	93	9	144	30.9	12.7	7.6	1.3	.467

YEAR	TEAM	GP	GS	MIN	PTS	FGM	FGA	FG%	3PM	3PA	3P%	FTM	FTA	FT%	ORB	DRB	TRB	AST	PF	DQ	STL	BLK	TO	MPG	PPG	RPG	APG	PCM
89-90	Milwaukee	16	7	381	112	43	118	.364	0	2	.000	26	33	.788	16	60	76	25	41	0	10	2	19	23.8	7.0	4.8	1.6	.290
91-92	Milwaukee	79	16	1848	713	293	660	.444	0	5	.000	127	169	.751	131	298	429	114	218	2	54	12	119	23.4	9.0	5.4	1.4	.391
92-93	Utah	71	0	1362	513	198	425	.466	0	1	.000	117	147	.796	74	205	279	68	181	1	42	13	64	19.2	7.2	3.9	1.0	.387
93-94	Orlando	34	11	682	173	71	148	.480	0	1	.000	31	39	.795	38	85	123	35	74	0	14	4	31	20.1	5.1	3.6	1.0	.298
94-95	Chicago	19	14	287	83	28	72	.389	0	0	.000	27	30	.900	19	40	59	26	34	0	9	2	25	15.1	4.4	3.1	1.4	.328
96-97	LA Lakers	3	0	11	3	1	2	.500	0	0	.000	1	2	.500	2	3	5	3	3	0	2	0	1	3.7	1.0	1.7	1.0	.818
NBA Season Totals		420	134	9097	3424	1294	2830	.457	5	36	.139	831	1046	.794	643	1408	2051	513	1048	4	264	62	526	21.7	8.2	4.9	1.2	....
87-88	Milwaukee	5	5	163	42	13	29	.448	0	0	.000	16	18	.889	13	21	34	7	17	0	4	0	5	32.6	8.4	6.8	1.4	.346
88-89	Milwaukee	8	8	239	85	29	68	.426	0	2	.000	27	31	.871	14	31	45	12	22	0	2	1	16	29.9	10.6	5.6	1.5	.332
90-91	Milwaukee	3	0	25	2	1	6	.167	0	0	.000	0	0	.000	0	3	3	2	3	0	1	0	0	8.3	0.7	1.0	0.7	.072
92-93	Utah	1	0	8	0	0	1	.000	0	0	.000	0	0	.000	1	1	2	0	1	0	0	0	1	8.0	0.0	2.0	0.0	-.058
93-94	Orlando	3	3	92	18	7	18	.389	0	0	.000	4	4	1.000	7	18	25	9	10	0	3	2	2	30.7	6.0	8.3	3.0	.421
NBA Playoff Totals		20	16	527	147	50	122	.410	0	2	.000	47	53	.887	35	74	109	30	53	0	10	3	24	26.4	7.4	5.5	1.5	....

• KRZOSKA, Ray

Ray Krzoska

Born: 1918. Height: 6'2". Weight: 190 lbs. Drafted: — College: Wisconsin (Milwaukee)

YEAR	TEAM	GP	GS	MIN	PTS	FGM	FGA	FG%	3PM	3PA	3P%	FTM	FTA	FT%	ORB	DRB	TRB	AST	PF	DQ	STL	BLK	TO	MPG	PPG	RPG	APG	PCM
42-43	Oshkosh-N	2	....	....	6	3	....	....	....	....	....	0													3.0			
44-45	Chicago-N	21	....	....	81	30	....	....	....	....	....	21													3.9			
NBL Season Totals		23	....	....	87	33						21													3.8			
44-45	Chicago-N	3	....	....	13	4						5													4.3			
NBL Playoff Totals		3	....	....	13	4						5													4.3			

• KUBERSKI, Steve

Stephen Paul Kuberski

Born: Nov. 6, 1947. Moline, IL, United States. Height: 6'8". Weight: 215 lbs. Drafted: 1969 College: Bradley

YEAR	TEAM	GP	GS	MIN	PTS	FGM	FGA	FG%	3PM	3PA	3P%	FTM	FTA	FT%	ORB	DRB	TRB	AST	PF	DQ	STL	BLK	TO	MPG	PPG	RPG	APG	PCM
69-70	Boston	51	....	797	324	130	335	.388	....	....	....	64	92	.696	....	....	257	29	87	0	....	....	....	15.6	6.4	5.0	0.6	.441
70-71	Boston	82	....	1867	759	313	745	.420	....	....	....	133	183	.727	....	....	538	78	198	1	....	....	....	22.8	9.3	6.6	1.0	.446
71-72	Boston	71	....	1128	450	185	444	.417	....	....	....	80	102	.784	....	....	320	46	130	1	....	....	....	15.9	6.3	4.5	0.6	.434
72-73	Boston	78	....	762	345	140	347	.403	....	....	....	65	84	.774	....	....	197	26	92	0	....	....	....	9.8	4.4	2.5	0.3	.418
73-74	Boston	78	....	985	400	157	368	.427	....	....	....	86	111	.775	96	141	237	38	125	0	7	7	....	12.6	5.1	3.0	0.5	.408
74-75	Milwaukee	59	....	517	168	62	159	.390	....	....	....	44	56	.786	52	71	123	35	59	0	11	3	....	8.8	2.8	2.1	0.6	.387
75-76	Buffalo	10	....	85	17	7	17	.412	....	....	....	3	3	1.000	4	21	25	3	10	0	1	2	....	8.5	1.7	2.5	0.3	.341
75-76	Boston	60	....	882	324	128	274	.467	....	....	....	68	76	.895	86	148	234	44	123	1	11	11	....	14.7	5.4	3.9	0.7	.446
76-77	Boston	76	....	860	325	131	312	.420	....	....	....	63	83	.759	76	133	209	39	89	0	7	5	....	11.3	4.3	2.8	0.5	.403
77-78	Boston	3	....	14	2	1	4	.250	....	....	....	0	0	.000	1	5	6	0	2	0	1	0	2	4.7	0.7	2.0	0.0	.205
NBA Season Totals		568	....	7897	3114	1254	3005	.417	....	....	....	606	790	.767	315	519	2146	338	915	3	38	28	2	13.9	5.5	3.8	0.6	....
71-72	Boston	11	....	218	128	48	87	.552	....	....	....	32	38	.842	....	....	63	3	23	0	....	....	....	19.8	11.6	5.7	0.3	.640
72-73	Boston	12	....	95	45	19	46	.413	....	....	....	7	10	.700	....	....	14	3	15	0	....	....	....	7.9	3.8	1.2	0.3	.311
73-74	Boston	9	....	69	15	5	25	.200	....	....	....	5	10	.500	8	12	20	2	9	0	1	1	....	7.7	1.7	2.2	0.2	.164
75-76	Boston	18	....	232	97	38	81	.469	....	....	....	21	26	.808	16	35	51	16	38	0	0	3	....	12.9	5.4	2.8	0.9	.447
NBA Playoff Totals		50	....	614	285	110	239	.460	....	....	....	65	84	.774	24	47	148	24	85	0	1	4	....	12.3	5.7	3.0	0.5	....

• KUBIAK, Leo

Leo R. Kubiak

Born: Dec. 25, 1927. Height: 5'11". Weight: 160 lbs. Drafted: 1948 College: Bowling Green

YEAR	TEAM	GP	GS	MIN	PTS	FGM	FGA	FG%	3PM	3PA	3P%	FTM	FTA	FT%	ORB	DRB	TRB	AST	PF	DQ	STL	BLK	TO	MPG	PPG	RPG	APG	PCM
48-49	Waterloo-N	62	....	....	462	177	....	....	....	....	....	108	142	.761	....	....	....	....	177	....	....	....	....	7.5			
49-50	Waterloo	62	....	....	710	259	794	.326	....	....	....	192	236	.814	....	....	....	201	250	....	....	....	....	11.5		3.2	
NBA Season Totals		62	....	....	710	259	794	.326	....	....	....	192	236	.814	....	....	....	201	250	....	....	....	....	11.5		3.2	
NBL Season Totals		62	....	....	462	177	....	....	....	....	....	108	142	....	....	....	....	....	177	....	....	....	....	7.5			
Career Totals		124	....	....	1172	436	794	....	....	....	....	300	378	....	....	....	....	201	427	....	....	....	....	9.5		1.6	

• KUBILUS, Vito

Vito Kubilus

Born: June 29, 1914. Died: Nov.1986. Height: 6'1". Weight: 180 lbs. Drafted: — College: Ohio College of Chiropody

YEAR	TEAM	GP	GS	MIN	PTS	FGM	FGA	FG%	3PM	3PA	3P%	FTM	FTA	FT%	ORB	DRB	TRB	AST	PF	DQ	STL	BLK	TO	MPG	PPG	RPG	APG	PCM
43-44	Cleveland-N	16	....	....	32	11	....	....	....	....	....	10													2.0			
NBL Season Totals		16	....	....	32	11	....	....	....	....	....	10													2.0			
43-44	Cleveland-N	1	....	....	2	1	....	....	....	....	....	0													2.0			
NBL Playoff Totals		1	....	....	2	1	....	....	....	....	....	0													2.0			

• KUBLIC, Les

Les Kublic

Born: 1912. Height: 6'3". Weight: 200 lbs. Drafted: — College: Beloit

YEAR	TEAM	GP	GS	MIN	PTS	FGM	FGA	FG%	3PM	3PA	3P%	FTM	FTA	FT%	ORB	DRB	TRB	AST	PF	DQ	STL	BLK	TO	MPG	PPG	RPG	APG	PCM
38-39	Sheboygan-N	26	....	....	34	14	....	....	....	....	....	6													1.3			
39-40	Sheboygan-N	13	....	....	13	6	....	....	....	....	....	1													1.0			
NBL Season Totals		39	....	....	47	20						7													1.2			
39-40	Sheboygan-N	1	....	....	0	0						0													0.0			
NBL Playoff Totals		1	....	....	0	0						0													0.0			

YEAR TEAM	GP	GS	MIN	PTS	FGM	FGA	FG%	3PM	3PA	3P%	FTM	FTA	FT%	ORB	DRB	TRB	AST	PF	DQ	STL	BLK	TO	MPG	PPG	RPG	APG	PCM

• KUCZENSKI, Bruce

Bruce John Kuczenski

Born: Feb. 3, 1961. Bristol, CT, United States. Height: 6'10". Weight: 230 lbs. Drafted: 1983 College: Connecticut

YEAR TEAM	GP	GS	MIN	PTS	FGM	FGA	FG%	3PM	3PA	3P%	FTM	FTA	FT%	ORB	DRB	TRB	AST	PF	DQ	STL	BLK	TO	MPG	PPG	RPG	APG	PCM
83-84 New Jersey	7	0	28	11	4	12	.333	0	0	.000	3	6	.500	3	5	8	4	3	0	0	0	1	4.0	1.6	1.1	0.6	.413
83-84 Philadelphia	3	2	40	3	1	8	.125	0	0	.000	1	2	.500	1	5	6	2	7	0	1	1	6	13.3	1.0	2.0	0.7	-.081
83-84 Indiana	5	0	51	14	5	17	.294	0	0	.000	4	4	1.000	3	6	9	2	8	0	0	0	8	10.2	2.8	1.8	0.4	.043
NBA Season Totals	15	2	119	28	10	37	.270	0	0	.000	8	12	.667	7	16	23	8	18	0	1	1	15	7.9	1.9	1.5	0.5	....

• KUDELKA, Frank

Frank Carl (Apples) Kudelka

Born: June 25, 1925. Died: May4, 1993. Height: 6'2". Weight: 193 lbs. Drafted: — College: St. Mary's (CA)

YEAR TEAM	GP	GS	MIN	PTS	FGM	FGA	FG%	3PM	3PA	3P%	FTM	FTA	FT%	ORB	DRB	TRB	AST	PF	DQ	STL	BLK	TO	MPG	PPG	RPG	APG	PCM
49-50 Chicago	65	....	....	433	172	528	.326	....	....	....	89	140	.636	....	....	....	132	198	....	....	....	....	....	6.7	....	2.0	....
50-51 Was/Bos	62	....	....	441	179	518	.346	....	....	....	83	119	.697	....	....	158	105	211	8	....	....	....	....	7.1	2.5	1.7	....
51-52 Baltimore	65	....	1583	606	204	614	.332	....	....	....	198	258	.767	....	....	275	183	220	11	....	....	....	24.4	9.3	4.2	2.8	.408
52-53 Bal/Phi	36	....	567	162	59	193	.306	....	....	....	44	68	.647	....	....	88	70	109	2	....	....	....	15.8	4.5	2.4	1.9	.300
NBA Season Totals	228	....	2150	1642	614	1853	.331	....	....	....	414	585	.708	....	....	521	490	738	21	....	....	....	9.4	7.2	2.3	2.1	....
49-50 Chicago	2	....	....	5	2	10	.200	....	....	....	1	2	.500	....	....	....	4	4	....	....	....	....	....	2.5	....	2.0	....
50-51 Boston	1	....	....	4	2	4	.500	....	....	....	0	3	.000	....	....	5	2	3	0	....	....	....	....	4.0	5.0	2.0	....
NBA Playoff Totals	3	....	....	9	4	14	.286	....	....	....	1	5	.200	....	....	5	6	7	0	....	....	....	....	3.0	1.7	2.0	....

• KUESTER, John

John Dewitt Kuester Jr.

Born: Feb. 6, 1955. Richmond, VA, United States. Height: 6'2". Weight: 180 lbs. Drafted: 1977 College: North Carolina

YEAR TEAM	GP	GS	MIN	PTS	FGM	FGA	FG%	3PM	3PA	3P%	FTM	FTA	FT%	ORB	DRB	TRB	AST	PF	DQ	STL	BLK	TO	MPG	PPG	RPG	APG	PCM
77-78 Kansas City	78	....	1215	377	145	319	.455	....	....	....	87	105	.829	19	95	114	252	143	1	58	1	94	15.6	4.8	1.5	3.2	.417
78-79 Denver	33	....	212	45	16	52	.308	....	....	....	13	14	.929	5	8	13	37	29	0	18	1	20	6.4	1.4	0.4	1.1	.239
79-80 Indiana	24	....	100	29	12	34	.353	0	1	.000	5	7	.714	3	11	14	16	8	0	7	1	5	4.2	1.2	0.6	0.7	.375
NBA Season Totals	135	....	1527	451	173	405	.427	0	1	.000	105	126	.833	27	114	141	305	180	1	83	3	119	11.3	3.3	1.0	2.3	....

• KUKA, Ray

Raphael Eugene (Cookie) Kuka

Born: Feb. 17, 1922. Havre, MT, United States. Died: Mar.27, 1990. Height: 6'3". Weight: 200 lbs. Drafted: — College: Notre Dame

YEAR TEAM	GP	GS	MIN	PTS	FGM	FGA	FG%	3PM	3PA	3P%	FTM	FTA	FT%	ORB	DRB	TRB	AST	PF	DQ	STL	BLK	TO	MPG	PPG	RPG	APG	PCM
47-48 New York	44	....	....	228	89	273	.326	....	....	....	50	84	.595	....	....	....	27	117	....	....	....	....	....	5.2	....	0.6	....
48-49 New York	8	....	....	25	10	36	.278	....	....	....	5	9	.556	....	....	....	11	16	....	....	....	....	....	3.1	....	1.4	....
NBA Season Totals	52	....	....	253	99	309	.320	....	....	....	55	93	.591	....	....	....	38	133	....	....	....	....	....	4.9	....	0.7	....
47-48 New York	3	....	....	8	3	10	.300	....	....	....	2	2	1.000	....	....	....	0	12	....	....	....	....	....	2.7	....	0.0	....
NBA Playoff Totals	3	....	....	8	3	10	.300	....	....	....	2	2	1.000	....	....	....	0	12	....	....	....	....	....	2.7	....	0.0	....

• KUKOC, Toni

Toni (The Waiter) Kukoc

Born: Sept. 18, 1968. Split, Croatia. Height: 6'10". Weight: 192 lbs. Drafted: 1990 College: none

YEAR TEAM	GP	GS	MIN	PTS	FGM	FGA	FG%	3PM	3PA	3P%	FTM	FTA	FT%	ORB	DRB	TRB	AST	PF	DQ	STL	BLK	TO	MPG	PPG	RPG	APG	PCM
93-94 Chicago	75	8	1808	814	313	726	.431	32	118	.271	156	210	.743	98	199	297	252	122	0	81	33	165	24.1	10.9	4.0	3.4	.472
94-95 Chicago	81	55	2584	1271	487	967	.504	62	198	.313	235	314	.748	155	285	440	372	163	1	102	16	162	31.9	15.7	5.4	4.6	.570
95-96 Chicago	81	20	2103	1065	386	787	.490	87	216	.403	206	267	.772	115	208	323	287	150	0	64	28	113	26.0	13.1	4.0	3.5	.560
96-97 Chicago	57	15	1610	754	285	605	.471	50	151	.331	134	174	.770	94	167	261	256	97	1	60	29	91	28.2	13.2	4.6	4.5	.563
97-98 Chicago	74	52	2235	984	383	841	.455	63	174	.362	155	219	.708	121	206	327	314	149	0	76	37	155	30.2	13.3	4.4	4.2	.478
98-99 Chicago	44	44	1654	828	315	750	.420	39	137	.285	159	215	.740	65	245	310	235	82	0	49	11	121	37.6	18.8	7.0	5.3	.521
99-00 Chicago	24	23	868	432	148	388	.381	18	78	.231	118	155	.761	37	93	130	124	51	0	44	19	75	36.2	18.0	5.4	5.2	.480
99-00 Philadelphia	32	8	916	398	149	340	.438	26	90	.289	74	110	.673	38	105	143	141	61	0	33	9	71	28.6	12.4	4.5	4.4	.478
00-01 Philadelphia	48	5	979	386	151	330	.458	32	78	.410	52	88	.591	47	115	162	93	62	0	35	6	60	20.4	8.0	3.4	1.9	.421
00-01 Atlanta	17	14	618	335	124	252	.492	38	79	.481	49	72	.681	19	78	97	106	36	0	13	5	51	36.4	19.7	5.7	6.2	.595
01-02 Atlanta	59	9	1494	584	211	504	.419	53	171	.310	109	153	.712	43	175	218	210	91	0	48	17	113	25.3	9.9	3.7	3.6	.429
02-03 Milwaukee	63	0	1704	730	249	577	.432	95	263	.361	137	194	.706	67	199	266	230	134	0	81	29	122	27.0	11.6	4.2	3.7	.485
NBA Season Totals	655	253	18573	8581	3201	7067	.453	595	1753	.339	1584	2171	.730	899	2075	2974	2620	1198	2	686	239	1299	28.4	13.1	4.5	4.0	....
93-94 Chicago	10	0	194	93	30	67	.448	8	19	.421	25	34	.735	11	29	40	36	15	0	5	3	17	19.4	9.3	4.0	3.6	.595
94-95 Chicago	10	10	372	138	53	111	.477	14	32	.438	18	26	.692	20	48	68	57	23	0	10	2	19	37.2	13.8	6.8	5.7	.502
95-96 Chicago	15	5	439	162	59	151	.391	13	68	.191	31	37	.838	19	44	63	58	33	0	14	4	26	29.3	10.8	4.2	3.9	.388
96-97 Chicago	19	0	423	150	45	125	.360	19	53	.358	41	58	.707	13	41	54	54	30	0	13	4	17	22.3	7.9	2.8	2.8	.382
97-98 Chicago	21	17	637	275	106	218	.486	23	61	.377	40	62	.645	24	57	81	60	57	1	26	10	27	30.3	13.1	3.9	2.9	.446
99-00 Philadelphia	10	0	257	93	36	93	.387	11	34	.324	10	17	.588	7	30	37	17	26	0	10	3	15	25.7	9.3	3.7	1.7	.298
02-03 Milwaukee	6	0	184	89	32	65	.492	11	29	.379	14	20	.700	6	19	25	22	12	0	13	1	11	30.7	14.8	4.2	3.7	.545
NBA Playoff Totals	91	32	2506	1000	361	830	.435	99	296	.334	179	254	.705	100	268	368	304	196	1	91	27	132	27.5	11.0	4.0	3.3	....

• KUNNERT, Kevin

Kevin Robert Kunnert

Born: Nov. 11, 1951. Dubuque, IA, United States. Height: 7' Weight: 230 lbs. Drafted: 1973 College: Iowa

YEAR TEAM	GP	GS	MIN	PTS	FGM	FGA	FG%	3PM	3PA	3P%	FTM	FTA	FT%	ORB	DRB	TRB	AST	PF	DQ	STL	BLK	TO	MPG	PPG	RPG	APG	PCM
73-74 Buffalo	39	....	340	109	49	101	.485	....	....	....	11	16	.688	43	63	106	25	83	0	5	25	....	8.7	2.8	2.7	0.6	.430
73-74 Houston	25	....	361	122	56	114	.491	....	....	....	10	17	.588	40	71	111	18	68	0	5	29	....	14.4	4.9	4.4	0.7	.432
74-75 Houston	75	....	1801	808	346	676	.512	....	....	....	116	169	.686	214	417	631	108	223	2	34	84	....	24.0	10.8	8.4	1.4	.595
75-76 Houston	80	....	2335	1032	465	954	.487	....	....	....	102	156	.654	267	520	787	155	315	14	57	105	....	29.2	12.9	9.8	1.9	.559
76-77 Houston	81	....	2050	759	333	685	.486	....	....	....	93	126	.738	210	459	669	154	361	17	35	105	....	25.3	9.4	8.3	1.9	.506
77-78 Houston	80	....	2152	829	368	842	.437	....	....	....	93	135	.689	262	431	693	97	315	13	44	90	144	26.9	10.4	8.7	1.2	.448
78-79 San Diego	81	....	1684	524	234	501	.467	....	....	....	56	85	.659	202	367	569	113	309	7	45	118	138	20.8	6.5	7.0	1.4	.469
79-80 Portland	18	....	302	126	50	114	.439	0	0	.000	26	43	.605	37	75	112	29	59	1	7	22	41	16.8	7.0	6.2	1.6	.516
80-81 Portland	55	....	842	244	101	216	.468	0	0	.000	42	54	.778	98	189	287	67	143	1	17	32	50	15.3	4.4	5.2	1.2	.478
81-82 Portland	21	0	237	49	20	48	.417	0	0	.000	9	17	.529	20	46	66	18	51	1	3	6	19	11.3	2.3	3.1	0.9	.283
NBA Season Totals	555	0	12104	4602	2022	4251	.476	0	0	.000	558	818	.682	1393	2638	4031	784	1927	56	252	616	392	21.8	8.3	7.3	1.4	....

YEAR	TEAM	GP	GS	MIN	PTS	FGM	FGA	FG%	3PM	3PA	3P%	FTM	FTA	FT%	ORB	DRB	TRB	AST	PF	DQ	STL	BLK	TO	MPG	PPG	RPG	APG	PCM
74-75	Houston	8	....	244	87	35	81	.432	....	....	....	17	26	.654	11	49	60	12	37	1	4	13	....	30.5	10.9	7.5	1.5	.382
76-77	Houston	12	....	328	114	51	104	.490	....	....	....	12	23	.522	48	59	107	14	51	2	2	8	....	27.3	9.5	8.9	1.2	.457
80-81	Portland	3	....	43	11	5	10	.500	0	1	.000	1	4	.250	2	7	9	1	7	0	1	0	3	14.3	3.7	3.0	0.3	.218
NBA Playoff Totals		23	....	615	212	91	195	.467	0	1	.000	30	53	.566	61	115	176	27	95	3	7	21	3	26.7	9.2	7.7	1.2	....

• KUNZE, Terry

Terry D. Kunze

Born: Mar. 11, 1943.   Height: 6'4".   Weight: 210 lbs.   Drafted: 1965   College: Minnesota

YEAR	TEAM	GP	GS	MIN	PTS	FGM	FGA	FG%	3PM	3PA	3P%	FTM	FTA	FT%	ORB	DRB	TRB	AST	PF	DQ	STL	BLK	TO	MPG	PPG	RPG	APG	PCM
67-68	Minnesota-A	46	....	662	230	83	245	.339	5	11	.455	59	102	.578	....	....	75	47	77	0	....	....	58	14.4	5.0	1.6	1.0	.246
ABA Season Totals		46	....	662	230	83	245	.339	5	11	.455	59	102	.578	....	....	75	47	77	0	....	....	58	14.4	5.0	1.6	1.0	....

• KUPCHAK, Mitch

Mitchell Kupchak

Born: May 24, 1954. Hicksville, NY, United States.   Height: 6'9".   Weight: 230 lbs.   Drafted: 1976   College: North Carolina

YEAR	TEAM	GP	GS	MIN	PTS	FGM	FGA	FG%	3PM	3PA	3P%	FTM	FTA	FT%	ORB	DRB	TRB	AST	PF	DQ	STL	BLK	TO	MPG	PPG	RPG	APG	PCM
76-77	Washington	82	....	1513	852	341	596	.572	....	....	....	170	246	.691	183	311	494	62	204	3	22	34	....	18.5	10.4	6.0	0.8	.666
77-78	Washington	67	....	1759	1066	393	768	.512	....	....	....	280	402	.697	162	298	460	71	196	1	28	42	181	26.3	15.9	6.9	1.1	.559
78-79	Washington	66	....	1604	961	369	685	.539	....	....	....	223	300	.743	152	278	430	88	141	0	23	23	119	24.3	14.6	6.5	1.3	.622
79-80	Washington	40	....	451	186	67	160	.419	0	2	.000	52	75	.693	32	73	105	16	49	1	8	8	40	11.3	4.7	2.6	0.4	.355
80-81	Washington	82	....	1934	1024	392	747	.525	0	1	.000	240	340	.706	198	371	569	62	195	1	36	26	164	23.6	12.5	6.9	0.8	.548
81-82	LA Lakers	26	26	821	371	153	267	.573	0	0	.000	65	98	.663	64	146	210	33	80	1	12	10	44	31.6	14.3	8.1	1.3	.515
83-84	LA Lakers	34	3	324	104	41	108	.380	0	1	.000	22	34	.647	35	52	87	7	46	0	4	6	20	9.5	3.1	2.6	0.2	.290
84-85	LA Lakers	58	3	716	306	123	244	.504	0	0	.000	60	91	.659	68	116	184	21	104	0	19	20	46	12.3	5.3	3.2	0.4	.444
85-86	LA Lakers	55	0	783	332	124	257	.482	0	1	.000	84	112	.750	69	122	191	17	102	0	12	7	66	14.2	6.0	3.5	0.3	.383
NBA Season Totals		510	32	9905	5202	2003	3832	.523	0	5	.000	1196	1698	.704	963	1767	2730	377	1117	7	164	176	680	19.4	10.2	5.4	0.7	....
76-77	Washington	9	....	252	146	53	90	.589	....	....	....	40	59	.678	28	40	68	10	34	0	2	3	....	28.0	16.2	7.6	1.1	.640
77-78	Washington	21	....	504	213	84	199	.422	....	....	....	45	69	.652	49	78	127	22	58	1	4	3	42	24.0	10.1	6.0	1.0	.361
78-79	Washington	8	....	137	52	21	52	.404	....	....	....	10	15	.667	16	18	34	3	12	0	2	0	5	17.1	6.5	4.3	0.4	.348
83-84	LA Lakers	9	0	69	18	5	17	.294	0	0	.000	8	14	.571	12	17	29	2	12	0	1	2	6	7.7	2.0	3.2	0.2	.359
84-85	LA Lakers	16	0	197	75	31	53	.585	0	1	.000	13	22	.591	11	37	48	5	42	0	2	7	10	12.3	4.7	3.0	0.3	.405
85-86	LA Lakers	5	0	56	20	8	15	.533	0	0	.000	4	6	.667	5	10	15	2	6	0	2	0	3	11.2	4.0	3.0	0.4	.445
NBA Playoff Totals		68	0	1215	524	202	426	.474	0	1	.000	120	185	.649	121	200	321	44	164	1	13	15	66	17.9	7.7	4.7	0.6	....

• KUPEC, C.J.

Charles J. (C.J.) Kupec

Born: Jan. 16, 1953. Oak Lawn, IL, United States.   Height: 6'6".   Weight: 220 lbs.   Drafted: 1975   College: Michigan

YEAR	TEAM	GP	GS	MIN	PTS	FGM	FGA	FG%	3PM	3PA	3P%	FTM	FTA	FT%	ORB	DRB	TRB	AST	PF	DQ	STL	BLK	TO	MPG	PPG	RPG	APG	PCM
75-76	LA Lakers	16	....	55	27	10	40	.250	....	....	....	7	11	.636	4	19	23	5	7	0	3	0	....	3.4	1.7	1.4	0.3	.400
76-77	LA Lakers	82	....	908	384	153	342	.447	....	....	....	78	101	.772	76	123	199	53	113	0	18	4	....	11.1	4.7	2.4	0.6	.434
77-78	Houston	49	....	626	195	84	197	.426	....	....	....	27	33	.818	27	64	91	50	54	0	10	3	25	12.8	4.0	1.9	1.0	.312
NBA Season Totals		147	....	1589	606	247	579	.427	....	....	....	112	145	.772	107	206	313	108	174	0	31	7	25	10.8	4.1	2.1	0.7	....
76-77	LA Lakers	11	....	57	21	8	18	.444	....	....	....	5	7	.714	3	13	16	4	7	0	3	0	....	5.2	1.9	1.5	0.4	.471
NBA Playoff Totals		11	....	57	21	8	18	.444	....	....	....	5	7	.714	3	13	16	4	7	0	3	0	....	5.2	1.9	1.5	0.4	....

• KWELLER, Ed

Ed Kweller

Born: 1915.   Height: 6'5".   Weight: 225 lbs.   Drafted: —   College: Duquesne

YEAR	TEAM	GP	GS	MIN	PTS	FGM	FGA	FG%	3PM	3PA	3P%	FTM	FTA	FT%	ORB	DRB	TRB	AST	PF	DQ	STL	BLK	TO	MPG	PPG	RPG	APG	PCM
37-38	Pittsburgh-N	8	....	....	13	4	....	....	....	....	....	5	....	....	....	....	....	....	....	....	....	....	....	....	1.6	....	....	....
38-39	Pittsburgh-N	13	....	....	42	14	....	....	....	....	....	14	....	....	....	....	....	....	....	....	....	....	....	....	3.2	....	....	....
NBL Season Totals		21	....	....	55	18	....	....	....	....	....	19	....	....	....	....	....	....	....	....	....	....	....	....	2.6	....	....	....

• LACEFIELD, Reggie

Reggie Lacefield

Born: Apr. 10, 1945. Gary, IN, United States.   Height: 6'5".   Weight: 230 lbs.   Drafted: 1968   College: Western Michigan

YEAR	TEAM	GP	GS	MIN	PTS	FGM	FGA	FG%	3PM	3PA	3P%	FTM	FTA	FT%	ORB	DRB	TRB	AST	PF	DQ	STL	BLK	TO	MPG	PPG	RPG	APG	PCM
68-69	Kentucky-A	8	....	48	24	11	22	.500	0	1	.000	2	4	.500	4	7	11	0	9	0	....	....	3	6.0	3.0	1.4	0.0	.402
ABA Season Totals		8	....	48	24	11	22	.500	0	1	.000	2	4	.500	4	7	11	0	9	0	....	....	3	6.0	3.0	1.4	0.0	....

• LACEY, Sam

Samuel Lacey

Born: Mar. 28, 1948. Indianaola, MS, United States.   Height: 6'10".   Weight: 235 lbs.   Drafted: 1970   College: New Mexico State

YEAR	TEAM	GP	GS	MIN	PTS	FGM	FGA	FG%	3PM	3PA	3P%	FTM	FTA	FT%	ORB	DRB	TRB	AST	PF	DQ	STL	BLK	TO	MPG	PPG	RPG	APG	PCM
70-71	Cincinnati	81	....	2648	1090	467	1117	.418	....	....	....	156	227	.687	....	....	913	117	270	8	....	....	....	32.7	13.5	11.3	1.4	.492
71-72	Cincinnati	81	....	2832	939	410	972	.422	....	....	....	119	169	.704	....	....	968	173	284	6	....	....	....	35.0	11.6	12.0	2.1	.474
72-73	Omaha	79	....	2930	1068	471	994	.474	....	....	....	126	178	.708	....	....	933	189	283	6	....	....	....	37.1	13.5	11.8	2.4	.509
73-74	Omaha	79	....	3107	1119	467	982	.476	....	....	....	185	247	.749	293	762	1055	299	254	3	126	184	....	39.3	14.2	13.4	3.8	.575
74-75	Omaha	81	....	3378	928	392	917	.427	....	....	....	144	191	.754	228	**921**	1149	428	274	4	139	168	....	41.7	11.5	14.2	5.3	.537
75-76	Kansas City	81	....	3083	1035	409	1019	.401	....	....	....	217	286	.759	218	806	1024	378	286	7	132	134	....	38.1	12.8	12.6	4.7	.542
76-77	Kansas City	82	....	2595	869	327	774	.422	....	....	....	215	282	.762	189	545	734	386	292	9	119	133	....	31.6	10.6	9.0	4.7	.540
77-78	Kansas City	77	....	2131	664	265	590	.449	....	....	....	134	187	.717	155	487	642	300	264	7	120	108	185	27.7	8.6	8.3	3.9	.553
78-79	Kansas City	82	....	2627	867	350	697	.502	....	....	....	167	226	.739	179	523	702	430	309	11	106	141	246	32.0	10.6	8.6	5.2	.569
79-80	Kansas City	81	....	2412	743	303	677	.448	0	1	.000	137	185	.741	172	473	645	460	307	8	111	109	211	29.8	9.2	8.0	5.7	.555
80-81	Kansas City	82	....	2228	567	237	536	.442	1	5	.200	92	117	.786	131	453	584	399	302	5	95	120	180	27.2	6.9	7.1	4.9	.514
81-82	Kansas City	2	1	20	6	3	5	.600	0	0	.000	0	2	.000	0	4	4	4	2	0	2	1	2	10.0	3.0	2.0	2.0	.562
81-82	New Jersey	54	6	650	155	64	149	.430	0	1	.000	27	35	.771	20	83	103	73	137	1	20	37	54	12.0	2.9	1.9	1.4	.287
82-83	Cleveland	60	33	1232	253	111	264	.420	2	9	.222	29	37	.784	62	169	231	118	209	3	29	25	96	20.5	4.2	3.9	2.0	.257
NBA Season Totals		1002	40	31873	10303	4276	9693	.441	3	16	.188	1748	2369	.738	1647	5226	9687	3754	3473	78	999	1160	974	31.8	10.3	9.7	3.7	....

Total Basketball

YEAR	TEAM	GP	GS	MIN	PTS	FGM	FGA	FG%	3PM	3PA	3P%	FTM	FTA	FT%	ORB	DRB	TRB	AST	PF	DQ	STL	BLK	TO	MPG	PPG	RPG	APG	PCM
74-75	Omaha	6	....	264	57	23	61	.377	....	....	....	11	18	.611	15	79	94	30	19	1	12	9	....	44.0	9.5	15.7	5.0	.485
78-79	Kansas City	5	....	176	47	16	42	.381	....	....	....	15	19	.789	17	34	51	21	20	2	9	10	19	35.2	9.4	10.2	4.2	.465
79-80	Kansas City	3	....	101	20	8	21	.381	1	1	1.000	3	4	.750	6	16	22	13	11	0	7	2	8	33.7	6.7	7.3	4.3	.375
80-81	Kansas City	15	....	533	150	60	143	.420	0	3	.000	30	35	.857	30	90	120	80	63	2	28	23	39	35.5	10.0	8.0	5.3	.471
NBA Playoff Totals		29	....	1074	274	107	267	.401	1	4	.250	59	76	.776	68	219	287	144	113	5	56	44	66	37.0	9.4	9.9	5.0	....

• LACKEY, Bob

Robert (Black Swan) Lackey

Born: Apr. 4, 1949. Evanston, IL, United States. Died: June2002.   Height: 6'5".   Weight: 200 lbs.   Drafted: 1972   College: Marquette

YEAR	TEAM	GP	GS	MIN	PTS	FGM	FGA	FG%	3PM	3PA	3P%	FTM	FTA	FT%	ORB	DRB	TRB	AST	PF	DQ	STL	BLK	TO	MPG	PPG	RPG	APG	PCM
72-73	New York-A	68	....	1185	407	153	350	.437	2	5	.400	99	167	.593	60	100	160	136	170	0	....	....	120	17.4	6.0	2.4	2.0	.351
73-74	New York-A	3	....	15	6	3	7	.429	0	0	.000	0	0	.000	3	1	4	1	2	....	1	0	1	5.0	2.0	1.3	0.3	.419
ABA Season Totals		71	....	1200	413	156	357	.437	2	5	.400	99	167	.593	63	101	164	137	172	0	1	0	121	16.9	5.8	2.3	1.9	....
72-73	New York-A	5	....	60	12	4	8	.500	0	2	.000	4	11	.364	3	5	8	5	10	0	....	....	7	12.0	2.4	1.6	1.0	.224
ABA Playoff Totals		5	....	60	12	4	8	.500	0	2	.000	4	11	.364	3	5	8	5	10	0	....	....	7	12.0	2.4	1.6	1.0	....

• LACOUR, Fred

Fred LaCour

Born: Feb. 7, 1938. Died: Aug.5, 1972.   Height: 6'5".   Weight: 210 lbs.   Drafted: —   College: San Francisco

YEAR	TEAM	GP	GS	MIN	PTS	FGM	FGA	FG%	3PM	3PA	3P%	FTM	FTA	FT%	ORB	DRB	TRB	AST	PF	DQ	STL	BLK	TO	MPG	PPG	RPG	APG	PCM
60-61	St. Louis	55	....	722	309	123	295	.417	....	....	....	63	84	.750	....	....	178	84	73	0	....	....	....	13.1	5.6	3.2	1.5	.529
61-62	St. Louis	73	....	1507	566	230	536	.429	....	....	....	106	130	.815	....	....	272	166	168	3	....	....	....	20.6	7.8	3.7	2.3	.442
62-63	San Francisco	16	....	171	65	28	73	.384	....	....	....	9	16	.563	....	....	24	19	27	0	....	....	....	10.7	4.1	1.5	1.2	.339
NBA Season Totals		144	....	2400	940	381	904	.421	....	....	....	178	230	.774	....	....	474	269	268	3	....	....	....	16.7	6.5	3.3	1.9	....
60-61	St. Louis	5	....	47	20	7	21	.333	....	....	....	6	7	.857	....	....	6	4	6	0	....	....	....	9.4	4.0	1.2	0.8	.345
NBA Playoff Totals		5	....	47	20	7	21	.333	....	....	....	6	7	.857	....	....	6	4	6	0	....	....	....	9.4	4.0	1.2	0.8	....

• LACY, Edgar

Edgar Eddie Lacy

Born: Aug. 2, 1944. Los Angeles, CA, United States.   Height: 6'6".   Weight: 190 lbs.   Drafted: 1968   College: UCLA

YEAR	TEAM	GP	GS	MIN	PTS	FGM	FGA	FG%	3PM	3PA	3P%	FTM	FTA	FT%	ORB	DRB	TRB	AST	PF	DQ	STL	BLK	TO	MPG	PPG	RPG	APG	PCM
68-69	Los Angeles-A	46	....	609	234	98	219	.447	0	2	.000	38	67	.567	70	110	180	30	92	1	....	....	63	13.2	5.1	3.9	0.7	.438
ABA Season Totals		46	....	609	234	98	219	.447	0	2	.000	38	67	.567	70	110	180	30	92	1	....	....	63	13.2	5.1	3.9	0.7	....

• LADNER, Wendell

Wendell Ladner

Born: Oct. 6, 1948. Necaise Crossing, MS, United States. Died: June24, 1975.   Height: 6'5".   Weight: 220 lbs.   Drafted: —   College: Southern Mississippi

YEAR	TEAM	GP	GS	MIN	PTS	FGM	FGA	FG%	3PM	3PA	3P%	FTM	FTA	FT%	ORB	DRB	TRB	AST	PF	DQ	STL	BLK	TO	MPG	PPG	RPG	APG	PCM
70-71	Memphis-A	77	....	2504	1306	572	1308	.437	8	29	.276	154	219	.703	337	538	875	160	**334**	**13**	....	....	170	32.5	17.0	11.4	2.1	.579
71-72	Carolina-A	43	....	1183	523	219	583	.376	34	139	.245	51	63	.810	106	318	424	88	**180**	6	....	....	90	27.5	12.2	9.9	2.0	.499
71-72	Memphis-A	39	....	1263	642	272	704	.386	27	97	.278	71	96	.740	138	271	409	78	**167**	9	....	....	125	32.4	16.5	10.5	2.0	.495
72-73	Kentucky-A	37	....	659	270	109	318	.343	8	38	.211	44	58	.759	57	124	181	72	132	2	....	....	52	17.8	7.3	4.9	1.9	.392
72-73	Memphis-A	15	....	273	89	37	128	.289	4	15	.267	11	15	.733	37	59	96	35	54	2	....	....	26	18.2	5.9	6.4	2.3	.388
73-74	Kentucky-A	34	....	928	338	154	418	.368	6	37	.162	24	41	.585	71	196	267	84	135	3	62	3	62	27.3	9.9	7.9	2.5	.400
73-74	New York-A	30	....	637	203	90	252	.357	18	53	.340	5	12	.417	39	122	161	65	98	....	46	3	62	21.2	6.8	5.4	2.2	.363
74-75	New York-A	25	....	436	103	45	173	.260	7	36	.194	6	10	.600	21	47	68	39	68	....	32	1	23	17.4	4.1	2.7	1.6	.140
ABA Season Totals		300	....	7883	3474	1498	3884	.386	112	444	.252	366	514	.712	806	1675	2481	621	1168	32	140	7	614	26.3	11.6	8.3	2.1	....
70-71	Memphis-A	4	....	143	41	19	72	.264	0	2	.000	3	8	.375	15	25	40	14	19	1	....	....	7	35.8	10.3	10.0	3.5	.264
72-73	Kentucky-A	19	....	269	136	55	142	.387	14	53	.264	12	14	.857	18	38	56	21	67	4	....	....	25	14.2	7.2	2.9	1.1	.373
73-74	New York-A	14	....	271	115	52	122	.426	6	24	.250	5	11	.455	15	55	70	34	49	....	25	0	19	19.4	8.2	5.0	2.4	.481
74-75	New York-A	3	....	35	13	5	23	.217	3	7	.429	0	0	.000	4	1	5	0	10	....	4	0	1	11.7	4.3	1.7	0.0	-.085
ABA Playoff Totals		40	....	718	305	131	359	.365	23	86	.267	20	33	.606	52	119	171	69	145	5	29	0	52	18.0	7.6	4.3	1.7	....

• LAETTNER, Christian

Christian Donald Laettner

Born: Aug. 17, 1969. Angola, NY, United States.   Height: 6'11".   Weight: 235 lbs.   Drafted: 1992   College: Duke

YEAR	TEAM	GP	GS	MIN	PTS	FGM	FGA	FG%	3PM	3PA	3P%	FTM	FTA	FT%	ORB	DRB	TRB	AST	PF	DQ	STL	BLK	TO	MPG	PPG	RPG	APG	PCM
92-93	Minnesota	81	81	2823	1472	503	1061	.474	4	40	.100	462	553	.835	171	537	708	223	290	4	105	83	275	34.9	18.2	8.7	2.8	.564
93-94	Minnesota	70	67	2428	1173	396	883	.448	6	25	.240	375	479	.783	160	442	602	307	264	6	87	86	259	34.7	16.8	8.6	4.4	.562
94-95	Minnesota	81	80	2770	1322	450	920	.489	13	40	.325	409	500	.818	164	449	613	234	302	4	101	87	227	34.2	16.3	7.6	2.9	.536
95-96	Minnesota	44	44	1518	792	283	582	.486	9	31	.290	217	266	.816	98	204	302	129	157	4	40	43	110	34.5	18.0	6.9	2.9	.533
95-96	Atlanta	30	27	977	425	159	325	.489	0	8	.000	107	130	.823	86	150	236	68	119	3	31	28	75	32.6	14.2	7.9	2.3	.492
96-97	Atlanta	82	82	3140	1486	548	1128	.486	31	88	.352	359	440	.816	212	508	720	223	277	8	102	64	221	38.3	18.1	8.8	2.7	.521
97-98	Atlanta	74	49	2282	1020	354	730	.485	6	27	.222	306	354	.864	142	345	487	190	246	6	71	73	185	30.8	13.8	6.6	2.6	.506
98-99	Detroit	16	0	337	121	38	106	.358	1	3	.333	44	57	.772	21	33	54	24	30	0	15	12	19	21.1	7.6	3.4	1.5	.366
99-00	Detroit	82	82	2443	1002	379	801	.473	7	24	.292	237	292	.812	175	378	553	186	326	10	83	45	186	29.8	12.2	6.7	2.3	.450
00-01	Dallas	53	35	930	398	165	323	.511	1	3	.333	67	82	.817	75	137	212	67	159	1	40	27	70	17.5	7.5	4.0	1.3	.473
00-01	Washington	25	13	733	330	112	228	.491	3	10	.300	103	122	.844	43	110	153	57	83	0	31	19	67	29.3	13.2	6.1	2.3	.498
01-02	Washington	57	48	1441	404	168	362	.464	2	10	.200	66	76	.868	74	227	301	151	129	1	60	25	85	25.3	7.1	5.3	2.6	.419
02-03	Washington	76	66	2219	632	255	516	.494	2	16	.125	120	144	.833	114	388	502	235	206	0	82	40	87	29.2	8.3	6.6	3.1	.466
NBA Season Totals		771	674	24041	10577	3810	7965	.478	85	325	.262	2872	3495	.822	1535	3908	5443	2094	2588	47	848	632	1866	31.2	13.7	7.1	2.7	....
95-96	Atlanta	10	10	334	157	59	122	.484	1	3	.333	38	54	.704	27	42	69	15	41	1	12	10	21	33.4	15.7	6.9	1.5	.457
96-97	Atlanta	10	10	403	176	62	153	.405	4	21	.190	48	56	.857	19	53	72	26	32	0	10	8	31	40.3	17.6	7.2	2.6	.385
97-98	Atlanta	4	0	87	39	12	35	.343	0	3	.000	15	17	.882	3	14	17	4	16	1	6	1	8	21.8	9.8	4.3	1.0	.330
98-99	Detroit	5	0	123	51	20	47	.426	0	0	.000	11	14	.786	6	8	14	11	14	0	4	1	3	24.6	10.2	2.8	2.2	.373
99-00	Detroit	3	3	75	20	7	17	.412	0	0	.000	6	8	.750	2	13	15	6	14	0	0	1	3	25.0	6.7	5.0	2.0	.293
NBA Playoff Totals		32	23	1022	443	160	374	.428	5	27	.185	118	149	.792	57	130	187	62	117	2	32	21	66	31.9	13.8	5.8	1.9	....

• LAFRENTZ, Raef

Raef Andrew LaFrentz

Born: May 29, 1976. Hampton, IA, United States. Height: 6'11". Weight: 240 lbs. Drafted: 1998 College: Kansas

YEAR	TEAM	GP	GS	MIN	PTS	FGM	FGA	FG%	3PM	3PA	3P%	FTM	FTA	FT%	ORB	DRB	TRB	AST	PF	DQ	STL	BLK	TO	MPG	PPG	RPG	APG	PCM
98-99	Denver	12	12	387	166	59	129	.457	12	31	.387	36	48	.750	33	58	91	8	38	2	9	17	9	32.3	13.8	7.6	0.7	.482
99-00	Denver	81	80	2435	1006	392	879	.446	60	183	.328	162	236	.686	170	471	641	97	292	6	42	180	96	30.1	12.4	7.9	1.2	.493
00-01	Denver	78	74	2457	1008	387	812	.477	51	139	.367	183	262	.698	173	434	607	107	290	9	37	206	97	31.5	12.9	7.8	1.4	.511
01-02	Denver	51	51	1668	759	307	659	.466	75	173	.434	70	105	.667	117	262	379	60	173	**5**	31	153	60	32.7	14.9	7.4	1.2	.520
01-02	Dallas	27	25	787	292	114	261	.437	29	95	.305	35	46	.761	59	141	200	29	108	**6**	24	60	34	29.1	10.8	7.4	1.1	.461
02-03	Dallas	69	43	1611	639	266	514	.518	47	116	.405	60	88	.682	125	205	330	54	264	8	35	91	46	23.3	9.3	4.8	0.8	.442
NBA Season Totals		318	285	9345	3870	1525	3254	.469	274	737	.372	546	785	.696	677	1571	2248	355	1165	36	178	707	342	29.4	12.2	7.1	1.1	....
01-02	Dallas	8	8	245	90	39	78	.500	6	18	.333	6	11	.545	18	43	61	5	39	2	2	22	6	30.6	11.3	7.6	0.6	.456
02-03	Dallas	20	16	491	160	68	157	.433	8	40	.200	16	19	.842	36	52	88	5	86	3	11	43	14	24.6	8.0	4.4	0.3	.327
NBA Playoff Totals		28	24	736	250	107	235	.455	14	58	.241	22	30	.733	54	95	149	10	125	5	13	65	20	26.3	8.9	5.3	0.4	....

• LAGARDE, Tom

Thomas Joseph LaGarde

Born: Feb. 10, 1955. Detroit, MI, United States. Height: 6'10". Weight: 220 lbs. Drafted: 1977 College: North Carolina

YEAR	TEAM	GP	GS	MIN	PTS	FGM	FGA	FG%	3PM	3PA	3P%	FTM	FTA	FT%	ORB	DRB	TRB	AST	PF	DQ	STL	BLK	TO	MPG	PPG	RPG	APG	PCM
77-78	Denver	77	....	868	306	96	237	.405	....	....	....	114	150	.760	75	139	214	47	146	1	17	17	100	11.3	4.0	2.8	0.6	.329
78-79	Seattle	23	....	575	253	98	181	.541	....	....	....	57	95	.600	61	129	190	32	75	2	6	18	46	25.0	11.0	8.3	1.4	.546
79-80	Seattle	82	....	1164	382	146	306	.477	0	0	.000	90	137	.657	127	185	312	91	206	2	19	34	98	14.2	4.7	3.8	1.1	.399
80-81	Dallas	82	....	2670	1122	417	888	.470	0	0	.000	288	444	.649	177	488	665	237	293	6	35	45	205	32.6	13.7	8.1	2.9	.464
81-82	Dallas	47	28	909	312	113	269	.420	0	2	.000	86	166	.518	63	147	210	49	138	3	17	17	80	19.3	6.6	4.5	1.0	.299
84-85	New Jersey	1	0	8	1	0	1	.000	0	0	.000	1	2	.500	1	1	2	0	2	0	0	0	1	8.0	1.0	2.0	0.0	-.050
NBA Season Totals		312	28	6194	2376	870	1882	.462	0	2	.000	636	994	.640	504	1089	1593	456	860	14	94	131	530	19.9	7.6	5.1	1.5	....
77-78	Denver	9	....	77	25	10	19	.526	....	....	....	5	7	.714	9	9	18	7	12	0	0	2	9	8.6	2.8	2.0	0.8	.370
79-80	Seattle	14	....	163	43	17	46	.370	0	0	.000	9	11	.818	13	27	40	12	25	0	2	0	7	11.6	3.1	2.9	0.9	.303
NBA Playoff Totals		23	....	240	68	27	65	.415	0	0	.000	14	18	.778	22	36	58	19	37	0	2	2	16	10.4	3.0	2.5	0.8	....

• LAIMBEER, Bill

William Laimbeer Jr.

Born: May 19, 1957. Boston, MA, United States. Height: 6'11". Weight: 245 lbs. Drafted: 1979 College: Notre Dame

YEAR	TEAM	GP	GS	MIN	PTS	FGM	FGA	FG%	3PM	3PA	3P%	FTM	FTA	FT%	ORB	DRB	TRB	AST	PF	DQ	STL	BLK	TO	MPG	PPG	RPG	APG	PCM
80-81	Cleveland	81	....	2460	791	337	670	.503	0	0	.000	117	153	.765	266	427	693	216	332	14	56	78	130	30.4	9.8	8.6	2.7	.484
81-82	Cleveland	50	4	894	334	119	253	.470	3	6	.500	93	120	.775	124	153	277	45	170	3	22	30	60	17.9	6.7	5.5	0.9	.466
81-82	Detroit	30	30	935	384	146	283	.516	1	7	.143	91	112	.813	110	230	340	55	126	2	17	34	60	31.2	12.8	11.3	1.8	.593
82-83	Detroit	82	82	2871	1119	436	877	.497	2	13	.154	245	310	.790	282	711	993	263	320	9	51	118	172	35.0	13.6	12.1	3.2	.602
83-84	Detroit	82	82	2864	1422	553	1044	.530	0	11	.000	316	365	.866	329	674	**1003**	149	273	4	49	84	148	34.9	17.3	12.2	1.8	.661
84-85	Detroit	82	82	2892	1438	595	1177	.506	4	18	.222	244	306	.797	295	718	1013	154	308	4	69	71	131	35.3	17.5	12.4	1.9	.636
85-86	Detroit	82	82	2891	1360	545	1107	.492	4	14	.286	266	319	.834	305	**770**	**1075**	146	291	4	59	65	131	35.3	16.6	**13.1**	1.8	.632
86-87	Detroit	82	82	2854	1263	506	1010	.501	6	21	.286	245	274	.894	243	712	955	151	283	4	72	69	123	34.8	15.4	11.6	1.8	.601
87-88	Detroit	82	82	2897	1110	455	923	.493	13	39	.333	187	214	.874	165	667	832	199	284	6	66	78	139	35.3	13.5	10.1	2.4	.525
88-89	Detroit	81	81	2640	1106	449	900	.499	30	86	.349	178	212	.840	138	638	776	177	259	2	51	100	130	32.6	13.7	9.6	2.2	.561
89-90	Detroit	81	81	2675	981	380	785	.484	57	158	.361	164	192	.854	166	614	780	171	278	4	57	84	97	33.0	12.1	9.6	2.1	.528
90-91	Detroit	82	81	2668	904	372	778	.478	37	125	.296	123	147	.837	173	564	737	157	242	3	38	56	98	32.5	11.0	9.0	1.9	.469
91-92	Detroit	81	46	2234	783	342	727	.470	32	85	.376	67	75	.893	104	347	451	160	225	0	51	54	105	27.6	9.7	5.6	2.0	.406
92-93	Detroit	79	41	1933	687	292	574	.509	10	27	.370	93	104	.894	110	309	419	127	212	4	46	40	55	24.5	8.7	5.3	1.6	.453
93-94	Detroit	11	5	248	108	47	90	.522	3	9	.333	11	13	.846	9	47	56	14	30	0	6	4	10	22.5	9.8	5.1	1.3	.486
NBA Season Totals		1068	861	33956	13790	5574	11198	.498	202	619	.326	2440	2916	.837	2819	7581	10400	2184	3633	63	710	965	1589	31.8	12.9	9.7	2.0	....
83-84	Detroit	5	5	165	76	29	51	.569	0	0	.000	18	20	.900	14	48	62	12	23	2	4	3	12	33.0	15.2	12.4	2.4	.665
84-85	Detroit	9	9	325	132	48	107	.449	0	2	.000	36	51	.706	36	60	96	15	32	1	7	7	16	36.1	14.7	10.7	1.7	.488
85-86	Detroit	4	4	168	90	34	68	.500	1	1	1.000	21	23	.913	20	36	56	1	19	1	2	3	8	42.0	22.5	14.0	0.3	.589
86-87	Detroit	15	15	543	184	84	163	.515	1	5	.200	15	24	.625	30	126	156	37	53	2	15	12	20	36.2	12.3	10.4	2.5	.503
87-88	Detroit	23	23	779	273	114	250	.456	5	17	.294	40	45	.889	43	178	221	44	77	2	18	19	30	33.9	11.9	9.6	1.9	.472
88-89	Detroit	17	17	497	172	66	142	.465	15	42	.357	25	31	.806	26	114	140	31	55	1	6	8	19	29.2	10.1	8.2	1.8	.466
89-90	Detroit	20	20	667	222	91	199	.457	15	43	.349	25	29	.862	41	170	211	28	77	3	23	18	16	33.4	11.1	10.6	1.4	.500
90-91	Detroit	15	15	446	164	66	148	.446	5	17	.294	27	31	.871	42	80	122	19	54	0	5	12	17	29.7	10.9	8.1	1.3	.436
91-92	Detroit	5	4	145	41	17	46	.370	2	10	.200	5	5	1.000	5	28	33	8	18	1	4	1	5	29.0	8.2	6.6	1.6	.310
NBA Playoff Totals		113	112	3735	1354	549	1174	.468	44	137	.321	212	259	.819	257	840	1097	195	408	13	84	83	143	33.1	12.0	9.7	1.7	....

• LALICH, Nick

Nick Lalich

Born: 1916. Height: 6'2". Weight: 220 lbs. Drafted: — College: Ohio University

YEAR	TEAM	GP	GS	MIN	PTS	FGM	FGA	FG%	3PM	3PA	3P%	FTM	FTA	FT%	ORB	DRB	TRB	AST	PF	DQ	STL	BLK	TO	MPG	PPG	RPG	APG	PCM
45-46	Youngstown-N	4	....	....	7	3	....	....	....	....	....	1	....	....	....	....	....	....	....	....	....	....	....	....	1.8	....	....	....
NBL Season Totals		4	....	....	7	3	....	....	....	....	....	1	....	....	....	....	....	....	....	....	....	....	....	....	1.8	....	....	....

• LALICH, Pete

Peter T. Lalich

Born: June 23, 1920. Height: 6'2". Weight: 190 lbs. Drafted: — College: Ohio University

YEAR	TEAM	GP	GS	MIN	PTS	FGM	FGA	FG%	3PM	3PA	3P%	FTM	FTA	FT%	ORB	DRB	TRB	AST	PF	DQ	STL	BLK	TO	MPG	PPG	RPG	APG	PCM
42-43	Sheboygan-N	1	....	....	0	0	....	....	....	....	....	0	....	....	....	....	....	....	....	....	....	....	....	....	0.0	....	....	....
43-44	Cleveland-N	17	....	....	109	44	....	....	....	....	....	21	....	....	....	....	....	....	....	....	....	....	....	....	6.4	....	....	....
44-45	Pittsburgh-N	9	....	....	20	8	....	....	....	....	....	4	....	....	....	....	....	....	....	....	....	....	....	....	2.2	....	....	....
45-46	Youngstown-N	11	....	....	7	2	....	....	....	....	....	3	....	....	....	....	....	....	....	....	....	....	....	....	0.6	....	....	....
46-47	Cleveland	1	....	....	0	0	1	.000	....	....	....	0	0	.000	....	....	....	0	1	....	....	....	....	....	0.0	....	0.0	....
NBA Season Totals		1	....	....	0	0	1	.000	....	....	....	0	0	.000	....	....	....	0	1	....	....	....	....	....	0.0	....	0.0	....
NBL Season Totals		38	....	....	136	54	....	....	....	....	....	28	....	....	....	....	....	....	....	....	....	....	....	....	3.6	....	....	....
Career Totals		39	....	....	136	54	1	....	....	....	....	28	0	....	....	....	....	0	1	....	....	....	....	....	3.5	....	0.0	....

YEAR	TEAM	GP	GS	MIN	PTS	FGM	FGA	FG%	3PM	3PA	3P%	FTM	FTA	FT%	ORB	DRB	TRB	AST	PF	DQ	STL	BLK	TO	MPG	PPG	RPG	APG	PCM
43-44	Cleveland-N	2	....	....	4	1	....	....	....	....	....	2	....	....	....	....	....	....	....	....	....	....	....	....	2.0	....	....	....
NBL Playoff Totals		2	....	....	4	1	....	....	....	....	....	2	....	....	....	....	....	....	....	....	....	....	....	....	2.0	....	....	....

• LALLEY, Gene
Gene Lalley

Born: 1922. Des Moines, IA, United States.   Height: 5'9".   Weight: 160 lbs.   Drafted: —   College: Creighton

YEAR	TEAM	GP	GS	MIN	PTS	FGM	FGA	FG%	3PM	3PA	3P%	FTM	FTA	FT%	ORB	DRB	TRB	AST	PF	DQ	STL	BLK	TO	MPG	PPG	RPG	APG	PCM
48-49	Denver-N	60	....	....	181	77	....	....	....	....	....	27	70	.386	....	....	....	....	198	....	....	....	....	....	3.0	....	....	....
NBL Season Totals		60	....	....	181	77	....	....	....	....	....	27	70		....	....	....	....	198	....	....	....	....	....	3.0	....	....	....

• LAMAR, Bo
Dwight (Bo) Lamar

Born: Apr. 7, 1951. Columbus, OH, United States.   Height: 6'1".   Weight: 180 lbs.   Drafted: 1973   College: Southwestern Louisiana

YEAR	TEAM	GP	GS	MIN	PTS	FGM	FGA	FG%	3PM	3PA	3P%	FTM	FTA	FT%	ORB	DRB	TRB	AST	PF	DQ	STL	BLK	TO	MPG	PPG	RPG	APG	PCM
73-74	San Diego-A	84	....	2824	1713	686	1726	.397	**69**	**247**	.279	272	350	.777	105	187	292	288	155	....	129	13	183	33.6	20.4	3.5	3.4	.460
74-75	San Diego-A	77	....	2917	1606	667	1571	.425	25	109	.229	247	315	.784	88	151	239	427	150	....	129	12	238	37.9	20.9	3.1	5.5	.478
75-76	Indiana-A	35	....	908	547	229	555	.413	21	78	.269	68	92	.739	37	61	98	135	46	....	36	1	75	25.9	15.6	2.8	3.9	.509
75-76	San Diego-A	6	....	222	110	48	113	.425	3	8	.375	11	14	.786	9	9	18	36	12	....	6	1	20	37.0	18.3	3.0	6.0	.457
76-77	LA Lakers	71	....	1165	502	228	561	.406	....	....	....	46	68	.676	30	62	92	177	73	0	59	3	....	16.4	7.1	1.3	2.5	.390
NBA Season Totals		71	....	1165	502	228	561	.406	....	....	....	46	68	.676	30	62	92	177	73	0	59	3	....	16.4	7.1	1.3	2.5	....
ABA Season Totals		202	....	6871	3976	1630	3965	.411	118	442	.267	598	771	.776	239	408	647	886	363	....	300	27	516	34.0	19.7	3.2	4.4	....
Career Totals		273	....	8036	4478	1858	4526	.411	118	442	.267	644	839	.768	269	470	739	1063	436	0	359	30	516	29.4	16.4	2.7	3.9	....
73-74	San Diego-A	6	....	241	165	71	161	.441	7	17	.412	16	19	.842	7	17	24	21	19	....	11	2	22	40.2	27.5	4.0	3.5	.510
76-77	LA Lakers	10	....	109	33	12	41	.293	....	....	....	9	10	.900	0	9	9	14	12	0	3	0	....	10.9	3.3	0.9	1.4	.239
NBA Playoff Totals		10	....	109	33	12	41	.293	....	....	....	9	10	.900	0	9	9	14	12	0	3	0	....	10.9	3.3	0.9	1.4	....
ABA Playoff Totals		6	....	241	165	71	161	.441	7	17	.412	16	19	.842	7	17	24	21	19	....	11	2	22	40.2	27.5	4.0	3.5	....
Career Playoff Totals		16	....	350	198	83	202	.411	7	17	.412	25	29	.862	7	26	33	35	31	0	14	2	22	21.9	12.4	2.1	2.2	....

• LAMBERT, John
John Edward Lambert

Born: Jan. 14, 1953. Berkeley, CA, United States.   Height: 6'10".   Weight: 225 lbs.   Drafted: 1975   College: USC

YEAR	TEAM	GP	GS	MIN	PTS	FGM	FGA	FG%	3PM	3PA	3P%	FTM	FTA	FT%	ORB	DRB	TRB	AST	PF	DQ	STL	BLK	TO	MPG	PPG	RPG	APG	PCM
75-76	Cleveland	54	....	333	123	49	110	.445	....	....	....	25	37	.676	37	65	102	16	54	0	8	12	....	6.2	2.3	1.9	0.3	.445
76-77	Cleveland	63	....	555	159	67	157	.427	....	....	....	25	36	.694	62	92	154	31	75	0	16	18	....	8.8	2.5	2.4	0.5	.383
77-78	Cleveland	76	....	1075	311	142	336	.423	....	....	....	27	48	.563	125	199	324	38	169	0	27	50	61	14.1	4.1	4.3	0.5	.371
78-79	Cleveland	70	....	1030	331	148	329	.450	....	....	....	35	55	.636	116	174	290	43	163	0	25	29	63	14.7	4.7	4.1	0.6	.375
79-80	Cleveland	74	....	1324	403	165	400	.413	0	3	.000	73	101	.723	138	214	352	56	203	4	47	42	67	17.9	5.4	4.8	0.8	.367
80-81	Cleveland	3	....	8	6	3	5	.600	0	0	.000	0	0	.000	1	2	3	3	2	0	0	0	0	2.7	2.0	1.0	1.0	1.158
80-81	Kansas City	43	....	475	148	65	160	.406	0	2	.000	18	23	.783	27	63	90	24	74	0	12	5	17	11.0	3.4	2.1	0.6	.281
81-82	Kansas City	42	1	493	142	60	139	.432	1	6	.167	21	28	.750	36	91	127	24	80	0	12	10	38	11.7	3.4	3.0	0.6	.319
81-82	San Antonio	21	6	271	65	26	58	.448	0	1	.000	13	14	.929	19	32	51	13	43	0	6	6	11	12.9	3.1	2.4	0.6	.285
NBA Season Totals		446	7	5564	1688	725	1694	.428	1	12	.083	237	342	.693	561	932	1493	248	863	4	153	172	257	12.5	3.8	3.3	0.6	....
75-76	Cleveland	6	....	34	12	5	13	.385	....	....	....	2	2	1.000	2	9	11	1	7	0	1	2	....	5.7	2.0	1.8	0.2	.374
76-77	Cleveland	3	....	19	4	2	4	.500	....	....	....	0	0	.000	2	1	3	0	4	0	2	0	....	6.3	1.3	1.0	0.0	.165
77-78	Cleveland	2	....	19	3	1	3	.333	....	....	....	1	2	.500	2	6	8	0	3	0	0	0	....	9.5	1.5	4.0	0.0	.342
80-81	Kansas City	15	....	175	49	22	54	.407	0	3	.000	5	6	.833	19	18	37	9	21	0	5	4	6	11.7	3.3	2.5	0.6	.320
81-82	San Antonio	2	0	3	0	0	1	.000	0	1	.000	0	0	.000	0	1	1	1	0	0	0	0	0	1.5	0.0	0.5	0.5	.360
NBA Playoff Totals		28	0	250	68	30	75	.400	0	4	.000	8	10	.800	25	35	60	11	35	0	8	6	6	8.9	2.4	2.1	0.4	....

• LAMME, Buck
Buck Lamme

Born: 1905.   Height: 6'2".   Weight: 180 lbs.   Drafted: —   College: Ohio Wesleyan

YEAR	TEAM	GP	GS	MIN	PTS	FGM	FGA	FG%	3PM	3PA	3P%	FTM	FTA	FT%	ORB	DRB	TRB	AST	PF	DQ	STL	BLK	TO	MPG	PPG	RPG	APG	PCM
37-38	Columbus-N	1	....	....	0	0	....	....	....	....	....	0	....	....	....	....	....	....	....	....	....	....	....	....	0.0	....	....	....
NBL Season Totals		1	....	....	0	0	....	....	....	....	....	0	....	....	....	....	....	....	....	....	....	....	....	....	0.0	....	....	....

• LAMP, Jeff
Jeffrey Alan Lamp

Born: Mar. 9, 1959. Minneapolis, MN, United States.   Height: 6'6".   Weight: 195 lbs.   Drafted: 1981   College: Virginia

YEAR	TEAM	GP	GS	MIN	PTS	FGM	FGA	FG%	3PM	3PA	3P%	FTM	FTA	FT%	ORB	DRB	TRB	AST	PF	DQ	STL	BLK	TO	MPG	PPG	RPG	APG	PCM
81-82	Portland	54	0	617	250	100	196	.510	0	1	.000	50	61	.820	24	40	64	28	83	0	16	1	43	11.4	4.6	1.2	0.5	.297
82-83	Portland	59	1	690	257	107	252	.425	1	6	.167	42	52	.808	25	51	76	58	67	0	20	3	35	11.7	4.4	1.3	1.0	.309
83-84	Portland	64	0	660	318	128	261	.490	2	13	.154	60	67	.896	23	40	63	51	67	0	22	4	51	10.3	5.0	1.0	0.8	.379
85-86	Milwaukee	44	1	701	276	109	243	.449	3	13	.231	55	64	.859	34	87	121	64	88	1	20	3	31	15.9	6.3	2.8	1.5	.399
85-86	San Antonio	30	1	620	332	136	271	.502	4	17	.235	56	69	.812	19	60	79	53	67	0	19	1	39	20.7	11.1	2.6	1.8	.455
87-88	LA Lakers	3	0	7	2	0	0	.000	0	0	.000	2	2	1.000	0	0	0	1	0	0	0	0	0	2.3	0.7	0.0	0.0	.219
88-89	LA Lakers	37	0	176	60	27	69	.391	2	4	.500	4	5	.800	6	28	34	15	27	0	8	2	15	4.8	1.6	0.9	0.4	.289
NBA Season Totals		291	3	3471	1495	607	1292	.470	12	54	.222	269	320	.841	131	306	437	269	400	1	105	14	214	11.9	5.1	1.5	0.9	....
82-83	Portland	1	0	1	2	1	2	.500	0	0	.000	0	0	.000	0	0	0	0	0	0	0	0	0	1.0	2.0	0.0	0.0	1.098
83-84	Portland	3	0	19	4	2	6	.333	0	0	.000	0	0	.000	0	0	0	1	0	0	0	0	1	6.3	1.3	0.0	0.0	-.059
85-86	San Antonio	3	0	45	15	7	18	.389	1	3	.333	0	0	.000	1	1	2	7	6	0	1	0	4	15.0	5.0	0.3	2.3	.170
88-89	LA Lakers	5	0	14	7	3	6	.500	0	0	.000	1	2	.500	2	1	3	1	3	0	0	0	1	2.8	1.4	0.6	0.2	.377
NBA Playoff Totals		12	0	79	28	13	32	.406	1	3	.333	1	2	.500	3	1	4	8	10	0	1	0	6	6.6	2.3	0.3	0.7	....

LAMPLEY, Jim
Jimmy D. Lampley

Born: July 2, 1960. Harrisburg, PA, United States.   Height: 6'10".   Weight: 230 lbs.   Drafted: 1983   College: Arkansas-Little Rock

YEAR	TEAM	GP	GS	MIN	PTS	FGM	FGA	FG%	3PM	3PA	3P%	FTM	FTA	FT%	ORB	DRB	TRB	AST	PF	DQ	STL	BLK	TO	MPG	PPG	RPG	APG	PCM
86-87	Philadelphia	1	0	16	3	1	3	.333	0	0	.000	1	2	.500	1	4	5	0	0	0	1	0	1	16.0	3.0	5.0	0.0	.333
NBA Season Totals		1	0	16	3	1	3	.333	0	0	.000	1	2	.500	1	4	5	0	0	0	1	0	1	16.0	3.0	5.0	0.0	....

LAMPLEY, Sean
Sean James Lampley

Born: Sept. 3, 1979. Harvey, IL, United States.   Height: 6'7".   Weight: 227 lbs.   Drafted: 2001   College: California

YEAR	TEAM	GP	GS	MIN	PTS	FGM	FGA	FG%	3PM	3PA	3P%	FTM	FTA	FT%	ORB	DRB	TRB	AST	PF	DQ	STL	BLK	TO	MPG	PPG	RPG	APG	PCM
02-03	Miami	35	0	487	169	56	129	.434	0	4	.000	57	82	.695	26	57	83	31	43	0	7	3	25	13.9	4.8	2.4	0.9	.344
NBA Season Totals		35	0	487	169	56	129	.434	0	4	.000	57	82	.695	26	57	83	31	43	0	7	3	25	13.9	4.8	2.4	0.9	....

LANDSBERGER, Mark
Mark Walter Landsberger

Born: May 21, 1955. Minot, ND, United States.   Height: 6'8".   Weight: 215 lbs.   Drafted: 1977   College: Arizona State

YEAR	TEAM	GP	GS	MIN	PTS	FGM	FGA	FG%	3PM	3PA	3P%	FTM	FTA	FT%	ORB	DRB	TRB	AST	PF	DQ	STL	BLK	TO	MPG	PPG	RPG	APG	PCM
77-78	Chicago	62	....	926	345	127	251	.506	....	....	....	91	157	.580	110	191	301	41	78	0	21	6	68	14.9	5.6	4.9	0.7	.483
78-79	Chicago	80	....	1959	647	278	585	.475	....	....	....	91	194	.469	292	450	742	68	125	0	27	22	152	24.5	8.1	9.3	0.9	.468
79-80	Chicago	54	....	1136	453	183	346	.529	0	0	.000	87	166	.524	157	293	450	32	113	1	23	17	76	21.0	8.4	8.3	0.6	.553
79-80	LA Lakers	23	....	374	161	66	137	.482	0	0	.000	29	56	.518	69	94	163	14	27	0	10	5	25	16.3	7.0	7.1	0.6	.605
80-81	LA Lakers	69	....	1086	390	164	327	.502	0	1	.000	62	116	.534	152	225	377	27	135	0	19	6	62	15.7	5.7	5.5	0.4	.455
81-82	LA Lakers	75	1	1134	321	144	329	.438	0	2	.000	33	65	.508	164	237	401	32	134	0	10	7	53	15.1	4.3	5.3	0.4	.392
82-83	LA Lakers	39	4	356	98	43	102	.422	0	0	.000	12	25	.480	55	73	128	12	48	0	8	4	20	9.1	2.5	3.3	0.3	.390
83-84	Atlanta	35	0	335	53	19	51	.373	0	0	.000	15	26	.577	42	77	119	10	32	0	6	3	21	9.6	1.5	3.4	0.3	.339
NBA Season Totals		437	5	7306	2468	1024	2128	.481	0	3	.000	420	805	.522	1041	1640	2681	236	692	1	124	70	477	16.7	5.6	6.1	0.5	....
79-80	LA Lakers	16	....	195	55	25	69	.362	0	1	.000	5	6	.833	25	44	69	2	35	0	3	2	10	12.2	3.4	4.3	0.1	.303
80-81	LA Lakers	3	....	32	5	2	7	.286	0	0	.000	1	1	1.000	9	6	15	0	5	0	1	0	1	10.7	1.7	5.0	0.0	.370
81-82	LA Lakers	9	0	60	10	3	9	.333	0	0	.000	4	9	.444	11	11	22	2	12	0	0	0	4	6.7	1.1	2.4	0.2	.256
82-83	LA Lakers	11	0	141	26	12	28	.429	0	1	.000	2	4	.500	19	25	44	3	24	0	0	2	6	12.8	2.4	4.0	0.3	.278
83-84	Atlanta	2	0	5	0	0	1	.000	0	0	.000	0	0	.000	1	0	1	0	1	0	0	0	0	2.5	0.0	0.5	0.0	-.093
NBA Playoff Totals		41	0	433	96	42	114	.368	0	2	.000	12	20	.600	65	86	151	7	77	0	4	4	21	10.6	2.3	3.7	0.2	....

LANE, Bill
Bill Lane

Born: 1916.   Height: 6'4".   Weight: 220 lbs.   Drafted: —   College: Michigan

YEAR	TEAM	GP	GS	MIN	PTS	FGM	FGA	FG%	3PM	3PA	3P%	FTM	FTA	FT%	ORB	DRB	TRB	AST	PF	DQ	STL	BLK	TO	MPG	PPG	RPG	APG	PCM
40-41	Detroit-N	3	....	....	0	0	....	....	....	....	....	0	....	....	....	....	....	....	....	....	....	....	....	0.0	....	....	....	
NBL Season Totals		3	....	....	0	0	....	....	....	....	....	0	....	....	....	....	....	....	....	....	....	....	....	0.0	....	....	....	

LANE, Jerome
Jerome Lane

Born: Dec. 4, 1966. Akron, OH, United States.   Height: 6'6".   Weight: 230 lbs.   Drafted: 1988   College: Pittsburgh

YEAR	TEAM	GP	GS	MIN	PTS	FGM	FGA	FG%	3PM	3PA	3P%	FTM	FTA	FT%	ORB	DRB	TRB	AST	PF	DQ	STL	BLK	TO	MPG	PPG	RPG	APG	PCM
88-89	Denver	54	1	550	261	109	256	.426	0	7	.000	43	112	.384	87	113	200	60	105	1	20	4	49	10.2	4.8	3.7	1.1	.492
89-90	Denver	67	46	956	334	145	309	.469	0	5	.000	44	120	.367	144	217	361	105	189	1	53	17	87	14.3	5.0	5.4	1.6	.513
90-91	Denver	62	25	1383	463	202	461	.438	1	4	.250	58	141	.411	280	298	578	123	192	1	51	14	105	22.3	7.5	9.3	2.0	.525
91-92	Denver	9	5	141	28	10	40	.250	0	0	.000	8	19	.421	22	22	44	13	18	0	2	1	10	15.7	3.1	4.9	1.4	.248
91-92	Indiana	3	0	30	6	3	5	.600	0	0	.000	0	6	.000	9	9	18	4	9	0	0	0	3	10.0	2.0	6.0	1.3	.513
91-92	Milwaukee	2	0	6	3	1	1	1.000	0	0	.000	1	2	.500	1	3	4	0	1	0	0	0	1	3.0	1.5	2.0	0.0	.810
92-93	Cleveland	21	2	149	59	27	54	.500	0	0	.000	5	20	.250	24	29	53	17	32	0	12	3	6	7.1	2.8	2.5	0.8	.590
NBA Season Totals		218	79	3215	1154	497	1126	.441	1	16	.063	159	420	.379	567	691	1258	322	546	3	138	39	261	14.7	5.3	5.8	1.5	....
88-89	Denver	2	0	21	6	2	7	.286	0	1	.000	2	2	1.000	1	5	6	2	4	0	0	0	0	10.5	3.0	3.0	1.0	.343
89-90	Denver	2	2	14	1	0	3	.000	0	0	.000	1	2	.500	0	1	1	2	4	0	0	0	2	7.0	0.5	0.5	1.0	-.212
NBA Playoff Totals		4	2	35	7	2	10	.200	0	1	.000	3	4	.750	1	6	7	4	8	0	0	0	2	8.8	1.8	1.8	1.0	....

LANG, Andrew
Andrew Charles Lang Jr.

Born: June 28, 1966. Pine Bluff, AR, United States.   Height: 6'11".   Weight: 245 lbs.   Drafted: 1988   College: Arkansas

YEAR	TEAM	GP	GS	MIN	PTS	FGM	FGA	FG%	3PM	3PA	3P%	FTM	FTA	FT%	ORB	DRB	TRB	AST	PF	DQ	STL	BLK	TO	MPG	PPG	RPG	APG	PCM
88-89	Phoenix	62	25	526	159	60	117	.513	0	0	.000	39	60	.650	54	93	147	9	112	1	17	48	31	8.5	2.6	2.4	0.1	.422
89-90	Phoenix	74	0	1011	258	97	174	.557	0	0	.000	64	98	.653	83	188	271	21	171	1	22	133	44	13.7	3.5	3.7	0.3	.465
90-91	Phoenix	63	18	1152	311	109	189	.577	0	1	.000	93	130	.715	113	190	303	27	168	2	17	127	44	18.3	4.9	4.8	0.4	.474
91-92	Phoenix	81	71	1965	622	248	475	.522	0	1	.000	126	164	.768	170	376	546	43	306	8	48	201	89	24.3	7.7	6.7	0.5	.485
92-93	Philadelphia	73	59	1861	386	149	351	.425	1	5	.200	87	114	.763	136	300	436	79	261	4	46	141	88	25.5	5.3	6.0	1.1	.347
93-94	Atlanta	82	0	1608	504	215	458	.469	1	4	.250	73	106	.689	126	187	313	51	192	2	38	87	82	19.6	6.1	3.8	0.6	.348
94-95	Atlanta	82	63	2068	794	320	677	.473	2	3	.667	152	188	.809	154	302	456	72	271	4	45	144	107	28.5	9.7	5.6	0.9	.383
95-96	Atlanta	51	51	1815	657	281	619	.454	0	3	.000	95	118	.805	111	223	334	62	178	4	35	85	92	35.6	12.9	6.5	1.2	.359
95-96	Minnesota	20	18	550	175	72	171	.421	1	2	.500	30	38	.789	42	79	121	3	63	0	7	41	30	27.5	8.8	6.1	0.2	.332
96-97	Milwaukee	52	52	1194	274	115	248	.464	0	0	.000	44	61	.721	94	184	278	25	140	4	26	47	42	23.0	5.3	5.3	0.5	.328
97-98	Milwaukee	57	0	692	152	54	143	.378	0	1	.000	44	57	.772	56	97	153	16	101	0	18	27	34	12.1	2.7	2.7	0.3	.269
98-99	Chicago	21	13	386	80	32	99	.323	0	0	.000	16	23	.696	33	60	93	13	43	0	5	12	17	18.4	3.8	4.4	0.6	.247
99-00	New York	19	10	244	59	28	64	.438	0	0	.000	7	7	.429	16	44	60	3	31	0	8	6	5	12.8	3.1	3.2	0.2	.313
NBA Season Totals		737	380	15344	4431	1780	3785	.470	5	20	.250	866	1164	.744	1188	2323	3511	424	2037	30	332	1099	705	20.8	6.0	4.8	0.6	....
88-89	Phoenix	4	0	8	0	0	2	.000	0	0	.000	0	0	.000	3	3	6	1	3	0	0	0	3	2.0	0.0	1.5	0.3	.076
89-90	Phoenix	13	0	93	16	6	9	.667	0	0	.000	4	7	.571	4	16	20	2	17	0	3	10	5	7.2	1.2	1.5	0.2	.346
90-91	Phoenix	4	0	55	26	6	11	.545	0	0	.000	14	17	.824	4	14	18	1	12	0	1	3	2	13.8	6.5	4.5	0.3	.619
91-92	Phoenix	8	8	192	45	15	40	.375	0	0	.000	15	19	.789	15	17	32	2	33	2	3	15	6	24.0	5.6	4.0	0.3	.238
93-94	Atlanta	11	0	234	75	29	63	.460	0	1	.000	17	22	.773	15	32	47	5	35	1	6	20	15	21.3	6.8	4.3	0.5	.359
94-95	Atlanta	3	3	101	31	12	28	.429	0	0	.000	7	9	.778	3	9	12	1	12	0	2	6	6	33.7	10.3	4.0	0.3	.197
NBA Playoff Totals		43	11	683	193	68	153	.444	0	1	.000	57	74	.770	44	91	135	12	112	3	15	50	39	15.9	4.5	3.1	0.3	....

• LANG, Antonio
Antonio Maurice Lang

Born: May 15, 1972. Mobile, AL, United States. Height: 6'8". Weight: 205 lbs. Drafted: 1994 College: Duke

YEAR	TEAM	GP	GS	MIN	PTS	FGM	FGA	FG%	3PM	3PA	3P%	FTM	FTA	FT%	ORB	DRB	TRB	AST	PF	DQ	STL	BLK	TO	MPG	PPG	RPG	APG	PCM
94-95	Phoenix	12	0	53	11	4	10	.400	0	0	.000	3	4	.750	3	1	4	1	11	0	0	2	5	4.4	0.9	0.3	0.1	.033
95-96	Cleveland	41	0	367	116	41	77	.532	0	2	.000	34	47	.723	17	36	53	12	61	0	14	12	25	9.0	2.8	1.3	0.3	.302
96-97	Cleveland	64	1	843	171	68	162	.420	0	6	.000	35	48	.729	52	75	127	33	111	0	33	30	51	13.2	2.7	2.0	0.5	.226
97-98	Miami	6	0	29	12	3	5	.600	0	0	.000	6	8	.750	2	3	5	1	3	0	2	0	4	4.8	2.0	0.8	0.2	.404
98-99	Cleveland	10	0	65	13	4	6	.667	0	0	.000	5	9	.556	6	10	16	1	13	0	2	1	4	6.5	1.3	1.6	0.1	.279
99-00	Toronto	7	0	32	3	0	5	.000	0	0	.000	3	4	.750	0	5	5	1	7	0	4	1	2	4.6	0.4	0.7	0.1	.100
99-00	Philadelphia	3	0	6	3	1	1	1.000	0	0	.000	1	1	1.000	0	0	0	1	1	0	0	0	0	2.0	1.0	0.0	0.3	.606
NBA Season Totals		143	1	1395	329	121	266	.455	0	8	.000	87	121	.719	80	130	210	50	207	0	55	46	91	9.8	2.3	1.5	0.3	....
95-96	Cleveland	1	0	2	0	0	0	.000	0	0	.000	0	0	.000	0	0	0	0	0	0	0	0	0	2.0	0.0	0.0	0.0	.000
NBA Playoff Totals		1	0	2	0	0	0	.000	0	0	.000	0	0	.000	0	0	0	0	0	0	0	0	0	2.0	0.0	0.0	0.0	....

• LANGDON, Trajan
Trajan Shaka Langdon

Born: May 13, 1976. Palo Alto, CA, United States. Height: 6'3". Weight: 197 lbs. Drafted: 1999 College: Duke

YEAR	TEAM	GP	GS	MIN	PTS	FGM	FGA	FG%	3PM	3PA	3P%	FTM	FTA	FT%	ORB	DRB	TRB	AST	PF	DQ	STL	BLK	TO	MPG	PPG	RPG	APG	PCM
99-00	Cleveland	10	0	145	49	15	40	.375	8	19	.421	11	11	1.000	4	11	15	11	16	0	5	0	6	14.5	4.9	1.5	1.1	.302
00-01	Cleveland	65	5	1116	389	135	313	.431	51	124	.411	68	76	.895	12	77	89	81	114	0	38	9	52	17.2	6.0	1.4	1.2	.304
01-02	Cleveland	44	0	477	209	70	176	.398	27	74	.365	42	46	.913	13	42	55	60	49	0	13	5	40	10.8	4.8	1.3	1.4	.387
NBA Season Totals		119	5	1738	647	220	529	.416	86	217	.396	121	133	.910	29	130	159	152	179	0	56	14	98	14.6	5.4	1.3	1.3	....

• LANGE, Dick
Dick Lange

Born: —. Height: — Weight: — Drafted: — College: —

YEAR	TEAM	GP	GS	MIN	PTS	FGM	FGA	FG%	3PM	3PA	3P%	FTM	FTA	FT%	ORB	DRB	TRB	AST	PF	DQ	STL	BLK	TO	MPG	PPG	RPG	APG	PCM
45-46	Oshkosh-N	4	....	....	2	1	....	....	....	....	....	0	0	.000	....	....	....	....	....	....	....	....	....	....	0.5	....	....	....
NBL Season Totals		4	....	....	2	1	....	....	....	....	....	0	0	....	....	....	....	....	....	....	....	....	....	....	0.5	....	....	....

• LANGHI, Dan
Daniel Matthew Langhi

Born: Nov. 28, 1977. Chicago, IL, United States. Height: 6'11". Weight: 220 lbs. Drafted: 2000 College: Vanderbilt

YEAR	TEAM	GP	GS	MIN	PTS	FGM	FGA	FG%	3PM	3PA	3P%	FTM	FTA	FT%	ORB	DRB	TRB	AST	PF	DQ	STL	BLK	TO	MPG	PPG	RPG	APG	PCM
00-01	Houston	33	0	241	90	37	99	.374	0	1	.000	16	29	.552	13	28	41	4	16	0	7	1	8	7.3	2.7	1.2	0.1	.259
01-02	Houston	34	8	434	107	49	125	.392	1	4	.250	8	11	.727	22	45	67	14	25	0	8	5	9	12.8	3.1	2.0	0.4	.242
02-03	Phoenix	60	0	540	183	81	202	.401	9	31	.290	12	20	.600	19	68	87	21	58	0	15	6	16	9.0	3.1	1.5	0.4	.277
NBA Season Totals		127	8	1215	380	167	426	.392	10	36	.278	36	60	.600	54	141	195	39	99	0	30	12	33	9.6	3.0	1.5	0.3	....

• LANIER, Bob
Robert Jerry Lanier Jr.

Born: Sept. 10, 1948. Buffalo, NY, United States. Height: 6'11". Weight: 250 lbs. Drafted: 1970 College: St. Bonaventure HOF: 1992

YEAR	TEAM	GP	GS	MIN	PTS	FGM	FGA	FG%	3PM	3PA	3P%	FTM	FTA	FT%	ORB	DRB	TRB	AST	PF	DQ	STL	BLK	TO	MPG	PPG	RPG	APG	PCM
70-71	Detroit	82	....	2017	1281	504	1108	.455	....	....	....	273	376	.726	....	....	665	146	272	4	....	....	....	24.6	15.6	8.1	1.8	.664
71-72	Detroit	80	....	3092	2056	834	1690	.493	....	....	....	388	505	.768	....	....	1132	248	297	6	....	....	....	38.7	25.7	14.2	3.1	.775
72-73	Detroit	81	....	3150	1927	810	1654	.490	....	....	....	307	397	.773	....	....	1205	260	278	4	....	....	....	38.9	23.8	14.9	3.2	.754
73-74	Detroit	81	....	3047	1822	748	1483	.504	....	....	....	326	409	.797	269	805	1074	343	273	7	110	247	....	37.6	22.5	13.3	4.2	.772
74-75	Detroit	76	....	2987	1823	731	1433	.510	....	....	....	361	450	.802	225	689	914	350	237	1	75	172	....	39.3	24.0	12.0	4.6	.759
75-76	Detroit	64	....	2363	1366	541	1017	.532	....	....	....	284	370	.768	217	529	746	217	203	2	79	86	....	36.9	21.3	11.7	3.4	.729
76-77	Detroit	64	....	2446	1616	678	1269	.534	....	....	....	260	318	.818	200	545	745	214	174	0	70	126	....	38.2	25.3	11.6	3.3	.774
77-78	Detroit	63	....	2311	1542	622	1159	.537	....	....	....	298	386	.772	197	518	715	216	185	2	82	93	227	36.7	24.5	11.3	3.4	.768
78-79	Detroit	53	....	1835	1253	489	950	.515	....	....	....	275	367	.749	164	330	494	140	181	5	50	75	175	34.6	23.6	9.3	2.6	.692
79-80	Detroit	37	....	1392	802	319	584	.546	0	5	.000	164	210	.781	108	265	373	122	130	2	38	60	115	37.6	21.7	10.1	3.3	.674
79-80	Milwaukee	26	....	739	408	147	283	.519	1	1	1.000	113	144	.785	44	135	179	62	70	1	36	29	49	28.4	15.7	6.9	2.4	.654
80-81	Milwaukee	67	....	1753	961	376	716	.525	1	1	1.000	208	277	.751	128	285	413	179	184	0	73	81	141	26.2	14.3	6.2	2.7	.638
81-82	Milwaukee	74	72	1986	996	407	729	.558	0	2	.000	182	242	.752	92	296	.388	219	211	3	72	56	163	26.8	13.5	5.2	3.0	.572
82-83	Milwaukee	39	35	978	417	163	332	.491	0	1	.000	91	133	.684	58	142	200	105	125	2	34	24	82	25.1	10.7	5.1	2.7	.474
83-84	Milwaukee	72	72	2007	978	392	685	.572	0	3	.000	194	274	.708	141	314	455	186	228	8	58	51	166	27.9	13.6	6.3	2.6	.564
NBA Season Totals		959	179	32103	19248	7761	15092	.514	2	13	.154	3724	4858	.767	1843	4853	9698	3007	3048	47	777	1100	1118	33.5	20.1	10.1	3.1	....
73-74	Detroit	7	....	303	184	77	152	.507	....	....	....	30	38	.789	26	81	107	21	28	1	4	14	....	43.3	26.3	15.3	3.0	.726
74-75	Detroit	3	....	128	61	26	51	.510	....	....	....	9	12	.750	5	27	32	19	10	0	4	12	....	42.7	20.3	10.7	6.3	.650
75-76	Detroit	9	....	359	235	95	152	.625	....	....	....	45	50	.900	39	75	114	30	34	1	8	21	....	39.9	26.1	12.7	3.3	.840
76-77	Detroit	3	....	118	84	34	54	.630	....	....	....	16	19	.842	13	37	50	6	10	0	3	7	....	39.3	28.0	16.7	2.0	.942
79-80	Milwaukee	7	....	256	135	52	101	.515	0	0	.000	31	42	.738	17	48	65	31	23	0	7	8	17	36.6	19.3	9.3	4.4	.649
80-81	Milwaukee	7	....	236	123	50	85	.588	0	0	.000	23	32	.719	12	40	52	28	18	0	12	8	15	33.7	17.6	7.4	4.0	.683
81-82	Milwaukee	6	6	212	96	41	80	.513	0	1	.000	14	25	.560	18	27	45	22	21	2	8	5	14	35.3	16.0	7.5	3.7	.517
82-83	Milwaukee	9	9	250	123	51	89	.573	0	0	.000	21	35	.600	17	46	63	23	32	2	5	14	21	27.8	13.7	7.0	2.6	.593
83-84	Milwaukee	16	16	499	203	82	171	.480	0	0	.000	39	44	.886	32	85	117	55	57	1	11	10	38	31.2	12.7	7.3	3.4	.487
NBA Playoff Totals		67	31	2361	1244	508	935	.543	0	1	.000	228	297	.768	179	466	645	235	233	7	62	99	105	35.2	18.6	9.6	3.5	....

• LANTZ, Stu
Stuart Burrell Lantz

Born: July 13, 1946. Uniontown, PA, United States. Height: 6'3". Weight: 175 lbs. Drafted: 1968 College: Nebraska

YEAR	TEAM	GP	GS	MIN	PTS	FGM	FGA	FG%	3PM	3PA	3P%	FTM	FTA	FT%	ORB	DRB	TRB	AST	PF	DQ	STL	BLK	TO	MPG	PPG	RPG	APG	PCM
68-69	San Diego	73	....	1378	569	220	482	.456	....	....	....	129	167	.772	....	....	236	99	178	0	....	....	....	18.9	7.8	3.2	1.4	.415
69-70	San Diego	82	....	2471	1188	455	1027	.443	....	....	....	278	361	.770	....	....	255	287	238	2	....	....	....	30.1	14.5	3.1	3.5	.441
70-71	San Diego	82	....	3102	1689	585	1305	.448	....	....	....	519	644	.806	....	....	406	344	230	3	....	....	....	37.8	20.6	5.0	4.2	.535
71-72	Houston	81	....	3097	1501	557	1279	.435	....	....	....	387	462	.838	....	....	345	337	211	2	....	....	....	38.2	18.5	4.3	4.2	.463
72-73	Detroit	51	....	1603	490	185	455	.407	....	....	....	120	150	.800	....	....	172	138	117	0	....	....	....	31.4	9.6	3.4	2.7	.312
73-74	Detroit	50	....	980	447	154	361	.427	....	....	....	139	164	.848	34	79	113	97	79	0	38	3	....	19.6	8.9	2.3	1.9	.443

YEAR	TEAM	GP	GS	MIN	PTS	FGM	FGA	FG%	3PM	3PA	3P%	FTM	FTA	FT%	ORB	DRB	TRB	AST	PF	DQ	STL	BLK	TO	MPG	PPG	RPG	APG	PCM
74-75	New Orleans	19	....	353	125	39	115	.339	....	....	....	47	53	.887	7	17	24	30	28	0	12	2	....	18.6	6.6	1.3	1.6	.285
74-75	LA Lakers	56	....	1430	523	189	446	.424	....	....	....	145	176	.824	81	89	170	158	134	1	44	10	....	25.5	9.3	3.0	2.8	.391
75-76	LA Lakers	53	....	853	250	85	204	.417	....	....	....	80	89	.899	28	71	99	76	105	1	27	3	....	16.1	4.7	1.9	1.4	.317
NBA Season Totals		547	....	15267	6782	2469	5674	.435	....	....	....	1844	2266	.814	150	256	1820	1566	1320	9	121	18	....	27.9	12.4	3.3	2.9	....
68-69	San Diego	6	....	208	81	30	69	.435	....	....	....	21	27	.778	....	....	21	10	22	0	....	....	....	34.7	13.5	3.5	1.7	.317
73-74	Detroit	7	....	227	84	28	59	.475	....	....	....	28	32	.875	10	19	29	14	19	0	2	0	....	32.4	12.0	4.1	2.0	.390
NBA Playoff Totals		13	....	435	165	58	128	.453	....	....	....	49	59	.831	10	19	50	24	41	0	2	0	....	33.5	12.7	3.8	1.8	....

• LARESE, York
York Bruno Larese

Born: July 18, 1938. New York, NY, United States.　　Height: 6'4".　　Weight: 183 lbs.　　Drafted: 1961　　College: North Carolina

YEAR	TEAM	GP	GS	MIN	PTS	FGM	FGA	FG%	3PM	3PA	3P%	FTM	FTA	FT%	ORB	DRB	TRB	AST	PF	DQ	STL	BLK	TO	MPG	PPG	RPG	APG	PCM
61-62	Chicago	8	....	57	25	10	21	.476	....	....	....	5	9	.556	....	....	6	9	8	0	....	....	....	7.1	3.1	0.8	1.1	.480
61-62	Philadelphia	51	....	646	277	112	306	.366	....	....	....	53	63	.841	....	....	71	85	96	0	....	....	....	12.7	5.4	1.4	1.7	.376
NBA Season Totals		59	....	703	302	122	327	.373	....	....	....	58	72	.806	....	....	77	94	104	0	....	....	....	11.9	5.1	1.3	1.6	....
61-62	Philadelphia	9	....	78	30	11	35	.314	....	....	....	8	12	.667	....	....	19	5	14	0	....	....	....	8.7	3.3	2.1	0.6	.323
NBA Playoff Totals		9	....	78	30	11	35	.314	....	....	....	8	12	.667	....	....	19	5	14	0	....	....	....	8.7	3.3	2.1	0.6	....

• LARUE, Rusty
Rusty LaRue

Born: Dec. 10, 1973. Winston-Salem, NC, United States.　　Height: 6'2".　　Weight: 210 lbs.　　Drafted: —　　College: Wake Forest

YEAR	TEAM	GP	GS	MIN	PTS	FGM	FGA	FG%	3PM	3PA	3P%	FTM	FTA	FT%	ORB	DRB	TRB	AST	PF	DQ	STL	BLK	TO	MPG	PPG	RPG	APG	PCM
97-98	Chicago	14	0	140	49	20	49	.408	4	16	.250	5	8	.625	1	7	8	5	12	0	3	1	6	10.0	3.5	0.6	0.4	.189
98-99	Chicago	43	6	732	203	78	217	.359	30	89	.337	17	17	1.000	9	47	56	63	66	0	33	3	34	17.0	4.7	1.3	1.5	.234
99-00	Chicago	4	1	129	37	15	43	.349	2	14	.143	5	7	.714	1	9	10	11	9	0	7	0	7	32.3	9.3	2.5	2.8	.215
01-02	Utah	33	0	541	193	73	185	.395	17	50	.340	30	35	.857	11	38	49	71	58	0	17	7	43	16.4	5.8	1.5	2.2	.310
NBA Season Totals		94	7	1542	482	186	494	.377	53	169	.314	57	67	.851	22	101	123	150	145	0	60	11	90	16.4	5.1	1.3	1.6	....
01-02	Utah	4	0	53	20	6	16	.375	2	5	.400	6	10	.600	0	6	6	6	6	0	1	0	4	13.3	5.0	1.5	1.5	.296
NBA Playoff Totals		4	0	53	20	6	16	.375	2	5	.400	6	10	.600	0	6	6	6	6	0	1	0	4	13.3	5.0	1.5	1.5	....

• LARUSSO, Rudy
Rudolph A, LaRusso

Born: Nov. 11, 1937. Brooklyn, NY, United States.　　Height: 6'7".　　Weight: 220 lbs.　　Drafted: 1959　　College: Dartmouth

YEAR	TEAM	GP	GS	MIN	PTS	FGM	FGA	FG%	3PM	3PA	3P%	FTM	FTA	FT%	ORB	DRB	TRB	AST	PF	DQ	STL	BLK	TO	MPG	PPG	RPG	APG	PCM
59-60	Minneapolis	71	....	2092	975	355	913	.389	....	....	....	265	357	.742	....	....	679	83	222	8	....	....	....	29.5	13.7	9.6	1.2	.502
60-61	LA Lakers	79	....	2593	1155	416	992	.419	....	....	....	323	409	.790	....	....	781	135	280	8	....	....	....	32.8	14.6	9.9	1.7	.516
61-62	LA Lakers	80	....	2754	1374	516	1108	.466	....	....	....	342	448	.763	....	....	828	179	255	5	....	....	....	34.4	17.2	10.4	2.2	.594
62-63	LA Lakers	75	....	2505	924	321	761	.422	....	....	....	282	393	.718	....	....	747	187	255	5	....	....	....	33.4	12.3	10.0	2.5	.498
63-64	LA Lakers	79	....	2746	972	337	776	.434	....	....	....	298	397	.751	....	....	800	190	268	5	....	....	....	34.8	12.3	10.1	2.4	.489
64-65	LA Lakers	77	....	2588	1083	381	827	.461	....	....	....	321	415	.773	....	....	725	198	258	3	....	....	....	33.6	14.1	9.4	2.6	.543
65-66	LA Lakers	76	....	2316	1170	410	897	.457	....	....	....	350	445	.787	....	....	660	165	261	9	....	....	....	30.5	15.4	8.7	2.2	.590
66-67	LA Lakers	45	....	1292	578	211	509	.415	....	....	....	156	224	.696	....	....	351	78	149	6	....	....	....	28.7	12.8	7.8	1.7	.486
67-68	San Francisco	79	....	2819	1726	602	1389	.433	....	....	....	522	661	.790	....	....	741	182	337	14	....	....	....	35.7	21.8	9.4	2.3	.609
68-69	San Francisco	75	....	2782	1550	553	1349	.410	....	....	....	444	559	.794	....	....	624	159	268	9	....	....	....	37.1	20.7	8.3	2.1	.514
NBA Season Totals		736	....	24487	11507	4102	9521	.431	....	....	....	3303	4308	.767	....	....	6936	1556	2553	72	....	....	....	33.3	15.6	9.4	2.1	....
59-60	Minneapolis	9	....	321	139	56	132	.424	....	....	....	27	35	.771	....	....	70	22	34	1	....	....	....	35.7	15.4	7.8	2.4	.455
60-61	LA Lakers	12	....	360	146	57	144	.396	....	....	....	32	48	.667	....	....	96	24	43	1	....	....	....	30.0	12.2	8.0	2.0	.445
61-62	LA Lakers	13	....	461	183	57	156	.365	....	....	....	69	91	.758	....	....	118	22	51	3	....	....	....	35.5	14.1	9.1	1.7	.425
62-63	LA Lakers	13	....	465	187	65	154	.422	....	....	....	57	75	.760	....	....	127	28	58	2	....	....	....	35.8	14.4	9.8	2.2	.475
63-64	LA Lakers	5	....	189	45	13	33	.394	....	....	....	19	22	.864	....	....	30	11	23	2	....	....	....	37.8	9.0	6.0	2.2	.297
64-65	LA Lakers	11	....	395	165	56	137	.409	....	....	....	53	74	.716	....	....	89	29	52	4	....	....	....	35.9	15.0	8.1	2.6	.453
65-66	LA Lakers	14	....	397	167	57	124	.460	....	....	....	53	67	.791	....	....	99	26	47	0	....	....	....	28.4	11.9	7.1	1.9	.503
67-68	San Francisco	10	....	385	203	72	182	.396	....	....	....	59	81	.728	....	....	99	17	35	0	....	....	....	38.5	20.3	9.9	1.7	.498
68-69	San Francisco	6	....	215	109	34	90	.378	....	....	....	41	53	.774	....	....	51	15	23	0	....	....	....	35.8	18.2	8.5	2.5	.501
NBA Playoff Totals		93	....	3188	1344	467	1152	.405	....	....	....	410	546	.751	....	....	779	194	366	13	....	....	....	34.3	14.5	8.4	2.1	....

• LASKOWSKI, John
John Laskowski

Born: June 7, 1953. South Bend, IN, United States.　　Height: 6'6".　　Weight: 185 lbs.　　Drafted: 1975　　College: Indiana

YEAR	TEAM	GP	GS	MIN	PTS	FGM	FGA	FG%	3PM	3PA	3P%	FTM	FTA	FT%	ORB	DRB	TRB	AST	PF	DQ	STL	BLK	TO	MPG	PPG	RPG	APG	PCM
75-76	Chicago	71	....	1570	655	284	690	.412	....	....	....	87	120	.725	52	167	219	55	90	0	56	10	....	22.1	9.2	3.1	0.8	.321
76-77	Chicago	47	....	562	177	75	212	.354	....	....	....	27	30	.900	16	47	63	44	22	0	32	2	....	12.0	3.8	1.3	0.9	.271
NBA Season Totals		118	....	2132	832	359	902	.398	....	....	....	114	150	.760	68	214	282	99	112	0	88	12	....	18.1	7.1	2.4	0.8	....

• LATTER, Dave
Dave Latter

Born: 1922.　　Height: 6'6".　　Weight: 210 lbs.　　Drafted: —　　College: none

YEAR	TEAM	GP	GS	MIN	PTS	FGM	FGA	FG%	3PM	3PA	3P%	FTM	FTA	FT%	ORB	DRB	TRB	AST	PF	DQ	STL	BLK	TO	MPG	PPG	RPG	APG	PCM
46-47	Detroit-N	41	....	....	321	123	....	....	....	....	....	75	132	.568	....	....	....	95	....	....	....	....	....	7.8	....	....	....
48-49	Detroit-N	13	....	....	90	26	....	....	....	....	....	38	66	.576	....	....	....	....	....	....	....	....	....	6.9	....	....	....
NBL Season Totals		54	....	....	411	149	....	....	....	....	....	113	198	....	....	....	....	95	....	....	....	....	....	7.6	....	....	....

• LATTIN, Dave
David (Big Daddy) Lattin

Born: Dec. 23, 1943. Houston, TX, United States.　　Height: 6'6".　　Weight: 225 lbs.　　Drafted: 1967　　College: Texas Western

YEAR	TEAM	GP	GS	MIN	PTS	FGM	FGA	FG%	3PM	3PA	3P%	FTM	FTA	FT%	ORB	DRB	TRB	AST	PF	DQ	STL	BLK	TO	MPG	PPG	RPG	APG	PCM
67-68	San Francisco	44	....	257	97	37	102	.363	....	....	....	23	33	.697	....	....	104	14	94	4	....	....	....	5.8	2.2	2.4	0.3	.403
68-69	Phoenix	68	....	987	409	150	366	.410	....	....	....	109	172	.634	....	....	323	48	163	5	....	....	....	14.5	6.0	4.8	0.7	.466
70-71	Pittsburgh-A	71	....	1135	462	177	377	.469	0	1	.000	108	177	.610	147	320	467	64	215	6	....	....	111	16.0	6.5	6.6	0.9	.563

YEAR	TEAM	GP	GS	MIN	PTS	FGM	FGA	FG%	3PM	3PA	3P%	FTM	FTA	FT%	ORB	DRB	TRB	AST	PF	DQ	STL	BLK	TO	MPG	PPG	RPG	APG	PCM
71-72	Pittsburgh-A	64	....	1482	806	329	605	.544	0	1	.000	148	242	.612	136	239	375	51	178	4	....	....	108	23.2	12.6	5.9	0.8	.560
72-73	Memphis-A	16	....	296	130	48	104	.462	0	1	.000	34	45	.756	21	42	63	7	45	0	....	....	32	18.5	8.1	3.9	0.4	.401
NBA Season Totals		112	....	1244	506	187	468	.400	....	....	....	132	205	.644	....	....	427	62	257	9	....	....	....	11.1	4.5	3.8	0.6	
ABA Season Totals		151	....	2913	1398	554	1086	.510	0	3	.000	290	464	.625	304	601	905	122	438	10	....	....	251	19.3	9.3	6.0	0.8	
Career Totals		263	....	4157	1904	741	1554	.477	0	3	.000	422	669	.631	304	601	1332	184	695	19	....	....	251	15.8	7.2	5.1	0.7	
67-68	San Francisco	5	....	27	7	1	5	.200	....	....	....	5	6	.833	....	....	5	1	9	0	....	....	....	5.4	1.4	1.0	0.2	.186
NBA Playoff Totals		5	....	27	7	1	5	.200	....	....	....	5	6	.833	....	....	5	1	9	0	....	....	....	5.4	1.4	1.0	0.2	

• LAUDERDALE, Priest

Priest Lauderdale

Born: Aug. 31, 1973. Chicago, IL, United States.   Height: 7'4".   Weight: 325 lbs.   Drafted: 1996   College: Central State (OH)

YEAR	TEAM	GP	GS	MIN	PTS	FGM	FGA	FG%	3PM	3PA	3P%	FTM	FTA	FT%	ORB	DRB	TRB	AST	PF	DQ	STL	BLK	TO	MPG	PPG	RPG	APG	PCM
96-97	Atlanta	35	0	180	111	49	89	.551	0	1	.000	13	23	.565	16	27	43	12	39	0	1	9	39	5.1	3.2	1.2	0.3	.426
97-98	Denver	39	0	345	144	53	127	.417	0	0	.000	38	69	.551	27	73	100	21	63	0	7	17	47	8.8	3.7	2.6	0.5	.367
NBA Season Totals		74	0	525	255	102	216	.472	0	1	.000	51	92	.554	43	100	143	33	102	0	8	26	86	7.1	3.4	1.9	0.4	
96-97	Atlanta	3	0	7	0	0	3	.000	0	0	.000	0	0	.000	1	1	2	0	1	0	0	0	3	2.3	0.0	0.7	0.0	-.599
NBA Playoff Totals		3	0	7	0	0	3	.000	0	0	.000	0	0	.000	1	1	2	0	1	0	0	0	3	2.3	0.0	0.7	0.0	

• LAUGHLIN, Bill

Bill Laughlin

Born: 1915.   Height: 6'2".   Weight: 185 lbs.   Drafted: —   College: Washington & Jefferson

YEAR	TEAM	GP	GS	MIN	PTS	FGM	FGA	FG%	3PM	3PA	3P%	FTM	FTA	FT%	ORB	DRB	TRB	AST	PF	DQ	STL	BLK	TO	MPG	PPG	RPG	APG	PCM
38-39	Cleveland-N	27	....	....	232	92	....	....	....	....	....	48													8.6			
NBL Season Totals		27	....	....	232	92	....	....	....	....	....	48													8.6			

• LAUREL, Rich

Richard Laurel

Born: July 11, 1954. Philadelphia, PA, United States.   Height: 6'6".   Weight: 190 lbs.   Drafted: 1977   College: Hofstra

YEAR	TEAM	GP	GS	MIN	PTS	FGM	FGA	FG%	3PM	3PA	3P%	FTM	FTA	FT%	ORB	DRB	TRB	AST	PF	DQ	STL	BLK	TO	MPG	PPG	RPG	APG	PCM
77-78	Milwaukee	10	....	57	24	10	31	.323	....	....	....	4	4	1.000	6	4	10	3	10	0	3	1	4	5.7	2.4	1.0	0.3	.235
NBA Season Totals		10	....	57	24	10	31	.323	....	....	....	4	4	1.000	6	4	10	3	10	0	3	1	4	5.7	2.4	1.0	0.3	

• LAURIE, Harry

Harry Laurie

Born: Nov. 2, 1944.   Height: 6'1".   Weight: 178 lbs.   Drafted: 1968   College: St. Peter's

YEAR	TEAM	GP	GS	MIN	PTS	FGM	FGA	FG%	3PM	3PA	3P%	FTM	FTA	FT%	ORB	DRB	TRB	AST	PF	DQ	STL	BLK	TO	MPG	PPG	RPG	APG	PCM
70-71	Pittsburgh-A	9	....	57	13	3	12	.250	0	0	.000	7	11	.636	7	8	15	8	16	0	....	....	10	6.3	1.4	1.7	0.9	.340
ABA Season Totals		9	....	57	13	3	12	.250	0	0	.000	7	11	.636	7	8	15	8	16	0	....	....	10	6.3	1.4	1.7	0.9	

• LAUTENBACH, Walt

Walter Henry Lautenbach

Born: Nov. 17, 1922.   Height: 6'2".   Weight: 185 lbs.   Drafted: —   College: Wisconsin

YEAR	TEAM	GP	GS	MIN	PTS	FGM	FGA	FG%	3PM	3PA	3P%	FTM	FTA	FT%	ORB	DRB	TRB	AST	PF	DQ	STL	BLK	TO	MPG	PPG	RPG	APG	PCM
47-48	Oshkosh-N	60	....	....	354	159	....	....	....	....	....	36	60	.600				....	130						5.9			
48-49	Oshkosh-N	61	....	....	234	104	....	....	....	....	....	26	45	.578				....	84						3.8			
49-50	Sheboygan	55	....	....	238	100	332	.301	....	....	....	38	55	.691				73	122						4.3		1.3	
NBA Season Totals		55	....	....	238	100	332	.301	....	....	....	38	55	.691				73	122						4.3		1.3	
NBL Season Totals		121	....	....	588	263	....	....	....	....	....	62	105	....				....	214						4.9			
Career Totals		176	....	....	826	363	332					100	160					73	336						4.7		0.4	
47-48	Oshkosh-N	4	....	....	33	14	....	....	....	....	....	5	6	.833											8.3			
48-49	Oshkosh-N	7	....	....	30	12	....	....	....	....	....	6	15	.400											4.3			
NBL Playoff Totals		11			63	26	....	....	....	....	....	11	21												5.7			

• LAUTENSCHLAGER, Rube

Reuben Lautenschlager

Born: 1915.   Height: 6'3".   Weight: 190 lbs.   Drafted: —   College: Wisconsin (Oshkosh)

YEAR	TEAM	GP	GS	MIN	PTS	FGM	FGA	FG%	3PM	3PA	3P%	FTM	FTA	FT%	ORB	DRB	TRB	AST	PF	DQ	STL	BLK	TO	MPG	PPG	RPG	APG	PCM
38-39	Sheboygan-N	27	....	....	204	83	....	....	....	....	....	38	....	....				....							7.6			
39-40	Sheboygan-N	28	....	....	184	76	....	....	....	....	....	32	....	....				....							6.6			
40-41	Sheboygan-N	23	....	....	88	31	....	....	....	....	....	26	....	....				....							3.8			
41-42	Sheboygan-N	24	....	....	155	67	....	....	....	....	....	21	....	....				....							6.5			
42-43	Sheboygan-N	23	....	....	212	88	....	....	....	....	....	36	....	....				....							9.2			
43-44	Sheboygan-N	21	....	....	164	68	....	....	....	....	....	28	....	....				....							7.8			
44-45	Sheboygan-N	30	....	....	194	83	....	....	....	....	....	28	....	....				....							6.5			
45-46	Sheboygan-N	3	....	....	17	8	....	....	....	....	....	1	....	....				....							5.7			
46-47	Sheboygan-N	43	....	....	224	94	....	....	....	....	....	36	65	.554				....	65						5.2			
NBL Season Totals		222	....	....	1442	598	....	....	....	....	....	246	65	....				....	65						6.5			
39-40	Sheboygan-N	3	....	....	16	5	....	....	....	....	....	6	....	....				....							5.3			
40-41	Sheboygan-N	6	....	....	16	5	....	....	....	....	....	6	....	....				....							2.7			
42-43	Sheboygan-N	5	....	....	56	22	....	....	....	....	....	12	....	....				....							11.2			
43-44	Sheboygan-N	4	....	....	8	3	....	....	....	....	....	2	....	....				....							2.0			
44-45	Sheboygan-N	8	....	....	45	16	....	....	....	....	....	13	....	....				....							5.6			
46-47	Sheboygan-N	5	....	....	34	11	....	....	....	....	....	12	21	.571				....							6.8			
NBL Playoff Totals		31	....	....	175	62	....	....	....	....	....	51	21					....							5.6			

• LAVELLI, Tony

Anthony Lavelli

Born: July 11, 1926. Somerville, MA, United States. Died: Jan.8, 1998. Height: 6'3". Weight: 185 lbs. Drafted: 1949 College: Yale

YEAR TEAM	GP	GS	MIN	PTS	FGM	FGA	FG%	3PM	3PA	3P%	FTM	FTA	FT%	ORB	DRB	TRB	AST	PF	DQ	STL	BLK	TO	MPG	PPG	RPG	APG	PCM
49-50 Boston	56	....	....	492	162	436	.372	....	....	....	168	197	.853	....	....	....	40	107	....	....	....	....	....	8.8	....	0.7	....
50-51 New York	30	....	....	99	32	93	.344	....	....	....	35	41	.854	....	....	59	23	56	1	....	....	....	....	3.3	2.0	0.8	....
NBA Season Totals	86	....	....	591	194	529	.367	....	....	....	203	238	.853	....	....	59	63	163	1	....	....	....	....	6.9	0.7	0.7	....
50-51 New York	2	....	....	4	1	5	.200	....	....	....	2	2	1.000	....	....	1	1	2	0	....	....	....	....	2.0	0.5	0.5	....
NBA Playoff Totals	2	....	....	4	1	5	.200	....	....	....	2	2	1.000	....	....	1	1	2	0	....	....	....	....	2.0	0.5	0.5	....

• LAVOY, Bob

Robert William Lavoy

Born: June 29, 1926. Height: 6'7". Weight: 185 lbs. Drafted: 1950 College: Western Kentucky

YEAR TEAM	GP	GS	MIN	PTS	FGM	FGA	FG%	3PM	3PA	3P%	FTM	FTA	FT%	ORB	DRB	TRB	AST	PF	DQ	STL	BLK	TO	MPG	PPG	RPG	APG	PCM
50-51 Indianapolis	63	....	....	526	221	619	.357	....	....	....	84	133	.632	....	....	310	76	190	2	....	....	....	....	8.3	4.9	1.2	....
51-52 Indianapolis	63	....	1829	648	240	604	.397	....	....	....	168	223	.753	....	....	479	107	210	5	....	....	....	29.0	10.3	7.6	1.7	.423
52-53 Indianapolis	70	....	2327	618	225	560	.402	....	....	....	168	242	.694	....	....	528	130	274	18	....	....	....	33.2	8.8	7.5	1.9	.343
53-54 Mil/Syr	68	....	1277	364	135	356	.379	....	....	....	94	129	.729	....	....	317	78	215	2	....	....	....	18.8	5.4	4.7	1.1	.348
NBA Season Totals	264	....	5433	2156	821	2139	.384	....	....	....	514	727	.707	....	....	1634	391	889	27	....	....	....	20.6	8.2	6.2	1.5	....
50-51 Indianapolis	3	....	....	3	0	7	.000	....	....	....	3	5	.600	....	....	6	4	6	0	....	....	....	....	1.0	2.0	1.3	....
51-52 Indianapolis	2	....	78	24	9	27	.333	....	....	....	6	8	.750	....	....	20	4	8	1	....	....	....	39.0	12.0	10.0	2.0	.346
52-53 Indianapolis	2	....	47	10	4	16	.250	....	....	....	2	5	.400	....	....	10	2	10	1	....	....	....	23.5	5.0	5.0	1.0	.136
53-54 Syracuse	13	....	358	118	37	95	.389	....	....	....	44	55	.800	....	....	85	20	50	0	....	....	....	27.5	9.1	6.5	1.5	.395
NBA Playoff Totals	20	....	483	155	50	145	.345	....	....	....	55	73	.753	....	....	121	30	74	2	....	....	....	24.2	7.8	6.1	1.5	....

• LAWRENCE, Edmund

Edmund Lawrence

Born: Dec. 8, 1952. Lake Charles, LA, United States. Height: 6'12". . Weight: 228 lbs. Drafted: 1980 College: McNeese State

YEAR TEAM	GP	GS	MIN	PTS	FGM	FGA	FG%	3PM	3PA	3P%	FTM	FTA	FT%	ORB	DRB	TRB	AST	PF	DQ	STL	BLK	TO	MPG	PPG	RPG	APG	PCM
80-81 Detroit	3	....	19	12	5	8	.625	0	0	.000	2	4	.500	2	2	4	1	6	0	1	0	1	6.3	4.0	1.3	0.3	.545
NBA Season Totals	3	....	19	12	5	8	.625	0	0	.000	2	4	.500	2	2	4	1	6	0	1	0	1	6.3	4.0	1.3	0.3	....

• LAWRY, Thomas

Thomas Lawry

Born: Aug. 1, 1911. Died: Sept.23, 1999. Height: 5'10". Weight: 155 lbs. Drafted: — College: Pittsburgh

YEAR TEAM	GP	GS	MIN	PTS	FGM	FGA	FG%	3PM	3PA	3P%	FTM	FTA	FT%	ORB	DRB	TRB	AST	PF	DQ	STL	BLK	TO	MPG	PPG	RPG	APG	PCM
37-38 Pittsburgh-N	9	....	....	26	9	....	....	....	....	....	8	....	....	....	....	....	....	....	....	....	....	....	....	2.9	....	....	....
NBL Season Totals	9	....	....	26	9	....	....	....	....	....	8	....	....	....	....	....	....	....	....	....	....	....	....	2.9	....	....	....

• LAWSON, Jason

Jason L. Lawson

Born: Sept. 2, 1974. Philadelphia, PA, United States. Height: 6'11". Weight: 240 lbs. Drafted: 1997 College: Villanova

YEAR TEAM	GP	GS	MIN	PTS	FGM	FGA	FG%	3PM	3PA	3P%	FTM	FTA	FT%	ORB	DRB	TRB	AST	PF	DQ	STL	BLK	TO	MPG	PPG	RPG	APG	PCM
97-98 Orlando	17	0	80	26	9	15	.600	0	0	.000	8	10	.800	8	19	27	5	14	1	4	4	2	4.7	1.5	1.6	0.3	.610
NBA Season Totals	17	0	80	26	9	15	.600	0	0	.000	8	10	.800	8	19	27	5	14	1	4	4	2	4.7	1.5	1.6	0.3	....

• LAYTON, Mo

Dennis (Mo) Layton

Born: Dec. 24, 1948. Newark, NJ, United States. Height: 6'1". Weight: 180 lbs. Drafted: 1971 College: USC

YEAR TEAM	GP	GS	MIN	PTS	FGM	FGA	FG%	3PM	3PA	3P%	FTM	FTA	FT%	ORB	DRB	TRB	AST	PF	DQ	STL	BLK	TO	MPG	PPG	RPG	APG	PCM
71-72 Phoenix	80	....	1849	730	304	717	.424	....	....	....	122	165	.739	....	....	164	247	219	0	....	....	....	23.1	9.1	2.1	3.1	.369
72-73 Phoenix	65	....	990	464	187	434	.431	....	....	....	90	119	.756	....	....	77	139	127	2	....	....	....	15.2	7.1	1.2	2.1	.414
73-74 Memphis-A	3	....	65	19	8	17	.471	0	0	.000	3	3	1.000	1	3	4	7	4	....	0	1	7	21.7	6.3	1.3	2.3	.323
73-74 Portland	22	....	327	124	55	112	.491	....	....	....	14	26	.538	7	26	33	51	45	0	9	1	....	14.9	5.6	1.5	2.3	.422
76-77 New York	56	....	765	326	134	277	.484	....	....	....	58	73	.795	11	36	47	154	87	0	21	6	....	13.7	5.8	0.8	2.8	.489
77-78 San Antonio	41	....	498	182	85	168	.506	....	....	....	12	13	.923	4	28	32	108	51	0	21	4	57	12.1	4.4	0.8	2.6	.418
NBA Season Totals	264	....	4429	1826	765	1708	.448	....	....	....	296	396	.747	22	90	353	699	529	2	51	11	57	16.8	6.9	1.3	2.6	....
ABA Season Totals	3	....	65	19	8	17	.471	0	0	.000	3	3	1.000	1	3	4	7	4	....	0	1	7	21.7	6.3	1.3	2.3	....
Career Totals	267	....	4494	1845	773	1725	.448	0	0	.000	299	399	.749	23	93	357	706	533	2	51	12	64	16.8	6.9	1.3	2.6	....

• LEAKS, Manny

Emanuel Leaks

Born: Nov. 27, 1945. Cleveland, OH, United States. Height: 6'8". Weight: 225 lbs. Drafted: 1968 College: Niagara

YEAR TEAM	GP	GS	MIN	PTS	FGM	FGA	FG%	3PM	3PA	3P%	FTM	FTA	FT%	ORB	DRB	TRB	AST	PF	DQ	STL	BLK	TO	MPG	PPG	RPG	APG	PCM
68-69 Dallas-A	27	....	702	286	115	229	.502	0	0	.000	56	81	.691	102	144	246	20	88	1	....	....	32	26.0	10.6	9.1	0.7	.532
68-69 Kentucky-A	31	....	674	222	88	238	.370	0	0	.000	46	67	.687	87	147	234	32	103	3	....	....	31	21.7	7.2	7.5	1.0	.412
68-69 New York-A	20	....	713	250	96	289	.332	0	1	.000	58	81	.716	133	150	283	40	62	0	....	....	34	35.7	12.5	14.2	2.0	.472
69-70 Dallas-A	84	....	3086	1577	636	1287	.494	0	2	.000	305	428	.713	427	620	1047	100	283	11	....	....	181	36.7	18.8	12.5	1.2	.602
70-71 New York-A	40	....	1427	678	274	553	.495	0	1	.000	130	179	.726	136	249	385	49	108	2	....	....	100	35.7	17.0	9.6	1.2	.532
70-71 Texas-A	40	....	1187	621	236	527	.448	0	0	.000	149	202	.738	181	289	470	55	103	3	....	....	70	29.7	15.5	11.8	1.4	.647
71-72 Florida-A	18	....	726	277	124	258	.481	0	1	.000	29	47	.617	51	125	176	26	55	1	....	....	39	40.3	15.4	9.8	1.4	.428
71-72 New York-A	9	....	142	54	24	71	.338	0	0	.000	6	9	.667	11	32	43	4	10	0	....	....	5	15.8	6.0	4.8	0.4	.347
71-72 Utah-A	42	....	575	223	92	251	.367	0	0	.000	39	65	.600	83	110	193	25	71	0	....	....	29	13.7	5.3	4.6	0.6	.414
72-73 Philadelphia	82	....	2530	898	377	933	.404	....	....	....	144	200	.720	....	....	677	95	191	5	....	....	....	30.9	11.0	8.3	1.2	.397
73-74 Washington	53	....	845	216	79	232	.341	....	....	....	58	83	.699	94	150	244	25	95	1	10	39	....	15.9	4.1	4.6	0.5	.321
NBA Season Totals	135	....	3375	1114	456	1165	.391	....	....	....	202	283	.714	94	150	921	120	286	6	10	39	....	25.0	8.3	6.8	0.9	....
ABA Season Totals	311	....	9232	4188	1685	3703	.455	0	5	.000	818	1159	.706	1211	1866	3077	351	883	21	....	....	521	29.7	13.5	9.9	1.1	....
Career Totals	446	....	12607	5302	2141	4868	.440	0	5	.000	1020	1442	.707	1305	2016	3998	471	1169	27	10	39	521	28.3	11.9	9.0	1.1	....

YEAR	TEAM	GP	GS	MIN	PTS	FGM	FGA	FG%	3PM	3PA	3P%	FTM	FTA	FT%	ORB	DRB	TRB	AST	PF	DQ	STL	BLK	TO	MPG	PPG	RPG	APG	PCM
68-69	Dallas-A	7	....	199	71	28	69	.406	0	0	.000	15	18	.833	25	38	63	8	25	0	....	....	15	28.4	10.1	9.0	1.1	.437
68-69	Dallas-A	6	....	237	121	48	98	.490	0	0	.000	25	35	.714	23	63	86	9	....	0	....	....	15	39.5	20.2	14.3	1.5	....
70-71	New York-A	6	....	204	76	35	69	.507	0	0	.000	6	12	.500	12	35	47	3	16	0	....	....	10	34.0	12.7	7.8	0.5	.398
73-74	Washington	2	....	5	2	1	2	.500	....	....	....	0	0	.000	1	1	2	0	1	0	0	0	....	2.5	1.0	1.0	0.0	.485
NBA Playoff Totals		2	....	5	2	1	2	.500	....	....	....	0	0	.000	1	1	2	0	1	0	0	0	....	2.5	1.0	1.0	0.0	....
ABA Playoff Totals		19	....	640	268	111	236	.470	0	0	.000	46	65	.708	60	136	196	20	41	0	....	....	40	33.7	14.1	10.3	1.1	....
Career Playoff Totals		21	....	645	270	112	238	.471	0	0	.000	46	65	.708	61	137	198	20	42	0	0	0	40	30.7	12.9	9.4	1.0	....

• LEAR, Hal
Harold C. (King) Lear Jr.

Born: Jan. 31, 1935. Philadelphia, PA, United States.   Height: 5'12".   Weight: 163 lbs.   Drafted: 1956   College: Temple

YEAR	TEAM	GP	GS	MIN	PTS	FGM	FGA	FG%	3PM	3PA	3P%	FTM	FTA	FT%	ORB	DRB	TRB	AST	PF	DQ	STL	BLK	TO	MPG	PPG	RPG	APG	PCM
56-57	Philadelphia	3	....	14	4	2	6	.333	....	....	....	0	0	.000	....	....	1	1	3	0	....	....	....	4.7	1.3	0.3	0.3	.136
NBA Season Totals		3	....	14	4	2	6	.333	....	....	....	0	0	.000	....	....	1	1	3	0	....	....	....	4.7	1.3	0.3	0.3	....

• LEAVELL, Allen
Allen Frazier Leavell

Born: May 27, 1957. Muncie, IN, United States.   Height: 6'1".   Weight: 170 lbs.   Drafted: 1979   College: Oklahoma City

YEAR	TEAM	GP	GS	MIN	PTS	FGM	FGA	FG%	3PM	3PA	3P%	FTM	FTA	FT%	ORB	DRB	TRB	AST	PF	DQ	STL	BLK	TO	MPG	PPG	RPG	APG	PCM
79-80	Houston	77	....	2123	843	330	656	.503	3	19	.158	180	221	.814	57	127	184	417	197	1	127	28	208	27.6	10.9	2.4	5.4	.478
80-81	Houston	79	....	1686	642	258	548	.471	2	17	.118	124	149	.832	30	104	134	384	160	1	97	15	190	21.3	8.1	1.7	4.9	.452
81-82	Houston	79	61	2150	864	370	793	.467	9	31	.290	115	135	.852	49	119	168	457	182	2	150	15	150	27.2	10.9	2.1	5.8	.485
82-83	Houston	79	76	2602	1167	439	1059	.415	42	175	.240	247	297	.832	64	131	195	530	215	0	165	14	198	32.9	14.8	2.5	6.7	.472
83-84	Houston	82	27	2009	947	349	731	.477	11	71	.155	238	286	.832	31	86	117	459	199	2	107	12	180	24.5	11.5	1.4	5.6	.508
84-85	Houston	42	0	536	228	88	209	.421	8	37	.216	44	57	.772	8	29	37	102	61	0	23	4	50	12.8	5.4	0.9	2.4	.378
85-86	Houston	74	12	1190	583	212	458	.463	24	67	.358	135	158	.854	6	61	67	234	126	1	58	8	89	16.1	7.9	0.9	3.2	.485
86-87	Houston	53	11	1175	412	147	358	.411	18	57	.316	100	119	.840	14	47	61	224	126	1	53	10	64	22.2	7.8	1.2	4.2	.377
87-88	Houston	80	54	2150	819	291	666	.437	19	88	.216	218	251	.869	22	126	148	405	162	1	124	9	128	26.9	10.2	1.9	5.1	.444
88-89	Houston	55	3	627	179	65	188	.346	5	41	.122	44	60	.733	13	40	53	127	61	0	25	5	61	11.4	3.3	1.0	2.3	.295
NBA Season Totals		700	244	16248	6684	2549	5666	.450	141	603	.234	1445	1733	.834	294	870	1164	3339	1489	9	929	120	1318	23.2	9.5	1.7	4.8	....
79-80	Houston	7	....	149	39	10	38	.263	0	4	.000	19	21	.905	2	10	12	24	12	0	6	0	6	21.3	5.6	1.7	3.4	.298
80-81	Houston	17	....	217	75	30	77	.390	0	0	.000	15	17	.882	5	12	17	44	26	0	18	4	20	12.8	4.4	1.0	2.6	.390
81-82	Houston	3	3	93	42	20	47	.426	0	1	.000	2	2	1.000	1	4	5	10	9	0	3	1	5	31.0	14.0	1.7	3.3	.295
84-85	Houston	5	0	16	6	2	6	.333	0	2	.000	2	2	1.000	1	2	3	3	2	0	0	0	1	3.2	1.2	0.6	0.6	.401
85-86	Houston	15	0	170	75	24	80	.300	7	15	.467	20	23	.870	3	12	15	40	12	0	9	0	9	11.3	5.0	1.0	2.7	.428
86-87	Houston	10	10	384	141	44	107	.411	4	16	.250	49	60	.817	6	19	25	72	42	2	19	3	28	38.4	14.1	2.5	7.2	.397
87-88	Houston	4	0	38	20	7	19	.368	2	6	.333	4	4	1.000	0	3	3	9	6	0	2	0	6	9.5	5.0	0.8	2.3	.387
88-89	Houston	2	0	5	4	1	3	.333	0	0	.000	2	2	1.000	0	0	0	1	0	0	0	0	0	2.5	2.0	0.0	0.5	.642
NBA Playoff Totals		63	13	1072	402	138	377	.366	13	44	.295	113	131	.863	18	62	80	203	109	2	57	8	75	17.0	6.4	1.3	3.2	....

• LEBO, Jeff
Jeffrey Brian Lebo

Born: Oct. 5, 1966. Carlisle, PA, United States.   Height: 6'2".   Weight: 180 lbs.   Drafted: —   College: North Carolina

YEAR	TEAM	GP	GS	MIN	PTS	FGM	FGA	FG%	3PM	3PA	3P%	FTM	FTA	FT%	ORB	DRB	TRB	AST	PF	DQ	STL	BLK	TO	MPG	PPG	RPG	APG	PCM
89-90	San Antonio	4	0	32	6	2	7	.286	0	0	.000	2	2	1.000	2	2	4	3	7	0	2	0	1	8.0	1.5	1.0	0.8	.185
NBA Season Totals		4	0	32	6	2	7	.286	0	0	.000	2	2	1.000	2	2	4	3	7	0	2	0	1	8.0	1.5	1.0	0.8	....

• LECKNER, Eric
Eric Charles Leckner

Born: May 27, 1966. Inglewood, CA, United States.   Height: 6'11".   Weight: 265 lbs.   Drafted: 1988   College: Wyoming

YEAR	TEAM	GP	GS	MIN	PTS	FGM	FGA	FG%	3PM	3PA	3P%	FTM	FTA	FT%	ORB	DRB	TRB	AST	PF	DQ	STL	BLK	TO	MPG	PPG	RPG	APG	PCM
88-89	Utah	75	0	779	319	120	220	.545	0	0	.000	79	113	.699	48	151	199	16	174	1	8	22	68	10.4	4.3	2.7	0.2	.380
89-90	Utah	77	0	764	331	125	222	.563	0	0	.000	81	109	.743	48	144	192	19	157	0	15	23	62	9.9	4.3	2.5	0.2	.433
90-91	Sacramento	32	0	378	94	39	96	.406	0	0	.000	16	27	.593	27	60	87	18	69	1	4	11	26	11.8	2.9	2.7	0.6	.248
90-91	Charlotte	40	2	744	230	92	198	.465	0	0	.000	46	84	.548	55	153	208	21	123	3	10	11	44	18.6	5.8	5.2	0.5	.337
91-92	Charlotte	59	2	716	196	79	154	.513	0	1	.000	38	51	.745	49	157	206	31	114	1	9	18	41	12.1	3.3	3.5	0.5	.390
93-94	Philadelphia	71	36	1163	362	139	286	.486	0	2	.000	84	130	.646	75	207	282	86	190	2	18	34	85	16.4	5.1	4.0	1.2	.379
94-95	Detroit	57	11	623	225	87	165	.527	0	2	.000	51	72	.708	47	127	174	14	122	1	15	15	40	10.9	3.9	3.1	0.2	.407
95-96	Detroit	18	8	155	44	18	29	.621	0	0	.000	8	13	.615	8	26	34	1	30	0	2	4	11	8.6	2.4	1.9	0.1	.294
96-97	Charlotte	1	0	11	0	0	3	.000	0	0	.000	0	0	.000	0	1	1	1	3	0	0	0	0	11.0	0.0	1.0	1.0	-.199
96-97	Vancouver	19	1	115	34	14	30	.467	0	0	.000	6	12	.500	5	30	35	4	32	0	3	2	10	6.1	1.8	1.8	0.2	.292
NBA Season Totals		449	60	5448	1835	713	1403	.508	0	5	.000	409	611	.669	362	1056	1418	211	1014	9	84	140	387	12.1	4.1	3.2	0.5	....
88-89	Utah	3	0	10	2	1	4	.250	0	0	.000	0	0	.000	1	1	2	0	2	0	0	0	3	3.3	0.7	0.7	0.0	-.265
89-90	Utah	3	0	28	18	6	10	.600	1	1	1.000	5	9	.556	2	6	8	2	8	0	0	0	1	9.3	6.0	2.7	0.7	.618
95-96	Detroit	1	0	3	0	0	0	.000	0	0	.000	0	0	.000	0	0	0	0	2	0	0	0	0	3.0	0.0	0.0	0.0	-.313
NBA Playoff Totals		7	0	41	20	7	14	.500	1	1	1.000	5	9	.556	3	7	10	2	12	0	0	0	4	5.9	2.9	1.4	0.3	....

• LEE, Butch
Alfred (Butch) Lee

Born: Dec. 5, 1956. Santurce, PR, Puerto Rico.   Height: 6'   Weight: 185 lbs.   Drafted: 1978   College: Marquette

YEAR	TEAM	GP	GS	MIN	PTS	FGM	FGA	FG%	3PM	3PA	3P%	FTM	FTA	FT%	ORB	DRB	TRB	AST	PF	DQ	STL	BLK	TO	MPG	PPG	RPG	APG	PCM
78-79	Atlanta	49	....	997	376	144	313	.460	....	....	....	88	117	.752	11	48	59	169	88	0	56	1	98	20.3	7.7	1.2	3.4	.375
78-79	Cleveland	33	....	782	379	146	321	.455	....	....	....	87	113	.770	22	45	67	126	58	0	30	0	59	23.7	11.5	2.0	3.8	.457
79-80	Cleveland	3	....	24	4	2	11	.182	0	0	.000	0	1	.000	3	0	3	3	0	0	0	0	3	8.0	1.3	1.0	1.0	-.055
79-80	LA Lakers	11	....	31	14	4	13	.308	0	0	.000	6	7	.857	4	4	8	9	2	0	1	0	7	2.8	1.3	0.7	0.8	.521
NBA Season Totals		96	....	1834	773	296	658	.450	0	0	.000	181	238	.761	40	97	137	307	148	0	87	1	167	19.1	8.1	1.4	3.2	....
79-80	LA Lakers	3	....	6	2	0	0	.000	0	0	.000	2	2	1.000	0	1	1	0	2	0	0	0	3	2.0	0.7	0.3	0.0	-.119
NBA Playoff Totals		3	....	6	2	0	0	.000	0	0	.000	2	2	1.000	0	1	1	0	2	0	0	0	3	2.0	0.7	0.3	0.0	....

• LEE, Clyde
Clyde Wayne Lee

Born: Mar. 14, 1944. Nashville, TN, United States.   Height: 6'10".   Weight: 205 lbs.   Drafted: 1966   College: Vanderbilt

YEAR	TEAM	GP	GS	MIN	PTS	FGM	FGA	FG%	3PM	3PA	3P%	FTM	FTA	FT%	ORB	DRB	TRB	AST	PF	DQ	STL	BLK	TO	MPG	PPG	RPG	APG	PCM
66-67	San Francisco	74	....	1247	515	205	503	.408	....	....	....	105	166	.633	....	....	551	77	168	5	....	....	....	16.9	7.0	7.4	1.0	.576
67-68	San Francisco	82	....	2699	975	373	894	.417	....	....	....	229	335	.684	....	....	1141	135	331	10	....	....	....	32.9	11.9	13.9	1.6	.540
68-69	San Francisco	65	....	2237	696	268	674	.398	....	....	....	160	256	.625	....	....	897	82	225	1	....	....	....	34.4	10.7	13.8	1.3	.477
69-70	San Francisco	82	....	2641	902	362	822	.440	....	....	....	178	300	.593	....	....	929	80	263	5	....	....	....	32.2	11.0	11.3	1.0	.468
70-71	San Francisco	82	....	1392	499	194	428	.453	....	....	....	111	199	.558	....	....	570	63	137	0	....	....	....	17.0	6.1	7.0	0.8	.548
71-72	Golden State	78	....	2674	632	256	544	.471	....	....	....	120	222	.541	....	....	1132	85	244	4	....	....	....	34.3	8.1	14.5	1.1	.489
72-73	Golden State	66	....	1476	414	170	365	.466	....	....	....	74	131	.565	....	....	598	34	183	5	....	....	....	22.4	6.3	9.1	0.5	.471
73-74	Golden State	54	....	1642	320	129	284	.454	....	....	....	62	107	.579	188	410	598	68	179	3	27	17	....	30.4	5.9	11.1	1.3	.414
74-75	Atlanta	9	....	177	56	12	36	.333	....	....	....	32	39	.821	24	46	70	8	25	0	1	4	....	19.7	6.2	7.8	0.9	.513
74-75	Philadelphia	71	....	2279	415	164	391	.419	....	....	....	87	138	.630	264	423	687	97	260	9	29	16	....	32.1	5.8	9.7	1.4	.345
75-76	Philadelphia	79	....	1421	309	123	282	.436	....	....	....	63	95	.663	164	289	453	59	188	0	23	27	....	18.0	3.9	5.7	0.7	.376
NBA Season Totals		742	....	19885	5733	2256	5223	.432	....	....	....	1221	1988	.614	640	1168	7626	788	2203	42	80	64	....	26.8	7.7	10.3	1.1	....
66-67	San Francisco	11	....	130	40	19	57	.333	....	....	....	2	10	.200	....	....	54	8	20	0	....	....	....	11.8	3.6	4.9	0.7	.394
67-68	San Francisco	10	....	405	114	48	117	.410	....	....	....	18	36	.500	....	....	132	22	38	2	....	....	....	40.5	11.4	13.2	2.2	.416
68-69	San Francisco	6	....	129	27	9	33	.273	....	....	....	9	11	.818	....	....	43	5	14	0	....	....	....	21.5	4.5	7.2	0.8	.326
70-71	San Francisco	5	....	93	24	10	24	.417	....	....	....	4	8	.500	....	....	37	2	13	0	....	....	....	18.6	4.8	7.4	0.4	.417
71-72	Golden State	5	....	175	24	8	28	.286	....	....	....	8	12	.667	....	....	64	7	14	0	....	....	....	35.0	4.8	12.8	1.4	.355
72-73	Golden State	11	....	413	117	48	103	.466	....	....	....	21	32	.656	....	....	173	16	43	1	....	....	....	37.5	10.6	15.7	1.5	.517
75-76	Philadelphia	3	....	53	14	4	6	.667	....	....	....	6	7	.857	4	12	16	1	15	0	0	1	....	17.7	4.7	5.3	0.3	.383
NBA Playoff Totals		51	....	1398	360	146	368	.397	....	....	....	68	116	.586	4	12	519	61	157	3	0	1	....	27.4	7.1	10.2	1.2	....

• LEE, David
David G. Lee

Born: Mar. 31, 1942. Modesto, CA, United States.   Height: 6'7".   Weight: 225 lbs.   Drafted: —   College: San Francisco

YEAR	TEAM	GP	GS	MIN	PTS	FGM	FGA	FG%	3PM	3PA	3P%	FTM	FTA	FT%	ORB	DRB	TRB	AST	PF	DQ	STL	BLK	TO	MPG	PPG	RPG	APG	PCM
67-68	Oakland-A	54	....	753	372	125	276	.453	2	6	.333	120	140	.857	....	....	184	20	83	2	....	....	42	13.9	6.9	3.4	0.4	.505
68-69	New Orleans-A	4	....	16	2	1	9	.111	0	0	.000	0	0	.000	3	0	3	0	0	0	....	....	2	4.0	0.5	0.8	0.0	-.143
ABA Season Totals		58	....	769	374	126	285	.442	2	6	.333	120	140	.857	3	0	187	20	83	2	....	....	44	13.3	6.4	3.2	0.3	....

• LEE, Dick
Richard (Dick) Lee

Born: —.   Height: —   Weight: —   Drafted: —   College: none

YEAR	TEAM	GP	GS	MIN	PTS	FGM	FGA	FG%	3PM	3PA	3P%	FTM	FTA	FT%	ORB	DRB	TRB	AST	PF	DQ	STL	BLK	TO	MPG	PPG	RPG	APG	PCM
67-68	Anaheim-A	2	....	2	0	0	0	.000	0	0	.000	0	0	.000	....	....	1	1	0	0	....	....	0	1.0	0.0	0.5	0.5	1.000
ABA Season Totals		2	....	2	0	0	0	.000	0	0	.000	0	0	.000	....	....	1	1	0	0	....	....	0	1.0	0.0	0.5	0.5	....

• LEE, Doug
Douglas Edward Lee

Born: Oct. 24, 1964. Washington, IL, United States.   Height: 6'5".   Weight: 200 lbs.   Drafted: 1987   College: Purdue

YEAR	TEAM	GP	GS	MIN	PTS	FGM	FGA	FG%	3PM	3PA	3P%	FTM	FTA	FT%	ORB	DRB	TRB	AST	PF	DQ	STL	BLK	TO	MPG	PPG	RPG	APG	PCM
91-92	New Jersey	46	0	307	120	50	116	.431	10	37	.270	10	19	.526	17	18	35	22	39	0	11	1	14	6.7	2.6	0.8	0.5	.295
92-93	New Jersey	5	0	33	5	2	7	.286	1	3	.333	0	0	.000	0	2	2	5	7	0	0	1	3	6.6	1.0	0.4	1.0	.073
94-95	Sacramento	22	0	75	43	9	25	.360	7	18	.389	18	21	.857	0	5	5	5	18	0	6	3	4	3.4	2.0	0.2	0.2	.438
NBA Season Totals		73	0	415	168	61	148	.412	18	58	.310	28	40	.700	17	25	42	32	64	0	17	5	21	5.7	2.3	0.6	0.4	....
91-92	New Jersey	2	0	6	0	0	3	.000	0	2	.000	0	0	.000	0	0	0	1	1	0	0	1	0	3.0	0.0	0.0	0.5	-.209
NBA Playoff Totals		2	0	6	0	0	3	.000	0	2	.000	0	0	.000	0	0	0	1	1	0	0	1	0	3.0	0.0	0.0	0.5	....

• LEE, George
George C. Lee

Born: Nov. 23, 1936.   Height: 6'4".   Weight: 200 lbs.   Drafted: 1959   College: Michigan

YEAR	TEAM	GP	GS	MIN	PTS	FGM	FGA	FG%	3PM	3PA	3P%	FTM	FTA	FT%	ORB	DRB	TRB	AST	PF	DQ	STL	BLK	TO	MPG	PPG	RPG	APG	PCM
60-61	Detroit	74	....	1735	896	310	776	.399	....	....	....	276	394	.701	....	....	490	89	158	1	....	....	....	23.4	12.1	6.6	1.2	.530
61-62	Detroit	75	....	1351	571	179	500	.358	....	....	....	213	280	.761	....	....	349	64	128	1	....	....	....	18.0	7.6	4.7	0.9	.440
62-63	San Francisco	64	....	1192	450	149	394	.378	....	....	....	152	193	.788	....	....	217	64	113	0	....	....	....	18.6	7.0	3.4	1.0	.373
63-64	San Francisco	54	....	522	175	64	169	.379	....	....	....	47	71	.662	....	....	97	25	67	0	....	....	....	9.7	3.2	1.8	0.5	.314
64-65	San Francisco	19	....	247	92	27	77	.351	....	....	....	38	52	.731	....	....	55	12	22	0	....	....	....	13.0	4.8	2.9	0.6	.392
66-67	San Francisco	1	....	5	12	3	4	.750	....	....	....	6	7	.857	....	....	0	0	0	0	....	....	....	5.0	12.0	0.0	0.0	2.161
67-68	San Francisco	10	....	106	33	8	35	.229	....	....	....	17	24	.708	....	....	27	4	16	0	....	....	....	10.6	3.3	2.7	0.4	.270
NBA Season Totals		297	....	5158	2229	740	1955	.379	....	....	....	749	1021	.734	....	....	1235	258	504	2	....	....	....	17.4	7.5	4.2	0.9	....
60-61	Detroit	5	....	135	78	29	70	.414	....	....	....	20	27	.741	....	....	34	14	11	0	....	....	....	27.0	15.6	6.8	2.8	.616
61-62	Detroit	6	....	50	26	10	20	.500	....	....	....	6	7	.857	....	....	8	1	6	0	....	....	....	8.3	4.3	1.3	0.2	.458
63-64	San Francisco	10	....	67	30	9	20	.450	....	....	....	12	20	.600	....	....	16	4	15	0	....	....	....	6.7	3.0	1.6	0.4	.445
NBA Playoff Totals		21	....	252	134	48	110	.436	....	....	....	38	54	.704	....	....	58	19	32	0	....	....	....	12.0	6.4	2.8	0.9	....

• LEE, Greg
Gregory Scott Lee

Born: Dec. 12, 1951. Reseda, CA, United States.   Height: 6'3".   Weight: 190 lbs.   Drafted: 1974   College: UCLA

YEAR	TEAM	GP	GS	MIN	PTS	FGM	FGA	FG%	3PM	3PA	3P%	FTM	FTA	FT%	ORB	DRB	TRB	AST	PF	DQ	STL	BLK	TO	MPG	PPG	RPG	APG	PCM
74-75	San Diego-A	5	....	63	18	8	15	.533	0	0	.000	2	2	1.000	1	2	3	13	6	....	4	0	6	12.6	3.6	0.6	2.6	.417
75-76	Portland	5	....	35	6	2	4	.500	....	....	....	2	2	1.000	0	2	2	11	6	0	2	0	....	7.0	1.2	0.4	2.2	.457
NBA Season Totals		5	....	35	6	2	4	.500	....	....	....	2	2	1.000	0	2	2	11	6	0	2	0	....	7.0	1.2	0.4	2.2	....
ABA Season Totals		5	....	63	18	8	15	.533	0	0	.000	2	2	1.000	1	2	3	13	6	....	4	0	6	12.6	3.6	0.6	2.6	....
Career Totals		10	....	98	24	10	19	.526	0	0	.000	4	4	1.000	1	4	5	24	12	0	6	0	6	9.8	2.4	0.5	2.4	....

YEAR	TEAM	GP	GS	MIN	PTS	FGM	FGA	FG%	3PM	3PA	3P%	FTM	FTA	FT%	ORB	DRB	TRB	AST	PF	DQ	STL	BLK	TO	MPG	PPG	RPG	APG	PCM

• LEE, Keith

Keith DeWayne Lee

Born: Dec. 28, 1962. West Memphis, AR, United States.   Height: 6'10".   Weight: 215 lbs.   Drafted: 1985   College: Memphis State

85-86	Cleveland	58	38	1197	431	177	380	.466	2	9	.222	75	96	.781	116	235	351	67	204	9	29	37	75	20.6	7.4	6.1	1.2	.441
86-87	Cleveland	67	1	870	412	170	374	.455	0	1	.000	72	101	.713	93	158	251	69	147	0	25	40	87	13.0	6.1	3.7	1.0	.491
88-89	New Jersey	57	4	840	271	109	258	.422	0	2	.000	53	71	.746	73	186	259	42	138	1	20	33	51	14.7	4.8	4.5	0.7	.414
NBA Season Totals		182	43	2907	1114	456	1012	.451	2	12	.167	200	268	.746	282	579	861	178	489	10	74	110	213	16.0	6.1	4.7	1.0	....

• LEE, Kurk

Kurk Lee

Born: June 3, 1967. Baltimore, MD, United States.   Height: 6'3".   Weight: 190 lbs.   Drafted: —   College: Towson State

| 90-91 | New Jersey | 48 | 0 | 265 | 66 | 19 | 71 | .268 | 3 | 15 | .200 | 25 | 28 | .893 | 7 | 23 | 30 | 34 | 39 | 0 | 11 | 2 | 19 | 5.5 | 1.4 | 0.6 | 0.7 | .213 |
| **NBA Season Totals** | | 48 | 0 | 265 | 66 | 19 | 71 | .268 | 3 | 15 | .200 | 25 | 28 | .893 | 7 | 23 | 30 | 34 | 39 | 0 | 11 | 2 | 19 | 5.5 | 1.4 | 0.6 | 0.7 | .... |

• LEE, Rock

Rock Alan Lee

Born: May 1, 1955. LaJolla, CA, United States.   Height: 6'10".   Weight: 220 lbs.   Drafted: —   College: San Diego State

| 81-82 | San Diego | 2 | 0 | 10 | 2 | 1 | 2 | .500 | 0 | 0 | .000 | 0 | 4 | .000 | 0 | 1 | 1 | 2 | 3 | 0 | 0 | 0 | 0 | 5.0 | 1.0 | 0.5 | 1.0 | .093 |
| **NBA Season Totals** | | 2 | 0 | 10 | 2 | 1 | 2 | .500 | 0 | 0 | .000 | 0 | 4 | .000 | 0 | 1 | 1 | 2 | 3 | 0 | 0 | 0 | 0 | 5.0 | 1.0 | 0.5 | 1.0 | .... |

• LEE, Ron

Ronald Henry (Ron) Lee

Born: Nov. 2, 1952. Boston, MA, United States.   Height: 6'4".   Weight: 193 lbs.   Drafted: 1976   College: Oregon

76-77	Phoenix	82	....	1849	836	347	786	.441	....	....	....	142	210	.676	99	200	299	263	276	10	156	33	....	22.5	10.2	3.6	3.2	.468
77-78	Phoenix	82	....	1928	1004	417	950	.439	....	....	....	170	228	.746	95	159	254	305	257	3	**225**	17	221	23.5	12.2	3.1	3.7	.510
78-79	Phoenix	43	....	948	420	173	383	.452	....	....	....	74	104	.712	42	71	113	132	138	2	69	4	116	22.0	9.8	2.6	3.1	.384
78-79	New Orleans	17	....	398	114	45	124	.363	....	....	....	24	37	.649	21	34	55	73	44	1	38	2	49	23.4	6.7	3.2	4.3	.350
79-80	Atlanta	30	....	364	67	29	91	.319	0	3	.000	9	17	.529	11	22	33	67	65	1	15	4	33	12.1	2.2	1.1	2.2	.188
79-80	Detroit	31	....	803	225	84	214	.393	22	56	.393	35	53	.660	29	61	90	174	107	4	84	13	68	25.9	7.3	2.9	5.6	.435
80-81	Detroit	82	....	1829	341	113	323	.350	2	13	.154	113	156	.724	65	155	220	362	260	4	166	29	172	22.3	4.2	2.7	4.4	.343
81-82	Detroit	81	7	1467	278	88	246	.358	18	59	.305	84	119	.706	35	120	155	312	221	3	116	20	122	18.1	3.4	1.9	3.9	.346
NBA Season Totals		448	7	9586	3285	1296	3117	.416	42	131	.321	651	924	.705	397	822	1219	1688	1368	28	869	122	781	21.4	7.3	2.7	3.8	....
77-78	Phoenix	2	....	41	12	5	16	.313	....	....	....	2	2	1.000	2	4	6	3	7	0	4	0	4	20.5	6.0	3.0	1.5	.194
NBA Playoff Totals		2	....	41	12	5	16	.313	....	....	....	2	2	1.000	2	4	6	3	7	0	4	0	4	20.5	6.0	3.0	1.5	....

• LEE, Russ

Russell E. (Russ) Lee

Born: Jan. 27, 1950. Boston, MA, United States.   Height: 6'5".   Weight: 185 lbs.   Drafted: 1972   College: Marshall

72-73	Milwaukee	46	....	277	130	49	127	.386	....	....	....	32	43	.744	....	....	43	38	36	0	....	....	....	6.0	2.8	0.9	0.8	.445
73-74	Milwaukee	36	....	166	87	38	94	.404	....	....	....	11	16	.688	16	24	40	20	29	0	11	0	....	4.6	2.4	1.1	0.6	.493
74-75	New Orleans	15	....	139	65	29	76	.382	....	....	....	7	14	.500	15	16	31	7	17	1	11	3	....	9.3	4.3	2.1	0.5	.354
NBA Season Totals		97	....	582	282	116	297	.391	....	....	....	50	73	.685	31	40	114	65	82	1	22	3	....	6.0	2.9	1.2	0.7	....
72-73	Milwaukee	5	....	13	16	8	14	.571	....	....	....	0	0	.000	....	....	4	2	1	0	....	....	....	2.6	3.2	0.8	0.4	1.241
73-74	Milwaukee	6	....	12	11	5	8	.625	....	....	....	1	4	.250	1	2	3	1	0	0	3	1	....	2.0	1.8	0.5	0.2	.906
NBA Playoff Totals		11	....	25	27	13	22	.591	....	....	....	1	4	.250	1	2	7	3	1	0	3	1	....	2.3	2.5	0.6	0.3	....

• LEEDE, Ed

Edward Horst (Ed) Leede

Born: July 17, 1927.   Height: 6'3".   Weight: 185 lbs.   Drafted: —   College: Dartmouth

49-50	Boston	64	....	....	571	174	507	.343	....	....	....	223	316	.706	....	....	....	130	167	....	....	....	....	8.9	....	2.0	....
50-51	Boston	57	....	....	378	119	370	.322	....	....	....	140	189	.741	....	....	118	95	144	3	....	....	....	6.6	2.1	1.7	....
NBA Season Totals		121	....	....	949	293	877	.334	....	....	....	363	505	.719	....	....	118	225	311	3	....	....	....	7.8	1.0	1.9	....
50-51	Boston	2	....	....	3	1	7	.143	....	....	....	1	1	1.000	....	....	0	2	3	0	....	....	....	1.5	0.0	1.0	....
NBA Playoff Totals		2	....	....	3	1	7	.143	....	....	....	1	1	1.000	....	....	0	2	3	0	....	....	....	1.5	0.0	1.0	....

• LEEKA, Sew

Sew Leeka

Born: 1907.   Height: 6'1".   Weight: 185 lbs.   Drafted: —   College: Iowa

37-38	Non-Skids-N	9	....	....	22	9	....	....	....	....	....	4	....	....	....	....	....	....	....	....	....	....	....	2.4	....	....	....
NBL Season Totals		9	....	....	22	9	....	....	....	....	....	4	....	....	....	....	....	....	....	....	....	....	....	2.4	....	....	....
37-38	Non-Skids-N	1	....	....	0	0	....	....	....	....	....	0	....	....	....	....	....	....	....	....	....	....	....	0.0	....	....	....
NBL Playoff Totals		1	....	....	0	0	....	....	....	....	....	0	....	....	....	....	....	....	....	....	....	....	....	0.0	....	....	....

• LEFKOWITZ, Hank

Henry A. (Hank) Lefkowitz

Born: Aug. 31, 1923.   Height: 6'2".   Weight: 190 lbs.   Drafted: —   College: Western Reserve

46-47	Cleveland	24	....	....	51	22	114	.193	....	....	....	7	13	.538	....	....	....	4	35	....	....	....	....	2.1	....	0.2	....
NBA Season Totals		24	....	....	51	22	114	.193	....	....	....	7	13	.538	....	....	....	4	35	....	....	....	....	2.1	....	0.2	....
46-47	Cleveland	2	....	....	9	4	18	.222	....	....	....	1	1	1.000	....	....	....	0	4	....	....	....	....	4.5	....	0.0	....
NBA Playoff Totals		2	....	....	9	4	18	.222	....	....	....	1	1	1.000	....	....	....	0	4	....	....	....	....	4.5	....	0.0	....

• LEGLER, Tim

Timothy Eugene (Tim) Legler

Born: Dec. 26, 1966. Washington, DC, United States.   Height: 6'4".   Weight: 200 lbs.   Drafted: —   College: LaSalle

YEAR	TEAM	GP	GS	MIN	PTS	FGM	FGA	FG%	3PM	3PA	3P%	FTM	FTA	FT%	ORB	DRB	TRB	AST	PF	DQ	STL	BLK	TO	MPG	PPG	RPG	APG	PCM
89-90	Phoenix	11	0	83	28	11	29	.379	0	1	.000	6	6	1.000	4	4	8	6	12	0	2	0	4	7.5	2.5	0.7	0.5	.211
90-91	Denver	10	0	148	58	25	72	.347	3	12	.250	5	6	.833	8	10	18	12	20	0	2	0	4	14.8	5.8	1.8	1.2	.217
92-93	Utah	3	0	5	2	1	3	.333	0	0	.000	0	0	.000	0	1	1	0	0	0	0	0	0	1.7	0.7	0.3	0.0	.213
92-93	Dallas	30	0	630	287	104	238	.437	22	65	.338	57	71	.803	25	33	58	46	63	0	24	6	27	21.0	9.6	1.9	1.5	.368
93-94	Dallas	79	0	1322	656	231	528	.438	52	139	.374	142	169	.840	36	92	128	120	133	0	52	13	63	16.7	8.3	1.6	1.5	.423
94-95	Golden State	24	0	371	176	60	115	.522	26	50	.520	30	34	.882	12	28	40	27	33	0	12	1	19	15.5	7.3	1.7	1.1	.452
95-96	Washington	77	0	1775	726	233	460	.507	128	245	.522	132	153	.863	29	111	140	136	141	0	45	12	46	23.1	9.4	1.8	1.8	.407
96-97	Washington	15	0	182	44	15	48	.313	8	29	.276	6	7	.857	0	21	21	7	21	0	3	5	9	12.1	2.9	1.4	0.5	.160
97-98	Washington	8	0	76	9	3	19	.158	0	6	.000	3	4	.750	2	2	4	3	11	0	1	0	4	9.5	1.1	0.5	0.4	-.092
98-99	Washington	30	0	377	119	51	115	.443	14	35	.400	3	6	.500	8	32	40	21	42	0	4	3	14	12.6	4.0	1.3	0.7	.251
99-00	Golden State	23	4	284	77	28	78	.359	7	21	.333	14	18	.778	4	19	23	24	33	0	4	1	6	12.3	3.3	1.0	1.0	.215
NBA Season Totals		310	4	5253	2182	762	1705	.447	260	603	.431	398	474	.840	128	353	481	402	509	0	149	41	196	16.9	7.0	1.6	1.3	....
96-97	Washington	3	0	19	1	0	2	.000	0	1	.000	1	2	.500	0	1	1	2	2	0	0	0	0	6.3	0.3	0.3	0.7	.042
NBA Playoff Totals		3	0	19	1	0	2	.000	0	1	.000	1	2	.500	0	1	1	2	2	0	0	0	0	6.3	0.3	0.3	0.7	....

• LEHMANN, George

George Lehmann

Born: May 1, 1942. Riverside, NJ, United States.   Height: 6'   Weight: 180 lbs.   Drafted: —   College: Campbell JC

YEAR	TEAM	GP	GS	MIN	PTS	FGM	FGA	FG%	3PM	3PA	3P%	FTM	FTA	FT%	ORB	DRB	TRB	AST	PF	DQ	STL	BLK	TO	MPG	PPG	RPG	APG	PCM
67-68	St. Louis	55	....	497	153	59	172	.343	....	....	....	35	43	.814	....	....	44	93	54	0	....	....	....	9.0	2.8	0.8	1.7	.372
68-69	Los Angeles-A	32	....	937	604	212	511	.415	48	137	.350	132	164	.805	25	48	73	159	96	1	....	....	122	29.3	18.9	2.3	5.0	.573
68-69	Atlanta	11	....	138	60	26	67	.388	....	....	....	8	12	.667	....	....	9	27	18	0	....	....	....	12.5	5.5	0.8	2.5	.402
69-70	Los Angeles-A	10	....	237	116	39	132	.295	5	20	.250	33	36	.917	0	12	12	28	26	0	....	....	24	23.7	11.6	1.2	2.8	.279
69-70	Miami-A	25	....	1078	448	168	415	.405	46	140	.329	66	81	.815	17	53	70	124	83	0	....	....	104	43.1	17.9	2.8	5.0	.367
69-70	New York-A	46	....	679	344	111	300	.370	41	126	.325	81	94	.862	18	21	39	104	80	0	....	....	73	14.8	7.5	0.8	2.3	.433
70-71	Carolina-A	83	....	2918	1438	535	1186	.451	**154**	**382**	**.403**	214	256	.836	53	150	203	464	221	1	....	....	309	35.2	17.3	2.4	5.6	.524
71-72	Carolina-A	38	....	1399	609	219	439	.499	49	125	.392	122	136	.897	16	55	71	295	114	1	....	....	168	36.8	16.0	1.9	7.8	.538
71-72	Memphis-A	15	....	522	237	84	224	.375	22	74	.297	47	56	.839	7	20	27	116	41	0	....	....	42	34.8	15.8	1.8	7.7	.471
72-73	Memphis-A	28	....	753	277	95	240	.396	26	67	.388	61	74	.824	7	27	34	150	74	1	....	....	65	26.9	9.9	1.2	5.4	.403
73-74	Memphis-A	33	....	554	172	68	177	.384	18	50	.360	18	19	.947	8	29	37	117	52	....	13	4	53	16.8	5.2	1.1	3.5	.399
NBA Season Totals		66	....	635	213	85	239	.356	....	....	....	43	55	.782	....	....	53	120	72	0	....	....	....	9.6	3.2	0.8	1.8	....
ABA Season Totals		310	....	9077	4245	1531	3624	.422	409	1121	.365	774	916	.845	151	415	566	1557	787	4	13	4	960	29.3	13.7	1.8	5.0	....
Career Totals		376	....	9712	4458	1616	3863	.418	409	1121	.365	817	971	.841	151	415	619	1677	859	4	13	4	960	25.8	11.9	1.6	4.5	....
67-68	St. Louis	1	....	2	0	0	1	.000	....	....	....	0	0	.000	....	....	0	2	1	0	....	....	....	2.0	0.0	0.0	2.0	.604
NBA Playoff Totals		1	....	2	0	0	1	.000	....	....	....	0	0	.000	....	....	0	2	1	0	....	....	....	2.0	0.0	0.0	2.0	....

• LENARD, Voshon

Voshon Kelan Lenard

Born: May 14, 1973. Detroit, MI, United States.   Height: 6'4".   Weight: 205 lbs.   Drafted: 1994   College: Minnesota

YEAR	TEAM	GP	GS	MIN	PTS	FGM	FGA	FG%	3PM	3PA	3P%	FTM	FTA	FT%	ORB	DRB	TRB	AST	PF	DQ	STL	BLK	TO	MPG	PPG	RPG	APG	PCM
95-96	Miami	30	0	323	176	53	141	.376	36	101	.356	34	43	.791	12	40	52	31	31	0	6	1	24	10.8	5.9	1.7	1.0	.434
96-97	Miami	73	47	2111	897	314	684	.459	183	442	.414	86	105	.819	38	179	217	161	168	1	50	18	110	28.9	12.3	3.0	2.2	.379
97-98	Miami	81	81	2621	1020	363	854	.425	153	378	.405	141	179	.788	72	220	292	180	219	0	58	16	97	32.4	12.6	3.6	2.2	.341
98-99	Miami	12	2	190	82	31	79	.392	12	35	.343	8	11	.727	4	12	16	10	18	0	3	1	7	15.8	6.8	1.3	0.8	.277
99-00	Miami	53	13	1434	629	228	560	.407	89	228	.390	84	106	.792	37	116	153	136	127	2	41	15	80	27.1	11.9	2.9	2.6	.366
00-01	Denver	80	58	2331	972	336	846	.397	147	382	.385	153	192	.797	47	184	231	190	170	1	65	18	102	29.1	12.2	2.9	2.4	.352
01-02	Denver	71	19	1665	813	315	769	.410	89	240	.371	94	120	.783	38	145	183	130	105	0	59	25	91	23.5	11.5	2.6	1.8	.387
02-03	Toronto	63	24	1930	898	325	809	.402	92	252	.365	156	194	.804	48	164	212	144	156	1	59	21	103	30.6	14.3	3.4	2.3	.362
NBA Season Totals		463	244	12605	5487	1965	4742	.414	801	2058	.389	756	950	.796	296	1060	1356	982	994	5	341	115	614	27.2	11.9	2.9	2.1	....
96-97	Miami	17	17	548	194	63	155	.406	36	91	.396	32	37	.865	12	38	50	36	49	0	11	3	30	32.2	11.4	2.9	2.1	.280
97-98	Miami	5	5	186	72	24	52	.462	9	26	.346	15	20	.750	1	18	19	7	20	0	1	2	11	37.2	14.4	3.8	1.4	.283
98-99	Miami	4	0	57	37	12	22	.545	9	14	.643	4	4	1.000	0	1	1	3	4	0	0	1	1	14.3	9.3	0.3	0.8	.536
NBA Playoff Totals		26	22	791	303	99	229	.432	54	131	.412	51	61	.836	13	57	70	46	73	0	12	6	42	30.4	11.7	2.7	1.8	....

• LENHART, Johnny

John Lenhart

Born: 1915.   Height: 6'4".   Weight: 180 lbs.   Drafted: —   College: Colgate

YEAR	TEAM	GP	GS	MIN	PTS	FGM	FGA	FG%	3PM	3PA	3P%	FTM	FTA	FT%	ORB	DRB	TRB	AST	PF	DQ	STL	BLK	TO	MPG	PPG	RPG	APG	PCM
37-38	Buffalo-N	3	....	....	0	0	....	....	....	....	....	0	....	....	....	....	....	....	....	....	....	....	....	0.0	....	....	....	....
NBL Season Totals		3	....	....	0	0	....	....	....	....	....	0	....	....	....	....	....	....	....	....	....	....	....	0.0	....	....	....	....

• LENTZ, Leary

Leary Lee Lentz

Born: Feb. 23, 1945. Clarkton, MO, United States.   Height: 6'6".   Weight: 200 lbs.   Drafted: —   College: Houston

YEAR	TEAM	GP	GS	MIN	PTS	FGM	FGA	FG%	3PM	3PA	3P%	FTM	FTA	FT%	ORB	DRB	TRB	AST	PF	DQ	STL	BLK	TO	MPG	PPG	RPG	APG	PCM
67-68	Houston-A	78	....	2504	833	343	845	.406	0	3	.000	147	221	.665	....	....	648	89	175	0	....	....	97	32.1	10.7	8.3	1.1	.381
68-69	Houston-A	44	....	687	217	87	208	.418	0	1	.000	43	74	.581	68	96	164	22	57	0	....	....	29	15.6	4.9	3.7	0.5	.351
68-69	New York-A	26	....	442	129	48	126	.381	0	0	.000	33	43	.767	40	67	107	9	46	1	....	....	25	17.0	5.0	4.1	0.3	.317
ABA Season Totals		148	....	3633	1179	478	1179	.405	0	4	.000	223	338	.660	108	163	919	120	278	1	....	....	151	24.5	8.0	6.2	0.8	....
67-68	Houston-A	3	....	73	25	12	26	.462	0	0	.000	1	3	.333	....	....	19	3	6	0	....	....	2	24.3	8.3	6.3	1.0	.402
ABA Playoff Totals		3	....	73	25	12	26	.462	0	0	.000	1	3	.333	....	....	19	3	6	0	....	....	2	24.3	8.3	6.3	1.0	....

YEAR	TEAM	GP	GS	MIN	PTS	FGM	FGA	FG%	3PM	3PA	3P%	FTM	FTA	FT%	ORB	DRB	TRB	AST	PF	DQ	STL	BLK	TO	MPG	PPG	RPG	APG	PCM

• LEONARD, Gary   Gary Francis Leonard

Born: Feb. 16, 1967. Belleville, IL, United States.   Height: 7'1".   Weight: 250 lbs.   Drafted: 1989   College: Missouri

YEAR	TEAM	GP	GS	MIN	PTS	FGM	FGA	FG%	3PM	3PA	3P%	FTM	FTA	FT%	ORB	DRB	TRB	AST	PF	DQ	STL	BLK	TO	MPG	PPG	RPG	APG	PCM
89-90	Minnesota	22	0	127	32	13	31	.419	0	1	.000	6	14	.429	10	17	27	1	26	0	3	9	9	5.8	1.5	1.2	0.0	.223
90-91	Atlanta	4	0	9	2	0	0	.000	0	0	.000	2	4	.500	0	2	2	0	2	0	1	0	3	2.3	0.5	0.5	0.0	.326
91-92	Atlanta	5	0	13	10	4	6	.667	0	0	.000	2	2	1.000	3	2	5	1	3	0	1	0	1	2.6	2.0	1.0	0.2	.959
NBA Season Totals		31	0	149	44	17	37	.459	0	1	.000	10	20	.500	13	21	34	2	31	0	4	10	10	4.8	1.4	1.1	0.1	....
90-91	Atlanta	2	0	5	4	2	2	1.000	0	0	.000	0	0	.000	0	2	2	0	0	0	0	0	0	2.5	2.0	1.0	0.0	1.173
NBA Playoff Totals		2	0	5	4	2	2	1.000	0	0	.000	0	0	.000	0	2	2	0	0	0	0	0	0	2.5	2.0	1.0	0.0	....

• LEONARD, Slick   William Robert (Slick) Leonard

Born: July 17, 1932. Terre Haute, IN, United States.   Height: 6'3".   Weight: 185 lbs.   Drafted: —   College: Indiana

YEAR	TEAM	GP	GS	MIN	PTS	FGM	FGA	FG%	3PM	3PA	3P%	FTM	FTA	FT%	ORB	DRB	TRB	AST	PF	DQ	STL	BLK	TO	MPG	PPG	RPG	APG	PCM
56-57	Minneapolis	72	....	1943	792	303	867	.349	....	....	....	186	241	.772	....	....	220	169	140	0	....	....	....	27.0	11.0	3.1	2.3	.347
57-58	Minneapolis	66	....	2074	737	266	794	.335	....	....	....	205	268	.765	....	....	237	218	145	0	....	....	....	31.4	11.2	3.6	3.3	.350
58-59	Minneapolis	58	....	1598	532	206	552	.373	....	....	....	120	160	.750	....	....	178	186	119	0	....	....	....	27.6	9.2	3.1	3.2	.362
59-60	Minneapolis	73	....	2074	598	231	717	.322	....	....	....	136	193	.705	....	....	245	252	171	3	....	....	....	28.4	8.2	3.4	3.5	.310
60-61	LA Lakers	55	....	600	193	61	207	.295	....	....	....	71	100	.710	....	....	70	81	70	0	....	....	....	10.9	3.5	1.3	1.5	.330
61-62	Chicago	70	....	2464	1125	423	1128	.375	....	....	....	279	371	.752	....	....	199	378	186	0	....	....	....	35.2	16.1	2.8	5.4	.439
62-63	Chicago	32	....	879	227	84	245	.343	....	....	....	59	85	.694	....	....	68	143	84	1	....	....	....	27.5	7.1	2.1	4.5	.322
NBA Season Totals		426	....	11632	4204	1574	4510	.349	....	....	....	1056	1418	.745	....	....	1217	1427	915	4	....	....	....	27.3	9.9	2.9	3.3	
56-57	Minneapolis	5	....	204	107	42	100	.420	....	....	....	23	26	.885	....	....	30	38	15	0	....	....	....	40.8	21.4	6.0	7.6	.623
58-59	Minneapolis	13	....	467	158	63	173	.364	....	....	....	32	40	.800	....	....	44	70	38	0	....	....	....	35.9	12.2	3.4	5.4	.382
59-60	Minneapolis	9	....	207	58	20	67	.299	....	....	....	18	28	.643	....	....	10	45	17	0	....	....	....	23.0	6.4	1.1	5.0	.366
60-61	LA Lakers	7	....	46	11	5	24	.208	....	....	....	1	4	.250	....	....	6	12	7	0	....	....	....	6.6	1.6	0.9	1.7	.265
NBA Playoff Totals		34	....	924	334	130	364	.357	....	....	....	74	98	.755	....	....	90	165	77	0	....	....	....	27.2	9.8	2.6	4.9	....

• LES, Jim   James Allen Les

Born: Aug. 18, 1963. Niles, IL, United States.   Height: 5'11".   Weight: 165 lbs.   Drafted: 1986   College: Bradley

YEAR	TEAM	GP	GS	MIN	PTS	FGM	FGA	FG%	3PM	3PA	3P%	FTM	FTA	FT%	ORB	DRB	TRB	AST	PF	DQ	STL	BLK	TO	MPG	PPG	RPG	APG	PCM
88-89	Utah	82	0	781	138	40	133	.301	1	14	.071	57	73	.781	23	64	87	215	88	0	27	5	90	9.5	1.7	1.1	2.6	.333
89-90	Utah	1	0	6	2	0	0	.000	0	0	.000	2	4	.500	0	0	0	1	3	0	0	0	3	6.0	2.0	0.0	1.0	-.348
89-90	LA Clippers	6	0	86	21	5	14	.357	0	1	.000	11	13	.846	3	4	7	20	6	0	3	0	7	14.3	3.5	1.2	3.3	.422
90-91	Sacramento	55	8	1399	395	119	268	.444	71	154	**.461**	86	103	.835	18	93	111	299	141	0	57	4	77	25.4	7.2	2.0	5.4	.422
91-92	Sacramento	62	5	712	231	74	192	.385	45	131	.344	38	47	.809	11	52	63	143	58	0	31	3	43	11.5	3.7	1.0	2.3	.412
92-93	Sacramento	73	0	881	328	110	259	.425	66	154	.429	42	50	.840	20	69	89	169	81	0	40	7	51	12.1	4.5	1.2	2.3	.462
93-94	Sacramento	18	0	169	45	13	34	.382	8	18	.444	11	13	.846	5	8	13	39	16	0	7	1	11	9.4	2.5	0.7	2.2	.408
94-95	Atlanta	24	0	188	50	11	38	.289	5	23	.217	23	27	.852	6	20	26	44	28	0	4	0	22	7.8	2.1	1.1	1.8	.340
NBA Season Totals		321	13	4222	1210	372	938	.397	196	495	.396	270	330	.818	86	310	396	930	421	0	169	20	304	13.2	3.8	1.2	2.9	....
88-89	Utah	3	0	5	0	0	0	.000	0	0	.000	0	0	.000	0	0	0	1	2	0	0	0	1	1.7	0.0	0.0	0.3	-.158
NBA Playoff Totals		3	0	5	0	0	0	.000	0	0	.000	0	0	.000	0	0	0	1	2	0	0	0	1	1.7	0.0	0.0	0.3	

• LESON, Joe   Joe Leson

Born: 1912.   Height: 6'2".   Weight: 210 lbs.   Drafted: —   College: Edinboro

YEAR	TEAM	GP	GS	MIN	PTS	FGM	FGA	FG%	3PM	3PA	3P%	FTM	FTA	FT%	ORB	DRB	TRB	AST	PF	DQ	STL	BLK	TO	MPG	PPG	RPG	APG	PCM
38-39	Cleveland-N	17	....	....	29	9	....	....	....	....	....	11	....	....	....	....	....	....	....	....	....	....	....	....	1.7	....	....	....
NBL Season Totals		17	....	....	29	9	....	....	....	....	....	11	....	....	....	....	....	....	....	....	....	....	....	....	1.7	....	....	....

• LESTER, Ronnie   Ronnie Lester

Born: Jan. 1, 1959. Canton, MS, United States.   Height: 6'2".   Weight: 175 lbs.   Drafted: 1980   College: Iowa

YEAR	TEAM	GP	GS	MIN	PTS	FGM	FGA	FG%	3PM	3PA	3P%	FTM	FTA	FT%	ORB	DRB	TRB	AST	PF	DQ	STL	BLK	TO	MPG	PPG	RPG	APG	PCM
80-81	Chicago	8	....	83	30	10	24	.417	0	0	.000	10	11	.909	3	3	6	7	5	0	2	0	9	10.4	3.8	0.8	0.9	.256
81-82	Chicago	75	74	2252	870	329	657	.501	4	8	.500	208	256	.813	75	138	213	362	158	2	80	14	188	30.0	11.6	2.8	4.8	.432
82-83	Chicago	65	38	1437	528	202	446	.453	0	5	.000	124	171	.725	46	126	172	332	121	2	51	6	137	22.1	8.1	2.6	5.1	.473
83-84	Chicago	43	3	687	232	78	188	.415	1	5	.200	75	87	.862	20	26	46	168	59	1	30	6	73	16.0	5.4	1.1	3.9	.415
84-85	LA Lakers	32	1	278	89	34	82	.415	0	1	.000	21	31	.677	4	22	26	80	25	0	15	3	32	8.7	2.8	0.8	2.5	.448
85-86	LA Lakers	27	0	222	67	26	52	.500	0	3	.000	15	19	.789	0	10	10	54	27	0	9	3	43	8.2	2.5	0.4	2.0	.301
NBA Season Totals		250	116	4959	1816	679	1449	.469	5	22	.227	453	575	.788	148	325	473	1003	395	5	187	32	482	19.8	7.3	1.9	4.0	....
80-81	Chicago	5	....	42	19	7	18	.389	0	1	.000	5	7	.714	5	1	6	4	4	0	2	0	5	8.4	3.8	1.2	0.8	.318
84-85	LA Lakers	9	0	54	19	6	15	.400	0	0	.000	7	9	.778	2	6	8	9	7	0	0	0	4	6.0	2.1	0.9	1.0	.366
NBA Playoff Totals		14	0	96	38	13	33	.394	0	1	.000	12	16	.750	7	7	14	13	11	0	2	0	9	6.9	2.7	1.0	0.9	....

• LETT, Clifford   Clifford Earl Lett

Born: Dec. 23, 1965. Pensacola, FL, United States.   Height: 6'3".   Weight: 170 lbs.   Drafted: —   College: Florida

YEAR	TEAM	GP	GS	MIN	PTS	FGM	FGA	FG%	3PM	3PA	3P%	FTM	FTA	FT%	ORB	DRB	TRB	AST	PF	DQ	STL	BLK	TO	MPG	PPG	RPG	APG	PCM
89-90	Chicago	4	0	28	4	2	8	.250	0	0	.000	0	0	.000	0	0	0	1	8	0	0	0	2	7.0	1.0	0.0	0.3	-.221
90-91	San Antonio	7	0	99	34	14	29	.483	0	1	.000	6	9	.667	1	6	7	7	9	0	2	1	8	14.1	4.9	1.0	1.0	.240
NBA Season Totals		11	0	127	38	16	37	.432	0	1	.000	6	9	.667	1	6	7	8	17	0	2	1	10	11.5	3.5	0.6	0.7	....

• LEVANE, Andrew   Andrew Joseph (Fuzzy) Levane

Born: Apr. 11, 1920. Brooklyn, NY, United States.   Height: 6'2".   Weight: 190 lbs.   Drafted: —   College: St. John's (NY)

YEAR	TEAM	GP	GS	MIN	PTS	FGM	FGA	FG%	3PM	3PA	3P%	FTM	FTA	FT%	ORB	DRB	TRB	AST	PF	DQ	STL	BLK	TO	MPG	PPG	RPG	APG	PCM
45-46	Rochester-N	22	....	....	112	52	....	....	....	....	....	8	19	.421	....	....	....	....	....	....	....	....	....	....	5.1	....	....	....
46-47	Rochester-N	39	....	....	315	133	....	....	....	....	....	49	87	.563	....	....	....	83	....	....	....	....	....	....	8.1	....	....	....

YEAR	TEAM	GP	GS	MIN	PTS	FGM	FGA	FG%	3PM	3PA	3P%	FTM	FTA	FT%	ORB	DRB	TRB	AST	PF	DQ	STL	BLK	TO	MPG	PPG	RPG	APG	PCM
47-48	Rochester-N	54	....	....	339	147	....	....	....	....	....	45	62	.726	....	....	....	....	100	....	....	....	....	....	6.3	....	....	....
48-49	Rochester	36	....	....	123	55	193	.285	....	....	....	13	21	.619	....	....	....	....	39	37	....	....	....	....	3.4	....	1.1	....
49-50	Syracuse	60	....	....	332	139	418	.333	....	....	....	54	85	.635	....	....	....	....	156	106	....	....	....	....	5.5	....	2.6	....
52-53	Milwaukee	7	....	68	8	3	24	.125	....	....	....	2	3	.667	....	....	....	9	9	15	0	....	....	....	9.7	1.1	1.3	1.3	.074
NBA Season Totals		103	....	68	463	197	635	.310	....	....	....	69	109	.633	....	....	....	9	204	158	0	....	....	....	0.7	4.5	0.1	2.0	....
NBL Season Totals		115	....	....	766	332	....	....	....	....	....	102	168	....	....	....	....	....	....	183	....	....	....	....	6.7	....	....	....	
Career Totals		218	....	68	1229	529	635	....	....	....	....	171	277	....	....	....	....	9	204	341	0	....	....	....	0.3	5.6	0.0	0.9	....
45-46	Rochester-N	3	....	....	2	0	....	....	....	....	....	2	2	1.000	....	....	....	....	....	....	....	....	....	....	0.7	....	....	....
46-47	Rochester-N	11	....	....	92	37	....	....	....	....	....	18	27	.667	....	....	....	....	....	....	....	....	....	....	8.4	....	....	....
47-48	Rochester-N	9	....	....	42	20	....	....	....	....	....	2	3	.667	....	....	....	....	....	....	....	....	....	....	4.7	....	....	....
49-50	Syracuse	9	....	....	31	13	37	.351	....	....	....	5	5	1.000	....	....	....	....	13	11	....	....	....	....	3.4	....	1.4	....
NBA Playoff Totals		9	....	....	31	13	37	.351	....	....	....	5	5	1.000	....	....	....	....	13	11	....	....	....	....	3.4	....	1.4	....
NBL Playoff Totals		23	....	....	136	57	....	....	....	....	....	22	32	....	....	....	....	....	....	....	....	....	....	....	5.9	....	....	....
Career Playoff Totals		32	....	....	167	70	37	....	....	....	....	27	37	....	....	....	....	....	13	11	....	....	....	....	5.2	....	0.4	....

• LEVER, Fat

Lafayette (Fat) Lever

Born: Aug. 18, 1960. Pine Bluff, AR, United States.　Height: 6'3".　Weight: 170 lbs.　Drafted: 1982　College: Arizona State

YEAR	TEAM	GP	GS	MIN	PTS	FGM	FGA	FG%	3PM	3PA	3P%	FTM	FTA	FT%	ORB	DRB	TRB	AST	PF	DQ	STL	BLK	TO	MPG	PPG	RPG	APG	PCM
82-83	Portland	81	45	2020	633	256	594	.431	5	15	.333	116	159	.730	85	140	225	426	179	2	153	15	138	24.9	7.8	2.8	5.3	.458
83-84	Portland	81	22	2010	788	313	701	.447	3	15	.200	159	214	.743	96	122	218	372	178	1	135	31	122	24.8	9.7	2.7	4.6	.478
84-85	Denver	82	82	2559	1051	424	985	.430	6	24	.250	197	256	.770	147	264	411	613	226	1	202	30	205	31.2	12.8	5.0	7.5	.570
85-86	Denver	78	77	2616	1080	468	1061	.441	12	38	.316	132	182	.725	136	284	420	584	204	3	178	15	211	33.5	13.8	5.4	7.5	.539
86-87	Denver	82	82	3054	1552	643	1370	.469	22	92	.239	244	312	.782	216	513	729	654	219	1	201	34	164	37.2	18.9	8.9	8.0	.716
87-88	Denver	82	82	3061	1546	643	1360	.473	12	57	.211	248	316	.785	203	462	665	639	214	0	223	21	180	37.3	18.9	8.1	7.8	.689
88-89	Denver	71	71	2745	1409	558	1221	.457	23	66	.348	270	344	.785	187	475	662	559	178	1	195	20	156	38.7	19.8	9.3	7.9	.708
89-90	Denver	79	79	2832	1443	568	1283	.443	36	87	.414	271	337	.804	230	504	734	517	172	1	168	13	158	35.8	18.3	9.3	6.5	.678
90-91	Dallas	4	0	86	29	9	23	.391	0	3	.000	11	14	.786	3	12	15	12	5	0	6	3	10	21.5	7.3	3.8	3.0	.443
91-92	Dallas	31	5	884	347	135	349	.387	17	52	.327	60	80	.750	56	105	161	107	73	0	46	12	37	28.5	11.2	5.2	3.5	.440
93-94	Dallas	81	54	1947	555	227	557	.408	26	74	.351	75	98	.765	83	200	283	213	155	1	159	15	89	24.0	6.9	3.5	2.6	.380
NBA Season Totals		752	599	23814	10433	4244	9504	.447	162	523	.310	1783	2312	.771	1442	3081	4523	4696	1803	11	1666	209	1470	31.7	13.9	6.0	6.2	....
82-83	Portland	7	0	134	42	19	42	.452	0	0	.000	4	5	.800	3	11	14	31	13	0	7	0	4	19.1	6.0	2.0	4.4	.480
83-84	Portland	5	0	75	26	8	30	.267	2	3	.667	8	10	.800	10	5	15	9	6	0	4	0	3	15.0	5.2	3.0	1.8	.351
84-85	Denver	11	8	342	146	49	122	.402	0	2	.000	48	63	.762	23	48	71	93	33	0	26	2	34	31.1	13.3	6.5	8.5	.630
85-86	Denver	10	10	347	143	59	131	.450	8	14	.571	17	24	.708	15	33	48	53	33	0	20	2	23	34.7	14.3	4.8	5.3	.455
86-87	Denver	3	3	99	46	19	50	.380	2	8	.250	6	9	.667	5	13	18	22	7	0	7	0	2	33.0	15.3	6.0	7.3	.580
87-88	Denver	7	7	273	119	45	98	.459	3	7	.429	26	33	.788	16	49	65	49	15	0	13	4	4	39.0	17.0	9.3	7.0	.675
88-89	Denver	2	2	58	22	9	24	.375	2	3	.667	2	2	1.000	2	11	13	19	4	0	4	0	6	29.0	11.0	6.5	9.5	.634
89-90	Denver	3	3	113	52	19	51	.373	1	7	.143	13	14	.929	11	21	32	21	7	0	8	1	5	37.7	17.3	10.7	7.0	.658
NBA Playoff Totals		48	33	1441	596	227	548	.414	18	44	.409	124	160	.775	85	191	276	297	118	0	89	9	81	30.0	12.4	5.8	6.2	....

• LEVINE, Sid

Sid Levine

Born: 1918.　Height: 5'7".　Weight: 185 lbs.　Drafted: —　College: none

YEAR	TEAM	GP	GS	MIN	PTS	FGM	FGA	FG%	3PM	3PA	3P%	FTM	FTA	FT%	ORB	DRB	TRB	AST	PF	DQ	STL	BLK	TO	MPG	PPG	RPG	APG	PCM
44-45	Pittsburgh-N	18	....	....	9	4	....	....	....	....	....	1	....	....	....	....	....	....	....	....	....	....	....	....	0.5	....	....	....
NBL Season Totals		18	....	....	9	4	....	....	....	....	....	1	....	....	....	....	....	....	....	....	....	....	....	....	0.5	....	....	....

• LEVINGSTON, Cliff

Clifford Eugene Levingston

Born: Jan. 4, 1961. San Diego, CA, United States.　Height: 6'8".　Weight: 210 lbs.　Drafted: 1982　College: Wichita State

YEAR	TEAM	GP	GS	MIN	PTS	FGM	FGA	FG%	3PM	3PA	3P%	FTM	FTA	FT%	ORB	DRB	TRB	AST	PF	DQ	STL	BLK	TO	MPG	PPG	RPG	APG	PCM
82-83	Detroit	62	5	879	346	131	270	.485	0	1	.000	84	147	.571	104	128	232	52	125	2	23	36	74	14.2	5.6	3.7	0.8	.442
83-84	Detroit	80	24	1746	583	229	436	.525	0	3	.000	125	186	.672	234	311	545	109	281	7	44	78	80	21.8	7.3	6.8	1.4	.512
84-85	Atlanta	74	53	2017	727	291	552	.527	0	2	.000	145	222	.653	230	336	566	104	231	3	70	69	133	27.3	9.8	7.6	1.4	.488
85-86	Atlanta	81	35	1945	752	294	551	.534	0	1	.000	164	242	.678	193	341	534	72	260	5	76	39	113	24.0	9.3	6.6	0.9	.479
86-87	Atlanta	82	10	1848	657	251	496	.506	0	3	.000	155	212	.731	219	314	533	40	261	4	48	68	74	22.5	8.0	6.5	0.5	.465
87-88	Atlanta	82	32	2135	819	314	564	.557	1	2	.500	190	246	.772	228	276	504	71	287	5	52	84	90	26.0	10.0	6.1	0.9	.475
88-89	Atlanta	80	52	2184	734	300	568	.528	1	5	.200	133	191	.696	194	304	498	75	270	4	97	70	104	27.3	9.2	6.2	0.9	.428
89-90	Atlanta	75	5	1706	516	216	424	.509	1	5	.200	83	122	.680	113	206	319	80	216	2	55	41	53	22.7	6.9	4.3	1.1	.367
90-91	Chicago	78	0	1013	314	127	282	.450	1	4	.250	59	91	.648	99	126	225	56	143	0	29	43	47	13.0	4.0	2.9	0.7	.376
91-92	Chicago	79	0	1020	311	125	251	.498	1	6	.167	60	96	.625	109	118	227	66	134	0	27	45	40	12.9	3.9	2.9	0.8	.418
94-95	Denver	57	0	469	129	55	130	.423	0	1	.000	19	45	.422	49	75	124	27	91	0	13	20	23	8.2	2.3	2.2	0.5	.337
NBA Season Totals		830	216	16962	5888	2333	4524	.516	5	33	.152	1217	1800	.676	1772	2535	4307	752	2299	32	534	593	831	20.4	7.1	5.2	0.9	....
83-84	Detroit	5	0	101	40	15	19	.789	0	0	.000	10	16	.625	11	13	24	1	15	0	1	2	3	20.2	8.0	4.8	0.2	.494
85-86	Atlanta	9	0	180	52	22	37	.595	1	1	1.000	7	9	.778	15	26	41	3	23	0	4	9	9	20.0	5.8	4.6	0.3	.397
86-87	Atlanta	9	0	108	28	7	18	.389	0	1	.000	14	18	.778	12	22	34	3	21	0	0	3	4	12.0	3.1	3.8	0.3	.371
87-88	Atlanta	12	0	163	60	24	50	.480	0	0	.000	12	16	.750	14	12	26	7	25	0	5	5	8	13.6	5.0	2.2	0.6	.342
88-89	Atlanta	5	0	77	16	3	11	.273	1	1	1.000	9	10	.900	6	11	17	2	15	0	0	3	3	15.4	3.2	3.4	0.4	.248
90-91	Chicago	17	0	192	45	21	41	.512	0	0	.000	3	6	.500	22	19	41	7	28	0	10	7	2	11.3	2.6	2.4	0.4	.373
91-92	Chicago	22	0	191	64	25	57	.439	0	1	.000	14	28	.500	17	24	41	9	31	0	4	6	11	8.7	2.9	1.9	0.4	.315
94-95	Denver	3	0	35	7	3	6	.500	0	0	.000	1	2	.500	6	3	9	1	4	0	3	2	2	11.7	2.3	3.0	0.3	.405
NBA Playoff Totals		82	0	1047	312	120	239	.502	2	4	.500	70	105	.667	103	130	233	33	162	0	27	37	42	12.8	3.8	2.8	0.4	....

• LEWINSKI, Ed

Ed (Gooch) Lewinski

Born: 1920.　Height: 6'4".　Weight: 210 lbs.　Drafted: —　College: Chicago

YEAR	TEAM	GP	GS	MIN	PTS	FGM	FGA	FG%	3PM	3PA	3P%	FTM	FTA	FT%	ORB	DRB	TRB	AST	PF	DQ	STL	BLK	TO	MPG	PPG	RPG	APG	PCM
45-46	Chicago-N	6	....	....	8	2	....	....	....	....	....	4	....	....	....	....	....	....	....	....	....	....	....	....	1.3	....	....	....
46-47	Anderson-N	27	....	....	189	82	....	....	....	....	....	25	48	.521	....	....	....	....	....	....	....	....	....	....	7.0	....	....	....
46-47	Tri-Cities-N	18	....	....	135	60	....	....	....	....	....	15	29	.517	....	....	....	....	....	....	....	....	....	....	7.5	....	....	....

YEAR	TEAM	GP	GS	MIN	PTS	FGM	FGA	FG%	3PM	3PA	3P%	FTM	FTA	FT%	ORB	DRB	TRB	AST	PF	DQ	STL	BLK	TO	MPG	PPG	RPG	APG	PCM
47-48	Tri-Cities-N	48	....	....	157	59	....	....	....	....	....	39	67	.582	....	....	....	....	71	....	....	....	....	....	3.3	....	....	....
48-49	Tri-Cities-N	3	....	....	2	1	....	....	....	....	....	0	0	.000	....	....	....	....	5	....	....	....	....	....	0.7	....	....	....
NBL Season Totals		102	....	....	491	204	....	....	....	....	....	83	144	....	....	....	....	....	76	....	....	....	....	....	4.8	....	....	....
47-48	Tri-Cities-N	6	....	....	27	13	....	....	....	....	....	1	3	.333	....	....	....	....	....	....	....	....	....	....	4.5	....	....	....
NBL Playoff Totals		6	....	....	27	13	....	....	....	....	....	1	3	....	....	....	....	....	....	....	....	....	....	....	4.5	....	....	....

• LEWIS, Bobby

Robert Franklin Lewis

Born: Mar. 20, 1945.   Height: 6'3".   Weight: 175 lbs.   Drafted: 1968   College: North Carolina

YEAR	TEAM	GP	GS	MIN	PTS	FGM	FGA	FG%	3PM	3PA	3P%	FTM	FTA	FT%	ORB	DRB	TRB	AST	PF	DQ	STL	BLK	TO	MPG	PPG	RPG	APG	PCM
67-68	San Francisco	41	....	342	179	59	151	.391				61	79	.772			56	41	40	0				8.3	4.4	1.4	1.0	.516
68-69	San Francisco	62	....	756	309	113	290	.390				83	113	.735			114	76	117	0				12.2	5.0	1.8	1.2	.375
69-70	San Francisco	73	....	1353	526	213	557	.382				100	152	.658			157	194	170	0				18.5	7.2	2.2	2.7	.356
70-71	Cleveland	79	....	1852	467	179	484	.370				109	152	.717			206	244	176	1				23.4	5.9	2.6	3.1	.306
NBA Season Totals		255	....	4303	1481	564	1482	.381				353	496	.712			533	555	503	1				16.9	5.8	2.1	2.2	
67-68	San Francisco	1	....	4	4	2	3	.667				0	0	.000			0	0	0	0				4.0	4.0	0.0	0.0	.801
68-69	San Francisco	5	....	59	23	11	28	.393				1	3	.333			5	6	12	0				11.8	4.6	1.0	1.2	.239
NBA Playoff Totals		6	....	63	27	13	31	.419				1	3	.333			5	6	12	0				10.5	4.5	0.8	1.0	

• LEWIS, Cedric

Cedric Lewis

Born: Sept. 24, 1969. Washington, DC, United States.   Height: 6'10".   Weight: 235 lbs.   Drafted: —   College: Maryland

YEAR	TEAM	GP	GS	MIN	PTS	FGM	FGA	FG%	3PM	3PA	3P%	FTM	FTA	FT%	ORB	DRB	TRB	AST	PF	DQ	STL	BLK	TO	MPG	PPG	RPG	APG	PCM
95-96	Washington	3	0	4	4	2	3	.667	0	0	.000	0	0	.000	2	0	2	0	0	0	1	0	0	1.3	1.3	0.7	0.0	1.470
NBA Season Totals		3	0	4	4	2	3	.667	0	0	.000	0	0	.000	2	0	2	0	0	0	1	0	0	1.3	1.3	0.7	0.0	

• LEWIS, Freddie

Frederick L. (Freddie, Fritz) Lewis

Born: July 1, 1943. Huntington, WV, United States.   Height: 6'   Weight: 175 lbs.   Drafted: 1966   College: Arizona State

YEAR	TEAM	GP	GS	MIN	PTS	FGM	FGA	FG%	3PM	3PA	3P%	FTM	FTA	FT%	ORB	DRB	TRB	AST	PF	DQ	STL	BLK	TO	MPG	PPG	RPG	APG	PCM
66-67	Cincinnati	32	....	334	149	60	153	.392				29	41	.707			44	40	49	1				10.4	4.7	1.4	1.3	.400
67-68	Indiana-A	76	....	2921	1565	542	1287	.421	16	74	.216	465	583	.798			440	183	217	2			209	38.4	20.6	5.8	2.4	.475
68-69	Indiana-A	78	....	3055	1585	572	1300	.440	22	83	.265	419	510	.822	119	255	374	346	289	5			224	39.2	20.3	4.8	4.4	.495
69-70	Indiana-A	81	....	2877	1326	448	1065	.421	47	177	.266	383	485	.790	118	159	277	289	294	5			190	35.5	16.4	3.4	3.6	.415
70-71	Indiana-A	81	....	3034	1525	547	1241	.441	59	194	.304	372	461	.807	169	167	336	433	249	1			202	37.5	18.8	4.1	5.3	.535
71-72	Indiana-A	77	....	2714	1182	405	947	.428	31	100	.310	341	396	.861	134	193	327	362	230	1			194	35.2	15.4	4.2	4.7	.469
72-73	Indiana-A	72	....	2217	1075	375	860	.436	38	110	.345	287	349	.822	97	131	228	288	204	4			173	30.8	14.9	3.2	4.0	.470
73-74	Indiana-A	78	....	2164	775	290	728	.398	13	72	.181	182	219	.831	84	117	201	322	169		99	11	169	27.7	9.9	2.6	4.1	.389
74-75	Memphis-A	6	....	227	106	45	111	.405	1	6	.167	15	16	.938	11	9	20	19	9		10		10	37.8	17.7	3.3	3.2	.361
74-75	St. Louis-A	63	....	2563	1425	534	1121	.476	17	61	.279	340	405	.840	100	145	245	348	152		137	3	196	40.7	22.6	3.9	5.5	.551
75-76	St. Louis-A	74	....	2266	1096	403	953	.423	31	106	.292	259	317	.817	67	146	213	293	183		109	7	193	30.6	14.8	2.9	4.0	.447
76-77	Indiana	32	....	552	224	81	199	.407				62	77	.805	17	30	47	56	58	0	18	2		17.3	7.0	1.5	1.8	.353
NBA Season Totals		64	....	886	373	141	352	.401				91	118	.771	17	30	91	96	107	1	18	2		13.8	5.8	1.4	1.5	
ABA Season Totals		686	....	24038	11660	4161	9613	.433	275	983	.280	3063	3741	.819	899	1322	2661	2883	2016	18	355	21	1760	35.0	17.0	3.9	4.2	
Career Totals		750	....	24924	12033	4302	9965	.432	275	983	.280	3154	3859	.817	916	1352	2752	2979	2123	19	373	23	1760	33.2	16.0	3.7	4.0	
66-67	Cincinnati	3	....	9	8	4	9	.444				0	0	.000			4	0	1	0				3.0	2.7	1.3	0.0	.756
67-68	Indiana-A	3	....	116	70	21	49	.429	0	9	.000	28	29	.966			19	7	10	0			10	38.7	23.3	6.3	2.3	.570
68-69	Indiana-A	17	....	727	409	144	327	.440	5	17	.294	116	133	.872			70	79	68	2			43	42.8	24.1	4.1	4.6	.503
69-70	Indiana-A	14	....	532	285	89	234	.380	10	28	.357	97	116	.836	27	30	57	54	50	1			34	38.0	20.4	4.1	3.9	.454
70-71	Indiana-A	11	....	384	109	39	107	.364	3	23	.130	28	37	.757	22	26	48	52	40	1			24	34.9	9.9	4.4	4.7	.353
71-72	Indiana-A	20	....	805	383	142	322	.441	7	34	.206	92	108	.852	32	49	81	87	70				45	40.3	19.2	4.1	4.4	.442
72-73	Indiana-A	18	....	637	279	102	260	.392	6	27	.222	69	80	.863	31	35	66	91	57	0			49	35.4	15.5	3.7	5.1	.417
73-74	Indiana-A	14	....	547	244	90	204	.441	6	19	.316	58	67	.866	20	30	50	62	35		24	1	33	39.1	17.4	3.6	4.4	.441
74-75	St. Louis-A	9	....	403	236	85	176	.483	6	18	.333	60	73	.822	21	25	46	26	18		16	1	23	44.8	26.2	5.1	2.9	.524
NBA Playoff Totals		3	....	9	8	4	9	.444				0	0	.000			4	0	1	0				3.0	2.7	1.3	0.0	
ABA Playoff Totals		106	....	4151	2015	712	1679	.424	43	175	.246	548	643	.852	153	195	437	458	348	4	40	2	261	39.2	19.0	4.1	4.3	
Career Playoff Totals		109	....	4160	2023	716	1688	.424	43	175	.246	548	643	.852	153	195	441	458	349	4	40	2	261	38.2	18.6	4.0	4.2	

• LEWIS, Freddie

Frederick B. Lewis Jr.

Born: Jan. 6, 1921. Died: Dec.27, 1994.   Height: 6'2".   Weight: 195 lbs.   Drafted: —   College: Eastern Kentucky

YEAR	TEAM	GP	GS	MIN	PTS	FGM	FGA	FG%	3PM	3PA	3P%	FTM	FTA	FT%	ORB	DRB	TRB	AST	PF	DQ	STL	BLK	TO	MPG	PPG	RPG	APG	PCM
46-47	Sheboygan-N	44	....	....	585	230						125	**1170**	.107					106					....	13.3	....	....	
47-48	Indianapolis-N	17	....	....	167	66						35	50	.700										....	9.8	....	....	
47-48	Sheboygan-N	27	....	....	272	103						66	87	.759										....	10.1	....	....	
48-49	Indianapolis	8	....	....	79	31	115	.270				17	24	.708				19	25					....	9.9	....	2.4	
48-49	Baltimore	53	....	....	603	241	719	.335				121	157	.771				88	142					....	11.4	....	1.7	
49-50	Baltimore	18	....	....	63	25	110	.227				13	19	.684				18	23					....	3.5	....	1.0	
49-50	Philadelphia	16	....	....	54	21	74	.284				12	13	.923				7	17					....	3.4	....	0.4	
NBA Season Totals		95	....	....	799	318	1018	.312				163	213	.765				132	207					....	8.4	....	1.4	
NBL Season Totals		88	....	....	1024	399						226	1307						106					....	11.6	....	....	
Career Totals		183	....	....	1823	717	1018					389	1520					132	313					....	10.0	....	0.7	
46-47	Sheboygan-N	5	....	....	55	23						9	15	.600										....	11.0	....	....	
47-48	Indianapolis-N	4	....	....	41	18						5	8	.625										....	10.3	....	....	
48-49	Baltimore	3	....	....	37	15	35	.429				7	10	.700				3	13					....	12.3	....	1.0	
NBA Playoff Totals		3	....	....	37	15	35	.429				7	10	.700				3	13					....	12.3	....	1.0	
NBL Playoff Totals		9	....	....	96	41						14	23											....	10.7	....	....	
Career Playoff Totals		12	....	....	133	56	35					21	33					3	13					....	11.1	....	0.3	

YEAR	TEAM	GP	GS	MIN	PTS	FGM	FGA	FG%	3PM	3PA	3P%	FTM	FTA	FT%	ORB	DRB	TRB	AST	PF	DQ	STL	BLK	TO	MPG	PPG	RPG	APG	PCM

• LEWIS, Garmon

Garmon Lewis

Born: —.   Height: —   Weight: —   Drafted: —   College: —

YEAR	TEAM	GP	GS	MIN	PTS	FGM	FGA	FG%	3PM	3PA	3P%	FTM	FTA	FT%	ORB	DRB	TRB	AST	PF	DQ	STL	BLK	TO	MPG	PPG	RPG	APG	PCM
39-40	Indianapolis-N	1	....	....	0	0	....	....	....	....	....	0	....	....	....	....	....	....	....	....	....	....	....	0.0	....	....	....
NBL Season Totals		1	....	....	0	0	....	....	....	....	....	0	....	....	....	....	....	....	....	....	....	....	....	0.0	....	....	....

• LEWIS, Grady

Grady W. Lewis

Born: Mar. 25, 1917. Boyd, TX, United States.   Height: 6'7".   Weight: 215 lbs.   Drafted: —   College: Oklahoma

YEAR	TEAM	GP	GS	MIN	PTS	FGM	FGA	FG%	3PM	3PA	3P%	FTM	FTA	FT%	ORB	DRB	TRB	AST	PF	DQ	STL	BLK	TO	MPG	PPG	RPG	APG	PCM
46-47	Detroit	60	....	....	287	106	520	.204	....	....	....	75	138	.543	....	....	54	166	....	....	....	....	....	4.8	....	0.9	....
47-48	St. Louis	24	....	....	166	59	238	.248	....	....	....	48	72	.667	....	....	13	85	....	....	....	....	....	6.9	....	0.5	....
47-48	Baltimore	21	....	....	149	55	187	.294	....	....	....	39	63	.619	....	....	28	66	....	....	....	....	....	7.1	....	1.3	....
48-49	St. Louis	34	....	....	148	53	137	.387	....	....	....	42	70	.600	....	....	37	104	....	....	....	....	....	4.4	....	1.1	....
NBA Season Totals		139	....	....	750	273	1082	.252	....	....	....	204	343	.595	....	....	132	421	....	....	....	....	....	5.4	....	0.9	....
47-48	Baltimore	11	....	....	68	23	109	.211	....	....	....	22	29	.759	....	....	9	49	....	....	....	....	....	6.2	....	0.8	....
NBA Playoff Totals		11	....	....	68	23	109	.211	....	....	....	22	29	.759	....	....	9	49	....	....	....	....	....	6.2	....	0.8	....

• LEWIS, Martin

Martin Lewis

Born: Apr. 28, 1975. Liberal, KS, United States.   Height: 6'5".   Weight: 210 lbs.   Drafted: 1995   College: Seward County CC

YEAR	TEAM	GP	GS	MIN	PTS	FGM	FGA	FG%	3PM	3PA	3P%	FTM	FTA	FT%	ORB	DRB	TRB	AST	PF	DQ	STL	BLK	TO	MPG	PPG	RPG	APG	PCM
95-96	Toronto	16	0	189	75	29	60	.483	2	7	.286	15	25	.600	15	14	29	3	21	0	8	3	14	11.8	4.7	1.8	0.2	.312
96-97	Toronto	9	0	50	14	6	14	.429	1	3	.333	1	2	.500	4	2	6	4	8	0	1	2	1	5.6	1.6	0.7	0.4	.282
NBA Season Totals		25	0	239	89	35	74	.473	3	10	.300	16	27	.593	19	16	35	7	29	0	9	5	15	9.6	3.6	1.4	0.3	....

• LEWIS, Mike

Michael J. Lewis

Born: Mar. 18, 1946. Missoula, MT, United States.   Height: 6'8".   Weight: 225 lbs.   Drafted: 1968   College: Duke

YEAR	TEAM	GP	GS	MIN	PTS	FGM	FGA	FG%	3PM	3PA	3P%	FTM	FTA	FT%	ORB	DRB	TRB	AST	PF	DQ	STL	BLK	TO	MPG	PPG	RPG	APG	PCM
68-69	Indiana-A	24	....	457	197	75	163	.460	0	2	.000	47	68	.691	78	103	181	29	68	1	....	....	49	19.0	8.2	7.5	1.2	.595
68-69	Minnesota-A	52	....	1160	450	172	405	.425	0	2	.000	106	167	.635	193	258	451	78	178	7	....	....	89	22.3	8.7	8.7	1.5	.538
69-70	Pittsburgh-A	78	....	2698	1267	499	1006	.496	0	0	.000	269	356	.755	370	684	1054	268	306	7	....	....	242	34.6	16.2	13.5	3.4	.695
70-71	Pittsburgh-A	83	....	2741	1075	420	825	.509	0	0	.000	235	306	.768	**435**	778	1213	268	332	8	....	....	238	33.0	13.0	14.6	3.2	.687
71-72	Pittsburgh-A	82	....	2618	935	385	713	.540	0	0	.000	165	226	.730	357	639	996	316	315	11	....	....	237	31.9	11.4	12.1	3.9	.654
72-73	Carolina-A	15	....	430	151	59	119	.496	0	0	.000	33	41	.805	44	78	122	41	48	1	....	....	27	28.7	10.1	8.1	2.7	.527
73-74	Carolina-A	3	....	14	6	3	8	.375	0	0	.000	0	0	.000	3	2	5	0	2	....	0	0	1	4.7	2.0	1.7	0.0	.367
ABA Season Totals		337	....	10118	4081	1613	3239	.498	0	4	.000	855	1164	.735	1480	2542	4022	1000	1249	35	0	0	883	30.0	12.1	11.9	3.0	....
68-69	Minnesota-A	7	....	131	50	20	52	.385	0	0	.000	10	19	.526	....	....	47	11	28	2	....	....	5	18.7	7.1	6.7	1.6	.455
ABA Playoff Totals		7	....	131	50	20	52	.385	0	0	.000	10	19	.526	....	....	47	11	28	2	....	....	5	18.7	7.1	6.7	1.6	....

• LEWIS, Quincy

Quincy Lavell Lewis

Born: June 26, 1977. Little Rock, AR, United States.   Height: 6'7".   Weight: 215 lbs.   Drafted: 1999   College: Minnesota

YEAR	TEAM	GP	GS	MIN	PTS	FGM	FGA	FG%	3PM	3PA	3P%	FTM	FTA	FT%	ORB	DRB	TRB	AST	PF	DQ	STL	BLK	TO	MPG	PPG	RPG	APG	PCM
99-00	Utah	74	0	896	283	111	298	.372	23	63	.365	38	52	.731	46	67	113	40	158	0	24	15	46	12.1	3.8	1.5	0.5	.195
00-01	Utah	35	2	402	124	50	123	.407	9	25	.360	15	21	.714	14	33	47	18	78	1	10	10	17	11.5	3.5	1.3	0.5	.213
01-02	Utah	36	19	490	144	64	143	.448	3	18	.167	13	20	.650	10	33	43	36	89	4	23	9	32	13.6	4.0	1.2	1.0	.219
NBA Season Totals		145	21	1788	551	225	564	.399	35	106	.330	66	93	.710	70	133	203	94	325	5	57	34	95	12.3	3.8	1.4	0.6	....
99-00	Utah	8	0	106	26	10	27	.370	2	6	.333	4	5	.800	2	13	15	2	24	0	3	7	3	13.3	3.3	1.9	0.3	.202
01-02	Utah	4	0	56	17	8	23	.348	1	5	.200	0	4	.000	1	2	3	2	10	0	2	1	3	14.0	4.3	0.8	0.5	.035
NBA Playoff Totals		12	0	162	43	18	50	.360	3	11	.273	4	9	.444	3	15	18	4	34	0	5	8	6	13.5	3.6	1.5	0.3	....

• LEWIS, Ralph

Ralph Adolphus Lewis

Born: Mar. 28, 1963. Philadelphia, PA, United States.   Height: 6'6".   Weight: 200 lbs.   Drafted: 1985   College: LaSalle

YEAR	TEAM	GP	GS	MIN	PTS	FGM	FGA	FG%	3PM	3PA	3P%	FTM	FTA	FT%	ORB	DRB	TRB	AST	PF	DQ	STL	BLK	TO	MPG	PPG	RPG	APG	PCM
87-88	Detroit	50	0	310	83	27	87	.310	0	1	.000	29	48	.604	17	34	51	14	36	0	13	4	20	6.2	1.7	1.0	0.3	.197
88-89	Charlotte	42	0	336	136	58	121	.479	1	3	.333	19	39	.487	35	26	61	15	28	0	11	3	25	8.0	3.2	1.5	0.4	.350
89-90	Detroit	4	0	6	0	0	1	.000	0	0	.000	0	0	.000	0	0	0	0	1	0	0	0	1	1.5	0.0	0.0	0.0	-.390
89-90	Charlotte	3	0	20	10	4	6	.667	0	0	.000	2	2	1.000	4	2	6	0	2	0	1	0	1	6.7	3.3	2.0	0.0	.641
NBA Season Totals		99	0	672	229	89	215	.414	1	4	.250	50	89	.562	56	62	118	29	67	0	25	7	47	6.8	2.3	1.2	0.3	....
87-88	Detroit	10	0	17	4	2	6	.333	0	1	.000	0	0	.000	3	5	8	1	2	0	0	0	0	1.7	0.4	0.8	0.1	.463
NBA Playoff Totals		10	0	17	4	2	6	.333	0	1	.000	0	0	.000	3	5	8	1	2	0	0	0	0	1.7	0.4	0.8	0.1	....

• LEWIS, Rashard

Rashard Quovon Lewis

Born: Aug. 8, 1979. Pineville, LA, United States.   Height: 6'10".   Weight: 215 lbs.   Drafted: 1998   College: none (HS: Alief Elsik, TX)

YEAR	TEAM	GP	GS	MIN	PTS	FGM	FGA	FG%	3PM	3PA	3P%	FTM	FTA	FT%	ORB	DRB	TRB	AST	PF	DQ	STL	BLK	TO	MPG	PPG	RPG	APG	PCM
98-99	Seattle	20	7	145	47	19	52	.365	1	6	.167	8	14	.571	13	12	25	4	19	0	8	1	20	7.3	2.4	1.3	0.2	.162
99-00	Seattle	82	8	1575	674	275	566	.486	40	120	.333	84	123	.683	127	209	336	70	163	0	62	36	78	19.2	8.2	4.1	0.9	.456
00-01	Seattle	78	78	2720	1151	426	887	.480	123	285	.432	176	213	.826	143	398	541	125	191	2	91	45	129	34.9	14.8	6.9	1.6	.465
01-02	Seattle	71	70	2584	1195	455	972	.468	123	316	.389	162	200	.810	139	359	498	123	174	3	104	40	97	36.4	16.8	7.0	1.7	.487
02-03	Seattle	77	77	3044	1396	519	1149	.452	75	217	.346	283	345	.820	152	351	503	133	205	1	99	35	143	39.5	18.1	6.5	1.7	.426
NBA Season Totals		328	240	10068	4463	1694	3626	.467	362	944	.383	713	895	.797	574	1329	1903	455	752	6	364	157	467	30.7	13.6	5.8	1.4	....
99-00	Seattle	5	5	157	77	26	59	.441	9	19	.474	16	20	.800	12	19	31	3	11	0	5	3	10	31.4	15.4	6.2	0.6	.445
01-02	Seattle	3	2	79	38	12	32	.375	1	6	.167	13	13	1.000	4	7	11	2	10	0	1	0	2	26.3	12.7	3.7	0.7	.337
NBA Playoff Totals		8	7	236	115	38	91	.418	10	25	.400	29	33	.879	16	26	42	5	21	0	6	3	12	29.5	14.4	5.3	0.6	....

• LEWIS, Reggie

Reggie Lewis

Born: Nov. 21, 1965. Baltimore, MD, United States. Died: July27, 1993. Height: 6'7". Weight: 195 lbs. Drafted: 1987 College: Northeastern

YEAR	TEAM	GP	GS	MIN	PTS	FGM	FGA	FG%	3PM	3PA	3P%	FTM	FTA	FT%	ORB	DRB	TRB	AST	PF	DQ	STL	BLK	TO	MPG	PPG	RPG	APG	PCM
87-88	Boston	49	0	405	220	90	193	.466	0	4	.000	40	57	.702	28	35	63	26	54	0	16	15	29	8.3	4.5	1.3	0.5	.443
88-89	Boston	81	57	2657	1495	604	1242	.486	3	22	.136	284	361	.787	116	261	377	218	258	5	124	72	146	32.8	18.5	4.7	2.7	.518
89-90	Boston	79	54	2522	1340	540	1089	.496	4	15	.267	256	317	.808	109	238	347	225	216	2	88	63	119	31.9	17.0	4.4	2.8	.512
90-91	Boston	79	79	2878	1478	598	1219	.491	1	13	.077	281	340	.826	119	291	410	201	234	1	98	85	150	36.4	18.7	5.2	2.5	.483
91-92	Boston	82	82	3070	1703	703	1397	.503	5	21	.238	292	343	.851	117	277	394	185	258	4	125	105	139	37.4	20.8	4.8	2.3	.509
92-93	Boston	80	80	3144	1666	663	1410	.470	14	60	.233	326	376	.867	88	259	347	298	248	1	118	77	136	39.3	20.8	4.3	3.7	.486
NBA Season Totals		450	352	14676	7902	3198	6550	.488	27	135	.200	1479	1794	.824	577	1361	1938	1153	1268	13	569	417	719	32.6	17.6	4.3	2.6	....
87-88	Boston	12	0	70	29	13	34	.382	0	1	.000	3	5	.600	9	7	16	4	13	0	3	2	0	5.8	2.4	1.3	0.3	.375
88-89	Boston	3	3	125	61	26	55	.473	0	2	.000	9	13	.692	5	16	21	11	11	0	5	0	8	41.7	20.3	7.0	3.7	.445
89-90	Boston	5	5	200	101	37	62	.597	0	1	.000	27	35	.771	9	16	25	22	14	0	7	2	12	40.0	20.2	5.0	4.4	.556
90-91	Boston	11	11	462	246	95	195	.487	0	4	.000	56	68	.824	18	50	68	32	33	1	12	6	20	42.0	22.4	6.2	2.9	.492
91-92	Boston	10	10	408	280	115	218	.528	2	6	.333	48	63	.762	11	32	43	39	38	2	24	8	16	40.8	28.0	4.3	3.9	.628
92-93	Boston	1	1	13	17	7	11	.636	0	1	.000	3	4	.750	2	0	2	1	1	0	0	1	1	13.0	17.0	2.0	1.0	1.174
NBA Playoff Totals		42	30	1278	734	293	575	.510	2	15	.133	146	188	.777	54	121	175	109	110	3	51	19	57	30.4	17.5	4.2	2.6	....

• LIBERTY, Marcus

Marcus (Doc) Liberty

Born: Oct. 27, 1968. Chicago, IL, United States. Height: 6'8". Weight: 205 lbs. Drafted: 1990 College: Illinois

YEAR	TEAM	GP	GS	MIN	PTS	FGM	FGA	FG%	3PM	3PA	3P%	FTM	FTA	FT%	ORB	DRB	TRB	AST	PF	DQ	STL	BLK	TO	MPG	PPG	RPG	APG	PCM
90-91	Denver	76	18	1171	507	216	513	.421	17	57	.298	58	92	.630	117	104	221	64	153	2	48	19	68	15.4	6.7	2.9	0.8	.355
91-92	Denver	75	13	1527	698	275	621	.443	17	50	.340	131	180	.728	144	164	308	58	166	3	66	29	90	20.4	9.3	4.1	0.8	.412
92-93	Denver	78	32	1585	628	252	620	.406	22	59	.373	102	156	.654	131	204	335	105	143	0	64	21	78	20.3	8.1	4.3	1.3	.394
93-94	Denver	3	0	11	9	4	7	.571	0	1	.000	1	2	.500	0	5	5	2	5	0	0	0	2	3.7	3.0	1.7	0.7	.765
93-94	Detroit	35	0	274	100	36	116	.310	10	27	.370	18	37	.486	26	30	56	15	29	0	11	4	21	7.8	2.9	1.6	0.4	.244
NBA Season Totals		267	63	4568	1942	783	1877	.417	66	194	.340	310	467	.664	418	507	925	244	496	5	189	73	259	17.1	7.3	3.5	0.9	....

• LICHTI, Todd

Todd Samuel Lichti

Born: Jan. 8, 1967. Walnut Creek, CA, United States. Height: 6'4". Weight: 205 lbs. Drafted: 1989 College: Stanford

YEAR	TEAM	GP	GS	MIN	PTS	FGM	FGA	FG%	3PM	3PA	3P%	FTM	FTA	FT%	ORB	DRB	TRB	AST	PF	DQ	STL	BLK	TO	MPG	PPG	RPG	APG	PCM
89-90	Denver	79	4	1326	630	250	514	.486	0	14	.000	130	174	.747	49	102	151	116	145	1	55	13	95	16.8	8.0	1.9	1.5	.402
90-91	Denver	29	25	860	405	166	378	.439	14	47	.298	59	69	.855	49	63	112	72	65	1	46	8	32	29.7	14.0	3.9	2.5	.435
91-92	Denver	68	10	1176	446	173	376	.460	1	9	.111	99	118	.839	36	82	118	74	130	0	43	12	75	17.3	6.6	1.7	1.1	.305
92-93	Denver	48	12	752	331	124	276	.449	2	6	.333	81	102	.794	35	67	102	52	60	0	28	11	48	15.7	6.9	2.1	1.1	.390
93-94	Orlando	4	0	20	8	4	9	.444	0	0	.000	0	0	.000	3	1	4	2	3	0	2	0	2	5.0	2.0	1.0	0.5	.394
93-94	Golden State	5	0	58	31	10	28	.357	2	2	1.000	9	11	.818	3	7	10	3	9	0	0	0	0	11.6	6.2	2.0	0.6	.377
93-94	Boston	4	0	48	19	6	14	.429	0	0	.000	7	14	.500	2	6	8	6	4	0	5	1	3	12.0	4.8	2.0	1.5	.483
NBA Season Totals		237	51	4240	1870	733	1595	.460	19	78	.244	385	488	.789	177	328	505	325	416	2	179	45	255	17.9	7.9	2.1	1.4	....
89-90	Denver	3	0	70	44	15	29	.517	0	1	.000	14	19	.737	5	13	18	9	6	0	1	0	8	23.3	14.7	6.0	3.0	.651
NBA Playoff Totals		3	0	70	44	15	29	.517	0	1	.000	14	19	.737	5	13	18	9	6	0	1	0	8	23.3	14.7	6.0	3.0	....

• LIEBERMAN, Sam

Sam Lieberman

Born: —. Height: 6'8". Weight: — Drafted: — College: Lawrence Tech

YEAR	TEAM	GP	GS	MIN	PTS	FGM	FGA	FG%	3PM	3PA	3P%	FTM	FTA	FT%	ORB	DRB	TRB	AST	PF	DQ	STL	BLK	TO	MPG	PPG	RPG	APG	PCM
46-47	Syracuse-N	2	....	....	1	0	....	....	....	....	....	1	2	.500	....	....	....	....	....	....	....	....	....	....	0.5	....	....	....
NBL Season Totals		2	....	....	1	0	....	....	....	....	....	1	2	....	....	....	....	....	....	....	....	....	....	....	0.5	....	....	....

• LIEBOWITZ, Barry

Barry Liebowitz

Born: Sept. 10, 1945. New York, NY, United States. Height: 6'2". Weight: 180 lbs. Drafted: — College: Long Island University

YEAR	TEAM	GP	GS	MIN	PTS	FGM	FGA	FG%	3PM	3PA	3P%	FTM	FTA	FT%	ORB	DRB	TRB	AST	PF	DQ	STL	BLK	TO	MPG	PPG	RPG	APG	PCM
67-68	New Jersey-A	24	....	707	273	98	287	.341	0	7	.000	77	96	.802	....	....	72	93	68	0	....	....	62	29.5	11.4	3.0	3.9	.352
67-68	Oakland-A	35	....	1014	401	139	379	.367	4	26	.154	119	152	.783	....	....	58	156	96	1	....	....	107	29.0	11.5	1.7	4.5	.374
67-68	Pittsburgh-A	23	....	447	220	83	207	.401	2	6	.333	52	60	.867	....	....	40	52	44	0	....	....	55	19.4	9.6	1.7	2.3	.424
ABA Season Totals		82	....	2168	894	320	873	.367	6	39	.154	248	308	.805	....	....	170	301	208	1	....	....	224	26.4	10.9	2.1	3.7	....

• LIGON, Bill

William N. Ligon

Born: May 29, 1952. Nashville, TN, United States. Height: 6'4". Weight: 180 lbs. Drafted: 1974 College: Vanderbilt

YEAR	TEAM	GP	GS	MIN	PTS	FGM	FGA	FG%	3PM	3PA	3P%	FTM	FTA	FT%	ORB	DRB	TRB	AST	PF	DQ	STL	BLK	TO	MPG	PPG	RPG	APG	PCM
74-75	Detroit	38	....	272	126	55	143	.385	....	....	....	16	25	.640	14	12	26	25	31	0	8	9	....	7.2	3.3	0.7	0.7	.312
NBA Season Totals		38	....	272	126	55	143	.385	....	....	....	16	25	.640	14	12	26	25	31	0	8	9	....	7.2	3.3	0.7	0.7	....
74-75	Detroit	2	....	7	2	1	1	1.000	....	....	....	0	0	.000	0	0	0	0	1	0	0	0	....	3.5	1.0	0.0	0.0	.225
NBA Playoff Totals		2	....	7	2	1	1	1.000	....	....	....	0	0	.000	0	0	0	0	1	0	0	0	....	3.5	1.0	0.0	0.0	....

• LIGON, Goose

Jim (Goose) Ligon

Born: Feb. 22, 1944. Kokomo, IN, United States. Height: 6'7". Weight: 210 lbs. Drafted: — College: none (HS: Kokomo, IN)

YEAR	TEAM	GP	GS	MIN	PTS	FGM	FGA	FG%	3PM	3PA	3P%	FTM	FTA	FT%	ORB	DRB	TRB	AST	PF	DQ	STL	BLK	TO	MPG	PPG	RPG	APG	PCM
67-68	Kentucky-A	78	....	2801	1262	428	942	.454	1	4	.250	405	595	.681	370	559	929	143	307	6	....	....	188	35.9	16.2	11.9	1.8	.560
68-69	Kentucky-A	75	....	2815	1120	391	879	.445	1	5	.200	337	510	.661	328	491	819	172	312	6	....	....	193	37.5	14.9	10.9	2.3	.495
69-70	Kentucky-A	84	....	3130	1301	507	1000	.507	0	2	.000	287	445	.645	399	695	1094	190	360	13	....	....	206	37.3	15.5	13.0	2.3	.579
70-71	Kentucky-A	84	....	2753	1072	429	795	.540	0	6	.000	214	391	.547	312	677	989	211	331	6	....	....	167	32.8	12.8	11.8	2.5	.589
71-72	Kentucky-A	16	....	400	95	37	72	.514	1	2	.500	20	33	.606	43	67	110	37	41	1	....	....	30	25.0	5.9	6.9	2.3	.447

YEAR	TEAM	GP	GS	MIN	PTS	FGM	FGA	FG%	3PM	3PA	3P%	FTM	FTA	FT%	ORB	DRB	TRB	AST	PF	DQ	STL	BLK	TO	MPG	PPG	RPG	APG	PCM
71-72	Pittsburgh-A	66	....	1941	473	176	356	.494	0	4	.000	121	184	.658	188	402	590	126	224	2	....	....	96	29.4	7.2	8.9	1.9	.437
72-73	Virginia-A	12	....	360	144	58	103	.563	0	0	.000	28	43	.651	36	58	94	20	40	0	....	....	21	30.0	12.0	7.8	1.7	.515
73-74	Virginia-A	19	....	360	93	37	85	.435	0	1	.000	19	25	.760	45	50	95	11	43	....	9	9	24	18.9	4.9	5.0	0.6	.347
ABA Season Totals		434	....	14560	5560	2063	4232	.487	3	24	.125	1431	2226	.643	1721	2999	4720	910	1658	34	9	9	925	33.5	12.8	10.9	2.1	....
67-68	Kentucky-A	5	....	173	72	20	46	.435	0	0	.000	32	42	.762	21	37	58	7	25	1	....	....	16	34.6	14.4	11.6	1.4	.533
68-69	Kentucky-A	7	....	260	98	34	78	.436	0	1	.000	30	41	.732	31	58	89	8	25	0	....	....	21	37.1	14.0	12.7	1.1	.501
69-70	Kentucky-A	12	....	475	212	73	134	.545	0	0	.000	66	99	.667	54	87	141	26	....	0	....	....	30	39.6	17.7	11.8	2.2	....
70-71	Kentucky-A	19	....	587	200	81	170	.476	0	0	.000	38	67	.567	76	143	219	35	74	4	....	....	21	30.9	10.5	11.5	1.8	.519
73-74	Virginia-A	3	....	23	6	3	11	.273	0	2	.000	0	0	.000	2	4	6	0	5	....	0	1	4	7.7	2.0	2.0	0.0	.093
ABA Playoff Totals		46	....	1518	588	211	439	.481	0	3	.000	166	249	.667	184	329	513	76	129	5	0	1	92	33.0	12.8	11.2	1.7	....

• LILLAGE, Carl

Carl Lillage

Born: —. Height: — Weight: — Drafted: — College: —

YEAR	TEAM	GP	GS	MIN	PTS	FGM	FGA	FG%	3PM	3PA	3P%	FTM	FTA	FT%	ORB	DRB	TRB	AST	PF	DQ	STL	BLK	TO	MPG	PPG	RPG	APG	PCM
39-40	Oshkosh-N	3	....	....	2	0	....	....	....	....	....	2	....	....	....	....	....	....	....	....	....	....	....	....	0.7	....	....	....
NBL Season Totals		3	....	....	2	0	....	....	....	....	....	2	....	....	....	....	....	....	....	....	....	....	....	....	0.7	....	....	....

• LINDBERG, Bud

Bud Lindberg

Born: 1911. Height: 6' Weight: 175 lbs. Drafted: — College: none

YEAR	TEAM	GP	GS	MIN	PTS	FGM	FGA	FG%	3PM	3PA	3P%	FTM	FTA	FT%	ORB	DRB	TRB	AST	PF	DQ	STL	BLK	TO	MPG	PPG	RPG	APG	PCM
37-38	Fort Wayne-N	18	....	....	80	30	....	....	....	....	....	20	....	....	....	....	....	....	....	....	....	....	....	....	4.4	....	....	....
NBL Season Totals		18	....	....	80	30	....	....	....	....	....	20	....	....	....	....	....	....	....	....	....	....	....	....	4.4	....	....	....

• LINGENFELTER, Steve

Steven Rodney Lingenfelter

Born: June 10, 1958. Eau Claire, WI, United States. Height: 6'9". Weight: 225 lbs. Drafted: 1981 College: South Dakota State

YEAR	TEAM	GP	GS	MIN	PTS	FGM	FGA	FG%	3PM	3PA	3P%	FTM	FTA	FT%	ORB	DRB	TRB	AST	PF	DQ	STL	BLK	TO	MPG	PPG	RPG	APG	PCM
82-83	Washington	7	0	53	8	4	6	.667	0	0	.000	0	4	.000	1	11	12	4	16	1	1	3	5	7.6	1.1	1.7	0.6	.217
83-84	San Antonio	3	0	14	2	1	1	1.000	0	0	.000	0	2	.000	3	1	4	1	6	0	0	0	1	4.7	0.7	1.3	0.3	.153
NBA Season Totals		10	0	67	10	5	7	.714	0	0	.000	0	6	.000	4	12	16	5	22	1	1	3	6	6.7	1.0	1.6	0.5	....

• LINS, Leroy

Leroy Lins

Born: June 21, 1913. Died: Aug.1986. Height: 6'1". Weight: 175 lbs. Drafted: — College: Rutgers

YEAR	TEAM	GP	GS	MIN	PTS	FGM	FGA	FG%	3PM	3PA	3P%	FTM	FTA	FT%	ORB	DRB	TRB	AST	PF	DQ	STL	BLK	TO	MPG	PPG	RPG	APG	PCM
37-38	Wingfoots-N	8	....	....	4	1	....	....	....	....	....	2	....	....	....	....	....	....	....	....	....	....	....	....	0.5	....	....	....
NBL Season Totals		8	....	....	4	1	....	....	....	....	....	2	....	....	....	....	....	....	....	....	....	....	....	....	0.5	....	....	....

• LINSKEY, Frank

Frank Linskey

Born: Aug. 18, 1913. Died: July3, 1999. Height: 6'2". Weight: 180 lbs. Drafted: — College: DePaul

YEAR	TEAM	GP	GS	MIN	PTS	FGM	FGA	FG%	3PM	3PA	3P%	FTM	FTA	FT%	ORB	DRB	TRB	AST	PF	DQ	STL	BLK	TO	MPG	PPG	RPG	APG	PCM
37-38	Oshkosh-N	11	....	....	47	16	....	....	....	....	....	15	....	....	....	....	....	....	....	....	....	....	....	....	4.3	....	....	....
38-39	Oshkosh-N	24	....	....	61	22	....	....	....	....	....	17	....	....	....	....	....	....	....	....	....	....	....	....	2.5	....	....	....
39-40	Chicago-N	27	....	....	97	38	....	....	....	....	....	21	....	....	....	....	....	....	....	....	....	....	....	....	3.6	....	....	....
40-41	Chicago-N	15	....	....	21	8	....	....	....	....	....	5	....	....	....	....	....	....	....	....	....	....	....	....	1.4	....	....	....
NBL Season Totals		77	....	....	226	84	....	....	....	....	....	58	....	....	....	....	....	....	....	....	....	....	....	....	2.9	....	....	....
37-38	Oshkosh-N	4	....	....	5	2	....	....	....	....	....	1	....	....	....	....	....	....	....	....	....	....	....	....	1.3	....	....	....
38-39	Oshkosh-N	4	....	....	12	5	....	....	....	....	....	2	....	....	....	....	....	....	....	....	....	....	....	....	3.0	....	....	....
NBL Playoff Totals		8	....	....	17	7	....	....	....	....	....	3	....	....	....	....	....	....	....	....	....	....	....	....	2.1	....	....	....

• LISTER, Alton

Alton Lavelle Lister

Born: Oct. 1, 1958. Dallas, TX, United States. Height: 7' Weight: 240 lbs. Drafted: 1981 College: Arizona State

YEAR	TEAM	GP	GS	MIN	PTS	FGM	FGA	FG%	3PM	3PA	3P%	FTM	FTA	FT%	ORB	DRB	TRB	AST	PF	DQ	STL	BLK	TO	MPG	PPG	RPG	APG	PCM
81-82	Milwaukee	80	23	1186	362	149	287	.519	0	0	.000	64	123	.520	108	279	387	84	239	4	18	118	128	14.8	4.5	4.8	1.1	.466
82-83	Milwaukee	80	37	1885	674	272	514	.529	0	0	.000	130	242	.537	168	400	568	111	328	18	50	177	184	23.6	8.4	7.1	1.4	.494
83-84	Milwaukee	82	72	1955	626	256	512	.500	0	0	.000	114	182	.626	156	447	603	110	327	11	41	140	156	23.8	7.6	7.4	1.3	.463
84-85	Milwaukee	81	80	2091	798	322	598	.538	0	1	.000	154	262	.588	219	428	647	127	287	5	49	167	186	25.8	9.9	8.0	1.6	.537
85-86	Milwaukee	81	19	1812	796	318	577	.551	0	2	.000	160	266	.602	199	393	592	101	300	8	49	142	162	22.4	9.8	7.3	1.2	.581
86-87	Seattle	75	75	2288	871	346	687	.504	0	1	.000	179	265	.675	223	482	705	110	289	11	32	180	173	30.5	11.6	9.4	1.5	.520
87-88	Seattle	82	55	1812	461	173	343	.504	1	2	.500	114	188	.606	200	427	627	58	319	8	27	140	90	22.1	5.6	7.6	0.7	.462
88-89	Seattle	82	82	1806	657	271	543	.499	0	0	.000	115	178	.646	207	338	545	54	310	3	28	180	115	22.0	8.0	6.6	0.7	.488
89-90	Golden State	3	0	40	12	4	8	.500	0	1	.000	4	7	.571	5	3	8	2	8	0	1	0	0	13.3	4.0	2.7	0.7	.341
90-91	Golden State	77	65	1552	491	188	393	.478	0	1	.000	115	202	.569	121	362	483	93	282	4	20	90	108	20.2	6.4	6.3	1.2	.438
91-92	Golden State	26	12	293	102	44	79	.557	0	0	.000	14	33	.424	21	71	92	14	61	0	5	16	21	11.3	3.9	3.5	0.5	.453
92-93	Golden State	20	9	174	45	19	42	.452	0	0	.000	7	13	.538	15	29	44	5	40	0	0	9	18	8.7	2.3	2.2	0.3	.230
94-95	Milwaukee	60	32	776	167	66	134	.493	0	1	.000	35	70	.500	67	169	236	12	146	3	16	57	36	12.9	2.8	3.9	0.2	.370
95-96	Milwaukee	7	5	88	10	4	9	.444	0	0	.000	2	2	1.000	7	22	29	4	15	0	0	3	4	12.6	1.4	4.1	0.6	.327
95-96	Boston	57	14	647	133	47	96	.490	0	0	.000	39	62	.629	60	191	251	15	121	1	6	39	46	11.4	2.3	4.4	0.3	.418
96-97	Boston	53	2	516	87	32	77	.416	0	0	.000	23	31	.742	66	102	168	13	95	1	8	14	32	9.7	1.6	3.2	0.2	.307
97-98	Portland	7	0	44	6	3	8	.375	0	0	.000	0	0	.000	2	9	11	1	12	0	1	1	2	6.3	0.9	1.6	0.1	.161
NBA Season Totals		953	582	18965	6298	2514	4907	.512	1	9	.111	1269	2126	.597	1844	4152	5996	914	3179	77	351	1473	1461	19.9	6.6	6.3	1.0	....
81-82	Milwaukee	6	5	112	33	14	24	.583	0	0	.000	5	7	.714	6	21	27	5	23	0	2	15	9	18.7	5.5	4.5	0.8	.446
82-83	Milwaukee	9	5	206	58	27	63	.429	0	1	.000	4	5	.800	21	40	61	11	30	1	9	15	17	22.9	6.4	6.8	1.2	.412
83-84	Milwaukee	16	12	368	108	39	78	.500	0	0	.000	30	48	.625	26	70	96	10	63	2	5	24	27	23.0	6.8	6.0	0.6	.369
84-85	Milwaukee	8	8	203	69	27	60	.450	0	0	.000	15	32	.469	27	35	62	15	36	1	6	15	16	25.4	8.6	7.8	1.9	.453
85-86	Milwaukee	14	1	335	167	66	103	.641	0	1	.000	35	58	.603	37	59	96	12	56	3	7	22	21	23.9	11.9	6.9	0.9	.613
86-87	Seattle	9	7	206	54	20	50	.400	0	0	.000	14	20	.700	29	27	56	7	37	3	7	13	10	22.9	6.0	6.2	0.8	.364
87-88	Seattle	5	5	77	28	12	17	.706	0	0	.000	4	5	.800	9	20	29	5	17	0	1	5	4	15.4	5.6	5.8	1.0	.639

YEAR	TEAM	GP	GS	MIN	PTS	FGM	FGA	FG%	3PM	3PA	3P%	FTM	FTA	FT%	ORB	DRB	TRB	AST	PF	DQ	STL	BLK	TO	MPG	PPG	RPG	APG	PCM
88-89	Seattle	8	8	160	56	17	39	.436	0	0	.000	22	26	.846	13	25	38	2	28	0	2	21	9	20.0	7.0	4.8	0.3	.445
90-91	Golden State	6	5	72	26	12	25	.480	0	0	.000	2	5	.400	7	21	28	2	15	0	0	7	8	12.0	4.3	4.7	0.3	.456
91-92	Golden State	4	3	47	16	6	15	.400	0	0	.000	4	5	.800	3	8	11	1	9	0	0	4	3	11.8	4.0	2.8	0.3	.324
97-98	Portland	2	0	11	2	1	3	.333	0	0	.000	0	0	.000	1	1	2	0	5	0	0	1	2	5.5	1.0	1.0	0.0	-.109
NBA Playoff Totals		87	59	1797	617	241	477	.505	0	2	.000	135	211	.640	179	327	506	70	319	10	39	142	126	20.7	7.1	5.8	0.8	....

• LITTLE, Samuel
Samuel Ray Little

Born: Mar. 29, 1946.   Height: 6'   Weight: 180 lbs.   Drafted: —   College: Delta State

YEAR	TEAM	GP	GS	MIN	PTS	FGM	FGA	FG%	3PM	3PA	3P%	FTM	FTA	FT%	ORB	DRB	TRB	AST	PF	DQ	STL	BLK	TO	MPG	PPG	RPG	APG	PCM
69-70	Kentucky-A	3	....	11	5	2	4	.500	0	1	.000	1	1	1.000	0	1	1	2	4	0	....	....	1	3.7	1.7	0.3	0.7	.428
ABA Season Totals		3	....	11	5	2	4	.500	0	1	.000	1	1	1.000	0	1	1	2	4	0	....	....	1	3.7	1.7	0.3	0.7	....

• LITTLES, Gene
Eugene Scape Littles

Born: June 29, 1943. Washington, DC, United States.   Height: 6'   Weight: 160 lbs.   Drafted: 1969   College: High Point

YEAR	TEAM	GP	GS	MIN	PTS	FGM	FGA	FG%	3PM	3PA	3P%	FTM	FTA	FT%	ORB	DRB	TRB	AST	PF	DQ	STL	BLK	TO	MPG	PPG	RPG	APG	PCM
69-70	Carolina-A	82	....	2832	1025	414	817	.507	0	3	.000	197	254	.776	154	261	415	282	255	0	....	....	157	34.5	12.5	5.1	3.4	.432
70-71	Carolina-A	70	....	1495	567	223	501	.445	4	14	.286	117	168	.696	81	124	205	173	175	3	....	....	80	21.4	8.1	2.9	2.5	.418
71-72	Carolina-A	69	....	2006	745	280	605	.463	7	26	.269	178	237	.751	122	154	276	237	180	1	....	....	104	29.1	10.8	4.0	3.4	.430
72-73	Carolina-A	84	....	2060	807	310	622	.498	8	30	.267	179	246	.728	104	158	262	245	198	0	120	....	125	24.5	9.6	3.1	2.9	.443
73-74	Carolina-A	84	....	2017	707	294	626	.470	4	23	.174	115	161	.714	87	144	231	280	159	....	105	17	122	24.0	8.4	2.8	3.3	.422
74-75	Kentucky-A	61	....	900	215	85	202	.421	2	8	.250	43	58	.741	30	56	86	119	81	....	52	4	62	14.8	3.5	1.4	2.0	.308
ABA Season Totals		450	....	11310	4066	1606	3373	.476	25	104	.240	829	1124	.738	578	897	1475	1336	1048	4	277	21	650	25.1	9.0	3.3	3.0	....
69-70	Carolina-A	4	....	133	42	18	33	.545	0	0	.000	6	9	.667	....	....	18	14	....	....	....	....	....	33.3	10.5	4.5	3.5	....
72-73	Carolina-A	12	....	223	80	30	67	.448	0	2	.000	20	32	.625	14	22	36	16	22	0	....	....	13	18.6	6.7	3.0	1.3	.365
73-74	Carolina-A	4	....	106	37	15	34	.441	4	7	.571	3	8	.375	4	7	11	18	7	....	6	0	2	26.5	9.3	2.8	4.5	.430
74-75	Kentucky-A	8	....	30	4	2	9	.222	0	0	.000	0	0	.000	4	1	5	4	0	....	1	0	1	3.8	0.5	0.6	0.5	.222
ABA Playoff Totals		28	....	492	163	65	143	.455	4	9	.444	29	49	.592	22	30	70	52	29	0	7	0	16	17.6	5.8	2.5	1.9	....

• LIVINGSTON, Randy
Randy Anthony Livingston

Born: Apr. 2, 1975. New Orleans, LA, United States.   Height: 6'4".   Weight: 209 lbs.   Drafted: 1996   College: Louisiana State

YEAR	TEAM	GP	GS	MIN	PTS	FGM	FGA	FG%	3PM	3PA	3P%	FTM	FTA	FT%	ORB	DRB	TRB	AST	PF	DQ	STL	BLK	TO	MPG	PPG	RPG	APG	PCM
96-97	Houston	64	0	981	251	100	229	.437	9	22	.409	42	65	.646	32	62	94	155	107	0	39	12	102	15.3	3.9	1.5	2.4	.281
97-98	Atlanta	12	0	82	10	3	12	.250	0	0	.000	4	5	.800	1	5	6	5	6	0	7	2	6	6.8	0.8	0.5	0.4	.149
98-99	Phoenix	1	0	22	12	5	8	.625	0	0	.000	2	2	1.000	0	2	2	3	1	0	2	0	1	22.0	12.0	2.0	3.0	.677
99-00	Phoenix	79	15	1081	381	155	373	.416	19	55	.345	52	62	.839	25	105	130	170	129	1	49	13	92	13.7	4.8	1.6	2.2	.367
00-01	Golden State	2	0	7	0	0	2	.000	0	1	.000	0	0	.000	0	1	1	1	0	0	0	0	0	3.5	0.0	0.5	0.5	.029
01-02	Seattle	13	0	176	41	15	54	.278	1	8	.125	10	11	.909	9	16	25	26	11	0	9	2	2	13.5	3.2	1.9	2.0	.338
02-03	New Orleans	2	0	12	6	2	4	.500	0	0	.000	2	2	1.000	0	0	0	1	0	0	0	0	0	6.0	3.0	0.0	0.5	.440
NBA Season Totals		173	15	2361	701	280	682	.411	29	86	.337	112	147	.762	67	191	258	361	254	1	106	29	203	13.6	4.1	1.5	2.1	....
96-97	Houston	2	0	15	3	1	4	.250	1	1	1.000	0	0	.000	0	0	0	4	1	0	1	0	1	7.5	1.5	0.0	2.0	.267
98-99	Phoenix	3	0	24	16	6	15	.400	0	1	.000	4	4	1.000	5	2	7	2	6	0	1	0	2	8.0	5.3	2.3	0.7	.537
99-00	Phoenix	7	3	63	14	6	27	.222	2	6	.333	0	0	.000	2	5	7	4	6	0	4	1	4	9.0	2.0	1.0	0.6	.061
01-02	Seattle	5	0	80	20	7	17	.412	1	3	.333	5	5	1.000	1	5	6	10	7	0	2	0	1	16.0	4.0	1.2	2.0	.313
NBA Playoff Totals		17	3	182	53	20	63	.317	4	11	.364	9	9	1.000	8	12	20	20	20	0	8	1	8	10.7	3.1	1.2	1.2	....

• LIVINGSTONE, Ron
George Ronald Livingstone

Born: Oct. 9, 1925.   Height: 6'10".   Weight: 220 lbs.   Drafted: 1949   College: St. Mary's (CA)

YEAR	TEAM	GP	GS	MIN	PTS	FGM	FGA	FG%	3PM	3PA	3P%	FTM	FTA	FT%	ORB	DRB	TRB	AST	PF	DQ	STL	BLK	TO	MPG	PPG	RPG	APG	PCM
49-50	Baltimore	16	....	....	85	25	102	.245	....	....	....	35	46	.761	....	....	....	24	54	....	....	....	....	5.3	....	1.5	....
49-50	Philadelphia	38	....	....	363	138	477	.289	....	....	....	87	131	.664	....	....	....	117	206	....	....	....	....	9.6	....	3.1	....
50-51	Philadelphia	63	....	....	284	104	353	.295	....	....	....	76	109	.697	....	297	76	220	10	....	....	....	....	4.5	4.7	1.2	....
NBA Season Totals		117	....	....	732	267	932	.286	....	....	....	198	286	.692	....	....	297	217	480	10	....	....	....	6.3	2.5	1.9	....
49-50	Philadelphia	2	....	....	16	6	16	.375	....	....	....	4	7	.571	....	....	....	5	12	....	....	....	....	8.0	....	2.5	....
50-51	Philadelphia	2	....	....	4	2	3	.667	....	....	....	0	0	.000	....	....	2	0	1	0	....	....	....	2.0	1.0	0.0	....
NBA Playoff Totals		4	....	....	20	8	19	.421	....	....	....	4	7	.571	....	....	2	5	13	0	....	....	....	5.0	0.5	1.3	....

• LLAMAS, Horacio
Horacio Llamas

Born: July 17, 1973. El Rosario, Mexico.   Height: 6'11".   Weight: 285 lbs.   Drafted: —   College: Grand Canyon

YEAR	TEAM	GP	GS	MIN	PTS	FGM	FGA	FG%	3PM	3PA	3P%	FTM	FTA	FT%	ORB	DRB	TRB	AST	PF	DQ	STL	BLK	TO	MPG	PPG	RPG	APG	PCM
96-97	Phoenix	20	2	101	34	15	28	.536	0	0	.000	4	8	.500	4	14	18	4	25	0	10	5	12	5.1	1.7	0.9	0.2	.319
97-98	Phoenix	8	0	42	24	8	21	.381	1	3	.333	7	10	.700	4	14	18	1	14	0	1	3	9	5.3	3.0	2.3	0.1	.412
NBA Season Totals		28	2	143	58	23	49	.469	1	3	.333	11	18	.611	8	28	36	5	39	0	11	8	21	5.1	2.1	1.3	0.2	....

• LLOYD, Bill
Bill Lloyd

Born: 1915.   Height: 6'2".   Weight: 180 lbs.   Drafted: —   College: St. John's (NY)

YEAR	TEAM	GP	GS	MIN	PTS	FGM	FGA	FG%	3PM	3PA	3P%	FTM	FTA	FT%	ORB	DRB	TRB	AST	PF	DQ	STL	BLK	TO	MPG	PPG	RPG	APG	PCM
39-40	Wingfoots-N	17	....	....	47	18	....	....	....	....	....	11	....	....	....	....	....	....	....	....	....	....	....	2.8	....	....	....
40-41	Wingfoots-N	2	....	....	3	1	....	....	....	....	....	1	....	....	....	....	....	....	....	....	....	....	....	1.5	....	....	....
NBL Season Totals		19	....	....	50	19	....	....	....	....	....	12	....	....	....	....	....	....	....	....	....	....	....	2.6	....	....	....

• LLOYD, Bobby
Robert E. Lloyd

Born: Jan. 3, 1946. Upper Darby, PA, United States. Height: 6'2". Weight: 184 lbs. Drafted: 1967 College: Rutgers

YEAR TEAM	GP	GS	MIN	PTS	FGM	FGA	FG%	3PM	3PA	3P%	FTM	FTA	FT%	ORB	DRB	TRB	AST	PF	DQ	STL	BLK	TO	MPG	PPG	RPG	APG	PCM
67-68 New Jersey-A	58	....	995	467	147	349	.421	3	8	.375	170	199	.854	....	....	108	93	114	1	....	....	74	17.2	8.1	1.9	1.6	.441
68-69 New York-A	67	....	1358	660	215	541	.397	12	31	.387	218	246	.886	25	87	112	136	176	1	....	....	95	20.3	9.9	1.7	2.0	.401
ABA Season Totals	125	....	2353	1127	362	890	.407	15	39	.385	388	445	.872	25	87	220	229	290	2	....	....	169	18.8	9.0	1.8	1.8	....

• LLOYD, Chuck
Charles P. (Chuck) Lloyd Jr.

Born: May 22, 1947. Height: 6'8". Weight: 220 lbs. Drafted: 1970 College: Yankton

YEAR TEAM	GP	GS	MIN	PTS	FGM	FGA	FG%	3PM	3PA	3P%	FTM	FTA	FT%	ORB	DRB	TRB	AST	PF	DQ	STL	BLK	TO	MPG	PPG	RPG	APG	PCM
70-71 Carolina-A	14	....	118	66	23	51	.451	0	0	.000	20	30	.667	14	11	25	6	25	0	....	....	2	8.4	4.7	1.8	0.4	.481
ABA Season Totals	14	....	118	66	23	51	.451	0	0	.000	20	30	.667	14	11	25	6	25	0	....	....	2	8.4	4.7	1.8	0.4	....

• LLOYD, Earl
Earl Francis (Big Cat, Moon Fixer) Lloyd

Born: Apr. 3, 1928. Height: 6'5". Weight: 200 lbs. Drafted: 1950 College: West Virginia State HOF: 2003

YEAR TEAM	GP	GS	MIN	PTS	FGM	FGA	FG%	3PM	3PA	3P%	FTM	FTA	FT%	ORB	DRB	TRB	AST	PF	DQ	STL	BLK	TO	MPG	PPG	RPG	APG	PCM
50-51 Washington	7	....	....	43	16	35	.457	....	....	....	11	13	.846	....	....	47	11	26	0	....	....	....	....	6.1	6.7	1.6	....
52-53 Syracuse	64	....	1806	472	156	453	.344	....	....	....	160	231	.693	....	....	444	64	241	6	....	....	....	28.2	7.4	6.9	1.0	.303
53-54 Syracuse	72	....	2206	654	249	666	.374	....	....	....	156	209	.746	....	....	529	115	**303**	**12**	....	....	....	30.6	9.1	7.3	1.6	.342
54-55 Syracuse	72	....	2212	731	286	784	.365	....	....	....	159	212	.750	....	....	553	151	283	4	....	....	....	30.7	10.2	7.7	2.1	.377
55-56 Syracuse	72	....	1837	612	213	636	.335	....	....	....	186	241	.772	....	....	492	116	267	6	....	....	....	25.5	8.5	6.8	1.6	.373
56-57 Syracuse	72	....	1965	646	256	687	.373	....	....	....	134	179	.749	....	....	435	114	282	10	....	....	....	27.3	9.0	6.0	1.6	.341
57-58 Syracuse	61	....	1045	317	119	359	.331	....	....	....	79	106	.745	....	....	287	60	179	3	....	....	....	17.1	5.2	4.7	1.0	.337
58-59 Detroit	72	....	1796	605	234	670	.349	....	....	....	137	182	.753	....	....	500	90	291	15	....	....	....	24.9	8.4	6.9	1.3	.356
59-60 Detroit	68	....	1610	602	237	665	.356	....	....	....	128	160	.800	....	....	322	89	226	1	....	....	....	23.7	8.9	4.7	1.3	.332
NBA Season Totals	560	....	14477	4682	1766	4955	.356	....	....	....	1150	1533	.750	....	....	3609	810	2098	57	....	....	....	25.9	8.4	6.4	1.4	....
52-53 Syracuse	2	....	73	15	4	17	.235	....	....	....	7	10	.700	....	....	9	5	10	0	....	....	....	36.5	7.5	4.5	2.5	.189
53-54 Syracuse	10	....	260	67	25	73	.342	....	....	....	17	26	.654	....	....	57	20	34	0	....	....	....	26.0	6.7	5.7	2.0	.323
54-55 Syracuse	11	....	355	127	44	122	.361	....	....	....	39	52	.750	....	....	89	35	41	0	....	....	....	32.3	11.5	8.1	3.2	.447
55-56 Syracuse	8	....	172	65	26	81	.321	....	....	....	13	14	.929	....	....	43	7	37	1	....	....	....	21.5	8.1	5.4	0.9	.291
56-57 Syracuse	5	....	83	31	12	30	.400	....	....	....	7	11	.636	....	....	21	5	18	0	....	....	....	16.6	6.2	4.2	1.0	.377
57-58 Syracuse	3	....	32	10	5	14	.357	....	....	....	0	0	.000	....	....	8	0	8	0	....	....	....	10.7	3.3	2.7	0.0	.199
58-59 Detroit	3	....	87	26	9	28	.321	....	....	....	8	8	1.000	....	....	18	7	12	0	....	....	....	29.0	8.7	6.0	2.3	.339
59-60 Detroit	2	....	53	17	6	24	.250	....	....	....	5	8	.625	....	....	9	3	11	1	....	....	....	26.5	8.5	4.5	1.5	.163
NBA Playoff Totals	44	....	1115	358	131	389	.337	....	....	....	96	129	.744	....	....	254	82	171	2	....	....	....	25.3	8.1	5.8	1.9	....

• LLOYD, Lewis
Lewis Kevin Lloyd

Born: Feb. 22, 1959. Philadelphia, PA, United States. Height: 6'6". Weight: 205 lbs. Drafted: 1981 College: Drake

YEAR TEAM	GP	GS	MIN	PTS	FGM	FGA	FG%	3PM	3PA	3P%	FTM	FTA	FT%	ORB	DRB	TRB	AST	PF	DQ	STL	BLK	TO	MPG	PPG	RPG	APG	PCM
81-82 Golden State	16	0	95	57	25	45	.556	0	0	.000	7	11	.636	9	7	16	6	20	0	5	1	14	5.9	3.6	1.0	0.4	.435
82-83 Golden State	73	24	1350	687	293	566	.518	1	4	.250	100	139	.719	77	183	260	130	109	0	61	31	117	18.5	9.4	3.6	1.8	.540
83-84 Houston	82	82	2578	1458	610	1182	.516	3	13	.231	235	298	.789	128	167	295	321	211	4	102	44	246	31.4	17.8	3.6	3.9	.513
84-85 Houston	82	58	2128	1077	457	869	.526	2	8	.250	161	220	.732	98	133	231	280	196	1	73	28	180	26.0	13.1	2.8	3.4	.477
85-86 Houston	82	82	2444	1386	592	1119	.529	3	15	.200	199	236	.843	155	169	324	300	216	0	102	24	197	29.8	16.9	4.0	3.7	.546
86-87 Houston	32	14	688	396	165	310	.532	1	7	.143	65	86	.756	13	35	48	90	69	0	19	5	51	21.5	12.4	1.5	2.8	.487
89-90 Philadelphia	2	0	10	2	1	2	.500	0	0	.000	0	0	.000	0	0	0	0	3	0	0	0	4	5.0	1.0	0.0	0.0	-.409
89-90 Houston	19	0	113	67	29	51	.569	0	0	.000	9	16	.563	8	10	18	11	9	0	3	0	15	5.9	3.5	0.9	0.6	.497
NBA Season Totals	388	260	9406	5130	2172	4144	.524	10	47	.213	776	1006	.771	488	704	1192	1138	833	5	365	133	824	24.2	13.2	3.1	2.9	....
84-85 Houston	5	5	174	86	38	77	.494	0	0	.000	10	14	.714	15	14	29	25	12	0	7	8	10	34.8	17.2	5.8	5.0	.578
85-86 Houston	20	20	589	281	116	241	.481	2	5	.400	47	58	.810	34	32	66	86	47	0	16	6	47	29.5	14.1	3.3	4.3	.455
NBA Playoff Totals	25	25	763	367	154	318	.484	2	5	.400	57	72	.792	49	46	95	111	59	0	23	14	57	30.5	14.7	3.8	4.4	....

• LLOYD, Scott
Scott G. Lloyd

Born: Dec. 19, 1952. Chicago, IL, United States. Height: 6'10". Weight: 230 lbs. Drafted: 1976 College: Arizona State

YEAR TEAM	GP	GS	MIN	PTS	FGM	FGA	FG%	3PM	3PA	3P%	FTM	FTA	FT%	ORB	DRB	TRB	AST	PF	DQ	STL	BLK	TO	MPG	PPG	RPG	APG	PCM
76-77 Milwaukee	69	....	1025	401	153	324	.472	....	....	....	95	126	.754	81	129	210	33	158	5	21	13	....	14.9	5.8	3.0	0.5	.381
77-78 Milwaukee	14	....	112	30	12	33	.364	....	....	....	6	10	.600	7	19	26	9	22	0	3	5	7	8.0	2.1	1.9	0.6	.304
77-78 Buffalo	56	....	566	179	68	160	.425	....	....	....	43	58	.741	45	74	119	35	83	1	11	9	34	10.1	3.2	2.1	0.6	.330
78-79 San Diego	5	....	31	0	0	2	.000	....	....	....	0	0	.000	1	2	3	0	6	0	1	0	8	6.2	0.0	0.6	0.0	-.261
78-79 Chicago	67	....	465	111	42	120	.350	....	....	....	27	47	.574	48	45	93	32	86	0	9	8	40	6.9	1.7	1.4	0.5	.197
80-81 Dallas	72	....	2186	637	245	547	.448	0	2	.000	147	205	.717	161	293	454	159	269	8	34	25	144	30.4	8.8	6.3	2.2	.330
81-82 Dallas	74	17	1047	287	108	285	.379	2	4	.500	69	91	.758	60	103	163	67	175	6	15	7	59	14.1	3.9	2.2	0.9	.212
82-83 Dallas	15	0	206	49	19	50	.380	0	1	.000	11	17	.647	19	27	46	21	24	0	6	6	6	13.7	3.3	3.1	1.4	.376
NBA Season Totals	372	17	5638	1694	647	1521	.425	2	7	.286	398	554	.718	422	692	1114	356	823	20	100	73	298	15.2	4.6	3.0	1.0	....

• LOCHMANN, Riney
Reinhold D. Lochmann

Born: May 26, 1944. Wichita, KS, United States. Height: 6'6". Weight: 215 lbs. Drafted: — College: Kansas

YEAR TEAM	GP	GS	MIN	PTS	FGM	FGA	FG%	3PM	3PA	3P%	FTM	FTA	FT%	ORB	DRB	TRB	AST	PF	DQ	STL	BLK	TO	MPG	PPG	RPG	APG	PCM
67-68 Dallas-A	63	....	808	266	108	285	.379	1	4	.250	49	79	.620	....	....	166	44	113	2	....	....	40	12.8	4.2	2.6	0.7	.308
68-69 Dallas-A	60	....	950	291	115	279	.412	1	4	.250	60	97	.619	75	129	204	59	138	4	....	....	50	15.8	4.9	3.4	1.0	.334
69-70 Dallas-A	47	....	447	174	73	166	.440	3	8	**.375**	25	45	.556	42	54	96	40	61	0	....	....	31	9.5	3.7	2.0	0.9	.419
ABA Season Totals	170	....	2205	731	296	730	.405	5	16	.313	134	221	.606	117	183	466	143	312	6	....	....	121	13.0	4.3	2.7	0.8	....
67-68 Dallas-A	5	....	33	7	2	6	.333	0	0	.000	3	3	1.000	....	....	3	0	5	0	....	....	0	6.6	1.4	0.6	0.0	.124
68-69 Dallas-A	3	....	18	6	3	8	.375	0	0	.000	0	0	.000	1	3	4	1	2	0	....	....	0	6.0	2.0	1.3	0.3	.301
ABA Playoff Totals	8	....	51	13	5	14	.357	0	0	.000	3	3	1.000	1	3	7	1	7	0	....	....	0	6.4	1.6	0.9	0.1	....

• LOCHMUELLER, Bob
Robert L. Lochmueller

Born: June 5, 1927.   Height: 6'5".   Weight: 185 lbs.   Drafted: —   College: Louisville

YEAR TEAM	GP	GS	MIN	PTS	FGM	FGA	FG%	3PM	3PA	3P%	FTM	FTA	FT%	ORB	DRB	TRB	AST	PF	DQ	STL	BLK	TO	MPG	PPG	RPG	APG	PCM
52-53 Syracuse	62	....	802	232	79	245	.322	....	....	....	74	122	.607	....	....	162	47	143	1	....	....	....	12.9	3.7	2.6	0.8	.274
NBA Season Totals	62	....	802	232	79	245	.322	....	....	....	74	122	.607	....	....	162	47	143	1	....	....	....	12.9	3.7	2.6	0.8	....
52-53 Syracuse	2	....	21	5	2	10	.200	....	....	....	1	4	.250	....	....	5	2	12	2	....	....	....	10.5	2.5	2.5	1.0	-.002
NBA Playoff Totals	2	....	21	5	2	10	.200	....	....	....	1	4	.250	....	....	5	2	12	2	....	....	....	10.5	2.5	2.5	1.0	....

• LOCK, Rob
Robert Alan Lock

Born: May 22, 1966. Reedley, CA, United States.   Height: 6'9".   Weight: 225 lbs.   Drafted: 1988   College: Kentucky

YEAR TEAM	GP	GS	MIN	PTS	FGM	FGA	FG%	3PM	3PA	3P%	FTM	FTA	FT%	ORB	DRB	TRB	AST	PF	DQ	STL	BLK	TO	MPG	PPG	RPG	APG	PCM
88-89 LA Clippers	20	0	110	30	9	32	.281	0	0	.000	12	15	.800	14	18	32	4	15	0	3	4	14	5.5	1.5	1.6	0.2	.252
NBA Season Totals	20	0	110	30	9	32	.281	0	0	.000	12	15	.800	14	18	32	4	15	0	3	4	14	5.5	1.5	1.6	0.2	....

• LOCKHART, Darrell
Darrell Lockhart

Born: Sept. 14, 1960. Thomaston, GA, United States.   Height: 6'9".   Weight: 245 lbs.   Drafted: 1983   College: Auburn

YEAR TEAM	GP	GS	MIN	PTS	FGM	FGA	FG%	3PM	3PA	3P%	FTM	FTA	FT%	ORB	DRB	TRB	AST	PF	DQ	STL	BLK	TO	MPG	PPG	RPG	APG	PCM
83-84 San Antonio	2	0	14	4	2	2	1.000	0	0	.000	0	0	.000	0	3	3	0	5	0	0	0	2	7.0	2.0	1.5	0.0	.186
NBA Season Totals	2	0	14	4	2	2	1.000	0	0	.000	0	0	.000	0	3	3	0	5	0	0	0	2	7.0	2.0	1.5	0.0	....

• LOCKHART, Ian
Ian DeWitt Lockhart

Born: June 25, 1967. Nassau, Bahamas.   Height: 6'8".   Weight: 240 lbs.   Drafted: —   College: Tennessee

YEAR TEAM	GP	GS	MIN	PTS	FGM	FGA	FG%	3PM	3PA	3P%	FTM	FTA	FT%	ORB	DRB	TRB	AST	PF	DQ	STL	BLK	TO	MPG	PPG	RPG	APG	PCM
90-91 Phoenix	1	0	2	4	1	1	1.000	0	0	.000	2	2	1.000	0	0	0	0	0	0	0	0	0	2.0	4.0	0.0	0.0	2.000
NBA Season Totals	1	0	2	4	1	1	1.000	0	0	.000	2	2	1.000	0	0	0	0	0	0	0	0	0	2.0	4.0	0.0	0.0	....

• LODER, Kevin
Kevin Allen Loder

Born: Mar. 15, 1959. Cassopolis, MI, United States.   Height: 6'6".   Weight: 205 lbs.   Drafted: 1981   College: Alabama State

YEAR TEAM	GP	GS	MIN	PTS	FGM	FGA	FG%	3PM	3PA	3P%	FTM	FTA	FT%	ORB	DRB	TRB	AST	PF	DQ	STL	BLK	TO	MPG	PPG	RPG	APG	PCM
81-82 Kansas City	71	13	1139	493	208	448	.464	0	11	.000	77	107	.720	69	126	195	88	147	0	35	30	71	16.0	6.9	2.7	1.2	.403
82-83 Kansas City	66	13	818	334	138	300	.460	5	9	.556	53	80	.663	37	88	125	72	98	0	29	8	66	12.4	5.1	1.9	1.1	.363
83-84 Kansas City	10	0	133	48	19	43	.442	1	3	.333	9	13	.692	7	11	18	14	15	0	3	5	11	13.3	4.8	1.8	1.4	.344
83-84 San Diego	1	0	4	0	0	0	.000	0	0	.000	0	0	.000	0	0	0	0	1	0	0	0	0	4.0	0.0	0.0	0.0	-.116
NBA Season Totals	148	26	2094	875	365	791	.461	6	23	.261	139	200	.695	113	225	338	174	261	0	67	43	148	14.1	5.9	2.3	1.2	....

• LOFGRAN, Don
Donald Lofgran

Born: Nov. 18, 1928. Oakland, CA, United States. Died: June17, 1976.   Height: 6'5".   Weight: 200 lbs.   Drafted: 1950   College: San Francisco

YEAR TEAM	GP	GS	MIN	PTS	FGM	FGA	FG%	3PM	3PA	3P%	FTM	FTA	FT%	ORB	DRB	TRB	AST	PF	DQ	STL	BLK	TO	MPG	PPG	RPG	APG	PCM
50-51 Syr/Ind	61	....	....	237	79	270	.293	....	....	....	79	127	.622	....	....	157	36	132	4	....	....	....	....	3.9	2.6	0.6	....
51-52 Indianapolis	63	....	1254	454	149	417	.357	....	....	....	156	219	.712	....	....	257	48	147	3	....	....	....	19.9	7.2	4.1	0.8	.346
52-53 Philadelphia	64	....	1788	472	173	525	.330	....	....	....	126	173	.728	....	....	339	106	178	6	....	....	....	27.9	7.4	5.3	1.7	.289
53-54 Milwaukee	21	....	380	102	35	112	.313	....	....	....	32	49	.653	....	....	64	26	34	0	....	....	....	18.1	4.9	3.0	1.2	.285
NBA Season Totals	209	....	3422	1265	436	1324	.329	....	....	....	393	568	.692	....	....	817	216	491	13	....	....	....	16.4	6.1	3.9	1.0	....
50-51 Indianapolis	1	....	....	5	2	6	.333	....	....	....	1	1	1.000	....	....	1	0	3	0	....	....	....	....	5.0	1.0	0.0	....
51-52 Indianapolis	2	....	10	0	0	3	.000	....	....	....	0	0	.000	....	....	0	0	3	0	....	....	....	5.0	0.0	0.0	0.0	-.320
NBA Playoff Totals	3	....	10	5	2	9	.222	....	....	....	1	1	1.000	....	....	1	0	6	0	....	....	....	3.3	1.7	0.3	0.0	....

• LOGAN, Henry
Charles Lee Logan

Born: 331224, 1946. Asheville, NC, United States. Died: Dec.1987.   Height: 6'   Weight: 180 lbs.   Drafted: 1968   College: Western Carolina

YEAR TEAM	GP	GS	MIN	PTS	FGM	FGA	FG%	3PM	3PA	3P%	FTM	FTA	FT%	ORB	DRB	TRB	AST	PF	DQ	STL	BLK	TO	MPG	PPG	RPG	APG	PCM
68-69 Oakland-A	76	....	1751	947	339	694	.488	1	4	.250	268	382	.702	105	182	287	185	226	4	....	....	188	23.0	12.5	3.8	2.4	.545
69-70 Washington-A	32	....	659	311	110	269	.409	0	3	.000	91	127	.717	40	49	89	59	93	3	....	....	63	20.6	9.7	2.8	1.8	.399
ABA Season Totals	108	....	2410	1258	449	963	.466	1	7	.143	359	509	.705	145	231	376	244	319	7	....	....	251	22.3	11.6	3.5	2.3	....
68-69 Oakland-A	16	....	380	217	75	176	.426	0	0	.000	67	99	.677	....	....	40	34	50	3	....	....	36	23.8	13.6	2.5	2.1	.443
70-71 Virginia-A	1	....	1	1	0	0	.000	0	0	.000	1	2	.500	0	0	0	0	0	0	....	....	0	1.0	1.0	0.0	0.0	.600
ABA Playoff Totals	17	....	381	218	75	176	.426	0	0	.000	68	101	.673	0	0	40	34	50	3	....	....	36	22.4	12.8	2.4	2.0	....

• LOGAN, John
John Arnold Logan

Born: Jan. 1, 1921. Richmond, IN, United States. Died: Sept.16, 1977.   Height: 6'2".   Weight: 175 lbs.   Drafted: —   College: Indiana

YEAR TEAM	GP	GS	MIN	PTS	FGM	FGA	FG%	3PM	3PA	3P%	FTM	FTA	FT%	ORB	DRB	TRB	AST	PF	DQ	STL	BLK	TO	MPG	PPG	RPG	APG	PCM
46-47 St. Louis	61	....	....	770	290	1043	.278	....	....	....	190	254	.748	....	....	....	78	136	....	....	....	....	....	12.6	....	1.3	....
47-48 St. Louis	48	....	....	644	221	734	.301	....	....	....	202	272	.743	....	....	....	62	141	....	....	....	....	....	13.4	....	1.3	....
48-49 St. Louis	57	....	....	803	282	816	.346	....	....	....	239	302	.791	....	....	....	276	191	....	....	....	....	....	14.1	....	4.8	....
49-50 St. Louis	62	....	....	755	251	759	.331	....	....	....	253	323	.783	....	....	....	240	206	....	....	....	....	....	12.2	....	3.9	....
50-51 Tri-Cities	29	....	....	224	81	257	.315	....	....	....	62	83	.747	....	....	134	127	66	2	....	....	....	....	7.7	4.6	4.4	....
NBA Season Totals	257	....	....	3196	1125	3609	.312	....	....	....	946	1234	.767	....	....	134	783	740	2	....	....	....	....	12.4	0.5	3.0	....
46-47 St. Louis	3	....	....	31	10	45	.222	....	....	....	11	15	.733	....	....	....	3	7	....	....	....	....	....	10.3	....	1.0	....
47-48 St. Louis	5	....	....	56	17	55	.309	....	....	....	22	28	.786	....	....	....	8	19	....	....	....	....	....	11.2	....	1.6	....
48-49 St. Louis	2	....	....	20	7	23	.304	....	....	....	6	9	.667	....	....	....	8	10	....	....	....	....	....	10.0	....	4.0	....
NBA Playoff Totals	10	....	....	107	34	123	.276	....	....	....	39	52	.750	....	....	....	19	36	....	....	....	....	....	10.7	....	1.9	....

YEAR TEAM	GP	GS	MIN	PTS	FGM	FGA	FG%	3PM	3PA	3P%	FTM	FTA	FT%	ORB	DRB	TRB	AST	PF	DQ	STL	BLK	TO	MPG	PPG	RPG	APG	PCM

• LOHAUS, Brad

Del Allen Lohaus

Born: Sept. 29, 1964. New Ulm, MN, United States. Height: 6'11". Weight: 230 lbs. Drafted: 1987 College: Iowa

YEAR TEAM	GP	GS	MIN	PTS	FGM	FGA	FG%	3PM	3PA	3P%	FTM	FTA	FT%	ORB	DRB	TRB	AST	PF	DQ	STL	BLK	TO	MPG	PPG	RPG	APG	PCM
87-88 Boston	70	4	718	297	122	246	.496	3	13	.231	50	62	.806	46	92	138	49	123	1	20	41	56	10.3	4.2	2.0	0.7	.424
88-89 Boston	48	15	738	269	117	270	.433	0	4	.000	35	46	.761	47	95	142	49	101	1	21	26	48	15.4	5.6	3.0	1.0	.350
88-89 Sacramento	29	10	476	233	93	216	.431	1	7	.143	46	57	.807	37	77	114	17	60	0	9	30	29	16.4	8.0	3.9	0.6	.460
89-90 Minnesota	28	24	590	210	94	202	.465	1	16	.063	21	26	.808	21	89	110	62	66	1	14	22	45	21.1	7.5	3.9	2.2	.400
89-90 Milwaukee	52	17	1353	522	211	461	.458	46	121	.380	54	77	.701	77	211	288	106	145	2	44	66	62	26.0	10.0	5.5	2.0	.470
90-91 Milwaukee	81	3	1219	428	179	415	.431	33	119	.277	37	54	.685	59	158	217	75	170	3	50	74	57	15.0	5.3	2.7	0.9	.382
91-92 Milwaukee	70	8	1081	408	162	360	.450	57	144	.396	27	41	.659	65	184	249	74	144	5	40	71	49	15.4	5.8	3.6	1.1	.480
92-93 Milwaukee	80	24	1766	724	283	614	.461	85	230	.370	73	101	.723	59	217	276	127	178	1	47	74	96	22.1	9.1	3.5	1.6	.416
93-94 Milwaukee	67	2	962	270	102	281	.363	46	134	.343	20	29	.690	33	117	150	62	142	3	30	55	60	14.4	4.0	2.2	0.9	.275
94-95 Miami	61	1	730	267	97	231	.420	63	155	.406	10	15	.667	28	74	102	43	85	2	20	25	31	12.0	4.4	1.7	0.7	.347
95-96 San Antonio	32	1	273	107	39	96	.406	27	65	.415	2	3	.667	5	28	33	17	34	0	2	7	10	8.5	3.3	1.0	0.5	.312
95-96 New York	23	7	325	90	32	79	.405	24	57	.421	2	2	1.000	2	29	31	27	36	0	8	10	12	14.1	3.9	1.3	1.2	.284
96-97 Toronto	6	0	45	10	4	15	.267	2	7	.286	0	0	.000	1	6	7	1	6	0	1	0	1	7.5	1.7	1.2	0.2	.101
97-98 San Antonio	9	0	102	19	7	21	.333	4	14	.286	1	3	.333	3	9	12	5	10	0	1	2	3	11.3	2.1	1.3	0.6	.168
NBA Season Totals	656	116	10378	3854	1542	3507	.440	392	1086	.361	378	516	.733	483	1386	1869	714	1300	19	307	503	559	15.8	5.9	2.8	1.1	....
87-88 Boston	9	0	26	16	8	11	.727	0	2	.000	0	0	.000	1	3	4	0	4	0	0	1	1	2.9	1.8	0.4	0.0	.580
89-90 Milwaukee	4	4	147	38	16	40	.400	6	16	.375	0	0	.000	4	23	27	5	17	1	8	9	9	36.8	9.5	6.8	1.3	.311
90-91 Milwaukee	3	0	41	14	5	16	.313	3	8	.375	1	2	.500	4	5	9	1	6	0	0	0	3	13.7	4.7	3.0	0.3	.174
97-98 San Antonio	4	0	10	0	0	1	.000	0	0	.000	0	0	.000	0	2	2	1	0	0	1	0	0	2.5	0.0	0.5	0.3	.292
NBA Playoff Totals	20	4	224	68	29	68	.426	9	26	.346	1	2	.500	9	33	42	7	27	1	9	10	13	11.2	3.4	2.1	0.4	....

• LONG, Art

Arthur Donnell Long

Born: Oct. 1, 1972. Rochester, NY, United States. Height: 6'9". Weight: 250 lbs. Drafted: — College: Cincinnati

YEAR TEAM	GP	GS	MIN	PTS	FGM	FGA	FG%	3PM	3PA	3P%	FTM	FTA	FT%	ORB	DRB	TRB	AST	PF	DQ	STL	BLK	TO	MPG	PPG	RPG	APG	PCM
00-01 Sacramento	9	0	20	0	0	4	.000	0	0	.000	0	2	.000	2	6	8	1	5	0	0	3	2	2.2	0.0	0.9	0.1	.122
01-02 Seattle	63	27	989	285	120	244	.492	0	0	.000	45	85	.529	107	144	251	41	180	4	22	28	63	15.7	4.5	4.0	0.7	.337
02-03 Philadelphia	19	0	131	40	19	50	.380	1	1	1.000	1	5	.200	13	27	40	2	22	0	2	8	9	6.9	2.1	2.1	0.1	.301
02-03 Toronto	7	0	80	20	9	25	.360	1	2	.500	1	5	.200	8	12	20	4	13	0	3	3	11	11.4	2.9	2.9	0.6	.197
NBA Season Totals	98	27	1220	345	148	323	.458	2	3	.667	47	97	.485	130	189	319	48	220	4	27	42	85	12.4	3.5	3.3	0.5	....

• LONG, Grant

Grant Andrew Long

Born: Mar. 12, 1966. Wayne, MI, United States. Height: 6'8". Weight: 225 lbs. Drafted: 1988 College: Eastern Michigan

YEAR TEAM	GP	GS	MIN	PTS	FGM	FGA	FG%	3PM	3PA	3P%	FTM	FTA	FT%	ORB	DRB	TRB	AST	PF	DQ	STL	BLK	TO	MPG	PPG	RPG	APG	PCM
88-89 Miami	82	73	2435	976	336	692	.486	0	5	.000	304	406	.749	240	306	546	149	**337**	13	122	48	205	29.7	11.9	6.7	1.8	.442
89-90 Miami	81	31	1856	686	257	532	.483	0	3	.000	172	241	.714	156	246	402	96	300	**11**	91	38	138	22.9	8.5	5.0	1.2	.391
90-91 Miami	80	66	2514	734	276	561	.492	1	6	.167	181	230	.787	225	343	568	176	295	10	119	43	152	31.4	9.2	7.1	2.2	.412
91-92 Miami	82	82	3063	1212	440	890	.494	6	22	.273	326	404	.807	259	432	691	225	248	2	139	40	189	37.4	14.8	8.4	2.7	.495
92-93 Miami	76	62	2730	1088	409	860	.476	8	30	.267	262	342	.766	197	366	563	181	262	8	105	31	137	35.9	14.3	7.4	2.4	.449
93-94 Miami	69	59	2201	788	300	672	.446	1	6	.167	187	238	.786	190	305	495	170	244	5	89	26	124	31.9	11.4	7.2	2.5	.428
94-95 Miami	2	2	62	16	5	12	.417	0	0	.000	6	10	.600	1	10	11	4	11	1	2	0	4	31.0	8.0	5.5	2.0	.243
94-95 Atlanta	79	77	2579	923	337	704	.479	11	31	.355	238	315	.756	190	405	595	127	232	3	107	34	150	32.6	11.7	7.5	1.6	.434
95-96 Atlanta	82	82	3008	1078	395	838	.471	31	86	.360	257	337	.763	248	540	788	183	233	3	108	34	156	36.7	13.1	9.6	2.2	.477
96-97 Detroit	65	24	1166	326	123	275	.447	17	47	.362	63	84	.750	88	134	222	39	106	0	43	6	46	17.9	5.0	3.4	0.6	.323
97-98 Detroit	40	17	739	141	50	117	.427	0	4	.000	41	57	.719	57	93	150	25	91	2	29	12	24	18.5	3.5	3.8	0.6	.285
98-99 Atlanta	50	13	1380	489	151	359	.421	3	18	.167	184	235	.783	100	196	296	53	143	0	57	16	74	27.6	9.8	5.9	1.1	.391
99-00 Vancouver	42	1	920	203	74	167	.443	0	4	.000	55	71	.775	86	148	234	43	108	0	45	10	49	21.9	4.8	5.6	1.0	.356
00-01 Vancouver	66	27	1507	396	140	319	.439	4	15	.267	112	157	.713	76	198	274	83	160	2	72	15	62	22.8	6.0	4.2	1.3	.334
01-02 Memphis	66	56	1868	417	164	385	.426	3	17	.176	86	123	.699	31	200	231	136	123	0	63	12	103	28.3	6.3	3.5	2.1	.255
02-03 Boston	41	1	488	72	27	70	.386	0	3	.000	18	23	.783	24	59	83	25	62	0	9	1	19	11.9	1.8	2.0	0.6	.199
NBA Season Totals	1003	673	28516	9545	3484	7453	.467	85	297	.286	2492	3273	.761	2168	3981	6149	1715	2955	59	1200	366	1632	28.4	9.5	6.1	1.7	....
91-92 Miami	3	3	120	37	15	36	.417	0	4	.000	7	10	.700	7	8	15	8	11	0	5	0	5	40.0	12.3	5.0	2.7	.279
93-94 Miami	4	2	110	49	14	36	.389	0	0	.000	21	27	.778	10	8	18	7	16	1	3	2	10	27.5	12.3	4.5	1.8	.348
94-95 Atlanta	3	3	110	41	14	28	.500	0	1	.000	13	18	.722	13	21	34	4	11	0	4	1	8	36.7	13.7	11.3	1.3	.488
95-96 Atlanta	10	10	362	114	44	111	.396	6	24	.250	20	25	.800	30	56	86	28	27	1	7	3	19	36.2	11.4	8.6	2.8	.381
96-97 Detroit	5	0	86	25	8	18	.444	0	2	.000	9	11	.818	4	7	11	3	11	0	4	0	0	17.2	5.0	2.2	0.6	.312
98-99 Atlanta	9	9	358	105	36	88	.409	1	4	.250	32	44	.727	28	46	74	8	27	0	18	4	23	39.8	11.7	8.2	0.9	.322
02-03 Boston	8	0	34	2	1	4	.250	0	0	.000	0	0	.000	3	2	5	1	1	0	0	0	1	4.3	0.3	0.6	0.1	.104
NBA Playoff Totals	42	27	1180	373	132	321	.411	7	35	.200	102	135	.756	95	148	243	59	104	2	41	10	66	28.1	8.9	5.8	1.4	....

• LONG, John

John Eddie Long

Born: Aug. 28, 1956. Romulus, MI, United States. Height: 6'5". Weight: 195 lbs. Drafted: 1978 College: Detroit

YEAR TEAM	GP	GS	MIN	PTS	FGM	FGA	FG%	3PM	3PA	3P%	FTM	FTA	FT%	ORB	DRB	TRB	AST	PF	DQ	STL	BLK	TO	MPG	PPG	RPG	APG	PCM
78-79 Detroit	82	....	2498	1319	581	1240	.469	....	....	....	157	190	.826	127	139	266	121	224	1	102	19	139	30.5	16.1	3.2	1.5	.387
79-80 Detroit	69	....	2364	1337	588	1164	.505	1	12	.083	160	194	.825	152	185	337	206	221	4	129	26	207	34.3	19.4	4.9	3.0	.501
80-81 Detroit	59	....	1750	1044	441	957	.461	2	11	.182	160	184	.870	95	102	197	106	164	3	95	22	153	29.7	17.7	3.3	1.8	.429
81-82 Detroit	69	66	2211	1514	637	1294	.492	2	15	.133	238	275	.865	95	162	257	148	173	0	65	25	166	32.0	21.9	3.7	2.1	.515
82-83 Detroit	70	30	1485	737	312	692	.451	2	7	.286	111	146	.760	56	124	180	105	130	1	44	12	147	21.2	10.5	2.6	1.5	.347
83-84 Detroit	82	82	2514	1334	545	1155	.472	1	5	.200	243	275	.884	139	150	289	205	199	1	93	18	139	30.7	16.3	3.5	2.5	.446
84-85 Detroit	66	55	1820	973	431	885	.487	5	15	.333	106	123	.862	81	109	190	130	139	0	71	14	99	27.6	14.7	2.9	2.0	.429
85-86 Detroit	62	30	1176	620	264	548	.482	3	16	.188	89	104	.856	47	51	98	82	92	0	41	13	62	19.0	10.0	1.6	1.3	.406
86-87 Indiana	80	68	2265	1218	490	1170	.419	19	67	.284	219	246	.890	75	142	217	258	167	1	96	8	152	28.3	15.2	2.7	3.2	.410
87-88 Indiana	81	81	2022	1034	417	879	.474	34	77	.442	166	183	.907	72	157	229	173	164	1	84	11	130	25.0	12.8	2.8	2.1	.438
88-89 Indiana	44	1	767	323	128	319	.401	8	20	.400	59	63	.937	16	50	66	65	68	1	29	1	48	17.4	7.3	1.5	1.5	.295
88-89 Detroit	24	0	152	49	19	40	.475	0	0	.000	11	13	.846	2	9	11	15	16	0	0	2	10	6.3	2.0	0.5	0.6	.263

YEAR	TEAM	GP	GS	MIN	PTS	FGM	FGA	FG%	3PM	3PA	3P%	FTM	FTA	FT%	ORB	DRB	TRB	AST	PF	DQ	STL	BLK	TO	MPG	PPG	RPG	APG	PCM
89-90	Atlanta	48	19	1030	404	174	384	.453	10	29	.345	46	55	.836	26	57	83	85	66	0	45	5	77	21.5	8.4	1.7	1.8	.306
90-91	Detroit	25	0	256	96	35	85	.412	2	6	.333	24	25	.960	9	23	32	18	17	0	9	2	15	10.2	3.8	1.3	0.7	.337
96-97	Toronto	32	0	370	129	46	117	.393	12	34	.353	25	28	.893	6	34	40	21	28	0	9	2	26	11.6	4.0	1.3	0.7	.254
NBA Season Totals		893	432	22680	12131	5108	10929	.467	101	314	.322	1814	2104	.862	998	1494	2492	1738	1868	13	912	180	1570	25.4	13.6	2.8	1.9	....
83-84	Detroit	5	5	149	55	20	55	.364	0	1	.000	15	15	1.000	7	4	11	2	15	0	7	0	10	29.8	11.0	2.2	0.4	.168
84-85	Detroit	9	9	255	112	48	105	.457	1	4	.250	15	15	1.000	10	7	17	13	22	0	14	2	11	28.3	12.4	1.9	1.4	.326
85-86	Detroit	1	0	13	7	2	5	.400	0	0	.000	3	3	1.000	0	1	1	0	1	0	1	0	2	13.0	7.0	1.0	0.0	.288
86-87	Indiana	4	4	109	44	16	52	.308	1	6	.167	11	13	.846	2	4	6	9	16	0	6	0	5	27.3	11.0	1.5	2.3	.167
88-89	Detroit	4	0	8	5	1	1	1.000	0	0	.000	3	3	1.000	0	0	0	0	0	0	0	0	0	2.0	1.3	0.0	0.0	.625
NBA Playoff Totals		23	18	534	223	87	218	.399	2	11	.182	47	49	.959	19	16	35	24	54	0	28	2	28	23.2	9.7	1.5	1.0	....

• LONG, Paul

Gene Richard Long

Born: Feb. 8, 1944. Louisville, KY, United States.　Height: 6'2".　Weight: 180 lbs.　Drafted: 1967　College: Virginia Tech

YEAR	TEAM	GP	GS	MIN	PTS	FGM	FGA	FG%	3PM	3PA	3P%	FTM	FTA	FT%	ORB	DRB	TRB	AST	PF	DQ	STL	BLK	TO	MPG	PPG	RPG	APG	PCM
67-68	Detroit	16	....	93	57	23	51	.451	....	....	....	11	15	.733	....	....	15	12	13	0	....	....	....	5.8	3.6	0.9	0.8	.584
68-69	Kentucky-A	9	....	82	35	9	40	.225	0	0	.000	17	21	.810	5	4	9	12	21	0	....	....	15	9.1	3.9	1.0	1.3	.233
69-70	Detroit	25	....	130	83	28	62	.452	....	....	....	27	38	.711	....	....	11	17	22	0	....	....	....	5.2	3.3	0.4	0.7	.518
70-71	Buffalo	30	....	213	134	57	120	.475	....	....	....	20	24	.833	....	....	31	25	23	0	....	....	....	7.1	4.5	1.0	0.8	.579
NBA Season Totals		71	....	436	274	108	233	.464	....	....	....	58	77	.753	....	....	57	54	58	0	....	....	....	6.1	3.9	0.8	0.8	....
ABA Season Totals		9	....	82	35	9	40	.225	0	0	.000	17	21	.810	5	4	9	12	21	0	....	....	15	9.1	3.9	1.0	1.3	....
Career Totals		80	....	518	309	117	273	.429	0	0	.000	75	98	.765	5	4	66	66	79	0	....	....	15	6.5	3.9	0.8	0.8	....
67-68	Detroit	1	....	4	6	3	3	1.000	....	....	....	0	0	.000	....	....	0	1	1	0	....	....	....	4.0	6.0	0.0	1.0	1.701
NBA Playoff Totals		1	....	4	6	3	3	1.000	....	....	....	0	0	.000	....	....	0	1	1	0	....	....	....	4.0	6.0	0.0	1.0	....

• LONG, Willie

Joseph Long

Born: Mar. 1, 1950. Fort Wayne, IN, United States.　Height: 6'8".　Weight: 225 lbs.　Drafted: 1971　College: New Mexico

YEAR	TEAM	GP	GS	MIN	PTS	FGM	FGA	FG%	3PM	3PA	3P%	FTM	FTA	FT%	ORB	DRB	TRB	AST	PF	DQ	STL	BLK	TO	MPG	PPG	RPG	APG	PCM
71-72	Florida-A	75	....	1925	878	336	761	.442	0	1	.000	206	291	.708	157	356	513	66	215	3	....	....	137	25.7	11.7	6.8	0.9	.466
72-73	Denver-A	56	....	1050	504	183	458	.400	0	2	.000	138	177	.780	99	191	290	43	147	3	....	....	95	18.8	9.0	5.2	0.8	.458
73-74	Denver-A	82	....	2058	1036	383	925	.414	0	2	.000	270	325	.831	197	269	466	100	244	....	54	13	157	25.1	12.6	5.7	1.2	.465
ABA Season Totals		213	....	5033	2418	902	2144	.421	0	5	.000	614	793	.774	453	816	1269	209	606	6	54	13	389	23.6	11.4	6.0	1.0	....
71-72	Florida-A	4	....	156	66	24	57	.421	0	0	.000	18	25	.720	14	26	40	4	16	....	....	....	9	39.0	16.5	10.0	1.0	.426
72-73	Denver-A	4	....	53	15	5	20	.250	0	0	.000	5	6	.833	4	5	9	1	13	1	....	....	11	13.3	3.8	2.3	0.3	.083
ABA Playoff Totals		8	....	209	81	29	77	.377	0	0	.000	23	31	.742	18	31	49	5	29	1	....	....	20	26.1	10.1	6.1	0.6	....

• LONGLEY, Luc

Sam James Longley

Born: Jan. 19, 1969. Melbourne, Australia.　Height: 7'2".　Weight: 265 lbs.　Drafted: 1991　College: New Mexico

YEAR	TEAM	GP	GS	MIN	PTS	FGM	FGA	FG%	3PM	3PA	3P%	FTM	FTA	FT%	ORB	DRB	TRB	AST	PF	DQ	STL	BLK	TO	MPG	PPG	RPG	APG	PCM
91-92	Minnesota	66	3	991	281	114	249	.458	0	0	.000	53	80	.663	67	190	257	53	157	0	35	64	86	15.0	4.3	3.9	0.8	.381
92-93	Minnesota	55	55	1045	319	133	292	.455	0	0	.000	53	74	.716	71	169	240	51	169	4	47	77	88	19.0	5.8	4.4	0.9	.377
93-94	Minnesota	49	29	989	324	134	289	.464	0	1	.000	56	80	.700	87	208	295	46	131	1	35	58	78	20.2	6.6	6.0	0.9	.450
93-94	Chicago	27	17	513	204	85	176	.483	0	0	.000	34	45	.756	42	96	138	63	85	2	10	21	41	19.0	7.6	5.1	2.3	.511
94-95	Chicago	55	0	1001	358	135	302	.447	0	2	.000	88	107	.822	82	181	263	73	177	5	24	45	88	18.2	6.5	4.8	1.3	.415
95-96	Chicago	62	62	1641	564	242	502	.482	0	0	.000	80	103	.777	104	214	318	119	223	4	22	84	112	26.5	9.1	5.1	1.9	.380
96-97	Chicago	59	59	1472	537	221	485	.456	0	2	.000	95	120	.792	121	211	332	141	191	5	23	66	112	24.9	9.1	5.6	2.4	.427
97-98	Chicago	58	58	1703	663	277	609	.455	0	0	.000	109	148	.736	113	228	341	161	206	7	34	62	128	29.4	11.4	5.9	2.8	.414
98-99	Phoenix	39	39	933	339	140	290	.483	0	0	.000	59	76	.776	59	162	221	45	119	0	23	21	53	23.9	8.7	5.7	1.2	.411
99-00	Phoenix	72	68	1417	452	186	399	.466	0	0	.000	80	97	.825	100	223	323	77	221	1	22	42	136	19.7	6.3	4.5	1.1	.326
00-01	New York	25	2	301	49	18	54	.333	0	0	.000	13	17	.765	26	40	66	7	51	0	3	9	22	12.0	2.0	2.6	0.3	.166
NBA Season Totals		567	362	12006	4090	1685	3647	.462	0	5	.000	720	947	.760	872	1922	2794	836	1730	29	278	549	944	21.2	7.2	4.9	1.5	....
93-94	Chicago	10	2	170	63	25	50	.500	0	0	.000	13	18	.722	13	32	45	18	38	0	6	8	21	17.0	6.3	4.5	1.8	.439
94-95	Chicago	10	8	204	56	24	50	.480	0	0	.000	8	10	.800	6	26	32	11	41	1	7	5	10	20.4	5.6	3.2	1.1	.270
95-96	Chicago	18	18	439	150	61	130	.469	0	0	.000	28	37	.757	34	48	82	28	83	4	7	25	38	24.4	8.3	4.6	1.6	.326
96-97	Chicago	19	19	432	124	57	104	.548	0	0	.000	10	26	.385	39	45	84	35	65	0	7	16	28	22.7	6.5	4.4	1.8	.355
97-98	Chicago	18	16	456	142	54	120	.450	0	0	.000	34	39	.872	34	56	90	35	73	2	12	15	36	25.3	7.9	5.0	1.9	.347
98-99	Phoenix	3	2	51	4	2	12	.167	0	0	.000	0	0	.000	2	7	9	1	2	0	3	0	2	17.0	1.3	3.0	0.3	.083
99-00	Phoenix	9	9	162	38	18	51	.353	0	0	.000	2	3	.667	12	18	30	8	36	1	4	4	10	18.0	4.2	3.3	0.9	.157
NBA Playoff Totals		87	74	1914	577	241	517	.466	0	0	.000	95	133	.714	140	232	372	136	338	8	46	73	145	22.0	6.6	4.3	1.6	....

• LONSDORF, Charles

Charles (Slim) Lonsdorf

Born: Mar. 22, 1905. Died: Dec.1987.　Height: 6'3".　Weight: 175 lbs.　Drafted: —　College: Marquette

YEAR	TEAM	GP	GS	MIN	PTS	FGM	FGA	FG%	3PM	3PA	3P%	FTM	FTA	FT%	ORB	DRB	TRB	AST	PF	DQ	STL	BLK	TO	MPG	PPG	RPG	APG	PCM
38-39	Sheboygan-N	17	....	....	20	5	....	....	....	....	....	10	....	....	....	....	....	....	....	....	....	....	....	....	1.2	....	....	....
NBL Season Totals		17	....	....	20	5	....	....	....	....	....	10	....	....	....	....	....	....	....	....	....	....	....	....	1.2	....	....	....

• LOPEZ, Felipe

Luis Felipe Lopez

Born: Dec. 19, 1974. Santo Domingo, Dominican Rep..　Height: 6'5".　Weight: 199 lbs.　Drafted: 1998　College: St. John's (NY)

YEAR	TEAM	GP	GS	MIN	PTS	FGM	FGA	FG%	3PM	3PA	3P%	FTM	FTA	FT%	ORB	DRB	TRB	AST	PF	DQ	STL	BLK	TO	MPG	PPG	RPG	APG	PCM
98-99	Vancouver	47	32	1218	437	169	379	.446	12	44	.273	87	135	.644	69	97	166	62	128	0	49	14	82	25.9	9.3	3.5	1.3	.305
97-98	Vancouver	65	0	781	292	111	261	.425	3	18	.167	67	109	.615	59	65	124	44	94	0	32	17	53	12.0	4.5	1.9	0.7	.321
00-01	Washington	47	38	1108	380	142	326	.436	6	29	.207	90	123	.732	30	130	160	73	110	0	41	18	56	23.6	8.1	3.4	1.6	.341
00-01	Minnesota	23	10	457	170	69	152	.454	13	23	.565	19	33	.576	25	49	74	34	46	0	21	12	27	19.9	7.4	3.2	1.5	.389
01-02	Minnesota	67	0	581	169	59	156	.378	14	33	.424	37	55	.673	29	51	80	39	73	0	18	1	36	8.7	2.5	1.2	0.6	.240
NBA Season Totals		249	80	4145	1448	550	1274	.432	48	147	.327	300	455	.659	212	392	604	252	451	0	161	62	254	16.6	5.8	2.4	1.0	....

YEAR	TEAM	GP	GS	MIN	PTS	FGM	FGA	FG%	3PM	3PA	3P%	FTM	FTA	FT%	ORB	DRB	TRB	AST	PF	DQ	STL	BLK	TO	MPG	PPG	RPG	APG	PCM
00-01	Minnesota	4	0	55	17	7	22	.318	1	5	.200	2	3	.667	4	7	11	5	5	0	4	0	2	13.8	4.3	2.8	1.3	.328
01-02	Minnesota	3	0	30	4	1	4	.250	1	2	.500	1	2	.500	1	0	1	1	6	0	1	0	1	10.0	1.3	0.3	0.3	.004
NBA Playoff Totals		**7**	**0**	**85**	**21**	**8**	**26**	**.308**	**2**	**7**	**.286**	**3**	**5**	**.600**	**5**	**7**	**12**	**6**	**11**	**0**	**5**	**0**	**3**	**12.1**	**3.0**	**1.7**	**0.9**	**....**

• LORANGER, Del

Del Loranger

Born: 1920. Height: 6'3". Weight: 175 lbs. Drafted: — College: Western Michigan

YEAR	TEAM	GP	GS	MIN	PTS	FGM	FGA	FG%	3PM	3PA	3P%	FTM	FTA	FT%	ORB	DRB	TRB	AST	PF	DQ	STL	BLK	TO	MPG	PPG	RPG	APG	PCM
46-47	Detroit-N	27	....	....	233	94	....	....	....	....	....	45	71	.634	....	....	....	....	71	....	....	....	....	....	8.6	....	....	....
47-48	Indianapolis-N	1	....	....	0	0	....	....	....	....	....	0	0	.000	....	....	....	....	....	....	....	....	....	....	0.0	....	....	....
48-49	Detroit-N	16	....	....	64	20	....	....	....	....	....	24	35	.686	....	....	....	....	....	....	....	....	....	....	4.0	....	....	....
NBL Season Totals		**44**	**....**	**....**	**297**	**114**	**....**	**....**	**....**	**....**	**....**	**69**	**106**	**....**	**....**	**....**	**....**	**....**	**71**	**....**	**....**	**....**	**....**	**....**	**6.8**	**....**	**....**	**....**

• LORD, Joe

Joseph Lord

Born: 1924. Height: 6'1". Weight: 175 lbs. Drafted: — College: Villanova

YEAR	TEAM	GP	GS	MIN	PTS	FGM	FGA	FG%	3PM	3PA	3P%	FTM	FTA	FT%	ORB	DRB	TRB	AST	PF	DQ	STL	BLK	TO	MPG	PPG	RPG	APG	PCM
47-48	Rochester-N	4	....	....	6	3	....	....	....	....	....	0	1	.000	....	....	....	....	3	....	....	....	....	....	1.5	....	....	....
NBL Season Totals		**4**	**....**	**....**	**6**	**3**	**....**	**....**	**....**	**....**	**....**	**0**	**1**	**....**	**....**	**....**	**....**	**....**	**3**	**....**	**....**	**....**	**....**	**....**	**1.5**	**....**	**....**	**....**

• LORENDO, Gene

Gene Lorendo

Born: 1921. Height: 6'3". Weight: 215 lbs. Drafted: — College: Georgia

YEAR	TEAM	GP	GS	MIN	PTS	FGM	FGA	FG%	3PM	3PA	3P%	FTM	FTA	FT%	ORB	DRB	TRB	AST	PF	DQ	STL	BLK	TO	MPG	PPG	RPG	APG	PCM
42-43	Oshkosh-N	9	....	....	17	7	....	....	....	....	....	3	....	....	....	....	....	....	....	....	....	....	....	....	1.9	....	....	....
NBL Season Totals		**9**	**....**	**....**	**17**	**7**	**....**	**....**	**....**	**....**	**....**	**3**	**....**	**....**	**....**	**....**	**....**	**....**	**....**	**....**	**....**	**....**	**....**	**....**	**1.9**	**....**	**....**	**....**

• LORTHRIDGE, Ryan

Ryan (Flyin' Ryan) Lorthridge

Born: July 27, 1972. Nashville, TN, United States. Height: 6'4". Weight: 190 lbs. Drafted: — College: Jackson State

YEAR	TEAM	GP	GS	MIN	PTS	FGM	FGA	FG%	3PM	3PA	3P%	FTM	FTA	FT%	ORB	DRB	TRB	AST	PF	DQ	STL	BLK	TO	MPG	PPG	RPG	APG	PCM
94-95	Golden State	37	2	672	272	106	223	.475	3	14	.214	57	88	.648	24	47	71	101	42	0	28	1	56	18.2	7.4	1.9	2.7	.412
NBA Season Totals		**37**	**2**	**672**	**272**	**106**	**223**	**.475**	**3**	**14**	**.214**	**57**	**88**	**.648**	**24**	**47**	**71**	**101**	**42**	**0**	**28**	**1**	**56**	**18.2**	**7.4**	**1.9**	**2.7**	**....**

• LOSCUTOFF, Jim

Robert (Jungle Jim, Luscy) Loscutoff Jr.

Born: Feb. 4, 1930. San Francisco, CA, United States. Height: 6'5". Weight: 220 lbs. Drafted: 1955 College: Oregon

YEAR	TEAM	GP	GS	MIN	PTS	FGM	FGA	FG%	3PM	3PA	3P%	FTM	FTA	FT%	ORB	DRB	TRB	AST	PF	DQ	STL	BLK	TO	MPG	PPG	RPG	APG	PCM
55-56	Boston	71	....	1582	591	226	628	.360	....	....	....	139	207	.671	....	....	622	65	213	4	....	....	....	22.3	8.3	8.8	0.9	.463
56-57	Boston	70	....	2220	744	306	888	.345	....	....	....	132	187	.706	....	....	730	89	244	5	....	....	....	31.7	10.6	10.4	1.3	.385
57-58	Boston	5	....	56	23	11	31	.355	....	....	....	1	3	.333	....	....	20	1	8	0	....	....	....	11.2	4.6	4.0	0.2	.368
58-59	Boston	66	....	1680	546	242	686	.353	....	....	....	62	84	.738	....	....	460	60	285	15	....	....	....	25.5	8.3	7.0	0.9	.308
59-60	Boston	28	....	536	154	66	205	.322	....	....	....	22	36	.611	....	....	108	12	108	6	....	....	....	19.1	5.5	3.9	0.4	.185
60-61	Boston	76	....	1153	337	144	478	.301	....	....	....	49	76	.645	....	....	291	25	238	5	....	....	....	15.2	4.4	3.8	0.3	.203
61-62	Boston	79	....	1146	421	188	519	.362	....	....	....	45	84	.536	....	....	329	51	185	3	....	....	....	14.5	5.3	4.2	0.6	.344
62-63	Boston	63	....	607	210	94	251	.375	....	....	....	22	42	.524	....	....	157	25	126	1	....	....	....	9.6	3.3	2.5	0.4	.301
63-64	Boston	53	....	451	130	56	182	.308	....	....	....	18	31	.581	....	....	131	25	90	1	....	....	....	8.5	2.5	2.5	0.5	.276
NBA Season Totals		**511**	**....**	**9431**	**3156**	**1333**	**3868**	**.345**	**....**	**....**	**....**	**490**	**750**	**.653**	**....**	**....**	**2848**	**353**	**1497**	**40**	**....**	**....**	**....**	**18.5**	**6.2**	**5.6**	**0.7**	**....**
55-56	Boston	3	....	89	29	11	31	.355	....	....	....	7	9	.778	....	....	26	4	8	0	....	....	....	29.7	9.7	8.7	1.3	.390
56-57	Boston	10	....	259	80	31	109	.284	....	....	....	18	28	.643	....	....	83	5	46	2	....	....	....	25.9	8.0	8.3	0.5	.267
58-59	Boston	11	....	260	89	39	113	.345	....	....	....	11	21	.524	....	....	73	13	49	1	....	....	....	23.6	8.1	6.6	1.2	.316
60-61	Boston	10	....	116	37	15	54	.278	....	....	....	7	9	.778	....	....	35	3	34	0	....	....	....	11.6	3.7	3.5	0.3	.207
61-62	Boston	14	....	212	66	31	86	.360	....	....	....	4	10	.400	....	....	59	6	59	5	....	....	....	15.1	4.7	4.2	0.4	.241
62-63	Boston	9	....	56	15	7	25	.280	....	....	....	1	2	.500	....	....	21	1	20	0	....	....	....	6.2	1.7	2.3	0.1	.184
63-64	Boston	1	....	5	4	2	2	1.000	....	....	....	0	0	.000	....	....	2	0	3	0	....	....	....	5.0	4.0	2.0	0.0	.878
NBA Playoff Totals		**58**	**....**	**997**	**320**	**136**	**420**	**.324**	**....**	**....**	**....**	**48**	**79**	**.608**	**....**	**....**	**299**	**32**	**219**	**8**	**....**	**....**	**....**	**17.2**	**5.5**	**5.2**	**0.6**	**....**

• LOTT, Plummer

Carl E. Lott

Born: Dec. 11, 1945. Height: 6'5". Weight: 210 lbs. Drafted: 1967 College: Seattle

YEAR	TEAM	GP	GS	MIN	PTS	FGM	FGA	FG%	3PM	3PA	3P%	FTM	FTA	FT%	ORB	DRB	TRB	AST	PF	DQ	STL	BLK	TO	MPG	PPG	RPG	APG	PCM
67-68	Seattle	44	....	478	111	46	148	.311	....	....	....	19	31	.613	....	....	93	36	65	1	....	....	....	10.9	2.5	2.1	0.8	.243
68-69	Seattle	23	....	160	36	17	66	.258	....	....	....	2	5	.400	....	....	30	7	9	0	....	....	....	7.0	1.6	1.3	0.3	.145
NBA Season Totals		**67**	**....**	**638**	**147**	**63**	**214**	**.294**	**....**	**....**	**....**	**21**	**36**	**.583**	**....**	**....**	**123**	**43**	**74**	**1**	**....**	**....**	**....**	**9.5**	**2.2**	**1.8**	**0.6**	**....**

• LOUCKS, Sam

Sam Loucks

Born: 1915. Height: 6'4". Weight: 195 lbs. Drafted: — College: Otterbein

YEAR	TEAM	GP	GS	MIN	PTS	FGM	FGA	FG%	3PM	3PA	3P%	FTM	FTA	FT%	ORB	DRB	TRB	AST	PF	DQ	STL	BLK	TO	MPG	PPG	RPG	APG	PCM
37-38	Columbus-N	9	....	....	37	15	....	....	....	....	....	7	....	....	....	....	....	....	....	....	....	....	....	....	4.1	....	....	....
NBL Season Totals		**9**	**....**	**....**	**37**	**15**	**....**	**....**	**....**	**....**	**....**	**7**	**....**	**....**	**....**	**....**	**....**	**....**	**....**	**....**	**....**	**....**	**....**	**....**	**4.1**	**....**	**....**	**....**

• LOUGHERY, Kevin

Kevin Michael (Murph) Loughery

Born: Mar. 28, 1940. Brooklyn, NY, United States. Height: 6'3". Weight: 190 lbs. Drafted: 1962 College: St. John's (NY)

YEAR	TEAM	GP	GS	MIN	PTS	FGM	FGA	FG%	3PM	3PA	3P%	FTM	FTA	FT%	ORB	DRB	TRB	AST	PF	DQ	STL	BLK	TO	MPG	PPG	RPG	APG	PCM
62-63	Detroit	57	....	845	363	146	397	.368	....	....	....	71	100	.710	....	....	109	104	135	1	....	....	....	14.8	6.4	1.9	1.8	.369
63-64	Detroit	1	....	2	2	1	4	.250	....	....	....	0	0	.000	....	....	0	0	2	0	....	....	....	2.0	2.0	0.0	0.0	-.556
63-64	Baltimore	65	....	1457	596	235	627	.375	....	....	....	126	177	.712	....	....	138	182	173	2	....	....	....	22.4	9.2	2.1	2.8	.366
64-65	Baltimore	80	....	2417	1024	406	957	.424	....	....	....	212	281	.754	....	....	235	296	320	13	....	....	....	30.2	12.8	2.9	3.7	.412
65-66	Baltimore	74	....	2455	1349	526	1264	.416	....	....	....	297	358	.830	....	....	227	356	273	8	....	....	....	33.2	18.2	3.1	4.8	.509
66-67	Baltimore	76	....	2577	1380	520	1306	.398	....	....	....	340	412	.825	....	....	349	288	294	10	....	....	....	33.9	18.2	4.6	3.8	.478
67-68	Baltimore	77	....	2297	1221	458	1127	.406	....	....	....	305	392	.778	....	....	247	256	301	13	....	....	....	29.8	15.9	3.2	3.3	.452

YEAR	TEAM	GP	GS	MIN	PTS	FGM	FGA	FG%	3PM	3PA	3P%	FTM	FTA	FT%	ORB	DRB	TRB	AST	PF	DQ	STL	BLK	TO	MPG	PPG	RPG	APG	PCM
68-69	Baltimore	80	....	3135	1806	717	1636	.438	....	....	....	372	463	.803	....	....	266	384	299	3	....	....	....	39.2	22.6	3.3	4.8	.493
69-70	Baltimore	55	....	2037	1207	477	1082	.441	....	....	....	253	298	.849	....	....	168	292	183	3	....	....	....	37.0	21.9	3.1	5.3	.515
70-71	Baltimore	82	....	2260	1237	481	1193	.403	....	....	....	275	331	.831	....	....	219	301	246	2	....	....	....	27.6	15.1	2.7	3.7	.454
71-72	Baltimore	2	....	42	13	4	17	.235	....	....	....	5	8	.625	....	....	5	8	5	0	....	....	....	21.0	6.5	2.5	4.0	.279
71-72	Philadelphia	74	....	1829	932	337	792	.426	....	....	....	258	312	.827	....	....	178	188	208	3	....	....	....	24.7	12.6	2.4	2.5	.434
72-73	Philadelphia	32	....	955	445	169	427	.396	....	....	....	107	130	.823	....	....	113	148	104	0	....	....	....	29.8	13.9	3.5	4.6	.456
NBA Season Totals		755	....	22308	11575	4477	10829	.413	....	....	....	2621	3262	.803	....	....	2254	2803	2543	58	....	....	....	29.5	15.3	3.0	3.7	....
62-63	Detroit	2	....	26	3	1	10	.100	....	....	....	1	1	1.000	....	....	0	4	3	0	....	....	....	13.0	1.5	0.0	2.0	-.018
64-65	Baltimore	10	....	297	140	53	137	.387	....	....	....	34	38	.895	....	....	34	30	36	0	....	....	....	29.7	14.0	3.4	3.0	.415
65-66	Baltimore	3	....	27	9	3	7	.429	....	....	....	3	6	.500	....	....	1	1	4	0	....	....	....	9.0	3.0	0.3	0.3	.190
68-69	Baltimore	4	....	173	81	29	79	.367	....	....	....	23	35	.657	....	....	18	21	16	0	....	....	....	43.3	20.3	4.5	5.3	.387
69-70	Baltimore	7	....	153	67	26	77	.338	....	....	....	15	21	.714	....	....	16	8	24	0	....	....	....	21.9	9.6	2.3	1.1	.209
70-71	Baltimore	17	....	500	232	84	212	.396	....	....	....	64	85	.753	....	....	38	52	57	2	....	....	....	29.4	13.6	2.2	3.1	.361
NBA Playoff Totals		43	....	1176	532	196	522	.375	....	....	....	140	186	.753	....	....	107	116	140	2	....	....	....	27.3	12.4	2.5	2.7	....

• LOVE, Bob
Robert (Butterbean, Bean) Love

Born: Dec. 8, 1942. Bastrop, LA, United States.   Height: 6'8".   Weight: 215 lbs.   Drafted: 1965   College: Southern University

YEAR	TEAM	GP	GS	MIN	PTS	FGM	FGA	FG%	3PM	3PA	3P%	FTM	FTA	FT%	ORB	DRB	TRB	AST	PF	DQ	STL	BLK	TO	MPG	PPG	RPG	APG	PCM
66-67	Cincinnati	66	....	1074	439	173	403	.429	....	....	....	93	147	.633	....	....	257	49	153	3	....	....	....	16.3	6.7	3.9	0.7	.407
67-68	Cincinnati	72	....	1068	464	193	455	.424	....	....	....	78	114	.684	....	....	209	55	141	1	....	....	....	14.8	6.4	2.9	0.8	.391
68-69	Milwaukee	14	....	227	107	39	106	.368	....	....	....	29	38	.763	....	....	64	3	22	0	....	....	....	16.2	7.6	4.6	0.2	.419
68-69	Chicago	35	....'	315	180	69	166	.416	....	....	....	42	58	.724	....	....	86	14	37	0	....	....	....	9.0	5.1	2.5	0.4	.524
69-70	Chicago	82	....	3123	1722	640	1373	.466	....	....	....	442	525	.842	....	....	712	148	260	2	....	....	....	38.1	21.0	8.7	1.8	.550
70-71	Chicago	81	....	3482	2043	765	1710	.447	....	....	....	513	619	.829	....	....	690	185	259	0	....	....	....	43.0	25.2	8.5	2.3	.539
71-72	Chicago	79	....	3108	2037	819	1854	.442	....	....	....	399	509	.784	....	....	518	125	235	2	....	....	....	39.3	25.8	6.6	1.6	.509
72-73	Chicago	82	....	3033	1895	774	1794	.431	....	....	....	347	421	.824	....	....	532	119	240	1	....	....	....	37.0	23.1	6.5	1.5	.487
73-74	Chicago	82	....	3292	1785	731	1752	.417	....	....	....	323	395	.818	183	309	492	130	221	1	84	28	....	40.1	21.8	6.0	1.6	.413
74-75	Chicago	61	....	2401	1342	539	1256	.429	....	....	....	264	318	.830	99	286	385	102	209	3	63	12	....	39.4	22.0	6.3	1.7	.443
75-76	Chicago	76	....	2823	1448	543	1391	.390	....	....	....	362	452	.801	191	319	510	145	233	3	63	10	....	37.1	19.1	6.7	1.9	.420
76-77	Chicago	14	....	496	171	68	201	.338	....	....	....	35	46	.761	38	35	73	23	47	1	8	2	....	35.4	12.2	5.2	1.6	.243
76-77	New York	13	....	228	131	49	106	.462	....	....	....	33	39	.846	15	23	38	4	23	0	1	2	....	17.5	10.1	2.9	0.3	.468
76-77	Seattle	32	....	450	131	45	121	.372	....	....	....	41	47	.872	26	61	87	21	50	0	13	2	....	14.1	4.1	2.7	0.7	.312
NBA Season Totals		789	....	25120	13895	5447	12688	.429	....	....	....	3001	3728	.805	552	1033	4653	1123	2130	17	232	56	....	31.8	17.6	5.9	1.4	....
69-70	Chicago	5	....	172	59	20	52	.385	....	....	....	19	24	.792	....	....	46	4	12	0	....	....	....	34.4	11.8	9.2	0.8	.397
70-71	Chicago	7	....	330	187	79	161	.491	....	....	....	29	36	.806	....	....	51	10	26	0	....	....	....	47.1	26.7	7.3	1.4	.477
71-72	Chicago	4	....	173	75	32	89	.360	....	....	....	11	13	.846	....	....	27	7	17	0	....	....	....	43.3	18.8	6.8	1.8	.282
72-73	Chicago	7	....	314	166	68	148	.459	....	....	....	30	41	.732	....	....	67	23	20	0	....	....	....	44.9	23.7	9.6	3.3	.534
73-74	Chicago	11	....	489	253	104	257	.405	....	....	....	45	59	.763	27	36	63	24	28	0	14	5	....	44.5	23.0	5.7	2.2	.381
74-75	Chicago	13	....	583	336	138	316	.437	....	....	....	60	77	.779	31	67	98	19	41	1	10	5	....	44.8	25.8	7.5	1.5	.454
NBA Playoff Totals		47	....	2061	1076	441	1023	.431	....	....	....	194	250	.776	58	103	352	87	144	1	24	10	....	43.9	22.9	7.5	1.9	....

• LOVE, Stan
Stanley S. Love

Born: Apr. 9, 1949. Los Angeles, CA, United States.   Height: 6'9".   Weight: 215 lbs.   Drafted: 1971   College: Oregon

YEAR	TEAM	GP	GS	MIN	PTS	FGM	FGA	FG%	3PM	3PA	3P%	FTM	FTA	FT%	ORB	DRB	TRB	AST	PF	DQ	STL	BLK	TO	MPG	PPG	RPG	APG	PCM
71-72	Baltimore	74	....	1327	587	242	536	.451	....	....	....	103	140	.736	....	....	338	52	202	0	....	....	....	17.9	7.9	4.6	0.7	.438
72-73	Baltimore	72	....	995	459	190	436	.436	....	....	....	79	100	.790	....	....	300	46	175	0	....	....	....	13.8	6.4	4.2	0.6	.476
73-74	LA Lakers	51	....	698	287	119	278	.428	....	....	....	49	64	.766	54	116	170	48	132	3	28	20	....	13.7	5.6	3.3	0.9	.414
74-75	San Antonio-A	12	....	64	29	13	30	.433	0	0	.000	3	4	.750	6	18	24	9	16	....	0	4	6	5.3	2.4	2.0	0.8	.589
74-75	LA Lakers	30	....	431	217	85	194	.438	....	....	....	47	66	.712	31	66	97	26	69	1	16	13	....	14.4	7.2	3.2	0.9	.462
NBA Season Totals		227	....	3451	1550	636	1444	.440	....	....	....	278	370	.751	85	182	905	172	578	4	44	33	....	15.2	6.8	4.0	0.8	....
ABA Season Totals		12	....	64	29	13	30	.433	0	0	.000	3	4	.750	6	18	24	9	16	....	0	4	6	5.3	2.4	2.0	0.8	....
Career Totals		239	....	3515	1579	649	1474	.440	0	0	.000	281	374	.751	91	200	929	181	594	4	44	37	6	14.7	6.6	3.9	0.8	....
71-72	Baltimore	4	....	14	2	1	4	.250	....	....	....	0	0	.000	....	....	6	1	3	0	....	....	....	3.5	0.5	1.5	0.3	.317
72-73	Baltimore	1	....	7	0	0	3	.000	....	....	....	0	0	.000	....	....	1	0	1	0	....	....	....	7.0	0.0	1.0	0.0	-.306
73-74	LA Lakers	2	....	9	6	2	3	.667	....	....	....	2	3	.667	1	2	3	1	0	0	1	0	....	4.5	3.0	1.5	0.5	.936
NBA Playoff Totals		7	....	30	8	3	10	.300	....	....	....	2	3	.667	1	2	10	2	4	0	1	0	....	4.3	1.1	1.4	0.3	....

• LOVELLETTE, Clyde
Clyde Edward Lovellette

Born: Sept. 7, 1929. Petersburg, IN, United States.   Height: 6'9".   Weight: 234 lbs.   Drafted: 1952   College: Kansas   HOF: 1988

YEAR	TEAM	GP	GS	MIN	PTS	FGM	FGA	FG%	3PM	3PA	3P%	FTM	FTA	FT%	ORB	DRB	TRB	AST	PF	DQ	STL	BLK	TO	MPG	PPG	RPG	APG	PCM
53-54	Minneapolis	72	....	1255	588	237	560	.423	....	....	....	114	164	.695	....	....	419	51	210	2	....	....	....	17.4	8.2	5.8	0.7	.502
54-55	Minneapolis	70	....	2361	1311	519	1192	.435	....	....	....	273	398	.686	....	....	802	100	262	6	....	....	....	33.7	18.7	11.5	1.4	.588
55-56	Minneapolis	71	....	2518	1526	594	1370	.434	....	....	....	338	469	.721	....	....	992	164	245	5	....	....	....	35.5	21.5	14.0	2.3	.695
56-57	Minneapolis	69	....	2492	1434	574	1348	.426	....	....	....	286	399	.717	....	....	932	139	251	4	....	....	....	36.1	20.8	13.5	2.0	.638
57-58	Cincinnati	71	....	2589	1659	**679**	1540	.441	....	....	....	301	405	.743	....	....	862	134	236	3	....	....	....	36.5	23.4	12.1	1.9	.659
58-59	St. Louis	70	....	1599	1009	402	885	.454	....	....	....	205	250	.820	....	....	605	91	216	1	....	....	....	22.8	14.4	8.6	1.3	.698
59-60	St. Louis	68	....	1953	1416	550	1174	.468	....	....	....	316	385	.821	....	....	721	127	248	6	....	....	....	28.7	20.8	10.6	1.9	.782
60-61	St. Louis	67	....	2111	1471	599	1321	.453	....	....	....	273	329	.830	....	....	677	172	248	4	....	....	....	31.5	22.0	10.1	2.6	.727
61-62	St. Louis	40	....	1192	837	341	724	.471	....	....	....	155	187	.829	....	....	350	68	136	4	....	....	....	29.8	20.9	8.8	1.7	.695
62-63	Boston	61	....	568	395	161	376	.428	....	....	....	73	98	.745	....	....	177	95	137	0	....	....	....	9.3	6.5	2.9	1.6	.732
63-64	Boston	45	....	437	301	128	305	.420	....	....	....	45	57	.789	....	....	126	24	100	0	....	....	....	9.7	6.7	2.8	0.5	.565
NBA Season Totals		704	....	19075	11947	4784	10795	.443	....	....	....	2379	3141	.757	....	....	6663	1165	2289	35	....	....	....	27.1	17.0	9.5	1.7	....
53-54	Minneapolis	13	....	265	136	54	120	.450	....	....	....	28	58	.483	....	....	126	7	37	0	....	....	....	20.4	10.5	9.7	0.5	.618
54-55	Minneapolis	7	....	197	117	44	98	.449	....	....	....	29	40	.725	....	....	64	3	32	1	....	....	....	28.1	16.7	9.1	0.4	.569
55-56	Minneapolis	3	....	69	57	19	39	.487	....	....	....	19	32	.594	....	....	25	6	13	1	....	....	....	23.0	19.0	8.3	2.0	.846
56-57	Minneapolis	5	....	181	121	51	118	.432	....	....	....	19	26	.731	....	....	47	11	21	1	....	....	....	36.2	24.2	9.4	2.2	.605
57-58	Cincinnati	2	....	72	33	12	31	.387	....	....	....	9	14	.643	....	....	21	1	9	0	....	....	....	36.0	16.5	10.5	0.5	.425
58-59	St. Louis	6	....	161	92	35	70	.500	....	....	....	22	28	.786	....	....	59	8	23	1	....	....	....	26.8	15.3	9.8	1.3	.678
59-60	St. Louis	14	....	426	246	95	242	.393	....	....	....	56	68	.824	....	....	151	39	53	0	....	....	....	30.4	17.6	10.8	2.8	.641

YEAR	TEAM	GP	GS	MIN	PTS	FGM	FGA	FG%	3PM	3PA	3P%	FTM	FTA	FT%	ORB	DRB	TRB	AST	PF	DQ	STL	BLK	TO	MPG	PPG	RPG	APG	PCM
60-61	St. Louis	8	....	191	123	46	114	.404	....	....	....	31	47	.660	....	....	52	11	23	0	....	....	....	23.9	15.4	6.5	1.4	.574
62-63	Boston	6	....	40	18	7	26	.269	....	....	....	4	6	.667	....	....	5	1	13	0	....	....	....	6.7	3.0	0.8	0.2	.055
63-64	Boston	5	....	40	20	8	34	.235	....	....	....	4	4	1.000	....	....	7	2	8	0	....	....	....	8.0	4.0	1.4	0.4	.114
NBA Playoff Totals		69	....	1642	963	371	892	.416	....	....	....	221	323	.684	....	....	557	89	232	4	....	....	....	23.8	14.0	8.1	1.3	....

• LOWE, Sidney

Sidney Rochell Lowe

Born: Jan. 21, 1960. Washington, DC, United States.　Height: 6'　Weight: 195 lbs.　Drafted: 1983　College: North Carolina State

YEAR	TEAM	GP	GS	MIN	PTS	FGM	FGA	FG%	3PM	3PA	3P%	FTM	FTA	FT%	ORB	DRB	TRB	AST	PF	DQ	STL	BLK	TO	MPG	PPG	RPG	APG	PCM
83-84	Indiana	78	2	1238	324	107	259	.413	2	18	.111	108	139	.777	30	92	122	269	112	0	93	5	109	15.9	4.2	1.6	3.4	.410
84-85	Detroit	6	0	31	4	2	7	.286	0	0	.000	0	0	.000	0	1	1	8	5	0	0	0	2	5.2	0.7	0.2	1.3	.149
84-85	Atlanta	15	0	159	24	8	20	.400	0	1	.000	8	8	1.000	4	11	15	42	23	0	11	0	11	10.6	1.6	1.0	2.8	.383
88-89	Charlotte	14	0	250	23	8	25	.320	0	2	.000	7	11	.636	6	28	34	93	28	0	14	0	8	17.9	1.6	2.4	6.6	.516
89-90	Minnesota	80	38	1744	187	73	229	.319	2	9	.222	39	54	.722	41	122	163	337	114	0	73	4	64	21.8	2.3	2.0	4.2	.289
NBA Season Totals		193	40	3422	562	198	540	.367	4	30	.133	162	212	.764	81	254	335	749	282	0	191	9	194	17.7	2.9	1.7	3.9	....

• LOWERY, Charlie

Charles P. (Chuck) Lowery

Born: Nov. 12, 1949.　Height: 6'3".　Weight: 185 lbs.　Drafted: 1971　College: Puget Sound

YEAR	TEAM	GP	GS	MIN	PTS	FGM	FGA	FG%	3PM	3PA	3P%	FTM	FTA	FT%	ORB	DRB	TRB	AST	PF	DQ	STL	BLK	TO	MPG	PPG	RPG	APG	PCM
71-72	Milwaukee	20	....	134	45	17	38	.447	....	....	....	11	18	.611	....	....	19	14	16	1	....	....	....	6.7	2.3	1.0	0.7	.367
NBA Season Totals		20	....	134	45	17	38	.447	....	....	....	11	18	.611	....	....	19	14	16	1	....	....	....	6.7	2.3	1.0	0.7	....
71-72	Milwaukee	7	....	26	6	2	8	.250	....	....	....	2	3	.667	....	....	3	1	4	0	....	....	....	3.7	0.9	0.4	0.1	.092
NBA Playoff Totals		7	....	26	6	2	8	.250	....	....	....	2	3	.667	....	....	3	1	4	0	....	....	....	3.7	0.9	0.4	0.1	....

• LOWTHER, Bobby

Robert Lowther

Born: 1923.　Height: 6'5".　Weight: 190 lbs.　Drafted: —　College: Louisiana State

YEAR	TEAM	GP	GS	MIN	PTS	FGM	FGA	FG%	3PM	3PA	3P%	FTM	FTA	FT%	ORB	DRB	TRB	AST	PF	DQ	STL	BLK	TO	MPG	PPG	RPG	APG	PCM
48-49	Tri-Cities-N	15	....	....	18	8	....	....	....	....	....	2	4	.500	....	....	....	....	....	....	....	....	....	....	1.2	....	....	....
48-49	Waterloo-N	9	....	....	27	11	....	....	....	....	....	5	7	.714	....	....	....	....	....	....	....	....	....	....	3.0	....	....	....
NBL Season Totals		24	....	....	45	19	....	....	....	....	....	7	11	....	....	....	....	....	....	....	....	....	....	....	1.9	....	....	....
48-49	Tri-Cities-N	4	....	....	4	1	....	....	....	....	....	2	2	1.000	....	....	....	....	....	....	....	....	....	....	1.0	....	....	....
NBL Playoff Totals		4	....	....	4	1	....	....	....	....	....	2	2	....	....	....	....	....	....	....	....	....	....	....	1.0	....	....	....

• LOYD, Carl

Carl Loyd

Born: 1925.　Height: 5'11".　Weight: 170 lbs.　Drafted: —　College: Notre Dame

YEAR	TEAM	GP	GS	MIN	PTS	FGM	FGA	FG%	3PM	3PA	3P%	FTM	FTA	FT%	ORB	DRB	TRB	AST	PF	DQ	STL	BLK	TO	MPG	PPG	RPG	APG	PCM
48-49	Hammond-N	29	....	....	97	43	....	....	....	....	....	11	23	.478	....	....	....	32	....	....	....	....	....	....	3.3	....	....	....
NBL Season Totals		29	....	....	97	43	....	....	....	....	....	11	23	....	....	....	....	32	....	....	....	....	....	....	3.3	....	....	....

• LUCAS, Al

Albert Thomas (Lukey) Lucas

Born: July 4, 1922. Died: Apr.26, 1995.　Height: 6'3".　Weight: 195 lbs.　Drafted: —　College: Fordham

YEAR	TEAM	GP	GS	MIN	PTS	FGM	FGA	FG%	3PM	3PA	3P%	FTM	FTA	FT%	ORB	DRB	TRB	AST	PF	DQ	STL	BLK	TO	MPG	PPG	RPG	APG	PCM
44-45	Sheboygan-N	26	....	....	150	57	....	....	....	....	....	36	....	....	....	....	....	....	....	....	....	....	....	....	5.8	....	....	....
45-46	Sheboygan-N	32	....	....	174	75	....	....	....	....	....	24	38	.632	....	....	....	....	....	....	....	....	....	....	5.4	....	....	....
46-47	Sheboygan-N	42	....	....	206	87	....	....	....	....	....	32	60	.533	....	....	....	74	....	....	....	....	....	....	4.9	....	....	....
47-48	Sheboygan-N	58	....	....	235	98	....	....	....	....	....	39	56	.696	....	....	....	135	....	....	....	....	....	....	4.1	....	....	....
48-49	Boston	2	....	....	2	1	3	.333	....	....	....	0	0	.000	....	....	....	2	0	....	....	....	....	....	1.0	....	1.0	....
NBA Season Totals		2	....	....	2	1	3	.333	....	....	....	0	0	.000	....	....	....	2	0	....	....	....	....	....	1.0	....	1.0	....
NBL Season Totals		158	....	....	765	317	....	....	....	....	....	131	154	....	....	....	....	209	....	....	....	....	....	....	4.8	....	....	....
Career Totals		160	....	....	767	318	3	....	....	....	....	131	154	....	....	....	....	2	209	....	....	....	....	....	4.8	....	0.0	....
44-45	Sheboygan-N	8	....	....	34	13	....	....	....	....	....	8	....	....	....	....	....	....	....	....	....	....	....	....	4.3	....	....	....
45-46	Sheboygan-N	3	....	....	7	3	....	....	....	....	....	1	2	.500	....	....	....	....	....	....	....	....	....	....	2.3	....	....	....
46-47	Sheboygan-N	5	....	....	36	15	....	....	....	....	....	6	7	.857	....	....	....	....	....	....	....	....	....	....	7.2	....	....	....
NBL Playoff Totals		16	....	....	77	31	....	....	....	....	....	15	9	....	....	....	....	....	....	....	....	....	....	....	4.8	....	....	....

• LUCAS, Jerry

Jerry Ray (Luke) Lucas

Born: Mar. 30, 1940. Middletown, OH, United States.　Height: 6'8".　Weight: 230 lbs.　Drafted: 1962　College: Ohio State　HOF: 1980

YEAR	TEAM	GP	GS	MIN	PTS	FGM	FGA	FG%	3PM	3PA	3P%	FTM	FTA	FT%	ORB	DRB	TRB	AST	PF	DQ	STL	BLK	TO	MPG	PPG	RPG	APG	PCM
63-64	Cincinnati	79	....	3273	1400	545	1035	**.527**	....	....	....	310	398	.779	....	....	1375	204	300	6	....	....	....	41.4	17.7	17.4	2.6	.668
64-65	Cincinnati	66	....	2864	1414	558	1121	.498	....	....	....	298	366	.814	....	....	1321	157	214	1	....	....	....	43.4	21.4	20.0	2.4	.727
65-66	Cincinnati	79	....	3517	1697	690	1523	.453	....	....	....	317	403	.787	....	....	1668	213	274	5	....	....	....	44.5	21.5	21.1	2.7	.702
66-67	Cincinnati	81	....	3558	1438	577	1257	.459	....	....	....	284	359	.791	....	....	1547	268	280	2	....	....	....	43.9	17.8	19.1	3.3	.649
67-68	Cincinnati	82	....	3619	1760	707	1361	.519	....	....	....	346	445	.778	....	....	1560	251	243	3	....	....	....	44.1	21.5	19.0	3.1	.732
68-69	Cincinnati	74	....	3075	1357	555	1007	.551	....	....	....	247	327	.755	....	....	1360	306	206	0	....	....	....	41.6	18.3	18.4	4.1	.765
69-70	Cincinnati	4	....	118	41	18	35	.514	....	....	....	5	7	.714	....	....	45	9	5	0	....	....	....	29.5	10.3	11.3	2.3	.616
69-70	San Francisco	63	....	2302	969	387	764	.507	....	....	....	195	248	.786	....	....	906	166	159	2	....	....	....	36.5	15.4	14.4	2.6	.663
70-71	San Francisco	80	....	3251	1535	623	1250	.498	....	....	....	289	367	.787	....	....	1265	293	197	0	....	....	....	40.6	19.2	15.8	3.7	.707
71-72	New York	77	....	2926	1283	543	1060	.512	....	....	....	197	249	.791	....	....	1011	318	218	1	....	....	....	38.0	16.7	13.1	4.1	.668
72-73	New York	71	....	2001	704	312	608	.513	....	....	....	80	100	.800	....	....	510	317	157	0	....	....	....	28.2	9.9	7.2	4.5	.587
73-74	New York	73	....	1627	455	194	420	.462	....	....	....	67	96	.698	62	312	374	230	134	0	28	24	....	22.3	6.2	5.1	3.2	.477
NBA Season Totals		829	....	32131	14053	5709	11441	.499	....	....	....	2635	3365	.783	62	312	12942	2732	2387	20	28	24	....	38.8	17.0	15.6	3.3	....
63-64	Cincinnati	10	....	370	122	48	123	.390	....	....	....	26	37	.703	....	....	125	34	37	1	....	....	....	37.0	12.2	12.5	3.4	.497
64-65	Cincinnati	4	....	195	93	38	75	.507	....	....	....	17	22	.773	....	....	84	9	12	0	....	....	....	48.8	23.3	21.0	2.3	.685
65-66	Cincinnati	5	....	231	107	40	85	.471	....	....	....	27	35	.771	....	....	101	14	14	0	....	....	....	46.2	21.4	20.2	2.8	.690
66-67	Cincinnati	4	....	183	50	24	55	.436	....	....	....	2	2	1.000	....	....	77	8	15	0	....	....	....	45.8	12.5	19.3	2.0	.493

YEAR	TEAM	GP	GS	MIN	PTS	FGM	FGA	FG%	3PM	3PA	3P%	FTM	FTA	FT%	ORB	DRB	TRB	AST	PF	DQ	STL	BLK	TO	MPG	PPG	RPG	APG	PCM
70-71	San Francisco	5	....	171	89	39	77	.506	....	....	....	11	16	.688	....	....	50	16	14	0	....	....	....	34.2	17.8	10.0	3.2	.640
71-72	New York	16	....	737	297	119	238	.500	....	....	....	59	71	.831	....	....	173	85	49	1	....	....	....	46.1	18.6	10.8	5.3	.562
72-73	New York	17	....	368	128	54	112	.482	....	....	....	20	23	.870	....	....	85	39	47	0	....	....	....	21.6	7.5	5.0	2.3	.474
73-74	New York	11	....	115	10	5	21	.238	....	....	....	0	0	.000	6	16	22	9	9	0	4	0	....	10.5	0.9	2.0	0.8	.188
NBA Playoff Totals		72	....	2370	896	367	786	.467	....	....	....	162	206	.786	6	16	717	214	197	2	4	0	....	32.9	12.4	10.0	3.0	....

• LUCAS, John

John Harding Lucas Jr.

Born: Oct. 31, 1953. Durham, NC, United States. Height: 6'3". Weight: 175 lbs. Drafted: 1976 College: Maryland

YEAR	TEAM	GP	GS	MIN	PTS	FGM	FGA	FG%	3PM	3PA	3P%	FTM	FTA	FT%	ORB	DRB	TRB	AST	PF	DQ	STL	BLK	TO	MPG	PPG	RPG	APG	PCM
76-77	Houston	82	....	2531	911	388	814	.477	....	....	....	135	171	.789	55	164	219	463	174	0	125	19	....	30.9	11.1	2.7	5.6	.462
77-78	Houston	82	....	2933	1017	412	947	.435	....	....	....	193	250	.772	51	204	255	768	208	1	160	9	213	35.8	12.4	3.1	9.4	.505
78-79	Golden State	82	....	3095	1324	530	1146	.462	....	....	....	264	321	.822	65	182	247	762	229	1	152	9	254	37.7	16.1	3.0	9.3	.524
79-80	Golden State	80	....	2763	1010	388	830	.467	12	42	.286	222	289	.768	61	159	220	602	196	2	138	3	184	34.5	12.6	2.8	7.5	.474
80-81	Golden State	66	....	1919	555	222	506	.439	4	24	.167	107	145	.738	34	120	154	464	140	1	83	2	185	29.1	8.4	2.3	7.0	.401
81-82	Washington	79	53	1940	666	263	618	.426	2	22	.091	138	176	.784	40	126	166	551	105	0	95	6	158	24.6	8.4	2.1	7.0	.499
82-83	Washington	35	0	386	145	62	131	.473	0	5	.000	21	42	.500	8	21	29	102	18	0	25	1	46	11.0	4.1	0.8	2.9	.480
83-84	San Antonio	63	39	1807	689	275	595	.462	19	69	.275	120	157	.764	23	157	180	673	123	1	92	5	145	28.7	10.9	2.9	10.7	.642
84-85	Houston	47	21	1158	536	206	446	.462	21	66	.318	103	129	.798	21	64	85	318	78	0	62	2	103	24.6	11.4	1.8	6.8	.558
85-86	Houston	65	65	2120	1006	365	818	.446	45	146	.308	231	298	.775	33	110	143	571	124	0	77	5	150	32.6	15.5	2.2	8.8	.555
86-87	Milwaukee	43	40	1358	753	285	624	.457	46	126	.365	137	174	.787	29	96	125	290	82	0	71	6	90	31.6	17.5	2.9	6.7	.586
87-88	Milwaukee	81	22	1766	743	281	631	.445	51	151	.338	130	162	.802	29	130	159	392	102	1	88	3	122	21.8	9.2	2.0	4.8	.505
88-89	Seattle	74	8	842	310	119	299	.398	18	68	.265	54	77	.701	22	57	79	260	53	0	60	1	67	11.4	4.2	1.1	3.5	.538
89-90	Houston	49	18	938	286	109	291	.375	26	87	.299	42	55	.764	19	71	90	238	59	0	45	2	83	19.1	5.8	1.8	4.9	.411
NBA Season Totals		928	266	25556	9951	3905	8696	.449	244	806	.303	1897	2446	.776	490	1661	2151	6454	1691	7	1273	73	1800	27.5	10.7	2.3	7.0	....
76-77	Houston	12	....	430	176	75	139	.540	....	....	....	26	34	.765	4	29	33	83	33	1	24	4	....	35.8	14.7	2.8	6.9	.525
81-82	Washington	7	0	74	31	14	26	.538	1	3	.333	2	3	.667	0	8	8	20	6	0	3	1	4	10.6	4.4	1.1	2.9	.617
84-85	Houston	5	4	152	68	26	80	.325	2	14	.143	14	22	.636	7	14	21	27	14	0	6	0	7	30.4	13.6	4.2	5.4	.361
86-87	Milwaukee	12	12	362	187	68	150	.453	12	36	.333	39	48	.813	4	21	25	62	17	0	14	1	20	30.2	15.6	2.1	5.2	.507
87-88	Milwaukee	5	0	80	29	10	27	.370	3	13	.231	6	9	.667	5	3	8	19	5	0	5	0	6	16.0	5.8	1.6	3.8	.453
88-89	Seattle	4	0	37	11	5	17	.294	0	3	.000	1	2	.500	0	1	1	8	5	0	0	0	2	9.3	2.8	0.3	2.0	.126
NBA Playoff Totals		45	16	1135	502	198	439	.451	18	69	.261	88	118	.746	20	76	96	219	80	1	52	6	39	25.2	11.2	2.1	4.9	....

• LUCAS, Maurice

Maurice D. (Luke) Lucas

Born: Feb. 18, 1952. Pittsburgh, PA, United States. Height: 6'9". Weight: 215 lbs. Drafted: 1974 College: Marquette

YEAR	TEAM	GP	GS	MIN	PTS	FGM	FGA	FG%	3PM	3PA	3P%	FTM	FTA	FT%	ORB	DRB	TRB	AST	PF	DQ	STL	BLK	TO	MPG	PPG	RPG	APG	PCM
74-75	St. Louis-A	80	....	2464	1058	438	937	.467	2	9	.222	180	229	.786	282	534	816	287	301	....	89	64	208	30.8	13.2	10.2	3.6	.610
75-76	Kentucky-A	58	....	1796	888	368	798	.461	3	7	.429	149	190	.784	191	357	548	147	228	....	56	36	186	31.0	15.3	9.4	2.5	.577
75-76	St. Louis-A	28	....	1065	572	252	548	.460	0	11	.000	68	93	.731	106	316	422	77	104	....	19	21	112	38.0	20.4	15.1	2.8	.669
76-77	Portland	79	....	2863	1599	632	1357	.466	....	....	....	335	438	.765	271	628	899	229	294	6	83	56	....	36.2	20.2	11.4	2.9	.642
77-78	Portland	68	....	2119	1113	453	989	.458	....	....	....	207	270	.767	186	435	621	173	221	3	61	56	190	31.2	16.4	9.1	2.5	.563
78-79	Portland	69	....	2462	1406	568	1208	.470	....	....	....	270	345	.783	192	524	716	215	254	3	66	81	235	35.7	20.4	10.4	3.1	.603
79-80	Portland	41	....	1176	588	243	552	.440	2	5	.400	100	137	.730	85	240	325	125	141	1	23	35	148	28.7	14.3	7.9	3.0	.491
79-80	New Jersey	22	....	708	335	128	261	.490	0	4	.000	79	102	.775	58	154	212	83	82	1	19	27	70	32.2	15.2	9.6	3.8	.605
80-81	New Jersey	68	....	2162	999	404	835	.484	0	2	.000	191	254	.752	153	422	575	173	260	3	57	59	177	31.8	14.7	8.5	2.5	.516
81-82	New York	80	74	2671	1263	505	1001	.504	0	3	.000	253	349	.725	274	629	903	179	309	4	68	70	176	33.4	15.8	11.3	2.2	.603
82-83	Phoenix	77	71	2586	1269	495	1045	.474	1	3	.333	278	356	.781	201	598	799	219	274	5	56	43	223	33.6	16.5	10.4	2.8	.566
83-84	Phoenix	75	69	2309	1195	451	908	.497	0	5	.000	293	383	.765	208	517	725	203	235	2	55	39	180	30.8	15.9	9.7	2.7	.619
84-85	Phoenix	63	22	1670	842	346	727	.476	0	4	.000	150	200	.750	138	419	557	145	183	0	39	17	151	26.5	13.4	8.8	2.3	.577
85-86	LA Lakers	77	8	1750	785	302	653	.462	1	2	.500	180	230	.783	164	402	566	84	253	1	45	24	123	22.7	10.2	7.4	1.1	.505
86-87	Seattle	63	0	1120	500	175	388	.451	0	5	.000	150	187	.802	88	219	307	65	171	1	34	21	76	17.8	7.9	4.9	1.0	.483
87-88	Portland	73	0	1191	445	168	373	.450	0	3	.000	109	148	.736	101	214	315	94	188	0	33	10	73	16.3	6.1	4.3	1.3	.432
NBA Season Totals		855	244	24787	12339	4870	10297	.473	4	36	.111	2595	3399	.763	2119	5401	7520	1987	2865	30	639	538	1822	29.0	14.4	8.8	2.3	....
ABA Season Totals		166	....	5325	2518	1058	2283	.463	5	27	.185	397	512	.775	579	1207	1786	511	633	....	164	121	506	32.1	15.2	10.8	3.1	....
Career Totals		1021	244	30112	14857	5928	12580	.471	9	63	.143	2992	3911	.765	2698	6608	9306	2498	3498	30	803	659	2328	29.5	14.6	9.1	2.4	....
74-75	St. Louis-A	10	....	375	163	68	153	.444	0	1	.000	27	41	.659	49	98	147	50	44	....	12	14	34	37.5	16.3	14.7	5.0	.661
75-76	Kentucky-A	10	....	330	171	78	152	.513	0	0	.000	15	19	.789	40	68	108	22	48	....	8	6	15	33.0	17.1	10.8	2.2	.614
76-77	Portland	19	....	731	403	164	316	.519	....	....	....	75	101	.743	43	145	188	79	79	3	28	23	....	38.5	21.2	9.9	4.2	.655
77-78	Portland	6	....	233	103	46	108	.426	....	....	....	11	19	.579	19	56	75	15	28	0	4	2	19	38.8	17.2	12.5	2.5	.447
78-79	Portland	3	....	104	33	14	41	.341	....	....	....	5	7	.714	2	30	32	18	12	0	3	1	11	34.7	11.0	10.7	6.0	.430
82-83	Phoenix	2	2	57	26	12	21	.571	0	0	.000	2	4	.500	5	7	12	8	5	0	3	0	4	28.5	13.0	6.0	4.0	.587
83-84	Phoenix	17	16	570	295	116	227	.511	0	0	.000	63	78	.808	42	127	169	61	66	2	12	8	29	33.5	17.4	9.9	3.6	.646
84-85	Phoenix	3	0	84	59	22	47	.468	0	0	.000	15	19	.789	12	21	33	10	12	0	2	2	8	28.0	19.7	11.0	3.3	.785
85-86	LA Lakers	14	0	319	132	59	112	.527	0	0	.000	14	19	.737	29	62	91	10	53	0	6	5	13	22.8	9.4	6.5	0.7	.468
86-87	Seattle	14	0	265	98	35	90	.389	0	1	.000	28	38	.737	19	46	65	19	43	1	12	5	18	18.9	7.0	4.6	1.4	.385
87-88	Portland	4	0	63	10	4	13	.308	0	0	.000	2	4	.500	9	16	25	5	12	0	1	0	5	15.8	2.5	6.3	1.3	.317
NBA Playoff Totals		82	18	2426	1159	472	975	.484	0	1	.000	215	289	.744	180	510	690	225	310	6	71	46	107	29.6	14.1	8.4	2.7	....
ABA Playoff Totals		20	....	705	334	146	305	.479	0	1	.000	42	60	.700	89	166	255	72	92	....	20	20	49	35.3	16.7	12.8	3.6	....
Career Playoff Totals		102	18	3131	1493	618	1280	.483	0	2	.000	257	349	.736	269	676	945	297	402	6	91	66	156	30.7	14.6	9.3	2.9	....

• LUCKENBILL, Ted

Theodore Luckenbill

Born: July 27, 1939. Height: 6'6". Weight: 205 lbs. Drafted: 1961 College: Houston

YEAR	TEAM	GP	GS	MIN	PTS	FGM	FGA	FG%	3PM	3PA	3P%	FTM	FTA	FT%	ORB	DRB	TRB	AST	PF	DQ	STL	BLK	TO	MPG	PPG	RPG	APG	PCM
61-62	Philadelphia	67	....	396	135	43	120	.358	....	....	....	49	76	.645	....	....	110	27	67	0	....	....	....	5.9	2.0	1.6	0.4	.396
62-63	San Francisco	20	....	201	61	26	68	.382	....	....	....	9	20	.450	....	....	56	8	34	0	....	....	....	10.1	3.1	2.8	0.4	.318
NBA Season Totals		87	....	597	196	69	188	.367	....	....	....	58	96	.604	....	....	166	35	101	0	....	....	....	6.9	2.3	1.9	0.4	....
61-62	Philadelphia	4	....	17	2	0	5	.000	....	....	....	2	5	.400	....	....	3	1	3	0	....	....	....	4.3	0.5	0.8	0.3	-.040
NBA Playoff Totals		4	....	17	2	0	5	.000	....	....	....	2	5	.400	....	....	3	1	3	0	....	....	....	4.3	0.5	0.8	0.3	....

• LUE, Tyronn
Tyronn Jamar Lue

Born: May 3, 1977. Mexico, MO, United States.   Height: 6'   Weight: 175 lbs.   Drafted: 1998   College: Nebraska

YEAR TEAM	GP	GS	MIN	PTS	FGM	FGA	FG%	3PM	3PA	3P%	FTM	FTA	FT%	ORB	DRB	TRB	AST	PF	DQ	STL	BLK	TO	MPG	PPG	RPG	APG	PCM
98-99 LA Lakers	15	0	188	75	28	65	.431	7	16	.438	12	21	.571	2	4	6	25	28	0	5	0	11	12.5	5.0	0.4	1.7	.284
99-00 LA Lakers	8	0	146	48	19	39	.487	4	8	.500	6	8	.750	2	10	12	17	17	0	3	0	9	18.3	6.0	1.5	2.1	.310
00-01 LA Lakers	38	1	468	130	50	117	.427	11	34	.324	19	24	.792	5	27	32	45	54	1	19	0	27	12.3	3.4	0.8	1.2	.245
01-02 Washington	71	0	1459	555	222	520	.427	63	141	.447	48	63	.762	14	108	122	246	120	2	49	0	96	20.5	7.8	1.7	3.5	.384
02-03 Washington	75	24	1986	647	248	573	.433	60	176	.341	91	104	.875	22	127	149	263	151	0	47	1	77	26.5	8.6	2.0	3.5	.339
NBA Season Totals	207	25	4247	1455	567	1314	.432	145	375	.387	176	220	.800	45	276	321	596	370	3	123	1	220	20.5	7.0	1.6	2.9	....
98-99 LA Lakers	3	0	33	14	7	17	.412	0	2	.000	0	0	.000	0	2	2	6	4	0	2	0	4	11.0	4.7	0.7	2.0	.303
00-01 LA Lakers	15	0	131	29	10	29	.345	5	13	.385	4	5	.800	1	9	10	10	11	0	12	1	8	8.7	1.9	0.7	0.7	.237
NBA Playoff Totals	18	0	164	43	17	46	.370	5	15	.333	4	5	.800	1	11	12	16	15	0	14	1	12	9.1	2.4	0.7	0.9	....

• LUISI, Jim
James A. Luisi

Born: Nov. 2, 1928.   Height: 6'2".   Weight: 180 lbs.   Drafted: 1951   College: St. Francis (NY)

YEAR TEAM	GP	GS	MIN	PTS	FGM	FGA	FG%	3PM	3PA	3P%	FTM	FTA	FT%	ORB	DRB	TRB	AST	PF	DQ	STL	BLK	TO	MPG	PPG	RPG	APG	PCM
53-54 Baltimore	31	....	367	89	31	95	.326	....	....	....	27	41	.659	....	....	25	35	45	0	....	....	....	11.8	2.9	0.8	1.1	.233
NBA Season Totals	31	....	367	89	31	95	.326	....	....	....	27	41	.659	....	....	25	35	45	0	....	....	....	11.8	2.9	0.8	1.1	

• LUJACK, Al
Bob R. Lujack

Born: Oct. 5, 1921.   Height: 6'3".   Weight: 220 lbs.   Drafted: —   College: Georgetown

YEAR TEAM	GP	GS	MIN	PTS	FGM	FGA	FG%	3PM	3PA	3P%	FTM	FTA	FT%	ORB	DRB	TRB	AST	PF	DQ	STL	BLK	TO	MPG	PPG	RPG	APG	PCM
46-47 Washington	5	....	....	4	1	8	.125	....	....	....	2	5	.400	....	....	....	0	6	....	....	....	....	....	0.8	....	0.0	....
NBA Season Totals	5	....	....	4	1	8	.125	....	....	....	2	5	.400	....	....	....	0	6	....	....	....	....	....	0.8	....	0.0	....

• LUMPKIN, Phil
Phil Lumpkin

Born: Dec. 20, 1951. Dayton, OH, United States.   Height: 6'   Weight: 165 lbs.   Drafted: 1974   College: Miami (OH)

YEAR TEAM	GP	GS	MIN	PTS	FGM	FGA	FG%	3PM	3PA	3P%	FTM	FTA	FT%	ORB	DRB	TRB	AST	PF	DQ	STL	BLK	TO	MPG	PPG	RPG	APG	PCM
74-75 Portland	48	....	792	202	86	190	.453	....	....	....	30	39	.769	10	49	59	177	80	1	20	3	....	16.5	4.2	1.2	3.7	.415
75-76 Phoenix	34	....	370	70	22	65	.338	....	....	....	26	30	.867	7	16	23	48	26	0	15	0	....	10.9	2.1	0.7	1.4	.256
NBA Season Totals	82	....	1162	272	108	255	.424	....	....	....	56	69	.812	17	65	82	225	106	1	35	3	....	14.2	3.3	1.0	2.7	....
75-76 Phoenix	17	....	136	31	10	30	.333	....	....	....	11	14	.786	5	8	13	21	8	0	2	0	....	8.0	1.8	0.8	1.2	.325
NBA Playoff Totals	17	....	136	31	10	30	.333	....	....	....	11	14	.786	5	8	13	21	8	0	2	0	....	8.0	1.8	0.8	1.2	

• LUMPP, Ray
Raymond G. Lumpp

Born: July 11, 1923. Brooklyn, NY, United States.   Height: 6'1".   Weight: 178 lbs.   Drafted: 1948   College: New York University

YEAR TEAM	GP	GS	MIN	PTS	FGM	FGA	FG%	3PM	3PA	3P%	FTM	FTA	FT%	ORB	DRB	TRB	AST	PF	DQ	STL	BLK	TO	MPG	PPG	RPG	APG	PCM
48-49 Indianapolis	37	....	....	453	162	489	.331	....	....	....	129	171	.754	....	....	....	124	99	....	....	....	....	....	12.2	....	3.4	....
48-49 New York	24	....	....	324	117	311	.376	....	....	....	90	112	.804	....	....	....	34	74	....	....	....	....	....	13.5	....	1.4	....
49-50 New York	58	....	....	268	91	283	.322	....	....	....	86	108	.796	....	....	....	90	117	....	....	....	....	....	4.6	....	1.6	....
50-51 New York	64	....	....	430	153	379	.404	....	....	....	124	160	.775	....	....	125	115	160	2	....	....	....	....	6.7	2.0	1.8	....
51-52 New York	62	....	1317	458	184	476	.387	....	....	....	90	119	.756	....	....	125	123	165	4	....	....	....	21.2	7.4	2.0	2.0	.326
52-53 New York	6	....	99	28	8	30	.267	....	....	....	12	12	1.000	....	....	18	12	18	0	....	....	....	16.5	4.7	3.0	2.0	.342
52-53 Baltimore	49	....	1323	501	180	476	.378	....	....	....	141	194	.727	....	....	123	156	160	5	....	....	....	27.0	10.2	2.5	3.2	.376
NBA Season Totals	300	....	2739	2462	895	2444	.366	....	....	....	672	876	.767	....	....	391	654	793	11	....	....	....	9.1	8.2	1.3	2.2	....
48-49 New York	6	....	....	69	21	73	.288	....	....	....	27	35	.771	....	....	....	11	26	....	....	....	....	....	11.5	....	1.8	....
49-50 New York	5	....	....	22	10	18	.556	....	....	....	2	3	.667	....	....	....	3	10	....	....	....	....	....	4.4	....	0.6	....
50-51 New York	13	....	....	68	24	67	.358	....	....	....	20	23	.870	....	....	20	23	40	3	....	....	....	5.2	1.5	1.8	....
51-52 New York	12	....	194	49	13	53	.245	....	....	....	23	25	.920	....	....	19	15	35	1	....	....	....	16.2	4.1	1.6	1.3	.207
52-53 Baltimore	2	....	75	21	7	33	.212	....	....	....	7	10	.700	....	....	8	5	8	0	....	....	....	37.5	10.5	4.0	2.5	.138
NBA Playoff Totals	38	....	269	229	75	244	.307	....	....	....	79	96	.823	....	....	47	57	119	4	....	....	....	7.1	6.0	1.2	1.5	....

• LYNAM, R.B.
Robert Bracey Lynam

Born: 1944.   Height: 6'1".   Weight: 190 lbs.   Drafted: 1966   College: Oklahoma Baptist

YEAR TEAM	GP	GS	MIN	PTS	FGM	FGA	FG%	3PM	3PA	3P%	FTM	FTA	FT%	ORB	DRB	TRB	AST	PF	DQ	STL	BLK	TO	MPG	PPG	RPG	APG	PCM
67-68 Denver-A	7	....	39	17	5	17	.294	0	1	.000	7	8	.875	....	....	5	0	10	0	....	....	5	5.6	2.4	0.7	0.0	.170
ABA Season Totals	7	....	39	17	5	17	.294	0	1	.000	7	8	.875	....	....	5	0	10	0	....	....	5	5.6	2.4	0.7	0.0	....

• LYNCH, George
George DeWitt Lynch III

Born: Sept. 3, 1970. Roanoke, VA, United States.   Height: 6'8".   Weight: 218 lbs.   Drafted: 1993   College: North Carolina

YEAR TEAM	GP	GS	MIN	PTS	FGM	FGA	FG%	3PM	3PA	3P%	FTM	FTA	FT%	ORB	DRB	TRB	AST	PF	DQ	STL	BLK	TO	MPG	PPG	RPG	APG	PCM
93-94 LA Lakers	71	46	1762	681	291	573	.508	0	5	.000	99	166	.596	220	190	410	96	177	1	102	27	85	24.8	9.6	5.8	1.4	.472
94-95 LA Lakers	56	15	953	341	138	295	.468	3	21	.143	62	86	.721	75	109	184	62	86	0	51	10	73	17.0	6.1	3.3	1.1	.388
95-96 LA Lakers	76	6	1012	291	117	272	.430	4	13	.308	53	80	.663	82	127	209	51	106	0	47	10	38	13.3	3.8	2.8	0.7	.347
96-97 Vancouver	41	27	1059	342	137	291	.471	8	31	.258	60	97	.619	98	163	261	76	97	1	63	17	66	25.8	8.3	6.4	1.9	.447
97-98 Vancouver	82	0	1493	616	248	516	.481	9	30	.300	111	158	.703	147	215	362	122	161	0	65	41	107	18.2	7.5	4.4	1.5	.495
98-99 Philadelphia	43	43	1315	356	147	349	.421	9	23	.391	53	84	.631	110	169	279	76	142	0	85	22	79	30.6	8.3	6.5	1.8	.347
99-00 Philadelphia	75	75	2416	722	297	644	.461	15	36	.417	113	183	.617	216	366	582	136	231	2	119	38	120	32.2	9.6	7.8	1.8	.406
00-01 Philadelphia	82	80	2649	686	274	616	.445	15	57	.263	123	183	.719	200	390	590	139	222	2	99	30	109	32.3	8.4	7.2	1.7	.362
01-02 Charlotte	45	18	892	172	73	198	.369	1	6	.167	25	40	.625	70	116	186	54	75	1	40	14	41	19.8	3.8	4.1	1.2	.289
02-03 New Orleans	81	32	1497	363	147	359	.409	28	79	.354	41	74	.554	139	214	353	104	136	1	66	19	52	18.5	4.5	4.4	1.3	.373
NBA Season Totals	652	342	15048	4570	1869	4113	.454	92	301	.306	740	1139	.650	1357	2059	3416	916	1433	10	737	228	770	23.1	7.0	5.2	1.4	....
94-95 LA Lakers	10	0	136	44	15	32	.469	1	5	.200	13	20	.650	13	17	30	7	22	0	8	0	9	13.6	4.4	3.0	0.7	.361
95-96 LA Lakers	2	0	15	4	2	4	.500	0	1	.000	0	0	.000	0	3	3	1	4	0	0	0	2	7.5	2.0	1.5	0.5	.149

Total Basketball

YEAR	TEAM	GP	GS	MIN	PTS	FGM	FGA	FG%	3PM	3PA	3P%	FTM	FTA	FT%	ORB	DRB	TRB	AST	PF	DQ	STL	BLK	TO	MPG	PPG	RPG	APG	PCM
98-99	Philadelphia	8	6	249	72	29	65	.446	2	6	.333	12	17	.706	28	25	53	16	30	1	18	2	13	31.1	9.0	6.6	2.0	.384
99-00	Philadelphia	10	10	293	59	22	65	.338	1	7	.143	14	18	.778	26	45	71	14	33	1	9	5	8	29.3	5.9	7.1	1.4	.302
00-01	Philadelphia	10	8	222	57	24	50	.480	0	1	.000	9	14	.643	20	31	51	12	30	0	13	2	13	22.2	5.7	5.1	1.2	.355
01-02	Charlotte	9	7	286	69	29	59	.492	2	6	.333	9	13	.692	32	44	76	14	26	0	10	6	10	31.8	7.7	8.4	1.6	.412
02-03	New Orleans	6	3	163	42	18	42	.429	5	18	.278	1	4	.250	10	27	37	10	14	0	6	5	8	27.2	7.0	6.2	1.7	.366
NBA Playoff Totals		55	34	1364	347	139	317	.438	11	44	.250	58	86	.674	129	192	321	74	159	2	64	20	63	24.8	6.3	5.8	1.3	....

• LYNCH, Kevin

John Joseph Lynch

Born: Dec. 24, 1968. Bloomington, MN, United States.　Height: 6'5".　Weight: 195 lbs.　Drafted: 1991　College: Minnesota

YEAR	TEAM	GP	GS	MIN	PTS	FGM	FGA	FG%	3PM	3PA	3P%	FTM	FTA	FT%	ORB	DRB	TRB	AST	PF	DQ	STL	BLK	TO	MPG	PPG	RPG	APG	PCM
91-92	Charlotte	55	3	819	224	93	223	.417	3	8	.375	35	46	.761	30	55	85	83	107	0	37	9	44	14.9	4.1	1.5	1.5	.266
92-93	Charlotte	40	8	324	86	30	59	.508	0	1	.000	26	38	.684	12	23	35	25	44	0	11	6	24	8.1	2.2	0.9	0.6	.264
NBA Season Totals		95	11	1143	310	123	282	.436	3	9	.333	61	84	.726	42	78	120	108	151	0	48	15	68	12.0	3.3	1.3	1.1	....
92-93	Charlotte	1	0	3	0	0	0	.000	0	0	.000	0	0	.000	0	0	0	1	0	0	0	0	0	3.0	0.0	0.0	1.0	.356
NBA Playoff Totals		1	0	3	0	0	0	.000	0	0	.000	0	0	.000	0	0	0	1	0	0	0	0	0	3.0	0.0	0.0	1.0	....

• LYNN, Lonnie

Lonnie Lynn

Born: May 24, 1943.　Height: 6'7".　Weight: 215 lbs.　Drafted: 1966　College: Wilberforce

YEAR	TEAM	GP	GS	MIN	PTS	FGM	FGA	FG%	3PM	3PA	3P%	FTM	FTA	FT%	ORB	DRB	TRB	AST	PF	DQ	STL	BLK	TO	MPG	PPG	RPG	APG	PCM
69-70	Denver-A	12	....	140	48	20	46	.435	0	0	.000	8	12	.667	15	35	50	4	18	0	....	....	7	11.7	4.0	4.2	0.3	.455
69-70	Pittsburgh-A	40	....	639	212	92	229	.402	0	3	.000	28	62	.452	68	140	208	39	102	1	....	....	61	16.0	5.3	5.2	1.0	.405
ABA Season Totals		52	....	779	260	112	275	.407	0	3	.000	36	74	.486	83	175	258	43	120	1	....	....	68	15.0	5.0	5.0	0.8	....

• LYNN, Mike

Michael Edward Lynn

Born: Nov. 25, 1945. Covina, CA, United States.　Height: 6'7".　Weight: 215 lbs.　Drafted: 1968　College: UCLA

YEAR	TEAM	GP	GS	MIN	PTS	FGM	FGA	FG%	3PM	3PA	3P%	FTM	FTA	FT%	ORB	DRB	TRB	AST	PF	DQ	STL	BLK	TO	MPG	PPG	RPG	APG	PCM
69-70	LA Lakers	44	....	403	119	44	133	.331	....	....	....	31	48	.646	....	....	64	30	87	4	....	....	....	9.2	2.7	1.5	0.7	.211
70-71	Buffalo	5	....	25	7	2	7	.286	....	....	....	3	3	1.000	....	....	4	1	9	0	....	....	....	5.0	1.4	0.8	0.2	.136
NBA Season Totals		49	....	428	126	46	140	.329	....	....	....	34	51	.667	....	....	68	31	96	4	....	....	....	8.7	2.6	1.4	0.6	....
69-70	LA Lakers	3	....	6	4	2	3	.667	....	....	....	0	0	.000	....	....	2	1	1	0	....	....	....	2.0	1.3	0.7	0.3	.927
NBA Playoff Totals		3	....	6	4	2	3	.667	....	....	....	0	0	.000	....	....	2	1	1	0	....	....	....	2.0	1.3	0.7	0.3	....

• LYTLE, Bob

Bob Lytle

Born: 1916.　Height: 6'4".　Weight: 180 lbs.　Drafted: —　College: Edinboro

YEAR	TEAM	GP	GS	MIN	PTS	FGM	FGA	FG%	3PM	3PA	3P%	FTM	FTA	FT%	ORB	DRB	TRB	AST	PF	DQ	STL	BLK	TO	MPG	PPG	RPG	APG	PCM
37-38	Warren-N	1	....	....	2	1	....	....	....	....	....	0	....	....	....	....	....	....	....	....	....	....	....	2.0	....	....	....
NBL Season Totals		1	....	....	2	1	....	....	....	....	....	0	....	....	....	....	....	....	....	....	....	....	....	2.0	....	....	....

• MACALUSO, Mike

Michael Emilius Macaluso

Born: July 20, 1951.　Height: 6'5".　Weight: 210 lbs.　Drafted: 1973　College: Canisius

YEAR	TEAM	GP	GS	MIN	PTS	FGM	FGA	FG%	3PM	3PA	3P%	FTM	FTA	FT%	ORB	DRB	TRB	AST	PF	DQ	STL	BLK	TO	MPG	PPG	RPG	APG	PCM
73-74	Buffalo	30	....	112	48	19	44	.432	....	....	....	10	17	.588	10	15	25	3	31	0	7	1	....	3.7	1.6	0.8	0.1	.315
NBA Season Totals		30	....	112	48	19	44	.432	....	....	....	10	17	.588	10	15	25	3	31	0	7	1	....	3.7	1.6	0.8	0.1	....

• MACAULEY, Ed

Charles Edward (Easy Ed) Macauley Jr.

Born: Mar. 22, 1928. St. Louis, MO, United States.　Height: 6'8".　Weight: 185 lbs.　Drafted: 1949　College: St. Louis　HOF: 1960

YEAR	TEAM	GP	GS	MIN	PTS	FGM	FGA	FG%	3PM	3PA	3P%	FTM	FTA	FT%	ORB	DRB	TRB	AST	PF	DQ	STL	BLK	TO	MPG	PPG	RPG	APG	PCM
49-50	St. Louis	67	....	....	1081	351	882	.398	....	....	....	379	528	.718	....	....	....	200	221	....	....	....	....	16.1	....	3.0	....
50-51	Boston	68	....	....	1384	459	985	.466	....	....	....	466	614	.759	....	....	616	252	205	4	....	....	....	20.4	9.1	3.7	....
51-52	Boston	66	....	2631	1264	384	888	.432	....	....	....	496	621	.799	....	....	529	232	174	0	....	....	39.9	19.2	8.0	3.5	.560
52-53	Boston	69	....	2902	1402	451	997	.452	....	....	....	500	667	.750	....	....	629	280	188	0	....	....	42.1	20.3	9.1	4.1	.583
53-54	Boston	71	....	2792	1344	462	950	.486	....	....	....	420	554	.758	....	....	571	271	168	1	....	....	39.3	18.9	8.0	3.8	.589
54-55	Boston	71	....	2706	1248	403	951	.424	....	....	....	442	558	.792	....	....	600	275	171	0	....	....	38.1	17.6	8.5	3.9	.563
55-56	Boston	71	....	2354	1240	420	995	.422	....	....	....	400	504	.794	....	....	422	211	158	2	....	....	33.2	17.5	5.9	3.0	.546
56-57	St. Louis	72	....	2582	1187	414	987	.419	....	....	....	359	479	.749	....	....	440	202	206	2	....	....	35.9	16.5	6.1	2.8	.472
57-58	St. Louis	72	....	1908	1019	376	879	.428	....	....	....	267	369	.724	....	....	478	143	156	2	....	....	26.5	14.2	6.6	2.0	.570
58-59	St. Louis	14	....	196	65	22	75	.293	....	....	....	21	35	.600	....	....	40	13	20	1	....	....	14.0	4.6	2.9	0.9	.299
NBA Season Totals		641	....	18071	11234	3742	8589	.436	....	....	....	3750	4929	.761	....	....	4325	2079	1667	12	....	....	28.2	17.5	6.7	3.2	....
50-51	Boston	2	....	....	44	17	36	.472	....	....	....	10	16	.625	....	....	18	8	4	0	....	....	....	22.0	9.0	4.0	....
51-52	Boston	3	....	129	70	27	49	.551	....	....	....	16	19	.842	....	....	33	11	11	1	....	....	43.0	23.3	11.0	3.7	.675
52-53	Boston	6	....	278	101	31	71	.437	....	....	....	39	54	.722	....	....	58	21	23	2	....	....	46.3	16.8	9.7	3.5	.457
53-54	Boston	5	....	127	25	8	22	.364	....	....	....	9	13	.692	....	....	21	21	14	0	....	....	25.4	5.0	4.2	4.2	.399
54-55	Boston	7	....	283	127	43	93	.462	....	....	....	41	54	.759	....	....	52	32	21	0	....	....	40.4	18.1	7.4	4.6	.550
55-56	Boston	3	....	73	31	12	30	.400	....	....	....	7	11	.636	....	....	15	5	6	0	....	....	24.3	10.3	5.0	1.7	.426
56-57	St. Louis	10	....	297	142	44	109	.404	....	....	....	54	74	.730	....	....	62	22	39	3	....	....	29.7	14.2	6.2	2.2	.489
57-58	St. Louis	11	....	227	108	36	89	.404	....	....	....	36	50	.720	....	....	62	18	23	0	....	....	20.6	9.8	5.6	1.6	.546
NBA Playoff Totals		47	....	1414	648	218	499	.437	....	....	....	212	291	.729	....	....	321	138	141	6	....	....	30.1	13.8	6.8	2.9	....

YEAR	TEAM	GP	GS	MIN	PTS	FGM	FGA	FG%	3PM	3PA	3P%	FTM	FTA	FT%	ORB	DRB	TRB	AST	PF	DQ	STL	BLK	TO	MPG	PPG	RPG	APG	PCM

• MACCULLOCH, Todd   Todd Carlyle MacCulloch

Born: Jan. 27, 1976. Winnipeg, MA, Canada.   Height: 7'   Weight: 280 lbs.   Drafted: 1999   College: Washington

YEAR	TEAM	GP	GS	MIN	PTS	FGM	FGA	FG%	3PM	3PA	3P%	FTM	FTA	FT%	ORB	DRB	TRB	AST	PF	DQ	STL	BLK	TO	MPG	PPG	RPG	APG	PCM
99-00	Philadelphia	56	6	528	206	89	161	.553	0	0	.000	28	54	.519	48	98	146	13	94	0	11	37	26	9.4	3.7	2.6	0.2	.479
00-01	Philadelphia	63	3	597	260	109	185	.589	0	0	.000	42	66	.636	69	99	168	10	96	0	7	19	27	9.5	4.1	2.7	0.2	.501
01-02	New Jersey	62	61	1502	604	247	465	.531	0	0	.000	110	164	.671	157	221	378	78	181	1	24	89	66	24.2	9.7	6.1	1.3	.513
02-03	Philadelphia	42	35	813	299	123	238	.517	0	0	.000	53	79	.671	66	130	196	20	107	0	19	32	35	19.4	7.1	4.7	0.5	.429
NBA Season Totals		223	105	3440	1369	568	1049	.541	0	0	.000	233	363	.642	340	548	888	121	478	1	61	177	154	15.4	6.1	4.0	0.5	....
99-00	Philadelphia	5	0	24	8	2	3	.667	0	0	.000	4	6	.667	3	6	9	0	2	0	0	0	0	4.8	1.6	1.8	0.0	.560
00-01	Philadelphia	18	0	109	56	24	38	.632	0	0	.000	8	10	.800	17	12	29	4	14	0	0	3	4	6.1	3.1	1.6	0.2	.604
01-02	New Jersey	20	20	384	123	52	106	.491	0	0	.000	19	31	.613	44	60	104	14	51	0	5	27	23	19.2	6.2	5.2	0.7	.425
NBA Playoff Totals		43	20	517	187	78	147	.531	0	0	.000	31	47	.660	64	78	142	18	67	0	5	30	27	12.0	4.3	3.3	0.4	....

• MACGILVRAY, Ronnie   Ronald MacGilvray

Born: July 20, 1930.   Height: 6'2".   Weight: 185 lbs.   Drafted: 1952   College: St. John's (NY)

YEAR	TEAM	GP	GS	MIN	PTS	FGM	FGA	FG%	3PM	3PA	3P%	FTM	FTA	FT%	ORB	DRB	TRB	AST	PF	DQ	STL	BLK	TO	MPG	PPG	RPG	APG	PCM
54-55	Milwaukee	6	....	57	8	2	12	.167	....	....	....	4	7	.571	....	....	9	11	5	0	....	....	....	9.5	1.3	1.5	1.8	.315
NBA Season Totals		6	....	57	8	2	12	.167	....	....	....	4	7	.571	....	....	9	11	5	0	....	....	....	9.5	1.3	1.5	1.8	....

• MACK, Ollie   Oliver Mack

Born: June 6, 1957. New York, NY, United States.   Height: 6'3".   Weight: 185 lbs.   Drafted: 1979   College: East Carolina

YEAR	TEAM	GP	GS	MIN	PTS	FGM	FGA	FG%	3PM	3PA	3P%	FTM	FTA	FT%	ORB	DRB	TRB	AST	PF	DQ	STL	BLK	TO	MPG	PPG	RPG	APG	PCM
79-80	LA Lakers	27	....	155	51	21	50	.420	0	1	.000	9	18	.500	7	15	22	20	16	0	4	0	8	5.7	1.9	0.8	0.7	.333
79-80	Chicago	23	....	526	183	77	149	.517	0	4	.000	29	33	.879	25	24	49	33	34	0	20	3	25	22.9	8.0	2.1	1.4	.341
80-81	Chicago	3	....	16	3	1	6	.167	0	0	.000	1	2	.500	0	1	1	1	3	0	1	0	0	5.3	1.0	0.3	0.3	-.029
80-81	Dallas	62	....	1666	635	278	600	.463	0	9	.000	79	123	.642	92	137	229	162	114	0	55	7	68	26.9	10.2	3.7	2.6	.390
81-82	Dallas	13	3	150	44	19	59	.322	0	2	.000	6	8	.750	8	10	18	14	6	0	5	1	4	11.5	3.4	1.4	1.1	.247
NBA Season Totals		128	3	2513	916	396	864	.458	0	16	.000	124	184	.674	132	187	319	230	173	0	85	11	105	19.6	7.2	2.5	1.8	....

• MACK, Sam   Sam Mack

Born: May 26, 1970. Chicago, IL, United States.   Height: 6'7".   Weight: 220 lbs.   Drafted: —   College: Houston

YEAR	TEAM	GP	GS	MIN	PTS	FGM	FGA	FG%	3PM	3PA	3P%	FTM	FTA	FT%	ORB	DRB	TRB	AST	PF	DQ	STL	BLK	TO	MPG	PPG	RPG	APG	PCM
92-93	San Antonio	40	0	267	142	47	118	.398	3	22	.136	45	58	.776	18	30	48	15	44	0	14	5	24	6.7	3.6	1.2	0.4	.394
95-96	Houston	31	20	868	335	121	287	.422	54	135	.400	39	46	.848	18	80	98	79	75	0	22	9	28	28.0	10.8	3.2	2.5	.368
96-97	Houston	52	10	904	292	105	262	.401	47	142	.331	35	42	.833	20	86	106	58	67	0	29	6	42	17.4	5.6	2.0	1.1	.294
97-98	Vancouver	57	54	1414	616	222	559	.397	110	269	.409	62	77	.805	30	103	133	101	117	0	41	11	68	24.8	10.8	2.3	1.8	.328
98-99	Vancouver	19	15	577	242	86	212	.406	42	108	.389	28	30	.933	7	46	53	23	53	1	20	1	20	30.4	12.7	2.8	1.2	.310
98-99	Houston	20	0	506	230	81	172	.471	45	111	.405	23	28	.821	7	35	42	32	41	0	15	3	13	20.2	9.2	1.7	1.3	.407
99-00	Golden State	23	5	333	114	37	122	.303	21	64	.328	19	20	.950	7	32	39	24	45	0	18	1	19	14.5	5.0	1.7	1.0	.233
01-02	Miami	12	1	159	40	14	49	.286	7	28	.250	5	7	.714	2	12	14	4	17	0	5	1	7	13.3	3.3	1.2	0.3	.100
NBA Season Totals		259	105	5028	2011	713	1781	.400	329	879	.374	256	308	.831	109	424	533	336	459	1	164	37	221	19.4	7.8	2.1	1.3	....
95-96	Houston	6	0	47	12	5	15	.333	2	9	.222	0	3	.000	0	9	9	1	1	0	1	0	2	7.8	2.0	1.5	0.2	.198
98-99	Houston	4	0	123	50	13	38	.342	10	26	.385	14	17	.824	1	8	9	7	11	0	4	0	5	30.8	12.5	2.3	1.8	.296
NBA Playoff Totals		10	0	170	62	18	53	.340	12	35	.343	14	20	.700	1	17	18	8	12	0	5	0	7	17.0	6.2	1.8	0.8	....

• MACKEY, Malcolm   Malcolm Malik Mackey

Born: July 11, 1970. Chattanooga, TN, United States.   Height: 6'9".   Weight: 248 lbs.   Drafted: 1993   College: Georgia Tech

YEAR	TEAM	GP	GS	MIN	PTS	FGM	FGA	FG%	3PM	3PA	3P%	FTM	FTA	FT%	ORB	DRB	TRB	AST	PF	DQ	STL	BLK	TO	MPG	PPG	RPG	APG	PCM
93-94	Phoenix	22	0	69	32	14	37	.378	0	2	.000	4	8	.500	12	12	24	1	9	0	0	3	2	3.1	1.5	1.1	0.0	.420
NBA Season Totals		22	0	69	32	14	37	.378	0	2	.000	4	8	.500	12	12	24	1	9	0	0	3	2	3.1	1.5	1.1	0.0	....

• MACKLIN, Rudy   Durand Macklin

Born: Feb. 19, 1958. Louisville, KY, United States.   Height: 6'7".   Weight: 205 lbs.   Drafted: 1981   College: Louisiana State

YEAR	TEAM	GP	GS	MIN	PTS	FGM	FGA	FG%	3PM	3PA	3P%	FTM	FTA	FT%	ORB	DRB	TRB	AST	PF	DQ	STL	BLK	TO	MPG	PPG	RPG	APG	PCM
81-82	Atlanta	79	32	1516	554	210	484	.434	0	3	.000	134	173	.775	113	150	263	47	225	5	40	20	111	19.2	7.0	3.3	0.6	.281
82-83	Atlanta	73	20	1171	441	170	360	.472	0	4	.000	101	131	.771	85	105	190	71	189	4	41	10	88	16.0	6.0	2.6	1.0	.330
83-84	New York	8	....	65	35	12	30	.400	0	0	.000	11	13	.846	5	6	11	3	17	0	1	0	6	8.1	4.4	1.4	0.4	.280
NBA Season Totals		160	52	2752	1030	392	874	.449	0	7	.000	246	317	.776	203	261	464	121	431	9	82	30	205	17.2	6.4	2.9	0.8	....
81-82	Atlanta	2	0	30	14	4	8	.500	0	1	.000	6	6	1.000	3	0	3	1	6	1	0	0	2	15.0	7.0	1.5	0.5	.318
82-83	Atlanta	3	3	78	30	11	24	.458	0	0	.000	8	10	.800	4	11	15	2	12	0	2	2	5	26.0	10.0	5.0	0.7	.343
NBA Playoff Totals		5	3	108	44	15	32	.469	0	1	.000	14	16	.875	7	11	18	3	18	1	2	2	7	21.6	8.8	3.6	0.6	....

• MACKNOWSKI, Johnny   John Andrew (Whitey, Mack) Macknowski

Born: Jan. 7, 1923.   Height: 6'   Weight: 180 lbs.   Drafted: 1948   College: Seton Hall

YEAR	TEAM	GP	GS	MIN	PTS	FGM	FGA	FG%	3PM	3PA	3P%	FTM	FTA	FT%	ORB	DRB	TRB	AST	PF	DQ	STL	BLK	TO	MPG	PPG	RPG	APG	PCM
48-49	Syracuse-N	62	....	....	420	146	....	....	....	....	....	128	178	.719	....	....	....	128	....	....	....	....	....	6.8	....	....	....	
49-50	Syracuse	59	....	....	439	154	463	.333	....	....	....	131	178	.736	....	65	128	....	....	....	....	....	....	7.4	....	1.1	....	
50-51	Syracuse	58	....	....	384	131	435	.301	....	....	....	122	170	.718	....	110	69	134	3	....	....	....	....	6.6	1.9	1.2	....	
NBA Season Totals		117	....	....	823	285	898	.317	....	....	....	253	348	.727	....	110	134	262	3	....	....	....	....	7.0	0.9	1.1	....	
NBL Season Totals		62	....	....	420	146	....	....	....	....	....	128	178		....	....	....	128	....	....	....	....	....	6.8	....	....	....	
Career Totals		179	....	....	1243	431	898	....	....	....	....	381	526	....	....	110	134	390	3	....	....	....	....	6.9	0.6	0.7	....	

YEAR	TEAM	GP	GS	MIN	PTS	FGM	FGA	FG%	3PM	3PA	3P%	FTM	FTA	FT%	ORB	DRB	TRB	AST	PF	DQ	STL	BLK	TO	MPG	PPG	RPG	APG	PCM
48-49	Syracuse-N	6	....	....	13	3	....	....	....	....	....	7	9	.778	....	....	....	....	21		....	....	....	....	2.2	....	....	....
49-50	Syracuse	11	....	....	117	39	100	.390	....	....	....	39	51	.765	....	....	....	....	21	18	....	....	....	....	10.6	....	1.9	....
50-51	Syracuse	2	....	....	13	6	13	.462	....	....	....	1	3	.333	....	....	7	4	5	0	....	....	....	....	6.5	3.5	2.0	....
NBA Playoff Totals		13	....	....	130	45	113	.398				40	54	.741	....	....	7	25	23	0	....	....	....	....	10.0	0.5	1.9	....
NBL Playoff Totals		6	....	....	13	3						7	9		....	....	....	....	21		....	....	....	....	2.2			....
Career Playoff Totals		19	....	....	143	48	113					47	63	....	....	....	7	25	23	0	....	....	....	....	7.5	0.4	1.3	....

• MACLEAN, Don

Donald James MacLean

Born: Jan. 16, 1970. Palo Alto, CA, United States.   Height: 6'10".   Weight: 235 lbs.   Drafted: 1992   College: UCLA

YEAR	TEAM	GP	GS	MIN	PTS	FGM	FGA	FG%	3PM	3PA	3P%	FTM	FTA	FT%	ORB	DRB	TRB	AST	PF	DQ	STL	BLK	TO	MPG	PPG	RPG	APG	PCM
92-93	Washington	62	4	674	407	157	361	.435	3	6	.500	90	111	.811	33	89	122	39	82	0	11	4	43	10.9	6.6	2.0	0.6	.442
93-94	Washington	75	69	2487	1365	517	1030	.502	3	21	.143	328	398	.824	140	327	467	160	169	0	47	22	150	33.2	18.2	6.2	2.1	.528
94-95	Washington	39	20	1052	430	158	361	.438	10	40	.250	104	136	.765	46	119	165	51	97	0	15	3	43	27.0	11.0	4.2	1.3	.347
95-96	Denver	56	5	1107	625	233	547	.426	14	49	.286	145	198	.732	62	143	205	89	105	1	21	5	67	19.8	11.2	3.7	1.6	.455
96-97	Philadelphia	37	2	733	402	163	365	.447	12	38	.316	64	97	.660	41	99	140	37	71	0	12	10	48	19.8	10.9	3.8	1.0	.424
97-98	New Jersey	9	0	42	3	1	10	.100	1	2	.500	0	0	.000	3	2	5	0	7	0	0	0	2	4.7	0.3	0.6	0.0	-.136
98-99	Seattle	17	10	365	185	63	159	.396	9	33	.273	50	80	.625	18	47	65	16	34	0	5	5	25	21.5	10.9	3.8	0.9	.366
99-00	Phoenix	16	0	143	42	18	49	.367	2	6	.333	4	6	.667	6	17	23	8	24	0	2	1	8	8.9	2.6	1.4	0.5	.190
00-01	Miami	8	1	76	31	10	20	.500	2	2	1.000	9	12	.750	7	11	18	4	9	0	5	1	10	9.5	3.9	2.3	0.5	.442
NBA Season Totals		319	111	6679	3490	1320	2902	.455	56	197	.284	794	1038	.765	356	854	1210	404	598	1	118	51	396	20.9	10.9	3.8	1.3	....

• MACLEOD, Robert

Robert Frederick (Wildfire) MacLeod

Born: Oct. 15, 1917. Glen Ellyn, IL, United States.   Height: 6'   Weight: 190 lbs.   Drafted: —   College: Dartmouth

YEAR	TEAM	GP	GS	MIN	PTS	FGM	FGA	FG%	3PM	3PA	3P%	FTM	FTA	FT%	ORB	DRB	TRB	AST	PF	DQ	STL	BLK	TO	MPG	PPG	RPG	APG	PCM
39-40	Chicago-N	9	....	....	11	4	....	....	....	....	....	3			....	....	....	....	....		....	....	....	1.2	....	....	....
NBL Season Totals		9	....	....	11	4	....	....	....	....	....	3			....	....	....	....	....		....	....	....	1.2	....	....	....

• MACON, Mark

Mark L. Macon

Born: Apr. 14, 1969. Saginaw, MI, United States.   Height: 6'4".   Weight: 185 lbs.   Drafted: 1991   College: Temple

YEAR	TEAM	GP	GS	MIN	PTS	FGM	FGA	FG%	3PM	3PA	3P%	FTM	FTA	FT%	ORB	DRB	TRB	AST	PF	DQ	STL	BLK	TO	MPG	PPG	RPG	APG	PCM
91-92	Denver	76	67	2304	805	333	889	.375	4	30	.133	135	185	.730	80	140	220	168	242	4	154	14	152	30.3	10.6	2.9	2.2	.240
92-93	Denver	48	27	1141	358	158	381	.415	0	6	.000	42	60	.700	33	70	103	126	135	2	69	3	72	23.8	7.5	2.1	2.6	.271
93-94	Denver	7	0	126	36	14	45	.311	0	3	.000	8	10	.800	3	4	7	11	17	0	6	1	14	18.0	5.1	1.0	1.6	.086
93-94	Detroit	35	1	370	127	55	139	.396	2	7	.286	15	24	.625	15	19	34	40	56	0	33	0	25	10.6	3.6	1.0	1.1	.276
94-95	Detroit	55	6	721	276	101	265	.381	20	62	.323	54	68	.794	29	47	76	63	97	1	67	1	39	13.1	5.0	1.4	1.1	.327
95-96	Detroit	23	0	287	74	29	67	.433	7	15	.467	9	11	.818	10	12	22	16	34	0	15	0	9	12.5	3.2	1.0	0.7	.225
98-99	Detroit	7	3	69	9	4	20	.200	1	3	.333	0	0	.000	3	2	5	4	6	0	5	1	6	9.9	1.3	0.7	0.6	.014
NBA Season Totals		251	104	5018	1685	694	1806	.384	34	126	.270	263	358	.735	173	294	467	428	587	7	349	20	317	20.0	6.7	1.9	1.7	....

• MACY, Kyle

Kyle Robert Macy

Born: Apr. 9, 1957. Fort Wayne, IN, United States.   Height: 6'3".   Weight: 175 lbs.   Drafted: 1979   College: Kentucky

YEAR	TEAM	GP	GS	MIN	PTS	FGM	FGA	FG%	3PM	3PA	3P%	FTM	FTA	FT%	ORB	DRB	TRB	AST	PF	DQ	STL	BLK	TO	MPG	PPG	RPG	APG	PCM
80-81	Phoenix	82	....	1469	663	272	532	.511	12	51	.235	107	119	.899	44	88	132	160	120	0	76	5	98	17.9	8.1	1.6	2.0	.439
81-82	Phoenix	82	72	2845	1163	486	945	.514	39	100	.390	152	169	**.899**	78	183	261	384	185	1	143	9	123	34.7	14.2	3.2	4.7	.467
82-83	Phoenix	82	9	1836	808	328	634	.517	23	76	.303	129	148	.872	41	124	165	278	130	0	64	8	90	22.4	9.9	2.0	3.4	.492
83-84	Phoenix	82	45	2402	832	357	713	.501	23	70	.329	95	114	.833	49	137	186	353	181	0	123	6	115	29.3	10.1	2.3	4.3	.405
84-85	Phoenix	65	52	2018	714	282	582	.485	23	85	.271	127	140	.907	33	146	179	380	128	0	83	3	111	31.0	11.0	2.8	5.8	.456
85-86	Chicago	82	79	2426	703	286	592	.483	58	141	.411	73	90	.811	41	137	178	446	201	1	81	11	115	29.6	8.6	2.2	5.4	.387
86-87	Indiana	76	0	1250	376	164	341	.481	14	46	.304	34	41	.829	25	88	113	197	136	0	59	7	61	16.4	4.9	1.5	2.6	.372
NBA Season Totals		551	257	14246	5259	2175	4339	.501	192	569	.337	717	821	.873	311	903	1214	2198	1081	2	631	49	713	25.9	9.5	2.2	4.0	....
80-81	Phoenix	7	....	102	49	19	36	.528	4	8	.500	7	7	1.000	2	11	13	11	8	0	5	0	7	14.6	7.0	1.9	1.6	.509
81-82	Phoenix	7	7	243	95	38	89	.427	4	11	.364	15	16	.938	11	11	22	28	21	0	7	1	13	34.7	13.6	3.1	4.0	.345
82-83	Phoenix	3	0	72	35	15	35	.429	0	3	.000	5	7	.714	2	6	8	9	6	0	1	0	1	24.0	11.7	2.7	3.0	.423
83-84	Phoenix	17	15	620	176	77	157	.490	10	22	.455	12	16	.750	14	40	54	98	43	0	22	2	25	36.5	10.4	3.2	5.8	.453
84-85	Phoenix	3	3	85	31	13	26	.500	1	4	.250	4	5	.800	3	5	8	9	5	0	6	0	6	28.3	10.3	2.7	3.0	.390
85-86	Chicago	3	3	87	12	5	14	.357	1	4	.250	1	1	1.000	2	2	4	10	9	0	2	0	1	29.0	4.0	1.3	3.3	.170
86-87	Indiana	4	0	49	4	2	6	.333	0	1	.000	0	1	.000	0	3	3	5	7	0	1	0	3	12.3	1.0	0.8	1.3	.058
NBA Playoff Totals		44	28	1258	402	169	363	.466	20	53	.377	44	53	.830	34	78	112	170	99	0	44	3	56	28.6	9.1	2.5	3.9	....

• MADDOX, Jack

Jack C. Maddox

Born: Dec. 10, 1921.   Height: 6'3".   Weight: 185 lbs.   Drafted: —   College: West Texas State

YEAR	TEAM	GP	GS	MIN	PTS	FGM	FGA	FG%	3PM	3PA	3P%	FTM	FTA	FT%	ORB	DRB	TRB	AST	PF	DQ	STL	BLK	TO	MPG	PPG	RPG	APG	PCM
46-47	Oshkosh-N	43	....	....	237	102	....	....	....	....	....	33	39	.846	....	....	....	....	53	....	....	....	....	5.5	....	....	....
47-48	Oshkosh-N	60	....	....	351	146	....	....	....	....	....	59	90	.656	....	....	....	....	112	....	....	....	....	5.9	....	....	....
48-49	Hammond-N	17	....	....	96	39	....	....	....	....	....	18	29	.621	....	....	....	....	28	....	....	....	....	5.6	....	....	....
48-49	Indianapolis	1	....	....	0	0	0	.000	....	....	....	0	0	.000	....	....	....	1	0	....	....	....	....	0.0	....	1.0	....
NBA Season Totals		1	....	....	0	0	0	.000				0	0	.000				1	0					0.0		1.0	....
NBL Season Totals		120	....	....	684	287						110	158		....	....	....	....	193		....	....	....	5.7	....	....	....
Career Totals		121	....	....	684	287	0					110	158	....				1	193					5.7	0.0		....
46-47	Oshkosh-N	7	....	....	7	3	....	....	....	....	....	1	2	.500	....	....	....	....		....	....	....	....	1.0	....	....	....
47-48	Oshkosh-N	4	....	....	9	4	....	....	....	....	....	1	1	1.000	....	....	....	....		....	....	....	....	2.3	....	....	....
NBL Playoff Totals		11	....	....	16	7	....	....	....	....	....	2	3	....	....	....	....	....		....	....	....	....	1.5	....	....	....

YEAR	TEAM	GP	GS	MIN	PTS	FGM	FGA	FG%	3PM	3PA	3P%	FTM	FTA	FT%	ORB	DRB	TRB	AST	PF	DQ	STL	BLK	TO	MPG	PPG	RPG	APG	PCM

• MADDOX, Tito
Theodore Maddox

Born: June 7, 1981. Compton, CA, United States.   Height: 6'4".   Weight: 190 lbs.   Drafted: 2002   College: Fresno State

YEAR	TEAM	GP	GS	MIN	PTS	FGM	FGA	FG%	3PM	3PA	3P%	FTM	FTA	FT%	ORB	DRB	TRB	AST	PF	DQ	STL	BLK	TO	MPG	PPG	RPG	APG	PCM
02-03	Houston	9	0	35	11	3	12	.250	0	3	.000	5	8	.625	1	6	7	5	4	0	3	1	3	3.9	1.2	0.8	0.6	.354
NBA Season Totals		9	0	35	11	3	12	.250	0	3	.000	5	8	.625	1	6	7	5	4	0	3	1	3	3.9	1.2	0.8	0.6	....

• MADKINS, Gerald
Gerald Madkins Jr.

Born: Apr. 18, 1969. Merced, CA, United States.   Height: 6'4".   Weight: 200 lbs.   Drafted: —   College: UCLA

YEAR	TEAM	GP	GS	MIN	PTS	FGM	FGA	FG%	3PM	3PA	3P%	FTM	FTA	FT%	ORB	DRB	TRB	AST	PF	DQ	STL	BLK	TO	MPG	PPG	RPG	APG	PCM
93-94	Cleveland	22	0	149	35	11	31	.355	5	15	.333	8	10	.800	1	10	11	19	16	0	9	0	13	6.8	1.6	0.5	0.9	.238
94-95	Cleveland	7	0	28	8	2	6	.333	1	2	.500	3	4	.750	0	0	0	1	2	0	2	0	3	4.0	1.1	0.0	0.1	.106
97-98	Golden State	19	0	243	37	13	34	.382	6	15	.400	5	7	.714	2	13	15	45	18	0	13	1	13	12.8	1.9	0.8	2.4	.297
NBA Season Totals		48	0	420	80	26	71	.366	12	32	.375	16	21	.762	3	23	26	65	36	0	24	1	29	8.8	1.7	0.5	1.4	....

• MADSEN, Mark
Mark Ellsworth Madsen

Born: Jan. 28, 1976. Walnut Creek, CA, United States.   Height: 6'9".   Weight: 240 lbs.   Drafted: 2000   College: Stanford

YEAR	TEAM	GP	GS	MIN	PTS	FGM	FGA	FG%	3PM	3PA	3P%	FTM	FTA	FT%	ORB	DRB	TRB	AST	PF	DQ	STL	BLK	TO	MPG	PPG	RPG	APG	PCM
00-01	LA Lakers	70	3	641	137	55	113	.487	1	1	1.000	26	37	.703	74	78	152	24	111	2	8	8	27	9.2	2.0	2.2	0.3	.286
01-02	LA Lakers	59	5	650	167	66	146	.452	0	2	.000	35	54	.648	89	73	162	44	104	0	16	13	22	11.0	2.8	2.7	0.7	.369
02-03	LA Lakers	54	22	781	174	69	163	.423	0	0	.000	36	61	.590	86	73	159	38	116	0	15	19	27	14.5	3.2	2.9	0.7	.278
NBA Season Totals		183	30	2072	478	190	422	.450	1	3	.333	97	152	.638	249	224	473	106	331	2	39	40	76	11.3	2.6	2.6	0.6	....
00-01	LA Lakers	13	0	48	5	1	13	.077	0	0	.000	3	5	.600	6	4	10	4	4	0	0	2	2	3.7	0.4	0.8	0.3	.102
01-02	LA Lakers	7	0	10	0	0	1	.000	0	1	.000	0	0	.000	0	2	2	1	0	0	0	1	1	1.4	0.0	0.3	0.0	-.045
02-03	LA Lakers	12	2	169	33	13	31	.419	0	1	.000	7	16	.438	14	14	28	12	32	0	3	2	8	14.1	2.8	2.3	1.0	.200
NBA Playoff Totals		32	2	227	38	14	45	.311	0	2	.000	10	21	.476	20	20	40	16	37	0	3	4	11	7.1	1.2	1.3	0.5	....

• MAGER, Norm
Norman Clifford (The Splinter) Mager

Born: Mar. 23, 1926.   Height: 6'5".   Weight: 185 lbs.   Drafted: 1950   College: CCNY

YEAR	TEAM	GP	GS	MIN	PTS	FGM	FGA	FG%	3PM	3PA	3P%	FTM	FTA	FT%	ORB	DRB	TRB	AST	PF	DQ	STL	BLK	TO	MPG	PPG	RPG	APG	PCM
50-51	Baltimore	22	....	....	101	32	126	.254	....	....	....	37	48	.771	....	....	44	22	56	3	....	....	....	....	4.6	2.0	1.0	....
NBA Season Totals		22	....	....	101	32	126	.254	....	....	....	37	48	.771	....	....	44	22	56	3	....	....	....	....	4.6	2.0	1.0	....

• MAGGETTE, Corey
Paul Antoine Maggette

Born: Feb. 1, 1979. Melrose Park, IL, United States. Died: Sept.1974.   Height: 6'6".   Weight: 218 lbs.   Drafted: 1999   College: Duke

YEAR	TEAM	GP	GS	MIN	PTS	FGM	FGA	FG%	3PM	3PA	3P%	FTM	FTA	FT%	ORB	DRB	TRB	AST	PF	DQ	STL	BLK	TO	MPG	PPG	RPG	APG	PCM
99-00	Orlando	77	5	1370	646	224	469	.478	2	11	.182	196	261	.751	123	180	303	61	169	1	24	26	138	17.8	8.4	3.9	0.8	.423
00-01	LA Clippers	69	9	1359	690	225	487	.462	17	56	.304	223	288	.774	88	203	291	82	140	1	35	9	106	19.7	10.0	4.2	1.2	.485
01-02	LA Clippers	63	52	1615	717	235	530	.443	46	139	.331	201	251	.801	54	177	231	112	155	0	41	19	116	25.6	11.4	3.7	1.8	.395
02-03	LA Clippers	64	57	2006	1073	343	773	.444	62	177	.350	325	405	.802	77	245	322	123	194	6	55	16	147	31.3	16.8	5.0	1.9	.457
NBA Season Totals		273	123	6350	3126	1027	2259	.455	127	383	.332	945	1205	.784	342	805	1147	378	658	8	155	70	507	23.3	11.5	4.2	1.4	....

• MAGLEY, George
Red John (Red) Magley

Born: May 3, 1959. South Bend, IN, United States. Died: Dec.1983.   Height: 6'8".   Weight: 202 lbs.   Drafted: 1982   College: Kansas

YEAR	TEAM	GP	GS	MIN	PTS	FGM	FGA	FG%	3PM	3PA	3P%	FTM	FTA	FT%	ORB	DRB	TRB	AST	PF	DQ	STL	BLK	TO	MPG	PPG	RPG	APG	PCM
82-83	Cleveland	14	0	56	12	4	16	.250	0	1	.000	4	8	.500	2	8	10	2	5	0	2	0	1	4.0	0.9	0.7	0.1	.165
NBA Season Totals		14	0	56	12	4	16	.250	0	1	.000	4	8	.500	2	8	10	2	5	0	2	0	1	4.0	0.9	0.7	0.1	....

• MAGLOIRE, Jamaal
Jamaal Dane Magloire

Born: May 21, 1978. Toronto, ON, Canada.   Height: 6'11".   Weight: 259 lbs.   Drafted: 2000   College: Kentucky

YEAR	TEAM	GP	GS	MIN	PTS	FGM	FGA	FG%	3PM	3PA	3P%	FTM	FTA	FT%	ORB	DRB	TRB	AST	PF	DQ	STL	BLK	TO	MPG	PPG	RPG	APG	PCM
00-01	Charlotte	74	0	1095	339	122	271	.450	0	2	.000	95	145	.655	103	192	295	27	139	0	18	78	61	14.8	4.6	4.0	0.4	.408
01-02	Charlotte	82	8	1549	699	228	414	.551	0	1	.000	243	333	.730	153	308	461	31	201	0	27	86	118	18.9	8.5	5.6	0.4	.546
02-03	New Orleans	82	82	2443	841	305	635	.480	0	3	.000	231	322	.717	260	464	724	88	276	4	49	111	158	29.8	10.3	8.8	1.1	.463
NBA Season Totals		238	90	5087	1879	655	1320	.496	0	6	.000	569	800	.711	516	964	1480	146	616	4	94	275	337	21.4	7.9	6.2	0.6	....
00-01	Charlotte	10	0	110	39	16	28	.571	0	0	.000	7	23	.304	8	20	28	3	20	0	0	6	4	11.0	3.9	2.8	0.3	.385
01-02	Charlotte	8	0	168	98	22	40	.550	0	0	.000	54	71	.761	17	28	45	5	30	1	0	15	17	21.0	12.3	5.6	0.6	.624
02-03	New Orleans	6	6	188	69	22	49	.449	0	0	.000	25	33	.758	17	33	50	2	15	0	4	6	9	31.3	11.5	8.3	0.3	.439
NBA Playoff Totals		24	6	466	206	60	117	.513	0	0	.000	86	127	.677	42	81	123	10	65	1	4	27	30	19.4	8.6	5.1	0.4	....

• MAHAFFEY, Randy
Randolph Mahaffey

Born: Sept. 28, 1945. LaGrange, GA, United States.   Height: 6'7".   Weight: 210 lbs.   Drafted: 1967   College: Clemson

YEAR	TEAM	GP	GS	MIN	PTS	FGM	FGA	FG%	3PM	3PA	3P%	FTM	FTA	FT%	ORB	DRB	TRB	AST	PF	DQ	STL	BLK	TO	MPG	PPG	RPG	APG	PCM
67-68	Kentucky-A	75	....	2325	1027	373	875	.426	0	2	.000	281	411	.684	259	425	684	129	278	15	....	....	224	31.0	13.7	9.1	1.7	.499
68-69	Kentucky-A	31	....	759	272	102	251	.406	0	1	.000	68	101	.673	57	127	184	35	99	4	....	....	94	24.5	8.8	5.9	1.1	.376
68-69	New York-A	48	....	1594	662	249	577	.432	0	1	.000	164	228	.719	137	250	387	64	162	4	....	....	149	33.2	13.8	8.1	1.3	.432
69-70	Carolina-A	84	....	2558	928	367	821	.447	0	4	.000	194	283	.686	212	469	681	164	205	7	....	....	240	30.5	11.0	8.1	2.0	.451
70-71	Carolina-A	83	....	2353	926	385	791	.487	0	8	.000	156	239	.653	215	403	618	115	304	12	....	....	170	28.3	11.2	7.4	1.4	.458
ABA Season Totals		321	....	9589	3815	1476	3315	.445	0	16	.000	863	1262	.684	880	1674	2554	507	1118	42	....	....	877	29.9	11.9	8.0	1.6	....
67-68	Kentucky-A	5	....	147	65	24	53	.453	0	0	.000	17	24	.708	....	....	23	3	16	1	....	....	16	29.4	13.0	4.6	0.6	.367
69-70	Carolina-A	4	....	91	48	19	38	.500	0	0	.000	10	14	.714	....	....	27	8	....	....	....	....	....	22.8	12.0	6.8	2.0	....
ABA Playoff Totals		9	....	238	113	43	91	.473	0	0	.000	27	38	.711	....	....	50	11	16	1	....	....	16	26.4	12.6	5.6	1.2	....

• MAHNKEN, John

John E. (Long John) Mahnken

Born: June 16, 1922. Height: 6'8". Weight: 220 lbs. Drafted: — College: Georgetown

YEAR TEAM	GP	GS	MIN	PTS	FGM	FGA	FG%	3PM	3PA	3P%	FTM	FTA	FT%	ORB	DRB	TRB	AST	PF	DQ	STL	BLK	TO	MPG	PPG	RPG	APG	PCM
45-46 Rochester-N	16	....	....	123	50	....	....	....	....	....	23	39	.590	....	....	....	....	....	....	....	....	....	....	7.7	....	....	....
46-47 Washington	60	....	....	557	223	876	.255	....	....	....	111	163	.681	....	....	....	60	181	....	....	....	....	....	9.3	....	1.0	....
47-48 Washington	48	....	....	316	131	526	.249	....	....	....	54	88	.614	....	....	....	31	151	....	....	....	....	....	6.6	....	0.6	....
48-49 Baltimore	7	....	....	53	21	80	.263	....	....	....	11	18	.611	....	....	....	9	32	....	....	....	....	....	7.6	....	1.3	....
48-49 Indianapolis	13	....	....	130	58	236	.246	....	....	....	14	30	.467	....	....	....	34	40	....	....	....	....	....	10.0	....	2.6	....
48-49 Fort Wayne	37	....	....	351	136	514	.265	....	....	....	79	119	.664	....	....	....	82	143	....	....	....	....	....	9.5	....	2.2	....
49-50 Fort Wayne	2	....	....	7	3	8	.375	....	....	....	1	3	.333	....	....	....	2	8	....	....	....	....	....	3.5	....	1.0	....
49-50 Tri-Cities	36	....	....	223	85	319	.266	....	....	....	53	76	.697	....	....	....	64	149	....	....	....	....	....	6.2	....	1.8	....
49-50 Boston	24	....	....	111	44	168	.262	....	....	....	23	36	.639	....	....	....	42	74	....	....	....	....	....	4.6	....	1.8	....
50-51 Bos/Ind	58	....	....	267	111	351	.316	....	....	....	45	70	.643	....	....	219	77	164	6	....	....	....	....	4.6	3.8	1.3	....
51-52 Boston	60	....	581	182	78	227	.344	....	....	....	26	43	.605	....	....	132	63	91	2	....	....	....	9.7	3.0	2.2	1.1	.366
52-53 Boston	69	....	771	191	76	252	.302	....	....	....	39	56	.696	....	....	182	75	110	1	....	....	....	11.2	2.8	2.6	1.1	.318
NBA Season Totals	414	....	1352	2388	966	3557	.272	....	....	....	456	702	.650	....	....	533	539	1143	9	....	....	....	3.3	5.8	1.3	1.3	....
NBL Season Totals	16	....	....	123	50	....	....	....	....	....	23	39	....	....	....	....	....	....	....	....	....	....	....	7.7	....	....	....
Career Totals	430	....	1352	2511	1016	3557	....	....	....	....	479	741	....	....	....	533	539	1143	9	....	....	....	3.1	5.8	1.2	1.3	....
45-46 Rochester-N	7	....	....	46	19	....	....	....	....	....	8	9	.889	....	....	....	....	....	....	....	....	....	....	6.6	....	....	....
46-47 Washington	6	....	....	62	23	96	.240	....	....	....	16	19	.842	....	....	....	1	25	....	....	....	....	....	10.3	....	0.2	....
50-51 Indianapolis	3	....	....	4	2	15	.133	....	....	....	0	0	.000	....	....	11	9	11	1	....	....	....	....	1.3	3.7	3.0	....
51-52 Boston	3	....	50	7	2	7	.286	....	....	....	3	6	.500	....	....	10	3	11	1	....	....	....	16.7	2.3	3.3	1.0	.189
52-53 Boston	6	....	72	5	0	10	.000	....	....	....	5	5	1.000	....	....	19	6	16	0	....	....	....	12.0	0.8	3.2	1.0	.186
NBA Playoff Totals	18	....	122	78	27	128	.211	....	....	....	24	30	.800	....	....	40	19	63	2	....	....	....	6.8	4.3	2.2	1.1	....
NBL Playoff Totals	7	....	....	46	19	....	....	....	....	....	8	9	....	....	....	....	....	....	....	....	....	....	....	6.6	....	....	....
Career Playoff Totals	25	....	122	124	46	128	....	....	....	....	32	39	....	....	....	40	19	63	2	....	....	....	4.9	5.0	1.6	0.8	....

• MAHONEY, Brian

Brian C. Mahoney

Born: Dec. 17, 1948. Height: 6'3". Weight: 175 lbs. Drafted: 1971 College: Manhattan

YEAR TEAM	GP	GS	MIN	PTS	FGM	FGA	FG%	3PM	3PA	3P%	FTM	FTA	FT%	ORB	DRB	TRB	AST	PF	DQ	STL	BLK	TO	MPG	PPG	RPG	APG	PCM
72-73 New York-A	19	....	181	58	17	57	.298	0	2	.000	24	40	.600	4	10	14	12	35	1	....	....	17	9.5	3.1	0.7	0.6	.138
ABA Season Totals	19	....	181	58	17	57	.298	0	2	.000	24	40	.600	4	10	14	12	35	1	....	....	17	9.5	3.1	0.7	0.6	....

• MAHONEY, Mo

Francis H. (Mo) Mahoney

Born: Nov. 20, 1927. Height: 6'2". Weight: 205 lbs. Drafted: 1950 College: Brown

YEAR TEAM	GP	GS	MIN	PTS	FGM	FGA	FG%	3PM	3PA	3P%	FTM	FTA	FT%	ORB	DRB	TRB	AST	PF	DQ	STL	BLK	TO	MPG	PPG	RPG	APG	PCM
52-53 Boston	6	....	34	12	4	10	.400	....	....	....	4	5	.800	....	....	7	1	7	0	....	....	....	5.7	2.0	1.2	0.2	.327
53-54 Baltimore	2	....	11	0	0	2	.000	....	....	....	0	0	.000	....	....	2	1	0	0	....	....	....	5.5	0.0	1.0	0.5	.117
NBA Season Totals	8	....	45	12	4	12	.333	....	....	....	4	5	.800	....	....	9	2	7	0	....	....	....	5.6	1.5	1.1	0.3	....
52-53 Boston	4	....	45	9	3	14	.214	....	....	....	3	5	.600	....	....	7	2	14	0	....	....	....	11.3	2.3	1.8	0.5	.064
NBA Playoff Totals	4	....	45	9	3	14	.214	....	....	....	3	5	.600	....	....	7	2	14	0	....	....	....	11.3	2.3	1.8	0.5	....

• MAHORN, Rick

Derrick Allen Mahorn

Born: Sept. 21, 1958. Hartford, CT, United States. Height: 6'10". Weight: 240 lbs. Drafted: 1980 College: Hampton Institute

YEAR TEAM	GP	GS	MIN	PTS	FGM	FGA	FG%	3PM	3PA	3P%	FTM	FTA	FT%	ORB	DRB	TRB	AST	PF	DQ	STL	BLK	TO	MPG	PPG	RPG	APG	PCM
80-81 Washington	52	....	696	249	111	219	.507	0	0	.000	27	40	.675	67	148	215	25	134	3	21	44	36	13.4	4.8	4.1	0.5	.479
81-82 Washington	80	80	2664	976	414	816	.507	0	3	.000	148	234	.632	149	555	704	150	349	12	57	138	160	33.3	12.2	8.8	1.9	.468
82-83 Washington	82	82	3023	898	376	768	.490	0	3	.000	146	254	.575	171	608	779	115	335	13	86	148	172	36.9	11.0	9.5	1.4	.407
83-84 Washington	82	82	2701	739	307	605	.507	0	0	.000	125	192	.651	169	569	738	131	358	14	62	123	139	32.9	9.0	9.0	1.6	.420
84-85 Washington	77	63	2072	483	206	413	.499	0	0	.000	71	104	.683	150	458	608	121	308	11	59	104	131	26.9	6.3	7.9	1.6	.414
85-86 Detroit	80	12	1442	395	157	345	.455	0	1	.000	81	119	.681	121	291	412	64	261	4	40	61	112	18.0	4.9	5.2	0.8	.362
86-87 Detroit	63	6	1278	384	144	322	.447	0	0	.000	96	117	.821	93	282	375	38	221	4	32	50	76	20.3	6.1	6.0	0.6	.392
87-88 Detroit	67	64	1963	717	276	481	.574	1	2	.500	164	217	.756	159	406	565	60	262	4	43	42	121	29.3	10.7	8.4	0.9	.477
88-89 Detroit	72	61	1795	522	203	393	.517	0	2	.000	116	155	.748	141	355	496	59	206	1	40	66	94	24.9	7.3	6.9	0.8	.427
89-90 Philadelphia	75	66	2271	811	313	630	.497	2	9	.222	183	256	.715	167	401	568	98	251	2	44	103	105	30.3	10.8	7.6	1.3	.457
90-91 Philadelphia	80	74	2439	711	261	559	.467	0	9	.000	189	240	.788	151	470	621	118	276	6	79	56	128	30.5	8.9	7.8	1.5	.407
92-93 New Jersey	74	9	1077	291	101	214	.472	1	3	.333	88	110	.800	93	186	279	33	156	0	19	31	59	14.6	3.9	3.8	0.4	.362
93-94 New Jersey	28	0	226	59	23	47	.489	0	1	.000	13	20	.650	16	38	54	5	38	0	3	5	8	8.1	2.1	1.9	0.2	.315
94-95 New Jersey	58	7	630	198	79	151	.523	1	3	.333	39	49	.796	45	117	162	26	93	0	11	12	35	10.9	3.4	2.8	0.4	.398
95-96 New Jersey	50	0	450	120	43	122	.352	0	1	.000	34	47	.723	31	79	110	16	72	0	14	13	30	9.0	2.4	2.2	0.3	.274
96-97 Detroit	22	7	218	56	20	54	.370	0	1	.000	16	22	.727	19	34	53	6	34	0	4	3	11	9.9	2.5	2.4	0.3	.265
97-98 Detroit	59	0	707	141	59	129	.457	0	0	.000	23	34	.676	65	130	195	15	123	0	14	7	35	12.0	2.4	3.3	0.3	.279
98-99 Philadelphia	16	0	127	13	5	18	.278	0	0	.000	3	8	.375	7	16	23	2	22	0	5	1	6	7.9	0.8	1.4	0.1	.095
NBA Season Totals	1117	613	25779	7763	3098	6286	.493	5	38	.132	1562	2218	.704	1814	5143	6957	1082	3499	74	633	1007	1458	23.1	6.9	6.2	1.0	....
81-82 Washington	7	7	242	74	32	73	.438	0	0	.000	10	14	.714	14	47	61	13	30	1	10	5	16	34.6	10.6	8.7	1.9	.371
83-84 Washington	4	4	154	38	15	25	.600	0	1	.000	8	10	.800	7	36	43	6	19	0	1	6	6	38.5	9.5	10.8	1.5	.430
84-85 Washington	4	1	41	12	4	8	.500	0	0	.000	4	4	1.000	2	5	7	0	9	0	0	3	1	10.3	3.0	1.8	0.0	.304
85-86 Detroit	4	0	61	12	5	13	.385	0	0	.000	2	2	1.000	3	9	12	0	14	0	1	0	3	15.3	3.0	3.0	0.0	.121
86-87 Detroit	15	15	483	146	59	109	.541	0	1	.000	28	35	.800	42	100	142	5	60	1	6	11	16	32.2	9.7	9.5	0.3	.428
87-88 Detroit	23	21	409	75	31	90	.344	0	0	.000	13	19	.684	19	70	89	13	64	2	5	10	16	17.8	3.3	3.9	0.6	.204
88-89 Detroit	17	17	360	97	40	69	.580	0	0	.000	17	26	.654	30	57	87	7	59	1	9	13	11	21.2	5.7	5.1	0.4	.381
89-90 Philadelphia	10	10	342	94	37	86	.430	0	1	.000	20	26	.769	18	52	70	10	41	1	7	8	13	34.2	9.4	7.0	1.0	.305
90-91 Philadelphia	8	8	208	51	20	36	.556	0	0	.000	11	14	.786	7	35	42	14	25	0	2	4	8	26.0	6.4	5.3	1.8	.362
92-93 New Jersey	4	2	63	8	4	10	.400	0	0	.000	0	0	.000	4	9	13	3	9	0	0	2	1	15.8	2.0	3.3	0.8	.230
93-94 New Jersey	3	0	19	0	0	1	.000	0	0	.000	0	0	.000	1	3	4	0	7	0	0	1	1	6.3	0.0	1.3	0.0	-.024

YEAR	TEAM	GP	GS	MIN	PTS	FGM	FGA	FG%	3PM	3PA	3P%	FTM	FTA	FT%	ORB	DRB	TRB	AST	PF	DQ	STL	BLK	TO	MPG	PPG	RPG	APG	PCM
96-97	Detroit	2	1	18	0	0	2	.000	0	0	.000	0	0	.000	1	0	1	0	5	0	0	0	0	9.0	0.0	0.5	0.0	-.181
98-99	Philadelphia	5	0	29	5	2	6	.333	0	0	.000	1	2	.500	2	6	8	1	6	0	1	0	1	5.8	1.0	1.6	0.2	.226
NBA Playoff Totals		106	86	2429	612	249	528	.472	0	3	.000	114	152	.750	150	429	579	72	348	6	42	63	93	22.9	5.8	5.5	0.7	....

• MAJERLE, Dan

Daniel Lewis (Thunder Dan) Majerle

Born: Sept. 9, 1965. Traverse City, MI, United States. Height: 6'6". Weight: 215 lbs. Drafted: 1988 College: Central Michigan

YEAR	TEAM	GP	GS	MIN	PTS	FGM	FGA	FG%	3PM	3PA	3P%	FTM	FTA	FT%	ORB	DRB	TRB	AST	PF	DQ	STL	BLK	TO	MPG	PPG	RPG	APG	PCM
88-89	Phoenix	54	5	1354	467	181	432	.419	27	82	.329	78	127	.614	62	147	209	130	139	1	63	14	49	25.1	8.6	3.9	2.4	.373
89-90	Phoenix	73	23	2244	809	296	698	.424	19	80	.238	198	260	.762	144	286	430	188	177	5	100	32	80	30.7	11.1	5.9	2.6	.433
90-91	Phoenix	77	7	2281	1051	397	821	.484	30	86	.349	227	298	.762	168	250	418	216	162	0	106	40	116	29.6	13.6	5.4	2.8	.524
91-92	Phoenix	82	15	2853	1418	551	1153	.478	87	228	.382	229	303	.756	148	335	483	274	158	0	131	43	98	34.8	17.3	5.9	3.3	.548
92-93	Phoenix	82	82	3199	1388	509	1096	.464	**167**	**438**	.381	203	261	.778	120	263	383	311	180	0	138	33	131	39.0	16.9	4.7	3.8	.455
93-94	Phoenix	80	76	3207	1320	476	1138	.418	**192**	**503**	.382	176	238	.739	120	229	349	275	153	0	129	43	136	40.1	16.5	4.4	3.4	.395
94-95	Phoenix	82	46	3091	1281	438	1031	.425	199	548	.363	206	282	.730	104	271	375	340	155	0	96	38	107	37.7	15.6	4.6	4.1	.438
95-96	Cleveland	82	15	2367	872	303	748	.405	146	414	.353	120	169	.710	70	235	305	214	131	0	81	34	90	28.9	10.6	3.7	2.6	.383
96-97	Miami	36	26	1264	390	141	347	.406	68	201	.338	40	59	.678	45	117	162	116	75	0	54	14	50	35.1	10.8	4.5	3.2	.353
97-98	Miami	72	22	1928	519	184	439	.419	111	295	.376	40	51	.784	48	220	268	157	139	2	68	15	65	26.8	7.2	3.7	2.2	.337
98-99	Miami	48	48	1624	337	118	298	.396	68	203	.335	33	46	.717	21	187	208	150	100	0	38	7	55	33.8	7.0	4.3	3.1	.289
99-00	Miami	69	69	2308	506	170	422	.403	110	304	.362	56	69	.812	27	306	333	206	156	1	89	17	62	33.4	7.3	4.8	3.0	.333
00-01	Miami	53	19	1306	267	87	259	.336	57	181	.315	36	44	.818	20	146	166	88	98	0	53	15	35	24.6	5.0	3.1	1.7	.261
01-02	Phoenix	65	1	1180	300	99	289	.343	79	235	.336	23	39	.590	28	148	176	90	104	0	48	15	35	18.2	4.6	2.7	1.4	.302
NBA Season Totals		955	454	30206	10925	3950	9171	.431	1360	3798	.358	1665	2246	.741	1125	3140	4265	2755	1927	9	1194	360	1109	31.6	11.4	4.5	2.9	....
88-89	Phoenix	12	0	352	172	63	144	.438	8	28	.286	38	48	.792	22	35	57	14	28	0	13	4	15	29.3	14.3	4.8	1.2	.423
89-90	Phoenix	16	0	479	201	73	150	.487	4	12	.333	51	65	.785	30	51	81	34	34	0	20	2	18	29.9	12.6	5.1	2.1	.464
90-91	Phoenix	4	0	110	42	12	32	.375	4	11	.364	14	19	.737	6	9	15	7	12	0	5	1	2	27.5	10.5	3.8	1.8	.369
91-92	Phoenix	7	0	266	130	48	111	.432	9	33	.273	25	26	.962	13	31	44	20	11	0	10	0	9	38.0	18.6	6.3	2.9	.485
92-93	Phoenix	24	24	1071	370	134	311	.431	54	137	.394	48	69	.696	29	111	140	88	57	0	33	28	32	44.6	15.4	5.8	3.7	.392
93-94	Phoenix	10	10	410	123	46	127	.362	20	59	.339	11	16	.688	15	28	43	24	23	0	11	4	10	41.0	12.3	4.3	2.4	.258
94-95	Phoenix	10	0	307	82	27	73	.370	16	44	.364	12	17	.706	8	23	31	17	24	0	14	3	9	30.7	8.2	3.1	1.7	.260
95-96	Cleveland	3	0	91	50	16	36	.444	10	23	.435	8	9	.889	2	10	12	9	6	0	4	2	3	30.3	16.7	4.0	3.0	.566
96-97	Miami	17	2	496	136	46	117	.393	25	74	.338	19	28	.679	16	56	72	43	31	0	21	4	13	29.2	8.0	4.2	2.5	.354
97-98	Miami	2	2	62	9	3	8	.375	2	6	.333	1	2	.500	1	4	5	5	3	0	4	1	1	31.0	4.5	2.5	2.5	.262
98-99	Miami	5	5	152	20	5	26	.192	5	22	.227	5	7	.714	3	26	29	6	15	0	5	2	3	30.4	4.0	5.8	1.2	.196
99-00	Miami	10	10	372	90	30	71	.423	20	50	.400	10	14	.714	5	65	70	32	34	0	21	1	11	37.2	9.0	7.0	3.2	.387
00-01	Miami	3	0	71	16	5	16	.313	4	14	.286	2	4	.500	3	7	10	5	7	0	3	0	2	23.7	5.3	3.3	1.7	.246
NBA Playoff Totals		123	53	4239	1441	508	1222	.416	181	513	.353	244	324	.753	153	456	609	304	285	0	164	52	128	34.5	11.7	5.0	2.5	....

• MAKI, Paul

Paul Maki

Born: Feb. 1, 1918. Died: Sept.1974. Height: 6'1". Weight: 175 lbs. Drafted: — College: Minnesota

YEAR	TEAM	GP	GS	MIN	PTS	FGM	FGA	FG%	3PM	3PA	3P%	FTM	FTA	FT%	ORB	DRB	TRB	AST	PF	DQ	STL	BLK	TO	MPG	PPG	RPG	APG	PCM
41-42	Sheboygan-N	8	....	....	35	13	....	....	....	....	....	9	....	....	....	....	....	....	....	....	....	....	....	....	4.4	....	....	....
NBL Season Totals		8	....	....	35	13	....	....	....	....	....	9	....	....	....	....	....	....	....	....	....	....	....	....	4.4	....	....	....

• MALACKANY, Red

George (Red) Malackany

Born: May 3, 1913. Died: Dec.1983. Height: 5'9". Weight: 165 lbs. Drafted: — College: Duquesne

YEAR	TEAM	GP	GS	MIN	PTS	FGM	FGA	FG%	3PM	3PA	3P%	FTM	FTA	FT%	ORB	DRB	TRB	AST	PF	DQ	STL	BLK	TO	MPG	PPG	RPG	APG	PCM
37-38	Warren-N	11	....	....	34	13	....	....	....	....	....	8	....	....	....	....	....	....	....	....	....	....	....	....	3.1	....	....	....
38-39	Pittsburgh-N	4	....	....	8	3	....	....	....	....	....	2	....	....	....	....	....	....	....	....	....	....	....	....	2.0	....	....	....
NBL Season Totals		15	....	....	42	16	....	....	....	....	....	10	....	....	....	....	....	....	....	....	....	....	....	....	2.8	....	....	....

• MALAMED, Lionel

Lionel Malamed

Born: Nov. 15, 1924. Died: Sept.17, 1989. Height: 5'9". Weight: 150 lbs. Drafted: — College: CCNY

YEAR	TEAM	GP	GS	MIN	PTS	FGM	FGA	FG%	3PM	3PA	3P%	FTM	FTA	FT%	ORB	DRB	TRB	AST	PF	DQ	STL	BLK	TO	MPG	PPG	RPG	APG	PCM
48-49	Rochester	9	....	....	30	12	31	.387	....	....	....	6	8	.750	....	....	....	6	9	....	....	....	....	....	3.3	....	0.7	....
48-49	Indianapolis	35	....	....	228	85	259	.328	....	....	....	58	69	.841	....	....	....	55	44	....	....	....	....	....	6.5	....	1.6	....
NBA Season Totals		44	....	....	258	97	290	.334	....	....	....	64	77	.831	....	....	....	61	53	....	....	....	....	....	5.9	....	1.4	....

• MALANOWICZ, Eddie

Edmund Malanowicz

Born: 1910. Buffalo, NY, United States. Height: 6'3". Weight: 220 lbs. Drafted: — College: Buffalo

YEAR	TEAM	GP	GS	MIN	PTS	FGM	FGA	FG%	3PM	3PA	3P%	FTM	FTA	FT%	ORB	DRB	TRB	AST	PF	DQ	STL	BLK	TO	MPG	PPG	RPG	APG	PCM
37-38	Buffalo-N	5	....	....	36	14	....	....	....	....	....	8	....	....	....	....	....	....	....	....	....	....	....	....	7.2	....	....	....
NBL Season Totals		5	....	....	36	14	....	....	....	....	....	8	....	....	....	....	....	....	....	....	....	....	....	....	7.2	....	....	....

• MALOKAS, Johnny

Johnny Malokas

Born: Aug. 1, 1916. Died: Apr.16, 2000. Height: 5'11". Weight: 195 lbs. Drafted: — College: Ohio University

YEAR	TEAM	GP	GS	MIN	PTS	FGM	FGA	FG%	3PM	3PA	3P%	FTM	FTA	FT%	ORB	DRB	TRB	AST	PF	DQ	STL	BLK	TO	MPG	PPG	RPG	APG	PCM
44-45	Cleveland-N	1	....	....	5	2	....	....	....	....	....	1	....	....	....	....	....	....	....	....	....	....	....	....	5.0	....	....	....
45-46	Cleveland-N	8	....	....	4	2	....	....	....	....	....	0	0	.000	....	....	....	....	....	....	....	....	....	....	0.5	....	....	....
NBL Season Totals		9	....	....	9	4	....	....	....	....	....	1	0	....	....	....	....	....	....	....	....	....	....	....	1.0	....	....	....

• MALONE, Jeff

Jeffrey Nigel Malone

Born: June 28, 1961. Mobile, AL, United States. Height: 6'4". Weight: 205 lbs. Drafted: 1983 College: Mississippi State

YEAR	TEAM	GP	GS	MIN	PTS	FGM	FGA	FG%	3PM	3PA	3P%	FTM	FTA	FT%	ORB	DRB	TRB	AST	PF	DQ	STL	BLK	TO	MPG	PPG	RPG	APG	PCM
83-84	Washington	81	2	1976	982	408	918	.444	24	74	.324	142	172	.826	57	98	155	151	162	1	23	13	113	24.4	12.1	1.9	1.9	.330
84-85	Washington	76	61	2613	1436	605	1213	.499	15	72	.208	211	250	.844	60	146	206	184	176	1	52	9	106	34.4	18.9	2.7	2.4	.427
85-86	Washington	80	80	2992	1795	735	1522	.483	3	17	.176	322	371	.868	66	222	288	191	180	2	70	12	168	37.4	22.4	3.6	2.4	.451

YEAR	TEAM	GP	GS	MIN	PTS	FGM	FGA	FG%	3PM	3PA	3P%	FTM	FTA	FT%	ORB	DRB	TRB	AST	PF	DQ	STL	BLK	TO	MPG	PPG	RPG	APG	PCM
86-87	Washington	80	79	2763	1758	689	1509	.457	4	26	.154	376	425	.885	50	168	218	298	154	0	75	13	184	34.5	22.0	2.7	3.7	.482
87-88	Washington	80	80	2655	1641	648	1360	.476	10	24	.417	335	380	.882	44	162	206	237	198	1	51	13	168	33.2	20.5	2.6	3.0	.457
88-89	Washington	76	75	2418	1651	677	1410	.480	1	19	.053	296	340	.871	55	124	179	219	155	0	39	14	167	31.8	21.7	2.4	2.9	.485
89-90	Washington	75	74	2567	1820	781	1592	.491	1	6	.167	257	293	.877	54	152	206	243	116	1	48	6	128	34.2	24.3	2.7	3.2	.534
90-91	Utah	69	69	2466	1282	525	1034	.508	1	6	.167	231	252	.917	36	170	206	143	128	0	50	6	110	35.7	18.6	3.0	2.1	.418
91-92	Utah	81	81	2922	1639	691	1353	.511	1	12	.083	256	285	.898	49	184	233	180	126	1	56	5	138	36.1	20.2	2.9	2.2	.441
92-93	Utah	79	59	2558	1429	595	1205	.494	3	9	.333	236	277	.852	31	142	173	128	117	0	42	4	126	32.4	18.1	2.2	1.6	.395
93-94	Utah	50	50	1657	808	338	692	.488	3	6	.500	129	153	.843	28	87	115	66	77	0	26	5	55	33.1	16.2	2.3	1.3	.357
93-94	Philadelphia	27	23	903	454	187	389	.481	4	6	.667	76	94	.809	23	61	84	59	46	0	14	0	27	33.4	16.8	3.1	2.2	.408
94-95	Philadelphia	19	19	660	350	144	284	.507	11	28	.393	51	59	.864	11	44	55	29	35	0	15	0	29	34.7	18.4	2.9	1.5	.406
95-96	Philadelphia	25	3	407	155	63	160	.394	5	16	.313	24	26	.923	8	24	32	19	19	0	13	0	20	16.3	6.2	1.3	0.8	.240
95-96	Miami	7	0	103	31	13	33	.394	0	0	.000	5	6	.833	0	8	8	7	6	0	3	0	3	14.7	4.4	1.1	1.0	.232
NBA Season Totals		905	755	29660	17231	7099	14674	.484	86	321	.268	2947	3383	.871	572	1792	2364	2154	1695	7	577	100	1542	32.8	19.0	2.6	2.4	....
83-84	Washington	4	0	71	24	12	26	.462	0	1	.000	0	0	.000	2	3	5	2	6	0	1	0	3	17.8	6.0	1.3	0.5	.185
84-85	Washington	4	4	126	65	27	56	.482	1	3	.333	10	13	.769	3	3	6	8	14	1	5	0	4	31.5	16.3	1.5	2.0	.358
85-86	Washington	5	5	197	110	42	103	.408	0	2	.000	26	29	.897	4	12	16	17	13	0	7	3	11	39.4	22.0	3.2	3.4	.396
86-87	Washington	3	3	105	45	17	46	.370	0	0	.000	11	11	1.000	1	6	7	9	8	0	1	0	11	35.0	15.0	2.3	3.0	.201
87-88	Washington	5	5	199	128	50	97	.515	0	1	.000	28	37	.757	3	14	17	11	16	0	5	5	14	39.8	25.6	3.4	2.2	.484
90-91	Utah	9	9	351	186	71	144	.493	0	2	.000	44	48	.917	7	28	35	29	22	0	9	1	12	39.0	20.7	3.9	3.2	.477
91-92	Utah	16	16	610	331	134	275	.487	1	3	.333	62	72	.861	12	27	39	31	33	0	8	2	26	38.1	20.7	2.4	1.9	.385
92-93	Utah	5	5	150	67	29	65	.446	0	0	.000	9	13	.692	3	13	16	3	11	0	3	1	9	30.0	13.4	3.2	0.6	.266
NBA Playoff Totals		51	47	1809	956	382	812	.470	2	12	.167	190	223	.852	35	106	141	110	123	1	39	12	90	35.5	18.7	2.8	2.2	....

• MALONE, Karl

Karl (The Mailman) Malone

Born: July 24, 1963. Summerfield, LA, United States. Height: 6'9". Weight: 250 lbs. Drafted: 1985 College: Louisiana Tech

85-86	Utah	81	76	2475	1203	504	1016	.496	0	2	.000	195	405	.481	174	544	718	236	295	2	105	44	275	30.6	14.9	8.9	2.9	.523
86-87	Utah	82	82	2857	1779	728	1422	.512	0	7	.000	323	540	.598	278	577	855	158	323	6	104	60	238	34.8	21.7	10.4	1.9	.622
87-88	Utah	82	82	3198	2268	858	1650	.520	0	5	.000	552	789	.700	277	709	986	199	296	2	117	50	**328**	39.0	27.7	12.0	2.4	.708
88-89	Utah	80	80	3126	2326	809	1559	.519	5	16	.313	**703**	**918**	.766	259	594	853	219	286	3	144	70	288	39.1	29.1	10.7	2.7	.753
89-90	Utah	82	82	3122	2540	914	1627	.562	16	43	.372	**696**	**913**	.762	232	679	911	226	259	1	121	50	303	38.1	31.0	11.1	2.8	.839
90-91	Utah	82	82	3302	2382	847	1608	.527	4	14	.286	**684**	**888**	.770	236	**731**	967	270	268	2	89	79	246	40.3	29.0	11.8	3.3	.778
91-92	Utah	81	81	3054	2272	798	1516	.526	3	17	.176	**673**	**865**	.778	225	684	909	241	226	2	108	51	251	37.7	28.0	11.2	3.0	.795
92-93	Utah	82	82	3099	2217	797	1443	.552	4	20	.200	**619**	**836**	.740	227	692	919	308	261	2	124	83	238	37.8	27.0	11.2	3.8	.822
93-94	Utah	82	82	3329	2063	772	1552	.497	8	32	.250	511	736	.694	235	705	940	328	268	2	125	126	238	40.6	25.2	11.5	4.0	.706
94-95	Utah	82	82	3126	2187	830	1548	.536	11	41	.268	516	695	.742	156	**715**	871	285	269	2	129	85	238	38.1	26.7	10.6	3.5	.768
95-96	Utah	82	82	3113	2106	789	1520	.519	16	40	.400	512	708	.723	175	629	804	345	245	1	138	56	197	38.0	25.7	9.8	4.2	.749
96-97	Utah	82	82	2998	2249	864	1571	.550	0	13	.000	**521**	**690**	.755	193	616	809	368	217	0	113	48	230	36.6	27.4	9.9	4.5	.832
97-98	Utah	81	81	3030	2190	780	1472	.530	2	6	.333	**628**	**825**	.761	189	645	834	316	237	0	96	70	243	37.4	27.0	10.3	3.9	.790
98-99	Utah	49	49	1832	1164	393	797	.493	0	1	.000	**378**	480	.788	107	356	463	201	134	0	62	28	162	37.4	23.8	9.4	4.1	.694
99-00	Utah	82	82	2947	2095	752	1476	.509	2	8	.250	589	739	.797	169	610	779	304	229	1	79	71	231	35.9	25.5	9.5	3.7	.757
00-01	Utah	81	81	2895	1878	670	1345	.498	2	5	.400	536	676	.793	114	555	669	361	216	0	93	62	244	35.7	23.2	8.3	4.5	.701
01-02	Utah	80	80	3040	1788	635	1399	.454	9	25	.360	509	639	.797	142	544	686	341	229	1	152	59	263	38.0	22.4	8.6	4.3	.619
02-03	Utah	81	81	2936	1667	595	1289	.462	3	14	.214	474	621	.763	113	515	628	379	204	0	136	31	210	36.2	20.6	7.8	4.7	.621
NBA Season Totals		1434	**1429**	53479	36374	13335	25810	.517	85	309	.275	**9619**	**12963**	.742	3501	**11100**	14601	5085	4462	27	2035	1123	**4423**	37.3	25.4	10.2	3.5	....
85-86	Utah	4	4	144	87	38	72	.528	0	0	.000	11	26	.423	6	24	30	4	18	1	8	0	6	36.0	21.8	7.5	1.0	.515
86-87	Utah	5	5	200	100	37	88	.420	0	0	.000	26	36	.722	15	33	48	6	20	1	11	4	17	40.0	20.0	9.6	1.2	.439
87-88	Utah	11	11	494	327	123	255	.482	0	1	.000	81	112	.723	33	97	130	17	35	0	13	7	39	44.9	29.7	11.8	1.5	.597
88-89	Utah	3	3	136	92	33	66	.500	0	0	.000	26	32	.813	22	27	49	4	16	1	3	1	13	45.3	30.7	16.3	1.3	.681
89-90	Utah	5	5	203	126	46	105	.438	0	1	.000	34	45	.756	16	35	51	11	22	1	11	5	12	40.6	25.2	10.2	2.2	.584
90-91	Utah	9	9	383	267	95	209	.455	0	8	.000	77	91	.846	23	97	120	29	35	0	9	11	26	42.6	29.7	13.3	3.2	.718
91-92	Utah	16	16	688	465	148	284	.521	0	2	.000	169	210	.805	43	138	181	42	57	0	22	19	46	43.0	29.1	11.3	2.6	.729
92-93	Utah	5	5	216	120	44	97	.454	1	2	.500	31	38	.816	12	40	52	10	21	0	6	2	20	43.2	24.0	10.4	2.0	.488
93-94	Utah	16	16	703	434	158	338	.467	0	4	.000	118	160	.738	52	146	198	54	59	2	23	13	34	43.9	27.1	12.4	3.4	.661
94-95	Utah	5	5	216	151	48	103	.466	1	3	.333	54	78	.692	15	51	66	19	18	0	7	2	14	43.2	30.2	13.2	3.8	.727
95-96	Utah	18	18	725	477	188	401	.469	0	3	.000	101	176	.574	47	139	186	79	60	0	34	10	45	40.3	26.5	10.3	4.4	.650
96-97	Utah	20	20	816	519	187	430	.435	1	2	.500	144	200	.720	60	168	228	57	59	0	27	15	54	40.8	26.0	11.4	2.9	.614
97-98	Utah	20	20	795	526	198	420	.471	0	3	.000	130	165	.788	47	170	217	68	69	0	22	20	60	39.8	26.3	10.9	3.4	.668
98-99	Utah	11	11	451	240	86	206	.417	0	1	.000	68	86	.791	36	88	124	52	37	0	13	8	40	41.0	21.8	11.3	4.7	.576
99-00	Utah	10	10	386	272	103	198	.520	2	2	1.000	64	79	.810	19	70	89	31	31	0	7	7	27	38.6	27.2	8.9	3.1	.694
00-01	Utah	5	5	199	138	49	121	.405	1	2	.500	39	49	.796	9	35	44	17	13	0	5	4	19	39.8	27.6	8.8	3.4	.564
01-02	Utah	4	4	163	80	30	73	.411	0	1	.000	20	28	.714	3	27	30	18	11	0	5	3	11	40.8	20.0	7.5	4.5	.470
02-03	Utah	5	5	191	98	34	84	.405	0	1	.000	30	41	.732	7	27	34	20	15	0	8	2	20	38.2	19.6	6.8	4.0	.442
NBA Playoff Totals		172	172	7109	4519	1645	3550	.463	6	36	.167	1223	1652	.740	465	**1412**	1877	538	596	6	234	133	503	41.3	26.3	10.9	3.1	....

• MALONE, Moses

Moses Eugene Malone

Born: Mar. 23, 1955. Petersburg, VA, United States. Height: 6'10". Weight: 215 lbs. Drafted: — College: none (HS: Petersburg, VA) HOF: 2001

74-75	Utah-A	83	....	3205	1557	591	1035	.571	0	1	.000	375	591	.635	**455**	754	1209	82	288	....	85	128	320	38.6	18.8	14.6	1.0	.656
75-76	St. Louis-A	43	....	1168	614	251	490	.512	0	2	.000	112	183	.612	196	217	413	58	113	....	25	28	140	27.2	14.3	9.6	1.3	.643
76-77	Buffalo	2	....	6	0	0	0	.000	....	....	....	0	0	.000	**0**	1	1	0	1	0	0	0	....	3.0	0.0	0.5	0.0	.072
76-77	Houston	80	....	2500	1083	389	810	.480	....	....	....	305	440	.693	**437**	634	1071	89	274	3	67	181	....	31.3	13.5	13.4	1.1	.627
77-78	Houston	59	....	2107	1144	413	828	.499	....	....	....	318	443	.718	**380**	506	886	31	179	2	48	76	218	35.7	19.4	15.0	0.5	.653
78-79	Houston	82	....	**3390**	2031	716	1325	.540	....	....	....	599	811	.739	**587**	**857**	**1444**	147	223	0	79	119	328	**41.3**	24.8	**17.6**	1.8	.776
79-80	Houston	82	....	3140	2119	778	1549	.502	0	6	.000	563	**783**	.719	**573**	617	1190	147	210	0	80	107	303	38.3	25.8	14.5	1.8	.751
80-81	Houston	80	....	3245	2222	806	1545	.522	1	3	.333	609	**804**	.757	**474**	706	**1180**	141	223	0	83	150	**312**	40.6	27.8	**14.8**	1.8	.775
81-82	Houston	81	81	**3398**	2520	945	1822	.519	0	6	.000	630	**827**	.762	**558**	630	**1188**	142	208	0	76	125	292	**42.0**	31.1	**14.7**	1.8	.791
82-83	Philadelphia	78	78	2922	1908	654	1305	.501	0	1	.000	**600**	**788**	.761	**445**	**749**	**1194**	101	206	0	89	157	265	37.5	24.5	**15.3**	1.3	.792
83-84	Philadelphia	71	71	2613	1609	532	1101	.483	0	4	.000	545	727	.750	352	598	950	96	188	0	71	110	249	36.8	22.7	**13.4**	1.4	.701
84-85	Philadelphia	79	79	2957	1941	602	1284	.469	0	2	.000	**737**	**904**	.815	385	646	**1031**	130	216	0	67	123	284	37.4	24.6	**13.1**	1.6	.723
85-86	Philadelphia	74	74	2706	1759	571	1246	.458	0	1	.000	617	784	.787	339	533	872	90	194	0	67	71	259	36.6	23.8	11.8	1.2	.650
86-87	Washington	73	70	2488	1760	595	1311	.454	0	11	.000	570	692	.824	340	484	824	120	139	0	59	92	204	34.1	24.1	11.3	1.6	.731

YEAR	TEAM	GP	GS	MIN	PTS	FGM	FGA	FG%	3PM	3PA	3P%	FTM	FTA	FT%	ORB	DRB	TRB	AST	PF	DQ	STL	BLK	TO	MPG	PPG	RPG	APG	PCM
87-88	Washington	79	78	2692	1607	531	1090	.487	2	7	.286	543	689	.788	372	512	884	112	160	0	59	72	253	34.1	20.3	11.2	1.4	.659
88-89	Atlanta	81	80	2878	1637	538	1096	.491	0	12	.000	561	711	.789	386	570	956	112	154	0	79	100	243	35.5	20.2	11.8	1.4	.669
89-90	Atlanta	81	81	2735	1528	517	1077	.480	1	9	.111	493	631	.781	**364**	448	812	130	158	0	47	84	235	33.8	18.9	10.0	1.6	.609
90-91	Atlanta	82	15	1912	869	280	598	.468	0	7	.000	309	372	.831	271	396	667	68	134	0	30	74	139	23.3	10.6	8.1	0.8	.598
91-92	Milwaukee	82	77	2511	1279	440	929	.474	3	8	.375	396	504	.786	320	424	744	93	136	0	74	64	148	30.6	15.6	9.1	1.1	.595
92-93	Milwaukee	11	0	104	50	13	42	.310	0	0	.000	24	31	.774	22	24	46	7	6	0	1	8	10	9.5	4.5	4.2	0.6	.638
93-94	Philadelphia	55	0	618	294	102	232	.440	0	1	.000	90	117	.769	106	120	226	34	52	0	11	17	61	11.2	5.3	4.1	0.6	.570
94-95	San Antonio	17	0	149	49	13	35	.371	1	2	.500	22	32	.688	20	26	46	6	15	0	2	3	10	8.8	2.9	2.7	0.4	.413
NBA Season Totals		1329	784	45071	27409	9435	19225	.491	8	80	.100	8531	11090	.769	**6731**	9481	16212	1796	3076	5	1089	1733	3813	33.9	20.6	12.2	1.4	....
ABA Season Totals		126	....	4373	2171	842	1525	.552	0	3	.000	487	774	.629	651	971	1622	140	401	....	110	156	460	34.7	17.2	12.9	1.1	....
Career Totals		1455	784	49444	29580	10277	20750	.495	8	83	.096	9018	11864	.760	7382	10452	17834	1936	3477	5	1199	1889	4273	34.0	20.3	12.3	1.3	....
74-75	Utah-A	6	....	235	136	51	80	.638	0	0	.000	34	51	.667	47	58	105	9	21	....	0	9	13	39.2	22.7	17.5	1.5	.837
76-77	Houston	12	....	518	225	81	162	.500	....	....	....	63	91	.692	84	119	203	7	42	0	13	21	....	43.2	18.8	16.9	0.6	.595
78-79	Houston	2	....	78	49	18	41	.439	....	....	....	13	18	.722	25	16	41	2	5	0	1	8	8	39.0	24.5	20.5	1.0	.818
79-80	Houston	7	....	275	181	74	138	.536	0	1	.000	33	43	.767	42	55	97	7	18	0	4	16	22	39.3	25.9	13.9	1.0	.742
80-81	Houston	21	....	955	562	207	432	.479	0	2	.000	148	208	.712	125	180	305	35	54	0	13	34	59	45.5	26.8	14.5	1.7	.639
81-82	Houston	3	3	136	72	29	67	.433	0	0	.000	14	15	.933	28	23	51	10	8	0	2	2	6	45.3	24.0	17.0	3.3	.653
82-83	Philadelphia	13	13	524	338	126	235	.536	0	1	.000	86	120	.717	70	136	206	20	40	0	19	25	40	40.3	26.0	15.8	1.5	.797
83-84	Philadelphia	5	5	212	107	38	83	.458	0	0	.000	31	32	.969	20	49	69	7	15	0	3	11	21	42.4	21.4	13.8	1.4	.580
84-85	Philadelphia	13	13	505	262	90	212	.425	0	1	.000	82	103	.796	36	102	138	24	39	0	17	22	23	38.8	20.2	10.6	1.8	.573
86-87	Washington	3	3	114	62	21	47	.447	0	0	.000	20	21	.952	15	23	38	5	5	0	0	3	8	38.0	20.7	12.7	1.7	.623
87-88	Washington	5	5	198	93	30	65	.462	0	1	.000	33	40	.825	22	34	56	7	9	0	3	4	15	39.6	18.6	11.2	1.4	.531
88-89	Atlanta	5	5	197	105	32	64	.500	1	1	1.000	33	41	.784	27	33	60	9	5	0	7	4	11	39.4	21.0	12.0	1.8	.676
90-91	Atlanta	5	0	84	21	4	20	.200	0	0	.000	13	14	.929	16	15	31	3	4	0	2	1	2	16.8	4.2	6.2	0.6	.438
NBA Playoff Totals		94	47	3796	2077	750	1566	.479	1	7	.143	576	756	.762	510	785	1295	136	244	0	84	151	215	40.4	22.1	13.8	1.4	....
ABA Playoff Totals		6	....	235	136	51	80	.638	0	0	.000	34	51	.667	47	58	105	9	21	....	0	9	13	39.2	22.7	17.5	1.5	....
Career Playoff Totals		100	47	4031	2213	801	1646	.487	1	7	.143	610	807	.756	557	843	1400	145	265	0	84	160	228	40.3	22.1	14.0	1.5	....

• MALONEY, Matt

Matthew Patrick Maloney

Born: Dec. 6, 1971. Silver Spring, MD, United States.   Height: 6'3".   Weight: 192 lbs.   Drafted: —   College: Pennsylvania

YEAR	TEAM	GP	GS	MIN	PTS	FGM	FGA	FG%	3PM	3PA	3P%	FTM	FTA	FT%	ORB	DRB	TRB	AST	PF	DQ	STL	BLK	TO	MPG	PPG	RPG	APG	PCM
96-97	Houston	82	82	2386	767	271	615	.441	154	381	.404	71	93	.763	19	141	160	303	125	0	82	1	123	29.1	9.4	2.0	3.7	.341
97-98	Houston	78	78	2217	669	239	586	.408	126	346	.364	65	78	.833	16	126	142	219	99	0	62	5	109	28.4	8.6	1.8	2.8	.284
98-99	Houston	15	7	186	21	5	28	.179	1	15	.067	10	11	.909	2	8	10	21	7	0	4	0	14	12.4	1.4	0.7	1.4	.109
99-00	Chicago	51	12	1175	327	114	318	.358	62	174	.356	37	45	.822	10	54	64	138	42	0	32	3	63	23.0	6.4	1.3	2.7	.257
00-01	Atlanta	55	27	1403	369	146	348	.420	51	142	.359	26	34	.765	14	103	117	154	94	1	56	5	70	25.5	6.7	2.1	2.8	.291
02-03	Atlanta	14	0	103	24	8	25	.320	5	15	.333	3	5	.600	1	6	7	17	9	0	4	0	5	7.4	1.7	0.5	1.2	.268
NBA Season Totals		295	206	7470	2177	783	1920	.408	399	1073	.372	212	266	.797	62	438	500	852	376	1	240	14	384	25.3	7.4	1.7	2.9	....
96-97	Houston	16	16	526	179	61	153	.399	43	108	.398	14	21	.667	1	18	19	50	31	0	10	3	38	32.9	11.2	1.2	3.1	.235
97-98	Houston	5	5	165	33	10	30	.333	5	20	.250	8	9	.889	0	8	8	18	11	0	2	2	4	33.0	6.6	1.6	3.6	.219
NBA Playoff Totals		21	21	691	212	71	183	.388	48	128	.375	22	30	.733	1	26	27	68	42	0	12	5	42	32.9	10.1	1.3	3.2	....

• MALOVIC, Steve

Stephen L. Malovic

Born: July 21, 1956. Cleveland, OH, United States.   Height: 6'10".   Weight: 230 lbs.   Drafted: 1978   College: San Diego State

YEAR	TEAM	GP	GS	MIN	PTS	FGM	FGA	FG%	3PM	3PA	3P%	FTM	FTA	FT%	ORB	DRB	TRB	AST	PF	DQ	STL	BLK	TO	MPG	PPG	RPG	APG	PCM
79-80	Washington	1	....	6	1	0	0	.000	0	0	.000	1	4	.250	0	0	0	0	0	0	1	0	2	6.0	1.0	0.0	0.0	-.210
79-80	San Diego	28	....	277	53	23	42	.548	0	0	.000	7	9	.778	27	31	58	12	35	0	5	1	14	9.9	1.9	2.1	0.4	.280
79-80	Detroit	10	....	162	26	8	25	.320	0	0	.000	10	14	.714	9	19	28	14	16	0	2	5	7	16.2	2.6	2.8	1.4	.261
NBA Season Totals		39	....	445	80	31	67	.463	0	0	.000	18	27	.667	36	50	86	26	51	0	8	6	23	11.4	2.1	2.2	0.7	....

• MALOY, Mike

Michael Alvin Maloy

Born: May 10, 1949. New York, NY, United States.   Height: 6'7".   Weight: 215 lbs.   Drafted: 1970   College: Davidson

YEAR	TEAM	GP	GS	MIN	PTS	FGM	FGA	FG%	3PM	3PA	3P%	FTM	FTA	FT%	ORB	DRB	TRB	AST	PF	DQ	STL	BLK	TO	MPG	PPG	RPG	APG	PCM
70-71	Virginia-A	55	....	725	396	149	334	.446	0	1	.000	98	139	.705	88	148	236	43	125	1	....	....	62	13.2	7.2	4.3	0.8	.582
71-72	Virginia-A	7	....	73	26	12	35	.343	0	0	.000	2	2	1.000	6	11	17	2	14	0	....	....	9	10.4	3.7	2.4	0.3	.230
72-73	Dallas-A	9	....	63	20	7	27	.259	0	0	.000	6	10	.600	6	9	15	3	14	0	....	....	4	7.0	2.2	1.7	0.3	.170
ABA Season Totals		71	....	861	442	168	396	.424	0	1	.000	106	151	.702	100	168	268	48	153	1	....	....	75	12.1	6.2	3.8	0.7	....
70-71	Virginia-A	1	....	2	2	1	3	.333	0	0	.000	0	0	.000	0	1	1	0	0	0	....	....	1	2.0	2.0	1.0	0.0	.600
ABA Playoff Totals		1	....	2	2	1	3	.333	0	0	.000	0	0	.000	0	1	1	0	0	0	....	....	1	2.0	2.0	1.0	0.0	....

• MANAKAS, Ted

Theodore Manakas

Born: Feb. 22, 1951.   Height: 6'2".   Weight: 180 lbs.   Drafted: 1973   College: Princeton

YEAR	TEAM	GP	GS	MIN	PTS	FGM	FGA	FG%	3PM	3PA	3P%	FTM	FTA	FT%	ORB	DRB	TRB	AST	PF	DQ	STL	BLK	TO	MPG	PPG	RPG	APG	PCM
73-74	Omaha	5	....	45	12	4	10	.400	....	....	....	4	4	1.000	0	3	3	2	4	0	1	0	....	9.0	2.4	0.6	0.4	.223
NBA Season Totals		5	....	45	12	4	10	.400	....	....	....	4	4	1.000	0	3	3	2	4	0	1	0	....	9.0	2.4	0.6	0.4	....

• MANDIC, John

John J. Mandic

Born: Oct. 3, 1919. Los Angeles, CA, United States. Height: 6'4". Weight: 205 lbs. Drafted: 1947 College: Oregon State

YEAR	TEAM	GP	GS	MIN	PTS	FGM	FGA	FG%	3PM	3PA	3P%	FTM	FTA	FT%	ORB	DRB	TRB	AST	PF	DQ	STL	BLK	TO	MPG	PPG	RPG	APG	PCM
47-48	Rochester-N	33	....	....	77	32	....	....	....	....	....	13	23	.565	....	....	....	....	57	....	....	....	....	....	2.3	....	....	....
48-49	Indianapolis	56	....	....	269	97	302	.321	....	....	....	75	115	.652	....	....	....	80	151	....	....	....	....	....	4.8	....	1.4	....
49-50	Washington	22	....	....	62	21	65	.323	....	....	....	20	30	.667	....	....	....	7	47	....	....	....	....	....	2.8	....	0.3	....
49-50	Baltimore	3	....	....	4	1	10	.100	....	....	....	2	2	1.000	....	....	....	1	7	....	....	....	....	....	1.3	....	0.3	....
NBA Season Totals		81	....	....	335	119	377	.316	....	....	....	97	147	.660	....	....	....	88	205	....	....	....	....	....	4.1	....	1.1	....
NBL Season Totals		33	....	....	77	32	....	....	....	....	....	13	23	....	....	....	....	....	57	....	....	....	....	....	2.3	....	....	....
Career Totals		114	....	....	412	151	377	....	....	....	....	110	170	....	....	....	....	88	262	....	....	....	....	....	3.6	....	0.8	....
47-48	Rochester-N	5	....	....	6	2	....	....	....	....	....	2	4	.500	....	....	....	....	....	....	....	....	....	....	1.2	....	....	....
NBL Playoff Totals		5	....	....	6	2	....	....	....	....	....	2	4	....	....	....	....	....	....	....	....	....	....	....	1.2	....	....	....

• MANGIAPANE, Frank

Francis E. Mangiapane

Born: Aug. 5, 1925. Height: 5'10". Weight: 195 lbs. Drafted: — College: New York University

YEAR	TEAM	GP	GS	MIN	PTS	FGM	FGA	FG%	3PM	3PA	3P%	FTM	FTA	FT%	ORB	DRB	TRB	AST	PF	DQ	STL	BLK	TO	MPG	PPG	RPG	APG	PCM
46-47	New York	6	....	....	5	2	13	.154	....	....	....	1	3	.333	....	....	....	0	6	....	....	....	....	....	0.8	....	0.0	....
NBA Season Totals		6	....	....	5	2	13	.154	....	....	....	1	3	.333	....	....	....	0	6	....	....	....	....	....	0.8	....	0.0	....

• MANNING, Danny

Daniel Ricardo (D) Manning

Born: May 17, 1966. Hattiesburg, MS, United States. Height: 6'10". Weight: 230 lbs. Drafted: 1988 College: Kansas

YEAR	TEAM	GP	GS	MIN	PTS	FGM	FGA	FG%	3PM	3PA	3P%	FTM	FTA	FT%	ORB	DRB	TRB	AST	PF	DQ	STL	BLK	TO	MPG	PPG	RPG	APG	PCM
88-89	LA Clippers	26	18	950	434	177	358	.494	1	5	.200	79	103	.767	70	101	171	81	89	1	44	25	94	36.5	16.7	6.6	3.1	.459
89-90	LA Clippers	71	42	2269	1154	440	826	.533	0	5	.000	274	370	.741	142	280	422	187	261	4	91	39	185	32.0	16.3	5.9	2.6	.515
90-91	LA Clippers	73	47	2197	1159	470	905	.519	0	3	.000	219	306	.716	169	257	426	196	281	5	117	62	190	30.1	15.9	5.8	2.7	.536
91-92	LA Clippers	82	82	2904	1579	650	1199	.542	0	5	.000	279	385	.725	229	335	564	285	293	5	135	122	213	35.4	19.3	6.9	3.5	.604
92-93	LA Clippers	79	77	2761	1800	702	1379	.509	8	30	.267	388	484	.802	198	322	520	207	323	8	108	101	229	34.9	22.8	6.6	2.6	.601
93-94	LA Clippers	42	41	1595	994	409	829	.493	2	14	.143	174	258	.674	82	214	296	176	167	2	53	57	147	38.0	23.7	7.0	4.2	.578
93-94	Atlanta	26	25	925	409	177	372	.476	1	3	.333	54	83	.651	49	120	169	85	93	0	46	25	86	35.6	15.7	6.5	3.3	.441
94-95	Phoenix	46	19	1510	822	340	622	.547	6	21	.286	136	202	.673	97	179	276	154	176	1	41	57	120	32.8	17.9	6.0	3.3	.560
95-96	Phoenix	33	4	816	441	178	388	.459	3	14	.214	82	109	.752	30	113	143	65	121	2	38	24	76	24.7	13.4	4.3	2.0	.446
96-97	Phoenix	77	17	2134	1040	426	795	.536	7	36	.194	181	251	.721	137	332	469	173	268	7	81	74	162	27.7	13.5	6.1	2.2	.541
97-98	Phoenix	70	11	1794	947	390	756	.516	0	7	.000	167	226	.739	110	282	392	139	201	2	71	46	98	25.6	13.5	5.6	2.0	.569
98-99	Phoenix	50	5	1184	453	187	386	.484	1	9	.111	78	112	.696	62	157	219	113	129	1	36	38	69	23.7	9.1	4.4	2.3	.446
99-00	Milwaukee	72	0	1217	333	149	339	.440	1	4	.250	34	52	.654	50	158	208	73	183	2	62	29	55	16.9	4.6	2.9	1.0	.304
00-01	Utah	82	0	1305	603	247	500	.494	7	28	.250	102	140	.729	66	148	214	92	219	0	47	29	96	15.9	7.4	2.6	1.1	.411
01-02	Dallas	41	10	552	165	71	149	.477	1	7	.143	22	33	.667	25	83	108	30	80	0	21	21	25	13.5	4.0	2.6	0.7	.361
02-03	Detroit	13	0	89	34	13	32	.406	3	8	.375	5	6	.833	7	11	18	7	11	0	9	3	7	6.8	2.6	1.4	0.5	.448
NBA Season Totals		883	398	24202	12367	5026	9835	.511	41	199	.206	2274	3120	.729	1523	3092	4615	2063	2895	40	1000	752	1852	27.4	14.0	5.2	2.3	....
91-92	LA Clippers	5	5	194	113	46	81	.568	1	3	.333	20	31	.645	15	13	28	14	21	1	5	4	13	38.8	22.6	5.6	2.8	.530
92-93	LA Clippers	5	5	171	91	35	85	.412	0	2	.000	21	26	.808	12	24	36	8	19	0	7	5	13	34.2	18.2	7.2	1.6	.435
93-94	Atlanta	11	11	426	220	84	172	.488	0	0	.000	52	66	.788	28	49	77	37	39	0	15	9	26	38.7	20.0	7.0	3.4	.525
95-96	Phoenix	4	0	90	49	22	48	.458	0	1	.000	5	8	.625	4	7	11	5	15	1	4	1	6	22.5	12.3	2.8	1.3	.342
96-97	Phoenix	5	0	116	66	26	45	.578	0	3	.000	14	15	.933	4	26	30	7	21	1	4	7	8	23.2	13.2	6.0	1.4	.658
98-99	Phoenix	3	1	79	38	14	24	.583	0	0	.000	10	13	.769	0	5	5	6	12	0	4	0	3	26.3	12.7	1.7	2.0	.436
99-00	Milwaukee	1	0	5	0	0	1	.000	0	0	.000	0	0	.000	0	1	1	0	0	0	0	0	0	5.0	0.0	1.0	0.0	.000
00-01	Utah	5	0	96	49	19	34	.559	2	2	1.000	9	12	.750	2	9	11	3	21	0	3	4	7	19.2	9.8	2.2	0.6	.395
02-03	Detroit	4	0	14	2	1	3	.333	0	1	.000	0	0	.000	1	2	3	0	4	0	0	1	0	3.5	0.5	0.8	0.0	.143
NBA Playoff Totals		43	22	1191	628	247	493	.501	3	12	.250	131	171	.766	66	136	202	80	152	3	42	31	76	27.7	14.6	4.7	1.9	....

• MANNING, Ed

Edward R. Manning

Born: Jan. 2, 1944. Summit, MS, United States. Height: 6'7". Weight: 210 lbs. Drafted: 1967 College: Jackson State

YEAR	TEAM	GP	GS	MIN	PTS	FGM	FGA	FG%	3PM	3PA	3P%	FTM	FTA	FT%	ORB	DRB	TRB	AST	PF	DQ	STL	BLK	TO	MPG	PPG	RPG	APG	PCM
67-68	Baltimore	71	....	951	284	112	259	.432	....	....	....	60	99	.606	....	....	375	32	153	3	....	....	....	13.4	4.0	5.3	0.5	.450
68-69	Baltimore	63	....	727	293	129	288	.448	....	....	....	35	54	.648	....	....	246	21	120	0	....	....	....	11.5	4.7	3.9	0.3	.457
69-70	Baltimore	29	....	161	69	32	66	.485	....	....	....	5	8	.625	....	....	35	2	33	0	....	....	....	5.6	2.4	1.2	0.1	.350
69-70	Chicago	38	....	616	211	87	255	.341	....	....	....	37	48	.771	....	....	197	34	89	1	....	....	....	16.2	5.6	5.2	0.9	.374
70-71	Portland	79	....	1558	561	243	559	.435	....	....	....	75	93	.806	....	....	411	111	198	3	....	....	....	19.7	7.1	5.2	1.4	.434
71-72	Carolina-A	77	....	1648	551	228	499	.457	0	3	.000	95	114	.833	117	324	441	58	227	4	....	....	83	21.4	7.2	5.7	0.8	.399
72-73	Carolina-A	83	....	1631	590	263	554	.475	0	1	.000	64	84	.762	110	283	393	64	247	4	....	....	84	19.7	7.1	4.7	0.8	.388
73-74	Carolina-A	82	....	1816	681	297	609	.488	1	2	.500	86	101	.851	105	265	370	100	210	....	93	16	95	22.1	8.3	4.5	1.2	.412
74-75	New York-A	70	....	992	241	103	243	.424	0	2	.000	35	42	.833	59	153	212	58	144	....	40	9	57	14.2	3.4	3.0	0.8	.305
75-76	Indiana-A	12	....	134	60	24	60	.400	0	0	.000	12	17	.706	15	22	37	14	18	....	4	2	7	11.2	5.0	3.1	1.2	.494
NBA Season Totals		280	....	4013	1418	603	1427	.423	....	....	....	212	302	.702	....	....	1264	200	593	7	....	....	....	14.3	5.1	4.5	0.7	....
ABA Season Totals		324	....	6221	2123	915	1965	.466	1	8	.125	292	358	.816	406	1047	1453	294	846	8	137	27	326	19.2	6.6	4.5	0.9	....
Career Totals		604	....	10234	3541	1518	3392	.448	1	8	.125	504	660	.764	406	1047	2717	494	1439	15	137	27	326	16.9	5.9	4.5	0.8	....
68-69	Baltimore	4	....	63	14	7	18	.389	....	....	....	0	0	.000	....	....	23	1	11	0	....	....	....	15.8	3.5	5.8	0.3	.327
69-70	Chicago	2	....	29	11	5	10	.500	....	....	....	1	2	.500	....	....	9	3	2	0	....	....	....	14.5	5.5	4.5	1.5	.571
72-73	Carolina-A	12	....	262	106	44	82	.537	0	0	.000	18	23	.783	18	39	57	8	40	0	....	....	14	21.8	8.8	4.8	0.7	.426
73-74	Carolina-A	4	....	81	42	18	37	.486	1	1	1.000	5	5	1.000	4	9	13	0	11	....	0	1	4	20.3	10.5	3.3	0.0	.397
74-75	New York-A	3	....	18	5	2	7	.286	0	1	.000	1	1	1.000	0	1	1	0	2	....	0	0	0	6.0	1.7	0.3	0.0	.031
NBA Playoff Totals		6	....	92	25	12	28	.429	....	....	....	1	2	.500	....	....	32	4	13	0	....	....	....	15.3	4.2	5.3	0.7	....
ABA Playoff Totals		19	....	361	153	64	126	.508	1	2	.500	24	29	.828	22	49	71	8	53	0	0	1	18	19.0	8.1	3.7	0.4	....
Career Playoff Totals		25	....	453	178	76	154	.494	1	2	.500	25	31	.806	22	49	103	12	66	0	0	1	18	18.1	7.1	4.1	0.5	....

YEAR	TEAM	GP	GS	MIN	PTS	FGM	FGA	FG%	3PM	3PA	3P%	FTM	FTA	FT%	ORB	DRB	TRB	AST	PF	DQ	STL	BLK	TO	MPG	PPG	RPG	APG	PCM

• MANNING, Guy

Guy R. Manning

Born: Feb. 4, 1944. Oakwood, TX, United States.   Height: 6'6".   Weight: 195 lbs.   Drafted: 1966   College: Prairie View A&M

YEAR	TEAM	GP	GS	MIN	PTS	FGM	FGA	FG%	3PM	3PA	3P%	FTM	FTA	FT%	ORB	DRB	TRB	AST	PF	DQ	STL	BLK	TO	MPG	PPG	RPG	APG	PCM
67-68	Houston-A	59	....	1107	529	206	502	.410	2	6	.333	115	199	.578	....	....	311	37	151	4	....	....	53	18.8	9.0	5.3	0.6	.440
68-69	Houston-A	14	....	167	75	27	95	.284	0	2	.000	21	37	.568	21	21	42	2	20	0	....	....	12	11.9	5.4	3.0	0.1	.237
ABA Season Totals		73	....	1274	604	233	597	.390	2	8	.250	136	236	.576	21	21	353	39	171	4	....	....	65	17.5	8.3	4.8	0.5	....
67-68	Houston-A	3	....	66	41	15	34	.441	0	0	.000	11	19	.579	....	....	19	2	11	0	....	....	5	22.0	13.7	6.3	0.7	.537
ABA Playoff Totals		3	....	66	41	15	34	.441	0	0	.000	11	19	.579	....	....	19	2	11	0	....	....	5	22.0	13.7	6.3	0.7	....

• MANNING, Rich

Richard Alan Manning

Born: June 23, 1970. Tacoma, WA, United States.   Height: 6'11".   Weight: 253 lbs.   Drafted: 1993   College: Washington

YEAR	TEAM	GP	GS	MIN	PTS	FGM	FGA	FG%	3PM	3PA	3P%	FTM	FTA	FT%	ORB	DRB	TRB	AST	PF	DQ	STL	BLK	TO	MPG	PPG	RPG	APG	PCM
95-96	Vancouver	29	0	311	107	49	113	.434	0	1	.000	9	14	.643	16	39	55	7	37	0	3	6	17	10.7	3.7	1.9	0.2	.253
96-97	Vancouver	16	1	128	44	18	48	.375	2	3	.667	6	8	.750	8	15	23	2	18	0	3	1	5	8.0	2.8	1.4	0.1	.229
96-97	LA Clippers	10	1	73	31	14	34	.412	0	1	.000	3	6	.500	8	8	16	1	11	0	1	1	2	7.3	3.1	1.6	0.1	.299
NBA Season Totals		55	2	512	182	81	195	.415	2	5	.400	18	28	.643	32	62	94	10	66	0	7	8	24	9.3	3.3	1.7	0.2	....
96-97	LA Clippers	3	0	21	9	2	9	.222	0	0	.000	5	6	.833	3	1	4	1	5	0	0	1	0	7.0	3.0	1.3	0.3	.258
NBA Playoff Totals		3	0	21	9	2	9	.222	0	0	.000	5	6	.833	3	1	4	1	5	0	0	1	0	7.0	3.0	1.3	0.3	....

• MANNION, Pace

Pace Shewan Mannion

Born: Sept. 22, 1960. Salt Lake City, UT, United States.   Height: 6'7".   Weight: 190 lbs.   Drafted: 1983   College: Utah

YEAR	TEAM	GP	GS	MIN	PTS	FGM	FGA	FG%	3PM	3PA	3P%	FTM	FTA	FT%	ORB	DRB	TRB	AST	PF	DQ	STL	BLK	TO	MPG	PPG	RPG	APG	PCM
83-84	Golden State	57	0	469	121	50	126	.397	3	13	.231	18	23	.783	23	36	59	47	63	0	25	2	23	8.2	2.1	1.0	0.8	.272
84-85	Utah	34	0	190	70	27	63	.429	0	1	.000	16	23	.696	12	11	23	27	17	0	16	3	17	5.6	2.1	0.7	0.8	.407
85-86	Utah	57	0	673	255	97	214	.453	8	42	.190	53	82	.646	26	56	82	55	68	0	32	5	40	11.8	4.5	1.4	1.0	.347
86-87	New Jersey	23	3	284	83	31	94	.330	3	9	.333	18	31	.581	10	29	39	45	32	0	18	4	23	12.3	3.6	1.7	2.0	.306
87-88	Milwaukee	35	1	477	123	48	118	.407	2	12	.167	25	37	.676	17	34	51	55	53	0	13	7	25	13.6	3.5	1.5	1.6	.271
88-89	Detroit	5	0	14	4	2	2	1.000	0	0	.000	0	0	.000	0	3	3	0	3	0	1	0	0	2.8	0.8	0.6	0.0	.452
88-89	Atlanta	5	0	18	4	2	6	.333	0	2	.000	0	0	.000	0	2	2	2	2	0	2	0	3	3.6	0.8	0.4	0.4	.134
NBA Season Totals		216	4	2125	660	257	623	.413	16	79	.203	130	196	.663	88	171	259	231	238	0	107	21	131	9.8	3.1	1.2	1.1	....
84-85	Utah	8	0	41	18	4	12	.333	0	1	.000	10	12	.833	3	4	7	4	5	0	1	2	7	5.1	2.3	0.9	0.5	.350
NBA Playoff Totals		8	0	41	18	4	12	.333	0	1	.000	10	12	.833	3	4	7	4	5	0	1	2	7	5.1	2.3	0.9	0.5	....

• MANTIS, Nick

Nicholas Mantis

Born: Dec. 7, 1935.   Height: 6'3".   Weight: 190 lbs.   Drafted: 1959   College: Northwestern

YEAR	TEAM	GP	GS	MIN	PTS	FGM	FGA	FG%	3PM	3PA	3P%	FTM	FTA	FT%	ORB	DRB	TRB	AST	PF	DQ	STL	BLK	TO	MPG	PPG	RPG	APG	PCM
59-60	Minneapolis	10	....	71	21	10	39	.256	....	....	....	1	2	.500	....	....	6	9	8	0	....	....	....	7.1	2.1	0.6	0.9	.161
62-63	St. Louis	9	....	58	19	8	20	.400	....	....	....	3	9	.333	....	....	6	7	13	0	....	....	....	6.4	2.1	0.7	0.8	.262
62-63	Chicago	33	....	626	196	86	224	.384	....	....	....	24	40	.600	....	....	79	75	81	0	....	....	....	19.0	5.9	2.4	2.3	.322
NBA Season Totals		52	....	755	236	104	283	.367	....	....	....	28	51	.549	....	....	91	91	102	0	....	....	....	14.5	4.5	1.8	1.8	....

• MARAVICH, Pete

Peter Press (Pistol Pete) Maravich

Born: June 22, 1947. Aliquippa, PA, United States. Died: Jan.5, 1988.   Height: 6'5".   Weight: 197 lbs.   Drafted: 1970   College: Louisiana State   HOF: 1987

YEAR	TEAM	GP	GS	MIN	PTS	FGM	FGA	FG%	3PM	3PA	3P%	FTM	FTA	FT%	ORB	DRB	TRB	AST	PF	DQ	STL	BLK	TO	MPG	PPG	RPG	APG	PCM
70-71	Atlanta	81	....	2926	1880	738	1613	.458	....	....	....	404	505	.800	....	....	298	355	238	1	....	....	....	36.1	23.2	3.7	4.4	.561
71-72	Atlanta	66	....	2302	1275	460	1077	.427	....	....	....	355	438	.811	....	....	256	393	207	0	....	....	....	34.9	19.3	3.9	6.0	.558
72-73	Atlanta	79	....	3089	2063	789	1788	.441	....	....	....	485	606	.800	....	....	346	546	245	1	....	....	....	39.1	26.1	4.4	6.9	.638
73-74	Atlanta	76	....	2903	2107	819	1791	.457	....	....	....	469	568	.826	98	276	374	396	261	4	111	13	....	38.2	27.7	4.9	5.2	.654
74-75	New Orleans	79	....	2853	1700	655	1562	.419	....	....	....	390	481	.811	93	329	422	488	227	4	120	18	....	36.1	21.5	5.3	6.2	.600
75-76	New Orleans	62	....	2373	1604	604	1316	.459	....	....	....	396	488	.811	46	254	300	332	197	3	87	23	....	38.3	25.9	4.8	5.4	.634
76-77	New Orleans	73	....	3041	2273	886	2047	.433	....	....	....	501	600	.835	90	284	374	392	191	1	84	22	....	41.7	31.1	5.1	5.4	.630
77-78	New Orleans	50	....	2041	1352	556	1253	.444	....	....	....	240	276	.870	49	129	178	335	116	1	101	8	250	40.8	27.0	3.6	6.7	.532
78-79	New Orleans	49	....	1824	1105	436	1035	.421	....	....	....	233	277	.841	33	88	121	243	104	2	60	18	201	37.2	22.6	2.5	5.0	.420
79-80	Utah	17	....	522	290	121	294	.412	7	11	.636	41	50	.820	7	33	40	54	30	0	15	4	44	30.7	17.1	2.4	3.2	.361
79-80	Boston	26	....	442	299	123	249	.494	3	4	.750	50	55	.909	10	28	38	29	49	1	9	2	36	17.0	11.5	1.5	1.1	.462
NBA Season Totals		658	....	24316	15948	6187	14025	.441	10	15	.667	3564	4344	.820	426	1421	2747	3563	1865	18	587	108	531	37.0	24.2	4.2	5.4	....
70-71	Atlanta	5	....	199	110	46	122	.377	....	....	....	18	26	.692	....	....	26	24	14	0	....	....	....	39.8	22.0	5.2	4.8	.427
71-72	Atlanta	6	....	219	166	54	121	.446	....	....	....	58	71	.817	....	....	32	28	24	0	....	....	....	36.5	27.7	5.3	4.7	.692
72-73	Atlanta	6	....	234	157	65	155	.419	....	....	....	27	34	.794	....	....	29	40	24	1	....	....	....	39.0	26.2	4.8	6.7	.586
79-80	Boston	9	....	104	54	25	51	.490	2	6	.333	2	3	.667	0	8	8	6	12	0	3	0	9	11.6	6.0	0.9	0.7	.317
NBA Playoff Totals		26	....	756	487	190	449	.423	2	6	.333	105	134	.784	0	8	95	98	74	1	3	0	9	29.1	18.7	3.7	3.8	....

• MARAVICH, Press

Peter (Press) Maravich

Born: Aug. 20, 1920. Died: Apr.15, 1987.   Height: 6'   Weight: 185 lbs.   Drafted: —   College: Davis & Elkins

YEAR	TEAM	GP	GS	MIN	PTS	FGM	FGA	FG%	3PM	3PA	3P%	FTM	FTA	FT%	ORB	DRB	TRB	AST	PF	DQ	STL	BLK	TO	MPG	PPG	RPG	APG	PCM
45-46	Youngstown-N	32	....	....	178	72	....	....	....	....	....	34	51	.667	....	....	....	....	....	....	....	....	....	5.6	....	....	....
46-47	Pittsburgh	51	....	....	234	102	375	.272	....	....	....	30	58	.517	....	....	6	102	....	....	....	....	....	4.6	....	0.1	....
NBA Season Totals		51	....	....	234	102	375	.272	....	....	....	30	58	.517	....	....	6	102	....	....	....	....	....	4.6	....	0.1	....
NBL Season Totals		32	....	....	178	72	....	....	....	....	....	34	51		....	....	....	....	....	....	....	....	....	5.6	....	....	....
Career Totals		83	....	....	412	174	375	....	....	....	....	64	109		....	....	6	102	....	....	....	....	....	5.0	....	0.1	....

• MARBLE, Roy

Roy Lane Marble Jr.

Born: Dec. 13, 1966. Flint, MI, United States. Height: 6'6". Weight: 190 lbs. Drafted: 1989 College: Iowa

YEAR TEAM	GP	GS	MIN	PTS	FGM	FGA	FG%	3PM	3PA	3P%	FTM	FTA	FT%	ORB	DRB	TRB	AST	PF	DQ	STL	BLK	TO	MPG	PPG	RPG	APG	PCM
89-90 Atlanta	24	0	162	51	16	58	.276	0	2	.000	19	29	.655	15	9	24	11	16	0	7	1	14	6.8	2.1	1.0	0.5	.173
93-94 Denver	5	0	32	4	2	12	.167	0	0	.000	0	3	.000	3	5	8	1	1	0	0	2	3	6.4	0.8	1.6	0.2	.016
NBA Season Totals	29	0	194	55	18	70	.257	0	2	.000	19	32	.594	18	14	32	12	17	0	7	3	17	6.7	1.9	1.1	0.4	....

• MARBURY, Stephon

Stephon Xzavier Marbury

Born: Feb. 20, 1977. Brooklyn, NY, United States. Height: 6'2". Weight: 180 lbs. Drafted: 1996 College: Georgia Tech

YEAR TEAM	GP	GS	MIN	PTS	FGM	FGA	FG%	3PM	3PA	3P%	FTM	FTA	FT%	ORB	DRB	TRB	AST	PF	DQ	STL	BLK	TO	MPG	PPG	RPG	APG	PCM
96-97 Minnesota	67	64	2324	1057	355	871	.408	102	288	.354	245	337	.727	54	130	184	522	159	2	67	19	208	34.7	15.8	2.7	7.8	.462
97-98 Minnesota	82	81	3112	1450	513	1237	.415	95	304	.313	329	450	.731	58	172	230	704	222	0	104	7	254	38.0	17.7	2.8	8.6	.474
98-99 Minnesota	18	18	661	319	124	304	.408	8	39	.205	63	87	.724	17	45	62	167	44	0	29	5	55	36.7	17.7	3.4	9.3	.531
98-99 New Jersey	31	31	1234	725	254	579	.439	58	158	.367	159	191	.832	20	60	80	270	81	0	30	3	109	39.8	23.4	2.6	8.7	.559
99-00 New Jersey	74	74	2881	1640	569	1317	.432	66	233	.283	436	536	.813	61	179	240	622	195	4	112	15	270	38.9	22.2	3.2	8.4	.553
00-01 New Jersey	67	67	2557	1598	563	1277	.441	110	335	.328	362	458	.790	53	152	205	506	150	1	79	5	197	38.2	23.9	3.1	7.6	.581
01-02 Phoenix	82	80	3187	1674	625	1413	.442	71	248	.286	353	452	.781	75	191	266	666	186	0	77	13	284	38.9	20.4	3.2	8.1	.510
02-03 Phoenix	81	81	3242	1806	671	1530	.439	89	296	.301	375	467	.803	53	210	263	654	200	1	108	20	263	40.0	22.3	3.2	8.1	.532
NBA Season Totals	502	496	19198	10269	3674	8528	.431	599	1901	.315	2322	2978	.780	391	1139	1530	4111	1237	8	606	87	1640	38.2	20.5	3.0	8.2	....
96-97 Minnesota	3	3	117	64	26	65	.400	6	20	.300	6	10	.600	2	10	12	23	9	0	2	0	9	39.0	21.3	4.0	7.7	.434
97-98 Minnesota	5	5	209	69	22	72	.306	7	25	.280	18	23	.783	5	11	16	38	16	0	12	0	18	41.8	13.8	3.2	7.6	.306
02-03 Phoenix	6	6	271	132	51	136	.375	5	22	.227	25	33	.758	6	18	24	34	26	1	7	0	23	45.2	22.0	4.0	5.7	.309
NBA Playoff Totals	14	14	597	265	99	273	.363	18	67	.269	49	66	.742	13	39	52	95	51	1	21	0	50	42.6	18.9	3.7	6.8	....

• MARCIULIONIS, Sarunas

Raimondas Sarunas (Rooney) Marciulionis

Born: June 13, 1964. Kaunas, Lithuania. Height: 6'5". Weight: 200 lbs. Drafted: 1987 College: State Univ. of Vilnius (LIT)

YEAR TEAM	GP	GS	MIN	PTS	FGM	FGA	FG%	3PM	3PA	3P%	FTM	FTA	FT%	ORB	DRB	TRB	AST	PF	DQ	STL	BLK	TO	MPG	PPG	RPG	APG	PCM
89-90 Golden State	75	3	1695	905	289	557	.519	10	39	.256	317	403	.787	84	137	221	121	230	5	94	7	135	22.6	12.1	2.9	1.6	.478
90-91 Golden State	50	10	987	545	183	365	.501	1	6	.167	178	246	.724	51	67	118	85	136	4	62	4	75	19.7	10.9	2.4	1.7	.479
91-92 Golden State	72	5	2117	1361	491	912	.538	3	10	.300	376	477	.788	68	140	208	243	237	4	116	10	194	29.4	18.9	2.9	3.4	.568
92-93 Golden State	30	8	836	521	178	328	.543	3	15	.200	162	213	.761	40	57	97	105	92	1	51	2	75	27.9	17.4	3.2	3.5	.594
94-95 Seattle	66	4	1194	612	216	457	.473	35	87	.402	145	198	.732	17	51	68	110	126	1	72	3	99	18.1	9.3	1.0	1.7	.385
95-96 Sacramento	53	0	1039	571	176	389	.452	64	157	.408	155	200	.775	20	57	77	118	112	1	52	4	95	19.6	10.8	1.5	2.2	.441
96-97 Denver	17	0	255	116	38	101	.376	11	30	.367	29	36	.806	12	18	30	25	38	0	12	1	41	15.0	6.8	1.8	1.5	.254
NBA Season Totals	363	30	8123	4631	1571	3109	.505	127	344	.369	1362	1773	.768	292	527	819	807	971	16	459	31	714	22.4	12.8	2.3	2.2	....
90-91 Golden State	9	0	206	119	42	84	.500	0	1	.000	35	39	.897	8	15	23	27	21	1	11	1	14	22.9	13.2	2.6	3.0	.566
91-92 Golden State	4	0	133	85	25	47	.532	1	2	.500	34	41	.829	3	6	9	20	15	0	3	1	4	33.3	21.3	2.3	5.0	.633
95-96 Sacramento	4	0	101	29	8	29	.276	4	18	.222	9	15	.600	4	3	7	14	4	0	10	0	10	25.3	7.3	1.8	3.5	.257
NBA Playoff Totals	17	0	440	233	75	160	.469	5	21	.238	78	95	.821	15	24	39	61	40	1	24	2	28	25.9	13.7	2.3	3.6	....

• MARIASCHIN, Saul

Saul George Mariaschin

Born: Sept. 1, 1924. Died: 1994. Height: 5'11". Weight: 165 lbs. Drafted: 1947 College: Harvard

YEAR TEAM	GP	GS	MIN	PTS	FGM	FGA	FG%	3PM	3PA	3P%	FTM	FTA	FT%	ORB	DRB	TRB	AST	PF	DQ	STL	BLK	TO	MPG	PPG	RPG	APG	PCM
47-48 Boston	43	....	....	333	125	463	.270	....	....	....	83	117	.709	....	....	....	60	121	....	....	....	....	....	7.7	....	1.4	....
NBA Season Totals	43	....	....	333	125	463	.270	....	....	....	83	117	.709	....	....	....	60	121	....	....	....	....	....	7.7	....	1.4	....
47-48 Boston	3	....	....	29	10	42	.238	....	....	....	9	14	.643	....	....	....	1	12	....	....	....	....	....	9.7	....	0.3	....
NBA Playoff Totals	3	....	....	29	10	42	.238	....	....	....	9	14	.643	....	....	....	1	12	....	....	....	....	....	9.7	....	0.3	....

• MARIN, Jack

John Warren Marin

Born: Oct. 12, 1944. Sharon, PA, United States. Height: 6'7". Weight: 200 lbs. Drafted: 1966 College: Duke

YEAR TEAM	GP	GS	MIN	PTS	FGM	FGA	FG%	3PM	3PA	3P%	FTM	FTA	FT%	ORB	DRB	TRB	AST	PF	DQ	STL	BLK	TO	MPG	PPG	RPG	APG	PCM
66-67 Baltimore	74	....	1323	711	283	632	.448	....	....	....	145	187	.775	....	....	313	75	199	6	....	....	....	17.9	9.6	4.2	1.0	.511
67-68 Baltimore	82	....	2037	1108	429	932	.460	....	....	....	250	314	.796	....	....	473	110	246	4	....	....	....	24.8	13.5	5.8	1.3	.536
68-69 Baltimore	82	....	2710	1302	505	1109	.455	....	....	....	292	352	.830	....	....	608	231	275	4	....	....	....	33.0	15.9	7.4	2.8	.529
69-70 Baltimore	82	....	2947	1618	666	1363	.489	....	....	....	286	339	.844	....	....	537	217	248	6	....	....	....	35.9	19.7	6.5	2.6	.539
70-71 Baltimore	82	....	2920	1542	626	1360	.460	....	....	....	290	342	.848	....	....	513	217	261	3	....	....	....	35.6	18.8	6.3	2.6	.502
71-72 Baltimore	78	....	2927	1736	690	1444	.478	....	....	....	356	398	**.894**	....	....	528	169	240	2	....	....	....	37.5	22.3	6.8	2.2	.550
72-73 Houston	81	....	3019	1496	624	1334	.468	....	....	....	248	292	.849	....	....	499	291	247	4	....	....	....	37.3	18.5	6.2	3.6	.504
73-74 Houston	47	....	1102	502	210	443	.474	....	....	....	82	98	.837	29	77	106	121	120	0	23	8	....	23.4	10.7	2.3	2.6	.431
73-74 Buffalo	27	....	680	361	145	266	.545	....	....	....	71	81	.877	30	92	122	46	93	0	23	18	....	25.2	13.4	4.5	1.7	.545
74-75 Buffalo	81	....	2147	953	380	836	.455	....	....	....	193	222	.869	104	259	363	133	238	7	51	16	....	26.5	11.8	4.5	1.6	.425
75-76 Buffalo	12	....	278	109	41	94	.436	....	....	....	27	33	.818	10	30	40	23	30	0	7	6	....	23.2	9.1	3.3	1.9	.391
75-76 Chicago	67	....	1631	738	302	718	.421	....	....	....	134	155	.865	59	153	212	118	134	0	38	5	....	24.3	11.0	3.2	1.8	.387
76-77 Chicago	54	....	869	365	167	359	.465	....	....	....	31	39	.795	27	64	91	62	85	0	13	6	....	16.1	6.8	1.7	1.1	.355
NBA Season Totals	849	....	24590	12541	5068	10890	.465	....	....	....	2405	2852	.843	259	675	4405	1813	2416	36	155	59	....	29.0	14.8	5.2	2.1	....
68-69 Baltimore	4	....	153	55	24	51	.471	....	....	....	7	11	.636	....	....	18	12	13	0	....	....	....	38.3	13.8	4.5	3.0	.355
69-70 Baltimore	7	....	265	125	48	114	.421	....	....	....	29	34	.853	....	....	47	22	27	1	....	....	....	37.9	17.9	6.7	3.1	.448
70-71 Baltimore	18	....	750	370	147	319	.461	....	....	....	76	93	.817	....	....	145	56	54	0	....	....	....	41.7	20.6	8.1	3.1	.507
71-72 Baltimore	6	....	229	103	31	78	.397	....	....	....	41	47	.872	....	....	36	12	22	1	....	....	....	38.2	17.2	6.0	2.0	.415
73-74 Buffalo	6	....	121	51	22	47	.468	....	....	....	7	9	.778	5	14	19	8	17	0	2	0	....	20.2	8.5	3.2	1.3	.388
74-75 Buffalo	7	....	108	37	12	27	.444	....	....	....	13	15	.867	5	12	17	8	12	0	7	1	....	15.4	5.3	2.4	1.1	.388
76-77 Chicago	3	....	53	16	8	13	.615	....	....	....	0	1	.000	0	1	1	2	6	0	0	0	....	17.7	5.3	0.3	0.7	.223
NBA Playoff Totals	51	....	1679	757	292	649	.450	....	....	....	173	210	.824	10	27	283	120	151	2	9	1	....	32.9	14.8	5.5	2.4	....

YEAR	TEAM	GP	GS	MIN	PTS	FGM	FGA	FG%	3PM	3PA	3P%	FTM	FTA	FT%	ORB	DRB	TRB	AST	PF	DQ	STL	BLK	TO	MPG	PPG	RPG	APG	PCM

• MARION, Shawn   Shawn Dwayne Marion

Born: May 7, 1978. Chicago, IL, United States.   Height: 6'7".   Weight: 220 lbs.   Drafted: 1999   College: UNLV

YEAR	TEAM	GP	GS	MIN	PTS	FGM	FGA	FG%	3PM	3PA	3P%	FTM	FTA	FT%	ORB	DRB	TRB	AST	PF	DQ	STL	BLK	TO	MPG	PPG	RPG	APG	PCM
99-00	Phoenix	51	38	1260	520	222	471	.471	4	22	.182	72	85	.847	105	227	332	69	113	0	38	53	51	24.7	10.2	6.5	1.4	.516
00-01	Phoenix	79	79	2857	1369	557	1160	.480	21	82	.256	234	289	.810	220	628	848	160	211	2	132	108	129	36.2	17.3	10.7	2.0	.611
01-02	Phoenix	81	81	3109	1547	654	1395	.469	48	122	.393	191	226	.845	211	592	803	162	214	0	149	86	144	38.4	19.1	9.9	2.0	.563
02-03	Phoenix	81	81	3373	1716	662	1466	.452	141	364	.387	251	295	.851	199	574	773	198	208	0	185	95	157	41.6	21.2	9.5	2.4	.564
NBA Season Totals		292	279	10599	5152	2095	4492	.466	214	590	.363	748	895	.836	735	2021	2756	589	746	2	504	342	481	36.3	17.6	9.4	2.0	....
99-00	Phoenix	9	9	281	82	36	86	.419	1	6	.167	9	11	.818	21	58	79	7	17	0	6	14	7	31.2	9.1	8.8	0.8	.424
00-01	Phoenix	4	4	139	59	23	62	.371	1	1	1.000	12	14	.857	10	23	33	3	13	0	6	6	6	34.8	14.8	8.3	0.8	.400
02-03	Phoenix	6	6	283	111	40	107	.374	9	28	.321	22	26	.846	21	49	70	12	17	0	11	11	13	47.2	18.5	11.7	2.0	.443
NBA Playoff Totals		19	19	703	252	99	255	.388	11	35	.314	43	51	.843	52	130	182	22	47	0	23	31	26	37.0	13.3	9.6	1.2	....

• MARKS, Sean   Sean Andrew Marks

Born: Aug. 23, 1975. Auckland, New Zealand.   Height: 6'10".   Weight: 250 lbs.   Drafted: 1998   College: California

YEAR	TEAM	GP	GS	MIN	PTS	FGM	FGA	FG%	3PM	3PA	3P%	FTM	FTA	FT%	ORB	DRB	TRB	AST	PF	DQ	STL	BLK	TO	MPG	PPG	RPG	APG	PCM
98-99	Toronto	8	0	28	11	5	8	.625	0	0	.000	1	2	.500	0	1	1	0	3	0	1	0	3	3.5	1.4	0.1	0.0	.202
99-00	Toronto	5	0	12	8	2	6	.333	0	1	.000	4	4	1.000	0	2	2	0	3	0	1	1	3	2.4	1.6	0.4	0.0	.326
01-02	Miami	21	6	319	96	38	88	.432	0	0	.000	20	34	.588	19	56	75	8	40	0	5	10	19	15.2	4.6	3.6	0.4	.311
02-03	Miami	23	0	223	54	22	59	.373	0	1	.000	10	15	.667	8	27	35	3	37	1	5	6	14	9.7	2.3	1.5	0.1	.151
NBA Season Totals		57	6	582	169	67	161	.416	0	2	.000	35	55	.636	27	86	113	11	83	1	12	17	39	10.2	3.0	2.0	0.2	....

• MARLATT, Harvey   Harvey W. Marlatt

Born: Aug. 26, 1948.   Height: 6'3".   Weight: 185 lbs.   Drafted: —   College: Eastern Michigan

YEAR	TEAM	GP	GS	MIN	PTS	FGM	FGA	FG%	3PM	3PA	3P%	FTM	FTA	FT%	ORB	DRB	TRB	AST	PF	DQ	STL	BLK	TO	MPG	PPG	RPG	APG	PCM
70-71	Detroit	23	....	214	65	25	80	.313	....	....	....	15	18	.833	....	....	23	30	27	0	....	....	....	9.3	2.8	1.0	1.3	.275
71-72	Detroit	31	....	506	156	60	149	.403	....	....	....	36	42	.857	....	....	62	60	64	1	....	....	....	16.3	5.0	2.0	1.9	.337
72-73	Detroit	7	....	26	4	2	4	.500	....	....	....	0	0	.000	....	....	1	4	1	0	....	....	....	3.7	0.6	0.1	0.6	.280
NBA Season Totals		61	....	746	225	87	233	.373	....	....	....	51	60	.850	....	....	86	94	92	1	....	....	....	12.2	3.7	1.4	1.5	....

• MARSH, Jim   James Marsh

Born: Apr. 26, 1946.   Height: 6'7".   Weight: 215 lbs.   Drafted: 1968   College: USC

YEAR	TEAM	GP	GS	MIN	PTS	FGM	FGA	FG%	3PM	3PA	3P%	FTM	FTA	FT%	ORB	DRB	TRB	AST	PF	DQ	STL	BLK	TO	MPG	PPG	RPG	APG	PCM
71-72	Portland	39	....	375	119	39	117	.333	....	....	....	41	59	.695	....	....	84	30	50	0	....	....	....	9.6	3.1	2.2	0.8	.344
NBA Season Totals		39	....	375	119	39	117	.333	....	....	....	41	59	.695	....	....	84	30	50	0	....	....	....	9.6	3.1	2.2	0.8	....

• MARSH, Ricky   Eric Clifton Marsh

Born: Mar. 10, 1954. New York, NY, United States.   Height: 6'3".   Weight: 200 lbs.   Drafted: —   College: Manhattan

YEAR	TEAM	GP	GS	MIN	PTS	FGM	FGA	FG%	3PM	3PA	3P%	FTM	FTA	FT%	ORB	DRB	TRB	AST	PF	DQ	STL	BLK	TO	MPG	PPG	RPG	APG	PCM
77-78	Golden State	60	....	851	269	123	289	.426	....	....	....	23	33	.697	16	59	75	90	111	0	29	19	48	14.2	4.5	1.3	1.5	.279
NBA Season Totals		60	....	851	269	123	289	.426	....	....	....	23	33	.697	16	59	75	90	111	0	29	19	48	14.2	4.5	1.3	1.5	....

• MARSHALL, Donny   Donny E. Marshall

Born: July 17, 1972. Detroit, MI, United States.   Height: 6'7".   Weight: 230 lbs.   Drafted: 1995   College: Connecticut

YEAR	TEAM	GP	GS	MIN	PTS	FGM	FGA	FG%	3PM	3PA	3P%	FTM	FTA	FT%	ORB	DRB	TRB	AST	PF	DQ	STL	BLK	TO	MPG	PPG	RPG	APG	PCM
95-96	Cleveland	34	0	208	77	24	68	.353	7	30	.233	22	35	.629	9	17	26	7	26	0	8	2	7	6.1	2.3	0.8	0.2	.250
96-97	Cleveland	56	0	548	175	52	160	.325	33	87	.379	38	54	.704	22	48	70	24	60	0	24	3	34	9.8	3.1	1.3	0.4	.225
99-00	Cleveland	6	0	39	11	3	11	.273	0	3	.000	5	6	.833	0	1	1	0	7	0	2	0	3	6.5	1.8	0.2	0.0	.003
01-02	New Jersey	20	0	118	30	8	29	.276	2	4	.500	12	18	.667	8	13	21	5	14	0	3	0	2	5.9	1.5	1.1	0.3	.223
02-03	New Jersey	3	0	6	0	0	3	.000	0	1	.000	0	0	.000	0	3	3	0	0	0	0	0	1	2.0	0.0	1.0	0.0	-.151
NBA Season Totals		119	0	919	293	87	271	.321	42	125	.336	77	113	.681	39	82	121	36	107	0	37	5	47	7.7	2.5	1.0	0.3	....
95-96	Cleveland	1	0	1	0	0	0	.000	0	0	.000	0	0	.000	0	0	0	0	0	0	0	0	0	1.0	0.0	0.0	0.0	.000
01-02	New Jersey	7	0	14	3	1	5	.200	0	4	.000	1	1	1.000	0	0	0	0	1	0	0	0	0	2.0	0.4	0.0	0.0	-.077
NBA Playoff Totals		8	0	15	3	1	5	.200	0	4	.000	1	1	1.000	0	0	0	0	1	0	0	0	0	1.9	0.4	0.0	0.0	....

• MARSHALL, Donyell   Donyell Lamar Marshall

Born: May 18, 1973. Reading, PA, United States.   Height: 6'9".   Weight: 218 lbs.   Drafted: 1994   College: Connecticut

YEAR	TEAM	GP	GS	MIN	PTS	FGM	FGA	FG%	3PM	3PA	3P%	FTM	FTA	FT%	ORB	DRB	TRB	AST	PF	DQ	STL	BLK	TO	MPG	PPG	RPG	APG	PCM
94-95	Minnesota	40	8	1036	431	158	423	.374	32	106	.302	83	122	.680	64	132	196	57	63	0	25	50	56	25.9	10.8	4.9	1.4	.383
94-95	Golden State	32	23	1050	475	187	453	.413	37	137	.270	64	100	.640	73	136	209	48	94	1	20	38	58	32.8	14.8	6.5	1.5	.392
95-96	Golden State	62	6	934	342	125	314	.398	28	94	.298	64	83	.771	65	148	213	49	83	0	22	31	50	15.1	5.5	3.4	0.8	.398
96-97	Golden State	61	20	1022	444	174	421	.413	35	111	.315	61	98	.622	92	184	276	54	96	0	25	46	55	16.8	7.3	4.5	0.9	.471
97-98	Golden State	73	73	2611	1123	451	1091	.413	63	201	.313	158	216	.731	210	418	628	159	226	1	95	73	146	35.8	15.4	8.6	2.2	.450
98-99	Golden State	48	20	1250	530	208	494	.421	26	72	.361	88	121	.727	115	227	342	66	123	1	47	37	80	26.0	11.0	7.1	1.4	.470
99-00	Golden State	64	51	2071	910	331	840	.394	49	138	.355	199	255	.780	189	448	637	167	180	1	68	68	123	32.4	14.2	10.0	2.6	.538
00-01	Utah	81	49	2326	1100	427	849	.503	41	128	.320	205	273	.751	172	394	566	133	196	0	85	78	128	28.7	13.6	7.0	1.6	.554
01-02	Utah	58	42	1750	859	343	661	.519	13	42	.310	160	226	.708	158	285	443	101	150	1	50	67	124	30.2	14.8	7.6	1.7	.559
02-03	Chicago	78	53	2379	1042	421	918	.459	33	87	.379	167	221	.756	234	465	699	137	234	3	95	85	135	30.5	13.4	9.0	1.8	.540
NBA Season Totals		597	345	16429	7256	2825	6464	.437	357	1116	.320	1249	1715	.728	1372	2837	4209	971	1445	8	532	573	955	27.5	12.2	7.1	1.6	....
00-01	Utah	5	5	160	52	22	54	.407	1	8	.125	7	9	.778	13	25	38	8	19	1	2	5	9	32.0	10.4	7.6	1.6	.344
01-02	Utah	4	0	124	57	21	50	.420	3	6	.500	12	16	.750	14	17	31	11	5	0	3	6	5	31.0	14.3	7.8	2.8	.568
NBA Playoff Totals		9	5	284	109	43	104	.413	4	14	.286	19	25	.760	27	42	69	19	24	1	5	11	14	31.6	12.1	7.7	2.1	....

YEAR	TEAM	GP	GS	MIN	PTS	FGM	FGA	FG%	3PM	3PA	3P%	FTM	FTA	FT%	ORB	DRB	TRB	AST	PF	DQ	STL	BLK	TO	MPG	PPG	RPG	APG	PCM

• MARSHALL, Tom

John Thomas Marshall

Born: Jan. 6, 1931.   Height: 6'4".   Weight: 215 lbs.   Drafted: 1954   College: Western Kentucky

YEAR	TEAM	GP	GS	MIN	PTS	FGM	FGA	FG%	3PM	3PA	3P%	FTM	FTA	FT%	ORB	DRB	TRB	AST	PF	DQ	STL	BLK	TO	MPG	PPG	RPG	APG	PCM
54-55	Rochester	72	....	1337	577	223	505	.442	....	....	....	131	194	.675	....	....	256	111	99	0	....	....	....	18.6	8.0	3.6	1.5	.475
56-57	Rochester	40	....	460	159	56	163	.344	....	....	....	47	58	.810	....	....	83	31	33	0	....	....	....	11.5	4.0	2.1	0.8	.356
57-58	Detroit	9	....	66	21	7	22	.318	....	....	....	7	8	.875	....	....	8	4	6	0	....	....	....	7.3	2.3	0.9	0.4	.279
57-58	Cincinnati	29	....	452	131	45	144	.313	....	....	....	41	55	.745	....	....	93	15	37	0	....	....	....	15.6	4.5	3.2	0.5	.281
58-59	Cincinnati	18	....	272	64	23	79	.291	....	....	....	18	29	.621	....	....	52	27	22	0	....	....	....	15.1	3.6	2.9	1.5	.303
NBA Season Totals		168	....	2587	952	354	913	.388	....	....	....	244	344	.709	....	....	492	188	197	0	....	....	....	15.4	5.7	2.9	1.1	....
54-55	Rochester	3	....	50	9	3	20	.150	....	....	....	3	5	.600	....	....	17	2	1	0	....	....	....	16.7	3.0	5.7	0.7	.207
57-58	Cincinnati	2	....	33	18	7	17	.412	....	....	....	4	5	.800	....	....	16	2	1	0	....	....	....	16.5	9.0	8.0	1.0	.733
NBA Playoff Totals		5	....	83	27	10	37	.270	....	....	....	7	10	.700	....	....	33	4	2	0	....	....	....	16.6	5.4	6.6	0.8	....

• MARSHALL, Vester

Vester Marshall

Born: Dec. 22, 1948.   Height: 6'7".   Weight: 200 lbs.   Drafted: —   College: Oklahoma

YEAR	TEAM	GP	GS	MIN	PTS	FGM	FGA	FG%	3PM	3PA	3P%	FTM	FTA	FT%	ORB	DRB	TRB	AST	PF	DQ	STL	BLK	TO	MPG	PPG	RPG	APG	PCM
73-74	Seattle	13	....	174	17	7	29	.241	....	....	....	3	7	.429	14	23	37	4	20	0	4	3	....	13.4	1.3	2.8	0.3	.139
NBA Season Totals		13	....	174	17	7	29	.241	....	....	....	3	7	.429	14	23	37	4	20	0	4	3	....	13.4	1.3	2.8	0.3	....

• MARTIN, Bill

William Martin

Born: Aug. 16, 1962. Washington, DC, United States.   Height: 6'7".   Weight: 205 lbs.   Drafted: 1985   College: Georgetown

YEAR	TEAM	GP	GS	MIN	PTS	FGM	FGA	FG%	3PM	3PA	3P%	FTM	FTA	FT%	ORB	DRB	TRB	AST	PF	DQ	STL	BLK	TO	MPG	PPG	RPG	APG	PCM
85-86	Indiana	66	0	691	332	143	298	.480	0	8	.000	46	54	.852	42	60	102	52	108	1	21	7	59	10.5	5.0	1.5	0.8	.370
86-87	New York	8	0	68	25	9	25	.360	0	0	.000	7	8	.875	2	5	7	0	5	0	4	2	7	8.5	3.1	0.9	0.0	.190
87-88	Phoenix	10	0	101	40	16	51	.314	0	1	.000	8	13	.615	9	18	27	6	16	0	5	0	9	10.1	4.0	2.7	0.6	.252
NBA Season Totals		84	0	860	397	168	374	.449	0	9	.000	61	75	.813	53	83	136	58	129	1	30	9	75	10.2	4.7	1.6	0.7	....

• MARTIN, Bob

Robert W. Martin

Born: Oct. 7, 1969. Minneapolis, MN, United States.   Height: 7'   Weight: 250 lbs.   Drafted: —   College: Minnesota

YEAR	TEAM	GP	GS	MIN	PTS	FGM	FGA	FG%	3PM	3PA	3P%	FTM	FTA	FT%	ORB	DRB	TRB	AST	PF	DQ	STL	BLK	TO	MPG	PPG	RPG	APG	PCM
93-94	LA Clippers	53	1	535	111	40	88	.455	0	0	.000	31	51	.608	36	81	117	17	106	1	8	33	27	10.1	2.1	2.2	0.3	.276
94-95	LA Clippers	1	0	14	2	1	5	.200	0	0	.000	0	0	.000	2	0	2	1	2	0	0	1	0	14.0	2.0	2.0	1.0	.085
NBA Season Totals		54	1	549	113	41	93	.441	0	0	.000	31	51	.608	38	81	119	18	108	1	8	34	27	10.2	2.1	2.2	0.3	....

• MARTIN, Brian

Brian Martin

Born: Aug. 18, 1962. Fort Smith, AR, United States.   Height: 6'9".   Weight: 212 lbs.   Drafted: 1984   College: Kansas

YEAR	TEAM	GP	GS	MIN	PTS	FGM	FGA	FG%	3PM	3PA	3P%	FTM	FTA	FT%	ORB	DRB	TRB	AST	PF	DQ	STL	BLK	TO	MPG	PPG	RPG	APG	PCM
85-86	Seattle	3	0	7	2	1	2	.500	0	0	.000	0	0	.000	1	3	4	0	2	0	0	1	2	2.3	0.7	1.3	0.0	.418
85-86	Portland	5	0	14	4	2	5	.400	0	0	.000	0	2	.000	0	0	0	0	5	0	0	0	0	2.8	0.8	0.0	0.0	-.146
NBA Season Totals		8	0	21	6	3	7	.429	0	0	.000	0	2	.000	1	3	4	0	7	0	0	1	2	2.6	0.8	0.5	0.0	....

• MARTIN, Cuonzo

Cuonzo LaMar Martin

Born: Sept. 23, 1971. St. Louis, MO, United States.   Height: 6'5".   Weight: 213 lbs.   Drafted: 1995   College: Purdue

YEAR	TEAM	GP	GS	MIN	PTS	FGM	FGA	FG%	3PM	3PA	3P%	FTM	FTA	FT%	ORB	DRB	TRB	AST	PF	DQ	STL	BLK	TO	MPG	PPG	RPG	APG	PCM
95-96	Vancouver	4	0	19	9	3	5	.600	3	3	1.000	0	2	.000	1	1	2	2	1	0	1	0	1	4.8	2.3	0.5	0.5	.511
96-97	Milwaukee	3	0	13	0	0	7	.000	0	2	.000	0	0	.000	1	0	1	1	1	0	0	0	1	4.3	0.0	0.3	0.3	-.456
NBA Season Totals		7	0	32	9	3	12	.250	3	5	.600	0	2	.000	2	1	3	3	2	0	1	0	2	4.6	1.3	0.4	0.4	....

• MARTIN, Darrick

Darrick Martin

Born: Mar. 6, 1971. Denver, CO, United States.   Height: 5'11".   Weight: 170 lbs.   Drafted: —   College: UCLA

YEAR	TEAM	GP	GS	MIN	PTS	FGM	FGA	FG%	3PM	3PA	3P%	FTM	FTA	FT%	ORB	DRB	TRB	AST	PF	DQ	STL	BLK	TO	MPG	PPG	RPG	APG	PCM
94-95	Minnesota	34	9	803	254	95	233	.408	7	38	.184	57	65	.877	14	50	64	133	88	0	34	0	61	23.6	7.5	1.9	3.9	.318
95-96	Vancouver	24	0	402	161	59	131	.450	5	22	.227	38	46	.826	13	25	38	61	47	0	27	1	36	16.8	6.7	1.6	2.5	.399
95-96	Minnesota	35	16	747	254	88	231	.381	15	47	.319	63	74	.851	3	41	44	156	76	0	26	2	70	21.3	7.3	1.3	4.5	.329
96-97	LA Clippers	82	64	1820	893	292	718	.407	91	234	.389	218	250	.872	26	87	113	339	165	1	57	2	123	22.2	10.9	1.4	4.1	.446
97-98	LA Clippers	82	63	2299	841	275	730	.377	107	293	.365	184	217	.848	19	145	164	331	198	2	82	10	156	28.0	10.3	2.0	4.0	.335
98-99	LA Clippers	37	25	941	296	102	278	.367	31	106	.292	61	76	.803	5	43	48	144	82	1	43	4	67	25.4	8.0	1.3	3.9	.299
99-00	Sacramento	71	1	893	402	133	350	.380	38	124	.306	98	119	.824	7	37	44	122	89	0	28	2	62	12.6	5.7	0.6	1.7	.335
00-01	Sacramento	31	0	176	103	29	76	.382	14	27	.519	31	35	.886	2	14	16	14	27	0	7	0	10	5.7	3.3	0.5	0.5	.420
01-02	Dallas	3	0	22	1	0	10	.000	0	2	.000	1	2	.500	0	1	1	3	4	0	2	0	1	7.3	0.3	0.3	1.0	-.238
NBA Season Totals		399	178	8103	3205	1073	2757	.389	308	893	.345	751	884	.850	89	443	532	1303	776	4	306	21	586	20.3	8.0	1.3	3.3	....
96-97	LA Clippers	3	3	77	33	11	25	.440	5	9	.556	6	9	.667	1	1	2	13	9	0	0	0	2	25.7	11.0	0.7	4.3	.367
99-00	Sacramento	2	0	21	10	3	9	.333	1	3	.333	3	4	.750	1	2	3	2	4	0	1	0	3	10.5	5.0	1.5	1.0	.256
00-01	Sacramento	2	0	9	0	0	6	.000	0	2	.000	0	0	.000	0	0	0	3	1	0	0	0	1	4.5	0.0	0.0	1.5	-.381
NBA Playoff Totals		7	3	107	43	14	40	.350	6	14	.429	9	13	.692	2	3	5	18	14	0	1	0	6	15.3	6.1	0.7	2.6	....

• MARTIN, Dino

Donald E. (Dino) Martin

Born: May 25, 1920.   Height: 5'8".   Weight: 160 lbs.   Drafted: —   College: Georgetown

YEAR	TEAM	GP	GS	MIN	PTS	FGM	FGA	FG%	3PM	3PA	3P%	FTM	FTA	FT%	ORB	DRB	TRB	AST	PF	DQ	STL	BLK	TO	MPG	PPG	RPG	APG	PCM
46-47	Providence	60	....	....	733	311	1022	.304	....	....	....	111	168	.661	....	....	....	59	98	....	....	....	....	12.2	....	1.0	....	....
47-48	Providence	32	....	....	101	46	193	.238	....	....	....	9	20	.450	....	....	....	14	17	....	....	....	....	3.2	....	0.4	....	....
NBA Season Totals		92	....	....	834	357	1215	.294	....	....	....	120	188	.638	....	....	....	73	115	....	....	....	....	9.1	....	0.8	....	....

• MARTIN, Don
James Donald Martin

Born: Feb. 7, 1920. Height: 6'7". Weight: 210 lbs. Drafted: — College: Central Missouri

YEAR TEAM	GP	GS	MIN	PTS	FGM	FGA	FG%	3PM	3PA	3P%	FTM	FTA	FT%	ORB	DRB	TRB	AST	PF	DQ	STL	BLK	TO	MPG	PPG	RPG	APG	PCM
46-47 St. Louis	54	....	....	191	89	304	.293	....	....	....	13	31	.419	....	....	....	9	75	....	....	....	....	....	3.5	....	0.2	....
47-48 St. Louis	39	....	....	85	35	150	.233	....	....	....	15	33	.455	....	....	....	2	61	....	....	....	....	....	2.2	....	0.1	....
48-49 St. Louis	37	....	....	129	50	161	.311	....	....	....	29	45	.644	....	....	....	21	101	....	....	....	....	....	3.5	....	0.6	....
48-49 Baltimore	7	....	....	5	2	9	.222	....	....	....	1	2	.500	....	....	....	4	14	....	....	....	....	....	0.7	....	0.6	....
NBA Season Totals	137	....	....	410	176	624	.282	....	....	....	58	111	.523	....	....	....	36	251	....	....	....	....	....	3.0	....	0.3	....
46-47 St. Louis	3	....	....	10	4	36	.111	....	....	....	2	2	1.000	....	....	....	1	10	....	....	....	....	....	3.3	....	0.3	....
47-48 St. Louis	5	....	....	11	5	20	.250	....	....	....	1	1	1.000	....	....	....	1	6	....	....	....	....	....	2.2	....	0.2	....
NBA Playoff Totals	8	....	....	21	9	56	.161	....	....	....	3	3	1.000	....	....	....	2	16	....	....	....	....	....	2.6	....	0.3	....

• MARTIN, Dugie
Slater Nelson (Dugie) Martin Jr.

Born: Oct. 22, 1925. El Mina, TX, United States. Height: 5'10". Weight: 170 lbs. Drafted: — College: Texas HOF: 1982

YEAR TEAM	GP	GS	MIN	PTS	FGM	FGA	FG%	3PM	3PA	3P%	FTM	FTA	FT%	ORB	DRB	TRB	AST	PF	DQ	STL	BLK	TO	MPG	PPG	RPG	APG	PCM
49-50 Minneapolis	67	....	....	271	106	302	.351	....	....	....	59	93	.634	....	....	....	148	162	....	....	....	....	....	4.0	....	2.2	....
50-51 Minneapolis	68	....	....	575	227	627	.362	....	....	....	121	177	.684	....	....	246	235	199	3	....	....	....	....	8.5	3.6	3.5	....
51-52 Minneapolis	66	....	2480	616	237	632	.375	....	....	....	142	190	.747	....	....	228	249	226	9	....	....	....	37.6	9.3	3.5	3.8	.291
52-53 Minneapolis	70	....	2556	744	260	634	.410	....	....	....	224	287	.780	....	....	186	250	246	4	....	....	....	36.5	10.6	2.7	3.6	.319
53-54 Minneapolis	69	....	2472	684	254	654	.388	....	....	....	176	243	.724	....	....	166	253	198	3	....	....	....	35.8	9.9	2.4	3.7	.303
54-55 Minneapolis	72	....	2784	976	350	919	.381	....	....	....	276	359	.769	....	....	260	427	221	7	....	....	....	38.7	13.6	3.6	5.9	.417
55-56 Minneapolis	72	....	2838	947	309	863	.358	....	....	....	329	395	.833	....	....	260	445	202	2	....	....	....	39.4	13.2	3.6	6.2	.413
56-57 New York	13	....	426	110	33	96	.344	....	....	....	44	53	.830	....	....	42	39	28	0	....	....	....	32.8	8.5	3.2	3.0	.304
56-57 St. Louis	53	....	1975	608	211	640	.330	....	....	....	186	238	.782	....	....	246	230	165	1	....	....	....	37.3	11.5	4.6	4.3	.344
57-58 St. Louis	60	....	2098	722	258	768	.336	....	....	....	206	276	.746	....	....	228	218	187	0	....	....	....	35.0	12.0	3.8	3.6	.334
58-59 St. Louis	71	....	2504	687	245	706	.347	....	....	....	197	254	.776	....	....	253	336	230	8	....	....	....	35.3	9.7	3.6	4.7	.336
59-60 St. Louis	64	....	1756	397	142	383	.371	....	....	....	113	155	.729	....	....	187	330	174	2	....	....	....	27.4	6.2	2.9	5.2	.390
NBA Season Totals	745	....	21889	7337	2632	7224	.364	....	....	....	2073	2720	.762	....	....	2302	3160	2238	39	....	....	....	29.4	9.8	3.1	4.2	....
49-50 Minneapolis	12	....	....	56	21	50	.420	....	....	....	14	24	.583	....	....	....	25	35	....	....	....	....	....	4.7	....	2.1	....
50-51 Minneapolis	7	....	....	50	18	51	.353	....	....	....	14	27	.519	....	....	42	25	20	0	....	....	....	....	7.1	6.0	3.6	....
51-52 Minneapolis	13	....	523	117	38	110	.345	....	....	....	41	56	.732	....	....	37	56	64	4	....	....	....	40.2	9.0	2.8	4.3	.260
52-53 Minneapolis	12	....	453	121	41	103	.398	....	....	....	39	51	.765	....	....	31	43	49	1	....	....	....	37.8	10.1	2.6	3.6	.290
53-54 Minneapolis	13	....	533	126	37	112	.330	....	....	....	52	70	.743	....	....	29	60	52	3	....	....	....	41.0	9.7	2.2	4.6	.274
54-55 Minneapolis	7	....	315	96	28	94	.298	....	....	....	40	49	.816	....	....	28	31	23	0	....	....	....	45.0	13.7	4.0	4.4	.299
55-56 Minneapolis	3	....	121	54	17	37	.459	....	....	....	20	24	.833	....	....	7	15	9	0	....	....	....	40.3	18.0	2.3	5.0	.477
56-57 St. Louis	10	....	439	166	55	155	.355	....	....	....	56	74	.757	....	....	42	49	39	2	....	....	....	43.9	16.6	4.2	4.9	.371
57-58 St. Louis	11	....	416	127	44	137	.321	....	....	....	39	63	.619	....	....	48	40	40	1	....	....	....	37.8	11.5	4.4	3.6	.293
58-59 St. Louis	1	....	18	8	4	5	.800	....	....	....	0	0	.000	....	....	3	2	2	0	....	....	....	18.0	8.0	3.0	2.0	.625
59-60 St. Louis	3	....	58	3	1	13	.077	....	....	....	1	4	.250	....	....	3	8	9	0	....	....	....	19.3	1.0	1.0	2.7	.028
NBA Playoff Totals	92	....	2876	924	304	867	.351	....	....	....	316	442	.715	....	....	270	354	342	11	....	....	....	31.3	10.0	2.9	3.8	....

• MARTIN, Fernando
Fernando Martin

Born: Mar. 25, 1962. Madrid, Spain. Died: Dec.3, 1989. Height: 6'9". Weight: 220 lbs. Drafted: 1985 College: none (HS: Estudiantes, ESP)

YEAR TEAM	GP	GS	MIN	PTS	FGM	FGA	FG%	3PM	3PA	3P%	FTM	FTA	FT%	ORB	DRB	TRB	AST	PF	DQ	STL	BLK	TO	MPG	PPG	RPG	APG	PCM
86-87 Portland	24	0	146	22	9	31	.290	0	1	.000	4	11	.364	8	20	28	9	24	0	7	1	19	6.1	0.9	1.2	0.4	.086
NBA Season Totals	24	0	146	22	9	31	.290	0	1	.000	4	11	.364	8	20	28	9	24	0	7	1	19	6.1	0.9	1.2	0.4	....
86-87 Portland	1	0	1	0	0	1	.000	0	0	.000	0	0	.000	0	0	0	0	0	0	0	0	0	1.0	0.0	0.0	0.0	-.931
NBA Playoff Totals	1	0	1	0	0	1	.000	0	0	.000	0	0	.000	0	0	0	0	0	0	0	0	0	1.0	0.0	0.0	0.0	....

• MARTIN, Jeff
Jeffery Allen Martin

Born: Jan. 14, 1967. Cherry Valley, AR, United States. Height: 6'5". Weight: 195 lbs. Drafted: 1989 College: Murray State

YEAR TEAM	GP	GS	MIN	PTS	FGM	FGA	FG%	3PM	3PA	3P%	FTM	FTA	FT%	ORB	DRB	TRB	AST	PF	DQ	STL	BLK	TO	MPG	PPG	RPG	APG	PCM
89-90 LA Clippers	69	23	1351	433	170	414	.411	2	15	.133	91	129	.705	78	81	159	44	97	0	41	16	48	19.6	6.3	2.3	0.6	.256
90-91 LA Clippers	74	26	1334	523	214	507	.422	27	88	.307	68	100	.680	53	78	131	65	104	0	37	31	52	18.0	7.1	1.8	0.9	.294
NBA Season Totals	143	49	2685	956	384	921	.417	29	103	.282	159	229	.694	131	159	290	109	201	0	78	47	100	18.8	6.7	2.0	0.8	....

• MARTIN, Kenyon
Kenyon Lee Martin

Born: Dec. 30, 1977. Saginaw, MI, United States. Height: 6'9". Weight: 234 lbs. Drafted: 2000 College: Cincinnati

YEAR TEAM	GP	GS	MIN	PTS	FGM	FGA	FG%	3PM	3PA	3P%	FTM	FTA	FT%	ORB	DRB	TRB	AST	PF	DQ	STL	BLK	TO	MPG	PPG	RPG	APG	PCM
00-01 New Jersey	68	68	2272	814	346	777	.445	1	11	.091	121	192	.630	137	365	502	131	281	**10**	78	113	138	33.4	12.0	7.4	1.9	.401
01-02 New Jersey	73	73	2503	1086	445	962	.463	15	67	.224	181	267	.678	113	275	388	192	261	8	90	121	172	34.3	14.9	5.3	2.6	.422
02-03 New Jersey	77	77	2629	1283	509	1082	.470	9	43	.209	256	392	.653	164	476	640	185	294	6	98	70	192	34.1	16.7	8.3	2.4	.505
NBA Season Totals	218	218	7404	3183	1300	2821	.461	25	121	.207	558	851	.656	414	1116	1530	508	836	24	266	304	502	34.0	14.6	7.0	2.3	....
01-02 New Jersey	20	20	749	336	129	304	.424	2	9	.222	76	110	.691	30	86	116	57	86	3	24	25	52	37.5	16.8	5.8	2.9	.384
02-03 New Jersey	20	20	777	378	149	329	.453	1	11	.091	79	114	.693	50	137	187	57	92	2	29	31	58	38.9	18.9	9.4	2.9	.503
NBA Playoff Totals	40	40	1526	714	278	633	.439	3	20	.150	155	224	.692	80	223	303	114	178	5	53	56	110	38.2	17.9	7.6	2.9	....

• MARTIN, LaRue
Larue Martin

Born: Mar. 30, 1950. Chicago, IL, United States. Height: 6'11". Weight: 208 lbs. Drafted: 1972 College: Loyola (IL)

YEAR TEAM	GP	GS	MIN	PTS	FGM	FGA	FG%	3PM	3PA	3P%	FTM	FTA	FT%	ORB	DRB	TRB	AST	PF	DQ	STL	BLK	TO	MPG	PPG	RPG	APG	PCM
72-73 Portland	77	....	996	340	145	366	.396	....	....	....	50	77	.649	....	....	358	42	162	0	....	....	....	12.9	4.4	4.6	0.5	.426
73-74 Portland	50	....	538	244	101	232	.435	....	....	....	42	66	.636	74	107	181	20	90	0	7	26	....	10.8	4.9	3.6	0.4	.485

YEAR	TEAM	GP	GS	MIN	PTS	FGM	FGA	FG%	3PM	3PA	3P%	FTM	FTA	FT%	ORB	DRB	TRB	AST	PF	DQ	STL	BLK	TO	MPG	PPG	RPG	APG	PCM
74-75	Portland	81	....	1372	571	236	522	.452	....	....	....	99	142	.697	136	272	408	69	239	5	33	49	....	16.9	7.0	5.0	0.9	.462
75-76	Portland	63	....	889	275	109	302	.361	....	....	....	57	77	.740	68	243	311	72	126	1	6	23	....	14.1	4.4	4.9	1.1	.445
NBA Season Totals		271	....	3795	1430	591	1422	.416	....	....	....	248	362	.685	278	622	1258	203	617	6	46	98	....	14.0	5.3	4.6	0.7	....

• MARTIN, Maurice

Maurice Martin

Born: July 2, 1964. Liberty, NY, United States. Height: 6'6". Weight: 200 lbs. Drafted: — College: St. Joseph's (PA)

YEAR	TEAM	GP	GS	MIN	PTS	FGM	FGA	FG%	3PM	3PA	3P%	FTM	FTA	FT%	ORB	DRB	TRB	AST	PF	DQ	STL	BLK	TO	MPG	PPG	RPG	APG	PCM
86-87	Denver	43	0	286	147	51	135	.378	3	15	.200	42	66	.636	12	29	41	35	48	0	13	6	34	6.7	3.4	1.0	0.8	.339
87-88	Denver	26	0	136	57	23	61	.377	1	4	.250	10	21	.476	13	11	24	14	21	0	6	3	10	5.2	2.2	0.9	0.5	.317
NBA Season Totals		69	0	422	204	74	196	.378	4	19	.211	52	87	.598	25	40	65	49	69	0	19	9	44	6.1	3.0	0.9	0.7	....
86-87	Denver	3	0	54	31	12	29	.414	0	1	.000	7	12	.583	4	5	9	10	12	0	0	1	5	18.0	10.3	3.0	3.3	.419
87-88	Denver	3	0	9	7	1	5	.200	0	1	.000	5	6	.833	0	1	1	0	1	0	0	1	1	3.0	2.3	0.3	0.0	.364
NBA Playoff Totals		6	0	63	38	13	34	.382	0	2	.000	12	18	.667	4	6	10	10	13	0	0	2	6	10.5	6.3	1.7	1.7	....

• MARTIN, Phil

Phillip Roger Martin

Born: Apr. 2, 1928. Height: 6'3". Weight: 190 lbs. Drafted: 1954 College: Toledo

YEAR	TEAM	GP	GS	MIN	PTS	FGM	FGA	FG%	3PM	3PA	3P%	FTM	FTA	FT%	ORB	DRB	TRB	AST	PF	DQ	STL	BLK	TO	MPG	PPG	RPG	APG	PCM
54-55	Milwaukee	7	....	47	12	5	19	.263	....	....	....	2	2	1.000	....	....	10	6	7	0	....	....	....	6.7	1.7	1.4	0.9	.295
NBA Season Totals		7	....	47	12	5	19	.263	....	....	....	2	2	1.000	....	....	10	6	7	0	....	....	....	6.7	1.7	1.4	0.9	....

• MARTIN, Whitey

Ronald Barry (Whitey) Martin

Born: Apr. 11, 1939. Height: 6'2". Weight: 185 lbs. Drafted: 1961 College: St. Bonaventure

YEAR	TEAM	GP	GS	MIN	PTS	FGM	FGA	FG%	3PM	3PA	3P%	FTM	FTA	FT%	ORB	DRB	TRB	AST	PF	DQ	STL	BLK	TO	MPG	PPG	RPG	APG	PCM
61-62	New York	66	....	1018	227	95	292	.325	....	....	....	37	55	.673	....	....	158	115	158	4	....	....	....	15.4	3.4	2.4	1.7	.263
NBA Season Totals		66	....	1018	227	95	292	.325	....	....	....	37	55	.673	....	....	158	115	158	4	....	....	....	15.4	3.4	2.4	1.7	....

• MASHBURN, Jamal

Jamal Mashburn

Born: Nov. 29, 1972. New York, NY, United States. Height: 6'8". Weight: 240 lbs. Drafted: 1993 College: Kentucky

YEAR	TEAM	GP	GS	MIN	PTS	FGM	FGA	FG%	3PM	3PA	3P%	FTM	FTA	FT%	ORB	DRB	TRB	AST	PF	DQ	STL	BLK	TO	MPG	PPG	RPG	APG	PCM
93-94	Dallas	79	73	2896	1513	561	1382	.406	85	299	.284	306	438	.699	107	246	353	266	205	0	89	14	245	36.7	19.2	4.5	3.4	.375
94-95	Dallas	80	80	2980	1926	683	1566	.436	113	344	.328	447	605	.739	116	215	331	298	190	0	82	8	232	37.3	24.1	4.1	3.7	.479
95-96	Dallas	18	18	669	422	145	383	.379	35	102	.343	97	133	.729	37	60	97	50	39	0	14	3	56	37.2	23.4	5.4	2.8	.404
96-97	Dallas	37	21	975	394	140	376	.372	42	131	.321	72	111	.649	28	87	115	93	69	0	35	5	56	26.4	10.6	3.1	2.5	.323
96-97	Miami	32	30	1189	428	146	367	.398	48	146	.329	88	117	.752	41	138	179	111	117	4	43	7	58	37.2	13.4	5.6	3.5	.363
97-98	Miami	48	48	1729	723	251	577	.435	37	122	.303	184	231	.797	72	164	236	132	137	1	43	14	110	36.0	15.1	4.9	2.8	.377
98-99	Miami	24	23	855	356	134	297	.451	13	30	.433	75	104	.721	24	122	146	75	58	0	20	3	60	35.6	14.8	6.1	3.1	.412
99-00	Miami	76	76	2828	1328	515	1158	.445	112	278	.403	186	239	.778	64	317	381	298	215	3	79	14	180	37.2	17.5	5.0	3.9	.430
00-01	Charlotte	76	76	2989	1528	573	1388	.413	103	289	.356	279	364	.766	92	484	576	411	185	1	85	13	211	39.3	20.1	7.6	5.4	.516
01-02	Charlotte	40	40	1601	858	303	744	.407	41	112	.366	211	241	.876	31	211	242	171	80	0	45	6	110	40.0	21.5	6.1	4.3	.476
02-03	New Orleans	82	81	3321	1772	670	1586	.422	119	306	.389	313	369	.848	66	432	498	462	196	0	83	17	230	40.5	21.6	6.1	5.6	.501
NBA Season Totals		592	566	22032	11248	4121	9824	.419	748	2159	.346	2258	2952	.765	678	2476	3154	2367	1491	9	618	104	1548	37.2	19.0	5.3	4.0	....
96-97	Miami	17	17	554	178	65	168	.387	22	62	.355	26	40	.650	22	62	84	35	58	2	17	2	30	32.6	10.5	4.9	2.1	.278
97-98	Miami	5	3	129	31	12	45	.267	4	11	.364	3	4	.750	4	18	22	9	21	2	3	1	9	25.8	6.2	4.4	1.8	.124
98-99	Miami	5	5	152	50	19	49	.388	6	14	.429	6	9	.667	4	9	13	10	11	0	2	0	10	30.4	10.0	2.6	2.0	.215
99-00	Miami	10	10	423	175	63	157	.401	13	33	.394	36	42	.857	9	37	46	32	30	0	11	2	24	42.3	17.5	4.6	3.2	.331
00-01	Charlotte	10	10	419	249	84	208	.404	7	21	.333	74	88	.841	18	44	62	57	24	0	12	3	30	41.9	24.9	6.2	5.7	.538
01-02	Charlotte	1	1	10	0	0	6	.000	0	1	.000	0	0	.000	0	1	1	1	0	0	0	0	0	10.0	0.0	1.0	1.0	-.344
02-03	New Orleans	4	4	162	99	34	79	.430	6	15	.400	25	35	.714	0	14	14	21	4	0	4	1	10	40.5	24.8	3.5	5.3	.512
NBA Playoff Totals		52	50	1849	782	277	712	.389	58	157	.369	170	218	.780	57	185	242	165	148	4	49	9	113	35.6	15.0	4.7	3.2	....

• MASINO, Al

Alfred Albert Masino

Born: Feb. 5, 1928. Height: 5'10". Weight: 174 lbs. Drafted: — College: Canisius

YEAR	TEAM	GP	GS	MIN	PTS	FGM	FGA	FG%	3PM	3PA	3P%	FTM	FTA	FT%	ORB	DRB	TRB	AST	PF	DQ	STL	BLK	TO	MPG	PPG	RPG	APG	PCM
52-53	Milwaukee	72	....	1773	396	134	400	.335	....	....	....	128	204	.627	....	....	177	160	252	12	....	....	....	24.6	5.5	2.5	2.2	.235
53-54	Rochester	11	....	80	23	8	16	.500	....	....	....	7	12	.583	....	....	12	7	20	0	....	....	....	7.3	2.1	1.1	0.6	.325
53-54	Syracuse	16	....	101	59	18	46	.391	....	....	....	23	37	.622	....	....	16	15	24	0	....	....	....	6.3	3.7	1.0	0.9	.558
NBA Season Totals		99	....	1954	478	160	462	.346	....	....	....	158	253	.625	....	....	205	182	296	12	....	....	....	19.7	4.8	2.1	1.8	....
53-54	Syracuse	13	....	96	21	7	20	.350	....	....	....	7	15	.467	....	....	6	7	23	0	....	....	....	7.4	1.6	0.5	0.5	.146
NBA Playoff Totals		13	....	96	21	7	20	.350	....	....	....	7	15	.467	....	....	6	7	23	0	....	....	....	7.4	1.6	0.5	0.5	....

• MASON, Anthony

Anthony George Douglas Mason

Born: Dec. 14, 1966. Miami, FL, United States. Height: 6'7". Weight: 250 lbs. Drafted: 1988 College: Tennessee State

YEAR	TEAM	GP	GS	MIN	PTS	FGM	FGA	FG%	3PM	3PA	3P%	FTM	FTA	FT%	ORB	DRB	TRB	AST	PF	DQ	STL	BLK	TO	MPG	PPG	RPG	APG	PCM
89-90	New Jersey	21	0	108	37	14	40	.350	0	0	.000	9	15	.600	11	23	34	7	20	0	2	2	11	5.1	1.8	1.6	0.3	.307
90-91	Denver	3	0	21	10	2	4	.500	0	0	.000	6	8	.750	3	2	5	0	6	0	1	0	0	7.0	3.3	1.7	0.0	.476
91-92	New York	82	0	2198	573	203	399	.509	0	0	.000	167	260	.642	216	357	573	106	229	0	46	20	98	26.8	7.0	7.0	1.3	.390
92-93	New York	81	0	2482	831	316	629	.502	0	0	.000	199	292	.682	231	409	640	170	240	2	43	19	138	30.6	10.3	7.9	2.1	.440
93-94	New York	73	12	1903	528	206	433	.476	0	1	.000	116	161	.720	158	269	427	151	190	2	31	9	110	26.1	7.2	5.8	2.1	.369
94-95	New York	77	11	2496	765	287	507	.566	0	1	.000	191	298	.641	182	468	650	240	253	3	69	21	123	32.4	9.9	8.4	3.1	.490
95-96	New York	82	82	**3457**	1196	449	798	.563	0	0	.000	298	414	.720	220	544	764	363	246	3	69	34	213	**42.2**	14.6	9.3	4.4	.491
96-97	Charlotte	73	73	3143	1186	433	825	.525	1	3	.333	319	428	.745	186	643	829	414	202	3	76	33	168	**43.1**	16.2	11.4	5.7	.584
97-98	Charlotte	81	80	3148	1039	389	764	.509	0	4	.000	261	402	.649	177	649	826	342	182	1	68	18	146	38.9	12.8	10.2	4.2	.515
99-00	Charlotte	82	81	3133	948	317	661	.480	0	1	.000	314	421	.746	145	554	699	367	220	0	74	29	160	38.2	11.6	8.5	4.5	.469

YEAR	TEAM	GP	GS	MIN	PTS	FGM	FGA	FG%	3PM	3PA	3P%	FTM	FTA	FT%	ORB	DRB	TRB	AST	PF	DQ	STL	BLK	TO	MPG	PPG	RPG	APG	PCM
00-01	Miami	80	80	3254	1290	460	954	.482	0	0	.000	370	474	.781	169	601	770	248	231	5	80	25	179	40.7	16.1	9.6	3.1	.490
01-02	Milwaukee	82	82	3143	787	316	626	.505	1	1	1.000	154	221	.697	124	522	646	346	187	0	57	22	130	38.3	9.6	7.9	4.2	.416
02-03	Milwaukee	65	58	2120	466	191	393	.486	0	1	.000	84	117	.718	90	326	416	209	147	0	32	12	79	32.6	7.2	6.4	3.2	.366
NBA Season Totals		882	559	30606	9656	3583	7033	.509	2	12	.167	2488	3511	.709	1912	5367	7279	2963	2353	19	648	244	1555	34.7	10.9	8.3	3.4	....
91-92	New York	12	0	288	60	19	43	.442	0	0	.000	22	28	.786	28	48	76	10	34	0	2	8	11	24.0	5.0	6.3	0.8	.346
92-93	New York	15	0	510	187	72	122	.590	0	0	.000	43	68	.632	55	54	109	41	50	2	10	6	23	34.0	12.5	7.3	2.7	.479
93-94	New York	25	0	660	189	67	137	.489	0	0	.000	55	77	.714	53	93	146	46	66	0	15	5	36	26.4	7.6	5.8	1.8	.384
94-95	New York	11	0	352	105	31	51	.608	0	1	.000	43	69	.623	23	45	68	24	28	0	6	6	26	32.0	9.5	6.2	2.2	.389
95-96	New York	8	8	350	101	41	78	.526	0	0	.000	19	28	.679	17	45	62	26	20	0	4	1	20	43.8	12.6	7.8	3.3	.355
96-97	Charlotte	3	3	131	39	16	38	.421	0	0	.000	7	13	.538	8	28	36	9	6	0	1	1	9	43.7	13.0	12.0	3.0	.378
97-98	Charlotte	9	9	367	139	57	99	.576	0	1	.000	25	42	.595	17	54	71	31	17	0	8	0	22	40.8	15.4	7.9	3.4	.465
99-00	Charlotte	4	4	179	50	18	38	.474	0	1	.000	14	20	.700	16	23	39	22	13	0	4	0	13	44.8	12.5	9.8	5.5	.416
00-01	Miami	3	3	98	16	5	13	.385	0	1	.000	6	6	1.000	1	8	9	4	6	0	1	0	7	32.7	5.3	3.0	1.3	.135
02-03	Milwaukee	6	0	157	23	7	17	.412	0	0	.000	9	13	.692	4	16	20	1	17	0	3	1	8	26.2	3.8	3.3	0.2	.127
NBA Playoff Totals		96	27	3092	909	333	636	.524	0	4	.000	243	364	.668	222	414	636	214	257	2	54	28	175	32.2	9.5	6.6	2.2	....

• MASON, Desmond
Desmond Tremaine Mason

Born: Oct. 11, 1977. Waxahachie, TX, United States.   Height: 6'7".   Weight: 224 lbs.   Drafted: 2000   College: Oklahoma State

YEAR	TEAM	GP	GS	MIN	PTS	FGM	FGA	FG%	3PM	3PA	3P%	FTM	FTA	FT%	ORB	DRB	TRB	AST	PF	DQ	STL	BLK	TO	MPG	PPG	RPG	APG	PCM
00-01	Seattle	78	14	1522	463	189	439	.431	18	67	.269	67	91	.736	72	177	249	63	146	0	39	20	53	19.5	5.9	3.2	0.8	.303
01-02	Seattle	75	20	2420	931	357	769	.464	16	59	.271	201	237	.848	92	259	351	104	170	0	67	27	104	32.3	12.4	4.7	1.4	.367
02-03	Seattle	52	15	1811	732	291	667	.436	16	55	.291	134	181	.740	88	247	335	95	136	1	47	21	74	34.8	14.1	6.4	1.8	.392
02-03	Milwaukee	28	25	952	415	166	350	.474	5	17	.294	78	102	.765	66	122	188	68	74	0	20	11	41	34.0	14.8	6.7	2.4	.461
NBA Season Totals		233	74	6705	2541	1003	2225	.451	55	198	.278	480	611	.786	318	805	1123	330	526	1	173	79	272	28.8	10.9	4.8	1.4	....
01-02	Seattle	5	5	205	59	24	57	.421	1	3	.333	10	17	.588	5	26	31	9	11	0	4	2	5	41.0	11.8	6.2	1.8	.292
02-03	Milwaukee	6	6	204	78	28	55	.509	0	4	.000	22	31	.710	6	36	42	5	19	1	6	4	7	34.0	13.0	7.0	0.8	.427
NBA Playoff Totals		11	11	409	137	52	112	.464	1	7	.143	32	48	.667	11	62	73	14	30	1	10	6	12	37.2	12.5	6.6	1.3	....

• MASON, Joel
Joel Gregory Mason   aka.: Joel Gregory Muleski

Born: Mar. 12, 1912. Iron River, MI, United States. Died: Oct.31, 1995.   Height: 6'   Weight: 195 lbs.   Drafted: —   College: Western Michigan

YEAR	TEAM	GP	GS	MIN	PTS	FGM	FGA	FG%	3PM	3PA	3P%	FTM	FTA	FT%	ORB	DRB	TRB	AST	PF	DQ	STL	BLK	TO	MPG	PPG	RPG	APG	PCM
42-43	Sheboygan-N	1	....	....	0	0	....	....	....	....	....	0	....	....	....	....	....	....	....	....	....	....	....	....	0.0	....	....	....
NBL Season Totals		1	....	....	0	0	....	....	....	....	....	0	....	....	....	....	....	....	....	....	....	....	....	....	0.0	....	....	....

• MASON, Roger
Roger Philip Mason Jr.

Born: Sept. 10, 1980. Washington, DC, United States.   Height: 6'5".   Weight: 200 lbs.   Drafted: 2002   College: Virginia

YEAR	TEAM	GP	GS	MIN	PTS	FGM	FGA	FG%	3PM	3PA	3P%	FTM	FTA	FT%	ORB	DRB	TRB	AST	PF	DQ	STL	BLK	TO	MPG	PPG	RPG	APG	PCM
02-03	Chicago	17	0	113	30	11	31	.355	6	18	.333	2	2	1.000	2	10	12	12	20	0	4	0	5	6.6	1.8	0.7	0.7	.229
NBA Season Totals		17	0	113	30	11	31	.355	6	18	.333	2	2	1.000	2	10	12	12	20	0	4	0	5	6.6	1.8	0.7	0.7	....

• MASSENBURG, Tony
Tony Arnel Massenburg

Born: July 13, 1967. Sussex, VA, United States.   Height: 6'9".   Weight: 220 lbs.   Drafted: 1990   College: Maryland

YEAR	TEAM	GP	GS	MIN	PTS	FGM	FGA	FG%	3PM	3PA	3P%	FTM	FTA	FT%	ORB	DRB	TRB	AST	PF	DQ	STL	BLK	TO	MPG	PPG	RPG	APG	PCM
90-91	San Antonio	35	0	161	82	27	60	.450	0	0	.000	28	45	.622	23	35	58	4	26	0	4	9	14	4.6	2.3	1.7	0.1	.550
91-92	San Antonio	1	0	9	2	1	5	.200	0	0	.000	0	0	.000	0	0	0	0	2	0	0	0	0	9.0	2.0	0.0	0.0	-.294
91-92	Charlotte	3	0	13	1	0	3	.000	0	0	.000	1	2	.500	1	3	4	0	2	0	1	0	4	4.3	0.3	1.3	0.0	-.173
91-92	Boston	7	0	46	10	4	9	.444	0	0	.000	2	4	.500	2	7	9	0	7	0	0	1	2	6.6	1.4	1.3	0.0	.187
91-92	Golden State	7	0	22	16	5	8	.625	0	0	.000	6	9	.667	4	8	12	0	10	0	0	0	3	3.1	2.3	1.7	0.0	.706
94-95	LA Clippers	80	50	2127	741	282	601	.469	0	3	.000	177	235	.753	160	295	455	67	253	2	48	58	120	26.6	9.3	5.7	0.8	.367
95-96	Toronto	24	20	659	243	100	196	.510	0	0	.000	43	65	.662	52	114	166	18	67	0	13	9	36	27.5	10.1	6.9	0.8	.414
95-96	Philadelphia	30	8	804	296	114	236	.483	0	3	.000	68	92	.739	75	111	186	12	73	0	15	11	39	26.8	9.9	6.2	0.4	.387
96-97	New Jersey	79	49	1954	568	219	452	.485	0	1	.000	130	206	.631	222	295	517	23	217	2	38	50	95	24.7	7.2	6.5	0.3	.366
97-98	Vancouver	61	13	894	396	148	309	.479	0	0	.000	100	137	.730	80	152	232	21	123	0	25	24	61	14.7	6.5	3.8	0.3	.447
98-99	Vancouver	43	35	1143	481	189	388	.487	0	2	.000	103	155	.665	83	174	257	23	108	0	26	39	64	26.6	11.2	6.0	0.5	.427
99-00	Houston	10	0	109	46	16	36	.444	0	0	.000	14	16	.875	7	20	27	3	13	0	2	5	9	10.9	4.6	2.7	0.3	.431
00-01	Vancouver	52	20	823	233	92	199	.462	0	0	.000	49	70	.700	75	135	210	9	122	0	10	28	48	15.8	4.5	4.0	0.2	.319
01-02	Memphis	73	31	1241	403	159	349	.456	1	1	1.000	84	117	.718	100	224	324	26	174	2	30	31	65	17.0	5.5	4.4	0.4	.367
02-03	Utah	58	1	792	273	104	232	.448	0	0	.000	65	84	.774	59	97	156	17	144	1	17	19	50	13.7	4.7	2.7	0.3	.291
NBA Season Totals		563	227	10797	3791	1460	3083	.474	1	10	.100	870	1237	.703	943	1670	2613	223	1341	7	229	284	610	19.2	6.7	4.6	0.4	....
90-91	San Antonio	1	0	1	0	0	0	.000	0	0	.000	0	0	.000	0	0	0	0	0	0	0	0	0	1.0	0.0	0.0	0.0	.000
02-03	Utah	5	0	70	25	10	21	.476	0	0	.000	5	9	.556	7	14	21	2	9	0	0	4	5	14.0	5.0	4.2	0.4	.421
NBA Playoff Totals		6	0	71	25	10	21	.476	0	0	.000	5	9	.556	7	14	21	2	9	0	0	4	5	11.8	4.2	3.5	0.3	....

• MAST, Eddie
Edward Mast

Born: Oct. 3, 1948. Philadelphia, PA, United States. Died: Oct.18, 1994.   Height: 6'9".   Weight: 220 lbs.   Drafted: 1969   College: Temple

YEAR	TEAM	GP	GS	MIN	PTS	FGM	FGA	FG%	3PM	3PA	3P%	FTM	FTA	FT%	ORB	DRB	TRB	AST	PF	DQ	STL	BLK	TO	MPG	PPG	RPG	APG	PCM
70-71	New York	30	....	164	61	25	66	.379	....	....	....	11	20	.550	....	....	56	4	25	0	....	....	....	5.5	2.0	1.9	0.1	.389
71-72	New York	40	....	270	103	39	112	.348	....	....	....	25	41	.610	....	....	73	10	39	0	....	....	....	6.8	2.6	1.8	0.3	.336
72-73	Atlanta	42	....	447	119	50	118	.424	....	....	....	19	30	.633	....	....	136	37	50	0	....	....	....	10.6	2.8	3.2	0.9	.433
NBA Season Totals		112	....	881	283	114	296	.385	....	....	....	55	91	.604	....	....	265	51	114	0	....	....	....	7.9	2.5	2.4	0.5	....
70-71	New York	3	....	11	4	2	5	.400	....	....	....	0	0	.000	....	....	3	0	2	0	....	....	....	3.7	1.3	1.0	0.0	.285
71-72	New York	9	....	23	9	4	7	.571	....	....	....	1	5	.200	....	....	7	1	4	0	....	....	....	2.6	1.0	0.8	0.1	.441
72-73	Atlanta	4	....	15	10	5	5	1.000	....	....	....	0	0	.000	....	....	5	1	1	0	....	....	....	3.8	2.5	1.3	0.3	1.000
NBA Playoff Totals		16	....	49	23	11	17	.647	....	....	....	1	5	.200	....	....	15	2	7	0	....	....	....	3.1	1.4	0.9	0.1	....

• MATHIS, Johnny

Johnny C. Mathis

Born: July 14, 1943. Eastman, GA, United States. Height: 6'6". Weight: 220 lbs. Drafted: — College: Savannah State

YEAR	TEAM	GP	GS	MIN	PTS	FGM	FGA	FG%	3PM	3PA	3P%	FTM	FTA	FT%	ORB	DRB	TRB	AST	PF	DQ	STL	BLK	TO	MPG	PPG	RPG	APG	PCM
67-68	New Jersey-A	51	....	656	173	69	186	.371	0	2	.000	35	55	.636	....	....	194	28	102	3	....	....	42	12.9	3.4	3.8	0.5	.334
ABA Season Totals		51	....	656	173	69	186	.371	0	2	.000	35	55	.636	....	....	194	28	102	3	....	....	42	12.9	3.4	3.8	0.5	....

• MATTHEWS, Wes

Wesley Joel Matthews

Born: Aug. 24, 1959. Sarasota, FL, United States. Height: 6'1". Weight: 170 lbs. Drafted: 1980 College: Wisconsin

YEAR	TEAM	GP	GS	MIN	PTS	FGM	FGA	FG%	3PM	3PA	3P%	FTM	FTA	FT%	ORB	DRB	TRB	AST	PF	DQ	STL	BLK	TO	MPG	PPG	RPG	APG	PCM
80-81	Washington	45	....	1161	552	224	449	.499	5	15	.333	99	129	.767	30	37	67	199	120	1	46	10	149	25.8	12.3	1.5	4.4	.406
80-81	Atlanta	34	....	1105	425	161	330	.488	0	6	.000	103	123	.837	16	56	72	212	122	1	61	7	112	32.5	12.5	2.1	6.2	.419
81-82	Atlanta	47	5	837	324	131	298	.440	2	8	.250	60	79	.759	19	39	58	139	129	3	53	2	61	17.8	6.9	1.2	3.0	.358
82-83	Atlanta	64	0	1187	442	171	424	.403	14	48	.292	86	112	.768	25	66	91	249	129	0	60	8	122	18.5	6.9	1.4	3.9	.380
83-84	Atlanta	6	0	96	50	16	30	.533	0	1	.000	18	22	.818	1	3	4	21	13	0	5	1	10	16.0	8.3	0.7	3.5	.537
83-84	Philadelphia	14	5	292	100	45	101	.446	1	7	.143	9	14	.643	6	17	23	62	32	0	11	2	29	20.9	7.1	1.6	4.4	.355
84-85	Chicago	78	38	1523	443	191	386	.495	2	16	.125	59	85	.694	16	51	67	354	133	0	73	12	125	19.5	5.7	0.9	4.5	.388
85-86	San Antonio	75	46	1853	817	320	603	.531	4	25	.160	173	211	.820	30	101	131	476	168	1	87	32	233	24.7	10.9	1.7	6.3	.531
86-87	LA Lakers	50	0	532	208	89	187	.476	1	3	.333	29	36	.806	13	34	47	100	53	0	23	4	50	10.6	4.2	0.9	2.0	.410
87-88	LA Lakers	51	8	706	289	114	248	.460	7	30	.233	54	65	.831	16	50	66	138	65	0	25	3	71	13.8	5.7	1.3	2.7	.421
89-90	Atlanta	1	0	13	4	1	3	.333	0	1	.000	2	2	1.000	0	0	0	5	0	0	0	0	0	13.0	4.0	0.0	5.0	.572
NBA Season Totals		465	102	9305	3654	1463	3059	.478	36	160	.225	692	878	.788	172	454	626	1955	964	6	444	81	962	20.0	7.9	1.3	4.2	....
81-82	Atlanta	2	0	28	8	2	10	.200	0	0	.000	4	4	1.000	0	0	0	4	4	0	0	1	2	14.0	4.0	0.0	2.0	.078
82-83	Atlanta	3	0	38	10	3	9	.333	0	1	.000	4	5	.800	0	0	0	11	5	0	0	1	3	12.7	3.3	0.0	3.7	.320
83-84	Philadelphia	4	0	23	10	4	8	.500	1	2	.500	1	2	.500	0	0	0	4	4	0	1	0	4	5.8	2.5	0.0	1.0	.237
84-85	Chicago	4	4	91	29	11	32	.344	0	3	.000	7	9	.778	2	4	6	12	10	0	3	0	7	22.8	7.3	1.5	3.0	.203
85-86	San Antonio	3	3	116	76	35	54	.648	0	1	.000	6	8	.750	1	6	7	24	7	0	6	0	11	38.7	25.3	2.3	8.0	.705
86-87	LA Lakers	12	0	61	28	11	23	.478	0	1	.000	6	7	.857	0	4	4	9	9	0	1	0	13	5.1	2.3	0.3	0.8	.235
87-88	LA Lakers	10	0	27	12	2	5	.400	0	1	.000	8	10	.800	0	1	1	2	4	0	1	0	3	2.7	1.2	0.1	0.2	.282
NBA Playoff Totals		38	7	384	173	68	141	.482	1	9	.111	36	45	.800	3	15	18	66	43	0	12	2	43	10.1	4.6	0.5	1.7	....

• MAUGHAN, Ariel

Ariel Leishman Maughan

Born: Feb. 23, 1923. Salt Lake City, UT, United States. Died: Aug.4, 1997. Height: 6'4". Weight: 190 lbs. Drafted: — College: Utah State

YEAR	TEAM	GP	GS	MIN	PTS	FGM	FGA	FG%	3PM	3PA	3P%	FTM	FTA	FT%	ORB	DRB	TRB	AST	PF	DQ	STL	BLK	TO	MPG	PPG	RPG	APG	PCM
46-47	Detroit	59	....	....	532	224	929	.241	....	....	....	84	114	.737	....	....	....	57	180	....	....	....	....	....	9.0	....	1.0	....
47-48	Providence	14	....	....	55	22	91	.242	....	....	....	11	16	.688	....	....	....	2	36	....	....	....	....	....	3.9	....	0.1	....
47-48	St. Louis	28	....	....	129	54	165	.327	....	....	....	21	37	.568	....	....	....	4	53	....	....	....	....	....	4.6	....	0.1	....
48-49	St. Louis	55	....	....	596	206	650	.317	....	....	....	184	285	.646	....	....	....	99	134	....	....	....	....	....	10.8	....	1.8	....
49-50	St. Louis	68	....	....	477	160	574	.279	....	....	....	157	205	.766	....	....	....	101	174	....	....	....	....	....	7.0	....	1.5	....
50-51	Washington	35	....	....	257	78	250	.312	....	....	....	101	120	.842	....	....	141	48	91	2	....	....	....	....	7.3	4.0	1.4	....
NBA Season Totals		259	....	....	2046	744	2659	.280	....	....	....	558	777	.718	....	....	141	311	668	2	....	....	....	....	7.9	0.5	1.2	....
47-48	St. Louis	7	....	....	80	32	122	.262	....	....	....	16	23	.696	....	....	....	1	22	....	....	....	....	....	11.4	....	0.1	....
48-49	St. Louis	2	....	....	2	0	6	.000	....	....	....	2	3	.667	....	....	....	3	3	....	....	....	....	....	1.0	....	1.5	....
NBA Playoff Totals		9	....	....	82	32	128	.250	....	....	....	18	26	.692	....	....	....	4	25	....	....	....	....	....	9.1	....	0.4	....

• MAURY, Frank

Frank ("X") Maury

Born: 1910. Height: 5'5". Weight: 155 lbs. Drafted: — College: none

YEAR	TEAM	GP	GS	MIN	PTS	FGM	FGA	FG%	3PM	3PA	3P%	FTM	FTA	FT%	ORB	DRB	TRB	AST	PF	DQ	STL	BLK	TO	MPG	PPG	RPG	APG	PCM
37-38	Warren-N	12	....	....	75	31	....	....	....	....	....	13	....	....	....	....	....	....	....	....	....	....	....	....	6.3	....	....	....
38-39	Cleveland-N	27	....	....	112	49	....	....	....	....	....	14	....	....	....	....	....	....	....	....	....	....	....	....	4.1	....	....	....
NBL Season Totals		39	....	....	187	80	....	....	....	....	....	27	....	....	....	....	....	....	....	....	....	....	....	....	4.8	....	....	....

• MAXEY, Marlon

Marlon Lee Maxey

Born: Feb. 19, 1969. Chicago, IL, United States. Height: 6'8". Weight: 250 lbs. Drafted: 1992 College: Texas (El Paso)

YEAR	TEAM	GP	GS	MIN	PTS	FGM	FGA	FG%	3PM	3PA	3P%	FTM	FTA	FT%	ORB	DRB	TRB	AST	PF	DQ	STL	BLK	TO	MPG	PPG	RPG	APG	PCM
92-93	Minnesota	43	3	520	231	93	169	.550	0	1	.000	45	70	.643	66	98	164	12	75	0	11	18	39	12.1	5.4	3.8	0.3	.519
93-94	Minnesota	55	2	626	248	89	167	.533	0	2	.000	70	98	.714	75	124	199	10	113	1	16	33	39	11.4	4.5	3.6	0.2	.502
NBA Season Totals		98	5	1146	479	182	336	.542	0	3	.000	115	168	.685	141	222	363	22	188	1	27	51	78	11.7	4.9	3.7	0.2	....

• MAXWELL, Cedric

Cedric Bryan (Cornbread) Maxwell

Born: Nov. 21, 1955. Kinston, NC, United States. Height: 6'8". Weight: 205 lbs. Drafted: 1977 College: North Carolina (Charlotte)

YEAR	TEAM	GP	GS	MIN	PTS	FGM	FGA	FG%	3PM	3PA	3P%	FTM	FTA	FT%	ORB	DRB	TRB	AST	PF	DQ	STL	BLK	TO	MPG	PPG	RPG	APG	PCM
77-78	Boston	72	....	1213	528	170	316	.538	....	....	....	188	250	.752	138	241	379	68	151	2	53	48	122	16.8	7.3	5.3	0.9	.574
78-79	Boston	80	....	2969	1518	472	808	**.584**	....	....	....	574	716	.802	272	519	791	228	266	4	98	74	272	37.1	19.0	9.9	2.9	.642
79-80	Boston	80	....	2744	1350	457	750	**.609**	0	0	.000	436	554	.787	284	420	704	199	266	6	76	61	232	34.3	16.9	8.8	2.5	.612
80-81	Boston	81	....	2730	1234	441	750	.588	0	1	.000	352	450	.782	222	303	525	219	256	5	79	68	178	33.7	15.2	6.5	2.7	.542
81-82	Boston	78	73	2590	1151	397	724	.548	0	3	.000	357	478	.747	218	281	499	183	263	6	79	49	172	33.2	14.8	6.4	2.3	.498
82-83	Boston	79	72	2252	942	331	663	.499	0	1	.000	280	345	.812	185	237	422	186	202	3	65	39	166	28.5	11.9	5.3	2.4	.467
83-84	Boston	80	78	2502	955	317	596	.532	1	6	.167	320	425	.753	201	260	461	205	224	4	63	24	200	31.3	11.9	5.8	2.6	.434
84-85	Boston	57	51	1495	633	201	377	.533	0	2	.000	231	278	.831	98	144	242	102	140	2	36	15	97	26.2	11.1	4.2	1.8	.450
85-86	LA Clippers	76	72	2458	1075	314	661	.475	0	3	.000	447	562	.795	241	383	624	215	252	2	61	29	205	32.3	14.1	8.2	2.8	.523
86-87	LA Clippers	35	0	1132	477	150	289	.519	0	0	.000	177	228	.776	103	148	251	122	102	1	26	9	88	32.3	13.6	7.2	3.5	.522
86-87	Houston	46	31	836	332	103	188	.548	0	1	.000	126	163	.773	72	112	184	75	76	0	13	5	46	18.2	7.2	4.0	1.6	.509
87-88	Houston	71	0	848	270	80	171	.468	0	2	.000	110	143	.769	74	105	179	60	75	0	22	12	57	11.9	3.8	2.5	0.8	.406
NBA Season Totals		835	377	23769	10465	3433	6293	.546	1	19	.053	3598	4592	.784	2108	3153	5261	1862	2273	35	671	433	1835	28.5	12.5	6.3	2.2	....
79-80	Boston	9	....	320	164	59	93	.634	0	0	.000	46	61	.754	31	59	90	19	25	0	5	10	22	35.6	18.2	10.0	2.1	.660
80-81	Boston	17	....	598	274	101	174	.580	0	0	.000	72	88	.818	61	64	125	46	53	0	12	16	43	35.2	16.1	7.4	2.7	.546
81-82	Boston	12	12	385	174	62	120	.517	0	0	.000	50	70	.714	37	50	87	26	40	0	18	11	24	32.1	14.5	7.3	2.2	.534

YEAR	TEAM	GP	GS	MIN	PTS	FGM	FGA	FG%	3PM	3PA	3P%	FTM	FTA	FT%	ORB	DRB	TRB	AST	PF	DQ	STL	BLK	TO	MPG	PPG	RPG	APG	PCM
82-83	Boston	7	7	246	90	29	55	.527	0	0	.000	32	38	.842	23	28	51	23	18	0	4	4	19	35.1	12.9	7.3	3.3	.476
83-84	Boston	23	23	752	274	84	167	.503	0	1	.000	106	136	.779	52	67	119	55	77	1	22	7	46	32.7	11.9	5.2	2.4	.400
84-85	Boston	20	0	238	76	21	43	.488	0	0	.000	34	43	.791	17	30	47	7	29	0	9	2	10	11.9	3.8	2.4	0.4	.378
86-87	Houston	10	0	177	62	18	34	.529	0	1	.000	26	35	.743	11	22	33	17	17	1	4	0	8	17.7	6.2	3.3	1.7	.453
87-88	Houston	4	0	15	2	1	2	.500	0	0	.000	0	0	.000	1	0	1	1	1	0	0	0	0	3.8	0.5	0.3	0.3	.173
NBA Playoff Totals		102	42	2731	1116	375	688	.545	0	2	.000	366	471	.777	233	320	553	194	260	2	74	50	172	26.8	10.9	5.4	1.9	....

• MAXWELL, Vernon

Vernon (Hawk, Mad Max) Maxwell

Born: Sept. 12, 1965. Gainesville, FL, United States.   Height: 6'4".   Weight: 180 lbs.   Drafted: 1988   College: Florida

YEAR	TEAM	GP	GS	MIN	PTS	FGM	FGA	FG%	3PM	3PA	3P%	FTM	FTA	FT%	ORB	DRB	TRB	AST	PF	DQ	STL	BLK	TO	MPG	PPG	RPG	APG	PCM
88-89	San Antonio	79	36	2065	927	357	827	.432	32	129	.248	181	243	.745	49	153	202	301	136	0	86	8	182	26.1	11.7	2.6	3.8	.400
89-90	San Antonio	49	2	1118	340	133	306	.435	15	52	.288	59	95	.621	35	106	141	146	79	0	42	5	69	22.8	6.9	2.9	3.0	.349
89-90	Houston	30	10	869	374	142	321	.442	13	53	.245	77	116	.664	15	72	87	150	69	0	42	5	72	29.0	12.5	2.9	5.0	.429
90-91	Houston	82	79	2870	1397	504	1247	.404	**172**	510	.337	217	296	.733	41	197	238	303	179	2	127	15	172	35.0	17.0	2.9	3.7	.384
91-92	Houston	80	80	2700	1372	502	1216	.413	**162**	**473**	.342	206	267	.772	37	206	243	326	200	3	104	28	176	33.8	17.2	3.0	4.1	.415
92-93	Houston	71	68	2251	982	349	858	.407	120	361	.332	164	228	.719	29	192	221	297	124	1	86	8	142	31.7	13.8	3.1	4.2	.399
93-94	Houston	75	73	2571	1023	380	976	.389	120	403	.298	143	191	.749	42	187	229	380	143	0	125	20	188	34.3	13.6	3.1	5.1	.378
94-95	Houston	64	54	2038	854	306	777	.394	143	441	.324	99	144	.688	18	146	164	274	157	1	75	13	134	31.8	13.3	2.6	4.3	.353
95-96	Philadelphia	75	57	2467	1217	410	1052	.390	146	460	.317	251	332	.756	39	190	229	330	182	1	96	12	218	32.9	16.2	3.1	4.4	.386
96-97	San Antonio	72	31	2068	929	340	906	.375	115	372	.309	134	180	.744	27	132	159	153	168	1	87	19	122	28.7	12.9	2.2	2.1	.289
97-98	Orlando	11	0	169	81	26	78	.333	6	26	.231	23	26	.885	5	8	13	12	20	0	2	1	12	15.4	7.4	1.2	1.1	.234
97-98	Charlotte	31	0	467	210	77	180	.428	31	86	.360	25	34	.735	9	35	44	40	51	1	14	3	28	15.1	6.8	1.4	1.3	.347
98-99	Sacramento	46	1	1007	492	164	421	.390	80	231	.346	84	114	.737	13	72	85	76	111	1	30	3	67	21.9	10.7	1.8	1.7	.328
99-00	Seattle	47	0	989	513	169	490	.345	67	223	.300	108	148	.730	15	64	79	75	83	0	38	9	53	21.0	10.9	1.7	1.6	.317
00-01	Philadelphia	24	6	375	120	42	125	.336	21	64	.328	15	22	.682	3	34	37	29	33	0	12	0	18	15.6	5.0	1.5	1.2	.233
00-01	Dallas	19	0	285	81	31	98	.316	13	47	.277	6	10	.600	1	28	29	20	31	0	9	3	17	15.0	4.3	1.5	1.1	.171
NBA Season Totals		855	497	24309	10912	3932	9878	.398	1256	3931	.320	1792	2446	.733	378	1822	2200	2912	1766	11	975	152	1670	28.4	12.8	2.6	3.4	....
89-90	Houston	4	4	159	79	30	81	.370	8	26	.308	11	21	.524	5	7	12	17	12	0	5	0	6	39.8	19.8	3.0	4.3	.310
90-91	Houston	3	3	113	56	23	56	.411	9	27	.333	1	2	.500	1	7	8	9	8	0	2	1	7	37.7	18.7	2.7	3.0	.304
92-93	Houston	9	7	308	126	47	117	.402	11	46	.239	21	24	.875	3	19	22	32	17	0	11	2	17	34.2	14.0	2.4	3.6	.332
93-94	Houston	23	23	880	318	118	314	.376	45	138	.326	37	54	.685	12	69	81	96	55	1	20	2	49	38.3	13.8	3.5	4.2	.294
94-95	Houston	1	0	16	3	1	7	.143	0	2	.000	1	1	1.000	0	3	3	1	1	0	0	0	1	16.0	3.0	3.0	1.0	-.010
98-99	Sacramento	5	0	129	56	19	60	.317	11	35	.314	7	10	.700	4	7	11	5	12	0	6	0	6	25.8	11.2	2.2	1.0	.219
00-01	Dallas	4	0	43	4	2	10	.200	0	5	.000	0	0	.000	1	5	6	5	6	0	0	0	2	10.8	1.0	1.5	1.3	.075
NBA Playoff Totals		49	37	1648	642	240	645	.372	84	279	.301	78	112	.696	26	117	143	165	111	1	44	5	88	33.6	13.1	2.9	3.4	....

• MAY, Don

Donald John May

Born: Jan. 3, 1946. Dayton, OH, United States.   Height: 6'4".   Weight: 200 lbs.   Drafted: 1968   College: Dayton

YEAR	TEAM	GP	GS	MIN	PTS	FGM	FGA	FG%	3PM	3PA	3P%	FTM	FTA	FT%	ORB	DRB	TRB	AST	PF	DQ	STL	BLK	TO	MPG	PPG	RPG	APG	PCM
68-69	New York	48	....	560	204	81	223	.363	....	....	....	42	58	.724	....	....	114	35	64	0	....	....	....	11.7	4.3	2.4	0.7	.336
69-70	New York	37	....	238	96	39	101	.386	....	....	....	18	19	.947	....	....	52	17	42	0	....	....	....	6.4	2.6	1.4	0.5	.367
70-71	Buffalo	76	....	2666	1535	629	1336	.471	....	....	....	277	350	.791	....	....	567	150	219	4	....	....	....	35.1	20.2	7.5	2.0	.548
71-72	Atlanta	75	....	1285	594	234	476	.492	....	....	....	126	164	.768	....	....	217	55	133	0	....	....	....	17.1	7.9	2.9	0.7	.437
72-73	Atlanta	32	....	317	144	61	134	.455	....	....	....	22	31	.710	....	....	67	21	55	0	....	....	....	9.9	4.5	2.1	0.7	.427
72-73	Philadelphia	26	....	602	309	128	290	.441	....	....	....	53	62	.855	....	....	143	43	80	0	....	....	....	23.2	11.9	5.5	1.7	.504
73-74	Philadelphia	56	....	812	393	152	367	.414	....	....	....	89	102	.873	25	111	136	63	137	0	25	8	....	14.5	7.0	2.4	1.1	.412
74-75	Omaha	29	....	139	64	27	54	.500	....	....	....	10	12	.833	4	9	13	5	21	0	4	2	....	4.8	2.2	0.4	0.2	.345
NBA Season Totals		379	....	6619	3339	1351	2981	.453	....	....	....	637	798	.798	29	120	1309	389	751	4	29	10	....	17.5	8.8	3.5	1.0	....
68-69	New York	9	....	88	25	9	30	.300	....	....	....	7	9	.778	....	....	23	8	7	0	....	....	....	9.8	2.8	2.6	0.9	.366
69-70	New York	2	....	7	4	2	3	.667	....	....	....	0	0	.000	....	....	0	0	2	0	....	....	....	3.5	2.0	0.0	0.0	.320
71-72	Atlanta	3	....	31	12	3	9	.333	....	....	....	6	8	.750	....	....	8	1	3	0	....	....	....	10.3	4.0	2.7	0.3	.410
NBA Playoff Totals		14	....	126	41	14	42	.333	....	....	....	13	17	.765	....	....	31	9	12	0	....	....	....	9.0	2.9	2.2	0.6	....

• MAY, Scott

Scott Glenn May

Born: Mar. 19, 1954. Sandusky, OH, United States.   Height: 6'7".   Weight: 215 lbs.   Drafted: 1976   College: Indiana

YEAR	TEAM	GP	GS	MIN	PTS	FGM	FGA	FG%	3PM	3PA	3P%	FTM	FTA	FT%	ORB	DRB	TRB	AST	PF	DQ	STL	BLK	TO	MPG	PPG	RPG	APG	PCM
76-77	Chicago	72	....	2369	1050	431	955	.451	....	....	....	188	227	.828	141	296	437	145	185	2	78	17	....	32.9	14.6	6.1	2.0	.440
77-78	Chicago	55	....	1802	735	280	617	.454	....	....	....	175	216	.810	118	214	332	114	170	4	50	6	127	32.8	13.4	6.0	2.1	.391
78-79	Chicago	37	....	403	148	59	136	.434	....	....	....	30	40	.750	14	50	64	39	51	0	22	1	52	10.9	4.0	1.7	1.1	.312
79-80	Chicago	54	....	1298	672	264	587	.450	0	4	.000	144	172	.837	78	140	218	104	126	2	45	5	76	24.0	12.4	4.0	1.9	.460
80-81	Chicago	63	....	815	443	165	338	.488	0	0	.000	113	149	.758	62	93	155	63	83	0	35	7	69	12.9	7.0	2.5	1.0	.511
81-82	Milwaukee	65	7	1187	583	212	417	.508	0	4	.000	159	193	.824	85	133	218	133	151	2	50	6	91	18.3	9.0	3.4	2.0	.523
82-83	Detroit	9	1	155	59	21	50	.420	0	0	.000	17	21	.810	10	16	26	12	24	1	5	2	13	17.2	6.6	2.9	1.3	.332
NBA Season Totals		355	8	8029	3690	1432	3100	.462	0	8	.000	826	1018	.811	508	942	1450	610	790	11	285	44	428	22.6	10.4	4.1	1.7	....
76-77	Chicago	3	....	97	32	10	26	.385	....	....	....	12	15	.800	6	8	14	3	10	0	8	2	....	32.3	10.7	4.7	1.0	.289
81-82	Milwaukee	4	0	50	17	4	20	.200	0	0	.000	9	14	.643	7	4	11	10	6	0	2	0	6	12.5	4.3	2.8	2.5	.289
NBA Playoff Totals		7	0	147	49	14	46	.304	0	0	.000	21	29	.724	13	12	25	13	16	0	10	2	6	21.0	7.0	3.6	1.9	....

• MAYBERRY, Lee

Orva Lee Mayberry Jr.

Born: June 12, 1970. Tulsa, OK, United States.   Height: 6'1".   Weight: 172 lbs.   Drafted: 1992   College: Arkansas

YEAR	TEAM	GP	GS	MIN	PTS	FGM	FGA	FG%	3PM	3PA	3P%	FTM	FTA	FT%	ORB	DRB	TRB	AST	PF	DQ	STL	BLK	TO	MPG	PPG	RPG	APG	PCM
92-93	Milwaukee	82	4	1503	424	171	375	.456	43	110	.391	39	68	.574	26	92	118	273	148	1	59	7	82	18.3	5.2	1.4	3.3	.358
93-94	Milwaukee	82	6	1472	433	167	402	.415	41	119	.345	58	84	.690	26	75	101	215	114	0	46	4	98	18.0	5.3	1.2	2.6	.295
94-95	Milwaukee	82	50	1744	474	172	408	.422	72	177	.407	58	83	.699	21	61	82	276	123	0	51	4	107	21.3	5.8	1.0	3.4	.289
95-96	Milwaukee	82	20	1705	422	153	364	.420	75	189	.397	41	68	.603	21	69	90	302	144	1	64	11	90	20.8	5.1	1.1	3.7	.313

YEAR	TEAM	GP	GS	MIN	PTS	FGM	FGA	FG%	3PM	3PA	3P%	FTM	FTA	FT%	ORB	DRB	TRB	AST	PF	DQ	STL	BLK	TO	MPG	PPG	RPG	APG	PCM
96-97	Vancouver	80	38	1952	410	149	370	.403	83	221	.376	29	46	.630	29	105	134	329	159	0	60	8	88	24.4	5.1	1.7	4.1	.297
97-98	Vancouver	79	32	1835	363	131	349	.375	63	180	.350	38	51	.745	19	95	114	349	164	1	65	10	111	23.2	4.6	1.4	4.4	.290
98-99	Vancouver	9	0	126	20	7	19	.368	2	10	.200	4	5	.800	0	3	3	23	13	0	7	0	11	14.0	2.2	0.3	2.6	.220
NBA Season Totals		496	150	10337	2546	950	2287	.415	379	1006	.377	267	405	.659	142	500	642	1767	865	3	352	44	587	20.8	5.1	1.3	3.6	....

• MAYES, Clyde
Clyde C. Mayes Jr.

Born: Mar. 17, 1953. Greenville, SC, United States.   Height: 6'8".   Weight: 225 lbs.   Drafted: 1975   College: Furman

YEAR	TEAM	GP	GS	MIN	PTS	FGM	FGA	FG%	3PM	3PA	3P%	FTM	FTA	FT%	ORB	DRB	TRB	AST	PF	DQ	STL	BLK	TO	MPG	PPG	RPG	APG	PCM
75-76	Milwaukee	65	....	948	284	114	248	.460	....	....	....	56	97	.577	97	166	263	37	154	7	9	42	....	14.6	4.4	4.0	0.6	.373
76-77	Indiana	2	....	21	7	3	7	.429	....	....	....	1	4	.250	4	3	7	3	5	0	0	2	....	10.5	3.5	3.5	1.5	.455
76-77	Buffalo	2	....	7	2	0	3	.000	....	....	....	2	3	.667	0	3	3	0	3	0	0	0	....	3.5	1.0	1.5	0.0	.101
76-77	Portland	5	....	24	4	2	9	.222	....	....	....	0	0	.000	6	0	6	0	5	0	0	2	....	4.8	0.8	1.2	0.0	.041
NBA Season Totals		74	....	1000	297	119	267	.446	....	....	....	59	104	.567	107	172	279	40	166	7	9	46	....	13.5	4.0	3.8	0.5	....
75-76	Milwaukee	3	....	41	5	1	5	.200	....	....	....	3	4	.750	0	6	6	1	6	1	1	1	....	13.7	1.7	2.0	0.3	.118
NBA Playoff Totals		3	....	41	5	1	5	.200	....	....	....	3	4	.750	0	6	6	1	6	1	1	1	....	13.7	1.7	2.0	0.3	

• MAYES, Tharon
Tharon R. Mayes

Born: Sept. 9, 1968. New Haven, CT, United States.   Height: 6'3".   Weight: 175 lbs.   Drafted: —   College: Florida State

YEAR	TEAM	GP	GS	MIN	PTS	FGM	FGA	FG%	3PM	3PA	3P%	FTM	FTA	FT%	ORB	DRB	TRB	AST	PF	DQ	STL	BLK	TO	MPG	PPG	RPG	APG	PCM
91-92	Philadelphia	21	0	215	90	28	94	.298	14	39	.359	20	30	.667	3	12	15	32	32	0	14	1	27	10.2	4.3	0.7	1.5	.215
91-92	LA Clippers	3	0	40	9	2	5	.400	1	2	.500	4	6	.667	0	1	1	3	9	0	2	1	3	13.3	3.0	0.3	1.0	.131
NBA Season Totals		24	0	255	99	30	99	.303	15	41	.366	24	36	.667	3	13	16	35	41	0	16	2	30	10.6	4.1	0.7	1.5	....

• MAYFIELD, Bill
William Henry Mayfield

Born: Oct. 17, 1957. Detroit, MI, United States.   Height: 6'7".   Weight: 205 lbs.   Drafted: —   College: Iowa

YEAR	TEAM	GP	GS	MIN	PTS	FGM	FGA	FG%	3PM	3PA	3P%	FTM	FTA	FT%	ORB	DRB	TRB	AST	PF	DQ	STL	BLK	TO	MPG	PPG	RPG	APG	PCM
80-81	Golden State	7	....	54	17	8	18	.444	0	0	.000	1	2	.500	7	2	9	1	8	0	0	1	3	7.7	2.4	1.3	0.1	.208
NBA Season Totals		7	....	54	17	8	18	.444	0	0	.000	1	2	.500	7	2	9	1	8	0	0	1	3	7.7	2.4	1.3	0.1	....

• MAYFIELD, Kenny
Kendall Mayfield

Born: May 11, 1948. Chicago, IL, United States.   Height: 6'2".   Weight: 185 lbs.   Drafted: 1971   College: Tuskegee

YEAR	TEAM	GP	GS	MIN	PTS	FGM	FGA	FG%	3PM	3PA	3P%	FTM	FTA	FT%	ORB	DRB	TRB	AST	PF	DQ	STL	BLK	TO	MPG	PPG	RPG	APG	PCM
75-76	New York	13	....	64	37	17	46	.370	....	....	....	3	3	1.000	1	7	8	4	18	0	0	0	....	4.9	2.8	0.6	0.3	.247
NBA Season Totals		13	....	64	37	17	46	.370	....	....	....	3	3	1.000	1	7	8	4	18	0	0	0	....	4.9	2.8	0.6	0.3	....

• MAYS, Travis
Travis Cortez Mays

Born: June 19, 1968. Ocala, FL, United States.   Height: 6'2".   Weight: 190 lbs.   Drafted: 1990   College: Texas

YEAR	TEAM	GP	GS	MIN	PTS	FGM	FGA	FG%	3PM	3PA	3P%	FTM	FTA	FT%	ORB	DRB	TRB	AST	PF	DQ	STL	BLK	TO	MPG	PPG	RPG	APG	PCM
90-91	Sacramento	64	55	2145	915	294	724	.406	72	197	.365	255	331	.770	54	124	178	253	169	1	81	11	160	33.5	14.3	2.8	4.0	.360
91-92	Atlanta	2	0	32	17	6	14	.429	3	6	.500	2	2	1.000	1	1	2	1	4	0	0	0	3	16.0	8.5	1.0	0.5	.245
92-93	Atlanta	49	9	787	341	129	309	.417	29	84	.345	54	82	.659	20	33	53	72	59	0	21	3	49	16.1	7.0	1.1	1.5	.299
NBA Season Totals		115	64	2964	1273	429	1047	.410	104	287	.362	311	415	.749	75	158	233	326	232	1	102	14	212	25.8	11.1	2.0	2.8	....
92-93	Atlanta	1	0	20	4	2	4	.500	0	1	.000	0	0	.000	0	1	1	0	3	0	0	0	1	20.0	4.0	1.0	0.0	.037
NBA Playoff Totals		1	0	20	4	2	4	.500	0	1	.000	0	0	.000	0	1	1	0	3	0	0	0	1	20.0	4.0	1.0	0.0	

• MAZZA, Matt
Matthew Anthony Mazza

Born: Sept. 23, 1923. Niagara Falls, NY, United States.   Height: 6'3".   Weight: 210 lbs.   Drafted: —   College: Michigan State

YEAR	TEAM	GP	GS	MIN	PTS	FGM	FGA	FG%	3PM	3PA	3P%	FTM	FTA	FT%	ORB	DRB	TRB	AST	PF	DQ	STL	BLK	TO	MPG	PPG	RPG	APG	PCM
49-50	Sheboygan	26	....	....	98	33	110	.300	....	....	....	32	45	.711	....	....	....	27	34	....	....	....	....	....	3.8	....	1.0	....
NBA Season Totals		26	....	....	98	33	110	.300	....	....	....	32	45	.711	....	....	....	27	34	....	....	....	....	....	3.8	....	1.0	....

• MCADAMS, Johnny
John McAdams

Born: 1915.   Height: 5'10".   Weight: 147 lbs.   Drafted: —   College: Ohio Wesleyan

YEAR	TEAM	GP	GS	MIN	PTS	FGM	FGA	FG%	3PM	3PA	3P%	FTM	FTA	FT%	ORB	DRB	TRB	AST	PF	DQ	STL	BLK	TO	MPG	PPG	RPG	APG	PCM
37-38	Wingfoots-N	6	....	....	13	6	....	....	....	....	....	1	....	....	....	....	....	....	....	....	....	....	....	2.2	....	....	....
39-40	Wingfoots-N	2	....	....	4	2	....	....	....	....	....	0	....	....	....	....	....	....	....	....	....	....	....	2.0	....	....	....
NBL Season Totals		8	....	....	17	8	....	....	....	....	....	1	....	....	....	....	....	....	....	....	....	....	....	2.1	....	....	....
37-38	Wingfoots-N	3	....	....	4	2	....	....	....	....	....	0	....	....	....	....	....	....	....	....	....	....	....	1.3	....	....	....
NBL Playoff Totals		3	....	....	4	2	....	....	....	....	....	0	....	....	....	....	....	....	....	....	....	....	....	1.3	....	....	....

• MCADOO, Bob
Robert Allen McAdoo Jr.

Born: Sept. 25, 1951. Greensboro, NC, United States.   Height: 6'9".   Weight: 210 lbs.   Drafted: 1972   College: North Carolina   HOF: 2000

YEAR	TEAM	GP	GS	MIN	PTS	FGM	FGA	FG%	3PM	3PA	3P%	FTM	FTA	FT%	ORB	DRB	TRB	AST	PF	DQ	STL	BLK	TO	MPG	PPG	RPG	APG	PCM
72-73	Buffalo	80	....	2562	1441	585	1293	.452	....	....	....	271	350	.774	....	....	728	139	256	....	....	....	....	32.0	18.0	9.1	1.7	.575
73-74	Buffalo	74	....	3185	**2261**	901	1647	**.547**	....	....	....	459	579	.793	281	836	1117	170	252	3	88	246	....	43.0	**30.6**	15.1	2.3	.821
74-75	Buffalo	82	....	**3539**	**2831**	**1095**	2138	.512	....	....	....	641	**796**	.805	307	848	**1155**	179	278	3	92	174	....	**43.2**	**34.5**	14.1	2.2	.833
75-76	Buffalo	78	....	3328	**2427**	934	1918	.487	....	....	....	**559**	734	.762	241	724	965	315	298	5	93	160	....	42.7	31.1	12.4	4.0	.771
76-77	Buffalo	20	....	767	474	182	400	.455	....	....	....	110	158	.696	66	198	264	65	74	1	16	34	....	38.4	23.7	13.2	3.3	.667
76-77	New York	52	....	2031	1387	558	1045	.534	....	....	....	271	358	.757	133	529	662	140	188	2	61	65	....	39.1	26.7	12.7	2.7	.777
77-78	New York	79	....	3182	2097	814	1564	.520	....	....	....	469	645	.727	236	774	1010	298	297	6	105	126	348	40.3	26.5	12.8	3.8	.739
78-79	New York	40	....	1594	1076	429	793	.541	....	....	....	218	335	.651	94	285	379	128	134	2	62	47	152	39.9	26.9	9.5	3.2	.677
78-79	Boston	20	....	637	411	167	334	.500	....	....	....	77	115	.670	36	105	141	40	55	1	12	20	64	31.9	20.6	7.1	2.0	.567
79-80	Detroit	58	....	2097	1222	492	1025	.480	3	24	.125	235	322	.730	100	367	467	200	178	3	73	65	238	36.2	21.1	8.1	3.4	.558

YEAR	TEAM	GP	GS	MIN	PTS	FGM	FGA	FG%	3PM	3PA	3P%	FTM	FTA	FT%	ORB	DRB	TRB	AST	PF	DQ	STL	BLK	TO	MPG	PPG	RPG	APG	PCM
80-81	Detroit	6	....	168	72	30	82	.366	0	0	.000	12	20	.600	9	32	41	20	16	0	8	7	18	28.0	12.0	6.8	3.3	.417
80-81	New Jersey	10	....	153	93	38	75	.507	0	1	.000	17	21	.810	8	18	26	10	22	0	9	6	14	15.3	9.3	2.6	1.0	.542
81-82	LA Lakers	41	0	746	392	151	330	.458	0	5	.000	90	126	.714	45	114	159	32	109	1	22	36	49	18.2	9.6	3.9	0.8	.469
82-83	LA Lakers	47	1	1019	703	292	562	.520	0	1	.000	119	163	.730	76	171	247	39	153	2	40	40	66	21.7	15.0	5.3	0.8	.637
83-84	LA Lakers	70	0	1456	916	352	748	.471	0	5	.000	212	264	.803	82	207	289	74	182	0	42	50	126	20.8	13.1	4.1	1.1	.519
84-85	LA Lakers	66	0	1254	690	284	546	.520	0	1	.000	122	162	.753	79	216	295	67	170	0	18	53	92	19.0	10.5	4.5	1.0	.538
85-86	Philadelphia	29	0	609	294	116	251	.462	0	0	.000	62	81	.765	25	78	103	35	64	0	10	18	49	21.0	10.1	3.6	1.2	.400
NBA Season Totals		852	1	28327	18787	7420	14751	.503	3	37	.081	3944	5229	.754	1818	5502	8048	1951	2726	35	751	1147	1216	33.2	22.1	9.4	2.3	....
73-74	Buffalo	6	....	271	190	76	159	.478	....	....	....	38	47	.809	14	68	82	9	25	1	6	13	....	45.2	31.7	13.7	1.5	.683
74-75	Buffalo	7	....	327	262	104	216	.481	....	....	....	54	73	.740	25	69	94	10	29	1	6	19	....	46.7	37.4	13.4	1.4	.727
75-76	Buffalo	9	....	406	252	97	215	.451	....	....	....	58	82	.707	31	97	128	29	37	3	7	18	....	45.1	28.0	14.2	3.2	.659
77-78	New York	6	....	238	143	61	126	.484	....	....	....	21	35	.600	11	47	58	23	19	0	7	12	23	39.7	23.8	9.7	3.8	.608
81-82	LA Lakers	14	0	388	234	101	179	.564	0	0	.000	32	47	.681	21	74	95	22	43	2	10	21	35	27.7	16.7	6.8	1.6	.626
82-83	LA Lakers	8	0	166	87	37	84	.440	2	6	.333	11	14	.786	15	31	46	5	23	0	11	10	10	20.8	10.9	5.8	0.6	.541
83-84	LA Lakers	20	0	447	279	111	215	.516	0	1	.000	57	81	.704	30	78	108	12	63	0	12	27	39	22.4	14.0	5.4	0.6	.571
84-85	LA Lakers	19	0	398	217	91	193	.472	0	1	.000	35	47	.745	25	61	86	15	66	2	9	26	32	20.9	11.4	4.5	0.8	.464
85-86	Philadelphia	5	0	73	54	20	36	.556	0	0	.000	14	16	.875	8	6	14	2	13	0	4	5	2	14.6	10.8	2.8	0.4	.737
NBA Playoff Totals		94	0	2714	1718	698	1423	.491	2	8	.250	320	442	.724	180	531	711	127	318	9	72	151	141	28.9	18.3	7.6	1.4	....

• MCBRIDE, Ken

Kenneth S. McBride

Born: 1931.   Height: 6'3".   Weight: 190 lbs.   Drafted: 1952   College: Maryland State

YEAR	TEAM	GP	GS	MIN	PTS	FGM	FGA	FG%	3PM	3PA	3P%	FTM	FTA	FT%	ORB	DRB	TRB	AST	PF	DQ	STL	BLK	TO	MPG	PPG	RPG	APG	PCM
54-55	Milwaukee	12	....	249	117	48	147	.327	....	....	....	21	29	.724	....	....	31	14	31	0	....	....	....	20.8	9.8	2.6	1.2	.276
NBA Season Totals		12	....	249	117	48	147	.327	....	....	....	21	29	.724	....	....	31	14	31	0	....	....	....	20.8	9.8	2.6	1.2	....

• MCCAHAN, Bill

William Glenn McCahan

Born: June 7, 1921. Philadelphia, PA, United States. Died: July3, 1986.   Height: 5'11".   Weight: 200 lbs.   Drafted: —   College: Duke

YEAR	TEAM	GP	GS	MIN	PTS	FGM	FGA	FG%	3PM	3PA	3P%	FTM	FTA	FT%	ORB	DRB	TRB	AST	PF	DQ	STL	BLK	TO	MPG	PPG	RPG	APG	PCM
46-47	Syracuse-N	27	....	....	94	35	....	....	....	....	....	24	46	.522	....	....	....	41	....	....	....	....	....	....	3.5	....	....	....
NBL Season Totals		27	....	....	94	35	....	....	....	....	....	24	46		....	....	....	41	....	....	....	....	....	....	3.5	....	....	....

• MCCALL, Paul

Paul McCall

Born: 1920.   Height: 6'2".   Weight: 195 lbs.   Drafted: —   College: Bradley

YEAR	TEAM	GP	GS	MIN	PTS	FGM	FGA	FG%	3PM	3PA	3P%	FTM	FTA	FT%	ORB	DRB	TRB	AST	PF	DQ	STL	BLK	TO	MPG	PPG	RPG	APG	PCM
45-46	Cleveland-N	6	....	....	37	15	....	....	....	....	....	7	....	....	....	....	....	....	....	....	....	....	....	....	6.2	....	....	....
NBL Season Totals		6	....	....	37	15	....	....	....	....	....	7	....	....	....	....	....	....	....	....	....	....	....	....	6.2	....	....	....

• MCCANN, Bob

Robert Glen McCann

Born: Apr. 22, 1964. Morristown, NJ, United States.   Height: 6'6".   Weight: 244 lbs.   Drafted: 1987   College: Morehead State

YEAR	TEAM	GP	GS	MIN	PTS	FGM	FGA	FG%	3PM	3PA	3P%	FTM	FTA	FT%	ORB	DRB	TRB	AST	PF	DQ	STL	BLK	TO	MPG	PPG	RPG	APG	PCM
89-90	Dallas	10	0	62	26	7	21	.333	0	0	.000	12	14	.857	4	8	12	6	7	0	2	2	6	6.2	2.6	1.2	0.6	.394
91-92	Detroit	26	0	129	30	13	33	.394	0	1	.000	4	13	.308	12	18	30	6	23	0	6	4	8	5.0	1.2	1.2	0.2	.254
92-93	Minnesota	79	7	1536	495	200	410	.488	0	2	.000	95	152	.625	92	192	284	68	200	2	50	58	79	19.4	6.3	3.6	0.9	.354
95-96	Washington	62	0	653	188	76	153	.497	1	2	.500	35	74	.473	46	97	143	24	116	0	21	15	43	10.5	3.0	2.3	0.4	.300
97-98	Toronto	1	0	5	0	0	1	.000	0	0	.000	0	0	.000	0	1	1	0	1	0	0	0	0	5.0	0.0	1.0	0.0	-.092
NBA Season Totals		178	7	2385	739	296	618	.479	1	5	.200	146	253	.577	154	316	470	104	347	2	79	79	136	13.4	4.2	2.6	0.6	....
91-92	Detroit	1	0	13	6	3	6	.500	0	0	.000	0	0	.000	1	1	2	0	2	0	0	1	2	13.0	6.0	2.0	0.0	.247
NBA Playoff Totals		1	0	13	6	3	6	.500	0	0	.000	0	0	.000	1	1	2	0	2	0	0	1	2	13.0	6.0	2.0	0.0	....

• MCCANN, Brendan

Brendan Michael (Blinky) McCann

Born: July 5, 1935. Brooklyn, NY, United States.   Height: 6'2".   Weight: 178 lbs.   Drafted: 1957   College: St. Bonaventure

YEAR	TEAM	GP	GS	MIN	PTS	FGM	FGA	FG%	3PM	3PA	3P%	FTM	FTA	FT%	ORB	DRB	TRB	AST	PF	DQ	STL	BLK	TO	MPG	PPG	RPG	APG	PCM
57-58	New York	36	....	295	69	22	100	.220	....	....	....	25	37	.676	....	....	45	54	34	0	....	....	....	8.2	1.9	1.3	1.5	.328
58-59	New York	1	....	7	0	0	3	.000	....	....	....	0	0	.000	....	....	1	1	1	0	....	....	....	7.0	0.0	1.0	1.0	-.090
59-60	New York	4	....	29	6	1	12	.083	....	....	....	4	4	1.000	....	....	7	9	3	0	....	....	....	7.3	1.5	1.8	2.3	.450
NBA Season Totals		41	....	331	75	23	115	.200	....	....	....	29	41	.707	....	....	53	64	38	0	....	....	....	8.1	1.8	1.3	1.6	....

• MCCANTS, Mel

Melvin Lamont McCants

Born: Aug. 19, 1967. Chicago, IL, United States.   Height: 6'8".   Weight: 240 lbs.   Drafted: —   College: Purdue

YEAR	TEAM	GP	GS	MIN	PTS	FGM	FGA	FG%	3PM	3PA	3P%	FTM	FTA	FT%	ORB	DRB	TRB	AST	PF	DQ	STL	BLK	TO	MPG	PPG	RPG	APG	PCM
89-90	LA Lakers	13	0	65	22	8	26	.308	0	0	.000	6	8	.750	1	5	6	2	11	0	3	1	1	5.0	1.7	0.5	0.2	.148
NBA Season Totals		13	0	65	22	8	26	.308	0	0	.000	6	8	.750	1	5	6	2	11	0	3	1	1	5.0	1.7	0.5	0.2	....
89-90	LA Lakers	2	0	5	0	0	0	.000	0	0	.000	0	0	.000	0	0	0	0	1	0	0	0	0	2.5	0.0	0.0	0.0	-.094
NBA Playoff Totals		2	0	5	0	0	0	.000	0	0	.000	0	0	.000	0	0	0	0	1	0	0	0	0	2.5	0.0	0.0	0.0	....

• MCCARRON, Mike

Michael McCarron

Born: Mar. 2, 1922. Died: Oct.2, 1991.   Height: 5'11".   Weight: 180 lbs.   Drafted: —   College: Seton Hall

YEAR	TEAM	GP	GS	MIN	PTS	FGM	FGA	FG%	3PM	3PA	3P%	FTM	FTA	FT%	ORB	DRB	TRB	AST	PF	DQ	STL	BLK	TO	MPG	PPG	RPG	APG	PCM
46-47	Toronto	60	....	....	649	236	838	.282	....	....	....	177	288	.615	....	....	....	59	184	....	....	....	....	....	10.8	....	1.0	....
49-50	St. Louis	5	....	....	5	2	10	.200	....	....	....	1	2	.500	....	....	....	2	0	....	....	....	....	....	1.0	....	0.4	....
49-50	Baltimore	3	....	....	4	1	5	.200	....	....	....	2	3	.667	....	....	....	1	5	....	....	....	....	....	1.3	....	0.3	....
NBA Season Totals		68	....	....	658	239	853	.280	....	....	....	180	293	.614	....	....	....	62	189	....	....	....	....	....	9.7	....	0.9	....

YEAR	TEAM	GP	GS	MIN	PTS	FGM	FGA	FG%	3PM	3PA	3P%	FTM	FTA	FT%	ORB	DRB	TRB	AST	PF	DQ	STL	BLK	TO	MPG	PPG	RPG	APG	PCM

• MCCARTER, Andre

Andre Eugene McCarter

Born: Aug. 25, 1953. Philadelphia, PA, United States.   Height: 6'3".   Weight: 190 lbs.   Drafted: 1976   College: UCLA

YEAR	TEAM	GP	GS	MIN	PTS	FGM	FGA	FG%	3PM	3PA	3P%	FTM	FTA	FT%	ORB	DRB	TRB	AST	PF	DQ	STL	BLK	TO	MPG	PPG	RPG	APG	PCM
76-77	Kansas City	59	....	725	270	119	257	.463	....	....	....	32	45	.711	16	39	55	99	63	0	23	0	....	12.3	4.6	0.9	1.7	.384
77-78	Kansas City	1	....	9	0	0	2	.000	....	....	....	0	0	.000	0	1	1	0	1	0	0	0	....	9.0	0.0	1.0	0.0	-.146
80-81	Washington	43	....	448	122	51	135	.378	2	8	.250	18	24	.750	16	23	39	73	36	0	14	0	26	10.4	2.8	0.9	1.7	.291
NBA Season Totals		103	....	1182	392	170	394	.431	2	8	.250	50	69	.725	32	63	95	172	100	0	37	0	26	11.5	3.8	0.9	1.7	....

• MCCARTER, Willie

Willie J. McCarter

Born: July 26, 1946. Gary, IN, United States.   Height: 6'3".   Weight: 175 lbs.   Drafted: 1969   College: Drake

YEAR	TEAM	GP	GS	MIN	PTS	FGM	FGA	FG%	3PM	3PA	3P%	FTM	FTA	FT%	ORB	DRB	TRB	AST	PF	DQ	STL	BLK	TO	MPG	PPG	RPG	APG	PCM
69-70	LA Lakers	40	....	861	307	132	349	.378	....	....	....	43	60	.717	....	....	83	93	71	0	....	....	....	21.5	7.7	2.1	2.3	.296
70-71	LA Lakers	76	....	1369	540	247	592	.417	....	....	....	46	77	.597	....	....	122	126	152	0	....	....	....	18.0	7.1	1.6	1.7	.302
71-72	Portland	39	....	612	243	103	257	.401	....	....	....	37	55	.673	....	....	43	85	58	0	....	....	....	15.7	6.2	1.1	2.2	.344
NBA Season Totals		155	....	2842	1090	482	1198	.402	....	....	....	126	192	.656	....	....	248	304	281	0	....	....	....	18.3	7.0	1.6	2.0	....
69-70	LA Lakers	5	....	14	7	3	7	.429	....	....	....	1	1	1.000	....	....	3	3	2	0	....	....	....	2.8	1.4	0.6	0.6	.614
70-71	LA Lakers	12	....	232	55	27	76	.355	....	....	....	1	6	.167	....	....	26	17	30	0	....	....	....	19.3	4.6	2.2	1.4	.170
NBA Playoff Totals		17	....	246	62	30	83	.361	....	....	....	2	7	.286	....	....	29	20	32	0	....	....	....	14.5	3.6	1.7	1.2	....

• MCCARTHY, Johnny

John Joseph McCarthy

Born: Apr. 25, 1934.   Height: 6'1".   Weight: 185 lbs.   Drafted: 1956   College: Canisius

YEAR	TEAM	GP	GS	MIN	PTS	FGM	FGA	FG%	3PM	3PA	3P%	FTM	FTA	FT%	ORB	DRB	TRB	AST	PF	DQ	STL	BLK	TO	MPG	PPG	RPG	APG	PCM
56-57	Rochester	72	....	1560	476	173	460	.376	....	....	....	130	193	.674	....	....	201	107	130	0	....	....	....	21.7	6.6	2.8	1.5	.304
58-59	Cincinnati	47	....	1827	606	245	657	.373	....	....	....	116	174	.667	....	....	227	225	158	4	....	....	....	38.9	12.9	4.8	4.8	.365
59-60	St. Louis	75	....	2383	629	240	730	.329	....	....	....	149	226	.659	....	....	301	328	233	3	....	....	....	31.8	8.4	4.0	4.4	.326
60-61	St. Louis	79	....	2519	654	266	746	.357	....	....	....	122	226	.540	....	....	325	430	272	8	....	....	....	31.9	8.3	4.1	5.4	.368
61-62	St. Louis	15	....	333	48	18	73	.247	....	....	....	12	27	.444	....	....	56	70	50	1	....	....	....	22.2	3.2	3.7	4.7	.327
63-64	Boston	28	....	206	37	16	48	.333	....	....	....	5	13	.385	....	....	35	24	42	0	....	....	....	7.4	1.3	1.3	0.9	.239
NBA Season Totals		316	....	8828	2450	958	2714	.353	....	....	....	534	859	.622	....	....	1145	1184	885	16	....	....	....	27.9	7.8	3.6	3.7	....
59-60	St. Louis	14	....	566	113	43	106	.406	....	....	....	27	36	.750	....	....	64	98	49	0	....	....	....	40.4	8.1	4.6	7.0	.378
60-61	St. Louis	12	....	236	44	19	55	.345	....	....	....	6	9	.667	....	....	31	33	29	0	....	....	....	19.7	3.7	2.6	2.8	.292
63-64	Boston	1	....	8	2	1	1	1.000	....	....	....	0	0	.000	....	....	1	1	0	0	....	....	....	8.0	2.0	1.0	1.0	.500
NBA Playoff Totals		27	....	810	159	63	162	.389	....	....	....	33	45	.733	....	....	96	132	78	0	....	....	....	30.0	5.9	3.6	4.9	....

• MCCARTY, Howie

Howard T. McCarty

Born: 1919. Died: 1973.   Height: 6'2".   Weight: 190 lbs.   Drafted: —   College: Wayne State (MI)

YEAR	TEAM	GP	GS	MIN	PTS	FGM	FGA	FG%	3PM	3PA	3P%	FTM	FTA	FT%	ORB	DRB	TRB	AST	PF	DQ	STL	BLK	TO	MPG	PPG	RPG	APG	PCM
45-46	Cleveland-N	13	....	....	93	40	....	....	....	....	....	13	....	....	....	....	....	....	....	....	....	....	....	7.2	....	....	....	....
46-47	Detroit-N	16	....	....	121	46	....	....	....	....	....	29	75	.387	....	....	....	....	....	....	....	....	....	7.6	....	....	....	....
46-47	Detroit	19	....	....	21	10	82	.122	....	....	....	1	10	.100	....	....	....	2	22	....	....	....	....	1.1	....	0.1	....	....
NBA Season Totals		19	....	....	21	10	82	.122	....	....	....	1	10	.100	....	....	....	2	22	....	....	....	....	1.1	....	0.1	....	....
NBL Season Totals		29	....	....	214	86	....	....	....	....	....	42	75	....	....	....	....	....	....	....	....	....	....	7.4	....	....	....	....
Career Totals		48	....	....	235	96	82	....	....	....	....	43	85	....	....	....	....	2	22	....	....	....	....	4.9	....	0.0	....	....

• MCCARTY, Kelly

Kelly Deshawn McCarty

Born: Aug. 24, 1975. Chicago, IL, United States.   Height: 6'7".   Weight: 200 lbs.   Drafted: —   College: Southern Mississippi

YEAR	TEAM	GP	GS	MIN	PTS	FGM	FGA	FG%	3PM	3PA	3P%	FTM	FTA	FT%	ORB	DRB	TRB	AST	PF	DQ	STL	BLK	TO	MPG	PPG	RPG	APG	PCM
98-99	Denver	2	0	4	4	2	3	.667	0	0	.000	0	0	.000	2	1	3	0	0	0	0	0	2	2.0	2.0	1.5	0.0	1.000
NBA Season Totals		2	0	4	4	2	3	.667	0	0	.000	0	0	.000	2	1	3	0	0	0	0	0	2	2.0	2.0	1.5	0.0	....

• MCCARTY, Walter

Walter Lee McCarty

Born: Feb. 1, 1974. Evansville, IN, United States.   Height: 6'10".   Weight: 230 lbs.   Drafted: 1996   College: Kentucky

YEAR	TEAM	GP	GS	MIN	PTS	FGM	FGA	FG%	3PM	3PA	3P%	FTM	FTA	FT%	ORB	DRB	TRB	AST	PF	DQ	STL	BLK	TO	MPG	PPG	RPG	APG	PCM
96-97	New York	35	0	192	64	26	68	.382	4	14	.286	8	14	.571	8	15	23	13	38	0	7	9	18	5.5	1.8	0.7	0.4	.197
97-98	Boston	82	64	2340	788	295	730	.404	54	175	.309	144	194	.742	141	223	364	177	274	6	110	44	139	28.5	9.6	4.4	2.2	.334
98-99	Boston	32	4	659	181	64	177	.362	13	50	.260	40	57	.702	36	79	115	40	88	0	24	13	40	20.6	5.7	3.6	1.3	.270
99-00	Boston	61	5	879	229	78	230	.339	34	110	.309	39	54	.722	33	77	110	70	83	1	24	23	16	14.4	3.8	1.8	1.1	.233
00-01	Boston	60	3	478	131	45	126	.357	19	56	.339	22	28	.786	24	57	81	39	82	0	14	7	20	8.0	2.2	1.4	0.7	.283
01-02	Boston	56	0	718	212	80	180	.444	39	99	.394	13	19	.684	32	96	128	41	83	0	18	7	22	12.8	3.8	2.3	0.7	.341
02-03	Boston	82	8	1949	498	173	418	.414	91	248	.367	61	98	.622	64	224	288	106	188	1	78	28	67	23.8	6.1	3.5	1.3	.301
NBA Season Totals		408	84	7215	2103	761	1929	.395	254	752	.338	327	464	.705	338	771	1109	486	836	8	275	131	373	17.7	5.2	2.7	1.2	....
96-97	New York	2	0	4	4	2	2	1.000	0	0	.000	0	0	.000	0	0	0	0	0	0	1	0	0	2.0	2.0	0.0	0.0	1.233
01-02	Boston	14	0	194	44	17	38	.447	3	18	.167	7	9	.778	8	26	34	4	19	0	4	0	4	13.9	3.1	2.4	0.3	.261
02-03	Boston	10	8	352	99	36	75	.480	21	52	.404	6	7	.857	10	33	43	22	35	0	8	5	11	35.2	9.9	4.3	2.2	.319
NBA Playoff Totals		26	8	550	147	55	115	.478	24	70	.343	13	16	.813	18	59	77	26	54	0	13	5	15	21.2	5.7	3.0	1.0	....

• MCCASKILL, Amal

Amal Omari McCaskill

Born: Oct. 28, 1973. Maywood, IL, United States.   Height: 6'11".   Weight: 235 lbs.   Drafted: 1996   College: Marquette

YEAR	TEAM	GP	GS	MIN	PTS	FGM	FGA	FG%	3PM	3PA	3P%	FTM	FTA	FT%	ORB	DRB	TRB	AST	PF	DQ	STL	BLK	TO	MPG	PPG	RPG	APG	PCM
96-97	Orlando	17	1	109	28	10	32	.313	0	2	.000	8	12	.667	4	18	22	7	7	0	3	5	10	6.4	1.6	1.3	0.4	.261
01-02	San Antonio	27	0	153	52	20	49	.408	0	0	.000	12	26	.462	16	20	36	4	23	0	6	10	14	5.7	1.9	1.3	0.1	.312
02-03	Atlanta	11	0	70	11	4	17	.235	0	0	.000	3	4	.750	7	15	22	5	13	0	3	1	2	6.4	1.0	2.0	0.5	.287
NBA Season Totals		55	1	332	91	34	98	.347	0	2	.000	23	42	.548	27	53	80	16	43	0	12	16	26	6.0	1.7	1.5	0.3	....

YEAR	TEAM	GP	GS	MIN	PTS	FGM	FGA	FG%	3PM	3PA	3P%	FTM	FTA	FT%	ORB	DRB	TRB	AST	PF	DQ	STL	BLK	TO	MPG	PPG	RPG	APG	PCM
96-97	Orlando	2	0	7	5	2	3	.667	0	0	.000	1	3	.333	0	3	3	1	1	0	0	0	0	3.5	2.5	1.5	0.5	.933
NBA Playoff Totals		2	0	7	5	2	3	.667	0	0	.000	1	3	.333	0	3	3	1	1	0	0	0	0	3.5	2.5	1.5	0.5	....

• MCCLAIN, Dwayne

Dwayne Edward McClain

Born: Feb. 7, 1963. Worcester, MA, United States.   Height: 6'6".   Weight: 185 lbs.   Drafted: 1985   College: Villanova

YEAR	TEAM	GP	GS	MIN	PTS	FGM	FGA	FG%	3PM	3PA	3P%	FTM	FTA	FT%	ORB	DRB	TRB	AST	PF	DQ	STL	BLK	TO	MPG	PPG	RPG	APG	PCM
85-86	Indiana	45	4	461	157	69	180	.383	1	9	.111	18	35	.514	14	16	30	67	61	0	38	4	41	10.2	3.5	0.7	1.5	.256
NBA Season Totals		45	4	461	157	69	180	.383	1	9	.111	18	35	.514	14	16	30	67	61	0	38	4	41	10.2	3.5	0.7	1.5	....

• MCCLAIN, Ted

Theodore (Hound Dog) McClain

Born: Aug. 30, 1946. Nashville, TN, United States.   Height: 6'1".   Weight: 180 lbs.   Drafted: 1971   College: Tennessee State

YEAR	TEAM	GP	GS	MIN	PTS	FGM	FGA	FG%	3PM	3PA	3P%	FTM	FTA	FT%	ORB	DRB	TRB	AST	PF	DQ	STL	BLK	TO	MPG	PPG	RPG	APG	PCM
71-72	Carolina-A	64	....	900	419	148	415	.357	13	53	.245	110	142	.775	44	76	120	120	144	5	....	....	116	14.1	6.5	1.9	1.9	.386
72-73	Carolina-A	84	....	1816	803	325	652	.498	8	24	.333	145	204	.711	108	155	263	225	256	1	120	....	185	21.6	9.6	3.1	2.7	.469
73-74	Carolina-A	84	....	2582	1099	423	872	.485	2	27	.074	251	325	.772	121	237	358	348	326	....	250	25	239	30.7	13.1	4.3	4.1	.483
74-75	Kentucky-A	72	....	1971	617	256	582	.440	1	8	.125	104	138	.754	65	203	268	365	231	....	130	15	167	27.4	8.6	3.7	5.1	.433
75-76	Kentucky-A	43	....	1231	333	139	328	.424	1	2	.500	54	69	.783	25	110	135	204	165	....	81	13	109	28.6	7.7	3.1	4.7	.350
75-76	New York-A	30	....	696	340	128	303	.422	2	10	.200	82	101	.812	27	46	73	106	112	....	57	10	85	23.2	11.3	2.4	3.5	.443
76-77	Denver	72	....	2002	589	245	551	.445	....	....	....	99	133	.744	52	177	229	324	255	9	106	13	....	27.8	8.2	3.2	4.5	.383
77-78	Buffalo	41	....	727	212	81	184	.440	....	....	....	50	63	.794	11	64	75	123	88	2	42	2	70	17.7	5.2	1.8	3.0	.356
77-78	Philadelphia	29	....	293	91	42	96	.438	....	....	....	7	10	.700	9	28	37	34	36	0	16	4	23	10.1	3.1	1.3	1.2	.323
78-79	Phoenix	36	....	465	166	62	132	.470	....	....	....	42	46	.913	25	44	69	60	51	0	19	0	54	12.9	4.6	1.9	1.7	.377
NBA Season Totals		178	....	3487	1058	430	963	.447	....	....	....	198	252	.786	97	313	410	541	430	11	183	19	147	19.6	5.9	2.3	3.0	....
ABA Season Totals		377	....	9196	3611	1419	3152	.450	27	124	.218	746	979	.762	390	827	1217	1368	1234	6	638	63	901	24.4	9.6	3.2	3.6	....
Career Totals		555	....	12683	4669	1849	4115	.449	27	124	.218	944	1231	.767	487	1140	1627	1909	1664	17	821	82	1048	22.9	8.4	2.9	3.4	....
72-73	Carolina-A	12	....	234	56	22	74	.297	1	5	.200	11	15	.733	21	22	43	22	39	1	....	....	23	19.5	4.7	3.6	1.8	.226
73-74	Carolina-A	4	....	133	51	22	53	.415	0	2	.000	7	12	.583	4	15	19	11	18	....	7	0	6	33.3	12.8	4.8	2.8	.326
74-75	Kentucky-A	15	....	544	180	74	177	.418	0	5	.000	32	41	.780	20	63	83	87	54	....	29	5	39	36.3	12.0	5.5	5.8	.425
75-76	New York-A	8	....	96	26	10	37	.270	0	1	.000	6	10	.600	5	6	11	7	19	....	5	1	10	12.0	3.3	1.4	0.9	.096
76-77	Denver	6	....	170	44	19	46	.413	....	....	....	6	8	.750	5	9	14	27	12	0	10	2	....	28.3	7.3	2.3	4.5	.338
77-78	Philadelphia	5	....	31	6	3	10	.300	....	....	....	0	0	.000	2	4	6	10	4	0	5	0	6	6.2	1.2	1.2	2.0	.472
78-79	Phoenix	14	....	103	43	15	34	.441	....	....	....	13	16	.813	5	11	16	13	20	0	6	0	16	7.4	3.1	1.1	0.9	.343
NBA Playoff Totals		25	....	304	93	37	90	.411	....	....	....	19	24	.792	12	24	36	50	36	0	21	2	21	12.2	3.7	1.4	2.0	....
ABA Playoff Totals		39	....	1007	313	128	341	.375	1	13	.077	56	78	.718	50	106	156	127	130	1	41	6	78	25.8	8.0	4.0	3.3	....
Career Playoff Totals		64	....	1311	406	165	431	.383	1	13	.077	75	102	.735	62	130	192	177	166	1	62	8	99	20.5	6.3	3.0	2.8	....

• MCCLINTOCK, Dan

Daniel Raymond McClintock

Born: Apr. 19, 1977. Fountain Valley, CA, United States.   Height: 7'   Weight: 270 lbs.   Drafted: 2000   College: Northern Arizona

YEAR	TEAM	GP	GS	MIN	PTS	FGM	FGA	FG%	3PM	3PA	3P%	FTM	FTA	FT%	ORB	DRB	TRB	AST	PF	DQ	STL	BLK	TO	MPG	PPG	RPG	APG	PCM
00-01	Denver	6	1	58	18	9	18	.500	0	0	.000	0	5	.000	10	7	17	1	11	1	0	2	3	9.7	3.0	2.8	0.2	.314
NBA Season Totals		6	1	58	18	9	18	.500	0	0	.000	0	5	.000	10	7	17	1	11	1	0	2	3	9.7	3.0	2.8	0.2	....

• MCCLOSKEY, Jack

John William McCloskey

Born: Sept. 19, 1925.   Height: 6'2".   Weight: 190 lbs.   Drafted: —   College: Pennsylvania

YEAR	TEAM	GP	GS	MIN	PTS	FGM	FGA	FG%	3PM	3PA	3P%	FTM	FTA	FT%	ORB	DRB	TRB	AST	PF	DQ	STL	BLK	TO	MPG	PPG	RPG	APG	PCM
52-53	Philadelphia	1	....	16	6	3	9	.333	....	....	....	0	0	.000	....	....	....	3	1	2	0	....	....	....	16.0	6.0	3.0	1.0	.274
NBA Season Totals		1	....	16	6	3	9	.333	....	....	....	0	0	.000	....	....	....	3	1	2	0	....	....	....	16.0	6.0	3.0	1.0	....

• MCCLOUD, George

George Aaron McCloud

Born: May 27, 1967. Daytona Beach, FL, United States.   Height: 6'6".   Weight: 205 lbs.   Drafted: 1989   College: Florida State

YEAR	TEAM	GP	GS	MIN	PTS	FGM	FGA	FG%	3PM	3PA	3P%	FTM	FTA	FT%	ORB	DRB	TRB	AST	PF	DQ	STL	BLK	TO	MPG	PPG	RPG	APG	PCM
89-90	Indiana	44	0	413	118	45	144	.313	13	40	.325	15	19	.789	12	30	42	45	56	0	19	3	35	9.4	2.7	1.0	1.0	.175
90-91	Indiana	74	0	1070	343	131	351	.373	43	124	.347	38	49	.776	35	83	118	150	141	1	40	11	89	14.5	4.6	1.6	2.0	.282
91-92	Indiana	51	5	892	338	128	313	.409	32	94	.340	50	64	.781	45	87	132	116	95	1	26	11	61	17.5	6.6	2.6	2.3	.381
92-93	Indiana	78	21	1500	565	216	525	.411	58	181	.320	75	102	.735	60	145	205	192	165	0	53	11	109	19.2	7.2	2.6	2.5	.361
94-95	Dallas	42	3	802	402	144	328	.439	34	89	.382	80	96	.833	82	65	147	53	71	0	23	9	42	19.1	9.6	3.5	1.3	.466
95-96	Dallas	79	63	2846	1497	530	1281	.414	257	**678**	.379	180	224	.804	116	263	379	212	212	1	113	38	166	36.0	18.9	4.8	2.7	.435
96-97	Dallas	41	26	1207	563	204	482	.423	78	205	.380	77	92	.837	29	114	143	92	106	1	52	8	53	29.4	13.7	3.5	2.2	.402
96-97	LA Lakers	23	2	286	95	34	96	.354	21	49	.429	6	9	.667	7	29	36	17	20	0	9	0	9	12.4	4.1	1.6	0.7	.273
97-98	Phoenix	63	13	1213	456	173	427	.405	71	208	.341	39	51	.765	45	173	218	84	132	1	54	13	63	19.3	7.2	3.5	1.3	.373
98-99	Phoenix	48	16	1245	428	142	324	.438	69	166	.416	75	87	.862	34	128	162	79	127	0	45	16	49	25.9	8.9	3.4	1.6	.358
99-00	Denver	78	11	2118	787	266	638	.417	107	283	.378	148	181	.818	72	213	285	246	180	2	48	26	134	27.2	10.1	3.7	3.2	.390
00-01	Denver	76	8	2007	729	250	655	.382	77	234	.329	152	181	.840	55	169	224	279	165	1	53	27	117	26.4	9.6	2.9	3.7	.375
01-02	Denver	69	26	1818	604	206	576	.358	60	222	.270	132	163	.810	67	184	251	204	175	3	58	19	144	26.3	8.8	3.6	3.0	.311
NBA Season Totals		766	194	17417	6925	2469	6140	.402	920	2573	.358	1067	1318	.810	659	1683	2342	1769	1645	11	593	190	1071	22.7	9.0	3.1	2.3	....
89-90	Indiana	1	0	4	2	1	2	.500	0	0	.000	0	0	.000	1	0	1	0	2	0	0	0	1	4.0	2.0	1.0	0.0	.032
91-92	Indiana	2	2	53	23	6	12	.500	3	6	.500	8	11	.727	0	2	2	6	5	0	2	1	3	26.5	11.5	1.0	3.0	.415
92-93	Indiana	4	0	79	19	8	23	.348	2	12	.167	1	4	.250	3	8	11	14	14	0	4	1	5	19.8	4.8	2.8	3.5	.282
97-98	Phoenix	4	3	126	57	21	41	.512	12	21	.571	3	4	.750	2	17	19	8	15	0	1	1	6	31.5	14.3	4.8	2.0	.427
98-99	Phoenix	3	0	80	42	13	30	.433	9	20	.450	7	10	.700	2	11	13	2	13	0	5	0	3	26.7	14.0	4.3	0.7	.442
NBA Playoff Totals		14	5	342	143	49	108	.454	26	59	.441	19	29	.655	8	38	46	30	49	0	12	3	18	24.4	10.2	3.3	2.1	....

YEAR	TEAM	GP	GS	MIN	PTS	FGM	FGA	FG%	3PM	3PA	3P%	FTM	FTA	FT%	ORB	DRB	TRB	AST	PF	DQ	STL	BLK	TO	MPG	PPG	RPG	APG	PCM

• MCCOMB, Gord — Gordon McComb

Born: Aug. 1, 1917. Died: Sept.1972.   Height: 5'10".   Weight: 160 lbs.   Drafted: —   College: Tennessee (Chatanooga)

YEAR	TEAM	GP	GS	MIN	PTS	FGM	FGA	FG%	3PM	3PA	3P%	FTM	FTA	FT%	ORB	DRB	TRB	AST	PF	DQ	STL	BLK	TO	MPG	PPG	RPG	APG	PCM
39-40	Hammond-N	2	....	....	3	1	....	....	....	....	....	1	....	....	....	....	....	....	....	....	....	....	....	....	1.5	....	....	....
NBL Season Totals		2	....	....	3	1	....	....	....	....	....	1	....	....	....	....	....	....	....	....	....	....	....	....	1.5	....	....	....

• MCCONATHY, John — John R. McConathy

Born: Apr. 9, 1930.   Height: 6'5".   Weight: 195 lbs.   Drafted: 1951   College: Northwestern Louisiana

YEAR	TEAM	GP	GS	MIN	PTS	FGM	FGA	FG%	3PM	3PA	3P%	FTM	FTA	FT%	ORB	DRB	TRB	AST	PF	DQ	STL	BLK	TO	MPG	PPG	RPG	APG	PCM
51-52	Milwaukee	11	....	106	14	4	29	.138	....	....	....	6	14	.429	....	....	20	8	7	0	....	....	....	9.6	1.3	1.8	0.7	.146
NBA Season Totals		11	....	106	14	4	29	.138	....	....	....	6	14	.429	....	....	20	8	7	0	....	....	....	9.6	1.3	1.8	0.7	....

• MCCONNELL, — — McConnell

Born: —.   Height: —   Weight: —   Drafted: —   College: Southern Illinois

YEAR	TEAM	GP	GS	MIN	PTS	FGM	FGA	FG%	3PM	3PA	3P%	FTM	FTA	FT%	ORB	DRB	TRB	AST	PF	DQ	STL	BLK	TO	MPG	PPG	RPG	APG	PCM
37-38	Columbus-N	5	....	....	5	2	....	....	....	....	....	1	....	....	....	....	....	....	....	....	....	....	....	....	1.0	....	....	....
NBL Season Totals		5	....	....	5	2	....	....	....	....	....	1	....	....	....	....	....	....	....	....	....	....	....	....	1.0	....	....	....

• MCCONNELL, Bucky — Paul Joseph (Bucky) McConnell

Born: July 1, 1928.   Height: 5'10".   Weight: 170 lbs.   Drafted: —   College: John Marshall

YEAR	TEAM	GP	GS	MIN	PTS	FGM	FGA	FG%	3PM	3PA	3P%	FTM	FTA	FT%	ORB	DRB	TRB	AST	PF	DQ	STL	BLK	TO	MPG	PPG	RPG	APG	PCM
52-53	Milwaukee	14	....	297	68	27	71	.380	....	....	....	14	29	.483	....	....	34	41	39	0	....	....	....	21.2	4.9	2.4	2.9	.315
NBA Season Totals		14	....	297	68	27	71	.380	....	....	....	14	29	.483	....	....	34	41	39	0	....	....	....	21.2	4.9	2.4	2.9	....

• MCCORD, Keith — Keith Rennae McCord

Born: June 22, 1957. Birmingham, AL, United States.   Height: 6'7".   Weight: 210 lbs.   Drafted: 1979   College: Alabama-Birmingham

YEAR	TEAM	GP	GS	MIN	PTS	FGM	FGA	FG%	3PM	3PA	3P%	FTM	FTA	FT%	ORB	DRB	TRB	AST	PF	DQ	STL	BLK	TO	MPG	PPG	RPG	APG	PCM
80-81	Washington	2	....	9	4	2	4	.500	0	0	.000	0	0	.000	1	1	2	1	0	0	0	0	2	4.5	2.0	1.0	0.5	.363
NBA Season Totals		2	....	9	4	2	4	.500	0	0	.000	0	0	.000	1	1	2	1	0	0	0	0	2	4.5	2.0	1.0	0.5	....

• MCCORMICK, Tim — Timothy Daniel McCormick

Born: Mar. 10, 1962. Detroit, MI, United States.   Height: 6'11".   Weight: 240 lbs.   Drafted: 1984   College: Michigan

YEAR	TEAM	GP	GS	MIN	PTS	FGM	FGA	FG%	3PM	3PA	3P%	FTM	FTA	FT%	ORB	DRB	TRB	AST	PF	DQ	STL	BLK	TO	MPG	PPG	RPG	APG	PCM
84-85	Seattle	78	27	1584	726	269	483	.557	0	1	.000	188	263	.715	146	252	398	78	207	2	18	33	117	20.3	9.3	5.1	1.0	.497
85-86	Seattle	77	42	1705	681	253	444	.570	1	2	.500	174	244	.713	140	263	403	83	219	4	19	28	108	22.1	8.8	5.2	1.1	.455
86-87	Philadelphia	81	79	2817	1033	391	718	.545	0	4	.000	251	349	.719	180	431	611	114	270	4	36	64	154	34.8	12.8	7.5	1.4	.425
87-88	Philadelphia	23	17	601	179	71	138	.514	0	0	.000	37	53	.698	49	95	144	26	75	1	14	8	35	26.1	7.8	6.3	1.1	.373
87-88	New Jersey	47	28	1513	662	277	510	.543	0	2	.000	108	162	.667	97	226	323	92	159	2	18	15	75	32.2	14.1	6.9	2.0	.466
88-89	Houston	81	0	1257	425	169	351	.481	0	4	.000	87	129	.674	87	174	261	54	193	0	18	24	65	15.5	5.2	3.2	0.7	.339
89-90	Houston	18	0	116	30	10	29	.345	0	0	.000	10	19	.526	8	19	27	3	24	0	3	1	11	6.4	1.7	1.5	0.2	.161
90-91	Atlanta	56	7	689	252	93	187	.497	0	3	.000	66	90	.733	56	109	165	32	91	1	11	14	45	12.3	4.5	2.9	0.6	.407
91-92	New York	22	0	108	42	14	33	.424	0	0	.000	14	21	.667	14	20	34	9	18	0	2	0	9	4.9	1.9	1.5	0.4	.439
NBA Season Totals		483	200	10390	4030	1547	2893	.535	1	16	.063	935	1330	.703	777	1589	2366	491	1256	14	139	187	619	21.5	8.3	4.9	1.0	....
86-87	Philadelphia	5	5	121	28	12	24	.500	0	0	.000	4	4	1.000	7	24	31	6	19	0	1	2	7	24.2	5.6	6.2	1.2	.327
88-89	Houston	4	0	53	22	7	13	.538	0	1	.000	8	9	.889	2	11	13	0	9	0	3	2	0	13.3	5.5	3.3	0.0	.538
89-90	Houston	3	0	21	3	1	3	.333	0	0	.000	1	2	.500	1	7	8	0	5	0	0	0	0	7.0	1.0	2.7	0.0	.277
90-91	Atlanta	2	0	13	6	2	7	.286	0	0	.000	2	3	.667	1	1	2	0	1	0	0	0	0	6.5	3.0	1.0	0.0	.174
91-92	New York	1	0	6	0	0	2	.000	0	0	.000	0	0	.000	0	3	3	0	1	0	0	0	0	6.0	0.0	3.0	0.0	.077
NBA Playoff Totals		15	5	214	59	22	49	.449	0	1	.000	15	18	.833	11	46	57	6	35	0	4	4	7	14.3	3.9	3.8	0.4	....

• MCCOY, Jelani — Jelani Marwan McCoy

Born: Dec. 6, 1977. Oakland, CA, United States.   Height: 6'10".   Weight: 245 lbs.   Drafted: 1998   College: UCLA

YEAR	TEAM	GP	GS	MIN	PTS	FGM	FGA	FG%	3PM	3PA	3P%	FTM	FTA	FT%	ORB	DRB	TRB	AST	PF	DQ	STL	BLK	TO	MPG	PPG	RPG	APG	PCM
98-99	Seattle	26	0	331	133	56	76	.737	0	0	.000	21	42	.500	27	52	79	4	42	0	11	20	10	12.7	5.1	3.0	0.2	.546
99-00	Seattle	58	2	746	249	102	177	.576	0	0	.000	45	91	.495	54	125	179	24	127	0	15	46	45	12.9	4.3	3.1	0.4	.410
00-01	Seattle	70	44	1143	317	138	264	.523	0	0	.000	41	93	.441	92	159	251	57	141	0	18	49	75	16.3	4.5	3.6	0.8	.348
01-02	LA Lakers	21	0	104	26	12	21	.571	0	0	.000	2	8	.250	8	17	25	7	14	0	0	5	8	5.0	1.2	1.2	0.3	.350
02-03	Toronto	67	25	1367	457	194	395	.491	0	0	.000	69	126	.548	95	260	355	43	162	2	28	60	96	20.4	6.8	5.3	0.6	.393
NBA Season Totals		242	71	3691	1182	502	933	.538	0	0	.000	178	360	.494	276	613	889	135	486	2	72	180	234	15.3	4.9	3.7	0.6	....
99-00	Seattle	3	0	26	4	2	5	.400	0	0	.000	0	3	.000	0	6	6	2	6	0	0	0	2	8.7	1.3	2.0	0.7	.116
NBA Playoff Totals		3	0	26	4	2	5	.400	0	0	.000	0	3	.000	0	6	6	2	6	0	0	0	2	8.7	1.3	2.0	0.7	....

• MCCRACKEN, Paul — Paul George McCracken

Born: Sept. 11, 1950. New York, NY, United States.   Height: 6'4".   Weight: 180 lbs.   Drafted: —   College: Northridge State

YEAR	TEAM	GP	GS	MIN	PTS	FGM	FGA	FG%	3PM	3PA	3P%	FTM	FTA	FT%	ORB	DRB	TRB	AST	PF	DQ	STL	BLK	TO	MPG	PPG	RPG	APG	PCM
72-73	Houston	24	....	305	111	44	89	.494	....	....	....	23	39	.590	....	....	51	17	32	0	....	....	....	12.7	4.6	2.1	0.7	.377
73-74	Houston	4	....	13	2	1	4	.250	....	....	....	0	0	.000	1	5	6	2	3	0	0	0	....	3.3	0.5	1.5	0.5	.429
76-77	Chicago	9	....	119	47	18	47	.383	....	....	....	11	18	.611	6	10	16	14	17	0	6	0	....	13.2	5.2	1.8	1.6	.347
NBA Season Totals		37	....	437	160	63	140	.450	....	....	....	34	57	.596	7	15	73	33	52	0	6	0	....	11.8	4.3	2.0	0.9	....

• MCCRAY, Rodney

Rodney Earl McCray

Born: Aug. 29, 1961. Mount Vernon, NY, United States. Height: 6'7". Weight: 220 lbs. Drafted: 1983 College: Louisville

YEAR	TEAM	GP	GS	MIN	PTS	FGM	FGA	FG%	3PM	3PA	3P%	FTM	FTA	FT%	ORB	DRB	TRB	AST	PF	DQ	STL	BLK	TO	MPG	PPG	RPG	APG	PCM
83-84	Houston	79	36	2081	853	335	672	.499	1	4	.250	182	249	.731	173	277	450	176	205	1	53	54	119	26.3	10.8	5.7	2.2	.485
84-85	Houston	82	82	3001	1183	476	890	.535	0	6	.000	231	313	.738	201	338	539	355	215	2	90	75	180	36.6	14.4	6.6	4.3	.509
85-86	Houston	82	82	2610	847	338	629	.537	0	3	.000	171	222	.770	159	361	520	292	197	2	50	58	131	31.8	10.3	6.3	3.6	.474
86-87	Houston	81	81	3136	1170	432	783	.552	0	9	.000	306	393	.779	190	388	578	434	172	2	88	53	211	38.7	14.4	7.1	5.4	.529
87-88	Houston	81	80	2689	1006	359	746	.481	0	4	.000	288	367	.785	232	399	631	264	166	2	57	51	146	33.2	12.4	7.8	3.3	.508
88-89	Sacramento	68	65	2435	854	340	729	.466	5	22	.227	169	234	.722	143	371	514	293	121	0	57	36	170	35.8	12.6	7.6	4.3	.462
89-90	Sacramento	82	82	**3238**	1358	537	1043	.515	11	42	.262	273	348	.784	192	477	669	377	176	0	60	70	172	**39.5**	16.6	8.2	4.6	.542
90-91	Dallas	74	68	2561	844	336	679	.495	13	39	.333	159	198	.803	153	407	560	259	203	3	70	51	126	34.6	11.4	7.6	3.5	.471
91-92	Dallas	75	48	2106	677	271	622	.436	25	85	.294	110	153	.719	149	319	468	219	180	2	48	30	113	28.1	9.0	6.2	2.9	.420
92-93	Chicago	64	5	1019	222	92	204	.451	2	5	.400	36	52	.692	53	105	158	81	99	0	12	15	51	15.9	3.5	2.5	1.3	.270
NBA Season Totals		**768**	**629**	**24876**	**9014**	**3516**	**6997**	**.503**	**57**	**219**	**.260**	**1925**	**2529**	**.761**	**1645**	**3442**	**5087**	**2750**	**1734**	**14**	**585**	**493**	**1419**	**32.4**	**11.7**	**6.6**	**3.6**	**....**
84-85	Houston	5	5	181	53	19	34	.559	0	0	.000	15	23	.652	9	21	30	11	17	0	6	1	13	36.2	10.6	6.0	2.2	.340
85-86	Houston	20	20	835	259	108	202	.535	0	3	.000	43	58	.741	23	95	118	125	45	0	18	19	37	41.8	13.0	5.9	6.3	.464
86-87	Houston	10	10	436	157	57	101	.564	0	2	.000	43	54	.796	32	51	83	56	21	0	5	9	26	43.6	15.7	8.3	5.6	.521
87-88	Houston	4	4	159	32	12	31	.387	0	1	.000	8	12	.667	15	12	27	9	12	0	4	3	7	39.8	8.0	6.8	2.3	.262
92-93	Chicago	7	0	39	2	1	6	.167	0	0	.000	0	0	.000	2	11	13	5	4	0	0	1	4	5.6	0.3	1.9	0.7	.260
NBA Playoff Totals		**46**	**39**	**1650**	**503**	**197**	**374**	**.527**	**0**	**6**	**.000**	**109**	**147**	**.741**	**81**	**190**	**271**	**206**	**99**	**0**	**33**	**33**	**87**	**35.9**	**10.9**	**5.9**	**4.5**	**....**

• MCCRAY, Scooter

Carlton Lamont (Scooter) McCray

Born: Feb. 8, 1960. Mount Vernon, NY, United States. Height: 6'9". Weight: 215 lbs. Drafted: 1983 College: Louisville

YEAR	TEAM	GP	GS	MIN	PTS	FGM	FGA	FG%	3PM	3PA	3P%	FTM	FTA	FT%	ORB	DRB	TRB	AST	PF	DQ	STL	BLK	TO	MPG	PPG	RPG	APG	PCM
83-84	Seattle	47	6	520	129	47	121	.388	0	0	.000	35	50	.700	45	70	115	44	73	1	11	19	33	11.1	2.7	2.4	0.9	.328
84-85	Seattle	6	0	93	15	6	10	.600	0	0	.000	3	4	.750	6	11	17	7	13	0	1	3	10	15.5	2.5	2.8	1.2	.242
86-87	Cleveland	24	2	279	80	30	65	.462	0	0	.000	20	41	.488	19	39	58	23	28	0	9	4	24	11.6	3.3	2.4	1.0	.333
NBA Season Totals		**77**	**8**	**892**	**224**	**83**	**196**	**.423**	**0**	**0**	**.000**	**58**	**95**	**.611**	**70**	**120**	**190**	**74**	**114**	**1**	**21**	**26**	**67**	**11.6**	**2.9**	**2.5**	**1.0**	**....**
83-84	Seattle	4	0	38	8	4	6	.667	0	1	.000	0	1	.000	3	3	6	3	8	0	1	0	0	9.5	2.0	1.5	0.8	.307
NBA Playoff Totals		**4**	**0**	**38**	**8**	**4**	**6**	**.667**	**0**	**1**	**.000**	**0**	**1**	**.000**	**3**	**3**	**6**	**3**	**8**	**0**	**1**	**0**	**0**	**9.5**	**2.0**	**1.5**	**0.8**	**....**

• MCCULLOUGH, John

John P. McCullough

Born: Oct. 5, 1956. Lima, OH, United States. Height: 6'4". Weight: 190 lbs. Drafted: 1979 College: Oklahoma

YEAR	TEAM	GP	GS	MIN	PTS	FGM	FGA	FG%	3PM	3PA	3P%	FTM	FTA	FT%	ORB	DRB	TRB	AST	PF	DQ	STL	BLK	TO	MPG	PPG	RPG	APG	PCM
81-82	Phoenix	8	0	23	21	9	13	.692	0	0	.000	3	5	.600	1	3	4	3	3	0	2	0	3	2.9	2.6	0.5	0.4	.914
NBA Season Totals		**8**	**0**	**23**	**21**	**9**	**13**	**.692**	**0**	**0**	**.000**	**3**	**5**	**.600**	**1**	**3**	**4**	**3**	**3**	**0**	**2**	**0**	**3**	**2.9**	**2.6**	**0.5**	**0.4**	**....**

• MCDANIEL, Clint

Clint McDaniel

Born: Feb. 26, 1972. Tulsa, OK, United States. Height: 6'4". Weight: 180 lbs. Drafted: — College: Arkansas

YEAR	TEAM	GP	GS	MIN	PTS	FGM	FGA	FG%	3PM	3PA	3P%	FTM	FTA	FT%	ORB	DRB	TRB	AST	PF	DQ	STL	BLK	TO	MPG	PPG	RPG	APG	PCM
95-96	Sacramento	12	0	71	30	8	23	.348	2	6	.333	12	16	.750	3	7	10	7	10	0	5	0	2	5.9	2.5	0.8	0.6	.408
NBA Season Totals		**12**	**0**	**71**	**30**	**8**	**23**	**.348**	**2**	**6**	**.333**	**12**	**16**	**.750**	**3**	**7**	**10**	**7**	**10**	**0**	**5**	**0**	**2**	**5.9**	**2.5**	**0.8**	**0.6**	**....**

• MCDANIEL, Xavier

Xavier Maurice (X, X-Man) McDaniel

Born: June 4, 1963. Columbia, SC, United States. Height: 6'7". Weight: 205 lbs. Drafted: 1985 College: Wichita State

YEAR	TEAM	GP	GS	MIN	PTS	FGM	FGA	FG%	3PM	3PA	3P%	FTM	FTA	FT%	ORB	DRB	TRB	AST	PF	DQ	STL	BLK	TO	MPG	PPG	RPG	APG	PCM
85-86	Seattle	82	80	2706	1404	576	1176	.490	2	10	.200	250	364	.687	307	348	655	193	305	8	101	37	246	33.0	17.1	8.0	2.4	.505
86-87	Seattle	82	82	3031	1890	806	1583	.509	3	14	.214	275	395	.696	338	367	705	207	300	4	115	52	238	37.0	23.0	8.6	2.5	.588
87-88	Seattle	78	77	2703	1669	687	1407	.488	14	50	.280	281	393	.715	206	312	518	263	230	2	96	52	226	34.7	21.4	6.6	3.4	.566
88-89	Seattle	82	10	2385	1677	677	1385	.489	11	36	.306	312	426	.732	177	256	433	134	231	0	84	40	213	29.1	20.5	5.3	1.6	.554
89-90	Seattle	69	67	2432	1471	611	1233	.496	5	17	.294	244	333	.733	165	282	447	171	231	2	73	36	186	35.2	21.3	6.5	2.5	.521
90-91	Seattle	15	15	529	327	139	290	.479	0	3	.000	49	69	.710	36	45	81	38	50	0	26	4	41	35.3	21.8	5.4	2.5	.490
90-91	Phoenix	66	64	2105	1046	451	896	.503	0	5	.000	144	198	.727	137	339	476	149	214	2	50	42	145	31.9	15.8	7.2	2.3	.503
91-92	New York	82	82	2344	1125	488	1021	.478	12	39	.308	137	192	.714	176	284	460	149	241	3	57	24	148	28.6	13.7	5.6	1.8	.434
92-93	Boston	82	27	2215	1111	457	924	.495	6	22	.273	191	241	.793	168	321	489	163	249	4	72	51	172	27.0	13.5	6.0	2.0	.506
93-94	Boston	82	5	1971	928	387	839	.461	10	41	.244	144	213	.676	142	258	400	126	193	0	48	39	115	24.0	11.3	4.9	1.5	.442
94-95	Boston	68	15	1430	587	246	546	.451	6	21	.286	89	125	.712	94	206	300	108	146	0	30	20	88	21.0	8.6	4.4	1.6	.406
96-97	New Jersey	62	5	1170	346	138	355	.389	5	25	.200	65	89	.730	124	194	318	65	144	0	36	17	68	18.9	5.6	5.1	1.0	.357
97-98	New Jersey	20	0	180	25	10	30	.333	0	0	.000	5	8	.625	12	19	31	9	23	0	3	2	8	9.0	1.3	1.6	0.5	.168
NBA Season Totals		**870**	**529**	**25201**	**13606**	**5673**	**11685**	**.485**	**74**	**283**	**.261**	**2186**	**3046**	**.718**	**2082**	**3231**	**5313**	**1775**	**2557**	**25**	**791**	**416**	**1894**	**29.0**	**15.6**	**6.1**	**2.0**	**....**
86-87	Seattle	14	14	528	284	124	254	.488	2	10	.200	34	56	.607	52	65	117	42	63	2	21	9	42	37.7	20.3	8.4	3.0	.504
87-88	Seattle	5	5	180	106	45	81	.556	4	8	.500	12	24	.500	14	34	48	25	15	0	3	1	11	36.0	21.2	9.6	5.0	.693
88-89	Seattle	8	8	281	150	58	144	.403	3	9	.333	31	41	.756	24	43	67	22	30	0	2	5	22	35.1	18.8	8.4	2.8	.439
90-91	Phoenix	4	4	101	38	17	41	.415	0	1	.000	4	6	.667	4	11	15	5	10	0	0	2	10	25.3	9.5	3.8	1.3	.217
91-92	New York	12	12	458	226	94	197	.477	2	8	.250	36	49	.735	43	43	86	23	34	1	9	2	27	38.2	18.8	7.2	1.9	.433
92-93	Boston	4	0	126	50	22	53	.415	0	2	.000	6	9	.667	6	12	18	9	16	0	1	3	7	31.5	12.5	4.5	2.3	.284
94-95	Boston	4	0	59	13	5	17	.294	0	1	.000	3	4	.750	2	4	6	5	5	0	0	0	6	14.8	3.3	1.5	1.3	.072
NBA Playoff Totals		**51**	**43**	**1733**	**867**	**365**	**787**	**.464**	**11**	**39**	**.282**	**126**	**189**	**.667**	**145**	**212**	**357**	**131**	**173**	**3**	**36**	**22**	**125**	**34.0**	**17.0**	**7.0**	**2.6**	**....**

• MCDANIELS, Jim

James Ronald McDaniels

Born: Apr. 2, 1948. Scottsville, KY, United States. Height: 6'11". Weight: 228 lbs. Drafted: 1971 College: Western Kentucky

YEAR	TEAM	GP	GS	MIN	PTS	FGM	FGA	FG%	3PM	3PA	3P%	FTM	FTA	FT%	ORB	DRB	TRB	AST	PF	DQ	STL	BLK	TO	MPG	PPG	RPG	APG	PCM
71-72	Carolina-A	58	....	2172	1552	659	1276	.516	0	0	.000	234	324	.722	249	565	814	97	251	10	....	....	167	37.4	26.8	14.0	1.7	.775
71-72	Seattle	12	....	235	113	51	123	.415	....	....	....	11	18	.611	....	....	82	9	26	0	....	....	....	19.6	9.4	6.8	0.8	.500
72-73	Seattle	68	....	1095	378	154	386	.399	....	....	....	70	100	.700	....	....	345	78	140	4	....	....	....	16.1	5.6	5.1	1.1	.448
73-74	Seattle	27	....	439	149	63	173	.364	....	....	....	23	43	.535	51	77	128	24	48	0	7	15	....	16.3	5.5	4.7	0.9	.371
75-76	Kentucky-A	29	....	365	179	78	165	.473	0	0	.000	23	28	.821	40	84	124	21	64	....	8	17	37	12.6	6.2	4.3	0.7	.560

YEAR	TEAM	GP	GS	MIN	PTS	FGM	FGA	FG%	3PM	3PA	3P%	FTM	FTA	FT%	ORB	DRB	TRB	AST	PF	DQ	STL	BLK	TO	MPG	PPG	RPG	APG	PCM
75-76	LA Lakers	35	....	242	91	41	102	.402	....	....	....	9	9	1.000	26	48	74	15	40	1	4	10	....	6.9	2.6	2.1	0.4	.422
77-78	Buffalo	42	....	694	236	100	234	.427	....	....	....	36	42	.857	46	135	181	44	112	3	4	37	50	16.5	5.6	4.3	1.0	.385
NBA Season Totals		184	....	2705	967	409	1018	.402	....	....	....	149	212	.703	123	260	810	170	366	8	15	62	50	14.7	5.3	4.4	0.9	
ABA Season Totals		87	....	2537	1731	737	1441	.511	0	0	.000	257	352	.730	289	649	938	118	315	10	8	17	204	29.2	19.9	10.8	1.4	
Career Totals		271	....	5242	2698	1146	2459	.466	0	0	.000	406	564	.720	412	909	1748	288	681	18	23	79	254	19.3	10.0	6.5	1.1	....
75-76	Kentucky-A	10	....	98	42	19	41	.463	0	0	.000	4	7	.571	9	26	35	5	16	....	3	5	4	9.8	4.2	3.5	0.5	.517
ABA Playoff Totals		10	....	98	42	19	41	.463	0	0	.000	4	7	.571	9	26	35	5	16	....	3	5	4	9.8	4.2	3.5	0.5	

• MCDERMOTT, Bobby

Bobby (Mr. Basketball Man) McDermott

Born: Jan. 7, 1914. Whitestone, NY, United States. Died: Oct.14, 1963.   Height: 5'11".   Weight: 180 lbs.   Drafted: —   College: none (HS: Flushing, NY)   HOF: 1988

YEAR	TEAM	GP	GS	MIN	PTS	FGM	FGA	FG%	3PM	3PA	3P%	FTM	FTA	FT%	ORB	DRB	TRB	AST	PF	DQ	STL	BLK	TO	MPG	PPG	RPG	APG	PCM
41-42	Fort Wayne-N	21	....	....	277	115	....	....	....	....		47	....	....											13.2			
42-43	Fort Wayne-N	23	....	....	316	132	....					52													13.7			
43-44	Fort Wayne-N	22	....	....	306	123	....					60													13.9			
44-45	Fort Wayne-N	30	....	....	603	258	....					87													20.1			
45-46	Fort Wayne-N	34	....	....	458	184	....					90	119	.756											13.5			
46-47	Chicago-N	27	....	....	304	123	....					58	81	.716											11.3			
46-47	Fort Wayne-N	14	....	....	159	59	....					41	60	.683											11.4			
47-48	Sheboygan-N	16	....	....	138	54	....					30	39	.769											8.6			
47-48	Tri-Cities-N	37	....	....	449	191	....					67	93	.720											12.1			
48-49	Hammond-N	18	....	....	149	56	....					37	51	.725											8.3			
48-49	Tri-Cities-N	45	....	....	424	170	....					84	113	.743											9.4			
NBL Season Totals		287	....		3583	1465	....					653	556												12.5			
41-42	Fort Wayne-N	6	....	....	72	28	....					16													12.0			
42-43	Fort Wayne-N	6	....	....	74	29	....					16													12.3			
43-44	Fort Wayne-N	5	....	....	67	27	....					13													13.4			
44-45	Fort Wayne-N	7	....	....	105	45	....					15													15.0			
45-46	Fort Wayne-N	4	....	....	24	7	....					10	12	.833											6.0			
46-47	Chicago-N	9	....	....	74	26	....					22	24	.917											8.2			
47-48	Tri-Cities-N	6	....	....	59	26	....					7	9	.778											9.8			
48-49	Hammond-N	2	....	....	19	7	....					5	5	1.000											9.5			
NBL Playoff Totals		45	....		494	195	....					104	50												11.0			

• MCDONALD, Ben

Benjamin McDonald

Born: July 20, 1962. Torrance, CA, United States.   Height: 6'8".   Weight: 210 lbs.   Drafted: 1984   College: California (Irvine)

YEAR	TEAM	GP	GS	MIN	PTS	FGM	FGA	FG%	3PM	3PA	3P%	FTM	FTA	FT%	ORB	DRB	TRB	AST	PF	DQ	STL	BLK	TO	MPG	PPG	RPG	APG	PCM
85-86	Cleveland	21	0	266	61	28	58	.483	0	1	.000	5	8	.625	15	23	38	9	30	0	7	1	11	12.7	2.9	1.8	0.4	.225
86-87	Golden State	63	34	1284	353	164	360	.456	1	8	.125	24	38	.632	63	120	183	84	200	5	27	8	44	20.4	5.6	2.9	1.3	.251
87-88	Golden State	81	41	2039	612	258	552	.467	9	35	.257	87	111	.784	133	202	335	138	246	4	39	8	89	25.2	7.6	4.1	1.7	.310
88-89	Golden State	11	0	103	35	13	19	.684	0	0	.000	9	15	.600	4	8	12	5	11	0	4	0	3	9.4	3.2	1.1	0.5	.378
NBA Season Totals		176	75	3692	1061	463	989	.468	10	44	.227	125	172	.727	215	353	568	236	487	9	77	17	147	21.0	6.0	3.2	1.3	....
86-87	Golden State	5	0	45	2	1	11	.091	0	2	.000	0	0	.000	2	4	6	9	7	0	2	0	0	9.0	0.4	1.2	1.8	.144
88-89	Golden State	5	0	40	6	2	10	.200	0	3	.000	2	4	.500	4	4	8	1	8	0	3	1	4	8.0	1.2	1.6	0.2	.061
NBA Playoff Totals		10	0	85	8	3	21	.143	0	5	.000	2	4	.500	6	8	14	10	15	0	5	1	4	8.5	0.8	1.4	1.0	....

• MCDONALD, Bill

Bill McDonald

Born: 1916.   Height: 6'3".   Weight: 190 lbs.   Drafted: —   College: Marquette

YEAR	TEAM	GP	GS	MIN	PTS	FGM	FGA	FG%	3PM	3PA	3P%	FTM	FTA	FT%	ORB	DRB	TRB	AST	PF	DQ	STL	BLK	TO	MPG	PPG	RPG	APG	PCM
40-41	Sheboygan-N	24	....	....	88	31	....					26													3.7			
41-42	Sheboygan-N	24	....	....	103	39	....					25													4.3			
42-43	Sheboygan-N	22	....	....	65	20	....					25													3.0			
43-44	Sheboygan-N	20	....	....	120	43	....					34													6.0			
44-45	Chicago-N	30	....	....	239	83	....					73													8.0			
46-47	Chicago-N	5	....	....	2	0	....					2	3	.667											0.4			
46-47	Oshkosh-N	21	....	....	56	18	....					20	26	.769											2.7			
47-48	Oshkosh-N	26	....	....	35	12	....					11	21	.524											1.3			
NBL Season Totals		172	....		708	246	....					216	50												4.1			
40-41	Sheboygan-N	6	....	....	29	12	....					5													4.8			
42-43	Sheboygan-N	5	....	....	16	5	....					6													3.2			
43-44	Sheboygan-N	6	....	....	28	8	....					12													4.7			
44-45	Chicago-N	3	....	....	11	1	....					9													3.7			
46-47	Oshkosh-N	7	....	....	28	10	....					8	9	.889											4.0			
NBL Playoff Totals		27	....		112	36	....					40	9												4.1			

• MCDONALD, Glenn

Glenn Stuart McDonald

Born: Mar. 18, 1952. Kewanee, IL, United States.   Height: 6'6".   Weight: 190 lbs.   Drafted: 1974   College: Long Beach State

YEAR	TEAM	GP	GS	MIN	PTS	FGM	FGA	FG%	3PM	3PA	3P%	FTM	FTA	FT%	ORB	DRB	TRB	AST	PF	DQ	STL	BLK	TO	MPG	PPG	RPG	APG	PCM
74-75	Boston	62	....	395	168	70	182	.385	....	....	....	28	37	.757	20	48	68	24	58	0	8	5	....	6.4	2.7	1.1	0.4	.328
75-76	Boston	75	....	1019	422	191	456	.419	....	....	....	40	56	.714	56	79	135	68	123	0	39	20	....	13.6	5.6	1.8	0.9	.322
76-77	Milwaukee	9	....	79	19	8	34	.235	....	....	....	3	4	.750	8	4	12	7	11	0	4	0	....	8.8	2.1	1.3	0.8	.123
NBA Season Totals		146	....	1493	609	269	672	.400	....	....	....	71	97	.732	84	131	215	99	192	0	51	25	....	10.2	4.2	1.5	0.7	....
74-75	Boston	6	....	30	5	2	12	.167	....	....	....	1	3	.333	1	5	6	2	4	0	1	0	....	5.0	0.8	1.0	0.3	.044
75-76	Boston	13	....	68	21	8	26	.308	....	....	....	5	6	.833	1	7	8	4	12	0	1	0	....	5.2	1.6	0.6	0.3	.168
NBA Playoff Totals		19	....	98	26	10	38	.263	....	....	....	6	9	.667	2	12	14	6	16	0	2	0	....	5.2	1.4	0.7	0.3	

• MCDONALD, Michael
Michael Dewayne McDonald

Born: Feb. 13, 1969. Longview, TX, United States.   Height: 6'10".   Weight: 232 lbs.   Drafted: 1995   College: New Orleans

YEAR	TEAM	GP	GS	MIN	PTS	FGM	FGA	FG%	3PM	3PA	3P%	FTM	FTA	FT%	ORB	DRB	TRB	AST	PF	DQ	STL	BLK	TO	MPC	PPG	RPG	APG	PCM
97-98	Charlotte	1	0	4	0	0	0	.000	0	0	.000	0	0	.000	1	0	1	0	1	0	0	0	2	4.0	0.0	1.0	0.0	-.343
NBA Season Totals		1	0	4	0	0	0	.000	0	0	.000	0	0	.000	1	0	1	0	1	0	0	0	2	4.0	0.0	1.0	0.0	....

• MCDONALD, Rod
Roderick William McDonald

Born: Apr. 9, 1945. Jacksonville, FL, United States. Died: Feb.7, 1994.   Height: 6'6".   Weight: 205 lbs.   Drafted: 1967   College: Whitworth

YEAR	TEAM	GP	GS	MIN	PTS	FGM	FGA	FG%	3PM	3PA	3P%	FTM	FTA	FT%	ORB	DRB	TRB	AST	PF	DQ	STL	BLK	TO	MPC	PPG	RPG	APG	PCM
70-71	Utah-A	29	....	206	117	50	109	.459	2	2	1.000	15	25	.600	40	53	93	7	41	1	....	....	17	7.1	4.0	3.2	0.2	.642
71-72	Utah-A	33	....	231	95	34	76	.447	0	2	.000	27	37	.730	32	42	74	18	40	0	....	....	23	7.0	2.9	2.2	0.5	.525
72-73	Utah-A	25	....	142	70	27	63	.429	1	4	.250	15	19	.789	13	17	30	15	19	0	....	....	14	5.7	2.8	1.2	0.6	.498
ABA Season Totals		87	....	579	282	111	248	.448	3	8	.375	57	81	.704	85	112	197	40	100	1	....	....	54	6.7	3.2	2.3	0.5	....
70-71	Utah-A	5	....	22	18	8	11	.727	1	1	1.000	1	2	.500	4	9	13	2	3	0	....	....	5	4.4	3.6	2.6	0.4	1.218
71-72	Utah-A	1	....	10	6	3	4	.750	0	0	.000	0	1	.000	0	0	0	0	3	0	....	....	0	10.0	6.0	0.0	0.0	.336
72-73	Utah-A	3	....	4	2	1	3	.333	0	1	.000	0	0	.000	1	0	1	0	0	0	....	....	0	1.3	0.7	0.3	0.0	.275
ABA Playoff Totals		9	....	36	26	12	18	.667	1	2	.500	1	3	.333	5	9	14	2	6	0	....	....	5	4.0	2.9	1.6	0.2	....

• MCDOWELL, Hank
Hank Leigh McDowell

Born: Nov. 13, 1959. Memphis, TN, United States.   Height: 6'9".   Weight: 215 lbs.   Drafted: 1981   College: Memphis State

YEAR	TEAM	GP	GS	MIN	PTS	FGM	FGA	FG%	3PM	3PA	3P%	FTM	FTA	FT%	ORB	DRB	TRB	AST	PF	DQ	STL	BLK	TO	MPC	PPG	RPG	APG	PCM
81-82	Golden State	30	1	335	95	34	84	.405	0	0	.000	27	41	.659	41	59	100	20	52	1	6	8	21	11.2	3.2	3.3	0.7	.375
82-83	Golden State	14	0	130	40	13	29	.448	0	0	.000	14	18	.778	15	15	30	4	26	0	2	4	8	9.3	2.9	2.1	0.3	.321
82-83	Portland	42	0	375	123	45	97	.464	0	2	.000	33	43	.767	39	50	89	20	58	0	6	7	34	8.9	2.9	2.1	0.5	.343
83-84	San Diego	57	0	611	208	85	197	.431	0	3	.000	38	56	.679	63	92	155	37	77	0	14	2	51	10.7	3.6	2.7	0.6	.345
84-85	Houston	34	0	132	47	20	42	.476	0	1	.000	7	10	.700	7	15	22	9	22	0	3	5	7	3.9	1.4	0.6	0.3	.348
85-86	Houston	22	0	204	65	24	42	.571	0	1	.000	17	25	.680	12	37	49	6	25	0	1	3	11	9.3	3.0	2.2	0.3	.384
86-87	Milwaukee	7	0	70	22	8	17	.471	0	0	.000	6	7	.857	9	10	19	2	14	0	2	0	3	10.0	3.1	2.7	0.3	.365
NBA Season Totals		206	1	1857	600	229	508	.451	0	7	.000	142	200	.710	186	278	464	98	274	1	34	29	135	9.0	2.9	2.3	0.5	....
82-83	Portland	2	0	4	0	0	1	.000	0	0	.000	0	0	.000	0	2	2	2	2	0	0	0	0	2.0	0.0	1.0	1.0	.549
85-86	Houston	13	0	33	9	2	7	.286	0	0	.000	5	8	.625	4	4	8	2	6	0	0	0	2	2.5	0.7	0.6	0.2	.239
NBA Playoff Totals		15	0	37	9	2	8	.250	0	0	.000	5	8	.625	4	6	10	4	8	0	0	0	2	2.5	0.6	0.7	0.3	....

• MCDYESS, Antonio
Antonio Keithflen McDyess

Born: Sept. 7, 1974. Quitman, MS, United States.   Height: 6'9".   Weight: 220 lbs.   Drafted: 1995   College: Alabama

YEAR	TEAM	GP	GS	MIN	PTS	FGM	FGA	FG%	3PM	3PA	3P%	FTM	FTA	FT%	ORB	DRB	TRB	AST	PF	DQ	STL	BLK	TO	MPC	PPG	RPG	APG	PCM
95-96	Denver	76	75	2280	1020	427	880	.485	0	4	.000	166	243	.683	229	343	572	75	250	4	54	114	152	30.0	13.4	7.5	1.0	.470
96-97	Denver	74	73	2565	1352	536	1157	.463	6	35	.171	274	387	.708	155	382	537	106	276	9	62	126	200	34.7	18.3	7.3	1.4	.466
97-98	Phoenix	81	81	2441	1225	497	927	.536	0	2	.000	231	329	.702	206	407	613	106	290	6	100	135	146	30.1	15.1	7.6	1.3	.578
98-99	Denver	50	50	1937	1061	415	882	.471	1	9	.111	230	338	.680	168	369	537	82	175	5	73	115	138	38.7	21.2	10.7	1.6	.585
99-00	Denver	81	81	2698	1551	614	1211	.507	0	2	.000	323	516	.626	234	451	685	159	316	12	69	139	230	33.3	19.1	8.5	2.0	.576
00-01	Denver	70	70	2555	1458	577	1165	.495	0	0	.000	304	434	.700	240	605	845	146	220	2	43	102	162	36.5	20.8	12.1	2.1	.656
01-02	Denver	10	10	236	113	43	75	.573	0	0	.000	27	33	.818	18	37	55	18	20	0	10	8	20	23.6	11.3	5.5	1.8	.593
NBA Season Totals		442	440	14712	7780	3109	6297	.494	7	52	.135	1555	2280	.682	1250	2594	3844	692	1549	38	411	739	1048	33.3	17.6	8.7	1.6	....
97-98	Phoenix	4	4	147	71	31	65	.477	0	0	.000	9	14	.643	18	35	53	4	12	0	2	6	5	36.8	17.8	13.3	1.0	.597
NBA Playoff Totals		4	4	147	71	31	65	.477	0	0	.000	9	14	.643	18	35	53	4	12	0	2	6	5	36.8	17.8	13.3	1.0	....

• MCELLIOTT, Bob
Robert McElliott

Born: July 10, 1915. Died: Feb.1975.   Height: —   Weight: —   Drafted: —   College: —

YEAR	TEAM	GP	GS	MIN	PTS	FGM	FGA	FG%	3PM	3PA	3P%	FTM	FTA	FT%	ORB	DRB	TRB	AST	PF	DQ	STL	BLK	TO	MPC	PPG	RPG	APG	PCM
38-39	Hammond-N	5	....	....	11	5	....	....	....	....	....	1	....	....	....	....	....	....	....	....	....	....	....	2.2	....	....	....
NBL Season Totals		5	....	....	11	5	....	....	....	....	....	1	....	....	....	....	....	....	....	....	....	....	....	2.2	....	....	....

• MCELROY, Jim
James Charles McElroy Jr.

Born: Oct. 4, 1953. Cotton Plant, AR, United States.   Height: 6'3".   Weight: 190 lbs.   Drafted: 1975   College: Central Michigan

YEAR	TEAM	GP	GS	MIN	PTS	FGM	FGA	FG%	3PM	3PA	3P%	FTM	FTA	FT%	ORB	DRB	TRB	AST	PF	DQ	STL	BLK	TO	MPC	PPG	RPG	APG	PCM
75-76	New Orleans	51	....	1134	383	151	296	.510	....	....	....	81	110	.736	34	76	110	107	70	0	44	4	....	22.2	7.5	2.2	2.1	.382
76-77	New Orleans	73	....	2029	771	301	640	.470	....	....	....	169	217	.779	55	128	183	260	119	3	60	8	....	27.8	10.6	2.5	3.6	.424
77-78	New Orleans	74	....	1760	697	287	607	.473	....	....	....	123	167	.737	44	104	148	292	110	0	58	34	141	23.8	9.4	2.0	3.9	.435
78-79	New Orleans	79	....	2698	1337	539	1097	.491	....	....	....	259	340	.762	61	154	215	453	183	1	148	49	237	34.2	16.9	2.7	5.7	.509
79-80	Detroit	36	....	1012	422	162	356	.455	3	14	.214	95	119	.798	12	38	50	162	78	1	25	14	86	28.1	11.7	1.4	4.5	.376
79-80	Atlanta	31	....	516	171	66	171	.386	2	7	.286	37	53	.698	20	29	49	65	45	1	21	5	43	16.6	5.5	1.6	2.1	.288
80-81	Atlanta	54	....	680	205	78	202	.386	1	8	.125	48	59	.814	10	38	48	84	62	0	20	9	81	12.6	3.8	0.9	1.6	.216
81-82	Atlanta	20	17	349	134	52	125	.416	1	5	.200	29	36	.806	6	11	17	39	44	0	8	3	22	17.5	6.7	0.9	2.0	.260
NBA Season Totals		418	17	10178	4120	1636	3494	.468	7	34	.206	841	1101	.764	242	578	820	1462	711	6	384	126	610	24.3	9.9	2.0	3.5	....
79-80	Atlanta	5	....	32	12	4	9	.444	0	1	.000	4	5	.800	1	1	2	4	1	0	0	0	2	6.4	2.4	0.4	0.8	.342
NBA Playoff Totals		5	....	32	12	4	9	.444	0	1	.000	4	5	.800	1	1	2	4	1	0	0	0	2	6.4	2.4	0.4	0.8	....

• MCFARLAND, Patrick

Patrick Aloysius McFarland

Born: Dec. 7, 1951. Willingboro, NJ, United States. Height: 6'5". Weight: 185 lbs. Drafted: 1973 College: St. Joseph's (PA)

YEAR TEAM	GP	GS	MIN	PTS	FGM	FGA	FG%	3PM	3PA	3P%	FTM	FTA	FT%	ORB	DRB	TRB	AST	PF	DQ	STL	BLK	TO	MPG	PPG	RPG	APG	PCM
73-74 Denver-A	67	....	757	361	159	359	.443	8	24	.333	35	52	.673	60	74	134	64	69	....	23	6	41	11.3	5.4	2.0	1.0	.450
74-75 Denver-A	70	....	945	454	200	424	.472	2	16	.125	52	66	.788	37	83	120	116	60	....	47	5	108	13.5	6.5	1.7	1.7	.484
75-76 San Diego-A	11	....	275	132	55	120	.458	1	2	.500	21	22	.955	17	27	44	39	20	....	6	1	29	25.0	12.0	4.0	3.5	.535
ABA Season Totals	148	....	1977	947	414	903	.458	11	42	.262	108	140	.771	114	184	298	219	149	....	76	12	178	13.4	6.4	2.0	1.5	....
74-75 Denver-A	5	....	30	6	2	8	.250	0	2	.000	2	2	1.000	1	2	3	2	3	....	0	0	6	6.0	1.2	0.6	0.4	.141
ABA Playoff Totals	5	....	30	6	2	8	.250	0	2	.000	2	2	1.000	1	2	3	2	3	....	0	0	6	6.0	1.2	0.6	0.4	....

• MCGAHA, Mel

Fred Melvin McGaha

Born: Sept. 26, 1926. Bastrop, LA, United States. Height: 6'1". Weight: 190 lbs. Drafted: 1948 College: Arkansas

YEAR TEAM	GP	GS	MIN	PTS	FGM	FGA	FG%	3PM	3PA	3P%	FTM	FTA	FT%	ORB	DRB	TRB	AST	PF	DQ	STL	BLK	TO	MPG	PPG	RPG	APG	PCM
48-49 New York	51	....	....	176	62	195	.318	....	....	....	52	88	.591	....	....	....	51	104	....	....	....	....	....	3.5	....	1.0	....
NBA Season Totals	51	....	....	176	62	195	.318	....	....	....	52	88	.591	....	....	....	51	104	....	....	....	....	....	3.5	....	1.0	....
48-49 New York	2	....	....	1	0	3	.000	....	....	....	1	2	.500	....	....	....	2	6	....	....	....	....	....	0.5	....	1.0	....
NBA Playoff Totals	2	....	....	1	0	3	.000	....	....	....	1	2	.500	....	....	....	2	6	....	....	....	....	....	0.5	....	1.0	....

• MCGEE, Mike

Michael Ray McGee

Born: July 29, 1959. Tyler, TX, United States. Height: 6'5". Weight: 190 lbs. Drafted: 1981 College: Michigan

YEAR TEAM	GP	GS	MIN	PTS	FGM	FGA	FG%	3PM	3PA	3P%	FTM	FTA	FT%	ORB	DRB	TRB	AST	PF	DQ	STL	BLK	TO	MPG	PPG	RPG	APG	PCM
81-82 LA Lakers	39	0	352	191	80	172	.465	0	4	.000	31	53	.585	34	15	49	16	59	0	18	3	35	9.0	4.9	1.3	0.4	.337
82-83 LA Lakers	39	7	381	156	69	163	.423	1	7	.143	17	23	.739	33	20	53	26	50	1	11	5	27	9.8	4.0	1.4	0.7	.295
83-84 LA Lakers	77	45	1425	757	347	584	.594	2	12	.167	61	113	.540	117	76	193	81	176	0	49	6	108	18.5	9.8	2.5	1.1	.454
84-85 LA Lakers	76	3	1170	774	329	612	.538	22	61	.361	94	160	.588	97	68	165	71	147	1	39	7	84	15.4	10.2	2.2	0.9	.517
85-86 LA Lakers	71	19	1213	587	252	544	.463	41	114	.360	42	64	.656	51	89	140	83	131	0	53	7	71	17.1	8.3	2.0	1.2	.374
86-87 Atlanta	76	6	1420	788	311	677	.459	86	229	.376	80	137	.584	71	88	159	149	156	1	61	2	106	18.7	10.4	2.1	2.0	.433
87-88 Atlanta	11	0	117	51	22	52	.423	5	19	.263	2	6	.333	4	12	16	13	6	0	5	0	7	10.6	4.6	1.5	1.2	.387
87-88 Sacramento	37	0	886	524	201	478	.421	48	141	.340	74	96	.771	51	61	112	58	75	0	47	6	59	23.9	14.2	3.0	1.6	.430
88-89 New Jersey	80	49	2027	1038	434	917	.473	93	255	.365	77	144	.535	73	116	189	116	184	1	80	12	128	25.3	13.0	2.4	1.5	.364
89-90 Phoenix	14	7	280	102	42	87	.483	8	23	.348	10	21	.476	11	25	36	16	28	0	8	1	14	20.0	7.3	2.6	1.1	.313
NBA Season Totals	520	136	9271	4968	2087	4286	.487	306	865	.354	488	817	.597	542	570	1112	629	1012	4	371	49	639	17.8	9.6	2.1	1.2	....
81-82 LA Lakers	4	0	10	12	6	13	.462	0	1	.000	0	0	.000	3	0	3	0	1	0	0	0	1	2.5	3.0	0.8	0.0	.693
82-83 LA Lakers	6	0	25	12	4	11	.364	1	1	1.000	3	4	.750	5	2	7	1	5	0	0	0	4	4.2	2.0	1.2	0.2	.271
83-84 LA Lakers	17	13	370	211	90	157	.573	6	17	.353	25	39	.641	22	12	34	23	52	0	11	1	27	21.8	12.4	2.0	1.4	.433
84-85 LA Lakers	17	0	260	190	76	142	.535	9	18	.500	29	42	.690	20	16	36	12	26	0	7	1	14	15.3	11.2	2.1	0.7	.581
85-86 LA Lakers	6	0	28	16	8	18	.444	0	3	.000	0	4	.000	3	2	5	2	3	0	0	0	2	4.7	2.7	0.8	0.3	.300
86-87 Atlanta	8	0	101	27	10	39	.256	2	14	.143	5	10	.500	9	11	20	15	7	0	4	0	4	12.6	3.4	2.5	1.9	.288
89-90 Phoenix	10	0	44	18	7	20	.350	3	7	.429	1	4	.250	1	3	4	2	6	0	1	1	2	4.4	1.8	0.4	0.2	.170
NBA Playoff Totals	68	13	838	486	201	400	.503	21	61	.344	63	103	.612	63	46	109	55	100	0	23	3	54	12.3	7.1	1.6	0.8	....

• MCGILL, Bill

Bill (The Hill) McGill

Born: Sept. 16, 1939. San Angelo, TX, United States. Height: 6'9". Weight: 225 lbs. Drafted: 1962 College: Utah

YEAR TEAM	GP	GS	MIN	PTS	FGM	FGA	FG%	3PM	3PA	3P%	FTM	FTA	FT%	ORB	DRB	TRB	AST	PF	DQ	STL	BLK	TO	MPG	PPG	RPG	APG	PCM
62-63 Chicago	60	....	590	442	181	353	.513	....	....	....	80	119	.672	....	....	161	38	118	1	....	....	....	9.8	7.4	2.7	0.6	.707
63-64 Baltimore	6	....	47	31	11	24	.458	....	....	....	9	11	.818	....	....	16	0	5	0	....	....	....	7.8	5.2	2.7	0.0	.651
63-64 New York	68	....	1737	1085	445	913	.487	....	....	....	195	271	.720	....	....	398	121	212	7	....	....	....	25.5	16.0	5.9	1.8	.614
64-65 St. Louis	16	....	96	40	14	45	.311	....	....	....	12	16	.750	....	....	24	6	26	1	....	....	....	6.0	2.5	1.5	0.4	.318
64-65 LA Lakers	8	....	37	15	7	20	.350	....	....	....	1	1	1.000	....	....	12	3	6	0	....	....	....	4.6	1.9	1.5	0.4	.422
68-69 Denver-A	78	....	1760	1002	411	745	**.552**	0	0	.000	180	264	.682	145	315	460	102	289	13	....	....	149	22.6	12.8	5.9	1.3	.606
69-70 Dallas-A	24	....	181	75	30	61	.492	0	0	.000	15	24	.625	13	44	57	17	41	0	....	....	24	7.5	3.1	2.4	0.7	.526
69-70 Los Angeles-A	27	....	492	310	131	232	.565	0	0	.000	48	63	.762	33	86	119	30	79	1	....	....	42	18.2	11.5	4.4	1.1	.649
69-70 Pittsburgh-A	8	....	157	94	40	76	.526	0	0	.000	14	21	.667	9	30	39	13	20	0	....	....	18	19.6	11.8	4.9	1.6	.636
NBA Season Totals	158	....	2507	1613	658	1355	.486	....	....	....	297	418	.711	....	....	611	168	367	9	....	....	....	15.9	10.2	3.9	1.1	....
ABA Season Totals	137	....	2590	1481	612	1114	.549	0	0	.000	257	372	.691	200	475	675	162	429	14	....	....	233	18.9	10.8	4.9	1.2	....
Career Totals	295	....	5097	3094	1270	2469	.514	0	0	.000	554	790	.701	200	475	1286	330	796	23	....	....	233	17.3	10.5	4.4	1.1	....
64-65 LA Lakers	5	....	34	11	5	9	.556	....	....	....	1	1	1.000	....	....	9	2	9	1	....	....	....	6.8	2.2	1.8	0.4	.407
68-69 Denver-A	7	....	96	47	19	39	.487	0	0	.000	9	10	.900	....	....	23	6	26	2	....	....	4	13.7	6.7	3.3	0.9	.467
NBA Playoff Totals	5	....	34	11	5	9	.556	....	....	....	1	1	1.000	....	....	9	2	9	1	....	....	....	6.8	2.2	1.8	0.4	....
ABA Playoff Totals	7	....	96	47	19	39	.487	0	0	.000	9	10	.900	....	....	23	6	26	2	....	....	4	13.7	6.7	3.3	0.9	....
Career Playoff Totals	12	....	130	58	24	48	.500	0	0	.000	10	11	.909	....	....	32	8	35	3	....	....	4	10.8	4.8	2.7	0.7	....

• MCGINNIS, George

George F. McGinnis

Born: Aug. 12, 1950. Indianapolis, IN, United States. Height: 6'8". Weight: 235 lbs. Drafted: 1973 College: Indiana

YEAR TEAM	GP	GS	MIN	PTS	FGM	FGA	FG%	3PM	3PA	3P%	FTM	FTA	FT%	ORB	DRB	TRB	AST	PF	DQ	STL	BLK	TO	MPG	PPG	RPG	APG	PCM
71-72 Indiana-A	73	....	2179	1234	465	999	.465	6	38	.158	298	462	.645	290	421	711	137	260	2	....	....	256	29.8	16.9	9.7	1.9	.623
72-73 Indiana-A	82	....	3347	2261	868	1755	.495	8	32	.250	517	**778**	.665	434	588	1022	205	348	9	160	....	**401**	40.8	27.6	12.5	2.5	.697
73-74 Indiana-A	80	....	3266	2071	789	1686	.468	5	34	.147	488	**715**	.683	422	775	1197	267	325	....	159	40	**393**	40.8	25.9	15.0	3.3	.734
74-75 Indiana-A	79	....	3193	**2353**	873	**1934**	.451	62	175	.354	**545**	**753**	.724	396	730	1126	495	303	....	206	56	**422**	40.4	**29.8**	14.3	6.3	.856
75-76 Philadelphia	77	....	2946	1769	647	1552	.417	....	....	....	475	642	.740	260	707	967	359	334	13	198	41	....	38.3	23.0	12.6	4.7	.685
76-77 Philadelphia	79	....	2769	1690	659	1439	.458	....	....	....	372	546	.681	324	587	911	302	299	4	163	37	....	35.1	21.4	11.5	3.8	.701
77-78 Philadelphia	78	....	2533	1587	588	1270	.463	....	....	....	411	574	.716	282	528	810	294	287	6	137	27	312	32.5	20.3	10.4	3.8	.672
78-79 Denver	76	....	2552	1715	603	1273	.474	....	....	....	509	765	.665	256	608	864	283	321	16	129	52	**350**	33.6	22.6	11.4	3.7	.702
79-80 Denver	45	....	1424	703	268	584	.459	1	7	.143	166	307	.541	134	328	462	221	187	**8**	69	17	189	31.6	15.6	10.3	4.9	.587

YEAR	TEAM	GP	GS	MIN	PTS	FGM	FGA	FG%	3PM	3PA	3P%	FTM	FTA	FT%	ORB	DRB	TRB	AST	PF	DQ	STL	BLK	TO	MPG	PPG	RPG	APG	PCM
79-80	Indiana	28	....	784	369	132	302	.437	1	8	.125	104	181	.575	88	149	237	112	116	4	32	6	92	28.0	13.2	8.5	4.0	.531
80-81	Indiana	69	....	1845	903	348	768	.453	0	7	.000	207	385	.538	164	364	528	210	242	3	99	28	221	26.7	13.1	7.7	3.0	.517
81-82	Indiana	76	4	1341	354	141	378	.373	0	3	.000	72	159	.453	93	305	398	204	198	4	96	28	129	17.6	4.7	5.2	2.7	.437
NBA Season Totals		528	4	16194	9090	3386	7566	.448	2	25	.080	2316	3559	.651	1601	3576	5177	1985	1984	58	923	236	1293	30.7	17.2	9.8	3.8	....
ABA Season Totals		314	....	11985	7919	2995	6374	.470	81	279	.290	1848	2708	.682	1542	2514	4056	1104	1236	11	525	96	1472	38.2	25.2	12.9	3.5	....
Career Totals		842	4	28179	17009	6381	13940	.458	83	304	.273	4164	6267	.664	3143	6090	9233	3089	3220	69	1448	332	2765	33.5	20.2	11.0	3.7	....
71-72	Indiana-A	20	....	633	310	106	261	.406	4	15	.267	94	150	.627	90	137	227	52	75	....	....	....	63	31.7	15.5	11.4	2.6	.591
72-73	Indiana-A	18	....	731	431	161	357	.451	0	5	.000	109	149	.732	92	130	222	39	78	1	....	....	61	40.6	23.9	12.3	2.2	.608
73-74	Indiana-A	14	....	585	336	119	261	.456	2	7	.286	96	129	.744	68	98	166	47	50	....	16	6	46	41.8	24.0	11.9	3.4	.640
74-75	Indiana-A	18	....	731	581	213	455	.468	23	73	.315	132	192	.688	95	191	286	148	88	....	36	10	111	40.6	32.3	15.9	8.2	.983
75-76	Philadelphia	3	....	120	69	29	61	.475	....	....	....	11	18	.611	9	32	41	12	14	1	1	4	....	40.0	23.0	13.7	4.0	.678
76-77	Philadelphia	19	....	603	269	102	273	.374	....	....	....	65	114	.570	62	136	198	69	83	2	23	6	....	31.7	14.2	10.4	3.6	.520
77-78	Philadelphia	10	....	273	147	53	125	.424	....	....	....	41	49	.837	24	54	78	30	40	1	15	1	38	27.3	14.7	7.8	3.0	.534
80-81	Indiana	2	....	39	10	3	15	.200	0	0	.000	4	8	.500	2	8	10	7	6	0	2	0	5	19.5	5.0	5.0	3.5	.218
NBA Playoff Totals		34	....	1035	495	187	474	.395	0	0	.000	121	189	.640	97	230	327	118	143	4	41	11	43	30.4	14.6	9.6	3.5	....
ABA Playoff Totals		70	....	2680	1658	599	1334	.449	29	100	.290	431	620	.695	345	556	901	286	291	1	52	16	281	38.3	23.7	12.9	4.1	....
Career Playoff Totals		104	....	3715	2153	786	1808	.435	29	100	.290	552	809	.682	442	786	1228	404	434	5	93	27	324	35.7	20.7	11.8	3.9	....

• MCGLOCKLIN, Jon
Jon P. McGlocklin

Born: June 10, 1943. Franklin, IN, United States.   Height: 6'5".   Weight: 205 lbs.   Drafted: 1965   College: Indiana

YEAR	TEAM	GP	GS	MIN	PTS	FGM	FGA	FG%	3PM	3PA	3P%	FTM	FTA	FT%	ORB	DRB	TRB	AST	PF	DQ	STL	BLK	TO	MPG	PPG	RPG	APG	PCM
65-66	Cincinnati	72	....	852	368	153	363	.421	....	....	....	62	79	.785	....	....	133	88	77	0	....	....	....	11.8	5.1	1.8	1.2	.443
66-67	Cincinnati	60	....	1194	508	217	493	.440	....	....	....	74	104	.712	....	....	164	93	84	0	....	....	....	19.9	8.5	2.7	1.6	.406
67-68	San Diego	65	....	1876	788	316	757	.417	....	....	....	156	180	.867	....	....	199	178	117	0	....	....	....	28.9	12.1	3.1	2.7	.401
68-69	Milwaukee	80	....	2888	1570	662	1358	.487	....	....	....	246	292	.842	....	....	343	312	186	1	....	....	....	36.1	19.6	4.3	3.9	.534
69-70	Milwaukee	82	....	2966	1447	639	1206	.530	....	....	....	169	198	.854	....	....	252	303	164	0	....	....	....	36.2	17.6	3.1	3.7	.480
70-71	Milwaukee	82	....	2891	1292	574	1073	.535	....	....	....	144	167	.862	....	....	223	305	189	0	....	....	....	35.3	15.8	2.7	3.7	.454
71-72	Milwaukee	80	....	2213	857	374	733	.510	....	....	....	109	126	.865	....	....	181	231	146	0	....	....	....	27.7	10.7	2.3	2.9	.405
72-73	Milwaukee	80	....	1951	765	351	699	.502	....	....	....	63	73	.863	....	....	158	236	119	0	....	....	....	24.4	9.6	2.0	3.0	.418
73-74	Milwaukee	79	....	1910	730	329	693	.475	....	....	....	72	80	.900	33	106	139	241	128	1	43	7	....	24.2	9.2	1.8	3.1	.397
74-75	Milwaukee	79	....	1853	709	323	651	.496	....	....	....	63	72	.875	25	94	119	255	142	2	51	6	....	23.5	9.0	1.5	3.2	.410
75-76	Milwaukee	33	....	336	135	63	148	.426	....	....	....	9	10	.900	3	14	17	38	18	0	8	0	....	10.2	4.1	0.5	1.2	.333
NBA Season Totals		792	....	20930	9169	4001	8174	.489	....	....	....	1167	1381	.845	61	214	1928	2280	1370	4	102	13	....	26.4	11.6	2.4	2.9	....
65-66	Cincinnati	4	....	66	30	14	29	.483	....	....	....	2	2	1.000	....	....	8	4	11	0	....	....	....	16.5	7.5	2.0	1.0	.380
69-70	Milwaukee	10	....	377	149	62	144	.431	....	....	....	25	31	.806	....	....	36	21	22	0	....	....	....	37.7	14.9	3.6	2.1	.318
70-71	Milwaukee	14	....	491	208	90	168	.536	....	....	....	28	33	.848	....	....	31	34	36	0	....	....	....	35.1	14.9	2.2	2.4	.384
71-72	Milwaukee	5	....	103	35	15	35	.429	....	....	....	5	6	.833	....	....	3	6	11	0	....	....	....	20.6	7.0	0.6	1.2	.213
72-73	Milwaukee	6	....	145	61	27	53	.509	....	....	....	7	8	.875	....	....	7	13	11	0	....	....	....	24.2	10.2	1.2	2.2	.375
73-74	Milwaukee	14	....	333	118	55	111	.495	....	....	....	8	11	.727	1	15	16	44	28	0	6	1	....	23.8	8.4	1.1	3.1	.364
75-76	Milwaukee	2	....	13	6	3	4	.750	....	....	....	0	0	.000	1	0	1	1	2	0	1	0	....	6.5	3.0	0.5	0.5	.483
NBA Playoff Totals		55	....	1528	607	266	544	.489	....	....	....	75	91	.824	2	15	102	123	121	0	7	1	....	27.8	11.0	1.9	2.2	....

• MCGOWAN, Vince
Vince McGowan

Born: Aug. 12, 1913. Died: Apr.1982.   Height: 6'6".   Weight: 208 lbs.   Drafted: —   College: DePaul

YEAR	TEAM	GP	GS	MIN	PTS	FGM	FGA	FG%	3PM	3PA	3P%	FTM	FTA	FT%	ORB	DRB	TRB	AST	PF	DQ	STL	BLK	TO	MPG	PPG	RPG	APG	PCM
37-38	Whiting-N	15	....	....	144	57	....	....	....	....	....	30	....	....	....	....	....	....	....	....	....	....	....	9.6	....	....	....	
38-39	Hammond-N	24	....	....	141	48	....	....	....	....	....	45	....	....	....	....	....	....	....	....	....	....	....	5.9	....	....	....	
39-40	Hammond-N	17	....	....	82	29	....	....	....	....	....	24	....	....	....	....	....	....	....	....	....	....	....	4.8	....	....	....	
40-41	Chicago-N	17	....	....	30	10	....	....	....	....	....	10	....	....	....	....	....	....	....	....	....	....	....	1.8	....	....	....	
41-42	Chicago-N	6	....	....	13	4	....	....	....	....	....	5	....	....	....	....	....	....	....	....	....	....	....	2.2	....	....	....	
44-45	Chicago-N	27	....	....	153	54	....	....	....	....	....	45	....	....	....	....	....	....	....	....	....	....	....	5.7	....	....	....	
NBL Season Totals		106	....	....	563	202	....	....	....	....	....	159	....	....	....	....	....	....	....	....	....	....	....	5.3	....	....	....	
37-38	Whiting-N	2	....	....	11	5	....	....	....	....	....	1	....	....	....	....	....	....	....	....	....	....	....	5.5	....	....	....	
44-45	Chicago-N	3	....	....	9	1	....	....	....	....	....	7	....	....	....	....	....	....	....	....	....	....	....	3.0	....	....	....	
NBL Playoff Totals		5	....	....	20	6	....	....	....	....	....	8	....	....	....	....	....	....	....	....	....	....	....	4.0	....	....	....	

• MCGRADY, Tracy
Tracy Lamar McGrady Jr.

Born: May 24, 1979. Bartow, FL, United States.   Height: 6'8".   Weight: 210 lbs.   Drafted: 1997   College: none (HS: Mount Zion Christian Academy, NC)

YEAR	TEAM	GP	GS	MIN	PTS	FGM	FGA	FG%	3PM	3PA	3P%	FTM	FTA	FT%	ORB	DRB	TRB	AST	PF	DQ	STL	BLK	TO	MPG	PPG	RPG	APG	PCM
97-98	Toronto	64	17	1179	451	179	398	.450	14	41	.341	79	111	.712	105	164	269	98	86	0	49	61	64	18.4	7.0	4.2	1.5	.501
98-99	Toronto	49	2	1106	458	168	385	.436	8	35	.229	114	157	.726	120	158	278	113	94	1	52	66	80	22.6	9.3	5.7	2.3	.552
99-00	Toronto	79	34	2462	1213	459	1018	.451	18	65	.277	277	392	.707	188	313	501	263	201	2	90	151	160	31.2	15.4	6.3	3.3	.560
00-01	Orlando	77	77	3087	2065	788	1724	.457	59	166	.355	430	587	.733	192	388	580	352	160	0	116	118	198	40.1	26.8	7.5	4.6	.655
01-02	Orlando	76	76	2912	1948	715	1586	.451	103	283	.364	415	555	.748	150	447	597	400	139	1	119	73	189	38.3	25.6	7.9	5.3	.692
02-03	Orlando	75	74	2954	2407	829	1813	.457	173	448	.386	576	726	.793	121	367	488	411	156	0	124	59	195	39.4	**32.1**	6.5	5.5	.764
NBA Season Totals		420	280	13700	8542	3138	6924	.453	375	1038	.361	1891	2528	.748	876	1837	2713	1637	836	4	550	528	886	32.6	20.3	6.5	3.9	....
99-00	Toronto	3	3	111	50	17	44	.386	2	7	.286	14	16	.875	10	11	21	9	10	0	3	3	10	37.0	16.7	7.0	3.0	.408
00-01	Orlando	4	4	178	135	51	123	.415	2	10	.200	31	38	.816	6	20	26	33	11	0	7	5	8	44.5	33.8	6.5	8.3	.705
01-02	Orlando	4	4	178	123	42	91	.462	5	16	.313	34	46	.739	6	19	25	22	11	0	2	7	13	44.5	30.8	6.3	5.5	.625
02-03	Orlando	7	7	308	222	74	165	.448	16	47	.340	58	75	.773	10	37	47	33	16	0	14	6	26	44.0	31.7	6.7	4.7	.642
NBA Playoff Totals		18	18	775	530	184	423	.435	25	80	.313	137	175	.783	32	87	119	97	48	0	26	21	57	43.1	29.4	6.6	5.4	....

• MCGREGOR, Gil
Gilbert Ray McGregor

Born: June 14, 1949. Height: 6'8". Weight: 240 lbs. Drafted: 1971 College: Wake Forest

YEAR	TEAM	GP	GS	MIN	PTS	FGM	FGA	FG%	3PM	3PA	3P%	FTM	FTA	FT%	ORB	DRB	TRB	AST	PF	DQ	STL	BLK	TO	MPG	PPG	RPG	APG	PCM
71-72	Cincinnati	42	....	532	171	66	182	.363	....	....	....	39	56	.696	....	....	148	18	120	4	....	....	....	12.7	4.1	3.5	0.4	.301
NBA Season Totals		42	....	532	171	66	182	.363	....	....	....	39	56	.696	....	....	148	18	120	4	....	....	....	12.7	4.1	3.5	0.4	....

• MCGRIFF, Elton
Elton Wayne (Mac) McGriff

Born: Aug. 21, 1942. Corsicana, TX, United States. Height: 6'9". Weight: 225 lbs. Drafted: 1965 College: Creighton

YEAR	TEAM	GP	GS	MIN	PTS	FGM	FGA	FG%	3PM	3PA	3P%	FTM	FTA	FT%	ORB	DRB	TRB	AST	PF	DQ	STL	BLK	TO	MPG	PPG	RPG	APG	PCM
67-68	Dallas-A	20	....	369	131	49	89	.551	0	0	.000	33	62	.532	....	....	114	2	65	3	....	....	21	18.5	6.6	5.7	0.1	.422
68-69	Dallas-A	24	....	377	174	66	146	.452	0	1	.000	42	70	.600	44	66	110	6	63	0	....	....	24	15.7	7.3	4.6	0.3	.444
68-69	Kentucky-A	9	....	107	29	7	20	.350	0	0	.000	15	20	.750	13	17	30	2	20	1	....	....	7	11.9	3.2	3.3	0.2	.328
68-69	New Orleans-A	3	....	11	4	2	5	.400	0	0	.000	0	0	.000	4	0	4	0	2	0	....	....	1	3.7	1.3	1.3	0.0	.364
ABA Season Totals		56	....	864	338	124	260	.477	0	1	.000	90	152	.592	61	83	258	10	150	4	....	....	53	15.4	6.0	4.6	0.2	....
67-68	Dallas-A	8	....	206	80	30	69	.435	0	0	.000	20	38	.526	....	....	72	6	32	1	....	....	22	25.8	10.0	9.0	0.8	.455
68-69	Kentucky-A	5	....	61	23	8	22	.364	0	0	.000	7	10	.700	....	....	27	2	17	2	....	....	4	12.2	4.6	5.4	0.4	.457
ABA Playoff Totals		13	....	267	103	38	91	.418	0	0	.000	27	48	.563	....	....	99	8	49	3	....	....	26	20.5	7.9	7.6	0.6	....

• MCGUIRE, Al
Alfred James McGuire

Born: Sept. 7, 1928. New York, NY, United States. Died: Jan.25, 2001. Height: 6'2". Weight: 180 lbs. Drafted: 1951 College: St. John's (NY)

YEAR	TEAM	GP	GS	MIN	PTS	FGM	FGA	FG%	3PM	3PA	3P%	FTM	FTA	FT%	ORB	DRB	TRB	AST	PF	DQ	STL	BLK	TO	MPG	PPG	RPG	APG	PCM
51-52	New York	59	....	788	208	72	167	.431	....	....	....	64	122	.525	....	....	121	107	136	8	....	....	....	13.4	3.5	2.1	1.8	.375
52-53	New York	58	....	1231	352	112	287	.390	....	....	....	128	201	.637	....	....	167	145	206	8	....	....	....	21.2	6.1	2.9	2.5	.349
53-54	New York	64	....	849	174	58	177	.328	....	....	....	58	133	.436	....	....	121	103	144	2	....	....	....	13.3	2.7	1.9	1.6	.272
54-55	Baltimore	10	....	98	23	9	32	.281	....	....	....	5	7	.714	....	....	9	8	15	0	....	....	....	9.8	2.3	0.9	0.8	.164
NBA Season Totals		191	....	2966	757	251	663	.379	....	....	....	255	463	.551	....	....	418	363	501	18	....	....	....	15.5	4.0	2.2	1.9	....
51-52	New York	13	....	208	60	20	51	.392	....	....	....	20	27	.741	....	....	17	14	34	1	....	....	....	16.0	4.6	1.3	1.1	.257
52-53	New York	7	....	62	6	3	14	.214	....	....	....	0	7	.000	....	....	7	9	11	0	....	....	....	8.9	0.9	1.0	1.3	.130
53-54	New York	4	....	69	18	8	18	.444	....	....	....	2	9	.222	....	....	4	7	15	2	....	....	....	17.3	4.5	1.0	1.8	.217
NBA Playoff Totals		24	....	339	84	31	83	.373	....	....	....	22	43	.512	....	....	28	30	60	3	....	....	....	14.1	3.5	1.2	1.3	....

• MCGUIRE, Allie
Alfred McGuire

Born: July 10, 1951. New York, NY, United States. Height: 6'3". Weight: 175 lbs. Drafted: 1973 College: Marquette

YEAR	TEAM	GP	GS	MIN	PTS	FGM	FGA	FG%	3PM	3PA	3P%	FTM	FTA	FT%	ORB	DRB	TRB	AST	PF	DQ	STL	BLK	TO	MPG	PPG	RPG	APG	PCM
73-74	New York	2	....	10	4	2	4	.500	....	....	....	0	0	.000	0	2	2	1	2	0	0	0	....	5.0	2.0	1.0	0.5	.430
NBA Season Totals		2	....	10	4	2	4	.500	....	....	....	0	0	.000	0	2	2	1	2	0	0	0	....	5.0	2.0	1.0	0.5	....

• MCGUIRE, Dick
Richard Joseph (Tricky Dick, Dick the Knick) McGuire

Born: Jan. 25, 1926. Huntington, NY, United States. Height: 6' Weight: 180 lbs. Drafted: 1949 College: St. John's (NY) HOF: 1993

YEAR	TEAM	GP	GS	MIN	PTS	FGM	FGA	FG%	3PM	3PA	3P%	FTM	FTA	FT%	ORB	DRB	TRB	AST	PF	DQ	STL	BLK	TO	MPG	PPG	RPG	APG	PCM
49-50	New York	68	....	....	584	190	563	.337	....	....	....	204	313	.652	....	....	....	**386**	160	....	....	....	....	....	8.6	....	5.7	....
50-51	New York	64	....	....	537	179	482	.371	....	....	....	179	276	.649	....	....	334	400	154	2	....	....	....	....	8.4	5.2	6.3	....
51-52	New York	64	....	2018	591	204	474	.430	....	....	....	183	290	.631	....	....	332	388	181	4	....	....	....	31.5	9.2	5.2	6.1	.512
52-53	New York	61	....	1783	437	142	373	.381	....	....	....	153	269	.569	....	....	280	296	172	3	....	....	....	29.2	7.2	4.6	4.9	.418
53-54	New York	68	....	2343	622	201	493	.408	....	....	....	220	345	.638	....	....	310	354	190	3	....	....	....	34.5	9.1	4.6	5.2	.418
54-55	New York	71	....	2310	647	226	581	.389	....	....	....	195	303	.644	....	....	322	542	143	0	....	....	....	32.5	9.1	4.5	7.6	.521
55-56	New York	62	....	1685	425	152	438	.347	....	....	....	121	193	.627	....	....	220	362	146	0	....	....	....	27.2	6.9	3.5	5.8	.439
56-57	New York	72	....	1191	385	140	366	.383	....	....	....	105	163	.644	....	....	146	222	103	0	....	....	....	16.5	5.3	2.0	3.1	.456
57-58	Detroit	69	....	2311	556	203	544	.373	....	....	....	150	225	.667	....	....	291	454	178	0	....	....	....	33.5	8.1	4.2	6.6	.435
58-59	Detroit	71	....	2063	655	232	543	.427	....	....	....	191	258	.740	....	....	285	443	147	1	....	....	....	29.1	9.2	4.0	6.2	.537
59-60	Detroit	68	....	1466	482	179	402	.445	....	....	....	124	201	.617	....	....	264	358	112	0	....	....	....	21.6	7.1	3.9	5.3	.605
NBA Season Totals		738	....	17170	5921	2048	5259	.389	....	....	....	1825	2836	.644	....	....	2784	4205	1686	13	....	....	....	23.3	8.0	3.8	5.7	....
49-50	New York	5	....	....	63	22	52	.423	....	....	....	19	26	.731	....	....	....	27	21	....	....	....	....	....	12.6	....	5.4	....
50-51	New York	14	....	....	74	25	80	.313	....	....	....	24	53	.453	....	....	83	78	50	1	....	....	....	....	5.3	5.9	5.6	....
51-52	New York	14	....	546	145	48	107	.449	....	....	....	49	86	.570	....	....	71	90	46	1	....	....	....	39.0	10.4	5.1	6.4	.440
52-53	New York	11	....	360	83	24	59	.407	....	....	....	35	55	.636	....	....	63	70	25	0	....	....	....	32.7	7.5	5.7	6.4	.490
53-54	New York	4	....	68	11	4	16	.250	....	....	....	3	5	.600	....	....	4	5	12	0	....	....	....	17.0	2.8	1.0	1.3	.100
54-55	New York	3	....	75	20	6	19	.316	....	....	....	8	12	.667	....	....	9	12	7	0	....	....	....	25.0	6.7	3.0	4.0	.371
57-58	Detroit	7	....	236	67	25	60	.417	....	....	....	17	24	.708	....	....	33	40	13	0	....	....	....	33.7	9.6	4.7	5.7	.462
58-59	Detroit	3	....	109	47	20	32	.625	....	....	....	7	11	.636	....	....	17	19	10	0	....	....	....	36.3	15.7	5.7	6.3	.635
59-60	Detroit	2	....	42	11	5	12	.417	....	....	....	1	3	.333	....	....	4	9	3	0	....	....	....	21.0	5.5	2.0	4.5	.429
NBA Playoff Totals		63	....	1436	521	179	437	.410	....	....	....	163	275	.593	....	....	284	350	187	2	....	....	....	22.8	8.3	4.5	5.6	....

• MCHALE, Kevin
Kevin Edward McHale

Born: Dec. 19, 1957. Hibbing, MN, United States. Height: 6'10". Weight: 210 lbs. Drafted: 1980 College: Minnesota HOF: 1999

YEAR	TEAM	GP	GS	MIN	PTS	FGM	FGA	FG%	3PM	3PA	3P%	FTM	FTA	FT%	ORB	DRB	TRB	AST	PF	DQ	STL	BLK	TO	MPG	PPG	RPG	APG	PCM
80-81	Boston	82	....	1645	818	355	666	.533	0	2	.000	108	159	.679	155	204	359	55	260	3	27	151	107	20.1	10.0	4.4	0.7	.513
81-82	Boston	82	33	2332	1117	465	875	.531	0	0	.000	187	248	.754	191	365	556	91	264	1	30	185	139	28.4	13.6	6.8	1.1	.545
82-83	Boston	82	13	2345	1159	483	893	.541	0	1	.000	193	269	.717	215	338	553	104	241	3	34	192	156	28.6	14.1	6.7	1.3	.564
83-84	Boston	82	10	2577	1511	587	1055	.556	1	3	.333	336	439	.765	208	402	610	104	243	5	23	126	148	31.4	18.4	7.4	1.3	.619
84-85	Boston	79	31	2653	1565	605	1062	.570	0	6	.000	355	467	.760	229	483	712	141	234	3	28	120	158	33.6	19.8	9.0	1.8	.672
85-86	Boston	68	62	2397	1448	561	978	.574	0	0	.000	326	420	.776	171	380	551	181	192	2	29	134	150	35.3	21.3	8.1	2.7	.687
86-87	Boston	77	77	3060	2008	790	1307	**.604**	0	4	.000	428	512	.836	247	516	763	198	240	1	38	172	200	39.7	26.1	9.9	2.6	.754
87-88	Boston	64	63	2390	1446	550	911	**.604**	0	0	.000	346	434	.797	159	377	536	171	179	1	27	92	141	37.3	22.6	8.4	2.7	.689
88-89	Boston	78	74	2876	1758	661	1211	.546	0	4	.000	436	533	.818	223	414	637	172	223	2	26	97	195	36.9	22.5	8.2	2.2	.628
89-90	Boston	82	25	2722	1712	648	1181	.549	23	69	.333	393	440	.893	201	476	677	172	250	3	30	157	180	33.2	20.9	8.3	2.1	.697
90-91	Boston	68	10	2067	1251	504	912	.553	15	37	.405	228	275	.829	145	335	480	126	194	2	25	146	143	30.4	18.4	7.1	1.9	.661

YEAR	TEAM	GP	GS	MIN	PTS	FGM	FGA	FG%	3PM	3PA	3P%	FTM	FTA	FT%	ORB	DRB	TRB	AST	PF	DQ	STL	BLK	TO	MPG	PPG	RPG	APG	PCM
91-92	Boston	56	1	1398	780	323	634	.509	0	13	.000	134	163	.822	119	211	330	82	112	1	11	59	84	25.0	13.9	5.9	1.5	.577
92-93	Boston	71	0	1656	762	298	649	.459	2	18	.111	164	195	.841	95	263	358	73	126	0	16	58	92	23.3	10.7	5.0	1.0	.457
NBA Season Totals		971	399	30118	17335	6830	12334	.554	41	157	.261	3634	4554	.798	2358	4764	7122	1670	2758	27	344	1689	1893	31.0	17.9	7.3	1.7	....
80-81	Boston	17	....	296	145	61	113	.540	0	0	.000	23	36	.639	29	30	59	14	51	1	4	25	15	17.4	8.5	3.5	0.8	.508
81-82	Boston	12	0	344	194	77	134	.575	0	0	.000	40	53	.755	41	44	85	11	44	0	5	27	16	28.7	16.2	7.1	0.9	.640
82-83	Boston	7	1	177	78	34	62	.548	0	1	.000	10	18	.556	15	27	42	5	16	0	3	7	10	25.3	11.1	6.0	0.7	.482
83-84	Boston	23	0	702	340	123	244	.504	0	3	.000	94	121	.777	62	81	143	27	75	1	3	35	38	30.5	14.8	6.2	1.2	.487
84-85	Boston	21	21	837	465	172	303	.568	0	0	.000	121	150	.807	74	134	208	32	73	3	13	46	60	39.9	22.1	9.9	1.5	.624
85-86	Boston	18	18	715	448	168	290	.579	0	1	.000	112	141	.794	51	104	155	48	64	0	8	43	48	39.7	24.9	8.6	2.7	.685
86-87	Boston	21	19	827	444	174	298	.584	0	1	.000	96	126	.762	66	128	194	39	71	2	7	30	54	39.4	21.1	9.2	1.9	.590
87-88	Boston	17	17	716	432	158	262	.603	1	1	1.000	115	137	.839	55	81	136	40	65	1	7	30	39	42.1	25.4	8.0	2.4	.645
88-89	Boston	3	3	115	57	20	41	.488	0	0	.000	17	23	.739	7	17	24	9	13	0	1	2	4	38.3	19.0	8.0	3.0	.519
89-90	Boston	5	5	192	110	42	69	.609	1	3	.333	25	29	.862	8	31	39	13	17	0	2	10	14	38.4	22.0	7.8	2.6	.642
90-91	Boston	11	1	376	228	78	148	.527	6	11	.545	66	80	.825	18	54	72	20	42	0	5	14	14	34.2	20.7	6.5	1.8	.611
91-92	Boston	10	0	306	165	65	126	.516	0	1	.000	35	44	.795	21	46	67	13	34	0	5	5	9	30.6	16.5	6.7	1.3	.541
92-93	Boston	4	0	113	76	32	55	.582	0	0	.000	12	14	.857	9	20	29	3	6	0	2	7	5	28.3	19.0	7.3	0.8	.750
NBA Playoff Totals		169	85	5716	3182	1204	2145	.561	8	21	.381	766	972	.788	456	797	1253	274	571	8	65	281	326	33.8	18.8	7.4	1.6	....

• MCHARTLEY, Maurice

Maurice Franklin (Reese, Toothpick) McHartley

Born: Aug. 1, 1942. Detroit, MI, United States.   Height: 6'3".   Weight: 185 lbs.   Drafted: 1964   College: North Carolina A&T

YEAR	TEAM	GP	GS	MIN	PTS	FGM	FGA	FG%	3PM	3PA	3P%	FTM	FTA	FT%	ORB	DRB	TRB	AST	PF	DQ	STL	BLK	TO	MPG	PPG	RPG	APG	PCM
67-68	Dallas-A	58	....	2175	888	330	825	.400	3	17	.176	225	324	.694	....	....	273	230	216	5	....		241	37.5	15.3	4.7	4.0	.387
68-69	Miami-A	52	....	1503	752	283	696	.407	6	23	.261	180	224	.804	38	97	135	193	165	4	....		189	28.9	14.5	2.6	3.7	.429
68-69	New York-A	24	....	645	297	107	266	.402	0	4	.000	83	107	.776	27	49	76	76	86	1	....		80	26.9	12.4	3.2	3.2	.411
69-70	Dallas-A	27	....	293	147	56	138	.406	4	28	.143	31	41	.756	15	29	44	42	59	1	....		44	10.9	5.4	1.6	1.6	.453
69-70	Miami-A	11	....	319	111	42	118	.356	0	3	.000	27	37	.730	11	21	32	45	51	1	....		46	29.0	10.1	2.9	4.1	.309
69-70	Pittsburgh-A	17	....	380	156	57	132	.432	2	5	.400	40	52	.769	16	23	39	55	48	1	....		59	22.4	9.2	2.3	3.2	.427
ABA Season Totals		189	....	5315	2351	875	2175	.402	15	80	.188	586	785	.746	107	219	599	641	625	13	....		659	28.1	12.4	3.2	3.4	....
67-68	Dallas-A	8	....	279	146	59	139	.424	0	2	.000	28	38	.737	....	....	45	28	40	2	....		35	34.9	18.3	5.6	3.5	.462
68-69	Miami-A	12	....	369	174	60	173	.347	0	4	.000	54	66	.818	....	....	42	50	48	1	....		44	30.8	14.5	3.5	4.2	.391
68-69	Dallas-A	5	....	51	26	8	25	.320	2	3	.667	8	10	.800	5	6	11	0	0	0	....		6	10.2	5.2	2.2	0.0	
ABA Playoff Totals		25	....	699	346	127	337	.377	2	9	.222	90	114	.789	5	6	98	78	88	3	....		85	28.0	13.8	3.9	3.1	....

• MCILVAINE, Jim

James Michael McIlvaine

Born: July 30, 1972. Racine, WI, United States.   Height: 7'1".   Weight: 240 lbs.   Drafted: 1994   College: Marquette

YEAR	TEAM	GP	GS	MIN	PTS	FGM	FGA	FG%	3PM	3PA	3P%	FTM	FTA	FT%	ORB	DRB	TRB	AST	PF	DQ	STL	BLK	TO	MPG	PPG	RPG	APG	PCM
94-95	Washington	55	0	534	96	34	71	.479	0	0	.000	28	41	.683	40	65	105	10	95	0	10	60	17	9.7	1.7	1.9	0.2	.317
95-96	Washington	80	6	1195	182	62	145	.428	0	0	.000	58	105	.552	66	164	230	11	171	0	21	166	40	14.9	2.3	2.9	0.1	.308
96-97	Seattle	82	79	1477	314	130	276	.471	1	7	.143	53	107	.495	132	198	330	23	247	4	39	164	66	18.0	3.8	4.0	0.3	.337
97-98	Seattle	78	72	1211	247	101	223	.453	0	3	.000	45	81	.556	96	163	259	19	240	3	24	137	55	15.5	3.2	3.3	0.2	.300
98-99	New Jersey	22	1	269	48	22	51	.431	0	0	.000	4	6	.667	31	23	54	2	59	1	9	32	13	12.2	2.2	2.5	0.1	.261
99-00	New Jersey	66	53	1048	157	64	154	.416	0	0	.000	29	56	.518	106	124	230	36	205	2	26	117	38	15.9	2.4	3.5	0.5	.299
00-01	New Jersey	18	3	193	28	10	28	.357	0	0	.000	8	12	.667	8	27	35	4	35	0	7	15	9	10.7	1.6	1.9	0.2	.217
NBA Season Totals		401	214	5927	1072	423	948	.446	1	10	.100	225	408	.551	479	764	1243	105	1052	10	136	691	238	14.8	2.7	3.1	0.3	....
96-97	Seattle	5	0	28	9	4	7	.571	0	0	.000	1	2	.500	1	1	2	0	7	0	1	2	1	5.6	1.8	0.4	0.0	.222
97-98	Seattle	6	4	59	13	6	20	.300	0	1	.000	1	2	.500	7	3	10	1	22	1	2	6	1	9.8	2.2	1.7	0.2	.107
NBA Playoff Totals		11	4	87	22	10	27	.370	0	1	.000	2	4	.500	8	4	12	1	29	1	3	8	2	7.9	2.0	1.1	0.1	....

• MCINNIS, Jeff

Jeff Lemans McInnis

Born: Oct. 22, 1974. Charlotte, NC, United States.   Height: 6'4".   Weight: 190 lbs.   Drafted: 1996   College: North Carolina

YEAR	TEAM	GP	GS	MIN	PTS	FGM	FGA	FG%	3PM	3PA	3P%	FTM	FTA	FT%	ORB	DRB	TRB	AST	PF	DQ	STL	BLK	TO	MPG	PPG	RPG	APG	PCM
96-97	Denver	13	0	117	65	23	49	.469	12	26	.462	7	10	.700	2	4	6	18	16	0	2	1	13	9.0	5.0	0.5	1.4	.405
98-99	Washington	35	6	427	130	50	134	.373	9	35	.257	21	28	.750	9	12	21	73	36	0	19	1	30	12.2	3.7	0.6	2.1	.298
99-00	LA Clippers	25	10	597	180	80	186	.430	7	21	.333	13	17	.765	18	54	72	89	55	0	15	2	27	23.9	7.2	2.9	3.6	.353
00-01	LA Clippers	81	81	2831	1046	432	933	.463	52	144	.361	130	161	.807	41	179	220	447	199	2	75	7	113	35.0	12.9	2.7	5.5	.408
01-02	LA Clippers	81	80	3030	1184	463	1121	.413	75	234	.321	183	219	.836	45	168	213	500	202	6	63	6	147	37.4	14.6	2.6	6.2	.379
02-03	Portland	75	1	1310	432	188	423	.444	6	35	.171	50	67	.746	22	75	97	170	117	1	21	2	75	17.5	5.8	1.3	2.3	.293
NBA Season Totals		310	178	8312	3037	1236	2846	.434	161	495	.325	404	502	.805	137	492	629	1297	625	5	195	19	405	26.8	9.8	2.0	4.2	....
02-03	Portland	7	0	99	21	9	26	.346	0	3	.000	3	4	.750	5	7	12	19	11	0	2	1	6	14.1	3.0	1.7	2.7	.293
NBA Playoff Totals		7	0	99	21	9	26	.346	0	3	.000	3	4	.750	5	7	12	19	11	0	2	1	6	14.1	3.0	1.7	2.7	

• MCINTOSH, Kenny

Kennedy McIntosh

Born: Jan. 21, 1949. Detroit, MI, United States.   Height: 6'7".   Weight: 225 lbs.   Drafted: 1971   College: Eastern Michigan

YEAR	TEAM	GP	GS	MIN	PTS	FGM	FGA	FG%	3PM	3PA	3P%	FTM	FTA	FT%	ORB	DRB	TRB	AST	PF	DQ	STL	BLK	TO	MPG	PPG	RPG	APG	PCM
71-72	Chicago	43	....	405	135	57	168	.339	....	....	....	21	44	.477	....	....	89	18	41	0	....			9.4	3.1	2.1	0.4	.269
72-73	Chicago	3	....	33	16	8	13	.615	....	....	....	0	2	.000	....	....	9	1	4	0	....			11.0	5.3	3.0	0.3	.545
72-73	Seattle	56	....	1105	254	107	328	.326	....	....	....	40	65	.615	....	....	222	53	98	0	....			19.7	4.5	4.0	0.9	.238
73-74	Seattle	69	....	2056	511	223	573	.389	....	....	....	65	107	.607	111	250	361	94	178	4	52	29	....	29.8	7.4	5.2	1.4	.260
74-75	Seattle	6	....	101	18	6	29	.207	....	....	....	6	9	.667	6	9	15	7	12	0	4	3	....	16.8	3.0	2.5	1.2	.127
NBA Season Totals		177	....	3700	934	401	1111	.361	....	....	....	132	227	.581	117	259	696	173	333	4	56	32	....	20.9	5.3	3.9	1.0	....

• MCINTYRE, Bob

Robert McIntyre

Born: Jan. 23, 1944. Height: 6'6". Weight: 215 lbs. Drafted: 1966 College: St. John's (NY)

YEAR	TEAM	GP	GS	MIN	PTS	FGM	FGA	FG%	3PM	3PA	3P%	FTM	FTA	FT%	ORB	DRB	TRB	AST	PF	DQ	STL	BLK	TO	MPG	PPG	RPG	APG	PCM
67-68	New Jersey-A	21	....	451	174	70	187	.374	0	1	.000	34	58	.586	....	....	101	11	27	0	....	....	27	21.5	8.3	4.8	0.5	.338
69-70	New York-A	7	....	94	25	12	32	.375	1	3	.333	0	1	.000	9	11	20	5	8	0	....	....	6	13.4	3.6	2.9	0.7	.286
ABA Season Totals		28	....	545	199	82	219	.374	1	4	.250	34	59	.576	9	11	121	16	35	0	....	....	33	19.5	7.1	4.3	0.6	....

• MCKEE, Jerry

Gerald McKee

Born: Aug. 4, 1946. Height: 6'3". Weight: 190 lbs. Drafted: 1969 College: Ohio University

YEAR	TEAM	GP	GS	MIN	PTS	FGM	FGA	FG%	3PM	3PA	3P%	FTM	FTA	FT%	ORB	DRB	TRB	AST	PF	DQ	STL	BLK	TO	MPG	PPG	RPG	APG	PCM
69-70	Indiana-A	1	....	3	0	0	1	.000	0	0	.000	0	0	.000	0	0	0	0	0	0	....	....	1	3.0	0.0	0.0	0.0	-.286
ABA Season Totals		1	....	3	0	0	1	.000	0	0	.000	0	0	.000	0	0	0	0	0	0	....	....	1	3.0	0.0	0.0	0.0	....

• MCKENNA, Kevin

Kevin Robert McKenna

Born: Jan. 8, 1959. St. Paul, MN, United States. Height: 6'5". Weight: 195 lbs. Drafted: 1981 College: Creighton

YEAR	TEAM	GP	GS	MIN	PTS	FGM	FGA	FG%	3PM	3PA	3P%	FTM	FTA	FT%	ORB	DRB	TRB	AST	PF	DQ	STL	BLK	TO	MPG	PPG	RPG	APG	PCM
81-82	LA Lakers	36	0	237	67	28	87	.322	0	2	.000	11	17	.647	18	11	29	14	45	0	10	2	22	6.6	1.9	0.8	0.4	.092
83-84	Indiana	61	13	923	387	152	371	.410	3	17	.176	80	98	.816	30	65	95	114	133	3	46	5	61	15.1	6.3	1.6	1.9	.340
84-85	New Jersey	29	7	535	165	61	134	.455	5	13	.385	38	43	.884	20	29	49	58	63	0	30	7	32	18.4	5.7	1.7	2.0	.332
85-86	Washington	30	1	430	174	61	166	.367	27	75	.360	25	30	.833	9	27	36	23	54	1	29	2	18	14.3	5.8	1.2	0.8	.277
86-87	New Jersey	56	3	942	401	153	337	.454	52	124	.419	43	57	.754	21	56	77	93	141	0	54	7	50	16.8	7.2	1.4	1.7	.360
87-88	New Jersey	31	2	393	126	43	109	.394	16	50	.320	24	25	.960	4	27	31	40	55	1	15	2	19	12.7	4.1	1.0	1.3	.275
NBA Season Totals		243	26	3460	1320	498	1204	.414	103	281	.367	221	270	.819	102	215	317	342	491	5	184	25	202	14.2	5.4	1.3	1.4	....
85-86	Washington	1	0	2	0	0	0	.000	0	0	.000	0	0	.000	0	0	0	0	0	0	0	0	0	2.0	0.0	0.0	0.0	.000
NBA Playoff Totals		1	0	2	0	0	0	.000	0	0	.000	0	0	.000	0	0	0	0	0	0	0	0	0	2.0	0.0	0.0	0.0	....

• MCKENZIE, Forrest

Forrest David Walton McKenzie

Born: Feb. 16, 1963. Camden, NJ, United States. Height: 6'7". Weight: 200 lbs. Drafted: 1986 College: Loyola Marymount

YEAR	TEAM	GP	GS	MIN	PTS	FGM	FGA	FG%	3PM	3PA	3P%	FTM	FTA	FT%	ORB	DRB	TRB	AST	PF	DQ	STL	BLK	TO	MPG	PPG	RPG	APG	PCM
86-87	San Antonio	6	0	42	17	7	28	.250	1	2	.500	2	2	1.000	2	5	7	1	9	0	1	0	3	7.0	2.8	1.2	0.2	-.024
NBA Season Totals		6	0	42	17	7	28	.250	1	2	.500	2	2	1.000	2	5	7	1	9	0	1	0	3	7.0	2.8	1.2	0.2	....

• MCKENZIE, Stan

Stanley McKenzie

Born: Oct. 6, 1944. Miami, FL, United States. Height: 6'5". Weight: 195 lbs. Drafted: 1966 College: New York University

YEAR	TEAM	GP	GS	MIN	PTS	FGM	FGA	FG%	3PM	3PA	3P%	FTM	FTA	FT%	ORB	DRB	TRB	AST	PF	DQ	STL	BLK	TO	MPG	PPG	RPG	APG	PCM
67-68	Baltimore	50	....	653	204	73	182	.401	....	....	....	58	88	.659	....	....	121	24	98	1	....	....	....	13.1	4.1	2.4	0.5	.293
68-69	Phoenix	80	....	1569	747	264	618	.427	....	....	....	219	287	.763	....	....	251	123	191	3	....	....	....	19.6	9.3	3.1	1.5	.443
69-70	Phoenix	58	....	525	220	81	206	.393	....	....	....	58	73	.795	....	....	93	52	67	1	....	....	....	9.1	3.8	1.6	0.9	.408
70-71	Portland	82	....	2290	1127	398	902	.441	....	....	....	331	396	.836	....	....	309	235	238	2	....	....	....	27.9	13.7	3.8	2.9	.479
71-72	Portland	82	....	2036	1135	410	834	.492	....	....	....	315	379	.831	....	....	272	148	240	2	....	....	....	24.8	13.8	3.3	1.8	.511
72-73	Portland	7	....	107	40	13	36	.361	....	....	....	14	16	.875	....	....	21	8	15	0	....	....	....	15.3	5.7	3.0	1.1	.375
72-73	Houston	26	....	187	86	35	83	.422	....	....	....	16	21	.762	....	....	34	15	28	0	....	....	....	7.2	3.3	1.3	0.6	.412
73-74	Houston	11	....	112	20	7	24	.292	....	....	....	6	8	.750	3	13	16	6	17	0	3	0	....	10.2	1.8	1.5	0.5	.160
NBA Season Totals		396	....	7479	3579	1281	2885	.444	....	....	....	1017	1268	.802	3	13	1117	611	894	9	3	0	....	18.9	9.0	2.8	1.5	....
69-70	Phoenix	7	....	71	20	8	29	.276	....	....	....	4	5	.800	....	....	9	3	14	0	....	....	....	10.1	2.9	1.3	0.4	.087
NBA Playoff Totals		7	....	71	20	8	29	.276	....	....	....	4	5	.800	....	....	9	3	14	0	....	....	....	10.1	2.9	1.3	0.4	....

• MCKEY, Derrick

Derrick Wayne (Heavy D) McKey

Born: Oct. 10, 1966. Meridian, MS, United States. Height: 6'9". Weight: 205 lbs. Drafted: 1987 College: Alabama

YEAR	TEAM	GP	GS	MIN	PTS	FGM	FGA	FG%	3PM	3PA	3P%	FTM	FTA	FT%	ORB	DRB	TRB	AST	PF	DQ	STL	BLK	TO	MPG	PPG	RPG	APG	PCM
87-88	Seattle	82	4	1706	694	255	519	.491	11	30	.367	173	224	.772	115	213	328	107	237	3	70	63	107	20.8	8.5	4.0	1.3	.444
88-89	Seattle	82	82	2804	1305	487	970	.502	30	89	.337	301	375	.803	167	297	464	219	264	4	105	70	189	34.2	15.9	5.7	2.7	.482
89-90	Seattle	80	80	2748	1254	468	949	.493	3	23	.130	315	403	.782	170	319	489	187	247	2	87	81	192	34.4	15.7	6.1	2.3	.466
90-91	Seattle	73	55	2503	1115	438	847	.517	4	19	.211	235	278	.845	172	251	423	169	220	2	91	56	161	34.3	15.3	5.8	2.3	.468
91-92	Seattle	52	44	1757	777	285	604	.472	19	50	.380	188	222	.847	95	173	268	120	142	2	61	47	114	33.8	14.9	5.2	2.3	.439
92-93	Seattle	77	68	2439	1034	387	780	.496	40	112	.357	220	297	.741	121	206	327	197	208	5	105	59	154	31.7	13.4	4.2	2.6	.434
93-94	Indiana	76	76	2613	911	355	710	.500	9	31	.290	192	254	.756	129	273	402	327	248	1	111	49	228	34.4	12.0	5.3	4.3	.422
94-95	Indiana	81	81	2805	1075	411	833	.493	32	89	.360	221	297	.744	125	269	394	276	260	5	125	49	170	34.6	13.3	4.9	3.4	.424
95-96	Indiana	75	75	2440	879	346	712	.486	17	68	.250	170	221	.769	123	238	361	262	246	4	83	44	143	32.5	11.7	4.8	3.5	.409
96-97	Indiana	50	49	1449	400	148	379	.391	15	58	.259	89	123	.724	80	161	241	135	141	1	47	30	85	29.0	8.0	4.8	2.7	.321
97-98	Indiana	57	4	1316	359	150	327	.459	4	17	.235	55	77	.714	74	137	211	88	156	1	57	30	80	23.1	6.3	3.7	1.5	.312
98-99	Indiana	13	0	244	60	23	52	.442	0	1	.000	14	17	.824	18	23	41	13	24	0	12	4	12	18.8	4.6	3.2	1.0	.314
99-00	Indiana	32	1	634	139	43	108	.398	10	23	.435	43	56	.768	29	106	135	35	81	0	29	13	19	19.8	4.3	4.2	1.1	.345
00-01	Indiana	66	20	987	145	60	136	.441	4	20	.200	21	27	.778	49	127	176	74	136	1	48	13	47	15.0	2.2	2.7	1.1	.269
01-02	Philadelphia	41	1	784	119	52	122	.426	5	12	.417	10	14	.714	48	79	127	45	90	0	41	4	22	19.1	2.9	3.1	1.1	.253
NBA Season Totals		937	640	27229	10266	3908	8048	.486	203	642	.316	2247	2885	.779	1515	2872	4387	2254	2700	31	1072	612	1723	29.1	11.0	4.7	2.4	....
87-88	Seattle	5	0	109	60	24	38	.632	2	6	.333	10	17	.588	7	13	20	8	12	0	3	5	5	21.8	12.0	4.0	1.6	.625
88-89	Seattle	8	8	286	106	44	89	.494	1	9	.111	17	21	.810	21	31	52	18	33	1	6	15	23	35.8	13.3	6.5	2.3	.394
90-91	Seattle	4	0	114	38	16	28	.571	0	1	.000	6	11	.545	7	16	23	8	13	0	3	0	6	28.5	9.5	5.8	2.0	.400
91-92	Seattle	9	9	315	147	52	99	.525	5	16	.313	38	45	.844	17	27	44	24	37	1	7	12	22	35.0	16.3	4.9	2.7	.466
92-93	Seattle	19	17	647	214	83	158	.525	2	5	.400	46	69	.667	51	47	98	71	51	0	12	17	36	34.1	11.3	5.2	3.7	.418
93-94	Indiana	16	16	587	155	58	142	.408	8	24	.333	31	47	.660	32	66	98	67	59	1	26	9	40	36.7	9.7	6.1	4.2	.343
94-95	Indiana	17	17	592	217	76	174	.437	11	35	.314	54	62	.871	29	52	81	64	65	2	17	11	36	34.8	12.8	4.8	3.8	.384
95-96	Indiana	5	5	180	64	24	57	.421	5	12	.417	11	13	.846	8	25	33	10	20	0	7	1	14	36.0	12.8	6.6	2.0	.326
97-98	Indiana	15	0	284	67	23	69	.333	3	10	.300	18	23	.783	8	32	40	11	50	0	9	8	11	18.9	4.5	2.7	0.7	.189
98-99	Indiana	13	0	245	47	15	40	.375	0	4	.000	17	26	.654	17	26	43	19	39	0	12	4	11	18.8	3.6	3.3	1.5	.274
99-00	Indiana	23	0	352	47	15	32	.469	1	6	.167	16	20	.800	25	54	79	14	45	0	7	4	19	15.3	2.0	3.4	0.6	.253

YEAR	TEAM	GP	GS	MIN	PTS	FGM	FGA	FG%	3PM	3PA	3P%	FTM	FTA	FT%	ORB	DRB	TRB	AST	PF	DQ	STL	BLK	TO	MPG	PPG	RPG	APG	PCM
00-01	Indiana	4	0	35	6	2	5	.400	1	1	1.000	1	2	.500	4	5	9	4	7	0	1	0	1	8.8	1.5	2.3	1.0	.349
01-02	Philadelphia	4	0	40	8	4	8	.500	0	0	.000	0	0	.000	3	3	6	1	5	0	1	2	1	10.0	2.0	1.5	0.3	.261
NBA Playoff Totals		142	72	3786	1176	436	939	.464	39	129	.302	265	356	.744	229	397	626	319	436	5	111	88	225	26.7	8.3	4.4	2.2	....

• MCKIE, Aaron

Aaron Fitzgerald McKie

Born: Oct. 2, 1972. Philadelphia, PA, United States. Height: 6'5". Weight: 209 lbs. Drafted: 1994 College: Temple

YEAR	TEAM	GP	GS	MIN	PTS	FGM	FGA	FG%	3PM	3PA	3P%	FTM	FTA	FT%	ORB	DRB	TRB	AST	PF	DQ	STL	BLK	TO	MPG	PPG	RPG	APG	PCM
94-95	Portland	45	20	827	293	116	261	.444	11	28	.393	50	73	.685	35	94	129	89	97	1	36	16	41	18.4	6.5	2.9	2.0	.395
95-96	Portland	81	73	2259	864	337	722	.467	38	117	.325	152	199	.764	86	218	304	205	205	5	92	21	138	27.9	10.7	3.8	2.5	.382
96-97	Portland	41	8	775	170	53	156	.340	23	55	.418	41	49	.837	13	80	93	84	61	1	34	15	49	18.9	4.1	2.3	2.0	.282
96-97	Detroit	42	3	850	263	97	209	.464	18	48	.375	51	61	.836	27	101	128	77	69	0	43	7	42	20.2	6.3	3.0	1.8	.389
97-98	Detroit	24	1	472	109	43	104	.413	3	17	.176	20	23	.870	24	44	68	38	47	0	23	1	24	19.7	4.5	2.8	1.6	.283
97-98	Philadelphia	57	31	1341	223	96	277	.347	9	46	.196	22	32	.688	34	129	163	137	117	0	78	12	51	23.5	3.9	2.9	2.4	.248
98-99	Philadelphia	50	4	959	240	95	237	.401	6	31	.194	44	62	.710	27	113	140	100	90	1	63	3	57	19.2	4.8	2.8	2.0	.323
99-00	Philadelphia	82	14	1952	653	244	593	.411	44	121	.364	121	146	.829	47	199	246	240	194	3	108	18	113	23.8	8.0	3.0	2.9	.376
00-01	Philadelphia	76	33	2394	878	338	714	.473	53	170	.312	149	194	.768	33	278	311	377	178	3	106	8	203	31.5	11.6	4.1	5.0	.441
01-02	Philadelphia	48	16	1470	587	220	490	.449	51	128	.398	96	122	.787	26	166	192	179	74	0	56	14	93	30.6	12.2	4.0	3.7	.439
02-03	Philadelphia	80	40	2375	721	286	666	.429	37	112	.330	112	134	.836	61	289	350	278	177	2	131	9	109	29.7	9.0	4.4	3.5	.394
NBA Season Totals		626	243	15674	5001	1925	4429	.435	293	873	.336	858	1095	.784	413	1711	2124	1804	1309	16	770	124	920	25.0	8.0	3.4	2.9	....
94-95	Portland	3	0	34	17	8	14	.571	1	2	.500	0	0	.000	0	2	2	1	4	0	3	0	0	11.3	5.7	0.7	0.3	.448
95-96	Portland	5	4	134	31	11	30	.367	2	8	.250	7	9	.778	4	14	18	9	13	0	6	2	9	26.8	6.2	3.6	1.8	.236
96-97	Detroit	5	0	97	15	7	20	.350	1	5	.200	0	0	.000	1	9	10	10	12	0	6	2	3	19.4	3.0	2.0	2.0	.226
98-99	Philadelphia	6	0	97	20	7	23	.304	0	1	.000	6	7	.857	4	11	15	11	17	0	4	0	1	16.2	3.3	2.5	1.8	.268
99-00	Philadelphia	10	6	331	138	50	103	.485	12	35	.343	26	31	.839	4	32	36	46	26	0	4	2	16	33.1	13.8	3.6	4.6	.452
00-01	Philadelphia	23	16	892	336	125	301	.415	27	64	.422	59	75	.787	24	95	119	121	67	0	34	3	46	38.8	14.6	5.2	5.3	.418
01-02	Philadelphia	5	0	146	53	20	46	.435	6	16	.375	7	10	.700	2	16	18	12	12	0	10	0	10	29.2	10.6	3.6	2.4	.357
02-03	Philadelphia	12	0	315	93	38	71	.535	5	9	.556	12	14	.857	5	38	43	22	31	0	10	2	15	26.3	7.8	3.6	1.8	.344
NBA Playoff Totals		69	26	2046	703	266	608	.438	54	140	.386	117	146	.801	44	217	261	232	182	0	77	11	100	29.7	10.2	3.8	3.4	....

• MCKINNEY, Billy

William Mervin (Billy) McKinney

Born: June 5, 1955. Waukegan, IL, United States. Height: 6' Weight: 160 lbs. Drafted: 1977 College: Northwestern

YEAR	TEAM	GP	GS	MIN	PTS	FGM	FGA	FG%	3PM	3PA	3P%	FTM	FTA	FT%	ORB	DRB	TRB	AST	PF	DQ	STL	BLK	TO	MPG	PPG	RPG	APG	PCM
78-79	Kansas City	78	....	1242	609	240	477	.503	....	....	....	129	162	.796	20	65	85	253	121	0	58	3	125	15.9	7.8	1.1	3.2	.503
79-80	Kansas City	76	....	1333	520	206	459	.449	1	10	.100	107	133	.805	20	66	86	248	87	0	58	5	91	17.5	6.8	1.1	3.3	.423
80-81	Utah	35	....	1032	293	124	233	.532	1	2	.500	44	48	.917	12	62	74	157	107	3	38	4	70	29.5	8.4	2.1	4.5	.345
80-81	Denver	49	....	1134	525	203	412	.493	1	10	.100	118	140	.843	24	86	110	203	124	0	61	7	88	23.1	10.7	2.2	4.1	.504
81-82	Denver	81	27	1963	875	369	699	.528	0	17	.000	137	170	.806	29	113	142	338	186	0	69	16	113	24.2	10.8	1.8	4.2	.479
82-83	Denver	68	38	1559	668	266	546	.487	0	7	.000	136	167	.814	21	100	121	288	142	0	39	5	102	22.9	9.8	1.8	4.2	.456
83-84	San Diego	80	0	843	311	136	305	.446	0	2	.000	39	46	.848	7	47	54	161	84	0	27	0	48	10.5	3.9	0.7	2.0	.373
85-86	Chicago	9	0	83	22	10	23	.435	0	0	.000	2	2	1.000	1	4	5	13	9	0	3	0	2	9.2	2.4	0.6	1.4	.304
NBA Season Totals		476	65	9189	3823	1554	3154	.493	3	48	.063	712	868	.820	134	543	677	1661	860	3	353	40	639	19.3	8.0	1.4	3.5	....
78-79	Kansas City	5	....	96	36	15	40	.375	....	....	....	6	7	.857	4	3	7	24	5	0	5	0	12	19.2	7.2	1.4	4.8	.389
79-80	Kansas City	3	....	34	4	2	5	.400	0	1	.000	0	0	.000	2	1	3	8	2	0	0	0	3	11.3	1.3	1.0	2.7	.269
81-82	Denver	3	3	91	42	16	27	.593	0	1	.000	10	12	.833	2	4	6	10	9	0	3	0	5	30.3	14.0	2.0	3.3	.454
82-83	Denver	8	0	113	62	26	46	.565	0	0	.000	10	18	.556	5	8	13	18	15	0	2	0	7	14.1	7.8	1.6	2.3	.536
NBA Playoff Totals		19	3	334	144	59	118	.500	0	2	.000	26	37	.703	13	16	29	60	31	0	10	0	27	17.6	7.6	1.5	3.2	....

• MCKINNEY, Bones

Horace Albert (Bones) McKinney

Born: Jan. 1, 1919. Lowlands, NC, United States. Died: May16, 1997. Height: 6'6". Weight: 185 lbs. Drafted: — College: North Carolina

YEAR	TEAM	GP	GS	MIN	PTS	FGM	FGA	FG%	3PM	3PA	3P%	FTM	FTA	FT%	ORB	DRB	TRB	AST	PF	DQ	STL	BLK	TO	MPG	PPG	RPG	APG	PCM
46-47	Washington	58	....	....	695	275	987	.279	....	....	....	145	210	.690	....	....	....	69	162	....	....	....	....	....	12.0	....	1.2	....
47-48	Washington	43	....	....	485	182	680	.268	....	....	....	121	188	.644	....	....	....	36	176	....	....	....	....	....	11.3	....	0.8	....
48-49	Washington	57	....	....	723	263	801	.328	....	....	....	197	279	.706	....	....	....	114	216	....	....	....	....	....	12.7	....	2.0	....
49-50	Washington	53	....	....	492	187	631	.296	....	....	....	118	152	.776	....	....	....	88	185	....	....	....	....	....	9.3	....	1.7	....
50-51	Was/Bos	44	....	....	262	102	327	.312	....	....	....	58	81	.716	....	....	198	85	136	6	....	....	....	....	6.0	4.5	1.9	....
51-52	Boston	63	....	1083	337	136	418	.325	....	....	....	65	80	.813	....	....	175	111	148	4	....	....	....	17.2	5.3	2.8	1.8	.320
NBA Season Totals		318	....	1083	2994	1145	3844	.298	....	....	....	704	990	.711	....	....	373	503	1023	10	....	....	....	3.4	9.4	1.2	1.6	....
46-47	Washington	6	....	....	58	18	85	.212	....	....	....	22	34	.647	....	....	....	3	17	....	....	....	....	....	9.7	....	0.5	....
48-49	Washington	10	....	....	128	45	127	.354	....	....	....	38	52	.731	....	....	....	9	36	....	....	....	....	....	12.8	....	0.9	....
49-50	Washington	2	....	....	16	6	22	.273	....	....	....	4	5	.800	....	....	....	3	11	....	....	....	....	....	8.0	....	1.5	....
50-51	Boston	2	....	....	26	11	25	.440	....	....	....	4	5	.800	....	....	10	8	9	0	....	....	....	....	13.0	5.0	4.0	....
51-52	Boston	3	....	20	4	2	9	.222	....	....	....	0	0	.000	....	....	6	2	9	0	....	....	....	6.7	1.3	2.0	0.7	.133
NBA Playoff Totals		23	....	20	232	82	268	.306	....	....	....	68	96	.708	....	....	16	25	82	0	....	....	....	0.9	10.1	0.7	1.1	....

• MCKINNEY, Carlton

Carlton B. McKinney

Born: Oct. 21, 1964. San Diego, CA, United States. Height: 6'4". Weight: 190 lbs. Drafted: — College: Southern Methodist

YEAR	TEAM	GP	GS	MIN	PTS	FGM	FGA	FG%	3PM	3PA	3P%	FTM	FTA	FT%	ORB	DRB	TRB	AST	PF	DQ	STL	BLK	TO	MPG	PPG	RPG	APG	PCM
89-90	LA Clippers	7	0	104	18	8	32	.250	0	1	.000	2	4	.500	4	8	12	7	15	1	6	1	7	14.9	2.6	1.7	1.0	.060
91-92	New York	2	0	9	4	2	9	.222	0	0	.000	0	0	.000	0	1	1	0	1	0	0	0	0	4.5	2.0	0.5	0.0	-.227
NBA Season Totals		9	0	113	22	10	41	.244	0	1	.000	2	4	.500	4	9	13	7	16	1	6	1	7	12.6	2.4	1.4	0.8	....

• MCLEMORE, McCoy

McCoy (Mac) McLemore Jr.

Born: Apr. 3, 1942. Houston, TX, United States. Height: 6'7". Weight: 230 lbs. Drafted: 1964 College: Drake

YEAR	TEAM	GP	GS	MIN	PTS	FGM	FGA	FG%	3PM	3PA	3P%	FTM	FTA	FT%	ORB	DRB	TRB	AST	PF	DQ	STL	BLK	TO	MPG	PPG	RPG	APG	PCM
64-65	San Francisco	78	....	1731	645	244	725	.337	....	....	....	157	220	.714	....	....	488	81	224	6	....	....	....	22.2	8.3	6.3	1.0	.370
65-66	San Francisco	80	....	1467	592	225	528	.426	....	....	....	142	191	.743	....	....	488	55	197	4	....	....	....	18.3	7.4	6.1	0.7	.482
66-67	Chicago	79	....	1382	726	258	670	.385	....	....	....	210	272	.772	....	....	374	62	189	2	....	....	....	17.5	9.2	4.7	0.8	.485

YEAR	TEAM	GP	GS	MIN	PTS	FGM	FGA	FG%	3PM	3PA	3P%	FTM	FTA	FT%	ORB	DRB	TRB	AST	PF	DQ	STL	BLK	TO	MPG	PPG	RPG	APG	PCM
67-68	Chicago	76	....	2100	963	374	940	.398	....	....	....	215	276	.779	....	....	430	130	219	4	....	....	....	27.6	12.7	5.7	1.7	.428
68-69	Phoenix	31	....	710	367	141	366	.385	....	....	....	85	110	.773	....	....	168	50	73	1	....	....	....	22.9	11.8	5.4	1.6	.474
68-69	Detroit	50	....	910	366	141	356	.396	....	....	....	84	104	.808	....	....	236	44	113	3	....	....	....	18.2	7.3	4.7	0.9	.417
69-70	Detroit	73	....	1421	585	233	500	.466	....	....	....	119	145	.821	....	....	336	83	159	3	....	....	....	19.5	8.0	4.6	1.1	.463
70-71	Cleveland	58	....	1839	678	254	654	.388	....	....	....	170	220	.773	....	....	463	176	169	1	....	....	....	31.7	11.7	8.0	3.0	.456
70-71	Milwaukee	28	....	415	132	49	133	.368	....	....	....	34	41	.829	....	....	105	30	66	1	....	....	....	14.8	4.7	3.8	1.1	.368
71-72	Milwaukee	10	....	99	29	9	28	.321	....	....	....	11	12	.917	....	....	34	12	18	0	....	....	....	9.9	2.9	3.4	1.2	.479
71-72	Houston	17	....	147	47	19	43	.442	....	....	....	9	12	.750	....	....	39	10	15	1	....	....	....	8.6	2.8	2.3	0.6	.432
NBA Season Totals		580	....	12221	5130	1947	4943	.394	....	....	....	1236	1603	.771	....	....	3161	733	1442	26	....	....	....	21.1	8.8	5.5	1.3	
66-67	Chicago	3	....	45	37	12	30	.400	....	....	....	13	15	.867	....	....	9	4	5	0	....	....	....	15.0	12.3	3.0	1.3	.708
67-68	Chicago	5	....	142	54	19	49	.388	....	....	....	16	21	.762	....	....	24	5	18	1	....	....	....	28.4	10.8	4.8	1.0	.324
70-71	Milwaukee	10	....	52	7	3	12	.250	....	....	....	1	2	.500	....	....	16	8	8	0	....	....	....	5.2	0.7	1.6	0.8	.351
NBA Playoff Totals		18	....	239	98	34	91	.374	....	....	....	30	38	.789	....	....	49	17	31	1	....	....	....	13.3	5.4	2.7	0.9	

• MCLEOD, George

George L. McLeod

Born: Jan. 3, 1931.   Height: 6'5".   Weight: 200 lbs.   Drafted: 1952   College: Texas Christian

YEAR	TEAM	GP	GS	MIN	PTS	FGM	FGA	FG%	3PM	3PA	3P%	FTM	FTA	FT%	ORB	DRB	TRB	AST	PF	DQ	STL	BLK	TO	MPG	PPG	RPG	APG	PCM
52-53	Baltimore	10	....	85	12	2	16	.125	....	....	....	8	15	.533	....	....	21	4	16	0	....	....	....	8.5	1.2	2.1	0.4	.163
NBA Season Totals		10	....	85	12	2	16	.125	....	....	....	8	15	.533	....	....	21	4	16	0	....	....	....	8.5	1.2	2.1	0.4	

• MCLEOD, Roshown

Roshown McLeod

Born: Nov. 17, 1975. Jersey City, NJ, United States.   Height: 6'8".   Weight: 221 lbs.   Drafted: 1998   College: Duke

YEAR	TEAM	GP	GS	MIN	PTS	FGM	FGA	FG%	3PM	3PA	3P%	FTM	FTA	FT%	ORB	DRB	TRB	AST	PF	DQ	STL	BLK	TO	MPG	PPG	RPG	APG	PCM
98-99	Atlanta	34	0	348	162	62	163	.380	1	10	.100	37	45	.822	12	38	50	14	24	0	2	1	23	10.2	4.8	1.5	0.4	.288
99-00	Atlanta	44	20	860	318	131	332	.395	2	13	.154	54	70	.771	41	97	138	52	84	0	16	5	59	19.5	7.2	3.1	1.2	.276
00-01	Atlanta	34	25	907	335	144	330	.436	2	21	.095	45	51	.882	37	81	118	58	88	0	23	8	57	26.7	9.9	3.5	1.7	.300
00-01	Philadelphia	1	0	15	2	1	2	.500	0	1	.000	0	0	.000	1	1	2	0	2	0	0	0	1	15.0	2.0	2.0	0.0	.073
NBA Season Totals		113	45	2130	817	338	827	.409	5	45	.111	136	166	.819	91	217	308	124	198	0	41	14	140	18.8	7.2	2.7	1.1	
98-99	Atlanta	6	0	49	26	11	21	.524	0	0	.000	4	4	1.000	1	2	3	1	3	0	1	1	1	8.2	4.3	0.5	0.2	.417
NBA Playoff Totals		6	0	49	26	11	21	.524	0	0	.000	4	4	1.000	1	2	3	1	3	0	1	1	1	8.2	4.3	0.5	0.2	

• MCMAHON, Curt

Curt McMahon

Born: Jan. 26, 1915. Died: Apr.1978.   Height: 6'   Weight: 150 lbs.   Drafted: —   College: none

YEAR	TEAM	GP	GS	MIN	PTS	FGM	FGA	FG%	3PM	3PA	3P%	FTM	FTA	FT%	ORB	DRB	TRB	AST	PF	DQ	STL	BLK	TO	MPG	PPG	RPG	APG	PCM
37-38	Dayton-N	10	....	....	19	8	....	....	....	....	....	3	....	....	....	....	....	....	....	....	....	....	....	....	1.9	....	....	....
NBL Season Totals		10	....	....	19	8	....	....	....	....	....	3	....	....	....	....	....	....	....	....	....	....	....	....	1.9	....	....	....

• MCMAHON, Jack

John Joseph McMahon

Born: Dec. 3, 1928. Died: June11, 1989.   Height: 6'1".   Weight: 185 lbs.   Drafted: 1952   College: St. John's (NY)

YEAR	TEAM	GP	GS	MIN	PTS	FGM	FGA	FG%	3PM	3PA	3P%	FTM	FTA	FT%	ORB	DRB	TRB	AST	PF	DQ	STL	BLK	TO	MPG	PPG	RPG	APG	PCM
52-53	Rochester	70	....	1665	507	176	534	.330	....	....	....	155	236	.657	....	....	183	186	253	16	....	....	....	23.8	7.2	2.6	2.7	.298
53-54	Rochester	71	....	1891	711	250	691	.362	....	....	....	211	303	.696	....	....	211	238	221	6	....	....	....	26.6	10.0	3.0	3.4	.393
54-55	Rochester	72	....	1807	645	251	721	.348	....	....	....	143	225	.636	....	....	211	246	179	1	....	....	....	25.1	9.0	2.9	3.4	.365
55-56	Rochester	34	....	856	255	100	307	.326	....	....	....	55	90	.611	....	....	85	115	85	0	....	....	....	25.2	7.5	2.5	3.4	.303
55-56	St. Louis	36	....	857	259	102	308	.331	....	....	....	55	95	.579	....	....	95	107	85	1	....	....	....	23.8	7.2	2.6	3.0	.303
56-57	St. Louis	72	....	2344	620	239	725	.330	....	....	....	142	225	.631	....	....	222	367	213	2	....	....	....	32.6	8.6	3.1	5.1	.330
57-58	St. Louis	72	....	2239	566	216	719	.300	....	....	....	134	221	.606	....	....	195	333	184	2	....	....	....	31.1	7.9	2.7	4.6	.297
58-59	St. Louis	72	....	2235	592	248	692	.358	....	....	....	96	156	.615	....	....	164	298	221	2	....	....	....	31.0	8.2	2.3	4.1	.290
59-60	St. Louis	25	....	334	82	33	93	.355	....	....	....	16	29	.552	....	....	24	49	42	1	....	....	....	13.4	3.3	1.0	2.0	.284
NBA Season Totals		524	....	14228	4237	1615	4790	.337	....	....	....	1007	1580	.637	....	....	1390	1939	1483	31	....	....	....	27.2	8.1	2.7	3.7	
52-53	Rochester	3	....	66	26	8	20	.400	....	....	....	10	14	.714	....	....	5	6	14	2	....	....	....	22.0	8.7	1.7	2.0	.334
53-54	Rochester	6	....	197	68	27	69	.391	....	....	....	14	25	.560	....	....	24	24	15	0	....	....	....	32.8	11.3	4.0	4.0	.391
54-55	Rochester	3	....	109	52	17	42	.405	....	....	....	18	28	.643	....	....	17	15	7	0	....	....	....	36.3	17.3	5.7	5.0	.535
55-56	St. Louis	8	....	162	43	19	55	.345	....	....	....	5	11	.455	....	....	9	15	18	0	....	....	....	20.3	5.4	1.1	1.9	.197
56-57	St. Louis	10	....	375	124	52	137	.380	....	....	....	20	36	.556	....	....	38	57	48	4	....	....	....	37.5	12.4	3.8	5.7	.364
57-58	St. Louis	11	....	332	86	36	88	.409	....	....	....	14	26	.538	....	....	37	51	36	0	....	....	....	30.2	7.8	3.4	4.6	.369
58-59	St. Louis	6	....	250	70	30	90	.333	....	....	....	10	19	.526	....	....	18	32	20	1	....	....	....	41.7	11.7	3.0	5.3	.270
59-60	St. Louis	2	....	27	4	2	4	.500	....	....	....	0	4	.000	....	....	1	3	5	0	....	....	....	13.5	2.0	0.5	1.5	.132
NBA Playoff Totals		49	....	1518	473	191	505	.378	....	....	....	91	163	.558	....	....	149	203	163	7	....	....	....	31.0	9.7	3.0	4.1	

• MCMICHAEL, Mike

Marcellus McMichael Jr.

Born: 1915. Des Moines, IA, United States.   Height: 6'2".   Weight: 195 lbs.   Drafted: —   College: Northwestern

YEAR	TEAM	GP	GS	MIN	PTS	FGM	FGA	FG%	3PM	3PA	3P%	FTM	FTA	FT%	ORB	DRB	TRB	AST	PF	DQ	STL	BLK	TO	MPG	PPG	RPG	APG	PCM
38-39	Wingfoots-N	11	....	....	43	17	....	....	....	....	....	9	....	....	....	....	....	....	....	....	....	....	....	....	3.9	....	....	....
NBL Season Totals		11	....	....	43	17	....	....	....	....	....	9	....	....	....	....	....	....	....	....	....	....	....	....	3.9	....	....	....

• MCMILLAN, Nate

Nathaniel (Mac) McMillan

Born: Aug. 3, 1964. Raleigh, NC, United States.   Height: 6'5".   Weight: 195 lbs.   Drafted: 1986   College: North Carolina State

YEAR	TEAM	GP	GS	MIN	PTS	FGM	FGA	FG%	3PM	3PA	3P%	FTM	FTA	FT%	ORB	DRB	TRB	AST	PF	DQ	STL	BLK	TO	MPG	PPG	RPG	APG	PCM
86-87	Seattle	71	50	1972	373	143	301	.475	0	7	.000	87	141	.617	101	230	331	583	238	4	125	45	156	27.8	5.3	4.7	8.2	.525
87-88	Seattle	82	82	2453	624	235	496	.474	9	24	.375	145	205	.707	117	221	338	702	238	1	169	47	189	29.9	7.6	4.1	8.6	.543
88-89	Seattle	75	74	2341	532	199	485	.410	15	70	.214	119	189	.630	143	245	388	696	236	3	156	42	210	31.2	7.1	5.2	9.3	.520
89-90	Seattle	82	69	2338	523	207	438	.473	11	31	.355	98	153	.641	127	276	403	598	289	7	140	37	189	28.5	6.4	4.9	7.3	.491
90-91	Seattle	78	0	1434	338	132	305	.433	17	48	.354	57	93	.613	71	180	251	371	211	0	104	20	125	18.4	4.3	3.2	4.8	.482
91-92	Seattle	72	30	1652	435	177	405	.437	27	98	.276	54	84	.643	92	160	252	359	218	4	129	29	115	22.9	6.0	3.5	5.0	.464
92-93	Seattle	73	25	1977	546	213	459	.464	25	65	.385	95	134	.709	84	222	306	384	240	6	173	32	139	27.1	7.5	4.2	5.3	.477

YEAR	TEAM	GP	GS	MIN	PTS	FGM	FGA	FG%	3PM	3PA	3P%	FTM	FTA	FT%	ORB	DRB	TRB	AST	PF	DQ	STL	BLK	TO	MPG	PPG	RPG	APG	PCM
93-94	Seattle	73	8	1887	437	177	396	.447	52	133	.391	31	55	.564	50	233	283	387	201	1	**216**	22	124	25.8	6.0	3.9	5.3	.486
94-95	Seattle	80	18	2070	419	166	397	.418	53	155	.342	34	58	.586	65	237	302	421	275	8	165	53	128	25.9	5.2	3.8	5.3	.424
95-96	Seattle	55	14	1261	275	100	238	.420	46	121	.380	29	41	.707	41	169	210	197	143	3	95	18	77	22.9	5.0	3.8	3.6	.406
96-97	Seattle	37	2	798	169	61	149	.409	28	84	.333	19	29	.655	15	103	118	140	78	0	58	6	33	21.6	4.6	3.2	3.8	.419
97-98	Seattle	18	1	279	62	23	67	.343	15	34	.441	1	1	1.000	13	27	40	55	41	0	14	4	13	15.5	3.4	2.2	3.1	.372
NBA Season Totals		796	373	20462	4733	1833	4136	.443	298	870	.343	769	1183	.650	919	2303	3222	4893	2408	37	1544	355	1498	25.7	5.9	4.0	6.1	....
86-87	Seattle	14	14	356	71	27	62	.435	0	0	.000	17	24	.708	13	41	54	112	42	1	14	10	26	25.4	5.1	3.9	8.0	.516
87-88	Seattle	5	5	127	33	12	35	.343	0	1	.000	9	14	.643	6	15	21	33	11	0	2	3	8	25.4	6.6	4.2	6.6	.442
88-89	Seattle	8	7	200	54	19	40	.475	0	2	.000	16	25	.640	9	16	25	63	21	0	10	5	19	25.0	6.8	3.1	7.9	.537
90-91	Seattle	5	0	95	14	6	23	.261	0	2	.000	2	4	.500	6	12	18	22	15	0	6	1	3	19.0	2.8	3.6	4.4	.360
91-92	Seattle	9	2	246	86	35	83	.422	6	26	.231	10	14	.714	14	19	33	63	35	1	16	3	22	27.3	9.6	3.7	7.0	.482
92-93	Seattle	19	2	415	91	35	103	.340	5	24	.208	16	30	.533	21	46	67	103	54	2	40	11	25	21.8	4.8	3.5	5.4	.464
93-94	Seattle	5	0	109	21	8	25	.320	4	11	.364	1	4	.250	6	10	16	10	18	1	6	1	5	21.8	4.2	3.2	2.0	.212
94-95	Seattle	4	4	113	19	8	23	.348	1	8	.125	2	2	1.000	7	11	18	29	13	0	10	2	7	28.3	4.8	4.5	7.3	.453
95-96	Seattle	19	0	385	84	28	69	.406	19	40	.475	9	14	.643	13	57	70	52	34	0	23	5	20	20.3	4.4	3.7	2.7	.404
96-97	Seattle	3	0	41	0	0	2	.000	0	2	.000	0	0	.000	1	4	5	3	11	0	1	0	2	13.7	0.0	1.7	1.0	-.001
97-98	Seattle	7	0	99	16	6	18	.333	2	12	.167	2	2	1.000	2	14	16	15	17	0	3	2	2	14.1	2.3	2.3	2.1	.312
NBA Playoff Totals		98	34	2186	489	184	483	.381	37	128	.289	84	133	.632	98	245	343	505	271	5	131	43	139	22.3	5.0	3.5	5.2	....

• MCMILLEN, Tom

Charles Thomas McMillen

Born: May 26, 1952. Mansfield, PA, United States. Height: 6'11". Weight: 215 lbs. Drafted: 1974 College: Maryland

YEAR	TEAM	GP	GS	MIN	PTS	FGM	FGA	FG%	3PM	3PA	3P%	FTM	FTA	FT%	ORB	DRB	TRB	AST	PF	DQ	STL	BLK	TO	MPG	PPG	RPG	APG	PCM
75-76	Buffalo	50	....	708	233	96	222	.432	....	....	....	41	54	.759	64	122	186	69	87	1	7	6	....	14.2	4.7	3.7	1.4	.453
76-77	Buffalo	20	....	270	116	45	92	.489	....	....	....	26	36	.722	29	43	72	16	29	0	1	2	....	13.5	5.8	3.6	0.8	.515
76-77	New York	56	....	1222	528	229	471	.486	....	....	....	70	87	.805	85	232	317	51	134	0	10	4	....	21.8	9.4	5.7	0.9	.479
77-78	Atlanta	68	....	1683	676	280	568	.493	....	....	....	116	145	.800	151	265	416	84	233	8	33	16	109	24.8	9.9	6.1	1.2	.425
78-79	Atlanta	82	....	1392	570	232	498	.466	....	....	....	106	119	.891	131	201	332	69	211	2	15	32	90	17.0	7.0	4.0	0.8	.407
79-80	Atlanta	53	....	1071	463	191	382	.500	0	1	.000	81	107	.757	70	150	220	62	126	2	36	14	64	20.2	8.7	4.2	1.2	.444
80-81	Atlanta	79	....	1564	587	253	519	.487	1	6	.167	80	108	.741	96	199	295	72	165	0	23	25	79	19.8	7.4	3.7	0.9	.368
81-82	Atlanta	73	23	1792	723	291	572	.509	1	3	.333	140	170	.824	102	234	336	129	202	1	25	24	124	24.5	9.9	4.6	1.8	.411
82-83	Atlanta	61	4	1364	504	198	424	.467	0	1	.000	108	133	.812	57	160	217	76	143	2	17	24	79	22.4	8.3	3.6	1.2	.344
83-84	Washington	62	5	1294	572	222	447	.497	1	6	.167	127	156	.814	64	135	199	73	162	0	14	17	68	20.9	9.2	3.2	1.2	.388
84-85	Washington	69	21	1547	616	252	534	.472	0	5	.000	112	135	.830	64	146	210	52	163	3	8	17	41	22.4	8.9	3.0	0.8	.325
85-86	Washington	56	1	863	326	131	285	.460	0	3	.000	64	79	.810	44	69	113	35	85	0	9	10	34	15.4	5.8	2.0	0.6	.307
NBA Season Totals		729	54	14770	5914	2420	5014	.483	3	25	.120	1071	1329	.806	957	1956	2913	788	1740	19	198	191	688	20.3	8.1	4.0	1.1	....
75-76	Buffalo	1	....	3	2	1	2	.500	....	....	....	0	0	.000	1	0	1	0	1	0	0	0	....	3.0	2.0	1.0	0.0	.524
77-78	Atlanta	2	....	75	26	13	23	.565	....	....	....	0	0	.000	7	15	22	1	9	0	1	0	3	37.5	13.0	11.0	0.5	.426
78-79	Atlanta	9	....	163	56	20	46	.435	....	....	....	16	19	.842	14	20	34	7	21	1	2	1	8	18.1	6.2	3.8	0.8	.341
81-82	Atlanta	2	0	47	20	8	13	.615	0	0	.000	4	6	.667	0	7	7	1	5	0	3	0	3	23.5	10.0	3.5	0.5	.419
82-83	Atlanta	3	0	39	10	4	12	.333	0	0	.000	2	2	1.000	3	4	7	2	5	0	1	2	3	13.0	3.3	2.3	0.7	.232
83-84	Washington	4	0	42	9	4	16	.250	0	0	.000	1	2	.500	1	1	2	3	6	0	0	0	1	10.5	2.3	0.5	0.8	-.030
84-85	Washington	1	0	7	0	0	4	.000	0	1	.000	0	0	.000	3	2	5	1	1	0	0	0	0	7.0	0.0	5.0	1.0	.219
85-86	Washington	4	0	54	16	8	16	.500	0	0	.000	0	0	.000	1	4	5	7	2	0	3	0	2	13.5	4.0	1.3	1.8	.384
NBA Playoff Totals		26	0	430	139	58	132	.439	0	1	.000	23	29	.793	30	53	83	22	50	1	10	3	20	16.5	5.3	3.2	0.8	....

• MCMILLIAN, Jim

James M. McMillian

Born: Mar. 11, 1948. Raeford, NC, United States. Height: 6'5". Weight: 215 lbs. Drafted: 1970 College: Columbia

YEAR	TEAM	GP	GS	MIN	PTS	FGM	FGA	FG%	3PM	3PA	3P%	FTM	FTA	FT%	ORB	DRB	TRB	AST	PF	DQ	STL	BLK	TO	MPG	PPG	RPG	APG	PCM
70-71	LA Lakers	81	....	1747	678	289	629	.459	....	....	....	100	130	.769	....	....	330	133	122	1	....	....	....	21.6	8.4	4.1	1.6	.433
71-72	LA Lakers	80	....	3050	1503	642	1331	.482	....	....	....	219	277	.791	....	....	522	209	209	0	....	....	....	38.1	18.8	6.5	2.6	.486
72-73	LA Lakers	81	....	2953	1533	655	1431	.458	....	....	....	223	264	.845	....	....	447	221	176	0	....	....	....	36.5	18.9	5.5	2.7	.477
73-74	Buffalo	82	....	3322	1525	600	1214	.494	....	....	....	325	379	.858	216	394	610	256	186	0	129	26	....	40.5	18.6	7.4	3.1	.516
74-75	Buffalo	62	....	2132	888	347	695	.499	....	....	....	194	231	.840	127	258	385	156	129	0	69	15	....	34.4	14.3	6.2	2.5	.482
75-76	Buffalo	74	....	2610	1172	492	918	.536	....	....	....	188	219	.858	134	256	390	205	141	0	88	14	....	35.3	15.8	5.3	2.8	.499
76-77	New York	67	....	2158	663	298	642	.464	....	....	....	67	86	.779	66	241	307	139	103	0	63	5	....	32.2	9.9	4.6	2.1	.341
77-78	New York	81	....	1977	691	288	623	.462	....	....	....	115	134	.858	80	209	289	205	116	0	76	17	105	24.4	8.5	3.6	2.5	.411
78-79	Portland	23	....	278	83	33	74	.446	....	....	....	17	21	.810	16	23	39	33	18	0	10	3	16	12.1	3.6	1.7	1.4	.378
NBA Season Totals		631	....	20227	8736	3644	7557	.482	....	....	....	1448	1741	.832	639	1381	3319	1557	1200	1	435	80	121	32.1	13.8	5.3	2.5	....
70-71	LA Lakers	12	....	522	181	79	181	.436	....	....	....	23	34	.676	....	....	65	22	27	0	....	....	....	43.5	15.1	5.4	1.8	.303
71-72	LA Lakers	15	....	624	286	113	253	.447	....	....	....	60	70	.857	....	....	85	22	43	0	....	....	....	41.6	19.1	5.7	1.5	.386
72-73	LA Lakers	17	....	630	341	143	307	.466	....	....	....	55	75	.733	....	....	82	37	41	0	....	....	....	37.1	20.1	4.8	2.2	.455
73-74	Buffalo	6	....	224	87	38	92	.413	....	....	....	11	16	.688	24	29	53	12	14	0	4	1	....	37.3	14.5	8.8	2.0	.410
74-75	Buffalo	7	....	240	91	39	86	.453	....	....	....	13	14	.929	10	24	34	14	12	0	11	2	....	34.3	13.0	4.9	2.0	.377
75-76	Buffalo	9	....	348	155	61	129	.473	....	....	....	33	38	.868	11	26	37	19	29	1	14	4	....	38.7	17.2	4.1	2.1	.389
77-78	New York	6	....	134	53	24	53	.453	....	....	....	5	6	.833	9	12	21	11	3	0	7	0	7	22.3	8.8	3.5	1.8	.423
NBA Playoff Totals		72	....	2722	1194	497	1101	.451	....	....	....	200	253	.791	54	91	377	137	169	1	36	7	7	37.8	16.6	5.2	1.9	....

• MCMILLON, Shellie

Shellie McMillon Jr.

Born: Mar. 11, 1936. Died: July11, 1980. Height: 6'5". Weight: 205 lbs. Drafted: 1958 College: Bradley

YEAR	TEAM	GP	GS	MIN	PTS	FGM	FGA	FG%	3PM	3PA	3P%	FTM	FTA	FT%	ORB	DRB	TRB	AST	PF	DQ	STL	BLK	TO	MPG	PPG	RPG	APG	PCM
58-59	Detroit	48	....	700	309	127	289	.439	....	....	....	55	104	.529	....	....	285	26	110	2	....	....	....	14.6	6.4	5.9	0.5	.535
59-60	Detroit	75	....	1416	666	267	627	.426	....	....	....	132	199	.663	....	....	431	49	198	3	....	....	....	18.9	8.9	5.7	0.7	.481
60-61	Detroit	78	....	1636	784	322	752	.428	....	....	....	140	201	.697	....	....	487	98	238	6	....	....	....	21.0	10.1	6.2	1.3	.510
61-62	Detroit	14	....	190	72	26	83	.313	....	....	....	20	36	.556	....	....	64	6	37	0	....	....	....	13.6	5.1	4.6	0.4	.337
61-62	St. Louis	48	....	1035	566	239	508	.470	....	....	....	88	146	.603	....	....	304	53	165	10	....	....	....	21.6	11.8	6.3	1.1	.552
NBA Season Totals		263	....	4977	2397	981	2259	.434	....	....	....	435	686	.634	....	....	1571	232	748	21	....	....	....	18.9	9.1	6.0	0.9	....

YEAR	TEAM	GP	GS	MIN	PTS	FGM	FGA	FG%	3PM	3PA	3P%	FTM	FTA	FT%	ORB	DRB	TRB	AST	PF	DQ	STL	BLK	TO	MPG	PPG	RPG	APG	PCM
58-59	Detroit	3	....	54	19	7	23	.304	....	....	....	5	6	.833	....	....	14	0	16	1	....	....	....	18.0	6.3	4.7	0.0	.206
59-60	Detroit	2	....	47	20	8	21	.381	....	....	....	4	5	.800	....	....	16	2	5	0	....	....	....	23.5	10.0	8.0	1.0	.478
60-61	Detroit	4	....	67	39	13	27	.481	....	....	....	13	18	.722	....	....	9	7	16	2	....	....	....	16.8	9.8	2.3	1.8	.535
NBA Playoff Totals		9	....	168	78	28	71	.394	....	....	....	22	29	.759	....	....	39	9	37	3	....	....	....	18.7	8.7	4.3	1.0	

• MCMULLAN, Mal

Malcolm H. McMullan

Born: Aug. 3, 1927. Died: Apr.13, 1995.   Height: 6'5".   Weight: 210 lbs.   Drafted: —   College: Xavier (OH)

YEAR	TEAM	GP	GS	MIN	PTS	FGM	FGA	FG%	3PM	3PA	3P%	FTM	FTA	FT%	ORB	DRB	TRB	AST	PF	DQ	STL	BLK	TO	MPG	PPG	RPG	APG	PCM
49-50	Indianapolis	58	....	....	323	123	380	.324	....	....	....	77	141	.546	....	....	....	87	212	....	....	....	....		5.6	....	1.5	....
50-51	Indianapolis	51	....	....	204	78	277	.282	....	....	....	48	82	.585	....	....	128	33	109	2	....	....	....		4.0	2.5	0.6	....
NBA Season Totals		109	....	....	527	201	657	.306	....	....	....	125	223	.561	....	....	128	120	321	2	....	....	....		4.8	1.2	1.1	
49-50	Indianapolis	6	....	....	14	4	21	.190	....	....	....	6	9	.667	....	....	....	9	19	....	....	....	....		2.3	....	1.5	
NBA Playoff Totals		6	....	....	14	4	21	.190	....	....	....	6	9	.667	....	....	....	9	19	....	....	....	....		2.3	....	1.5	

• MCNABB, Chet

Chester McNabb

Born: 1921.   Height: 6'2".   Weight: 200 lbs.   Drafted: —   College: Arizona State

YEAR	TEAM	GP	GS	MIN	PTS	FGM	FGA	FG%	3PM	3PA	3P%	FTM	FTA	FT%	ORB	DRB	TRB	AST	PF	DQ	STL	BLK	TO	MPG	PPG	RPG	APG	PCM
47-48	Baltimore	2	....		0	0	1	.000	....	....	....	0	0	.000	....	....		0	1	....	....	....	....		0.0	....	0.0	
NBA Season Totals		2	....	....	0	0	1	.000	....	....	....	0	0	.000	....	....		0	1	....	....	....	....		0.0	....	0.0	

• MCNAMARA, Mark

Mark Robert McNamara

Born: June 8, 1959. San Jose, CA, United States.   Height: 6'11".   Weight: 235 lbs.   Drafted: 1982   College: California

YEAR	TEAM	GP	GS	MIN	PTS	FGM	FGA	FG%	3PM	3PA	3P%	FTM	FTA	FT%	ORB	DRB	TRB	AST	PF	DQ	STL	BLK	TO	MPG	PPG	RPG	APG	PCM
82-83	Philadelphia	36	2	182	78	29	64	.453	0	0	.000	20	45	.444	34	42	76	7	42	1	3	3	36	5.1	2.2	2.1	0.2	.359
83-84	San Antonio	70	3	1037	388	157	253	.621	0	0	.000	74	157	.471	137	180	317	31	138	2	14	12	91	14.8	5.5	4.5	0.4	.447
84-85	San Antonio	12	0	63	33	12	18	.667	0	0	.000	9	18	.500	7	10	17	0	5	0	2	1	6	5.3	2.8	1.4	0.0	.539
84-85	Kansas City	33	0	210	79	28	58	.483	0	0	.000	23	44	.523	24	33	57	6	22	0	5	7	13	6.4	2.4	1.7	0.2	.427
86-87	Philadelphia	11	1	113	35	14	30	.467	0	0	.000	7	19	.368	17	19	36	2	17	0	1	0	8	10.3	3.2	3.3	0.2	.316
87-88	Philadelphia	42	18	581	152	52	133	.391	0	0	.000	48	66	.727	66	91	157	18	67	0	4	12	25	13.8	3.6	3.7	0.4	.334
88-89	LA Lakers	39	0	318	113	32	64	.500	0	0	.000	49	78	.628	38	62	100	10	51	0	4	3	23	8.2	2.9	2.6	0.3	.424
89-90	LA Lakers	33	1	190	102	38	86	.442	0	0	.000	26	40	.650	22	41	63	3	31	1	2	1	20	5.8	3.1	1.9	0.1	.433
90-91	Orlando	2	0	13	0	0	1	.000	0	0	.000	0	0	.000	0	4	4	0	1	0	0	0	0	6.5	0.0	2.0	0.0	.179
NBA Season Totals		278	25	2707	980	362	707	.512	0	0	.000	256	467	.548	345	482	827	77	374	4	35	39	222	9.7	3.5	3.0	0.3	
82-83	Philadelphia	2	0	2	4	2	2	1.000	0	0	.000	0	0	.000	0	1	1	0	0	0	0	0	0	1.0	2.0	0.5	0.0	2.451
86-87	Philadelphia	1	0	2	2	1	1	1.000	0	0	.000	0	0	.000	0	1	1	0	0	0	0	0	0	2.0	2.0	1.0	0.0	1.466
88-89	LA Lakers	3	0	7	3	1	2	.500	0	0	.000	1	2	.500	0	1	1	0	0	0	0	0	0	2.3	1.0	0.3	0.0	.362
89-90	LA Lakers	2	0	5	2	1	4	.250	0	0	.000	0	0	.000	0	1	1	0	1	0	0	0	0	2.5	1.0	0.5	0.0	-.069
NBA Playoff Totals		8	0	16	11	5	9	.556	0	0	.000	1	2	.500	0	4	4	0	1	0	0	0	0	2.0	1.4	0.5	0.0	

• MCNAMEE, Joe

John Joseph McNamee

Born: Sept. 24, 1926.   Height: 6'6".   Weight: 210 lbs.   Drafted: 1950   College: San Francisco

YEAR	TEAM	GP	GS	MIN	PTS	FGM	FGA	FG%	3PM	3PA	3P%	FTM	FTA	FT%	ORB	DRB	TRB	AST	PF	DQ	STL	BLK	TO	MPG	PPG	RPG	APG	PCM
50-51	Rochester	60	....	....	123	48	167	.287	....	....	....	27	42	.643	....	....	101	18	88	2	....	....	....		2.1	1.7	0.3	
51-52	Roc/Bal	58	....	695	166	68	222	.306	....	....	....	30	50	.600	....	....	137	40	108	4	....	....	....	12.0	2.9	2.4	0.7	.230
NBA Season Totals		118	....	695	289	116	389	.298	....	....	....	57	92	.620	....	....	238	58	196	6	....	....	....		5.9	2.4	2.0	0.5	
50-51	Rochester	13	....	....	33	12	41.	.293	....	....	....	9	12	.750	....	....	35	9	26	0	....	....	....		2.5	2.7	0.7	
NBA Playoff Totals		13	....	....	33	12	41	.293	....	....	....	9	12	.750	....	....	35	9	26	0	....	....	....		2.5	2.7	0.7	

• MCNEALY, Chris

Christopher McNealy

Born: July 15, 1961. Fresno, CA, United States.   Height: 6'7".   Weight: 210 lbs.   Drafted: 1983   College: San Jose State

YEAR	TEAM	GP	GS	MIN	PTS	FGM	FGA	FG%	3PM	3PA	3P%	FTM	FTA	FT%	ORB	DRB	TRB	AST	PF	DQ	STL	BLK	TO	MPG	PPG	RPG	APG	PCM
85-86	New York	30	6	627	171	70	144	.486	0	0	.000	31	47	.660	62	141	203	41	88	2	38	12	36	20.9	5.7	6.8	1.4	.478
86-87	New York	59	16	972	228	88	179	.492	0	0	.000	52	80	.650	74	153	227	46	136	1	36	16	65	16.5	3.9	3.8	0.8	.324
87-88	New York	19	0	265	67	23	74	.311	0	0	.000	21	31	.677	24	40	64	23	50	1	16	2	17	13.9	3.5	3.4	1.2	.289
NBA Season Totals		108	22	1864	466	181	397	.456	0	0	.000	104	158	.658	160	334	494	110	274	4	90	30	118	17.3	4.3	4.6	1.0	

• MCNEILL, Bob

Robert J. McNeill

Born: Oct. 22, 1938. Philadelphia, PA, United States.   Height: 6'1".   Weight: 170 lbs.   Drafted: 1960   College: St. Joseph's (PA)

YEAR	TEAM	GP	GS	MIN	PTS	FGM	FGA	FG%	3PM	3PA	3P%	FTM	FTA	FT%	ORB	DRB	TRB	AST	PF	DQ	STL	BLK	TO	MPG	PPG	RPG	APG	PCM
60-61	New York	75	....	1387	437	166	427	.389	....	....	....	105	126	.833	....	....	123	238	148	2	....	....	....	18.5	5.8	1.6	3.2	.406
61-62	Philadelphia	21	....	212	86	34	76	.447	....	....	....	18	22	.818	....	....	33	49	21	0	....	....	....	10.1	4.1	1.6	2.3	.608
61-62	LA Lakers	29	....	229	52	22	60	.367	....	....	....	8	12	.667	....	....	23	40	25	0	....	....	....	7.9	1.8	0.8	1.4	.339
NBA Season Totals		125	....	1828	575	222	563	.394	....	....	....	131	160	.819	....	....	179	327	194	2	....	....	....	14.6	4.6	1.4	2.6	
61-62	LA Lakers	5	....	20	9	4	7	.571	....	....	....	1	2	.500	....	....	6	5	6	0	....	....	....	4.0	1.8	1.2	1.0	.735
NBA Playoff Totals		5	....	20	9	4	7	.571	....	....	....	1	2	.500	....	....	6	5	6	0	....	....	....	4.0	1.8	1.2	1.0	

• MCNEILL, Larry

Larry (The Hawk) McNeill

Born: Jan. 31, 1951. Hoke, NC, United States.   Height: 6'9".   Weight: 195 lbs.   Drafted: 1973   College: Marquette

YEAR	TEAM	GP	GS	MIN	PTS	FGM	FGA	FG%	3PM	3PA	3P%	FTM	FTA	FT%	ORB	DRB	TRB	AST	PF	DQ	STL	BLK	TO	MPG	PPG	RPG	APG	PCM
73-74	Omaha	54	....	516	311	106	220	.482	....	....	....	99	140	.707	60	86	146	24	76	0	35	6	....	9.6	5.8	2.7	0.4	.612
74-75	Omaha	80	....	1749	781	296	645	.459	....	....	....	189	241	.784	149	348	497	73	229	1	69	27	....	21.9	9.8	6.2	0.9	.498
75-76	Kansas City	82	....	1613	797	295	610	.484	....	....	....	207	273	.758	157	353	510	72	244	2	51	32	....	19.7	9.7	6.2	0.9	.566
76-77	New York	8	....	93	60	18	51	.353	....	....	....	24	30	.800	10	16	26	3	13	1	4	1	....	11.6	7.5	3.3	0.4	.529

YEAR	TEAM	GP	GS	MIN	PTS	FGM	FGA	FG%	3PM	3PA	3P%	FTM	FTA	FT%	ORB	DRB	TRB	AST	PF	DQ	STL	BLK	TO	MPG	PPG	RPG	APG	PCM
76-77	Golden State	16	....	137	86	29	61	.475	....	....	....	28	31	.903	18	31	49	3	19	0	6	1	....	8.6	5.4	3.1	0.2	.690
77-78	Golden State	9	....	67	27	6	18	.333	....	....	....	15	19	.789	2	12	14	2	14	0	0	1	7	7.4	3.0	1.6	0.2	.267
77-78	Buffalo	37	....	873	442	156	338	.462	....	....	....	130	156	.833	78	110	188	45	100	1	18	10	59	23.6	11.9	5.1	1.2	.476
78-79	Detroit	11	....	46	29	9	20	.450	....	....	....	11	12	.917	3	7	10	3	7	0	0	0	4	4.2	2.6	0.9	0.3	.527
NBA Season Totals		297	....	5094	2533	915	1963	.466	....	....	....	703	902	.779	477	963	1440	225	702	5	183	78	70	17.2	8.5	4.8	0.8	....
74-75	Omaha	6	....	103	61	22	34	.647	....	....	....	17	20	.850	7	19	26	2	21	2	2	2	....	17.2	10.2	4.3	0.3	.631
76-77	Golden State	6	....	21	16	7	10	.700	....	....	....	2	4	.500	2	0	2	0	2	0	1	0	....	3.5	2.7	0.3	0.0	.639
NBA Playoff Totals		12	....	124	77	29	44	.659	....	....	....	19	24	.792	9	19	28	2	23	2	3	2	....	10.3	6.4	2.3	0.2	....

• MCNULTY, Carl
Carl Edwin McNulty

Born: Feb. 14, 1930.   Height: 6'3".   Weight: 185 lbs.   Drafted: 1952   College: Purdue

YEAR	TEAM	GP	GS	MIN	PTS	FGM	FGA	FG%	3PM	3PA	3P%	FTM	FTA	FT%	ORB	DRB	TRB	AST	PF	DQ	STL	BLK	TO	MPG	PPG	RPG	APG	PCM
54-55	Milwaukee	1	....	14	2	1	6	.167	....	....	....	0	0	.000	....	....	0	0	1	0	....	....	....	14.0	2.0	0.0	0.0	-.153
NBA Season Totals		1	....	14	2	1	6	.167	....	....	....	0	0	.000	....	....	0	0	1	0	....	....	....	14.0	2.0	0.0	0.0	....

• MCPHERSON, Paul
Paul McPherson

Born: July 3, 1978. Chicago, IL, United States.   Height: 6'4".   Weight: 210 lbs.   Drafted: —   College: DePaul

YEAR	TEAM	GP	GS	MIN	PTS	FGM	FGA	FG%	3PM	3PA	3P%	FTM	FTA	FT%	ORB	DRB	TRB	AST	PF	DQ	STL	BLK	TO	MPG	PPG	RPG	APG	PCM
00-01	Phoenix	33	0	308	112	47	96	.490	0	6	.000	18	24	.750	20	28	48	16	48	0	12	3	23	9.3	3.4	1.5	0.5	.316
00-01	Golden State	22	0	287	150	62	120	.517	2	6	.333	24	34	.706	20	11	31	22	32	0	13	1	24	13.0	6.8	1.4	1.0	.426
NBA Season Totals		55	0	595	262	109	216	.505	2	12	.167	42	58	.724	40	39	79	38	80	0	25	4	47	10.8	4.8	1.4	0.7	....

• MCPIPE, Roy
Roy McPipe

Born: May 5, 1950. Hammond, IN, United States.   Height: 6'3".   Weight: 205 lbs.   Drafted: 1974   College: Eastern Montana

YEAR	TEAM	GP	GS	MIN	PTS	FGM	FGA	FG%	3PM	3PA	3P%	FTM	FTA	FT%	ORB	DRB	TRB	AST	PF	DQ	STL	BLK	TO	MPG	PPG	RPG	APG	PCM
74-75	Utah-A	5	....	44	21	8	24	.333	2	4	.500	3	4	.750	2	3	5	1	5	....	1	0	10	8.8	4.2	1.0	0.2	.220
ABA Season Totals		5	....	44	21	8	24	.333	2	4	.500	3	4	.750	2	3	5	1	5	....	1	0	10	8.8	4.2	1.0	0.2	....

• MCQUEEN, Cozell
Cozell McQueen

Born: Jan. 18, 1962. Paris, France.   Height: 6'11".   Weight: 235 lbs.   Drafted: 1985   College: North Carolina State

YEAR	TEAM	GP	GS	MIN	PTS	FGM	FGA	FG%	3PM	3PA	3P%	FTM	FTA	FT%	ORB	DRB	TRB	AST	PF	DQ	STL	BLK	TO	MPG	PPG	RPG	APG	PCM
86-87	Detroit	3	0	7	6	3	3	1.000	0	0	.000	0	0	.000	3	5	8	0	1	0	0	1	0	2.3	2.0	2.7	0.0	1.988
NBA Season Totals		3	0	7	6	3	3	1.000	0	0	.000	0	0	.000	3	5	8	0	1	0	0	1	0	2.3	2.0	2.7	0.0	....

• MCREYNOLDS, Thales
Thales McReynolds

Born: June 8, 1943. Birmingham, AL, United States. Died: July 3, 1988.   Height: 6'3".   Weight: 185 lbs.   Drafted: 1965   College: Miles

YEAR	TEAM	GP	GS	MIN	PTS	FGM	FGA	FG%	3PM	3PA	3P%	FTM	FTA	FT%	ORB	DRB	TRB	AST	PF	DQ	STL	BLK	TO	MPG	PPG	RPG	APG	PCM
65-66	Baltimore	5	....	28	3	1	12	.083	....	....	....	1	2	.500	....	....	6	1	0	0	....	....	....	5.6	0.6	1.2	0.2	-.003
NBA Season Totals		5	....	28	3	1	12	.083	....	....	....	1	2	.500	....	....	6	1	0	0	....	....	....	5.6	0.6	1.2	0.2	....

• MCWILLIAMS, Eric
Eric Lee McWilliams

Born: Apr. 18, 1950. Denver, CO, United States.   Height: 6'8".   Weight: 200 lbs.   Drafted: 1972   College: Long Beach State

YEAR	TEAM	GP	GS	MIN	PTS	FGM	FGA	FG%	3PM	3PA	3P%	FTM	FTA	FT%	ORB	DRB	TRB	AST	PF	DQ	STL	BLK	TO	MPG	PPG	RPG	APG	PCM
72-73	Houston	44	....	245	86	34	98	.347	....	....	....	18	37	.486	....	....	60	5	46	0	....	....	....	5.6	2.0	1.4	0.1	.247
NBA Season Totals		44	....	245	86	34	98	.347	....	....	....	18	37	.486	....	....	60	5	46	0	....	....	....	5.6	2.0	1.4	0.1	....

• MEALY, Dean
Dean Mealy

Born: May 7, 1915. Died: Apr. 1973.   Height: 6'4".   Weight: 195 lbs.   Drafted: —   College: Muskingum

YEAR	TEAM	GP	GS	MIN	PTS	FGM	FGA	FG%	3PM	3PA	3P%	FTM	FTA	FT%	ORB	DRB	TRB	AST	PF	DQ	STL	BLK	TO	MPG	PPG	RPG	APG	PCM
37-38	Wingfoots-N	8	....	....	28	6	....	....	....	....	....	16	....	....	....	....	....	....	....	....	....	....	....	....	3.5	....	....	....
38-39	Wingfoots-N	10	....	....	44	15	....	....	....	....	....	14	....	....	....	....	....	....	....	....	....	....	....	....	4.4	....	....	....
39-40	Oshkosh-N	1	....	....	0	0	....	....	....	....	....	0	....	....	....	....	....	....	....	....	....	....	....	....	0.0	....	....	....
NBL Season Totals		19	....	....	72	21	....	....	....	....	....	30	....	....	....	....	....	....	....	....	....	....	....	....	3.8	....	....	....
37-38	Wingfoots-N	3	....	....	9	2	....	....	....	....	....	5	....	....	....	....	....	....	....	....	....	....	....	....	3.0	....	....	....
NBL Playoff Totals		3	....	....	9	2	....	....	....	....	....	5	....	....	....	....	....	....	....	....	....	....	....	....	3.0	....	....	....

• MEARNS, George
George Mearns

Born: Apr. 18, 1922.   Height: 6'3".   Weight: 175 lbs.   Drafted: —   College: Rhode Island

YEAR	TEAM	GP	GS	MIN	PTS	FGM	FGA	FG%	3PM	3PA	3P%	FTM	FTA	FT%	ORB	DRB	TRB	AST	PF	DQ	STL	BLK	TO	MPG	PPG	RPG	APG	PCM
46-47	Providence	57	....	....	382	128	478	.268	....	....	....	126	175	.720	....	....	....	35	137	....	....	....	....	....	6.7	....	0.6	....
47-48	Providence	24	....	....	61	23	115	.200	....	....	....	15	31	.484	....	....	....	10	65	....	....	....	....	....	2.5	....	0.4	....
NBA Season Totals		81	....	....	443	151	593	.255	....	....	....	141	206	.684	....	....	....	45	202	....	....	....	....	....	5.5	....	0.6	....

• MECHLING, Gene
Gene Mechling

Born: 1909.   Height: 6'1".   Weight: 215 lbs.   Drafted: —   College: Capital

YEAR	TEAM	GP	GS	MIN	PTS	FGM	FGA	FG%	3PM	3PA	3P%	FTM	FTA	FT%	ORB	DRB	TRB	AST	PF	DQ	STL	BLK	TO	MPG	PPG	RPG	APG	PCM
37-38	Cincinnati-N	3	....	....	18	8	....	....	....	....	....	2	....	....	....	....	....	....	....	....	....	....	....	....	6.0	....	....	....
NBL Season Totals		3	....	....	18	8	....	....	....	....	....	2	....	....	....	....	....	....	....	....	....	....	....	....	6.0	....	....	....

MEDVEDENKO, Stanislav

Stanislav Medvedenko

Born: Apr. 4, 1979. Budivelnik-Horda, Ukraine.   Height: 6'10".   Weight: 250 lbs.   Drafted: —   College: none

YEAR TEAM	GP	GS	MIN	PTS	FGM	FGA	FG%	3PM	3PA	3P%	FTM	FTA	FT%	ORB	DRB	TRB	AST	PF	DQ	STL	BLK	TO	MPG	PPG	RPG	APG	PCM
00-01 LA Lakers	7	0	39	32	12	25	.480	1	1	1.000	7	12	.583	1	8	9	2	9	0	1	1	3	5.6	4.6	1.3	0.3	.601
01-02 LA Lakers	71	6	729	331	145	303	.479	0	4	.000	41	62	.661	85	73	158	43	119	0	29	11	42	10.3	4.7	2.2	0.6	.429
02-03 LA Lakers	58	10	620	255	112	258	.434	0	2	.000	31	43	.721	66	75	141	18	118	0	11	8	37	10.7	4.4	2.4	0.3	.314
NBA Season Totals	136	16	1388	618	269	586	.459	1	7	.143	79	117	.675	152	156	308	63	246	0	41	20	82	10.2	4.5	2.3	0.5	....
01-02 LA Lakers	7	0	21	6	3	5	.600	0	0	.000	0	0	.000	1	3	4	0	8	0	0	0	1	3.0	0.9	0.6	0.0	.156
02-03 LA Lakers	9	0	73	34	15	27	.556	0	0	.000	4	6	.667	4	14	18	1	14	0	1	1	3	8.1	3.8	2.0	0.1	.443
NBA Playoff Totals	16	0	94	40	18	32	.563	0	0	.000	4	6	.667	5	17	22	1	22	0	1	1	4	5.9	2.5	1.4	0.1	....

MEE, Darnell

LaFarrell Darnell Mee

Born: Feb. 11, 1971. Cleveland, TN, United States.   Height: 6'5".   Weight: 175 lbs.   Drafted: 1993   College: Western Kentucky

YEAR TEAM	GP	GS	MIN	PTS	FGM	FGA	FG%	3PM	3PA	3P%	FTM	FTA	FT%	ORB	DRB	TRB	AST	PF	DQ	STL	BLK	TO	MPG	PPG	RPG	APG	PCM
93-94 Denver	38	0	285	73	28	88	.318	5	24	.208	12	27	.444	17	18	35	16	34	0	15	13	19	7.5	1.9	0.9	0.4	.187
94-95 Denver	2	0	8	3	1	5	.200	1	3	.333	0	0	.000	0	1	1	2	0	0	1	0	0	4.0	1.5	0.5	1.0	.406
NBA Season Totals	40	0	293	76	29	93	.312	6	27	.222	12	27	.444	17	19	36	18	34	0	16	13	19	7.3	1.9	0.9	0.5	....
93-94 Denver	3	0	30	7	3	6	.500	1	4	.250	0	0	.000	0	2	2	2	4	0	3	0	3	10.0	2.3	0.7	0.7	.214
NBA Playoff Totals	3	0	30	7	3	6	.500	1	4	.250	0	0	.000	0	2	2	2	4	0	3	0	3	10.0	2.3	0.7	0.7	....

MEEHAN, Chick

Don (Chick) Meehan

Born: 1917.   Height: 6'1".   Weight: 195 lbs.   Drafted: —   College: Syracuse

YEAR TEAM	GP	GS	MIN	PTS	FGM	FGA	FG%	3PM	3PA	3P%	FTM	FTA	FT%	ORB	DRB	TRB	AST	PF	DQ	STL	BLK	TO	MPG	PPG	RPG	APG	PCM
46-47 Syracuse-N	29	....	....	209	83	....	....	....	....	....	43	63	.683	....	....	....	....	58	....	....	....	....	....	7.2	....	....	....
47-48 Syracuse-N	22	....	....	42	16	....	....	....	....	....	10	16	.625	....	....	....	....	....	....	....	....	....	....	1.9	....	....	....
NBL Season Totals	51	....	....	251	99	....	....	....	....	....	53	79	....	....	....	....	....	58	....	....	....	....	....	4.9	....	....	....

MEELY, Cliff

Cliff Meely

Born: July 10, 1947. Rosedale, MS, United States.   Height: 6'8".   Weight: 215 lbs.   Drafted: 1971   College: Colorado

YEAR TEAM	GP	GS	MIN	PTS	FGM	FGA	FG%	3PM	3PA	3P%	FTM	FTA	FT%	ORB	DRB	TRB	AST	PF	DQ	STL	BLK	TO	MPG	PPG	RPG	APG	PCM
71-72 Houston	77	....	1815	763	315	776	.406	....	....	....	133	197	.675	....	....	507	119	254	9	....	....	....	23.6	9.9	6.6	1.5	.441
72-73 Houston	82	....	1694	628	268	657	.408	....	....	....	92	137	.672	....	....	496	91	263	6	....	....	....	20.7	7.7	6.0	1.1	.408
73-74 Houston	77	....	1754	750	330	773	.427	....	....	....	90	140	.643	103	336	439	124	234	5	53	77	....	22.8	9.7	5.7	1.6	.438
74-75 Houston	48	....	753	380	156	349	.447	....	....	....	68	94	.723	55	109	164	45	117	4	21	21	....	15.7	7.9	3.4	0.9	.459
75-76 Houston	14	....	174	73	32	81	.395	....	....	....	9	16	.563	12	40	52	10	31	1	9	4	....	12.4	5.2	3.7	0.7	.406
75-76 LA Lakers	20	....	139	64	20	51	.392	....	....	....	24	32	.750	10	35	45	9	30	0	5	4	....	7.0	3.2	2.3	0.5	.504
NBA Season Totals	318	....	6329	2658	1121	2687	.417	....	....	....	416	616	.675	180	520	1703	398	929	25	88	106	....	19.9	8.4	5.4	1.3	....

MEENTS, Scott

Scott E. Meents

Born: Jan. 4, 1964. Kankakee, IL, United States.   Height: 6'10".   Weight: 225 lbs.   Drafted: —   College: Illinois

YEAR TEAM	GP	GS	MIN	PTS	FGM	FGA	FG%	3PM	3PA	3P%	FTM	FTA	FT%	ORB	DRB	TRB	AST	PF	DQ	STL	BLK	TO	MPG	PPG	RPG	APG	PCM
89-90 Seattle	26	0	148	55	19	44	.432	0	0	.000	17	23	.739	7	23	30	7	12	0	4	3	8	5.7	2.1	1.2	0.3	.390
90-91 Seattle	13	0	53	17	7	28	.250	1	1	1.000	2	4	.500	3	7	10	8	5	0	7	4	7	4.1	1.3	0.8	0.6	.297
NBA Season Totals	39	0	201	72	26	72	.361	1	1	1.000	19	27	.704	10	30	40	15	17	0	11	7	15	5.2	1.8	1.0	0.4	....
90-91 Seattle	2	0	8	4	2	4	.500	0	0	.000	0	1	.000	0	1	1	0	1	0	1	0	0	4.0	2.0	0.5	0.0	.383
NBA Playoff Totals	2	0	8	4	2	4	.500	0	0	.000	0	1	.000	0	1	1	0	1	0	1	0	0	4.0	2.0	0.5	0.0	....

MEHEN, Bernie

Bernie Mehen

Born: 1918.   Height: 6'4".   Weight: 185 lbs.   Drafted: —   College: Tennessee

YEAR TEAM	GP	GS	MIN	PTS	FGM	FGA	FG%	3PM	3PA	3P%	FTM	FTA	FT%	ORB	DRB	TRB	AST	PF	DQ	STL	BLK	TO	MPG	PPG	RPG	APG	PCM
46-47 Toledo-N	4	....	....	24	10	....	....	....	....	....	4	7	.571	....	....	....	....	....	....	....	....	....	....	6.0	....	....	....
46-47 Youngstown-N	36	....	....	345	140	....	....	....	....	....	65	91	.714	....	....	....	....	....	....	....	....	....	....	9.6	....	....	....
47-48 Toledo-N	55	....	....	282	118	....	....	....	....	....	46	72	.639	....	....	....	....	60	....	....	....	....	....	5.1	....	....	....
NBL Season Totals	95	....	....	651	268	....	....	....	....	....	115	170	....	....	....	....	....	60	....	....	....	....	....	6.9	....	....	....
46-47 Toledo-N	5	....	....	33	11	....	....	....	....	....	11	14	.786	....	....	....	....	....	....	....	....	....	....	6.6	....	....	....
NBL Playoff Totals	5	....	....	33	11	....	....	....	....	....	11	14	....	....	....	....	....	....	....	....	....	....	....	6.6	....	....	....

MEHEN, Dick

Richard P. Mehen

Born: May 20, 1922. Died: Dec. 14, 1986.   Height: 6'5".   Weight: 195 lbs.   Drafted: —   College: Tennessee

YEAR TEAM	GP	GS	MIN	PTS	FGM	FGA	FG%	3PM	3PA	3P%	FTM	FTA	FT%	ORB	DRB	TRB	AST	PF	DQ	STL	BLK	TO	MPG	PPG	RPG	APG	PCM
47-48 Toledo-N	57	....	....	387	151	....	....	....	....	....	85	125	.680	....	....	....	....	95	....	....	....	....	....	6.8	....	....	....
48-49 Waterloo-N	62	....	....	841	**315**	....	....	....	....	....	211	304	.694	....	....	....	....	195	....	....	....	....	....	13.6	....	....	....
49-50 Waterloo	62	....	....	892	347	826	.420	....	....	....	198	281	.705	....	....	....	191	203	....	....	....	....	....	14.4	....	3.1	....
50-51 Baltimore	16	....	....	151	57	170	.335	....	....	....	37	51	.725	....	....	76	55	42	2	....	....	....	....	9.4	4.8	3.4	....
50-51 Bos/FtW	50	....	....	323	135	362	.373	....	....	....	53	72	.736	....	....	147	133	107	2	....	....	....	....	6.5	2.9	2.7	....
51-52 Milwaukee	65	....	2294	703	293	824	.356	....	....	....	117	167	.701	....	....	282	171	209	10	....	....	....	35.3	10.8	4.3	2.6	.285
NBA Season Totals	193	....	2294	2069	832	2182	.381	....	....	....	405	571	.709	....	....	505	550	561	14	....	....	....	11.9	10.7	2.6	2.8	....
NBL Season Totals	119	....	....	1228	466	....	....	....	....	....	296	429	....	....	....	....	....	290	....	....	....	....	....	10.3	....	....	....
Career Totals	312	....	2294	3297	1298	2182	....	....	....	....	701	1000	....	....	....	505	550	851	14	....	....	....	7.4	10.6	1.6	1.8	....
50-51 Fort Wayne	3	....	....	26	12	29	.414	....	....	....	2	4	.500	....	....	14	3	9	0	....	....	....	....	8.7	4.7	1.0	....
NBA Playoff Totals	3	....	....	26	12	29	.414	....	....	....	2	4	.500	....	....	14	3	9	0	....	....	....	....	8.7	4.7	1.0	....

MEINEKE, Monk
Donald E. (Monk) Meineke

Born: Oct. 30, 1930. Dayton, OH, United States. Height: 6'7". Weight: 208 lbs. Drafted: 1952 College: Dayton

YEAR	TEAM	GP	GS	MIN	PTS	FGM	FGA	FG%	3PM	3PA	3P%	FTM	FTA	FT%	ORB	DRB	TRB	AST	PF	DQ	STL	BLK	TO	MPG	PPG	RPG	APG	PCM
52-53	Fort Wayne	68	....	2250	725	240	630	.381	....	....	....	245	313	.783	....	....	466	148	334	26	....	....	....	33.1	10.7	6.9	2.2	.366
53-54	Fort Wayne	71	....	1466	406	135	393	.344	....	....	....	136	169	.805	....	....	372	81	214	6	....	....	....	20.6	5.7	5.2	1.1	.344
54-55	Fort Wayne	68	....	1026	391	136	366	.372	....	....	....	119	170	.700	....	....	246	64	153	1	....	....	....	15.1	5.8	3.6	0.9	.396
55-56	Rochester	69	....	1248	489	154	414	.372	....	....	....	181	232	.780	....	....	316	102	191	4	....	....	....	18.1	7.1	4.6	1.5	.453
57-58	Cincinnati	67	....	792	327	125	351	.356	....	....	....	77	119	.647	....	....	226	38	155	3	....	....	....	11.8	4.9	3.4	0.6	.383
NBA Season Totals		343	....	6782	2338	790	2154	.367	....	....	....	758	1003	.756	....	....	1626	433	1047	40	....	....	....	19.8	6.8	4.7	1.3	....
52-53	Fort Wayne	8	....	227	60	15	40	.375	....	....	....	30	44	.682	....	....	26	10	37	4	....	....	....	28.4	7.5	3.3	1.3	.242
53-54	Fort Wayne	4	....	87	19	6	23	.261	....	....	....	7	11	.636	....	....	15	6	11	1	....	....	....	21.8	4.8	3.8	1.5	.230
54-55	Fort Wayne	11	....	162	59	18	40	.450	....	....	....	23	25	.920	....	....	48	9	22	0	....	....	....	14.7	5.4	4.4	0.8	.499
57-58	Cincinnati	2	....	32	8	1	11	.091	....	....	....	6	8	.750	....	....	11	1	3	0	....	....	....	16.0	4.0	5.5	0.5	.256
NBA Playoff Totals		25	....	508	146	40	114	.351	....	....	....	66	88	.750	....	....	100	26	73	5	....	....	....	20.3	5.8	4.0	1.0	....

MEINHOLD, Carl
Carl Marvin (Red) Meinhold

Born: Mar. 29, 1926. Height: 6'2". Weight: 185 lbs. Drafted: — College: Long Island University

YEAR	TEAM	GP	GS	MIN	PTS	FGM	FGA	FG%	3PM	3PA	3P%	FTM	FTA	FT%	ORB	DRB	TRB	AST	PF	DQ	STL	BLK	TO	MPG	PPG	RPG	APG	PCM
47-48	Baltimore	48	....	....	253	108	356	.303	....	....	....	37	60	.617	....	....	16	64	....	....	....	....	....	....	5.3	....	0.3	
48-49	Chicago	15	....	....	41	16	36	.444	....	....	....	9	13	.692	....	....	9	12	....	....	....	....	....	....	2.7	....	0.6	
48-49	Providence	35	....	....	222	85	270	.315	....	....	....	52	83	.627	....	....	38	48	....	....	....	....	....	....	6.3	....	1.1	
NBA Season Totals		98	....	....	516	209	662	.316	....	....	....	98	156	.628	....	....	63	124	....	....	....	....	....	....	5.3	....	0.6	
47-48	Baltimore	11	....	....	40	17	67	.254	....	....	....	6	13	.462	....	....	0	6	....	....	....	....	....	....	3.6	....	0.0	
NBA Playoff Totals		11	....	....	40	17	67	.254	....	....	....	6	13	.462	....	....	0	6	....	....	....	....	....	....	3.6	....	0.0	

MEKULES, Frank
Frank Mekules

Born: 1919. Height: 6'4". Weight: 218 lbs. Drafted: — College: Michigan State

YEAR	TEAM	GP	GS	MIN	PTS	FGM	FGA	FG%	3PM	3PA	3P%	FTM	FTA	FT%	ORB	DRB	TRB	AST	PF	DQ	STL	BLK	TO	MPG	PPG	RPG	APG	PCM
46-47	Detroit-N	3	....	....	6	3	....	....	....	....	....	0	1	.000	....	....	....	....	....	....	....	....	....	2.0	....	....	....	
NBL Season Totals		3	....	....	6	3	....	....	....	....	....	0	1		....	....	....	....	....	....	....	....	....	2.0	....	....	....	

MELCHIONNI, Bill
William P. Melchionni

Born: Oct. 19, 1944. Philadelphia, PA, United States. Height: 6'1". Weight: 165 lbs. Drafted: 1966 College: Villanova

YEAR	TEAM	GP	GS	MIN	PTS	FGM	FGA	FG%	3PM	3PA	3P%	FTM	FTA	FT%	ORB	DRB	TRB	AST	PF	DQ	STL	BLK	TO	MPG	PPG	RPG	APG	PCM
66-67	Philadelphia	73	....	692	315	138	353	.391	....	....	....	39	60	.650	....	....	98	98	73	0	....	....	....	9.5	4.3	1.3	1.3	.437
67-68	Philadelphia	71	....	758	325	146	336	.435	....	....	....	33	47	.702	....	....	104	105	75	0	....	....	....	10.7	4.6	1.5	1.5	.458
69-70	New York-A	80	....	3157	1218	479	1030	.465	5	28	.179	255	311	.820	66	164	230	457	282	7	....	....	186	39.5	15.2	2.9	5.7	.418
70-71	New York-A	81	....	3284	1425	561	1244	.451	2	22	.091	301	370	.814	49	188	237	**672**	273	4	....	....	300	40.5	17.6	2.9	**8.3**	**.529**
71-72	New York-A	80	....	3326	1682	672	1346	.499	2	19	.105	336	416	.808	51	197	248	**669**	275	7	....	....	314	41.6	21.0	3.1	**8.4**	**.572**
72-73	New York-A	61	....	1849	751	291	646	.450	6	15	.400	163	194	.840	19	108	127	453	155	0	....	....	184	30.3	12.3	2.1	**7.4**	.520
73-74	New York-A	56	....	1146	296	116	276	.420	5	23	.217	59	71	.831	13	64	77	207	94	....	51	5	86	20.5	5.3	1.4	3.7	.363
74-75	New York-A	77	....	1384	472	201	413	.487	8	27	.296	62	78	.795	12	63	75	320	105	....	69	7	106	18.0	6.1	1.0	4.2	.471
75-76	New York-A	67	....	1191	386	149	358	.416	9	23	.391	79	93	.849	13	75	88	266	66	....	52	8	95	17.8	5.8	1.3	4.0	.451
NBA Season Totals		144	....	1450	640	284	689	.412	....	....	....	72	107	.673	....	....	202	203	148	0	....	....	....	10.1	4.4	1.4	1.4	....
ABA Season Totals		502	....	15337	6230	2469	5313	.465	37	157	.236	1255	1533	.819	223	859	1082	3044	1250	18	172	20	1271	30.6	12.4	2.2	6.1	....
Career Totals		646	....	16787	6870	2753	6002	.459	37	157	.236	1327	1640	.809	223	859	1284	3247	1398	18	172	20	1271	26.0	10.6	2.0	5.0	....
66-67	Philadelphia	1	....	5	0	0	2	.000	....	....	....	0	2	.000	....	....	3	1	0	0	....	....	....	5.0	0.0	3.0	1.0	.241
67-68	Philadelphia	9	....	50	18	8	24	.333	....	....	....	2	4	.500	....	....	4	10	4	0	....	....	....	5.6	2.0	0.4	1.1	.361
69-70	New York-A	7	....	316	128	48	104	.462	1	3	.333	31	38	.816	....	....	22	33	....	0	....	....	....	45.1	18.3	3.1	4.7	
70-71	New York-A	5	....	205	112	44	82	.537	0	0	.000	24	26	.923	1	6	7	41	16	0	....	....	18	41.0	22.4	1.4	8.2	.630
71-72	New York-A	11	....	376	159	61	152	.401	0	2	.000	37	46	.804	....	....	26	69	32	....	....	....	32	34.2	14.5	2.4	6.3	.429
72-73	New York-A	5	....	174	66	24	43	.558	1	3	.333	17	21	.810	0	10	10	31	25	2	....	....	20	34.8	13.2	2.0	6.2	.454
73-74	New York-A	6	....	60	18	8	16	.500	0	0	.000	2	2	1.000	2	7	9	16	5	....	1	0	4	10.0	3.0	1.5	2.7	.583
74-75	New York-A	5	....	108	34	14	39	.359	1	6	.167	5	7	.714	3	9	12	32	10	....	1	1	6	21.6	6.8	2.4	6.4	.488
75-76	New York-A	6	....	36	10	4	14	.286	0	4	.000	2	2	1.000	1	4	5	5	3	....	2	0	3	6.0	1.7	0.8	0.8	.271
NBA Playoff Totals		10	....	55	18	8	26	.308	....	....	....	2	6	.333	....	....	7	11	4	0	....	....	....	5.5	1.8	0.7	1.1	....
ABA Playoff Totals		45	....	1275	527	203	450	.451	3	18	.167	118	142	.831	7	36	91	227	91	2	4	1	83	28.3	11.7	2.0	5.0	....
Career Playoff Totals		55	....	1330	545	211	476	.443	3	18	.167	120	148	.811	7	36	98	238	95	2	4	1	83	24.2	9.9	1.8	4.3	....

MELCHIONNI, Gary
Gary Dennis Melchionni

Born: Jan. 19, 1951. Camden, NJ, United States. Height: 6'2". Weight: 185 lbs. Drafted: 1973 College: Duke

YEAR	TEAM	GP	GS	MIN	PTS	FGM	FGA	FG%	3PM	3PA	3P%	FTM	FTA	FT%	ORB	DRB	TRB	AST	PF	DQ	STL	BLK	TO	MPG	PPG	RPG	APG	PCM
73-74	Phoenix	69	....	1251	496	202	439	.460	....	....	....	92	107	.860	46	96	142	142	85	1	41	9	....	18.1	7.2	2.1	2.1	.428
74-75	Phoenix	68	....	1529	578	232	539	.430	....	....	....	114	141	.809	45	142	187	156	116	1	48	12	....	22.5	8.5	2.8	2.3	.388
NBA Season Totals		137	....	2780	1074	434	978	.444	....	....	....	206	248	.831	91	238	329	298	201	2	89	21	....	20.3	7.8	2.4	2.2	....

MELVIN, Ed
Edward H. Melvin   aka.: Ed Milkovich

Born: Feb. 13, 1916. Height: 5'9". Weight: 170 lbs. Drafted: — College: Duquesne

YEAR	TEAM	GP	GS	MIN	PTS	FGM	FGA	FG%	3PM	3PA	3P%	FTM	FTA	FT%	ORB	DRB	TRB	AST	PF	DQ	STL	BLK	TO	MPG	PPG	RPG	APG	PCM
46-47	Pittsburgh	57	....	....	281	99	376	.263	....	....	....	83	127	.654	....	....	37	150	....	....	....	....	....	4.9	....	0.6	....	
NBA Season Totals		57	....	....	281	99	376	.263	....	....	....	83	127	.654	....	....	37	150	....	....	....	....	....	4.9	....	0.6	....	

YEAR	TEAM	GP	GS	MIN	PTS	FGM	FGA	FG%	3PM	3PA	3P%	FTM	FTA	FT%	ORB	DRB	TRB	AST	PF	DQ	STL	BLK	TO	MPG	PPG	RPG	APG	PCM

• MEMINGER, Dean
Dean P. (The Dream) Meminger

Born: May 13, 1948. Walterboro, SC, United States.   Height: 6'   Weight: 175 lbs.   Drafted: 1971   College: Marquette

YEAR	TEAM	GP	GS	MIN	PTS	FGM	FGA	FG%	3PM	3PA	3P%	FTM	FTA	FT%	ORB	DRB	TRB	AST	PF	DQ	STL	BLK	TO	MPG	PPG	RPG	APG	PCM
71-72	New York	78	....	1173	357	139	293	.474	....	....	....	79	140	.564	....	....	185	103	137	0	....	....	....	15.0	4.6	2.4	1.3	.354
72-73	New York	80	....	1453	457	188	365	.515	....	....	....	81	129	.628	....	....	229	133	109	1	....	....	....	18.2	5.7	2.9	1.7	.403
73-74	New York	78	....	2079	651	274	539	.508	....	....	....	103	160	.644	125	156	281	162	161	0	62	8	....	26.7	8.3	3.6	2.1	.365
74-75	Atlanta	80	....	2177	634	233	500	.466	....	....	....	168	263	.639	84	130	214	397	160	0	118	11	....	27.2	7.9	2.7	5.0	.430
75-76	Atlanta	68	....	1418	410	155	379	.409	....	....	....	100	152	.658	65	86	151	222	116	0	54	8	....	20.9	6.0	2.2	3.3	.373
76-77	New York	32	....	254	43	15	36	.417	....	....	....	13	23	.565	12	14	26	29	17	0	8	1	....	7.9	1.3	0.8	0.9	.270
NBA Season Totals		416	....	8554	2552	1004	2112	.475	....	....	....	544	867	.627	286	386	1086	1046	700	1	242	28	....	20.6	6.1	2.6	2.5	....
71-72	New York	16	....	277	65	24	57	.421	....	....	....	17	27	.630	....	....	43	20	37	0	....	....	....	17.3	4.1	2.7	1.3	.275
72-73	New York	17	....	323	81	31	56	.554	....	....	....	19	34	.559	....	....	37	37	29	1	....	....	....	19.0	4.8	2.2	2.2	.355
73-74	New York	12	....	179	23	11	32	.344	....	....	....	1	5	.200	9	15	24	25	19	0	4	0	....	14.9	1.9	2.0	2.1	.249
NBA Playoff Totals		45	....	779	169	66	145	.455	....	....	....	37	66	.561	9	15	104	82	85	1	4	0	....	17.3	3.8	2.3	1.8	....

• MENCEL, Chuck
Charles J. (Chuck) Mencel

Born: Apr. 21, 1933. Phillips, WI, United States.   Height: 6'   Weight: 168 lbs.   Drafted: 1955   College: Minnesota

YEAR	TEAM	GP	GS	MIN	PTS	FGM	FGA	FG%	3PM	3PA	3P%	FTM	FTA	FT%	ORB	DRB	TRB	AST	PF	DQ	STL	BLK	TO	MPG	PPG	RPG	APG	PCM
55-56	Minneapolis	69	....	973	318	120	375	.320	....	....	....	78	96	.813	....	....	110	132	74	1	....	....	....	14.1	4.6	1.6	1.9	.346
56-57	Minneapolis	72	....	1848	665	243	688	.353	....	....	....	179	240	.746	....	....	237	201	95	0	....	....	....	25.7	9.2	3.3	2.8	.381
NBA Season Totals		141	....	2821	983	363	1063	.341	....	....	....	257	336	.765	....	....	347	333	169	1	....	....	....	20.0	7.0	2.5	2.4	....
55-56	Minneapolis	3	....	52	26	10	19	.526	....	....	....	6	7	.857	....	....	5	8	4	0	....	....	....	17.3	8.7	1.7	2.7	.595
56-57	Minneapolis	5	....	98	25	9	36	.250	....	....	....	7	9	.778	....	....	13	6	7	0	....	....	....	19.6	5.0	2.6	1.2	.191
NBA Playoff Totals		8	....	150	51	19	55	.345	....	....	....	13	16	.813	....	....	18	14	11	0	....	....	....	18.8	6.4	2.3	1.8	....

• MENDENHALL, Murray
Murray (Bud) Mendenhall Jr.

Born: 1925.   Height: 5'10".   Weight: 155 lbs.   Drafted: —   College: Indiana

YEAR	TEAM	GP	GS	MIN	PTS	FGM	FGA	FG%	3PM	3PA	3P%	FTM	FTA	FT%	ORB	DRB	TRB	AST	PF	DQ	STL	BLK	TO	MPG	PPG	RPG	APG	PCM
48-49	Anderson-N	60	....	....	168	64	....	....	....	....	....	40	70	.571	....	....	....	114	....	....	....	....	....	2.8	....	....	....
NBL Season Totals		60	....	....	168	64	....	....	....	....	....	40	70	....	....	....	....	114	....	....	....	....	....	2.8	....	....	....
48-49	Anderson-N	7	....	....	9	3	....	....	....	....	....	3	7	.429	....	....	....	....	....	....	....	....	....	1.3	....	....	....
NBL Playoff Totals		7	....	....	9	3	....	....	....	....	....	3	7	....	....	....	....	....	....	....	....	....	....	1.3	....	....	....

• MENGELT, John
John P. (Crash) Mengelt

Born: Oct. 16, 1949. Lacrosse, WI, United States.   Height: 6'2".   Weight: 195 lbs.   Drafted: 1971   College: Auburn

YEAR	TEAM	GP	GS	MIN	PTS	FGM	FGA	FG%	3PM	3PA	3P%	FTM	FTA	FT%	ORB	DRB	TRB	AST	PF	DQ	STL	BLK	TO	MPG	PPG	RPG	APG	PCM
71-72	Cincinnati	78	....	1438	782	287	605	.474	....	....	....	208	252	.825	....	....	148	146	163	0	....	....	....	18.4	10.0	1.9	1.9	.495
72-73	Omaha	12	....	212	63	26	68	.382	....	....	....	11	19	.579	....	....	22	25	24	0	....	....	....	17.7	5.3	1.8	2.1	.286
72-73	Detroit	67	....	1435	704	294	583	.504	....	....	....	116	141	.823	....	....	159	128	124	0	....	....	....	21.4	10.5	2.4	1.9	.470
73-74	Detroit	77	....	1555	680	249	558	.446	....	....	....	182	229	.795	40	166	206	148	164	2	68	7	....	20.2	8.8	2.7	1.9	.433
74-75	Detroit	80	....	1995	883	336	701	.479	....	....	....	211	248	.851	38	153	191	201	198	2	72	4	....	24.9	11.0	2.4	2.5	.434
75-76	Detroit	67	....	1105	720	264	540	.489	....	....	....	192	237	.810	27	88	115	108	138	1	40	5	....	16.5	10.7	1.7	1.6	.567
76-77	Chicago	61	....	1178	507	209	458	.456	....	....	....	89	113	.788	29	81	110	114	102	2	37	4	....	19.3	8.3	1.8	1.9	.392
77-78	Chicago	81	....	1767	834	325	675	.481	....	....	....	184	238	.773	41	88	129	232	169	0	51	4	122	21.8	10.3	1.6	2.9	.422
78-79	Chicago	75	....	1705	826	338	689	.491	....	....	....	150	182	.824	25	93	118	187	148	1	46	4	120	22.7	11.0	1.6	2.5	.398
79-80	Chicago	36	....	387	219	90	166	.542	0	6	.000	39	49	.796	3	20	23	38	54	0	10	0	36	10.8	6.1	0.6	1.1	.414
80-81	Golden State	2	....	11	0	0	4	.000	0	0	.000	0	0	.000	0	0	0	2	0	0	0	0	0	5.5	0.0	0.0	1.0	-.133
NBA Season Totals		636	....	12788	6218	2418	5047	.479	0	6	.000	1382	1708	.809	203	689	1221	1329	1284	8	324	28	278	20.1	9.8	1.9	2.1	....
73-74	Detroit	4	....	39	17	5	14	.357	....	....	....	7	8	.875	2	5	7	6	6	0	2	0	....	9.8	4.3	1.8	1.5	.493
74-75	Detroit	3	....	65	25	9	23	.391	....	....	....	7	9	.778	2	6	8	9	9	1	1	1	....	21.7	8.3	2.7	3.0	.393
75-76	Detroit	9	....	119	87	34	56	.607	....	....	....	19	27	.704	2	12	14	10	22	0	4	1	....	13.2	9.7	1.6	1.1	.661
76-77	Chicago	3	....	67	38	14	26	.538	....	....	....	10	11	.909	0	4	4	8	3	0	4	0	....	22.3	12.7	1.3	2.7	.574
NBA Playoff Totals		19	....	290	167	62	119	.521	....	....	....	43	55	.782	6	27	33	33	40	0	11	2	....	15.3	8.8	1.7	1.7	....

• MENKE, Ken
Kenneth H. (Angles) Menke

Born: Oct. 2, 1922.   Height: 6'   Weight: 168 lbs.   Drafted: —   College: Illinois

YEAR	TEAM	GP	GS	MIN	PTS	FGM	FGA	FG%	3PM	3PA	3P%	FTM	FTA	FT%	ORB	DRB	TRB	AST	PF	DQ	STL	BLK	TO	MPG	PPG	RPG	APG	PCM
47-48	Fort Wayne-N	44	....	....	123	39	....	....	....	....	....	45	57	.789	....	....	....	49	....	....	....	....	....	2.8	....	....	....
49-50	Waterloo	6	....	....	15	6	17	.353	....	....	....	3	8	.375	....	....	7	7	....	....	....	....	....	2.5	....	1.2	....
NBA Season Totals		6	....	....	15	6	17	.353	....	....	....	3	8	.375	....	....	7	7	....	....	....	....	....	2.5	....	1.2	....
NBL Season Totals		44	....	....	123	39	....	....	....	....	....	45	57	....	....	....	....	49	....	....	....	....	....	2.8	....	....	....
Career Totals		50	....	....	138	45	17	....	....	....	....	48	65	....	....	....	7	56	....	....	....	....	....	2.8	....	0.1	....
47-48	Fort Wayne-N	1	....	....	2	1	....	....	....	....	....	0	0	.000	....	....	....	....	....	....	....	....	....	2.0	....	....	....
NBL Playoff Totals		1	....	....	2	1	....	....	....	....	....	0	0	....	....	....	....	....	....	....	....	....	....	2.0	....	....	....

• MENYARD, Dewitt

Dewitt Menyard

Born: 1944. Height: 6'10". Weight: 210 lbs. Drafted: — College: Utah

YEAR TEAM	GP	GS	MIN	PTS	FGM	FGA	FG%	3PM	3PA	3P%	FTM	FTA	FT%	ORB	DRB	TRB	AST	PF	DQ	STL	BLK	TO	MPG	PPG	RPG	APG	PCM
67-68 Houston-A	71	....	1756	643	256	692	.370	0	0	.000	131	197	.665	....	....	551	84	218	5	....	....	99	24.7	9.1	7.8	1.2	.409
ABA Season Totals	71	....	1756	643	256	692	.370	0	0	.000	131	197	.665	....	....	551	84	218	5	....	....	99	24.7	9.1	7.8	1.2	....
67-68 Houston-A	3	....	64	15	7	18	.389	0	1	.000	1	3	.333	....	....	11	0	8	0	....	....	3	21.3	5.0	3.7	0.0	.170
ABA Playoff Totals	3	....	64	15	7	18	.389	0	1	.000	1	3	.333	....	....	11	0	8	0	....	....	3	21.3	5.0	3.7	0.0	....

• MERCER, Ron

Ronald Eugene Mercer

Born: May 18, 1976. Nashville, TN, United States. Height: 6'7". Weight: 210 lbs. Drafted: 1997 College: Kentucky

YEAR TEAM	GP	GS	MIN	PTS	FGM	FGA	FG%	3PM	3PA	3P%	FTM	FTA	FT%	ORB	DRB	TRB	AST	PF	DQ	STL	BLK	TO	MPG	PPG	RPG	APG	PCM
97-98 Boston	80	62	2662	1221	515	1145	.450	3	28	.107	188	224	.839	109	171	280	176	213	2	125	17	128	33.3	15.3	3.5	2.2	.372
98-99 Boston	41	40	1551	698	305	707	.431	5	30	.167	83	105	.790	37	118	155	104	81	1	67	12	89	37.8	17.0	3.8	2.5	.348
99-00 Denver	37	37	1408	678	272	612	.444	15	39	.385	119	151	.788	29	123	152	104	75	0	33	15	87	38.1	18.3	4.1	2.8	.381
99-00 Orlando	31	31	969	470	188	468	.402	0	9	.000	94	119	.790	35	63	98	54	76	2	42	8	64	31.3	15.2	3.2	1.7	.315
00-01 Chicago	61	61	2535	1202	500	1121	.446	14	46	.304	188	228	.825	72	164	236	201	148	3	78	27	129	41.6	19.7	3.9	3.3	.383
01-02 Chicago	40	40	1503	673	286	717	.399	17	57	.298	84	108	.778	44	111	155	118	86	1	30	10	79	37.6	16.8	3.9	3.0	.311
01-02 Indiana	13	1	213	62	25	67	.373	1	5	.200	11	11	1.000	6	17	23	10	22	0	2	3	9	16.4	4.8	1.8	0.8	.198
02-03 Indiana	72	3	1660	556	244	597	.409	3	16	.188	65	81	.802	32	122	154	112	123	1	49	14	54	23.1	7.7	2.1	1.6	.267
NBA Season Totals	375	275	12501	5560	2335	5434	.430	58	230	.252	832	1027	.810	364	889	1253	879	824	10	426	106	639	33.3	14.8	3.3	2.3	....
01-02 Indiana	5	0	117	39	18	36	.500	0	0	.000	3	4	.750	0	10	10	4	9	0	1	1	3	23.4	7.8	2.0	0.8	.262
02-03 Indiana	6	0	135	39	16	49	.327	0	0	.000	7	8	.875	2	11	13	7	11	0	6	1	5	22.5	6.5	2.2	1.2	.184
NBA Playoff Totals	11	0	252	78	34	85	.400	0	0	.000	10	12	.833	2	21	23	11	20	0	7	2	8	22.9	7.1	2.1	1.0	....

• MERIWEATHER, Joe

Joe C. Meriweather

Born: Oct. 26, 1953. Phenix City, AL, United States. Height: 6'10". Weight: 215 lbs. Drafted: 1975 College: Southern Illinois

YEAR TEAM	GP	GS	MIN	PTS	FGM	FGA	FG%	3PM	3PA	3P%	FTM	FTA	FT%	ORB	DRB	TRB	AST	PF	DQ	STL	BLK	TO	MPG	PPG	RPG	APG	PCM
75-76 Houston	81	....	2042	830	338	684	.494	....	....	....	154	239	.644	163	353	516	82	219	4	36	120	....	25.2	10.2	6.4	1.0	.460
76-77 Atlanta	74	....	2068	820	319	607	.526	....	....	....	182	255	.714	216	380	596	82	324	**21**	41	82	....	27.9	11.1	8.1	1.1	.487
77-78 New Orleans	54	....	1277	475	194	411	.472	....	....	....	87	133	.654	135	237	372	58	188	8	18	118	92	23.6	8.8	6.9	1.1	.479
78-79 New Orleans	36	....	640	219	84	187	.449	....	....	....	51	78	.654	62	122	184	31	105	2	17	41	47	17.8	6.1	5.1	0.9	.432
78-79 New York	41	....	1053	391	158	313	.505	....	....	....	75	109	.688	81	144	225	48	178	8	23	53	86	25.7	9.5	5.5	1.2	.382
79-80 New York	65	....	1565	582	252	477	.528	0	1	.000	78	121	.645	122	228	350	66	239	8	37	120	111	24.1	9.0	5.4	1.0	.435
80-81 Kansas City	74	....	1514	560	206	415	.496	0	0	.000	148	213	.695	126	267	393	77	219	4	27	80	126	20.5	7.6	5.3	1.0	.439
81-82 Kansas City	18	10	380	125	47	91	.516	0	0	.000	31	40	.775	25	63	88	17	68	1	13	21	25	21.1	6.9	4.9	0.9	.412
82-83 Kansas City	78	74	1706	618	258	453	.570	0	0	.000	102	163	.626	150	274	424	64	285	4	47	86	117	21.9	7.9	5.4	0.8	.442
83-84 Kansas City	73	31	1501	480	193	363	.532	0	0	.000	94	123	.764	111	242	353	51	247	8	35	61	80	20.6	6.6	4.8	0.7	.394
84-85 Kansas City	76	4	1061	339	121	243	.498	1	2	.500	96	124	.774	94	169	263	27	181	1	17	28	53	14.0	4.5	3.5	0.4	.372
NBA Season Totals	670	119	14807	5439	2170	4244	.511	1	3	.333	1098	1598	.687	1285	2479	3764	603	2253	69	311	810	737	22.1	8.1	5.6	0.9	....
80-81 Kansas City	10	....	199	56	24	49	.490	0	0	.000	8	14	.571	12	19	31	5	31	1	5	7	9	19.9	5.6	3.1	0.5	.265
NBA Playoff Totals	10	....	199	56	24	49	.490	0	0	.000	8	14	.571	12	19	31	5	31	1	5	7	9	19.9	5.6	3.1	0.5	....

• MERIWETHER, Porter

Porter L. Meriwether

Born: Mar. 16, 1940. Height: 6'2". Weight: 180 lbs. Drafted: 1962 College: Tennessee State

YEAR TEAM	GP	GS	MIN	PTS	FGM	FGA	FG%	3PM	3PA	3P%	FTM	FTA	FT%	ORB	DRB	TRB	AST	PF	DQ	STL	BLK	TO	MPG	PPG	RPG	APG	PCM
62-63 Syracuse	31	....	268	119	48	122	.393	....	....	....	23	33	.697	....	....	29	43	19	0	....	....	....	8.6	3.8	0.9	1.4	.462
NBA Season Totals	31	....	268	119	48	122	.393	....	....	....	23	33	.697	....	....	29	43	19	0	....	....	....	8.6	3.8	0.9	1.4	....

• MESCHERY, Tom

Thomas N. Meschery

Born: Oct. 26, 1938. Harbin Manchuria, China. Height: 6'6". Weight: 215 lbs. Drafted: 1961 College: St. Mary's (CA)

YEAR TEAM	GP	GS	MIN	PTS	FGM	FGA	FG%	3PM	3PA	3P%	FTM	FTA	FT%	ORB	DRB	TRB	AST	PF	DQ	STL	BLK	TO	MPG	PPG	RPG	APG	PCM
61-62 Philadelphia	80	....	2509	966	375	929	.404	....	....	....	216	262	.824	....	....	729	145	**330**	15	....	....	....	31.4	12.1	9.1	1.8	.451
62-63 San Francisco	64	....	2245	1022	397	935	.425	....	....	....	228	313	.728	....	....	624	104	249	11	....	....	....	35.1	16.0	9.8	1.6	.483
63-64 San Francisco	80	....	2422	1079	436	951	.458	....	....	....	207	295	.702	....	....	612	149	288	6	....	....	....	30.3	13.5	7.7	1.9	.491
64-65 San Francisco	79	....	2408	1000	361	917	.394	....	....	....	278	370	.751	....	....	655	106	279	6	....	....	....	30.5	12.7	8.3	1.3	.442
65-66 San Francisco	80	....	2383	1026	401	895	.448	....	....	....	224	293	.765	....	....	716	81	285	7	....	....	....	29.8	12.8	9.0	1.0	.487
66-67 San Francisco	72	....	1846	761	293	706	.415	....	....	....	175	244	.717	....	....	549	94	264	8	....	....	....	25.6	10.6	7.6	1.3	.460
67-68 Seattle	82	....	2857	1190	473	1008	.469	....	....	....	244	345	.707	....	....	840	193	323	14	....	....	....	34.8	14.5	10.2	2.4	.524
68-69 Seattle	82	....	2673	1144	462	1019	.453	....	....	....	220	299	.736	....	....	822	194	304	7	....	....	....	32.6	14.0	10.0	2.4	.535
69-70 Seattle	80	....	2294	984	394	818	.482	....	....	....	196	248	.790	....	....	666	157	317	13	....	....	....	28.7	12.3	8.3	2.0	.528
70-71 Seattle	79	....	1822	732	285	615	.463	....	....	....	162	216	.750	....	....	485	108	202	2	....	....	....	23.1	9.3	6.1	1.4	.482
NBA Season Totals	778	....	23459	9904	3877	8793	.441	....	....	....	2150	2885	.745	....	....	6698	1331	2841	89	....	....	....	30.2	12.7	8.6	1.7	....
61-62 Philadelphia	12	....	508	241	89	224	.397	....	....	....	63	73	.863	....	....	138	32	48	2	....	....	....	42.3	20.1	11.5	2.7	.511
63-64 San Francisco	12	....	405	202	80	181	.442	....	....	....	42	54	.778	....	....	87	21	37	0	....	....	....	33.8	16.8	7.3	1.8	.488
66-67 San Francisco	15	....	408	193	79	175	.451	....	....	....	35	46	.761	....	....	119	25	68	5	....	....	....	27.2	12.9	7.9	1.7	.515
NBA Playoff Totals	39	....	1321	636	248	580	.428	....	....	....	140	173	.809	....	....	344	78	153	7	....	....	....	33.9	16.3	8.8	2.0	....

• MEYER, Big Moose

Big Moose Meyer

Born: —. Height: 6'7". Weight: — Drafted: — College: Gallagher Business School

YEAR TEAM	GP	GS	MIN	PTS	FGM	FGA	FG%	3PM	3PA	3P%	FTM	FTA	FT%	ORB	DRB	TRB	AST	PF	DQ	STL	BLK	TO	MPG	PPG	RPG	APG	PCM
37-38 Kankakee-N	9	....	....	30	14	....	....	....	....	....	2	....	....	....	....	....	....	....	....	....	....	....	....	3.3	....	....	....
NBL Season Totals	9	....	....	30	14	....	....	....	....	....	2	....	....	....	....	....	....	....	....	....	....	....	....	3.3	....	....	....

YEAR	TEAM	GP	GS	MIN	PTS	FGM	FGA	FG%	3PM	3PA	3P%	FTM	FTA	FT%	ORB	DRB	TRB	AST	PF	DQ	STL	BLK	TO	MPG	PPG	RPG	APG	PCM

• MEYER, Bill — William Joseph Meyer

Born: Aug. 30, 1943.   Height: 6'3".   Weight: 195 lbs.   Drafted: 1965   College: Hiram Scott

YEAR	TEAM	GP	GS	MIN	PTS	FGM	FGA	FG%	3PM	3PA	3P%	FTM	FTA	FT%	ORB	DRB	TRB	AST	PF	DQ	STL	BLK	TO	MPG	PPG	RPG	APG	PCM
67-68	Pittsburgh-A	7	....	45	22	10	22	.455	0	0	.000	2	2	1.000	....	....	5	1	7	0	....	....	2	6.4	3.1	0.7	0.1	.321
ABA Season Totals		7	....	45	22	10	22	.455	0	0	.000	2	2	1.000	....	....	5	1	7	0	....	....	2	6.4	3.1	0.7	0.1	....

• MEYER, Little Moose — Little Moose Meyer

Born: 1916.   Height: 6'   Weight: —   Drafted: —   College: Gallagher Business School

YEAR	TEAM	GP	GS	MIN	PTS	FGM	FGA	FG%	3PM	3PA	3P%	FTM	FTA	FT%	ORB	DRB	TRB	AST	PF	DQ	STL	BLK	TO	MPG	PPG	RPG	APG	PCM
37-38	Kankakee-N	3	....	....	7	3	....	....	....	....	....	1	....	....	....	....	....	....	....	....	....	....	....	....	2.3	....	....	....
NBL Season Totals		3	....	....	7	3	....	....	....	....	....	1	....	....	....	....	....	....	....	....	....	....	....	....	2.3	....	....	....

• MEYER, Loren — Loren Henry Meyer

Born: Dec. 30, 1972. Emmetsburg, IA, United States.   Height: 6'10".   Weight: 257 lbs.   Drafted: 1995   College: Iowa State

YEAR	TEAM	GP	GS	MIN	PTS	FGM	FGA	FG%	3PM	3PA	3P%	FTM	FTA	FT%	ORB	DRB	TRB	AST	PF	DQ	STL	BLK	TO	MPG	PPG	RPG	APG	PCM
95-96	Dallas	72	21	1266	363	145	330	.439	3	11	.273	70	102	.686	114	205	319	57	224	6	20	32	65	17.6	5.0	4.4	0.8	.329
96-97	Dallas	19	16	259	78	34	78	.436	1	2	.500	9	12	.750	14	35	49	7	52	1	6	3	27	13.6	4.1	2.6	0.4	.184
96-97	Phoenix	35	17	449	188	74	166	.446	3	5	.600	37	52	.712	39	57	96	12	73	2	5	12	35	12.8	5.4	2.7	0.3	.327
98-99	Denver	14	0	70	16	7	28	.250	1	5	.200	1	2	.500	4	12	16	1	22	0	0	3	4	5.0	1.1	1.1	0.1	.022
NBA Season Totals		140	54	2044	645	260	602	.432	8	23	.348	117	168	.696	171	309	480	77	371	9	31	50	131	14.6	4.6	3.4	0.6	....
96-97	Phoenix	3	0	14	0	0	4	.000	0	1	.000	0	0	.000	2	4	6	1	0	0	0	2	3	4.7	0.0	2.0	0.3	.143
NBA Playoff Totals		3	0	14	0	0	4	.000	0	1	.000	0	0	.000	2	4	6	1	0	0	0	2	3	4.7	0.0	2.0	0.3	....

• MEYER, Tom — Tom Meyer

Born: —.   Height: 6'4".   Weight: 214 lbs.   Drafted: —   College: Detroit

YEAR	TEAM	GP	GS	MIN	PTS	FGM	FGA	FG%	3PM	3PA	3P%	FTM	FTA	FT%	ORB	DRB	TRB	AST	PF	DQ	STL	BLK	TO	MPG	PPG	RPG	APG	PCM
46-47	Detroit-N	24	....	....	188	77	....	....	....	....	....	34	53	.642	....	....	....	....	24	....	....	....	....	....	7.8	....	....	....
NBL Season Totals		24	....	....	188	77	....	....	....	....	....	34	53	....	....	....	....	....	24	....	....	....	....	....	7.8	....	....	....

• MEYERS, Dave — David William Meyers

Born: Apr. 21, 1953. San Diego, CA, United States.   Height: 6'8".   Weight: 215 lbs.   Drafted: 1975   College: UCLA

YEAR	TEAM	GP	GS	MIN	PTS	FGM	FGA	FG%	3PM	3PA	3P%	FTM	FTA	FT%	ORB	DRB	TRB	AST	PF	DQ	STL	BLK	TO	MPG	PPG	RPG	APG	PCM
75-76	Milwaukee	72	....	1589	531	198	472	.419	....	....	....	135	210	.643	121	324	445	100	145	0	72	25	....	22.1	7.4	6.2	1.4	.439
76-77	Milwaukee	50	....	1262	485	179	383	.467	....	....	....	127	192	.661	122	219	341	86	152	4	42	32	....	25.2	9.7	6.8	1.7	.481
77-78	Milwaukee	80	....	2416	1178	432	938	.461	....	....	....	314	435	.722	144	393	537	241	240	2	86	46	216	30.2	14.7	6.7	3.0	.515
79-80	Milwaukee	79	....	2204	955	399	830	.481	1	5	.200	156	246	.634	140	308	448	225	218	3	72	40	182	27.9	12.1	5.7	2.8	.460
NBA Season Totals		281	....	7471	3149	1208	2623	.461	1	5	.200	732	1083	.676	527	1244	1771	652	755	9	272	143	398	26.6	11.2	6.3	2.3	....
75-76	Milwaukee	3	....	54	24	5	11	.455	....	....	....	14	17	.824	2	12	14	2	8	0	1	0	....	18.0	8.0	4.7	0.7	.526
77-78	Milwaukee	9	....	279	116	44	99	.444	....	....	....	28	42	.667	27	47	74	35	32	0	7	11	25	31.0	12.9	8.2	3.9	.522
79-80	Milwaukee	7	....	195	66	26	62	.419	0	3	.000	14	30	.467	16	19	35	14	25	1	9	6	15	27.9	9.4	5.0	2.0	.317
NBA Playoff Totals		19	....	528	206	75	172	.436	0	3	.000	56	89	.629	45	78	123	51	65	1	17	17	40	27.8	10.8	6.5	2.7	....

• MEYERS, Ward — Ward Meyers

Born: 1908.   Height: 6'1".   Weight: 185 lbs.   Drafted: —   College: none

YEAR	TEAM	GP	GS	MIN	PTS	FGM	FGA	FG%	3PM	3PA	3P%	FTM	FTA	FT%	ORB	DRB	TRB	AST	PF	DQ	STL	BLK	TO	MPG	PPG	RPG	APG	PCM
39-40	Indianapolis-N	2	....	....	4	1	....	....	....	....	....	2	....	....	....	....	....	....	....	....	....	....	....	....	2.0	....	....	....
NBL Season Totals		2	....	....	4	1	....	....	....	....	....	2	....	....	....	....	....	....	....	....	....	....	....	....	2.0	....	....	....

• MIASEK, Stan — Stanley Miasek

Born: Aug. 8, 1924. Died: Oct.18, 1989.   Height: 6'5".   Weight: 210 lbs.   Drafted: —   College: none (HS: Textile, NY)

YEAR	TEAM	GP	GS	MIN	PTS	FGM	FGA	FG%	3PM	3PA	3P%	FTM	FTA	FT%	ORB	DRB	TRB	AST	PF	DQ	STL	BLK	TO	MPG	PPG	RPG	APG	PCM
46-47	Detroit	60	....	....	895	331	1154	.287	....	....	....	233	385	.605	....	....	....	93	**208**	....	....	....	....	....	14.9	....	1.6	....
47-48	Chicago	48	....	....	716	263	867	.303	....	....	....	190	310	.613	....	....	....	31	192	....	....	....	....	....	14.9	....	0.6	....
48-49	Chicago	58	....	....	451	169	488	.346	....	....	....	113	216	.523	....	....	....	57	208	....	....	....	....	....	7.8	....	1.0	....
49-50	Chicago	68	....	....	498	176	462	.381	....	....	....	146	221	.661	....	....	....	75	264	....	....	....	....	....	7.3	....	1.1	....
51-52	Baltimore	66	....	2174	779	288	707	.365	....	....	....	263	372	.707	....	....	639	140	257	12	....	....	....	32.9	11.8	9.7	2.1	.444
52-53	Bal/Mil	65	....	1584	512	178	488	.365	....	....	....	156	248	.629	....	....	360	122	229	13	....	....	....	24.4	7.9	5.5	1.9	.371
NBA Season Totals		365	....	3758	3851	1375	4166	.330	....	....	....	1101	1752	.628	....	....	999	518	1358	25	....	....	....	10.3	10.6	2.7	1.4	....
47-48	Chicago	5	....	....	73	28	76	.368	....	....	....	17	30	.567	....	....	....	3	27	....	....	....	....	....	14.6	....	0.6	....
48-49	Chicago	2	....	....	19	6	16	.375	....	....	....	7	11	.636	....	....	....	1	9	....	....	....	....	....	9.5	....	0.5	....
49-50	Chicago	1	....	....	5	2	4	.500	....	....	....	1	1	1.000	....	....	....	0	2	....	....	....	....	....	5.0	....	0.0	....
NBA Playoff Totals		8	....	....	97	36	96	.375	....	....	....	25	42	.595	....	....	....	4	38	....	....	....	....	....	12.1	....	0.5	....

• MICHEAUX, Larry — Larry Wayne Micheaux

Born: Mar. 24, 1960. Houston, TX, United States.   Height: 6'9".   Weight: 220 lbs.   Drafted: 1983   College: Houston

YEAR	TEAM	GP	GS	MIN	PTS	FGM	FGA	FG%	3PM	3PA	3P%	FTM	FTA	FT%	ORB	DRB	TRB	AST	PF	DQ	STL	BLK	TO	MPG	PPG	RPG	APG	PCM
83-84	Kansas City	39	0	332	119	49	90	.544	0	0	.000	21	39	.538	40	73	113	19	46	0	21	11	20	8.5	3.1	2.9	0.5	.565
84-85	Milwaukee	18	0	171	46	17	35	.486	0	0	.000	12	17	.706	18	26	44	13	26	0	8	7	7	9.5	2.6	2.4	0.7	.451
84-85	Houston	39	0	394	165	74	122	.607	0	3	.000	17	26	.654	44	55	99	17	49	0	12	14	27	10.1	4.2	2.5	0.4	.515
NBA Season Totals		96	0	897	330	140	247	.567	0	3	.000	50	82	.610	102	154	256	49	121	0	41	32	54	9.3	3.4	2.7	0.5	....

YEAR	TEAM	GP	GS	MIN	PTS	FGM	FGA	FG%	3PM	3PA	3P%	FTM	FTA	FT%	ORB	DRB	TRB	AST	PF	DQ	STL	BLK	TO	MPG	PPG	RPG	APG	PCM
83-84	Kansas City	3	0	65	30	12	18	.667	0	0	.000	6	10	.600	12	9	21	3	10	0	0	5	2	21.7	10.0	7.0	1.0	.668
84-85	Houston	5	0	57	16	6	19	.316	0	1	.000	4	10	.400	12	9	21	0	8	0	0	2	3	11.4	3.2	4.2	0.0	.281
NBA Playoff Totals		8	0	122	46	18	37	.486	0	1	.000	10	20	.500	24	18	42	3	18	0	0	7	5	15.3	5.8	5.3	0.4	....

• MIGDAL, Ted

Ted Migdal

Born: Feb. 14, 1918. Died: Nov.1, 1999.   Height: 5'9".   Weight: 140 lbs.   Drafted: —   College: Miami (OH)

YEAR	TEAM	GP	GS	MIN	PTS	FGM	FGA	FG%	3PM	3PA	3P%	FTM	FTA	FT%	ORB	DRB	TRB	AST	PF	DQ	STL	BLK	TO	MPG	PPG	RPG	APG	PCM
38-39	Non-Skids-N	2	....	....	18	8	....	....	....	....	....	2	....	....	....	....	....	....	....	....	....	....	....	....	9.0	....	....	....
NBL Season Totals		2	....	....	18	8	....	....	....	....	....	2	....	....	....	....	....	....	....	....	....	....	....	....	9.0	....	....	....
38-39	Non-Skids-N	1	....	....	0	0	....	....	....	....	....	0	....	....	....	....	....	....	....	....	....	....	....	....	0.0	....	....	....
NBL Playoff Totals		1	....	....	0	0	....	....	....	....	....	0	....	....	....	....	....	....	....	....	....	....	....	....	0.0	....	....	....

• MIHALIK, Red

Zigmund John (Red) Mihalik

Born: Sept. 22, 1916. Ford City, PA, United States. Died: Oct.25, 1996.   Height: 6'   Weight: 180 lbs.   Drafted: —   College: none (HS: Ford City, PA)

YEAR	TEAM	GP	GS	MIN	PTS	FGM	FGA	FG%	3PM	3PA	3P%	FTM	FTA	FT%	ORB	DRB	TRB	AST	PF	DQ	STL	BLK	TO	MPG	PPG	RPG	APG	PCM
46-47	Youngstown-N	31	....	....	94	41	....	....	....	....	....	12	29	.414											3.0	....	....	....
46-47	Pittsburgh	7	....	....	6	3	9	.333	....	....	....	0	0	.000			0		10						0.9	....	0.0	....
NBA Season Totals		7	....	....	6	3	9	.333	....	....	....	0	0	.000			0		10						0.9	....	0.0	....
NBL Season Totals		31	....	....	94	41	....	....	....	....	....	12	29												3.0	....	....	....
Career Totals		38	....	....	100	44	9	....	....	....	....	12	29				0		10						2.6	....	0.0	....

• MIHM, Chris

Christopher Steven Mihm

Born: July 16, 1979. Milwaukee, WI, United States.   Height: 7'   Weight: 265 lbs.   Drafted: 2000   College: Texas

YEAR	TEAM	GP	GS	MIN	PTS	FGM	FGA	FG%	3PM	3PA	3P%	FTM	FTA	FT%	ORB	DRB	TRB	AST	PF	DQ	STL	BLK	TO	MPG	PPG	RPG	APG	PCM
00-01	Cleveland	59	43	1166	446	173	391	.442	0	1	.000	100	126	.794	106	174	280	16	156	2	20	53	80	19.8	7.6	4.7	0.3	.370
01-02	Cleveland	74	60	1659	569	221	526	.420	3	7	.429	124	179	.693	133	259	392	24	260	7	18	89	97	22.4	7.7	5.3	0.3	.326
02-03	Cleveland	52	0	809	308	116	287	.404	0	3	.000	76	105	.724	93	138	231	28	124	0	18	38	48	15.6	5.9	4.4	0.5	.409
NBA Season Totals		185	103	3634	1323	510	1204	.424	3	11	.273	300	410	.732	332	571	903	68	540	9	56	180	225	19.6	7.2	4.9	0.4	....

• MIKAN, Ed

Edward Anton Mikan

Born: Oct. 20, 1925. Died: Oct.22, 1999.   Height: 6'8".   Weight: 230 lbs.   Drafted: 1948   College: DePaul

YEAR	TEAM	GP	GS	MIN	PTS	FGM	FGA	FG%	3PM	3PA	3P%	FTM	FTA	FT%	ORB	DRB	TRB	AST	PF	DQ	STL	BLK	TO	MPG	PPG	RPG	APG	PCM
48-49	Chicago	60	....	....	594	229	729	.314	....	....	....	136	183	.743	....	....	....	62	191						9.9	....	1.0	....
49-50	Chicago	21	....	....	107	31	127	.244	....	....	....	45	58	.776	....	....	....	14	48						5.1	....	0.7	....
49-50	Rochester	44	....	....	163	58	194	.299	....	....	....	47	62	.758	....	....	....	28	95						3.7	....	0.6	....
50-51	Rochester	10	....	....	43	17	62	.274	....	....	....	9	12	.750			60	2	21	0					4.3	6.0	0.2	....
50-51	Was/Phi	51	....	....	480	176	494	.356	....	....	....	128	177	.723			284	61	173	6					9.4	5.6	1.2	....
51-52	Philadelphia	66	....	1781	520	202	571	.354	....	....	....	116	148	.784			492	87	252	7					27.0	7.9	7.5	1.3	.347
52-53	Phi/Ind	62	....	927	235	78	292	.267	....	....	....	79	98	.806			237	39	124	0					15.0	3.8	3.8	0.6	.269
53-54	Boston	9	....	71	21	8	24	.333	....	....	....	5	9	.556			20	3	15	0					7.9	2.3	2.2	0.3	.295
NBA Season Totals		323	....	2779	2163	799	2493	.320	....	....	....	565	747	.756	....	....	1093	296	919	13					8.6	6.7	3.4	0.9	....
48-49	Chicago	2	....	....	16	8	38	.211	....	....	....	0	3	.000	....	....	....	1	6						8.0	....	0.5	....
49-50	Rochester	2	....	....	26	8	24	.333	....	....	....	10	11	.909	....	....	....	2	8						13.0	10.5	1.0	....
50-51	Philadelphia	2	....	....	22	6	26	.231	....	....	....	10	11	.909			21	3	6	0					11.0	11.0	1.5	....
51-52	Philadelphia	3	....	74	20	7	22	.318	....	....	....	6	7	.857			20	2	15	0					24.7	6.7	6.7	0.7	.276
52-53	Indianapolis	2	....	32	7	2	10	.200	....	....	....	3	3	1.000			7	0	1	0					16.0	3.5	3.5	0.0	.185
NBA Playoff Totals		11	....	106	91	31	120	.258	....	....	....	29	35	.829	....	....	48	8	36	0					9.6	8.3	4.4	0.7	....

• MIKAN, George

George Lawrence (Mr. Basketball) Mikan Jr.

Born: June 18, 1924. Joliet, IL, United States.   Height: 6'10".   Weight: 245 lbs.   Drafted: —   College: DePaul   HOF: 1959

YEAR	TEAM	GP	GS	MIN	PTS	FGM	FGA	FG%	3PM	3PA	3P%	FTM	FTA	FT%	ORB	DRB	TRB	AST	PF	DQ	STL	BLK	TO	MPG	PPG	RPG	APG	PCM
46-47	Chicago-N	25	....	....	413	147	....	....	....	....	....	119	164	.726	....	....	....		96						16.5	....	....	....
47-48	Minneapolis-N	56	....	....	**1195**	406	....	....	....	....	....	**383**	509	.752	....	....	....		210						**21.3**	....	....	....
48-49	Minneapolis	60	....	....	**1698**	583	1403	.416	....	....	....	**532**	689	.772	....	....	218	260							**28.3**	....	3.6	....
49-50	Minneapolis	68	....	....	**1865**	649	1595	.407	....	....	....	**567**	728	.779	....	....	197	297							**27.4**	....	2.9	....
50-51	Minneapolis	68	....	....	**1932**	678	1584	.428	....	....	....	**576**	717	.803			958	208	**308**	14					**28.4**	14.1	3.1	....
51-52	Minneapolis	64	....	2572	1523	545	**1414**	.385	....	....	....	433	555	.780			866	194	286	14					40.2	23.8	**13.5**	3.0	.632
52-53	Minneapolis	70	....	2651	1442	500	1252	.399	....	....	....	442	567	.780			**1007**	201	290	12					37.9	20.6	**14.4**	2.9	.654
53-54	Minneapolis	72	....	2362	1306	441	1160	.380	....	....	....	424	546	.777			1028	174	268	4					32.8	18.1	14.3	2.4	.682
55-56	Minneapolis	37	....	765	390	148	375	.395	....	....	....	94	122	.770			308	53	153	6					20.7	10.5	8.3	1.4	.586
NBA Season Totals		439	....	8350	10156	3544	8783	.404	....	....	....	3068	3924	.782	....	....	4167	1245	1862	50					19.0	23.1	9.5	2.8	
NBL Season Totals		81	....	....	1608	553	....	....	....	....	....	502	673						306							19.9	....	....	
Career Totals		520	....	8350	11764	4097	8783		....	....	....	3570	4597		....	....	4167	1245	2168	50					16.1	22.6	8.0	2.4	
46-47	Chicago-N	11	....	....	217	72	....	....	....	....	....	73	96	.760	....	....	....								19.7	....	....	....
47-48	Minneapolis-N	10	....	....	244	88	....	....	....	....	....	68	96	.708	....	....	....								24.4	....	....	....
48-49	Minneapolis	10	....	....	303	103	227	.454	....	....	....	97	121	.802	....	....	21	44							30.3	....	2.1	....
49-50	Minneapolis	12	....	....	376	121	316	.383	....	....	....	134	170	.788	....	....	36	47							31.3	....	3.0	....
50-51	Minneapolis	7	....	....	168	62	152	.408	....	....	....	44	55	.800			74	9	25	1					24.0	10.6	1.3	....
51-52	Minneapolis	13	....	553	307	99	261	.379	....	....	....	109	138	.790			207	36	63	3					42.5	23.6	15.9	2.8	.638
52-53	Minneapolis	12	....	463	238	78	213	.366	....	....	....	82	112	.732			185	23	56	5					38.6	19.8	15.4	1.9	.588

YEAR	TEAM	GP	GS	MIN	PTS	FGM	FGA	FG%	3PM	3PA	3P%	FTM	FTA	FT%	ORB	DRB	TRB	AST	PF	DQ	STL	BLK	TO	MPG	PPG	RPG	APG	PCM
53-54	Minneapolis	13	....	424	252	87	190	.458	....	....	....	78	96	.813	....	....	171	25	56	1	....	....	....	32.6	19.4	13.2	1.9	.722
55-56	Minneapolis	3	....	60	36	13	35	.371	....	....	....	10	13	.769	....	....	28	5	14	0	....	....	....	20.0	12.0	9.3	1.7	.672
NBA Playoff Totals		70	....	1500	1680	563	1394	.404	....	....	....	554	705	.786	....	....	665	155	305	10	....	....	....	21.4	24.0	9.5	2.2	....
NBL Playoff Totals		21	....	....	461	160	....	....	....	....	....	141	192	....	....	....	....	....	....	....	....	....	....	22.0	....	....	....	....
Career Playoff Totals		91	....	1500	2141	723	1394	....	....	....	....	695	897	....	....	....	665	155	305	10	....	....	....	16.5	23.5	7.3	1.7	....

• MIKAN, Larry

George Lawrence Mikan III

Born: Apr. 8, 1948. Height: 6'7". Weight: 210 lbs. Drafted: 1970 College: Minnesota

YEAR	TEAM	GP	GS	MIN	PTS	FGM	FGA	FG%	3PM	3PA	3P%	FTM	FTA	FT%	ORB	DRB	TRB	AST	PF	DQ	STL	BLK	TO	MPG	PPG	RPG	APG	PCM
70-71	Cleveland	53	....	536	158	62	186	.333	....	....	....	34	55	.618	....	....	139	41	56	1	....	....	....	10.1	3.0	2.6	0.8	.344
NBA Season Totals		53	....	536	158	62	186	.333	....	....	....	34	55	.618	....	....	139	41	56	1	....	....	....	10.1	3.0	2.6	0.8	....

• MIKKELSEN, Vern

Arild Verner Agerskov Mikkelsen

Born: Oct. 21, 1928. Fresno, CA, United States. Height: 6'7". Weight: 230 lbs. Drafted: 1949 College: Hamline HOF: 1995

YEAR	TEAM	GP	GS	MIN	PTS	FGM	FGA	FG%	3PM	3PA	3P%	FTM	FTA	FT%	ORB	DRB	TRB	AST	PF	DQ	STL	BLK	TO	MPG	PPG	RPG	APG	PCM
49-50	Minneapolis	68	....	....	791	288	722	.399	....	....	....	215	286	.752	....	....	....	123	222	....	....	....	....	11.6	....	1.8	....	
50-51	Minneapolis	64	....	....	904	359	893	.402	....	....	....	186	275	.676	....	....	655	181	260	13	....	....	....	14.1	10.2	2.8	....	
51-52	Minneapolis	66	....	2345	1009	363	866	.419	....	....	....	283	372	.761	....	....	681	180	282	16	....	....	35.5	15.3	10.3	2.7	.527	
52-53	Minneapolis	70	....	2465	1047	378	868	.435	....	....	....	291	387	.752	....	....	654	148	289	14	....	....	35.2	15.0	9.3	2.1	.493	
53-54	Minneapolis	72	....	2247	797	288	771	.374	....	....	....	221	298	.742	....	....	615	119	264	7	....	....	31.2	11.1	8.5	1.7	.411	
54-55	Minneapolis	71	....	2559	1327	440	1043	.422	....	....	....	447	598	.747	....	....	722	145	**319**	14	....	....	36.0	18.7	10.2	2.0	.555	
55-56	Minneapolis	72	....	2100	962	317	821	.386	....	....	....	328	408	.804	....	....	608	173	**319**	**17**	....	....	29.2	13.4	8.4	2.4	.526	
56-57	Minneapolis	72	....	2198	986	322	854	.377	....	....	....	342	424	.807	....	....	630	121	**312**	**18**	....	....	30.5	13.7	8.8	1.7	.484	
57-58	Minneapolis	72	....	2390	1248	439	1070	.410	....	....	....	370	471	.786	....	....	805	166	299	**20**	....	....	33.2	17.3	11.2	2.3	.603	
58-59	Minneapolis	72	....	2139	992	353	904	.390	....	....	....	286	355	.806	....	....	570	159	246	8	....	....	29.7	13.8	7.9	2.2	.508	
NBA Season Totals		699	....	18443	10063	3547	8812	.403	....	....	....	2969	3874	.766	....	....	5940	1515	2812	**127**	....	....	26.4	14.4	8.5	2.2	....	
49-50	Minneapolis	12	....	....	156	55	149	.369	....	....	....	46	60	.767	....	....	....	18	52	....	....	....	....	13.0	....	1.5	....	
50-51	Minneapolis	7	....	....	109	39	96	.406	....	....	....	31	47	.660	....	....	67	17	35	3	....	....	....	15.6	9.6	2.4	....	
51-52	Minneapolis	13	....	495	173	60	139	.432	....	....	....	53	64	.828	....	....	110	20	66	4	....	....	38.1	13.3	8.5	1.5	.391	
52-53	Minneapolis	12	....	400	144	44	133	.331	....	....	....	56	66	.848	....	....	104	24	59	3	....	....	33.3	12.0	8.7	2.0	.401	
53-54	Minneapolis	13	....	375	133	51	111	.459	....	....	....	31	36	.861	....	....	73	17	52	1	....	....	28.8	10.2	5.6	1.3	.384	
54-55	Minneapolis	7	....	209	96	30	85	.353	....	....	....	36	46	.783	....	....	78	13	36	4	....	....	29.9	13.7	11.1	1.9	.537	
55-56	Minneapolis	3	....	90	40	11	26	.423	....	....	....	18	20	.900	....	....	17	2	14	2	....	....	30.0	13.3	5.7	0.7	.421	
56-57	Minneapolis	5	....	162	88	33	83	.398	....	....	....	22	34	.647	....	....	43	17	29	4	....	....	32.4	17.6	8.6	3.4	.548	
58-59	Minneapolis	13	....	371	202	73	177	.412	....	....	....	56	73	.767	....	....	93	24	54	3	....	....	28.5	15.5	7.2	1.8	.531	
NBA Playoff Totals		85	....	2102	1141	396	999	.396	....	....	....	349	446	.783	....	....	585	152	397	24	....	....	24.7	13.4	6.9	1.8	....	

• MIKSIS, Al

Alfonse K. Miksis

Born: Feb. 2, 1928. Height: 6'7". Weight: 210 lbs. Drafted: — College: Western Illinois

YEAR	TEAM	GP	GS	MIN	PTS	FGM	FGA	FG%	3PM	3PA	3P%	FTM	FTA	FT%	ORB	DRB	TRB	AST	PF	DQ	STL	BLK	TO	MPG	PPG	RPG	APG	PCM
49-50	Waterloo	8	....	....	27	5	21	.238	....	....	....	17	21	.810	....	....	....	4	22	....	....	....	....	3.4	....	0.5	....	
NBA Season Totals		8	....	....	27	5	21	.238	....	....	....	17	21	.810	....	....	....	4	22	....	....	....	....	3.4	....	0.5	....	

• MILES, Darius

Darius LaVar Miles

Born: Oct. 9, 1981. Belleville, IL, United States. Height: 6'9". Weight: 210 lbs. Drafted: 2000 College: none

YEAR	TEAM	GP	GS	MIN	PTS	FGM	FGA	FG%	3PM	3PA	3P%	FTM	FTA	FT%	ORB	DRB	TRB	AST	PF	DQ	STL	BLK	TO	MPG	PPG	RPG	APG	PCM
00-01	LA Clippers	81	21	2133	761	318	630	.505	1	19	.053	124	238	.521	127	350	477	99	191	1	51	125	147	26.3	9.4	5.9	1.2	.425
01-02	LA Clippers	82	8	2228	779	309	642	.481	3	19	.158	158	255	.620	109	344	453	184	184	2	71	103	160	27.2	9.5	5.5	2.2	.437
02-03	Cleveland	67	62	2007	618	263	642	.410	0	14	.000	92	155	.594	113	250	363	176	159	3	67	69	178	30.0	9.2	5.4	2.6	.327
NBA Season Totals		230	91	6368	2158	890	1914	.465	4	52	.077	374	648	.577	349	944	1293	459	534	6	189	297	485	27.7	9.4	5.6	2.0	....

• MILES, Eddie

Edward (the Man with the Golden Arm) Miles Jr.

Born: July 5, 1940. North Little Rock, AR, United States. Height: 6'4". Weight: 195 lbs. Drafted: 1963 College: Seattle

YEAR	TEAM	GP	GS	MIN	PTS	FGM	FGA	FG%	3PM	3PA	3P%	FTM	FTA	FT%	ORB	DRB	TRB	AST	PF	DQ	STL	BLK	TO	MPG	PPG	RPG	APG	PCM
63-64	Detroit	60	....	811	324	131	371	.353	....	....	....	62	87	.713	....	....	95	58	92	0	....	....	....	13.5	5.4	1.6	1.0	.292
64-65	Detroit	76	....	2074	1044	439	994	.442	....	....	....	166	223	.744	....	....	258	157	201	1	....	....	....	27.3	13.7	3.4	2.1	.439
65-66	Detroit	80	....	2788	1566	634	1418	.447	....	....	....	298	402	.741	....	....	302	221	203	2	....	....	....	34.9	19.6	3.8	2.8	.479
66-67	Detroit	81	....	2419	1425	582	1363	.427	....	....	....	261	338	.772	....	....	298	181	216	2	....	....	....	29.9	17.6	3.7	2.2	.472
67-68	Detroit	76	....	2303	1404	561	1180	.475	....	....	....	282	369	.764	....	....	264	215	200	3	....	....	....	30.3	18.5	3.5	2.8	.549
68-69	Detroit	80	....	2252	1064	441	983	.449	....	....	....	182	273	.667	....	....	283	180	201	0	....	....	....	28.2	13.3	3.5	2.3	.415
69-70	Detroit	44	....	1243	592	231	531	.435	....	....	....	130	170	.765	....	....	173	82	99	0	....	....	....	28.3	13.5	3.9	1.9	.411
69-70	Baltimore	3	....	52	17	7	10	.700	....	....	....	3	5	.600	....	....	4	4	8	0	....	....	....	17.3	5.7	1.3	1.3	.345
70-71	Baltimore	63	....	1541	622	252	591	.426	....	....	....	118	147	.803	....	....	167	110	119	0	....	....	....	24.5	9.9	2.7	1.7	.348
71-72	New York	42	....	198	62	23	64	.359	....	....	....	16	18	.889	....	....	16	17	46	0	....	....	....	4.7	1.5	0.4	0.4	.197
NBA Season Totals		605	....	15681	8120	3301	7505	.440	....	....	....	1518	2032	.747	....	....	1860	1225	1385	8	....	....	....	25.9	13.4	3.1	2.0	....
67-68	Detroit	6	....	197	87	39	95	.411	....	....	....	9	12	.750	....	....	22	15	16	0	....	....	....	32.8	14.5	3.7	2.5	.357
69-70	Baltimore	5	....	63	8	4	10	.400	....	....	....	0	0	.000	....	....	5	0	5	0	....	....	....	12.6	1.6	1.0	0.0	.078
71-72	New York	9	....	17	4	0	6	.000	....	....	....	4	5	.800	....	....	8	1	2	0	....	....	....	1.9	0.4	0.9	0.1	.328
NBA Playoff Totals		20	....	277	99	43	111	.387	....	....	....	13	17	.765	....	....	35	16	23	0	....	....	....	13.9	5.0	1.8	0.8	....

YEAR	TEAM	GP	GS	MIN	PTS	FGM	FGA	FG%	3PM	3PA	3P%	FTM	FTA	FT%	ORB	DRB	TRB	AST	PF	DQ	STL	BLK	TO	MPG	PPG	RPG	APG	PCM

• MILIC, Marko

Marko Milic

Born: May 7, 1977. Kranj, Slovakia.　　Height: 6'6".　　Weight: 235 lbs.　　Drafted: 1997　　College: none (HS: Kranj, SLV)

YEAR	TEAM	GP	GS	MIN	PTS	FGM	FGA	FG%	3PM	3PA	3P%	FTM	FTA	FT%	ORB	DRB	TRB	AST	PF	DQ	STL	BLK	TO	MPG	PPG	RPG	APG	PCM
97-98	Phoenix	33	0	163	92	39	64	.609	3	6	.500	11	17	.647	10	15	25	12	17	0	10	0	20	4.9	2.8	0.8	0.4	.524
98-99	Phoenix	11	0	53	16	8	20	.400	0	1	.000	0	0	.000	3	2	5	2	7	0	3	1	6	4.8	1.5	0.5	0.2	.134
NBA Season Totals		44	0	216	108	47	84	.560	3	7	.429	11	17	.647	13	17	30	14	24	0	13	1	26	4.9	2.5	0.7	0.3	....
97-98	Phoenix	2	0	4	4	2	3	.667	0	0	.000	0	0	.000	0	1	1	0	1	0	1	0	0	2.0	2.0	0.5	0.0	1.114
NBA Playoff Totals		2	0	4	4	2	3	.667	0	0	.000	0	0	.000	0	1	1	0	1	0	1	0	0	2.0	2.0	0.5	0.0	....

• MILITZOK, Nat

Nathan Militzok

Born: May 3, 1923.　　Height: 6'3".　　Weight: 195 lbs.　　Drafted: —　　College: Cornell

YEAR	TEAM	GP	GS	MIN	PTS	FGM	FGA	FG%	3PM	3PA	3P%	FTM	FTA	FT%	ORB	DRB	TRB	AST	PF	DQ	STL	BLK	TO	MPG	PPG	RPG	APG	PCM
46-47	New York	36	....	....	144	52	214	.243	....	....	....	40	73	.548	....	....	....	28	91	....	....	....	....	4.0	....	0.8	....
46-47	Toronto	21	....	....	100	38	129	.295	....	....	....	24	39	.615	....	....	....	14	29	....	....	....	....	4.8	....	0.7	....
NBA Season Totals		57	....	....	244	90	343	.262	....	....	....	64	112	.571	....	....	....	42	120	....	....	....	....	4.3	....	0.7	....

• MILLER, —

Miller

Born: —.　　Height: —　　Weight: —　　Drafted: —　　College: —

YEAR	TEAM	GP	GS	MIN	PTS	FGM	FGA	FG%	3PM	3PA	3P%	FTM	FTA	FT%	ORB	DRB	TRB	AST	PF	DQ	STL	BLK	TO	MPG	PPG	RPG	APG	PCM
37-38	Columbus-N	1			0	0						0												0.0				
NBL Season Totals		1	....	....	0	0	....	....	....	....	....	0	....	....	....	....	....	....	....	....	....	....	....	0.0	....	....	....	

• MILLER, Andre

Andre Lloyd Miller

Born: Mar. 19, 1976. Los Angeles, CA, United States.　　Height: 6'2".　　Weight: 200 lbs.　　Drafted: 1999　　College: Utah

YEAR	TEAM	GP	GS	MIN	PTS	FGM	FGA	FG%	3PM	3PA	3P%	FTM	FTA	FT%	ORB	DRB	TRB	AST	PF	DQ	STL	BLK	TO	MPG	PPG	RPG	APG	PCM
99-00	Cleveland	82	36	2093	914	339	755	.449	10	49	.204	226	292	.774	85	195	280	476	194	1	84	17	166	25.5	11.1	3.4	5.8	.541
00-01	Cleveland	82	82	2848	1296	452	999	.452	17	64	.266	375	450	.833	94	266	360	657	229	0	119	28	265	34.7	15.8	4.4	8.0	.565
01-02	Cleveland	81	81	3023	1335	474	1045	.454	22	87	.253	365	447	.817	108	271	379	**882**	228	1	126	34	245	37.3	16.5	4.7	**10.9**	**.631**
02-03	LA Clippers	80	80	2914	1088	377	928	.406	23	108	.213	311	391	.795	84	232	316	537	203	3	99	11	206	36.4	13.6	4.0	6.7	.427
NBA Season Totals		325	279	10878	4633	1642	3727	.441	72	308	.234	1277	1580	.808	371	964	1335	2552	854	5	428	90	882	33.5	14.3	4.1	7.9	....

• MILLER, Anthony

Anthony (Pig) Miller

Born: Oct. 22, 1971. Benton Harbor, MI, United States.　　Height: 6'9".　　Weight: 225 lbs.　　Drafted: 1994　　College: Michigan State

YEAR	TEAM	GP	GS	MIN	PTS	FGM	FGA	FG%	3PM	3PA	3P%	FTM	FTA	FT%	ORB	DRB	TRB	AST	PF	DQ	STL	BLK	TO	MPG	PPG	RPG	APG	PCM
94-95	LA Lakers	46	1	527	189	70	132	.530	2	5	.400	47	76	.618	67	85	152	35	77	2	20	7	37	11.5	4.1	3.3	0.8	.477
95-96	LA Lakers	27	0	123	36	15	35	.429	0	2	.000	6	10	.600	11	14	25	4	19	0	4	1	8	4.6	1.3	0.9	0.1	.255
96-97	Atlanta	1	0	14	0	0	5	.000	0	0	.000	0	0	.000	2	5	7	0	2	0	0	0	0	14.0	0.0	7.0	0.0	.067
97-98	Atlanta	37	0	228	79	29	52	.558	0	0	.000	21	39	.538	30	40	70	3	41	0	15	3	15	6.2	2.1	1.9	0.1	.443
98-99	Houston	29	0	249	70	28	60	.467	0	1	.000	14	22	.636	26	41	67	7	34	0	7	5	9	8.6	2.4	2.3	0.2	.373
99-00	Houston	35	14	476	130	52	97	.536	0	0	.000	26	51	.510	49	115	164	16	68	1	11	10	19	13.6	3.7	4.7	0.5	.452
00-01	Atlanta	2	0	6	2	1	2	.500	0	0	.000	0	0	.000	0	2	2	0	0	0	0	0	1	3.0	1.0	1.0	0.0	.333
00-01	Houston	1	0	3	0	0	0	.000	0	0	.000	0	0	.000	0	0	0	1	0	0	0	0	0	3.0	0.0	0.0	0.0	-.150
00-01	Philadelphia	1	0	2	0	0	0	.000	0	0	.000	0	0	.000	0	0	0	0	0	0	0	0	0	2.0	0.0	0.0	0.0	....
NBA Season Totals		179	15	1628	506	195	383	.509	2	8	.250	114	198	.576	185	302	487	65	242	3	57	26	89	9.1	2.8	2.7	0.4	....
94-95	LA Lakers	4	0	15	0	0	2	.000	0	0	.000	0	0	.000	2	4	6	1	2	0	1	0	1	3.8	0.0	1.5	0.3	.258
97-98	Atlanta	4	0	33	8	3	8	.375	0	0	.000	2	2	1.000	5	4	9	1	5	0	2	1	3	8.3	2.0	2.3	0.3	.317
NBA Playoff Totals		8	0	48	8	3	10	.300	0	0	.000	2	2	1.000	7	8	15	2	7	0	3	1	4	6.0	1.0	1.9	0.3	....

• MILLER, Bill

William Ralph Miller

Born: Nov. 24, 1924.　　Height: 6'3".　　Weight: 190 lbs.　　Drafted: —　　College: North Carolina

YEAR	TEAM	GP	GS	MIN	PTS	FGM	FGA	FG%	3PM	3PA	3P%	FTM	FTA	FT%	ORB	DRB	TRB	AST	PF	DQ	STL	BLK	TO	MPG	PPG	RPG	APG	PCM
48-49	Chicago	14	....	....	14	5	23	.217	....	....	....	4	9	.444	....	....	....	8	17	....	....	....	....	1.0	....	0.6	....
48-49	St. Louis	14	....	....	39	16	49	.327	....	....	....	7	11	.636	....	....	....	12	15	....	....	....	....	2.8	....	0.9	....
NBA Season Totals		28	....	....	53	21	72	.292	....	....	....	11	20	.550	....	....	....	20	32	....	....	....	....	1.9	....	0.7	....
48-49	St. Louis	1	....	....	0	0	0	.000	....	....	....	0	2	.000	....	....	....	0	0	....	....	....	....	0.0	....	0.0	....
NBA Playoff Totals		1	....	....	0	0	0	.000	....	....	....	0	2	.000	....	....	....	0	0	....	....	....	....	0.0	....	0.0	....

• MILLER, Bob

Robert E. Miller

Born: July 9, 1956. Louisville, KY, United States.　　Height: 6'10".　　Weight: 230 lbs.　　Drafted: 1978　　College: Cincinnati

YEAR	TEAM	GP	GS	MIN	PTS	FGM	FGA	FG%	3PM	3PA	3P%	FTM	FTA	FT%	ORB	DRB	TRB	AST	PF	DQ	STL	BLK	TO	MPG	PPG	RPG	APG	PCM
83-84	San Antonio	2	0	8	4	2	3	.667	0	0	.000	0	0	.000	2	3	5	1	5	0	0	1	0	4.0	2.0	2.5	0.5	.924
NBA Season Totals		2	0	8	4	2	3	.667	0	0	.000	0	0	.000	2	3	5	1	5	0	0	1	0	4.0	2.0	2.5	0.5	....

• MILLER, Brad

Bradley Alan Miller

Born: Apr. 12, 1976. Fort Wayne, IN, United States.　　Height: 6'11".　　Weight: 244 lbs.　　Drafted: —　　College: Purdue

YEAR	TEAM	GP	GS	MIN	PTS	FGM	FGA	FG%	3PM	3PA	3P%	FTM	FTA	FT%	ORB	DRB	TRB	AST	PF	DQ	STL	BLK	TO	MPG	PPG	RPG	APG	PCM
98-99	Charlotte	38	0	469	238	78	138	.565	1	2	.500	81	102	.794	35	82	117	22	65	0	9	18	32	12.3	6.3	3.1	0.6	.577
99-00	Charlotte	55	4	961	423	135	293	.461	0	2	.000	153	195	.785	113	180	293	45	111	1	23	35	48	17.5	7.7	5.3	0.8	.556
00-01	Chicago	57	45	1434	505	168	386	.435	1	5	.200	168	226	.743	144	275	419	107	176	5	33	38	73	25.2	8.9	7.4	1.9	.486
01-02	Chicago	48	47	1391	608	208	452	.460	2	4	.500	190	253	.751	176	225	401	101	156	2	52	29	74	29.0	12.7	8.4	2.1	.552

YEAR	TEAM	GP	GS	MIN	PTS	FGM	FGA	FG%	3PM	3PA	3P%	FTM	FTA	FT%	ORB	DRB	TRB	AST	PF	DQ	STL	BLK	TO	MPG	PPG	RPG	APG	PCM
01-02	Indiana	28	28	872	424	158	281	.562	1	3	.333	107	130	.823	76	144	220	51	88	1	24	12	41	31.1	15.1	7.9	1.8	.588
02-03	Indiana	73	72	2271	955	329	667	.493	5	16	.313	292	357	.818	185	418	603	193	203	0	65	43	118	31.1	13.1	8.3	2.6	.562
NBA Season Totals		299	196	7398	3153	1076	2217	.485	10	32	.313	991	1263	.785	729	1324	2053	519	799	9	206	175	386	24.7	10.5	6.9	1.7	....
99-00	Charlotte	4	0	62	30	9	17	.529	0	0	.000	12	15	.800	8	5	13	3	11	0	0	3	9	15.5	7.5	3.3	0.8	.420
01-02	Indiana	5	5	180	56	20	44	.455	0	0	.000	16	20	.800	17	32	49	7	16	0	4	2	7	36.0	11.2	9.8	1.4	.424
02-03	Indiana	6	6	135	52	18	40	.450	0	0	.000	16	22	.727	10	23	33	15	17	1	5	0	9	22.5	8.7	5.5	2.5	.476
NBA Playoff Totals		15	11	377	138	47	101	.465	0	0	.000	44	57	.772	35	60	95	25	44	1	9	5	25	25.1	9.2	6.3	1.7	....

• MILLER, Dick

Richard Mathias Miller

Born: Apr. 26, 1958. Milwaukee, WI, United States.   Height: 6'6".   Weight: 215 lbs.   Drafted: 1980   College: Toledo

YEAR	TEAM	GP	GS	MIN	PTS	FGM	FGA	FG%	3PM	3PA	3P%	FTM	FTA	FT%	ORB	DRB	TRB	AST	PF	DQ	STL	BLK	TO	MPG	PPG	RPG	APG	PCM
80-81	Indiana	5	....	34	4	2	6	.333	0	1	.000	0	0	.000	1	3	4	4	2	0	3	0	4	6.8	0.8	0.8	0.8	.192
80-81	Utah	3	....	19	4	2	3	.667	0	0	.000	0	0	.000	1	2	3	1	3	0	1	0	4	6.3	1.3	1.0	0.3	.148
NBA Season Totals		8	....	53	8	4	9	.444	0	1	.000	0	0	.000	2	5	7	5	5	0	4	0	8	6.6	1.0	0.9	0.6	....

• MILLER, Eddie

Edwin B. Miller

Born: June 18, 1931.   Height: 6'8".   Weight: 225 lbs.   Drafted: 1952   College: Syracuse

YEAR	TEAM	GP	GS	MIN	PTS	FGM	FGA	FG%	3PM	3PA	3P%	FTM	FTA	FT%	ORB	DRB	TRB	AST	PF	DQ	STL	BLK	TO	MPG	PPG	RPG	APG	PCM
52-53	Mil/Bal	70	....	2018	733	273	781	.350	....	....	....	187	287	.652	....	....	669	115	250	12	....	....	....	28.8	10.5	9.6	1.6	.431
53-54	Baltimore	72	....	1657	719	244	600	.407	....	....	....	231	317	.729	....	....	537	95	194	0	....	....	....	23.0	10.0	7.5	1.3	.525
NBA Season Totals		142	....	3675	1452	517	1381	.374	....	....	....	418	604	.692	....	....	1206	210	444	12	....	....	....	25.9	10.2	8.5	1.5	....
52-53	Baltimore	2	....	93	33	13	34	.382	....	....	....	7	16	.438	....	....	36	5	9	0	....	....	....	46.5	16.5	18.0	2.5	.470
NBA Playoff Totals		2	....	93	33	13	34	.382	....	....	....	7	16	.438	....	....	36	5	9	0	....	....	....	46.5	16.5	18.0	2.5	....

• MILLER, Harry

Harry David (Moose) Miller

Born: July 28, 1923.   Height: 6'4".   Weight: 230 lbs.   Drafted: —   College: North Carolina

YEAR	TEAM	GP	GS	MIN	PTS	FGM	FGA	FG%	3PM	3PA	3P%	FTM	FTA	FT%	ORB	DRB	TRB	AST	PF	DQ	STL	BLK	TO	MPG	PPG	RPG	APG	PCM
46-47	Toronto	53	....	....	152	58	260	.223	....	....	....	36	82	.439	....	....	....	42	119	....	....	....	....	....	2.9	....	0.8	....
NBA Season Totals		53	....	....	152	58	260	.223	....	....	....	36	82	.439	....	....	....	42	119	....	....	....	....	....	2.9	....	0.8	....

• MILLER, Jay

Jay Julian (Jay Jay) Miller

Born: July 19, 1943. St. Louis, MO, United States. Died: Apr.5, 2001.   Height: 6'5".   Weight: 205 lbs.   Drafted: —   College: Notre Dame

YEAR	TEAM	GP	GS	MIN	PTS	FGM	FGA	FG%	3PM	3PA	3P%	FTM	FTA	FT%	ORB	DRB	TRB	AST	PF	DQ	STL	BLK	TO	MPG	PPG	RPG	APG	PCM
67-68	St. Louis	8	....	52	20	8	31	.258	....	....	....	4	7	.571	....	....	7	1	11	0	....	....	....	6.5	2.5	0.9	0.1	.055
68-69	Indiana-A	41	....	494	283	103	229	.450	0	0	.000	77	112	.688	42	39	81	20	65	2	....	....	55	12.0	6.9	2.0	0.5	.454
68-69	Los Angeles-A	11	....	248	138	44	127	.346	0	0	.000	50	64	.781	18	14	32	9	38	0	....	....	16	22.5	12.5	2.9	0.8	.332
68-69	Milwaukee	3	....	27	9	2	10	.200	....	....	....	5	7	.714	....	....	2	0	4	0	....	....	....	9.0	3.0	0.7	0.0	.055
69-70	Indiana-A	52	....	415	191	75	167	.449	0	1	.000	41	57	.719	43	37	80	16	72	2	....	....	28	8.0	3.7	1.5	0.3	.388
70-71	Indiana-A	2	....	9	8	4	5	.800	0	0	.000	0	0	.000	3	0	3	1	1	0	....	....	1	4.5	4.0	1.5	0.5	1.156
NBA Season Totals		11	....	79	29	10	41	.244	....	....	....	9	14	.643	....	....	9	1	15	0	....	....	....	7.2	2.6	0.8	0.1	....
ABA Season Totals		106	....	1166	620	226	528	.428	0	1	.000	168	233	.721	106	90	196	46	176	4	....	....	100	11.0	5.8	1.8	0.4	....
Career Totals		117	....	1245	649	236	569	.415	0	1	.000	177	247	.717	106	90	205	47	191	4	....	....	100	10.6	5.5	1.8	0.4	....
68-69	Indiana-A	11	....	62	34	15	33	.455	0	0	.000	4	10	.400	....	....	21	2	14	0	....	....	5	5.6	3.1	1.9	0.2	.488
69-70	Indiana-A	3	....	10	2	1	5	.200	0	0	.000	0	0	.000	3	1	4	0	4	0	....	....	1	3.3	0.7	1.3	0.0	.028
ABA Playoff Totals		14	....	72	36	16	38	.421	0	0	.000	4	10	.400	3	1	25	2	18	0	....	....	6	5.1	2.6	1.8	0.1	....

• MILLER, Larry

Lawrence James (Mills) Miller

Born: Apr. 4, 1946. Allentown, PA, United States.   Height: 6'4".   Weight: 190 lbs.   Drafted: 1968   College: North Carolina

YEAR	TEAM	GP	GS	MIN	PTS	FGM	FGA	FG%	3PM	3PA	3P%	FTM	FTA	FT%	ORB	DRB	TRB	AST	PF	DQ	STL	BLK	TO	MPG	PPG	RPG	APG	PCM
68-69	Los Angeles-A	78	....	2871	1328	473	1162	.407	42	139	.302	340	475	.716	196	403	599	177	193	0	....	....	182	36.8	17.0	7.7	2.3	.457
69-70	Carolina-A	59	....	1383	579	223	510	.437	6	36	.167	127	197	.645	89	178	267	100	117	0	....	....	83	23.4	9.8	4.5	1.7	.431
69-70	Los Angeles-A	21	....	654	293	94	248	.379	9	38	.237	96	134	.716	43	104	147	47	56	0	....	....	64	31.1	14.0	7.0	2.2	.459
70-71	Carolina-A	77	....	2140	938	364	795	.458	13	61	.213	197	272	.724	171	286	457	167	181	2	....	....	130	27.8	12.2	5.9	2.2	.494
71-72	Carolina-A	83	....	3199	1529	562	1228	.458	12	47	.255	393	497	.791	177	222	399	235	232	2	....	....	191	38.5	18.4	4.8	2.8	.441
72-73	Carolina-A	83	....	2700	1206	450	1080	.417	0	7	.000	306	422	.725	171	184	355	281	174	1	....	....	168	32.5	14.5	4.3	3.4	.421
73-74	San Diego-A	7	....	68	17	5	13	.385	0	0	.000	7	10	.700	3	6	9	8	5	....	5	0	5	9.7	2.4	1.3	1.1	.347
73-74	Virginia-A	73	....	1900	696	276	625	.442	0	3	.000	144	218	.661	84	116	200	136	133	....	51	6	115	26.0	9.5	2.7	1.9	.334
74-75	Utah-A	5	....	26	9	3	9	.333	0	0	.000	3	3	1.000	1	0	1	4	0	....	1	0	2	5.2	1.8	0.2	0.8	.346
ABA Season Totals		486	....	14941	6595	2450	5670	.432	82	331	.248	1613	2228	.724	935	1499	2434	1155	1091	5	57	6	940	30.7	13.6	5.0	2.4	....
69-70	Carolina-A	4	....	79	37	11	33	.333	2	4	.500	13	17	.765	....	....	10	13	....	....	....	....	....	19.8	9.3	2.5	3.3	....
72-73	San Diego-A	4	....	71	24	9	28	.321	0	1	.000	6	6	1.000	8	2	10	6	3	0	....	....	7	17.8	6.0	2.5	1.5	.298
73-74	Virginia-A	1	....	3	0	0	0	.000	0	0	.000	0	0	.000	0	0	0	1	0	....	0	0	0	3.0	0.0	0.0	1.0	.381
ABA Playoff Totals		9	....	153	61	20	61	.328	2	5	.400	19	23	.826	8	2	20	20	3	0	0	0	7	17.0	6.8	2.2	2.2	....

• MILLER, Mike

Michael Lloyd Miller

Born: Feb. 19, 1980. Mitchell, SD, United States.   Height: 6'8".   Weight: 218 lbs.   Drafted: 2000   College: Florida

YEAR	TEAM	GP	GS	MIN	PTS	FGM	FGA	FG%	3PM	3PA	3P%	FTM	FTA	FT%	ORB	DRB	TRB	AST	PF	DQ	STL	BLK	TO	MPG	PPG	RPG	APG	PCM
00-01	Orlando	82	62	2390	975	368	845	.436	148	364	.407	91	128	.711	66	261	327	140	200	2	51	19	97	29.1	11.9	4.0	1.7	.361
01-02	Orlando	63	53	2123	956	351	802	.438	116	303	.383	138	181	.762	49	224	273	198	145	0	47	23	108	33.7	15.2	4.3	3.1	.420
02-03	Orlando	49	39	1826	806	296	708	.418	87	256	.340	127	150	.847	40	246	286	139	139	1	36	16	99	37.3	16.4	5.8	2.8	.398
02-03	Memphis	16	13	360	205	77	151	.510	22	44	.500	29	36	.806	6	49	55	31	34	1	6	5	26	22.5	12.8	3.4	1.9	.526
NBA Season Totals		210	167	6699	2942	1092	2506	.436	373	967	.386	385	495	.778	161	780	941	508	518	4	140	63	330	31.9	14.0	4.5	2.4	....

YEAR TEAM	GP	GS	MIN	PTS	FGM	FGA	FG%	3PM	3PA	3P%	FTM	FTA	FT%	ORB	DRB	TRB	AST	PF	DQ	STL	BLK	TO	MPG	PPG	RPG	APG	PCM
00-01 Orlando	4	4	112	48	19	48	.396	7	18	.389	3	4	.750	5	13	18	7	13	0	0	3	3	28.0	12.0	4.5	1.8	.353
01-02 Orlando	4	1	72	19	7	21	.333	1	8	.125	4	4	1.000	0	5	5	5	8	0	4	0	4	18.0	4.8	1.3	1.3	.176
NBA Playoff Totals	8	5	184	67	26	69	.377	8	26	.308	7	8	.875	5	18	23	12	21	0	4	3	7	23.0	8.4	2.9	1.5	....

• MILLER, Oliver

Oliver J. Miller

Born: Apr. 6, 1970. Fort Worth, TX, United States. Height: 6'9". Weight: 280 lbs. Drafted: 1992 College: Arkansas

YEAR TEAM	GP	GS	MIN	PTS	FGM	FGA	FG%	3PM	3PA	3P%	FTM	FTA	FT%	ORB	DRB	TRB	AST	PF	DQ	STL	BLK	TO	MPG	PPG	RPG	APG	PCM
92-93 Phoenix	56	1	1069	313	121	255	.475	0	3	.000	71	100	.710	70	205	275	118	145	0	37	100	106	19.1	5.6	4.9	2.1	.485
93-94 Phoenix	69	30	1786	636	277	455	.609	2	9	.222	80	137	.584	140	336	476	244	230	1	83	156	166	25.9	9.2	6.9	3.5	.621
94-95 Detroit	64	22	1558	545	232	418	.555	3	13	.231	78	124	.629	162	313	475	93	217	1	60	116	115	24.3	8.5	7.4	1.5	.545
95-96 Toronto	76	72	2516	982	418	795	.526	0	11	.000	146	221	.661	177	385	562	219	277	4	108	143	205	33.1	12.9	7.4	2.9	.503
96-97 Dallas	42	0	836	180	76	154	.494	0	1	.000	28	53	.528	82	151	233	58	133	1	34	50	71	19.9	4.3	5.5	1.4	.389
96-97 Toronto	19	8	316	114	47	84	.560	0	1	.000	20	26	.769	23	50	73	29	48	0	13	13	21	16.6	6.0	3.8	1.5	.500
97-98 Toronto	64	53	1628	401	170	369	.461	0	4	.000	61	101	.604	146	254	400	196	184	1	58	72	128	25.4	6.3	6.3	3.1	.428
98-99 Sacramento	4	0	35	10	5	11	.455	0	0	.000	0	0	.000	7	1	8	0	3	0	0	2	4	8.8	2.5	2.0	0.0	.248
99-00 Phoenix	51	9	1088	323	137	233	.588	0	0	.000	49	73	.671	87	174	261	68	132	1	42	80	74	21.3	6.3	5.1	1.3	.478
NBA Season Totals	445	195	10832	3504	1483	2774	.535	5	42	.119	533	835	.638	894	1869	2763	1025	1369	9	435	732	890	24.3	7.9	6.2	2.3	....
92-93 Phoenix	24	0	513	173	71	121	.587	0	2	.000	31	55	.564	33	91	124	51	76	0	21	59	42	21.4	7.2	5.2	2.1	.556
93-94 Phoenix	10	4	146	35	16	27	.593	0	0	.000	3	7	.429	14	30	44	13	22	0	6	12	13	14.6	3.5	4.4	1.3	.493
99-00 Phoenix	7	0	37	6	2	9	.222	0	3	.000	2	4	.500	2	6	8	1	8	0	0	2	2	5.3	0.9	1.1	0.1	.094
NBA Playoff Totals	41	4	696	214	89	157	.567	0	5	.000	36	66	.545	49	127	176	65	106	0	27	73	57	17.0	5.2	4.3	1.6	....

• MILLER, Reggie

Reginald Wayne Miller

Born: Aug. 24, 1965. Riverside, CA, United States. Height: 6'7". Weight: 185 lbs. Drafted: 1987 College: UCLA

YEAR TEAM	GP	GS	MIN	PTS	FGM	FGA	FG%	3PM	3PA	3P%	FTM	FTA	FT%	ORB	DRB	TRB	AST	PF	DQ	STL	BLK	TO	MPG	PPG	RPG	APG	PCM
87-88 Indiana	82	1	1840	822	306	627	.488	61	172	.355	149	186	.801	95	95	190	132	157	0	53	19	98	22.4	10.0	2.3	1.6	.395
88-89 Indiana	74	70	2536	1181	398	831	.479	98	244	.402	287	340	.844	73	219	292	227	170	2	93	29	141	34.3	16.0	3.9	3.1	.462
89-90 Indiana	82	82	3192	2016	661	1287	.514	150	362	.414	544	627	.868	95	200	295	311	175	1	110	18	221	38.9	24.6	3.6	3.8	.573
90-91 Indiana	82	82	2972	1855	596	1164	.512	112	322	.348	551	600	**.918**	81	200	281	331	165	1	109	13	164	36.2	22.6	3.4	4.0	.606
91-92 Indiana	82	82	3120	1695	562	1121	.501	129	341	.378	442	515	.858	82	236	318	314	210	1	105	26	156	38.0	20.7	3.9	3.8	.530
92-93 Indiana	82	82	2954	1736	571	1193	.479	**167**	419	.399	427	485	.880	67	191	258	262	182	0	120	26	148	36.0	21.2	3.1	3.2	.529
93-94 Indiana	79	79	2638	1574	524	1042	.503	123	292	.421	403	444	.908	30	182	212	248	193	2	119	24	174	33.4	19.9	2.7	3.1	.541
94-95 Indiana	81	81	2665	1588	505	1092	.462	195	470	.415	383	427	.897	30	180	210	242	157	0	98	16	154	32.9	19.6	2.6	3.0	.510
95-96 Indiana	76	76	2621	1606	504	1066	.473	168	410	.410	430	498	.863	38	176	214	253	175	0	77	13	190	34.5	21.1	2.8	3.3	.511
96-97 Indiana	81	81	2966	1751	552	1244	.444	**229**	536	.427	418	475	.880	53	233	286	273	172	1	75	25	162	36.6	21.6	3.5	3.4	.506
97-98 Indiana	81	81	2795	1578	516	1081	.477	164	382	.429	382	440	.868	46	186	232	171	148	2	78	11	130	34.5	19.5	2.9	2.1	.475
98-99 Indiana	50	50	1787	920	294	671	.438	106	275	.385	226	247	**.915**	25	110	135	112	101	1	37	9	76	35.7	18.4	2.7	2.2	.419
99-00 Indiana	81	81	2987	1470	466	1041	.448	165	404	.408	373	406	.919	50	189	239	187	126	0	85	25	129	36.9	18.1	3.0	2.3	.428
00-01 Indiana	81	81	3181	1527	517	1176	.440	170	464	.366	323	348	**.928**	38	247	285	260	162	0	81	15	133	39.3	18.9	3.5	3.2	.428
01-02 Indiana	79	79	2889	1304	414	913	.453	180	443	.406	296	325	**.911**	23	196	219	253	143	0	88	10	120	36.6	16.5	2.8	3.2	.425
02-03 Indiana	70	70	2119	882	281	637	.441	113	318	.355	207	230	.900	21	151	172	170	89	0	62	4	66	30.3	12.6	2.5	2.4	.401
NBA Season Totals	1243	1158	43262	23505	7667	16186	.474	**2330**	**5854**	.398	5841	6593	.886	847	2991	3838	3746	2525	11	1390	283	2262	34.8	18.9	3.1	3.0	....
89-90 Indiana	3	3	125	62	20	35	.571	3	7	.429	19	21	.905	1	11	12	6	6	0	3	0	3	41.7	20.7	4.0	2.0	.495
90-91 Indiana	5	5	193	108	34	70	.486	8	19	.421	32	37	.865	5	11	16	14	14	0	8	2	12	38.6	21.6	3.2	2.8	.485
91-92 Indiana	3	3	130	81	25	43	.581	7	11	.636	24	30	.800	4	3	7	14	12	1	4	0	4	43.3	27.0	2.3	4.7	.595
92-93 Indiana	4	4	175	126	40	75	.533	10	19	.526	36	38	.947	4	8	12	11	11	0	3	0	10	43.8	31.5	3.0	2.8	.592
93-94 Indiana	16	16	576	371	121	270	.448	35	83	.422	94	112	.839	11	37	48	46	34	0	21	4	32	36.0	23.2	3.0	2.9	.517
94-95 Indiana	17	17	641	434	138	290	.476	54	128	.422	104	121	.860	9	52	61	36	35	0	15	4	39	37.7	25.5	3.6	2.1	.536
95-96 Indiana	1	1	31	29	7	17	.412	2	6	.333	13	15	.867	1	0	1	1	1	0	1	0	0	31.0	29.0	1.0	1.0	.682
97-98 Indiana	16	16	628	319	98	230	.426	38	95	.400	85	94	.904	5	23	28	32	26	0	19	3	27	39.3	19.9	1.8	2.0	.379
98-99 Indiana	13	13	481	263	79	199	.397	28	84	.333	77	86	.895	13	38	51	34	26	0	9	3	21	37.0	20.2	3.9	2.6	.449
99-00 Indiana	22	22	892	527	174	385	.452	58	147	.395	121	129	.938	9	44	53	60	37	0	23	10	28	40.5	24.0	2.4	2.7	.486
00-01 Indiana	4	4	177	125	41	90	.456	15	35	.429	28	30	.933	7	13	20	10	3	0	3	2	11	44.3	31.3	5.0	2.5	.578
01-02 Indiana	5	5	198	118	42	83	.506	13	31	.419	21	24	.875	0	16	16	14	10	0	8	1	14	39.6	23.6	3.2	2.8	.506
02-03 Indiana	6	6	176	55	15	53	.283	4	25	.160	21	23	.913	1	13	14	14	10	0	1	1	7	29.3	9.2	2.3	2.3	.219
NBA Playoff Totals	115	115	4423	2618	834	1840	.453	**275**	**690**	.399	675	760	.888	70	269	339	292	225	1	118	30	208	38.5	22.8	2.9	2.5	....

• MILLER, Walt

Walter P. Miller

Born: July 30, 1915. Died: Jan.21, 2001. Height: 6'2". Weight: 190 lbs. Drafted: — College: Duquesne

YEAR TEAM	GP	GS	MIN	PTS	FGM	FGA	FG%	3PM	3PA	3P%	FTM	FTA	FT%	ORB	DRB	TRB	AST	PF	DQ	STL	BLK	TO	MPG	PPG	RPG	APG	PCM
37-38 Pittsburgh-N	9	....	....	46	18	....	....	....	....	....	10	....	....	....	....	....	....	....	....	....	....	....	....	5.1	....	....	....
38-39 Pittsburgh-N	19	....	....	148	52	....	....	....	....	....	44	....	....	....	....	....	....	....	....	....	....	....	....	7.8	....	....	....
45-46 Youngstown-N	10	....	....	13	4	....	....	....	....	....	5	....	....	....	....	....	....	....	....	....	....	....	....	1.3	....	....	....
46-47 Pittsburgh	12	....	....	23	7	21	.333	....	....	....	9	18	.500	....	....	....	6	16	....	....	....	....	....	1.9	....	0.5	....
NBA Season Totals	12	....	....	23	7	21	.333	....	....	....	9	18	.500	....	....	....	6	16	....	....	....	....	....	1.9	....	0.5	....
NBL Season Totals	38	....	....	207	74	....	....	....	....	....	59	....	....	....	....	....	....	....	....	....	....	....	....	5.4	....	....	....
Career Totals	50	....	....	230	81	21	....	....	....	....	68	18	....	....	....	....	6	16	....	....	....	....	....	4.6	....	0.1	....

• MILLS, Chris

Christopher Lemonte Mills

Born: Jan. 25, 1970. Los Angeles, CA, United States. Height: 6'6". Weight: 215 lbs. Drafted: 1993 College: Arizona

YEAR TEAM	GP	GS	MIN	PTS	FGM	FGA	FG%	3PM	3PA	3P%	FTM	FTA	FT%	ORB	DRB	TRB	AST	PF	DQ	STL	BLK	TO	MPG	PPG	RPG	APG	PCM
93-94 Cleveland	79	18	2022	743	284	677	.419	38	122	.311	137	176	.778	134	267	401	128	232	3	54	50	87	25.6	9.4	5.1	1.6	.386
94-95 Cleveland	80	79	2814	986	359	855	.420	94	240	.392	174	213	.817	99	267	366	154	242	2	59	35	120	35.2	12.3	4.6	1.9	.310
95-96 Cleveland	80	80	3060	1205	454	971	.468	79	210	.376	218	263	.829	112	331	443	188	241	1	73	52	120	38.3	15.1	5.5	2.4	.394
96-97 Cleveland	80	79	3167	1072	405	894	.453	86	220	.391	176	209	.842	118	379	497	198	222	1	86	41	120	39.6	13.4	6.2	2.5	.372
97-98 New York	80	29	2183	776	292	675	.433	40	137	.292	152	189	.804	120	288	408	133	218	3	45	30	104	27.3	9.7	5.1	1.7	.366
98-99 Golden State	47	24	1395	483	186	453	.411	32	115	.278	79	96	.823	49	188	237	103	125	1	39	14	58	29.7	10.3	5.0	2.2	.361
99-00 Golden State	20	11	649	322	123	292	.421	8	30	.267	68	84	.810	46	77	123	47	60	0	18	4	25	32.5	16.1	6.2	2.4	.454
00-01 Golden State	15	8	493	180	71	191	.372	7	25	.280	31	36	.861	24	69	93	18	43	1	9	5	20	32.9	12.0	6.2	1.2	.302

YEAR	TEAM	GP	GS	MIN	PTS	FGM	FGA	FG%	3PM	3PA	3P%	FTM	FTA	FT%	ORB	DRB	TRB	AST	PF	DQ	STL	BLK	TO	MPG	PPG	RPG	APG	PCM
01-02	Golden State	66	0	1237	489	178	427	.417	48	127	.378	85	107	.794	51	139	190	72	120	0	31	13	56	18.7	7.4	2.9	1.1	.355
02-03	Golden State	21	0	262	101	39	106	.368	7	25	.280	16	18	.889	19	31	50	22	29	0	7	3	10	12.5	4.8	2.4	1.0	.365
NBA Season Totals		568	328	17282	6357	2391	5541	.432	439	1251	.351	1136	1391	.817	772	2036	2808	1063	1532	12	421	247	720	30.4	11.2	4.9	1.9	....
93-94	Cleveland	3	1	112	51	19	38	.500	4	5	.800	9	11	.818	10	13	23	8	9	0	7	1	5	37.3	17.0	7.7	2.7	.545
94-95	Cleveland	4	4	139	53	20	37	.541	8	14	.571	5	5	1.000	2	14	16	11	18	1	3	2	6	34.8	13.3	4.0	2.8	.391
95-96	Cleveland	3	3	105	23	11	33	.333	0	5	.000	1	1	1.000	5	11	16	5	10	0	2	2	3	35.0	7.7	5.3	1.7	.180
97-98	New York	9	2	168	44	15	35	.429	4	10	.400	10	12	.833	8	19	27	5	21	0	8	2	6	18.7	4.9	3.0	0.6	.291
NBA Playoff Totals		19	10	524	171	65	143	.455	16	34	.471	25	29	.862	25	57	82	29	58	1	20	7	20	27.6	9.0	4.3	1.5	

• MILLS, Ed

Ed Mills

Born: 1922.   Height: 6'8".   Weight: 225 lbs.   Drafted: 1948   College: Wisconsin

YEAR	TEAM	GP	GS	MIN	PTS	FGM	FGA	FG%	3PM	3PA	3P%	FTM	FTA	FT%	ORB	DRB	TRB	AST	PF	DQ	STL	BLK	TO	MPG	PPG	RPG	APG	PCM
48-49	Oshkosh-N	8	....	....	23	8	....	....	....	....	....	7	12	.583	....	....	....	....	7	....	....	....	....	....	2.9	....	....	....
NBL Season Totals		8	....	....	23	8	....	....	....	....	....	7	12		....	....	....	....	7	....	....	....	....	....	2.9	....	....	....

• MILLS, Jack

Jack Mills

Born: 1918.   Height: 6'4".   Weight: 210 lbs.   Drafted: —   College: Mt. Union

YEAR	TEAM	GP	GS	MIN	PTS	FGM	FGA	FG%	3PM	3PA	3P%	FTM	FTA	FT%	ORB	DRB	TRB	AST	PF	DQ	STL	BLK	TO	MPG	PPG	RPG	APG	PCM
46-47	Youngstown-N	8	....	....	18	5	....	....	....	....	....	8	10	.800	....	....	....	....	....	....	....	....	....	2.3		....	....	....
NBL Season Totals		8	....	....	18	5						8	10												2.3	....	....	....

• MILLS, John

John (Long John) Mills

Born: Sept. 7, 1919.   Height: 6'8".   Weight: 203 lbs.   Drafted: 1947   College: Western Kentucky

YEAR	TEAM	GP	GS	MIN	PTS	FGM	FGA	FG%	3PM	3PA	3P%	FTM	FTA	FT%	ORB	DRB	TRB	AST	PF	DQ	STL	BLK	TO	MPG	PPG	RPG	APG	PCM
44-45	Cleveland-N	29	....	....	100	29	....	....	....	....	....	42	....	....	....	....	....	....	....	....	....	....	....	3.4	....	....		
45-46	Cleveland-N	19	....	....	51	13	....	....	....	....	....	25	....	....	....	....	....	....	....	....	....	....	....	2.7	....	....		
46-47	Pittsburgh	47	....	....	181	55	187	.294	....	....	....	71	129	.550	....	....	....	9	94	....	....	....	....	3.9	....	0.2		
NBA Season Totals		47	....	....	181	55	187	.294				71	129	.550				9	94					3.9	....	0.2		
NBL Season Totals		48	....	....	151	42	....					67												3.1				
Career Totals		95	....	....	332	97	187					138	129					9	94					3.5	....	0.1		
44-45	Cleveland-N	2	....	....	12	3	....	....	....	....	....	6	....	....	....	....	....	....	....	....	....	....	....	6.0	....	....		
NBL Playoff Totals		2	....	....	12	3	....	....				6												6.0	....	....		

• MILLS, Terry

Terry Richard (T) Mills

Born: Dec. 21, 1967. Romulus, MI, United States.   Height: 6'10".   Weight: 230 lbs.   Drafted: 1990   College: Michigan

YEAR	TEAM	GP	GS	MIN	PTS	FGM	FGA	FG%	3PM	3PA	3P%	FTM	FTA	FT%	ORB	DRB	TRB	AST	PF	DQ	STL	BLK	TO	MPG	PPG	RPG	APG	PCM
90-91	Denver	17	0	279	128	56	120	.467	0	2	.000	16	22	.727	31	57	88	16	44	0	16	9	19	16.4	7.5	5.2	0.9	.537
90-91	New Jersey	38	2	540	187	78	168	.464	0	2	.000	31	44	.705	51	90	141	17	56	0	19	20	27	14.2	4.9	3.7	0.4	.429
91-92	New Jersey	82	24	1714	742	310	670	.463	8	23	.348	114	152	.750	187	266	453	84	200	3	48	41	82	20.9	9.0	5.5	1.0	.475
92-93	Detroit	81	46	2183	1199	494	1073	.460	10	36	.278	201	254	.791	176	296	472	111	282	6	44	50	146	27.0	14.8	5.8	1.4	.464
93-94	Detroit	80	74	2773	1381	588	1151	.511	24	73	.329	181	227	.797	193	479	672	177	309	6	64	62	152	34.7	17.3	8.4	2.2	.536
94-95	Detroit	72	69	2514	1118	417	933	.447	109	285	.382	175	219	.799	124	434	558	160	253	5	68	33	144	34.9	15.5	7.8	2.2	.457
95-96	Detroit	82	5	1656	769	283	675	.419	82	207	.396	121	157	.771	108	244	352	98	197	0	42	20	98	20.2	9.4	4.3	1.2	.418
96-97	Detroit	79	5	1997	857	312	702	.444	175	415	.422	58	70	.829	68	309	377	99	161	1	35	27	87	25.3	10.8	4.8	1.3	.424
97-98	Miami	50	0	782	212	81	206	.393	25	81	.309	25	33	.758	34	118	152	39	129	1	19	9	45	15.6	4.2	3.0	0.8	.257
98-99	Miami	1	0	29	9	3	8	.375	2	4	.500	1	2	.500	3	1	4	0	3	0	1	0	3	29.0	9.0	4.0	0.0	.157
99-00	Detroit	82	78	1842	548	214	488	.439	95	242	.393	25	34	.735	50	340	390	85	242	1	38	24	46	22.5	6.7	4.8	1.0	.351
00-01	Indiana	14	0	113	25	11	34	.324	9	17	.176	0	0	.000	4	17	21	5	20	1	3	1	10	8.1	1.8	1.5	0.4	.127
NBA Season Totals		678	303	16422	7175	2847	6228	.457	533	1387	.384	948	1214	.781	1029	2651	3680	891	1896	27	397	296	859	24.2	10.6	5.4	1.3	....
91-92	New Jersey	4	0	77	27	10	27	.370	0	1	.000	7	11	.636	9	15	24	8	18	0	1	2	7	19.3	6.8	6.0	2.0	.365
95-96	Detroit	3	0	48	16	5	20	.250	1	8	.125	5	6	.833	3	2	5	4	6	0	1	0	1	16.0	5.3	1.7	1.3	.157
96-97	Detroit	5	4	196	59	24	55	.436	9	26	.346	2	4	.500	4	31	35	7	14	0	6	0	4	39.2	11.8	7.0	1.4	.330
97-98	Miami	2	0	11	4	1	5	.200	1	4	.250	1	2	.500	0	3	3	0	3	0	0	0	0	5.5	2.0	1.5	0.0	.114
99-00	Detroit	3	3	77	25	9	15	.600	6	9	.667	1	2	.500	0	6	6	1	12	1	2	0	2	25.7	8.3	2.0	0.3	.262
NBA Playoff Totals		17	7	409	131	49	122	.402	17	48	.354	16	25	.640	16	57	73	20	53	1	10	2	14	24.1	7.7	4.3	1.2	

• MINER, Harold

Harold David (Baby Jordan) Miner

Born: May 5, 1971. Inglewood, CA, United States.   Height: 6'5".   Weight: 210 lbs.   Drafted: 1992   College: USC

YEAR	TEAM	GP	GS	MIN	PTS	FGM	FGA	FG%	3PM	3PA	3P%	FTM	FTA	FT%	ORB	DRB	TRB	AST	PF	DQ	STL	BLK	TO	MPG	PPG	RPG	APG	PCM
92-93	Miami	73	0	1383	750	292	615	.475	3	9	.333	163	214	.762	74	73	147	73	130	2	34	8	95	18.9	10.3	2.0	1.0	.383
93-94	Miami	63	31	1358	661	254	532	.477	4	6	.667	149	180	.828	75	81	156	95	132	0	31	13	95	21.6	10.5	2.5	1.5	.391
94-95	Miami	45	16	871	329	123	305	.403	14	49	.286	69	95	.726	38	79	117	69	85	0	15	6	77	19.4	7.3	2.6	1.5	.272
95-96	Cleveland	19	0	136	61	23	52	.442	2	10	.200	13	13	1.000	4	8	12	8	23	1	0	0	13	7.2	3.2	0.6	0.4	.224
NBA Season Totals		200	47	3748	1801	692	1504	.460	23	74	.311	394	502	.785	191	241	432	245	370	3	80	27	280	18.7	9.0	2.2	1.2	....
93-94	Miami	4	0	57	32	12	26	.462	0	0	.000	8	11	.727	3	5	8	2	4	0	1	0	2	14.3	8.0	2.0	0.5	.430
NBA Playoff Totals		4	0	57	32	12	26	.462	0	0	.000	8	11	.727	3	5	8	2	4	0	1	0	2	14.3	8.0	2.0	0.5	

• MING, Yao

Yao Ming

Born: Sept. 12, 1980. Shanghai, China.   Height: 7'5".   Weight: 296 lbs.   Drafted: 2002   College: none

YEAR	TEAM	GP	GS	MIN	PTS	FGM	FGA	FG%	3PM	3PA	3P%	FTM	FTA	FT%	ORB	DRB	TRB	AST	PF	DQ	STL	BLK	TO	MPG	PPG	RPG	APG	PCM
02-03	Houston	82	72	2383	1104	401	805	.498	1	2	.500	301	371	.811	196	479	675	137	230	1	31	147	173	29.1	13.5	8.2	1.7	.574
NBA Season Totals		82	72	2383	1104	401	805	.498	1	2	.500	301	371	.811	196	479	675	137	230	1	31	147	173	29.1	13.5	8.2	1.7	....

YEAR	TEAM	GP	GS	MIN	PTS	FGM	FGA	FG%	3PM	3PA	3P%	FTM	FTA	FT%	ORB	DRB	TRB	AST	PF	DQ	STL	BLK	TO	MPG	PPG	RPG	APG	PCM

• MINNIEFIELD, Dirk
Dirk DeWayne Minniefield

Born: Jan. 17, 1961. Lexington, KY, United States.　Height: 6'3".　Weight: 180 lbs.　Drafted: 1983　College: Kentucky

YEAR	TEAM	GP	GS	MIN	PTS	FGM	FGA	FG%	3PM	3PA	3P%	FTM	FTA	FT%	ORB	DRB	TRB	AST	PF	DQ	STL	BLK	TO	MPG	PPG	RPG	APG	PCM
85-86	Cleveland	76	2	1131	417	167	347	.481	10	37	.270	73	93	.785	43	88	131	269	165	1	65	1	106	14.9	5.5	1.7	3.5	.474
86-87	Cleveland	11	0	122	27	13	42	.310	0	5	.000	1	4	.250	1	9	10	13	8	0	6	1	12	11.1	2.5	0.9	1.2	.110
86-87	Houston	63	52	1478	482	205	440	.466	11	34	.324	61	86	.709	28	102	130	335	166	2	66	6	145	23.5	7.7	2.1	5.3	.396
87-88	Golden State	11	0	202	65	25	48	.521	1	5	.200	14	23	.609	8	13	21	38	26	0	15	0	17	18.4	5.9	1.9	3.5	.423
87-88	Boston	61	6	868	196	83	173	.480	3	11	.273	27	32	.844	22	53	75	190	107	0	44	3	79	14.2	3.2	1.2	3.1	.349
NBA Season Totals		222	60	3801	1187	493	1050	.470	25	92	.272	176	238	.739	102	265	367	845	472	3	196	11	359	17.1	5.3	1.7	3.8	....
86-87	Houston	8	0	27	14	4	8	.500	0	1	.000	6	6	1.000	2	0	2	2	8	0	1	0	4	3.4	1.8	0.3	0.3	.287
87-88	Boston	11	0	50	16	6	14	.429	2	4	.500	2	2	1.000	1	1	2	11	13	0	2	0	10	4.5	1.5	0.2	1.0	.173
NBA Playoff Totals		19	0	77	30	10	22	.455	2	5	.400	8	8	1.000	3	1	4	13	21	0	3	0	14	4.1	1.6	0.2	0.7	....

• MINOR, Dave
Davage (Wheelhorse of Steel City) Minor

Born: Feb. 23, 1922. MO, United States.　Height: 6'2".　Weight: 185 lbs.　Drafted: —　College: UCLA

YEAR	TEAM	GP	GS	MIN	PTS	FGM	FGA	FG%	3PM	3PA	3P%	FTM	FTA	FT%	ORB	DRB	TRB	AST	PF	DQ	STL	BLK	TO	MPG	PPG	RPG	APG	PCM
51-52	Baltimore	57	....	1558	471	185	522	.354	....	....	....	101	132	.765	....	....	275	160	161	2	....	....	....	27.3	8.3	4.8	2.8	.363
52-53	Bal/Mil	59	....	1610	406	154	420	.367	....	....	....	98	132	.742	....	....	252	128	211	....	....	....	....	27.3	6.9	4.3	2.2	.292
NBA Season Totals		116	....	3168	877	339	942	.360	....	....	....	199	264	.754	....	....	527	288	372	2	....	....	....	27.3	7.6	4.5	2.5	....

• MINOR, Greg
Greg Magado Minor

Born: Sept. 18, 1971. Sandersville, GA, United States.　Height: 6'6".　Weight: 210 lbs.　Drafted: 1994　College: Louisville

YEAR	TEAM	GP	GS	MIN	PTS	FGM	FGA	FG%	3PM	3PA	3P%	FTM	FTA	FT%	ORB	DRB	TRB	AST	PF	DQ	STL	BLK	TO	MPG	PPG	RPG	APG	PCM
94-95	Boston	63	8	945	377	155	301	.515	2	12	.167	65	78	.833	49	88	137	66	89	0	32	16	44	15.0	6.0	2.2	1.0	.418
95-96	Boston	78	47	1761	746	320	640	.500	7	27	.259	99	130	.762	93	164	257	146	161	0	36	11	78	22.6	9.6	3.3	1.9	.410
96-97	Boston	23	15	547	220	94	196	.480	1	8	.125	31	36	.861	30	50	80	34	45	0	15	2	23	23.8	9.6	3.5	1.5	.378
97-98	Boston	69	16	1126	345	140	321	.436	6	31	.194	59	86	.686	55	95	150	88	100	0	53	11	41	16.3	5.0	2.2	1.3	.333
98-99	Boston	44	7	765	214	85	204	.417	8	28	.286	36	48	.750	31	86	117	50	69	1	20	6	38	17.4	4.9	2.7	1.1	.289
NBA Season Totals		277	93	5144	1902	794	1662	.478	24	106	.226	290	378	.767	258	483	741	384	464	1	156	46	224	18.6	6.9	2.7	1.4	....
94-95	Boston	4	0	37	11	5	13	.385	0	0	.000	1	1	1.000	1	0	1	2	3	0	1	1	1	9.3	2.8	0.3	0.5	.165
NBA Playoff Totals		4	0	37	11	5	13	.385	0	0	.000	1	1	1.000	1	0	1	2	3	0	1	1	1	9.3	2.8	0.3	0.5	....

• MINOR, Mark
Mark William Minor

Born: May 14, 1950.　Height: 6'6".　Weight: 215 lbs.　Drafted: —　College: Ohio State

YEAR	TEAM	GP	GS	MIN	PTS	FGM	FGA	FG%	3PM	3PA	3P%	FTM	FTA	FT%	ORB	DRB	TRB	AST	PF	DQ	STL	BLK	TO	MPG	PPG	RPG	APG	PCM
72-73	Boston	4	....	20	5	1	4	.250	....	....	....	3	4	.750	....	....	4	2	5	0	....	....	....	5.0	1.3	1.0	0.5	.278
NBA Season Totals		4	....	20	5	1	4	.250	....	....	....	3	4	.750	....	....	4	2	5	0	....	....	....	5.0	1.3	1.0	0.5	....

• MISAKA, Wat
Wataru Misaka

Born: Dec. 21, 1923. Ogden, UT, United States.　Height: 5'7".　Weight: 150 lbs.　Drafted: 1947　College: Utah

YEAR	TEAM	GP	GS	MIN	PTS	FGM	FGA	FG%	3PM	3PA	3P%	FTM	FTA	FT%	ORB	DRB	TRB	AST	PF	DQ	STL	BLK	TO	MPG	PPG	RPG	APG	PCM
47-48	New York	3	....	....	7	3	13	.231	....	....	....	1	3	.333	....	....	0	7	....	....	....	....	....	....	2.3	....	0.0	....
NBA Season Totals		3	....	....	7	3	13	.231	....	....	....	1	3	.333	....	....	0	7	....	....	....	....	....	....	2.3	....	0.0	....

• MISKIRI, Jason
Jason Miskiri

Born: Aug. 19, 1975. Georgetown, Guyana.　Height: 6'2".　Weight: 175 lbs.　Drafted: —　College: George Mason

YEAR	TEAM	GP	GS	MIN	PTS	FGM	FGA	FG%	3PM	3PA	3P%	FTM	FTA	FT%	ORB	DRB	TRB	AST	PF	DQ	STL	BLK	TO	MPG	PPG	RPG	APG	PCM
99-00	Charlotte	1	0	3	0	0	1	.000	0	1	.000	0	0	.000	0	0	0	1	2	0	0	0	0	3.0	0.0	0.0	1.0	-.241
NBA Season Totals		1	0	3	0	0	1	.000	0	1	.000	0	0	.000	0	0	0	1	2	0	0	0	0	3.0	0.0	0.0	1.0	....

• MITCHELL, Guy
Guy Mitchell

Born: 1924. Hutchinson, KS, United States.　Height: 6'3".　Weight: 190 lbs.　Drafted: —　College: Pittsburg State

YEAR	TEAM	GP	GS	MIN	PTS	FGM	FGA	FG%	3PM	3PA	3P%	FTM	FTA	FT%	ORB	DRB	TRB	AST	PF	DQ	STL	BLK	TO	MPG	PPG	RPG	APG	PCM
48-49	Denver-N	57	....	....	171	67	....	....	....	....	....	37	75	.493	....	....	....	80	....	....	....	....	....	....	3.0	....	....	....
NBL Season Totals		57	....	....	171	67	....	....	....	....	....	37	75		....	....	....	80	....	....	....	....	....	....	3.0	....	....	....

• MITCHELL, Leland
Leland Mitchell

Born: Feb. 22, 1941. Kiln, MS, United States.　Height: 6'4".　Weight: 210 lbs.　Drafted: 1963　College: Mississippi State

YEAR	TEAM	GP	GS	MIN	PTS	FGM	FGA	FG%	3PM	3PA	3P%	FTM	FTA	FT%	ORB	DRB	TRB	AST	PF	DQ	STL	BLK	TO	MPG	PPG	RPG	APG	PCM
67-68	New Orleans-A	78	....	1091	321	122	350	.349	21	76	.276	56	85	.659	....	....	182	73	159	1	....	....	108	14.0	4.1	2.3	0.9	.266
ABA Season Totals		78	....	1091	321	122	350	.349	21	76	.276	56	85	.659	....	....	182	73	159	1	....	....	108	14.0	4.1	2.3	0.9	....
67-68	New Orleans-A	7	....	57	3	1	9	.111	0	4	.000	1	2	.500	....	....	3	3	8	0	....	....	5	8.1	0.4	0.4	0.4	-.024
ABA Playoff Totals		7	....	57	3	1	9	.111	0	4	.000	1	2	.500	....	....	3	3	8	0	....	....	5	8.1	0.4	0.4	0.4	....

• MITCHELL, Mike
Michael Anthony Mitchell

Born: Jan. 1, 1956. Atlanta, GA, United States.　Height: 6'7".　Weight: 215 lbs.　Drafted: 1978　College: Auburn

YEAR	TEAM	GP	GS	MIN	PTS	FGM	FGA	FG%	3PM	3PA	3P%	FTM	FTA	FT%	ORB	DRB	TRB	AST	PF	DQ	STL	BLK	TO	MPG	PPG	RPG	APG	PCM
78-79	Cleveland	80	....	1576	855	362	706	.513	....	....	....	131	178	.736	127	202	329	60	215	6	51	29	104	19.7	10.7	4.1	0.8	.488
79-80	Cleveland	82	....	2802	1820	775	1482	.523	0	6	.000	270	343	.787	206	385	591	93	259	4	70	77	172	34.2	22.2	7.2	1.1	.587
80-81	Cleveland	82	....	3194	2012	853	**1791**	.476	4	9	.444	302	385	.784	215	287	502	139	199	0	63	52	172	39.0	24.5	6.1	1.7	.496
81-82	Cleveland	27	0	973	530	229	504	.454	0	6	.000	72	100	.720	71	70	141	39	77	0	27	15	54	36.0	19.6	5.2	1.4	.400
81-82	San Antonio	57	0	2090	1196	524	973	.539	0	1	.000	148	202	.733	173	276	449	43	200	4	33	28	97	36.7	21.0	7.9	0.8	.523

YEAR	TEAM	GP	GS	MIN	PTS	FGM	FGA	FG%	3PM	3PA	3P%	FTM	FTA	FT%	ORB	DRB	TRB	AST	PF	DQ	STL	BLK	TO	MPG	PPG	RPG	APG	PCM
82-83	San Antonio	80	79	2803	1591	686	1342	.511	0	3	.000	219	289	.758	188	349	537	98	248	6	57	52	128	35.0	19.9	6.7	1.2	.510
83-84	San Antonio	79	79	2853	1839	779	1597	.488	6	14	.429	275	353	.779	188	382	570	93	251	6	62	73	142	36.1	23.3	7.2	1.2	.543
84-85	San Antonio	82	82	2853	1824	775	1558	.497	5	23	.217	269	346	.777	145	272	417	151	219	1	61	27	148	34.8	22.2	5.1	1.8	.508
85-86	San Antonio	82	82	2970	1921	802	1697	.473	0	12	.000	317	392	.809	134	275	409	188	175	0	56	25	180	36.2	23.4	5.0	2.3	.493
86-87	San Antonio	40	18	922	509	208	478	.435	1	2	.500	92	112	.821	38	65	103	38	68	0	19	9	52	23.1	12.7	2.6	1.0	.359
87-88	San Antonio	68	20	1501	919	378	784	.482	3	12	.250	160	194	.825	54	144	198	68	101	0	31	13	54	22.1	13.5	2.9	1.0	.483
NBA Season Totals		759	360	24537	15016	6371	12912	.493	19	88	.216	2255	2894	.779	1539	2707	4246	1010	2012	27	530	400	1303	32.3	19.8	5.6	1.3	....
81-82	San Antonio	9	9	365	223	90	169	.533	0	0	.000	43	57	.754	28	45	73	7	22	0	5	1	24	40.6	24.8	8.1	0.8	.526
82-83	San Antonio	11	11	422	230	102	200	.510	1	2	.500	25	33	.758	33	72	105	12	34	0	7	19	25	38.4	20.9	9.5	1.1	.548
84-85	San Antonio	5	5	180	109	44	78	.564	0	1	.000	21	24	.875	5	14	19	12	19	1	3	4	9	36.0	21.8	3.8	2.4	.532
85-86	San Antonio	3	3	107	47	21	52	.404	0	0	.000	5	10	.500	3	6	9	10	8	1	3	3	10	35.7	15.7	3.0	3.3	.257
87-88	San Antonio	3	3	74	31	13	37	.351	0	0	.000	5	6	.833	6	9	15	4	5	0	1	1	5	24.7	10.3	5.0	1.3	.288
89-90	San Antonio	4	0	15	6	3	8	.375	0	0	.000	0	0	.000	1	2	3	2	2	0	0	0	2	3.8	1.5	0.8	0.5	.229
NBA Playoff Totals		35	31	1163	646	273	544	.502	1	3	.333	99	130	.762	76	148	224	47	90	2	19	28	75	33.2	18.5	6.4	1.3	....

• MITCHELL, Murray

Murray C. Mitchell

Born: Mar. 19, 1923.   Height: 6'6".   Weight: —   Drafted: 1948   College: Sam Houston State

YEAR	TEAM	GP	GS	MIN	PTS	FGM	FGA	FG%	3PM	3PA	3P%	FTM	FTA	FT%	ORB	DRB	TRB	AST	PF	DQ	STL	BLK	TO	MPG	PPG	RPG	APG	PCM
49-50	Anderson	2	....		2	1	3	.333	....	....	....	0	0	.000	....	....		2	1	....	....	....		1.0	....	1.0	....
NBA Season Totals		2	....		2	1	3	.333	....	....	....	0	0	.000	....	....		2	1	....	....	....		1.0	....	1.0	....

• MITCHELL, Sam

Samuel E. Mitchell Jr.

Born: Sept. 2, 1963. Columbus, GA, United States.   Height: 6'6".   Weight: 210 lbs.   Drafted: 1985   College: Mercer (GA)

YEAR	TEAM	GP	GS	MIN	PTS	FGM	FGA	FG%	3PM	3PA	3P%	FTM	FTA	FT%	ORB	DRB	TRB	AST	PF	DQ	STL	BLK	TO	MPG	PPG	RPG	APG	PCM
89-90	Minnesota	80	30	2414	1012	372	834	.446	0	9	.000	268	349	.768	180	282	462	89	301	7	66	54	96	30.2	12.7	5.8	1.1	.394
90-91	Minnesota	82	60	3121	1197	445	1010	.441	0	9	.000	307	396	.775	188	332	520	133	**338**	13	66	57	107	38.1	14.6	6.3	1.6	.357
91-92	Minnesota	82	63	2151	825	307	725	.423	2	11	.182	209	266	.786	158	315	473	94	230	3	53	39	98	26.2	10.1	5.8	1.1	.390
92-93	Indiana	81	1	1402	584	215	483	.445	4	23	.174	150	185	.811	93	155	248	76	207	1	23	10	49	17.3	7.2	3.1	0.9	.370
93-94	Indiana	75	18	1084	362	140	306	.458	0	5	.000	82	110	.745	71	119	190	65	152	1	33	9	53	14.5	4.8	2.5	0.9	.334
94-95	Indiana	81	12	1377	529	201	413	.487	1	10	.100	126	174	.724	95	148	243	61	206	0	43	20	57	17.0	6.5	3.0	0.8	.370
95-96	Minnesota	78	42	2145	844	303	618	.490	1	18	.056	237	291	.814	107	232	339	74	220	3	49	26	86	27.5	10.8	4.3	0.9	.376
96-97	Minnesota	82	5	2044	766	269	603	.446	4	25	.160	224	295	.759	112	214	326	79	232	1	51	20	90	24.9	9.3	4.0	1.0	.335
97-98	Minnesota	81	33	2239	1000	371	800	.464	15	43	.349	243	292	.832	118	267	385	107	200	0	64	22	65	27.6	12.3	4.8	1.3	.438
98-99	Minnesota	50	20	1344	561	213	522	.408	9	38	.237	126	165	.764	55	127	182	98	111	1	35	16	34	26.9	11.2	3.6	2.0	.376
99-00	Minnesota	66	24	1227	427	168	376	.447	10	23	.435	81	92	.880	28	110	138	111	116	0	27	14	44	18.6	6.5	2.1	1.7	.346
00-01	Minnesota	82	4	983	285	118	289	.408	9	43	.209	40	55	.727	28	95	123	57	117	0	26	10	36	12.0	3.5	1.5	0.7	.250
01-02	Minnesota	74	10	725	244	98	227	.432	10	35	.286	38	49	.776	18	64	82	45	79	0	12	4	26	9.8	3.3	1.1	0.6	.277
NBA Season Totals		994	322	22256	8636	3220	7206	.447	65	292	.223	2131	2719	.784	1251	2460	3711	1089	2509	30	548	301	841	22.4	8.7	3.7	1.1	....
92-93	Indiana	4	0	25	12	5	8	.625	0	0	.000	2	2	1.000	0	1	1	0	4	0	0	0	2	6.3	3.0	0.3	0.0	.256
93-94	Indiana	15	0	99	21	9	26	.346	0	1	.000	3	4	.750	5	12	17	5	22	0	2	2	4	6.6	1.4	1.1	0.3	.160
94-95	Indiana	17	0	223	68	23	64	.359	0	2	.000	22	28	.786	17	31	48	6	41	0	3	1	14	13.1	4.0	2.8	0.4	.222
96-97	Minnesota	3	0	47	17	6	13	.462	0	0	.000	5	8	.625	2	5	7	1	9	0	1	1	1	15.7	5.7	2.3	0.3	.285
97-98	Minnesota	5	5	177	72	26	58	.448	3	14	.214	17	19	.895	7	20	27	8	18	0	1	1	5	35.4	14.4	5.4	1.6	.363
98-99	Minnesota	4	1	131	40	15	40	.375	1	6	.167	9	12	.750	5	9	14	6	13	0	1	2	8	32.8	10.0	3.5	1.5	.193
99-00	Minnesota	4	0	68	23	9	18	.500	2	5	.400	3	3	1.000	2	5	7	2	5	0	0	1	4	17.0	5.8	1.8	0.5	.270
00-01	Minnesota	4	0	50	6	2	10	.200	0	1	.000	2	2	1.000	1	6	7	3	5	0	1	0	1	12.5	1.5	1.8	0.8	.123
01-02	Minnesota	3	2	34	8	3	9	.333	0	0	.000	2	2	1.000	0	2	2	3	5	0	1	1	0	11.3	2.7	0.7	1.0	.212
NBA Playoff Totals		59	8	854	267	98	246	.398	6	29	.207	65	80	.813	39	91	130	34	122	0	10	9	39	14.5	4.5	2.2	0.6	....

• MITCHELL, Todd

Ernest Todd Mitchell

Born: July 26, 1966. Toledo, OH, United States.   Height: 6'7".   Weight: 205 lbs.   Drafted: 1988   College: Purdue

YEAR	TEAM	GP	GS	MIN	PTS	FGM	FGA	FG%	3PM	3PA	3P%	FTM	FTA	FT%	ORB	DRB	TRB	AST	PF	DQ	STL	BLK	TO	MPG	PPG	RPG	APG	PCM
88-89	Miami	22	0	320	118	41	88	.466	0	0	.000	36	60	.600	17	30	47	20	49	0	15	2	29	14.5	5.4	2.1	0.9	.295
88-89	San Antonio	2	0	33	5	2	9	.222	0	0	.000	1	4	.250	1	2	3	1	2	0	1	0	4	16.5	2.5	1.5	0.5	-.084
NBA Season Totals		24	0	353	123	43	97	.443	0	0	.000	37	64	.578	18	32	50	21	51	0	16	2	33	14.7	5.1	2.1	0.9	....

• MIX, Steve

Steven Charles Mix

Born: Dec. 30, 1947. Toledo, OH, United States.   Height: 6'7".   Weight: 215 lbs.   Drafted: 1969   College: Toledo

YEAR	TEAM	GP	GS	MIN	PTS	FGM	FGA	FG%	3PM	3PA	3P%	FTM	FTA	FT%	ORB	DRB	TRB	AST	PF	DQ	STL	BLK	TO	MPG	PPG	RPG	APG	PCM
69-70	Detroit	18	....	276	119	48	100	.480	....	....	....	23	39	.590	....	....	64	15	31	0	....	....		15.3	6.6	3.6	0.8	.455
70-71	Detroit	35	....	731	290	111	249	.446	....	....	....	68	89	.764	....	....	164	34	72	0	....	....		20.9	8.3	4.7	1.0	.426
71-72	Denver-A	1	....	4	2	1	1	1.000	0	0	.000	0	0	.000	1	0	1	0	1	0	....	....	0	4.0	2.0	1.0	0.0	.610
71-72	Detroit	8	....	104	37	15	47	.319	....	....	....	7	12	.583	....	....	23	4	7	0	....	....		13.0	4.6	2.9	0.5	.275
73-74	Philadelphia	82	....	2969	1218	495	1042	.475	....	....	....	228	288	.792	305	559	864	152	305	9	212	37	....	36.2	14.9	10.5	1.9	.508
74-75	Philadelphia	46	....	1748	719	280	582	.481	....	....	....	159	205	.776	155	345	500	99	175	6	79	21	....	38.0	15.6	10.9	2.2	.519
75-76	Philadelphia	81	....	3039	1129	421	844	.499	....	....	....	287	351	.818	215	447	662	216	288	6	158	29	....	37.5	13.9	8.2	2.7	.470
76-77	Philadelphia	75	....	1958	791	288	551	.523	....	....	....	215	263	.817	127	249	376	152	167	0	90	20	....	26.1	10.5	5.0	2.0	.495
77-78	Philadelphia	82	....	1819	757	291	560	.520	....	....	....	175	220	.795	96	201	297	174	158	1	87	3	131	22.2	9.2	3.6	2.1	.469
78-79	Philadelphia	74	....	1269	691	265	493	.538	....	....	....	161	201	.801	109	184	293	121	112	0	57	16	104	17.1	9.3	4.0	1.6	.620
79-80	Philadelphia	81	....	1543	937	363	703	.516	4	10	.400	207	249	.831	114	176	290	149	114	0	67	9	130	19.0	11.6	3.6	1.8	.606
80-81	Philadelphia	72	....	1327	776	288	575	.501	0	3	.000	200	240	.833	105	159	264	114	107	0	59	18	86	18.4	10.8	3.7	1.6	.606
81-82	Philadelphia	75	0	1235	541	202	399	.506	1	4	.250	136	172	.791	92	133	225	93	86	0	42	17	68	16.5	7.2	3.0	1.2	.488
82-83	Milwaukee	57	20	792	341	133	273	.487	1	4	.250	74	87	.851	37	99	136	68	70	0	33	3	46	13.9	6.0	2.4	1.2	.462
82-83	LA Lakers	1	0	17	9	4	10	.400	0	0	.000	1	1	1.000	1	0	1	2	1	0	0	0	0	17.0	9.0	1.0	2.0	.367
NBA Season Totals		787	20	18827	8355	3204	6428	.498	6	21	.286	1941	2417	.803	1356	2552	4159	1393	1693	22	884	173	565	23.9	10.6	5.3	1.8	....
ABA Season Totals		1	....	4	2	1	1	1.000	0	0	.000	0	0	.000	1	0	1	0	1	0	....	....	0	4.0	2.0	1.0	0.0	....
Career Totals		788	20	18831	8357	3205	6429	.499	6	21	.286	1941	2417	.803	1357	2552	4160	1393	1694	22	884	173	565	23.9	10.6	5.3	1.8	....

YEAR	TEAM	GP	GS	MIN	PTS	FGM	FGA	FG%	3PM	3PA	3P%	FTM	FTA	FT%	ORB	DRB	TRB	AST	PF	DQ	STL	BLK	TO	MPG	PPG	RPG	APG	PCM
75-76	Philadelphia	3	....	134	44	18	46	.391	....	....	....	8	10	.800	6	12	18	12	13	1	11	2	....	44.7	14.7	6.0	4.0	.319
76-77	Philadelphia	19	....	412	149	56	107	.523	....	....	....	37	45	.822	22	42	64	44	39	0	21	3	....	21.7	7.8	3.4	2.3	.461
77-78	Philadelphia	10	....	235	136	49	82	.598	....	....	....	38	43	.884	17	29	46	36	22	0	15	1	12	23.5	13.6	4.6	3.6	.764
78-79	Philadelphia	9	....	179	75	31	59	.525	....	....	....	13	15	.867	12	23	35	16	20	0	6	0	11	19.9	8.3	3.9	1.8	.472
79-80	Philadelphia	17	....	200	113	44	96	.458	0	0	.000	25	28	.893	10	21	31	13	22	0	8	5	15	11.8	6.6	1.8	0.8	.476
80-81	Philadelphia	16	....	206	88	32	77	.416	0	1	.000	24	26	.923	19	23	42	10	16	0	4	2	11	12.9	5.5	2.6	0.6	.405
81-82	Philadelphia	7	0	50	30	12	22	.545	1	1	1.000	5	7	.714	4	7	11	6	5	0	0	0	4	7.1	4.3	1.6	0.9	.610
82-83	LA Lakers	8	0	26	7	2	5	.400	0	0	.000	3	3	1.000	0	1	1	0	6	0	0	0	0	3.3	0.9	0.1	0.0	.096
NBA Playoff Totals		89	0	1442	642	244	494	.494	1	2	.500	153	177	.864	90	158	248	137	143	1	65	13	53	16.2	7.2	2.8	1.5	....

• MLKVY, Bill

William P. (The Owl without a Vowel) Mlkvy

Born: Jan. 19, 1931. Palmerton, PA, United States. Height: 6'4". Weight: 190 lbs. Drafted: 1952 College: Temple

YEAR	TEAM	GP	GS	MIN	PTS	FGM	FGA	FG%	3PM	3PA	3P%	FTM	FTA	FT%	ORB	DRB	TRB	AST	PF	DQ	STL	BLK	TO	MPG	PPG	RPG	APG	PCM
52-53	Philadelphia	31	....	608	181	75	246	.305	....	....	....	31	48	.646	....	....	101	62	54	1	....	....	....	19.6	5.8	3.3	2.0	.302
NBA Season Totals		31	....	608	181	75	246	.305	....	....	....	31	48	.646	....	....	101	62	54	1	....	....	....	19.6	5.8	3.3	2.0	....

• MOBLEY, Cuttino

Cuttino Rashawn Mobley

Born: Sept. 1, 1974. Philadelphia, PA, United States. Height: 6'4". Weight: 190 lbs. Drafted: 1998 College: Rhode Island

YEAR	TEAM	GP	GS	MIN	PTS	FGM	FGA	FG%	3PM	3PA	3P%	FTM	FTA	FT%	ORB	DRB	TRB	AST	PF	DQ	STL	BLK	TO	MPG	PPG	RPG	APG	PCM
98-99	Houston	49	37	1456	487	172	405	.425	53	148	.358	90	110	.818	22	89	111	121	98	0	44	23	79	29.7	9.9	2.3	2.5	.309
99-00	Houston	81	8	2496	1277	437	1016	.430	104	292	.356	299	353	.847	59	229	288	208	171	0	87	32	186	30.8	15.8	3.6	2.6	.431
00-01	Houston	79	49	3002	1538	527	1214	.434	90	252	.357	394	474	.831	83	314	397	195	169	1	84	26	165	38.0	19.5	5.0	2.5	.443
01-02	Houston	74	74	3117	1606	595	1358	.438	149	377	.395	267	314	.850	63	237	300	187	189	3	109	37	180	**42.1**	21.7	4.1	2.5	.402
02-03	Houston	73	73	3044	1280	463	1067	.434	112	318	.352	242	282	.858	70	233	303	208	185	0	95	36	166	41.7	17.5	4.2	2.8	.361
NBA Season Totals		356	241	13115	6188	2194	5060	.434	508	1387	.366	1292	1533	.843	297	1102	1399	919	812	4	419	154	776	36.8	17.4	3.9	2.6	....
98-99	Houston	4	4	94	28	7	15	.467	4	7	.571	10	11	.909	0	4	4	11	11	0	2	0	5	23.5	7.0	1.0	2.8	.305
NBA Playoff Totals		4	4	94	28	7	15	.467	4	7	.571	10	11	.909	0	4	4	11	11	0	2	0	5	23.5	7.0	1.0	2.8	....

• MOBLEY, Eric

Eric Mobley

Born: Feb. 1, 1970. Bronx, NY, United States. Height: 6'11". Weight: 235 lbs. Drafted: 1994 College: Pittsburgh

YEAR	TEAM	GP	GS	MIN	PTS	FGM	FGA	FG%	3PM	3PA	3P%	FTM	FTA	FT%	ORB	DRB	TRB	AST	PF	DQ	STL	BLK	TO	MPG	PPG	RPG	APG	PCM
94-95	Milwaukee	46	26	587	180	78	132	.591	2	2	1.000	22	45	.489	55	98	153	21	63	0	8	27	23	12.8	3.9	3.3	0.5	.453
95-96	Milwaukee	5	3	65	6	2	7	.286	0	0	.000	2	4	.500	3	9	12	0	5	0	1	1	1	13.0	1.2	2.4	0.0	.157
95-96	Vancouver	34	1	611	182	72	131	.550	1	2	.500	37	83	.446	51	77	128	22	82	1	13	23	48	18.0	5.4	3.8	0.6	.325
96-97	Vancouver	28	8	307	72	28	63	.444	0	0	.000	16	30	.533	30	28	58	14	44	0	5	10	28	11.0	2.6	2.1	0.5	.226
NBA Season Totals		113	38	1570	440	180	333	.541	3	4	.750	77	162	.475	139	212	351	57	194	1	27	61	100	13.9	3.9	3.1	0.5	....

• MOE, Douglas

Douglas Edwin Moe

Born: Sept. 21, 1938. Brooklyn, NY, United States. Height: 6'5". Weight: 215 lbs. Drafted: 1960 College: North Carolina

YEAR	TEAM	GP	GS	MIN	PTS	FGM	FGA	FG%	3PM	3PA	3P%	FTM	FTA	FT%	ORB	DRB	TRB	AST	PF	DQ	STL	BLK	TO	MPG	PPG	RPG	APG	PCM
67-68	New Orleans-A	78	....	3113	**1884**	665	1610	.413	3	22	.136	551	693	.795	249	546	795	202	282	4	....	....	199	39.9	24.2	10.2	2.6	.585
68-69	Oakland-A	75	....	2528	1423	529	1227	.431	5	14	.357	360	444	.811	249	365	614	151	266	9	....	....	181	33.7	19.0	8.2	2.0	.543
69-70	Carolina-A	80	....	2671	1382	535	1254	.427	8	34	.235	304	399	.762	142	295	437	425	282	8	....	....	265	33.4	17.3	5.5	5.3	.548
70-71	Virginia-A	78	....	2297	1017	397	871	.456	2	10	.200	221	259	.853	175	298	473	270	284	6	....	....	183	29.4	13.0	6.1	3.5	.527
71-72	Virginia-A	67	....	1472	455	175	415	.422	1	9	.111	104	129	.806	80	161	241	149	172	1	....	....	112	22.0	6.8	3.6	2.2	.364
ABA Season Totals		378	....	12081	6161	2301	5377	.428	19	89	.213	1540	1924	.800	895	1665	2560	1197	1286	28	....	....	940	32.0	16.3	6.8	3.2	....
67-68	New Orleans-A	17	....	715	399	144	346	.416	4	11	.364	107	149	.718	47	122	169	40	71	2	....	....	54	42.1	23.5	9.9	2.4	.520
68-69	Oakland-A	16	....	593	317	115	284	.405	0	4	.000	87	111	.784	....	....	124	31	67	1	....	....	43	37.1	19.8	7.8	1.9	.463
69-70	Carolina-A	4	....	168	62	25	76	.329	0	4	.000	12	16	.750	....	....	26	25	....	....	....	....	....	42.0	15.5	6.5	6.3	....
70-71	Virginia-A	12	....	421	212	90	177	.508	1	3	.333	31	41	.756	22	35	57	37	43	1	....	....	17	35.1	17.7	4.8	3.1	.501
71-72	Virginia-A	11	....	245	96	37	85	.435	0	1	.000	22	25	.880	23	20	43	27	40	1	....	....	25	22.3	8.7	3.9	2.5	.420
ABA Playoff Totals		60	....	2142	1086	411	968	.425	5	23	.217	259	342	.757	92	177	419	160	221	5	....	....	139	35.7	18.1	7.0	2.7	....

• MOELLER, Ed

Ed Moeller

Born: 1919. Height: 6' Weight: 175 lbs. Drafted: —• College: Ohio State

YEAR	TEAM	GP	GS	MIN	PTS	FGM	FGA	FG%	3PM	3PA	3P%	FTM	FTA	FT%	ORB	DRB	TRB	AST	PF	DQ	STL	BLK	TO	MPG	PPG	RPG	APG	PCM
46-47	Tri-Cities-N	3	....	....	0	0	....	....	....	....	....	0	0	.000	....	....	....	....	....	....	....	....	....	....	0.0	....	....	....
46-47	Youngstown-N	19	....	....	39	13	....	....	....	....	....	13	14	.929	....	....	....	....	....	....	....	....	....	....	2.1	....	....	....
NBL Season Totals		22	....	....	39	13	....	....	....	....	....	13	14	....	....	....	....	....	....	....	....	....	....	....	1.8	....	....	....

• MOFFETT, Larry

Larry Moffett

Born: Nov. 5, 1954. Mobile, AL, United States. Height: 6'8". Weight: 210 lbs. Drafted: 1977 College: UNLV

YEAR	TEAM	GP	GS	MIN	PTS	FGM	FGA	FG%	3PM	3PA	3P%	FTM	FTA	FT%	ORB	DRB	TRB	AST	PF	DQ	STL	BLK	TO	MPG	PPG	RPG	APG	PCM
77-78	Houston	20	....	110	16	5	17	.294	....	....	....	6	10	.600	10	11	21	7	16	0	2	2	8	5.5	0.8	1.1	0.4	.177
NBA Season Totals		20	....	110	16	5	17	.294	....	....	....	6	10	.600	10	11	21	7	16	0	2	2	8	5.5	0.8	1.1	0.4	....

• MOGUS, Leo

Leo Mogus

Born: Apr. 13, 1921. Died: 1975. Height: 6'4". Weight: 190 lbs. Drafted: — College: Youngstown State

YEAR	TEAM	GP	GS	MIN	PTS	FGM	FGA	FG%	3PM	3PA	3P%	FTM	FTA	FT%	ORB	DRB	TRB	AST	PF	DQ	STL	BLK	TO	MPG	PPG	RPG	APG	PCM
45-46	Youngstown-N	16	....	....	188	61	....	....	....	....	....	66	98	.673	....	....	....	....	....	....	....	....	....	....	11.8	....	....	....
46-47	Cleveland	17	....	....	209	73	226	.323	....	....	....	63	88	.716	....	....	....	28	50	....	....	....	....	....	12.3	....	1.6	....
46-47	Toronto	41	....	....	544	186	653	.285	....	....	....	172	237	.726	....	....	....	56	126	....	....	....	....	....	13.3	....	1.4	....
48-49	Baltimore	13	....	....	45	10	50	.200	....	....	....	25	36	.694	....	....	....	3	29	....	....	....	....	....	3.5	....	0.2	....
48-49	Fort Wayne	20	....	....	173	59	176	.335	....	....	....	55	74	.743	....	....	....	27	66	....	....	....	....	....	8.7	....	1.4	....
48-49	Indianapolis	19	....	....	303	103	283	.364	....	....	....	97	133	.729	....	....	....	74	75	....	....	....	....	....	15.9	....	3.9	....

YEAR	TEAM	GP	GS	MIN	PTS	FGM	FGA	FG%	3PM	3PA	3P%	FTM	FTA	FT%	ORB	DRB	TRB	AST	PF	DQ	STL	BLK	TO	MPG	PPG	RPG	APG	PCM
49-50	Philadelphia	64	....	....	562	172	434	.396	....	....	....	218	300	.727	....	....	....	99	169		....	....	....	....	8.8		1.5	....
50-51	Philadelphia	57	....	....	139	43	122	.352	....	....	....	53	86	.616	....	....	102	32	60	0	....	....	....	....	2.4	1.8	0.6	....
NBA Season Totals		231	....	....	1975	646	1944	.332	....	....	....	683	954	.716	....	....	102	319	575	0	....	....	....	....	8.5	0.4	1.4	
NBL Season Totals		16	....	....	188	61						66	98												11.8			
Career Totals		247	....	....	2163	707	1944					749	1052				102	319	575	0					8.8	0.4	1.3	
49-50	Philadelphia	2	....	....	10	3	18	.167	....	....	....	4	7	.571	....	....		7	10		....	....	....	....	5.0	....	3.5	
50-51	Philadelphia	1	....	....	0	0	0	.000	....	....	....	0	0	.000	....	....	0	0	0	0	....	....	....	....	0.0	0.0	0.0	
NBA Playoff Totals		3	....	....	10	3	18	.167	....	....	....	4	7	.571	....	....	0	7	10	0	....	....	....	....	3.3	0.0	2.3	

• MOHAMMED, Nazr

Nazr Tahiru Mohammed

Born: Sept. 5, 1977. Chicago, IL, United States.   Height: 6'10".   Weight: 221 lbs.   Drafted: 1998   College: Kentucky

YEAR	TEAM	GP	GS	MIN	PTS	FGM	FGA	FG%	3PM	3PA	3P%	FTM	FTA	FT%	ORB	DRB	TRB	AST	PF	DQ	STL	BLK	TO	MPG	PPG	RPG	APG	PCM
98-99	Philadelphia	26	0	121	42	15	42	.357	0	0	.000	12	21	.571	18	19	37	2	22	0	5	4	12	4.7	1.6	1.4	0.1	.303
99-00	Philadelphia	28	3	190	54	21	54	.389	0	0	.000	12	22	.545	16	34	50	2	29	0	4	12	18	6.8	1.9	1.8	0.1	.274
00-01	Philadelphia	30	3	196	96	41	88	.466	0	0	.000	14	28	.500	18	37	55	2	40	0	6	7	9	6.5	3.2	1.8	0.1	.432
00-01	Atlanta	28	19	716	345	135	281	.480	0	1	.000	75	98	.765	97	155	252	17	73	0	23	28	55	25.6	12.3	9.0	0.6	.576
01-02	Atlanta	82	73	2168	795	329	713	.461	0	1	.000	137	222	.617	242	409	651	33	252	2	63	61	118	26.4	9.7	7.9	0.4	.427
02-03	Atlanta	35	0	449	160	67	159	.421	0	0	.000	26	41	.634	47	82	129	6	79	0	16	21	25	12.8	4.6	3.7	0.2	.375
NBA Season Totals		229	98	3840	1492	608	1337	.455	0	2	.000	276	432	.639	438	736	1174	62	495	2	117	133	237	16.8	6.5	5.1	0.3	....
98-99	Philadelphia	3	0	3	0	0	0	.000	0	0	.000	0	0	.000	0	0	0	0	0	0	0	0	0	1.0	0.0	0.0	0.0	.000
NBA Playoff Totals		3	0	3	0	0	0	.000	0	0	.000	0	0	.000	0	0	0	0	0	0	0	0	0	1.0	0.0	0.0	0.0	....

• MOIR, John

John Moir

Born: May 22, 1917. Rutherglen, Scotland.   Height: 6'2".   Weight: 184 lbs.   Drafted: —   College: Notre Dame

YEAR	TEAM	GP	GS	MIN	PTS	FGM	FGA	FG%	3PM	3PA	3P%	FTM	FTA	FT%	ORB	DRB	TRB	AST	PF	DQ	STL	BLK	TO	MPG	PPG	RPG	APG	PCM
38-39	Non-Skids-N	23	....	....	182	78	....	....	....	....	....	26													7.9			
39-40	Non-Skids-N	27	....	....	165	59	....	....	....	....	....	47													6.1			
40-41	Non-Skids-N	24	....	....	153	59	....	....	....	....	....	35													6.4			
45-46	Cleveland-N	13	....	....	62	27	....	....	....	....	....	8													4.8			
NBL Season Totals		87	....	....	562	223	....	....	....	....	....	116													6.5			
38-39	Non-Skids-N	5	....	....	44	18	....	....	....	....	....	8													8.8			
39-40	Non-Skids-N	7	....	....	78	31	....	....	....	....	....	16													11.1			
40-41	Non-Skids-N	2	....	....	12	5	....	....	....	....	....	2													6.0			
NBL Playoff Totals		14	....	....	134	54	....	....	....	....	....	26													9.6			

• MOISEICHICK, John

John Moiseichick

Born: 1920.   Height: 5'11".   Weight: 180 lbs.   Drafted: —   College: Cortland State

YEAR	TEAM	GP	GS	MIN	PTS	FGM	FGA	FG%	3PM	3PA	3P%	FTM	FTA	FT%	ORB	DRB	TRB	AST	PF	DQ	STL	BLK	TO	MPG	PPG	RPG	APG	PCM
46-47	Syracuse-N	9	....	....	16	6	....	....	....	....	....	4	9	.444											1.8			
NBL Season Totals		9	....	....	16	6	....	....	....	....	....	4	9												1.8			

• MOISO, Jerome

Jerome Moiso

Born: June 15, 1978. Paris, France.   Height: 6'10".   Weight: 235 lbs.   Drafted: 2000   College: UCLA

YEAR	TEAM	GP	GS	MIN	PTS	FGM	FGA	FG%	3PM	3PA	3P%	FTM	FTA	FT%	ORB	DRB	TRB	AST	PF	DQ	STL	BLK	TO	MPG	PPG	RPG	APG	PCM
00-01	Boston	24	0	135	35	12	30	.400	0	1	.000	11	26	.423	12	30	42	3	29	0	3	4	18	5.6	1.5	1.8	0.1	.224
01-02	Charlotte	15	0	76	16	8	20	.400	0	0	.000	0	0	.000	4	21	25	4	12	0	3	2	8	5.1	1.1	1.7	0.3	.316
02-03	New Orleans	51	1	644	205	89	171	.520	0	0	.000	27	41	.659	59	119	178	22	87	1	19	44	46	12.6	4.0	3.5	0.4	.444
NBA Season Totals		90	1	855	256	109	221	.493	0	1	.000	38	67	.567	75	170	245	29	128	1	25	50	72	9.5	2.8	2.7	0.3	....
02-03	New Orleans	4	0	60	23	10	16	.625	0	0	.000	3	4	.750	8	8	16	5	9	0	0	7	4	15.0	5.8	4.0	1.3	.595
NBA Playoff Totals		4	0	60	23	10	16	.625	0	0	.000	3	4	.750	8	8	16	5	9	0	0	7	4	15.0	5.8	4.0	1.3	....

• MOKESKI, Paul

Paul Keen (Mo) Mokeski

Born: Jan. 3, 1957. Spokane, WA, United States.   Height: 7'   Weight: 250 lbs.   Drafted: 1979   College: Kansas

YEAR	TEAM	GP	GS	MIN	PTS	FGM	FGA	FG%	3PM	3PA	3P%	FTM	FTA	FT%	ORB	DRB	TRB	AST	PF	DQ	STL	BLK	TO	MPG	PPG	RPG	APG	PCM
79-80	Houston	12	....	113	29	11	33	.333	0	0	.000	7	9	.778	14	15	29	2	24	0	1	6	10	9.4	2.4	2.4	0.2	.204
80-81	Detroit	80	....	1815	568	224	458	.489	0	1	.000	120	200	.600	141	277	418	135	267	7	38	73	160	22.7	7.1	5.2	1.7	.375
81-82	Detroit	39	3	523	123	49	111	.441	0	1	.000	25	33	.758	35	87	122	24	103	2	13	23	39	13.4	3.2	3.1	0.6	.287
81-82	Cleveland	28	1	345	93	35	82	.427	0	2	.000	23	30	.767	24	62	86	11	68	0	20	17	17	12.3	3.3	3.1	0.4	.361
82-83	Cleveland	23	18	539	126	55	121	.455	0	0	.000	16	26	.615	47	91	138	26	85	6	12	23	28	23.4	5.5	6.0	1.1	.383
82-83	Milwaukee	50	1	589	162	64	139	.460	0	1	.000	34	42	.810	29	93	122	23	138	3	9	21	40	11.8	3.2	2.4	0.5	.263
83-84	Milwaukee	68	4	838	255	102	213	.479	1	3	.333	50	72	.694	51	115	166	44	168	1	11	29	41	12.3	3.8	2.4	0.6	.315
84-85	Milwaukee	79	6	1586	491	205	429	.478	0	2	.000	81	116	.698	107	303	410	99	266	6	28	35	87	20.1	6.2	5.2	1.3	.383
85-86	Milwaukee	45	0	521	143	59	139	.424	0	0	.000	25	34	.735	36	103	139	30	92	1	6	6	27	11.6	3.2	3.1	0.7	.325
86-87	Milwaukee	62	3	626	150	52	129	.403	0	1	.000	46	64	.719	45	93	138	22	126	0	18	13	25	10.1	2.4	2.2	0.4	.270
87-88	Milwaukee	60	0	848	251	100	476	.476	0	4	.000	51	72	.708	70	151	221	22	194	5	27	27	48	14.1	4.2	3.7	0.4	.334
88-89	Milwaukee	74	0	690	165	59	164	.360	7	26	.269	40	51	.784	63	124	187	36	153	0	29	21	37	9.3	2.2	2.5	0.5	.312
89-90	Cleveland	38	1	449	151	63	150	.420	0	1	.000	25	36	.694	27	72	99	17	76	0	8	10	27	11.8	4.0	2.6	0.4	.292
90-91	Golden State	36	1	257	57	21	59	.356	3	9	.333	12	15	.800	20	47	67	9	58	0	8	3	7	7.1	1.6	1.9	0.3	.268
NBA Season Totals		694	38	9739	2764	1099	2437	.451	11	51	.216	555	800	.694	709	1633	2342	500	1818	31	228	307	593	14.0	4.0	3.4	0.7	....
82-83	Milwaukee	4	0	12	4	2	4	.500	0	0	.000	0	0	.000	1	1	2	1	1	0	1	0	0	3.0	1.0	0.5	0.3	.462
83-84	Milwaukee	16	0	322	98	34	63	.540	0	2	.000	30	45	.667	20	68	88	6	62	0	9	11	10	20.1	6.1	5.5	0.4	.417
84-85	Milwaukee	8	0	154	44	16	36	.444	0	0	.000	12	12	1.000	8	26	34	12	28	1	2	4	12	19.3	5.5	4.3	1.5	.333
85-86	Milwaukee	14	0	101	34	14	27	.519	0	0	.000	6	9	.667	5	19	24	8	27	1	6	3	7	7.2	2.4	1.7	0.6	.403
86-87	Milwaukee	12	0	107	28	8	22	.364	0	1	.000	12	15	.800	12	17	29	2	22	1	3	2	5	8.9	2.3	2.4	0.2	.303

YEAR	TEAM	GP	GS	MIN	PTS	FGM	FGA	FG%	3PM	3PA	3P%	FTM	FTA	FT%	ORB	DRB	TRB	AST	PF	DQ	STL	BLK	TO	MPG	PPG	RPG	APG	PCM
87-88	Milwaukee	4	0	40	14	5	14	.357	0	0	.000	4	6	.667	5	4	9	0	4	0	3	2	2	10.0	3.5	2.3	0.0	.350
88-89	Milwaukee	5	0	61	23	8	14	.571	1	1	1.000	6	8	.750	8	9	17	3	16	0	0	0	2	12.2	4.6	3.4	0.6	.430
89-90	Cleveland	3	0	10	4	1	2	.500	0	0	.000	2	2	1.000	0	2	2	0	2	0	1	1	0	3.3	1.3	0.7	0.0	.587
90-91	Golden State	3	0	8	2	1	1	1.000	0	0	.000	0	0	.000	0	2	2	1	4	0	1	0	1	2.7	0.7	0.7	0.3	.383
NBA Playoff Totals		69	0	815	251	89	183	.486	1	4	.250	72	97	.742	59	148	207	33	166	3	26	23	39	11.8	3.6	3.0	0.5	....

• MOLINAS, Jack

Jacob L. Molinas

Born: Jan. 1931. Died: Aug.3, 1975. Height: 6'6". Weight: 200 lbs. Drafted: 1953 College: Columbia

YEAR	TEAM	GP	GS	MIN	PTS	FGM	FGA	FG%	3PM	3PA	3P%	FTM	FTA	FT%	ORB	DRB	TRB	AST	PF	DQ	STL	BLK	TO	MPG	PPG	RPG	APG	PCM
53-54	Fort Wayne	29	....	993	350	108	278	.388	....	....	....	134	176	.761	....	....	209	47	74	2	....	....	....	34.2	12.1	7.2	1.6	.400
NBA Season Totals		29	....	993	350	108	278	.388	....	....	....	134	176	.761	....	....	209	47	74	2	....	....	....	34.2	12.1	7.2	1.6	....

• MOLIS, Wayne

Wayne J. Molis

Born: Apr. 17, 1943. Chicago, IL, United States. Height: 6'8". Weight: 230 lbs. Drafted: 1965 College: Lewis

YEAR	TEAM	GP	GS	MIN	PTS	FGM	FGA	FG%	3PM	3PA	3P%	FTM	FTA	FT%	ORB	DRB	TRB	AST	PF	DQ	STL	BLK	TO	MPG	PPG	RPG	APG	PCM
66-67	New York	13	....	75	45	19	51	.373	....	....	....	7	13	.538	....	....	22	2	9	0	....	....	....	5.8	3.5	1.7	0.2	.446
67-68	Houston-A	41	....	489	221	91	212	.429	2	3	.667	37	57	.649	....	....	160	36	46	1	....	....	23	11.9	5.4	3.9	0.9	.548
67-68	Oakland-A	5	....	46	14	5	13	.385	0	0	.000	4	4	1.000	....	....	10	3	3	0	....	....	3	9.2	2.8	2.0	0.6	.390
NBA Season Totals		13	....	75	45	19	51	.373	....	....	....	7	13	.538	....	....	22	2	9	0	....	....	....	5.8	3.5	1.7	0.2	....
ABA Season Totals		46	....	535	235	96	225	.427	2	3	.667	41	61	.672	....	....	170	39	49	1	....	....	26	11.6	5.1	3.7	0.8	....
Career Totals		59	....	610	280	115	276	.417	2	3	.667	48	74	.649	....	....	192	41	58	1	....	....	26	10.3	4.7	3.3	0.7	....
66-67	New York	1	....	10	0	0	2	.000	....	....	....	0	0	.000	....	....	1	1	1	0	....	....	....	10.0	0.0	1.0	1.0	.001
NBA Playoff Totals		1	....	10	0	0	2	.000	....	....	....	0	0	.000	....	....	1	1	1	0	....	....	....	10.0	0.0	1.0	1.0	....

• MONCRIEF, Sidney

Sidney A. (The Squid) Moncrief

Born: Sept. 21, 1957. Little Rock, AR, United States. Height: 6'3". Weight: 180 lbs. Drafted: 1979 College: Arkansas

YEAR	TEAM	GP	GS	MIN	PTS	FGM	FGA	FG%	3PM	3PA	3P%	FTM	FTA	FT%	ORB	DRB	TRB	AST	PF	DQ	STL	BLK	TO	MPG	PPG	RPG	APG	PCM
79-80	Milwaukee	77	....	1557	654	211	451	.468	0	1	.000	232	292	.795	154	184	338	133	106	0	72	16	116	20.2	8.5	4.4	1.7	.506
80-81	Milwaukee	80	....	2417	1122	400	739	.541	2	9	.222	320	398	.804	186	220	406	264	156	1	90	37	144	30.2	14.0	5.1	3.3	.558
81-82	Milwaukee	80	80	2980	1581	556	1063	.523	1	14	.071	468	573	.817	221	313	534	382	206	3	138	22	208	37.3	19.8	6.7	4.8	.614
82-83	Milwaukee	76	76	2710	1712	606	1156	.524	1	10	.100	499	604	.826	192	245	437	300	180	1	113	23	198	35.7	22.5	5.8	3.9	.648
83-84	Milwaukee	79	79	3075	1654	560	1125	.498	5	18	.278	529	624	.848	215	313	528	358	204	2	108	27	213	38.9	20.9	6.7	4.5	.582
84-85	Milwaukee	73	72	2734	1585	561	1162	.483	9	33	.273	454	548	.828	149	242	391	382	197	1	117	39	183	37.5	21.7	5.4	5.2	.599
85-86	Milwaukee	73	72	2567	1471	470	962	.489	33	103	.320	498	580	.859	115	219	334	357	178	1	103	18	175	35.2	20.2	4.6	4.9	.598
86-87	Milwaukee	39	30	992	460	158	324	.488	8	31	.258	136	162	.840	57	70	127	121	73	0	27	10	62	25.4	11.8	3.3	3.1	.488
87-88	Milwaukee	56	51	1428	603	217	444	.489	5	31	.161	164	196	.837	58	122	180	204	109	0	41	14	84	25.5	10.8	3.2	3.6	.479
88-89	Milwaukee	62	50	1594	752	261	532	.491	25	73	.342	205	237	.865	46	126	172	188	114	1	65	13	93	25.7	12.1	2.8	3.0	.489
90-91	Atlanta	72	3	1096	337	117	240	.488	21	64	.328	82	105	.781	31	97	128	104	112	0	50	9	65	15.2	4.7	1.8	1.4	.350
NBA Season Totals		767	513	23150	11931	4117	8198	.502	110	387	.284	3587	4319	.831	1424	2151	3575	2793	1635	10	924	228	1541	30.2	15.6	4.7	3.6	....
79-80	Milwaukee	7	....	182	87	30	51	.588	0	0	.000	27	31	.871	17	14	31	11	14	0	5	1	14	26.0	12.4	4.4	1.6	.509
80-81	Milwaukee	7	....	277	98	30	69	.435	0	0	.000	38	51	.745	19	28	47	20	24	0	12	3	20	39.6	14.0	6.7	2.9	.381
81-82	Milwaukee	6	6	252	92	31	74	.419	0	1	.000	30	38	.789	15	15	30	24	22	1	9	2	12	42.0	15.3	5.0	4.0	.362
82-83	Milwaukee	9	9	377	170	62	142	.437	0	1	.000	46	61	.754	28	32	60	33	25	1	18	3	27	41.9	18.9	6.7	3.7	.437
83-84	Milwaukee	16	16	618	305	99	191	.518	1	4	.250	106	134	.791	44	67	111	68	54	1	28	9	61	38.6	19.1	6.9	4.3	.542
84-85	Milwaukee	8	7	319	184	55	99	.556	4	10	.400	70	75	.933	10	24	34	40	26	0	5	4	20	39.9	23.0	4.3	5.0	.604
85-86	Milwaukee	9	9	327	152	52	122	.426	4	14	.286	44	63	.698	15	26	41	44	30	0	5	5	21	36.3	16.9	4.6	4.9	.426
86-87	Milwaukee	12	10	426	233	78	165	.473	4	14	.286	73	90	.811	21	33	54	36	43	0	13	6	24	35.5	19.4	4.5	3.0	.489
87-88	Milwaukee	5	5	173	75	24	50	.480	1	1	1.000	26	27	.963	6	13	19	26	14	0	3	1	11	34.6	15.0	3.8	5.2	.478
88-89	Milwaukee	9	9	184	55	19	48	.396	2	7	.286	15	16	.938	8	18	26	13	17	0	5	2	11	20.4	6.1	2.9	1.4	.294
90-91	Atlanta	5	0	91	36	11	22	.500	1	6	.167	13	16	.813	6	10	16	2	16	0	3	0	3	18.2	7.2	3.2	0.4	.373
NBA Playoff Totals		93	71	3226	1487	491	1033	.475	17	58	.293	488	602	.811	189	280	469	317	285	3	106	36	224	34.7	16.0	5.0	3.4	....

• MONEY, Eric

Eric V. Money

Born: Feb. 6, 1955. Detroit, MI, United States. Height: 6' Weight: 170 lbs. Drafted: 1974 College: Arizona

YEAR	TEAM	GP	GS	MIN	PTS	FGM	FGA	FG%	3PM	3PA	3P%	FTM	FTA	FT%	ORB	DRB	TRB	AST	PF	DQ	STL	BLK	TO	MPG	PPG	RPG	APG	PCM
74-75	Detroit	66	....	889	319	144	319	.451	....	....	....	31	45	.689	27	61	88	101	121	3	33	2	....	13.5	4.8	1.3	1.5	.341
75-76	Detroit	80	....	2267	1043	449	947	.474	....	....	....	145	180	.806	77	130	207	338	243	4	137	11	....	28.3	13.0	2.6	4.2	.468
76-77	Detroit	73	....	1586	748	329	631	.521	....	....	....	90	114	.789	43	81	124	243	199	3	91	14	....	21.7	10.2	1.7	3.3	.488
77-78	Detroit	76	....	2557	1414	600	1200	.500	....	....	....	214	298	.718	90	119	209	356	237	5	123	12	319	33.6	18.6	2.8	4.7	.458
78-79	New Jersey	47	....	1434	786	325	676	.481	....	....	....	136	183	.743	55	70	125	249	132	0	74	10	165	30.5	16.7	2.7	5.3	.491
78-79	Philadelphia	23	....	545	272	119	217	.548	....	....	....	34	54	.630	15	22	37	82	70	2	13	2	69	23.7	11.8	1.6	3.6	.401
79-80	Philadelphia	6	....	82	30	14	36	.389	0	0	.000	2	2	1.000	3	4	7	16	11	0	0	1	12	13.7	5.0	1.2	2.7	.232
79-80	Detroit	55	....	1467	599	259	510	.508	0	0	.000	81	104	.779	28	69	97	238	135	3	53	10	143	26.7	10.9	1.8	4.3	.393
NBA Season Totals		426	....	10827	5211	2239	4536	.494	0	0	.000	733	980	.748	338	556	894	1623	1148	20	524	62	708	25.4	12.2	2.1	3.8	....
75-76	Detroit	9	....	273	113	48	105	.457	....	....	....	17	21	.810	10	12	22	51	36	1	14	1	....	30.3	12.6	2.4	5.7	.454
76-77	Detroit	3	....	103	55	22	44	.500	....	....	....	11	13	.846	2	7	9	20	9	0	6	0	....	34.3	18.3	3.0	6.7	.600
78-79	Philadelphia	8	....	129	54	26	61	.426	....	....	....	2	4	.500	6	5	11	22	17	0	3	0	22	16.1	6.8	1.4	2.8	.241
NBA Playoff Totals		20	....	505	222	96	210	.457	....	....	....	30	38	.789	18	24	42	93	62	1	23	1	22	25.3	11.1	2.1	4.7	....

• MONROE, Earl

Vernon Earl (The Pearl) Monroe

Born: Nov. 21, 1944. Philadelphia, PA, United States. Height: 6'3". Weight: 185 lbs. Drafted: 1967 College: Winston-Salem State HOF: 1990

YEAR	TEAM	GP	GS	MIN	PTS	FGM	FGA	FG%	3PM	3PA	3P%	FTM	FTA	FT%	ORB	DRB	TRB	AST	PF	DQ	STL	BLK	TO	MPG	PPG	RPG	APG	PCM
67-68	Baltimore	82	....	3012	1991	742	1637	.453	....	....	....	507	649	.781	....	....	465	349	282	3	....	....	....	36.7	24.3	5.7	4.3	.630
68-69	Baltimore	80	....	3075	2065	809	1837	.440	....	....	....	447	582	.768	....	....	280	392	261	1	....	....	....	38.4	25.8	3.5	4.9	.563
69-70	Baltimore	82	....	3051	1922	695	1557	.446	....	....	....	532	641	.830	....	....	257	402	258	3	....	....	....	37.2	23.4	3.1	4.9	.550
70-71	Baltimore	81	....	2843	1732	663	1501	.442	....	....	....	406	506	.802	....	....	213	354	220	3	....	....	....	35.1	21.4	2.6	4.4	.514
71-72	Baltimore	3	....	103	65	26	64	.406	....	....	....	13	18	.722	....	....	8	10	9	0	....	....	....	34.3	21.7	2.7	3.3	.431

YEAR	TEAM	GP	GS	MIN	PTS	FGM	FGA	FG%	3PM	3PA	3P%	FTM	FTA	FT%	ORB	DRB	TRB	AST	PF	DQ	STL	BLK	TO	MPG	PPG	RPG	APG	PCM
71-72	New York	60	....	1234	684	261	598	.436	....	....	....	162	206	.786	....	....	92	132	130	1	....	....	....	20.6	11.4	1.5	2.2	.443
72-73	New York	75	....	2370	1163	496	1016	.488	....	....	....	171	208	.822	....	....	245	288	195	1	....	....	....	31.6	15.5	3.3	3.8	.488
73-74	New York	41	....	1194	573	240	513	.468	....	....	....	93	113	.823	22	99	121	110	97	0	34	19	....	29.1	14.0	3.0	2.7	.436
74-75	New York	78	....	2814	1633	668	1462	.457	....	....	....	297	359	.827	56	271	327	270	200	0	108	29	....	36.1	20.9	4.2	3.5	.509
75-76	New York	76	....	2889	1574	647	1354	.478	....	....	....	280	356	.787	48	225	273	304	209	1	111	22	....	38.0	20.7	3.6	4.0	.494
76-77	New York	77	....	2656	1533	613	1185	.517	....	....	....	307	366	.839	45	178	223	366	197	0	91	23	....	34.5	19.9	2.9	4.8	.579
77-78	New York	76	....	2369	1354	556	1123	.495	....	....	....	242	291	.832	47	135	182	361	189	0	60	19	182	31.2	17.8	2.4	4.8	.519
78-79	New York	64	....	1393	787	329	699	.471	....	....	....	129	154	.838	26	48	74	189	123	0	48	6	96	21.8	12.3	1.2	3.0	.449
79-80	New York	51	....	633	378	161	352	.457	0	0	.000	56	64	.875	16	20	36	67	46	0	21	3	26	12.4	7.4	0.7	1.3	.450
NBA Season Totals		926	....	29636	17454	6906	14898	.464	0	0	.000	3642	4513	.807	260	976	2796	3594	2416	13	473	121	304	32.0	18.8	3.0	3.9	....
68-69	Baltimore	4	....	171	113	44	114	.386	....	....	....	25	31	.806	....	....	21	16	10	0	....	....	....	42.8	28.3	5.3	4.0	.491
69-70	Baltimore	7	....	299	196	74	154	.481	....	....	....	48	60	.800	....	....	23	28	23	0	....	....	....	42.7	28.0	3.3	4.0	.541
70-71	Baltimore	18	....	671	397	145	356	.407	....	....	....	107	135	.793	....	....	64	74	56	0	....	....	....	37.3	22.1	3.6	4.1	.475
71-72	New York	16	....	429	197	76	185	.411	....	....	....	45	57	.789	....	....	45	47	41	0	....	....	....	26.8	12.3	2.8	2.9	.401
72-73	New York	16	....	504	258	111	211	.526	....	....	....	36	48	.750	....	....	51	51	39	0	....	....	....	31.5	16.1	3.2	3.2	.501
73-74	New York	12	....	407	209	81	165	.491	....	....	....	47	55	.855	8	40	48	25	26	0	8	9	....	33.9	17.4	4.0	2.1	.473
74-75	New York	3	....	89	42	12	45	.267	....	....	....	18	22	.818	1	8	9	6	6	0	4	2	....	29.7	14.0	3.0	2.0	.271
77-78	New York	6	....	145	59	24	62	.387	....	....	....	11	18	.611	1	4	5	17	15	0	6	0	6	24.2	9.8	0.8	2.8	.273
NBA Playoff Totals		82	....	2715	1471	567	1292	.439	....	....	....	337	426	.791	10	52	266	264	216	0	18	11	6	33.1	17.9	3.2	3.2	

• MONROE, Rodney

Rodney Eugene Monroe

Born: Apr. 16, 1968. Baltimore, MD, United States.   Height: 6'3".   Weight: 185 lbs.   Drafted: 1991   College: North Carolina State

YEAR	TEAM	GP	GS	MIN	PTS	FGM	FGA	FG%	3PM	3PA	3P%	FTM	FTA	FT%	ORB	DRB	TRB	AST	PF	DQ	STL	BLK	TO	MPG	PPG	RPG	APG	PCM
91-92	Atlanta	38	0	313	131	53	144	.368	6	27	.222	19	23	.826	12	21	33	27	19	0	12	2	23	8.2	3.4	0.9	0.7	.278
NBA Season Totals		38	0	313	131	53	144	.368	6	27	.222	19	23	.826	12	21	33	27	19	0	12	2	23	8.2	3.4	0.9	0.7	....

• MONTGOMERY, Howie

Howard Montgomery

Born: Aug. 22, 1940.   Height: 6'5".   Weight: 220 lbs.   Drafted: 1962   College: Pan American

YEAR	TEAM	GP	GS	MIN	PTS	FGM	FGA	FG%	3PM	3PA	3P%	FTM	FTA	FT%	ORB	DRB	TRB	AST	PF	DQ	STL	BLK	TO	MPG	PPG	RPG	APG	PCM
62-63	San Francisco	20	....	364	144	65	153	.425	....	....	....	14	23	.609	....	....	69	21	35	1	....	....	....	18.2	7.2	3.5	1.1	.376
NBA Season Totals		20	....	364	144	65	153	.425	....	....	....	14	23	.609	....	....	69	21	35	1	....	....	....	18.2	7.2	3.5	1.1	....

• MONTGOMERY, Jim

Jim Montgomery

Born: 1917.   Height: 6'3".   Weight: 190 lbs.   Drafted: —   College: Villanova

YEAR	TEAM	GP	GS	MIN	PTS	FGM	FGA	FG%	3PM	3PA	3P%	FTM	FTA	FT%	ORB	DRB	TRB	AST	PF	DQ	STL	BLK	TO	MPG	PPG	RPG	APG	PCM
39-40	Wingfoots-N	26	....	....	117	41	....	....	....	....	....	35	....	....	....	....	....	....	....	....	....	....	....	4.5	....	....	....
40-41	Wingfoots-N	15	....	....	19	3	....	....	....	....	....	13	....	....	....	....	....	....	....	....	....	....	....	1.3	....	....	....
NBL Season Totals		41	....	....	136	44	....	....	....	....	....	48	....	....	....	....	....	....	....	....	....	....	....	3.3	....	....	....

• MONTROSS, Eric

Eric Scott Montross

Born: Sept. 23, 1971. Indianapolis, IN, United States.   Height: 7'   Weight: 270 lbs.   Drafted: 1994   College: North Carolina

YEAR	TEAM	GP	GS	MIN	PTS	FGM	FGA	FG%	3PM	3PA	3P%	FTM	FTA	FT%	ORB	DRB	TRB	AST	PF	DQ	STL	BLK	TO	MPG	PPG	RPG	APG	PCM
94-95	Boston	78	75	2315	781	307	575	.534	0	1	.000	167	263	.635	196	370	566	36	299	10	29	61	109	29.7	10.0	7.3	0.5	.387
95-96	Boston	61	59	1432	442	196	346	.566	0	0	.000	50	133	.376	119	233	352	43	181	1	19	29	85	23.5	7.2	5.8	0.7	.362
96-97	Dallas	47	46	984	182	86	187	.460	0	0	.000	10	34	.294	66	170	236	32	150	2	9	34	52	20.9	3.9	5.0	0.7	.257
96-97	New Jersey	31	31	844	157	73	162	.451	0	0	.000	11	28	.393	115	167	282	29	118	3	11	39	25	27.2	5.1	9.1	0.9	.389
97-98	Philadelphia	20	20	337	67	30	76	.395	0	0	.000	7	19	.368	28	64	92	7	61	0	7	12	16	16.9	3.4	4.6	0.4	.255
97-98	Detroit	28	10	354	71	31	68	.456	0	0	.000	9	21	.429	41	66	107	4	66	1	6	15	14	12.6	2.5	3.8	0.1	.311
98-99	Detroit	46	2	577	95	42	80	.525	0	1	.000	11	32	.344	45	94	139	14	107	1	12	27	16	12.5	2.1	3.0	0.3	.284
99-00	Detroit	51	0	332	40	17	55	.309	0	0	.000	6	12	.500	18	54	72	7	81	0	6	9	22	6.5	0.8	1.4	0.1	.098
00-01	Detroit	42	20	568	107	50	121	.413	0	0	.000	7	26	.269	43	101	144	15	100	0	8	23	37	13.5	2.5	3.4	0.4	.229
00-01	Toronto	12	1	81	13	6	17	.353	0	0	.000	1	5	.200	9	20	29	4	15	0	3	3	4	6.8	1.1	2.4	0.3	.331
01-02	Toronto	49	24	656	116	53	132	.402	0	1	.000	10	31	.323	36	104	140	16	92	1	12	23	25	13.4	2.4	2.9	0.3	.224
NBA Season Totals		465	288	8480	2071	891	1819	.490	0	3	.000	289	604	.478	716	1443	2159	207	1270	19	122	275	405	18.2	4.5	4.6	0.4	....
94-95	Boston	4	4	62	13	5	11	.455	0	0	.000	3	6	.500	7	2	9	0	13	0	0	0	8	15.5	3.3	2.3	0.0	.013
98-99	Detroit	5	0	70	7	3	6	.500	0	0	.000	1	2	.500	3	10	13	0	15	0	0	2	0	14.0	1.4	2.6	0.0	.151
99-00	Detroit	2	0	5	0	0	0	.000	0	0	.000	0	0	.000	0	2	2	0	2	0	0	0	0	2.5	0.0	1.0	0.0	.182
00-01	Toronto	5	0	31	4	2	5	.400	0	0	.000	0	0	.000	5	5	10	1	6	0	0	3	2	6.2	0.8	2.0	0.2	.309
NBA Playoff Totals		16	4	168	24	10	22	.455	0	0	.000	4	8	.500	15	19	34	1	36	0	0	5	10	10.5	1.5	2.1	0.1	....

• MOODLER, Bud

Bud Moodler

Born: 1911.   Height: 6'3".   Weight: 215 lbs.   Drafted: —   College: Defiance

YEAR	TEAM	GP	GS	MIN	PTS	FGM	FGA	FG%	3PM	3PA	3P%	FTM	FTA	FT%	ORB	DRB	TRB	AST	PF	DQ	STL	BLK	TO	MPG	PPG	RPG	APG	PCM
37-38	Dayton-N	7	....	....	17	4	....	....	....	....	....	9	....	....	....	....	....	....	....	....	....	....	....	2.4	....	....	....
39-40	Detroit-N	11	....	....	20	4	....	....	....	....	....	12	....	....	....	....	....	....	....	....	....	....	....	1.8	....	....	....
NBL Season Totals		18	....	....	37	8	....	....	....	....	....	21	....	....	....	....	....	....	....	....	....	....	....	2.1	....	....	....

• MOONEY, Jim

James J. Mooney

Born: July 8, 1930.   Height: 6'5".   Weight: 215 lbs.   Drafted: —   College: Villanova

YEAR	TEAM	GP	GS	MIN	PTS	FGM	FGA	FG%	3PM	3PA	3P%	FTM	FTA	FT%	ORB	DRB	TRB	AST	PF	DQ	STL	BLK	TO	MPG	PPG	RPG	APG	PCM
52-53	Philadelphia	18	....	529	135	54	148	.365	....	....	....	27	40	.675	....	....	70	35	50	1	....	....	....	29.4	7.5	3.9	1.9	.264
NBA Season Totals		18	....	529	135	54	148	.365	....	....	....	27	40	.675	....	....	70	35	50	1	....	....	....	29.4	7.5	3.9	1.9	....

MOORE, Andre
Andre M. Moore

Born: July 2, 1964. Chicago, IL, United States.   Height: 6'9".   Weight: 215 lbs.   Drafted: 1987   College: Loyola (IL)

YEAR	TEAM	GP	GS	MIN	PTS	FGM	FGA	FG%	3PM	3PA	3P%	FTM	FTA	FT%	ORB	DRB	TRB	AST	PF	DQ	STL	BLK	TO	MPG	PPG	RPG	APG	PCM
87-88	Denver	7	0	34	20	7	24	.292	0	0	.000	6	6	1.000	5	7	12	5	4	0	2	1	3	4.9	2.9	1.7	0.7	.553
87-88	Milwaukee	3	0	16	4	2	3	.667	0	0	.000	0	2	.000	1	1	2	1	2	0	0	0	1	5.3	1.3	0.7	0.3	.200
NBA Season Totals		10	0	50	24	9	27	.333	0	0	.000	6	8	.750	6	8	14	6	6	0	2	1	4	5.0	2.4	1.4	0.6	....

MOORE, Donald
Donald (Dudey) Moore

Born: Apr. 5, 1910. Died: Apr.8, 1984.   Height: 5'9".   Weight: 180 lbs.   Drafted: —   College: Duquesne

YEAR	TEAM	GP	GS	MIN	PTS	FGM	FGA	FG%	3PM	3PA	3P%	FTM	FTA	FT%	ORB	DRB	TRB	AST	PF	DQ	STL	BLK	TO	MPG	PPG	RPG	APG	PCM
37-38	Pittsburgh-N	8	....	....	25	10	....	....	....	....	....	....	5	....	....	....	....	....	....	....	....	....	....	....	3.1	....	....	....
38-39	Pittsburgh-N	13	....	....	47	20	....	....	....	....	....	....	7	....	....	....	....	....	....	....	....	....	....	....	3.6	....	....	....
NBL Season Totals		21	....	....	72	30	....	....	....	....	....	....	12	....	....	....	....	....	....	....	....	....	....	....	3.4	....	....	....

MOORE, Gene
Eugene Wilbert Moore

Born: July 29, 1945. St. Louis, MO, United States.   Height: 6'9".   Weight: 225 lbs.   Drafted: 1968   College: St. Louis

YEAR	TEAM	GP	GS	MIN	PTS	FGM	FGA	FG%	3PM	3PA	3P%	FTM	FTA	FT%	ORB	DRB	TRB	AST	PF	DQ	STL	BLK	TO	MPG	PPG	RPG	APG	PCM
68-69	Kentucky-A	76	....	2026	1038	417	920	.453	0	2	.000	204	290	.703	318	499	817	90	311	18	....	....	160	26.7	13.7	10.8	1.2	.612
69-70	Kentucky-A	83	....	2613	1471	630	1390	.453	2	4	.500	209	311	.672	345	657	1002	188	382	25	....	....	304	31.5	17.7	12.1	2.3	.645
70-71	Texas-A	84	....	2243	1125	467	972	.480	2	6	.333	189	280	.675	285	565	850	101	303	8	....	....	231	26.7	13.4	10.1	1.2	.608
71-72	Dallas-A	9	....	263	94	41	100	.410	0	0	.000	12	14	.857	30	44	74	13	43	1	....	....	24	29.2	10.4	8.2	1.4	.388
71-72	New York-A	68	....	1149	502	212	445	.476	1	3	.333	77	106	.726	149	260	409	40	178	2	....	....	126	16.9	7.4	6.0	0.6	.531
72-73	San Diego-A	83	....	2481	984	400	804	.498	4	11	.364	180	260	.692	324	550	874	152	369	22	....	149	227	29.9	11.9	10.5	1.8	.553
73-74	San Diego-A	49	....	897	350	154	340	.453	1	7	.143	41	85	.482	96	196	292	59	133	....	26	51	74	18.3	7.1	6.0	1.2	.482
74-75	St. Louis-A	13	....	108	30	13	32	.406	0	0	.000	4	4	1.000	15	27	42	5	11	....	4	7	12	8.3	2.3	3.2	0.4	.473
ABA Season Totals		465	....	11780	5594	2334	5003	.467	10	33	.303	916	1350	.679	1562	2798	4360	648	1730	76	30	207	1158	25.3	12.0	9.4	1.4	....
68-69	Kentucky-A	7	....	204	114	44	100	.440	0	0	.000	26	34	.765	25	76	101	15	37	2	....	....	21	29.1	16.3	14.4	2.1	.737
69-70	Kentucky-A	12	....	369	229	97	202	.480	0	1	.000	35	49	.714	57	93	150	26	....	6	....	....	45	30.8	19.1	12.5	2.2	....
70-71	Texas-A	4	....	137	62	26	55	.473	0	0	.000	10	13	.769	17	30	47	5	14	1	....	....	8	34.3	15.5	11.8	1.3	.552
71-72	New York-A	18	....	111	39	16	36	.444	0	0	.000	7	8	.875	....	....	29	2	21	....	....	....	10	6.2	2.2	1.6	0.1	.356
72-73	San Diego-A	4	....	107	33	12	44	.273	0	0	.000	9	16	.563	21	17	38	4	18	2	....	....	8	26.8	8.3	9.5	1.0	.295
74-75	St. Louis-A	2	....	5	2	1	3	.333	0	0	.000	0	0	.000	0	1	1	0	2	....	0	0	0	2.5	1.0	0.5	0.0	.045
ABA Playoff Totals		47	....	933	479	196	440	.445	0	1	.000	87	120	.725	120	217	366	52	92	11	0	0	92	19.9	10.2	7.8	1.1	....

MOORE, Jackie
John T. (Jackie) Moore

Born: Sept. 24, 1932.   Height: 6'5".   Weight: 180 lbs.   Drafted: —   College: LaSalle

YEAR	TEAM	GP	GS	MIN	PTS	FGM	FGA	FG%	3PM	3PA	3P%	FTM	FTA	FT%	ORB	DRB	TRB	AST	PF	DQ	STL	BLK	TO	MPG	PPG	RPG	APG	PCM
54-55	Syr/Mil/Phi	23	....	376	110	44	115	.383	....	....	....	22	47	.468	....	....	105	20	62	2	....	....	....	16.3	4.8	4.6	0.9	.340
55-56	Philadelphia	54	....	402	132	50	129	.388	....	....	....	32	53	.604	....	....	117	26	80	1	....	....	....	7.4	2.4	2.2	0.5	.385
56-57	Philadelphia	57	....	400	123	43	106	.406	....	....	....	37	46	.804	....	....	116	21	75	1	....	....	....	7.0	2.2	2.0	0.4	.394
NBA Season Totals		134	....	1178	365	137	350	.391	....	....	....	91	146	.623	....	....	338	67	217	4	....	....	....	8.8	2.7	2.5	0.5	....
55-56	Philadelphia	8	....	52	18	8	20	.400	....	....	....	2	6	.333	....	....	17	2	14	0	....	....	....	6.5	2.3	2.1	0.3	.335
56-57	Philadelphia	1	....	1	0	0	0	.000	....	....	....	0	0	.000	....	....	0	0	0	0	....	....	....	1.0	0.0	0.0	0.0	.000
NBA Playoff Totals		9	....	53	18	8	20	.400	....	....	....	2	6	.333	....	....	17	2	14	0	....	....	....	5.9	2.0	1.9	0.2	....

MOORE, Johnny
John Brian Moore

Born: Mar. 3, 1958. Altoona, PA, United States.   Height: 6'1".   Weight: 175 lbs.   Drafted: 1979   College: Texas

YEAR	TEAM	GP	GS	MIN	PTS	FGM	FGA	FG%	3PM	3PA	3P%	FTM	FTA	FT%	ORB	DRB	TRB	AST	PF	DQ	STL	BLK	TO	MPG	PPG	RPG	APG	PCM
80-81	San Antonio	82	....	1578	604	249	520	.479	1	19	.053	105	172	.610	58	138	196	373	178	0	120	22	156	19.2	7.4	2.4	4.5	.518
81-82	San Antonio	79	78	2294	741	309	667	.463	1	21	.048	122	182	.670	62	213	275	762	254	6	163	12	174	29.0	9.4	3.5	9.6	.585
82-83	San Antonio	77	73	2552	941	394	841	.468	5	22	.227	148	199	.744	65	212	277	753	247	2	194	32	223	33.1	12.2	3.6	9.8	.581
83-84	San Antonio	59	42	1650	595	231	518	.446	28	87	.322	105	139	.755	37	141	178	566	168	2	123	20	142	28.0	10.1	3.0	9.6	.610
84-85	San Antonio	82	82	2689	1046	416	910	.457	25	89	.281	189	248	.762	94	284	378	816	247	3	229	18	238	32.8	12.8	4.6	10.0	.623
85-86	San Antonio	28	23	856	363	150	303	.495	4	22	.182	59	86	.686	25	61	86	252	78	0	70	6	81	30.6	13.0	3.1	9.0	.604
86-87	San Antonio	55	27	1234	474	198	448	.442	22	79	.278	56	70	.800	32	68	100	250	97	0	83	3	105	22.4	8.6	1.8	4.5	.431
87-88	San Antonio	4	0	51	8	4	9	.444	0	1	.000	0	0	.000	1	3	4	11	1	0	3	0	4	12.8	2.0	1.0	2.8	.342
87-88	New Jersey	1	0	10	0	0	1	.000	0	0	.000	0	0	.000	0	1	1	1	0	0	0	0	3	10.0	0.0	1.0	1.0	-.173
89-90	San Antonio	53	8	516	118	47	126	.373	8	34	.235	16	27	.593	16	36	52	82	55	0	32	3	37	9.7	2.2	1.0	1.5	.285
NBA Season Totals		520	333	13430	4890	1998	4343	.460	94	374	.251	800	1123	.712	390	1157	1547	3866	1325	13	1017	116	1163	25.8	9.4	3.0	7.4	....
80-81	San Antonio	7	....	124	42	18	37	.486	0	3	.000	6	8	.750	8	5	13	27	14	0	10	1	8	17.7	6.0	1.9	3.9	.495
81-82	San Antonio	9	9	292	94	39	82	.476	0	3	.000	16	27	.593	9	22	31	93	38	0	15	6	15	32.4	10.4	3.4	10.3	.569
82-83	San Antonio	11	11	414	247	105	197	.533	9	17	.529	28	35	.800	8	39	47	161	41	0	28	3	28	37.6	22.5	4.3	14.6	.880
84-85	San Antonio	5	5	168	66	25	54	.463	1	3	.333	15	23	.652	13	17	30	42	17	0	10	2	16	33.6	13.2	6.0	8.4	.574
89-90	San Antonio	9	0	86	16	6	24	.250	0	6	.000	4	8	.500	3	8	11	21	11	0	7	1	7	9.6	1.8	1.2	2.3	.299
NBA Playoff Totals		41	25	1084	465	193	394	.490	10	32	.313	69	101	.683	41	91	132	344	121	0	70	13	74	26.4	11.3	3.2	8.4	....

MOORE, Larry
Lawrence Moore

Born: 1944.   Height: 6'7".   Weight: 215 lbs.   Drafted: —   College: none

YEAR	TEAM	GP	GS	MIN	PTS	FGM	FGA	FG%	3PM	3PA	3P%	FTM	FTA	FT%	ORB	DRB	TRB	AST	PF	DQ	STL	BLK	TO	MPG	PPG	RPG	APG	PCM
67-68	Anaheim-A	12	....	78	27	8	33	.242	0	5	.000	11	13	.846	....	....	16	1	17	0	....	....	7	6.5	2.3	1.3	0.1	.164
ABA Season Totals		12	....	78	27	8	33	.242	0	5	.000	11	13	.846	....	....	16	1	17	0	....	....	7	6.5	2.3	1.3	0.1	....

MOORE, Lowes
Lowes Lee Moore

Born: May 5, 1957. Plymouth, SC, United States. Height: 6'1". Weight: 170 lbs. Drafted: 1980 College: West Virginia

YEAR	TEAM	GP	GS	MIN	PTS	FGM	FGA	FG%	3PM	3PA	3P%	FTM	FTA	FT%	ORB	DRB	TRB	AST	PF	DQ	STL	BLK	TO	MPG	PPG	RPG	APG	PCM
80-81	New Jersey	71	....	1406	497	212	478	.444	4	27	.148	69	92	.750	43	125	168	228	179	1	61	17	107	19.8	7.0	2.4	3.2	.382
81-82	Cleveland	4	0	70	45	19	38	.500	1	5	.200	6	8	.750	1	3	4	15	15	0	6	1	5	17.5	11.3	1.0	3.8	.591
82-83	San Diego	37	1	642	210	81	190	.426	6	23	.261	42	56	.750	15	40	55	73	72	3	22	1	44	17.4	5.7	1.5	2.0	.286
NBA Season Totals		112	1	2118	752	312	706	.442	11	55	.200	117	156	.750	59	168	227	316	266	4	89	19	156	18.9	6.7	2.0	2.8	....

MOORE, Mikki
Mikki Moore

Born: Nov. 4, 1975. Orangeburg, SC, United States. Height: 6'11". Weight: 225 lbs. Drafted: — College: Nebraska

YEAR	TEAM	GP	GS	MIN	PTS	FGM	FGA	FG%	3PM	3PA	3P%	FTM	FTA	FT%	ORB	DRB	TRB	AST	PF	DQ	STL	BLK	TO	MPG	PPG	RPG	APG	PCM
98-99	Detroit	2	0	6	4	1	1	1.000	0	0	.000	2	2	1.000	0	1	1	0	0	0	0	0	0	3.0	2.0	0.5	0.0	.815
99-00	Detroit	29	0	488	228	87	140	.621	0	0	.000	54	68	.794	44	68	112	17	104	5	9	31	23	16.8	7.9	3.9	0.6	.537
00-01	Detroit	81	2	1154	359	132	268	.493	0	1	.000	95	130	.731	121	195	316	33	202	2	24	61	74	14.2	4.4	3.9	0.4	.399
01-02	Detroit	30	0	217	79	29	61	.475	1	2	.500	20	26	.769	22	31	53	11	35	0	7	9	14	7.2	2.6	1.8	0.4	.430
02-03	Boston	3	0	12	0	0	1	.000	0	0	.000	0	0	.000	1	0	1	0	6	0	0	2	0	4.0	0.0	0.3	0.0	-.076
02-03	Atlanta	5	0	31	18	5	12	.417	0	0	.000	8	10	.800	5	2	7	3	1	0	0	2	2	6.2	3.6	1.4	0.6	.642
NBA Season Totals		150	2	1908	688	254	483	.526	1	3	.333	179	236	.758	193	297	490	64	348	7	40	105	113	12.7	4.6	3.3	0.4	....
99-00	Detroit	3	0	42	18	5	12	.417	0	0	.000	8	8	1.000	7	5	12	3	9	0	1	0	4	14.0	6.0	4.0	1.0	.453
NBA Playoff Totals		3	0	42	18	5	12	.417	0	0	.000	8	8	1.000	7	5	12	3	9	0	1	0	4	14.0	6.0	4.0	1.0	....

MOORE, Otto
Otto George (Say No Moore) Moore

Born: Aug. 27, 1946. Miami, FL, United States. Height: 6'11". Weight: 205 lbs. Drafted: 1968 College: Pan American

YEAR	TEAM	GP	GS	MIN	PTS	FGM	FGA	FG%	3PM	3PA	3P%	FTM	FTA	FT%	ORB	DRB	TRB	AST	PF	DQ	STL	BLK	TO	MPG	PPG	RPG	APG	PCM
68-69	Detroit	74	....	1605	570	241	544	.443	....	....	....	88	168	.524	....	....	524	68	182	2	....	....	....	21.7	7.7	7.1	0.9	.451
69-70	Detroit	81	....	2523	960	383	805	.476	....	....	....	194	305	.636	....	....	900	104	232	3	....	....	....	31.1	11.9	11.1	1.3	.534
70-71	Detroit	82	....	1926	741	310	696	.445	....	....	....	121	219	.553	....	....	700	88	180	0	....	....	....	23.5	9.0	8.5	1.1	.515
71-72	Phoenix	81	....	1624	614	260	597	.436	....	....	....	94	156	.603	....	....	540	88	212	2	....	....	....	20.0	7.6	6.7	1.1	.475
72-73	Houston	82	....	2712	963	418	859	.487	....	....	....	127	211	.602	....	....	868	167	239	4	....	....	....	33.1	11.7	10.6	2.0	.509
73-74	Houston	13	....	313	68	32	69	.464	....	....	....	4	8	.500	20	64	84	18	37	0	10	18	....	24.1	5.2	6.5	1.4	.355
73-74	Omaha	65	....	633	211	88	171	.515	....	....	....	35	54	.648	60	140	200	47	62	0	16	31	....	9.7	3.2	3.1	0.7	.521
74-75	Detroit	2	....	11	3	1	4	.250	....	....	....	1	2	.500	0	2	2	1	2	0	0	1	....	5.5	1.5	1.0	0.5	.183
74-75	New Orleans	40	....	1055	279	117	258	.453	....	....	....	45	67	.672	92	236	328	82	146	3	21	39	....	26.4	7.0	8.2	2.1	.437
75-76	New Orleans	81	....	2407	730	293	672	.436	....	....	....	144	226	.637	162	631	793	216	250	3	85	136	....	29.7	9.0	9.8	2.7	.494
76-77	New Orleans	81	....	2084	477	193	477	.405	....	....	....	91	134	.679	170	466	636	181	231	3	54	117	....	25.7	5.9	7.9	2.2	.417
NBA Season Totals		682	....	16893	5616	2336	5152	.453	....	....	....	944	1550	.609	504	1539	5575	1060	1775	20	186	342	....	24.8	8.2	8.2	1.6	....

MOORE, Richard
Richard L. Moore

Born: 1945. Height: 6'2". Weight: 190 lbs. Drafted: 1967 College: Hiram Scott

YEAR	TEAM	GP	GS	MIN	PTS	FGM	FGA	FG%	3PM	3PA	3P%	FTM	FTA	FT%	ORB	DRB	TRB	AST	PF	DQ	STL	BLK	TO	MPG	PPG	RPG	APG	PCM
67-68	Denver-A	18	....	211	69	24	71	.338	0	2	.000	21	28	.750	....	....	19	8	16	0	....	....	24	11.7	3.8	1.1	0.4	.216
ABA Season Totals		18	....	211	69	24	71	.338	0	2	.000	21	28	.750	....	....	19	8	16	0	....	....	24	11.7	3.8	1.1	0.4	....

MOORE, Ron
Ronald Keith Moore

Born: Jan. 16, 1962. New York, NY, United States. Height: 7'. Weight: 260 lbs. Drafted: 1987 College: West Virginia State

YEAR	TEAM	GP	GS	MIN	PTS	FGM	FGA	FG%	3PM	3PA	3P%	FTM	FTA	FT%	ORB	DRB	TRB	AST	PF	DQ	STL	BLK	TO	MPG	PPG	RPG	APG	PCM
87-88	Detroit	9	0	25	10	4	13	.308	0	0	.000	2	4	.500	2	0	2	1	8	0	2	0	3	2.8	1.1	0.2	0.1	-.042
87-88	Phoenix	5	0	34	14	5	16	.313	0	0	.000	4	4	1.000	0	6	6	0	13	0	3	0	1	6.8	2.8	1.2	0.0	.151
NBA Season Totals		14	0	59	24	9	29	.310	0	0	.000	6	8	.750	2	6	8	1	21	0	5	0	4	4.2	1.7	0.6	0.1	....

MOORE, Tracy
Tracy Lamont Moore

Born: Dec. 28, 1965. Oklahoma City, OK, United States. Height: 6'4". Weight: 200 lbs. Drafted: — College: Tulsa

YEAR	TEAM	GP	GS	MIN	PTS	FGM	FGA	FG%	3PM	3PA	3P%	FTM	FTA	FT%	ORB	DRB	TRB	AST	PF	DQ	STL	BLK	TO	MPG	PPG	RPG	APG	PCM
91-92	Dallas	42	2	782	355	130	325	.400	30	84	.357	65	78	.833	31	51	82	48	97	0	32	4	42	18.6	8.5	2.0	1.1	.313
92-93	Dallas	39	1	510	282	103	249	.414	23	67	.343	53	61	.869	23	29	52	47	54	0	21	4	31	13.1	7.2	1.3	1.2	.412
93-94	Detroit	3	0	10	6	2	3	.667	0	0	.000	2	2	1.000	0	1	1	0	0	0	2	0	0	3.3	2.0	0.3	0.0	.783
95-96	Houston	8	0	190	91	30	76	.395	13	30	.433	18	19	.947	10	12	22	6	16	0	2	0	8	23.8	11.4	2.8	0.8	.322
96-97	Houston	27	1	237	99	33	85	.388	11	43	.256	22	31	.710	11	15	26	20	19	0	5	0	14	8.8	3.7	1.0	0.7	.315
NBA Season Totals		119	6	1729	833	298	738	.404	77	224	.344	160	191	.838	75	108	183	121	186	0	62	8	95	14.5	7.0	1.5	1.0	....

MORELAND, Jackie
Jack Moreland

Born: Mar. 11, 1938. Minden, LA, United States. Died: Dec.19, 1971. Height: 6'7". Weight: 215 lbs. Drafted: 1960 College: Louisiana Tech

YEAR	TEAM	GP	GS	MIN	PTS	FGM	FGA	FG%	3PM	3PA	3P%	FTM	FTA	FT%	ORB	DRB	TRB	AST	PF	DQ	STL	BLK	TO	MPG	PPG	RPG	APG	PCM
60-61	Detroit	64	....	1003	468	191	477	.400	....	....	....	86	132	.652	....	....	315	52	174	3	....	....	....	15.7	7.3	4.9	0.8	.469
61-62	Detroit	74	....	1219	549	205	487	.421	....	....	....	139	186	.747	....	....	427	76	179	2	....	....	....	16.5	7.4	5.8	1.0	.547
62-63	Detroit	78	....	1516	687	271	622	.436	....	....	....	145	214	.678	....	....	449	114	226	5	....	....	....	19.4	8.8	5.8	1.5	.518
63-64	Detroit	78	....	1780	708	272	639	.426	....	....	....	164	210	.781	....	....	405	121	268	9	....	....	....	22.8	9.1	5.2	1.6	.429
64-65	Detroit	54	....	732	272	103	296	.348	....	....	....	66	104	.635	....	....	183	69	151	4	....	....	....	13.6	5.0	3.4	1.3	.378
67-68	New Orleans-A	76	....	2332	1112	459	1051	.437	2	4	.500	192	263	.730	....	....	619	138	289	13	....	....	124	30.7	14.6	8.1	1.8	.492
68-69	New Orleans-A	78	....	2714	1159	468	1109	.422	2	8	.250	221	313	.706	264	369	633	207	310	11	....	....	171	34.8	14.9	8.1	2.7	.448
69-70	New Orleans-A	80	....	2321	775	317	765	.414	2	8	.250	139	176	.790	150	236	386	160	250	8	....	....	152	29.0	9.7	4.8	2.0	.337
NBA Season Totals		348	....	6250	2684	1042	2521	.413	....	....	....	600	846	.709	....	....	1779	432	998	23	....	....	....	18.0	7.7	5.1	1.2	....
ABA Season Totals		234	....	7367	3046	1244	2925	.425	6	20	.300	552	752	.734	414	605	1638	505	849	32	....	....	447	31.5	13.0	7.0	2.2	....
Career Totals		582	....	13617	5730	2286	5446	.420	6	20	.300	1152	1598	.721	414	605	3417	937	1847	55	....	....	447	23.4	9.8	5.9	1.6	....
60-61	Detroit	3	....	45	32	14	31	.452	....	....	....	4	5	.800	....	....	18	3	10	0	....	....	....	15.0	10.7	6.0	1.0	.718
61-62	Detroit	7	....	96	38	17	33	.515	....	....	....	4	7	.571	....	....	24	7	22	0	....	....	....	13.7	5.4	3.4	1.0	.448

YEAR	TEAM	GP	GS	MIN	PTS	FGM	FGA	FG%	3PM	3PA	3P%	FTM	FTA	FT%	ORB	DRB	TRB	AST	PF	DQ	STL	BLK	TO	MPG	PPG	RPG	APG	PCM
62-63	Detroit	4	....	82	33	13	26	.500	....	....	....	7	10	.700	....	....	20	6	18	1	....	....	....	20.5	8.3	5.0	1.5	.457
67-68	New Orleans-A	17	....	487	208	84	193	.435	0	2	.000	40	59	.678	....	....	114	43	74	1	....	....	27	28.6	12.2	6.7	2.5	.460
68-69	New Orleans-A	11	....	342	139	59	149	.396	0	0	.000	21	33	.636	....	....	79	27	49	3	....	....	19	31.1	12.6	7.2	2.5	.392
NBA Playoff Totals		14	....	223	103	44	90	.489	....	....	....	15	22	.682	....	....	62	16	50	1	....	....	....	15.9	7.4	4.4	1.1	....
ABA Playoff Totals		28	....	829	347	143	342	.418	0	2	.000	61	92	.663	....	....	193	70	123	4	....	....	46	29.6	12.4	6.9	2.5	....
Career Playoff Totals		42	....	1052	450	187	432	.433	0	2	.000	76	114	.667	....	....	255	86	173	5	....	....	46	25.0	10.7	6.1	2.0	....

• MOREY, Dale

Dale Morey

Born: 1916.   Height: 6'1".   Weight: 180 lbs.   Drafted: —   College: Louisiana State

YEAR	TEAM	GP	GS	MIN	PTS	FGM	FGA	FG%	3PM	3PA	3P%	FTM	FTA	FT%	ORB	DRB	TRB	AST	PF	DQ	STL	BLK	TO	MPG	PPG	RPG	APG	PCM
46-47	Anderson-N	24	....	....	77	32	....	....	....	....	....	13	18	.722	....	....	....	....	....	....	....	....	....	....	3.2	....	....	....
NBL Season Totals		24	....	....	77	32	....	....	....	....	....	13	18		....	....	....	....	....	....	....	....	....	....	3.2	....	....	....

• MORGAN, Guy

Munden Guy Morgan

Born: Aug. 23, 1960. Virginia Beach, VA, United States.   Height: 6'8".   Weight: 205 lbs.   Drafted: 1982   College: Wake Forest

YEAR	TEAM	GP	GS	MIN	PTS	FGM	FGA	FG%	3PM	3PA	3P%	FTM	FTA	FT%	ORB	DRB	TRB	AST	PF	DQ	STL	BLK	TO	MPG	PPG	RPG	APG	PCM
82-83	Indiana	8	0	46	15	7	24	.292	0	0	.000	1	4	.250	6	11	17	7	7	0	2	0	2	5.8	1.9	2.1	0.9	.395
NBA Season Totals		8	0	46	15	7	24	.292	0	0	.000	1	4	.250	6	11	17	7	7	0	2	0	2	5.8	1.9	2.1	0.9	....

• MORGAN, Rex

Rex Morgan

Born: Oct. 27, 1948. Charleston, IL, United States.   Height: 6'5".   Weight: 190 lbs.   Drafted: 1970   College: Jacksonville

YEAR	TEAM	GP	GS	MIN	PTS	FGM	FGA	FG%	3PM	3PA	3P%	FTM	FTA	FT%	ORB	DRB	TRB	AST	PF	DQ	STL	BLK	TO	MPG	PPG	RPG	APG	PCM
70-71	Boston	34	....	266	117	41	102	.402	....	....	....	35	54	.648	....	....	61	22	58	2	....	....	....	7.8	3.4	1.8	0.6	.410
71-72	Boston	28	....	150	55	16	50	.320	....	....	....	23	31	.742	....	....	30	17	34	0	....	....	....	5.4	2.0	1.1	0.6	.351
NBA Season Totals		62	....	416	172	57	152	.375	....	....	....	58	85	.682	....	....	91	39	92	2	....	....	....	6.7	2.8	1.5	0.6	....
71-72	Boston	4	....	10	3	1	7	.143	....	....	....	1	3	.333	....	....	5	0	6	0	....	....	....	2.5	0.8	1.3	0.0	-.132
NBA Playoff Totals		4	....	10	3	1	7	.143	....	....	....	1	3	.333	....	....	5	0	6	0	....	....	....	2.5	0.8	1.3	0.0	....

• MORGENTHALER, Elmore

Elmore Robert Morgenthaler

Born: Aug. 3, 1922.   Height: 6'9".   Weight: 230 lbs.   Drafted: —   College: New Mexico Mines

YEAR	TEAM	GP	GS	MIN	PTS	FGM	FGA	FG%	3PM	3PA	3P%	FTM	FTA	FT%	ORB	DRB	TRB	AST	PF	DQ	STL	BLK	TO	MPG	PPG	RPG	APG	PCM
46-47	Providence	11	....	....	15	4	13	.308	....	....	....	7	12	.583	....	....	3	3	....	....	....	....	....	1.4	....	0.3	....	....
48-49	Philadelphia	20	....	....	42	15	39	.385	....	....	....	12	18	.667	....	....	7	18	....	....	....	....	....	2.1	....	0.4	....	....
NBA Season Totals		31	....	....	57	19	52	.365	....	....	....	19	30	.633	....	....	10	21	....	....	....	....	....	1.8	....	0.3	....	....

• MORNINGSTAR, Darren

Darren Morningstar

Born: Apr. 22, 1969. Stevenson, WA, United States.   Height: 6'10".   Weight: 235 lbs.   Drafted: 1992   College: Pittsburgh

YEAR	TEAM	GP	GS	MIN	PTS	FGM	FGA	FG%	3PM	3PA	3P%	FTM	FTA	FT%	ORB	DRB	TRB	AST	PF	DQ	STL	BLK	TO	MPG	PPG	RPG	APG	PCM
93-94	Dallas	22	15	363	94	38	81	.469	0	0	.000	18	30	.600	31	49	80	15	69	1	14	2	20	16.5	4.3	3.6	0.7	.285
93-94	Utah	1	0	4	2	1	1	1.000	0	0	.000	0	0	.000	0	1	1	0	1	0	0	0	0	4.0	2.0	1.0	0.0	.615
NBA Season Totals		23	15	367	96	39	82	.476	0	0	.000	18	30	.600	31	50	81	15	70	1	14	2	20	16.0	4.2	3.5	0.7	....

• MORRIS, —

Morris

Born: —.   Height: —   Weight: —   Drafted: —   College: —

YEAR	TEAM	GP	GS	MIN	PTS	FGM	FGA	FG%	3PM	3PA	3P%	FTM	FTA	FT%	ORB	DRB	TRB	AST	PF	DQ	STL	BLK	TO	MPG	PPG	RPG	APG	PCM
41-42	Chicago-N	1	....	....	0	0	....	....	....	....	....	0	....	....	....	....	....	....	....	....	....	....	....	....	0.0	....	....	....
NBL Season Totals		1	....	....	0	0	....	....	....	....	....	0	....	....	....	....	....	....	....	....	....	....	....	....	0.0	....	....	....

• MORRIS, Chris

Christopher Vernard Morris

Born: Jan. 20, 1966. Atlanta, GA, United States.   Height: 6'8".   Weight: 210 lbs.   Drafted: 1988   College: Auburn

YEAR	TEAM	GP	GS	MIN	PTS	FGM	FGA	FG%	3PM	3PA	3P%	FTM	FTA	FT%	ORB	DRB	TRB	AST	PF	DQ	STL	BLK	TO	MPG	PPG	RPG	APG	PCM
88-89	New Jersey	76	48	2096	1074	414	905	.457	64	175	.366	182	254	.717	188	209	397	119	250	4	102	60	190	27.6	14.1	5.2	1.6	.448
89-90	New Jersey	80	76	2449	1187	449	1065	.422	61	193	.316	228	316	.722	194	228	422	143	219	1	130	79	184	30.6	14.8	5.3	1.8	.423
90-91	New Jersey	79	68	2553	1042	409	962	.425	45	179	.251	179	244	.734	210	311	521	220	248	5	138	96	166	32.3	13.2	6.6	2.8	.456
91-92	New Jersey	77	74	2394	879	346	726	.477	22	110	.200	165	231	.714	199	295	494	197	211	2	129	81	169	31.1	11.4	6.4	2.6	.462
92-93	New Jersey	77	57	2302	1086	436	907	.481	17	76	.224	197	248	.794	227	227	454	106	171	2	144	51	116	29.9	14.1	5.9	1.4	.501
93-94	New Jersey	50	27	1349	544	203	454	.447	53	147	.361	85	118	.720	91	137	228	83	120	2	55	49	50	27.0	10.9	4.6	1.7	.439
94-95	New Jersey	71	49	2131	950	351	856	.410	106	317	.334	142	195	.728	181	221	402	147	155	0	86	51	114	30.0	13.4	5.7	2.1	.438
95-96	Utah	66	33	1424	691	265	606	.437	63	197	.320	98	127	.772	100	129	229	77	140	1	63	20	73	21.6	10.5	3.5	1.2	.419
96-97	Utah	73	1	977	314	122	299	.408	31	113	.274	39	54	.722	37	125	162	43	121	3	29	24	44	13.4	4.3	2.2	0.6	.298
97-98	Utah	54	1	538	233	85	207	.411	19	62	.306	44	61	.721	35	79	114	24	61	0	25	17	32	10.0	4.3	2.1	0.4	.419
98-99	Phoenix	44	2	535	184	64	149	.430	16	56	.286	40	46	.870	54	67	121	23	54	0	16	11	21	12.2	4.2	2.8	0.5	.412
NBA Season Totals		747	436	18748	8184	3144	7136	.441	497	1625	.306	1399	1894	.739	1516	2028	3544	1182	1750	20	917	539	1159	25.1	11.0	4.7	1.6	....
91-92	New Jersey	4	4	135	75	32	58	.552	4	10	.400	7	9	.778	11	9	20	5	11	0	7	7	8	33.8	18.8	5.0	1.3	.550
92-93	New Jersey	5	4	163	85	34	61	.557	6	16	.375	11	12	.917	13	19	32	7	8	0	8	6	3	32.6	17.0	6.4	1.4	.633
93-94	New Jersey	4	3	98	37	12	43	.279	3	20	.150	10	10	1.000	11	11	22	7	14	0	5	5	6	24.5	9.3	5.5	1.8	.343
95-96	Utah	18	13	321	112	45	106	.425	10	37	.270	12	16	.750	24	46	70	19	25	0	13	8	14	17.8	6.2	3.9	1.1	.416
96-97	Utah	20	0	175	57	20	50	.400	8	25	.320	9	15	.600	5	27	32	5	18	0	8	3	6	8.8	2.9	1.6	0.3	.330
97-98	Utah	17	0	240	77	28	69	.406	7	23	.304	14	20	.700	8	39	47	10	38	0	5	3	8	14.1	4.5	2.8	0.6	.305
98-99	Phoenix	1	0	10	5	2	2	1.000	1	1	1.000	0	2	.000	0	1	1	0	1	0	0	0	0	10.0	5.0	1.0	0.0	.456
NBA Playoff Totals		69	24	1142	448	173	389	.445	39	132	.295	63	84	.750	72	152	224	53	115	0	46	32	45	16.6	6.5	3.2	0.8	....

YEAR	TEAM	GP	GS	MIN	PTS	FGM	FGA	FG%	3PM	3PA	3P%	FTM	FTA	FT%	ORB	DRB	TRB	AST	PF	DQ	STL	BLK	TO	MPG	PPG	RPG	APG	PCM

• MORRIS, Isaiah
Isaiah Butch Morris

Born: Apr. 2, 1969. Richmond, VA, United States.   Height: 6'8".   Weight: 229 lbs.   Drafted: 1992   College: Arkansas

YEAR	TEAM	GP	GS	MIN	PTS	FGM	FGA	FG%	3PM	3PA	3P%	FTM	FTA	FT%	ORB	DRB	TRB	AST	PF	DQ	STL	BLK	TO	MPG	PPG	RPG	APG	PCM
92-93*	Detroit	25	0	102	55	26	57	.456	0	0	.000	3	4	.750	6	6	12	4	14	0	3	1	8	4.1	2.2	0.5	0.2	.302
NBA Season Totals		25	0	102	55	26	57	.456	0	0	.000	3	4	.750	6	6	12	4	14	0	3	1	8	4.1	2.2	0.5	0.2	....

• MORRIS, Max
Glen Max Morris

Born: Mar. 14, 1925. Died: Jan.8, 1998.   Height: 6'2".   Weight: 195 lbs.   Drafted: —   College: Northwestern

YEAR	TEAM	GP	GS	MIN	PTS	FGM	FGA	FG%	3PM	3PA	3P%	FTM	FTA	FT%	ORB	DRB	TRB	AST	PF	DQ	STL	BLK	TO	MPG	PPG	RPG	APG	PCM
46-47	Chicago-N	33	....	....	121	44	....	....	....	....	....	33	63	.524	....	....	....	....	59						3.7	....	....	....
47-48	Sheboygan-N	39	....	....	396	132	....	....	....	....	....	132	215	.614	....	....	....	....	107						10.2	....	....	....
48-49	Sheboygan-N	41	....	....	208	70	....	....	....	....	....	68	104	.654	....	....	....	....	83						5.1	....	....	....
49-50	Sheboygan	62	....	....	781	252	694	.363	....	....	....	277	415	.667	....	....	....	194	172						12.6	....	3.1	....
NBA Season Totals		62	....	....	781	252	694	.363				277	415	.667				194	172						12.6	....	3.1	....
NBL Season Totals		113	....	....	725	246	....	....				233	382	....				....	249						6.4	....	....	....
Career Totals		175	....	....	1506	498	694					510	797	....				194	421						8.6	....	1.1	....
46-47	Chicago-N	10	....	....	18	8	....	....				2	6	.333											1.8	....	....	....
48-49	Sheboygan-N	2	....	....	10	4	....	....				2	3	.667											5.0	....	....	....
49-50	Sheboygan	3	....	....	43	14	40	.350				15	26	.577				14	8						14.3	....	4.7	....
NBA Playoff Totals		3	....	....	43	14	40	.350				15	26	.577				14	8						14.3	....	4.7	....
NBL Playoff Totals		12	....	....	28	12	....	....				4	9	....				....							2.3	....	....	....
Career Playoff Totals		15	....	....	71	26	40	....				19	35	....				14	8						4.7	....	0.9	....

• MORRIS, Terence
Terence Darea Morris

Born: Jan. 11, 1979. Frederick, MD, United States.   Height: 6'9".   Weight: 221 lbs.   Drafted: 2001   College: Maryland

YEAR	TEAM	GP	GS	MIN	PTS	FGM	FGA	FG%	3PM	3PA	3P%	FTM	FTA	FT%	ORB	DRB	TRB	AST	PF	DQ	STL	BLK	TO	MPG	PPG	RPG	APG	PCM
01-02	Houston	68	12	1110	255	111	289	.384	15	78	.192	18	28	.643	77	134	211	64	72	1	21	27	45	16.3	3.8	3.1	0.9	.289
02-03	Houston	49	0	632	182	82	176	.466	7	32	.219	11	14	.786	40	88	128	25	35	0	8	17	29	12.9	3.7	2.6	0.5	.347
NBA Season Totals		117	12	1742	437	193	465	.415	22	110	.200	29	42	.690	117	222	339	89	107	1	29	44	74	14.9	3.7	2.9	0.8	....

• MORRISON, Emmett
Emmett W. Morrison

Born: Aug. 24, 1915. Died: Feb.2, 1993.   Height: 6'3".   Weight: 180 lbs.   Drafted: —   College: Pittsburgh

YEAR	TEAM	GP	GS	MIN	PTS	FGM	FGA	FG%	3PM	3PA	3P%	FTM	FTA	FT%	ORB	DRB	TRB	AST	PF	DQ	STL	BLK	TO	MPG	PPG	RPG	APG	PCM
37-38	Warren-N	11	....	....	19	5	....	....	....	....	....	9	....	....	....	....	....	....	....	....	....	....	....	1.7	....	....	....
NBL Season Totals		11	....	....	19	5	....	....				9	....	....	....	....	....	....	....	....	....	....	....	1.7	....	....	....

• MORRISON, John
John Russell Morrison

Born: May 2, 1945.   Height: 6'2".   Weight: 190 lbs.   Drafted: 1967   College: Canisius

YEAR	TEAM	GP	GS	MIN	PTS	FGM	FGA	FG%	3PM	3PA	3P%	FTM	FTA	FT%	ORB	DRB	TRB	AST	PF	DQ	STL	BLK	TO	MPG	PPG	RPG	APG	PCM
67-68	Denver-A	9	....	76	27	10	34	.294	1	6	.167	6	9	.667	....	....	9	7	15	0	....	....	9	8.4	3.0	1.0	0.8	.201
ABA Season Totals		9	....	76	27	10	34	.294	1	6	.167	6	9	.667	....	....	9	7	15	0	....	....	9	8.4	3.0	1.0	0.8	....

• MORRISON, Mike
Michael Fitzgerald Morrison

Born: Aug. 16, 1967. Washington, DC, United States.   Height: 6'4".   Weight: 195 lbs.   Drafted: 1989   College: Loyola (MD)

YEAR	TEAM	GP	GS	MIN	PTS	FGM	FGA	FG%	3PM	3PA	3P%	FTM	FTA	FT%	ORB	DRB	TRB	AST	PF	DQ	STL	BLK	TO	MPG	PPG	RPG	APG	PCM
89-90	Phoenix	36	1	153	72	23	68	.338	2	7	.286	24	30	.800	7	13	20	11	20	0	2	0	22	4.3	2.0	0.6	0.3	.192
NBA Season Totals		36	1	153	72	23	68	.338	2	7	.286	24	30	.800	7	13	20	11	20	0	2	0	22	4.3	2.0	0.6	0.3	....

• MORRISON, Red
Dwight W. (Red) Morrison

Born: Apr. 26, 1932.   Height: 6'8".   Weight: 220 lbs.   Drafted: 1954   College: Idaho

YEAR	TEAM	GP	GS	MIN	PTS	FGM	FGA	FG%	3PM	3PA	3P%	FTM	FTA	FT%	ORB	DRB	TRB	AST	PF	DQ	STL	BLK	TO	MPG	PPG	RPG	APG	PCM
54-55	Boston	71	....	1227	312	120	284	.423	....	....	....	72	115	.626	....	....	451	82	222	10	....	....	....	17.3	4.4	6.4	1.2	.432
55-56	Boston	71	....	910	222	89	240	.371	....	....	....	44	89	.494	....	....	345	53	159	5	....	....	....	12.8	3.1	4.9	0.7	.393
57-58	St. Louis	13	....	79	21	9	26	.346	....	....	....	3	4	.750	....	....	26	0	12	0	....	....	....	6.1	1.6	2.0	0.0	.289
NBA Season Totals		155	....	2216	555	218	550	.396	....	....	....	119	208	.572	....	....	822	135	393	15	....	....	....	14.3	3.6	5.3	0.9	....
54-55	Boston	7	....	42	7	3	8	.375	....	....	....	1	3	.333	....	....	14	1	22	1	....	....	....	6.0	1.0	2.0	0.1	.143
55-56	Boston	3	....	23	4	2	7	.286	....	....	....	0	4	.000	....	....	11	0	5	0	....	....	....	7.7	1.3	3.7	0.0	.224
NBA Playoff Totals		10	....	65	11	5	15	.333	....	....	....	1	7	.143	....	....	25	1	27	1	....	....	....	6.5	1.1	2.5	0.1	....

• MORSE, George
George Morse

Born: 1919.   Height: —   Weight: —   Drafted: —   College: Marquette

YEAR	TEAM	GP	GS	MIN	PTS	FGM	FGA	FG%	3PM	3PA	3P%	FTM	FTA	FT%	ORB	DRB	TRB	AST	PF	DQ	STL	BLK	TO	MPG	PPG	RPG	APG	PCM
41-42	Chicago-N	2	....	....	2	0	....	....	....	....	....	2	....	....	....	....	....	....	....	....	....	....	....	1.0	....	....	....
NBL Season Totals		2	....	....	2	0	....	....				2	....	....	....	....	....	....	....	....	....	....	....	1.0	....	....	....

YEAR	TEAM	GP	GS	MIN	PTS	FGM	FGA	FG%	3PM	3PA	3P%	FTM	FTA	FT%	ORB	DRB	TRB	AST	PF	DQ	STL	BLK	TO	MPG	PPG	RPG	APG	PCM

• MORSTADT, Ray

Ray Morstadt

Born: 1913.   Height: 6'2".   Weight: 220 lbs.   Drafted: —   College: Marquette

YEAR	TEAM	GP	GS	MIN	PTS	FGM	FGA	FG%	3PM	3PA	3P%	FTM	FTA	FT%	ORB	DRB	TRB	AST	PF	DQ	STL	BLK	TO	MPG	PPG	RPG	APG	PCM
37-38	Wingfoots-N	9	....	....	73	25	....	....	....	....	....	23	....	....	....	....	....	....	....	....	....	....	....	....	8.1	....	....	....
38-39	Wingfoots-N	23	....	....	54	21	....	....	....	....	....	12	....	....	....	....	....	....	....	....	....	....	....	....	2.3	....	....	....
39-40	Wingfoots-N	25	....	....	75	29	....	....	....	....	....	17	....	....	....	....	....	....	....	....	....	....	....	....	3.0	....	....	....
NBL Season Totals		57	....	....	202	75	....	....	....	....	....	52	....	....	....	....	....	....	....	....	....	....	....	....	3.5	....	....	....

• MORTON, Dwayne

Dwayne Lamont Morton

Born: Aug. 8, 1971. Louisville, KY, United States.   Height: 6'7".   Weight: 195 lbs.   Drafted: 1994   College: Louisville

YEAR	TEAM	GP	GS	MIN	PTS	FGM	FGA	FG%	3PM	3PA	3P%	FTM	FTA	FT%	ORB	DRB	TRB	AST	PF	DQ	STL	BLK	TO	MPG	PPG	RPG	APG	PCM
94-95	Golden State	41	6	395	167	50	129	.388	9	25	.360	58	85	.682	21	37	58	18	45	1	11	15	29	9.6	4.1	1.4	0.4	.329
NBA Season Totals		41	6	395	167	50	129	.388	9	25	.360	58	85	.682	21	37	58	18	45	1	11	15	29	9.6	4.1	1.4	0.4	....

• MORTON, John

John (Salt) Morton Jr.

Born: May 18, 1967. Bronx, NY, United States.   Height: 6'3".   Weight: 180 lbs.   Drafted: 1989   College: Seton Hall

YEAR	TEAM	GP	GS	MIN	PTS	FGM	FGA	FG%	3PM	3PA	3P%	FTM	FTA	FT%	ORB	DRB	TRB	AST	PF	DQ	STL	BLK	TO	MPG	PPG	RPG	APG	PCM
89-90	Cleveland	37	3	402	146	48	161	.298	7	30	.233	43	62	.694	7	25	32	67	30	0	18	4	52	10.9	3.9	0.9	1.8	.225
90-91	Cleveland	66	2	1207	357	120	274	.438	4	12	.333	113	139	.813	41	62	103	243	112	1	61	18	106	18.3	5.4	1.6	3.7	.397
91-92	Cleveland	4	0	54	14	3	12	.250	0	1	.000	8	9	.889	3	4	7	5	3	0	1	0	4	13.5	3.5	1.8	1.3	.238
91-92	Miami	21	0	216	92	33	81	.407	2	15	.133	24	29	.828	3	16	19	27	20	0	12	1	23	10.3	4.4	0.9	1.3	.338
NBA Season Totals		128	5	1879	609	204	528	.386	13	58	.224	188	239	.787	54	107	161	342	165	1	92	23	185	14.7	4.8	1.3	2.7	....
89-90	Cleveland	2	0	9	6	2	5	.400	0	0	.000	2	2	1.000	0	0	0	0	1	0	0	0	1	4.5	3.0	0.0	0.0	.198
91-92	Miami	1	0	2	2	0	0	.000	0	0	.000	2	2	1.000	0	0	0	0	0	0	0	0	1	2.0	2.0	0.0	0.0	.536
NBA Playoff Totals		3	0	11	8	2	5	.400	0	0	.000	4	4	1.000	0	0	0	0	1	0	0	0	2	3.7	2.7	0.0	0.0	....

• MORTON, Richard

Richard Morton

Born: Feb. 2, 1966. San Francisco, CA, United States.   Height: 6'3".   Weight: 190 lbs.   Drafted: —   College: Fullerton State

YEAR	TEAM	GP	GS	MIN	PTS	FGM	FGA	FG%	3PM	3PA	3P%	FTM	FTA	FT%	ORB	DRB	TRB	AST	PF	DQ	STL	BLK	TO	MPG	PPG	RPG	APG	PCM
88-89	Indiana	2	0	11	6	3	4	.750	0	0	.000	0	0	.000	0	0	0	1	2	0	0	0	1	5.5	3.0	0.0	0.5	.389
NBA Season Totals		2	0	11	6	3	4	.750	0	0	.000	0	0	.000	0	0	0	1	2	0	0	0	1	5.5	3.0	0.0	0.5	....

• MOSCHETTI, Al

Al Moschetti

Born: 1920.   Height: 6'1".   Weight: 180 lbs.   Drafted: —   College: St. John's (NY)

YEAR	TEAM	GP	GS	MIN	PTS	FGM	FGA	FG%	3PM	3PA	3P%	FTM	FTA	FT%	ORB	DRB	TRB	AST	PF	DQ	STL	BLK	TO	MPG	PPG	RPG	APG	PCM
44-45	Sheboygan-N	24	....	....	121	43	....	....	....	....	....	35	....	....	....	....	....	....	....	....	....	....	....	....	5.0	....	....	....
NBL Season Totals		24	....	....	121	43	....	....	....	....	....	35	....	....	....	....	....	....	....	....	....	....	....	....	5.0	....	....	....
44-45	Sheboygan-N	2	....	....	5	2	....	....	....	....	....	1	....	....	....	....	....	....	....	....	....	....	....	....	2.5	....	....	....
NBL Playoff Totals		2	....	....	5	2	....	....	....	....	....	1	....	....	....	....	....	....	....	....	....	....	....	....	2.5	....	....	....

• MOSLEY, Glenn

Glenn E. Mosley

Born: Dec. 26, 1955. Newark, NJ, United States.   Height: 6'8".   Weight: 195 lbs.   Drafted: 1977   College: Seton Hall

YEAR	TEAM	GP	GS	MIN	PTS	FGM	FGA	FG%	3PM	3PA	3P%	FTM	FTA	FT%	ORB	DRB	TRB	AST	PF	DQ	STL	BLK	TO	MPG	PPG	RPG	APG	PCM
77-78	Philadelphia	6	....	21	13	5	13	.385	....	....	....	3	7	.429	0	5	5	2	5	0	0	0	5	3.5	2.2	0.8	0.3	.205
78-79	San Antonio	26	....	221	85	31	75	.413	....	....	....	23	38	.605	27	37	64	19	35	0	8	10	21	8.5	3.3	2.5	0.7	.447
NBA Season Totals		32	....	242	98	36	88	.409	....	....	....	26	45	.578	27	42	69	21	40	0	8	10	26	7.6	3.1	2.2	0.7	....
78-79	San Antonio	3	....	6	5	2	3	.667	....	....	....	1	3	.333	0	1	1	1	0	0	0	1	0	2.0	1.7	0.3	0.3	1.017
NBA Playoff Totals		3	....	6	5	2	3	.667	....	....	....	1	3	.333	0	1	1	1	0	0	0	1	0	2.0	1.7	0.3	0.3	....

• MOSS, Perry

Perry Victor Moss

Born: Nov. 11, 1958. Tucson, AZ, United States.   Height: 6'2".   Weight: 185 lbs.   Drafted: 1982   College: Northeastern

YEAR	TEAM	GP	GS	MIN	PTS	FGM	FGA	FG%	3PM	3PA	3P%	FTM	FTA	FT%	ORB	DRB	TRB	AST	PF	DQ	STL	BLK	TO	MPG	PPG	RPG	APG	PCM
85-86	Washington	12	0	160	55	21	53	.396	2	7	.286	11	15	.733	9	16	25	19	26	1	6	3	18	13.3	4.6	2.1	1.6	.291
85-86	Philadelphia	60	0	852	249	95	239	.397	5	25	.200	54	74	.730	25	65	90	59	106	0	50	12	60	14.2	4.2	1.5	1.0	.241
86-87	Golden State	64	0	698	232	91	207	.440	1	14	.071	49	69	.710	29	66	95	90	96	0	42	3	58	10.9	3.6	1.5	1.4	.348
NBA Season Totals		136	0	1710	536	207	499	.415	8	46	.174	114	158	.722	63	147	210	168	228	1	98	18	136	12.6	3.9	1.5	1.2	....
85-86	Philadelphia	7	0	28	5	2	8	.250	0	1	.000	1	1	1.000	0	3	3	2	6	0	0	1	4	4.0	0.7	0.4	0.3	-.044
86-87	Golden State	8	0	45	25	8	14	.571	1	1	1.000	8	9	.889	2	3	5	5	5	0	6	0	3	5.6	3.1	0.6	0.6	.654
NBA Playoff Totals		15	0	73	30	10	22	.455	1	2	.500	9	10	.900	2	6	8	7	11	0	6	1	7	4.9	2.0	0.5	0.5	....

• MOTEN, Lawrence

Lawrence Edward Moten III

Born: Mar. 25, 1972. Washington, DC, United States.   Height: 6'5".   Weight: 185 lbs.   Drafted: 1995   College: Syracuse

YEAR	TEAM	GP	GS	MIN	PTS	FGM	FGA	FG%	3PM	3PA	3P%	FTM	FTA	FT%	ORB	DRB	TRB	AST	PF	DQ	STL	BLK	TO	MPG	PPG	RPG	APG	PCM
95-96	Vancouver	44	3	573	291	112	247	.453	18	55	.327	49	75	.653	36	25	61	50	54	0	29	8	44	13.0	6.6	1.4	1.1	.402
96-97	Vancouver	67	18	1214	447	171	441	.388	41	141	.291	64	99	.646	43	76	119	129	83	0	48	24	80	18.1	6.7	1.8	1.9	.314
97-98	Washington	8	0	27	9	3	13	.231	0	1	.000	3	4	.750	1	0	1	3	6	0	0	0	1	3.4	1.1	0.1	0.4	-.004
NBA Season Totals		119	21	1814	747	286	701	.408	59	197	.299	116	178	.652	80	101	181	182	143	0	77	32	125	15.2	6.3	1.5	1.5	....

YEAR	TEAM	GP	GS	MIN	PTS	FGM	FGA	FG%	3PM	3PA	3P%	FTM	FTA	FT%	ORB	DRB	TRB	AST	PF	DQ	STL	BLK	TO	MPG	PPG	RPG	APG	PCM

• MOTTOLA, Hanno
Hanno Aleksanteri Mottola

Born: Sept. 9, 1976. Helsinki, Finland. Height: 6'11". Weight: 247 lbs. Drafted: 2000 College: Utah

YEAR	TEAM	GP	GS	MIN	PTS	FGM	FGA	FG%	3PM	3PA	3P%	FTM	FTA	FT%	ORB	DRB	TRB	AST	PF	DQ	STL	BLK	TO	MPG	PPG	RPG	APG	PCM
00-01	Atlanta	73	3	989	319	123	277	.444	0	3	.000	73	90	.811	49	125	174	25	163	3	11	9	67	13.5	4.4	2.4	0.3	.244
01-02	Atlanta	82	14	1371	396	169	384	.440	1	13	.077	57	76	.750	81	187	268	50	174	5	20	19	70	16.7	4.8	3.3	0.6	.280
NBA Season Totals		155	17	2360	715	292	661	.442	1	16	.063	130	166	.783	130	312	442	75	337	8	31	28	137	15.2	4.6	2.9	0.5	....

• MOUNT, Pete
Paul W. Mount

Born: 1925. Height: 6'4". Weight: 185 lbs. Drafted: — College: none

YEAR	TEAM	GP	GS	MIN	PTS	FGM	FGA	FG%	3PM	3PA	3P%	FTM	FTA	FT%	ORB	DRB	TRB	AST	PF	DQ	STL	BLK	TO	MPG	PPG	RPG	APG	PCM
46-47	Sheboygan-N	10	....		15	6						3	5	.600				....							1.5			
NBL Season Totals		10	....		15	6						3	5					....							1.5			

• MOUNT, Richard
Richard Carl (The Rocket) Mount

Born: Jan. 5, 1947. Lebanon, IN, United States. Height: 6'3". Weight: 175 lbs. Drafted: 1970 College: Purdue

YEAR	TEAM	GP	GS	MIN	PTS	FGM	FGA	FG%	3PM	3PA	3P%	FTM	FTA	FT%	ORB	DRB	TRB	AST	PF	DQ	STL	BLK	TO	MPG	PPG	RPG	APG	PCM
70-71	Indiana-A	66	....	832	437	149	402	.371	23	79	.291	116	145	.800	28	43	71	107	127	0	....	....	78	12.6	6.6	1.1	1.6	.429
71-72	Indiana-A	78	....	2126	1113	420	949	.443	57	180	.317	216	261	.828	48	107	155	230	233	4	....	....	142	27.3	14.3	2.0	2.9	.433
72-73	Kentucky-A	61	....	1780	906	369	804	.459	9	30	.300	159	198	.803	50	88	138	194	172	0	....	....	119	29.2	14.9	2.3	3.2	.426
73-74	Kentucky-A	18	....	276	131	55	151	.364	2	13	.154	19	25	.760	7	13	20	27	37	....	7	0	21	15.3	7.3	1.1	1.5	.283
73-74	Utah-A	34	....	477	298	124	259	.479	10	33	.303	40	46	.870	20	20	40	39	40	....	20	1	27	14.0	8.8	1.2	1.1	.506
74-75	Memphis-A	26	....	895	445	181	431	.420	20	47	.426	63	73	.863	14	37	51	79	44	....	28	7	41	34.4	17.1	2.0	3.0	.371
ABA Season Totals		283	....	6386	3330	1298	2996	.433	121	382	.317	613	748	.820	167	308	475	676	653	4	55	8	428	22.6	11.8	1.7	2.4	....
70-71	Indiana-A	10	....	129	60	25	73	.342	5	17	.294	5	7	.714	5	5	10	9	13	0	....	....	6	12.9	6.0	1.0	0.9	.266
71-72	Indiana-A	20	....	387	177	68	178	.382	8	30	.267	33	39	.846	10	13	23	31	49	....	....	....	23	19.4	8.9	1.2	1.6	.287
72-73	Kentucky-A	19	....	676	321	119	293	.406	10	22	.455	73	87	.839	21	26	47	49	48	0	....	....	42	35.6	16.9	2.5	2.6	.345
73-74	Utah-A	16	....	306	170	78	170	.459	5	16	.313	9	10	.900	7	17	24	17	18	....	9	6	10	19.1	10.6	1.5	1.1	.402
ABA Playoff Totals		65	....	1498	728	290	714	.406	28	85	.329	120	143	.839	43	61	104	106	128	0	9	6	81	23.0	11.2	1.6	1.6	....

• MOURNING, Alonzo
Alonzo (Zo) Mourning

Born: Feb. 8, 1970. Chesapeake, VA, United States. Height: 6'10". Weight: 240 lbs. Drafted: 1992 College: Georgetown

YEAR	TEAM	GP	GS	MIN	PTS	FGM	FGA	FG%	3PM	3PA	3P%	FTM	FTA	FT%	ORB	DRB	TRB	AST	PF	DQ	STL	BLK	TO	MPG	PPG	RPG	APG	PCM
92-93	Charlotte	78	78	2644	1639	572	1119	.511	0	3	.000	495	634	.781	263	542	805	76	286	6	27	271	234	33.9	21.0	10.3	1.0	.689
93-94	Charlotte	60	59	2018	1287	427	845	.505	0	2	.000	433	568	.762	177	433	610	86	207	3	27	188	198	33.6	21.5	10.2	1.4	.701
94-95	Charlotte	77	77	2941	1643	571	1101	.519	11	34	.324	490	644	.761	200	561	761	111	275	5	49	225	239	38.2	21.3	9.9	1.4	.615
95-96	Miami	70	70	2671	1623	563	1076	.523	9	30	.300	488	712	.685	218	509	727	159	245	5	70	189	259	38.2	23.2	10.4	2.3	.664
96-97	Miami	66	65	2320	1310	473	885	.534	1	9	.111	363	565	.642	189	467	656	104	272	9	56	189	224	35.2	19.8	9.9	1.6	.624
97-98	Miami	58	56	1939	1115	403	732	.551	0	0	.000	309	465	.665	193	365	558	52	208	4	40	130	180	33.4	19.2	9.6	0.9	.622
98-99	Miami	46	46	1753	924	324	634	.511	0	2	.000	276	423	.652	166	341	507	74	161	1	34	**180**	139	38.1	20.1	11.0	1.6	.634
99-00	Miami	79	78	2748	1718	652	1184	.551	0	4	.000	414	582	.711	215	538	753	123	308	9	40	**294**	217	34.8	21.7	9.5	1.6	.707
00-01	Miami	13	3	306	177	73	141	.518	0	1	.000	31	55	.564	35	66	101	12	24	0	4	31	28	23.5	13.6	7.8	0.9	.669
01-02	Miami	75	74	2455	1178	447	866	.516	1	3	.333	283	431	.657	182	450	632	87	258	7	27	186	182	32.7	15.7	8.4	1.2	.534
NBA Season Totals		622	606	21795	12614	4505	8583	.525	22	88	.250	3582	5079	.705	1838	4272	6110	884	2244	49	374	1883	1900	35.0	20.3	9.8	1.4	....
92-93	Charlotte	9	9	367	214	71	148	.480	0	2	.000	72	93	.774	28	61	89	13	37	1	6	31	37	40.8	23.8	9.9	1.4	.578
94-95	Charlotte	4	4	174	88	24	57	.421	4	8	.500	36	43	.837	14	39	53	11	17	0	3	13	14	43.5	22.0	13.3	2.8	.627
95-96	Miami	3	3	92	54	17	35	.486	0	0	.000	20	28	.714	3	15	18	4	13	1	2	3	16	30.7	18.0	6.0	1.3	.413
96-97	Miami	17	17	630	303	107	218	.491	3	8	.375	86	155	.555	44	129	173	18	73	2	11	46	70	37.1	17.8	10.2	1.1	.479
97-98	Miami	4	4	138	77	29	56	.518	0	0	.000	19	29	.655	10	24	34	5	18	0	3	10	8	34.5	19.3	8.5	1.3	.584
98-99	Miami	5	5	194	108	38	73	.521	0	0	.000	32	49	.653	7	34	41	4	19	0	8	14	12	38.8	21.6	8.2	0.8	.570
99-00	Miami	10	10	376	216	76	157	.484	0	1	.000	64	96	.667	31	69	100	14	40	1	2	33	24	37.6	21.6	10.0	1.4	.601
00-01	Miami	3	3	91	35	12	25	.480	0	0	.000	11	19	.579	3	13	16	3	9	0	0	5	5	30.3	11.7	5.3	1.0	.367
NBA Playoff Totals		55	55	2062	1095	374	769	.486	7	19	.368	340	512	.664	140	384	524	72	226	5	35	155	186	37.5	19.9	9.5	1.3	....

• MRAZOVICH, Chuck
Charles Mrazovich

Born: Feb. 26, 1924. Height: 6'5". Weight: 185 lbs. Drafted: 1950 College: Eastern Kentucky

YEAR	TEAM	GP	GS	MIN	PTS	FGM	FGA	FG%	3PM	3PA	3P%	FTM	FTA	FT%	ORB	DRB	TRB	AST	PF	DQ	STL	BLK	TO	MPG	PPG	RPG	APG	PCM
50-51	Indianapolis	23	....		76	24	73	.329				28	46	.609	....		33	12	48	1	....	....	....		3.3	1.4	0.5	....
NBA Season Totals		23	....		76	24	73	.329				28	46	.609	....		33	12	48	1	....	....	....		3.3	1.4	0.5	....

• MUELLER, Erwin
Erwin L. Mueller

Born: Mar. 12, 1944. Height: 6'8". Weight: 230 lbs. Drafted: 1966 College: San Francisco

YEAR	TEAM	GP	GS	MIN	PTS	FGM	FGA	FG%	3PM	3PA	3P%	FTM	FTA	FT%	ORB	DRB	TRB	AST	PF	DQ	STL	BLK	TO	MPG	PPG	RPG	APG	PCM
66-67	Chicago	80	....	2136	1015	422	957	.441				171	260	.658	....		497	131	223	2	....	....	....	26.7	12.7	6.2	1.6	.477
67-68	Chicago	35	....	815	228	91	235	.387				46	82	.561	....		167	76	78	1	....	....	....	23.3	6.5	4.8	2.2	.359
67-68	LA Lakers	39	....	973	325	132	254	.520				61	103	.592	....		222	78	86	2	....	....	....	24.9	8.3	5.7	2.0	.460
68-69	Chicago	52	....	872	196	75	224	.335				46	90	.511	....		193	124	98	1	....	....	....	16.8	3.8	3.7	2.4	.364
68-69	Seattle	26	....	483	181	69	160	.431				43	72	.597	....		104	62	45	0	....	....	....	18.6	7.0	4.0	2.4	.483
69-70	Seattle	4	....	69	30	13	32	.406				4	9	.444	....		14	6	6	0	....	....	....	17.3	7.5	3.5	1.5	.398
69-70	Detroit	74	....	2284	759	287	614	.467				185	254	.728	....		469	199	186	1	....	....	....	30.9	10.3	6.3	2.7	.435
70-71	Detroit	52	....	1224	312	126	309	.408				60	108	.556	....		223	113	99	0	....	....	....	23.5	6.0	4.3	2.2	.337
71-72	Detroit	42	....	605	179	68	197	.345				43	74	.581	....		147	57	64	0	....	....	....	14.4	4.3	3.5	1.4	.361

YEAR	TEAM	GP	GS	MIN	PTS	FGM	FGA	FG%	3PM	3PA	3P%	FTM	FTA	FT%	ORB	DRB	TRB	AST	PF	DQ	STL	BLK	TO	MPG	PPG	RPG	APG	PCM
72-73	Virginia-A	17	....	205	37	17	53	.321	0	0	.000	3	10	.300	17	30	47	26	24	0	....	....	22	12.1	2.2	2.8	1.5	.300
72-73	Detroit	21	....	80	23	9	31	.290	....	....	....	5	7	.714	....	....	14	7	13	0	....	....	....	3.8	1.1	0.7	0.3	.221
73-74	Memphis-A	3	....	20	2	0	4	.000	0	0	.000	2	5	.400	0	3	3	2	5	....	0	0	3	6.7	0.7	1.0	0.7	.000
NBA Season Totals		425	....	9541	3248	1292	3013	.429	....	....	....	664	1059	.627	....	....	2050	853	898	7	....	....	....	22.4	7.6	4.8	2.0	....
ABA Season Totals		20	....	225	39	17	57	.298	0	0	.000	5	15	.333	17	33	50	28	29	0	0	0	25	11.3	2.0	2.5	1.4	....
Career Totals		445	....	9766	3287	1309	3070	.426	0	0	.000	669	1074	.623	17	33	2100	881	927	7	0	0	25	21.9	7.4	4.7	2.0	....
66-67	Chicago	3	....	84	26	8	26	.308	....	....	....	10	14	.714	....	....	14	9	7	0	....	....	....	28.0	8.7	4.7	3.0	.348
67-68	LA Lakers	14	....	250	45	20	59	.339	....	....	....	5	14	.357	....	....	54	18	32	0	....	....	....	17.9	3.2	3.9	1.3	.249
72-73	Virginia-A	5	....	112	17	5	18	.278	1	1	1.000	6	7	.857	7	12	19	15	10	0	....	....	11	22.4	3.4	3.8	3.0	.303
NBA Playoff Totals		17	....	334	71	28	85	.329	....	....	....	15	28	.536	....	....	68	27	39	0	....	....	....	19.6	4.2	4.0	1.6	....
ABA Playoff Totals		5	....	112	17	5	18	.278	1	1	1.000	6	7	.857	7	12	19	15	10	0	....	....	11	22.4	3.4	3.8	3.0	....
Career Playoff Totals		22	....	446	88	33	103	.320	1	1	1.000	21	35	.600	7	12	87	42	49	0	....	....	11	20.3	4.0	4.0	1.9	....

• MUELLER, Tex

Tex Mueller

Born: 1916. Height: 6'1". Weight: 175 lbs. Drafted: — College: Western State (CO)

YEAR	TEAM	GP	GS	MIN	PTS	FGM	FGA	FG%	3PM	3PA	3P%	FTM	FTA	FT%	ORB	DRB	TRB	AST	PF	DQ	STL	BLK	TO	MPG	PPG	RPG	APG	PCM
39-40	Oshkosh-N	20	....	....	19	6	....	....	....	....	....	7	....	....	....	....	....	....	....	....	....	....	....	....	1.0	....	....	....
40-41	Oshkosh-N	7	....	....	8	4	....	....	....	....	....	0	....	....	....	....	....	....	....	....	....	....	....	....	1.1	....	....	....
42-43	Oshkosh-N	1	....	....	0	0	....	....	....	....	....	0	....	....	....	....	....	....	....	....	....	....	....	....	0.0	....	....	....
NBL Season Totals		28	....	....	27	10	....	....	....	....	....	7	....	....	....	....	....	....	....	....	....	....	....	....	1.0	....	....	....
39-40	Oshkosh-N	2	....	....	4	2	....	....	....	....	....	0	....	....	....	....	....	....	....	....	....	....	....	....	2.0	....	....	....
40-41	Oshkosh-N	1	....	....	0	0	....	....	....	....	....	0	....	....	....	....	....	....	....	....	....	....	....	....	0.0	....	....	....
NBL Playoff Totals		3	....	....	4	2	....	....	....	....	....	0	....	....	....	....	....	....	....	....	....	....	....	....	1.3	....	....	....

• MULLANEY, Joe

Joseph A. Mullaney

Born: Nov. 17, 1925. Long Island, NY, United States. Died: Mar.8, 2000. Height: 6' Weight: 165 lbs. Drafted: 1949 College: Holy Cross

YEAR	TEAM	GP	GS	MIN	PTS	FGM	FGA	FG%	3PM	3PA	3P%	FTM	FTA	FT%	ORB	DRB	TRB	AST	PF	DQ	STL	BLK	TO	MPG	PPG	RPG	APG	PCM
49-50	Boston	37	....	....	30	9	70	.129	....	....	....	12	15	.800	....	....	....	52	30	....	....	....	....	....	0.8	....	1.4	....
NBA Season Totals		37	....	....	30	9	70	.129	....	....	....	12	15	.800	....	....	....	52	30	....	....	....	....	....	0.8	....	1.4	....

• MULLEN, Ed

Ed Mullen

Born: 1913. Height: 6'3". Weight: 185 lbs. Drafted: — College: Marquette

YEAR	TEAM	GP	GS	MIN	PTS	FGM	FGA	FG%	3PM	3PA	3P%	FTM	FTA	FT%	ORB	DRB	TRB	AST	PF	DQ	STL	BLK	TO	MPG	PPG	RPG	APG	PCM
37-38	Oshkosh-N	9	....	....	16	8	....	....	....	....	....	0	....	....	....	....	....	....	....	....	....	....	....	....	1.8	....	....	....
38-39	Oshkosh-N	26	....	....	61	25	....	....	....	....	....	11	....	....	....	....	....	....	....	....	....	....	....	....	2.3	....	....	....
39-40	Oshkosh-N	7	....	....	4	1	....	....	....	....	....	2	....	....	....	....	....	....	....	....	....	....	....	....	0.6	....	....	....
NBL Season Totals		42	....	....	81	34	....	....	....	....	....	13	....	....	....	....	....	....	....	....	....	....	....	....	1.9	....	....	....
37-38	Oshkosh-N	5	....	....	8	1	....	....	....	....	....	6	....	....	....	....	....	....	....	....	....	....	....	....	1.6	....	....	....
38-39	Oshkosh-N	5	....	....	3	0	....	....	....	....	....	3	....	....	....	....	....	....	....	....	....	....	....	....	0.6	....	....	....
NBL Playoff Totals		10	....	....	11	1	....	....	....	....	....	9	....	....	....	....	....	....	....	....	....	....	....	....	1.1	....	....	....

• MULLENS, Bob

Robert J. Mullens

Born: Nov. 1, 1922. Died: July22, 1989. Height: 6'1". Weight: 175 lbs. Drafted: — College: Fordham

YEAR	TEAM	GP	GS	MIN	PTS	FGM	FGA	FG%	3PM	3PA	3P%	FTM	FTA	FT%	ORB	DRB	TRB	AST	PF	DQ	STL	BLK	TO	MPG	PPG	RPG	APG	PCM
46-47	New York	26	....	....	76	27	104	.260	....	....	....	22	34	.647	....	....	....	18	32	....	....	....	....	....	2.9	....	0.7	....
46-47	Toronto	28	....	....	238	98	341	.287	....	....	....	42	68	.618	....	....	....	36	62	....	....	....	....	....	8.5	....	1.3	....
NBA Season Totals		54	....	....	314	125	445	.281	....	....	....	64	102	.627	....	....	....	54	94	....	....	....	....	....	5.8	....	1.0	....

• MULLIN, Chris

Christopher Paul Mullin

Born: July 30, 1963. New York, NY, United States. Height: 6'6". Weight: 200 lbs. Drafted: 1985 College: St. John's (NY)

YEAR	TEAM	GP	GS	MIN	PTS	FGM	FGA	FG%	3PM	3PA	3P%	FTM	FTA	FT%	ORB	DRB	TRB	AST	PF	DQ	STL	BLK	TO	MPG	PPG	RPG	APG	PCM
85-86	Golden State	55	30	1391	768	287	620	.463	5	27	.185	189	211	.896	42	73	115	105	130	1	70	23	77	25.3	14.0	2.1	1.9	.447
86-87	Golden State	82	82	2377	1242	477	928	.514	19	63	.302	269	326	.825	39	142	181	261	217	1	98	36	156	29.0	15.1	2.2	3.2	.472
87-88	Golden State	60	55	2033	1213	470	926	.508	34	97	.351	239	270	.885	58	147	205	290	136	3	113	32	156	33.9	20.2	3.4	4.8	.591
88-89	Golden State	82	82	3093	2176	830	1630	.509	23	100	.230	493	553	.892	152	331	483	415	178	1	176	39	295	37.7	26.5	5.9	5.1	.692
89-90	Golden State	78	78	2830	1956	682	1272	.536	87	234	.372	505	568	.889	130	333	463	319	142	1	123	45	242	36.3	25.1	5.9	4.1	.711
90-91	Golden State	82	82	**3315**	2107	777	1449	.536	40	133	.301	513	580	.884	141	302	443	329	176	2	173	63	246	**40.4**	25.7	5.4	4.0	.640
91-92	Golden State	81	81	**3346**	2074	830	1584	.524	64	175	.366	350	420	.833	127	323	450	286	171	1	173	62	203	**41.3**	25.6	5.6	3.5	.602
92-93	Golden State	46	46	1902	1191	474	930	.510	60	133	.451	183	226	.810	42	190	232	166	76	0	68	41	138	41.3	25.9	5.0	3.6	.566
93-94	Golden State	62	39	2324	1040	410	869	.472	55	151	.364	165	219	.753	64	281	345	315	114	0	107	53	180	37.5	16.8	5.6	5.1	.508
94-95	Golden State	25	23	890	476	170	348	.489	42	93	.452	94	107	.879	25	90	115	125	53	0	38	19	93	35.6	19.0	4.6	5.0	.545
95-96	Golden State	55	19	1617	734	269	539	.499	59	150	.393	137	160	.856	44	115	159	194	127	0	75	32	121	29.4	13.3	2.9	3.5	.465
96-97	Golden State	79	63	2733	1143	438	792	.553	83	202	.411	184	213	.864	75	242	317	322	155	0	130	33	190	34.6	14.5	4.0	4.1	.491
97-98	Indiana	82	82	2177	927	333	692	.481	107	243	.440	154	164	**.939**	38	211	249	186	186	0	95	39	115	26.5	11.3	3.0	2.3	.439
98-99	Indiana	50	50	1179	507	177	371	.477	73	157	.465	80	92	.870	25	135	160	81	101	0	47	13	60	23.6	10.1	3.2	1.6	.438
99-00	Indiana	47	2	582	242	80	187	.428	45	110	.409	37	41	.902	14	62	76	37	60	0	28	9	28	12.4	5.1	1.6	0.8	.401
00-01	Golden State	20	8	374	115	36	106	.340	19	52	.365	24	28	.857	10	31	41	19	28	0	16	10	19	18.7	5.8	2.1	1.0	.272
NBA Season Totals		986	822	32163	17911	6740	13243	.509	815	2120	.384	3616	4178	.865	1026	3008	4034	3450	2050	10	1530	549	2319	32.6	18.2	4.1	3.5	....
86-87	Golden State	10	10	262	113	49	98	.500	3	4	.750	12	16	.750	2	13	15	23	31	0	9	2	16	26.2	11.3	1.5	2.3	.324
88-89	Golden State	8	8	341	235	88	163	.540	1	8	.125	58	67	.866	11	36	47	36	19	0	14	11	32	42.6	29.4	5.9	4.5	.668
90-91	Golden State	8	8	366	190	69	131	.527	9	13	.692	43	50	.860	9	49	58	23	23	0	15	12	25	45.8	23.8	7.3	2.9	.543
91-92	Golden State	4	4	168	71	27	63	.429	4	12	.333	13	14	.929	3	9	12	12	8	0	5	2	8	42.0	17.8	3.0	3.0	.336
93-94	Golden State	3	3	135	76	30	51	.588	6	12	.500	10	11	.909	4	10	14	11	4	0	0	5	7	45.0	25.3	4.7	3.7	.573

YEAR	TEAM	GP	GS	MIN	PTS	FGM	FGA	FG%	3PM	3PA	3P%	FTM	FTA	FT%	ORB	DRB	TRB	AST	PF	DQ	STL	BLK	TO	MPG	PPG	RPG	APG	PCM
97-98	Indiana	16	16	412	142	52	113	.460	20	52	.385	18	21	.857	13	44	57	23	32	0	15	9	24	25.8	8.9	3.6	1.4	.357
98-99	Indiana	13	13	283	124	41	100	.410	22	55	.400	20	23	.870	2	18	20	15	21	0	10	3	20	21.8	9.5	1.5	1.2	.315
99-00	Indiana	9	1	90	31	10	21	.476	2	8	.250	9	11	.818	2	12	14	5	7	0	6	1	4	10.0	3.4	1.6	0.6	.420
NBA Playoff Totals		71	63	2057	982	366	740	.495	67	164	.409	183	213	.859	46	191	237	148	145	0	74	45	136	29.0	13.8	3.3	2.1	....

• MULLINS, Jeff

Jeffrey Vincent (Pork Chop) Mullins Jr.

Born: Mar. 18, 1942. Astoria, NY, United States.　Height: 6'4".　Weight: 190 lbs.　Drafted: 1964　College: Duke

YEAR	TEAM	GP	GS	MIN	PTS	FGM	FGA	FG%	3PM	3PA	3P%	FTM	FTA	FT%	ORB	DRB	TRB	AST	PF	DQ	STL	BLK	TO	MPG	PPG	RPG	APG	PCM
64-65	St. Louis	44	....	492	215	87	209	.416	....	....	....	41	61	.672	....	....	102	44	60	0	....	....	....	11.2	4.9	2.3	1.0	.454
65-66	St. Louis	44	....	587	255	113	296	.382	....	....	....	29	36	.806	....	....	69	66	68	1	....	....	....	13.3	5.8	1.6	1.5	.369
66-67	San Francisco	77	....	1835	992	421	919	.458	....	....	....	150	214	.701	....	....	388	226	195	5	....	....	....	23.8	12.9	5.0	2.9	.585
67-68	San Francisco	79	....	2805	1493	610	1391	.439	....	....	....	273	344	.794	....	....	447	351	271	2	....	....	....	35.5	18.9	5.7	4.4	.539
68-69	San Francisco	78	....	2916	1775	697	1517	.459	....	....	....	381	452	.843	....	....	460	339	251	4	....	....	....	37.4	22.8	5.9	4.3	.595
69-70	San Francisco	74	....	2861	1632	656	1426	.460	....	....	....	320	378	.847	....	....	382	360	240	4	....	....	....	38.7	22.1	5.2	4.9	.546
70-71	San Francisco	75	....	2909	1562	630	1308	.482	....	....	....	302	358	.844	....	....	341	332	246	5	....	....	....	38.8	20.8	4.5	4.4	.523
71-72	Golden State	80	....	3214	1720	685	1466	.467	....	....	....	350	441	.794	....	....	444	471	260	5	....	....	....	40.2	21.5	5.6	5.9	.564
72-73	Golden State	81	....	3005	1445	651	1321	.493	....	....	....	143	172	.831	....	....	363	337	201	2	....	....	....	37.1	17.8	4.5	4.2	.488
73-74	Golden State	77	....	2498	1250	541	1144	.473	....	....	....	168	192	.875	86	190	276	305	214	2	69	22	....	32.4	16.2	3.6	4.0	.489
74-75	Golden State	66	....	1141	539	234	514	.455	....	....	....	71	87	.816	46	77	123	153	123	0	57	14	....	17.3	8.2	1.9	2.3	.457
75-76	Golden State	29	....	311	139	58	120	.483	....	....	....	23	29	.793	12	20	32	39	36	0	14	1	....	10.7	4.8	1.1	1.3	.449
NBA Season Totals		804	....	24574	13017	5383	11631	.463	....	....	....	2251	2764	.814	144	287	3427	3023	2165	30	140	37	....	30.6	16.2	4.3	3.8	
64-65	St. Louis	2	....	11	8	4	8	.500	....	....	....	0	0	.000	....	....	6	1	0	0	....	....	....	5.5	4.0	3.0	0.5	.979
65-66	St. Louis	4	....	13	3	1	9	.111	....	....	....	1	2	.500	....	....	4	0	5	0	....	....	....	3.3	0.8	1.0	0.0	-.191
66-67	San Francisco	15	....	498	265	109	242	.450	....	....	....	47	59	.797	....	....	91	58	53	3	....	....	....	33.2	17.7	6.1	3.9	.553
67-68	San Francisco	10	....	390	251	110	211	.521	....	....	....	31	43	.721	....	....	44	49	36	2	....	....	....	39.0	25.1	4.4	4.9	.629
68-69	San Francisco	6	....	180	86	39	96	.406	....	....	....	8	11	.727	....	....	18	23	16	0	....	....	....	30.0	14.3	3.0	3.8	.401
70-71	San Francisco	5	....	205	82	30	85	.353	....	....	....	22	25	.880	....	....	32	24	13	0	....	....	....	41.0	16.4	6.4	4.8	.403
71-72	Golden State	5	....	203	74	31	72	.431	....	....	....	12	13	.923	....	....	24	29	11	0	....	....	....	40.6	14.8	4.8	5.8	.429
72-73	Golden State	11	....	409	165	72	168	.429	....	....	....	21	29	.724	....	....	46	43	32	0	....	....	....	37.2	15.0	4.2	3.9	.377
74-75	Golden State	17	....	313	138	60	123	.488	....	....	....	18	31	.581	16	19	35	29	43	0	10	1	....	18.4	8.1	2.1	1.7	.395
75-76	Golden State	8	....	33	12	6	16	.375	....	....	....	0	0	.000	3	1	4	3	8	0	2	1	....	4.1	1.5	0.5	0.4	.207
NBA Playoff Totals		83	....	2255	1084	462	1030	.449	....	....	....	160	213	.751	19	20	304	259	217	5	12	2	....	27.2	13.1	3.7	3.1	....

• MULVIHILL, Bob

Bob Mulvihill

Born: 1924.　Height: 6'1".　Weight: 185 lbs.　Drafted: —　College: Fordham

YEAR	TEAM	GP	GS	MIN	PTS	FGM	FGA	FG%	3PM	3PA	3P%	FTM	FTA	FT%	ORB	DRB	TRB	AST	PF	DQ	STL	BLK	TO	MPG	PPG	RPG	APG	PCM
48-49	Oshkosh-N	34	....	....	30	8	....	....	....	....	....	14	24	.583	....	....	....	39	....	....	....	....	....	....	0.9	....	....	....
NBL Season Totals		34	....	....	30	8	....	....	....	....	....	14	24		....	....	....	39	....	....	....	....	....	....	0.9	....	....	....
48-49	Oshkosh-N	3	....	....	0	0	....	....	....	....	....	0	0	.000	....	....	....	....	....	....	....	....	....	....	0.0	....	....	....
NBL Playoff Totals		3	....	....	0	0	....	....	....	....	....	0	0		....	....	....	....	....	....	....	....	....	....	0.0	....	....	....

• MUNDT, Todd

Todd Mundt

Born: May 17, 1970. Iowa City, IA, United States.　Height: 7'　Weight: 250 lbs.　Drafted: —　College: Delta State

YEAR	TEAM	GP	GS	MIN	PTS	FGM	FGA	FG%	3PM	3PA	3P%	FTM	FTA	FT%	ORB	DRB	TRB	AST	PF	DQ	STL	BLK	TO	MPG	PPG	RPG	APG	PCM
95-96	Atlanta	24	0	118	31	13	32	.406	0	0	.000	5	8	.625	10	15	25	2	23	0	1	4	2	4.9	1.3	1.0	0.1	.249
95-96	Boston	9	0	33	6	3	9	.333	0	0	.000	0	0	.000	1	2	3	1	6	0	1	1	0	3.7	0.7	0.3	0.1	.100
NBA Season Totals		33	0	151	37	16	41	.390	0	0	.000	5	8	.625	11	17	28	3	29	0	2	5	2	4.6	1.1	0.8	0.1	....

• MUNK, Chris

Christian Munk

Born: Aug. 5, 1967. San Francisco, CA, United States.　Height: 6'9".　Weight: 225 lbs.　Drafted: —　College: USC

YEAR	TEAM	GP	GS	MIN	PTS	FGM	FGA	FG%	3PM	3PA	3P%	FTM	FTA	FT%	ORB	DRB	TRB	AST	PF	DQ	STL	BLK	TO	MPG	PPG	RPG	APG	PCM
90-91	Utah	11	0	29	13	3	7	.429	0	0	.000	7	12	.583	5	9	14	1	5	0	1	2	6	2.6	1.2	1.3	0.1	.549
NBA Season Totals		11	0	29	13	3	7	.429	0	0	.000	7	12	.583	5	9	14	1	5	0	1	2	6	2.6	1.2	1.3	0.1	....

• MUNROE, George

George B. Munroe

Born: Jan. 5, 1922.　Height: 5'11".　Weight: 170 lbs.　Drafted: —　College: Dartmouth

YEAR	TEAM	GP	GS	MIN	PTS	FGM	FGA	FG%	3PM	3PA	3P%	FTM	FTA	FT%	ORB	DRB	TRB	AST	PF	DQ	STL	BLK	TO	MPG	PPG	RPG	APG	PCM
46-47	St. Louis	59	....	....	414	164	623	.263	....	....	....	86	133	.647	....	....	....	17	91	....	....	....	....	....	7.0	....	0.3	....
47-48	Boston	21	....	....	71	27	91	.297	....	....	....	17	26	.654	....	....	....	3	20	....	....	....	....	....	3.4	....	0.1	....
NBA Season Totals		80	....	....	485	191	714	.268	....	....	....	103	159	.648	....	....	....	20	111	....	....	....	....	....	6.1	....	0.3	....
46-47	St. Louis	3	....	....	34	15	31	.484	....	....	....	4	7	.571	....	....	....	0	8	....	....	....	....	....	11.3	....	0.0	....
47-48	Boston	3	....	....	4	1	5	.200	....	....	....	2	2	1.000	....	....	....	1	2	....	....	....	....	....	1.3	....	0.3	....
NBA Playoff Totals		6	....	....	38	16	36	.444	....	....	....	6	9	.667	....	....	....	1	10	....	....	....	....	....	6.3	....	0.2	....

• MURDOCK, Eric

Eric Lloyd Murdock

Born: June 14, 1968. Somerville, NJ, United States.　Height: 6'1".　Weight: 190 lbs.　Drafted: 1991　College: Providence

YEAR	TEAM	GP	GS	MIN	PTS	FGM	FGA	FG%	3PM	3PA	3P%	FTM	FTA	FT%	ORB	DRB	TRB	AST	PF	DQ	STL	BLK	TO	MPG	PPG	RPG	APG	PCM
91-92	Utah	50	0	478	203	76	183	.415	5	26	.192	46	61	.754	21	33	54	92	52	0	30	7	50	9.6	4.1	1.1	1.8	.437
92-93	Milwaukee	79	78	2437	1138	438	936	.468	31	119	.261	231	296	.780	95	189	284	603	177	2	174	7	205	30.8	14.4	3.6	7.6	.594
93-94	Milwaukee	82	76	2533	1257	477	1019	.468	69	168	.411	234	288	.813	91	170	261	546	189	2	197	12	205	30.9	15.3	3.2	6.7	.585
94-95	Milwaukee	75	32	2158	977	338	814	.415	90	240	.375	211	267	.790	48	166	214	482	139	0	113	12	195	28.8	13.0	2.9	6.4	.503
95-96	Milwaukee	9	0	193	62	24	66	.364	6	23	.261	8	12	.667	5	9	14	35	16	0	6	0	12	21.4	6.9	1.6	3.9	.299
95-96	Vancouver	64	14	1480	585	220	521	.422	39	122	.320	106	131	.809	21	134	155	292	124	0	129	9	122	23.1	9.1	2.4	4.6	.475
96-97	Denver	12	0	114	45	15	33	.455	4	10	.400	11	12	.917	1	10	11	24	9	0	9	2	11	9.5	3.8	0.9	2.0	.521

YEAR	TEAM	GP	GS	MIN	PTS	FGM	FGA	FG%	3PM	3PA	3P%	FTM	FTA	FT%	ORB	DRB	TRB	AST	PF	DQ	STL	BLK	TO	MPG	PPG	RPG	APG	PCM
97-98	Miami	82	1	1395	507	177	419	.422	28	91	.308	125	156	.801	39	117	156	219	173	1	103	13	107	17.0	6.2	1.9	2.7	.416
98-99	New Jersey	15	8	401	119	45	114	.395	8	22	.364	21	26	.808	3	32	35	66	35	1	22	2	29	26.7	7.9	2.3	4.4	.349
99-00	LA Clippers	40	15	693	225	79	205	.385	16	42	.381	51	80	.638	15	62	77	108	67	0	47	5	58	17.3	5.6	1.9	2.7	.360
NBA Season Totals		508	224	11882	5118	1889	4310	.438	296	863	.343	1044	1329	.786	339	922	1261	2467	981	6	830	69	994	23.4	10.1	2.5	4.9	....
91-92	Utah	3	0	11	8	3	5	.600	0	1	.000	2	2	1.000	0	3	3	1	1	0	1	1	3	3.7	2.7	1.0	0.3	.782
97-98	Miami	5	0	125	47	11	32	.344	2	9	.222	23	28	.821	3	17	20	15	11	0	7	0	4	25.0	9.4	4.0	3.0	.462
NBA Playoff Totals		8	0	136	55	14	37	.378	2	10	.200	25	30	.833	3	20	23	16	12	0	8	1	7	17.0	6.9	2.9	2.0	....

• MURESAN, Gheorghe
Gheorghe Muresan

Born: Feb. 14, 1971. Triteni, Romania.   Height: 7'7".   Weight: 303 lbs.   Drafted: 1993   College: Cluj University (ROM)

YEAR	TEAM	GP	GS	MIN	PTS	FGM	FGA	FG%	3PM	3PA	3P%	FTM	FTA	FT%	ORB	DRB	TRB	AST	PF	DQ	STL	BLK	TO	MPG	PPG	RPG	APG	PCM
93-94	Washington	54	2	650	304	128	235	.545	0	0	.000	48	71	.676	66	126	192	18	120	1	28	48	54	12.0	5.6	3.6	0.3	.548
94-95	Washington	73	58	1720	730	303	541	.560	0	0	.000	124	175	.709	179	309	488	38	259	6	48	127	117	23.6	10.0	6.7	0.5	.531
95-96	Washington	76	76	2242	1104	466	798	**.584**	0	1	.000	172	278	.619	248	480	728	56	297	8	52	172	144	29.5	14.5	9.6	0.7	.634
96-97	Washington	73	69	1849	777	327	541	**.604**	0	0	.000	123	199	.618	141	340	481	29	230	3	43	96	117	25.3	10.6	6.6	0.4	.506
98-99	New Jersey	1	0	1	0	0	1	.000	0	0	.000	0	0	.000	0	0	0	0	0	0	0	0	1	1.0	0.0	0.0	0.0	-1.78
99-00	New Jersey	30	2	267	105	41	90	.456	0	0	.000	23	38	.605	24	44	68	9	52	0	0	12	16	8.9	3.5	2.3	0.3	.367
NBA Season Totals		307	207	6729	3020	1265	2206	.573	0	1	.000	490	761	.644	658	1299	1957	150	958	18	171	455	449	21.9	9.8	6.4	0.5	....
96-97	Washington	3	3	70	15	4	9	.444	0	0	.000	7	8	.875	2	16	18	0	6	0	0	4	11	23.3	5.0	6.0	0.0	.248
NBA Playoff Totals		3	3	70	15	4	9	.444	0	0	.000	7	8	.875	2	16	18	0	6	0	0	4	11	23.3	5.0	6.0	0.0	....

• MURPHY, Allen
Allen Murphy

Born: July 15, 1952. Birmingham, AL, United States.   Height: 6'5".   Weight: 190 lbs.   Drafted: 1975   College: Louisville

YEAR	TEAM	GP	GS	MIN	PTS	FGM	FGA	FG%	3PM	3PA	3P%	FTM	FTA	FT%	ORB	DRB	TRB	AST	PF	DQ	STL	BLK	TO	MPG	PPG	RPG	APG	PCM
75-76	Kentucky-A	29	....	248	113	43	114	.377	0	1	.000	27	37	.730	24	23	47	13	52	....	10	8	27	8.6	3.9	1.6	0.4	.316
76-77	LA Lakers	2	....	18	5	1	5	.200	....	....	....	3	7	.429	3	1	4	0	5	0	0	0	....	9.0	2.5	2.0	0.0	.062
NBA Season Totals		2	....	18	5	1	5	.200	....	....	....	3	7	.429	3	1	4	0	5	0	0	0	....	9.0	2.5	2.0	0.0	
ABA Season Totals		29	....	248	113	43	114	.377	0	1	.000	27	37	.730	24	23	47	13	52	....	10	8	27	8.6	3.9	1.6	0.4	
Career Totals		31	....	266	118	44	119	.370	0	1	.000	30	44	.682	27	24	51	13	57	0	10	8	27	8.6	3.8	1.6	0.4	

• MURPHY, Calvin
Calvin Jerome Murphy

Born: May 9, 1948. Norwalk, CT, United States.   Height: 5'9".   Weight: 165 lbs.   Drafted: 1970   College: Niagara   HOF: 1993

YEAR	TEAM	GP	GS	MIN	PTS	FGM	FGA	FG%	3PM	3PA	3P%	FTM	FTA	FT%	ORB	DRB	TRB	AST	PF	DQ	STL	BLK	TO	MPG	PPG	RPG	APG	PCM
70-71	San Diego	82	....	2020	1298	471	1029	.458	....	....	....	356	434	.820	....	....	245	329	263	4	....	....	....	24.6	15.8	3.0	4.0	.622
71-72	Houston	82	....	2538	1491	571	1255	.455	....	....	....	349	392	.890	....	....	258	393	298	6	....	....	....	31.0	18.2	3.1	4.8	.560
72-73	Houston	77	....	1697	1001	381	820	.465	....	....	....	239	269	.888	....	....	149	262	211	3	....	....	....	22.0	13.0	1.9	3.4	.559
73-74	Houston	81	....	2922	1652	671	1285	.522	....	....	....	310	357	.868	51	137	188	603	310	8	157	4	....	36.1	20.4	2.3	7.4	.626
74-75	Houston	78	....	2513	1455	557	1152	.484	....	....	....	341	386	.883	52	121	173	381	281	8	128	4	....	32.2	18.7	2.2	4.9	.554
75-76	Houston	82	....	2995	1722	675	1369	.493	....	....	....	372	410	.907	52	157	209	596	294	3	151	6	....	36.5	21.0	2.5	7.3	.616
76-77	Houston	82	....	2764	1464	596	1216	.490	....	....	....	272	307	.886	54	118	172	386	281	6	144	8	....	33.7	17.9	2.1	4.7	.499
77-78	Houston	76	....	2900	1949	852	**1737**	.491	....	....	....	245	267	.918	57	107	164	259	241	4	112	3	175	38.2	25.6	2.2	3.4	.497
78-79	Houston	82	....	2941	1660	707	1424	.496	....	....	....	246	265	.928	78	95	173	351	288	5	117	6	189	35.9	20.2	2.1	4.3	.463
79-80	Houston	76	....	2676	1520	624	1267	.493	1	25	.040	271	302	.897	68	82	150	299	269	3	143	9	160	35.2	20.0	2.0	3.9	.470
80-81	Houston	76	....	2014	1266	528	1074	.492	4	17	.235	206	215	**.958**	33	54	87	222	209	0	111	6	129	26.5	16.7	1.1	2.9	.486
81-82	Houston	64	....	1204	655	277	648	.427	1	16	.063	100	110	.909	20	41	61	163	142	0	43	1	83	18.8	10.2	1.0	2.5	.365
82-83	Houston	64	0	1423	816	337	754	.447	4	14	.286	138	150	**.920**	34	40	74	158	163	3	59	4	90	22.2	12.8	1.2	2.5	.405
NBA Season Totals		1002	0	30607	17949	7247	15030	.482	10	72	.139	3445	3864	.892	499	952	2103	4402	3250	53	1165	51	826	30.5	17.9	2.1	4.4	....
74-75	Houston	8	....	305	195	72	156	.462	....	....	....	51	57	.895	9	10	19	45	36	2	14	1	....	38.1	24.4	2.4	5.6	.568
76-77	Houston	12	....	420	232	102	213	.479	....	....	....	28	30	.933	7	12	19	75	47	1	19	2	....	35.0	19.3	1.6	6.3	.516
78-79	Houston	2	....	73	26	9	31	.290	....	....	....	8	9	.889	2	1	3	6	9	0	8	1	2	36.5	13.0	1.5	3.0	.238
79-80	Houston	7	....	265	131	58	108	.537	2	4	.500	13	13	1.000	4	6	10	26	29	1	11	0	16	37.9	18.7	1.4	3.7	.399
80-81	Houston	19	....	540	344	142	287	.495	2	7	.286	58	60	.967	7	17	24	57	69	0	26	0	42	28.4	18.1	1.3	3.0	.461
81-82	Houston	3	0	57	17	5	22	.227	0	3	.000	7	8	.875	2	1	3	4	7	0	1	0	4	19.0	5.7	1.0	1.3	.035
NBA Playoff Totals		51	0	1660	945	388	817	.475	4	14	.286	165	177	.932	31	47	78	213	197	4	79	4	64	32.5	18.5	1.5	4.2	....

• MURPHY, Dick
Richard D. Murphy

Born: Mar. 10, 1921. Died: Oct.22, 1973.   Height: 6'1".   Weight: 175 lbs.   Drafted: —   College: Marshall

YEAR	TEAM	GP	GS	MIN	PTS	FGM	FGA	FG%	3PM	3PA	3P%	FTM	FTA	FT%	ORB	DRB	TRB	AST	PF	DQ	STL	BLK	TO	MPG	PPG	RPG	APG	PCM
46-47	New York	24	....	....	32	14	58	.241	....	....	....	4	5	.800	....	....	....	5	9	....	....	....	....		1.3		0.2	
46-47	Boston	7	....	....	2	1	17	.059	....	....	....	0	4	.000	....	....	....	3	6	....	....	....	....		0.3		0.4	
NBA Season Totals		31	....	....	34	15	75	.200	....	....	....	4	9	.444	....	....	....	8	15	....	....	....	....		1.1		0.3	

• MURPHY, Jay
Jay Dennis Murphy

Born: June 26, 1962. Meriden, CT, United States.   Height: 6'9".   Weight: 220 lbs.   Drafted: 1984   College: Boston College

YEAR	TEAM	GP	GS	MIN	PTS	FGM	FGA	FG%	3PM	3PA	3P%	FTM	FTA	FT%	ORB	DRB	TRB	AST	PF	DQ	STL	BLK	TO	MPG	PPG	RPG	APG	PCM
84-85	LA Clippers	23	0	149	28	8	50	.160	0	1	.000	12	21	.571	6	35	41	4	21	0	1	2	7	6.5	1.2	1.8	0.2	.091
85-86	LA Clippers	14	0	100	41	16	45	.356	0	2	.000	9	14	.643	7	8	15	3	12	0	4	3	6	7.1	2.9	1.1	0.2	.242
86-87	Washington	21	0	141	71	31	72	.431	0	0	.000	9	16	.563	17	22	39	5	21	0	3	2	6	6.7	3.4	1.9	0.2	.429
87-88	Washington	9	0	46	20	8	23	.348	0	0	.000	4	5	.800	4	12	16	1	5	0	0	0	5	5.1	2.2	1.8	0.1	.316
NBA Season Totals		67	0	436	160	63	190	.332	0	3	.000	34	56	.607	34	77	111	13	59	0	8	7	24	6.5	2.4	1.7	0.2	....

YEAR	TEAM	GP	GS	MIN	PTS	FGM	FGA	FG%	3PM	3PA	3P%	FTM	FTA	FT%	ORB	DRB	TRB	AST	PF	DQ	STL	BLK	TO	MPG	PPG	RPG	APG	PCM

• MURPHY, John

John Francis Murphy

Born: Sept. 13, 1924.　Height: 6'2".　Weight: 175 lbs.　Drafted: —　College: none

YEAR	TEAM	GP	GS	MIN	PTS	FGM	FGA	FG%	3PM	3PA	3P%	FTM	FTA	FT%	ORB	DRB	TRB	AST	PF	DQ	STL	BLK	TO	MPG	PPG	RPG	APG	PCM
46-47	New York	9	....	....	24	8	25	.320	....	....	....	8	12	.667	....	....	....	0	3	....	....	....	....	....	2.7	....	0.0	....
46-47	Philadelphia	11	....	....	8	3	15	.200	....	....	....	2	3	.667	....	....	....	0	5	....	....	....	....	....	0.7	....	0.0	....
NBA Season Totals		20	....	....	32	11	40	.275	....	....	....	10	15	.667	....	....	....	0	8	....	....	....	....	....	1.6	....	0.0	....

• MURPHY, Ronnie

Ronald T. Murphy

Born: July 29, 1964. Dover, DE, United States.　Height: 6'5".　Weight: 225 lbs.　Drafted: 1987　College: Jacksonville

YEAR	TEAM	GP	GS	MIN	PTS	FGM	FGA	FG%	3PM	3PA	3P%	FTM	FTA	FT%	ORB	DRB	TRB	AST	PF	DQ	STL	BLK	TO	MPG	PPG	RPG	APG	PCM
87-88	Portland	18	0	89	36	14	49	.286	1	4	.250	7	11	.636	5	6	11	6	14	0	5	1	7	4.9	2.0	0.6	0.3	.120
NBA Season Totals		18	0	89	36	14	49	.286	1	4	.250	7	11	.636	5	6	11	6	14	0	5	1	7	4.9	2.0	0.6	0.3	....

• MURPHY, Tod

Tod James Murphy

Born: Dec. 24, 1963. Long Beach, CA, United States.　Height: 6'9".　Weight: 220 lbs.　Drafted: 1986　College: California (Irvine)

YEAR	TEAM	GP	GS	MIN	PTS	FGM	FGA	FG%	3PM	3PA	3P%	FTM	FTA	FT%	ORB	DRB	TRB	AST	PF	DQ	STL	BLK	TO	MPG	PPG	RPG	APG	PCM
87-88	LA Clippers	1	0	19	5	1	1	1.000	0	0	.000	3	4	.750	1	1	2	2	2	0	1	0	0	19.0	5.0	2.0	2.0	.449
89-90	Minnesota	82	59	2493	680	260	552	.471	16	43	.372	144	203	.709	207	357	564	106	229	2	76	60	57	30.4	8.3	6.9	1.3	.396
90-91	Minnesota	52	19	1063	251	90	227	.396	1	17	.059	70	105	.667	92	163	255	60	101	1	25	20	31	20.4	4.8	4.9	1.2	.353
91-92	Minnesota	47	3	429	98	39	80	.488	1	2	.500	19	34	.559	36	74	110	11	40	0	9	8	19	9.1	2.1	2.3	0.2	.341
93-94	Detroit	7	0	57	15	6	12	.500	0	0	.000	3	6	.500	4	5	9	3	8	0	2	0	1	8.1	2.1	1.3	0.4	.296
93-94	Golden State	2	0	10	0	0	0	.000	0	0	.000	0	0	.000	0	1	1	1	2	0	0	0	0	5.0	0.0	0.5	0.5	.108
NBA Season Totals		191	81	4071	1049	396	872	.454	18	62	.290	239	352	.679	340	601	941	183	382	3	113	88	108	21.3	5.5	4.9	1.0	....

• MURPHY, Troy

Troy Brandon Murphy

Born: May 2, 1980. Morristown, NJ, United States.　Height: 6'11".　Weight: 245 lbs.　Drafted: 2001　College: Notre Dame

YEAR	TEAM	GP	GS	MIN	PTS	FGM	FGA	FG%	3PM	3PA	3P%	FTM	FTA	FT%	ORB	DRB	TRB	AST	PF	DQ	STL	BLK	TO	MPG	PPG	RPG	APG	PCM
01-02	Golden State	82	4	1448	480	178	423	.421	3	9	.333	121	156	.776	99	223	322	70	217	2	36	21	84	17.7	5.9	3.9	0.9	.337
02-03	Golden State	79	79	2510	923	338	749	.451	3	14	.214	244	290	.841	228	578	806	106	246	1	65	30	111	31.8	11.7	10.2	1.3	.498
NBA Season Totals		161	83	3958	1403	516	1172	.440	6	23	.261	365	446	.818	327	801	1128	176	463	3	101	51	195	24.6	8.7	7.0	1.1	....

• MURRAY, Ken

Kenneth Stanley Murray Jr.

Born: Apr. 20, 1928.　Height: 6'2".　Weight: 190 lbs.　Drafted: 1950　College: St. Bonaventure

YEAR	TEAM	GP	GS	MIN	PTS	FGM	FGA	FG%	3PM	3PA	3P%	FTM	FTA	FT%	ORB	DRB	TRB	AST	PF	DQ	STL	BLK	TO	MPG	PPG	RPG	APG	PCM
50-51	Baltimore	52	....	....	716	255	735	.347	....	....	....	206	281	.733	....	....	290	150	140	5	....	....	....	....	13.8	5.6	2.9	....
50-51	Fort Wayne	14	....	....	134	46	152	.303	....	....	....	42	51	.824	....	....	65	52	24	2	....	....	....	....	9.6	4.6	3.7	....
53-54	Fort Wayne	49	....	528	149	53	195	.272	....	....	....	43	60	.717	....	....	65	56	60	0	....	....	....	10.8	3.0	1.3	1.1	.264
54-55	Bal/Phi	66	....	1590	472	187	535	.350	....	....	....	98	129	.760	....	....	179	224	126	1	....	....	....	24.1	7.2	2.7	3.4	.356
NBA Season Totals		181	....	2118	1471	541	1617	.335	....	....	....	389	521	.747	....	....	599	482	350	8	....	....	....	11.7	8.1	3.3	2.7	....
50-51	Fort Wayne	3	....	....	26	11	48	.229	....	....	....	4	5	.800	....	....	14	10	7	0	....	....	....	8.7	4.7	3.3	....
53-54	Fort Wayne	3	....	15	14	6	10	.600	....	....	....	2	2	1.000	....	....	0	0	6	0	....	....	....	5.0	4.7	0.0	0.0	.602
NBA Playoff Totals		6	....	15	40	17	58	.293	....	....	....	6	7	.857	....	....	14	10	13	0	....	....	....	2.5	6.7	2.3	1.7	....

• MURRAY, Lamond

Lamond Maurice Murray

Born: Apr. 20, 1973. Pasadena, CA, United States.　Height: 6'7".　Weight: 236 lbs.　Drafted: 1994　College: California

YEAR	TEAM	GP	GS	MIN	PTS	FGM	FGA	FG%	3PM	3PA	3P%	FTM	FTA	FT%	ORB	DRB	TRB	AST	PF	DQ	STL	BLK	TO	MPG	PPG	RPG	APG	PCM
94-95	LA Clippers	81	61	2556	1142	439	1093	.402	65	218	.298	199	264	.754	132	222	354	133	180	3	72	55	162	31.6	14.1	4.4	1.6	.334
95-96	LA Clippers	77	32	1816	650	257	575	.447	37	116	.319	99	132	.750	89	157	246	84	151	0	61	25	108	23.6	8.4	3.2	1.1	.311
96-97	LA Clippers	74	1	1295	549	181	435	.416	31	91	.341	156	211	.739	85	148	233	57	113	3	53	29	89	17.5	7.4	3.1	0.8	.390
97-98	LA Clippers	79	65	2579	1220	473	984	.481	54	153	.353	220	294	.748	172	312	484	142	193	3	118	54	174	32.6	15.4	6.1	1.8	.475
98-99	LA Clippers	50	13	1317	612	226	578	.391	34	103	.330	126	157	.803	59	136	195	61	107	1	58	20	99	26.3	12.2	3.9	1.2	.349
99-00	Cleveland	74	72	2365	1175	460	1019	.451	51	139	.367	204	268	.761	127	296	423	132	208	2	105	36	184	32.0	15.9	5.7	1.8	.437
00-01	Cleveland	78	46	2225	998	391	925	.423	61	165	.370	155	211	.735	104	236	340	124	173	0	83	27	141	28.5	12.8	4.4	1.6	.373
01-02	Cleveland	71	68	2312	1176	430	986	.436	101	238	.424	215	263	.817	81	291	372	157	148	1	70	43	141	32.6	16.6	5.2	2.2	.461
NBA Season Totals		584	358	16465	7522	2857	6595	.433	434	1223	.355	1374	1800	.763	849	1798	2647	890	1273	13	620	289	1098	28.2	12.9	4.5	1.5	....
96-97	LA Clippers	3	0	65	21	6	20	.300	2	8	.250	7	7	1.000	2	9	11	3	7	0	2	3	4	21.7	7.0	3.7	1.0	.294
NBA Playoff Totals		3	0	65	21	6	20	.300	2	8	.250	7	7	1.000	2	9	11	3	7	0	2	3	4	21.7	7.0	3.7	1.0	....

• MURRAY, Ronald

Ronald Murray

Born: July 29, 1979. Philadelphia, PA, United States.　Height: 6'4".　Weight: 190 lbs.　Drafted: 2002　College: Shaw

YEAR	TEAM	GP	GS	MIN	PTS	FGM	FGA	FG%	3PM	3PA	3P%	FTM	FTA	FT%	ORB	DRB	TRB	AST	PF	DQ	STL	BLK	TO	MPG	PPG	RPG	APG	PCM
02-03	Milwaukee	12	0	42	23	9	26	.346	0	4	.000	5	8	.625	0	1	1	3	0	0	4	0	4	3.5	1.9	0.1	0.3	.247
02-03	Seattle	2	0	20	4	2	5	.400	0	1	.000	0	0	.000	0	3	3	2	0	0	0	0	4	10.0	2.0	1.5	1.0	.128
NBA Season Totals		14	0	62	27	11	31	.355	0	5	.000	5	8	.625	0	4	4	5	0	0	4	0	8	4.4	1.9	0.3	0.4	....

• MURRAY, Tracy

Tracy Lamonte Murray

Born: July 25, 1971. Los Angeles, CA, United States.　Height: 6'7".　Weight: 225 lbs.　Drafted: 1992　College: UCLA

YEAR	TEAM	GP	GS	MIN	PTS	FGM	FGA	FG%	3PM	3PA	3P%	FTM	FTA	FT%	ORB	DRB	TRB	AST	PF	DQ	STL	BLK	TO	MPG	PPG	RPG	APG	PCM
92-93	Portland	48	14	495	272	108	260	.415	21	70	.300	35	40	.875	40	43	83	11	59	0	8	5	29	10.3	5.7	1.7	0.2	.353
93-94	Portland	66	1	820	434	167	355	.470	50	109	.459	50	72	.694	43	68	111	31	76	0	21	20	40	12.4	6.6	1.7	0.5	.430
94-95	Portland	29	3	313	170	63	153	.412	16	41	.390	28	34	.824	18	19	37	14	42	0	7	1	20	10.8	5.9	1.3	0.5	.324
94-95	Houston	25	0	203	88	32	80	.400	19	45	.422	5	8	.625	2	20	22	5	31	0	7	3	15	8.1	3.5	0.9	0.2	.238
95-96	Toronto	82	37	2458	1325	496	1092	.454	151	358	.422	182	219	.831	114	238	352	131	208	2	87	40	131	30.0	16.2	4.3	1.6	.454
96-97	Washington	82	1	1814	817	288	678	.425	106	300	.353	135	161	.839	84	169	253	78	150	1	69	19	82	22.1	10.0	3.1	1.0	.384
97-98	Washington	82	12	2227	1238	449	1007	.446	158	403	.392	182	209	.871	75	202	277	84	167	0	67	25	98	27.2	15.1	3.4	1.0	.439

YEAR	TEAM	GP	GS	MIN	PTS	FGM	FGA	FG%	3PM	3PA	3P%	FTM	FTA	FT%	ORB	DRB	TRB	AST	PF	DQ	STL	BLK	TO	MPG	PPG	RPG	APG	PCM
98-99	Washington	36	0	653	233	83	237	.350	33	103	.320	34	42	.810	18	63	81	27	65	0	21	6	29	18.1	6.5	2.3	0.8	.251
99-00	Washington	80	8	1831	813	290	670	.433	113	263	.430	120	141	.851	63	208	271	72	185	0	45	24	84	22.9	10.2	3.4	0.9	.374
00-01	Denver	13	0	135	50	17	55	.309	7	23	.304	9	10	.900	4	18	22	9	8	0	4	1	6	10.4	3.8	1.7	0.7	.301
00-01	Toronto	38	1	453	207	77	193	.399	29	80	.363	24	32	.750	18	41	59	14	45	0	8	6	20	11.9	5.4	1.6	0.4	.314
01-02	Toronto	40	3	473	227	85	207	.411	40	104	.385	17	21	.810	18	35	53	19	38	0	11	8	25	11.8	5.7	1.3	0.5	.340
02-03	LA Lakers	31	0	193	61	23	71	.324	8	38	.211	7	9	.778	5	18	23	12	22	0	5	3	14	6.2	2.0	0.7	0.4	.182
NBA Season Totals		652	80	12068	5935	2178	5058	.431	751	1937	.388	828	998	.830	502	1142	1644	507	1096	3	360	161	593	18.5	9.1	2.5	0.8	....
93-94	Portland	2	0	11	6	3	6	.500	0	1	.000	0	0	.000	3	0	3	1	3	0	1	0	0	5.5	3.0	1.5	0.5	.602
96-97	Washington	3	0	87	55	17	30	.567	5	10	.500	16	17	.941	3	6	9	2	10	0	4	2	0	29.0	18.3	3.0	0.7	.619
00-01	Toronto	2	0	5	2	1	3	.333	0	2	.000	0	0	.000	0	0	0	0	1	0	1	0	2	2.5	1.0	0.0	0.0	-.229
NBA Playoff Totals		7	0	103	63	21	39	.538	5	13	.385	16	17	.941	6	6	12	3	14	0	6	2	2	14.7	9.0	1.7	0.4	....

• MURRELL, Willie

Willie Vernon Murrell

Born: Sept. 13, 1941. Taft, OK, United States. Height: 6'6". Weight: 225 lbs. Drafted: 1964 College: Kansas State

YEAR	TEAM	GP	GS	MIN	PTS	FGM	FGA	FG%	3PM	3PA	3P%	FTM	FTA	FT%	ORB	DRB	TRB	AST	PF	DQ	STL	BLK	TO	MPG	PPG	RPG	APG	PCM
67-68	Denver-A	71	....	2495	1165	498	1069	.466	3	11	.273	166	236	.703	....	....	637	64	200	1	....	....	116	35.1	16.4	9.0	0.9	.474
68-69	Miami-A	75	....	2493	1147	476	1019	.467	4	18	.222	191	269	.710	186	380	566	103	239	5	....	....	159	33.2	15.3	7.5	1.4	.461
69-70	Kentucky-A	35	....	438	118	48	118	.407	4	7	.571	18	28	.643	47	94	141	10	68	0	....	....	25	12.5	3.4	4.0	0.3	.358
69-70	Miami-A	47	....	1321	558	228	478	.477	3	10	.300	99	126	.786	74	237	311	56	133	2	....	....	87	28.1	11.9	6.6	1.2	.458
ABA Season Totals		228	....	6747	2988	1250	2684	.466	14	46	.304	474	659	.719	307	711	1655	233	640	8	....	....	387	29.6	13.1	7.3	1.0	....
67-68	Denver-A	5	....	198	112	45	88	.511	0	1	.000	22	26	.846	....	....	47	7	24	1	....	....	8	39.6	22.4	9.4	1.4	.565
68-69	Miami-A	12	....	456	197	82	179	.458	1	4	.250	32	38	.842	....	....	101	21	38	0	....	....	19	38.0	16.4	8.4	1.8	.451
69-70	Kentucky-A	7	....	35	8	3	11	.273	0	1	.000	2	5	.400	3	8	11	1	....	0	....	....	6	5.0	1.1	1.6	0.1	....
ABA Playoff Totals		24	....	689	317	130	278	.468	1	6	.167	56	69	.812	3	8	159	29	62	1	....	....	33	28.7	13.2	6.6	1.2	....

• MURREY, Dorie

Dorie S. Murrey

Born: Sept. 7, 1943. Height: 6'8". Weight: 215 lbs. Drafted: 1966 College: Detroit

YEAR	TEAM	GP	GS	MIN	PTS	FGM	FGA	FG%	3PM	3PA	3P%	FTM	FTA	FT%	ORB	DRB	TRB	AST	PF	DQ	STL	BLK	TO	MPG	PPG	RPG	APG	PCM
66-67	Detroit	35	....	311	98	33	82	.402	....	....	....	32	54	.593	....	....	102	12	57	2	....	....	....	8.9	2.8	2.9	0.3	.396
67-68	Seattle	81	....	1494	590	211	484	.436	....	....	....	168	244	.689	....	....	600	68	273	7	....	....	....	18.4	7.3	7.4	0.8	.531
68-69	Seattle	38	....	465	212	75	194	.387	....	....	....	62	97	.639	....	....	149	21	81	1	....	....	....	12.2	5.6	3.9	0.6	.458
69-70	Seattle	81	....	1079	442	153	343	.446	....	....	....	136	186	.731	....	....	357	76	191	4	....	....	....	13.3	5.5	4.4	0.9	.526
70-71	Portland	2	....	20	11	1	6	.167	....	....	....	9	11	.818	....	....	7	1	3	0	....	....	....	10.0	5.5	3.5	0.5	.586
70-71	Baltimore	69	....	696	220	77	172	.448	....	....	....	66	101	.653	....	....	214	31	146	4	....	....	....	10.1	3.2	3.1	0.4	.402
71-72	Baltimore	51	....	421	110	43	113	.381	....	....	....	24	39	.615	....	....	126	17	76	2	....	....	....	8.3	2.2	2.5	0.3	.329
NBA Season Totals		357	....	4486	1683	593	1394	.425	....	....	....	497	732	.679	....	....	1555	226	827	20	....	....	....	12.6	4.7	4.4	0.6	....
70-71	Baltimore	16	....	92	33	13	27	.481	....	....	....	7	11	.636	....	....	33	1	6	0	....	....	....	5.8	2.1	2.1	0.1	.502
71-72	Baltimore	1	....	1	0	0	0	.000	....	....	....	0	0	.000	....	....	0	0	0	0	....	....	....	1.0	0.0	0.0	0.0	.000
NBA Playoff Totals		17	....	93	33	13	27	.481	....	....	....	7	11	.636	....	....	33	1	6	0	....	....	....	5.5	1.9	1.9	0.1	....

• MUSI, Angelo

Angelo Musi Jr.

Born: July 25, 1918. Height: 5'9". Weight: 145 lbs. Drafted: — College: Temple

YEAR	TEAM	GP	GS	MIN	PTS	FGM	FGA	FG%	3PM	3PA	3P%	FTM	FTA	FT%	ORB	DRB	TRB	AST	PF	DQ	STL	BLK	TO	MPG	PPG	RPG	APG	PCM
46-47	Philadelphia	60	....	....	562	230	818	.281	....	....	....	102	123	.829	....	....	....	26	120	....	....	....	....	....	9.4	....	0.4	....
47-48	Philadelphia	43	....	....	319	134	485	.276	....	....	....	51	73	.699	....	....	....	10	56	....	....	....	....	....	7.4	....	0.2	....
48-49	Philadelphia	58	....	....	478	194	618	.314	....	....	....	90	119	.756	....	....	....	81	108	....	....	....	....	....	8.2	....	1.4	....
NBA Season Totals		161	....	....	1359	558	1921	.290	....	....	....	243	315	.771	....	....	....	117	284	....	....	....	....	....	8.4	....	0.7	....
46-47	Philadelphia	10	....	....	117	48	160	.300	....	....	....	21	29	.724	....	....	....	5	27	....	....	....	....	....	11.7	....	0.5	....
47-48	Philadelphia	13	....	....	73	26	129	.202	....	....	....	21	28	.750	....	....	....	11	30	....	....	....	....	....	5.6	....	0.8	....
48-49	Philadelphia	2	....	....	8	3	17	.176	....	....	....	2	2	1.000	....	....	....	0	1	....	....	....	....	....	4.0	....	0.0	....
NBA Playoff Totals		25	....	....	198	77	306	.252	....	....	....	44	59	.746	....	....	....	16	58	....	....	....	....	....	7.9	....	0.6	....

• MUSTAF, Jerrod

Terrah Jerrod Mustaf

Born: Oct. 28, 1969. Whiteville, NC, United States. Height: 6'10". Weight: 238 lbs. Drafted: 1990 College: Maryland

YEAR	TEAM	GP	GS	MIN	PTS	FGM	FGA	FG%	3PM	3PA	3P%	FTM	FTA	FT%	ORB	DRB	TRB	AST	PF	DQ	STL	BLK	TO	MPG	PPG	RPG	APG	PCM
90-91	New York	62	5	825	268	106	228	.465	0	1	.000	56	87	.644	51	118	169	36	109	0	15	14	62	13.3	4.3	2.7	0.6	.308
91-92	Phoenix	52	3	550	233	92	193	.477	0	0	.000	49	71	.690	45	100	145	45	59	0	21	16	52	10.6	4.5	2.8	0.9	.492
92-93	Phoenix	32	9	336	147	57	130	.438	0	1	.000	33	53	.623	29	54	83	10	40	0	15	11	22	10.5	4.6	2.6	0.3	.425
93-94	Phoenix	33	2	196	73	30	84	.357	0	0	.000	13	22	.591	20	35	55	8	29	0	4	5	10	5.9	2.2	1.7	0.2	.328
NBA Season Totals		179	19	1907	721	285	635	.449	0	2	.000	151	233	.648	145	307	452	99	237	0	55	46	146	10.7	4.0	2.5	0.6	....
90-91	New York	3	0	22	12	4	5	.800	0	0	.000	4	5	.800	3	2	5	0	2	0	0	1	1	7.3	4.0	1.7	0.0	.651
92-93	Phoenix	7	0	10	6	3	5	.600	0	0	.000	0	0	.000	0	2	2	0	0	0	0	1	0	1.4	0.9	0.3	0.0	.693
NBA Playoff Totals		10	0	32	18	7	10	.700	0	0	.000	4	5	.800	3	4	7	0	2	0	0	2	1	3.2	1.8	0.7	0.0	....

• MUTOMBO, Dikembe

Dikembe Mpolondo Jean-Jacque Mutombo

Born: June 25, 1966. Kinshasa, Zaire. Height: 7'2". Weight: 245 lbs. Drafted: 1991 College: Georgetown

YEAR	TEAM	GP	GS	MIN	PTS	FGM	FGA	FG%	3PM	3PA	3P%	FTM	FTA	FT%	ORB	DRB	TRB	AST	PF	DQ	STL	BLK	TO	MPG	PPG	RPG	APG	PCM
91-92	Denver	71	71	2716	1177	428	869	.493	0	0	.000	321	500	.642	316	554	870	156	273	1	43	210	249	38.3	16.6	12.3	2.2	.566
92-93	Denver	82	82	3029	1131	398	781	.510	0	0	.000	335	492	.681	344	726	1070	147	284	5	43	287	213	36.9	13.8	13.0	1.8	.605
93-94	Denver	82	82	2853	986	365	642	.569	0	1	.000	256	439	.583	286	685	971	127	262	2	59	**336**	205	34.8	12.0	11.8	1.5	.606
94-95	Denver	82	82	3100	946	349	628	.556	0	0	.000	248	379	.654	319	710	**1029**	113	284	2	40	**321**	189	37.8	11.5	12.5	1.4	.560
95-96	Denver	74	74	2713	814	284	569	.499	0	1	.000	246	354	.695	249	622	871	108	258	4	38	**332**	148	36.7	11.0	11.8	1.5	.559
96-97	Atlanta	80	80	2973	1066	380	721	.527	0	0	.000	306	434	.705	268	661	**929**	110	249	3	49	**264**	184	37.2	13.3	11.6	1.4	.564
97-98	Atlanta	82	82	2917	1101	399	743	.537	0	0	.000	303	452	.670	276	656	932	82	254	1	34	**277**	164	35.6	13.4	11.4	1.0	.575
98-99	Atlanta	50	50	1829	541	173	338	.512	0	0	.000	195	285	.684	192	**418**	**610**	57	145	2	16	147	94	36.6	10.8	12.2	1.1	.523

YEAR	TEAM	GP	GS	MIN	PTS	FGM	FGA	FG%	3PM	3PA	3P%	FTM	FTA	FT%	ORB	DRB	TRB	AST	PF	DQ	STL	BLK	TO	MPG	PPG	RPG	APG	PCM
99-00	Atlanta	82	82	2984	942	322	573	.562	0	0	.000	298	421	.708	304	**853**	**1157**	105	248	3	27	269	174	36.4	11.5	**14.1**	1.3	.610
00-01	Atlanta	49	49	1716	445	169	354	.477	0	0	.000	107	154	.695	**188**	505	693	54	139	2	20	137	92	35.0	9.1	**14.1**	1.1	.545
00-01	Philadelphia	26	26	875	304	100	202	.495	0	0	.000	104	137	.759	**119**	203	322	22	65	0	9	66	52	33.7	11.7	**12.4**	0.8	.574
01-02	Philadelphia	80	80	2907	920	321	641	.501	0	0	.000	278	364	.764	254	609	863	83	242	2	29	190	156	36.3	11.5	10.8	1.0	.485
02-03	New Jersey	24	16	514	138	49	131	.374	0	0	.000	40	55	.727	54	99	153	19	54	0	4	37	34	21.4	5.8	6.4	0.8	.386
NBA Season Totals		864	856	31126	10511	3737	7192	.520	0	2	.000	3037	4466	.680	3169	7301	10470	1183	2757	27	411	2873	1954	36.0	12.2	12.1	1.4	....
93-94	Denver	12	12	511	159	50	108	.463	0	0	.000	59	98	.602	40	104	144	21	42	0	8	69	30	42.6	13.3	12.0	1.8	.522
94-95	Denver	3	3	84	18	6	10	.600	0	0	.000	6	9	.667	4	15	19	1	7	1	0	7	7	28.0	6.0	6.3	0.3	.294
96-97	Atlanta	10	10	415	154	54	86	.628	0	0	.000	46	64	.719	37	86	123	13	30	0	1	26	20	41.5	15.4	12.3	1.3	.571
97-98	Atlanta	4	4	136	32	11	24	.458	0	0	.000	10	16	.625	13	38	51	1	10	0	1	9	8	34.0	8.0	12.8	0.3	.459
98-99	Atlanta	9	9	380	113	40	71	.563	0	0	.000	33	47	.702	36	89	125	11	28	0	5	23	18	42.2	12.6	13.9	1.2	.524
00-01	Philadelphia	23	23	981	319	102	208	.490	0	1	.000	115	148	.777	113	203	316	17	56	1	15	72	36	42.7	13.9	13.7	0.7	.542
01-02	Philadelphia	5	5	173	44	14	31	.452	0	0	.000	16	26	.615	14	39	53	3	16	0	2	9	11	34.6	8.8	10.6	0.6	.394
02-03	New Jersey	10	0	115	18	7	15	.467	0	0	.000	4	4	1.000	8	19	27	6	21	0	3	9	8	11.5	1.8	2.7	0.6	.312
NBA Playoff Totals		76	66	2795	857	284	553	.514	0	1	.000	289	412	.701	265	593	858	73	218	2	35	224	138	36.8	11.3	11.3	1.0	....

• MUURSEPP, Martin

Martin Muursepp

Born: Sept. 26, 1974. Estonia.   Height: 6'9".   Weight: 235 lbs.   Drafted: 1996   College: —

YEAR	TEAM	GP	GS	MIN	PTS	FGM	FGA	FG%	3PM	3PA	3P%	FTM	FTA	FT%	ORB	DRB	TRB	AST	PF	DQ	STL	BLK	TO	MPG	PPG	RPG	APG	PCM
96-97	Miami	10	0	27	17	5	14	.357	1	4	.250	6	14	.429	2	3	5	3	3	0	0	1	3	2.7	1.7	0.5	0.3	.351
96-97	Dallas	32	0	321	139	49	117	.419	3	20	.150	38	56	.679	33	29	62	17	55	1	12	10	16	10.0	4.3	1.9	0.5	.384
97-98	Dallas	41	7	603	233	83	191	.435	16	38	.421	51	67	.761	46	68	114	30	96	1	29	14	29	14.7	5.7	2.8	0.7	.386
NBA Season Totals		83	7	951	389	137	322	.425	20	62	.323	95	137	.693	81	100	181	50	154	2	41	25	48	11.5	4.7	2.2	0.6	....

• MYERS, Pete

Peter E. (Skeeter Hawk) Myers

Born: Sept. 15, 1963. Mobile, AL, United States.   Height: 6'6".   Weight: 180 lbs.   Drafted: 1986   College: Arkansas-Little Rock

YEAR	TEAM	GP	GS	MIN	PTS	FGM	FGA	FG%	3PM	3PA	3P%	FTM	FTA	FT%	ORB	DRB	TRB	AST	PF	DQ	STL	BLK	TO	MPG	PPG	RPG	APG	PCM
86-87	Chicago	29	0	155	66	19	52	.365	0	6	.000	28	43	.651	8	9	17	21	25	0	14	2	9	5.3	2.3	0.6	0.7	.396
87-88	San Antonio	22	0	328	112	43	95	.453	0	4	.000	26	39	.667	11	26	37	48	30	0	17	6	33	14.9	5.1	1.7	2.2	.366
88-89	Philadelphia	4	0	40	14	6	12	.500	0	0	.000	2	4	.500	3	7	10	2	3	0	3	0	4	10.0	3.5	2.5	0.5	.415
88-89	New York	29	0	230	81	25	61	.410	0	2	.000	31	44	.705	12	11	23	46	41	0	17	2	29	7.9	2.8	0.8	1.6	.400
89-90	New York	24	0	208	46	15	45	.333	0	1	.000	16	31	.516	10	18	28	35	39	0	15	2	29	8.7	1.9	1.2	1.5	.215
89-90	New Jersey	28	2	543	198	74	180	.411	0	6	.000	50	69	.725	23	45	68	100	70	0	20	9	48	19.4	7.1	2.4	3.6	.385
90-91	San Antonio	8	1	103	29	10	23	.435	0	1	.000	9	11	.818	2	16	18	14	14	0	3	3	14	12.9	3.6	2.3	1.8	.327
93-94	Chicago	82	81	2030	650	253	556	.455	8	29	.276	136	194	.701	54	127	181	245	195	1	78	20	139	24.8	7.9	2.2	3.0	.320
94-95	Chicago	71	14	1270	318	119	287	.415	10	39	.256	70	114	.614	57	82	139	148	125	1	58	15	85	17.9	4.5	2.0	2.1	.281
95-96	Miami	39	1	639	184	62	160	.388	11	42	.262	49	76	.645	21	52	73	97	75	1	14	11	55	16.4	4.7	1.9	2.5	.293
95-96	Charlotte	32	1	453	92	29	87	.333	3	16	.188	31	46	.674	14	53	67	48	57	0	20	6	26	14.2	2.9	2.1	1.5	.259
97-98	New York	9	0	40	14	5	10	.500	0	0	.000	4	6	.667	5	5	10	3	7	0	4	0	4	4.4	1.6	1.1	0.3	.443
NBA Season Totals		377	100	6039	1804	660	1568	.421	32	146	.219	452	677	.668	220	451	671	807	681	3	263	76	466	16.0	4.8	1.8	2.1	....
86-87	Chicago	1	0	1	0	0	1	.000	0	0	.000	0	0	.000	0	0	0	0	0	0	0	0	0	1.0	0.0	0.0	0.0	-.931
88-89	New York	4	0	14	4	0	0	.000	0	0	.000	4	6	.667	1	2	3	1	2	0	1	0	1	3.5	1.0	0.8	0.3	.495
93-94	Chicago	10	10	235	70	29	56	.518	0	4	.000	12	21	.571	10	9	19	28	21	0	8	4	17	23.5	7.0	1.9	2.8	.318
94-95	Chicago	9	0	79	13	5	14	.357	1	2	.500	2	6	.333	6	4	10	8	10	0	4	1	4	8.8	1.4	1.1	0.9	.213
NBA Playoff Totals		24	10	329	87	34	71	.479	1	6	.167	18	33	.545	17	15	32	37	33	0	12	6	21	13.7	3.6	1.3	1.5	....

• NABER, Bob

Robert E. Naber

Born: Sept. 3, 1929.   Height: 6'3".   Weight: 185 lbs.   Drafted: —   College: Louisville

YEAR	TEAM	GP	GS	MIN	PTS	FGM	FGA	FG%	3PM	3PA	3P%	FTM	FTA	FT%	ORB	DRB	TRB	AST	PF	DQ	STL	BLK	TO	MPG	PPG	RPG	APG	PCM
52-53	Indianapolis	4	....	11	1	0	4	.000	....	....	....	1	2	.500	....	....	5	1	6	0	....	....	....	2.8	0.3	1.3	0.3	.042
NBA Season Totals		4	....	11	1	0	4	.000	....	....	....	1	2	.500	....	....	5	1	6	0	....	....	....	2.8	0.3	1.3	0.3	....

• NACHAMKIN, Boris

Boris Alexander Nachamkin

Born: Dec. 6, 1933.   Height: 6'6".   Weight: 210 lbs.   Drafted: 1954   College: New York University

YEAR	TEAM	GP	GS	MIN	PTS	FGM	FGA	FG%	3PM	3PA	3P%	FTM	FTA	FT%	ORB	DRB	TRB	AST	PF	DQ	STL	BLK	TO	MPG	PPG	RPG	APG	PCM
54-55	Rochester	6	....	59	20	6	20	.300	....	....	....	8	13	.615	....	....	19	3	6	0	....	....	....	9.8	3.3	3.2	0.5	.396
NBA Season Totals		6	....	59	20	6	20	.300	....	....	....	8	13	.615	....	....	19	3	6	0	....	....	....	9.8	3.3	3.2	0.5	....

• NACHBAR, Bostjan

Bostjan Nachbar

Born: July 3, 1980. Slovenj Gradec, Slovakia.   Height: 6'9".   Weight: 221 lbs.   Drafted: 2002   College: none

YEAR	TEAM	GP	GS	MIN	PTS	FGM	FGA	FG%	3PM	3PA	3P%	FTM	FTA	FT%	ORB	DRB	TRB	AST	PF	DQ	STL	BLK	TO	MPG	PPG	RPG	APG	PCM
02-03	Houston	14	1	77	29	11	31	.355	2	10	.200	5	10	.500	3	8	11	3	13	0	2	2	6	5.5	2.1	0.8	0.2	.183
NBA Season Totals		14	1	77	29	11	31	.355	2	10	.200	5	10	.500	3	8	11	3	13	0	2	2	6	5.5	2.1	0.8	0.2	....

• NAGEL, Jerry

Gerald R. Nagel

Born: May 18, 1928. Chicago, IL, United States.   Height: 6'   Weight: 190 lbs.   Drafted: —   College: Loyola (IL)

YEAR	TEAM	GP	GS	MIN	PTS	FGM	FGA	FG%	3PM	3PA	3P%	FTM	FTA	FT%	ORB	DRB	TRB	AST	PF	DQ	STL	BLK	TO	MPG	PPG	RPG	APG	PCM
49-50	Fort Wayne	14	....	....	13	6	28	.214	....	....	....	1	4	.250	....	....	....	18	11	....	....	....	....	0.9	....	1.3	....	....
NBA Season Totals		14	....	....	13	6	28	.214	....	....	....	1	4	.250	....	....	....	18	11	....	....	....	....	0.9	....	1.3	....	....

YEAR	TEAM	GP	GS	MIN	PTS	FGM	FGA	FG%	3PM	3PA	3P%	FTM	FTA	FT%	ORB	DRB	TRB	AST	PF	DQ	STL	BLK	TO	MPG	PPG	RPG	APG	PCM

● NAGODE, Jake — Jake Nagode

Born: July 11, 1915. Died: Jan.1976. Height: 6'2". Weight: 170 lbs. Drafted: — College: Northwestern

YEAR	TEAM	GP	GS	MIN	PTS	FGM	FGA	FG%	3PM	3PA	3P%	FTM	FTA	FT%	ORB	DRB	TRB	AST	PF	DQ	STL	BLK	TO	MPG	PPG	RPG	APG	PCM
39-40	Wingfoots-N	25	....	....	78	33	....	....	....	....	....	12	....		....	....	....	....	....		....	....	....		3.1	....	....	....
40-41	Wingfoots-N	18	....	....	47	19	....	....	....	....	....	9	....		....	....	....	....	....		....	....	....		2.6	....	....	....
NBL Season Totals		43	....	....	125	52	....	....	....	....	....	21	....		....	....	....	....	....		....	....	....		2.9	....	....	....

● NAGY, Fritz — Frederick Karl (Fritz) Nagy

Born: Jan. 3, 1924. Died: June5, 1989. Height: 6'2". Weight: 185 lbs. Drafted: 1947 College: Akron

YEAR	TEAM	GP	GS	MIN	PTS	FGM	FGA	FG%	3PM	3PA	3P%	FTM	FTA	FT%	ORB	DRB	TRB	AST	PF	DQ	STL	BLK	TO	MPG	PPG	RPG	APG	PCM
47-48	Indianapolis-N	39	....	....	126	42	....	....	....	....	....	42	63	.667	....	....	....	....	53		....	....	....		3.2	....	....	
48-49	Indianapolis	50	....	....	253	94	271	.347	....	....	....	65	97	.670	....	....	....	68	84		....	....	....		5.1	....	1.4	
NBA Season Totals		50	....	....	253	94	271	.347	....	....	....	65	97	.670	....	....	....	68	84	....	....	....	....		5.1	....	1.4	
NBL Season Totals		39	....	....	126	42	....	....	....	....	....	42	63		....	....	....		53		....	....	....		3.2	....	....	
Career Totals		89	....	....	379	136	271		....	....	....	107	160		....	....	....	68	137	....	....	....	....		4.3	....	0.8	
47-48	Indianapolis-N	4	....	....	8	1	....	....	....	....	....	6	8	.750	....	....	....	....	....		....	....	....		2.0	....	....	
NBL Playoff Totals		4	....	....	8	1	....	....	....	....	....	6	8		....	....	....		....		....	....	....		2.0	....	....	

● NAILON, Lee — Lee Nailon

Born: Feb. 22, 1975. South Bend, IN, United States. Height: 6'9". Weight: 238 lbs. Drafted: 1999 College: Texas Christian

YEAR	TEAM	GP	GS	MIN	PTS	FGM	FGA	FG%	3PM	3PA	3P%	FTM	FTA	FT%	ORB	DRB	TRB	AST	PF	DQ	STL	BLK	TO	MPG	PPG	RPG	APG	PCM
00-01	Charlotte	42	0	469	164	66	136	.485	0	1	.000	32	43	.744	29	63	92	24	60	0	9	5	27	11.2	3.9	2.2	0.6	.355
01-02	Charlotte	79	41	1911	851	369	764	.483	1	2	.500	112	150	.747	103	188	291	94	175	1	59	17	96	24.2	10.8	3.7	1.2	.390
02-03	New York	38	0	405	210	84	190	.442	0	1	.000	42	51	.824	32	38	70	26	46	0	6	3	32	10.7	5.5	1.8	0.7	.395
NBA Season Totals		159	41	2785	1225	519	1090	.476	1	4	.250	186	244	.762	164	289	453	144	281	1	74	25	155	17.5	7.7	2.8	0.9	....
01-02	Charlotte	9	1	160	69	27	59	.458	0	1	.000	15	19	.789	10	14	24	6	17	0	3	0	7	17.8	7.7	2.7	0.7	.345
NBA Playoff Totals		9	1	160	69	27	59	.458	0	1	.000	15	19	.789	10	14	24	6	17	0	3	0	7	17.8	7.7	2.7	0.7	....

● NAJERA, Eduardo — Eduardo Alonso Najera

Born: July 11, 1976. Meoqui, Mexico. Height: 6'8". Weight: 240 lbs. Drafted: 2000 College: Oklahoma

YEAR	TEAM	GP	GS	MIN	PTS	FGM	FGA	FG%	3PM	3PA	3P%	FTM	FTA	FT%	ORB	DRB	TRB	AST	PF	DQ	STL	BLK	TO	MPG	PPG	RPG	APG	PCM
00-01	Dallas	40	4	431	131	58	111	.523	1	3	.333	14	33	.424	41	54	95	27	48	0	13	8	17	10.8	3.3	2.4	0.7	.399
01-02	Dallas	62	11	1357	400	150	300	.500	0	2	.000	100	148	.676	149	193	342	38	156	2	56	30	40	21.9	6.5	5.5	0.6	.416
02-03	Dallas	48	12	1102	320	129	231	.558	0	1	.000	62	91	.681	90	133	223	47	129	1	40	22	23	23.0	6.7	4.6	1.0	.404
NBA Season Totals		150	27	2890	851	337	642	.525	1	6	.167	176	272	.647	280	380	660	112	333	3	109	60	80	19.3	5.7	4.4	0.7	....
00-01	Dallas	7	0	44	21	9	17	.529	3	4	.750	0	0	.000	7	8	15	1	8	0	1	1	1	6.3	3.0	2.1	0.1	.584
01-02	Dallas	8	4	122	37	16	23	.696	0	0	.000	5	8	.625	3	10	13	1	22	0	3	0	2	15.3	4.6	1.6	0.1	.271
02-03	Dallas	19	5	394	116	39	86	.453	0	0	.000	38	48	.792	36	38	74	15	53	1	14	4	16	20.7	6.1	3.9	0.8	.330
NBA Playoff Totals		34	9	560	174	64	126	.508	3	4	.750	43	56	.768	46	56	102	17	83	1	18	5	19	16.5	5.1	3.0	0.5	....

● NANCE, Larry — Larry Donell Nance

Born: Feb. 12, 1959. Anderson, SC, United States. Height: 6'10". Weight: 205 lbs. Drafted: 1981 College: Clemson

YEAR	TEAM	GP	GS	MIN	PTS	FGM	FGA	FG%	3PM	3PA	3P%	FTM	FTA	FT%	ORB	DRB	TRB	AST	PF	DQ	STL	BLK	TO	MPG	PPG	RPG	APG	PCM
81-82	Phoenix	80	0	1186	529	227	436	.521	0	1	.000	75	117	.641	95	161	256	82	169	2	42	71	104	14.8	6.6	3.2	1.0	.482
82-83	Phoenix	82	82	2914	1370	588	1069	.550	1	3	.333	193	287	.672	239	471	710	197	254	4	99	217	189	35.5	16.7	8.7	2.4	.601
83-84	Phoenix	82	82	2899	1451	601	1044	.576	0	7	.000	249	352	.707	227	451	678	214	274	5	86	174	180	35.4	17.7	8.3	2.6	.620
84-85	Phoenix	61	55	2202	1211	515	877	.587	1	2	.500	180	254	.709	195	341	536	159	185	2	88	104	134	36.1	19.9	8.8	2.6	.670
85-86	Phoenix	73	69	2484	1474	582	1001	.581	0	8	.000	310	444	.698	169	449	618	240	247	6	70	130	212	34.0	20.2	8.5	3.3	.696
86-87	Phoenix	69	67	2569	1552	585	1062	.551	1	5	.200	381	493	.773	188	411	599	233	223	4	86	148	152	37.2	22.5	8.7	3.4	.714
87-88	Phoenix	40	34	1477	843	327	616	.531	2	5	.400	187	249	.751	119	275	394	123	152	7	45	96	104	36.9	21.1	9.9	3.1	.682
87-88	Cleveland	27	26	906	437	160	304	.526	0	1	.000	117	141	.830	74	139	213	84	90	3	18	63	49	33.6	16.2	7.9	3.1	.627
88-89	Cleveland	73	72	2526	1259	496	920	.539	0	4	.000	267	334	.799	156	425	581	159	186	0	57	206	117	34.6	17.2	8.0	2.2	.631
89-90	Cleveland	62	53	2065	1011	412	807	.511	1	1	1.000	186	239	.778	162	354	516	161	185	3	54	122	112	33.3	16.3	8.3	2.6	.602
90-91	Cleveland	80	78	2927	1537	635	1211	.524	2	8	.250	265	330	.803	201	485	686	237	219	3	66	200	128	36.6	19.2	8.6	3.0	.645
91-92	Cleveland	81	81	2880	1375	556	1032	.539	0	6	.000	263	320	.822	213	457	670	232	200	2	80	243	89	35.6	17.0	8.3	2.9	.660
92-93	Cleveland	77	77	2753	1268	533	971	.549	0	4	.000	202	247	.818	184	484	668	223	223	3	54	198	108	35.8	16.5	8.7	2.9	.628
93-94	Cleveland	33	19	909	370	153	314	.487	0	0	.000	64	85	.753	77	150	227	49	96	1	27	55	40	27.5	11.2	6.9	1.5	.515
NBA Season Totals		920	795	30697	15687	6370	11664	.546	8	55	.145	2939	3892	.755	2299	5053	7352	2393	2703	45	872	2027	1718	33.4	17.1	8.0	2.6	....
81-82	Phoenix	7	0	128	54	25	41	.610	0	0	.000	4	8	.500	13	19	32	7	15	1	10	11	12	18.3	7.7	4.6	1.0	.592
82-83	Phoenix	3	3	103	36	14	35	.400	0	0	.000	8	10	.800	10	15	25	3	12	1	3	6	6	34.3	12.0	8.3	1.0	.381
83-84	Phoenix	17	17	633	287	118	200	.590	0	0	.000	51	76	.671	51	97	148	40	59	1	16	34	31	37.2	16.9	8.7	2.4	.584
87-88	Cleveland	5	5	200	84	34	64	.531	0	0	.000	16	18	.889	10	26	36	18	13	0	2	11	14	40.0	16.8	7.2	3.6	.504
88-89	Cleveland	5	5	195	97	38	69	.551	0	0	.000	21	32	.656	16	23	39	16	12	0	3	12	9	39.0	19.4	7.8	3.2	.597
89-90	Cleveland	5	5	159	61	26	45	.578	0	0	.000	9	12	.750	4	20	24	12	20	0	3	10	4	31.8	12.2	4.8	2.4	.479
91-92	Cleveland	17	17	681	306	124	251	.494	0	1	.000	58	70	.829	45	112	157	43	56	1	14	46	26	40.1	18.0	9.2	2.5	.558
92-93	Cleveland	9	9	329	145	61	108	.565	0	0	.000	23	30	.767	35	39	74	21	33	1	8	14	6	36.6	16.1	8.2	2.3	.574
NBA Playoff Totals		68	61	2428	1070	440	813	.541	0	1	.000	190	256	.742	184	351	535	160	220	5	59	144	108	35.7	15.7	7.9	2.4	....

• NAPOLITANO, Paul

Paul Wally Napolitano

Born: Feb. 3, 1923. Height: 6'2". Weight: 185 lbs. Drafted: 1947 College: San Francisco

YEAR	TEAM	GP	GS	MIN	PTS	FGM	FGA	FG%	3PM	3PA	3P%	FTM	FTA	FT%	ORB	DRB	TRB	AST	PF	DQ	STL	BLK	TO	MPG	PPG	RPG	APG	PCM
47-48	Minneapolis-N	52	....	....	155	72	....	....	....	....	....	11	21	.524	....	....	....	....	48	....	....	....	....	....	3.0	....	....	....
48-49	Indianapolis	1	....	....	0	0	0	.000	....	....	....	0	0	.000	....	....	....	0	0	....	....	....	....	....	0.0	....	0.0	....
NBA Season Totals		1	....	....	0	0	0	.000	....	....	....	0	0	.000	....	....	....	0	0	....	....	....	....	....	0.0	....	0.0	....
NBL Season Totals		52	....	....	155	72	....	....	....	....	....	11	21	....	....	....	....	....	48	....	....	....	....	....	3.0	....	....	....
Career Totals		53	....	....	155	72	0	....	....	....	....	11	21	....	....	....	....	0	48	....	....	....	....	....	2.9	....	0.0	....
47-48	Minneapolis-N	9	....	....	20	8	....	....	....	....	....	4	5	.800	....	....	....	....	....	....	....	....	....	....	2.2	....	....	....
NBL Playoff Totals		9	....	....	20	8	....	....	....	....	....	4	5	....	....	....	....	....	....	....	....	....	....	....	2.2	....	....	....

• NASH, Bob

Robert Lee Nash Jr.

Born: Aug. 24, 1950. Hartford, CT, United States. Height: 6'8". Weight: 195 lbs. Drafted: 1972 College: Hawaii

YEAR	TEAM	GP	GS	MIN	PTS	FGM	FGA	FG%	3PM	3PA	3P%	FTM	FTA	FT%	ORB	DRB	TRB	AST	PF	DQ	STL	BLK	TO	MPG	PPG	RPG	APG	PCM
72-73	Detroit	36	....	169	43	16	72	.222	....	....	....	11	17	.647	....	....	34	16	30	0	....	....	....	4.7	1.2	0.9	0.4	.159
73-74	Detroit	35	....	281	106	41	115	.357	....	....	....	24	39	.615	31	43	74	14	35	0	3	10	....	8.0	3.0	2.1	0.4	.359
74-75	San Diego-A	17	....	175	67	27	78	.346	0	2	.000	13	18	.722	20	35	55	12	30	....	4	2	16	10.3	3.9	3.2	0.7	.391
77-78	Kansas City	66	....	800	364	157	304	.516	....	....	....	50	69	.725	75	94	169	46	75	0	27	18	46	12.1	5.5	2.6	0.7	.491
78-79	Kansas City	82	....	1307	523	227	522	.435	....	....	....	69	86	.802	76	130	206	71	135	0	29	15	82	15.9	6.4	2.5	0.9	.321
NBA Season Totals		219	....	2557	1036	441	1013	.435	....	....	....	154	211	.730	182	267	483	147	275	0	59	43	128	11.7	4.7	2.2	0.7	....
ABA Season Totals		17	....	175	67	27	78	.346	0	2	.000	13	18	.722	20	35	55	12	30	....	4	2	16	10.3	3.9	3.2	0.7	....
Career Totals		236	....	2732	1103	468	1091	.429	0	2	.000	167	229	.729	202	302	538	159	305	0	63	45	144	11.6	4.7	2.3	0.7	....
78-79	Kansas City	5	....	64	24	8	27	.296	....	....	....	8	10	.800	6	5	11	0	10	0	0	4	7	12.8	4.8	2.2	0.0	.136
NBA Playoff Totals		5	....	64	24	8	27	.296	....	....	....	8	10	.800	6	5	11	0	10	0	0	4	7	12.8	4.8	2.2	0.0	....

• NASH, Cotton

Charles Francis (Cotton) Nash

Born: July 24, 1942. Jersey City, NJ, United States. Height: 6'5". Weight: 215 lbs. Drafted: 1964 College: Kentucky

YEAR	TEAM	GP	GS	MIN	PTS	FGM	FGA	FG%	3PM	3PA	3P%	FTM	FTA	FT%	ORB	DRB	TRB	AST	PF	DQ	STL	BLK	TO	MPG	PPG	RPG	APG	PCM
64-65	LA Lakers	25	....	167	53	14	57	.246	....	....	....	25	32	.781	....	....	35	10	30	0	....	....	....	6.7	2.1	1.4	0.4	.269
64-65	San Francisco	20	....	190	84	33	88	.375	....	....	....	18	20	.900	....	....	48	9	27	0	....	....	....	9.5	4.2	2.4	0.5	.414
67-68	Kentucky-A	39	....	786	333	106	305	.348	0	1	.000	121	162	.747	....	....	190	46	63	0	....	....	49	20.2	8.5	4.9	1.2	.428
NBA Season Totals		45	....	357	137	47	145	.324	....	....	....	43	52	.827	....	....	83	19	57	0	....	....	....	7.9	3.0	1.8	0.4	....
ABA Season Totals		39	....	786	333	106	305	.348	0	1	.000	121	162	.747	....	....	190	46	63	0	....	....	49	20.2	8.5	4.9	1.2	....
Career Totals		84	....	1143	470	153	450	.340	0	1	.000	164	214	.766	....	....	273	65	120	0	....	....	49	13.6	5.6	3.3	0.8	....

• NASH, Steve

Stephen John Nash

Born: Feb. 7, 1974. Johannesburg, South Africa. Height: 6'3". Weight: 195 lbs. Drafted: 1996 College: Santa Clara

YEAR	TEAM	GP	GS	MIN	PTS	FGM	FGA	FG%	3PM	3PA	3P%	FTM	FTA	FT%	ORB	DRB	TRB	AST	PF	DQ	STL	BLK	TO	MPG	PPG	RPG	APG	PCM
96-97	Phoenix	65	2	684	213	74	175	.423	23	55	.418	42	51	.824	16	47	63	138	92	1	20	0	65	10.5	3.3	1.0	2.1	.345
97-98	Phoenix	76	9	1664	691	268	584	.459	81	195	.415	74	86	.860	32	128	160	262	145	1	63	4	99	21.9	9.1	2.1	3.4	.440
98-99	Dallas	40	40	1269	315	114	314	.363	49	131	.374	38	46	.826	32	82	114	219	98	2	37	2	83	31.7	7.9	2.9	5.5	.312
99-00	Dallas	56	27	1532	481	173	363	.477	60	149	.403	75	85	.882	34	87	121	272	122	1	37	3	102	27.4	8.6	2.2	4.9	.391
00-01	Dallas	70	70	2387	1092	386	792	.487	89	219	.406	231	258	.895	46	177	223	509	158	0	72	5	205	34.1	15.6	3.2	7.3	.541
01-02	Dallas	82	82	2838	1466	525	1088	.483	156	343	.455	260	293	.887	50	204	254	634	164	0	53	4	229	34.6	17.9	3.1	7.7	.576
02-03	Dallas	82	82	2711	1455	518	1114	.465	111	269	.413	308	339	.909	63	171	234	598	134	0	85	6	192	33.1	17.7	2.9	7.3	.595
NBA Season Totals		471	312	13085	5713	2058	4430	.465	569	1361	.418	1028	1158	.888	273	896	1169	2632	913	5	367	24	975	27.8	12.1	2.5	5.6	....
96-97	Phoenix	4	0	15	5	2	9	.222	1	4	.250	0	0	.000	1	0	1	1	5	0	1	1	2	3.8	1.3	0.3	0.3	-.124
97-98	Phoenix	4	1	51	22	8	18	.444	1	5	.200	5	8	.625	2	8	10	7	7	0	2	0	3	12.8	5.5	2.5	1.8	.473
00-01	Dallas	10	10	370	136	45	108	.417	16	39	.410	30	34	.882	6	26	32	64	19	0	6	1	25	37.0	13.6	3.2	6.4	.411
01-02	Dallas	8	8	323	156	51	118	.432	20	45	.444	34	35	.971	7	25	32	70	20	0	4	0	30	40.4	19.5	4.0	8.8	.520
02-03	Dallas	20	20	729	322	115	257	.447	37	76	.487	55	63	.873	15	55	70	145	46	0	17	1	51	36.5	16.1	3.5	7.3	.494
NBA Playoff Totals		46	39	1488	641	221	510	.433	75	169	.444	124	140	.886	31	114	145	287	97	0	30	3	111	32.3	13.9	3.2	6.2	....

• NATER, Swen

Swen Eric Nater aka.: Swen Langeberg

Born: Jan. 14, 1950. Denhelder, Netherlands. Height: 6'11". Weight: 240 lbs. Drafted: 1973 College: UCLA

YEAR	TEAM	GP	GS	MIN	PTS	FGM	FGA	FG%	3PM	3PA	3P%	FTM	FTA	FT%	ORB	DRB	TRB	AST	PF	DQ	STL	BLK	TO	MPG	PPG	RPG	APG	PCM
73-74	San Antonio-A	62	....	2001	900	383	695	**.551**	0	1	.000	134	181	.740	248	596	844	112	177	....	26	48	153	32.3	14.5	13.6	1.8	.694
73-74	Virginia-A	17	....	374	214	84	151	**.556**	0	0	.000	46	73	.630	38	116	154	17	37	....	6	15	47	22.0	12.6	9.1	1.0	.750
74-75	San Antonio-A	78	....	2713	1175	495	914	.542	0	1	.000	185	246	.752	369	910	1279	97	240	....	43	87	185	34.8	15.1	**16.4**	1.2	.705
75-76	New York-A	43	....	1016	376	160	330	.485	0	3	.000	56	78	.718	139	302	441	19	142	....	18	26	94	23.6	8.7	10.3	0.4	.557
75-76	Virginia-A	33	....	774	372	160	321	.498	0	1	.000	52	77	.675	90	235	325	36	96	....	13	25	76	23.5	11.3	9.8	1.1	.651
76-77	Milwaukee	72	....	1960	938	383	725	.528	....	....	....	172	228	.754	266	599	865	108	214	6	54	51	....	27.2	13.0	12.0	1.5	.712
77-78	Buffalo	78	....	2778	1210	501	994	.504	....	....	....	208	272	.765	278	751	1029	216	274	3	40	47	226	35.6	15.5	13.2	2.8	.595
78-79	San Diego	79	....	2006	846	357	627	.569	....	....	....	132	165	.800	218	483	701	140	244	6	38	29	174	25.4	10.7	8.9	1.8	.582
79-80	San Diego	81	....	2860	1082	443	799	.554	0	2	.000	196	273	.718	352	**864**	**1216**	233	259	3	45	37	259	35.3	13.4	**15.0**	2.9	.630
80-81	San Diego	82	....	2809	1278	517	935	.553	0	0	.000	244	307	.795	295	**722**	1017	199	295	8	49	46	213	34.3	15.6	12.4	2.4	.630
81-82	San Diego	21	7	575	262	101	175	.577	1	1	1.000	59	79	.747	46	146	192	30	64	1	6	9	48	27.4	12.5	9.1	1.4	.581
82-83	San Diego	7	0	51	16	6	20	.300	0	0	.000	4	4	1.000	2	11	13	1	1	0	1	0	3	7.3	2.3	1.9	0.1	.273
83-84	LA Lakers	69	0	829	311	124	253	.490	0	1	.000	63	91	.692	81	183	264	27	150	0	25	7	69	12.0	4.5	3.8	0.4	.420
NBA Season Totals		489	7	13868	5943	2432	4528	.537	1	4	.250	1078	1419	.760	1538	3759	5297	954	1501	27	258	226	992	28.4	12.2	10.8	2.0	....
ABA Season Totals		233	....	6878	3037	1282	2411	.532	0	6	.000	473	655	.722	884	2159	3043	281	692	....	106	201	555	29.5	13.0	13.1	1.2	....
Career Totals		722	7	20746	8980	3714	6939	.535	1	10	.100	1551	2074	.748	2422	5918	8340	1235	2193	27	364	427	1547	28.7	12.4	11.6	1.7	....

YEAR	TEAM	GP	GS	MIN	PTS	FGM	FGA	FG%	3PM	3PA	3P%	FTM	FTA	FT%	ORB	DRB	TRB	AST	PF	DQ	STL	BLK	TO	MPG	PPG	RPG	APG	PCM
73-74	San Antonio-A	7	....	211	104	47	85	.553	0	0	.000	10	14	.714	27	55	82	15	21	....	3	5	8	30.1	14.9	11.7	2.1	.702
74-75	San Antonio-A	6	....	234	89	40	84	.476	0	0	.000	9	21	.429	24	75	99	6	18	....	1	6	16	39.0	14.8	16.5	1.0	.561
83-84	LA Lakers	17	0	146	58	19	38	.500	0	0	.000	20	26	.769	16	24	40	1	27	0	1	2	8	8.6	3.4	2.4	0.1	.401
NBA Playoff Totals		17	0	146	58	19	38	.500	0	0	.000	20	26	.769	16	24	40	1	27	0	1	2	8	8.6	3.4	2.4	0.1	....
ABA Playoff Totals		13	....	445	193	87	169	.515	0	0	.000	19	35	.543	51	130	181	21	39	....	4	11	24	34.2	14.8	13.9	1.6	....
Career Playoff Totals		30	0	591	251	106	207	.512	0	0	.000	39	61	.639	67	154	221	22	66	0	5	13	32	19.7	8.4	7.4	0.7	....

• NATHAN, Howard

Howard Nathan

Born: Jan. 21, 1972. Peoria, IL, United States. Height: 5'11". Weight: 175 lbs. Drafted: — College: Northeast Louisiana

YEAR	TEAM	GP	GS	MIN	PTS	FGM	FGA	FG%	3PM	3PA	3P%	FTM	FTA	FT%	ORB	DRB	TRB	AST	PF	DQ	STL	BLK	TO	MPG	PPG	RPG	APG	PCM
95-96	Atlanta	5	0	15	13	5	9	.556	0	1	.000	3	4	.750	0	0	0	2	2	0	3	0	8	3.0	2.6	0.0	0.4	.350
NBA Season Totals		5	0	15	13	5	9	.556	0	1	.000	3	4	.750	0	0	0	2	2	0	3	0	8	3.0	2.6	0.0	0.4	....

• NATT, Calvin

Calvin Leon Natt

Born: Jan. 8, 1957. Monroe, LA, United States. Height: 6'6". Weight: 220 lbs. Drafted: 1979 College: Northeast Louisiana

YEAR	TEAM	GP	GS	MIN	PTS	FGM	FGA	FG%	3PM	3PA	3P%	FTM	FTA	FT%	ORB	DRB	TRB	AST	PF	DQ	STL	BLK	TO	MPG	PPG	RPG	APG	PCM
79-80	New Jersey	53	....	2046	1042	421	879	.479	1	5	.200	199	280	.711	173	340	513	112	148	1	78	22	133	38.6	19.7	9.7	2.1	.528
79-80	Portland	25	....	811	511	201	419	.480	2	4	.500	107	139	.770	66	112	178	57	57	0	24	12	65	32.4	20.4	7.1	2.3	.580
80-81	Portland	74	....	2111	994	395	794	.497	4	8	.500	200	283	.707	149	282	431	159	188	2	73	18	163	28.5	13.4	5.8	2.1	.477
81-82	Portland	75	71	2599	1326	515	894	.576	2	8	.250	294	392	.750	193	420	613	150	175	1	62	36	143	34.7	17.7	8.2	2.0	.591
82-83	Portland	80	80	2879	1630	644	1187	.543	3	20	.150	339	428	.792	214	385	599	171	184	2	63	29	200	36.0	20.4	7.5	2.1	.572
83-84	Portland	79	74	2638	1277	500	857	.583	2	17	.118	275	345	.797	166	310	476	179	218	3	69	22	166	33.4	16.2	6.0	2.3	.521
84-85	Denver	78	76	2657	1817	685	1255	.546	0	3	.000	447	564	.793	209	401	610	238	182	1	75	33	187	34.1	23.3	7.8	3.1	.713
85-86	Denver	69	62	2007	1218	469	930	.504	2	6	.333	278	347	.801	125	311	436	164	143	0	58	13	131	29.1	17.7	6.3	2.4	.606
86-87	Denver	1	1	20	10	4	10	.400	0	0	.000	2	2	1.000	2	3	5	2	2	0	1	0	1	20.0	10.0	5.0	2.0	.514
87-88	Denver	27	7	533	258	102	208	.490	0	1	.000	54	73	.740	35	61	96	47	43	0	13	3	30	19.7	9.6	3.6	1.7	.482
88-89	Denver	14	0	168	66	22	50	.440	0	1	.000	22	31	.710	12	34	46	7	13	0	6	1	11	12.0	4.7	3.3	0.5	.454
88-89	San Antonio	10	0	185	85	25	66	.379	0	0	.000	35	48	.729	16	16	32	11	19	0	2	2	19	18.5	8.5	3.2	1.1	.322
89-90	Indiana	14	0	164	57	20	31	.645	0	0	.000	17	22	.773	10	25	35	9	14	0	1	0	6	11.7	4.1	2.5	0.6	.460
NBA Season Totals		599	371	18818	10291	4003	7580	.528	16	73	.219	2269	2954	.768	1370	2700	4070	1306	1386	10	525	191	1255	31.4	17.2	6.8	2.2	....
79-80	Portland	3	....	125	48	21	48	.438	0	2	.000	6	10	.600	9	15	24	2	7	0	2	1	10	41.7	16.0	8.0	0.7	.289
80-81	Portland	3	....	95	32	14	31	.452	0	0	.000	4	8	.500	6	14	20	1	4	0	1	1	7	31.7	10.7	6.7	0.3	.291
82-83	Portland	7	7	274	132	50	102	.490	1	2	.500	31	48	.646	22	42	64	11	14	0	8	1	9	39.1	18.9	9.1	1.6	.514
83-84	Portland	5	5	195	99	37	72	.514	0	3	.000	25	36	.694	11	27	38	9	10	0	6	1	10	39.0	19.8	7.6	1.8	.507
84-85	Denver	15	15	508	334	131	238	.550	0	0	.000	72	89	.809	31	68	99	57	35	0	8	5	31	33.9	22.3	6.6	3.8	.682
85-86	Denver	10	6	293	179	66	142	.465	1	2	.500	46	59	.780	17	62	79	28	25	0	2	3	22	29.3	17.9	7.9	2.8	.609
89-90	Indiana	2	0	14	2	1	3	.333	0	0	.000	0	0	.000	1	1	2	1	5	0	0	0	2	7.0	1.0	1.0	0.5	-.082
NBA Playoff Totals		45	33	1504	826	320	636	.503	2	9	.222	184	250	.736	97	229	326	109	100	0	27	12	91	33.4	18.4	7.2	2.4	....

• NATT, Kenny

Kenneth Wayne Natt

Born: Oct. 5, 1958. Monroe, LA, United States. Height: 6'3". Weight: 185 lbs. Drafted: 1980 College: Northeast Louisiana

YEAR	TEAM	GP	GS	MIN	PTS	FGM	FGA	FG%	3PM	3PA	3P%	FTM	FTA	FT%	ORB	DRB	TRB	AST	PF	DQ	STL	BLK	TO	MPG	PPG	RPG	APG	PCM
80-81	Indiana	19	....	149	59	25	77	.325	2	8	.250	7	11	.636	9	6	15	10	18	0	5	1	10	7.8	3.1	0.8	0.5	.151
82-83	Utah	22	0	210	85	38	73	.521	0	2	.000	9	14	.643	6	16	22	28	36	0	5	0	22	9.5	3.9	1.0	1.3	.334
84-85	Utah	4	0	13	6	2	5	.400	0	0	.000	2	4	.500	1	1	2	0	2	0	1	0	0	3.3	1.5	0.5	0.0	.318
84-85	Kansas City	4	0	16	0	0	1	.000	0	0	.000	0	0	.000	1	0	1	3	1	0	1	0	3	4.0	0.0	0.3	0.8	.055
NBA Season Totals		49	0	388	150	65	156	.417	2	10	.200	18	29	.621	17	23	40	41	57	0	12	1	35	7.9	3.1	0.8	0.8	....

• NAULLS, Willie

William Dean (The Whale) Naulls

Born: Oct. 7, 1934. Dallas, TX, United States. Height: 6'6". Weight: 225 lbs. Drafted: 1956 College: UCLA

YEAR	TEAM	GP	GS	MIN	PTS	FGM	FGA	FG%	3PM	3PA	3P%	FTM	FTA	FT%	ORB	DRB	TRB	AST	PF	DQ	STL	BLK	TO	MPG	PPG	RPG	APG	PCM
56-57	St. Louis	19	....	438	195	77	211	.365	....	....	....	41	60	.683	....	....	167	22	57	1	....	....	....	23.1	10.3	8.8	1.2	.500
56-57	New York	52	....	1340	523	216	609	.355	....	....	....	91	135	.674	....	....	450	62	129	0	....	....	....	25.8	10.1	8.7	1.2	.432
57-58	New York	68	....	2369	1228	472	1189	.397	....	....	....	284	344	.826	....	....	799	97	220	4	....	....	....	34.8	18.1	11.8	1.4	.553
58-59	New York	68	....	2061	1068	405	1072	.378	....	....	....	258	311	.830	....	....	723	102	233	8	....	....	....	30.3	15.7	10.6	1.5	.548
59-60	New York	65	....	2250	1388	551	1286	.428	....	....	....	286	342	.836	....	....	921	138	214	4	....	....	....	34.6	21.4	14.2	2.1	.710
60-61	New York	79	....	2976	1846	737	1723	.428	....	....	....	372	456	.816	....	....	1055	191	268	5	....	....	....	37.7	23.4	13.4	2.4	.672
61-62	New York	75	....	2978	1877	747	1798	.415	....	....	....	383	455	.842	....	....	867	192	260	6	....	....	....	39.7	25.0	11.6	2.6	.617
62-63	New York	23	....	676	388	155	375	.413	....	....	....	78	96	.813	....	....	200	44	42	0	....	....	....	29.4	16.9	8.7	1.9	.594
62-63	San Francisco	47	....	1225	518	215	512	.420	....	....	....	88	111	.793	....	....	315	58	163	3	....	....	....	26.1	11.0	6.7	1.2	.432
63-64	Boston	78	....	1409	767	321	769	.417	....	....	....	125	157	.796	....	....	356	64	208	0	....	....	....	18.1	9.8	4.6	0.8	.483
64-65	Boston	71	....	1465	747	302	786	.384	....	....	....	143	176	.813	....	....	336	72	225	5	....	....	....	20.6	10.5	4.7	1.0	.425
65-66	Boston	71	....	1433	760	328	815	.402	....	....	....	104	131	.794	....	....	319	72	197	4	....	....	....	20.2	10.7	4.5	1.0	.438
NBA Season Totals		716	....	20620	11305	4526	11145	.406	....	....	....	2253	2774	.812	....	....	6508	1114	2216	40	....	....	....	28.8	15.8	9.1	1.6	....
58-59	New York	2	....	63	34	14	42	.333	....	....	....	6	8	.750	....	....	21	3	11	1	....	....	....	31.5	17.0	10.5	1.5	.438
63-64	Boston	10	....	167	91	37	95	.389	....	....	....	17	23	.739	....	....	46	8	31	1	....	....	....	16.7	9.1	4.6	0.8	.461
64-65	Boston	12	....	180	88	39	95	.411	....	....	....	10	15	.667	....	....	51	9	27	0	....	....	....	15.0	7.3	4.3	0.8	.461
65-66	Boston	11	....	75	35	9	35	.257	....	....	....	17	21	.810	....	....	16	1	23	0	....	....	....	6.8	3.2	1.5	0.1	.237
NBA Playoff Totals		35	....	485	248	99	267	.371	....	....	....	50	67	.746	....	....	134	21	92	2	....	....	....	13.9	7.1	3.8	0.6	....

• N'DIAYE, Makhtar

Makhtar Vincent N'diaye

Born: Dec. 12, 1973. Dakar, Senegal. Height: 6'8". Weight: 245 lbs. Drafted: — College: North Carolina

YEAR	TEAM	GP	GS	MIN	PTS	FGM	FGA	FG%	3PM	3PA	3P%	FTM	FTA	FT%	ORB	DRB	TRB	AST	PF	DQ	STL	BLK	TO	MPG	PPG	RPG	APG	PCM
98-99	Vancouver	4	0	27	5	1	4	.250	0	0	.000	3	4	.750	3	2	5	1	9	0	0	1	1	6.8	1.3	1.3	0.3	.128
NBA Season Totals		4	0	27	5	1	4	.250	0	0	.000	3	4	.750	3	2	5	1	9	0	0	1	1	6.8	1.3	1.3	0.3	....

YEAR	TEAM	GP	GS	MIN	PTS	FGM	FGA	FG%	3PM	3PA	3P%	FTM	FTA	FT%	ORB	DRB	TRB	AST	PF	DQ	STL	BLK	TO	MPG	PPG	RPG	APG	PCM
• N'DIAYE, Mamadou																												Mamadou N'diaye

Born: June 16, 1975. Dakar, Senegal.   Height: 7'   Weight: 255 lbs.   Drafted: —   College: Auburn

YEAR	TEAM	GP	GS	MIN	PTS	FGM	FGA	FG%	3PM	3PA	3P%	FTM	FTA	FT%	ORB	DRB	TRB	AST	PF	DQ	STL	BLK	TO	MPG	PPG	RPG	APG	PCM
00-01	Toronto	3	0	10	4	1	4	.250	0	0	.000	2	2	1.000	1	1	2	0	3	0	0	0	0	3.3	1.3	0.7	0.0	.176
01-02	Toronto	5	0	46	20	6	10	.600	0	0	.000	8	10	.800	6	5	11	0	6	0	0	2	1	9.2	4.0	2.2	0.0	.514
02-03	Toronto	22	8	364	120	43	96	.448	0	0	.000	34	47	.723	29	53	82	7	58	0	8	32	21	16.5	5.5	3.7	0.3	.382
NBA Season Totals		30	8	420	144	50	110	.455	0	0	.000	44	59	.746	36	59	95	7	67	0	8	34	22	14.0	4.8	3.2	0.2	....

| **• NEAL, Craig** | | | | | | | | | | | | | | | | | | | | | | | | | | | | Craig Duane Neal |

Born: Feb. 16, 1964. Muncie, IN, United States.   Height: 6'5".   Weight: 165 lbs.   Drafted: 1988   College: Georgia Tech

YEAR	TEAM	GP	GS	MIN	PTS	FGM	FGA	FG%	3PM	3PA	3P%	FTM	FTA	FT%	ORB	DRB	TRB	AST	PF	DQ	STL	BLK	TO	MPG	PPG	RPG	APG	PCM
88-89	Portland	21	0	159	25	11	35	.314	2	9	.222	1	2	.500	3	8	11	32	24	0	9	0	15	7.6	1.2	0.5	1.5	.188
88-89	Miami	32	0	341	89	34	88	.386	4	25	.320	13	21	.619	4	14	18	86	46	0	15	4	42	10.7	2.8	0.6	2.7	.296
90-91	Denver	10	0	125	44	14	35	.400	3	9	.333	13	22	.591	2	14	16	37	26	1	4	0	19	12.5	4.4	1.6	3.7	.388
NBA Season Totals		63	0	625	158	59	158	.373	13	43	.302	27	45	.600	9	36	45	155	96	1	28	4	76	9.9	2.5	0.7	2.5	....

| **• NEAL, Jim** | | | | | | | | | | | | | | | | | | | | | | | | | | | | James Ellerbe Neal |

Born: May 21, 1930.   Height: 6'11".   Weight: 235 lbs.   Drafted: —   College: Wofford

YEAR	TEAM	GP	GS	MIN	PTS	FGM	FGA	FG%	3PM	3PA	3P%	FTM	FTA	FT%	ORB	DRB	TRB	AST	PF	DQ	STL	BLK	TO	MPG	PPG	RPG	APG	PCM
53-54	Syracuse	67	....	899	312	117	369	.317	....	....	....	78	132	.591	....	....	257	24	139	0	....	....	....	13.4	4.7	3.8	0.4	.309
54-55	Baltimore	13	....	194	38	12	59	.203	....	....	....	14	21	.667	....	....	47	9	22	0	....	....	....	14.9	2.9	3.6	0.7	.198
NBA Season Totals		80	....	1093	350	129	428	.301	....	....	....	92	153	.601	....	....	304	33	161	0	....	....	....	13.7	4.4	3.8	0.4	....
53-54	Syracuse	11	....	100	31	13	35	.371	....	....	....	5	13	.385	....	....	27	2	14	0	....	....	....	9.1	2.8	2.5	0.2	.293
NBA Playoff Totals		11	....	100	31	13	35	.371	....	....	....	5	13	.385	....	....	27	2	14	0	....	....	....	9.1	2.8	2.5	0.2	....

| **• NEAL, Lloyd** | | | | | | | | | | | | | | | | | | | | | | | | | | | | Lloyd Neal |

Born: Dec. 10, 1950. Talbottom, GA, United States.   Height: 6'7".   Weight: 225 lbs.   Drafted: 1972   College: Tennessee State

YEAR	TEAM	GP	GS	MIN	PTS	FGM	FGA	FG%	3PM	3PA	3P%	FTM	FTA	FT%	ORB	DRB	TRB	AST	PF	DQ	STL	BLK	TO	MPG	PPG	RPG	APG	PCM
72-73	Portland	82	....	2723	1097	455	921	.494	....	....	....	187	293	.638	....	....	967	146	305	6	....	....	....	33.2	13.4	11.8	1.8	.557
73-74	Portland	80	....	1517	609	246	502	.490	....	....	....	117	168	.696	150	344	494	89	190	0	45	73	....	19.0	7.6	6.2	1.1	.535
74-75	Portland	82	....	2278	1007	409	869	.471	....	....	....	189	295	.641	186	501	687	139	239	2	43	87	....	27.8	12.3	8.4	1.7	.532
75-76	Portland	68	....	2320	1056	435	904	.481	....	....	....	186	268	.694	145	440	585	118	254	4	53	107	....	34.1	15.5	8.6	1.7	.494
76-77	Portland	58	....	955	397	160	340	.471	....	....	....	77	114	.675	87	168	255	58	148	0	8	35	....	16.5	6.8	4.4	1.0	.469
77-78	Portland	61	....	1174	671	272	540	.504	....	....	....	127	177	.718	116	257	373	81	128	0	29	21	98	19.2	11.0	6.1	1.3	.625
78-79	Portland	4	....	48	9	4	11	.364	....	....	....	1	1	1.000	2	7	9	1	7	0	0	1	6	12.0	2.3	2.3	0.3	.089
NBA Season Totals		435	....	11015	4846	1981	4087	.485	....	....	....	884	1316	.672	686	1717	3370	632	1271	12	178	324	104	25.3	11.1	7.7	1.5	....
76-77	Portland	19	....	206	77	30	63	.476	....	....	....	17	26	.654	21	49	70	17	34	0	2	8	....	10.8	4.1	3.7	0.9	.533
77-78	Portland	3	....	47	15	7	21	.333	....	....	....	1	1	1.000	2	9	11	2	5	0	0	4	6	15.7	5.0	3.7	0.7	.227
NBA Playoff Totals		22	....	253	92	37	84	.440	....	....	....	18	27	.667	23	58	81	19	39	0	2	12	6	11.5	4.2	3.7	0.9	....

| **• NEALY, Ed** | | | | | | | | | | | | | | | | | | | | | | | | | | | | Eddie Carl Nealy |

Born: Feb. 19, 1960. Pittsburg, KS, United States.   Height: 6'7".   Weight: 238 lbs.   Drafted: 1982   College: Kansas State

YEAR	TEAM	GP	GS	MIN	PTS	FGM	FGA	FG%	3PM	3PA	3P%	FTM	FTA	FT%	ORB	DRB	TRB	AST	PF	DQ	STL	BLK	TO	MPG	PPG	RPG	APG	PCM
82-83	Kansas City	82	61	1643	364	147	247	.595	0	0	.000	70	114	.614	170	315	485	62	247	4	68	12	49	20.0	4.4	5.9	0.8	.411
83-84	Kansas City	71	1	960	174	63	126	.500	0	0	.000	48	60	.800	73	149	222	50	138	1	41	9	36	13.5	2.5	3.1	0.7	.332
84-85	Kansas City	22	0	225	62	26	44	.591	0	0	.000	10	19	.526	15	29	44	18	26	0	3	1	11	10.2	2.8	2.0	0.8	.367
86-87	San Antonio	60	7	980	223	84	192	.438	4	31	.129	51	69	.739	96	188	284	83	144	1	40	11	36	16.3	3.7	4.7	1.4	.423
87-88	San Antonio	68	1	837	142	50	109	.459	1	2	.500	41	63	.651	82	140	222	49	94	0	29	5	27	12.3	2.1	3.3	0.7	.357
88-89	Chicago	13	0	94	11	5	7	.714	0	0	.000	1	2	.500	4	19	23	6	23	0	3	1	1	7.2	0.8	1.8	0.5	.304
88-89	Phoenix	30	0	164	19	8	29	.276	0	2	.000	3	7	.429	18	37	55	8	22	0	4	0	6	5.5	0.6	1.8	0.3	.276
89-90	Chicago	46	0	503	104	39	70	.529	0	2	.000	30	41	.732	46	92	138	28	67	0	16	4	18	10.9	2.3	3.0	0.6	.393
90-91	Phoenix	55	0	573	123	45	97	.464	5	16	.313	28	38	.737	44	107	151	36	46	0	24	4	17	10.4	2.2	2.7	0.7	.415
91-92	Phoenix	52	4	505	160	62	121	.512	20	50	.400	16	24	.667	25	86	111	37	45	0	16	2	16	9.7	3.1	2.1	0.7	.446
92-93	Golden State	30	4	229	46	16	46	.348	7	22	.318	7	10	.700	8	40	48	13	35	0	9	1	6	7.6	1.5	1.6	0.4	.274
92-93	Chicago	11	0	79	23	10	23	.435	1	5	.200	2	2	1.000	4	12	16	2	6	0	3	1	2	7.2	2.1	1.5	0.2	.342
NBA Season Totals		540	78	6792	1451	553	1111	.498	38	130	.292	307	449	.684	585	1214	1799	392	893	6	256	51	225	12.6	2.7	3.3	0.7	....
83-84	Kansas City	2	0	19	6	2	2	1.000	0	0	.000	2	2	1.000	2	4	6	2	1	0	0	0	1	9.5	3.0	3.0	1.0	.649
87-88	San Antonio	2	0	36	4	2	4	.500	0	0	.000	0	0	.000	3	4	7	4	6	0	1	0	1	18.0	2.0	3.5	2.0	.282
88-89	Phoenix	4	0	6	2	1	3	.333	0	0	.000	0	0	.000	1	2	3	0	0	0	0	0	0	1.5	0.5	0.8	0.0	.488
89-90	Chicago	15	0	228	47	17	36	.472	0	1	.000	13	21	.619	16	36	52	5	45	1	10	1	7	15.2	3.1	3.5	0.3	.273
90-91	Phoenix	2	0	20	2	1	5	.200	0	1	.000	0	0	.000	2	3	5	0	2	0	0	0	1	10.0	1.0	2.5	0.0	.053
91-92	Phoenix	8	0	67	23	7	18	.389	5	13	.385	4	4	1.000	4	14	18	4	12	0	3	0	0	8.4	2.9	2.3	0.5	.463
NBA Playoff Totals		33	0	376	84	30	68	.441	5	15	.333	19	27	.704	28	63	91	15	66	1	14	1	10	11.4	2.5	2.8	0.5	....

| **• NEAT, Lyle** | | | | | | | | | | | | | | | | | | | | | | | | | | | | Lyle Neat |

Born: 1916.   Height: 6'   Weight: 180 lbs.   Drafted: —   College: —

YEAR	TEAM	GP	GS	MIN	PTS	FGM	FGA	FG%	3PM	3PA	3P%	FTM	FTA	FT%	ORB	DRB	TRB	AST	PF	DQ	STL	BLK	TO	MPG	PPG	RPG	APG	PCM
46-47	Fort Wayne-N	1	....	....	0	0	....	....	....	....	....	0	0	.000	....	....	....	....	....	....	....	....	....	0.0	....	....	....	....
NBL Season Totals		1	....	....	0	0	....	....	....	....	....	0	0	....	....	....	....	....	....	....	....	....	....	0.0	....	....	....	....

• NEGRATTI, Al
Albert Edward Negratti

Born: June 12, 1921. Died: Jan.19, 1998.   Height: 6'3".   Weight: 200 lbs.   Drafted: —   College: Seton Hall

YEAR TEAM	GP	GS	MIN	PTS	FGM	FGA	FG%	3PM	3PA	3P%	FTM	FTA	FT%	ORB	DRB	TRB	AST	PF	DQ	STL	BLK	TO	MPG	PPG	RPG	APG	PCM
45-46 Rochester-N	16			48	19						10													3.0			
46-47 Rochester-N	33			44	15						14	24	.583											1.3			
46-47 Washington	11			31	13	69	.188				5	8	.625				5	20						2.8		0.5	
NBA Season Totals	11			31	13	69	.188				5	8	.625				5	20						2.8		0.5	
NBL Season Totals	49			92	34						24	24												1.9			
Career Totals	60			123	47	69					29	32					5	20						2.1		0.1	
45-46 Rochester-N	7			25	9						7	14	.500											3.6			
46-47 Rochester-N	11			10	3						4	7	.571											0.9			
NBL Playoff Totals	18			35	12						11	21												1.9			

• NELMARK, George
George Nelmark

Born: 1917.   Height: 6'1".   Weight: 180 lbs.   Drafted: —   College: California (Santa Barbara)

YEAR TEAM	GP	GS	MIN	PTS	FGM	FGA	FG%	3PM	3PA	3P%	FTM	FTA	FT%	ORB	DRB	TRB	AST	PF	DQ	STL	BLK	TO	MPG	PPG	RPG	APG	PCM
41-42 Toledo-N	21			112	40						32													5.3			
46-47 Syracuse-N	37			265	107						51	92	.554				102							7.2			
47-48 Syracuse-N	52			203	76						51	85	.600				124							3.9			
NBL Season Totals	110			580	223						134	177					226							5.3			
46-47 Syracuse-N	4			31	13						5	7	.714											7.8			
47-48 Syracuse-N	3			2	1						0	1	.000											0.7			
NBL Playoff Totals	7			33	14						5	8												4.7			

• NELSON, Barry
Barry G. Nelson

Born: Sept. 19, 1949.   Height: 6'10".   Weight: 230 lbs.   Drafted: 1971   College: Duquesne

YEAR TEAM	GP	GS	MIN	PTS	FGM	FGA	FG%	3PM	3PA	3P%	FTM	FTA	FT%	ORB	DRB	TRB	AST	PF	DQ	STL	BLK	TO	MPG	PPG	RPG	APG	PCM
71-72 Milwaukee	28		102	35	15	36	.417				5	10	.500			20	7	21	0					3.6	1.3	0.7	0.3	.303
NBA Season Totals	28		102	35	15	36	.417				5	10	.500			20	7	21	0					3.6	1.3	0.7	0.3	
71-72 Milwaukee	2		5	0	0	0	.000				0	0	.000			1	1	1	0					2.5	0.0	0.5	0.5	.314
NBA Playoff Totals	2		5	0	0	0	.000				0	0	.000			1	1	1	0					2.5	0.0	0.5	0.5	

• NELSON, Don
Donald Arvid (Nellie) Nelson

Born: May 15, 1940. Muskegon, MI, United States.   Height: 6'6".   Weight: 210 lbs.   Drafted: 1962   College: Iowa

YEAR TEAM	GP	GS	MIN	PTS	FGM	FGA	FG%	3PM	3PA	3P%	FTM	FTA	FT%	ORB	DRB	TRB	AST	PF	DQ	STL	BLK	TO	MPG	PPG	RPG	APG	PCM
62-63 Chicago	62		1071	419	129	293	.440				161	221	.729			279	72	136	3					17.3	6.8	4.5	1.2	.485
63-64 LA Lakers	80		1406	419	135	323	.418				149	201	.741			323	76	181	1					17.6	5.2	4.0	1.0	.374
64-65 LA Lakers	39		238	92	36	85	.424				20	26	.769			73	24	40	1					6.1	2.4	1.9	0.6	.514
65-66 Boston	75		1765	765	271	618	.439				223	326	.684			403	79	187	1					23.5	10.2	5.4	1.1	.448
66-67 Boston	79		1202	595	227	509	.446				141	190	.742			295	65	143	0					15.2	7.5	3.7	0.8	.505
67-68 Boston	82		1498	819	312	632	.494				195	268	.728			431	103	178	1					18.3	10.0	5.3	1.3	.622
68-69 Boston	82		1773	949	374	771	.485				201	259	.776			458	92	198	2					21.6	11.6	5.6	1.1	.564
69-70 Boston	82		2224	1259	461	920	.501				337	435	.775			601	148	238	3					27.1	15.4	7.3	1.8	.630
70-71 Boston	82		2254	1141	412	881	.468				317	426	.744			565	153	232	2					27.5	13.9	6.9	1.9	.555
71-72 Boston	82		2086	1134	389	811	.480				356	452	.788			453	192	220	3					25.4	13.8	5.5	2.3	.596
72-73 Boston	72		1425	777	309	649	.476				159	188	.846			315	102	155	1					19.8	10.8	4.4	1.4	.557
73-74 Boston	82		1748	943	364	717	.508				215	273	.788	90	255	345	162	189	1	19	13		21.3	11.5	4.2	2.0	.582
74-75 Boston	79		2052	1109	423	785	**.539**				263	318	.827	127	342	469	181	239	2	32	15		26.0	14.0	5.9	2.3	.625
75-76 Boston	75		943	477	175	379	.462				127	161	.789	56	126	182	77	115	0	14	7		12.6	6.4	2.4	1.0	.511
NBA Season Totals	1053		21685	10898	4017	8373	.480				2864	3744	.765	273	723	5192	1526	2451	21	65	35		20.6	10.3	4.9	1.4	
63-64 LA Lakers	5		56	17	7	13	.538				3	3	1.000			13	2	11	1				11.2	3.4	2.6	0.4	.368	
64-65 LA Lakers	11		212	67	24	53	.453				19	25	.760			59	19	31	0				19.3	6.1	5.4	1.7	.468	
65-66 Boston	17		316	142	50	118	.424				42	52	.808			85	13	50	0				18.6	8.4	5.0	0.8	.467	
66-67 Boston	9		142	64	27	59	.458				10	17	.588			42	9	12	0				15.8	7.1	4.7	1.0	.530	
67-68 Boston	19		468	237	91	175	.520				55	74	.743			143	32	49	0				24.6	12.5	7.5	1.7	.631	
68-69 Boston	18		348	224	87	168	.518				50	60	.833			83	21	51	0				19.3	12.4	4.6	1.2	.645	
71-72 Boston	11		308	145	52	99	.525				41	48	.854			61	21	30	0				28.0	13.2	5.5	1.9	.536	
72-73 Boston	13		303	143	47	101	.465				49	56	.875			38	15	29	0				23.3	11.0	2.9	1.2	.432	
73-74 Boston	18		467	205	82	164	.500				41	53	.774	25	72	97	35	54	2	8	3		25.9	11.4	5.4	1.9	.492
74-75 Boston	11		274	169	66	117	.564				37	41	.902	18	27	45	26	36	1	2	2		24.9	15.4	4.1	2.4	.645
75-76 Boston	18		315	164	52	108	.481				60	69	.870	17	36	53	17	46	1	3	2		17.5	9.1	2.9	0.9	.499
NBA Playoff Totals	150		3209	1577	585	1175	.498				407	498	.817	60	135	719	210	399	5	13	7		21.4	10.5	4.8	1.4	

• NELSON, Louie
Louis (Sweets) Nelson

Born: May 28, 1951. Los Angeles, CA, United States.   Height: 6'3".   Weight: 190 lbs.   Drafted: 1973   College: Washington

YEAR TEAM	GP	GS	MIN	PTS	FGM	FGA	FG%	3PM	3PA	3P%	FTM	FTA	FT%	ORB	DRB	TRB	AST	PF	DQ	STL	BLK	TO	MPG	PPG	RPG	APG	PCM
73-74 Washington	49		556	239	93	215	.433				53	73	.726	26	44	70	52	62	0	31	2		11.3	4.9	1.4	1.1	.395
74-75 New Orleans	72		1898	806	307	679	.452				192	250	.768	75	121	196	178	186	1	65	6		26.4	11.2	2.7	2.5	.398
75-76 New Orleans	66		2030	823	327	755	.433				169	230	.735	81	121	202	169	147	1	82	6		30.8	12.5	3.1	2.6	.361
76-77 San Antonio	4		57	18	7	14	.500				4	7	.571	2	5	7	3	9	0	2	0		14.3	4.5	1.8	0.8	.285
77-78 Kansas City	8		53	15	3	14	.214				9	11	.818	1	2	3	5	5	0	2	1	8	6.6	1.9	0.4	0.6	.117
77-78 New Jersey	25		353	212	82	197	.416				48	73	.658	12	37	49	29	28	0	20	6	40	14.1	8.5	2.0	1.2	.429
NBA Season Totals	224		4947	2113	819	1874	.437				475	644	.738	197	330	527	436	437	2	202	21	48	22.1	9.4	2.4	1.9	

YEAR	TEAM	GP	GS	MIN	PTS	FGM	FGA	FG%	3PM	3PA	3P%	FTM	FTA	FT%	ORB	DRB	TRB	AST	PF	DQ	STL	BLK	TO	MPG	PPG	RPG	APG	PCM

• NELSON, Ron
Ron Nelson

Born: Oct. 7, 1946. Height: 6'2". Weight: 175 lbs. Drafted: 1968 College: New Mexico

YEAR	TEAM	GP	GS	MIN	PTS	FGM	FGA	FG%	3PM	3PA	3P%	FTM	FTA	FT%	ORB	DRB	TRB	AST	PF	DQ	STL	BLK	TO	MPG	PPG	RPG	APG	PCM
70-71	Florida-A	59	....	490	186	72	172	.419	1	3	.333	41	54	.759	19	34	53	47	95	0	....	....	46	8.3	3.2	0.9	0.8	.329
ABA Season Totals		59	....	490	186	72	172	.419	1	3	.333	41	54	.759	19	34	53	47	95	0	....	....	46	8.3	3.2	0.9	0.8	
70-71	Florida-A	1	....	2	0	0	1	.000	0	0	.000	0	0	.000	0	1	1	0	0	0	....	....	2	2.0	0.0	1.0	0.0	.000
ABA Playoff Totals		1	....	2	0	0	1	.000	0	0	.000	0	0	.000	0	1	1	0	0	0	....	....	2	2.0	0.0	1.0	0.0	

• NEMBHARD, Ruben
Ruben R. Nembhard

Born: Feb. 20, 1972. Bronx, NY, United States. Height: 6'3". Weight: 208 lbs. Drafted: — College: Weber State

YEAR	TEAM	GP	GS	MIN	PTS	FGM	FGA	FG%	3PM	3PA	3P%	FTM	FTA	FT%	ORB	DRB	TRB	AST	PF	DQ	STL	BLK	TO	MPG	PPG	RPG	APG	PCM
96-97	Utah	8	0	94	32	12	29	.414	0	4	.000	8	10	.800	3	5	8	12	9	0	6	0	3	11.8	4.0	1.0	1.5	.363
96-97	Portland	2	0	19	8	4	8	.500	0	2	.000	0	0	.000	0	0	0	5	3	0	3	0	5	9.5	4.0	0.0	2.5	.334
NBA Season Totals		10	0	113	40	16	37	.432	0	6	.000	8	10	.800	3	5	8	17	12	0	9	0	8	11.3	4.0	0.8	1.7	....

• NEMELKA, Dick
Richard S. Nemelka

Born: Oct. 1, 1943. Height: 6' Weight: 175 lbs. Drafted: 1966 College: Brigham Young

YEAR	TEAM	GP	GS	MIN	PTS	FGM	FGA	FG%	3PM	3PA	3P%	FTM	FTA	FT%	ORB	DRB	TRB	AST	PF	DQ	STL	BLK	TO	MPG	PPG	RPG	APG	PCM
70-71	Utah-A	39	....	504	216	82	213	.385	20	62	.323	32	49	.653	24	35	59	57	60	0	....	....	41	12.9	5.5	1.5	1.5	.389
ABA Season Totals		39	....	504	216	82	213	.385	20	62	.323	32	49	.653	24	35	59	57	60	0	....	....	41	12.9	5.5	1.5	1.5	
70-71	Utah-A	9	....	51	19	7	21	.333	1	9	.111	4	5	.800	2	7	9	9	12	0	....	....	4	5.7	2.1	1.0	1.0	.404
ABA Playoff Totals		9	....	51	19	7	21	.333	1	9	.111	4	5	.800	2	7	9	9	12	0	....	....	4	5.7	2.1	1.0	1.0	

• NESBY, Tyrone
Tyrone Lamont Nesby

Born: Jan. 31, 1976. Cairo, IL, United States. Height: 6'6". Weight: 225 lbs. Drafted: — College: UNLV

YEAR	TEAM	GP	GS	MIN	PTS	FGM	FGA	FG%	3PM	3PA	3P%	FTM	FTA	FT%	ORB	DRB	TRB	AST	PF	DQ	STL	BLK	TO	MPG	PPG	RPG	APG	PCM
98-99	LA Clippers	50	36	1288	503	182	405	.449	35	96	.365	104	133	.782	57	118	175	82	143	2	77	20	53	25.8	10.1	3.5	1.6	.399
99-00	LA Clippers	73	39	2317	973	364	915	.398	94	281	.335	151	191	.791	82	193	275	121	205	5	75	31	102	31.7	13.3	3.8	1.7	.322
00-01	LA Clippers	14	12	333	108	40	123	.325	10	46	.217	18	23	.783	16	26	42	11	28	0	10	4	10	23.8	7.7	3.0	0.8	.216
00-01	Washington	48	22	1223	404	149	407	.366	39	134	.291	67	83	.807	35	96	131	65	127	1	41	16	55	25.5	8.4	2.7	1.4	.245
01-02	Washington	70	9	1497	443	183	421	.435	13	47	.277	64	93	.688	105	213	318	91	164	1	61	22	49	21.4	6.3	4.5	1.3	.373
NBA Season Totals		255	118	6658	2431	918	2271	.404	191	604	.316	404	523	.772	295	646	941	370	667	9	264	93	269	26.1	9.5	3.7	1.5	....

• NESSLEY, Martin
Martin Scott Nessley

Born: Feb. 16, 1965. Columbus, OH, United States. Height: 7'2". Weight: 260 lbs. Drafted: 1987 College: Duke

YEAR	TEAM	GP	GS	MIN	PTS	FGM	FGA	FG%	3PM	3PA	3P%	FTM	FTA	FT%	ORB	DRB	TRB	AST	PF	DQ	STL	BLK	TO	MPG	PPG	RPG	APG	PCM
87-88	LA Clippers	35	0	295	43	18	49	.367	0	0	.000	7	14	.500	20	53	73	16	78	1	7	11	21	8.4	1.2	2.1	0.5	.193
87-88	Sacramento	9	0	41	5	2	3	.667	0	0	.000	1	4	.250	3	6	9	0	11	0	1	1	2	4.6	0.6	1.0	0.0	.145
NBA Season Totals		44	0	336	48	20	52	.385	0	0	.000	8	18	.444	23	59	82	16	89	1	8	12	23	7.6	1.1	1.9	0.4	....

• NESTEROVIC, Rados
Radoslav Nesterovic

Born: May 30, 1976. Ljubljana, Slovakia. Height: 7' Weight: 248 lbs. Drafted: 1998 College: —

YEAR	TEAM	GP	GS	MIN	PTS	FGM	FGA	FG%	3PM	3PA	3P%	FTM	FTA	FT%	ORB	DRB	TRB	AST	PF	DQ	STL	BLK	TO	MPG	PPG	RPG	APG	PCM
98-99	Minnesota	2	0	30	8	3	12	.250	0	0	.000	2	2	1.000	3	5	8	1	5	0	0	0	1	15.0	4.0	4.0	0.5	.170
99-00	Minnesota	82	55	1723	471	206	433	.476	0	2	.000	59	103	.573	135	244	379	93	262	9	21	85	71	21.0	5.7	4.6	1.1	.350
00-01	Minnesota	73	39	1233	328	147	319	.461	0	1	.000	34	65	.523	99	187	286	45	189	3	25	63	55	16.9	4.5	3.9	0.6	.333
01-02	Minnesota	82	82	2218	687	324	657	.493	0	1	.000	39	71	.549	200	334	534	75	262	3	45	109	94	27.0	8.4	6.5	0.9	.393
02-03	Minnesota	77	77	2338	861	400	762	.525	0	2	.000	61	95	.642	146	358	504	114	256	9	39	116	99	30.4	11.2	6.5	1.5	.442
NBA Season Totals		316	253	7542	2355	1080	2183	.495	0	6	.000	195	336	.580	583	1128	1711	328	974	24	130	373	320	23.9	7.5	5.4	1.0	....
98-99	Minnesota	3	0	29	8	4	8	.500	0	0	.000	0	0	.000	4	3	7	3	4	0	0	0	1	9.7	2.7	2.3	1.0	.391
99-00	Minnesota	4	4	126	25	11	25	.440	0	0	.000	3	6	.500	5	8	13	6	20	1	3	7	4	31.5	6.3	3.3	1.5	.204
00-01	Minnesota	4	2	49	10	5	13	.385	0	0	.000	0	0	.000	5	7	12	3	9	0	1	3	3	12.3	2.5	3.0	0.8	.281
01-02	Minnesota	3	3	92	34	15	31	.484	0	0	.000	4	9	.444	6	14	20	3	10	0	1	0	4	30.7	11.3	6.7	1.0	.341
02-03	Minnesota	6	6	169	42	19	38	.500	0	0	.000	4	6	.667	9	21	30	4	28	1	1	4	5	28.2	7.0	5.0	0.7	.253
NBA Playoff Totals		20	15	465	119	54	115	.470	0	0	.000	11	21	.524	29	53	82	19	71	2	6	14	17	23.3	6.0	4.1	1.0	....

• NETOLICKY, Bob
Robert (Neto) Netolicky

Born: Aug. 2, 1942. San Francisco, CA, United States. Height: 6'9". Weight: 220 lbs. Drafted: 1967 College: Drake

YEAR	TEAM	GP	GS	MIN	PTS	FGM	FGA	FG%	3PM	3PA	3P%	FTM	FTA	FT%	ORB	DRB	TRB	AST	PF	DQ	STL	BLK	TO	MPG	PPG	RPG	APG	PCM
67-68	Indiana-A	71	....	2385	1156	468	928	.504	0	1	.000	220	369	.596	313	506	819	69	162	0	....	....	143	33.6	16.3	11.5	1.0	.589
68-69	Indiana-A	78	....	2721	1472	583	1145	.509	0	5	.000	306	491	.623	313	485	798	87	231	4	....	....	178	34.9	18.9	10.2	1.1	.586
69-70	Indiana-A	82	....	3222	1691	673	1393	.483	2	7	.286	343	502	.683	337	539	876	123	206	2	....	....	185	39.3	20.6	10.7	1.5	.561
70-71	Indiana-A	82	....	3137	1541	651	1305	.499	2	8	.250	237	333	.712	267	507	774	104	192	2	....	....	138	38.3	18.8	9.4	1.3	.525
71-72	Indiana-A	83	....	2905	1250	522	1090	.479	4	19	.211	202	279	.724	264	500	764	83	185	0	....	....	166	35.0	15.1	9.2	1.0	.482
72-73	Dallas-A	84	....	3409	1569	650	1347	.483	0	4	.000	269	404	.666	338	513	851	239	166	1	....	....	214	40.6	18.7	10.1	2.8	.538
73-74	Indiana-A	56	....	1157	507	214	449	.477	2	6	.333	77	118	.647	130	162	292	50	92	....	21	22	64	20.7	9.1	5.2	0.9	.480
73-74	San Antonio-A	19	....	488	229	100	195	.513	0	0	.000	29	46	.630	43	58	101	44	21	....	7	11	34	25.7	12.1	5.3	2.3	.549
74-75	Indiana-A	59	....	1077	442	189	375	.504	2	12	.167	62	98	.633	98	133	231	49	108	....	9	18	55	18.3	7.5	3.9	0.8	.439
75-76	Indiana-A	4	....	53	19	8	21	.381	0	0	.000	3	3	1.000	7	5	12	0	2	....	0	1	5	13.3	4.8	3.0	0.0	.325
ABA Season Totals		618	....	20554	9876	4058	8248	.492	12	62	.194	1748	2644	.661	2110	3408	5518	848	1365	9	37	52	1182	33.3	16.0	8.9	1.4	....
67-68	Indiana-A	3	....	117	67	29	51	.569	0	0	.000	9	16	.563	....	....	22	6	10	0	....	....	3	39.0	22.3	7.3	2.0	.572
68-69	Indiana-A	17	....	702	383	161	303	.531	0	3	.000	61	97	.629	86	128	214	17	55	2	....	....	27	41.3	22.5	12.6	1.0	.606
69-70	Indiana-A	15	....	603	304	124	249	.498	0	0	.000	56	82	.683	70	124	194	20	43	0	....	....	39	40.2	20.3	12.9	1.3	.591
70-71	Indiana-A	11	....	380	161	67	143	.469	0	0	.000	27	37	.730	31	61	92	5	26	0	....	....	12	34.5	14.6	8.4	0.5	.435

YEAR	TEAM	GP	GS	MIN	PTS	FGM	FGA	FG%	3PM	3PA	3P%	FTM	FTA	FT%	ORB	DRB	TRB	AST	PF	DQ	STL	BLK	TO	MPG	PPG	RPG	APG	PCM
71-72	Indiana-A	20	....	552	218	91	191	.476	0	1	.000	36	61	.590	42	76	118	12	36	....	....	....	22	27.6	10.9	5.9	0.6	.399
74-75	Indiana-A	7	....	31	10	3	8	.375	0	0	.000	4	4	1.000	2	3	5	1	7	....	0	1	0	4.4	1.4	0.7	0.1	.258
ABA Playoff Totals		73	....	2385	1143	475	945	.503	0	4	.000	193	297	.650	231	392	645	61	177	2	0	1	103	32.7	15.7	8.8	0.8	....

• NEU, Bobby

Robert Neu

Born: June 28, 1917. Chicago, IL, United States. Died: Feb.7, 1971. Height: 6'1". Weight: 175 lbs. Drafted: — College: DePaul

YEAR	TEAM	GP	GS	MIN	PTS	FGM	FGA	FG%	3PM	3PA	3P%	FTM	FTA	FT%	ORB	DRB	TRB	AST	PF	DQ	STL	BLK	TO	MPG	PPG	RPG	APG	PCM
39-40	Hammond-N	24	....	....	159	44	....	....	....	....	....	71	....	....	....	....	....	....	....	....	....	....	....	....	6.6	....	....	....
40-41	Hammond-N	22	....	....	195	66	....	....	....	....	....	63	....	....	....	....	....	....	....	....	....	....	....	....	8.9	....	....	....
44-45	Pittsburgh-N	3	....	....	1	0	....	....	....	....	....	1	....	....	....	....	....	....	....	....	....	....	....	....	0.3	....	....	....
45-46	Chicago-N	31	....	....	178	61	....	....	....	....	....	56	83	.675	....	....	....	....	....	....	....	....	....	....	5.7	....	....	....
NBL Season Totals		80	....	....	533	171	....	....	....	....	....	191	83	....	....	....	....	....	....	....	....	....	....	....	6.7	....	....	....

• NEUMANN, Johnny

Johnny Neumann

Born: Sept. 11, 1951. Memphis, TN, United States. Height: 6'6". Weight: 200 lbs. Drafted: 1973 College: Mississippi

YEAR	TEAM	GP	GS	MIN	PTS	FGM	FGA	FG%	3PM	3PA	3P%	FTM	FTA	FT%	ORB	DRB	TRB	AST	PF	DQ	STL	BLK	TO	MPG	PPG	RPG	APG	PCM
71-72	Memphis-A	77	....	1969	1409	545	1328	.410	26	128	.203	293	385	.761	196	126	322	147	285	7	....	....	239	25.6	18.3	4.2	1.9	.509
72-73	Memphis-A	79	....	2787	1548	605	1283	.472	9	51	.176	329	423	.778	146	164	310	470	304	5	....	....	345	35.3	19.6	3.9	5.9	.558
73-74	Memphis-A	43	....	1300	704	292	665	.439	7	35	.200	113	145	.779	66	70	136	178	160	....	56	13	157	30.2	16.4	3.2	4.1	.478
73-74	Utah-A	44	....	756	444	190	405	.469	11	39	.282	53	70	.757	42	48	90	76	123	....	39	13	91	17.2	10.1	2.0	1.7	.481
74-75	Indiana-A	48	....	835	398	164	378	.434	21	73	.288	49	67	.731	34	44	78	123	118	....	22	10	74	17.4	8.3	1.6	2.6	.424
74-75	Virginia-A	4	....	96	47	22	67	.328	0	5	.000	3	8	.375	8	3	11	12	13	....	4	1	8	24.0	11.8	2.8	3.0	.231
75-76	Kentucky-A	42	....	812	426	171	399	.429	29	86	.337	55	77	.714	39	70	109	104	107	....	31	10	93	19.3	10.1	2.6	2.5	.465
75-76	Virginia-A	35	....	777	582	222	550	.404	42	122	.344	96	112	.857	41	51	92	67	115	....	37	16	81	22.2	16.6	2.6	1.9	.499
76-77	Buffalo	4	....	49	35	15	34	.441	....	....	....	5	6	.833	5	4	9	4	7	0	3	2	....	12.3	8.8	2.3	1.0	.561
76-77	LA Lakers	59	....	888	346	146	363	.402	....	....	....	54	81	.667	19	44	63	137	127	2	28	8	....	15.1	5.9	1.1	2.3	.341
77-78	Indiana	20	....	216	83	35	86	.407	....	....	....	13	18	.722	5	9	14	27	24	0	6	1	22	10.8	4.2	0.7	1.4	.255
NBA Season Totals		83	....	1153	464	196	483	.406	....	....	....	72	105	.686	29	57	86	168	158	2	37	11	22	13.9	5.6	1.0	2.0	....
ABA Season Totals		372	....	9332	5558	2211	5075	.436	145	539	.269	991	1287	.770	572	576	1148	1177	1225	12	189	63	1088	25.1	14.9	3.1	3.2	....
Career Totals		455	....	10485	6022	2407	5558	.433	145	539	.269	1063	1392	.764	601	633	1234	1345	1383	14	226	74	1110	23.0	13.2	2.7	3.0	....
73-74	Utah-A	15	....	173	82	34	92	.370	1	9	.111	13	13	1.000	16	16	32	15	21	....	4	2	18	11.5	5.5	2.1	1.0	.392
75-76	Kentucky-A	8	....	112	82	33	76	.434	5	13	.385	11	14	.786	2	2	4	7	20	....	6	1	8	14.0	10.3	0.5	0.9	.400
76-77	LA Lakers	6	....	68	24	11	29	.379	....	....	....	2	4	.500	0	2	2	9	14	0	3	2	....	11.3	4.0	0.3	1.5	.199
NBA Playoff Totals		6	....	68	24	11	29	.379	....	....	....	2	4	.500	0	2	2	9	14	0	3	2	....	11.3	4.0	0.3	1.5	....
ABA Playoff Totals		23	....	285	164	67	168	.399	6	22	.273	24	27	.889	18	18	36	22	41	....	10	3	26	12.4	7.1	1.6	1.0	....
Career Playoff Totals		29	....	353	188	78	197	.396	6	22	.273	26	31	.839	18	20	38	31	55	0	13	5	26	12.2	6.5	1.3	1.1	....

• NEUMANN, Paul

Paul R. Neumann

Born: Jan. 30, 1938. Height: 6'1". Weight: 175 lbs. Drafted: 1959 College: Stanford

YEAR	TEAM	GP	GS	MIN	PTS	FGM	FGA	FG%	3PM	3PA	3P%	FTM	FTA	FT%	ORB	DRB	TRB	AST	PF	DQ	STL	BLK	TO	MPG	PPG	RPG	APG	PCM
61-62	Syracuse	77	....	1265	477	172	401	.429	....	....	....	133	172	.773	....	....	194	176	203	3	....	....	....	16.4	6.2	2.5	2.3	.450
62-63	Syracuse	80	....	1581	655	237	503	.471	....	....	....	181	222	.815	....	....	200	227	221	5	....	....	....	19.8	8.2	2.5	2.8	.489
63-64	Philadelphia	74	....	1973	858	324	732	.443	....	....	....	210	266	.789	....	....	246	291	211	1	....	....	....	26.7	11.6	3.3	3.9	.499
64-65	Philadelphia	40	....	1100	574	213	434	.491	....	....	....	148	184	.804	....	....	102	139	119	1	....	....	....	27.5	14.4	2.6	3.5	.540
64-65	San Francisco	36	....	934	390	152	338	.450	....	....	....	86	119	.723	....	....	96	94	99	2	....	....	....	25.9	10.8	2.7	2.6	.413
65-66	San Francisco	66	....	1729	951	343	817	.420	....	....	....	265	317	.836	....	....	208	184	174	0	....	....	....	26.2	14.4	3.2	2.8	.508
66-67	San Francisco	78	....	2421	1084	386	911	.424	....	....	....	312	390	.800	....	....	272	342	266	4	....	....	....	31.0	13.9	3.5	4.4	.478
NBA Season Totals		451	....	11003	4989	1827	4136	.442	....	....	....	1335	1670	.799	....	....	1318	1453	1293	16	....	....	....	24.4	11.1	2.9	3.2	....
61-62	Syracuse	5	....	124	28	12	29	.414	....	....	....	4	6	.667	....	....	17	14	13	0	....	....	....	24.8	5.6	3.4	2.8	.316
62-63	Syracuse	4	....	65	16	8	18	.444	....	....	....	0	1	.000	....	....	14	9	11	0	....	....	....	16.3	4.0	3.5	2.3	.389
63-64	Philadelphia	5	....	165	80	27	59	.458	....	....	....	26	31	.839	....	....	13	25	13	0	....	....	....	33.0	16.0	2.6	5.0	.538
66-67	San Francisco	15	....	254	93	29	88	.330	....	....	....	35	47	.745	....	....	17	34	50	0	....	....	....	16.9	6.2	1.1	2.3	.298
NBA Playoff Totals		29	....	608	217	76	194	.392	....	....	....	65	85	.765	....	....	61	82	87	0	....	....	....	21.0	7.5	2.1	2.8	....

• NEVITT, Chuck

Charles Goodrich Nevitt

Born: June 13, 1959. Cortez, CO, United States. Height: 7'5". Weight: 217 lbs. Drafted: 1982 College: North Carolina State

YEAR	TEAM	GP	GS	MIN	PTS	FGM	FGA	FG%	3PM	3PA	3P%	FTM	FTA	FT%	ORB	DRB	TRB	AST	PF	DQ	STL	BLK	TO	MPG	PPG	RPG	APG	PCM
82-83	Houston	6	0	64	23	11	15	.733	0	0	.000	1	4	.250	6	11	17	0	14	0	1	12	7	10.7	3.8	2.8	0.0	.507
84-85	LA Lakers	11	0	59	12	5	17	.294	0	0	.000	2	8	.250	5	15	20	3	20	0	0	15	10	5.4	1.1	1.8	0.3	.258
85-86	LA Lakers	4	0	25	10	3	11	.273	0	0	.000	4	6	.667	3	4	7	2	6	0	2	2	5	6.3	2.5	1.8	0.5	.263
85-86	Detroit	25	0	101	39	12	32	.375	0	0	.000	15	20	.750	10	15	25	5	29	0	2	17	8	4.0	1.6	1.0	0.2	.430
86-87	Detroit	41	0	267	76	31	63	.492	0	0	.000	14	24	.583	36	47	83	4	73	0	7	30	21	6.5	1.9	2.0	0.1	.390
87-88	Detroit	17	0	63	17	7	21	.333	0	0	.000	3	6	.500	4	14	18	0	12	0	1	5	2	3.7	1.0	1.1	0.0	.277
88-89	Houston	43	0	228	65	27	62	.435	0	0	.000	11	16	.688	17	47	64	3	51	1	5	29	22	5.3	1.5	1.5	0.1	.352
89-90	Houston	3	0	9	4	2	2	1.000	0	0	.000	0	0	.000	0	3	3	1	3	0	0	1	2	3.0	1.3	1.0	0.3	.615
91-92	Chicago	4	0	9	2	1	3	.333	0	0	.000	0	0	.000	0	1	1	1	2	0	0	0	3	2.3	0.5	0.3	0.3	-.175
93-94	San Antonio	1	0	1	3	0	0	.000	0	0	.000	3	6	.500	1	0	1	0	1	0	0	0	1	1.0	3.0	1.0	0.0	1.166
NBA Season Totals		155	0	826	251	99	226	.438	0	0	.000	53	90	.589	82	157	239	19	211	1	18	111	81	5.3	1.6	1.5	0.1	....
84-85	LA Lakers	7	0	37	10	3	9	.333	0	0	.000	4	8	.500	3	3	6	1	11	0	4	6	2	5.3	1.4	0.9	0.1	.312
85-86	Detroit	1	0	1	0	0	0	.000	0	0	.000	0	0	.000	0	0	0	0	0	0	0	0	0	1.0	0.0	0.0	0.0	.000
86-87	Detroit	3	0	10	4	1	5	.200	0	0	.000	2	2	1.000	1	5	6	0	1	0	0	3	3	3.3	1.3	2.0	0.0	.540
87-88	Detroit	3	0	4	2	1	2	.500	0	0	.000	0	0	.000	2	1	3	0	1	0	0	0	1	1.3	0.7	1.0	0.0	.617
88-89	Houston	2	0	3	0	0	0	.000	0	0	.000	0	0	.000	0	1	1	0	0	0	0	0	0	1.5	0.0	0.5	0.0	.310
NBA Playoff Totals		16	0	55	16	5	16	.313	0	0	.000	6	10	.600	6	10	16	1	13	0	4	9	6	3.4	1.0	1.0	0.1	....

• NEWBERN, Melvin

Melvin Newbern

Born: June 11, 1967. Toledo, OH, United States. Height: 6'4". Weight: 200 lbs. Drafted: — College: Minnesota

YEAR	TEAM	GP	GS	MIN	PTS	FGM	FGA	FG%	3PM	3PA	3P%	FTM	FTA	FT%	ORB	DRB	TRB	AST	PF	DQ	STL	BLK	TO	MPG	PPG	RPG	APG	PCM
92-93	Detroit	33	1	311	119	42	113	.372	1	8	.125	34	60	.567	19	18	37	57	42	0	23	1	33	9.4	3.6	1.1	1.7	.347
NBA Season Totals		33	1	311	119	42	113	.372	1	8	.125	34	60	.567	19	18	37	57	42	0	23	1	33	9.4	3.6	1.1	1.7	....

• NEWBILL, Ivano

Ivano Miguel Newbill

Born: Dec. 12, 1970. Sedalia, MO, United States. Height: 6'9". Weight: 245 lbs. Drafted: — College: Georgia Tech

YEAR	TEAM	GP	GS	MIN	PTS	FGM	FGA	FG%	3PM	3PA	3P%	FTM	FTA	FT%	ORB	DRB	TRB	AST	PF	DQ	STL	BLK	TO	MPG	PPG	RPG	APG	PCM
94-95	Detroit	34	0	331	40	16	45	.356	0	0	.000	8	22	.364	40	41	81	17	60	0	12	11	14	9.7	1.2	2.4	0.5	.243
96-97	Atlanta	72	2	850	100	40	91	.440	0	0	.000	20	52	.385	76	128	204	24	115	1	28	15	43	11.8	1.4	2.8	0.3	.235
97-98	Vancouver	28	2	249	58	20	57	.351	1	1	1.000	17	30	.567	24	45	69	9	38	0	10	3	17	8.9	2.1	2.5	0.3	.281
NBA Season Totals		134	4	1430	198	76	193	.394	1	1	1.000	45	104	.433	140	214	354	50	213	1	50	29	74	10.7	1.5	2.6	0.4	....
96-97	Atlanta	3	0	5	0	0	0	.000	0	0	.000	0	0	.000	0	1	1	1	2	0	0	0	1	1.7	0.0	0.3	0.3	.027
NBA Playoff Totals		3	0	5	0	0	0	.000	0	0	.000	0	0	.000	0	1	1	1	2	0	0	0	1	1.7	0.0	0.3	0.3	....

• NEWBLE, Ira

Ira Newble

Born: Jan. 20, 1975. Southfield, MI, United States. Height: 6'7". Weight: 220 lbs. Drafted: — College: Miami (OH)

YEAR	TEAM	GP	GS	MIN	PTS	FGM	FGA	FG%	3PM	3PA	3P%	FTM	FTA	FT%	ORB	DRB	TRB	AST	PF	DQ	STL	BLK	TO	MPG	PPG	RPG	APG	PCM
00-01	San Antonio	27	6	184	54	21	55	.382	4	9	.444	8	16	.500	13	22	35	6	18	0	2	4	7	6.8	2.0	1.3	0.2	.266
01-02	Atlanta	42	35	1273	338	131	263	.498	1	7	.143	75	88	.852	80	142	222	45	117	2	38	20	49	30.3	8.0	5.3	1.1	.328
02-03	Atlanta	73	45	1932	564	231	467	.495	32	84	.381	70	90	.778	86	185	271	99	174	1	50	26	69	26.5	7.7	3.7	1.4	.322
NBA Season Totals		142	86	3389	956	383	785	.488	37	100	.370	153	194	.789	179	349	528	150	309	3	90	50	125	23.9	6.7	3.7	1.1	....

• NEWLIN, Mike

Michael F. Newlin

Born: Jan. 2, 1949. Portland, OR, United States. Height: 6'4". Weight: 200 lbs. Drafted: 1971 College: Utah

YEAR	TEAM	GP	GS	MIN	PTS	FGM	FGA	FG%	3PM	3PA	3P%	FTM	FTA	FT%	ORB	DRB	TRB	AST	PF	DQ	STL	BLK	TO	MPG	PPG	RPG	APG	PCM
71-72	Houston	82	....	1495	620	256	618	.414	....	....	....	108	144	.750	....	....	228	135	233	6	....	....	....	18.2	7.6	2.8	1.6	.362
72-73	Houston	82	....	2658	1395	534	1206	.443	....	....	....	327	369	.886	....	....	340	409	301	5	....	....	....	32.4	17.0	4.1	5.0	.538
73-74	Houston	76	....	2591	1400	510	1139	.448	....	....	....	380	444	.856	77	185	262	363	259	5	87	9	....	34.1	18.4	3.4	4.8	.528
74-75	Houston	79	....	2709	1137	436	905	.482	....	....	....	265	305	.869	55	205	260	403	288	4	111	7	....	34.3	14.4	3.3	5.1	.473
75-76	Houston	82	....	3065	1523	569	1123	.507	....	....	....	385	445	.865	72	264	336	457	263	5	106	5	....	37.4	18.6	4.1	5.6	.561
76-77	Houston	82	....	2119	1043	387	850	.455	....	....	....	269	304	.885	53	151	204	320	226	2	60	3	....	25.8	12.7	2.5	3.9	.505
77-78	Houston	45	....	1181	584	216	495	.436	....	....	....	152	174	.874	36	84	120	203	128	1	52	9	122	26.2	13.0	2.7	4.5	.469
78-79	Houston	76	....	1828	778	283	581	.487	....	....	....	212	243	.872	51	119	170	291	218	3	51	79	175	24.1	10.2	2.2	3.8	.455
79-80	New Jersey	78	....	2510	1634	611	1329	.460	45	152	.296	367	415	.884	101	163	264	314	195	1	115	4	234	32.2	20.9	3.4	4.0	.539
80-81	New Jersey	79	....	2911	1688	632	1272	.497	10	30	.333	414	466	.888	78	141	219	299	237	2	87	9	245	36.8	21.4	2.8	3.8	.468
81-82	New York	76	32	1507	705	286	615	.465	7	23	.304	126	147	.857	36	55	91	170	194	2	33	3	106	19.8	9.3	1.2	2.2	.336
NBA Season Totals		837	32	24574	12507	4720	10133	.466	62	205	.302	3005	3456	.870	559	1367	2494	3364	2542	36	702	128	882	29.4	14.9	3.0	4.0	....
74-75	Houston	8	....	299	130	52	107	.486	....	....	....	26	29	.897	11	22	33	45	25	0	12	0	....	37.4	16.3	4.1	5.6	.505
76-77	Houston	12	....	316	171	75	143	.524	....	....	....	21	28	.750	8	26	34	53	37	0	15	0	....	26.3	14.3	2.8	4.4	.579
78-79	Houston	2	....	67	24	8	20	.400	....	....	....	8	8	1.000	2	4	6	5	10	1	1	1	6	33.5	12.0	3.0	2.5	.239
NBA Playoff Totals		22	....	682	325	135	270	.500	....	....	....	55	65	.846	21	52	73	103	72	1	28	1	6	31.0	14.8	3.3	4.7	....

• NEWMAN, Johnny

John Sylvester (J. New) Newman Jr.

Born: Nov. 28, 1963. Danville, VA, United States. Height: 6'7". Weight: 190 lbs. Drafted: 1986 College: Richmond

YEAR	TEAM	GP	GS	MIN	PTS	FGM	FGA	FG%	3PM	3PA	3P%	FTM	FTA	FT%	ORB	DRB	TRB	AST	PF	DQ	STL	BLK	TO	MPG	PPG	RPG	APG	PCM
86-87	Cleveland	59	0	630	293	113	275	.411	1	22	.045	66	76	.868	36	34	70	27	67	0	20	7	47	10.7	5.0	1.2	0.5	.288
87-88	New York	77	25	1589	773	270	620	.435	26	93	.280	207	246	.841	87	72	159	62	204	5	72	11	100	20.6	10.0	2.1	0.8	.335
88-89	New York	81	80	2336	1293	455	957	.475	97	287	.338	286	351	.815	93	113	206	162	259	4	111	23	154	28.8	16.0	2.5	2.0	.437
89-90	New York	80	69	2277	1032	374	786	.476	45	142	.317	239	299	.799	60	131	191	180	254	3	95	22	144	28.5	12.9	2.4	2.3	.371
90-91	Charlotte	81	81	2477	1371	478	1017	.470	30	84	.357	385	476	.809	94	160	254	188	278	7	100	17	186	30.6	16.9	3.1	2.3	.432
91-92	Charlotte	55	55	1651	839	295	618	.477	13	46	.283	236	308	.766	71	108	179	146	181	4	70	14	127	30.0	15.3	3.3	2.7	.426
92-93	Charlotte	64	27	1471	764	279	534	.522	12	45	.267	194	240	.808	72	71	143	117	154	1	45	19	90	23.0	11.9	2.2	1.8	.453
93-94	Charlotte	18	18	429	234	91	174	.523	4	16	.250	48	59	.814	21	37	58	29	44	1	18	5	29	23.8	13.0	3.2	1.6	.494
93-94	New Jersey	63	0	1268	598	222	490	.453	20	74	.270	134	166	.807	65	57	122	43	152	2	51	22	63	20.1	9.5	1.9	0.7	.343
94-95	Milwaukee	82	11	1896	634	226	488	.463	45	128	.352	137	171	.801	72	101	173	91	234	3	69	13	82	23.1	7.7	2.1	1.1	.275
95-96	Milwaukee	82	82	2690	889	321	649	.495	61	162	.377	186	232	.802	66	134	200	154	257	4	90	15	107	32.8	10.8	2.4	1.9	.293
96-97	Milwaukee	82	4	2060	715	246	547	.450	34	98	.347	189	247	.765	66	120	186	116	257	4	73	17	115	25.1	8.7	2.3	1.4	.273
97-98	Denver	74	15	2176	1089	344	799	.431	36	105	.343	365	445	.820	50	91	141	138	208	2	77	24	148	29.4	14.7	1.9	1.9	.357
98-99	Cleveland	50	2	949	303	106	251	.422	23	61	.377	68	84	.810	15	60	75	41	126	2	28	12	41	19.0	6.1	1.5	0.8	.234
99-00	New Jersey	82	9	1763	820	278	623	.446	72	190	.379	192	229	.838	39	115	154	65	207	0	53	11	89	21.5	10.0	1.9	0.8	.331
00-01	New Jersey	82	17	2049	895	291	695	.419	59	176	.335	254	297	.855	34	142	176	115	229	3	63	10	106	25.0	10.9	2.1	1.4	.325
01-02	Dallas	47	17	724	198	67	148	.453	22	57	.386	42	58	.724	9	40	49	14	88	2	29	4	21	15.4	4.2	1.0	0.3	.205
NBA Season Totals		1159	512	28435	12740	4456	9671	.461	600	1786	.336	3228	3984	.810	950	1586	2536	1688	3199	47	1064	246	1649	24.5	11.0	2.2	1.5	....
87-88	New York	4	2	113	76	31	68	.456	0	9	.000	14	16	.875	8	3	11	7	16	0	6	1	6	28.3	19.0	2.8	1.8	.458
88-89	New York	9	9	258	145	50	107	.467	7	28	.250	38	49	.776	13	12	25	17	27	1	8	1	18	28.7	16.1	2.8	1.9	.416
89-90	New York	10	0	231	117	38	85	.447	4	10	.400	37	49	.755	11	10	21	10	41	1	9	3	17	23.1	11.7	2.1	1.0	.319
92-93	Charlotte	9	9	173	68	28	55	.509	1	5	.200	11	16	.688	7	12	19	18	19	0	10	1	15	19.2	7.6	2.1	2.0	.375
93-94	New Jersey	4	0	54	12	3	13	.231	1	4	.250	5	7	.714	2	3	5	2	11	0	2	2	3	13.5	3.0	1.3	0.5	.084
01-02	Dallas	3	2	22	3	1	7	.143	1	6	.167	0	0	.000	0	0	0	2	5	0	0	0	0	7.3	1.0	0.0	0.7	-.114
NBA Playoff Totals		39	22	851	421	151	335	.451	14	62	.226	105	137	.766	41	40	81	56	119	2	35	8	59	21.8	10.8	2.1	1.4	....

YEAR	TEAM	GP	GS	MIN	PTS	FGM	FGA	FG%	3PM	3PA	3P%	FTM	FTA	FT%	ORB	DRB	TRB	AST	PF	DQ	STL	BLK	TO	MPG	PPG	RPG	APG	PCM

• NEWMARK, Dave
David L. (Shorty) Newmark

Born: Sept. 11, 1946. Brooklyn, NY, United States.   Height: 7'   Weight: 240 lbs.   Drafted: 1968   College: Columbia

YEAR	TEAM	GP	GS	MIN	PTS	FGM	FGA	FG%	3PM	3PA	3P%	FTM	FTA	FT%	ORB	DRB	TRB	AST	PF	DQ	STL	BLK	TO	MPG	PPG	RPG	APG	PCM
68-69	Chicago	81	....	1159	456	185	475	.389	....	....	....	86	139	.619	....	....	347	58	205	7	....	....	....	14.3	5.6	4.3	0.7	.400
69-70	Atlanta	64	....	612	313	127	296	.429	....	....	....	59	77	.766	....	....	174	42	128	3	....	....	....	9.6	4.9	2.7	0.7	.491
70-71	Carolina-A	31	....	457	234	100	209	.478	0	0	.000	34	60	.567	46	111	157	28	84	1	....	....	41	14.7	7.5	5.1	0.9	.573
NBA Season Totals		145	....	1771	769	312	771	.405	....	....	....	145	216	.671	....	....	521	100	333	10	....	....	....	12.2	5.3	3.6	0.7	....
ABA Season Totals		31	....	457	234	100	209	.478	0	0	.000	34	60	.567	46	111	157	28	84	1	....	....	41	14.7	7.5	5.1	0.9	....
Career Totals		176	....	2228	1003	412	980	.420	0	0	.000	179	276	.649	46	111	678	128	417	11	....	....	41	12.7	5.7	3.9	0.7	....
69-70	Atlanta	6	....	42	34	15	33	.455	....	....	....	4	4	1.000	....	....	12	2	8	0	....	....	....	7.0	5.7	2.0	0.3	.653
NBA Playoff Totals		6	....	42	34	15	33	.455	....	....	....	4	4	1.000	....	....	12	2	8	0	....	....	....	7.0	5.7	2.0	0.3	

• NEWTON, Bill
Bill R. Newton

Born: Dec. 22, 1950. Rockville, IN, United States.   Height: 6'9".   Weight: 220 lbs.   Drafted: —   College: Louisiana State

YEAR	TEAM	GP	GS	MIN	PTS	FGM	FGA	FG%	3PM	3PA	3P%	FTM	FTA	FT%	ORB	DRB	TRB	AST	PF	DQ	STL	BLK	TO	MPG	PPG	RPG	APG	PCM
72-73	Indiana-A	24	....	117	58	24	56	.429	1	2	.500	9	18	.500	21	26	47	9	40	1	....	....	10	4.9	2.4	2.0	0.4	.507
73-74	Indiana-A	11	....	73	15	7	15	.467	0	0	.000	1	2	.500	1	17	18	5	12	....	2	0	7	6.6	1.4	1.6	0.5	.325
ABA Season Totals		35	....	190	73	31	71	.437	1	2	.500	10	20	.500	22	43	65	14	52	1	2	0	17	5.4	2.1	1.9	0.4	....
72-73	Indiana-A	4	....	7	4	2	5	.400	0	1	.000	0	0	.000	2	3	5	0	3	0	....	....	1	1.8	1.0	1.3	0.0	.636
ABA Playoff Totals		4	....	7	4	2	5	.400	0	1	.000	0	0	.000	2	3	5	0	3	0	....	....	1	1.8	1.0	1.3	0.0	

• NICHOLS, Jack
Jack Edward Nichols

Born: Apr. 9, 1926. Died: Dec.24, 1992.   Height: 6'7".   Weight: 222 lbs.   Drafted: 1948   College: Washington

YEAR	TEAM	GP	GS	MIN	PTS	FGM	FGA	FG%	3PM	3PA	3P%	FTM	FTA	FT%	ORB	DRB	TRB	AST	PF	DQ	STL	BLK	TO	MPG	PPG	RPG	APG	PCM
48-49	Washington	34	....	....	398	153	392	.390	....	....	....	92	126	.730	....	....	....	56	118	....	....	....	....	11.7	....	1.6	....	
49-50	Washington	49	....	....	643	228	629	.362	....	....	....	187	254	.736	....	....	....	81	118	....	....	....	....	13.1	....	1.7	....	
49-50	Tri-Cities	18	....	236	82	219	.374	....	....	....	72	90	.800	....	....	....	61	61	....	....	....	....	13.1	....	3.4	....		
50-51	Tri-Cities	5	....	46	18	48	.375	....	....	....	10	13	.769	52	14	18	0	....	....	....	....	9.2	10.4	2.8			
52-53	Milwaukee	69	....	2626	1090	425	1170	.363	....	....	....	240	339	.708	....	....	533	196	237	9	....	....	....	38.1	15.8	7.7	2.8	.406
53-54	Mil/Bos	75	....	1607	439	163	528	.309	....	....	....	113	152	.743	....	....	363	104	187	2	....	....	....	21.4	5.9	4.8	1.4	.306
54-55	Boston	64	....	1910	636	249	656	.380	....	....	....	138	177	.780	....	....	533	144	238	10	....	....	....	29.8	9.9	8.3	2.3	.422
55-56	Boston	60	....	1964	860	330	799	.413	....	....	....	200	253	.791	....	....	625	160	228	7	....	....	....	32.7	14.3	10.4	2.7	.545
56-57	Boston	61	....	1372	498	195	537	.363	....	....	....	108	136	.794	....	....	374	85	185	4	....	....	....	22.5	8.2	6.1	1.4	.400
57-58	Boston	69	....	1224	399	170	484	.351	....	....	....	59	80	.738	....	....	302	63	123	1	....	....	....	17.7	5.8	4.4	0.9	.341
NBA Season Totals		504	....	10703	5245	2013	5462	.369	....	....	....	1219	1620	.752	....	....	2782	964	1513	33	....	....	....	21.2	10.4	5.5	1.9	....
48-49	Washington	11	....	....	158	62	152	.408	....	....	....	34	51	.667	....	....	....	27	44	....	....	....	....	14.4	....	2.5	....	
49-50	Tri-Cities	3	....	....	59	19	60	.300	....	....	....	23	31	.742	....	....	....	11	11	....	....	....	....	19.7	....	3.7	....	
53-54	Boston	6	....	211	100	35	72	.486	....	....	....	30	38	.789	....	....	62	31	24	0	....	....	....	35.2	16.7	10.3	5.2	.694
54-55	Boston	7	....	231	73	30	81	.370	....	....	....	13	16	.813	....	....	49	23	28	1	....	....	....	33.0	10.4	7.0	3.3	.383
55-56	Boston	3	....	100	41	16	43	.372	....	....	....	9	10	.900	....	....	36	10	13	0	....	....	....	33.3	13.7	12.0	3.3	.549
56-57	Boston	10	....	117	35	16	40	.400	....	....	....	3	5	.600	....	....	17	7	23	0	....	....	....	11.7	3.5	1.7	0.7	.250
57-58	Boston	11	....	148	53	23	66	.348	....	....	....	7	10	.700	....	....	45	8	21	1	....	....	....	13.5	4.8	4.1	0.7	.378
NBA Playoff Totals		51	....	807	519	200	514	.389	....	....	....	119	161	.739	....	....	209	117	164	2	....	....	....	15.8	10.2	4.1	2.3	

• NICHOLS, Oren
Oren Nichols

Born: 1923.   Height: 6'3".   Weight: 185 lbs.   Drafted: —   College: none

YEAR	TEAM	GP	GS	MIN	PTS	FGM	FGA	FG%	3PM	3PA	3P%	FTM	FTA	FT%	ORB	DRB	TRB	AST	PF	DQ	STL	BLK	TO	MPG	PPG	RPG	APG	PCM
45-46	Indianapolis-N	5	....	....	11	4	....	....	....	....	....	3	....	....	....	....	....	....	....	....	....	....	....	2.2	....	....	....	
NBL Season Totals		5	....	....	11	4	....	....	....	....	....	3	....	....	....	....	....	....	....	....	....	....	....	2.2	....	....	....	

• NICKERSON, Gaylon
Gaylon H. Nickerson

Born: Feb. 5, 1969. Osecola, AR, United States.   Height: 6'3".   Weight: 190 lbs.   Drafted: 1994   College: Northwest Oklahoma State

YEAR	TEAM	GP	GS	MIN	PTS	FGM	FGA	FG%	3PM	3PA	3P%	FTM	FTA	FT%	ORB	DRB	TRB	AST	PF	DQ	STL	BLK	TO	MPG	PPG	RPG	APG	PCM
96-97	San Antonio	3	0	36	13	3	9	.333	0	1	.000	7	7	1.000	1	3	4	1	1	0	0	1	0	12.0	4.3	1.3	0.3	.352
96-97	Washington	1	0	6	2	1	3	.333	0	1	.000	0	0	.000	0	1	1	0	0	0	1	0	1	6.0	2.0	1.0	0.0	.178
NBA Season Totals		4	0	42	15	4	12	.333	0	2	.000	7	7	1.000	1	4	5	1	1	0	1	1	1	10.5	3.8	1.3	0.3	....

• NICKS, Carl
Orlando Carl Nicks

Born: Oct. 6, 1958. Chicago, IL, United States.   Height: 6'1".   Weight: 175 lbs.   Drafted: 1980   College: Indiana State

YEAR	TEAM	GP	GS	MIN	PTS	FGM	FGA	FG%	3PM	3PA	3P%	FTM	FTA	FT%	ORB	DRB	TRB	AST	PF	DQ	STL	BLK	TO	MPG	PPG	RPG	APG	PCM
80-81	Denver	27	....	493	165	65	149	.436	0	1	.000	35	59	.593	13	36	49	80	52	0	28	2	62	18.3	6.1	1.8	3.0	.317
80-81	Utah	40	....	616	250	107	210	.510	0	3	.000	36	67	.537	24	37	61	69	89	0	32	1	52	15.4	6.3	1.5	1.7	.349
81-82	Utah	80	1	1322	589	252	555	.454	0	5	.000	85	150	.567	67	94	161	89	184	0	66	4	104	16.5	7.4	2.0	1.1	.309
82-83	Cleveland	9	2	148	63	26	59	.441	0	1	.000	11	17	.647	8	18	26	11	17	0	6	0	11	16.4	7.0	2.9	1.2	.364
NBA Season Totals		156	3	2579	1067	450	973	.462	0	10	.000	167	293	.570	112	185	297	249	342	0	132	7	229	16.5	6.8	1.9	1.6	....

• NIEMANN, Rich
Richard W. Niemann

Born: July 2, 1946. St. Louis, MO, United States.   Height: 7'   Weight: 245 lbs.   Drafted: 1968   College: St. Louis

YEAR	TEAM	GP	GS	MIN	PTS	FGM	FGA	FG%	3PM	3PA	3P%	FTM	FTA	FT%	ORB	DRB	TRB	AST	PF	DQ	STL	BLK	TO	MPG	PPG	RPG	APG	PCM
68-69	Detroit	16	....	123	48	20	47	.426	....	....	....	8	10	.800	....	....	41	9	30	0	....	....	....	7.7	3.0	2.6	0.6	.462
68-69	Milwaukee	18	....	149	59	24	59	.407	....	....	....	11	15	.733	....	....	59	7	31	1	....	....	....	8.3	3.3	3.3	0.4	.487
69-70	Carolina-A	63	....	1466	711	285	601	.474	0	0	.000	141	192	.734	171	392	563	87	219	7	....	....	141	23.3	11.3	8.9	1.4	.618

YEAR TEAM	GP	GS	MIN	PTS	FGM	FGA	FG%	3PM	3PA	3P%	FTM	FTA	FT%	ORB	DRB	TRB	AST	PF	DQ	STL	BLK	TO	MPG	PPG	RPG	APG	PCM
69-70 Boston	6	....	18	6	2	5	.400				2	2	1.000	....	....	6	2	10	0	....	....	....	3.0	1.0	1.0	0.3	.360
70-71 Florida-A	51	....	642	285	121	241	.502	0	0	.000	43	60	.717	74	181	255	29	137	6	....	....	57	12.6	5.6	5.0	0.6	.570
71-72 Dallas-A	33	....	524	121	48	98	.490	0	0	.000	25	34	.735	46	109	155	24	87	4	....	....	27	15.9	3.7	4.7	0.7	.378
NBA Season Totals	40	....	290	113	46	111	.414	....	....	....	21	27	.778	....	....	106	18	71	1	....	....	....	7.3	2.8	2.7	0.5	
ABA Season Totals	147	....	2632	1117	454	940	.483	0	0	.000	209	286	.731	291	682	973	140	443	17	....	....	225	17.9	7.6	6.6	1.0	
Career Totals	187	....	2922	1230	500	1051	.476	0	0	.000	230	313	.735	291	682	1079	158	514	18	....	....	225	15.6	6.6	5.8	0.8	
69-70 Carolina-A	4	....	51	15	6	16	.375	0	0	.000	3	3	1.000	....	....	12	0	....	....	....	....	....	12.8	3.8	3.0	0.0	
70-71 Florida-A	1	....	2	2	1	2	.500	0	0	.000	0	0	.000	0	0	0	0	0	0	....	....	0	2.0	2.0	0.0	0.0	.600
ABA Playoff Totals	5	....	53	17	7	18	.389	0	0	.000	3	3	1.000	0	0	12	0	0	0	....	....	0	10.6	3.4	2.4	0.0	

• NIEMIERA, Richie

John Richard Niemiera

Born: May 26, 1921.   Height: 6'1".   Weight: 165 lbs.   Drafted: —   College: Notre Dame

YEAR TEAM	GP	GS	MIN	PTS	FGM	FGA	FG%	3PM	3PA	3P%	FTM	FTA	FT%	ORB	DRB	TRB	AST	PF	DQ	STL	BLK	TO	MPG	PPG	RPG	APG	PCM
46-47 Fort Wayne-N	13	....	....	73	28	....	....	....				17	23	.739				....	....					5.6				
47-48 Fort Wayne-N	59	....	....	333	118	....	....	....				97	135	.719				....	113					5.6				
48-49 Fort Wayne	55	....	....	362	115	331	.347					132	165	.800				96	115					6.6			1.7	
49-50 Fort Wayne	31	....	....	174	59	207	.285					56	73	.767				61	42					5.6			2.0	
49-50 Anderson	29	....	....	150	51	143	.357					48	66	.727				55	35					5.2			1.9	
NBA Season Totals	115	....	....	686	225	681	.330					236	304	.776				212	192					6.0			1.8	
NBL Season Totals	72	....	....	406	146	....	....	....				114	158	....				....	113					5.6				
Career Totals	187	....	....	1092	371	681						350	462					212	305					5.8			1.1	
46-47 Fort Wayne-N	6	....	....	27	11	....	....	....				5	8	.625										4.5				
47-48 Fort Wayne-N	4	....	....	27	10	....	....	....				7	8	.875										6.8				
49-50 Anderson	8	....	....	28	11	27	.407					6	8	.750				8	10					3.5			1.0	
NBA Playoff Totals	8	....	....	28	11	27	.407					6	8	.750				8	10					3.5			1.0	
NBL Playoff Totals	10	....	....	54	21	....	....	....				12	16											5.4				
Career Playoff Totals	18	....	....	82	32	27						18	24					8	10					4.6			0.4	

• NILES, Mike

Michael Donnell Niles

Born: Mar. 31, 1955. Los Angeles, CA, United States.   Height: 6'6".   Weight: 225 lbs.   Drafted: 1979   College: Cal State Fullerton

YEAR TEAM	GP	GS	MIN	PTS	FGM	FGA	FG%	3PM	3PA	3P%	FTM	FTA	FT%	ORB	DRB	TRB	AST	PF	DQ	STL	BLK	TO	MPG	PPG	RPG	APG	PCM
80-81 Phoenix	44	....	231	115	48	138	.348	2	4	.500	17	37	.459	26	32	58	15	41	0	8	1	26	5.3	2.6	1.3	0.3	.255
NBA Season Totals	44	....	231	115	48	138	.348	2	4	.500	17	37	.459	26	32	58	15	41	0	8	1	26	5.3	2.6	1.3	0.3	
80-81 Phoenix	2	....	4	0	0	5	.000	0	0	.000	0	0	.000	0	0	0	0	0	0	1	0	0	2.0	0.0	0.0	0.0	-.911
NBA Playoff Totals	2	....	4	0	0	5	.000	0	0	.000	0	0	.000	0	0	0	0	0	0	1	0	0	2.0	0.0	0.0	0.0	

• NIMPHIUS, Kurt

Kurt Allen Nimphius

Born: Mar. 13, 1958. Milwaukee, WI, United States.   Height: 6'10".   Weight: 218 lbs.   Drafted: 1980   College: Arizona State

YEAR TEAM	GP	GS	MIN	PTS	FGM	FGA	FG%	3PM	3PA	3P%	FTM	FTA	FT%	ORB	DRB	TRB	AST	PF	DQ	STL	BLK	TO	MPG	PPG	RPG	APG	PCM
81-82 Dallas	63	27	1085	337	137	297	.461	0	0	.000	63	108	.583	92	203	295	61	190	5	17	82	57	17.2	5.3	4.7	1.0	.422
82-83 Dallas	81	12	1515	426	174	355	.490	1	1	1.000	77	140	.550	157	247	404	115	287	11	24	111	65	18.7	5.3	5.0	1.4	.435
83-84 Dallas	82	46	2284	646	272	523	.520	1	4	.250	101	162	.623	182	331	513	176	283	5	41	144	98	27.9	7.9	6.3	2.1	.437
84-85 Dallas	82	40	2010	500	196	434	.452	0	6	.000	108	140	.771	136	272	408	183	262	4	30	126	98	24.5	6.1	5.0	2.2	.384
85-86 Dallas	13	4	280	91	37	72	.514	0	1	.000	17	29	.586	23	37	60	14	38	1	3	12	13	21.5	7.0	4.6	1.1	.385
85-86 LA Clippers	67	62	1946	805	314	622	.505	0	2	.000	177	233	.760	129	264	393	48	229	7	30	93	107	29.0	12.0	5.9	0.7	.420
86-87 LA Clippers	38	6	811	295	119	252	.472	0	3	.000	57	88	.648	58	75	133	18	118	1	16	41	46	21.3	7.8	3.5	0.5	.315
86-87 Detroit	28	5	277	96	36	78	.462	0	1	.000	24	32	.750	22	32	54	7	38	0	4	13	17	9.9	3.4	1.9	0.3	.337
87-88 San Antonio	72	7	919	316	128	257	.498	0	1	.000	60	83	.723	62	91	153	53	141	2	22	56	50	12.8	4.4	2.1	0.7	.375
89-90 Philadelphia	38	1	314	90	38	91	.418	0	1	.000	14	30	.467	22	39	61	6	45	0	4	18	11	8.3	2.4	1.6	0.2	.273
NBA Season Totals	564	210	11441	3602	1451	2981	.487	2	20	.100	698	1045	.668	883	1591	2474	681	1631	36	191	696	562	20.3	6.4	4.4	1.2	
83-84 Dallas	10	0	178	42	14	33	.424	0	0	.000	14	17	.824	20	33	53	13	24	0	0	14	9	17.8	4.2	5.3	1.3	.447
84-85 Dallas	4	0	50	6	3	6	.500	0	0	.000	0	0	.000	3	3	6	3	10	0	1	1	2	12.5	1.5	1.5	0.8	.147
86-87 Detroit	4	0	30	8	3	9	.333	0	0	.000	2	4	.500	5	5	10	0	10	0	0	2	3	7.5	2.0	2.5	0.0	.174
87-88 San Antonio	3	0	30	12	5	10	.500	0	0	.000	2	2	1.000	3	5	8	2	7	0	0	1	0	10.0	4.0	2.7	0.7	.487
89-90 Philadelphia	4	0	18	2	1	7	.143	0	0	.000	0	0	.000	3	1	4	0	1	0	1	1	0	4.5	0.5	1.0	0.0	.085
NBA Playoff Totals	25	0	306	70	26	65	.400	0	0	.000	18	23	.783	34	47	81	18	52	0	2	19	14	12.2	2.8	3.2	0.7	

• NIMZ, Fred

Fred Nimz

Born: Apr. 22, 1914. Died: May 9, 1992.   Height: 6'3".   Weight: 200 lbs.   Drafted: —   College: Wisconsin (Stevens Point)

YEAR TEAM	GP	GS	MIN	PTS	FGM	FGA	FG%	3PM	3PA	3P%	FTM	FTA	FT%	ORB	DRB	TRB	AST	PF	DQ	STL	BLK	TO	MPG	PPG	RPG	APG	PCM
42-43 Oshkosh-N	5	....	....	11	4	....	....	....				3						....						2.2				
NBL Season Totals	5	....	....	11	4	....	....	....				3						....						2.2				

• NISBET, Tommy

Thomas Nisbet

Born: 1917.   Height: 5'10".   Weight: 165 lbs.   Drafted: —   College: Illinois

YEAR TEAM	GP	GS	MIN	PTS	FGM	FGA	FG%	3PM	3PA	3P%	FTM	FTA	FT%	ORB	DRB	TRB	AST	PF	DQ	STL	BLK	TO	MPG	PPG	RPG	APG	PCM
38-39 Hammond-N	5	....	....	36	16	....	....	....				4												7.2				
39-40 Hammond-N	5	....	....	16	4	....	....	....				8												3.2				
40-41 Oshkosh-N	24	....	....	58	21	....	....	....				16												2.4				
41-42 Oshkosh-N	24	....	....	76	24	....	....	....				28												3.2				
42-43 Oshkosh-N	9	....	....	22	7	....	....	....				8												2.4				
NBL Season Totals	67	....	....	208	72	....	....	....				64												3.1				

YEAR	TEAM	GP	GS	MIN	PTS	FGM	FGA	FG%	3PM	3PA	3P%	FTM	FTA	FT%	ORB	DRB	TRB	AST	PF	DQ	STL	BLK	TO	MPG	PPG	RPG	APG	PCM
40-41	Oshkosh-N	5	....	....	10	3	....	....	....	....	....	4	....	....	....	....	....	....	....	....	....	....	....	....	2.0	....	....	....
41-42	Oshkosh-N	5	....	....	31	11	....	....	....	....	....	9	....	....	....	....	....	....	....	....	....	....	....	....	6.2	....	....	....
42-43	Oshkosh-N	2	....	....	9	3	....	....	....	....	....	3	....	....	....	....	....	....	....	....	....	....	....	....	4.5	....	....	....
NBL Playoff Totals		12	....	....	50	17	....	....	....	....	....	16	....	....	....	....	....	....	....	....	....	....	....	....	4.2	....	....	....

• NIX, Dyron

Dyron Patrick Nix

Born: Feb. 11, 1967. Meridian, MS, United States. Height: 6'7". Weight: 210 lbs. Drafted: 1989 College: Tennessee

YEAR	TEAM	GP	GS	MIN	PTS	FGM	FGA	FG%	3PM	3PA	3P%	FTM	FTA	FT%	ORB	DRB	TRB	AST	PF	DQ	STL	BLK	TO	MPG	PPG	RPG	APG	PCM
89-90	Indiana	20	0	109	39	14	39	.359	0	0	.000	11	16	.688	8	18	26	5	15	0	3	1	6	5.5	2.0	1.3	0.3	.312
NBA Season Totals		20	0	109	39	14	39	.359	0	0	.000	11	16	.688	8	18	26	5	15	0	3	1	6	5.5	2.0	1.3	0.3	....

• NIXON, Norm

Norman Ellard Nixon

Born: Oct. 11, 1955. Macon, GA, United States. Height: 6'2". Weight: 170 lbs. Drafted: 1977 College: Duquesne

YEAR	TEAM	GP	GS	MIN	PTS	FGM	FGA	FG%	3PM	3PA	3P%	FTM	FTA	FT%	ORB	DRB	TRB	AST	PF	DQ	STL	BLK	TO	MPG	PPG	RPG	APG	PCM
77-78	LA Lakers	81	....	2779	1107	496	998	.497	....	....	....	115	161	.714	41	198	239	553	259	3	138	7	251	34.3	13.7	3.0	6.8	.458
78-79	LA Lakers	82	....	3145	1404	623	1149	.542	....	....	....	158	204	.775	48	183	231	737	250	6	**201**	17	230	38.4	17.1	2.8	9.0	.575
79-80	LA Lakers	82	....	**3226**	1446	624	1209	.516	1	8	.125	197	253	.779	52	177	229	642	241	1	147	14	287	**39.3**	17.6	2.8	7.8	.489
80-81	LA Lakers	79	....	2962	1350	576	1210	.476	2	12	.167	196	252	.778	64	168	232	696	226	2	146	11	284	37.5	17.1	2.9	8.8	.506
81-82	LA Lakers	82	82	3024	1440	628	1274	.493	3	12	.250	181	224	.808	38	138	176	652	264	3	132	7	238	36.9	17.6	2.1	8.0	.489
82-83	LA Lakers	79	79	2711	1191	533	1123	.475	0	13	.000	125	168	.744	61	144	205	566	176	1	104	4	237	34.3	15.1	2.6	7.2	.461
83-84	San Diego	82	82	3053	1391	587	1270	.462	11	46	.239	206	271	.760	56	147	203	**914**	180	1	94	4	254	37.2	17.0	2.5	11.1	**.545**
84-85	LA Clippers	81	81	2894	1395	596	1281	.465	33	99	.333	170	218	.780	55	163	218	711	175	2	95	4	275	35.7	17.2	2.7	8.8	.501
85-86	LA Clippers	67	62	2138	979	403	921	.438	42	121	.347	131	162	.809	45	135	180	576	143	0	84	3	188	31.9	14.6	2.7	8.6	.518
88-89	LA Clippers	53	30	1318	362	153	370	.414	8	29	.276	48	65	.738	13	65	78	339	69	0	46	0	117	24.9	6.8	1.5	6.4	.371
NBA Season Totals		768	416	27250	12065	5219	10805	.483	100	340	.294	1527	1978	.772	473	1518	1991	6386	1983	19	1187	71	2361	35.5	15.7	2.6	8.3	....
77-78	LA Lakers	3	....	92	24	11	24	.458	....	....	....	2	3	.667	4	5	9	16	13	0	4	1	5	30.7	8.0	3.0	5.3	.352
78-79	LA Lakers	8	....	327	123	56	119	.471	....	....	....	11	15	.733	6	22	28	94	37	1	11	0	24	40.9	15.4	3.5	11.8	.505
79-80	LA Lakers	16	....	648	270	114	239	.477	1	5	.200	41	51	.804	13	43	56	125	59	0	32	3	49	40.5	16.9	3.5	7.8	.464
80-81	LA Lakers	3	....	133	58	25	49	.510	0	0	.000	8	10	.800	1	10	11	26	9	0	1	1	5	44.3	19.3	3.7	8.7	.502
81-82	LA Lakers	14	14	549	286	121	253	.478	1	3	.333	43	57	.754	13	30	43	114	43	0	23	2	34	39.2	20.4	3.1	8.1	.533
82-83	LA Lakers	14	14	538	266	113	237	.477	3	7	.429	37	50	.740	13	35	48	90	40	0	18	1	34	38.4	19.0	3.4	6.4	.481
NBA Playoff Totals		58	28	2287	1027	440	921	.478	5	15	.333	142	186	.763	50	145	195	465	201	1	89	8	151	39.4	17.7	3.4	8.0	....

• NOBLE, Chuck

Charles E. Noble

Born: July 24, 1931. Height: 6'4". Weight: 190 lbs. Drafted: 1954 College: Louisville

YEAR	TEAM	GP	GS	MIN	PTS	FGM	FGA	FG%	3PM	3PA	3P%	FTM	FTA	FT%	ORB	DRB	TRB	AST	PF	DQ	STL	BLK	TO	MPG	PPG	RPG	APG	PCM
55-56	Fort Wayne	72	....	2013	686	270	767	.352	....	....	....	146	195	.749	....	....	261	282	253	3	....	....	....	28.0	9.5	3.6	3.9	.368
56-57	Fort Wayne	54	....	1260	476	200	556	.360	....	....	....	76	102	.745	....	....	135	180	161	2	....	....	....	23.3	8.8	2.5	3.3	.371
57-58	Detroit	61	....	1363	454	199	601	.331	....	....	....	56	77	.727	....	....	140	153	166	0	....	....	....	22.3	7.4	2.3	2.5	.286
58-59	Detroit	65	....	939	461	189	560	.338	....	....	....	83	113	.735	....	....	115	114	126	0	....	....	....	14.4	7.1	1.8	1.8	.375
59-60	Detroit	58	....	1621	653	276	774	.357	....	....	....	101	138	.732	....	....	201	265	172	2	....	....	....	27.9	11.3	3.5	4.6	.419
60-61	Detroit	75	....	1665	474	196	566	.346	....	....	....	82	115	.713	....	....	180	287	195	4	....	....	....	22.2	6.3	2.4	3.8	.359
61-62	Detroit	26	....	361	72	32	113	.283	....	....	....	8	15	.533	....	....	43	63	55	1	....	....	....	13.9	2.8	1.7	2.4	.263
NBA Season Totals		411	....	9222	3276	1362	3937	.346	....	....	....	552	755	.731	....	....	1075	1344	1128	12	....	....	....	22.4	8.0	2.6	3.3	....
55-56	Fort Wayne	10	....	261	74	29	92	.315	....	....	....	16	17	.941	....	....	30	41	30	1	....	....	....	26.1	7.4	3.0	4.1	.337
56-57	Fort Wayne	2	....	45	21	10	26	.385	....	....	....	1	2	.500	....	....	3	4	5	0	....	....	....	22.5	10.5	1.5	2.0	.313
57-58	Detroit	7	....	72	20	8	38	.211	....	....	....	4	8	.500	....	....	13	6	9	0	....	....	....	10.3	2.9	1.9	0.9	.146
58-59	Detroit	3	....	28	12	5	17	.294	....	....	....	2	2	1.000	....	....	0	1	3	0	....	....	....	9.3	4.0	0.0	0.3	.111
59-60	Detroit	2	....	61	14	7	26	.269	....	....	....	0	0	.000	....	....	9	13	6	0	....	....	....	30.5	7.0	4.5	6.5	.334
60-61	Detroit	5	....	124	45	20	45	.444	....	....	....	5	7	.714	....	....	8	21	18	1	....	....	....	24.8	9.0	1.6	4.2	.407
NBA Playoff Totals		29	....	591	186	79	244	.324	....	....	....	28	36	.778	....	....	63	86	71	2	....	....	....	20.4	6.4	2.2	3.0	....

• NOEL, Paul

Paul Wendel Noel

Born: Aug. 4, 1924. Midway, KY, United States. Height: 6'4". Weight: 185 lbs. Drafted: — College: Kentucky

YEAR	TEAM	GP	GS	MIN	PTS	FGM	FGA	FG%	3PM	3PA	3P%	FTM	FTA	FT%	ORB	DRB	TRB	AST	PF	DQ	STL	BLK	TO	MPG	PPG	RPG	APG	PCM
47-48	New York	29	....	....	99	40	138	.290	....	....	....	19	30	.633	....	....	....	3	41	....	....	....	....	....	3.4	....	0.1	....
48-49	New York	47	....	....	177	70	277	.253	....	....	....	37	60	.617	....	....	....	33	84	....	....	....	....	....	3.8	....	0.7	....
49-50	New York	65	....	....	249	98	291	.337	....	....	....	53	87	.609	....	....	....	67	132	....	....	....	....	....	3.8	....	1.0	....
50-51	Rochester	52	....	....	130	49	174	.282	....	....	....	32	45	.711	....	....	81	34	61	1	....	....	....	....	2.5	1.6	0.7	....
51-52	Rochester	8	....	32	6	2	9	.222	....	....	....	2	3	.667	....	....	4	3	6	0	....	....	....	4.0	0.8	0.5	0.4	.164
NBA Season Totals		201	....	32	661	259	889	.291	....	....	....	143	225	.636	....	....	85	140	324	1	....	....	....	0.2	3.3	0.4	0.7	....
47-48	New York	3	....	....	0	0	7	.000	....	....	....	0	1	.000	....	....	....	0	4	....	....	....	....	....	0.0	....	0.0	....
48-49	New York	3	....	....	14	5	12	.417	....	....	....	4	5	.800	....	....	....	2	12	....	....	....	....	....	4.7	....	0.7	....
49-50	New York	5	....	....	3	1	7	.143	....	....	....	1	3	.333	....	....	....	1	8	....	....	....	....	....	0.6	....	0.2	....
50-51	Rochester	9	....	....	19	7	18	.389	....	....	....	5	7	.714	....	....	9	1	11	0	....	....	....	....	2.1	1.0	0.1	....
NBA Playoff Totals		20	....	....	36	13	44	.295	....	....	....	10	16	.625	....	....	9	4	35	0	....	....	....	....	1.8	0.5	0.2	....

• NOLAN, Jim

James S. Nolan

Born: June 9, 1927. Macon, GA, United States. Died: Apr.19, 1983. Height: 6'8". Weight: 210 lbs. Drafted: 1949 College: Georgia Tech

YEAR	TEAM	GP	GS	MIN	PTS	FGM	FGA	FG%	3PM	3PA	3P%	FTM	FTA	FT%	ORB	DRB	TRB	AST	PF	DQ	STL	BLK	TO	MPG	PPG	RPG	APG	PCM
49-50	Philadelphia	5	....	....	8	4	21	.190	....	....	....	0	0	.000	....	....	....	4	14	....	....	....	....	....	1.6	....	0.8	....
NBA Season Totals		5	....	....	8	4	21	.190	....	....	....	0	0	.000	....	....	....	4	14	....	....	....	....	....	1.6	....	0.8	....

YEAR TEAM	GP	GS	MIN	PTS	FGM	FGA	FG%	3PM	3PA	3P%	FTM	FTA	FT%	ORB	DRB	TRB	AST	PF	DQ	STL	BLK	TO	MPG	PPG	RPG	APG	PCM

• NOLEN, Paul

Paul E. Nolen

Born: Sept. 3, 1929. Height: 6'10". Weight: — Drafted: 1953 College: Texas Tech

YEAR TEAM	GP	GS	MIN	PTS	FGM	FGA	FG%	3PM	3PA	3P%	FTM	FTA	FT%	ORB	DRB	TRB	AST	PF	DQ	STL	BLK	TO	MPG	PPG	RPG	APG	PCM
53-54 Baltimore	1	....	2	0	0	1	.000	....	....	....	0	0	.000	....	....	1	0	1	0	....	....	....	2.0	0.0	1.0	0.0	-.178
NBA Season Totals	1	....	2	0	0	1	.000	....	....	....	0	0	.000	....	....	1	0	1	0	....	....	....	2.0	0.0	1.0	0.0	....

• NORDGAARD, Jeff

Jeff Wallace Nordgaard

Born: Feb. 23, 1973. Dawson, MN, United States. Height: 6'7". Weight: 225 lbs. Drafted: 1996 College: Wisconsin (Green Bay)

YEAR TEAM	GP	GS	MIN	PTS	FGM	FGA	FG%	3PM	3PA	3P%	FTM	FTA	FT%	ORB	DRB	TRB	AST	PF	DQ	STL	BLK	TO	MPG	PPG	RPG	APG	PCM
97-98 Milwaukee	13	0	48	18	5	18	.278	0	0	.000	8	9	.889	4	10	14	3	7	0	2	0	3	3.7	1.4	1.1	0.2	.367
NBA Season Totals	13	0	48	18	5	18	.278	0	0	.000	8	9	.889	4	10	14	3	7	0	2	0	3	3.7	1.4	1.1	0.2	....

• NORDMANN, Bevo

Robert (Bevo) Nordmann

Born: Dec. 11, 1939. St. Louis, MO, United States. Height: 6'10". Weight: 225 lbs. Drafted: 1961 College: St. Louis

YEAR TEAM	GP	GS	MIN	PTS	FGM	FGA	FG%	3PM	3PA	3P%	FTM	FTA	FT%	ORB	DRB	TRB	AST	PF	DQ	STL	BLK	TO	MPG	PPG	RPG	APG	PCM
61-62 Cincinnati	58	....	344	131	51	126	.405	....	....	....	29	57	.509	....	....	128	18	81	1	....	....	....	5.9	2.3	2.2	0.3	.441
62-63 St. Louis	27	....	271	93	36	80	.450	....	....	....	21	39	.538	....	....	85	8	49	0	....	....	....	10.0	3.4	3.1	0.3	.401
62-63 New York	26	....	729	278	120	239	.502	....	....	....	38	83	.458	....	....	231	39	107	6	....	....	....	28.0	10.7	8.9	1.5	.485
63-64 New York	7	....	106	34	13	25	.520	....	....	....	8	14	.571	....	....	25	1	18	0	....	....	....	15.1	4.9	3.6	0.1	.340
63-64 St. Louis	12	....	153	29	14	41	.341	....	....	....	1	5	.200	....	....	40	4	33	1	....	....	....	12.8	2.4	3.3	0.3	.194
64-65 Boston	3	....	25	6	3	5	.600	....	....	....	0	0	.000	....	....	8	3	5	0	....	....	....	8.3	2.0	2.7	1.0	.495
NBA Season Totals	133	....	1628	571	237	516	.459	....	....	....	97	198	.490	....	....	517	73	293	8	....	....	....	12.2	4.3	3.9	0.5	....
61-62 Cincinnati	2	....	5	0	0	1	.000	....	....	....	0	0	.000	....	....	2	0	1	0	....	....	....	2.5	0.0	1.0	0.0	.078
NBA Playoff Totals	2	....	5	0	0	1	.000	....	....	....	0	0	.000	....	....	2	0	1	0	....	....	....	2.5	0.0	1.0	0.0	....

• NOREN, Irving

Irving Arnold Noren

Born: Nov. 29, 1924. Jamestown, NY, United States. Height: 6' Weight: 180 lbs. Drafted: — College: Pasadena City

YEAR TEAM	GP	GS	MIN	PTS	FGM	FGA	FG%	3PM	3PA	3P%	FTM	FTA	FT%	ORB	DRB	TRB	AST	PF	DQ	STL	BLK	TO	MPG	PPG	RPG	APG	PCM
46-47 Chicago-N	3	....	....	1	0	....	....	....	....	....	1	2	.500	....	....	....	....	....	....	....	....	....	0.3	....	....	....	....
NBL Season Totals	3	....	....	1	0	....	....	....	....	....	1	2	....	....	....	....	....	....	....	....	....	....	0.3	....	....	....	....

• NORLANDER, Johnny

John A. Norlander

Born: Mar. 5, 1921. Virginia, MN, United States. Height: 6'3". Weight: 180 lbs. Drafted: — College: Hamline

YEAR TEAM	GP	GS	MIN	PTS	FGM	FGA	FG%	3PM	3PA	3P%	FTM	FTA	FT%	ORB	DRB	TRB	AST	PF	DQ	STL	BLK	TO	MPG	PPG	RPG	APG	PCM
46-47 Washington	60	....	....	626	223	698	.319	....	....	....	180	276	.652	....	....	....	50	122	....	....	....	....	10.4	....	0.8	....	....
47-48 Washington	48	....	....	469	167	543	.308	....	....	....	135	182	.742	....	....	....	44	102	....	....	....	....	9.8	....	0.9	....	....
48-49 Washington	60	....	....	444	164	454	.361	....	....	....	116	171	.678	....	....	....	86	124	....	....	....	....	7.4	....	1.4	....	....
49-50 Washington	40	....	....	251	99	293	.338	....	....	....	53	85	.624	....	....	....	33	71	....	....	....	....	6.3	....	0.8	....	....
50-51 Washington	9	....	21	6	19	.316	....	....	....	9	14	.643	....	....	9	5	14	0	....	....	....	2.3	1.0	0.6	....	....	
NBA Season Totals	217	....	....	1811	659	2007	.328	....	....	....	493	728	.677	....	....	9	218	433	0	....	....	....	8.3	0.0	1.0	....	....
46-47 Washington	6	....	....	41	14	50	.280	....	....	....	13	17	.765	....	....	....	2	11	....	....	....	....	6.8	....	0.3	....	....
48-49 Washington	11	....	....	70	25	73	.342	....	....	....	20	26	.769	....	....	....	7	27	....	....	....	....	6.4	....	0.6	....	....
NBA Playoff Totals	17	....	....	111	39	123	.317	....	....	....	33	43	.767	....	....	....	9	38	....	....	....	....	6.5	....	0.5	....	....

• NORMAN, Connie

Coniel Norman

Born: Sept. 24, 1953. Detroit, MI, United States. Height: 6'3". Weight: 175 lbs. Drafted: 1974 College: Arizona

YEAR TEAM	GP	GS	MIN	PTS	FGM	FGA	FG%	3PM	3PA	3P%	FTM	FTA	FT%	ORB	DRB	TRB	AST	PF	DQ	STL	BLK	TO	MPG	PPG	RPG	APG	PCM
74-75 Philadelphia	12	....	72	48	23	44	.523	....	....	....	2	3	.667	3	9	12	4	9	0	3	1	....	6.0	4.0	1.0	0.3	.565
75-76 Philadelphia	65	....	818	386	183	422	.434	....	....	....	20	24	.833	51	50	101	66	87	1	28	7	....	12.6	5.9	1.6	1.0	.372
78-79 San Diego	22	....	323	161	71	165	.430	....	....	....	19	23	.826	13	19	32	24	35	0	10	3	22	14.7	7.3	1.5	1.1	.329
NBA Season Totals	99	....	1213	595	277	631	.439	....	....	....	41	50	.820	67	78	145	94	131	1	41	11	22	12.3	6.0	1.5	0.9	....
75-76 Philadelphia	1	....	1	2	1	1	1.000	....	....	....	0	0	.000	0	1	1	0	0	0	0	0	....	1.0	2.0	1.0	0.0	2.858
NBA Playoff Totals	1	....	1	2	1	1	1.000	....	....	....	0	0	.000	0	1	1	0	0	0	0	0	....	1.0	2.0	1.0	0.0	....

• NORMAN, Ken

Kenneth Darnel (Snake) Norman   aka.: Ken Colliers

Born: Sept. 5, 1964. Chicago, IL, United States. Height: 6'8". Weight: 215 lbs. Drafted: 1987 College: Illinois

YEAR TEAM	GP	GS	MIN	PTS	FGM	FGA	FG%	3PM	3PA	3P%	FTM	FTA	FT%	ORB	DRB	TRB	AST	PF	DQ	STL	BLK	TO	MPG	PPG	RPG	APG	PCM
87-88 LA Clippers	66	28	1435	569	241	500	.482	0	10	.000	87	170	.512	100	163	263	78	123	0	44	34	106	21.7	8.6	4.0	1.2	.372
88-89 LA Clippers	80	79	3020	1450	638	1271	.502	4	21	.190	170	270	.630	245	422	667	277	223	2	106	66	208	37.8	18.1	8.3	3.5	.528
89-90 LA Clippers	70	64	2334	1128	484	949	.510	7	16	.438	153	242	.632	143	327	470	160	196	0	78	59	189	33.3	16.1	6.7	2.3	.480
90-91 LA Clippers	70	45	2309	1219	520	1037	.501	6	32	.188	173	275	.629	177	320	497	159	192	0	63	63	140	33.0	17.4	7.1	2.3	.528
91-92 LA Clippers	77	24	2009	929	402	821	.490	4	28	.143	121	226	.535	158	290	448	125	145	0	53	66	100	26.1	12.1	5.8	1.6	.493
92-93 LA Clippers	76	71	2477	1137	498	975	.511	10	38	.263	131	220	.595	209	362	571	165	156	0	59	57	122	32.6	15.0	7.5	2.2	.517
93-94 Milwaukee	82	75	2539	979	412	919	.448	63	189	.333	92	183	.503	169	331	500	222	209	2	58	46	148	31.0	11.9	6.1	2.7	.408
94-95 Atlanta	74	28	1879	938	388	856	.453	98	285	.344	64	140	.457	103	259	362	94	154	0	34	20	96	25.4	12.7	4.9	1.3	.421
95-96 Atlanta	34	28	770	304	127	273	.465	33	84	.393	17	48	.354	40	92	132	63	68	0	15	16	48	22.6	8.9	3.9	1.9	.383
96-97 Atlanta	17	0	220	64	27	94	.287	6	38	.158	4	12	.333	8	31	39	12	17	0	7	3	19	12.9	3.8	2.3	0.7	.139
NBA Season Totals	646	441	18992	8717	3737	7695	.486	231	741	.312	1012	1786	.567	1352	2597	3949	1355	1483	4	517	430	1176	29.4	13.5	6.1	2.1	....
91-92 LA Clippers	5	5	184	63	27	53	.509	0	2	.000	9	17	.529	19	30	49	15	18	0	4	3	6	36.8	12.6	9.8	3.0	.485
92-93 LA Clippers	5	5	164	64	25	67	.373	3	8	.375	11	22	.500	14	27	41	12	8	0	4	0	1	32.8	12.8	8.2	2.4	.426
94-95 Atlanta	3	0	42	16	7	18	.389	1	8	.125	1	7	.143	2	7	9	3	13	1	0	1	3	14.0	5.3	3.0	1.0	.155
NBA Playoff Totals	13	10	390	143	59	138	.428	4	18	.222	21	46	.457	35	64	99	30	39	1	8	4	10	30.0	11.0	7.6	2.3	....

YEAR	TEAM	GP	GS	MIN	PTS	FGM	FGA	FG%	3PM	3PA	3P%	FTM	FTA	FT%	ORB	DRB	TRB	AST	PF	DQ	STL	BLK	TO	MPG	PPG	RPG	APG	PCM

• NORRIS, Audie
Audie James Norris

Born: Dec. 18, 1960. Jackson, MS, United States.   Height: 6'9".   Weight: 230 lbs.   Drafted: 1982   College: Jackson State

YEAR	TEAM	GP	GS	MIN	PTS	FGM	FGA	FG%	3PM	3PA	3P%	FTM	FTA	FT%	ORB	DRB	TRB	AST	PF	DQ	STL	BLK	TO	MPG	PPG	RPG	APG	PCM
82-83	Portland	30	0	311	66	26	63	.413	0	0	.000	14	30	.467	25	44	69	24	61	0	13	2	33	10.4	2.2	2.3	0.8	.226
83-84	Portland	79	1	1157	352	124	246	.504	0	0	.000	104	149	.698	82	175	257	76	231	2	30	34	111	14.6	4.5	3.3	1.0	.334
84-85	Portland	78	13	1117	401	133	245	.543	0	3	.000	135	203	.665	90	160	250	47	221	7	42	33	101	14.3	5.1	3.2	0.6	.377
NBA Season Totals		187	14	2585	819	283	554	.511	0	3	.000	253	382	.662	197	379	576	147	513	9	85	69	245	13.8	4.4	3.1	0.8	....
82-83	Portland	7	0	53	15	7	13	.538	0	0	.000	1	2	.500	3	9	12	5	5	0	2	2	2	7.6	2.1	1.7	0.7	.472
83-84	Portland	5	0	52	17	6	10	.600	0	0	.000	5	8	.625	6	10	16	4	13	1	1	1	5	10.4	3.4	3.2	0.8	.427
84-85	Portland	8	0	109	47	19	32	.594	0	0	.000	9	22	.409	22	21	43	3	25	0	4	5	11	13.6	5.9	5.4	0.4	.538
NBA Playoff Totals		20	0	214	79	32	55	.582	0	0	.000	15	32	.469	31	40	71	12	43	1	7	8	18	10.7	4.0	3.6	0.6	....

• NORRIS, Moochie
Martyn (Moochie) Norris

Born: July 27, 1973. Washington, DC, United States.   Height: 6'1".   Weight: 175 lbs.   Drafted: 1996   College: West Florida

YEAR	TEAM	GP	GS	MIN	PTS	FGM	FGA	FG%	3PM	3PA	3P%	FTM	FTA	FT%	ORB	DRB	TRB	AST	PF	DQ	STL	BLK	TO	MPG	PPG	RPG	APG	PCM
96-97	Vancouver	8	0	89	12	4	22	.182	2	10	.200	2	5	.400	3	9	12	23	5	0	4	0	5	11.1	1.5	1.5	2.9	.296
98-99	Seattle	12	0	140	38	13	40	.325	6	15	.400	6	16	.375	4	16	20	24	17	0	7	0	16	11.7	3.2	1.7	2.0	.275
99-00	Houston	30	0	502	207	69	159	.434	12	29	.414	57	73	.781	16	52	68	94	32	0	23	1	30	16.7	6.9	2.3	3.1	.523
00-01	Houston	82	6	1654	544	184	413	.446	25	89	.281	151	194	.778	44	154	198	283	84	0	69	2	107	20.2	6.6	2.4	3.5	.447
01-02	Houston	82	26	2250	665	251	631	.398	36	134	.269	127	169	.751	73	173	246	403	130	0	81	4	156	27.4	8.1	3.0	4.9	.374
02-03	Houston	82	3	1375	357	134	330	.406	11	45	.244	78	114	.684	37	122	159	196	72	0	55	4	86	16.8	4.4	1.9	2.4	.337
NBA Season Totals		296	35	6010	1823	655	1595	.411	92	322	.286	421	571	.737	177	526	703	1023	340	0	239	11	400	20.3	6.2	2.4	3.5	....

• NORRIS, Sylvester
Sylvester Norris

Born: Feb. 18, 1957. Jackson, MS, United States.   Height: 6'11".   Weight: 220 lbs.   Drafted: 1979   College: Jackson State

YEAR	TEAM	GP	GS	MIN	PTS	FGM	FGA	FG%	3PM	3PA	3P%	FTM	FTA	FT%	ORB	DRB	TRB	AST	PF	DQ	STL	BLK	TO	MPG	PPG	RPG	APG	PCM
79-80	San Antonio	17	....	189	40	18	43	.419	0	0	.000	4	6	.667	10	33	43	6	41	1	3	12	19	11.1	2.4	2.5	0.4	.210
NBA Season Totals		17	....	189	40	18	43	.419	0	0	.000	4	6	.667	10	33	43	6	41	1	3	12	19	11.1	2.4	2.5	0.4	

• NORRIS, Woody
Woody Norris

Born: 1919.   Height: 6'1".   Weight: 170 lbs.   Drafted: —   College: Butler

YEAR	TEAM	GP	GS	MIN	PTS	FGM	FGA	FG%	3PM	3PA	3P%	FTM	FTA	FT%	ORB	DRB	TRB	AST	PF	DQ	STL	BLK	TO	MPG	PPG	RPG	APG	PCM
41-42	Indianapolis-N	7	....	....	43	20	....	....	....	....	....	3	....	....	....	....	....	....	....	....	....	....	....	6.1	....	....	....
45-46	Indianapolis-N	21	....	....	188	83	....	....	....	....	....	22	29	.759	....	....	....	....	....	....	....	....	....	9.0	....	....	....
46-47	Indianapolis-N	38	....	....	102	42	....	....	....	....	....	18	36	.500	....	....	....	31	....	....	....	....	....	2.7	....	....	....
47-48	Indianapolis-N	10	....	....	25	9	....	....	....	....	....	7	11	.636	....	....	....	....	....	....	....	....	....	2.5	....	....	....
NBL Season Totals		76	....	....	358	154	....	....	....	....	....	50	76		....	....	....	31	....	....	....	....	....	4.7	....	....	....
41-42	Indianapolis-N	2	....	....	9	2	....	....	....	....	....	5	....	....	....	....	....	....	....	....	....	....	....	4.5	....	....	....
46-47	Indianapolis-N	3	....	....	2	1	....	....	....	....	....	0	0	.000	....	....	....	....	....	....	....	....	....	0.7	....	....	....
NBL Playoff Totals		5	....	....	11	3	....	....	....	....	....	5	0		....	....	....	....	....	....	....	....	....	2.2	....	....	....

• NORWOOD, Willie
Willie B. Norwood

Born: Aug. 8, 1947. Carrolton, MS, United States.   Height: 6'7".   Weight: 220 lbs.   Drafted: 1969   College: Alcorn A&M

YEAR	TEAM	GP	GS	MIN	PTS	FGM	FGA	FG%	3PM	3PA	3P%	FTM	FTA	FT%	ORB	DRB	TRB	AST	PF	DQ	STL	BLK	TO	MPG	PPG	RPG	APG	PCM
71-72	Detroit	78	....	1272	584	222	440	.505	....	....		140	215	.651	....	....	316	43	229	4	....	....	....	16.3	7.5	4.1	0.6	.461
72-73	Detroit	79	....	1282	652	249	504	.494	....	....		154	225	.684	....	....	324	56	182	0	....	....	....	16.2	8.3	4.1	0.7	.520
73-74	Detroit	74	....	1178	589	247	484	.510	....	....		95	143	.664	95	134	229	58	156	2	60	9	....	15.9	8.0	3.1	0.8	.477
74-75	Detroit	24	....	347	159	64	123	.520	....	....		31	42	.738	31	57	88	16	51	0	23	0	....	14.5	6.6	3.7	0.7	.506
75-76	Seattle	64	....	1004	444	146	301	.485	....	....		152	203	.749	91	138	229	59	139	3	42	4	....	15.7	6.9	3.6	0.9	.491
76-77	Seattle	76	....	1647	583	216	461	.469	....	....		151	206	.733	127	165	292	99	191	1	62	6	....	21.7	7.7	3.8	1.3	.382
77-78	Detroit	16	....	260	88	34	82	.415	....	....		20	29	.690	27	27	54	14	45	0	13	3	18	16.3	5.5	3.4	0.9	.322
77-78	Portland	19	....	351	110	40	99	.404	....	....		30	46	.652	22	43	65	19	56	1	18	0	40	18.5	5.8	3.4	1.0	.245
NBA Season Totals		430	....	7341	3209	1218	2494	.488	....	....		773	1109	.697	393	564	1597	364	1049	11	218	22	58	17.1	7.5	3.7	0.8	....
73-74	Detroit	5	....	31	18	7	11	.636	....	....		4	4	1.000	1	2	3	1	7	0	1	1	....	6.2	3.6	0.6	0.2	.494
75-76	Seattle	6	....	215	59	24	58	.414	....	....		11	18	.611	20	18	38	8	25	3	7	1	....	35.8	9.8·	6.3	1.3	.269
77-78	Portland	3	....	44	15	7	12	.583	....	....		1	1	1.000	1	3	4	4	11	1	0	1	2	14.7	5.0	1.3	1.3	.294
NBA Playoff Totals		14	....	290	92	38	81	.469	....	....		16	23	.696	22	23	45	13	43	4	8	3	2	20.7	6.6	3.2	0.9	....

• NOSTRAND, George
George Thomas Nostrand

Born: Jan. 25, 1924. Uniondale, NY, United States. Died: Nov.8, 1981.   Height: 6'8".   Weight: 195 lbs.   Drafted: —   College: Wyoming

YEAR	TEAM	GP	GS	MIN	PTS	FGM	FGA	FG%	3PM	3PA	3P%	FTM	FTA	FT%	ORB	DRB	TRB	AST	PF	DQ	STL	BLK	TO	MPG	PPG	RPG	APG	PCM
46-47	Toronto	13	....	....	116	46	136	.338	....	....		24	61	.393	....	....	10	22	....	....	....	....	....	8.9	....	0.8	....
46-47	Cleveland	48	....	....	366	146	520	.281	....	....		74	149	.497	....	....	21	123	....	....	....	....	....	7.6	....	0.4	....
47-48	Providence	45	....	....	521	196	660	.297	....	....		129	239	.540	....	....	30	148	....	....	....	....	....	11.6	....	0.7	....
48-49	Providence	33	....	....	324	121	384	.315	....	....		82	149	.550	....	....	56	90	....	....	....	....	....	9.8	....	1.7	....
48-49	Boston	27	....	....	265	91	267	.341	....	....		83	135	.615	....	....	38	74	....	....	....	....	....	9.8	....	1.4	....
49-50	Boston	18	....	....	108	36	120	.300	....	....		36	59	.610	....	....	17	46	....	....	....	....	....	6.0	....	0.9	....
49-50	Tri-Cities	1	....	....	12	5	10	.500	....	....		2	5	.400	....	....	1	1	....	....	....	....	....	12.0	....	1.0	....
49-50	Chicago	36	....	....	92	37	125	.296	....	....		18	35	.514	....	....	11	71	....	....	....	....	....	2.6	....	0.3	....
NBA Season Totals		221	....	....	1804	678	2222	.305	....	....		448	832	.538	....	....	184	575	....	....	....	....	....	8.2	....	0.8	....
46-47	Cleveland	3	....	....	33	14	40	.350	....	....		5	7	.714	....	....	3	10	....	....	....	....	....	11.0	....	1.0	....
NBA Playoff Totals		3	....	....	33	14	40	.350	....	....		5	7	.714	....	....	3	10	....	....	....	....	....	11.0	....	1.0	....

YEAR	TEAM	GP	GS	MIN	PTS	FGM	FGA	FG%	3PM	3PA	3P%	FTM	FTA	FT%	ORB	DRB	TRB	AST	PF	DQ	STL	BLK	TO	MPG	PPG	RPG	APG	PCM

• NOSZKA, Stan   Stanley M. Noszka

Born: Sept. 9, 1920. Died: Nov.15, 1991.   Height: 6'1".   Weight: 185 lbs.   Drafted: —   College: Duquesne

YEAR	TEAM	GP	GS	MIN	PTS	FGM	FGA	FG%	3PM	3PA	3P%	FTM	FTA	FT%	ORB	DRB	TRB	AST	PF	DQ	STL	BLK	TO	MPG	PPG	RPG	APG	PCM
45-46	Youngstown-N	2	....	....	1	0	....	....	....	....	....	1							....	....					0.5	....	....	....
46-47	Pittsburgh	58	....	....	507	199	693	.287	....	....	....	109	157	.694					39	163					8.7	....	0.7	....
47-48	Boston	22	....	....	78	27	97	.278	....	....	....	24	35	.686					4	52					3.5	....	0.2	....
48-49	Boston	30	....	....	75	30	123	.244	....	....	....	15	30	.500					25	56					2.5	....	0.8	....
NBA Season Totals		110	....	....	660	256	913	.280	....	....	....	148	222	.667					68	271					6.0	....	0.6	....
NBL Season Totals		2	....	....	1	0	....	....	....	....	....	1													0.5	....	....	....
Career Totals		112	....	....	661	256	913	....	....	....	....	149	222						68	271					5.9	....	0.6	....
47-48	Boston	3	....	....	25	10	30	.333	....	....	....	5	8	.625					2	11					8.3	....	0.7	....
NBA Playoff Totals		3	....	....	25	10	30	.333	....	....	....	5	8	.625					2	11					8.3	....	0.7	....

• NOVAK, Mike   Michael D. Novak

Born: Apr. 23, 1915. Chicago, IL, United States. Died: Aug.15, 1978.   Height: 6'9".   Weight: 219 lbs.   Drafted: —   College: Loyola (IL)

YEAR	TEAM	GP	GS	MIN	PTS	FGM	FGA	FG%	3PM	3PA	3P%	FTM	FTA	FT%	ORB	DRB	TRB	AST	PF	DQ	STL	BLK	TO	MPG	PPG	RPG	APG	PCM
39-40	Chicago-N	28	....	....	293	114	....	....	....	....	....	65													10.5	....	....	....
40-41	Chicago-N	23	....	....	146	56	....	....	....	....	....	34													6.3	....	....	....
41-42	Chicago-N	19	....	....	147	58	....	....	....	....	....	31													7.7	....	....	....
42-43	Chicago-N	18	....	....	135	50	....	....	....	....	....	35													7.5	....	....	....
43-44	Sheboygan-N	22	....	....	92	39	....	....	....	....	....	14													4.2	....	....	....
44-45	Sheboygan-N	27	....	....	233	88	....	....	....	....	....	57													8.6	....	....	....
45-46	Sheboygan-N	34	....	....	310	111	....	....	....	....	....	88	144	.611											9.1	....	....	....
46-47	Sheboygan-N	3	....	....	10	3	....	....	....	....	....	4	7	.571											3.3	....	....	....
46-47	Syracuse-N	33	....	....	369	150	....	....	....	....	....	69	129	.535											11.2	....	....	....
47-48	Syracuse-N	60	....	....	546	211	....	....	....	....	....	124	201	.617					....	201					9.1	....	....	....
48-49	Rochester	60	....	....	320	124	363	.342	....	....	....	72	124	.581				112	188						5.3	....	1.9	....
49-50	Rochester	5	....	....	3	1	11	.091	....	....	....	1	1	1.000				4	10						0.6	....	0.8	....
49-50	Philadelphia	55	....	....	96	36	138	.261	....	....	....	24	46	.522				57	129						1.7	....	1.0	....
53-54	Syracuse	5	24	....	1	0	7	.000	....	....	....	1	2	.500		2	2	9	0				4.8	0.2	0.4	0.4	-.147
NBA Season Totals		125	24	....	420	161	519	.310	....	....	....	98	173	.566		....	2	175	336	0		....		0.2	3.4	0.0	1.4	....
NBL Season Totals		267	....	....	2281	880	....	....	....	....	....	521	481				....	201						8.5	....	....	....
Career Totals		392	....	24	2701	1041	519	....	....	....	....	619	654			....	2	175	537	0		....		0.1	6.9	0.0	0.4	....
42-43	Chicago-N	3	....	....	13	3	....	....	....	....	....	7	....											4.3	....	....	....
43-44	Sheboygan-N	6	....	....	16	6	....	....	....	....	....	4												2.7	....	....	....
44-45	Sheboygan-N	8	....	....	64	24	....	....	....	....	....	16												8.0	....	....	....
45-46	Sheboygan-N	8	....	....	65	22	....	....	....	....	....	21	34	.618										8.1	....	....	....
46-47	Syracuse-N	4	....	....	65	26	....	....	....	....	....	13	21	.619										16.3	....	....	....
47-48	Syracuse-N	3	....	....	22	9	....	....	....	....	....	4	5	.800										7.3	....	....	....
48-49	Rochester	4	....	....	13	6	22	.273	....	....	....	1	1	1.000				10	13					3.3	....	2.5	....
NBA Playoff Totals		4	....	....	13	6	22	.273	....	....	....	1	1	1.000				10	13					3.3	....	2.5	....
NBL Playoff Totals		32	....	....	245	90	....	....	....	....	....	65	60											7.7	....	....	....
Career Playoff Totals		36	....	....	258	96	22	....	....	....	....	66	61					10	13					7.2	....	0.3	....

• NOVOTNY, John   John Novotny

Born: 1918.   Height: 5'10".   Weight: 165 lbs.   Drafted: —   College: Appalachian State

YEAR	TEAM	GP	GS	MIN	PTS	FGM	FGA	FG%	3PM	3PA	3P%	FTM	FTA	FT%	ORB	DRB	TRB	AST	PF	DQ	STL	BLK	TO	MPG	PPG	RPG	APG	PCM
44-45	Pittsburgh-N	1	....	....	4	2	....	....	....	....	....	0													4.0	....	....	....
NBL Season Totals		1	....	....	4	2	....	....	....	....	....	0	....												4.0	....	....	....

• NOWAK, Paul   Paul (Butch, Giz) Nowak

Born: Mar. 15, 1914. South Bend, IN, United States. Died: Jan.10, 1983.   Height: 6'5".   Weight: 205 lbs.   Drafted: —   College: Notre Dame

YEAR	TEAM	GP	GS	MIN	PTS	FGM	FGA	FG%	3PM	3PA	3P%	FTM	FTA	FT%	ORB	DRB	TRB	AST	PF	DQ	STL	BLK	TO	MPG	PPG	RPG	APG	PCM
38-39	Non-Skids-N	15	....	....	80	33	....	....	....	....	....	14	....						....	....					5.3	....	....	....
39-40	Non-Skids-N	26	....	....	124	45	....	....	....	....	....	34													4.8	....	....	....
40-41	Non-Skids-N	18	....	....	45	13	....	....	....	....	....	19													2.5	....	....	....
41-42	Toledo-N	1	....	....	0	0	....	....	....	....	....	0													0.0	....	....	....
NBL Season Totals		60	....	....	249	91	....	....	....	....	....	67													4.2	....	....	....
39-40	Non-Skids-N	8	....	....	34	13	....	....	....	....	....	8													4.3	....	....	....
40-41	Non-Skids-N	2	....	....	7	1	....	....	....	....	....	5													3.5	....	....	....
NBL Playoff Totals		10	....	....	41	14	....	....	....	....	....	13													4.1	....	....	....

• NOWELL, Mel   Melvyn P. Nowell

Born: Dec. 27, 1939.   Height: 6'2".   Weight: 170 lbs.   Drafted: 1962   College: Ohio State

YEAR	TEAM	GP	GS	MIN	PTS	FGM	FGA	FG%	3PM	3PA	3P%	FTM	FTA	FT%	ORB	DRB	TRB	AST	PF	DQ	STL	BLK	TO	MPG	PPG	RPG	APG	PCM
62-63	Chicago	39	....	589	232	92	237	.388	....	....	....	48	66	.727			67	84	86	0		....		15.1	5.9	1.7	2.2	.392
67-68	New Jersey-A	76	....	1555	731	273	679	.402	9	32	.281	176	213	.826			193	155	188	1		....	142	20.5	9.6	2.5	2.0	.413
NBA Season Totals		39	....	589	232	92	237	.388	....	....	....	48	66	.727			67	84	86	0		....		15.1	5.9	1.7	2.2	....
ABA Season Totals		76	....	1555	731	273	679	.402	9	32	.281	176	213	.826			193	155	188	1		....	142	20.5	9.6	2.5	2.0	....
Career Totals		115	....	2144	963	365	916	.398	9	32	.281	224	279	.803			260	239	274	1		....	142	18.6	8.4	2.3	2.1	....

NOWITZKI, Dirk

Dirk Nowitzki

Born: June 19, 1978. Wurzburg, Germany.   Height: 6'11".   Weight: 237 lbs.   Drafted: 1998   College: none (HS: Rontgen Gymnasium, GER)

YEAR	TEAM	GP	GS	MIN	PTS	FGM	FGA	FG%	3PM	3PA	3P%	FTM	FTA	FT%	ORB	DRB	TRB	AST	PF	DQ	STL	BLK	TO	MPG	PPG	RPG	APG	PCM
98-99	Dallas	47	24	958	385	136	336	.405	14	68	.206	99	128	.773	41	121	162	47	105	5	29	27	73	20.4	8.2	3.4	1.0	.343
99-00	Dallas	82	81	2938	1435	515	1118	.461	116	306	.379	289	348	.830	102	430	532	203	256	4	63	68	141	35.8	17.5	6.5	2.5	.490
00-01	Dallas	82	82	3125	1784	591	1247	.474	151	390	.387	451	538	.838	119	635	754	173	245	1	79	101	156	38.1	21.8	9.2	2.1	.619
01-02	Dallas	76	76	2891	1779	600	1258	.477	139	350	.397	440	516	.853	120	635	755	186	222	2	83	77	145	38.0	23.4	9.9	2.4	.674
02-03	Dallas	80	80	3118	2011	690	1489	.463	148	390	.379	483	548	.881	81	710	791	239	206	2	111	82	152	39.0	25.1	9.9	3.0	.699
NBA Season Totals		367	343	13030	7394	2532	5448	.465	568	1504	.378	1762	2078	.848	463	2531	2994	848	1034	14	365	355	667	35.5	20.1	8.2	2.3	....
00-01	Dallas	10	10	399	234	69	163	.423	13	46	.283	83	94	.883	14	67	81	14	37	1	11	8	14	39.9	23.4	8.1	1.4	.553
01-02	Dallas	8	8	357	227	73	164	.445	16	28	.571	65	74	.878	17	88	105	18	27	1	16	6	22	44.6	28.4	13.1	2.3	.681
02-03	Dallas	17	17	722	430	150	313	.479	27	61	.443	103	113	.912	15	181	196	37	52	0	21	16	40	42.5	25.3	11.5	2.2	.650
NBA Playoff Totals		35	35	1478	891	292	640	.456	56	135	.415	251	281	.893	46	336	382	69	116	2	48	30	76	42.2	25.5	10.9	2.0	....

NUGENT, Bob

Bob Nugent

Born: 1915.   Height: 5'11".   Weight: 170 lbs.   Drafted: —   College: none

YEAR	TEAM	GP	GS	MIN	PTS	FGM	FGA	FG%	3PM	3PA	3P%	FTM	FTA	FT%	ORB	DRB	TRB	AST	PF	DQ	STL	BLK	TO	MPG	PPG	RPG	APG	PCM
46-47	Syracuse-N	31	....	....	109	39	....	....	....	....	....	31	45	.689	....	....	....	....	56	....	....	....	....	....	3.5	....	....	....
NBL Season Totals		31	....	....	109	39	....	....	....	....	....	31	45	....	....	....	....	....	56	....	....	....	....	....	3.5	....	....	....
46-47	Syracuse-N	4	....	....	17	6	....	....	....	....	....	5	6	.833	....	....	....	....	....	....	....	....	....	....	4.3	....	....	....
NBL Playoff Totals		4	....	....	17	6	....	....	....	....	....	5	6	....	....	....	....	....	....	....	....	....	....	....	4.3	....	....	....

NUTT, Dennis

Dennis Clay Nutt

Born: Mar. 25, 1963. Little Rock, AR, United States.   Height: 6'2".   Weight: 170 lbs.   Drafted: —   College: Texas Christian

YEAR	TEAM	GP	GS	MIN	PTS	FGM	FGA	FG%	3PM	3PA	3P%	FTM	FTA	FT%	ORB	DRB	TRB	AST	PF	DQ	STL	BLK	TO	MPG	PPG	RPG	APG	PCM
86-87	Dallas	25	0	91	57	16	40	.400	5	17	.294	20	22	.909	1	7	8	16	6	0	7	0	10	3.6	2.3	0.3	0.6	.579
NBA Season Totals		25	0	91	57	16	40	.400	5	17	.294	20	22	.909	1	7	8	16	6	0	7	0	10	3.6	2.3	0.3	0.6	....
86-87	Dallas	1	0	10	2	1	5	.200	0	2	.000	0	0	.000	1	1	2	1	0	0	0	0	1	10.0	2.0	2.0	1.0	.028
NBA Playoff Totals		1	0	10	2	1	5	.200	0	2	.000	0	0	.000	1	1	2	1	0	0	0	0	1	10.0	2.0	2.0	1.0	....

NWOSU, Julius

Obinna Julius Nwosu

Born: May 1, 1971. Nkwere, Nigeria.   Height: 6'10".   Weight: 255 lbs.   Drafted: —   College: Liberty

YEAR	TEAM	GP	GS	MIN	PTS	FGM	FGA	FG%	3PM	3PA	3P%	FTM	FTA	FT%	ORB	DRB	TRB	AST	PF	DQ	STL	BLK	TO	MPG	PPG	RPG	APG	PCM
94-95	San Antonio	23	0	84	31	9	28	.321	0	0	.000	13	17	.765	11	13	24	3	20	0	0	3	9	3.7	1.3	1.0	0.1	.262
NBA Season Totals		23	0	84	31	9	28	.321	0	0	.000	13	17	.765	11	13	24	3	20	0	0	3	9	3.7	1.3	1.0	0.1	....
94-95	San Antonio	2	0	7	0	0	2	.000	0	0	.000	0	0	.000	1	1	2	0	1	0	0	0	1	3.5	0.0	1.0	0.0	-.201
NBA Playoff Totals		2	0	7	0	0	2	.000	0	0	.000	0	0	.000	1	1	2	0	1	0	0	0	1	3.5	0.0	1.0	0.0	....

OAKLEY, Charles

Charles Oakley

Born: Dec. 18, 1963. Cleveland, OH, United States.   Height: 6'8".   Weight: 225 lbs.   Drafted: 1985   College: Virginia Union

YEAR	TEAM	GP	GS	MIN	PTS	FGM	FGA	FG%	3PM	3PA	3P%	FTM	FTA	FT%	ORB	DRB	TRB	AST	PF	DQ	STL	BLK	TO	MPG	PPG	RPG	APG	PCM
85-86	Chicago	77	30	1772	740	281	541	.519	0	3	.000	178	269	.662	255	409	664	133	250	9	68	30	177	23.0	9.6	8.6	1.7	.579
86-87	Chicago	82	81	2980	1192	468	1052	.445	11	30	.367	245	357	.686	299	775	1074	296	315	4	85	36	295	36.3	14.5	13.1	3.6	.538
87-88	Chicago	82	82	2816	1014	375	776	.483	3	12	.250	261	359	.727	326	740	1066	248	272	2	68	28	238	34.3	12.4	13.0	3.0	.566
88-89	New York	82	82	2604	1061	426	835	.510	12	48	.250	197	255	.773	343	518	861	187	270	1	104	14	246	31.8	12.9	10.5	2.3	.541
89-90	New York	61	61	2196	889	336	641	.524	0	3	.000	217	285	.761	258	469	727	146	220	3	64	16	165	36.0	14.6	11.9	2.4	.558
90-91	New York	76	74	2739	853	307	595	.516	0	2	.000	239	305	.784	305	615	920	204	288	4	62	17	213	36.0	11.2	12.1	2.7	.500
91-92	New York	82	82	2309	506	210	402	.522	0	3	.000	86	117	.735	256	444	700	133	258	4	67	15	123	28.2	6.2	8.5	1.6	.411
92-93	New York	82	82	2230	565	219	431	.508	0	1	.000	127	176	.722	288	420	708	126	289	5	85	15	123	27.2	6.9	8.6	1.5	.441
93-94	New York	82	82	2932	969	363	760	.478	0	3	.000	243	313	.776	349	616	965	218	293	4	110	18	197	35.8	11.8	11.8	2.7	.510
94-95	New York	50	49	1567	506	192	393	.489	3	12	.250	119	150	.793	155	290	445	126	179	3	60	7	105	31.3	10.1	8.9	2.5	.469
95-96	New York	53	51	1775	604	211	448	.471	7	26	.269	175	210	.833	162	298	460	137	195	6	58	14	106	33.5	11.4	8.7	2.6	.461
96-97	New York	80	80	2873	864	339	694	.488	5	19	.263	181	224	.808	246	535	781	221	305	4	111	21	168	35.9	10.8	9.8	2.8	.453
97-98	New York	79	79	2734	711	307	698	.440	0	6	.000	97	114	.851	218	506	724	201	280	4	123	22	126	34.6	9.0	9.2	2.5	.408
98-99	Toronto	50	50	1633	348	140	327	.428	1	5	.200	67	83	.807	96	278	374	168	182	4	46	21	96	32.7	7.0	7.5	3.4	.360
99-00	Toronto	80	80	2431	548	234	560	.418	14	41	.341	66	85	.776	117	423	540	253	294	6	102	45	154	30.4	6.9	6.8	3.2	.358
00-01	Toronto	78	77	2767	748	305	786	.388	11	49	.224	127	152	.836	142	599	741	264	258	0	76	48	139	35.5	9.6	9.5	3.4	.409
01-02	Chicago	57	36	1383	216	97	263	.369	1	6	.167	21	28	.750	72	271	343	114	175	2	49	11	87	24.3	3.8	6.0	2.0	.285
02-03	Washington	42	1	514	74	23	55	.418	0	0	.000	28	34	.824	37	70	107	40	90	0	13	6	21	12.2	1.8	2.5	1.0	.273
NBA Season Totals		1275	1159	40255	12408	4833	10257	.471	68	269	.253	2674	3516	.761	3924	8276	12200	3215	4413	63	1351	384	2779	31.6	9.7	9.6	2.5	....
85-86	Chicago	3	3	88	30	11	21	.524	0	0	.000	8	13	.615	10	20	30	3	13	0	6	2	5	29.3	10.0	10.0	1.0	.525
86-87	Chicago	3	3	129	60	19	50	.380	2	4	.500	20	24	.833	17	29	46	6	13	0	4	1	8	43.0	20.0	15.3	2.0	.540
87-88	Chicago	10	10	373	101	40	91	.440	0	2	.000	21	24	.875	39	89	128	32	33	0	6	4	18	37.3	10.1	12.8	3.2	.490
88-89	New York	9	9	299	87	35	73	.479	1	2	.500	16	24	.667	43	58	101	11	31	1	12	1	22	33.2	9.7	11.2	1.2	.438
89-90	New York	10	8	336	121	43	84	.512	1	1	1.000	34	52	.654	39	71	110	27	33	1	11	2	22	33.6	12.1	11.0	2.7	.542
90-91	New York	3	3	100	23	10	21	.476	0	0	.000	3	6	.500	15	16	31	3	10	0	2	1	7	33.3	7.7	10.3	1.0	.337
91-92	New York	12	12	354	64	22	58	.379	0	0	.000	20	27	.741	44	64	108	8	36	0	8	5	5	29.5	5.3	9.0	0.7	.332
92-93	New York	15	15	507	166	63	131	.481	0	0	.000	40	55	.727	71	94	165	17	51	1	16	2	36	33.8	11.1	11.0	1.1	.448
93-94	New York	25	25	992	329	125	262	.477	0	0	.000	79	102	.775	116	176	292	59	87	1	35	5	65	39.7	13.2	11.7	2.4	.465
94-95	New York	11	11	421	144	49	109	.450	4	10	.400	42	51	.824	31	62	93	41	42	0	19	6	24	38.3	13.1	8.5	3.7	.464
95-96	New York	8	8	308	105	39	78	.500	2	6	.333	25	36	.694	28	41	69	14	33	1	8	0	18	38.5	13.1	8.6	1.8	.352
96-97	New York	10	10	358	98	38	86	.442	0	1	.000	22	29	.759	23	65	88	16	37	0	22	3	18	35.8	9.8	8.8	1.6	.387

YEAR	TEAM	GP	GS	MIN	PTS	FGM	FGA	FG%	3PM	3PA	3P%	FTM	FTA	FT%	ORB	DRB	TRB	AST	PF	DQ	STL	BLK	TO	MPG	PPG	RPG	APG	PCM
97-98	New York	10	10	342	81	29	71	.408	0	0	.000	23	25	.920	21	64	85	14	38	1	11	2	13	34.2	8.1	8.5	1.4	.343
99-00	Toronto	3	3	110	30	14	29	.483	2	7	.286	0	1	.000	2	21	23	11	14	0	6	1	5	36.7	10.0	7.7	3.7	.403
00-01	Toronto	12	12	391	111	47	108	.435	3	8	.375	14	17	.824	20	56	76	21	29	0	12	7	22	32.6	9.3	6.3	1.8	.334
NBA Playoff Totals		144	142	5108	1550	584	1272	.459	15	41	.366	367	486	.755	519	926	1445	283	503	6	178	42	308	35.5	10.8	10.0	2.0	

• O'BANNON, Charles

Charles Edward O'Bannon

Born: Feb. 22, 1975. Bellflower, CA, United States.   Height: 6'5".   Weight: 209 lbs.   Drafted: 1997   College: UCLA

YEAR	TEAM	GP	GS	MIN	PTS	FGM	FGA	FG%	3PM	3PA	3P%	FTM	FTA	FT%	ORB	DRB	TRB	AST	PF	DQ	STL	BLK	TO	MPG	PPG	RPG	APG	PCM
97-98	Detroit	30	0	234	64	26	69	.377	0	3	.000	12	15	.800	14	19	33	17	15	0	9	1	9	7.8	2.1	1.1	0.6	.282
98-99	Detroit	18	1	165	56	24	56	.429	0	1	.000	8	8	1.000	18	16	34	12	22	0	2	3	8	9.2	3.1	1.9	0.7	.356
NBA Season Totals		48	1	399	120	50	125	.400	0	4	.000	20	23	.870	32	35	67	29	37	0	11	4	17	8.3	2.5	1.4	0.6	....
98-99	Detroit	4	0	9	4	2	3	.667	0	0	.000	0	0	.000	1	0	1	1	0	0	0	0	3	2.3	1.0	0.3	0.3	.272
NBA Playoff Totals		4	0	9	4	2	3	.667	0	0	.000	0	0	.000	1	0	1	1	0	0	0	0	3	2.3	1.0	0.3	0.3	

• O'BANNON, Ed

Edward Charles O'Bannon Jr.

Born: Aug. 14, 1972. Los Angeles, CA, United States.   Height: 6'8".   Weight: 222 lbs.   Drafted: 1995   College: UCLA

YEAR	TEAM	GP	GS	MIN	PTS	FGM	FGA	FG%	3PM	3PA	3P%	FTM	FTA	FT%	ORB	DRB	TRB	AST	PF	DQ	STL	BLK	TO	MPG	PPG	RPG	APG	PCM
95-96	New Jersey	64	29	1253	399	156	400	.390	10	56	.179	77	108	.713	65	103	168	63	95	0	44	11	64	19.6	6.2	2.6	1.0	.261
96-97	New Jersey	45	5	634	189	76	207	.367	17	60	.283	20	23	.870	41	71	112	28	78	0	24	10	14	14.1	4.2	2.5	0.6	.287
96-97	Dallas	19	0	175	46	17	72	.236	1	10	.100	11	12	.917	9	27	36	11	19	0	5	2	6	9.2	2.4	1.9	0.6	.181
NBA Season Totals		128	34	2062	634	249	679	.367	28	126	.222	108	143	.755	115	201	316	102	192	0	73	23	84	16.1	5.0	2.5	0.8	....

• OBERBRUNNER, Red

Red Oberbrunner

Born: Oct. 5, 1918. Died: Sept.6, 1991.   Height: 5'11".   Weight: 175 lbs.   Drafted: —   College: Notre Dame

YEAR	TEAM	GP	GS	MIN	PTS	FGM	FGA	FG%	3PM	3PA	3P%	FTM	FTA	FT%	ORB	DRB	TRB	AST	PF	DQ	STL	BLK	TO	MPG	PPG	RPG	APG	PCM
41-42	Fort Wayne-N	19	....	....	42	17	....	....	....	....	....	8													2.2			
NBL Season Totals		19	....	....	42	17	....	....	....	....	....	8													2.2			
41-42	Fort Wayne-N	6	....	....	12	4	....	....	....	....	....	4													2.0			
NBL Playoff Totals		6	....	....	12	4	....	....	....	....	....	4													2.0			

• OBERST, Jack

Jack Oberst

Born: 1918.   Height: 5'11".   Weight: 175 lbs.   Drafted: —   College: Baldwin-Wallace

YEAR	TEAM	GP	GS	MIN	PTS	FGM	FGA	FG%	3PM	3PA	3P%	FTM	FTA	FT%	ORB	DRB	TRB	AST	PF	DQ	STL	BLK	TO	MPG	PPG	RPG	APG	PCM
45-46	Cleveland-N	9	....	....	10	2	....	....	....	....	....	6													1.1			
NBL Season Totals		9	....	....	10	2	....	....	....	....	....	6													1.1			

• O'BOYLE, John

John W. O'Boyle

Born: Mar. 7, 1928.   Height: 6'2".   Weight: 185 lbs.   Drafted: —   College: Colorado State

YEAR	TEAM	GP	GS	MIN	PTS	FGM	FGA	FG%	3PM	3PA	3P%	FTM	FTA	FT%	ORB	DRB	TRB	AST	PF	DQ	STL	BLK	TO	MPG	PPG	RPG	APG	PCM
52-53	Milwaukee	5	....	97	21	8	26	.308	....	....	....	5	7	.714	....	....	10	5	20	1	....	....	....	19.4	4.2	2.0	1.0	.140
NBA Season Totals		5	....	97	21	8	26	.308	....	....	....	5	7	.714	....	....	10	5	20	1	....	....	....	19.4	4.2	2.0	1.0	

• O'BRIEN, Bill

Bill O'Brien

Born: 1918.   Height: 6'4".   Weight: 185 lbs.   Drafted: —   College: Loyola (IL)

YEAR	TEAM	GP	GS	MIN	PTS	FGM	FGA	FG%	3PM	3PA	3P%	FTM	FTA	FT%	ORB	DRB	TRB	AST	PF	DQ	STL	BLK	TO	MPG	PPG	RPG	APG	PCM
40-41	Chicago-N	19	....	....	20	5	....	....	....	....	....	10													1.1			
NBL Season Totals		19	....	....	20	5	....	....	....	....	....	10													1.1			

• O'BRIEN, Bob

Robert O'Brien

Born: Jan. 26, 1927.   Height: 6'4".   Weight: 190 lbs.   Drafted: —   College: Pepperdine

YEAR	TEAM	GP	GS	MIN	PTS	FGM	FGA	FG%	3PM	3PA	3P%	FTM	FTA	FT%	ORB	DRB	TRB	AST	PF	DQ	STL	BLK	TO	MPG	PPG	RPG	APG	PCM
47-48	Philadelphia	22	....	....	49	17	81	.210	....	....	....	15	26	.577	....	....	....	1	40	....	....	....	....	2.2		0.0		
48-49	Philadelphia	16	....	....	15	5	32	.156	....	....	....	5	14	.357	....	....	....	8	21	....	....	....	....	0.9		0.5		
48-49	St. Louis	8	....	....	17	5	18	.278	....	....	....	7	18	.389	....	....	....	1	11	....	....	....	....	2.1		0.1		
NBA Season Totals		46	....	....	81	27	131	.206	....	....	....	27	58	.466	....	....	....	10	72	....	....	....	....	1.8		0.2		
47-48	Philadelphia	9	....	....	28	9	38	.237	....	....	....	10	15	.667	....	....	....	3	13	....	....	....	....	3.1		0.3		
NBA Playoff Totals		9	....	....	28	9	38	.237	....	....	....	10	15	.667	....	....	....	3	13	....	....	....	....	3.1		0.3		

• O'BRIEN, Jack

John J. O'Brien Jr.

Born: 1916.   Height: 6'1".   Weight: 180 lbs.   Drafted: —   College: Columbia

YEAR	TEAM	GP	GS	MIN	PTS	FGM	FGA	FG%	3PM	3PA	3P%	FTM	FTA	FT%	ORB	DRB	TRB	AST	PF	DQ	STL	BLK	TO	MPG	PPG	RPG	APG	PCM
41-42	Wingfoots-N	7	....	....	17	5	....	....	....	....	....	7													2.4			
NBL Season Totals		7	....	....	17	5	....	....	....	....	....	7													2.4			
41-42	Wingfoots-N	3	....	....	11	2	....	....	....	....	....	7													3.7			
NBL Playoff Totals		3	....	....	11	2	....	....	....	....	....	7													3.7			

YEAR	TEAM	GP	GS	MIN	PTS	FGM	FGA	FG%	3PM	3PA	3P%	FTM	FTA	FT%	ORB	DRB	TRB	AST	PF	DQ	STL	BLK	TO	MPG	PPG	RPG	APG	PCM

● O'BRIEN, Jim

James M. O'Brien

Born: Nov. 7, 1951. Falls Church, VA, United States.　　Height: 6'7".　　Weight: 200 lbs.　　Drafted: 1973　　College: Maryland

YEAR	TEAM	GP	GS	MIN	PTS	FGM	FGA	FG%	3PM	3PA	3P%	FTM	FTA	FT%	ORB	DRB	TRB	AST	PF	DQ	STL	BLK	TO	MPG	PPG	RPG	APG	PCM
73-74	New York-A	11	....	54	39	15	37	.405	0	4	.000	9	15	.600	13	4	17	6	5	....	3	3	8	4.9	3.5	1.5	0.5	.682
74-75	Memphis-A	47	....	611	229	88	203	.433	6	26	.231	47	60	.783	45	76	121	81	56	....	38	23	73	13.0	4.9	2.6	1.7	.481
ABA Season Totals		58	....	665	268	103	240	.429	6	30	.200	56	75	.747	58	80	138	87	61	....	41	26	81	11.5	4.6	2.4	1.5	....
73-74	New York-A	4	....	9	8	4	10	.400	0	0	.000	0	0	.000	1	1	2	3	1	....	0	0	0	2.3	2.0	0.5	0.8	.841
74-75	Memphis-A	3	....	33	6	2	9	.222	0	1	.000	2	2	1.000	1	5	6	5	2	....	3	0	1	11.0	2.0	2.0	1.7	.296
ABA Playoff Totals		7	....	42	14	6	19	.316	0	1	.000	2	2	1.000	2	6	8	8	3	....	3	0	1	6.0	2.0	1.1	1.1	....

● O'BRIEN, Jimmy

James J. O'Brien

Born: Apr. 9, 1949. New York, NY, United States.　　Height: 6'1".　　Weight: 170 lbs.　　Drafted: 1971　　College: Boston College

YEAR	TEAM	GP	GS	MIN	PTS	FGM	FGA	FG%	3PM	3PA	3P%	FTM	FTA	FT%	ORB	DRB	TRB	AST	PF	DQ	STL	BLK	TO	MPG	PPG	RPG	APG	PCM
71-72	Kentucky-A	66	....	1424	336	139	354	.393	4	23	.174	54	66	.818	46	128	174	299	152	0	....	....	114	21.6	5.1	2.6	4.5	.395
71-72	Pittsburgh-A	18	....	354	82	34	82	.415	3	9	.333	11	14	.786	13	19	32	74	37	0	....	....	38	19.7	4.6	1.8	4.1	.377
72-73	Kentucky-A	68	....	1014	320	126	317	.397	0	9	.000	68	89	.764	27	65	92	174	103	0	....	....	77	14.9	4.7	1.4	2.6	.362
73-74	Kentucky-A	46	....	761	285	119	284	.419	2	10	.200	45	54	.833	32	53	85	139	47	0	34	1	70	16.5	6.2	1.8	3.0	.461
73-74	San Diego-A	26	....	559	223	92	229	.402	5	17	.294	34	41	.829	17	32	49	115	32	....	29	0	43	21.5	8.6	1.9	4.4	.469
74-75	San Diego-A	79	....	2036	549	210	525	.400	4	34	.118	125	142	.880	50	136	186	443	147	....	89	2	192	25.8	6.9	2.4	5.6	.420
ABA Season Totals		303	....	6148	1795	720	1791	.402	18	102	.176	337	406	.830	185	433	618	1244	518	0	152	3	534	20.3	5.9	2.0	4.1	....
71-72	Kentucky-A	5	....	23	9	3	7	.429	0	1	.000	3	3	1.000	...	...	3	3	0	....	....	0	4.6	1.8	0.6	0.6	.499
72-73	Kentucky-A	19	....	435	106	33	93	.355	1	3	.333	39	45	.867	9	25	34	82	35	0	....	....	33	22.9	5.6	1.8	4.3	.355
73-74	San Diego-A	6	....	152	47	21	48	.438	1	3	.333	4	7	.571	1	8	9	26	6	....	3	1	7	25.3	7.8	1.5	4.3	.378
ABA Playoff Totals		30	....	610	162	57	148	.385	2	7	.286	46	55	.836	10	33	46	111	41	0	3	1	40	20.3	5.4	1.5	3.7	....

● O'BRIEN, Ralph

Ralph E. (Buckshot, Buck) O'Brien

Born: Apr. 8, 1928. Henshaw, KY, United States.　　Height: 5'9".　　Weight: 160 lbs.　　Drafted: 1950　　College: Butler

YEAR	TEAM	GP	GS	MIN	PTS	FGM	FGA	FG%	3PM	3PA	3P%	FTM	FTA	FT%	ORB	DRB	TRB	AST	PF	DQ	STL	BLK	TO	MPG	PPG	RPG	APG	PCM
51-52	Indianapolis	64	....	1577	578	228	613	.372	....	....	....	122	149	.819	....	....	122	124	115	0	....	....	....	24.6	9.0	1.9	1.9	.317
52-53	Ind/FtW/Bal	55	....	758	270	96	286	.336	....	....	....	78	92	.848	....	....	70	56	74	0	....	....	....	13.8	4.9	1.3	1.0	.294
NBA Season Totals		119	....	2335	848	324	899	.360	....	....	....	200	241	.830	....	....	192	180	189	0	....	....	....	19.6	7.1	1.6	1.5	....
51-52	Indianapolis	2	....	49	15	5	11	.455	....	....	....	5	5	1.000	....	....	3	3	1	0	....	....	....	24.5	7.5	1.5	1.5	.334
52-53	Baltimore	1	....	18	2	0	2	.000	....	....	....	2	2	1.000	....	....	1	0	2	0	....	....	....	18.0	2.0	1.0	0.0	.031
NBA Playoff Totals		3	....	67	17	5	13	.385	....	....	....	7	7	1.000	....	....	4	3	3	0	....	....	....	22.3	5.7	1.3	1.0	....

● O'BRIEN, Tommy

Thomas O'Brien

Born: 1916.　　Height: —　　Weight: —　　Drafted: —　　College: George Washington

YEAR	TEAM	GP	GS	MIN	PTS	FGM	FGA	FG%	3PM	3PA	3P%	FTM	FTA	FT%	ORB	DRB	TRB	AST	PF	DQ	STL	BLK	TO	MPG	PPG	RPG	APG	PCM
39-40	Non-Skids-N	13	....	....	21	9	....	....	....	....	....	3	....	....	....	....	....	....	....	....	....	....	....	1.6	....	....	....	....
40-41	Non-Skids-N	15	....	....	34	13	....	....	....	....	....	8	....	....	....	....	....	....	....	....	....	....	....	2.3	....	....	....	....
NBL Season Totals		28	....	....	55	22	....	....	....	....	....	11	....	....	....	....	....	....	....	....	....	....	....	2.0	....	....	....	....
39-40	Non-Skids-N	6	....	....	24	11	....	....	....	....	....	2	....	....	....	....	....	....	....	....	....	....	....	4.0	....	....	....	....
40-41	Non-Skids-N	1	....	....	2	1	....	....	....	....	....	0	....	....	....	....	....	....	....	....	....	....	....	2.0	....	....	....	....
NBL Playoff Totals		7	....	....	26	12	....	....	....	....	....	2	....	....	....	....	....	....	....	....	....	....	....	3.7	....	....	....	....

● OCHSENHIRT, Russ

Russ Ochsenhirt

Born: Feb. 7, 1912. Died: Dec.1974.　　Height: 6'3".　　Weight: 195 lbs.　　Drafted: —　　College: Pittsburgh

YEAR	TEAM	GP	GS	MIN	PTS	FGM	FGA	FG%	3PM	3PA	3P%	FTM	FTA	FT%	ORB	DRB	TRB	AST	PF	DQ	STL	BLK	TO	MPG	PPG	RPG	APG	PCM
37-38	Wingfoots-N	17	....	....	69	24	....	....	....	....	....	21	....	....	....	....	....	....	....	....	....	....	....	4.1	....	....	....	....
38-39	Wingfoots-N	24	....	....	103	40	....	....	....	....	....	23	....	....	....	....	....	....	....	....	....	....	....	4.3	....	....	....	....
NBL Season Totals		41	....	....	172	64	....	....	....	....	....	44	....	....	....	....	....	....	....	....	....	....	....	4.2	....	....	....	....
37-38	Wingfoots-N	5	....	....	26	9	....	....	....	....	....	8	....	....	....	....	....	....	....	....	....	....	....	5.2	....	....	....	....
NBL Playoff Totals		5	....	....	26	9	....	....	....	....	....	8	....	....	....	....	....	....	....	....	....	....	....	5.2	....	....	....	....

● O'CONNELL, Dermie

Dermott F. (Dermie) O'Connell

Born: Apr. 13, 1928. Died: Oct.5, 1988.　　Height: 6'　　Weight: 174 lbs.　　Drafted: —　　College: Holy Cross

YEAR	TEAM	GP	GS	MIN	PTS	FGM	FGA	FG%	3PM	3PA	3P%	FTM	FTA	FT%	ORB	DRB	TRB	AST	PF	DQ	STL	BLK	TO	MPG	PPG	RPG	APG	PCM
48-49	Boston	21	....	....	204	87	315	.276	....	....	....	30	56	.536	....	....	....	65	40	....	....	....	....	....	9.7	....	3.1	....
49-50	Boston	37	....	....	177	72	275	.262	....	....	....	33	58	.569	....	....	....	64	62	....	....	....	....	....	4.8	....	1.7	....
49-50	St. Louis	24	....	....	92	39	150	.260	....	....	....	14	31	.452	....	....	....	27	29	....	....	....	....	....	3.8	....	1.1	....
NBA Season Totals		82	....	....	473	198	740	.268	....	....	....	77	145	.531	....	....	....	156	131	....	....	....	....	....	5.8	....	1.9	....

● O'CONNOR, Connie

Connie O'Connor

Born: 1924.　　Height: 6'1".　　Weight: —　　Drafted: —　　College: South Dakota

YEAR	TEAM	GP	GS	MIN	PTS	FGM	FGA	FG%	3PM	3PA	3P%	FTM	FTA	FT%	ORB	DRB	TRB	AST	PF	DQ	STL	BLK	TO	MPG	PPG	RPG	APG	PCM
46-47	Detroit-N	36	....	....	196	82	....	....	....	....	....	32	78	.410	....	....	....	42	....	....	....	....	....	....	5.4	....	....	....
NBL Season Totals		36	....	....	196	82	....	....	....	....	....	32	78	....	....	....	....	42	....	....	....	....	....	....	5.4	....	....	....

YEAR	TEAM	GP	GS	MIN	PTS	FGM	FGA	FG%	3PM	3PA	3P%	FTM	FTA	FT%	ORB	DRB	TRB	AST	PF	DQ	STL	BLK	TO	MPG	PPG	RPG	APG	PCM

• ODOM, Lamar

Lamar Joseph Odom

Born: Nov. 6, 1979. Jamaica, NY, United States.　Height: 6'10".　Weight: 220 lbs.　Drafted: 1999　College: Rhode Island

YEAR	TEAM	GP	GS	MIN	PTS	FGM	FGA	FG%	3PM	3PA	3P%	FTM	FTA	FT%	ORB	DRB	TRB	AST	PF	DQ	STL	BLK	TO	MPG	PPG	RPG	APG	PCM
99-00	LA Clippers	76	70	2767	1259	449	1024	.438	59	164	.360	302	420	.719	159	436	595	317	291	13	91	95	258	36.4	16.6	7.8	4.2	.496
00-01	LA Clippers	76	74	2836	1304	481	1046	.460	80	253	.316	262	386	.679	110	482	592	392	236	4	74	122	264	37.3	17.2	7.8	5.2	.542
01-02	LA Clippers	29	25	999	379	151	360	.419	16	84	.190	61	93	.656	31	145	176	171	91	3	23	36	97	34.4	13.1	6.1	5.9	.446
02-03	LA Clippers	49	47	1679	714	268	611	.439	42	129	.326	136	175	.777	59	267	326	178	181	6	42	41	140	34.3	14.6	6.7	3.6	.442
NBA Season Totals		230	216	8281	3656	1349	3041	.444	197	630	.313	761	1074	.709	359	1330	1689	1058	799	26	230	294	759	36.0	15.9	7.3	4.6	

• O'DONNELL, Andy

Andrew J. O'Donnell

Born: Mar. 10, 1925.　Height: 6'1".　Weight: 180 lbs.　Drafted: —　College: Loyola (MD)

YEAR	TEAM	GP	GS	MIN	PTS	FGM	FGA	FG%	3PM	3PA	3P%	FTM	FTA	FT%	ORB	DRB	TRB	AST	PF	DQ	STL	BLK	TO	MPG	PPG	RPG	APG	PCM
49-50	Baltimore	25	....	....	90	38	108	.352	....	....	....	14	18	.778	....	....	....	17	32	....	....	....	....	....	3.6	....	0.7	....
NBA Season Totals		25	....	....	90	38	108	.352	....	....	....	14	18	.778	....	....	....	17	32	....	....	....	....	....	3.6	....	0.7	....

• O'DONNELL, Jim

James O'Donnell

Born: 1912.　Height: 6'1".　Weight: 180 lbs.　Drafted: —　College: Canisius

YEAR	TEAM	GP	GS	MIN	PTS	FGM	FGA	FG%	3PM	3PA	3P%	FTM	FTA	FT%	ORB	DRB	TRB	AST	PF	DQ	STL	BLK	TO	MPG	PPG	RPG	APG	PCM
37-38	Buffalo-N	8	....	....	10	3	....	....	....	....	....	4	....	....	....	....	....	....	....	....	....	....	....	....	1.3	....	....	....
NBL Season Totals		8	....	....	10	3	....	....	....	....	....	4	....	....	....	....	....	....	....	....	....	....	....	....	1.3	....	....	....

• O'DONNELL, Neil

Neil O'Donnell

Born: 1914.　Height: 6'5".　Weight: 210 lbs.　Drafted: —　College: Canisius

YEAR	TEAM	GP	GS	MIN	PTS	FGM	FGA	FG%	3PM	3PA	3P%	FTM	FTA	FT%	ORB	DRB	TRB	AST	PF	DQ	STL	BLK	TO	MPG	PPG	RPG	APG	PCM
37-38	Buffalo-N	9	....	....	35	14	....	....	....	....	....	7	....	....	....	....	....	....	....	....	....	....	....	....	3.9	....	....	....
NBL Season Totals		9	....	....	35	14	....	....	....	....	....	7	....	....	....	....	....	....	....	....	....	....	....	....	3.9	....	....	....

• OGDEN, Bud

Carlos Ogden

Born: Dec. 29, 1946. San Luis Obispo, CA, United States.　Height: 6'6".　Weight: 215 lbs.　Drafted: 1969　College: Santa Clara

YEAR	TEAM	GP	GS	MIN	PTS	FGM	FGA	FG%	3PM	3PA	3P%	FTM	FTA	FT%	ORB	DRB	TRB	AST	PF	DQ	STL	BLK	TO	MPG	PPG	RPG	APG	PCM
69-70	Philadelphia	47	....	357	191	82	172	.477	....	....	....	27	39	.692	....	....	86	31	62	2	....	....	....	7.6	4.1	1.8	0.7	.531
70-71	Philadelphia	27	....	133	66	24	66	.364	....	....	....	18	26	.692	....	....	20	17	21	0	....	....	....	4.9	2.4	0.7	0.6	.406
NBA Season Totals		74	....	490	257	106	238	.445	....	....	....	45	65	.692	....	....	106	48	83	2	....	....	....	6.6	3.5	1.4	0.6	
69-70	Philadelphia	1	....	12	12	5	9	.556	....	....	....	2	4	.500	....	....	1	6	0	0	....	....	....	12.0	12.0	1.0	6.0	1.267
70-71	Philadelphia	1	....	4	0	0	2	.000	....	....	....	0	0	.000	....	....	2	0	1	0	....	....	....	4.0	0.0	2.0	0.0	-.108
NBA Playoff Totals		2	....	16	12	5	11	.455	....	....	....	2	4	.500	....	....	3	6	1	0	....	....	....	8.0	6.0	1.5	3.0	....

• OGDEN, Ralph

Ralph Ogden

Born: Jan. 25, 1948.　Height: 6'5".　Weight: 205 lbs.　Drafted: 1970　College: Santa Clara

YEAR	TEAM	GP	GS	MIN	PTS	FGM	FGA	FG%	3PM	3PA	3P%	FTM	FTA	FT%	ORB	DRB	TRB	AST	PF	DQ	STL	BLK	TO	MPG	PPG	RPG	APG	PCM
70-71	San Francisco	32	....	162	42	17	71	.239	....	....	....	8	12	.667	....	....	32	9	17	0	....	....	....	5.1	1.3	1.0	0.3	.150
NBA Season Totals		32	....	162	42	17	71	.239	....	....	....	8	12	.667	....	....	32	9	17	0	....	....	....	5.1	1.3	1.0	0.3	....
70-71	San Francisco	2	....	15	6	1	5	.200	....	....	....	4	4	1.000	....	....	4	1	0	0	....	....	....	7.5	3.0	2.0	0.5	.476
NBA Playoff Totals		2	....	15	6	1	5	.200	....	....	....	4	4	1.000	....	....	4	1	0	0	....	....	....	7.5	3.0	2.0	0.5	....

• OGG, Alan

Raymond Alan Ogg

Born: July 5, 1967. Lancaster, OH, United States.　Height: 7'2".　Weight: 240 lbs.　Drafted: —　College: Alabama-Birmingham

YEAR	TEAM	GP	GS	MIN	PTS	FGM	FGA	FG%	3PM	3PA	3P%	FTM	FTA	FT%	ORB	DRB	TRB	AST	PF	DQ	STL	BLK	TO	MPG	PPG	RPG	APG	PCM
90-91	Miami	31	1	261	54	24	55	.436	0	2	.000	6	10	.600	15	34	49	2	53	1	6	27	9	8.4	1.7	1.6	0.1	.263
91-92	Miami	43	0	367	108	46	84	.548	0	0	.000	16	30	.533	30	44	74	7	73	0	5	28	17	8.5	2.5	1.7	0.2	.336
92-93	Milwaukee	3	0	26	8	3	9	.333	0	0	.000	2	2	1.000	1	5	6	4	6	0	1	3	3	8.7	2.7	2.0	1.3	.400
92-93	Washington	3	0	3	5	2	4	.500	0	0	.000	1	2	.500	2	2	4	0	0	0	0	0	0	1.0	1.7	1.3	0.0	2.133
NBA Season Totals		80	1	657	175	75	152	.493	0	2	.000	25	44	.568	48	85	133	13	132	1	12	58	29	8.2	2.2	1.7	0.2	....
91-92	Miami	3	0	15	3	1	3	.333	0	0	.000	1	2	.500	0	1	1	0	3	0	1	3	0	5.0	1.0	0.3	0.0	.262
NBA Playoff Totals		3	0	15	3	1	3	.333	0	0	.000	1	2	.500	0	1	1	0	3	0	1	3	0	5.0	1.0	0.3	0.0	....

• O'GRADY, Buddy

Francis David (Buddy) O'Grady

Born: Jan. 19, 1920. Died: Feb.29, 1992.　Height: 5'11".　Weight: 160 lbs.　Drafted: —　College: Georgetown

YEAR	TEAM	GP	GS	MIN	PTS	FGM	FGA	FG%	3PM	3PA	3P%	FTM	FTA	FT%	ORB	DRB	TRB	AST	PF	DQ	STL	BLK	TO	MPG	PPG	RPG	APG	PCM
45-46	Rochester-N	1	....	....	0	0	....	....	....	....	....	0	....	....	....	....	....	....	....	....	....	....	....	....	0.0	....	....	....
46-47	Washington	55	....	....	148	55	231	.238	....	....	....	38	53	.717	....	....	....	20	60	....	....	....	....	....	2.7	....	0.4	....
47-48	St. Louis	44	....	....	170	67	257	.261	....	....	....	36	54	.667	....	....	....	9	61	....	....	....	....	....	3.9	....	0.2	....
48-49	St. Louis	30	....	....	138	52	176	.295	....	....	....	34	46	.739	....	....	....	43	36	....	....	....	....	....	4.6	....	1.4	....
48-49	Providence	17	....	....	81	33	117	.282	....	....	....	15	25	.600	....	....	....	25	21	....	....	....	....	....	4.8	....	1.5	....
NBA Season Totals		146	....	....	537	207	781	.265	....	....	....	123	178	.691	....	....	....	97	178	....	....	....	....	....	3.7	....	0.7	....
NBL Season Totals		1	....	....	0	0	....	....	....	....	....	0	....	....	....	....	....	....	....	....	....	....	....	....	0.0	....	....	....
Career Totals		147	....	....	537	207	781	....	....	....	....	123	178	....	....	....	....	97	178	....	....	....	....	....	3.7	....	0.7	....
46-47	Washington	6	....	....	9	2	20	.100	....	....	....	5	5	1.000	....	....	....	0	5	....	....	....	....	....	1.5	....	0.0	....
47-48	St. Louis	7	....	....	25	11	33	.333	....	....	....	3	3	1.000	....	....	....	0	5	....	....	....	....	....	3.6	....	0.0	....
NBA Playoff Totals		13	....	....	34	13	53	.245	....	....	....	8	8	1.000	....	....	....	0	10	....	....	....	....	....	2.6	....	0.0	....

YEAR	TEAM	GP	GS	MIN	PTS	FGM	FGA	FG%	3PM	3PA	3P%	FTM	FTA	FT%	ORB	DRB	TRB	AST	PF	DQ	STL	BLK	TO	MPG	PPG	RPG	APG	PCM

• O'HANLON, Francis
Francis Brian O'Hanlon

Born: Aug. 24, 1948.   Height: 6'1".   Weight: 175 lbs.   Drafted: 1970   College: Villanova

| 70-71 | Florida-A | 14 | .... | 101 | 22 | 8 | 22 | .364 | 0 | 1 | .000 | 6 | 9 | .667 | 2 | 2 | 4 | 13 | 18 | 0 | .... | .... | 22 | 7.2 | 1.6 | 0.3 | 0.9 | .210 |
| **ABA Season Totals** | | 14 | .... | 101 | 22 | 8 | 22 | .364 | 0 | 1 | .000 | 6 | 9 | .667 | 2 | 2 | 4 | 13 | 18 | 0 | .... | .... | 22 | 7.2 | 1.6 | 0.3 | 0.9 | .... |

• OHL, Don
Donald Jay Ohl

Born: Apr. 18, 1936. Murphysboro, IL, United States.   Height: 6'3".   Weight: 190 lbs.   Drafted: 1958   College: Illinois

60-61	Detroit	79	....	2173	1054	427	1085	.394	....	....	....	200	278	.719	....	....	256	265	224	3	....	....	....	27.5	13.3	3.2	3.4	.442
61-62	Detroit	77	....	2526	1311	555	1250	.444	....	....	....	201	280	.718	....	....	267	244	173	2	....	....	....	32.8	17.0	3.5	3.2	.465
62-63	Detroit	80	....	2961	1547	636	1450	.439	....	....	....	275	380	.724	....	....	239	325	234	3	....	....	....	37.0	19.3	3.0	4.1	.456
63-64	Detroit	71	....	2366	1225	500	1224	.408	....	....	....	225	331	.680	....	....	180	225	219	3	....	....	....	33.3	17.3	2.5	3.2	.402
64-65	Baltimore	77	....	2821	1420	568	1297	.438	....	....	....	284	388	.732	....	....	336	250	274	7	....	....	....	36.6	18.4	4.4	3.2	.454
65-66	Baltimore	73	....	2645	1502	593	1334	.445	....	....	....	316	430	.735	....	....	280	290	208	1	....	....	....	36.2	20.6	3.8	4.0	.517
66-67	Baltimore	58	....	2024	1180	452	1002	.451	....	....	....	276	354	.780	....	....	189	168	153	1	....	....	....	34.9	20.3	3.3	2.9	.495
67-68	Baltimore	39	....	1096	578	232	536	.433	....	....	....	114	148	.770	....	....	113	84	91	0	....	....	....	28.1	14.8	2.9	2.2	.435
67-68	St. Louis	31	....	823	405	161	355	.454	....	....	....	83	106	.783	....	....	62	73	93	1	....	....	....	26.5	13.1	2.0	2.4	.414
68-69	Atlanta	76	....	1995	917	385	901	.427	....	....	....	147	208	.707	....	....	170	221	232	5	....	....	....	26.3	12.1	2.2	2.9	.382
69-70	Atlanta	66	....	984	410	176	372	.473	....	....	....	58	72	.806	....	....	71	98	113	1	....	....	....	14.9	6.2	1.1	1.5	.360
NBA Season Totals		727	....	22414	11549	4685	10806	.434	....	....	....	2179	2975	.732	....	....	2163	2243	2014	27	....	....	....	30.8	15.9	3.0	3.1	....
60-61	Detroit	5	....	130	63	25	78	.321	....	....	....	13	19	.684	....	....	19	14	13	0	....	....	....	26.0	12.6	3.8	2.8	.363
61-62	Detroit	8	....	317	164	71	171	.415	....	....	....	22	27	.815	....	....	27	25	22	0	....	....	....	39.6	20.5	3.4	3.1	.400
62-63	Detroit	4	....	155	85	33	83	.398	....	....	....	19	22	.864	....	....	12	19	18	0	....	....	....	38.8	21.3	3.0	4.8	.449
64-65	Baltimore	10	....	432	261	100	208	.481	....	....	....	61	78	.782	....	....	64	27	46	1	....	....	....	43.2	26.1	6.4	2.7	.547
65-66	Baltimore	3	....	111	80	34	67	.507	....	....	....	12	16	.750	....	....	14	8	13	1	....	....	....	37.0	26.7	4.7	2.7	.614
67-68	St. Louis	6	....	143	69	27	56	.482	....	....	....	15	22	.682	....	....	12	21	17	4	....	....	....	23.8	11.5	2.0	3.5	.497
68-69	Atlanta	11	....	194	73	30	86	.349	....	....	....	13	22	.591	....	....	13	16	25	0	....	....	....	17.6	6.6	1.2	1.5	.214
NBA Playoff Totals		47	....	1482	795	320	749	.427	....	....	....	155	206	.752	....	....	161	130	154	3	....	....	....	31.5	16.9	3.4	2.8	....

• O'KEEFE, Dick
Richard T. O'Keefe

Born: Sept. 29, 1923.   Height: 6'2".   Weight: 185 lbs.   Drafted: 1947   College: Santa Clara

47-48	Washington	37	....	....	156	63	257	.245	....	....	....	30	59	.508	....	....	....	18	85	....	....	....	....	4.2	....	0.5	....
48-49	Washington	50	....	....	191	70	274	.255	....	....	....	51	99	.515	....	....	....	43	119	....	....	....	....	3.8	....	0.9	....
49-50	Washington	68	....	....	474	162	529	.306	....	....	....	150	203	.739	....	....	....	74	217	....	....	....	....	7.0	....	1.1	....
50-51	Washington	17	....	....	67	21	102	.206	....	....	....	25	39	.641	37	....	....	25	48	0	....	....	....	3.9	2.2	1.5	....
NBA Season Totals		172	....	....	888	316	1162	.272	....	....	....	256	400	.640	....	....	37	160	469	0	....	....	....	5.2	0.2	0.9	....
48-49	Washington	11	....	....	57	22	60	.367	....	....	....	13	20	.650	....	....	....	11	37	....	....	....	....	5.2	....	1.0	....
49-50	Washington	2	....	....	15	4	13	.308	....	....	....	7	8	.875	....	....	....	5	10	....	....	....	....	7.5	....	2.5	....
NBA Playoff Totals		13	....	....	72	26	73	.356	....	....	....	20	28	.714	....	....	....	16	47	....	....	....	....	5.5	....	1.2	....

• O'KEEFE, Tommy
Thomas V. O'Keefe

Born: July 16, 1926.   Height: 6'2".   Weight: 185 lbs.   Drafted: 1950   College: Georgetown

| 50-51 | Was/Bal | 6 | .... | .... | 23 | 10 | 28 | .357 | .... | .... | .... | 3 | 4 | .750 | .... | .... | 7 | 10 | 5 | 0 | .... | .... | .... | 3.8 | 1.2 | 1.7 | .... |
| **NBA Season Totals** | | 6 | .... | .... | 23 | 10 | 28 | .357 | .... | .... | .... | 3 | 4 | .750 | .... | .... | 7 | 10 | 5 | 0 | .... | .... | .... | 3.8 | 1.2 | 1.7 | .... |

• O'KEEFFE, Hank
Henry (Handsome Hank) O'Keeffe

Born: 1923.   Height: 6'3".   Weight: 195 lbs.   Drafted: —   College: Canisius

48-49	Syracuse-N	56	....	....	240	94	....	....	....	....	....	52	90	.578	....	....	....	102	....	....	....	....	....	4.3	....	....	....
NBL Season Totals		56	....	....	240	94	....	....	....	....	....	52	90		....	....	....	102	....	....	....	....	....	4.3	....	....	....
48-49	Syracuse-N	5	....	....	6	2	....	....	....	....	....	2	2	1.000	....	....	....	....	....	....	....	....	....	1.2	....	....	....
NBL Playoff Totals		5	....	....	6	2	....	....	....	....	....	2	2		....	....	....	....	....	....	....	....	....	1.2	....	....	....

• O'KOREN, Mike
Michael F. O'Koren

Born: Feb. 7, 1958. Jersey City, NJ, United States.   Height: 6'7".   Weight: 207 lbs.   Drafted: 1980   College: North Carolina

80-81	New Jersey	79	....	2473	870	365	751	.486	5	18	.278	135	212	.637	179	299	478	252	243	8	86	27	142	31.3	11.0	6.1	3.2	.427
81-82	New Jersey	80	32	2018	909	383	778	.492	8	23	.348	135	189	.714	111	194	305	192	175	0	83	13	144	25.2	11.4	3.8	2.4	.438
82-83	New Jersey	46	14	803	308	136	259	.525	2	9	.222	34	48	.708	42	72	114	82	67	0	42	11	60	17.5	6.7	2.5	1.8	.432
83-84	New Jersey	73	25	1191	430	186	385	.483	5	28	.179	53	87	.609	71	104	175	95	148	3	34	11	73	16.3	5.9	2.4	1.3	.335
84-85	New Jersey	43	29	1119	438	194	393	.494	8	21	.381	42	67	.627	46	120	166	102	115	1	32	16	52	26.0	10.2	3.9	2.4	.400
85-86	New Jersey	67	11	1031	350	160	336	.476	7	27	.259	23	39	.590	33	102	135	118	134	3	29	9	54	15.4	5.2	2.0	1.8	.343
86-87	Washington	15	0	123	32	16	42	.381	0	2	.000	0	2	.000	6	8	14	13	10	0	2	0	6	8.2	2.1	0.9	0.9	.207
87-88	New Jersey	4	0	52	18	9	16	.563	0	1	.000	0	4	.000	1	3	4	2	2	0	3	2	0	13.0	4.5	1.0	0.5	.369
NBA Season Totals		407	111	8810	3355	1449	2960	.490	35	129	.271	422	648	.651	489	902	1391	856	894	15	311	89	531	21.6	8.2	3.4	2.1	....
81-82	New Jersey	2	0	44	7	3	11	.273	0	1	.000	1	2	.500	0	8	8	3	8	1	1	0	2	22.0	3.5	4.0	1.5	.118
82-83	New Jersey	2	0	18	4	2	8	.250	0	0	.000	0	0	.000	1	5	6	3	3	0	0	0	2	9.0	2.0	3.0	1.5	.230
83-84	New Jersey	11	11	216	55	25	59	.424	0	1	.000	5	6	.833	18	17	35	21	37	1	3	4	12	19.6	5.0	3.2	1.9	.260
84-85	New Jersey	3	0	34	6	3	7	.429	0	0	.000	0	2	.000	1	9	10	4	6	0	0	0	1	11.3	2.0	3.3	1.3	.330
85-86	New Jersey	2	0	21	2	1	6	.167	0	1	.000	0	0	.000	1	1	2	2	5	0	2	1	3	10.5	1.0	1.0	1.0	-.046
NBA Playoff Totals		20	11	333	74	34	91	.374	0	3	.000	6	10	.600	21	40	61	33	59	2	6	5	20	16.7	3.7	3.1	1.7	....

• OKUR, Mehmet

Okur Okur

Born: May 26, 1979. Yalova, Turkey. Height: 6'11". Weight: 249 lbs. Drafted: 2001 College: none

YEAR	TEAM	GP	GS	MIN	PTS	FGM	FGA	FG%	3PM	3PA	3P%	FTM	FTA	FT%	ORB	DRB	TRB	AST	PF	DQ	STL	BLK	TO	MPG	PPG	RPG	APG	PCM
02-03	Detroit	72	9	1367	494	180	423	.426	38	112	.339	96	131	.733	117	218	335	71	167	0	25	39	66	19.0	6.9	4.7	1.0	.411
NBA Season Totals		72	9	1367	494	180	423	.426	38	112	.339	96	131	.733	117	218	335	71	167	0	25	39	66	19.0	6.9	4.7	1.0	....
02-03	Detroit	17	0	323	94	35	80	.438	7	13	.538	17	32	.531	24	46	70	13	39	0	12	12	14	19.0	5.5	4.1	0.8	.357
NBA Playoff Totals		17	0	323	94	35	80	.438	7	13	.538	17	32	.531	24	46	70	13	39	0	12	12	14	19.0	5.5	4.1	0.8	....

• OLAJUWON, Hakeem

Hakeem Abdul (The Dream) Olajuwon aka.: Akeem Abdul Olajuwon

Born: Jan. 21, 1963. Lagos, Nigeria. Height: 7' Weight: 250 lbs. Drafted: 1984 College: Houston

YEAR	TEAM	GP	GS	MIN	PTS	FGM	FGA	FG%	3PM	3PA	3P%	FTM	FTA	FT%	ORB	DRB	TRB	AST	PF	DQ	STL	BLK	TO	MPG	PPG	RPG	APG	PCM
84-85	Houston	82	82	2914	1692	677	1258	.538	0	0	.000	338	551	.613	**440**	534	974	111	**344**	10	99	220	238	35.5	20.6	11.9	1.4	.684
85-86	Houston	68	68	2467	1597	625	1188	.526	0	0	.000	347	538	.645	333	448	781	137	271	9	134	231	197	36.3	23.5	11.5	2.0	.765
86-87	Houston	75	75	2760	1755	677	1332	.508	1	5	.200	400	570	.702	315	543	858	220	294	8	140	254	225	36.8	23.4	11.4	2.9	.768
87-88	Houston	79	79	2825	1805	712	1385	.514	0	4	.000	381	548	.695	302	657	959	163	324	7	162	214	245	35.8	22.8	12.1	2.1	.757
88-89	Houston	82	82	3024	2034	790	1556	.508	0	10	.000	454	652	.696	338	**767**	**1105**	149	329	10	213	282	279	36.9	24.8	**13.5**	1.8	.815
89-90	Houston	82	82	3124	1995	806	1609	.501	1	6	.167	382	536	.713	299	**850**	**1149**	234	314	6	174	**376**	320	38.1	24.3	**14.0**	2.9	.821
90-91	Houston	56	50	2062	1187	487	959	.508	0	4	.000	213	277	.769	219	551	770	131	221	5	121	221	174	36.8	21.2	13.8	2.3	.790
91-92	Houston	70	69	2636	1510	591	1177	.502	0	1	.000	328	428	.766	246	599	845	157	263	7	127	304	189	37.7	21.6	12.1	2.2	.749
92-93	Houston	82	82	3242	2140	848	1603	.529	0	8	.000	444	570	.779	283	785	1068	291	305	5	150	**342**	262	39.5	26.1	13.0	3.5	.850
93-94	Houston	80	80	3277	2184	894	**1694**	.528	8	19	.421	388	542	.716	229	726	955	287	289	4	128	297	272	41.0	27.3	11.9	3.6	.786
94-95	Houston	72	72	2853	2005	798	1545	.517	3	16	.188	406	537	.756	172	603	775	255	250	3	133	242	238	39.6	27.8	10.8	3.5	.789
95-96	Houston	72	72	2797	1936	768	1494	.514	3	14	.214	397	548	.724	176	608	784	257	242	0	113	207	245	38.8	26.9	10.9	3.6	.768
96-97	Houston	78	78	2852	1810	727	1426	.510	5	16	.313	351	446	.787	173	543	716	236	249	3	117	173	281	36.6	23.2	9.2	3.0	.675
97-98	Houston	47	45	1633	772	306	633	.483	0	3	.000	160	212	.755	116	344	460	143	152	0	84	96	127	34.7	16.4	9.8	3.0	.615
98-99	Houston	50	50	1784	945	373	725	.514	4	13	.308	195	272	.717	106	371	477	88	160	3	82	123	139	35.7	18.9	9.5	1.8	.621
99-00	Houston	44	28	1049	455	193	421	.458	0	2	.000	69	112	.616	65	209	274	61	88	0	41	70	73	23.8	10.3	6.2	1.4	.513
00-01	Houston	58	55	1545	689	283	568	.498	0	1	.000	123	198	.621	124	307	431	72	141	0	70	88	81	26.6	11.9	7.4	1.2	.564
01-02	Toronto	61	37	1378	435	194	418	.464	0	2	.000	47	84	.560	98	268	366	66	147	0	74	90	98	22.6	7.1	6.0	1.1	.444
NBA Season Totals		1238	1186	44222	26946	10749	20991	.512	25	124	.202	5423	7621	.712	4034	9713	13747	3058	4383	80	2162	**3830**	3683	35.7	21.8	11.1	2.5	....
84-85	Houston	5	5	187	106	42	88	.477	0	0	.000	22	46	.478	33	32	65	7	22	0	7	13	11	37.4	21.2	13.0	1.4	.632
85-86	Houston	20	20	766	537	205	387	.530	0	1	.000	127	199	.638	101	135	236	39	87	3	40	69	43	38.3	26.9	11.8	2.0	.805
86-87	Houston	10	10	389	292	110	179	.615	0	1	.000	72	97	.742	39	74	113	25	44	1	13	43	36	38.9	29.2	11.3	2.5	.890
87-88	Houston	4	4	162	150	56	98	.571	0	1	.000	38	43	.884	20	47	67	7	14	0	9	11	9	40.5	37.5	16.8	1.8	1.125
88-89	Houston	4	4	162	101	42	81	.519	0	0	.000	17	25	.680	14	38	52	12	17	0	10	11	10	40.5	25.3	13.0	3.0	.769
89-90	Houston	4	4	161	74	31	70	.443	0	0	.000	12	17	.706	15	31	46	8	19	0	10	23	11	40.3	18.5	11.5	2.0	.611
90-91	Houston	3	3	129	66	26	45	.578	0	1	.000	14	17	.824	12	32	44	6	11	0	4	8	8	43.0	22.0	14.7	2.0	.720
92-93	Houston	12	12	518	308	123	238	.517	0	1	.000	62	75	.827	52	116	168	57	37	0	21	59	45	43.2	25.7	14.0	4.8	.825
93-94	Houston	23	23	989	664	267	514	.519	2	4	.500	128	161	.795	55	199	254	98	82	0	40	92	83	43.0	28.9	11.0	4.3	.777
94-95	Houston	22	22	929	725	306	576	.531	2	4	.500	111	163	.681	44	183	227	98	95	0	26	62	69	42.2	33.0	10.3	4.5	.794
95-96	Houston	8	8	329	179	75	147	.510	0	1	.000	29	40	.725	17	56	73	31	28	1	15	17	29	41.1	22.4	9.1	3.9	.600
96-97	Houston	16	16	629	370	147	249	.590	0	3	.000	76	104	.731	46	128	174	54	61	0	33	41	46	39.3	23.1	10.9	3.4	.762
97-98	Houston	5	5	190	102	39	99	.394	0	1	.000	24	33	.727	9	45	54	12	18	0	5	16	13	38.0	20.4	10.8	2.4	.550
98-99	Houston	4	4	123	53	23	54	.426	0	0	.000	7	8	.875	5	24	29	2	18	0	5	3	5	30.8	13.3	7.3	0.5	.388
01-02	Toronto	5	0	86	28	12	22	.545	0	0	.000	4	6	.667	9	10	19	2	9	0	7	4	6	17.2	5.6	3.8	0.4	.441
NBA Playoff Totals		145	140	5749	3755	1504	2847	.528	4	18	.222	743	1034	.719	471	1150	1621	458	562	5	245	472	424	39.6	25.9	11.2	3.2	....

• OLBERDING, Mark

Mark Allen Olberding

Born: Apr. 21, 1956. Melrose, MN, United States. Height: 6'8". Weight: 225 lbs. Drafted: — College: Minnesota

YEAR	TEAM	GP	GS	MIN	PTS	FGM	FGA	FG%	3PM	3PA	3P%	FTM	FTA	FT%	ORB	DRB	TRB	AST	PF	DQ	STL	BLK	TO	MPG	PPG	RPG	APG	PCM
75-76	San Antonio-A	70	....	1621	627	233	463	.503	0	0	.000	161	204	.789	149	276	425	124	197	....	40	30	114	23.2	9.0	6.1	1.8	.513
75-76	San Diego-A	11	....	434	168	69	144	.479	0	0	.000	30	43	.698	35	70	105	18	52	....	10	7	27	39.5	15.3	9.5	1.6	.428
76-77	San Antonio	82	....	1949	853	301	598	.503	....	....	....	251	316	.794	162	287	449	119	277	6	59	29	....	23.8	10.4	5.5	1.5	.499
77-78	San Antonio	79	....	1773	646	231	480	.481	....	....	....	184	227	.811	104	269	373	131	235	1	45	26	119	22.4	8.2	4.7	1.7	.416
78-79	San Antonio	80	....	1885	755	261	551	.474	....	....	....	233	290	.803	96	333	429	211	282	2	53	18	160	23.6	9.4	5.4	2.6	.467
79-80	San Antonio	75	....	2111	792	291	609	.478	0	3	.000	210	264	.795	83	335	418	327	274	7	67	22	180	28.1	10.6	5.6	4.4	.478
80-81	San Antonio	82	....	2408	1012	348	685	.508	1	7	.143	315	380	.829	146	325	471	277	307	6	75	31	205	29.4	12.3	5.7	3.4	.488
81-82	San Antonio	68	63	2098	941	333	705	.472	2	12	.167	273	338	.808	118	321	439	202	253	5	57	29	136	30.9	13.8	6.5	3.0	.490
82-83	Chicago	80	31	1817	698	251	522	.481	2	12	.167	194	248	.782	108	250	358	131	246	3	50	9	152	22.7	8.7	4.5	1.6	.386
83-84	Kansas City	81	81	2160	759	249	504	.494	0	1	.000	261	318	.821	119	326	445	192	291	2	50	28	162	26.7	9.4	5.5	2.4	.417
84-85	Kansas City	81	62	2277	823	265	528	.502	0	3	.000	293	352	.832	139	374	513	243	298	8	56	11	186	28.1	10.2	6.3	3.0	.456
85-86	Sacramento	81	64	2157	612	225	403	.558	0	2	.000	162	210	.771	113	310	423	266	276	3	43	23	146	26.6	7.6	5.2	3.3	.417
86-87	Sacramento	76	0	1002	254	69	165	.418	0	1	.000	116	131	.885	50	135	185	91	144	0	18	9	53	13.2	3.3	2.4	1.2	.335
NBA Season Totals		865	301	21637	8145	2824	5750	.491	5	41	.122	2492	3074	.811	1238	3265	4503	2190	2883	43	573	235	1499	25.0	9.4	5.2	2.5	....
ABA Season Totals		81	....	2055	795	302	607	.498	0	0	.000	191	247	.773	184	346	530	142	249	....	50	37	141	25.4	9.8	6.5	1.8	....
Career Totals		946	301	23692	8940	3126	6357	.492	5	41	.122	2683	3321	.808	1422	3611	5033	2332	3132	43	623	272	1640	25.0	9.5	5.3	2.5	....
75-76	San Antonio-A	7	....	73	13	5	15	.333	0	0	.000	3	6	.500	7	15	22	3	15	....	3	2	4	10.4	1.9	3.1	0.4	.260
76-77	San Antonio	2	....	42	13	5	9	.556	....	....	....	3	6	.500	2	5	7	2	8	0	0	1	....	21.0	6.5	3.5	1.0	.312
77-78	San Antonio	6	....	152	63	25	51	.490	....	....	....	13	15	.867	9	21	30	14	23	0	6	6	8	25.3	10.5	5.0	2.3	.492
78-79	San Antonio	14	....	359	111	41	103	.398	....	....	....	29	37	.784	12	57	69	33	53	2	12	5	29	25.6	7.9	4.9	2.4	.322
79-80	San Antonio	3	....	97	29	13	23	.565	0	0	.000	3	4	.750	5	17	22	11	14	1	2	1	3	32.3	9.7	7.3	3.7	.465
80-81	San Antonio	7	....	254	138	58	105	.552	1	3	.333	21	25	.840	11	30	41	30	31	1	4	0	17	36.3	19.7	5.9	4.3	.541
81-82	San Antonio	9	9	328	132	53	120	.442	0	1	.000	26	31	.839	20	38	58	32	39	1	9	6	27	36.4	14.7	6.4	3.6	.387
83-84	Kansas City	3	3	60	20	6	15	.400	0	0	.000	8	14	.571	4	11	15	6	6	0	0	0	4	20.0	6.7	5.0	2.0	.378
85-86	Sacramento	3	3	74	15	3	9	.333	0	0	.000	9	12	.750	4	9	13	3	9	0	2	1	7	24.7	5.0	4.3	1.0	.208
NBA Playoff Totals		47	15	1366	521	204	435	.469	1	4	.250	112	144	.778	67	188	255	131	183	5	35	20	95	29.1	11.1	5.4	2.8	....
ABA Playoff Totals		7	....	73	13	5	15	.333	0	0	.000	3	6	.500	7	15	22	3	15	....	3	2	4	10.4	1.9	3.1	0.4	....
Career Playoff Totals		54	15	1439	534	209	450	.464	1	4	.250	115	150	.767	74	203	277	134	198	5	38	22	99	26.6	9.9	5.1	2.5	....

YEAR	TEAM	GP	GS	MIN	PTS	FGM	FGA	FG%	3PM	3PA	3P%	FTM	FTA	FT%	ORB	DRB	TRB	AST	PF	DQ	STL	BLK	TO	MPG	PPG	RPG	APG	PCM

• OLDHAM, Jawann
Jawann Oldham

Born: July 4, 1957. Chicago, IL, United States.   Height: 7'   Weight: 215 lbs.   Drafted: 1980   College: Seattle

YEAR	TEAM	GP	GS	MIN	PTS	FGM	FGA	FG%	3PM	3PA	3P%	FTM	FTA	FT%	ORB	DRB	TRB	AST	PF	DQ	STL	BLK	TO	MPG	PPG	RPG	APG	PCM
80-81	Denver	4	....	21	4	2	6	.333	0	0	.000	0	0	.000	3	2	5	0	3	0	0	2	2	5.3	1.0	1.3	0.0	.169
81-82	Houston	22	0	124	34	13	36	.361	0	0	.000	8	14	.571	7	17	24	3	28	0	2	10	7	5.6	1.5	1.1	0.1	.219
82-83	Chicago	16	0	171	74	31	58	.534	0	0	.000	12	22	.545	18	29	47	5	30	1	5	13	13	10.7	4.6	2.9	0.3	.491
83-84	Chicago	64	0	870	259	110	218	.505	0	0	.000	39	66	.591	75	158	233	33	139	2	15	76	83	13.6	4.0	3.6	0.5	.392
84-85	Chicago	63	0	993	212	89	192	.464	0	1	.000	34	50	.680	79	157	236	31	166	3	11	127	57	15.8	3.4	3.7	0.5	.362
85-86	Chicago	52	47	1276	387	167	323	.517	0	1	.000	53	91	.582	112	194	306	37	206	6	28	134	88	24.5	7.4	5.9	0.7	.409
86-87	New York	44	9	776	173	71	174	.408	0	1	.000	31	57	.544	51	128	179	19	95	1	22	71	48	17.6	3.9	4.1	0.4	.322
87-88	Sacramento	54	13	946	297	119	250	.476	0	0	.000	59	87	.678	82	222	304	33	143	2	12	110	59	17.5	5.5	5.6	0.6	.499
89-90	Orlando	3	0	36	4	1	3	.333	0	0	.000	2	5	.400	4	11	15	0	6	0	2	3	3	12.0	1.3	5.0	0.0	.384
89-90	LA Lakers	3	0	9	5	2	3	.667	0	0	.000	1	2	.500	1	1	1	1	3	0	0	1	1	3.0	1.7	0.3	0.3	.361
90-91	Indiana	4	0	19	6	3	6	.500	0	0	.000	0	0	.000	0	3	3	0	1	0	0	0	0	4.8	1.5	0.8	0.0	.291
NBA Season Totals		329	69	5241	1455	608	1269	.479	0	3	.000	239	394	.607	431	922	1353	162	820	15	97	546	361	15.9	4.4	4.1	0.5	....
84-85	Chicago	4	0	91	14	7	15	.467	0	0	.000	0	0	.000	8	14	22	3	19	1	6	7	11	22.8	3.5	5.5	0.8	.256
85-86	Chicago	1	0	4	0	0	1	.000	0	0	.000	0	0	.000	1	1	2	0	0	0	0	0	1	4.0	0.0	2.0	0.0	.000
NBA Playoff Totals		5	0	95	14	7	16	.438	0	0	.000	0	0	.000	9	15	24	3	19	1	6	7	12	19.0	2.8	4.8	0.6	....

• OLDHAM, John
John O. Oldham

Born: June 22, 1923. Beaver Dam, KY, United States.   Height: 6'3".   Weight: 175 lbs.   Drafted: 1949   College: Western Kentucky

YEAR	TEAM	GP	GS	MIN	PTS	FGM	FGA	FG%	3PM	3PA	3P%	FTM	FTA	FT%	ORB	DRB	TRB	AST	PF	DQ	STL	BLK	TO	MPG	PPG	RPG	APG	PCM
49-50	Fort Wayne	59	....	....	357	127	426	.298	....	....	....	103	145	.710	....	....	99	192							6.1	....	1.7	
50-51	Fort Wayne	68	....	....	569	199	597	.333	....	....	....	171	292	.586	....	....	242	127	242	15					8.4	3.6	1.9	
NBA Season Totals		127	....	....	926	326	1023	.319	....	....	....	274	437	.627	....	....	242	226	434	15					7.3	1.9	1.8	
49-50	Fort Wayne	4	....	....	37	12	27	.444	....	....	....	13	17	.765	....	....	0	4	15	....					9.3	0.0	1.0	
50-51	Fort Wayne	3	....	....	17	6	16	.375	....	....	....	5	10	.500	....	....	5	5	13	0					5.7	1.7	1.7	
NBA Playoff Totals		7	....	....	54	18	43	.419	....	....	....	18	27	.667	....	....	5	9	28	0					7.7	0.7	1.3	

• OLEYNICK, Frank
Frank (Magic) Oleynick

Born: Feb. 20, 1955. Bridgeport, CT, United States.   Height: 6'2".   Weight: 185 lbs.   Drafted: 1975   College: Seattle

YEAR	TEAM	GP	GS	MIN	PTS	FGM	FGA	FG%	3PM	3PA	3P%	FTM	FTA	FT%	ORB	DRB	TRB	AST	PF	DQ	STL	BLK	TO	MPG	PPG	RPG	APG	PCM
75-76	Seattle	52	....	650	307	127	316	.402	....	....	....	53	77	.688	10	35	45	53	62	0	21	6	....	12.5	5.9	0.9	1.0	.319
76-77	Seattle	50	....	516	201	81	223	.363	....	....	....	39	53	.736	13	32	45	60	48	0	13	4	....	10.3	4.0	0.9	1.2	.308
NBA Season Totals		102	....	1166	508	208	539	.386	....	....	....	92	130	.708	23	67	90	113	110	0	34	10	....	11.4	5.0	0.9	1.1	....

• OLIVE, John
John Olive

Born: Mar. 1, 1955. Philadelphia, PA, United States.   Height: 6'7".   Weight: 210 lbs.   Drafted: 1977   College: Villanova

YEAR	TEAM	GP	GS	MIN	PTS	FGM	FGA	FG%	3PM	3PA	3P%	FTM	FTA	FT%	ORB	DRB	TRB	AST	PF	DQ	STL	BLK	TO	MPG	PPG	RPG	APG	PCM
78-79	San Diego	34	....	189	44	13	40	.325	....	....	....	18	23	.783	3	16	19	3	32	0	4	0	14	5.6	1.3	0.6	0.1	.077
79-80	San Diego	1	....	15	0	0	2	.000	0	0	.000	0	0	.000	0	1	1	0	2	0	0	0	2	15.0	0.0	1.0	0.0	-.241
NBA Season Totals		35	....	204	44	13	42	.310	0	0	.000	18	23	.783	3	17	20	3	34	0	4	0	16	5.8	1.3	0.6	0.1	....

• OLIVER, Brian
Brian Darnell Oliver

Born: June 1, 1968. Chicago, IL, United States.   Height: 6'4".   Weight: 210 lbs.   Drafted: 1990   College: Georgia Tech

YEAR	TEAM	GP	GS	MIN	PTS	FGM	FGA	FG%	3PM	3PA	3P%	FTM	FTA	FT%	ORB	DRB	TRB	AST	PF	DQ	STL	BLK	TO	MPG	PPG	RPG	APG	PCM
90-91	Philadelphia	73	4	800	279	111	272	.408	5	18	.278	52	71	.732	18	62	80	88	76	0	34	4	51	11.0	3.8	1.1	1.2	.301
91-92	Philadelphia	34	0	279	81	33	100	.330	0	4	.000	15	22	.682	10	20	30	20	33	0	10	2	24	8.2	2.4	0.9	0.6	.137
94-95	Washington	6	0	42	14	4	9	.444	0	0	.000	6	8	.750	0	4	4	4	8	0	0	0	3	7.0	2.3	0.7	0.7	.233
97-98	Atlanta	5	0	61	15	7	19	.368	0	0	.000	1	4	.250	3	6	9	2	4	0	1	0	1	12.2	3.0	1.8	0.4	.184
NBA Season Totals		118	4	1182	389	155	400	.388	5	22	.227	74	105	.705	31	92	123	114	121	0	45	6	79	10.0	3.3	1.0	1.0	....
90-91	Philadelphia	4	0	15	6	2	6	.333	0	0	.000	2	2	1.000	0	0	0	1	4	0	1	0	0	3.8	1.5	0.0	0.3	.160
NBA Playoff Totals		4	0	15	6	2	6	.333	0	0	.000	2	2	1.000	0	0	0	1	4	0	1	0	0	3.8	1.5	0.0	0.3	....

• OLIVER, Dean
Dean Oliver

Born: Nov. 5, 1978. Quincy, IL, United States.   Height: 5'11".   Weight: 1975 lbs.   Drafted: —   College: Iowa

YEAR	TEAM	GP	GS	MIN	PTS	FGM	FGA	FG%	3PM	3PA	3P%	FTM	FTA	FT%	ORB	DRB	TRB	AST	PF	DQ	STL	BLK	TO	MPG	PPG	RPG	APG	PCM
01-02	Golden State	20	0	139	42	17	46	.370	2	13	.154	6	9	.667	0	8	8	21	16	1	3	0	11	7.0	2.1	0.4	1.1	.216
02-03	Golden State	15	0	93	22	7	29	.241	1	6	.167	7	8	.875	8	8	16	23	9	0	7	0	10	6.2	1.5	1.1	1.5	.370
NBA Season Totals		35	0	232	64	24	75	.320	3	19	.158	13	17	.765	8	16	24	44	25	1	10	0	21	6.6	1.8	0.7	1.3	....

• OLIVER, Jimmy
Jimmy Allen Oliver

Born: July 12, 1969. Menifee, AR, United States.   Height: 6'5".   Weight: 205 lbs.   Drafted: 1991   College: Purdue

YEAR	TEAM	GP	GS	MIN	PTS	FGM	FGA	FG%	3PM	3PA	3P%	FTM	FTA	FT%	ORB	DRB	TRB	AST	PF	DQ	STL	BLK	TO	MPG	PPG	RPG	APG	PCM
91-92	Cleveland	27	8	252	96	39	98	.398	1	9	.111	17	22	.773	9	18	27	20	22	0	9	2	8	9.3	3.6	1.0	0.7	.309
93-94	Boston	44	6	540	216	89	214	.416	13	32	.406	25	33	.758	8	38	46	33	39	0	16	1	22	12.3	4.9	1.0	0.8	.284
96-97	Toronto	4	0	43	11	4	13	.308	1	6	.167	2	2	1.000	1	4	5	1	2	0	2	0	3	10.8	2.8	1.3	0.3	.151
97-98	Washington	1	0	10	5	2	4	.500	1	2	.500	0	0	.000	0	2	2	1	1	0	0	0	0	10.0	5.0	2.0	1.0	.563
98-99	Phoenix	2	0	11	3	1	3	.333	1	1	1.000	0	0	.000	0	0	0	0	2	0	0	0	0	5.5	1.5	0.0	0.0	.030
NBA Season Totals		78	14	856	331	135	332	.407	17	50	.340	44	57	.772	18	62	80	55	66	0	27	3	33	11.0	4.2	1.0	0.7	....

YEAR	TEAM	GP	GS	MIN	PTS	FGM	FGA	FG%	3PM	3PA	3P%	FTM	FTA	FT%	ORB	DRB	TRB	AST	PF	DQ	STL	BLK	TO	MPG	PPG	RPG	APG	PCM

● OLIVER, Vince

Vince Oliver

Born: 1915. Height: 5'10". Weight: 185 lbs. Drafted: — College: Indiana

YEAR	TEAM	GP	GS	MIN	PTS	FGM	FGA	FG%	3PM	3PA	3P%	FTM	FTA	FT%	ORB	DRB	TRB	AST	PF	DQ	STL	BLK	TO	MPG	PPG	RPG	APG	PCM
38-39	Hammond-N	5	....	....	2	1	....	....	....	....	....	0	....	....	....	....	....	....	....	....	....	....	....	0.4	....	....	....
NBL Season Totals		5	....	....	2	1	....	....	....	....	....	0	....	....	....	....	....	....	....	....	....	....	....	0.4	....	....	....

● OLLIE, Kevin

Kevin Jermaine Ollie

Born: Dec. 27, 1972. Dallas, TX, United States. Height: 6'4". Weight: 195 lbs. Drafted: — College: Connecticut

YEAR	TEAM	GP	GS	MIN	PTS	FGM	FGA	FG%	3PM	3PA	3P%	FTM	FTA	FT%	ORB	DRB	TRB	AST	PF	DQ	STL	BLK	TO	MPG	PPG	RPG	APG	PCM
97-98	Dallas	16	0	214	46	14	42	.333	0	0	.000	18	25	.720	6	15	21	32	16	0	6	0	16	13.4	2.9	1.3	2.0	.255
97-98	Orlando	19	0	216	77	23	56	.411	0	1	.000	31	45	.689	3	15	18	33	15	0	7	0	29	11.4	4.1	0.9	1.7	.304
98-99	Sacramento	7	0	68	12	4	13	.308	0	0	.000	4	5	.800	0	6	6	3	8	0	3	1	3	9.7	1.7	0.9	0.4	.141
98-99	Orlando	1	0	4	1	0	1	.000	0	0	.000	1	2	.500	0	1	1	0	1	0	0	0	0	4.0	1.0	1.0	0.0	.028
99-00	Philadelphia	40	0	290	72	22	49	.449	0	0	.000	28	37	.757	4	27	31	46	27	0	10	0	10	7.3	1.8	0.8	1.2	.378
00-01	New Jersey	19	0	161	22	5	27	.185	0	0	.000	12	19	.632	3	20	23	25	14	0	5	0	9	8.5	1.2	1.2	1.3	.232
00-01	Philadelphia	51	0	764	194	71	165	.430	1	3	.333	51	70	.729	13	59	72	121	70	0	25	1	40	15.0	3.8	1.4	2.4	.334
01-02	Chicago	52	17	1146	304	97	253	.383	1	2	.500	109	130	.838	18	110	128	193	64	1	36	1	80	22.0	5.8	2.5	3.7	.360
01-02	Indiana	29	0	577	158	40	100	.400	0	0	.000	78	97	.804	7	49	56	98	33	0	26	1	26	19.9	5.4	1.9	3.4	.414
02-03	Milwaukee	53	4	1127	303	117	255	.459	1	5	.200	68	91	.747	12	87	99	181	71	0	37	4	36	21.3	5.7	1.9	3.4	.379
02-03	Seattle	29	1	770	231	82	186	.441	1	1	1.000	66	87	.759	13	70	83	110	51	0	32	1	36	26.6	8.0	2.9	3.8	.385
NBA Season Totals		316	26	5337	1420	475	1147	.414	4	12	.333	466	608	.766	79	459	538	842	370	1	187	9	285	16.9	4.5	1.7	2.7	....
99-00	Philadelphia	10	0	65	20	6	12	.500	0	0	.000	8	9	.889	0	5	5	12	5	0	2	0	3	6.5	2.0	0.5	1.2	.439
00-01	Philadelphia	23	0	123	33	10	27	.370	0	0	.000	13	14	.929	2	7	9	23	12	0	0	0	8	5.3	1.4	0.4	1.0	.310
01-02	Indiana	5	0	118	29	11	26	.423	1	2	.500	6	6	1.000	0	12	12	23	6	0	3	0	5	23.6	5.8	2.4	4.6	.398
NBA Playoff Totals		38	0	306	82	27	65	.415	1	2	.500	27	29	.931	2	24	26	58	23	0	5	0	16	8.1	2.2	0.7	1.5	....

● OLLRICH, Gene

Gene W. (Moe) Ollrich

Born: June 30, 1922. Whiting, IN, United States. Height: 5'11". Weight: 160 lbs. Drafted: — College: Drake

YEAR	TEAM	GP	GS	MIN	PTS	FGM	FGA	FG%	3PM	3PA	3P%	FTM	FTA	FT%	ORB	DRB	TRB	AST	PF	DQ	STL	BLK	TO	MPG	PPG	RPG	APG	PCM
49-50	Waterloo	14	....	....	44	17	72	.236	....	....	....	10	14	.714	....	....	....	24	34	....	....	....	....	....	3.1	....	1.7	....
NBA Season Totals		14	....	....	44	17	72	.236	....	....	....	10	14	.714	....	....	....	24	34	....	....	....	....	....	3.1	....	1.7	....

● OLOWOKANDI, Michael

Michael (Kandi) Olowokandi

Born: Apr. 3, 1975. Lagos, Nigeria. Height: 7' Weight: 269 lbs. Drafted: 1998 College: Pacific

YEAR	TEAM	GP	GS	MIN	PTS	FGM	FGA	FG%	3PM	3PA	3P%	FTM	FTA	FT%	ORB	DRB	TRB	AST	PF	DQ	STL	BLK	TO	MPG	PPG	RPG	APG	PCM
98-99	LA Clippers	45	36	1279	401	172	399	.431	0	0	.000	57	118	.483	120	237	357	25	137	2	27	55	85	28.4	8.9	7.9	0.6	.355
99-00	LA Clippers	80	77	2493	783	330	756	.437	0	0	.000	123	189	.651	194	462	656	38	304	10	35	140	177	31.2	9.8	8.2	0.5	.346
00-01	LA Clippers	82	82	2127	701	308	708	.435	0	0	.000	85	156	.545	168	357	525	46	250	4	30	108	169	25.9	8.5	6.4	0.6	.325
01-02	LA Clippers	80	80	2569	885	384	886	.433	0	0	.000	117	188	.622	164	547	711	90	217	1	55	145	175	32.1	11.1	8.9	1.1	.415
02-03	LA Clippers	36	36	1369	441	186	436	.427	0	0	.000	69	105	.657	57	271	328	47	110	5	18	79	98	38.0	12.3	9.1	1.3	.362
NBA Season Totals		323	311	9837	3211	1380	3185	.433	0	0	.000	451	756	.597	703	1874	2577	246	1018	22	165	527	704	30.5	9.9	8.0	0.8	....

● OLSEN, Bud

Enoch Eli (Bud) Olsen III

Born: July 25, 1940. Height: 6'8". Weight: 220 lbs. Drafted: 1962 College: Louisville

YEAR	TEAM	GP	GS	MIN	PTS	FGM	FGA	FG%	3PM	3PA	3P%	FTM	FTA	FT%	ORB	DRB	TRB	AST	PF	DQ	STL	BLK	TO	MPG	PPG	RPG	APG	PCM
62-63	Cincinnati	52	....	373	113	43	133	.323	....	....	....	27	39	.692	....	....	105	42	78	0	....	....	....	7.2	2.2	2.0	0.8	.375
63-64	Cincinnati	49	....	513	202	85	210	.405	....	....	....	32	57	.561	....	....	149	29	78	0	....	....	....	10.5	4.1	3.0	0.6	.421
64-65	Cincinnati	79	....	1372	592	224	512	.438	....	....	....	144	195	.738	....	....	333	84	203	5	....	....	....	17.4	7.5	4.2	1.1	.461
65-66	Cincinnati	4	....	36	7	3	8	.375	....	....	....	1	3	.333	....	....	13	2	4	0	....	....	....	9.0	1.8	3.3	0.5	.371
65-66	San Francisco	55	....	566	194	78	185	.422	....	....	....	38	85	.447	....	....	179	18	77	1	....	....	....	10.3	3.5	3.3	0.3	.395
66-67	San Francisco	40	....	348	173	75	167	.449	....	....	....	23	58	.397*	....	....	103	32	51	1	....	....	....	8.7	4.3	2.6	0.8	.534
67-68	Seattle	73	....	897	277	130	285	.456	....	....	....	17	62	.274	....	....	204	75	136	1	....	....	....	12.3	3.8	2.8	1.0	.372
68-69	Boston	7	....	43	14	7	19	.368	....	....	....	0	6	.000	....	....	14	4	6	0	....	....	....	6.1	2.0	2.0	0.6	.356
68-69	Detroit	10	....	70	20	8	23	.348	....	....	....	4	12	.333	....	....	11	7	8	0	....	....	....	7.0	2.0	1.1	0.7	.259
69-70	Kentucky-A	84	....	1375	343	158	330	.479	1	4	.250	26	73	.356	140	234	374	249	234	5	....	....	113	16.4	4.1	4.5	3.0	.495
NBA Season Totals		369	....	4218	1592	653	1542	.423	....	....	....	286	517	.553	....	....	1111	293	641	8	....	....	....	11.4	4.3	3.0	0.8	....
ABA Season Totals		84	....	1375	343	158	330	.479	1	4	.250	26	73	.356	140	234	374	249	234	5	....	....	113	16.4	4.1	4.5	3.0	....
Career Totals		453	....	5593	1935	811	1872	.433	1	4	.250	312	590	.529	140	234	1485	542	875	13	....	....	113	12.3	4.3	3.3	1.2	....
62-63	Cincinnati	5	....	21	15	7	9	.778	....	....	....	1	5	.200	....	....	10	3	4	0	....	....	....	4.2	3.0	2.0	0.6	1.038
63-64	Cincinnati	2	....	10	6	3	6	.500	....	....	....	0	0	.000	....	....	4	1	2	0	....	....	....	5.0	3.0	2.0	0.5	.722
64-65	Cincinnati	4	....	39	17	7	17	.412	....	....	....	3	5	.600	....	....	9	1	8	0	....	....	....	9.8	4.3	2.3	0.3	.349
66-67	San Francisco	4	....	14	8	4	13	.308	....	....	....	0	2	.000	....	....	9	1	2	0	....	....	....	3.5	2.0	2.3	0.3	.544
69-70	Kentucky-A	12	....	211	37	18	43	.419	0	1	.000	1	7	.143	22	39	61	0	....	2	....	....	14	17.6	3.1	5.1	0.0	....
NBA Playoff Totals		15	....	84	46	21	45	.467	....	....	....	4	12	.333	....	....	32	6	16	0	....	....	....	5.6	3.1	2.1	0.4	....
ABA Playoff Totals		12	....	211	37	18	43	.419	0	1	.000	1	7	.143	22	39	61	0	....	2	....	....	14	17.6	3.1	5.1	0.0	....
Career Playoff Totals		27	....	295	83	39	88	.443	0	1	.000	5	19	.263	22	39	93	6	16	2	....	....	14	10.9	3.1	3.4	0.2	....

● OLSEN, Jim

Jim Olsen

Born: 1921. Height: 6'6". Weight: 205 lbs. Drafted: — College: Dartmouth

YEAR	TEAM	GP	GS	MIN	PTS	FGM	FGA	FG%	3PM	3PA	3P%	FTM	FTA	FT%	ORB	DRB	TRB	AST	PF	DQ	STL	BLK	TO	MPG	PPG	RPG	APG	PCM
45-46	Chicago-N	9	....	....	26	9	....	....	....	....	....	8	....	....	....	....	....	....	....	....	....	....	....	2.9	....	....	....
NBL Season Totals		9	....	....	26	9	....	....	....	....	....	8	....	....	....	....	....	....	....	....	....	....	....	2.9	....	....	....

• OLSON, Oscar

Oscar (Sonny) Olson

Born: 1917. Height: 6' Weight: 165 lbs. Drafted: — College: Carleton

YEAR TEAM	GP	GS	MIN	PTS	FGM	FGA	FG%	3PM	3PA	3P%	FTM	FTA	FT%	ORB	DRB	TRB	AST	PF	DQ	STL	BLK	TO	MPG	PPG	RPG	APG	PCM
39-40 Oshkosh-N	2	....	....	4	1	....	....	....	....	....	2	....	....	....	....	....	....	....	....	....	....	....	....	2.0	....	....	....
NBL Season Totals	2	....	....	4	1	....	....	....	....	....	2	....	....	....	....	....	....	....	....	....	....	....	....	2.0	....	....	....

• O'MALLEY, Grady

V. Grady O'Malley

Born: Apr. 25, 1948. Boston, MA, United States. Height: 6'5". Weight: 205 lbs. Drafted: 1969 College: Manhattan

YEAR TEAM	GP	GS	MIN	PTS	FGM	FGA	FG%	3PM	3PA	3P%	FTM	FTA	FT%	ORB	DRB	TRB	AST	PF	DQ	STL	BLK	TO	MPG	PPG	RPG	APG	PCM
69-70 Atlanta	24	....	113	50	21	60	.350	....	....	....	8	19	.421	....	....	26	10	12	0	....	....	....	4.7	2.1	1.1	0.4	.351
NBA Season Totals	24	....	113	50	21	60	.350	....	....	....	8	19	.421	....	....	26	10	12	0	....	....	....	4.7	2.1	1.1	0.4	....

• O'NEAL, Jermaine

Jermaine O'Neal

Born: Oct. 13, 1978. Columbia, SC, United States. Height: 6'11". Weight: 226 lbs. Drafted: 1996 College: none (HS: Eau Claire, SC)

YEAR TEAM	GP	GS	MIN	PTS	FGM	FGA	FG%	3PM	3PA	3P%	FTM	FTA	FT%	ORB	DRB	TRB	AST	PF	DQ	STL	BLK	TO	MPG	PPG	RPG	APG	PCM
96-97 Portland	45	0	458	185	69	153	.451	0	1	.000	47	78	.603	39	85	124	8	46	0	2	26	27	10.2	4.1	2.8	0.2	.428
97-98 Portland	60	9	808	269	112	231	.485	0	2	.000	45	89	.506	80	121	201	17	101	0	15	58	54	13.5	4.5	3.4	0.3	.388
98-99 Portland	35	1	310	90	36	83	.434	0	1	.000	18	35	.514	42	55	97	13	41	0	4	14	14	8.9	2.6	2.8	0.4	.409
99-00 Portland	70	8	859	273	108	222	.486	0	1	.000	57	98	.582	97	132	229	18	127	1	11	55	47	12.3	3.9	3.3	0.3	.394
00-01 Indiana	81	80	2641	1041	404	868	.465	0	5	.000	233	388	.601	249	545	794	98	280	5	49	**228**	161	32.6	12.9	9.8	1.2	.513
01-02 Indiana	72	72	2709	1371	543	1133	.479	1	14	.071	284	413	.688	188	569	757	118	269	4	45	166	174	37.6	19.0	10.5	1.6	.555
02-03 Indiana	77	76	2863	1600	610	1260	.484	7	21	.333	373	510	.731	202	594	796	155	277	5	66	178	180	37.2	20.8	10.3	2.0	.619
NBA Season Totals	440	246	10648	4829	1882	3950	.476	8	45	.178	1057	1611	.656	897	2101	2998	427	1141	15	192	725	657	24.2	11.0	6.8	1.0	....
96-97 Portland	2	0	4	0	0	2	.000	0	1	.000	0	2	.000	0	1	1	0	0	0	0	1	0	2.0	0.0	0.5	0.0	-.233
97-98 Portland	1	0	3	0	0	3	.000	0	1	.000	0	0	.000	1	0	1	0	1	0	0	2	0	3.0	0.0	1.0	0.0	-.153
98-99 Portland	9	0	55	14	4	10	.400	0	0	.000	6	12	.500	8	9	17	1	11	0	0	3	2	6.1	1.6	1.9	0.1	.331
99-00 Portland	8	0	38	12	3	11	.273	0	0	.000	6	9	.667	2	5	7	1	9	0	0	3	0	4.8	1.5	0.9	0.1	.249
00-01 Indiana	4	4	157	39	17	39	.436	0	1	.000	5	10	.500	12	38	50	7	13	0	0	10	7	39.3	9.8	12.5	1.8	.423
01-02 Indiana	5	5	191	86	34	76	.447	0	1	.000	18	24	.750	6	32	38	5	24	1	4	8	14	38.2	17.2	7.6	1.0	.379
02-03 Indiana	6	6	272	137	43	92	.467	0	3	.000	51	65	.785	24	81	105	4	22	0	3	18	18	45.3	22.8	17.5	0.7	.657
NBA Playoff Totals	35	15	720	288	101	233	.433	0	7	.000	86	122	.705	53	166	219	18	80	1	7	45	41	20.6	8.2	6.3	0.5	....

• O'NEAL, Shaquille

Shaquille Rashaun (Shaq) O'Neal

Born: Mar. 6, 1972. Newark, NJ, United States. Height: 7'1". Weight: 300 lbs. Drafted: 1992 College: Louisiana State

YEAR TEAM	GP	GS	MIN	PTS	FGM	FGA	FG%	3PM	3PA	3P%	FTM	FTA	FT%	ORB	DRB	TRB	AST	PF	DQ	STL	BLK	TO	MPG	PPG	RPG	APG	PCM
92-93 Orlando	81	81	3071	1893	733	1304	.562	0	2	.000	427	721	.592	342	780	1122	152	321	8	60	286	**308**	37.9	23.4	13.9	1.9	.755
93-94 Orlando	81	81	3224	2377	**953**	1591	**.599**	0	2	.000	471	850	.554	384	688	1072	195	281	3	76	231	219	39.8	29.3	13.2	2.4	.857
94-95 Orlando	79	79	2923	**2315**	**930**	**1594**	.583	0	5	.000	455	**854**	.533	328	573	901	214	258	1	73	192	205	37.0	**29.3**	11.4	2.7	.860
95-96 Orlando	54	52	1946	1434	592	1033	.573	1	2	.500	249	511	.487	182	414	596	155	193	1	34	115	157	36.0	26.6	11.0	2.9	.782
96-97 LA Lakers	51	51	1941	1336	552	991	.557	0	4	.000	232	479	.484	195	445	640	159	180	2	46	147	148	38.1	26.2	12.5	3.1	.791
97-98 LA Lakers	60	57	2175	1699	670	1147	**.584**	0	0	.000	359	681	.527	208	473	681	142	193	1	39	144	174	36.3	28.3	11.4	2.4	.833
98-99 LA Lakers	49	49	1705	**1289**	**510**	885	**.576**	0	1	.000	269	**498**	.540	187	338	525	114	155	4	36	82	122	34.8	26.3	10.7	2.3	.806
99-00 LA Lakers	79	79	3163	**2344**	**956**	1665	**.574**	0	1	.000	432	**824**	.524	336	742	1078	299	255	2	36	239	223	40.0	**29.7**	13.6	3.8	.872
00-01 LA Lakers	74	74	2924	2125	**813**	1422	**.572**	0	2	.000	499	**972**	.513	291	649	940	277	256	6	47	204	218	39.5	28.7	12.7	3.7	.831
01-02 LA Lakers	67	66	2423	1822	712	1229	**.579**	0	1	.000	398	**717**	.555	235	480	715	200	199	2	41	137	171	36.2	27.2	10.7	3.0	.822
02-03 LA Lakers	67	66	2535	1841	695	1211	.574	0	0	.000	451	725	.622	259	483	742	206	229	4	38	159	196	37.8	27.5	11.1	3.1	.806
NBA Season Totals	742	735	28030	20475	8116	14072	.577	1	20	.050	4242	7832	.542	2947	6065	9012	2113	2520	34	526	1936	2141	37.8	27.6	12.1	2.8	....
93-94 Orlando	3	3	126	62	23	45	.511	0	0	.000	16	34	.471	17	23	40	7	13	0	2	9	10	42.0	20.7	13.3	2.3	.578
94-95 Orlando	21	21	805	539	195	338	.577	0	0	.000	149	261	.571	95	155	250	70	84	1	18	40	73	38.3	25.7	11.9	3.3	.755
95-96 Orlando	12	12	459	310	131	216	.606	0	0	.000	48	122	.393	49	71	120	55	40	0	9	15	44	38.3	25.8	10.0	4.6	.716
96-97 LA Lakers	9	9	326	242	89	173	.514	0	0	.000	64	105	.610	38	57	95	29	37	1	5	17	22	36.2	26.9	10.6	3.2	.757
97-98 LA Lakers	13	13	501	396	158	258	.612	0	0	.000	80	159	.503	48	84	132	38	41	1	7	34	43	38.5	30.5	10.2	2.9	.818
98-99 LA Lakers	8	8	315	213	79	155	.510	0	0	.000	55	118	.466	44	49	93	18	29	0	7	23	18	39.4	26.6	11.6	2.3	.692
99-00 LA Lakers	23	23	1000	707	286	505	.566	0	0	.000	135	296	.456	119	236	355	71	67	1	13	55	56	43.5	30.7	15.4	3.1	.815
00-01 LA Lakers	16	16	676	487	191	344	.555	0	0	.000	105	200	.525	91	156	247	51	55	2	7	38	57	42.3	30.4	15.4	3.2	.813
01-02 LA Lakers	19	19	776	541	203	384	.529	0	0	.000	135	208	.649	67	172	239	54	62	1	10	48	62	40.8	28.5	12.6	2.8	.758
02-03 LA Lakers	12	12	481	324	121	226	.535	0	0	.000	82	132	.621	63	115	178	44	34	1	7	34	35	40.1	27.0	14.8	3.7	.843
NBA Playoff Totals	136	136	5465	3821	1476	2644	.558	0	0	.000	869	1635	.531	**631**	1118	1749	437	462	8	85	313	420	40.2	28.1	12.9	3.2	....

• O'NEILL, Mike

Mike O'Neill

Born: 1927. Height: 6'3". Weight: 210 lbs. Drafted: — College: California

YEAR TEAM	GP	GS	MIN	PTS	FGM	FGA	FG%	3PM	3PA	3P%	FTM	FTA	FT%	ORB	DRB	TRB	AST	PF	DQ	STL	BLK	TO	MPG	PPG	RPG	APG	PCM
52-53 Milwaukee	4	....	50	12	4	17	.235	....	....	....	4	4	1.000	....	....	9	3	10	1	....	....	....	12.5	3.0	2.3	0.8	.186
NBA Season Totals	4	....	50	12	4	17	.235	....	....	....	4	4	1.000	....	....	9	3	10	1	....	....	....	12.5	3.0	2.3	0.8	....

• OPPER, Bernie

Bernard Opper

Born: Sept. 1, 1915. New York, NY, United States. Died: Feb.24, 2000. Height: 6' Weight: 185 lbs. Drafted: — College: Kentucky

YEAR TEAM	GP	GS	MIN	PTS	FGM	FGA	FG%	3PM	3PA	3P%	FTM	FTA	FT%	ORB	DRB	TRB	AST	PF	DQ	STL	BLK	TO	MPG	PPG	RPG	APG	PCM
39-40 Detroit-N	27	....	....	104	42	....	....	....	....	....	20	....	....	....	....	....	....	....	....	....	....	....	....	3.9	....	....	....
40-41 Detroit-N	5	....	....	6	3	....	....	....	....	....	0	....	....	....	....	....	....	....	....	....	....	....	....	1.2	....	....	....
NBL Season Totals	32	....	....	110	45	....	....	....	....	....	20	....	....	....	....	....	....	....	....	....	....	....	....	3.4	....	....	....
39-40 Detroit-N	3	....	....	15	6	....	....	....	....	....	3	....	....	....	....	....	....	....	....	....	....	....	....	5.0	....	....	....
NBL Playoff Totals	3	....	....	15	6	....	....	....	....	....	3	....	....	....	....	....	....	....	....	....	....	....	....	5.0	....	....	....

YEAR TEAM	GP	GS	MIN	PTS	FGM	FGA	FG%	3PM	3PA	3P%	FTM	FTA	FT%	ORB	DRB	TRB	AST	PF	DQ	STL	BLK	TO	MPG	PPG	RPG	APG	PCM

• ORAM, Eddie — Edward Oram

Born: 1914. Height: 6'3". Weight: 175 lbs. Drafted: — College: USC

YEAR TEAM	GP	GS	MIN	PTS	FGM	FGA	FG%	3PM	3PA	3P%	FTM	FTA	FT%	ORB	DRB	TRB	AST	PF	DQ	STL	BLK	TO	MPG	PPG	RPG	APG	PCM
39-40 Chicago-N	18	....	....	53	18	....	....	....	....	....	17	....	....	....	....	....	....	....	....	....	....	....	....	2.9	....	....	....
47-48 Syracuse-N	24	....	....	107	39	....	....	....	....	....	29	44	.659	....	....	....	....	....	....	....	....	....	....	4.5	....	....	....
NBL Season Totals	42	....	....	160	57	....	....	....	....	....	46	44	....	....	....	....	....	....	....	....	....	....	....	3.8	....	....	....

• ORMS, Barry — Barry D. Orms

Born: May 1, 1946. St. Louis, MO, United States. Height: 6'3". Weight: 190 lbs. Drafted: 1968 College: St. Louis

YEAR TEAM	GP	GS	MIN	PTS	FGM	FGA	FG%	3PM	3PA	3P%	FTM	FTA	FT%	ORB	DRB	TRB	AST	PF	DQ	STL	BLK	TO	MPG	PPG	RPG	APG	PCM
68-69 Baltimore	64	....	916	181	76	246	.309	....	....	....	29	60	.483	....	....	158	49	155	3	....	....	....	14.3	2.8	2.5	0.8	.164
69-70 Indiana-A	9	....	143	51	17	40	.425	0	3	.000	17	26	.654	13	24	37	13	30	1	....	....	8	15.9	5.7	4.1	1.4	.427
69-70 Pittsburgh-A	68	....	1948	650	255	655	.389	5	23	.217	135	250	.540	127	183	310	119	185	2	....	....	140	28.6	9.6	4.6	1.8	.298
NBA Season Totals	64	....	916	181	76	246	.309	....	....	....	29	60	.483	....	....	158	49	155	3	....	....	....	14.3	2.8	2.5	0.8	....
ABA Season Totals	77	....	2091	701	272	695	.391	5	26	.192	152	276	.551	140	207	347	132	215	3	....	....	148	27.2	9.1	4.5	1.7	....
Career Totals	141	....	3007	882	348	941	.370	5	26	.192	181	336	.539	140	207	505	181	370	6	....	....	148	21.3	6.3	3.6	1.3	....
68-69 Baltimore	3	....	10	0	0	0	.000	....	....	....	0	0	.000	....	....	1	0	2	0	....	....	....	3.3	0.0	0.3	0.0	.000
NBA Playoff Totals	3	....	10	0	0	0	.000	....	....	....	0	0	.000	....	....	1	0	2	0	....	....	....	3.3	0.0	0.3	0.0	....

• O'ROURKE, Bud — Bud O'Rourke

Born: 1919. Height: 6'4". Weight: 170 lbs. Drafted: — College: DePaul

YEAR TEAM	GP	GS	MIN	PTS	FGM	FGA	FG%	3PM	3PA	3P%	FTM	FTA	FT%	ORB	DRB	TRB	AST	PF	DQ	STL	BLK	TO	MPG	PPG	RPG	APG	PCM
45-46 Chicago-N	6	....	....	2	1	....	....	....	....	....	0	0	.000	....	....	....	....	....	....	....	....	....	0.3	....	....	....
NBL Season Totals	6	....	....	2	1	....	....	....	....	....	0	0	....	....	....	....	....	....	....	....	....	....	0.3	....	....	....

• ORR, Johnny — John M. Orr

Born: June 10, 1927. Yale, KS, United States. Height: 6'3". Weight: 195 lbs. Drafted: 1948 College: Beloit

YEAR TEAM	GP	GS	MIN	PTS	FGM	FGA	FG%	3PM	3PA	3P%	FTM	FTA	FT%	ORB	DRB	TRB	AST	PF	DQ	STL	BLK	TO	MPG	PPG	RPG	APG	PCM
42-43 Chicago-N	20	....	....	57	26	....	....	....	....	....	5	....	....	....	....	....	....	....	....	....	....	....	2.9	....	....	....
43-44 Sheboygan-N	19	....	....	28	10	....	....	....	....	....	8	....	....	....	....	....	....	....	....	....	....	....	1.5	....	....	....
44-45 Chicago-N	18	....	....	24	11	....	....	....	....	....	2	....	....	....	....	....	....	....	....	....	....	....	1.3	....	....	....
45-46 Chicago-N	22	....	....	36	13	....	....	....	....	....	10	....	....	....	....	....	....	....	....	....	....	....	1.6	....	....	....
49-50 St. Louis	21	....	....	40	17	47	.362	....	....	....	6	7	.857	....	....	....	6	19	....	....	....	....	1.9	....	0.3	....
49-50 Waterloo	13	....	....	52	23	71	.324	....	....	....	6	7	.857	....	....	....	14	15	....	....	....	....	4.0	....	1.1	....
NBA Season Totals	34	....	....	92	40	118	.339	....	....	....	12	14	.857	....	....	....	20	34	....	....	....	....	2.7	....	0.6	....
NBL Season Totals	79	....	....	145	60	....	....	....	....	....	25	....	....	....	....	....	....	....	....	....	....	....	1.8	....	....	....
Career Totals	113	....	....	237	100	118	....	....	....	....	37	14	....	....	....	....	20	34	....	....	....	....	2.1	....	0.2	....
43-44 Sheboygan-N	5	....	....	4	1	....	....	....	....	....	2	....	....	....	....	....	....	....	....	....	....	....	0.8	....	....	....
44-45 Chicago-N	3	....	....	2	1	....	....	....	....	....	0	....	....	....	....	....	....	....	....	....	....	....	0.7	....	....	....
NBL Playoff Totals	8	....	....	6	2	....	....	....	....	....	2	....	....	....	....	....	....	....	....	....	....	....	0.8	....	....	....

• ORR, Louis — Louis M. Orr

Born: May 7, 1958. Cincinnati, OH, United States. Height: 6'8". Weight: 175 lbs. Drafted: 1980 College: Syracuse

YEAR TEAM	GP	GS	MIN	PTS	FGM	FGA	FG%	3PM	3PA	3P%	FTM	FTA	FT%	ORB	DRB	TRB	AST	PF	DQ	STL	BLK	TO	MPG	PPG	RPG	APG	PCM
80-81 Indiana	82	....	1787	859	348	709	.491	0	6	.000	163	202	.807	172	189	361	132	153	0	55	25	123	21.8	10.5	4.4	1.6	.490
81-82 Indiana	80	41	1951	918	357	719	.497	1	8	.125	203	254	.799	127	204	331	134	182	1	56	26	136	24.4	11.5	4.1	1.7	.450
82-83 New York	82	14	1666	688	274	593	.462	0	2	.000	140	175	.800	94	134	228	94	134	0	64	24	90	20.3	8.4	2.8	1.1	.379
83-84 New York	78	20	1640	697	262	572	.458	0	0	.000	173	211	.820	101	127	228	61	142	0	66	17	94	21.0	8.9	2.9	0.8	.361
84-85 New York	79	31	2452	1007	372	766	.486	1	10	.100	262	334	.784	171	220	391	134	195	1	100	27	134	31.0	12.7	4.9	1.7	.415
85-86 New York	74	64	2237	878	330	741	.445	0	4	.000	218	278	.784	123	189	312	179	177	4	61	26	118	30.2	11.9	4.2	2.4	.375
86-87 New York	65	8	1440	458	166	389	.427	1	5	.200	125	172	.727	102	130	232	110	123	0	47	18	72	22.2	7.0	3.6	1.7	.346
87-88 New York	29	0	180	40	16	50	.320	0	1	.000	8	16	.500	13	21	34	9	27	0	6	0	15	6.2	1.4	1.2	0.3	.138
NBA Season Totals	569	178	13353	5545	2125	4539	.468	3	36	.083	1292	1642	.787	903	1214	2117	853	1133	6	455	163	782	23.5	9.7	3.7	1.5	....
80-81 Indiana	2	....	56	24	9	25	.360	0	0	.000	6	7	.857	6	4	10	4	4	0	5	1	6	28.0	12.0	5.0	2.0	.368
82-83 New York	6	0	105	46	18	47	.383	0	0	.000	10	10	1.000	8	13	21	3	10	0	5	4	8	17.5	7.7	3.5	0.5	.366
83-84 New York	12	0	229	73	29	70	.414	0	0	.000	15	19	.789	22	28	50	6	32	1	4	1	10	19.1	6.1	4.2	0.5	.290
87-88 New York	2	0	3	1	0	1	.000	0	0	.000	1	2	.500	1	1	2	0	0	0	0	0	0	1.5	0.5	1.0	0.0	.489
NBA Playoff Totals	22	0	393	144	56	143	.392	0	0	.000	32	38	.842	37	46	83	13	46	1	14	6	24	17.9	6.5	3.8	0.6	....

• ORTIZ, Jose — Jose Rafael Ortiz

Born: Oct. 25, 1963. Albonito, PR, Puerto Rico. Height: 6'10". Weight: 225 lbs. Drafted: 1987 College: Oregon State

YEAR TEAM	GP	GS	MIN	PTS	FGM	FGA	FG%	3PM	3PA	3P%	FTM	FTA	FT%	ORB	DRB	TRB	AST	PF	DQ	STL	BLK	TO	MPG	PPG	RPG	APG	PCM
88-89 Utah	51	15	327	141	55	125	.440	0	1	.000	31	52	.596	30	28	58	11	40	0	8	7	36	6.4	2.8	1.1	0.2	.287
89-90 Utah	13	0	64	42	19	42	.452	1	2	.500	3	5	.600	8	7	15	7	15	0	2	1	5	4.9	3.2	1.2	0.5	.502
NBA Season Totals	64	15	391	183	74	167	.443	1	3	.333	34	57	.596	38	35	73	18	55	0	10	8	41	6.1	2.9	1.1	0.3	....

• OSBORNE, Chuck — Charles H. Osborne

Born: Jan. 21, 1939. Died: Apr.1979. Height: 6'6". Weight: 210 lbs. Drafted: 1961 College: Western Kentucky

YEAR TEAM	GP	GS	MIN	PTS	FGM	FGA	FG%	3PM	3PA	3P%	FTM	FTA	FT%	ORB	DRB	TRB	AST	PF	DQ	STL	BLK	TO	MPG	PPG	RPG	APG	PCM
61-62 Syracuse	4	....	21	5	1	8	.125	....	....	....	3	4	.750	....	....	9	1	3	0	....	....	....	5.3	1.3	2.3	0.3	.296
NBA Season Totals	4	....	21	5	1	8	.125	....	....	....	3	4	.750	....	....	9	1	3	0	....	....	....	5.3	1.3	2.3	0.3	....

• O'SHAUGHNESSY, Bob

Robert O'Shaughnessy

Born: 1921. Height: 6' Weight: 175 lbs. Drafted: — College: Nevada

YEAR	TEAM	GP	GS	MIN	PTS	FGM	FGA	FG%	3PM	3PA	3P%	FTM	FTA	FT%	ORB	DRB	TRB	AST	PF	DQ	STL	BLK	TO	MPG	PPG	RPG	APG	PCM
47-48	Syracuse-N	25	....	....	101	41	....	....	....	....	....	19	31	.613	....	....	....	....	....	....	....	....	....	....	4.0	....	....	....
NBL Season Totals		25	....	....	101	41	....	....	....	....	....	19	31	....	....	....	....	....	....	....	....	....	....	....	4.0	....	....	....

• O'SHEA, Kevin

Kevin Christopher O'Shea

Born: July 10, 1925. San Francisco, CA, United States. Died: Feb.21, 2003. Height: 6'2". Weight: 175 lbs. Drafted: 1950 College: Notre Dame

YEAR	TEAM	GP	GS	MIN	PTS	FGM	FGA	FG%	3PM	3PA	3P%	FTM	FTA	FT%	ORB	DRB	TRB	AST	PF	DQ	STL	BLK	TO	MPG	PPG	RPG	APG	PCM
50-51	Minneapolis	63	....	....	271	87	267	.326	....	....	....	97	134	.724	....	....	125	100	99	1	....	....	....	....	4.3	2.0	1.6	....
51-52	Mil/Bal	65	....	1725	450	153	466	.328	....	....	....	144	210	.686	....	....	201	171	175	7	....	....	....	26.5	6.9	3.1	2.6	.293
52-53	Baltimore	46	....	643	190	71	189	.376	....	....	....	48	81	.593	....	....	76	87	82	1	....	....	....	14.0	4.1	1.7	1.9	.356
NBA Season Totals		174	....	2368	911	311	922	.337	....	....	....	289	425	.680	....	....	402	358	356	9	....	....	....	13.6	5.2	2.3	2.1	....
50-51	Minneapolis	5	....	....	5	1	7	.143	....	....	....	3	4	.750	....	....	5	1	8	0	....	....	....	....	1.0	1.0	0.2	....
NBA Playoff Totals		5	....	....	5	1	7	.143	....	....	....	3	4	.750	....	....	5	1	8	0	....	....	....	....	1.0	1.0	0.2	....

• O'SHIELDS, Garland

Garland L. (Mule) O'Shields

Born: May 23, 1921. Height: 6'1". Weight: 195 lbs. Drafted: — College: Tennessee

YEAR	TEAM	GP	GS	MIN	PTS	FGM	FGA	FG%	3PM	3PA	3P%	FTM	FTA	FT%	ORB	DRB	TRB	AST	PF	DQ	STL	BLK	TO	MPG	PPG	RPG	APG	PCM
46-47	Chicago	9	....	....	4	2	11	.182	....	....	....	0	2	.000	....	....	....	1	8	....	....	....	....	....	0.4	....	0.1	....
47-48	Syracuse-N	5	....	....	9	3	....	....	....	....	....	3	4	.750	....	....	....	....	....	....	....	....	....	....	1.8	....	....	....
NBA Season Totals		9	....	....	4	2	11	.182	....	....	....	0	2	.000	....	....	....	1	8	....	....	....	....	....	0.4	....	0.1	....
NBL Season Totals		5	....	....	9	3	....	....	....	....	....	3	4	....	....	....	....	....	....	....	....	....	....	....	1.8	....	....	....
Career Totals		14	....	....	13	5	11	....	....	....	....	3	6	....	....	....	....	1	8	....	....	....	....	....	0.9	....	0.1	....

• OSIEWALSKI, Leo

Leo Osiewalski

Born: Sept. 25, 1921. Died: Feb.1985. Height: 6'4". Weight: 190 lbs. Drafted: — College: none

YEAR	TEAM	GP	GS	MIN	PTS	FGM	FGA	FG%	3PM	3PA	3P%	FTM	FTA	FT%	ORB	DRB	TRB	AST	PF	DQ	STL	BLK	TO	MPG	PPG	RPG	APG	PCM
43-44	Oshkosh-N	4	....	....	2	1	....	....	....	....	....	0	....	....	....	....	....	....	....	....	....	....	....	....	0.5	....	....	....
NBL Season Totals		4	....	....	2	1	....	....	....	....	....	0	....	....	....	....	....	....	....	....	....	....	....	....	0.5	....	....	....

• OSTERKORN, Wally

Walter Raymond (Ox) Osterkorn

Born: July 6, 1928. Height: 6'5". Weight: 215 lbs. Drafted: 1950 College: Illinois

YEAR	TEAM	GP	GS	MIN	PTS	FGM	FGA	FG%	3PM	3PA	3P%	FTM	FTA	FT%	ORB	DRB	TRB	AST	PF	DQ	STL	BLK	TO	MPG	PPG	RPG	APG	PCM
51-52	Syracuse	66	....	1721	489	145	413	.351	....	....	....	199	335	.594	....	....	444	117	226	8	....	....	....	26.1	7.4	6.7	1.8	.370
52-53	Syracuse	49	....	1016	276	85	262	.324	....	....	....	106	168	.631	....	....	217	61	129	2	....	....	....	20.7	5.6	4.4	1.2	.309
53-54	Syracuse	70	....	2164	615	203	586	.346	....	....	....	209	361	.579	....	....	487	151	209	1	....	....	....	30.9	8.8	7.0	2.2	.349
54-55	Syracuse	19	....	286	56	20	97	.206	....	....	....	16	32	.500	....	....	70	17	32	0	....	....	....	15.1	2.9	3.7	0.9	.188
NBA Season Totals		204	....	5187	1436	453	1358	.334	....	....	....	530	896	.592	....	....	1218	346	596	11	....	....	....	25.4	7.0	6.0	1.7	....
51-52	Syracuse	7	....	249	74	23	67	.343	....	....	....	28	47	.596	....	....	57	20	32	1	....	....	....	35.6	10.6	8.1	2.9	.365
52-53	Syracuse	2	....	42	9	4	9	.444	....	....	....	1	3	.333	....	....	4	2	11	1	....	....	....	21.0	4.5	2.0	1.0	.146
53-54	Syracuse	13	....	542	140	45	122	.369	....	....	....	50	90	.556	....	....	125	37	40	1	....	....	....	41.7	10.8	9.6	2.8	.357
54-55	Syracuse	11	....	75	35	11	34	.324	....	....	....	13	17	.765	....	....	21	11	14	0	....	....	....	6.8	3.2	1.9	1.0	.539
NBA Playoff Totals		33	....	908	258	83	232	.358	....	....	....	92	157	.586	....	....	207	70	97	3	....	....	....	27.5	7.8	6.3	2.1	....

• OSTERTAG, Greg

Gregory Donovan Ostertag

Born: Mar. 6, 1973. Dallas, TX, United States. Height: 7'2". Weight: 280 lbs. Drafted: 1995 College: Kansas

YEAR	TEAM	GP	GS	MIN	PTS	FGM	FGA	FG%	3PM	3PA	3P%	FTM	FTA	FT%	ORB	DRB	TRB	AST	PF	DQ	STL	BLK	TO	MPG	PPG	RPG	APG	PCM
95-96	Utah	57	10	661	208	86	182	.473	0	0	.000	36	54	.667	57	118	175	5	91	1	5	63	23	11.6	3.6	3.1	0.1	.422
96-97	Utah	77	70	1818	559	210	408	.515	0	4	.000	139	205	.678	180	385	565	27	233	2	24	152	77	23.6	7.3	7.3	0.4	.486
97-98	Utah	63	23	1288	297	115	239	.481	0	0	.000	67	140	.479	134	240	374	25	166	1	28	132	76	20.4	4.7	5.9	0.4	.404
98-99	Utah	48	48	1340	273	99	208	.476	0	0	.000	75	121	.620	105	243	348	23	140	2	12	131	45	27.9	5.7	7.3	0.5	.385
99-00	Utah	81	3	1606	367	124	267	.464	0	1	.000	119	187	.636	172	310	482	18	196	2	20	172	79	19.8	4.5	6.0	0.2	.422
00-01	Utah	81	3	1491	363	139	281	.495	1	2	.500	84	151	.556	164	251	415	22	215	3	22	142	63	18.4	4.5	5.1	0.3	.400
01-02	Utah	74	14	1107	245	91	201	.453	0	0	.000	63	130	.485	125	188	313	50	152	1	15	109	51	15.0	3.3	4.2	0.7	.407
02-03	Utah	81	74	1926	438	169	326	.518	0	0	.000	100	196	.510	180	323	503	55	235	4	20	147	104	23.8	5.4	6.2	0.7	.373
NBA Season Totals		562	245	11237	2750	1033	2112	.489	1	7	.143	683	1184	.577	1117	2058	3175	225	1428	16	146	1048	518	20.0	4.9	5.6	0.4	....
95-96	Utah	15	0	212	53	20	45	.444	0	0	.000	13	21	.619	18	32	50	1	28	0	2	21	4	14.1	3.5	3.3	0.1	.370
96-97	Utah	20	20	459	94	34	83	.410	0	0	.000	26	35	.743	52	85	137	6	76	3	10	47	18	23.0	4.7	6.9	0.3	.390
97-98	Utah	19	1	336	64	26	46	.565	0	0	.000	12	25	.480	25	56	81	5	51	0	7	37	12	17.7	3.4	4.3	0.3	.373
98-99	Utah	11	11	261	44	13	35	.371	0	0	.000	18	28	.643	18	47	65	6	27	0	2	24	8	23.7	4.0	5.9	0.5	.339
99-00	Utah	8	0	172	30	10	19	.526	0	0	.000	10	22	.455	19	26	45	2	20	0	2	17	8	21.5	3.8	5.6	0.3	.351
00-01	Utah	5	0	64	8	4	11	.364	0	0	.000	0	4	.000	6	12	18	1	10	1	0	2	2	12.8	1.6	3.6	0.2	.198
01-02	Utah	4	0	87	27	13	21	.619	0	0	.000	1	10	.100	19	15	34	2	14	1	2	6	6	21.8	6.8	8.5	0.5	.507
02-03	Utah	5	5	151	46	16	36	.444	0	0	.000	14	19	.737	19	24	43	8	17	0	3	9	8	30.2	9.2	8.6	1.6	.459
NBA Playoff Totals		87	37	1742	366	136	296	.459	0	0	.000	94	164	.573	176	297	473	31	243	5	28	163	66	20.0	4.2	5.4	0.4	....

• O'SULLIVAN, Dan

Daniel James O'Sullivan

Born: Mar. 3, 1968. Bronx, NY, United States. Height: 6'10". Weight: 250 lbs. Drafted: — College: Fordham

YEAR	TEAM	GP	GS	MIN	PTS	FGM	FGA	FG%	3PM	3PA	3P%	FTM	FTA	FT%	ORB	DRB	TRB	AST	PF	DQ	STL	BLK	TO	MPG	PPG	RPG	APG	PCM
90-91	Utah	21	0	85	21	7	16	.438	0	0	.000	7	11	.636	5	12	17	4	18	0	1	1	4	4.0	1.0	0.8	0.2	.242
92-93	New Jersey	3	0	10	4	2	3	.667	0	0	.000	0	0	.000	2	2	4	0	1	0	0	0	0	3.3	1.3	1.3	0.0	.633
92-93	Milwaukee	3	0	7	5	1	2	.500	0	0	.000	3	4	.750	0	2	2	1	3	0	1	0	0	2.3	1.7	0.7	0.3	.867

YEAR	TEAM	GP	GS	MIN	PTS	FGM	FGA	FG%	3PM	3PA	3P%	FTM	FTA	FT%	ORB	DRB	TRB	AST	PF	DQ	STL	BLK	TO	MPG	PPG	RPG	APG	PCM
93-94	Detroit	13	0	56	17	4	12	.333	0	0	.000	9	12	.750	2	8	10	3	10	0	0	0	3	4.3	1.3	0.8	0.2	.239
95-96	Toronto	5	2	139	33	13	35	.371	0	1	.000	7	8	.875	13	19	32	2	13	0	2	4	5	27.8	6.6	6.4	0.4	.280
NBA Season Totals		45	2	297	80	27	68	.397	0	1	.000	26	35	.743	22	43	65	10	45	0	4	5	12	6.6	1.8	1.4	0.2	....

• OTHICK, Matt

Matthew Brian Othick

Born: Mar. 16, 1969. Clovis, NM, United States.   Height: 6'2".   Weight: 165 lbs.   Drafted: —   College: Arizona

YEAR	TEAM	GP	GS	MIN	PTS	FGM	FGA	FG%	3PM	3PA	3P%	FTM	FTA	FT%	ORB	DRB	TRB	AST	PF	DQ	STL	BLK	TO	MPG	PPG	RPG	APG	PCM
92-93	San Antonio	4	0	39	8	3	5	.600	2	4	.500	0	2	.000	1	1	2	7	7	0	1	0	4	9.8	2.0	0.5	1.8	.217
NBA Season Totals		4	0	39	8	3	5	.600	2	4	.500	0	2	.000	1	1	2	7	7	0	1	0	4	9.8	2.0	0.5	1.8	....

• O'TOOLE, Tom

Thomas O'Toole

Born: —.   Height: —   Weight: —   Drafted: —   College: —

YEAR	TEAM	GP	GS	MIN	PTS	FGM	FGA	FG%	3PM	3PA	3P%	FTM	FTA	FT%	ORB	DRB	TRB	AST	PF	DQ	STL	BLK	TO	MPG	PPG	RPG	APG	PCM
40-41	Hammond-N	1	....	....	0	0	....	....	....	....	....	0	....	....	....	....	....	....	....	....	....	....	....	0.0	....	....	....	
NBL Season Totals		1	....	....	0	0	....					0												0.0				

• OTTEN, Don

Donald F. (Big Don) Otten

Born: Apr. 18, 1921. Bellefontaine, OH, United States. Died: Sept.18, 1985.   Height: 6'10".   Weight: 240 lbs.   Drafted: —   College: Bowling Green

YEAR	TEAM	GP	GS	MIN	PTS	FGM	FGA	FG%	3PM	3PA	3P%	FTM	FTA	FT%	ORB	DRB	TRB	AST	PF	DQ	STL	BLK	TO	MPG	PPG	RPG	APG	PCM
46-47	Tri-Cities-N	44	....	....	569	200	....	....				169	261	.648	....		98								12.9			
47-48	Tri-Cities-N	60	....	....	824	282	....	....				260	392	.663	....		184								13.7			
48-49	Tri-Cities-N	64	....	....	**899**	301	....	....				297	424	.700	....		205								14.0			
49-50	Tri-Cities	46	....	....	556	165	451	.366				226	315	.717		73	180								12.1	1.6		
49-50	Washington	18	....	....	269	77	197	.391				115	148	.777		18	66								14.9	1.0		
50-51	Baltimore	2	....	....	11	3	15	.200				5	9	.556		3	3	5	0						5.5	1.5	1.5	
50-51	Was/FtW	65	....	....	559	159	464	.343				241	299	.806		401	59	250	15						8.6	6.2	0.9	
51-52	FtW/Mil	64	....	1789	767	222	636	.349				323	418	.773		435	123	218	11						28.0	12.0	6.8	1.9	.464
52-53	Milwaukee	24	....	384	132	34	87	.391				64	91	.703		89	21	68	4						16.0	5.5	3.7	0.9	.392
NBA Season Totals		219	....	2173	2294	660	1850	.357				974	1280	.761		928	297	787	30						9.9	10.5	4.2	1.4	
NBL Season Totals		168	....		2292	783						726	1077				487								13.6			
Career Totals		387	....	2173	4586	1443	1850					1700	2357			928	297	1274	30						5.6	11.9	2.4	0.8
47-48	Tri-Cities-N	6	....	....	98	34						30	38	.789											16.3			
48-49	Tri-Cities-N	6	....	....	91	24						43	55	.782											15.2			
49-50	Washington	2	....	....	41	10	25	.400				21	26	.808			6	7							20.5		3.0	
50-51	Fort Wayne	3	....	....	29	8	26	.308				13	16	.813		19	8	15	1						9.7	6.3	2.7	
NBA Playoff Totals		5	....	....	70	18	51	.353				34	42	.810		19	14	22	1						14.0	3.8	2.8	
NBL Playoff Totals		12	....	....	189	58						73	93												15.8			
Career Playoff Totals		17	....	....	259	76	51					107	135			19	14	22	1						15.2	1.1	0.8	

• OTTEN, Mac

Mac William Otten

Born: Dec. 16, 1925.   Height: 6'7".   Weight: 220 lbs.   Drafted: 1949   College: Bowling Green

YEAR	TEAM	GP	GS	MIN	PTS	FGM	FGA	FG%	3PM	3PA	3P%	FTM	FTA	FT%	ORB	DRB	TRB	AST	PF	DQ	STL	BLK	TO	MPG	PPG	RPG	APG	PCM
49-50	Tri-Cities	12	....	....	39	12	34	.353				15	22	.682				11	27						3.3		0.9	
49-50	St. Louis	47	....	....	103	39	121	.322				25	59	.424				25	92						2.2		0.5	
NBA Season Totals		59	....	....	142	51	155	.329				40	81	.494				36	119						2.4		0.6	

• OTWAY, Frank

Frank Otway

Born: 1923.   Height: 6'4".   Weight: 205 lbs.   Drafted: —   College: Chicago

YEAR	TEAM	GP	GS	MIN	PTS	FGM	FGA	FG%	3PM	3PA	3P%	FTM	FTA	FT%	ORB	DRB	TRB	AST	PF	DQ	STL	BLK	TO	MPG	PPG	RPG	APG	PCM
44-45	Chicago-N	1	....	....	0	0	....					0													0.0			
NBL Season Totals		1	....	....	0	0	....					0													0.0			

• OUTLAW, Bo

Charles (Bo) Outlaw

Born: Apr. 13, 1971. San Antonio, TX, United States.   Height: 6'8".   Weight: 210 lbs.   Drafted: —   College: Houston

YEAR	TEAM	GP	GS	MIN	PTS	FGM	FGA	FG%	3PM	3PA	3P%	FTM	FTA	FT%	ORB	DRB	TRB	AST	PF	DQ	STL	BLK	TO	MPG	PPG	RPG	APG	PCM
93-94	LA Clippers	37	14	871	257	98	167	.587	0	2	.000	61	103	.592	81	131	212	36	94	1	36	37	30	23.5	6.9	5.7	1.0	.464
94-95	LA Clippers	81	31	1655	422	170	325	.523	0	5	.000	82	186	.441	121	192	313	84	227	4	90	151	81	20.4	5.2	3.9	1.0	.395
95-96	LA Clippers	80	3	985	286	107	186	.575	0	3	.000	72	162	.444	87	113	200	50	127	0	44	91	48	12.3	3.6	2.5	0.6	.439
96-97	LA Clippers	82	25	2195	625	254	417	.609	0	8	.000	117	232	.504	174	280	454	157	227	5	94	142	107	26.8	7.6	5.5	1.9	.467
97-98	Orlando	82	76	2953	783	301	543	.554	1	4	.250	180	313	.575	255	382	637	216	260	1	107	181	172	36.0	9.5	7.8	2.6	.442
98-99	Orlando	31	22	851	203	84	154	.545	0	3	.000	35	81	.432	54	113	167	56	79	1	40	43	58	27.5	6.5	5.4	1.8	.374
99-00	Orlando	82	55	2336	491	206	343	.601	0	3	.000	79	159	.497	204	336	540	245	201	0	114	148	129	28.5	6.0	6.6	3.0	.478
00-01	Orlando	80	69	2534	582	226	368	.614	1	2	.500	129	225	.573	211	408	619	225	241	4	105	137	141	31.7	7.3	7.7	2.8	.473
01-02	Orlando	10	0	160	34	13	21	.619	0	0	.000	8	18	.444	15	14	29	5	23	0	9	9	11	16.0	3.4	2.9	0.5	.312
01-02	Phoenix	73	36	1768	342	153	278	.550	1	2	.500	35	84	.417	132	203	335	122	182	1	61	83	85	24.2	4.7	4.6	1.7	.348
02-03	Phoenix	80	20	1800	378	153	278	.550	0	2	.000	72	116	.621	134	234	368	112	194	1	50	71	76	22.5	4.7	4.6	1.4	.363
NBA Season Totals		718	351	18108	4403	1765	3080	.573	3	34	.088	870	1679	.518	1468	2406	3874	1308	1855	18	750	1093	938	25.2	6.1	5.4	1.8	....
96-97	LA Clippers	3	0	66	15	6	11	.545	0	1	.000	3	10	.300	6	8	14	4	5	0	1	2	3	22.0	5.0	4.7	1.3	.334
98-99	Orlando	4	0	83	18	6	10	.600	0	0	.000	6	13	.462	3	12	15	2	9	0	1	8	6	20.8	4.5	3.8	0.5	.308
00-01	Orlando	4	4	134	34	16	26	.615	0	0	.000	2	11	.182	11	31	42	9	15	0	5	6	9	33.5	8.5	10.5	2.3	.475
02-03	Phoenix	6	0	70	4	1	10	.100	0	0	.000	2	4	.500	6	7	13	5	19	1	1	1	6	11.7	0.7	2.2	0.8	-.001
NBA Playoff Totals		17	4	353	71	29	57	.509	0	1	.000	13	38	.342	26	58	84	20	48	1	8	17	24	20.8	4.2	4.9	1.2	....

YEAR	TEAM	GP	GS	MIN	PTS	FGM	FGA	FG%	3PM	3PA	3P%	FTM	FTA	FT%	ORB	DRB	TRB	AST	PF	DQ	STL	BLK	TO	MPG	PPG	RPG	APG	PCM

• OVERTON, Claude
Claudell Overton

Born: Dec. 16, 1927.   Height: 6'2".   Weight: 195 lbs.   Drafted: 1950   College: East Central Oklahoma

YEAR	TEAM	GP	GS	MIN	PTS	FGM	FGA	FG%	3PM	3PA	3P%	FTM	FTA	FT%	ORB	DRB	TRB	AST	PF	DQ	STL	BLK	TO	MPG	PPG	RPG	APG	PCM
52-53	Philadelphia	15	....	182	58	19	75	.253	....	....	....	20	30	.667	....	....	25	15	25	0	....	....	....	12.1	3.9	1.7	1.0	.231
NBA Season Totals		**15**	....	**182**	**58**	**19**	**75**	**.253**	....	....	....	**20**	**30**	**.667**	....	....	**25**	**15**	**25**	**0**	....	....	....	**12.1**	**3.9**	**1.7**	**1.0**	

• OVERTON, Doug
Douglas M. Overton

Born: Aug. 3, 1969. Philadelphia, PA, United States.   Height: 6'3".   Weight: 190 lbs.   Drafted: 1991   College: LaSalle

YEAR	TEAM	GP	GS	MIN	PTS	FGM	FGA	FG%	3PM	3PA	3P%	FTM	FTA	FT%	ORB	DRB	TRB	AST	PF	DQ	STL	BLK	TO	MPG	PPG	RPG	APG	PCM
92-93	Washington	45	13	990	366	152	323	.471	3	13	.231	59	81	.728	25	81	106	157	81	0	31	6	72	22.0	8.1	2.4	3.5	.396
93-94	Washington	61	1	749	218	87	216	.403	1	11	.091	43	52	.827	19	50	69	92	48	0	21	1	55	12.3	3.6	1.1	1.5	.275
94-95	Washington	82	20	1704	576	207	498	.416	53	125	.424	109	125	.872	26	117	143	246	126	1	53	2	107	20.8	7.0	1.7	3.0	.342
95-96	Denver	55	0	607	182	67	178	.376	8	26	.308	40	55	.727	8	55	63	106	49	0	13	5	39	11.0	3.3	1.1	1.9	.329
96-97	Philadelphia	61	4	634	217	81	190	.426	10	40	.250	45	48	.938	18	50	68	101	44	0	24	0	37	10.4	3.6	1.1	1.7	.398
97-98	Philadelphia	23	2	277	62	24	63	.381	0	3	.000	14	16	.875	2	12	14	37	34	0	8	1	23	12.0	2.7	0.6	1.6	.180
98-99	Orlando	6	0	33	18	6	12	.500	0	2	.000	6	6	1.000	1	1	2	3	2	0	1	0	3	5.5	3.0	0.3	0.5	.458
98-99	New Jersey	8	1	174	64	25	57	.439	2	4	.500	12	14	.857	6	11	17	16	14	0	3	1	15	21.8	8.0	2.1	2.0	.296
98-99	Philadelphia	10	0	37	10	5	15	.333	0	1	.000	0	0	.000	0	2	2	4	2	0	1	0	2	3.7	1.0	0.2	0.4	.150
99-00	Boston	48	0	432	152	61	154	.396	10	28	.357	20	21	.952	14	19	33	53	46	0	10	0	20	9.0	3.2	0.7	1.1	.289
00-01	Boston	7	1	144	38	15	44	.341	1	4	.250	7	11	.636	3	12	15	19	15	0	4	0	13	20.6	5.4	2.1	2.7	.207
00-01	Charlotte	2	0	15	4	2	2	1.000	0	0	.000	0	0	.000	0	0	0	0	2	0	1	0	3	7.5	2.0	0.0	0.0	.087
00-01	New Jersey	12	9	316	83	35	93	.376	10	32	.313	3	5	.600	1	23	24	53	20	0	3	0	15	26.3	6.9	2.0	4.4	.286
01-02	LA Clippers	18	0	131	39	14	44	.318	7	27	.259	4	7	.571	1	11	12	13	10	0	3	1	12	7.3	2.2	0.7	0.7	.182
NBA Season Totals		**438**	**51**	**6243**	**2029**	**781**	**1889**	**.413**	**105**	**316**	**.332**	**362**	**441**	**.821**	**124**	**444**	**568**	**900**	**493**	**1**	**176**	**17**	**416**	**14.3**	**4.6**	**1.3**	**2.1**	

• OWENS, Billy
Billy Eugene Owens

Born: May 1, 1969. Carlisle, PA, United States.   Height: 6'8".   Weight: 220 lbs.   Drafted: 1991   College: Syracuse

YEAR	TEAM	GP	GS	MIN	PTS	FGM	FGA	FG%	3PM	3PA	3P%	FTM	FTA	FT%	ORB	DRB	TRB	AST	PF	DQ	STL	BLK	TO	MPG	PPG	RPG	APG	PCM
91-92	Golden State	80	77	2510	1141	468	891	.525	1	9	.111	204	312	.654	243	396	639	188	276	4	90	65	176	31.4	14.3	8.0	2.4	.536
92-93	Golden State	37	37	1201	612	247	493	.501	1	11	.091	117	183	.639	108	156	264	144	105	1	35	28	107	32.5	16.5	7.1	3.9	.551
93-94	Golden State	79	72	2738	1186	492	971	.507	3	15	.200	199	326	.610	230	410	640	326	269	5	83	60	213	34.7	15.0	8.1	4.1	.526
94-95	Miami	70	60	2296	1002	403	820	.491	2	22	.091	194	313	.620	203	299	502	246	205	6	80	30	203	32.8	14.3	7.2	3.5	.481
95-96	Miami	40	40	1388	590	239	473	.505	0	6	.000	112	177	.633	94	192	286	134	132	1	30	22	112	34.7	14.8	7.2	3.4	.455
95-96	Sacramento	22	11	594	218	84	200	.420	5	12	.417	45	70	.643	49	76	125	70	60	1	19	16	51	27.0	9.9	5.7	3.2	.414
96-97	Sacramento	66	56	1995	724	299	640	.467	25	72	.347	101	145	.697	134	258	392	187	187	4	62	25	132	30.2	11.0	5.9	2.8	.412
97-98	Sacramento	78	78	2348	818	338	728	.464	26	70	.371	116	197	.589	170	412	582	219	231	5	93	38	156	30.1	10.5	7.5	2.8	.454
98-99	Seattle	21	19	451	163	65	165	.394	5	11	.455	28	35	.800	35	45	80	38	37	0	12	4	33	21.5	7.8	3.8	1.8	.339
99-00	Philadelphia	46	7	919	271	112	258	.434	9	27	.333	38	64	.594	63	129	192	59	119	1	26	16	61	20.0	5.9	4.2	1.3	.320
99-00	Golden State	16	4	386	103	38	100	.380	2	7	.286	25	42	.595	36	73	109	38	47	0	7	5	24	24.1	6.4	6.8	2.4	.381
00-01	Detroit	45	14	793	198	88	230	.383	3	20	.150	19	40	.475	84	121	205	55	93	0	32	12	39	17.6	4.4	4.6	1.2	.339
NBA Season Totals		**600**	**475**	**17619**	**7026**	**2873**	**5969**	**.481**	**82**	**282**	**.291**	**1198**	**1904**	**.629**	**1449**	**2567**	**4016**	**1704**	**1761**	**28**	**569**	**321**	**1307**	**29.4**	**11.7**	**6.7**	**2.8**	
91-92	Golden State	4	4	157	77	30	57	.526	0	0	.000	17	27	.630	13	20	33	13	14	0	8	2	6	39.3	19.3	8.3	3.3	.567
93-94	Golden State	3	3	127	59	25	50	.500	0	1	.000	9	12	.750	12	18	30	13	11	0	4	2	7	42.3	19.7	10.0	4.3	.554
95-96	Sacramento	4	4	131	33	15	34	.441	0	4	.000	3	6	.500	5	21	26	14	17	1	4	1	11	32.8	8.3	6.5	3.5	.301
NBA Playoff Totals		**11**	**11**	**415**	**169**	**70**	**141**	**.496**	**0**	**5**	**.000**	**29**	**45**	**.644**	**30**	**59**	**89**	**40**	**42**	**1**	**16**	**5**	**24**	**37.7**	**15.4**	**8.1**	**3.6**	

• OWENS, Chris
Haywood Chris Owens

Born: Mar. 1, 1979. Akron, OH, United States.   Height: 6'7".   Weight: 245 lbs.   Drafted: 2002   College: Texas

YEAR	TEAM	GP	GS	MIN	PTS	FGM	FGA	FG%	3PM	3PA	3P%	FTM	FTA	FT%	ORB	DRB	TRB	AST	PF	DQ	STL	BLK	TO	MPG	PPG	RPG	APG	PCM
02-03	Memphis	1	0	6	4	2	3	.667	0	0	.000	0	0	.000	1	0	1	0	0	0	0	0	1	6.0	4.0	1.0	0.0	.515
NBA Season Totals		**1**	**0**	**6**	**4**	**2**	**3**	**.667**	**0**	**0**	**.000**	**0**	**0**	**.000**	**1**	**0**	**1**	**0**	**0**	**0**	**0**	**0**	**1**	**6.0**	**4.0**	**1.0**	**0.0**	

• OWENS, Eddie
Eddie Owens

Born: Dec. 26, 1953.   Height: 6'7".   Weight: 210 lbs.   Drafted: 1977   College: UNLV

YEAR	TEAM	GP	GS	MIN	PTS	FGM	FGA	FG%	3PM	3PA	3P%	FTM	FTA	FT%	ORB	DRB	TRB	AST	PF	DQ	STL	BLK	TO	MPG	PPG	RPG	APG	PCM
77-78	Buffalo	8	....	63	21	9	21	.429	....	....	....	3	6	.500	5	5	10	5	9	0	1	0	3	7.9	2.6	1.3	0.6	.284
NBA Season Totals		**8**	....	**63**	**21**	**9**	**21**	**.429**	....	....	....	**3**	**6**	**.500**	**5**	**5**	**10**	**5**	**9**	**0**	**1**	**0**	**3**	**7.9**	**2.6**	**1.3**	**0.6**	

• OWENS, Jim
Jim Owens

Born: May 1, 1950. Los Angeles, CA, United States.   Height: 6'5".   Weight: 200 lbs.   Drafted: 1973   College: Arizona State

YEAR	TEAM	GP	GS	MIN	PTS	FGM	FGA	FG%	3PM	3PA	3P%	FTM	FTA	FT%	ORB	DRB	TRB	AST	PF	DQ	STL	BLK	TO	MPG	PPG	RPG	APG	PCM
73-74	Phoenix	17	....	101	53	21	39	.538	....	....	....	11	14	.786	1	8	9	15	6	0	5	0	....	5.9	3.1	0.5	0.9	.582
74-75	Phoenix	41	....	432	124	56	145	.386	....	....	....	12	16	.750	7	36	43	49	27	0	16	2	....	10.5	3.0	1.0	1.2	.296
NBA Season Totals		**58**	....	**533**	**177**	**77**	**184**	**.418**	....	....	....	**23**	**30**	**.767**	**8**	**44**	**52**	**64**	**33**	**0**	**21**	**2**	....	**9.2**	**3.1**	**0.9**	**1.1**	

• OWENS, Keith
Keith Kensel Owens

Born: May 31, 1969. San Francisco, CA, United States.   Height: 6'7".   Weight: 225 lbs.   Drafted: —   College: UCLA

YEAR	TEAM	GP	GS	MIN	PTS	FGM	FGA	FG%	3PM	3PA	3P%	FTM	FTA	FT%	ORB	DRB	TRB	AST	PF	DQ	STL	BLK	TO	MPG	PPG	RPG	APG	PCM
91-92	LA Lakers	20	0	80	26	9	32	.281	0	0	.000	8	10	.800	8	7	15	3	11	0	5	4	2	4.0	1.3	0.8	0.2	.278
NBA Season Totals		**20**	**0**	**80**	**26**	**9**	**32**	**.281**	**0**	**0**	**.000**	**8**	**10**	**.800**	**8**	**7**	**15**	**3**	**11**	**0**	**5**	**4**	**2**	**4.0**	**1.3**	**0.8**	**0.2**	

YEAR TEAM	GP	GS	MIN	PTS	FGM	FGA	FG%	3PM	3PA	3P%	FTM	FTA	FT%	ORB	DRB	TRB	AST	PF	DQ	STL	BLK	TO	MPG	PPG	RPG	APG	PCM
• OWENS, Red																											James L. (Red) Owens
Born: Sept. 2, 1925. Died: Oct.11, 1988. Height: 6'3". Weight: 185 lbs. Drafted: 1949 College: Baylor																											
49-50 Tri-Cities	26	....	....	124	42	137	.307	....	....	....	40	59	.678	....	....	....	32	65	....	....	....	....	....	4.8	....	1.2	....
49-50 Anderson	35	....	....	116	44	151	.291	....	....	....	28	42	.667	....	....	....	41	87	....	....	....	....	....	3.3	....	1.2	....
51-52 Bal/Mil	29	....	626	230	83	252	.329	....	....	....	64	114	.561	....	....	102	64	92	5	....	....	....	21.6	7.9	3.5	2.2	.342
NBA Season Totals	90	....	626	470	169	540	.313	....	....	....	132	215	.614	....	....	102	137	244	5	....	....	....	7.0	5.2	1.1	1.5	....
49-50 Anderson	8	....	....	80	26	89	.292	....	....	....	28	41	.683	....	....	....	19	37	....	....	....	....	....	10.0	....	2.4	....
NBA Playoff Totals	8	....	....	80	26	89	.292	....	....	....	28	41	.683	....	....	....	19	37	....	....	....	....	....	10.0	....	2.4	....
• OWENS, Tom																											Thomas William Owens
Born: June 28, 1949. Bronx, NY, United States. Height: 6'10". Weight: 215 lbs. Drafted: 1971 College: South Carolina																											
71-72 Carolina-A	31	....	501	254	99	193	.513	1	3	.333	55	87	.632	77	114	191	21	81	1	....	....	32	16.2	8.2	6.2	0.7	.625
71-72 Memphis-A	38	....	617	250	98	209	.469	0	2	.000	54	88	.614	86	113	199	30	89	0	....	....	51	16.2	6.6	5.2	0.8	.497
72-73 Carolina-A	83	....	2209	979	393	727	.541	0	2	.000	193	284	.680	229	417	646	94	318	10	....	....	173	26.6	11.8	7.8	1.1	.534
73-74 Carolina-A	81	....	2284	1116	444	843	.527	2	6	.333	226	294	.769	301	416	717	127	308	....	54	41	171	28.2	13.8	8.9	1.6	.601
74-75 Memphis-A	77	....	2558	1206	497	943	.527	0	2	.000	212	280	.757	285	594	879	201	252	....	34	79	147	33.2	15.7	11.4	2.6	.654
74-75 St. Louis-A	5	....	89	33	14	26	.538	0	0	.000	5	9	.556	11	15	26	7	9	....	2	3	6	17.8	6.6	5.2	1.4	.533
75-76 Indiana-A	16	....	243	104	42	82	.512	0	0	.000	20	25	.800	28	41	69	9	53	....	2	11	19	15.2	6.5	4.3	0.6	.469
75-76 Kentucky-A	19	....	326	118	46	105	.438	0	0	.000	26	44	.591	33	60	93	19	50	....	6	17	26	17.2	6.2	4.9	1.0	.427
75-76 San Antonio-A	39	....	538	226	90	182	.495	0	0	.000	46	60	.767	54	101	155	41	97	....	3	13	29	13.8	5.8	4.0	1.1	.517
76-77 Houston	46	....	462	188	68	135	.504	....	....	....	52	76	.684	47	95	142	18	96	2	4	13	....	10.0	4.1	3.1	0.4	.479
77-78 Portland	82	....	1714	832	313	639	.490	....	....	....	206	278	.741	195	346	541	160	263	7	33	37	156	20.9	10.1	6.6	2.0	.571
78-79 Portland	82	....	2791	1520	600	1095	.548	....	....	....	320	403	.794	263	477	740	301	329	15	59	58	246	34.0	18.5	9.0	3.7	.634
79-80 Portland	76	....	2337	1250	518	1008	.514	1	2	.500	213	283	.753	189	384	573	194	270	5	45	53	175	30.8	16.4	7.5	2.6	.562
80-81 Portland	79	....	1843	835	322	630	.511	0	4	.000	191	250	.764	165	291	456	140	273	10	36	47	126	23.3	10.6	5.8	1.8	.506
81-82 Indiana	74	40	1599	780	299	636	.470	1	2	.500	181	226	.801	142	230	372	127	259	7	41	37	141	21.6	10.5	5.0	1.7	.470
82-83 Detroit	49	4	725	207	81	192	.422	0	0	.000	45	66	.682	66	120	186	44	115	0	12	14	49	14.8	4.2	3.8	0.9	.332
NBA Season Totals	488	44	11471	5612	2201	4335	.508	2	8	.250	1208	1582	.764	1067	1943	3010	984	1605	46	230	259	893	23.5	11.5	6.2	2.0	....
ABA Season Totals	389	....	9365	4286	1723	3310	.521	3	15	.200	837	1171	.715	1104	1871	2975	549	1257	11	101	164	654	24.1	11.0	7.6	1.4	....
Career Totals	877	44	20836	9898	3924	7645	.513	5	23	.217	2045	2753	.743	2171	3814	5985	1533	2862	57	331	423	1547	23.8	11.3	6.8	1.7	....
72-73 Carolina-A	12	....	377	175	65	127	.512	0	0	.000	45	60	.750	53	84	137	19	49	3	....	....	19	31.4	14.6	11.4	1.6	.622
73-74 Carolina-A	4	....	78	31	15	36	.417	0	0	.000	1	3	.333	7	8	15	5	18	....	1	0	4	19.5	7.8	3.8	1.3	.295
74-75 Memphis-A	5	....	207	109	48	87	.552	0	0	.000	13	19	.684	19	43	62	10	20	....	3	1	7	41.4	21.8	12.4	2.0	.623
75-76 San Antonio-A	7	....	89	23	8	24	.333	0	1	.000	7	14	.500	11	13	24	2	15	....	2	2	3	12.7	3.3	3.4	0.3	.253
76-77 Houston	3	....	7	0	0	1	.000	....	....	....	0	0	.000	0	2	2	0	1	0	1	0	....	2.3	0.0	0.7	0.0	.062
77-78 Portland	6	....	200	91	38	69	.551	....	....	....	15	21	.714	13	26	39	26	30	1	5	7	7	33.3	15.2	6.5	4.3	.579
78-79 Portland	3	....	80	35	15	31	.484	....	....	....	5	8	.625	9	10	19	5	16	1	4	1	7	26.7	11.7	6.3	1.7	.411
79-80 Portland	3	....	83	33	14	26	.538	0	0	.000	5	8	.625	13	8	21	2	14	1	1	2	5	27.7	11.0	7.0	0.7	.408
80-81 Portland	1	....	5	0	0	0	.000	0	0	.000	0	0	.000	0	1	1	0	1	0	0	0	0	5.0	0.0	1.0	0.0	.091
NBA Playoff Totals	16	....	375	159	67	127	.528	0	0	.000	25	37	.676	35	47	82	33	62	3	11	10	19	23.4	9.9	5.1	2.1	....
ABA Playoff Totals	28	....	751	338	136	274	.496	0	1	.000	66	96	.688	90	148	238	36	102	3	6	3	33	26.8	12.1	8.5	1.3	....
Career Playoff Totals	44	....	1126	497	203	401	.506	0	1	.000	91	133	.684	125	195	320	69	164	6	17	13	52	25.6	11.3	7.3	1.6	....
• OWES, Ray																											Raymond Owes
Born: Dec. 11, 1972. San Bernardino, CA, United States. Height: 6'9". Weight: 224 lbs. Drafted: — College: Arizona																											
96-97 Golden State	57	1	592	177	75	180	.417	1	5	.200	26	46	.565	64	99	163	15	86	1	15	20	23	10.4	3.1	2.9	0.3	.353
NBA Season Totals	57	1	592	177	75	180	.417	1	5	.200	26	46	.565	64	99	163	15	86	1	15	20	23	10.4	3.1	2.9	0.3	....
• OYEDEJI, Olumide																											Olumide Oyedeji
Born: May 11, 1981. Ibadan, Nigeria. Height: 6'10". Weight: 240 lbs. Drafted: 2000 College: none (HS: Community, NIG)																											
00-01 Seattle	30	1	221	45	18	37	.486	0	0	.000	9	12	.750	24	43	67	2	40	0	7	10	11	7.4	1.5	2.2	0.1	.346
01-02 Seattle	36	1	221	55	22	41	.537	0	0	.000	11	18	.611	27	52	79	4	36	0	4	2	14	6.1	1.5	2.2	0.1	.394
02-03 Orlando	27	3	145	27	10	23	.435	0	0	.000	7	11	.636	10	40	50	5	30	0	5	3	5	5.4	1.0	1.9	0.2	.368
NBA Season Totals	93	5	587	127	50	101	.495	0	0	.000	27	41	.659	61	135	196	11	106	0	16	15	30	6.3	1.4	2.1	0.1	....
01-02 Seattle	3	0	17	9	4	5	.800	0	0	.000	1	5	.200	4	2	6	1	2	0	0	0	1	5.7	3.0	2.0	0.3	.647
NBA Playoff Totals	3	0	17	9	4	5	.800	0	0	.000	1	5	.200	4	2	6	1	2	0	0	0	1	5.7	3.0	2.0	0.3	....
• OZBURN, Jack																											Jack Ozburn
Born: Jan. 4, 1913. Died: Feb.14, 1969. Height: 6'1". Weight: 170 lbs. Drafted: — College: Monmouth																											
37-38 Non-Skids-N	15	....	....	144	59	....	....	....	....	....	26	....	....	....	....	....	....	....	....	....	....	....	....	9.6	....	....	....
38-39 Non-Skids-N	19	....	....	184	75	....	....	....	....	....	34	....	....	....	....	....	....	....	....	....	....	....	....	9.7	....	....	....
39-40 Non-Skids-N	26	....	....	264	102	....	....	....	....	....	60	....	....	....	....	....	....	....	....	....	....	....	....	10.2	....	....	....
40-41 Non-Skids-N	24	....	....	211	88	....	....	....	....	....	35	....	....	....	....	....	....	....	....	....	....	....	....	8.8	....	....	....
41-42 Toledo-N	3	....	....	15	7	....	....	....	....	....	1	....	....	....	....	....	....	....	....	....	....	....	....	5.0	....	....	....
NBL Season Totals	87	....	....	818	331	....	....	....	....	....	156	....	....	....	....	....	....	....	....	....	....	....	....	9.4	....	....	....
37-38 Non-Skids-N	2	....	....	15	6	....	....	....	....	....	3	....	....	....	....	....	....	....	....	....	....	....	....	7.5	....	....	....
38-39 Non-Skids-N	5	....	....	47	18	....	....	....	....	....	11	....	....	....	....	....	....	....	....	....	....	....	....	9.4	....	....	....
39-40 Non-Skids-N	8	....	....	80	30	....	....	....	....	....	20	....	....	....	....	....	....	....	....	....	....	....	....	10.0	....	....	....
40-41 Non-Skids-N	2	....	....	3	1	....	....	....	....	....	1	....	....	....	....	....	....	....	....	....	....	....	....	1.5	....	....	....
NBL Playoff Totals	17	....	....	145	55	....	....	....	....	....	35	....	....	....	....	....	....	....	....	....	....	....	....	8.5	....	....	....

The Player Register PAGE • 1219

YEAR	TEAM	GP	GS	MIN	PTS	FGM	FGA	FG%	3PM	3PA	3P%	FTM	FTA	FT%	ORB	DRB	TRB	AST	PF	DQ	STL	BLK	TO	MPG	PPG	RPG	APG	PCM

• **PACE, Joe** — Joseph Pace

Born: Dec. 18, 1953. New Brunswick, NJ, United States. Height: 6'10". Weight: 220 lbs. Drafted: 1976 College: Maryland Eastern Shore

76-77	Washington	30	....	119	64	24	55	.436	....	....	....	16	29	.552	16	18	34	4	29	0	2	17	....	4.0	2.1	1.1	0.1	.445
77-78	Washington	49	....	438	191	67	140	.479	....	....	....	57	93	.613	50	84	134	23	86	1	12	21	44	8.9	3.9	2.7	0.5	.473
NBA Season Totals		79	....	557	255	91	195	.467	....	....	....	73	122	.598	66	102	168	27	115	1	14	38	44	7.1	3.2	2.1	0.3	....
77-78	Washington	9	....	52	25	7	10	.700	....	....	....	11	15	.733	5	15	20	1	17	1	1	6	5	5.8	2.8	2.2	0.1	.645
NBA Playoff Totals		9	....	52	25	7	10	.700	....	....	....	11	15	.733	5	15	20	1	17	1	1	6	5	5.8	2.8	2.2	0.1	....

• **PACK, Robert** — Robert John Pack Jr.

Born: Feb. 3, 1969. New Orleans, LA, United States. Height: 6'2". Weight: 180 lbs. Drafted: — College: USC

91-92	Portland	72	0	894	332	115	272	.423	0	10	.000	102	127	.803	32	65	97	140	101	0	40	4	94	12.4	4.6	1.3	1.9	.359
92-93	Denver	77	1	1579	810	285	606	.470	1	8	.125	239	311	.768	52	108	160	335	182	1	81	10	185	20.5	10.5	2.1	4.4	.514
93-94	Denver	66	4	1382	631	223	503	.443	6	29	.207	179	236	.758	25	98	123	356	147	1	81	9	205	20.9	9.6	1.9	5.4	.487
94-95	Denver	42	32	1144	507	170	395	.430	30	72	.417	137	175	.783	19	94	113	290	101	1	61	6	134	27.2	12.1	2.7	6.9	.509
95-96	Washington	31	31	1084	560	190	444	.428	26	98	.265	154	182	.846	29	103	132	242	68	0	62	1	115	35.0	18.1	4.3	7.8	.561
96-97	New Jersey	34	31	1185	542	193	474	.407	22	74	.297	134	170	.788	15	71	86	325	83	0	59	3	150	34.9	15.9	2.5	9.6	.481
96-97	Dallas	20	11	597	229	79	219	.361	9	38	.237	62	73	.849	13	47	60	127	56	0	35	3	68	29.9	11.5	3.0	6.4	.387
97-98	Dallas	12	10	292	94	33	98	.337	3	6	.500	25	36	.694	8	26	34	42	17	0	20	1	38	24.3	7.8	2.8	3.5	.284
98-99	Dallas	25	0	468	222	75	174	.431	0	4	.000	72	88	.818	9	27	36	81	41	0	20	1	49	18.7	8.9	1.4	3.2	.440
99-00	Dallas	29	22	665	259	96	230	.417	4	11	.364	63	78	.808	7	35	42	168	44	0	31	3	76	22.9	8.9	1.4	5.8	.442
00-01	Denver	74	11	1260	479	181	426	.425	12	31	.387	105	137	.766	30	107	137	293	114	0	65	1	135	17.0	6.5	1.9	4.0	.458
01-02	Minnesota	16	0	252	62	25	68	.368	1	4	.250	11	15	.733	7	16	23	49	32	0	13	0	20	15.8	3.9	1.4	3.1	.297
02-03	New Orleans	28	4	440	145	52	129	.403	0	5	.000	41	55	.745	11	40	51	81	35	0	25	0	40	15.7	5.2	1.8	2.9	.395
NBA Season Totals		526	157	11242	4872	1717	4038	.425	114	390	.292	1324	1683	.787	257	837	1094	2529	1021	3	593	42	1309	21.4	9.3	2.1	4.8	....
91-92	Portland	14	0	52	11	4	18	.222	0	0	.000	3	4	.750	2	4	6	7	10	0	5	1	3	3.7	0.8	0.4	0.5	.168
93-94	Denver	12	0	332	141	48	118	.407	6	20	.300	39	55	.709	5	23	28	51	41	0	18	6	46	27.7	11.8	2.3	4.3	.336
01-02	Minnesota	3	0	10	3	1	5	.200	0	1	.000	1	1	1.000	0	0	0	0	5	0	0	0	1	3.3	1.0	0.0	0.0	-.380
02-03	New Orleans	4	0	42	15	6	13	.462	0	0	.000	3	3	1.000	0	1	1	4	9	0	0	0	1	10.5	3.8	0.3	1.0	.213
NBA Playoff Totals		33	0	436	170	59	154	.383	6	21	.286	46	63	.730	7	28	35	62	65	0	23	7	51	13.2	5.2	1.1	1.9	....

• **PACK, Wayne** — Wayne (Six-Pack) Pack

Born: July 5, 1950. Indianapolis, IN, United States. Height: 6' Weight: 165 lbs. Drafted: — College: Tennessee Tech

| 74-75 | Indiana-A | 21 | .... | 189 | 61 | 23 | 60 | .383 | 5 | 17 | .294 | 10 | 12 | .833 | 7 | 13 | 20 | 13 | 21 | .... | 6 | 0 | 13 | 9.0 | 2.9 | 1.0 | 0.6 | .265 |
| **ABA Season Totals** | | 21 | .... | 189 | 61 | 23 | 60 | .383 | 5 | 17 | .294 | 10 | 12 | .833 | 7 | 13 | 20 | 13 | 21 | .... | 6 | 0 | 13 | 9.0 | 2.9 | 1.0 | 0.6 | .... |

• **PADDIO, Gerald** — Gerald James Paddio

Born: Apr. 21, 1965. Lafayette, LA, United States. Height: 6'7". Weight: 205 lbs. Drafted: 1988 College: UNLV

90-91	Cleveland	70	22	1181	504	212	506	.419	6	24	.250	74	93	.796	38	80	118	90	71	0	20	6	70	16.9	7.2	1.7	1.3	.299
92-93	Seattle	41	3	307	158	71	159	.447	2	8	.250	14	21	.667	17	33	50	33	24	0	14	6	16	7.5	3.9	1.2	0.8	.479
93-94	Indiana	7	1	55	19	9	23	.391	0	0	.000	1	2	.500	0	5	5	4	2	0	1	0	4	7.9	2.7	0.7	0.6	.199
93-94	New York	3	0	8	4	2	5	.400	0	0	.000	0	0	.000	0	0	0	0	3	0	0	0	0	2.7	1.3	0.0	0.0	-.016
93-94	Washington	8	0	74	30	11	32	.344	0	1	.000	8	14	.571	5	6	11	7	4	0	3	0	2	9.3	3.8	1.4	0.9	.334
NBA Season Totals		129	26	1625	715	305	725	.421	8	33	.242	97	130	.746	60	124	184	134	104	0	38	12	92	12.6	5.5	1.4	1.0	....
92-93	Seattle	9	0	30	14	7	14	.500	0	1	.000	0	0	.000	1	2	3	4	1	0	2	1	2	3.3	1.6	0.3	0.4	.500
NBA Playoff Totals		9	0	30	14	7	14	.500	0	1	.000	0	0	.000	1	2	3	4	1	0	2	1	2	3.3	1.6	0.3	0.4	....

• **PADGETT, Scott** — Scott Anthony Padgett

Born: Apr. 19, 1976. Louisville, KY, United States. Height: 6'9". Weight: 240 lbs. Drafted: 1999 College: Kentucky

99-00	Utah	47	9	432	120	44	140	.314	13	44	.295	19	27	.704	24	64	88	25	55	1	14	8	22	9.2	2.6	1.9	0.5	.258
00-01	Utah	27	0	127	56	18	43	.419	5	9	.556	15	20	.750	19	20	39	5	21	0	6	3	10	4.7	2.1	1.4	0.2	.484
01-02	Utah	75	1	1295	500	188	395	.476	49	113	.434	75	102	.735	111	174	285	82	140	0	43	13	69	17.3	6.7	3.8	1.1	.442
02-03	Utah	82	2	1321	466	170	423	.402	45	133	.338	81	107	.757	83	189	272	86	148	1	41	24	70	16.1	5.7	3.3	1.0	.374
NBA Season Totals		231	12	3175	1142	420	1001	.420	112	299	.375	190	256	.742	237	447	684	198	364	2	104	48	171	13.7	4.9	3.0	0.9	....
99-00	Utah	8	0	59	15	6	16	.375	3	9	.333	0	0	.000	3	14	17	5	10	0	1	2	4	7.4	1.9	2.1	0.6	.362
01-02	Utah	4	0	47	16	6	13	.462	0	3	.000	4	5	.800	7	7	14	2	6	0	1	1	5	11.8	4.0	3.5	0.5	.397
02-03	Utah	4	0	53	19	8	19	.421	2	7	.286	1	2	.500	6	3	9	4	6	0	3	0	5	13.3	4.8	2.3	1.0	.312
NBA Playoff Totals		16	0	159	50	20	48	.417	5	19	.263	5	7	.714	16	24	40	11	22	0	5	3	14	9.9	3.1	2.5	0.7	....

• **PAGE, —** — Page

Born: —. Height: — Weight: — Drafted: — College: —

| 40-41 | Detroit-N | 1 | .... | .... | 0 | 0 | .... | .... | .... | .... | 0 | .... | .... | .... | .... | .... | .... | .... | .... | .... | .... | .... | 0.0 | .... | .... | .... | .... |
| **NBL Season Totals** | | 1 | .... | .... | 0 | 0 | .... | .... | .... | .... | 0 | .... | .... | .... | .... | .... | .... | .... | .... | .... | .... | .... | .... | 0.0 | .... | .... | .... | .... |

YEAR	TEAM	GP	GS	MIN	PTS	FGM	FGA	FG%	3PM	3PA	3P%	FTM	FTA	FT%	ORB	DRB	TRB	AST	PF	DQ	STL	BLK	TO	MPG	PPG	RPG	APG	PCM

• PAGETT, Dana

Dana P. Pagett

Born: Mar. 29, 1949. Height: 6'2". Weight: 180 lbs. Drafted: 1971 College: USC

YEAR	TEAM	GP	GS	MIN	PTS	FGM	FGA	FG%	3PM	3PA	3P%	FTM	FTA	FT%	ORB	DRB	TRB	AST	PF	DQ	STL	BLK	TO	MPG	PPG	RPG	APG	PCM
71-72	Virginia-A	5	....	34	5	1	9	.111	1	3	.333	2	3	.667	1	2	3	6	8	0	....	....	3	6.8	1.0	0.6	1.2	.099
ABA Season Totals		5	....	34	5	1	9	.111	1	3	.333	2	3	.667	1	2	3	6	8	0	....	....	3	6.8	1.0	0.6	1.2	

• PAINE, Fred

Frederick Vincent Paine Jr.

Born: Dec. 7, 1925. Height: 6'5". Weight: 210 lbs. Drafted: — College: Westminster (PA)

YEAR	TEAM	GP	GS	MIN	PTS	FGM	FGA	FG%	3PM	3PA	3P%	FTM	FTA	FT%	ORB	DRB	TRB	AST	PF	DQ	STL	BLK	TO	MPG	PPG	RPG	APG	PCM
48-49	Providence	3	....	....	7	3	19	.158	....	....	....	1	5	.200	....	....	....	1	3	....	....	....	....	2.3	....	0.3	....
NBA Season Totals		3	....	....	7	3	19	.158	....	....	....	1	5	.200	....	....	....	1	3	....	....	....	....	2.3	....	0.3	....

• PALACIO, Milt

Milton S. Palacio

Born: Feb. 7, 1978. Los Angeles, CA, United States. Height: 6'3". Weight: 195 lbs. Drafted: — College: Colorado State

YEAR	TEAM	GP	GS	MIN	PTS	FGM	FGA	FG%	3PM	3PA	3P%	FTM	FTA	FT%	ORB	DRB	TRB	AST	PF	DQ	STL	BLK	TO	MPG	PPG	RPG	APG	PCM
99-00	Vancouver	53	0	394	108	43	98	.439	0	2	.000	22	37	.595	17	34	51	48	32	0	20	0	44	7.4	2.0	1.0	0.9	.288
00-01	Boston	58	6	1141	342	126	267	.472	12	36	.333	78	92	.848	25	77	102	151	83	0	48	0	80	19.7	5.9	1.8	2.6	.352
01-02	Boston	41	0	518	152	52	135	.385	12	34	.353	36	51	.706	8	42	50	54	38	0	21	3	24	12.6	3.7	1.2	1.3	.303
01-02	Phoenix	28	1	272	79	30	79	.380	1	7	.143	18	23	.783	3	20	23	29	23	0	9	1	16	9.7	2.8	0.8	1.0	.254
02-03	Cleveland	80	46	1976	397	162	388	.418	8	37	.216	65	87	.747	48	187	235	259	168	2	68	16	131	24.7	5.0	2.9	3.2	.283
NBA Season Totals		260	53	4301	1078	413	967	.427	33	116	.284	219	290	.755	101	360	461	541	344	2	166	20	295	16.5	4.1	1.8	2.1	....

• PALAZZI, Togo

Togo Anthony Palazzi

Born: Aug. 8, 1932. Union Hill, NJ, United States. Height: 6'4". Weight: 205 lbs. Drafted: 1954 College: Holy Cross

YEAR	TEAM	GP	GS	MIN	PTS	FGM	FGA	FG%	3PM	3PA	3P%	FTM	FTA	FT%	ORB	DRB	TRB	AST	PF	DQ	STL	BLK	TO	MPG	PPG	RPG	APG	PCM
54-55	Boston	53	....	504	247	101	253	.399	....	....	....	45	60	.750	....	....	146	30	60	1	....	....	....	9.5	4.7	2.8	0.6	.499
55-56	Boston	63	....	703	375	145	373	.389	....	....	....	85	124	.685	....	....	182	42	87	0	....	....	....	11.2	6.0	2.9	0.7	.489
56-57	Boston	21	....	233	105	41	118	.347	....	....	....	23	32	.719	....	....	75	8	23	0	....	....	....	11.1	5.0	3.6	0.4	.436
56-57	Syracuse	42	....	780	451	169	453	.373	....	....	....	113	143	.790	....	....	187	41	94	1	....	....	....	18.6	10.7	4.5	1.0	.492
57-58	Syracuse	67	....	1001	579	228	579	.394	....	....	....	123	171	.719	....	....	243	42	125	0	....	....	....	14.9	8.6	3.6	0.6	.490
58-59	Syracuse	71	....	1053	595	240	612	.392	....	....	....	115	158	.728	....	....	266	67	174	5	....	....	....	14.8	8.4	3.7	0.9	.491
59-60	Syracuse	7	....	70	30	13	41	.317	....	....	....	4	8	.500	....	....	14	3	7	0	....	....	....	10.0	4.3	2.0	0.4	.271
NBA Season Totals		324	....	4344	2382	937	2429	.386	....	....	....	508	696	.730	....	....	1113	233	570	7	....	....	....	13.4	7.4	3.4	0.7	....
54-55	Boston	5	....	30	29	12	24	.500	....	....	....	5	10	.500	....	....	14	1	7	0	....	....	....	6.0	5.8	2.8	0.2	.908
55-56	Boston	2	....	7	2	1	5	.200	....	....	....	0	0	.000	....	....	2	0	1	0	....	....	....	3.5	1.0	1.0	0.0	.014
56-57	Syracuse	5	....	87	45	19	49	.388	....	....	....	7	9	.778	....	....	18	5	11	0	....	....	....	17.4	9.0	3.6	1.0	.431
57-58	Syracuse	3	....	25	9	3	14	.214	....	....	....	3	6	.500	....	....	4	0	4	0	....	....	....	8.3	3.0	1.3	0.0	.054
58-59	Syracuse	8	....	67	36	13	44	.295	....	....	....	10	14	.714	....	....	21	6	10	0	....	....	....	8.4	4.5	2.6	0.8	.458
NBA Playoff Totals		23	....	216	121	48	136	.353	....	....	....	25	39	.641	....	....	59	12	33	0	....	....	....	9.4	5.3	2.6	0.5	....

• PALMER, Bud

John S. (Bud) Palmer

Born: Sept. 14, 1921. Hollywood, CA, United States. Height: 6'4". Weight: 180 lbs. Drafted: — College: Princeton

YEAR	TEAM	GP	GS	MIN	PTS	FGM	FGA	FG%	3PM	3PA	3P%	FTM	FTA	FT%	ORB	DRB	TRB	AST	PF	DQ	STL	BLK	TO	MPG	PPG	RPG	APG	PCM
46-47	New York	42	....	....	401	160	521	.307	....	....	....	81	121	.669	....	....	....	34	110	....	....	....	....	9.5	....	0.8	....
47-48	New York	48	....	....	622	224	710	.315	....	....	....	174	234	.744	....	....	....	45	149	....	....	....	....	13.0	....	0.9	....
48-49	New York	58	....	....	714	240	685	.350	....	....	....	234	307	.762	....	....	....	108	206	....	....	....	....	12.3	....	1.9	....
NBA Season Totals		148	....	....	1737	624	1916	.326	....	....	....	489	662	.739	....	....	....	187	465	....	....	....	....	11.7	....	1.3	....
46-47	New York	5	....	....	78	33	94	.351	....	....	....	12	20	.600	....	....	....	4	8	....	....	....	....	15.6	....	0.8	....
47-48	New York	3	....	....	42	16	38	.421	....	....	....	10	13	.769	....	....	....	0	17	....	....	....	....	14.0	....	0.0	....
48-49	New York	6	....	....	81	27	64	.422	....	....	....	27	35	.771	....	....	....	10	31	....	....	....	....	13.5	....	1.7	....
NBA Playoff Totals		14	....	....	201	76	196	.388	....	....	....	49	68	.721	....	....	....	14	56	....	....	....	....	14.4	....	1.0	....

• PALMER, Errol

Errol Palmer

Born: 1945. Height: 6'5". Weight: 195 lbs. Drafted: — College: DePaul

YEAR	TEAM	GP	GS	MIN	PTS	FGM	FGA	FG%	3PM	3PA	3P%	FTM	FTA	FT%	ORB	DRB	TRB	AST	PF	DQ	STL	BLK	TO	MPG	PPG	RPG	APG	PCM
67-68	Minnesota-A	63	....	1191	500	165	453	.364	0	0	.000	170	253	.672	....	....	471	91	169	2	....	....	78	18.9	7.9	7.5	1.4	.549
ABA Season Totals		63	....	1191	500	165	453	.364	0	0	.000	170	253	.672	....	....	471	91	169	2	....	....	78	18.9	7.9	7.5	1.4	....
67-68	Minnesota-A	6	....	75	28	10	25	.400	0	0	.000	8	10	.800	....	....	27	7	17	0	....	....	7	12.5	4.7	4.5	1.2	.510
ABA Playoff Totals		6	....	75	28	10	25	.400	0	0	.000	8	10	.800	....	....	27	7	17	0	....	....	7	12.5	4.7	4.5	1.2	....

• PALMER, Jim

James G. (Keok) Palmer

Born: June 8, 1933. Keokee, VA, United States. Height: 6'8". Weight: 224 lbs. Drafted: 1957 College: Dayton

YEAR	TEAM	GP	GS	MIN	PTS	FGM	FGA	FG%	3PM	3PA	3P%	FTM	FTA	FT%	ORB	DRB	TRB	AST	PF	DQ	STL	BLK	TO	MPG	PPG	RPG	APG	PCM
58-59	Cincinnati	67	....	1624	690	256	633	.404	....	....	....	178	246	.724	....	....	472	65	211	7	....	....	....	24.2	10.3	7.0	1.0	.454
59-60	Cincinnati	20	....	400	181	71	155	.458	....	....	....	39	55	.709	....	....	111	17	65	1	....	....	....	20.0	9.1	5.6	0.9	.480
59-60	New York	54	....	1082	430	175	419	.418	....	....	....	80	119	.672	....	....	278	53	159	5	....	....	....	20.0	8.0	5.1	1.0	.413
60-61	New York	55	....	688	294	125	310	.403	....	....	....	44	65	.677	....	....	179	30	128	0	....	....	....	12.5	5.3	3.3	0.5	.392
NBA Season Totals		196	....	3794	1595	627	1517	.413	....	....	....	341	485	.703	....	....	1040	165	563	13	....	....	....	19.4	8.1	5.3	0.8	....

YEAR	TEAM	GP	GS	MIN	PTS	FGM	FGA	FG%	3PM	3PA	3P%	FTM	FTA	FT%	ORB	DRB	TRB	AST	PF	DQ	STL	BLK	TO	MPG	PPG	RPG	APG	PCM

• PALMER, Walter

Walter Scott Palmer

Born: Oct. 23, 1968. Ithaca, NY, United States. Height: 7'1". Weight: 215 lbs. Drafted: 1990 College: Dartmouth

YEAR	TEAM	GP	GS	MIN	PTS	FGM	FGA	FG%	3PM	3PA	3P%	FTM	FTA	FT%	ORB	DRB	TRB	AST	PF	DQ	STL	BLK	TO	MPG	PPG	RPG	APG	PCM
90-91	Utah	28	0	85	40	15	45	.333	0	1	.000	10	15	.667	6	15	21	6	20	0	3	4	6	3.0	1.4	0.8	0.2	.321
92-93	Dallas	20	0	124	60	27	57	.474	0	0	.000	6	9	.667	12	32	44	5	29	0	1	5	10	6.2	3.0	2.2	0.3	.482
NBA Season Totals		48	0	209	100	42	102	.412	0	1	.000	16	24	.667	18	47	65	11	49	0	4	9	16	4.4	2.1	1.4	0.2	....
90-91	Utah	2	0	6	2	1	4	.250	0	0	.000	0	0	.000	0	1	1	0	3	0	0	0	1	3.0	1.0	0.5	0.0	-.366
NBA Playoff Totals		2	0	6	2	1	4	.250	0	0	.000	0	0	.000	0	1	1	0	3	0	0	0	1	3.0	1.0	0.5	0.0	....

• PANKO, Andy

Andy Panko

Born: Nov. 27, 1977. Harrisburg, PA, United States. Height: 6'9". Weight: 222 lbs. Drafted: — College: Lebanon Valley

YEAR	TEAM	GP	GS	MIN	PTS	FGM	FGA	FG%	3PM	3PA	3P%	FTM	FTA	FT%	ORB	DRB	TRB	AST	PF	DQ	STL	BLK	TO	MPG	PPG	RPG	APG	PCM
00-01	Atlanta	1	0	1	0	0	0	.000	0	0	.000	0	0	.000	0	0	0	0	0	0	0	0	0	1.0	0.0	0.0	0.0	.000
NBA Season Totals		1	0	1	0	0	0	.000	0	0	.000	0	0	.000	0	0	0	0	0	0	0	0	0	1.0	0.0	0.0	0.0	....

• PARGO, Jannero

Jannero Pargo

Born: Sept. 22, 1979. Chicago, IL, United States. Height: 6'1". Weight: 175 lbs. Drafted: — College: Arkansas

YEAR	TEAM	GP	GS	MIN	PTS	FGM	FGA	FG%	3PM	3PA	3P%	FTM	FTA	FT%	ORB	DRB	TRB	AST	PF	DQ	STL	BLK	TO	MPG	PPG	RPG	APG	PCM
02-03	LA Lakers	34	0	342	85	37	93	.398	7	24	.292	4	4	1.000	9	28	37	39	45	0	13	2	23	10.1	2.5	1.1	1.1	.242
NBA Season Totals		34	0	342	85	37	93	.398	7	24	.292	4	4	1.000	9	28	37	39	45	0	13	2	23	10.1	2.5	1.1	1.1	....
02-03	LA Lakers	11	0	129	23	8	24	.333	4	15	.267	3	4	.750	3	6	9	14	22	0	8	1	7	11.7	2.1	0.8	1.3	.181
NBA Playoff Totals		11	0	129	23	8	24	.333	4	15	.267	3	4	.750	3	6	9	14	22	0	8	1	7	11.7	2.1	0.8	1.3	....

• PARHAM, Easy

Estes Foster (Easy) Parham

Born: Dec. 27, 1921. Fort Worth, TX, United States. Died: Oct.1982. Height: 6'3". Weight: 200 lbs. Drafted: 1948 College: Texas Wesleyan

YEAR	TEAM	GP	GS	MIN	PTS	FGM	FGA	FG%	3PM	3PA	3P%	FTM	FTA	FT%	ORB	DRB	TRB	AST	PF	DQ	STL	BLK	TO	MPG	PPG	RPG	APG	PCM
48-49	St. Louis	60	....	....	344	124	404	.307	....	....	....	96	172	.558	....	....	....	151	134	....	....	....	....	....	5.7	....	2.5	....
49-50	St. Louis	66	....	....	362	137	421	.325	....	....	....	88	178	.494	....	....	....	132	158	....	....	....	....	....	5.5	....	2.0	....
50-51	Philadelphia	7	....	....	10	3	7	.429	....	....	....	4	9	.444	....	....	12	3	5	0	....	....	....	....	1.4	1.7	0.4	....
NBA Season Totals		133	....	....	716	264	832	.317	....	....	....	188	359	.524	....	....	12	286	297	0	....	....	....	....	5.4	0.1	2.2	....
48-49	St. Louis	2	....	....	10	5	13	.385	....	....	....	0	0	.000	....	....	....	6	6	....	....	....	....	....	5.0	....	3.0	....
NBA Playoff Totals		2	....	....	10	5	13	.385	....	....	....	0	0	.000	....	....	....	6	6	....	....	....	....	....	5.0	....	3.0	....

• PARISH, Robert

Robert Lee (Chief) Parish

Born: Aug. 30, 1953. Shreveport, LA, United States. Height: 7' Weight: 230 lbs. Drafted: 1976 College: Centenary HOF: 2003

YEAR	TEAM	GP	GS	MIN	PTS	FGM	FGA	FG%	3PM	3PA	3P%	FTM	FTA	FT%	ORB	DRB	TRB	AST	PF	DQ	STL	BLK	TO	MPG	PPG	RPG	APG	PCM
76-77	Golden State	77	....	1384	697	288	573	.503	....	....	....	121	171	.708	201	342	543	74	224	7	55	94	....	18.0	9.1	7.1	1.0	.640
77-78	Golden State	82	....	1969	1025	430	911	.472	....	....	....	165	264	.625	211	469	680	95	291	10	79	123	205	24.0	12.5	8.3	1.2	.575
78-79	Golden State	76	....	2411	1304	554	1110	.499	....	....	....	196	281	.698	265	651	916	115	303	10	100	217	236	31.7	17.2	12.1	1.5	.685
79-80	Golden State	72	....	2119	1223	510	1006	.507	0	1	.000	203	284	.715	247	536	783	122	248	6	58	115	223	29.4	17.0	10.9	1.7	.671
80-81	Boston	82	....	2298	1552	635	1166	.545	0	1	.000	282	397	.710	245	532	777	144	310	9	81	214	189	28.0	18.9	9.5	1.8	.799
81-82	Boston	80	78	2534	1590	669	1235	.542	0	0	.000	252	355	.710	288	578	866	140	267	5	68	192	224	31.7	19.9	10.8	1.8	.742
82-83	Boston	78	76	2459	1509	619	1125	.550	0	1	.000	271	388	.698	260	567	827	141	222	4	79	148	187	31.5	19.3	10.6	1.8	.747
83-84	Boston	80	79	2867	1520	623	1140	.546	0	0	.000	274	368	.745	243	614	857	139	266	7	55	116	184	35.8	19.0	10.7	1.7	.630
84-85	Boston	79	78	2850	1394	551	1016	.542	0	0	.000	292	393	.743	263	577	840	125	223	2	56	101	190	36.1	17.6	10.6	1.6	.595
85-86	Boston	81	80	2567	1305	530	966	.549	0	0	.000	245	335	.731	246	524	770	145	215	3	65	116	186	31.7	16.1	9.5	1.8	.633
86-87	Boston	80	80	2995	1403	588	1057	.556	0	1	.000	227	309	.735	254	597	851	173	266	5	64	144	192	37.4	17.5	10.6	2.2	.600
87-88	Boston	74	73	2312	1061	442	750	.589	0	1	.000	177	241	.734	173	455	628	115	198	5	55	84	155	31.2	14.3	8.5	1.6	.582
88-89	Boston	80	80	2840	1486	596	1045	.570	0	0	.000	294	409	.719	342	654	996	175	209	2	79	116	200	35.5	18.6	12.5	2.2	.714
89-90	Boston	79	78	2396	1243	505	871	.580	0	0	.000	233	312	.747	259	537	796	103	189	2	38	69	166	30.3	15.7	10.1	1.3	.657
90-91	Boston	81	81	2441	1207	485	811	.598	0	1	.000	237	309	.767	271	585	856	66	197	1	66	103	154	30.1	14.9	10.6	0.8	.680
91-92	Boston	79	79	2285	1115	468	874	.535	0	0	.000	179	232	.772	219	486	705	70	172	2	68	97	134	28.9	14.1	8.9	0.9	.609
92-93	Boston	79	79	2146	994	416	777	.535	0	0	.000	162	235	.689	246	494	740	61	201	3	57	107	119	27.2	12.6	9.4	0.8	.618
93-94	Boston	74	74	1987	866	356	725	.491	0	0	.000	154	208	.740	141	401	542	82	190	3	42	96	111	26.9	11.7	7.3	1.1	.517
94-95	Charlotte	81	4	1352	389	159	372	.427	0	0	.000	71	101	.703	93	257	350	44	132	0	27	36	65	16.7	4.8	4.3	0.5	.360
95-96	Charlotte	74	34	1086	290	120	241	.498	0	0	.000	50	71	.704	89	214	303	29	80	0	21	54	52	14.7	3.9	4.1	0.4	.429
96-97	Chicago	43	3	406	161	70	143	.490	0	0	.000	21	31	.677	42	47	89	22	40	0	6	19	30	9.4	3.7	2.1	0.5	.422
NBA Season Totals		1611	1056	45704	23334	9614	17914	.537	0	6	.000	4106	5694	.721	4598	10117	14715	2180	4443	86	1219	2361	3202	28.4	14.5	9.1	1.4	....
76-77	Golden State	10	....	239	121	52	108	.481	....	....	....	17	26	.654	43	60	103	11	42	1	7	11	....	23.9	12.1	10.3	1.1	.636
80-81	Boston	17	....	492	255	108	219	.493	0	0	.000	39	58	.672	50	96	146	19	74	2	21	39	44	28.9	15.0	8.6	1.1	.569
81-82	Boston	12	12	426	255	102	209	.488	0	0	.000	51	75	.680	43	92	135	18	47	1	5	48	39	35.5	21.3	11.3	1.5	.658
82-83	Boston	7	7	249	103	43	89	.483	0	0	.000	17	20	.850	21	53	74	9	18	0	5	9	17	35.6	14.7	10.6	1.3	.506
83-84	Boston	23	23	869	342	139	291	.478	0	0	.000	64	99	.646	76	172	248	27	100	6	23	41	45	37.8	14.9	10.8	1.2	.478
84-85	Boston	21	21	803	359	136	276	.493	0	0	.000	87	111	.784	57	162	219	31	68	0	21	34	50	38.2	17.1	10.4	1.5	.532
85-86	Boston	18	18	591	270	106	225	.471	0	0	.000	58	89	.652	52	106	158	25	47	1	9	30	44	32.8	15.0	8.8	1.4	.494
86-87	Boston	21	21	734	377	149	263	.567	0	1	.000	79	103	.767	59	139	198	28	79	4	18	35	38	35.0	18.0	9.4	1.3	.615
87-88	Boston	17	17	626	250	100	188	.532	0	0	.000	50	61	.820	51	117	168	21	42	0	11	19	38	36.8	14.7	9.9	1.2	.503
88-89	Boston	3	3	112	47	20	44	.455	0	0	.000	7	9	.778	6	20	26	6	5	0	4	2	6	37.3	15.7	8.7	2.0	.465
89-90	Boston	5	5	170	79	31	54	.574	0	0	.000	17	18	.944	23	27	50	13	21	0	5	7	12	34.0	15.8	10.0	2.6	.634
90-91	Boston	10	10	296	158	58	97	.598	0	0	.000	42	61	.689	33	59	92	6	34	1	8	7	16	29.6	15.8	9.2	0.6	.636
91-92	Boston	10	10	335	120	50	101	.495	0	0	.000	20	28	.714	38	59	97	14	22	0	7	15	9	33.5	12.0	9.7	1.4	.525
92-93	Boston	4	4	146	68	31	57	.544	0	0	.000	6	7	.857	13	25	38	5	14	0	1	6	6	36.5	17.0	9.5	1.3	.537
94-95	Charlotte	4	0	71	14	6	11	.545	0	0	.000	2	5	.400	4	5	9	1	2	0	0	3	1	17.8	3.5	2.3	0.3	.258
96-97	Chicago	2	0	18	2	1	7	.143	0	0	.000	0	0	.000	2	2	4	0	2	0	0	3	0	9.0	1.0	2.0	0.0	.111
NBA Playoff Totals		184	151	6177	2820	1132	2239	.506	0	1	.000	556	770	.722	571	1194	1765	234	617	16	145	309	365	33.6	15.3	9.6	1.3	....

• PARK, Med

Medford R. Park

Born: Apr. 11, 1933. Britton, SD, United States. Died: July23, 1998.   Height: 6'2".   Weight: 205 lbs.   Drafted: —   College: Missouri

YEAR	TEAM	GP	GS	MIN	PTS	FGM	FGA	FG%	3PM	3PA	3P%	FTM	FTA	FT%	ORB	DRB	TRB	AST	PF	DQ	STL	BLK	TO	MPG	PPG	RPG	APG	PCM
55-56	St. Louis	40	....	424	150	53	152	.349	....	....	....	44	70	.629	....	....	94	40	64	0	....	....	....	10.6	3.8	2.4	1.0	.381
56-57	St. Louis	66	....	1130	344	118	324	.364	....	....	....	108	146	.740	....	....	200	94	137	2	....	....	....	17.1	5.2	3.0	1.4	.347
57-58	St. Louis	71	....	1103	384	133	363	.366	....	....	....	118	162	.728	....	....	184	76	106	0	....	....	....	15.5	5.4	2.6	1.1	.356
58-59	St. Louis	29	....	228	86	34	84	.405	....	....	....	18	24	.750	....	....	38	28	22	0	....	....	....	7.9	3.0	1.3	1.0	.445
58-59	Cincinnati	33	....	898	319	111	277	.401	....	....	....	97	126	.770	....	....	150	80	71	0	....	....	....	27.2	9.7	4.5	2.4	.411
59-60	Cincinnati	74	....	1849	641	226	582	.388	....	....	....	189	260	.727	....	....	301	214	180	2	....	....	....	25.0	8.7	4.1	2.9	.417
NBA Season Totals		313	....	5632	1924	675	1782	.379	....	....	....	574	788	.728	....	....	967	532	580	4	....	....	....	18.0	6.1	3.1	1.7	....
55-56	St. Louis	6	....	88	38	7	30	.233	....	....	....	24	33	.727	....	....	17	11	19	1	....	....	....	14.7	6.3	2.8	1.8	.414
56-57	St. Louis	10	....	183	44	14	49	.286	....	....	....	16	22	.727	....	....	33	12	18	0	....	....	....	18.3	4.4	3.3	1.2	.266
57-58	St. Louis	10	....	147	47	17	42	.405	....	....	....	13	22	.591	....	....	24	12	24	0	....	....	....	14.7	4.7	2.4	1.2	.337
NBA Playoff Totals		26	....	418	129	38	121	.314	....	....	....	53	77	.688	....	....	74	35	61	1	....	....	....	16.1	5.0	2.8	1.3	....

• PARKER, Anthony

Anthony Michael Parker

Born: June 19, 1975. Naperville, IL, United States.   Height: 6'6".   Weight: 215 lbs.   Drafted: 1997   College: Bradley

YEAR	TEAM	GP	GS	MIN	PTS	FGM	FGA	FG%	3PM	3PA	3P%	FTM	FTA	FT%	ORB	DRB	TRB	AST	PF	DQ	STL	BLK	TO	MPG	PPG	RPG	APG	PCM
97-98	Philadelphia	37	0	196	72	25	63	.397	9	28	.321	13	20	.650	8	18	26	19	17	0	11	3	11	5.3	1.9	0.7	0.5	.374
98-99	Philadelphia	2	0	3	2	1	1	1.000	0	0	.000	0	0	.000	0	0	0	0	0	0	0	0	0	1.5	1.0	0.0	0.0	.667
99-00	Orlando	16	0	187	57	24	57	.421	1	14	.071	8	11	.727	5	22	27	10	13	0	8	4	11	11.7	3.6	1.7	0.6	.300
NBA Season Totals		55	0	386	131	50	121	.413	10	42	.238	21	31	.677	13	40	53	29	30	0	19	7	22	7.0	2.4	1.0	0.5	....
01-02	San Antonio	10	10	341	155	62	136	.456	10	27	.370	21	28	.750	5	24	29	40	22	0	9	1	22	34.1	15.5	2.9	4.0	.393
NBA Playoff Totals		10	10	341	155	62	136	.456	10	27	.370	21	28	.750	5	24	29	40	22	0	9	1	22	34.1	15.5	2.9	4.0	....

• PARKER, Smush

William (Smush) Parker

Born: June 1, 1981. New York, NY, United States.   Height: 6'4".   Weight: 190 lbs.   Drafted: —   College: Fordham

YEAR	TEAM	GP	GS	MIN	PTS	FGM	FGA	FG%	3PM	3PA	3P%	FTM	FTA	FT%	ORB	DRB	TRB	AST	PF	DQ	STL	BLK	TO	MPG	PPG	RPG	APG	PCM
02-03	Cleveland	66	18	1103	408	136	338	.402	38	118	.322	98	118	.831	29	90	119	162	106	1	48	12	133	16.7	6.2	1.8	2.5	.350
NBA Season Totals		66	18	1103	408	136	338	.402	38	118	.322	98	118	.831	29	90	119	162	106	1	48	12	133	16.7	6.2	1.8	2.5	....

• PARKER, Sonny

Robert S. (Sonny) Parker Jr.

Born: Mar. 22, 1955. Chicago, IL, United States.   Height: 6'6".   Weight: 200 lbs.   Drafted: 1976   College: Texas A&M

YEAR	TEAM	GP	GS	MIN	PTS	FGM	FGA	FG%	3PM	3PA	3P%	FTM	FTA	FT%	ORB	DRB	TRB	AST	PF	DQ	STL	BLK	TO	MPG	PPG	RPG	APG	PCM
76-77	Golden State	65	....	889	379	154	292	.527	....	....	....	71	92	.772	85	88	173	59	77	0	53	26	....	13.7	5.8	2.7	0.9	.488
77-78	Golden State	82	....	2069	934	406	783	.519	....	....	....	122	173	.705	167	222	389	155	186	0	135	36	131	25.2	11.4	4.7	1.9	.508
78-79	Golden State	79	....	2893	1199	512	1019	.502	....	....	....	175	222	.788	164	280	444	291	187	0	144	33	190	36.6	15.2	5.6	3.7	.465
79-80	Golden State	82	....	2849	1203	483	988	.489	0	2	.000	237	302	.785	166	298	464	254	195	2	173	32	164	34.7	14.7	5.7	3.1	.479
80-81	Golden State	73	....	1317	476	191	388	.492	0	0	.000	94	128	.734	101	93	194	106	112	0	67	13	88	18.0	6.5	2.7	1.5	.391
81-82	Golden State	71	0	899	280	116	245	.473	0	0	.000	48	72	.667	73	104	177	89	101	0	39	11	50	12.7	3.9	2.5	1.3	.403
NBA Season Totals		452	0	10916	4471	1862	3715	.501	0	2	.000	747	989	.755	756	1085	1841	954	858	2	611	151	623	24.2	9.9	4.1	2.1	....
76-77	Golden State	10	....	120	42	19	36	.528	....	....	....	4	4	1.000	9	19	28	9	9	0	5	2	....	12.0	4.2	2.8	0.9	.482
NBA Playoff Totals		10	....	120	42	19	36	.528	....	....	....	4	4	1.000	9	19	28	9	9	0	5	2	....	12.0	4.2	2.8	0.9	....

• PARKER, Tony

William Anthony Parker

Born: May 17, 1982. Bruges, Belgium.   Height: 6'2".   Weight: 180 lbs.   Drafted: 2001   College: none (HS:INSEP, FRA)

YEAR	TEAM	GP	GS	MIN	PTS	FGM	FGA	FG%	3PM	3PA	3P%	FTM	FTA	FT%	ORB	DRB	TRB	AST	PF	DQ	STL	BLK	TO	MPG	PPG	RPG	APG	PCM
01-02	San Antonio	77	72	2267	705	268	639	.419	61	189	.323	108	160	.675	33	164	197	334	166	1	89	7	151	29.4	9.2	2.6	4.3	.337
02-03	San Antonio	82	82	2774	1269	484	1043	.464	82	243	.337	219	290	.755	33	183	216	432	174	2	71	4	198	33.8	15.5	2.6	5.3	.435
NBA Season Totals		159	154	5041	1974	752	1682	.447	143	432	.331	327	450	.727	66	347	413	766	340	3	160	11	349	31.7	12.4	2.6	4.8	....
02-03	San Antonio	24	24	814	352	135	335	.403	15	56	.268	67	94	.713	8	58	66	85	51	0	22	3	47	33.9	14.7	2.8	3.5	.329
NBA Playoff Totals		24	24	814	352	135	335	.403	15	56	.268	67	94	.713	8	58	66	85	51	0	22	3	47	33.9	14.7	2.8	3.5	....

• PARKHILL, Barry

Barry Parkhill

Born: May 10, 1951. Philadelphia, PA, United States.   Height: 6'4".   Weight: 185 lbs.   Drafted: 1973   College: Virginia

YEAR	TEAM	GP	GS	MIN	PTS	FGM	FGA	FG%	3PM	3PA	3P%	FTM	FTA	FT%	ORB	DRB	TRB	AST	PF	DQ	STL	BLK	TO	MPG	PPG	RPG	APG	PCM
73-74	Virginia-A	60	....	869	283	115	310	.371	3	16	.188	50	61	.820	13	52	65	96	151	....	28	12	80	14.5	4.7	1.1	1.6	.243
74-75	Virginia-A	78	....	1870	607	266	638	.417	0	8	.000	75	100	.750	27	106	133	226	228	....	50	11	170	24.0	7.8	1.7	2.9	.285
75-76	St. Louis-A	35	....	377	80	37	100	.370	1	11	.091	5	8	.625	2	24	26	64	46	....	9	7	29	10.8	2.3	0.7	1.8	.255
ABA Season Totals		173	....	3116	970	418	1048	.399	4	35	.114	130	169	.769	42	182	224	386	425	....	87	30	279	18.0	5.6	1.3	2.2	....
73-74	Virginia-A	3	....	9	6	3	7	.429	0	0	.000	0	0	.000	0	1	1	2	0	....	1	0	0	3.0	2.0	0.3	0.7	.634
ABA Playoff Totals		3	....	9	6	3	7	.429	0	0	.000	0	0	.000	0	1	1	2	0	....	1	0	0	3.0	2.0	0.3	0.7	....

• PARKINSON, Jack

Jack Gordon Parkinson

Born: Mar. 4, 1924. Yorktown, IN, United States.   Height: 6'   Weight: 174 lbs.   Drafted: 1948   College: Kentucky

YEAR	TEAM	GP	GS	MIN	PTS	FGM	FGA	FG%	3PM	3PA	3P%	FTM	FTA	FT%	ORB	DRB	TRB	AST	PF	DQ	STL	BLK	TO	MPG	PPG	RPG	APG	PCM
49-50	Indianapolis	4	....	....	3	1	12	.083	....	....	....	1	1	1.000	....	....	2	3	....	....	....	....	....	0.8	....	0.5	....	....
NBA Season Totals		4	....	....	3	1	12	.083	....	....	....	1	1	1.000	....	....	2	3	....	....	....	....	....	0.8	....	0.5	....	....

YEAR	TEAM	GP	GS	MIN	PTS	FGM	FGA	FG%	3PM	3PA	3P%	FTM	FTA	FT%	ORB	DRB	TRB	AST	PF	DQ	STL	BLK	TO	MPG	PPG	RPG	APG	PCM

• PARKS, Charles

Charles Parks

Born: 1946. Height: 6'5". Weight: 210 lbs. Drafted: — College: Idaho State

| 68-69 | Denver-A | 2 | .... | 5 | 0 | 0 | 1 | .000 | 0 | 0 | .000 | 0 | 0 | .000 | 0 | 0 | 0 | 0 | 1 | 0 | .... | .... | 0 | 2.5 | 0.0 | 0.0 | 0.0 | -.257 |
| **ABA Season Totals** | | 2 | .... | 5 | 0 | 0 | 1 | .000 | 0 | 0 | .000 | 0 | 0 | .000 | 0 | 0 | 0 | 0 | 1 | 0 | .... | .... | 0 | 2.5 | 0.0 | 0.0 | 0.0 | .... |

• PARKS, Cherokee

Cherokee Bryan Parks

Born: Oct. 11, 1972. Huntington Beach, CA, United States. Height: 6'11". Weight: 235 lbs. Drafted: 1995 College: Duke

95-96	Dallas	64	3	869	250	101	247	.409	7	26	.269	41	62	.661	66	150	216	29	100	0	25	32	32	13.6	3.9	3.4	0.5	.360
96-97	Minnesota	76	0	961	252	103	202	.510	0	1	.000	46	76	.605	83	112	195	34	150	2	41	48	30	12.6	3.3	2.6	0.4	.363
97-98	Minnesota	79	43	1703	558	224	449	.499	0	1	.000	110	169	.651	140	297	437	53	237	4	36	86	63	21.6	7.1	5.5	0.7	.428
98-99	Vancouver	48	41	1118	266	118	275	.429	0	1	.000	30	55	.545	75	168	243	36	114	0	28	28	49	23.3	5.5	5.1	0.8	.292
99-00	Vancouver	56	14	808	168	72	145	.497	0	1	.000	24	37	.649	55	128	183	35	115	0	29	45	28	14.4	3.0	3.3	0.6	.359
00-01	Washington	13	0	178	48	18	38	.474	0	0	.000	12	17	.706	13	27	40	7	20	0	6	11	10	13.7	3.7	3.1	0.5	.386
00-01	LA Clippers	52	31	876	251	116	236	.492	0	6	.000	19	27	.704	58	131	189	39	102	0	19	25	31	16.8	4.8	3.6	0.8	.363
01-02	San Antonio	42	1	234	63	30	83	.361	0	0	.000	3	8	.375	24	34	58	10	34	0	7	8	14	5.6	1.5	1.4	0.2	.264
02-03	LA Clippers	30	18	648	188	82	163	.503	1	2	.500	23	38	.605	46	86	132	21	52	0	16	20	18	21.6	6.3	4.4	0.7	.375
NBA Season Totals		460	151	7395	2044	864	1838	.470	8	38	.211	308	489	.630	560	1133	1693	264	924	6	207	303	275	16.1	4.4	3.7	0.6	....
96-97	Minnesota	1	0	11	4	2	3	.667	0	0	.000	0	0	.000	0	5	5	0	5	0	1	0	0	11.0	4.0	5.0	0.0	.575
97-98	Minnesota	1	0	1	0	0	0	.000	0	0	.000	0	0	.000	0	0	0	0	0	0	0	0	0	1.0	0.0	0.0	0.0	.000
01-02	San Antonio	5	0	43	8	4	14	.286	0	0	.000	0	1	.000	3	8	11	0	6	0	0	2	2	8.6	1.6	2.2	0.0	.133
NBA Playoff Totals		7	0	55	12	6	17	.353	0	0	.000	0	1	.000	3	13	16	0	11	0	1	2	2	7.9	1.7	2.3	0.0	....

• PARKS, Richard

Richard E. Parks

Born: Oct. 28, 1943. Died: Aug.1978. Height: 6'7". Weight: 235 lbs. Drafted: 1966 College: St. Louis

67-68	Pittsburgh-A	40	....	374	131	59	133	.444	1	3	.333	12	21	.571	....	....	116	14	68	3	....	....	19	9.4	3.3	2.9	0.4	.402
ABA Season Totals		40	....	374	131	59	133	.444	1	3	.333	12	21	.571	....	....	116	14	68	3	....	....	19	9.4	3.3	2.9	0.4	....
67-68	Pittsburgh-A	5	....	7	1	0	2	.000	0	1	.000	1	4	.250	....	....	2	0	3	0	....	....	0	1.4	0.2	0.4	0.0	-.213
ABA Playoff Totals		5	....	7	1	0	2	.000	0	1	.000	1	4	.250	....	....	2	0	3	0	....	....	0	1.4	0.2	0.4	0.0	....

• PARR, Jack

Jack Parr

Born: Mar. 13, 1936. Louisville, KY, United States. Height: 6'9". Weight: 220 lbs. Drafted: 1958 College: Kansas State

| 58-59 | Cincinnati | 66 | .... | 1037 | 262 | 109 | 307 | .355 | .... | .... | .... | 44 | 73 | .603 | .... | .... | 278 | 51 | 138 | 1 | .... | .... | .... | 15.7 | 4.0 | 4.2 | 0.8 | .311 |
| **NBA Season Totals** | | 66 | .... | 1037 | 262 | 109 | 307 | .355 | .... | .... | .... | 44 | 73 | .603 | .... | .... | 278 | 51 | 138 | 1 | .... | .... | .... | 15.7 | 4.0 | 4.2 | 0.8 | .... |

• PARRACK, Doyle

Doyle Kenneth Parrack

Born: Dec. 6, 1921. Height: 6' Weight: 165 lbs. Drafted: — College: Oklahoma A&M

46-47	Chicago	58	....	....	272	110	413	.266	....	....	....	52	80	.650	....	....	....	20	77	....	....	....	....	4.7	....	0.3	....
NBA Season Totals		58	....	....	272	110	413	.266	....	....	....	52	80	.650	....	....	....	20	77	....	....	....	....	4.7	....	0.3	....
46-47	Chicago	7	....	....	3	0	9	.000	....	....	....	3	3	1.000	....	....	....	1	3	....	....	....	....	0.4	....	0.1	....
NBA Playoff Totals		7	....	....	3	0	9	.000	....	....	....	3	3	1.000	....	....	....	1	3	....	....	....	....	0.4	....	0.1	....

• PARRY, Ed

Ed Parry

Born: 1918. Height: 6'2". Weight: 175 lbs. Drafted: — College: none

39-40	Detroit-N	3	....	....	2	1	....	....	....	....	....	0	....	....	....	....	....	....	....	....	....	....	....	0.7	....	....	....
40-41	Detroit-N	24	....	....	105	34	....	....	....	....	....	37	....	....	....	....	....	....	....	....	....	....	....	4.4	....	....	....
46-47	Detroit-N	34	....	....	235	81	....	....	....	....	....	73	113	.646	....	....	....	....	94	....	....	....	....	6.9	....	....	....
NBL Season Totals		61	....	....	342	116	....	....	....	....	....	110	113	....	....	....	....	....	94	....	....	....	....	5.6	....	....	....
39-40	Detroit-N	3	....	....	7	3	....	....	....	....	....	1	....	....	....	....	....	....	....	....	....	....	....	2.3	....	....	....
40-41	Detroit-N	3	....	....	12	4	....	....	....	....	....	4	....	....	....	....	....	....	....	....	....	....	....	4.0	....	....	....
NBL Playoff Totals		6	....	....	19	7	....	....	....	....	....	5	....	....	....	....	....	....	....	....	....	....	....	3.2	....	....	....

• PARSLEY, Charlie

Charles H. Parsley

Born: Oct. 13, 1925. Height: 6'2". Weight: 175 lbs. Drafted: — College: Western Kentucky

| 49-50 | Philadelphia | 9 | .... | .... | 22 | 8 | 31 | .258 | .... | .... | .... | 6 | 7 | .857 | .... | .... | .... | 8 | 7 | .... | .... | .... | .... | 2.4 | .... | 0.9 | .... |
| **NBA Season Totals** | | 9 | .... | .... | 22 | 8 | 31 | .258 | .... | .... | .... | 6 | 7 | .857 | .... | .... | .... | 8 | 7 | .... | .... | .... | .... | 2.4 | .... | 0.9 | .... |

YEAR TEAM	GP	GS	MIN	PTS	FGM	FGA	FG%	3PM	3PA	3P%	FTM	FTA	FT%	ORB	DRB	TRB	AST	PF	DQ	STL	BLK	TO	MPG	PPG	RPG	APG	PCM

• PARSONS, Bob
Robert Parsons

Born: 1915. Height: 6'1". Weight: 175 lbs. Drafted: — College: Nebraska

YEAR TEAM	GP	GS	MIN	PTS	FGM	FGA	FG%	3PM	3PA	3P%	FTM	FTA	FT%	ORB	DRB	TRB	AST	PF	DQ	STL	BLK	TO	MPG	PPG	RPG	APG	PCM
38-39 Wingfoots-N	11	....	....	26	11	....	....	....	....	....	4	....	....											2.4	....	....	....
41-42 Wingfoots-N	15	....	....	28	12	....	....	....	....	....	4	....	....											1.9	....	....	....
NBL Season Totals	26	....	....	54	23	....	....	....	....	....	8	....	....											2.1	....	....	....
41-42 Wingfoots-N	3	....	....	4	1	....	....	....	....	....	2	....	....											1.3	....	....	....
NBL Playoff Totals	3	....	....	4	1	....	....	....	....	....	2	....	....											1.3	....	....	....

• PASKO, Pete
Pete Pasko

Born: 1923. Height: 6'2". Weight: 190 lbs. Drafted: — College: East Stroudsburg

YEAR TEAM	GP	GS	MIN	PTS	FGM	FGA	FG%	3PM	3PA	3P%	FTM	FTA	FT%	ORB	DRB	TRB	AST	PF	DQ	STL	BLK	TO	MPG	PPG	RPG	APG	PCM
44-45 Oshkosh-N	26	....	....	228	89	....	....	....	....	....	50	....	....											8.8	....	....	....
45-46 Oshkosh-N	17	....	....	33	12	....	....	....	....	....	9	....	....											1.9	....	....	....
NBL Season Totals	43	....	....	261	101	....	....	....	....	....	59	....	....											6.1	....	....	....

• PASPALJ, Zarko
Zarko Paspalj

Born: Mar. 27, 1966. Pljevlja, Yugoslavia. Height: 6'9". Weight: 215 lbs. Drafted: — College: none

YEAR TEAM	GP	GS	MIN	PTS	FGM	FGA	FG%	3PM	3PA	3P%	FTM	FTA	FT%	ORB	DRB	TRB	AST	PF	DQ	STL	BLK	TO	MPG	PPG	RPG	APG	PCM
89-90 San Antonio	28	1	181	72	27	79	.342	0	1	.000	18	22	.818	15	15	30	10	37	0	3	7	22	6.5	2.6	1.1	0.4	.174
NBA Season Totals	28	1	181	72	27	79	.342	0	1	.000	18	22	.818	15	15	30	10	37	0	3	7	22	6.5	2.6	1.1	0.4	....

• PASSAGLIA, Marty
Martin Harold Passaglia

Born: Apr. 22, 1919. Height: 6'1". Weight: 170 lbs. Drafted: — College: Santa Clara

YEAR TEAM	GP	GS	MIN	PTS	FGM	FGA	FG%	3PM	3PA	3P%	FTM	FTA	FT%	ORB	DRB	TRB	AST	PF	DQ	STL	BLK	TO	MPG	PPG	RPG	APG	PCM
46-47 Washington	43	....	....	120	51	221	.231	....	....	....	18	32	.563				9	44	....					2.8	....	0.2	....
48-49 Indianapolis	10	....	....	31	14	57	.246	....	....	....	3	4	.750				17	17	....					3.1	....	1.7	....
NBA Season Totals	53	....	....	151	65	278	.234	....	....	....	21	36	.583				26	61	....					2.8	....	0.5	....
46-47 Washington	6	....	....	5	2	14	.143	....	....	....	1	3	.333				0	10	....					0.8	....	0.0	....
NBA Playoff Totals	6	....	....	5	2	14	.143	....	....	....	1	3	.333				0	10	....					0.8	....	0.0	....

• PASTUSHOK, George
George A. Pastushok

Born: 1923. Height: 6'1". Weight: 195 lbs. Drafted: — College: St. John's (NY)

YEAR TEAM	GP	GS	MIN	PTS	FGM	FGA	FG%	3PM	3PA	3P%	FTM	FTA	FT%	ORB	DRB	TRB	AST	PF	DQ	STL	BLK	TO	MPG	PPG	RPG	APG	PCM
46-47 Providence	39	....	....	121	48	183	.262	....	....	....	25	46	.543				15	42	....					3.1	....	0.4	....
NBA Season Totals	39	....	....	121	48	183	.262	....	....	....	25	46	.543				15	42	....					3.1	....	0.4	....

• PATANELLI, Joe
Joe (Pat) Patanelli

Born: 1919. Height: 6'3". Weight: 205 lbs. Drafted: — College: none

YEAR TEAM	GP	GS	MIN	PTS	FGM	FGA	FG%	3PM	3PA	3P%	FTM	FTA	FT%	ORB	DRB	TRB	AST	PF	DQ	STL	BLK	TO	MPG	PPG	RPG	APG	PCM
46-47 Toledo-N	35	....	....	87	29	....	....	....	....	....	29	40	.725											2.5	....	....	....
47-48 Minneapolis-N	5	....	....	4	1	....	....	....	....	....	2	5	.400											0.8	....	....	....
NBL Season Totals	40	....	....	91	30	....	....	....	....	....	31	45												2.3	....	....	....
46-47 Toledo-N	5	....	....	18	4	....	....	....	....	....	10	21	.476											3.6	....	....	....
NBL Playoff Totals	5	....	....	18	4	....	....	....	....	....	10	21												3.6	....	....	....

• PATRICK, Myles
Myles Patrick

Born: Nov. 19, 1954. Macon, GA, United States. Height: 6'8". Weight: 220 lbs. Drafted: — College: Auburn

YEAR TEAM	GP	GS	MIN	PTS	FGM	FGA	FG%	3PM	3PA	3P%	FTM	FTA	FT%	ORB	DRB	TRB	AST	PF	DQ	STL	BLK	TO	MPG	PPG	RPG	APG	PCM
80-81 LA Lakers	3	....	9	5	2	5	.400	0	0	.000	1	2	.500	1	1	2	1	3	0	0	0	1	3.0	1.7	0.7	0.3	.272
NBA Season Totals	3	....	9	5	2	5	.400	0	0	.000	1	2	.500	1	1	2	1	3	0	0	0	1	3.0	1.7	0.7	0.3	....

• PATRICK, Stan
Stanley A. Patrick

Born: May 5, 1922. Died: Jan.1, 2000. Height: 6'2". Weight: 185 lbs. Drafted: — College: Illinois

YEAR TEAM	GP	GS	MIN	PTS	FGM	FGA	FG%	3PM	3PA	3P%	FTM	FTA	FT%	ORB	DRB	TRB	AST	PF	DQ	STL	BLK	TO	MPG	PPG	RPG	APG	PCM
44-45 Chicago-N	28	....	....	458	187	....	....	....	....	....	84	....	....				....	....	....					16.4	....	....	....
45-46 Chicago-N	33	....	....	312	123	....	....	....	....	....	66	100	.660				....	....	....					9.5	....	....	....
46-47 Chicago-N	42	....	....	180	72	....	....	....	....	....	36	67	.537				....	61	....					4.3	....	....	....
47-48 Flint-N	48	....	....	388	149	....	....	....	....	....	90	144	.625				....	104	....					8.1	....	....	....
48-49 Hammond-N	61	....	....	427	150	....	....	....	....	....	127	192	.661				....	97	....					7.0	....	....	....
49-50 Waterloo	34	....	....	228	79	187	.422	....	....	....	70	108	.648				41	43	....					6.7	....	1.2	....
49-50 Sheboygan	19	....	....	93	37	107	.346	....	....	....	19	39	.487				33	33	....					4.9	....	1.7	....
NBA Season Totals	53	....	....	321	116	294	.395	....	....	....	89	147	.605				74	76	....					6.1	....	1.4	....
NBL Season Totals	212	....	....	1765	681	....	....	....	....	....	403	503					....	262	....					8.3	....	....	....
Career Totals	265	....	....	2086	797	294	....	....	....	....	492	650					74	338	....					7.9	....	0.3	....
44-45 Chicago-N	3	....	....	19	7	....	....	....	....	....	5	....	....				....	....	....					6.3	....	....	....
46-47 Chicago-N	11	....	....	70	30	....	....	....	....	....	10	15	.667				....	....	....					6.4	....	....	....

YEAR	TEAM	GP	GS	MIN	PTS	FGM	FGA	FG%	3PM	3PA	3P%	FTM	FTA	FT%	ORB	DRB	TRB	AST	PF	DQ	STL	BLK	TO	MPG	PPG	RPG	APG	PCM
48-49	Hammond-N	2	....	....	5	2	....	....	....	....	....	1	2	.500	....	....	....	....	....	....	....	....	....	2.5	....	....	....
49-50	Sheboygan	3	....	....	10	4	7	.571	....	....	....	2	3	.667	....	....	....	1	2	....	....	....	....	3.3	....	0.3	....
NBA Playoff Totals		3	....	....	10	4	7	.571	....	....	....	2	3	.667	....	....	....	1	2	....	....	....	....	3.3	....	0.3	....
NBL Playoff Totals		16	....	....	94	39	....	....	....	....	....	16	17	....	....	....	....	....	....	....	....	....	....	5.9	....	....	....
Career Playoff Totals		19	....	....	104	43	7	....	....	....	....	18	20	....	....	....	....	1	2	....	....	....	....	5.5	....	0.1	....

• PATTERSON, Andrae

Andrae Malone Patterson

Born: Nov. 12, 1975. Riverside, CA, United States.   Height: 6'9".   Weight: 238 lbs.   Drafted: 1998   College: Indiana

YEAR	TEAM	GP	GS	MIN	PTS	FGM	FGA	FG%	3PM	3PA	3P%	FTM	FTA	FT%	ORB	DRB	TRB	AST	PF	DQ	STL	BLK	TO	MPG	PPG	RPG	APG	PCM
98-99	Minnesota	35	0	284	114	43	97	.443	0	5	.000	28	36	.778	30	35	65	15	62	1	19	7	22	8.1	3.3	1.9	0.4	.397
99-00	Minnesota	5	0	20	6	3	4	.750	0	0	.000	0	0	.000	1	1	2	1	4	0	1	0	1	4.0	1.2	0.4	0.2	.309
NBA Season Totals		40	0	304	120	46	101	.455	0	5	.000	28	36	.778	31	36	67	16	66	1	20	7	23	7.6	3.0	1.7	0.4	....
98-99	Minnesota	2	0	7	0	0	0	.000	0	0	.000	0	0	.000	1	3	4	2	1	0	0	0	1	3.5	0.0	2.0	1.0	.635
NBA Playoff Totals		2	0	7	0	0	0	.000	0	0	.000	0	0	.000	1	3	4	2	1	0	0	0	1	3.5	0.0	2.0	1.0	....

• PATTERSON, George

George Patterson

Born: Nov. 26, 1939.   Height: 6'8".   Weight: 230 lbs.   Drafted: 1961   College: Toledo

YEAR	TEAM	GP	GS	MIN	PTS	FGM	FGA	FG%	3PM	3PA	3P%	FTM	FTA	FT%	ORB	DRB	TRB	AST	PF	DQ	STL	BLK	TO	MPG	PPG	RPG	APG	PCM
67-68	Detroit	59	....	559	120	44	133	.331	....	....	....	32	38	.842	....	....	159	51	85	0	....	....	....	9.5	2.0	2.7	0.9	.359
NBA Season Totals		59	....	559	120	44	133	.331	....	....	....	32	38	.842	....	....	159	51	85	0	....	....	....	9.5	2.0	2.7	0.9	....
67-68	Detroit	1	....	4	0	0	0	.000	....	....	....	0	0	.000	....	....	1	1	0	0	....	....	....	4.0	0.0	1.0	1.0	.500
NBA Playoff Totals		1	....	4	0	0	0	.000	....	....	....	0	0	.000	....	....	1	1	0	0	....	....	....	4.0	0.0	1.0	1.0	....

• PATTERSON, Ray

Ray Patterson

Born: 1923.   Height: 6'2".   Weight: 195 lbs.   Drafted: —   College: Wisconsin

YEAR	TEAM	GP	GS	MIN	PTS	FGM	FGA	FG%	3PM	3PA	3P%	FTM	FTA	FT%	ORB	DRB	TRB	AST	PF	DQ	STL	BLK	TO	MPG	PPG	RPG	APG	PCM
47-48	Flint-N	56	....	....	366	147	....	....	....	....	....	72	117	.615	....	....	....	130	....	....	....	....	....	6.5	....	....	....
NBL Season Totals		56	....	....	366	147	....	....	....	....	....	72	117	....	....	....	....	130	....	....	....	....	....	6.5	....	....	....

• PATTERSON, Ruben

Ruben Nathaniel Patterson

Born: July 31, 1975. Cleveland, OH, United States.   Height: 6'5".   Weight: 224 lbs.   Drafted: 1998   College: Cincinnati

YEAR	TEAM	GP	GS	MIN	PTS	FGM	FGA	FG%	3PM	3PA	3P%	FTM	FTA	FT%	ORB	DRB	TRB	AST	PF	DQ	STL	BLK	TO	MPG	PPG	RPG	APG	PCM
98-99	LA Lakers	24	2	144	65	21	51	.412	1	6	.167	22	31	.710	17	13	30	2	16	0	5	3	12	6.0	2.7	1.3	0.1	.365
99-00	Seattle	81	74	2097	942	354	661	.536	12	27	.444	222	321	.692	218	216	434	126	190	0	94	40	144	25.9	11.6	5.4	1.6	.503
00-01	Seattle	76	22	2059	988	370	749	.494	2	36	.056	246	361	.681	183	199	382	161	176	1	103	45	155	27.1	13.0	5.0	2.1	.501
01-02	Portland	75	13	1765	839	319	619	.515	9	36	.250	192	274	.701	155	143	298	107	140	1	79	37	114	23.5	11.2	4.0	1.4	.485
02-03	Portland	78	17	1656	649	254	516	.492	3	20	.150	138	220	.627	120	144	264	101	161	0	73	29	117	21.2	8.3	3.4	1.3	.385
NBA Season Totals		334	128	7721	3483	1318	2596	.508	27	125	.216	820	1207	.679	693	715	1408	497	683	2	354	154	542	23.1	10.4	4.2	1.5	....
98-99	LA Lakers	3	0	5	0	0	1	.000	0	0	.000	0	0	.000	0	0	0	0	0	0	0	0	1	1.7	0.0	0.0	0.0	-.356
99-00	Seattle	5	0	84	41	14	26	.538	0	2	.000	13	15	.867	9	6	15	2	6	0	3	2	8	16.8	8.2	3.0	0.4	.471
01-02	Portland	3	0	65	16	5	15	.333	0	1	.000	6	8	.750	2	5	7	1	7	0	3	1	3	21.7	5.3	2.3	0.3	.172
02-03	Portland	7	0	155	70	25	52	.481	0	4	.000	20	29	.690	14	12	26	11	10	0	4	1	10	22.1	10.0	3.7	1.6	.438
NBA Playoff Totals		18	0	309	127	44	94	.468	0	7	.000	39	52	.750	25	23	48	14	23	0	10	4	22	17.2	7.1	2.7	0.8	....

• PATTERSON, Steve

Steven J. Patterson

Born: June 24, 1948. Riverside, CA, United States.   Height: 6'9".   Weight: 225 lbs.   Drafted: 1971   College: UCLA

YEAR	TEAM	GP	GS	MIN	PTS	FGM	FGA	FG%	3PM	3PA	3P%	FTM	FTA	FT%	ORB	DRB	TRB	AST	PF	DQ	STL	BLK	TO	MPG	PPG	RPG	APG	PCM
71-72	Cleveland	65	....	775	211	94	263	.357	....	....	....	23	46	.500	....	....	228	54	80	0	....	....	....	11.9	3.2	3.5	0.8	.360
72-73	Cleveland	62	....	710	176	71	198	.359	....	....	....	34	65	.523	....	....	228	51	79	1	....	....	....	11.5	2.8	3.7	0.8	.386
73-74	Cleveland	76	....	1910	593	262	599	.437	....	....	....	69	112	.616	223	396	619	165	193	3	48	58	....	25.1	7.8	8.1	2.2	.483
74-75	Cleveland	81	....	1269	370	161	387	.416	....	....	....	48	73	.658	112	217	329	93	128	1	21	20	....	15.7	4.6	4.1	1.1	.393
75-76	Cleveland	14	....	136	38	15	38	.395	....	....	....	8	10	.800	7	21	28	9	11	0	3	5	....	9.7	2.7	2.0	0.6	.346
75-76	Chicago	52	....	782	164	69	182	.379	....	....	....	26	44	.591	73	127	200	71	82	1	13	11	....	15.0	3.2	3.8	1.4	.354
NBA Season Totals		350	....	5582	1552	672	1667	.403	....	....	....	208	350	.594	415	761	1632	443	573	6	85	94	....	15.9	4.4	4.7	1.3	....

• PATTERSON, Tom

Tommie J. Patterson

Born: Oct. 15, 1948.   Height: 6'6".   Weight: 220 lbs.   Drafted: 1972   College: Ouachita Baptist

YEAR	TEAM	GP	GS	MIN	PTS	FGM	FGA	FG%	3PM	3PA	3P%	FTM	FTA	FT%	ORB	DRB	TRB	AST	PF	DQ	STL	BLK	TO	MPG	PPG	RPG	APG	PCM
72-73	Baltimore	23	....	92	55	21	49	.429	....	....	....	13	16	.813	....	....	22	3	18	0	....	....	....	4.0	2.4	1.0	0.1	.481
73-74	Washington	2	....	8	1	0	1	.000	....	....	....	1	2	.500	1	1	2	2	0	0	0	0	....	4.0	0.5	1.0	1.0	.465
NBA Season Totals		25	....	100	56	21	50	.420	....	....	....	14	18	.778	1	1	24	5	18	0	0	0	....	4.0	2.2	1.0	0.2	....
72-73	Baltimore	1	....	1	0	0	0	.000	....	....	....	0	0	.000	....	....	0	0	0	0	....	....	....	1.0	0.0	0.0	0.0	.000
NBA Playoff Totals		1	....	1	0	0	0	.000	....	....	....	0	0	.000	....	....	0	0	0	0	....	....	....	1.0	0.0	0.0	0.0	....

• PATTERSON, Worthy

Worthington R. Patterson

Born: June 17, 1931. New Haven, CT, United States.   Height: 6'2".   Weight: 175 lbs.   Drafted: —   College: Connecticut

YEAR	TEAM	GP	GS	MIN	PTS	FGM	FGA	FG%	3PM	3PA	3P%	FTM	FTA	FT%	ORB	DRB	TRB	AST	PF	DQ	STL	BLK	TO	MPG	PPG	RPG	APG	PCM
57-58	St. Louis	4	....	13	7	3	8	.375	....	....	....	1	2	.500	....	....	2	2	3	0	....	....	....	3.3	1.8	0.5	0.5	.454
NBA Season Totals		4	....	13	7	3	8	.375	....	....	....	1	2	.500	....	....	2	2	3	0	....	....	....	3.3	1.8	0.5	0.5	....

PAULK, Charlie
Charles Paulk

Born: June 14, 1946. Fitzgerald, GA, United States.　　Height: 6'8".　　Weight: 219 lbs.　　Drafted: 1968　　College: Northeast Oklahoma State

YEAR	TEAM	GP	GS	MIN	PTS	FGM	FGA	FG%	3PM	3PA	3P%	FTM	FTA	FT%	ORB	DRB	TRB	AST	PF	DQ	STL	BLK	TO	MPG	PPG	RPG	APG	PCM
68-69	Milwaukee	17	....	217	51	19	84	.226	....	....	....	13	23	.565	....	....	78	3	26	0	....	....	....	12.8	3.0	4.6	0.2	.232
70-71	Cincinnati	68	....	1213	627	274	637	.430	....	....	....	79	131	.603	....	....	320	27	186	6	....	....	....	17.8	9.2	4.7	0.4	.427
71-72	Chicago	7	....	60	23	8	28	.286	....	....	....	7	9	.778	....	....	15	4	7	0	....	....	....	8.6	3.3	2.1	0.6	.322
71-72	New York	28	....	151	40	16	60	.267	....	....	....	8	12	.667	....	....	49	7	24	0	....	....	....	5.4	1.4	1.8	0.3	.266
NBA Season Totals		120	....	1641	741	317	809	.392	....	....	....	107	175	.611	....	....	462	41	243	6	....	....	....	13.7	6.2	3.9	0.3	
71-72	New York	7	....	13	6	3	10	.300	....	....	....	0	0	.000	....	....	5	0	5	0	....	....	....	1.9	0.9	0.7	0.0	.162
NBA Playoff Totals		7	....	13	6	3	10	.300	....	....	....	0	0	.000	....	....	5	0	5	0	....	....	....	1.9	0.9	0.7	0.0	

PAULSON, Jerry
Gerald Arthur Paulson

Born: July 21, 1935. Died: Mar.6, 1986.　　Height: 6'2".　　Weight: 185 lbs.　　Drafted: 1957　　College: Manhattan

YEAR	TEAM	GP	GS	MIN	PTS	FGM	FGA	FG%	3PM	3PA	3P%	FTM	FTA	FT%	ORB	DRB	TRB	AST	PF	DQ	STL	BLK	TO	MPG	PPG	RPG	APG	PCM
57-58	Cincinnati	6	....	68	20	8	23	.348	....	....	....	4	6	.667	....	....	10	4	5	0	....	....	....	11.3	3.3	1.7	0.7	.278
NBA Season Totals		6	....	68	20	8	23	.348	....	....	....	4	6	.667	....	....	10	4	5	0	....	....	....	11.3	3.3	1.7	0.7	

PAULTZ, Billy
William Edward (The Whopper) Paultz

Born: July 30, 1948. River Edge, NJ, United States.　　Height: 6'11".　　Weight: 235 lbs.　　Drafted: 1970　　College: St. John's (NY)

YEAR	TEAM	GP	GS	MIN	PTS	FGM	FGA	FG%	3PM	3PA	3P%	FTM	FTA	FT%	ORB	DRB	TRB	AST	PF	DQ	STL	BLK	TO	MPG	PPG	RPG	APG	PCM
70-71	New York-A	83	....	2758	1221	510	973	.524	0	2	.000	201	269	.747	239	701	940	160	274	6	....	....	206	33.2	14.7	11.3	1.9	.601
71-72	New York-A	83	....	2824	1203	498	1021	.488	0	3	.000	207	299	.692	263	772	1035	128	298	9	....	....	214	34.0	14.5	12.5	1.5	.575
72-73	New York-A	81	....	2800	1351	532	1027	.518	0	2	.000	287	405	.709	279	736	1015	189	259	5	....	214	213	34.6	16.7	12.5	2.3	.663
73-74	New York-A	77	....	2596	1260	519	1051	.494	0	1	.000	222	308	.721	211	571	782	167	238	....	60	147	175	33.7	16.4	10.2	2.2	.588
74-75	New York-A	80	....	2826	1262	524	1080	.485	0	3	.000	214	286	.748	174	598	772	179	273	....	59	137	149	35.3	15.8	9.7	2.2	.531
75-76	San Antonio-A	83	....	2958	1370	566	1124	.504	0	2	.000	238	324	.735	210	652	862	340	232	....	61	**253**	231	35.6	16.5	10.4	4.1	.634
76-77	San Antonio	82	....	2694	1280	521	1102	.473	....	....	....	238	320	.744	192	495	687	223	262	5	55	173	....	32.9	15.6	8.4	2.7	.548
77-78	San Antonio	80	....	2479	1266	518	979	.529	....	....	....	230	306	.752	172	503	675	213	222	3	42	194	168	31.0	15.8	8.4	2.7	.654
78-79	San Antonio	79	....	2122	912	399	758	.526	....	....	....	114	194	.588	169	456	625	178	204	4	35	125	158	26.9	11.5	7.9	2.3	.576
79-80	San Antonio	47	....	1213	444	189	381	.496	0	1	.000	66	100	.660	95	226	321	118	127	3	47	45	56	25.8	9.4	6.8	2.5	.536
79-80	Houston	37	....	980	319	138	292	.473	0	0	.000	43	82	.524	92	173	265	70	86	0	22	39	56	26.5	8.6	7.2	1.9	.453
80-81	Houston	81	....	1659	599	262	517	.507	0	3	.000	75	153	.490	111	280	391	105	182	1	28	72	89	20.5	7.4	4.8	1.3	.439
81-82	Houston	65	3	807	212	89	226	.394	0	0	.000	34	65	.523	54	126	180	41	99	0	15	22	46	12.4	3.3	2.8	0.6	.282
82-83	Houston	57	0	695	204	89	200	.445	0	0	.000	26	57	.456	54	113	167	57	95	0	12	12	40	12.2	3.6	2.9	1.0	.354
82-83	San Antonio	7	0	125	25	12	27	.444	0	0	.000	1	2	.500	10	23	33	4	14	0	5	6	6	17.9	3.6	4.7	0.6	.347
83-84	Atlanta	40	4	486	89	36	88	.409	0	0	.000	17	33	.515	35	78	113	18	57	0	8	7	24	12.2	2.2	2.8	0.5	.252
84-85	Utah	62	0	370	82	32	87	.368	0	0	.000	18	28	.643	24	72	96	16	51	0	6	11	31	6.0	1.3	1.5	0.3	.259
NBA Season Totals		637	7	13630	5432	2285	4657	.491	0	4	.000	862	1340	.643	1008	2545	3553	1043	1399	16	275	706	674	21.4	8.5	5.6	1.6	....
ABA Season Totals		487	....	16762	7667	3149	6276	.502	0	13	.000	1369	1891	.724	1376	4030	5406	1163	1574	20	180	751	1188	34.4	15.7	11.1	2.4	....
Career Totals		1124	7	30392	13099	5434	10933	.497	0	17	.000	2231	3231	.690	2384	6575	8959	2206	2973	36	455	1457	1862	27.0	11.7	8.0	2.0	....
70-71	New York-A	6	....	239	121	45	76	.592	1	1	1.000	30	40	.750	17	73	90	18	29	0	....	....	25	39.8	20.2	15.0	3.0	.729
71-72	New York-A	19	....	809	337	140	276	.507	0	2	.000	57	90	.633	78	210	288	29	74	....	....	....	51	42.6	17.7	15.2	1.5	.564
72-73	New York-A	5	....	172	95	34	56	.607	0	0	.000	27	43	.628	12	43	55	10	17	0	....	....	14	34.4	19.0	11.0	2.0	.703
73-74	New York-A	14	....	520	207	81	169	.479	0	0	.000	45	57	.789	27	105	132	28	49	....	10	20	25	37.1	14.8	9.4	2.0	.482
74-75	New York-A	5	....	178	70	29	59	.492	0	0	.000	12	15	.800	10	35	45	11	18	....	1	16	11	35.6	14.0	9.0	2.2	.484
75-76	San Antonio-A	7	....	254	121	43	97	.443	0	0	.000	35	40	.875	15	57	72	19	29	....	2	16	14	36.3	17.3	10.3	2.7	.563
76-77	San Antonio	2	....	74	34	12	24	.500	....	....	....	10	13	.769	1	16	17	5	3	0	2	1	....	37.0	17.0	8.5	2.5	.560
77-78	San Antonio	6	....	191	69	29	63	.460	....	....	....	11	17	.647	7	34	41	14	10	0	5	5	6	31.8	11.5	6.8	2.3	.457
78-79	San Antonio	13	....	299	82	30	80	.375	....	....	....	22	33	.667	24	74	98	30	33	0	4	13	14	23.0	6.3	7.5	2.3	.472
79-80	Houston	7	....	128	30	13	40	.325	0	0	.000	4	7	.571	12	21	33	8	13	0	1	3	11	18.3	4.3	4.7	1.1	.289
80-81	Houston	21	....	720	254	111	246	.451	0	1	.000	32	48	.667	53	94	147	35	69	1	13	27	27	34.3	12.1	7.0	1.7	.384
81-82	Houston	3	0	34	7	3	9	.333	0	0	.000	1	3	.333	2	2	4	1	4	0	0	2	1	11.3	2.3	1.3	0.3	.129
82-83	San Antonio	11	0	133	30	13	32	.406	0	0	.000	4	4	1.000	11	21	32	11	18	0	4	2	6	12.1	2.7	2.9	1.0	.344
83-84	Atlanta	2	0	7	2	1	3	.333	0	0	.000	0	0	.000	0	0	0	0	0	0	0	0	0	3.5	1.0	0.0	0.0	.020
84-85	Utah	5	0	30	7	3	8	.375	0	0	.000	1	4	.250	3	5	8	2	7	0	1	1	2	6.0	1.4	1.6	0.4	.242
NBA Playoff Totals		70	0	1616	515	215	505	.426	0	1	.000	85	129	.659	113	267	380	106	157	1	30	54	67	23.1	7.4	5.4	1.5	....
ABA Playoff Totals		56	....	2172	951	372	733	.508	1	3	.333	206	285	.723	159	523	682	115	216	0	13	52	140	38.8	17.0	12.2	2.1	....
Career Playoff Totals		126	0	3788	1466	587	1238	.474	1	4	.250	291	414	.703	272	790	1062	221	373	1	43	106	207	30.1	11.6	8.4	1.8	....

PAWK, Johnny
John Pawk

Born: 1910.　　Height: 6'2".　　Weight: 210 lbs.　　Drafted: —　　College: Westminster (PA)

YEAR	TEAM	GP	GS	MIN	PTS	FGM	FGA	FG%	3PM	3PA	3P%	FTM	FTA	FT%	ORB	DRB	TRB	AST	PF	DQ	STL	BLK	TO	MPG	PPG	RPG	APG	PCM
37-38	Warren-N	12	....	....	54	22	....	....	....	....	....	10	....	....	....	....	....	....	....	....	....	....	....	....	4.5	....	....	....
38-39	Cleveland-N	2	....	....	4	1	....	....	....	....	....	2	....	....	....	....	....	....	....	....	....	....	....	....	2.0	....	....	....
NBL Season Totals		14	....	....	58	23	....	....	....	....	....	12	....	....	....	....	....	....	....	....	....	....	....	....	4.1	....	....	....

PAWK, Steve
Steve Pawk

Born: 1914.　　Height: 6'4".　　Weight: 175 lbs.　　Drafted: —　　College: none

YEAR	TEAM	GP	GS	MIN	PTS	FGM	FGA	FG%	3PM	3PA	3P%	FTM	FTA	FT%	ORB	DRB	TRB	AST	PF	DQ	STL	BLK	TO	MPG	PPG	RPG	APG	PCM
37-38	Warren-N	6	....	....	21	8	....	....	....	....	....	5	....	....	....	....	....	....	....	....	....	....	....	....	3.5	....	....	....
NBL Season Totals		6	....	....	21	8	....	....	....	....	....	5	....	....	....	....	....	....	....	....	....	....	....	....	3.5	....	....	....

• PAXSON, Jim

James Edward Paxson

Born: Dec. 19, 1932. Height: 6'6". Weight: 200 lbs. Drafted: 1956 College: Dayton

YEAR TEAM	GP	GS	MIN	PTS	FGM	FGA	FG%	3PM	3PA	3P%	FTM	FTA	FT%	ORB	DRB	TRB	AST	PF	DQ	STL	BLK	TO	MPG	PPG	RPG	APG	PCM
56-57 Minneapolis	71	....	1274	446	138	485	.285	....	....	....	170	236	.720	....	....	266	86	163	3	....	....	....	17.9	6.3	3.7	1.2	.320
57-58 Cincinnati	67	....	1795	659	225	639	.352	....	....	....	209	285	.733	....	....	350	139	183	2	....	....	....	26.8	9.8	5.2	2.1	.387
NBA Season Totals	138	....	3069	1105	363	1124	.323	....	....	....	379	521	.727	....	....	616	225	346	5	....	....	....	22.2	8.0	4.5	1.6	....
56-57 Minneapolis	5	....	54	25	9	27	.333	....	....	....	7	14	.500	....	....	14	3	4	0	....	....	....	10.8	5.0	2.8	0.6	.401
57-58 Cincinnati	2	....	30	12	3	20	.150	....	....	....	6	8	.750	....	....	8	5	7	0	....	....	....	15.0	6.0	4.0	2.5	.284
NBA Playoff Totals	7	....	84	37	12	47	.255	....	....	....	13	22	.591	....	....	22	8	11	0	....	....	....	12.0	5.3	3.1	1.1	....

• PAXSON, Jim

James Joseph Paxson

Born: July 9, 1957. Kettering, OH, United States. Height: 6'6". Weight: 200 lbs. Drafted: 1979 College: Dayton

YEAR TEAM	GP	GS	MIN	PTS	FGM	FGA	FG%	3PM	3PA	3P%	FTM	FTA	FT%	ORB	DRB	TRB	AST	PF	DQ	STL	BLK	TO	MPG	PPG	RPG	APG	PCM
79-80 Portland	72	....	1270	443	189	460	.411	1	22	.045	64	90	.711	25	84	109	144	97	0	48	5	94	17.6	6.2	1.5	2.0	.284
80-81 Portland	79	....	2701	1354	585	1092	.536	2	30	.067	182	248	.734	74	137	211	299	172	1	140	9	134	34.2	17.1	2.7	3.8	.487
81-82 Portland	82	82	2756	1552	662	1258	.526	8	35	.229	220	287	.767	75	146	221	276	159	0	129	12	148	33.6	18.9	2.7	3.4	.506
82-83 Portland	81	81	2740	1756	682	1323	.515	4	25	.160	388	478	.812	68	106	174	231	160	0	140	17	154	33.8	21.7	2.1	2.9	.540
83-84 Portland	81	81	2686	1722	680	1322	.514	17	59	.288	345	410	.841	68	105	173	251	165	0	122	10	146	33.2	21.3	2.1	3.1	.534
84-85 Portland	68	57	2253	1218	508	988	.514	6	39	.154	196	248	.790	69	153	222	264	115	0	101	5	109	33.1	17.9	3.3	3.9	.523
85-86 Portland	75	31	1931	981	372	792	.470	20	62	.323	217	244	.889	42	106	148	278	156	3	94	5	113	25.7	13.1	2.0	3.7	.481
86-87 Portland	72	1	1798	874	337	733	.460	26	98	.265	174	216	.806	41	98	139	237	134	0	76	12	108	25.0	12.1	1.9	3.3	.438
87-88 Portland	17	1	263	103	43	107	.402	3	8	.375	14	18	.778	8	10	18	27	29	0	7	1	10	15.5	6.1	1.1	1.6	.273
87-88 Boston	28	2	538	244	94	191	.492	2	13	.154	54	61	.885	7	20	27	49	44	0	23	4	28	19.2	8.7	1.0	1.8	.384
88-89 Boston	57	7	1138	492	202	445	.454	4	24	.167	84	103	.816	18	56	74	107	96	0	38	8	57	20.0	8.6	1.3	1.9	.339
89-90 Boston	72	25	1283	460	191	422	.453	5	20	.250	73	90	.811	24	53	77	137	115	0	33	5	58	17.8	6.4	1.1	1.9	.297
NBA Season Totals	784	368	21357	11199	4545	9133	.498	98	435	.225	2011	2493	.807	519	1074	1593	2300	1442	4	951	93	1159	27.2	14.3	2.0	2.9	....
79-80 Portland	3	....	44	16	5	16	.313	0	0	.000	6	6	1.000	0	4	4	3	2	0	2	1	2	14.7	5.3	1.3	1.0	.294
80-81 Portland	1	....	4	0	0	3	.000	0	0	.000	0	0	.000	0	0	0	0	0	0	0	0	0	4.0	0.0	0.0	0.0	-.683
82-83 Portland	7	7	260	163	68	116	.586	2	4	.500	25	33	.758	4	11	15	18	11	0	9	1	15	37.1	23.3	2.1	2.6	.538
83-84 Portland	5	5	172	114	40	78	.513	1	5	.200	33	40	.825	11	8	19	12	13	0	2	0	9	34.4	22.8	3.8	2.4	.543
84-85 Portland	9	0	212	116	47	101	.465	3	10	.300	19	24	.792	6	14	20	21	16	0	6	0	5	23.6	12.9	2.2	2.3	.462
85-86 Portland	4	0	71	42	14	37	.378	2	6	.333	12	15	.800	1	3	4	15	12	1	3	0	6	17.8	10.5	1.0	3.8	.432
86-87 Portland	4	0	94	34	13	32	.406	0	2	.000	8	9	.889	4	5	9	13	8	0	5	0	4	23.5	8.5	2.3	3.3	.376
87-88 Boston	15	0	188	50	17	59	.288	0	2	.000	16	20	.800	1	8	9	11	18	0	6	2	12	12.5	3.3	0.6	0.7	.090
89-90 Boston	5	0	62	19	8	16	.500	0	1	.000	3	4	.750	0	0	0	7	1	0	5	0	3	12.4	3.8	0.0	1.4	.321
NBA Playoff Totals	53	12	1107	554	212	458	.463	8	30	.267	122	151	.808	27	53	80	100	81	1	38	4	56	20.9	10.5	1.5	1.9	....

• PAXSON, John

John MacBeth Paxson

Born: Sept. 29, 1960. Dayton, OH, United States. Height: 6'2". Weight: 185 lbs. Drafted: 1983 College: Notre Dame

YEAR TEAM	GP	GS	MIN	PTS	FGM	FGA	FG%	3PM	3PA	3P%	FTM	FTA	FT%	ORB	DRB	TRB	AST	PF	DQ	STL	BLK	TO	MPG	PPG	RPG	APG	PCM
83-84 San Antonio	49	0	458	142	61	137	.445	4	22	.182	16	26	.615	4	29	33	149	47	0	10	2	34	9.3	2.9	0.7	3.0	.468
84-85 San Antonio	78	1	1259	486	196	385	.509	10	34	.294	84	100	.840	19	49	68	215	117	0	45	3	78	16.1	6.2	0.9	2.8	.407
85-86 Chicago	75	3	1570	395	153	328	.466	15	50	.300	74	92	.804	18	76	94	274	172	2	55	2	60	20.9	5.3	1.3	3.7	.333
86-87 Chicago	82	64	2689	930	386	793	.487	52	140	.371	106	131	.809	22	117	139	467	207	1	66	8	107	32.8	11.3	1.7	5.7	.387
87-88 Chicago	81	30	1888	640	287	582	.493	33	95	.347	33	45	.733	16	88	104	303	154	2	49	1	65	23.3	7.9	1.3	3.7	.368
88-89 Chicago	78	20	1738	567	246	513	.480	44	133	.331	31	36	.861	13	81	94	308	162	1	53	6	70	22.3	7.3	1.2	3.9	.373
89-90 Chicago	82	82	2365	819	365	708	.516	33	92	.359	56	68	.824	27	92	119	335	176	1	83	6	82	28.8	10.0	1.5	4.1	.374
90-91 Chicago	82	82	1971	710	317	578	.548	42	96	.438	34	41	.829	15	76	91	297	136	0	62	3	66	24.0	8.7	1.1	3.6	.406
91-92 Chicago	79	79	1946	555	257	487	.528	12	44	.273	29	37	.784	21	75	96	241	142	0	49	9	47	24.6	7.0	1.2	3.1	.323
92-93 Chicago	59	8	1030	246	105	233	.451	19	41	.463	17	20	.850	9	39	48	136	99	0	38	2	30	17.5	4.2	0.8	2.3	.270
93-94 Chicago	27	0	343	70	30	68	.441	9	22	.409	1	2	.500	3	17	20	33	18	0	7	2	5	12.7	2.6	0.7	1.2	.245
NBA Season Totals	772	369	17257	5560	2403	4812	.499	273	769	.355	481	598	.804	167	739	906	2758	1430	7	517	44	644	22.4	7.2	1.2	3.6	....
84-85 San Antonio	5	0	114	51	21	42	.500	2	9	.222	7	9	.778	0	5	5	21	9	0	5	0	5	22.8	10.2	1.0	4.2	.468
85-86 Chicago	3	0	80	27	7	15	.467	0	0	.000	13	17	.765	0	0	0	5	9	0	3	0	3	26.7	9.0	0.0	1.7	.236
86-87 Chicago	3	3	87	26	11	22	.500	3	7	.429	1	1	1.000	0	3	3	11	9	0	2	0	5	29.0	8.7	1.0	3.7	.268
87-88 Chicago	10	0	165	46	20	53	.377	2	12	.167	4	4	1.000	0	4	4	30	24	1	1	1	5	16.5	4.6	0.4	3.0	.224
88-89 Chicago	16	0	302	93	37	78	.474	5	19	.263	14	16	.875	2	8	10	34	35	1	12	0	15	18.9	5.8	0.6	2.1	.267
89-90 Chicago	15	15	395	92	37	87	.425	4	9	.444	14	14	1.000	2	20	22	54	42	3	9	0	15	26.3	6.1	1.5	3.6	.248
90-91 Chicago	17	17	487	140	62	117	.530	2	14	.143	14	14	1.000	2	21	23	53	32	0	11	0	6	28.6	8.2	1.4	3.1	.321
91-92 Chicago	22	22	598	174	73	139	.525	12	27	.444	16	19	.842	0	22	22	61	53	1	14	1	13	27.2	7.9	1.0	2.8	.291
92-93 Chicago	19	0	331	93	35	60	.583	15	24	.625	8	11	.727	5	14	19	32	30	0	6	1	4	17.4	4.9	1.0	1.7	.329
93-94 Chicago	9	0	58	6	3	7	.429	0	1	.000	0	0	.000	0	1	1	5	6	0	2	0	0	6.4	0.7	0.1	0.6	.134
NBA Playoff Totals	119	57	2617	748	306	620	.494	45	122	.369	91	105	.867	11	98	109	306	249	6	65	3	71	22.0	6.3	0.9	2.6	....

• PAYAK, Johnny

John Payak Jr.

Born: Nov. 20, 1926. Height: 6'4". Weight: 174 lbs. Drafted: — College: Bowling Green

YEAR TEAM	GP	GS	MIN	PTS	FGM	FGA	FG%	3PM	3PA	3P%	FTM	FTA	FT%	ORB	DRB	TRB	AST	PF	DQ	STL	BLK	TO	MPG	PPG	RPG	APG	PCM
49-50 Philadelphia	17	....	....	37	12	32	.375	....	....	....	13	21	.619	....	....	....	8	18	....	....	....	....	....	2.2	....	0.5	....
49-50 Waterloo	35	....	....	280	86	299	.288	....	....	....	108	152	.711	....	....	....	78	95	....	....	....	....	....	8.0	....	2.2	....
52-53 Milwaukee	68	....	1470	436	128	373	.343	....	....	....	180	248	.726	....	....	114	140	194	7	....	....	....	21.6	6.4	1.7	2.1	.289
NBA Season Totals	120	....	1470	753	226	704	.321	....	....	....	301	421	.715	....	....	114	226	307	7	....	....	....	12.3	6.3	1.0	1.9	....

• PAYNE, Kenny

Kenneth Victor Payne

Born: Nov. 25, 1966. Laurel, MS, United States. Height: 6'8". Weight: 195 lbs. Drafted: 1989 College: Louisville

YEAR TEAM	GP	GS	MIN	PTS	FGM	FGA	FG%	3PM	3PA	3P%	FTM	FTA	FT%	ORB	DRB	TRB	AST	PF	DQ	STL	BLK	TO	MPG	PPG	RPG	APG	PCM
89-90 Philadelphia	35	4	216	114	47	108	.435	4	10	.400	16	18	.889	11	15	26	10	37	0	7	6	21	6.2	3.3	0.7	0.3	.306
90-91 Philadelphia	47	6	444	166	68	189	.360	4	18	.222	26	29	.897	17	49	66	16	43	0	10	6	19	9.4	3.5	1.4	0.3	.242

YEAR	TEAM	GP	GS	MIN	PTS	FGM	FGA	FG%	3PM	3PA	3P%	FTM	FTA	FT%	ORB	DRB	TRB	AST	PF	DQ	STL	BLK	TO	MPG	PPG	RPG	APG	PCM
91-92	Philadelphia	49	3	353	144	65	145	.448	5	12	.417	9	13	.692	13	41	54	17	34	0	16	8	20	7.2	2.9	1.1	0.3	.352
92-93	Philadelphia	13	0	154	84	38	90	.422	4	18	.222	4	4	1.000	4	20	24	18	15	0	5	2	7	11.8	6.5	1.8	1.4	.455
NBA Season Totals		144	13	1167	508	218	532	.410	17	58	.293	55	64	.859	45	125	170	61	129	0	38	22	67	8.1	3.5	1.2	0.4	....
89-90	Philadelphia	3	0	10	6	2	5	.400	0	2	.000	2	2	1.000	1	1	2	0	3	0	0	0	1	3.3	2.0	0.7	0.0	.272
NBA Playoff Totals		3	0	10	6	2	5	.400	0	2	.000	2	2	1.000	1	1	2	0	3	0	0	0	1	3.3	2.0	0.7	0.0	....

• PAYNE, Tom

Tom Payne

Born: Nov. 19, 1950. Louisville, KY, United States.   Height: 7'2".   Weight: 240 lbs.   Drafted: 1971   College: Kentucky

YEAR	TEAM	GP	GS	MIN	PTS	FGM	FGA	FG%	3PM	3PA	3P%	FTM	FTA	FT%	ORB	DRB	TRB	AST	PF	DQ	STL	BLK	TO	MPG	PPG	RPG	APG	PCM
71-72	Atlanta	29	....	227	119	45	103	.437	....	....	....	29	46	.630			69	15	40	0	....	....	....	7.8	4.1	2.4	0.5	.533
NBA Season Totals		29	....	227	119	45	103	.437	....	....	....	29	46	.630			69	15	40	0				7.8	4.1	2.4	0.5	
71-72	Atlanta	1	....	5	4	1	1	1.000	....	....	....	2	5	.400			4	0	1	0	....	....	....	5.0	4.0	4.0	0.0	1.146
NBA Playoff Totals		1	....	5	4	1	1	1.000	....	....	....	2	5	.400			4	0	1	0				5.0	4.0	4.0	0.0	

• PAYTON, Gary

Gary Dwayne (The Glove) Payton

Born: July 23, 1968. Oakland, CA, United States.   Height: 6'4".   Weight: 180 lbs.   Drafted: 1990   College: Oregon State

YEAR	TEAM	GP	GS	MIN	PTS	FGM	FGA	FG%	3PM	3PA	3P%	FTM	FTA	FT%	ORB	DRB	TRB	AST	PF	DQ	STL	BLK	TO	MPG	PPG	RPG	APG	PCM
90-91	Seattle	82	82	2244	588	259	575	.450	1	13	.077	69	97	.711	108	135	243	528	249	3	165	15	180	27.4	7.2	3.0	6.4	.425
91-92	Seattle	81	79	2549	764	331	734	.451	3	23	.130	99	148	.669	123	172	295	506	248	0	147	21	170	31.5	9.4	3.6	6.2	.418
92-93	Seattle	82	78	2548	1110	476	963	.494	7	34	.206	151	196	.770	95	186	281	399	250	1	177	21	148	31.1	13.5	3.4	4.9	.492
93-94	Seattle	82	82	2881	1349	584	1159	.504	15	54	.278	166	279	.595	105	164	269	494	227	0	188	19	172	35.1	16.5	3.3	6.0	.514
94-95	Seattle	82	82	3015	1689	685	1345	.509	70	232	.302	249	348	.716	108	173	281	583	206	1	204	13	205	36.8	20.6	3.4	7.1	.604
95-96	Seattle	81	81	3162	1563	618	1276	.484	98	299	.328	229	306	.748	104	235	339	608	221	1	231	19	259	39.0	19.3	4.2	7.5	.556
96-97	Seattle	82	82	3213	1785	706	1482	.476	119	380	.313	254	355	.715	106	272	378	583	208	0	197	13	213	39.2	21.8	4.6	7.1	.588
97-98	Seattle	82	82	3145	1571	579	1278	.453	134	397	.338	279	375	.744	77	299	376	679	195	0	185	18	230	38.4	19.2	4.6	8.3	.590
98-99	Seattle	50	50	2008	1084	401	923	.434	83	281	.295	199	276	.721	62	182	244	436	115	0	109	12	154	40.2	21.7	4.9	8.7	.601
99-00	Seattle	82	82	3425	1982	747	1666	.448	**177**	**520**	.340	311	423	.735	100	429	529	**732**	178	0	153	18	224	41.8	24.2	6.5	8.9	**.656**
00-01	Seattle	79	79	3244	1823	725	1591	.456	102	272	.375	271	354	.766	73	288	361	642	184	0	127	26	209	41.1	23.1	4.6	8.1	.588
01-02	Seattle	82	82	3301	1815	737	1578	.467	74	236	.314	267	335	.797	80	316	396	737	179	0	131	26	209	40.3	22.1	4.8	9.0	.624
02-03	Seattle	52	52	2123	1084	444	992	.448	34	114	.298	162	234	.692	56	192	248	457	117	0	93	12	131	40.8	20.8	4.8	8.8	.566
02-03	Milwaukee	28	28	1085	550	221	474	.466	20	68	.294	88	118	.746	23	63	86	206	64	0	40	8	56	38.8	19.6	3.1	7.4	.528
NBA Season Totals		1027	1021	37943	18757	7513	16036	.469	937	2923	.321	2794	3844	.727	1220	3106	4326	7590	2641	7	2147	241	2560	36.9	18.3	4.2	7.4	
90-91	Seattle	5	5	135	24	11	27	.407	0	1	.000	2	2	1.000	5	8	13	32	16	0	8	1	9	27.0	4.8	2.6	6.4	.355
91-92	Seattle	8	8	221	61	27	58	.466	0	2	.000	7	12	.583	6	15	21	38	26	1	8	2	10	27.6	7.6	2.6	4.8	.353
92-93	Seattle	19	19	605	234	104	235	.443	1	6	.167	25	37	.676	22	41	63	70	64	1	34	3	34	31.8	12.3	3.3	3.7	.351
93-94	Seattle	5	5	181	79	34	69	.493	3	9	.333	8	19	.421	6	11	17	28	15	0	8	2	8	36.2	15.8	3.4	5.6	.457
94-95	Seattle	4	4	172	71	32	67	.478	2	10	.200	5	12	.417	6	4	10	21	13	0	5	0	8	43.0	17.8	2.5	5.3	.335
95-96	Seattle	21	21	911	434	162	334	.485	41	100	.410	69	109	.633	19	89	108	143	69	0	37	7	62	43.4	20.7	5.1	6.8	.502
96-97	Seattle	12	12	546	285	105	255	.412	25	75	.333	50	61	.820	20	45	65	104	26	0	26	4	35	45.5	23.8	5.4	8.7	.540
97-98	Seattle	10	10	428	240	87	183	.475	19	50	.380	47	50	.940	9	25	34	70	31	1	18	1	26	42.8	24.0	3.4	7.0	.554
99-00	Seattle	5	5	221	129	50	113	.442	9	23	.391	20	26	.769	8	30	38	37	16	0	9	1	18	44.2	25.8	7.6	7.4	.586
01-02	Seattle	5	5	207	111	45	106	.425	4	15	.267	17	29	.586	10	33	43	29	12	0	3	2	13	41.4	22.2	8.6	5.8	.523
02-03	Milwaukee	6	6	251	111	48	112	.429	1	15	.067	14	20	.700	4	14	18	52	18	0	8	1	13	41.8	18.5	3.0	8.7	.444
NBA Playoff Totals		100	100	3878	1779	705	1559	.452	105	306	.343	264	377	.700	115	315	430	624	306	3	164	24	236	38.8	17.8	4.3	6.2	....

• PAYTON, Mel

Melvin E. Payton

Born: July 16, 1926.   Height: 6'4".   Weight: 185 lbs.   Drafted: 1951   College: Tulane

YEAR	TEAM	GP	GS	MIN	PTS	FGM	FGA	FG%	3PM	3PA	3P%	FTM	FTA	FT%	ORB	DRB	TRB	AST	PF	DQ	STL	BLK	TO	MPG	PPG	RPG	APG	PCM
51-52	Philadelphia	45	....	471	129	54	140	.386	....	....	....	21	28	.750	....	....	83	45	68	2	....	....	....	10.5	2.9	1.8	1.0	.336
52-53	Indianapolis	66	....	1424	466	173	485	.357	....	....	....	120	161	.745	....	....	313	81	118	0	....	....	....	21.6	7.1	4.7	1.2	.360
NBA Season Totals		111	....	1895	595	227	625	.363	....	....	....	141	189	.746	....	....	396	126	186	2	....	....	....	17.1	5.4	3.6	1.1	
51-52	Philadelphia	3	....	18	4	1	2	.500	....	....	....	2	2	1.000	....	....	3	1	6	0	....	....	....	6.0	1.3	1.0	0.3	.254
52-53	Indianapolis	2	....	36	21	7	17	.412	....	....	....	7	8	.875	....	....	6	0	7	0	....	....	....	18.0	10.5	3.0	0.0	.422
NBA Playoff Totals		5	....	54	25	8	19	.421	....	....	....	9	10	.900	....	....	9	1	13	0	....	....	....	10.8	5.0	1.8	0.2	

• PEARCY, George

George W. (Wig) Pearcy

Born: July 2, 1919.   Height: 6'1".   Weight: 165 lbs.   Drafted: —   College: Indiana State

YEAR	TEAM	GP	GS	MIN	PTS	FGM	FGA	FG%	3PM	3PA	3P%	FTM	FTA	FT%	ORB	DRB	TRB	AST	PF	DQ	STL	BLK	TO	MPG	PPG	RPG	APG	PCM
46-47	Detroit	37	....	....	94	31	130	.238	....	....	....	32	44	.727	....	....		13	68	....	....	....	....		2.5	....	0.4	....
NBA Season Totals		37	....	....	94	31	130	.238	....	....	....	32	44	.727	....	....		13	68	....	....	....	....		2.5	....	0.4	

• PEARCY, Henry

Henry Earl Pearcy

Born: July 21, 1922.   Height: 6'1".   Weight: 170 lbs.   Drafted: —   College: Indiana State

YEAR	TEAM	GP	GS	MIN	PTS	FGM	FGA	FG%	3PM	3PA	3P%	FTM	FTA	FT%	ORB	DRB	TRB	AST	PF	DQ	STL	BLK	TO	MPG	PPG	RPG	APG	PCM
46-47	Detroit	29	....	....	73	24	108	.222	....	....	....	25	34	.735	....	....		7	20	....	....	....	....		2.5	....	0.2	....
NBA Season Totals		29	....	....	73	24	108	.222	....	....	....	25	34	.735	....	....		7	20	....	....	....	....		2.5	....	0.2	

• PECK, Wiley

Wiley J. Peck

Born: Sept. 15, 1957. Montgomery, AL, United States. Height: 6'7". Weight: 220 lbs. Drafted: 1979 College: Mississippi State

YEAR TEAM	GP	GS	MIN	PTS	FGM	FGA	FG%	3PM	3PA	3P%	FTM	FTA	FT%	ORB	DRB	TRB	AST	PF	DQ	STL	BLK	TO	MPG	PPG	RPG	APG	PCM
79-80 San Antonio	52	....	628	180	73	169	.432	0	2	.000	34	55	.618	66	117	183	33	100	2	17	23	47	12.1	3.5	3.5	0.6	.372
NBA Season Totals	52	....	628	180	73	169	.432	0	2	.000	34	55	.618	66	117	183	33	100	2	17	23	47	12.1	3.5	3.5	0.6	....
79-80 San Antonio	2	....	9	0	0	3	.000	0	0	.000	0	0	.000	0	3	3	0	1	0	0	1	0	4.5	0.0	1.5	0.0	.050
NBA Playoff Totals	2	....	9	0	0	3	.000	0	0	.000	0	0	.000	0	3	3	0	1	0	0	1	0	4.5	0.0	1.5	0.0	....

• PEDERSON, Pete

Willard (Pete) Pederson

Born: 1912. Height: 6'4". Weight: — Drafted: — College: Western State (CO)

YEAR TEAM	GP	GS	MIN	PTS	FGM	FGA	FG%	3PM	3PA	3P%	FTM	FTA	FT%	ORB	DRB	TRB	AST	PF	DQ	STL	BLK	TO	MPG	PPG	RPG	APG	PCM
39-40 Oshkosh-N	26	....	....	78	33	....	....	....	....	....	12	....	....	....	....	....	....	....	....	....	....	....	....	3.0	....	....	....
41-42 Toledo-N	9	....	....	32	12	....	....	....	....	....	8	....	....	....	....	....	....	....	....	....	....	....	....	3.6	....	....	....
NBL Season Totals	35	....	....	110	45	....	....	....	....	....	20	....	....	....	....	....	....	....	....	....	....	....	....	3.1	....	....	....
39-40 Oshkosh-N	8	....	....	39	15	....	....	....	....	....	9	....	....	....	....	....	....	....	....	....	....	....	....	4.9	....	....	....
NBL Playoff Totals	8	....	....	39	15	....	....	....	....	....	9	....	....	....	....	....	....	....	....	....	....	....	....	4.9	....	....	....

• PEEK, Richard

Richard Shelby Peek

Born: Oct. 28, 1943. Miami, FL, United States. Height: 6'11". Weight: 230 lbs. Drafted: 1967 College: Florida

YEAR TEAM	GP	GS	MIN	PTS	FGM	FGA	FG%	3PM	3PA	3P%	FTM	FTA	FT%	ORB	DRB	TRB	AST	PF	DQ	STL	BLK	TO	MPG	PPG	RPG	APG	PCM
67-68 Dallas-A	51	....	759	237	101	209	.483	0	0	.000	35	65	.538	....	....	197	22	94	1	....	....	49	14.9	4.6	3.9	0.4	.376
ABA Season Totals	51	....	759	237	101	209	.483	0	0	.000	35	65	.538	....	....	197	22	94	1	....	....	49	14.9	4.6	3.9	0.4	....
67-68 Dallas-A	8	....	137	43	18	37	.486	0	0	.000	7	15	.467	....	....	42	3	17	1	....	....	10	17.1	5.4	5.3	0.4	.403
ABA Playoff Totals	8	....	137	43	18	37	.486	0	0	.000	7	15	.467	....	....	42	3	17	1	....	....	10	17.1	5.4	5.3	0.4	....

• PEELER, Anthony

Anthony Eugene Peeler

Born: Nov. 25, 1969. Kansas City, MO, United States. Height: 6'4". Weight: 208 lbs. Drafted: 1992 College: Missouri

YEAR TEAM	GP	GS	MIN	PTS	FGM	FGA	FG%	3PM	3PA	3P%	FTM	FTA	FT%	ORB	DRB	TRB	AST	PF	DQ	STL	BLK	TO	MPG	PPG	RPG	APG	PCM
92-93 LA Lakers	77	11	1655	802	297	634	.468	46	118	.390	162	206	.786	64	115	179	166	193	0	60	14	123	21.5	10.4	2.3	2.2	.408
93-94 LA Lakers	30	30	923	423	176	409	.430	14	63	.222	57	71	.803	48	61	109	94	93	0	43	8	60	30.8	14.1	3.6	3.1	.383
94-95 LA Lakers	73	24	1559	756	285	659	.432	84	216	.389	102	128	.797	62	106	168	122	143	1	52	13	80	21.4	10.4	2.3	1.7	.384
95-96 LA Lakers	73	12	1608	710	272	602	.452	105	254	.413	61	86	.709	45	92	137	117	139	0	59	10	58	22.0	9.7	1.9	1.6	.364
96-97 Vancouver	72	57	2291	1041	402	1011	.398	128	343	.373	109	133	.820	54	193	247	256	168	0	105	17	158	31.8	14.5	3.4	3.6	.373
97-98 Vancouver	8	8	202	79	35	72	.486	5	19	.263	4	6	.667	6	14	20	23	16	0	9	0	6	25.3	9.9	2.5	2.9	.410
97-98 Minnesota	30	24	991	390	155	348	.445	48	106	.453	32	41	.780	31	72	103	114	81	0	52	6	45	33.0	13.0	3.4	3.8	.406
98-99 Minnesota	28	28	810	270	103	272	.379	34	114	.298	30	41	.732	30	54	84	78	60	0	35	6	38	28.9	9.6	3.0	2.8	.311
99-00 Minnesota	82	22	2073	804	316	725	.436	85	255	.333	87	109	.798	58	174	232	195	171	1	62	10	85	25.3	9.8	2.8	2.4	.365
00-01 Minnesota	75	41	2126	791	308	732	.421	100	256	.391	75	87	.862	44	148	192	192	166	1	91	18	105	28.3	10.5	2.6	2.6	.338
01-02 Minnesota	82	0	2060	737	288	684	.421	111	283	.392	50	58	.862	37	169	206	177	137	0	61	11	76	25.1	9.0	2.5	2.2	.335
02-03 Minnesota	82	39	2245	630	252	609	.414	87	212	.410	39	50	.780	40	201	241	244	161	0	72	13	82	27.4	7.7	2.9	3.0	.319
NBA Season Totals	712	296	18543	7433	2889	6757	.428	847	2239	.378	808	1016	.795	519	1399	1918	1778	1528	3	701	126	916	26.0	10.4	2.7	2.5	....
94-95 LA Lakers	10	10	268	89	32	79	.405	8	31	.258	17	22	.773	8	20	28	25	23	0	10	2	12	26.8	8.9	2.8	2.5	.316
95-96 LA Lakers	3	0	72	28	9	27	.333	6	14	.429	4	4	1.000	2	6	8	3	6	0	6	0	3	24.0	9.3	2.7	1.0	.303
97-98 Minnesota	5	5	213	81	31	77	.403	15	31	.484	4	4	1.000	16	22	38	18	15	0	10	3	8	42.6	16.2	7.6	3.6	.427
98-99 Minnesota	4	4	125	27	11	35	.314	5	13	.385	0	0	.000	7	9	16	6	12	1	4	0	4	31.3	6.8	4.0	1.5	.170
99-00 Minnesota	4	0	90	30	11	24	.458	2	10	.200	6	8	.750	2	7	9	5	9	0	3	1	1	22.5	7.5	2.3	1.3	.328
00-01 Minnesota	4	4	137	34	14	53	.264	6	17	.353	0	0	.000	3	11	14	7	10	0	7	1	6	34.3	8.5	3.5	1.8	.121
01-02 Minnesota	3	0	67	27	9	20	.450	5	9	.556	4	6	.667	1	12	13	2	5	0	4	0	6	22.3	9.0	4.3	0.7	.388
02-03 Minnesota	6	5	166	29	13	38	.342	2	16	.125	1	2	.500	5	16	21	18	14	0	4	1	4	27.7	4.8	3.5	3.0	.236
NBA Playoff Totals	39	28	1138	345	130	353	.368	49	141	.348	36	46	.783	44	103	147	84	94	1	48	8	44	29.2	8.8	3.8	2.2	....

• PEEPLES, George

George Albert Peeples

Born: Oct. 30, 1943. GA, United States. Height: 6'7". Weight: 190 lbs. Drafted: 1966 College: Iowa

YEAR TEAM	GP	GS	MIN	PTS	FGM	FGA	FG%	3PM	3PA	3P%	FTM	FTA	FT%	ORB	DRB	TRB	AST	PF	DQ	STL	BLK	TO	MPG	PPG	RPG	APG	PCM
67-68 Indiana-A	65	....	1203	391	138	339	.407	0	3	.000	115	188	.612	....	....	378	29	136	1	....	....	71	18.5	6.0	5.8	0.4	.403
68-69 Indiana-A	64	....	1111	345	122	278	.439	0	0	.000	101	142	.711	126	232	358	33	137	2	....	....	73	17.4	5.4	5.6	0.5	.432
69-70 Carolina-A	83	....	2220	767	279	682	.409	0	7	.000	209	315	.663	229	456	685	123	232	0	....	....	145	26.7	9.2	8.3	1.5	.452
70-71 Carolina-A	82	....	2220	956	377	773	.488	0	1	.000	202	335	.603	265	506	771	110	279	7	....	....	193	27.1	11.7	9.4	1.3	.551
71-72 Dallas-A	6	....	125	29	11	25	.440	0	0	.000	7	11	.636	15	20	35	5	10	0	....	....	9	20.8	4.8	5.8	0.8	.375
72-73 Indiana-A	9	....	56	14	4	14	.286	0	0	.000	6	11	.545	3	12	15	4	14	0	....	....	6	6.2	1.6	1.7	0.4	.256
ABA Season Totals	309	....	6935	2502	931	2111	.441	0	11	.000	640	1002	.639	638	1226	2242	304	808	10	....	....	497	22.4	8.1	7.3	1.0	....
67-68 Indiana-A	3	....	62	26	12	21	.571	0	0	.000	2	3	.667	....	....	31	4	9	1	....	....	4	20.7	8.7	10.3	1.3	.722
68-69 Indiana-A	17	....	419	102	32	81	.395	0	1	.000	38	57	.667	....	....	116	11	41	0	....	....	15	24.6	6.0	6.8	0.6	.349
69-70 Carolina-A	4	....	126	39	15	42	.357	0	0	.000	9	13	.692	15	39	54	4	....	....	....	....	....	31.5	9.8	13.5	1.0	....
ABA Playoff Totals	24	....	607	167	59	144	.410	0	1	.000	49	73	.671	15	39	201	19	50	1	....	....	19	25.3	7.0	8.4	0.8	....

• PELKINGTON, Jake

John Francis Robert (Pelky) Pelkington Jr.

Born: Jan. 3, 1916. Died: May1, 1982. Height: 6'6". Weight: 220 lbs. Drafted: — College: Manhattan

YEAR TEAM	GP	GS	MIN	PTS	FGM	FGA	FG%	3PM	3PA	3P%	FTM	FTA	FT%	ORB	DRB	TRB	AST	PF	DQ	STL	BLK	TO	MPG	PPG	RPG	APG	PCM
40-41 Wingfoots-N	24	....	....	184	57	....	....	....	....	....	70	....	....	....	....	....	....	....	....	....	....	....	....	7.7	....	....	....
42-43 Fort Wayne-N	23	....	....	236	83	....	....	....	....	....	70	....	....	....	....	....	....	....	....	....	....	....	....	10.3	....	....	....
43-44 Fort Wayne-N	20	....	....	132	46	....	....	....	....	....	40	....	....	....	....	....	....	....	....	....	....	....	....	6.6	....	....	....
44-45 Fort Wayne-N	30	....	....	246	85	....	....	....	....	....	76	....	....	....	....	....	....	....	....	....	....	....	....	8.2	....	....	....
45-46 Fort Wayne-N	33	....	....	264	94	....	....	....	....	....	76	104	.731	....	....	....	....	....	....	....	....	....	....	8.0	....	....	....

YEAR	TEAM	GP	GS	MIN	PTS	FGM	FGA	FG%	3PM	3PA	3P%	FTM	FTA	FT%	ORB	DRB	TRB	AST	PF	DQ	STL	BLK	TO	MPG	PPG	RPG	APG	PCM
46-47	Fort Wayne-N	42	....	....	383	129	....	....	....	....	....	125	166	.753	....	....	....	....	117	....	....	....	....	....	9.1	....	....	....
47-48	Fort Wayne-N	54	....	....	504	174	....	....	....	....	....	156	214	.729	....	....	....	....	156	....	....	....	....	....	9.3	....	....	....
48-49	Fort Wayne	14	....	....	124	33	104	.317	....	....	....	58	75	.773	....	....	....	32	54	....	....	....	....	....	8.9	....	2.3	....
48-49	Baltimore	40	....	....	473	160	365	.438	....	....	....	153	192	.797	....	....	....	99	162	....	....	....	....	....	11.8	....	2.5	....
NBA Season Totals		54	....	....	597	193	469	.412	....	....	....	211	267	.790	....	....	....	131	216	....	....	....	....	....	11.1	....	2.4	....
NBL Season Totals		226	....	....	1949	668	....	....	....	....	....	613	484	....	....	....	....	....	273	....	....	....	....	....	8.6	....	....	....
Career Totals		280	....	....	2546	861	469	....	....	....	....	824	751	....	....	....	....	131	489	....	....	....	....	....	9.1	....	0.5	....
42-43	Fort Wayne-N	6	....	....	39	12	....	....	....	....	....	15	....	....	....	....	....	....	....	....	....	....	....	....	6.5	....	....	....
43-44	Fort Wayne-N	5	....	....	32	11	....	....	....	....	....	10	....	....	....	....	....	....	....	....	....	....	....	....	6.4	....	....	....
44-45	Fort Wayne-N	7	....	....	56	19	....	....	....	....	....	18	....	....	....	....	....	....	....	....	....	....	....	....	8.0	....	....	....
45-46	Fort Wayne-N	4	....	....	21	8	....	....	....	....	....	5	5	1.000	....	....	....	....	....	....	....	....	....	....	5.3	....	....	....
46-47	Fort Wayne-N	8	....	....	55	18	....	....	....	....	....	19	25	.760	....	....	....	....	....	....	....	....	....	....	6.9	....	....	....
47-48	Fort Wayne-N	4	....	....	34	14	....	....	....	....	....	6	13	.462	....	....	....	....	....	....	....	....	....	....	8.5	....	....	....
48-49	Baltimore	3	....	....	53	13	33	.394	....	....	....	27	35	.771	....	....	....	3	13	....	....	....	....	....	17.7	....	1.0	....
NBA Playoff Totals		3	....	....	53	13	33	.394	....	....	....	27	35	.771	....	....	....	3	13	....	....	....	....	....	17.7	....	1.0	....
NBL Playoff Totals		34	....	....	237	82	....	....	....	....	....	73	43	....	....	....	....	....	....	....	....	....	....	....	7.0	....	....	....
Career Playoff Totals		37	....	....	290	95	33	....	....	....	....	100	78	....	....	....	....	3	13	....	....	....	....	....	7.8	....	0.1	....

• PELLOM, Sam

Samuel Troy Pellom

Born: Oct. 2, 1951. Wilmington, NC, United States. Height: 6'9". Weight: 225 lbs. Drafted: — College: SUNY Buffalo

79-80	Atlanta	44	....	373	109	44	108	.407	0	0	.000	21	30	.700	28	64	92	18	70	0	12	12	18	8.5	2.5	2.1	0.4	.332
80-81	Atlanta	77	....	1472	453	186	380	.489	0	1	.000	81	116	.698	122	234	356	48	228	6	50	92	100	19.1	5.9	4.6	0.6	.388
81-82	Atlanta	69	4	1037	289	114	251	.454	0	1	.000	61	79	.772	90	139	229	28	164	0	29	47	55	15.0	4.2	3.3	0.4	.327
82-83	Atlanta	2	0	9	4	2	6	.333	0	0	.000	0	0	.000	0	0	0	1	0	0	0	0	0	4.5	2.0	0.0	0.5	.166
82-83	Milwaukee	4	0	20	8	4	10	.400	0	0	.000	0	0	.000	2	6	8	0	3	0	0	0	2	5.0	2.0	2.0	0.0	.332
NBA Season Totals		196	4	2911	863	350	755	.464	0	2	.000	163	225	.724	242	443	685	95	465	6	91	151	175	14.9	4.4	3.5	0.5	....
79-80	Atlanta	4	....	18	1	0	3	.000	0	0	.000	1	3	.333	0	0	0	1	3	0	0	1	0	4.5	0.3	0.0	0.3	-.110
81-82	Atlanta	1	0	4	2	1	3	.333	0	0	.000	0	0	.000	1	0	1	0	0	0	0	0	0	4.0	2.0	1.0	0.0	.270
NBA Playoff Totals		5	0	22	3	1	6	.167	0	0	.000	1	3	.333	1	0	1	1	3	0	0	1	0	4.4	0.6	0.2	0.2	....

• PENBERTHY, Mike

Michael Penberthy

Born: Nov. 29, 1974. Los Gatos, CA, United States. Height: 6'3". Weight: 185 lbs. Drafted: — College: Master's College

00-01	LA Lakers	53	0	851	267	92	222	.414	55	139	.396	28	31	.903	10	53	63	71	57	0	22	2	34	16.1	5.0	1.2	1.3	.293
01-02	LA Lakers	3	0	12	5	1	2	.500	0	0	.000	3	4	.750	0	2	2	2	0	0	2	0	0	4.0	1.7	0.7	0.7	.788
NBA Season Totals		56	0	863	272	93	224	.415	55	139	.396	31	35	.886	10	55	65	73	57	0	24	2	34	15.4	4.9	1.2	1.3	....

• PENDER, Jerry

Jerry Lee Pender

Born: Feb. 12, 1950. Height: 6'2". Weight: 185 lbs. Drafted: 1972 College: Fresno State

73-74	San Diego-A	11	....	68	27	8	30	.267	1	3	.333	10	13	.769	3	2	5	4	11	....	6	0	9	6.2	2.5	0.5	0.4	.161
ABA Season Totals		11	....	68	27	8	30	.267	1	3	.333	10	13	.769	3	2	5	4	11	....	6	0	9	6.2	2.5	0.5	0.4	....

• PEPLOWSKI, Mike

Michael Walter Peplowski

Born: Oct. 15, 1970. Detroit, MI, United States. Height: 6'10". Weight: 270 lbs. Drafted: 1993 College: Michigan State

93-94	Sacramento	55	19	667	176	76	141	.539	0	1	.000	24	44	.545	49	120	169	24	131	2	17	25	33	12.1	3.2	3.1	0.4	.354
94-95	Detroit	6	0	21	11	5	5	1.000	0	0	.000	1	2	.500	1	2	3	1	10	0	1	0	2	3.5	1.8	0.5	0.2	.418
95-96	Washington	2	0	5	0	0	0	.000	0	0	.000	0	0	.000	0	0	0	0	4	0	0	0	0	2.5	0.0	0.0	0.0	-.376
95-96	Milwaukee	5	0	12	7	3	5	.600	0	0	.000	1	3	.333	1	3	4	1	6	0	1	2	2	2.4	1.4	0.8	0.2	.593
NBA Season Totals		68	19	705	194	84	151	.556	0	1	.000	26	49	.531	51	125	176	26	151	2	19	27	37	10.4	2.9	2.6	0.4	....

• PERDUE, Will

William Edward Perdue III

Born: Aug. 29, 1965. Melbourne, FL, United States. Height: 7' Weight: 240 lbs. Drafted: 1988 College: Vanderbilt

88-89	Chicago	30	0	190	66	29	72	.403	0	0	.000	8	14	.571	18	27	45	11	38	0	4	6	15	6.3	2.2	1.5	0.4	.287
89-90	Chicago	77	11	884	294	111	268	.414	0	5	.000	72	104	.692	88	126	214	46	150	0	19	26	62	11.5	3.8	2.8	0.6	.334
90-91	Chicago	74	3	972	307	116	235	.494	0	3	.000	75	112	.670	122	214	336	47	147	1	23	57	74	13.1	4.1	4.5	0.6	.493
91-92	Chicago	77	7	1007	350	152	278	.547	1	2	.500	45	91	.495	108	204	312	80	133	1	16	43	69	13.1	4.5	4.1	1.0	.512
92-93	Chicago	72	16	998	341	137	246	.557	0	1	.000	67	111	.604	103	184	287	74	139	2	22	47	72	13.9	4.7	4.0	1.0	.499
93-94	Chicago	43	6	397	117	47	112	.420	0	1	.000	23	32	.719	40	86	126	34	61	0	8	11	43	9.2	2.7	2.9	0.8	.392
94-95	Chicago	78	78	1592	621	254	459	.553	0	1	.000	113	194	.582	211	311	522	90	220	3	26	56	117	20.4	8.0	6.7	1.2	.528
95-96	San Antonio	80	22	1396	413	173	331	.523	0	1	.000	67	125	.536	175	310	485	33	183	0	28	74	88	17.5	5.2	6.1	0.4	.469
96-97	San Antonio	65	34	1918	565	233	410	.568	0	0	.000	99	171	.579	251	387	638	38	184	2	32	102	85	29.5	8.7	9.8	0.6	.501
97-98	San Antonio	79	30	1491	394	162	295	.549	0	1	.000	70	133	.526	177	358	535	57	137	0	22	50	79	18.9	5.0	6.8	0.7	.487
98-99	San Antonio	37	1	445	90	38	60	.633	0	0	.000	14	26	.538	33	105	138	18	63	0	9	10	22	12.0	2.4	3.7	0.5	.398
99-00	Chicago	67	15	1012	168	59	168	.351	0	0	.000	50	105	.476	88	174	262	65	126	1	14	42	78	15.1	2.5	3.9	1.0	.272
00-01	Portland	13	0	58	14	6	9	.667	0	0	.000	2	4	.500	6	12	18	2	8	0	3	2	0	4.5	1.1	1.4	0.2	.512
NBA Season Totals		792	223	12360	3740	1517	2943	.515	1	15	.067	705	1222	.577	1420	2498	3918	595	1589	10	226	526	804	15.6	4.7	4.9	0.8	....
88-89	Chicago	3	0	22	14	6	9	.667	0	1	.000	2	3	.667	3	3	6	2	4	0	0	0	0	7.3	4.7	2.0	0.7	.755
89-90	Chicago	13	0	78	40	13	28	.464	1	2	.500	13	18	.722	7	12	19	2	13	0	0	5	4	6.0	3.1	1.5	0.2	.492
90-91	Chicago	17	0	198	70	29	53	.547	0	0	.000	12	22	.545	32	33	65	4	41	1	2	8	14	11.6	4.1	3.8	0.2	.429
91-92	Chicago	18	0	157	45	18	37	.486	0	1	.000	9	20	.450	18	22	40	9	34	1	3	10	12	8.7	2.5	2.2	0.5	.345
92-93	Chicago	13	0	101	25	10	20	.500	0	0	.000	5	10	.500	15	15	30	5	18	0	1	2	8	7.8	1.9	2.3	0.4	.333
94-95	Chicago	10	2	176	50	19	37	.514	0	0	.000	12	21	.571	18	30	48	6	27	0	1	3	10	17.6	5.0	4.8	0.6	.352

YEAR TEAM	GP	GS	MIN	PTS	FGM	FGA	FG%	3PM	3PA	3P%	FTM	FTA	FT%	ORB	DRB	TRB	AST	PF	DQ	STL	BLK	TO	MPG	PPG	RPG	APG	PCM
95-96 San Antonio	10	2	242	74	29	42	.690	0	0	.000	16	20	.800	26	53	79	5	24	0	2	4	11	24.2	7.4	7.9	0.5	.510
97-98 San Antonio	9	7	191	36	9	27	.333	0	0	.000	18	21	.857	24	36	60	1	26	0	6	9	11	21.2	4.0	6.7	0.1	.345
98-99 San Antonio	12	0	86	13	6	11	.545	0	0	.000	1	2	.500	9	19	28	0	19	0	0	1	3	7.2	1.1	2.3	0.0	.265
00-01 Portland	3	0	5	0	0	0	.000	0	0	.000	0	2	.000	1	1	2	0	0	0	0	0	0	1.7	0.0	0.7	0.0	.180
NBA Playoff Totals	108	11	1256	367	139	264	.527	1	4	.250	88	139	.633	153	224	377	34	206	2	15	42	73	11.6	3.4	3.5	0.3	....

• PERIGO, Bill

Bill Perigo

Born: Sept. 17, 1911. Died: Feb.7, 1990. Height: 6' Weight: 180 lbs. Drafted: — College: Western Michigan

YEAR TEAM	GP	GS	MIN	PTS	FGM	FGA	FG%	3PM	3PA	3P%	FTM	FTA	FT%	ORB	DRB	TRB	AST	PF	DQ	STL	BLK	TO	MPG	PPG	RPG	APG	PCM
37-38 Whiting-N	15	....	....	55	22	....	....	....	....	....	11	....	....	....	....	....	....	....	....	....	....	....	....	3.7	....	....	....
38-39 Hammond-N	4	....	....	10	2	....	....	....	....	....	6	....	....	....	....	....	....	....	....	....	....	....	....	2.5	....	....	....
NBL Season Totals	19	....	....	65	24	....	....	....	....	....	17	....	....	....	....	....	....	....	....	....	....	....	....	3.4	....	....	....
37-38 Whiting-N	1	....	....	0	0	....	....	....	....	....	0	....	....	....	....	....	....	....	....	....	....	....	....	0.0	....	....	....
NBL Playoff Totals	1	....	....	0	0	....	....	....	....	....	0	....	....	....	....	....	....	....	....	....	....	....	....	0.0	....	....	....

• PERKINS, Sam

Samuel Bruce Perkins

Born: June 14, 1961. Brooklyn, NY, United States. Height: 6'9". Weight: 235 lbs. Drafted: 1984 College: North Carolina

YEAR TEAM	GP	GS	MIN	PTS	FGM	FGA	FG%	3PM	3PA	3P%	FTM	FTA	FT%	ORB	DRB	TRB	AST	PF	DQ	STL	BLK	TO	MPG	PPG	RPG	APG	PCM
84-85 Dallas	82	42	2317	903	347	736	.471	9	36	.250	200	244	.820	189	416	605	135	236	1	63	63	98	28.3	11.0	7.4	1.6	.494
85-86 Dallas	80	79	2626	1234	458	910	.503	11	33	.333	307	377	.814	195	490	685	153	212	2	75	94	144	32.8	15.4	8.6	1.9	.574
86-87 Dallas	80	80	2687	1186	461	957	.482	19	54	.352	245	296	.828	197	419	616	146	269	6	109	77	128	33.6	14.8	7.7	1.8	.506
87-88 Dallas	75	75	2499	1066	394	876	.450	5	30	.167	273	332	.822	201	400	601	118	227	2	74	54	120	33.3	14.2	8.0	1.6	.471
88-89 Dallas	78	77	2860	1171	445	959	.464	7	38	.184	274	329	.833	235	453	688	127	224	1	76	92	140	36.7	15.0	8.8	1.6	.477
89-90 Dallas	76	70	2668	1206	435	883	.493	6	28	.214	330	424	.778	209	363	572	175	225	4	88	64	144	35.1	15.9	7.5	2.3	.512
90-91 LA Lakers	73	66	2504	983	368	744	.495	18	64	.281	229	279	.821	167	371	538	108	247	2	64	78	102	34.3	13.5	7.4	1.5	.459
91-92 LA Lakers	63	63	2332	1041	361	803	.450	15	69	.217	304	372	.817	192	364	556	141	192	1	64	62	82	37.0	16.5	8.8	2.2	.522
92-93 LA Lakers	49	49	1589	673	242	527	.459	5	29	.172	184	222	.829	111	268	379	128	139	0	40	51	78	32.4	13.7	7.7	2.6	.520
92-93 Seattle	30	13	762	363	139	272	.511	19	42	.452	66	83	.795	52	93	145	28	86	0	20	31	33	25.4	12.1	4.8	0.9	.489
93-94 Seattle	81	41	2170	999	341	779	.438	99	270	.367	218	272	.801	120	246	366	111	197	0	67	31	105	26.8	12.3	4.5	1.4	.429
94-95 Seattle	82	37	2356	1043	346	742	.466	136	343	.397	215	269	.799	96	302	398	135	186	0	72	45	74	28.7	12.7	4.9	1.6	.474
95-96 Seattle	82	20	2169	970	325	797	.408	129	363	.355	191	241	.793	101	266	367	120	174	1	83	48	82	26.5	11.8	4.5	1.5	.433
96-97 Seattle	81	4	1976	889	290	661	.439	122	309	.395	187	229	.817	74	226	300	103	134	0	69	49	81	24.4	11.0	3.7	1.3	.448
97-98 Seattle	81	0	1675	580	196	471	.416	87	222	.392	101	128	.789	53	202	255	113	158	0	62	29	65	20.7	7.2	3.1	1.4	.372
98-99 Indiana	48	0	789	238	80	200	.400	35	90	.389	43	60	.717	36	102	138	25	74	0	15	14	22	16.4	5.0	2.9	0.5	.314
99-00 Indiana	81	0	1620	537	184	441	.417	89	218	.408	80	97	.825	64	225	289	68	136	0	31	33	63	20.0	6.6	3.6	0.8	.353
00-01 Indiana	64	41	999	242	86	226	.381	38	110	.345	32	38	.842	32	136	168	41	61	0	33	18	19	15.6	3.8	2.6	0.6	.311
NBA Season Totals	1286	757	36598	15324	5498	11984	.459	849	2348	.362	3479	4292	.811	2324	5342	7666	1975	3177	20	1105	933	1580	28.5	11.9	6.0	1.5	....
84-85 Dallas	4	4	169	75	24	49	.490	1	4	.250	26	34	.765	16	35	51	11	13	1	2	1	3	42.3	18.8	12.8	2.8	.599
85-86 Dallas	10	10	347	149	57	133	.429	2	8	.250	33	43	.767	30	53	83	24	32	0	9	14	16	34.7	14.9	8.3	2.4	.485
86-87 Dallas	4	4	133	68	26	52	.500	0	4	.000	16	23	.696	12	22	34	5	16	0	4	1	9	33.3	17.0	8.5	1.3	.499
87-88 Dallas	17	17	572	230	88	195	.451	1	7	.143	53	66	.803	39	73	112	31	51	1	25	17	30	33.6	13.5	6.6	1.8	.436
89-90 Dallas	3	3	118	45	16	36	.444	0	1	.000	13	17	.765	10	12	22	8	17	2	3	2	7	39.3	15.0	7.3	2.7	.370
90-91 LA Lakers	19	19	752	336	121	221	.548	11	30	.367	83	109	.761	41	116	157	33	69	0	15	27	37	39.6	17.7	8.3	1.7	.512
92-93 Seattle	19	17	626	274	98	225	.436	30	79	.380	48	55	.873	33	100	133	37	55	0	19	25	21	32.9	14.4	7.0	1.9	.498
93-94 Seattle	5	0	141	49	14	42	.333	6	14	.429	15	17	.882	6	30	36	4	15	0	4	2	6	28.2	9.8	7.2	0.8	.375
94-95 Seattle	4	2	141	54	21	48	.438	10	22	.455	2	2	1.000	6	25	31	13	12	0	3	5	9	35.3	13.5	7.8	3.3	.461
95-96 Seattle	21	1	654	258	90	196	.459	32	87	.368	46	61	.754	21	69	90	35	44	0	15	6	30	31.1	12.3	4.3	1.7	.373
96-97 Seattle	12	6	340	101	31	92	.337	14	45	.311	25	29	.862	15	38	53	15	34	1	12	12	13	28.3	8.4	4.4	1.3	.300
97-98 Seattle	10	1	210	54	16	42	.381	10	24	.417	12	20	.600	6	26	32	14	22	0	3	5	11	21.0	5.4	3.2	1.4	.277
98-99 Indiana	13	0	146	53	18	35	.514	11	24	.458	6	9	.667	2	23	25	6	13	0	0	3	7	11.2	4.1	1.9	0.5	.384
99-00 Indiana	23	0	417	110	34	105	.324	23	66	.348	19	21	.905	17	56	73	10	45	1	4	6	8	18.1	4.8	3.2	0.4	.248
00-01 Indiana	3	0	19	5	2	8	.250	1	4	.250	0	0	.000	1	3	4	0	3	0	0	0	0	6.3	1.7	1.3	0.0	.098
NBA Playoff Totals	167	84	4785	1861	656	1479	.444	152	419	.363	397	506	.785	255	681	936	246	441	6	118	126	207	28.7	11.1	5.6	1.5	....

• PERKINS, Warren

Warren C. (Red) Perkins

Born: Feb. 2, 1924. Height: 6'3". Weight: 190 lbs. Drafted: — College: Tulane

YEAR TEAM	GP	GS	MIN	PTS	FGM	FGA	FG%	3PM	3PA	3P%	FTM	FTA	FT%	ORB	DRB	TRB	AST	PF	DQ	STL	BLK	TO	MPG	PPG	RPG	APG	PCM
49-50 Tri-Cities	60	....	....	371	128	422	.303	....	....	....	115	195	.590	....	....	....	114	260	....	....	....	....	....	6.2	....	1.9	....
50-51 Tri-Cities	66	....	....	396	135	428	.315	....	....	....	126	195	.646	....	....	319	143	232	13	....	....	....	....	6.0	4.8	2.2	....
NBA Season Totals	126	....	....	767	263	850	.309	....	....	....	241	390	.618	....	....	319	257	492	13	....	....	....	....	6.1	2.5	2.0	....
49-50 Tri-Cities	2	....	....	4	1	1	1.000	....	....	....	2	2	1.000	....	....	....	0	2	....	....	....	....	....	2.0	....	0.0	....
NBA Playoff Totals	2	....	....	4	1	1	1.000	....	....	....	2	2	1.000	....	....	....	0	2	....	....	....	....	....	2.0	....	0.0	....

• PERRY, —

Perry

Born: —. Height: — Weight: — Drafted: — College: —

YEAR TEAM	GP	GS	MIN	PTS	FGM	FGA	FG%	3PM	3PA	3P%	FTM	FTA	FT%	ORB	DRB	TRB	AST	PF	DQ	STL	BLK	TO	MPG	PPG	RPG	APG	PCM
46-47 Detroit-N	5	....	....	15	4	....	....	....	....	....	7	14	.500	....	....	....	....	....	....	....	....	....	....	3.0	....	....	....
NBL Season Totals	5	....	....	15	4	....	....	....	....	....	7	14	....	....	....	....	....	....	....	....	....	....	....	3.0	....	....	....

• PERRY, Aulcie

Aulcie Perry

Born: July 3, 1950. Newark, NJ, United States. Height: 6'10". Weight: 210 lbs. Drafted: — College: Bethune-Cookman

YEAR TEAM	GP	GS	MIN	PTS	FGM	FGA	FG%	3PM	3PA	3P%	FTM	FTA	FT%	ORB	DRB	TRB	AST	PF	DQ	STL	BLK	TO	MPG	PPG	RPG	APG	PCM
74-75 Virginia-A	21	....	415	181	81	186	.435	0	1	.000	19	30	.633	40	65	105	20	58	....	12	16	34	19.8	8.6	5.0	1.0	.416
ABA Season Totals	21	....	415	181	81	186	.435	0	1	.000	19	30	.633	40	65	105	20	58	....	12	16	34	19.8	8.6	5.0	1.0	....

• PERRY, Curtis
Curtis R. Perry

Born: Sept. 13, 1948. Washington, DC, United States. Height: 6'7". Weight: 220 lbs. Drafted: 1970 College: Southwest Missouri State

YEAR	TEAM	GP	GS	MIN	PTS	FGM	FGA	FG%	3PM	3PA	3P%	FTM	FTA	FT%	ORB	DRB	TRB	AST	PF	DQ	STL	BLK	TO	MPG	PPG	RPG	APG	PCM
70-71	San Diego	18	....	100	53	21	48	.438	....	....	....	11	20	.550	....	....	30	5	22	0	....	....	....	5.6	2.9	1.7	0.3	.480
71-72	Houston	25	....	355	88	38	115	.330	....	....	....	12	24	.500	....	....	122	22	47	**1**	....	....	....	14.2	3.5	4.9	0.9	.356
71-72	Milwaukee	50	....	1471	350	143	371	.385	....	....	....	64	95	.674	....	....	471	78	214	**13**	....	....	....	29.4	7.0	9.4	1.6	.369
72-73	Milwaukee	67	....	2094	613	265	575	.461	....	....	....	83	126	.659	....	....	644	123	246	6	....	....	....	31.3	9.1	9.6	1.8	.437
73-74	Milwaukee	81	....	2386	728	325	729	.446	....	....	....	78	134	.582	242	461	703	183	301	8	104	97	....	29.5	9.0	8.7	2.3	.436
74-75	Phoenix	79	....	2688	1058	437	917	.477	....	....	....	184	256	.719	347	593	940	186	288	10	108	78	....	34.0	13.4	11.9	2.4	.562
75-76	Phoenix	71	....	2353	947	386	776	.497	....	....	....	175	239	.732	197	487	684	182	269	5	84	66	....	33.1	13.3	9.6	2.6	.537
76-77	Phoenix	44	....	1391	470	179	414	.432	....	....	....	112	142	.789	149	246	395	79	163	3	49	28	....	31.6	10.7	9.0	1.8	.442
77-78	Phoenix	45	....	818	271	110	243	.453	....	....	....	51	65	.785	87	163	250	48	120	2	34	22	63	18.2	6.0	5.6	1.1	.443
NBA Season Totals		480	....	13656	4578	1904	4188	.455	....	....	....	770	1101	.699	1022	1950	4239	906	1670	48	379	291	63	28.5	9.5	8.8	1.9	....
71-72	Milwaukee	11	....	397	104	43	91	.473	....	....	....	18	23	.783	....	....	141	14	45	2	....	....	....	36.1	9.5	12.8	1.3	.450
72-73	Milwaukee	6	....	238	53	25	52	.481	....	....	....	3	6	.500	....	....	69	13	23	1	....	....	....	39.7	8.8	11.5	2.2	.390
73-74	Milwaukee	16	....	296	99	46	92	.500	....	....	....	7	12	.583	34	47	81	12	43	1	10	2	....	18.5	6.2	5.1	0.8	.413
75-76	Phoenix	19	....	615	242	99	218	.454	....	....	....	44	68	.647	63	83	146	36	78	3	12	17	....	32.4	12.7	7.7	1.9	.427
NBA Playoff Totals		52	....	1546	498	213	453	.470	....	....	....	72	109	.661	97	130	437	75	189	7	22	19	....	29.7	9.6	8.4	1.4	....

• PERRY, Elliot
Elliot Lamonte (Socks) Perry

Born: Mar. 28, 1969. Memphis, TN, United States. Height: 6' Weight: 150 lbs. Drafted: 1991 College: Memphis State

YEAR	TEAM	GP	GS	MIN	PTS	FGM	FGA	FG%	3PM	3PA	3P%	FTM	FTA	FT%	ORB	DRB	TRB	AST	PF	DQ	STL	BLK	TO	MPG	PPG	RPG	APG	PCM
91-92	LA Clippers	10	0	66	13	6	15	.400	0	2	.000	1	2	.500	2	5	7	14	10	0	9	1	13	6.6	1.3	0.7	1.4	.276
91-92	Charlotte	40	0	371	113	43	114	.377	1	5	.200	26	39	.667	12	20	32	64	26	0	25	2	36	9.3	2.8	0.8	1.6	.320
93-94	Phoenix	27	9	432	105	42	113	.372	0	3	.000	21	28	.750	12	27	39	125	36	0	25	1	43	16.0	3.9	1.4	4.6	.407
94-95	Phoenix	82	51	1977	795	306	588	.520	25	60	.417	158	195	.810	51	100	151	394	142	0	156	4	164	24.1	9.7	1.8	4.8	.507
95-96	Phoenix	81	26	1668	697	261	549	.475	24	59	.407	151	194	.778	34	102	136	353	140	1	87	5	146	20.6	8.6	1.7	4.4	.475
96-97	Milwaukee	82	3	1595	562	217	458	.474	49	137	.358	79	106	.745	24	100	124	247	117	0	98	3	115	19.5	6.9	1.5	3.0	.399
97-98	Milwaukee	81	33	1752	591	241	561	.430	17	50	.340	92	109	.844	21	87	108	230	129	1	90	2	130	21.6	7.3	1.3	2.8	.311
98-99	Milwaukee	5	0	47	20	9	17	.529	1	1	1.000	1	2	.500	1	7	8	12	3	0	4	0	2	9.4	4.0	1.6	2.4	.709
98-99	New Jersey	30	0	243	78	30	86	.349	9	23	.391	9	12	.750	6	20	26	35	22	0	16	0	32	8.1	2.6	0.9	1.2	.267
99-00	New Jersey	60	5	803	317	128	294	.435	11	39	.282	50	62	.806	13	48	61	139	47	0	39	1	60	13.4	5.3	1.0	2.3	.409
00-01	Orlando	6	0	39	10	5	11	.455	0	1	.000	0	0	.000	1	3	4	5	1	0	3	0	6	6.5	1.7	0.7	0.8	.271
00-01	Phoenix	43	6	460	137	60	129	.465	1	4	.250	16	22	.727	8	34	42	74	28	0	19	1	32	10.7	3.2	1.0	1.7	.366
01-02	Memphis	2	0	48	11	5	10	.500	0	0	.000	1	2	.500	0	4	4	7	6	0	3	0	7	24.0	5.5	2.0	3.5	.228
NBA Season Totals		549	133	9501	3449	1353	2945	.459	138	384	.359	605	773	.783	185	557	742	1699	707	2	574	20	786	17.3	6.3	1.4	3.1	....
93-94	Phoenix	4	0	13	2	1	7	.143	0	0	.000	0	0	.000	0	0	0	1	2	0	1	0	1	3.3	0.5	0.0	0.3	-.257
94-95	Phoenix	9	0	106	62	20	42	.476	2	5	.400	20	25	.800	3	7	10	12	8	0	5	0	9	11.8	6.9	1.1	1.3	.506
95-96	Phoenix	4	0	51	14	7	14	.500	0	0	.000	0	1	.000	0	2	2	12	3	0	2	0	0	12.8	3.5	0.5	3.0	.432
00-01	Phoenix	2	0	17	13	6	10	.600	0	1	.000	1	1	1.000	1	3	4	4	0	0	2	0	0	8.5	6.5	2.0	2.0	1.130
NBA Playoff Totals		19	0	187	91	34	73	.466	2	6	.333	21	27	.778	4	12	16	29	13	0	10	0	10	9.8	4.8	0.8	1.5	....

• PERRY, Ron
Ron Perry

Born: Dec. 29, 1943. Garrisonville, VA, United States. Height: 6'3". Weight: 190 lbs. Drafted: 1967 College: Virginia Tech

YEAR	TEAM	GP	GS	MIN	PTS	FGM	FGA	FG%	3PM	3PA	3P%	FTM	FTA	FT%	ORB	DRB	TRB	AST	PF	DQ	STL	BLK	TO	MPG	PPG	RPG	APG	PCM
67-68	Minnesota-A	67	....	2125	858	339	878	.386	62	178	.348	118	179	.659	....	....	223	139	151	2	....	....	169	31.7	12.8	3.3	2.1	.315
68-69	Indiana-A	27	....	865	365	137	336	.408	33	91	.363	58	70	.829	24	49	73	97	108	3	....	....	67	32.0	13.5	2.7	3.6	.366
68-69	Miami-A	24	....	708	274	100	299	.334	12	44	.273	62	91	.681	27	46	73	62	66	0	....	....	61	29.5	11.4	3.0	2.6	.277
68-69	New York-A	23	....	812	444	165	425	.388	22	57	.386	92	131	.702	32	63	95	85	81	5	....	....	73	35.3	19.3	4.1	3.7	.429
69-70	Carolina-A	19	....	221	118	42	103	.408	2	10	.200	32	43	.744	4	14	18	18	34	1	....	....	19	11.6	6.2	0.9	0.9	.373
69-70	New Orleans-A	27	....	301	169	62	169	.367	8	25	.320	37	54	.685	20	15	35	19	44	0	....	....	32	11.1	6.3	1.3	0.7	.341
ABA Season Totals		187	....	5032	2228	845	2210	.382	139	405	.343	399	568	.702	107	187	517	420	484	11	....	....	421	26.9	11.9	2.8	2.2	....
68-69	Indiana-A	17	....	202	97	34	114	.298	11	38	.289	18	27	.667	....	....	21	18	33	0	....	....	19	11.9	5.7	1.2	1.1	.242
ABA Playoff Totals		17	....	202	97	34	114	.298	11	38	.289	18	27	.667	....	....	21	18	33	0	....	....	19	11.9	5.7	1.2	1.1	....

• PERRY, Tim
Timothy D. Perry

Born: June 4, 1965. Freehold, NJ, United States. Height: 6'9". Weight: 200 lbs. Drafted: 1988 College: Temple

YEAR	TEAM	GP	GS	MIN	PTS	FGM	FGA	FG%	3PM	3PA	3P%	FTM	FTA	FT%	ORB	DRB	TRB	AST	PF	DQ	STL	BLK	TO	MPG	PPG	RPG	APG	PCM
88-89	Phoenix	62	15	614	257	108	201	.537	1	4	.250	40	65	.615	61	71	132	18	47	0	19	32	37	9.9	4.1	2.1	0.3	.476
89-90	Phoenix	60	18	612	254	100	195	.513	1	1	1.000	53	90	.589	79	73	152	17	76	0	21	22	48	10.2	4.2	2.5	0.3	.438
90-91	Phoenix	46	2	587	193	75	144	.521	0	5	.000	43	70	.614	53	73	126	27	60	1	23	43	32	12.8	4.2	2.7	0.6	.453
91-92	Phoenix	80	69	2483	982	413	789	.523	3	8	.375	153	215	.712	204	347	551	134	237	2	44	116	144	31.0	12.3	6.9	1.7	.469
92-93	Philadelphia	81	51	2104	731	287	613	.468	10	49	.204	147	207	.710	154	255	409	126	159	0	40	91	122	26.0	9.0	5.0	1.6	.404
93-94	Philadelphia	80	68	2336	719	272	625	.435	73	200	.365	102	176	.580	117	287	404	94	154	1	60	82	80	29.2	9.0	5.1	1.2	.351
94-95	Philadelphia	42	1	446	76	27	78	.346	0	14	.000	22	40	.550	38	51	89	12	51	0	10	15	21	10.6	1.8	2.1	0.3	.215
95-96	Philadelphia	8	0	87	19	8	18	.444	1	1	1.000	2	3	.667	6	7	13	2	5	0	2	3	3	10.9	2.4	1.6	0.3	.264
95-96	New Jersey	22	1	167	52	23	47	.489	3	7	.429	3	6	.500	15	20	35	6	11	0	2	10	7	7.6	2.4	1.6	0.3	.400
NBA Season Totals		481	225	9436	3283	1313	2710	.485	92	289	.318	565	872	.648	727	1184	1911	436	800	4	221	414	494	19.6	6.8	4.0	0.9	....
88-89	Phoenix	4	0	17	4	2	4	.500	0	0	.000	0	2	.000	1	1	2	0	1	0	2	1	1	4.3	1.0	0.5	0.0	.263
89-90	Phoenix	11	0	100	34	13	25	.520	0	0	.000	8	18	.444	10	11	21	2	19	0	3	6	5	9.1	3.1	1.9	0.2	.347
91-92	Phoenix	8	8	185	99	38	63	.603	0	0	.000	23	32	.719	12	27	39	11	24	1	3	6	14	23.1	12.4	4.9	1.4	.561
NBA Playoff Totals		23	8	302	137	53	92	.576	0	0	.000	31	52	.596	23	39	62	13	44	1	8	13	20	13.1	6.0	2.7	0.6	....

• PERSON, Chuck
Chuck Connors (The Rifleman) Person

Born: June 27, 1964. Brantley, AL, United States.   Height: 6'8".   Weight: 220 lbs.   Drafted: 1986   College: Auburn

YEAR	TEAM	GP	GS	MIN	PTS	FGM	FGA	FG%	3PM	3PA	3P%	FTM	FTA	FT%	ORB	DRB	TRB	AST	PF	DQ	STL	BLK	TO	MPG	PPG	RPG	APG	PCM
86-87	Indiana	82	78	2956	1541	635	1358	.468	49	138	.355	222	297	.747	168	509	677	295	310	4	90	16	213	36.0	18.8	8.3	3.6	.519
87-88	Indiana	79	71	2807	1341	575	1252	.459	59	177	.333	132	197	.670	171	365	536	309	266	4	73	9	213	35.5	17.0	6.8	3.9	.450
88-89	Indiana	80	79	3012	1728	711	1453	.489	63	205	.307	243	307	.792	144	372	516	289	280	12	83	18	312	37.7	21.6	6.5	3.6	.488
89-90	Indiana	77	73	2714	1515	605	1242	.487	94	253	.372	211	270	.781	126	319	445	230	217	1	53	20	169	35.2	19.7	5.8	3.0	.501
90-91	Indiana	80	79	2566	1474	620	1231	.504	69	203	.340	165	229	.721	121	296	417	238	221	1	56	17	184	32.1	18.4	5.2	3.0	.511
91-92	Indiana	81	81	2923	1497	616	1284	.480	132	354	.373	133	197	.675	114	312	426	382	247	5	68	18	219	36.1	18.5	5.3	4.7	.484
92-93	Minnesota	78	75	2985	1309	541	1248	.433	118	332	.355	109	168	.649	98	335	433	343	198	2	67	30	218	38.3	16.8	5.6	4.4	.398
93-94	Minnesota	77	37	2029	894	356	843	.422	100	272	.368	82	108	.759	55	198	253	185	164	1	45	12	123	26.4	11.6	3.3	2.4	.361
94-95	San Antonio	81	1	2033	872	317	750	.423	172	445	.387	66	102	.647	49	209	258	106	198	0	45	12	105	25.1	10.8	3.2	1.3	.327
95-96	San Antonio	80	16	2131	873	308	705	.437	190	463	.410	67	104	.644	76	337	413	100	197	2	49	26	88	26.6	10.9	5.2	1.3	.409
97-98	San Antonio	61	11	1455	409	143	398	.359	95	276	.344	28	37	.757	17	187	204	86	121	1	29	10	67	23.9	6.7	3.3	1.4	.255
98-99	Charlotte	50	21	990	303	112	289	.388	55	157	.350	24	32	.750	17	115	132	60	90	0	20	8	41	19.8	6.1	2.6	1.2	.277
99-00	Seattle	37	0	340	102	37	123	.301	24	95	.253	4	8	.500	6	47	53	22	56	1	5	2	12	9.2	2.8	1.4	0.6	.189
NBA Season Totals		943	622	28941	13858	5576	12176	.458	1220	3370	.362	1486	2056	.723	1162	3601	4763	2645	2565	33	683	198	1964	30.7	14.7	5.1	2.8	....
86-87	Indiana	4	4	159	108	38	74	.514	2	8	.250	30	39	.769	6	27	33	20	14	0	5	2	15	39.8	27.0	8.3	5.0	.682
89-90	Indiana	3	3	123	40	17	45	.378	1	10	.100	5	12	.417	6	14	20	12	11	0	1	0	4	41.0	13.3	6.7	4.0	.277
90-91	Indiana	5	5	192	130	48	90	.533	17	31	.548	17	21	.810	3	25	28	16	15	1	5	0	12	38.4	26.0	5.6	3.2	.618
91-92	Indiana	3	3	118	51	19	47	.404	5	15	.333	8	12	.667	1	8	9	7	11	0	2	0	6	39.3	17.0	3.0	2.3	.256
94-95	San Antonio	15	0	258	75	27	77	.351	13	45	.289	8	11	.727	2	25	27	8	22	0	4	7	6	17.2	5.0	1.8	0.5	.213
95-96	San Antonio	10	0	284	121	41	77	.532	25	47	.532	14	17	.824	5	35	40	16	32	0	2	3	11	28.4	12.1	4.0	1.6	.421
97-98	San Antonio	9	0	196	52	18	53	.340	14	40	.350	2	2	1.000	0	27	27	7	15	1	4	0	6	21.8	5.8	3.0	0.8	.222
99-00	Seattle	2	0	2	0	0	1	.000	0	1	.000	0	0	.000	0	0	0	0	0	0	0	0	0	1.0	0.0	0.0	0.0	-.454
NBA Playoff Totals		51	15	1332	577	208	464	.448	77	197	.391	84	114	.737	23	161	184	86	120	2	23	12	60	26.1	11.3	3.6	1.7	....

• PERSON, Wesley
Wesley Lavon Person

Born: Mar. 28, 1971. Crenshaw, AL, United States.   Height: 6'6".   Weight: 195 lbs.   Drafted: 1994   College: Auburn

YEAR	TEAM	GP	GS	MIN	PTS	FGM	FGA	FG%	3PM	3PA	3P%	FTM	FTA	FT%	ORB	DRB	TRB	AST	PF	DQ	STL	BLK	TO	MPG	PPG	RPG	APG	PCM
94-95	Phoenix	78	56	1800	814	309	638	.484	116	266	.436	80	101	.792	67	134	201	105	149	0	48	24	78	23.1	10.4	2.6	1.3	.400
95-96	Phoenix	82	47	2609	1045	390	877	.445	117	313	.374	148	192	.771	56	265	321	138	148	0	55	22	90	31.8	12.7	3.9	1.7	.358
96-97	Phoenix	80	42	2326	1080	409	903	.453	117	414	.413	91	114	.798	68	224	292	123	102	0	86	19	72	29.1	13.5	3.7	1.5	.428
97-98	Cleveland	82	82	3198	1204	440	957	.460	**192**	**447**	.430	132	170	.776	65	298	363	188	108	0	129	49	107	39.0	14.7	4.4	2.3	.396
98-99	Cleveland	45	42	1342	503	198	437	.453	75	200	.375	32	53	.604	19	123	142	80	52	0	37	16	41	29.8	11.2	3.2	1.8	.361
99-00	Cleveland	79	38	2056	727	280	654	.428	106	250	.424	61	77	.792	44	223	267	146	119	1	40	19	60	26.0	9.2	3.4	1.8	.354
00-01	Cleveland	44	22	958	314	128	292	.438	34	84	.405	24	30	.800	11	119	130	64	62	0	27	11	40	21.8	7.1	3.0	1.5	.336
01-02	Cleveland	78	78	2793	1176	467	944	.495	143	322	.444	99	124	.798	50	244	294	173	93	0	77	37	74	35.8	15.1	3.8	2.2	.423
02-03	Memphis	66	44	1941	727	274	601	.456	100	231	.433	79	97	.814	24	168	192	112	64	0	42	19	56	29.4	11.0	2.9	1.7	.358
NBA Season Totals		634	451	19023	7590	2895	6303	.459	1054	2527	.417	746	958	.779	404	1798	2202	1129	897	1	541	216	618	30.0	12.0	3.5	1.8	....
94-95	Phoenix	10	10	247	96	34	83	.410	17	45	.378	11	12	.917	9	12	21	11	19	0	3	2	9	24.7	9.6	2.1	1.1	.276
95-96	Phoenix	4	4	183	57	22	56	.393	9	29	.310	4	5	.800	8	15	23	3	7	0	3	1	5	45.8	14.3	5.8	0.8	.247
96-97	Phoenix	5	1	163	78	25	53	.472	14	33	.424	14	18	.778	5	28	33	6	5	0	4	3	4	32.6	15.6	6.6	1.2	.538
97-98	Cleveland	4	4	136	32	11	29	.379	7	19	.368	3	4	.750	2	7	9	10	5	0	3	0	1	34.0	8.0	2.3	2.5	.248
NBA Playoff Totals		23	19	729	263	92	221	.416	47	126	.373	32	39	.821	24	62	86	30	36	0	13	6	19	31.7	11.4	3.7	1.3	....

• PETERSEN, Jim
James Richard (Pete) Petersen

Born: Feb. 22, 1962. Minneapolis, MN, United States.   Height: 6'10".   Weight: 235 lbs.   Drafted: 1984   College: Minnesota

YEAR	TEAM	GP	GS	MIN	PTS	FGM	FGA	FG%	3PM	3PA	3P%	FTM	FTA	FT%	ORB	DRB	TRB	AST	PF	DQ	STL	BLK	TO	MPG	PPG	RPG	APG	PCM
84-85	Houston	60	0	714	190	70	144	.486	0	0	.000	50	66	.758	44	103	147	29	125	1	14	32	72	11.9	3.2	2.5	0.5	.279
85-86	Houston	82	20	1664	505	196	411	.477	0	3	.000	113	160	.706	149	247	396	85	231	2	38	54	82	20.3	6.2	4.8	1.0	.387
86-87	Houston	82	56	2403	924	386	755	.511	0	4	.000	152	209	.727	177	380	557	127	268	5	43	102	156	29.3	11.3	6.8	1.5	.447
87-88	Houston	69	50	1793	613	249	488	.510	1	6	.167	114	153	.745	145	291	436	106	203	3	36	40	117	26.0	8.9	6.3	1.5	.423
88-89	Sacramento	66	40	1633	671	278	606	.459	0	8	.000	115	154	.747	121	292	413	81	236	8	47	68	145	24.7	10.2	6.3	1.2	.417
89-90	Golden State	43	19	592	172	60	141	.426	0	1	.000	52	73	.712	49	111	160	23	103	0	17	20	34	13.8	4.0	3.7	0.5	.363
90-91	Golden State	62	21	834	279	114	236	.483	1	4	.250	50	76	.658	69	131	200	27	153	2	13	41	50	13.5	4.5	3.2	0.4	.361
91-92	Golden State	27	2	169	43	18	40	.450	0	2	.000	7	10	.700	12	33	45	9	35	0	5	6	5	6.3	1.6	1.7	0.3	.366
NBA Season Totals		491	208	9802	3397	1371	2821	.486	2	28	.071	653	901	.725	766	1588	2354	487	1354	21	213	363	661	20.0	6.9	4.8	1.0	....
84-85	Houston	3	0	8	2	1	1	1.000	0	0	.000	0	0	.000	1	1	2	1	2	0	0	0	1	2.7	0.7	0.7	0.3	.384
85-86	Houston	20	0	378	111	44	108	.407	0	0	.000	23	33	.697	47	64	111	21	58	1	9	9	16	18.9	5.6	5.6	1.1	.390
86-87	Houston	10	0	187	68	28	51	.549	0	0	.000	12	16	.727	14	32	46	6	26	1	5	2	10	18.7	6.8	4.6	0.6	.418
87-88	Houston	4	0	98	31	12	23	.522	0	0	.000	7	12	.583	7	14	21	6	11	1	1	2	4	24.5	7.8	5.3	1.5	.391
90-91	Golden State	9	4	117	29	12	17	.706	0	0	.000	5	8	.625	4	23	27	3	35	1	2	4	2	13.0	3.2	3.0	0.3	.331
NBA Playoff Totals		46	4	788	241	97	200	.485	0	0	.000	47	71	.662	73	134	207	37	132	4	17	17	33	17.1	5.2	4.5	0.8	....

• PETERSEN, Loy
Loy M. Petersen

Born: July 26, 1945.   Height: 6'5".   Weight: 205 lbs.   Drafted: 1968   College: Oregon State

YEAR	TEAM	GP	GS	MIN	PTS	FGM	FGA	FG%	3PM	3PA	3P%	FTM	FTA	FT%	ORB	DRB	TRB	AST	PF	DQ	STL	BLK	TO	MPG	PPG	RPG	APG	PCM
68-69	Chicago	38	....	299	107	44	109	.404	....	....	....	19	27	.704	....	....	41	25	39	0	....	....	....	7.9	2.8	1.1	0.7	.322
69-70	Chicago	31	....	231	92	33	90	.367	....	....	....	26	39	.667	....	....	26	23	22	0	....	....	....	7.5	3.0	0.8	0.7	.325
NBA Season Totals		69	....	530	199	77	199	.387	....	....	....	45	66	.682	....	....	67	48	61	0	....	....	....	7.7	2.9	1.0	0.7	....

PETERSON, Bob

Robert (Blinky) Peterson

Born: Jan. 25, 1932. San Mateo, CA, United States. Height: 6'5". Weight: 210 lbs. Drafted: 1953 College: Oregon

YEAR	TEAM	GP	GS	MIN	PTS	FGM	FGA	FG%	3PM	3PA	3P%	FTM	FTA	FT%	ORB	DRB	TRB	AST	PF	DQ	STL	BLK	TO	MPG	PPG	RPG	APG	PCM
53-54	Bal/Mil	8	....	60	15	3	10	.300	....	....	....	9	11	.818	....	....	12	3	15	1	....	....	....	7.5	1.9	1.5	0.4	.273
54-55	New York	37	....	503	154	62	169	.367	....	....	....	30	45	.667	....	....	154	31	80	2	....	....	....	13.6	4.2	4.2	0.8	.382
55-56	New York	58	....	779	310	121	303	.399	....	....	....	68	104	.654	....	....	223	44	123	0	....	....	....	13.4	5.3	3.8	0.8	.430
NBA Season Totals		103	....	1342	479	186	482	.386	....	....	....	107	160	.669	....	....	389	78	218	3	....	....	....	13.0	4.7	3.8	0.8	....
54-55	New York	3	....	71	24	7	15	.467	....	....	....	10	11	.909	....	....	16	5	3	0	....	....	....	23.7	8.0	5.3	1.7	.489
NBA Playoff Totals		3	....	71	24	7	15	.467	....	....	....	10	11	.909	....	....	16	5	3	0	....	....	....	23.7	8.0	5.3	1.7	....

PETERSON, Ed

Edward T. Peterson

Born: June 27, 1924. Died: Mar.20, 1984. Height: 6'9". Weight: 220 lbs. Drafted: 1948 College: Cornell

YEAR	TEAM	GP	GS	MIN	PTS	FGM	FGA	FG%	3PM	3PA	3P%	FTM	FTA	FT%	ORB	DRB	TRB	AST	PF	DQ	STL	BLK	TO	MPG	PPG	RPG	APG	PCM
48-49	Syracuse-N	63	....	....	434	165	....	....	....	....	....	104	177	.588	....	....	203	....	....	....	....	....	....	6.9	....	....	....	....
49-50	Syracuse	62	....	....	445	167	390	.428	....	....	....	111	185	.600	....	33	198	....	....	....	....	....	....	7.2	....	0.5	....	....
50-51	Syr/Tri	53	....	....	359	130	384	.339	....	....	....	99	150	.660	....	....	288	66	188	9	....	....	....	6.8	5.4	1.2	....	....
NBA Season Totals		115	....	....	804	297	774	.384	....	....	....	210	335	.627	....	....	288	99	386	9	....	....	....	7.0	2.5	0.9	....	....
NBL Season Totals		63	....	....	434	165	....	....	....	....	....	104	177	....	....	....	203	....	....	....	....	....	....	6.9	....	....	....	....
Career Totals		178	....	....	1238	462	774	....	....	....	....	314	512	....	....	....	288	99	589	9	....	....	....	7.0	1.6	0.6	....	....
48-49	Syracuse-N	6	....	....	44	14	....	....	....	....	....	16	28	.571	....	....	....	....	....	....	....	....	....	7.3	....	....	....	....
49-50	Syracuse	11	....	....	44	18	43	.419	....	....	....	8	14	.571	....	....	....	1	33	....	....	....	....	4.0	....	0.1	....	....
NBA Playoff Totals		11	....	....	44	18	43	.419	....	....	....	8	14	.571	....	....	....	1	33	....	....	....	....	4.0	....	0.1	....	....
NBL Playoff Totals		6	....	....	44	14	....	....	....	....	....	16	28	....	....	....	....	....	....	....	....	....	....	7.3	....	....	....	....
Career Playoff Totals		17	....	....	88	32	43	....	....	....	....	24	42	....	....	....	....	1	33	....	....	....	....	5.2	....	0.1	....	....

PETERSON, Mel

Melvin Lowell Peterson

Born: Mar. 23, 1938. Thief River Falls, MN, United States. Height: 6'4". Weight: 185 lbs. Drafted: 1960 College: Wheaton

YEAR	TEAM	GP	GS	MIN	PTS	FGM	FGA	FG%	3PM	3PA	3P%	FTM	FTA	FT%	ORB	DRB	TRB	AST	PF	DQ	STL	BLK	TO	MPG	PPG	RPG	APG	PCM
63-64	Baltimore	2	....	3	2	1	1	1.000	....	....	....	0	0	.000	....	....	1	0	2	0	....	....	....	1.5	1.0	0.5	0.0	.667
67-68	Oakland-A	77	....	1589	731	323	756	.427	9	34	.265	76	93	.817	....	....	451	104	161	1	....	....	114	20.6	9.5	5.9	1.4	.500
68-69	Oakland-A	51	....	709	276	132	263	.502	0	2	.000	12	15	.800	62	108	170	55	61	0	....	....	43	13.9	5.4	3.3	1.1	.486
69-70	Los Angeles-A	4	....	53	23	10	35	.286	0	4	.000	3	3	1.000	5	8	13	1	4	0	....	....	4	13.3	5.8	3.3	0.3	.229
NBA Season Totals		2	....	3	2	1	1	1.000	....	....	....	0	0	.000	....	....	1	0	2	0	....	....	....	1.5	1.0	0.5	0.0	....
ABA Season Totals		132	....	2351	1030	465	1054	.441	9	40	.225	91	111	.820	67	116	634	160	226	1	....	....	161	17.8	7.8	4.8	1.2	....
Career Totals		134	....	2354	1032	466	1055	.442	9	40	.225	91	111	.820	67	116	635	160	228	1	....	....	161	17.6	7.7	4.7	1.2	....
68-69	Oakland-A	14	....	98	44	18	30	.600	1	2	.500	7	12	.583	....	....	28	4	11	0	....	....	6	7.0	3.1	2.0	0.3	.566
69-70	Los Angeles-A	4	....	22	7	3	6	.500	0	0	.000	1	2	.500	....	....	6	0	0	0	....	....	0	5.5	1.8	1.5	0.0	....
ABA Playoff Totals		18	....	120	51	21	36	.583	1	2	.500	8	14	.571	....	....	34	4	11	0	....	....	6	6.7	2.8	1.9	0.2	....

PETERSON, Morris

Morris Peterson

Born: Aug. 26, 1977. Flint, MI, United States. Height: 6'7". Weight: 218 lbs. Drafted: 2000 College: Michigan State

YEAR	TEAM	GP	GS	MIN	PTS	FGM	FGA	FG%	3PM	3PA	3P%	FTM	FTA	FT%	ORB	DRB	TRB	AST	PF	DQ	STL	BLK	TO	MPG	PPG	RPG	APG	PCM
00-01	Toronto	80	49	1809	747	290	673	.431	63	165	.382	104	145	.717	112	147	259	105	164	0	63	20	78	22.6	9.3	3.2	1.3	.367
01-02	Toronto	63	56	1989	883	336	768	.438	84	231	.364	127	169	.751	91	132	223	153	174	2	73	11	86	31.6	14.0	3.5	2.4	.383
02-03	Toronto	82	80	2949	1153	421	1073	.392	116	344	.337	195	247	.789	97	266	363	188	232	1	88	32	128	36.0	14.1	4.4	2.3	.325
NBA Season Totals		225	185	6747	2783	1047	2514	.416	263	740	.355	426	561	.759	300	545	845	446	570	3	224	63	292	30.0	12.4	3.8	2.0	....
00-01	Toronto	8	3	110	43	18	35	.514	4	9	.444	3	4	.750	2	10	12	15	10	0	6	0	6	13.8	5.4	1.5	1.9	.455
01-02	Toronto	5	5	154	46	18	49	.367	2	17	.118	8	10	.800	3	11	14	11	17	0	5	3	7	30.8	9.2	2.8	2.2	.227
NBA Playoff Totals		13	8	264	89	36	84	.429	6	26	.231	11	14	.786	5	21	26	26	27	0	11	3	13	20.3	6.8	2.0	2.0	....

PETRIE, Geoff

Geoffrey Michael Petrie

Born: Apr. 17, 1948. Darby, PA, United States. Height: 6'4". Weight: 190 lbs. Drafted: 1970 College: Princeton

YEAR	TEAM	GP	GS	MIN	PTS	FGM	FGA	FG%	3PM	3PA	3P%	FTM	FTA	FT%	ORB	DRB	TRB	AST	PF	DQ	STL	BLK	TO	MPG	PPG	RPG	APG	PCM
70-71	Portland	82	....	3032	2031	784	1770	.443	....	....	....	463	600	.772	....	....	280	390	196	1	....	....	....	37.0	24.8	3.4	4.8	.569
71-72	Portland	60	....	2155	1132	465	1115	.417	....	....	....	202	256	.789	....	....	133	248	108	0	....	....	....	35.9	18.9	2.2	4.1	.416
72-73	Portland	79	....	3134	1970	836	1801	.464	....	....	....	298	383	.778	....	....	273	350	163	2	....	....	....	39.7	24.9	3.5	4.4	.533
73-74	Portland	73	....	2800	1771	740	1537	.481	....	....	....	291	341	.853	64	144	208	315	199	2	84	15	....	38.4	24.3	2.8	4.3	.545
74-75	Portland	80	....	3109	1465	602	1319	.456	....	....	....	261	311	.839	38	171	209	424	215	1	81	13	....	38.9	18.3	2.6	5.3	.452
75-76	Portland	72	....	2557	1363	543	1177	.461	....	....	....	277	334	.829	38	130	168	330	194	0	82	5	....	35.5	18.9	2.3	4.6	.482
NBA Season Totals		446	....	16787	9732	3970	8719	.455	....	....	....	1792	2225	.805	140	445	1271	2057	1075	6	247	33	....	37.6	21.8	2.8	4.6	....

PETROVIC, Drazen

Drazen Petrovic

Born: Oct. 22, 1964. Sibenik, Croatia. Died: June7, 1993. Height: 6'5". Weight: 195 lbs. Drafted: 1986 College: Zagreb (Croatia) HOF: 2002

YEAR	TEAM	GP	GS	MIN	PTS	FGM	FGA	FG%	3PM	3PA	3P%	FTM	FTA	FT%	ORB	DRB	TRB	AST	PF	DQ	STL	BLK	TO	MPG	PPG	RPG	APG	PCM
89-90	Portland	77	0	967	583	207	427	.485	34	74	.459	135	160	.844	50	61	111	116	134	0	23	2	92	12.6	7.6	1.4	1.5	.483
90-91	Portland	18	0	133	80	32	71	.451	1	6	.167	15	22	.682	10	8	18	20	21	0	6	0	13	7.4	4.4	1.0	1.1	.467
90-91	New Jersey	43	0	882	543	211	422	.500	22	59	.373	99	115	.861	41	51	92	66	111	0	37	1	69	20.5	12.6	2.1	1.5	.470
91-92	New Jersey	82	82	3027	1691	668	1315	.508	123	277	.444	232	287	.808	97	161	258	252	248	3	105	11	213	36.9	20.6	3.1	3.1	.452
92-93	New Jersey	70	67	2660	1564	587	1134	.518	75	167	.449	315	362	.870	42	148	190	247	237	5	94	13	203	38.0	22.3	2.7	3.5	.478
NBA Season Totals		290	149	7669	4461	1705	3369	.506	255	583	.437	796	946	.841	240	429	669	701	751	8	265	27	590	26.4	15.4	2.3	2.4	....

YEAR	TEAM	GP	GS	MIN	PTS	FGM	FGA	FG%	3PM	3PA	3P%	FTM	FTA	FT%	ORB	DRB	TRB	AST	PF	DQ	STL	BLK	TO	MPG	PPG	RPG	APG	PCM
89-90	Portland	20	0	253	122	48	109	.440	5	16	.313	21	36	.583	10	22	32	20	37	0	6	0	20	12.7	6.1	1.6	1.0	.311
91-92	New Jersey	4	4	163	97	41	76	.539	4	12	.333	11	13	.846	4	6	10	13	13	0	4	1	8	40.8	24.3	2.5	3.3	.478
92-93	New Jersey	5	5	193	78	30	66	.455	2	6	.333	16	20	.800	2	7	9	9	18	0	2	0	22	38.6	15.6	1.8	1.8	.174
NBA Playoff Totals		29	9	609	297	119	251	.474	11	34	.324	48	69	.696	16	35	51	42	68	0	12	1	50	21.0	10.2	1.8	1.4	....

• PETRUSKA, Richard
Richard Petruska

Born: Jan. 25, 1969. Levice, Czechoslovakia.   Height: 6'10".   Weight: 260 lbs.   Drafted: 1993   College: UCLA

YEAR	TEAM	GP	GS	MIN	PTS	FGM	FGA	FG%	3PM	3PA	3P%	FTM	FTA	FT%	ORB	DRB	TRB	AST	PF	DQ	STL	BLK	TO	MPG	PPG	RPG	APG	PCM
93-94	Houston	22	0	92	53	20	46	.435	7	15	.467	6	8	.750	9	22	31	1	15	0	2	3	15	4.2	2.4	1.4	0.0	.453
NBA Season Totals		22	0	92	53	20	46	.435	7	15	.467	6	8	.750	9	22	31	1	15	0	2	3	15	4.2	2.4	1.4	0.0	....

• PETTIT, Bob
Robert E. Lee Pettit Jr.

Born: Dec. 12, 1932. Baton Rouge, LA, United States.   Height: 6'9".   Weight: 205 lbs.   Drafted: 1954   College: Louisiana State   HOF: 1971

YEAR	TEAM	GP	GS	MIN	PTS	FGM	FGA	FG%	3PM	3PA	3P%	FTM	FTA	FT%	ORB	DRB	TRB	AST	PF	DQ	STL	BLK	TO	MPG	PPG	RPG	APG	PCM
54-55	Milwaukee	72	....	2659	1466	520	1279	.407	....	....	....	426	567	.751	....	....	994	229	258	5	....	....	....	36.9	20.4	13.8	3.2	.669
55-56	St. Louis	72	....	2794	1849	646	1507	.429	....	....	....	557	757	.736	....	....	1164	189	202	1	....	....	....	38.8	25.7	16.2	2.6	.773
56-57	St. Louis	71	....	2491	1755	613	1477	.415	....	....	....	529	684	.773	....	....	1037	133	181	1	....	....	....	35.1	24.7	14.6	1.9	.773
57-58	St. Louis	70	....	2528	1719	581	1418	.410	....	....	....	557	744	.749	....	....	1216	157	222	6	....	....	....	36.1	24.6	17.4	2.2	.809
58-59	St. Louis	72	....	2873	2105	719	1640	.438	....	....	....	667	879	.759	....	....	1182	221	200	3	....	....	....	39.9	29.2	16.4	3.1	.843
59-60	St. Louis	72	....	2896	1882	669	1526	.438	....	....	....	544	722	.753	....	....	1221	257	204	1	....	....	....	40.2	26.1	17.0	3.6	.805
60-61	St. Louis	76	....	3027	2120	769	1720	.447	....	....	....	582	804	.724	....	....	1540	262	217	1	....	....	....	39.8	27.9	20.3	3.4	.900
61-62	St. Louis	78	....	3282	2429	867	1928	.450	....	....	....	695	901	.771	....	....	1459	289	296	4	....	....	....	42.1	31.1	18.7	3.7	.882
62-63	St. Louis	79	....	3090	2241	778	1746	.446	....	....	....	685	885	.774	....	....	1191	245	282	8	....	....	....	39.1	28.4	15.1	3.1	.816
63-64	St. Louis	80	....	3296	2190	791	1708	.463	....	....	....	608	771	.789	....	....	1224	259	300	3	....	....	....	41.2	27.4	15.3	3.2	.778
64-65	St. Louis	50	....	1754	1124	396	923	.429	....	....	....	332	405	.820	....	....	621	128	167	0	....	....	....	35.1	22.5	12.4	2.6	.719
NBA Season Totals		792	....	30690	20880	7349	16872	.436	....	....	....	6182	8119	.761	....	....	12849	2369	2529	32	....	....	....	38.8	26.4	16.2	3.0	....
55-56	St. Louis	8	....	274	153	47	128	.367	....	....	....	59	70	.843	....	....	84	18	20	0	....	....	....	34.3	19.1	10.5	2.3	.605
56-57	St. Louis	10	....	430	298	98	237	.414	....	....	....	102	133	.767	....	....	168	25	33	0	....	....	....	43.0	29.8	16.8	2.5	.761
57-58	St. Louis	11	....	430	266	90	230	.391	....	....	....	86	118	.729	....	....	181	20	31	0	....	....	....	39.1	24.2	16.5	1.8	.694
58-59	St. Louis	6	....	257	167	58	137	.423	....	....	....	51	65	.785	....	....	75	14	20	0	....	....	....	42.8	27.8	12.5	2.3	.656
59-60	St. Louis	14	....	576	365	129	292	.442	....	....	....	107	142	.754	....	....	221	52	43	1	....	....	....	41.1	26.1	15.8	3.7	.771
60-61	St. Louis	12	....	526	343	117	284	.412	....	....	....	109	144	.757	....	....	211	38	42	0	....	....	....	43.8	28.6	17.6	3.2	.750
62-63	St. Louis	11	....	463	350	119	259	.459	....	....	....	112	144	.778	....	....	166	33	34	0	....	....	....	42.1	31.8	15.1	3.0	.830
63-64	St. Louis	12	....	494	252	93	226	.412	....	....	....	66	79	.835	....	....	174	33	44	0	....	....	....	41.2	21.0	14.5	2.8	.611
64-65	St. Louis	4	....	95	46	15	41	.366	....	....	....	16	20	.800	....	....	24	8	10	0	....	....	....	23.8	11.5	6.0	2.0	.515
NBA Playoff Totals		88	....	3545	2240	766	1834	.418	....	....	....	708	915	.774	....	....	1304	241	277	1	....	....	....	40.3	25.5	14.8	2.7	....

• PETTWAY, Jerry
Jerry Pettway

Born: Feb. 13, 1944. Detroit, MI, United States.   Height: 6'3".   Weight: 185 lbs.   Drafted: 1967   College: Northwood Institute

YEAR	TEAM	GP	GS	MIN	PTS	FGM	FGA	FG%	3PM	3PA	3P%	FTM	FTA	FT%	ORB	DRB	TRB	AST	PF	DQ	STL	BLK	TO	MPG	PPG	RPG	APG	PCM
67-68	Houston-A	76	....	1572	713	289	838	.345	16	57	.281	119	183	.650	....	....	274	103	132	2	....	....	82	20.7	9.4	3.6	1.4	.333
68-69	Houston-A	11	....	264	79	37	123	.301	0	5	.000	5	7	.714	13	16	29	17	19	0	....	....	16	24.0	7.2	2.6	1.5	.153
ABA Season Totals		87	....	1836	792	326	961	.339	16	62	.258	124	190	.653	13	16	303	120	151	2	....	....	98	21.1	9.1	3.5	1.4	....
67-68	Houston-A	3	....	62	29	12	29	.414	1	2	.500	4	5	.800	....	....	14	5	5	0	....	....	2	20.7	9.7	4.7	1.7	.482
ABA Playoff Totals		3	....	62	29	12	29	.414	1	2	.500	4	5	.800	....	....	14	5	5	0	....	....	2	20.7	9.7	4.7	1.7	....

• PEYTON, Tony
Tony Peyton

Born: 1921.   Height: 6'2".   Weight: 200 lbs.   Drafted: —   College: Michigan

YEAR	TEAM	GP	GS	MIN	PTS	FGM	FGA	FG%	3PM	3PA	3P%	FTM	FTA	FT%	ORB	DRB	TRB	AST	PF	DQ	STL	BLK	TO	MPG	PPG	RPG	APG	PCM
42-43	Chicago-N	18	....	....	43	17	....	....	....	....	....	9	....	....	....	....	....	....	....	....	....	....	....	....	2.4	....	....	....
NBL Season Totals		18	....	....	43	17	....	....	....	....	....	9	....	....	....	....	....	....	....	....	....	....	....	....	2.4	....	....	....

• PHARES, Jack
Jack (Squint) Phares

Born: Dec. 31, 1915. Died: Aug.1974.   Height: 5'10".   Weight: —   Drafted: —   College: West Virginia

YEAR	TEAM	GP	GS	MIN	PTS	FGM	FGA	FG%	3PM	3PA	3P%	FTM	FTA	FT%	ORB	DRB	TRB	AST	PF	DQ	STL	BLK	TO	MPG	PPG	RPG	APG	PCM
38-39	Pittsburgh-N	7	....	....	48	18	....	....	....	....	....	12	....	....	....	....	....	....	....	....	....	....	....	....	6.9	....	....	....
NBL Season Totals		7	....	....	48	18	....	....	....	....	....	12	....	....	....	....	....	....	....	....	....	....	....	....	6.9	....	....	....

• PHEGLEY, Roger
Roger Dale Phegley

Born: Oct. 16, 1956. East Peoria, IL, United States.   Height: 6'6".   Weight: 205 lbs.   Drafted: 1978   College: Bradley

YEAR	TEAM	GP	GS	MIN	PTS	FGM	FGA	FG%	3PM	3PA	3P%	FTM	FTA	FT%	ORB	DRB	TRB	AST	PF	DQ	STL	BLK	TO	MPG	PPG	RPG	APG	PCM
78-79	Washington	29	....	153	80	28	78	.359	....	....	....	24	29	.828	5	17	22	15	21	0	5	2	17	5.3	2.8	0.8	0.5	.332
79-80	Washington	50	....	971	554	224	473	.474	2	5	.400	104	120	.867	49	66	115	70	106	1	19	3	70	19.4	11.1	2.3	1.4	.423
79-80	New Jersey	28	....	541	327	126	260	.485	2	4	.500	73	83	.880	26	44	70	32	52	0	15	4	50	19.3	11.7	2.5	1.1	.458
80-81	Cleveland	82	....	2269	1180	474	965	.491	8	28	.286	224	267	.839	90	156	246	184	262	7	65	15	164	27.7	14.4	3.0	2.2	.415
81-82	Cleveland	27	0	566	248	104	214	.486	4	13	.308	36	45	.800	28	43	71	53	61	0	16	2	32	21.0	9.2	2.6	2.0	.396
81-82	San Antonio	54	0	617	308	129	293	.440	1	18	.056	49	64	.766	33	50	83	61	91	0	20	6	32	11.4	5.7	1.5	1.1	.397
82-83	San Antonio	62	4	599	286	120	267	.449	3	14	.214	43	56	.768	39	45	84	60	92	0	30	8	50	9.7	4.6	1.4	1.0	.395
83-84	San Antonio	3	0	11	7	2	4	.500	1	1	1.000	2	2	1.000	0	2	2	2	1	0	0	0	1	3.7	2.3	0.7	0.7	.704
83-84	Dallas	10	0	76	21	9	31	.290	1	4	.250	2	2	1.000	2	7	9	9	10	0	1	0	5	7.6	2.1	0.9	0.9	.134
NBA Season Totals		345	4	5803	3011	1216	2585	.470	22	87	.253	557	668	.834	272	430	702	486	696	8	171	40	421	16.8	8.7	2.0	1.4	....

YEAR	TEAM	GP	GS	MIN	PTS	FGM	FGA	FG%	3PM	3PA	3P%	FTM	FTA	FT%	ORB	DRB	TRB	AST	PF	DQ	STL	BLK	TO	MPG	PPG	RPG	APG	PCM
81-82	San Antonio	5	0	6	0	0	2	.000	0	1	.000	0	0	.000	0	0	0	0	1	0	0	0	3	1.2	0.0	0.0	0.0	-.844
82-83	San Antonio	8	0	38	24	9	17	.529	3	4	.750	3	4	.750	1	7	8	1	6	0	0	0	1	4.8	3.0	1.0	0.1	.554
83-84	Dallas	1	0	5	2	0	4	.000	0	1	.000	2	2	1.000	0	0	0	1	0	0	2	0	0	5.0	2.0	0.0	1.0	.242
NBA Playoff Totals		14	0	49	26	9	23	.391	3	6	.500	5	6	.833	1	7	8	2	7	0	2	0	4	3.5	1.9	0.6	0.1	....

• PHELAN, Jack

John Edward Phelan

Born: Nov. 6, 1925. Chicago, IL, United States.   Height: 6'5".   Weight: 195 lbs.   Drafted: —   College: DePaul

YEAR	TEAM	GP	GS	MIN	PTS	FGM	FGA	FG%	3PM	3PA	3P%	FTM	FTA	FT%	ORB	DRB	TRB	AST	PF	DQ	STL	BLK	TO	MPG	PPG	RPG	APG	PCM
49-50	Waterloo	15	....	....	61	24	69	.348	....	....	....	13	24	.542	....	....		16	48	....	....	....	....		4.1	....	1.1	....
49-50	Sheboygan	40	....	....	165	63	199	.317	....	....	....	39	66	.591	....	....		41	103	....	....	....	....		4.1	....	1.0	....
NBA Season Totals		55	....	....	226	87	268	.325	....	....	....	52	90	.578	....	....		57	151	....	....	....	....		4.1	....	1.0	....
49-50	Sheboygan	3	....	....	10	4	10	.400	....	....	....	2	3	.667	....	....		3	10	....	....	....	....		3.3	....	1.0	....
NBA Playoff Totals		3	....	....	10	4	10	.400	....	....	....	2	3	.667	....	....		3	10	....	....	....	....		3.3	....	1.0	....

• PHELAN, James

James J. Phelan

Born: Mar. 19, 1929.   Height: 6'1".   Weight: 175 lbs.   Drafted: 1951   College: LaSalle

YEAR	TEAM	GP	GS	MIN	PTS	FGM	FGA	FG%	3PM	3PA	3P%	FTM	FTA	FT%	ORB	DRB	TRB	AST	PF	DQ	STL	BLK	TO	MPG	PPG	RPG	APG	PCM
53-54	Philadelphia	4	....	33	3	0	6	.000	....	....	....	3	6	.500	....	....	5	2	9	0	....	....	....	8.3	0.8	1.3	0.5	.018
NBA Season Totals		4	....	33	3	0	6	.000	....	....	....	3	6	.500	....	....	5	2	9	0	....	....	....	8.3	0.8	1.3	0.5	....

• PHELPS, Derrick

Derrick Michael Phelps

Born: July 31, 1972. Queens, NY, United States.   Height: 6'4".   Weight: 181 lbs.   Drafted: —   College: North Carolina

YEAR	TEAM	GP	GS	MIN	PTS	FGM	FGA	FG%	3PM	3PA	3P%	FTM	FTA	FT%	ORB	DRB	TRB	AST	PF	DQ	STL	BLK	TO	MPG	PPG	RPG	APG	PCM
94-95	Sacramento	3	0	5	0	0	1	.000	0	0	.000	0	2	.000	0	0	0	1	3	0	0	0	0	1.7	0.0	0.0	0.3	-.444
NBA Season Totals		3	0	5	0	0	1	.000	0	0	.000	0	2	.000	0	0	0	1	3	0	0	0	0	1.7	0.0	0.0	0.3	....

• PHELPS, Michael

Michael Phelps

Born: Oct. 3, 1961. Vicksburg, MS, United States.   Height: 6'4".   Weight: 180 lbs.   Drafted: 1985   College: Alcorn State

YEAR	TEAM	GP	GS	MIN	PTS	FGM	FGA	FG%	3PM	3PA	3P%	FTM	FTA	FT%	ORB	DRB	TRB	AST	PF	DQ	STL	BLK	TO	MPG	PPG	RPG	APG	PCM
85-86	Seattle	70	18	880	279	117	286	.409	1	12	.083	44	74	.595	29	60	89	71	86	0	45	1	63	12.6	4.0	1.3	1.0	.240
86-87	Seattle	60	6	469	182	75	176	.426	1	10	.100	31	44	.705	16	34	50	64	60	0	21	2	30	7.8	3.0	0.8	1.1	.346
87-88	LA Clippers	2	0	23	9	3	7	.429	0	0	.000	3	4	.750	0	2	2	3	1	0	5	0	2	11.5	4.5	1.0	1.5	.531
NBA Season Totals		132	24	1372	470	195	469	.416	2	22	.091	78	122	.639	45	96	141	138	147	0	71	3	95	10.4	3.6	1.1	1.0	....

• PHILLIP, Andy

Andrew Michael Phillip

Born: Mar. 7, 1922. Granite City, IL, United States.   Height: 6'2".   Weight: 195 lbs.   Drafted: 1947   College: Illinois   HOF: 1961

YEAR	TEAM	GP	GS	MIN	PTS	FGM	FGA	FG%	3PM	3PA	3P%	FTM	FTA	FT%	ORB	DRB	TRB	AST	PF	DQ	STL	BLK	TO	MPG	PPG	RPG	APG	PCM
47-48	Chicago	32	....	....	346	143	425	.336	....	....	....	60	103	.583	....	....	....	74	75	....	....	....	....	10.8	....	2.3	....
48-49	Chicago	60	....	....	718	285	818	.348	....	....	....	148	219	.676	....	....	....	319	205	....	....	....	....	12.0	....	5.3	....
49-50	Chicago	65	....	....	758	284	814	.349	....	....	....	190	270	.704	....	....	....	377	210	....	....	....	....	11.7	....	**5.8**	....
50-51	Philadelphia	66	....	....	740	275	690	.399	....	....	....	190	253	.751	446	**414**	221	8	....	....	....	....	11.2	6.8	**6.3**	....
51-52	Philadelphia	66	....	2933	790	279	762	.366	....	....	....	232	308	.753	434	**539**	218	6	....	....	....	44.4	12.0	6.6	**8.2**	.459
52-53	Phi/FtW	70	....	2690	722	250	629	.397	....	....	....	222	301	.738	364	397	229	9	....	....	....	38.4	10.3	5.2	5.7	.411
53-54	Fort Wayne	71	....	2705	751	255	680	.375	....	....	....	241	330	.730	265	449	204	4	....	....	....	38.1	10.6	3.7	6.3	.411
54-55	Fort Wayne	64	....	2332	617	202	545	.371	....	....	....	213	308	.692	290	491	166	1	....	....	....	36.4	9.6	4.5	7.7	.468
55-56	Fort Wayne	70	....	2078	408	148	405	.365	....	....	....	112	199	.563	257	410	155	2	....	....	....	29.7	5.8	3.7	5.9	.396
56-57	Boston	67	....	1476	298	105	277	.379	....	....	....	88	137	.642	181	168	121	1	....	....	....	22.0	4.4	2.7	2.5	.306
57-58	Boston	70	....	1164	236	97	273	.355	....	....	....	42	71	.592	158	121	121	0	....	....	....	16.6	3.4	2.3	1.7	.277
NBA Season Totals		701	....	15378	6384	2323	6318	.368	....	....	....	1738	2499	.695	....	2395	3759	1925	31	....	....	....	21.9	9.1	3.4	5.4	....
47-48	Chicago	5	....	....	36	13	46	.283	....	....	....	10	14	.714	....	....		4	11	....	....	....	....	7.2	....	0.8	....
48-49	Chicago	2	....	....	39	14	36	.389	....	....	....	11	11	1.000	....	....		12	9	....	....	....	....	19.5	....	6.0	....
49-50	Chicago	2	....	....	24	7	27	.259	....	....	....	10	13	.769	....	....		12	8	....	....	....	....	12.0	....	6.0	....
50-51	Philadelphia	2	....	....	15	6	15	.400	....	....	....	3	6	.500	15	14	9	0	....	....	....	7.5	7.5	7.0	....
51-52	Philadelphia	3	....	122	35	8	19	.421	....	....	....	19	24	.792	14	22	16	1	....	....	....	40.7	11.7	4.7	7.3	.476
52-53	Fort Wayne	8	....	329	82	24	71	.338	....	....	....	34	51	.667	32	30	23	1	....	....	....	41.1	10.3	4.0	3.8	.289
53-54	Fort Wayne	4	....	136	35	13	38	.342	....	....	....	9	12	.750	12	17	9	0	....	....	....	34.0	8.8	3.0	4.3	.319
54-55	Fort Wayne	11	....	445	94	30	93	.323	....	....	....	34	40	.850	60	78	37	0	....	....	....	40.5	8.5	5.5	7.1	.389
55-56	Fort Wayne	10	....	173	29	9	27	.333	....	....	....	11	25	.440	26	35	16	0	....	....	....	17.3	2.9	2.6	3.5	.388
56-57	Boston	10	....	128	22	8	22	.364	....	....	....	6	15	.400	20	17	18	0	....	....	....	12.8	2.2	2.0	1.7	.295
57-58	Boston	10	....	91	17	5	21	.238	....	....	....	7	9	.778	14	7	20	0	....	....	....	9.1	1.7	1.4	0.7	.180
NBA Playoff Totals		67	....	1424	428	137	415	.330	....	....	....	154	220	.700	....	193	248	176	2	....	....	....	21.3	6.4	2.9	3.7	....

• PHILLIPS, Bob

Robert Phillips

Born: 1916.   Height: —   Weight: —   Drafted: —   College: —

YEAR	TEAM	GP	GS	MIN	PTS	FGM	FGA	FG%	3PM	3PA	3P%	FTM	FTA	FT%	ORB	DRB	TRB	AST	PF	DQ	STL	BLK	TO	MPG	PPG	RPG	APG	PCM
38-39	Indianapolis-N	1	....	....	0	0	....	....	....	....	....	0	....	....	....	....	....	....	....	....	....	....		0.0	....	....	....
NBL Season Totals		1	....	....	0	0	....	....	....	....	....	0	....	....	....	....	....	....	....	....	....	....		0.0	....	....	....

• PHILLIPS, Eddie
Eddie Lee Phillips

Born: Sept. 29, 1961. Birmingham, AL, United States. Height: 6'7". Weight: 225 lbs. Drafted: 1982 College: Alabama

YEAR TEAM	GP	GS	MIN	PTS	FGM	FGA	FG%	3PM	3PA	3P%	FTM	FTA	FT%	ORB	DRB	TRB	AST	PF	DQ	STL	BLK	TO	MPG	PPG	RPG	APG	PCM
82-83 New Jersey	48	0	416	152	56	138	.406	0	2	.000	40	59	.678	27	50	77	29	58	0	14	8	48	8.7	3.2	1.6	0.6	.291
NBA Season Totals	48	0	416	152	56	138	.406	0	2	.000	40	59	.678	27	50	77	29	58	0	14	8	48	8.7	3.2	1.6	0.6	....
82-83 New Jersey	2	0	12	7	3	6	.500	0	2	.000	1	4	.250	3	2	5	3	2	0	0	0	1	6.0	3.5	2.5	1.5	.745
NBA Playoff Totals	2	0	12	7	3	6	.500	0	2	.000	1	4	.250	3	2	5	3	2	0	0	0	1	6.0	3.5	2.5	1.5	....

• PHILLIPS, Gary
Gary A. (The Ghost) Phillips

Born: Dec. 7, 1939. Quincy, IL, United States. Height: 6'3". Weight: 189 lbs. Drafted: 1961 College: Houston

YEAR TEAM	GP	GS	MIN	PTS	FGM	FGA	FG%	3PM	3PA	3P%	FTM	FTA	FT%	ORB	DRB	TRB	AST	PF	DQ	STL	BLK	TO	MPG	PPG	RPG	APG	PCM
61-62 Boston	67	....	693	270	110	310	.355	....	....	....	50	86	.581	....	....	107	64	109	0	....	....	....	10.3	4.0	1.6	1.0	.316
62-63 San Francisco	75	....	1801	609	256	643	.398	....	....	....	97	152	.638	....	....	225	137	185	7	....	....	....	24.0	8.1	3.0	1.8	.306
63-64 San Francisco	66	....	2010	658	256	691	.370	....	....	....	146	218	.670	....	....	248	203	245	8	....	....	....	30.5	10.0	3.8	3.1	.317
64-65 San Francisco	73	....	1541	516	198	553	.358	....	....	....	120	199	.603	....	....	189	148	184	3	....	....	....	21.1	7.1	2.6	2.0	.305
65-66 San Francisco	67	....	867	266	106	303	.350	....	....	....	54	87	.621	....	....	134	113	97	0	....	....	....	12.9	4.0	2.0	1.7	.350
NBA Season Totals	348	....	6912	2319	926	2500	.370	....	....	....	467	742	.629	....	....	903	665	820	18	....	....	....	19.9	6.7	2.6	1.9	....
61-62 Boston	6	....	32	10	1	16	.063	....	....	....	8	11	.727	....	....	3	1	6	0	....	....	....	5.3	1.7	0.5	0.2	-.052
63-64 San Francisco	11	....	256	96	35	97	.361	....	....	....	26	40	.650	....	....	24	20	36	2	....	....	....	23.3	8.7	2.2	1.8	.279
NBA Playoff Totals	17	....	288	106	36	113	.319	....	....	....	34	51	.667	....	....	27	21	42	2	....	....	....	16.9	6.2	1.6	1.2	....

• PHILLIPS, Gene
Donald Eugene Phillips

Born: Oct. 25, 1948. Livingston, TX, United States. Height: 6'4". Weight: 175 lbs. Drafted: 1971 College: Southern Methodist

YEAR TEAM	GP	GS	MIN	PTS	FGM	FGA	FG%	3PM	3PA	3P%	FTM	FTA	FT%	ORB	DRB	TRB	AST	PF	DQ	STL	BLK	TO	MPG	PPG	RPG	APG	PCM
71-72 Dallas-A	28	....	174	78	30	76	.395	7	17	.412	11	14	.786	4	17	21	13	23	0	....	....	8	6.2	2.8	0.8	0.5	.340
72-73 Dallas-A	3	....	10	0	0	5	.000	0	3	.000	0	0	.000	0	0	0	1	3	0	....	....	0	3.3	0.0	0.0	0.3	-.474
ABA Season Totals	31	....	184	78	30	81	.370	7	20	.350	11	14	.786	4	17	21	14	26	0	....	....	8	5.9	2.5	0.7	0.5	....
71-72 Dallas-A	1	....	2	0	0	0	.000	0	0	.000	0	0	.000	0	0	0	0	0	0	....	....	0	2.0	0.0	0.0	0.0	.000
ABA Playoff Totals	1	....	2	0	0	0	.000	0	0	.000	0	0	.000	0	0	0	0	0	0	....	....	0	2.0	0.0	0.0	0.0	....

• PHILLIPS, Willie
William Phillips

Born: 1915. Height: 5'8". Weight: 175 lbs. Drafted: — College: DePaul

YEAR TEAM	GP	GS	MIN	PTS	FGM	FGA	FG%	3PM	3PA	3P%	FTM	FTA	FT%	ORB	DRB	TRB	AST	PF	DQ	STL	BLK	TO	MPG	PPG	RPG	APG	PCM
39-40 Chicago-N	28	....	....	49	16	....	....	....	....	....	17	....	....	....	....	....	....	....	....	....	....	....	....	1.8	....	....	....
NBL Season Totals	28	....	....	49	16	....	....	....	....	....	17	....	....	....	....	....	....	....	....	....	....	....	....	1.8	....	....	....

• PHILLS, Bobby
Bobby Ray Phills II

Born: Dec. 20, 1969. Baton Rouge, LA, United States. Died: Jan.12, 2000. Height: 6'5". Weight: 210 lbs. Drafted: 1991 College: Southern (LA)

YEAR TEAM	GP	GS	MIN	PTS	FGM	FGA	FG%	3PM	3PA	3P%	FTM	FTA	FT%	ORB	DRB	TRB	AST	PF	DQ	STL	BLK	TO	MPG	PPG	RPG	APG	PCM
91-92 Cleveland	10	0	65	31	12	28	.429	0	2	.000	7	11	.636	4	4	8	4	3	0	3	1	8	6.5	3.1	0.8	0.4	.321
92-93 Cleveland	31	0	139	93	38	82	.463	2	5	.400	15	25	.600	6	11	17	10	19	0	10	2	19	4.5	3.0	0.5	0.3	.420
93-94 Cleveland	72	53	1531	598	242	514	.471	1	12	.083	113	157	.720	71	141	212	133	135	1	67	12	65	21.3	8.3	2.9	1.8	.404
94-95 Cleveland	80	79	2500	878	338	816	.414	19	55	.345	183	235	.779	90	175	265	180	206	0	115	25	112	31.3	11.0	3.3	2.3	.310
95-96 Cleveland	72	69	2530	1051	386	826	.467	93	211	.441	186	240	.775	62	199	261	271	192	3	102	27	130	35.1	14.6	3.6	3.8	.416
96-97 Cleveland	69	65	2375	866	328	766	.428	85	216	.394	125	174	.718	63	182	245	233	174	1	113	21	138	34.4	12.6	3.6	3.4	.348
97-98 Charlotte	62	61	1887	642	246	552	.446	44	114	.386	106	140	.757	59	157	216	187	181	2	81	18	105	30.4	10.4	3.5	3.0	.349
98-99 Charlotte	43	43	1574	613	215	497	.433	68	172	.395	115	168	.685	39	135	174	149	124	1	60	25	92	36.6	14.3	4.0	3.5	.380
99-00 Charlotte	28	9	825	381	152	335	.454	30	91	.330	47	65	.723	17	54	71	79	72	2	41	8	48	29.5	13.6	2.5	2.8	.395
NBA Season Totals	467	379	13426	5153	1957	4416	.443	342	878	.390	897	1215	.738	411	1058	1469	1246	1106	10	592	139	717	28.7	11.0	3.1	2.7	....
91-92 Cleveland	5	0	12	11	4	9	.444	0	1	.000	3	4	.750	2	4	6	5	1	0	1	0	2	2.4	2.2	1.2	1.0	1.286
92-93 Cleveland	2	0	9	4	1	3	.333	0	0	.000	2	2	1.000	0	0	0	0	0	0	0	0	1	4.5	2.0	0.0	0.0	.133
93-94 Cleveland	3	2	68	20	9	24	.375	1	1	1.000	1	2	.500	5	9	14	7	11	0	2	0	5	22.7	6.7	4.7	2.3	.271
94-95 Cleveland	4	4	146	57	19	43	.442	4	7	.571	15	20	.750	3	9	12	6	8	0	9	0	9	36.5	14.3	3.0	1.5	.315
95-96 Cleveland	3	3	96	29	13	35	.371	2	10	.200	1	4	.250	5	9	14	6	4	0	2	1	5	32.0	9.7	4.7	2.0	.236
97-98 Charlotte	9	9	269	57	25	64	.391	5	17	.294	2	8	.250	4	19	23	24	24	0	10	2	13	29.9	6.3	2.6	2.7	.200
NBA Playoff Totals	26	18	600	178	71	178	.399	12	36	.333	24	40	.600	19	50	69	48	48	0	24	3	35	23.1	6.8	2.7	1.8	....

• PIANA, Jack
Jack Piana

Born: 1918. Died: July10, 2001. Height: 6'2". Weight: 190 lbs. Drafted: — College: Detroit

YEAR TEAM	GP	GS	MIN	PTS	FGM	FGA	FG%	3PM	3PA	3P%	FTM	FTA	FT%	ORB	DRB	TRB	AST	PF	DQ	STL	BLK	TO	MPG	PPG	RPG	APG	PCM
40-41 Detroit-N	2	....	....	0	0	....	....	....	....	....	0	....	....	....	....	....	....	....	....	....	....	....	....	0.0	....	....	....
NBL Season Totals	2	....	....	0	0	....	....	....	....	....	0	....	....	....	....	....	....	....	....	....	....	....	....	0.0	....	....	....
40-41 Detroit-N	1	....	....	0	0	....	....	....	....	....	0	....	....	....	....	....	....	....	....	....	....	....	....	0.0	....	....	....
NBL Playoff Totals	1	....	....	0	0	....	....	....	....	....	0	....	....	....	....	....	....	....	....	....	....	....	....	0.0	....	....	....

• PIATKOWSKI, Eric
Eric Todd (Pike) Piatkowski

Born: Sept. 30, 1970. Steubenville, OH, United States. Height: 6'7". Weight: 215 lbs. Drafted: 1994 College: Nebraska

YEAR TEAM	GP	GS	MIN	PTS	FGM	FGA	FG%	3PM	3PA	3P%	FTM	FTA	FT%	ORB	DRB	TRB	AST	PF	DQ	STL	BLK	TO	MPG	PPG	RPG	APG	PCM
94-95 LA Clippers	81	11	1208	566	201	456	.441	74	198	.374	90	115	.783	63	70	133	77	150	1	37	15	65	14.9	7.0	1.6	1.0	.363
95-96 LA Clippers	65	1	784	301	98	242	.405	38	114	.333	67	82	.817	40	63	103	48	83	0	24	10	46	12.1	4.6	1.6	0.7	.327
96-97 LA Clippers	65	0	747	388	134	298	.450	51	120	.425	69	84	.821	49	56	105	52	85	0	33	10	46	11.5	6.0	1.6	0.8	.454
97-98 LA Clippers	67	35	1740	760	257	568	.452	106	259	.409	140	170	.824	70	166	236	85	137	0	51	12	80	26.0	11.3	3.5	1.3	.397
98-99 LA Clippers	49	38	1242	513	180	417	.432	65	165	.394	88	102	.863	39	101	140	53	86	0	44	6	53	25.3	10.5	2.9	1.1	.353

YEAR TEAM	GP	GS	MIN	PTS	FGM	FGA	FG%	3PM	3PA	3P%	FTM	FTA	FT%	ORB	DRB	TRB	AST	PF	DQ	STL	BLK	TO	MPG	PPG	RPG	APG	PCM
99-00 LA Clippers	75	23	1712	654	238	573	.415	93	243	.383	85	100	.850	74	148	222	81	140	0	44	13	57	22.8	8.7	3.0	1.1	.333
00-01 LA Clippers	81	40	2144	860	291	672	.433	120	297	.404	158	181	.873	54	187	241	96	123	0	46	19	76	26.5	10.6	3.0	1.2	.357
01-02 LA Clippers	71	61	1718	626	207	471	.439	111	238	.466	101	113	.894	43	141	184	112	110	0	41	12	64	24.2	8.8	2.6	1.6	.356
02-03 LA Clippers	62	26	1360	601	210	446	.471	80	201	.398	101	122	.828	44	112	156	70	92	0	33	9	56	21.9	9.7	2.5	1.1	.398
NBA Season Totals	616	235	12655	5269	1816	4143	.438	738	1835	.402	899	1069	.841	476	1044	1520	674	1006	1	353	106	543	20.5	8.6	2.5	1.1	....
96-97 LA Clippers	3	0	38	16	4	11	.364	2	5	.400	6	7	.857	1	1	2	0	5	0	1	0	0	12.7	5.3	0.7	0.0	.249
NBA Playoff Totals	3	0	38	16	4	11	.364	2	5	.400	6	7	.857	1	1	2	0	5	0	1	0	0	12.7	5.3	0.7	0.0	....

• PIATKOWSKI, Walter

Walter Piatkowski Jr.

Born: June 11, 1945. Toledo, OH, United States. Height: 6'8". Weight: 220 lbs. Drafted: — College: Bowling Green

YEAR TEAM	GP	GS	MIN	PTS	FGM	FGA	FG%	3PM	3PA	3P%	FTM	FTA	FT%	ORB	DRB	TRB	AST	PF	DQ	STL	BLK	TO	MPG	PPG	RPG	APG	PCM
68-69 Denver-A	77	....	1819	942	399	956	.417	27	82	.329	117	151	.775	147	216	363	46	226	2	....	....	100	23.6	12.2	4.7	0.6	.394
69-70 Denver-A	74	....	1302	517	215	535	.402	11	50	.220	76	99	.768	106	146	252	41	180	1	....	....	75	17.6	7.0	3.4	0.6	.321
71-72 Florida-A	6	....	28	6	3	16	.188	0	0	.000	0	0	.000	1	1	2	2	2	0	....	....	3	4.7	1.0	0.3	0.3	-.082
ABA Season Totals	157	....	3149	1465	617	1507	.409	38	132	.288	193	250	.772	254	363	617	89	408	3	....	....	178	20.1	9.3	3.9	0.6	....
68-69 Denver-A	7	....	201	107	48	111	.432	1	9	.111	10	11	.909	....	....	29	6	32	1	....	....	13	28.7	15.3	4.1	0.9	.351
69-70 Denver-A	6	....	50	27	12	24	.500	1	4	.250	2	4	.500	9	2	11	4	9	0	....	....	2	8.3	4.5	1.8	0.7	.520
ABA Playoff Totals	13	....	251	134	60	135	.444	2	13	.154	12	15	.800	9	2	40	10	41	1	....	....	15	19.3	10.3	3.1	0.8	....

• PIERCE, Paul

Paul Anthony Pierce

Born: Oct. 13, 1977. Oakland, CA, United States. Height: 6'6". Weight: 230 lbs. Drafted: 1998 College: Kansas

YEAR TEAM	GP	GS	MIN	PTS	FGM	FGA	FG%	3PM	3PA	3P%	FTM	FTA	FT%	ORB	DRB	TRB	AST	PF	DQ	STL	BLK	TO	MPG	PPG	RPG	APG	PCM
98-99 Boston	48	47	1632	791	284	647	.439	84	204	.412	139	195	.713	117	192	309	115	139	1	82	50	113	34.0	16.5	6.4	2.4	.491
99-00 Boston	73	72	2583	1427	486	1099	.442	96	280	.343	359	450	.798	83	313	396	221	237	5	152	62	178	35.4	19.5	5.4	3.0	.525
00-01 Boston	82	82	3120	2071	687	1513	.454	147	384	.383	550	738	.745	94	428	522	253	251	3	138	69	262	38.0	25.3	6.4	3.1	.587
01-02 Boston	82	82	3302	**2144**	707	1598	.442	210	520	.404	520	643	.809	81	485	566	261	237	1	154	86	241	40.3	26.1	6.9	3.2	.597
02-03 Boston	79	79	3096	2048	663	1592	.416	118	391	.302	**604**	**753**	.802	106	472	578	349	227	2	139	62	288	39.2	25.9	7.3	4.4	.601
NBA Season Totals	364	362	13733	8481	2827	6449	.438	655	1779	.368	2172	2779	.782	481	1890	2371	1199	1091	12	665	329	1082	37.7	23.3	6.5	3.3	....
01-02 Boston	16	16	672	394	122	303	.403	30	104	.288	120	157	.764	27	110	137	66	52	0	27	20	61	42.0	24.6	8.6	4.1	.556
02-03 Boston	10	10	445	271	77	193	.399	16	45	.356	101	117	.863	11	79	90	67	38	0	21	8	44	44.5	27.1	9.0	6.7	.635
NBA Playoff Totals	26	26	1117	665	199	496	.401	46	149	.309	221	274	.807	38	189	227	133	90	0	48	28	105	43.0	25.6	8.7	5.1	....

• PIERCE, Ricky

Ricky Charles Pierce

Born: Aug. 19, 1959. Dallas, TX, United States. Height: 6'4". Weight: 205 lbs. Drafted: 1982 College: Rice

YEAR TEAM	GP	GS	MIN	PTS	FGM	FGA	FG%	3PM	3PA	3P%	FTM	FTA	FT%	ORB	DRB	TRB	AST	PF	DQ	STL	BLK	TO	MPG	PPG	RPG	APG	PCM
82-83 Detroit	39	1	265	85	33	88	.375	1	7	.143	18	32	.563	15	20	35	14	42	0	8	4	20	6.8	2.2	0.9	0.4	.188
83-84 San Diego	69	35	1280	685	268	570	.470	0	9	.000	149	173	.861	59	76	135	60	143	1	27	13	83	18.6	9.9	2.0	0.9	.372
84-85 Milwaukee	44	3	882	433	165	307	.537	1	4	.250	102	124	.823	49	68	117	94	117	0	34	5	62	20.0	9.8	2.7	2.1	.481
85-86 Milwaukee	81	8	2147	1127	429	798	.538	3	23	.130	266	310	.858	94	137	231	177	252	6	83	6	105	26.5	13.9	2.9	2.2	.483
86-87 Milwaukee	79	31	2505	1540	575	1077	.534	3	28	.107	387	440	.880	117	149	266	144	222	0	64	24	119	31.7	19.5	3.4	1.8	.526
87-88 Milwaukee	37	0	965	606	248	486	.510	3	14	.214	107	122	.877	30	53	83	73	94	0	21	7	56	26.1	16.4	2.2	2.0	.479
88-89 Milwaukee	75	4	2078	1317	527	1018	.518	8	36	.222	255	297	.859	82	115	197	156	193	1	77	19	113	27.7	17.6	2.6	2.1	.522
89-90 Milwaukee	59	0	1709	1359	503	987	.510	46	133	.346	307	366	.839	64	103	167	133	158	2	50	7	130	29.0	23.0	2.8	2.3	.605
90-91 Milwaukee	46	0	1327	1037	359	720	.499	37	93	.398	282	311	.907	37	80	117	96	90	0	38	11	92	28.8	22.5	2.5	2.1	.615
90-91 Seattle	32	2	840	561	202	436	.463	9	23	.391	148	160	.925	30	44	74	72	80	1	22	2	54	26.3	17.5	2.3	2.3	.497
91-92 Seattle	78	78	2658	1690	620	1306	.475	33	123	.268	417	455	.916	93	140	233	241	213	2	86	20	187	34.1	21.7	3.0	3.1	.502
92-93 Seattle	77	72	2218	1403	524	1072	.489	42	113	.372	313	352	.889	58	134	192	220	167	0	100	7	162	28.8	18.2	2.5	2.9	.522
93-94 Seattle	51	0	1022	739	272	577	.471	6	32	.188	189	211	.896	29	54	83	91	84	0	42	5	66	20.0	14.5	1.6	1.8	.556
94-95 Golden State	27	6	673	338	111	254	.437	23	70	.329	93	106	.877	12	52	64	40	38	0	22	2	24	24.9	12.5	2.4	1.5	.420
95-96 Indiana	76	2	1404	737	264	590	.447	35	104	.337	174	205	.849	40	96	136	101	188	1	57	6	91	18.5	9.7	1.8	1.3	.382
96-97 Denver	33	10	600	335	120	260	.462	12	39	.308	83	92	.902	17	36	53	31	49	0	14	5	40	18.2	10.2	1.6	0.9	.401
96-97 Charlotte	27	17	650	324	119	237	.502	30	56	.536	56	63	.889	19	49	68	49	48	0	14	4	30	24.1	12.0	2.5	1.8	.451
97-98 Milwaukee	39	0	442	151	52	143	.364	4	13	.308	43	52	.827	19	26	45	34	35	0	9	0	20	11.3	3.9	1.2	0.9	.262
NBA Season Totals	969	269	23665	14467	5391	10926	.493	296	920	.322	3389	3871	.875	864	1432	2296	1826	2213	14	768	147	1454	24.4	14.9	2.4	1.9	....
84-85 Milwaukee	8	1	198	79	36	73	.493	0	2	.000	7	9	.778	8	10	18	15	26	0	3	1	17	24.8	9.9	2.3	1.9	.263
85-86 Milwaukee	13	0	322	144	52	113	.460	0	2	.000	40	45	.889	20	16	36	20	42	0	8	3	15	24.8	11.1	2.8	1.5	.362
86-87 Milwaukee	12	2	317	191	68	142	.479	0	0	.000	55	67	.821	12	16	28	16	39	0	10	5	19	26.4	15.9	2.3	1.3	.435
87-88 Milwaukee	5	0	105	59	25	53	.472	1	5	.200	8	9	.889	6	8	14	9	9	0	1	2	4	21.0	11.8	2.8	1.8	.476
88-89 Milwaukee	9	0	292	201	77	141	.546	6	8	.750	41	47	.872	5	20	25	25	31	1	11	2	9	32.4	22.3	2.8	2.8	.610
89-90 Milwaukee	4	0	122	89	28	60	.467	5	10	.500	28	31	.903	6	3	9	6	14	0	5	0	3	30.5	22.3	2.3	1.5	.555
90-91 Seattle	5	0	112	57	19	57	.333	3	10	.300	16	17	.941	6	8	14	4	12	1	4	1	11	22.4	11.4	2.8	0.8	.243
91-92 Seattle	9	9	316	176	63	131	.481	3	11	.273	47	54	.870	9	13	22	28	24	0	5	1	24	35.1	19.6	2.4	3.1	.418
92-93 Seattle	19	19	578	337	123	270	.456	12	30	.400	79	88	.898	17	29	46	42	40	0	12	4	28	30.4	17.7	2.4	2.2	.439
93-94 Seattle	5	0	74	40	14	31	.452	0	0	.000	12	17	.706	4	1	5	3	8	0	1	0	9	14.8	8.0	1.0	0.6	.256
95-96 Indiana	5	4	133	51	16	47	.340	2	8	.250	17	20	.850	3	1	4	15	13	0	8	1	12	26.6	10.2	0.8	3.0	.234
96-97 Charlotte	3	2	87	23	11	24	.458	1	7	.143	0	0	.000	1	7	8	4	8	0	2	0	3	29.0	7.7	2.7	1.3	.206
NBA Playoff Totals	97	37	2656	1447	532	1142	.466	33	93	.355	350	404	.866	97	132	229	187	266	2	70	20	154	27.4	14.9	2.4	1.9	....

• PIETKIEWICZ, Stan

Stanley Thomas Pietkiewicz

Born: July 14, 1956. Huntsville, AL, United States. Height: 6'5". Weight: 200 lbs. Drafted: 1978 College: Auburn

YEAR TEAM	GP	GS	MIN	PTS	FGM	FGA	FG%	3PM	3PA	3P%	FTM	FTA	FT%	ORB	DRB	TRB	AST	PF	DQ	STL	BLK	TO	MPG	PPG	RPG	APG	PCM
78-79 San Diego	4	....	32	4	1	8	.125	....	....	....	2	2	1.000	0	6	6	3	5	0	1	0	1	8.0	1.0	1.5	0.8	.130
79-80 San Diego	50	....	577	228	91	179	.508	9	36	.250	37	46	.804	26	19	45	94	52	1	25	4	50	11.5	4.6	0.9	1.9	.425
80-81 San Diego	6	....	30	4	2	5	.400	0	0	.000	0	0	.000	0	1	1	2	2	0	0	0	5	5.0	0.7	0.2	0.3	-.037
80-81 Dallas	36	....	431	140	55	133	.414	19	48	.396	11	14	.786	13	28	41	75	26	0	15	2	18	12.0	3.9	1.1	2.1	.403
NBA Season Totals	96	....	1070	376	149	325	.458	28	84	.333	50	62	.806	39	54	93	174	85	1	41	6	74	11.1	3.9	1.0	1.8	....

• PILCH, John
John A. Pilch

Born: July 11, 1925. Sheridan, WY, United States. Height: 6'3". Weight: 185 lbs. Drafted: 1950 College: Wyoming

YEAR	TEAM	GP	GS	MIN	PTS	FGM	FGA	FG%	3PM	3PA	3P%	FTM	FTA	FT%	ORB	DRB	TRB	AST	PF	DQ	STL	BLK	TO	MPG	PPG	RPG	APG	PCM
51-52	Minneapolis	9	....	41	5	1	10	.100	....	....	....	3	6	.500	....	....	9	2	10	0	....	....	....	4.6	0.6	1.0	0.2	.072
NBA Season Totals		9	....	41	5	1	10	.100	....	....	....	3	6	.500	....	....	9	2	10	0	....	....	....	4.6	0.6	1.0	0.2	....

• PINCKNEY, Ed
Edward Lewis (E-Z Ed) Pinckney

Born: Mar. 27, 1963. Bronx, NY, United States. Height: 6'9". Weight: 195 lbs. Drafted: 1985 College: Villanova

YEAR	TEAM	GP	GS	MIN	PTS	FGM	FGA	FG%	3PM	3PA	3P%	FTM	FTA	FT%	ORB	DRB	TRB	AST	PF	DQ	STL	BLK	TO	MPG	PPG	RPG	APG	PCM
85-86	Phoenix	80	24	1602	681	255	457	.558	0	2	.000	171	254	.673	95	213	308	90	190	3	71	37	152	20.0	8.5	3.9	1.1	.442
86-87	Phoenix	80	65	2250	837	290	497	.584	0	2	.000	257	348	.739	179	401	580	116	196	1	86	54	136	28.1	10.5	7.3	1.5	.524
87-88	Sacramento	79	7	1177	491	179	343	.522	0	2	.000	133	178	.747	94	136	230	66	118	0	39	32	79	14.9	6.2	2.9	0.8	.458
88-89	Sacramento	51	24	1334	625	224	446	.502	0	6	.000	177	221	.801	106	195	301	74	125	1	54	43	82	26.2	12.3	5.9	1.5	.534
88-89	Boston	29	9	678	293	95	176	.540	0	0	.000	103	129	.798	60	88	148	44	77	1	29	23	38	23.4	10.1	5.1	1.5	.542
89-90	Boston	77	50	1082	362	135	249	.542	0	1	.000	92	119	.773	93	132	225	68	126	1	34	42	54	14.1	4.7	2.9	0.9	.450
90-91	Boston	70	16	1165	366	131	243	.539	0	1	.000	104	116	.897	155	186	341	45	147	0	61	43	42	16.6	5.2	4.9	0.6	.525
91-92	Boston	81	36	1917	613	203	378	.537	0	1	.000	207	255	.812	252	312	564	62	158	1	70	56	73	23.7	7.6	7.0	0.8	.519
92-93	Boston	7	5	151	32	10	24	.417	0	0	.000	12	13	.923	14	29	43	1	13	0	4	7	8	21.6	4.6	6.1	0.1	.373
93-94	Boston	76	35	1524	394	151	289	.522	0	0	.000	92	125	.736	160	318	478	62	131	0	58	44	61	20.1	5.2	6.3	0.8	.482
94-95	Milwaukee	62	17	835	140	48	97	.495	0	0	.000	44	62	.710	65	146	211	21	64	0	34	17	25	13.5	2.3	3.4	0.3	.360
95-96	Toronto	47	24	1031	328	117	233	.502	0	3	.000	94	124	.758	115	167	282	50	101	0	31	17	52	21.9	7.0	6.0	1.1	.458
95-96	Philadelphia	27	23	679	150	54	102	.529	0	0	.000	42	55	.764	74	102	176	22	55	1	33	11	24	25.1	5.6	6.5	0.8	.413
96-97	Miami	27	0	273	66	23	43	.535	0	0	.000	20	25	.800	25	40	65	6	30	0	8	9	19	10.1	2.4	2.4	0.2	.352
NBA Season Totals		793	335	15698	5378	1915	3577	.535	0	18	.000	1548	2024	.765	1487	2465	3952	727	1531	9	612	435	845	19.8	6.8	5.0	0.9	....
88-89	Boston	3	0	45	8	3	12	.250	0	0	.000	2	2	1.000	2	3	5	1	7	0	1	1	4	15.0	2.7	1.7	0.3	.005
89-90	Boston	4	0	25	19	6	7	.857	0	0	.000	7	9	.778	2	4	6	0	3	0	0	0	2	6.3	4.8	1.5	0.0	.779
90-91	Boston	11	0	170	49	16	21	.762	0	0	.000	17	21	.810	23	17	40	2	17	0	6	2	2	15.5	4.5	3.6	0.2	.468
91-92	Boston	10	8	314	96	35	58	.603	0	1	.000	26	31	.839	36	48	84	7	30	0	12	9	13	31.4	9.6	8.4	0.7	.482
96-97	Miami	2	0	6	4	2	3	.667	0	0	.000	0	0	.000	0	0	0	1	0	0	0	0	0	3.0	2.0	0.0	0.5	.689
NBA Playoff Totals		30	8	560	176	62	101	.614	0	1	.000	52	63	.825	63	72	135	11	57	0	19	12	21	18.7	5.9	4.5	0.4	....

• PINONE, John
John Gabriel Pinone Jr.

Born: Feb. 19, 1961. Hartford, CT, United States. Height: 6'8". Weight: 230 lbs. Drafted: 1983 College: Villanova

YEAR	TEAM	GP	GS	MIN	PTS	FGM	FGA	FG%	3PM	3PA	3P%	FTM	FTA	FT%	ORB	DRB	TRB	AST	PF	DQ	STL	BLK	TO	MPG	PPG	RPG	APG	PCM
83-84	Atlanta	7	0	65	20	7	13	.538	0	0	.000	6	10	.600	0	10	10	3	11	0	2	1	5	9.3	2.9	1.4	0.4	.278
NBA Season Totals		7	0	65	20	7	13	.538	0	0	.000	6	10	.600	0	10	10	3	11	0	2	1	5	9.3	2.9	1.4	0.4	....

• PIONTEK, Dave
David Vincent Piontek

Born: Aug. 27, 1934. Height: 6'6". Weight: 230 lbs. Drafted: 1956 College: Xavier (OH)

YEAR	TEAM	GP	GS	MIN	PTS	FGM	FGA	FG%	3PM	3PA	3P%	FTM	FTA	FT%	ORB	DRB	TRB	AST	PF	DQ	STL	BLK	TO	MPG	PPG	RPG	APG	PCM
56-57	Rochester	71	....	1759	636	257	637	.403	....	....	....	122	183	.667	....	....	351	108	141	1	....	....	....	24.8	9.0	4.9	1.5	.383
57-58	Cincinnati	71	....	1032	395	150	397	.378	....	....	....	95	151	.629	....	....	254	52	134	2	....	....	....	14.5	5.6	3.6	0.7	.385
58-59	Cincinnati	72	....	1674	766	305	813	.375	....	....	....	156	227	.687	....	....	385	124	162	3	....	....	....	23.3	10.6	5.3	1.7	.442
59-60	Cincinnati	52	....	1111	518	217	531	.409	....	....	....	84	122	.689	....	....	341	84	143	2	....	....	....	21.4	10.0	6.6	1.6	.517
59-60	St. Louis	25	....	722	195	75	197	.381	....	....	....	45	80	.563	....	....	120	34	68	3	....	....	....	28.9	7.8	4.8	1.4	.273
60-61	St. Louis	29	....	254	110	47	96	.490	....	....	....	16	31	.516	....	....	68	19	31	0	....	....	....	8.8	3.8	2.3	0.7	.514
61-62	Chicago	45	....	614	205	83	225	.369	....	....	....	39	59	.661	....	....	155	31	89	1	....	....	....	13.6	4.6	3.4	0.7	.343
62-63	Cincinnati	48	....	457	130	60	158	.380	....	....	....	10	16	.625	....	....	96	26	67	0	....	....	....	9.5	2.7	2.0	0.5	.287
NBA Season Totals		413	....	7623	2955	1194	3054	.391	....	....	....	567	869	.652	....	....	1770	478	835	12	....	....	....	18.5	7.2	4.3	1.2	....
57-58	Cincinnati	2	....	27	10	4	10	.400	....	....	....	2	5	.400	....	....	10	0	7	1	....	....	....	13.5	5.0	5.0	0.0	.343
59-60	St. Louis	14	....	220	72	27	79	.342	....	....	....	18	25	.720	....	....	41	18	28	0	....	....	....	15.7	5.1	2.9	1.3	.331
60-61	St. Louis	1	....	10	2	1	7	.143	....	....	....	0	0	.000	....	....	3	1	2	0	....	....	....	10.0	2.0	3.0	1.0	.020
62-63	Cincinnati	8	....	68	20	8	17	.471	....	....	....	4	7	.571	....	....	16	1	7	0	....	....	....	8.5	2.5	2.0	0.1	.335
NBA Playoff Totals		25	....	325	104	40	113	.354	....	....	....	24	37	.649	....	....	70	20	44	1	....	....	....	13.0	4.2	2.8	0.8	....

• PIOTROWSKI, Tom
Thomas Tracy Piotrowski

Born: Oct. 17, 1960. West Chester, PA, United States. Height: 7'1". Weight: 240 lbs. Drafted: 1983 College: LaSalle

YEAR	TEAM	GP	GS	MIN	PTS	FGM	FGA	FG%	3PM	3PA	3P%	FTM	FTA	FT%	ORB	DRB	TRB	AST	PF	DQ	STL	BLK	TO	MPG	PPG	RPG	APG	PCM
83-84	Portland	18	0	78	30	12	26	.462	0	0	.000	6	6	1.000	6	10	16	5	22	0	1	3	5	4.3	1.7	0.9	0.3	.334
NBA Season Totals		18	0	78	30	12	26	.462	0	0	.000	6	6	1.000	6	10	16	5	22	0	1	3	5	4.3	1.7	0.9	0.3	....

• PIPPEN, Scottie
Scottie Pippen

Born: Sept. 25, 1965. Hamburg, AR, United States. Height: 6'7". Weight: 210 lbs. Drafted: 1987 College: Central Arkansas

YEAR	TEAM	GP	GS	MIN	PTS	FGM	FGA	FG%	3PM	3PA	3P%	FTM	FTA	FT%	ORB	DRB	TRB	AST	PF	DQ	STL	BLK	TO	MPG	PPG	RPG	APG	PCM
87-88	Chicago	79	0	1650	625	261	564	.463	4	23	.174	99	172	.576	115	183	298	169	214	3	91	52	134	20.9	7.9	3.8	2.1	.409
88-89	Chicago	73	56	2413	1048	413	867	.476	21	77	.273	201	301	.668	138	307	445	256	261	8	139	61	197	33.1	14.4	6.1	3.5	.476
89-90	Chicago	82	82	3148	1351	562	1150	.489	28	112	.250	199	295	.675	150	397	547	444	298	6	211	101	279	38.4	16.5	6.7	5.4	.518
90-91	Chicago	82	82	3014	1461	600	1153	.520	21	68	.309	240	340	.706	163	432	595	511	270	3	193	93	230	36.8	17.8	7.3	6.2	.639
91-92	Chicago	82	82	3164	1720	687	1359	.506	16	80	.200	330	434	.760	185	445	630	572	242	2	155	93	254	38.6	21.0	7.7	7.0	.672
92-93	Chicago	81	81	3123	1510	628	1327	.473	22	93	.237	232	350	.663	203	418	621	507	219	3	173	72	243	38.6	18.6	7.7	6.3	.584
93-94	Chicago	72	72	2759	1587	627	1278	.491	63	197	.320	270	409	.660	173	456	629	403	227	1	211	58	230	38.3	22.0	8.7	5.6	.678
94-95	Chicago	79	79	3014	1692	634	1320	.480	109	316	.345	315	440	.716	175	464	639	409	238	4	**232**	89	269	38.2	21.4	8.1	5.2	.651
95-96	Chicago	77	77	2825	1496	563	1216	.463	150	401	.374	220	324	.679	152	344	496	452	198	0	133	57	208	36.7	19.4	6.4	5.9	.591
96-97	Chicago	82	82	3095	1656	648	1366	.474	156	424	.368	204	291	.701	160	371	531	467	213	2	154	45	213	37.7	20.2	6.5	5.7	.591
97-98	Chicago	44	44	1652	841	315	704	.447	61	192	.318	150	193	.777	53	174	227	254	116	0	79	43	110	37.5	19.1	5.2	5.8	.549
98-99	Houston	50	50	2011	726	261	604	.432	72	212	.340	132	183	.721	63	260	323	293	118	0	98	37	159	40.2	14.5	6.5	5.9	.466
99-00	Portland	82	82	2749	1022	388	860	.451	86	263	.327	160	223	.717	114	399	513	406	208	0	117	41	208	33.5	12.5	6.3	5.0	.485
00-01	Portland	64	60	2133	721	269	596	.451	64	186	.344	119	161	.739	70	263	333	294	158	2	94	35	154	33.3	11.3	5.2	4.6	.440

YEAR	TEAM	GP	GS	MIN	PTS	FGM	FGA	FG%	3PM	3PA	3P%	FTM	FTA	FT%	ORB	DRB	TRB	AST	PF	DQ	STL	BLK	TO	MPG	PPG	RPG	APG	PCM
01-02	Portland	62	60	1996	659	246	599	.411	54	177	.305	113	146	.774	77	244	321	363	162	3	101	35	171	32.2	10.6	5.2	5.9	.454
02-03	Portland	64	58	1911	689	265	597	.444	38	133	.286	121	148	.818	57	221	278	285	149	0	105	25	164	29.9	10.8	4.3	4.5	.440
NBA Season Totals		1155	1047	40657	18804	7367	15560	.473	965	2954	.327	3105	4410	.704	2048	5378	7426	6085	3291	37	2286	937	3223	35.2	16.3	6.4	5.3	....
87-88	Chicago	10	6	294	100	46	99	.465	3	6	.500	5	7	.714	24	28	52	24	33	1	8	8	26	29.4	10.0	5.2	2.4	.337
88-89	Chicago	17	17	619	222	84	182	.462	22	56	.393	32	50	.640	34	95	129	67	63	2	23	16	41	36.4	13.1	7.6	3.9	.457
89-90	Chicago	15	14	612	289	104	210	.495	10	31	.323	71	100	.710	33	75	108	83	62	0	31	19	49	40.8	19.3	7.2	5.5	.551
90-91	Chicago	17	17	704	368	142	282	.504	4	17	.235	80	101	.792	37	114	151	99	58	1	42	19	55	41.4	21.6	8.9	5.8	.643
91-92	Chicago	22	22	899	428	152	325	.468	6	24	.250	118	155	.761	59	134	193	147	72	1	41	25	70	40.9	19.5	8.8	6.7	.611
92-93	Chicago	19	19	789	381	152	327	.465	3	17	.176	74	116	.638	37	95	132	107	62	0	41	13	71	41.5	20.1	6.9	5.6	.495
93-94	Chicago	10	10	384	228	85	196	.434	12	45	.267	46	52	.885	17	66	83	46	33	1	24	7	37	38.4	22.8	8.3	4.6	.596
94-95	Chicago	10	10	396	178	58	131	.443	14	38	.368	48	71	.676	24	62	86	58	40	1	14	10	27	39.6	17.8	8.6	5.8	.554
95-96	Chicago	18	18	742	305	112	287	.390	30	105	.286	51	80	.638	62	91	153	107	51	0	47	16	41	41.2	16.9	8.5	5.9	.513
96-97	Chicago	19	19	753	365	129	309	.417	39	113	.345	68	86	.791	36	93	129	72	49	0	28	18	55	39.6	19.2	6.8	3.8	.471
97-98	Chicago	21	21	836	353	122	294	.415	18	79	.228	91	134	.679	49	101	150	110	66	1	45	20	51	39.8	16.8	7.1	5.2	.497
98-99	Houston	4	4	172	73	23	70	.329	6	22	.273	21	26	.808	20	27	47	22	12	0	7	3	13	43.0	18.3	11.8	5.5	.507
99-00	Portland	16	16	614	239	83	198	.419	21	70	.300	52	70	.743	22	92	114	69	49	1	32	7	37	38.4	14.9	7.1	4.3	.464
00-01	Portland	3	3	117	41	16	38	.421	3	17	.176	6	9	.667	2	15	17	7	14	1	8	2	12	39.0	13.7	5.7	2.3	.297
01-02	Portland	3	3	99	49	18	39	.462	6	11	.545	7	8	.875	8	20	28	17	14	1	4	2	10	33.0	16.3	9.3	5.7	.642
02-03	Portland	4	1	75	23	9	22	.409	3	9	.333	2	2	1.000	2	9	11	13	8	0	0	0	7	18.8	5.8	2.8	3.3	.339
NBA Playoff Totals		208	200	8105	3642	1335	3009	.444	200	660	.303	772	1067	.724	466	1117	1583	1048	686	11	395	185	602	39.0	17.5	7.6	5.0	....

• PITTMAN, Charles

Charles E. Pittman

Born: Mar. 23, 1958. Rocky Mount, NC, United States.   Height: 6'8".   Weight: 220 lbs.   Drafted: 1982   College: Maryland

YEAR	TEAM	GP	GS	MIN	PTS	FGM	FGA	FG%	3PM	3PA	3P%	FTM	FTA	FT%	ORB	DRB	TRB	AST	PF	DQ	STL	BLK	TO	MPG	PPG	RPG	APG	PCM
82-83	Phoenix	28	0	170	63	19	40	.475	0	1	.000	25	37	.676	13	18	31	7	41	0	2	7	22	6.1	2.3	1.1	0.3	.259
83-84	Phoenix	69	8	989	321	126	209	.603	0	2	.000	69	101	.683	76	138	214	70	129	1	16	22	83	14.3	4.7	3.1	1.0	.405
84-85	Phoenix	68	3	1001	323	107	227	.471	0	2	.000	109	146	.747	90	137	227	69	144	1	20	21	102	14.7	4.8	3.3	1.0	.355
85-86	Phoenix	69	17	1132	353	127	218	.583	0	0	.000	99	141	.702	99	147	246	58	140	2	37	23	110	16.4	5.1	3.6	0.8	.378
NBA Season Totals		234	28	3292	1060	379	694	.546	0	5	.000	302	425	.711	278	440	718	204	454	4	75	73	317	14.1	4.5	3.1	0.9	....
82-83	Phoenix	1	0	1	0	0	0	.000	0	0	.000	0	0	.000	0	0	0	0	0	0	0	0	0	1.0	0.0	0.0	0.0	.000
83-84	Phoenix	17	1	253	74	28	51	.549	0	1	.000	18	29	.621	25	39	64	12	31	0	5	5	16	14.9	4.4	3.8	0.7	.395
84-85	Phoenix	3	3	82	40	14	23	.609	0	0	.000	12	17	.706	6	13	19	9	10	0	0	3	9	27.3	13.3	6.3	3.0	.565
NBA Playoff Totals		21	4	336	114	42	74	.568	0	1	.000	30	46	.652	31	52	83	21	41	0	5	8	25	16.0	5.4	4.0	1.0	....

• PITZER, Woody

Woody Pitzer

Born: 1910.   Height: 6'   Weight: 160 lbs.   Drafted: —   College: Wittenberg

YEAR	TEAM	GP	GS	MIN	PTS	FGM	FGA	FG%	3PM	3PA	3P%	FTM	FTA	FT%	ORB	DRB	TRB	AST	PF	DQ	STL	BLK	TO	MPG	PPG	RPG	APG	PCM
37-38	Columbus-N	11	....	....	50	20	....	....	....	....	....	10	....	....	....	....	....	....	....	....	....	....	....	....	4.5	....	....	....
NBL Season Totals		11	....	....	50	20	....	....	....	....	....	10	....	....	....	....	....	....	....	....	....	....	....	....	4.5	....	....	....

• PLAHNA, Eric

Eric Plahna

Born: 1921.   Height: —   Weight: —   Drafted: —   College: Wisconsin (Milwaukee)

YEAR	TEAM	GP	GS	MIN	PTS	FGM	FGA	FG%	3PM	3PA	3P%	FTM	FTA	FT%	ORB	DRB	TRB	AST	PF	DQ	STL	BLK	TO	MPG	PPG	RPG	APG	PCM
43-44	Oshkosh-N	9	....	....	14	7	....	....	....	....	....	0	....	....	....	....	....	....	....	....	....	....	....	....	1.6	....	....	....
NBL Season Totals		9	....	....	14	7	....	....	....	....	....	0	....	....	....	....	....	....	....	....	....	....	....	....	1.6	....	....	....
43-44	Oshkosh-N	3	....	....	6	2	....	....	....	....	....	2	....	....	....	....	....	....	....	....	....	....	....	....	2.0	....	....	....
NBL Playoff Totals		3	....	....	6	2	....	....	....	....	....	2	....	....	....	....	....	....	....	....	....	....	....	....	2.0	....	....	....

• PLUMMER, Gary

Gary Plummer

Born: Feb. 21, 1962. Highland Park, MI, United States.   Height: 6'9".   Weight: 215 lbs.   Drafted: 1984   College: Boston University

YEAR	TEAM	GP	GS	MIN	PTS	FGM	FGA	FG%	3PM	3PA	3P%	FTM	FTA	FT%	ORB	DRB	TRB	AST	PF	DQ	STL	BLK	TO	MPG	PPG	RPG	APG	PCM
84-85	Golden State	66	0	702	250	92	232	.397	1	4	.250	65	92	.707	54	80	134	26	127	1	15	14	53	10.6	3.8	2.0	0.4	.254
92-93	Denver	60	0	737	281	106	228	.465	0	3	.000	69	95	.726	53	120	173	40	141	1	14	11	78	12.3	4.7	2.9	0.7	.331
NBA Season Totals		126	0	1439	531	198	460	.430	1	7	.143	134	187	.717	107	200	307	66	268	2	29	25	131	11.4	4.2	2.4	0.5	....

• POLEE, Dwayne

Dwayne L. Polee

Born: Mar. 2, 1963. Los Angeles, CA, United States.   Height: 6'5".   Weight: 180 lbs.   Drafted: 1986   College: Pepperdine

YEAR	TEAM	GP	GS	MIN	PTS	FGM	FGA	FG%	3PM	3PA	3P%	FTM	FTA	FT%	ORB	DRB	TRB	AST	PF	DQ	STL	BLK	TO	MPG	PPG	RPG	APG	PCM
86-87	LA Clippers	1	0	6	2	1	4	.250	0	3	.000	0	0	.000	0	0	0	0	3	0	1	0	1	6.0	2.0	0.0	0.0	-.365
NBA Season Totals		1	0	6	2	1	4	.250	0	3	.000	0	0	.000	0	0	0	0	3	0	1	0	1	6.0	2.0	0.0	0.0	....

• POLLARD, Jim

James Clifford (The Kangaroo Kid) Pollard

Born: July 9, 1922. Oakland, CA, United States. Died: Jan.22, 1993.   Height: 6'4".   Weight: 185 lbs.   Drafted: 1947   College: Stanford   HOF: 1978

YEAR	TEAM	GP	GS	MIN	PTS	FGM	FGA	FG%	3PM	3PA	3P%	FTM	FTA	FT%	ORB	DRB	TRB	AST	PF	DQ	STL	BLK	TO	MPG	PPG	RPG	APG	PCM
47-48	Minneapolis-N	59	....	....	760	310	....	....	....	....	....	140	207	.676	....	....	....	147	....	....	....	....	....	....	12.9	....	....	....
48-49	Minneapolis	53	....	....	784	314	792	.396	....	....	....	156	227	.687	....	....	....	142	144	....	....	....	....	....	14.8	....	2.7	....
49-50	Minneapolis	66	....	....	973	394	1140	.346	....	....	....	185	242	.764	....	....	....	252	143	....	....	....	....	....	14.7	....	3.8	....
50-51	Minneapolis	54	....	....	629	256	728	.352	....	....	....	117	156	.750	....	484	....	184	157	4	....	....	....	....	11.6	9.0	3.4	....
51-52	Minneapolis	65	....	2545	1005	411	1155	.356	....	....	....	183	260	.704	....	593	....	234	199	4	....	....	....	....	39.2	15.5	9.1	3.6	.433
52-53	Minneapolis	66	....	2403	859	333	933	.357	....	....	....	193	251	.769	....	452	....	231	194	3	....	....	....	....	36.4	13.0	6.8	3.5	.398

YEAR	TEAM	GP	GS	MIN	PTS	FGM	FGA	FG%	3PM	3PA	3P%	FTM	FTA	FT%	ORB	DRB	TRB	AST	PF	DQ	STL	BLK	TO	MPG	PPG	RPG	APG	PCM
53-54	Minneapolis	71	....	2483	831	326	882	.370	....	....	....	179	230	.778	....	....	500	214	161	0	....	....	....	35.0	11.7	7.0	3.0	.400
54-55	Minneapolis	63	....	1960	681	265	749	.354	....	....	....	151	186	.812	....	....	458	160	147	3	....	....	....	31.1	10.8	7.3	2.5	.404
NBA Season Totals		438	....	9391	5762	2299	6379	.360	....	....	....	1164	1552	.750	....	....	2487	1417	1145	14	....	....	....	21.4	13.2	5.7	3.2	....
NBL Season Totals		59	....	....	760	310	....	....	....	....	....	140	207	....	....	....	....	....	147	....	....	....	....	....	12.9	....	....	....
Career Totals		497	...	9391	6522	2609	6379	....	....	....	....	1304	1759	....	....	....	2487	1417	1292	14	....	....	....	18.9	13.1	5.0	2.9	....
47-48	Minneapolis-N	10	....	....	123	48	....	....	....	....	....	27	41	.659	....	....	....	....	....	....	....	....	....	12.3	....	....	....
48-49	Minneapolis	10	....	....	130	43	147	.293	....	....	....	44	62	.710	....	....	....	39	31	....	....	....	....	13.0	....	3.9	....
49-50	Minneapolis	12	....	....	144	50	175	.286	....	....	....	44	62	.710	....	....	....	56	36	....	....	....	....	12.0	....	4.7	....
50-51	Minneapolis	7	....	....	95	35	108	.324	....	....	....	25	30	.833	....	....	62	27	27	1	....	....	....	13.6	8.9	3.9	....
51-52	Minneapolis	11	....	469	177	70	173	.405	....	....	....	37	50	.740	....	....	71	33	34	1	....	....	....	42.6	16.1	6.5	3.0	.384
52-53	Minneapolis	12	....	455	172	62	167	.371	....	....	....	48	62	.774	....	....	86	49	37	2	....	....	....	37.9	14.3	7.2	4.1	.445
53-54	Minneapolis	13	....	543	160	56	155	.361	....	....	....	48	60	.800	....	....	110	41	27	0	....	....	....	41.8	12.3	8.5	3.2	.381
54-55	Minneapolis	7	....	257	99	33	104	.317	....	....	....	33	46	.717	....	....	78	14	13	0	....	....	....	36.7	14.1	11.1	2.0	.436
NBA Playoff Totals		72	....	1724	977	349	1029	.339	....	....	....	279	372	.750	....	....	407	259	205	4	....	....	....	23.9	13.6	5.7	3.6	....
NBL Playoff Totals		10	....	....	123	48	....	....	....	....	....	27	41	....	....	....	....	....	....	....	....	....	....	12.3	....	....	....
Career Playoff Totals		82	....	1724	1100	397	1029	....	....	....	....	306	413	....	....	....	407	259	205	4	....	....	....	21.0	13.4	5.0	3.2	....

• POLLARD, Scot

Scot Pollard

Born: Feb. 12, 1975. Murray, UT, United States.   Height: 6'11".   Weight: 265 lbs.   Drafted: 1997   College: Kansas

YEAR	TEAM	GP	GS	MIN	PTS	FGM	FGA	FG%	3PM	3PA	3P%	FTM	FTA	FT%	ORB	DRB	TRB	AST	PF	DQ	STL	BLK	TO	MPG	PPG	RPG	APG	PCM
97-98	Detroit	33	0	317	89	35	70	.500	0	0	.000	19	23	.826	34	40	74	9	48	0	8	10	13	9.6	2.7	2.2	0.3	.364
98-99	Sacramento	16	5	259	82	33	61	.541	0	0	.000	16	23	.696	38	44	82	4	41	0	8	18	5	16.2	5.1	5.1	0.3	.509
99-00	Sacramento	76	5	1336	412	149	283	.527	0	0	.000	114	159	.717	168	236	404	43	213	3	55	59	50	17.6	5.4	5.3	0.6	.483
00-01	Sacramento	77	8	1658	498	185	395	.468	0	2	.000	128	171	.749	173	292	465	47	206	4	48	97	66	21.5	6.5	6.0	0.6	.445
01-02	Sacramento	80	29	1881	509	197	358	.550	0	0	.000	115	166	.693	188	377	565	53	202	1	70	76	68	23.5	6.4	7.1	0.7	.473
02-03	Sacramento	23	0	325	103	40	87	.460	0	0	.000	23	38	.605	46	60	106	6	50	0	13	15	15	14.1	4.5	4.6	0.3	.447
NBA Season Totals		305	47	5776	1693	639	1254	.510	0	2	.000	415	580	.716	647	1049	1696	162	760	8	202	275	217	18.9	5.6	5.6	0.5	....
98-99	Sacramento	5	0	74	15	6	9	.667	0	0	.000	3	5	.600	5	6	11	1	13	0	4	6	2	14.8	3.0	2.2	0.2	.320
99-00	Sacramento	5	0	70	20	9	16	.563	0	0	.000	2	6	.333	6	10	16	1	18	1	2	1	3	14.0	4.0	3.2	0.2	.275
00-01	Sacramento	8	0	141	48	19	30	.633	0	0	.000	10	17	.588	23	32	55	2	30	0	1	7	6	17.6	6.0	6.9	0.3	.531
01-02	Sacramento	15	0	193	50	21	40	.525	0	0	.000	8	12	.667	29	24	53	3	36	1	7	5	3	12.9	3.3	3.5	0.2	.384
02-03	Sacramento	8	0	91	24	7	24	.292	0	0	.000	10	13	.769	17	13	30	2	15	1	1	7	7	11.4	3.0	3.8	0.3	.338
NBA Playoff Totals		41	0	569	157	62	119	.521	0	0	.000	33	53	.623	80	85	165	9	112	3	15	26	21	13.9	3.8	4.0	0.2	....

• POLSON, Ralph

Ralph M. Polson

Born: Oct. 26, 1929.   Height: 6'7".   Weight: 200 lbs.   Drafted: 1952   College: Whitworth

YEAR	TEAM	GP	GS	MIN	PTS	FGM	FGA	FG%	3PM	3PA	3P%	FTM	FTA	FT%	ORB	DRB	TRB	AST	PF	DQ	STL	BLK	TO	MPG	PPG	RPG	APG	PCM
52-53	New York	3	....	37	10	3	9	.333	....	....	....	4	6	.667	....	....	8	2	8	1	....	....	....	12.3	3.3	2.7	0.7	.281
52-53	Philadelphia	46	....	773	181	62	170	.365	....	....	....	57	90	.633	....	....	203	22	94	4	....	....	....	16.8	3.9	4.4	0.5	.300
NBA Season Totals		49	....	810	191	65	179	.363	....	....	....	61	96	.635	....	....	211	24	102	5	....	....	....	16.5	3.9	4.3	0.5	....

• POLYNICE, Olden

Olden (O.P.) Polynice

Born: Nov. 21, 1964. Port-au-Prince, Haiti.   Height: 6'11".   Weight: 220 lbs.   Drafted: 1987   College: Virginia

YEAR	TEAM	GP	GS	MIN	PTS	FGM	FGA	FG%	3PM	3PA	3P%	FTM	FTA	FT%	ORB	DRB	TRB	AST	PF	DQ	STL	BLK	TO	MPG	PPG	RPG	APG	PCM
87-88	Seattle	82	0	1080	337	118	254	.465	0	2	.000	101	158	.639	122	208	330	33	215	1	32	26	82	13.2	4.1	4.0	0.4	.374
88-89	Seattle	80	0	835	233	91	180	.506	0	2	.000	51	86	.593	98	108	206	21	164	0	37	30	48	10.4	2.9	2.6	0.3	.347
89-90	Seattle	79	7	1085	360	156	289	.540	1	2	.500	47	99	.475	128	172	300	15	187	0	25	21	32	13.7	4.6	3.8	0.2	.400
90-91	Seattle	48	0	960	397	165	303	.545	0	0	.000	67	114	.588	114	156	270	16	94	0	26	19	53	20.0	8.3	5.6	0.3	.483
90-91	LA Clippers	31	30	1132	381	151	261	.579	0	1	.000	79	138	.572	106	177	283	26	98	1	17	13	34	36.5	12.3	9.1	0.8	.436
91-92	LA Clippers	76	65	1834	613	244	470	.519	0	1	.000	125	201	.622	195	341	536	46	165	0	45	20	84	24.1	8.1	7.1	0.6	.447
92-93	Detroit	67	18	1299	486	210	428	.491	0	1	.000	66	142	.465	181	237	418	29	126	0	31	21	54	19.4	7.3	6.2	0.4	.468
93-94	Detroit	37	36	1350	486	222	406	.547	0	1	.000	42	92	.457	148	308	456	22	108	1	24	36	48	36.5	13.1	12.3	0.6	.517
93-94	Sacramento	31	29	1052	303	124	256	.484	0	1	.000	55	99	.556	151	202	353	19	81	1	18	31	48	33.9	9.8	11.4	0.6	.464
94-95	Sacramento	81	81	2534	877	376	691	.544	1	1	1.000	124	194	.639	277	448	725	62	238	0	48	52	113	31.3	10.8	9.0	0.8	.462
95-96	Sacramento	81	80	2441	985	431	818	.527	1	3	.333	122	203	.601	257	507	764	58	250	3	52	66	130	30.1	12.2	9.4	0.7	.506
96-97	Sacramento	82	82	2893	1025	442	967	.457	0	6	.000	141	251	.562	272	500	772	178	298	4	46	80	140	35.3	12.5	9.4	2.2	.422
97-98	Sacramento	70	25	1458	550	249	542	.459	0	1	.000	52	115	.452	173	266	439	107	158	0	37	45	98	20.8	7.9	6.3	1.5	.469
98-99	Seattle	48	47	1481	368	169	358	.472	1	1	1.000	29	94	.309	184	241	425	43	150	0	20	30	49	30.9	7.7	8.9	0.9	.358
99-00	Utah	82	79	1819	435	203	398	.510	1	2	.500	28	90	.311	166	287	453	37	260	1	30	84	70	22.2	5.3	5.5	0.5	.332
00-01	Utah	81	79	1619	429	206	415	.496	0	1	.000	17	65	.262	157	221	378	31	241	2	27	77	78	20.0	5.3	4.7	0.4	.314
NBA Season Totals		1056	658	24872	8265	3557	7036	.506	5	26	.192	1146	2141	.535	2729	4379	7108	743	2833	14	515	651	1165	23.6	7.8	6.7	0.7	....
87-88	Seattle	5	0	44	10	5	11	.455	0	0	.000	0	2	.000	2	6	8	0	6	0	3	0	1	8.8	2.0	1.6	0.0	.227
88-89	Seattle	8	0	162	57	25	41	.610	0	0	.000	7	13	.538	27	35	62	1	32	1	6	4	5	20.3	7.1	7.8	0.1	.542
91-92	LA Clippers	5	0	63	16	7	12	.583	0	0	.000	2	6	.333	2	16	18	2	11	0	1	1	1	12.6	3.2	3.6	0.4	.384
95-96	Sacramento	4	4	141	55	24	46	.522	1	1	1.000	6	9	.667	16	32	48	3	15	0	1	7	3	35.3	13.8	12.0	0.8	.559
99-00	Utah	10	10	260	59	28	52	.538	0	0	.000	3	6	.500	24	42	66	5	36	1	3	8	13	26.0	5.9	6.6	0.5	.320
00-01	Utah	5	5	100	39	16	30	.533	0	1	.000	7	10	.700	16	3	19	1	12	0	1	2	6	20.0	7.8	3.8	0.2	.352
NBA Playoff Totals		37	19	770	236	105	192	.547	1	2	.500	25	46	.543	87	134	221	12	112	2	15	22	29	20.8	6.4	6.0	0.3	....

YEAR	TEAM	GP	GS	MIN	PTS	FGM	FGA	FG%	3PM	3PA	3P%	FTM	FTA	FT%	ORB	DRB	TRB	AST	PF	DQ	STL	BLK	TO	MPG	PPG	RPG	APG	PCM

• PONCAR, John

John Poncar

Born: 1913. Height: 6'3". Weight: 190 lbs. Drafted: — College: none

YEAR	TEAM	GP	GS	MIN	PTS	FGM	FGA	FG%	3PM	3PA	3P%	FTM	FTA	FT%	ORB	DRB	TRB	AST	PF	DQ	STL	BLK	TO	MPG	PPG	RPG	APG	PCM
43-44	Cleveland-N	18	....	....	30	11	....	....	....	....	....	8	....	....	....	....	....	....	....	....	....	....	....	....	1.7	....	....	....
NBL Season Totals		18	....	....	30	11	....	....	....	....	....	8	....	....	....	....	....	....	....	....	....	....	....	....	1.7	....	....	....
43-44	Cleveland-N	2	....	....	1	0	....	....	....	....	....	1	....	....	....	....	....	....	....	....	....	....	....	....	0.5	....	....	....
NBL Playoff Totals		2	....	....	1	0	....	....	....	....	....	1	....	....	....	....	....	....	....	....	....	....	....	....	0.5	....	....	....

• PONDEXTER, Cliff

Clifton Pondexter

Born: Sept. 15, 1954. Fresno, CA, United States. Height: 6'9". Weight: 233 lbs. Drafted: 1974 College: Long Beach State

YEAR	TEAM	GP	GS	MIN	PTS	FGM	FGA	FG%	3PM	3PA	3P%	FTM	FTA	FT%	ORB	DRB	TRB	AST	PF	DQ	STL	BLK	TO	MPG	PPG	RPG	APG	PCM
75-76	Chicago	75	....	1326	434	156	380	.411	....	....	....	122	182	.670	113	268	381	90	134	4	28	26	....	17.7	5.8	5.1	1.2	.444
76-77	Chicago	78	....	996	256	107	257	.416	....	....	....	42	65	.646	77	159	236	41	82	0	34	11	....	12.8	3.3	3.0	0.5	.333
77-78	Chicago	44	....	534	88	37	85	.435	....	....	....	14	20	.700	36	94	130	87	66	0	19	15	31	12.1	2.0	3.0	2.0	.428
NBA Season Totals		197	....	2856	778	300	722	.416	....	....	....	178	267	.667	226	521	747	218	282	4	81	52	31	14.5	3.9	3.8	1.1	....
76-77	Chicago	3	....	12	2	0	1	.000	....	....	....	2	2	1.000	0	3	3	1	0	0	0	0	....	4.0	0.7	1.0	0.3	.405
NBA Playoff Totals		3	....	12	2	0	1	.000	....	....	....	2	2	1.000	0	3	3	1	0	0	0	0	....	4.0	0.7	1.0	0.3	

• POPE, David

David Pope

Born: Apr. 15, 1962. Newport News, VA, United States. Height: 6'7". Weight: 220 lbs. Drafted: 1984 College: Norfolk State

YEAR	TEAM	GP	GS	MIN	PTS	FGM	FGA	FG%	3PM	3PA	3P%	FTM	FTA	FT%	ORB	DRB	TRB	AST	PF	DQ	STL	BLK	TO	MPG	PPG	RPG	APG	PCM
84-85	Kansas City	22	0	129	41	17	53	.321	0	1	.000	7	13	.538	9	9	18	5	30	0	3	3	7	5.9	1.9	0.8	0.2	.092
85-86	Seattle	11	0	74	21	9	20	.450	1	1	1.000	2	4	.500	6	5	11	4	11	0	2	1	2	6.7	1.9	1.0	0.4	.273
NBA Season Totals		33	0	203	62	26	73	.356	1	2	.500	9	17	.529	15	14	29	9	41	0	5	4	9	6.2	1.9	0.9	0.3	....

• POPE, Mark

Mark Edward Pope

Born: Sept. 11, 1972. Omaha, NE, United States. Height: 6'10". Weight: 235 lbs. Drafted: 1996 College: Kentucky

YEAR	TEAM	GP	GS	MIN	PTS	FGM	FGA	FG%	3PM	3PA	3P%	FTM	FTA	FT%	ORB	DRB	TRB	AST	PF	DQ	STL	BLK	TO	MPG	PPG	RPG	APG	PCM
97-98	Indiana	28	0	193	39	14	41	.341	1	3	.333	10	17	.588	9	17	26	7	36	0	3	6	11	6.9	1.4	0.9	0.3	.125
98-99	Indiana	4	0	26	2	1	7	.143	0	4	.000	0	1	.000	2	2	4	0	6	0	0	0	1	6.5	0.5	1.0	0.0	-.145
00-01	Milwaukee	63	45	942	151	62	142	.437	5	24	.208	22	35	.629	56	91	147	38	140	2	16	26	17	15.0	2.4	2.3	0.6	.220
01-02	Milwaukee	45	12	429	87	36	91	.396	4	25	.160	11	21	.524	20	53	73	17	47	0	11	11	15	9.5	1.9	1.6	0.4	.239
NBA Season Totals		140	57	1590	279	113	281	.402	10	56	.179	43	74	.581	87	163	250	62	229	2	30	43	44	11.4	2.0	1.8	0.4	....
97-98	Indiana	7	0	42	9	4	6	.667	0	1	.000	1	1	1.000	2	3	5	1	8	0	1	0	1	6.0	1.3	0.7	0.1	.218
00-01	Milwaukee	6	3	46	10	5	10	.500	0	1	.000	0	0	.000	5	7	12	2	6	0	2	0	0	7.7	1.7	2.0	0.3	.382
NBA Playoff Totals		13	3	88	19	9	16	.563	0	2	.000	1	1	1.000	7	10	17	3	14	0	3	0	1	6.8	1.5	1.3	0.2	....

• POPSON, Dave

David G. Popson

Born: May 17, 1964. Kingston, PA, United States. Height: 6'10". Weight: 220 lbs. Drafted: 1987 College: North Carolina

YEAR	TEAM	GP	GS	MIN	PTS	FGM	FGA	FG%	3PM	3PA	3P%	FTM	FTA	FT%	ORB	DRB	TRB	AST	PF	DQ	STL	BLK	TO	MPG	PPG	RPG	APG	PCM
88-89	LA Clippers	10	0	68	23	11	25	.440	0	0	.000	1	2	.500	5	11	16	6	9	0	1	2	6	6.8	2.3	1.6	0.6	.351
88-89	Miami	7	0	38	11	5	15	.333	0	0	.000	1	2	.500	7	4	11	2	8	0	0	1	4	5.4	1.6	1.6	0.3	.187
90-91	Boston	19	0	64	35	13	32	.406	0	0	.000	9	10	.900	7	7	14	2	12	0	1	2	6	3.4	1.8	0.7	0.1	.369
91-92	Milwaukee	5	0	26	7	3	7	.429	0	1	.000	1	2	.500	2	3	5	3	5	0	2	1	4	5.2	1.4	1.0	0.6	.286
NBA Season Totals		41	0	196	76	32	79	.405	0	1	.000	12	16	.750	21	25	46	13	34	0	4	6	20	4.8	1.9	1.1	0.3	....

• POQUETTE, Ben

Benedict Jay (Gentle Ben) Poquette

Born: May 7, 1955. Ann Arbor, MI, United States. Height: 6'9". Weight: 235 lbs. Drafted: 1977 College: Central Michigan

YEAR	TEAM	GP	GS	MIN	PTS	FGM	FGA	FG%	3PM	3PA	3P%	FTM	FTA	FT%	ORB	DRB	TRB	AST	PF	DQ	STL	BLK	TO	MPG	PPG	RPG	APG	PCM
77-78	Detroit	52	....	626	232	95	225	.422	....	....	....	42	60	.700	50	95	145	20	69	1	10	22	42	12.0	4.5	2.8	0.4	.353
78-79	Detroit	76	....	1337	507	198	464	.427	....	....	....	111	142	.782	99	237	336	57	198	4	38	98	68	17.6	6.7	4.4	0.8	.442
79-80	Utah	82	....	2349	731	296	566	.523	0	2	.000	139	167	.832	124	436	560	131	283	8	45	162	107	28.6	8.9	6.8	1.6	.463
80-81	Utah	82	....	2808	777	324	614	.528	3	6	.500	126	162	.778	160	469	629	161	**342**	**18**	67	174	123	34.2	9.5	7.7	2.0	.426
81-82	Utah	82	56	1698	540	220	428	.514	3	10	.300	97	120	.808	117	294	411	94	235	4	51	65	66	20.7	6.6	5.0	1.1	.445
82-83	Utah	75	50	2331	825	329	697	.472	1	5	.200	166	221	.751	155	366	521	168	264	6	64	116	98	31.1	11.0	6.9	2.2	.462
83-84	Cleveland	51	4	858	185	75	171	.439	1	5	.200	34	43	.791	57	125	182	49	114	1	20	33	26	16.8	3.6	3.6	1.0	.333
84-85	Cleveland	79	6	1656	532	210	457	.460	3	17	.176	109	137	.796	148	325	473	79	220	3	47	58	71	21.0	6.7	6.0	1.0	.449
85-86	Cleveland	81	3	1496	406	166	348	.477	2	10	.200	72	100	.720	121	252	373	78	187	2	33	32	65	18.5	5.0	4.6	1.0	.379
86-87	Cleveland	37	1	437	113	41	82	.500	0	3	.000	31	39	.795	20	57	77	28	51	1	6	22	19	11.8	3.1	2.1	0.8	.360
86-87	Chicago	21	1	167	51	21	40	.525	0	1	.000	9	11	.818	10	14	24	7	26	0	3	12	4	8.0	2.4	1.1	0.3	.361
NBA Season Totals		718	121	15763	4899	1975	4092	.483	13	59	.220	936	1202	.779	1061	2670	3731	872	1989	47	384	794	689	22.0	6.8	5.2	1.2	....
84-85	Cleveland	4	0	91	30	13	21	.619	0	0	.000	4	5	.800	4	10	14	1	16	2	2	6	4	22.8	7.5	3.5	0.3	.357
NBA Playoff Totals		4	0	91	30	13	21	.619	0	0	.000	4	5	.800	4	10	14	1	16	2	2	6	4	22.8	7.5	3.5	0.3	....

• PORTER, Chris

Chris Porter

Born: May 9, 1978. Abbeville, AL, United States. Height: 6'7". Weight: 218 lbs. Drafted: 2000 College: Auburn

YEAR	TEAM	GP	GS	MIN	PTS	FGM	FGA	FG%	3PM	3PA	3P%	FTM	FTA	FT%	ORB	DRB	TRB	AST	PF	DQ	STL	BLK	TO	MPG	PPG	RPG	APG	PCM
00-01	Golden State	51	35	1147	440	173	445	.389	0	5	.000	94	141	.667	89	100	189	61	111	2	45	6	59	22.5	8.6	3.7	1.2	.309
NBA Season Totals		51	35	1147	440	173	445	.389	0	5	.000	94	141	.667	89	100	189	61	111	2	45	6	59	22.5	8.6	3.7	1.2	....

• PORTER, Howard

Howard (Geezer) Porter

Born: Aug. 31, 1948. Stuart, FL, United States. Height: 6'8". Weight: 220 lbs. Drafted: 1971 College: Villanova

YEAR	TEAM	GP	GS	MIN	PTS	FGM	FGA	FG%	3PM	3PA	3P%	FTM	FTA	FT%	ORB	DRB	TRB	AST	PF	DQ	STL	BLK	TO	MPG	PPG	RPG	APG	PCM
71-72	Chicago	67	....	730	401	171	403	.424	....	....	....	59	77	.766	....	....	183	24	88	0	....	....	....	10.9	6.0	2.7	0.4	.466
72-73	Chicago	43	....	407	218	98	217	.452	....	....	....	22	29	.759	....	....	118	16	52	1	....	....	....	9.5	5.1	2.7	0.4	.516
73-74	Chicago	73	....	1229	684	296	658	.450	....	....	....	92	115	.800	86	199	285	32	116	0	23	39	....	16.8	9.4	3.9	0.4	.485
74-75	New York	17	....	133	33	13	36	.361	....	....	....	7	9	.778	13	25	38	2	17	0	3	1	....	7.8	1.9	2.2	0.1	.301
74-75	Detroit	41	....	1030	435	188	376	.500	....	....	....	59	70	.843	66	150	216	17	76	0	20	25	....	25.1	10.6	5.3	0.4	.428
75-76	Detroit	75	....	1482	669	298	635	.469	....	....	....	73	97	.753	81	214	295	25	133	0	31	36	....	19.8	8.9	3.9	0.3	.401
76-77	Detroit	78	....	2200	1033	465	962	.483	....	....	....	103	120	.858	155	303	458	53	202	0	50	73	....	28.2	13.2	5.9	0.7	.439
77-78	Detroit	8	....	107	36	16	43	.372	....	....	....	4	7	.571	5	12	17	2	15	0	3	5	5	13.4	4.5	2.1	0.3	.227
77-78	New Jersey	55	....	1216	706	293	592	.495	....	....	....	120	148	.811	95	167	262	40	119	0	26	33	50	22.1	12.8	4.8	0.7	.545
NBA Season Totals		457	....	8534	4215	1838	3922	.469	....	....	....	539	672	.802	501	1070	1872	211	818	1	156	212	55	18.7	9.2	4.1	0.5	....
71-72	Chicago	4	....	31	19	9	21	.429	....	....	....	1	1	1.000	....	....	11	3	3	0	....	....	....	7.8	4.8	2.8	0.8	.653
72-73	Chicago	6	....	79	27	12	34	.353	....	....	....	3	4	.750	....	....	18	2	5	0	....	....	....	13.2	4.5	3.0	0.3	.295
73-74	Chicago	11	....	150	60	27	88	.307	....	....	....	6	6	1.000	15	29	44	5	15	0	4	5	....	13.6	5.5	4.0	0.5	.299
74-75	Detroit	3	....	92	52	23	42	.548	....	....	....	6	7	.857	8	12	20	0	5	0	5	1	....	30.7	17.3	6.7	0.0	.547
75-76	Detroit	9	....	213	117	51	97	.526	....	....	....	15	17	.882	22	20	42	6	24	0	7	5	....	23.7	13.0	4.7	0.7	.513
76-77	Detroit	3	....	98	60	29	47	.617	....	....	....	2	4	.500	6	11	17	2	7	0	2	4	....	32.7	20.0	5.7	0.7	.587
NBA Playoff Totals		36	....	663	335	151	329	.459	....	....	....	33	39	.846	51	72	152	18	59	0	18	15	....	18.4	9.3	4.2	0.5	....

• PORTER, Kevin

Kevin Porter

Born: Apr. 17, 1950. Chicago, IL, United States. Height: 6' Weight: 170 lbs. Drafted: 1972 College: St. Francis (PA)

YEAR	TEAM	GP	GS	MIN	PTS	FGM	FGA	FG%	3PM	3PA	3P%	FTM	FTA	FT%	ORB	DRB	TRB	AST	PF	DQ	STL	BLK	TO	MPG	PPG	RPG	APG	PCM
72-73	Baltimore	71	....	1217	472	205	451	.455	....	....	....	62	101	.614	....	....	72	237	206	5	....	....	....	17.1	6.6	1.0	3.3	.401
73-74	Washington	81	....	2339	1134	477	997	.478	....	....	....	180	249	.723	79	100	179	469	**319**	14	95	9	....	28.9	14.0	2.2	5.8	.521
74-75	Washington	81	....	2589	943	406	827	.491	....	....	....	131	186	.704	55	97	152	**650**	320	**12**	152	11	....	32.0	11.6	1.9	**8.0**	**.502**
75-76	Detroit	19	....	687	240	99	235	.421	....	....	....	42	56	.750	14	30	44	193	83	3	35	3	....	36.2	12.6	2.3	10.2	.495
76-77	Detroit	81	....	2117	717	310	605	.512	....	....	....	97	133	.729	28	70	98	592	271	8	88	8	....	26.1	8.9	1.2	7.3	.514
77-78	Detroit	8	....	127	37	14	31	.452	....	....	....	9	13	.692	5	10	15	**36**	18	0	5	0	12	15.9	4.6	1.9	**4.5**	**.472**
77-78	New Jersey	74	....	2686	1197	481	1024	.470	....	....	....	235	307	.765	48	151	199	**801**	265	6	118	15	348	36.3	16.2	2.7	**10.8**	**.544**
78-79	Detroit	82	....	3064	1260	534	1110	.481	....	....	....	192	266	.722	62	147	209	**1099**	302	5	158	5	336	37.4	15.4	2.5	**13.4**	**.593**
79-80	Washington	70	....	1494	512	201	438	.459	0	4	.000	110	137	.803	25	57	82	457	180	1	59	11	161	21.3	7.3	1.2	6.5	.466
80-81	Washington	81	....	2577	1086	446	859	.519	3	12	.250	191	247	.773	35	89	124	**734**	257	4	110	10	251	31.8	13.4	1.5	**9.1**	**.528**
82-83	Washington	11	0	210	47	21	40	.525	0	0	.000	5	6	.833	2	3	5	46	30	0	10	0	21	19.1	4.3	0.5	4.2	.290
NBA Season Totals		659	0	19107	7645	3194	6617	.483	3	16	.188	1254	1701	.737	353	754	1179	5314	2251	58	830	72	1129	29.0	11.6	1.8	8.1	....
72-73	Baltimore	4	....	41	12	6	12	.500	....	....	....	0	0	.000	....	....	2	9	11	0	....	....	....	10.3	3.0	0.5	2.3	.345
73-74	Washington	7	....	195	75	33	85	.388	....	....	....	9	14	.643	10	7	17	32	30	2	8	0	....	27.9	10.7	2.4	4.6	.344
74-75	Washington	17	....	625	244	99	197	.503	....	....	....	46	69	.667	13	28	41	124	73	3	21	0	....	36.8	14.4	2.4	7.3	.475
76-77	Detroit	3	....	61	16	5	14	.357	....	....	....	6	9	.667	1	5	6	17	7	0	1	0	....	20.3	5.3	2.0	5.7	.466
79-80	Washington	2	....	49	16	7	16	.438	0	1	.000	2	5	.400	2	0	2	9	7	0	3	0	4	24.5	8.0	1.0	4.5	.288
NBA Playoff Totals		33	....	971	363	150	324	.463	0	1	.000	63	97	.649	26	40	68	191	128	5	33	0	4	29.4	11.0	2.1	5.8	....

• PORTER, Terry

Terry Porter

Born: Apr. 8, 1963. Milwaukee, WI, United States. Height: 6'3". Weight: 195 lbs. Drafted: 1985 College: Wisconsin (Stevens Point)

YEAR	TEAM	GP	GS	MIN	PTS	FGM	FGA	FG%	3PM	3PA	3P%	FTM	FTA	FT%	ORB	DRB	TRB	AST	PF	DQ	STL	BLK	TO	MPG	PPG	RPG	APG	PCM
85-86	Portland	79	3	1214	562	212	447	.474	13	42	.310	125	155	.806	35	82	117	198	136	0	81	1	103	15.4	7.1	1.5	2.5	.468
86-87	Portland	80	80	2714	1045	376	770	.488	13	60	.217	280	334	.838	70	267	337	715	192	0	159	9	256	33.9	13.1	4.2	8.9	.575
87-88	Portland	82	82	2991	1222	462	890	.519	24	69	.348	274	324	.846	65	313	378	831	204	1	150	16	246	36.5	14.9	4.6	10.1	.625
88-89	Portland	81	81	3102	1431	540	1146	.471	79	219	.361	272	324	.840	85	282	367	770	187	1	146	8	251	38.3	17.7	4.5	9.5	.590
89-90	Portland	80	80	2781	1406	448	969	.462	89	238	.374	421	472	.892	59	213	272	726	150	0	151	4	248	34.8	17.6	3.4	9.1	.634
90-91	Portland	81	81	2665	1381	486	944	.515	130	313	.415	279	339	.823	52	230	282	649	151	2	158	12	186	32.9	17.0	3.5	8.0	.674
91-92	Portland	82	82	2784	1485	521	1129	.461	128	324	.395	315	368	.856	51	204	255	477	155	1	127	12	189	34.0	18.1	3.1	5.8	.548
92-93	Portland	81	81	2883	1476	503	1108	.454	143	345	.414	327	388	.843	58	258	316	419	122	0	101	10	203	35.6	18.2	3.9	5.2	.514
93-94	Portland	77	34	2074	1010	348	836	.416	110	282	.390	204	234	.872	45	170	215	401	132	0	79	18	169	26.9	13.1	2.8	5.2	.508
94-95	Portland	35	9	770	312	105	267	.393	44	114	.386	58	82	.707	18	63	81	133	60	0	30	2	60	22.0	8.9	2.3	3.8	.405
95-96	Minnesota	82	40	2072	773	269	608	.442	71	226	.314	164	209	.785	36	176	212	452	154	0	89	15	172	25.3	9.4	2.6	5.5	.471
96-97	Minnesota	82	20	1568	568	187	449	.416	67	200	.335	127	166	.765	31	145	176	295	104	0	54	11	131	19.1	6.9	2.1	3.6	.430
97-98	Minnesota	82	8	1786	777	259	577	.449	92	233	.395	167	195	.856	37	131	168	271	103	0	63	16	107	21.8	9.5	2.0	3.3	.475
98-99	Miami	50	1	1365	525	172	370	.465	58	141	.411	123	148	.831	13	127	140	146	97	0	48	11	74	27.3	10.5	2.8	2.9	.416
99-00	San Antonio	68	8	1613	641	207	463	.447	90	207	.435	137	170	.806	24	167	191	221	79	0	50	9	100	23.7	9.4	2.8	3.3	.456
00-01	San Antonio	80	42	1678	573	197	440	.448	87	205	.424	92	116	.793	24	177	201	251	88	1	52	11	104	21.0	7.2	2.5	3.1	.432
01-02	San Antonio	72	0	1294	399	136	321	.424	59	142	.415	68	83	.819	12	152	164	205	89	0	45	16	85	18.0	5.5	2.3	2.8	.414
NBA Season Totals		1274	732	35354	15586	5428	11734	.463	1297	3360	.386	3433	4107	.836	715	3157	3872	7160	2203	6	1583	181	2684	27.8	12.2	3.0	5.6	....
85-86	Portland	4	0	68	27	12	27	.444	1	6	.167	2	4	.500	1	4	5	12	10	0	3	2	6	17.0	6.8	1.3	3.0	.354
86-87	Portland	4	4	150	68	24	50	.480	2	5	.400	18	20	.900	1	18	19	40	14	0	10	2	13	37.5	17.0	4.8	10.0	.639
87-88	Portland	4	4	149	68	29	52	.558	1	3	.333	9	13	.692	4	10	14	28	13	0	10	0	13	37.3	17.0	3.5	7.0	.529
88-89	Portland	3	3	124	66	26	52	.500	4	11	.364	10	12	.833	6	12	18	25	8	0	1	1	7	41.3	22.0	6.0	8.3	.613
89-90	Portland	21	21	815	433	127	274	.464	40	102	.392	139	165	.842	9	52	61	155	51	1	28	3	62	38.8	20.6	2.9	7.4	.555
90-91	Portland	16	16	595	289	102	204	.500	17	47	.362	68	79	.861	8	36	44	105	32	0	24	1	32	37.2	18.1	2.8	6.6	.538
91-92	Portland	21	21	870	450	147	285	.516	37	78	.474	119	143	.832	25	72	97	141	49	0	22	3	46	41.4	21.4	4.6	6.7	.586
92-93	Portland	4	4	152	66	27	68	.397	3	19	.158	9	11	.818	4	16	20	8	10	0	4	0	6	38.0	16.5	5.0	2.0	.312
93-94	Portland	4	0	76	41	12	35	.343	6	14	.429	11	14	.786	1	11	12	9	3	0	4	0	2	19.0	10.3	3.0	2.3	.523
94-95	Portland	3	0	21	19	7	13	.538	2	5	.400	3	5	.600	1	1	2	4	6	0	0	0	1	7.0	6.3	0.7	1.3	.705
96-97	Minnesota	3	0	46	16	5	13	.385	3	9	.333	3	4	.750	1	2	3	9	2	0	2	2	2	15.3	5.3	1.0	3.0	.466
97-98	Minnesota	5	4	188	79	27	63	.429	10	25	.400	15	18	.833	7	18	25	16	10	0	5	0	4	37.6	15.8	5.0	3.2	.432
98-99	Miami	5	0	139	45	15	32	.469	3	12	.250	12	15	.800	3	16	19	15	8	0	3	0	8	27.8	9.0	3.8	3.0	.389

YEAR	TEAM	GP	GS	MIN	PTS	FGM	FGA	FG%	3PM	3PA	3P%	FTM	FTA	FT%	ORB	DRB	TRB	AST	PF	DQ	STL	BLK	TO	MPG	PPG	RPG	APG	PCM
99-00	San Antonio	4	0	89	20	8	31	.258	4	14	.286	0	0	.000	0	1	1	5	4	0	6	0	7	22.3	5.0	0.3	1.3	.031
00-01	San Antonio	13	13	326	108	39	86	.453	13	39	.333	17	22	.773	1	23	24	44	15	0	11	0	22	25.1	8.3	1.8	3.4	.359
01-02	San Antonio	10	0	131	33	13	35	.371	5	17	.294	2	4	.500	1	8	9	8	10	0	4	0	5	13.1	3.3	0.9	0.8	.180
NBA Playoff Totals		124	90	3939	1828	620	1320	.470	151	406	.372	437	529	.826	73	300	373	624	245	1	137	14	236	31.8	14.7	3.0	5.0	....

• PORTER, Willie
Willie William Porter

Born: July 3, 1942. Winston-Salem, NC, United States.   Height: 6'7".   Weight: 205 lbs.   Drafted: 1965   College: Tennessee A&I

YEAR	TEAM	GP	GS	MIN	PTS	FGM	FGA	FG%	3PM	3PA	3P%	FTM	FTA	FT%	ORB	DRB	TRB	AST	PF	DQ	STL	BLK	TO	MPG	PPG	RPG	APG	PCM
67-68	Oakland-A	43	....	1123	565	199	472	.422	0	0	.000	167	246	.679	....	....	380	50	162	11	....	....	140	26.1	13.1	8.8	1.2	.545
67-68	Pittsburgh-A	13	....	171	84	26	74	.351	0	0	.000	32	48	.667	....	....	69	9	28	0	....	....	15	13.2	6.5	5.3	0.7	.548
68-69	Houston-A	2	....	11	10	3	7	.429	0	0	.000	4	4	1.000	3	4	7	0	0	0	....	....	1	5.5	5.0	3.5	0.1	1.143
68-69	Minnesota-A	11	....	137	63	25	45	.556	0	0	.000	13	27	.481	24	24	48	6	23	0	....	....	10	12.5	5.7	4.4	0.5	.569
ABA Season Totals		69	....	1442	722	253	598	.423	0	0	.000	216	325	.665	27	28	504	65	213	11	....	....	166	20.9	10.5	7.3	0.9	....
67-68	Pittsburgh-A	14	....	167	58	19	43	.442	0	0	.000	20	29	.690	....	....	69	6	43	0	....	....	18	11.9	4.1	4.9	0.4	.484
ABA Playoff Totals		14	....	167	58	19	43	.442	0	0	.000	20	29	.690	....	....	69	6	43	0	....	....	18	11.9	4.1	4.9	0.4	....

• PORTMAN, Bob
Robert M. Portman

Born: Mar. 22, 1947. San Francisco, CA, United States.   Height: 6'5".   Weight: 200 lbs.   Drafted: 1969   College: Creighton

YEAR	TEAM	GP	GS	MIN	PTS	FGM	FGA	FG%	3PM	3PA	3P%	FTM	FTA	FT%	ORB	DRB	TRB	AST	PF	DQ	STL	BLK	TO	MPG	PPG	RPG	APG	PCM
69-70	San Francisco	60	....	813	420	177	398	.445	....	....	....	66	85	.776	....	....	224	28	77	0	....	....	....	13.6	7.0	3.7	0.5	.506
70-71	San Francisco	68	....	1395	519	221	483	.458	....	....	....	77	106	.726	....	....	321	67	130	0	....	....	....	20.5	7.6	4.7	1.0	.414
71-72	Golden State	61	....	553	231	89	221	.403	....	....	....	53	60	.883	....	....	133	26	69	0	....	....	....	9.1	3.8	2.2	0.4	.413
72-73	Golden State	32	....	176	84	32	70	.457	....	....	....	20	26	.769	....	....	51	7	16	0	....	....	....	5.5	2.6	1.6	0.2	.532
NBA Season Totals		221	....	2937	1254	519	1172	.443	....	....	....	216	277	.780	....	....	729	128	292	0	....	....	....	13.3	5.7	3.3	0.6	....
70-71	San Francisco	5	....	110	46	20	39	.513	....	....	....	6	9	.667	....	....	20	2	9	0	....	....	....	22.0	9.2	4.0	0.4	.400
71-72	Golden State	3	....	22	5	2	12	.167	....	....	....	1	1	1.000	....	....	5	0	5	0	....	....	....	7.3	1.7	1.7	0.0	-.067
72-73	Golden State	3	....	17	8	2	10	.200	....	....	....	4	4	1.000	....	....	5	1	0	0	....	....	....	5.7	2.7	1.7	0.3	.386
NBA Playoff Totals		11	....	149	59	24	61	.393	....	....	....	11	14	.786	....	....	30	3	14	0	....	....	....	13.5	5.4	2.7	0.3	....

• POSEWITZ, Johnny
John Posewitz

Born: Aug. 9, 1906. Died: Apr.11, 1994.   Height: 6'   Weight: 185 lbs.   Drafted: —   College: none

YEAR	TEAM	GP	GS	MIN	PTS	FGM	FGA	FG%	3PM	3PA	3P%	FTM	FTA	FT%	ORB	DRB	TRB	AST	PF	DQ	STL	BLK	TO	MPG	PPG	RPG	APG	PCM
38-39	Sheboygan-N	24	....	....	56	25	....	....	....	....	....	6	....	....	....	....	....	....	....	....	....	....	....	2.3	....	....	....	....
39-40	Sheboygan-N	12	....	....	34	15	....	....	....	....	....	4	....	....	....	....	....	....	....	....	....	....	....	2.8	....	....	....	....
44-45	Sheboygan-N	1	....	....	0	0	....	....	....	....	....	0	....	....	....	....	....	....	....	....	....	....	....	0.0	....	....	....	....
NBL Season Totals		37	....	....	90	40	....	....	....	....	....	10	....	....	....	....	....	....	....	....	....	....	....	2.4	....	....	....	....

• POSEWITZ, Scoop
Joe (Scoop) Posewitz

Born: Sept. 12, 1908. Died: Sept.25, 1993.   Height: 5'11".   Weight: 180 lbs.   Drafted: —   College: none

YEAR	TEAM	GP	GS	MIN	PTS	FGM	FGA	FG%	3PM	3PA	3P%	FTM	FTA	FT%	ORB	DRB	TRB	AST	PF	DQ	STL	BLK	TO	MPG	PPG	RPG	APG	PCM
38-39	Sheboygan-N	22	....	....	43	15	....	....	....	....	....	13	....	....	....	....	....	....	....	....	....	....	....	2.0	....	....	....	....
39-40	Sheboygan-N	5	....	....	2	0	....	....	....	....	....	2	....	....	....	....	....	....	....	....	....	....	....	0.4	....	....	....	....
NBL Season Totals		27	....	....	45	15	....	....	....	....	....	15	....	....	....	....	....	....	....	....	....	....	....	1.7	....	....	....	....

• POSEY, James
James Mikley Mantell Posey

Born: Jan. 13, 1977. Cleveland, OH, United States.   Height: 6'8".   Weight: 215 lbs.   Drafted: 1999   College: Xavier

YEAR	TEAM	GP	GS	MIN	PTS	FGM	FGA	FG%	3PM	3PA	3P%	FTM	FTA	FT%	ORB	DRB	TRB	AST	PF	DQ	STL	BLK	TO	MPG	PPG	RPG	APG	PCM
99-00	Denver	81	77	2052	662	230	536	.429	82	220	.373	120	150	.800	85	232	317	146	207	1	98	33	95	25.3	8.2	3.9	1.8	.369
00-01	Denver	82	82	2255	666	243	590	.412	65	217	.300	115	141	.816	125	306	431	163	226	2	93	40	102	27.5	8.1	5.3	2.0	.371
01-02	Denver	73	63	2238	782	277	736	.376	67	237	.283	161	203	.793	109	320	429	180	224	3	114	39	127	30.7	10.7	5.9	2.5	.382
02-03	Denver	25	24	872	352	121	324	.373	24	88	.273	86	102	.843	38	107	145	82	67	1	29	6	66	34.9	14.1	5.8	3.1	.368
02-03	Houston	58	47	1646	541	188	428	.439	46	141	.326	119	144	.826	52	229	281	106	134	0	77	9	78	28.4	9.3	4.8	1.8	.382
NBA Season Totals		319	293	9063	3003	1059	2614	.405	284	903	.315	601	740	.812	409	1194	1603	673	854	7	411	127	468	28.4	9.4	5.0	2.1	....

• POSSNER, Lou
Louis Possner

Born: Aug. 11, 1917. Died: Mar.6, 1990.   Height: 6'3".   Weight: 180 lbs.   Drafted: —   College: DePaul

YEAR	TEAM	GP	GS	MIN	PTS	FGM	FGA	FG%	3PM	3PA	3P%	FTM	FTA	FT%	ORB	DRB	TRB	AST	PF	DQ	STL	BLK	TO	MPG	PPG	RPG	APG	PCM
41-42	Chicago-N	4	....	....	5	2	....	....	....	....	....	1	....	....	....	....	....	....	....	....	....	....	....	1.3	....	....	....	....
46-47	Syracuse-N	3	....	....	9	4	....	....	....	....	....	1	2	.500	....	....	....	....	....	....	....	....	....	3.0	....	....	....	....
NBL Season Totals		7	....	....	14	6	....	....	....	....	....	2	2	....	....	....	....	....	....	....	....	....	....	2.0	....	....	....	....

• POSTELL, Lavor
Andre Lavor Postell

Born: Feb. 26, 1978. Albany, GA, United States.   Height: 6'5".   Weight: 215 lbs.   Drafted: 2000   College: St. John's (NY)

YEAR	TEAM	GP	GS	MIN	PTS	FGM	FGA	FG%	3PM	3PA	3P%	FTM	FTA	FT%	ORB	DRB	TRB	AST	PF	DQ	STL	BLK	TO	MPG	PPG	RPG	APG	PCM
00-01	New York	26	0	169	59	17	54	.315	3	11	.273	22	27	.815	8	17	25	5	12	0	4	2	17	6.5	2.3	1.0	0.2	.214
01-02	New York	23	0	179	93	28	84	.333	6	26	.231	31	41	.756	2	14	16	5	7	0	6	0	11	7.8	4.0	0.7	0.2	.279
02-03	New York	12	0	98	43	14	38	.368	2	7	.286	13	15	.867	1	3	4	3	9	0	2	0	7	8.2	3.6	0.3	0.3	.190
NBA Season Totals		61	0	446	195	59	176	.335	11	44	.250	66	83	.795	11	34	45	13	28	0	12	2	35	7.3	3.2	0.7	0.2	....

YEAR	TEAM	GP	GS	MIN	PTS	FGM	FGA	FG%	3PM	3PA	3P%	FTM	FTA	FT%	ORB	DRB	TRB	AST	PF	DQ	STL	BLK	TO	MPG	PPG	RPG	APG	PCM

• POSTLEY, John

John Postley

Born: May 30, 1940. Died: July 1970.   Height: 6'5".   Weight: 220 lbs.   Drafted: —   College: Bethune-Cookman

YEAR	TEAM	GP	GS	MIN	PTS	FGM	FGA	FG%	3PM	3PA	3P%	FTM	FTA	FT%	ORB	DRB	TRB	AST	PF	DQ	STL	BLK	TO	MPG	PPG	RPG	APG	PCM
67-68	Pittsburgh-A	1	....	6	2	1	3	.333	0	0	.000	0	0	.000	....	....	6	1	1	0	....	....	1	6.0	2.0	6.0	1.0	1.013
ABA Season Totals		1	....	6	2	1	3	.333	0	0	.000	0	0	.000	....	....	6	1	1	0	....	....	1	6.0	2.0	6.0	1.0	....

• POTAPENKO, Vitaly

Vitaly Nikolaevich Potapenko

Born: Mar. 21, 1975. Kiev, Ukraine.   Height: 6'10".   Weight: 280 lbs.   Drafted: 1996   College: Wright State

YEAR	TEAM	GP	GS	MIN	PTS	FGM	FGA	FG%	3PM	3PA	3P%	FTM	FTA	FT%	ORB	DRB	TRB	AST	PF	DQ	STL	BLK	TO	MPG	PPG	RPG	APG	PCM
96-97	Cleveland	80	3	1238	465	186	423	.440	1	2	.500	92	125	.736	105	112	217	40	216	3	26	34	112	15.5	5.8	2.7	0.5	.262
97-98	Cleveland	80	0	1412	570	234	488	.480	0	1	.000	102	144	.708	110	203	313	57	198	2	27	28	128	17.7	7.1	3.9	0.7	.361
98-99	Cleveland	17	12	467	143	55	126	.437	0	1	.000	33	49	.673	23	71	94	16	53	2	11	16	28	27.5	8.4	5.5	0.9	.320
98-99	Boston	33	32	927	356	149	286	.521	0	0	.000	58	106	.547	91	147	238	59	116	2	24	20	72	28.1	10.8	7.2	1.8	.446
99-00	Boston	79	72	1797	723	307	615	.499	0	1	.000	109	160	.681	182	317	499	77	239	4	41	29	145	22.7	9.2	6.3	1.0	.434
00-01	Boston	82	7	1901	611	248	521	.476	0	0	.000	115	158	.728	206	289	495	64	228	2	52	23	105	23.2	7.5	6.0	0.8	.385
01-02	Boston	79	9	1343	363	137	301	.455	0	0	.000	89	120	.742	167	180	347	30	174	0	37	18	63	17.0	4.6	4.4	0.4	.344
02-03	Seattle	26	2	403	104	41	93	.441	0	0	.000	22	29	.759	25	64	89	4	46	0	9	8	25	15.5	4.0	3.4	0.2	.275
NBA Season Totals		476	137	9488	3335	1357	2853	.476	1	5	.200	620	891	.696	909	1383	2292	347	1270	15	227	176	678	19.9	7.0	4.8	0.7	....
97-98	Cleveland	4	0	70	17	6	15	.400	0	0	.000	5	10	.500	3	8	11	3	8	0	2	0	6	17.5	4.3	2.8	0.8	.178
NBA Playoff Totals		4	0	70	17	6	15	.400	0	0	.000	5	10	.500	3	8	11	3	8	0	2	0	6	17.5	4.3	2.8	0.8	....

• POWELL, Cincy

Cincinnatus Powell

Born: Feb. 25, 1942. Baton Rouge, LA, United States.   Height: 6'7".   Weight: 220 lbs.   Drafted: 1965   College: Portland

YEAR	TEAM	GP	GS	MIN	PTS	FGM	FGA	FG%	3PM	3PA	3P%	FTM	FTA	FT%	ORB	DRB	TRB	AST	PF	DQ	STL	BLK	TO	MPG	PPG	RPG	APG	PCM
67-68	Dallas-A	77	....	2524	1410	533	1089	.489	1	4	.250	343	496	.692	....	....	694	106	254	7	....	....	190	32.8	18.3	9.0	1.4	.586
68-69	Dallas-A	75	....	2573	1454	555	1179	.471	2	7	.286	342	470	.728	203	468	671	173	275	5	....	....	212	34.3	19.4	8.9	2.3	.590
69-70	Dallas-A	76	....	2624	1528	562	1200	.468	2	12	.167	402	519	.775	193	489	682	192	250	6	....	....	251	34.5	20.1	9.0	2.5	.620
70-71	Kentucky-A	81	....	2933	1462	578	1173	.493	4	16	.250	302	398	.759	311	579	890	255	323	8	....	....	235	36.2	18.0	11.0	3.1	.626
71-72	Kentucky-A	65	....	2288	1049	430	907	.474	4	13	.308	185	256	.723	158	342	500	237	219	3	....	....	178	35.2	16.1	7.7	3.6	.528
72-73	Utah-A	83	....	1985	1016	423	853	.496	3	13	.231	167	240	.696	135	285	420	137	249	7	....	....	137	23.9	12.2	5.1	1.7	.510
73-74	Virginia-A	82	....	2485	1275	528	1167	.452	10	31	.323	209	296	.706	171	348	519	136	270	....	46	32	186	30.3	15.5	6.3	1.7	.473
74-75	Virginia-A	60	....	1224	552	214	530	.404	5	17	.294	119	180	.661	74	132	206	94	138	....	27	8	91	20.4	9.2	3.4	1.6	.384
ABA Season Totals		599	....	18636	9746	3823	8098	.472	31	113	.274	2069	2855	.725	1245	2643	4582	1330	1978	36	73	40	1480	31.1	16.3	7.6	2.2	....
67-68	Dallas-A	8	....	334	187	63	144	.438	0	2	.000	61	73	.836	....	....	87	17	30	0	....	....	28	41.8	23.4	10.9	2.1	.582
68-69	Dallas-A	7	....	227	140	51	114	.447	1	1	1.000	37	43	.860	16	52	68	10	21	0	....	....	22	32.4	20.0	9.7	1.4	.635
68-69	Dallas-A	6	....	219	131	51	108	.472	0	3	.000	29	41	.707	24	57	81	29	....	0	....	....	26	36.5	21.8	13.5	4.8	....
70-71	Kentucky-A	19	....	702	350	138	382	.361	3	7	.429	71	102	.696	77	171	248	47	83	2	....	....	51	36.9	18.4	13.1	2.5	.518
71-72	Kentucky-A	6	....	169	71	28	52	.538	0	1	.000	15	19	.789	....	....	24	9	17	....	....	....	13	28.2	11.8	4.0	1.5	.425
72-73	Utah-A	10	....	192	92	37	89	.416	0	1	.000	18	29	.621	12	25	37	6	30	1	....	....	17	19.2	9.2	3.7	0.6	.347
73-74	Virginia-A	5	....	176	100	44	100	.440	1	3	.333	11	14	.786	18	30	48	5	21	....	3	1	17	35.2	20.0	9.6	1.0	.503
ABA Playoff Totals		61	....	2019	1071	412	989	.417	5	18	.278	242	321	.754	147	335	593	123	202	3	3	1	174	33.1	17.6	9.7	2.0	....

• POWELL, Robert

Robert (Longie) Powell

Born: —. Gary, IN, United States.   Height: 6'4".   Weight: —   Drafted: —   College: —

YEAR	TEAM	GP	GS	MIN	PTS	FGM	FGA	FG%	3PM	3PA	3P%	FTM	FTA	FT%	ORB	DRB	TRB	AST	PF	DQ	STL	BLK	TO	MPG	PPG	RPG	APG	PCM
48-49	Dayton-N	6	....	....	30	11	....	....	....	....	....	8	13	.615	....	....	....	....	....	....	....	....	....	5.0	....	....	....
NBL Season Totals		6	....	....	30	11	....	....	....	....	....	8	13		....	....	....	....	....	....	....	....	....	5.0	....	....	....

• PRADD, Marl

Marlbert Pradd

Born: Nov. 17, 1944. Chicago, IL, United States.   Height: 6'3".   Weight: 170 lbs.   Drafted: 1965   College: Dillard

YEAR	TEAM	GP	GS	MIN	PTS	FGM	FGA	FG%	3PM	3PA	3P%	FTM	FTA	FT%	ORB	DRB	TRB	AST	PF	DQ	STL	BLK	TO	MPG	PPG	RPG	APG	PCM
67-68	New Orleans-A	29	....	125	74	27	60	.450	0	0	.000	20	27	.741	....	....	26	3	22	0	....	....	18	4.3	2.6	0.9	0.1	.477
68-69	New Orleans-A	50	....	323	258	81	186	.435	3	13	.231	93	119	.782	34	16	50	23	60	0	....	....	34	6.5	5.2	1.0	0.5	.620
ABA Season Totals		79	....	448	332	108	246	.439	3	13	.231	113	146	.774	34	16	76	26	82	0	....	....	52	5.7	4.2	1.0	0.3	....
67-68	New Orleans-A	6	....	18	12	3	9	.333	0	0	.000	6	11	.545	....	....	5	0	3	0	....	....	3	3.0	2.0	0.8	0.0	.436
68-69	New Orleans-A	7	....	39	28	10	22	.455	4	6	.667	4	7	.571	....	....	4	1	7	0	....	....	4	5.6	4.0	0.6	0.1	.461
ABA Playoff Totals		13	....	57	40	13	31	.419	4	6	.667	10	18	.556	....	....	9	1	10	0	....	....	7	4.4	3.1	0.7	0.1	....

• PRASSE, Erv

Erwin Prasse

Born: 1917.   Height: 6'2".   Weight: 190 lbs.   Drafted: —   College: Iowa

YEAR	TEAM	GP	GS	MIN	PTS	FGM	FGA	FG%	3PM	3PA	3P%	FTM	FTA	FT%	ORB	DRB	TRB	AST	PF	DQ	STL	BLK	TO	MPG	PPG	RPG	APG	PCM
40-41	Oshkosh-N	24	....	....	77	25	....	....	....	....	....	27			....	....	....	....	....	....	....	....	....	3.2	....	....	....
41-42	Oshkosh-N	5	....	....	7	3	....	....	....	....	....	1			....	....	....	....	....	....	....	....	....	1.4	....	....	....
45-46	Oshkosh-N	9	....	....	9	2	....	....	....	....	....	5			....	....	....	....	....	....	....	....	....	1.0	....	....	....
NBL Season Totals		38	....	....	93	30	....	....	....	....	....	33			....	....	....	....	....	....	....	....	....	2.4	....	....	....
40-41	Oshkosh-N	5	....	....	10	2	....	....	....	....	....	6			....	....	....	....	....	....	....	....	....	2.0	....	....	....
41-42	Oshkosh-N	5	....	....	13	4	....	....	....	....	....	5			....	....	....	....	....	....	....	....	....	2.6	....	....	....
45-46	Oshkosh-N	5	....	....	5	1	....	....	....	....	....	3	4	.750	....	....	....	....	....	....	....	....	....	1.0	....	....	....
NBL Playoff Totals		15	....	....	28	7	....	....	....	....	....	14	4		....	....	....	....	....	....	....	....	....	1.9	....	....	....

YEAR	TEAM	GP	GS	MIN	PTS	FGM	FGA	FG%	3PM	3PA	3P%	FTM	FTA	FT%	ORB	DRB	TRB	AST	PF	DQ	STL	BLK	TO	MPG	PPG	RPG	APG	PCM

• PRATT, Mike
Michael P. Pratt

Born: Aug. 4, 1948. Dayton, OH, United States.   Height: 6'4".   Weight: 195 lbs.   Drafted: —   College: Kentucky

YEAR	TEAM	GP	GS	MIN	PTS	FGM	FGA	FG%	3PM	3PA	3P%	FTM	FTA	FT%	ORB	DRB	TRB	AST	PF	DQ	STL	BLK	TO	MPG	PPG	RPG	APG	PCM
70-71	Kentucky-A	78	....	1213	440	173	416	.416	3	11	.273	91	121	.752	91	134	225	188	135	0	....	....	124	15.6	5.6	2.9	2.4	.482
71-72	Kentucky-A	65	....	889	366	133	301	.442	16	40	.400	84	98	.857	67	91	158	98	81	1	....	....	81	13.7	5.6	2.4	1.5	.478
ABA Season Totals		143	....	2102	806	306	717	.427	19	51	.373	175	219	.799	158	225	383	286	216	1	....	....	205	14.7	5.6	2.7	2.0	....
70-71	Kentucky-A	19	....	318	131	47	124	.379	0	2	.000	37	47	.787	37	29	66	53	30	0	....	....	29	16.7	6.9	3.5	2.8	.534
71-72	Kentucky-A	6	....	170	72	33	63	.524	1	4	.250	5	5	1.000	....	....	17	15	23	....	....	....	11	28.3	12.0	2.8	2.5	.396
ABA Playoff Totals		25	....	488	203	80	187	.428	1	6	.167	42	52	.808	37	29	83	68	53	0	....	....	40	19.5	8.1	3.3	2.7	....

• PREBOSKI, Pete
Pete Preboski

Born: 1914.   Height: 6'1".   Weight: 195 lbs.   Drafted: —   College: Wisconsin

YEAR	TEAM	GP	GS	MIN	PTS	FGM	FGA	FG%	3PM	3PA	3P%	FTM	FTA	FT%	ORB	DRB	TRB	AST	PF	DQ	STL	BLK	TO	MPG	PPG	RPG	APG	PCM
37-38	Oshkosh-N	11	....	....	63	25	....	....	....	....	....	13	....	....	....	....	....	....	....	....	....	....	....	....	5.7	....	....	....
38-39	Oshkosh-N	27	....	....	188	76	....	....	....	....	....	36	....	....	....	....	....	....	....	....	....	....	....	....	7.0	....	....	....
NBL Season Totals		38	....	....	251	101	....	....	....	....	....	49	....	....	....	....	....	....	....	....	....	....	....	....	6.6	....	....	....
37-38	Oshkosh-N	5	....	....	31	10	....	....	....	....	....	11	....	....	....	....	....	....	....	....	....	....	....	....	6.2	....	....	....
38-39	Oshkosh-N	5	....	....	19	4	....	....	....	....	....	11	....	....	....	....	....	....	....	....	....	....	....	....	3.8	....	....	....
NBL Playoff Totals		10	....	....	50	14	....	....	....	....	....	22	....	....	....	....	....	....	....	....	....	....	....	....	5.0	....	....	....

• PRESSEY, Paul
Paul Matthew Pressey

Born: Dec. 24, 1958. Richmond, VA, United States.   Height: 6'5".   Weight: 185 lbs.   Drafted: 1982   College: Tulsa

YEAR	TEAM	GP	GS	MIN	PTS	FGM	FGA	FG%	3PM	3PA	3P%	FTM	FTA	FT%	ORB	DRB	TRB	AST	PF	DQ	STL	BLK	TO	MPG	PPG	RPG	APG	PCM
82-83	Milwaukee	79	18	1528	532	213	466	.457	1	9	.111	105	176	.597	83	198	281	207	174	2	99	47	166	19.3	6.7	3.6	2.6	.429
83-84	Milwaukee	81	18	1730	674	276	528	.523	2	9	.222	120	200	.600	102	180	282	252	241	6	86	50	154	21.4	8.3	3.5	3.1	.466
84-85	Milwaukee	80	80	2876	1284	480	928	.517	7	20	.350	317	418	.758	149	280	429	543	258	4	129	56	248	36.0	16.1	5.4	6.8	.563
85-86	Milwaukee	80	80	2704	1146	411	843	.488	8	44	.182	316	392	.806	127	272	399	623	247	4	168	71	240	33.8	14.3	5.0	7.8	.603
86-87	Milwaukee	61	60	2057	846	294	616	.477	16	55	.291	242	328	.738	98	198	296	441	213	4	110	47	183	33.7	13.9	4.9	7.2	.549
87-88	Milwaukee	75	75	2484	983	345	702	.491	8	39	.205	285	357	.798	130	245	375	523	233	6	112	34	195	33.1	13.1	5.0	7.0	.552
88-89	Milwaukee	67	62	2170	813	307	648	.474	12	55	.218	187	241	.776	73	189	262	439	221	2	119	44	181	32.4	12.1	3.9	6.6	.491
89-90	Milwaukee	57	2	1400	628	239	506	.472	6	43	.140	144	190	.758	59	113	172	244	149	3	71	23	108	24.6	11.0	3.0	4.3	.496
90-91	San Antonio	70	18	1683	528	201	426	.472	16	57	.281	110	133	.827	50	126	176	271	174	1	63	32	133	24.0	7.5	2.5	3.9	.383
91-92	San Antonio	56	7	759	151	60	161	.373	3	21	.143	28	41	.683	22	73	95	142	86	0	29	19	62	13.6	2.7	1.7	2.5	.314
92-93	Golden State	18	0	268	79	29	66	.439	0	4	.000	21	27	.778	8	23	31	30	36	0	11	5	23	14.9	4.4	1.7	1.7	.296
NBA Season Totals		724	420	19659	7664	2855	5890	.485	79	356	.222	1875	2503	.749	901	1897	2798	3715	2032	32	997	428	1693	27.2	10.6	3.9	5.1	....
82-83	Milwaukee	9	6	150	46	19	47	.404	0	1	.000	8	20	.400	14	19	33	14	23	0	9	6	18	16.7	5.1	3.7	1.6	.316
83-84	Milwaukee	16	1	351	142	52	100	.520	0	3	.000	38	56	.679	17	42	59	50	53	1	22	9	38	21.9	8.9	3.7	3.1	.474
84-85	Milwaukee	8	8	296	122	45	88	.511	1	3	.333	31	38	.816	15	33	48	61	27	1	18	5	32	37.0	15.3	6.0	7.6	.566
85-86	Milwaukee	14	14	530	225	76	157	.484	6	18	.333	67	88	.761	19	41	60	110	48	0	18	13	50	37.9	16.1	4.3	7.9	.516
86-87	Milwaukee	12	12	465	171	68	146	.466	1	8	.125	34	46	.739	28	34	62	103	51	3	28	8	35	38.8	14.3	5.2	8.6	.511
87-88	Milwaukee	5	5	178	70	23	50	.460	1	3	.333	23	30	.767	6	13	19	33	21	0	4	3	16	35.6	14.0	3.8	6.6	.429
89-90	Milwaukee	4	2	129	59	19	44	.432	0	3	.000	21	26	.808	8	13	21	30	14	0	6	1	7	32.3	14.8	5.3	7.5	.607
90-91	San Antonio	4	0	124	33	13	32	.406	1	4	.250	6	9	.667	5	6	11	16	15	0	8	3	6	31.0	8.3	2.8	4.0	.314
91-92	San Antonio	3	2	46	13	6	18	.333	1	2	.500	0	0	.000	1	2	3	3	9	1	3	1	5	15.3	4.3	1.0	1.0	.060
NBA Playoff Totals		75	50	2269	881	321	682	.471	11	45	.244	228	313	.728	113	203	316	420	261	6	116	49	207	30.3	11.7	4.2	5.6	....

• PRESSLEY, Dominic
Dominic Ivan Pressley

Born: May 30, 1964. Washington, DC, United States.   Height: 6'2".   Weight: 170 lbs.   Drafted: 1986   College: Boston College

YEAR	TEAM	GP	GS	MIN	PTS	FGM	FGA	FG%	3PM	3PA	3P%	FTM	FTA	FT%	ORB	DRB	TRB	AST	PF	DQ	STL	BLK	TO	MPG	PPG	RPG	APG	PCM
88-89	Washington	10	0	107	21	8	25	.320	0	0	.000	5	9	.556	3	11	14	22	9	0	4	0	11	10.7	2.1	1.4	2.2	.273
88-89	Chicago	3	0	17	2	1	6	.167	0	2	.000	0	0	.000	0	1	1	4	2	0	0	0	0	5.7	0.7	0.3	1.3	.096
NBA Season Totals		13	0	124	23	9	31	.290	0	2	.000	5	9	.556	3	12	15	26	11	0	4	0	11	9.5	1.8	1.2	2.0	....

• PRESSLEY, Harold
Harold Pressley

Born: July 14, 1963. Bronx, NY, United States.   Height: 6'7".   Weight: 210 lbs.   Drafted: 1986   College: Villanova

YEAR	TEAM	GP	GS	MIN	PTS	FGM	FGA	FG%	3PM	3PA	3P%	FTM	FTA	FT%	ORB	DRB	TRB	AST	PF	DQ	STL	BLK	TO	MPG	PPG	RPG	APG	PCM
86-87	Sacramento	67	23	913	310	134	317	.423	7	28	.250	35	48	.729	68	108	176	120	96	1	40	21	60	13.6	4.6	2.6	1.8	.418
87-88	Sacramento	80	49	2029	775	318	702	.453	36	110	.327	103	130	.792	139	230	369	185	211	4	84	55	136	25.4	9.7	4.6	2.3	.419
88-89	Sacramento	80	36	2257	981	383	873	.439	119	295	.403	96	123	.780	216	269	485	174	215	1	93	76	128	28.2	12.3	6.1	2.2	.482
89-90	Sacramento	72	10	1603	636	240	566	.424	46	148	.311	110	141	.780	94	215	309	149	148	0	58	36	86	22.3	8.8	4.3	2.1	.438
NBA Season Totals		299	118	6802	2702	1075	2458	.437	208	581	.358	344	442	.778	517	822	1339	628	670	6	275	188	410	22.7	9.0	4.5	2.1	....

• PRESSLEY, Louis
Louis (Babe) Pressley

Born: 1916.   Height: 6'2".   Weight: 195 lbs.   Drafted: —   College: Xavier (LA)

YEAR	TEAM	GP	GS	MIN	PTS	FGM	FGA	FG%	3PM	3PA	3P%	FTM	FTA	FT%	ORB	DRB	TRB	AST	PF	DQ	STL	BLK	TO	MPG	PPG	RPG	APG	PCM
42-43	Chicago-N	3	....	....	12	4	....	....	....	....	....	4	....	....	....	....	....	....	....	....	....	....	....	....	4.0	....	....	....
NBL Playoff Totals		3	....	....	12	4	....	....	....	....	....	4	....	....	....	....	....	....	....	....	....	....	....	....	4.0	....	....	....

YEAR	TEAM	GP	GS	MIN	PTS	FGM	FGA	FG%	3PM	3PA	3P%	FTM	FTA	FT%	ORB	DRB	TRB	AST	PF	DQ	STL	BLK	TO	MPG	PPG	RPG	APG	PCM

• PREVIS, Stephen
Stephen Richard Previs

Born: Feb. 9, 1950. Bethel Park, PA, United States.   Height: 6'3".   Weight: 183 lbs.   Drafted: 1972   College: North Carolina

YEAR	TEAM	GP	GS	MIN	PTS	FGM	FGA	FG%	3PM	3PA	3P%	FTM	FTA	FT%	ORB	DRB	TRB	AST	PF	DQ	STL	BLK	TO	MPG	PPG	RPG	APG	PCM
72-73	Carolina-A	30	....	147	55	23	60	.383	1	8	.125	8	15	.533	6	8	14	24	26	0	....	....	13	4.9	1.8	0.5	0.8	.312
ABA Season Totals		30	....	147	55	23	60	.383	1	8	.125	8	15	.533	6	8	14	24	26	0	....	....	13	4.9	1.8	0.5	0.8	....
72-73	Carolina-A	2	....	11	3	1	7	.143	1	2	.500	0	0	.000	1	2	3	3	2	0	....	....	4	5.5	1.5	1.5	1.5	.246
ABA Playoff Totals		2	....	11	3	1	7	.143	1	2	.500	0	0	.000	1	2	3	3	2	0	....	....	4	5.5	1.5	1.5	1.5	....

• PRICE, Al
Al Price

Born: 1917.   Height: 6'   Weight: 180 lbs.   Drafted: —   College: Toledo

YEAR	TEAM	GP	GS	MIN	PTS	FGM	FGA	FG%	3PM	3PA	3P%	FTM	FTA	FT%	ORB	DRB	TRB	AST	PF	DQ	STL	BLK	TO	MPG	PPG	RPG	APG	PCM
42-43	Toledo-N	3	....	....	8	3	....	....	....	....	....	2	....	....	....	....	....	....	....	....	....	....	....	....	2.7	....	....	....
NBL Season Totals		3	....	....	8	3	....	....	....	....	....	2	....	....	....	....	....	....	....	....	....	....	....	....	2.7	....	....	....

• PRICE, Bernie
Bernard (Bernie) Price

Born: 1915.   Height: 6'3".   Weight: 180 lbs.   Drafted: —   College: none

YEAR	TEAM	GP	GS	MIN	PTS	FGM	FGA	FG%	3PM	3PA	3P%	FTM	FTA	FT%	ORB	DRB	TRB	AST	PF	DQ	STL	BLK	TO	MPG	PPG	RPG	APG	PCM
42-43	Chicago-N	22	....	....	197	60	....	....	....	....	....	**77**	....	....	....	....	....	....	....	....	....	....	....	....	9.0	....	....	....
NBL Season Totals		22	....	....	197	60	....	....	....	....	....	77	....	....	....	....	....	....	....	....	....	....	....	....	9.0	....	....	....
42-43	Chicago-N	3	....	....	23	7	....	....	....	....	....	9	....	....	....	....	....	....	....	....	....	....	....	....	7.7	....	....	....
NBL Playoff Totals		3	....	....	23	7	....	....	....	....	....	9	....	....	....	....	....	....	....	....	....	....	....	....	7.7	....	....	....

• PRICE, Brent
Hartley Brent Price

Born: Dec. 9, 1968. Shawnee, OK, United States.   Height: 6'1".   Weight: 165 lbs.   Drafted: 1992   College: Oklahoma

YEAR	TEAM	GP	GS	MIN	PTS	FGM	FGA	FG%	3PM	3PA	3P%	FTM	FTA	FT%	ORB	DRB	TRB	AST	PF	DQ	STL	BLK	TO	MPG	PPG	RPG	APG	PCM
92-93	Washington	68	9	859	262	100	279	.358	8	48	.167	54	68	.794	28	75	103	154	90	0	56	3	88	12.6	3.9	1.5	2.3	.326
93-94	Washington	65	13	1035	400	141	326	.433	50	150	.333	68	87	.782	31	59	90	213	114	1	55	2	117	15.9	6.2	1.4	3.3	.413
95-96	Washington	81	50	2042	810	252	534	.472	139	301	.462	167	191	.874	38	190	228	416	184	3	78	4	154	25.2	10.0	2.8	5.1	.507
96-97	Houston	25	0	390	126	44	105	.419	17	53	.321	21	21	1.000	10	19	29	65	34	0	17	0	33	15.6	5.0	1.2	2.6	.346
97-98	Houston	72	2	1332	406	128	310	.413	73	187	.390	77	98	.786	37	70	107	192	163	3	52	4	108	18.5	5.6	1.5	2.7	.311
98-99	Houston	40	6	806	292	100	207	.483	46	112	.411	46	61	.754	18	60	78	113	90	0	33	1	65	20.2	7.3	2.0	2.8	.394
99-00	Vancouver	41	0	424	141	41	119	.345	25	68	.368	34	39	.872	8	29	37	69	63	0	17	1	47	10.3	3.4	0.9	1.7	.288
00-01	Vancouver	6	0	30	13	3	11	.273	1	4	.250	6	7	.857	1	3	4	5	8	0	2	0	4	5.0	2.2	0.7	0.8	.303
01-02	Sacramento	20	0	89	31	9	27	.333	4	15	.267	9	13	.692	4	4	8	9	13	0	3	1	10	4.5	1.6	0.4	0.5	.210
NBA Season Totals		418	80	7007	2481	818	1918	.426	363	938	.387	482	585	.824	175	509	684	1236	759	7	313	16	626	16.8	5.9	1.6	3.0	....
97-98	Houston	5	0	75	19	6	15	.400	5	13	.385	2	3	.667	1	8	9	6	12	1	4	0	6	15.0	3.8	1.8	1.2	.236
98-99	Houston	4	0	98	33	11	24	.458	5	14	.357	6	6	1.000	3	5	8	14	5	0	4	1	6	24.5	8.3	2.0	3.5	.418
NBA Playoff Totals		9	0	173	52	17	39	.436	10	27	.370	8	9	.889	4	13	17	20	17	1	8	1	12	19.2	5.8	1.9	2.2	....

• PRICE, Jim
James E. Price

Born: Nov. 27, 1949. Russellville, KY, United States.   Height: 6'3".   Weight: 195 lbs.   Drafted: 1972   College: Louisville

YEAR	TEAM	GP	GS	MIN	PTS	FGM	FGA	FG%	3PM	3PA	3P%	FTM	FTA	FT%	ORB	DRB	TRB	AST	PF	DQ	STL	BLK	TO	MPG	PPG	RPG	APG	PCM
72-73	LA Lakers	59	....	828	376	158	359	.440	....	....	....	60	73	.822	....	....	115	97	119	1	....	....	....	14.0	6.4	1.9	1.6	.430
73-74	LA Lakers	82	....	2628	1263	538	1197	.449	....	....	....	187	234	.799	120	258	378	369	229	2	157	29	....	32.0	15.4	4.6	4.5	.506
74-75	LA Lakers	9	....	339	191	75	167	.449	....	....	....	41	45	.911	17	26	43	63	36	1	21	3	....	37.7	21.2	4.8	7.0	.603
74-75	Milwaukee	41	....	1531	612	242	550	.440	....	....	....	128	149	.859	45	110	155	223	146	0	90	21	....	37.3	14.9	3.8	5.4	.435
75-76	Milwaukee	80	....	2525	937	398	958	.415	....	....	....	141	166	.849	74	187	261	395	264	3	148	32	....	31.6	11.7	3.3	4.9	.399
76-77	Milwaukee	6	....	111	49	21	41	.512	....	....	....	7	9	.778	4	9	13	15	14	0	7	1	....	18.5	8.2	2.2	2.5	.478
76-77	Buffalo	20	....	333	105	44	104	.423	....	....	....	17	20	.850	5	29	34	38	52	0	25	5	....	16.7	5.3	1.7	1.9	.306
76-77	Denver	55	....	1384	435	188	422	.445	....	....	....	59	74	.797	41	143	184	208	181	3	96	14	....	25.2	7.9	3.3	3.8	.393
77-78	Denver	49	....	1090	333	141	293	.481	....	....	....	51	66	.773	30	129	159	158	118	0	69	4	103	22.2	6.8	3.2	3.2	.397
77-78	Detroit	34	....	839	390	153	363	.421	....	....	....	84	103	.816	27	74	101	102	82	0	45	5	75	24.7	11.5	3.0	3.0	.409
78-79	LA Lakers	75	....	1207	397	171	344	.497	....	....	....	55	79	.696	26	97	123	218	128	0	66	12	98	16.1	5.3	1.6	2.9	.419
NBA Season Totals		510	....	12815	5088	2129	4798	.444	....	....	....	830	1018	.815	389	1062	1566	1886	1369	10	724	126	276	25.1	10.0	3.1	3.7	....
72-73	LA Lakers	3	....	16	6	3	11	.273	....	....	....	0	0	.000	....	....	4	2	2	0	....	....	....	5.3	2.0	1.3	0.7	.250
73-74	LA Lakers	5	....	161	59	25	66	.379	....	....	....	9	13	.692	8	11	19	13	21	1	7	0	....	32.2	11.8	3.8	2.6	.277
75-76	Milwaukee	1	....	19	10	3	8	.375	....	....	....	4	7	.571	0	0	0	4	1	0	1	0	....	19.0	10.0	0.0	4.0	.451
76-77	Denver	6	....	158	43	19	53	.358	....	....	....	5	8	.625	6	18	24	25	18	0	12	1	....	26.3	7.2	4.0	4.2	.340
78-79	LA Lakers	8	....	128	20	9	30	.300	....	....	....	2	4	.500	1	7	8	18	19	0	5	0	8	16.0	2.5	1.0	2.3	.125
NBA Playoff Totals		23	....	482	138	59	168	.351	....	....	....	20	32	.625	15	36	55	62	61	1	25	1	8	21.0	6.0	2.4	2.7	....

• PRICE, Mark
William Mark Price

Born: Feb. 15, 1964. Bartlesville, OK, United States.   Height: 6'   Weight: 170 lbs.   Drafted: 1986   College: Georgia Tech

YEAR	TEAM	GP	GS	MIN	PTS	FGM	FGA	FG%	3PM	3PA	3P%	FTM	FTA	FT%	ORB	DRB	TRB	AST	PF	DQ	STL	BLK	TO	MPG	PPG	RPG	APG	PCM
86-87	Cleveland	67	0	1217	464	173	424	.408	23	70	.329	95	114	.833	33	84	117	202	75	1	43	4	107	18.2	6.9	1.7	3.0	.374
87-88	Cleveland	80	79	2626	1279	493	974	.506	72	148	.486	221	252	.877	54	126	180	480	119	1	99	12	184	32.8	16.0	2.3	6.0	.523
88-89	Cleveland	75	74	2728	1414	529	1006	.526	93	211	.441	263	292	.901	48	178	226	631	98	0	115	7	210	36.4	18.9	3.0	8.4	.629
89-90	Cleveland	73	73	2706	1430	489	1066	.459	152	374	.406	300	338	.888	66	185	251	666	89	0	114	5	212	37.1	19.6	3.4	9.1	.623
90-91	Cleveland	16	16	571	271	97	195	.497	18	53	.340	59	62	.952	8	37	45	166	23	0	42	2	56	35.7	16.9	2.8	10.4	.657
91-92	Cleveland	72	72	2138	1247	438	897	.488	101	261	.387	270	285	**.947**	38	135	173	535	113	0	94	12	158	29.7	17.3	2.4	7.4	.677
92-93	Cleveland	75	74	2380	1365	477	986	.484	122	293	.416	289	305	**.948**	37	164	201	597	105	0	89	11	195	31.7	18.2	2.7	8.0	.659
93-94	Cleveland	76	73	2386	1316	480	1005	.478	118	297	.397	238	268	.888	39	189	228	589	93	0	103	11	190	31.4	17.3	3.0	7.8	.652
94-95	Cleveland	48	34	1375	757	253	612	.413	103	253	.407	148	162	.914	25	87	112	335	50	0	35	4	144	28.6	15.8	2.3	7.0	.547

YEAR	TEAM	GP	GS	MIN	PTS	FGM	FGA	FG%	3PM	3PA	3P%	FTM	FTA	FT%	ORB	DRB	TRB	AST	PF	DQ	STL	BLK	TO	MPG	PPG	RPG	APG	PCM
95-96	Washington	7	1	127	56	18	60	.300	10	30	.333	10	10	1.000	1	6	7	18	7	0	6	0	10	18.1	8.0	1.0	2.6	.277
96-97	Golden State	70	49	1876	793	263	589	.447	112	283	.396	155	171	**.906**	36	143	179	342	100	0	67	3	161	26.8	11.3	2.6	4.9	.470
97-98	Orlando	63	33	1430	597	229	531	.431	52	155	.335	87	103	.845	24	105	129	297	92	0	53	5	164	22.7	9.5	2.0	4.7	.430
NBA Season Totals		722	578	21560	10989	3939	8345	.472	976	2428	.402	2135	2362	**.904**	409	1439	1848	4858	964	2	860	76	1791	29.9	15.2	2.6	6.7	....
87-88	Cleveland	5	5	205	105	38	67	.567	5	12	.417	24	25	.960	3	15	18	38	11	1	3	0	8	41.0	21.0	3.6	7.6	.610
88-89	Cleveland	4	4	158	64	22	57	.386	6	16	.375	14	15	.933	4	9	13	22	3	0	3	0	19	39.5	16.0	3.3	5.5	.319
89-90	Cleveland	5	5	192	100	32	61	.525	6	17	.353	30	30	1.000	0	14	14	44	9	0	9	1	15	38.4	20.0	2.8	8.8	.645
91-92	Cleveland	17	17	603	327	118	238	.496	25	69	.362	66	73	.904	10	32	42	128	34	0	24	4	56	35.5	19.2	2.5	7.5	.575
92-93	Cleveland	9	9	288	117	43	97	.443	8	26	.308	23	24	.958	1	18	19	55	13	0	15	0	33	32.0	13.0	2.1	6.1	.416
93-94	Cleveland	3	3	102	45	15	43	.349	2	9	.222	13	14	.929	1	5	6	14	6	0	4	0	9	34.0	15.0	2.0	4.7	.316
94-95	Cleveland	4	4	143	60	12	40	.300	4	17	.235	32	33	.970	2	10	12	26	5	0	6	0	18	35.8	15.0	3.0	6.5	.409
NBA Playoff Totals		47	47	1691	818	280	603	.464	56	166	.337	202	214	.944	21	103	124	327	81	1	64	5	158	36.0	17.4	2.6	7.0	....

• PRICE, Mike

Michael Price

Born: Sept. 11, 1948. Russellville, KY, United States.   Height: 6'3".   Weight: 200 lbs.   Drafted: 1970   College: Illinois

YEAR	TEAM	GP	GS	MIN	PTS	FGM	FGA	FG%	3PM	3PA	3P%	FTM	FTA	FT%	ORB	DRB	TRB	AST	PF	DQ	STL	BLK	TO	MPG	PPG	RPG	APG	PCM
70-71	New York	56	....	251	84	30	81	.370	....	....	....	24	34	.706	....	....	29	12	57	0	....	....	....	4.5	1.5	0.5	0.2	.199
71-72	Indiana-A	4	....	25	6	3	9	.333	0	0	.000	0	0	.000	1	4	5	1	4	0	....	....	4	6.3	1.5	1.3	0.3	.179
71-72	New York	6	....	40	19	5	14	.357	....	....	....	9	11	.818	....	....	6	6	10	0	....	....	....	6.7	3.2	1.0	1.0	.451
72-73	Philadelphia	57	....	751	288	125	301	.415	....	....	....	38	47	.809	....	....	117	71	106	0	....	....	....	13.2	5.1	2.1	1.2	.358
NBA Season Totals		119	....	1042	391	160	396	.404	....	....	....	71	92	.772	....	....	152	89	173	0	....	....	....	8.8	3.3	1.3	0.7	
ABA Season Totals		4	....	25	6	3	9	.333	0	0	.000	0	0	.000	1	4	5	1	4	0	....	....	4	6.3	1.5	1.3	0.3	
Career Totals		123	....	1067	397	163	405	.402	0	0	.000	71	92	.772	1	4	157	90	177	0	....	....	4	8.7	3.2	1.3	0.7	
70-71	New York	8	....	26	12	4	11	.364	....	....	....	4	6	.667	....	....	5	5	11	0	....	....	....	3.3	1.5	0.6	0.6	.400
NBA Playoff Totals		8	....	26	12	4	11	.364	....	....	....	4	6	.667	....	....	5	5	11	0	....	....	....	3.3	1.5	0.6	0.6	

• PRICE, Paul

Paul Price

Born: 1914.   Height: —   Weight: —   Drafted: —   College: Notre Dame

YEAR	TEAM	GP	GS	MIN	PTS	FGM	FGA	FG%	3PM	3PA	3P%	FTM	FTA	FT%	ORB	DRB	TRB	AST	PF	DQ	STL	BLK	TO	MPG	PPG	RPG	APG	PCM
40-41	Hammond-N	1	....	....	6	3	....	....	....	....	....	0	....	....	....	....	....	....	....	....	....	....	....	6.0				
NBL Season Totals		1	....	....	6	3	....	....	....	....	....	0	....	....	....	....	....	....	....	....	....	....	....	6.0				

• PRICE, Tony

Anthony Price

Born: Jan. 5, 1957. Bronx, NY, United States.   Height: 6'6".   Weight: 190 lbs.   Drafted: 1979   College: Pennsylvania

YEAR	TEAM	GP	GS	MIN	PTS	FGM	FGA	FG%	3PM	3PA	3P%	FTM	FTA	FT%	ORB	DRB	TRB	AST	PF	DQ	STL	BLK	TO	MPG	PPG	RPG	APG	PCM
80-81	San Diego	5	....	29	4	2	7	.286	0	0	.000	0	0	.000	0	0	0	3	3	0	2	1	2	5.8	0.8	0.0	0.6	.078
NBA Season Totals		5	....	29	4	2	7	.286	0	0	.000	0	0	.000	0	0	0	3	3	0	2	1	2	5.8	0.8	0.0	0.6	

• PRIDDY, Bob

Robert B. Priddy

Born: Mar. 24, 1930.   Height: 6'3".   Weight: 190 lbs.   Drafted: 1952   College: New Mexico A&M

YEAR	TEAM	GP	GS	MIN	PTS	FGM	FGA	FG%	3PM	3PA	3P%	FTM	FTA	FT%	ORB	DRB	TRB	AST	PF	DQ	STL	BLK	TO	MPG	PPG	RPG	APG	PCM
52-53	Baltimore	16	....	149	36	14	38	.368	....	....	....	8	14	.571	....	....	36	7	36	3	....	....	....	9.3	2.3	2.3	0.4	.258
NBA Season Totals		16	....	149	36	14	38	.368	....	....	....	8	14	.571	....	....	36	7	36	3	....	....	....	9.3	2.3	2.3	0.4	
52-53	Baltimore	1	....	1	0	0	0	.000	....	....	....	0	0	.000	....	....	0	0	1	0	....	....	....	1.0	0.0	0.0	0.0	-.362
NBA Playoff Totals		1	....	1	0	0	0	.000	....	....	....	0	0	.000	....	....	0	0	1	0	....	....	....	1.0	0.0	0.0	0.0	

• PRINCE, Tayshaun

Tayshaun Durell Prince

Born: Feb. 18, 1980. Compton, CA, United States.   Height: 6'9".   Weight: 215 lbs.   Drafted: 2002   College: Kentucky

YEAR	TEAM	GP	GS	MIN	PTS	FGM	FGA	FG%	3PM	3PA	3P%	FTM	FTA	FT%	ORB	DRB	TRB	AST	PF	DQ	STL	BLK	TO	MPG	PPG	RPG	APG	PCM
02-03	Detroit	42	5	435	137	53	118	.449	20	47	.426	11	17	.647	5	40	45	24	25	0	10	14	21	10.4	3.3	1.1	0.6	.307
NBA Season Totals		42	5	435	137	53	118	.449	20	47	.426	11	17	.647	5	40	45	24	25	0	10	14	21	10.4	3.3	1.1	0.6	
02-03	Detroit	15	3	382	141	49	115	.426	14	48	.292	29	38	.763	11	46	57	23	20	0	8	13	16	25.5	9.4	3.8	1.5	.391
NBA Playoff Totals		15	3	382	141	49	115	.426	14	48	.292	29	38	.763	11	46	57	23	20	0	8	13	16	25.5	9.4	3.8	1.5	

• PRITCHARD, John

John D. Pritchard

Born: Jan. 23, 1927.   Height: 6'9".   Weight: 220 lbs.   Drafted: 1949   College: Drake

YEAR	TEAM	GP	GS	MIN	PTS	FGM	FGA	FG%	3PM	3PA	3P%	FTM	FTA	FT%	ORB	DRB	TRB	AST	PF	DQ	STL	BLK	TO	MPG	PPG	RPG	APG	PCM
49-50	Waterloo	7	....	....	22	9	29	.310	....	....	....	4	11	.364	....	....	....	8	14	....	....	....	....	3.1	....	1.1	....	
NBA Season Totals		7	....	....	22	9	29	.310	....	....	....	4	11	.364	....	....	....	8	14	....	....	....	....	3.1	....	1.1	....	

• PRITCHARD, Kevin

Kevin Lee Pritchard

Born: July 17, 1967. Bloomington, IN, United States.   Height: 6'3".   Weight: 180 lbs.   Drafted: 1990   College: Kansas

YEAR	TEAM	GP	GS	MIN	PTS	FGM	FGA	FG%	3PM	3PA	3P%	FTM	FTA	FT%	ORB	DRB	TRB	AST	PF	DQ	STL	BLK	TO	MPG	PPG	RPG	APG	PCM
90-91	Golden State	62	1	773	243	88	229	.384	5	31	.161	62	77	.805	16	49	65	81	104	1	30	8	62	12.5	3.9	1.0	1.3	.234
91-92	Boston	11	0	136	46	16	34	.471	0	3	.000	14	18	.778	1	10	11	30	17	0	3	4	11	12.4	4.2	1.0	2.7	.428
94-95	Philadelphia	5	0	36	1	0	3	.000	0	3	.000	1	4	.250	0	1	1	11	3	0	0	0	5	7.2	0.2	0.2	2.2	.092
94-95	Miami	14	0	158	43	13	29	.448	2	5	.400	15	17	.882	0	11	11	23	19	0	2	1	7	11.3	3.1	0.8	1.6	.311
95-96	Washington	2	0	22	7	2	3	.667	1	1	1.000	2	3	.667	0	2	2	7	3	0	2	0	0	11.0	3.5	1.0	3.5	.698
NBA Season Totals		94	1	1125	340	119	298	.399	8	43	.186	94	119	.790	17	73	90	152	146	1	37	13	85	12.0	3.6	1.0	1.6	....

YEAR	TEAM	GP	GS	MIN	PTS	FGM	FGA	FG%	3PM	3PA	3P%	FTM	FTA	FT%	ORB	DRB	TRB	AST	PF	DQ	STL	BLK	TO	MPG	PPG	RPG	APG	PCM

• PROCTOR, Lorvin

Lorvin Proctor

Born: —.　Height: —　Weight: —　Drafted: —　College: none

YEAR	TEAM	GP	GS	MIN	PTS	FGM	FGA	FG%	3PM	3PA	3P%	FTM	FTA	FT%	ORB	DRB	TRB	AST	PF	DQ	STL	BLK	TO	MPG	PPG	RPG	APG	PCM
38-39	Indianapolis-N	3	....	....	8	4	....	....	....	....	....	0	....	....	....	....	....	....	....	....	....	....	....	....	2.7	....	....	....
NBL Season Totals		3	....	....	8	4	....	....	....	....	....	0	....	....	....	....	....	....	....	....	....	....	....	....	2.7	....	....	....

• PROFIT, Laron

Bronta Laron Profit

Born: Aug. 5, 1977. Charleston, SC, United States.　Height: 6'5".　Weight: 204 lbs.　Drafted: 1999　College: Maryland

YEAR	TEAM	GP	GS	MIN	PTS	FGM	FGA	FG%	3PM	3PA	3P%	FTM	FTA	FT%	ORB	DRB	TRB	AST	PF	DQ	STL	BLK	TO	MPG	PPG	RPG	APG	PCM
99-00	Washington	33	1	225	49	21	59	.356	3	17	.176	4	10	.400	2	24	26	25	26	0	7	4	19	6.8	1.5	0.8	0.8	.194
00-01	Washington	35	12	605	152	56	142	.394	7	26	.269	33	45	.733	18	46	64	89	43	0	36	11	46	17.3	4.3	1.8	2.5	.341
NBA Season Totals		68	13	830	201	77	201	.383	10	43	.233	37	55	.673	20	70	90	114	69	0	43	15	65	12.2	3.0	1.3	1.7	....

• PROFITT, Cy

Cy Profitt

Born: 1911.　Height: 6'3".　Weight: 190 lbs.　Drafted: —　College: Butler

YEAR	TEAM	GP	GS	MIN	PTS	FGM	FGA	FG%	3PM	3PA	3P%	FTM	FTA	FT%	ORB	DRB	TRB	AST	PF	DQ	STL	BLK	TO	MPG	PPG	RPG	APG	PCM
37-38	Indianapolis-N	12	....	....	51	19	....	....	....	....	....	13	....	....	....	....	....	....	....	....	....	....	....	....	4.3	....	....	....
NBL Season Totals		12	....	....	51	19	....	....	....	....	....	13	....	....	....	....	....	....	....	....	....	....	....	....	4.3	....	....	....

• PROKSA, Joe

Joe Proksa

Born: June 30, 1914. Died: Oct.25, 1999.　Height: 6'1".　Weight: 185 lbs.　Drafted: —　College: Penn State

YEAR	TEAM	GP	GS	MIN	PTS	FGM	FGA	FG%	3PM	3PA	3P%	FTM	FTA	FT%	ORB	DRB	TRB	AST	PF	DQ	STL	BLK	TO	MPG	PPG	RPG	APG	PCM
44-45	Pittsburgh-N	1	....	....	7	2	....	....	....	....	....	3	....	....	....	....	....	....	....	....	....	....	....	....	7.0	....	....	....
NBL Season Totals		1	....	....	7	2	....	....	....	....	....	3	....	....	....	....	....	....	....	....	....	....	....	....	7.0	....	....	....

• PRYOR, Leroy

Leroy (Red) Pryor

Born: 1923.　Height: 6'3".　Weight: 180 lbs.　Drafted: —　College: DePaul

YEAR	TEAM	GP	GS	MIN	PTS	FGM	FGA	FG%	3PM	3PA	3P%	FTM	FTA	FT%	ORB	DRB	TRB	AST	PF	DQ	STL	BLK	TO	MPG	PPG	RPG	APG	PCM
48-49	Dayton-N	10	....	....	12	6	....	....	....	....	....	0	3	.000	....	....	....	....	....	....	....	....	....	....	1.2	....	....	....
NBL Season Totals		10	....	....	12	6	....	....	....	....	....	0	3		....	....	....	....	....	....	....	....	....	....	1.2	....	....	....

• PRZYBILLA, Joel

Joel Anthony Przybilla

Born: Oct. 10, 1979. Monticello, MN, United States.　Height: 7'1".　Weight: 255 lbs.　Drafted: 2000　College: Minnesota

YEAR	TEAM	GP	GS	MIN	PTS	FGM	FGA	FG%	3PM	3PA	3P%	FTM	FTA	FT%	ORB	DRB	TRB	AST	PF	DQ	STL	BLK	TO	MPG	PPG	RPG	APG	PCM
00-01	Milwaukee	33	13	270	27	12	35	.343	0	0	.000	3	11	.273	29	42	71	2	56	0	3	30	13	8.2	0.8	2.2	0.1	.228
01-02	Milwaukee	71	62	1127	190	76	142	.535	0	1	.000	38	90	.422	78	205	283	21	199	3	20	118	43	15.9	2.7	4.0	0.3	.339
02-03	Milwaukee	32	17	545	48	18	46	.391	0	0	.000	12	24	.500	48	97	145	12	85	1	10	45	19	17.0	1.5	4.5	0.4	.286
NBA Season Totals		136	92	1942	265	106	223	.475	0	1	.000	53	125	.424	155	344	499	35	340	4	33	193	75	14.3	1.9	3.7	0.3	....
00-01	Milwaukee	1	0	2	0	0	0	.000	0	0	.000	0	0	.000	0	0	0	0	0	0	0	0	0	2.0	0.0	0.0	0.0	.000
02-03	Milwaukee	4	3	33	2	1	1	1.000	0	0	.000	0	0	.000	2	8	10	1	11	0	0	2	1	8.3	0.5	2.5	0.3	.245
NBA Playoff Totals		5	3	35	2	1	1	1.000	0	0	.000	0	0	.000	2	8	10	1	11	0	0	2	1	7.0	0.4	2.0	0.2	....

• PUGH, Les

Leslie Pugh

Born: Sept. 18, 1923.　Height: 6'7".　Weight: 190 lbs.　Drafted: —　College: Ohio State

YEAR	TEAM	GP	GS	MIN	PTS	FGM	FGA	FG%	3PM	3PA	3P%	FTM	FTA	FT%	ORB	DRB	TRB	AST	PF	DQ	STL	BLK	TO	MPG	PPG	RPG	APG	PCM
48-49	Providence	60	....	....	461	168	556	.302	....	....	....	125	167	.749	....	....	....	59	168	....	....	....	....	7.7	....	1.0	....
49-50	Baltimore	56	....	....	251	68	273	.249	....	....	....	115	136	.846	....	....	....	16	118	....	....	....	....	4.5	....	0.3	....
NBA Season Totals		116	....	....	712	236	829	.285	....	....	....	240	303	.792	....	....	....	75	286	....	....	....	....	6.1	....	0.6	....

• PUGH, Roy

Roy Pugh

Born: Mar. 21, 1923. Died: Feb.17, 2001.　Height: 6'6".　Weight: 210 lbs.　Drafted: 1948　College: Southern Methodist

YEAR	TEAM	GP	GS	MIN	PTS	FGM	FGA	FG%	3PM	3PA	3P%	FTM	FTA	FT%	ORB	DRB	TRB	AST	PF	DQ	STL	BLK	TO	MPG	PPG	RPG	APG	PCM
47-48	Indianapolis-N	4	....	....	4	1	....	....	....	....	....	2	4	.500	....	....	....	....	....	....	....	....	....	1.0	....	....	....
48-49	Philadelphia	13	....	....	20	8	36	.222	....	....	....	4	10	.400	....	....	....	6	12	....	....	....	....	1.5	....	0.5	....
48-49	Fort Wayne	4	....	....	9	4	8	.500	....	....	....	1	4	.250	....	....	....	1	3	....	....	....	....	2.3	....	0.3	....
48-49	Indianapolis	6	....	....	3	1	7	.143	....	....	....	1	5	.200	....	....	....	2	2	....	....	....	....	0.5	....	0.3	....
NBA Season Totals		23	....	....	32	13	51	.255	....	....	....	6	19	.316	....	....	....	9	17	....	....	....	....	1.4	....	0.4	....
NBL Season Totals		4	....	....	4	1	....	....	....	....	....	2	4		....	....	....	....	....	....	....	....	....	1.0	....	....	....
Career Totals		27	....	....	36	14	51		....	....	....	8	23		....	....	....	9	17	....	....	....	....	1.3	....	0.3	....

• PULLARD, Anthony

Anthony Quinn Pullard

Born: June 23, 1966. DeQuincy, LA, United States.　Height: 6'10".　Weight: 245 lbs.　Drafted: —　College: McNeese State

YEAR	TEAM	GP	GS	MIN	PTS	FGM	FGA	FG%	3PM	3PA	3P%	FTM	FTA	FT%	ORB	DRB	TRB	AST	PF	DQ	STL	BLK	TO	MPG	PPG	RPG	APG	PCM
92-93	Milwaukee	8	0	37	17	8	18	.444	0	0	.000	1	3	.333	2	6	8	2	5	0	2	2	5	4.6	2.1	1.0	0.3	.353
NBA Season Totals		8	0	37	17	8	18	.444	0	0	.000	1	3	.333	2	6	8	2	5	0	2	2	5	4.6	2.1	1.0	0.3	....

• PUTMAN, Don

James Donald Putman

Born: Nov. 13, 1922.　Height: 6'1".　Weight: 170 lbs.　Drafted: —　College: Denver

YEAR	TEAM	GP	GS	MIN	PTS	FGM	FGA	FG%	3PM	3PA	3P%	FTM	FTA	FT%	ORB	DRB	TRB	AST	PF	DQ	STL	BLK	TO	MPG	PPG	RPG	APG	PCM
46-47	St. Louis	58	....	....	380	156	635	.246	....	....	....	68	105	.648	....	....	....	30	106	....	....	....	....	6.6	....	0.5	....
47-48	St. Louis	42	....	....	267	105	399	.263	....	....	....	57	84	.679	....	....	....	25	95	....	....	....	....	6.4	....	0.6	....

YEAR	TEAM	GP	GS	MIN	PTS	FGM	FGA	FG%	3PM	3PA	3P%	FTM	FTA	FT%	ORB	DRB	TRB	AST	PF	DQ	STL	BLK	TO	MPG	PPG	RPG	APG	PCM
48-49	St. Louis	59	....	....	248	98	330	.297	....	....	....	52	97	.536	....	....	....	140	132	....	....	....	....		4.2	....	2.4	
49-50	St. Louis	57	....	....	135	51	200	.255	....	....	....	33	52	.635	....	....	....	90	116	....	....	....	....		2.4	....	1.6	
NBA Season Totals		216	....	....	1030	410	1564	.262	....	....	....	210	338	.621	....	....	....	285	449	....	....	....	....		4.8	....	1.3	
46-47	St. Louis	3	....	....	15	7	24	.292	....	....	....	1	4	.250	....	....	....	1	7	....	....	....	....		5.0	....	0.3	
47-48	St. Louis	7	....	....	23	8	44	.182	....	....	....	7	12	.583	....	....	....	5	15	....	....	....	....		3.3	....	0.7	
48-49	St. Louis	2	....	....	4	2	11	.182	....	....	....	0	3	.000	....	....	....	4	6	....	....	....	....		2.0	....	2.0	
NBA Playoff Totals		12	....	....	42	17	79	.215	....	....	....	8	19	.421	....	....	....	10	28	....	....	....	....		3.5	....	0.8	

● PUTNAM, Scoop

Scoop Putnam

Born: 1947.   Height: 6'.   Weight: 175 lbs.   Drafted: —   College: Tennessee

YEAR	TEAM	GP	GS	MIN	PTS	FGM	FGA	FG%	3PM	3PA	3P%	FTM	FTA	FT%	ORB	DRB	TRB	AST	PF	DQ	STL	BLK	TO	MPG	PPG	RPG	APG	PCM
39-40	Oshkosh-N	8	....	....	14	6	....	....	....	....	....	2	....	....	....	....	....	....	....	....	....	....	....		1.8	....	....	
40-41	Oshkosh-N	22	....	....	97	40	....	....	....	....	....	17	....	....	....	....	....	....	....	....	....	....	....		4.4	....	....	
41-42	Toledo-N	20	....	....	83	36	....	....	....	....	....	11	....	....	....	....	....	....	....	....	....	....	....		4.2	....	....	
NBL Season Totals		50	....	....	194	82	....	....	....	....	....	30	....	....	....	....	....	....	....	....	....	....	....		3.9	....	....	
39-40	Oshkosh-N	5	....	....	5	2	....	....	....	....	....	1	....	....	....	....	....	....	....	....	....	....	....		1.0	....	....	
40-41	Oshkosh-N	3	....	....	10	5	....	....	....	....	....	0	....	....	....	....	....	....	....	....	....	....	....		3.3	....	....	
NBL Playoff Totals		8	....	....	15	7	....	....	....	....	....	1	....	....	....	....	....	....	....	....	....	....	....		1.9	....	....	

● QUABIUS, Dave

David Quabius

Born: Mar. 16, 1916. Died: June19, 1983.   Height: 6'   Weight: 185 lbs.   Drafted: —   College: Marquette

YEAR	TEAM	GP	GS	MIN	PTS	FGM	FGA	FG%	3PM	3PA	3P%	FTM	FTA	FT%	ORB	DRB	TRB	AST	PF	DQ	STL	BLK	TO	MPG	PPG	RPG	APG	PCM
38-39	Sheboygan-N	1	....	....	0	0	....	....	....	....	....	0	....	....	....	....	....	....	....	....	....	....	....		0.0	....	....	
39-40	Sheboygan-N	27	....	....	115	42	....	....	....	....	....	31	....	....	....	....	....	....	....	....	....	....	....		4.3	....	....	
40-41	Sheboygan-N	24	....	....	152	56	....	....	....	....	....	40	....	....	....	....	....	....	....	....	....	....	....		6.3	....	....	
42-43	Oshkosh-N	13	....	....	39	15	....	....	....	....	....	9	....	....	....	....	....	....	....	....	....	....	....		3.0	....	....	
NBL Season Totals		65	....	....	306	113	....	....	....	....	....	80	....	....	....	....	....	....	....	....	....	....	....		4.7	....	....	
39-40	Sheboygan-N	3	....	....	16	4	....	....	....	....	....	8	....	....	....	....	....	....	....	....	....	....	....		5.3	....	....	
40-41	Sheboygan-N	6	....	....	32	13	....	....	....	....	....	6	....	....	....	....	....	....	....	....	....	....	....		5.3	....	....	
42-43	Oshkosh-N	1	....	....	2	1	....	....	....	....	....	0	....	....	....	....	....	....	....	....	....	....	....		2.0	....	....	
NBL Playoff Totals		10	....	....	50	18	....	....	....	....	....	14	....	....	....	....	....	....	....	....	....	....	....		5.0	....	....	

● QUICK, Bob

Robert L. Quick

Born: Mar. 5, 1946. Thornton, MS, United States.   Height: 6'5".   Weight: 215 lbs.   Drafted: 1968   College: Xavier (OH)

YEAR	TEAM	GP	GS	MIN	PTS	FGM	FGA	FG%	3PM	3PA	3P%	FTM	FTA	FT%	ORB	DRB	TRB	AST	PF	DQ	STL	BLK	TO	MPG	PPG	RPG	APG	PCM
68-69	Baltimore	28	....	154	87	30	73	.411	....	....	....	27	44	.614	....	....	25	12	14	0	....	....	....	5.5	3.1	0.9	0.4	.474
69-70	Baltimore	15	....	67	40	14	28	.500	....	....	....	12	18	.667	....	....	12	3	9	0	....	....	....	4.5	2.7	0.8	0.2	.522
69-70	Detroit	19	....	297	135	49	111	.441	....	....	....	37	53	.698	....	....	63	11	41	0	....	....	....	15.6	7.1	3.3	0.6	.415
70-71	Detroit	56	....	1146	448	155	341	.455	....	....	....	138	176	.784	....	....	230	56	142	1	....	....	....	20.5	8.0	4.1	1.0	.412
71-72	Dallas-A	6	....	57	26	8	15	.533	0	0	.000	10	10	1.000	6	8	14	1	9	0	....	....	4	9.5	4.3	2.3	0.2	.514
71-72	Detroit	18	....	204	112	39	82	.476	....	....	....	34	45	.756	....	....	51	11	29	0	....	....	....	11.3	6.2	2.8	0.6	.559
NBA Season Totals		136	....	1868	822	287	635	.452	....	....	....	248	336	.738	....	....	381	93	235	1	....	....	....	13.7	6.0	2.8	0.7	....
ABA Season Totals		6	....	57	26	8	15	.533	0	0	.000	10	10	1.000	6	8	14	1	9	0	....	....	4	9.5	4.3	2.3	0.2	....
Career Totals		142	....	1925	848	295	650	.454	0	0	.000	258	346	.746	6	8	395	94	244	1	....	....	4	13.6	6.0	2.8	0.7	....
68-69	Baltimore	2	....	9	4	2	3	.667	....	....	....	0	2	.000	....	....	1	0	1	0	....	....	....	4.5	2.0	0.5	0.0	.305
NBA Playoff Totals		2	....	9	4	2	3	.667	....	....	....	0	2	.000	....	....	1	0	1	0	....	....	....	4.5	2.0	0.5	0.0	

● QUINLAN, Jim

Jim Quinlan

Born: 1922.   Height: 6'4".   Weight: 205 lbs.   Drafted: —   College: Canisius

YEAR	TEAM	GP	GS	MIN	PTS	FGM	FGA	FG%	3PM	3PA	3P%	FTM	FTA	FT%	ORB	DRB	TRB	AST	PF	DQ	STL	BLK	TO	MPG	PPG	RPG	APG	PCM
46-47	Rochester-N	3	....	....	1	0	....	....	....	....	....	1	2	.500	....	....	....	....	....	....	....	....	....		0.3	....	....	
NBL Season Totals		3	....	....	1	0	....	....	....	....	....	1	2	....	....	....	....	....	....	....	....	....	....		0.3	....	....	

● QUINN, Bart

Bart Quinn

Born: 1917.   Height: 6'2".   Weight: 210 lbs.   Drafted: —   College: Toledo

YEAR	TEAM	GP	GS	MIN	PTS	FGM	FGA	FG%	3PM	3PA	3P%	FTM	FTA	FT%	ORB	DRB	TRB	AST	PF	DQ	STL	BLK	TO	MPG	PPG	RPG	APG	PCM
37-38	Fort Wayne-N	18	....	....	170	71	....	....	....	....	....	28	....	....	....	....	....	....	....	....	....	....	....		9.4	....	....	
NBL Season Totals		18	....	....	170	71	....	....	....	....	....	28	....	....	....	....	....	....	....	....	....	....	....		9.4	....	....	

● QUINNETT, Brian

Brian Ralph Quinnett

Born: May 30, 1966. Pullman, WA, United States.   Height: 6'8".   Weight: 235 lbs.   Drafted: 1989   College: Washington State

YEAR	TEAM	GP	GS	MIN	PTS	FGM	FGA	FG%	3PM	3PA	3P%	FTM	FTA	FT%	ORB	DRB	TRB	AST	PF	DQ	STL	BLK	TO	MPG	PPG	RPG	APG	PCM
89-90	New York	31	0	193	40	19	58	.328	0	2	.000	2	3	.667	9	19	28	11	27	0	3	4	3	6.2	1.3	0.9	0.4	.166
90-91	New York	68	5	1011	319	139	303	.459	15	43	.349	26	36	.722	65	80	145	53	100	0	22	13	54	14.9	4.7	2.1	0.8	.286
91-92	New York	24	0	190	74	28	73	.384	10	26	.385	8	14	.571	9	15	24	7	21	0	7	6	7	7.9	3.1	1.0	0.3	.290
91-92	Dallas	15	0	136	41	15	51	.294	3	15	.200	8	12	.667	7	20	27	5	11	0	9	2	8	9.1	2.7	1.8	0.3	.249
NBA Season Totals		138	5	1530	474	201	485	.414	28	86	.326	44	65	.677	90	134	224	76	159	0	41	25	72	11.1	3.4	1.6	0.6	....
89-90	New York	3	0	16	5	2	4	.500	1	1	1.000	0	0	.000	5	3	8	2	2	0	0	0	1	5.3	1.7	2.7	0.7	.680
90-91	New York	3	0	36	9	4	8	.500	1	3	.333	0	0	.000	0	1	1	3	2	0	1	0	2	12.0	3.0	0.3	1.0	.209
NBA Playoff Totals		6	0	52	14	6	12	.500	2	4	.500	0	0	.000	5	4	9	5	4	0	1	0	3	8.7	2.3	1.5	0.8	

YEAR	TEAM	GP	GS	MIN	PTS	FGM	FGA	FG%	3PM	3PA	3P%	FTM	FTA	FT%	ORB	DRB	TRB	AST	PF	DQ	STL	BLK	TO	MPG	PPG	RPG	APG	PCM

• RACKLEY, Luther
Luther Rackley Jr.

Born: June 11, 1946. Bainbridge, GA, United States.   Height: 6'10".   Weight: 220 lbs.   Drafted: 1969   College: Xavier (OH)

YEAR	TEAM	GP	GS	MIN	PTS	FGM	FGA	FG%	3PM	3PA	3P%	FTM	FTA	FT%	ORB	DRB	TRB	AST	PF	DQ	STL	BLK	TO	MPG	PPG	RPG	APG	PCM
69-70	Cincinnati	66	....	1256	504	190	423	.449	....	....	....	124	195	.636	....	....	378	56	204	5	....	....	....	19.0	7.6	5.7	0.8	.456
70-71	Cleveland	74	....	1434	559	219	470	.466	....	....	....	121	190	.637	....	....	394	66	186	3	....	....	....	19.4	7.6	5.3	0.9	.452
71-72	Cleveland	9	....	65	23	11	25	.440	....	....	....	1	4	.250	....	....	21	3	3	0	....	....	....	7.2	2.6	2.3	0.3	.459
71-72	New York	62	....	618	233	92	215	.428	....	....	....	49	84	.583	....	....	187	18	104	0	....	....	....	10.0	3.8	3.0	0.3	.402
72-73	Memphis-A	57	....	893	418	170	344	.494	0	1	.000	78	120	.650	90	197	287	36	130	2	....	....	50	15.7	7.3	5.0	0.6	.540
72-73	New York	1	....	2	0	0	0	.000	....	....	....	0	0	.000	....	....	1	0	2	0	....	....	....	2.0	0.0	1.0	0.0	.000
73-74	Philadelphia	9	....	68	18	5	13	.385	....	....	....	8	11	.727	5	17	22	0	11	0	3	4	....	7.6	2.0	2.4	0.0	.352
NBA Season Totals		221	....	3443	1337	517	1146	.451	....	....	....	303	484	.626	5	17	1003	143	510	8	3	4	....	15.6	6.0	4.5	0.6	....
ABA Season Totals		57	....	893	418	170	344	.494	0	1	.000	78	120	.650	90	197	287	36	130	2	....	....	50	15.7	7.3	5.0	0.6	....
Career Totals		278	....	4336	1755	687	1490	.461	0	1	.000	381	604	.631	95	214	1290	179	640	10	3	4	50	15.6	6.3	4.6	0.6	....
71-72	New York	11	....	29	8	2	14	.143	....	....	....	4	4	1.000	....	....	7	1	7	0	....	....	....	2.6	0.7	0.6	0.1	.062
NBA Playoff Totals		11	....	29	8	2	14	.143	....	....	....	4	4	1.000	....	....	7	1	7	0	....	....	....	2.6	0.7	0.6	0.1	....

• RADER, Howie
Howard Rader

Born: Mar. 29, 1921. Died: Feb.2, 1991.   Height: 6'1".   Weight: 190 lbs.   Drafted: —   College: Long Island University

YEAR	TEAM	GP	GS	MIN	PTS	FGM	FGA	FG%	3PM	3PA	3P%	FTM	FTA	FT%	ORB	DRB	TRB	AST	PF	DQ	STL	BLK	TO	MPG	PPG	RPG	APG	PCM
46-47	Tri-Cities-N	41	....	....	195	76	....	....	....	....	....	43	64	.672	....	....	....	93	....	....	....	....	....	4.8	....	....	....	
47-48	Tri-Cities-N	45	....	....	117	44	....	....	....	....	....	29	54	.537	....	....	....	90	....	....	....	....	....	2.6	....	....	....	
48-49	Baltimore	13	....	....	17	7	45	.156	....	....	....	3	10	.300	....	....	14	25	....	....	....	....	....	1.3	....	1.1	....	
NBA Season Totals		13	....	....	17	7	45	.156	....	....	....	3	10	.300	....	....	14	25	....	....	....	....	....	1.3	....	1.1	....	
NBL Season Totals		86	....	....	312	120	....	....	....	....	....	72	118	....	....	....	....	183	....	....	....	....	....	3.6	....	....	....	
Career Totals		99	....	....	329	127	45	....	....	....	....	75	128	....	....	....	14	208	....	....	....	....	....	3.3	....	0.1	....	
47-48	Tri-Cities-N	6	....	....	22	8	....	....	....	....	....	6	12	.500	....	....	....	....	....	....	....	....	....	3.7	....	....	....	
NBL Playoff Totals		6	....	....	22	8	....	....	....	....	....	6	12	....	....	....	....	....	....	....	....	....	....	3.7	....	....	....	

• RADER, Len
Len Rader

Born: 1921.   Height: 6'2".   Weight: 185 lbs.   Drafted: —   College: Long Island University

YEAR	TEAM	GP	GS	MIN	PTS	FGM	FGA	FG%	3PM	3PA	3P%	FTM	FTA	FT%	ORB	DRB	TRB	AST	PF	DQ	STL	BLK	TO	MPG	PPG	RPG	APG	PCM
46-47	Tri-Cities-N	20	....	....	69	27	....	....	....	....	....	15	30	.500	....	....	....	....	....	....	....	....	....	3.5	....	....	....	
48-49	Hammond-N	14	....	....	53	15	....	....	....	....	....	23	34	.676	....	....	....	33	....	....	....	....	....	3.8	....	....	....	
NBL Season Totals		34	....	....	122	42	....	....	....	....	....	38	64	....	....	....	....	33	....	....	....	....	....	3.6	....	....	....	
48-49	Hammond-N	2	....	....	5	2	....	....	....	....	....	1	1	1.000	....	....	....	....	....	....	....	....	....	2.5	....	....	....	
NBL Playoff Totals		2	....	....	5	2	....	....	....	....	....	1	1	....	....	....	....	....	....	....	....	....	....	2.5	....	....	....	

• RADFORD, Mark
Mark Jeffrey Radford

Born: July 5, 1959. Tacoma, WA, United States.   Height: 6'4".   Weight: 190 lbs.   Drafted: 1981   College: Oregon State

YEAR	TEAM	GP	GS	MIN	PTS	FGM	FGA	FG%	3PM	3PA	3P%	FTM	FTA	FT%	ORB	DRB	TRB	AST	PF	DQ	STL	BLK	TO	MPG	PPG	RPG	APG	PCM
81-82	Seattle	43	0	369	145	54	100	.540	2	3	.667	35	69	.507	13	16	29	57	65	0	16	2	43	8.6	3.4	0.7	1.3	.331
82-83	Seattle	54	2	439	202	84	172	.488	4	18	.222	30	73	.411	12	35	47	104	78	0	34	4	76	8.1	3.7	0.9	1.9	.434
NBA Season Totals		97	2	808	347	138	272	.507	6	21	.286	65	142	.458	25	51	76	161	143	0	50	6	119	8.3	3.6	0.8	1.7	....

• RADFORD, Wayne
Wayne Radford

Born: May 29, 1956. Indianapolis, IN, United States.   Height: 6'3".   Weight: 205 lbs.   Drafted: 1978   College: Indiana

YEAR	TEAM	GP	GS	MIN	PTS	FGM	FGA	FG%	3PM	3PA	3P%	FTM	FTA	FT%	ORB	DRB	TRB	AST	PF	DQ	STL	BLK	TO	MPG	PPG	RPG	APG	PCM
78-79	Indiana	52	....	649	202	83	175	.474	....	....	....	36	45	.800	25	43	68	57	61	0	30	1	47	12.5	3.9	1.3	1.1	.304
NBA Season Totals		52	....	649	202	83	175	.474	....	....	....	36	45	.800	25	43	68	57	61	0	30	1	47	12.5	3.9	1.3	1.1	....

• RADJA, Dino
Dino Radja

Born: Apr. 24, 1967. Split, Croatia.   Height: 6'11".   Weight: 225 lbs.   Drafted: 1989   College: none (HS: Technical School Ctr, CRO)

YEAR	TEAM	GP	GS	MIN	PTS	FGM	FGA	FG%	3PM	3PA	3P%	FTM	FTA	FT%	ORB	DRB	TRB	AST	PF	DQ	STL	BLK	TO	MPG	PPG	RPG	APG	PCM
93-94	Boston	80	47	2303	1208	491	942	.521	0	1	.000	226	301	.751	191	386	577	114	276	2	70	67	152	28.8	15.1	7.2	1.4	.552
94-95	Boston	66	48	2147	1133	450	919	.490	0	1	.000	233	307	.759	149	424	573	111	232	5	60	86	158	32.5	17.2	8.7	1.7	.556
95-96	Boston	53	52	1984	1043	426	852	.500	0	0	.000	191	275	.695	113	409	522	83	161	2	48	81	117	37.4	19.7	9.8	1.6	.563
96-97	Boston	25	25	874	349	149	339	.440	0	1	.000	51	71	.718	44	167	211	48	76	2	23	48	70	35.0	14.0	8.4	1.9	.430
NBA Season Totals		224	172	7308	3733	1516	3052	.497	0	3	.000	701	954	.735	497	1386	1883	356	745	11	201	282	497	32.6	16.7	8.4	1.6	....
94-95	Boston	4	3	153	60	20	50	.400	0	0	.000	20	28	.714	4	24	28	9	19	0	4	5	9	38.3	15.0	7.0	2.3	.360
NBA Playoff Totals		4	3	153	60	20	50	.400	0	0	.000	20	28	.714	4	24	28	9	19	0	4	5	9	38.3	15.0	7.0	2.3	....

• RADMANOVIC, Vladimir
Vladimir Radmanovic

Born: Nov. 19, 1980. Trebinje Srpska, Bosnia.   Height: 6'10".   Weight: 227 lbs.   Drafted: 2001   College: none

YEAR	TEAM	GP	GS	MIN	PTS	FGM	FGA	FG%	3PM	3PA	3P%	FTM	FTA	FT%	ORB	DRB	TRB	AST	PF	DQ	STL	BLK	TO	MPG	PPG	RPG	APG	PCM
01-02	Seattle	61	16	1230	407	146	354	.412	66	157	.420	49	72	.681	45	185	230	81	119	0	56	24	72	20.2	6.7	3.8	1.3	.373
02-03	Seattle	72	16	1910	724	274	668	.410	104	293	.355	72	102	.706	76	247	323	97	136	0	64	22	100	26.5	10.1	4.5	1.3	.355
NBA Season Totals		133	32	3140	1131	420	1022	.411	170	450	.378	121	174	.695	121	432	553	178	255	0	120	46	172	23.6	8.5	4.2	1.3	....
01-02	Seattle	5	2	113	38	14	32	.438	7	13	.538	3	3	1.000	6	12	18	5	11	0	1	1	5	22.6	7.6	3.6	1.0	.317
NBA Playoff Totals		5	2	113	38	14	32	.438	7	13	.538	3	3	1.000	6	12	18	5	11	0	1	1	5	22.6	7.6	3.6	1.0	....

YEAR	TEAM	GP	GS	MIN	PTS	FGM	FGA	FG%	3PM	3PA	3P%	FTM	FTA	FT%	ORB	DRB	TRB	AST	PF	DQ	STL	BLK	TO	MPG	PPG	RPG	APG	PCM

• RADOJEVIC, Alex
Aleksandar Radojevic

Born: Aug. 8, 1976. Trebinje, Bosnia,   Height: 7'3".   Weight: 242 lbs.   Drafted: 1999   College: Barton County CC

YEAR	TEAM	GP	GS	MIN	PTS	FGM	FGA	FG%	3PM	3PA	3P%	FTM	FTA	FT%	ORB	DRB	TRB	AST	PF	DQ	STL	BLK	TO	MPG	PPG	RPG	APG	PCM
99-00	Toronto	3	0	24	7	2	7	.286	0	0	.000	3	6	.500	2	6	8	1	5	0	2	1	5	8.0	2.3	2.7	0.3	.224
NBA Season Totals		3	0	24	7	2	7	.286	0	0	.000	3	6	.500	2	6	8	1	5	0	2	1	5	8.0	2.3	2.7	0.3	....

• RADOVICH, Frank
Frank Raymond Radovich

Born: Mar. 3, 1938.   Height: 6'8".   Weight: 235 lbs.   Drafted: —   College: Indiana

YEAR	TEAM	GP	GS	MIN	PTS	FGM	FGA	FG%	3PM	3PA	3P%	FTM	FTA	FT%	ORB	DRB	TRB	AST	PF	DQ	STL	BLK	TO	MPG	PPG	RPG	APG	PCM
61-62	Philadelphia	37	....	175	87	37	93	.398	....	....	....	13	26	.500	....	....	51	4	27	0	....	....	....	4.7	2.4	1.4	0.1	.413
NBA Season Totals		37	....	175	87	37	93	.398	....	....	....	13	26	.500	....	....	51	4	27	0	....	....	....	4.7	2.4	1.4	0.1	
61-62	Philadelphia	2	....	12	4	1	6	.167	....	....	....	2	4	.500	....	....	3	0	2	0	....	....	....	6.0	2.0	1.5	0.0	.073
NBA Playoff Totals		2	....	12	4	1	6	.167	....	....	....	2	4	.500	....	....	3	0	2	0	....	....	....	6.0	2.0	1.5	0.0	

• RADOVICH, Moe
George Lewis (Moe) Radovich

Born: May 5, 1929.   Height: 6'   Weight: 160 lbs.   Drafted: 1952   College: Wyoming

YEAR	TEAM	GP	GS	MIN	PTS	FGM	FGA	FG%	3PM	3PA	3P%	FTM	FTA	FT%	ORB	DRB	TRB	AST	PF	DQ	STL	BLK	TO	MPG	PPG	RPG	APG	PCM
52-53	Philadelphia	4	....	33	14	5	13	.385	....	....	....	4	4	1.000	....	....	1	8	5	0	....	....	....	8.3	3.5	0.3	2.0	.525
NBA Season Totals		4	....	33	14	5	13	.385	....	....	....	4	4	1.000	....	....	1	8	5	0	....	....	....	8.3	3.5	0.3	2.0	

• RADZISZEWSKI, Ray
Raymond A. Radziszewski

Born: Mar. 1, 1935.   Height: 6'5".   Weight: 210 lbs.   Drafted: 1957   College: St. Joseph's (PA)

YEAR	TEAM	GP	GS	MIN	PTS	FGM	FGA	FG%	3PM	3PA	3P%	FTM	FTA	FT%	ORB	DRB	TRB	AST	PF	DQ	STL	BLK	TO	MPG	PPG	RPG	APG	PCM
57-58	Philadelphia	1	....	6	0	0	3	.000	....	....	....	0	0	.000	....	....	2	1	1	0	....	....	....	6.0	0.0	2.0	1.0	.030
NBA Season Totals		1	....	6	0	0	3	.000	....	....	....	0	0	.000	....	....	2	1	1	0	....	....	....	6.0	0.0	2.0	1.0	

• RAE, Jim
Jim Rae

Born: 1917.   Height: 6'4".   Weight: 200 lbs.   Drafted: —   College: Michigan

YEAR	TEAM	GP	GS	MIN	PTS	FGM	FGA	FG%	3PM	3PA	3P%	FTM	FTA	FT%	ORB	DRB	TRB	AST	PF	DQ	STL	BLK	TO	MPG	PPG	RPG	APG	PCM
41-42	Toledo-N	3	....	....	10	5	....	....	....	....	....	0	....	....	....	....	....	....	....	....	....	....	....	....	3.3	....	....	....
NBL Season Totals		3	....	....	10	5	....	....	....	....	....	0	....	....	....	....	....	....	....	....	....	....	....	....	3.3	....	....	....

• RAGELIS, Ray
Raymond Ernest Ragelis

Born: Dec. 10, 1928. Died: Sept.19, 1983.   Height: 6'4".   Weight: 205 lbs.   Drafted: 1951   College: Northwestern

YEAR	TEAM	GP	GS	MIN	PTS	FGM	FGA	FG%	3PM	3PA	3P%	FTM	FTA	FT%	ORB	DRB	TRB	AST	PF	DQ	STL	BLK	TO	MPG	PPG	RPG	APG	PCM
51-52	Rochester	51	....	337	68	25	96	.260	....	....	....	18	29	.621	....	....	76	31	62	1	....	....	....	6.6	1.3	1.5	0.6	.254
NBA Season Totals		51	....	337	68	25	96	.260	....	....	....	18	29	.621	....	....	76	31	62	1	....	....	....	6.6	1.3	1.5	0.6	
51-52	Rochester	3	....	7	0	0	1	.000	....	....	....	0	0	.000	....	....	1	1	0	0	....	....	....	2.3	0.0	0.3	0.3	.184
NBA Playoff Totals		3	....	7	0	0	1	.000	....	....	....	0	0	.000	....	....	1	1	0	0	....	....	....	2.3	0.0	0.3	0.3	

• RAIKEN, Sherwin
Sherwin H. Raiken

Born: Oct. 29, 1928.   Height: 6'2".   Weight: 185 lbs.   Drafted: —   College: Villanova

YEAR	TEAM	GP	GS	MIN	PTS	FGM	FGA	FG%	3PM	3PA	3P%	FTM	FTA	FT%	ORB	DRB	TRB	AST	PF	DQ	STL	BLK	TO	MPG	PPG	RPG	APG	PCM
52-53	New York	6	....	63	9	3	21	.143	....	....	....	3	8	.375	....	....	8	6	10	0	....	....	....	10.5	1.5	1.3	1.0	.063
NBA Season Totals		6	....	63	9	3	21	.143	....	....	....	3	8	.375	....	....	8	6	10	0	....	....	....	10.5	1.5	1.3	1.0	
52-53	New York	4	....	19	8	4	5	.800	....	....	....	0	1	1.000	....	....	1	2	3	0	....	....	....	4.8	2.0	0.3	0.5	.479
NBA Playoff Totals		4	....	19	8	4	5	.800	....	....	....	0	1	1.000	....	....	1	2	3	0	....	....	....	4.8	2.0	0.3	0.5	

• RAIMAN, Stan
Stan Raiman

Born: Mar. 22, 1914. Died: Jan.30, 1997.   Height: 5'9".   Weight: 140 lbs.   Drafted: —   College: Canisius

YEAR	TEAM	GP	GS	MIN	PTS	FGM	FGA	FG%	3PM	3PA	3P%	FTM	FTA	FT%	ORB	DRB	TRB	AST	PF	DQ	STL	BLK	TO	MPG	PPG	RPG	APG	PCM
37-38	Buffalo-N	9	....	....	22	10	....	....	....	....	....	2	....	....	....	....	....	....	....	....	....	....	....	....	2.4	....	....	....
NBL Season Totals		9	....	....	22	10	....	....	....	....	....	2	....	....	....	....	....	....	....	....	....	....	....	....	2.4	....	....	....

• RAINS, Ed
Edward Eugene Rains

Born: Dec. 24, 1956. Ocala, FL, United States.   Height: 6'7".   Weight: 190 lbs.   Drafted: 1981   College: South Alabama

YEAR	TEAM	GP	GS	MIN	PTS	FGM	FGA	FG%	3PM	3PA	3P%	FTM	FTA	FT%	ORB	DRB	TRB	AST	PF	DQ	STL	BLK	TO	MPG	PPG	RPG	APG	PCM
81-82	San Antonio	49	15	637	192	77	177	.435	0	2	.000	38	64	.594	37	43	80	40	74	0	18	2	25	13.0	3.9	1.6	0.8	.261
82-83	San Antonio	34	1	292	95	33	83	.398	0	1	.000	29	43	.674	25	19	44	22	35	0	10	1	24	8.6	2.8	1.3	0.6	.274
NBA Season Totals		83	16	929	287	110	260	.423	0	3	.000	67	107	.626	62	62	124	62	109	0	28	3	49	11.2	3.5	1.5	0.7	....
81-82	San Antonio	5	0	30	10	3	6	.500	0	0	.000	4	9	.444	3	5	8	1	5	0	1	0	1	6.0	2.0	1.6	0.2	.369
82-83	San Antonio	3	0	11	4	2	5	.400	0	1	.000	0	0	.000	1	0	1	1	0	0	0	0	1	3.7	1.3	0.3	0.3	.217
NBA Playoff Totals		8	0	41	14	5	11	.455	0	1	.000	4	9	.444	4	5	9	2	5	0	1	0	2	5.1	1.8	1.1	0.3	....

YEAR	TEAM	GP	GS	MIN	PTS	FGM	FGA	FG%	3PM	3PA	3P%	FTM	FTA	FT%	ORB	DRB	TRB	AST	PF	DQ	STL	BLK	TO	MPG	PPG	RPG	APG	PCM

• RAKOCEVIC, Igor

Igor Rakocevic

Born: Mar. 29, 1978. Belgrade, Yugoslavia. Height: 6'3". Weight: 183 lbs. Drafted: 2000 College: none

YEAR	TEAM	GP	GS	MIN	PTS	FGM	FGA	FG%	3PM	3PA	3P%	FTM	FTA	FT%	ORB	DRB	TRB	AST	PF	DQ	STL	BLK	TO	MPG	PPG	RPG	APG	PCM
02-03	Minnesota	42	0	244	78	22	58	.379	5	12	.417	29	36	.806	4	13	17	33	25	0	4	0	23	5.8	1.9	0.4	0.8	.266
NBA Season Totals		42	0	244	78	22	58	.379	5	12	.417	29	36	.806	4	13	17	33	25	0	4	0	23	5.8	1.9	0.4	0.8	....

• RAMBIS, Kurt

Darrell Kurt (Rambo) Rambis

Born: Feb. 25, 1958. Cupertino, CA, United States. Height: 6'8". Weight: 213 lbs. Drafted: 1980 College: Santa Clara

YEAR	TEAM	GP	GS	MIN	PTS	FGM	FGA	FG%	3PM	3PA	3P%	FTM	FTA	FT%	ORB	DRB	TRB	AST	PF	DQ	STL	BLK	TO	MPG	PPG	RPG	APG	PCM
81-82	LA Lakers	64	43	1131	295	118	228	.518	0	1	.000	59	117	.504	116	232	348	56	167	2	60	76	77	17.7	4.6	5.4	0.9	.464
82-83	LA Lakers	78	77	1806	584	235	413	.569	0	2	.000	114	166	.687	164	367	531	90	233	2	105	63	148	23.2	7.5	6.8	1.2	.493
83-84	LA Lakers	47	31	743	168	63	113	.558	0	0	.000	42	66	.636	82	184	266	34	108	0	30	14	56	15.8	3.6	5.7	0.7	.448
84-85	LA Lakers	82	46	1617	430	181	327	.554	0	0	.000	68	103	.660	164	364	528	69	211	0	82	47	98	19.7	5.2	6.4	0.8	.479
85-86	LA Lakers	74	74	1573	408	160	269	.595	0	0	.000	88	122	.721	156	361	517	69	198	0	66	33	96	21.3	5.5	7.0	0.9	.481
86-87	LA Lakers	78	10	1514	446	163	313	.521	0	0	.000	120	157	.764	159	294	453	63	201	1	74	41	101	19.4	5.7	5.8	0.8	.461
87-88	LA Lakers	70	20	845	277	102	186	.548	0	0	.000	73	93	.785	103	165	268	54	103	0	39	13	56	12.1	4.0	3.8	0.8	.527
88-89	Charlotte	75	75	2233	832	325	627	.518	0	3	.000	182	248	.734	269	434	703	159	208	4	100	57	150	29.8	11.1	9.4	2.1	.562
89-90	Charlotte	16	16	448	146	58	116	.500	0	1	.000	30	55	.545	48	72	120	28	45	0	32	10	29	28.0	9.1	7.5	1.8	.476
89-90	Phoenix	58	45	1456	316	132	257	.514	0	2	.000	52	72	.722	108	297	405	107	163	0	68	27	75	25.1	5.4	7.0	1.8	.429
90-91	Phoenix	62	17	900	226	83	167	.497	0	2	.000	60	85	.706	77	189	266	64	107	1	25	11	43	14.5	3.6	4.3	1.0	.440
91-92	Phoenix	28	5	381	90	38	82	.463	0	0	.000	14	18	.778	23	83	106	37	46	0	12	14	25	13.6	3.2	3.8	1.3	.433
92-93	Phoenix	5	0	41	9	4	7	.571	0	0	.000	1	2	.500	2	4	6	1	3	0	3	0	6	8.2	1.8	1.2	0.2	.200
92-93	Sacramento	67	1	781	168	63	122	.516	0	2	.000	42	63	.667	75	146	221	52	119	0	40	18	34	11.7	2.5	3.3	0.8	.425
93-94	LA Lakers	50	1	635	164	59	114	.518	0	1	.000	46	71	.648	84	105	189	32	89	0	22	23	25	12.7	3.3	3.8	0.6	.453
94-95	LA Lakers	26	1	195	44	18	35	.514	0	0	.000	8	12	.667	10	24	34	16	35	0	3	9	8	7.5	1.7	1.3	0.6	.320
NBA Season Totals		880	462	16299	4603	1802	3376	.534	0	14	.000	999	1450	.689	1640	3321	4961	931	2036	10	761	456	1027	18.5	5.2	5.6	1.1	....
81-82	LA Lakers	14	14	279	82	33	64	.516	0	0	.000	16	26	.615	32	54	86	11	47	0	8	12	17	19.9	5.9	6.1	0.8	.434
82-83	LA Lakers	15	15	377	113	45	79	.570	0	0	.000	23	35	.657	27	63	90	19	51	0	13	16	23	25.1	7.5	6.0	1.3	.428
83-84	LA Lakers	21	21	428	141	60	92	.652	0	0	.000	21	33	.636	33	88	121	14	57	0	10	10	22	20.4	6.7	5.8	0.7	.479
84-85	LA Lakers	19	19	375	115	48	81	.593	0	0	.000	19	28	.679	42	87	129	17	52	0	18	9	19	19.7	6.1	6.8	0.9	.538
85-86	LA Lakers	14	14	267	67	27	45	.600	0	0	.000	13	18	.722	26	57	83	14	39	0	10	7	18	19.1	4.8	5.9	1.0	.453
86-87	LA Lakers	17	0	215	79	24	41	.585	0	0	.000	31	34	.912	16	51	67	9	42	0	8	3	13	12.6	4.6	3.9	0.5	.523
87-88	LA Lakers	19	6	186	51	21	34	.618	0	0	.000	9	13	.692	13	38	51	9	28	0	5	2	8	9.8	2.7	2.7	0.5	.431
89-90	Phoenix	16	16	385	67	24	54	.444	0	1	.000	19	28	.679	39	84	123	22	51	0	8	8	17	24.1	4.2	7.7	1.4	.386
90-91	Phoenix	4	0	53	4	2	5	.400	0	0	.000	0	0	.000	8	6	14	4	6	0	5	1	4	13.3	1.0	3.5	1.0	.332
NBA Playoff Totals		139	105	2565	719	284	495	.574	0	1	.000	151	215	.702	236	528	764	119	373	0	85	68	141	18.5	5.2	5.5	0.9	....

• RAMSEY, Cal

Calvin Ramsey

Born: July 13, 1937. Selma, AL, United States. Height: 6'4". Weight: 200 lbs. Drafted: 1959 College: New York University

YEAR	TEAM	GP	GS	MIN	PTS	FGM	FGA	FG%	3PM	3PA	3P%	FTM	FTA	FT%	ORB	DRB	TRB	AST	PF	DQ	STL	BLK	TO	MPG	PPG	RPG	APG	PCM
59-60	St. Louis	4	....	35	17	7	19	.368	....	....	....	3	4	.750	....	....	19	0	4	0	....	....	....	8.8	4.3	4.8	0.0	.583
59-60	New York	7	....	160	80	32	77	.416	....	....	....	16	29	.552	....	....	47	9	21	1	....	....	....	22.9	11.4	6.7	1.3	.499
60-61	Syracuse	2	....	27	6	2	11	.182	....	....	....	2	4	.500	....	....	7	3	7	0	....	....	....	13.5	3.0	3.5	1.5	.177
NBA Season Totals		13	....	222	103	41	107	.383	....	....	....	21	37	.568	....	....	73	12	32	1	....	....	....	17.1	7.9	5.6	0.9	....

• RAMSEY, Frank

Frank Vernon (The Kentucky Colonel) Ramsey Jr.

Born: July 13, 1931. Corydon, KY, United States. Height: 6'3". Weight: 190 lbs. Drafted: 1953 College: Kentucky HOF: 1982

YEAR	TEAM	GP	GS	MIN	PTS	FGM	FGA	FG%	3PM	3PA	3P%	FTM	FTA	FT%	ORB	DRB	TRB	AST	PF	DQ	STL	BLK	TO	MPG	PPG	RPG	APG	PCM
54-55	Boston	64	....	1754	715	236	592	.399	....	....	....	243	322	.755	....	....	402	185	250	11	....	....	....	27.4	11.2	6.3	2.9	.488
56-57	Boston	35	....	807	418	137	349	.393	....	....	....	144	182	.791	....	....	178	67	113	3	....	....	....	23.1	11.9	5.1	1.9	.521
57-58	Boston	69	....	2047	1137	377	900	.419	....	....	....	383	472	.811	....	....	504	167	245	8	....	....	....	29.7	16.5	7.3	2.4	.593
58-59	Boston	72	....	2013	1107	383	1013	.378	....	....	....	341	436	.782	....	....	491	147	266	11	....	....	....	28.0	15.4	6.8	2.0	.522
59-60	Boston	73	....	2009	1117	422	1062	.397	....	....	....	273	347	.787	....	....	506	137	251	10	....	....	....	27.5	15.3	6.9	1.9	.529
60-61	Boston	79	....	2019	1191	448	1100	.407	....	....	....	295	354	.833	....	....	431	146	284	14	....	....	....	25.6	15.1	5.5	1.8	.532
61-62	Boston	79	....	1913	1206	436	1019	.428	....	....	....	334	405	.825	....	....	387	109	245	10	....	....	....	24.2	15.3	4.9	1.4	.555
62-63	Boston	77	....	1541	839	284	743	.382	....	....	....	271	332	.816	....	....	288	95	259	**13**	....	....	....	20.0	10.9	3.7	1.2	.449
63-64	Boston	75	....	1227	648	226	604	.374	....	....	....	196	233	.841	....	....	223	81	245	7	....	....	....	16.4	8.6	3.0	1.1	.421
NBA Season Totals		623	....	15330	8378	2949	7382	.399	....	....	....	2480	3083	.804	....	....	3410	1134	2158	87	....	....	....	24.6	13.4	5.5	1.8	....
54-55	Boston	7	....	154	75	28	54	.519	....	....	....	19	26	.731	....	....	35	16	27	0	....	....	....	22.0	10.7	5.0	2.3	.578
56-57	Boston	10	....	229	122	38	82	.463	....	....	....	46	59	.780	....	....	43	17	36	1	....	....	....	22.9	12.2	4.3	1.7	.543
57-58	Boston	11	....	352	202	74	174	.425	....	....	....	54	59	.915	....	....	90	16	50	3	....	....	....	32.0	18.4	8.2	1.5	.554
58-59	Boston	11	....	303	255	95	192	.495	....	....	....	65	81	.802	....	....	68	20	52	4	....	....	....	27.5	23.2	6.2	1.8	.768
59-60	Boston	13	....	459	217	81	196	.413	....	....	....	55	63	.873	....	....	100	27	51	1	....	....	....	35.3	16.7	7.7	2.1	.473
60-61	Boston	10	....	300	171	55	136	.404	....	....	....	61	75	.813	....	....	64	23	40	0	....	....	....	30.0	17.1	6.4	2.3	.553
61-62	Boston	13	....	210	119	39	104	.375	....	....	....	41	45	.911	....	....	38	10	38	3	....	....	....	16.2	9.2	2.9	0.8	.446
62-63	Boston	13	....	251	108	37	104	.356	....	....	....	34	47	.723	....	....	35	12	43	1	....	....	....	19.3	8.3	2.7	0.9	.299
63-64	Boston	10	....	138	62	22	63	.349	....	....	....	18	21	.857	....	....	21	10	25	0	....	....	....	13.8	6.2	2.1	1.0	.346
NBA Playoff Totals		98	....	2396	1331	469	1105	.424	....	....	....	393	476	.826	....	....	494	151	362	13	....	....	....	24.4	13.6	5.0	1.5	....

• RAMSEY, Ray

Raymond Leroy Ramsey

Born: July 18, 1921. Height: 6'2". Weight: 165 lbs. Drafted: — College: Bradley

YEAR	TEAM	GP	GS	MIN	PTS	FGM	FGA	FG%	3PM	3PA	3P%	FTM	FTA	FT%	ORB	DRB	TRB	AST	PF	DQ	STL	BLK	TO	MPG	PPG	RPG	APG	PCM
47-48	Tri-Cities-N	2	....	....	0	0	....	....	....	....	....	0	0	.000	....	....	....	....	....	....	....	....	....	....	0.0	....	....	....
48-49	Baltimore	2	....	....	2	0	1	.000	....	....	....	2	2	1.000	....	....	....	0	0	....	....	....	....	....	1.0	....	0.0	....
NBA Season Totals		2	....	....	2	0	1	.000	....	....	....	2	2	1.000	....	....	....	0	0	....	....	....	....	....	1.0	....	0.0	....
NBL Season Totals		2	....	....	0	0	....	....	....	....	....	0	0	....	....	....	....	....	....	....	....	....	....	....	0.0	....	....	....
Career Totals		4	....	....	2	0	1	....	....	....	....	2	2	....	....	....	....	0	0	....	....	....	....	....	0.5	....	0.0	....

YEAR	TEAM	GP	GS	MIN	PTS	FGM	FGA	FG%	3PM	3PA	3P%	FTM	FTA	FT%	ORB	DRB	TRB	AST	PF	DQ	STL	BLK	TO	MPG	PPG	RPG	APG	PCM

• RANDALL, Mark
Mark Christopher Randall

Born: Sept. 30, 1967. Edina, MN, United States.   Height: 6'8".   Weight: 235 lbs.   Drafted: 1991   College: Kansas

YEAR	TEAM	GP	GS	MIN	PTS	FGM	FGA	FG%	3PM	3PA	3P%	FTM	FTA	FT%	ORB	DRB	TRB	AST	PF	DQ	STL	BLK	TO	MPG	PPG	RPG	APG	PCM
91-92	Chicago	15	0	67	26	10	22	.455	0	2	.000	6	8	.750	4	5	9	7	8	0	0	0	6	4.5	1.7	0.6	0.5	.306
91-92	Minnesota	39	0	374	145	58	127	.457	3	14	.214	26	35	.743	35	27	62	26	31	0	12	3	20	9.6	3.7	1.6	0.7	.383
92-93	Minnesota	2	0	8	0	0	1	.000	0	1	.000	0	0	.000	0	0	0	1	1	0	0	0	1	4.0	0.0	0.0	0.5	-.158
92-93	Detroit	35	0	240	97	40	79	.506	1	7	.143	16	26	.615	27	28	55	10	32	0	4	2	18	6.9	2.8	1.6	0.3	.383
93-94	Denver	28	0	155	58	17	50	.340	2	14	.143	22	28	.786	9	13	22	11	18	0	8	3	11	5.5	2.1	0.8	0.4	.315
94-95	Denver	8	0	39	6	3	10	.300	0	1	.000	0	0	.000	4	8	12	1	5	0	0	0	1	4.9	0.8	1.5	0.1	.217
NBA Season Totals		127	0	883	332	128	289	.443	6	39	.154	70	97	.722	79	81	160	56	95	0	24	8	57	7.0	2.6	1.3	0.4	....
93-94	Denver	2	0	6	0	0	1	.000	0	0	.000	0	0	.000	1	4	5	0	1	0	0	1	1	3.0	0.0	2.5	0.0	.535
NBA Playoff Totals		2	0	6	0	0	1	.000	0	0	.000	0	0	.000	1	4	5	0	1	0	0	1	1	3.0	0.0	2.5	0.0	

• RANDOLPH, Zach
Zachary Randolph

Born: July 16, 1981. Marion, IN, United States.   Height: 6'9".   Weight: 253 lbs.   Drafted: 2001   College: Michigan State

YEAR	TEAM	GP	GS	MIN	PTS	FGM	FGA	FG%	3PM	3PA	3P%	FTM	FTA	FT%	ORB	DRB	TRB	AST	PF	DQ	STL	BLK	TO	MPG	PPG	RPG	APG	PCM
01-02	Portland	41	0	238	114	48	107	.449	0	0	.000	18	27	.667	31	38	69	13	29	0	7	4	15	5.8	2.8	1.7	0.3	.489
02-03	Portland	77	11	1301	650	264	515	.513	0	5	.000	122	161	.758	139	204	343	41	141	0	42	14	62	16.9	8.4	4.5	0.5	.531
NBA Season Totals		118	11	1539	764	312	622	.502	0	5	.000	140	188	.745	170	242	412	54	170	0	49	18	77	13.0	6.5	3.5	0.5	....
01-02	Portland	1	0	1	0	0	0	.000	0	0	.000	0	0	.000	0	0	0	0	0	0	0	0	0	1.0	0.0	0.0	0.0	.000
02-03	Portland	7	4	205	97	32	61	.525	0	0	.000	33	37	.892	22	39	61	11	17	0	3	2	13	29.3	13.9	8.7	1.6	.592
NBA Playoff Totals		8	4	206	97	32	61	.525	0	0	.000	33	37	.892	22	39	61	11	17	0	3	2	13	25.8	12.1	7.6	1.4	

• RANK, Wally
Wallace Aliifua Rank

Born: Mar. 1, 1958. Fort Ord, CA, United States.   Height: 6'6".   Weight: 220 lbs.   Drafted: 1980   College: San Jose State

YEAR	TEAM	GP	GS	MIN	PTS	FGM	FGA	FG%	3PM	3PA	3P%	FTM	FTA	FT%	ORB	DRB	TRB	AST	PF	DQ	STL	BLK	TO	MPG	PPG	RPG	APG	PCM
80-81	San Diego	25	....	153	55	21	57	.368	0	0	.000	13	28	.464	17	13	30	17	33	1	7	1	25	6.1	2.2	1.2	0.7	.201
NBA Season Totals		25	....	153	55	21	57	.368	0	0	.000	13	28	.464	17	13	30	17	33	1	7	1	25	6.1	2.2	1.2	0.7	

• RANSEY, Kelvin
Kelvin Ransey

Born: May 3, 1958. Toledo, OH, United States.   Height: 6'1".   Weight: 170 lbs.   Drafted: 1980   College: Ohio State

YEAR	TEAM	GP	GS	MIN	PTS	FGM	FGA	FG%	3PM	3PA	3P%	FTM	FTA	FT%	ORB	DRB	TRB	AST	PF	DQ	STL	BLK	TO	MPG	PPG	RPG	APG	PCM
80-81	Portland	80	....	2431	1217	525	1162	.452	3	31	.097	164	219	.749	42	153	195	555	201	1	88	9	232	30.4	15.2	2.4	6.9	.485
81-82	Portland	78	68	2418	1253	504	1095	.460	3	38	.079	242	318	.761	39	147	186	555	169	1	97	4	226	31.0	16.1	2.4	7.1	.517
82-83	Dallas	76	4	1607	840	343	746	.460	2	16	.125	152	199	.764	44	103	147	280	109	1	58	4	129	21.1	11.1	1.9	3.7	.489
83-84	New Jersey	80	50	1937	760	304	700	.434	7	32	.219	145	183	.792	28	99	127	483	182	2	91	6	144	24.2	9.5	1.6	6.0	.455
84-85	New Jersey	81	29	1689	724	300	654	.459	2	11	.182	122	142	.859	40	90	130	355	134	0	87	7	113	20.9	8.9	1.6	4.4	.477
85-86	New Jersey	79	15	1504	586	231	505	.457	3	24	.125	121	148	.818	34	82	116	252	128	0	51	4	111	19.0	7.4	1.5	3.2	.389
NBA Season Totals		474	166	11586	5380	2207	4862	.454	20	152	.132	946	1209	.782	227	674	901	2480	923	5	472	34	955	24.4	11.4	1.9	5.2	
80-81	Portland	3	....	131	49	23	65	.354	0	1	.000	3	6	.500	5	7	12	25	8	0	6	1	11	43.7	16.3	4.0	8.3	.307
83-84	New Jersey	5	0	44	13	6	14	.429	1	1	1.000	0	0	.000	0	1	1	10	6	0	0	1	5	8.8	2.6	0.2	2.0	.243
84-85	New Jersey	3	3	63	17	6	16	.375	0	0	.000	5	5	1.000	0	5	5	17	10	0	2	1	2	21.0	5.7	1.7	5.7	.425
85-86	New Jersey	3	3	68	27	10	22	.455	1	3	.333	6	8	.750	3	4	7	12	9	0	1	0	4	22.7	9.0	2.3	4.0	.402
NBA Playoff Totals		14	6	306	106	45	117	.385	2	5	.400	14	19	.737	8	17	25	64	33	0	9	3	22	21.9	7.6	1.8	4.6	....

• RANZINO, Sam
Samuel Salvador Ranzino

Born: June 21, 1927. Gary, IN, United States.   Height: 6'1".   Weight: 185 lbs.   Drafted: 1951   College: North Carolina State

YEAR	TEAM	GP	GS	MIN	PTS	FGM	FGA	FG%	3PM	3PA	3P%	FTM	FTA	FT%	ORB	DRB	TRB	AST	PF	DQ	STL	BLK	TO	MPG	PPG	RPG	APG	PCM
51-52	Rochester	39	....	234	86	30	90	.333	....	....	....	26	37	.703	....	....	39	25	63	2	....	....	....	6.0	2.2	1.0	0.6	.329
NBA Season Totals		39	....	234	86	30	90	.333	....	....	....	26	37	.703	....	....	39	25	63	2	....	....	....	6.0	2.2	1.0	0.6	

• RASCOE, Bobby
Robert B. Rascoe

Born: July 22, 1940. Trigg County, KY, United States.   Height: 6'4".   Weight: 205 lbs.   Drafted: 1962   College: Western Kentucky

YEAR	TEAM	GP	GS	MIN	PTS	FGM	FGA	FG%	3PM	3PA	3P%	FTM	FTA	FT%	ORB	DRB	TRB	AST	PF	DQ	STL	BLK	TO	MPG	PPG	RPG	APG	PCM
67-68	Kentucky-A	77	....	1606	680	245	563	.435	0	5	.000	190	249	.763	....	....	284	102	158	2	....	....	86	20.9	8.8	3.7	1.3	.424
68-69	Kentucky-A	78	....	1247	534	201	477	.421	3	15	.200	129	167	.772	56	94	150	105	131	1	....	....	93	16.0	6.8	1.9	1.3	.380
69-70	Kentucky-A	4	....	34	14	4	21	.190	0	1	.000	6	7	.857	1	3	4	1	3	0	....	....	2	8.5	3.5	1.0	0.3	.067
ABA Season Totals		159	....	2887	1228	450	1061	.424	3	21	.143	325	423	.768	57	97	438	208	292	3	....	....	181	18.2	7.7	2.8	1.3	....
67-68	Kentucky-A	5	....	51	28	12	27	.444	0	1	.000	4	4	1.000	....	....	5	3	7	0	....	....	5	10.2	5.6	1.0	0.6	.398
68-69	Kentucky-A	7	....	200	90	30	63	.476	0	0	.000	30	32	.938	....	....	20	10	25	0	....	....	5	28.6	12.9	2.9	1.4	.393
ABA Playoff Totals		12	....	251	118	42	90	.467	0	1	.000	34	36	.944	....	....	25	13	32	0	....	....	10	20.9	9.8	2.1	1.1	

• RASMUSSEN, Blair
Blair Allen Rasmussen

Born: Nov. 13, 1962. Auburn, WA, United States.   Height: 7'   Weight: 250 lbs.   Drafted: 1985   College: Oregon

YEAR	TEAM	GP	GS	MIN	PTS	FGM	FGA	FG%	3PM	3PA	3P%	FTM	FTA	FT%	ORB	DRB	TRB	AST	PF	DQ	STL	BLK	TO	MPG	PPG	RPG	APG	PCM
85-86	Denver	48	1	330	153	61	150	.407	0	0	.000	31	39	.795	37	60	97	16	63	0	3	10	38	6.9	3.2	2.0	0.3	.368
86-87	Denver	74	23	1421	705	268	570	.470	0	0	.000	169	231	.732	183	282	465	60	224	6	24	58	81	19.2	9.5	6.3	0.8	.555
87-88	Denver	79	45	1779	1002	435	884	.492	0	0	.000	132	170	.776	130	307	437	78	241	1	22	81	71	22.5	12.7	5.5	1.0	.547
88-89	Denver	77	22	1308	583	257	577	.445	0	0	.000	69	81	.852	105	182	287	49	194	2	29	41	46	17.0	7.6	3.7	0.6	.406
89-90	Denver	81	55	1995	1001	445	895	.497	0	1	.000	111	134	.828	174	420	594	82	300	10	40	104	73	24.6	12.4	7.3	1.0	.571

YEAR TEAM	GP	GS	MIN	PTS	FGM	FGA	FG%	3PM	3PA	3P%	FTM	FTA	FT%	ORB	DRB	TRB	AST	PF	DQ	STL	BLK	TO	MPG	PPG	RPG	APG	PCM
90-91 Denver	70	69	2325	875	405	885	.458	2	5	.400	63	93	.677	170	508	678	70	307	**15**	52	132	84	33.2	12.5	9.7	1.0	.460
91-92 Atlanta	81	61	1968	729	347	726	.478	5	23	.217	30	40	.750	94	299	393	107	233	1	35	48	49	24.3	9.0	4.9	1.3	.394
92-93 Atlanta	22	6	283	71	30	80	.375	2	6	.333	9	13	.692	20	35	55	5	61	2	5	10	11	12.9	3.2	2.5	0.2	.192
NBA Season Totals	532	282	11409	5119	2248	4767	.472	9	35	.257	614	801	.767	913	2093	3006	467	1623	37	210	484	453	21.4	9.6	5.7	0.9	....
85-86 Denver	10	4	175	111	39	96	.406	0	0	.000	33	41	.805	27	33	60	10	28	1	5	9	7	17.5	11.1	6.0	1.0	.653
86-87 Denver	3	3	92	49	22	45	.489	0	0	.000	5	10	.500	8	15	23	7	12	0	2	2	5	30.7	16.3	7.7	2.3	.518
87-88 Denver	11	11	277	138	60	127	.472	0	0	.000	18	20	.900	25	46	71	7	33	0	1	12	6	25.2	12.5	6.5	0.6	.503
88-89 Denver	2	0	4	0	0	0	.000	0	0	.000	0	0	.000	0	0	0	0	1	0	0	0	1	2.0	0.0	0.0	0.0	-.349
89-90 Denver	3	0	84	47	19	48	.396	0	0	.000	9	10	.900	8	18	26	1	10	0	2	4	2	28.0	15.7	8.7	0.3	.522
NBA Playoff Totals	29	18	632	345	140	316	.443	0	0	.000	65	81	.802	68	112	180	25	84	1	10	27	21	21.8	11.9	6.2	0.9	....

• RATKOVICZ, George

George Ratkovicz

Born: Nov. 13, 1922. Chicago, IL, United States. Height: 6'6". Weight: 220 lbs. Drafted: — College: none

YEAR TEAM	GP	GS	MIN	PTS	FGM	FGA	FG%	3PM	3PA	3P%	FTM	FTA	FT%	ORB	DRB	TRB	AST	PF	DQ	STL	BLK	TO	MPG	PPG	RPG	APG	PCM
41-42 Chicago-N	13	....	....	32	9	....	....	....	....	....	14	....	....	....	....	....	....	....	....	....	....	....	....	2.5	....	....	....
45-46 Chicago-N	33	....	....	226	80	....	....	....	....	....	66	113	.584	....	....	....	....	....	....	....	....	....	....	6.8	....	....	....
46-47 Chicago-N	37	....	....	112	43	....	....	....	....	....	26	58	.448	....	....	....	....	68	....	....	....	....	....	3.0	....	....	....
47-48 Rochester-N	53	....	....	234	79	....	....	....	....	....	76	119	.639	....	....	....	....	135	....	....	....	....	....	4.4	....	....	....
48-49 Tri-Cities-N	64	....	....	324	109	....	....	....	....	....	106	175	.606	....	....	....	....	207	....	....	....	....	....	5.1	....	....	....
49-50 Syracuse	62	....	....	535	162	439	.369	....	....	....	211	348	.606	....	....	....	124	201	....	....	....	....	....	8.6	....	2.0	....
50-51 Syracuse	66	....	....	849	264	636	.415	....	....	....	321	439	.731	....	....	547	193	256	11	....	....	....	....	12.9	8.3	2.9	....
51-52 Syracuse	66	....	1356	493	165	473	.349	....	....	....	163	242	.674	....	....	328	90	235	8	....	....	....	20.5	7.5	5.0	1.4	.377
52-53 Bal/Mil	71	....	2235	678	208	619	.336	....	....	....	262	373	.702	....	....	522	217	287	16	....	....	....	31.5	9.5	7.4	3.1	.399
53-54 Milwaukee	69	....	2170	570	197	501	.393	....	....	....	176	273	.645	....	....	523	154	255	11	....	....	....	31.4	8.3	7.6	2.2	.368
54-55 Milwaukee	9	....	102	16	3	19	.158	....	....	....	10	23	.435	....	....	17	13	15	0	....	....	....	11.3	1.8	1.9	1.4	.220
NBA Season Totals	343	....	5863	3141	999	2687	.372	....	....	....	1143	1698	.673	....	....	1937	791	1249	46	....	....	....	17.1	9.2	5.6	2.3	....
NBL Season Totals	200	....	....	928	320	....	....	....	....	....	288	465	....	....	....	....	....	410	....	....	....	....	....	4.6	....	....	....
Career Totals	543	....	5863	4069	1319	2687	....	....	....	....	1431	2163	....	....	....	1937	791	1659	46	....	....	....	10.8	7.5	3.6	1.5	....
46-47 Chicago-N	10	....	....	20	6	....	....	....	....	....	8	9	.889	....	....	....	....	....	....	....	....	....	....	2.0	....	....	....
47-48 Rochester-N	11	....	....	60	22	....	....	....	....	....	16	28	.571	....	....	....	....	....	....	....	....	....	....	5.5	....	....	....
48-49 Tri-Cities-N	6	....	....	38	11	....	....	....	....	....	16	22	.727	....	....	....	....	....	....	....	....	....	....	6.3	....	....	....
49-50 Syracuse	11	....	....	144	47	121	.388	....	....	....	50	73	.685	....	....	....	21	45	....	....	....	....	....	13.1	....	1.9	....
50-51 Syracuse	7	....	....	97	28	59	.475	....	....	....	41	55	.745	....	....	63	14	33	0	....	....	....	....	13.9	9.0	2.0	....
51-52 Syracuse	6	....	59	18	5	15	.333	....	....	....	8	20	.400	....	....	22	3	16	0	....	....	....	9.8	3.0	3.7	0.5	.347
NBA Playoff Totals	24	....	59	259	80	195	.410	....	....	....	99	148	.669	....	....	85	38	94	0	....	....	....	2.5	10.8	3.5	1.6	....
NBL Playoff Totals	27	....	....	118	39	....	....	....	....	....	40	59	....	....	....	....	....	....	....	....	....	....	....	4.4	....	....	....
Career Playoff Totals	51	....	59	377	119	195	....	....	....	....	139	207	....	....	....	85	38	94	0	....	....	....	1.2	7.4	1.7	0.7	....

• RATLEFF, Ed

William Edward Ratleff

Born: Mar. 29, 1950. Bellefontaine, OH, United States. Height: 6'6". Weight: 195 lbs. Drafted: 1973 College: Long Beach State

YEAR TEAM	GP	GS	MIN	PTS	FGM	FGA	FG%	3PM	3PA	3P%	FTM	FTA	FT%	ORB	DRB	TRB	AST	PF	DQ	STL	BLK	TO	MPG	PPG	RPG	APG	PCM
73-74 Houston	81	....	1773	611	254	585	.434	....	....	....	103	129	.798	93	193	286	181	182	2	90	27	....	21.9	7.5	3.5	2.2	.390
74-75 Houston	80	....	2563	941	392	851	.461	....	....	....	157	190	.826	185	274	459	259	231	5	146	51	....	32.0	11.8	5.7	3.2	.439
75-76 Houston	72	....	2401	796	314	647	.485	....	....	....	168	206	.816	107	272	379	260	234	4	114	37	....	33.3	11.1	5.3	3.6	.423
76-77 Houston	37	....	533	166	70	161	.435	....	....	....	26	42	.619	24	53	77	43	45	0	20	6	....	14.4	4.5	2.1	1.2	.331
77-78 Houston	68	....	1163	299	130	310	.419	....	....	....	39	47	.830	56	106	162	153	109	0	60	22	68	17.1	4.4	2.4	2.3	.358
NBA Season Totals	338	....	8433	2813	1160	2554	.454	....	....	....	493	614	.803	465	898	1363	896	801	11	430	143	68	24.9	8.3	4.0	2.7	....
74-75 Houston	8	....	291	89	36	87	.414	....	....	....	17	20	.850	24	29	53	35	31	0	14	1	....	36.4	11.1	6.6	4.4	.400
NBA Playoff Totals	8	....	291	89	36	87	.414	....	....	....	17	20	.850	24	29	53	35	31	0	14	1	....	36.4	11.1	6.6	4.4	....

• RATLIFF, Mike

Michael D. Ratliff

Born: June 7, 1951. New Albany, MS, United States. Height: 6'10". Weight: 230 lbs. Drafted: 1972 College: Eau Claire State

YEAR TEAM	GP	GS	MIN	PTS	FGM	FGA	FG%	3PM	3PA	3P%	FTM	FTA	FT%	ORB	DRB	TRB	AST	PF	DQ	STL	BLK	TO	MPG	PPG	RPG	APG	PCM
72-73 Omaha	58	....	681	241	98	235	.417	....	....	....	45	84	.536	....	....	194	38	111	1	....	....	....	11.7	4.2	3.3	0.7	.395
73-74 Omaha	2	....	4	0	0	0	.000	....	....	....	0	0	.000	0	0	0	0	0	0	0	0	....	2.0	0.0	0.0	0.0	.000
NBA Season Totals	60	....	685	241	98	235	.417	....	....	....	45	84	.536	0	0	194	38	111	1	0	0	....	11.4	4.0	3.2	0.6	....

• RATLIFF, Theo

Theo Curtis Ratliff

Born: Apr. 17, 1973. Demopolis, AL, United States. Height: 6'10". Weight: 225 lbs. Drafted: 1995 College: Wyoming

YEAR TEAM	GP	GS	MIN	PTS	FGM	FGA	FG%	3PM	3PA	3P%	FTM	FTA	FT%	ORB	DRB	TRB	AST	PF	DQ	STL	BLK	TO	MPG	PPG	RPG	APG	PCM
95-96 Detroit	75	2	1305	341	128	230	.557	0	1	.000	85	120	.708	110	187	297	13	144	1	16	116	53	17.4	4.5	4.0	0.2	.405
96-97 Detroit	76	38	1292	439	179	337	.531	0	0	.000	81	116	.698	109	147	256	13	181	2	29	111	53	17.0	5.8	3.4	0.2	.406
97-98 Detroit	24	12	586	157	57	111	.514	0	0	.000	43	63	.683	46	75	121	15	83	2	12	55	34	24.4	6.5	5.0	0.6	.371
97-98 Philadelphia	58	55	1861	652	249	486	.512	0	0	.000	154	218	.706	175	251	426	42	209	6	38	203	81	32.1	11.2	7.3	0.7	.479
98-99 Philadelphia	50	50	1627	560	197	419	.470	0	0	.000	166	229	.725	139	268	407	30	180	8	45	149	92	32.5	11.2	8.1	0.6	.455
99-00 Philadelphia	57	56	1795	676	247	491	.503	0	0	.000	182	236	.771	140	295	435	36	185	4	32	171	108	31.5	11.9	7.6	0.6	.483
00-01 Philadelphia	50	50	1800	621	228	457	.499	0	0	.000	165	217	.760	125	288	413	58	165	3	30	187	126	36.0	12.4	8.3	1.2	.464
01-02 Atlanta	3	2	82	26	10	20	.500	0	0	.000	6	11	.545	5	11	16	1	8	0	1	8	7	27.3	8.7	5.3	0.3	.347
02-03 Atlanta	81	81	2518	706	276	595	.464	0	0	.000	154	214	.720	154	453	607	73	271	3	56	**262**	137	31.1	8.7	7.5	0.9	.421
NBA Season Totals	474	346	12866	4178	1571	3146	.499	0	1	.000	1036	1424	.728	1003	1975	2978	281	1426	29	259	1262	691	27.1	8.8	6.3	0.6	....
95-96 Detroit	1	0	4	0	0	0	.000	0	0	.000	0	0	.000	0	0	0	0	0	0	0	0	0	4.0	0.0	0.0	0.0	.000
96-97 Detroit	3	0	18	8	3	4	.750	0	0	.000	2	4	.500	2	2	4	1	5	0	1	4	3	6.0	2.7	1.3	0.3	.581
98-99 Philadelphia	7	7	204	51	20	43	.465	0	0	.000	11	19	.579	23	28	51	6	19	0	5	18	7	29.1	7.3	7.3	0.9	.416
99-00 Philadelphia	10	10	374	130	48	101	.475	0	0	.000	34	47	.723	28	51	79	9	35	1	10	30	17	37.4	13.0	7.9	0.9	.435
NBA Playoff Totals	21	17	600	189	71	148	.480	0	0	.000	47	70	.671	53	81	134	16	59	1	16	52	27	28.6	9.0	6.4	0.8	....

• RAUTINS, Leo

Leo R. Rautins

Born: Mar. 20, 1960. Toronto, ON, Canada. Height: 6'8". Weight: 215 lbs. Drafted: 1983 College: Syracuse

YEAR	TEAM	GP	GS	MIN	PTS	FGM	FGA	FG%	3PM	3PA	3P%	FTM	FTA	FT%	ORB	DRB	TRB	AST	PF	DQ	STL	BLK	TO	MPG	PPG	RPG	APG	PCM
83-84	Philadelphia	28	3	196	48	21	58	.362	0	0	.000	6	10	.600	9	24	33	29	31	0	9	2	20	7.0	1.7	1.2	1.0	.258
84-85	Atlanta	4	0	12	0	0	2	.000	0	0	.000	0	0	.000	1	1	2	3	3	0	0	0	1	3.0	0.0	0.5	0.8	.073
NBA Season Totals		32	3	208	48	21	60	.350	0	0	.000	6	10	.600	10	25	35	32	34	0	9	2	21	6.5	1.5	1.1	1.0	....
83-84	Philadelphia	3	0	5	3	1	3	.333	1	2	.500	0	0	.000	2	0	2	1	2	0	1	0	0	1.7	1.0	0.7	0.3	.814
NBA Playoff Totals		3	0	5	3	1	3	.333	1	2	.500	0	0	.000	2	0	2	1	2	0	1	0	0	1.7	1.0	0.7	0.3	....

• RAY, Clifford

Clifford Ray

Born: Jan. 21, 1949. Union, SC, United States. Height: 6'9". Weight: 230 lbs. Drafted: 1971 College: Oklahoma

YEAR	TEAM	GP	GS	MIN	PTS	FGM	FGA	FG%	3PM	3PA	3P%	FTM	FTA	FT%	ORB	DRB	TRB	AST	PF	DQ	STL	BLK	TO	MPG	PPG	RPG	APG	PCM
71-72	Chicago	82	....	1872	578	222	445	.499	....	....	....	134	218	.615	....	....	869	254	296	5	....	....	....	22.8	7.0	10.6	3.1	.673
72-73	Chicago	73	....	2009	625	254	516	.492	....	....	....	117	189	.619	....	....	797	271	232	5	....	....	....	27.5	8.6	10.9	3.7	.629
73-74	Chicago	80	....	2632	747	313	612	.511	....	....	....	121	199	.608	285	692	977	246	281	5	58	173	....	32.9	9.3	12.2	3.1	.552
74-75	Golden State	82	....	2519	769	299	573	.522	....	....	....	171	284	.602	259	611	870	178	305	9	95	116	....	30.7	9.4	10.6	2.2	.517
75-76	Golden State	82	....	2184	564	212	404	.525	....	....	....	140	230	.609	270	506	776	149	247	2	78	83	....	26.6	6.9	9.5	1.8	.499
76-77	Golden State	77	....	2018	631	263	450	.584	....	....	....	105	199	.528	199	416	615	112	242	5	74	81	....	26.2	8.2	8.0	1.5	.487
77-78	Golden State	79	....	2268	692	272	476	.571	....	....	....	148	243	.609	236	522	758	147	291	9	74	90	150	28.7	8.8	9.6	1.9	.523
78-79	Golden State	82	....	1917	568	231	439	.526	....	....	....	106	190	.558	213	395	608	136	264	4	47	50	156	23.4	6.9	7.4	1.7	.453
79-80	Golden State	81	....	1683	490	203	383	.530	0	2	.000	84	149	.564	122	344	466	183	266	6	51	32	154	20.8	6.0	5.8	2.3	.437
80-81	Golden State	66	....	838	157	64	152	.421	0	0	.000	29	62	.468	73	144	217	52	194	2	24	13	73	12.7	2.4	3.3	0.8	.233
NBA Season Totals		784	....	19940	5821	2333	4450	.524	0	2	.000	1155	1963	.588	1657	3630	6953	1728	2618	52	501	638	533	25.4	7.4	8.9	2.2	....
71-72	Chicago	4	....	161	61	27	51	.529	....	....	....	7	9	.778	....	....	66	16	15	0	....	....	....	40.3	15.3	16.5	4.0	.672
72-73	Chicago	5	....	36	6	3	8	.375	....	....	....	0	0	.000	....	....	9	1	2	0	....	....	....	7.2	1.2	1.8	0.2	.270
73-74	Chicago	11	....	362	107	51	102	.500	....	....	....	5	15	.333	44	78	122	35	45	0	14	21	....	32.9	9.7	11.1	3.2	.509
74-75	Golden State	17	....	495	104	36	69	.522	....	....	....	32	53	.604	55	111	166	38	60	0	14	21	....	29.1	6.1	9.8	2.2	.458
75-76	Golden State	13	....	377	118	48	79	.608	....	....	....	22	34	.647	43	87	130	20	47	2	19	19	....	29.0	9.1	10.0	1.5	.532
76-77	Golden State	10	....	304	100	42	76	.553	....	....	....	16	28	.571	54	61	115	15	37	0	4	9	....	30.4	10.0	11.5	1.5	.545
NBA Playoff Totals		60	....	1735	496	207	385	.538	....	....	....	82	139	.590	196	337	608	125	206	2	51	70	....	28.9	8.3	10.1	2.1	....

• RAY, Don

Donald L. (Duck) Ray

Born: July 8, 1921. Mt. Juliet, TN, United States. Died: Nov.23, 1998. Height: 6'5". Weight: 190 lbs. Drafted: 1948 College: Western Kentucky

YEAR	TEAM	GP	GS	MIN	PTS	FGM	FGA	FG%	3PM	3PA	3P%	FTM	FTA	FT%	ORB	DRB	TRB	AST	PF	DQ	STL	BLK	TO	MPG	PPG	RPG	APG	PCM
48-49	Tri-Cities-N	46	....	....	326	123	....	....	....	....	....	80	117	.684	....	....	....	....	103	....	....	....	....	....	7.1	....	....	....
49-50	Tri-Cities	61	....	....	364	130	403	.323	....	....	....	104	149	.698	....	....	....	60	147	....	....	....	....	....	6.0	....	1.0	....
NBA Season Totals		61	....	....	364	130	403	.323	....	....	....	104	149	.698	....	....	....	60	147	....	....	....	....	....	6.0	....	1.0	....
NBL Season Totals		46	....	....	326	123	....	....	....	....	....	80	117	....	....	....	....	....	103	....	....	....	....	....	7.1	....	....	....
Career Totals		107	....	....	690	253	403	....	....	....	....	184	266	....	....	....	....	60	250	....	....	....	....	....	6.4	....	0.6	....
48-49	Tri-Cities-N	6	....	....	49	16	....	....	....	....	....	17	21	.810	....	....	....	....	....	....	....	....	....	....	8.2	....	....	....
49-50	Tri-Cities	3	....	....	18	4	13	.308	....	....	....	10	11	.909	....	....	....	0	7	....	....	....	....	....	6.0	....	0.0	....
NBA Playoff Totals		3	....	....	18	4	13	.308	....	....	....	10	11	.909	....	....	....	0	7	....	....	....	....	....	6.0	....	0.0	....
NBL Playoff Totals		6	....	....	49	16	....	....	....	....	....	17	21	....	....	....	....	....	....	....	....	....	....	....	8.2	....	....	....
Career Playoff Totals		9	....	....	67	20	13	....	....	....	....	27	32	....	....	....	....	0	7	....	....	....	....	....	7.4	....	0.0	....

• RAY, James

James Earl Ray

Born: July 27, 1957. New Orleans, LA, United States. Height: 6'8". Weight: 215 lbs. Drafted: 1980 College: Jacksonville

YEAR	TEAM	GP	GS	MIN	PTS	FGM	FGA	FG%	3PM	3PA	3P%	FTM	FTA	FT%	ORB	DRB	TRB	AST	PF	DQ	STL	BLK	TO	MPG	PPG	RPG	APG	PCM
80-81	Denver	18	....	148	37	15	49	.306	0	1	.000	7	10	.700	13	24	37	11	31	0	4	4	13	8.2	2.1	2.1	0.6	.214
81-82	Denver	40	4	262	124	51	116	.440	1	1	1.000	21	36	.583	18	47	65	26	59	0	10	16	36	6.6	3.1	1.6	0.7	.415
82-83	Denver	45	3	433	173	70	153	.458	0	1	.000	33	51	.647	37	89	126	39	83	2	24	19	50	9.6	3.8	2.8	0.9	.468
NBA Season Totals		103	7	843	334	136	318	.428	1	3	.333	61	97	.629	68	160	228	76	173	2	38	39	99	8.2	3.2	2.2	0.7	....
81-82	Denver	1	0	2	0	0	0	.000	0	0	.000	0	0	.000	0	0	0	0	1	0	0	1	0	2.0	0.0	0.0	0.0	.230
82-83	Denver	3	0	18	3	1	6	.167	0	0	.000	1	4	.250	1	2	3	0	3	0	0	1	0	6.0	1.0	1.0	0.0	-.034
NBA Playoff Totals		4	0	20	3	1	6	.167	0	0	.000	1	4	.250	1	2	3	0	4	0	0	2	0	5.0	0.8	0.8	0.0	....

• RAY, Jim

James E. Ray

Born: Jan. 12, 1934. Height: 6'1". Weight: 180 lbs. Drafted: 1956 College: Toledo

YEAR	TEAM	GP	GS	MIN	PTS	FGM	FGA	FG%	3PM	3PA	3P%	FTM	FTA	FT%	ORB	DRB	TRB	AST	PF	DQ	STL	BLK	TO	MPG	PPG	RPG	APG	PCM
56-57	Syracuse	4	....	43	7	2	11	.182	....	....	....	3	5	.600	....	....	5	3	4	0	....	....	....	10.8	1.8	1.3	0.8	.129
59-60	Syracuse	4	....	21	2	1	6	.167	....	....	....	0	0	.000	....	....	0	2	3	0	....	....	....	5.3	0.5	0.0	0.5	-.020
NBA Season Totals		8	....	64	9	3	17	.176	....	....	....	3	5	.600	....	....	5	5	7	0	....	....	....	8.0	1.1	0.6	0.6	....

• RAYL, Jimmy

James R. (The Splendid Splinter) Rayl

Born: June 21, 1941. Kokomo, IN, United States. Height: 6'2". Weight: 175 lbs. Drafted: 1963 College: Indiana

YEAR	TEAM	GP	GS	MIN	PTS	FGM	FGA	FG%	3PM	3PA	3P%	FTM	FTA	FT%	ORB	DRB	TRB	AST	PF	DQ	STL	BLK	TO	MPG	PPG	RPG	APG	PCM
67-68	Indiana-A	74	....	2193	886	317	819	.387	57	175	.326	195	243	.802	....	....	238	210	197	1	....	....	193	29.6	12.0	3.2	2.8	.370
68-69	Indiana-A	27	....	567	239	72	202	.356	34	92	.370	61	68	.897	25	42	67	63	80	2	....	....	50	21.0	8.9	2.5	2.3	.387
ABA Season Totals		101	....	2760	1125	389	1021	.381	91	267	.341	256	311	.823	25	42	305	273	277	3	....	....	243	27.3	11.1	3.0	2.7	....
67-68	Indiana-A	3	....	118	39	15	42	.357	4	14	.286	5	7	.714			10	14	14	0	....	....	9	39.3	13.0	3.3	4.7	.293
ABA Playoff Totals		3	....	118	39	15	42	.357	4	14	.286	5	7	.714	....	....	10	14	14	0	....	....	9	39.3	13.0	3.3	4.7	....

YEAR	TEAM	GP	GS	MIN	PTS	FGM	FGA	FG%	3PM	3PA	3P%	FTM	FTA	FT%	ORB	DRB	TRB	AST	PF	DQ	STL	BLK	TO	MPG	PPG	RPG	APG	PCM

• RAYMOND, Craig
Craig Milford Raymond

Born: Apr. 5, 1945. Aberdeen, WA, United States.　　Height: 6'11".　　Weight: 235 lbs.　　Drafted: 1967　　College: Brigham Young

YEAR	TEAM	GP	GS	MIN	PTS	FGM	FGA	FG%	3PM	3PA	3P%	FTM	FTA	FT%	ORB	DRB	TRB	AST	PF	DQ	STL	BLK	TO	MPG	PPG	RPG	APG	PCM
68-69	Philadelphia	27	....	177	55	22	64	.344	....	....	....	11	17	.647	....	....	68	8	46	2	....	....	....	6.6	2.0	2.5	0.3	.363
69-70	Los Angeles-A	46	....	1567	710	286	583	.491	0	1	.000	138	206	.670	105	435	540	99	174	6	....	....	137	34.1	15.4	11.7	2.2	.592
69-70	Pittsburgh-A	34	....	789	252	100	229	.437	0	0	.000	52	98	.531	41	215	256	55	100	2	....	....	110	23.2	7.4	7.5	1.6	.458
70-71	Memphis-A	56	....	1102	351	142	330	.430	0	1	.000	67	106	.632	63	226	289	91	124	2	....	....	102	19.7	6.3	5.2	1.6	.432
71-72	Florida-A	64	....	889	256	104	227	.458	0	3	.000	48	76	.632	63	221	284	67	108	0	....	....	91	13.9	4.0	4.4	1.0	.464
72-73	Indiana-A	6	....	33	5	2	8	.250	0	0	.000	1	2	.500	3	7	10	1	8	0	....	....	3	5.5	0.8	1.7	0.2	.171
72-73	San Diego-A	8	....	135	29	10	31	.323	0	0	.000	9	12	.750	20	43	63	6	16	0	....	....	12	16.9	3.6	7.9	0.8	.480
NBA Season Totals		27	....	177	55	22	64	.344	....	....	....	11	17	.647	....	....	68	8	46	2	....	....	....	6.6	2.0	2.5	0.3	....
ABA Season Totals		214	....	4515	1603	644	1408	.457	0	5	.000	315	500	.630	295	1147	1442	319	530	10	....	....	455	21.1	7.5	6.7	1.5	....
Career Totals		241	....	4692	1658	666	1472	.452	0	5	.000	326	517	.631	295	1147	1510	327	576	12	....	....	455	19.5	6.9	6.3	1.4	....
69-70	Los Angeles-A	17	....	664	296	113	240	.471	0	0	.000	70	91	.769	45	209	254	41	....	2	....	....	75	39.1	17.4	14.9	2.4	....
70-71	Memphis-A	2	....	17	8	3	7	.429	0	0	.000	2	2	1.000	2	2	4	1	1	0	....	....	2	8.5	4.0	2.0	0.5	.518
71-72	Florida-A	4	....	62	32	15	23	.652	0	0	.000	2	3	.667	....	....	22	2	6	....	....	....	1	15.5	8.0	5.5	0.5	.701
ABA Playoff Totals		23	....	743	336	131	270	.485	0	0	.000	74	96	.771	47	211	280	44	7	2	....	....	78	32.3	14.6	12.2	1.9	....

• REA, Connie
Connie Mack Rea

Born: Jan. 27, 1935.　　Height: 6'3".　　Weight: 175 lbs.　　Drafted: 1953　　College: Centenary

YEAR	TEAM	GP	GS	MIN	PTS	FGM	FGA	FG%	3PM	3PA	3P%	FTM	FTA	FT%	ORB	DRB	TRB	AST	PF	DQ	STL	BLK	TO	MPG	PPG	RPG	APG	PCM
53-54	Baltimore	20	....	154	23	9	43	.209	....	....	....	5	16	.313	....	....	31	16	13	0	....	....	....	7.7	1.2	1.6	0.8	.214
NBA Season Totals		20	....	154	23	9	43	.209	....	....	....	5	16	.313	....	....	31	16	13	0	....	....	....	7.7	1.2	1.6	0.8	....

• REAVES, Joe
Joe L. Reaves

Born: May 27, 1950.　　Height: 6'5".　　Weight: 210 lbs.　　Drafted: 1973　　College: Bethel (TN)

YEAR	TEAM	GP	GS	MIN	PTS	FGM	FGA	FG%	3PM	3PA	3P%	FTM	FTA	FT%	ORB	DRB	TRB	AST	PF	DQ	STL	BLK	TO	MPG	PPG	RPG	APG	PCM
73-74	Memphis-A	12	....	172	64	30	70	.429	0	0	.000	4	6	.667	17	29	46	6	23	....	2	7	17	14.3	5.3	3.8	0.5	.380
73-74	Phoenix	7	....	38	16	6	11	.545	0	0	.000	4	11	.364	2	6	8	1	6	0	0	2	....	5.4	2.3	1.1	0.1	.373
NBA Season Totals		7	....	38	16	6	11	.545	0	0	.000	4	11	.364	2	6	8	1	6	0	0	2	....	5.4	2.3	1.1	0.1	....
ABA Season Totals		12	....	172	64	30	70	.429	0	0	.000	4	6	.667	17	29	46	6	23	....	2	7	17	14.3	5.3	3.8	0.5	....
Career Totals		19	....	210	80	36	81	.444	0	0	.000	8	17	.471	19	35	54	7	29	0	2	9	17	11.1	4.2	2.8	0.4	....

• REBRACA, Zeljko
Zeljko Rebraca

Born: Apr. 9, 1972. Apatin, Yugoslavia.　　Height: 7'　　Weight: 257 lbs.　　Drafted: 1994　　College: none

YEAR	TEAM	GP	GS	MIN	PTS	FGM	FGA	FG%	3PM	3PA	3P%	FTM	FTA	FT%	ORB	DRB	TRB	AST	PF	DQ	STL	BLK	TO	MPG	PPG	RPG	APG	PCM
01-02	Detroit	74	4	1179	513	189	374	.505	0	0	.000	135	175	.771	84	206	290	38	192	0	28	73	84	15.9	6.9	3.9	0.5	.475
02-03	Detroit	30	12	488	198	80	145	.552	0	0	.000	38	48	.792	27	65	92	9	79	1	6	17	29	16.3	6.6	3.1	0.3	.382
NBA Season Totals		104	16	1667	711	269	519	.518	0	0	.000	173	223	.776	111	271	382	47	271	1	34	90	113	16.0	6.8	3.7	0.5	....
01-02	Detroit	5	0	69	21	5	11	.455	0	0	.000	11	14	.786	4	6	10	0	14	0	1	1	4	13.8	4.2	2.0	0.0	.219
02-03	Detroit	4	0	29	17	6	17	.353	0	0	.000	5	7	.714	2	3	5	0	9	1	0	0	1	7.3	4.3	1.3	0.0	.195
NBA Playoff Totals		9	0	98	38	11	28	.393	0	0	.000	16	21	.762	6	9	15	0	23	1	1	1	5	10.9	4.2	1.7	0.0	....

• RECASNER, Eldridge
Eldridge David Recasner

Born: Dec. 14, 1967. New Orleans, LA, United States.　　Height: 6'3".　　Weight: 190 lbs.　　Drafted: —　　College: Washington

YEAR	TEAM	GP	GS	MIN	PTS	FGM	FGA	FG%	3PM	3PA	3P%	FTM	FTA	FT%	ORB	DRB	TRB	AST	PF	DQ	STL	BLK	TO	MPG	PPG	RPG	APG	PCM
94-95	Denver	3	0	13	6	1	6	.167	0	1	.000	4	4	1.000	0	2	2	1	0	0	3	0	2	4.3	2.0	0.7	0.3	.399
95-96	Houston	63	27	1275	436	149	359	.415	81	191	.424	57	66	.864	31	113	144	170	111	1	23	5	63	20.2	6.9	2.3	2.7	.365
96-97	Atlanta	71	4	1207	405	148	350	.423	58	140	.414	51	58	.879	35	80	115	94	97	0	38	4	64	17.0	5.7	1.6	1.3	.294
97-98	Atlanta	59	14	1454	548	206	452	.456	62	148	.419	74	79	.937	32	110	142	117	94	0	41	1	89	24.6	9.3	2.4	2.0	.338
98-99	Charlotte	44	2	708	222	82	184	.446	24	60	.400	34	39	.872	20	57	77	91	66	0	17	1	58	16.1	5.0	1.8	2.1	.330
99-00	Charlotte	7	0	28	7	3	7	.429	1	4	.250	0	0	.000	0	4	4	5	1	0	0	0	4	4.0	1.0	0.6	0.7	.429
00-01	Charlotte	43	0	403	103	38	114	.333	13	39	.333	14	18	.778	13	37	50	39	30	0	6	1	27	9.4	2.4	1.2	0.9	.222
01-02	Charlotte	1	0	2	0	0	0	.000	0	0	.000	0	0	.000	0	0	0	0	1	0	0	0	0	2.0	0.0	0.0	0.0	-.227
01-02	LA Clippers	5	0	31	5	2	6	.333	0	1	.000	1	1	1.000	0	0	0	5	3	0	1	0	1	6.2	1.0	0.0	1.0	.177
NBA Season Totals		296	47	5121	1732	629	1478	.426	239	584	.409	235	265	.887	131	403	534	522	403	1	129	12	304	17.3	5.9	1.8	1.8	....
95-96	Houston	1	0	8	0	0	3	.000	0	1	.000	0	0	.000	0	1	1	2	0	0	0	0	1	8.0	0.0	1.0	2.0	-.088
96-97	Atlanta	10	0	121	31	11	26	.423	4	11	.364	5	8	.625	3	8	11	9	9	0	2	0	7	12.1	3.1	1.1	0.9	.220
97-98	Atlanta	4	0	89	29	10	25	.400	7	12	.583	2	2	1.000	0	4	4	8	7	0	2	0	2	22.3	7.3	1.0	2.0	.274
00-01	Charlotte	2	0	9	3	0	1	.000	0	0	.000	3	4	.750	0	1	1	2	0	0	0	0	1	4.5	1.5	0.5	1.0	.429
NBA Playoff Totals		17	0	227	63	21	55	.382	11	24	.458	10	14	.714	3	14	17	21	16	0	4	0	11	13.4	3.7	1.0	1.2	....

• REDD, Michael
Michael Wesley Redd

Born: Aug. 24, 1979. Columbus, OH, United States.　　Height: 6'6".　　Weight: 220 lbs.　　Drafted: 2000　　College: Ohio State

YEAR	TEAM	GP	GS	MIN	PTS	FGM	FGA	FG%	3PM	3PA	3P%	FTM	FTA	FT%	ORB	DRB	TRB	AST	PF	DQ	STL	BLK	TO	MPG	PPG	RPG	APG	PCM
00-01	Milwaukee	6	0	35	13	5	19	.263	0	3	.000	3	6	.500	3	1	4	1	2	0	1	0	1	5.8	2.2	0.7	0.2	.082
01-02	Milwaukee	67	8	1417	767	294	609	.483	88	198	.444	91	115	.791	77	147	224	91	96	0	42	7	57	21.1	11.4	3.3	1.4	.510
02-03	Milwaukee	82	14	2315	1241	455	971	.469	182	416	.438	149	185	.805	98	273	371	117	143	0	100	13	74	28.2	15.1	4.5	1.4	.515
NBA Season Totals		155	22	3767	2021	754	1599	.472	270	617	.438	243	306	.794	178	421	599	209	241	0	143	20	132	24.3	13.0	3.9	1.3	....
02-03	Milwaukee	6	0	128	58	21	52	.404	3	12	.250	13	14	.929	9	12	21	11	15	0	2	1	7	21.3	9.7	3.5	1.8	.391
NBA Playoff Totals		6	0	128	58	21	52	.404	3	12	.250	13	14	.929	9	12	21	11	15	0	2	1	7	21.3	9.7	3.5	1.8	....

YEAR	TEAM	GP	GS	MIN	PTS	FGM	FGA	FG%	3PM	3PA	3P%	FTM	FTA	FT%	ORB	DRB	TRB	AST	PF	DQ	STL	BLK	TO	MPG	PPG	RPG	APG	PCM

• REDDOUT, Frank
Franklin P. Reddout

Born: 1931.   Height: 6'5".   Weight: 195 lbs.   Drafted: —   College: Syracuse

YEAR TEAM	GP	GS	MIN	PTS	FGM	FGA	FG%	3PM	3PA	3P%	FTM	FTA	FT%	ORB	DRB	TRB	AST	PF	DQ	STL	BLK	TO	MPG	PPG	RPG	APG	PCM
53-54 Rochester	7	....	18	13	5	6	.833	....	....	....	3	4	.750	....	....	9	0	6	0	....	....	....	2.6	1.9	1.3	0.0	.900
NBA Season Totals	7	....	18	13	5	6	.833	....	....	....	3	4	.750	....	....	9	0	6	0	....	....	....	2.6	1.9	1.3	0.0	....

• REDMOND, Marlon
Marlon Bernard Redmond

Born: Apr. 15, 1955. San Francisco, CA, United States.   Height: 6'6".   Weight: 188 lbs.   Drafted: 1977   College: San Francisco

YEAR TEAM	GP	GS	MIN	PTS	FGM	FGA	FG%	3PM	3PA	3P%	FTM	FTA	FT%	ORB	DRB	TRB	AST	PF	DQ	STL	BLK	TO	MPG	PPG	RPG	APG	PCM
78-79 Kansas City	49	....	736	355	162	375	.432	....	....	....	31	50	.620	57	51	108	57	93	2	28	16	54	15.0	7.2	2.2	1.2	.359
78-79 Philadelphia	4	....	23	2	1	12	.083	....	....	....	0	0	.000	0	1	1	1	3	0	0	0	1	5.8	0.5	0.3	0.3	-.353
79-80 Kansas City	24	....	298	142	59	138	.428	0	9	.000	24	34	.706	18	34	52	19	27	0	4	9	19	12.4	5.9	2.2	0.8	.390
NBA Season Totals	77	....	1057	499	222	525	.423	0	9	.000	55	84	.655	75	86	161	77	123	2	32	25	74	13.7	6.5	2.1	1.0	....
78-79 Philadelphia	1	....	2	0	0	2	.000	....	....	....	0	0	.000	0	0	0	0	0	0	0	0	0	2.0	0.0	0.0	0.0	-.898
NBA Playoff Totals	1	....	2	0	0	2	.000	....	....	....	0	0	.000	0	0	0	0	0	0	0	0	0	2.0	0.0	0.0	0.0	....

• REED, Billy
Billy Reed

Born: —.   Height: 5'11".   Weight: 185 lbs.   Drafted: —   College: Notre Dame

YEAR TEAM	GP	GS	MIN	PTS	FGM	FGA	FG%	3PM	3PA	3P%	FTM	FTA	FT%	ORB	DRB	TRB	AST	PF	DQ	STL	BLK	TO	MPG	PPG	RPG	APG	PCM
46-47 Oshkosh-N	17	....	....	45	20	....	....	....	....	....	5	18	.278	....	....	....	....	....	....	....	....	....	....	2.6	....	....	....
NBL Season Totals	17	....	....	45	20	....	....	....	....	....	5	18	....	....	....	....	....	....	....	....	....	....	....	2.6	....	....	....

• REED, Hub
Hubert F. Reed

Born: Oct. 4, 1936. Harrah, OK, United States.   Height: 6'9".   Weight: 215 lbs.   Drafted: 1958   College: Oklahoma City

YEAR TEAM	GP	GS	MIN	PTS	FGM	FGA	FG%	3PM	3PA	3P%	FTM	FTA	FT%	ORB	DRB	TRB	AST	PF	DQ	STL	BLK	TO	MPG	PPG	RPG	APG	PCM
58-59 St. Louis	65	....	950	325	136	317	.429	....	....	....	53	71	.746	....	....	317	32	171	2	....	....	....	14.6	5.0	4.9	0.5	.417
59-60 St. Louis	2	....	17	2	1	3	.333	....	....	....	0	0	.000	....	....	2	0	2	0	....	....	....	8.5	1.0	1.0	0.0	.073
59-60 Cincinnati	69	....	1803	672	269	598	.450	....	....	....	134	184	.728	....	....	612	69	228	6	....	....	....	26.1	9.7	8.9	1.0	.481
60-61 Cincinnati	75	....	1216	397	156	364	.429	....	....	....	85	122	.697	....	....	367	69	199	7	....	....	....	16.2	5.3	4.9	0.9	.422
61-62 Cincinnati	80	....	1446	466	203	460	.441	....	....	....	60	82	.732	....	....	440	53	267	9	....	....	....	18.1	5.8	5.5	0.7	.388
62-63 Cincinnati	80	....	1299	472	199	427	.466	....	....	....	74	98	.755	....	....	398	83	261	7	....	....	....	16.2	5.9	5.0	1.0	.457
63-64 LA Lakers	46	....	386	76	33	91	.363	....	....	....	10	15	.667	....	....	107	23	73	0	....	....	....	8.4	1.7	2.3	0.5	.290
64-65 Detroit	62	....	753	208	84	221	.380	....	....	....	40	58	.690	....	....	206	38	136	2	....	....	....	12.1	3.4	3.3	0.6	.330
NBA Season Totals	479	....	7870	2618	1081	2481	.436	....	....	....	456	630	.724	....	....	2449	367	1337	33	....	....	....	16.4	5.5	5.1	0.8	....
58-59 St. Louis	4	....	48	11	4	11	.364	....	....	....	3	6	.500	....	....	17	1	7	0	....	....	....	12.0	2.8	4.3	0.3	.334
61-62 Cincinnati	4	....	69	21	9	21	.429	....	....	....	3	4	.750	....	....	20	5	9	0	....	....	....	17.3	5.3	5.0	1.3	.427
62-63 Cincinnati	12	....	187	71	28	70	.400	....	....	....	15	18	.833	....	....	64	10	38	0	....	....	....	15.6	5.9	5.3	0.8	.451
63-64 LA Lakers	1	....	12	4	2	4	.500	....	....	....	0	2	.000	....	....	2	0	2	0	....	....	....	12.0	4.0	2.0	0.0	.204
NBA Playoff Totals	21	....	316	107	43	106	.406	....	....	....	21	30	.700	....	....	103	16	56	0	....	....	....	15.0	5.1	4.9	0.8	....

• REED, Ron
Ronald Lee Reed

Born: Nov. 2, 1942. La Porte, IN, United States.   Height: 6'5".   Weight: 205 lbs.   Drafted: 1965   College: Notre Dame

YEAR TEAM	GP	GS	MIN	PTS	FGM	FGA	FG%	3PM	3PA	3P%	FTM	FTA	FT%	ORB	DRB	TRB	AST	PF	DQ	STL	BLK	TO	MPG	PPG	RPG	APG	PCM
65-66 Detroit	57	....	997	426	186	524	.355	....	....	....	54	100	.540	....	....	339	92	133	1	....	....	....	17.5	7.5	5.9	1.6	.470
66-67 Detroit	62	....	1248	525	223	600	.372	....	....	....	79	133	.594	....	....	423	81	145	2	....	....	....	20.1	8.5	6.8	1.3	.465
NBA Season Totals	119	....	2245	951	409	1124	.364	....	....	....	133	233	.571	....	....	762	173	278	3	....	....	....	18.9	8.0	6.4	1.5	....

• REED, Willis
Willis (The Captain) Reed Jr.

Born: June 25, 1942. Hico, LA, United States.   Height: 6'9".   Weight: 235 lbs.   Drafted: 1964   College: Grambling   HOF: 1982

YEAR TEAM	GP	GS	MIN	PTS	FGM	FGA	FG%	3PM	3PA	3P%	FTM	FTA	FT%	ORB	DRB	TRB	AST	PF	DQ	STL	BLK	TO	MPG	PPG	RPG	APG	PCM
64-65 New York	80	....	3042	1560	629	1457	.432	....	....	....	302	407	.742	....	....	1175	133	339	14	....	....	....	38.0	19.5	14.7	1.7	.598
65-66 New York	76	....	2537	1178	438	1009	.434	....	....	....	302	399	.757	....	....	883	91	323	13	....	....	....	33.4	15.5	11.6	1.2	.539
66-67 New York	78	....	2824	1628	635	1298	.489	....	....	....	358	487	.735	....	....	1136	126	293	9	....	....	....	36.2	20.9	14.6	1.6	.704
67-68 New York	81	....	2879	1685	659	1346	.490	....	....	....	367	509	.721	....	....	1073	159	343	12	....	....	....	35.5	20.8	13.2	2.0	.691
68-69 New York	82	....	3108	1733	704	1351	.521	....	....	....	325	435	.747	....	....	1191	190	314	7	....	....	....	37.9	21.1	14.5	2.3	.718
69-70 New York	81	....	3089	1755	702	1385	.507	....	....	....	351	464	.756	....	....	1126	161	287	2	....	....	....	38.1	21.7	13.9	2.0	.696
70-71 New York	73	....	2855	1527	614	1330	.462	....	....	....	299	381	.785	....	....	1003	148	228	1	....	....	....	39.1	20.9	13.7	2.0	.634
71-72 New York	11	....	363	147	60	137	.438	....	....	....	27	39	.692	....	....	96	22	30	0	....	....	....	33.0	13.4	8.7	2.0	.469
72-73 New York	69	....	1876	760	334	705	.474	....	....	....	92	124	.742	....	....	590	126	205	0	....	....	....	27.2	11.0	8.6	1.8	.528
73-74 New York	19	....	500	210	84	184	.457	....	....	....	42	53	.792	47	94	141	30	49	0	12	21	....	26.3	11.1	7.4	1.6	.508
NBA Season Totals	650	....	23073	12183	4859	10202	.476	....	....	....	2465	3298	.747	47	94	8414	1186	2411	58	12	21	....	35.5	18.7	12.9	1.8	....
66-67 New York	4	....	148	110	43	80	.538	....	....	....	24	25	.960	....	....	55	7	19	1	....	....	....	37.0	27.5	13.8	1.8	.843
67-68 New York	6	....	210	128	53	98	.541	....	....	....	22	30	.733	....	....	62	11	24	1	....	....	....	35.0	21.3	10.3	1.8	.676
68-69 New York	10	....	429	257	101	198	.510	....	....	....	55	70	.786	....	....	141	19	40	1	....	....	....	42.9	25.7	14.1	1.9	.683
69-70 New York	18	....	732	426	178	378	.471	....	....	....	70	95	.737	....	....	248	51	60	0	....	....	....	40.7	23.7	13.8	2.8	.667
70-71 New York	12	....	504	188	81	196	.413	....	....	....	26	39	.667	....	....	144	27	41	0	....	....	....	42.0	15.7	12.0	2.3	.438
72-73 New York	17	....	486	212	97	208	.466	....	....	....	18	21	.857	....	....	129	30	65	1	....	....	....	28.6	12.5	7.6	1.8	.478
73-74 New York	11	....	132	37	17	45	.378	....	....	....	3	5	.600	4	18	22	4	26	0	2	0	....	12.0	3.4	2.0	0.4	.186
NBA Playoff Totals	78	....	2641	1358	570	1203	.474	....	....	....	218	285	.765	4	18	801	149	275	4	2	0	....	33.9	17.4	10.3	1.9	....

YEAR	TEAM	GP	GS	MIN	PTS	FGM	FGA	FG%	3PM	3PA	3P%	FTM	FTA	FT%	ORB	DRB	TRB	AST	PF	DQ	STL	BLK	TO	MPG	PPG	RPG	APG	PCM

• REEVES, Bill
Bill Reeves

Born: 1904. Height: 5'10". Weight: 165 lbs. Drafted: — College: Indiana Central

YEAR	TEAM	GP	GS	MIN	PTS	FGM	FGA	FG%	3PM	3PA	3P%	FTM	FTA	FT%	ORB	DRB	TRB	AST	PF	DQ	STL	BLK	TO	MPG	PPG	RPG	APG	PCM
37-38	Non-Skids-N	8	....	....	14	5	....	....	....	....	....	4	....	....	....	....	....	....	....	....	....	....	....	....	1.8	....	....	....
NBL Season Totals		8	....	....	14	5	....	....	....	....	....	4	....	....	....	....	....	....	....	....	....	....	....	....	1.8	....	....	....
37-38	Non-Skids-N	1	....	....	0	0	....	....	....	....	....	0	....	....	....	....	....	....	....	....	....	....	....	....	0.0	....	....	....
NBL Playoff Totals		1	....	....	0	0	....	....	....	....	....	0	....	....	....	....	....	....	....	....	....	....	....	....	0.0	....	....	....

• REEVES, Bryant
Bryant (Big Country) Reeves

Born: June 8, 1973. Fort Smith, AR, United States. Height: 7' Weight: 275 lbs. Drafted: 1995 College: Oklahoma State

YEAR	TEAM	GP	GS	MIN	PTS	FGM	FGA	FG%	3PM	3PA	3P%	FTM	FTA	FT%	ORB	DRB	TRB	AST	PF	DQ	STL	BLK	TO	MPG	PPG	RPG	APG	PCM
95-96	Vancouver	77	63	2460	1021	401	877	.457	0	3	.000	219	299	.732	178	392	570	109	226	2	43	55	154	31.9	13.3	7.4	1.4	.418
96-97	Vancouver	75	75	2777	1213	498	1025	.486	1	11	.091	216	307	.704	174	436	610	160	270	3	29	67	173	37.0	16.2	8.1	2.1	.440
97-98	Vancouver	74	74	2527	1207	492	941	.523	0	4	.000	223	316	.706	196	389	585	155	278	6	39	80	155	34.1	16.3	7.9	2.1	.513
98-99	Vancouver	25	14	702	271	102	251	.406	0	1	.000	67	116	.578	50	88	138	37	103	3	13	8	47	28.1	10.8	5.5	1.5	.301
99-00	Vancouver	69	67	1773	611	252	562	.448	0	4	.000	107	165	.648	126	264	390	82	245	0	33	38	119	25.7	8.9	5.7	1.2	.334
00-01	Vancouver	75	48	1832	622	254	552	.460	1	4	.250	113	142	.796	132	320	452	80	243	5	43	54	90	24.4	8.3	6.0	1.1	.400
NBA Season Totals		395	341	12071	4945	1999	4208	.475	2	27	.074	945	1345	.703	856	1889	2745	623	1365	19	200	302	738	30.6	12.5	6.9	1.6	....

• REEVES, Khalid
Khalid Reeves

Born: July 15, 1972. Queens, NY, United States. Height: 6'3". Weight: 199 lbs. Drafted: 1994 College: Arizona

YEAR	TEAM	GP	GS	MIN	PTS	FGM	FGA	FG%	3PM	3PA	3P%	FTM	FTA	FT%	ORB	DRB	TRB	AST	PF	DQ	STL	BLK	TO	MPG	PPG	RPG	APG	PCM
94-95	Miami	67	17	1462	619	206	465	.443	67	171	.392	140	196	.714	52	134	186	288	139	1	77	10	134	21.8	9.2	2.8	4.3	.493
95-96	Charlotte	20	5	418	162	54	118	.458	11	36	.306	43	51	.843	11	29	40	72	46	0	16	1	30	20.9	8.1	2.0	3.6	.426
95-96	New Jersey	31	7	415	117	41	109	.376	17	55	.309	18	31	.581	7	32	39	46	69	2	21	2	34	13.4	3.8	1.3	1.5	.216
96-97	New Jersey	50	18	1048	414	141	359	.393	76	192	.396	56	75	.747	22	66	88	170	119	3	23	7	80	21.0	8.3	1.8	3.4	.347
96-97	Dallas	13	12	384	102	43	111	.387	7	35	.200	9	12	.750	12	19	31	56	40	0	11	2	26	29.5	7.8	2.4	4.3	.248
97-98	Dallas	82	54	1950	717	248	593	.418	56	152	.368	165	213	.775	54	131	185	230	195	3	80	10	131	23.8	8.7	2.3	2.8	.344
98-99	Detroit	11	0	112	25	8	21	.381	1	3	.333	8	14	.571	3	4	7	11	13	0	4	0	7	10.2	2.3	0.6	1.0	.185
99-00	Chicago	3	0	48	11	3	12	.250	0	3	.000	5	5	1.000	2	2	4	13	8	0	2	0	6	16.0	3.7	1.3	4.3	.279
NBA Season Totals		277	113	5837	2167	744	1788	.416	235	647	.363	444	597	.744	163	417	580	886	629	9	234	32	448	21.1	7.8	2.1	3.2	....

• REGAN, Richie
Richard Joseph Regan

Born: Nov. 30, 1930. Newark, NJ, United States. Height: 6'2". Weight: 180 lbs. Drafted: 1953 College: Seton Hall

YEAR	TEAM	GP	GS	MIN	PTS	FGM	FGA	FG%	3PM	3PA	3P%	FTM	FTA	FT%	ORB	DRB	TRB	AST	PF	DQ	STL	BLK	TO	MPG	PPG	RPG	APG	PCM
55-56	Rochester	72	....	1746	565	240	681	.352	....	....	....	85	133	.639	....	....	174	222	179	4	....	....	....	24.3	7.8	2.4	3.1	.315
56-57	Rochester	71	....	2100	696	257	780	.329	....	....	....	182	235	.774	....	....	205	222	179	1	....	....	....	29.6	9.8	2.9	3.1	.310
57-58	Cincinnati	72	....	1648	524	202	569	.355	....	....	....	120	172	.698	....	....	175	185	174	0	....	....	....	22.9	7.3	2.4	2.6	.326
NBA Season Totals		215	....	5494	1785	699	2030	.344	....	....	....	387	540	.717	....	....	554	629	532	5	....	....	....	25.6	8.3	2.6	2.9	....
57-58	Cincinnati	2	....	63	24	12	26	.462	....	....	....	0	1	.000	....	....	9	3	5	0	....	....	....	31.5	12.0	4.5	1.5	.349
NBA Playoff Totals		2	....	63	24	12	26	.462	....	....	....	0	1	.000	....	....	9	3	5	0	....	....	....	31.5	12.0	4.5	1.5	....

• REGH, Bob
Bob Regh

Born: Oct. 22, 1912. Died: June 24, 1999. Height: 6'2". Weight: — Drafted: — College: —

YEAR	TEAM	GP	GS	MIN	PTS	FGM	FGA	FG%	3PM	3PA	3P%	FTM	FTA	FT%	ORB	DRB	TRB	AST	PF	DQ	STL	BLK	TO	MPG	PPG	RPG	APG	PCM
42-43	Sheboygan-N	11	....	....	24	10	....	....	....	....	....	4	....	....	....	....	....	....	....	....	....	....	....	2.2	....	....	....
43-44	Sheboygan-N	1	....	....	0	0	....	....	....	....	....	0	....	....	....	....	....	....	....	....	....	....	....	0.0	....	....	....
NBL Season Totals		12	....	....	24	10	....	....	....	....	....	4	....	....	....	....	....	....	....	....	....	....	....	2.0	....	....	....
42-43	Sheboygan-N	4	....	....	4	2	....	....	....	....	....	0	....	....	....	....	....	....	....	....	....	....	....	1.0	....	....	....
NBL Playoff Totals		4	....	....	4	2	....	....	....	....	....	0	....	....	....	....	....	....	....	....	....	....	....	1.0	....	....	....

• REHFELDT, Don
Donald Rehfeldt

Born: Jan. 7, 1927. Chicago, IL, United States. Died: Oct. 17, 1980. Height: 6'6". Weight: 210 lbs. Drafted: 1950 College: Wisconsin

YEAR	TEAM	GP	GS	MIN	PTS	FGM	FGA	FG%	3PM	3PA	3P%	FTM	FTA	FT%	ORB	DRB	TRB	AST	PF	DQ	STL	BLK	TO	MPG	PPG	RPG	APG	PCM
50-51	Baltimore	59	....	....	431	164	426	.385	....	....	....	103	139	.741	....	....	251	68	146	4	....	....	....	....	7.3	4.3	1.2	....
51-52	Bal/Mil	39	....	788	261	99	285	.347	....	....	....	63	80	.788	....	....	243	50	102	2	....	....	....	20.2	6.7	6.2	1.3	.411
NBA Season Totals		98	....	788	692	263	711	.370	....	....	....	166	219	.758	....	....	494	118	248	6	....	....	....	8.0	7.1	5.0	1.2	....

• REHM, Fred
Fred Rehm

Born: 1921. Height: 6'3". Weight: 195 lbs. Drafted: — College: Wisconsin

YEAR	TEAM	GP	GS	MIN	PTS	FGM	FGA	FG%	3PM	3PA	3P%	FTM	FTA	FT%	ORB	DRB	TRB	AST	PF	DQ	STL	BLK	TO	MPG	PPG	RPG	APG	PCM
45-46	Oshkosh-N	32	....	....	90	36	....	....	....	....	....	18	....	....	....	....	....	....	....	....	....	....	....	2.8	....	....	....
47-48	Flint-N	14	....	....	61	19	....	....	....	....	....	23	30	.767	....	....	....	....	....	....	....	....	....	4.4	....	....	....
47-48	Oshkosh-N	26	....	....	72	21	....	....	....	....	....	30	42	.714	....	....	....	....	....	....	....	....	....	2.8	....	....	....
NBL Season Totals		72	....	....	223	76	....	....	....	....	....	71	72	....	....	....	....	....	....	....	....	....	....	3.1	....	....	....
45-46	Oshkosh-N	5	....	....	20	9	....	....	....	....	....	2	2	1.000	....	....	....	....	....	....	....	....	....	4.0	....	....	....
47-48	Oshkosh-N	4	....	....	17	4	....	....	....	....	....	9	10	.900	....	....	....	....	....	....	....	....	....	4.3	....	....	....
NBL Playoff Totals		9	....	....	37	13	....	....	....	....	....	11	12	....	....	....	....	....	....	....	....	....	....	4.1	....	....	....

• REID, Billy

William Jennings Reid Jr.

Born: Sept. 10, 1957. New York, NY, United States. Height: 6'5". Weight: 190 lbs. Drafted: 1980 College: San Francisco

YEAR	TEAM	GP	GS	MIN	PTS	FGM	FGA	FG%	3PM	3PA	3P%	FTM	FTA	FT%	ORB	DRB	TRB	AST	PF	DQ	STL	BLK	TO	MPG	PPG	RPG	APG	PCM
80-81	Golden State	59	....	597	190	84	185	.454	0	5	.000	22	39	.564	27	33	60	71	111	0	33	5	77	10.1	3.2	1.0	1.2	.228
NBA Season Totals		59	....	597	190	84	185	.454	0	5	.000	22	39	.564	27	33	60	71	111	0	33	5	77	10.1	3.2	1.0	1.2	....

• REID, Don

Don Cory Reid

Born: Dec. 30, 1973. Washington, DC, United States. Height: 6'8". Weight: 250 lbs. Drafted: 1995 College: Georgetown

YEAR	TEAM	GP	GS	MIN	PTS	FGM	FGA	FG%	3PM	3PA	3P%	FTM	FTA	FT%	ORB	DRB	TRB	AST	PF	DQ	STL	BLK	TO	MPG	PPG	RPG	APG	PCM
95-96	Detroit	69	46	997	263	106	187	.567	0	0	.000	51	77	.662	78	125	203	11	199	2	47	40	41	14.4	3.8	2.9	0.2	.328
96-97	Detroit	47	14	462	132	54	112	.482	0	1	.000	24	32	.750	36	65	101	14	105	1	16	15	24	9.8	2.8	2.1	0.3	.305
97-98	Detroit	68	44	994	238	94	176	.534	0	0	.000	50	71	.704	77	98	175	26	183	2	25	55	27	14.6	3.5	2.6	0.4	.308
98-99	Detroit	47	30	935	242	97	174	.557	0	0	.000	48	79	.608	66	104	170	33	156	2	27	43	36	19.9	5.1	3.6	0.7	.330
99-00	Detroit	21	3	165	35	16	34	.471	0	0	.000	3	6	.500	5	20	25	1	45	1	5	12	11	7.9	1.7	1.2	0.0	.158
99-00	Washington	17	0	333	109	44	78	.564	0	0	.000	21	28	.750	26	51	77	10	73	4	19	19	12	19.6	6.4	4.5	0.6	.439
00-01	Orlando	65	7	764	210	82	145	.566	0	0	.000	46	75	.613	84	158	242	21	190	4	23	54	48	11.8	3.2	3.7	0.3	.421
01-02	Orlando	68	5	714	224	90	190	.474	0	0	.000	44	68	.647	65	111	176	27	180	2	20	44	54	10.5	3.3	2.6	0.4	.335
02-03	Detroit	1	0	10	1	0	3	.000	0	0	.000	1	2	.500	0	0	0	0	4	0	0	0	0	10.0	1.0	0.0	0.0	-.399
NBA Season Totals		403	149	5374	1454	583	1099	.530	0	1	.000	288	438	.658	437	732	1169	143	1135	18	182	282	253	13.3	3.6	2.9	0.4	....
95-96	Detroit	3	0	26	3	1	3	.333	0	0	.000	1	3	.333	0	1	1	1	8	0	0	2	1	8.7	1.0	0.3	0.3	-.025
96-97	Detroit	1	0	3	4	0	0	.000	0	0	.000	4	4	1.000	0	1	1	0	0	0	0	0	0	3.0	4.0	1.0	0.0	1.644
98-99	Detroit	4	0	21	4	2	3	.667	0	0	.000	0	0	.000	2	2	4	1	2	0	0	0	0	5.3	1.0	1.0	0.3	.328
00-01	Orlando	3	0	25	10	4	5	.800	0	1	.000	2	6	.333	5	6	11	0	9	0	1	2	2	8.3	3.3	3.7	0.0	.562
01-02	Orlando	4	0	38	9	4	6	.667	0	0	.000	1	2	.500	3	3	6	0	15	0	1	2	0	9.5	2.3	1.5	0.0	.213
NBA Playoff Totals		15	0	113	30	11	17	.647	0	1	.000	8	15	.533	10	13	23	2	34	0	2	6	3	7.5	2.0	1.5	0.1	....

• REID, J.R.

Herman (J.R.) Reid Jr.

Born: Mar. 31, 1968. Virginia Beach, VA, United States. Height: 6'9". Weight: 247 lbs. Drafted: 1989 College: North Carolina

YEAR	TEAM	GP	GS	MIN	PTS	FGM	FGA	FG%	3PM	3PA	3P%	FTM	FTA	FT%	ORB	DRB	TRB	AST	PF	DQ	STL	BLK	TO	MPG	PPG	RPG	APG	PCM
89-90	Charlotte	82	82	2757	908	358	814	.440	0	5	.000	192	289	.664	199	492	691	101	292	7	92	54	172	33.6	11.1	8.4	1.2	.373
90-91	Charlotte	80	80	2467	902	360	773	.466	0	2	.000	182	259	.703	154	348	502	89	286	6	87	47	152	30.8	11.3	6.3	1.1	.362
91-92	Charlotte	51	7	1257	560	213	435	.490	0	3	.000	134	190	.705	96	221	317	81	159	0	49	23	82	24.6	11.0	6.2	1.6	.498
92-93	Charlotte	17	1	295	127	42	98	.429	0	1	.000	43	58	.741	20	50	70	24	49	1	11	5	24	17.4	7.5	4.1	1.4	.435
92-93	San Antonio	66	24	1592	653	241	497	.485	0	4	.000	171	222	.770	100	286	386	56	217	2	36	26	99	24.1	9.9	5.8	0.8	.424
93-94	San Antonio	70	11	1344	627	260	530	.491	0	3	.000	107	153	.699	91	129	220	73	165	0	43	25	84	19.2	9.0	3.1	1.0	.408
94-95	San Antonio	81	37	1566	563	201	396	.508	1	2	.500	160	233	.687	120	273	393	55	230	2	60	32	113	19.3	7.0	4.9	0.7	.412
95-96	San Antonio	32	5	643	208	72	164	.439	0	1	.000	64	87	.736	35	88	123	14	98	0	25	10	48	20.1	6.5	3.8	0.4	.284
95-96	New York	33	16	670	219	88	160	.550	0	0	.000	43	55	.782	38	94	132	28	89	0	18	7	30	20.3	6.6	4.0	0.8	.377
97-98	Charlotte	79	1	1109	384	146	318	.459	3	8	.375	89	122	.730	72	138	210	51	172	1	35	19	63	14.0	4.9	2.7	0.6	.336
98-99	Charlotte	16	16	556	243	88	169	.521	0	0	.000	67	84	.798	21	92	113	25	63	2	22	10	28	34.8	15.2	7.1	1.6	.481
98-99	LA Lakers	25	10	473	126	44	108	.407	0	1	.000	38	53	.717	24	75	99	23	72	1	15	0	23	18.9	5.0	4.0	0.9	.289
99-00	Milwaukee	34	7	602	150	53	127	.417	1	7	.143	43	56	.768	29	88	117	18	81	2	19	5	20	17.7	4.4	3.4	0.5	.282
00-01	Cleveland	6	0	39	10	2	5	.400	0	0	.000	6	8	.750	5	3	8	1	4	0	2	1	1	6.5	1.7	1.3	0.2	.377
NBA Season Totals		672	297	15370	5680	2168	4594	.472	5	37	.135	1339	1869	.716	1004	2377	3381	639	1977	24	514	264	939	22.9	8.5	5.0	1.0	....
92-93	San Antonio	10	2	220	85	29	60	.483	0	2	.000	27	35	.771	16	34	50	15	31	0	8	8	13	22.0	8.5	5.0	1.5	.470
93-94	San Antonio	4	0	56	15	6	21	.286	0	0	.000	3	5	.600	3	9	12	3	10	0	1	2	1	14.0	3.8	3.0	0.8	.211
94-95	San Antonio	15	1	209	91	29	59	.492	0	0	.000	33	39	.846	14	28	42	9	36	0	7	4	15	13.9	6.1	2.8	0.6	.423
95-96	New York	1	0	7	2	1	1	1.000	0	0	.000	0	0	.000	0	1	1	1	2	0	0	0	1	7.0	2.0	1.0	1.0	.303
97-98	Charlotte	9	0	114	30	11	28	.393	0	1	.000	8	10	.800	7	13	20	2	23	0	3	2	11	12.7	3.3	2.2	0.2	.158
98-99	LA Lakers	8	8	178	26	10	28	.357	0	0	.000	6	8	.750	9	33	42	3	33	1	4	5	2	22.3	3.3	5.3	0.4	.232
NBA Playoff Totals		47	11	784	249	86	197	.437	0	3	.000	77	97	.794	49	118	167	33	135	1	23	21	43	16.7	5.3	3.6	0.7	....

• REID, Jim

James Reid

Born: Aug. 3, 1945. Height: 6'6". Weight: 210 lbs. Drafted: 1967 College: Winston-Salem State

YEAR	TEAM	GP	GS	MIN	PTS	FGM	FGA	FG%	3PM	3PA	3P%	FTM	FTA	FT%	ORB	DRB	TRB	AST	PF	DQ	STL	BLK	TO	MPG	PPG	RPG	APG	PCM
67-68	Philadelphia	6	....	52	21	10	20	.500	....	....	....	1	5	.200	....	....	11	3	6	0	....	....	....	8.7	3.5	1.8	0.5	.412
NBA Season Totals		6	....	52	21	10	20	.500	....	....	....	1	5	.200	....	....	11	3	6	0	....	....	....	8.7	3.5	1.8	0.5	....

• REID, Robert

Robert Keith Reid

Born: Aug. 30, 1955. Atlanta, GA, United States. Height: 6'8". Weight: 205 lbs. Drafted: 1977 College: St. Mary's (TX)

YEAR	TEAM	GP	GS	MIN	PTS	FGM	FGA	FG%	3PM	3PA	3P%	FTM	FTA	FT%	ORB	DRB	TRB	AST	PF	DQ	STL	BLK	TO	MPG	PPG	RPG	APG	PCM
77-78	Houston	80	....	1849	585	261	574	.455	....	....	....	63	96	.656	111	248	359	121	277	8	67	51	80	23.1	7.3	4.5	1.5	.356
78-79	Houston	82	....	2259	895	382	777	.492	....	....	....	131	186	.704	129	354	483	230	302	7	75	48	131	27.5	10.9	5.9	2.8	.469
79-80	Houston	76	....	2304	991	419	861	.487	0	3	.000	153	208	.736	140	301	441	244	281	2	132	57	167	30.3	13.0	5.8	3.2	.488
80-81	Houston	82	....	2963	1301	536	1113	.482	0	4	.000	229	303	.756	164	419	583	344	325	4	163	66	197	36.1	15.9	7.1	4.2	.516
81-82	Houston	77	75	2913	1035	437	958	.456	1	10	.100	160	214	.748	175	336	511	314	297	2	115	48	154	37.8	13.4	6.6	4.1	.416
83-84	Houston	64	28	1936	895	406	857	.474	2	8	.250	81	123	.659	97	244	341	217	243	5	88	30	90	30.3	14.0	5.3	3.4	.474
84-85	Houston	82	0	1763	713	312	648	.481	1	16	.063	88	126	.698	81	192	273	171	196	1	48	22	98	21.5	8.7	3.3	2.1	.398
85-86	Houston	82	5	2157	986	409	881	.464	6	33	.182	162	214	.757	67	234	301	222	231	3	91	16	98	26.3	12.0	3.7	2.7	.437
86-87	Houston	75	63	2594	1029	420	1006	.417	53	162	.327	136	177	.768	47	242	289	323	232	2	75	21	105	34.6	13.7	3.9	4.3	.371
87-88	Houston	62	31	980	393	165	356	.463	13	34	.382	50	63	.794	38	87	125	67	118	0	27	5	43	15.8	6.3	2.0	1.1	.339
88-89	Charlotte	82	54	2152	1207	519	1214	.428	17	52	.327	152	196	.776	82	220	302	153	235	2	53	20	107	26.2	14.7	3.7	1.9	.392
89-90	Portland	12	1	85	31	13	33	.394	1	3	.333	4	8	.500	1	7	8	8	17	0	2	2	1	7.1	2.6	0.7	0.7	.250
89-90	Charlotte	60	27	1117	383	162	414	.391	9	29	.310	50	78	.641	33	110	143	82	136	0	36	14	42	18.6	6.4	2.4	1.4	.267
90-91	Philadelphia	3	0	37	4	2	14	.143	0	0	.000	0	0	.000	2	7	9	4	3	0	1	3	3	12.3	1.3	3.0	1.3	.135
NBA Season Totals		919	284	25109	10448	4443	9706	.458	103	354	.291	1459	1992	.732	1167	3001	4168	2500	2893	36	973	403	1316	27.3	11.4	4.5	2.7	....
78-79	Houston	2	....	45	20	7	17	.412	....	....	....	6	9	.667	5	4	9	2	7	0	1	2	5	22.5	10.0	4.5	1.0	.334
79-80	Houston	7	....	266	126	52	102	.510	0	1	.000	22	26	.846	14	41	55	26	28	0	6	7	19	38.0	18.0	7.9	3.7	.523

YEAR	TEAM	GP	GS	MIN	PTS	FGM	FGA	FG%	3PM	3PA	3P%	FTM	FTA	FT%	ORB	DRB	TRB	AST	PF	DQ	STL	BLK	TO	MPG	PPG	RPG	APG	PCM
80-81	Houston	21	....	868	339	139	303	.459	0	2	.000	61	92	.663	56	86	142	98	80	2	50	24	44	41.3	16.1	6.8	4.7	.464
81-82	Houston	3	3	115	34	15	31	.484	0	0	.000	4	5	.800	9	17	26	9	10	0	5	2	0	38.3	11.3	8.7	3.0	.472
84-85	Houston	5	0	87	38	19	45	.422	0	4	.000	0	0	.000	3	14	17	5	22	0	4	2	6	17.4	7.6	3.4	1.0	.284
85-86	Houston	20	20	773	298	124	288	.431	3	21	.143	47	59	.797	13	70	83	137	74	1	27	1	42	38.7	14.9	4.2	6.9	.409
86-87	Houston	10	10	431	129	56	155	.361	2	17	.118	15	23	.652	6	30	36	48	36	0	10	3	27	43.1	12.9	3.6	4.8	.205
87-88	Houston	4	4	114	35	15	33	.455	3	7	.429	2	3	.667	3	12	15	8	13	0	2	0	3	28.5	8.8	3.8	2.0	.292
90-91	Philadelphia	7	0	41	6	3	9	.333	0	1	.000	0	0	.000	1	7	8	2	7	0	1	0	2	5.9	0.9	1.1	0.3	.142
NBA Playoff Totals		79	37	2740	1025	430	983	.437	8	53	.151	157	217	.724	110	281	391	335	277	3	106	41	148	34.7	13.0	4.9	4.2	....

• REISER, Chick

Joseph Francis (Chick) Reiser

Born: Dec. 17, 1914. Died: July30, 1996. Height: 5'11". Weight: 165 lbs. Drafted: 1947 College: New York University

YEAR	TEAM	GP	GS	MIN	PTS	FGM	FGA	FG%	3PM	3PA	3P%	FTM	FTA	FT%	ORB	DRB	TRB	AST	PF	DQ	STL	BLK	TO	MPG	PPG	RPG	APG	PCM
43-44	Fort Wayne-N	22	....	....	81	28	....	....	....	....	....	25	....	....	....	....	....	....	....	....	....	....	....	....	3.7	....	....	....
44-45	Fort Wayne-N	30	....	....	217	82	....	....	....	....	....	53	....	....	....	....	....	....	....	....	....	....	....	....	7.2	....	....	....
45-46	Fort Wayne-N	34	....	....	233	90	....	....	....	....	....	53	80	.663	....	....	....	....	....	....	....	....	....	....	6.9	....	....	....
46-47	Fort Wayne-N	44	....	....	410	153	....	....	....	....	....	104	139	.748	....	....	....	....	**153**	....	....	....	....	....	9.3	....	....	....
47-48	Baltimore	47	....	....	541	202	628	.322	....	....	....	137	185	.741	....	....	....	40	175	....	....	....	....	....	11.5	....	0.9	....
48-49	Baltimore	57	....	....	626	219	653	.335	....	....	....	188	257	.732	....	....	....	132	202	....	....	....	....	....	11.0	....	2.3	....
49-50	Washington	67	....	....	606	197	646	.305	....	....	....	212	254	.835	....	....	....	174	223	....	....	....	....	....	9.0	....	2.6	....
NBA Season Totals		171	....	....	1773	618	1927	.321	....	....	....	537	696	.772	....	....	....	346	600	....	....	....	....	....	10.4	....	2.0	....
NBL Season Totals		130	....	....	941	353	....	....	....	....	....	235	219	....	....	....	....	....	153	....	....	....	....	....	7.2	....	....	....
Career Totals		301	....	....	2714	971	1927	....	....	....	....	772	915	....	....	....	....	346	753	....	....	....	....	....	9.0	....	1.1	....
43-44	Fort Wayne-N	5	....	....	34	13	....	....	....	....	....	8	....	....	....	....	....	....	....	....	....	....	....	....	6.8	....	....	....
44-45	Fort Wayne-N	7	....	....	58	23	....	....	....	....	....	12	....	....	....	....	....	....	....	....	....	....	....	....	8.3	....	....	....
45-46	Fort Wayne-N	4	....	....	34	15	....	....	....	....	....	4	8	.500	....	....	....	....	....	....	....	....	....	....	8.5	....	....	....
46-47	Fort Wayne-N	8	....	....	72	26	....	....	....	....	....	20	29	.690	....	....	....	....	....	....	....	....	....	....	9.0	....	....	....
47-48	Baltimore	11	....	....	103	36	139	.259	....	....	....	31	42	.738	....	....	....	7	46	....	....	....	....	....	9.4	....	0.6	....
48-49	Baltimore	3	....	....	30	6	25	.240	....	....	....	18	20	.900	....	....	....	8	15	....	....	....	....	....	10.0	....	2.7	....
49-50	Washington	2	....	....	23	7	27	.259	....	....	....	9	11	.818	....	....	....	5	11	....	....	....	....	....	11.5	....	2.5	....
NBA Playoff Totals		16	....	....	156	49	191	.257	....	....	....	58	73	.795	....	....	....	20	72	....	....	....	....	....	9.8	....	1.3	....
NBL Playoff Totals		24	....	....	198	77	....	....	....	....	....	44	37	....	....	....	....	....	....	....	....	....	....	....	8.3	....	....	....
Career Playoff Totals		40	....	....	354	126	191	....	....	....	....	102	110	....	....	....	....	20	72	....	....	....	....	....	8.9	....	0.5	....

• REISWERG, Rube

Ruben Reiswerg

Born: Aug. 10, 1912. Died: Mar.22, 1998. Height: 5'8". Weight: 175 lbs. Drafted: — College: none

YEAR	TEAM	GP	GS	MIN	PTS	FGM	FGA	FG%	3PM	3PA	3P%	FTM	FTA	FT%	ORB	DRB	TRB	AST	PF	DQ	STL	BLK	TO	MPG	PPG	RPG	APG	PCM
39-40	Indianapolis-N	4	....	....	1	0	....	....	....	....	....	1	....	....	....	....	....	....	....	....	....	....	....	....	0.3	....	....	....
NBL Season Totals		4	....	....	1	0	....	....	....	....	....	1	....	....	....	....	....	....	....	....	....	....	....	....	0.3	....	....	....

• REITER, Marty

Marty Reiter

Born: Aug. 25, 1911. Died: Feb.1986. Height: 5'7". Weight: 160 lbs. Drafted: — College: Duquesne

YEAR	TEAM	GP	GS	MIN	PTS	FGM	FGA	FG%	3PM	3PA	3P%	FTM	FTA	FT%	ORB	DRB	TRB	AST	PF	DQ	STL	BLK	TO	MPG	PPG	RPG	APG	PCM
37-38	Pittsburgh-N	1	....	....	7	3	....	....	....	....	....	1	....	....	....	....	....	....	....	....	....	....	....	....	7.0	....	....	....
38-39	Pittsburgh-N	17	....	....	79	30	....	....	....	....	....	19	....	....	....	....	....	....	....	....	....	....	....	....	4.6	....	....	....
NBL Season Totals		18	....	....	86	33	....	....	....	....	....	20	....	....	....	....	....	....	....	....	....	....	....	....	4.8	....	....	....

• RELLFORD, Richard

Richard Allen Rellford

Born: Feb. 16, 1964. Riviera Beach, FL, United States. Height: 6'6". Weight: 230 lbs. Drafted: 1986 College: Michigan

YEAR	TEAM	GP	GS	MIN	PTS	FGM	FGA	FG%	3PM	3PA	3P%	FTM	FTA	FT%	ORB	DRB	TRB	AST	PF	DQ	STL	BLK	TO	MPG	PPG	RPG	APG	PCM
87-88	San Antonio	4	0	42	16	5	8	.625	0	0	.000	6	8	.750	2	5	7	1	3	0	0	3	4	10.5	4.0	1.8	0.3	.417
NBA Season Totals		4	0	42	16	5	8	.625	0	0	.000	6	8	.750	2	5	7	1	3	0	0	3	4	10.5	4.0	1.8	0.3	....

• RENCHER, Terrence

Terrence Lamont Rencher

Born: Feb. 19, 1973. Bronx, NY, United States. Height: 6'3". Weight: 185 lbs. Drafted: 1995 College: Texas

YEAR	TEAM	GP	GS	MIN	PTS	FGM	FGA	FG%	3PM	3PA	3P%	FTM	FTA	FT%	ORB	DRB	TRB	AST	PF	DQ	STL	BLK	TO	MPG	PPG	RPG	APG	PCM
95-96	Miami	34	1	397	103	32	99	.323	9	29	.310	30	43	.698	9	33	42	54	36	0	16	1	41	11.7	3.0	1.2	1.6	.230
95-96	Phoenix	2	0	8	3	1	1	1.000	0	0	.000	1	3	.333	0	2	2	0	1	0	0	1	2	4.0	1.5	1.0	0.0	.316
NBA Season Totals		36	1	405	106	33	100	.330	9	29	.310	31	46	.674	9	35	44	54	37	0	16	2	43	11.3	2.9	1.2	1.5	....

• RENNICKE, John

John W. Rennicke

Born: Aug. 11, 1929. Height: 6'2". Weight: 185 lbs. Drafted: 1951 College: Drake

YEAR	TEAM	GP	GS	MIN	PTS	FGM	FGA	FG%	3PM	3PA	3P%	FTM	FTA	FT%	ORB	DRB	TRB	AST	PF	DQ	STL	BLK	TO	MPG	PPG	RPG	APG	PCM
51-52	Milwaukee	6	....	54	11	4	18	.222	....	....	....	3	9	.333	....	....	9	1	7	0	....	....	....	9.0	1.8	1.5	0.2	.076
NBA Season Totals		6	....	54	11	4	18	.222	....	....	....	3	9	.333	....	....	9	1	7	0	....	....	....	9.0	1.8	1.5	0.2	....

• RENSBERGER, Rob

Robert Lamar Rensberger

Born: Mar. 7, 1921. Height: 6'2". Weight: 170 lbs. Drafted: — College: Notre Dame

YEAR	TEAM	GP	GS	MIN	PTS	FGM	FGA	FG%	3PM	3PA	3P%	FTM	FTA	FT%	ORB	DRB	TRB	AST	PF	DQ	STL	BLK	TO	MPG	PPG	RPG	APG	PCM
45-46	Chicago-N	16	....	....	15	6	....	....	....	....	....	3	....	....	....	....	....	....	....	....	....	....	....	....	0.9	....	....	....
46-47	Chicago	3	....	....	0	0	7	.000	....	....	....	0	0	.000	....	....	....	0	4	....	....	....	....	....	0.0	....	0.0	....
NBA Season Totals		3	....	....	0	0	7	.000	....	....	....	0	0	.000	....	....	....	0	4	....	....	....	....	....	0.0	....	0.0	....
NBL Season Totals		16	....	....	15	6	....	....	....	....	....	3	....	....	....	....	....	....	....	....	....	....	....	....	0.9	....	....	....
Career Totals		19	....	....	15	6	7	....	....	....	....	3	0	....	....	....	....	0	4	....	....	....	....	....	0.8	....	0.0	....

YEAR	TEAM	GP	GS	MIN	PTS	FGM	FGA	FG%	3PM	3PA	3P%	FTM	FTA	FT%	ORB	DRB	TRB	AST	PF	DQ	STL	BLK	TO	MPG	PPG	RPG	APG	PCM

• RENTZIAS, Efthimi
Efthimi Rentzias

Born: Jan. 11, 1976. Trikala, Greece.　Height: 6'11".　Weight: 250 lbs.　Drafted: 1996　College: none

YEAR	TEAM	GP	GS	MIN	PTS	FGM	FGA	FG%	3PM	3PA	3P%	FTM	FTA	FT%	ORB	DRB	TRB	AST	PF	DQ	STL	BLK	TO	MPG	PPG	RPG	APG	PCM
02-03	Philadelphia	35	0	143	52	20	59	.339	4	8	.500	8	9	.889	10	16	26	7	21	0	6	2	4	4.1	1.5	0.7	0.2	.290
NBA Season Totals		35	0	143	52	20	59	.339	4	8	.500	8	9	.889	10	16	26	7	21	0	6	2	4	4.1	1.5	0.7	0.2	....

• RESPERT, Shawn
Shawn Christopher Respert

Born: Feb. 6, 1972. Detroit, MI, United States.　Height: 6'1".　Weight: 195 lbs.　Drafted: 1995　College: Michigan State

YEAR	TEAM	GP	GS	MIN	PTS	FGM	FGA	FG%	3PM	3PA	3P%	FTM	FTA	FT%	ORB	DRB	TRB	AST	PF	DQ	STL	BLK	TO	MPG	PPG	RPG	APG	PCM
95-96	Milwaukee	62	0	845	303	113	292	.387	42	122	.344	35	42	.833	28	46	74	68	67	0	32	4	43	13.6	4.9	1.2	1.1	.278
96-97	Milwaukee	14	0	83	20	6	19	.316	1	9	.111	7	7	1.000	3	4	7	8	5	0	0	0	8	5.9	1.4	0.5	0.6	.159
96-97	Toronto	27	0	412	152	53	120	.442	19	48	.396	27	32	.844	11	21	32	32	35	0	20	2	22	15.3	5.6	1.2	1.2	.327
97-98	Toronto	47	4	696	257	94	209	.450	25	67	.373	44	54	.815	30	43	73	44	58	0	29	1	33	14.8	5.5	1.6	0.9	.334
97-98	Dallas	10	0	215	82	36	84	.429	6	26	.231	4	7	.571	7	20	27	17	17	0	5	0	15	21.5	8.2	2.7	1.7	.293
98-99	Phoenix	12	1	99	37	13	36	.361	4	13	.308	7	10	.700	2	11	13	8	10	0	5	0	5	8.3	3.1	1.1	0.7	.315
NBA Season Totals		172	5	2350	851	315	760	.414	97	285	.340	124	152	.816	81	145	226	177	192	0	91	7	126	13.7	4.9	1.3	1.0	....

• RESTANI, Kevin
Kevin Gilbert (Big Bird) Restani

Born: Dec. 23, 1951. San, CA, United States.　Height: 6'9".　Weight: 225 lbs.　Drafted: 1974　College: San Francisco

YEAR	TEAM	GP	GS	MIN	PTS	FGM	FGA	FG%	3PM	3PA	3P%	FTM	FTA	FT%	ORB	DRB	TRB	AST	PF	DQ	STL	BLK	TO	MPG	PPG	RPG	APG	PCM
74-75	Milwaukee	76	....	1755	411	188	427	.440	....	....	....	35	49	.714	131	272	403	119	172	1	36	19	....	23.1	5.4	5.3	1.6	.346
75-76	Milwaukee	82	....	1650	492	234	493	.475	....	....	....	24	42	.571	115	261	376	96	151	3	36	12	....	20.1	6.0	4.6	1.2	.382
76-77	Milwaukee	64	....	1116	358	173	334	.518	....	....	....	12	24	.500	81	181	262	88	102	0	33	11	....	17.4	5.6	4.1	1.4	.444
77-78	Milwaukee	8	....	84	26	13	28	.464	....	....	....	0	2	.000	4	10	14	9	4	0	0	1	2	10.5	3.3	1.8	1.1	.378
77-78	Kansas City	46	....	463	127	59	139	.424	....	....	....	9	11	.818	32	62	94	21	37	0	5	4	14	10.1	2.8	2.0	0.5	.305
78-79	Milwaukee	81	....	1598	575	262	529	.495	....	....	....	51	73	.699	141	244	385	122	155	0	30	27	97	19.7	7.1	4.8	1.5	.438
79-80	San Antonio	82	....	1966	874	369	727	.508	5	29	.172	131	161	.814	142	244	386	189	186	0	54	12	131	24.0	10.7	4.7	2.3	.483
80-81	San Antonio	64	....	999	449	192	369	.520	3	8	.375	62	88	.705	71	103	174	81	103	0	16	14	70	15.6	7.0	2.7	1.3	.440
81-82	San Antonio	13	0	145	21	9	28	.321	0	1	.000	3	4	.750	8	27	35	7	16	0	1	4	7	11.2	1.6	2.7	0.5	.232
81-82	Cleveland	34	0	338	53	23	60	.383	0	1	.000	7	12	.583	31	46	77	15	40	0	10	7	14	9.9	1.6	2.3	0.4	.261
NBA Season Totals		550	0	10114	3386	1522	3134	.486	8	39	.205	334	466	.717	756	1450	2206	747	966	4	221	111	335	18.4	6.2	4.0	1.4	....
75-76	Milwaukee	3	....	33	2	1	5	.200	....	....	....	0	0	.000	0	5	5	1	0	0	1	0	....	11.0	0.7	1.7	0.3	.121
79-80	San Antonio	3	....	74	38	17	28	.607	0	1	.000	4	9	.444	8	8	16	3	8	0	0	1	2	24.7	12.7	5.3	1.0	.527
80-81	San Antonio	3	....	11	2	1	3	.333	0	0	.000	0	0	.000	0	2	2	0	2	0	0	1	1	3.7	0.7	0.7	0.0	.099
NBA Playoff Totals		9	....	118	42	19	36	.528	0	1	.000	4	9	.444	8	15	23	4	10	0	1	2	3	13.1	4.7	2.6	0.4	....

• REYNOLDS, George
George Reynolds

Born: Nov. 23, 1947.　Height: 6'4".　Weight: 195 lbs.　Drafted: 1969　College: Houston

YEAR	TEAM	GP	GS	MIN	PTS	FGM	FGA	FG%	3PM	3PA	3P%	FTM	FTA	FT%	ORB	DRB	TRB	AST	PF	DQ	STL	BLK	TO	MPG	PPG	RPG	APG	PCM
69-70	Detroit	10	....	44	21	8	19	.421	....	....	....	5	7	.714	....	....	14	12	10	0	....	....	....	4.4	2.1	1.4	1.2	.723
NBA Season Totals		10	....	44	21	8	19	.421	....	....	....	5	7	.714	....	....	14	12	10	0	....	....	....	4.4	2.1	1.4	1.2	....

• REYNOLDS, Jerry
Jerry (Ice) Reynolds

Born: Dec. 23, 1962. Brooklyn, NY, United States.　Height: 6'8".　Weight: 200 lbs.　Drafted: 1985　College: Louisiana State

YEAR	TEAM	GP	GS	MIN	PTS	FGM	FGA	FG%	3PM	3PA	3P%	FTM	FTA	FT%	ORB	DRB	TRB	AST	PF	DQ	STL	BLK	TO	MPG	PPG	RPG	APG	PCM
85-86	Milwaukee	55	8	508	203	72	162	.444	1	2	.500	58	104	.558	37	43	80	86	57	0	43	19	50	9.2	3.7	1.5	1.6	.490
86-87	Milwaukee	58	24	963	404	140	356	.393	6	18	.333	118	184	.641	72	101	173	106	91	0	50	30	81	16.6	7.0	3.0	1.8	.419
87-88	Milwaukee	62	21	1161	498	188	419	.449	3	7	.429	119	154	.773	70	90	160	104	97	0	74	32	105	18.7	8.0	2.6	1.7	.415
88-89	Seattle	56	0	737	428	149	357	.417	3	15	.200	127	167	.760	49	51	100	62	58	0	53	26	56	13.2	7.6	1.8	1.1	.502
89-90	Orlando	67	40	1817	858	309	741	.417	1	14	.071	239	322	.742	91	232	323	180	162	1	93	64	141	27.1	12.8	4.8	2.7	.466
90-91	Orlando	80	9	1843	1034	344	793	.434	10	34	.294	336	419	.802	88	211	299	203	123	0	95	56	168	23.0	12.9	3.7	2.5	.542
91-92	Orlando	46	16	1159	555	197	518	.380	3	24	.125	158	189	.836	47	102	149	151	69	0	63	17	97	25.2	12.1	3.2	3.3	.427
95-96	Milwaukee	19	0	191	56	21	53	.396	1	10	.100	13	21	.619	13	20	33	12	20	0	15	6	15	10.1	2.9	1.7	0.6	.325
NBA Season Totals		443	118	8379	4036	1420	3399	.418	28	124	.226	1168	1560	.749	467	850	1317	904	677	1	486	250	713	18.9	9.1	3.0	2.0	....
85-86	Milwaukee	7	0	40	20	7	17	.412	0	1	.000	6	11	.545	3	6	9	4	5	0	4	3	4	5.7	2.9	1.3	0.6	.537
86-87	Milwaukee	4	0	5	3	1	3	.333	0	1	.000	1	2	.500	1	0	1	2	0	0	3	0	0	1.3	0.8	0.3	0.5	1.307
87-88	Milwaukee	3	0	12	8	4	6	.667	0	0	.000	0	0	.000	0	1	1	1	1	0	0	0	1	4.0	2.7	0.3	0.3	.562
88-89	Seattle	4	0	40	22	7	22	.318	1	4	.250	7	10	.700	1	4	5	1	6	0	2	6	4	10.0	5.5	1.3	0.3	.333
NBA Playoff Totals		18	0	97	53	19	48	.396	1	6	.167	14	23	.609	5	11	16	8	12	0	9	9	9	5.4	2.9	0.9	0.4	....

• RHINE, Kendall
Kendall Lee Rhine

Born: Feb. 13, 1943. Eldorado, IL, United States.　Height: 6'10".　Weight: 230 lbs.　Drafted: 1964　College: Rice

YEAR	TEAM	GP	GS	MIN	PTS	FGM	FGA	FG%	3PM	3PA	3P%	FTM	FTA	FT%	ORB	DRB	TRB	AST	PF	DQ	STL	BLK	TO	MPG	PPG	RPG	APG	PCM
67-68	Kentucky-A	52	....	552	127	50	158	.316	0	1	.000	27	56	.482	....	....	235	31	120	2	....	....	36	10.6	2.4	4.5	0.6	.375
68-69	Houston-A	73	....	2116	659	255	629	.405	0	1	.000	149	265	.562	307	497	804	150	321	16	....	....	119	29.0	9.0	11.0	2.1	.478
ABA Season Totals		125	....	2668	786	305	787	.388	0	2	.000	176	321	.548	307	497	1039	181	441	18	....	....	155	21.3	6.3	8.3	1.4	....
67-68	Kentucky-A	5	....	62	10	5	17	.294	0	0	.000	0	7	.000	....	....	15	4	16	0	....	....	4	12.4	2.0	3.0	0.8	.123
ABA Playoff Totals		5	....	62	10	5	17	.294	0	0	.000	0	7	.000	....	....	15	4	16	0	....	....	4	12.4	2.0	3.0	0.8	....

• RHODES, Gene

Eugene Stephen Rhodes

Born: Sept. 2, 1927. Height: 6'1". Weight: 170 lbs. Drafted: 1952 College: Western Kentucky

YEAR	TEAM	GP	GS	MIN	PTS	FGM	FGA	FG%	3PM	3PA	3P%	FTM	FTA	FT%	ORB	DRB	TRB	AST	PF	DQ	STL	BLK	TO	MPG	PPG	RPG	APG	PCM
52-53	Indianapolis	65	....	1162	337	109	342	.319	....	....	....	119	169	.704	....	....	98	91	78	2	....	....	....	17.9	5.2	1.5	1.4	.266
NBA Season Totals		65	....	1162	337	109	342	.319	....	....	....	119	169	.704	....	....	98	91	78	2	....	....	....	17.9	5.2	1.5	1.4	....
52-53	Indianapolis	2	....	51	9	4	14	.286	....	....	....	1	4	.250	....	....	7	5	5	0	....	....	....	25.5	4.5	3.5	2.5	.202
NBA Playoff Totals		2	....	51	9	4	14	.286	....	....	....	1	4	.250	....	....	7	5	5	0	....	....	....	25.5	4.5	3.5	2.5	....

• RHODES, Rodrick

Rodrick Rhodes

Born: Sept. 24, 1973. Jersey City, NJ, United States. Height: 6'6". Weight: 225 lbs. Drafted: 1997 College: Southern California

YEAR	TEAM	GP	GS	MIN	PTS	FGM	FGA	FG%	3PM	3PA	3P%	FTM	FTA	FT%	ORB	DRB	TRB	AST	PF	DQ	STL	BLK	TO	MPG	PPG	RPG	APG	PCM
97-98	Houston	58	13	1070	337	112	305	.367	2	8	.250	111	180	.617	28	42	70	110	125	0	62	10	99	18.4	5.8	1.2	1.9	.215
98-99	Houston	3	0	33	9	2	8	.250	0	0	.000	5	6	.833	2	2	4	1	5	0	1	0	5	11.0	3.0	1.3	0.3	.064
98-99	Vancouver	10	1	123	34	11	44	.250	1	7	.143	11	19	.579	7	6	13	10	16	0	4	2	15	12.3	3.4	1.3	1.0	.070
99-00	Dallas	1	0	8	0	0	3	.000	0	0	.000	0	0	.000	1	0	1	0	0	0	2	0	2	8.0	0.0	1.0	0.0	-.227
NBA Season Totals		72	14	1234	380	125	360	.347	3	15	.200	127	205	.620	38	50	88	121	146	0	69	12	121	17.1	5.3	1.2	1.7	....
97-98	Houston	3	0	7	6	2	3	.667	0	0	.000	2	4	.500	0	1	1	0	0	0	1	0	1	2.3	2.0	0.3	0.0	.726
NBA Playoff Totals		3	0	7	6	2	3	.667	0	0	.000	2	4	.500	0	1	1	0	0	0	1	0	1	2.3	2.0	0.3	0.0	....

• RICE, Del

Delbert Rice

Born: Oct. 27, 1922. Portsmouth, OH, United States. Died: Jan.26, 1983. Height: 6'2". Weight: 190 lbs. Drafted: — College: none (HS: Portsmouth, OH)

YEAR	TEAM	GP	GS	MIN	PTS	FGM	FGA	FG%	3PM	3PA	3P%	FTM	FTA	FT%	ORB	DRB	TRB	AST	PF	DQ	STL	BLK	TO	MPG	PPG	RPG	APG	PCM
45-46	Rochester-N	11	....	....	22	8	....	....	....	....	....	6	....	....	....	....	....	....	....	....	....	....	....	....	2.0	....	....	....
NBL Season Totals		11	....	....	22	8	....	....	....	....	....	6	....	....	....	....	....	....	....	....	....	....	....	....	2.0	....	....	....

• RICE, Glen

Glen Anthony Rice

Born: May 28, 1967. Flint, MI, United States. Height: 6'7". Weight: 215 lbs. Drafted: 1989 College: Michigan

YEAR	TEAM	GP	GS	MIN	PTS	FGM	FGA	FG%	3PM	3PA	3P%	FTM	FTA	FT%	ORB	DRB	TRB	AST	PF	DQ	STL	BLK	TO	MPG	PPG	RPG	APG	PCM
89-90	Miami	77	60	2311	1048	470	1071	.439	17	69	.246	91	124	.734	100	252	352	138	198	1	67	27	116	30.0	13.6	4.6	1.8	.360
90-91	Miami	77	77	2646	1342	550	1193	.461	71	184	.386	171	209	.818	85	296	381	189	216	0	101	26	169	34.4	17.4	4.9	2.5	.431
91-92	Miami	79	79	3007	1765	672	1432	.469	155	396	.391	266	318	.836	84	310	394	184	170	0	90	35	142	38.1	22.3	5.0	2.3	.500
92-93	Miami	82	82	3080	1527	570	1311	.435	146	382	.382	241	294	.820	92	337	429	181	203	0	91	25	156	37.6	18.6	5.2	2.2	.413
93-94	Miami	81	81	2999	1708	663	1421	.467	132	346	.382	250	284	.880	76	358	434	184	186	0	110	32	130	37.0	21.1	5.4	2.3	.507
94-95	Miami	82	82	3014	1831	667	1403	.475	185	451	.410	312	365	.855	99	279	378	192	203	1	112	14	156	36.8	22.3	4.6	2.3	.515
95-96	Charlotte	79	79	3142	1710	610	1296	.471	171	403	.424	319	381	.837	86	292	378	232	217	1	91	19	166	39.8	21.6	4.8	2.9	.472
96-97	Charlotte	79	78	**3362**	2115	722	1513	.477	207	440	**.470**	464	535	.867	67	251	318	160	190	0	72	26	174	42.6	26.8	4.0	2.0	.492
97-98	Charlotte	82	82	3295	1826	634	1386	.457	130	300	.433	428	504	.849	89	264	353	182	200	0	77	22	180	40.2	22.3	4.3	2.2	.442
98-99	LA Lakers	27	25	985	472	171	396	.432	53	135	.393	77	90	.856	9	90	99	71	67	1	17	6	45	36.5	17.5	3.7	2.6	.390
99-00	LA Lakers	80	80	2530	1272	421	980	.430	84	229	.367	346	396	.874	56	271	327	176	179	0	47	12	114	31.6	15.9	4.1	2.2	.435
00-01	New York	75	25	2212	899	331	752	.440	82	211	.389	155	182	.852	61	246	307	89	179	1	41	13	96	29.5	12.0	4.1	1.2	.346
01-02	Houston	20	20	606	172	65	167	.389	18	64	.281	24	30	.800	5	42	47	31	34	0	12	3	24	30.3	8.6	2.4	1.6	.214
02-03	Houston	62	26	1532	556	196	457	.429	101	254	.398	63	83	.759	28	126	154	65	99	0	23	5	55	24.7	9.0	2.5	1.0	.295
NBA Season Totals		982	876	34721	18243	6742	14778	.456	1552	3864	.402	3207	3795	.845	937	3414	4351	2074	2341	5	951	265	1723	35.4	18.6	4.4	2.1	....
91-92	Miami	3	3	119	57	24	64	.375	3	12	.250	6	7	.857	3	7	10	5	7	0	2	0	6	39.7	19.0	3.3	1.7	.227
93-94	Miami	5	5	195	65	26	68	.382	7	23	.304	6	8	.750	6	30	36	10	14	0	11	2	14	39.0	13.0	7.2	2.0	.318
96-97	Charlotte	3	3	137	83	28	57	.491	6	16	.375	21	23	.913	1	10	11	11	11	0	4	1	4	45.7	27.7	3.7	3.7	.532
97-98	Charlotte	9	9	369	205	82	173	.474	11	36	.306	30	36	.833	11	40	51	13	26	0	5	3	13	41.0	22.8	5.7	1.4	.443
98-99	LA Lakers	7	7	307	128	45	101	.446	10	28	.357	28	29	.966	4	23	27	11	15	0	5	1	9	43.9	18.3	3.9	1.6	.341
99-00	LA Lakers	23	23	766	285	93	228	.408	28	67	.418	71	89	.798	10	82	92	48	50	0	15	4	36	33.3	12.4	4.0	2.1	.329
00-01	New York	5	0	144	61	24	52	.462	6	14	.429	7	8	.875	3	19	22	3	10	0	3	1	7	28.8	12.2	4.4	0.6	.356
NBA Playoff Totals		55	50	2037	884	322	743	.433	71	196	.362	169	200	.845	38	211	249	101	133	0	45	12	89	37.0	16.1	4.5	1.8	....

• RICH, Tommy

Tommy Rich

Born: 1916. Height: 6'3". Weight: 185 lbs. Drafted: — College: Cornell

YEAR	TEAM	GP	GS	MIN	PTS	FGM	FGA	FG%	3PM	3PA	3P%	FTM	FTA	FT%	ORB	DRB	TRB	AST	PF	DQ	STL	BLK	TO	MPG	PPG	RPG	APG	PCM
45-46	Rochester-N	17	....	....	44	18	....	....	....	....	....	8	....	....	....	....	....	....	....	....	....	....	....	....	2.6	....	....	....
NBL Season Totals		17	....	....	44	18	....	....	....	....	....	8	....	....	....	....	....	....	....	....	....	....	....	....	2.6	....	....	....

• RICHARDSON, Clint

Clint Dewitt Richardson

Born: Aug. 7, 1956. Seattle, WA, United States. Height: 6'3". Weight: 195 lbs. Drafted: 1979 College: Seattle

YEAR	TEAM	GP	GS	MIN	PTS	FGM	FGA	FG%	3PM	3PA	3P%	FTM	FTA	FT%	ORB	DRB	TRB	AST	PF	DQ	STL	BLK	TO	MPG	PPG	RPG	APG	PCM
79-80	Philadelphia	52	....	988	347	159	348	.457	1	3	.333	28	45	.622	55	68	123	107	97	0	24	15	62	19.0	6.7	2.4	2.1	.336
80-81	Philadelphia	77	....	1313	538	227	464	.489	0	1	.000	84	108	.778	83	93	176	152	102	0	36	10	108	17.1	7.0	2.3	2.0	.407
81-82	Philadelphia	77	0	1040	351	140	310	.452	2	2	1.000	69	88	.784	55	63	118	109	109	0	36	9	77	13.5	4.6	1.5	1.4	.320
82-83	Philadelphia	77	1	1755	589	259	559	.463	0	6	.000	71	111	.640	98	149	247	168	164	0	71	18	100	22.8	7.6	3.2	2.2	.355
83-84	Philadelphia	69	12	1571	521	221	473	.467	0	4	.000	79	103	.767	62	103	165	155	145	0	49	23	97	22.8	7.6	2.4	2.2	.321
84-85	Philadelphia	74	20	1531	443	183	404	.453	1	3	.333	76	89	.854	60	95	155	157	143	0	37	15	81	20.7	6.0	2.1	2.1	.294
85-86	Indiana	82	61	2224	794	335	736	.455	1	9	.111	123	147	.837	69	182	251	372	153	1	58	8	139	27.1	9.7	3.1	4.5	.406
86-87	Indiana	78	14	1396	501	218	467	.467	6	17	.353	59	74	.797	51	92	143	241	106	0	49	7	86	17.9	6.4	1.8	3.1	.412
NBA Season Totals		586	108	11818	4084	1742	3761	.463	11	45	.244	589	765	.770	533	845	1378	1461	1019	1	360	105	750	20.2	7.0	2.4	2.5	....
79-80	Philadelphia	3	....	3	2	1	3	.333	0	2	.000	0	0	.000	0	0	0	0	0	0	1	0	1	1.0	0.7	0.0	0.0	.063
80-81	Philadelphia	13	....	181	49	20	38	.526	0	0	.000	9	17	.529	9	12	21	12	15	0	6	3	8	13.9	3.8	1.6	0.9	.305
81-82	Philadelphia	21	0	415	111	47	104	.452	0	0	.000	17	30	.567	29	40	69	40	48	0	13	5	21	19.8	5.3	3.3	1.9	.324
82-83	Philadelphia	13	1	319	88	37	83	.446	0	0	.000	14	17	.824	14	25	39	23	37	0	15	3	14	24.5	6.8	3.0	1.8	.290

YEAR	TEAM	GP	GS	MIN	PTS	FGM	FGA	FG%	3PM	3PA	3P%	FTM	FTA	FT%	ORB	DRB	TRB	AST	PF	DQ	STL	BLK	TO	MPG	PPG	RPG	APG	PCM
83-84	Philadelphia	5	0	115	37	13	23	.565	0	0	.000	11	12	.917	4	12	16	10	17	0	3	1	4	23.0	7.4	3.2	2.0	.391
84-85	Philadelphia	13	0	281	115	53	94	.564	0	0	.000	9	10	.900	14	24	38	27	23	0	10	2	17	21.6	8.8	2.9	2.1	.446
86-87	Indiana	4	0	73	16	7	12	.583	0	1	.000	2	4	.500	3	7	10	8	12	0	0	0	5	18.3	4.0	2.5	2.0	.247
NBA Playoff Totals		72	1	1387	418	178	357	.499	0	3	.000	62	90	.689	73	120	193	120	152	0	48	14	70	19.3	5.8	2.7	1.7	....

• RICHARDSON, Jason

Jason Anthony Richardson

Born: Jan. 20, 1981. Saginaw, MI, United States.   Height: 6'6".   Weight: 220 lbs.   Drafted: 2001   College: Michigan State

YEAR	TEAM	GP	GS	MIN	PTS	FGM	FGA	FG%	3PM	3PA	3P%	FTM	FTA	FT%	ORB	DRB	TRB	AST	PF	DQ	STL	BLK	TO	MPG	PPG	RPG	APG	PCM
01-02	Golden State	80	75	2629	1151	464	1090	.426	82	246	.333	141	210	.671	124	216	340	236	195	2	106	31	160	32.9	14.4	4.3	3.0	.384
02-03	Golden State	82	82	2696	1282	476	1161	.410	123	334	.368	207	271	.764	111	267	378	247	201	1	90	23	179	32.9	15.6	4.6	3.0	.405
NBA Season Totals		162	157	5325	2433	940	2251	.418	205	580	.353	348	481	.723	235	483	718	483	396	3	196	54	339	32.9	15.0	4.4	3.0	....

• RICHARDSON, Michael Ray

Micheal Ray (Sugar Ray) Richardson

Born: Apr. 11, 1955. Lubbock, TX, United States.   Height: 6'5".   Weight: 189 lbs.   Drafted: 1978   College: Montana

YEAR	TEAM	GP	GS	MIN	PTS	FGM	FGA	FG%	3PM	3PA	3P%	FTM	FTA	FT%	ORB	DRB	TRB	AST	PF	DQ	STL	BLK	TO	MPG	PPG	RPG	APG	PCM
78-79	New York	72	....	1218	469	200	483	.414	....	....	....	69	128	.539	78	155	233	213	188	2	100	18	144	16.9	6.5	3.2	3.0	.431
79-80	New York	82	....	3060	1254	502	1063	.472	27	110	.245	223	338	.660	151	388	539	**832**	260	3	**265**	35	**361**	37.3	15.3	6.6	**10.1**	**.628**
80-81	New York	79	....	3175	1293	523	1116	.469	23	102	.225	224	338	.663	173	372	545	627	258	2	**232**	35	300	40.2	16.4	6.9	7.9	.546
81-82	New York	82	79	3044	1469	619	1343	.461	19	101	.188	212	303	.700	177	388	565	572	317	3	**213**	41	287	37.1	17.9	6.9	7.0	.566
82-83	Golden State	33	25	1074	411	176	427	.412	4	31	.129	55	87	.632	45	100	145	245	124	2	101	9	139	32.5	12.5	4.4	7.4	.454
82-83	New Jersey	31	26	1002	395	170	388	.438	4	20	.200	51	76	.671	68	82	150	187	116	2	81	15	109	32.3	12.7	4.8	6.0	.463
83-84	New Jersey	48	25	1285	576	243	528	.460	14	58	.241	76	108	.704	56	116	172	214	156	4	103	20	120	26.8	12.0	3.6	4.5	.479
84-85	New Jersey	82	82	3127	1649	690	1470	.469	29	115	.252	240	313	.767	156	301	457	669	277	3	**243**	22	246	38.1	20.1	5.6	8.2	.613
85-86	New Jersey	47	39	1604	737	296	661	.448	4	27	.148	141	179	.788	77	173	250	340	163	2	125	11	150	34.1	15.7	5.3	7.2	.554
NBA Season Totals		556	276	18589	8253	3419	7479	.457	124	564	.220	1291	1870	.690	981	2075	3056	3899	1859	23	1463	206	1856	33.4	14.8	5.5	7.0	....
80-81	New York	2	....	86	23	8	33	.242	0	4	.000	7	12	.583	6	13	19	11	8	0	7	0	8	43.0	11.5	9.5	5.5	.264
82-83	New Jersey	2	2	58	19	8	21	.381	0	1	.000	3	5	.600	2	6	8	5	3	0	5	0	4	29.0	9.5	4.0	2.5	.321
83-84	New Jersey	11	11	443	185	69	169	.408	6	22	.273	41	56	.732	20	34	54	79	40	1	34	4	30	40.3	16.8	4.9	7.2	.471
84-85	New Jersey	3	3	125	55	23	57	.404	0	2	.000	9	14	.643	4	14	18	34	12	0	4	0	8	41.7	18.3	6.0	11.3	.518
NBA Playoff Totals		18	16	712	282	108	280	.386	6	29	.207	60	87	.690	32	67	99	129	63	1	50	4	50	39.6	15.7	5.5	7.2	....

• RICHARDSON, Norm

Norm Richardson

Born: July 24, 1979. Brooklyn, NY, United States.   Height: 6'5".   Weight: 190 lbs.   Drafted: —   College: Hofstra

YEAR	TEAM	GP	GS	MIN	PTS	FGM	FGA	FG%	3PM	3PA	3P%	FTM	FTA	FT%	ORB	DRB	TRB	AST	PF	DQ	STL	BLK	TO	MPG	PPG	RPG	APG	PCM
01-02	Indiana	3	0	4	0	0	3	.000	0	0	.000	0	0	.000	1	0	1	1	0	0	0	0	0	1.3	0.0	0.3	0.3	-.180
01-02	Chicago	8	0	63	30	10	23	.435	4	8	.500	6	9	.667	2	5	7	1	5	0	0	0	3	7.9	3.8	0.9	0.1	.307
NBA Season Totals		11	0	67	30	10	26	.385	4	8	.500	6	9	.667	3	5	8	2	5	0	0	0	3	6.1	2.7	0.7	0.2	....

• RICHARDSON, Pooh

Jerome (Pooh) Richardson Jr.

Born: May 14, 1966. Philadelphia, PA, United States.   Height: 6'1".   Weight: 180 lbs.   Drafted: 1989   College: UCLA

YEAR	TEAM	GP	GS	MIN	PTS	FGM	FGA	FG%	3PM	3PA	3P%	FTM	FTA	FT%	ORB	DRB	TRB	AST	PF	DQ	STL	BLK	TO	MPG	PPG	RPG	APG	PCM
89-90	Minnesota	82	48	2581	938	426	925	.461	23	83	.277	63	107	.589	55	162	217	554	143	0	133	25	139	31.5	11.4	2.6	6.8	.462
90-91	Minnesota	82	82	3154	1401	635	1350	.470	42	128	.328	89	165	.539	82	204	286	734	114	0	131	13	172	38.5	17.1	3.5	9.0	.529
91-92	Minnesota	82	82	2922	1350	587	1261	.466	53	155	.342	123	178	.691	91	210	301	685	152	0	119	25	205	35.6	16.5	3.7	8.4	.542
92-93	Indiana	74	73	2396	769	337	703	.479	3	29	.103	92	124	.742	63	204	267	573	132	1	94	12	170	32.4	10.4	3.6	7.7	.481
93-94	Indiana	37	25	1022	370	160	354	.452	3	12	.250	47	77	.610	28	82	110	237	78	0	32	3	89	27.6	10.0	3.0	6.4	.441
94-95	LA Clippers	80	77	2864	874	353	897	.394	87	244	.357	81	125	.648	38	223	261	632	218	1	129	12	168	35.8	10.9	3.3	7.9	.395
95-96	LA Clippers	63	61	2013	734	281	664	.423	94	245	.384	78	105	.743	35	123	158	340	134	0	77	13	95	32.0	11.7	2.5	5.4	.399
96-97	LA Clippers	59	18	1065	330	131	344	.381	42	128	.328	26	43	.605	25	73	98	169	82	0	54	5	65	18.1	5.6	1.7	2.9	.330
97-98	LA Clippers	69	17	1252	289	124	333	.372	11	57	.193	30	43	.698	17	79	96	226	71	0	44	3	55	18.1	4.2	1.4	3.3	.308
98-99	LA Clippers	11	0	130	28	12	36	.333	0	6	.000	4	4	1.000	1	12	13	30	5	0	4	0	9	11.8	2.5	1.2	2.7	.345
NBA Season Totals		639	483	19399	7083	3046	6867	.444	358	1087	.329	633	971	.652	435	1372	1807	4180	1129	2	817	111	1167	30.4	11.1	2.8	6.5	....
92-93	Indiana	4	1	95	17	6	15	.400	1	1	1.000	4	6	.667	1	10	11	23	7	1	2	0	6	23.8	4.3	2.8	5.8	.373
96-97	LA Clippers	2	0	18	4	2	4	.500	0	1	.000	0	1	.000	0	0	0	3	4	0	1	0	1	9.0	2.0	0.0	1.5	.167
NBA Playoff Totals		6	1	113	21	8	19	.421	1	2	.500	4	7	.571	1	10	11	26	11	1	3	0	7	18.8	3.5	1.8	4.3	....

• RICHARDSON, Quentin

Quentin L. Richardson

Born: Apr. 13, 1980. Chicago, IL, United States.   Height: 6'6".   Weight: 223 lbs.   Drafted: 2000   College: DePaul

YEAR	TEAM	GP	GS	MIN	PTS	FGM	FGA	FG%	3PM	3PA	3P%	FTM	FTA	FT%	ORB	DRB	TRB	AST	PF	DQ	STL	BLK	TO	MPG	PPG	RPG	APG	PCM
00-01	LA Clippers	76	28	1358	613	232	525	.442	50	151	.331	99	158	.627	105	152	257	62	98	0	42	7	64	17.9	8.1	3.4	0.8	.416
01-02	LA Clippers	81	0	2152	1076	400	926	.432	133	349	.381	143	187	.765	113	221	334	128	142	2	78	21	102	26.6	13.3	4.1	1.6	.444
02-03	LA Clippers	59	13	1368	552	203	546	.372	61	198	.308	85	124	.685	98	183	281	52	92	0	35	10	64	23.2	9.4	4.8	0.9	.348
NBA Season Totals		216	41	4878	2241	835	1997	.418	244	698	.350	327	469	.697	316	556	872	242	332	2	155	38	230	22.6	10.4	4.0	1.1	....

• RICHIE, Ocie

Ocie (Eyes) Richie

Born: 1921.   Height: 6'3".   Weight: 195 lbs.   Drafted: —   College: Northwestern Louisiana

YEAR	TEAM	GP	GS	MIN	PTS	FGM	FGA	FG%	3PM	3PA	3P%	FTM	FTA	FT%	ORB	DRB	TRB	AST	PF	DQ	STL	BLK	TO	MPG	PPG	RPG	APG	PCM
47-48	Rochester-N	1	....	....	1	0	....	....	....	....	....	1	1	1.000	....	....	....	0	....	....	....	....	....	1.0	....	....	....	....
NBL Season Totals		1	....	....	1	0	....	....	....	....	....	1	1	....	....	....	....	0	....	....	....	....	....	1.0	....	....	....	....

• RICHMOND, Mitch

Mitchell James (Rock) Richmond

Born: June 30, 1965. Fort Lauderdale, FL, United States.   Height: 6'5".   Weight: 215 lbs.   Drafted: 1988   College: Kansas State

YEAR	TEAM	GP	GS	MIN	PTS	FGM	FGA	FG%	3PM	3PA	3P%	FTM	FTA	FT%	ORB	DRB	TRB	AST	PF	DQ	STL	BLK	TO	MPG	PPG	RPG	APG	PCM
88-89	Golden State	79	79	2717	1741	649	1386	.468	33	90	.367	410	506	.810	158	310	468	334	223	5	82	13	269	34.4	22.0	5.9	4.2	.566
89-90	Golden State	78	78	2799	1720	640	1287	.497	34	95	.358	406	469	.866	98	262	360	223	210	3	98	24	203	35.9	22.1	4.6	2.9	.530

YEAR	TEAM	GP	GS	MIN	PTS	FGM	FGA	FG%	3PM	3PA	3P%	FTM	FTA	FT%	ORB	DRB	TRB	AST	PF	DQ	STL	BLK	TO	MPG	PPG	RPG	APG	PCM
90-91	Golden State	77	77	3027	1840	703	1424	.494	40	115	.348	394	465	.847	147	305	452	238	207	0	126	34	231	39.3	23.9	5.9	3.1	.544
91-92	Sacramento	80	80	3095	1803	685	1465	.468	103	268	.384	330	406	.813	62	257	319	411	231	1	92	34	248	38.7	22.5	4.0	5.1	.504
92-93	Sacramento	45	45	1728	987	371	782	.474	48	130	.369	197	233	.845	18	136	154	221	137	3	53	9	131	38.4	21.9	3.4	4.9	.485
93-94	Sacramento	78	78	2897	1823	635	1428	.445	127	312	.407	426	511	.834	70	216	286	313	211	3	103	17	218	37.1	23.4	3.7	4.0	.508
94-95	Sacramento	82	82	3172	1867	668	1497	.446	156	424	.368	375	445	.843	69	288	357	311	227	2	91	29	238	38.7	22.8	4.4	3.8	.474
95-96	Sacramento	81	81	2946	1872	611	1368	.447	225	515	.437	425	491	.866	54	215	269	255	233	6	125	19	219	36.4	23.1	3.3	3.1	.500
96-97	Sacramento	81	81	3125	2095	717	1578	.454	204	477	.428	457	531	.861	59	260	319	338	211	1	118	24	235	38.6	25.9	3.9	4.2	.554
97-98	Sacramento	70	70	2569	1623	543	1220	.445	130	334	.389	407	471	.864	50	179	229	279	154	0	88	15	182	36.7	23.2	3.3	4.0	.523
98-99	Washington	50	50	1912	983	331	803	.412	70	221	.317	251	293	.857	30	142	172	122	121	1	64	10	136	38.2	19.7	3.4	2.4	.379
99-00	Washington	74	69	2397	1285	447	1049	.426	93	241	.386	298	340	.876	37	176	213	185	191	1	110	13	154	32.4	17.4	2.9	2.5	.417
00-01	Washington	37	30	1216	598	205	504	.407	45	133	.338	143	160	.894	15	94	109	111	86	0	43	7	84	32.9	16.2	2.9	3.0	.389
01-02	LA Lakers	64	2	709	260	100	247	.405	18	62	.290	42	44	.955	14	80	94	57	61	0	18	6	40	11.1	4.1	1.5	0.9	.326
NBA Season Totals		976	902	34309	20497	7305	16038	.455	1326	3417	.388	4561	5365	.850	881	2920	3801	3398	2503	26	1211	254	2588	35.2	21.0	3.9	3.5	....
88-89	Golden State	8	8	314	161	62	135	.459	3	16	.188	34	38	.895	10	48	58	35	25	0	14	1	24	39.3	20.1	7.3	4.4	.518
90-91	Golden State	9	9	372	201	85	169	.503	8	24	.333	23	24	.958	10	37	47	22	28	1	5	6	17	41.3	22.3	5.2	2.4	.459
95-96	Sacramento	4	4	146	84	24	54	.444	8	23	.348	28	35	.800	3	14	17	12	11	0	3	0	15	36.5	21.0	4.3	3.0	.444
01-02	LA Lakers	2	0	4	3	1	1	1.000	0	0	.000	1	2	.500	0	1	1	0	0	0	0	0	1	2.0	1.5	0.5	0.0	.637
NBA Playoff Totals		23	21	836	449	172	359	.479	19	63	.302	86	99	.869	23	100	123	69	64	1	22	7	57	36.3	19.5	5.3	3.0	....

• RICHTER, John

John Fritz Richter

Born: Mar. 12, 1937. Height: 6'9". Weight: 225 lbs. Drafted: 1959 College: North Carolina State

YEAR	TEAM	GP	GS	MIN	PTS	FGM	FGA	FG%	3PM	3PA	3P%	FTM	FTA	FT%	ORB	DRB	TRB	AST	PF	DQ	STL	BLK	TO	MPG	PPG	RPG	APG	PCM
59-60	Boston	66	....	808	285	113	332	.340	....	....	....	59	117	.504	....	....	312	27	158	1	....	....	....	12.2	4.3	4.7	0.4	.380
NBA Season Totals		66	....	808	285	113	332	.340	....	....	....	59	117	.504	....	....	312	27	158	1	....	....	....	12.2	4.3	4.7	0.4	....
59-60	Boston	8	....	95	35	15	38	.395	....	....	....	5	14	.357	....	....	29	2	18	1	....	....	....	11.9	4.4	3.6	0.3	.335
NBA Playoff Totals		8	....	95	35	15	38	.395	....	....	....	5	14	.357	....	....	29	2	18	1	....	....	....	11.9	4.4	3.6	0.3	....

• RICKETTS, Dick

Richard James Ricketts Jr.

Born: Dec. 4, 1933. Pottstown, PA, United States. Died: Mar.6, 1988. Height: 6'7". Weight: 215 lbs. Drafted: 1955 College: Duquesne

YEAR	TEAM	GP	GS	MIN	PTS	FGM	FGA	FG%	3PM	3PA	3P%	FTM	FTA	FT%	ORB	DRB	TRB	AST	PF	DQ	STL	BLK	TO	MPG	PPG	RPG	APG	PCM
55-56	St. Louis	29	....	777	243	94	301	.312	....	....	....	55	78	.705	....	....	196	82	115	6	....	....	....	26.8	8.4	6.8	2.8	.365
55-56	Rochester	39	....	1166	365	141	451	.313	....	....	....	83	117	.709	....	....	294	124	172	8	....	....	....	29.9	9.4	7.5	3.2	.367
56-57	Rochester	72	....	2114	804	299	869	.344	....	....	....	206	297	.694	....	....	437	127	307	12	....	....	....	29.4	11.2	6.1	1.8	.338
57-58	Cincinnati	72	....	1620	562	215	664	.324	....	....	....	132	196	.673	....	....	410	114	277	8	....	....	....	22.5	7.8	5.7	1.6	.342
NBA Season Totals		212	....	5677	1974	749	2285	.328	....	....	....	476	688	.692	....	....	1337	447	871	34	....	....	....	26.8	9.3	6.3	2.1	....
57-58	Cincinnati	2	....	31	15	5	15	.333	....	....	....	5	5	1.000	....	....	10	2	9	0	....	....	....	15.5	7.5	5.0	1.0	.460
NBA Playoff Totals		2	....	31	15	5	15	.333	....	....	....	5	5	1.000	....	....	10	2	9	0	....	....	....	15.5	7.5	5.0	1.0	....

• RIDER, Isaiah

Isaiah Rider Jr.

Born: Mar. 12, 1971. Oakland, CA, United States. Height: 6'5". Weight: 215 lbs. Drafted: 1993 College: UNLV

YEAR	TEAM	GP	GS	MIN	PTS	FGM	FGA	FG%	3PM	3PA	3P%	FTM	FTA	FT%	ORB	DRB	TRB	AST	PF	DQ	STL	BLK	TO	MPG	PPG	RPG	APG	PCM
93-94	Minnesota	79	60	2415	1313	522	1115	.468	54	150	.360	215	265	.811	118	197	315	202	194	0	54	28	221	30.6	16.6	4.0	2.6	.430
94-95	Minnesota	75	67	2645	1532	558	1249	.447	139	396	.351	277	339	.817	90	159	249	245	194	3	69	23	233	35.3	20.4	3.3	3.3	.425
95-96	Minnesota	75	68	2594	1470	560	1206	.464	102	275	.371	248	296	.838	99	210	309	213	204	2	48	23	203	34.6	19.6	4.1	2.8	.438
96-97	Portland	76	68	2563	1223	456	983	.464	99	257	.385	212	261	.812	94	210	304	198	199	2	45	19	213	33.7	16.1	4.0	2.6	.379
97-98	Portland	74	66	2786	1458	551	1302	.423	135	420	.321	221	267	.828	99	247	346	231	188	1	55	19	185	37.6	19.7	4.7	3.1	.405
98-99	Portland	47	41	1385	651	249	605	.412	42	111	.378	111	147	.755	59	137	196	104	100	0	25	9	95	29.5	13.9	4.2	2.2	.368
99-00	Atlanta	60	47	2084	1158	449	1072	.419	56	180	.311	204	260	.785	63	195	258	219	132	3	41	6	168	34.7	19.3	4.3	3.7	.418
00-01	LA Lakers	67	6	1206	507	201	472	.426	34	92	.370	71	83	.855	44	112	156	111	105	0	27	7	98	18.0	7.6	2.3	1.7	.345
01-02	Denver	10	1	173	93	37	81	.457	6	15	.400	13	17	.765	10	23	33	12	11	0	3	2	14	17.3	9.3	3.3	1.2	.469
NBA Season Totals		563	424	17851	9405	3583	8085	.443	667	1896	.352	1572	1935	.812	676	1490	2166	1535	1327	11	367	136	1430	31.7	16.7	3.8	2.7	....
96-97	Portland	4	4	161	53	16	43	.372	6	16	.375	15	17	.882	1	7	8	17	11	0	3	0	12	40.3	13.3	2.0	4.3	.242
97-98	Portland	4	4	166	77	28	67	.418	1	11	.091	20	26	.769	7	13	20	17	11	0	5	0	16	41.5	19.3	5.0	4.3	.363
98-99	Portland	13	13	426	214	70	163	.429	11	26	.423	63	71	.887	17	33	50	31	30	0	11	0	33	32.8	16.5	3.8	2.4	.408
NBA Playoff Totals		21	21	753	344	114	273	.418	18	53	.340	98	114	.860	25	53	78	65	52	0	19	0	61	35.9	16.4	3.7	3.1	....

• RIDGLE, Jackie

Jackie Lendell Ridgle

Born: Feb. 13, 1948. Height: 6'4". Weight: 195 lbs. Drafted: 1971 College: California

YEAR	TEAM	GP	GS	MIN	PTS	FGM	FGA	FG%	3PM	3PA	3P%	FTM	FTA	FT%	ORB	DRB	TRB	AST	PF	DQ	STL	BLK	TO	MPG	PPG	RPG	APG	PCM
71-72	Cleveland	32	....	107	57	19	44	.432	....	....	....	19	26	.731	....	....	15	7	15	0	....	....	....	3.3	1.8	0.5	0.2	.437
NBA Season Totals		32	....	107	57	19	44	.432	....	....	....	19	26	.731	....	....	15	7	15	0	....	....	....	3.3	1.8	0.5	0.2	....

• RIEBE, Bill

Bill Riebe

Born: 1917. Height: 5'11". Weight: 175 lbs. Drafted: — College: none

YEAR	TEAM	GP	GS	MIN	PTS	FGM	FGA	FG%	3PM	3PA	3P%	FTM	FTA	FT%	ORB	DRB	TRB	AST	PF	DQ	STL	BLK	TO	MPG	PPG	RPG	APG	PCM
43-44	Cleveland-N	18	....	....	111	44	....	....	....	....	....	23	....	....	....	....	....	....	....	....	....	....	....	....	6.2	....	....	....
44-45	Cleveland-N	24	....	....	70	24	....	....	....	....	....	22	....	....	....	....	....	....	....	....	....	....	....	....	2.9	....	....	....
45-46	Cleveland-N	22	....	....	42	13	....	....	....	....	....	16	....	....	....	....	....	....	....	....	....	....	....	....	1.9	....	....	....
NBL Season Totals		64	....	....	223	81	....	....	....	....	....	61	....	....	....	....	....	....	....	....	....	....	....	....	3.5	....	....	....
43-44	Cleveland-N	2	....	....	11	3	....	....	....	....	....	5	....	....	....	....	....	....	....	....	....	....	....	....	5.5	....	....	....
44-45	Cleveland-N	2	....	....	5	0	....	....	....	....	....	5	....	....	....	....	....	....	....	....	....	....	....	....	2.5	....	....	....
NBL Playoff Totals		4	....	....	16	3	....	....	....	....	....	10	....	....	....	....	....	....	....	....	....	....	....	....	4.0	....	....	....

RIEBE, Mel — Melvin Russell (Mouse) Riebe

Born: July 12, 1916. Died: July 25, 1977. Height: 5'11". Weight: 180 lbs. Drafted: — College: Wooster

YEAR TEAM	GP	GS	MIN	PTS	FGM	FGA	FG%	3PM	3PA	3P%	FTM	FTA	FT%	ORB	DRB	TRB	AST	PF	DQ	STL	BLK	TO	MPG	PPG	RPG	APG	PCM
43-44 Cleveland-N	18	....	....	**323**	113	....	....	....	....	....	....	97	....	....	....	....	....	....	....	....	....	....	....	17.9	....	....	....
44-45 Cleveland-N	30	....	....	**607**	223	....	....	....	....	....	....	161	....	....	....	....	....	....	....	....	....	....	....	20.2	....	....	....
45-46 Cleveland-N	5	....	....	72	23	....	....	....	....	....	....	26	....	....	....	....	....	....	....	....	....	....	....	14.4	....	....	....
46-47 Cleveland	55	....	....	663	276	898	.307	....	....	....	....	111	173	.642	....	....	....	67	169	....	....	....	....	12.1	....	1.2	....
47-48 Boston	48	....	....	489	202	653	.309	....	....	....	....	85	137	.620	....	....	....	41	137	....	....	....	....	10.2	....	0.9	....
48-49 Boston	33	....	....	362	146	501	.291	....	....	....	....	70	116	.603	....	....	....	95	97	....	....	....	....	11.0	....	2.9	....
48-49 Providence	10	....	....	61	26	88	.295	....	....	....	....	9	17	.529	....	....	....	9	13	....	....	....	....	6.1	....	0.9	....
NBA Season Totals	146	....	....	1575	650	2140	.304	....	....	....	....	275	443	.621	....	....	....	212	416	....	....	....	....	10.8	....	1.5	....
NBL Season Totals	53	....	....	1002	359	....	....	....	....	....	....	284	....	....	....	....	....	....	....	....	....	....	....	18.9	....	....	....
Career Totals	199	....	....	2577	1009	2140	....	....	....	....	....	559	443	....	....	....	....	212	416	....	....	....	....	12.9	....	1.1	....
43-44 Cleveland-N	2	....	....	25	8	....	....	....	....	....	....	9	....	....	....	....	....	....	....	....	....	....	....	12.5	....	....	....
44-45 Cleveland-N	2	....	....	41	15	....	....	....	....	....	....	11	....	....	....	....	....	....	....	....	....	....	....	20.5	....	....	....
46-47 Cleveland	3	....	....	21	9	37	.243	....	....	....	....	3	6	.500	....	....	....	2	3	....	....	....	....	7.0	....	0.7	....
47-48 Boston	3	....	....	42	14	43	.326	....	....	....	....	14	20	.700	....	....	....	3	10	....	....	....	....	14.0	....	1.0	....
NBA Playoff Totals	6	....	....	63	23	80	.288	....	....	....	....	17	26	.654	....	....	....	5	13	....	....	....	....	10.5	....	0.8	....
NBL Playoff Totals	4	....	....	66	23	....	....	....	....	....	....	20	....	....	....	....	....	....	....	....	....	....	....	16.5	....	....	....
Career Playoff Totals	10	....	....	129	46	80	....	....	....	....	....	37	26	....	....	....	....	5	13	....	....	....	....	12.9	....	0.5	....

RIEDY, Bob — Robert F. Riedy

Born: Aug. 26, 1945. Height: 6'6". Weight: 215 lbs. Drafted: 1967 College: Duke

YEAR TEAM	GP	GS	MIN	PTS	FGM	FGA	FG%	3PM	3PA	3P%	FTM	FTA	FT%	ORB	DRB	TRB	AST	PF	DQ	STL	BLK	TO	MPG	PPG	RPG	APG	PCM
67-68 Houston-A	23	....	331	131	45	129	.349	0	0	.000	41	67	.612	....	....	68	5	27	0	....	....	21	14.4	5.7	3.0	0.2	.307
ABA Season Totals	23	....	331	131	45	129	.349	0	0	.000	41	67	.612	....	....	68	5	27	0	....	....	21	14.4	5.7	3.0	0.2	....

RIFFEY, Jim — James R. Riffey

Born: Dec. 14, 1923. Height: 6'4". Weight: 200 lbs. Drafted: 1950 College: Tulane

YEAR TEAM	GP	GS	MIN	PTS	FGM	FGA	FG%	3PM	3PA	3P%	FTM	FTA	FT%	ORB	DRB	TRB	AST	PF	DQ	STL	BLK	TO	MPG	PPG	RPG	APG	PCM
50-51 Fort Wayne	35	....	....	150	65	185	.351	....	....	....	....	20	26	.769	....	....	....	61	16	54	0	....	....	....	4.3	1.7	0.5	....
NBA Season Totals	35	....	....	150	65	185	.351	....	....	....	....	20	26	.769	....	....	....	61	16	54	0	....	....	....	4.3	1.7	0.5	....

RIGAUDEAU, Antoine

Born: Dec. 17, 1971. Cholet, France. Height: 6'7". Weight: 210 lbs. Drafted: — College: none

YEAR TEAM	GP	GS	MIN	PTS	FGM	FGA	FG%	3PM	3PA	3P%	FTM	FTA	FT%	ORB	DRB	TRB	AST	PF	DQ	STL	BLK	TO	MPG	PPG	RPG	APG	PCM
02-03 Dallas	11	0	91	17	8	35	.229	1	5	.200	0	0	.000	4	4	8	6	11	0	3	0	6	8.3	1.5	0.7	0.5	-.016
NBA Season Totals	11	0	91	17	8	35	.229	1	5	.200	0	0	.000	4	4	8	6	11	0	3	0	6	8.3	1.5	0.7	0.5	....

RIGG, Ted — Ted Rigg

Born: 1913. Height: 6'. Weight: 175 lbs. Drafted: — College: Carnegie-Mellon

YEAR TEAM	GP	GS	MIN	PTS	FGM	FGA	FG%	3PM	3PA	3P%	FTM	FTA	FT%	ORB	DRB	TRB	AST	PF	DQ	STL	BLK	TO	MPG	PPG	RPG	APG	PCM
37-38 Pittsburgh-N	11	....	....	47	18	....	....	....	....	....	....	11	....	....	....	....	....	....	....	....	....	....	....	....	4.3	....	....	....
NBL Season Totals	11	....	....	47	18	....	....	....	....	....	....	11	....	....	....	....	....	....	....	....	....	....	....	....	4.3	....	....	....

RIKER, Tom — Thomas E. Riker

Born: Feb. 28, 1950. Rockville Centre, NY, United States. Height: 6'10". Weight: 225 lbs. Drafted: 1972 College: South Carolina

YEAR TEAM	GP	GS	MIN	PTS	FGM	FGA	FG%	3PM	3PA	3P%	FTM	FTA	FT%	ORB	DRB	TRB	AST	PF	DQ	STL	BLK	TO	MPG	PPG	RPG	APG	PCM
72-73 New York	14	....	65	35	10	24	.417	....	....	....	....	15	24	.625	....	....	16	2	15	0	....	....	....	4.6	2.5	1.1	0.1	.442
73-74 New York	17	....	57	38	13	29	.448	....	....	....	....	12	17	.706	9	6	15	3	6	0	0	0	....	3.4	2.2	0.9	0.2	.630
74-75 New York	51	....	483	152	53	147	.361	....	....	....	....	46	82	.561	40	67	107	19	64	0	15	5	....	9.5	3.0	2.1	0.4	.294
NBA Season Totals	82	....	605	225	76	200	.380	....	....	....	....	73	123	.593	49	73	138	24	85	0	15	5	....	7.4	2.7	1.7	0.3	....
74-75 New York	1	....	8	2	1	2	.500	....	....	....	....	0	0	.000	1	1	2	1	1	0	0	0	....	8.0	2.0	2.0	1.0	.447
NBA Playoff Totals	1	....	8	2	1	2	.500	....	....	....	....	0	0	.000	1	1	2	1	1	0	0	0	....	8.0	2.0	2.0	1.0	....

RILEY, Bob — Robert J. Riley

Born: July 6, 1948. Height: 6'9". Weight: 235 lbs. Drafted: 1970 College: Mount St. Mary's

YEAR TEAM	GP	GS	MIN	PTS	FGM	FGA	FG%	3PM	3PA	3P%	FTM	FTA	FT%	ORB	DRB	TRB	AST	PF	DQ	STL	BLK	TO	MPG	PPG	RPG	APG	PCM
70-71 Atlanta	7	....	39	13	4	9	.444	....	....	....	....	5	9	.556	....	....	12	1	5	0	....	....	....	5.6	1.9	1.7	0.1	.418
NBA Season Totals	7	....	39	13	4	9	.444	....	....	....	....	5	9	.556	....	....	12	1	5	0	....	....	....	5.6	1.9	1.7	0.1	....

RILEY, Eric — Eric Kendall Riley

Born: June 2, 1970. Cleveland, OH, United States. Height: 7'. Weight: 245 lbs. Drafted: 1993 College: Michigan

YEAR TEAM	GP	GS	MIN	PTS	FGM	FGA	FG%	3PM	3PA	3P%	FTM	FTA	FT%	ORB	DRB	TRB	AST	PF	DQ	STL	BLK	TO	MPG	PPG	RPG	APG	PCM
93-94 Houston	47	2	219	88	34	70	.486	0	1	.000	20	37	.541	24	35	59	9	30	0	5	9	14	4.7	1.9	1.3	0.2	.444
94-95 LA Clippers	40	4	434	177	65	145	.448	0	1	.000	47	64	.734	45	67	112	11	78	1	17	35	32	10.9	4.4	2.8	0.3	.444
95-96 Minnesota	25	10	310	92	35	74	.473	0	1	.000	22	28	.786	32	44	76	5	42	0	8	16	18	12.4	3.7	3.0	0.2	.371
97-98 Dallas	39	14	544	139	56	135	.415	0	1	.000	27	36	.750	43	90	133	22	80	0	15	46	35	13.9	3.6	3.4	0.6	.359
98-99 Boston	35	11	337	78	28	54	.519	0	0	.000	22	31	.710	36	63	99	13	73	2	9	26	26	9.6	2.2	2.8	0.4	.382
NBA Season Totals	186	41	1844	574	218	478	.456	0	4	.000	138	196	.704	180	299	479	60	303	3	54	132	125	9.9	3.1	2.6	0.3	....

• RILEY, Pat

Patrick James Riley

Born: Mar. 20, 1945. Rome, NY, United States. Height: 6'4". Weight: 205 lbs. Drafted: 1967 College: Kentucky

YEAR	TEAM	GP	GS	MIN	PTS	FGM	FGA	FG%	3PM	3PA	3P%	FTM	FTA	FT%	ORB	DRB	TRB	AST	PF	DQ	STL	BLK	TO	MPG	PPG	RPG	APG	PCM
67-68	San Diego	80	....	1263	628	250	660	.379	....	....	....	128	202	.634	....	....	177	138	205	1	....	....	....	15.8	7.9	2.2	1.7	.393
68-69	San Diego	56	....	1027	494	202	498	.406	....	....	....	90	134	.672	....	....	112	136	146	1	....	....	....	18.3	8.8	2.0	2.4	.408
69-70	San Diego	36	....	474	190	75	180	.417	....	....	....	40	55	.727	....	....	57	85	68	0	....	....	....	13.2	5.3	1.6	2.4	.436
70-71	LA Lakers	54	....	506	266	105	254	.413	....	....	....	56	87	.644	....	....	54	72	84	0	....	....	....	9.4	4.9	1.0	1.3	.429
71-72	LA Lakers	67	....	926	449	197	441	.447	....	....	....	55	74	.743	....	....	127	75	110	0	....	....	....	13.8	6.7	1.9	1.1	.408
72-73	LA Lakers	55	....	801	399	167	390	.428	....	....	....	65	82	.793	....	....	65	81	126	0	....	....	....	14.6	7.3	1.2	1.5	.368
73-74	LA Lakers	72	....	1361	684	287	667	.430	....	....	....	110	144	.764	38	90	128	148	173	1	54	3	....	18.9	9.5	1.8	2.1	.405
74-75	LA Lakers	46	....	1016	507	219	523	.419	....	....	....	69	93	.742	25	60	85	121	128	0	36	4	....	22.1	11.0	1.8	2.6	.388
75-76	LA Lakers	2	....	23	11	5	13	.385	....	....	....	1	3	.333	1	2	3	0	5	0	1	1	....	11.5	5.5	1.5	0.0	.161
75-76	Phoenix	60	....	790	278	112	288	.389	....	....	....	54	74	.730	15	32	47	57	107	0	21	5	....	13.2	4.6	0.8	1.0	.225
NBA Season Totals		528	....	8187	3906	1619	3914	.414	....	....	....	668	948	.705	79	184	855	913	1152	3	112	13	....	15.5	7.4	1.6	1.7	....
68-69	San Diego	5	....	76	37	16	37	.432	....	....	....	5	6	.833	....	....	11	2	13	0	....	....	....	15.2	7.4	2.2	0.4	.330
70-71	LA Lakers	7	....	135	66	29	69	.420	....	....	....	8	11	.727	....	....	15	14	12	0	....	....	....	19.3	9.4	2.1	2.0	.400
71-72	LA Lakers	15	....	244	78	33	99	.333	....	....	....	12	16	.750	....	....	29	14	37	0	....	....	....	16.3	5.2	1.9	0.9	.181
72-73	LA Lakers	7	....	53	18	9	27	.333	....	....	....	0	0	.000	....	....	5	7	10	0	....	....	....	7.6	2.6	0.7	1.0	.199
73-74	LA Lakers	5	....	106	39	18	50	.360	....	....	....	3	4	.750	3	3	6	10	11	0	4	0	....	21.2	7.8	1.2	2.0	.219
75-76	Phoenix	5	....	27	13	6	15	.400	....	....	....	1	1	1.000	0	0	0	5	3	0	0	0	....	5.4	2.6	0.0	1.0	.359
NBA Playoff Totals		44	....	641	251	111	297	.374	....	....	....	29	38	.763	3	3	66	52	86	0	4	0	....	14.6	5.7	1.5	1.2	....

• RILEY, Ron

Ronald Jay Riley

Born: Nov. 11, 1950. Los Angeles, CA, United States. Height: 6'8". Weight: 195 lbs. Drafted: 1972 College: USC

YEAR	TEAM	GP	GS	MIN	PTS	FGM	FGA	FG%	3PM	3PA	3P%	FTM	FTA	FT%	ORB	DRB	TRB	AST	PF	DQ	STL	BLK	TO	MPG	PPG	RPG	APG	PCM
72-73	Omaha	74	....	1634	625	273	634	.431	....	....	....	79	116	.681	....	....	507	76	226	3	....	....	....	22.1	8.4	6.9	1.0	.443
73-74	Omaha	12	....	170	62	24	57	.421	....	....	....	14	24	.583	13	43	56	8	27	0	3	2	....	14.2	5.2	4.7	0.7	.441
73-74	Houston	36	....	421	124	57	145	.393	....	....	....	10	14	.714	35	86	121	29	68	0	15	22	....	11.7	3.4	3.4	0.8	.368
74-75	Houston	77	....	1578	463	196	470	.417	....	....	....	71	97	.732	137	243	380	130	197	3	56	22	....	20.5	6.0	4.9	1.7	.385
75-76	Houston	65	....	1049	268	115	280	.411	....	....	....	38	56	.679	91	213	304	75	137	1	32	21	....	16.1	4.1	4.7	1.2	.387
NBA Season Totals		264	....	4852	1542	665	1586	.419	....	....	....	212	307	.691	276	585	1368	318	655	7	106	67	....	18.4	5.8	5.2	1.2	....
74-75	Houston	8	....	152	56	25	42	.595	....	....	....	6	16	.375	12	24	36	15	18	0	9	2	....	19.0	7.0	4.5	1.9	.510
NBA Playoff Totals		8	....	152	56	25	42	.595	....	....	....	6	16	.375	12	24	36	15	18	0	9	2	....	19.0	7.0	4.5	1.9	....

• RINALDI, Rich

Richard P. Rinaldi

Born: Aug. 3, 1949. Height: 6'3". Weight: 195 lbs. Drafted: 1971 College: St. Peter's

YEAR	TEAM	GP	GS	MIN	PTS	FGM	FGA	FG%	3PM	3PA	3P%	FTM	FTA	FT%	ORB	DRB	TRB	AST	PF	DQ	STL	BLK	TO	MPG	PPG	RPG	APG	PCM
71-72	Baltimore	39	....	159	104	42	104	.404	....	....	....	20	30	.667	....	....	18	15	25	0	....	....	....	4.1	2.7	0.5	0.4	.427
72-73	Baltimore	33	....	646	280	116	284	.408	....	....	....	48	64	.750	....	....	68	48	40	0	....	....	....	19.6	8.5	2.1	1.5	.348
73-74	New York-A	5	....	28	12	4	14	.286	0	1	.000	4	4	1.000	5	0	5	1	3	....	2	0	1	5.6	2.4	1.0	0.2	.270
73-74	Washington	7	....	48	9	3	22	.136	....	....	....	3	4	.750	2	5	7	10	7	0	3	1	....	6.9	1.3	1.0	1.4	.143
NBA Season Totals		79	....	853	393	161	410	.393	....	....	....	71	98	.724	2	5	93	73	72	0	3	1	....	10.8	5.0	1.2	0.9	....
ABA Season Totals		5	....	28	12	4	14	.286	0	1	.000	4	4	1.000	5	0	5	1	3	....	2	0	1	5.6	2.4	1.0	0.2	....
Career Totals		84	....	881	405	165	424	.389	0	1	.000	75	102	.735	7	5	98	74	75	0	5	1	1	10.5	4.8	1.2	0.9	....
71-72	Baltimore	3	....	6	2	1	2	.500	....	....	....	0	0	.000	....	....	0	1	3	0	....	....	....	2.0	0.7	0.0	0.3	.163
NBA Playoff Totals		3	....	6	2	1	2	.500	....	....	....	0	0	.000	....	....	0	1	3	0	....	....	....	2.0	0.7	0.0	0.3	....

• RIORDAN, Mike

Michael W. Riordan

Born: July 9, 1945. New York, NY, United States. Height: 6'4". Weight: 200 lbs. Drafted: 1967 College: Providence

YEAR	TEAM	GP	GS	MIN	PTS	FGM	FGA	FG%	3PM	3PA	3P%	FTM	FTA	FT%	ORB	DRB	TRB	AST	PF	DQ	STL	BLK	TO	MPG	PPG	RPG	APG	PCM
68-69	New York	54	....	397	126	49	144	.340	....	....	....	28	42	.667	....	....	57	46	93	1	....	....	....	7.4	2.3	1.1	0.9	.260
69-70	New York	81	....	1677	624	255	549	.464	....	....	....	114	165	.691	....	....	194	201	192	1	....	....	....	20.7	7.7	2.4	2.5	.390
70-71	New York	82	....	1320	391	162	388	.418	....	....	....	67	108	.620	....	....	169	121	151	0	....	....	....	16.1	4.8	2.1	1.5	.301
71-72	New York	4	....	33	8	4	11	.364	....	....	....	0	1	.000	....	....	1	2	2	0	....	....	....	8.3	2.0	0.3	0.5	.115
71-72	Baltimore	54	....	1344	542	229	488	.469	....	....	....	84	123	.683	....	....	127	124	127	0	....	....	....	24.9	10.0	2.4	2.3	.370
72-73	Baltimore	82	....	3466	1483	652	1278	.510	....	....	....	179	218	.821	....	....	404	426	216	0	....	....	....	42.3	18.1	4.9	5.2	.482
73-74	Washington	81	....	3230	1290	577	1223	.472	....	....	....	136	174	.782	120	260	380	264	237	2	102	14	....	39.9	15.9	4.7	3.3	.387
74-75	Washington	74	....	2191	1138	520	1057	.492	....	....	....	98	117	.838	90	194	284	198	238	4	72	6	....	29.6	15.4	3.8	2.7	.475
75-76	Washington	78	....	1943	653	291	662	.440	....	....	....	71	96	.740	44	143	187	122	201	2	54	13	....	24.9	8.4	2.4	1.6	.277
76-77	Washington	49	....	289	79	34	94	.362	....	....	....	11	15	.733	7	20	27	20	33	0	3	2	....	5.9	1.6	0.6	0.4	.198
NBA Season Totals		639	....	15890	6334	2773	5894	.470	....	....	....	788	1059	.744	261	617	1830	1524	1490	10	231	35	....	24.9	9.9	2.9	2.4	....
68-69	New York	10	....	108	52	20	39	.513	....	....	....	12	16	.750	....	....	17	3	27	0	....	....	....	10.8	5.2	1.7	0.3	.378
69-70	New York	19	....	296	131	53	109	.486	....	....	....	25	35	.714	....	....	46	27	33	0	....	....	....	15.6	6.9	2.4	1.4	.451
70-71	New York	12	....	168	46	20	52	.385	....	....	....	6	8	.750	....	....	30	9	26	0	....	....	....	14.0	3.8	2.5	0.8	.253
71-72	Baltimore	6	....	161	83	33	57	.579	....	....	....	17	21	.810	....	....	15	11	18	0	....	....	....	26.8	13.8	2.5	1.8	.486
72-73	Baltimore	5	....	231	75	28	62	.452	....	....	....	19	24	.792	....	....	18	15	16	0	....	....	....	46.2	15.0	3.6	3.0	.300
73-74	Washington	7	....	267	86	36	87	.414	....	....	....	14	16	.875	7	17	24	17	28	0	4	2	....	38.1	12.3	3.4	2.4	.261
74-75	Washington	17	....	378	134	60	151	.397	....	....	....	14	18	.778	12	29	41	27	49	1	16	2	....	22.2	7.9	2.4	1.6	.264
75-76	Washington	6	....	31	6	3	8	.375	....	....	....	0	0	.000	1	5	6	1	5	0	0	0	....	5.2	1.0	1.0	0.2	.189
76-77	Washington	2	....	8	0	0	2	.000	....	....	....	0	0	.000	0	2	2	1	1	0	0	0	....	4.0	0.0	1.0	0.5	.088
NBA Playoff Totals		84	....	1648	613	253	567	.446	....	....	....	107	138	.775	20	53	199	111	203	1	20	4	....	19.6	7.3	2.4	1.3	....

• RISEN, Arnie

Arnold D. (Stilts) Risen

Born: Oct. 9, 1924. Williamstown, KY, United States. Height: 6'9". Weight: 200 lbs. Drafted: — College: Ohio State HOF: 1998

YEAR	TEAM	GP	GS	MIN	PTS	FGM	FGA	FG%	3PM	3PA	3P%	FTM	FTA	FT%	ORB	DRB	TRB	AST	PF	DQ	STL	BLK	TO	MPG	PPG	RPG	APG	PCM
45-46	Indianapolis-N	18	....	....	219	77	....	....	....	....	....	65	110	.591	....	....	....	....	....	....	....	....	....	....	12.2	....	....	....
46-47	Indianapolis-N	44	....	....	582	204	....	....	....	....	....	174	276	.630	....	....	....	....	150	....	....	....	....	....	13.2	....	....	....

YEAR	TEAM	GP	GS	MIN	PTS	FGM	FGA	FG%	3PM	3PA	3P%	FTM	FTA	FT%	ORB	DRB	TRB	AST	PF	DQ	STL	BLK	TO	MPG	PPG	RPG	APG	PCM
47-48	Indianapolis-N	33	....	....	398	137	....	....	....	....	....	124	191	.649	....	....	....	....	....	....	....	....		....	12.1	....	....	....
47-48	Rochester-N	28	....	....	407	145	....	....	....	....	....	117	161	.727	....	....	....	....	....	....	....	....		....	14.5	....	....	....
48-49	Rochester	60	....	....	995	345	816	.423	....	....	....	305	462	.660	....	....	....	100	216	....	....	....		....	16.6	....	1.7	....
49-50	Rochester	62	....	....	625	206	598	.344	....	....	....	213	321	.664	....	....	....	92	228	....	....	....		....	10.1	....	1.5	....
50-51	Rochester	66	....	....	1077	377	940	.401	....	....	....	323	440	.734	....	....	795	158	278	9	....	....		....	16.3	12.0	2.4	....
51-52	Rochester	66	....	2396	1032	365	926	.394	....	....	....	302	431	.701	....	....	841	150	258	3	....	....		36.3	15.6	12.7	2.3	.537
52-53	Rochester	68	....	2288	884	295	802	.368	....	....	....	294	429	.685	....	....	745	135	274	10	....	....		33.6	13.0	11.0	2.0	.472
53-54	Rochester	72	....	2385	949	321	872	.368	....	....	....	307	430	.714	....	....	728	120	284	9	....	....		33.1	13.2	10.1	1.7	.455
54-55	Rochester	69	....	1970	797	259	699	.371	....	....	....	279	375	.744	....	....	703	112	253	10	....	....		28.6	11.6	10.2	1.6	.509
55-56	Boston	68	....	1597	548	189	493	.383	....	....	....	170	240	.708	....	....	553	88	300	17	....	....		23.5	8.1	8.1	1.3	.442
56-57	Boston	43	....	935	344	119	307	.388	....	....	....	106	156	.679	....	....	286	53	163	4	....	....		21.7	8.0	6.7	1.2	.432
57-58	Boston	63	....	1119	382	134	397	.338	....	....	....	114	167	.683	....	....	360	50	195	5	....	....		17.8	6.1	5.7	0.8	.381
NBA Season Totals		637	....	12690	7633	2610	6850	.381	....	....	....	2413	3451	.699	....	....	5011	1058	2449	67	....	....		19.9	12.0	7.9	1.7	
NBL Season Totals		123	....		1606	563	....		....	....	....	480	738	....	....	....			150		....	....			13.1			
Career Totals		760	....	12690	9239	3173	6850		....	....	....	2893	4189	....	....	....	5011	1058	2599	67	....	....			16.7	12.2	6.6	1.4
46-47	Indianapolis-N	5	....	....	95	32	....	....	....	....	....	31	40	.775	....	....	....	....	....	....					19.0			
47-48	Rochester-N	7	....	....	100	35	....	....	....	....	....	30	44	.682	....	....	....	....	....	....					14.3			
48-49	Rochester	4	....	....	66	22	53	.415	....	....	....	22	33	.667	....	....	....	10	16	....					16.5	....	2.5	
49-50	Rochester	2	....	....	23	7	19	.368	....	....	....	9	15	.600	....	....	....	4	7	....					11.5	....	2.0	
50-51	Rochester	14	....	....	273	93	239	.389	....	....	....	87	135	.644	....	....	196	33	59	2					19.5	14.0	2.4	
51-52	Rochester	6	....	229	94	33	81	.407	....	....	....	28	40	.700	....	....	75	9	24	0				38.2	15.7	12.5	1.5	.489
52-53	Rochester	3	....	109	39	11	38	.289	....	....	....	17	24	.708	....	....	35	2	16	1				36.3	13.0	11.7	0.7	.358
53-54	Rochester	6	....	200	89	28	67	.418	....	....	....	33	44	.750	....	....	54	4	25	0				33.3	14.8	9.0	0.7	.460
54-55	Rochester	3	....	77	48	17	38	.447	....	....	....	14	19	.737	....	....	37	5	13	0				25.7	16.0	12.3	1.7	.773
55-56	Boston	3	....	88	37	12	34	.353	....	....	....	13	18	.722	....	....	44	2	15	0				29.3	12.3	14.7	0.7	.552
56-57	Boston	10	....	152	75	28	63	.444	....	....	....	19	29	.655	....	....	58	8	48	5				15.2	7.5	5.8	0.8	.530
57-58	Boston	10	....	168	46	12	52	.231	....	....	....	22	33	.667	....	....	62	9	32	1				16.8	4.6	6.2	0.9	.344
NBA Playoff Totals		61	....	1023	790	263	684	.385	....	....	....	264	390	.677	....	....	561	86	255	9					16.8	13.0	9.2	1.4
NBL Playoff Totals		12	....		195	67	....		....	....	....	61	84												16.3			
Career Playoff Totals		73	....	1023	985	330	684		....	....	....	325	474				561	86	255	9					14.0	13.5	7.7	1.2

• RISKA, Eddie

Edward Riska

Born: Oct. 4, 1919. Died: Aug.3, 1992.   Height: 6'   Weight: 175 lbs.   Drafted: —   College: Notre Dame

YEAR	TEAM	GP	GS	MIN	PTS	FGM	FGA	FG%	3PM	3PA	3P%	FTM	FTA	FT%	ORB	DRB	TRB	AST	PF	DQ	STL	BLK	TO	MPG	PPG	RPG	APG	PCM
41-42	Oshkosh-N	16	....	....	63	24	....	....	....	....	....	15	....	....											3.9			
45-46	Oshkosh-N	32	....	....	123	38	....	....	....	....	....	47	69	.681					....						3.8			
46-47	Oshkosh-N	44	....	....	233	81	....	....	....	....	....	71	102	.696					105						5.3			
47-48	Oshkosh-N	18	....	....	57	21	....	....	....	....	....	15	24	.625					28						3.2			
48-49	Oshkosh-N	42	....	....	145	42	....	....	....	....	....	61	93	.656					103						3.5			
NBL Season Totals		152	....	....	621	206			....	....	....	209	288	....					236		....	....			4.1	....	....	
41-42	Oshkosh-N	5	....	....	18	3	....	....	....	....	....	12	....	....											3.6			
45-46	Oshkosh-N	5	....	....	12	4	....	....	....	....	....	4	5	.800											2.4			
46-47	Oshkosh-N	7	....	....	54	16	....	....	....	....	....	22	27	.815											7.7			
47-48	Oshkosh-N	4	....	....	10	1	....	....	....	....	....	8	10	.800											2.5			
NBL Playoff Totals		21	....	....	94	24	....		....	....	....	46	42	....							....	....			4.5	....	....	

• RISKIND, —

Riskind

Born: —.   Height: —   Weight: —   Drafted: —   College: —

YEAR	TEAM	GP	GS	MIN	PTS	FGM	FGA	FG%	3PM	3PA	3P%	FTM	FTA	FT%	ORB	DRB	TRB	AST	PF	DQ	STL	BLK	TO	MPG	PPG	RPG	APG	PCM
39-40	Chicago-N	1	....	....	0	0	....	....	....	....	....	0	....	....											0.0			
NBL Season Totals		1	....	....	0	0			....	....	....	0													0.0			

• RITTER, Tex

Goebel Franklin (Tex) Ritter

Born: Feb. 26, 1924. Richmond, KY, United States.   Height: 6'2".   Weight: 185 lbs.   Drafted: 1948   College: Eastern Kentucky

YEAR	TEAM	GP	GS	MIN	PTS	FGM	FGA	FG%	3PM	3PA	3P%	FTM	FTA	FT%	ORB	DRB	TRB	AST	PF	DQ	STL	BLK	TO	MPG	PPG	RPG	APG	PCM
48-49	New York	55	....	....	337	123	353	.348	....	....	....	91	146	.623	....	....	....	57	71	....	....				6.1	....	1.0	
49-50	New York	62	....	....	325	100	297	.337	....	....	....	125	176	.710	....	....	....	51	101	....	....				5.2	....	0.8	
50-51	New York	34	....	....	127	39	103	.379	....	....	....	49	71	.690	....	....	65	37	52	1	....				3.7	1.9	1.1	
NBA Season Totals		151	....	....	789	262	753	.348	....	....	....	265	393	.674	....	....	65	145	224	1	....	....			5.2	0.4	1.0	....
48-49	New York	5	....	....	31	10	33	.303	....	....	....	11	20	.550	....	....	....	2	15	....	....				6.2	....	0.4	
49-50	New York	5	....	....	45	10	33	.303	....	....	....	25	28	.893	....	....	....	8	22	....	....				9.0	....	1.6	
50-51	New York	3	....	....	3	1	5	.200	....	....	....	1	1	1.000	....	....	2	0	5	0	....				1.0	0.7	0.0	
NBA Playoff Totals		13	....	....	79	21	71	.296	....	....	....	37	49	.755	....	....	2	10	42	0	....	....			6.1	0.2	0.8	....

• RIVAS, Ramon

Ramon Rivas

Born: June 3, 1966. Carolina, PR, Puerto Rico.   Height: 6'10".   Weight: 260 lbs.   Drafted: —   College: Temple

YEAR	TEAM	GP	GS	MIN	PTS	FGM	FGA	FG%	3PM	3PA	3P%	FTM	FTA	FT%	ORB	DRB	TRB	AST	PF	DQ	STL	BLK	TO	MPG	PPG	RPG	APG	PCM
88-89	Boston	28	0	91	40	12	31	.387	0	1	.000	16	25	.640	9	15	24	3	21	0	4	1	8	3.3	1.4	0.9	0.1	.342
NBA Season Totals		28	0	91	40	12	31	.387	0	1	.000	16	25	.640	9	15	24	3	21	0	4	1	8	3.3	1.4	0.9	0.1	....

• RIVERS, David
David Lee Rivers

Born: Jan. 20, 1965. Jersey City, NJ, United States. Height: 6' Weight: 170 lbs. Drafted: 1988 College: Notre Dame

YEAR	TEAM	GP	GS	MIN	PTS	FGM	FGA	FG%	3PM	3PA	3P%	FTM	FTA	FT%	ORB	DRB	TRB	AST	PF	DQ	STL	BLK	TO	MPG	PPG	RPG	APG	PCM
88-89	LA Lakers	47	0	440	134	49	122	.402	1	6	.167	35	42	.833	13	30	43	106	50	0	23	9	61	9.4	2.9	0.9	2.3	.377
89-90	LA Clippers	52	11	724	219	80	197	.406	0	5	.000	59	78	.756	30	55	85	155	53	0	31	0	88	13.9	4.2	1.6	3.0	.368
91-92	LA Clippers	15	0	122	30	10	30	.333	0	1	.000	10	11	.909	10	9	19	21	14	0	7	1	17	8.1	2.0	1.3	1.4	.297
NBA Season Totals		114	11	1286	383	139	349	.398	1	12	.083	104	131	.794	53	94	147	282	117	0	61	10	166	11.3	3.4	1.3	2.5	....
88-89	LA Lakers	6	0	33	15	4	12	.333	0	2	.000	7	8	.875	1	3	4	6	6	0	0	0	4	5.5	2.5	0.7	1.0	.325
NBA Playoff Totals		6	0	33	15	4	12	.333	0	2	.000	7	8	.875	1	3	4	6	6	0	0	0	4	5.5	2.5	0.7	1.0	....

• RIVERS, Doc
Glenn Anton (Doc) Rivers

Born: Oct. 13, 1961. Chicago, IL, United States. Height: 6'4". Weight: 185 lbs. Drafted: 1983 College: Marquette

YEAR	TEAM	GP	GS	MIN	PTS	FGM	FGA	FG%	3PM	3PA	3P%	FTM	FTA	FT%	ORB	DRB	TRB	AST	PF	DQ	STL	BLK	TO	MPG	PPG	RPG	APG	PCM
83-84	Atlanta	81	47	1938	757	250	541	.462	2	12	.167	255	325	.785	72	148	220	314	286	8	127	30	170	23.9	9.3	2.7	3.9	.438
84-85	Atlanta	69	58	2126	974	334	701	.476	15	36	.417	291	378	.770	66	148	214	410	250	7	163	53	179	30.8	14.1	3.1	5.9	.539
85-86	Atlanta	53	50	1571	612	220	464	.474	0	16	.000	172	283	.608	49	113	162	443	185	2	120	13	143	29.6	11.5	3.1	8.4	.550
86-87	Atlanta	82	82	2590	1053	342	758	.451	4	21	.190	365	441	.828	83	216	299	823	287	5	171	30	213	31.6	12.8	3.6	10.0	.635
87-88	Atlanta	80	80	2502	1134	403	890	.453	9	33	.273	319	421	.758	83	283	366	747	272	3	140	41	208	31.3	14.2	4.6	9.3	.647
88-89	Atlanta	76	76	2462	1032	371	816	.455	43	124	.347	247	287	.861	89	197	286	525	263	6	181	40	160	32.4	13.6	3.8	6.9	.553
89-90	Atlanta	48	44	1526	598	218	480	.454	24	66	.364	138	170	.812	47	153	200	264	151	2	116	22	96	31.8	12.5	4.2	5.5	.507
90-91	Atlanta	79	79	2586	1197	444	1020	.435	88	262	.336	221	262	.844	47	206	253	340	216	2	148	47	126	32.7	15.2	3.2	4.3	.465
91-92	LA Clippers	59	25	1657	641	226	533	.424	26	92	.283	163	196	.832	23	124	147	233	166	2	111	19	94	28.1	10.9	2.5	3.9	.412
92-93	New York	77	45	1886	604	216	494	.437	39	123	.317	133	162	.821	26	166	192	397	215	2	125	9	116	24.5	7.8	2.5	5.2	.451
93-94	New York	19	19	499	143	55	127	.433	19	52	.365	14	22	.636	4	35	39	100	44	0	25	5	29	26.3	7.5	2.1	5.3	.397
94-95	New York	3	0	47	19	4	13	.308	3	5	.600	8	11	.727	2	7	9	8	8	1	4	0	4	15.7	6.3	3.0	2.7	.475
94-95	San Antonio	60	0	942	302	104	289	.360	42	122	.344	52	71	.732	13	87	100	154	142	1	61	21	54	15.7	5.0	1.7	2.6	.357
95-96	San Antonio	78	0	1235	311	108	290	.372	47	137	.343	48	64	.750	30	108	138	123	175	0	73	21	55	15.8	4.0	1.8	1.6	.281
NBA Season Totals		864	605	23567	9377	3295	7416	.444	361	1101	.328	2426	3093	.784	634	1991	2625	4881	2660	41	1565	351	1647	27.3	10.9	3.0	5.6	....
83-84	Atlanta	5	4	130	68	16	32	.500	0	3	.000	36	41	.878	7	3	10	16	16	0	12	4	9	26.0	13.6	2.0	3.2	.587
85-86	Atlanta	9	9	262	114	40	92	.435	3	6	.500	31	42	.738	10	32	42	78	38	2	18	0	26	29.1	12.7	4.7	8.7	.603
86-87	Atlanta	8	8	245	62	18	47	.383	0	0	.000	26	52	.500	6	21	27	90	32	0	9	3	25	30.6	7.8	3.4	11.3	.479
87-88	Atlanta	12	12	409	188	71	139	.511	7	22	.318	39	43	.907	8	51	59	115	40	1	25	2	25	34.1	15.7	4.9	9.6	.694
88-89	Atlanta	5	5	191	67	22	57	.386	6	19	.316	17	24	.708	4	20	24	34	22	2	7	2	12	38.2	13.4	4.8	6.8	.402
90-91	Atlanta	5	5	173	78	30	64	.469	1	11	.091	17	19	.895	6	14	20	15	14	0	5	2	4	34.6	15.6	4.0	3.0	.441
91-92	LA Clippers	5	4	187	76	25	56	.446	4	8	.500	22	27	.815	4	15	19	21	16	0	6	0	3	37.4	15.2	3.8	4.2	.430
92-93	New York	15	15	458	153	48	106	.453	11	31	.355	46	60	.767	6	33	39	86	44	0	29	1	30	30.5	10.2	2.6	5.7	.437
94-95	San Antonio	15	0	318	117	37	95	.389	17	46	.370	26	31	.839	3	26	29	24	40	0	14	9	18	21.2	7.8	1.9	1.6	.311
95-96	San Antonio	2	0	20	3	1	3	.333	1	2	.500	0	0	.000	0	1	1	0	3	0	0	0	1	10.0	1.5	0.5	0.0	-.015
NBA Playoff Totals		81	62	2393	926	308	691	.446	50	148	.338	260	339	.767	54	216	270	479	265	5	125	23	153	29.5	11.4	3.3	5.9	....

• RIVLIN, Julie
Julie Rivlin

Born: 1917. Height: 5'11". Weight: 160 lbs. Drafted: — College: Marshall

YEAR	TEAM	GP	GS	MIN	PTS	FGM	FGA	FG%	3PM	3PA	3P%	FTM	FTA	FT%	ORB	DRB	TRB	AST	PF	DQ	STL	BLK	TO	MPG	PPG	RPG	APG	PCM
40-41	Wingfoots-N	21	....	....	51	20	....	....	....	....	....	11	....	....	....	....	....	....	....	....	....	....	....	....	2.4	....	....	....
46-47	Toledo-N	44	....	....	280	105	....	....	....	....	....	70	90	.778	....	....	....	....	80	....	....	....	....	....	6.4	....	....	....
47-48	Toledo-N	40	....	....	72	28	....	....	....	....	....	16	25	.640	....	....	....	....	34	....	....	....	....	....	1.8	....	....	....
NBL Season Totals		105	....	....	403	153	....	....	....	....	....	97	115	....	....	....	....	....	114	....	....	....	....	....	3.8	....	....	....
46-47	Toledo-N	5	....	....	27	8	....	....	....	....	....	11	13	.846	....	....	....	....	....	....	....	....	....	....	5.4	....	....	....
NBL Playoff Totals		5	....	....	27	8	....	....	....	....	....	11	13	....	....	....	....	....	....	....	....	....	....	....	5.4	....	....	....

• RIZZO, Jerry
Jerry Rizzo

Born: Apr. 21, 1919. Astoria, NY, United States. Height: 5'8". Weight: 150 lbs. Drafted: — College: Fordham

YEAR	TEAM	GP	GS	MIN	PTS	FGM	FGA	FG%	3PM	3PA	3P%	FTM	FTA	FT%	ORB	DRB	TRB	AST	PF	DQ	STL	BLK	TO	MPG	PPG	RPG	APG	PCM
46-47	Syracuse-N	44	....	....	479	155	....	....	....	....	....	169	238	.710	....	....	....	....	125	....	....	....	....	....	10.9	....	....	....
47-48	Syracuse-N	60	....	....	537	160	....	....	....	....	....	217	303	.716	....	....	....	....	156	....	....	....	....	....	9.0	....	....	....
48-49	Syracuse-N	45	....	....	240	67	....	....	....	....	....	106	150	.707	....	....	....	....	106	....	....	....	....	....	5.3	....	....	....
NBL Season Totals		149	....	....	1256	382	....	....	....	....	....	492	691	....	....	....	....	....	387	....	....	....	....	....	8.4	....	....	....
46-47	Syracuse-N	4	....	....	51	16	....	....	....	....	....	19	26	.731	....	....	....	....	....	....	....	....	....	....	12.8	....	....	....
47-48	Syracuse-N	3	....	....	28	6	....	....	....	....	....	16	18	.889	....	....	....	....	....	....	....	....	....	....	9.3	....	....	....
48-49	Syracuse-N	6	....	....	44	13	....	....	....	....	....	18	22	.818	....	....	....	....	....	....	....	....	....	....	7.3	....	....	....
NBL Playoff Totals		13	....	....	123	35	....	....	....	....	....	53	66	....	....	....	....	....	....	....	....	....	....	....	9.5	....	....	....

• ROBBINS, Lee
Lee Roy Robbins

Born: Feb. 11, 1922. Died: Apr.8, 1968. Height: 6'3". Weight: 175 lbs. Drafted: — College: Colorado

YEAR	TEAM	GP	GS	MIN	PTS	FGM	FGA	FG%	3PM	3PA	3P%	FTM	FTA	FT%	ORB	DRB	TRB	AST	PF	DQ	STL	BLK	TO	MPG	PPG	RPG	APG	PCM
47-48	Providence	31	....	....	195	72	260	.277	....	....	....	51	93	.548	....	....	....	7	93	....	....	....	....	....	6.3	....	0.2	....
48-49	Providence	16	....	....	29	9	25	.360	....	....	....	11	17	.647	....	....	....	12	24	....	....	....	....	....	1.8	....	0.8	....
NBA Season Totals		47	....	....	224	81	285	.284				62	110	.564	....	....	....	19	117	....	....	....	....	....	4.8	....	0.4	....

• ROBBINS, Red
Austin (Red) Robbins

Born: Sept. 30, 1944. Leesburg, FL, United States. Height: 6'8". Weight: 190 lbs. Drafted: 1966 College: Tennessee

YEAR	TEAM	GP	GS	MIN	PTS	FGM	FGA	FG%	3PM	3PA	3P%	FTM	FTA	FT%	ORB	DRB	TRB	AST	PF	DQ	STL	BLK	TO	MPG	PPG	RPG	APG	PCM
67-68	New Orleans-A	73	....	2159	1143	448	918	.488	2	6	.333	245	308	.795	366	528	894	73	157	0	....	....	115	29.6	15.7	12.2	1.0	.690
68-69	New Orleans-A	76	....	2736	1210	456	1035	.441	7	29	.241	291	361	.806	368	656	1024	142	200	1	....	....	121	36.0	15.9	13.5	1.9	.599
69-70	New Orleans-A	82	....	3266	1342	525	1091	.481	7	23	.304	285	366	.779	427	905	1332	182	251	1	....	....	148	39.8	16.4	16.2	2.2	.632
70-71	Utah-A	82	....	2995	1030	396	908	.436	11	44	.250	227	272	.835	303	673	976	178	203	0	....	....	127	36.5	12.6	11.9	2.2	.506

YEAR	TEAM	GP	GS	MIN	PTS	FGM	FGA	FG%	3PM	3PA	3P%	FTM	FTA	FT%	ORB	DRB	TRB	AST	PF	DQ	STL	BLK	TO	MPG	PPG	RPG	APG	PCM
71-72	Utah-A	78	....	2567	954	379	752	.504	29	71	.408	167	201	.831	216	495	711	124	171	0	....	....	86	32.9	12.2	9.1	1.6	.506
72-73	San Diego-A	58	....	1618	576	218	525	.415	9	30	.300	131	155	.845	159	258	417	99	134	2	....	....	85	27.9	9.9	7.2	1.7	.441
73-74	Kentucky-A	34	....	615	235	97	201	.483	0	5	.000	41	49	.837	53	87	140	31	38	....	8	7	29	18.1	6.9	4.1	0.9	.458
73-74	San Diego-A	46	....	1012	434	179	376	.476	1	8	.125	75	87	.862	91	155	246	58	74	....	32	27	60	22.0	9.4	5.3	1.3	.499
74-75	Kentucky-A	4	....	29	30	12	21	.571	0	0	.000	6	6	1.000	8	3	11	1	4	....	2	1	2	7.3	7.5	2.8	0.3	1.073
74-75	Virginia-A	53	....	1748	749	295	618	.477	3	10	.300	156	181	.862	145	259	404	113	102	....	29	30	95	33.0	14.1	7.6	2.1	.509
ABA Season Totals		586	....	18745	7703	3005	6445	.466	69	226	.305	1624	1986	.818	2136	4019	6155	1001	1334	4	71	65	868	32.0	13.1	10.5	1.7	....
67-68	New Orleans-A	17	....	621	296	115	252	.456	0	6	.000	66	93	.710	83	151	234	28	45	0	....	....	40	36.5	17.4	13.8	1.6	.611
68-69	New Orleans-A	11	....	410	185	71	146	.486	2	5	.400	41	53	.774	67	108	175	17	32	0	....	....	20	37.3	16.8	15.9	1.5	.662
70-71	Utah-A	18	....	566	222	94	170	.553	5	11	.455	29	41	.707	49	134	183	40	44	0	....	....	24	31.4	12.3	10.2	2.2	.589
71-72	Utah-A	9	....	227	53	20	56	.357	0	6	.000	13	16	.813	14	47	61	14	12	0	....	....	5	25.2	5.9	6.8	1.6	.370
72-73	San Diego-A	4	....	147	64	19	55	.345	2	4	.500	24	27	.889	17	27	44	5	16	0	....	....	10	36.8	16.0	11.0	1.3	.464
73-74	Kentucky-A	8	....	108	45	16	27	.593	0	0	.000	13	14	.929	5	27	32	5	6	....	4	5	9	13.5	5.6	4.0	0.6	.609
ABA Playoff Totals		67	....	2079	865	335	706	.475	9	32	.281	186	244	.762	235	494	729	109	155	0	4	5	108	31.0	12.9	10.9	1.6	....

• ROBERSON, Rick

Rick Roberson

Born: July 7, 1947. Memphis, TN, United States. Height: 6'9". Weight: 231 lbs. Drafted: 1969 College: Cincinnati

YEAR	TEAM	GP	GS	MIN	PTS	FGM	FGA	FG%	3PM	3PA	3P%	FTM	FTA	FT%	ORB	DRB	TRB	AST	PF	DQ	STL	BLK	TO	MPG	PPG	RPG	APG	PCM
69-70	LA Lakers	74	....	2005	644	262	586	.447	....	....	....	120	212	.566	....	....	672	92	256	7	....	....	....	27.1	8.7	9.1	1.2	.449
70-71	LA Lakers	65	....	909	338	125	301	.415	....	....	....	88	143	.615	....	....	304	47	125	1	....	....	....	14.0	5.2	4.7	0.7	.467
71-72	Cleveland	63	....	2207	823	304	688	.442	....	....	....	215	366	.587	....	....	801	109	251	7	....	....	....	35.0	13.1	12.7	1.7	.514
72-73	Cleveland	62	....	2127	781	307	709	.433	....	....	....	167	290	.576	....	....	693	134	249	5	....	....	....	34.3	12.6	11.2	2.2	.481
73-74	Portland	69	....	2060	933	364	797	.457	....	....	....	205	316	.649	251	450	701	133	252	4	65	55	....	29.9	13.5	10.2	1.9	.563
74-75	New Orleans	16	....	339	119	48	108	.444	....	....	....	23	40	.575	39	79	118	23	49	0	7	8	....	21.2	7.4	7.4	1.4	.492
75-76	Kansas City	74	....	709	188	73	180	.406	....	....	....	42	103	.408	74	159	233	53	126	1	18	17	....	9.6	2.5	3.1	0.7	.390
NBA Season Totals		423	....	10356	3826	1483	3369	.440	....	....	....	860	1470	.585	364	688	3522	591	1308	25	90	80	....	24.5	9.0	8.3	1.4	....
69-70	LA Lakers	9	....	61	22	8	18	.444	....	....	....	6	10	.600	....	....	16	0	13	0	....	....	....	6.8	2.4	1.8	0.0	.325
70-71	LA Lakers	9	....	93	24	10	29	.345	....	....	....	4	7	.571	....	....	26	4	14	0	....	....	....	10.3	2.7	2.9	0.4	.293
NBA Playoff Totals		18	....	154	46	18	47	.383	....	....	....	10	17	.588	....	....	42	4	27	0	....	....	....	8.6	2.6	2.3	0.2	....

• ROBERSON, Terrance

Terrance Roberson

Born: Dec. 30, 1976. Saginaw, MI, United States. Height: 6'7". Weight: 215 lbs. Drafted: — College: Fresno State

YEAR	TEAM	GP	GS	MIN	PTS	FGM	FGA	FG%	3PM	3PA	3P%	FTM	FTA	FT%	ORB	DRB	TRB	AST	PF	DQ	STL	BLK	TO	MPG	PPG	RPG	APG	PCM
00-01	Charlotte	3	0	13	0	0	2	.000	0	1	.000	0	0	.000	0	1	1	1	3	0	0	0	2	4.3	0.0	0.3	0.3	-.226
NBA Season Totals		3	0	13	0	0	2	.000	0	1	.000	0	0	.000	0	1	1	1	3	0	0	0	2	4.3	0.0	0.3	0.3	....

• ROBERTS, Anthony

Anthony Jerome Roberts

Born: Apr. 15, 1955. Chattanooga, TN, United States. Died: Mar.29, 1998. Height: 6'5". Weight: 185 lbs. Drafted: 1977 College: Oral Roberts

YEAR	TEAM	GP	GS	MIN	PTS	FGM	FGA	FG%	3PM	3PA	3P%	FTM	FTA	FT%	ORB	DRB	TRB	AST	PF	DQ	STL	BLK	TO	MPG	PPG	RPG	APG	PCM
77-78	Denver	82	....	1598	775	311	736	.423	....	....	....	153	212	.722	135	216	351	105	212	1	40	7	115	19.5	9.5	4.3	1.3	.407
78-79	Denver	63	....	1236	498	211	498	.424	....	....	....	76	110	.691	106	152	258	107	142	2	20	2	63	19.6	7.9	4.1	1.7	.384
79-80	Denver	23	....	486	177	69	181	.381	0	1	.000	39	60	.650	54	55	109	20	52	1	13	3	28	21.1	7.7	4.7	0.9	.313
80-81	Washington	26	....	350	127	54	144	.375	0	0	.000	19	29	.655	18	50	68	20	52	0	11	0	29	13.5	4.9	2.6	0.8	.240
83-84	Denver	19	0	197	81	34	91	.374	0	0	.000	13	18	.722	20	31	51	13	43	1	5	1	17	10.4	4.3	2.7	0.7	.288
NBA Season Totals		213	0	3867	1658	679	1650	.412	0	1	.000	300	429	.699	333	504	837	265	501	5	89	13	252	18.2	7.8	3.9	1.2	....
77-78	Denver	13	....	400	212	86	199	.432	....	....	....	40	50	.800	45	63	108	30	57	3	11	6	27	30.8	16.3	8.3	2.3	.508
78-79	Denver	3	....	80	33	13	33	.394	....	....	....	7	11	.636	5	8	13	6	9	0	2	1	3	26.7	11.0	4.3	2.0	.344
NBA Playoff Totals		16	....	480	245	99	232	.427	....	....	....	47	61	.770	50	71	121	36	66	3	13	7	30	30.0	15.3	7.6	2.3	....

• ROBERTS, Bill

William Roberts

Born: Mar. 3, 1925. Fort Wayne, IN, United States. Height: 6'9". Weight: 210 lbs. Drafted: — College: Wyoming

YEAR	TEAM	GP	GS	MIN	PTS	FGM	FGA	FG%	3PM	3PA	3P%	FTM	FTA	FT%	ORB	DRB	TRB	AST	PF	DQ	STL	BLK	TO	MPG	PPG	RPG	APG	PCM
48-49	Chicago	2	....	....	2	1	3	.333	....	....	....	0	0	.000	....	....	....	0	2	....	....	....	....	....	1.0	....	0.0	....
48-49	Boston	26	....	....	81	36	109	.330	....	....	....	9	19	.474	....	....	....	13	34	....	....	....	....	....	3.1	....	0.5	....
48-49	St. Louis	22	....	....	139	52	155	.335	....	....	....	35	44	.795	....	....	....	28	77	....	....	....	....	....	6.3	....	1.3	....
49-50	St. Louis	67	....	....	182	77	222	.347	....	....	....	28	39	.718	....	....	....	24	90	....	....	....	....	....	2.7	....	0.4	....
NBA Season Totals		117	....	....	404	166	489	.339	....	....	....	72	102	.706	....	....	....	65	203	....	....	....	....	....	3.5	....	0.6	....
48-49	St. Louis	2	....	....	22	10	29	.345	....	....	....	2	5	.400	....	....	....	2	10	....	....	....	....	....	11.0	....	1.0	....
NBA Playoff Totals		2	....	....	22	10	29	.345	....	....	....	2	5	.400	....	....	....	2	10	....	....	....	....	....	11.0	....	1.0	....

• ROBERTS, Fred

Frederick Clark Roberts

Born: Aug. 14, 1960. Provo, UT, United States. Height: 6'10". Weight: 218 lbs. Drafted: 1982 College: Brigham Young

YEAR	TEAM	GP	GS	MIN	PTS	FGM	FGA	FG%	3PM	3PA	3P%	FTM	FTA	FT%	ORB	DRB	TRB	AST	PF	DQ	STL	BLK	TO	MPG	PPG	RPG	APG	PCM
83-84	San Antonio	79	8	1531	573	214	399	.536	1	4	.250	144	172	.837	102	202	304	98	219	4	52	38	103	19.4	7.3	3.8	1.2	.432
84-85	San Antonio	22	0	305	117	44	98	.449	0	0	.000	29	38	.763	10	25	35	22	45	0	10	12	22	13.9	5.3	1.6	1.0	.320
84-85	Utah	52	0	873	450	164	320	.513	1	1	1.000	121	144	.840	68	83	151	65	96	0	18	10	68	16.8	8.7	2.9	1.3	.483
85-86	Utah	58	0	469	216	74	167	.443	1	2	.500	67	87	.770	31	49	80	27	72	0	8	6	52	8.1	3.7	1.4	0.5	.330
86-87	Boston	73	11	1079	402	139	270	.515	0	3	.000	124	153	.810	54	136	190	62	129	1	22	20	88	14.8	5.5	2.6	0.8	.377
87-88	Boston	74	14	1032	450	161	330	.488	0	6	.000	128	165	.776	60	102	162	81	118	0	16	15	67	13.9	6.1	2.2	1.1	.411
88-89	Milwaukee	71	3	1251	417	155	319	.486	3	14	.214	104	129	.806	68	141	209	66	126	0	36	23	78	17.6	5.9	2.9	0.9	.353
89-90	Milwaukee	82	66	2235	857	330	666	.495	2	11	.182	195	249	.783	107	204	311	147	210	5	56	25	131	27.3	10.5	3.8	1.8	.367
90-91	Milwaukee	82	82	2114	888	357	670	.533	4	25	.160	170	209	.813	107	174	281	135	190	2	63	29	131	25.8	10.8	3.4	1.6	.406
91-92	Milwaukee	80	63	1746	769	311	645	.482	19	37	.514	128	171	.749	103	154	257	122	177	0	52	40	120	21.8	9.6	3.2	1.5	.401
92-93	Milwaukee	79	5	1488	599	226	428	.528	12	29	.414	135	169	.799	91	146	237	118	138	0	57	27	63	18.8	7.6	3.0	1.5	.468

YEAR	TEAM	GP	GS	MIN	PTS	FGM	FGA	FG%	3PM	3PA	3P%	FTM	FTA	FT%	ORB	DRB	TRB	AST	PF	DQ	STL	BLK	TO	MPG	PPG	RPG	APG	PCM
94-95	Cleveland	21	0	223	80	28	72	.389	4	11	.364	20	26	.769	13	21	34	8	26	1	6	3	6	10.6	3.8	1.6	0.4	.300
95-96	LA Lakers	33	1	317	122	48	97	.495	4	14	.286	22	28	.786	18	29	47	26	24	0	16	4	23	9.6	3.7	1.4	0.8	.412
96-97	Dallas	12	0	40	22	6	15	.400	0	0	.000	10	14	.714	2	8	10	0	2	0	0	1	5	3.3	1.8	0.8	0.0	.410
NBA Season Totals		818	253	14703	5962	2257	4496	.502	51	157	.325	1397	1754	.796	834	1474	2308	977	1572	13	412	253	957	18.0	7.3	2.8	1.2	....
84-85	Utah	10	0	130	54	19	43	.442	0	0	.000	16	20	.800	6	11	17	9	16	0	7	3	14	13.0	5.4	1.7	0.9	.339
85-86	Utah	4	0	31	22	7	15	.467	0	0	.000	8	9	.889	4	3	7	3	5	0	0	0	6	7.8	5.5	1.8	0.8	.514
86-87	Boston	20	4	265	91	30	59	.508	0	0	.000	31	44	.705	15	18	33	12	47	0	6	3	12	13.3	4.6	1.7	0.6	.290
87-88	Boston	15	0	100	29	11	21	.524	0	0	.000	7	11	.636	8	8	16	3	20	1	3	0	6	6.7	1.9	1.1	0.2	.238
88-89	Milwaukee	9	5	345	132	49	100	.490	0	3	.000	34	40	.850	11	28	39	20	29	1	5	4	13	38.3	14.7	4.3	2.2	.354
89-90	Milwaukee	4	4	79	39	13	20	.650	0	1	.000	13	16	.813	5	3	8	3	9	0	0	1	5	19.8	9.8	2.0	0.8	.427
90-91	Milwaukee	3	3	103	34	16	35	.457	0	1	.000	2	2	1.000	4	11	15	7	5	0	2	1	5	34.3	11.3	5.0	2.3	.326
94-95	Cleveland	1	0	7	6	3	4	.750	0	0	.000	0	2	.000	1	1	2	0	0	0	0	0	1	7.0	6.0	2.0	0.0	.723
95-96	LA Lakers	1	0	3	0	0	2	.000	0	0	.000	0	0	.000	2	1	3	0	0	0	0	0	1	3.0	0.0	3.0	0.0	.000
NBA Playoff Totals		67	16	1063	407	148	299	.495	0	5	.000	111	144	.771	56	84	140	57	131	2	23	12	63	15.9	6.1	2.1	0.9	....

• ROBERTS, Glenn

Glenn Roberts

Born: 1912. Died: May21, 1980. Height: 6'5". Weight: 200 lbs. Drafted: — College: Emory & Henry

YEAR	TEAM	GP	GS	MIN	PTS	FGM	FGA	FG%	3PM	3PA	3P%	FTM	FTA	FT%	ORB	DRB	TRB	AST	PF	DQ	STL	BLK	TO	MPG	PPG	RPG	APG	PCM
37-38	Dayton-N	8	....	....	39	14	....	....	....	....	....	11	....	....	....	....	....	....	....	....	....	....	....	....	4.9	....	....	....
38-39	Non-Skids-N	15	....	....	46	20	....	....	....	....	....	6	....	....	....	....	....	....	....	....	....	....	....	....	3.1	....	....	....
41-42	Toledo-N	1	....	....	2	1	....	....	....	....	....	0	....	....	....	....	....	....	....	....	....	....	....	....	2.0	....	....	....
NBL Season Totals		24	....	....	87	35	....	....	....	....	....	17	....	....	....	....	....	....	....	....	....	....	....	....	3.6	....	....	....
38-39	Non-Skids-N	2	....	....	1	0	....	....	....	....	....	1	....	....	....	....	....	....	....	....	....	....	....	....	0.5	....	....	....
NBL Playoff Totals		2	....	....	1	0	....	....	....	....	....	1	....	....	....	....	....	....	....	....	....	....	....	....	0.5	....	....	....

• ROBERTS, Joe

Joseph Roberts

Born: May 18, 1936. Height: 6'6". Weight: 214 lbs. Drafted: 1960 College: Ohio State

YEAR	TEAM	GP	GS	MIN	PTS	FGM	FGA	FG%	3PM	3PA	3P%	FTM	FTA	FT%	ORB	DRB	TRB	AST	PF	DQ	STL	BLK	TO	MPG	PPG	RPG	APG	PCM
60-61	Syracuse	68	....	800	322	130	351	.370	....	....	....	62	104	.596	....	....	243	43	125	0	....	....	....	11.8	4.7	3.6	0.6	.411
61-62	Syracuse	80	....	1642	615	243	619	.393	....	....	....	129	194	.665	....	....	538	50	230	4	....	....	....	20.5	7.7	6.7	0.6	.419
62-63	Syracuse	33	....	466	181	73	196	.372	....	....	....	35	51	.686	....	....	155	16	66	1	....	....	....	14.1	5.5	4.7	0.5	.415
67-68	Kentucky-A	37	....	564	137	54	146	.370	1	3	.333	28	50	.560	....	....	139	14	64	1	....	....	30	15.2	3.7	3.8	0.4	.278
NBA Season Totals		181	....	2908	1118	446	1166	.383	....	....	....	226	349	.648	....	....	936	109	421	5	....	....	....	16.1	6.2	5.2	0.6	....
ABA Season Totals		37	....	564	137	54	146	.370	1	3	.333	28	50	.560	....	....	139	14	64	1	....	....	30	15.2	3.7	3.8	0.4	....
Career Totals		218	....	3472	1255	500	1312	.381	1	3	.333	254	399	.637	....	....	1075	123	485	6	....	....	30	15.9	5.8	4.9	0.6	....
60-61	Syracuse	5	....	20	6	3	10	.300	....	....	....	0	0	.000	....	....	4	0	3	0	....	....	....	4.0	1.2	0.8	0.0	.129
61-62	Syracuse	4	....	64	26	8	22	.364	....	....	....	10	14	.714	....	....	28	0	9	0	....	....	....	16.0	6.5	7.0	0.0	.498
67-68	Kentucky-A	5	....	63	12	5	15	.333	0	0	.000	2	6	.333	....	....	15	1	13	0	....	....	3	12.6	2.4	3.0	0.2	.163
NBA Playoff Totals		9	....	84	32	11	32	.344	....	....	....	10	14	.714	....	....	32	0	12	0	....	....	....	9.3	3.6	3.6	0.0	....
ABA Playoff Totals		5	....	63	12	5	15	.333	0	0	.000	2	6	.333	....	....	15	1	13	0	....	....	3	12.6	2.4	3.0	0.2	....
Career Playoff Totals		14	....	147	44	16	47	.340	0	0	.000	12	20	.600	....	....	47	1	25	0	....	....	3	10.5	3.1	3.4	0.1	....

• ROBERTS, Marv

Marvin James Roberts

Born: Jan. 29, 1950. Brooklyn, NY, United States. Height: 6'8". Weight: 200 lbs. Drafted: 1971 College: Utah State

YEAR	TEAM	GP	GS	MIN	PTS	FGM	FGA	FG%	3PM	3PA	3P%	FTM	FTA	FT%	ORB	DRB	TRB	AST	PF	DQ	STL	BLK	TO	MPG	PPG	RPG	APG	PCM
71-72	Denver-A	68	....	1047	521	217	533	.407	1	4	.250	86	120	.717	121	173	294	61	150	3	....	....	77	15.4	7.7	4.3	0.9	.467
72-73	Denver-A	77	....	1959	950	374	807	.463	1	3	.333	201	255	.788	180	218	398	95	194	3	....	....	110	25.4	12.3	5.2	1.2	.465
73-74	Carolina-A	39	....	954	401	160	361	.443	0	0	.000	81	102	.794	103	137	240	75	81	....	34	5	52	24.5	10.3	6.2	1.9	.499
73-74	Denver-A	35	....	645	261	106	237	.447	1	1	1.000	48	62	.774	58	73	131	44	72	....	13	2	48	18.4	7.5	3.7	1.3	.425
74-75	Kentucky-A	83	....	1370	529	201	467	.430	0	1	.000	127	164	.774	91	155	246	103	200	....	27	4	100	16.5	6.4	3.0	1.2	.380
75-76	Kentucky-A	40	....	1003	428	170	385	.442	0	0	.000	88	113	.779	74	85	159	78	96	....	21	6	68	25.1	10.7	4.0	2.0	.409
75-76	Virginia-A	32	....	556	197	89	236	.377	0	0	.000	19	24	.792	30	47	77	42	55	....	15	2	32	17.4	6.2	2.4	1.3	.278
76-77	LA Lakers	28	....	209	58	27	76	.355	....	....	....	4	6	.667	9	16	25	19	34	0	4	2	....	7.5	2.1	0.9	0.7	.207
NBA Season Totals		28	....	209	58	27	76	.355	....	....	....	4	6	.667	9	16	25	19	34	0	4	2	....	7.5	2.1	0.9	0.7	....
ABA Season Totals		374	....	7534	3287	1317	3026	.435	3	9	.333	650	840	.774	657	888	1545	498	848	6	110	19	487	20.1	8.8	4.1	1.3	....
Career Totals		402	....	7743	3345	1344	3102	.433	3	9	.333	654	846	.773	666	904	1570	517	882	6	114	21	487	19.3	8.3	3.9	1.3	....
71-72	Denver-A	3	....	20	6	2	7	.286	0	1	.000	2	2	1.000	....	....	2	0	1	0	....	....	2	6.7	2.0	0.7	0.0	.146
72-73	Denver-A	2	....	24	10	4	8	.500	0	0	.000	2	2	1.000	0	3	3	1	5	0	....	....	0	12.0	5.0	1.5	0.5	.331
73-74	Carolina-A	4	....	119	50	20	48	.417	0	0	.000	10	12	.833	11	14	25	7	10	....	2	1	2	29.8	12.5	6.3	1.8	.422
74-75	Kentucky-A	15	....	259	151	60	115	.522	0	0	.000	31	41	.756	27	27	54	23	29	....	3	0	18	17.3	10.1	3.6	1.5	.611
ABA Playoff Totals		24	....	422	217	86	178	.483	0	1	.000	45	57	.789	38	44	84	31	45	0	5	1	22	17.6	9.0	3.5	1.3	....

• ROBERTS, Stanley

Stanley Corvet Roberts

Born: Feb. 7, 1970. Hopkins, SC, United States. Height: 7' Weight: 285 lbs. Drafted: 1991 College: Louisiana State

YEAR	TEAM	GP	GS	MIN	PTS	FGM	FGA	FG%	3PM	3PA	3P%	FTM	FTA	FT%	ORB	DRB	TRB	AST	PF	DQ	STL	BLK	TO	MPG	PPG	RPG	APG	PCM
91-92	Orlando	55	34	1118	573	236	446	.529	0	1	.000	101	196	.515	113	223	336	39	221	7	22	83	77	20.3	10.4	6.1	0.7	.547
92-93	LA Clippers	77	76	1816	870	375	711	.527	0	0	.000	120	246	.488	181	297	478	59	**332**	**15**	34	141	123	23.6	11.3	6.2	0.8	.496
93-94	LA Clippers	14	14	350	104	43	100	.430	0	0	.000	18	44	.409	27	66	93	11	54	2	6	25	24	25.0	7.4	6.6	0.8	.339
95-96	LA Clippers	51	7	795	356	141	304	.464	0	0	.000	74	133	.556	42	120	162	41	153	3	15	39	46	15.6	7.0	3.2	0.8	.385
96-97	LA Clippers	18	2	378	171	63	148	.426	0	0	.000	45	64	.703	24	67	91	9	57	2	8	23	23	21.0	9.5	5.1	0.5	.419
97-98	Minnesota	74	44	1328	457	191	386	.495	0	0	.000	75	156	.481	109	254	363	27	226	5	24	72	67	17.9	6.2	4.9	0.4	.396
98-99	Houston	6	0	33	14	5	13	.385	0	0	.000	4	8	.500	4	7	11	0	2	0	0	1	4	5.5	2.3	1.8	0.0	.343
99-00	Philadelphia	5	1	51	10	5	16	.313	0	1	.000	0	3	.000	6	9	15	3	15	0	1	1	2	10.2	2.0	3.0	0.6	.171
NBA Season Totals		300	178	5869	2555	1059	2124	.499	0	2	.000	437	850	.514	506	1043	1549	189	1060	34	110	385	366	19.6	8.5	5.2	0.6	....

YEAR	TEAM	GP	GS	MIN	PTS	FGM	FGA	FG%	3PM	3PA	3P%	FTM	FTA	FT%	ORB	DRB	TRB	AST	PF	DQ	STL	BLK	TO	MPG	PPG	RPG	APG	PCM
92-93	LA Clippers	5	5	149	57	26	50	.520	0	1	.000	5	18	.278	17	24	41	1	24	2	3	3	10	29.8	11.4	8.2	0.2	.355
97-98	Minnesota	1	0	8	1	0	1	.000	0	0	.000	1	2	.500	1	1	2	0	0	0	0	0	1	8.0	1.0	2.0	0.0	.068
98-99	Houston	3	0	20	1	0	6	.000	0	0	.000	1	2	.500	0	3	3	0	5	0	0	4	0	6.7	0.3	1.0	0.0	-.039
NBA Playoff Totals		9	5	177	59	26	57	.456	0	1	.000	7	22	.318	18	28	46	1	29	2	3	7	11	19.7	6.6	5.1	0.1	....

• ROBERTS, Wyman

Wyman Roberts

Born: 1916. Height: 5'11". Weight: 160 lbs. Drafted: — College: none

YEAR	TEAM	GP	GS	MIN	PTS	FGM	FGA	FG%	3PM	3PA	3P%	FTM	FTA	FT%	ORB	DRB	TRB	AST	PF	DQ	STL	BLK	TO	MPG	PPG	RPG	APG	PCM
37-38	Dayton-N	2	....	....	6	2	....	....	....	....	....	2	....	....	....	....	....	....	....	....	....	....	....	....	3.0	....	....	....
NBL Season Totals		2	....	....	6	2	....	....	....	....	....	2	....	....	....	....	....	....	....	....	....	....	....	....	3.0	....	....	....

• ROBERTSON, Alvin

Alvin Cyrrale Robertson

Born: July 22, 1962. Barberton, OH, United States. Height: 6'3". Weight: 185 lbs. Drafted: 1984 College: Arkansas

YEAR	TEAM	GP	GS	MIN	PTS	FGM	FGA	FG%	3PM	3PA	3P%	FTM	FTA	FT%	ORB	DRB	TRB	AST	PF	DQ	STL	BLK	TO	MPG	PPG	RPG	APG	PCM
84-85	San Antonio	79	9	1685	726	299	600	.498	4	11	.364	124	169	.734	116	149	265	275	217	1	127	24	166	21.3	9.2	3.4	3.5	.504
85-86	San Antonio	82	82	2878	1392	562	1093	.514	8	29	.276	260	327	.795	184	332	516	448	296	4	**301**	40	254	35.1	17.0	6.3	5.5	.615
86-87	San Antonio	81	78	2697	1435	589	1264	.466	13	48	.271	244	324	.753	186	238	424	421	264	2	**260**	35	243	33.3	17.7	5.2	5.2	.571
87-88	San Antonio	82	82	2978	1610	655	1408	.465	27	95	.284	273	365	.748	165	333	498	557	300	4	243	69	254	36.3	19.6	6.1	6.8	.617
88-89	San Antonio	65	65	2287	1122	465	962	.483	9	45	.200	183	253	.723	157	227	384	393	259	6	197	36	234	35.2	17.3	5.9	6.0	.561
89-90	Milwaukee	81	81	2599	1153	476	946	.503	4	26	.154	197	266	.741	230	329	559	445	280	2	207	17	219	32.1	14.2	6.9	5.5	.597
90-91	Milwaukee	81	81	2598	1098	438	904	.485	23	63	.365	199	263	.757	191	268	459	444	273	5	**246**	16	211	32.1	13.6	5.7	5.5	.560
91-92	Milwaukee	82	79	2463	1010	396	922	.430	67	210	.319	151	198	.763	175	175	350	360	263	5	210	32	221	30.0	12.3	4.3	4.4	.450
92-93	Milwaukee	39	32	1065	339	139	290	.479	17	55	.309	44	70	.629	47	90	137	156	120	0	90	9	78	27.3	8.7	3.5	4.0	.417
92-93	Detroit	30	22	941	279	108	249	.434	23	67	.343	40	58	.690	60	72	132	108	99	1	64	9	57	31.4	9.3	4.4	3.6	.368
95-96	Toronto	77	69	2478	718	285	607	.470	41	151	.272	107	158	.677	110	232	342	323	268	5	166	36	185	32.2	9.3	4.4	4.2	.381
NBA Season Totals		779	680	24669	10882	4412	9245	.477	236	800	.295	1822	2451	.743	1621	2445	4066	3930	2639	35	2111	323	2122	31.7	14.0	5.2	5.0	....
85-86	San Antonio	3	3	98	27	8	29	.276	0	0	.000	11	13	.846	5	9	14	19	10	0	7	1	5	32.7	9.0	4.7	6.3	.388
87-88	San Antonio	3	3	119	70	30	53	.566	3	7	.429	7	9	.778	5	9	14	28	15	1	12	1	9	39.7	23.3	4.7	9.3	.734
89-90	Milwaukee	4	4	155	94	35	67	.522	0	1	.000	24	34	.706	10	13	23	19	16	0	9	0	15	38.8	23.5	5.8	4.8	.567
90-91	Milwaukee	3	3	118	71	29	49	.592	3	9	.333	10	13	.769	7	11	18	15	12	0	8	0	10	39.3	23.7	6.0	5.0	.646
NBA Playoff Totals		13	13	490	262	102	198	.515	6	17	.353	52	69	.754	27	42	69	81	53	1	36	2	39	37.7	20.2	5.3	6.2	....

• ROBERTSON, Oscar

Oscar Palmer (The Big O, Horse, Donut) Robertson

Born: Nov. 24, 1938. Charlotte, TN, United States. Height: 6'5". Weight: 205 lbs. Drafted: 1960 College: Cincinnati HOF: 1980

YEAR	TEAM	GP	GS	MIN	PTS	FGM	FGA	FG%	3PM	3PA	3P%	FTM	FTA	FT%	ORB	DRB	TRB	AST	PF	DQ	STL	BLK	TO	MPG	PPG	RPG	APG	PCM
60-61	Cincinnati	71	....	3032	2165	756	1600	.473	....	....	....	653	794	.822	....	....	716	**690**	219	3	....	....	....	42.7	30.5	10.1	**9.7**	**.919**
61-62	Cincinnati	79	....	3503	2432	866	1810	.478	....	....	....	700	872	.803	....	....	985	**899**	258	1	....	....	....	44.3	30.8	12.5	**11.4**	**.968**
62-63	Cincinnati	80	....	3521	2264	825	1593	.518	....	....	....	614	758	.810	....	....	835	758	293	1	....	....	....	44.0	28.3	10.4	9.5	.869
63-64	Cincinnati	79	....	3559	2480	840	1740	.483	....	....	....	**800**	938	**.853**	....	....	783	**868**	280	3	....	....	....	45.1	31.4	9.9	**11.0**	**.924**
64-65	Cincinnati	75	....	3421	2279	807	1681	.480	....	....	....	**665**	793	.839	....	....	674	**861**	205	2	....	....	....	**45.6**	30.4	9.0	**11.5**	**.894**
65-66	Cincinnati	76	....	3493	2378	818	1723	.475	....	....	....	742	881	.842	....	....	586	**847**	227	1	....	....	....	46.0	31.3	7.7	**11.1**	**.863**
66-67	Cincinnati	79	....	3468	2412	838	1699	.493	....	....	....	736	843	.873	....	....	486	845	226	2	....	....	....	43.9	30.5	6.2	10.7	.864
67-68	Cincinnati	65	....	2765	1896	660	1321	.500	....	....	....	**576**	660	**.873**	....	....	391	633	199	2	....	....	....	42.5	29.2	6.0	9.7	.842
68-69	Cincinnati	79	....	3461	1955	656	1351	.486	....	....	....	**643**	767	.838	....	....	502	**772**	231	2	....	....	....	43.8	24.7	6.4	**9.8**	**.735**
69-70	Cincinnati	69	....	2865	1748	647	1267	.511	....	....	....	454	561	.809	....	....	422	558	175	1	....	....	....	41.5	25.3	6.1	8.1	.724
70-71	Milwaukee	81	....	3194	1569	592	1193	.496	....	....	....	385	453	.850	....	....	462	668	203	0	....	....	....	39.4	19.4	5.7	8.2	.656
71-72	Milwaukee	64	....	2390	1114	419	887	.472	....	....	....	276	330	.836	....	....	323	491	116	0	....	....	....	37.3	17.4	5.0	7.7	.616
72-73	Milwaukee	73	....	2737	1130	446	983	.454	....	....	....	238	281	.847	....	....	360	551	167	0	....	....	....	37.5	15.5	4.9	7.5	.554
73-74	Milwaukee	70	....	2477	888	338	772	.438	....	....	....	212	254	.835	71	208	279	446	132	0	77	4	....	35.4	12.7	4.0	6.4	.482
NBA Season Totals		1040	....	43886	26710	9508	19620	.485	....	....	....	7694	9185	.838	71	208	7804	9887	2931	18	77	4	....	42.2	25.7	7.5	9.5	....
61-62	Cincinnati	4	....	185	115	42	81	.519	....	....	....	31	39	.795	....	....	44	44	18	1	....	....	....	46.3	28.8	11.0	11.0	.878
62-63	Cincinnati	12	....	570	381	124	264	.470	....	....	....	133	154	.864	....	....	156	108	41	0	....	....	....	47.5	31.8	13.0	9.0	.877
63-64	Cincinnati	10	....	471	293	92	202	.455	....	....	....	109	127	.858	....	....	89	84	30	0	....	....	....	47.1	29.3	8.9	8.4	.766
64-65	Cincinnati	4	....	195	112	38	89	.427	....	....	....	36	39	.923	....	....	19	48	14	0	....	....	....	48.8	28.0	4.8	12.0	.718
65-66	Cincinnati	5	....	224	159	49	120	.408	....	....	....	61	68	.897	....	....	38	39	20	1	....	....	....	44.8	31.8	7.6	7.8	.759
66-67	Cincinnati	4	....	183	99	33	64	.516	....	....	....	33	37	.892	....	....	16	45	9	0	....	....	....	45.8	24.8	4.0	11.3	.743
70-71	Milwaukee	14	....	520	256	102	210	.486	....	....	....	52	69	.754	....	....	70	124	39	0	....	....	....	37.1	18.3	5.0	8.9	.655
71-72	Milwaukee	11	....	380	144	57	140	.407	....	....	....	30	36	.833	....	....	64	83	29	0	....	....	....	34.5	13.1	5.8	7.5	.544
72-73	Milwaukee	6	....	256	127	48	96	.500	....	....	....	31	34	.912	....	....	28	45	21	1	....	....	....	42.7	21.2	4.7	7.5	.590
73-74	Milwaukee	16	....	689	224	90	200	.450	....	....	....	44	52	.846	15	39	54	149	46	0	15	4	....	43.1	14.0	3.4	9.3	.471
NBA Playoff Totals		86	....	3673	1910	675	1466	.460	....	....	....	560	655	.855	15	39	578	769	267	3	15	4	....	42.7	22.2	6.7	8.9	....

• ROBERTSON, Ryan

Ryan Ashley Robertson

Born: Oct. 2, 1976. Lawton, OK, United States. Height: 6'5". Weight: 190 lbs. Drafted: 1999 College: Kansas

YEAR	TEAM	GP	GS	MIN	PTS	FGM	FGA	FG%	3PM	3PA	3P%	FTM	FTA	FT%	ORB	DRB	TRB	AST	PF	DQ	STL	BLK	TO	MPG	PPG	RPG	APG	PCM
99-00	Sacramento	1	0	25	5	2	6	.333	0	2	.000	1	1	1.000	0	0	0	0	0	0	0	0	0	25.0	5.0	0.0	0.0	.055
NBA Season Totals		1	0	25	5	2	6	.333	0	2	.000	1	1	1.000	0	0	0	0	0	0	0	0	0	25.0	5.0	0.0	0.0	....

• ROBERTSON, Tony

Tony Robertson

Born: Jan. 1, 1956. Detroit, MI, United States. Height: 6'4". Weight: 195 lbs. Drafted: 1977 College: West Virginia

YEAR	TEAM	GP	GS	MIN	PTS	FGM	FGA	FG%	3PM	3PA	3P%	FTM	FTA	FT%	ORB	DRB	TRB	AST	PF	DQ	STL	BLK	TO	MPG	PPG	RPG	APG	PCM
77-78	Atlanta	63	....	929	373	168	381	.441	....	....	....	37	53	.698	15	55	70	103	133	2	74	5	88	14.7	5.9	1.1	1.6	.313
78-79	Golden State	12	....	74	36	15	40	.375	....	....	....	6	9	.667	6	4	10	4	10	0	8	0	8	6.2	3.0	0.8	0.3	.285
NBA Season Totals		75	....	1003	409	183	421	.435	....	....	....	43	62	.694	21	59	80	107	143	2	82	5	96	13.4	5.5	1.1	1.4	....
77-78	Atlanta	2	....	12	5	2	6	.333	....	....	....	1	2	.500	0	0	0	0	3	0	0	0	0	6.0	2.5	0.0	0.0	-.021
NBA Playoff Totals		2	....	12	5	2	6	.333	....	....	....	1	2	.500	0	0	0	0	3	0	0	0	0	6.0	2.5	0.0	0.0	....

• ROBEY, Rick
Frederick Robert Robey

Born: Jan. 30, 1956. Coral Gables, FL, United States. Height: 6'11". Weight: 230 lbs. Drafted: 1978 College: Kentucky

YEAR	TEAM	GP	GS	MIN	PTS	FGM	FGA	FG%	3PM	3PA	3P%	FTM	FTA	FT%	ORB	DRB	TRB	AST	PF	DQ	STL	BLK	TO	MPG	PPG	RPG	APG	PCM
78-79	Indiana	43	....	849	370	140	295	.475	....	....	....	90	121	.744	80	174	254	53	111	1	25	12	90	19.7	8.6	5.9	1.2	.478
78-79	Boston	36	....	914	448	182	378	.481	....	....	....	84	103	.816	88	171	259	79	121	3	23	3	76	25.4	12.4	7.2	2.2	.529
79-80	Boston	82	....	1918	942	379	727	.521	0	1	.000	184	269	.684	209	321	530	92	244	2	53	15	148	23.4	11.5	6.5	1.1	.514
80-81	Boston	82	....	1569	740	298	547	.545	0	1	.000	144	251	.574	132	258	390	126	204	0	38	19	139	19.1	9.0	4.8	1.5	.503
81-82	Boston	80	4	1186	454	185	375	.493	0	2	.000	84	157	.535	114	181	295	68	183	2	27	14	88	14.8	5.7	3.7	0.9	.390
82-83	Boston	59	6	855	245	100	214	.467	0	0	.000	45	78	.577	79	140	219	65	131	1	13	8	71	14.5	4.2	3.7	1.1	.342
83-84	Phoenix	61	4	856	342	140	257	.545	1	1	1.000	61	88	.693	80	118	198	65	120	0	20	14	79	14.0	5.6	3.2	1.1	.440
84-85	Phoenix	4	0	48	5	2	9	.222	0	0	.000	1	2	.500	3	5	8	5	7	0	2	0	8	12.0	1.3	2.0	1.3	.041
85-86	Phoenix	46	1	629	177	72	191	.377	0	3	.000	33	48	.688	40	108	148	58	92	1	19	5	64	13.7	3.8	3.2	1.3	.285
NBA Season Totals		493	15	8824	3723	1498	2993	.501	1	8	.125	726	1117	.650	825	1476	2301	611	1213	10	220	90	763	17.9	7.6	4.7	1.2	....
79-80	Boston	9	....	151	55	24	53	.453	0	1	.000	7	14	.500	13	19	32	10	27	0	7	3	8	16.8	6.1	3.6	1.1	.365
80-81	Boston	17	....	265	86	35	81	.432	0	0	.000	16	35	.457	19	41	60	12	44	0	2	5	19	15.6	5.1	3.5	0.7	.272
81-82	Boston	12	0	122	55	21	40	.525	0	0	.000	13	17	.765	13	16	29	4	27	0	2	3	11	10.2	4.6	2.4	0.3	.399
82-83	Boston	5	0	29	2	0	4	.000	0	1	.000	2	4	.500	3	5	8	1	4	0	0	0	2	5.8	0.4	1.6	0.2	.076
83-84	Phoenix	10	0	43	18	7	16	.438	0	1	.000	4	8	.500	7	3	10	2	5	0	2	0	4	4.3	1.8	1.0	0.2	.349
NBA Playoff Totals		53	0	610	216	87	194	.448	0	3	.000	42	78	.538	55	84	139	29	107	0	13	11	44	11.5	4.1	2.6	0.5	....

• ROBINSON, Chris
Chris Sean Robinson

Born: Apr. 2, 1974. Columbus, GA, United States. Height: 6'5". Weight: 200 lbs. Drafted: 1996 College: Western Kentucky

YEAR	TEAM	GP	GS	MIN	PTS	FGM	FGA	FG%	3PM	3PA	3P%	FTM	FTA	FT%	ORB	DRB	TRB	AST	PF	DQ	STL	BLK	TO	MPG	PPG	RPG	APG	PCM
96-97	Vancouver	41	6	681	188	69	182	.379	34	89	.382	16	26	.615	23	48	71	65	85	2	28	9	33	16.6	4.6	1.7	1.6	.261
97-98	Vancouver	16	0	143	54	23	63	.365	7	24	.292	1	2	.500	0	13	13	10	21	0	7	1	14	8.9	3.4	0.8	0.6	.172
97-98	Sacramento	19	0	271	108	42	111	.378	17	42	.405	7	14	.500	9	24	33	29	29	0	12	3	17	14.3	5.7	1.7	1.5	.326
NBA Season Totals		76	6	1095	350	134	356	.376	58	155	.374	24	42	.571	32	85	117	104	135	2	47	13	64	14.4	4.6	1.5	1.4	....

• ROBINSON, Cliff
Clifford Trent Robinson

Born: Mar. 13, 1960. Oakland, CA, United States. Height: 6'9". Weight: 220 lbs. Drafted: 1979 College: USC

YEAR	TEAM	GP	GS	MIN	PTS	FGM	FGA	FG%	3PM	3PA	3P%	FTM	FTA	FT%	ORB	DRB	TRB	AST	PF	DQ	STL	BLK	TO	MPG	PPG	RPG	APG	PCM
79-80	New Jersey	70	....	1661	951	391	833	.469	1	4	.250	168	242	.694	174	332	506	98	178	1	61	34	140	23.7	13.6	7.2	1.4	.579
80-81	New Jersey	63	....	1822	1229	525	1070	.491	1	1	1.000	178	248	.718	120	361	481	105	216	6	58	52	183	28.9	19.5	7.6	1.7	.597
81-82	Kansas City	38	30	1229	769	322	708	.455	0	3	.000	125	180	.694	83	239	322	71	120	1	46	60	87	32.3	20.2	8.5	1.9	.589
81-82	Cleveland	30	29	946	489	196	435	.451	0	1	.000	97	133	.729	91	196	287	49	102	3	42	43	63	31.5	16.3	9.6	1.6	.574
82-83	Cleveland	77	75	2601	1387	587	1230	.477	0	5	.000	213	301	.708	190	666	856	145	272	7	61	58	223	33.8	18.0	11.1	1.9	.570
83-84	Cleveland	73	70	2402	1301	533	1185	.450	1	2	.500	234	334	.701	156	597	753	185	195	2	51	32	190	32.9	17.8	10.3	2.5	.565
84-85	Washington	60	37	1870	1003	422	896	.471	1	3	.333	158	213	.742	141	405	546	149	187	4	51	47	162	31.2	16.7	9.1	2.5	.565
85-86	Washington	78	78	2563	1460	595	1255	.474	1	4	.250	269	353	.762	180	500	680	186	217	2	98	44	203	32.9	18.7	8.7	2.4	.578
86-87	Philadelphia	55	30	1586	815	338	729	.464	0	4	.000	139	184	.755	86	221	307	89	150	1	86	30	121	28.8	14.8	5.6	1.6	.464
87-88	Philadelphia	62	51	2110	1178	483	1041	.464	2	9	.222	210	293	.717	116	289	405	131	192	4	79	39	161	34.0	19.0	6.5	2.1	.477
88-89	Philadelphia	14	13	416	212	90	187	.481	0	1	.000	32	44	.727	19	56	75	32	37	0	17	2	34	29.7	15.1	5.4	2.3	.454
91-92	LA Lakers	9	0	78	29	11	27	.407	0	1	.000	7	8	.875	7	12	19	9	4	0	5	0	7	8.7	3.2	2.1	1.0	.478
NBA Season Totals		629	413	19284	10823	4493	9596	.468	7	38	.184	1830	2533	.722	1363	3874	5237	1249	1870	31	655	441	1574	30.7	17.2	8.3	2.0	....
84-85	Washington	4	4	123	59	25	56	.446	0	0	.000	9	12	.750	12	18	30	4	14	0	4	2	3	30.8	14.8	7.5	1.0	.465
85-86	Washington	5	5	177	107	46	93	.495	0	0	.000	15	31	.484	17	26	43	17	19	1	10	3	15	35.4	21.4	8.6	3.4	.584
86-87	Philadelphia	5	5	138	73	30	61	.492	0	0	.000	13	15	.867	10	33	43	6	15	0	3	7	8	27.6	14.6	8.6	1.2	.613
91-92	LA Lakers	3	0	24	11	3	10	.300	0	0	.000	5	8	.625	2	4	6	1	6	0	3	1	2	8.0	3.7	2.0	0.3	.367
NBA Playoff Totals		17	14	462	250	104	220	.473	0	0	.000	42	66	.636	41	81	122	28	54	1	20	13	28	27.2	14.7	7.2	1.6	....

• ROBINSON, Clifford
Clifford Ralph Robinson

Born: Dec. 16, 1966. Buffalo, NY, United States. Height: 6'10". Weight: 225 lbs. Drafted: 1989 College: Connecticut

YEAR	TEAM	GP	GS	MIN	PTS	FGM	FGA	FG%	3PM	3PA	3P%	FTM	FTA	FT%	ORB	DRB	TRB	AST	PF	DQ	STL	BLK	TO	MPG	PPG	RPG	APG	PCM
89-90	Portland	82	0	1565	746	298	751	.397	12	44	.273	138	251	.550	110	198	308	72	226	4	53	53	131	19.1	9.1	3.8	0.9	.322
90-91	Portland	82	11	1940	957	373	806	.463	6	19	.316	205	314	.653	123	226	349	151	263	2	78	76	131	23.7	11.7	4.3	1.8	.458
91-92	Portland	82	7	2124	1016	398	854	.466	1	11	.091	219	330	.664	140	276	416	137	274	11	85	107	156	25.9	12.4	5.1	1.7	.461
92-93	Portland	82	12	2575	1570	632	1336	.473	19	77	.247	287	416	.690	165	377	542	182	287	8	98	161	172	31.4	19.1	6.6	2.2	.583
93-94	Portland	82	64	2853	1647	641	1404	.457	13	53	.245	352	460	.765	164	386	550	159	263	0	118	111	172	34.8	20.1	6.7	1.9	.528
94-95	Portland	75	73	2725	1601	597	1320	.452	142	383	.371	265	382	.694	152	271	423	198	240	3	79	82	158	36.3	21.3	5.6	2.6	.501
95-96	Portland	78	76	2980	1644	553	1306	.423	178	471	.378	360	542	.664	123	320	443	190	248	3	86	68	195	38.2	21.1	5.7	2.4	.441
96-97	Portland	81	79	3077	1224	444	1043	.426	121	350	.346	215	309	.696	90	231	321	261	251	6	99	66	170	38.0	15.1	4.0	3.2	.350
97-98	Phoenix	80	64	2359	1133	429	895	.479	27	84	.321	248	360	.689	152	258	410	170	249	5	92	90	144	29.5	14.2	5.1	2.1	.481
98-99	Phoenix	50	35	1740	819	299	629	.475	58	139	.417	163	234	.697	69	158	227	128	154	2	75	59	88	34.8	16.4	4.5	2.6	.466
99-00	Phoenix	80	67	2839	1478	530	1142	.464	120	324	.370	298	381	.782	105	254	359	224	239	3	90	61	166	35.5	18.5	4.5	2.8	.470
00-01	Phoenix	82	82	2751	1345	501	1186	.422	90	249	.361	253	357	.709	105	229	334	237	258	6	87	82	186	33.5	16.4	4.1	2.9	.405
01-02	Detroit	80	80	2853	1169	455	1070	.425	116	305	.380	143	206	.694	79	307	386	202	243	4	89	95	151	35.7	14.6	4.8	2.5	.376
02-03	Detroit	81	69	2825	992	372	935	.398	87	259	.336	161	238	.676	81	237	318	268	259	5	87	88	158	34.9	12.2	3.9	3.3	.327
NBA Season Totals		1097	719	35206	17341	6522	14677	.444	990	2768	.358	3307	4780	.692	1658	3728	5386	2579	3454	62	1216	1199	2178	32.1	15.8	4.9	2.4	....
89-90	Portland	21	6	391	137	54	151	.358	0	4	.000	29	52	.558	32	55	87	23	71	1	19	24	25	18.6	6.5	4.1	1.1	.319
90-91	Portland	16	0	354	165	63	117	.538	1	3	.333	38	69	.551	24	39	63	18	47	1	7	16	25	22.1	10.3	3.9	1.1	.436
91-92	Portland	21	0	522	227	91	197	.462	1	6	.167	44	77	.571	25	63	88	43	84	3	22	21	28	24.9	10.8	4.2	2.0	.414
92-93	Portland	4	0	131	41	16	61	.262	0	1	.000	9	22	.409	10	7	17	6	17	1	6	7	8	32.8	10.3	4.3	1.5	.091
93-94	Portland	4	4	149	65	28	68	.412	2	9	.222	7	8	.875	11	14	25	10	13	0	3	6	11	37.3	16.3	6.3	2.5	.361
94-95	Portland	3	3	119	47	17	47	.362	4	17	.235	9	16	.563	7	12	19	8	13	0	2	1	8	39.7	15.7	6.3	2.7	.261
95-96	Portland	5	5	181	76	21	61	.344	6	23	.261	28	37	.757	4	14	18	8	19	0	7	5	16	36.2	15.2	3.6	1.6	.259
96-97	Portland	4	4	161	48	17	47	.362	3	16	.188	11	16	.688	12	15	27	12	13	0	2	4	10	40.3	12.0	6.8	3.0	.285
97-98	Phoenix	4	4	92	25	9	33	.273	0	1	.000	7	9	.778	6	6	12	3	19	1	3	2	5	23.0	6.3	3.0	0.8	.083
98-99	Phoenix	3	3	117	47	19	40	.475	2	9	.222	7	11	.636	7	9	16	8	12	1	6	1	7	39.0	15.7	5.3	2.7	.379
99-00	Phoenix	9	9	333	158	56	145	.386	13	40	.325	33	45	.733	18	36	54	19	35	0	11	7	18	37.0	17.6	6.0	2.1	.377
00-01	Phoenix	4	4	114	60	21	50	.420	4	16	.250	14	22	.636	6	10	16	4	14	0	6	2	9	28.5	15.0	4.0	1.0	.368

YEAR	TEAM	GP	GS	MIN	PTS	FGM	FGA	FG%	3PM	3PA	3P%	FTM	FTA	FT%	ORB	DRB	TRB	AST	PF	DQ	STL	BLK	TO	MPG	PPG	RPG	APG	PCM
01-02	Detroit	10	10	409	132	45	124	.363	18	53	.340	24	30	.800	5	25	30	29	28	0	18	19	21	40.9	13.2	3.0	2.9	.290
02-03	Detroit	17	17	524	158	57	159	.358	22	59	.373	22	37	.595	14	32	46	49	62	1	16	13	28	30.8	9.3	2.7	2.9	.242
NBA Playoff Totals		125	69	3597	1386	514	1300	.395	76	257	.296	282	451	.625	181	337	518	240	447	9	128	128	219	28.8	11.1	4.1	1.9	....

• ROBINSON, David
David Maurice (The Admiral) Robinson

Born: Aug. 6, 1965. Key West, FL, United States.　Height: 7'1".　Weight: 235 lbs.　Drafted: 1987　College: Navy

YEAR	TEAM	GP	GS	MIN	PTS	FGM	FGA	FG%	3PM	3PA	3P%	FTM	FTA	FT%	ORB	DRB	TRB	AST	PF	DQ	STL	BLK	TO	MPG	PPG	RPG	APG	PCM
89-90	San Antonio	82	81	3002	1993	690	1300	.531	0	2	.000	613	837	.732	303	680	983	164	259	3	138	319	254	36.6	24.3	12.0	2.0	.826
90-91	San Antonio	82	81	3095	2101	754	1366	.552	1	7	.143	592	777	.762	335	728	**1063**	208	264	5	127	**320**	271	37.7	25.6	**13.0**	2.5	.872
91-92	San Antonio	68	68	2564	1578	592	1074	.551	1	8	.125	393	561	.701	261	568	829	181	219	2	158	**305**	184	37.7	23.2	12.2	2.7	.848
92-93	San Antonio	82	82	3211	1916	676	1348	.501	3	17	.176	561	766	.732	229	727	956	301	239	5	127	264	238	39.2	23.4	11.7	3.7	.759
93-94	San Antonio	80	80	3241	**2383**	840	1658	.507	10	29	.345	**693**	**925**	.749	241	614	855	381	228	3	139	265	256	40.5	**29.8**	10.7	4.8	.850
94-95	San Antonio	81	81	3074	2238	788	1487	.530	6	20	.300	**656**	847	.774	234	643	877	236	230	2	134	262	235	38.0	27.6	10.8	2.9	.849
95-96	San Antonio	82	82	3019	2051	711	1378	.516	3	9	.333	**626**	**823**	.761	319	**681**	**1000**	247	262	1	111	271	189	36.8	25.0	12.2	3.0	.858
96-97	San Antonio	6	6	147	106	36	72	.500	0	0	.000	34	52	.654	19	32	51	8	9	0	6	6	8	24.5	17.7	8.5	1.3	.814
97-98	San Antonio	73	73	2457	1574	544	1065	.511	1	4	.250	485	660	.735	239	536	775	199	204	2	64	192	204	33.7	21.6	10.6	2.7	.772
98-99	San Antonio	49	49	1554	775	268	527	.509	0	1	.000	239	363	.658	148	344	492	103	143	0	69	119	108	31.7	15.8	10.0	2.1	.675
99-00	San Antonio	80	80	2557	1427	528	1031	.512	0	2	.000	371	511	.726	193	577	770	142	247	1	97	183	164	32.0	17.8	9.6	1.8	.686
00-01	San Antonio	80	80	2371	1151	400	823	.486	0	1	.000	351	470	.747	208	483	691	116	212	1	80	197	122	29.6	14.4	8.6	1.5	.637
01-02	San Antonio	78	78	2303	951	341	672	.507	0	0	.000	269	395	.681	191	456	647	94	193	3	86	140	104	29.5	12.2	8.3	1.2	.567
02-03	San Antonio	64	64	1677	546	197	420	.469	0	0	.000	152	214	.710	163	345	508	61	126	1	52	111	83	26.2	8.5	7.9	1.0	.512
NBA Season Totals		987	985	34272	20790	7365	14221	.518	25	100	.250	6035	8201	.736	3083	7414	10497	2441	2835	29	1388	2954	2420	34.7	21.1	10.6	2.5	....
89-90	San Antonio	10	10	375	243	89	167	.533	0	0	.000	65	96	.677	36	84	120	23	35	1	11	40	24	37.5	24.3	12.0	2.3	.803
90-91	San Antonio	4	4	166	103	35	51	.686	0	1	.000	33	38	.868	11	43	54	8	11	0	6	15	15	41.5	25.8	13.5	2.0	.874
92-93	San Antonio	10	10	421	231	79	170	.465	0	1	.000	73	110	.664	29	97	126	40	39	0	10	36	25	42.1	23.1	12.6	4.0	.690
93-94	San Antonio	4	4	146	80	30	73	.411	0	1	.000	20	27	.741	13	27	40	14	14	0	3	10	9	36.5	20.0	10.0	3.5	.592
94-95	San Antonio	15	15	623	380	129	289	.446	1	5	.200	121	149	.812	57	125	182	47	63	1	22	39	56	41.5	25.3	12.1	3.1	.662
95-96	San Antonio	10	10	353	236	83	161	.516	0	0	.000	70	105	.667	37	64	101	24	38	2	15	25	24	35.3	23.6	10.1	2.4	.747
97-98	San Antonio	9	9	353	175	57	134	.425	0	0	.000	61	96	.635	41	86	127	23	28	1	11	30	25	39.2	19.4	14.1	2.6	.656
98-99	San Antonio	17	17	600	265	87	180	.483	0	0	.000	91	126	.722	36	132	168	43	61	1	28	40	40	35.3	15.6	9.9	2.5	.603
99-00	San Antonio	4	4	155	94	31	83	.373	0	1	.000	32	42	.762	17	38	55	10	15	0	7	12	8	38.8	23.5	13.8	2.5	.686
00-01	San Antonio	13	13	409	216	75	159	.472	0	1	.000	66	95	.695	39	114	153	22	42	0	17	31	28	31.5	16.6	11.8	1.7	.705
01-02	San Antonio	4	4	81	18	9	19	.474	0	0	.000	0	4	.000	6	17	23	5	14	0	3	3	2	20.3	4.5	5.8	1.3	.379
02-03	San Antonio	23	23	539	180	64	118	.542	0	0	.000	52	78	.667	45	107	152	21	63	3	18	31	24	23.4	7.8	6.6	0.9	.509
NBA Playoff Totals		123	123	4221	2221	768	1604	.479	1	10	.100	684	966	.708	367	934	1301	280	423	9	151	312	280	34.3	18.1	10.6	2.3	....

• ROBINSON, Eddie
Eddie B. Robinson Jr.

Born: Apr. 10, 1976. Flint, MI, United States.　Height: 6'8".　Weight: 210 lbs.　Drafted: —　College: Central Oklahoma

YEAR	TEAM	GP	GS	MIN	PTS	FGM	FGA	FG%	3PM	3PA	3P%	FTM	FTA	FT%	ORB	DRB	TRB	AST	PF	DQ	STL	BLK	TO	MPG	PPG	RPG	APG	PCM
99-00	Charlotte	67	8	1112	471	212	386	.549	0	4	.000	47	64	.734	54	130	184	32	67	0	48	25	39	16.6	7.0	2.7	0.5	.457
00-01	Charlotte	67	6	1201	498	216	407	.531	2	4	.500	64	88	.727	60	138	198	59	66	0	50	32	43	17.9	7.4	3.0	0.9	.470
01-02	Chicago	29	12	653	262	112	247	.453	2	5	.400	36	48	.750	24	54	78	37	35	0	23	11	36	22.5	9.0	2.7	1.3	.349
02-03	Chicago	64	18	1354	364	155	315	.492	3	14	.214	51	63	.810	76	124	200	66	120	2	62	13	52	21.2	5.7	3.1	1.0	.320
NBA Season Totals		227	44	4320	1595	695	1355	.513	7	27	.259	198	263	.753	214	446	660	194	288	2	183	81	170	19.0	7.0	2.9	0.9	....
99-00	Charlotte	4	0	45	12	5	12	.417	0	0	.000	2	2	1.000	1	2	3	4	2	0	2	1	1	11.3	3.0	0.8	1.0	.303
00-01	Charlotte	10	0	192	69	31	60	.517	1	3	.333	6	6	1.000	9	24	33	9	12	0	4	4	5	19.2	6.9	3.3	0.9	.416
NBA Playoff Totals		14	0	237	81	36	72	.500	1	3	.333	8	8	1.000	10	26	36	13	14	0	6	5	6	16.9	5.8	2.6	0.9	....

• ROBINSON, Flynn
Flynn James (Electric Eye) Robinson

Born: Apr. 28, 1941. Elgin, IL, United States.　Height: 6'1".　Weight: 185 lbs.　Drafted: 1965　College: Wyoming

YEAR	TEAM	GP	GS	MIN	PTS	FGM	FGA	FG%	3PM	3PA	3P%	FTM	FTA	FT%	ORB	DRB	TRB	AST	PF	DQ	STL	BLK	TO	MPG	PPG	RPG	APG	PCM
66-67	Cincinnati	76	....	1140	668	274	599	.457	....	....	....	120	154	.779	....	....	133	110	197	3	....	....	....	15.0	8.8	1.8	1.4	.487
67-68	Cincinnati	2	....	16	9	3	10	.300	....	....	....	3	7	.429	....	....	4	5	4	0	....	....	....	8.0	4.5	2.0	2.5	.589
67-68	Chicago	73	....	2030	1167	441	1000	.441	....	....	....	285	344	.828	....	....	268	214	180	1	....	....	....	27.8	16.0	3.7	2.9	.540
68-69	Chicago	18	....	550	343	124	293	.423	....	....	....	95	114	.833	....	....	69	57	52	1	....	....	....	30.6	19.1	3.8	3.2	.538
68-69	Milwaukee	65	....	2066	1319	501	1149	.436	....	....	....	317	377	.841	....	....	237	320	209	6	....	....	....	31.8	20.3	3.6	4.9	.598
69-70	Milwaukee	81	....	2762	1765	663	1391	.477	....	....	....	439	489	**.898**	....	....	263	449	254	5	....	....	....	34.1	21.8	3.2	5.5	.625
70-71	Cincinnati	71	....	1368	943	374	817	.458	....	....	....	195	228	.855	....	....	143	138	161	0	....	....	....	19.3	13.3	2.0	1.9	.555
71-72	LA Lakers	64	....	1007	635	262	535	.490	....	....	....	111	129	.860	....	....	115	138	139	2	....	....	....	15.7	9.9	1.8	2.2	.583
72-73	LA Lakers	6	....	47	34	14	28	.500	....	....	....	6	8	.750	....	....	7	8	11	0	....	....	....	7.8	5.7	1.2	1.3	.671
72-73	Baltimore	38	....	583	264	119	260	.458	....	....	....	26	31	.839	....	....	55	77	60	0	....	....	....	15.3	6.9	1.4	2.0	.429
73-74	San Diego-A	49	....	779	430	185	405	.457	8	30	.267	52	68	.765	28	50	78	112	72	....	23	2	50	15.9	8.8	1.6	2.3	.511
NBA Season Totals		494	....	11569	7147	2775	6082	.456	....	....	....	1597	1881	.849	....	....	1294	1516	1267	18	....	....	....	23.4	14.5	2.6	3.1	....
ABA Season Totals		49	....	779	430	185	405	.457	8	30	.267	52	68	.765	28	50	78	112	72	....	23	2	50	15.9	8.8	1.6	2.3	....
Career Totals		543	....	12348	7577	2960	6487	.456	8	30	.267	1649	1949	.846	28	50	1372	1628	1339	18	23	2	50	22.7	14.0	2.5	3.0	....
66-67	Cincinnati	4	....	72	50	24	47	.511	....	....	....	2	4	.500	....	....	7	8	8	0	....	....	....	18.0	12.5	1.8	2.0	.596
67-68	Chicago	5	....	180	101	42	98	.429	....	....	....	17	24	.708	....	....	10	13	14	0	....	....	....	36.0	20.2	2.0	2.6	.397
69-70	Milwaukee	10	....	300	128	42	129	.326	....	....	....	44	50	.880	....	....	23	50	22	0	....	....	....	30.0	12.8	2.3	5.0	.385
71-72	LA Lakers	7	....	72	45	19	41	.463	....	....	....	7	10	.700	....	....	13	5	13	0	....	....	....	10.3	6.4	1.9	0.7	.500
72-73	Baltimore	1	....	2	4	2	3	.667	....	....	....	0	0	.000	....	....	1	0	0	0	....	....	....	2.0	4.0	1.0	0.0	2.000
NBA Playoff Totals		27	....	626	328	129	318	.406	....	....	....	70	88	.795	....	....	54	76	57	0	....	....	....	23.2	12.1	2.0	2.8	....

• ROBINSON, Glenn
Glenn A. (Big Dog) Robinson

Born: Jan. 10, 1973. Gary, IN, United States.　Height: 6'7".　Weight: 225 lbs.　Drafted: 1994　College: Purdue

YEAR	TEAM	GP	GS	MIN	PTS	FGM	FGA	FG%	3PM	3PA	3P%	FTM	FTA	FT%	ORB	DRB	TRB	AST	PF	DQ	STL	BLK	TO	MPG	PPG	RPG	APG	PCM
94-95	Milwaukee	80	76	2958	1755	636	1410	.451	86	268	.321	397	499	.796	169	344	513	197	234	2	115	22	**312**	37.0	21.9	6.4	2.5	.473
95-96	Milwaukee	82	82	3249	1660	627	1382	.454	90	263	.342	316	389	.812	136	368	504	293	236	2	95	42	279	39.6	20.2	6.1	3.6	.448
96-97	Milwaukee	80	79	3114	1689	669	1438	.465	63	180	.350	288	364	.791	130	372	502	248	225	5	103	68	272	38.9	21.1	6.3	3.1	.472

YEAR	TEAM	GP	GS	MIN	PTS	FGM	FGA	FG%	3PM	3PA	3P%	FTM	FTA	FT%	ORB	DRB	TRB	AST	PF	DQ	STL	BLK	TO	MPG	PPG	RPG	APG	PCM
97-98	Milwaukee	56	56	2294	1308	534	1136	.470	25	65	.385	215	266	.808	82	225	307	158	164	2	69	34	202	41.0	23.4	5.5	2.8	.445
98-99	Milwaukee	47	47	1579	865	347	756	.459	31	79	.392	140	161	.870	73	203	276	100	114	1	46	41	106	33.6	18.4	5.9	2.1	.495
99-00	Milwaukee	81	81	2909	1693	690	1461	.472	86	237	.363	227	283	.802	107	378	485	193	212	3	78	41	223	35.9	20.9	6.0	2.4	.491
00-01	Milwaukee	76	74	2813	1674	684	1460	.468	55	184	.299	251	306	.820	124	402	526	252	191	2	86	62	219	37.0	22.0	6.9	3.3	.552
01-02	Milwaukee	66	63	2346	1366	536	1147	.467	58	178	.326	236	282	.837	70	336	406	168	173	1	97	41	174	35.5	20.7	6.2	2.5	.525
02-03	Atlanta	69	68	2591	1436	539	1248	.432	90	263	.342	268	306	.876	86	371	457	205	183	0	91	26	248	37.6	20.8	6.6	3.0	.468
NBA Season Totals		637	626	23853	13446	5262	11438	.460	584	1717	.340	2338	2856	.819	977	2999	3976	1814	1732	18	780	377	2035	37.4	21.1	6.2	2.8	....
98-99	Milwaukee	3	3	118	62	21	51	.412	4	8	.500	16	18	.889	4	21	25	5	5	0	3	2	10	39.3	20.7	8.3	1.7	.471
99-00	Milwaukee	5	5	174	77	32	79	.405	2	7	.286	11	13	.846	0	21	21	13	18	0	8	4	15	34.8	15.4	4.2	2.6	.321
00-01	Milwaukee	18	18	687	350	138	322	.429	24	62	.387	50	56	.893	26	90	116	60	43	1	11	24	46	38.2	19.4	6.4	3.3	.470
NBA Playoff Totals		26	26	979	489	191	452	.423	30	77	.390	77	87	.885	30	132	162	78	66	1	22	30	71	37.7	18.8	6.2	3.0	....

• ROBINSON, Jackie

Jackie Robinson

Born: May 20, 1955. Los Angeles, CA, United States. Height: 6'6". Weight: 210 lbs. Drafted: 1978 College: UNLV

YEAR	TEAM	GP	GS	MIN	PTS	FGM	FGA	FG%	3PM	3PA	3P%	FTM	FTA	FT%	ORB	DRB	TRB	AST	PF	DQ	STL	BLK	TO	MPG	PPG	RPG	APG	PCM
78-79	Seattle	12	....	105	46	19	41	.463	....	....	....	8	15	.533	9	10	19	13	9	0	5	1	11	8.8	3.8	1.6	1.1	.438
79-80	Detroit	7	....	51	27	9	17	.529	0	1	.000	9	11	.818	3	2	5	0	8	0	3	3	2	7.3	3.9	0.7	0.0	.458
81-82	Chicago	3	0	29	10	3	9	.333	0	0	.000	4	4	1.000	3	0	3	0	1	0	0	0	1	9.7	3.3	1.0	0.0	.202
NBA Season Totals		22	0	185	83	31	67	.463	0	1	.000	21	30	.700	15	12	27	13	18	0	8	4	14	8.4	3.8	1.2	0.6	....

• ROBINSON, Jamal

Jamal Robinson

Born: Dec. 27, 1973. Jamaica, NY, United States. Height: 6'7". Weight: 212 lbs. Drafted: — College: Virginia

YEAR	TEAM	GP	GS	MIN	PTS	FGM	FGA	FG%	3PM	3PA	3P%	FTM	FTA	FT%	ORB	DRB	TRB	AST	PF	DQ	STL	BLK	TO	MPG	PPG	RPG	APG	PCM
00-01	Miami	6	0	72	6	3	22	.136	0	2	.000	0	0	.000	3	8	11	2	7	0	6	0	3	12.0	1.0	1.8	0.3	.008
NBA Season Totals		6	0	72	6	3	22	.136	0	2	.000	0	0	.000	3	8	11	2	7	0	6	0	3	12.0	1.0	1.8	0.3	....

• ROBINSON, James

James (Hollywood) Robinson

Born: Aug. 31, 1970. Jackson, MS, United States. Height: 6'2". Weight: 180 lbs. Drafted: 1993 College: Alabama

YEAR	TEAM	GP	GS	MIN	PTS	FGM	FGA	FG%	3PM	3PA	3P%	FTM	FTA	FT%	ORB	DRB	TRB	AST	PF	DQ	STL	BLK	TO	MPG	PPG	RPG	APG	PCM
93-94	Portland	58	3	673	276	104	285	.365	23	73	.315	45	67	.672	34	44	78	68	69	0	30	15	52	11.6	4.8	1.3	1.2	.308
94-95	Portland	71	25	1539	651	255	624	.409	76	223	.341	65	110	.591	42	90	132	180	142	0	48	13	128	21.7	9.2	1.9	2.5	.305
95-96	Portland	76	5	1627	649	229	574	.399	102	284	.359	89	135	.659	44	113	157	150	146	0	34	16	114	21.4	8.5	2.1	2.0	.296
96-97	Minnesota	69	5	1309	572	196	482	.407	102	267	.382	78	114	.684	24	88	112	126	125	1	30	8	69	19.0	8.3	1.6	1.8	.337
97-98	LA Clippers	70	13	1231	541	195	501	.389	74	225	.329	77	107	.720	37	74	111	135	100	0	37	10	98	17.6	7.7	1.6	1.9	.327
98-99	LA Clippers	14	0	280	106	39	98	.398	8	30	.267	20	27	.741	10	17	27	18	29	0	14	3	16	20.0	7.6	1.9	1.3	.294
98-99	Minnesota	17	0	226	77	28	87	.322	13	44	.295	8	14	.571	8	27	35	38	31	0	8	5	28	13.3	4.5	2.1	2.2	.301
00-01	Orlando	6	0	50	10	4	11	.364	2	5	.400	0	0	.000	0	8	8	0	5	0	4	1	4	8.3	1.7	1.3	0.0	.191
NBA Season Totals		381	51	6935	2882	1050	2662	.394	400	1151	.348	382	574	.666	199	461	660	715	647	1	205	71	509	18.2	7.6	1.7	1.9	....
93-94	Portland	4	0	28	10	4	10	.400	1	2	.500	1	2	.500	2	1	3	6	2	0	1	1	0	7.0	2.5	0.8	1.5	.507
94-95	Portland	2	0	4	6	2	3	.667	2	3	.667	0	0	.000	0	0	0	1	0	0	0	0	0	2.0	3.0	0.0	0.5	1.531
95-96	Portland	2	0	26	8	3	10	.300	2	6	.333	0	0	.000	0	1	1	3	4	0	1	1	3	13.0	4.0	0.5	1.5	.105
96-97	Minnesota	2	0	31	14	5	12	.417	4	10	.400	0	0	.000	1	2	3	3	4	0	2	0	1	15.5	7.0	1.5	1.5	.405
98-99	Minnesota	4	0	10	3	1	4	.250	1	3	.333	0	0	.000	0	1	1	0	3	0	0	0	3	2.5	0.8	0.3	0.0	-.278
NBA Playoff Totals		14	0	99	41	15	39	.385	10	24	.417	1	2	.500	3	5	8	13	13	0	4	2	7	7.1	2.9	0.6	0.9	....

• ROBINSON, Larry

Larry Robinson

Born: Jan. 11, 1968. Bossier City, LA, United States. Height: 6'3". Weight: 180 lbs. Drafted: — College: Centenary

YEAR	TEAM	GP	GS	MIN	PTS	FGM	FGA	FG%	3PM	3PA	3P%	FTM	FTA	FT%	ORB	DRB	TRB	AST	PF	DQ	STL	BLK	TO	MPG	PPG	RPG	APG	PCM
90-91	Golden State	24	0	170	56	24	59	.407	0	0	.000	8	15	.533	15	8	23	11	23	0	9	1	17	7.1	2.3	1.0	0.5	.212
90-91	Washington	12	10	255	83	38	91	.418	0	1	.000	7	12	.583	14	14	28	24	26	0	7	0	11	21.3	6.9	2.3	2.0	.263
91-92	Boston	1	0	6	2	1	5	.200	0	0	.000	0	0	.000	2	0	2	1	3	0	0	0	1	6.0	2.0	2.0	1.0	-.185
92-93	Washington	4	0	33	15	6	16	.375	0	1	.000	3	5	.600	1	2	3	3	0	0	1	1	1	8.3	3.8	0.8	0.8	.354
93-94	Houston	6	0	55	25	10	20	.500	2	8	.250	3	8	.375	4	6	10	6	8	0	7	0	10	9.2	4.2	1.7	1.0	.414
97-98	Vancouver	6	0	41	17	6	19	.316	3	6	.500	2	2	1.000	2	10	12	1	0	0	4	0	2	6.8	2.8	2.0	0.2	.463
00-01	Cleveland	1	0	1	0	0	0	.000	0	0	.000	0	0	.000	0	0	0	0	0	0	0	0	1	1.0	0.0	0.0	0.0	-.898
00-01	Atlanta	33	1	631	199	67	184	.364	44	116	.379	21	24	.875	23	64	87	36	46	0	28	2	24	19.1	6.0	2.6	1.1	.309
01-02	New York	2	0	10	3	1	4	.250	1	2	.500	0	0	.000	0	2	2	0	1	0	0	0	0	5.0	1.5	1.0	0.0	.164
NBA Season Totals		89	11	1202	400	153	398	.384	50	134	.373	44	66	.667	61	106	167	82	107	0	56	4	67	13.5	4.5	1.9	0.9	....

• ROBINSON, Oliver

Oliver Leon Robinson Jr.

Born: Mar. 13, 1960. Birmingham, AL, United States. Height: 6'4". Weight: 180 lbs. Drafted: 1982 College: Alabama-Birmingham

YEAR	TEAM	GP	GS	MIN	PTS	FGM	FGA	FG%	3PM	3PA	3P%	FTM	FTA	FT%	ORB	DRB	TRB	AST	PF	DQ	STL	BLK	TO	MPG	PPG	RPG	APG	PCM
82-83	San Antonio	35	0	147	101	35	97	.361	1	11	.091	30	45	.667	6	11	17	21	18	0	4	2	14	4.2	2.9	0.5	0.6	.417
NBA Season Totals		35	0	147	101	35	97	.361	1	11	.091	30	45	.667	6	11	17	21	18	0	4	2	14	4.2	2.9	0.5	0.6	....

• ROBINSON, Ronnie

Ronnie Robinson

Born: Mar. 9, 1951. Memphis, TN, United States. Height: 6'8". Weight: 200 lbs. Drafted: 1973 College: Memphis State

YEAR	TEAM	GP	GS	MIN	PTS	FGM	FGA	FG%	3PM	3PA	3P%	FTM	FTA	FT%	ORB	DRB	TRB	AST	PF	DQ	STL	BLK	TO	MPG	PPG	RPG	APG	PCM
73-74	Memphis-A	40	....	862	287	128	282	.454	0	1	.000	31	46	.674	85	132	217	37	90	....	12	7	45	21.6	7.2	5.4	0.9	.392
73-74	Utah-A	22	....	308	110	46	112	.411	0	0	.000	18	27	.667	18	46	64	12	33	....	8	2	23	14.0	5.0	2.9	0.5	.338
74-75	Memphis-A	10	....	102	40	18	38	.474	0	0	.000	4	6	.667	10	17	27	4	14	....	5	0	7	10.2	4.0	2.7	0.4	.427
ABA Season Totals		72	....	1272	437	192	432	.444	0	1	.000	53	79	.671	113	195	308	53	137	....	25	9	75	17.7	6.1	4.3	0.7	....

• ROBINSON, Rumeal
Rumeal James (Meal Time) Robinson

Born: Nov. 13, 1966. Mandeville, Jamaica. Height: 6'2". Weight: 195 lbs. Drafted: 1990 College: Michigan

YEAR	TEAM	GP	GS	MIN	PTS	FGM	FGA	FG%	3PM	3PA	3P%	FTM	FTA	FT%	ORB	DRB	TRB	AST	PF	DQ	STL	BLK	TO	MPG	PPG	RPG	APG	PCM
90-91	Atlanta	47	16	674	265	108	242	.446	2	11	.182	47	80	.588	20	51	71	132	65	0	32	8	75	14.3	5.6	1.5	2.8	.399
91-92	Atlanta	81	64	2220	1055	423	928	.456	34	104	.327	175	275	.636	64	155	219	446	178	0	105	24	203	27.4	13.0	2.7	5.5	.482
92-93	New Jersey	80	28	1585	672	270	638	.423	20	56	.357	112	195	.574	49	110	159	323	169	2	96	12	144	19.8	8.4	2.0	4.0	.423
93-94	New Jersey	17	0	301	101	42	119	.353	7	15	.467	10	20	.500	4	20	24	45	33	0	15	3	26	17.7	5.9	1.4	2.6	.246
93-94	Charlotte	14	0	95	30	13	33	.394	1	5	.200	3	9	.333	2	6	8	18	15	0	3	0	18	6.8	2.1	0.6	1.3	.159
95-96	Portland	43	14	715	247	92	221	.416	30	79	.380	33	51	.647	19	59	78	142	79	1	26	5	73	16.6	5.7	1.8	3.3	.370
96-97	LA Lakers	15	3	126	45	17	48	.354	6	23	.261	5	8	.625	2	8	10	13	12	0	5	2	11	8.4	3.0	0.7	0.9	.227
96-97	Phoenix	12	0	87	36	16	34	.471	3	10	.300	1	4	.250	1	6	7	8	8	0	1	0	5	7.3	3.0	0.6	0.7	.292
96-97	Portland	27	0	295	95	33	82	.402	9	23	.391	20	23	.870	3	27	30	52	40	0	18	0	27	10.9	3.5	1.1	1.9	.354
NBA Season Totals		336	125	6098	2546	1014	2345	.432	112	326	.344	406	665	.611	164	442	606	1179	599	3	301	54	582	18.1	7.6	1.8	3.5	....
90-91	Atlanta	2	0	13	2	1	4	.250	0	0	.000	0	0	.000	0	1	1	1	1	0	1	0	4	6.5	1.0	0.5	0.5	-.159
92-93	New Jersey	5	5	136	49	21	49	.429	2	7	.286	5	7	.714	4	8	12	35	18	0	5	0	20	27.2	9.8	2.4	7.0	.354
95-96	Portland	5	0	43	21	8	19	.421	4	9	.444	1	4	.250	0	2	2	3	8	0	3	0	3	8.6	4.2	0.4	0.6	.245
96-97	Portland	4	0	24	5	2	6	.333	0	2	.000	1	1	1.000	0	1	1	5	6	0	1	0	1	6.0	1.3	0.3	1.3	.198
NBA Playoff Totals		16	5	216	77	32	78	.410	6	18	.333	7	12	.583	4	12	16	44	33	0	10	0	28	13.5	4.8	1.0	2.8	....

• ROBINSON, Samuel
Samuel Lee Robinson

Born: Jan. 1, 1948. Los Angeles, CA, United States. Height: 6'7". Weight: 190 lbs. Drafted: 1970 College: Long Beach State

YEAR	TEAM	GP	GS	MIN	PTS	FGM	FGA	FG%	3PM	3PA	3P%	FTM	FTA	FT%	ORB	DRB	TRB	AST	PF	DQ	STL	BLK	TO	MPG	PPG	RPG	APG	PCM
70-71	Florida-A	83	....	2172	917	405	896	.452	4	19	.211	103	134	.769	143	267	410	112	182	1	....	....	94	26.2	11.0	4.9	1.3	.415
71-72	Florida-A	51	....	686	306	126	300	.420	0	2	.000	54	68	.794	58	78	136	48	70	0	....	....	24	13.5	6.0	2.7	0.9	.422
ABA Season Totals		134	....	2858	1223	531	1196	.444	4	21	.190	157	202	.777	201	345	546	160	252	1	....	....	118	21.3	9.1	4.1	1.2	....
70-71	Florida-A	6	....	111	62	24	53	.453	0	0	.000	14	16	.875	7	12	19	6	17	1	....	....	5	18.5	10.3	3.2	1.0	.483
71-72	Florida-A	4	....	81	43	18	37	.486	0	0	.000	7	7	1.000	....	....	22	2	11	....	....	....	3	20.3	10.8	5.5	0.5	.531
ABA Playoff Totals		10	....	192	105	42	90	.467	0	0	.000	21	23	.913	7	12	41	8	28	1	....	....	8	19.2	10.5	4.1	0.8	....

• ROBINSON, Truck
Leonard Eugene (Truck) Robinson

Born: Oct. 4, 1951. Jacksonville, FL, United States. Height: 6'7". Weight: 225 lbs. Drafted: 1974 College: Tennessee State

YEAR	TEAM	GP	GS	MIN	PTS	FGM	FGA	FG%	3PM	3PA	3P%	FTM	FTA	FT%	ORB	DRB	TRB	AST	PF	DQ	STL	BLK	TO	MPG	PPG	RPG	APG	PCM
74-75	Washington	76	....	995	442	191	393	.486	....	....	....	60	115	.522	94	207	301	40	132	0	36	32	....	13.1	5.8	4.0	0.5	.495
75-76	Washington	82	....	2055	919	354	779	.454	....	....	....	211	314	.672	139	418	557	113	239	3	42	107	....	25.1	11.2	6.8	1.4	.494
76-77	Washington	41	....	1328	656	264	552	.478	....	....	....	128	189	.677	119	247	366	45	123	0	28	18	....	32.4	16.0	8.9	1.1	.523
76-77	Atlanta	36	....	1449	806	310	648	.478	....	....	....	186	241	.772	133	329	462	97	130	3	38	20	....	40.3	22.4	12.8	2.7	.651
77-78	New Orleans	82	....	**3638**	1862	748	1683	.444	....	....	....	366	572	.640	298	**990**	**1288**	171	265	5	73	79	303	**44.4**	22.7	**15.7**	2.1	.557
78-79	New Orleans	43	....	1781	1039	397	819	.485	....	....	....	245	339	.723	139	438	577	74	130	1	29	63	142	41.4	24.2	13.4	1.7	.626
78-79	Phoenix	26	....	756	417	169	333	.508	....	....	....	79	123	.642	56	169	225	39	76	1	17	12	91	29.1	16.0	8.7	1.5	.536
79-80	Phoenix	82	....	2710	1415	545	1064	.512	0	0	.000	325	487	.667	213	557	770	142	262	2	58	59	254	33.0	17.3	9.4	1.7	.547
80-81	Phoenix	82	....	3088	1543	647	1280	.505	0	0	.000	249	396	.629	216	573	789	206	220	1	68	38	246	37.7	18.8	9.6	2.5	.523
81-82	Phoenix	74	72	2745	1414	579	1128	.513	1	1	1.000	255	371	.687	202	519	721	179	215	2	42	28	200	37.1	19.1	9.7	2.4	.544
82-83	New York	81	76	2426	770	326	706	.462	0	0	.000	118	201	.587	199	458	657	145	241	4	57	24	186	30.0	9.5	8.1	1.8	.387
83-84	New York	65	63	2135	701	284	581	.489	0	0	.000	133	206	.646	171	374	545	94	217	6	43	27	163	32.8	10.8	8.4	1.4	.380
84-85	New York	2	1	35	4	2	5	.400	0	0	.000	0	2	.000	6	3	9	3	3	0	2	3	5	17.5	2.0	4.5	1.5	.299
NBA Season Totals		772	212	25141	11988	4816	9971	.483	1	1	1.000	2355	3556	.662	1985	5282	7267	1348	2253	28	533	510	1590	32.6	15.5	9.4	1.7	....
74-75	Washington	17	....	130	35	14	42	.333	....	....	....	7	14	.500	11	29	40	6	21	0	6	10	....	7.6	2.1	2.4	0.4	.309
75-76	Washington	7	....	137	49	16	37	.432	....	....	....	17	21	.810	8	25	33	5	27	0	5	8	....	19.6	7.0	4.7	0.7	.377
78-79	Phoenix	15	....	392	157	56	139	.403	....	....	....	45	69	.652	38	83	121	10	52	0	6	12	31	26.1	10.5	8.1	0.7	.399
79-80	Phoenix	3	....	64	17	6	16	.375	0	0	.000	5	7	.714	5	15	20	4	6	0	3	2	8	21.3	5.7	6.7	1.3	.376
80-81	Phoenix	7	....	233	74	27	77	.351	0	0	.000	20	34	.588	23	52	75	13	15	0	5	2	13	33.3	10.6	10.7	1.9	.396
81-82	Phoenix	7	7	213	93	45	80	.563	0	0	.000	3	10	.300	14	39	53	19	17	0	5	1	10	30.4	13.3	7.6	2.7	.542
82-83	New York	6	6	205	94	39	73	.534	0	0	.000	16	28	.571	21	45	66	13	25	1	10	2	14	34.2	15.7	11.0	2.2	.579
83-84	New York	12	12	362	85	38	74	.514	0	0	.000	9	15	.600	31	66	97	7	41	2	7	9	27	30.2	7.1	8.1	0.6	.324
NBA Playoff Totals		74	25	1736	604	241	538	.448	0	0	.000	122	198	.616	151	354	505	77	204	3	47	46	103	23.5	8.2	6.8	1.0	....

• ROBINSON, Wayne
Wayne Howard Robinson

Born: Apr. 19, 1958. Greensboro, NC, United States. Height: 6'8". Weight: 217 lbs. Drafted: 1980 College: Virginia Tech

YEAR	TEAM	GP	GS	MIN	PTS	FGM	FGA	FG%	3PM	3PA	3P%	FTM	FTA	FT%	ORB	DRB	TRB	AST	PF	DQ	STL	BLK	TO	MPG	PPG	RPG	APG	PCM
80-81	Detroit	81	....	1592	643	234	509	.460	0	6	.000	175	240	.729	117	177	294	112	186	2	46	24	146	19.7	7.9	3.6	1.4	.376
NBA Season Totals		81	....	1592	643	234	509	.460	0	6	.000	175	240	.729	117	177	294	112	186	2	46	24	146	19.7	7.9	3.6	1.4	....

• ROBINSON, Will
Wilbert Robinson Jr.

Born: Dec. 25, 1949. Uniontown, PA, United States. Height: 6'2". Weight: 175 lbs. Drafted: 1972 College: West Virginia

YEAR	TEAM	GP	GS	MIN	PTS	FGM	FGA	FG%	3PM	3PA	3P%	FTM	FTA	FT%	ORB	DRB	TRB	AST	PF	DQ	STL	BLK	TO	MPG	PPG	RPG	APG	PCM
73-74	Memphis-A	45	....	956	389	166	402	.413	0	6	.000	57	67	.851	28	51	79	132	124	....	51	9	92	21.2	8.6	1.8	2.9	.364
ABA Season Totals		45	....	956	389	166	402	.413	0	6	.000	57	67	.851	28	51	79	132	124	....	51	9	92	21.2	8.6	1.8	2.9	....

• ROBINZINE, Bill
William Clintard Robinzine

Born: Jan. 20, 1953. Chicago, IL, United States. Died: Sept.16, 1982. Height: 6'7". Weight: 230 lbs. Drafted: 1975 College: DePaul

YEAR	TEAM	GP	GS	MIN	PTS	FGM	FGA	FG%	3PM	3PA	3P%	FTM	FTA	FT%	ORB	DRB	TRB	AST	PF	DQ	STL	BLK	TO	MPG	PPG	RPG	APG	PCM
75-76	Kansas City	75	....	1327	603	229	499	.459	....	....	....	145	198	.732	128	227	355	60	290	**19**	80	8	....	17.7	8.0	4.7	0.8	.450
76-77	Kansas City	75	....	1594	773	307	677	.453	....	....	....	159	216	.736	164	310	474	95	283	7	86	13	....	21.3	10.3	6.3	1.3	.517
77-78	Kansas City	82	....	1748	816	305	677	.451	....	....	....	206	271	.760	173	366	539	72	281	5	74	11	172	21.3	10.0	6.6	0.9	.467
78-79	Kansas City	82	....	2179	1098	459	837	.548	....	....	....	180	246	.732	218	420	638	104	**367**	16	105	15	180	26.6	13.4	7.8	1.3	.550
79-80	Kansas City	81	....	1917	925	362	723	.501	1	2	.500	200	274	.730	184	342	526	62	311	5	106	23	146	23.7	11.4	6.5	0.8	.497
80-81	Cleveland	8	....	84	33	14	32	.438	0	0	.000	5	8	.625	4	9	13	5	19	1	4	0	10	10.5	4.1	1.6	0.6	.219

YEAR TEAM	GP	GS	MIN	PTS	FGM	FGA	FG%	3PM	3PA	3P%	FTM	FTA	FT%	ORB	DRB	TRB	AST	PF	DQ	STL	BLK	TO	MPG	PPG	RPG	APG	PCM
80-81 Dallas	70	....	1932	970	378	794	.476	1	6	.167	213	273	.780	164	356	520	113	256	5	71	9	175	27.6	13.9	7.4	1.6	.496
81-82 Utah	56	9	651	323	131	294	.446	0	0	.000	61	75	.813	56	88	144	49	156	5	37	5	84	11.6	5.8	2.6	0.9	.371
NBA Season Totals	529	9	11432	5541	2185	4533	.482	2	8	.250	1169	1561	.749	1091	2118	3209	560	1963	63	563	84	767	21.6	10.5	6.1	1.1	....
78-79 Kansas City	5	....	118	50	22	51	.431	....	....	....	6	8	.750	15	21	36	3	20	1	13	0	8	23.6	10.0	7.2	0.6	.459
79-80 Kansas City	3	....	69	33	13	24	.542	0	0	.000	7	10	.700	7	11	18	0	6	0	3	0	6	23.0	11.0	6.0	0.0	.472
NBA Playoff Totals	8	....	187	83	35	75	.467	0	0	.000	13	18	.722	22	32	54	3	26	1	16	0	14	23.4	10.4	6.8	0.4	....

• ROBISCH, Dave

David George (Robo) Robisch

Born: Dec. 22, 1949. Cincinnati, OH, United States. Height: 6'10". Weight: 235 lbs. Drafted: 1971 College: Kansas

YEAR TEAM	GP	GS	MIN	PTS	FGM	FGA	FG%	3PM	3PA	3P%	FTM	FTA	FT%	ORB	DRB	TRB	AST	PF	DQ	STL	BLK	TO	MPG	PPG	RPG	APG	PCM
71-72 Denver-A	84	....	2420	1304	505	1138	.444	0	5	.000	294	419	.702	287	517	804	201	251	6	....	....	113	28.8	15.5	9.6	2.4	.626
72-73 Denver-A	83	....	2647	1351	521	1010	.516	0	1	.000	309	409	.756	248	496	744	170	271	8	....	....	134	31.9	16.3	9.0	2.0	.605
73-74 Denver-A	84	....	2469	1216	449	950	.473	0	0	.000	318	411	.774	217	491	708	152	225	....	45	66	103	29.4	14.5	8.4	1.8	.579
74-75 Denver-A	84	....	1899	1088	392	779	.503	0	1	.000	304	346	.879	161	342	503	153	205	....	46	48	108	22.6	13.0	6.0	1.8	.659
75-76 Indiana-A	76	....	2415	1015	376	899	.418	0	2	.000	263	311	.846	230	442	672	145	183	....	65	48	96	31.8	13.4	8.8	1.9	.499
75-76 San Diego-A	11	....	374	181	60	134	.448	0	1	.000	61	70	.871	51	71	122	21	17	....	6	11	17	34.0	16.5	11.1	1.9	.630
76-77 Indiana	80	....	1966	951	369	811	.455	....	....	....	213	256	.832	171	383	554	158	169	1	55	37	....	24.6	11.9	6.9	2.0	.578
77-78 Indiana	23	....	598	196	73	181	.403	....	....	....	50	64	.781	47	126	173	49	59	1	20	15	35	26.0	8.5	7.5	2.1	.462
77-78 LA Lakers	55	....	679	258	104	249	.418	....	....	....	50	65	.769	53	126	179	40	71	0	19	14	39	12.3	4.7	3.3	0.7	.427
78-79 LA Lakers	80	....	1219	386	150	336	.446	....	....	....	86	115	.748	82	203	285	97	108	0	20	25	56	15.2	4.8	3.6	1.2	.419
79-80 Cleveland	82	....	2670	1255	489	940	.520	0	3	.000	277	329	.842	225	433	658	192	211	2	53	53	139	32.6	15.3	8.0	2.3	.563
80-81 Cleveland	11	....	372	103	37	98	.378	0	0	.000	29	36	.806	27	58	85	44	21	0	7	6	14	33.8	9.4	7.7	4.0	.428
80-81 Denver	73	....	1744	757	293	642	.456	0	0	.000	171	211	.810	130	284	414	129	152	0	30	28	66	23.9	10.4	5.7	1.8	.494
81-82 Denver	12	0	257	144	48	106	.453	0	0	.000	48	55	.873	14	49	63	32	29	0	3	4	13	21.4	12.0	5.3	2.7	.627
82-83 Denver	61	0	711	284	96	251	.382	0	1	.000	92	118	.780	34	117	151	53	61	0	10	9	43	11.7	4.7	2.5	0.9	.391
83-84 Denver	19	0	141	37	13	40	.325	0	0	.000	11	13	.846	1	20	21	13	13	0	0	1	11	7.4	1.9	1.1	0.7	.206
83-84 San Antonio	4	0	37	8	4	8	.500	0	0	.000	0	0	.000	2	6	8	1	8	1	0	0	1	9.3	2.0	2.0	0.3	.220
83-84 Kansas City	8	0	162	47	18	48	.375	0	0	.000	11	13	.846	12	17	29	6	15	0	3	1	0	20.3	5.9	3.6	0.8	.298
NBA Season Totals	508	0	10556	4426	1694	3710	.457	0	4	.000	1038	1275	.814	798	1822	2620	814	917	5	220	193	417	20.8	8.7	5.2	1.6	....
ABA Season Totals	422	....	12224	6155	2303	4910	.469	0	10	.000	1549	1966	.788	1194	2359	3553	842	1152	14	162	173	571	29.0	14.6	8.4	2.0	....
Career Totals	930	0	22780	10581	3997	8620	.464	0	14	.000	2587	3241	.798	1992	4181	6173	1656	2069	19	382	366	988	24.5	11.4	6.6	1.8	....
71-72 Denver-A	7	....	288	137	50	138	.362	0	0	.000	37	52	.712	32	67	99	15	25	0	....	....	15	41.1	19.6	14.1	2.1	.507
72-73 Denver-A	5	....	184	101	40	85	.471	0	0	.000	21	31	.677	30	38	68	8	21	1	....	....	1	36.8	20.2	13.6	1.6	.633
74-75 Denver-A	13	....	354	192	73	151	.483	0	0	.000	46	53	.868	27	48	75	22	31	....	11	8	13	27.2	14.8	5.8	1.7	.556
75-76 Indiana-A	3	....	83	34	11	27	.407	0	0	.000	12	16	.750	8	12	20	8	8	....	3	0	1	27.7	11.3	6.7	2.7	.495
77-78 LA Lakers	3	....	47	30	13	24	.542	....	....	....	4	5	.800	8	4	12	1	6	0	1	1	0	15.7	10.0	4.0	0.3	.653
78-79 LA Lakers	5	....	32	8	3	5	.600	....	....	....	2	2	1.000	0	10	10	2	4	0	0	0	3	6.4	1.6	2.0	0.4	.403
82-83 Denver	3	0	22	2	1	7	.143	0	0	.000	0	2	.000	3	6	9	1	2	0	0	1	0	7.3	0.7	3.0	0.3	.223
83-84 Kansas City	3	0	51	9	4	12	.333	0	0	.000	1	2	.500	6	9	15	2	6	0	1	0	5	17.0	3.0	5.0	0.7	.209
NBA Playoff Totals	14	0	152	49	21	48	.438	0	0	.000	7	11	.636	17	29	46	6	18	0	2	2	8	10.9	3.5	3.3	0.4	....
ABA Playoff Totals	28	....	909	464	174	401	.434	0	0	.000	116	152	.763	97	165	262	53	85	1	14	8	30	32.5	16.6	9.4	1.9	....
Career Playoff Totals	42	0	1061	513	195	449	.434	0	0	.000	123	163	.755	114	194	308	59	103	1	16	10	38	25.3	12.2	7.3	1.4	....

• ROCHA, Red

Ephraim J. (The Thin Man) Rocha

Born: Sept. 18, 1923. Hilo, HI, United States. Height: 6'9". Weight: 185 lbs. Drafted: 1947 College: Oregon State

YEAR TEAM	GP	GS	MIN	PTS	FGM	FGA	FG%	3PM	3PA	3P%	FTM	FTA	FT%	ORB	DRB	TRB	AST	PF	DQ	STL	BLK	TO	MPG	PPG	RPG	APG	PCM
47-48 St. Louis	48	....	....	611	232	740	.314	....	....	....	147	213	.690	....	....	....	39	209	....	....	....	....	....	12.7	....	0.8	....
48-49 St. Louis	58	....	....	608	223	574	.389	....	....	....	162	211	.768	....	....	....	157	251	....	....	....	....	....	10.5	....	2.7	....
49-50 St. Louis	65	....	....	770	275	679	.405	....	....	....	220	313	.703	....	....	....	155	257	....	....	....	....	....	11.8	....	2.4	....
50-51 Baltimore	64	....	....	836	297	843	.352	....	....	....	242	299	.809	....	....	511	147	242	9	....	....	....	....	13.1	8.0	2.3	....
51-52 Syracuse	66	....	2543	854	300	749	.401	....	....	....	254	330	.770	....	....	549	128	249	4	....	....	....	38.5	12.9	8.3	1.9	.383
52-53 Syracuse	69	....	2454	770	268	690	.388	....	....	....	234	310	.755	....	....	510	137	257	5	....	....	....	35.6	11.2	7.4	2.0	.362
54-55 Syracuse	72	....	2473	812	295	801	.368	....	....	....	222	284	.782	....	....	489	178	242	5	....	....	....	34.3	11.3	6.8	2.5	.367
55-56 Syracuse	72	....	1883	720	250	692	.361	....	....	....	220	281	.783	....	....	416	131	244	6	....	....	....	26.2	10.0	5.8	1.8	.396
56-57 Fort Wayne	72	....	1154	381	136	390	.349	....	....	....	109	144	.757	....	....	272	81	162	1	....	....	....	16.0	5.3	3.8	1.1	.366
NBA Season Totals	586	....	10507	6362	2276	6158	.370	....	....	....	1810	2385	.759	....	....	2747	1153	2113	30	....	....	....	17.9	10.9	4.7	2.0	....
47-48 St. Louis	7	....	....	80	29	118	.246	....	....	....	22	30	.733	....	....	....	6	30	....	....	....	....	....	11.4	....	0.9	....
48-49 St. Louis	2	....	....	36	16	36	.444	....	....	....	4	5	.800	....	....	....	6	6	....	....	....	....	....	18.0	....	3.0	....
51-52 Syracuse	7	....	276	119	41	95	.432	....	....	....	37	51	.725	....	....	48	10	36	3	....	....	....	39.4	17.0	6.9	1.4	.398
52-53 Syracuse	2	....	107	31	10	26	.385	....	....	....	11	14	.786	....	....	17	7	11	1	....	....	....	53.5	15.5	8.5	3.5	.333
54-55 Syracuse	11	....	371	136	46	110	.418	....	....	....	44	58	.759	....	....	74	14	45	1	....	....	....	33.7	12.4	6.7	1.3	.374
55-56 Syracuse	8	....	189	68	23	68	.338	....	....	....	22	26	.846	....	....	52	15	37	3	....	....	....	23.6	8.5	6.5	1.9	.404
56-57 Fort Wayne	2	....	18	4	0	5	.000	....	....	....	4	6	.667	....	....	6	0	4	0	....	....	....	9.0	2.0	3.0	0.0	.139
NBA Playoff Totals	39	....	961	474	165	458	.360	....	....	....	144	190	.758	....	....	197	58	169	8	....	....	....	24.6	12.2	5.1	1.5	....

• ROCHE, John

John Michael Roche

Born: Sept. 26, 1949. New York, NY, United States. Height: 6'3". Weight: 170 lbs. Drafted: 1971 College: South Carolina

YEAR TEAM	GP	GS	MIN	PTS	FGM	FGA	FG%	3PM	3PA	3P%	FTM	FTA	FT%	ORB	DRB	TRB	AST	PF	DQ	STL	BLK	TO	MPG	PPG	RPG	APG	PCM
71-72 New York-A	82	....	2593	1058	403	859	.469	12	35	.343	240	311	.772	45	127	172	259	211	1	....	....	188	31.6	12.9	2.1	3.2	.376
72-73 New York-A	77	....	2615	1107	404	912	.443	34	103	.330	265	347	.764	33	113	146	348	170	0	....	....	207	34.0	14.4	1.9	4.5	.402
73-74 Kentucky-A	34	....	926	408	173	369	.469	10	37	.270	52	63	.825	18	45	63	155	71	....	16	9	78	27.2	12.0	1.9	4.6	.471
73-74 New York-A	50	....	1254	570	224	460	.487	26	68	.382	96	114	.842	16	43	59	208	86	....	41	6	106	25.1	11.4	1.2	4.2	.487
74-75 Kentucky-A	19	....	258	74	29	79	.367	1	7	.143	15	18	.833	4	5	9	34	23	....	8	1	18	13.6	3.9	0.5	1.8	.248
74-75 Utah-A	39	....	1129	506	212	430	.493	12	37	.324	70	88	.795	17	67	84	157	80	....	41	6	87	28.9	13.0	2.2	4.0	.459
75-76 Utah-A	16	....	484	264	112	212	.528	9	26	.346	31	41	.756	5	20	25	79	47	....	14	1	51	30.3	16.5	1.6	4.9	.536
75-76 LA Lakers	15	....	52	8	3	14	.214	....	....	....	2	4	.500	0	3	3	6	7	0	0	0	....	3.5	0.5	0.2	0.4	.079

YEAR	TEAM	GP	GS	MIN	PTS	FGM	FGA	FG%	3PM	3PA	3P%	FTM	FTA	FT%	ORB	DRB	TRB	AST	PF	DQ	STL	BLK	TO	MPG	PPG	RPG	APG	PCM
79-80	Denver	82	....	2286	932	354	741	.478	49	129	.380	175	202	.866	24	91	115	405	139	0	82	12	156	27.9	11.4	1.4	4.9	.437
80-81	Denver	26	....	611	231	82	179	.458	9	27	.333	58	77	.753	5	32	37	140	44	0	17	8	52	23.5	8.9	1.4	5.4	.451
81-82	Denver	39	2	501	187	68	150	.453	23	52	.442	28	38	.737	4	19	23	89	40	0	15	2	27	12.8	4.8	0.6	2.3	.392
NBA Season Totals		162	2	3450	1358	507	1084	.468	81	208	.389	263	321	.819	33	145	178	640	230	0	114	22	235	21.3	8.4	1.1	4.0	....
ABA Season Totals		317	....	9259	3987	1557	3321	.469	104	313	.332	769	982	.783	138	420	558	1240	688	1	120	23	735	29.2	12.6	1.8	3.9	....
Career Totals		479	2	12709	5345	2064	4405	.469	185	521	.355	1032	1303	.792	171	565	736	1880	918	1	234	45	970	26.5	11.2	1.5	3.9	....
71-72	New York-A	18	....	763	425	163	343	.475	10	30	.333	89	118	.754	....	....	31	84	42	....	....	....	53	42.4	23.6	1.7	4.7	.468
72-73	New York-A	4	....	83	41	16	33	.485	2	6	.333	7	12	.583	0	1	1	10	7	0	....	....	7	20.8	10.3	0.3	2.5	.388
73-74	Kentucky-A	8	....	197	91	39	85	.459	7	14	.500	6	11	.545	3	6	9	27	6	....	3	2	23	24.6	11.4	1.1	3.4	.433
74-75	Utah-A	6	....	196	103	41	82	.500	8	15	.533	13	15	.867	8	7	15	43	16	....	9	2	12	32.7	17.2	2.5	7.2	.611
ABA Playoff Totals		36	....	1239	660	259	543	.477	27	65	.415	115	156	.737	11	14	56	164	71	0	12	4	95	34.4	18.3	1.6	4.6	....

• ROCK, Gene

Eugene Rock

Born: Nov. 4, 1921. Height: 5'9". Weight: 155 lbs. Drafted: — College: USC

YEAR	TEAM	GP	GS	MIN	PTS	FGM	FGA	FG%	3PM	3PA	3P%	FTM	FTA	FT%	ORB	DRB	TRB	AST	PF	DQ	STL	BLK	TO	MPG	PPG	RPG	APG	PCM
47-48	Chicago	11	....	....	10	4	18	.222	....	....	....	2	4	.500	....	....	....	0	8	....	....	....	....	....	0.9	....	0.0	....
NBA Season Totals		11	....	....	10	4	18	.222	....	....	....	2	4	.500	....	....	....	0	8	....	....	....	....	....	0.9	....	0.0	....
47-48	Chicago	2	....	....	0	0	0	.000	....	....	....	0	1	.000	....	....	....	0	0	....	....	....	....	....	0.0	....	0.0	....
NBA Playoff Totals		2	....	....	0	0	0	.000	....	....	....	0	1	.000	....	....	....	0	0	....	....	....	....	....	0.0	....	0.0	....

• ROCKER, Jack

Jack L. Rocker

Born: Aug. 12, 1922. Height: 6'5". Weight: 185 lbs. Drafted: — College: California

YEAR	TEAM	GP	GS	MIN	PTS	FGM	FGA	FG%	3PM	3PA	3P%	FTM	FTA	FT%	ORB	DRB	TRB	AST	PF	DQ	STL	BLK	TO	MPG	PPG	RPG	APG	PCM
47-48	Minneapolis-N	5	....	....	4	2	....	....	....	....	....	0	0	.000	....	....	....	....	....	....	....	....	....	....	0.8	....	....	....
47-48	Philadelphia	9	....	....	17	8	22	.364	....	....	....	1	1	1.000	....	....	....	3	2	....	....	....	....	....	1.9	....	0.3	....
NBA Season Totals		9	....	....	17	8	22	.364	....	....	....	1	1	1.000	....	....	....	3	2	....	....	....	....	....	1.9	....	0.3	....
NBL Season Totals		5	....	....	4	2	....	....	....	....	....	0	0	....	....	....	....	....	....	....	....	....	....	....	0.8	....	....	....
Career Totals		14	....	....	21	10	22	....	....	....	....	1	1	....	....	....	....	3	2	....	....	....	....	....	1.5	....	0.2	....

• RODGERS, Guy

Guy William Rodgers Jr.

Born: Sept. 1, 1935. Philadelphia, PA, United States. Died: Feb.19, 2001. Height: 6' Weight: 185 lbs. Drafted: 1958 College: Temple

YEAR	TEAM	GP	GS	MIN	PTS	FGM	FGA	FG%	3PM	3PA	3P%	FTM	FTA	FT%	ORB	DRB	TRB	AST	PF	DQ	STL	BLK	TO	MPG	PPG	RPG	APG	PCM
58-59	Philadelphia	45	....	1565	483	211	535	.394	....	....	....	61	112	.545	....	....	281	261	132	1	....	....	....	34.8	10.7	6.2	5.8	.452
59-60	Philadelphia	68	....	2483	787	338	870	.389	....	....	....	111	181	.613	....	....	391	482	196	3	....	....	....	36.5	11.6	5.8	7.1	.475
60-61	Philadelphia	78	....	2905	1000	397	1029	.386	....	....	....	206	300	.687	....	....	509	677	262	3	....	....	....	37.2	12.8	6.5	8.7	.554
61-62	Philadelphia	80	....	2648	655	267	749	.356	....	....	....	121	182	.665	....	....	348	643	312	12	....	....	....	33.1	8.2	4.4	8.0	.449
62-63	San Francisco	79	....	3249	1098	445	1150	.387	....	....	....	208	286	.727	....	....	394	**825**	296	7	....	....	....	41.1	13.9	5.0	**10.4**	**.524**
63-64	San Francisco	79	....	2695	872	337	923	.365	....	....	....	198	280	.707	....	....	328	556	245	4	....	....	....	34.1	11.0	4.2	7.0	.454
64-65	San Francisco	79	....	2699	1153	465	1225	.380	....	....	....	223	325	.686	....	....	323	565	256	4	....	....	....	34.2	14.6	4.1	7.2	.510
65-66	San Francisco	79	....	2902	1468	586	1571	.373	....	....	....	296	407	.727	....	....	421	846	241	6	....	....	....	36.7	18.6	5.3	10.7	.660
66-67	Chicago	81	....	3063	1459	538	1377	.391	....	....	....	383	475	.806	....	....	346	**908**	243	1	....	....	....	37.8	18.0	4.3	**11.2**	**.661**
67-68	Chicago	4	....	129	41	16	54	.296	....	....	....	9	11	.818	....	....	14	28	11	0	....	....	....	32.3	10.3	3.5	7.0	.390
67-68	Cincinnati	75	....	1417	362	132	372	.355	....	....	....	98	122	.803	....	....	136	352	156	1	....	....	....	18.9	4.8	1.8	4.7	.445
68-69	Milwaukee	81	....	2157	834	325	862	.377	....	....	....	184	232	.793	....	....	226	561	207	2	....	....	....	26.6	10.3	2.8	6.9	.519
69-70	Milwaukee	64	....	749	203	68	191	.356	....	....	....	67	90	.744	....	....	74	213	73	1	....	....	....	11.7	3.2	1.2	3.3	.476
NBA Season Totals		892	....	28661	10415	4125	10908	.378	....	....	....	2165	3003	.721	....	....	3791	6917	2630	45	....	....	....	32.1	11.7	4.3	7.8	....
59-60	Philadelphia	9	....	370	118	49	136	.360	....	....	....	20	36	.556	....	....	77	54	39	3	....	....	....	41.1	13.1	8.6	6.0	.424
60-61	Philadelphia	3	....	121	53	21	57	.368	....	....	....	11	20	.550	....	....	21	15	16	2	....	....	....	40.3	17.7	7.0	5.0	.419
61-62	Philadelphia	12	....	482	139	52	145	.359	....	....	....	35	55	.636	....	....	71	88	57	3	....	....	....	40.2	11.6	5.9	7.3	.413
63-64	San Francisco	12	....	419	147	57	173	.329	....	....	....	33	47	.702	....	....	58	90	46	1	....	....	....	34.9	12.3	4.8	7.5	.450
66-67	Chicago	3	....	97	34	15	40	.375	....	....	....	4	5	.800	....	....	6	18	11	0	....	....	....	32.3	11.3	2.0	6.0	.368
69-70	Milwaukee	7	....	68	17	4	14	.286	....	....	....	9	12	.750	....	....	4	21	7	0	....	....	....	9.7	2.4	0.6	3.0	.454
NBA Playoff Totals		46	....	1557	508	198	565	.350	....	....	....	112	175	.640	....	....	237	286	176	9	....	....	....	33.8	11.0	5.2	6.2	....

• RODGERS, Willie

Willie Daniel (Willie D.) Rodgers

Born: Sept. 11, 1945. Nacogdoches, TX, United States. Height: 6'3". Weight: 185 lbs. Drafted: 1968 College: Oklahoma

YEAR	TEAM	GP	GS	MIN	PTS	FGM	FGA	FG%	3PM	3PA	3P%	FTM	FTA	FT%	ORB	DRB	TRB	AST	PF	DQ	STL	BLK	TO	MPG	PPG	RPG	APG	PCM
68-69	Denver-A	40	....	294	85	27	80	.338	0	3	.000	31	52	.596	17	30	47	16	51	1	....	....	30	7.4	2.1	1.2	0.4	.229
ABA Season Totals		40	....	294	85	27	80	.338	0	3	.000	31	52	.596	17	30	47	16	51	1	....	....	30	7.4	2.1	1.2	0.4	....

• RODMAN, Dennis

Dennis Keith (Worm) Rodman

Born: May 13, 1961. Trenton, NJ, United States. Height: 6'7". Weight: 210 lbs. Drafted: 1986 College: Southeast Oklahoma State

YEAR	TEAM	GP	GS	MIN	PTS	FGM	FGA	FG%	3PM	3PA	3P%	FTM	FTA	FT%	ORB	DRB	TRB	AST	PF	DQ	STL	BLK	TO	MPG	PPG	RPG	APG	PCM
86-87	Detroit	77	1	1155	500	213	391	.545	0	1	.000	74	126	.587	163	169	332	56	166	1	38	48	92	15.0	6.5	4.3	0.7	.516
87-88	Detroit	82	32	2147	953	398	709	.561	5	17	.294	152	284	.535	318	397	715	110	273	5	75	45	156	26.2	11.6	8.7	1.3	.570
88-89	Detroit	82	8	2208	735	316	531	**.595**	6	26	.231	97	155	.626	327	445	772	99	292	4	55	76	123	26.9	9.0	9.4	1.2	.545
89-90	Detroit	82	43	2377	719	288	496	.581	1	9	.111	142	217	.654	336	456	792	72	276	2	52	60	90	29.0	8.8	9.7	0.9	.504
90-91	Detroit	82	77	2747	669	276	560	.493	6	30	.200	111	176	.631	**361**	665	1026	85	281	7	65	55	90	33.5	8.2	12.5	1.0	.480
91-92	Detroit	82	80	3301	800	342	635	.539	32	101	.317	84	140	.600	**523**	**1007**	**1530**	191	248	0	68	70	139	40.3	9.8	**18.7**	2.3	.609
92-93	Detroit	62	55	2410	468	183	429	.427	15	73	.205	87	163	.534	**367**	765	**1132**	102	201	0	48	45	105	38.9	7.5	**18.3**	1.6	.524
93-94	San Antonio	79	51	2989	370	156	292	.534	5	24	.208	53	102	.520	**453**	**914**	**1367**	184	229	0	52	32	134	37.8	4.7	**17.3**	2.3	.510
94-95	San Antonio	49	26	1568	349	137	240	.571	0	2	.000	75	111	.676	274	549	823	97	159	1	31	23	98	32.0	7.1	**16.8**	2.0	.634
95-96	Chicago	64	57	2088	351	146	304	.480	3	27	.111	56	106	.528	**356**	596	952	160	196	1	36	27	141	32.6	5.5	**14.9**	2.5	.516
96-97	Chicago	55	54	1947	311	128	286	.448	5	19	.263	50	88	.568	**320**	563	883	170	172	1	32	19	110	35.4	5.7	**16.1**	3.1	.522

YEAR	TEAM	GP	GS	MIN	PTS	FGM	FGA	FG%	3PM	3PA	3P%	FTM	FTA	FT%	ORB	DRB	TRB	AST	PF	DQ	STL	BLK	TO	MPG	PPG	RPG	APG	PCM
97-98	Chicago	80	66	2856	375	155	360	.431	4	23	.174	61	111	.550	421	780	1201	230	238	2	47	18	144	35.7	4.7	**15.0**	2.9	.466
98-99	LA Lakers	23	11	657	49	16	46	.348	0	2	.000	17	39	.436	62	196	258	30	71	0	10	12	31	28.6	2.1	11.2	1.3	.359
99-00	Dallas	12	12	389	34	12	31	.387	0	1	.000	10	14	.714	48	123	171	14	41	2	2	1	19	32.4	2.8	14.3	1.2	.392
NBA Season Totals		911	573	28839	6683	2766	5310	.521	82	355	.231	1069	1832	.584	4329	7625	11954	1600	2843	26	611	531	1472	31.7	7.3	13.1	1.8	....
86-87	Detroit	15	0	245	98	40	74	.541	0	0	.000	18	32	.563	32	39	71	3	48	0	6	17	17	16.3	6.5	4.7	0.2	.459
87-88	Detroit	23	0	474	164	71	136	.522	0	2	.000	22	54	.407	51	85	136	21	87	1	14	14	31	20.6	7.1	5.9	0.9	.410
88-89	Detroit	17	0	409	98	37	70	.529	0	4	.000	24	35	.686	56	114	170	16	58	0	6	12	24	24.1	5.8	10.0	0.9	.501
89-90	Detroit	19	17	560	126	54	95	.568	0	0	.000	18	35	.514	55	106	161	17	62	1	9	13	31	29.5	6.6	8.5	0.9	.377
90-91	Detroit	15	14	495	94	41	91	.451	2	9	.222	10	24	.417	67	110	177	14	55	1	11	10	13	33.0	6.3	11.8	0.9	.410
91-92	Detroit	5	5	156	36	16	27	.593	0	2	.000	4	8	.500	16	35	51	9	17	0	4	2	7	31.2	7.2	10.2	1.8	.462
93-94	San Antonio	3	3	114	25	12	24	.500	0	5	.000	1	6	.167	24	24	48	2	14	0	6	4	6	38.0	8.3	16.0	0.7	.484
94-95	San Antonio	14	12	459	124	52	96	.542	0	5	.000	20	35	.571	69	138	207	18	51	1	12	0	25	32.8	8.9	14.8	1.3	.551
95-96	Chicago	18	15	620	135	50	103	.485	0	0	.000	35	59	.593	98	149	247	37	76	1	14	8	41	34.4	7.5	13.7	2.1	.471
96-97	Chicago	19	14	535	79	30	81	.370	4	16	.250	15	26	.577	59	101	160	27	74	3	10	4	28	28.2	4.2	8.4	1.4	.293
97-98	Chicago	21	9	722	102	39	105	.371	1	4	.250	23	38	.605	99	149	248	41	88	4	14	13	35	34.4	4.9	11.8	2.0	.358
NBA Playoff Totals		169	89	4789	1081	442	902	.490	7	47	.149	190	352	.540	626	1050	1676	205	630	12	106	97	258	28.3	6.4	9.9	1.2	....

• RODRIGUES, Abel

Abel Rodrigues

Born: 1922. Height: 6' Weight: 175 lbs. Drafted: — College: San Francisco

YEAR	TEAM	GP	GS	MIN	PTS	FGM	FGA	FG%	3PM	3PA	3P%	FTM	FTA	FT%	ORB	DRB	TRB	AST	PF	DQ	STL	BLK	TO	MPG	PPG	RPG	APG	PCM
47-48	Oshkosh-N	8	....	....	9	4	....	....	....	....	....	1	2	.500	....	....	....	....	....	....	....	....	....	1.1	....	....	....	
NBL Season Totals		8	....	....	9	4	....	....	....	....	....	1	2	....	....	....	....	....	....	....	....	....	....	1.1	....	....	....	

• ROE, Lou

Louis M. Roe

Born: July 14, 1972. Atlantic City, NJ, United States. Height: 6'7". Weight: 220 lbs. Drafted: 1995 College: Massachusetts

YEAR	TEAM	GP	GS	MIN	PTS	FGM	FGA	FG%	3PM	3PA	3P%	FTM	FTA	FT%	ORB	DRB	TRB	AST	PF	DQ	STL	BLK	TO	MPG	PPG	RPG	APG	PCM
95-96	Detroit	49	2	372	90	32	90	.356	2	9	.222	24	32	.750	30	48	78	15	42	0	10	8	15	7.6	1.8	1.6	0.3	.280
96-97	Golden State	17	0	107	40	14	48	.292	3	11	.273	9	19	.474	7	7	14	6	10	0	3	1	10	6.3	2.4	0.8	0.4	.120
NBA Season Totals		66	2	479	130	46	138	.333	5	20	.250	33	51	.647	37	55	92	21	52	0	13	9	25	7.3	2.0	1.4	0.3	....
95-96	Detroit	2	0	7	0	0	1	.000	0	0	.000	0	0	.000	1	1	2	0	1	0	1	0	0	3.5	0.0	1.0	0.0	.201
NBA Playoff Totals		2	0	7	0	0	1	.000	0	0	.000	0	0	.000	1	1	2	0	1	0	1	0	0	3.5	0.0	1.0	0.0	....

• ROGERS, Carlos

Carlos Deon (Bonz) Rogers

Born: Feb. 6, 1971. Detroit, MI, United States. Height: 6'11". Weight: 220 lbs. Drafted: 1994 College: Tennessee State

YEAR	TEAM	GP	GS	MIN	PTS	FGM	FGA	FG%	3PM	3PA	3P%	FTM	FTA	FT%	ORB	DRB	TRB	AST	PF	DQ	STL	BLK	TO	MPG	PPG	RPG	APG	PCM
94-95	Golden State	49	18	1017	438	180	340	.529	2	14	.143	76	146	.521	108	170	278	37	124	2	22	52	83	20.8	8.9	5.7	0.8	.480
95-96	Toronto	56	18	1043	430	178	344	.517	3	21	.143	71	130	.546	80	90	170	35	87	0	25	48	62	18.6	7.7	3.0	0.6	.396
96-97	Toronto	56	3	1397	551	212	404	.525	25	66	.379	102	170	.600	120	184	304	37	140	1	42	69	50	24.9	9.8	5.4	0.7	.469
97-98	Toronto	18	0	351	108	45	87	.517	0	1	.000	18	32	.563	34	31	65	16	34	0	9	8	13	19.5	6.0	3.6	0.9	.365
97-98	Portland	3	0	25	4	2	4	.500	0	1	.000	1	0	.000	1	1	2	2	1	0	1	0	1	8.3	1.3	0.7	0.7	.229
98-99	Portland	2	0	8	5	2	2	1.000	0	0	.000	1	4	.250	0	1	1	1	2	0	0	0	0	4.0	2.5	0.5	0.5	.597
99-00	Houston	53	15	1101	422	170	324	.525	1	14	.071	81	137	.591	98	177	275	42	77	0	14	34	63	20.8	8.0	5.2	0.8	.458
00-01	Houston	39	0	544	179	75	110	.682	0	1	.000	29	52	.558	48	91	139	9	33	0	10	18	17	13.9	4.6	3.6	0.2	.491
01-02	Indiana	22	1	168	59	24	43	.558	1	6	.167	10	19	.526	14	24	38	3	17	0	5	6	5	7.6	2.7	1.7	0.1	.435
NBA Season Totals		298	55	5654	2196	888	1658	.536	32	124	.258	388	690	.562	503	769	1272	182	515	3	128	235	294	19.0	7.4	4.3	0.6	....

• ROGERS, Harry

Harry J. (Tree) Rogers

Born: Dec. 31, 1950. Height: 6'7". Weight: 195 lbs. Drafted: 1973 College: St. Louis

YEAR	TEAM	GP	GS	MIN	PTS	FGM	FGA	FG%	3PM	3PA	3P%	FTM	FTA	FT%	ORB	DRB	TRB	AST	PF	DQ	STL	BLK	TO	MPG	PPG	RPG	APG	PCM
75-76	St. Louis-A	18	....	298	137	60	124	.484	0	2	.000	17	24	.708	38	58	96	15	34	....	12	6	21	16.6	7.6	5.3	0.8	.550
ABA Season Totals		18	....	298	137	60	124	.484	0	2	.000	17	24	.708	38	58	96	15	34	....	12	6	21	16.6	7.6	5.3	0.8	....

• ROGERS, Johnny

John Bernard Rogers

Born: Dec. 30, 1963. Fullerton, CA, United States. Height: 6'10". Weight: 225 lbs. Drafted: 1986 College: California (Irvine)

YEAR	TEAM	GP	GS	MIN	PTS	FGM	FGA	FG%	3PM	3PA	3P%	FTM	FTA	FT%	ORB	DRB	TRB	AST	PF	DQ	STL	BLK	TO	MPG	PPG	RPG	APG	PCM
86-87	Sacramento	45	15	468	189	90	185	.486	0	5	.000	9	15	.600	30	47	77	26	66	0	9	8	18	10.4	4.2	1.7	0.6	.354
87-88	Cleveland	24	0	168	62	26	61	.426	0	2	.000	10	13	.769	8	19	27	3	23	0	4	3	10	7.0	2.6	1.1	0.1	.255
NBA Season Totals		69	15	636	251	116	246	.472	0	7	.000	19	28	.679	38	66	104	29	89	0	13	11	28	9.2	3.6	1.5	0.4	....

• ROGERS, Marshall

Marshall Lee Rogers

Born: Aug. 27, 1953. St. Louis, MO, United States. Height: 6'1". Weight: 190 lbs. Drafted: 1976 College: Pan American

YEAR	TEAM	GP	GS	MIN	PTS	FGM	FGA	FG%	3PM	3PA	3P%	FTM	FTA	FT%	ORB	DRB	TRB	AST	PF	DQ	STL	BLK	TO	MPG	PPG	RPG	APG	PCM
76-77	Golden State	26	....	176	100	43	116	.371	....	....	....	14	15	.933	6	5	11	10	33	0	8	3	....	6.8	3.8	0.4	0.4	.245
NBA Season Totals		26	....	176	100	43	116	.371	....	....	....	14	15	.933	6	5	11	10	33	0	8	3	....	6.8	3.8	0.4	0.4	
76-77	Golden State	1	....	3	2	0	2	.000	....	....	....	2	2	1.000	0	1	1	0	0	0	0	0	....	3.0	2.0	1.0	0.0	.379
NBA Playoff Totals		1	....	3	2	0	2	.000	....	....	....	2	2	1.000	0	1	1	0	0	0	0	0	....	3.0	2.0	1.0	0.0	....

• ROGERS, Rodney

Rodney Ray Rogers Jr.

Born: June 20, 1971. Durham, NC, United States. Height: 6'7". Weight: 235 lbs. Drafted: 1993 College: Wake Forest

YEAR	TEAM	GP	GS	MIN	PTS	FGM	FGA	FG%	3PM	3PA	3P%	FTM	FTA	FT%	ORB	DRB	TRB	AST	PF	DQ	STL	BLK	TO	MPG	PPG	RPG	APG	PCM
93-94	Denver	79	14	1406	640	239	545	.439	35	92	.380	127	189	.672	90	136	226	101	195	3	63	48	134	17.8	8.1	2.9	1.3	.382
94-95	Denver	80	77	2142	979	375	769	.488	50	148	.338	179	275	.651	132	253	385	161	281	7	95	46	176	26.8	12.2	4.8	2.0	.435
95-96	LA Clippers	67	51	1950	774	306	641	.477	49	153	.320	113	180	.628	113	173	286	167	216	2	75	35	141	29.1	11.6	4.3	2.5	.381
96-97	LA Clippers	81	62	2480	1072	408	884	.462	65	180	.361	191	288	.663	137	274	411	222	272	5	88	61	219	30.6	13.2	5.1	2.7	.408

YEAR	TEAM	GP	GS	MIN	PTS	FGM	FGA	FG%	3PM	3PA	3P%	FTM	FTA	FT%	ORB	DRB	TRB	AST	PF	DQ	STL	BLK	TO	MPG	PPG	RPG	APG	PCM
97-98	LA Clippers	76	70	2499	1149	426	935	.456	72	212	.340	225	328	.686	155	269	424	202	242	5	93	38	190	32.9	15.1	5.6	2.7	.432
98-99	LA Clippers	47	7	968	348	131	297	.441	18	63	.286	68	101	.673	65	114	179	77	140	2	47	22	66	20.6	7.4	3.8	1.6	.383
99-00	Phoenix	82	7	2286	1130	428	881	.486	115	262	.439	159	249	.639	138	309	447	170	290	5	94	47	163	27.9	13.8	5.5	2.1	.489
00-01	Phoenix	82	3	2183	998	377	876	.430	56	189	.296	188	247	.761	94	265	359	180	269	5	97	47	157	26.6	12.2	4.4	2.2	.418
01-02	Phoenix	50	7	1254	629	249	534	.466	49	140	.350	82	99	.828	95	146	241	72	148	2	50	17	66	25.1	12.6	4.8	1.4	.474
01-02	Boston	27	1	626	288	107	222	.482	39	95	.411	35	50	.700	34	73	107	40	78	1	16	12	42	23.2	10.7	4.0	1.5	.431
02-03	New Jersey	68	0	1303	478	183	455	.402	44	132	.333	68	90	.756	61	202	263	107	192	2	50	31	91	19.2	7.0	3.9	1.6	.369
NBA Season Totals		739	299	19097	8485	3229	7039	.459	592	1666	.355	1435	2096	.685	1114	2214	3328	1499	2323	39	768	404	1445	25.8	11.5	4.5	2.0	....
93-94	Denver	12	0	190	61	19	49	.388	6	19	.316	17	27	.630	8	13	21	16	25	0	7	6	8	15.8	5.1	1.8	1.3	.308
94-95	Denver	3	3	76	26	12	22	.545	1	4	.250	1	4	.250	1	11	12	5	13	1	3	4	5	25.3	8.7	4.0	1.7	.363
96-97	LA Clippers	3	3	85	32	12	29	.414	2	10	.200	6	8	.750	3	4	7	6	13	0	4	3	7	28.3	10.7	2.3	2.0	.260
99-00	Phoenix	9	0	263	127	48	115	.417	8	36	.222	23	31	.742	16	45	61	14	31	1	10	10	15	29.2	14.1	6.8	1.6	.470
00-01	Phoenix	4	0	82	35	12	40	.300	2	10	.200	9	14	.643	3	11	14	2	16	0	2	3	5	20.5	8.8	3.5	0.5	.185
01-02	Boston	16	0	394	142	46	108	.426	19	52	.365	31	35	.886	28	60	88	34	42	1	16	7	22	24.6	8.9	5.5	2.1	.464
02-03	New Jersey	20	0	350	134	45	121	.372	17	42	.405	27	38	.711	22	34	56	27	51	0	6	3	25	17.5	6.7	2.8	1.4	.293
NBA Playoff Totals		67	6	1440	557	194	484	.401	55	173	.318	114	157	.726	81	178	259	104	191	3	48	36	87	21.5	8.3	3.9	1.6	....

• ROGERS, Roy

Roy Rogers Jr.

Born: Aug. 19, 1973. Linden, AL, United States. Height: 6'10". Weight: 235 lbs. Drafted: 1996 College: Alabama

YEAR	TEAM	GP	GS	MIN	PTS	FGM	FGA	FG%	3PM	3PA	3P%	FTM	FTA	FT%	ORB	DRB	TRB	AST	PF	DQ	STL	BLK	TO	MPG	PPG	RPG	APG	PCM
96-97	Vancouver	82	50	1848	543	244	483	.505	1	1	1.000	54	94	.574	139	247	386	46	214	1	21	161	82	22.5	6.6	4.7	0.6	.381
97-98	Boston	9	0	37	7	3	8	.375	0	0	.000	1	2	.500	0	5	5	1	6	0	2	4	1	4.1	0.8	0.6	0.1	.256
97-98	Toronto	6	0	69	13	6	17	.353	0	0	.000	1	4	.250	8	4	12	1	12	0	1	4	4	11.5	2.2	2.0	0.2	.131
99-00	Denver	40	0	355	89	35	88	.398	0	1	.000	19	41	.463	33	47	80	9	36	0	2	38	10	8.9	2.2	2.0	0.2	.350
NBA Season Totals		137	50	2309	652	288	596	.483	1	2	.500	75	141	.532	180	303	483	57	268	1	26	207	97	16.9	4.8	3.5	0.4	....

• ROGES, Al

Albert A. Roges

Born: Oct. 25, 1930. Height: 6'4". Weight: 195 lbs. Drafted: — College: Long Island University

YEAR	TEAM	GP	GS	MIN	PTS	FGM	FGA	FG%	3PM	3PA	3P%	FTM	FTA	FT%	ORB	DRB	TRB	AST	PF	DQ	STL	BLK	TO	MPG	PPG	RPG	APG	PCM
53-54	Baltimore	67	....	1937	570	220	614	.358	....	....	....	130	179	.726	....	....	213	160	177	1	....	....	....	28.9	8.5	3.2	2.4	.293
54-55	Bal/FtW	17	....	201	61	23	61	.377	....	....	....	15	24	.625	....	....	24	19	20	0	....	....	....	11.8	3.6	1.4	1.1	.315
NBA Season Totals		84	....	2138	631	243	675	.360	....	....	....	145	203	.714	....	....	237	179	197	1	....	....	....	25.5	7.5	2.8	2.1	....

• ROHLOFF, Ken

Kenneth Lawrance (Ken) Rohloff

Born: Apr. 18, 1939. Height: 6' Weight: 195 lbs. Drafted: 1963 College: North Carolina State

YEAR	TEAM	GP	GS	MIN	PTS	FGM	FGA	FG%	3PM	3PA	3P%	FTM	FTA	FT%	ORB	DRB	TRB	AST	PF	DQ	STL	BLK	TO	MPG	PPG	RPG	APG	PCM
63-64	St. Louis	2	....	7	0	0	1	.000	....	....	....	0	0	.000	....	....	0	1	4	0	....	....	....	3.5	0.0	0.0	0.5	-.159
NBA Season Totals		2	....	7	0	0	1	.000	....	....	....	0	0	.000	....	....	0	1	4	0	....	....	....	3.5	0.0	0.0	0.5	....

• ROLLINS, Kenny

Kenneth Herman Rollins

Born: Sept. 14, 1923. Charlestown, MO, United States. Height: 6' Weight: 168 lbs. Drafted: 1948 College: Kentucky

YEAR	TEAM	GP	GS	MIN	PTS	FGM	FGA	FG%	3PM	3PA	3P%	FTM	FTA	FT%	ORB	DRB	TRB	AST	PF	DQ	STL	BLK	TO	MPG	PPG	RPG	APG	PCM
48-49	Chicago	59	....	....	365	144	520	.277	....	....	....	77	104	.740	....	....	....	167	150	....	....	....	....	....	6.2	....	2.8	....
49-50	Chicago	66	....	....	354	144	421	.342	....	....	....	66	89	.742	....	....	....	131	129	....	....	....	....	....	5.4	....	2.0	....
52-53	Boston	43	....	426	98	38	115	.330	....	....	....	22	27	.815	....	....	45	46	63	1	....	....	....	9.9	2.3	1.0	1.1	.256
NBA Season Totals		168	....	426	817	326	1056	.309	....	....	....	165	220	.750	....	....	45	344	342	1	....	....	....	2.5	4.9	0.3	2.0	....
48-49	Chicago	2	....	....	0	0	6	.000	....	....	....	0	0	.000	....	....	....	2	2	....	....	....	....	....	0.0	....	1.0	....
49-50	Chicago	2	....	....	0	0	3	.000	....	....	....	0	0	.000	....	....	....	0	4	....	....	....	....	....	0.0	....	0.0	....
52-53	Boston	6	....	65	20	6	15	.400	....	....	....	8	8	1.000	....	....	8	7	14	0	....	....	....	10.8	3.3	1.3	1.2	.356
NBA Playoff Totals		10	....	65	20	6	24	.250	....	....	....	8	8	1.000	....	....	8	9	20	0	....	....	....	6.5	2.0	0.8	0.9	....

• ROLLINS, Phil

Philip Lee Rollins

Born: Jan. 19, 1934. Wickliffe, KY, United States. Height: 6'2". Weight: 185 lbs. Drafted: 1956 College: Louisville

YEAR	TEAM	GP	GS	MIN	PTS	FGM	FGA	FG%	3PM	3PA	3P%	FTM	FTA	FT%	ORB	DRB	TRB	AST	PF	DQ	STL	BLK	TO	MPG	PPG	RPG	APG	PCM
58-59	Philadelphia	23	....	251	86	29	77	.377	....	....	....	28	45	.622	....	....	41	44	19	0	....	....	....	10.9	3.7	1.8	1.9	.487
58-59	Cincinnati	21	....	440	143	54	144	.375	....	....	....	35	45	.778	....	....	87	58	30	0	....	....	....	21.0	6.8	4.1	2.8	.450
59-60	Cincinnati	72	....	1235	393	158	386	.409	....	....	....	77	127	.606	....	....	180	233	150	1	....	....	....	17.2	5.5	2.5	3.2	.462
60-61	Cincinnati	14	....	86	20	10	32	.313	....	....	....	0	7	.000	....	....	9	11	13	0	....	....	....	6.1	1.4	0.6	0.8	.188
60-61	St. Louis	7	....	90	13	3	29	.103	....	....	....	7	7	1.000	....	....	6	15	2	0	....	....	....	12.9	1.9	0.9	2.1	.173
60-61	New York	40	....	640	243	96	232	.414	....	....	....	51	74	.689	....	....	82	97	106	1	....	....	....	16.0	6.1	2.1	2.4	.427
NBA Season Totals		177	....	2742	898	350	900	.389	....	....	....	198	305	.649	....	....	405	458	320	2	....	....	....	15.5	5.1	2.3	2.6	....

• ROLLINS, Tree

Wayne Monte (Tree) Rollins

Born: June 16, 1955. Winter Haven, FL, United States. Height: 7'1". Weight: 235 lbs. Drafted: 1977 College: Clemson

YEAR	TEAM	GP	GS	MIN	PTS	FGM	FGA	FG%	3PM	3PA	3P%	FTM	FTA	FT%	ORB	DRB	TRB	AST	PF	DQ	STL	BLK	TO	MPG	PPG	RPG	APG	PCM
77-78	Atlanta	80	....	1795	610	253	520	.487	....	....	....	104	148	.703	179	373	552	79	326	16	57	218	120	22.4	7.6	6.9	1.0	.514
78-79	Atlanta	81	....	1900	683	297	555	.535	....	....	....	89	141	.631	219	369	588	49	328	**19**	46	254	89	23.5	8.4	7.3	0.6	.554
79-80	Atlanta	82	....	2123	731	287	514	.558	0	0	.000	157	220	.714	283	491	774	76	322	**12**	54	244	98	25.9	8.9	9.4	0.9	.620
80-81	Atlanta	40	....	1044	278	116	210	.552	0	1	.000	46	57	.807	102	184	286	35	151	7	29	117	56	26.1	7.0	7.2	0.9	.478
81-82	Atlanta	79	39	2018	483	202	346	.584	0	0	.000	79	129	.612	168	443	611	59	285	4	35	224	79	25.5	6.1	7.7	0.7	.490
82-83	Atlanta	80	80	2472	620	261	512	.510	0	1	.000	98	135	.726	210	533	743	75	294	7	49	**343**	96	30.9	7.8	9.3	0.9	.511
83-84	Atlanta	77	76	2351	666	274	529	.518	0	0	.000	118	190	.621	200	393	593	62	297	9	35	277	100	30.5	8.6	7.7	0.8	.456
84-85	Atlanta	70	60	1750	439	186	339	.549	0	0	.000	67	93	.720	113	329	442	52	213	6	35	167	77	25.0	6.3	6.3	0.7	.439
85-86	Atlanta	74	61	1781	415	173	347	.499	0	1	.000	69	90	.767	131	327	458	41	239	5	38	167	89	24.1	5.6	6.2	0.6	.399
86-87	Atlanta	75	58	1764	405	171	313	.546	0	0	.000	63	87	.724	155	333	488	22	240	1	43	140	60	23.5	5.4	6.5	0.3	.421
87-88	Atlanta	76	59	1765	336	133	260	.512	0	0	.000	70	80	.875	142	317	459	20	229	2	31	132	53	23.2	4.4	6.0	0.3	.373
88-89	Cleveland	60	2	583	136	62	138	.449	0	1	.000	12	19	.632	38	101	139	19	89	0	11	38	24	9.7	2.3	2.3	0.3	.332

YEAR	TEAM	GP	GS	MIN	PTS	FGM	FGA	FG%	3PM	3PA	3P%	FTM	FTA	FT%	ORB	DRB	TRB	AST	PF	DQ	STL	BLK	TO	MPG	PPG	RPG	APG	PCM
89-90	Cleveland	48	19	674	125	57	125	.456	0	1	.000	11	16	.688	58	95	153	24	83	3	13	53	34	14.0	2.6	3.2	0.5	.325
90-91	Detroit	37	0	202	36	14	33	.424	0	0	.000	8	14	.571	13	29	42	4	35	0	2	20	15	5.5	1.0	1.1	0.1	.243
91-92	Houston	59	5	697	118	46	86	.535	0	0	.000	26	30	.867	61	110	171	15	85	0	14	62	18	11.8	2.0	2.9	0.3	.385
92-93	Houston	42	0	247	31	11	41	.268	0	2	.000	9	12	.750	12	48	60	10	43	0	6	15	8	5.9	0.7	1.4	0.2	.244
93-94	Orlando	45	1	384	76	29	53	.547	0	0	.000	18	30	.600	33	63	96	9	55	1	7	35	14	8.5	1.7	2.1	0.2	.382
94-95	Orlando	51	3	478	61	20	42	.476	0	0	.000	21	31	.677	31	64	95	9	63	0	7	36	26	9.4	1.2	1.9	0.2	.253
NBA Season Totals		1156	463	24028	6249	2592	4963	.522	0	7	.000	1065	1522	.700	2148	4602	6750	660	3377	92	512	2542	1056	20.8	5.4	5.8	0.6	....
77-78	Atlanta	2	....	51	16	7	12	.583	....	....	....	2	8	.250	3	6	9	1	8	1	1	4	3	25.5	8.0	4.5	0.5	.319
78-79	Atlanta	9	....	212	51	21	51	.412	....	....	....	9	13	.692	19	52	71	5	29	1	3	24	14	23.6	5.7	7.9	0.6	.425
79-80	Atlanta	5	....	134	42	18	31	.581	0	0	.000	6	10	.600	18	20	38	3	25	3	2	14	6	26.8	8.4	7.6	0.6	.476
81-82	Atlanta	2	2	65	7	2	6	.333	0	0	.000	3	4	.750	5	3	8	2	8	1	0	6	5	32.5	3.5	4.0	1.0	.148
82-83	Atlanta	3	3	118	29	13	27	.481	0	0	.000	3	9	.333	10	20	30	3	12	1	1	10	6	39.3	9.7	10.0	1.0	.365
83-84	Atlanta	5	5	152	25	10	25	.400	0	0	.000	5	8	.625	10	24	34	1	23	1	2	10	11	30.4	5.0	6.8	0.2	.214
85-86	Atlanta	9	9	248	59	26	47	.553	0	0	.000	7	11	.636	18	60	78	3	32	2	2	15	12	27.6	6.6	8.7	0.3	.416
86-87	Atlanta	9	9	221	40	15	28	.536	0	0	.000	10	14	.714	19	34	53	3	33	0	3	16	7	24.6	4.4	5.9	0.3	.337
87-88	Atlanta	12	12	333	53	20	36	.556	0	0	.000	13	15	.867	23	48	71	6	46	0	10	19	5	27.8	4.4	5.9	0.5	.332
88-89	Cleveland	5	0	74	15	6	8	.750	0	0	.000	3	5	.600	5	11	16	1	10	0	3	7	1	14.8	3.0	3.2	0.2	.431
89-90	Cleveland	3	0	38	8	1	3	.333	0	0	.000	6	8	.750	0	8	8	1	7	0	2	1	3	12.7	2.7	2.7	0.3	.275
90-91	Detroit	6	0	32	4	2	2	1.000	0	0	.000	0	0	.000	1	2	3	0	6	1	1	2	1	5.3	0.7	0.5	0.0	.125
92-93	Houston	6	0	16	0	0	3	.000	0	1	.000	0	0	.000	1	3	4	0	2	0	2	0	2	2.7	0.0	0.7	0.0	.117
93-94	Orlando	3	0	29	4	2	5	.400	0	0	.000	0	0	.000	3	0	3	0	9	0	1	1	0	9.7	1.3	1.0	0.0	.059
94-95	Orlando	14	0	81	7	3	5	.600	0	0	.000	1	4	.250	4	2	6	0	19	0	0	6	4	5.8	0.5	0.4	0.0	.029
NBA Playoff Totals		93	40	1804	360	146	289	.505	0	1	.000	68	109	.624	139	293	432	29	269	10	33	134	79	19.4	3.9	4.6	0.3	....

• ROMAR, Lorenzo

Lorenzo Romar

Born: Nov. 13, 1958. South Gate, CA, United States.   Height: 6'1".   Weight: 175 lbs.   Drafted: 1980   College: Washington

YEAR	TEAM	GP	GS	MIN	PTS	FGM	FGA	FG%	3PM	3PA	3P%	FTM	FTA	FT%	ORB	DRB	TRB	AST	PF	DQ	STL	BLK	TO	MPG	PPG	RPG	APG	PCM
80-81	Golden State	53	....	726	219	87	211	.412	2	6	.333	43	63	.683	10	46	56	136	64	0	27	3	53	13.7	4.1	1.1	2.6	.339
81-82	Golden State	79	11	1259	488	203	403	.504	3	15	.200	79	96	.823	12	86	98	226	103	0	60	13	87	15.9	6.2	1.2	2.9	.453
82-83	Golden State	82	64	2130	620	266	572	.465	10	33	.303	78	105	.743	23	115	138	455	142	0	98	5	139	26.0	7.6	1.7	5.5	.403
83-84	Golden State	3	0	15	6	2	5	.400	0	1	.000	2	4	.500	0	1	1	1	1	0	0	0	0	5.0	2.0	0.3	0.3	.254
83-84	Milwaukee	65	9	1007	387	159	346	.460	4	32	.125	65	90	.722	21	71	92	192	76	0	55	8	65	15.5	6.0	1.4	3.0	.452
84-85	Milwaukee	4	0	16	2	1	8	.125	0	1	.000	0	0	.000	0	0	0	2	2	0	0	0	0	4.0	0.5	0.0	0.5	-.208
84-85	Detroit	5	0	35	9	2	8	.250	0	2	.000	5	5	1.000	0	0	0	10	5	0	4	0	5	7.0	1.8	0.0	2.0	.309
NBA Season Totals		291	84	5188	1731	720	1553	.464	19	90	.211	272	363	.749	66	319	385	1022	393	0	244	29	349	17.8	5.9	1.3	3.5	....
83-84	Milwaukee	13	0	67	25	9	20	.450	0	3	.000	7	11	.636	0	3	3	15	9	0	0	0	5	5.2	1.9	0.2	1.2	.342
NBA Playoff Totals		13	0	67	25	9	20	.450	0	3	.000	7	11	.636	0	3	3	15	9	0	0	0	5	5.2	1.9	0.2	1.2	....

• ROOK, Jerry

Jerry G. Rook

Born: Oct. 27, 1943. Jonesboro, AR, United States.   Height: 6'5".   Weight: 219 lbs.   Drafted: 1965   College: Arkansas State

YEAR	TEAM	GP	GS	MIN	PTS	FGM	FGA	FG%	3PM	3PA	3P%	FTM	FTA	FT%	ORB	DRB	TRB	AST	PF	DQ	STL	BLK	TO	MPG	PPG	RPG	APG	PCM
69-70	New Orleans-A	28	....	155	85	37	82	.451	0	2	.000	11	13	.846	12	19	31	10	21	0	....	....	16	5.5	3.0	1.1	0.4	.481
ABA Season Totals		28	....	155	85	37	82	.451	0	2	.000	11	13	.846	12	19	31	10	21	0	....	....	16	5.5	3.0	1.1	0.4	....

• ROOKS, Sean

Sean Lester Rooks

Born: Sept. 9, 1969. New York, NY, United States.   Height: 6'10".   Weight: 250 lbs.   Drafted: 1992   College: Arizona

YEAR	TEAM	GP	GS	MIN	PTS	FGM	FGA	FG%	3PM	3PA	3P%	FTM	FTA	FT%	ORB	DRB	TRB	AST	PF	DQ	STL	BLK	TO	MPG	PPG	RPG	APG	PCM
92-93	Dallas	72	68	2087	970	368	747	.493	0	2	.000	234	389	.602	196	340	536	95	204	2	38	81	158	29.0	13.5	7.4	1.3	.486
93-94	Dallas	47	28	1255	536	193	393	.491	0	1	.000	150	210	.714	84	175	259	49	109	0	21	44	80	26.7	11.4	5.5	1.0	.440
94-95	Minnesota	80	70	2405	868	289	615	.470	0	5	.000	290	381	.761	165	321	486	97	208	1	29	71	144	30.1	10.9	6.1	1.2	.391
95-96	Minnesota	49	7	902	331	112	227	.493	1	6	.167	106	159	.667	60	144	204	38	106	0	19	28	49	18.4	6.8	4.2	0.8	.419
95-96	Atlanta	16	0	215	93	32	58	.552	0	1	.000	29	43	.674	21	30	51	9	35	0	4	14	30	13.4	5.8	3.2	0.6	.427
96-97	LA Lakers	69	3	735	265	87	185	.470	0	1	.000	91	130	.700	56	107	163	42	123	1	17	38	48	10.7	3.8	2.4	0.6	.410
97-98	LA Lakers	41	1	425	139	46	101	.455	0	0	.000	47	79	.595	46	72	118	24	68	0	2	23	21	10.4	3.4	2.9	0.6	.425
98-99	LA Lakers	36	0	315	98	32	79	.405	0	2	.000	34	48	.708	33	39	72	9	61	0	2	9	21	8.8	2.7	2.0	0.3	.279
99-00	Dallas	71	13	1001	309	122	283	.431	0	0	.000	65	89	.730	82	166	248	68	169	0	29	52	70	14.1	4.4	3.5	1.0	.384
00-01	LA Clippers	82	0	1553	446	169	395	.428	1	2	.500	107	143	.748	91	212	303	77	197	2	34	64	73	18.9	5.4	3.7	0.9	.333
01-02	LA Clippers	61	2	727	183	81	194	.418	0	0	.000	21	29	.724	32	92	124	25	114	1	12	21	20	11.9	3.0	2.0	0.4	.243
02-03	LA Clippers	70	38	1344	297	125	297	.421	0	1	.000	47	58	.810	53	163	216	69	174	3	34	44	66	19.2	4.2	3.1	1.0	.252
NBA Season Totals		694	230	12964	4535	1656	3574	.463	2	21	.095	1221	1758	.695	919	1861	2780	602	1568	10	241	489	780	18.7	6.5	4.0	0.9	....
95-96	Atlanta	10	0	140	45	16	28	.571	0	0	.000	13	21	.619	13	14	27	7	35	0	4	4	9	14.0	4.5	2.7	0.7	.324
96-97	LA Lakers	8	0	54	14	4	9	.444	0	0	.000	6	8	.750	5	7	12	1	10	0	3	3	3	6.8	1.8	1.5	0.1	.348
97-98	LA Lakers	4	0	11	4	2	6	.333	0	0	.000	0	0	.000	1	0	1	0	2	0	0	3	0	2.8	1.0	0.3	0.0	.280
98-99	LA Lakers	7	0	48	9	2	6	.333	0	0	.000	5	6	.833	1	1	2	3	13	0	0	1	1	6.9	1.3	0.3	0.4	.090
NBA Playoff Totals		29	0	253	72	24	49	.490	0	0	.000	24	35	.686	20	22	42	11	60	0	7	11	13	8.7	2.5	1.4	0.4	....

• ROONEY, Pat

Pat Rooney

Born: 1926.   Height: 6'3".   Weight: —   Drafted: —   College: —

YEAR	TEAM	GP	GS	MIN	PTS	FGM	FGA	FG%	3PM	3PA	3P%	FTM	FTA	FT%	ORB	DRB	TRB	AST	PF	DQ	STL	BLK	TO	MPG	PPG	RPG	APG	PCM
46-47	Detroit-N	5	....	....	11	4	....	....	....	....	....	3	7	.429	....	....	....	....	....	....	....	....	....	....	2.2	....	....	....
46-47	Tri-Cities-N	5	....	....	4	2	....	....	....	....	....	0	0	.000	....	....	....	....	....	....	....	....	....	....	0.8	....	....	....
NBL Season Totals		10	....	....	15	6	....	....	....	....	....	3	7		....	....	....	....	....	....	....	....	....	....	1.5	....	....	....

ROOS, Swede
Harry (Swede) Roos

Born: 1913. Height: 6'1". Weight: 180 lbs. Drafted: — College: none

YEAR TEAM	GP	GS	MIN	PTS	FGM	FGA	FG%	3PM	3PA	3P%	FTM	FTA	FT%	ORB	DRB	TRB	AST	PF	DQ	STL	BLK	TO	MPG	PPG	RPG	APG	PCM
44-45 Chicago-N	22	....	....	70	24	....	....	....	....	....	22	....	....	....	....	....	....	....	....	....	....	....	3.2	....	....	....
NBL Season Totals	22	....	....	70	24	....	....	....	....	....	22	....	....	....	....	....	....	....	....	....	....	....	3.2	....	....	....

ROSE, Jalen
Jalen Rose

Born: Jan. 30, 1973. Detroit, MI, United States. Height: 6'8". Weight: 210 lbs. Drafted: 1994 College: Michigan

YEAR TEAM	GP	GS	MIN	PTS	FGM	FGA	FG%	3PM	3PA	3P%	FTM	FTA	FT%	ORB	DRB	TRB	AST	PF	DQ	STL	BLK	TO	MPG	PPG	RPG	APG	PCM
94-95 Denver	81	37	1798	663	227	500	.454	36	114	.316	173	234	.739	57	160	217	389	206	0	65	22	162	22.2	8.2	2.7	4.8	.461
95-96 Denver	80	37	2134	803	290	604	.480	32	108	.296	191	277	.690	46	214	260	495	229	3	53	39	232	26.7	10.0	3.3	6.2	.467
96-97 Indiana	66	6	1188	482	172	377	.456	21	72	.292	117	156	.750	27	94	121	155	136	1	57	18	106	18.0	7.3	1.8	2.3	.386
97-98 Indiana	82	0	1706	771	290	607	.478	25	73	.342	166	228	.728	28	167	195	155	171	0	56	14	131	20.8	9.4	2.4	1.9	.390
98-99 Indiana	49	1	1238	542	200	496	.403	17	65	.262	125	158	.791	34	120	154	93	128	0	50	15	72	25.3	11.1	3.1	1.9	.356
99-00 Indiana	80	80	2978	1457	563	1196	.471	77	196	.393	254	307	.827	42	345	387	320	234	1	84	49	188	37.2	18.2	4.8	4.0	.471
00-01 Indiana	72	72	2943	1478	567	1242	.457	59	174	.339	285	344	.828	37	322	359	435	230	2	65	43	211	40.9	20.5	5.0	6.0	.493
01-02 Indiana	53	53	1937	982	387	871	.444	52	146	.356	156	186	.839	29	220	249	197	148	1	45	29	105	36.5	18.5	4.7	3.7	.452
01-02 Chicago	30	30	1216	714	276	587	.470	37	100	.370	125	149	.839	14	110	124	158	103	1	33	16	96	40.5	23.8	4.1	5.3	.508
02-03 Chicago	82	82	3352	1816	642	1583	.406	133	359	.370	399	467	.854	68	283	351	395	271	2	72	23	285	40.9	22.1	4.3	4.8	.413
NBA Season Totals	675	398	20490	9708	3614	8063	.448	489	1407	.348	1991	2506	.794	382	2035	2417	2792	1856	11	580	268	1588	30.4	14.4	3.6	4.1	....
94-95 Denver	3	3	99	30	13	28	.464	1	4	.250	3	5	.600	4	7	11	18	9	0	3	2	9	33.0	10.0	3.7	6.0	.368
97-98 Indiana	15	0	293	122	48	100	.480	6	16	.375	20	27	.741	1	26	27	28	37	0	11	6	25	19.5	8.1	1.8	1.9	.348
98-99 Indiana	13	0	355	158	61	138	.442	8	23	.348	28	34	.824	11	20	31	32	39	0	13	5	25	27.3	12.2	2.4	2.5	.356
99-00 Indiana	23	23	964	479	171	391	.437	30	70	.429	107	133	.805	10	91	101	78	71	0	16	11	50	41.9	20.8	4.4	3.4	.406
00-01 Indiana	4	4	164	72	30	79	.380	5	16	.313	7	7	1.000	3	15	18	11	18	0	6	1	9	41.0	18.0	4.5	2.8	.283
NBA Playoff Totals	58	30	1875	861	323	736	.439	50	129	.388	165	206	.801	29	159	188	167	174	0	49	25	118	32.3	14.8	3.2	2.9	....

ROSE, Malik
Malik Jabari Rose

Born: Nov. 23, 1974. Philadelphia, PA, United States. Height: 6'7". Weight: 250 lbs. Drafted: 1996 College: Drexel

YEAR TEAM	GP	GS	MIN	PTS	FGM	FGA	FG%	3PM	3PA	3P%	FTM	FTA	FT%	ORB	DRB	TRB	AST	PF	DQ	STL	BLK	TO	MPG	PPG	RPG	APG	PCM
96-97 Charlotte	54	1	525	160	61	128	.477	0	2	.000	38	62	.613	70	94	164	32	114	3	28	17	43	9.7	3.0	3.0	0.6	.423
97-98 San Antonio	53	0	429	158	59	136	.434	1	3	.333	39	61	.639	40	50	90	19	79	1	21	7	42	8.1	3.0	1.7	0.4	.307
98-99 San Antonio	47	0	608	284	93	201	.463	0	1	.000	98	146	.671	90	92	182	29	120	0	40	22	56	12.9	6.0	3.9	0.6	.514
99-00 San Antonio	74	3	1341	496	176	385	.457	1	3	.333	143	198	.722	133	202	335	47	232	2	35	52	99	18.1	6.7	4.5	0.6	.388
00-01 San Antonio	57	9	1219	437	160	368	.435	3	17	.176	114	160	.713	95	213	308	48	148	1	59	40	74	21.4	7.7	5.4	0.8	.423
01-02 San Antonio	82	1	1725	772	293	633	.463	1	12	.083	185	257	.720	172	320	492	61	208	2	70	42	140	21.0	9.4	6.0	0.7	.478
02-03 San Antonio	79	13	1934	822	289	630	.459	2	5	.400	242	306	.791	148	358	506	124	206	2	57	40	170	24.5	10.4	6.4	1.6	.475
NBA Season Totals	446	27	7781	3129	1131	2481	.456	8	43	.186	859	1190	.722	748	1329	2077	360	1107	11	310	220	624	17.4	7.0	4.7	0.8	....
96-97 Charlotte	2	0	12	4	2	4	.500	0	0	.000	0	0	.000	4	1	5	1	2	0	0	0	2	6.0	2.0	2.5	0.5	.422
97-98 San Antonio	5	0	18	10	4	6	.667	0	0	.000	2	4	.500	3	4	7	1	2	0	1	0	4	3.6	2.0	1.4	0.2	.616
98-99 San Antonio	17	0	194	46	14	38	.368	0	0	.000	18	26	.692	17	22	39	3	52	0	7	4	10	11.4	2.7	2.3	0.2	.190
99-00 San Antonio	4	0	83	21	8	18	.444	0	0	.000	5	9	.556	5	14	19	1	12	0	2	3	7	20.8	5.3	4.8	0.3	.255
00-01 San Antonio	13	0	215	64	23	55	.418	1	3	.333	17	20	.850	16	33	49	4	38	0	3	1	10	16.5	4.9	3.8	0.3	.278
01-02 San Antonio	10	3	292	129	46	96	.479	0	1	.000	37	50	.740	27	52	79	14	30	0	10	5	12	29.2	12.9	7.9	1.4	.527
02-03 San Antonio	24	0	560	222	75	179	.419	0	3	.000	72	94	.766	49	89	138	24	72	0	16	11	43	23.3	9.3	5.8	1.0	.396
NBA Playoff Totals	75	3	1374	496	172	396	.434	1	7	.143	151	203	.744	121	215	336	48	208	0	39	24	88	18.3	6.6	4.5	0.6	....

ROSE, Rob
Robert Paul Rose

Born: Dec. 27, 1964. Rochester, NY, United States. Height: 6'5". Weight: 180 lbs. Drafted: — College: George Mason

YEAR TEAM	GP	GS	MIN	PTS	FGM	FGA	FG%	3PM	3PA	3P%	FTM	FTA	FT%	ORB	DRB	TRB	AST	PF	DQ	STL	BLK	TO	MPG	PPG	RPG	APG	PCM
88-89 LA Clippers	2	0	3	0	0	1	.000	0	0	.000	0	0	.000	1	1	2	0	0	0	0	0	0	1.5	0.0	1.0	0.0	.310
NBA Season Totals	2	0	3	0	0	1	.000	0	0	.000	0	0	.000	1	1	2	0	0	0	0	0	0	1.5	0.0	1.0	0.0	....

ROSENBERG, Petey
Alexander (Pete) Rosenberg

Born: Apr. 7, 1918. Died: June 29, 1997. Height: 5'10". Weight: 165 lbs. Drafted: — College: St. Joseph's (PA)

YEAR TEAM	GP	GS	MIN	PTS	FGM	FGA	FG%	3PM	3PA	3P%	FTM	FTA	FT%	ORB	DRB	TRB	AST	PF	DQ	STL	BLK	TO	MPG	PPG	RPG	APG	PCM
46-47 Philadelphia	51	....	....	150	60	287	.209	....	....	....	30	49	.612	....	....	....	27	64	....	....	....	....	....	2.9	....	0.5	....
NBA Season Totals	51	....	....	150	60	287	.209	....	....	....	30	49	.612	....	....	....	27	64	....	....	....	....	....	2.9	....	0.5	....
46-47 Philadelphia	9	....	....	2	1	12	.083	....	....	....	0	3	.000	....	....	....	3	4	....	....	....	....	....	0.2	....	0.3	....
NBA Playoff Totals	9	....	....	2	1	12	.083	....	....	....	0	3	.000	....	....	....	3	4	....	....	....	....	....	0.2	....	0.3	....

ROSENBLUTH, Lennie
Leonard Robert Rosenbluth

Born: Jan. 22, 1933. New York, NY, United States. Height: 6'4". Weight: 190 lbs. Drafted: 1957 College: North Carolina

YEAR TEAM	GP	GS	MIN	PTS	FGM	FGA	FG%	3PM	3PA	3P%	FTM	FTA	FT%	ORB	DRB	TRB	AST	PF	DQ	STL	BLK	TO	MPG	PPG	RPG	APG	PCM
57-58 Philadelphia	53	....	373	235	91	265	.343	....	....	....	53	84	.631	....	....	91	23	39	0	....	....	....	7.0	4.4	1.7	0.4	.478
58-59 Philadelphia	29	....	205	107	43	145	.297	....	....	....	21	29	.724	....	....	54	6	20	0	....	....	....	7.1	3.7	1.9	0.2	.331
NBA Season Totals	82	....	578	342	134	410	.327	....	....	....	74	113	.655	....	....	145	29	59	0	....	....	....	7.0	4.2	1.8	0.4	....
57-58 Philadelphia	4	....	11	8	3	9	.333	....	....	....	2	3	.667	....	....	3	0	0	0	....	....	....	2.8	2.0	0.8	0.0	.495
NBA Playoff Totals	4	....	11	8	3	9	.333	....	....	....	2	3	.667	....	....	3	0	0	0	....	....	....	2.8	2.0	0.8	0.0	....

YEAR	TEAM	GP	GS	MIN	PTS	FGM	FGA	FG%	3PM	3PA	3P%	FTM	FTA	FT%	ORB	DRB	TRB	AST	PF	DQ	STL	BLK	TO	MPG	PPG	RPG	APG	PCM

● ROSENSTEIN, Hank — Henry Rosenstein

Born: June 16, 1920.   Height: 6'4".   Weight: 185 lbs.   Drafted: —   College: CCNY (DNP)

YEAR	TEAM	GP	GS	MIN	PTS	FGM	FGA	FG%	3PM	3PA	3P%	FTM	FTA	FT%	ORB	DRB	TRB	AST	PF	DQ	STL	BLK	TO	MPG	PPG	RPG	APG	PCM
46-47	New York	31	....	....	133	38	145	.262	....	....	....	57	95	.600	....	....	....	19	71	....	....	....	....	....	4.3	....	0.6	....
46-47	Providence	29	....	....	249	81	245	.331	....	....	....	87	130	.669	....	....	....	17	101	....	....	....	....	....	8.6	....	0.6	....
NBA Season Totals		60	....	....	382	119	390	.305	....	....	....	144	225	.640	....	....	....	36	172	....	....	....	....	....	6.4	....	0.6	....

● ROSENTHAL, Dick — Richard Anthony Rosenthal

Born: Jan. 20, 1930.   Height: 6'5".   Weight: 205 lbs.   Drafted: 1954   College: Notre Dame

YEAR	TEAM	GP	GS	MIN	PTS	FGM	FGA	FG%	3PM	3PA	3P%	FTM	FTA	FT%	ORB	DRB	TRB	AST	PF	DQ	STL	BLK	TO	MPG	PPG	RPG	APG	PCM
54-55	Fort Wayne	67	....	1406	524	197	523	.377	....	....	....	130	181	.718	....	....	300	153	179	2	....	....	....	21.0	7.8	4.5	2.3	.433
56-57	Fort Wayne	18	....	188	51	21	79	.266	....	....	....	9	17	.529	....	....	52	17	22	0	....	....	....	10.4	2.8	2.9	0.9	.301
NBA Season Totals		85	....	1594	575	218	602	.362	....	....	....	139	198	.702	....	....	352	170	201	2	....	....	....	18.8	6.8	4.1	2.0	....
54-55	Fort Wayne	11	....	209	82	27	84	.321	....	....	....	28	39	.718	....	....	48	26	39	1	....	....	....	19.0	7.5	4.4	2.4	.425
NBA Playoff Totals		11	....	209	82	27	84	.321	....	....	....	28	39	.718	....	....	48	26	39	1	....	....	....	19.0	7.5	4.4	2.4	

● ROSENTHAL, Gene — Gene Rosenthal

Born: 1914.   Height: 5'11".   Weight: 175 lbs.   Drafted: —   College: Carnegie-Mellon

YEAR	TEAM	GP	GS	MIN	PTS	FGM	FGA	FG%	3PM	3PA	3P%	FTM	FTA	FT%	ORB	DRB	TRB	AST	PF	DQ	STL	BLK	TO	MPG	PPG	RPG	APG	PCM
38-39	Pittsburgh-N	9	....	....	30	13	...	....	....	....	....	4	....	....	....	....	....	....	....	....	....	....	....	....	3.3	....	....	....
NBL Season Totals		9	....	....	30	13	....	....	....	....	....	4	....	....	....	....	....	....	....	....	....	....	....	....	3.3	....	....	....

● ROTH, Carl — Carl Roth

Born: 1909.   Height: 6'2".   Weight: 200 lbs.   Drafted: —   College: Wisconsin

YEAR	TEAM	GP	GS	MIN	PTS	FGM	FGA	FG%	3PM	3PA	3P%	FTM	FTA	FT%	ORB	DRB	TRB	AST	PF	DQ	STL	BLK	TO	MPG	PPG	RPG	APG	PCM
38-39	Sheboygan-N	14	....	....	29	14	....	....	....	....	....	1	....	....	....	....	....	....	....	....	....	....	....	....	2.1	....	....	....
NBL Season Totals		14	....	....	29	14	....	....	....	....	....	1	....	....	....	....	....	....	....	....	....	....	....	....	2.1	....	....	....

● ROTH, Doug — Douglas Keith Roth

Born: Aug. 24, 1967. Knoxville, TN, United States.   Height: 6'11".   Weight: 255 lbs.   Drafted: 1989   College: Tennessee

YEAR	TEAM	GP	GS	MIN	PTS	FGM	FGA	FG%	3PM	3PA	3P%	FTM	FTA	FT%	ORB	DRB	TRB	AST	PF	DQ	STL	BLK	TO	MPG	PPG	RPG	APG	PCM
89-90	Washington	42	0	412	81	37	86	.430	0	1	.000	7	14	.500	44	76	120	20	70	1	8	13	17	9.8	1.9	2.9	0.5	.331
NBA Season Totals		42	0	412	81	37	86	.430	0	1	.000	7	14	.500	44	76	120	20	70	1	8	13	17	9.8	1.9	2.9	0.5	....

● ROTH, Scott — Scott Edward Roth

Born: June 3, 1963. Cleveland, OH, United States.   Height: 6'8".   Weight: 212 lbs.   Drafted: 1985   College: Wisconsin

YEAR	TEAM	GP	GS	MIN	PTS	FGM	FGA	FG%	3PM	3PA	3P%	FTM	FTA	FT%	ORB	DRB	TRB	AST	PF	DQ	STL	BLK	TO	MPG	PPG	RPG	APG	PCM
87-88	Utah	26	0	201	84	30	74	.405	2	11	.182	22	30	.733	7	21	28	16	37	0	12	0	10	7.7	3.2	1.1	0.6	.334
88-89	Utah	16	0	72	23	7	24	.292	1	6	.167	8	11	.727	0	8	8	7	14	0	5	1	6	4.5	1.4	0.5	0.4	.197
88-89	San Antonio	47	3	464	158	52	143	.364	2	10	.200	52	76	.684	20	36	56	48	55	0	19	4	33	9.9	3.4	1.2	1.0	.282
89-90	Minnesota	71	3	1061	486	159	420	.379	18	52	.346	150	201	.746	34	78	112	115	144	1	51	6	85	14.9	6.8	1.6	1.6	.331
NBA Season Totals		160	6	1798	751	248	661	.375	23	79	.291	232	318	.730	61	143	204	186	250	1	87	11	134	11.2	4.7	1.3	1.2	....
87-88	Utah	6	0	10	2	1	3	.333	0	0	.000	0	0	.000	0	0	0	0	0	0	2	0	0	1.7	0.3	0.0	0.0	.200
NBA Playoff Totals		6	0	10	2	1	3	.333	0	0	.000	0	0	.000	0	0	0	0	0	0	2	0	0	1.7	0.3	0.0	0.0	....

● ROTHENBERG, Irv — Irwin P. Rothenberg

Born: Dec. 31, 1921.   Height: 6'7".   Weight: 215 lbs.   Drafted: 1947   College: Long Island University

YEAR	TEAM	GP	GS	MIN	PTS	FGM	FGA	FG%	3PM	3PA	3P%	FTM	FTA	FT%	ORB	DRB	TRB	AST	PF	DQ	STL	BLK	TO	MPG	PPG	RPG	APG	PCM
46-47	Cleveland	29	....	....	102	36	167	.216	....	....	....	30	54	.556	....	....	....	15	62	....	....	....	....	....	3.5	....	0.5	....
47-48	Washington	11	....	....	46	15	60	.250	....	....	....	16	21	.762	....	....	....	1	22	....	....	....	....	....	4.2	....	0.1	....
47-48	Baltimore	14	....	....	61	25	86	.291	....	....	....	11	23	.478	....	....	....	2	24	....	....	....	....	....	4.4	....	0.1	....
47-48	St. Louis	24	....	....	186	63	218	.289	....	....	....	60	106	.566	....	....	....	4	69	....	....	....	....	....	7.8	....	0.2	....
48-49	New York	53	....	....	314	101	367	.275	....	....	....	112	174	.644	....	....	....	68	174	....	....	....	....	....	5.9	....	1.3	....
NBA Season Totals		131	....	....	709	240	898	.267	....	....	....	229	378	.606	....	....	....	90	351	....	....	....	....	....	5.4	....	0.7	....
47-48	St. Louis	5	....	....	14	5	34	.147	....	....	....	4	7	.571	....	....	....	0	9	....	....	....	....	....	2.8	....	0.0	....
48-49	New York	6	....	....	10	4	19	.211	....	....	....	2	10	.200	....	....	....	2	12	....	....	....	....	....	1.7	....	0.3	....
NBA Playoff Totals		11	....	....	24	9	53	.170	....	....	....	6	17	.353	....	....	....	2	21	....	....	....	....	....	2.2	....	0.2	....

● ROTHMAN, Les — Les Rothman

Born: 1926.   Height: 6'1".   Weight: 195 lbs.   Drafted: —   College: Long Island University

YEAR	TEAM	GP	GS	MIN	PTS	FGM	FGA	FG%	3PM	3PA	3P%	FTM	FTA	FT%	ORB	DRB	TRB	AST	PF	DQ	STL	BLK	TO	MPG	PPG	RPG	APG	PCM
46-47	Chicago-N	1	....	....	0	0	....	....	....	....	....	0	0	.000	....	....	....	....	....	....	....	....	....	....	0.0	....	....	....
46-47	Syracuse-N	13	....	....	63	24	....	....	....	....	....	15	21	.714	....	....	....	....	....	....	....	....	....	....	4.8	....	....	....
NBL Season Totals		14	....	....	63	24	....	....	....	....	....	15	21	....	....	....	....	....	....	....	....	....	....	....	4.5	....	....	....

• ROTTNER, Mickey
Marvin (Mickey) Rottner

Born: Mar. 23, 1919. Height: 5'10". Weight: 180 lbs. Drafted: — College: Loyola (IL)

YEAR	TEAM	GP	GS	MIN	PTS	FGM	FGA	FG%	3PM	3PA	3P%	FTM	FTA	FT%	ORB	DRB	TRB	AST	PF	DQ	STL	BLK	TO	MPG	PPG	RPG	APG	PCM
45-46	Sheboygan-N	5	....	....	20	10	....	....	....	....	....	0	0	.000	....	....	....	....	....	....	....	....	....	....	4.0	....	....	....
46-47	Chicago	56	....	....	423	190	655	.290	....	....	....	43	79	.544	....	....	....	93	109	....	....	....	....	....	7.6	....	1.7	....
47-48	Chicago	44	....	....	117	53	184	.288	....	....	....	11	34	.324	....	....	....	46	49	....	....	....	....	....	2.7	....	1.0	....
NBA Season Totals		100	....	....	540	243	839	.290	....	....	....	54	113	.478	....	....	....	139	158	....	....	....	....	....	5.4	....	1.4	....
NBL Season Totals		5	....	....	20	10	....	....	....	....	....	0	0	....	....	....	....	....	....	....	....	....	....	....	4.0	....	....	....
Career Totals		105	....	....	560	253	839	....	....	....	....	54	113	....	....	....	....	139	158	....	....	....	....	....	5.3	....	1.3	....
45-46	Sheboygan-N	8	....	....	24	10	....	....	....	....	....	4	9	.444	....	....	....	....	....	....	....	....	....	....	3.0	....	....	....
46-47	Chicago	10	....	....	11	5	43	.116	....	....	....	1	4	.250	....	....	....	3	10	....	....	....	....	....	1.1	....	0.3	....
47-48	Chicago	4	....	....	7	3	15	.200	....	....	....	1	3	.333	....	....	....	2	13	....	....	....	....	....	1.8	....	0.5	....
NBA Playoff Totals		14	....	....	18	8	58	.138	....	....	....	2	7	.286	....	....	....	5	23	....	....	....	....	....	1.3	....	0.4	....
NBL Playoff Totals		8	....	....	24	10	....	....	....	....	....	4	9	....	....	....	....	....	....	....	....	....	....	....	3.0	....	....	....
Career Playoff Totals		22	....	....	42	18	58	....	....	....	....	6	16	....	....	....	....	5	23	....	....	....	....	....	1.9	....	0.2	....

• ROUNDFIELD, Dan
Danny Thomas (Rounds, Dr. Rounds) Roundfield

Born: May 26, 1953. Detroit, MI, United States. Height: 6'8". Weight: 205 lbs. Drafted: 1975 College: Central Michigan

YEAR	TEAM	GP	GS	MIN	PTS	FGM	FGA	FG%	3PM	3PA	3P%	FTM	FTA	FT%	ORB	DRB	TRB	AST	PF	DQ	STL	BLK	TO	MPG	PPG	RPG	APG	PCM
75-76	Indiana-A	67	....	767	339	131	309	.424	0	2	.000	77	122	.631	131	128	259	35	161	....	31	43	64	11.4	5.1	3.9	0.5	.467
76-77	Indiana	61	....	1645	848	342	734	.466	....	....	....	164	239	.686	179	339	518	69	243	8	61	131	....	27.0	13.9	8.5	1.1	.546
77-78	Indiana	79	....	2423	1060	421	861	.489	....	....	....	218	300	.727	275	527	802	196	297	4	81	149	198	30.7	13.4	10.2	2.5	.602
78-79	Atlanta	80	....	2539	1224	462	916	.504	....	....	....	300	420	.714	326	539	865	131	358	16	87	176	208	31.7	15.3	10.8	1.6	.619
79-80	Atlanta	81	....	2588	1334	502	1007	.499	0	4	.000	330	465	.710	293	544	837	184	317	6	101	139	235	32.0	16.5	10.3	2.3	.632
80-81	Atlanta	63	....	2128	1108	426	808	.527	0	1	.000	256	355	.721	231	403	634	161	258	8	76	119	176	33.8	17.6	10.1	2.6	.643
81-82	Atlanta	61	58	2217	1134	424	910	.466	1	5	.200	285	375	.760	227	494	721	162	210	3	64	93	183	36.3	18.6	11.8	2.7	.615
82-83	Atlanta	77	76	2811	1464	561	1193	.470	5	27	.185	337	450	.749	259	621	880	225	239	1	60	115	246	36.5	19.0	11.4	2.9	.609
83-84	Atlanta	73	72	2610	1380	503	1038	.485	0	11	.000	374	486	.770	206	515	721	184	221	2	61	74	204	35.8	18.9	9.9	2.5	.587
84-85	Detroit	56	43	1492	611	236	505	.467	0	2	.000	139	178	.781	175	278	453	102	147	0	26	54	123	26.6	10.9	8.1	1.8	.513
85-86	Washington	79	21	2321	917	322	660	.488	0	6	.000	273	362	.754	210	432	642	167	194	1	36	51	190	29.4	11.6	8.1	2.1	.496
86-87	Washington	36	0	669	238	90	220	.409	1	5	.200	57	72	.792	64	106	170	39	77	0	11	16	50	18.6	6.6	4.7	1.1	.378
NBA Season Totals		746	270	23443	11318	4289	8852	.485	7	61	.115	2733	3702	.738	2445	4798	7243	1620	2561	49	664	1117	1813	31.4	15.2	9.7	2.2	....
ABA Season Totals		67	....	767	339	131	309	.424	0	2	.000	77	122	.631	131	128	259	35	161	....	31	43	64	11.4	5.1	3.9	0.5	....
Career Totals		813	270	24210	11657	4420	9161	.482	7	63	.111	2810	3824	.735	2576	4926	7502	1655	2722	49	695	1160	1877	29.8	14.3	9.2	2.0	....
75-76	Indiana-A	2	....	25	22	7	12	.583	0	0	.000	8	9	.889	4	6	10	0	6	....	2	4	0	12.5	11.0	5.0	0.0	.933
78-79	Atlanta	9	....	338	158	61	133	.459	....	....	....	36	45	.800	44	62	106	25	44	3	8	23	23	37.6	17.6	11.8	2.8	.590
79-80	Atlanta	5	....	174	86	32	69	.464	0	1	.000	22	35	.629	25	33	58	11	22	1	4	8	11	34.8	17.2	11.6	2.2	.587
81-82	Atlanta	2	2	85	42	17	36	.472	0	0	.000	8	14	.571	6	16	22	2	8	0	2	4	6	42.5	21.0	11.0	1.0	.476
82-83	Atlanta	3	3	124	53	24	50	.480	0	1	.000	5	11	.455	6	36	42	10	5	0	4	4	11	41.3	17.7	14.0	3.3	.571
83-84	Atlanta	5	5	191	86	30	69	.435	1	1	1.000	25	35	.714	12	32	44	8	16	1	2	7	19	38.2	17.2	8.8	1.6	.407
84-85	Detroit	9	8	215	82	33	68	.485	0	0	.000	16	17	.941	19	41	60	15	21	0	4	6	15	23.9	9.1	6.7	1.7	.495
85-86	Washington	5	0	177	70	28	53	.528	0	1	.000	14	17	.824	14	32	46	10	17	0	2	4	13	35.4	14.0	9.2	2.0	.477
NBA Playoff Totals		38	18	1304	577	225	478	.471	1	4	.250	126	174	.724	126	252	378	81	133	5	26	56	98	34.3	15.2	9.9	2.1	....
ABA Playoff Totals		2	....	25	22	7	12	.583	0	0	.000	8	9	.889	4	6	10	0	6	....	2	4	0	12.5	11.0	5.0	0.0	....
Career Playoff Totals		40	18	1329	599	232	490	.473	1	4	.250	134	183	.732	130	258	388	81	139	5	28	60	98	33.2	15.0	9.7	2.0	....

• ROUX, Giff
Gifford H. Roux

Born: June 28, 1923. Height: 6'5". Weight: 195 lbs. Drafted: — College: Kansas

YEAR	TEAM	GP	GS	MIN	PTS	FGM	FGA	FG%	3PM	3PA	3P%	FTM	FTA	FT%	ORB	DRB	TRB	AST	PF	DQ	STL	BLK	TO	MPG	PPG	RPG	APG	PCM
46-47	St. Louis	60	....	....	354	142	478	.297	....	....	....	70	160	.438	....	....	....	17	95	....	....	....	....	....	5.9	....	0.3	....
47-48	St. Louis	46	....	....	176	68	258	.264	....	....	....	40	68	.588	....	....	....	12	60	....	....	....	....	....	3.8	....	0.3	....
48-49	St. Louis	19	....	....	37	11	44	.250	....	....	....	15	17	.882	....	....	....	11	12	....	....	....	....	....	1.9	....	0.6	....
48-49	Providence	26	....	....	50	18	74	.243	....	....	....	14	27	.519	....	....	....	9	18	....	....	....	....	....	1.9	....	0.3	....
NBA Season Totals		151	....	....	617	239	854	.280	....	....	....	139	272	.511	....	....	....	49	185	....	....	....	....	....	4.1	....	0.3	....
46-47	St. Louis	3	....	....	22	11	29	.379	....	....	....	0	2	.000	....	....	....	0	6	....	....	....	....	....	7.3	....	0.0	....
47-48	St. Louis	5	....	....	7	2	24	.083	....	....	....	3	7	.429	....	....	....	0	3	....	....	....	....	....	1.4	....	0.0	....
NBA Playoff Totals		8	....	....	29	13	53	.245	....	....	....	3	9	.333	....	....	....	0	9	....	....	....	....	....	3.6	....	0.0	....

• ROWAN, Ron
Ronald Lewis Rowan

Born: Apr. 23, 1962. New Brighton, PA, United States. Height: 6'5". Weight: 200 lbs. Drafted: 1986 College: St. John's (NY)

YEAR	TEAM	GP	GS	MIN	PTS	FGM	FGA	FG%	3PM	3PA	3P%	FTM	FTA	FT%	ORB	DRB	TRB	AST	PF	DQ	STL	BLK	TO	MPG	PPG	RPG	APG	PCM
86-87	Portland	7	0	16	12	4	9	.444	1	1	1.000	3	4	.750	1	0	1	1	1	0	4	0	3	2.3	1.7	0.1	0.1	.584
NBA Season Totals		7	0	16	12	4	9	.444	1	1	1.000	3	4	.750	1	0	1	1	1	0	4	0	3	2.3	1.7	0.1	0.1	....

• ROWE, Curtis
Curtis Rowe Jr.

Born: July 2, 1949. Bessemer, AL, United States. Height: 6'7". Weight: 225 lbs. Drafted: 1971 College: UCLA

YEAR	TEAM	GP	GS	MIN	PTS	FGM	FGA	FG%	3PM	3PA	3P%	FTM	FTA	FT%	ORB	DRB	TRB	AST	PF	DQ	STL	BLK	TO	MPG	PPG	RPG	APG	PCM
71-72	Detroit	82	....	2661	930	369	802	.460	....	....	....	192	287	.669	....	....	699	99	171	1	....	....	....	32.5	11.3	8.5	1.2	.435
72-73	Detroit	81	....	3009	1304	547	1053	.519	....	....	....	210	327	.642	....	....	760	172	191	0	....	....	....	37.1	16.1	9.4	2.1	.527
73-74	Detroit	82	....	2499	878	380	769	.494	....	....	....	118	169	.698	167	348	515	136	177	1	49	36	....	30.5	10.7	6.3	1.7	.418
74-75	Detroit	82	....	2787	1015	422	874	.483	....	....	....	171	227	.753	174	411	585	121	190	0	50	44	....	34.0	12.4	7.1	1.5	.417
75-76	Detroit	80	....	2998	1280	514	1098	.468	....	....	....	252	342	.737	231	466	697	183	209	3	47	45	....	37.5	16.0	8.7	2.3	.486

YEAR	TEAM	GP	GS	MIN	PTS	FGM	FGA	FG%	3PM	3PA	3P%	FTM	FTA	FT%	ORB	DRB	TRB	AST	PF	DQ	STL	BLK	TO	MPG	PPG	RPG	APG	PCM
76-77	Boston	79	....	2190	800	315	632	.498	....	....	....	170	240	.708	188	375	563	107	215	3	24	47	....	27.7	10.1	7.1	1.4	.462
77-78	Boston	51	....	911	312	123	273	.451	....	....	....	66	89	.742	74	129	203	45	94	1	14	8	77	17.9	6.1	4.0	0.9	.340
78-79	Boston	53	....	1222	354	151	346	.436	....	....	....	52	75	.693	79	163	242	69	105	2	15	13	90	23.1	6.7	4.6	1.3	.294
NBA Season Totals		590	....	18277	6873	2821	5847	.482	....	....	....	1231	1756	.701	913	1892	4264	932	1352	11	199	193	167	31.0	11.6	7.2	1.6	....
73-74	Detroit	7	....	229	58	25	52	.481	....	....	....	8	13	.615	16	36	52	11	23	0	3	6	....	32.7	8.3	7.4	1.6	.349
74-75	Detroit	3	....	115	44	17	33	.515	....	....	....	10	19	.526	8	18	26	15	6	0	1	5	....	38.3	14.7	8.7	5.0	.551
75-76	Detroit	9	....	346	135	53	111	.477	....	....	....	29	34	.853	25	45	70	26	27	1	6	8	....	38.4	15.0	7.8	2.9	.466
76-77	Boston	9	....	237	86	32	68	.471	....	....	....	22	29	.759	29	43	72	10	29	1	1	4	....	26.3	9.6	8.0	1.1	.476
NBA Playoff Totals		28	....	927	323	127	264	.481	....	....	....	69	95	.726	78	142	220	62	85	2	11	23	....	33.1	11.5	7.9	2.2	....

• ROWINSKI, Jim
James Rowinski

Born: Jan. 4, 1961. Long Island, NY, United States.   Height: 6'8".   Weight: 250 lbs.   Drafted: 1984   College: Purdue

YEAR	TEAM	GP	GS	MIN	PTS	FGM	FGA	FG%	3PM	3PA	3P%	FTM	FTA	FT%	ORB	DRB	TRB	AST	PF	DQ	STL	BLK	TO	MPG	PPG	RPG	APG	PCM
88-89	Detroit	6	0	8	4	0	2	.000	0	0	.000	4	4	1.000	0	2	2	0	0	0	0	0	0	1.3	0.7	0.3	0.0	.500
88-89	Philadelphia	3	0	7	3	1	2	.500	0	0	.000	1	2	.500	1	2	3	0	0	0	0	0	0	2.3	1.0	1.0	0.0	.628
89-90	Miami	14	0	112	50	14	32	.438	0	0	.000	22	26	.846	17	12	29	5	19	0	1	2	10	8.0	3.6	2.1	0.4	.431
NBA Season Totals		23	0	127	57	15	36	.417	0	0	.000	27	32	.844	18	16	34	5	19	0	1	2	10	5.5	2.5	1.5	0.2	....

• ROWLAND, Derrick
Derrick Rowland

Born: June 21, 1959. Brookhaven, NY, United States.   Height: 6'5".   Weight: 195 lbs.   Drafted: 1981   College: SUNY Potsdam

YEAR	TEAM	GP	GS	MIN	PTS	FGM	FGA	FG%	3PM	3PA	3P%	FTM	FTA	FT%	ORB	DRB	TRB	AST	PF	DQ	STL	BLK	TO	MPG	PPG	RPG	APG	PCM
85-86	Milwaukee	2	0	9	3	1	3	.333	0	0	.000	1	2	.500	0	1	1	1	1	0	0	0	0	4.5	1.5	0.5	0.5	.246
NBA Season Totals		2	0	9	3	1	3	.333	0	0	.000	1	2	.500	0	1	1	1	1	0	0	0	0	4.5	1.5	0.5	0.5	....

• ROWSOM, Brian
Brian Maurice Rowsom

Born: Oct. 23, 1965. Newark, NJ, United States.   Height: 6'9".   Weight: 220 lbs.   Drafted: 1987   College: North Carolina (Wilmington)

YEAR	TEAM	GP	GS	MIN	PTS	FGM	FGA	FG%	3PM	3PA	3P%	FTM	FTA	FT%	ORB	DRB	TRB	AST	PF	DQ	STL	BLK	TO	MPG	PPG	RPG	APG	PCM
87-88	Indiana	4	0	16	6	0	6	.000	0	0	.000	6	6	1.000	1	4	5	1	3	0	1	0	1	4.0	1.5	1.3	0.3	.296
88-89	Charlotte	34	0	517	226	80	162	.494	1	1	1.000	65	81	.802	56	81	137	24	69	1	10	12	17	15.2	6.6	4.0	0.7	.518
89-90	Charlotte	44	2	559	225	78	179	.436	1	2	.500	68	83	.819	44	87	131	22	58	0	18	11	26	12.7	5.1	3.0	0.5	.438
NBA Season Totals		82	2	1092	457	158	347	.455	2	3	.667	139	170	.818	101	172	273	47	130	1	29	23	44	13.3	5.6	3.3	0.6	....

• ROYAL, Donald
Donald Adam (D. Rock) Royal

Born: May 22, 1966. New Orleans, LA, United States.   Height: 6'8".   Weight: 210 lbs.   Drafted: 1987   College: Notre Dame

YEAR	TEAM	GP	GS	MIN	PTS	FGM	FGA	FG%	3PM	3PA	3P%	FTM	FTA	FT%	ORB	DRB	TRB	AST	PF	DQ	STL	BLK	TO	MPG	PPG	RPG	APG	PCM
89-90	Minnesota	66	0	746	387	117	255	.459	0	1	.000	153	197	.777	69	68	137	43	107	0	32	8	79	11.3	5.9	2.1	0.7	.435
91-92	San Antonio	60	4	718	252	80	178	.449	0	0	.000	92	133	.692	65	59	124	34	73	0	25	7	42	12.0	4.2	2.1	0.6	.349
92-93	Orlando	77	0	1636	706	194	391	.496	0	3	.000	318	390	.815	116	179	295	80	179	4	36	25	116	21.2	9.2	3.8	1.0	.437
93-94	Orlando	74	0	1357	547	174	347	.501	0	2	.000	199	269	.740	94	154	248	61	121	1	50	16	74	18.3	7.4	3.4	0.8	.433
94-95	Orlando	70	0	1841	635	196	434	.475	0	4	.000	223	299	.746	83	196	279	198	156	0	45	16	126	26.3	9.1	4.0	2.8	.393
95-96	Orlando	64	7	963	337	106	216	.491	0	2	.000	125	164	.762	57	96	153	42	97	0	29	15	51	15.0	5.3	2.4	0.7	.365
96-97	Golden State	36	1	509	136	37	96	.385	0	2	.000	62	78	.795	33	62	95	14	55	0	11	9	22	14.1	3.8	2.6	0.4	.294
96-97	Orlando	1	1	29	12	4	10	.400	0	0	.000	4	4	1.000	1	0	1	1	3	0	0	0	3	29.0	12.0	1.0	1.0	.145
96-97	Charlotte	25	2	320	70	21	40	.525	0	0	.000	28	35	.800	18	40	58	10	42	0	12	2	23	12.8	2.8	2.3	0.4	.268
97-98	Orlando	2	0	18	5	1	6	.167	0	0	.000	3	4	.750	2	2	4	1	5	0	1	0	3	9.0	2.5	2.0	0.5	.033
97-98	Charlotte	29	5	305	74	24	63	.381	0	0	.000	26	29	.897	16	21	37	16	30	0	6	1	6	10.5	2.6	1.3	0.6	.247
NBA Season Totals		504	88	8442	3161	964	2036	.473	0	14	.000	1233	1602	.770	554	877	1431	500	868	5	247	99	545	16.8	6.3	2.8	1.0	....
91-92	San Antonio	3	2	57	15	5	9	.556	0	0	.000	5	9	.556	5	7	12	0	7	0	2	2	6	19.0	5.0	4.0	0.0	.271
93-94	Orlando	3	0	45	21	6	14	.429	0	0	.000	9	12	.750	1	3	4	5	3	0	1	0	2	15.0	7.0	1.3	1.7	.424
94-95	Orlando	18	6	198	37	11	33	.333	0	0	.000	15	20	.750	6	13	19	9	22	0	3	0	13	11.0	2.1	1.1	0.5	.110
95-96	Orlando	7	0	92	25	7	12	.583	0	0	.000	11	16	.688	4	7	11	1	7	0	0	1	2	13.1	3.6	1.6	0.1	.273
96-97	Charlotte	1	0	4	0	0	1	.000	0	0	.000	0	0	.000	0	2	2	0	1	0	0	0	0	4.0	0.0	2.0	0.0	.117
97-98	Charlotte	4	0	28	9	3	7	.429	0	0	.000	3	4	.750	0	4	4	1	4	0	0	0	1	7.0	2.3	1.0	0.3	.246
NBA Playoff Totals		36	8	424	107	32	76	.421	0	0	.000	43	61	.705	16	36	52	16	44	0	6	3	24	11.8	3.0	1.4	0.4	....

• ROYALS, Reggie
Reggie Royals

Born: Sept. 18, 1954. Whiteville, NC, United States.   Height: 6'10".   Weight: 200 lbs.   Drafted: 1973   College: Florida State

YEAR	TEAM	GP	GS	MIN	PTS	FGM	FGA	FG%	3PM	3PA	3P%	FTM	FTA	FT%	ORB	DRB	TRB	AST	PF	DQ	STL	BLK	TO	MPG	PPG	RPG	APG	PCM
74-75	San Diego-A	2	....	11	4	2	4	.500	0	0	.000	0	0	.000	0	0	0	0	1	....	0	0	0	5.5	2.0	0.0	0.0	.162
ABA Season Totals		2	....	11	4	2	4	.500	0	0	.000	0	0	.000	0	0	0	0	1	....	0	0	0	5.5	2.0	0.0	0.0	....

• ROYER, Bob
Robert D. Royer

Born: Oct. 15, 1927. Died: May 30, 1973.   Height: 5'10".   Weight: 155 lbs.   Drafted: —   College: Indiana State

YEAR	TEAM	GP	GS	MIN	PTS	FGM	FGA	FG%	3PM	3PA	3P%	FTM	FTA	FT%	ORB	DRB	TRB	AST	PF	DQ	STL	BLK	TO	MPG	PPG	RPG	APG	PCM
49-50	Denver	42	....	....	197	78	231	.338	....	....	....	41	58	.707	....	....	....	85	72	....	....	....	....	4.7		2.0		....
NBA Season Totals		42	....	....	197	78	231	.338	....	....	....	41	58	.707	....	....	....	85	72	....	....	....	....	4.7	....	2.0	....	....

• ROZIER, Clifford
Clifford Glen Rozier II

Born: Oct. 31, 1972. Bradenton, FL, United States.   Height: 6'11".   Weight: 245 lbs.   Drafted: 1994   College: Louisville

YEAR	TEAM	GP	GS	MIN	PTS	FGM	FGA	FG%	3PM	3PA	3P%	FTM	FTA	FT%	ORB	DRB	TRB	AST	PF	DQ	STL	BLK	TO	MPG	PPG	RPG	APG	PCM
94-95	Golden State	66	34	1494	448	189	390	.485	2	7	.286	68	152	.447	200	286	486	45	196	2	35	39	86	22.6	6.8	7.4	0.7	.415
95-96	Golden State	59	1	723	184	79	135	.585	0	2	.000	26	55	.473	71	100	171	22	135	0	19	30	41	12.3	3.1	2.9	0.4	.340

YEAR	TEAM	GP	GS	MIN	PTS	FGM	FGA	FG%	3PM	3PA	3P%	FTM	FTA	FT%	ORB	DRB	TRB	AST	PF	DQ	STL	BLK	TO	MPG	PPG	RPG	APG	PCM
96-97	Golden State	1	0	5	0	0	1	.000	0	0	.000	0	0	.000	0	0	0	0	0	0	0	0	0	5.0	0.0	0.0	0.0	-.186
96-97	Toronto	41	29	732	189	79	173	.457	0	2	.000	31	61	.508	102	132	234	31	97	2	24	44	29	17.9	4.6	5.7	0.8	.450
97-98	Minnesota	6	0	30	6	3	6	.500	0	0	.000	0	1	.000	3	3	6	0	7	0	0	0	4	5.0	1.0	1.0	0.0	.048
NBA Season Totals		173	64	2984	827	350	705	.496	2	11	.182	125	269	.465	376	521	897	98	435	4	78	113	160	17.2	4.8	5.2	0.6	....

• RUCKER, Guy

Guy Rucker

Born: July 27, 1977. Inkster, MI, United States.   Height: 6'11".   Weight: 265 lbs.   Drafted: —   College: Iowa

YEAR	TEAM	GP	GS	MIN	PTS	FGM	FGA	FG%	3PM	3PA	3P%	FTM	FTA	FT%	ORB	DRB	TRB	AST	PF	DQ	STL	BLK	TO	MPG	PPG	RPG	APG	PCM
02-03	Golden State	3	0	4	0	0	0	.000	0	0	.000	0	0	.000	0	1	1	1	1	0	0	0	0	1.3	0.0	0.3	0.3	.387
NBA Season Totals		3	0	4	0	0	0	.000	0	0	.000	0	0	.000	0	1	1	1	1	0	0	0	0	1.3	0.0	0.3	0.3	....

• RUDD, Delaney

Edward Delaney Rudd

Born: Nov. 8, 1962. Halifax, NC, United States.   Height: 6'2".   Weight: 180 lbs.   Drafted: 1985   College: Wake Forest

YEAR	TEAM	GP	GS	MIN	PTS	FGM	FGA	FG%	3PM	3PA	3P%	FTM	FTA	FT%	ORB	DRB	TRB	AST	PF	DQ	STL	BLK	TO	MPG	PPG	RPG	APG	PCM
89-90	Utah	77	2	850	273	111	259	.429	16	56	.286	35	53	.660	12	43	55	177	81	0	22	1	85	11.0	3.5	0.7	2.3	.317
90-91	Utah	82	0	874	324	124	285	.435	17	61	.279	59	71	.831	14	52	66	216	92	0	36	2	98	10.7	4.0	0.8	2.6	.413
91-92	Utah	65	0	538	193	75	188	.399	11	47	.234	32	42	.762	15	39	54	109	64	0	15	1	52	8.3	3.0	0.8	1.7	.348
92-93	Portland	15	1	95	26	7	36	.194	1	11	.091	11	14	.786	4	5	9	17	7	0	1	0	11	6.3	1.7	0.6	1.1	.121
NBA Season Totals		239	3	2357	816	317	768	.413	45	175	.257	137	180	.761	45	139	184	519	244	0	74	4	246	9.9	3.4	0.8	2.2	....
89-90	Utah	5	0	45	18	8	23	.348	1	7	.143	1	2	.500	1	2	3	13	10	0	1	0	3	9.0	3.6	0.6	2.6	.301
90-91	Utah	9	0	58	24	9	21	.429	4	12	.333	2	4	.500	2	0	2	17	6	0	3	0	3	6.4	2.7	0.2	1.9	.501
91-92	Utah	10	0	84	25	10	21	.476	2	7	.286	3	4	.750	0	4	4	19	11	0	3	0	4	8.4	2.5	0.4	1.9	.385
NBA Playoff Totals		24	0	187	67	27	65	.415	7	26	.269	6	10	.600	3	6	9	49	27	0	7	0	10	7.8	2.8	0.4	2.0	....

• RUDD, John

John William Rudd

Born: Aug. 7, 1955. DeRidder, LA, United States.   Height: 6'7".   Weight: 230 lbs.   Drafted: 1978   College: McNeese State

YEAR	TEAM	GP	GS	MIN	PTS	FGM	FGA	FG%	3PM	3PA	3P%	FTM	FTA	FT%	ORB	DRB	TRB	AST	PF	DQ	STL	BLK	TO	MPG	PPG	RPG	APG	PCM
78-79	New York	58	....	723	184	59	133	.444	....	....	....	66	93	.710	69	98	167	35	95	1	17	8	58	12.5	3.2	2.9	0.6	.307
NBA Season Totals		58	....	723	184	59	133	.444	....	....	....	66	93	.710	69	98	167	35	95	1	17	8	58	12.5	3.2	2.9	0.6	....

• RUDICEL, Rex

Rex Rudicel

Born: Sept. 6, 1912. Died: Mar.20, 2000.   Height: 5'6".   Weight: 150 lbs.   Drafted: —   College: Ball State

YEAR	TEAM	GP	GS	MIN	PTS	FGM	FGA	FG%	3PM	3PA	3P%	FTM	FTA	FT%	ORB	DRB	TRB	AST	PF	DQ	STL	BLK	TO	MPG	PPG	RPG	APG	PCM
38-39	Indianapolis-N	3	....	....	4	2	....	....	....	....	....	0	....	....	....	....	....	....	....	....	....	....	....	1.3	....	....	....	....
NBL Season Totals		3	....	....	4	2	....	....	....	....	....	0	....	....	....	....	....	....	....	....	....	....	....	1.3	....	....	....	....

• RUDOMETKIN, John

John (Rudo) Rudometkin

Born: June 6, 1940. Santa Maria, CA, United States.   Height: 6'6".   Weight: 205 lbs.   Drafted: 1962   College: USC

YEAR	TEAM	GP	GS	MIN	PTS	FGM	FGA	FG%	3PM	3PA	3P%	FTM	FTA	FT%	ORB	DRB	TRB	AST	PF	DQ	STL	BLK	TO	MPG	PPG	RPG	APG	PCM
62-63	New York	56	....	572	289	108	307	.352	....	....	....	73	95	.768	....	....	149	30	58	0	....	....	....	10.2	5.2	2.7	0.5	.444
63-64	New York	52	....	696	395	154	326	.472	....	....	....	87	116	.750	....	....	164	26	86	0	....	....	....	13.4	7.6	3.2	0.5	.540
64-65	New York	1	....	22	6	3	8	.375	....	....	....	0	0	.000	....	....	7	0	5	0	....	....	....	22.0	6.0	7.0	0.0	.255
64-65	San Francisco	22	....	354	132	49	146	.336	....	....	....	34	50	.680	....	....	92	16	49	0	....	....	....	16.1	6.0	4.2	0.7	.347
NBA Season Totals		131	....	1644	822	314	787	.399	....	....	....	194	261	.743	....	....	412	72	198	0	....	....	....	12.5	6.3	3.1	0.5	....

• RUFFIN, Michael

Michael David Ruffin

Born: Jan. 21, 1977. Denver, CO, United States.   Height: 6'9".   Weight: 246 lbs.   Drafted: 1999   College: Tulsa

YEAR	TEAM	GP	GS	MIN	PTS	FGM	FGA	FG%	3PM	3PA	3P%	FTM	FTA	FT%	ORB	DRB	TRB	AST	PF	DQ	STL	BLK	TO	MPG	PPG	RPG	APG	PCM
99-00	Chicago	71	6	975	159	58	138	.420	0	0	.000	43	88	.489	117	133	250	44	170	1	26	26	59	13.7	2.2	3.5	0.6	.264
00-01	Chicago	45	16	879	119	40	90	.444	0	0	.000	39	77	.506	101	161	262	39	131	2	30	38	46	19.5	2.6	5.8	0.9	.337
01-02	Philadelphia	15	0	170	16	7	26	.269	0	0	.000	2	8	.250	23	28	51	5	23	0	5	8	11	11.3	1.1	3.4	0.3	.230
NBA Season Totals		131	22	2024	294	105	254	.413	0	0	.000	84	173	.486	241	322	563	88	324	3	61	72	116	15.5	2.2	4.3	0.7	....

• RUFFIN, Trevor

Trevor Ruffin

Born: Sept. 26, 1970. Buffalo, NY, United States.   Height: 6'1".   Weight: 185 lbs.   Drafted: —   College: Hawaii

YEAR	TEAM	GP	GS	MIN	PTS	FGM	FGA	FG%	3PM	3PA	3P%	FTM	FTA	FT%	ORB	DRB	TRB	AST	PF	DQ	STL	BLK	TO	MPG	PPG	RPG	APG	PCM
94-95	Phoenix	49	1	319	233	84	197	.426	38	99	.384	27	38	.711	8	15	23	48	52	0	14	2	49	6.5	4.8	0.5	1.0	.436
95-96	Philadelphia	61	23	1551	778	263	648	.406	104	284	.366	148	182	.813	21	111	132	269	132	0	43	2	146	25.4	12.8	2.2	4.4	.421
NBA Season Totals		110	24	1870	1011	347	845	.411	142	383	.371	175	220	.795	29	126	155	317	184	0	57	4	195	17.0	9.2	1.4	2.9	....
94-95	Phoenix	5	0	16	12	5	12	.417	1	4	.250	1	5	.200	1	3	4	2	0	0	1	0	0	3.2	2.4	0.8	0.4	.648
NBA Playoff Totals		5	0	16	12	5	12	.417	1	4	.250	1	5	.200	1	3	4	2	0	0	1	0	0	3.2	2.4	0.8	0.4	....

• RUFFNER, Paul

Paul Ruffner

Born: Oct. 15, 1948. Downey, CA, United States.   Height: 6'10".   Weight: 225 lbs.   Drafted: 1970   College: Brigham Young

YEAR	TEAM	GP	GS	MIN	PTS	FGM	FGA	FG%	3PM	3PA	3P%	FTM	FTA	FT%	ORB	DRB	TRB	AST	PF	DQ	STL	BLK	TO	MPG	PPG	RPG	APG	PCM
70-71	Chicago	10	....	60	34	15	35	.429	....	....	....	4	8	.500	....	....	16	2	10	0	....	....	....	6.0	3.4	1.6	0.2	.447
71-72	Pittsburgh-A	79	....	1059	448	182	381	.478	0	0	.000	84	115	.730	118	223	341	52	178	0	....	....	69	13.4	5.7	4.3	0.7	.509
73-74	Buffalo	20	....	51	30	11	27	.407	....	....	....	8	13	.615	4	7	11	0	10	0	1	1	....	2.6	1.5	0.6	0.0	.380

YEAR	TEAM	GP	GS	MIN	PTS	FGM	FGA	FG%	3PM	3PA	3P%	FTM	FTA	FT%	ORB	DRB	TRB	AST	PF	DQ	STL	BLK	TO	MPG	PPG	RPG	APG	PCM
74-75	Buffalo	22	....	103	45	22	47	.468	....	....	....	1	5	.200	12	10	22	7	22	0	3	3	....	4.7	2.0	1.0	0.3	.382
75-76	St. Louis-A	2	....	5	4	2	3	.667	0	0	.000	0	0	.000	1	2	3	0	0	....	0	0	0	2.5	2.0	1.5	0.0	1.156
NBA Season Totals		52	....	214	109	48	109	.440				13	26	.500	16	17	49	9	42	0	4	4	....	4.1	2.1	0.9	0.2	....
ABA Season Totals		81	....	1064	452	184	384	.479	0	0	.000	84	115	.730	119	225	344	52	178	0	0	0	69	13.1	5.6	4.2	0.6	....
Career Totals		133	....	1278	561	232	493	.471	0	0	.000	97	141	.688	135	242	393	61	220	0	4	4	69	9.6	4.2	3.0	0.5	....
70-71	Chicago	1	....	3	0	0	5	.000	....	....	....	0	0	.000	....	....	2	0	0	0	....	....	....	3.0	0.0	2.0	0.0	-.860
74-75	Buffalo	1	....	4	0	0	1	.000	....	....	....	0	0	.000	0	2	2	0	0	0	0	0	....	4.0	0.0	2.0	0.0	.213
NBA Playoff Totals		2	....	7	0	0	6	.000				0	0	.000	0	2	4	0	0	0	0	0	....	3.5	0.0	2.0	0.0	....

• RUH, Clem
Clemens Ruh

Born: Oct. 31, 1915. Died: Oct.5, 1973.   Height: 5'10".   Weight: 165 lbs.   Drafted: —   College: Southern California

YEAR	TEAM	GP	GS	MIN	PTS	FGM	FGA	FG%	3PM	3PA	3P%	FTM	FTA	FT%	ORB	DRB	TRB	AST	PF	DQ	STL	BLK	TO	MPG	PPG	RPG	APG	PCM
40-41	Hammond-N	21	....	....	77	26	....	....	....	....	....	25	....	....	....	....	....	....	....	....	....	....	....	....	3.7	....	....	....
NBL Season Totals		21	....	....	77	26	....	....	....	....	....	25	....	....	....	....	....	....	....	....	....	....	....	....	3.7	....	....	....

• RUKLICK, Joe
Joseph Ruklick

Born: Aug. 3, 1938. Princeton, IL, United States.   Height: 6'9".   Weight: 220 lbs.   Drafted: 1959   College: Northwestern

YEAR	TEAM	GP	GS	MIN	PTS	FGM	FGA	FG%	3PM	3PA	3P%	FTM	FTA	FT%	ORB	DRB	TRB	AST	PF	DQ	STL	BLK	TO	MPG	PPG	RPG	APG	PCM
59-60	Philadelphia	39	....	384	196	85	214	.397	....	....	....	26	36	.722	....	....	137	24	70	0	....	....	....	9.8	5.0	3.5	0.6	.525
60-61	Philadelphia	29	....	223	94	43	120	.358	....	....	....	8	13	.615	....	....	62	10	38	0	....	....	....	7.7	3.2	2.1	0.3	.353
61-62	Philadelphia	46	....	302	108	48	147	.327	....	....	....	12	26	.462	....	....	87	14	56	1	....	....	....	6.6	2.3	1.9	0.3	.293
NBA Season Totals		114	....	909	398	176	481	.366				46	75	.613			286	48	164	1				8.0	3.5	2.5	0.4	....
59-60	Philadelphia	4	....	15	4	2	9	.222	....	....	....	0	0	.000	....	....	5	0	3	0	....	....	....	3.8	1.0	1.3	0.0	.090
61-62	Philadelphia	2	....	8	3	1	4	.250	....	....	....	1	2	.500	....	....	4	0	2	0	....	....	....	4.0	1.5	2.0	0.0	.326
NBA Playoff Totals		6	....	23	7	3	13	.231				1	2	.500			9	0	5	0				3.8	1.2	1.5	0.0	....

• RULAND, Jeff
Jeffrey Alan Ruland

Born: Dec. 16, 1958. Bayshore, NY, United States.   Height: 6'10".   Weight: 240 lbs.   Drafted: 1980   College: Iona

YEAR	TEAM	GP	GS	MIN	PTS	FGM	FGA	FG%	3PM	3PA	3P%	FTM	FTA	FT%	ORB	DRB	TRB	AST	PF	DQ	STL	BLK	TO	MPG	PPG	RPG	APG	PCM
81-82	Washington	82	0	2214	1183	420	749	.561	1	3	.333	342	455	.752	253	509	762	134	319	7	44	58	238	27.0	14.4	9.3	1.6	.633
82-83	Washington	79	47	2862	1536	580	1051	.552	1	3	.333	375	544	.689	293	578	871	234	312	12	74	77	300	36.2	19.4	11.0	3.0	.630
83-84	Washington	75	75	**3082**	1665	599	1035	.579	1	7	.143	466	636	.733	265	657	922	296	285	8	68	72	**345**	41.1	22.2	12.3	3.9	.659
84-85	Washington	37	36	1436	700	250	439	.569	0	2	.000	200	292	.685	127	283	410	162	128	2	31	27	178	38.8	18.9	11.1	4.4	.602
85-86	Washington	30	24	1114	569	212	383	.554	0	4	.000	145	200	.725	107	213	320	159	100	1	23	25	120	37.1	19.0	10.7	5.3	.663
86-87	Philadelphia	5	2	116	47	19	28	.679	0	0	.000	9	12	.750	12	16	28	10	13	0	4	0	10	23.2	9.4	5.6	2.0	.537
91-92	Philadelphia	13	5	209	51	20	38	.526	0	0	.000	11	16	.688	16	31	47	5	45	0	7	4	20	16.1	3.9	3.6	0.4	.247
92-93	Detroit	11	0	55	12	5	11	.455	0	0	.000	2	4	.500	9	9	18	2	16	0	2	0	6	5.0	1.1	1.6	0.2	.240
NBA Season Totals		332	189	11088	5763	2105	3734	.564	3	19	.158	1550	2159	.718	1082	2296	3378	1002	1218	30	249	267	1217	33.4	17.4	10.2	3.0	....
81-82	Washington	7	0	237	119	38	79	.481	0	1	.000	43	56	.768	29	37	66	5	24	1	3	4	23	33.9	17.0	9.4	0.7	.488
83-84	Washington	4	4	187	96	37	71	.521	0	1	.000	22	27	.815	16	35	51	31	15	0	2	3	19	46.8	24.0	12.8	7.8	.656
84-85	Washington	4	3	162	70	28	47	.596	0	2	.000	14	20	.700	12	22	34	21	15	0	9	4	23	40.5	17.5	8.5	5.3	.539
85-86	Washington	2	0	54	28	7	14	.500	0	0	.000	14	17	.824	5	7	12	10	6	0	0	2	6	27.0	14.0	6.0	5.0	.657
NBA Playoff Totals		17	7	640	313	110	211	.521	0	4	.000	93	120	.775	62	101	163	67	60	1	14	13	71	37.6	18.4	9.6	3.9	....

• RULE, Bob
Bobby Frank (Golden) Rule

Born: June 29, 1944. Riverside, CA, United States.   Height: 6'9".   Weight: 220 lbs.   Drafted: 1967   College: Colorado State

YEAR	TEAM	GP	GS	MIN	PTS	FGM	FGA	FG%	3PM	3PA	3P%	FTM	FTA	FT%	ORB	DRB	TRB	AST	PF	DQ	STL	BLK	TO	MPG	PPG	RPG	APG	PCM
67-68	Seattle	82	....	2424	1484	568	1162	.489	....	....	....	348	529	.658	....	....	776	99	316	10	....	....	....	29.6	18.1	9.5	1.2	.639
68-69	Seattle	82	....	3104	1965	776	1655	.469	....	....	....	413	606	.682	....	....	941	141	322	8	....	....	....	37.9	24.0	11.5	1.7	.633
69-70	Seattle	80	....	2959	1965	789	1705	.463	....	....	....	387	542	.714	....	....	825	144	278	6	....	....	....	37.0	24.6	10.3	1.8	.627
70-71	Seattle	4	....	142	119	47	98	.480	....	....	....	25	30	.833	....	....	46	7	14	0	....	....	....	35.5	29.8	11.5	1.8	.806
71-72	Seattle	16	....	243	113	45	124	.363	....	....	....	23	43	.535	....	....	55	6	27	0	....	....	....	15.2	7.1	3.4	0.4	.324
71-72	Philadelphia	60	....	1987	1035	416	934	.445	....	....	....	203	292	.695	....	....	479	110	162	4	....	....	....	33.1	17.3	8.0	1.8	.512
72-73	Philadelphia	3	....	12	0	0	1	.000	....	....	....	0	0	.000	....	....	2	1	2	0	....	....	....	4.0	0.0	0.7	0.3	.095
72-73	Cleveland	49	....	440	140	60	157	.382	....	....	....	20	31	.645	....	....	106	37	66	0	....	....	....	9.0	2.9	2.2	0.8	.357
73-74	Cleveland	26	....	540	186	76	192	.396	....	....	....	34	46	.739	43	60	103	47	71	0	12	10	....	20.8	7.2	4.0	1.8	.359
74-75	Milwaukee	1	....	11	0	0	1	.000	....	....	....	0	0	.000	0	0	0	2	2	0	0	0	....	11.0	0.0	0.0	2.0	.053
NBA Season Totals		403	....	11862	7007	2777	6029	.461	....		....	1453	2119	.686	43	60	3333	594	1260	28	12	10	....	29.4	17.4	8.3	1.5	....

• RULLO, Jerry
Generoso Charles Rullo

Born: June 23, 1923.   Height: 5'10".   Weight: 165 lbs.   Drafted: —   College: Temple

YEAR	TEAM	GP	GS	MIN	PTS	FGM	FGA	FG%	3PM	3PA	3P%	FTM	FTA	FT%	ORB	DRB	TRB	AST	PF	DQ	STL	BLK	TO	MPG	PPG	RPG	APG	PCM
46-47	Philadelphia	50	....	....	127	52	174	.299	....	....	....	23	47	.489	....	....	....	20	61	....	....	....	....	....	2.5	....	0.4	....
47-48	Baltimore	2	....	....	0	0	4	.000	....	....	....	0	0	.000	....	....	....	0	1	....	....	....	....	....	0.0	....	0.0	....
48-49	Philadelphia	39	....	....	137	53	183	.290	....	....	....	31	45	.689	....	....	....	48	71	....	....	....	....	....	3.5	....	1.2	....
49-50	Philadelphia	4	....	....	7	3	9	.333	....	....	....	1	1	1.000	....	....	....	2	2	....	....	....	....	....	1.8	....	0.5	....
NBA Season Totals		95	....	....	271	108	370	.292				55	93	.591				70	135	....				....	2.9	....	0.7	....
46-47	Philadelphia	7	....	....	7	3	13	.231	....	....	....	1	1	1.000	....	....	....	0	1	....	....	....	....	....	1.0	....	0.0	....
48-49	Philadelphia	2	....	....	6	2	8	.250	....	....	....	2	2	1.000	....	....	....	1	9	....	....	....	....	....	3.0	....	0.5	....
NBA Playoff Totals		9	....	....	13	5	21	.238				3	3	1.000				1	10	....				....	1.4	....	0.1	....

YEAR	TEAM	GP	GS	MIN	PTS	FGM	FGA	FG%	3PM	3PA	3P%	FTM	FTA	FT%	ORB	DRB	TRB	AST	PF	DQ	STL	BLK	TO	MPG	PPG	RPG	APG	PCM

• RUNG, George

George Rung

Born: May 27, 1916. Died: Sept.29, 1996. Height: 6' Weight: 185 lbs. Drafted: — College: Miami (OH)

45-46	Cleveland-N	10	....	....	12	4	....	....	....	....	....	4	....	....	....	....	....	....	....	....	....	....	....	....	1.2	....	....	....
45-46	Indianapolis-N	3	....	....	8	4	....	....	....	....	....	0	0	.000	....	....	....	....	....	....	....	....	....	....	2.7	....	....	....
NBL Season Totals		13	....	....	20	8	....	....	....	....	....	4	0	....	....	....	....	....	....	....	....	....	....	....	1.5	....	....	....

• RUSCONI, Stefano

Stefano (Rusca) Rusconi

Born: Oct. 2, 1968. Bassanod'Grappa, Italy. Height: 6'9". Weight: 240 lbs. Drafted: 1990 College: —

95-96	Phoenix	7	0	30	8	3	9	.333	0	0	.000	2	5	.400	3	3	6	3	10	0	0	2	3	4.3	1.1	0.9	0.4	.138
NBA Season Totals		7	0	30	8	3	9	.333	0	0	.000	2	5	.400	3	3	6	3	10	0	0	2	3	4.3	1.1	0.9	0.4	....

• RUSH, Kareem

Kareem Lamar Rush

Born: Oct. 30, 1980. Kansas City, MO, United States. Height: 6'6". Weight: 215 lbs. Drafted: 2002 College: Missouri

02-03	LA Lakers	76	0	872	227	96	244	.393	19	68	.279	16	23	.696	26	68	94	68	71	0	10	11	63	11.5	3.0	1.2	0.9	.205
NBA Season Totals		76	0	872	227	96	244	.393	19	68	.279	16	23	.696	26	68	94	68	71	0	10	11	63	11.5	3.0	1.2	0.9	....
02-03	LA Lakers	9	0	64	30	11	29	.379	4	11	.364	4	4	1.000	2	1	3	2	2	0	1	0	3	7.1	3.3	0.3	0.2	.248
NBA Playoff Totals		9	0	64	30	11	29	.379	4	11	.364	4	4	1.000	2	1	3	2	2	0	1	0	3	7.1	3.3	0.3	0.2	....

• RUSH, Mal

Mal Rush

Born: Apr. 2, 1909. Died: Jan.1, 1989. Height: 6' Weight: 170 lbs. Drafted: — College: Bethany (WV)

37-38	Wingfoots-N	7	....	....	18	6	....	....	....	....	....	6	....	....	....	....	....	....	....	....	....	....	....	....	2.6	....	....	....
NBL Season Totals		7	....	....	18	6	....	....	....	....	....	6	....	....	....	....	....	....	....	....	....	....	....	....	2.6	....	....	....
37-38	Wingfoots-N	4	....	....	11	4	....	....	....	....	....	3	....	....	....	....	....	....	....	....	....	....	....	....	2.8	....	....	....
NBL Playoff Totals		4	....	....	11	4	....	....	....	....	....	3	....	....	....	....	....	....	....	....	....	....	....	....	2.8	....	....	....

• RUSSELL, Bill

William Felton Russell

Born: Feb. 12, 1934. Monroe, LA, United States. Height: 6'9". Weight: 215 lbs. Drafted: 1956 College: San Francisco HOF: 1975

56-57	Boston	48	....	1695	706	277	649	.427	....	....	....	152	309	.492	....	....	943	88	143	2	....	....	....	35.3	14.7	19.6	1.8	.667
57-58	Boston	69	....	2640	1142	456	1032	.442	....	....	....	230	443	.519	....	....	**1564**	202	181	2	....	....	....	38.3	16.6	**22.7**	2.9	.748
58-59	Boston	70	....	**2979**	1168	456	997	.457	....	....	....	256	428	.598	....	....	**1612**	222	161	3	....	....	....	**42.6**	16.7	**23.0**	3.2	.713
59-60	Boston	74	....	3146	1350	555	1189	.467	....	....	....	240	392	.612	....	....	1778	277	210	0	....	....	....	42.5	18.2	24.0	3.7	.770
60-61	Boston	78	....	3458	1322	532	1250	.426	....	....	....	258	469	.550	....	....	1868	268	155	0	....	....	....	44.3	16.9	23.9	3.4	.691
61-62	Boston	76	....	3433	1436	575	1258	.457	....	....	....	286	481	.595	....	....	1790	341	207	3	....	....	....	45.2	18.9	23.6	4.5	.745
62-63	Boston	78	....	3500	1309	511	1182	.432	....	....	....	287	517	.555	....	....	1843	348	189	1	....	....	....	44.9	16.8	23.6	4.5	.712
63-64	Boston	78	....	3482	1168	466	1077	.433	....	....	....	236	429	.550	....	....	**1930**	370	190	0	....	....	....	44.6	15.0	**24.7**	4.7	.717
64-65	Boston	78	....	**3466**	1102	429	980	.438	....	....	....	244	426	.573	....	....	**1878**	410	204	1	....	....	....	44.4	14.1	**24.1**	5.3	.715
65-66	Boston	78	....	3386	1005	391	943	.415	....	....	....	223	405	.551	....	....	1779	371	221	4	....	....	....	43.4	12.9	22.8	4.8	.667
66-67	Boston	81	....	3297	1075	395	870	.454	....	....	....	285	467	.610	....	....	1700	472	258	4	....	....	....	40.7	13.3	21.0	5.8	.741
67-68	Boston	78	....	2953	977	365	858	.425	....	....	....	247	460	.537	....	....	1451	357	242	2	....	....	....	37.9	12.5	18.6	4.6	.674
68-69	Boston	77	....	3291	762	279	645	.433	....	....	....	204	388	.526	....	....	1484	374	231	2	....	....	....	42.7	9.9	19.3	4.9	.595
NBA Season Totals		963	....	40726	14522	5687	12930	.440	....	....	....	3148	5614	.561	....	....	21620	4100	2592	24	....	....	....	42.3	15.1	22.5	4.3	....
56-57	Boston	10	....	409	139	54	148	.365	....	....	....	31	61	.508	....	....	244	32	41	1	....	....	....	40.9	13.9	24.4	3.2	.647
57-58	Boston	9	....	355	136	48	133	.361	....	....	....	40	66	.606	....	....	221	24	24	0	....	....	....	39.4	15.1	24.6	2.7	.697
58-59	Boston	11	....	496	171	65	159	.409	....	....	....	41	67	.612	....	....	305	40	28	1	....	....	....	45.1	15.5	27.7	3.6	.724
59-60	Boston	13	....	572	241	94	206	.456	....	....	....	53	75	.707	....	....	336	38	38	1	....	....	....	44.0	18.5	25.8	2.9	.760
60-61	Boston	10	....	462	191	73	171	.427	....	....	....	45	86	.523	....	....	299	48	24	0	....	....	....	46.2	19.1	29.9	4.8	.820
61-62	Boston	14	....	672	314	116	253	.458	....	....	....	82	113	.726	....	....	370	70	49	0	....	....	....	48.0	22.4	26.4	5.0	.819
62-63	Boston	13	....	617	264	96	212	.453	....	....	....	72	109	.661	....	....	326	66	36	0	....	....	....	47.5	20.3	25.1	5.1	.780
63-64	Boston	10	....	451	131	47	132	.356	....	....	....	37	67	.552	....	....	272	44	23	0	....	....	....	45.1	13.1	27.2	4.4	.687
64-65	Boston	12	....	561	198	79	150	.527	....	....	....	40	76	.526	....	....	302	76	43	2	....	....	....	46.8	16.5	25.2	6.3	.782
65-66	Boston	17	....	814	324	124	261	.475	....	....	....	76	123	.618	....	....	428	85	60	0	....	....	....	47.9	19.1	25.2	5.0	.754
66-67	Boston	9	....	390	95	31	86	.360	....	....	....	33	52	.635	....	....	198	50	32	1	....	....	....	43.3	10.6	22.0	5.6	.638
67-68	Boston	19	....	869	274	99	242	.409	....	....	....	76	130	.585	....	....	434	99	73	1	....	....	....	45.7	14.4	22.8	5.2	.661
68-69	Boston	18	....	829	195	77	182	.423	....	....	....	41	81	.506	....	....	369	98	65	1	....	....	....	46.1	10.8	20.5	5.4	.586
NBA Playoff Totals		165	....	7497	2673	1003	2335	.430	....	....	....	667	1106	.603	....	....	**4104**	770	536	8	....	....	....	45.4	16.2	**24.9**	4.7	....

• RUSSELL, Bryon

Bryon Demetrise Russell

Born: Dec. 31, 1970. San Bernardino, CA, United States. Height: 6'7". Weight: 225 lbs. Drafted: 1993 College: Long Beach State

93-94	Utah	67	48	1121	334	135	279	.484	2	22	.091	62	101	.614	61	120	181	54	138	0	68	19	54	16.7	5.0	2.7	0.8	.335
94-95	Utah	63	15	860	283	104	238	.437	13	44	.295	62	93	.667	44	97	141	34	101	0	48	11	44	13.7	4.5	2.2	0.5	.323
95-96	Utah	59	9	577	174	56	142	.394	14	40	.350	48	67	.716	28	62	90	29	66	0	29	8	35	9.8	2.9	1.5	0.5	.295
96-97	Utah	81	81	2525	873	297	620	.479	108	264	.409	171	244	.701	79	252	331	123	237	2	129	27	97	31.2	10.8	4.1	1.5	.365
97-98	Utah	82	7	2219	738	226	525	.430	73	214	.341	213	278	.766	78	248	326	101	229	2	90	31	82	27.1	9.0	4.0	1.2	.349
98-99	Utah	50	50	1770	622	217	468	.464	52	147	.354	136	171	.795	65	201	266	74	154	3	76	15	76	35.4	12.4	5.3	1.5	.365
99-00	Utah	82	70	2900	1159	408	914	.446	106	268	.396	237	316	.750	99	328	427	158	255	3	128	23	101	35.4	14.1	5.2	1.9	.398
00-01	Utah	78	46	2473	933	308	700	.440	95	230	.413	222	285	.779	94	236	330	160	229	1	96	20	113	31.7	12.0	4.2	2.1	.374
01-02	Utah	66	40	1998	636	222	584	.380	77	226	.341	115	140	.821	79	216	295	136	205	1	64	19	110	30.3	9.6	4.5	2.1	.298
02-03	Washington	70	23	1387	315	108	306	.353	46	140	.329	53	69	.768	43	165	208	72	130	1	70	7	55	19.8	4.5	3.0	1.0	.257
NBA Season Totals		698	389	17830	6067	2081	4776	.436	586	1595	.367	1319	1764	.748	670	1925	2595	941	1744	13	798	180	767	25.5	8.7	3.7	1.3	....

YEAR	TEAM	GP	GS	MIN	PTS	FGM	FGA	FG%	3PM	3PA	3P%	FTM	FTA	FT%	ORB	DRB	TRB	AST	PF	DQ	STL	BLK	TO	MPG	PPG	RPG	APG	PCM
93-94	Utah	6	0	36	16	4	10	.400	2	3	.667	6	6	1.000	4	5	9	3	3	0	0	0	1	6.0	2.7	1.5	0.5	.547
94-95	Utah	2	0	13	11	4	7	.571	2	4	.500	1	2	.500	1	1	2	3	2	0	1	0	0	6.5	5.5	1.0	1.5	.983
95-96	Utah	18	0	459	172	58	124	.468	25	53	.472	31	38	.816	17	58	75	22	43	0	23	9	10	25.5	9.6	4.2	1.2	.438
96-97	Utah	20	20	758	245	89	193	.461	36	101	.356	31	43	.721	18	74	92	27	59	1	21	6	20	37.9	12.3	4.6	1.4	.311
97-98	Utah	20	13	698	219	69	147	.469	23	63	.365	58	81	.716	12	81	93	22	49	0	21	5	17	34.9	11.0	4.7	1.1	.332
98-99	Utah	11	11	387	133	49	115	.426	9	36	.250	26	36	.722	17	50	67	13	37	0	20	2	11	35.2	12.1	6.1	1.2	.355
99-00	Utah	10	10	371	140	48	114	.421	13	45	.289	31	41	.756	9	43	52	21	27	0	16	5	15	37.1	14.0	5.2	2.1	.374
00-01	Utah	5	5	214	71	25	56	.446	10	22	.455	11	12	.917	4	32	36	15	13	0	3	1	2	42.8	14.2	7.2	3.0	.409
01-02	Utah	4	4	120	28	9	36	.250	6	15	.400	4	4	1.000	6	11	17	7	15	1	4	0	9	30.0	7.0	4.3	1.8	.127
NBA Playoff Totals		96	63	3056	1035	355	802	.443	126	342	.368	199	263	.757	88	355	443	133	248	2	109	28	85	31.8	10.8	4.6	1.4	....

• RUSSELL, Campy

Michael Campanella (Campy, Mr. Moves) Russell

Born: Jan. 12, 1952. Jackson, TN, United States.   Height: 6'8".   Weight: 215 lbs.   Drafted: 1974   College: Michigan

YEAR	TEAM	GP	GS	MIN	PTS	FGM	FGA	FG%	3PM	3PA	3P%	FTM	FTA	FT%	ORB	DRB	TRB	AST	PF	DQ	STL	BLK	TO	MPG	PPG	RPG	APG	PCM
74-75	Cleveland	68	....	754	424	150	365	.411	....	....	....	124	165	.752	43	109	152	45	100	0	21	3	....	11.1	6.2	2.2	0.7	.480
75-76	Cleveland	82	....	1961	1232	483	1003	.482	....	....	....	266	344	.773	134	211	345	107	231	5	69	10	....	23.9	15.0	4.2	1.3	.546
76-77	Cleveland	70	....	2109	1158	435	1003	.434	....	....	....	288	370	.778	144	275	419	189	196	3	70	24	....	30.1	16.5	6.0	2.7	.533
77-78	Cleveland	72	....	2520	1398	523	1168	.448	....	....	....	352	469	.751	154	304	458	278	193	3	88	12	209	35.0	19.4	6.4	3.9	.522
78-79	Cleveland	74	....	2859	1623	603	1268	.476	....	....	....	417	523	.797	147	356	503	348	222	2	98	25	259	38.6	21.9	6.8	4.7	.557
79-80	Cleveland	41	....	1331	747	284	630	.451	1	9	.111	178	239	.745	76	149	225	173	113	1	72	20	148	32.5	18.2	5.5	4.2	.524
80-81	New York	79	....	2865	1292	508	1095	.464	8	26	.308	268	343	.781	109	244	353	257	248	2	99	8	213	36.3	16.4	4.5	3.3	.389
81-82	New York	77	63	2358	1073	410	858	.478	25	57	**.439**	228	294	.776	86	150	236	284	221	1	77	12	193	30.6	13.9	3.1	3.7	.406
84-85	Cleveland	3	0	24	6	2	7	.286	0	1	.000	2	3	.667	0	5	5	3	3	0	0	0	5	8.0	2.0	1.7	1.0	.112
NBA Season Totals		566	63	16781	8953	3398	7397	.459	34	93	.366	2123	2750	.772	893	1803	2696	1684	1527	17	594	114	1027	29.6	15.8	4.8	3.0	....
75-76	Cleveland	13	....	328	177	65	161	.404	....	....	....	47	55	.855	25	46	71	14	51	0	8	7	....	25.2	13.6	5.5	1.1	.446
76-77	Cleveland	3	....	100	53	21	54	.389	....	....	....	11	15	.733	10	16	26	10	10	0	3	1	....	33.3	17.7	8.7	3.3	.523
77-78	Cleveland	2	....	88	55	19	39	.487	....	....	....	17	21	.810	7	8	15	11	9	0	3	1	10	44.0	27.5	7.5	5.5	.592
80-81	New York	2	....	89	46	15	34	.441	0	2	.000	16	17	.941	1	8	9	9	9	0	4	1	8	44.5	23.0	4.5	4.5	.443
NBA Playoff Totals		20	....	605	331	120	288	.417	0	2	.000	91	108	.843	43	78	121	44	79	0	18	10	18	30.3	16.6	6.1	2.2	....

• RUSSELL, Cazzie

Cazzie Lee Russell Jr.

Born: June 7, 1944. Chicago, IL, United States.   Height: 6'5".   Weight: 218 lbs.   Drafted: 1966   College: Michigan

YEAR	TEAM	GP	GS	MIN	PTS	FGM	FGA	FG%	3PM	3PA	3P%	FTM	FTA	FT%	ORB	DRB	TRB	AST	PF	DQ	STL	BLK	TO	MPG	PPG	RPG	APG	PCM
66-67	New York	77	....	1696	867	344	789	.436	....	....	....	179	228	.785	....	....	251	187	174	1	....	....	....	22.0	11.3	3.3	2.4	.500
67-68	New York	82	....	2296	1384	551	1192	.462	....	....	....	282	349	.808	....	....	374	195	223	2	....	....	....	28.0	16.9	4.6	2.4	.562
68-69	New York	50	....	1645	915	362	804	.450	....	....	....	191	240	.796	....	....	209	115	140	1	....	....	....	32.9	18.3	4.2	2.3	.471
69-70	New York	78	....	1563	894	385	773	.498	....	....	....	124	160	.775	....	....	236	135	137	0	....	....	....	20.0	11.5	3.0	1.7	.534
70-71	New York	57	....	1056	524	216	504	.429	....	....	....	92	119	.773	....	....	192	77	74	0	....	....	....	18.5	9.2	3.4	1.4	.460
71-72	Golden State	79	....	2902	1693	689	1514	.455	....	....	....	315	378	.833	....	....	428	248	176	0	....	....	....	36.7	21.4	5.4	3.1	.527
72-73	Golden State	80	....	2429	1254	541	1182	.458	....	....	....	172	199	.864	....	....	350	187	171	0	....	....	....	30.4	15.7	4.4	2.3	.466
73-74	Golden State	82	....	2574	1684	738	1531	.482	....	....	....	208	249	.835	142	211	353	192	194	1	54	17	....	31.4	20.5	4.3	2.3	.556
74-75	LA Lakers	40	....	1055	629	264	580	.455	....	....	....	101	113	.894	34	81	115	109	56	0	27	2	....	26.4	15.7	2.9	2.7	.525
75-76	LA Lakers	74	....	1625	874	371	802	.463	....	....	....	132	148	.892	50	133	183	122	122	0	53	3	....	22.0	11.8	2.5	1.6	.456
76-77	LA Lakers	82	....	2583	1344	578	1179	.490	....	....	....	188	219	.858	86	208	294	210	163	1	86	7	....	31.5	16.4	3.6	2.6	.478
77-78	Chicago	36	....	789	315	133	304	.438	....	....	....	49	57	.860	31	52	83	61	63	1	19	4	36	21.9	8.8	2.3	1.7	.335
NBA Season Totals		817	....	22213	12377	5172	11154	.464	....	....	....	2033	2459	.827	343	685	3068	1838	1693	7	239	33	36	27.2	15.1	3.8	2.2	....
66-67	New York	4	....	89	62	26	66	.394	....	....	....	10	13	.769	....	....	19	11	16	1	....	....	....	22.3	15.5	4.8	2.8	.572
67-68	New York	6	....	209	130	55	98	.561	....	....	....	20	24	.833	....	....	23	10	16	0	....	....	....	34.8	21.7	3.8	1.7	.565
68-69	New York	5	....	36	12	5	21	.238	....	....	....	2	2	1.000	....	....	5	1	4	0	....	....	....	7.2	2.4	1.0	0.2	.064
69-70	New York	19	....	306	178	80	165	.485	....	....	....	18	19	.947	....	....	47	16	31	0	....	....	....	16.1	9.4	2.5	0.8	.485
70-71	New York	11	....	120	62	25	64	.391	....	....	....	12	12	1.000	....	....	22	8	14	0	....	....	....	10.9	5.6	2.0	0.7	.421
71-72	Golden State	5	....	161	71	31	63	.492	....	....	....	9	12	.750	....	....	22	9	13	0	....	....	....	32.2	14.2	4.4	1.8	.408
72-73	Golden State	11	....	263	163	72	147	.490	....	....	....	19	22	.864	....	....	36	17	24	0	....	....	....	23.9	14.8	3.3	1.5	.522
76-77	LA Lakers	11	....	382	174	65	157	.414	....	....	....	44	50	.880	22	26	48	25	33	0	16	1	....	34.7	15.8	4.4	2.3	.386
NBA Playoff Totals		72	....	1566	852	359	781	.460	....	....	....	134	154	.870	22	26	222	97	151	1	16	1	....	21.8	11.8	3.1	1.3	....

• RUSSELL, Frank

Frank Russell

Born: Apr. 17, 1949.   Height: 6'3".   Weight: 180 lbs.   Drafted: 1972   College: Detroit

YEAR	TEAM	GP	GS	MIN	PTS	FGM	FGA	FG%	3PM	3PA	3P%	FTM	FTA	FT%	ORB	DRB	TRB	AST	PF	DQ	STL	BLK	TO	MPG	PPG	RPG	APG	PCM
72-73	Chicago	23	....	131	74	29	77	.377	....	....	....	16	18	.889	....	....	17	15	12	0	....	....	....	5.7	3.2	0.7	0.7	.447
NBA Season Totals		23	....	131	74	29	77	.377	....	....	....	16	18	.889	....	....	17	15	12	0	....	....	....	5.7	3.2	0.7	0.7	

• RUSSELL, Pierre

Pierre Angelo Russell

Born: Dec. 13, 1949. Kansas City, KS, United States.   Height: 6'4".   Weight: 190 lbs.   Drafted: 1971   College: Kansas

YEAR	TEAM	GP	GS	MIN	PTS	FGM	FGA	FG%	3PM	3PA	3P%	FTM	FTA	FT%	ORB	DRB	TRB	AST	PF	DQ	STL	BLK	TO	MPG	PPG	RPG	APG	PCM
71-72	Kentucky-A	51	....	397	146	65	153	.425	0	3	.000	16	21	.762	40	53	93	51	56	1	....	....	33	7.8	2.9	1.8	1.0	.455
72-73	Kentucky-A	59	....	618	289	119	266	.447	2	17	.118	49	78	.628	54	75	129	61	80	0	....	....	33	10.5	4.9	2.2	1.0	.471
ABA Season Totals		110	....	1015	435	184	419	.439	2	20	.100	65	99	.657	94	128	222	112	136	1	....	....	66	9.2	4.0	2.0	1.0	....
72-73	Kentucky-A	12	....	37	17	7	12	.583	0	0	.000	3	6	.500	5	7	12	2	5	0	....	....	1	3.1	1.4	1.0	0.2	.592
ABA Playoff Totals		12	....	37	17	7	12	.583	0	0	.000	3	6	.500	5	7	12	2	5	0	....	....	1	3.1	1.4	1.0	0.2	....

YEAR	TEAM	GP	GS	MIN	PTS	FGM	FGA	FG%	3PM	3PA	3P%	FTM	FTA	FT%	ORB	DRB	TRB	AST	PF	DQ	STL	BLK	TO	MPG	PPG	RPG	APG	PCM

• RUSSELL, Rubin

Rubin B. Russell Jr.

Born: Nov. 7, 1944. Fort Worth, TX, United States.   Height: 6'2".   Weight: 180 lbs.   Drafted: 1967   College: North Texas State

YEAR	TEAM	GP	GS	MIN	PTS	FGM	FGA	FG%	3PM	3PA	3P%	FTM	FTA	FT%	ORB	DRB	TRB	AST	PF	DQ	STL	BLK	TO	MPG	PPG	RPG	APG	PCM
67-68	Dallas-A	16	....	157	65	27	80	.338	2	13	.154	9	18	.500	....	....	23	6	18	0	....	....	23	9.8	4.1	1.4	0.4	.229
67-68	Kentucky-A	10	....	112	76	29	78	.372	2	9	.222	16	23	.696	....	....	29	1	22	0	....	....	9	11.2	7.6	2.9	0.1	.433
ABA Season Totals		26	....	269	141	56	158	.354	4	22	.182	25	41	.610	....	....	52	7	40	0	....	....	32	10.3	5.4	2.0	0.3	....

• RUSSELL, Walker

Walker D. Russell

Born: Oct. 26, 1960. Pontiac, MI, United States.   Height: 6'5".   Weight: 195 lbs.   Drafted: 1982   College: Western Michigan

YEAR	TEAM	GP	GS	MIN	PTS	FGM	FGA	FG%	3PM	3PA	3P%	FTM	FTA	FT%	ORB	DRB	TRB	AST	PF	DQ	STL	BLK	TO	MPG	PPG	RPG	APG	PCM
82-83	Detroit	68	1	757	183	67	184	.364	2	18	.111	47	58	.810	19	54	73	131	71	0	16	1	95	11.1	2.7	1.1	1.9	.238
83-84	Atlanta	16	0	119	41	14	42	.333	1	2	.500	12	13	.923	6	13	19	22	25	0	4	0	10	7.4	2.6	1.2	1.4	.324
84-85	Atlanta	21	2	377	83	34	63	.540	1	1	1.000	14	17	.824	8	32	40	66	37	1	17	4	40	18.0	4.0	1.9	3.1	.338
85-86	Detroit	1	0	2	0	0	1	.000	0	0	.000	0	0	.000	0	0	0	1	0	0	0	0	0	2.0	0.0	0.0	1.0	.071
86-87	Indiana	48	0	511	157	64	165	.388	2	16	.125	27	37	.730	18	37	55	129	62	0	20	5	62	10.6	3.3	1.1	2.7	.360
87-88	Detroit	1	0	1	0	0	1	.000	0	1	.000	0	0	.000	0	0	0	1	0	0	0	0	0	1.0	0.0	0.0	1.0	.136
NBA Season Totals		155	3	1767	464	179	456	.393	6	38	.158	100	125	.800	51	136	187	350	195	1	57	10	207	11.4	3.0	1.2	2.3	....
87-88	Detroit	7	0	10	6	2	5	.400	0	0	.000	2	2	1.000	0	0	0	1	1	0	1	0	1	1.4	0.9	0.0	0.1	.381
NBA Playoff Totals		7	0	10	6	2	5	.400	0	0	.000	2	2	1.000	0	0	0	1	1	0	1	0	1	1.4	0.9	0.0	0.1	....

• RUTTER, Lou

Lou Rutter

Born: Aug. 14, 1914. Died: Nov.1971.   Height: 6'2".   Weight: 180 lbs.   Drafted: —   College: Otterbein

YEAR	TEAM	GP	GS	MIN	PTS	FGM	FGA	FG%	3PM	3PA	3P%	FTM	FTA	FT%	ORB	DRB	TRB	AST	PF	DQ	STL	BLK	TO	MPG	PPG	RPG	APG	PCM
37-38	Dayton-N	8	....	....	80	30	....	....	....	....	....	20	....	....	....	....	....	....	....	....	....	....	....	10.0	....	....	....	....
NBL Season Totals		8	....	....	80	30	....	....	....	....	....	20	....	....	....	....	....	....	....	....	....	....	....	10.0	....	....	....	....

• SABO, Frank

Frank Sabo

Born: 1922.   Height: 6'1".   Weight: 190 lbs.   Drafted: —   College: Wayne State (MI)

YEAR	TEAM	GP	GS	MIN	PTS	FGM	FGA	FG%	3PM	3PA	3P%	FTM	FTA	FT%	ORB	DRB	TRB	AST	PF	DQ	STL	BLK	TO	MPG	PPG	RPG	APG	PCM
46-47	Detroit-N	3	....	....	16	7	....	....	....	....	....	2	3	.667	....	....	....	....	....	....	....	....	....	5.3	....	....	....	....
NBL Season Totals		3	....	....	16	7	....	....	....	....	....	2	3	....	....	....	....	....	....	....	....	....	....	5.3	....	....	....	....

• SABONIS, Arvydas

Arvydas Sabonis

Born: Dec. 19, 1964. Kaunas, Lithuania.   Height: 7'3".   Weight: 279 lbs.   Drafted: —   College: none

YEAR	TEAM	GP	GS	MIN	PTS	FGM	FGA	FG%	3PM	3PA	3P%	FTM	FTA	FT%	ORB	DRB	TRB	AST	PF	DQ	STL	BLK	TO	MPG	PPG	RPG	APG	PCM
95-96	Portland	73	21	1735	1058	394	723	.545	39	104	.375	231	305	.757	147	441	588	130	211	2	64	78	153	23.8	14.5	8.1	1.8	.746
96-97	Portland	69	68	1762	928	328	658	.498	49	132	.371	223	287	.777	114	433	547	146	203	4	63	84	152	25.5	13.4	7.9	2.1	.657
97-98	Portland	73	73	2333	1167	407	826	.493	30	115	.261	323	405	.798	149	580	729	218	267	7	65	80	190	32.0	16.0	10.0	3.0	.637
98-99	Portland	50	48	1349	606	232	478	.485	7	24	.292	135	175	.771	88	305	393	119	147	2	34	63	85	27.0	12.1	7.9	2.4	.590
99-00	Portland	66	61	1688	778	302	598	.505	7	19	.368	167	198	.843	97	416	513	118	184	3	43	78	97	25.6	11.8	7.8	1.8	.609
00-01	Portland	61	42	1299	616	247	516	.479	1	15	.067	121	156	.776	51	280	331	91	137	2	40	62	85	21.3	10.1	5.4	1.5	.547
02-03	Portland	78	1	1209	476	172	361	.476	3	6	.500	129	164	.787	88	247	335	142	141	0	61	49	75	15.5	6.1	4.3	1.8	.592
NBA Season Totals		470	314	11375	5629	2082	4160	.500	136	415	.328	1329	1690	.786	734	2702	3436	964	1290	20	370	494	837	24.2	12.0	7.3	2.1	....
95-96	Portland	5	5	177	118	35	81	.432	5	9	.556	43	60	.717	12	39	51	9	17	0	4	3	10	35.4	23.6	10.2	1.8	.641
96-97	Portland	4	4	108	45	18	42	.429	2	8	.250	7	8	.875	8	18	26	9	19	1	3	3	9	27.0	11.3	6.5	2.3	.411
97-98	Portland	4	4	107	49	18	40	.450	1	2	.500	12	14	.857	7	24	31	6	19	1	7	3	10	26.8	12.3	7.8	1.5	.506
98-99	Portland	13	13	392	130	45	113	.398	1	5	.200	39	43	.907	12	102	114	29	35	0	15	15	19	30.2	10.0	8.8	2.2	.499
99-00	Portland	16	16	493	181	68	150	.453	6	21	.286	39	49	.796	19	88	107	31	59	2	14	13	26	30.8	11.3	6.7	1.9	.420
00-01	Portland	3	3	104	34	14	29	.483	0	2	.000	6	8	.750	8	17	25	8	12	0	1	7	2	34.7	11.3	8.3	2.7	.489
02-03	Portland	6	1	86	60	24	36	.667	0	0	.000	12	15	.800	6	18	24	5	14	1	4	4	6	14.3	10.0	4.0	0.8	.819
NBA Playoff Totals		51	46	1467	617	222	491	.452	15	47	.319	158	197	.802	72	306	378	97	175	5	48	48	82	28.8	12.1	7.4	1.9	....

• SACHS, Ed

Ed Sachs

Born: 1918.   Height: 6'2".   Weight: 175 lbs.   Drafted: —   College: DePaul

YEAR	TEAM	GP	GS	MIN	PTS	FGM	FGA	FG%	3PM	3PA	3P%	FTM	FTA	FT%	ORB	DRB	TRB	AST	PF	DQ	STL	BLK	TO	MPG	PPG	RPG	APG	PCM
41-42	Chicago-N	8	....	....	20	8	....	....	....	....	....	4	....	....	....	....	....	....	....	....	....	....	....	2.5	....	....	....	....
NBL Season Totals		8	....	....	20	8	....	....	....	....	....	4	....	....	....	....	....	....	....	....	....	....	....	2.5	....	....	....	....

• SACHSE, Frank

Francis Marion (Butch) Sachse

Born: July 24, 1917. Brice, TX, United States. Died: Oct.1, 1989.   Height: 6'   Weight: 197 lbs.   Drafted: —   College: Texas Tech

YEAR	TEAM	GP	GS	MIN	PTS	FGM	FGA	FG%	3PM	3PA	3P%	FTM	FTA	FT%	ORB	DRB	TRB	AST	PF	DQ	STL	BLK	TO	MPG	PPG	RPG	APG	PCM
43-44	Oshkosh-N	22	....	....	96	42	....	....	....	....	....	12	....	....	....	....	....	....	....	....	....	....	....	4.4	....	....	....	....
44-45	Oshkosh-N	8	....	....	39	16	....	....	....	....	....	7	....	....	....	....	....	....	....	....	....	....	....	4.9	....	....	....	....
NBL Season Totals		30	....	....	135	58	....	....	....	....	....	19	....	....	....	....	....	....	....	....	....	....	....	4.5	....	....	....	....
43-44	Oshkosh-N	3	....	....	6	2	....	....	....	....	....	2	....	....	....	....	....	....	....	....	....	....	....	2.0	....	....	....	....
NBL Playoff Totals		3	....	....	6	2	....	....	....	....	....	2	....	....	....	....	....	....	....	....	....	....	....	2.0	....	....	....	....

• SACK, Leo

Leo Sack

Born: May 18, 1914. Died: Jan.1987.   Height: 5'8".   Weight: 145 lbs.   Drafted: —   College: Xavier (OH)

YEAR	TEAM	GP	GS	MIN	PTS	FGM	FGA	FG%	3PM	3PA	3P%	FTM	FTA	FT%	ORB	DRB	TRB	AST	PF	DQ	STL	BLK	TO	MPG	PPG	RPG	APG	PCM
37-38	Cincinnati-N	6	....	....	43	20	....	....	....	....	....	3	....	....	....	....	....	....	....	....	....	....	....	7.2	....	....	....	....
NBL Season Totals		6	....	....	43	20	....	....	....	....	....	3	....	....	....	....	....	....	....	....	....	....	....	7.2	....	....	....	....

• SADOWSKI, Ed

Edward Frank (Big Ed) Sadowski

Born: July 11, 1917. Died: Sept.18, 1990. Height: 6'5". Weight: 240 lbs. Drafted: — College: Seton Hall

YEAR	TEAM	GP	GS	MIN	PTS	FGM	FGA	FG%	3PM	3PA	3P%	FTM	FTA	FT%	ORB	DRB	TRB	AST	PF	DQ	STL	BLK	TO	MPG	PPG	RPG	APG	PCM
39-40	Indianapolis-N	12	....	....	38	17	....	....	....	....	....	4	....	....	....	....	....	....	....	....	....	....	....	....	3.2	....	....	....
40-41	Detroit-N	24	....	....	256	95	....	....	....	....	....	66	....	....	....	....	....	....	....	....	....	....	....	....	10.7	....	....	....
41-42	Indianapolis-N	22	....	....	127	52	....	....	....	....	....	23	....	....	....	....	....	....	....	....	....	....	....	....	5.8	....	....	....
42-43	Sheboygan-N	8	....	....	43	16	....	....	....	....	....	11	....	....	....	....	....	....	....	....	....	....	....	....	5.4	....	....	....
42-43	Toledo-N	2	....	....	8	4	....	....	....	....	....	0	....	....	....	....	....	....	....	....	....	....	....	....	4.0	....	....	....
44-45	Fort Wayne-N	1	....	....	10	4	....	....	....	....	....	2	....	....	....	....	....	....	....	....	....	....	....	....	10.0	....	....	....
45-46	Fort Wayne-N	34	....	....	326	122	....	....	....	....	....	82	120	.683	....	....	....	....	....	....	....	....	....	....	9.6	....	....	....
45-46	Indianapolis-N	1	....	....	2	1	....	....	....	....	....	0	0	.000	....	....	....	....	....	....	....	....	....	....	2.0	....	....	....
46-47	Toronto	10	....	....	191	73	209	.349	....	....	....	45	66	.682	....	....	....	8	42	....	....	....	....	....	19.1	....	0.8	....
46-47	Cleveland	43	....	....	686	256	682	.375	....	....	....	174	262	.664	....	....	....	38	152	....	....	....	....	....	16.0	....	0.9	....
47-48	Boston	47	....	....	910	308	953	.323	....	....	....	294	**422**	.697	....	....	....	74	182	....	....	....	....	....	19.4	....	1.6	....
48-49	Philadelphia	60	....	....	920	340	839	.405	....	....	....	240	350	.686	....	....	....	160	**273**	....	....	....	....	....	15.3	....	2.7	....
49-50	Philadelphia	17	....	....	146	47	153	.307	....	....	....	52	75	.693	....	....	....	39	63	....	....	....	....	....	8.6	....	2.3	....
49-50	Baltimore	52	....	....	726	252	769	.328	....	....	....	222	298	.745	....	....	....	97	181	....	....	....	....	....	14.0	....	1.9	....
NBA Season Totals		229	....	....	3579	1276	3605	.354	....	....	....	1027	1473	.697	....	....	....	416	893	....	....	....	....	....	15.6	....	1.8	....
NBL Season Totals		104	....	....	810	311	....	....	....	....	....	188	120	....	....	....	....	....	....	....	....	....	....	....	7.8	....	....	....
Career Totals		333	....	....	4389	1587	3605	....	....	....	....	1215	1593	....	....	....	....	416	893	....	....	....	....	....	13.2	....	1.2	....
40-41	Detroit-N	3	....	....	23	7	....	....	....	....	....	9	....	....	....	....	....	....	....	....	....	....	....	....	7.7	....	....	....
41-42	Indianapolis-N	2	....	....	5	2	....	....	....	....	....	1	....	....	....	....	....	....	....	....	....	....	....	....	2.5	....	....	....
42-43	Sheboygan-N	2	....	....	3	1	....	....	....	....	....	1	....	....	....	....	....	....	....	....	....	....	....	....	1.5	....	....	....
44-45	Fort Wayne-N	7	....	....	45	17	....	....	....	....	....	11	....	....	....	....	....	....	....	....	....	....	....	....	6.4	....	....	....
45-46	Fort Wayne-N	4	....	....	57	20	....	....	....	....	....	17	23	.739	....	....	....	....	....	....	....	....	....	....	14.3	....	....	....
46-47	Cleveland	3	....	....	71	22	56	.393	....	....	....	27	34	.794	....	....	....	5	10	....	....	....	....	....	23.7	....	1.7	....
47-48	Boston	3	....	....	61	19	55	.345	....	....	....	23	38	.605	....	....	....	6	17	....	....	....	....	....	20.3	....	2.0	....
48-49	Philadelphia	2	....	....	20	6	28	.214	....	....	....	8	13	.615	....	....	....	3	6	....	....	....	....	....	10.0	....	1.5	....
NBA Playoff Totals		8	....	....	152	47	139	.338	....	....	....	58	85	.682	....	....	....	14	33	....	....	....	....	....	19.0	....	1.8	....
NBL Playoff Totals		18	....	....	133	47	....	....	....	....	....	39	23	....	....	....	....	....	....	....	....	....	....	....	7.4	....	....	....
Career Playoff Totals		26	....	....	285	94	139	....	....	....	....	97	108	....	....	....	....	14	33	....	....	....	....	....	11.0	....	0.5	....

• SAFFER, Junior

Junior Saffer

Born: 1917. Height: — Weight: — Drafted: — College: none

YEAR	TEAM	GP	GS	MIN	PTS	FGM	FGA	FG%	3PM	3PA	3P%	FTM	FTA	FT%	ORB	DRB	TRB	AST	PF	DQ	STL	BLK	TO	MPG	PPG	RPG	APG	PCM
37-38	Cincinnati-N	1	....	....	0	0	....	....	....	....	....	0	....	....	....	....	....	....	....	....	....	....	....	....	0.0	....	....	....
NBL Season Totals		1	....	....	0	0	....	....	....	....	....	0	....	....	....	....	....	....	....	....	....	....	....	....	0.0	....	....	....

• SAILORS, Kenny

Kenneth L. Sailors

Born: Jan. 14, 1922. Hillsdale, WY, United States. Height: 5'10". Weight: 175 lbs. Drafted: — College: Wyoming

YEAR	TEAM	GP	GS	MIN	PTS	FGM	FGA	FG%	3PM	3PA	3P%	FTM	FTA	FT%	ORB	DRB	TRB	AST	PF	DQ	STL	BLK	TO	MPG	PPG	RPG	APG	PCM
46-47	Cleveland	58	....	....	577	229	741	.309	....	....	....	119	200	.595	....	....	....	134	177	....	....	....	....	....	9.9	....	2.3	....
47-48	Chicago	1	....	....	0	0	3	.000	....	....	....	0	0	.000	....	....	....	0	1	....	....	....	....	....	0.0	....	0.0	....
47-48	Philadelphia	2	....	....	4	2	3	.667	....	....	....	0	0	.000	....	....	....	0	4	....	....	....	....	....	2.0	....	0.0	....
47-48	Providence	41	....	....	520	205	683	.300	....	....	....	110	159	.692	....	....	....	59	157	....	....	....	....	....	12.7	....	1.4	....
48-49	Providence	57	....	....	899	309	906	.341	....	....	....	281	367	.766	....	....	....	209	239	....	....	....	....	....	15.8	....	3.7	....
49-50	Denver	57	....	....	987	329	944	.349	....	....	....	329	456	.721	....	....	....	229	242	....	....	....	....	....	17.3	....	4.0	....
50-51	Bos/Bal	60	....	....	493	181	533	.340	....	....	....	131	180	.728	....	....	120	150	196	8	....	....	....	....	8.2	2.0	2.5	....
NBA Season Totals		276	....	....	3480	1255	3813	.329	....	....	....	970	1362	.712	....	....	120	781	1016	8	....	....	....	....	12.6	0.4	2.8	....
46-47	Cleveland	2	....	....	15	6	16	.375	....	....	....	3	4	.750	....	....	....	4	8	....	....	....	....	....	7.5	....	2.0	....
NBA Playoff Totals		2	....	....	15	6	16	.375	....	....	....	3	4	.750	....	....	....	4	8	....	....	....	....	....	7.5	....	2.0	....

• SALLEY, John

John Thomas (Spider) Salley

Born: May 16, 1964. Brooklyn, NY, United States. Height: 6'11". Weight: 230 lbs. Drafted: 1986 College: Georgia Tech

YEAR	TEAM	GP	GS	MIN	PTS	FGM	FGA	FG%	3PM	3PA	3P%	FTM	FTA	FT%	ORB	DRB	TRB	AST	PF	DQ	STL	BLK	TO	MPG	PPG	RPG	APG	PCM
86-87	Detroit	82	2	1463	431	163	290	.562	0	1	.000	105	171	.614	108	188	296	54	256	5	44	125	74	17.8	5.3	3.6	0.7	.400
87-88	Detroit	82	16	2003	701	258	456	.566	0	0	.000	185	261	.709	166	236	402	113	294	4	53	137	123	24.4	8.5	4.9	1.4	.450
88-89	Detroit	67	21	1458	467	166	333	.498	0	2	.000	135	195	.692	134	201	335	75	197	3	40	72	101	21.8	7.0	5.0	1.1	.408
89-90	Detroit	82	12	1914	593	209	408	.512	1	4	.250	174	244	.713	154	285	439	67	282	7	51	153	98	23.3	7.2	5.4	0.8	.430
90-91	Detroit	74	1	1649	544	179	377	.475	0	1	.000	186	256	.727	137	190	327	70	240	7	52	112	89	22.3	7.4	4.4	0.9	.403
91-92	Detroit	72	38	1774	684	249	486	.512	0	3	.000	186	260	.715	106	190	296	116	222	1	49	110	101	24.6	9.5	4.1	1.6	.439
92-93	Miami	51	34	1422	423	154	307	.502	0	0	.000	115	144	.799	113	200	313	83	192	7	32	70	102	27.9	8.3	6.1	1.6	.392
93-94	Miami	76	45	1910	582	208	436	.477	2	3	.667	164	225	.729	132	275	407	135	260	4	56	78	91	25.1	7.7	5.4	1.8	.411
94-95	Miami	75	50	1955	547	197	395	.499	0	0	.000	153	207	.739	110	226	336	123	279	5	47	85	98	26.1	7.3	4.5	1.6	.349
95-96	Toronto	25	6	482	149	51	105	.486	0	0	.000	47	65	.723	26	71	97	39	72	3	11	12	40	19.3	6.0	3.9	1.6	.358
95-96	Chicago	17	0	191	36	12	35	.343	0	0	.000	12	20	.600	20	23	43	15	38	0	8	15	15	11.2	2.1	2.5	0.9	.296
99-00	LA Lakers	45	3	303	71	25	69	.362	0	0	.000	21	28	.750	20	45	65	26	67	1	8	14	18	6.7	1.6	1.4	0.6	.292
NBA Season Totals		748	228	16524	5228	1871	3697	.506	3	14	.214	1483	2076	.714	1226	2130	3356	916	2399	47	451	983	950	22.1	7.0	4.5	1.2	....
86-87	Detroit	15	0	311	93	33	66	.500	0	0	.000	27	42	.643	30	42	72	11	60	1	3	17	14	20.7	6.2	4.8	0.7	.359
87-88	Detroit	23	0	623	161	56	104	.538	0	1	.000	49	69	.710	64	91	155	21	88	2	15	37	23	27.1	7.0	6.7	0.9	.417
88-89	Detroit	17	0	392	152	58	99	.586	0	0	.000	36	54	.667	34	45	79	9	58	0	9	25	12	23.1	8.9	4.6	0.5	.465
89-90	Detroit	20	0	547	190	58	122	.475	0	0	.000	74	98	.755	57	60	117	20	76	2	9	33	22	27.4	9.5	5.9	1.0	.426
90-91	Detroit	15	0	308	112	38	70	.543	0	0	.000	36	60	.600	20	42	62	11	58	1	6	20	13	20.5	7.5	4.1	0.7	.408
91-92	Detroit	5	1	149	63	20	44	.455	0	1	.000	23	28	.821	10	20	30	14	18	0	3	14	9	29.8	12.6	6.0	2.8	.539
93-94	Miami	5	5	201	55	22	57	.386	0	0	.000	11	16	.688	16	24	40	8	21	1	2	5	6	40.2	11.0	8.0	1.6	.285

YEAR	TEAM	GP	GS	MIN	PTS	FGM	FGA	FG%	3PM	3PA	3P%	FTM	FTA	FT%	ORB	DRB	TRB	AST	PF	DQ	STL	BLK	TO	MPG	PPG	RPG	APG	PCM
95-96	Chicago	16	0	85	14	6	11	.545	0	0	.000	2	7	.286	4	7	11	6	25	0	1	2	4	5.3	0.9	0.7	0.4	.129
99-00	LA Lakers	18	0	78	17	5	13	.385	0	0	.000	7	10	.700	9	13	22	4	16	0	1	6	4	4.3	0.9	1.2	0.2	.361
NBA Playoff Totals		134	6	2694	857	296	586	.505	0	2	.000	265	384	.690	244	344	588	104	420	7	49	159	107	20.1	6.4	4.4	0.8	....

• SALMONS, John
John Rashall Salmons

Born: Dec. 12, 1979. Philadelphia, PA, United States.   Height: 6'7".   Weight: 210 lbs.   Drafted: 2002   College: Miami (FL)

YEAR	TEAM	GP	GS	MIN	PTS	FGM	FGA	FG%	3PM	3PA	3P%	FTM	FTA	FT%	ORB	DRB	TRB	AST	PF	DQ	STL	BLK	TO	MPG	PPG	RPG	APG	PCM
02-03	Philadelphia	64	1	502	132	48	116	.414	10	31	.323	26	35	.743	16	43	59	47	53	1	17	6	29	7.8	2.1	0.9	0.7	.282
NBA Season Totals		64	1	502	132	48	116	.414	10	31	.323	26	35	.743	16	43	59	47	53	1	17	6	29	7.8	2.1	0.9	0.7	....
02-03	Philadelphia	6	0	16	0	0	1	.000	0	1	.000	0	2	.000	0	3	3	0	0	0	0	0	2	2.7	0.0	0.5	0.0	-.057
NBA Playoff Totals		6	0	16	0	0	1	.000	0	1	.000	0	2	.000	0	3	3	0	0	0	0	0	2	2.7	0.0	0.5	0.0	....

• SALVADORI, Al
Albert Julian Salvadori

Born: May 6, 1945. Wheeling, WV, United States.   Height: 6'9".   Weight: 220 lbs.   Drafted: 1967   College: South Carolina

YEAR	TEAM	GP	GS	MIN	PTS	FGM	FGA	FG%	3PM	3PA	3P%	FTM	FTA	FT%	ORB	DRB	TRB	AST	PF	DQ	STL	BLK	TO	MPG	PPG	RPG	APG	PCM
67-68	Oakland-A	17	....	186	54	21	58	.362	1	1	1.000	11	16	.688	....	....	46	4	28	0	....	....	12	10.9	3.2	2.7	0.2	.282
ABA Season Totals		17	....	186	54	21	58	.362	1	1	1.000	11	16	.688	....	....	46	4	28	0	....	....	12	10.9	3.2	2.7	0.2	....

• SALVADORI, Kevin
Kevin Michael Salvadori

Born: Dec. 30, 1970. Wheeling, WV, United States.   Height: 7'   Weight: 231 lbs.   Drafted: —   College: North Carolina

YEAR	TEAM	GP	GS	MIN	PTS	FGM	FGA	FG%	3PM	3PA	3P%	FTM	FTA	FT%	ORB	DRB	TRB	AST	PF	DQ	STL	BLK	TO	MPG	PPG	RPG	APG	PCM
96-97	Sacramento	23	0	154	37	12	33	.364	0	0	.000	13	18	.722	6	19	25	10	17	0	2	13	12	6.7	1.6	1.1	0.4	.285
97-98	Sacramento	16	0	87	5	1	13	.077	0	0	.000	3	6	.500	5	15	20	3	12	0	0	11	5	5.4	0.3	1.3	0.2	.163
NBA Season Totals		39	0	241	42	13	46	.283	0	0	.000	16	24	.667	11	34	45	13	29	0	2	24	17	6.2	1.1	1.2	0.3	....

• SAMAKE, Soumaila
Soumaila Samake

Born: Mar. 18, 1978. Bougouni, Malaysia.   Height: 7'   Weight: 230 lbs.   Drafted: 2000   College: none

YEAR	TEAM	GP	GS	MIN	PTS	FGM	FGA	FG%	3PM	3PA	3P%	FTM	FTA	FT%	ORB	DRB	TRB	AST	PF	DQ	STL	BLK	TO	MPG	PPG	RPG	APG	PCM
00-01	New Jersey	34	0	226	46	18	48	.375	0	0	.000	10	24	.417	22	31	53	1	23	0	2	14	4	6.6	1.4	1.6	0.0	.274
02-03	LA Lakers	13	1	77	22	10	24	.417	0	0	.000	2	2	1.000	10	13	23	4	13	0	0	5	2	5.9	1.7	1.8	0.3	.407
NBA Season Totals		47	1	303	68	28	72	.389	0	0	.000	12	26	.462	32	44	76	5	36	0	2	19	6	6.4	1.4	1.6	0.1	....

• SAMPSON, Jamal
Jamal Wesley Sampson

Born: May 15, 1983. Inglewood, CA, United States.   Height: 6'11".   Weight: 235 lbs.   Drafted: 2002   College: California

YEAR	TEAM	GP	GS	MIN	PTS	FGM	FGA	FG%	3PM	3PA	3P%	FTM	FTA	FT%	ORB	DRB	TRB	AST	PF	DQ	STL	BLK	TO	MPG	PPG	RPG	APG	PCM
02-03	Milwaukee	5	0	8	0	0	2	.000	0	0	.000	0	0	.000	1	1	2	1	0	0	1	0	0	1.6	0.0	0.4	0.2	.250
NBA Season Totals		5	0	8	0	0	2	.000	0	0	.000	0	0	.000	1	1	2	1	0	0	1	0	0	1.6	0.0	0.4	0.2	....

• SAMPSON, Ralph
Ralph Lee Sampson

Born: July 7, 1960. Harrisonburg, VA, United States.   Height: 7'4".   Weight: 228 lbs.   Drafted: 1983   College: Virginia

YEAR	TEAM	GP	GS	MIN	PTS	FGM	FGA	FG%	3PM	3PA	3P%	FTM	FTA	FT%	ORB	DRB	TRB	AST	PF	DQ	STL	BLK	TO	MPG	PPG	RPG	APG	PCM
83-84	Houston	82	82	2693	1720	716	1369	.523	1	4	.250	287	434	.661	293	620	913	163	339	16	70	197	295	32.8	21.0	11.1	2.0	.700
84-85	Houston	82	82	3086	1809	753	1499	.502	0	6	.000	303	448	.676	227	626	853	224	306	10	81	168	**328**	37.6	22.1	10.4	2.7	.604
85-86	Houston	79	76	2864	1491	624	1280	.488	2	15	.133	241	376	.641	258	621	879	283	308	12	99	129	284	36.3	18.9	11.1	3.6	.609
86-87	Houston	43	32	1326	672	277	566	.489	0	3	.000	118	189	.624	88	284	372	120	169	6	40	58	125	30.8	15.6	8.7	2.8	.559
87-88	Houston	19	19	705	303	119	271	.439	2	6	.333	63	85	.741	58	114	172	37	63	1	17	33	63	37.1	15.9	9.1	1.9	.439
87-88	Golden State	29	25	958	446	180	411	.438	0	5	.000	86	111	.775	82	208	290	85	101	2	24	55	110	33.0	15.4	10.0	2.9	.526
88-89	Golden State	61	36	1086	393	164	365	.449	3	8	.375	62	95	.653	105	202	307	77	170	3	31	65	92	17.8	6.4	5.0	1.3	.445
89-90	Sacramento	26	7	417	109	48	129	.372	1	4	.250	12	23	.522	11	73	84	28	66	1	14	22	34	16.0	4.2	3.2	1.1	.257
90-91	Sacramento	25	4	348	74	34	93	.366	1	5	.200	5	19	.263	41	70	111	17	54	0	11	17	28	13.9	3.0	4.4	0.7	.313
91-92	Washington	10	0	108	22	9	29	.310	0	2	.000	4	6	.667	11	19	30	4	14	1	3	8	10	10.8	2.2	3.0	0.4	.269
NBA Season Totals		456	363	13591	7039	2924	6012	.486	10	58	.172	1181	1786	.661	1174	2837	4011	1038	1590	52	390	752	1369	29.8	15.4	8.8	2.3	....
84-85	Houston	5	5	193	106	43	100	.430	1	1	1.000	19	37	.514	25	58	83	7	23	2	2	8	17	38.6	21.2	16.6	1.4	.581
85-86	Houston	20	20	741	399	156	301	.518	1	1	1.000	86	118	.729	66	149	215	80	79	1	30	35	71	37.1	20.0	10.8	4.0	.665
86-87	Houston	10	10	330	186	75	146	.514	1	2	.500	35	43	.814	27	61	88	21	47	1	2	12	31	33.0	18.6	8.8	2.1	.554
88-89	Golden State	3	1	43	20	9	22	.409	0	4	.000	2	4	.500	6	8	14	1	8	0	1	2	4	14.3	6.7	4.7	0.3	.382
NBA Playoff Totals		38	36	1307	711	283	569	.497	3	8	.375	142	202	.703	124	276	400	109	157	4	35	57	123	34.4	18.7	10.5	2.9	....

• SANCHEZ, Pepe
Juan Ignacio Sanchez

Born: May 8, 1977. Bahia Blanca, Argentina.   Height: 6'4".   Weight: 195 lbs.   Drafted: —   College: Temple

YEAR	TEAM	GP	GS	MIN	PTS	FGM	FGA	FG%	3PM	3PA	3P%	FTM	FTA	FT%	ORB	DRB	TRB	AST	PF	DQ	STL	BLK	TO	MPG	PPG	RPG	APG	PCM
00-01	Atlanta	5	0	34	0	0	7	.000	0	0	.000	0	0	.000	1	0	1	5	3	0	2	0	3	6.8	0.0	0.2	1.0	-.062
00-01	Philadelphia	24	0	116	20	9	21	.429	0	1	.000	2	2	1.000	2	12	14	36	18	0	9	1	3	4.8	0.8	0.6	1.5	.514
02-03	Detroit	9	0	37	0	0	5	.000	0	0	.000	0	0	.000	4	2	6	8	3	0	5	0	2	4.1	0.0	0.7	0.9	.297
NBA Season Totals		38	0	187	20	9	33	.273	0	1	.000	2	2	1.000	7	14	21	49	24	0	16	1	8	4.9	0.5	0.6	1.3	....

• SANDERS, Al
Albert T. (Apple) Sanders III

Born: Jan. 1, 1950. Baton Rouge, LA, United States. Died: May4, 1994.   Height: 6'7".   Weight: 240 lbs.   Drafted: —   College: Louisiana State

YEAR	TEAM	GP	GS	MIN	PTS	FGM	FGA	FG%	3PM	3PA	3P%	FTM	FTA	FT%	ORB	DRB	TRB	AST	PF	DQ	STL	BLK	TO	MPG	PPG	RPG	APG	PCM
72-73	Virginia-A	4	....	25	8	2	2	1.000	0	0	.000	4	6	.667	0	5	5	0	4	0	....	....	3	6.3	2.0	1.3	0.0	.392
ABA Season Totals		4	....	25	8	2	2	1.000	0	0	.000	4	6	.667	0	5	5	0	4	0	....	....	3	6.3	2.0	1.3	0.0	....

• SANDERS, Frankie

Frankie J. Sanders

Born: Jan. 23, 1957. Dayton, OH, United States. Height: 6'6". Weight: 200 lbs. Drafted: 1978 College: Southern

YEAR	TEAM	GP	GS	MIN	PTS	FGM	FGA	FG%	3PM	3PA	3P%	FTM	FTA	FT%	ORB	DRB	TRB	AST	PF	DQ	STL	BLK	TO	MPG	PPG	RPG	APG	PCM
78-79	San Antonio	22	....	263	132	50	127	.394	....	....	....	32	41	.780	13	46	59	35	44	1	14	3	33	12.0	6.0	2.7	1.6	.442
78-79	Boston	24	....	216	132	55	119	.462	....	....	....	22	27	.815	22	29	51	17	25	0	7	3	24	9.0	5.5	2.1	0.7	.523
80-81	Kansas City	23	....	186	88	34	77	.442	0	0	.000	20	22	.909	6	15	21	17	20	0	16	1	21	8.1	3.8	0.9	0.7	.391
NBA Season Totals		69	....	665	352	139	323	.430	0	0	.000	74	90	.822	41	90	131	69	89	1	37	7	78	9.6	5.1	1.9	1.0	....
80-81	Kansas City	9	....	50	23	9	18	.500	1	2	.500	4	4	1.000	4	1	5	2	8	0	3	0	8	5.6	2.6	0.6	0.2	.267
NBA Playoff Totals		9	....	50	23	9	18	.500	1	2	.500	4	4	1.000	4	1	5	2	8	0	3	0	8	5.6	2.6	0.6	0.2	....

• SANDERS, Jeff

Jeffery Raynard Sanders

Born: Jan. 14, 1966. Augusta, GA, United States. Height: 6'8". Weight: 225 lbs. Drafted: 1989 College: Georgia Southern

YEAR	TEAM	GP	GS	MIN	PTS	FGM	FGA	FG%	3PM	3PA	3P%	FTM	FTA	FT%	ORB	DRB	TRB	AST	PF	DQ	STL	BLK	TO	MPG	PPG	RPG	APG	PCM
89-90	Chicago	31	0	182	28	13	40	.325	0	0	.000	2	4	.500	17	22	39	9	27	0	4	4	16	5.9	0.9	1.3	0.3	.152
90-91	Charlotte	3	0	43	13	6	14	.429	0	0	.000	1	2	.500	3	6	9	1	6	0	1	1	1	14.3	4.3	3.0	0.3	.295
91-92	Atlanta	12	0	117	47	20	45	.444	0	0	.000	7	9	.778	9	17	26	9	15	0	5	3	5	9.8	3.9	2.2	0.8	.448
92-93	Atlanta	9	0	120	24	10	25	.400	0	0	.000	4	8	.500	12	17	29	6	16	0	8	1	11	13.3	2.7	3.2	0.7	.269
NBA Season Totals		55	0	462	112	49	124	.395	0	0	.000	14	23	.609	41	62	103	25	64	0	18	9	33	8.4	2.0	1.9	0.5	....
89-90	Chicago	3	0	3	2	1	1	1.000	0	0	.000	0	0	.000	0	0	0	0	0	0	0	0	0	1.0	0.7	0.0	0.0	.667
NBA Playoff Totals		3	0	3	2	1	1	1.000	0	0	.000	0	0	.000	0	0	0	0	0	0	0	0	0	1.0	0.7	0.0	0.0	....

• SANDERS, Mike

Michael Anthony Sanders

Born: May 7, 1960. Vidalia, LA, United States. Height: 6'6". Weight: 210 lbs. Drafted: 1982 College: UCLA

YEAR	TEAM	GP	GS	MIN	PTS	FGM	FGA	FG%	3PM	3PA	3P%	FTM	FTA	FT%	ORB	DRB	TRB	AST	PF	DQ	STL	BLK	TO	MPG	PPG	RPG	APG	PCM
82-83	San Antonio	26	0	393	183	76	157	.484	0	2	.000	31	43	.721	31	63	94	19	57	0	18	6	29	15.1	7.0	3.6	0.7	.458
83-84	Phoenix	50	0	586	223	97	203	.478	0	0	.000	29	42	.690	40	63	103	44	101	0	23	12	45	11.7	4.5	2.1	0.9	.350
84-85	Phoenix	21	11	418	215	85	175	.486	0	0	.000	45	59	.763	38	51	89	29	59	0	23	4	34	19.9	10.2	4.2	1.4	.489
85-86	Phoenix	82	5	1644	905	347	676	.513	3	15	.200	208	257	.809	104	169	273	150	236	3	76	31	139	20.0	11.0	3.3	1.8	.518
86-87	Phoenix	82	4	1655	859	357	722	.494	2	17	.118	143	183	.781	101	170	271	126	210	1	61	23	107	20.2	10.5	3.3	1.5	.464
87-88	Phoenix	35	5	466	203	82	171	.480	0	1	.000	39	53	.736	28	34	62	30	73	0	18	4	28	13.3	5.8	1.8	0.9	.351
87-88	Cleveland	24	11	417	162	71	132	.538	0	0	.000	20	23	.870	10	37	47	26	58	1	13	5	24	17.4	6.8	2.0	1.1	.342
88-89	Cleveland	82	82	2102	764	332	733	.453	3	10	.300	97	135	.719	98	209	307	133	230	2	89	32	107	25.6	9.3	3.7	1.6	.336
89-90	Indiana	82	13	1531	510	225	479	.470	5	14	.357	55	75	.733	78	152	230	89	220	1	43	23	82	18.7	6.2	2.8	1.1	.297
90-91	Indiana	80	7	1357	463	206	494	.417	4	20	.200	47	57	.825	73	112	185	106	198	1	37	26	64	17.0	5.8	2.3	1.3	.282
91-92	Indiana	10	0	81	27	11	22	.500	0	0	.000	5	6	.833	0	8	8	11	8	0	2	1	6	8.1	2.7	0.8	1.1	.358
91-92	Cleveland	21	20	552	194	81	139	.583	1	3	.333	31	41	.756	27	61	88	42	75	1	22	9	17	26.3	9.2	4.2	2.0	.435
92-93	Cleveland	53	51	1189	454	197	396	.497	1	4	.250	59	78	.756	52	118	170	75	150	2	39	30	58	22.4	8.6	3.2	1.4	.369
NBA Season Totals		648	209	12391	5162	2167	4499	.482	19	86	.221	809	1052	.769	680	1247	1927	880	1675	12	464	206	740	19.1	8.0	3.0	1.4	....
82-83	San Antonio	6	0	25	14	7	13	.538	0	0	.000	0	0	.000	2	7	9	4	3	0	0	0	0	4.2	2.3	1.5	0.7	.790
83-84	Phoenix	15	0	152	60	22	46	.478	0	0	.000	16	17	.941	10	10	20	7	31	0	6	4	14	10.1	4.0	1.3	0.5	.297
84-85	Phoenix	3	3	91	52	22	37	.595	0	0	.000	8	10	.800	8	7	15	10	8	0	5	0	9	30.3	17.3	5.0	3.3	.597
87-88	Cleveland	5	5	134	64	28	52	.538	0	1	.000	8	10	.800	11	14	25	7	21	0	3	2	11	26.8	12.8	5.0	1.4	.419
88-89	Cleveland	5	3	87	33	15	30	.500	0	0	.000	3	5	.600	6	10	16	4	11	0	2	1	10	17.4	6.6	3.2	0.8	.295
89-90	Indiana	3	0	24	11	5	11	.455	1	1	1.000	0	0	.000	5	1	6	2	4	0	0	0	2	8.0	3.7	2.0	0.7	.391
90-91	Indiana	5	0	41	15	6	10	.600	1	2	.500	2	4	.500	0	4	4	4	9	0	4	2	1	8.2	3.0	0.8	0.8	.459
91-92	Cleveland	17	17	418	130	56	115	.487	1	3	.333	17	21	.810	20	35	55	37	62	0	15	12	23	24.6	7.6	3.2	2.2	.332
92-93	Cleveland	8	7	145	46	20	48	.417	0	2	.000	6	10	.600	8	10	18	10	17	0	8	1	3	18.1	5.8	2.3	1.3	.298
NBA Playoff Totals		67	35	1117	425	181	362	.500	3	9	.333	60	77	.779	70	98	168	85	166	0	43	22	73	16.7	6.3	2.5	1.3	....

• SANDERS, Tom

Thomas Ernest (Satch) Sanders

Born: Nov. 8, 1938. Height: 6'6". Weight: 210 lbs. Drafted: 1960 College: New York University

YEAR	TEAM	GP	GS	MIN	PTS	FGM	FGA	FG%	3PM	3PA	3P%	FTM	FTA	FT%	ORB	DRB	TRB	AST	PF	DQ	STL	BLK	TO	MPG	PPG	RPG	APG	PCM
60-61	Boston	68	....	1084	363	148	352	.420	....	....	....	67	100	.670	....	....	385	44	131	1	....	....	....	15.9	5.3	5.7	0.6	.455
61-62	Boston	80	....	2325	897	350	804	.435	....	....	....	197	263	.749	....	....	762	74	279	9	....	....	....	29.1	11.2	9.5	0.9	.470
62-63	Boston	80	....	2148	864	339	744	.456	....	....	....	186	252	.738	....	....	576	95	262	5	....	....	....	26.9	10.8	7.2	1.2	.458
63-64	Boston	80	....	2370	911	349	836	.417	....	....	....	213	280	.761	....	....	667	102	277	6	....	....	....	29.6	11.4	8.3	1.3	.440
64-65	Boston	80	....	2459	941	374	871	.429	....	....	....	193	259	.745	....	....	661	92	318	**15**	....	....	....	30.7	11.8	8.3	1.2	.420
65-66	Boston	72	....	1896	909	349	816	.428	....	....	....	211	276	.764	....	....	508	90	317	**19**	....	....	....	26.3	12.6	7.1	1.3	.475
66-67	Boston	81	....	1926	824	323	755	.428	....	....	....	178	218	.817	....	....	439	91	304	6	....	....	....	23.8	10.2	5.4	1.1	.416
67-68	Boston	78	....	1981	792	296	691	.428	....	....	....	200	255	.784	....	....	454	100	300	12	....	....	....	25.4	10.2	5.8	1.3	.413
68-69	Boston	82	....	2184	915	364	847	.430	....	....	....	187	255	.733	....	....	574	110	293	9	....	....	....	26.6	11.2	7.0	1.3	.443
69-70	Boston	57	....	1616	653	246	555	.443	....	....	....	161	183	.880	....	....	314	92	199	5	....	....	....	28.4	11.5	5.5	1.6	.410
70-71	Boston	17	....	121	39	16	44	.364	....	....	....	7	8	.875	....	....	17	11	25	0	....	....	....	7.1	2.3	1.0	0.6	.255
71-72	Boston	82	....	1631	541	215	524	.410	....	....	....	111	136	.816	....	....	353	98	257	7	....	....	....	19.9	6.6	4.3	1.2	.349
72-73	Boston	59	....	423	117	47	149	.315	....	....	....	23	35	.657	....	....	88	27	82	0	....	....	....	7.2	2.0	1.5	0.5	.226
NBA Season Totals		916	....	22164	8766	3416	7988	.428	....	....	....	1934	2520	.767	....	....	5798	1026	3044	94	....	....	....	24.2	9.6	6.3	1.1	....
60-61	Boston	10	....	216	89	37	75	.493	....	....	....	15	24	.625	....	....	84	7	42	2	....	....	....	21.6	8.9	8.4	0.7	.524
61-62	Boston	14	....	439	141	56	130	.431	....	....	....	29	36	.806	....	....	115	14	65	4	....	....	....	31.4	10.1	8.2	1.0	.369
62-63	Boston	13	....	387	128	52	119	.437	....	....	....	24	31	.774	....	....	96	19	61	4	....	....	....	29.8	9.8	7.4	1.5	.380
63-64	Boston	10	....	302	91	34	94	.362	....	....	....	23	34	.676	....	....	71	6	45	5	....	....	....	30.2	9.1	7.1	0.6	.282
64-65	Boston	12	....	365	159	64	152	.421	....	....	....	31	43	.721	....	....	102	19	58	4	....	....	....	30.4	13.3	8.5	1.6	.456
65-66	Boston	17	....	500	230	97	201	.483	....	....	....	36	48	.750	....	....	110	27	70	2	....	....	....	29.4	13.5	6.5	1.6	.471
66-67	Boston	9	....	144	44	21	61	.344	....	....	....	2	5	.400	....	....	43	5	31	1	....	....	....	16.0	4.9	4.8	0.6	.270
67-68	Boston	14	....	289	116	50	99	.505	....	....	....	16	21	.762	....	....	63	12	53	4	....	....	....	20.6	8.3	4.5	0.9	.410
68-69	Boston	15	....	197	87	32	73	.438	....	....	....	23	31	.742	....	....	48	7	40	0	....	....	....	13.1	5.8	3.2	0.5	.411

YEAR	TEAM	GP	GS	MIN	PTS	FGM	FGA	FG%	3PM	3PA	3P%	FTM	FTA	FT%	ORB	DRB	TRB	AST	PF	DQ	STL	BLK	TO	MPG	PPG	RPG	APG	PCM
71-72	Boston	11	....	186	47	17	53	.321	....	....	....	13	21	.619	....	....	26	10	36	0	....	....	....	16.9	4.3	2.4	0.9	.165
72-73	Boston	5	....	24	10	5	9	.556	....	....	....	0	2	.000	....	....	5	1	7	0	....	....	....	4.8	2.0	1.0	0.2	.339
NBA Playoff Totals		130	....	3049	1142	465	1066	.436	....	....	....	212	296	.716	....	....	763	127	508	**26**	....	....	....	23.5	8.8	5.9	1.0	

• SANFORD, Ron
Ron Sanford

Born: June 11, 1946.　Height: 6'9".　Weight: 215 lbs.　Drafted: 1970　College: New Mexico

YEAR	TEAM	GP	GS	MIN	PTS	FGM	FGA	FG%	3PM	3PA	3P%	FTM	FTA	FT%	ORB	DRB	TRB	AST	PF	DQ	STL	BLK	TO	MPG	PPG	RPG	APG	PCM
71-72	Dallas-A	1	....	2	0	0	0	.000	0	0	.000	0	0	.000	0	0	0	0	1	0	....	....	0	2.0	0.0	0.0	0.0	-.220
ABA Season Totals		1	....	2	0	0	0	.000	0	0	.000	0	0	.000	0	0	0	0	1	0	....	....	0	2.0	0.0	0.0	0.0	....

• SANTIAGO, Dan
Daniel Gregg Santiago

Born: June 24, 1976. Lubbock, TX, United States.　Height: 7'1".　Weight: 256 lbs.　Drafted: —　College: St. Vincent

YEAR	TEAM	GP	GS	MIN	PTS	FGM	FGA	FG%	3PM	3PA	3P%	FTM	FTA	FT%	ORB	DRB	TRB	AST	PF	DQ	STL	BLK	TO	MPG	PPG	RPG	APG	PCM
00-01	Phoenix	54	2	581	170	64	134	.478	0	0	.000	42	61	.689	35	67	102	11	101	1	17	21	47	10.8	3.1	1.9	0.2	.256
01-02	Phoenix	3	0	24	8	4	8	.500	0	0	.000	0	0	.000	0	7	7	2	4	0	0	1	2	8.0	2.7	2.3	0.7	.425
NBA Season Totals		57	2	605	178	68	142	.479	0	0	.000	42	61	.689	35	74	109	13	105	1	17	22	49	10.6	3.1	1.9	0.2	....
00-01	Phoenix	1	0	12	2	1	2	.500	0	0	.000	0	0	.000	1	4	5	0	2	0	0	2	1	12.0	2.0	5.0	0.0	.466
NBA Playoff Totals		1	0	12	2	1	2	.500	0	0	.000	0	0	.000	1	4	5	0	2	0	0	2	1	12.0	2.0	5.0	0.0	....

• SANTINI, Bob
Robert Santini

Born: Feb. 17, 1935. Bronx, NY, United States.　Height: 6'5".　Weight: 190 lbs.　Drafted: 1953　College: Iona

YEAR	TEAM	GP	GS	MIN	PTS	FGM	FGA	FG%	3PM	3PA	3P%	FTM	FTA	FT%	ORB	DRB	TRB	AST	PF	DQ	STL	BLK	TO	MPG	PPG	RPG	APG	PCM
55-56	New York	4	....	23	11	5	10	.500	....	....	....	1	2	.500	....	....	3	1	4	0	....	....	....	5.8	2.8	0.8	0.3	.383
NBA Season Totals		4	....	23	11	5	10	.500	....	....	....	1	2	.500	....	....	3	1	4	0	....	....	....	5.8	2.8	0.8	0.3	

• SAPPLETON, Wayne
Wayne B. Sappleton

Born: Nov. 17, 1960. Kingston, Jamaica.　Height: 6'9".　Weight: 215 lbs.　Drafted: 1982　College: Loyola (IL)

YEAR	TEAM	GP	GS	MIN	PTS	FGM	FGA	FG%	3PM	3PA	3P%	FTM	FTA	FT%	ORB	DRB	TRB	AST	PF	DQ	STL	BLK	TO	MPG	PPG	RPG	APG	PCM
84-85	New Jersey	33	0	298	96	41	87	.471	0	0	.000	14	34	.412	28	47	75	7	50	0	7	4	20	9.0	2.9	2.3	0.2	.300
NBA Season Totals		33	0	298	96	41	87	.471	0	0	.000	14	34	.412	28	47	75	7	50	0	7	4	20	9.0	2.9	2.3	0.2	....

• SASSER, Jason
Jason Jermane Sasser

Born: Jan. 13, 1974. Denton, TX, United States.　Height: 6'7".　Weight: 225 lbs.　Drafted: 1996　College: Texas Tech

YEAR	TEAM	GP	GS	MIN	PTS	FGM	FGA	FG%	3PM	3PA	3P%	FTM	FTA	FT%	ORB	DRB	TRB	AST	PF	DQ	STL	BLK	TO	MPG	PPG	RPG	APG	PCM
96-97	San Antonio	6	0	62	17	8	19	.421	1	2	.500	0	0	.000	0	7	7	1	11	0	2	0	2	10.3	2.8	1.2	0.2	.149
96-97	Dallas	2	0	7	2	1	4	.250	0	1	.000	0	0	.000	1	0	1	1	0	0	1	0	0	3.5	1.0	0.5	0.5	.305
98-99	Vancouver	6	0	39	11	5	11	.455	0	0	.000	1	2	.500	2	5	7	2	4	0	2	0	2	6.5	1.8	1.2	0.3	.305
NBA Season Totals		14	0	108	30	14	34	.412	1	3	.333	1	2	.500	3	12	15	4	15	0	5	0	4	7.7	2.1	1.1	0.3	....

• SASSER, Jeryl
Jeryl Henry Brazton Sasser Jr.

Born: Feb. 13, 1979. Dallas, TX, United States.　Height: 6'6".　Weight: 200 lbs.　Drafted: 2001　College: Southern Methodist

YEAR	TEAM	GP	GS	MIN	PTS	FGM	FGA	FG%	3PM	3PA	3P%	FTM	FTA	FT%	ORB	DRB	TRB	AST	PF	DQ	STL	BLK	TO	MPG	PPG	RPG	APG	PCM
01-02	Orlando	7	0	36	10	3	14	.214	0	0	.000	4	5	.800	3	4	7	2	3	0	3	0	2	5.1	1.4	1.0	0.3	.213
02-03	Orlando	75	4	1023	194	64	207	.309	13	44	.295	53	78	.679	64	120	184	65	91	0	45	12	39	13.6	2.6	2.5	0.9	.260
NBA Season Totals		82	4	1059	204	67	221	.303	13	44	.295	57	83	.687	67	124	191	67	94	0	48	12	41	12.9	2.5	2.3	0.8	....
02-03	Orlando	6	0	25	5	2	7	.286	1	4	.250	0	0	.000	1	4	5	1	1	0	1	1	1	4.2	0.8	0.8	0.2	.262
NBA Playoff Totals		6	0	25	5	2	7	.286	1	4	.250	0	0	.000	1	4	5	1	1	0	1	1	1	4.2	0.8	0.8	0.2	....

• SATTERFIELD, Kenny
Kenneth Satterfield Satterfield

Born: Apr. 10, 1981. New York, NY, United States.　Height: 6'2".　Weight: 186 lbs.　Drafted: 2001　College: Cincinnati

YEAR	TEAM	GP	GS	MIN	PTS	FGM	FGA	FG%	3PM	3PA	3P%	FTM	FTA	FT%	ORB	DRB	TRB	AST	PF	DQ	STL	BLK	TO	MPG	PPG	RPG	APG	PCM
01-02	Denver	36	4	560	189	73	199	.367	7	27	.259	36	46	.783	17	35	52	108	43	0	31	1	53	15.6	5.3	1.4	3.0	.352
02-03	Denver	22	6	420	123	51	165	.309	5	28	.179	16	23	.696	12	23	35	53	30	0	18	2	36	19.1	5.6	1.6	2.4	.185
02-03	Philadelphia	17	0	82	9	4	18	.222	0	0	.000	1	2	.500	4	4	8	15	6	0	2	0	7	4.8	0.5	0.5	0.9	.149
NBA Season Totals		75	10	1062	321	128	382	.335	12	55	.218	53	71	.746	33	62	95	176	79	0	51	3	96	14.2	4.3	1.3	2.3	....

• SATTLER, Bill
William Sattler

Born: 1916.　Height: 6'8".　Weight: 197 lbs.　Drafted: —　College: Ohio State

YEAR	TEAM	GP	GS	MIN	PTS	FGM	FGA	FG%	3PM	3PA	3P%	FTM	FTA	FT%	ORB	DRB	TRB	AST	PF	DQ	STL	BLK	TO	MPG	PPG	RPG	APG	PCM
46-47	Youngstown-N	42	....	....	220	85	....	....	....	....	....	50	105	.476	....	....	....	112	....	....	....	....	....	5.2	....	....	....	
47-48	Flint-N	7	....	....	45	15	....	....	....	....	....	15	25	.600	....	....	....	....	....	....	....	....	....	6.4	....	....	....	
NBL Season Totals		49	....	....	265	100	....	....	....	....	....	65	130	....	....	....	....	112	....	....	....	....	....	5.4	....	....	....	

• SAUER, Louie
Louie Sauer

Born: Sept. 3, 1915. Died: Sept.1985.　Height: 6'6".　Weight: 235 lbs.　Drafted: —　College: Valparaiso

YEAR	TEAM	GP	GS	MIN	PTS	FGM	FGA	FG%	3PM	3PA	3P%	FTM	FTA	FT%	ORB	DRB	TRB	AST	PF	DQ	STL	BLK	TO	MPG	PPG	RPG	APG	PCM
37-38	Kankakee-N	12	....	....	79	31	....	....	....	....	....	17	....	....	....	....	....	....	....	....	....	....	....	6.6	....	....	....	
NBL Season Totals		12	....	....	79	31	....	....	....	....	....	17	....	....	....	....	....	....	....	....	....	....	....	6.6	....	....	....	

• SAUL, Pep

Frank Benjamin (Pep) Saul Jr.

Born: Feb. 16, 1924. Height: 6'2". Weight: 185 lbs. Drafted: 1949 College: Seton Hall

YEAR	TEAM	GP	GS	MIN	PTS	FGM	FGA	FG%	3PM	3PA	3P%	FTM	FTA	FT%	ORB	DRB	TRB	AST	PF	DQ	STL	BLK	TO	MPG	PPG	RPG	APG	PCM
49-50	Rochester	49	....	....	182	74	183	.404	....	....	....	34	47	.723	....	....	....	28	33	....	....	....	....	....	3.7	....	0.6	....
50-51	Rochester	65	....	....	282	105	310	.339	....	....	....	72	105	.686	....	....	84	68	85	0	....	....	....	....	4.3	1.3	1.0	....
51-52	Bal/Min	64	....	1479	433	157	436	.360	....	....	....	119	153	.778	....	....	165	147	120	3	....	....	....	23.1	6.8	2.6	2.3	.329
52-53	Minneapolis	70	....	1796	516	187	471	.397	....	....	....	142	200	.710	....	....	141	110	174	3	....	....	....	25.7	7.4	2.0	1.6	.261
53-54	Minneapolis	71	....	1805	452	162	467	.347	....	....	....	128	170	.753	....	....	159	139	149	3	....	....	....	25.4	6.4	2.2	2.0	.255
54-55	Milwaukee	65	....	1139	287	96	303	.317	....	....	....	95	123	.772	....	....	134	104	126	0	....	....	....	17.5	4.4	2.1	1.6	.267
NBA Season Totals		384	....	6219	2152	781	2170	.360	....	....	....	590	798	.739	....	....	683	596	687	9	....	....	....	16.2	5.6	1.8	1.6	....
49-50	Rochester	2	....	....	18	7	13	.538	....	....	....	4	5	.800	....	....	....	4	8	....	....	....	....	....	9.0	....	2.0	....
50-51	Rochester	9	....	....	9	4	12	.333	....	....	....	1	2	.500	....	....	3	6	2	0	....	....	....	....	1.0	0.3	0.7	....
51-52	Minneapolis	13	....	530	147	56	121	.463	....	....	....	35	48	.729	....	....	36	45	42	1	....	....	....	40.8	11.3	2.8	3.5	.311
52-53	Minneapolis	12	....	297	86	31	74	.419	....	....	....	24	33	.727	....	....	28	18	40	1	....	....	....	24.8	7.2	2.3	1.5	.271
53-54	Minneapolis	13	....	227	61	18	51	.353	....	....	....	25	34	.735	....	....	27	14	27	0	....	....	....	17.5	4.7	2.1	1.1	.273
NBA Playoff Totals		49	....	1054	321	116	271	.428	....	....	....	89	122	.730	....	....	94	87	119	2	....	....	....	21.5	6.6	1.9	1.8	....

• SAULDSBERRY, Woody

Woodrow Sauldsberry Jr.

Born: July 11, 1934. Winnsboro, LA, United States. Height: 6'7". Weight: 220 lbs. Drafted: 1957 College: Texas Southern

YEAR	TEAM	GP	GS	MIN	PTS	FGM	FGA	FG%	3PM	3PA	3P%	FTM	FTA	FT%	ORB	DRB	TRB	AST	PF	DQ	STL	BLK	TO	MPG	PPG	RPG	APG	PCM
57-58	Philadelphia	71	....	2377	912	389	1082	.360	....	....	....	134	218	.615	....	....	729	58	245	3	....	....	....	33.5	12.8	10.3	0.8	.375
58-59	Philadelphia	72	....	2743	1112	501	1380	.363	....	....	....	110	176	.625	....	....	826	71	276	12	....	....	....	38.1	15.4	11.5	1.0	.376
59-60	Philadelphia	71	....	1848	705	325	974	.334	....	....	....	55	103	.534	....	....	447	112	203	2	....	....	....	26.0	9.9	6.3	1.6	.323
60-61	St. Louis	69	....	1491	516	230	768	.299	....	....	....	56	100	.560	....	....	491	74	197	3	....	....	....	21.6	7.5	7.1	1.1	.322
61-62	StL/Chi	63	....	1765	675	298	869	.343	....	....	....	79	123	.642	....	....	536	90	179	5	....	....	....	28.0	10.7	8.5	1.4	.380
62-63	Chicago	54	....	1664	697	304	792	.384	....	....	....	89	130	.685	....	....	367	66	171	3	....	....	....	30.8	12.9	6.8	1.2	.359
62-63	St. Louis	23	....	370	142	62	174	.356	....	....	....	18	33	.545	....	....	80	12	59	0	....	....	....	16.1	6.2	3.5	0.5	.275
65-66	Boston	39	....	530	171	80	249	.321	....	....	....	11	22	.500	....	....	142	15	94	0	....	....	....	13.6	4.4	3.6	0.4	.239
NBA Season Totals		462	....	12788	4930	2189	6288	.348	....	....	....	552	905	.610	....	....	3618	498	1424	28	....	....	....	27.7	10.7	7.8	1.1	....
57-58	Philadelphia	8	....	290	103	45	131	.344	....	....	....	13	23	.565	....	....	87	6	27	0	....	....	....	36.3	12.9	10.9	0.8	.337
59-60	Philadelphia	9	....	298	116	54	159	.340	....	....	....	8	14	.571	....	....	64	12	40	3	....	....	....	33.1	12.9	7.1	1.3	.277
60-61	St. Louis	12	....	407	164	75	206	.364	....	....	....	14	25	.560	....	....	108	34	51	1	....	....	....	33.9	13.7	9.0	2.8	.405
NBA Playoff Totals		29	....	995	383	174	496	.351	....	....	....	35	62	.565	....	....	259	52	118	4	....	....	....	34.3	13.2	8.9	1.8	....

• SAULTERS, Glynn

Glynn Saulters

Born: Feb. 10, 1945. Minden, LA, United States. Height: 6'2". Weight: 175 lbs. Drafted: 1968 College: Northeast Louisiana

YEAR	TEAM	GP	GS	MIN	PTS	FGM	FGA	FG%	3PM	3PA	3P%	FTM	FTA	FT%	ORB	DRB	TRB	AST	PF	DQ	STL	BLK	TO	MPG	PPG	RPG	APG	PCM
68-69	New Orleans-A	22	....	120	59	22	70	.314	0	1	.000	15	22	.682	7	12	19	11	25	0	....	....	11	5.5	2.7	0.9	0.5	.275
ABA Season Totals		22	....	120	59	22	70	.314	0	1	.000	15	22	.682	7	12	19	11	25	0	....	....	11	5.5	2.7	0.9	0.5	....

• SAUNDERS, Fred

James Frederick Saunders

Born: June 13, 1951. Columbus, OH, United States. Height: 6'7". Weight: 210 lbs. Drafted: 1974 College: Syracuse

YEAR	TEAM	GP	GS	MIN	PTS	FGM	FGA	FG%	3PM	3PA	3P%	FTM	FTA	FT%	ORB	DRB	TRB	AST	PF	DQ	STL	BLK	TO	MPG	PPG	RPG	APG	PCM
74-75	Phoenix	69	....	1059	418	176	406	.433	....	....	....	66	95	.695	82	171	253	80	151	3	41	15	....	15.3	6.1	3.7	1.2	.427
75-76	Phoenix	17	....	146	62	28	64	.438	....	....	....	6	11	.545	11	26	37	13	23	0	5	1	....	8.6	3.6	2.2	0.8	.450
76-77	Boston	68	....	1051	403	184	395	.466	....	....	....	35	53	.660	73	150	223	85	191	3	26	7	....	15.5	5.9	3.3	1.3	.399
77-78	Boston	26	....	243	74	30	91	.330	....	....	....	14	17	.824	11	26	37	11	34	0	7	4	21	9.3	2.8	1.4	0.4	.166
77-78	New Orleans	30	....	400	150	69	143	.483	....	....	....	12	19	.632	27	47	74	35	72	3	14	10	21	13.3	5.0	2.5	1.2	.394
NBA Season Totals		210	....	2899	1107	487	1099	.443	....	....	....	133	195	.682	204	420	624	224	471	9	93	37	42	13.8	5.3	3.0	1.1	....
76-77	Boston	9	....	66	29	12	33	.364	....	....	....	5	6	.833	1	8	9	5	21	0	1	0	....	7.3	3.2	1.0	0.6	.225
NBA Playoff Totals		9	....	66	29	12	33	.364	....	....	....	5	6	.833	1	8	9	5	21	0	1	0	....	7.3	3.2	1.0	0.6	....

• SAUNDERS, Rusty

Russell Collier Saunders

Born: Mar. 12, 1906. Trenton, NJ, United States. Died: Nov.24, 1967. Height: 6'2". Weight: 205 lbs. Drafted: — College: none (HS: Central, NJ)

YEAR	TEAM	GP	GS	MIN	PTS	FGM	FGA	FG%	3PM	3PA	3P%	FTM	FTA	FT%	ORB	DRB	TRB	AST	PF	DQ	STL	BLK	TO	MPG	PPG	RPG	APG	PCM
40-41	Detroit-N	14	....	....	21	6	....	....	....	....	....	9	....	....	....	....	....	....	....	....	....	....	....	....	1.5	....	....	....
45-46	Indianapolis-N	5	....	....	3	0	....	....	....	....	....	3	....	....	....	....	....	....	....	....	....	....	....	....	0.6	....	....	....
NBL Season Totals		19	....	....	24	6	....	....	....	....	....	12	....	....	....	....	....	....	....	....	....	....	....	....	1.3	....	....	....

• SAVAGE, Don

Donald Joseph Savage

Born: Apr. 9, 1928. Height: 6'3". Weight: 205 lbs. Drafted: 1951 College: LeMoyne (NY)

YEAR	TEAM	GP	GS	MIN	PTS	FGM	FGA	FG%	3PM	3PA	3P%	FTM	FTA	FT%	ORB	DRB	TRB	AST	PF	DQ	STL	BLK	TO	MPG	PPG	RPG	APG	PCM
51-52	Syracuse	12	....	118	36	9	43	.209	....	....	....	18	28	.643	....	....	24	12	22	0	....	....	....	9.8	3.0	2.0	1.0	.280
56-57	Syracuse	5	....	55	18	6	19	.316	....	....	....	6	7	.857	....	....	7	2	7	0	....	....	....	11.0	3.6	1.4	0.4	.237
NBA Season Totals		17	....	173	54	15	62	.242	....	....	....	24	35	.686	....	....	31	14	29	0	....	....	....	10.2	3.2	1.8	0.8	....

• SAVOVIC, Predrag

Predrag Savovic

Born: May 21, 1976. Pula, Yugoslavia. Height: 6'6". Weight: 225 lbs. Drafted: — College: Hawaii

YEAR	TEAM	GP	GS	MIN	PTS	FGM	FGA	FG%	3PM	3PA	3P%	FTM	FTA	FT%	ORB	DRB	TRB	AST	PF	DQ	STL	BLK	TO	MPG	PPG	RPG	APG	PCM
02-03	Denver	27	0	256	83	29	93	.312	4	26	.154	21	29	.724	9	16	25	22	33	0	14	1	21	9.5	3.1	0.9	0.8	.186
NBA Season Totals		27	0	256	83	29	93	.312	4	26	.154	21	29	.724	9	16	25	22	33	0	14	1	21	9.5	3.1	0.9	0.8	....

YEAR	TEAM	GP	GS	MIN	PTS	FGM	FGA	FG%	3PM	3PA	3P%	FTM	FTA	FT%	ORB	DRB	TRB	AST	PF	DQ	STL	BLK	TO	MPG	PPG	RPG	APG	PCM

• SAWYER, Alan

Alan Leigh Sawyer

Born: Jan. 1, 1928.   Height: 6'5".   Weight: 195 lbs.   Drafted: 1950   College: UCLA

YEAR	TEAM	GP	GS	MIN	PTS	FGM	FGA	FG%	3PM	3PA	3P%	FTM	FTA	FT%	ORB	DRB	TRB	AST	PF	DQ	STL	BLK	TO	MPG	PPG	RPG	APG	PCM
50-51	Washington	33	....	....	217	87	215	.405	....	....	....	43	54	.796	....	....	125	25	75	1	....	....	....	....	6.6	3.8	0.8	....
NBA Season Totals		33	....	....	217	87	215	.405	....	....	....	43	54	.796	....	....	125	25	75	1	....	....	....	....	6.6	3.8	0.8	....

• SCALABRINE, Brian

Brain David Scalabrine

Born: Mar. 18, 1978. Long Beach, CA, United States.   Height: 6'9".   Weight: 241 lbs.   Drafted: 2001   College: Southern California

YEAR	TEAM	GP	GS	MIN	PTS	FGM	FGA	FG%	3PM	3PA	3P%	FTM	FTA	FT%	ORB	DRB	TRB	AST	PF	DQ	STL	BLK	TO	MPG	PPG	RPG	APG	PCM
01-02	New Jersey	28	0	290	60	23	67	.343	3	10	.300	11	15	.733	12	39	51	21	39	0	9	2	24	10.4	2.1	1.8	0.8	.200
02-03	New Jersey	59	7	724	180	68	169	.402	14	39	.359	30	36	.833	40	101	141	46	77	0	16	18	46	12.3	3.1	2.4	0.8	.301
NBA Season Totals		87	7	1014	240	91	236	.386	17	49	.347	41	51	.804	52	140	192	67	116	0	25	20	70	11.7	2.8	2.2	0.8	
01-02	New Jersey	6	0	14	2	1	3	.333	0	1	.000	0	0	.000	1	2	3	0	0	0	0	1	1	2.3	0.3	0.5	0.0	.208
02-03	New Jersey	7	0	20	4	2	4	.500	0	1	.000	0	0	.000	1	3	4	0	3	0	0	0	1	2.9	0.6	0.6	0.0	.177
NBA Playoff Totals		13	0	34	6	3	7	.429	0	2	.000	0	0	.000	2	5	7	0	3	0	0	1	2	2.6	0.5	0.5	0.0	....

• SCALES, DeWayne

DeWayne Jay (Hot Man) Scales

Born: Dec. 28, 1958. Dallas, TX, United States.   Height: 6'8".   Weight: 208 lbs.   Drafted: 1980   College: Louisiana State

YEAR	TEAM	GP	GS	MIN	PTS	FGM	FGA	FG%	3PM	3PA	3P%	FTM	FTA	FT%	ORB	DRB	TRB	AST	PF	DQ	STL	BLK	TO	MPG	PPG	RPG	APG	PCM
80-81	New York	44	....	484	215	94	225	.418	1	6	.167	26	39	.667	47	85	132	10	54	0	12	4	31	11.0	4.9	3.0	0.2	.377
81-82	New York	3	0	24	3	1	5	.200	0	0	.000	1	2	.500	2	3	5	0	3	0	1	1	2	8.0	1.0	1.7	0.0	.087
83-84	Washington	2	0	13	6	3	5	.600	0	0	.000	0	2	.000	0	3	3	0	1	0	1	0	2	6.5	3.0	1.5	0.0	.354
NBA Season Totals		49	0	521	224	98	235	.417	1	6	.167	27	43	.628	49	91	140	10	58	0	14	5	35	10.6	4.6	2.9	0.2	

• SCALISSI, Ted

Theodore Glenn Scalissi

Born: Oct. 26, 1921. Madison, WI, United States. Died: Jan.6, 1987.   Height: 5'8".   Weight: 160 lbs.   Drafted: —   College: Ripon

YEAR	TEAM	GP	GS	MIN	PTS	FGM	FGA	FG%	3PM	3PA	3P%	FTM	FTA	FT%	ORB	DRB	TRB	AST	PF	DQ	STL	BLK	TO	MPG	PPG	RPG	APG	PCM
47-48	Oshkosh-N	7	....	....	5	1	....	....	....	....	....	3	3	1.000	....	....	....	....	....	....	....	....	....	....	0.7	....	....	....
NBL Season Totals		7	....	....	5	1	....	....	....	....	....	3	3		....	....	....	....	....	....	....	....	....	....	0.7	....	....	....

• SCARRY, Jack

Jack Scarry

Born: 1917.   Height: 6'3".   Weight: 195 lbs.   Drafted: —   College: Duquesne

YEAR	TEAM	GP	GS	MIN	PTS	FGM	FGA	FG%	3PM	3PA	3P%	FTM	FTA	FT%	ORB	DRB	TRB	AST	PF	DQ	STL	BLK	TO	MPG	PPG	RPG	APG	PCM
44-45	Pittsburgh-N	6	....	....	7	3	....	....	....	....	....	1	....	....	....	....	....	....	....	....	....	....	....	....	1.2	....	....	....
NBL Season Totals		6	....	....	7	3	....	....	....	....	....	1	....	....	....	....	....	....	....	....	....	....	....	....	1.2	....	....	....

• SCHADE, Frank

Frank Schade

Born: Jan. 22, 1950. Wausau, WI, United States.   Height: 6'1".   Weight: 170 lbs.   Drafted: 1972   College: Texas (El Paso)

YEAR	TEAM	GP	GS	MIN	PTS	FGM	FGA	FG%	3PM	3PA	3P%	FTM	FTA	FT%	ORB	DRB	TRB	AST	PF	DQ	STL	BLK	TO	MPG	PPG	RPG	APG	PCM
72-73	Omaha	9	....	76	10	2	7	.286	....	....	....	6	6	1.000	....	....	6	10	12	0	....	....	....	8.4	1.1	0.7	1.1	.225
NBA Season Totals		9	....	76	10	2	7	.286	....	....	....	6	6	1.000	....	....	6	10	12	0	....	....	....	8.4	1.1	0.7	1.1	

• SCHADLER, Ben

Bernard R. Schadler

Born: Mar. 9, 1924.   Height: 6'   Weight: 185 lbs.   Drafted: 1947   College: Northwestern

YEAR	TEAM	GP	GS	MIN	PTS	FGM	FGA	FG%	3PM	3PA	3P%	FTM	FTA	FT%	ORB	DRB	TRB	AST	PF	DQ	STL	BLK	TO	MPG	PPG	RPG	APG	PCM
47-48	Chicago	37	....	....	56	23	116	.198	....	....	....	10	13	.769	....	....	....	6	40	....	....	....	....	....	1.5	....	0.2	....
48-49	Detroit-N	13	....	....	136	58	....	....	....	....	....	20	28	.714	....	....	....	....	....	....	....	....	....	....	10.5	....	....	....
48-49	Waterloo-N	40	....	....	222	92	....	....	....	....	....	38	61	.623	....	....	....	....	129	....	....	....	....	....	5.6	....	....	....
NBA Season Totals		37	....	....	56	23	116	.198	....	....	....	10	13	.769	....	....	....	6	40	....	....	....	....	....	1.5	....	0.2	....
NBL Season Totals		53	....	....	358	150	....	....	....	....	....	58	89		....	....	....	....	129	....	....	....	....	....	6.8	....	....	....
Career Totals		90	....	....	414	173	116	....	....	....	....	68	102		....	....	....	6	169	....	....	....	....	....	4.6	....	0.1	....
47-48	Chicago	4	....	....	10	5	23	.217	....	....	....	0	2	.000	....	....	....	1	4	....	....	....	....	....	2.5	....	0.3	....
NBA Playoff Totals		4	....	....	10	5	23	.217	....	....	....	0	2	.000	....	....	....	1	4	....	....	....	....	....	2.5	....	0.3	....

• SCHAEFER, Herm

Herman H. Schaefer

Born: Dec. 20, 1919. Died: Mar.21, 1980.   Height: 6'   Weight: 175 lbs.   Drafted: —   College: Indiana

YEAR	TEAM	GP	GS	MIN	PTS	FGM	FGA	FG%	3PM	3PA	3P%	FTM	FTA	FT%	ORB	DRB	TRB	AST	PF	DQ	STL	BLK	TO	MPG	PPG	RPG	APG	PCM
41-42	Fort Wayne-N	24	....	....	207	85	....	....	....	....	....	37	....	....	....	....	....	....	....	....	....	....	....	....	8.6	....	....	....
42-43	Fort Wayne-N	21	....	....	84	36	....	....	....	....	....	12	....	....	....	....	....	....	....	....	....	....	....	....	4.0	....	....	....
45-46	Fort Wayne-N	15	....	....	23	10	....	....	....	....	....	3	....	....	....	....	....	....	....	....	....	....	....	....	1.5	....	....	....
46-47	Indianapolis-N	44	....	....	359	147	....	....	....	....	....	65	90	.722	....	....	....	....	45	....	....	....	....	....	8.2	....	....	....
47-48	Indianapolis-N	3	....	....	10	2	....	....	....	....	....	6	6	1.000	....	....	....	....	....	....	....	....	....	....	3.3	....	....	....
47-48	Minneapolis-N	54	....	....	288	108	....	....	....	....	....	72	90	.800	....	....	....	....	....	....	....	....	....	....	5.3	....	....	....
48-49	Minneapolis	58	....	....	602	214	572	.374	....	....	....	174	213	.817	....	....	....	185	121	....	....	....	....	....	10.4	....	3.2	....
49-50	Minneapolis	65	....	....	330	122	314	.389	....	....	....	86	101	.851	....	....	....	203	104	....	....	....	....	....	5.1	....	3.1	....
NBA Season Totals		123	....	....	932	336	886	.379	....	....	....	260	314	.828	....	....	....	388	225	....	....	....	....	....	7.6	....	3.2	....
NBL Season Totals		161	....	....	971	388	....	....	....	....	....	195	186		....	....	....	....	45	....	....	....	....	....	6.0	....	....	....
Career Totals		284	....	....	1903	724	886	....	....	....	....	455	500		....	....	....	388	270	....	....	....	....	....	6.7	....	1.4	....
41-42	Fort Wayne-N	6	....	....	31	13	....	....	....	....	....	5	....	....	....	....	....	....	....	....	....	....	....	....	5.2	....	....	....
42-43	Fort Wayne-N	5	....	....	15	6	....	....	....	....	....	3	....	....	....	....	....	....	....	....	....	....	....	....	3.0	....	....	....
46-47	Indianapolis-N	5	....	....	58	22	....	....	....	....	....	14	18	.778	....	....	....	....	....	....	....	....	....	....	11.6	....	....	....
47-48	Minneapolis-N	10	....	....	133	51	....	....	....	....	....	31	38	.816	....	....	....	....	....	....	....	....	....	....	13.3	....	....	....

YEAR	TEAM	GP	GS	MIN	PTS	FGM	FGA	FG%	3PM	3PA	3P%	FTM	FTA	FT%	ORB	DRB	TRB	AST	PF	DQ	STL	BLK	TO	MPG	PPG	RPG	APG	PCM
48-49	Minneapolis	10	....	....	124	48	104	.462	....	....	....	28	32	.875	....	....	....		31	22	....	....	....	....	12.4	....	3.1	....
49-50	Minneapolis	12	....	....	51	16	42	.381	....	....	....	19	22	.864	....	....	....		16	12	....	....	....	....	4.3	....	1.3	....
NBA Playoff Totals		22	....	....	175	64	146	.438	....	....	....	47	54	.870	....	....	....		47	34	....	....	....	....	8.0	....	2.1	....
NBL Playoff Totals		26	....	....	237	92	....					53	56													9.1		
Career Playoff Totals		48	....	....	412	156	146					100	110						47	34					8.6	....	1.0	....

• SCHAEFFER, Billy

William G. Schaeffer

Born: Dec. 11, 1951. Bellerose, NY, United States.   Height: 6'5".   Weight: 200 lbs.   Drafted: 1973   College: St. John's (NY)

YEAR	TEAM	GP	GS	MIN	PTS	FGM	FGA	FG%	3PM	3PA	3P%	FTM	FTA	FT%	ORB	DRB	TRB	AST	PF	DQ	STL	BLK	TO	MPG	PPG	RPG	APG	PCM
73-74	New York-A	59	....	871	385	171	344	.497	2	9	.222	41	54	.759	49	92	141	37	140	....	24	9	53	14.8	6.5	2.4	0.6	.384
74-75	New York-A	27	....	280	139	61	131	.466	2	7	.286	15	25	.600	15	22	37	20	36	....	9	2	18	10.4	5.1	1.4	0.7	.398
75-76	New York-A	20	....	119	72	31	77	.403	2	9	.222	8	9	.889	10	12	22	9	15	....	6	2	7	6.0	3.6	1.1	0.5	.449
75-76	Virginia-A	31	....	518	206	83	181	.459	0	1	.000	40	54	.741	29	60	89	28	57	....	13	7	28	16.7	6.6	2.9	0.9	.381
ABA Season Totals		137	....	1788	802	346	733	.472	6	26	.231	104	142	.732	103	186	289	94	248	....	52	20	106	13.1	5.9	2.1	0.7	....
73-74	New York-A	5	....	23	19	8	16	.500	0	0	.000	3	4	.750	6	3	9	3	3	....	0	0	1	4.6	3.8	1.8	0.6	.938
ABA Playoff Totals		5	....	23	19	8	16	.500	0	0	.000	3	4	.750	6	3	9	3	3	....	0	0	1	4.6	3.8	1.8	0.6	....

• SCHAFER, Bob

Robert Thomas Schafer

Born: 1933.   Height: 6'3".   Weight: 195 lbs.   Drafted: 1955   College: Villanova

YEAR	TEAM	GP	GS	MIN	PTS	FGM	FGA	FG%	3PM	3PA	3P%	FTM	FTA	FT%	ORB	DRB	TRB	AST	PF	DQ	STL	BLK	TO	MPG	PPG	RPG	APG	PCM
55-56	Philadelphia	12	....	82	31	12	35	.343	....	....	....	7	12	.583			13	9	14	0	....	....	....	6.8	2.6	1.1	0.8	.333
55-56	St. Louis	42	....	496	193	69	235	.294	....	....	....	55	69	.797			58	44	61	0	....	....	....	11.8	4.6	1.4	1.0	.276
56-57	Syracuse	11	....	167	49	19	66	.288	....	....	....	11	13	.846			11	15	16	0	....	....	....	15.2	4.5	1.0	1.4	.205
NBA Season Totals		65	....	745	273	100	336	.298	....	....	....	73	94	.777			82	68	91	0	....	....	....	11.5	4.2	1.3	1.0	....
55-56	St. Louis	4	....	39	11	3	20	.150	....	....	....	5	6	.833			9	1	8	1	....	....	....	9.8	2.8	2.3	0.3	.070
NBA Playoff Totals		4	....	39	11	3	20	.150	....	....	....	5	6	.833			9	1	8	1	....	....	....	9.8	2.8	2.3	0.3	....

• SCHALL, Benny

Benny Schall

Born: 1917.   Height: 5'11".   Weight: 170 lbs.   Drafted: —   College: Toledo

YEAR	TEAM	GP	GS	MIN	PTS	FGM	FGA	FG%	3PM	3PA	3P%	FTM	FTA	FT%	ORB	DRB	TRB	AST	PF	DQ	STL	BLK	TO	MPG	PPG	RPG	APG	PCM
41-42	Toledo-N	2	....	....	1	0	....					1	....	....											0.5		
46-47	Toledo-N	5	....	....	2	1	....					0	0	.000											0.4		
NBL Season Totals		7	....	....	3	1	....					1	0												0.4		

• SCHARNUS, Ben

Benedict Michael (Whitey) Scharnus

Born: Dec. 11, 1917. Died: Mar.19, 1982.   Height: 6'2".   Weight: 173 lbs.   Drafted: —   College: Seton Hall

YEAR	TEAM	GP	GS	MIN	PTS	FGM	FGA	FG%	3PM	3PA	3P%	FTM	FTA	FT%	ORB	DRB	TRB	AST	PF	DQ	STL	BLK	TO	MPG	PPG	RPG	APG	PCM
46-47	Cleveland	51	....	....	103	33	165	.200	....	....	....	37	59	.627	....	....		19	83						2.0		0.4	
48-49	Providence	1	....	....	0	0	1	.000	....	....	....	0	1	.000	....	....		0	0						0.0		0.0	
NBA Season Totals		52	....	....	103	33	166	.199	....	....	....	37	60	.617	....	....		19	83						2.0		0.4	
46-47	Cleveland	3	....	....	17	6	21	.286	....	....	....	5	9	.556	....	....		2	10						5.7		0.7	
NBA Playoff Totals		3	....	....	17	6	21	.286	....	....	....	5	9	.556	....	....		2	10						5.7		0.7	

• SCHATZMAN, Marv

Marvin J. Schatzman

Born: Feb. 18, 1927.   Height: 6'5".   Weight: 200 lbs.   Drafted: 1949   College: St. Louis

YEAR	TEAM	GP	GS	MIN	PTS	FGM	FGA	FG%	3PM	3PA	3P%	FTM	FTA	FT%	ORB	DRB	TRB	AST	PF	DQ	STL	BLK	TO	MPG	PPG	RPG	APG	PCM
49-50	Baltimore	34	....	....	115	43	174	.247	....	....	....	29	50	.580	....	....		38	49						3.4		1.1	
NBA Season Totals		34	....	....	115	43	174	.247	....	....	....	29	50	.580	....	....		38	49						3.4		1.1	

• SCHAUS, Fred

Frederick Appleton Schaus

Born: June 30, 1925. Newark, OH, United States.   Height: 6'5".   Weight: 205 lbs.   Drafted: —   College: West Virginia

YEAR	TEAM	GP	GS	MIN	PTS	FGM	FGA	FG%	3PM	3PA	3P%	FTM	FTA	FT%	ORB	DRB	TRB	AST	PF	DQ	STL	BLK	TO	MPG	PPG	RPG	APG	PCM
49-50	Fort Wayne	68	....	....	972	351	996	.352	....	....	....	270	330	.818	....	....		176	232	....					14.3	....	2.6	
50-51	Fort Wayne	68	....	....	1028	312	918	.340	....	....	....	404	484	.835	....	....	495	184	240	11					15.1	7.3	2.7	
51-52	Fort Wayne	62	....	2581	872	281	778	.361	....	....	....	310	372	.833	....	....	434	247	221	7				41.6	14.1	7.0	4.0	.405
52-53	Fort Wayne	69	....	2541	723	240	719	.334	....	....	....	243	296	.821	....	....	413	245	261	11				36.8	10.5	6.0	3.6	.344
53-54	FtW/NY	67	....	1515	475	161	415	.388	....	....	....	153	195	.785	....	....	267	109	176	3				22.6	7.1	4.0	1.6	.361
NBA Season Totals		334	....	6637	4070	1345	3826	.352	....	....	....	1380	1677	.823	....	....	1609	961	1130	32				19.9	12.2	4.8	2.9	....
49-50	Fort Wayne	4	....	....	74	24	66	.364	....	....	....	26	31	.839	....	....		11	9	....					18.5	....	2.8	
50-51	Fort Wayne	3	....	....	43	17	44	.386	....	....	....	9	11	.818	....	....	16	10	10	0					14.3	5.3	3.3	
51-52	Fort Wayne	2	....	90	31	12	35	.343	....	....	....	7	8	.875	....	....	15	14	9	0				45.0	15.5	7.5	7.0	.442
52-53	Fort Wayne	8	....	244	71	18	60	.300	....	....	....	35	46	.761	....	....	42	12	40	2				30.5	8.9	5.3	1.5	.278
53-54	New York	4	....	119	28	7	25	.280	....	....	....	14	15	.933	....	....	12	8	18	2				29.8	7.0	3.0	2.0	.230
NBA Playoff Totals		21	....	453	247	78	230	.339	....	....	....	91	111	.820	....	....	85	55	86	4				21.6	11.8	4.0	2.6	....

• SCHAYES, Danny

Daniel Leslie (Danny) Schayes

Born: May 10, 1959. Syracuse, NY, United States.   Height: 6'11".   Weight: 235 lbs.   Drafted: 1981   College: Syracuse

YEAR	TEAM	GP	GS	MIN	PTS	FGM	FGA	FG%	3PM	3PA	3P%	FTM	FTA	FT%	ORB	DRB	TRB	AST	PF	DQ	STL	BLK	TO	MPG	PPG	RPG	APG	PCM
81-82	Utah	82	20	1623	644	252	524	.481	0	1	.000	140	185	.757	131	296	427	146	292	4	46	72	148	19.8	7.9	5.2	1.8	.469
82-83	Utah	50	50	1638	619	231	514	.449	0	1	.000	157	195	.805	137	312	449	165	216	7	39	68	195	32.8	12.4	9.0	3.3	.462
82-83	Denver	32	0	646	293	111	235	.472	0	0	.000	71	100	.710	63	123	186	40	109	1	15	30	58	20.2	9.2	5.8	1.3	.494
83-84	Denver	82	15	1420	581	183	371	.493	0	2	.000	215	272	.790	145	288	433	91	308	5	32	60	123	17.3	7.1	5.3	1.1	.498

YEAR	TEAM	GP	GS	MIN	PTS	FGM	FGA	FG%	3PM	3PA	3P%	FTM	FTA	FT%	ORB	DRB	TRB	AST	PF	DQ	STL	BLK	TO	MPG	PPG	RPG	APG	PCM
84-85	Denver	56	0	542	199	60	129	.465	0	0	.000	79	97	.814	48	96	144	38	98	2	20	25	45	9.7	3.6	2.6	0.7	.471
85-86	Denver	80	13	1654	658	221	440	.502	0	1	.000	216	278	.777	154	285	439	79	298	7	42	63	104	20.7	8.2	5.5	1.0	.472
86-87	Denver	76	41	1556	649	210	405	.519	0	0	.000	229	294	.779	120	260	380	85	266	5	20	74	99	20.5	8.5	5.0	1.1	.484
87-88	Denver	81	74	2166	1129	361	668	.540	0	2	.000	407	487	.836	200	462	662	106	323	9	62	92	154	26.7	13.9	8.2	1.3	.640
88-89	Denver	76	64	1918	969	317	607	.522	3	9	.333	332	402	.826	142	358	500	105	320	8	42	81	160	25.2	12.8	6.6	1.4	.553
89-90	Denver	53	22	1194	551	163	330	.494	0	4	.000	225	264	.852	117	225	342	61	200	7	41	45	74	22.5	10.4	6.5	1.2	.569
90-91	Milwaukee	82	38	2228	870	298	597	.499	0	5	.000	274	328	.835	174	361	535	98	264	4	55	61	107	27.2	10.6	6.5	1.2	.473
91-92	Milwaukee	43	4	726	240	83	199	.417	0	0	.000	74	96	.771	58	110	168	34	98	0	19	19	43	16.9	5.6	3.9	0.8	.364
92-93	Milwaukee	70	7	1124	322	105	263	.399	0	3	.000	112	137	.818	72	177	249	78	148	1	36	36	63	16.1	4.6	3.6	1.1	.372
93-94	Milwaukee	23	6	230	49	14	46	.304	0	0	.000	21	22	.955	16	29	45	5	27	0	5	8	14	10.0	2.1	2.0	0.2	.229
93-94	LA Lakers	13	0	133	36	14	38	.368	0	0	.000	8	10	.800	15	19	34	8	18	0	5	2	9	10.2	2.8	2.6	0.6	.322
94-95	Phoenix	69	27	823	303	126	248	.508	1	1	1.000	50	69	.725	57	151	208	89	170	0	20	37	62	11.9	4.4	3.0	1.3	.468
95-96	Miami	32	6	399	101	32	94	.340	0	0	.000	37	46	.804	29	60	89	9	60	0	11	16	22	12.5	3.2	2.8	0.3	.271
96-97	Orlando	45	6	540	133	47	120	.392	0	1	.000	39	52	.750	41	84	125	14	74	0	15	16	27	12.0	3.0	2.8	0.3	.296
97-98	Orlando	74	33	1272	406	155	371	.418	0	0	.000	96	119	.807	97	145	242	44	182	0	34	33	59	17.2	5.5	3.3	0.6	.307
98-99	Orlando	19	1	143	28	11	29	.379	0	0	.000	6	8	.750	3	11	14	4	23	0	1	2	8	7.5	1.5	0.7	0.2	.093
NBA Season Totals		1138	427	21975	8780	2994	6228	.481	4	30	.133	2788	3461	.806	1819	3852	5671	1299	3494	60	560	840	1574	19.3	7.7	5.0	1.1	....
82-83	Denver	8	0	163	57	21	43	.488	0	0	.000	15	15	1.000	11	29	40	14	25	0	2	5	17	20.4	7.1	5.0	1.8	.419
83-84	Denver	5	0	81	28	11	18	.611	0	0	.000	6	8	.750	3	21	24	4	20	0	4	3	7	16.2	5.6	4.8	0.8	.467
84-85	Denver	9	0	118	36	11	26	.423	0	0	.000	14	20	.700	8	22	30	12	22	0	3	4	5	13.1	4.0	3.3	1.3	.437
85-86	Denver	10	6	295	116	46	86	.535	0	0	.000	24	30	.800	34	48	82	9	37	1	4	17	21	29.5	11.6	8.2	0.9	.490
86-87	Denver	3	0	75	30	12	17	.706	0	0	.000	6	9	.667	6	11	17	2	10	0	1	2	3	25.0	10.0	5.7	0.7	.497
87-88	Denver	11	11	314	180	55	88	.625	0	0	.000	70	83	.843	30	49	79	18	46	1	3	10	24	28.5	16.4	7.2	1.6	.651
88-89	Denver	2	0	36	8	1	7	.143	0	0	.000	6	8	.750	2	9	11	1	4	0	1	1	1	18.0	4.0	5.5	0.5	.329
90-91	Milwaukee	3	3	71	28	9	23	.391	0	1	.000	10	11	.909	4	8	12	3	8	0	3	1	6	23.7	9.3	4.0	1.0	.328
94-95	Phoenix	10	0	146	29	11	29	.379	0	1	.000	7	8	.875	4	16	20	8	38	0	3	3	8	14.6	2.9	2.0	0.8	.132
95-96	Miami	2	0	17	7	3	4	.750	0	0	.000	1	2	.500	2	2	4	0	1	0	0	0	2	8.5	3.5	2.0	0.0	.412
96-97	Orlando	5	2	92	22	9	23	.391	0	0	.000	4	4	1.000	4	8	12	5	16	0	2	1	4	18.4	4.4	2.4	1.0	.186
98-99	Orlando	1	0	8	0	0	1	.000	0	0	.000	0	0	.000	0	0	0	0	0	0	0	0	0	8.0	0.0	0.0	0.0	-.111
NBA Playoff Totals		69	22	1416	541	189	365	.518	0	2	.000	163	198	.823	108	223	331	76	227	2	26	47	98	20.5	7.8	4.8	1.1	....

• SCHAYES, Dolph

Adolph Schayes

Born: May 19, 1928. New York, NY, United States. Height: 6'7". Weight: 195 lbs. Drafted: 1948 College: New York University HOF: 1973

YEAR	TEAM	GP	GS	MIN	PTS	FGM	FGA	FG%	3PM	3PA	3P%	FTM	FTA	FT%	ORB	DRB	TRB	AST	PF	DQ	STL	BLK	TO	MPG	PPG	RPG	APG	PCM
48-49	Syracuse-N	63	....	....	809	271	....	....	....	....	....	267	370	.722	....	....	....	....	217	....	....	....	....	....	12.8	....	....	....
49-50	Syracuse	64	....	....	1072	348	903	.385	....	....	....	376	486	.774	....	....	....	259	225	....	....	....	....	....	16.8	....	4.0	....
50-51	Syracuse	66	....	....	1121	332	930	.357	....	....	....	457	608	.752	....	....	**1080**	251	271	9	....	....	....	....	17.0	**16.4**	3.8	....
51-52	Syracuse	63	....	2004	868	263	740	.355	....	....	....	342	424	.807	....	....	773	182	213	5	....	....	....	31.8	13.8	12.3	2.9	.603
52-53	Syracuse	71	....	2668	1262	375	1022	.367	....	....	....	512	619	.827	....	....	920	227	271	9	....	....	....	37.6	17.8	13.0	3.2	.604
53-54	Syracuse	72	....	2655	1228	370	973	.380	....	....	....	488	590	.827	....	....	870	214	232	4	....	....	....	36.9	17.1	12.1	3.0	.593
54-55	Syracuse	72	....	2526	1333	422	1103	.383	....	....	....	489	587	.833	....	....	887	213	247	6	....	....	....	35.1	18.5	12.3	3.0	.643
55-56	Syracuse	72	....	2517	1472	465	1202	.387	....	....	....	542	632	.858	....	....	891	200	251	9	....	....	....	35.0	20.4	12.4	2.8	.678
56-57	Syracuse	72	....	**2851**	1617	496	1308	.379	....	....	....	**625**	691	.904	....	....	1008	229	219	5	....	....	....	**39.6**	22.5	14.0	3.2	.682
57-58	Syracuse	72	....	**2918**	1791	581	1458	.398	....	....	....	629	696	**.904**	....	....	1022	224	244	6	....	....	....	**40.5**	24.9	14.2	3.1	.709
58-59	Syracuse	72	....	2645	1534	504	1304	.387	....	....	....	526	609	.864	....	....	962	178	280	9	....	....	....	36.7	21.3	13.4	2.5	.658
59-60	Syracuse	75	....	2741	1689	578	1440	.401	....	....	....	533	597	**.893**	....	....	959	256	263	10	....	....	....	36.5	22.5	12.8	3.4	.714
60-61	Syracuse	79	....	3007	1868	594	1595	.372	....	....	....	**680**	783	.868	....	....	960	296	296	9	....	....	....	38.1	23.6	12.2	3.7	.682
61-62	Syracuse	56	....	1480	822	268	751	.357	....	....	....	286	319	**.897**	....	....	439	120	167	4	....	....	....	26.4	14.7	7.8	2.1	.578
62-63	Syracuse	66	....	1438	627	223	575	.388	....	....	....	181	206	.879	....	....	375	175	177	2	....	....	....	21.8	9.5	5.7	2.7	.540
63-64	Philadelphia	24	....	350	134	44	143	.308	....	....	....	46	57	.807	....	....	110	48	76	3	....	....	....	14.6	5.6	4.6	2.0	.478
NBA Season Totals		996	....	29800	18438	5863	15447	.380	....	....	....	6712	7904	.849	....	....	11256	3072	3432	90	....	....	....	29.9	18.5	11.3	3.1	....
NBL Season Totals		63	....	....	809	271	....	....	....	....	....	267	370	....	....	....	....	....	217	....	....	....	....	....	12.8	....	....	....
Career Totals		1059	....	29800	19247	6134	15447	....	....	....	....	6979	8274	....	....	....	11256	3072	3649	90	....	....	....	28.1	18.2	10.6	2.9	....
48-49	Syracuse-N	6	....	....	86	27	....	....	....	....	....	32	41	.780	....	....	....	....	....	....	....	....	....	....	14.3	....	....	....
49-50	Syracuse	11	....	....	188	57	148	.385	....	....	....	74	101	.733	....	....	....	28	43	....	....	....	....	....	17.1	....	2.5	....
50-51	Syracuse	7	....	....	143	47	105	.448	....	....	....	49	64	.766	....	....	102	20	28	2	....	....	....	....	20.4	14.6	2.9	....
51-52	Syracuse	7	....	248	142	41	91	.451	....	....	....	60	78	.769	....	....	90	15	34	2	....	....	....	35.4	20.3	12.9	2.1	.691
52-53	Syracuse	2	....	58	18	4	16	.250	....	....	....	10	13	.769	....	....	17	1	7	0	....	....	....	29.0	9.0	8.5	0.5	.332
53-54	Syracuse	13	....	374	208	64	140	.457	....	....	....	80	108	.741	....	....	136	24	40	1	....	....	....	28.8	16.0	10.5	1.8	.688
54-55	Syracuse	11	....	363	209	60	167	.359	....	....	....	89	106	.840	....	....	141	40	48	3	....	....	....	33.0	19.0	12.8	3.6	.716
55-56	Syracuse	8	....	310	177	52	142	.366	....	....	....	73	83	.880	....	....	111	27	27	0	....	....	....	38.8	22.1	13.9	3.4	.685
56-57	Syracuse	5	....	215	107	29	95	.305	....	....	....	49	55	.891	....	....	90	14	18	0	....	....	....	43.0	21.4	18.0	2.8	.621
57-58	Syracuse	3	....	131	80	25	64	.391	....	....	....	30	36	.833	....	....	45	6	10	0	....	....	....	43.7	26.7	15.0	2.0	.658
58-59	Syracuse	9	....	351	254	78	195	.400	....	....	....	98	107	.916	....	....	117	41	36	0	....	....	....	39.0	28.2	13.0	4.6	.821
59-60	Syracuse	3	....	126	88	30	66	.455	....	....	....	28	30	.933	....	....	48	8	10	0	....	....	....	42.0	29.3	16.0	2.7	.813
60-61	Syracuse	8	....	308	165	51	152	.336	....	....	....	63	70	.900	....	....	91	21	32	2	....	....	....	38.5	20.6	11.4	2.6	.547
61-62	Syracuse	5	....	95	57	24	66	.364	....	....	....	9	13	.692	....	....	35	5	21	0	....	....	....	19.0	11.4	7.0	1.0	.504
62-63	Syracuse	5	....	108	51	20	44	.455	....	....	....	11	12	.917	....	....	28	7	17	0	....	....	....	21.6	10.2	5.6	1.4	.514
NBA Playoff Totals		97	....	2687	1887	582	1491	.390	....	....	....	723	876	.825	....	....	1051	257	371	10	....	....	....	27.7	19.5	10.8	2.6	....
NBL Playoff Totals		6	....	....	86	27	....	....	....	....	....	32	41	....	....	....	....	....	....	....	....	....	....	....	14.3	....	....	....
Career Playoff Totals		103	....	2687	1973	609	1491	....	....	....	....	755	917	....	....	....	1051	257	371	10	....	....	....	26.1	19.2	10.2	2.5	....

• SCHECTMAN, Ossie

Oscar B. (Ossie) Schectman

Born: Mar. 30, 1919. Kew Gardens, NY, United States. Height: 6' Weight: 175 lbs. Drafted: — College: Long Island University

YEAR	TEAM	GP	GS	MIN	PTS	FGM	FGA	FG%	3PM	3PA	3P%	FTM	FTA	FT%	ORB	DRB	TRB	AST	PF	DQ	STL	BLK	TO	MPG	PPG	RPG	APG	PCM
46-47	New York	54	....	....	435	162	588	.276	....	....	....	111	179	.620	....	....	....	109	115	....	....	....	....	....	8.1	....	2.0	....
NBA Season Totals		54	....	....	435	162	588	.276	....	....	....	111	179	.620	....	....	....	109	115	....	....	....	....	....	8.1	....	2.0	....

YEAR	TEAM	GP	GS	MIN	PTS	FGM	FGA	FG%	3PM	3PA	3P%	FTM	FTA	FT%	ORB	DRB	TRB	AST	PF	DQ	STL	BLK	TO	MPG	PPG	RPG	APG	PCM

• SCHEFFLER, Herb

Herb Scheffler

Born: 1917. Height: 6'4". Weight: 220 lbs. Drafted: — College: Northwestern Illinois

YEAR	TEAM	GP	GS	MIN	PTS	FGM	FGA	FG%	3PM	3PA	3P%	FTM	FTA	FT%	ORB	DRB	TRB	AST	PF	DQ	STL	BLK	TO	MPG	PPG	RPG	APG	PCM
46-47	Detroit-N	33	....	....	126	43	....	....	....	....	....	40	67	.597	....	....	....	....	85	....	....	....	....	....	3.8	....	....	....
NBL Season Totals		33	....	....	126	43	....	....	....	....	....	40	67	....	....	....	....	....	85	....	....	....	....	....	3.8	....	....	....

• SCHEFFLER, Steve

Stephen Robert Scheffler

Born: Sept. 3, 1967. Grand Rapids, MI, United States. Height: 6'9". Weight: 250 lbs. Drafted: 1990 College: Purdue

YEAR	TEAM	GP	GS	MIN	PTS	FGM	FGA	FG%	3PM	3PA	3P%	FTM	FTA	FT%	ORB	DRB	TRB	AST	PF	DQ	STL	BLK	TO	MPG	PPG	RPG	APG	PCM
90-91	Charlotte	39	0	227	59	20	39	.513	0	0	.000	19	21	.905	21	24	45	9	20	0	6	2	4	5.8	1.5	1.2	0.2	.380
91-92	Sacramento	4	0	15	9	2	2	1.000	0	0	.000	5	6	.833	2	1	3	0	2	0	0	1	0	3.8	2.3	0.8	0.0	.755
91-92	Denver	7	0	46	12	4	7	.571	0	0	.000	4	6	.667	8	3	11	0	8	0	3	0	1	6.6	1.7	1.6	0.0	.362
92-93	Seattle	29	5	166	66	25	48	.521	0	0	.000	16	24	.667	15	21	36	5	37	0	6	1	6	5.7	2.3	1.2	0.2	.382
93-94	Seattle	35	1	152	75	28	46	.609	0	0	.000	19	20	.950	11	15	26	6	25	0	7	0	7	4.3	2.1	0.7	0.2	.506
94-95	Seattle	18	0	102	39	12	23	.522	0	0	.000	15	18	.833	8	15	23	4	9	0	2	2	4	5.7	2.2	1.3	0.2	.479
95-96	Seattle	35	2	181	58	24	45	.533	1	5	.200	9	19	.474	15	18	33	2	25	0	6	2	7	5.2	1.7	0.9	0.1	.309
96-97	Seattle	7	0	29	13	6	7	.857	0	0	.000	1	2	.500	1	2	3	0	5	0	0	0	5	4.1	1.9	0.4	0.0	.255
NBA Season Totals		174	8	918	331	121	217	.558	1	5	.200	88	116	.759	81	99	180	26	131	0	30	8	34	5.3	1.9	1.0	0.1	
92-93	Seattle	9	0	22	14	5	10	.500	0	0	.000	4	4	1.000	6	4	10	1	1	0	2	0	0	2.4	1.6	1.1	0.1	.961
93-94	Seattle	1	0	9	2	1	1	1.000	0	0	.000	0	2	.000	0	3	3	0	1	0	1	0	1	9.0	2.0	3.0	0.0	.375
94-95	Seattle	1	0	1	2	1	1	1.000	0	0	.000	0	0	.000	0	1	1	0	0	0	0	0	0	1.0	2.0	1.0	0.0	2.938
95-96	Seattle	8	0	22	0	0	4	.000	0	0	.000	0	2	.000	2	4	6	2	2	0	1	0	1	2.8	0.0	0.8	0.3	.096
NBA Playoff Totals		19	0	54	18	7	16	.438	0	0	.000	4	8	.500	8	12	20	3	4	0	4	0	2	2.8	0.9	1.1	0.2	

• SCHEFFLER, Tom

Thomas Mark Scheffler

Born: Oct. 27, 1954. St. Joseph, MI, United States. Height: 6'11". Weight: 240 lbs. Drafted: 1977 College: Purdue

YEAR	TEAM	GP	GS	MIN	PTS	FGM	FGA	FG%	3PM	3PA	3P%	FTM	FTA	FT%	ORB	DRB	TRB	AST	PF	DQ	STL	BLK	TO	MPG	PPG	RPG	APG	PCM
84-85	Portland	39	0	268	52	21	51	.412	0	0	.000	10	20	.500	18	58	76	11	48	0	8	11	16	6.9	1.3	1.9	0.3	.307
NBA Season Totals		39	0	268	52	21	51	.412	0	0	.000	10	20	.500	18	58	76	11	48	0	8	11	16	6.9	1.3	1.9	0.3	
84-85	Portland	3	0	10	7	2	3	.667	0	0	.000	3	4	.750	3	2	5	0	0	0	1	0	1	3.3	2.3	1.7	0.0	1.026
NBA Playoff Totals		3	0	10	7	2	3	.667	0	0	.000	3	4	.750	3	2	5	0	0	0	1	0	1	3.3	2.3	1.7	0.0	

• SCHEIWE, Ed

Ed Scheiwe

Born: Feb. 25, 1918. Died: June19, 1997. Height: 5'11". Weight: 170 lbs. Drafted: — College: Wisconsin

YEAR	TEAM	GP	GS	MIN	PTS	FGM	FGA	FG%	3PM	3PA	3P%	FTM	FTA	FT%	ORB	DRB	TRB	AST	PF	DQ	STL	BLK	TO	MPG	PPG	RPG	APG	PCM
43-44	Oshkosh-N	16	....	....	72	28	....	....	....	....	....	16	....	....	....	....	....	....	....	....	....	....	....	....	4.5	....	....	....
44-45	Chicago-N	16	....	....	16	6	....	....	....	....	....	4	....	....	....	....	....	....	....	....	....	....	....	....	1.0	....	....	....
NBL Season Totals		32	....	....	88	34	....	....	....	....	....	20	....	....	....	....	....	....	....	....	....	....	....	....	2.8	....	....	....
43-44	Oshkosh-N	3	....	....	3	1	....	....	....	....	....	1	....	....	....	....	....	....	....	....	....	....	....	....	1.0	....	....	....
44-45	Chicago-N	2	....	....	1	0	....	....	....	....	....	1	....	....	....	....	....	....	....	....	....	....	....	....	0.5	....	....	....
NBL Playoff Totals		5	....	....	4	1	....	....	....	....	....	2	....	....	....	....	....	....	....	....	....	....	....	....	0.8	....	....	....

• SCHELLHASE, Dave

David Gene Schellhase Jr.

Born: Oct. 14, 1944. Evansville, IN, United States. Height: 6'3". Weight: 205 lbs. Drafted: 1966 College: Purdue

YEAR	TEAM	GP	GS	MIN	PTS	FGM	FGA	FG%	3PM	3PA	3P%	FTM	FTA	FT%	ORB	DRB	TRB	AST	PF	DQ	STL	BLK	TO	MPG	PPG	RPG	APG	PCM
66-67	Chicago	31	....	212	94	40	111	.360	....	....	....	14	22	.636	....	....	29	23	27	0	....	....	....	6.8	3.0	0.9	0.7	.350
67-68	Chicago	42	....	301	114	47	138	.341	....	....	....	20	38	.526	....	....	47	37	43	0	....	....	....	7.2	2.7	1.1	0.9	.329
NBA Season Totals		73	....	513	208	87	249	.349	....	....	....	34	60	.567	....	....	76	60	70	0	....	....	....	7.0	2.8	1.0	0.8	
66-67	Chicago	2	....	3	1	0	2	.000	....	....	....	1	2	.500	....	....	1	0	0	0	....	....	....	1.5	0.5	0.5	0.0	-.065
67-68	Chicago	1	....	5	2	1	3	.333	....	....	....	0	0	.000	....	....	0	0	0	0	....	....	....	5.0	2.0	0.0	0.0	.081
NBA Playoff Totals		3	....	8	3	1	5	.200	....	....	....	1	2	.500	....	....	1	0	0	0	....	....	....	2.7	1.0	0.3	0.0	

• SCHERER, Herb

Herbert Frederick Scherer

Born: Dec. 21, 1929. Height: 6'9". Weight: 212 lbs. Drafted: 1950 College: Long Island University

YEAR	TEAM	GP	GS	MIN	PTS	FGM	FGA	FG%	3PM	3PA	3P%	FTM	FTA	FT%	ORB	DRB	TRB	AST	PF	DQ	STL	BLK	TO	MPG	PPG	RPG	APG	PCM
50-51	Tri-Cities	20	....	....	68	24	84	.286	....	....	....	20	35	.571	....	....	50	17	56	1	....	....	....	....	3.4	2.5	0.9	....
51-52	New York	12	....	167	47	19	65	.292	....	....	....	9	14	.643	....	....	26	6	25	0	....	....	....	13.9	3.9	2.2	0.5	.179
NBA Season Totals		32	....	167	115	43	149	.289	....	....	....	29	49	.592	....	....	76	23	81	1	....	....	....	5.2	3.6	2.4	0.7	

• SCHICK, John

John Schick

Born: 1916. Height: 6'6". Weight: 230 lbs. Drafted: — College: Ohio State

YEAR	TEAM	GP	GS	MIN	PTS	FGM	FGA	FG%	3PM	3PA	3P%	FTM	FTA	FT%	ORB	DRB	TRB	AST	PF	DQ	STL	BLK	TO	MPG	PPG	RPG	APG	PCM
46-47	Toledo-N	42	....	....	209	86	....	....	....	....	....	37	69	.536	....	....	....	....	148	....	....	....	....	....	5.0	....	....	....
47-48	Toledo-N	55	....	....	151	64	....	....	....	....	....	23	37	.622	....	....	....	....	106	....	....	....	....	....	2.7	....	....	....
NBL Season Totals		97	....	....	360	150	....	....	....	....	....	60	106	....	....	....	....	....	254	....	....	....	....	....	3.7	....	....	....
46-47	Toledo-N	5	....	....	6	2	....	....	....	....	....	2	6	.333	....	....	....	....	....	....	....	....	....	....	1.2	....	....	....
NBL Playoff Totals		5	....	....	6	2	....	....	....	....	....	2	6	....	....	....	....	....	....	....	....	....	....	....	1.2	....	....	....

YEAR	TEAM	GP	GS	MIN	PTS	FGM	FGA	FG%	3PM	3PA	3P%	FTM	FTA	FT%	ORB	DRB	TRB	AST	PF	DQ	STL	BLK	TO	MPG	PPG	RPG	APG	PCM

• SCHINTZIUS, Dwayne
Dwayne Kenneth Schintzius

Born: Oct. 14, 1968. Brandon, FL, United States.   Height: 7'1".   Weight: 260 lbs.   Drafted: 1990   College: Florida

YEAR	TEAM	GP	GS	MIN	PTS	FGM	FGA	FG%	3PM	3PA	3P%	FTM	FTA	FT%	ORB	DRB	TRB	AST	PF	DQ	STL	BLK	TO	MPG	PPG	RPG	APG	PCM
90-91	San Antonio	42	7	398	158	68	155	.439	0	2	.000	22	40	.550	28	93	121	17	64	0	2	29	34	9.5	3.8	2.9	0.4	.419
91-92	Sacramento	33	0	400	110	50	117	.427	0	4	.000	10	12	.833	43	75	118	20	67	1	6	28	20	12.1	3.3	3.6	0.6	.399
92-93	New Jersey	5	0	35	7	2	7	.286	0	0	.000	3	3	1.000	2	6	8	2	4	0	2	2	0	7.0	1.4	1.6	0.4	.394
93-94	New Jersey	30	7	319	68	29	84	.345	0	0	.000	10	17	.588	26	63	89	13	49	1	7	17	12	10.6	2.3	3.0	0.4	.309
94-95	New Jersey	43	11	318	88	41	108	.380	0	0	.000	6	11	.545	29	52	81	15	45	0	3	17	17	7.4	2.0	1.9	0.3	.303
95-96	Indiana	33	8	297	111	49	110	.445	0	0	.000	13	21	.619	23	55	78	14	53	0	9	12	20	9.0	3.4	2.4	0.4	.384
96-97	LA Clippers	15	0	116	34	13	36	.361	1	2	.500	7	8	.875	9	13	22	4	22	0	1	9	8	7.7	2.3	1.5	0.3	.246
98-99	Boston	16	0	67	11	4	16	.250	0	0	.000	3	4	.750	7	12	19	8	17	0	0	3	10	4.2	0.7	1.2	0.5	.177
NBA Season Totals		217	33	1950	587	256	633	.404	1	8	.125	74	116	.638	167	369	536	93	321	2	30	117	121	9.0	2.7	2.5	0.4	....
92-93	New Jersey	5	0	106	29	13	29	.448	0	0	.000	3	6	.500	6	19	25	4	12	0	1	6	3	21.2	5.8	5.0	0.8	.362
NBA Playoff Totals		5	0	106	29	13	29	.448	0	0	.000	3	6	.500	6	19	25	4	12	0	1	6	3	21.2	5.8	5.0	0.8	

• SCHLECHTY, Glenn
Glenn Schlechty

Born: Mar. 31, 1912. Died: Apr. 1962.   Height: 6'6".   Weight: 185 lbs.   Drafted: —   College: Findlay

YEAR	TEAM	GP	GS	MIN	PTS	FGM	FGA	FG%	3PM	3PA	3P%	FTM	FTA	FT%	ORB	DRB	TRB	AST	PF	DQ	STL	BLK	TO	MPG	PPG	RPG	APG	PCM
37-38	Dayton-N	4	....		7	3	....	....	....	....	....	1	....	....	....	....	....	....	....	....	....	....	....		1.8	....	....	....
NBL Season Totals		4	....		7	3	....	....	....	....	....	1	....	....	....	....	....	....	....	....	....	....	....		1.8	....	....	....

• SCHLUETER, Dale
Dale Wayne Schlueter

Born: Nov. 12, 1945. Tacoma, WA, United States.   Height: 6'10".   Weight: 225 lbs.   Drafted: 1967   College: Colorado State

YEAR	TEAM	GP	GS	MIN	PTS	FGM	FGA	FG%	3PM	3PA	3P%	FTM	FTA	FT%	ORB	DRB	TRB	AST	PF	DQ	STL	BLK	TO	MPG	PPG	RPG	APG	PCM
68-69	San Francisco	31	....	559	181	68	157	.433	....	....	....	45	82	.549	....	....	216	30	81	3	....	....	....	18.0	5.8	7.0	1.0	.488
69-70	San Francisco	63	....	685	224	82	167	.491	....	....	....	60	97	.619	....	....	231	25	108	0	....	....	....	10.9	3.6	3.7	0.4	.462
70-71	Portland	80	....	1823	657	257	527	.488	....	....	....	143	218	.656	....	....	629	192	265	4	....	....	....	22.8	8.2	7.9	2.4	.570
71-72	Portland	81	....	2693	947	353	672	.525	....	....	....	241	326	.739	....	....	860	285	277	3	....	....	....	33.2	11.7	10.6	3.5	.587
72-73	Philadelphia	78	....	1136	418	166	317	.524	....	....	....	86	123	.699	....	....	354	103	166	0	....	....	....	14.6	5.4	4.5	1.3	.548
73-74	Atlanta	57	....	547	164	63	135	.467	....	....	....	38	50	.760	54	101	153	45	84	0	25	22	....	9.6	2.9	2.7	0.8	.449
74-75	Buffalo	76	....	962	268	92	178	.517	....	....	....	84	121	.694	78	186	264	104	163	0	18	42	....	12.7	3.5	3.5	1.4	.472
75-76	Buffalo	71	....	773	176	61	122	.500	....	....	....	54	81	.667	58	166	224	80	141	1	13	17	....	10.9	2.5	3.2	1.1	.434
76-77	Phoenix	39	....	337	70	26	72	.361	....	....	....	18	31	.581	30	50	80	38	62	0	8	8	....	8.6	1.8	2.1	1.0	.327
77-78	Portland	10	....	109	25	8	19	.421	....	....	....	9	18	.500	5	16	21	18	20	0	3	2	15	10.9	2.5	2.1	1.8	.299
NBA Season Totals		586	....	9624	3130	1176	2366	.497	....	....	....	778	1147	.678	225	519	3034	920	1367	11	67	91	15	16.4	5.3	5.2	1.6	
68-69	San Francisco	3	....	25	13	3	9	.333	....	....	....	7	15	.467	....	....	22	1	4	0	....	....	....	8.3	4.3	7.3	0.3	.901
74-75	Buffalo	6	....	40	13	6	10	.600	....	....	....	1	3	.333	5	8	13	1	6	0	1	0	....	6.7	2.2	2.2	0.2	.460
75-76	Buffalo	8	....	44	15	5	7	.714	....	....	....	5	6	.833	2	6	8	2	11	0	1	3	....	5.5	1.9	1.0	0.3	.393
NBA Playoff Totals		17	....	109	41	14	26	.538	....	....	....	13	24	.542	7	14	43	4	21	0	2	3	....	6.4	2.4	2.5	0.2	

• SCHNELLBACHER, Otto
Otto Ole (The Claw) Schnellbacher

Born: Apr. 15, 1923. Sublette, KS, United States.   Height: 6'4".   Weight: 185 lbs.   Drafted: —   College: Kansas

YEAR	TEAM	GP	GS	MIN	PTS	FGM	FGA	FG%	3PM	3PA	3P%	FTM	FTA	FT%	ORB	DRB	TRB	AST	PF	DQ	STL	BLK	TO	MPG	PPG	RPG	APG	PCM
48-49	Providence	23	....	....	102	34	118	.288	....	....	....	34	54	.630	....	....	....	19	48	....	....	....	....	4.4	....	0.8	
48-49	St. Louis	20	....	....	173	59	162	.364	....	....	....	55	79	.696	....	....	....	45	61	....	....	....	....	8.7	....	2.3	
NBA Season Totals		43	....	....	275	93	280	.332	....	....	....	89	133	.669	....	....	....	64	109	....	....	....	....	6.4	....	1.5	
48-49	St. Louis	2	....	....	18	6	20	.300	....	....	....	6	12	.500	....	....	....	6	9	....	....	....	....	9.0	....	3.0	
NBA Playoff Totals		2	....	....	18	6	20	.300	....	....	....	6	12	.500	....	....	....	6	9	....	....	....	....	9.0	....	3.0	

• SCHNITTKER, Dick
Richard D. Schnittker

Born: May 27, 1928. Kelleys Island, OH, United States.   Height: 6'5".   Weight: 200 lbs.   Drafted: 1950   College: Ohio State

YEAR	TEAM	GP	GS	MIN	PTS	FGM	FGA	FG%	3PM	3PA	3P%	FTM	FTA	FT%	ORB	DRB	TRB	AST	PF	DQ	STL	BLK	TO	MPG	PPG	RPG	APG	PCM
50-51	Washington	29	....	....	293	85	219	.388	....	....	....	123	139	.885	....	....	153	42	76	0	....	....	....	10.1	5.3	1.4	
53-54	Minneapolis	71	....	1040	330	122	307	.397	....	....	....	86	132	.652	....	....	178	59	178	3	....	....	....	14.6	4.6	2.5	0.8	.309
54-55	Minneapolis	72	....	1798	750	226	583	.388	....	....	....	298	362	.823	....	....	349	114	231	7	....	....	....	25.0	10.4	4.8	1.6	.431
55-56	Minneapolis	72	....	1930	812	254	647	.393	....	....	....	304	355	.856	....	....	296	142	253	4	....	....	....	26.8	11.3	4.1	2.0	.414
56-57	Minneapolis	70	....	997	386	113	351	.322	....	....	....	160	193	.829	....	....	185	52	144	3	....	....	....	14.2	5.5	2.6	0.7	.347
57-58	Minneapolis	50	....	979	457	128	357	.359	....	....	....	201	237	.848	....	....	211	71	126	5	....	....	....	19.6	9.1	4.2	1.4	.485
NBA Season Totals		364	....	6744	3028	928	2464	.377	....	....	....	1172	1418	.827	....	....	1372	480	1008	22	....	....	....	18.5	8.3	3.8	1.3	
52-53	Minneapolis	7	....	29	9	1	8	.125	....	....	....	7	11	.636	....	....	4	0	8	0	....	....	....	4.1	1.3	0.6	0.0	.086
53-54	Minneapolis	13	....	163	34	11	32	.344	....	....	....	12	20	.600	....	....	21	5	32	0	....	....	....	12.5	2.6	1.6	0.4	.161
54-55	Minneapolis	7	....	140	53	14	51	.275	....	....	....	25	36	.694	....	....	31	7	23	1	....	....	....	20.0	7.6	4.4	1.0	.317
55-56	Minneapolis	3	....	87	43	13	23	.565	....	....	....	17	20	.850	....	....	15	5	14	2	....	....	....	29.0	14.3	5.0	1.7	.535
56-57	Minneapolis	5	....	83	27	6	21	.286	....	....	....	15	17	.882	....	....	12	8	6	0	....	....	....	16.6	5.4	2.4	1.6	.383
NBA Playoff Totals		35	....	502	166	45	135	.333	....	....	....	76	104	.731	....	....	83	25	83	3	....	....	....	14.3	4.7	2.4	0.7	....

• SCHOENE, Russ
Russell Schoene

Born: Apr. 16, 1960. Trenton, IL, United States.   Height: 6'10".   Weight: 210 lbs.   Drafted: 1982   College: Tennessee (Chatanooga)

YEAR	TEAM	GP	GS	MIN	PTS	FGM	FGA	FG%	3PM	3PA	3P%	FTM	FTA	FT%	ORB	DRB	TRB	AST	PF	DQ	STL	BLK	TO	MPG	PPG	RPG	APG	PCM
82-83	Philadelphia	46	2	702	233	106	207	.512	0	1	.000	21	28	.750	52	102	154	32	118	2	13	9	46	15.3	5.1	3.3	0.7	.339
82-83	Indiana	31	5	520	243	101	228	.443	1	3	.333	40	55	.727	44	57	101	27	74	1	12	14	34	16.8	7.8	3.3	0.9	.388
86-87	Seattle	63	0	579	173	71	190	.374	2	13	.154	29	46	.630	52	65	117	27	94	1	20	11	44	9.2	2.7	1.9	0.4	.235

YEAR	TEAM	GP	GS	MIN	PTS	FGM	FGA	FG%	3PM	3PA	3P%	FTM	FTA	FT%	ORB	DRB	TRB	AST	PF	DQ	STL	BLK	TO	MPG	PPG	RPG	APG	PCM
87-88	Seattle	81	2	973	484	208	454	.458	17	58	.293	51	63	.810	78	120	198	53	151	0	39	13	57	12.0	6.0	2.4	0.7	.427
88-89	Seattle	69	1	774	358	135	349	.387	42	110	.382	46	57	.807	58	107	165	36	136	1	37	24	48	11.2	5.2	2.4	0.5	.381
NBA Season Totals		290	10	3548	1491	621	1428	.435	62	185	.335	187	249	.751	284	451	735	175	573	5	121	71	229	12.2	5.1	2.5	0.6	....
86-87	Seattle	14	0	123	31	10	28	.357	2	6	.333	9	12	.750	6	20	26	3	16	1	1	4	2	8.8	2.2	1.9	0.2	.289
87-88	Seattle	5	0	39	16	7	12	.583	2	4	.500	0	0	.000	1	6	7	2	8	0	1	0	2	7.8	3.2	1.4	0.4	.393
88-89	Seattle	3	0	43	13	4	17	.235	0	7	.000	5	6	.833	3	2	5	2	7	0	2	0	0	14.3	4.3	1.7	0.7	.136
NBA Playoff Totals		22	0	205	60	21	57	.368	4	17	.235	14	18	.778	10	28	38	7	31	1	4	4	4	9.3	2.7	1.7	0.3	....

• SCHOLZ, Dave

David A. Scholz

Born: Apr. 12, 1948.   Height: 6'8".   Weight: 220 lbs.   Drafted: 1969   College: Illinois

YEAR	TEAM	GP	GS	MIN	PTS	FGM	FGA	FG%	3PM	3PA	3P%	FTM	FTA	FT%	ORB	DRB	TRB	AST	PF	DQ	STL	BLK	TO	MPG	PPG	RPG	APG	PCM
69-70	Philadelphia	1	....	1	2	1	1	1.000	....	....	....	0	0	.000	....	....	0	0	0	0	....	....	....	1.0	2.0	0.0	0.0	2.000
NBA Season Totals		1	....	1	2	1	1	1.000	....	....	....	0	0	.000	....	....	0	0	0	0	....	....	....	1.0	2.0	0.0	0.0	

• SCHOLZ, Gene

Gene Scholz

Born: 1917.   Height: 5'8".   Weight: 160 lbs.   Drafted: —   College: Capital

YEAR	TEAM	GP	GS	MIN	PTS	FGM	FGA	FG%	3PM	3PA	3P%	FTM	FTA	FT%	ORB	DRB	TRB	AST	PF	DQ	STL	BLK	TO	MPG	PPG	RPG	APG	PCM
37-38	Columbus-N	3	....	....	2	1	....	....	....	....	....	0	....	....	....	....	....	....	....	....	....	....	....	0.7	....	....	....	
NBL Season Totals		3	....	....	2	1	....	....	....	....	....	0	....	....	....	....	....	....	....	....	....	....	....	0.7	....	....	....	

• SCHOON, Milt

Milton W. Schoon

Born: Feb. 25, 1922.   Height: 6'7".   Weight: 230 lbs.   Drafted: —   College: Valparaiso

YEAR	TEAM	GP	GS	MIN	PTS	FGM	FGA	FG%	3PM	3PA	3P%	FTM	FTA	FT%	ORB	DRB	TRB	AST	PF	DQ	STL	BLK	TO	MPG	PPG	RPG	APG	PCM
46-47	Detroit	41	....	....	120	43	199	.216	....	....	....	34	80	.425	....	....	....	12	75	....	....	....	....	2.9	....	0.3	....	
47-48	Flint-N	55	....	....	348	114	....	....	....	....	....	120	214	.561	....	....	....	....	194	....	....	....	....	6.3	....	....	....	
48-49	Sheboygan-N	57	....	....	271	81	....	....	....	....	....	109	184	.592	....	....	....	....	143	....	....	....	....	4.8	....	....	....	
49-50	Sheboygan	62	....	....	496	150	366	.410	....	....	....	196	300	.653	....	....	....	84	190	....	....	....	....	8.0	....	1.4	....	
NBA Season Totals		103	....	....	616	193	565	.342	....	....	....	230	380	.605	....	....	....	96	265	....	....	....	....	6.0	....	0.9	....	
NBL Season Totals		112	....	....	619	195	....	....	....	....	....	229	398	....	....	....	....	....	337	....	....	....	....	5.5	....	....	....	
Career Totals		215	....	....	1235	388	565	....	....	....	....	459	778	....	....	....	....	96	602	....	....	....	....	5.7	....	0.4	....	
48-49	Sheboygan-N	2	....	....	6	2	....	....	....	....	....	2	5	.400	....	....	....	....	....	....	....	....	....	3.0	....	....	....	
49-50	Sheboygan	3	....	....	17	5	17	.294	....	....	....	7	10	.700	....	....	....	3	6	....	....	....	....	5.7	....	1.0	....	
NBA Playoff Totals		3	....	....	17	5	17	.294	....	....	....	7	10	.700	....	....	....	3	6	....	....	....	....	5.7	....	1.0	....	
NBL Playoff Totals		2	....	....	6	2	....	....	....	....	....	2	5	....	....	....	....	....	....	....	....	....	....	3.0	....	....	....	
Career Playoff Totals		5	....	....	23	7	17	....	....	....	....	9	15	....	....	....	....	3	6	....	....	....	....	4.6	....	0.6	....	

• SCHRADER, Bill

Bill Schrader

Born: 1911.   Height: 6'7".   Weight: 210 lbs.   Drafted: —   College: Notre Dame

YEAR	TEAM	GP	GS	MIN	PTS	FGM	FGA	FG%	3PM	3PA	3P%	FTM	FTA	FT%	ORB	DRB	TRB	AST	PF	DQ	STL	BLK	TO	MPG	PPG	RPG	APG	PCM
37-38	Indianapolis-N	8	....	....	14	6	....	....	....	....	....	2	....	....	....	....	....	....	....	....	....	....	....	1.8	....	....	....	
NBL Season Totals		8	....	....	14	6	....	....	....	....	....	2	....	....	....	....	....	....	....	....	....	....	....	1.8	....	....	....	

• SCHRAGE, Warren

Warren Schrage

Born: July 30, 1920. Died: Jan.19, 1999.   Height: 6'5".   Weight: 190 lbs.   Drafted: —   College: Wisconsin

YEAR	TEAM	GP	GS	MIN	PTS	FGM	FGA	FG%	3PM	3PA	3P%	FTM	FTA	FT%	ORB	DRB	TRB	AST	PF	DQ	STL	BLK	TO	MPG	PPG	RPG	APG	PCM
42-43	Sheboygan-N	10	....	....	2	1	....	....	....	....	....	0	....	....	....	....	....	....	....	....	....	....	....	0.2	....	....	....	
NBL Season Totals		10	....	....	2	1	....	....	....	....	....	0	....	....	....	....	....	....	....	....	....	....	....	0.2	....	....	....	
42-43	Sheboygan-N	1	....	....	3	1	....	....	....	....	....	1	....	....	....	....	....	....	....	....	....	....	....	3.0	....	....	....	
NBL Playoff Totals		1	....	....	3	1	....	....	....	....	....	1	....	....	....	....	....	....	....	....	....	....	....	3.0	....	....	....	

• SCHRECKER, Al

Al Schrecker

Born: July 23, 1917. Died: Jan.4, 2000.   Height: 6'1".   Weight: 160 lbs.   Drafted: —   College: none

YEAR	TEAM	GP	GS	MIN	PTS	FGM	FGA	FG%	3PM	3PA	3P%	FTM	FTA	FT%	ORB	DRB	TRB	AST	PF	DQ	STL	BLK	TO	MPG	PPG	RPG	APG	PCM
44-45	Pittsburgh-N	1	....	....	7	3	....	....	....	....	....	1	....	....	....	....	....	....	....	....	....	....	....	7.0	....	....	....	
NBL Season Totals		1	....	....	7	3	....	....	....	....	....	1	....	....	....	....	....	....	....	....	....	....	....	7.0	....	....	....	

• SCHREMPF, Detlef

Detlef Schrempf

Born: Jan. 21, 1963. Leverkusen, Germany.   Height: 6'9".   Weight: 214 lbs.   Drafted: 1985   College: Washington

YEAR	TEAM	GP	GS	MIN	PTS	FGM	FGA	FG%	3PM	3PA	3P%	FTM	FTA	FT%	ORB	DRB	TRB	AST	PF	DQ	STL	BLK	TO	MPG	PPG	RPG	APG	PCM
85-86	Dallas	64	12	969	397	142	315	.451	3	7	.429	110	152	.724	70	128	198	88	166	1	23	10	83	15.1	6.2	3.1	1.4	.383
86-87	Dallas	81	5	1711	756	265	561	.472	33	69	.478	193	260	.742	87	216	303	161	224	2	50	16	113	21.1	9.3	3.7	2.0	.442
87-88	Dallas	82	4	1587	698	246	539	.456	5	32	.156	201	266	.756	102	177	279	159	189	0	42	32	107	19.4	8.5	3.4	1.9	.445
88-89	Dallas	37	1	845	353	112	263	.426	2	16	.125	127	161	.789	56	110	166	86	118	3	24	9	56	22.8	9.5	4.5	2.3	.434
88-89	Indiana	32	12	1005	475	162	315	.514	5	19	.263	146	189	.772	70	159	229	93	102	0	29	10	77	31.4	14.8	7.2	2.9	.540
89-90	Indiana	78	18	2573	1267	424	822	.516	17	48	.354	402	490	.820	149	471	620	247	271	6	59	16	179	33.0	16.2	7.9	3.2	.572
90-91	Indiana	82	3	2632	1320	432	831	.520	15	40	.375	441	539	.818	178	482	660	301	262	3	58	22	172	32.1	16.1	8.0	3.7	.620
91-92	Indiana	80	4	2605	1380	496	925	.536	23	71	.324	365	441	.828	202	568	770	312	286	4	62	37	192	32.6	17.3	9.6	3.9	.682
92-93	Indiana	82	60	3098	1567	517	1085	.476	8	52	.154	525	653	.804	210	570	780	493	305	2	79	27	246	37.8	19.1	9.5	6.0	.632
93-94	Seattle	81	80	2728	1212	445	903	.493	22	68	.324	300	390	.769	144	310	454	275	273	3	73	9	170	33.7	15.0	5.6	3.4	.462
94-95	Seattle	82	82	2886	1572	521	997	.523	93	181	.514	437	521	.839	135	373	508	310	252	0	93	35	172	35.2	19.2	6.2	3.8	.600
95-96	Seattle	63	60	2200	1080	360	740	.486	73	179	.408	287	370	.776	73	255	328	276	179	0	56	8	145	34.9	17.1	5.2	4.4	.511
96-97	Seattle	61	60	2192	1022	356	724	.492	57	161	.354	253	316	.801	87	307	394	266	151	0	63	16	153	35.9	16.8	6.5	4.4	.530
97-98	Seattle	78	78	2742	1232	437	898	.487	61	147	.415	297	352	.844	135	419	554	341	205	0	60	19	172	35.2	15.8	7.1	4.4	.541

YEAR	TEAM	GP	GS	MIN	PTS	FGM	FGA	FG%	3PM	3PA	3P%	FTM	FTA	FT%	ORB	DRB	TRB	AST	PF	DQ	STL	BLK	TO	MPG	PPG	RPG	APG	PCM
98-99	Seattle	50	39	1765	752	259	549	.472	34	86	.395	200	243	.823	77	293	370	184	152	0	41	26	103	35.3	15.0	7.4	3.7	.515
99-00	Portland	77	6	1662	574	187	433	.432	21	52	.404	179	215	.833	79	253	332	197	182	0	37	17	100	21.6	7.5	4.3	2.6	.437
00-01	Portland	26	0	397	104	39	95	.411	3	8	.375	23	27	.852	17	61	78	44	43	0	7	3	28	15.3	4.0	3.0	1.7	.340
NBA Season Totals		1136	524	33597	15761	5400	10995	.491	475	1236	.384	4486	5585	.803	1871	5152	7023	3833	3360	25	856	312	2268	29.6	13.9	6.2	3.4	....
85-86	Dallas	10	0	120	37	13	28	.464	0	1	.000	11	17	.647	7	16	23	14	24	0	2	1	10	12.0	3.7	2.3	1.4	.325
86-87	Dallas	4	0	97	31	13	35	.371	0	3	.000	5	11	.455	4	8	12	6	13	0	3	2	6	24.3	7.8	3.0	1.5	.189
87-88	Dallas	15	0	274	117	40	86	.465	1	3	.333	36	51	.706	25	30	55	24	29	0	8	7	21	18.3	7.8	3.7	1.6	.456
89-90	Indiana	3	3	125	61	23	47	.489	0	3	.000	15	16	.938	5	17	22	5	13	0	2	1	10	41.7	20.3	7.3	1.7	.411
90-91	Indiana	5	0	179	79	27	57	.474	0	4	.000	25	30	.833	10	26	36	11	17	0	2	0	11	35.8	15.8	7.2	2.2	.434
91-92	Indiana	3	0	120	63	18	47	.383	2	4	.500	25	28	.893	12	27	39	7	10	0	2	1	7	40.0	21.0	13.0	2.3	.584
92-93	Indiana	4	4	165	78	25	54	.463	0	2	.000	28	36	.778	3	20	23	29	14	0	1	2	17	41.3	19.5	5.8	7.3	.485
93-94	Seattle	5	5	174	93	26	50	.520	2	6	.333	39	45	.867	8	19	27	10	21	1	1	3	8	34.8	18.6	5.4	2.0	.520
94-95	Seattle	4	4	153	75	23	57	.404	10	18	.556	19	24	.792	2	17	19	12	12	0	3	2	11	38.3	18.8	4.8	3.0	.393
95-96	Seattle	21	21	789	336	123	259	.475	21	57	.368	69	92	.750	19	86	105	67	63	1	14	5	67	37.6	16.0	5.0	3.2	.371
96-97	Seattle	12	12	459	203	67	142	.472	16	29	.552	53	65	.815	20	49	69	41	40	0	13	1	18	38.3	16.9	5.8	3.4	.465
97-98	Seattle	10	10	375	161	64	125	.512	2	14	.143	31	38	.816	18	59	77	39	21	0	7	1	22	37.5	16.1	7.7	3.9	.513
99-00	Portland	15	0	276	84	22	56	.393	1	6	.167	39	47	.830	10	43	53	30	29	0	4	0	15	18.4	5.6	3.5	2.0	.389
00-01	Portland	3	0	32	14	4	6	.667	2	3	.667	4	6	.667	0	5	5	1	3	0	0	0	2	10.7	4.7	1.7	0.3	.430
NBA Playoff Totals		114	59	3338	1432	488	1049	.465	57	153	.373	399	506	.789	143	422	565	296	309	2	62	26	225	29.3	12.6	5.0	2.6	....

• SCHROEDER, William

William Henry Schroeder

Born: Apr. 11, 1923. Sheboygan, WI, United States. Height: 6' Weight: 190 lbs. Drafted: — College: Wisconsin

46-47	Sheboygan-N	9	....	....	15	5	....	....	....	....	....	5	8	.625	....	....	....	....	....	....	....	....	....	....	1.7	....	....	....
NBL Season Totals		9	....	....	15	5	....	....	....	....	....	5	8	....	....	....	....	....	....	....	....	....	....	....	1.7	....	....	....

• SCHU, Wilbur

Wilbur Schu

Born: Dec. 18, 1922. Versailles, KY, United States. Died: Nov.1, 1980. Height: 6'3". Weight: 190 lbs. Drafted: — College: Kentucky

46-47	Tri-Cities-N	22	....	....	26	8	....	....	....	....	....	10	17	.588	....	....	....	....	....	....	....	....	....	....	1.2	....	....	....
46-47	Youngstown-N	11	....	....	20	7	....	....	....	....	....	6	9	.667	....	....	....	....	....	....	....	....	....	....	1.8	....	....	....
NBL Season Totals		33	....	....	46	15	....	....	....	....	....	16	26	....	....	....	....	....	....	....	....	....	....	....	1.4	....	....	....

• SCHUESSLER, Herm

Herm Schuessler

Born: July 20, 1914. Died: July5, 1997. Height: 6'8". Weight: 210 lbs. Drafted: — College: none

38-39	Indianapolis-N	19	....	....	70	28	....	....	....	....	....	14	....	....	....	....	....	....	....	....	....	....	....	....	3.7	....	....	....
NBL Season Totals		19	....	....	70	28	....	....	....	....	....	14	....	....	....	....	....	....	....	....	....	....	....	....	3.7	....	....	....

• SCHULTZ, Howie

Howard Henry (Stretch, Steeple) Schultz

Born: July 3, 1922. St. Paul, MN, United States. Height: 6'6". Weight: 200 lbs. Drafted: — College: Hamline

46-47	Anderson-N	41	....	....	457	155	....	....	....	....	....	147	213	.690	....	....	....	....	124	....	....	....	....	....	11.1	....	....	....
47-48	Anderson-N	60	....	....	605	213	....	....	....	....	....	179	258	.694	....	....	....	....	194	....	....	....	....	....	10.1	....	....	....
48-49	Anderson-N	64	....	....	538	176	....	....	....	....	....	186	256	.727	....	....	....	....	204	....	....	....	....	....	8.4	....	....	....
49-50	Anderson	35	....	....	283	83	316	.263	....	....	....	117	160	.731	....	....	....	88	125	....	....	....	....	....	8.1	....	2.5	....
49-50	Fort Wayne	32	....	....	271	96	355	.270	....	....	....	79	122	.648	....	....	....	81	119	....	....	....	....	....	8.5	....	2.5	....
51-52	Minneapolis	66	....	1301	268	89	315	.283	....	....	....	90	119	.756	....	....	246	102	197	13	....	....	....	19.7	4.1	3.7	1.5	.256
52-53	Minneapolis	40	....	474	91	24	90	.267	....	....	....	43	62	.694	....	....	80	29	73	1	....	....	....	11.9	2.3	2.0	0.7	.221
NBA Season Totals		173	....	1775	913	292	1076	.271	....	....	....	329	463	.711	....	....	326	300	514	14	....	....	....	10.3	5.3	1.9	1.7	....
NBL Season Totals		165	....	....	1600	544	....	....	....	....	....	512	727	....	....	....	....	....	522	....	....	....	....	....	9.7	....	....	....
Career Totals		338	....	1775	2513	836	1076	....	....	....	....	841	1190	....	....	....	326	300	1036	14	....	....	....	5.3	7.4	1.0	0.9	....
47-48	Anderson-N	6	....	....	55	23	....	....	....	....	....	9	18	.500	....	....	....	....	....	....	....	....	....	....	9.2	....	....	....
48-49	Anderson-N	7	....	....	64	13	....	....	....	....	....	38	52	.731	....	....	....	....	....	....	....	....	....	....	9.1	....	....	....
49-50	Fort Wayne	4	....	....	43	15	61	.246	....	....	....	13	17	.765	....	....	....	4	15	....	....	....	....	....	10.8	....	1.0	....
51-52	Minneapolis	12	....	99	18	6	18	.333	....	....	....	6	10	.600	....	....	19	5	18	1	....	....	....	8.3	1.5	1.6	0.4	.218
NBA Playoff Totals		16	....	99	61	21	79	.266	....	....	....	19	27	.704	....	....	19	9	33	1	....	....	....	6.2	3.8	1.2	0.6	....
NBL Playoff Totals		13	....	....	119	36	....	....	....	....	....	47	70	....	....	....	....	....	....	....	....	....	....	....	9.2	....	....	....
Career Playoff Totals		29	....	99	180	57	79	....	....	....	....	66	97	....	....	....	19	9	33	1	....	....	....	3.4	6.2	0.7	0.3	....

• SCHULZ, Dick

Richard A. Schulz

Born: Jan. 3, 1917. Died: June26, 1998. Height: 6'2". Weight: 192 lbs. Drafted: — College: Wisconsin

42-43	Sheboygan-N	1	....	....	0	0	....	....	....	....	....	0	....	....	....	....	....	....	....	....	....	....	....	....	0.0	....	....	....
43-44	Sheboygan-N	20	....	....	46	18	....	....	....	....	....	10	....	....	....	....	....	....	....	....	....	....	....	....	2.3	....	....	....
44-45	Sheboygan-N	29	....	....	243	86	....	....	....	....	....	71	....	....	....	....	....	....	....	....	....	....	....	....	8.4	....	....	....
45-46	Sheboygan-N	29	....	....	178	56	....	....	....	....	....	66	94	.702	....	....	....	....	....	....	....	....	....	....	6.1	....	....	....
46-47	Cleveland	16	....	....	106	43	176	.244	....	....	....	20	31	.645	....	....	....	17	29	....	....	....	....	....	6.6	....	1.1	....
46-47	Toronto	41	....	....	248	87	372	.234	....	....	....	74	107	.692	....	....	....	39	94	....	....	....	....	....	6.0	....	1.0	....
47-48	Baltimore	48	....	....	383	133	469	.284	....	....	....	117	160	.731	....	....	....	28	116	....	....	....	....	....	8.0	....	0.6	....
48-49	Washington	50	....	....	195	65	278	.234	....	....	....	65	91	.714	....	....	....	53	107	....	....	....	....	....	3.9	....	1.1	....
49-50	Washington	13	....	....	43	12	45	.267	....	....	....	19	28	.679	....	....	....	10	27	....	....	....	....	....	3.3	....	0.8	....

YEAR	TEAM	GP	GS	MIN	PTS	FGM	FGA	FG%	3PM	3PA	3P%	FTM	FTA	FT%	ORB	DRB	TRB	AST	PF	DQ	STL	BLK	TO	MPG	PPG	RPG	APG	PCM
49-50	Tri-Cities	8			41	13	45	.289				15	21	.714					8	12						5.1		1.0	
49-50	Sheboygan	29			125	38	122	.311				49	61	.803					48	67						4.3		1.7	
NBA Season Totals		205			1141	391	1507	.259				359	499	.719					203	452						5.6		1.0	
NBL Season Totals		79			467	160						147	94													5.9			
Career Totals		284			1608	551	1507					506	593						203	452						5.7		0.7	
42-43	Sheboygan-N	1			0	0						0														0.0			
43-44	Sheboygan-N	5			48	17						14														9.6			
44-45	Sheboygan-N	8			76	22						32														9.5			
45-46	Sheboygan-N	8			47	12						23	30	.767												5.9			
47-48	Baltimore	11			82	22	114	.193				38	51	.745					7	30						7.5		0.6	
48-49	Washington	11			54	17	74	.230				20	35	.571					27	36						4.9		2.5	
49-50	Sheboygan	3			12	1	9	.111				10	10	1.000					2	12						4.0		0.7	
NBA Playoff Totals		25			148	40	197	.203				68	96	.708					36	78						5.9		1.4	
NBL Playoff Totals		22			171	51						69	30													7.8			
Career Playoff Totals		47			319	91	197					137	126						36	78						6.8		0.8	

• SCHUMACHER, Wilbur
Wilbur Schumacher

Born: Mar. 6, 1920. Died: Sept.3, 1971.   Height: —   Weight: —   Drafted: —   College: Butler

YEAR	TEAM	GP	GS	MIN	PTS	FGM	FGA	FG%	3PM	3PA	3P%	FTM	FTA	FT%	ORB	DRB	TRB	AST	PF	DQ	STL	BLK	TO	MPG	PPG	RPG	APG	PCM
45-46	Indianapolis-N	5			10	4						2														2.0			
NBL Season Totals		5			10	4						2														2.0			

• SCHURIG, Roger
Roger Paul Schurig

Born: Apr. 3, 1942.   Height: 6'3".   Weight: 185 lbs.   Drafted: —   College: Vanderbilt

YEAR	TEAM	GP	GS	MIN	PTS	FGM	FGA	FG%	3PM	3PA	3P%	FTM	FTA	FT%	ORB	DRB	TRB	AST	PF	DQ	STL	BLK	TO	MPG	PPG	RPG	APG	PCM
67-68	Houston-A	21		252	100	35	94	.372	3	8	.375	27	36	.750			29	18	38	0			23	12.0	4.8	1.4	0.9	.304
ABA Season Totals		21		252	100	35	94	.372	3	8	.375	27	36	.750			29	18	38	0			23	12.0	4.8	1.4	0.9	

• SCHWARTZ, Bob
Bob Schwartz

Born: —.   Height: 6'3".   Weight: —   Drafted: —   College: Wisconsin

YEAR	TEAM	GP	GS	MIN	PTS	FGM	FGA	FG%	3PM	3PA	3P%	FTM	FTA	FT%	ORB	DRB	TRB	AST	PF	DQ	STL	BLK	TO	MPG	PPG	RPG	APG	PCM
42-43	Sheboygan-N	13			73	32						9														5.6			
NBL Season Totals		13			73	32						9														5.6			
42-43	Sheboygan-N	4			12	6						0														3.0			
NBL Playoff Totals		4			12	6						0														3.0			

• SCHWEITZ, John
John Elwood Schweitz

Born: Apr. 19, 1960. Waterloo, NY, United States.   Height: 6'6".   Weight: 210 lbs.   Drafted: 1982   College: Richmond

YEAR	TEAM	GP	GS	MIN	PTS	FGM	FGA	FG%	3PM	3PA	3P%	FTM	FTA	FT%	ORB	DRB	TRB	AST	PF	DQ	STL	BLK	TO	MPG	PPG	RPG	APG	PCM
84-85	Seattle	19	0	110	57	25	74	.338	0	4	.000	7	10	.700	6	15	21	18	12	0	0	1	13	5.8	3.0	1.1	0.9	.290
86-87	Detroit	3	0	7	0	0	1	.000	0	0	.000	0	0	.000	0	1	1	0	2	0	0	0	2	2.3	0.0	0.3	0.0	-.399
NBA Season Totals		22	0	117	57	25	75	.333	0	4	.000	7	10	.700	6	16	22	18	14	0	0	1	15	5.3	2.6	1.0	0.8	

• SCOLARI, Fred
Fred J. (Fat Freddie, Blubber) Scolari

Born: Mar. 1, 1922. Died: Oct.17, 2002.   Height: 5'10".   Weight: 180 lbs.   Drafted: —   College: San Francisco

YEAR	TEAM	GP	GS	MIN	PTS	FGM	FGA	FG%	3PM	3PA	3P%	FTM	FTA	FT%	ORB	DRB	TRB	AST	PF	DQ	STL	BLK	TO	MPG	PPG	RPG	APG	PCM
46-47	Washington	58			728	291	989	.294				146	180	**.811**					58	159						12.6		1.0	
47-48	Washington	47			589	229	780	.294				131	179	.732					58	153						12.5		1.2	
48-49	Washington	48			538	196	633	.310				146	183	.798					100	150						11.2		2.1	
49-50	Was/Syr	66			860	312	910	.343				236	287	.822					175	181						13.0		2.7	
50-51	Was/Syr	66			883	302	923	.327				279	331	.843			218	255	183	1					13.4	3.3	3.9	
51-52	Baltimore	64		2242	933	290	867	.334				353	423	.835			214	303	213	6			35.0	14.6	3.3	4.7	.430
52-53	Bal/FtW	62		2123	830	277	809	.342				276	327	.844			209	233	212	4			34.2	13.4	3.4	3.8	.376
53-54	Fort Wayne	64		1589	462	159	491	.324				144	180	.800			139	131	155	1			24.8	7.2	2.2	2.0	.268
54-55	Boston	59		619	191	76	249	.305				39	49	.796			77	93	76	0			10.5	3.2	1.3	1.6	.327
NBA Season Totals		534		6573	6014	2132	6651	.321				1750	2139	.818			857	1406	1482	12				12.3	11.3	1.6	2.6	
46-47	Washington	6			71	22	95	.232				27	34	.794					5	17						11.8		0.8	
48-49	Washington	9			82	27	100	.270				28	40	.700					16	24						9.1		1.8	
49-50	Washington	2			37	13	27	.481				11	11	1.000					3	6						18.5		1.5	
50-51	Syracuse	7			88	33	93	.355				22	27	.815			41	16	23	1				12.6	5.9	2.3	
52-53	Fort Wayne	8		268	107	29	90	.322				49	61	.803			25	21	31	0			33.5	13.4	3.1	2.6	.344
53-54	Fort Wayne	4		60	12	6	24	.250				0	0	.000			7	6	8	0			15.0	3.0	1.8	1.5	.152
54-55	Boston	5		29	12	4	15	.267				4	5	.800			5	3	7	0			5.8	2.4	1.0	0.6	.284
NBA Playoff Totals		41		357	409	134	444	.302				141	178	.792			78	70	116	1				8.7	10.0	1.9	1.7	

• SCOTT, Alvin
Alvin Leroy Scott

Born: Sept. 14, 1955. Cleveland, TN, United States.   Height: 6'7".   Weight: 185 lbs.   Drafted: 1977   College: Oral Roberts

YEAR	TEAM	GP	GS	MIN	PTS	FGM	FGA	FG%	3PM	3PA	3P%	FTM	FTA	FT%	ORB	DRB	TRB	AST	PF	DQ	STL	BLK	TO	MPG	PPG	RPG	APG	PCM
77-78	Phoenix	81		1538	492	180	369	.488				132	191	.691	135	222	357	88	158	0	52	40	81	19.0	6.1	4.4	1.1	.424
78-79	Phoenix	81		1737	544	212	396	.535				120	168	.714	104	256	360	126	139	2	80	62	97	21.4	6.7	4.4	1.6	.459
79-80	Phoenix	79		1303	350	127	301	.422	1	3	.333	95	122	.779	89	139	228	98	101	0	47	53	95	16.5	4.4	2.9	1.2	.347
80-81	Phoenix	82		1423	444	173	348	.497	1	6	.167	97	127	.764	101	167	268	114	124	0	60	70	74	17.4	5.4	3.3	1.4	.445
81-82	Phoenix	81	38	1740	486	189	380	.497	0	2	.000	108	148	.730	97	197	294	149	169	0	59	70	97	21.5	6.0	3.6	1.8	.388
82-83	Phoenix	81	9	1139	329	124	259	.479	0	2	.000	81	110	.736	60	164	224	97	133	0	48	31	65	14.1	4.1	2.8	1.2	.400

1304 • SCOTT **Total Basketball**

YEAR	TEAM	GP	GS	MIN	PTS	FGM	FGA	FG%	3PM	3PA	3P%	FTM	FTA	FT%	ORB	DRB	TRB	AST	PF	DQ	STL	BLK	TO	MPG	PPG	RPG	APG	PCM
83-84	Phoenix	65	5	735	167	55	124	.444	1	2	.500	56	72	.778	29	71	100	48	85	0	19	20	39	11.3	2.6	1.5	0.7	.272
84-85	Phoenix	77	18	1238	276	111	259	.429	1	5	.200	53	74	.716	46	115	161	127	125	0	39	25	62	16.1	3.6	2.1	1.6	.289
NBA Season Totals		627	70	10853	3088	1171	2436	.481	4	20	.200	742	1012	.733	661	1331	1992	847	1034	2	404	371	610	17.3	4.9	3.2	1.4	....
77-78	Phoenix	2	....	37	13	4	8	.500	....	....	....	5	6	.833	2	4	6	3	3	0	2	0	2	18.5	6.5	3.0	1.5	.443
78-79	Phoenix	15	....	217	53	20	52	.385	....	....	....	13	21	.619	14	28	42	22	20	0	6	16	14	14.5	3.5	2.8	1.5	.373
79-80	Phoenix	8	....	140	38	17	33	.515	0	2	.000	4	8	.500	8	14	22	10	8	0	4	5	7	17.5	4.8	2.8	1.3	.363
80-81	Phoenix	7	....	120	38	14	30	.467	0	0	.000	10	15	.667	8	11	19	7	6	0	4	6	7	17.1	5.4	2.7	1.0	.384
81-82	Phoenix	7	0	127	32	14	32	.438	0	4	.000	4	8	.500	8	8	16	14	12	0	8	13	5	18.1	4.6	2.3	2.0	.414
82-83	Phoenix	3	1	62	14	6	13	.462	0	0	.000	2	2	1.000	4	8	12	5	6	0	2	5	4	20.7	4.7	4.0	1.7	.387
83-84	Phoenix	16	0	111	25	10	26	.385	1	1	1.000	4	6	.667	10	14	24	7	14	0	2	2	7	6.9	1.6	1.5	0.4	.268
84-85	Phoenix	3	0	64	11	3	12	.250	0	1	.000	5	6	.833	3	5	8	10	8	0	1	4	6	21.3	3.7	2.7	3.3	.244
NBA Playoff Totals		61	1	878	224	88	206	.427	1	8	.125	47	72	.653	57	92	149	78	77	0	29	51	52	14.4	3.7	2.4	1.3	....

• SCOTT, Brent

Brent Steven Scott

Born: June 15, 1971. Jackson, MI, United States. Height: 6'10". Weight: 250 lbs. Drafted: — College: Rice

YEAR	TEAM	GP	GS	MIN	PTS	FGM	FGA	FG%	3PM	3PA	3P%	FTM	FTA	FT%	ORB	DRB	TRB	AST	PF	DQ	STL	BLK	TO	MPG	PPG	RPG	APG	PCM
96-97	Indiana	16	0	55	19	8	17	.471	0	0	.000	3	6	.500	3	6	9	3	14	0	1	1	5	3.4	1.2	0.6	0.2	.209
NBA Season Totals		16	0	55	19	8	17	.471	0	0	.000	3	6	.500	3	6	9	3	14	0	1	1	5	3.4	1.2	0.6	0.2	....

• SCOTT, Byron

Byron Antom Scott

Born: Mar. 28, 1961. Ogden, UT, United States. Height: 6'3". Weight: 195 lbs. Drafted: 1983 College: Arizona State

YEAR	TEAM	GP	GS	MIN	PTS	FGM	FGA	FG%	3PM	3PA	3P%	FTM	FTA	FT%	ORB	DRB	TRB	AST	PF	DQ	STL	BLK	TO	MPG	PPG	RPG	APG	PCM
83-84	LA Lakers	74	49	1637	788	334	690	.484	8	34	.235	112	139	.806	50	114	164	177	174	0	81	19	118	22.1	10.6	2.2	2.4	.421
84-85	LA Lakers	81	65	2305	1295	541	1003	.539	26	60	**.433**	187	228	.820	57	153	210	244	197	1	100	17	138	28.5	16.0	2.6	3.0	.516
85-86	LA Lakers	76	62	2190	1174	507	989	.513	22	61	.361	138	176	.784	55	134	189	164	167	0	85	15	106	28.8	15.4	2.5	2.2	.446
86-87	LA Lakers	82	82	2729	1397	554	1134	.489	65	149	.436	224	251	.892	63	223	286	281	163	0	125	18	148	33.3	17.0	3.5	3.4	.488
87-88	LA Lakers	81	81	3048	1754	710	1348	.527	62	179	.346	272	317	.858	76	257	333	335	204	2	155	27	162	37.6	21.7	4.1	4.1	.568
88-89	LA Lakers	74	73	2605	1448	588	1198	.491	77	193	.399	195	226	.863	72	230	302	231	181	1	114	27	155	35.2	19.6	4.1	3.1	.498
89-90	LA Lakers	77	77	2593	1197	472	1005	.470	93	220	.423	160	209	.766	51	191	242	274	180	2	77	31	123	33.7	15.5	3.1	3.6	.422
90-91	LA Lakers	82	82	2630	1191	501	1051	.477	71	219	.324	118	148	.797	54	192	246	177	146	0	95	21	82	32.1	14.5	3.0	2.2	.398
91-92	LA Lakers	82	82	2679	1218	460	1005	.458	54	157	.344	244	291	.838	74	236	310	226	140	0	105	28	123	32.7	14.9	3.8	2.8	.435
92-93	LA Lakers	58	53	1678	792	296	659	.449	44	135	.326	156	184	.848	27	107	134	157	98	0	55	13	70	28.9	13.7	2.3	2.7	.408
93-94	Indiana	67	2	1197	696	256	548	.467	27	74	.365	157	195	.805	19	91	110	133	80	0	62	9	101	17.9	10.4	1.6	2.0	.494
94-95	Indiana	80	1	1528	802	265	583	.455	79	203	.389	193	227	.850	18	133	151	108	123	1	61	13	120	19.1	10.0	1.9	1.4	.421
95-96	Vancouver	80	0	1894	819	271	676	.401	74	221	.335	203	243	.835	40	152	192	123	126	0	63	22	104	23.7	10.2	2.4	1.5	.345
96-97	LA Lakers	79	8	1440	526	163	379	.430	73	188	.388	127	151	.841	21	97	118	99	72	0	46	16	55	18.2	6.7	1.5	1.3	.349
NBA Season Totals		1073	717	30153	15097	5918	12268	.482	775	2093	.370	2486	2985	.833	677	2310	2987	2729	2051	7	1224	276	1605	28.1	14.1	2.8	2.5	....
83-84	LA Lakers	20	0	404	171	74	161	.460	2	10	.200	21	35	.600	11	26	37	34	39	1	18	2	26	20.2	8.6	1.9	1.7	.323
84-85	LA Lakers	19	19	585	321	138	267	.517	10	21	.476	35	44	.795	16	36	52	50	47	0	41	4	24	30.8	16.9	2.7	2.6	.506
85-86	LA Lakers	14	14	470	224	90	181	.497	6	17	.353	38	42	.905	15	40	55	42	38	0	19	2	30	33.6	16.0	3.9	3.0	.442
86-87	LA Lakers	18	18	608	266	103	210	.490	7	34	.206	53	67	.791	20	42	62	57	52	0	19	4	25	33.8	14.8	3.4	3.2	.415
87-88	LA Lakers	24	24	897	470	178	357	.499	24	55	.436	90	104	.865	26	74	100	60	65	0	34	5	47	37.4	19.6	4.2	2.5	.464
88-89	LA Lakers	11	11	402	219	79	160	.494	15	39	.385	46	55	.836	10	35	45	25	31	0	18	2	20	36.5	19.9	4.1	2.3	.482
89-90	LA Lakers	9	9	325	121	49	106	.462	13	34	.382	10	13	.769	7	30	37	23	32	1	20	3	13	36.1	13.4	4.1	2.6	.368
90-91	LA Lakers	18	18	678	237	95	186	.511	20	38	.526	27	34	.794	13	44	57	29	53	0	23	4	17	37.7	13.2	3.2	1.6	.321
91-92	LA Lakers	4	4	148	75	22	44	.500	7	12	.583	24	27	.889	3	7	10	14	10	0	6	1	5	37.0	18.8	2.5	3.5	.504
92-93	LA Lakers	5	5	177	68	21	42	.500	8	15	.533	18	23	.783	0	11	11	9	11	0	5	0	4	35.4	13.6	2.2	1.8	.349
93-94	Indiana	16	0	239	125	38	96	.396	9	19	.474	40	51	.784	10	23	33	20	22	0	12	2	25	14.9	7.8	2.1	1.3	.412
94-95	Indiana	17	0	298	103	32	94	.340	9	34	.265	30	34	.882	5	20	25	16	30	0	10	1	22	17.5	6.1	1.5	0.9	.198
96-97	LA Lakers	8	0	134	51	15	33	.455	4	11	.364	17	19	.895	0	12	12	11	15	0	1	0	8	16.8	6.4	1.5	1.4	.319
NBA Playoff Totals		183	122	5365	2451	934	1937	.482	134	339	.395	449	548	.819	136	400	536	390	445	2	226	30	266	29.3	13.4	2.9	2.1	....

• SCOTT, Charlie

Charles Thomas Scott

Born: Dec. 15, 1948. New York, NY, United States. Height: 6'5". Weight: 175 lbs. Drafted: 1970 College: North Carolina

YEAR	TEAM	GP	GS	MIN	PTS	FGM	FGA	FG%	3PM	3PA	3P%	FTM	FTA	FT%	ORB	DRB	TRB	AST	PF	DQ	STL	BLK	TO	MPG	PPG	RPG	APG	PCM
70-71	Virginia-A	84	....	3185	2276	902	1947	.463	16	65	.246	456	611	.746	150	288	438	472	298	7	....	....	319	37.9	27.1	5.2	5.6	.683
71-72	Virginia-A	73	....	3061	2524	**985**	**2192**	.449	29	110	.264	525	654	.803	174	200	374	347	261	2	....	....	340	41.9	**34.6**	5.1	4.8	.656
71-72	Phoenix	6	....	177	113	48	113	.425	....	....	....	17	21	.810	....	....	23	26	19	0	....	....	....	29.5	18.8	3.8	4.3	.544
72-73	Phoenix	81	....	3062	2048	806	1809	.446	....	....	....	436	556	.784	....	....	342	495	306	5	....	....	....	37.8	25.3	4.2	6.1	.609
73-74	Phoenix	52	....	2003	1322	538	1171	.459	....	....	....	246	315	.781	64	158	222	271	194	6	99	22	....	38.5	25.4	4.3	5.2	.585
74-75	Phoenix	69	....	2592	1680	703	1594	.441	....	....	....	274	351	.781	72	201	273	311	296	11	111	24	....	37.6	24.3	4.0	4.5	.521
75-76	Boston	82	....	2913	1443	588	1309	.449	....	....	....	267	335	.797	106	252	358	341	**356**	17	103	24	....	35.5	17.6	4.4	4.2	.460
76-77	Boston	43	....	1581	781	326	734	.444	....	....	....	129	173	.746	52	139	191	196	155	3	60	12	....	36.8	18.2	4.4	4.6	.462
77-78	Boston	31	....	1080	504	210	485	.433	....	....	....	84	118	.712	24	77	101	143	97	2	51	6	105	34.8	16.3	3.3	4.6	.383
77-78	LA Lakers	48	....	1393	560	225	509	.442	....	....	....	110	142	.775	38	110	148	235	155	4	59	11	134	29.0	11.7	3.1	4.9	.407
78-79	Denver	79	....	2617	947	393	854	.460	....	....	....	161	215	.749	54	156	210	428	284	12	78	30	253	33.1	12.0	2.7	5.4	.348
79-80	Denver	69	....	1860	639	276	688	.401	2	11	.182	85	118	.720	51	115	166	250	197	3	47	23	166	27.0	9.3	2.4	3.6	.268
NBA Season Totals		560	....	19278	10037	4113	9266	.444	2	11	.182	1809	2344	.772	461	1208	2034	2696	2059	63	608	152	658	34.4	17.9	3.6	4.8	....
ABA Season Totals		157	....	6246	4800	1887	4139	.456	45	175	.257	981	1265	.775	324	488	812	819	559	9	....	....	659	39.8	30.6	5.2	5.2	....
Career Totals		717	....	25524	14837	6000	13405	.448	47	186	.253	2790	3609	.773	785	1696	2846	3515	2618	72	608	152	1317	35.6	20.7	4.0	4.9	....
70-71	Virginia-A	12	....	504	321	115	281	.409	8	31	.258	83	110	.755	25	54	79	82	45	2	....	....	44	42.0	26.8	6.6	6.8	.636
75-76	Boston	18	....	632	277	111	284	.391	....	....	....	55	72	.764	23	53	76	71	97	11	21	8	....	35.1	15.4	4.2	3.9	.358
76-77	Boston	9	....	338	148	52	108	.481	....	....	....	44	52	.846	15	23	38	38	41	3	13	2	....	37.6	16.4	4.2	4.2	.457
77-78	LA Lakers	3	....	103	30	12	40	.300	....	....	....	6	8	.750	6	7	13	14	9	0	4	0	11	34.3	10.0	4.3	4.7	.211
78-79	Denver	3	....	104	48	20	42	.476	....	....	....	8	14	.571	2	12	14	10	11	0	2	2	10	34.7	16.0	4.7	3.3	.373
NBA Playoff Totals		33	....	1177	503	195	474	.411	....	....	....	113	146	.774	46	95	141	133	158	14	40	12	21	35.7	15.2	4.3	4.0	....
ABA Playoff Totals		12	....	504	321	115	281	.409	8	31	.258	83	110	.755	25	54	79	82	45	2	....	....	44	42.0	26.8	6.6	**6.8**	....
Career Playoff Totals		45	....	1681	824	310	755	.411	8	31	.258	196	256	.766	71	149	220	215	203	16	40	12	65	37.4	18.3	4.9	4.8	....

• SCOTT, Dennis

Dennis Eugene Scott

Born: Sept. 5, 1968. Hagerstown, MD, United States. Height: 6'8". Weight: 229 lbs. Drafted: 1990 College: Georgia Tech

YEAR	TEAM	GP	GS	MIN	PTS	FGM	FGA	FG%	3PM	3PA	3P%	FTM	FTA	FT%	ORB	DRB	TRB	AST	PF	DQ	STL	BLK	TO	MPG	PPG	RPG	APG	PCM
90-91	Orlando	82	73	2336	1284	503	1183	.425	125	334	.374	153	204	.750	62	173	235	134	203	1	62	25	123	28.5	15.7	2.9	1.6	.368
91-92	Orlando	18	15	608	359	133	331	.402	29	89	.326	64	71	.901	14	52	66	35	49	1	20	9	31	33.8	19.9	3.7	1.9	.405
92-93	Orlando	54	43	1759	858	329	763	.431	108	268	.403	92	117	.786	38	148	186	136	131	3	57	18	103	32.6	15.9	3.4	2.5	.383
93-94	Orlando	82	37	2283	1046	384	949	.405	155	388	.399	123	159	.774	54	164	218	216	161	0	81	32	90	27.8	12.8	2.7	2.6	.391
94-95	Orlando	62	10	1499	802	283	645	.439	150	352	.426	86	114	.754	25	121	146	131	119	1	45	14	56	24.2	12.9	2.4	2.1	.449
95-96	Orlando	82	82	3041	1431	491	1117	.440	**267**	628	.425	182	222	.820	63	246	309	243	169	1	90	29	123	37.1	17.5	3.8	3.0	.424
96-97	Orlando	66	62	2166	823	298	749	.398	147	373	.394	80	101	.792	40	163	203	139	138	2	74	19	79	32.8	12.5	3.1	2.1	.314
97-98	Dallas	52	42	1797	707	258	666	.387	94	273	.344	97	118	.822	39	158	197	129	121	1	43	32	94	34.6	13.6	3.8	2.5	.318
97-98	Phoenix	29	3	493	181	71	162	.438	31	69	.449	8	12	.667	8	42	50	24	31	0	10	7	12	17.0	6.2	1.7	0.8	.321
98-99	New York	15	0	206	43	17	56	.304	8	29	.276	1	4	.250	3	17	20	8	17	0	3	1	5	13.7	2.9	1.3	0.5	.122
98-99	Minnesota	21	9	532	191	70	157	.446	29	68	.426	22	27	.815	5	33	38	32	32	0	12	2	14	25.3	9.1	1.8	1.5	.313
99-00	Vancouver	66	0	1263	369	125	333	.375	71	189	.376	48	57	.842	16	90	106	69	104	0	28	9	30	19.1	5.6	1.6	1.0	.243
NBA Season Totals		629	376	17983	8094	2962	7111	.417	1214	3060	.397	956	1206	.793	367	1407	1774	1296	1275	10	525	197	760	28.6	12.9	2.8	2.1	....
93-94	Orlando	3	3	99	43	14	41	.341	7	22	.318	8	10	.800	1	5	6	3	7	0	2	3	8	33.0	14.3	2.0	1.0	.203
94-95	Orlando	21	15	746	308	109	264	.413	56	151	.371	34	40	.850	9	54	63	45	62	0	22	5	33	35.5	14.7	3.0	2.1	.311
95-96	Orlando	12	12	446	136	48	116	.414	26	69	.377	14	22	.636	9	34	43	23	37	0	9	1	15	37.2	11.3	3.6	1.9	.249
96-97	Orlando	5	1	94	15	6	23	.261	3	11	.273	0	0	.000	2	7	9	5	8	0	2	0	2	18.8	3.0	1.8	1.0	.097
97-98	Phoenix	4	0	62	17	7	17	.412	3	8	.375	0	0	.000	2	6	8	1	2	0	1	0	2	15.5	4.3	2.0	0.3	.233
NBA Playoff Totals		45	31	1447	519	184	461	.399	95	261	.364	56	72	.778	23	106	129	77	116	0	36	9	60	32.2	11.5	2.9	1.7	....

• SCOTT, James

James Lamont Scott

Born: June 6, 1972. Paterson, NJ, United States. Height: 6'6". Weight: 180 lbs. Drafted: — College: St. John's (NY)

YEAR	TEAM	GP	GS	MIN	PTS	FGM	FGA	FG%	3PM	3PA	3P%	FTM	FTA	FT%	ORB	DRB	TRB	AST	PF	DQ	STL	BLK	TO	MPG	PPG	RPG	APG	PCM
96-97	Miami	8	0	32	1	0	8	.000	0	4	.000	1	2	.500	1	5	6	3	5	0	2	0	2	4.0	0.1	0.8	0.4	-.014
NBA Season Totals		8	0	32	1	0	8	.000	0	4	.000	1	2	.500	1	5	6	3	5	0	2	0	2	4.0	0.1	0.8	0.4	....

• SCOTT, Joe

Joe Scott

Born: 1918. Height: — Weight: — Drafted: — College: Case Reserve

YEAR	TEAM	GP	GS	MIN	PTS	FGM	FGA	FG%	3PM	3PA	3P%	FTM	FTA	FT%	ORB	DRB	TRB	AST	PF	DQ	STL	BLK	TO	MPG	PPG	RPG	APG	PCM
45-46	Cleveland-N	15	....	....	37	14	....	....	....	....	....	9	....	....	....	....	....	....	....	....	....	....	....	....	2.5	....	....	....
NBL Season Totals		15	....	....	37	14	....	....	....	....	....	9	....	....	....	....	....	....	....	....	....	....	....	....	2.5	....	....	....

• SCOTT, Ray

John Raymond (Chink) Scott

Born: July 12, 1938. Philadelphia, PA, United States. Height: 6'9". Weight: 215 lbs. Drafted: 1961 College: Portland

YEAR	TEAM	GP	GS	MIN	PTS	FGM	FGA	FG%	3PM	3PA	3P%	FTM	FTA	FT%	ORB	DRB	TRB	AST	PF	DQ	STL	BLK	TO	MPG	PPG	RPG	APG	PCM
61-62	Detroit	75	....	2087	995	370	956	.387	....	....	....	255	388	.657	....	....	865	132	232	6	....	....	....	27.8	13.3	11.5	1.8	.590
62-63	Detroit	76	....	2538	1228	460	1110	.414	....	....	....	308	457	.674	....	....	772	191	263	9	....	....	....	33.4	16.2	10.2	2.5	.549
63-64	Detroit	80	....	2964	1406	539	1307	.412	....	....	....	328	456	.719	....	....	1078	244	296	7	....	....	....	37.1	17.6	13.5	3.1	.601
64-65	Detroit	66	....	2167	1024	402	1092	.368	....	....	....	220	314	.701	....	....	634	239	209	5	....	....	....	32.8	15.5	9.6	3.6	.535
65-66	Detroit	79	....	2652	1411	544	1309	.416	....	....	....	323	435	.743	....	....	755	238	209	1	....	....	....	33.6	17.9	9.6	3.0	.591
66-67	Detroit	45	....	1477	660	252	681	.370	....	....	....	156	206	.757	....	....	404	84	132	1	....	....	....	32.8	14.7	9.0	1.9	.453
66-67	Baltimore	27	....	969	512	206	463	.445	....	....	....	100	160	.625	....	....	356	76	83	1	....	....	....	35.9	19.0	13.2	2.8	.645
67-68	Baltimore	81	....	2924	1328	490	1189	.412	....	....	....	348	447	.779	....	....	1111	167	252	2	....	....	....	36.1	16.4	13.7	2.1	.587
68-69	Baltimore	82	....	2168	967	386	929	.416	....	....	....	195	257	.759	....	....	722	133	212	1	....	....	....	26.4	11.8	8.8	1.6	.534
69-70	Baltimore	73	....	1393	653	257	605	.425	....	....	....	139	173	.803	....	....	457	114	147	0	....	....	....	19.1	8.9	6.3	1.6	.572
70-71	Virginia-A	72	....	1552	1028	420	933	.450	1	1	1.000	187	236	.792	163	410	573	123	180	3	....	....	137	21.6	14.3	8.0	1.7	.729
71-72	Virginia-A	55	....	818	417	163	393	.415	2	4	.500	89	114	.781	71	181	252	40	90	0	....	....	55	14.9	7.6	4.6	0.7	.526
NBA Season Totals		684	....	21339	10184	3906	9641	.405	....	....	....	2372	3293	.720	....	....	7154	1618	2035	33	....	....	....	31.2	14.9	10.5	2.4	....
ABA Season Totals		127	....	2370	1445	583	1326	.440	3	5	.600	276	350	.789	234	591	825	163	270	3	....	....	192	18.7	11.4	6.5	1.3	....
Career Totals		811	....	23709	11629	4489	10967	.409	3	5	.600	2648	3643	.727	234	591	7979	1781	2305	36	....	....	192	29.2	14.3	9.8	2.2	....
61-62	Detroit	10	....	400	173	69	170	.406	....	....	....	35	67	.522	....	....	145	43	39	2	....	....	....	40.0	17.3	14.5	4.3	.580
62-63	Detroit	4	....	155	63	27	77	.351	....	....	....	9	13	.692	....	....	48	9	19	0	....	....	....	38.8	15.8	12.0	2.3	.408
68-69	Baltimore	4	....	137	53	23	52	.442	....	....	....	7	8	.875	....	....	32	4	16	0	....	....	....	34.3	13.3	8.0	1.0	.387
69-70	Baltimore	7	....	90	32	11	34	.324	....	....	....	10	14	.714	....	....	21	4	8	0	....	....	....	12.9	4.6	3.0	0.6	.327
70-71	Virginia-A	12	....	264	207	80	157	.510	0	0	.000	47	56	.839	19	59	78	21	43	0	....	....	12	22.0	17.3	6.5	1.8	.804
71-72	Virginia-A	11	....	212	132	52	105	.495	0	0	.000	28	38	.737	12	46	58	17	25	0	....	....	16	19.3	12.0	5.3	1.5	.661
NBA Playoff Totals		25	....	782	321	130	333	.390	....	....	....	61	102	.598	....	....	246	60	82	2	....	....	....	31.3	12.8	9.8	2.4	....
ABA Playoff Totals		23	....	476	339	132	262	.504	0	0	.000	75	94	.798	31	105	136	38	68	0	....	....	28	20.7	14.7	5.9	1.7	....
Career Playoff Totals		48	....	1258	660	262	595	.440	0	0	.000	136	196	.694	31	105	382	98	150	2	....	....	28	26.2	13.8	8.0	2.0	....

• SCOTT, Shawnelle

Shawnelle Scott

Born: June 16, 1972. New York, NY, United States. Height: 6'10". Weight: 250 lbs. Drafted: 1994 College: St. John's (NY)

YEAR	TEAM	GP	GS	MIN	PTS	FGM	FGA	FG%	3PM	3PA	3P%	FTM	FTA	FT%	ORB	DRB	TRB	AST	PF	DQ	STL	BLK	TO	MPG	PPG	RPG	APG	PCM
96-97	Cleveland	16	0	50	20	8	16	.500	0	0	.000	4	11	.364	8	8	16	0	6	0	0	3	0	3.1	1.3	1.0	0.0	.484
97-98	Cleveland	41	0	188	44	16	36	.444	0	0	.000	12	18	.667	20	39	59	8	45	0	6	8	8	4.6	1.1	1.4	0.2	.375
00-01	San Antonio	27	1	144	43	17	41	.415	0	0	.000	9	22	.409	23	27	50	4	23	0	5	6	11	5.3	1.6	1.9	0.1	.379
01-02	Denver	21	10	252	82	37	75	.493	0	0	.000	8	20	.400	53	50	103	8	49	0	3	6	15	12.0	3.9	4.9	0.4	.463
NBA Season Totals		105	11	634	189	78	168	.464	0	0	.000	33	71	.465	104	124	228	20	123	0	14	23	34	6.0	1.8	2.2	0.2	....
97-98	Cleveland	1	0	3	2	1	2	.500	0	0	.000	0	0	.000	0	0	0	0	0	0	0	1	1	3.0	2.0	0.0	0.0	.362
00-01	San Antonio	7	0	13	3	1	4	.250	0	2	.000	1	1	1.000	0	2	2	0	2	0	0	0	3	1.9	0.4	0.3	0.0	-.115
NBA Playoff Totals		8	0	16	5	2	6	.333	0	2	.000	1	1	1.000	0	2	2	0	2	0	0	1	4	2.0	0.6	0.3	0.0	....

YEAR	TEAM	GP	GS	MIN	PTS	FGM	FGA	FG%	3PM	3PA	3P%	FTM	FTA	FT%	ORB	DRB	TRB	AST	PF	DQ	STL	BLK	TO	MPG	PPG	RPG	APG	PCM

• SCOTT, Willie
Willie Scott

Born: May 22, 1947. Gadsden, AL, United States.   Height: 6'5".   Weight: 210 lbs.   Drafted: 1969   College: Alabama State

YEAR	TEAM	GP	GS	MIN	PTS	FGM	FGA	FG%	3PM	3PA	3P%	FTM	FTA	FT%	ORB	DRB	TRB	AST	PF	DQ	STL	BLK	TO	MPG	PPG	RPG	APG	PCM
69-70	Dallas-A	8	....	51	13	6	15	.400	0	0	.000	1	6	.167	2	2	4	2	16	0	....	....	8	6.4	1.6	0.5	0.3	.039
ABA Season Totals		8	....	51	13	6	15	.400	0	0	.000	1	6	.167	2	2	4	2	16	0	....	....	8	6.4	1.6	0.5	0.3	....

• SCRANTON, Paul
Paul Earl Scranton Jr.

Born: Apr. 30, 1944. Los Angeles, CA, United States.   Height: 6'5".   Weight: 230 lbs.   Drafted: —   College: Cal Poly Pomona

YEAR	TEAM	GP	GS	MIN	PTS	FGM	FGA	FG%	3PM	3PA	3P%	FTM	FTA	FT%	ORB	DRB	TRB	AST	PF	DQ	STL	BLK	TO	MPG	PPG	RPG	APG	PCM
67-68	Anaheim-A	5	....	41	9	4	9	.444	0	0	.000	1	4	.250	....	....	16	1	5	0	....	....	1	8.2	1.8	3.2	0.2	.390
ABA Season Totals		5	....	41	9	4	9	.444	0	0	.000	1	4	.250	....	....	16	1	5	0	....	....	1	8.2	1.8	3.2	0.2	....

• SCURRY, Carey
Carey Scurry

Born: Dec. 4, 1962. Brooklyn, NY, United States.   Height: 6'7".   Weight: 188 lbs.   Drafted: 1985   College: Long Island University

YEAR	TEAM	GP	GS	MIN	PTS	FGM	FGA	FG%	3PM	3PA	3P%	FTM	FTA	FT%	ORB	DRB	TRB	AST	PF	DQ	STL	BLK	TO	MPG	PPG	RPG	APG	PCM
85-86	Utah	78	0	1168	363	142	301	.472	1	11	.091	78	126	.619	97	145	242	85	171	2	78	66	94	15.0	4.7	3.1	1.1	.407
86-87	Utah	69	5	753	344	123	247	.498	4	13	.308	94	134	.701	97	101	198	57	124	1	55	54	55	10.9	5.0	2.9	0.8	.595
87-88	Utah	29	0	447	138	54	116	.466	3	8	.375	27	39	.692	29	52	81	49	78	0	47	22	41	15.4	4.8	2.8	1.7	.430
87-88	New York	4	0	8	2	1	2	.500	0	0	.000	0	0	.000	1	2	3	1	3	0	2	1	2	2.0	0.5	0.8	0.3	.558
NBA Season Totals		180	5	2376	847	320	666	.480	8	32	.250	199	299	.666	224	300	524	192	376	3	182	143	192	13.2	4.7	2.9	1.1	....
85-86	Utah	4	0	54	17	8	20	.400	0	2	.000	1	2	.500	10	6	16	3	12	0	1	4	2	13.5	4.3	4.0	0.8	.383
86-87	Utah	4	0	57	24	10	22	.455	1	2	.500	3	7	.429	7	7	14	0	10	0	4	5	2	14.3	6.0	3.5	0.0	.454
NBA Playoff Totals		8	0	111	41	18	42	.429	1	4	.250	4	9	.444	17	13	30	3	22	0	5	9	4	13.9	5.1	3.8	0.4	....

• SEALS, Bruce
Bruce A. Seals

Born: June 18, 1953. New Orleans, LA, United States.   Height: 6'8".   Weight: 210 lbs.   Drafted: 1975   College: Xavier (LA)

YEAR	TEAM	GP	GS	MIN	PTS	FGM	FGA	FG%	3PM	3PA	3P%	FTM	FTA	FT%	ORB	DRB	TRB	AST	PF	DQ	STL	BLK	TO	MPG	PPG	RPG	APG	PCM
73-74	Utah-A	78	....	1358	545	229	605	.379	19	90	.211	68	108	.630	100	179	279	54	199	....	57	57	81	17.4	7.0	3.6	0.7	.310
74-75	Utah-A	35	....	371	140	60	142	.423	0	3	.000	20	26	.769	43	54	97	13	67	....	15	16	24	10.6	4.0	2.8	0.4	.365
75-76	Seattle	81	....	2435	957	388	889	.436	....	....	....	181	267	.678	157	350	507	119	314	11	64	44	....	30.1	11.8	6.3	1.5	.380
76-77	Seattle	81	....	1977	894	378	851	.444	....	....	....	138	195	.708	118	236	354	93	262	6	49	58	....	24.4	11.0	4.4	1.1	.384
77-78	Seattle	73	....	1322	571	230	551	.417	....	....	....	111	175	.634	62	164	226	81	210	4	41	33	102	18.1	7.8	3.1	1.1	.329
NBA Season Totals		235	....	5734	2422	996	2291	.435	....	....	....	430	637	.675	337	750	1087	293	786	21	154	135	102	24.4	10.3	4.6	1.2	....
ABA Season Totals		113	....	1729	685	289	747	.387	19	93	.204	88	134	.657	143	233	376	67	266	....	72	73	105	15.3	6.1	3.3	0.6	....
Career Totals		348	....	7463	3107	1285	3038	.423	19	93	.204	518	771	.672	480	983	1463	360	1052	21	226	208	207	21.4	8.9	4.2	1.0	....
73-74	Utah-A	15	....	260	91	41	98	.418	2	10	.200	7	14	.500	22	30	52	14	40	....	6	4	15	17.3	6.1	3.5	0.9	.317
74-75	Utah-A	3	....	41	24	9	14	.643	0	0	.000	6	9	.667	6	5	11	0	8	....	1	0	2	13.7	8.0	3.7	0.0	.596
75-76	Seattle	6	....	181	78	30	68	.441	....	....	....	18	26	.692	14	22	36	3	22	0	5	6	....	30.2	13.0	6.0	0.5	.369
77-78	Seattle	9	....	92	27	12	37	.324	....	....	....	3	7	.429	8	12	20	8	14	0	2	2	6	10.2	3.0	2.2	0.9	.239
NBA Playoff Totals		15	....	273	105	42	105	.400	....	....	....	21	33	.636	22	34	56	11	36	0	7	8	6	18.2	7.0	3.7	0.7	....
ABA Playoff Totals		18	....	301	115	50	112	.446	2	10	.200	13	23	.565	28	35	63	14	48	....	7	4	17	16.7	6.4	3.5	0.8	....
Career Playoff Totals		33	....	574	220	92	217	.424	2	10	.200	34	56	.607	50	69	119	25	84	0	14	12	23	17.4	6.7	3.6	0.8	....

• SEALS, Shea
Shea Seals

Born: Aug. 26, 1975. Tulsa, OK, United States.   Height: 6'5".   Weight: 210 lbs.   Drafted: —   College: Tulsa

YEAR	TEAM	GP	GS	MIN	PTS	FGM	FGA	FG%	3PM	3PA	3P%	FTM	FTA	FT%	ORB	DRB	TRB	AST	PF	DQ	STL	BLK	TO	MPG	PPG	RPG	APG	PCM
97-98	LA Lakers	4	0	9	4	1	8	.125	0	3	.000	2	4	.500	3	1	4	0	1	0	1	0	0	2.3	1.0	1.0	0.0	.089
NBA Season Totals		4	0	9	4	1	8	.125	0	3	.000	2	4	.500	3	1	4	0	1	0	1	0	0	2.3	1.0	1.0	0.0	....

• SEALY, Malik
Malik Sealy

Born: Feb. 1, 1970. Bronx, NY, United States. Died: May 20, 2000.   Height: 6'8".   Weight: 190 lbs.   Drafted: 1992   College: St. John's (NY)

YEAR	TEAM	GP	GS	MIN	PTS	FGM	FGA	FG%	3PM	3PA	3P%	FTM	FTA	FT%	ORB	DRB	TRB	AST	PF	DQ	STL	BLK	TO	MPG	PPG	RPG	APG	PCM
92-93	Indiana	58	2	672	330	136	319	.426	7	31	.226	51	74	.689	60	52	112	47	74	0	36	7	58	11.6	5.7	1.9	0.8	.379
93-94	Indiana	43	5	623	285	111	274	.405	4	16	.250	59	87	.678	43	75	118	48	84	0	31	8	52	14.5	6.6	2.7	1.1	.373
94-95	LA Clippers	60	41	1604	778	291	669	.435	22	73	.301	174	223	.780	77	137	214	107	173	2	72	25	84	26.7	13.0	3.6	1.8	.403
95-96	LA Clippers	62	48	1601	712	272	655	.415	21	100	.210	147	184	.799	76	164	240	116	150	2	84	28	112	25.8	11.5	3.9	1.9	.383
96-97	LA Clippers	80	79	2456	1079	373	942	.396	79	222	.356	254	290	.876	59	179	238	165	185	4	124	45	152	30.7	13.5	3.0	2.1	.350
97-98	Detroit	77	10	1641	591	216	505	.428	9	41	.220	150	182	.824	48	171	219	100	156	2	65	20	77	21.3	7.7	2.8	1.3	.339
98-99	Minnesota	31	7	731	251	95	231	.411	6	23	.261	55	61	.902	23	69	92	36	68	0	30	5	33	23.6	8.1	3.0	1.2	.302
99-00	Minnesota	82	61	2392	929	371	780	.476	10	35	.286	177	218	.812	119	233	352	197	197	1	76	19	110	29.2	11.3	4.3	2.4	.406
NBA Season Totals		493	253	11720	4955	1865	4375	.426	158	541	.292	1067	1319	.809	505	1080	1585	816	1087	11	518	157	678	23.8	10.1	3.2	1.7	....
92-93	Indiana	3	0	18	2	0	5	.000	0	1	.000	2	2	1.000	2	0	2	0	1	0	0	0	1	6.0	0.7	0.7	0.0	-.122
96-97	LA Clippers	3	3	79	36	12	25	.480	1	5	.200	11	15	.733	1	2	3	5	10	1	0	0	5	26.3	12.0	1.0	1.7	.264
98-99	Minnesota	4	0	70	20	8	23	.348	0	0	.000	4	5	.800	2	4	6	3	4	0	1	1	2	17.5	5.0	1.5	0.8	.187
99-00	Minnesota	4	4	122	50	19	41	.463	1	3	.333	11	16	.688	5	13	18	5	10	0	2	0	8	30.5	12.5	4.5	1.3	.324
NBA Playoff Totals		14	7	289	108	39	94	.415	2	9	.222	28	38	.737	10	19	29	13	25	1	3	1	16	20.6	7.7	2.1	0.9	....

• SEALY, Tom
Tom Sealy

Born: 1921.   Height: 6'1".   Weight: 190 lbs.   Drafted: —   College: Brooklyn

YEAR	TEAM	GP	GS	MIN	PTS	FGM	FGA	FG%	3PM	3PA	3P%	FTM	FTA	FT%	ORB	DRB	TRB	AST	PF	DQ	STL	BLK	TO	MPG	PPG	RPG	APG	PCM
48-49	Dayton-N	40	....	....	260	100	....	....	....	....	....	60	92	.652	....	....	....	....	....	....	....	....	....	6.5	....	....	....
NBL Season Totals		40	....	....	260	100	....	....	....	....	....	60	92	....	....	....	....	....	....	....	....	....	....	6.5	....	....	....

• SEARCY, Ed

Edwin Searcy

Born: Apr. 17, 1952. New York, NY, United States. Height: 6'6". Weight: 210 lbs. Drafted: 1974 College: St. John's (NY)

YEAR TEAM	GP	GS	MIN	PTS	FGM	FGA	FG%	3PM	3PA	3P%	FTM	FTA	FT%	ORB	DRB	TRB	AST	PF	DQ	STL	BLK	TO	MPG	PPG	RPG	APG	PCM
75-76 Boston	4	....	12	6	2	6	.333	....	....	....	2	2	1.000	0	0	0	1	4	0	0	0	....	3.0	1.5	0.0	0.3	.166
NBA Season Totals	4	....	12	6	2	6	.333	....	....	....	2	2	1.000	0	0	0	1	4	0	0	0	....	3.0	1.5	0.0	0.3	....

• SEARS, Kenny

Kenneth Robert (Kenny, Big Cat) Sears

Born: Aug. 17, 1933. Watsonville, CA, United States. Height: 6'9". Weight: 198 lbs. Drafted: 1955 College: Santa Clara

YEAR TEAM	GP	GS	MIN	PTS	FGM	FGA	FG%	3PM	3PA	3P%	FTM	FTA	FT%	ORB	DRB	TRB	AST	PF	DQ	STL	BLK	TO	MPG	PPG	RPG	APG	PCM
55-56 New York	70	....	2069	896	319	728	.438	....	....	....	258	324	.796	....	....	616	114	201	4	....	....	....	29.6	12.8	8.8	1.6	.528
56-57 New York	72	....	2516	1069	343	821	.418	....	....	....	383	485	.790	....	....	614	101	226	2	....	....	....	34.9	14.8	8.5	1.4	.467
57-58 New York	72	....	2685	1342	445	1014	.439	....	....	....	452	550	.822	....	....	785	126	251	7	....	....	....	37.3	18.6	10.9	1.8	.571
58-59 New York	71	....	2498	1488	491	1002	**.490**	....	....	....	506	588	.861	....	....	658	136	237	6	....	....	....	35.2	21.0	9.3	1.9	.660
59-60 New York	64	....	2099	1187	412	863	**.477**	....	....	....	363	418	.868	....	....	876	127	191	2	....	....	....	32.8	18.5	13.7	2.0	.750
60-61 New York	52	....	1396	750	241	568	.424	....	....	....	268	325	.825	....	....	293	102	165	6	....	....	....	26.8	14.4	5.6	2.0	.549
62-63 New York	23	....	359	122	48	92	.522	....	....	....	26	46	.565	....	....	67	40	29	0	....	....	....	15.6	5.3	2.9	1.7	.471
62-63 San Francisco	54	....	782	331	113	212	.533	....	....	....	105	122	.861	....	....	139	55	99	0	....	....	....	14.5	6.1	2.6	1.0	.490
63-64 San Francisco	51	....	519	170	53	120	.442	....	....	....	64	79	.810	....	....	94	42	71	0	....	....	....	10.2	3.3	1.8	0.8	.402
NBA Season Totals	529	....	14923	7355	2465	5420	.455	....	....	....	2425	2937	.826	....	....	4142	843	1470	27	....	....	....	28.2	13.9	7.8	1.6	....
58-59 New York	2	....	64	33	10	27	.370	....	....	....	13	15	.867	....	....	17	6	6	0	....	....	....	32.0	16.5	8.5	3.0	.586
63-64 San Francisco	7	....	24	12	6	10	.600	....	....	....	0	0	.000	....	....	12	3	4	0	....	....	....	3.4	1.7	1.7	0.4	.847
NBA Playoff Totals	9	....	88	45	16	37	.432	....	....	....	13	15	.867	....	....	29	9	10	0	....	....	....	9.8	5.0	3.2	1.0	....

• SEBASTIAN, Johnny

John Sebastian

Born: 1921. Odin, IL, United States. Height: 6' Weight: 185 lbs. Drafted: — College: Southern Illinois

YEAR TEAM	GP	GS	MIN	PTS	FGM	FGA	FG%	3PM	3PA	3P%	FTM	FTA	FT%	ORB	DRB	TRB	AST	PF	DQ	STL	BLK	TO	MPG	PPG	RPG	APG	PCM
47-48 Syracuse-N	1	....	....	0	0	....	....	....	....	....	0	0	.000	....	....	....	....	1	....	....	....	....	....	0.0	....	....	....
48-49 Detroit-N	19	....	....	234	86	....	....	....	....	....	62	101	.614	....	....	....	....	....	....	....	....	....	....	12.3	....	....	....
48-49 Hammond-N	42	....	....	262	99	....	....	....	....	....	64	105	.610	....	....	....	....	149	....	....	....	....	....	6.2	....	....	....
NBL Season Totals	62	....	....	496	185	....	....	....	....	....	126	206	....	....	....	....	....	150	....	....	....	....	....	8.0	....	....	....
48-49 Hammond-N	2	....	....	15	6	....	....	....	....	....	3	4	.750	....	....	....	....	....	....	....	....	....	....	7.5	....	....	....
NBL Playoff Totals	2	....	....	15	6	....	....	....	....	....	3	4	....	....	....	....	....	....	....	....	....	....	....	7.5	....	....	....

• SEE, Wayne

Marshall Wayne See

Born: Nov. 3, 1923. Clemenceau, AZ, United States. Height: 6'3". Weight: 190 lbs. Drafted: — College: Northern Arizona

YEAR TEAM	GP	GS	MIN	PTS	FGM	FGA	FG%	3PM	3PA	3P%	FTM	FTA	FT%	ORB	DRB	TRB	AST	PF	DQ	STL	BLK	TO	MPG	PPG	RPG	APG	PCM
49-50 Waterloo	61	....	....	320	113	303	.373	....	....	....	94	135	.696	....	....	....	143	147	....	....	....	....	....	5.2	....	2.3	....
NBA Season Totals	61	....	....	320	113	303	.373	....	....	....	94	135	.696	....	....	....	143	147	....	....	....	....	....	5.2	....	2.3	....

• SEIKALY, Rony

Ronald F. Seikaly

Born: May 10, 1965. Beirut, Lebanon. Height: 6'11". Weight: 230 lbs. Drafted: 1988 College: Syracuse

YEAR TEAM	GP	GS	MIN	PTS	FGM	FGA	FG%	3PM	3PA	3P%	FTM	FTA	FT%	ORB	DRB	TRB	AST	PF	DQ	STL	BLK	TO	MPG	PPG	RPG	APG	PCM
88-89 Miami	78	62	1962	848	333	744	.448	1	4	.250	181	354	.511	204	345	549	55	258	8	46	96	203	25.2	10.9	7.0	0.7	.397
89-90 Miami	74	72	2409	1228	486	968	.502	0	1	.000	256	431	.594	253	513	766	78	258	8	78	124	237	32.6	16.6	10.4	1.1	.557
90-91 Miami	64	59	2171	1050	395	822	.481	2	6	.333	258	417	.619	207	502	709	95	213	2	51	86	205	33.9	16.4	11.1	1.5	.542
91-92 Miami	79	78	2800	1296	463	947	.489	0	3	.000	370	505	.733	307	627	934	109	278	2	40	121	213	35.4	16.4	11.8	1.4	.568
92-93 Miami	72	64	2456	1232	417	868	.480	1	8	.125	397	540	.735	259	587	846	100	260	3	38	83	202	34.1	17.1	11.8	1.4	.588
93-94 Miami	72	60	2410	1088	392	803	.488	0	2	.000	304	422	.720	244	496	740	136	279	8	59	100	194	33.5	15.1	10.3	1.9	.549
94-95 Golden State	36	35	1035	435	162	314	.516	0	0	.000	111	160	.694	77	189	266	45	122	1	20	37	104	28.8	12.1	7.4	1.3	.450
95-96 Golden State	64	60	1813	776	285	568	.502	2	3	.667	204	282	.723	166	333	499	71	219	5	40	69	179	28.3	12.1	7.8	1.1	.468
96-97 Orlando	74	68	2615	1277	460	907	.507	0	3	.000	357	500	.714	274	427	701	92	275	4	49	107	215	35.3	17.3	9.5	1.2	.521
97-98 Orlando	47	47	1484	704	237	538	.441	0	2	.000	230	305	.754	130	227	357	69	137	2	25	39	136	31.6	15.0	7.6	1.5	.450
97-98 New Jersey	9	2	152	42	13	41	.317	0	0	.000	16	27	.593	16	20	36	8	27	0	3	4	12	16.9	4.7	4.0	0.9	.237
98-99 New Jersey	9	0	88	15	4	20	.200	0	0	.000	7	18	.389	5	16	21	2	15	0	4	6	10	9.8	1.7	2.3	0.2	.115
NBA Season Totals	678	607	21395	9991	3647	7540	.484	6	32	.188	2691	3961	.679	2142	4282	6424	860	2341	43	453	872	1910	31.6	14.7	9.5	1.3	....
91-92 Miami	3	3	117	62	19	35	.543	0	0	.000	24	32	.750	11	19	30	4	15	1	1	5	9	39.0	20.7	10.0	1.3	.563
93-94 Miami	5	3	165	41	14	32	.438	0	0	.000	13	23	.565	19	28	47	8	22	0	4	7	11	33.0	8.2	9.4	1.6	.373
96-97 Orlando	3	3	86	19	7	22	.318	0	0	.000	5	7	.714	5	11	16	0	10	0	1	3	4	28.7	6.3	5.3	0.0	.167
97-98 New Jersey	3	0	37	18	7	9	.778	0	0	.000	4	6	.667	3	6	9	0	4	0	1	0	4	12.3	6.0	3.0	0.0	.511
NBA Playoff Totals	14	9	405	140	47	98	.480	0	0	.000	46	68	.676	38	64	102	12	51	1	7	15	28	28.9	10.0	7.3	0.9	....

• SELBO, Glen

Glen L. Selbo

Born: Mar. 29, 1926. Height: 6'3". Weight: 196 lbs. Drafted: 1947 College: Wisconsin

YEAR TEAM	GP	GS	MIN	PTS	FGM	FGA	FG%	3PM	3PA	3P%	FTM	FTA	FT%	ORB	DRB	TRB	AST	PF	DQ	STL	BLK	TO	MPG	PPG	RPG	APG	PCM
47-48 Oshkosh-N	59	....	....	376	157	....	....	....	....	....	62	100	.620	....	....	....	....	85	....	....	....	....	....	6.4	....	....	....
48-49 Oshkosh-N	60	....	....	315	119	....	....	....	....	....	77	114	.675	....	....	....	....	94	....	....	....	....	....	5.3	....	....	....
49-50 Sheboygan	13	....	....	42	10	51	.196	....	....	....	22	29	.759	....	....	....	23	15	....	....	....	....	....	3.2	....	1.8	....
NBA Season Totals	13	....	....	42	10	51	.196	....	....	....	22	29	.759	....	....	....	23	15	....	....	....	....	....	3.2	....	1.8	....
NBL Season Totals	119	....	....	691	276	....	....	....	....	....	139	214	....	....	....	....	....	179	....	....	....	....	....	5.8	....	....	....
Career Totals	132	....	....	733	286	51	....	....	....	....	161	243	....	....	....	....	23	194	....	....	....	....	....	5.6	....	0.2	....
47-48 Oshkosh-N	4	....	....	15	5	....	....	....	....	....	5	5	1.000	....	....	....	....	....	....	....	....	....	....	3.8	....	....	....
NBL Playoff Totals	4	....	....	15	5	....	....	....	....	....	5	5	....	....	....	....	....	....	....	....	....	....	....	3.8	....	....	....

YEAR	TEAM	GP	GS	MIN	PTS	FGM	FGA	FG%	3PM	3PA	3P%	FTM	FTA	FT%	ORB	DRB	TRB	AST	PF	DQ	STL	BLK	TO	MPG	PPG	RPG	APG	PCM

• SELLERS, Brad
Bradley Donn Sellers

Born: Dec. 17, 1962. WarrensvilleHts, OH, United States.　Height: 7'　Weight: 210 lbs.　Drafted: 1986　College: Ohio State

YEAR	TEAM	GP	GS	MIN	PTS	FGM	FGA	FG%	3PM	3PA	3P%	FTM	FTA	FT%	ORB	DRB	TRB	AST	PF	DQ	STL	BLK	TO	MPG	PPG	RPG	APG	PCM
86-87	Chicago	80	17	1751	680	276	606	.455	2	10	.200	126	173	.728	155	218	373	102	194	1	44	68	88	21.9	8.5	4.7	1.3	.422
87-88	Chicago	82	76	2212	777	326	714	.457	1	7	.143	124	157	.790	107	143	250	141	174	0	34	66	90	27.0	9.5	3.0	1.7	.322
88-89	Chicago	80	25	1732	551	231	476	.485	3	6	.500	86	101	.851	85	142	227	99	176	2	35	69	72	21.7	6.9	2.8	1.2	.336
89-90	Seattle	45	0	587	217	84	198	.424	0	3	.000	49	61	.803	31	39	70	32	63	1	11	19	36	13.0	4.8	1.6	0.7	.288
89-90	Minnesota	14	0	113	47	19	56	.339	0	2	.000	9	12	.750	8	11	19	1	11	0	6	3	13	8.1	3.4	1.4	0.1	.185
91-92	Detroit	43	1	226	102	41	88	.466	0	1	.000	20	26	.769	15	27	42	14	20	0	1	10	13	5.3	2.4	1.0	0.3	.435
92-93	Minnesota	54	4	533	135	49	130	.377	0	1	.000	37	39	.949	27	56	83	46	40	0	6	10	27	9.9	2.5	1.5	0.9	.293
NBA Season Totals		398	123	7154	2509	1026	2268	.452	6	30	.200	451	569	.793	428	636	1064	435	678	4	137	245	339	18.0	6.3	2.7	1.1	....
86-87	Chicago	3	0	68	15	6	19	.316	0	0	.000	3	3	1.000	2	5	7	3	8	0	0	1	1	22.7	5.0	2.3	1.0	.131
87-88	Chicago	10	4	144	45	15	43	.349	0	0	.000	15	17	.882	10	11	21	8	18	0	2	5	5	14.4	4.5	2.1	0.8	.275
88-89	Chicago	13	0	177	54	22	58	.379	0	0	.000	10	12	.833	15	16	31	15	21	0	3	4	6	13.6	4.2	2.4	1.2	.314
91-92	Detroit	2	0	13	6	2	4	.500	0	0	.000	2	2	1.000	0	0	0	2	0	0	0	2	0	6.5	3.0	0.0	1.0	.626
NBA Playoff Totals		28	4	402	120	45	124	.363	0	0	.000	30	34	.882	27	32	59	28	47	0	5	12	12	14.4	4.3	2.1	1.0	....

• SELLERS, Phil
Phillip Sellers Jr.

Born: Nov. 20, 1953. Brooklyn, NY, United States.　Height: 6'4".　Weight: 195 lbs.　Drafted: 1976　College: Rutgers

YEAR	TEAM	GP	GS	MIN	PTS	FGM	FGA	FG%	3PM	3PA	3P%	FTM	FTA	FT%	ORB	DRB	TRB	AST	PF	DQ	STL	BLK	TO	MPG	PPG	RPG	APG	PCM
76-77	Detroit	44	....	329	198	73	190	.384	....	....	....	52	72	.722	19	22	41	25	56	0	22	0	....	7.5	4.5	0.9	0.6	.389
NBA Season Totals		44	....	329	198	73	190	.384	....	....	....	52	72	.722	19	22	41	25	56	0	22	0		7.5	4.5	0.9	0.6	
76-77	Detroit	1	....	6	3	1	4	.250	....	....	....	1	4	.250	1	1	2	0	2	0	0	0	....	6.0	3.0	2.0	0.0	-.003
NBA Playoff Totals		1	....	6	3	1	4	.250	....	....	....	1	4	.250	1	1	2	0	2	0	0	0	....	6.0	3.0	2.0	0.0	....

• SELTZ, Rollie
Rolland A. Seltz

Born: Jan. 25, 1924. McIntosh, MN, United States.　Height: 5'10".　Weight: 165 lbs.　Drafted: —　College: Hamline

YEAR	TEAM	GP	GS	MIN	PTS	FGM	FGA	FG%	3PM	3PA	3P%	FTM	FTA	FT%	ORB	DRB	TRB	AST	PF	DQ	STL	BLK	TO	MPG	PPG	RPG	APG	PCM
46-47	Anderson-N	41	....	....	350	123	....	....	....	....	....	104	143	.727	....	....	....	97	....	....	....	....	....	8.5	....	....	....
47-48	Anderson-N	59	....	....	326	118	....	....	....	....	....	90	119	.756	....	....	....	110	....	....	....	....	....	5.5	....	....	....
48-49	Waterloo-N	62	....	....	503	188	....	....	....	....	....	127	174	.730	....	....	....	139	....	....	....	....	....	8.1	....	....	....
49-50	Anderson	34	....	266	93	309	....	.301	....	....	....	80	104	.769	....	....	64	72	....	....	....	....	....	7.8	....	1.9	....
NBA Season Totals		34	....	266	93	309		.301	....	....	....	80	104	.769	....	....	64	72	....	....	....	....	....	7.8		1.9	
NBL Season Totals		162	....	....	1179	429	....	....	....	....	....	321	436	....	....	....	....	346	....	....	....	....	....	7.3	....	....	....
Career Totals		196	....	....	1445	522	309	....	....	....	....	401	540	....	....	....	64	418	....	....	....	....	....	7.4	....	0.3	....
47-48	Anderson-N	6	....	....	26	11	....	....	....	....	....	4	4	1.000	....	....	....	....	....	....	....	....	....	4.3	....	....	....
NBL Playoff Totals		6	....	....	26	11	....	....	....	....	....	4	4		....	....	....	....	....	....	....	....	....	4.3			

• SELVAGE, Lester
Lester Revell (Lightning) Selvage

Born: Mar. 7, 1943. St. Louis, MO, United States.　Height: 6'1".　Weight: 175 lbs.　Drafted: —　College: Kirksville State

YEAR	TEAM	GP	GS	MIN	PTS	FGM	FGA	FG%	3PM	3PA	3P%	FTM	FTA	FT%	ORB	DRB	TRB	AST	PF	DQ	STL	BLK	TO	MPG	PPG	RPG	APG	PCM
67-68	Anaheim-A	78	....	2432	1095	371	1044	.355	147	461	.319	206	278	.741	....	....	217	247	239	3	....	....	195	31.2	14.0	2.8	3.2	.360
69-70	Los Angeles-A	4	....	17	8	4	14	.286	0	4	.000	0	0	.000	0	2	2	5	2	0	....	....	1	4.3	2.0	0.5	1.3	.352
ABA Season Totals		82	....	2449	1103	375	1058	.354	147	465	.316	206	278	.741	0	2	219	252	241	3	....	....	196	29.9	13.5	2.7	3.1	....
69-70	Los Angeles-A	1	....	1	0	0	0	.000	0	0	.000	0	0	.000	0	0	0	0	....	0	....	....	0	1.0	0.0	0.0	0.0	....
ABA Playoff Totals		1	....	1	0	0	0	.000	0	0	.000	0	0	.000	0	0	0	0	....	0	....	....	0	1.0	0.0	0.0	0.0	....

• SELVY, Frank
Franklin Delano Selvy

Born: Nov. 9, 1932. Corbin, KY, United States.　Height: 6'3".　Weight: 180 lbs.　Drafted: 1954　College: Furman

YEAR	TEAM	GP	GS	MIN	PTS	FGM	FGA	FG%	3PM	3PA	3P%	FTM	FTA	FT%	ORB	DRB	TRB	AST	PF	DQ	STL	BLK	TO	MPG	PPG	RPG	APG	PCM
54-55	Bal/Mil	71	....	2668	1348	452	1195	.378	....	....	....	444	610	.728	....	....	394	245	230	3	....	....	....	37.6	19.0	5.5	3.5	.466
55-56	St. Louis	17	....	444	187	67	183	.366	....	....	....	53	71	.746	....	....	54	35	38	1	....	....	....	26.1	11.0	3.2	2.1	.365
57-58	St. Louis	26	....	195	59	16	83	.193	....	....	....	27	48	.563	....	....	53	16	23	0	....	....	....	7.5	2.3	2.0	0.6	.272
57-58	Minneapolis	12	....	231	76	28	84	.333	....	....	....	20	29	.690	....	....	35	19	21	0	....	....	....	19.3	6.3	2.9	1.6	.320
58-59	New York	68	....	1448	667	233	605	.385	....	....	....	201	262	.767	....	....	248	96	113	1	....	....	....	21.3	9.8	3.6	1.4	.434
59-60	Syracuse	19	....	217	103	36	94	.383	....	....	....	31	48	.646	....	....	47	20	25	1	....	....	....	11.4	5.4	2.5	1.1	.478
59-60	Minneapolis	43	....	1091	460	169	427	.396	....	....	....	122	160	.763	....	....	127	81	76	0	....	....	....	25.4	10.7	3.0	1.9	.384
60-61	LA Lakers	77	....	2153	832	311	767	.405	....	....	....	210	279	.753	....	....	299	246	219	3	....	....	....	28.0	10.8	3.9	3.2	.422
61-62	LA Lakers	79	....	2806	1164	433	1032	.420	....	....	....	298	404	.738	....	....	412	381	232	0	....	....	....	35.5	14.7	5.2	4.8	.481
62-63	LA Lakers	80	....	2369	826	317	747	.424	....	....	....	192	269	.714	....	....	289	281	149	0	....	....	....	29.6	10.3	3.6	3.5	.407
63-64	LA Lakers	73	....	1286	398	160	423	.378	....	....	....	78	122	.639	....	....	139	149	115	1	....	....	....	17.6	5.5	1.9	2.0	.328
NBA Season Totals		565	....	14908	6120	2222	5640	.394	....	....	....	1676	2302	.728	....	....	2097	1569	1241	10	....	....	....	26.4	10.8	3.7	2.8	....
58-59	New York	2	....	43	29	10	20	.500	....	....	....	9	11	.818	....	....	4	3	6	0	....	....	....	21.5	14.5	2.0	1.5	.587
59-60	Minneapolis	9	....	330	141	55	153	.359	....	....	....	31	44	.705	....	....	55	29	21	0	....	....	....	36.7	15.7	6.1	3.2	.399
60-61	LA Lakers	12	....	371	123	43	111	.387	....	....	....	37	48	.771	....	....	44	50	42	1	....	....	....	30.9	10.3	3.7	4.2	.395
61-62	LA Lakers	13	....	478	165	66	152	.434	....	....	....	33	39	.846	....	....	73	65	34	0	....	....	....	36.8	12.7	5.6	5.0	.457
62-63	LA Lakers	13	....	317	103	32	81	.395	....	....	....	39	48	.813	....	....	45	36	36	0	....	....	....	24.4	7.9	3.5	2.8	.396
63-64	LA Lakers	3	....	69	28	13	27	.481	....	....	....	2	2	1.000	....	....	5	6	8	0	....	....	....	23.0	9.3	1.7	2.0	.365
NBA Playoff Totals		52	....	1608	589	219	544	.403	....	....	....	151	192	.786	....	....	226	189	147	1	....	....	....	30.9	11.3	4.3	3.6	....

YEAR	TEAM	GP	GS	MIN	PTS	FGM	FGA	FG%	3PM	3PA	3P%	FTM	FTA	FT%	ORB	DRB	TRB	AST	PF	DQ	STL	BLK	TO	MPG	PPG	RPG	APG	PCM

• SEMINOFF, Jim

James Seminoff

Born: Sept. 1, 1922.   Height: 6'2".   Weight: 190 lbs.   Drafted: —   College: USC

YEAR	TEAM	GP	GS	MIN	PTS	FGM	FGA	FG%	3PM	3PA	3P%	FTM	FTA	FT%	ORB	DRB	TRB	AST	PF	DQ	STL	BLK	TO	MPG	PPG	RPG	APG	PCM
46-47	Chicago	60	....	....	439	184	586	.314	....	....	....	71	130	.546	....	....	....	63	155	....	....	....	....	....	7.3	....	1.1	....
47-48	Chicago	48	....	....	299	113	381	.297	....	....	....	73	105	.695	....	....	....	89	105	....	....	....	....	....	6.2	....	1.9	....
48-49	Boston	58	....	....	457	153	487	.314	....	....	....	151	219	.689	....	....	....	229	195	....	....	....	....	....	7.9	....	3.9	....
49-50	Boston	65	....	....	312	85	283	.300	....	....	....	142	188	.755	....	....	....	249	154	....	....	....	....	....	4.8	....	3.8	....
NBA Season Totals		231	....	....	1507	535	1737	.308	....	....	....	437	642	.681	....	....	....	630	609	....	....	....	....	....	6.5	....	2.7	....
46-47	Chicago	11	....	....	75	31	132	.235	....	....	....	13	19	.684	....	....	....	8	27	....	....	....	....	....	6.8	....	0.7	....
47-48	Chicago	5	....	....	49	16	62	.258	....	....	....	17	26	.654	....	....	....	8	21	....	....	....	....	....	9.8	....	1.6	....
NBA Playoff Totals		16	....	....	124	47	194	.242	....	....	....	30	45	.667	....	....	....	16	48	....	....	....	....	....	7.8	....	1.0	....

• SENESKY, George

George Lawrence Senesky

Born: Apr. 4, 1922. Mahanoy City, PA, United States.   Height: 6'2".   Weight: 179 lbs.   Drafted: —   College: St. Joseph's (PA)

YEAR	TEAM	GP	GS	MIN	PTS	FGM	FGA	FG%	3PM	3PA	3P%	FTM	FTA	FT%	ORB	DRB	TRB	AST	PF	DQ	STL	BLK	TO	MPG	PPG	RPG	APG	PCM
46-47	Philadelphia	58	....	....	366	142	531	.267	....	....	....	82	124	.661	....	....	....	34	83	....	....	....	....	....	6.3	....	0.6	....
47-48	Philadelphia	47	....	....	414	158	570	.277	....	....	....	98	147	.667	....	....	....	52	90	....	....	....	....	....	8.8	....	1.1	....
48-49	Philadelphia	60	....	....	387	138	516	.267	....	....	....	111	152	.730	....	....	....	233	133	....	....	....	....	....	6.5	....	3.9	....
49-50	Philadelphia	68	....	....	611	227	709	.320	....	....	....	157	223	.704	....	....	....	264	164	....	....	....	....	....	9.0	....	3.9	....
50-51	Philadelphia	65	....	....	679	249	703	.354	....	....	....	181	238	.761	326		342	144	1	....	....	....	....	10.4	5.0	5.3		
51-52	Philadelphia	57	....	1925	474	164	454	.361	....	....	....	146	194	.753	232		280	123	0	....	....	....	33.8	8.3	4.1	4.9	.381
52-53	Philadelphia	69	....	2336	413	160	485	.330	....	....	....	93	146	.637	254		264	166	1	....	....	....	33.9	6.0	3.7	3.8	.265
53-54	Philadelphia	58	....	771	111	41	119	.345	....	....	....	29	53	.547	66		84	79	0	....	....	....	13.3	1.9	1.1	1.4	.226
NBA Season Totals		482	....	5032	3455	1279	4087	.313	....	....	....	897	1277	.702	....		878	1553	982	2	....	....	....	10.4	7.2	1.8	3.2	
46-47	Philadelphia	10	....	....	109	44	139	.317	....	....	....	21	26	.808	....	....	8	15	....	....	....	....	....	10.9	....	0.8	....
47-48	Philadelphia	13	....	....	129	50	159	.314	....	....	....	29	45	.644	....	....	10	33	....	....	....	....	....	9.9	....	0.8	....
48-49	Philadelphia	2	....	....	12	3	22	.136	....	....	....	6	8	.750	....	....	4	6	....	....	....	....	....	6.0	....	2.0	....
49-50	Philadelphia	2	....	....	14	6	16	.375	....	....	....	2	4	.500	....	....	3	2	....	....	....	....	....	7.0	....	1.5	....
50-51	Philadelphia	2	....	....	15	4	22	.182	....	....	....	7	9	.778	7		15	6	0	....	....	....	7.5	3.5	7.5	....
51-52	Philadelphia	3	....	120	43	18	33	.545	....	....	....	7	11	.636	12		11	9	0	....	....	....	40.0	14.3	4.0	3.7	.420
NBA Playoff Totals		32	....	120	322	125	391	.320	....	....	....	72	103	.699	....		19	51	71	0	....	....	....	3.8	10.1	0.6	1.6	

• SESAY, Ansu

Ansu Martin Sesay

Born: July 29, 1976. Greensboro, NC, United States.   Height: 6'9".   Weight: 225 lbs.   Drafted: 1998   College: Mississippi

YEAR	TEAM	GP	GS	MIN	PTS	FGM	FGA	FG%	3PM	3PA	3P%	FTM	FTA	FT%	ORB	DRB	TRB	AST	PF	DQ	STL	BLK	TO	MPG	PPG	RPG	APG	PCM
01-02	Seattle	9	0	142	58	22	44	.500	0	0	.000	14	20	.700	7	13	20	8	18	0	3	2	2	15.8	6.4	2.2	0.9	.400
02-03	Seattle	45	4	448	94	41	107	.383	0	0	.000	12	21	.571	34	39	73	23	62	1	14	5	25	10.0	2.1	1.6	0.5	.196
NBA Season Totals		54	4	590	152	63	151	.417	0	0	.000	26	41	.634	41	52	93	31	80	1	17	7	27	10.9	2.8	1.7	0.6	....
01-02	Seattle	4	0	60	7	3	8	.375	0	0	.000	1	1	1.000	2	12	14	4	8	0	0	4	2	15.0	1.8	3.5	1.0	.295
NBA Playoff Totals		4	0	60	7	3	8	.375	0	0	.000	1	1	1.000	2	12	14	4	8	0	0	4	2	15.0	1.8	3.5	1.0	....

• SEWELL, Tom

Tom Sewell

Born: Mar. 11, 1962. Pensacola, FL, United States.   Height: 6'5".   Weight: 185 lbs.   Drafted: 1984   College: Lamar

YEAR	TEAM	GP	GS	MIN	PTS	FGM	FGA	FG%	3PM	3PA	3P%	FTM	FTA	FT%	ORB	DRB	TRB	AST	PF	DQ	STL	BLK	TO	MPG	PPG	RPG	APG	PCM
84-85	Washington	21	0	87	20	9	36	.250	0	2	.000	2	4	.500	2	2	4	6	13	0	3	1	6	4.1	1.0	0.2	0.3	-.045
NBA Season Totals		21	0	87	20	9	36	.250	0	2	.000	2	4	.500	2	2	4	6	13	0	3	1	6	4.1	1.0	0.2	0.3	....

• SEYMOUR, Paul

Paul Norman Seymour

Born: Jan. 30, 1928. Toledo, OH, United States. Died: May5, 1998.   Height: 6'1".   Weight: 180 lbs.   Drafted: —   College: Toledo

YEAR	TEAM	GP	GS	MIN	PTS	FGM	FGA	FG%	3PM	3PA	3P%	FTM	FTA	FT%	ORB	DRB	TRB	AST	PF	DQ	STL	BLK	TO	MPG	PPG	RPG	APG	PCM
46-47	Toledo-N	33	....	....	99	41						17	30	.567											3.0			
47-48	Syracuse-N	30	....	....	205	79						47	64	.734					54						6.8			
47-48	Baltimore	22	....	....	76	27	101	.267				22	37	.595				6	34						3.5		0.3	
48-49	Syracuse-N	63	....	....	310	120						70	106	.660					145						4.9			
49-50	Syracuse	62	....	....	476	175	524	.334				126	176	.716				189	157						7.7		3.0	
50-51	Syracuse	51	....	....	367	125	385	.325				117	159	.736	194		187	138	0					7.2	3.8	3.7	
51-52	Syracuse	66	....	2209	598	206	615	.335				186	245	.759	225		220	165	4				33.5	9.1	3.4	3.3	.304
52-53	Syracuse	67	....	2684	952	306	798	.383				340	416	.817	246		294	210	3				40.1	14.2	3.7	4.4	.390
53-54	Syracuse	71	....	2727	931	316	838	.377				299	368	.813	291		364	187	2				38.4	13.1	4.1	5.1	.420
54-55	Syracuse	72	....	2950	1050	375	1036	.362				300	370	.811	309		483	137	0				41.0	14.6	4.3	6.7	.444
55-56	Syracuse	57	....	1826	642	227	670	.339				188	233	.807	152		276	130	1				32.0	11.3	2.7	4.8	.381
56-57	Syracuse	65	....	1235	387	143	442	.324				101	123	.821	130		193	91	0				19.0	6.0	2.0	3.0	.373
57-58	Syracuse	64	....	763	267	107	315	.340				53	63	.841	107		93	88	0				11.9	4.2	1.7	1.5	.362
58-59	Syracuse	21	....	266	90	32	98	.327				26	29	.897	39		36	25	0				12.7	4.3	1.9	1.7	.391
59-60	Syracuse	4	....	7	0	0	4	.000				0	0	.000	1		0	1	0				1.8	0.0	0.3	0.0	-.378
NBA Season Totals		622	....	14667	5836	2039	5826	.350				1758	2219	.792	....		1694	2341	1363	10				23.6	9.4	2.7	3.8	....
NBL Season Totals		126	....	....	614	240						134	200						199						4.9			
Career Totals		748	....	14667	6450	2279	5826					1892	2419				1694	2341	1562	10				19.6	8.6	2.3	3.1	
46-47	Toledo-N	5	....	....	10	2						6	10	.600											2.0			
47-48	Syracuse-N	3	....	....	29	12						5	7	.714											9.7			
48-49	Syracuse-N	6	....	....	51	21						9	10	.900											8.5			
49-50	Syracuse	11	....	....	78	27	93	.290				24	28	.857				32	34						7.1		2.9	
50-51	Syracuse	7	....	....	34	10	48	.208				14	21	.667	26		25	22	1				7.0		3.6	
51-52	Syracuse	7	....	270	85	25	60	.417				35	43	.814	26		25	33	1				38.6	12.1	3.7	3.6	.356
52-53	Syracuse	2	....	112	36	9	24	.375				18	19	.947	10		8	11	1				56.0	18.0	5.0	4.0	.341
53-54	Syracuse	13	....	559	194	59	143	.413				76	94	.809	34		60	39	1				43.0	14.9	2.6	4.6	.386
54-55	Syracuse	11	....	410	137	46	149	.309				45	50	.900	43		75	21	0				37.3	12.5	3.9	6.8	.429

YEAR	TEAM	GP	GS	MIN	PTS	FGM	FGA	FG%	3PM	3PA	3P%	FTM	FTA	FT%	ORB	DRB	TRB	AST	PF	DQ	STL	BLK	TO	MPG	PPG	RPG	APG	PCM
55-56	Syracuse	7	....	153	47	16	55	.291	....	....	....	15	20	.750	....	....	11	18	11	0	....	....	....	21.9	6.7	1.6	2.6	.274
56-57	Syracuse	5	....	98	21	8	37	.216	....	....	....	5	6	.833	....	....	10	8	11	0	....	....	....	19.6	4.2	2.0	1.6	.126
57-58	Syracuse	3	....	50	18	8	23	.348	....	....	....	2	3	.667	....	....	4	4	5	0	....	....	....	16.7	6.0	1.3	1.3	.258
NBA Playoff Totals		66	....	1652	650	208	632	.329	....	....	....	234	284	.824	....	....	164	255	187	4	....	....	....	25.0	9.8	2.5	3.9	....
NBL Playoff Totals		14	....	....	90	35	....	....	....	....	....	20	27	....	....	....	....	....	....	....	....	....	....	....	6.4	....	....	....
Career Playoff Totals		80	....	1652	740	243	632	....	....	....	....	254	311	....	....	....	164	255	187	4	....	....	....	20.7	9.3	2.1	3.2	....

• SHABACK, Nick
Nicholas Shaback

Born: Sept. 10, 1918.   Height: 5'11".   Weight: 180 lbs.   Drafted: —   College: none (HS: James Monroe, NY)

YEAR	TEAM	GP	GS	MIN	PTS	FGM	FGA	FG%	3PM	3PA	3P%	FTM	FTA	FT%	ORB	DRB	TRB	AST	PF	DQ	STL	BLK	TO	MPG	PPG	RPG	APG	PCM
46-47	Cleveland	53	....	....	242	102	385	.265	....	....	....	38	53	.717	....	....	....	29	75	....	....	....	....	....	4.6	....	0.5	....
NBA Season Totals		53	....	....	242	102	385	.265	....	....	....	38	53	.717	....	....	....	29	75	....	....	....	....	....	4.6	....	0.5	....
46-47	Cleveland	3	....	....	15	6	22	.273	....	....	....	3	5	.600	....	....	....	0	6	....	....	....	....	....	5.0	....	0.0	....
NBA Playoff Totals		3	....	....	15	6	22	.273	....	....	....	3	5	.600	....	....	....	0	6	....	....	....	....	....	5.0	....	0.0	....

• SHACKELFORD, Ray
Ray Lynn Shackelford

Born: Aug. 27, 1947.   Height: 6'5".   Weight: 190 lbs.   Drafted: 1969   College: UCLA

YEAR	TEAM	GP	GS	MIN	PTS	FGM	FGA	FG%	3PM	3PA	3P%	FTM	FTA	FT%	ORB	DRB	TRB	AST	PF	DQ	STL	BLK	TO	MPG	PPG	RPG	APG	PCM
69-70	Miami-A	22	....	183	58	22	72	.306	4	13	.308	10	13	.769	11	16	27	11	34	0	....	....	9	8.3	2.6	1.2	0.5	.191
ABA Season Totals		22	....	183	58	22	72	.306	4	13	.308	10	13	.769	11	16	27	11	34	0	....	....	9	8.3	2.6	1.2	0.5	....

• SHACKLEFORD, Charles
Charles Edward Shackleford

Born: Apr. 22, 1966. Kinston, NC, United States.   Height: 6'10".   Weight: 225 lbs.   Drafted: 1988   College: North Carolina State

YEAR	TEAM	GP	GS	MIN	PTS	FGM	FGA	FG%	3PM	3PA	3P%	FTM	FTA	FT%	ORB	DRB	TRB	AST	PF	DQ	STL	BLK	TO	MPG	PPG	RPG	APG	PCM
88-89	New Jersey	60	0	484	187	83	168	.494	0	1	.000	21	42	.500	50	103	153	21	71	0	15	18	30	8.1	3.1	2.6	0.4	.481
89-90	New Jersey	70	37	1557	573	247	535	.462	0	1	.000	79	115	.687	180	299	479	56	183	1	40	35	119	22.2	8.2	6.8	0.8	.429
91-92	Philadelphia	72	62	1399	473	205	422	.486	0	1	.000	63	95	.663	145	270	415	46	205	3	38	51	65	19.4	6.6	5.8	0.6	.442
92-93	Philadelphia	48	0	568	191	80	164	.488	0	2	.000	31	49	.633	65	140	205	26	92	1	13	25	38	11.8	4.0	4.3	0.5	.494
94-95	Minnesota	21	2	239	94	39	65	.600	0	0	.000	16	20	.800	16	51	67	8	47	0	8	6	8	11.4	4.5	3.2	0.4	.513
98-99	Charlotte	32	4	367	107	44	90	.489	0	0	.000	19	29	.655	41	88	129	13	66	1	5	13	27	11.5	3.3	4.0	0.4	.418
NBA Season Totals		303	105	4614	1625	698	1444	.483	0	5	.000	229	350	.654	497	951	1448	170	664	6	119	148	287	15.2	5.4	4.8	0.6	....

• SHADDOCK, Bob
Bob Shaddock

Born: Nov. 15, 1920. Died: Apr.22, 1991.   Height: 6'1".   Weight: 160 lbs.   Drafted: —   College: Syracuse

YEAR	TEAM	GP	GS	MIN	PTS	FGM	FGA	FG%	3PM	3PA	3P%	FTM	FTA	FT%	ORB	DRB	TRB	AST	PF	DQ	STL	BLK	TO	MPG	PPG	RPG	APG	PCM
46-47	Syracuse-N	2	....	....	0	0	....	....	....	....	....	0	0	.000	....	....	....	....	....	....	....	....	....	0.0	....	....	....
NBL Season Totals		2	....	....	0	0	....	....	....	....	....	0	0	....	....	....	....	....	....	....	....	....	....	0.0	....	....	....

• SHAEFFER, Carl
Carl Edgel Shaeffer

Born: Oct. 25, 1924. Delphi, IN, United States. Died: Oct.25, 1974.   Height: 6'3".   Weight: 185 lbs.   Drafted: —   College: Alabama

YEAR	TEAM	GP	GS	MIN	PTS	FGM	FGA	FG%	3PM	3PA	3P%	FTM	FTA	FT%	ORB	DRB	TRB	AST	PF	DQ	STL	BLK	TO	MPG	PPG	RPG	APG	PCM
49-50	Indianapolis	43	....	....	150	59	160	.369	....	....	....	32	57	.561	....	....	....	40	103	....	....	....	....	....	3.5	....	0.9	....
50-51	Indianapolis	10	....	....	15	6	22	.273	....	....	....	3	3	1.000	....	....	10	6	15	0	....	....	....	....	1.5	1.0	0.6	....
NBA Season Totals		53	....	....	165	65	182	.357	....	....	....	35	60	.583	....	....	10	46	118	0	....	....	....	....	3.1	0.2	0.9	....
49-50	Indianapolis	6	....	....	21	7	21	.333	....	....	....	7	14	.500	....	....	....	7	20	....	....	....	....	....	3.5	....	1.2	....
NBA Playoff Totals		6	....	....	21	7	21	.333	....	....	....	7	14	.500	....	....	....	7	20	....	....	....	....	....	3.5	....	1.2	....

• SHAFFER, Jack
Jack Shaffer

Born: —.   Height: 6'3".   Weight: 190 lbs.   Drafted: —   College: Nebraska

YEAR	TEAM	GP	GS	MIN	PTS	FGM	FGA	FG%	3PM	3PA	3P%	FTM	FTA	FT%	ORB	DRB	TRB	AST	PF	DQ	STL	BLK	TO	MPG	PPG	RPG	APG	PCM
37-38	Non-Skids-N	6	....	....	34	16	....	....	....	....	....	2	....	....	....	....	....	....	....	....	....	....	....	....	5.7	....	....	....
NBL Season Totals		6	....	....	34	16	....	....	....	....	....	2	....	....	....	....	....	....	....	....	....	....	....	....	5.7	....	....	....

• SHAFFER, Lee
Lee Philip Shaffer II

Born: Feb. 23, 1939. Chicago, IL, United States.   Height: 6'7".   Weight: 220 lbs.   Drafted: 1960   College: North Carolina

YEAR	TEAM	GP	GS	MIN	PTS	FGM	FGA	FG%	3PM	3PA	3P%	FTM	FTA	FT%	ORB	DRB	TRB	AST	PF	DQ	STL	BLK	TO	MPG	PPG	RPG	APG	PCM
61-62	Syracuse	75	....	2093	1267	514	1180	.436	....	....	....	239	310	.771	....	....	511	99	266	6	....	....	....	27.9	16.9	6.8	1.3	.542
62-63	Syracuse	80	....	2392	1488	597	1393	.429	....	....	....	294	375	.784	....	....	524	97	249	5	....	....	....	29.9	18.6	6.6	1.2	.527
63-64	Philadelphia	41	....	1013	536	217	587	.370	....	....	....	102	133	.767	....	....	205	36	116	1	....	....	....	24.7	13.1	5.0	0.9	.389
NBA Season Totals		196	....	5498	3291	1328	3160	.420	....	....	....	635	818	.776	....	....	1240	232	631	12	....	....	....	28.1	16.8	6.3	1.2	....
61-62	Syracuse	5	....	174	94	35	99	.354	....	....	....	24	31	.774	....	....	55	7	17	0	....	....	....	34.8	18.8	11.0	1.4	.495
62-63	Syracuse	5	....	173	136	56	117	.479	....	....	....	24	30	.800	....	....	23	6	19	0	....	....	....	34.6	27.2	4.6	1.2	.597
63-64	Philadelphia	3	....	40	17	8	22	.364	....	....	....	1	2	.500	....	....	4	2	5	0	....	....	....	13.3	5.7	1.3	0.7	.233
NBA Playoff Totals		13	....	387	247	99	238	.416	....	....	....	49	63	.778	....	....	82	15	41	0	....	....	....	29.8	19.0	6.3	1.2	....

• SHAMEL, Frank
Frank Shamel

Born: Dec. 6, 1912. Died: Nov.2, 1994.   Height: 6'   Weight: 200 lbs.   Drafted: —   College: Earlham

YEAR	TEAM	GP	GS	MIN	PTS	FGM	FGA	FG%	3PM	3PA	3P%	FTM	FTA	FT%	ORB	DRB	TRB	AST	PF	DQ	STL	BLK	TO	MPG	PPG	RPG	APG	PCM
37-38	Cincinnati-N	3	....	....	10	5	....	....	....	....	....	0	....	....	....	....	....	....	....	....	....	....	....	....	3.3	....	....	....
NBL Season Totals		3	....	....	10	5	....	....	....	....	....	0	....	....	....	....	....	....	....	....	....	....	....	....	3.3	....	....	....

• SHAMMGOD, God
God Shammgod

Born: Apr. 29, 1976. New York, NY, United States. Height: 6' Weight: 169 lbs. Drafted: 1997 College: Providence

YEAR	TEAM	GP	GS	MIN	PTS	FGM	FGA	FG%	3PM	3PA	3P%	FTM	FTA	FT%	ORB	DRB	TRB	AST	PF	DQ	STL	BLK	TO	MPG	PPG	RPG	APG	PCM
97-98	Washington	20	0	146	61	19	58	.328	0	2	.000	23	30	.767	2	5	7	36	27	0	7	1	22	7.3	3.1	0.4	1.8	.291
NBA Season Totals		20	0	146	61	19	58	.328	0	2	.000	23	30	.767	2	5	7	36	27	0	7	1	22	7.3	3.1	0.4	1.8	....

• SHANKLIN, Chuck
Charles Shanklin

Born: —. Height: 5'9". Weight: — Drafted: — College: —

YEAR	TEAM	GP	GS	MIN	PTS	FGM	FGA	FG%	3PM	3PA	3P%	FTM	FTA	FT%	ORB	DRB	TRB	AST	PF	DQ	STL	BLK	TO	MPG	PPG	RPG	APG	PCM
44-45	Oshkosh-N	30	....	....	97	42	....	....	....	....	....	13	....	....	....	....	....	....	....	....	....	....	....	....	3.2	....	....	....
NBL Season Totals		30	....	....	97	42	....	....	....	....	....	13	....	....	....	....	....	....	....	....	....	....	....	....	3.2	....	....	....

• SHANNON, Earl
Earl F. Shannon

Born: Nov. 23, 1921. Height: 5'11". Weight: 170 lbs. Drafted: — College: Rhode Island

YEAR	TEAM	GP	GS	MIN	PTS	FGM	FGA	FG%	3PM	3PA	3P%	FTM	FTA	FT%	ORB	DRB	TRB	AST	PF	DQ	STL	BLK	TO	MPG	PPG	RPG	APG	PCM
46-47	Providence	57	....	....	687	245	722	.339	....	....	....	197	348	.566	....	....	....	84	169	....	....	....	....	....	12.1	....	1.5	....
47-48	Providence	45	....	....	362	123	469	.262	....	....	....	116	183	.634	....	....	....	49	106	....	....	....	....	....	8.0	....	1.1	....
48-49	Providence	27	....	....	102	32	116	.276	....	....	....	38	54	.704	....	....	....	40	31	....	....	....	....	....	3.8	....	1.5	....
48-49	Boston	5	....	....	5	2	11	.182	....	....	....	1	4	.250	....	....	....	4	2	....	....	....	....	....	1.0	....	0.8	....
NBA Season Totals		134	....	....	1156	402	1318	.305	....	....	....	352	589	.598	....	....	....	177	308	....	....	....	....	....	8.6	....	1.3	....

• SHANNON, Frank
Frank Shannon

Born: 1917. Height: 5'11". Weight: 178 lbs. Drafted: — College: Wittenberg

YEAR	TEAM	GP	GS	MIN	PTS	FGM	FGA	FG%	3PM	3PA	3P%	FTM	FTA	FT%	ORB	DRB	TRB	AST	PF	DQ	STL	BLK	TO	MPG	PPG	RPG	APG	PCM
46-47	Youngstown-N	29	....	....	124	55	....	....	....	....	....	14	20	.700	....	....	....	....	53	....	....	....	....	....	4.3	....	....	....
NBL Season Totals		29	....	....	124	55	....	....	....	....	....	14	20	....	....	....	....	....	53	....	....	....	....	....	4.3	....	....	....

• SHANNON, Howie
Howard Payne Shannon

Born: June 10, 1923. Manhattan, KS, United States. Height: 6'2". Weight: 175 lbs. Drafted: 1949 College: Kansas State

YEAR	TEAM	GP	GS	MIN	PTS	FGM	FGA	FG%	3PM	3PA	3P%	FTM	FTA	FT%	ORB	DRB	TRB	AST	PF	DQ	STL	BLK	TO	MPG	PPG	RPG	APG	PCM
48-49	Providence	55	....	....	736	292	802	.364	....	....	....	152	189	.804	....	....	....	125	154	....	....	....	....	....	13.4	....	2.3	....
49-50	Boston	67	....	....	587	222	646	.344	....	....	....	143	182	.786	....	....	....	174	148	....	....	....	....	....	8.8	....	2.6	....
NBA Season Totals		122	....	....	1323	514	1448	.355	....	....	....	295	371	.795	....	....	....	299	302	....	....	....	....	....	10.8	....	2.5	....

• SHARE, Chuck
Charles Edward (Charlie) Share

Born: Mar. 14, 1927. Height: 6'11". Weight: 235 lbs. Drafted: 1950 College: Bowling Green

YEAR	TEAM	GP	GS	MIN	PTS	FGM	FGA	FG%	3PM	3PA	3P%	FTM	FTA	FT%	ORB	DRB	TRB	AST	PF	DQ	STL	BLK	TO	MPG	PPG	RPG	APG	PCM
51-52	Fort Wayne	63	....	882	248	76	236	.322	....	....	....	96	155	.619	....	....	331	66	141	9	....	....	....	14.0	3.9	5.3	1.0	.435
52-53	Fort Wayne	67	....	1044	354	91	254	.358	....	....	....	172	234	.735	....	....	373	74	213	13	....	....	....	15.6	5.3	5.6	1.1	.480
53-54	FtW/Mil	68	....	1576	564	188	493	.381	....	....	....	188	275	.684	....	....	555	80	210	8	....	....	....	23.2	8.3	8.2	1.2	.469
54-55	Milwaukee	69	....	1685	821	235	577	.407	....	....	....	351	492	.713	....	....	684	84	273	**17**	....	....	....	24.4	11.9	9.9	1.2	.610
55-56	St. Louis	72	....	1975	976	315	733	.430	....	....	....	346	498	.695	....	....	774	131	318	13	....	....	....	27.4	13.6	10.8	1.8	.623
56-57	St. Louis	72	....	1673	739	235	535	.439	....	....	....	269	393	.684	....	....	642	79	269	15	....	....	....	23.2	10.3	8.9	1.1	.566
57-58	St. Louis	72	....	1824	622	216	545	.396	....	....	....	190	293	.648	....	....	749	130	279	15	....	....	....	25.3	8.6	10.4	1.8	.523
58-59	St. Louis	72	....	1713	433	147	381	.386	....	....	....	139	184	.755	....	....	657	103	261	6	....	....	....	23.8	6.0	9.1	1.4	.446
59-60	StL/Min	41	....	651	171	59	151	.391	....	....	....	53	80	.663	....	....	221	62	142	9	....	....	....	15.9	4.2	5.4	1.5	.433
NBA Season Totals		596	....	13023	4928	1562	3905	.400	....	....	....	1804	2604	.693	....	....	4986	809	2106	105	....	....	....	21.9	8.3	8.4	1.4	....
51-52	Fort Wayne	2	....	35	19	8	11	.727	....	....	....	3	5	.600	....	....	10	3	8	0	....	....	....	17.5	9.5	5.0	1.5	.694
52-53	Fort Wayne	8	....	198	48	11	27	.407	....	....	....	26	39	.667	....	....	52	12	45	5	....	....	....	24.8	6.0	6.5	1.5	.345
55-56	St. Louis	8	....	231	103	36	73	.493	....	....	....	31	48	.646	....	....	73	13	41	4	....	....	....	28.9	12.9	9.1	1.6	.539
56-57	St. Louis	10	....	168	92	31	72	.431	....	....	....	30	50	.600	....	....	63	6	39	2	....	....	....	16.8	9.2	6.3	0.6	.559
57-58	St. Louis	11	....	199	73	24	61	.393	....	....	....	25	38	.658	....	....	68	11	49	4	....	....	....	18.1	6.6	6.2	1.0	.437
58-59	St. Louis	6	....	122	26	8	27	.296	....	....	....	10	14	.714	....	....	52	9	16	1	....	....	....	20.3	4.3	8.7	1.5	.447
59-60	Minneapolis	9	....	123	22	6	14	.429	....	....	....	10	11	.909	....	....	34	5	26	1	....	....	....	13.7	2.4	3.8	0.6	.306
NBA Playoff Totals		54	....	1076	383	124	285	.435	....	....	....	135	205	.659	....	....	352	59	224	17	....	....	....	19.9	7.1	6.5	1.1	....

• SHARKEY, Steve
Steve Sharkey

Born: 1918. Height: 6' Weight: 190 lbs. Drafted: — College: none

YEAR	TEAM	GP	GS	MIN	PTS	FGM	FGA	FG%	3PM	3PA	3P%	FTM	FTA	FT%	ORB	DRB	TRB	AST	PF	DQ	STL	BLK	TO	MPG	PPG	RPG	APG	PCM
45-46	Sheboygan-N	22	....	....	50	18	....	....	....	....	....	14	....	....	....	....	....	....	....	....	....	....	....	....	2.3	....	....	....
46-47	Sheboygan-N	1	....	....	0	0	....	....	....	....	....	0	0	.000	....	....	....	....	0	....	....	....	....	....	0.0	....	....	....
46-47	Syracuse-N	37	....	....	237	99	....	....	....	....	....	39	52	.750	....	....	....	....	61	....	....	....	....	....	6.4	....	....	....
47-48	Syracuse-N	60	....	....	280	108	....	....	....	....	....	64	110	.582	....	....	....	....	104	....	....	....	....	....	4.7	....	....	....
NBL Season Totals		120	....	....	567	225	....	....	....	....	....	117	162	....	....	....	....	....	165	....	....	....	....	....	4.7	....	....	....
45-46	Sheboygan-N	7	....	....	51	20	....	....	....	....	....	11	16	.688	....	....	....	....	....	....	....	....	....	....	7.3	....	....	....
46-47	Syracuse-N	4	....	....	40	15	....	....	....	....	....	10	12	.833	....	....	....	....	....	....	....	....	....	....	10.0	....	....	....
47-48	Syracuse-N	3	....	....	10	4	....	....	....	....	....	2	3	.667	....	....	....	....	....	....	....	....	....	....	3.3	....	....	....
NBL Playoff Totals		14	....	....	101	39	....	....	....	....	....	23	31	....	....	....	....	....	....	....	....	....	....	....	7.2	....	....	....

• SHARMAN, Bill
William Walton Sharman

Born: May 25, 1926. Abilene, TX, United States. Height: 6'1". Weight: 175 lbs. Drafted: 1950 College: USC HOF: 1976

YEAR	TEAM	GP	GS	MIN	PTS	FGM	FGA	FG%	3PM	3PA	3P%	FTM	FTA	FT%	ORB	DRB	TRB	AST	PF	DQ	STL	BLK	TO	MPG	PPG	RPG	APG	PCM
50-51	Washington	31	....	....	378	141	361	.391	....	....	....	96	108	.889	....	....	96	39	86	3	....	....	....	....	12.2	3.1	1.3	....
51-52	Boston	63	....	1389	671	244	628	.389	....	....	....	183	213	.859	....	....	221	151	181	3	....	....	....	22.0	10.7	3.5	2.4	.486
52-53	Boston	71	....	2333	1147	403	925	.436	....	....	....	341	401	**.850**	....	....	288	191	240	7	....	....	....	32.9	16.2	4.1	2.7	.477

YEAR	TEAM	GP	GS	MIN	PTS	FGM	FGA	FG%	3PM	3PA	3P%	FTM	FTA	FT%	ORB	DRB	TRB	AST	PF	DQ	STL	BLK	TO	MPG	PPG	RPG	APG	PCM
53-54	Boston	72	....	2467	1155	412	915	.450	....	....	....	331	392	**.844**	....	....	255	229	211	4	....	....	....	34.3	16.0	3.5	3.2	.477
54-55	Boston	68	....	2453	1253	453	1062	.427	....	....	....	347	387	**.897**	....	....	302	280	212	2	....	....	....	36.1	18.4	4.4	4.1	.521
55-56	Boston	72	....	2698	1434	538	1229	.438	....	....	....	358	413	**.867**	....	....	259	339	197	1	....	....	....	37.5	19.9	3.6	4.7	.530
56-57	Boston	67	....	2403	1413	516	1241	.416	....	....	....	381	421	**.905**	....	....	286	236	188	1	....	....	....	35.9	21.1	4.3	3.5	.539
57-58	Boston	63	....	2214	1402	550	1297	.424	....	....	....	302	338	.893	....	....	295	167	156	3	....	....	....	35.1	22.3	4.7	2.7	.549
58-59	Boston	72	....	2382	1466	562	1377	.408	....	....	....	342	367	**.932**	....	....	292	179	173	1	....	....	....	33.1	20.4	4.1	2.5	.513
59-60	Boston	71	....	1916	1370	559	1225	.456	....	....	....	252	291	.866	....	....	262	144	154	2	....	....	....	27.0	19.3	3.7	2.0	.611
60-61	Boston	61	....	1538	976	383	908	.422	....	....	....	210	228	**.921**	....	....	223	146	127	0	....	....	....	25.2	16.0	3.7	2.4	.567
NBA Season Totals		711	....	21793	12665	4761	11168	.426	....	....	....	3143	3559	.883	....	....	2779	2101	1925	27	....	....	....	30.7	17.8	3.9	3.0	....
51-52	Boston	1	....	27	15	7	12	.583	....	....	....	1	1	1.000	....	....	3	7	4	0	....	....	....	27.0	15.0	3.0	7.0	.784
52-53	Boston	6	....	201	70	20	60	.333	....	....	....	30	32	.938	....	....	15	15	26	1	....	....	....	33.5	11.7	2.5	2.5	.303
53-54	Boston	6	....	206	113	35	81	.432	....	....	....	43	50	.860	....	....	25	10	29	2	....	....	....	34.3	18.8	4.2	1.7	.477
54-55	Boston	7	....	290	145	55	110	.500	....	....	....	35	38	.921	....	....	38	38	24	1	....	....	....	41.4	20.7	5.4	5.4	.584
55-56	Boston	3	....	119	52	18	46	.391	....	....	....	16	17	.941	....	....	7	12	7	0	....	....	....	39.7	17.3	2.3	4.0	.402
56-57	Boston	10	....	377	211	75	197	.381	....	....	....	61	64	.953	....	....	35	29	23	1	....	....	....	37.7	21.1	3.5	2.9	.458
57-58	Boston	11	....	406	232	90	221	.407	....	....	....	52	56	.929	....	....	54	25	28	0	....	....	....	36.9	21.1	4.9	2.3	.483
58-59	Boston	11	....	322	221	82	193	.425	....	....	....	57	59	.966	....	....	36	28	35	0	....	....	....	29.3	20.1	3.3	2.5	.576
59-60	Boston	13	....	364	219	88	209	.421	....	....	....	43	53	.811	....	....	45	20	22	1	....	....	....	28.0	16.8	3.5	1.5	.479
60-61	Boston	10	....	261	168	68	133	.511	....	....	....	32	36	.889	....	....	27	17	22	0	....	....	....	26.1	16.8	2.7	1.7	.576
NBA Playoff Totals		78	....	2573	1446	538	1262	.426	....	....	....	370	406	.911	....	....	285	201	220	6	....	....	....	33.0	18.5	3.7	2.6	....

• SHASKY, John

John Paul Shasky

Born: July 31, 1964. Birmingham, MI, United States. Height: 6'11". Weight: 235 lbs. Drafted: 1986 College: Minnesota

YEAR	TEAM	GP	GS	MIN	PTS	FGM	FGA	FG%	3PM	3PA	3P%	FTM	FTA	FT%	ORB	DRB	TRB	AST	PF	DQ	STL	BLK	TO	MPG	PPG	RPG	APG	PCM
88-89	Miami	65	4	944	357	121	248	.488	0	2	.000	115	167	.689	96	136	232	22	94	0	14	13	46	14.5	5.5	3.6	0.3	.416
89-90	Golden State	14	0	51	10	4	14	.286	0	0	.000	2	6	.333	4	9	13	1	10	0	1	2	1	3.6	0.7	0.9	0.1	.180
90-91	Dallas	57	0	510	150	51	116	.440	0	0	.000	48	79	.608	58	76	134	11	75	0	14	20	29	8.9	2.6	2.4	0.2	.356
NBA Season Totals		136	4	1505	517	176	378	.466	0	2	.000	165	252	.655	158	221	379	34	179	0	29	35	76	11.1	3.8	2.8	0.3	....

• SHAVLIK, Ron

Ronald Dean (Ronnie) Shavlik

Born: Dec. 4, 1933. Denver, CO, United States. Died: June27, 1983. Height: 6'8". Weight: 200 lbs. Drafted: 1956 College: North Carolina State

YEAR	TEAM	GP	GS	MIN	PTS	FGM	FGA	FG%	3PM	3PA	3P%	FTM	FTA	FT%	ORB	DRB	TRB	AST	PF	DQ	STL	BLK	TO	MPG	PPG	RPG	APG	PCM
56-57	New York	7	....	7	10	4	22	.182	....	....	....	2	5	.400	....	....	22	0	12	0	....	....	....	1.0	1.4	3.1	0.0	1.056
57-58	New York	1	....	2	0	0	1	.000	....	....	....	0	0	.000	....	....	1	0	0	0	....	....	....	2.0	0.0	1.0	0.0	.000
NBA Season Totals		8	....	9	10	4	23	.174	....	....	....	2	5	.400	....	....	23	0	12	0	....	....	....	1.1	1.3	2.9	0.0	....

• SHAW, Brian

Brian K. Shaw

Born: Mar. 22, 1966. Oakland, CA, United States. Height: 6'6". Weight: 190 lbs. Drafted: 1988 College: Cal State Santa Barbara

YEAR	TEAM	GP	GS	MIN	PTS	FGM	FGA	FG%	3PM	3PA	3P%	FTM	FTA	FT%	ORB	DRB	TRB	AST	PF	DQ	STL	BLK	TO	MPG	PPG	RPG	APG	PCM
88-89	Boston	82	54	2301	703	297	686	.433	0	13	.000	109	132	.826	119	257	376	472	211	1	78	27	189	28.1	8.6	4.6	5.8	.439
90-91	Boston	79	79	2772	1091	442	942	.469	3	27	.111	204	249	.819	104	266	370	602	206	1	105	34	221	35.1	13.8	4.7	7.6	.512
91-92	Boston	17	3	436	175	70	164	.427	0	7	.000	35	40	.875	11	58	69	89	29	0	12	10	32	25.6	10.3	4.1	5.2	.509
91-92	Miami	46	23	987	320	139	349	.398	5	16	.313	37	51	.725	39	96	135	161	86	0	45	12	69	21.5	7.0	2.9	3.5	.370
92-93	Miami	68	45	1603	498	197	501	.393	43	130	.331	61	78	.782	70	187	257	235	163	2	48	19	95	23.6	7.3	3.8	3.5	.371
93-94	Miami	77	52	2037	693	278	667	.417	73	216	.338	64	89	.719	104	246	350	385	195	1	71	21	169	26.5	9.0	4.5	5.0	.443
94-95	Orlando	78	9	1836	502	192	494	.389	48	184	.261	70	95	.737	52	189	241	406	184	1	73	18	187	23.5	6.4	3.1	5.2	.375
95-96	Orlando	75	1	1679	496	182	486	.374	41	144	.285	91	114	.798	58	166	224	336	160	1	58	11	173	22.4	6.6	3.0	4.5	.353
96-97	Orlando	77	31	1867	552	189	516	.366	63	194	.325	111	140	.793	47	147	194	319	197	3	67	26	169	24.2	7.2	2.5	4.1	.317
97-98	Golden State	39	32	1028	251	103	307	.336	21	67	.313	24	33	.727	20	131	151	173	93	3	35	14	74	26.4	6.4	3.9	4.4	.312
97-98	Philadelphia	20	2	502	121	51	139	.367	7	28	.250	12	19	.632	17	47	64	88	55	1	14	3	24	25.1	6.1	3.2	4.4	.318
98-99	Portland	1	0	5	0	0	1	.000	0	0	.000	0	0	.000	0	1	1	1	1	0	0	0	1	5.0	0.0	1.0	1.0	-.045
99-00	LA Lakers	74	2	1249	305	123	322	.382	18	58	.310	41	54	.759	45	171	216	201	105	0	35	14	75	16.9	4.1	2.9	2.7	.370
00-01	LA Lakers	80	28	1833	421	164	411	.399	42	135	.311	51	64	.797	48	256	304	258	159	1	49	27	97	22.9	5.3	3.8	3.2	.360
01-02	LA Lakers	58	0	631	169	61	173	.353	29	88	.330	18	26	.692	19	93	112	89	43	0	25	3	32	10.9	2.9	1.9	1.5	.380
02-03	LA Lakers	72	0	900	250	101	261	.387	38	109	.349	10	15	.667	20	99	119	103	62	0	32	13	54	12.5	3.5	1.7	1.4	.319
NBA Season Totals		943	361	21666	6547	2589	6419	.403	431	1416	.304	938	1199	.782	773	2410	3183	3918	1949	15	747	252	1661	23.0	6.9	3.4	4.2	....
88-89	Boston	3	3	124	51	22	43	.512	0	1	.000	7	9	.778	2	15	17	19	11	0	3	0	6	41.3	17.0	5.7	6.3	.474
90-91	Boston	11	11	316	121	47	100	.470	1	3	.333	26	30	.867	8	30	38	51	34	0	10	1	25	28.7	11.0	3.5	4.6	.413
91-92	Miami	3	3	85	36	14	30	.467	3	5	.600	5	8	.625	2	11	13	12	13	0	2	0	7	28.3	12.0	4.3	4.0	.400
93-94	Miami	5	5	112	39	16	41	.390	0	13	.000	7	12	.583	3	17	20	9	8	0	4	1	13	22.4	7.8	4.0	1.8	.276
94-95	Orlando	21	0	355	138	48	123	.390	22	57	.386	20	32	.625	17	45	62	66	49	0	11	4	26	16.9	6.6	3.0	3.1	.442
95-96	Orlando	10	0	217	47	18	52	.346	8	22	.364	3	4	.750	6	15	21	46	27	0	5	0	19	21.7	4.7	2.1	4.6	.264
96-97	Orlando	5	4	82	10	3	19	.158	2	6	.333	2	4	.500	1	8	9	8	5	0	1	1	8	16.4	2.0	1.8	1.6	.039
99-00	LA Lakers	22	1	408	119	45	107	.421	16	48	.333	13	16	.813	7	44	51	67	46	1	11	4	17	18.5	5.4	2.3	3.0	.388
00-01	LA Lakers	16	0	290	70	27	72	.375	10	29	.345	6	9	.667	10	45	55	43	37	0	10	1	16	18.1	4.4	3.4	2.7	.358
01-02	LA Lakers	19	0	238	55	21	63	.333	9	32	.281	4	4	1.000	9	26	35	30	16	0	5	6	8	12.5	2.9	1.8	1.6	.323
02-03	LA Lakers	12	1	215	38	15	49	.306	6	26	.231	2	3	.667	1	37	38	24	18	0	4	5	9	17.9	3.2	3.2	2.0	.275
NBA Playoff Totals		127	28	2442	724	276	699	.395	77	242	.318	95	131	.725	66	293	359	375	264	1	66	23	154	19.2	5.7	2.8	3.0	....

• SHAW, Casey

Joseph Casey Shaw

Born: July 20, 1975. Lebanon, OH, United States. Height: 6'11". Weight: 260 lbs. Drafted: 1998 College: Toledo

YEAR	TEAM	GP	GS	MIN	PTS	FGM	FGA	FG%	3PM	3PA	3P%	FTM	FTA	FT%	ORB	DRB	TRB	AST	PF	DQ	STL	BLK	TO	MPG	PPG	RPG	APG	PCM
98-99	Philadelphia	9	0	14	2	1	8	.125	0	0	.000	0	0	.000	3	0	3	0	2	0	0	0	2	1.6	0.2	0.3	0.0	-.302
NBA Season Totals		9	0	14	2	1	8	.125	0	0	.000	0	0	.000	3	0	3	0	2	0	0	0	2	1.6	0.2	0.3	0.0	....

YEAR	TEAM	GP	GS	MIN	PTS	FGM	FGA	FG%	3PM	3PA	3P%	FTM	FTA	FT%	ORB	DRB	TRB	AST	PF	DQ	STL	BLK	TO	MPG	PPG	RPG	APG	PCM

• SHAW, Robert

Robert Shaw

Born: May 22, 1921. Richmond, OH, United States.   Height: 6'4".   Weight: 225 lbs.   Drafted: —   College: Ohio State

YEAR	TEAM	GP	GS	MIN	PTS	FGM	FGA	FG%	3PM	3PA	3P%	FTM	FTA	FT%	ORB	DRB	TRB	AST	PF	DQ	STL	BLK	TO	MPG	PPG	RPG	APG	PCM
45-46	Cleveland-N	12	....	....	122	43	....	....	....	....	....	....	36	....	....	....	....	....	....	....	....	....	....	....	....	10.2	....	....	....
45-46	Youngstown-N	1	....	....	0	0	....	....	....	....	....	....	0	0	.000	....	....	....	....	....	....	....	....	....	....	0.0	....	....	....
46-47	Toledo-N	8	....	....	19	6	....	....	....	....	....	....	7	10	.700	....	....	....	....	....	....	....	....	....	....	2.4	....	....	....
NBL Season Totals		21	....	....	141	49	....	....	....	....	....	....	43	10	....	....	....	....	....	....	....	....	....	....	....	6.7	....	....	....

• SHEA, Bob

Robert F. Shea

Born: Sept. 11, 1924.   Height: 6'2".   Weight: 194 lbs.   Drafted: —   College: Rhode Island

YEAR	TEAM	GP	GS	MIN	PTS	FGM	FGA	FG%	3PM	3PA	3P%	FTM	FTA	FT%	ORB	DRB	TRB	AST	PF	DQ	STL	BLK	TO	MPG	PPG	RPG	APG	PCM
46-47	Providence	43	....	....	93	37	153	.242	....	....	....	19	33	.576	....	....	....	6	42	....	....	....	....	....	2.2	....	0.1	....
NBA Season Totals		43	....	....	93	37	153	.242	....	....	....	19	33	.576	....	....	....	6	42	....	....	....	....	....	2.2	....	0.1	....

• SHEFFIELD, Fred

Frederick J. Sheffield

Born: Nov. 5, 1923.   Height: 6'2".   Weight: 165 lbs.   Drafted: —   College: Utah

YEAR	TEAM	GP	GS	MIN	PTS	FGM	FGA	FG%	3PM	3PA	3P%	FTM	FTA	FT%	ORB	DRB	TRB	AST	PF	DQ	STL	BLK	TO	MPG	PPG	RPG	APG	PCM
46-47	Philadelphia	22	....	....	74	29	146	.199	....	....	....	16	26	.615	....	....	....	4	34	....	....	....	....	....	3.4	....	0.2	....
NBA Season Totals		22	....	....	74	29	146	.199	....	....	....	16	26	.615	....	....	....	4	34	....	....	....	....	....	3.4	....	0.2	....

• SHELTON, Craig

Craig Anthony Shelton

Born: May 1, 1957. Washington, DC, United States.   Height: 6'7".   Weight: 210 lbs.   Drafted: 1980   College: Georgetown

YEAR	TEAM	GP	GS	MIN	PTS	FGM	FGA	FG%	3PM	3PA	3P%	FTM	FTA	FT%	ORB	DRB	TRB	AST	PF	DQ	STL	BLK	TO	MPG	PPG	RPG	APG	PCM
80-81	Atlanta	55	....	586	235	100	219	.457	0	1	.000	35	58	.603	59	79	138	27	128	1	18	5	61	10.7	4.3	2.5	0.5	.304
81-82	Atlanta	4	0	21	5	2	6	.333	0	0	.000	1	2	.500	1	2	3	0	3	0	1	0	0	5.3	1.3	0.8	0.0	.150
NBA Season Totals		59	0	607	240	102	225	.453	0	1	.000	36	60	.600	60	81	141	27	131	1	19	5	61	10.3	4.1	2.4	0.5	....

• SHELTON, Lonnie

Lonnie Jewel Shelton

Born: Oct. 19, 1955. Bakersfield, CA, United States.   Height: 6'8".   Weight: 240 lbs.   Drafted: 1976   College: Oregon State

YEAR	TEAM	GP	GS	MIN	PTS	FGM	FGA	FG%	3PM	3PA	3P%	FTM	FTA	FT%	ORB	DRB	TRB	AST	PF	DQ	STL	BLK	TO	MPG	PPG	RPG	APG	PCM
76-77	New York	82	....	2104	955	398	836	.476	....	....	....	159	225	.707	220	413	633	149	**363**	10	125	98	....	25.7	11.6	7.7	1.8	.526
77-78	New York	82	....	2319	1219	508	988	.514	....	....	....	203	276	.736	204	376	580	195	**350**	11	109	112	230	28.3	14.9	7.1	2.4	.575
78-79	Seattle	76	....	2158	1023	446	859	.519	....	....	....	131	189	.693	182	286	468	110	266	7	76	75	190	28.4	13.5	6.2	1.4	.469
79-80	Seattle	76	....	2243	1035	425	802	.530	1	5	.200	184	241	.763	199	383	582	145	292	11	92	79	167	29.5	13.6	7.7	1.9	.546
80-81	Seattle	14	....	440	182	73	174	.420	0	0	.000	36	55	.655	31	47	78	35	48	0	22	3	41	31.4	13.0	5.6	2.5	.350
81-82	Seattle	81	81	2667	1204	508	1046	.486	0	8	.000	188	240	.783	161	348	509	252	317	12	99	43	203	32.9	14.9	6.3	3.1	.459
82-83	Seattle	82	79	2572	1016	437	915	.478	1	6	.167	141	187	.754	158	337	495	237	310	8	75	72	172	31.4	12.4	6.0	2.9	.431
83-84	Cleveland	79	78	2101	850	371	779	.476	1	5	.200	107	140	.764	140	241	381	179	279	9	76	55	166	26.6	10.8	4.8	2.3	.399
84-85	Cleveland	57	14	1244	367	158	363	.435	0	5	.000	51	77	.662	82	185	267	96	187	3	44	18	74	21.8	6.4	4.7	1.7	.335
85-86	Cleveland	44	1	682	198	92	188	.489	0	2	.000	14	16	.875	38	105	143	61	128	2	21	4	48	15.5	4.5	3.3	1.4	.330
NBA Season Totals		673	253	18530	8049	3416	6950	.492	3	31	.097	1214	1646	.738	1415	2721	4136	1459	2540	73	739	559	1291	27.5	12.0	6.1	2.2	....
77-78	New York	6	....	151	66	30	56	.536	....	....	....	6	8	.750	18	26	44	17	29	1	2	5	14	25.2	11.0	7.3	2.8	.538
78-79	Seattle	17	....	566	220	101	209	.483	....	....	....	18	26	.692	61	81	142	34	80	4	19	18	31	33.3	12.9	8.4	2.0	.449
79-80	Seattle	15	....	469	180	74	146	.507	0	1	.000	32	51	.627	35	90	125	25	54	0	23	12	37	31.3	12.0	8.3	1.7	.470
81-82	Seattle	8	8	266	102	40	85	.471	0	0	.000	22	32	.688	24	35	59	16	38	3	5	7	20	33.3	12.8	7.4	2.0	.386
82-83	Seattle	2	2	53	10	4	23	.174	0	3	.000	2	5	.400	13	8	21	5	7	0	1	0	2	26.5	5.0	10.5	2.5	.224
84-85	Cleveland	4	0	106	46	19	34	.559	0	0	.000	8	10	.800	6	16	22	4	20	2	2	1	6	26.5	11.5	5.5	1.0	.413
NBA Playoff Totals		52	10	1611	624	268	553	.485	0	4	.000	88	132	.667	157	256	413	101	228	10	52	43	110	31.0	12.0	7.9	1.9	....

• SHEPHERD, Billy

Billy L. Shepherd

Born: Nov. 18, 1949. Bedford, IN, United States.   Height: 5'10".   Weight: 160 lbs.   Drafted: —   College: Butler

YEAR	TEAM	GP	GS	MIN	PTS	FGM	FGA	FG%	3PM	3PA	3P%	FTM	FTA	FT%	ORB	DRB	TRB	AST	PF	DQ	STL	BLK	TO	MPG	PPG	RPG	APG	PCM
72-73	Virginia-A	16	....	68	27	7	35	.200	4	16	.250	9	10	.900	2	3	5	8	12	0	....	....	8	4.3	1.7	0.3	0.5	.137
73-74	San Diego-A	84	....	1738	507	200	530	.377	65	202	.322	42	66	.636	22	85	107	371	102	....	97	10	120	20.7	6.0	1.3	4.4	.394
74-75	Memphis-A	69	....	1315	434	161	386	.417	60	143	**.420**	52	72	.722	14	65	79	278	68	....	66	9	91	19.1	6.3	1.1	4.0	.437
ABA Season Totals		169	....	3121	968	368	951	.387	129	361	.357	103	148	.696	38	153	191	657	182	0	163	19	219	18.5	5.7	1.1	3.9	....
73-74	San Diego-A	6	....	152	45	17	56	.304	8	23	.348	3	3	1.000	2	9	11	21	11	....	8	1	14	25.3	7.5	1.8	3.5	.265
74-75	Memphis-A	5	....	75	29	10	30	.333	3	16	.188	6	6	1.000	1	4	5	12	3	....	3	1	5	15.0	5.8	1.0	2.4	.369
ABA Playoff Totals		11	....	227	74	27	86	.314	11	39	.282	9	9	1.000	3	13	16	33	14	....	11	2	19	20.6	6.7	1.5	3.0	....

• SHEPPARD, Jeffrey

Jeffrey Kyle Sheppard

Born: Sept. 29, 1974. Marietta, GA, United States.   Height: 6'3".   Weight: 190 lbs.   Drafted: —   College: Kentucky

YEAR	TEAM	GP	GS	MIN	PTS	FGM	FGA	FG%	3PM	3PA	3P%	FTM	FTA	FT%	ORB	DRB	TRB	AST	PF	DQ	STL	BLK	TO	MPG	PPG	RPG	APG	PCM
98-99	Atlanta	18	5	185	40	15	39	.385	2	7	.286	8	13	.615	6	16	22	16	12	0	3	0	7	10.3	2.2	1.2	0.9	.243
NBA Season Totals		18	5	185	40	15	39	.385	2	7	.286	8	13	.615	6	16	22	16	12	0	3	0	7	10.3	2.2	1.2	0.9	....
98-99	Atlanta	4	0	12	0	0	3	.000	0	0	.000	0	0	.000	2	0	2	2	0	0	1	0	0	3.0	0.0	0.5	0.5	.185
NBA Playoff Totals		4	0	12	0	0	3	.000	0	0	.000	0	0	.000	2	0	2	2	0	0	1	0	0	3.0	0.0	0.5	0.5	....

• SHEPPARD, Steve
Steve Sheppard

Born: Mar. 21, 1954. New York, NY, United States. Height: 6'6". Weight: 215 lbs. Drafted: 1977 College: Maryland

YEAR	TEAM	GP	GS	MIN	PTS	FGM	FGA	FG%	3PM	3PA	3P%	FTM	FTA	FT%	ORB	DRB	TRB	AST	PF	DQ	STL	BLK	TO	MPG	PPG	RPG	APG	PCM
77-78	Chicago	64	....	698	275	119	262	.454	....	....	....	37	56	.661	67	64	131	43	72	0	14	3	45	10.9	4.3	2.0	0.7	.356
78-79	Chicago	22	....	203	60	24	51	.471	....	....	....	12	19	.632	16	12	28	15	16	0	5	0	22	9.2	2.7	1.3	0.7	.255
78-79	Detroit	20	....	76	32	12	25	.480	....	....	....	8	15	.533	9	10	19	4	10	0	3	1	4	3.8	1.6	1.0	0.2	.450
NBA Season Totals		106	....	977	367	155	338	.459	....	....	....	57	90	.633	92	86	178	62	98	0	22	4	71	9.2	3.5	1.7	0.6	....

• SHEROD, Ed
Edmund Sherod

Born: Sept. 13, 1959. Richmond, VA, United States. Height: 6'2". Weight: 170 lbs. Drafted: 1981 College: Virginia Commonwealth

YEAR	TEAM	GP	GS	MIN	PTS	FGM	FGA	FG%	3PM	3PA	3P%	FTM	FTA	FT%	ORB	DRB	TRB	AST	PF	DQ	STL	BLK	TO	MPG	PPG	RPG	APG	PCM
82-83	New York	64	37	1624	395	171	421	.406	1	13	.077	52	80	.650	43	106	149	311	112	2	96	14	102	25.4	6.2	2.3	4.9	.363
NBA Season Totals		64	37	1624	395	171	421	.406	1	13	.077	52	80	.650	43	106	149	311	112	2	96	14	102	25.4	6.2	2.3	4.9	....
81-82	New Jersey	2	0	8	0	0	1	.000	0	0	.000	0	0	.000	1	0	1	1	1	0	1	0	0	4.0	0.0	0.5	0.5	.192
82-83	New York	4	0	15	2	1	4	.250	0	0	.000	0	0	.000	0	1	1	3	2	0	3	0	1	3.8	0.5	0.3	0.8	.293
NBA Playoff Totals		6	0	23	2	1	5	.200	0	0	.000	0	0	.000	1	1	2	4	3	0	4	0	1	3.8	0.3	0.3	0.7	....

• SHIPP, Charley
Charles William (Jo-Jo) Shipp

Born: Dec. 3, 1913. Died: Mar.21, 1988. Height: 6'1". Weight: 200 lbs. Drafted: — College: Catholic

YEAR	TEAM	GP	GS	MIN	PTS	FGM	FGA	FG%	3PM	3PA	3P%	FTM	FTA	FT%	ORB	DRB	TRB	AST	PF	DQ	STL	BLK	TO	MPG	PPG	RPG	APG	PCM
37-38	Wingfoots-N	16	....	....	90	38	....	....	....	....	....	14	....	....	....	....	....	....	....	....	....	....	....	....	5.6	....	....	....
38-39	Wingfoots-N	24	....	....	142	59	....	....	....	....	....	24	....	....	....	....	....	....	....	....	....	....	....	....	5.9	....	....	....
39-40	Oshkosh-N	28	....	....	174	74	....	....	....	....	....	26	....	....	....	....	....	....	....	....	....	....	....	....	6.2	....	....	....
40-41	Oshkosh-N	22	....	....	113	46	....	....	....	....	....	21	....	....	....	....	....	....	....	....	....	....	....	....	5.1	....	....	....
41-42	Oshkosh-N	24	....	....	178	70	....	....	....	....	....	38	....	....	....	....	....	....	....	....	....	....	....	....	7.4	....	....	....
42-43	Oshkosh-N	23	....	....	140	52	....	....	....	....	....	36	....	....	....	....	....	....	....	....	....	....	....	....	6.1	....	....	....
43-44	Oshkosh-N	20	....	....	150	57	....	....	....	....	....	36	....	....	....	....	....	....	....	....	....	....	....	....	7.5	....	....	....
44-45	Fort Wayne-N	30	....	....	78	31	....	....	....	....	....	16	....	....	....	....	....	....	....	....	....	....	....	....	2.6	....	....	....
45-46	Fort Wayne-N	34	....	....	98	42	....	....	....	....	....	14	24	.583	....	....	....	....	....	....	....	....	....	....	2.9	....	....	....
46-47	Anderson-N	30	....	....	201	77	....	....	....	....	....	47	67	.701	....	....	....	....	....	....	....	....	....	....	6.7	....	....	....
46-47	Fort Wayne-N	14	....	....	35	12	....	....	....	....	....	11	16	.688	....	....	....	....	....	....	....	....	....	....	2.5	....	....	....
47-48	Anderson-N	55	....	....	269	103	....	....	....	....	....	63	95	.663	....	....	....	....	136	....	....	....	....	....	4.9	....	....	....
48-49	Waterloo-N	56	....	....	267	104	....	....	....	....	....	59	90	.656	....	....	....	....	105	....	....	....	....	....	4.8	....	....	....
49-50	Waterloo	23	....	....	107	35	137	.255	....	....	....	37	51	.725	....	....	....	46	46	....	....	....	....	....	4.7	....	2.0	....
NBA Season Totals		23	....	....	107	35	137	.255	....	....	....	37	51	.725	....	....	....	46	46	....	....	....	....	....	4.7	....	2.0	....
NBL Season Totals		376	....	....	1935	765	....	....	....	....	....	405	292	....	....	....	....	....	241	....	....	....	....	....	5.1	....	....	....
Career Totals		399	....	....	2042	800	137	....	....	....	....	442	343	....	....	....	....	46	287	....	....	....	....	....	5.1	....	0.1	....
37-38	Wingfoots-N	5	....	....	17	5	....	....	....	....	....	7	....	....	....	....	....	....	....	....	....	....	....	....	3.4	....	....	....
39-40	Oshkosh-N	8	....	....	38	13	....	....	....	....	....	12	....	....	....	....	....	....	....	....	....	....	....	....	4.8	....	....	....
40-41	Oshkosh-N	5	....	....	20	7	....	....	....	....	....	6	....	....	....	....	....	....	....	....	....	....	....	....	4.0	....	....	....
41-42	Oshkosh-N	4	....	....	16	5	....	....	....	....	....	6	....	....	....	....	....	....	....	....	....	....	....	....	4.0	....	....	....
42-43	Oshkosh-N	2	....	....	10	4	....	....	....	....	....	2	....	....	....	....	....	....	....	....	....	....	....	....	5.0	....	....	....
43-44	Oshkosh-N	3	....	....	13	3	....	....	....	....	....	7	....	....	....	....	....	....	....	....	....	....	....	....	4.3	....	....	....
44-45	Fort Wayne-N	7	....	....	13	4	....	....	....	....	....	5	....	....	....	....	....	....	....	....	....	....	....	....	1.9	....	....	....
45-46	Fort Wayne-N	4	....	....	0	0	....	....	....	....	....	0	1	.000	....	....	....	....	....	....	....	....	....	....	0.0	....	....	....
47-48	Anderson-N	2	....	....	7	2	....	....	....	....	....	3	4	.750	....	....	....	....	....	....	....	....	....	....	3.5	....	....	....
NBL Playoff Totals		40	....	....	134	43	....	....	....	....	....	48	5	....	....	....	....	....	....	....	....	....	....	....	3.4	....	....	....

• SHIRLEY, Paul
Paul Shirley

Born: Dec. 23, 1977. Meriden, KS, United States. Height: 6'10". Weight: 230 lbs. Drafted: — College: Iowa State

YEAR	TEAM	GP	GS	MIN	PTS	FGM	FGA	FG%	3PM	3PA	3P%	FTM	FTA	FT%	ORB	DRB	TRB	AST	PF	DQ	STL	BLK	TO	MPG	PPG	RPG	APG	PCM
02-03	Atlanta	2	0	5	0	0	4	.000	0	0	.000	0	0	.000	0	1	1	0	0	0	0	0	0	2.5	0.0	0.5	0.0	-.545
NBA Season Totals		2	0	5	0	0	4	.000	0	0	.000	0	0	.000	0	1	1	0	0	0	0	0	0	2.5	0.0	0.5	0.0	....

• SHOAFF, Oliver
Oliver (Ollie) Shoaff

Born: 1923. Height: 5'10". Weight: 165 lbs. Drafted: — College: Southern Illinois

YEAR	TEAM	GP	GS	MIN	PTS	FGM	FGA	FG%	3PM	3PA	3P%	FTM	FTA	FT%	ORB	DRB	TRB	AST	PF	DQ	STL	BLK	TO	MPG	PPG	RPG	APG	PCM
48-49	Detroit-N	19	....	....	260	108	....	....	....	....	....	44	59	.746	....	....	....	....	....	....	....	....	....	....	13.7	....	....	....
48-49	Hammond-N	42	....	....	255	103	....	....	....	....	....	49	66	.742	....	....	....	....	147	....	....	....	....	....	6.1	....	....	....
NBL Season Totals		61	....	....	515	211	....	....	....	....	....	93	125	....	....	....	....	....	147	....	....	....	....	....	8.4	....	....	....
48-49	Hammond-N	2	....	....	20	9	....	....	....	....	....	2	3	.667	....	....	....	....	....	....	....	....	....	....	10.0	....	....	....
NBL Playoff Totals		2	....	....	20	9	....	....	....	....	....	2	3	....	....	....	....	....	....	....	....	....	....	....	10.0	....	....	....

• SHORT, Gene
Eugene Short

Born: Aug. 7, 1953. Macon, MS, United States. Height: 6'6". Weight: 200 lbs. Drafted: 1975 College: Jackson State

YEAR	TEAM	GP	GS	MIN	PTS	FGM	FGA	FG%	3PM	3PA	3P%	FTM	FTA	FT%	ORB	DRB	TRB	AST	PF	DQ	STL	BLK	TO	MPG	PPG	RPG	APG	PCM
75-76	Seattle	7	....	37	13	6	11	.545	....	....	....	1	2	.500	2	5	7	2	5	0	0	0	....	5.3	1.9	1.0	0.3	.390
75-76	New York	27	....	185	71	26	80	.325	....	....	....	19	30	.633	17	24	41	8	31	0	8	3	....	6.9	2.6	1.5	0.3	.275
NBA Season Totals		34	....	222	84	32	91	.352	....	....	....	20	32	.625	19	29	48	10	36	0	8	3	....	6.5	2.5	1.4	0.3	....

• SHORT, Purvis

Purvis Short

Born: July 2, 1957. Hattiesburg, MS, United States. Height: 6'7". Weight: 210 lbs. Drafted: 1978 College: Jackson State

YEAR	TEAM	GP	GS	MIN	PTS	FGM	FGA	FG%	3PM	3PA	3P%	FTM	FTA	FT%	ORB	DRB	TRB	AST	PF	DQ	STL	BLK	TO	MPG	PPG	RPG	APG	PCM
78-79	Golden State	75	....	1703	795	369	771	.479	....	....	....	57	85	.671	127	220	347	97	233	6	54	12	113	22.7	10.6	4.6	1.3	.407
79-80	Golden State	62	....	1636	1056	461	916	.503	0	6	.000	134	165	.812	119	197	316	123	186	4	63	9	124	26.4	17.0	5.1	2.0	.562
80-81	Golden State	79	....	2309	1269	549	1157	.475	3	17	.176	168	205	.820	151	240	391	249	244	3	78	19	142	29.2	16.1	4.9	3.2	.508
81-82	Golden State	76	8	1782	1095	456	935	.488	6	28	.214	177	221	.801	123	143	266	209	220	3	65	10	122	23.4	14.4	3.5	2.8	.538
82-83	Golden State	67	57	2397	1437	589	1209	.487	4	15	.267	255	308	.828	145	209	354	228	242	3	94	14	194	35.8	21.4	5.3	3.4	.516
83-84	Golden State	79	76	2945	1803	714	1509	.473	22	72	.306	353	445	.793	184	254	438	246	252	2	103	11	229	37.3	22.8	5.5	3.1	.498
84-85	Golden State	78	77	3081	2186	819	1780	.460	47	150	.313	501	613	.817	157	241	398	234	255	4	116	27	242	39.5	28.0	5.1	3.0	.535
85-86	Golden State	64	63	2427	1632	633	1313	.482	15	49	.306	351	406	.865	126	203	329	237	229	5	92	22	186	37.9	25.5	5.1	3.7	.561
86-87	Golden State	34	15	950	621	240	501	.479	4	17	.235	137	160	.856	55	82	137	86	103	1	45	7	68	27.9	18.3	4.0	2.5	.552
87-88	Houston	81	11	1949	1159	474	986	.481	5	21	.238	206	240	.858	71	151	222	162	197	0	58	14	122	24.1	14.3	2.7	2.0	.466
88-89	Houston	65	16	1157	482	198	480	.413	9	33	.273	77	89	.865	65	114	179	107	116	1	44	13	72	17.8	7.4	2.8	1.6	.369
89-90	New Jersey	82	24	2213	1072	432	950	.455	10	35	.286	198	237	.835	101	147	248	145	202	2	66	20	123	27.0	13.1	3.0	1.8	.373
NBA Season Totals		842	347	24549	14607	5934	12507	.474	125	443	.282	2614	3174	.824	1424	2201	3625	2123	2479	34	878	178	1737	29.2	17.3	4.3	2.5	....
86-87	Golden State	10	2	253	146	57	123	.463	0	2	.000	32	36	.889	12	21	33	27	34	0	12	2	21	25.3	14.6	3.3	2.7	.474
87-88	Houston	4	0	71	22	7	26	.269	0	1	.000	8	8	1.000	4	5	9	1	8	0	1	0	4	17.8	5.5	2.3	0.3	.102
88-89	Houston	4	0	37	19	8	21	.381	0	2	.000	3	5	.600	6	3	9	1	7	0	0	0	1	9.3	4.8	2.3	0.3	.304
NBA Playoff Totals		18	2	361	187	72	170	.424	0	5	.000	43	49	.878	22	29	51	29	49	0	13	2	26	20.1	10.4	2.8	1.6	....

• SHOUN, Milas

Milas (Slim) Shoun

Born: Oct. 4, 1904. Died: Oct.10, 1983. Height: 6'11". Weight: 175 lbs. Drafted: — College: Carson-Newman

YEAR	TEAM	GP	GS	MIN	PTS	FGM	FGA	FG%	3PM	3PA	3P%	FTM	FTA	FT%	ORB	DRB	TRB	AST	PF	DQ	STL	BLK	TO	MPG	PPG	RPG	APG	PCM
37-38	Non-Skids-N	13	....	....	41	15	....	....	....	....	....	11	....	....	....	....	....	....	....	....	....	....	....	....	3.2	....	....	....
38-39	Non-Skids-N	6	....	....	38	13	....	....	....	....	....	12	....	....	....	....	....	....	....	....	....	....	....	....	6.3	....	....	....
NBL Season Totals		19	....	....	79	28	....	....	....	....	....	23	....	....	....	....	....	....	....	....	....	....	....	....	4.2	....	....	....
37-38	Non-Skids-N	2	....	....	4	2	....	....	....	....	....	0	....	....	....	....	....	....	....	....	....	....	....	....	2.0	....	....	....
38-39	Non-Skids-N	2	....	....	4	2	....	....	....	....	....	0	....	....	....	....	....	....	....	....	....	....	....	....	2.0	....	....	....
NBL Playoff Totals		4	....	....	8	4	....	....	....	....	....	0	....	....	....	....	....	....	....	....	....	....	....	....	2.0	....	....	....

• SHOUSE, Dexter

Dexter Wayne Shouse

Born: Mar. 24, 1963. Terre Haute, IN, United States. Height: 6'2". Weight: 200 lbs. Drafted: 1985 College: South Alabama

YEAR	TEAM	GP	GS	MIN	PTS	FGM	FGA	FG%	3PM	3PA	3P%	FTM	FTA	FT%	ORB	DRB	TRB	AST	PF	DQ	STL	BLK	TO	MPG	PPG	RPG	APG	PCM
89-90	Philadelphia	3	0	18	0	0	4	.000	0	1	.000	0	0	.000	0	0	0	2	2	0	1	1	2	6.0	0.0	0.0	0.7	-.142
NBA Season Totals		3	0	18	0	0	4	.000	0	1	.000	0	0	.000	0	0	0	2	2	0	1	1	2	6.0	0.0	0.0	0.7	....

• SHRIDER, Dick

Richard G. Shrider

Born: Feb. 7, 1923. Height: 6'2". Weight: 190 lbs. Drafted: 1948 College: Ohio University

YEAR	TEAM	GP	GS	MIN	PTS	FGM	FGA	FG%	3PM	3PA	3P%	FTM	FTA	FT%	ORB	DRB	TRB	AST	PF	DQ	STL	BLK	TO	MPG	PPG	RPG	APG	PCM
48-49	Detroit-N	3	....	....	9	3	....	....	....	....	....	3	6	.500	....	....	....	....	....	....	....	....	....	....	3.0	....	....	....
48-49	New York	4	....	....	1	0	0	.000	....	....	....	1	3	.333	....	....	....	2	2	....	....	....	....	....	0.3	....	0.5	....
NBA Season Totals		4	....	....	1	0	0	.000	....	....	....	1	3	.333	....	....	....	2	2	....	....	....	....	....	0.3	....	0.5	....
NBL Season Totals		3	....	....	9	3	....	....	....	....	....	3	6	....	....	....	....	....	....	....	....	....	....	....	3.0	....	....	....
Career Totals		7	....	....	10	3	0	....	....	....	....	4	9	....	....	....	....	2	2	....	....	....	....	....	1.4	....	0.3	....

• SHUE, Gene

Eugene William Shue

Born: Dec. 18, 1931. Baltimore, MD, United States. Height: 6'2". Weight: 170 lbs. Drafted: 1954 College: Maryland

YEAR	TEAM	GP	GS	MIN	PTS	FGM	FGA	FG%	3PM	3PA	3P%	FTM	FTA	FT%	ORB	DRB	TRB	AST	PF	DQ	STL	BLK	TO	MPG	PPG	RPG	APG	PCM
54-55	Philadelphia	6	....	65	11	3	15	.200	....	....	....	5	6	.833	....	....	10	11	4	0	....	....	....	10.8	1.8	1.7	1.8	.328
54-55	New York	56	....	882	248	97	274	.354	....	....	....	54	72	.750	....	....	144	78	60	0	....	....	....	15.8	4.4	2.6	1.4	.330
55-56	New York	72	....	1750	661	240	625	.384	....	....	....	181	237	.764	....	....	212	179	111	0	....	....	....	24.3	9.2	2.9	2.5	.393
56-57	Fort Wayne	72	....	2470	787	273	710	.385	....	....	....	241	316	.763	....	....	421	238	137	0	....	....	....	34.3	10.9	5.8	3.3	.403
57-58	Detroit	63	....	2333	982	353	919	.384	....	....	....	276	327	.844	....	....	333	172	150	1	....	....	....	37.0	15.6	5.3	2.7	.410
58-59	Detroit	72	....	2745	1266	464	1197	.388	....	....	....	338	421	.803	....	....	335	231	129	1	....	....	....	38.1	17.6	4.7	3.2	.428
59-60	Detroit	75	....	**3338**	1712	620	1501	.413	....	....	....	472	541	.872	....	....	409	295	146	2	....	....	....	44.5	22.8	5.5	3.9	.492
60-61	Detroit	78	....	3361	1765	650	1545	.421	....	....	....	465	543	.856	....	....	334	530	207	1	....	....	....	43.1	22.6	4.3	6.8	.561
61-62	Detroit	80	....	3143	1522	580	1422	.408	....	....	....	362	447	.810	....	....	372	465	192	1	....	....	....	39.3	19.0	4.7	5.8	.513
62-63	New York	78	....	2288	916	354	894	.396	....	....	....	208	302	.689	....	....	191	259	171	0	....	....	....	29.3	11.7	2.4	3.3	.371
63-64	Baltimore	47	....	963	198	81	276	.293	....	....	....	36	61	.590	....	....	94	150	98	2	....	....	....	20.5	4.2	2.0	3.2	.265
NBA Season Totals		699	....	23338	10068	3715	9378	.396	....	....	....	2638	3273	.806	....	....	2855	2608	1405	8	....	....	....	33.4	14.4	4.1	3.7	....
54-55	New York	3	....	49	22	8	17	.471	....	....	....	6	7	.857	....	....	12	4	5	0	....	....	....	16.3	7.3	4.0	1.3	.551
56-57	Fort Wayne	2	....	79	32	14	27	.519	....	....	....	4	4	1.000	....	....	7	8	3	0	....	....	....	39.5	16.0	3.5	4.0	.461
57-58	Detroit	7	....	281	130	45	123	.366	....	....	....	40	43	.930	....	....	46	33	15	0	....	....	....	40.1	18.6	6.6	4.7	.506
58-59	Detroit	3	....	118	83	28	60	.467	....	....	....	27	33	.818	....	....	14	10	7	0	....	....	....	39.3	27.7	4.7	3.3	.653
59-60	Detroit	2	....	89	48	15	38	.395	....	....	....	18	20	.900	....	....	12	6	5	0	....	....	....	44.5	24.0	6.0	3.0	.500
60-61	Detroit	5	....	186	93	35	72	.486	....	....	....	23	29	.793	....	....	12	22	11	0	....	....	....	37.2	18.6	2.4	4.4	.509
61-62	Detroit	10	....	363	161	62	151	.411	....	....	....	37	48	.771	....	....	30	49	29	0	....	....	....	36.3	16.1	3.0	4.9	.438
NBA Playoff Totals		32	....	1165	569	207	488	.424	....	....	....	155	184	.842	....	....	133	132	75	0	....	....	....	36.4	17.8	4.2	4.1	....

• SHUMATE, John

John H. Shumate

Born: Apr. 6, 1952. Greenville, SC, United States. Height: 6'9". Weight: 235 lbs. Drafted: 1974 College: Notre Dame

YEAR	TEAM	GP	GS	MIN	PTS	FGM	FGA	FG%	3PM	3PA	3P%	FTM	FTA	FT%	ORB	DRB	TRB	AST	PF	DQ	STL	BLK	TO	MPG	PPG	RPG	APG	PCM
75-76	Phoenix	43	....	930	487	186	338	.550	....	....	....	115	183	.628	61	179	240	62	76	1	44	16	....	21.6	11.3	5.6	1.4	.615
75-76	Buffalo	32	....	1046	389	146	254	.575	....	....	....	97	143	.678	82	232	314	65	83	1	38	18	....	32.7	12.2	9.8	2.0	.559
76-77	Buffalo	74	....	2601	1116	407	810	.502	....	....	....	302	450	.671	163	538	701	159	197	1	90	84	....	35.1	15.1	9.5	2.1	.540

YEAR	TEAM	GP	GS	MIN	PTS	FGM	FGA	FG%	3PM	3PA	3P%	FTM	FTA	FT%	ORB	DRB	TRB	AST	PF	DQ	STL	BLK	TO	MPG	PPG	RPG	APG	PCM
77-78	Buffalo	18	....	590	224	75	151	.497	....	....	....	74	99	.747	32	96	128	58	58	1	14	9	47	32.8	12.4	7.1	3.2	.470
77-78	Detroit	62	....	2170	958	316	622	.508	....	....	....	326	409	.797	125	429	554	122	142	1	76	43	186	35.0	15.5	8.9	2.0	.532
79-80	Detroit	9	....	228	87	35	65	.538	0	0	.000	17	25	.680	18	52	70	9	16	0	9	5	14	25.3	9.7	7.8	1.0	.536
79-80	Houston	29	....	332	101	34	64	.531	0	0	.000	33	44	.750	25	54	79	23	39	0	8	9	26	11.4	3.5	2.7	0.8	.421
79-80	San Antonio	27	....	777	391	138	263	.525	0	1	.000	115	147	.782	65	149	214	52	71	1	23	31	51	28.8	14.5	7.9	1.9	.624
80-81	San Antonio	22	....	519	165	56	128	.438	0	0	.000	53	73	.726	33	54	87	24	46	0	21	9	42	23.6	7.5	4.0	1.1	.316
80-81	Seattle	2	....	8	2	0	3	.000	0	0	.000	2	3	.667	1	0	1	0	3	0	0	0	1	4.0	1.0	0.5	0.0	-.319
NBA Season Totals		318	....	9201	3920	1393	2698	.516	0	1	.000	1134	1576	.720	605	1783	2388	574	731	6	323	224	367	28.9	12.3	7.5	1.8	
75-76	Buffalo	9	....	362	127	54	92	.587	....	....	....	19	38	.500	25	52	77	25	29	0	9	13	....	40.2	14.1	8.6	2.8	.465
79-80	San Antonio	3	....	78	21	9	20	.450	0	0	.000	3	3	1.000	7	6	13	5	9	0	4	4	5	26.0	7.0	4.3	1.7	.345
NBA Playoff Totals		12	....	440	148	63	112	.563	0	0	.000	22	41	.537	32	58	90	30	38	0	13	17	5	36.7	12.3	7.5	2.5	

• SIBERT, Sam

Sam Lewis Sibert

Born: Feb. 11, 1949.   Height: 6'7".   Weight: 215 lbs.   Drafted: 1972   College: Kentucky State

YEAR	TEAM	GP	GS	MIN	PTS	FGM	FGA	FG%	3PM	3PA	3P%	FTM	FTA	FT%	ORB	DRB	TRB	AST	PF	DQ	STL	BLK	TO	MPG	PPG	RPG	APG	PCM
72-73	Omaha	5	....	26	12	4	13	.308	....	....	....	4	5	.800	....	....	4	0	4	0	....	....	....	5.2	2.4	0.8	0.0	.214
NBA Season Totals		5	....	26	12	4	13	.308	....	....	....	4	5	.800	....	....	4	0	4	0	....	....	....	5.2	2.4	0.8	0.0	

• SIBLEY, Mark

Donald Mark Sibley

Born: Nov. 13, 1950.   Height: 6'2".   Weight: 175 lbs.   Drafted: 1973   College: Northwestern

YEAR	TEAM	GP	GS	MIN	PTS	FGM	FGA	FG%	3PM	3PA	3P%	FTM	FTA	FT%	ORB	DRB	TRB	AST	PF	DQ	STL	BLK	TO	MPG	PPG	RPG	APG	PCM
73-74	Portland	28	....	124	46	20	56	.357	....	....	....	6	7	.857	9	16	25	13	23	0	4	1	....	4.4	1.6	0.9	0.5	.334
NBA Season Totals		28	....	124	46	20	56	.357	....	....	....	6	7	.857	9	16	25	13	23	0	4	1	....	4.4	1.6	0.9	0.5	

• SICHTING, Jerry

Jerry Lee Sichting

Born: Nov. 29, 1956. Martinsville, IN, United States.   Height: 6'1".   Weight: 168 lbs.   Drafted: 1979   College: Purdue

YEAR	TEAM	GP	GS	MIN	PTS	FGM	FGA	FG%	3PM	3PA	3P%	FTM	FTA	FT%	ORB	DRB	TRB	AST	PF	DQ	STL	BLK	TO	MPG	PPG	RPG	APG	PCM
80-81	Indiana	47	....	450	93	34	95	.358	0	5	.000	25	32	.781	11	32	43	70	38	0	23	1	28	9.6	2.0	0.9	1.5	.286
81-82	Indiana	51	0	800	212	91	194	.469	1	9	.111	29	38	.763	14	41	55	117	63	0	33	1	41	15.7	4.2	1.1	2.3	.318
82-83	Indiana	78	58	2435	727	316	661	.478	3	18	.167	92	107	.860	33	122	155	433	185	0	104	2	140	31.2	9.3	2.0	5.6	.374
83-84	Indiana	80	80	2497	917	397	746	.532	6	20	.300	117	135	.867	44	127	171	457	179	0	90	8	144	31.2	11.5	2.1	5.7	.443
84-85	Indiana	70	25	1808	771	325	624	.521	9	37	.243	112	128	.875	24	90	114	264	116	0	47	4	105	25.8	11.0	1.6	3.8	.425
85-86	Boston	82	7	1596	537	235	412	.570	6	16	.375	61	66	.924	27	77	104	188	118	0	50	0	74	19.5	6.5	1.3	2.3	.370
86-87	Boston	78	15	1566	448	202	398	.508	7	26	.269	37	42	.881	22	69	91	187	124	0	40	1	62	20.1	5.7	1.2	2.4	.300
87-88	Boston	24	1	370	98	44	82	.537	2	8	.250	8	12	.667	5	16	21	60	30	0	14	0	14	15.4	4.1	0.9	2.5	.352
87-88	Portland	28	0	324	115	49	90	.544	8	14	.571	9	11	.818	4	11	15	33	30	0	7	0	8	11.6	4.1	0.5	1.2	.340
88-89	Portland	25	1	390	102	46	104	.442	3	12	.250	7	8	.875	9	20	29	59	17	0	15	0	15	15.6	4.1	1.2	2.4	.309
89-90	Charlotte	34	8	469	118	50	119	.420	3	12	.250	15	18	.833	3	16	19	92	39	0	16	2	20	13.8	3.5	0.6	2.7	.314
89-90	Milwaukee	1	0	27	3	0	6	.000	0	0	.000	3	4	.750	0	0	0	2	1	0	0	0	0	27.0	3.0	0.0	2.0	-.053
NBA Season Totals		598	195	12732	4141	1789	3531	.507	48	177	.271	515	601	.857	196	621	817	1962	940	0	439	19	661	21.3	6.9	1.4	3.3	
80-81	Indiana	1	....	1	0	0	0	.000	0	0	.000	0	0	.000	0	0	0	0	1	0	1	0	0	1.0	0.0	0.0	0.0	.911
85-86	Boston	18	0	274	57	27	61	.443	0	1	.000	3	7	.429	5	11	16	40	18	0	5	0	8	15.2	3.2	0.9	2.2	.256
86-87	Boston	23	4	338	79	35	82	.427	1	6	.167	8	10	.800	5	15	20	33	36	0	9	0	10	14.7	3.4	0.9	1.4	.209
87-88	Portland	4	0	31	4	2	7	.286	0	0	.000	0	0	.000	1	1	2	5	4	0	1	0	0	7.8	1.0	0.5	1.3	.181
88-89	Portland	1	0	11	0	0	3	.000	0	0	.000	0	0	.000	0	0	0	1	1	0	0	0	0	11.0	0.0	0.0	1.0	-.199
NBA Playoff Totals		47	4	655	140	64	153	.418	1	7	.143	11	17	.647	11	27	38	79	59	0	16	0	18	13.9	3.0	0.8	1.7	

• SICKY, —

Sicky

Born: —.   Height: —   Weight: —   Drafted: —   College: —

YEAR	TEAM	GP	GS	MIN	PTS	FGM	FGA	FG%	3PM	3PA	3P%	FTM	FTA	FT%	ORB	DRB	TRB	AST	PF	DQ	STL	BLK	TO	MPG	PPG	RPG	APG	PCM
38-39	Hammond-N	1	....	....	0	0	....	....	....	....	....	0	....	....	....	....	....	0	....	....	....	....	....	....	0.0	....	....	....
NBL Season Totals		1	....	....	0	0	....	....	....	....	....	0	....	....	....	....	....	0	....	....	....	....	....	....	0.0	....	....	

• SIDLE, Donald

Donald Roy Sidle

Born: June 21, 1946. Dallas, TX, United States. Died: May 1987.   Height: 6'8".   Weight: 215 lbs.   Drafted: 1968   College: Oklahoma

YEAR	TEAM	GP	GS	MIN	PTS	FGM	FGA	FG%	3PM	3PA	3P%	FTM	FTA	FT%	ORB	DRB	TRB	AST	PF	DQ	STL	BLK	TO	MPG	PPG	RPG	APG	PCM
68-69	Miami-A	77	....	1984	931	305	656	.465	0	4	.000	321	450	.713	223	328	551	73	212	3	....	....	142	25.8	12.1	7.2	0.9	.524
69-70	Miami-A	84	....	3493	1748	639	1320	.484	1	6	.167	469	634	.740	432	650	1082	129	272	3	....	....	250	41.6	20.8	12.9	1.5	.587
70-71	Denver-A	54	....	1623	870	339	694	.488	0	5	.000	192	257	.747	213	275	488	66	167	0	....	....	123	30.1	16.1	9.0	1.2	.593
70-71	Indiana-A	30	....	528	223	86	157	.548	2	4	.500	49	74	.662	73	74	147	31	66	1	....	....	33	17.6	7.4	4.9	1.0	.539
71-72	Indiana-A	27	....	394	175	72	143	.503	0	1	.000	31	49	.633	44	51	95	10	39	0	....	....	20	14.6	6.5	3.5	0.4	.463
71-72	Memphis-A	42	....	566	300	103	241	.427	1	9	.111	93	146	.637	71	68	139	16	57	0	....	....	36	13.5	7.1	3.3	0.4	.478
ABA Season Totals		314	....	8588	4247	1544	3211	.481	4	29	.138	1155	1610	.717	1056	1446	2502	325	813	7	....	....	604	27.4	13.5	8.0	1.0	
68-69	Miami-A	12	....	340	163	60	117	.513	0	0	.000	43	60	.717	....	....	100	16	35	1	....	....	23	28.3	13.6	8.3	1.3	.576
70-71	Indiana-A	8	....	68	26	8	24	.333	0	1	.000	10	16	.625	13	9	22	4	8	0	....	....	2	8.5	3.3	2.8	0.5	.441
ABA Playoff Totals		20	....	408	189	68	141	.482	0	1	.000	53	76	.697	13	9	122	20	43	1	....	....	25	20.4	9.5	6.1	1.0	

• SIEGEL, Vic

Vic Siegel

Born: 1920.   Height: 5'10".   Weight: 160 lbs.   Drafted: —   College: Iowa

YEAR	TEAM	GP	GS	MIN	PTS	FGM	FGA	FG%	3PM	3PA	3P%	FTM	FTA	FT%	ORB	DRB	TRB	AST	PF	DQ	STL	BLK	TO	MPG	PPG	RPG	APG	PCM
46-47	Tri-Cities-N	8	....	....	11	3	....	....	....	....	....	5	5	1.000	....	....	....	....	....	....	....	....	....	....	1.4	....	....	....
NBL Season Totals		8	....	....	11	3	....	....	....	....	....	5	5	....	....	....	....	....	....	....	....	....	....	....	1.4	....	....	

YEAR	TEAM	GP	GS	MIN	PTS	FGM	FGA	FG%	3PM	3PA	3P%	FTM	FTA	FT%	ORB	DRB	TRB	AST	PF	DQ	STL	BLK	TO	MPG	PPG	RPG	APG	PCM

• SIEGFRIED, Larry

Larry E. Siegfried

Born: May 22, 1939. Shelby, OH, United States. Height: 6'3". Weight: 190 lbs. Drafted: 1961 College: Ohio State

YEAR	TEAM	GP	GS	MIN	PTS	FGM	FGA	FG%	3PM	3PA	3P%	FTM	FTA	FT%	ORB	DRB	TRB	AST	PF	DQ	STL	BLK	TO	MPG	PPG	RPG	APG	PCM
63-64	Boston	31	....	261	101	35	110	.318	....	....	....	31	39	.795	....	....	51	40	33	0	....	....	....	8.4	3.3	1.6	1.3	.442
64-65	Boston	72	....	996	455	173	417	.415	....	....	....	109	140	.779	....	....	134	119	108	1	....	....	....	13.8	6.3	1.9	1.7	.466
65-66	Boston	71	....	1675	972	349	825	.423	....	....	....	274	311	**.881**	....	....	196	165	157	1	....	....	....	23.6	13.7	2.8	2.3	.524
66-67	Boston	73	....	1891	1030	368	833	.442	....	....	....	294	347	.847	....	....	228	250	207	1	....	....	....	25.9	14.1	3.1	3.4	.549
67-68	Boston	62	....	1937	758	261	629	.415	....	....	....	236	272	.868	....	....	215	289	194	2	....	....	....	31.2	12.2	3.5	4.7	.460
68-69	Boston	79	....	2560	1120	392	1031	.380	....	....	....	336	389	**.864**	....	....	282	370	222	0	....	....	....	32.4	14.2	3.6	4.7	.444
69-70	Boston	78	....	2081	984	382	902	.424	....	....	....	220	257	.856	....	....	212	299	187	2	....	....	....	26.7	12.6	2.7	3.8	.456
70-71	San Diego	53	....	1673	422	146	378	.386	....	....	....	130	153	.850	....	....	207	346	146	0	....	....	....	31.6	8.0	3.9	6.5	.432
71-72	Houston	10	....	223	48	18	46	.391	....	....	....	12	14	.857	....	....	10	20	21	0	....	....	....	22.3	4.8	1.0	2.0	.203
71-72	Atlanta	21	....	335	70	25	77	.325	....	....	....	20	23	.870	....	....	32	52	32	0	....	....	....	16.0	3.3	1.5	2.5	.289
NBA Season Totals		550	....	13632	5960	2149	5248	.409	....	....	....	1662	1945	.854	....	....	1567	1950	1307	7	....	....	....	24.8	10.8	2.8	3.5	....
63-64	Boston	4	....	24	7	2	6	.333	....	....	....	3	6	.500	....	....	4	1	4	0	....	....	....	6.0	1.8	1.0	0.3	.229
64-65	Boston	12	....	163	84	30	79	.380	....	....	....	24	28	.857	....	....	25	21	25	0	....	....	....	13.6	7.0	2.1	1.8	.493
65-66	Boston	17	....	452	224	81	193	.420	....	....	....	62	75	.827	....	....	42	41	52	0	....	....	....	26.6	13.2	2.5	2.4	.428
66-67	Boston	9	....	260	111	38	102	.373	....	....	....	35	43	.814	....	....	40	44	33	1	....	....	....	28.9	12.3	4.4	4.9	.494
67-68	Boston	19	....	535	233	78	201	.388	....	....	....	77	85	.906	....	....	50	56	75	3	....	....	....	28.2	12.3	2.6	2.9	.391
68-69	Boston	18	....	392	199	72	172	.419	....	....	....	55	70	.786	....	....	38	46	60	1	....	....	....	21.8	11.1	2.1	2.6	.432
NBA Playoff Totals		79	....	1826	858	301	753	.400	....	....	....	256	307	.834	....	....	199	209	249	5	....	....	....	23.1	10.9	2.5	2.6	....

• SIEWERT, Ralph

Ralph Paul Siewert

Born: Dec. 31, 1923. Died: Nov.21, 1990. Height: 7'1". Weight: 230 lbs. Drafted: — College: Dakota Wesleyan

YEAR	TEAM	GP	GS	MIN	PTS	FGM	FGA	FG%	3PM	3PA	3P%	FTM	FTA	FT%	ORB	DRB	TRB	AST	PF	DQ	STL	BLK	TO	MPG	PPG	RPG	APG	PCM
46-47	St. Louis	7	....	....	4	1	13	.077	....	....	....	2	5	.400	....	....	....	0	8	....	....	....	....	....	0.6	....	0.0	....
46-47	Toronto	14	....	....	16	5	31	.161	....	....	....	6	10	.600	....	....	....	4	10	....	....	....	....	....	1.1	....	0.3	....
NBA Season Totals		21	....	....	20	6	44	.136	....	....	....	8	15	.533	....	....	....	4	18	....	....	....	....	....	1.0	....	0.2	....

• SIKMA, Jack

Jack Wayne Sikma

Born: Nov. 14, 1955. Kankankee, IL, United States. Height: 6'11". Weight: 230 lbs. Drafted: 1977 College: Illinois Wesleyan

YEAR	TEAM	GP	GS	MIN	PTS	FGM	FGA	FG%	3PM	3PA	3P%	FTM	FTA	FT%	ORB	DRB	TRB	AST	PF	DQ	STL	BLK	TO	MPG	PPG	RPG	APG	PCM
77-78	Seattle	82	....	2238	876	342	752	.455	....	....	....	192	247	.777	196	482	678	134	300	6	68	40	189	27.3	10.7	8.3	1.6	.462
78-79	Seattle	82	....	2958	1281	476	1034	.460	....	....	....	329	404	.814	232	781	1013	261	295	4	82	67	254	36.1	15.6	12.4	3.2	.580
79-80	Seattle	82	....	2793	1175	470	989	.475	0	1	.000	235	292	.805	198	710	908	279	232	5	68	77	205	34.1	14.3	11.1	3.4	.590
80-81	Seattle	82	....	2920	1530	595	1311	.454	0	5	.000	340	413	.823	184	668	852	248	282	5	78	93	205	35.6	18.7	10.4	3.0	.593
81-82	Seattle	82	82	3049	1611	581	1212	.479	2	13	.154	447	523	.855	223	**815**	1038	277	268	5	102	107	213	37.2	19.6	12.7	3.4	.696
82-83	Seattle	75	71	2564	1368	484	1043	.464	0	8	.000	400	478	.837	213	645	858	233	263	4	87	65	188	34.2	18.2	11.4	3.1	.666
83-84	Seattle	82	82	2993	1563	576	1155	.499	0	2	.000	411	480	.856	225	**686**	911	327	301	6	95	92	238	36.5	19.1	11.1	4.0	.669
84-85	Seattle	68	68	2402	1259	461	943	.489	2	10	.200	335	393	.852	164	559	723	285	239	1	83	91	163	35.3	18.5	10.6	4.2	.691
85-86	Seattle	80	78	2790	1371	508	1100	.462	0	13	.000	355	411	.864	146	602	748	301	293	4	92	73	216	34.9	17.1	9.4	3.8	.584
86-87	Milwaukee	82	82	2536	1045	390	842	.463	0	2	.000	265	313	.847	208	614	822	203	328	14	88	90	164	30.9	12.7	10.0	2.5	.570
87-88	Milwaukee	82	82	2923	1352	514	1058	.486	3	14	.214	321	348	**.922**	195	514	709	279	316	**11**	93	80	156	35.6	16.5	8.6	3.4	.568
88-89	Milwaukee	80	80	2587	1068	360	835	.431	82	216	.380	266	294	.905	141	482	623	289	300	6	85	61	144	32.3	13.4	7.8	3.6	.527
89-90	Milwaukee	71	70	2250	986	344	827	.416	68	199	.342	230	260	.885	109	383	492	229	244	5	76	48	142	31.7	13.9	6.9	3.2	.486
90-91	Milwaukee	77	44	1940	802	295	691	.427	46	135	.341	166	197	.843	108	333	441	143	218	4	65	64	131	25.2	10.4	5.7	1.9	.453
NBA Season Totals		1107	739	36943	17287	6396	13792	.464	203	618	.328	4292	5053	.849	2542	8274	10816	3488	3879	80	1162	1048	2608	33.4	15.6	9.8	3.2	....
77-78	Seattle	22	....	701	301	115	247	.466	....	....	....	71	91	.780	50	128	178	27	101	7	18	11	35	31.9	13.7	8.1	1.2	.447
78-79	Seattle	17	....	655	252	103	224	.460	....	....	....	46	61	.754	39	160	199	43	70	2	16	24	40	38.5	14.8	11.7	2.5	.506
79-80	Seattle	15	....	534	176	65	163	.399	0	2	.000	46	54	.852	30	96	126	55	55	1	17	5	35	35.6	11.7	8.4	3.7	.414
81-82	Seattle	8	8	315	164	57	128	.445	0	0	.000	50	58	.862	21	76	97	24	34	1	9	8	16	39.4	20.5	12.1	3.0	.620
82-83	Seattle	2	2	75	30	11	31	.355	0	1	.000	8	12	.667	6	20	26	11	7	0	2	2	5	37.5	15.0	13.0	5.5	.555
83-84	Seattle	5	5	193	110	49	98	.500	0	1	.000	12	14	.857	11	40	51	5	22	1	3	7	9	38.6	22.0	10.2	1.0	.554
86-87	Milwaukee	12	12	426	194	73	150	.487	0	1	.000	48	49	.980	33	97	130	23	56	3	15	10	18	35.5	16.2	10.8	1.9	.582
87-88	Milwaukee	5	5	190	95	35	76	.461	0	3	.000	25	30	.833	24	38	62	13	23	0	2	4	15	38.0	19.0	12.4	2.6	.563
88-89	Milwaukee	9	9	301	105	37	94	.394	8	28	.286	23	28	.821	9	41	50	30	41	2	8	4	21	33.4	11.7	5.6	3.3	.335
89-90	Milwaukee	4	4	117	20	6	23	.261	2	7	.286	6	8	.750	0	14	14	7	19	0	2	4	12	29.3	5.0	3.5	1.8	.078
90-91	Milwaukee	3	0	51	14	6	15	.400	1	2	.500	1	2	.500	3	9	12	6	4	0	5	1	3	17.0	4.7	4.0	2.0	.464
NBA Playoff Totals		102	45	3558	1461	557	1249	.446	11	45	.244	336	407	.826	226	719	945	244	432	17	97	80	209	34.9	14.3	9.3	2.4	....

• SILAS, James

James Edward (Captain Late) Silas

Born: Feb. 11, 1949. Tallulah, LA, United States. Height: 6'1". Weight: 180 lbs. Drafted: 1972 College: Stephen F. Austin State

YEAR	TEAM	GP	GS	MIN	PTS	FGM	FGA	FG%	3PM	3PA	3P%	FTM	FTA	FT%	ORB	DRB	TRB	AST	PF	DQ	STL	BLK	TO	MPG	PPG	RPG	APG	PCM
72-73	Dallas-A	78	....	2417	1071	341	679	.502	0	0	.000	389	467	.833	109	227	336	244	262	2	....	....	192	31.0	13.7	4.3	3.1	.490
73-74	San Antonio-A	84	....	3096	1321	486	1017	.478	0	1	.000	349	420	.831	83	260	343	319	256	....	90	8	220	36.9	15.7	4.1	3.8	.447
74-75	San Antonio-A	82	....	3105	1586	578	1136	.509	0	2	.000	430	486	.885	73	237	310	398	232	....	111	17	230	37.9	19.3	3.8	4.9	.541
75-76	San Antonio-A	84	....	3112	2000	718	1384	.519	0	2	.000	**564**	647	.872	111	224	335	452	263	....	155	24	254	37.0	23.8	4.0	5.4	.659
76-77	San Antonio	22	....	356	209	61	142	.430	....	....	....	87	107	.813	7	25	32	50	36	0	13	3	....	16.2	9.5	1.5	2.3	.560
77-78	San Antonio	37	....	311	146	43	97	.443	....	....	....	60	73	.822	4	19	23	38	29	0	11	1	30	8.4	3.9	0.6	1.0	.410
78-79	San Antonio	79	....	2171	1266	466	922	.505	....	....	....	334	402	.831	35	148	183	273	215	1	76	20	198	27.5	16.0	2.3	3.5	.508
79-80	San Antonio	77	....	2293	1365	513	999	.514	0	4	.000	339	382	.887	45	122	167	347	206	2	61	14	193	29.8	17.7	2.2	4.5	.539
80-81	San Antonio	75	....	2055	1326	476	997	.477	0	2	.000	374	440	.850	44	187	231	285	129	0	51	12	158	27.4	17.7	3.1	3.8	.582
81-82	Cleveland	67	34	1447	748	251	573	.438	0	5	.000	246	286	.860	26	83	109	222	109	0	40	6	107	21.6	11.2	1.6	3.3	.461
NBA Season Totals		357	34	8633	5060	1810	3730	.485	0	11	.000	1440	1690	.852	161	584	745	1215	724	3	252	56	686	24.2	14.2	2.1	3.4	....
ABA Season Totals		328	....	11730	5978	2123	4216	.504	0	5	.000	1732	2020	.857	376	948	1324	1413	1013	2	356	49	896	35.8	18.2	4.0	4.3	....
Career Totals		685	34	20363	11038	3933	7946	.495	0	16	.000	3172	3710	.855	537	1532	2069	2628	1737	5	608	105	1582	29.7	16.1	3.0	3.8	....
73-74	San Antonio-A	7	....	294	124	49	105	.467	0	1	.000	26	38	.684	8	30	38	32	15	....	14	1	21	42.0	17.7	5.4	4.6	.454
74-75	San Antonio-A	6	....	271	113	41	87	.471	0	0	.000	31	40	.775	6	12	18	60	27	....	9	1	16	45.2	18.8	3.0	10.0	.512
75-76	San Antonio-A	1	....	26	10	3	10	.300	0	0	.000	4	4	1.000	2	2	4	0	3	....	1	0	2	26.0	10.0	4.0	0.0	.230

YEAR	TEAM	GP	GS	MIN	PTS	FGM	FGA	FG%	3PM	3PA	3P%	FTM	FTA	FT%	ORB	DRB	TRB	AST	PF	DQ	STL	BLK	TO	MPG	PPG	RPG	APG	PCM
77-78	San Antonio	3	....	19	7	3	10	.300	....	....	....	1	2	.500	0	0	0	1	1	0	1	0	1	6.3	2.3	0.0	0.3	.059
78-79	San Antonio	14	....	475	267	102	215	.474	....	....	....	63	80	.788	12	30	42	66	39	0	21	1	36	33.9	19.1	3.0	4.7	.502
79-80	San Antonio	3	....	90	43	16	36	.444	0	0	.000	11	11	1.000	1	6	7	9	8	0	6	1	5	30.0	14.3	2.3	3.0	.436
80-81	San Antonio	7	....	161	80	27	69	.391	0	0	.000	26	32	.813	5	10	15	19	9	0	4	0	18	23.0	11.4	2.1	2.7	.351
NBA Playoff Totals		27	....	745	397	148	330	.448	0	0	.000	101	125	.808	18	46	64	95	57	0	32	2	60	27.6	14.7	2.4	3.5	....
ABA Playoff Totals		14	....	591	247	93	202	.460	0	1	.000	61	82	.744	16	44	60	92	45	....	24	2	39	42.2	17.6	4.3	6.6	....
Career Playoff Totals		41	....	1336	644	241	532	.453	0	1	.000	162	207	.783	34	90	124	187	102	0	56	4	99	32.6	15.7	3.0	4.6	....

• SILAS, Paul

Paul Theron Silas

Born: July 12, 1943. Prescott, AZ, United States. Height: 6'7". Weight: 220 lbs. Drafted: 1964 College: Creighton

YEAR	TEAM	GP	GS	MIN	PTS	FGM	FGA	FG%	3PM	3PA	3P%	FTM	FTA	FT%	ORB	DRB	TRB	AST	PF	DQ	STL	BLK	TO	MPG	PPG	RPG	APG	PCM
64-65	St. Louis	79	....	1243	363	140	375	.373	....	....	....	83	164	.506	....	....	576	48	161	1	....	....	....	15.7	4.6	7.3	0.6	.476
65-66	St. Louis	46	....	586	175	70	173	.405	....	....	....	35	61	.574	....	....	236	22	72	0	....	....	....	12.7	3.8	5.1	0.5	.457
66-67	St. Louis	77	....	1570	527	207	482	.429	....	....	....	113	213	.531	....	....	669	74	208	4	....	....	....	20.4	6.8	8.7	1.0	.514
67-68	St. Louis	82	....	2652	1097	399	871	.458	....	....	....	299	424	.705	....	....	958	162	243	4	....	....	....	32.3	13.4	11.7	2.0	.578
68-69	Atlanta	79	....	1853	686	241	575	.419	....	....	....	204	333	.613	....	....	745	140	166	0	....	....	....	23.5	8.7	9.4	1.8	.577
69-70	Phoenix	78	....	2836	996	373	804	.464	....	....	....	250	412	.607	....	....	916	214	266	5	....	....	....	36.4	12.8	11.7	2.7	.520
70-71	Phoenix	81	....	2944	961	338	789	.428	....	....	....	285	416	.685	....	....	1015	247	227	3	....	....	....	36.3	11.9	12.5	3.0	.535
71-72	Phoenix	80	....	3082	1403	485	1031	.470	....	....	....	433	560	.773	....	....	955	343	201	2	....	....	....	38.5	17.5	11.9	4.3	.650
72-73	Boston	80	....	2618	1066	400	851	.470	....	....	....	266	380	.700	....	....	1039	251	197	1	....	....	....	32.7	13.3	13.0	3.1	.658
73-74	Boston	82	....	2599	944	340	772	.440	....	....	....	264	337	.783	334	581	915	186	246	3	63	20	....	31.7	11.5	11.2	2.3	.551
74-75	Boston	82	....	2661	868	312	749	.417	....	....	....	244	344	.709	348	677	1025	224	229	3	60	22	....	32.5	10.6	12.5	2.7	.559
75-76	Boston	81	....	2662	866	315	740	.426	....	....	....	236	333	.709	**365**	660	1025	203	227	3	56	33	....	32.9	10.7	12.7	2.5	.554
76-77	Denver	81	....	1959	582	206	572	.360	....	....	....	170	255	.667	236	370	606	132	183	0	58	23	....	24.2	7.2	7.5	1.6	.420
77-78	Seattle	82	....	2172	477	184	464	.397	....	....	....	109	186	.586	289	377	666	145	182	0	65	16	156	26.5	5.8	8.1	1.8	.368
78-79	Seattle	82	....	1957	456	170	402	.423	....	....	....	116	194	.598	259	316	575	115	177	3	31	19	98	23.9	5.6	7.0	1.4	.375
79-80	Seattle	82	....	1595	315	113	299	.378	0	0	.000	89	136	.654	204	232	436	66	120	0	25	5	82	19.5	3.8	5.3	0.8	.308
NBA Season Totals		1254	....	34989	11782	4293	9949	.432	0	0	.000	3196	4748	.673	2035	3213	12357	2572	3105	32	358	138	336	27.9	9.4	9.9	2.1	....
64-65	St. Louis	4	....	42	11	4	10	.400	....	....	....	3	4	.750	....	....	18	1	6	0	....	....	....	10.5	2.8	4.5	0.3	.447
65-66	St. Louis	7	....	80	18	5	18	.278	....	....	....	8	11	.727	....	....	34	2	11	0	....	....	....	11.4	2.6	4.9	0.3	.393
66-67	St. Louis	8	....	122	29	9	36	.250	....	....	....	11	18	.611	....	....	52	6	17	0	....	....	....	15.3	3.6	6.5	0.8	.382
67-68	St. Louis	6	....	178	71	22	51	.431	....	....	....	27	38	.711	....	....	57	21	17	0	....	....	....	29.7	11.8	9.5	3.5	.603
68-69	Atlanta	11	....	258	61	21	58	.362	....	....	....	19	37	.514	....	....	92	21	32	0	....	....	....	23.5	5.5	8.4	1.9	.428
69-70	Phoenix	7	....	286	113	46	109	.422	....	....	....	21	32	.656	....	....	111	30	29	1	....	....	....	40.9	16.1	15.9	4.3	.599
72-73	Boston	13	....	512	125	47	120	.392	....	....	....	31	50	.620	....	....	196	39	39	0	....	....	....	39.4	9.6	15.1	3.0	.489
73-74	Boston	18	....	574	144	50	126	.397	....	....	....	44	53	.830	53	138	191	47	51	2	13	9	....	31.9	8.0	10.6	2.6	.471
74-75	Boston	11	....	405	100	42	92	.457	....	....	....	16	25	.640	46	84	130	40	45	1	12	2	....	36.8	9.1	11.8	3.6	.472
75-76	Boston	18	....	741	194	69	154	.448	....	....	....	56	69	.812	78	168	246	42	67	1	24	6	....	41.2	10.8	13.7	2.3	.467
76-77	Denver	6	....	141	41	14	33	.424	....	....	....	13	24	.542	16	24	40	16	23	1	2	4	....	23.5	6.8	6.7	2.7	.444
77-78	Seattle	22	....	605	107	33	94	.351	....	....	....	41	60	.683	73	114	187	36	59	0	12	6	30	27.5	4.9	8.5	1.6	.352
78-79	Seattle	17	....	418	73	21	54	.389	....	....	....	31	46	.674	40	58	98	19	44	1	9	5	34	24.6	4.3	5.8	1.1	.258
79-80	Seattle	15	....	257	37	13	43	.302	0	0	.000	11	13	.846	33	42	75	15	29	0	9	2	9	17.1	2.5	5.0	1.0	.319
NBA Playoff Totals		163	....	4619	1124	396	998	.397	0	0	.000	332	480	.692	339	628	1527	335	469	7	81	34	73	28.3	6.9	9.4	2.1	....

• SILLIMAN, Mike

Michael Barnwell Silliman

Born: May 5, 1944. Louisville, KY, United States. Height: 6'6". Weight: 225 lbs. Drafted: 1966 College: Army

YEAR	TEAM	GP	GS	MIN	PTS	FGM	FGA	FG%	3PM	3PA	3P%	FTM	FTA	FT%	ORB	DRB	TRB	AST	PF	DQ	STL	BLK	TO	MPG	PPG	RPG	APG	PCM
70-71	Buffalo	36	....	366	91	36	79	.456	....	....	....	19	39	.487	....	....	62	23	37	0	....	....	....	10.2	2.5	1.7	0.6	.298
NBA Season Totals		36	....	366	91	36	79	.456	....	....	....	19	39	.487	....	....	62	23	37	0	....	....	....	10.2	2.5	1.7	0.6	....

• SIMMONS, Bobby

Bobby (Boo Silky) Simmons

Born: June 2, 1980. Chicago, IL, United States. Height: 6'7". Weight: 210 lbs. Drafted: 2001 College: DePaul

YEAR	TEAM	GP	GS	MIN	PTS	FGM	FGA	FG%	3PM	3PA	3P%	FTM	FTA	FT%	ORB	DRB	TRB	AST	PF	DQ	STL	BLK	TO	MPG	PPG	RPG	APG	PCM
01-02	Washington	30	3	343	112	43	95	.453	4	14	.286	22	30	.733	25	27	52	17	31	1	13	5	14	11.4	3.7	1.7	0.6	.340
02-03	Washington	36	2	378	120	44	112	.393	0	5	.000	32	35	.914	33	44	77	20	51	0	10	3	8	10.5	3.3	2.1	0.6	.344
NBA Season Totals		66	5	721	232	87	207	.420	4	19	.211	54	65	.831	58	71	129	37	82	1	23	8	22	10.9	3.5	2.0	0.6	....

• SIMMONS, Connie

Cornelius Leo Simmons

Born: Mar. 15, 1925. Newark, NJ, United States. Died: Apr.15, 1989. Height: 6'8". Weight: 222 lbs. Drafted: — College: none (HS: Flushing, NY)

YEAR	TEAM	GP	GS	MIN	PTS	FGM	FGA	FG%	3PM	3PA	3P%	FTM	FTA	FT%	ORB	DRB	TRB	AST	PF	DQ	STL	BLK	TO	MPG	PPG	RPG	APG	PCM
46-47	Boston	60	....	....	620	246	768	.320	....	....	....	128	189	.677	....	....	....	62	130	....	....	....	....	....	10.3	....	1.0	....
47-48	Boston	32	....	....	248	108	366	.295	....	....	....	32	54	.593	....	....	....	17	82	....	....	....	....	....	7.8	....	0.5	....
47-48	Baltimore	13	....	....	138	54	179	.302	....	....	....	30	54	.556	....	....	....	7	40	....	....	....	....	....	10.6	....	0.5	....
48-49	Baltimore	60	....	....	779	299	794	.377	....	....	....	181	265	.683	....	....	....	116	215	....	....	....	....	....	13.0	....	1.9	....
49-50	New York	60	....	....	680	241	729	.331	....	....	....	198	299	.662	....	....	....	102	203	....	....	....	....	....	11.3	....	1.7	....
50-51	New York	66	....	....	604	229	613	.374	....	....	....	146	208	.702	....	....	426	117	222	8	....	....	....	....	9.2	6.5	1.8	....
51-52	New York	66	....	1558	629	227	600	.378	....	....	....	175	254	.689	....	....	471	121	214	8	....	....	....	23.6	9.5	7.1	1.8	.482
52-53	New York	65	....	1707	729	240	637	.377	....	....	....	249	340	.732	....	....	458	127	252	9	....	....	....	26.3	11.2	7.0	2.0	.475
53-54	New York	72	....	2006	720	255	713	.358	....	....	....	210	305	.689	....	....	484	128	234	1	....	....	....	27.9	10.0	6.7	1.8	.392
54-55	Bal/Syr	36	....	862	346	137	384	.357	....	....	....	72	114	.632	....	....	220	61	109	2	....	....	....	23.9	9.6	6.1	1.7	.400
55-56	Rochester	68	....	903	366	144	428	.336	....	....	....	78	129	.605	....	....	235	82	142	2	....	....	....	13.3	5.4	3.5	1.2	.395
NBA Season Totals		598	....	7036	5859	2180	6211	.351	....	....	....	1499	2211	.678	....	....	2294	940	1843	30	....	....	....	11.8	9.8	3.8	1.6	....
47-48	Baltimore	11	....	....	188	65	175	.371	....	....	....	58	78	.744	....	....	....	11	42	....	....	....	....	....	17.1	....	1.0	....
48-49	Baltimore	3	....	....	48	13	37	.351	....	....	....	22	29	.759	....	....	....	7	12	....	....	....	....	....	16.0	....	2.3	....
49-50	New York	5	....	....	42	11	40	.275	....	....	....	20	21	.952	....	....	....	7	21	....	....	....	....	....	8.4	....	1.4	....
50-51	New York	14	....	....	152	55	151	.364	....	....	....	42	68	.618	....	....	94	24	61	1	....	....	....	....	10.9	6.7	1.7	....

YEAR	TEAM	GP	GS	MIN	PTS	FGM	FGA	FG%	3PM	3PA	3P%	FTM	FTA	FT%	ORB	DRB	TRB	AST	PF	DQ	STL	BLK	TO	MPG	PPG	RPG	APG	PCM
51-52	New York	14	....	427	222	77	166	.464	....	....	....	68	89	.764	....	....	108	12	55	3	....	....	....	30.5	15.9	7.7	0.9	.524
52-53	New York	11	....	341	145	47	128	.367	....	....	....	51	70	.729	....	....	82	25	48	1	....	....	....	31.0	13.2	7.5	2.3	.450
53-54	New York	4	....	111	45	10	31	.323	....	....	....	25	36	.694	....	....	33	10	17	1	....	....	....	27.8	11.3	8.3	2.5	.509
NBA Playoff Totals		62	....	879	842	278	728	.382	....	....	....	286	391	.731	....	....	317	96	256	6	....	....	....	14.2	13.6	5.1	1.5	....

• SIMMONS, Grant

Grant M. Simmons

Born: Mar. 7, 1943. New Orleans, LA, United States. Height: 6'3". Weight: 190 lbs. Drafted: 1966 College: Nebraska

YEAR	TEAM	GP	GS	MIN	PTS	FGM	FGA	FG%	3PM	3PA	3P%	FTM	FTA	FT%	ORB	DRB	TRB	AST	PF	DQ	STL	BLK	TO	MPG	PPG	RPG	APG	PCM
67-68	Denver-A	78	....	2264	793	292	688	.424	1	22	.045	208	295	.705	....	....	240	182	236	3	....	....	153	29.0	10.2	3.1	2.3	.328
68-69	Denver-A	17	....	252	65	22	59	.373	1	2	.500	20	29	.690	6	20	26	15	42	2	....	....	17	14.8	3.8	1.5	0.9	.202
ABA Season Totals		95	....	2516	858	314	747	.420	2	24	.083	228	324	.704	6	20	266	197	278	5	....	....	170	26.5	9.0	2.8	2.1	....
67-68	Denver-A	5	....	145	38	13	36	.361	0	1	.000	12	16	.750	....	....	22	15	20	1	....	....	10	29.0	7.6	4.4	3.0	.309
68-69	Denver-A	2	....	9	0	0	1	.000	0	0	.000	0	0	.000	....	....	0	0	1	0	....	....	0	4.5	0.0	0.0	0.0	-.143
ABA Playoff Totals		7	....	154	38	13	37	.351	0	1	.000	12	16	.750	....	....	22	15	21	1	....	....	10	22.0	5.4	3.1	2.1	....

• SIMMONS, Johnny

John Earl Simmons

Born: July 7, 1924. Birmingham, AL, United States. Height: 6'1". Weight: 184 lbs. Drafted: — College: New York University

YEAR	TEAM	GP	GS	MIN	PTS	FGM	FGA	FG%	3PM	3PA	3P%	FTM	FTA	FT%	ORB	DRB	TRB	AST	PF	DQ	STL	BLK	TO	MPG	PPG	RPG	APG	PCM
46-47	Boston	60	....	....	318	120	429	.280	....	....	....	78	127	.614	....	....	....	29	78	....	....	....	....	....	5.3	....	0.5	....
NBA Season Totals		60	....	....	318	120	429	.280	....	....	....	78	127	.614	....	....	....	29	78	....	....	....	....	....	5.3	....	0.5	....

• SIMMONS, Lionel

Lionel James (Train, L-Train) Simmons

Born: Nov. 14, 1968. Philadelphia, PA, United States. Height: 6'7". Weight: 210 lbs. Drafted: 1990 College: LaSalle

YEAR	TEAM	GP	GS	MIN	PTS	FGM	FGA	FG%	3PM	3PA	3P%	FTM	FTA	FT%	ORB	DRB	TRB	AST	PF	DQ	STL	BLK	TO	MPG	PPG	RPG	APG	PCM
90-91	Sacramento	79	79	2978	1421	549	1301	.422	3	11	.273	320	435	.736	193	504	697	315	249	0	113	85	229	37.7	18.0	8.8	4.0	.506
91-92	Sacramento	78	78	2895	1336	527	1162	.454	1	5	.200	281	365	.770	149	485	634	337	205	0	135	132	218	37.1	17.1	8.1	4.3	.555
92-93	Sacramento	69	68	2502	1235	468	1055	.444	1	11	.091	298	364	.819	156	339	495	312	197	4	95	38	193	36.3	17.9	7.2	4.5	.521
93-94	Sacramento	75	74	2702	1129	436	996	.438	6	17	.353	251	323	.777	168	394	562	305	189	2	104	50	180	36.0	15.1	7.5	4.1	.488
94-95	Sacramento	58	3	1064	327	131	312	.420	6	16	.375	59	84	.702	61	135	196	89	118	0	28	23	70	18.3	5.6	3.4	1.5	.330
95-96	Sacramento	54	5	810	246	86	217	.396	19	51	.373	55	75	.733	41	104	145	83	85	0	31	20	49	15.0	4.6	2.7	1.5	.370
96-97	Sacramento	41	0	521	139	45	136	.331	7	30	.233	42	48	.875	30	74	104	57	63	0	8	13	33	12.7	3.4	2.5	1.4	.324
NBA Season Totals		454	307	13472	5833	2242	5179	.433	43	141	.305	1306	1694	.771	798	2035	2833	1498	1106	6	514	361	972	29.7	12.8	6.2	3.3	....
95-96	Sacramento	4	0	77	38	15	33	.455	3	9	.333	5	7	.714	4	8	12	8	12	0	6	2	6	19.3	9.5	3.0	2.0	.469
NBA Playoff Totals		4	0	77	38	15	33	.455	3	9	.333	5	7	.714	4	8	12	8	12	0	6	2	6	19.3	9.5	3.0	2.0	....

• SIMON, Miles

Miles Julian Simon

Born: Nov. 21, 1975. Stockholm, Sweden. Height: 6'3". Weight: 202 lbs. Drafted: 1998 College: Arizona

YEAR	TEAM	GP	GS	MIN	PTS	FGM	FGA	FG%	3PM	3PA	3P%	FTM	FTA	FT%	ORB	DRB	TRB	AST	PF	DQ	STL	BLK	TO	MPG	PPG	RPG	APG	PCM
98-99	Orlando	5	0	19	2	1	5	.200	0	2	.000	0	0	.000	1	1	2	0	1	0	1	0	3	3.8	0.4	0.4	0.0	-.105
NBA Season Totals		5	0	19	2	1	5	.200	0	2	.000	0	0	.000	1	1	2	0	1	0	1	0	3	3.8	0.4	0.4	0.0	....

• SIMON, Walter

Walter J. Simon

Born: Dec. 1, 1939. Delcambre, LA, United States. Died: Oct.10, 1997. Height: 6'6". Weight: 200 lbs. Drafted: 1968 College: Benedict

YEAR	TEAM	GP	GS	MIN	PTS	FGM	FGA	FG%	3PM	3PA	3P%	FTM	FTA	FT%	ORB	DRB	TRB	AST	PF	DQ	STL	BLK	TO	MPG	PPG	RPG	APG	PCM
67-68	New Jersey-A	78	....	2518	1036	433	955	.453	1	15	.067	169	266	.635	....	....	524	212	272	8	....	....	173	32.3	13.3	6.7	2.7	.450
68-69	New York-A	68	....	2750	1436	570	1296	.440	6	27	.222	290	417	.695	181	373	554	234	289	5	....	....	183	40.4	21.1	8.1	3.4	.501
69-70	New York-A	81	....	2696	1162	454	1030	.441	1	20	.050	253	338	.749	152	322	474	294	296	5	....	....	197	33.3	14.3	5.9	3.6	.462
70-71	Kentucky-A	84	....	1411	649	274	578	.474	1	11	.091	100	156	.641	102	213	315	156	253	2	....	....	128	16.8	7.7	3.8	1.9	.511
71-72	Kentucky-A	67	....	1111	596	243	464	.524	1	10	.100	109	156	.699	72	161	233	137	157	3	....	....	72	16.6	8.9	3.5	2.0	.603
72-73	Kentucky-A	83	....	2403	1010	433	897	.483	1	17	.059	143	191	.749	122	273	395	336	271	6	....	....	156	29.0	12.2	4.8	4.0	.489
73-74	Kentucky-A	80	....	1164	525	233	492	.474	2	13	.154	57	68	.838	62	147	209	117	133	....	38	10	77	14.6	6.6	2.6	1.5	.476
ABA Season Totals		541	....	14053	6414	2640	5712	.462	13	113	.115	1121	1592	.704	691	1489	2704	1486	1671	29	38	10	986	26.0	11.9	5.0	2.7	....
69-70	New York-A	7	....	222	101	39	78	.500	0	6	.000	23	28	.821	....	....	53	21	....	1	....	....	....	31.7	14.4	7.6	3.0	....
70-71	Kentucky-A	19	....	385	174	70	155	.452	0	6	.000	34	49	.694	34	63	97	52	67	3	....	....	26	20.3	9.2	5.1	2.7	.554
71-72	Kentucky-A	6	....	99	39	16	39	.410	0	0	.000	7	8	.875	....	....	12	3	21	....	....	....	2	16.5	6.5	2.0	0.5	.233
72-73	Kentucky-A	19	....	639	211	92	207	.444	0	4	.000	27	31	.871	19	74	93	79	67	1	....	....	38	33.6	11.1	4.9	4.2	.385
73-74	Kentucky-A	8	....	90	30	14	35	.400	0	2	.000	2	2	1.000	3	6	9	7	17	....	4	3	5	11.3	3.8	1.1	0.9	.227
ABA Playoff Totals		59	....	1435	555	231	514	.449	0	18	.000	93	118	.788	56	143	264	162	172	5	4	3	71	24.3	9.4	4.5	2.7	....

• SIMPKINS, Dickey

LuBara Dixon (Dickey) Simpkins

Born: Apr. 6, 1972. Fort Washington, MD, United States. Height: 6'9". Weight: 248 lbs. Drafted: 1994 College: Providence

YEAR	TEAM	GP	GS	MIN	PTS	FGM	FGA	FG%	3PM	3PA	3P%	FTM	FTA	FT%	ORB	DRB	TRB	AST	PF	DQ	STL	BLK	TO	MPG	PPG	RPG	APG	PCM
94-95	Chicago	59	5	586	206	78	184	.424	0	0	.000	50	72	.694	60	91	151	37	72	0	10	7	47	9.9	3.5	2.6	0.6	.367
95-96	Chicago	60	12	685	216	77	160	.481	1	1	1.000	61	97	.629	66	90	156	38	78	0	9	8	54	11.4	3.6	2.6	0.6	.345
96-97	Chicago	48	0	395	91	31	93	.333	1	4	.250	28	40	.700	36	56	92	31	44	0	5	5	34	8.2	1.9	1.9	0.6	.262
97-98	Golden State	19	0	196	54	22	48	.458	0	1	.000	10	26	.385	19	27	46	16	19	0	5	2	19	10.3	2.8	2.4	0.8	.320
97-98	Chicago	21	0	237	78	26	41	.634	0	1	.000	26	44	.591	8	23	31	17	35	0	4	3	13	11.3	3.7	1.5	0.8	.343
98-99	Chicago	50	35	1448	456	150	324	.463	0	1	.000	156	242	.645	110	229	339	65	128	1	36	13	72	29.0	9.1	6.8	1.3	.386
99-00	Chicago	69	48	1651	287	111	274	.405	0	1	.000	65	120	.542	124	248	372	100	217	4	22	22	128	23.9	4.2	5.4	1.4	.234
01-02	Atlanta	1	0	3	0	0	0	.000	0	0	.000	0	0	.000	0	0	0	1	0	0	0	0	0	3.0	0.0	0.0	1.0	.365
NBA Season Totals		327	100	5201	1388	495	1124	.440	2	9	.222	396	641	.618	423	764	1187	305	593	5	91	60	367	15.9	4.2	3.6	0.9	....
97-98	Chicago	13	0	74	16	6	16	.375	0	0	.000	4	9	.444	4	9	13	3	10	0	2	1	3	5.7	1.2	1.0	0.2	.205
NBA Playoff Totals		13	0	74	16	6	16	.375	0	0	.000	4	9	.444	4	9	13	3	10	0	2	1	3	5.7	1.2	1.0	0.2	....

YEAR	TEAM	GP	GS	MIN	PTS	FGM	FGA	FG%	3PM	3PA	3P%	FTM	FTA	FT%	ORB	DRB	TRB	AST	PF	DQ	STL	BLK	TO	MPG	PPG	RPG	APG	PCM

• SIMPSON, Ralph

Ralph Derek Simpson

Born: Aug. 10, 1949. Detroit, MI, United States.   Height: 6'5".   Weight: 200 lbs.   Drafted: 1972   College: Michigan State

YEAR	TEAM	GP	GS	MIN	PTS	FGM	FGA	FG%	3PM	3PA	3P%	FTM	FTA	FT%	ORB	DRB	TRB	AST	PF	DQ	STL	BLK	TO	MPG	PPG	RPG	APG	PCM
70-71	Denver-A	81	....	1820	1152	460	1108	.415	17	60	.283	215	285	.754	125	106	231	168	152	1	....	....	186	22.5	14.2	2.9	2.1	.511
71-72	Denver-A	84	....	3006	2300	920	2000	.460	3	22	.136	457	568	.805	171	227	398	258	244	3	....	....	266	35.8	27.4	4.7	3.1	.610
72-73	Denver-A	81	....	2589	1890	732	1670	.438	5	24	.208	421	556	.757	140	231	371	222	241	2	127	....	283	32.0	23.3	4.6	2.7	.562
73-74	Denver-A	75	....	2244	1404	597	1395	.428	2	24	.083	208	276	.754	113	213	326	326	191	....	103	12	196	29.9	18.7	4.3	2.5	.493
74-75	Denver-A	82	....	2863	1692	694	1374	.505	1	12	.083	303	402	.754	108	283	391	442	214	....	166	19	314	34.9	20.6	4.8	5.4	.624
75-76	Denver-A	84	....	3121	1515	619	1211	.511	4	24	.167	273	350	.780	121	333	454	597	183	....	153	23	**360**	37.2	18.0	5.4	7.1	.621
76-77	Detroit	77	....	1597	850	356	834	.427	....	....	....	138	195	.708	48	133	181	180	100	0	68	5	....	20.7	11.0	2.4	2.3	.457
77-78	Detroit	32	....	739	340	143	346	.413	....	....	....	54	64	.844	27	55	82	87	48	1	32	3	77	23.1	10.6	2.6	2.7	.365
77-78	Denver	32	....	584	177	73	230	.317	....	....	....	31	40	.775	26	49	75	72	42	0	43	4	48	18.3	5.5	2.3	2.3	.279
78-79	Philadelphia	37	....	452	202	87	196	.444	....	....	....	28	40	.700	16	19	35	58	27	0	25	1	48	12.2	5.5	0.9	1.6	.359
78-79	New Jersey	32	....	527	222	87	237	.367	....	....	....	48	71	.676	19	42	61	68	30	0	12	4	54	16.5	6.9	1.9	2.1	.302
79-80	New Jersey	8	....	81	41	18	47	.383	0	2	.000	5	10	.500	6	5	11	14	3	0	9	0	12	10.1	5.1	1.4	1.8	.416
NBA Season Totals		218	....	3980	1832	764	1890	.404	0	2	.000	304	420	.724	142	303	445	479	250	1	189	17	239	18.3	8.4	2.0	2.2	....
ABA Season Totals		487	....	15643	9953	4022	8758	.459	32	166	.193	1877	2437	.770	778	1393	2171	1878	1224	6	549	54	1605	32.1	20.4	4.5	3.9	....
Career Totals		705	....	19623	11785	4786	10648	.449	32	168	.190	2181	2857	.763	920	1696	2616	2357	1474	7	738	71	1844	27.8	16.7	3.7	3.3	....
71-72	Denver-A	7	....	291	187	70	162	.432	0	2	.000	47	57	.825	....	....	32	24	21	0	....	....	18	41.6	26.7	4.6	3.4	.507
72-73	Denver-A	5	....	197	132	51	138	.370	2	6	.333	28	37	.757	8	16	24	14	20	1	....	....	15	39.4	26.4	4.8	2.8	.395
74-75	Denver-A	13	....	471	258	102	214	.477	1	6	.167	53	68	.779	18	47	65	74	30	....	22	3	55	36.2	19.8	5.0	5.7	.591
75-76	Denver-A	13	....	542	257	99	217	.456	1	2	.500	58	64	.906	17	44	61	73	33	....	21	4	58	41.7	19.8	4.7	5.6	.498
76-77	Detroit	2	....	17	0	0	9	.000	....	....	....	0	0	.000	1	2	3	1	1	0	0	0	....	8.5	0.0	1.5	0.5	-.263
77-78	Denver	13	....	225	102	43	95	.453	....	....	....	16	23	.696	5	14	19	38	20	0	4	2	21	17.3	7.8	1.5	2.9	.404
78-79	New Jersey	2	....	10	4	2	5	.400	....	....	....	0	0	.000	0	2	2	2	0	0	0	0	1	5.0	2.0	1.0	1.0	.441
NBA Playoff Totals		17	....	252	106	45	109	.413	....	....	....	16	23	.696	6	18	24	41	21	0	4	2	22	14.8	6.2	1.4	2.4	....
ABA Playoff Totals		38	....	1501	834	322	731	.440	4	16	.250	186	226	.823	43	107	182	185	104	1	43	7	146	39.5	21.9	4.8	4.9	....
Career Playoff Totals		55	....	1753	940	367	840	.437	4	16	.250	202	249	.811	49	125	206	226	125	1	47	9	168	31.9	17.1	3.7	4.1	....

• SIMS, Alvin

Alvin Sims

Born: Oct. 18, 1974. Paris, KY, United States.   Height: 6'4".   Weight: 235 lbs.   Drafted: —   College: Louisville

YEAR	TEAM	GP	GS	MIN	PTS	FGM	FGA	FG%	3PM	3PA	3P%	FTM	FTA	FT%	ORB	DRB	TRB	AST	PF	DQ	STL	BLK	TO	MPG	PPG	RPG	APG	PCM
98-99	Phoenix	4	0	25	11	4	10	.400	1	1	1.000	2	5	.400	3	1	4	5	2	0	2	0	6	6.3	2.8	1.0	1.3	.360
NBA Season Totals		4	0	25	11	4	10	.400	1	1	1.000	2	5	.400	3	1	4	5	2	0	2	0	6	6.3	2.8	1.0	1.3	....

• SIMS, Bob

Robert Antell (Bobby) Sims Jr.

Born: Oct. 9, 1938.   Height: 6'5".   Weight: 220 lbs.   Drafted: 1960   College: Pepperdine

YEAR	TEAM	GP	GS	MIN	PTS	FGM	FGA	FG%	3PM	3PA	3P%	FTM	FTA	FT%	ORB	DRB	TRB	AST	PF	DQ	STL	BLK	TO	MPG	PPG	RPG	APG	PCM
61-62	LA Lakers	19	....	171	63	22	59	.373	....	....	....	19	39	.487	....	....	27	12	40	1	....	....	....	9.0	3.3	1.4	0.6	.271
61-62	St. Louis	46	....	1174	446	171	432	.396	....	....	....	104	177	.588	....	....	156	142	147	3	....	....	....	25.5	9.7	3.4	3.1	.384
67-68	Anaheim-A	2	....	19	8	2	7	.286	0	0	.000	4	6	.667	....	....	1	2	6	1	....	....	0	9.5	4.0	0.5	1.0	.195
NBA Season Totals		65	....	1345	509	193	491	.393	....	....	....	123	216	.569	....	....	183	154	187	4	....	....	....	20.7	7.8	2.8	2.4	....
ABA Season Totals		2	....	19	8	2	7	.286	0	0	.000	4	6	.667	....	....	1	2	6	1	....	....	0	9.5	4.0	0.5	1.0	....
Career Totals		67	....	1364	517	195	498	.392	0	0	.000	127	222	.572	....	....	184	156	193	5	....	....	0	20.4	7.7	2.7	2.3	....
46-47	Sheboygan-N	1	....	....	2	1	....	....	....	....	....	0	0	.000	....	....	....	....	....	....	....	....	....	2.0	....	....	....	
NBL Playoff Totals		1	....	....	2	1	....	....	....	....	....	0	0	....	....	....	....	....	....	....	....	....	....	2.0	....	....	....	....

• SIMS, Bob

Bob Sims

Born: 1915.   Height: 6'6".   Weight: 220 lbs.   Drafted: —   College: Western Michigan

YEAR	TEAM	GP	GS	MIN	PTS	FGM	FGA	FG%	3PM	3PA	3P%	FTM	FTA	FT%	ORB	DRB	TRB	AST	PF	DQ	STL	BLK	TO	MPG	PPG	RPG	APG	PCM
46-47	Sheboygan-N	13	....	....	15	4	....	....	....	....	....	7	11	.636	....	....	....	....	....	....	....	....	....	1.2	....	....	....	
46-47	Tri-Cities-N	10	....	....	31	10	....	....	....	....	....	11	14	.786	....	....	....	....	....	....	....	....	....	3.1	....	....	....	
NBL Season Totals		23	....	....	46	14	....	....	....	....	....	18	25	....	....	....	....	....	....	....	....	....	....	2.0	....	....	....	....

• SIMS, Doug

H. Douglas Sims

Born: June 29, 1943. Elba, AL, United States.   Height: 6'7".   Weight: 195 lbs.   Drafted: —   College: Kent State

YEAR	TEAM	GP	GS	MIN	PTS	FGM	FGA	FG%	3PM	3PA	3P%	FTM	FTA	FT%	ORB	DRB	TRB	AST	PF	DQ	STL	BLK	TO	MPG	PPG	RPG	APG	PCM
68-69	Cincinnati	4	....	12	4	2	5	.400	....	....	....	0	0	.000	....	....	4	0	4	0	....	....	....	3.0	1.0	1.0	0.0	.264
NBA Season Totals		4	....	12	4	2	5	.400	....	....	....	0	0	.000	....	....	4	0	4	0	....	....	....	3.0	1.0	1.0	0.0	....

• SIMS, Scott

Scott Alan Sims

Born: Apr. 18, 1955. Kirksville, MO, United States.   Height: 6'1".   Weight: 170 lbs.   Drafted: 1977   College: Missouri

YEAR	TEAM	GP	GS	MIN	PTS	FGM	FGA	FG%	3PM	3PA	3P%	FTM	FTA	FT%	ORB	DRB	TRB	AST	PF	DQ	STL	BLK	TO	MPG	PPG	RPG	APG	PCM
77-78	San Antonio	12	....	95	30	10	26	.385	....	....	....	10	15	.667	5	8	13	20	16	0	3	0	19	7.9	2.5	1.1	1.7	.281
NBA Season Totals		12	....	95	30	10	26	.385	....	....	....	10	15	.667	5	8	13	20	16	0	3	0	19	7.9	2.5	1.1	1.7	....

• SINES, Johnny

John Sines

Born: Aug. 17, 1917. Died: Apr.1978.   Height: 6'1".   Weight: 190 lbs.   Drafted: —   College: Purdue

YEAR	TEAM	GP	GS	MIN	PTS	FGM	FGA	FG%	3PM	3PA	3P%	FTM	FTA	FT%	ORB	DRB	TRB	AST	PF	DQ	STL	BLK	TO	MPG	PPG	RPG	APG	PCM
38-39	Indianapolis-N	23	....	....	215	86	....	....	....	....	....	43	....	....	....	....	....	....	....	....	....	....	....	9.3	....	....	....	
39-40	Indianapolis-N	16	....	....	101	34	....	....	....	....	....	33	....	....	....	....	....	....	....	....	....	....	....	6.3	....	....	....	
41-42	Indianapolis-N	10	....	....	37	14	....	....	....	....	....	9	....	....	....	....	....	....	....	....	....	....	....	3.7	....	....	....	
NBL Season Totals		49	....	....	353	134	....	....	....	....	....	85	....	....	....	....	....	....	....	....	....	....	....	7.2	....	....	....	....

YEAR	TEAM	GP	GS	MIN	PTS	FGM	FGA	FG%	3PM	3PA	3P%	FTM	FTA	FT%	ORB	DRB	TRB	AST	PF	DQ	STL	BLK	TO	MPG	PPG	RPG	APG	PCM

• SINGLETON, McKinley
McKinley Singleton

Born: Oct. 29, 1961. Memphis, TN, United States.   Height: 6'5".   Weight: 175 lbs.   Drafted: 1984   College: Alabama-Birmingham

YEAR	TEAM	GP	GS	MIN	PTS	FGM	FGA	FG%	3PM	3PA	3P%	FTM	FTA	FT%	ORB	DRB	TRB	AST	PF	DQ	STL	BLK	TO	MPG	PPG	RPG	APG	PCM
86-87	New York	2	0	10	4	2	3	.667	0	1	.000	0	0	.000	0	0	0	1	1	0	0	0	0	5.0	2.0	0.0	0.5	.367
NBA Season Totals		2	0	10	4	2	3	.667	0	1	.000	0	0	.000	0	0	0	1	1	0	0	0	0	5.0	2.0	0.0	0.5	

• SINICOLA, Zeke
Emilio J. (Zeke) Sinicola

Born: Jan. 25, 1929.   Height: 5'10".   Weight: 165 lbs.   Drafted: 1951   College: Niagara

YEAR	TEAM	GP	GS	MIN	PTS	FGM	FGA	FG%	3PM	3PA	3P%	FTM	FTA	FT%	ORB	DRB	TRB	AST	PF	DQ	STL	BLK	TO	MPG	PPG	RPG	APG	PCM
51-52	Fort Wayne	3	....	15	2	1	4	.250	....	....	....	0	2	.000	....	....	1	0	2	0	....	....	....	5.0	0.7	0.3	0.0	-.056
53-54	Fort Wayne	9	....	53	11	4	16	.250	....	....	....	3	6	.500	....	....	1	3	8	0	....	....	....	5.9	1.2	0.1	0.3	.060
NBA Season Totals		12	....	68	13	5	20	.250	....	....	....	3	8	.375	....	....	2	3	10	0	....	....	....	5.7	1.1	0.2	0.3	

• SITKO, Steve
Steven Joseph Sitko

Born: Nov. 18, 1917. Fort Wayne, IN, United States. Died: Jan.8, 2003.   Height: 6'   Weight: 185 lbs.   Drafted: —   College: Notre Dame

YEAR	TEAM	GP	GS	MIN	PTS	FGM	FGA	FG%	3PM	3PA	3P%	FTM	FTA	FT%	ORB	DRB	TRB	AST	PF	DQ	STL	BLK	TO	MPG	PPG	RPG	APG	PCM
40-41	Wingfoots-N	8	....	....	6	3	....	....	....	....	....	0	....	....	....	....	....	....	....	....	....	....	....	0.8	....	....	....
44-45	Cleveland-N	1	....	....	0	0	....	....	....	....	....	0	....	....	....	....	....	....	....	....	....	....	....	0.0	....	....	....
NBL Season Totals		9	....	....	6	3	....	....	....	....	....	0	....	....	....	....	....	....	....	....	....	....	....	0.7	....	....	....

• SITTON, Charlie
Charles E. Sitton

Born: July 3, 1962. McMinnville, OR, United States.   Height: 6'8".   Weight: 210 lbs.   Drafted: 1984   College: Oregon State

YEAR	TEAM	GP	GS	MIN	PTS	FGM	FGA	FG%	3PM	3PA	3P%	FTM	FTA	FT%	ORB	DRB	TRB	AST	PF	DQ	STL	BLK	TO	MPG	PPG	RPG	APG	PCM
84-85	Dallas	43	0	304	91	39	94	.415	0	2	.000	13	25	.520	24	36	60	26	50	0	7	6	17	7.1	2.1	1.4	0.6	.299
NBA Season Totals		43	0	304	91	39	94	.415	0	2	.000	13	25	.520	24	36	60	26	50	0	7	6	17	7.1	2.1	1.4	0.6	

• SKARDA, Bob
Robert Skarda

Born: 1925.   Height: 6'3".   Weight: 190 lbs.   Drafted: —   College: Tufts

YEAR	TEAM	GP	GS	MIN	PTS	FGM	FGA	FG%	3PM	3PA	3P%	FTM	FTA	FT%	ORB	DRB	TRB	AST	PF	DQ	STL	BLK	TO	MPG	PPG	RPG	APG	PCM
47-48	Tri-Cities-N	8	....	....	10	5	....	....	....	....	....	0	1	.000	....	....	....	2	....	....	....	....	....	1.3	....	....	....
NBL Season Totals		8	....	....	10	5	....	....	....	....	....	0	1		....	....	....	2	....	....	....	....	....	1.3	....	....	....
47-48	Tri-Cities-N	6	....	....	3	1	....	....	....	....	....	1	2	.500	....	....	....	....	....	....	....	....	....	0.5	....	....	....
NBL Playoff Totals		6	....	....	3	1	....	....	....	....	....	1	2		....	....	....	....	....	....	....	....	....	0.5	....	....	....

• SKILES, Scott
Scott Allen Skiles

Born: Mar. 5, 1964. LaPorte, IN, United States.   Height: 6'1".   Weight: 180 lbs.   Drafted: 1986   College: Michigan State

YEAR	TEAM	GP	GS	MIN	PTS	FGM	FGA	FG%	3PM	3PA	3P%	FTM	FTA	FT%	ORB	DRB	TRB	AST	PF	DQ	STL	BLK	TO	MPG	PPG	RPG	APG	PCM
86-87	Milwaukee	13	0	205	49	18	62	.290	3	14	.214	10	12	.833	6	20	26	45	18	0	5	1	21	15.8	3.8	2.0	3.5	.278
87-88	Indiana	51	2	760	223	86	209	.411	6	20	.300	45	54	.833	11	55	66	180	97	0	22	3	77	14.9	4.4	1.3	3.5	.348
88-89	Indiana	80	13	1571	546	198	442	.448	20	75	.267	130	144	.903	21	128	149	390	151	1	64	2	176	19.6	6.8	1.9	4.9	.443
89-90	Orlando	70	32	1460	536	190	464	.409	52	132	.394	104	119	.874	23	136	159	334	126	0	36	4	91	20.9	7.7	2.3	4.8	.459
90-91	Orlando	79	66	2714	1357	462	1039	.445	93	228	.408	340	377	.902	57	213	270	660	192	2	89	4	253	34.4	17.2	3.4	8.4	.560
91-92	Orlando	75	63	2377	1057	359	868	.414	91	250	.364	248	277	.895	36	166	202	544	188	0	74	5	233	31.7	14.1	2.7	7.3	.467
92-93	Orlando	78	78	3086	1201	416	891	.467	80	235	.340	289	324	.892	52	238	290	735	244	4	86	2	265	39.6	15.4	3.7	9.4	.492
93-94	Orlando	82	46	2303	815	276	644	.429	68	165	.412	195	222	.878	42	147	189	503	171	1	47	2	197	28.1	9.9	2.3	6.1	.421
94-95	Washington	62	62	2077	805	265	583	.455	96	228	.421	179	202	.886	26	133	159	452	135	2	70	6	174	33.5	13.0	2.6	7.3	.467
95-96	Philadelphia	10	9	236	63	20	57	.351	15	34	.441	8	10	.800	1	15	16	38	21	0	7	0	16	23.6	6.3	1.6	3.8	.272
NBA Season Totals		600	371	16789	6652	2290	5259	.435	524	1381	.379	1548	1741	.889	275	1251	1526	3881	1343	10	500	29	1503	28.0	11.1	2.5	6.5	
93-94	Orlando	2	0	23	9	4	8	.500	0	2	.000	1	1	1.000	1	0	1	3	2	0	0	0	5	11.5	4.5	0.5	1.5	.174
NBA Playoff Totals		2	0	23	9	4	8	.500	0	2	.000	1	1	1.000	1	0	1	3	2	0	0	0	5	11.5	4.5	0.5	1.5	

• SKINNER, Al
Albert L. Skinner Jr.

Born: June 16, 1952. Mount Vernon, NY, United States.   Height: 6'3".   Weight: 190 lbs.   Drafted: 1974   College: Massachusetts

YEAR	TEAM	GP	GS	MIN	PTS	FGM	FGA	FG%	3PM	3PA	3P%	FTM	FTA	FT%	ORB	DRB	TRB	AST	PF	DQ	STL	BLK	TO	MPG	PPG	RPG	APG	PCM
74-75	New York-A	51	....	773	333	130	266	.489	1	3	.333	72	94	.766	42	78	120	121	111	....	29	13	68	15.2	6.5	2.4	2.4	.510
75-76	New York-A	83	....	2082	865	330	702	.470	2	8	.250	203	241	.842	96	211	307	280	252	....	91	50	169	25.1	10.4	3.7	3.4	.475
76-77	New York	79	....	2256	995	382	887	.431	....	....	....	231	292	.791	112	251	363	289	279	7	103	53	....	28.6	12.6	4.6	3.7	.467
77-78	New Jersey	8	....	277	121	41	101	.406	....	....	....	39	44	.886	14	38	52	33	34	2	13	5	29	34.6	15.1	6.5	4.1	.449
77-78	Detroit	69	....	1274	485	181	387	.468	....	....	....	123	159	.774	53	119	172	113	208	4	52	15	131	18.5	7.0	2.5	1.6	.329
78-79	New Jersey	23	....	334	182	55	125	.440	....	....	....	72	82	.878	12	30	42	49	53	0	22	2	39	14.5	7.9	1.8	2.1	.506
78-79	Philadelphia	22	....	309	99	36	89	.404	....	....	....	27	32	.844	15	29	44	40	61	2	18	1	33	14.0	4.5	2.0	1.8	.300
79-80	Philadelphia	2	....	10	2	1	2	.500	0	0	.000	0	0	.000	0	0	0	2	1	0	0	0	2	5.0	1.0	0.0	1.0	.102
NBA Season Totals		203	....	4460	1884	696	1591	.437	0	0	.000	492	609	.808	206	467	673	526	636	15	208	76	234	22.0	9.3	3.3	2.6	
ABA Season Totals		134	....	2855	1198	460	968	.475	3	11	.273	275	335	.821	138	289	427	401	363	....	120	63	237	21.3	8.9	3.2	3.0	
Career Totals		337	....	7315	3082	1156	2559	.452	3	11	.273	767	944	.813	344	756	1100	927	999	15	328	139	471	21.7	9.1	3.3	2.8	
74-75	New York-A	1	....	9	5	1	2	.500	0	0	.000	3	4	.750	1	1	2	0	1	....	0	0	1	9.0	5.0	2.0	0.0	.556
75-76	New York-A	13	....	287	128	44	101	.436	1	1	1.000	39	50	.780	24	24	48	28	45	....	21	2	25	22.1	9.8	3.7	2.2	.439
78-79	Philadelphia	5	....	47	18	6	17	.353	....	....	....	6	8	.750	5	5	10	11	6	0	3	1	6	9.4	3.6	2.0	2.2	.507
NBA Playoff Totals		5	....	47	18	6	17	.353	....	....	....	6	8	.750	5	5	10	11	6	0	3	1	6	9.4	3.6	2.0	2.2	
ABA Playoff Totals		14	....	296	133	45	103	.437	1	1	1.000	42	54	.778	25	25	50	28	46	....	21	2	26	21.1	9.5	3.6	2.0	
Career Playoff Totals		19	....	343	151	51	120	.425	1	1	1.000	48	62	.774	30	30	60	39	52	0	24	3	32	18.1	7.9	3.2	2.1	

SKINNER, Brian — Brian Skinner

Born: May 19, 1976. Temple, TX, United States. Height: 6'9". Weight: 255 lbs. Drafted: 1998 College: Baylor

YEAR	TEAM	GP	GS	MIN	PTS	FGM	FGA	FG%	3PM	3PA	3P%	FTM	FTA	FT%	ORB	DRB	TRB	AST	PF	DQ	STL	BLK	TO	MPG	PPG	RPG	APG	PCM
98-99	LA Clippers	21	0	258	86	33	71	.465	0	0	.000	20	33	.606	20	33	53	1	20	0	10	13	19	12.3	4.1	2.5	0.0	.346
99-00	LA Clippers	33	9	775	179	68	134	.507	0	0	.000	43	65	.662	63	138	201	11	75	0	16	44	37	23.5	5.4	6.1	0.3	.375
00-01	LA Clippers	39	23	584	160	64	161	.398	0	0	.000	32	59	.542	55	113	168	18	61	0	14	11	32	15.0	4.1	4.3	0.5	.339
01-02	Cleveland	65	8	1107	224	88	162	.543	0	0	.000	48	79	.608	93	188	281	17	130	1	24	61	42	17.0	3.4	4.3	0.3	.358
02-03	Philadelphia	77	9	1382	461	182	331	.550	0	0	.000	97	161	.602	136	230	366	19	176	1	47	53	62	17.9	6.0	4.8	0.2	.437
NBA Season Totals		235	49	4106	1110	435	859	.506	0	0	.000	240	397	.605	367	702	1069	66	462	2	111	182	192	17.5	4.7	4.5	0.3	....
02-03	Philadelphia	8	0	38	6	1	6	.167	0	1	.000	4	4	1.000	3	3	6	0	6	0	0	1	2	4.8	0.8	0.8	0.0	.086
NBA Playoff Totals		8	0	38	6	1	6	.167	0	1	.000	4	4	1.000	3	3	6	0	6	0	0	1	2	4.8	0.8	0.8	0.0	....

SKINNER, Tal — Talvin (Tab) Skinner

Born: Sept. 10, 1952. Berlin, MD, United States. Height: 6'5". Weight: 195 lbs. Drafted: 1974 College: Maryland Eastern Shore

YEAR	TEAM	GP	GS	MIN	PTS	FGM	FGA	FG%	3PM	3PA	3P%	FTM	FTA	FT%	ORB	DRB	TRB	AST	PF	DQ	STL	BLK	TO	MPG	PPG	RPG	APG	PCM
74-75	Seattle	73	....	1574	347	142	347	.409	....	....	....	63	97	.649	135	209	344	85	161	0	49	17	....	21.6	4.8	4.7	1.2	.305
75-76	Seattle	72	....	1224	313	132	285	.463	....	....	....	49	80	.613	89	175	264	67	116	1	50	7	....	17.0	4.3	3.7	0.9	.345
NBA Season Totals		145	....	2798	660	274	632	.434	....	....	....	112	177	.633	224	384	608	152	277	1	99	24	....	19.3	4.6	4.2	1.0	....
74-75	Seattle	9	....	211	56	21	45	.467	....	....	....	14	19	.737	11	27	38	12	26	0	9	2	....	23.4	6.2	4.2	1.3	.325
75-76	Seattle	6	....	86	19	4	14	.286	....	....	....	11	15	.733	6	9	15	7	9	0	5	2	....	14.3	3.2	2.5	1.2	.299
NBA Playoff Totals		15	....	297	75	25	59	.424	....	....	....	25	34	.735	17	36	53	19	35	0	14	4	....	19.8	5.0	3.5	1.3	....

SKOOG, Whitey — Myer Upton (Whitey) Skoog

Born: Nov. 2, 1926. Duluth, MN, United States. Height: 5'11". Weight: 180 lbs. Drafted: 1951 College: Minnesota

YEAR	TEAM	GP	GS	MIN	PTS	FGM	FGA	FG%	3PM	3PA	3P%	FTM	FTA	FT%	ORB	DRB	TRB	AST	PF	DQ	STL	BLK	TO	MPG	PPG	RPG	APG	PCM
51-52	Minneapolis	35	....	988	234	102	296	.345	....	....	....	30	38	.789	....		122	60	94	4			....	28.2	6.7	3.5	1.7	.227
52-53	Minneapolis	68	....	996	250	102	264	.386	....	....	....	46	61	.754	....		121	82	137	2			....	14.6	3.7	1.8	1.2	.271
53-54	Minneapolis	71	....	1877	496	212	530	.400	....	....	....	72	97	.742	....		224	179	234	5			....	26.4	7.0	3.2	2.5	.303
54-55	Minneapolis	72	....	2365	785	330	836	.395	....	....	....	125	155	.806	....		303	251	265	10			....	32.8	10.9	4.2	3.5	.353
55-56	Minneapolis	72	....	2311	835	340	854	.398	....	....	....	155	193	.803	....		291	255	232	5			....	32.1	11.6	4.0	3.5	.380
56-57	Minneapolis	23	....	656	200	78	220	.355	....	....	....	44	47	.936	....		72	76	65	1			....	28.5	8.7	3.1	3.3	.332
NBA Season Totals		341	....	9193	2800	1164	3000	.388	....	....	....	472	591	.799	....		1133	903	1027	27			....	27.0	8.2	3.3	2.6	....
52-53	Minneapolis	11	....	198	64	24	56	.429	....	....	....	16	20	.800	....		23	13	29	1			....	18.0	5.8	2.1	1.2	.314
53-54	Minneapolis	13	....	402	96	42	107	.393	....	....	....	12	21	.571	....		47	23	60	3			....	30.9	7.4	3.6	1.8	.220
54-55	Minneapolis	7	....	241	91	36	92	.391	....	....	....	19	21	.905	....		37	16	30	1			....	34.4	13.0	5.3	2.3	.351
55-56	Minneapolis	3	....	90	29	13	31	.419	....	....	....	3	11	.273	....		18	18	11	0			....	30.0	9.7	6.0	6.0	.490
NBA Playoff Totals		34	....	931	280	115	286	.402	....	....	....	50	73	.685	....		125	70	130	5			....	27.4	8.2	3.7	2.1	....

SLACK, Pres — Pres Slack

Born: 1911. Height: 6'2". Weight: 180 lbs. Drafted: — College: none

YEAR	TEAM	GP	GS	MIN	PTS	FGM	FGA	FG%	3PM	3PA	3P%	FTM	FTA	FT%	ORB	DRB	TRB	AST	PF	DQ	STL	BLK	TO	MPG	PPG	RPG	APG	PCM
37-38	Fort Wayne-N	16	....	....	86	38	....	....	....	....	....	10	....	....	....	....	....	....	....	....	....	....	....		5.4	....	....	....
38-39	Sheboygan-N	7	....	....	12	5	....	....	....	....	....	2	....	....	....	....	....	....	....	....	....	....	....		1.7	....	....	....
NBL Season Totals		23	....	....	98	43	....	....	....	....	....	12	....	....	....	....	....	....	....	....	....	....	....		4.3	....	....	....

SLADE, Jeff — Jeffrey Alan Slade

Born: Mar. 1, 1941. Height: 6'6". Weight: 220 lbs. Drafted: 1962 College: Kenyon

YEAR	TEAM	GP	GS	MIN	PTS	FGM	FGA	FG%	3PM	3PA	3P%	FTM	FTA	FT%	ORB	DRB	TRB	AST	PF	DQ	STL	BLK	TO	MPG	PPG	RPG	APG	PCM
62-63	Chicago	3	....	20	4	2	5	.400	....	....	....	0	1	.000	....	....	7	0	3	0	....	....	....	6.7	1.3	2.3	0.0	.279
NBA Season Totals		3	....	20	4	2	5	.400	....	....	....	0	1	.000	....	....	7	0	3	0	....	....	....	6.7	1.3	2.3	0.0	....

SLATER, Reggie — Reginald Dwayne Slater

Born: Aug. 27, 1970. Houston, TX, United States. Height: 6'7". Weight: 215 lbs. Drafted: — College: Wyoming

YEAR	TEAM	GP	GS	MIN	PTS	FGM	FGA	FG%	3PM	3PA	3P%	FTM	FTA	FT%	ORB	DRB	TRB	AST	PF	DQ	STL	BLK	TO	MPG	PPG	RPG	APG	PCM
94-95	Denver	25	0	236	120	40	81	.494	0	0	.000	40	55	.727	21	36	57	12	47	0	7	3	25	9.4	4.8	2.3	0.5	.443
95-96	Portland	4	0	20	6	3	5	.600	0	0	.000	0	0	.000	0	3	3	0	1	0	1	2	3	5.0	1.5	0.8	0.0	.324
95-96	Denver	4	0	26	14	6	11	.545	0	0	.000	2	5	.400	3	4	7	2	4	0	1	1	3	6.5	3.5	1.8	0.5	.530
95-96	Dallas	3	0	26	11	5	11	.455	0	0	.000	1	2	.500	1	4	5	0	6	0	0	0	3	8.7	3.7	1.7	0.0	.152
96-97	Toronto	26	0	406	203	82	149	.550	0	2	.000	39	75	.520	40	55	95	21	34	0	9	6	29	15.6	7.8	3.7	0.8	.507
97-98	Toronto	78	28	1662	625	211	459	.460	0	0	.000	203	322	.630	134	171	305	74	201	4	45	30	101	21.3	8.0	3.9	0.9	.353
98-99	Toronto	30	0	263	115	31	81	.383	0	0	.000	53	85	.624	36	34	70	5	50	0	3	3	25	8.8	3.8	2.3	0.2	.323
00-01	Minnesota	55	16	686	254	90	175	.514	0	0	.000	74	110	.673	78	108	186	26	126	1	18	9	43	12.5	4.6	3.4	0.5	.417
01-02	New Jersey	4	0	10	5	2	2	1.000	0	0	.000	1	1	1.000	0	2	2	0	1	0	0	0	1	2.5	1.3	0.5	0.0	.545
01-02	Atlanta	4	0	37	16	5	13	.385	0	0	.000	6	9	.667	5	2	7	1	2	0	1	1	0	9.3	4.0	1.8	0.3	.425
02-03	Minnesota	26	0	141	81	27	50	.540	0	0	.000	27	45	.600	18	13	31	4	31	0	6	1	9	5.4	3.1	1.2	0.2	.486
NBA Season Totals		259	44	3513	1450	502	1037	.484	0	2	.000	446	709	.629	336	432	768	145	503	5	91	56	242	13.6	5.6	3.0	0.6	....
00-01	Minnesota	4	0	52	13	6	16	.375	0	0	.000	1	2	.500	5	9	14	0	15	1	2	3	3	13.0	3.3	3.5	0.0	.215
NBA Playoff Totals		4	0	52	13	6	16	.375	0	0	.000	1	2	.500	5	9	14	0	15	1	2	3	3	13.0	3.3	3.5	0.0	....

YEAR TEAM	GP	GS	MIN	PTS	FGM	FGA	FG%	3PM	3PA	3P%	FTM	FTA	FT%	ORB	DRB	TRB	AST	PF	DQ	STL	BLK	TO	MPG	PPG	RPG	APG	PCM

• SLAUGHTER, Jim
James W. Slaughter

Born: May 13, 1928. Died: Aug.2, 1999.   Height: 6'11".   Weight: 210 lbs.   Drafted: 1951   College: South Carolina

YEAR TEAM	GP	GS	MIN	PTS	FGM	FGA	FG%	3PM	3PA	3P%	FTM	FTA	FT%	ORB	DRB	TRB	AST	PF	DQ	STL	BLK	TO	MPG	PPG	RPG	APG	PCM
51-52 Baltimore	28	....	525	147	53	165	.321	....	....	....	41	68	.603	....	....	148	25	81	0	....	....	....	18.8	5.3	5.3	0.9	.317
NBA Season Totals	28	....	525	147	53	165	.321	....	....	....	41	68	.603	....	....	148	25	81	0	....	....	....	18.8	5.3	5.3	0.9	....

• SLAUGHTER, Jose
Jose Dan Slaughter

Born: Sept. 9, 1960. Los Angeles, CA, United States.   Height: 6'5".   Weight: 205 lbs.   Drafted: 1982   College: Portland

YEAR TEAM	GP	GS	MIN	PTS	FGM	FGA	FG%	3PM	3PA	3P%	FTM	FTA	FT%	ORB	DRB	TRB	AST	PF	DQ	STL	BLK	TO	MPG	PPG	RPG	APG	PCM
82-83 Indiana	63	1	515	225	89	238	.374	9	41	.220	38	59	.644	34	34	68	52	93	0	36	7	44	8.2	3.6	1.1	0.8	.304
NBA Season Totals	63	1	515	225	89	238	.374	9	41	.220	38	59	.644	34	34	68	52	93	0	36	7	44	8.2	3.6	1.1	0.8	....

• SLAY, Tamar
Tamar Ulysses Slay

Born: Apr. 2, 1980. Beckley, WV, United States.   Height: 6'8".   Weight: 215 lbs.   Drafted: 2002   College: Marshall

YEAR TEAM	GP	GS	MIN	PTS	FGM	FGA	FG%	3PM	3PA	3P%	FTM	FTA	FT%	ORB	DRB	TRB	AST	PF	DQ	STL	BLK	TO	MPG	PPG	RPG	APG	PCM
02-03 New Jersey	36	0	274	92	39	103	.379	7	25	.280	7	10	.700	8	23	31	14	31	0	14	3	20	7.6	2.6	0.9	0.4	.216
NBA Season Totals	36	0	274	92	39	103	.379	7	25	.280	7	10	.700	8	23	31	14	31	0	14	3	20	7.6	2.6	0.9	0.4	....
02-03 New Jersey	6	0	11	3	1	4	.250	1	1	1.000	0	0	.000	0	0	0	0	1	0	0	0	2	1.8	0.5	0.0	0.0	-.181
NBA Playoff Totals	6	0	11	3	1	4	.250	1	1	1.000	0	0	.000	0	0	0	0	1	0	0	0	2	1.8	0.5	0.0	0.0	....

• SLOAN, Jerry
Gerald Eugene (Spider) Sloan

Born: Mar. 28, 1942. McLeansboro, IL, United States.   Height: 6'5".   Weight: 195 lbs.   Drafted: 1965   College: Evansville

YEAR TEAM	GP	GS	MIN	PTS	FGM	FGA	FG%	3PM	3PA	3P%	FTM	FTA	FT%	ORB	DRB	TRB	AST	PF	DQ	STL	BLK	TO	MPG	PPG	RPG	APG	PCM
65-66 Baltimore	59	....	952	338	120	289	.415	....	....	....	98	139	.705	....	....	230	110	176	7	....	....	....	16.1	5.7	3.9	1.9	.456
66-67 Chicago	80	....	2942	1390	525	1214	.432	....	....	....	340	427	.796	....	....	726	170	293	7	....	....	....	36.8	17.4	9.1	2.1	.501
67-68 Chicago	77	....	2454	1027	369	959	.385	....	....	....	289	386	.749	....	....	591	229	291	11	....	....	....	31.9	13.3	7.7	3.0	.468
68-69 Chicago	78	....	2939	1309	488	1170	.417	....	....	....	333	447	.745	....	....	619	276	313	6	....	....	....	37.7	16.8	7.9	3.5	.476
69-70 Chicago	53	....	1822	827	310	737	.421	....	....	....	207	318	.651	....	....	372	165	179	3	....	....	....	34.4	15.6	7.0	3.1	.459
70-71 Chicago	80	....	3140	1462	592	1342	.441	....	....	....	278	389	.715	....	....	701	281	289	5	....	....	....	39.3	18.3	8.8	3.5	.499
71-72 Chicago	82	....	3035	1328	535	1206	.444	....	....	....	258	391	.660	....	....	691	211	309	8	....	....	....	37.0	16.2	8.4	2.6	.459
72-73 Chicago	69	....	2412	696	301	733	.411	....	....	....	94	133	.707	....	....	475	151	235	5	....	....	....	35.0	10.1	6.9	2.2	.327
73-74 Chicago	77	....	2860	1018	412	921	.447	....	....	....	194	273	.711	150	406	556	149	273	3	183	10	....	37.1	13.2	7.2	1.9	.377
74-75 Chicago	78	....	2577	953	380	865	.439	....	....	....	193	258	.748	177	361	538	161	265	5	171	17	....	33.0	12.2	6.9	2.1	.404
75-76 Chicago	22	....	617	223	84	210	.400	....	....	....	55	78	.705	40	76	116	22	77	1	27	5	....	28.0	10.1	5.3	1.0	.319
NBA Season Totals	755	....	25750	10571	4116	9646	.427	....	....	....	2339	3239	.722	367	843	5615	1925	2700	61	381	32	....	34.1	14.0	7.4	2.5	....
65-66 Baltimore	2	....	34	13	5	12	.417	....	....	....	3	4	.750	....	....	16	6	6	1	....	....	....	17.0	6.5	8.0	3.0	.724
66-67 Chicago	3	....	71	30	12	31	.387	....	....	....	6	9	.667	....	....	10	1	7	0	....	....	....	23.7	10.0	3.3	0.3	.282
67-68 Chicago	5	....	137	43	12	37	.324	....	....	....	19	25	.760	....	....	32	12	19	0	....	....	....	27.4	8.6	6.4	2.4	.387
69-70 Chicago	5	....	190	74	29	74	.392	....	....	....	16	25	.640	....	....	39	11	18	0	....	....	....	38.0	14.8	7.8	2.2	.364
70-71 Chicago	7	....	284	119	51	117	.436	....	....	....	17	23	.739	....	....	63	17	25	1	....	....	....	40.6	17.0	9.0	2.4	.431
71-72 Chicago	4	....	170	63	26	64	.406	....	....	....	11	19	.579	....	....	35	10	18	1	....	....	....	42.5	15.8	8.8	2.5	.356
72-73 Chicago	7	....	292	104	45	103	.437	....	....	....	14	19	.737	....	....	59	14	31	1	....	....	....	41.7	14.9	8.4	2.0	.361
73-74 Chicago	6	....	240	100	39	88	.443	....	....	....	22	29	.759	18	44	62	12	17	0	7	1	....	40.0	16.7	10.3	2.0	.478
74-75 Chicago	13	....	470	170	75	163	.460	....	....	....	20	36	.556	24	72	96	26	46	0	20	0	....	36.2	13.1	7.4	2.0	.383
NBA Playoff Totals	52	....	1888	716	294	689	.427	....	....	....	128	189	.677	42	116	412	109	187	4	27	1	....	36.3	13.8	7.9	2.1	....

• SLUBY, Tom
Tom Griffin Sluby

Born: Feb. 18, 1962. Washington, DC, United States.   Height: 6'4".   Weight: 200 lbs.   Drafted: 1984   College: Notre Dame

YEAR TEAM	GP	GS	MIN	PTS	FGM	FGA	FG%	3PM	3PA	3P%	FTM	FTA	FT%	ORB	DRB	TRB	AST	PF	DQ	STL	BLK	TO	MPG	PPG	RPG	APG	PCM
84-85 Dallas	31	0	151	73	30	58	.517	0	2	.000	13	21	.619	5	7	12	16	18	0	3	0	12	4.9	2.4	0.4	0.5	.362
NBA Season Totals	31	0	151	73	30	58	.517	0	2	.000	13	21	.619	5	7	12	16	18	0	3	0	12	4.9	2.4	0.4	0.5	....

• SMART, Keith
Jonathan Keith Smart

Born: Sept. 21, 1964. Baton Rouge, LA, United States.   Height: 6'1".   Weight: 175 lbs.   Drafted: 1988   College: Indiana

YEAR TEAM	GP	GS	MIN	PTS	FGM	FGA	FG%	3PM	3PA	3P%	FTM	FTA	FT%	ORB	DRB	TRB	AST	PF	DQ	STL	BLK	TO	MPG	PPG	RPG	APG	PCM
88-89 San Antonio	2	0	12	2	0	2	.000	0	1	.000	2	2	1.000	0	1	1	2	0	0	0	0	2	6.0	1.0	0.5	1.0	.113
NBA Season Totals	2	0	12	2	0	2	.000	0	1	.000	2	2	1.000	0	1	1	2	0	0	0	0	2	6.0	1.0	0.5	1.0	....

• SMAWLEY, Belus
Belus Van Smawley

Born: Mar. 20, 1918. Golden Valley, NC, United States.   Height: 6'1".   Weight: 195 lbs.   Drafted: —   College: Appalachian State

YEAR TEAM	GP	GS	MIN	PTS	FGM	FGA	FG%	3PM	3PA	3P%	FTM	FTA	FT%	ORB	DRB	TRB	AST	PF	DQ	STL	BLK	TO	MPG	PPG	RPG	APG	PCM
46-47 St. Louis	22	....	....	262	113	352	.321	....	....	....	36	47	.766	....	....	....	10	37	....	....	....	....	11.9	....	0.5	....
47-48 St. Louis	48	....	....	535	212	688	.308	....	....	....	111	150	.740	....	....	....	18	88	....	....	....	....	11.1	....	0.4	....
48-49 St. Louis	59	....	....	914	352	946	.372	....	....	....	210	281	.747	....	....	....	183	145	....	....	....	....	15.5	....	3.1	....
49-50 St. Louis	61	....	....	834	287	832	.345	....	....	....	260	314	.828	....	....	....	215	160	....	....	....	....	13.7	....	3.5	....
50-51 Syr/Bal	60	....	....	731	252	663	.380	....	....	....	227	267	.850	....	178	....	161	145	4	....	....	....	12.2	3.0	2.7	....
51-52 Baltimore	11	....	....	40	13	63	.206	....	....	....	14	17	.824	....	....	18	8	9	0	....	....	....	3.6	1.6	0.7	....
NBA Season Totals	261	....	0	3316	1229	3544	.347	....	....	....	858	1076	.797	....	....	196	595	584	4	....	....	....	0.0	12.7	0.8	2.3	....
46-47 St. Louis	3	....	....	52	23	71	.324	....	....	....	6	11	.545	....	....	....	1	12	....	....	....	....	17.3	....	0.3	....
47-48 St. Louis	6	....	....	66	26	86	.302	....	....	....	14	18	.778	....	....	....	2	15	....	....	....	....	11.0	....	0.3	....
48-49 St. Louis	2	....	....	10	5	12	.417	....	....	....	0	0	.000	....	....	....	0	4	....	....	....	....	5.0	....	0.0	....
NBA Playoff Totals	11	....	....	128	54	169	.320	....	....	....	20	29	.690	....	....	....	3	31	....	....	....	....	11.6	....	0.3	....

• SMICK, Danny
Daniel Smick

Born: 1918. Height: 6'5". Weight: 215 lbs. Drafted: — College: Michigan

YEAR TEAM	GP	GS	MIN	PTS	FGM	FGA	FG%	3PM	3PA	3P%	FTM	FTA	FT%	ORB	DRB	TRB	AST	PF	DQ	STL	BLK	TO	MPG	PPG	RPG	APG	PCM
47-48 Flint-N	35	....	....	76	26	....	....	....	....	....	24	43	.558	....	....	....	....	63	....	....	....	....	....	2.2	....	....	....
NBL Season Totals	35	....	....	76	26	....	....	....	....	....	24	43	....	....	....	....	....	63	....	....	....	....	....	2.2	....	....	....

• SMILEY, Jack
A. John (Smiles) Smiley

Born: Dec. 22, 1922. Died: July30, 2000. Height: 6'3". Weight: 190 lbs. Drafted: — College: Illinois

YEAR TEAM	GP	GS	MIN	PTS	FGM	FGA	FG%	3PM	3PA	3P%	FTM	FTA	FT%	ORB	DRB	TRB	AST	PF	DQ	STL	BLK	TO	MPG	PPG	RPG	APG	PCM
47-48 Fort Wayne-N	60	....	....	300	105	....	....	....	....	....	90	135	.667	....	....	....	....	168	....	....	....	....	....	5.0	....	....	....
48-49 Fort Wayne	59	....	....	394	141	571	.247	....	....	....	112	164	.683	....	....	....	138	202	....	....	....	....	....	6.7	....	2.3	....
49-50 Anderson	12	....	....	24	6	50	.120	....	....	....	12	24	.500	....	....	....	14	35	....	....	....	....	....	2.0	....	1.2	....
49-50 Waterloo	47	....	....	308	92	314	.293	....	....	....	124	177	.701	....	....	....	147	158	....	....	....	....	....	6.6	....	3.1	....
NBA Season Totals	118	....	....	726	239	935	.256	....	....	....	248	365	.679	....	....	....	299	395	....	....	....	....	....	6.2	....	2.5	....
NBL Season Totals	60	....	....	300	105	....	....	....	....	....	90	135	....	....	....	....	....	168	....	....	....	....	....	5.0	....	....	....
Career Totals	178	....	....	1026	344	935	....	....	....	....	338	500	....	....	....	....	299	563	....	....	....	....	....	5.8	....	1.7	....
47-48 Fort Wayne-N	4	....	....	20	7	....	....	....	....	....	6	8	.750	....	....	....	....	....	....	....	....	....	....	5.0	....	....	....
NBL Playoff Totals	4	....	....	20	7	....	....	....	....	....	6	8	....	....	....	....	....	....	....	....	....	....	....	5.0	....	....	....

• SMITH, Adrian
Adrian Howard (Odie) Smith

Born: Oct. 5, 1936. Farmington, KY, United States. Height: 6'1". Weight: 180 lbs. Drafted: — College: Kentucky

YEAR TEAM	GP	GS	MIN	PTS	FGM	FGA	FG%	3PM	3PA	3P%	FTM	FTA	FT%	ORB	DRB	TRB	AST	PF	DQ	STL	BLK	TO	MPG	PPG	RPG	APG	PCM
61-62 Cincinnati	80	....	1462	576	202	499	.405	....	....	....	172	222	.775	....	....	151	167	101	0	....	....	....	18.3	7.2	1.9	2.1	.415
62-63 Cincinnati	79	....	1522	705	241	544	.443	....	....	....	223	275	.811	....	....	174	141	157	1	....	....	....	19.3	8.9	2.2	1.8	.454
63-64 Cincinnati	66	....	1524	622	234	576	.406	....	....	....	154	197	.782	....	....	147	145	164	1	....	....	....	23.1	9.4	2.2	2.2	.372
64-65 Cincinnati	80	....	2745	1210	463	1016	.456	....	....	....	284	342	.830	....	....	220	240	199	2	....	....	....	34.3	15.1	2.8	3.0	.419
65-66 Cincinnati	80	....	2982	1470	531	1310	.405	....	....	....	408	480	.850	....	....	287	256	276	1	....	....	....	37.3	18.4	3.6	3.2	.422
66-67 Cincinnati	81	....	2636	1347	502	1147	.438	....	....	....	343	380	**.903**	....	....	205	187	272	0	....	....	....	32.5	16.6	2.5	2.3	.417
67-68 Cincinnati	82	....	2783	1280	480	1035	.464	....	....	....	320	386	.829	....	....	185	272	259	6	....	....	....	33.9	15.6	2.3	3.3	.425
68-69 Cincinnati	73	....	1336	703	243	562	.432	....	....	....	217	269	.807	....	....	105	127	166	1	....	....	....	18.3	9.6	1.4	1.7	.435
69-70 Cincinnati	32	....	453	172	60	148	.405	....	....	....	52	60	.867	....	....	33	45	56	0	....	....	....	14.2	5.4	1.0	1.4	.322
69-70 San Francisco	45	....	634	286	93	268	.347	....	....	....	100	110	.909	....	....	49	87	66	0	....	....	....	14.1	6.4	1.1	1.9	.377
70-71 San Francisco	21	....	247	111	38	89	.427	....	....	....	35	41	.854	....	....	24	30	24	0	....	....	....	11.8	5.3	1.1	1.4	.442
71-72 Virginia-A	53	....	686	268	87	195	.446	2	11	.182	92	103	.893	14	32	46	42	89	0	....	....	34	12.9	5.1	0.9	0.8	.316
NBA Season Totals	719	....	18324	8482	3087	7194	.429	....	....	....	2308	2762	.836	....	....	1580	1697	1740	12	....	....	....	25.5	11.8	2.2	2.4	....
ABA Season Totals	53	....	686	268	87	195	.446	2	11	.182	92	103	.893	14	32	46	42	89	0	....	....	34	12.9	5.1	0.9	0.8	....
Career Totals	772	....	19010	8750	3174	7389	.430	2	11	.182	2400	2865	.838	14	32	1626	1739	1829	12	....	....	34	24.6	11.3	2.1	2.3	....
61-62 Cincinnati	4	....	53	21	8	19	.421	....	....	....	5	5	1.000	....	....	5	3	2	0	....	....	....	13.3	5.3	1.3	0.8	.362
62-63 Cincinnati	12	....	200	97	33	82	.402	....	....	....	31	44	.705	....	....	16	28	19	0	....	....	....	16.7	8.1	1.3	2.3	.460
63-64 Cincinnati	7	....	66	21	8	26	.308	....	....	....	5	7	.714	....	....	9	4	8	0	....	....	....	9.4	3.0	1.3	0.6	.227
64-65 Cincinnati	4	....	150	57	18	48	.375	....	....	....	21	22	.955	....	....	11	21	11	0	....	....	....	37.5	14.3	2.8	5.3	.424
65-66 Cincinnati	5	....	157	65	22	59	.373	....	....	....	21	22	.955	....	....	12	13	12	0	....	....	....	31.4	13.0	2.4	2.6	.357
66-67 Cincinnati	4	....	120	45	18	48	.375	....	....	....	9	12	.750	....	....	8	11	8	0	....	....	....	30.0	11.3	2.0	2.8	.303
71-72 Virginia-A	11	....	297	125	46	95	.484	1	5	.200	32	37	.865	2	17	19	17	28	0	....	....	11	27.0	11.4	1.7	1.5	.347
NBA Playoff Totals	36	....	746	306	107	282	.379	....	....	....	92	112	.821	....	....	61	80	60	0	....	....	....	20.7	8.5	1.7	2.2	....
ABA Playoff Totals	11	....	297	125	46	95	.484	1	5	.200	32	37	.865	2	17	19	17	28	0	....	....	11	27.0	11.4	1.7	1.5	....
Career Playoff Totals	47	....	1043	431	153	377	.406	1	5	.200	124	149	.832	2	17	80	97	88	0	....	....	11	22.2	9.2	1.7	2.1	....

• SMITH, Al
Alan Richard Smith

Born: Jan. 15, 1947. Peoria, IL, United States. Height: 6'1". Weight: 185 lbs. Drafted: 1971 College: Bradley

YEAR TEAM	GP	GS	MIN	PTS	FGM	FGA	FG%	3PM	3PA	3P%	FTM	FTA	FT%	ORB	DRB	TRB	AST	PF	DQ	STL	BLK	TO	MPG	PPG	RPG	APG	PCM
71-72 Denver-A	83	....	1764	769	292	675	.433	32	107	.299	153	211	.725	85	141	226	249	244	4	....	....	163	21.3	9.3	2.7	3.0	.441
72-73 Denver-A	83	....	2343	919	315	767	.411	17	90	.189	272	352	.773	68	146	214	477	295	7	....	....	261	28.2	11.1	2.6	5.7	.453
73-74 Denver-A	76	....	2435	831	311	779	.399	22	72	.306	187	242	.773	56	185	241	**619**	257	....	100	7	273	32.0	10.9	3.2	**8.1**	**.497**
74-75 Utah-A	80	....	2037	641	227	582	.390	30	94	.319	157	193	.813	39	108	147	375	230	....	59	3	201	25.5	8.0	1.8	4.7	.371
75-76 Utah-A	15	....	392	138	42	105	.400	6	17	.353	48	59	.814	13	24	37	73	45	....	10	2	29	26.1	9.2	2.5	4.9	.436
ABA Season Totals	337	....	8971	3298	1187	2908	.408	107	380	.282	817	1057	.773	261	604	865	1793	1071	11	169	12	927	26.6	9.8	2.6	5.3	....
71-72 Denver-A	7	....	99	30	12	27	.444	2	3	.667	4	5	.800	....	....	18	7	14	0	....	....	7	14.1	4.3	2.6	1.0	.342
72-73 Denver-A	5	....	185	48	15	54	.278	0	2	.000	18	20	.900	10	15	25	26	17	0	....	....	18	37.0	9.6	5.0	5.2	.300
74-75 Utah-A	6	....	165	84	32	73	.438	3	11	.273	17	20	.850	2	10	12	35	24	....	2	0	22	27.5	14.0	2.0	5.8	.516
ABA Playoff Totals	18	....	449	162	59	154	.383	5	16	.313	39	45	.867	12	25	55	68	55	0	2	0	47	24.9	9.0	3.1	3.8	....

• SMITH, Bill
William F. Smith

Born: Apr. 26, 1939. Height: 6'5". Weight: 190 lbs. Drafted: 1961 College: St. Peter's

YEAR TEAM	GP	GS	MIN	PTS	FGM	FGA	FG%	3PM	3PA	3P%	FTM	FTA	FT%	ORB	DRB	TRB	AST	PF	DQ	STL	BLK	TO	MPG	PPG	RPG	APG	PCM
61-62 New York	9	....	83	23	8	33	.242	....	....	....	7	8	.875	....	....	16	7	6	0	....	....	....	9.2	2.6	1.8	0.8	.262
NBA Season Totals	9	....	83	23	8	33	.242	....	....	....	7	8	.875	....	....	16	7	6	0	....	....	....	9.2	2.6	1.8	0.8	....

• SMITH, Bingo
Robert (Bingo) Smith

Born: Feb. 26, 1946. Memphis, TN, United States. Height: 6'5". Weight: 195 lbs. Drafted: 1969 College: Tulsa

YEAR TEAM	GP	GS	MIN	PTS	FGM	FGA	FG%	3PM	3PA	3P%	FTM	FTA	FT%	ORB	DRB	TRB	AST	PF	DQ	STL	BLK	TO	MPG	PPG	RPG	APG	PCM
69-70 San Diego	75	....	1198	550	242	567	.427	....	....	....	66	96	.688	....	....	328	75	119	0	....	....	....	16.0	7.3	4.4	1.0	.477
70-71 Cleveland	77	....	2332	1168	495	1106	.448	....	....	....	178	234	.761	....	....	429	258	175	4	....	....	....	30.3	15.2	5.6	3.4	.517
71-72 Cleveland	82	....	2734	1232	527	1190	.443	....	....	....	178	224	.795	....	....	502	247	222	3	....	....	....	33.3	15.0	6.1	3.0	.460
72-73 Cleveland	73	....	1068	600	268	603	.444	....	....	....	64	81	.790	....	....	199	108	80	0	....	....	....	14.6	8.2	2.7	1.5	.529

YEAR	TEAM	GP	GS	MIN	PTS	FGM	FGA	FG%	3PM	3PA	3P%	FTM	FTA	FT%	ORB	DRB	TRB	AST	PF	DQ	STL	BLK	TO	MPG	PPG	RPG	APG	PCM
73-74	Cleveland	82	....	2612	1211	536	1179	.455	....	....	....	139	169	.822	134	301	435	198	242	4	89	30	....	31.9	14.8	5.3	2.4	.439
74-75	Cleveland	82	....	2636	1302	585	1212	.483	....	....	....	132	160	.825	108	299	407	229	227	1	80	26	....	32.1	15.9	5.0	2.8	.481
75-76	Cleveland	81	....	2338	1101	495	1121	.442	....	....	....	111	136	.816	83	258	341	155	231	0	58	36	....	28.9	13.6	4.2	1.9	.395
76-77	Cleveland	81	....	2135	1174	513	1149	.446	....	....	....	148	181	.818	92	225	317	152	211	3	61	30	....	26.4	14.5	3.9	1.9	.453
77-78	Cleveland	82	....	1581	846	369	840	.439	....	....	....	108	135	.800	65	142	207	91	155	1	38	21	82	19.3	10.3	2.5	1.1	.391
78-79	Cleveland	72	....	1650	805	361	784	.460	....	....	....	83	106	.783	77	129	206	121	188	2	43	7	72	22.9	11.2	2.9	1.7	.381
79-80	Cleveland	8	....	135	74	33	72	.458	1	5	.200	7	8	.875	2	12	14	7	21	0	3	2	9	16.9	9.3	1.8	0.9	.337
79-80	San Diego	70	....	1988	819	352	819	.430	22	76	.289	93	107	.869	92	153	245	93	188	4	59	15	70	28.4	11.7	3.5	1.3	.318
NBA Season Totals		865	....	22407	10882	4776	10642	.449	23	81	.284	1307	1637	.798	653	1519	3630	1734	2059	22	431	167	233	25.9	12.6	4.2	2.0	....
75-76	Cleveland	13	....	379	164	71	164	.433	....	....	....	22	25	.880	11	32	43	30	41	1	11	3	....	29.2	12.6	3.3	2.3	.360
76-77	Cleveland	3	....	57	21	9	39	.231	....	....	....	3	3	1.000	3	5	8	4	5	0	3	1	....	19.0	7.0	2.7	1.3	.077
77-78	Cleveland	2	....	34	16	8	13	.615	....	....	....	0	0	.000	2	1	3	1	2	0	0	0	1	17.0	8.0	1.5	0.5	.401
NBA Playoff Totals		18	....	470	201	88	216	.407	....	....	....	25	28	.893	16	38	54	35	48	1	14	4	1	26.1	11.2	3.0	1.9	....

• SMITH, Bobby
Robert Joseph Smith

Born: Aug. 20, 1937. Height: 6'4". Weight: 190 lbs. Drafted: 1959 College: West Virginia

YEAR	TEAM	GP	GS	MIN	PTS	FGM	FGA	FG%	3PM	3PA	3P%	FTM	FTA	FT%	ORB	DRB	TRB	AST	PF	DQ	STL	BLK	TO	MPG	PPG	RPG	APG	PCM
59-60	Minneapolis	10	....	130	37	13	54	.241	....	....	....	11	16	.688	....	....	33	14	10	0	....	....	....	13.0	3.7	3.3	1.4	.328
61-62	LA Lakers	3	....	7	0	0	1	.000	....	....	....	0	0	.000	....	....	0	0	1	0	....	....	....	2.3	0.0	0.0	0.0	-.167
NBA Season Totals		13	....	137	37	13	55	.236	....	....	....	11	16	.688	....	....	33	14	11	0	....	....	....	10.5	2.8	2.5	1.1	....

• SMITH, Charles
Charles Daniel Smith

Born: July 16, 1965. Bridgeport, CT, United States.   Height: 6'10".   Weight: 230 lbs.   Drafted: 1988   College: Pittsburgh

YEAR	TEAM	GP	GS	MIN	PTS	FGM	FGA	FG%	3PM	3PA	3P%	FTM	FTA	FT%	ORB	DRB	TRB	AST	PF	DQ	STL	BLK	TO	MPG	PPG	RPG	APG	PCM
88-89	LA Clippers	71	56	2161	1155	435	878	.495	0	3	.000	285	393	.725	173	292	465	103	273	6	68	89	149	30.4	16.3	6.5	1.5	.516
89-90	LA Clippers	78	76	2732	1645	595	1145	.520	1	12	.083	454	572	.794	177	347	524	114	294	6	86	119	164	35.0	21.1	6.7	1.5	.581
90-91	LA Clippers	74	74	2703	1480	548	1168	.469	0	7	.000	384	484	.793	216	392	608	134	267	4	81	145	163	36.5	20.0	8.2	1.8	.555
91-92	LA Clippers	49	25	1310	714	251	539	.466	0	6	.000	212	270	.785	95	206	301	56	159	2	41	98	69	26.7	14.6	6.1	1.1	.573
92-93	New York	81	68	2172	1003	358	764	.469	0	2	.000	287	367	.782	170	262	432	142	254	4	48	96	154	26.8	12.4	5.3	1.8	.467
93-94	New York	43	21	1105	447	176	397	.443	8	16	.500	87	121	.719	66	99	165	50	144	4	26	45	95	25.7	10.4	3.8	1.2	.338
94-95	New York	76	58	2150	966	352	747	.471	7	31	.226	255	322	.792	144	180	324	120	286	6	49	95	144	28.3	12.7	4.3	1.6	.401
95-96	New York	41	4	890	303	114	294	.388	2	15	.133	73	103	.709	59	101	160	29	124	2	18	51	62	21.7	7.4	3.9	0.7	.280
95-96	San Antonio	32	30	826	306	130	284	.458	0	0	.000	46	60	.767	74	128	202	36	100	1	32	29	45	25.8	9.6	6.3	1.1	.425
96-97	San Antonio	19	7	329	88	34	84	.405	0	1	.000	20	26	.769	18	47	65	14	44	0	13	22	23	17.3	4.6	3.4	0.7	.319
NBA Season Totals		564	419	16378	8107	2993	6300	.475	18	93	.194	2103	2718	.774	1192	2054	3246	798	1945	35	462	789	1038	29.0	14.4	5.8	1.4	....
91-92	LA Clippers	5	5	148	58	22	56	.393	0	0	.000	14	15	.933	10	18	28	9	24	2	4	12	10	29.6	11.6	5.6	1.8	.379
92-93	New York	15	15	388	167	65	138	.471	0	0	.000	37	50	.740	27	33	60	20	52	1	9	14	29	25.9	11.1	4.0	1.3	.362
93-94	New York	25	18	612	221	85	177	.480	0	3	.000	51	70	.729	34	61	95	25	92	0	12	24	32	24.5	8.8	3.8	1.0	.333
94-95	New York	11	11	303	119	51	95	.537	0	2	.000	17	30	.567	20	22	42	13	44	1	13	17	24	27.5	10.8	3.8	1.2	.362
95-96	San Antonio	10	8	165	51	24	48	.500	0	0	.000	3	8	.375	11	26	37	10	28	0	7	10	8	16.5	5.1	3.7	1.0	.405
NBA Playoff Totals		66	57	1616	616	247	514	.481	0	5	.000	122	173	.705	102	160	262	77	240	4	45	77	103	24.5	9.3	4.0	1.2	....

• SMITH, Charles
Charles Cornelius Smith

Born: Aug. 22, 1975. Fort Worth, TX, United States.   Height: 6'4".   Weight: 194 lbs.   Drafted: 1997   College: New Mexico

YEAR	TEAM	GP	GS	MIN	PTS	FGM	FGA	FG%	3PM	3PA	3P%	FTM	FTA	FT%	ORB	DRB	TRB	AST	PF	DQ	STL	BLK	TO	MPG	PPG	RPG	APG	PCM
97-98	Miami	11	0	32	10	4	18	.222	1	3	.333	1	2	.500	5	3	8	2	3	0	2	1	6	2.9	0.9	0.7	0.2	.066
97-98	LA Clippers	23	0	260	109	45	107	.421	14	44	.318	5	9	.556	8	11	19	19	21	0	10	5	21	11.3	4.7	0.8	0.8	.282
98-99	LA Clippers	23	10	317	84	35	97	.361	7	33	.212	7	16	.438	7	17	24	13	35	0	17	14	20	13.8	3.7	1.0	0.6	.173
01-02	San Antonio	60	22	1141	441	182	428	.425	35	131	.267	42	65	.646	34	99	133	80	114	1	52	44	59	19.0	7.4	2.2	1.3	.348
02-03	Portland	3	0	13	5	1	4	.250	0	1	.000	3	4	.750	0	0	0	1	3	0	1	0	1	4.3	1.7	0.0	0.3	.119
NBA Season Totals		120	32	1763	649	267	654	.408	57	212	.269	58	96	.604	54	130	184	115	176	1	82	64	107	14.7	5.4	1.5	1.0	....
01-02	San Antonio	4	0	19	5	2	3	.667	0	0	.000	1	2	.500	2	1	3	2	5	0	2	1	3	4.8	1.3	0.8	0.5	.331
NBA Playoff Totals		4	0	19	5	2	3	.667	0	0	.000	1	2	.500	2	1	3	2	5	0	2	1	3	4.8	1.3	0.8	0.5	....

• SMITH, Charles
Charles Edward Smith IV

Born: Nov. 29, 1967. Washington, DC, United States.   Height: 6'1".   Weight: 160 lbs.   Drafted: —   College: Georgetown

YEAR	TEAM	GP	GS	MIN	PTS	FGM	FGA	FG%	3PM	3PA	3P%	FTM	FTA	FT%	ORB	DRB	TRB	AST	PF	DQ	STL	BLK	TO	MPG	PPG	RPG	APG	PCM
89-90	Boston	60	0	519	171	59	133	.444	0	7	.000	53	76	.697	14	55	69	103	75	0	35	3	36	8.7	2.9	1.2	1.7	.447
90-91	Boston	5	0	30	9	3	7	.429	0	0	.000	3	5	.600	0	2	2	6	7	0	1	0	3	6.0	1.8	0.4	1.2	.249
95-96	Minnesota	8	0	39	6	3	10	.300	0	3	.000	0	2	.000	0	5	5	6	7	0	1	0	5	4.9	0.8	0.6	0.8	.064
NBA Season Totals		73	0	588	186	65	150	.433	0	10	.000	56	83	.675	14	62	76	115	89	0	37	3	44	8.1	2.5	1.0	1.6	....
89-90	Boston	3	0	9	2	1	2	.500	0	0	.000	0	0	.000	1	0	1	3	0	0	1	0	0	3.0	0.7	0.3	1.0	.681
NBA Playoff Totals		3	0	9	2	1	2	.500	0	0	.000	0	0	.000	1	0	1	3	0	0	1	0	0	3.0	0.7	0.3	1.0	....

• SMITH, Chris
Chris G. Smith

Born: May 17, 1970. Bridgeport, CT, United States.   Height: 6'3".   Weight: 190 lbs.   Drafted: 1992   College: Connecticut

YEAR	TEAM	GP	GS	MIN	PTS	FGM	FGA	FG%	3PM	3PA	3P%	FTM	FTA	FT%	ORB	DRB	TRB	AST	PF	DQ	STL	BLK	TO	MPG	PPG	RPG	APG	PCM
92-93	Minnesota	80	6	1266	347	125	289	.433	2	14	.143	95	120	.792	32	64	96	196	96	1	48	15	64	15.8	4.3	1.2	2.5	.344
93-94	Minnesota	80	16	1617	473	184	423	.435	10	39	.256	95	141	.674	15	107	122	285	131	1	38	18	104	20.2	5.9	1.5	3.6	.340
94-95	Minnesota	64	17	1073	320	116	265	.438	47	108	.435	41	63	.651	14	59	73	146	119	0	32	22	51	16.8	5.0	1.1	2.3	.317
NBA Season Totals		224	39	3956	1140	425	977	.435	59	161	.366	231	324	.713	61	230	291	627	346	2	118	55	219	17.7	5.1	1.3	2.8	....

Total Basketball

YEAR	TEAM	GP	GS	MIN	PTS	FGM	FGA	FG%	3PM	3PA	3P%	FTM	FTA	FT%	ORB	DRB	TRB	AST	PF	DQ	STL	BLK	TO	MPG	PPG	RPG	APG	PCM

• SMITH, Clinton
Clinton Smith

Born: Jan. 19, 1964. Cleveland, OH, United States. Height: 6'6". Weight: 210 lbs. Drafted: 1986 College: Cleveland State

YEAR	TEAM	GP	GS	MIN	PTS	FGM	FGA	FG%	3PM	3PA	3P%	FTM	FTA	FT%	ORB	DRB	TRB	AST	PF	DQ	STL	BLK	TO	MPG	PPG	RPG	APG	PCM
86-87	Golden State	41	0	341	127	50	117	.427	0	2	.000	27	36	.750	26	30	56	45	36	0	13	1	25	8.3	3.1	1.4	1.1	.392
90-91	Washington	5	0	45	7	2	4	.500	0	0	.000	3	6	.500	2	2	4	4	3	0	1	0	1	9.0	1.4	0.8	0.8	.230
NBA Season Totals		46	0	386	134	52	121	.430	0	2	.000	30	42	.714	28	32	60	49	39	0	14	1	26	8.4	2.9	1.3	1.1	....

• SMITH, Deb
Delbert Bower Smith

Born: Jan. 7, 1920. Height: 6'3". Weight: 180 lbs. Drafted: — College: Utah

YEAR	TEAM	GP	GS	MIN	PTS	FGM	FGA	FG%	3PM	3PA	3P%	FTM	FTA	FT%	ORB	DRB	TRB	AST	PF	DQ	STL	BLK	TO	MPG	PPG	RPG	APG	PCM
46-47	St. Louis	48	....	....	73	32	119	.269	....	....	....	9	21	.429	....	....	....	6	47	....	....	....	....	....	1.5	....	0.1	
NBA Season Totals		48	....	....	73	32	119	.269	....	....	....	9	21	.429	....	....	....	6	47	....	....	....	....	....	1.5	....	0.1	
46-47	St. Louis	1	....	....	0	0	0	.000	....	....	....	0	1	.000	....	....	....	0	1	....	....	....	....	....	0.0	....	0.0	
NBA Playoff Totals		1	....	....	0	0	0	.000	....	....	....	0	1	.000	....	....	....	0	1	....	....	....	....	....	0.0	....	0.0	

• SMITH, Derek
Derek Ervin Smith

Born: Nov. 1, 1961. Hogansville, GA, United States. Died: Aug.10, 1996. Height: 6'6". Weight: 205 lbs. Drafted: 1982 College: Louisville

YEAR	TEAM	GP	GS	MIN	PTS	FGM	FGA	FG%	3PM	3PA	3P%	FTM	FTA	FT%	ORB	DRB	TRB	AST	PF	DQ	STL	BLK	TO	MPG	PPG	RPG	APG	PCM
82-83	Golden State	27	0	154	59	21	51	.412	0	2	.000	17	25	.680	10	28	38	2	40	0	0	4	11	5.7	2.2	1.4	0.1	.263
83-84	San Diego	61	20	1297	600	238	436	.546	1	6	.167	123	163	.755	54	116	170	82	165	2	33	22	79	21.3	9.8	2.8	1.3	.419
84-85	LA Clippers	80	80	2762	1767	682	1271	.537	3	19	.158	400	504	.794	174	253	427	216	317	8	77	52	232	34.5	22.1	5.3	2.7	.563
85-86	LA Clippers	11	9	339	259	100	181	.552	1	2	.500	58	84	.690	20	21	41	31	35	2	9	13	33	30.8	23.5	3.7	2.8	.639
86-87	Sacramento	52	42	1658	863	338	757	.446	9	33	.273	178	228	.781	60	122	182	204	184	3	46	23	125	31.9	16.6	3.5	3.9	.422
87-88	Sacramento	35	18	899	443	174	364	.478	8	23	.348	87	113	.770	35	68	103	89	108	2	21	17	49	25.7	12.7	2.9	2.5	.427
88-89	Sacramento	29	20	600	289	111	276	.402	3	15	.200	64	95	.674	30	51	81	60	64	1	19	8	44	20.7	10.0	2.8	2.1	.358
88-89	Philadelphia	36	18	695	279	105	220	.477	4	16	.250	65	93	.699	31	55	86	68	100	3	24	15	43	19.3	7.8	2.4	1.9	.376
89-90	Philadelphia	75	7	1405	668	261	514	.508	16	36	.444	130	186	.699	62	110	172	109	198	2	35	20	83	18.7	8.9	2.3	1.5	.401
90-91	Boston	2	0	16	5	1	4	.250	0	1	.000	3	4	.750	0	0	0	5	3	0	1	1	1	8.0	2.5	0.0	2.5	.413
NBA Season Totals		408	214	9825	5232	2031	4074	.499	45	153	.294	1125	1495	.753	476	824	1300	866	1214	23	265	175	700	24.1	12.8	3.2	2.1	....
88-89	Philadelphia	3	3	48	19	9	14	.643	0	0	.000	1	2	.500	2	5	7	3	9	0	1	0	6	16.0	6.3	2.3	1.0	.308
89-90	Philadelphia	1	0	15	11	5	8	.625	0	1	.000	1	2	.500	0	0	0	1	3	0	1	0	1	15.0	11.0	0.0	1.0	.492
90-91	Boston	10	0	86	29	9	21	.429	0	1	.000	11	14	.786	2	7	9	5	20	0	3	1	8	8.6	2.9	0.9	0.5	.199
NBA Playoff Totals		14	3	149	59	23	43	.535	0	2	.000	13	18	.722	4	12	16	9	32	0	5	1	15	10.6	4.2	1.1	0.6	....

• SMITH, Don
Donald E. Smith

Born: July 27, 1920. Height: 6'2". Weight: 190 lbs. Drafted: 1947 College: Minnesota

YEAR	TEAM	GP	GS	MIN	PTS	FGM	FGA	FG%	3PM	3PA	3P%	FTM	FTA	FT%	ORB	DRB	TRB	AST	PF	DQ	STL	BLK	TO	MPG	PPG	RPG	APG	PCM
37-38	Pittsburgh-N	13	....	....	53	16	....	....	....	....	....	21	....	....	....	....	....	....	....	....	....	....	....	....	4.1	....	....	....
38-39	Non-Skids-N	1	....	....	2	1	....	....	....	....	....	0	....	....	....	....	....	....	....	....	....	....	....	....	2.0	....	....	....
42-43	Oshkosh-N	13	....	....	59	22	....	....	....	....	....	15	....	....	....	....	....	....	....	....	....	....	....	....	4.5	....	....	....
45-46	Oshkosh-N	9	....	....	8	1	....	....	....	....	....	6	....	....	....	....	....	....	....	....	....	....	....	....	0.9	....	....	....
46-47	Indianapolis-N	2	....	....	3	1	....	....	....	....	....	1	2	.500	....	....	....	....	....	....	....	....	....	....	1.5	....	....	....
46-47	Oshkosh-N	10	....	....	12	4	....	....	....	....	....	4	6	.667	....	....	....	....	....	....	....	....	....	....	1.2	....	....	....
47-48	Minneapolis-N	57	....	....	200	69	....	....	....	....	....	62	94	.660	....	....	....	....	98	....	....	....	....	....	3.5	....	....	....
48-49	Minneapolis	8	....	....	6	2	13	.154	....	....	....	2	3	.667	....	....	....	2	6	....	....	....	....	....	0.8	....	0.3	
NBA Season Totals		8	....	....	6	2	13	.154	....	....	....	2	3	.667	....	....	....	2	6	....	....	....	....	....	0.8	....	0.3	
NBL Season Totals		105	....	....	337	114	....	....	....	....	....	109	102	....	....	....	....	....	98	....	....	....	....	....	3.2	....	....	
Career Totals		113	....	....	343	116	13	....	....	....	....	111	105	....	....	....	....	2	104	....	....	....	....	....	3.0	....	0.0	
42-43	Oshkosh-N	2	....	....	4	1	....	....	....	....	....	2	....	....	....	....	....	....	....	....	....	....	....	....	2.0	....	....	
47-48	Minneapolis-N	10	....	....	35	13	....	....	....	....	....	9	12	.750	....	....	....	....	....	....	....	....	....	....	3.5	....	....	
NBL Playoff Totals		12	....	....	39	14	....	....	....	....	....	11	12	....	....	....	....	....	....	....	....	....	....	....	3.3	....	....	

• SMITH, Don
Donald Smith

Born: Oct. 10, 1951. Dayton, OH, United States. Height: 6' Weight: 160 lbs. Drafted: 1974 College: Dayton

YEAR	TEAM	GP	GS	MIN	PTS	FGM	FGA	FG%	3PM	3PA	3P%	FTM	FTA	FT%	ORB	DRB	TRB	AST	PF	DQ	STL	BLK	TO	MPG	PPG	RPG	APG	PCM
74-75	Philadelphia	54	....	538	283	131	321	.408	....	....	....	21	21	1.000	14	16	30	47	45	0	20	3	....	10.0	5.2	0.6	0.9	.337
NBA Season Totals		54	....	538	283	131	321	.408	....	....	....	21	21	1.000	14	16	30	47	45	0	20	3	....	10.0	5.2	0.6	0.9	....

• SMITH, Doug
Douglas Smith

Born: Sept. 17, 1969. Detroit, MI, United States. Height: 6'10". Weight: 220 lbs. Drafted: 1991 College: Missouri

YEAR	TEAM	GP	GS	MIN	PTS	FGM	FGA	FG%	3PM	3PA	3P%	FTM	FTA	FT%	ORB	DRB	TRB	AST	PF	DQ	STL	BLK	TO	MPG	PPG	RPG	APG	PCM
91-92	Dallas	76	32	1707	671	291	702	.415	0	11	.000	89	121	.736	129	262	391	129	259	5	62	34	99	22.5	8.8	5.1	1.7	.382
92-93	Dallas	61	42	1524	634	289	666	.434	0	4	.000	56	74	.757	96	232	328	104	280	12	48	52	116	25.0	10.4	5.4	1.7	.358
93-94	Dallas	79	42	1684	698	295	678	.435	2	9	.222	106	127	.835	114	235	349	119	287	3	82	38	95	21.3	8.8	4.4	1.5	.402
94-95	Dallas	63	0	826	320	131	314	.417	1	12	.083	57	75	.760	43	101	144	44	132	1	29	26	38	13.1	5.1	2.3	0.7	.334
95-96	Boston	17	2	92	33	14	39	.359	0	0	.000	5	8	.625	12	10	22	4	21	0	3	0	10	5.4	1.9	1.3	0.2	.180
NBA Season Totals		296	118	5833	2356	1020	2399	.425	3	36	.083	313	405	.773	394	840	1234	400	979	21	224	150	358	19.7	8.0	4.2	1.4	....

• SMITH, Ed
Edward Bernard Smith

Born: July 5, 1929. West Jefferson, OH, United States. Height: 6'6". Weight: 180 lbs. Drafted: 1951 College: Harvard

YEAR	TEAM	GP	GS	MIN	PTS	FGM	FGA	FG%	3PM	3PA	3P%	FTM	FTA	FT%	ORB	DRB	TRB	AST	PF	DQ	STL	BLK	TO	MPG	PPG	RPG	APG	PCM
53-54	New York	11	....	104	28	11	45	.244	....	....	....	6	10	.600	....	....	26	9	15	0	....	....	....	9.5	2.5	2.4	0.8	.261
NBA Season Totals		11	....	104	28	11	45	.244	....	....	....	6	10	.600	....	....	26	9	15	0	....	....	....	9.5	2.5	2.4	0.8	....

• SMITH, Elmore

Elmore Smith

Born: May 9, 1949. Macon, GA, United States. Height: 7'. Weight: 250 lbs. Drafted: 1971 College: Kentucky State

YEAR	TEAM	GP	GS	MIN	PTS	FGM	FGA	FG%	3PM	3PA	3P%	FTM	FTA	FT%	ORB	DRB	TRB	AST	PF	DQ	STL	BLK	TO	MPG	PPG	RPG	APG	PCM
71-72	Buffalo	78	....	3186	1352	579	1275	.454	....	....	....	194	363	.534	....	....	1184	111	306	10	....	....	....	40.8	17.3	15.2	1.4	.532
72-73	Buffalo	76	....	2829	1388	600	1244	.482	....	....	....	188	337	.558	....	....	946	192	295	**16**	....	....	....	37.2	18.3	12.4	2.5	.592
73-74	LA Lakers	81	....	2922	1015	434	949	.457	....	....	....	147	249	.590	204	702	906	150	309	8	71	**393**	....	36.1	12.5	11.2	1.9	.460
74-75	LA Lakers	74	....	2341	804	346	702	.493	....	....	....	112	231	.485	210	600	810	145	255	6	84	**216**	....	31.6	10.9	10.9	2.0	.512
75-76	Milwaukee	78	....	2809	1218	498	962	.518	....	....	....	222	351	.632	201	692	893	97	268	7	78	238	....	36.0	15.6	11.4	1.2	.543
76-77	Milwaukee	34	....	789	287	113	253	.447	....	....	....	61	105	.581	52	156	208	30	109	2	19	69	....	23.2	8.4	6.1	0.9	.398
76-77	Cleveland	36	....	675	312	128	254	.504	....	....	....	56	108	.519	62	169	231	13	98	2	16	75	....	18.8	8.7	6.4	0.4	.522
77-78	Cleveland	81	....	1996	1009	402	809	.497	....	....	....	205	309	.663	178	500	678	57	241	4	50	176	138	24.6	12.5	8.4	0.7	.619
78-79	Cleveland	24	....	332	156	69	130	.531	....	....	....	18	26	.692	45	61	106	13	60	0	7	16	43	13.8	6.5	4.4	0.5	.489
NBA Season Totals		562	....	17879	7541	3169	6578	.482	....	....	....	1203	2079	.579	952	2880	5962	808	1941	55	325	1183	181	31.8	13.4	10.6	1.4	....
73-74	LA Lakers	5	....	171	96	42	88	.477	....	....	....	12	17	.706	19	34	53	6	20	0	7	8	....	34.2	19.2	10.6	1.2	.574
75-76	Milwaukee	3	....	104	44	15	27	.556	....	....	....	14	21	.667	5	17	22	1	14	0	2	11	....	34.7	14.7	7.3	0.3	.430
76-77	Cleveland	3	....	56	41	18	33	.545	....	....	....	5	8	.625	6	18	24	1	10	0	5	3	....	18.7	13.7	8.0	0.3	.791
77-78	Cleveland	2	....	56	25	11	24	.458	....	....	....	3	6	.500	6	13	19	0	9	0	3	3	5	28.0	12.5	9.5	0.0	.462
NBA Playoff Totals		13	....	387	206	86	172	.500	....	....	....	34	52	.654	36	82	118	8	53	0	17	25	5	29.8	15.8	9.1	0.6	....

• SMITH, Garfield

Garfield Smith

Born: Nov. 18, 1945. Campbellsville, KY, United States. Height: 6'9". Weight: 235 lbs. Drafted: 1968 College: Eastern Kentucky

YEAR	TEAM	GP	GS	MIN	PTS	FGM	FGA	FG%	3PM	3PA	3P%	FTM	FTA	FT%	ORB	DRB	TRB	AST	PF	DQ	STL	BLK	TO	MPG	PPG	RPG	APG	PCM
70-71	Boston	37	....	281	106	42	116	.362	....	....	....	22	56	.393	....	....	95	9	53	0	....	....	....	7.6	2.9	2.6	0.2	.345
71-72	Boston	26	....	134	62	28	66	.424	....	....	....	6	31	.194	....	....	37	8	22	0	....	....	....	5.2	2.4	1.4	0.3	.373
72-73	San Diego-A	71	....	1055	260	116	244	.475	0	0	.000	28	93	.301	140	166	306	39	197	4	....	....	33	14.9	3.7	4.3	0.5	.327
NBA Season Totals		63	....	415	168	70	182	.385	....	....	....	28	87	.322	....	....	132	17	75	0	....	....	....	6.6	2.7	2.1	0.3	....
ABA Season Totals		71	....	1055	260	116	244	.475	0	0	.000	28	93	.301	140	166	306	39	197	4	....	....	33	14.9	3.7	4.3	0.5	....
Career Totals		134	....	1470	428	186	426	.437	0	0	.000	56	180	.311	140	166	438	56	272	4	....	....	33	11.0	3.2	3.3	0.4	....
71-72	Boston	4	....	6	2	1	5	.200	....	....	....	0	3	.000	....	....	1	0	1	0	....	....	....	1.5	0.5	0.3	0.0	-.387
72-73	San Diego-A	4	....	63	12	5	17	.294	0	0	.000	2	7	.286	12	9	21	1	9	0	....	....	1	15.8	3.0	5.3	0.3	.236
NBA Playoff Totals		4	....	6	2	1	5	.200	....	....	....	0	3	.000	....	....	1	0	1	0	....	....	....	1.5	0.5	0.3	0.0	....
ABA Playoff Totals		4	....	63	12	5	17	.294	0	0	.000	2	7	.286	12	9	21	1	9	0	....	....	1	15.8	3.0	5.3	0.3	....
Career Playoff Totals		8	....	69	14	6	22	.273	0	0	.000	2	10	.200	12	9	22	1	10	0	....	....	1	8.6	1.8	2.8	0.1	....

• SMITH, Greg

Gregory Darnell Smith

Born: Jan. 28, 1947. Princeton, KY, United States. Height: 6'5". Weight: 195 lbs. Drafted: 1968 College: Western Kentucky

YEAR	TEAM	GP	GS	MIN	PTS	FGM	FGA	FG%	3PM	3PA	3P%	FTM	FTA	FT%	ORB	DRB	TRB	AST	PF	DQ	STL	BLK	TO	MPG	PPG	RPG	APG	PCM
68-69	Milwaukee	79	....	2207	643	276	613	.450	....	....	....	91	155	.587	....	....	804	137	264	12	....	....	....	27.9	8.1	10.2	1.7	.478
69-70	Milwaukee	82	....	2368	803	339	664	.511	....	....	....	125	174	.718	....	....	712	156	304	8	....	....	....	28.9	9.8	8.7	1.9	.491
70-71	Milwaukee	82	....	2428	959	409	799	.512	....	....	....	141	213	.662	....	....	589	227	284	5	....	....	....	29.6	11.7	7.2	2.8	.509
71-72	Milwaukee	28	....	737	235	97	198	.490	....	....	....	41	58	.707	....	....	161	63	92	1	....	....	....	26.3	8.4	5.8	2.3	.422
71-72	Houston	54	....	1519	494	212	473	.448	....	....	....	70	110	.636	....	....	322	159	167	3	....	....	....	28.1	9.1	6.0	2.9	.420
72-73	Houston	4	....	41	10	5	16	.313	....	....	....	0	0	.000	....	....	8	5	8	0	....	....	....	10.3	2.5	2.0	1.3	.237
72-73	Portland	72	....	1569	533	229	469	.488	....	....	....	75	128	.586	....	....	375	117	210	0	....	....	....	21.8	7.4	5.2	1.6	.427
73-74	Portland	67	....	878	246	99	228	.434	....	....	....	48	79	.608	65	124	189	78	126	1	41	6	....	13.1	3.7	2.8	1.2	.364
74-75	Portland	55	....	519	174	71	146	.486	....	....	....	32	48	.667	29	60	89	27	96	1	22	6	....	9.4	3.2	1.6	0.5	.326
75-76	Portland	1	....	3	0	0	1	.000	....	....	....	0	0	.000	0	0	0	0	2	0	0	0	....	3.0	0.0	0.0	0.0	-.572
NBA Season Totals		524	....	12269	4097	1737	3607	.482	....	....	....	623	965	.646	94	184	3249	969	1553	31	63	12	....	23.4	7.8	6.2	1.8	....
69-70	Milwaukee	7	....	82	30	11	19	.579	....	....	....	8	10	.800	....	....	26	4	5	0	....	....	....	11.7	4.3	3.7	0.6	.576
69-70	Milwaukee	10	....	329	107	47	94	.500	....	....	....	13	22	.591	....	....	85	22	34	1	....	....	....	32.9	10.7	8.5	2.2	.444
70-71	Milwaukee	14	....	454	162	70	128	.547	....	....	....	22	40	.550	....	....	120	36	45	0	....	....	....	32.4	11.6	8.6	2.6	.505
NBA Playoff Totals		31	....	865	299	128	241	.531	....	....	....	43	72	.597	....	....	231	62	84	1	....	....	....	27.9	9.6	7.5	2.0	....

• SMITH, Jabari

Jabari Montsho Smith

Born: Feb. 12, 1977. Atlanta, GA, United States. Height: 6'11". Weight: 250 lbs. Drafted: 2000 College: Louisiana State

YEAR	TEAM	GP	GS	MIN	PTS	FGM	FGA	FG%	3PM	3PA	3P%	FTM	FTA	FT%	ORB	DRB	TRB	AST	PF	DQ	STL	BLK	TO	MPG	PPG	RPG	APG	PCM
00-01	Sacramento	9	0	66	26	11	22	.500	0	0	.000	4	6	.667	1	7	8	6	7	0	4	0	3	7.3	2.9	0.9	0.7	.406
01-02	Sacramento	12	0	71	18	6	21	.286	0	1	.000	6	12	.500	2	12	14	6	12	0	2	4	2	5.9	1.5	1.2	0.5	.269
01-02	Philadelphia	11	0	110	55	20	42	.476	0	2	.000	15	20	.750	6	8	14	5	19	1	4	2	3	10.0	5.0	1.3	0.5	.410
NBA Season Totals		32	0	247	99	37	85	.435	0	3	.000	25	38	.658	9	27	36	17	38	1	10	6	8	7.7	3.1	1.1	0.5	....

• SMITH, Jim

James Oliver Smith

Born: Apr. 12, 1958. Cleveland, OH, United States. Height: 6'9". Weight: 225 lbs. Drafted: 1981 College: Ohio State

YEAR	TEAM	GP	GS	MIN	PTS	FGM	FGA	FG%	3PM	3PA	3P%	FTM	FTA	FT%	ORB	DRB	TRB	AST	PF	DQ	STL	BLK	TO	MPG	PPG	RPG	APG	PCM
81-82	San Diego	72	3	858	211	86	169	.509	0	0	.000	39	85	.459	72	110	182	46	185	5	22	51	50	11.9	2.9	2.5	0.6	.311
82-83	Detroit	4	0	18	8	3	4	.750	0	0	.000	2	4	.500	0	5	5	0	4	0	0	0	0	4.5	2.0	1.3	0.0	.495
NBA Season Totals		76	3	876	219	89	173	.514	0	0	.000	41	89	.461	72	115	187	46	189	5	22	51	50	11.5	2.9	2.5	0.6	....

• SMITH, Joe

Joseph Leynard Smith

Born: July 26, 1975. Norfolk, VA, United States. Height: 6'10". Weight: 225 lbs. Drafted: 1995 College: Maryland

YEAR	TEAM	GP	GS	MIN	PTS	FGM	FGA	FG%	3PM	3PA	3P%	FTM	FTA	FT%	ORB	DRB	TRB	AST	PF	DQ	STL	BLK	TO	MPG	PPG	RPG	APG	PCM
95-96	Golden State	82	82	2821	1251	469	1024	.458	10	28	.357	303	392	.773	300	417	717	79	224	5	85	134	139	34.4	15.3	8.7	1.0	.502
96-97	Golden State	80	80	3086	1493	587	1293	.454	12	46	.261	307	377	.814	261	418	679	125	244	3	74	86	192	38.6	18.7	8.5	1.6	.462
97-98	Golden State	49	49	1645	846	343	800	.429	0	7	.000	160	208	.769	141	197	338	67	169	2	44	38	108	33.6	17.3	6.9	1.4	.417
97-98	Philadelphia	30	6	699	309	121	270	.448	0	1	.000	67	85	.788	58	75	133	27	94	0	18	13	51	23.3	10.3	4.4	0.9	.364

YEAR	TEAM	GP	GS	MIN	PTS	FGM	FGA	FG%	3PM	3PA	3P%	FTM	FTA	FT%	ORB	DRB	TRB	AST	PF	DQ	STL	BLK	TO	MPG	PPG	RPG	APG	PCM
98-99	Minnesota	43	42	1418	588	223	522	.427	0	3	.000	142	188	.755	154	200	354	68	147	3	32	66	66	33.0	13.7	8.2	1.6	.462
99-00	Minnesota	78	9	1975	774	289	623	.464	1	1	1.000	195	258	.756	186	298	484	88	302	8	45	85	119	25.3	9.9	6.2	1.1	.431
00-01	Detroit	69	59	1941	847	308	765	.403	0	5	.000	231	287	.805	160	331	491	79	258	5	47	50	88	28.1	12.3	7.1	1.1	.428
01-02	Minnesota	72	63	1921	767	297	581	.511	2	3	.667	171	206	.830	152	301	453	82	250	2	39	59	86	26.7	10.7	6.3	1.1	.464
02-03	Minnesota	54	21	1117	404	151	328	.460	0	2	.000	102	131	.779	111	159	270	38	171	2	14	55	43	20.7	7.5	5.0	0.7	.414
NBA Season Totals		557	411	16623	7279	2788	6206	.449	25	96	.260	1678	2132	.787	1523	2396	3919	653	1859	30	398	586	892	29.8	13.1	7.0	1.2	....
98-99	Minnesota	4	4	120	30	11	37	.297	0	0	.000	8	11	.727	10	16	26	5	15	0	2	8	5	30.0	7.5	6.5	1.3	.267
99-00	Minnesota	4	0	79	18	8	17	.471	0	1	.000	2	2	1.000	7	5	12	1	15	0	3	1	4	19.8	4.5	3.0	0.3	.190
01-02	Minnesota	3	1	43	13	3	7	.429	0	0	.000	7	8	.875	4	7	11	0	8	0	0	1	1	14.3	4.3	3.7	0.0	.355
02-03	Minnesota	5	1	40	14	4	6	.667	0	0	.000	6	6	1.000	0	6	6	0	14	0	1	1	3	8.0	2.8	1.2	0.0	.259
NBA Playoff Totals		16	6	282	75	26	67	.388	0	1	.000	23	27	.852	21	34	55	6	52	0	6	11	13	17.6	4.7	3.4	0.4	....

• SMITH, John

John Smith Jr.

Born: May 24, 1944. Columbus, MS, United States. Height: 7' Weight: 235 lbs. Drafted: 1968 College: Southern Colorado

YEAR	TEAM	GP	GS	MIN	PTS	FGM	FGA	FG%	3PM	3PA	3P%	FTM	FTA	FT%	ORB	DRB	TRB	AST	PF	DQ	STL	BLK	TO	MPG	PPG	RPG	APG	PCM
68-69	Dallas-A	77	....	2172	608	246	623	.395	0	0	.000	116	214	.542	271	538	809	58	**328**	**19**	....	....	117	28.2	7.9	10.5	0.8	.397
69-70	Dallas-A	48	....	966	232	92	232	.397	0	1	.000	48	78	.615	101	228	329	52	149	5	....	....	68	20.1	4.8	6.9	1.1	.390
69-70	New York-A	16	....	165	23	9	40	.225	0	1	.000	5	7	.714	27	33	60	3	30	0	....	....	13	10.3	1.4	3.8	0.2	.228
69-70	Pittsburgh-A	6	....	59	11	4	12	.333	0	0	.000	3	9	.333	2	13	15	3	6	0	....	....	4	9.8	1.8	2.5	0.5	.259
ABA Season Totals		147	....	3362	874	351	907	.387	0	2	.000	172	308	.558	401	812	1213	116	513	24	....	....	202	22.9	5.9	8.3	0.8	....
68-69	Dallas-A	7	....	131	39	16	31	.516	0	0	.000	7	13	.538	14	28	42	8	19	0	....	....	4	18.7	5.6	6.0	1.1	.462
69-70	New York-A	2	....	10	0	0	3	.000	0	1	.000	0	0	.000	....	....	2	0	....	0	....	....	....	5.0	0.0	1.0	0.0	....
ABA Playoff Totals		9	....	141	39	16	34	.471	0	1	.000	7	13	.538	14	28	44	8	19	0	....	....	4	15.7	4.3	4.9	0.9	....

• SMITH, Keith

Keith LeWayne Smith

Born: Mar. 9, 1964. Flint, MI, United States. Height: 6'3". Weight: 180 lbs. Drafted: 1986 College: Loyola Marymount

YEAR	TEAM	GP	GS	MIN	PTS	FGM	FGA	FG%	3PM	3PA	3P%	FTM	FTA	FT%	ORB	DRB	TRB	AST	PF	DQ	STL	BLK	TO	MPG	PPG	RPG	APG	PCM
86-87	Milwaukee	42	4	461	138	57	150	.380	3	9	.333	21	28	.750	13	19	32	43	74	0	25	3	29	11.0	3.3	0.8	1.0	.192
NBA Season Totals		42	4	461	138	57	150	.380	3	9	.333	21	28	.750	13	19	32	43	74	0	25	3	29	11.0	3.3	0.8	1.0	....

• SMITH, Ken

Kenneth Wayne (Grasshopper) Smith

Born: July 12, 1953. Height: 6'7". Weight: 185 lbs. Drafted: 1975 College: Tulsa

YEAR	TEAM	GP	GS	MIN	PTS	FGM	FGA	FG%	3PM	3PA	3P%	FTM	FTA	FT%	ORB	DRB	TRB	AST	PF	DQ	STL	BLK	TO	MPG	PPG	RPG	APG	PCM
75-76	San Antonio-A	19	....	164	82	34	83	.410	1	5	.200	13	16	.813	9	15	24	7	22	....	4	0	8	8.6	4.3	1.3	0.4	.344
ABA Season Totals		19	....	164	82	34	83	.410	1	5	.200	13	16	.813	9	15	24	7	22	....	4	0	8	8.6	4.3	1.3	0.4	....

• SMITH, Kenny

Kenneth Smith

Born: Mar. 8, 1965. Queens, NY, United States. Height: 6'3". Weight: 170 lbs. Drafted: 1987 College: North Carolina

YEAR	TEAM	GP	GS	MIN	PTS	FGM	FGA	FG%	3PM	3PA	3P%	FTM	FTA	FT%	ORB	DRB	TRB	AST	PF	DQ	STL	BLK	TO	MPG	PPG	RPG	APG	PCM
87-88	Sacramento	61	60	2170	841	331	694	.477	12	39	.308	167	204	.819	40	98	138	434	140	1	92	8	183	35.6	13.8	2.3	7.1	.431
88-89	Sacramento	81	81	3145	1403	547	1183	.462	46	128	.359	263	357	.737	49	177	226	621	173	0	102	7	251	38.8	17.3	2.8	7.7	.455
89-90	Sacramento	46	46	1747	688	280	607	.461	22	59	.373	106	131	.809	11	109	120	303	98	0	57	7	124	38.0	15.0	2.6	6.6	.402
89-90	Atlanta	33	5	674	255	98	204	.480	4	24	.167	55	65	.846	7	30	37	142	45	0	22	1	46	20.4	7.7	1.1	4.3	.436
90-91	Houston	78	78	2699	1380	522	1003	.520	49	135	.363	287	340	.844	36	127	163	554	131	0	106	11	234	34.6	17.7	2.1	7.1	.548
91-92	Houston	81	80	2735	1137	432	910	.475	54	137	.394	219	253	.866	34	143	177	562	112	0	104	7	227	33.8	14.0	2.2	6.9	.469
92-93	Houston	82	82	2422	1065	387	744	.520	96	219	.438	195	222	.878	28	132	160	446	110	0	80	7	164	29.5	13.0	2.0	5.4	.504
93-94	Houston	78	78	2209	906	341	711	.480	89	220	.405	135	155	.871	24	114	138	327	121	0	59	4	125	28.3	11.6	1.8	4.2	.419
94-95	Houston	81	81	2030	842	287	593	.484	142	331	.429	126	148	.851	27	128	155	323	109	1	71	10	122	25.1	10.4	1.9	4.0	.465
95-96	Houston	68	56	1617	580	201	464	.433	91	238	.382	87	106	.821	21	75	96	245	116	1	47	3	102	23.8	8.5	1.4	3.6	.353
96-97	Detroit	9	0	64	23	8	20	.400	5	10	.500	2	2	1.000	0	5	5	10	2	0	1	0	3	7.1	2.6	0.6	1.1	.381
96-97	Orlando	6	0	47	17	6	13	.462	3	5	.600	2	2	1.000	1	1	2	4	3	0	0	0	6	7.8	2.8	0.3	0.7	.205
96-97	Denver	33	3	654	260	87	206	.422	51	120	.425	35	41	.854	3	34	37	102	25	0	18	0	63	19.8	7.9	1.1	3.1	.361
NBA Season Totals		737	650	22213	9397	3527	7352	.480	664	1665	.399	1679	2026	.829	281	1173	1454	4073	1185	3	759	65	1650	30.1	12.8	2.0	5.5	....
90-91	Houston	3	3	113	46	18	38	.474	2	4	.500	8	9	.889	4	4	8	24	5	0	4	1	6	37.7	15.3	2.7	8.0	.502
92-93	Houston	12	12	391	177	63	128	.492	23	46	.500	28	36	.778	2	22	24	50	18	0	9	1	26	32.6	14.8	2.0	4.2	.422
93-94	Houston	23	23	696	248	86	189	.455	34	76	.447	42	52	.808	5	49	54	94	40	0	22	4	33	30.3	10.8	2.3	4.1	.396
94-95	Houston	22	22	652	238	78	178	.438	46	104	.442	36	40	.900	7	42	49	99	46	0	14	3	31	29.6	10.8	2.2	4.5	.397
95-96	Houston	8	8	191	71	23	53	.434	12	31	.387	13	13	1.000	4	8	12	38	14	0	5	0	8	23.9	8.9	1.5	4.8	.445
NBA Playoff Totals		68	68	2043	780	268	586	.457	117	261	.448	127	150	.847	22	125	147	305	123	0	54	9	104	30.0	11.5	2.2	4.5	....

• SMITH, LaBradford

LaBradford Corvey (L.A.) Smith

Born: Apr. 3, 1969. Bay City, TX, United States. Height: 6'3". Weight: 200 lbs. Drafted: 1991 College: Louisville

YEAR	TEAM	GP	GS	MIN	PTS	FGM	FGA	FG%	3PM	3PA	3P%	FTM	FTA	FT%	ORB	DRB	TRB	AST	PF	DQ	STL	BLK	TO	MPG	PPG	RPG	APG	PCM
91-92	Washington	48	5	708	247	100	246	.407	2	21	.095	45	56	.804	30	51	81	99	98	0	44	1	62	14.8	5.1	1.7	2.1	.320
92-93	Washington	69	33	1546	639	261	570	.458	8	23	.348	109	127	.858	26	80	106	186	178	2	58	9	104	22.4	9.3	1.5	2.7	.338
93-94	Washington	7	0	48	31	8	18	.444	0	0	.000	15	20	.750	5	3	8	5	8	0	3	1	1	6.9	4.4	1.1	0.7	.654
93-94	Sacramento	59	2	829	301	116	288	.403	21	60	.350	48	64	.750	29	47	76	104	88	2	37	4	47	14.1	5.1	1.3	1.8	.329
NBA Season Totals		183	40	3131	1218	485	1122	.432	31	104	.298	217	267	.813	90	181	271	394	372	4	142	15	214	17.1	6.7	1.5	2.2	....

• SMITH, Larry

Larry (Mr. Mean) Smith

Born: Jan. 18, 1958. Rolling Fork, MS, United States. Height: 6'8". Weight: 215 lbs. Drafted: 1980 College: Alcorn State

YEAR	TEAM	GP	GS	MIN	PTS	FGM	FGA	FG%	3PM	3PA	3P%	FTM	FTA	FT%	ORB	DRB	TRB	AST	PF	DQ	STL	BLK	TO	MPG	PPG	RPG	APG	PCM
80-81	Golden State	82	....	2578	785	304	594	.512	0	0	.000	177	301	.588	433	561	994	93	316	10	70	63	148	31.4	9.6	12.1	1.1	.510
81-82	Golden State	74	55	2213	528	220	412	.534	0	1	.000	88	159	.553	279	534	813	83	291	7	65	54	104	29.9	7.1	11.0	1.1	.468
82-83	Golden State	49	41	1433	413	180	306	.588	0	0	.000	53	99	.535	209	276	485	46	186	5	36	20	83	29.2	8.4	9.9	0.9	.459
83-84	Golden State	75	63	2091	582	244	436	.560	0	0	.000	94	168	.560	282	390	672	72	274	6	61	22	128	27.9	7.8	9.0	1.0	.431

YEAR	TEAM	GP	GS	MIN	PTS	FGM	FGA	FG%	3PM	3PA	3P%	FTM	FTA	FT%	ORB	DRB	TRB	AST	PF	DQ	STL	BLK	TO	MPG	PPG	RPG	APG	PCM
84-85	Golden State	80	78	2497	887	366	690	.530	0	0	.000	155	256	.605	405	464	869	96	285	5	78	54	160	31.2	11.1	10.9	1.2	.517
85-86	Golden State	77	74	2441	740	314	586	.536	0	1	.000	112	227	.493	**384**	472	856	95	286	7	62	50	139	31.7	9.6	11.1	1.2	.481
86-87	Golden State	80	78	2374	707	297	544	.546	0	1	.000	113	197	.574	366	551	917	95	295	7	71	56	136	29.7	8.8	11.5	1.2	.525
87-88	Golden State	20	10	499	127	58	123	.472	0	1	.000	11	27	.407	79	103	182	25	63	1	12	11	36	25.0	6.4	9.1	1.3	.428
88-89	Golden State	80	78	1897	456	219	397	.552	0	0	.000	18	58	.310	272	380	652	118	248	2	61	54	112	23.7	5.7	8.2	1.5	.470
89-90	Houston	74	0	1300	222	101	213	.474	0	2	.000	20	55	.364	180	272	452	69	203	3	56	28	67	17.6	3.0	6.1	0.9	.399
90-91	Houston	81	28	1923	268	128	263	.487	0	0	.000	12	50	.240	302	407	709	88	265	6	83	22	89	23.7	3.3	8.8	1.1	.401
91-92	Houston	45	7	800	104	50	92	.543	0	1	.000	4	11	.364	107	149	256	33	121	3	21	7	45	17.8	2.3	5.7	0.7	.329
92-93	San Antonio	66	13	833	85	38	87	.437	0	0	.000	9	22	.409	103	165	268	28	133	2	23	16	40	12.6	1.3	4.1	0.4	.300
NBA Season Totals		883	525	22879	5904	2519	4743	.531	0	7	.000	866	1630	.531	3401	4724	8125	941	2966	64	699	457	1287	25.9	6.7	9.2	1.1	....
86-87	Golden State	10	10	329	103	43	81	.531	0	0	.000	17	24	.708	61	76	137	17	39	0	12	6	14	32.9	10.3	13.7	1.7	.595
88-89	Golden State	8	8	148	8	4	16	.250	0	0	.000	0	0	.000	17	23	40	16	24	0	6	11	6	18.5	1.0	5.0	2.0	.339
89-90	Houston	4	0	73	12	6	8	.750	0	0	.000	0	0	.000	7	6	13	5	11	0	4	0	5	18.3	3.0	3.3	1.3	.295
90-91	Houston	3	0	57	2	1	4	.250	0	1	.000	0	1	1.000	6	7	13	4	11	0	1	1	2	19.0	0.7	4.3	1.3	.175
92-93	San Antonio	6	0	50	7	2	3	.667	0	0	.000	3	4	.750	8	8	16	1	16	0	4	2	1	8.3	1.2	2.7	0.2	.376
NBA Playoff Totals		31	18	657	132	56	112	.500	0	1	.000	20	29	.690	99	120	219	43	101	0	27	20	28	21.2	4.3	7.1	1.4	....

• SMITH, Leon

Leon Smith

Born: Nov. 2, 1980. Chicago, IL, United States.   Height: 6'10".   Weight: 235 lbs.   Drafted: 1999   College: none (HS: Mount Carmel, Martin Luther King, IL)

YEAR	TEAM	GP	GS	MIN	PTS	FGM	FGA	FG%	3PM	3PA	3P%	FTM	FTA	FT%	ORB	DRB	TRB	AST	PF	DQ	STL	BLK	TO	MPG	PPG	RPG	APG	PCM
01-02	Atlanta	14	0	100	31	10	26	.385	0	0	.000	11	17	.647	10	21	31	3	12	0	5	1	3	7.1	2.2	2.2	0.2	.424
NBA Season Totals		14	0	100	31	10	26	.385	0	0	.000	11	17	.647	10	21	31	3	12	0	5	1	3	7.1	2.2	2.2	0.2	....

• SMITH, Michael

Michael John Smith

Born: May 19, 1965. Rochester, NY, United States.   Height: 6'10".   Weight: 225 lbs.   Drafted: 1989   College: Brigham Young

YEAR	TEAM	GP	GS	MIN	PTS	FGM	FGA	FG%	3PM	3PA	3P%	FTM	FTA	FT%	ORB	DRB	TRB	AST	PF	DQ	STL	BLK	TO	MPG	PPG	RPG	APG	PCM
89-90	Boston	65	7	620	327	136	286	.476	2	28	.071	53	64	.828	40	60	100	79	51	0	9	1	52	9.5	5.0	1.5	1.2	.477
90-91	Boston	47	3	389	218	95	200	.475	6	24	.250	22	27	.815	21	35	56	43	27	0	6	2	38	8.3	4.6	1.2	0.9	.451
94-95	LA Clippers	29	0	319	153	63	134	.470	1	8	.125	26	30	.867	13	43	56	20	41	0	6	2	17	11.0	5.3	1.9	0.7	.409
NBA Season Totals		141	10	1328	698	294	620	.474	9	60	.150	101	121	.835	74	138	212	142	119	0	21	5	107	9.4	5.0	1.5	1.0	....
89-90	Boston	4	0	16	17	5	8	.625	0	2	.000	7	7	1.000	0	0	0	0	1	0	1	0	1	4.0	4.3	0.0	0.0	.858
90-91	Boston	2	0	6	2	1	2	.500	0	1	.000	0	0	.000	0	0	0	1	2	0	0	0	0	3.0	1.0	0.0	0.5	.200
95-96	Sacramento	4	0	87	19	7	12	.583	0	0	.000	5	11	.455	7	15	22	8	14	0	1	2	2	21.8	4.8	5.5	2.0	.402
NBA Playoff Totals		10	0	109	38	13	22	.591	0	3	.000	12	18	.667	7	15	22	9	17	0	2	2	3	10.9	3.8	2.2	0.9	....

• SMITH, Mike

Mike Smith

Born: Apr. 15, 1976.   Height: 6'7".   Weight: 205 lbs.   Drafted: —   College: Louisiana-Monroe

YEAR	TEAM	GP	GS	MIN	PTS	FGM	FGA	FG%	3PM	3PA	3P%	FTM	FTA	FT%	ORB	DRB	TRB	AST	PF	DQ	STL	BLK	TO	MPG	PPG	RPG	APG	PCM
00-01	Washington	17	0	180	51	19	59	.322	3	18	.167	10	16	.625	10	12	22	10	8	0	5	3	7	10.6	3.0	1.3	0.6	.225
NBA Season Totals		17	0	180	51	19	59	.322	3	18	.167	10	16	.625	10	12	22	10	8	0	5	3	7	10.6	3.0	1.3	0.6	....

• SMITH, Otis

Otis Fitzgerald Smith

Born: Jan. 30, 1964. Jacksonville, FL, United States.   Height: 6'5".   Weight: 210 lbs.   Drafted: 1986   College: Jacksonville

YEAR	TEAM	GP	GS	MIN	PTS	FGM	FGA	FG%	3PM	3PA	3P%	FTM	FTA	FT%	ORB	DRB	TRB	AST	PF	DQ	STL	BLK	TO	MPG	PPG	RPG	APG	PCM
86-87	Denver	28	0	168	78	33	79	.418	0	2	.000	12	21	.571	17	17	34	22	30	0	1	1	20	6.0	2.8	1.2	0.8	.330
87-88	Denver	15	6	191	93	37	93	.398	0	0	.000	21	28	.750	16	14	30	11	23	0	5	6	12	12.7	6.3	2.0	0.7	.354
87-88	Golden State	57	12	1358	746	288	569	.506	13	41	.317	157	201	.781	110	107	217	144	137	0	86	36	97	23.8	13.1	3.8	2.5	.574
88-89	Golden State	80	5	1597	803	311	715	.435	7	37	.189	174	218	.798	128	202	330	140	165	1	88	40	128	20.0	10.0	4.1	1.8	.493
89-90	Orlando	65	35	1644	875	348	708	.492	10	40	.250	169	222	.761	117	183	300	147	174	0	76	57	104	25.3	13.5	4.6	2.3	.545
90-91	Orlando	75	39	1885	1044	407	902	.451	9	46	.196	221	301	.734	176	213	389	169	190	1	85	35	143	25.1	13.9	5.2	2.3	.519
91-92	Orlando	55	5	877	310	116	318	.365	8	21	.381	70	91	.769	40	76	116	57	85	1	36	13	61	15.9	5.6	2.1	1.0	.263
NBA Season Totals		375	102	7720	3951	1540	3384	.455	47	187	.251	824	1082	.762	604	812	1416	690	804	3	377	188	565	20.6	10.5	3.8	1.8	....
86-87	Denver	3	0	19	10	2	6	.333	0	0	.000	6	9	.667	1	4	5	4	1	0	0	2	4	6.3	3.3	1.7	1.3	.604
88-89	Golden State	4	0	49	19	9	24	.375	0	0	.000	1	2	.500	6	7	13	6	5	0	2	1	2	12.3	4.8	3.3	1.5	.443
NBA Playoff Totals		7	0	68	29	11	30	.367	0	0	.000	7	11	.636	7	11	18	10	6	0	2	3	6	9.7	4.1	2.6	1.4	....

• SMITH, Pete

Pete Smith

Born: 1947.   Height: 6'6".   Weight: 205 lbs.   Drafted: 1971   College: Pepperdine

YEAR	TEAM	GP	GS	MIN	PTS	FGM	FGA	FG%	3PM	3PA	3P%	FTM	FTA	FT%	ORB	DRB	TRB	AST	PF	DQ	STL	BLK	TO	MPG	PPG	RPG	APG	PCM
72-73	San Diego-A	5	....	32	4	2	12	.167	0	2	.000	0	0	.000	3	5	8	1	5	0	....	....	5	6.4	0.8	1.6	0.2	.033
ABA Season Totals		5	....	32	4	2	12	.167	0	2	.000	0	0	.000	3	5	8	1	5	0	....	....	5	6.4	0.8	1.6	0.2	....

• SMITH, Phil

Philip Arnold Smith

Born: Apr. 22, 1952. San Francisco, CA, United States. Died: July29, 2002.   Height: 6'4".   Weight: 185 lbs.   Drafted: 1974   College: San Francisco

YEAR	TEAM	GP	GS	MIN	PTS	FGM	FGA	FG%	3PM	3PA	3P%	FTM	FTA	FT%	ORB	DRB	TRB	AST	PF	DQ	STL	BLK	TO	MPG	PPG	RPG	APG	PCM
74-75	Golden State	74	....	1055	569	221	464	.476	....	....	....	127	158	.804	51	89	140	135	141	0	62	0	....	14.3	7.7	1.9	1.8	.533
75-76	Golden State	82	....	2793	1641	659	1383	.477	....	....	....	323	410	.788	133	243	376	362	223	0	108	18	....	34.1	20.0	4.6	4.4	.581
76-77	Golden State	82	....	2880	1557	631	1318	.479	....	....	....	295	376	.785	101	231	332	328	227	0	98	29	....	35.1	19.0	4.0	4.0	.518
77-78	Golden State	82	....	2940	1612	648	1373	.472	....	....	....	316	389	.812	100	200	300	393	219	2	108	27	262	35.9	19.7	3.7	4.8	.491
78-79	Golden State	59	....	2288	1172	489	977	.501	....	....	....	194	255	.761	48	164	212	261	159	3	101	23	171	38.8	19.9	3.6	4.4	.468
79-80	Golden State	51	....	1552	792	325	685	.474	7	22	.318	135	171	.789	28	118	146	187	154	1	62	15	122	30.4	15.5	2.9	3.7	.436
80-81	San Diego	76	....	2378	1279	519	1057	.491	4	18	.222	237	313	.757	49	107	156	372	231	1	84	18	175	31.3	16.8	2.1	4.9	.475

YEAR	TEAM	GP	GS	MIN	PTS	FGM	FGA	FG%	3PM	3PA	3P%	FTM	FTA	FT%	ORB	DRB	TRB	AST	PF	DQ	STL	BLK	TO	MPG	PPG	RPG	APG	PCM
81-82	San Diego	48	39	1446	634	253	575	.440	5	24	.208	123	168	.732	34	83	117	233	151	0	45	19	115	30.1	13.2	2.4	4.9	.387
81-82	Seattle	26	2	596	214	87	186	.468	0	3	.000	40	55	.727	17	52	69	74	62	0	22	8	39	22.9	8.2	2.7	2.8	.373
82-83	Seattle	79	17	1238	454	175	400	.438	3	8	.375	101	133	.759	27	103	130	216	113	0	44	8	103	15.7	5.7	1.6	2.7	.399
NBA Season Totals		**659**	**58**	**19166**	**9924**	**4007**	**8418**	**.476**	**19**	**75**	**.253**	**1891**	**2428**	**.779**	**588**	**1390**	**1978**	**2561**	**1680**	**7**	**734**	**165**	**987**	**29.1**	**15.1**	**3.0**	**3.9**	**....**
74-75	Golden State	16	....	235	103	39	104	.375	....	....	....	25	40	.625	7	21	28	30	30	0	9	7	....	14.7	6.4	1.8	1.9	.369
75-76	Golden State	13	....	493	312	127	245	.518	....	....	....	58	79	.734	23	38	61	60	33	1	21	6	....	37.9	24.0	4.7	4.6	.626
76-77	Golden State	10	....	371	142	53	132	.402	....	....	....	36	45	.800	10	40	50	45	24	0	14	4	....	37.1	14.2	5.0	4.5	.415
81-82	Seattle	8	0	92	25	12	30	.400	0	1	.000	1	3	.333	3	5	8	7	11	0	5	1	4	11.5	3.1	1.0	0.9	.209
82-83	Seattle	2	0	19	6	3	6	.500	0	0	.000	0	0	.000	0	3	3	1	1	0	0	0	2	9.5	3.0	1.5	0.5	.255
NBA Playoff Totals		**49**	**0**	**1210**	**588**	**234**	**517**	**.453**	**0**	**1**	**.000**	**120**	**167**	**.719**	**43**	**107**	**150**	**143**	**99**	**1**	**49**	**18**	**6**	**24.7**	**12.0**	**3.1**	**2.9**	**....**

• SMITH, Randy

Randolph Smith

Born: Dec. 12, 1948. Bellport, NY, United States. Height: 6'3". Weight: 180 lbs. Drafted: 1971 College: Buffalo State

YEAR	TEAM	GP	GS	MIN	PTS	FGM	FGA	FG%	3PM	3PA	3P%	FTM	FTA	FT%	ORB	DRB	TRB	AST	PF	DQ	STL	BLK	TO	MPG	PPG	RPG	APG	PCM
71-72	Buffalo	76	....	2094	1022	432	896	.482	....	....	....	158	254	.622	....	....	368	189	202	2	....	....	....	27.6	13.4	4.8	2.5	.490
72-73	Buffalo	82	....	2603	1214	511	1154	.443	....	....	....	192	264	.727	....	....	391	422	247	1	....	....	....	31.7	14.8	4.8	5.1	.516
73-74	Buffalo	82	....	2745	1267	531	1079	.492	....	....	....	205	288	.712	87	228	315	383	261	4	203	4	....	33.5	15.5	3.8	4.7	.496
74-75	Buffalo	82	....	3001	1456	610	1261	.484	....	....	....	236	295	.800	95	249	344	534	247	2	137	3	....	36.6	17.8	4.2	6.5	.559
75-76	Buffalo	82	....	3167	1787	702	1422	.494	....	....	....	383	469	.817	104	313	417	484	274	5	153	4	....	38.6	21.8	5.1	5.9	.608
76-77	Buffalo	82	....	3094	1698	702	1504	.467	....	....	....	294	386	.762	134	323	457	441	264	2	176	8	....	37.7	20.7	5.6	5.4	.565
77-78	Buffalo	82	....	3314	2021	789	1697	.465	....	....	....	443	554	.800	110	200	310	458	224	2	172	11	287	40.4	24.6	3.8	5.6	.536
78-79	San Diego	82	....	3111	1678	693	1523	.455	....	....	....	292	359	.813	102	193	295	395	177	1	177	5	254	37.9	20.5	3.6	4.8	.469
79-80	Cleveland	82	....	2677	1441	599	1326	.452	10	53	.189	233	283	.823	93	163	256	363	190	1	125	7	197	32.6	17.6	3.1	4.4	.465
80-81	Cleveland	82	....	2199	1194	486	1043	.466	1	28	.036	221	271	.815	46	147	193	357	132	0	113	14	197	26.8	14.6	2.4	4.4	.502
81-82	New York	82	40	2033	821	348	748	.465	3	11	.273	122	151	.808	53	102	155	255	199	1	91	1	123	24.8	10.0	1.9	3.1	.362
82-83	San Diego	65	16	1264	592	244	499	.489	3	16	.188	101	117	.863	35	53	88	192	122	1	54	0	91	19.4	9.1	1.4	3.0	.440
82-83	Atlanta	15	0	142	71	29	66	.439	0	2	.000	13	14	.929	2	6	8	14	17	0	2	0	9	9.5	4.7	0.5	0.9	.322
NBA Season Totals		**976**	**56**	**31444**	**16262**	**6676**	**14218**	**.470**	**17**	**110**	**.155**	**2893**	**3705**	**.781**	**861**	**1977**	**3597**	**4487**	**2556**	**22**	**1403**	**57**	**1158**	**32.2**	**16.7**	**3.7**	**4.6**	**....**
73-74	Buffalo	6	....	227	85	36	90	.400	....	....	....	13	20	.650	5	21	26	27	21	1	10	1	....	37.8	14.2	4.3	4.5	.354
74-75	Buffalo	7	....	286	126	50	105	.476	....	....	....	26	30	.867	8	22	30	49	23	0	18	1	....	40.9	18.0	4.3	7.0	.522
75-76	Buffalo	9	....	386	203	81	161	.503	....	....	....	41	49	.837	5	47	52	77	35	0	14	0	....	42.9	22.6	5.8	8.6	.644
82-83	Atlanta	2	0	15	6	1	5	.200	0	0	.000	4	4	1.000	0	1	1	4	1	0	1	0	0	7.5	3.0	0.5	2.0	.542
NBA Playoff Totals		**24**	**0**	**914**	**420**	**168**	**361**	**.465**	**0**	**0**	**.000**	**84**	**103**	**.816**	**18**	**91**	**109**	**157**	**80**	**1**	**43**	**2**	**0**	**38.1**	**17.5**	**4.5**	**6.5**	**....**

• SMITH, Reggie

Reginald D. Smith

Born: Aug. 21, 1970. San Jose, CA, United States. Height: 6'10". Weight: 240 lbs. Drafted: 1992 College: Texas Christian

YEAR	TEAM	GP	GS	MIN	PTS	FGM	FGA	FG%	3PM	3PA	3P%	FTM	FTA	FT%	ORB	DRB	TRB	AST	PF	DQ	STL	BLK	TO	MPG	PPG	RPG	APG	PCM
92-93	Portland	23	0	68	23	10	27	.370	0	1	.000	3	14	.214	15	6	21	1	16	0	4	1	5	3.0	1.0	0.9	0.0	.224
93-94	Portland	43	9	316	76	29	72	.403	0	0	.000	18	38	.474	40	59	99	4	47	0	12	6	13	7.3	1.8	2.3	0.1	.334
NBA Season Totals		**66**	**9**	**384**	**99**	**39**	**99**	**.394**	**0**	**1**	**.000**	**21**	**52**	**.404**	**55**	**65**	**120**	**5**	**63**	**0**	**16**	**7**	**18**	**5.8**	**1.5**	**1.8**	**0.1**	**....**

• SMITH, Robert

Robert Leroy Smith

Born: Mar. 10, 1955. Los Angeles, CA, United States. Height: 5'11". Weight: 165 lbs. Drafted: 1977 College: UNLV

YEAR	TEAM	GP	GS	MIN	PTS	FGM	FGA	FG%	3PM	3PA	3P%	FTM	FTA	FT%	ORB	DRB	TRB	AST	PF	DQ	STL	BLK	TO	MPG	PPG	RPG	APG	PCM
77-78	Denver	45	....	378	121	50	97	.515	....	....	....	21	24	.875	6	30	36	39	52	0	18	3	18	8.4	2.7	0.8	0.9	.354
78-79	Denver	82	....	1479	527	184	436	.422	....	....	....	159	180	.883	41	105	146	208	165	1	58	13	98	18.0	6.4	1.8	2.5	.374
79-80	Utah	6	....	73	15	5	15	.333	0	0	.000	5	5	1.000	3	0	3	7	3	0	4	0	1	12.2	2.5	0.5	1.2	.242
79-80	New Jersey	59	....	736	309	113	254	.445	8	26	.308	75	87	.862	17	59	76	85	102	1	22	4	53	12.5	5.2	1.3	1.4	.363
80-81	Cleveland	1	....	20	8	2	5	.400	0	0	.000	4	4	1.000	1	2	3	3	6	1	0	0	3	20.0	8.0	3.0	3.0	.290
81-82	Milwaukee	17	1	316	116	52	110	.473	2	10	.200	10	12	.833	1	13	14	44	35	0	10	1	14	18.6	6.8	0.8	2.6	.326
82-83	San Diego	5	0	43	11	2	13	.154	0	1	.000	7	8	.875	1	2	3	6	7	0	4	0	3	8.6	2.2	0.6	1.2	.178
82-83	San Antonio	7	0	25	12	5	11	.455	0	1	.000	2	2	1.000	0	3	3	2	6	0	1	0	3	3.6	1.7	0.4	0.3	.279
84-85	Cleveland	7	0	48	16	4	17	.235	0	4	.000	8	10	.800	0	4	4	7	6	0	2	0	3	6.9	2.3	0.6	1.0	.217
NBA Season Totals		**229**	**1**	**3118**	**1135**	**417**	**958**	**.435**	**10**	**42**	**.238**	**291**	**332**	**.877**	**70**	**218**	**288**	**401**	**382**	**3**	**119**	**21**	**196**	**13.6**	**5.0**	**1.3**	**1.8**	**....**
77-78	Denver	11	....	96	39	17	26	.654	....	....	....	5	7	.714	5	4	9	17	13	0	6	0	8	8.7	3.5	0.8	1.5	.519
78-79	Denver	3	....	25	2	0	7	.000	....	....	....	2	2	1.000	1	1	2	4	2	0	2	0	2	8.3	0.7	0.7	1.3	.041
81-82	Milwaukee	6	0	68	29	10	26	.385	2	7	.286	7	8	.875	1	6	7	12	8	0	1	0	1	11.3	4.8	1.2	2.0	.434
82-83	San Antonio	6	0	19	10	4	9	.444	0	1	.000	2	2	1.000	3	2	5	6	2	0	1	0	1	3.2	1.7	0.8	1.0	.826
NBA Playoff Totals		**26**	**0**	**208**	**80**	**31**	**68**	**.456**	**2**	**8**	**.250**	**16**	**19**	**.842**	**10**	**13**	**23**	**39**	**25**	**0**	**10**	**0**	**12**	**8.0**	**3.1**	**0.9**	**1.5**	**....**

• SMITH, Sam

Sam Smith

Born: Jan. 27, 1944. Hazard, KY, United States. Height: 6'7". Weight: 230 lbs. Drafted: 1967 College: Kentucky Wesleyan

YEAR	TEAM	GP	GS	MIN	PTS	FGM	FGA	FG%	3PM	3PA	3P%	FTM	FTA	FT%	ORB	DRB	TRB	AST	PF	DQ	STL	BLK	TO	MPG	PPG	RPG	APG	PCM
67-68	Minnesota-A	77	....	2175	755	284	750	.379	2	6	.333	185	280	.661	....	....	586	81	171	1	....	....	94	28.2	9.8	7.6	1.1	.386
68-69	Kentucky-A	62	....	1421	461	173	437	.396	1	10	.100	114	172	.663	169	221	390	64	143	0	....	....	70	22.9	7.4	6.3	1.0	.391
69-70	Kentucky-A	81	....	2405	778	307	724	.424	1	4	.250	163	249	.655	301	418	719	109	202	4	....	....	123	29.7	9.6	8.9	1.3	.432
70-71	Kentucky-A	25	....	259	88	33	73	.452	0	2	.000	22	35	.629	29	39	68	16	34	0	....	....	18	10.4	3.5	2.7	0.6	.428
70-71	Utah-A	10	....	43	15	6	20	.300	1	3	.333	2	4	.500	10	3	13	4	8	0	....	....	1	4.3	1.5	1.3	0.4	.349
ABA Season Totals		**255**	**....**	**6303**	**2097**	**803**	**2004**	**.401**	**5**	**25**	**.200**	**486**	**740**	**.657**	**509**	**681**	**1776**	**274**	**558**	**5**	**....**	**....**	**306**	**24.7**	**8.2**	**7.0**	**1.1**	**....**
67-68	Minnesota-A	10	....	374	147	56	142	.394	0	0	.000	35	51	.686	....	....	81	12	39	0	....	....	15	37.4	14.7	8.1	1.2	.358
68-69	Kentucky-A	7	....	157	45	19	57	.333	0	2	.000	7	16	.438	....	....	42	9	24	0	....	....	8	22.4	6.4	6.0	1.3	.284
69-70	Kentucky-A	12	....	354	136	54	99	.545	0	0	.000	28	38	.737	41	55	96	12	....	0	....	....	25	29.5	11.3	8.0	1.0	....
70-71	Utah-A	3	....	10	4	2	6	.333	0	2	.000	0	0	.000	2	1	3	1	1	0	....	....	0	3.3	1.3	1.0	0.3	.400
ABA Playoff Totals		**32**	**....**	**895**	**332**	**131**	**304**	**.431**	**0**	**4**	**.000**	**70**	**105**	**.667**	**43**	**56**	**222**	**34**	**64**	**0**	**....**	**....**	**48**	**28.0**	**10.4**	**6.9**	**1.1**	**....**

YEAR	TEAM	GP	GS	MIN	PTS	FGM	FGA	FG%	3PM	3PA	3P%	FTM	FTA	FT%	ORB	DRB	TRB	AST	PF	DQ	STL	BLK	TO	MPG	PPG	RPG	APG	PCM

• SMITH, Sam

Sam Smith

Born: Jan. 8, 1955. Ferriday, LA, United States.   Height: 6'4".   Weight: 200 lbs.   Drafted: 1977   College: UNLV

YEAR	TEAM	GP	GS	MIN	PTS	FGM	FGA	FG%	3PM	3PA	3P%	FTM	FTA	FT%	ORB	DRB	TRB	AST	PF	DQ	STL	BLK	TO	MPG	PPG	RPG	APG	PCM
78-79	Milwaukee	16	....	125	56	19	47	.404	....	....	....	18	24	.750	0	9	9	16	12	0	8	7	8	7.8	3.5	0.6	1.0	.438
79-80	Chicago	30	....	496	259	97	230	.422	8	35	.229	57	63	.905	22	32	54	42	54	0	25	7	33	16.5	8.6	1.8	1.4	.414
NBA Season Totals		46	....	621	315	116	277	.419	8	35	.229	75	87	.862	22	41	63	58	66	0	33	14	41	13.5	6.8	1.4	1.3	....

• SMITH, Steve

Steven Delano Smith

Born: Mar. 31, 1969. Highland Park, MI, United States.   Height: 6'7".   Weight: 200 lbs.   Drafted: 1991   College: Michigan State

YEAR	TEAM	GP	GS	MIN	PTS	FGM	FGA	FG%	3PM	3PA	3P%	FTM	FTA	FT%	ORB	DRB	TRB	AST	PF	DQ	STL	BLK	TO	MPG	PPG	RPG	APG	PCM
91-92	Miami	61	59	1806	729	297	654	.454	40	125	.320	95	127	.748	81	107	188	278	162	1	59	19	153	29.6	12.0	3.1	4.6	.393
92-93	Miami	48	43	1610	766	279	619	.451	53	132	.402	155	197	.787	56	141	197	267	148	3	50	15	130	33.5	16.0	4.1	5.6	.477
93-94	Miami	78	77	2776	1346	491	1076	.456	91	262	.347	273	327	.835	156	196	352	394	217	6	84	35	203	35.6	17.3	4.5	5.1	.489
94-95	Miami	2	2	62	41	11	29	.379	2	12	.167	17	22	.773	4	2	6	7	9	0	2	1	4	31.0	20.5	3.0	3.5	.479
94-95	Atlanta	78	59	2603	1264	417	976	.427	135	404	.334	295	349	.845	100	170	270	267	216	2	60	32	148	33.4	16.2	3.5	3.4	.422
95-96	Atlanta	80	80	2856	1446	494	1143	.432	140	423	.331	318	385	.826	124	202	326	224	207	1	68	17	152	35.7	18.1	4.1	2.8	.416
96-97	Atlanta	72	72	2818	1445	491	1145	.429	130	388	.335	333	393	.847	90	148	238	305	173	2	62	23	173	39.1	20.1	3.3	4.2	.423
97-98	Atlanta	73	73	2857	1464	489	1101	.444	97	276	.351	389	455	.855	133	176	309	292	219	4	75	29	175	39.1	20.1	4.2	4.0	.458
98-99	Atlanta	36	36	1314	672	217	540	.402	47	139	.338	191	225	.849	50	101	151	118	100	2	36	11	99	36.5	18.7	4.2	3.3	.414
99-00	Portland	82	81	2689	1225	420	900	.467	96	241	.398	289	340	.850	123	190	313	209	214	0	71	31	117	32.8	14.9	3.8	2.5	.434
00-01	Portland	81	36	2542	1105	359	788	.456	78	230	.339	309	347	.890	87	185	272	213	203	0	48	24	137	31.4	13.6	3.4	2.6	.406
01-02	San Antonio	77	76	2212	895	310	682	.455	116	246	**.472**	159	181	.878	45	148	193	151	158	0	54	15	108	28.7	11.6	2.5	2.0	.353
02-03	San Antonio	53	18	1032	360	113	291	.388	39	118	.331	95	114	.833	21	78	99	70	79	0	28	9	43	19.5	6.8	1.9	1.3	.305
NBA Season Totals		821	712	27177	12758	4388	9944	.441	1064	2996	.355	2918	3462	.843	1070	1844	2914	2795	2105	21	697	261	1642	33.1	15.5	3.5	3.4	....
91-92	Miami	3	3	100	48	18	34	.529	7	11	.636	5	6	.833	3	3	6	15	2	0	4	1	3	33.3	16.0	2.0	5.0	.552
93-94	Miami	5	5	192	96	33	80	.413	9	22	.409	21	25	.840	17	13	30	11	12	0	4	2	10	38.4	19.2	6.0	2.2	.424
94-95	Atlanta	3	3	108	57	17	43	.395	7	18	.389	16	19	.842	1	7	8	6	14	0	6	1	3	36.0	19.0	2.7	2.0	.391
95-96	Atlanta	10	10	421	217	75	171	.439	25	61	.410	42	52	.808	15	26	41	32	31	0	13	13	16	42.1	21.7	4.1	3.2	.450
96-97	Atlanta	10	10	421	189	55	139	.396	18	55	.327	61	74	.824	12	27	39	17	38	0	4	1	28	42.1	18.9	3.9	1.7	.285
97-98	Atlanta	4	4	160	99	39	68	.574	10	20	.500	11	16	.688	2	9	11	9	17	1	2	3	5	40.0	24.8	2.8	2.3	.514
98-99	Atlanta	9	9	356	156	54	153	.353	9	33	.273	39	43	.907	14	17	31	30	32	0	14	2	21	39.6	17.3	3.4	3.3	.305
99-00	Portland	16	16	604	274	88	181	.486	29	53	.547	69	78	.885	13	27	40	44	44	0	19	4	27	37.8	17.1	2.5	2.8	.408
00-01	Portland	3	3	122	51	16	34	.471	4	11	.364	15	16	.938	5	8	13	7	3	0	2	1	10	40.7	17.0	4.3	2.3	.378
01-02	San Antonio	10	10	298	103	32	87	.368	10	38	.263	29	30	.967	14	20	34	17	20	0	8	1	7	29.8	10.3	3.4	1.7	.318
02-03	San Antonio	9	0	66	16	5	24	.208	2	12	.167	4	4	1.000	1	6	7	6	3	0	1	0	2	7.3	1.8	0.8	0.7	.142
NBA Playoff Totals		82	73	2848	1306	432	1014	.426	130	334	.389	312	363	.860	97	163	260	194	216	1	77	29	132	34.7	15.9	3.2	2.4	....

• SMITH, Stevin

Stevin L. (Hedake) Smith

Born: Jan. 24, 1972. Dallas, TX, United States.   Height: 6'2".   Weight: 208 lbs.   Drafted: —   College: Arizona State

YEAR	TEAM	GP	GS	MIN	PTS	FGM	FGA	FG%	3PM	3PA	3P%	FTM	FTA	FT%	ORB	DRB	TRB	AST	PF	DQ	STL	BLK	TO	MPG	PPG	RPG	APG	PCM
96-97	Dallas	8	0	60	14	6	18	.333	1	6	.167	1	1	1.000	2	8	10	4	9	0	1	0	4	7.5	1.8	1.3	0.5	.157
NBA Season Totals		8	0	60	14	6	18	.333	1	6	.167	1	1	1.000	2	8	10	4	9	0	1	0	4	7.5	1.8	1.3	0.5	....

• SMITH, Tony

Charles Anton Smith

Born: June 14, 1968. Wauwatosa, WI, United States.   Height: 6'3".   Weight: 185 lbs.   Drafted: 1990   College: Marquette

YEAR	TEAM	GP	GS	MIN	PTS	FGM	FGA	FG%	3PM	3PA	3P%	FTM	FTA	FT%	ORB	DRB	TRB	AST	PF	DQ	STL	BLK	TO	MPG	PPG	RPG	APG	PCM
90-91	LA Lakers	64	1	695	234	97	220	.441	0	7	.000	40	57	.702	24	47	71	135	80	0	28	12	70	10.9	3.7	1.1	2.1	.369
91-92	LA Lakers	63	0	820	275	113	283	.399	0	11	.000	49	75	.653	31	45	76	109	91	0	39	8	50	13.0	4.4	1.2	1.7	.302
92-93	LA Lakers	55	9	752	330	133	275	.484	2	11	.182	62	82	.756	46	41	87	63	72	1	50	7	39	13.7	6.0	1.6	1.1	.425
93-94	LA Lakers	73	31	1617	645	272	617	.441	16	50	.320	85	119	.714	106	89	195	148	128	1	59	14	73	22.2	8.8	2.7	2.0	.367
94-95	LA Lakers	61	4	1024	340	132	309	.427	32	91	.352	44	63	.698	43	64	107	102	111	0	46	7	49	16.8	5.6	1.8	1.7	.318
95-96	Phoenix	34	2	528	189	70	173	.405	25	77	.325	24	37	.649	24	32	56	86	60	0	21	5	41	15.5	5.6	1.6	2.5	.355
95-96	Miami	25	1	410	109	46	101	.455	13	39	.333	4	9	.444	6	33	39	68	46	1	16	5	25	16.4	4.4	1.6	2.7	.337
96-97	Charlotte	69	39	1291	346	138	337	.409	32	99	.323	38	59	.644	38	56	94	150	110	2	48	19	76	18.7	5.0	1.4	2.2	.263
97-98	Milwaukee	7	0	80	19	8	24	.333	0	4	.000	3	4	.750	4	3	7	10	7	0	5	2	9	11.4	2.7	1.0	1.4	.202
00-01	Atlanta	6	0	78	17	8	23	.348	0	2	.000	1	2	.500	2	1	3	10	12	0	7	0	9	13.0	2.8	0.5	1.7	.123
NBA Season Totals		457	87	7295	2504	1017	2362	.431	120	391	.307	350	507	.690	324	411	735	881	717	6	319	79	441	16.0	5.5	1.6	1.9	....
90-91	LA Lakers	7	0	40	14	6	13	.462	0	0	.000	2	3	.667	3	0	3	2	6	1	1	0	6	5.7	2.0	0.4	0.3	.112
91-92	LA Lakers	4	0	40	7	3	10	.300	0	2	.000	1	2	.500	1	1	2	5	5	0	4	0	3	10.0	1.8	0.5	1.3	.146
92-93	LA Lakers	5	0	73	34	13	25	.520	2	4	.500	6	9	.667	5	3	8	2	14	0	1	1	3	14.6	6.8	1.6	0.4	.322
94-95	LA Lakers	6	0	27	9	3	13	.231	3	10	.300	0	2	.000	1	2	3	3	1	0	0	0	4	4.5	1.5	0.5	0.5	.017
95-96	Miami	3	0	61	22	9	19	.474	4	10	.400	0	0	.000	3	1	4	8	7	0	4	0	3	20.3	7.3	1.3	2.7	.369
96-97	Charlotte	2	0	9	1	0	1	.000	0	1	.000	1	2	.500	0	1	1	2	1	0	1	0	3	4.5	0.5	0.5	1.0	.038
NBA Playoff Totals		27	0	250	87	34	81	.420	9	27	.333	10	18	.556	13	8	21	22	34	1	11	1	22	9.3	3.2	0.8	0.8	....

• SMITH, William

William A. Smith

Born: Feb. 14, 1949.   Height: 7'.   Weight: 220 lbs.   Drafted: 1971   College: Syracuse

YEAR	TEAM	GP	GS	MIN	PTS	FGM	FGA	FG%	3PM	3PA	3P%	FTM	FTA	FT%	ORB	DRB	TRB	AST	PF	DQ	STL	BLK	TO	MPG	PPG	RPG	APG	PCM
71-72	Portland	22	....	448	182	72	173	.416	....	....	....	38	64	.594	....	....	135	19	73	3	....	....	....	20.4	8.3	6.1	0.9	.425
72-73	Portland	8	....	43	23	9	15	.600	....	....	....	5	8	.625	....	....	8	1	8	0	....	....	....	5.4	2.9	1.0	0.1	.492
NBA Season Totals		30	....	491	205	81	188	.431	....	....	....	43	72	.597	....	....	143	20	81	3	....	....	....	16.4	6.8	4.8	0.7	....
43-44	Cleveland-N	2	....	....	17	5	....	....	....	....	....	7	....	....	....	....	....	....	....	....	....	....	....	....	8.5	....	....	....
NBL Playoff Totals		2	....	....	17	5	....	....	....	....	....	7	....	....	....	....	....	....	....	....	....	....	....	....	8.5	....	....	....

• SMITH, William

William Smith

Born: 1911. Height: 6'5". Weight: 230 lbs. Drafted: — College: none

YEAR	TEAM	GP	GS	MIN	PTS	FGM	FGA	FG%	3PM	3PA	3P%	FTM	FTA	FT%	ORB	DRB	TRB	AST	PF	DQ	STL	BLK	TO	MPG	PPG	RPG	APG	PCM
43-44	Cleveland-N	4	....	....	24	9	....	....	....	....	....	6	....	....	....	....	....	....	....	....	....	....	....	....	6.0	....	....	....
48-49	Dayton-N	32	....	....	127	45	....	....	....	....	....	37	49	.755	....	....	....	....	....	....	....	....	....	....	4.0	....	....	....
NBL Season Totals		36	....	....	151	54	....	....	....	....	....	43	49	....	....	....	....	....	....	....	....	....	....	....	4.2	....	....	....

• SMITH, Willie

William C. Smith

Born: Oct. 26, 1953. Las Vegas, NV, United States. Height: 6'2". Weight: 170 lbs. Drafted: 1976 College: Missouri

YEAR	TEAM	GP	GS	MIN	PTS	FGM	FGA	FG%	3PM	3PA	3P%	FTM	FTA	FT%	ORB	DRB	TRB	AST	PF	DQ	STL	BLK	TO	MPG	PPG	RPG	APG	PCM
76-77	Chicago	2	....	11	0	0	1	.000	....	....	....	0	0	.000	0	0	0	0	1	0	0	0	....	5.5	0.0	0.0	0.0	-.118
77-78	Indiana	1	....	7	0	0	0	.000	....	....	....	0	0	.000	0	0	0	1	1	0	0	0	0	7.0	0.0	0.0	1.0	.098
78-79	Portland	13	....	131	58	23	44	.523	....	....	....	12	17	.706	7	6	13	17	19	0	10	1	14	10.1	4.5	1.0	1.3	.428
79-80	Cleveland	62	....	1051	299	121	315	.384	17	71	.239	40	52	.769	56	65	121	259	110	1	75	1	93	17.0	4.8	2.0	4.2	.424
NBA Season Totals		78	....	1200	357	144	360	.400	17	71	.239	52	69	.754	63	71	134	277	131	1	85	2	107	15.4	4.6	1.7	3.6	....

• SMITS, Rik

Rik (The Dunking Dutchman) Smits

Born: Aug. 23, 1966. Eindhoven, Netherlands. Height: 7'4". Weight: 250 lbs. Drafted: 1988 College: Marist

YEAR	TEAM	GP	GS	MIN	PTS	FGM	FGA	FG%	3PM	3PA	3P%	FTM	FTA	FT%	ORB	DRB	TRB	AST	PF	DQ	STL	BLK	TO	MPG	PPG	RPG	APG	PCM
88-89	Indiana	82	71	2041	956	386	746	.517	0	1	.000	184	255	.722	185	315	500	70	310	**14**	37	151	131	24.9	11.7	6.1	0.9	.508
89-90	Indiana	82	82	2404	1271	515	967	.533	0	1	.000	241	297	.811	135	377	512	142	**328**	**11**	45	169	139	29.3	15.5	6.2	1.7	.569
90-91	Indiana	76	38	1690	828	342	705	.485	0	0	.000	144	189	.762	116	241	357	84	246	3	24	111	84	22.2	10.9	4.7	1.1	.487
91-92	Indiana	74	55	1772	1024	436	855	.510	0	2	.000	152	193	.788	124	293	417	116	231	4	29	100	133	23.9	13.8	5.6	1.6	.574
92-93	Indiana	81	81	2072	1155	494	1017	.486	0	0	.000	167	228	.732	126	306	432	121	285	5	27	74	146	25.6	14.3	5.3	1.5	.481
93-94	Indiana	78	75	2113	1224	493	923	.534	0	1	.000	238	300	.793	135	348	483	156	281	**11**	49	82	148	27.1	15.7	6.2	2.0	.600
94-95	Indiana	78	78	2381	1400	558	1060	.526	0	2	.000	284	377	.753	192	409	601	111	278	6	40	79	187	30.5	17.9	7.7	1.4	.577
95-96	Indiana	63	63	1901	1164	466	894	.521	1	5	.200	231	293	.788	119	314	433	110	226	5	21	45	158	30.2	18.5	6.9	1.7	.559
96-97	Indiana	52	52	1518	887	356	733	.486	2	8	.250	173	217	.797	105	256	361	67	175	3	22	59	125	29.2	17.1	6.9	1.3	.527
97-98	Indiana	73	69	2085	1216	514	1038	.495	0	3	.000	188	240	.783	127	378	505	101	243	9	40	88	131	28.6	16.7	6.9	1.4	.561
98-99	Indiana	49	49	1271	728	310	633	.490	0	2	.000	108	132	.818	73	202	275	52	159	1	18	52	75	25.9	14.9	5.6	1.1	.517
99-00	Indiana	79	79	1852	1018	431	890	.484	0	1	.000	156	211	.739	94	307	401	85	249	1	20	100	108	23.4	12.9	5.1	1.1	.503
NBA Season Totals		867	792	23100	12871	5301	10461	.507	3	26	.115	2266	2932	.773	1531	3746	5277	1215	3011	73	372	1110	1565	26.6	14.8	6.1	1.4	....
89-90	Indiana	3	3	96	37	14	28	.500	0	0	.000	9	11	.818	4	12	16	3	12	0	2	4	5	32.0	12.3	5.3	1.0	.380
90-91	Indiana	5	0	88	49	21	37	.568	0	0	.000	7	8	.875	4	14	18	2	23	1	1	7	5	17.6	9.8	3.6	0.4	.507
91-92	Indiana	3	1	28	10	4	11	.364	0	0	.000	2	2	1.000	3	3	6	0	7	0	2	1	3	9.3	3.3	2.0	0.0	.208
92-93	Indiana	4	4	143	90	37	64	.578	0	1	.000	16	22	.727	13	19	32	7	18	1	5	4	8	35.8	22.5	8.0	1.8	.642
93-94	Indiana	16	16	450	256	103	218	.472	0	0	.000	50	62	.806	23	61	84	31	64	1	10	9	43	28.1	16.0	5.3	1.9	.454
94-95	Indiana	17	17	546	341	127	232	.547	1	1	1.000	86	107	.804	32	87	119	34	73	2	5	14	34	32.1	20.1	7.0	2.0	.608
95-96	Indiana	5	5	166	95	42	77	.545	0	0	.000	11	14	.786	13	24	37	8	20	1	2	2	14	33.2	19.0	7.4	1.6	.513
97-98	Indiana	16	16	476	265	105	209	.502	0	1	.000	55	64	.859	17	68	85	20	67	3	8	14	21	29.8	16.6	5.3	1.3	.495
98-99	Indiana	13	13	293	153	67	147	.456	0	0	.000	19	20	.950	16	49	65	9	51	3	6	15	25	22.5	11.8	5.0	0.7	.420
99-00	Indiana	22	21	461	241	103	207	.498	0	1	.000	35	40	.875	24	54	78	21	84	1	10	20	27	21.0	11.0	3.5	1.0	.440
NBA Playoff Totals		104	96	2747	1537	623	1230	.507	1	4	.250	290	350	.829	149	391	540	135	419	13	51	90	185	26.4	14.8	5.2	1.3	....

• SMREK, Mike

Michael Frank Smrek

Born: Aug. 31, 1962. Welland, ON, Canada. Height: 7' Weight: 250 lbs. Drafted: 1985 College: Canisius

YEAR	TEAM	GP	GS	MIN	PTS	FGM	FGA	FG%	3PM	3PA	3P%	FTM	FTA	FT%	ORB	DRB	TRB	AST	PF	DQ	STL	BLK	TO	MPG	PPG	RPG	APG	PCM
85-86	Chicago	38	5	408	108	46	122	.377	0	2	.000	16	29	.552	46	64	110	19	95	0	6	23	30	10.7	2.8	2.9	0.5	.267
86-87	LA Lakers	35	3	233	76	30	60	.500	0	0	.000	16	25	.640	13	24	37	5	70	1	4	13	18	6.7	2.2	1.1	0.1	.215
87-88	LA Lakers	48	2	421	132	44	103	.427	0	0	.000	44	66	.667	27	58	85	8	105	3	7	42	29	8.8	2.8	1.8	0.2	.295
88-89	San Antonio	43	18	623	193	72	153	.471	0	0	.000	49	76	.645	42	87	129	12	102	2	13	58	47	14.5	4.5	3.0	0.3	.342
89-90	Golden State	13	3	107	21	10	24	.417	0	0	.000	1	6	.167	11	23	34	1	18	0	4	11	9	8.2	1.6	2.6	0.1	.333
90-91	Golden State	5	0	25	14	6	11	.545	0	0	.000	2	4	.500	3	4	7	1	9	0	2	0	2	5.0	2.8	1.4	0.2	.472
90-91	LA Clippers	10	0	70	10	3	16	.188	0	0	.000	4	8	.500	4	15	19	3	18	1	1	3	1	7.0	1.0	1.9	0.3	.162
91-92	Golden State	2	0	3	0	0	0	.000	0	0	.000	0	0	.000	0	1	1	0	0	0	0	0	0	1.5	0.0	0.5	0.0	.310
NBA Season Totals		194	31	1890	554	211	489	.431	0	2	.000	132	214	.617	146	276	422	49	417	7	37	150	136	9.7	2.9	2.2	0.3	....
85-86	Chicago	3	0	5	0	0	1	.000	0	0	.000	0	0	.000	0	0	0	0	2	0	0	1	0	1.7	0.0	0.0	0.0	-.186
86-87	LA Lakers	10	0	33	8	2	10	.200	0	0	.000	4	6	.667	3	4	7	0	15	0	0	6	1	3.3	0.8	0.7	0.0	.115
87-88	LA Lakers	8	0	34	3	1	5	.200	0	0	.000	1	3	.333	1	5	6	0	4	0	1	3	2	4.3	0.4	0.8	0.0	.116
NBA Playoff Totals		21	0	72	11	3	16	.188	0	0	.000	5	9	.556	4	9	13	0	21	0	1	10	3	3.4	0.5	0.6	0.0	....

• SMYTH, Joe

Joseph George Smyth

Born: May 22, 1929. Height: 6'3". Weight: 215 lbs. Drafted: 1953 College: Niagara

YEAR	TEAM	GP	GS	MIN	PTS	FGM	FGA	FG%	3PM	3PA	3P%	FTM	FTA	FT%	ORB	DRB	TRB	AST	PF	DQ	STL	BLK	TO	MPG	PPG	RPG	APG	PCM
53-54	New York	8	....	59	15	5	15	.333	....	....	....	5	9	.556	....	....	10	2	9	0	....	....	....	7.4	1.9	1.3	0.3	.220
53-54	Baltimore	32	....	436	116	43	123	.350	....	....	....	30	56	.536	....	....	88	47	44	0	....	....	....	13.6	3.6	2.8	1.5	.361
NBA Season Totals		40	....	495	131	48	138	.348	....	....	....	35	65	.538	....	....	98	49	53	0	....	....	....	12.4	3.3	2.5	1.2	....

• SNOW, Eric

Eric Snow

Born: Apr. 24, 1973. Canton, OH, United States. Height: 6'3". Weight: 190 lbs. Drafted: 1995 College: Michigan State

YEAR	TEAM	GP	GS	MIN	PTS	FGM	FGA	FG%	3PM	3PA	3P%	FTM	FTA	FT%	ORB	DRB	TRB	AST	PF	DQ	STL	BLK	TO	MPG	PPG	RPG	APG	PCM
95-96	Seattle	43	1	389	115	42	100	.420	2	10	.200	29	49	.592	9	34	43	73	53	0	28	0	39	9.0	2.7	1.0	1.7	.344
96-97	Seattle	67	0	775	199	74	164	.451	4	15	.267	47	66	.712	17	53	70	159	94	0	37	3	47	11.6	3.0	1.0	2.4	.375
97-98	Seattle	17	0	74	25	10	23	.435	0	1	.000	5	10	.500	0	4	4	13	15	0	0	1	12	4.4	1.5	0.2	0.8	.158
97-98	Philadelphia	47	0	844	184	69	161	.429	2	16	.125	44	61	.721	19	58	77	164	99	0	60	4	52	18.0	3.9	1.6	3.5	.363
98-99	Philadelphia	48	48	1716	413	149	348	.428	5	21	.238	110	150	.733	25	137	162	301	149	2	100	1	111	35.8	8.6	3.4	6.3	.362
99-00	Philadelphia	82	80	2866	651	257	597	.430	11	45	.244	126	177	.712	42	219	261	624	243	2	140	8	162	35.0	7.9	3.2	7.6	.389
00-01	Philadelphia	50	50	1740	491	182	435	.418	5	19	.263	122	154	.792	27	139	166	369	123	1	77	7	124	34.8	9.8	3.3	7.4	.410

YEAR	TEAM	GP	GS	MIN	PTS	FGM	FGA	FG%	3PM	3PA	3P%	FTM	FTA	FT%	ORB	DRB	TRB	AST	PF	DQ	STL	BLK	TO	MPG	PPG	RPG	APG	PCM
01-02	Philadelphia	61	61	2225	738	276	624	.442	3	27	.111	183	227	.806	33	182	215	400	167	1	95	9	138	36.5	12.1	3.5	6.6	.417
02-03	Philadelphia	82	82	3108	1054	361	799	.452	7	32	.219	325	379	.858	71	230	301	544	235	2	133	11	194	37.9	12.9	3.7	6.6	.433
NBA Season Totals		497	322	13737	3870	1420	3251	.437	39	186	.210	991	1273	.778	243	1056	1299	2647	1178	8	670	44	879	27.6	7.8	2.6	5.3	....
95-96	Seattle	10	0	24	2	1	7	.143	0	2	.000	0	0	.000	0	4	4	6	3	0	2	0	4	2.4	0.2	0.4	0.6	.133
96-97	Seattle	8	0	48	13	5	11	.455	2	4	.500	1	2	.500	0	2	2	12	7	0	4	0	0	6.0	1.6	0.3	1.5	.460
98-99	Philadelphia	8	8	306	99	37	88	.420	3	13	.231	22	27	.815	3	30	33	57	26	0	8	1	25	38.3	12.4	4.1	7.1	.387
99-00	Philadelphia	5	4	138	37	15	31	.484	3	4	.750	4	4	1.000	0	10	10	35	14	0	4	1	7	27.6	7.4	2.0	7.0	.446
00-01	Philadelphia	23	9	717	214	87	210	.414	0	7	.000	40	55	.727	26	60	86	104	63	0	27	2	45	31.2	9.3	3.7	4.5	.343
01-02	Philadelphia	5	5	171	54	18	56	.321	1	6	.167	17	22	.773	3	19	22	27	13	0	6	0	15	34.2	10.8	4.4	5.4	.308
02-03	Philadelphia	12	12	415	138	43	102	.422	1	10	.100	51	58	.879	9	31	40	67	47	1	18	0	30	34.6	11.5	3.3	5.6	.382
NBA Playoff Totals		71	38	1819	557	206	505	.408	10	46	.217	135	168	.804	41	156	197	308	173	1	69	4	126	25.6	7.8	2.8	4.3	....

• SNYDER, Bello

Bello Snyder

Born: 1912. Height: 5'9". Weight: 185 lbs. Drafted: — College: none

YEAR	TEAM	GP	GS	MIN	PTS	FGM	FGA	FG%	3PM	3PA	3P%	FTM	FTA	FT%	ORB	DRB	TRB	AST	PF	DQ	STL	BLK	TO	MPG	PPG	RPG	APG	PCM
37-38	Buffalo-N	8	....	....	46	18	....	....	....	....	....	10	....	....	....	....	....	....	....	....	....	....	....	....	5.8	....	....	....
NBL Season Totals		8	....	....	46	18	....	....	....	....	....	10	....	....	....	....	....	....	....	....	....	....	....	....	5.8	....	....	....

• SNYDER, Dick

Richard J. Snyder Jr.

Born: Feb. 1, 1944. North Canton, OH, United States. Height: 6'5". Weight: 207 lbs. Drafted: 1966 College: Davidson

YEAR	TEAM	GP	GS	MIN	PTS	FGM	FGA	FG%	3PM	3PA	3P%	FTM	FTA	FT%	ORB	DRB	TRB	AST	PF	DQ	STL	BLK	TO	MPG	PPG	RPG	APG	PCM
66-67	St. Louis	55	....	676	334	144	333	.432	....	....	....	46	61	.754	....	....	91	59	82	1	....	....	....	12.3	6.1	1.7	1.1	.426
67-68	St. Louis	75	....	1622	643	257	613	.419	....	....	....	129	167	.772	....	....	194	164	215	5	....	....	....	21.6	8.6	2.6	2.2	.376
68-69	Phoenix	81	....	2108	983	399	846	.472	....	....	....	185	255	.725	....	....	328	211	213	2	....	....	....	26.0	12.1	4.0	2.6	.480
69-70	Phoenix	6	....	147	51	22	45	.489	....	....	....	7	8	.875	....	....	15	9	20	1	....	....	....	24.5	8.5	2.5	1.5	.305
69-70	Seattle	76	....	2290	1030	434	818	.531	....	....	....	162	200	.810	....	....	308	333	257	7	....	....	....	30.1	13.6	4.1	4.4	.527
70-71	Seattle	82	....	2824	1592	645	1215	.531	....	....	....	302	361	.837	....	....	257	352	249	6	....	....	....	34.4	19.4	3.1	4.3	.564
71-72	Seattle	73	....	2534	1210	496	937	.529	....	....	....	218	259	.842	....	....	228	283	200	3	....	....	....	34.7	16.6	3.1	3.9	.491
72-73	Seattle	82	....	3060	1132	473	1022	.463	....	....	....	186	216	.861	....	....	323	311	216	2	....	....	....	37.3	13.8	3.9	3.8	.388
73-74	Seattle	74	....	2670	1338	572	1189	.481	....	....	....	194	224	.866	90	216	306	265	257	4	90	26	....	36.1	18.1	4.1	3.6	.470
74-75	Cleveland	82	....	2590	1161	498	988	.504	....	....	....	165	195	.846	37	201	238	281	226	3	69	43	....	31.6	14.2	2.9	3.4	.448
75-76	Cleveland	82	....	2274	1037	441	881	.501	....	....	....	155	188	.824	50	148	198	220	215	0	59	33	....	27.7	12.6	2.4	2.7	.428
76-77	Cleveland	82	....	1685	759	316	693	.456	....	....	....	127	149	.852	47	102	149	160	177	2	45	30	....	20.5	9.3	1.8	2.0	.391
77-78	Cleveland	58	....	660	280	112	252	.444	....	....	....	56	64	.875	9	40	49	56	74	0	23	19	46	11.4	4.8	0.8	1.0	.339
78-79	Seattle	56	....	536	205	81	187	.433	....	....	....	43	51	.843	15	33	48	63	52	0	14	6	34	9.6	3.7	0.9	1.1	.341
NBA Season Totals		964	....	25676	11755	4890	10019	.488	....	....	....	1975	2398	.824	248	740	2732	2767	2453	36	300	157	80	26.6	12.2	2.8	2.9	....
66-67	St. Louis	1	....	2	0	0	0	.000	....	....	....	0	0	.000	....	....	0	0	0	0	....	....	....	2.0	0.0	0.0	0.0	.000
67-68	St. Louis	4	....	62	24	10	22	.455	....	....	....	4	5	.800	....	....	5	4	6	0	....	....	....	15.5	6.0	1.3	1.0	.330
75-76	Cleveland	13	....	364	156	69	153	.451	....	....	....	18	22	.818	10	19	29	31	35	1	11	6	....	28.0	12.0	2.2	2.4	.350
76-77	Cleveland	3	....	53	18	8	27	.296	....	....	....	2	5	.400	2	3	5	4	6	0	1	2	....	17.7	6.0	1.7	1.3	.124
77-78	Cleveland	1	....	3	0	0	0	.000	....	....	....	0	0	.000	0	0	0	0	0	0	0	0	1	3.0	0.0	0.0	0.0	-.292
78-79	Seattle	9	....	88	26	10	31	.323	....	....	....	6	9	.667	2	9	11	10	8	0	4	3	7	9.8	2.9	1.2	1.1	.263
NBA Playoff Totals		31	....	572	224	97	233	.416	....	....	....	30	41	.732	14	31	50	49	55	1	16	11	8	18.5	7.2	1.6	1.6	....

• SOBEK, Chips

George Edward (Chips) Sobek

Born: Feb. 10, 1920. Died: Apr.9, 1990. Height: 6' Weight: 180 lbs. Drafted: — College: Notre Dame

YEAR	TEAM	GP	GS	MIN	PTS	FGM	FGA	FG%	3PM	3PA	3P%	FTM	FTA	FT%	ORB	DRB	TRB	AST	PF	DQ	STL	BLK	TO	MPG	PPG	RPG	APG	PCM
45-46	Indianapolis-N	1	....	....	5	2	....	....	....	....	....	1	....	....	....	....	....	....	....	....	....	....	....	....	5.0	....	....	....
46-47	Toledo-N	42	....	....	551	186	....	....	....	....	....	**179**	248	.722	....	....	....	....	106	....	....	....	....	....	13.1	....	....	....
47-48	Toledo-N	48	....	....	360	118	....	....	....	....	....	124	170	.729	....	....	....	....	110	....	....	....	....	....	7.5	....	....	....
48-49	Hammond-N	57	....	....	518	143	....	....	....	....	....	232	322	.720	....	....	....	....	167	....	....	....	....	....	9.1	....	....	....
49-50	Sheboygan	60	....	....	346	95	251	.378	....	....	....	156	205	.761	....	....	....	95	158	....	....	....	....	....	5.8	....	1.6	....
NBA Season Totals		60	....	....	346	95	251	.378	....	....	....	156	205	.761	....	....	....	95	158	....	....	....	....	....	5.8	....	1.6	....
NBL Season Totals		148	....	....	1434	449	....	....	....	....	....	536	740	....	....	....	....	....	383	....	....	....	....	....	9.7	....	....	....
Career Totals		208	....	....	1780	544	251	....	....	....	....	692	945	....	....	....	....	95	541	....	....	....	....	....	8.6	....	0.5	....
46-47	Toledo-N	5	....	....	47	14	....	....	....	....	....	19	26	.731	....	....	....	....	....	....	....	....	....	....	9.4	....	....	....
48-49	Hammond-N	2	....	....	9	4	....	....	....	....	....	1	1	1.000	....	....	....	....	....	....	....	....	....	....	4.5	....	....	....
49-50	Sheboygan	3	....	....	32	10	20	.500	....	....	....	12	16	.750	....	....	....	3	15	....	....	....	....	....	10.7	....	1.0	....
NBA Playoff Totals		3	....	....	32	10	20	.500	....	....	....	12	16	.750	....	....	....	3	15	....	....	....	....	....	10.7	....	1.0	....
NBL Playoff Totals		7	....	....	56	18	....	....	....	....	....	20	27	....	....	....	....	....	....	....	....	....	....	....	8.0	....	....	....
Career Playoff Totals		10	....	....	88	28	20	....	....	....	....	32	43	....	....	....	....	3	15	....	....	....	....	....	8.8	....	0.3	....

• SOBERS, Ricky

Ricky Brad Sobers

Born: Jan. 15, 1953. Bronx, NY, United States. Height: 6'3". Weight: 198 lbs. Drafted: 1975 College: UNLV

YEAR	TEAM	GP	GS	MIN	PTS	FGM	FGA	FG%	3PM	3PA	3P%	FTM	FTA	FT%	ORB	DRB	TRB	AST	PF	DQ	STL	BLK	TO	MPG	PPG	RPG	APG	PCM
75-76	Phoenix	78	....	1898	718	280	623	.449	....	....	....	158	192	.823	80	179	259	215	253	6	106	7	....	24.3	9.2	3.3	2.8	.405
76-77	Phoenix	79	....	2005	1071	414	834	.496	....	....	....	243	289	.841	82	152	234	238	258	3	93	14	....	25.4	13.6	3.0	3.0	.524
77-78	Indiana	79	....	3019	1436	553	1221	.453	....	....	....	330	400	.825	92	235	327	584	308	10	170	23	356	38.2	18.2	4.1	7.4	.492
78-79	Indiana	81	....	2825	1404	553	1194	.463	....	....	....	298	338	.882	118	183	301	450	315	8	138	23	308	34.9	17.3	3.7	5.6	.461
79-80	Chicago	82	....	2673	1161	470	1002	.469	21	68	.309	200	239	.837	75	167	242	426	294	4	136	17	279	32.6	14.2	3.0	5.2	.412
80-81	Chicago	71	....	1803	958	355	769	.462	17	66	.258	231	247	.935	46	98	144	284	225	3	98	17	206	25.4	13.5	2.0	4.0	.460
81-82	Chicago	80	6	1938	940	363	801	.453	19	76	.250	195	254	.768	37	105	142	301	238	6	73	18	216	24.2	11.8	1.8	3.8	.382
82-83	Washington	41	39	1438	645	234	534	.438	23	55	.418	154	185	.832	35	67	102	218	158	3	61	14	148	35.1	15.7	2.5	5.3	.386

YEAR TEAM	GP	GS	MIN	PTS	FGM	FGA	FG%	3PM	3PA	3P%	FTM	FTA	FT%	ORB	DRB	TRB	AST	PF	DQ	STL	BLK	TO	MPG	PPG	RPG	APG	PCM
83-84 Washington	81	81	2624	1266	508	1115	.456	29	111	.261	221	264	.837	51	128	179	377	278	10	117	17	219	32.4	15.6	2.2	4.7	.397
84-85 Seattle	71	12	1490	700	280	628	.446	8	28	.286	132	162	.815	27	76	103	252	156	0	49	9	156	21.0	9.9	1.5	3.5	.378
85-86 Seattle	78	0	1279	603	240	541	.444	13	43	.302	110	125	.880	29	70	99	180	139	1	44	2	86	16.4	7.7	1.3	2.3	.390
NBA Season Totals	821	138	22992	10902	4250	9262	.459	130	447	.291	2272	2695	.843	672	1460	2132	3525	2622	54	1085	161	1974	28.0	13.3	2.6	4.3	....
75-76 Phoenix	19	....	563	247	96	205	.468	....	....	....	55	66	.833	20	43	63	79	77	3	18	6	....	29.6	13.0	3.3	4.2	.462
80-81 Chicago	6	....	162	79	35	81	.432	1	6	.167	8	9	.889	3	8	11	22	26	1	4	0	15	27.0	13.2	1.8	3.7	.301
83-84 Washington	4	4	150	61	25	57	.439	3	10	.300	8	10	.800	2	3	5	16	19	1	5	2	9	37.5	15.3	1.3	4.0	.276
NBA Playoff Totals	29	4	875	387	156	343	.455	4	16	.250	71	85	.835	25	54	79	117	122	5	27	8	24	30.2	13.3	2.7	4.0	....

• SOBIE, Ron

Ronald Charles Sobie aka.: Ronald Charles Sobieszczyk

Born: Sept. 21, 1934. Chicago, IL, United States. Height: 6'3". Weight: 185 lbs. Drafted: 1956 College: DePaul

YEAR TEAM	GP	GS	MIN	PTS	FGM	FGA	FG%	3PM	3PA	3P%	FTM	FTA	FT%	ORB	DRB	TRB	AST	PF	DQ	STL	BLK	TO	MPG	PPG	RPG	APG	PCM
56-57 New York	71	....	1378	484	166	442	.376	....	....	....	152	199	.764	....	....	326	129	158	0	....	....	....	19.4	6.8	4.6	1.8	.440
57-58 New York	55	....	1399	630	217	539	.403	....	....	....	196	239	.820	....	....	263	125	147	3	....	....	....	25.4	11.5	4.8	2.3	.484
58-59 New York	50	....	857	400	144	400	.360	....	....	....	112	133	.842	....	....	154	78	84	0	....	....	....	17.1	8.0	3.1	1.6	.445
59-60 New York	15	....	221	103	36	104	.346	....	....	....	31	36	.861	....	....	46	19	28	0	....	....	....	14.7	6.9	3.1	1.3	.441
59-60 Minneapolis	1	....	13	2	1	4	.250	....	....	....	0	1	.000	....	....	2	2	4	0	....	....	....	13.0	2.0	2.0	2.0	.142
NBA Season Totals	192	....	3868	1619	564	1489	.379	....	....	....	491	608	.808	....	....	791	353	421	3	....	....	....	20.1	8.4	4.1	1.8	....

• SOJOURNER, Mike

Mike Sojourner

Born: Oct. 16, 1953. Germantown, PA, United States. Height: 6'9". Weight: 225 lbs. Drafted: 1974 College: Utah

YEAR TEAM	GP	GS	MIN	PTS	FGM	FGA	FG%	3PM	3PA	3P%	FTM	FTA	FT%	ORB	DRB	TRB	AST	PF	DQ	STL	BLK	TO	MPG	PPG	RPG	APG	PCM
74-75 Atlanta	73	....	2129	851	378	775	.488	....	....	....	95	146	.651	196	446	642	93	217	10	35	57	....	29.2	11.7	8.8	1.3	.494
75-76 Atlanta	67	....	1602	576	248	524	.473	....	....	....	80	119	.672	126	323	449	58	174	2	38	40	....	23.9	8.6	6.7	0.9	.437
76-77 Atlanta	51	....	551	231	95	203	.468	....	....	....	41	57	.719	49	97	146	21	66	0	15	9	....	10.8	4.5	2.9	0.4	.458
NBA Season Totals	191	....	4282	1658	721	1502	.480	....	....	....	216	322	.671	371	866	1237	172	457	12	88	106	....	22.4	8.7	6.5	0.9	....

• SOJOURNER, Willard

Willard (Rainbow) Sojourner

Born: Sept. 10, 1948. Philadelphia, PA, United States. Height: 6'8". Weight: 225 lbs. Drafted: 1971 College: Weber State

YEAR TEAM	GP	GS	MIN	PTS	FGM	FGA	FG%	3PM	3PA	3P%	FTM	FTA	FT%	ORB	DRB	TRB	AST	PF	DQ	STL	BLK	TO	MPG	PPG	RPG	APG	PCM
71-72 Virginia-A	84	....	1313	568	222	448	.496	0	0	.000	124	193	.642	185	329	514	56	222	6	....	....	86	15.6	6.8	6.1	0.7	.576
72-73 Virginia-A	64	....	1065	482	199	410	.485	0	0	.000	84	128	.656	121	243	364	75	187	4	....	....	80	16.6	7.5	5.7	1.2	.562
73-74 New York-A	82	....	1316	458	202	419	.482	0	3	.000	54	64	.844	110	225	335	54	205	....	24	88	85	16.0	5.6	4.1	0.7	.402
74-75 New York-A	79	....	1020	360	155	324	.478	1	3	.333	49	70	.700	94	181	275	42	190	....	16	64	63	12.9	4.6	3.5	0.5	.399
ABA Season Totals	309	....	4714	1868	778	1601	.486	1	6	.167	311	455	.684	510	978	1488	227	804	10	40	152	314	15.3	6.0	4.8	0.7	....
71-72 Virginia-A	10	....	58	26	11	21	.524	0	0	.000	4	4	1.000	8	15	23	6	11	0	....	....	11	5.8	2.6	2.3	0.6	.678
72-73 Virginia-A	3	....	20	10	4	7	.571	0	0	.000	2	2	1.000	3	3	6	2	2	0	....	....	2	6.7	3.3	2.0	0.7	.700
73-74 New York-A	14	....	154	39	17	41	.415	0	0	.000	5	9	.556	16	18	34	8	26	....	2	12	12	11.0	2.8	2.4	0.6	.285
74-75 New York-A	5	....	65	27	12	22	.545	0	0	.000	3	5	.600	8	5	13	2	13	....	0	9	5	13.0	5.4	2.6	0.4	.388
ABA Playoff Totals	32	....	297	102	44	91	.484	0	0	.000	14	20	.700	35	41	76	18	52	0	2	21	30	9.3	3.2	2.4	0.6	....

• SOKODY, Paul

Paul Sokody

Born: Aug. 18, 1914. Died: May12, 1992. Height: 6'2". Weight: 170 lbs. Drafted: — College: Marquette

YEAR TEAM	GP	GS	MIN	PTS	FGM	FGA	FG%	3PM	3PA	3P%	FTM	FTA	FT%	ORB	DRB	TRB	AST	PF	DQ	STL	BLK	TO	MPG	PPG	RPG	APG	PCM
38-39 Sheboygan-N	28	....	....	223	88	....	....	....	....	....	47	....	....	....	....	....	....	....	....	....	....	....	....	8.0	....	....	....
39-40 Sheboygan-N	28	....	....	133	51	....	....	....	....	....	31	....	....	....	....	....	....	....	....	....	....	....	....	4.8	....	....	....
40-41 Sheboygan-N	24	....	....	114	43	....	....	....	....	....	28	....	....	....	....	....	....	....	....	....	....	....	....	4.8	....	....	....
41-42 Sheboygan-N	24	....	....	126	52	....	....	....	....	....	22	....	....	....	....	....	....	....	....	....	....	....	....	5.3	....	....	....
42-43 Chicago-N	14	....	....	26	10	....	....	....	....	....	6	....	....	....	....	....	....	....	....	....	....	....	....	1.9	....	....	....
NBL Season Totals	118	....	....	622	244	....	....	....	....	....	134	....	....	....	....	....	....	....	....	....	....	....	....	5.3	....	....	....
39-40 Sheboygan-N	3	....	....	18	6	....	....	....	....	....	6	....	....	....	....	....	....	....	....	....	....	....	....	6.0	....	....	....
40-41 Sheboygan-N	6	....	....	25	10	....	....	....	....	....	5	....	....	....	....	....	....	....	....	....	....	....	....	4.2	....	....	....
NBL Playoff Totals	9	....	....	43	16	....	....	....	....	....	11	....	....	....	....	....	....	....	....	....	....	....	....	4.8	....	....	....

• SOLOMON, Willie

William James Solomon

Born: July 20, 1978. Hartford, CT, United States. Height: 6'1". Weight: 185 lbs. Drafted: 2001 College: Clemson

YEAR TEAM	GP	GS	MIN	PTS	FGM	FGA	FG%	3PM	3PA	3P%	FTM	FTA	FT%	ORB	DRB	TRB	AST	PF	DQ	STL	BLK	TO	MPG	PPG	RPG	APG	PCM
01-02 Memphis	62	4	881	321	113	331	.341	46	162	.284	49	73	.671	12	56	68	92	76	0	35	7	62	14.2	5.2	1.1	1.5	.252
NBA Season Totals	62	4	881	321	113	331	.341	46	162	.284	49	73	.671	12	56	68	92	76	0	35	7	62	14.2	5.2	1.1	1.5	....

• SOMERSET, Willie

Willard F. Somerset

Born: Mar. 17, 1942. Sharon, PA, United States. Height: 5'8". Weight: 170 lbs. Drafted: 1965 College: Duquesne

YEAR TEAM	GP	GS	MIN	PTS	FGM	FGA	FG%	3PM	3PA	3P%	FTM	FTA	FT%	ORB	DRB	TRB	AST	PF	DQ	STL	BLK	TO	MPG	PPG	RPG	APG	PCM
65-66 Baltimore	8	....	98	45	18	43	.419	....	....	....	9	11	.818	....	....	15	9	21	0	....	....	....	12.3	5.6	1.9	1.1	.399
67-68 Houston-A	61	....	2334	1326	467	1042	.448	33	107	.308	359	460	.780	....	....	305	225	211	5	....	....	164	38.3	21.7	5.0	3.7	.529
68-69 Houston-A	43	....	1793	1011	337	853	.395	17	75	.227	320	383	.836	79	118	197	174	158	3	....	....	123	41.7	23.5	4.6	4.0	.469
68-69 New York-A	31	....	1325	747	282	657	.429	19	64	.297	164	200	.820	62	73	135	106	103	1	....	....	92	42.7	24.1	4.4	3.4	.455
NBA Season Totals	8	....	98	45	18	43	.419	....	....	....	9	11	.818	....	....	15	9	21	0	....	....	....	12.3	5.6	1.9	1.1	....
ABA Season Totals	135	....	5452	3084	1086	2552	.426	69	246	.280	843	1043	.808	141	191	637	505	472	9	....	....	379	40.4	22.8	4.7	3.7	....
Career Totals	143	....	5550	3129	1104	2595	.425	69	246	.280	852	1054	.808	141	191	652	514	493	9	....	....	379	38.8	21.9	4.6	3.6	....
67-68 Houston-A	3	....	131	91	30	73	.411	4	14	.286	27	34	.794	....	....	25	9	11	0	....	....	16	43.7	30.3	8.3	3.0	.604
ABA Playoff Totals	3	....	131	91	30	73	.411	4	14	.286	27	34	.794	....	....	25	9	11	0	....	....	16	43.7	30.3	8.3	3.0	....

YEAR	TEAM	GP	GS	MIN	PTS	FGM	FGA	FG%	3PM	3PA	3P%	FTM	FTA	FT%	ORB	DRB	TRB	AST	PF	DQ	STL	BLK	TO	MPG	PPG	RPG	APG	PCM

• SORENSEN, Harry

Harry Sorensen

Born: 1914. Height: 6'4". Weight: 200 lbs. Drafted: — College: Nebraska

YEAR	TEAM	GP	GS	MIN	PTS	FGM	FGA	FG%	3PM	3PA	3P%	FTM	FTA	FT%	ORB	DRB	TRB	AST	PF	DQ	STL	BLK	TO	MPG	PPG	RPG	APG	PCM
39-40	Non-Skids-N	17	....	....	30	11	....	....	....	....	....	8	....	....	....	....	....	....	....	....	....	....	....	1.8	....	....	....	....
40-41	Non-Skids-N	7	....	....	7	3	....	....	....	....	....	1	....	....	....	....	....	....	....	....	....	....	....	1.0	....	....	....	....
NBL Season Totals		24	....	....	37	14	....	....	....	....	....	9	....	....	....	....	....	....	....	....	....	....	....	1.5	....	....	....	....
39-40	Non-Skids-N	5	....	....	5	1	....	....	....	....	....	3	....	....	....	....	....	....	....	....	....	....	....	1.0	....	....	....	....
NBL Playoff Totals		5	....	....	5	1	....	....	....	....	....	3	....	....	....	....	....	....	....	....	....	....	....	1.0	....	....	....	....

• SORENSON, Dave

David Lowell (Sunshine) Sorenson

Born: July 8, 1948. Height: 6'8". Weight: 225 lbs. Drafted: 1970 College: Ohio State

YEAR	TEAM	GP	GS	MIN	PTS	FGM	FGA	FG%	3PM	3PA	3P%	FTM	FTA	FT%	ORB	DRB	TRB	AST	PF	DQ	STL	BLK	TO	MPG	PPG	RPG	APG	PCM
70-71	Cleveland	79	....	1940	890	353	794	.445	....	....	....	184	229	.803	....	....	486	163	181	3	....	....	....	24.6	11.3	6.2	2.1	.524
71-72	Cleveland	76	....	1162	532	213	475	.448	....	....	....	106	136	.779	....	....	301	81	120	1	....	....	....	15.3	7.0	4.0	1.1	.510
72-73	Cleveland	10	....	129	27	11	45	.244	....	....	....	5	11	.455	....	....	37	5	16	0	....	....	....	12.9	2.7	3.7	0.5	.200
72-73	Philadelphia	48	....	626	285	113	248	.456	....	....	....	59	79	.747	....	....	173	31	91	0	....	....	....	13.0	5.9	3.6	0.6	.488
NBA Season Totals		213	....	3857	1734	690	1562	.442	....	....	....	354	455	.778	....	....	997	280	408	4	....	....	....	18.1	8.1	4.7	1.3	....

• SOTAK, Joe

Joe Sotak

Born: Apr. 22, 1914. Died: Oct.1984. Height: 6'2". Weight: 210 lbs. Drafted: — College: none

YEAR	TEAM	GP	GS	MIN	PTS	FGM	FGA	FG%	3PM	3PA	3P%	FTM	FTA	FT%	ORB	DRB	TRB	AST	PF	DQ	STL	BLK	TO	MPG	PPG	RPG	APG	PCM
37-38	Whiting-N	5	....	....	5	2	....	....	....	....	....	1	....	....	....	....	....	....	....	....	....	....	....	1.0	....	....	....
38-39	Hammond-N	23	....	....	142	47	....	....	....	....	....	48	....	....	....	....	....	....	....	....	....	....	....	6.2	....	....	....
39-40	Hammond-N	23	....	....	61	21	....	....	....	....	....	19	....	....	....	....	....	....	....	....	....	....	....	2.7	....	....	....
40-41	Hammond-N	4	....	....	17	8	....	....	....	....	....	1	....	....	....	....	....	....	....	....	....	....	....	4.3	....	....	....
NBL Season Totals		55	....	....	225	78	....	....	....	....	....	69	....	....	....	....	....	....	....	....	....	....	....	4.1	....	....	....
37-38	Whiting-N	2	....	....	4	1	....	....	....	....	....	2	....	....	....	....	....	....	....	....	....	....	....	2.0	....	....	....
NBL Playoff Totals		2	....	....	4	1	....	....	....	....	....	2	....	....	....	....	....	....	....	....	....	....	....	2.0	....	....	....

• SOTNIK, —

Sotnik

Born: —. Height: — Weight: — Drafted: — College: —

YEAR	TEAM	GP	GS	MIN	PTS	FGM	FGA	FG%	3PM	3PA	3P%	FTM	FTA	FT%	ORB	DRB	TRB	AST	PF	DQ	STL	BLK	TO	MPG	PPG	RPG	APG	PCM
46-47	Youngstown-N	4	....	....	2	1	....	....	....	....	....	0	0	.000	....	....	....	....	....	....	....	....	....	0.5	....	....	....
NBL Season Totals		4	....	....	2	1	....	....	....	....	....	0	0	....	....	....	....	....	....	....	....	....	....	0.5	....	....	....

• SOVRAN, Gino

Gino Sovran

Born: Dec. 17, 1924. Windsor, ON, Canada. Height: 6'2". Weight: 175 lbs. Drafted: — College: Detroit

YEAR	TEAM	GP	GS	MIN	PTS	FGM	FGA	FG%	3PM	3PA	3P%	FTM	FTA	FT%	ORB	DRB	TRB	AST	PF	DQ	STL	BLK	TO	MPG	PPG	RPG	APG	PCM
46-47	Toronto	6	....	....	11	5	15	.333	....	....	....	1	2	.500	....	....	....	1	5	....	....	....	....	1.8	....	0.2	....
NBA Season Totals		6	....	....	11	5	15	.333	....	....	....	1	2	.500	....	....	....	1	5	....	....	....	....	1.8	....	0.2	....

• SPAIN, Ken

John Kenneth Spain

Born: Oct. 6, 1946. Houston, TX, United States. Died: Oct.1990. Height: 6'9". Weight: 225 lbs. Drafted: 1969 College: Houston

YEAR	TEAM	GP	GS	MIN	PTS	FGM	FGA	FG%	3PM	3PA	3P%	FTM	FTA	FT%	ORB	DRB	TRB	AST	PF	DQ	STL	BLK	TO	MPG	PPG	RPG	APG	PCM
70-71	Pittsburgh-A	11	....	112	24	8	22	.364	0	0	.000	8	17	.471	11	29	40	2	17	0	....	....	9	10.2	2.2	3.6	0.2	.329
ABA Season Totals		11	....	112	24	8	22	.364	0	0	.000	8	17	.471	11	29	40	2	17	0	....	....	9	10.2	2.2	3.6	0.2	....

• SPANARKEL, Jim

James Gerard Spanarkel

Born: June 28, 1957. Jersey City, NJ, United States. Height: 6'5". Weight: 190 lbs. Drafted: 1979 College: Duke

YEAR	TEAM	GP	GS	MIN	PTS	FGM	FGA	FG%	3PM	3PA	3P%	FTM	FTA	FT%	ORB	DRB	TRB	AST	PF	DQ	STL	BLK	TO	MPG	PPG	RPG	APG	PCM
79-80	Philadelphia	40	....	442	198	72	153	.471	0	2	.000	54	65	.831	27	27	54	51	58	0	12	6	56	11.1	5.0	1.4	1.3	.371
80-81	Dallas	82	....	2317	1184	404	866	.467	1	10	.100	375	423	.887	142	155	297	232	230	3	117	20	172	28.3	14.4	3.6	2.8	.487
81-82	Dallas	82	1	1755	827	270	564	.479	8	24	.333	279	327	.853	99	111	210	206	140	0	86	9	115	21.4	10.1	2.6	2.5	.494
82-83	Dallas	48	4	722	272	91	197	.462	2	10	.200	88	113	.779	27	57	84	78	59	0	27	3	53	15.0	5.7	1.8	1.6	.387
83-84	Dallas	7	0	54	24	7	16	.438	1	2	.500	9	13	.692	5	2	7	5	8	0	6	0	4	7.7	3.4	1.0	0.7	.440
NBA Season Totals		259	5	5290	2505	844	1796	.470	12	48	.250	805	941	.855	300	352	652	572	495	3	248	38	400	20.4	9.7	2.5	2.2	....
79-80	Philadelphia	5	....	8	2	0	2	.000	0	0	.000	2	2	1.000	0	1	1	1	1	0	0	0	0	1.6	0.4	0.2	0.2	.217
NBA Playoff Totals		5	....	8	2	0	2	.000	0	0	.000	2	2	1.000	0	1	1	1	1	0	0	0	0	1.6	0.4	0.2	0.2	....

• SPARKS, Daniel

Daniel E. Sparks

Born: Apr. 17, 1945. Bloomington, IN, United States. Height: 6'8". Weight: 200 lbs. Drafted: 1968 College: Weber State

YEAR	TEAM	GP	GS	MIN	PTS	FGM	FGA	FG%	3PM	3PA	3P%	FTM	FTA	FT%	ORB	DRB	TRB	AST	PF	DQ	STL	BLK	TO	MPG	PPG	RPG	APG	PCM
68-69	Miami-A	64	....	1138	419	153	396	.386	0	0	.000	113	165	.685	138	149	287	43	171	5	....	....	70	17.8	6.5	4.5	0.7	.360
69-70	Miami-A	3	....	52	19	7	18	.389	0	0	.000	5	6	.833	9	7	16	2	7	0	....	....	4	17.3	6.3	5.3	0.7	.426
ABA Season Totals		67	....	1190	438	160	414	.386	0	0	.000	118	171	.690	147	156	303	45	178	5	....	....	74	17.8	6.5	4.5	0.7	....
68-69	Miami-A	12	....	251	77	29	65	.446	0	0	.000	19	30	.633	....	....	57	8	35	0	....	....	14	20.9	6.4	4.8	0.7	.336
ABA Playoff Totals		12	....	251	77	29	65	.446	0	0	.000	19	30	.633	....	....	57	8	35	0	....	....	14	20.9	6.4	4.8	0.7	....

• SPARROW, Guy

Guy Paul Joseph (The Bird) Sparrow

Born: Nov. 2, 1932. Pontiac, MI, United States. Height: 6'6". Weight: 218 lbs. Drafted: 1955 College: Detroit

YEAR	TEAM	GP	GS	MIN	PTS	FGM	FGA	FG%	3PM	3PA	3P%	FTM	FTA	FT%	ORB	DRB	TRB	AST	PF	DQ	STL	BLK	TO	MPG	PPG	RPG	APG	PCM
57-58	New York	72	....	1661	801	318	838	.379	....	....	....	165	257	.642	....	....	461	69	232	6	....	....	....	23.1	11.1	6.4	1.0	.438
58-59	New York	44	....	607	249	96	308	.312	....	....	....	57	98	.582	....	....	187	45	115	3	....	....	....	13.8	5.7	4.3	1.0	.375
58-59	Philadelphia	23	....	235	87	33	98	.337	....	....	....	21	40	.525	....	....	57	22	43	0	....	....	....	10.2	3.8	2.5	1.0	.362
59-60	Philadelphia	11	....	80	30	14	45	.311	....	....	....	2	8	.250	....	....	23	6	20	0	....	....	....	7.3	2.7	2.1	0.5	.270
NBA Season Totals		150	....	2583	1167	461	1289	.358	....	....	....	245	403	.608	....	....	728	142	410	9	....	....	....	17.2	7.8	4.9	0.9	....

• SPARROW, Rory

Rory Darnell Sparrow

Born: June 12, 1958. Suffolk, VA, United States. Height: 6'2". Weight: 175 lbs. Drafted: 1980 College: Villanova

YEAR	TEAM	GP	GS	MIN	PTS	FGM	FGA	FG%	3PM	3PA	3P%	FTM	FTA	FT%	ORB	DRB	TRB	AST	PF	DQ	STL	BLK	TO	MPG	PPG	RPG	APG	PCM
80-81	New Jersey	15	....	212	56	22	63	.349	0	0	.000	12	16	.750	7	11	18	32	15	0	13	3	18	14.1	3.7	1.2	2.1	.280
81-82	Atlanta	82	82	2610	857	366	730	.501	1	15	.067	124	148	.838	53	171	224	424	240	2	87	13	148	31.8	10.5	2.7	5.2	.391
82-83	Atlanta	49	49	1548	615	264	512	.516	3	15	.200	84	113	.743	39	102	141	238	162	2	70	1	127	31.6	12.6	2.9	4.9	.415
82-83	New York	32	9	880	321	128	298	.430	2	7	.286	63	86	.733	22	67	89	159	93	2	37	4	70	27.5	10.0	2.8	5.0	.391
83-84	New York	79	74	2436	818	350	738	.474	10	39	.256	108	131	.824	48	141	189	539	230	4	100	8	213	30.8	10.4	2.4	6.8	.408
84-85	New York	79	41	2292	781	326	662	.492	7	31	.226	122	141	.865	38	131	169	557	200	2	81	9	150	29.0	9.9	2.1	7.1	.463
85-86	New York	74	74	2344	796	345	723	.477	5	20	.250	101	127	.795	50	120	170	472	182	1	85	14	155	31.7	10.8	2.3	6.4	.409
86-87	New York	80	30	1951	608	263	590	.446	11	42	.262	71	89	.798	29	86	115	432	160	0	67	6	144	24.4	7.6	1.4	5.4	.371
87-88	New York	3	0	52	10	5	19	.263	0	1	.000	0	0	.000	1	1	2	5	7	0	4	0	6	17.3	3.3	0.7	1.7	-.019
87-88	Chicago	55	25	992	250	112	274	.409	2	12	.167	24	33	.727	14	56	70	162	72	1	37	3	50	18.0	4.5	1.3	2.9	.293
88-89	Miami	80	79	2613	1000	444	982	.452	18	74	.243	94	107	.879	55	161	216	429	168	0	103	17	200	32.7	12.5	2.7	5.4	.383
89-90	Miami	82	25	1756	487	210	510	.412	8	40	.200	59	77	.766	37	101	138	298	140	0	49	4	98	21.4	5.9	1.7	3.6	.305
90-91	Sacramento	80	74	2375	831	371	756	.491	31	78	.397	58	83	.699	45	141	186	362	189	1	83	16	128	29.7	10.4	2.3	4.5	.381
91-92	Chicago	4	0	18	3	1	8	.125	1	2	.500	0	0	.000	0	1	1	4	2	0	0	0	2	4.5	0.8	0.3	1.0	-.060
91-92	LA Lakers	42	0	471	124	57	143	.399	2	13	.154	8	13	.615	3	24	27	79	55	0	12	5	29	11.2	3.0	0.6	1.9	.244
NBA Season Totals		836	562	22550	7557	3264	7008	.466	101	389	.260	928	1164	.797	441	1314	1755	4192	1915	15	828	103	1538	27.0	9.0	2.1	5.0	....
81-82	Atlanta	2	2	69	14	5	12	.417	0	1	.000	4	4	1.000	2	6	8	11	7	0	2	0	7	34.5	7.0	4.0	5.5	.275
82-83	New York	6	6	202	78	30	71	.423	1	5	.200	17	21	.810	3	10	13	42	18	1	7	0	13	33.7	13.0	2.2	7.0	.413
83-84	New York	12	12	389	134	54	121	.446	2	6	.333	24	30	.800	10	16	26	86	41	2	12	1	30	32.4	11.2	2.2	7.2	.386
87-88	Chicago	7	0	106	26	10	32	.313	2	4	.500	4	6	.667	0	3	3	18	11	0	4	0	4	15.1	3.7	0.4	2.6	.202
91-92	LA Lakers	3	0	16	5	1	4	.250	0	0	.000	3	4	.750	1	0	1	4	5	0	1	0	0	5.3	1.7	0.3	1.3	.348
NBA Playoff Totals		30	20	782	257	100	240	.417	5	16	.313	52	65	.800	16	35	51	161	82	3	26	1	54	26.1	8.6	1.7	5.4	....

• SPEARS, Odie

Marion Odicca Spears

Born: June 26, 1925. Died: Mar.28, 1985. Height: 6'5". Weight: 205 lbs. Drafted: 1948 College: Western Kentucky

YEAR	TEAM	GP	GS	MIN	PTS	FGM	FGA	FG%	3PM	3PA	3P%	FTM	FTA	FT%	ORB	DRB	TRB	AST	PF	DQ	STL	BLK	TO	MPG	PPG	RPG	APG	PCM
48-49	Chicago	57	....	....	531	200	631	.317	....	....	....	131	197	.665	....	....	....	97	200	....	....	....	....	....	9.3	....	1.7	....
49-50	Chicago	68	....	....	712	277	775	.357	....	....	....	158	230	.687	....	....	....	159	250	....	....	....	....	....	10.5	....	2.3	....
51-52	Rochester	66	....	1673	566	225	570	.395	....	....	....	116	152	.763	....	....	303	163	225	8	....	....	....	25.3	8.6	4.6	2.5	.391
52-53	Rochester	62	....	1414	595	198	494	.401	....	....	....	199	243	.819	....	....	251	113	227	15	....	....	....	22.8	9.6	4.0	1.8	.430
53-54	Rochester	72	....	1633	551	184	505	.364	....	....	....	183	238	.769	....	....	310	109	211	5	....	....	....	22.7	7.7	4.3	1.5	.361
54-55	Rochester	71	....	1888	672	226	585	.386	....	....	....	220	271	.812	....	....	299	148	252	6	....	....	....	26.6	9.5	4.2	2.1	.370
55-56	Fort Wayne	72	....	1378	491	166	468	.355	....	....	....	159	201	.791	....	....	231	121	191	2	....	....	....	19.1	6.8	3.2	1.7	.362
56-57	FtW/StL	11	....	118	43	12	38	.316	....	....	....	19	22	.864	....	....	15	7	24	0	....	....	....	10.7	3.9	1.4	0.6	.284
NBA Season Totals		479	....	8104	4161	1488	4066	.366	....	....	....	1185	1554	.763	....	....	1409	917	1580	36	....	....	....	16.9	8.7	2.9	1.9	....
48-49	Chicago	2	....	....	18	7	26	.269	....	....	....	4	7	.571	....	....	....	2	9	....	....	....	....	....	9.0	....	1.0	....
49-50	Chicago	2	....	....	23	9	22	.409	....	....	....	5	10	.500	....	....	....	1	11	....	....	....	....	....	11.5	....	0.5	....
51-52	Rochester	6	....	123	29	10	33	.303	....	....	....	9	16	.563	....	....	21	9	18	0	....	....	....	20.5	4.8	3.5	1.5	.246
52-53	Rochester	3	....	62	20	8	19	.421	....	....	....	4	5	.800	....	....	12	0	12	1	....	....	....	20.7	6.7	4.0	0.0	.258
53-54	Rochester	6	....	121	28	8	28	.286	....	....	....	12	14	.857	....	....	13	8	17	1	....	....	....	20.2	4.7	2.2	1.3	.220
54-55	Rochester	3	....	90	35	12	45	.267	....	....	....	11	16	.688	....	....	14	10	14	1	....	....	....	30.0	11.7	4.7	3.3	.289
55-56	Fort Wayne	10	....	177	53	20	62	.323	....	....	....	13	23	.565	....	....	29	14	33	0	....	....	....	17.7	5.3	2.9	1.4	.249
NBA Playoff Totals		32	....	573	206	74	235	.315	....	....	....	58	91	.637	....	....	89	44	114	3	....	....	....	17.9	6.4	2.8	1.4	....

• SPECTOR, Art

Arthur Edward (Speed) Spector

Born: Oct. 17, 1920. Philadelphia, PA, United States. Died: June18, 1987. Height: 6'4". Weight: 200 lbs. Drafted: — College: Villanova

YEAR	TEAM	GP	GS	MIN	PTS	FGM	FGA	FG%	3PM	3PA	3P%	FTM	FTA	FT%	ORB	DRB	TRB	AST	PF	DQ	STL	BLK	TO	MPG	PPG	RPG	APG	PCM
46-47	Boston	55	....	....	329	123	460	.267	....	....	....	83	150	.553	....	....	....	46	130	....	....	....	....	....	6.0	....	0.8	....
47-48	Boston	48	....	....	194	67	243	.276	....	....	....	60	92	.652	....	....	....	17	106	....	....	....	....	....	4.0	....	0.4	....
48-49	Boston	59	....	....	324	130	434	.300	....	....	....	64	116	.552	....	....	....	77	111	....	....	....	....	....	5.5	....	1.3	....
49-50	Boston	7	....	....	5	2	12	.167	....	....	....	1	4	.250	....	....	....	3	4	....	....	....	....	....	0.7	....	0.4	....
NBA Season Totals		169	....	....	852	322	1149	.280	....	....	....	208	362	.575	....	....	....	143	351	....	....	....	....	....	5.0	....	0.8	....
47-48	Boston	3	....	....	6	2	9	.222	....	....	....	2	4	.500	....	....	....	0	9	....	....	....	....	....	2.0	....	0.0	....
NBA Playoff Totals		3	....	....	6	2	9	.222	....	....	....	2	4	.500	....	....	....	0	9	....	....	....	....	....	2.0	....	0.0	....

• SPENCER, Andre

Andre Spencer

Born: July 20, 1964. Stockton, CA, United States. Height: 6'6". Weight: 210 lbs. Drafted: — College: Northern Arizona

YEAR	TEAM	GP	GS	MIN	PTS	FGM	FGA	FG%	3PM	3PA	3P%	FTM	FTA	FT%	ORB	DRB	TRB	AST	PF	DQ	STL	BLK	TO	MPG	PPG	RPG	APG	PCM
92-93	Atlanta	3	0	15	0	0	3	.000	0	0	.000	0	0	.000	0	1	1	0	3	0	2	0	2	5.0	0.0	0.3	0.0	-.218
92-93	Golden State	17	1	407	187	73	160	.456	0	2	.000	41	54	.759	38	42	80	24	61	0	15	10	24	23.9	11.0	4.7	1.4	.424
93-94	Golden State	5	1	63	21	9	18	.500	0	0	.000	3	4	.750	4	8	12	3	6	0	1	2	2	12.6	4.2	2.4	0.6	.392
93-94	Sacramento	23	0	286	138	43	100	.430	0	0	.000	52	73	.712	26	35	61	19	37	0	18	5	18	12.4	6.0	2.7	0.8	.490
NBA Season Totals		48	2	771	346	125	281	.445	0	2	.000	96	131	.733	68	86	154	46	107	0	36	17	46	16.1	7.2	3.2	1.0	....

YEAR	TEAM	GP	GS	MIN	PTS	FGM	FGA	FG%	3PM	3PA	3P%	FTM	FTA	FT%	ORB	DRB	TRB	AST	PF	DQ	STL	BLK	TO	MPG	PPG	RPG	APG	PCM

• SPENCER, Elmore

Elmore Spencer

Born: Dec. 6, 1969. Atlanta, GA, United States.　　Height: 7'　　Weight: 270 lbs.　　Drafted: 1992　　College: UNLV

YEAR	TEAM	GP	GS	MIN	PTS	FGM	FGA	FG%	3PM	3PA	3P%	FTM	FTA	FT%	ORB	DRB	TRB	AST	PF	DQ	STL	BLK	TO	MPG	PPG	RPG	APG	PCM
92-93	LA Clippers	44	4	280	104	44	82	.537	0	0	.000	16	32	.500	17	45	62	8	54	0	8	18	26	6.4	2.4	1.4	0.2	.365
93-94	LA Clippers	76	63	1930	673	288	540	.533	0	2	.000	97	162	.599	96	319	415	75	208	3	30	127	167	25.4	8.9	5.5	1.0	.399
94-95	LA Clippers	19	8	368	132	52	118	.441	0	1	.000	28	50	.560	11	54	65	25	62	0	14	23	48	19.4	6.9	3.4	1.3	.293
95-96	Denver	6	0	21	0	0	1	.000	0	0	.000	0	0	.000	1	3	4	0	8	1	0	0	3	3.5	0.0	0.7	0.0	-.179
95-96	Portland	11	0	37	14	5	12	.417	0	0	.000	4	6	.667	2	7	9	1	4	0	0	2	3	3.4	1.3	0.8	0.1	.356
96-97	Seattle	1	0	5	0	0	1	.000	0	0	.000	0	0	.000	0	0	0	0	0	0	1	0	1	5.0	0.0	0.0	0.0	-.186
NBA Season Totals		157	75	2641	923	389	754	.516	0	3	.000	145	250	.580	127	428	555	109	336	4	53	170	248	16.8	5.9	3.5	0.7	....
92-93	LA Clippers	2	0	4	0	0	2	.000	0	0	.000	0	0	.000	1	0	1	0	1	0	0	0	0	2.0	0.0	0.5	0.0	-.350
95-96	Portland	1	0	1	0	0	0	.000	0	0	.000	0	2	.000	0	0	0	0	0	0	0	0	0	1.0	0.0	0.0	0.0	-.940
NBA Playoff Totals		3	0	5	0	0	2	.000	0	0	.000	0	2	.000	1	0	1	0	1	0	0	0	0	1.7	0.0	0.3	0.0	....

• SPENCER, Felton

Felton LaFrance Spencer

Born: Jan. 15, 1968. Louisville, KY, United States.　　Height: 7'　　Weight: 265 lbs.　　Drafted: 1990　　College: Louisville

YEAR	TEAM	GP	GS	MIN	PTS	FGM	FGA	FG%	3PM	3PA	3P%	FTM	FTA	FT%	ORB	DRB	TRB	AST	PF	DQ	STL	BLK	TO	MPG	PPG	RPG	APG	PCM
90-91	Minnesota	81	46	2099	572	195	381	.512	0	1	.000	182	252	.722	272	369	641	25	337	14	48	121	81	25.9	7.1	7.9	0.3	.436
91-92	Minnesota	61	54	1481	405	141	331	.426	0	0	.000	123	178	.691	167	268	435	53	241	7	27	79	67	24.3	6.6	7.1	0.9	.397
92-93	Minnesota	71	48	1296	293	105	226	.465	0	0	.000	83	127	.654	134	190	324	17	243	10	23	66	71	18.3	4.1	4.6	0.2	.296
93-94	Utah	79	79	2210	677	256	507	.505	0	0	.000	165	272	.607	235	423	658	43	304	5	41	67	126	28.0	8.6	8.3	0.5	.404
94-95	Utah	34	34	905	317	105	215	.488	0	0	.000	107	135	.793	90	170	260	17	131	3	12	32	68	26.6	9.3	7.6	0.5	.418
95-96	Utah	71	70	1267	396	146	281	.520	0	0	.000	104	151	.689	100	206	306	11	240	1	20	54	78	17.8	5.6	4.3	0.2	.339
96-97	Orlando	1	1	19	4	2	2	1.000	0	0	.000	0	0	.000	5	1	6	1	2	0	0	0	1	19.0	4.0	6.0	1.0	.463
96-97	Golden State	72	64	1539	368	137	282	.486	0	0	.000	94	161	.584	152	258	410	21	273	7	34	50	86	21.4	5.1	5.7	0.3	.310
97-98	Golden State	68	0	813	162	59	129	.457	0	0	.000	44	79	.557	93	133	226	17	175	3	23	37	48	12.0	2.4	3.3	0.3	.293
98-99	Golden State	26	0	159	42	15	33	.455	0	0	.000	12	26	.462	18	28	46	0	41	0	5	10	9	6.1	1.6	1.8	0.0	.300
99-00	San Antonio	26	0	149	50	15	33	.455	0	0	.000	20	30	.667	15	24	39	3	32	0	6	8	9	5.7	1.9	1.5	0.1	.388
00-01	New York	18	0	113	39	12	20	.600	0	0	.000	15	25	.600	16	19	35	2	24	0	2	2	11	6.3	2.2	1.9	0.1	.388
01-02	New York	32	8	248	29	6	26	.231	0	0	.000	17	33	.515	16	34	50	3	73	0	7	8	12	7.8	0.9	1.6	0.1	.088
NBA Season Totals		640	404	12298	3354	1194	2466	.484	0	1	.000	966	1469	.658	1313	2123	3436	213	2116	50	248	534	667	19.2	5.2	5.4	0.3	....
93-94	Utah	16	16	492	127	47	105	.448	0	0	.000	33	50	.660	61	74	135	7	73	3	3	20	24	30.8	7.9	8.4	0.4	.331
95-96	Utah	18	18	276	51	23	53	.434	0	1	.000	5	9	.556	26	28	54	2	58	0	5	22	19	15.3	2.8	3.0	0.1	.196
00-01	New York	2	0	4	0	0	0	.000	0	0	.000	0	0	.000	0	0	0	0	2	0	0	0	0	2.0	0.0	0.0	0.0	-.225
NBA Playoff Totals		36	34	772	178	70	158	.443	0	1	.000	38	59	.644	87	102	189	9	133	3	8	42	43	21.4	4.9	5.3	0.3	....

• SPENCER, Jack

Jack Spencer

Born: 1923.　　Height: 6'3".　　Weight: 160 lbs.　　Drafted: —　　College: Iowa

YEAR	TEAM	GP	GS	MIN	PTS	FGM	FGA	FG%	3PM	3PA	3P%	FTM	FTA	FT%	ORB	DRB	TRB	AST	PF	DQ	STL	BLK	TO	MPG	PPG	RPG	APG	PCM
48-49	Waterloo-N	11	....	....	16	6	....	....	....	....	....	4	4	1.000	....	....	....	12	....	....	....	....	....	1.5	....	....	....
NBL Season Totals		11	....	....	16	6	....	....	....	....	....	4	4	....	....	....	....	12	....	....	....	....	....	1.5	....	....	....

• SPICER, Lou

Lewis G. Spicer

Born: Nov. 12, 1922. Died: June 23, 1981.　　Height: 6'2".　　Weight: 195 lbs.　　Drafted: —　　College: Syracuse

YEAR	TEAM	GP	GS	MIN	PTS	FGM	FGA	FG%	3PM	3PA	3P%	FTM	FTA	FT%	ORB	DRB	TRB	AST	PF	DQ	STL	BLK	TO	MPG	PPG	RPG	APG	PCM
46-47	Providence	4	....	....	1	0	7	.000	....	....	....	1	2	.500	....	....	0	3	....	....	....	....	....	0.3	....	0.0	....
NBA Season Totals		4	....	....	1	0	7	.000	....	....	....	1	2	.500	....	....	0	3	....	....	....	....	....	0.3	....	0.0	....

• SPITZER, Craig

Craig W. Spitzer

Born: Dec. 18, 1945.　　Height: 7'　　Weight: 225 lbs.　　Drafted: —　　College: Tulane

YEAR	TEAM	GP	GS	MIN	PTS	FGM	FGA	FG%	3PM	3PA	3P%	FTM	FTA	FT%	ORB	DRB	TRB	AST	PF	DQ	STL	BLK	TO	MPG	PPG	RPG	APG	PCM
67-68	Chicago	10	....	44	18	8	21	.381	....	....	....	2	3	.667	....	....	24	0	4	0	....	....	....	4.4	1.8	2.4	0.0	.563
NBA Season Totals		10	....	44	18	8	21	.381	....	....	....	2	3	.667	....	....	24	0	4	0	....	....	....	4.4	1.8	2.4	0.0	....
67-68	Chicago	1	....	3	0	0	3	.000	....	....	....	0	0	.000	....	....	3	1	0	0	....	....	....	3.0	0.0	3.0	1.0	.401
NBA Playoff Totals		1	....	3	0	0	3	.000	....	....	....	0	0	.000	....	....	3	1	0	0	....	....	....	3.0	0.0	3.0	1.0	....

• SPOELSTRA, Art

Arthur Cornelius Spoelstra

Born: Sept. 11, 1932.　　Height: 6'9".　　Weight: 220 lbs.　　Drafted: 1954　　College: Western Kentucky

YEAR	TEAM	GP	GS	MIN	PTS	FGM	FGA	FG%	3PM	3PA	3P%	FTM	FTA	FT%	ORB	DRB	TRB	AST	PF	DQ	STL	BLK	TO	MPG	PPG	RPG	APG	PCM
54-55	Rochester	70	....	1127	426	159	399	.398	....	....	....	108	156	.692	....	....	285	58	170	2	....	....	....	16.1	6.1	4.1	0.8	.400
55-56	Rochester	72	....	1640	615	226	576	.392	....	....	....	163	238	.685	....	....	436	95	248	11	....	....	....	22.8	8.5	6.1	1.3	.412
56-57	Rochester	69	....	1176	522	217	559	.388	....	....	....	88	120	.733	....	....	220	56	168	5	....	....	....	17.0	7.6	3.2	0.8	.363
57-58	Minneapolis	50	....	1098	382	141	353	.399	....	....	....	100	150	.667	....	....	281	51	183	10	....	....	....	22.0	7.6	5.6	1.0	.375
57-58	New York	17	....	207	67	20	66	.303	....	....	....	27	37	.730	....	....	51	6	42	1	....	....	....	12.2	3.9	3.0	0.4	.287
NBA Season Totals		278	....	5248	2012	763	1953	.391	....	....	....	486	701	.693	....	....	1273	266	811	29	....	....	....	18.9	7.2	4.6	1.0	....
54-55	Rochester	3	....	28	15	7	14	.500	....	....	....	1	1	1.000	....	....	9	0	11	0	....	....	....	9.3	5.0	3.0	0.0	.442
NBA Playoff Totals		3	....	28	15	7	14	.500	....	....	....	1	1	1.000	....	....	9	0	11	0	....	....	....	9.3	5.0	3.0	0.0	....

• SPOTOVICH, Ed

Edward Spotovich

Born: 1916.　　Height: 6'2".　　Weight: 190 lbs.　　Drafted: —　　College: Pittsburgh

YEAR	TEAM	GP	GS	MIN	PTS	FGM	FGA	FG%	3PM	3PA	3P%	FTM	FTA	FT%	ORB	DRB	TRB	AST	PF	DQ	STL	BLK	TO	MPG	PPG	RPG	APG	PCM
38-39	Pittsburgh-N	3	....	....	13	6	....	....	....	....	....	1	....	....	....	....	....	....	....	....	....	....	....	4.3	....	....	....
NBL Season Totals		3	....	....	13	6	....	....	....	....	....	1	....	....	....	....	....	....	....	....	....	....	....	4.3	....	....	....

YEAR	TEAM	GP	GS	MIN	PTS	FGM	FGA	FG%	3PM	3PA	3P%	FTM	FTA	FT%	ORB	DRB	TRB	AST	PF	DQ	STL	BLK	TO	MPG	PPG	RPG	APG	PCM

• SPRAGGINS, Bruce
Warren Bruce Spraggins

Born: 1940. Williamsburg, VA, United States.   Height: 6'5".   Weight: 188 lbs.   Drafted: 1961   College: Virginia Union

YEAR	TEAM	GP	GS	MIN	PTS	FGM	FGA	FG%	3PM	3PA	3P%	FTM	FTA	FT%	ORB	DRB	TRB	AST	PF	DQ	STL	BLK	TO	MPG	PPG	RPG	APG	PCM
67-68	New Jersey-A	70	....	1590	852	306	686	.446	2	5	.400	238	336	.708	....	....	329	66	173	2	....	....	81	22.7	12.2	4.7	0.9	.487
ABA Season Totals		70	....	1590	852	306	686	.446	2	5	.400	238	336	.708	....	....	329	66	173	2	....	....	81	22.7	12.2	4.7	0.9	....

• SPREWELL, Latrell
Latrell Fontaine Sprewell

Born: Sept. 8, 1970. Milwaukee, WI, United States.   Height: 6'5".   Weight: 190 lbs.   Drafted: 1992   College: Alabama

YEAR	TEAM	GP	GS	MIN	PTS	FGM	FGA	FG%	3PM	3PA	3P%	FTM	FTA	FT%	ORB	DRB	TRB	AST	PF	DQ	STL	BLK	TO	MPG	PPG	RPG	APG	PCM
92-93	Golden State	77	69	2741	1182	449	968	.464	73	198	.369	211	283	.746	79	192	271	295	166	2	126	49	200	35.6	15.4	3.5	3.8	.413
93-94	Golden State	82	82	**3533**	1720	613	1417	.433	141	391	.361	353	456	.774	80	321	401	385	158	0	180	76	230	**43.1**	21.0	4.9	4.7	.473
94-95	Golden State	69	69	2771	1420	490	1171	.418	90	326	.276	350	448	.781	58	198	256	279	108	0	112	46	228	40.2	20.6	3.7	4.0	.417
95-96	Golden State	78	78	3064	1473	515	1202	.428	91	282	.323	352	446	.789	124	256	380	328	150	1	127	45	218	39.3	18.9	4.9	4.2	.448
96-97	Golden State	80	79	3353	1938	649	1444	.449	147	415	.354	493	585	.843	58	308	366	507	153	0	132	45	320	41.9	24.2	4.6	6.3	.546
97-98	Golden State	14	13	547	299	110	277	.397	9	48	.188	70	94	.745	7	44	51	68	26	0	19	5	43	39.1	21.4	3.6	4.9	.414
98-99	New York	37	4	1233	606	215	518	.415	21	77	.273	155	191	.812	41	115	156	91	65	0	46	2	79	33.3	16.4	4.2	2.5	.409
99-00	New York	82	82	3276	1524	568	1305	.435	44	127	.346	344	397	.866	49	300	349	332	184	0	109	22	226	40.0	18.6	4.3	4.0	.409
00-01	New York	77	77	3017	1364	524	1219	.430	41	135	.304	275	351	.783	49	298	347	269	159	1	106	28	218	39.2	17.7	4.5	3.5	.387
01-02	New York	81	81	3326	1575	573	1419	.404	145	403	.360	284	346	.821	59	239	298	313	161	0	94	14	223	41.1	19.4	3.7	3.9	.366
02-03	New York	74	73	2858	1215	454	1127	.403	134	360	.372	173	218	.794	45	240	285	332	134	2	102	22	172	38.6	16.4	3.9	4.5	.385
NBA Season Totals		751	707	29719	14316	5160	12067	.428	936	2762	.339	3060	3815	.802	649	2511	3160	3199	1464	6	1153	354	2157	39.6	19.1	4.2	4.3	....
93-94	Golden State	3	3	122	68	26	60	.433	8	23	.348	8	12	.667	1	8	9	21	15	0	2	3	9	40.7	22.7	3.0	7.0	.454
98-99	New York	20	8	743	407	145	346	.419	4	25	.160	113	133	.850	24	72	96	43	40	1	19	6	58	37.2	20.4	4.8	2.2	.411
99-00	New York	16	16	700	299	110	266	.414	10	30	.333	69	88	.784	12	58	70	58	28	0	18	5	37	43.8	18.7	4.4	3.6	.357
00-01	New York	5	5	212	92	35	86	.407	3	14	.214	19	25	.760	3	12	15	17	17	0	5	1	20	42.4	18.4	3.0	3.4	.262
NBA Playoff Totals		44	32	1777	866	316	758	.417	25	92	.272	209	258	.810	40	150	190	139	100	1	44	15	124	40.4	19.7	4.3	3.2	....

• SPRIGGS, Larry
Larry Michael Spriggs

Born: Sept. 8, 1959. Cheverly, MD, United States.   Height: 6'7".   Weight: 230 lbs.   Drafted: 1981   College: Howard

YEAR	TEAM	GP	GS	MIN	PTS	FGM	FGA	FG%	3PM	3PA	3P%	FTM	FTA	FT%	ORB	DRB	TRB	AST	PF	DQ	STL	BLK	TO	MPG	PPG	RPG	APG	PCM
81-82	Houston	4	0	37	14	7	11	.636	0	0	.000	0	2	.000	2	4	6	4	7	0	2	0	4	9.3	3.5	1.5	1.0	.383
82-83	Chicago	9	0	39	21	8	20	.400	0	0	.000	5	7	.714	2	7	9	3	3	0	1	2	2	4.3	2.3	1.0	0.3	.359
83-84	LA Lakers	38	0	363	124	44	82	.537	0	2	.000	36	50	.720	16	45	61	30	55	0	12	4	34	9.6	3.3	1.6	0.8	.354
84-85	LA Lakers	75	32	1292	500	194	354	.548	0	3	.000	112	146	.767	77	150	227	132	195	2	47	13	113	17.2	6.7	3.0	1.8	.424
85-86	LA Lakers	43	7	471	214	88	192	.458	0	1	.000	38	49	.776	28	53	81	49	78	0	18	9	56	11.0	5.0	1.9	1.1	.375
NBA Season Totals		169	39	2202	873	341	659	.517	0	6	.000	191	254	.752	125	259	384	218	338	2	80	28	209	13.0	5.2	2.3	1.3	....
81-82	Houston	2	0	9	6	3	4	.750	0	0	.000	0	1	.000	0	1	1	2	3	0	0	0	0	4.5	3.0	0.5	1.0	.702
83-84	LA Lakers	9	0	45	25	7	19	.368	0	0	.000	11	11	1.000	4	5	9	3	11	0	0	1	7	5.0	2.8	1.0	0.3	.327
84-85	LA Lakers	16	0	230	98	40	77	.519	0	2	.000	18	29	.621	16	35	51	33	36	0	4	5	26	14.4	6.1	3.2	2.1	.472
85-86	LA Lakers	3	0	13	20	5	6	.833	0	0	.000	10	10	1.000	1	6	7	2	0	0	1	0	0	4.3	6.7	2.3	0.7	2.203
NBA Playoff Totals		30	0	297	149	55	106	.519	0	2	.000	39	51	.765	21	47	68	40	50	0	5	6	33	9.9	5.0	2.3	1.3	....

• SPRINGER, Jim
James E. Springer

Born: June 17, 1926. New Winchester, OH, United States.   Height: 6'9".   Weight: 235 lbs.   Drafted: —   College: Canterbury

YEAR	TEAM	GP	GS	MIN	PTS	FGM	FGA	FG%	3PM	3PA	3P%	FTM	FTA	FT%	ORB	DRB	TRB	AST	PF	DQ	STL	BLK	TO	MPG	PPG	RPG	APG	PCM
47-48	Anderson-N	6	....	....	17	4	....	....	....	....	....	9	14	.643	....	....	....	....	....	....	....	....	....	....	2.8	....	....	....
47-48	Indianapolis-N	19	....	....	32	8	....	....	....	....	....	16	26	.615	....	....	....	....	....	....	....	....	....	....	1.7	....	....	....
48-49	Indianapolis	2	....	....	1	0	0	.000	....	....	....	1	1	1.000	....	....	0	0	....	....	....	....	....	....	0.5	....	0.0	....
NBA Season Totals		2	....	....	1	0	0	.000	....	....	....	1	1	1.000	....	....	0	0	....	....	....	....	....	....	0.5	....	0.0	....
NBL Season Totals		25	....	....	49	12	....	....	....	....	....	25	40	....	....	....	....	....	....	....	....	....	....	....	2.0	....	....	....
Career Totals		27	....	....	50	12	0	....	....	....	....	26	41	....	....	....	0	0	....	....	....	....	....	....	1.9	....	0.0	....
47-48	Indianapolis-N	3	....	....	0	0	....	....	....	....	....	0	2	.000	....	....	....	....	....	....	....	....	....	....	0.0	....	....	....
NBL Playoff Totals		3	....	....	0	0	....	....	....	....	....	0	2	....	....	....	....	....	....	....	....	....	....	....	0.0	....	....	....

• SPRUILL, Jim
James Winfred Spruill

Born: Feb. 26, 1923. Dublin, TX, United States.   Height: 6'2".   Weight: 225 lbs.   Drafted: —   College: Rice

YEAR	TEAM	GP	GS	MIN	PTS	FGM	FGA	FG%	3PM	3PA	3P%	FTM	FTA	FT%	ORB	DRB	TRB	AST	PF	DQ	STL	BLK	TO	MPG	PPG	RPG	APG	PCM
48-49	Indianapolis	1	....	....	2	1	3	.333	....	....	....	0	0	.000	....	....	0	3	....	....	....	....	....	....	2.0	....	0.0	....
NBA Season Totals		1	....	....	2	1	3	.333	....	....	....	0	0	.000	....	....	0	3	....	....	....	....	....	....	2.0	....	0.0	....

• SPUDICH, —
Spudich

Born: —.   Height: —   Weight: —   Drafted: —   College: —

YEAR	TEAM	GP	GS	MIN	PTS	FGM	FGA	FG%	3PM	3PA	3P%	FTM	FTA	FT%	ORB	DRB	TRB	AST	PF	DQ	STL	BLK	TO	MPG	PPG	RPG	APG	PCM
39-40	Hammond-N	2	....	....	2	1	....	....	....	....	....	0	....	....	....	....	....	....	....	....	....	....	....	....	1.0	....	....	....
NBL Season Totals		2	....	....	2	1	....	....	....	....	....	0	....	....	....	....	....	....	....	....	....	....	....	....	1.0	....	....	....

• STACK, Joe

Joe Stack

Born: 1913. Height: 5'10". Weight: 185 lbs. Drafted: — College: none

YEAR TEAM	GP	GS	MIN	PTS	FGM	FGA	FG%	3PM	3PA	3P%	FTM	FTA	FT%	ORB	DRB	TRB	AST	PF	DQ	STL	BLK	TO	MPG	PPG	RPG	APG	PCM
37-38 Whiting-N	14	....	....	60	23	....	....	....	....	....	14	....	....	....	....	....	....	....	....	....	....	....	....	4.3	....	....	....
38-39 Hammond-N	15	....	....	74	26	....	....	....	....	....	22	....	....	....	....	....	....	....	....	....	....	....	....	4.9	....	....	....
NBL Season Totals	29	....	....	134	49	....	....	....	....	....	36	....	....	....	....	....	....	....	....	....	....	....	....	4.6	....	....	....
37-38 Whiting-N	2	....	....	0	0	....	....	....	....	....	0	....	....	....	....	....	....	....	....	....	....	....	....	0.0	....	....	....
NBL Playoff Totals	2	....	....	0	0	....	....	....	....	....	0	....	....	....	....	....	....	....	....	....	....	....	....	0.0	....	....	....

• STACK, Ryan

Ryan Eugene Stack

Born: July 24, 1975. Nashville, TN, United States. Height: 6'11". Weight: 215 lbs. Drafted: 1998 College: South Carolina

YEAR TEAM	GP	GS	MIN	PTS	FGM	FGA	FG%	3PM	3PA	3P%	FTM	FTA	FT%	ORB	DRB	TRB	AST	PF	DQ	STL	BLK	TO	MPG	PPG	RPG	APG	PCM
98-99 Cleveland	18	0	199	47	14	37	.378	0	0	.000	19	20	.950	19	15	34	5	31	0	2	11	9	11.1	2.6	1.9	0.3	.260
99-00 Cleveland	25	0	198	52	17	51	.333	0	1	.000	18	27	.667	15	30	45	5	47	3	4	11	17	7.9	2.1	1.8	0.2	.203
NBA Season Totals	43	0	397	99	31	88	.352	0	1	.000	37	47	.787	34	45	79	10	78	3	6	22	26	9.2	2.3	1.8	0.2	....

• STACKHOUSE, Jerry

Jerry Darnell Stackhouse

Born: Nov. 5, 1974. Kinston, NC, United States. Height: 6'6". Weight: 218 lbs. Drafted: 1995 College: North Carolina

YEAR TEAM	GP	GS	MIN	PTS	FGM	FGA	FG%	3PM	3PA	3P%	FTM	FTA	FT%	ORB	DRB	TRB	AST	PF	DQ	STL	BLK	TO	MPG	PPG	RPG	APG	PCM
95-96 Philadelphia	72	71	2701	1384	452	1091	.414	93	292	.318	387	518	.747	90	175	265	278	179	0	76	79	252	37.5	19.2	3.7	3.9	.404
96-97 Philadelphia	81	81	3166	1679	533	1308	.407	102	342	.298	511	667	.766	156	182	338	253	219	2	93	63	316	39.1	20.7	4.2	3.1	.385
97-98 Philadelphia	22	22	748	353	128	283	.452	16	46	.348	81	101	.802	28	48	76	67	56	1	31	21	75	34.0	16.0	3.5	3.0	.398
97-98 Detroit	57	15	1797	896	296	692	.428	31	149	.208	273	349	.782	77	113	190	174	119	1	58	38	148	31.5	15.7	3.3	3.1	.423
98-99 Detroit	42	9	1188	607	181	488	.371	35	126	.278	210	247	.850	26	81	107	118	79	0	34	19	121	28.3	14.5	2.5	2.8	.377
99-00 Detroit	82	82	3148	1939	619	1447	.428	83	288	.288	**618**	758	.815	118	197	315	365	188	1	103	36	**311**	38.4	23.6	3.8	4.5	.498
00-01 Detroit	80	80	3215	**2380**	774	**1927**	.402	166	473	.351	**666**	810	.822	99	216	315	410	160	1	97	54	**326**	40.2	29.8	3.9	5.1	.555
01-02 Detroit	76	76	2685	1629	524	1319	.397	86	300	.287	495	577	.858	77	238	315	403	163	0	77	37	266	35.3	21.4	4.1	5.3	.516
02-03 Washington	70	70	2748	1508	491	1201	.409	71	245	.290	455	518	.878	61	197	258	316	130	1	65	28	193	39.3	21.5	3.7	4.5	.460
NBA Season Totals	582	506	21396	12375	3998	9756	.410	683	2261	.302	3696	4545	.813	732	1447	2179	2384	1293	7	634	375	2008	36.8	21.3	3.7	4.1	....
98-99 Detroit	5	0	124	50	18	46	.391	2	8	.250	12	14	.857	3	5	8	6	11	0	2	1	10	24.8	10.0	1.6	1.2	.217
99-00 Detroit	3	3	120	74	24	59	.407	3	7	.429	23	31	.742	1	11	12	10	4	0	2	0	14	40.0	24.7	4.0	3.3	.397
01-02 Detroit	10	10	361	176	53	165	.321	18	53	.340	52	63	.825	9	34	43	43	26	0	6	6	27	36.1	17.6	4.3	4.3	.361
NBA Playoff Totals	18	13	605	300	95	270	.352	23	68	.338	87	108	.806	13	50	63	59	41	0	10	7	51	33.6	16.7	3.5	3.3	....

• STACOM, Kevin

Kevin M. Stacom

Born: Sept. 4, 1951. New York, NY, United States. Height: 6'3". Weight: 185 lbs. Drafted: 1973 College: Providence

YEAR TEAM	GP	GS	MIN	PTS	FGM	FGA	FG%	3PM	3PA	3P%	FTM	FTA	FT%	ORB	DRB	TRB	AST	PF	DQ	STL	BLK	TO	MPG	PPG	RPG	APG	PCM
74-75 Boston	61	....	447	173	72	159	.453	....	....	....	29	33	.879	30	25	55	49	65	0	11	3	....	7.3	2.8	0.9	0.8	.386
75-76 Boston	77	....	1114	408	170	387	.439	....	....	....	68	91	.747	62	99	161	128	117	0	23	5	....	14.5	5.3	2.1	1.7	.400
76-77 Boston	79	....	1051	404	179	438	.409	....	....	....	46	58	.793	40	57	97	117	65	0	19	3	....	13.3	5.1	1.2	1.5	.346
77-78 Boston	55	....	1006	466	206	484	.426	....	....	....	54	71	.761	26	80	106	111	60	0	28	3	72	18.3	8.5	1.9	2.0	.369
78-79 Indiana	44	....	571	183	76	209	.364	....	....	....	31	41	.756	20	41	61	77	29	0	14	1	44	13.0	4.2	1.4	1.8	.280
78-79 Boston	24	....	260	117	52	133	.391	....	....	....	13	19	.684	10	14	24	35	18	0	15	0	36	10.8	4.9	1.0	1.5	.288
81-82 Milwaukee	7	0	90	30	14	34	.412	1	2	.500	1	2	.500	2	5	7	7	6	0	1	0	9	12.9	4.3	1.0	1.0	.167
NBA Season Totals	347	0	4539	1781	769	1844	.417	1	2	.500	242	315	.768	190	321	511	524	360	0	111	15	161	13.1	5.1	1.5	1.5	....
74-75 Boston	4	....	7	0	0	2	.000	....	....	....	0	0	.000	0	0	0	1	0	0	0	0	....	1.8	0.0	0.0	0.3	-.080
75-76 Boston	17	....	195	34	13	45	.289	....	....	....	8	11	.727	9	8	17	16	21	0	5	0	....	11.5	2.0	1.0	0.9	.149
76-77 Boston	5	....	25	7	3	6	.500	....	....	....	1	1	1.000	0	2	2	4	3	0	0	0	....	5.0	1.4	0.4	0.8	.376
NBA Playoff Totals	26	....	227	41	16	53	.302	....	....	....	9	12	.750	9	10	19	21	24	0	5	0	....	8.7	1.6	0.7	0.8	....

• STAGGS, Erv

James Ervin Staggs

Born: 1948. Philadelphia, PA, United States. Height: 6'6". Weight: 195 lbs. Drafted: — College: Cheyney State

YEAR TEAM	GP	GS	MIN	PTS	FGM	FGA	FG%	3PM	3PA	3P%	FTM	FTA	FT%	ORB	DRB	TRB	AST	PF	DQ	STL	BLK	TO	MPG	PPG	RPG	APG	PCM
69-70 Miami-A	53	....	1058	453	189	474	.399	2	7	.286	73	114	.640	35	87	122	76	155	7	....	....	113	20.0	8.5	2.3	1.4	.299
ABA Season Totals	53	....	1058	453	189	474	.399	2	7	.286	73	114	.640	35	87	122	76	155	7	....	....	113	20.0	8.5	2.3	1.4	....

• STALLWORTH, Bud

Isaac (Bud) Stallworth

Born: Jan. 18, 1950. Hartselle, AL, United States. Height: 6'5". Weight: 190 lbs. Drafted: 1972 College: Kansas

YEAR TEAM	GP	GS	MIN	PTS	FGM	FGA	FG%	3PM	3PA	3P%	FTM	FTA	FT%	ORB	DRB	TRB	AST	PF	DQ	STL	BLK	TO	MPG	PPG	RPG	APG	PCM
72-73 Seattle	77	....	1225	482	198	522	.379	....	....	....	86	114	.754	....	....	225	58	138	0	....	....	....	15.9	6.3	2.9	0.8	.320
73-74 Seattle	67	....	1019	424	188	479	.392	....	....	....	48	77	.623	51	123	174	33	129	0	21	12	....	15.2	6.3	2.6	0.5	.290
74-75 New Orleans	73	....	1668	721	298	710	.420	....	....	....	125	182	.687	78	168	246	46	208	4	59	11	....	22.8	9.9	3.4	0.6	.311
75-76 New Orleans	56	....	1051	507	211	483	.437	....	....	....	85	124	.685	42	103	145	53	135	1	30	17	....	18.8	9.1	2.6	0.9	.365
76-77 New Orleans	40	....	526	269	126	272	.463	....	....	....	17	29	.586	19	52	71	23	76	1	19	11	....	13.2	6.7	1.8	0.6	.366
NBA Season Totals	313	....	5489	2403	1021	2466	.414	....	....	....	361	526	.686	190	446	861	213	686	6	129	51	....	17.5	7.7	2.8	0.7	....

• STALLWORTH, Dave

David A. (The Rave) Stallworth

Born: Dec. 20, 1941. Dallas, TX, United States. Height: 6'7". Weight: 200 lbs. Drafted: 1965 College: Wichita State

YEAR TEAM	GP	GS	MIN	PTS	FGM	FGA	FG%	3PM	3PA	3P%	FTM	FTA	FT%	ORB	DRB	TRB	AST	PF	DQ	STL	BLK	TO	MPG	PPG	RPG	APG	PCM
65-66 New York	80	....	1893	1004	373	820	.455	....	....	....	258	376	.686	....	....	492	186	237	4	....	....	....	23.7	12.6	6.2	2.3	.595
66-67 New York	76	....	1889	989	380	816	.466	....	....	....	229	320	.716	....	....	472	144	226	4	....	....	....	24.9	13.0	6.2	1.9	.564
69-70 New York	82	....	1375	639	239	557	.429	....	....	....	161	225	.716	....	....	323	139	194	2	....	....	....	16.8	7.8	3.9	1.7	.499
70-71 New York	81	....	1565	759	295	685	.431	....	....	....	169	230	.735	....	....	352	106	175	1	....	....	....	19.3	9.4	4.3	1.3	.476
71-72 New York	14	....	225	95	33	88	.375	....	....	....	29	35	.829	....	....	35	25	31	0	....	....	....	16.1	6.8	2.5	1.8	.401
71-72 Baltimore	64	....	1815	729	303	690	.439	....	....	....	123	153	.804	....	....	398	133	186	3	....	....	....	28.4	11.4	6.2	2.1	.439

YEAR	TEAM	GP	GS	MIN	PTS	FGM	FGA	FG%	3PM	3PA	3P%	FTM	FTA	FT%	ORB	DRB	TRB	AST	PF	DQ	STL	BLK	TO	MPG	PPG	RPG	APG	PCM
72-73	Baltimore	73	....	1217	438	180	435	.414	....	....	....	78	101	.772	....	....	236	112	139	1	....	....	....	16.7	6.0	3.2	1.5	.394
73-74	Washington	45	....	458	197	75	187	.401	....	....	....	47	55	.855	52	73	125	25	61	0	28	4	....	10.2	4.4	2.8	0.6	.453
74-75	New York	7	....	57	10	5	18	.278	....	....	....	0	0	.000	6	14	20	2	10	0	3	3	....	8.1	1.4	2.9	0.3	.246
NBA Season Totals		522	....	10494	4860	1883	4296	.438	....	....	....	1094	1495	.732	58	87	2453	872	1259	15	31	7	....	20.1	9.3	4.7	1.7	....
69-70	New York	19	....	275	137	61	133	.459	....	....	....	15	16	.938	....	....	77	20	35	0	....	....	....	14.5	7.2	4.1	1.1	.538
70-71	New York	12	....	185	64	18	68	.265	....	....	....	28	39	.718	....	....	42	10	27	0	....	....	....	15.4	5.3	3.5	0.8	.282
71-72	Baltimore	6	....	105	33	12	28	.429	....	....	....	9	13	.692	....	....	15	5	14	0	....	....	....	17.5	5.5	2.5	0.8	.286
72-73	Baltimore	3	....	14	2	1	1	1.000	....	....	....	0	0	.000	....	....	3	1	3	0	....	....	....	4.7	0.7	1.0	0.3	.316
NBA Playoff Totals		40	....	579	236	92	230	.400	....	....	....	52	68	.765	....	....	137	36	79	0	....	....	....	14.5	5.9	3.4	0.9	

• STAMMLER, Howard

Howard Stammler

Born: July 23, 1911. Died: June 1977.   Height: 5'10".   Weight: 155 lbs.   Drafted: —   College: Ohio Wesleyan

YEAR	TEAM	GP	GS	MIN	PTS	FGM	...	FTM	...	PPG	...
37-38	Dayton-N	4	....		20	9		2		5.0	
NBL Season Totals		4	....	....	20	9		2		5.0	

• STAMPF, Joe

Joseph Stampf

Born: Dec. 16, 1919. Died: Apr. 1985.   Height: 6'4".   Weight: 210 lbs.   Drafted: —   College: Chicago

YEAR	TEAM	GP	GS	MIN	PTS	FGM	...	FTM	...	PPG	...
44-45	Chicago-N	7	....	....	21	8		5		3.0	
NBL Season Totals		7	....	....	21	8		5		3.0	

• STANCZAK, Ed

Edmund A. Stanczak

Born: Aug. 15, 1921.   Height: 6'1".   Weight: 185 lbs.   Drafted: —   College: none (HS: Central, IN)

YEAR	TEAM	GP	GS	MIN	PTS	FGM	FGA	FG%	...	FTM	FTA	FT%	...	AST	PF	DQ	...	PPG	RPG	APG	...
46-47	Anderson-N	44	....	....	402	142				118	201	.587		....	109			9.1			
47-48	Anderson-N	55	....	....	207	73				61	102	.598		....	95			3.8			
48-49	Anderson-N	64	....	....	584	191				202	275	.735		....	209			9.1			
49-50	Anderson	57	....	....	521	159	456	.349		203	270	.752		67	166			9.1		1.2	
50-51	Boston	17	....	....	57	11	48	.229		35	43	.814	34	6	6	0		3.4	2.0	0.4	
NBA Season Totals		74	....	....	578	170	504	.337		238	313	.760	34	73	172	0		7.8	0.5	1.0	
NBL Season Totals		163	....	....	1193	406				381	578			....	413			7.3			
Career Totals		237	....	....	1771	576	504			619	891		34	73	585	0		7.5	0.1	0.3	
47-48	Anderson-N	6	....	....	25	7				11	18	.611		....				4.2			
48-49	Anderson-N	7	....	....	36	10				16	27	.593		....	0			5.1			
49-50	Anderson	8	....	....	51	14	48	.292		23	30	.767		10	26			6.4		1.3	
NBA Playoff Totals		8	....	....	51	14	48	.292		23	30	.767		10	26			6.4		1.3	
NBL Playoff Totals		13	....	....	61	17				27	45			....	0			4.7			
Career Playoff Totals		21	....	....	112	31	48			50	75			10	26			5.3		0.5	

• STANKEY, Walt

Walt Stankey

Born: 1911.   Height: 6'3".   Weight: 200 lbs.   Drafted: —   College: none

YEAR	TEAM	GP	GS	MIN	PTS	FGM	...	FTM	...	PPG	...
37-38	Warren-N	9	....	....	59	21		17		6.6	
38-39	Cleveland-N	27	....	....	219	97		25		8.1	
39-40	Detroit-N	16	....	....	54	24		6		3.4	
39-40	Oshkosh-N	11	....	....	25	12		1		2.3	
NBL Season Totals		63	....	....	357	154		49		5.7	
39-40	Oshkosh-N	8	....	....	15	6		3		1.9	
NBL Playoff Totals		8	....	....	15	6		3		1.9	

• STANSBURY, Terence

Terence R. Stansbury

Born: Feb. 27, 1961. Los Angeles, CA, United States.   Height: 6'5".   Weight: 170 lbs.   Drafted: 1984   College: Temple

YEAR	TEAM	GP	GS	MIN	PTS	FGM	FGA	FG%	3PM	3PA	3P%	FTM	FTA	FT%	ORB	DRB	TRB	AST	PF	DQ	STL	BLK	TO	MPG	PPG	RPG	APG	PCM
84-85	Indiana	74	14	1278	526	210	458	.459	4	25	.160	102	126	.810	39	75	114	127	205	2	47	12	81	17.3	7.1	1.5	1.7	.320
85-86	Indiana	74	17	1331	498	191	441	.433	9	53	.170	107	132	.811	29	110	139	206	200	2	59	8	141	18.0	6.7	1.9	2.8	.332
86-87	Seattle	44	0	375	176	67	156	.429	11	29	.379	31	50	.620	8	16	24	57	78	0	13	0	31	8.5	4.0	0.5	1.3	.305
NBA Season Totals		192	31	2984	1200	468	1055	.444	24	107	.224	240	308	.779	76	201	277	390	483	4	119	20	253	15.5	6.3	1.4	2.0	....

• STANTON, Jack

Jack Stanton

Born: 1921.   Height: 6'   Weight: 175 lbs.   Drafted: —   College: Loyola (IL)

YEAR	TEAM	GP	GS	MIN	PTS	FGM	...	FTM	FTA	FT%	...	PPG	...
46-47	Anderson-N	7	....	....	22	10		2	7	.286		3.1	
NBL Season Totals		7	....	....	22	10		2	7			3.1	

• STARK, Clovis

Clovis Stark

Born: Dec. 7, 1914. Died: Jan. 1981.   Height: 6'4".   Weight: 175 lbs.   Drafted: —   College: Ohio Wesleyan

YEAR	TEAM	GP	GS	MIN	PTS	FGM	...	FTM	...	PPG	...
37-38	Dayton-N	9	....	....	38	14		10		4.2	
NBL Season Totals		9	....	....	38	14		10		4.2	

• STARKS, John

John Levell Starks

Born: Aug. 10, 1965. Tulsa, OK, United States. Height: 6'3". Weight: 180 lbs. Drafted: — College: Oklahoma State

YEAR	TEAM	GP	GS	MIN	PTS	FGM	FGA	FG%	3PM	3PA	3P%	FTM	FTA	FT%	ORB	DRB	TRB	AST	PF	DQ	STL	BLK	TO	MPG	PPG	RPG	APG	PCM
88-89	Golden State	36	0	316	146	51	125	.408	10	26	.385	34	52	.654	15	26	41	27	36	0	23	3	40	8.8	4.1	1.1	0.8	.336
90-91	New York	61	10	1173	466	180	410	.439	27	93	.290	79	105	.752	30	101	131	204	137	1	59	17	73	19.2	7.6	2.1	3.3	.442
91-92	New York	82	0	2118	1139	405	902	.449	94	270	.348	235	302	.778	45	146	191	276	231	4	103	18	148	25.8	13.9	2.3	3.4	.466
92-93	New York	80	51	2477	1397	513	1199	.428	108	336	.321	263	331	.795	54	150	204	404	234	3	91	12	176	31.0	17.5	2.6	5.1	.472
93-94	New York	59	54	2057	1120	410	977	.420	113	337	.335	187	248	.754	37	148	185	348	191	4	95	6	183	34.9	19.0	3.1	5.9	.465
94-95	New York	80	78	2725	1223	419	1062	.395	**217**	**611**	.355	168	228	.737	34	185	219	411	257	3	92	4	160	34.1	15.3	2.7	5.1	.386
95-96	New York	81	71	2491	1024	375	846	.443	143	396	.361	131	174	.753	31	206	237	315	226	2	103	11	154	30.8	12.6	2.9	3.9	.391
96-97	New York	77	1	2042	1061	369	856	.431	150	407	.369	173	225	.769	36	169	205	217	196	2	90	11	162	26.5	13.8	2.7	2.8	.420
97-98	New York	82	10	2188	1059	372	947	.393	130	398	.327	185	235	.787	48	182	230	219	205	2	78	5	139	26.7	12.9	2.8	2.7	.372
98-99	Golden State	50	50	1686	690	269	728	.370	78	269	.290	74	100	.740	33	130	163	235	135	3	69	5	83	33.7	13.8	3.3	4.7	.361
99-00	Golden State	33	30	1108	485	192	508	.378	56	161	.348	45	54	.833	10	81	91	170	93	1	37	3	64	33.6	14.7	2.8	5.2	.359
99-00	Chicago	4	0	82	30	11	34	.324	3	10	.300	5	5	1.000	0	10	10	11	9	0	5	1	3	20.5	7.5	2.5	2.8	.352
00-01	Utah	75	64	2122	699	273	686	.398	64	182	.352	89	111	.802	29	125	154	178	217	2	73	10	94	28.3	9.3	2.1	2.4	.257
01-02	Utah	66	1	929	290	114	310	.368	29	95	.305	33	41	.805	15	53	68	70	126	1	33	0	52	14.1	4.4	1.0	1.1	.186
NBA Season Totals		866	420	23514	10829	3953	9590	.412	1222	3591	.340	1701	2211	.769	417	1712	2129	3085	2293	28	951	106	1531	27.2	12.5	2.5	3.6	....
90-91	New York	3	0	28	6	2	5	.400	0	0	.000	2	2	1.000	1	2	3	6	4	0	0	0	6	9.3	2.0	1.0	2.0	.176
91-92	New York	12	0	295	145	46	123	.374	11	46	.239	42	52	.808	7	23	30	38	45	1	17	0	22	24.6	12.1	2.5	3.2	.379
92-93	New York	15	15	575	247	88	200	.440	28	75	.373	43	60	.717	4	48	52	96	57	0	15	3	55	38.3	16.5	3.5	6.4	.390
93-94	New York	25	18	840	364	110	289	.381	47	132	.356	97	126	.770	9	49	58	114	86	1	35	2	57	33.6	14.6	2.3	4.6	.364
94-95	New York	11	11	380	172	58	129	.450	30	73	.411	26	42	.619	2	23	25	57	40	0	13	1	26	34.5	15.6	2.3	5.2	.400
95-96	New York	8	8	314	128	39	87	.448	21	45	.467	29	39	.744	3	26	29	33	26	0	13	1	25	39.3	16.0	3.6	4.1	.375
96-97	New York	9	1	253	126	44	99	.444	13	41	.317	25	31	.806	7	24	31	25	25	1	10	0	20	28.1	14.0	3.4	2.8	.421
97-98	New York	10	2	314	164	59	125	.472	25	59	.424	21	24	.875	4	36	40	23	35	1	16	1	11	31.4	16.4	4.0	2.3	.488
00-01	Utah	3	0	36	11	4	12	.333	1	4	.250	2	2	1.000	0	3	3	1	5	0	1	1	2	12.0	3.7	1.0	0.3	.149
NBA Playoff Totals		96	55	3035	1363	450	1069	.421	176	475	.371	287	378	.759	37	234	271	393	323	4	120	9	224	31.6	14.2	2.8	4.1	....

• STARR, Keith

Keith Edward Starr

Born: Mar. 14, 1954. Sewickley, PA, United States. Height: 6'6". Weight: 190 lbs. Drafted: 1976 College: Pittsburgh

YEAR	TEAM	GP	GS	MIN	PTS	FGM	FGA	FG%	3PM	3PA	3P%	FTM	FTA	FT%	ORB	DRB	TRB	AST	PF	DQ	STL	BLK	TO	MPG	PPG	RPG	APG	PCM
76-77	Chicago	17	....	65	14	6	24	.250	....	....	....	2	2	1.000	6	4	10	6	11	0	1	0	....	3.8	0.8	0.6	0.4	.141
NBA Season Totals		17	....	65	14	6	24	.250	....	....	....	2	2	1.000	6	4	10	6	11	0	1	0	....	3.8	0.8	0.6	0.4	....

• STARZYK, Dick

Dick Starzyk

Born: 1921. Height: 5'10". Weight: 180 lbs. Drafted: — College: DePaul

YEAR	TEAM	GP	GS	MIN	PTS	FGM	FGA	FG%	3PM	3PA	3P%	FTM	FTA	FT%	ORB	DRB	TRB	AST	PF	DQ	STL	BLK	TO	MPG	PPG	RPG	APG	PCM
46-47	Tri-Cities-N	9	....	....	12	4	....	....	....	....	....	4	5	.800	....	....	....	....	....	....	....	....	....	....	1.3	....	....	....
NBL Season Totals		9	....	....	12	4	....	....	....	....	....	4	5	....	....	....	....	....	....	....	....	....	....	....	1.3	....	....	....

• STAVERMAN, Larry

Larry Joseph Staverman

Born: Oct. 11, 1936. Height: 6'7". Weight: 205 lbs. Drafted: 1958 College: Villa Madonna

YEAR	TEAM	GP	GS	MIN	PTS	FGM	FGA	FG%	3PM	3PA	3P%	FTM	FTA	FT%	ORB	DRB	TRB	AST	PF	DQ	STL	BLK	TO	MPG	PPG	RPG	APG	PCM
58-59	Cincinnati	57	....	681	247	101	215	.470	....	....	....	45	59	.763	....	....	218	54	103	0	....	....	....	11.9	4.3	3.8	0.9	.512
59-60	Cincinnati	49	....	479	187	70	149	.470	....	....	....	47	64	.734	....	....	180	36	98	0	....	....	....	9.8	3.8	3.7	0.7	.553
60-61	Cincinnati	66	....	944	301	111	249	.446	....	....	....	79	93	.849	....	....	287	86	164	4	....	....	....	14.3	4.6	4.3	1.3	.480
62-63	Chicago	33	....	602	237	94	194	.485	....	....	....	49	62	.790	....	....	158	43	94	3	....	....	....	18.2	7.2	4.8	1.3	.486
63-64	Baltimore	6	....	99	16	6	14	.429	....	....	....	4	4	1.000	....	....	13	2	7	0	....	....	....	16.5	2.7	2.2	0.3	.198
63-64	Detroit	20	....	255	114	44	82	.537	....	....	....	26	39	.667	....	....	69	12	50	2	....	....	....	12.8	5.7	3.5	0.6	.503
63-64	Cincinnati	34	....	320	135	48	116	.414	....	....	....	39	47	.830	....	....	94	18	61	1	....	....	....	9.4	4.0	2.8	0.5	.470
NBA Season Totals		265	....	3380	1237	474	1019	.465	....	....	....	289	368	.785	....	....	1019	251	577	10	....	....	....	12.8	4.7	3.8	0.9	....
63-64	Cincinnati	7	....	70	37	11	23	.478	....	....	....	15	19	.789	....	....	26	5	16	0	....	....	....	10.0	5.3	3.7	0.7	.660
NBA Playoff Totals		7	....	70	37	11	23	.478	....	....	....	15	19	.789	....	....	26	5	16	0	....	....	....	10.0	5.3	3.7	0.7	....

• STEELE, Larry

Larry Nelson Steele

Born: May 5, 1949. Greencastle, IN, United States. Height: 6'5". Weight: 180 lbs. Drafted: 1971 College: Kentucky

YEAR	TEAM	GP	GS	MIN	PTS	FGM	FGA	FG%	3PM	3PA	3P%	FTM	FTA	FT%	ORB	DRB	TRB	AST	PF	DQ	STL	BLK	TO	MPG	PPG	RPG	APG	PCM
71-72	Portland	72	....	1311	366	148	308	.481	....	....	....	70	97	.722	....	....	282	161	198	8	....	....	....	18.2	5.1	3.9	2.2	.425
72-73	Portland	66	....	1301	389	159	329	.483	....	....	....	71	89	.798	....	....	154	156	181	4	....	....	....	19.7	5.9	2.3	2.4	.360
73-74	Portland	81	....	2648	785	325	680	.478	....	....	....	135	171	.789	89	221	310	323	295	10	**217**	32	....	32.7	9.7	3.8	4.0	.369
74-75	Portland	76	....	2389	652	265	484	.548	....	....	....	122	146	.836	86	140	226	287	254	6	183	16	....	31.4	8.6	3.0	3.8	.364
75-76	Portland	81	....	2382	798	322	651	.495	....	....	....	154	203	.759	77	215	292	324	289	8	170	19	....	29.4	9.9	3.6	4.0	.416
76-77	Portland	81	....	1680	835	326	652	.500	....	....	....	183	227	.806	71	117	188	172	216	3	118	13	....	20.7	10.3	2.3	2.1	.476
77-78	Portland	65	....	1132	520	210	447	.470	....	....	....	100	122	.820	34	79	113	87	138	2	59	5	65	17.4	8.0	1.7	1.3	.387
78-79	Portland	72	....	1488	518	203	483	.420	....	....	....	112	136	.824	58	113	171	142	208	4	74	10	94	20.7	7.2	2.4	2.0	.311
79-80	Portland	16	....	446	146	62	146	.425	0	4	.000	22	27	.815	13	32	45	67	53	0	25	1	34	27.9	9.1	2.8	4.2	.338
NBA Season Totals		610	....	14777	5009	2020	4180	.483	0	4	.000	969	1218	.796	428	917	1781	1719	1832	45	846	96	193	24.2	8.2	2.9	2.8	....
76-77	Portland	18	....	261	76	26	70	.371	....	....	....	24	32	.750	12	15	27	18	30	0	9	0	....	14.5	4.2	1.5	1.0	.251
77-78	Portland	6	....	191	69	25	60	.417	....	....	....	19	21	.905	8	18	26	14	22	0	7	2	12	31.8	11.5	4.3	2.3	.334
78-79	Portland	3	....	73	40	16	28	.571	....	....	....	8	9	.889	6	5	11	7	8	0	10	0	3	24.3	13.3	3.7	2.3	.672
NBA Playoff Totals		27	....	525	185	67	158	.424	....	....	....	51	62	.823	26	38	64	39	60	0	26	2	15	19.4	6.9	2.4	1.4	....

YEAR	TEAM	GP	GS	MIN	PTS	FGM	FGA	FG%	3PM	3PA	3P%	FTM	FTA	FT%	ORB	DRB	TRB	AST	PF	DQ	STL	BLK	TO	MPG	PPG	RPG	APG	PCM

• STEGE, Ed
Ed Stege

Born: 1913.   Height: 6'6".   Weight: 220 lbs.   Drafted: —   College: Wisconsin

YEAR	TEAM	GP	GS	MIN	PTS	FGM	FGA	FG%	3PM	3PA	3P%	FTM	FTA	FT%	ORB	DRB	TRB	AST	PF	DQ	STL	BLK	TO	MPG	PPG	RPG	APG	PCM
37-38	Oshkosh-N	2	....	....	0	0	....	....	....	....	....	....	0	....	....	....	....	....	....	....	....	....	....	....	0.0	....	....	....
NBL Season Totals		2	....	....	0	0	....	....	....	....	....	....	0	....	....	....	....	....	....	....	....	....	....	....	0.0	....	....	....

• STEIGENGA, Matt
Matthew Todd Steigenga

Born: Mar. 27, 1970. Grand Rapids, MI, United States.   Height: 6'7".   Weight: 225 lbs.   Drafted: 1992   College: Michigan State

YEAR	TEAM	GP	GS	MIN	PTS	FGM	FGA	FG%	3PM	3PA	3P%	FTM	FTA	FT%	ORB	DRB	TRB	AST	PF	DQ	STL	BLK	TO	MPG	PPG	RPG	APG	PCM
96-97	Chicago	2	0	12	3	1	4	.250	0	2	.000	1	2	.500	0	3	3	2	1	0	1	1	2	6.0	1.5	1.5	1.0	.350
NBA Season Totals		2	0	12	3	1	4	.250	0	2	.000	1	2	.500	0	3	3	2	1	0	1	1	2	6.0	1.5	1.5	1.0	

• STEINER, Jerry
Jerome Steiner

Born: 1918.   Height: 5'7".   Weight: 160 lbs.   Drafted: —   College: Butler

YEAR	TEAM	GP	GS	MIN	PTS	FGM	FGA	FG%	3PM	3PA	3P%	FTM	FTA	FT%	ORB	DRB	TRB	AST	PF	DQ	STL	BLK	TO	MPG	PPG	RPG	APG	PCM
45-46	Indianapolis-N	30	....	....	270	106	....	....	....	....	....	58	94	.617	....	....	....	....	....	....	....	....	....	....	9.0	....	....	....
46-47	Fort Wayne-N	16	....	....	29	12	....	....	....	....	....	5	9	.556	....	....	....	....	....	....	....	....	....	....	1.8	....	....	....
NBL Season Totals		46	....	....	299	118	....	....	....	....	....	63	103	....	....	....	....	....	....	....	....	....	....	....	6.5	....	....	....
46-47	Fort Wayne-N	4	....	....	3	1	....	....	....	....	....	1	4	.250	....	....	....	....	....	....	....	....	....	....	0.8	....	....	....
NBL Playoff Totals		4	....	....	3	1	....	....	....	....	....	1	4	....	....	....	....	....	....	....	....	....	....	....	0.8	....	....	....

• STEPANIA, Vladimir
Vladimir Stepania

Born: Aug. 5, 1976. Tbilisi, Georgia.   Height: 7'   Weight: 236 lbs.   Drafted: 1998   College: —

YEAR	TEAM	GP	GS	MIN	PTS	FGM	FGA	FG%	3PM	3PA	3P%	FTM	FTA	FT%	ORB	DRB	TRB	AST	PF	DQ	STL	BLK	TO	MPG	PPG	RPG	APG	PCM
98-99	Seattle	23	6	313	127	53	125	.424	0	3	.000	21	40	.525	27	48	75	12	58	0	10	23	32	13.6	5.5	3.3	0.5	.350
99-00	Seattle	30	1	202	75	29	79	.367	0	6	.000	17	36	.472	21	26	47	3	44	0	10	11	22	6.7	2.5	1.6	0.1	.228
00-01	New Jersey	29	0	280	82	28	88	.318	1	4	.250	25	34	.735	35	74	109	16	47	0	10	11	19	9.7	2.8	3.8	0.6	.430
01-02	Miami	67	4	884	285	117	249	.470	1	2	.500	50	104	.481	100	170	270	16	103	1	24	44	52	13.2	4.3	4.0	0.2	.420
02-03	Miami	79	6	1594	441	185	427	.433	0	0	.000	71	134	.530	211	343	554	24	169	0	45	40	69	20.2	5.6	7.0	0.3	.414
NBA Season Totals		228	17	3273	1010	412	968	.426	2	15	.133	184	348	.529	394	661	1055	71	421	1	99	129	194	14.4	4.4	4.6	0.3	

• STEPHANS, John
John Stephans

Born: —.   Height: 5'6".   Weight: —   Drafted: —   College: none

YEAR	TEAM	GP	GS	MIN	PTS	FGM	FGA	FG%	3PM	3PA	3P%	FTM	FTA	FT%	ORB	DRB	TRB	AST	PF	DQ	STL	BLK	TO	MPG	PPG	RPG	APG	PCM
44-45	Pittsburgh-N	1	....	....	4	2	....	....	....	....	....	0	....	....	....	....	....	....	....	....	....	....	....	....	4.0	....	....	....
NBL Season Totals		1	....	....	4	2	....	....	....	....	....	0	....	....	....	....	....	....	....	....	....	....	....	....	4.0	....	....	....

• STEPHENS, Ben
Ben Stephens

Born: 1917.   Height: 6'   Weight: 175 lbs.   Drafted: —   College: Iowa

YEAR	TEAM	GP	GS	MIN	PTS	FGM	FGA	FG%	3PM	3PA	3P%	FTM	FTA	FT%	ORB	DRB	TRB	AST	PF	DQ	STL	BLK	TO	MPG	PPG	RPG	APG	PCM
39-40	Wingfoots-N	28	....	....	295	91	....	....	....	....	....	113	....	....	....	....	....	....	....	....	....	....	....	....	10.5	....	....	....
40-41	Wingfoots-N	24	....	....	**265**	**98**	....	....	....	....	....	69	....	....	....	....	....	....	....	....	....	....	....	....	11.0	....	....	....
41-42	Wingfoots-N	24	....	....	222	81	....	....	....	....	....	60	....	....	....	....	....	....	....	....	....	....	....	....	9.3	....	....	....
NBL Season Totals		76	....	....	782	270	....	....	....	....	....	242	....	....	....	....	....	....	....	....	....	....	....	....	10.3	....	....	....
41-42	Wingfoots-N	3	....	....	39	13	....	....	....	....	....	13	....	....	....	....	....	....	....	....	....	....	....	....	13.0	....	....	....
NBL Playoff Totals		3	....	....	39	13	....	....	....	....	....	13	....	....	....	....	....	....	....	....	....	....	....	....	13.0	....	....	....

• STEPHENS, Everette
Everette Louis Stephens

Born: Oct. 21, 1966. Evanston, IL, United States.   Height: 6'2".   Weight: 175 lbs.   Drafted: 1988   College: Purdue

YEAR	TEAM	GP	GS	MIN	PTS	FGM	FGA	FG%	3PM	3PA	3P%	FTM	FTA	FT%	ORB	DRB	TRB	AST	PF	DQ	STL	BLK	TO	MPG	PPG	RPG	APG	PCM
88-89	Indiana	35	0	209	65	23	72	.319	2	10	.200	17	22	.773	11	12	23	37	22	0	9	4	28	6.0	1.9	0.7	1.1	.258
90-91	Milwaukee	3	0	6	6	2	3	.667	0	0	.000	2	2	1.000	0	0	0	2	0	0	0	0	0	2.0	2.0	0.0	0.7	1.200
NBA Season Totals		38	0	215	71	25	75	.333	2	10	.200	19	24	.792	11	12	23	39	22	0	9	4	28	5.7	1.9	0.6	1.0	

• STEPHENS, Jack
John Francis (Junior) Stephens

Born: May 18, 1933.   Height: 6'3".   Weight: 185 lbs.   Drafted: 1955   College: Notre Dame

YEAR	TEAM	GP	GS	MIN	PTS	FGM	FGA	FG%	3PM	3PA	3P%	FTM	FTA	FT%	ORB	DRB	TRB	AST	PF	DQ	STL	BLK	TO	MPG	PPG	RPG	APG	PCM
55-56	St. Louis	72	....	2219	743	248	643	.386	....	....	....	247	357	.692	....	....	377	207	144	6	....	....	....	30.8	10.3	5.2	2.9	.401
NBA Season Totals		72	....	2219	743	248	643	.386	....	....	....	247	357	.692	....	....	377	207	144	6	....	....	....	30.8	10.3	5.2	2.9	
55-56	St. Louis	7	....	116	39	12	41	.293	....	....	....	15	25	.600	....	....	23	9	9	0	....	....	....	16.6	5.6	3.3	1.3	.331
NBA Playoff Totals		7	....	116	39	12	41	.293	....	....	....	15	25	.600	....	....	23	9	9	0	....	....	....	16.6	5.6	3.3	1.3	

• STEPHENS, Joe
Joe Stephens

Born: Jan. 28, 1973. Riverside, CA, United States.   Height: 6'7".   Weight: 210 lbs.   Drafted: —   College: Arkansas-Little Rock

YEAR	TEAM	GP	GS	MIN	PTS	FGM	FGA	FG%	3PM	3PA	3P%	FTM	FTA	FT%	ORB	DRB	TRB	AST	PF	DQ	STL	BLK	TO	MPG	PPG	RPG	APG	PCM
96-97	Houston	2	0	9	3	1	5	.200	1	3	.333	0	0	.000	2	1	3	0	3	0	3	0	3	4.5	1.5	1.5	0.0	.074
97-98	Houston	7	0	37	27	10	28	.357	3	10	.300	4	6	.667	3	3	6	1	2	0	2	0	2	5.3	3.9	0.9	0.1	.413
99-00	Vancouver	13	0	181	41	19	51	.373	0	8	.000	3	4	.750	13	23	36	11	9	0	7	3	6	13.9	3.2	2.8	0.8	.308
NBA Season Totals		22	0	227	71	30	84	.357	4	21	.190	7	10	.700	18	27	45	12	14	0	12	3	11	10.3	3.2	2.0	0.5	

YEAR	TEAM	GP	GS	MIN	PTS	FGM	FGA	FG%	3PM	3PA	3P%	FTM	FTA	FT%	ORB	DRB	TRB	AST	PF	DQ	STL	BLK	TO	MPG	PPG	RPG	APG	PCM

• STEPPE, Brook — Michael Holbrook (Brook) Steppe

Born: Nov. 7, 1959. Chapel Hill, NC, United States.   Height: 6'5".   Weight: 195 lbs.   Drafted: 1982   College: Georgia Tech

YEAR	TEAM	GP	GS	MIN	PTS	FGM	FGA	FG%	3PM	3PA	3P%	FTM	FTA	FT%	ORB	DRB	TRB	AST	PF	DQ	STL	BLK	TO	MPG	PPG	RPG	APG	PCM
82-83	Kansas City	62	6	606	245	84	176	.477	1	7	.143	76	100	.760	25	48	73	68	92	0	26	3	56	9.8	4.0	1.2	1.1	.373
83-84	Indiana	61	13	857	430	148	314	.471	0	3	.000	134	161	.832	43	79	122	79	93	0	34	6	85	14.0	7.0	2.0	1.3	.439
84-85	Detroit	54	0	486	253	83	178	.466	0	1	.000	87	104	.837	25	32	57	36	61	0	16	4	43	9.0	4.7	1.1	0.7	.408
86-87	Sacramento	34	7	665	266	95	199	.477	3	9	.333	73	88	.830	21	40	61	81	56	0	18	3	54	19.6	7.8	1.8	2.4	.374
88-89	Portland	27	2	244	103	33	78	.423	5	9	.556	32	37	.865	13	19	32	16	32	0	11	1	14	9.0	3.8	1.2	0.6	.365
NBA Season Totals		238	28	2858	1297	443	945	.469	9	29	.310	402	490	.820	127	218	345	280	334	0	105	17	252	12.0	5.4	1.4	1.2	....
84-85	Detroit	4	0	20	8	2	7	.286	0	1	.000	4	6	.667	1	2	3	2	3	0	0	0	2	5.0	2.0	0.8	0.5	.204
NBA Playoff Totals		4	0	20	8	2	7	.286	0	1	.000	4	6	.667	1	2	3	2	3	0	0	0	2	5.0	2.0	0.8	0.5	....

• STERLING, Jack — Jack Sterling

Born: 1917.   Height: 6'5".   Weight: —   Drafted: —   College: Geneva

YEAR	TEAM	GP	GS	MIN	PTS	FGM	FGA	FG%	3PM	3PA	3P%	FTM	FTA	FT%	ORB	DRB	TRB	AST	PF	DQ	STL	BLK	TO	MPG	PPG	RPG	APG	PCM
37-38	Warren-N	6	....	....	36	13	....	....	....	....	....	10	....	....	....	....	....	....	....	....	....	....	....	....	6.0	....	....	....
38-39	Pittsburgh-N	12	....	....	3	1	....	....	....	....	....	1	....	....	....	....	....	....	....	....	....	....	....	....	0.3	....	....	....
NBL Season Totals		18	....	....	39	14	....	....	....	....	....	11	....	....	....	....	....	....	....	....	....	....	....	....	2.2	....	....	....

• STEVENS, Barry — Barry Wayne Stevens

Born: Jan. 17, 1963. Flint, MI, United States.   Height: 6'5".   Weight: 195 lbs.   Drafted: 1985   College: Iowa State

YEAR	TEAM	GP	GS	MIN	PTS	FGM	FGA	FG%	3PM	3PA	3P%	FTM	FTA	FT%	ORB	DRB	TRB	AST	PF	DQ	STL	BLK	TO	MPG	PPG	RPG	APG	PCM
92-93	Golden State	2	0	6	2	1	2	.500	0	0	.000	0	0	.000	2	0	2	0	1	0	0	0	0	3.0	1.0	1.0	0.0	.411
NBA Season Totals		2	0	6	2	1	2	.500	0	0	.000	0	0	.000	2	0	2	0	1	0	0	0	0	3.0	1.0	1.0	0.0	....

• STEVENS, Wayne — Wayne Stevens

Born: June 19, 1936.   Height: 6'3".   Weight: 185 lbs.   Drafted: 1958   College: Cincinnati

YEAR	TEAM	GP	GS	MIN	PTS	FGM	FGA	FG%	3PM	3PA	3P%	FTM	FTA	FT%	ORB	DRB	TRB	AST	PF	DQ	STL	BLK	TO	MPG	PPG	RPG	APG	PCM
59-60	Cincinnati	8	....	49	13	3	19	.158	....	....	....	7	10	.700	....	....	16	4	4	0	....	....	....	6.1	1.6	2.0	0.5	.313
NBA Season Totals		8	....	49	13	3	19	.158	....	....	....	7	10	.700	....	....	16	4	4	0	....	....	....	6.1	1.6	2.0	0.5	....

• STEVENSON, DeShawn — DeShawn Stevenson

Born: Apr. 3, 1981. Fresno, CA, United States.   Height: 6'5".   Weight: 210 lbs.   Drafted: 2000   College: none (HS: Washington Union, CA)

YEAR	TEAM	GP	GS	MIN	PTS	FGM	FGA	FG%	3PM	3PA	3P%	FTM	FTA	FT%	ORB	DRB	TRB	AST	PF	DQ	STL	BLK	TO	MPG	PPG	RPG	APG	PCM
00-01	Utah	40	2	293	89	31	91	.341	1	12	.083	26	38	.684	9	19	28	18	29	0	10	2	28	7.3	2.2	0.7	0.5	.162
01-02	Utah	67	23	1134	325	143	371	.385	2	25	.080	37	53	.698	44	87	131	116	82	0	29	24	68	16.9	4.9	2.0	1.7	.270
02-03	Utah	61	8	760	279	114	284	.401	4	12	.333	47	68	.691	22	63	85	40	57	0	22	8	49	12.5	4.6	1.4	0.7	.254
NBA Season Totals		168	33	2187	693	288	746	.386	7	49	.143	110	159	.692	75	169	244	174	168	0	61	34	145	13.0	4.1	1.5	1.0	....
00-01	Utah	1	0	8	2	1	2	.500	0	0	.000	0	0	.000	0	1	1	0	0	0	0	0	1	8.0	2.0	1.0	0.0	.138
02-03	Utah	4	0	37	18	6	15	.400	0	2	.000	6	6	1.000	2	5	7	4	3	0	1	0	0	9.3	4.5	1.8	1.0	.543
NBA Playoff Totals		5	0	45	20	7	17	.412	0	2	.000	6	6	1.000	2	6	8	4	3	0	1	0	1	9.0	4.0	1.6	0.8	....

• STEWART, Dennis — Dennis Edward Stewart

Born: Apr. 11, 1947.   Height: 6'6".   Weight: 220 lbs.   Drafted: 1969   College: Michigan

YEAR	TEAM	GP	GS	MIN	PTS	FGM	FGA	FG%	3PM	3PA	3P%	FTM	FTA	FT%	ORB	DRB	TRB	AST	PF	DQ	STL	BLK	TO	MPG	PPG	RPG	APG	PCM
70-71	Florida-A	10	....	66	36	15	44	.341	1	3	.333	5	7	.714	4	10	14	1	12	0	....	....	9	6.6	3.6	1.4	0.1	.297
70-71	Baltimore	2	....	6	4	1	4	.250	....	....	....	2	2	1.000	....	....	3	1	0	0	....	....	....	3.0	2.0	1.5	0.5	.857
NBA Season Totals		2	....	6	4	1	4	.250	....	....	....	2	2	1.000	....	....	3	1	0	0	....	....	....	3.0	2.0	1.5	0.5	....
ABA Season Totals		10	....	66	36	15	44	.341	1	3	.333	5	7	.714	4	10	14	1	12	0	....	....	9	6.6	3.6	1.4	0.1	....
Career Totals		12	....	72	40	16	48	.333	1	3	.333	7	9	.778	4	10	17	2	12	0	....	....	9	6.0	3.3	1.4	0.2	....

• STEWART, Kebu — Kebu Stewart

Born: Dec. 19, 1973. Brooklyn, NY, United States.   Height: 6'8".   Weight: 239 lbs.   Drafted: 1997   College: Cal State Bakersfield

YEAR	TEAM	GP	GS	MIN	PTS	FGM	FGA	FG%	3PM	3PA	3P%	FTM	FTA	FT%	ORB	DRB	TRB	AST	PF	DQ	STL	BLK	TO	MPG	PPG	RPG	APG	PCM
97-98	Philadelphia	15	0	110	40	12	26	.462	0	0	.000	16	25	.640	9	22	31	2	13	0	5	2	8	7.3	2.7	2.1	0.1	.425
NBA Season Totals		15	0	110	40	12	26	.462	0	0	.000	16	25	.640	9	22	31	2	13	0	5	2	8	7.3	2.7	2.1	0.1	....

• STEWART, Larry — Larry Stewart

Born: Sept. 21, 1968. Philadelphia, PA, United States.   Height: 6'8".   Weight: 220 lbs.   Drafted: —   College: Coppin State

YEAR	TEAM	GP	GS	MIN	PTS	FGM	FGA	FG%	3PM	3PA	3P%	FTM	FTA	FT%	ORB	DRB	TRB	AST	PF	DQ	STL	BLK	TO	MPG	PPG	RPG	APG	PCM
91-92	Washington	76	43	2229	794	303	590	.514	0	3	.000	188	233	.807	186	263	449	120	225	3	51	44	114	29.3	10.4	5.9	1.6	.417
92-93	Washington	81	8	1823	796	306	564	.543	0	2	.000	184	253	.727	154	229	383	146	191	1	47	29	154	22.5	9.8	4.7	1.8	.480
93-94	Washington	3	0	35	13	3	8	.375	0	0	.000	7	10	.700	1	6	7	2	4	0	2	1	2	11.7	4.3	2.3	0.7	.420
94-95	Washington	40	0	346	102	41	89	.461	0	2	.000	20	30	.667	28	39	67	18	52	0	16	9	16	8.7	2.6	1.7	0.5	.342
96-97	Seattle	70	21	982	300	112	252	.444	9	37	.243	67	93	.720	75	96	171	52	108	0	31	23	63	14.0	4.3	2.4	0.7	.319
NBA Season Totals		270	72	5415	2005	765	1503	.509	9	44	.205	466	619	.753	444	633	1077	338	580	4	147	106	349	20.1	7.4	4.0	1.3	....
96-97	Seattle	4	0	16	13	5	6	.833	1	2	.500	2	2	1.000	0	1	1	2	4	0	2	1	2	4.0	3.3	0.3	0.5	.888
NBA Playoff Totals		4	0	16	13	5	6	.833	1	2	.500	2	2	1.000	0	1	1	2	4	0	2	1	2	4.0	3.3	0.3	0.5	....

YEAR	TEAM	GP	GS	MIN	PTS	FGM	FGA	FG%	3PM	3PA	3P%	FTM	FTA	FT%	ORB	DRB	TRB	AST	PF	DQ	STL	BLK	TO	MPG	PPG	RPG	APG	PCM

• STEWART, Michael

Michael Curtis (Yogi) Stewart

Born: Apr. 24, 1975. CutqTrepiedStel, France.   Height: 6'10".   Weight: 230 lbs.   Drafted: —   College: California

YEAR	TEAM	GP	GS	MIN	PTS	FGM	FGA	FG%	3PM	3PA	3P%	FTM	FTA	FT%	ORB	DRB	TRB	AST	PF	DQ	STL	BLK	TO	MPG	PPG	RPG	APG	PCM
97-98	Sacramento	81	37	1761	375	155	323	.480	0	0	.000	65	142	.458	197	339	536	61	251	6	29	195	81	21.7	4.6	6.6	0.8	.431
98-99	Toronto	42	2	394	61	22	53	.415	0	0	.000	17	25	.680	43	56	99	5	76	0	4	28	12	9.4	1.5	2.4	0.1	.273
99-00	Toronto	42	1	389	58	20	53	.377	0	0	.000	18	32	.563	33	61	94	6	81	3	5	19	17	9.3	1.4	2.2	0.1	.214
00-01	Toronto	26	0	123	33	11	34	.324	0	0	.000	11	18	.611	16	13	29	2	19	0	4	3	5	4.7	1.3	1.1	0.1	.250
01-02	Toronto	11	0	93	22	8	23	.348	0	0	.000	6	11	.545	12	13	25	3	22	0	4	3	4	8.5	2.0	2.3	0.3	.267
02-03	Cleveland	47	0	251	36	14	37	.378	0	0	.000	8	12	.667	19	36	55	6	42	0	2	15	10	5.3	0.8	1.2	0.1	.227
NBA Season Totals		249	40	3011	585	230	523	.440	0	0	.000	125	240	.521	320	518	838	83	491	9	48	263	129	12.1	2.3	3.4	0.3	....
00-01	Toronto	2	0	4	0	0	1	.000	0	0	.000	0	0	.000	1	0	1	0	0	0	0	0	0	2.0	0.0	0.5	0.0	.000
01-02	Toronto	1	0	8	4	2	2	1.000	0	0	.000	0	0	.000	0	3	3	0	2	0	0	1	1	8.0	4.0	3.0	0.0	.727
NBA Playoff Totals		3	0	12	4	2	3	.667	0	0	.000	0	0	.000	1	3	4	0	2	0	0	1	1	4.0	1.3	1.3	0.0	....

• STEWART, Norm

Norman E. Stewart

Born: Jan. 20, 1935. Leonard, MO, United States.   Height: 6'5".   Weight: 205 lbs.   Drafted: 1956   College: Missouri

YEAR	TEAM	GP	GS	MIN	PTS	FGM	FGA	FG%	3PM	3PA	3P%	FTM	FTA	FT%	ORB	DRB	TRB	AST	PF	DQ	STL	BLK	TO	MPG	PPG	RPG	APG	PCM
56-57	St. Louis	5	....	37	10	4	15	.267	....	....	....	2	6	.333	....	....	5	2	9	0	....	....	....	7.4	2.0	1.0	0.4	.086
NBA Season Totals		5	....	37	10	4	15	.267	....	....	....	2	6	.333	....	....	5	2	9	0	....	....	....	7.4	2.0	1.0	0.4	....

• STIPANOVICH, Steve

Stephen Samuel Stipanovich

Born: Nov. 17, 1960. St. Louis, MO, United States.   Height: 6'11".   Weight: 245 lbs.   Drafted: 1983   College: Missouri

YEAR	TEAM	GP	GS	MIN	PTS	FGM	FGA	FG%	3PM	3PA	3P%	FTM	FTA	FT%	ORB	DRB	TRB	AST	PF	DQ	STL	BLK	TO	MPG	PPG	RPG	APG	PCM
83-84	Indiana	81	73	2426	970	392	816	.480	3	16	.188	183	243	.753	116	446	562	170	303	4	73	67	162	30.0	12.0	6.9	2.1	.450
84-85	Indiana	82	66	2315	1126	414	871	.475	4	11	.091	297	372	.798	141	473	614	199	265	4	71	78	180	28.2	13.7	7.5	2.4	.560
85-86	Indiana	79	65	2397	1076	416	885	.470	2	10	.200	242	315	.768	173	450	623	206	261	1	75	69	142	30.3	13.6	7.9	2.6	.537
86-87	Indiana	81	81	2761	1072	382	760	.503	1	4	.250	307	367	.837	184	486	670	180	304	9	106	97	130	34.1	13.2	8.3	2.2	.520
87-88	Indiana	80	80	2692	1079	411	828	.496	3	15	.200	254	314	.809	157	505	662	183	302	8	90	69	152	33.7	13.5	8.3	2.3	.498
NBA Season Totals		403	365	12591	5323	2015	4160	.484	10	56	.179	1283	1611	.796	771	2360	3131	938	1435	26	415	380	766	31.2	13.2	7.8	2.3	....
86-87	Indiana	4	4	149	55	21	38	.553	0	1	.000	13	19	.684	7	23	30	3	14	0	3	2	4	37.3	13.8	7.5	0.8	.416
NBA Playoff Totals		4	4	149	55	21	38	.553	0	1	.000	13	19	.684	7	23	30	3	14	0	3	2	4	37.3	13.8	7.5	0.8	....

• STITH, Bryant

Bryant Lamonica Stith

Born: Dec. 10, 1970. Emporia, VA, United States.   Height: 6'5".   Weight: 208 lbs.   Drafted: 1992   College: Virginia

YEAR	TEAM	GP	GS	MIN	PTS	FGM	FGA	FG%	3PM	3PA	3P%	FTM	FTA	FT%	ORB	DRB	TRB	AST	PF	DQ	STL	BLK	TO	MPG	PPG	RPG	APG	PCM
92-93	Denver	39	12	865	347	124	278	.446	0	4	.000	99	119	.832	39	85	124	49	82	0	24	5	43	22.2	8.9	3.2	1.3	.359
93-94	Denver	82	82	2853	1023	365	811	.450	2	9	.222	291	351	.829	119	230	349	199	165	0	116	16	131	34.8	12.5	4.3	2.4	.367
94-95	Denver	81	51	2329	911	312	661	.472	20	68	.294	267	324	.824	95	173	268	153	142	0	91	18	113	28.8	11.2	3.3	1.9	.387
95-96	Denver	82	77	2810	1119	379	912	.416	41	148	.277	320	379	.844	125	275	400	241	187	3	114	16	156	34.3	13.6	4.9	2.9	.395
96-97	Denver	52	52	1788	774	251	603	.416	70	182	.385	202	234	.863	74	143	217	133	119	1	60	20	99	34.4	14.9	4.2	2.6	.393
97-98	Denver	31	15	718	235	75	225	.333	10	48	.208	75	86	.872	15	50	65	50	52	0	21	8	34	23.2	7.6	2.1	1.6	.248
98-99	Denver	46	32	1194	320	114	290	.393	31	106	.292	61	71	.859	30	77	107	82	65	0	28	15	45	26.0	7.0	2.3	1.8	.264
99-00	Denver	45	6	691	253	86	189	.455	17	56	.304	64	77	.831	23	61	84	61	56	0	18	12	33	15.4	5.6	1.9	1.4	.388
00-01	Boston	78	74	2504	756	245	611	.401	91	242	.376	175	207	.845	65	219	284	168	182	0	93	14	90	32.1	9.7	3.6	2.2	.314
01-02	Cleveland	50	5	665	208	70	188	.372	24	68	.353	44	52	.846	20	65	85	42	42	0	29	6	30	13.3	4.2	1.7	0.8	.310
NBA Season Totals		586	406	16417	5946	2021	4768	.424	306	931	.329	1598	1900	.841	605	1378	1983	1178	1092	4	594	130	774	28.0	10.1	3.4	2.0	....
93-94	Denver	12	12	413	136	43	102	.422	0	1	.000	50	60	.833	23	33	56	26	23	0	11	2	14	34.4	11.3	4.7	2.2	.352
94-95	Denver	3	1	85	50	17	32	.531	1	6	.167	15	19	.789	3	6	9	7	7	0	1	1	0	28.3	16.7	3.0	2.3	.571
NBA Playoff Totals		15	13	498	186	60	134	.448	1	7	.143	65	79	.823	26	39	65	33	30	0	12	3	14	33.2	12.4	4.3	2.2	....

• STITH, Sam

Samuel Elwood Stith

Born: July 22, 1937. Greenville Co., VA, United States.   Height: 6'2".   Weight: 185 lbs.   Drafted: 1960   College: St. Bonaventure

YEAR	TEAM	GP	GS	MIN	PTS	FGM	FGA	FG%	3PM	3PA	3P%	FTM	FTA	FT%	ORB	DRB	TRB	AST	PF	DQ	STL	BLK	TO	MPG	PPG	RPG	APG	PCM
61-62	New York	32	....	440	141	59	162	.364	....	....	....	23	38	.605	....	....	51	60	55	0	....	....	....	13.8	4.4	1.6	1.9	.332
NBA Season Totals		32	....	440	141	59	162	.364	....	....	....	23	38	.605	....	....	51	60	55	0	....	....	....	13.8	4.4	1.6	1.9	....

• STITH, Tom

Thomas Alvin Stith

Born: Jan. 21, 1939. Greenville Co., VA, United States.   Height: 6'5".   Weight: 210 lbs.   Drafted: 1961   College: St. Bonaventure

YEAR	TEAM	GP	GS	MIN	PTS	FGM	FGA	FG%	3PM	3PA	3P%	FTM	FTA	FT%	ORB	DRB	TRB	AST	PF	DQ	STL	BLK	TO	MPG	PPG	RPG	APG	PCM
62-63	New York	25	....	209	77	37	110	.336	....	....	....	3	10	.300	....	....	39	18	23	0	....	....	....	8.4	3.1	1.6	0.7	.287
NBA Season Totals		25	....	209	77	37	110	.336	....	....	....	3	10	.300	....	....	39	18	23	0	....	....	....	8.4	3.1	1.6	0.7	....

• STIVRINS, Alex

Alex Frank Stivrins

Born: Nov. 29, 1962. Lincoln, NE, United States.   Height: 6'8".   Weight: 220 lbs.   Drafted: 1985   College: Colorado

YEAR	TEAM	GP	GS	MIN	PTS	FGM	FGA	FG%	3PM	3PA	3P%	FTM	FTA	FT%	ORB	DRB	TRB	AST	PF	DQ	STL	BLK	TO	MPG	PPG	RPG	APG	PCM
85-86	Seattle	3	0	14	3	1	4	.250	0	0	.000	1	4	.250	3	0	3	1	2	0	0	0	3	4.7	1.0	1.0	0.3	-.074
92-93	Atlanta	5	0	15	8	4	9	.444	0	1	.000	0	0	.000	2	3	5	0	0	0	0	1	0	3.0	1.6	1.0	0.0	.596
92-93	LA Clippers	1	0	1	0	0	1	.000	0	0	.000	0	0	.000	0	0	0	0	0	0	0	0	0	1.0	0.0	0.0	0.0	-.933
92-93	Milwaukee	3	0	25	11	4	11	.364	0	0	.000	3	4	.750	3	3	6	2	4	0	1	0	2	8.3	3.7	2.0	0.7	.357
92-93	Phoenix	10	0	35	22	11	18	.611	0	1	.000	0	0	.000	2	6	8	1	7	0	1	1	5	3.5	2.2	0.8	0.1	.512
NBA Season Totals		22	0	90	44	20	43	.465	0	2	.000	4	8	.500	10	12	22	4	13	0	2	2	10	4.1	2.0	1.0	0.2	....

• STOCKTON, John

John Houston (Stock) Stockton

Born: Mar. 26, 1962. Spokane, WA, United States. Height: 6'1". Weight: 170 lbs. Drafted: 1984 College: Gonzaga

YEAR	TEAM	GP	GS	MIN	PTS	FGM	FGA	FG%	3PM	3PA	3P%	FTM	FTA	FT%	ORB	DRB	TRB	AST	PF	DQ	STL	BLK	TO	MPG	PPG	RPG	APG	PCM
84-85	Utah	82	5	1490	458	157	333	.471	2	11	.182	142	193	.736	26	79	105	415	203	3	109	11	148	18.2	5.6	1.3	5.1	.463
85-86	Utah	82	38	1935	630	228	466	.489	2	15	.133	172	205	.839	33	146	179	610	227	2	157	10	164	23.6	7.7	2.2	7.4	.574
86-87	Utah	82	2	1858	648	231	463	.499	7	39	.179	179	229	.782	32	119	151	670	224	1	177	14	164	22.7	7.9	1.8	8.2	.639
87-88	Utah	82	79	2842	1204	454	791	.574	24	67	.358	272	324	.840	54	183	237	**1128**	247	5	242	16	262	34.7	14.7	2.9	**13.8**	**.764**
88-89	Utah	82	82	3171	1400	497	923	.538	16	66	.242	390	452	.863	83	165	248	**1118**	241	3	**263**	14	312	38.7	17.1	3.0	**13.6**	**.712**
89-90	Utah	78	78	2915	1345	472	918	.514	47	113	.416	354	432	.819	57	149	206	**1134**	233	3	207	18	273	37.4	17.2	2.6	**14.5**	**.732**
90-91	Utah	82	82	3103	1413	496	978	.507	58	168	.345	363	434	.836	46	191	237	**1164**	233	1	234	16	295	37.8	17.2	2.9	**14.2**	**.723**
91-92	Utah	82	82	3002	1297	453	939	.482	83	204	.407	308	366	.842	68	202	270	**1126**	234	3	**244**	22	**287**	36.6	15.8	3.3	**13.7**	**.715**
92-93	Utah	82	82	2863	1239	437	899	.486	72	187	.385	293	367	.798	64	173	237	**987**	224	2	199	21	262	34.9	15.1	2.9	**12.0**	**.665**
93-94	Utah	82	82	2969	1236	458	868	.528	48	149	.322	272	338	.805	72	186	258	**1031**	236	3	199	22	262	36.2	15.1	3.1	**12.6**	**.686**
94-95	Utah	82	82	2867	1206	429	791	.542	102	227	.449	246	306	.804	57	194	251	**1011**	215	3	194	22	271	35.0	14.7	3.1	**12.3**	**.696**
95-96	Utah	82	82	2915	1209	440	818	.538	95	225	.422	234	282	.830	54	172	226	**916**	207	1	140	15	246	35.5	14.7	2.8	**11.2**	**.628**
96-97	Utah	82	82	2896	1183	416	759	.548	76	180	.422	275	325	.846	45	183	228	860	194	2	166	15	246	35.3	14.4	2.8	10.5	.628
97-98	Utah	64	64	1858	770	270	511	.528	39	91	.429	191	231	.827	35	131	166	543	138	0	89	10	160	29.0	12.0	2.6	8.5	.621
98-99	Utah	50	50	1410	553	200	410	.488	16	50	.320	137	169	.811	31	115	146	374	107	0	81	13	110	28.2	11.1	2.9	7.5	.593
99-00	Utah	82	82	2432	990	363	725	.501	43	121	.355	221	257	.860	45	170	215	703	192	0	143	15	179	29.7	12.1	2.6	8.6	.617
00-01	Utah	82	82	2397	944	328	651	.504	61	132	.462	227	278	.817	54	173	227	713	194	1	132	21	203	29.2	11.5	2.8	8.7	.621
01-02	Utah	82	82	2566	1102	401	775	.517	25	78	.321	275	321	.857	59	204	263	674	209	1	152	24	208	31.3	13.4	3.2	8.2	.621
02-03	Utah	82	82	2275	884	309	640	.483	29	80	.363	237	287	.826	51	150	201	629	184	1	137	16	182	27.7	10.8	2.5	7.7	.580
NBA Season Totals		1504	1300	47764	19711	7039	13658	.515	845	2203	.384	4788	5796	.826	966	3085	4051	**15806**	3942	35	**3265**	315	4234	31.8	13.1	2.7	10.5	....
84-85	Utah	10	0	186	68	21	45	.467	0	2	.000	26	35	.743	7	21	28	43	30	0	11	2	16	18.6	6.8	2.8	4.3	.520
85-86	Utah	4	0	73	27	9	17	.529	1	1	1.000	8	9	.889	3	3	6	14	10	0	5	0	4	18.3	6.8	1.5	3.5	.493
86-87	Utah	5	2	157	50	18	29	.621	4	5	.800	10	13	.769	2	9	11	40	18	0	15	1	11	31.4	10.0	2.2	8.0	.558
87-88	Utah	11	11	478	215	68	134	.507	4	14	.286	75	91	.824	14	31	45	163	36	0	37	3	48	43.5	19.5	4.1	14.8	.707
88-89	Utah	3	3	139	82	30	59	.508	3	4	.750	19	21	.905	2	8	10	41	15	0	11	5	11	46.3	27.3	3.3	13.7	.755
89-90	Utah	5	5	194	75	29	69	.420	1	13	.077	16	20	.800	4	12	16	75	20	0	6	0	14	38.8	15.0	3.2	15.0	.585
90-91	Utah	9	9	373	164	58	108	.537	11	27	.407	37	44	.841	10	32	42	124	33	0	20	2	32	41.4	18.2	4.7	13.8	.699
91-92	Utah	16	16	623	237	77	182	.423	18	58	.310	65	78	.833	10	37	47	217	38	0	34	5	58	38.9	14.8	2.9	13.6	.601
92-93	Utah	5	5	193	66	23	51	.451	5	13	.385	15	18	.833	5	7	12	55	16	0	12	0	15	38.6	13.2	2.4	11.0	.508
93-94	Utah	16	16	597	231	88	193	.456	4	24	.167	51	63	.810	14	38	52	157	44	0	27	8	40	37.3	14.4	3.3	9.8	.540
94-95	Utah	5	5	193	89	34	74	.459	8	20	.400	13	17	.765	6	11	17	51	13	0	7	1	14	38.6	17.8	3.4	10.2	.560
95-96	Utah	18	18	679	199	70	157	.446	11	38	.289	48	59	.814	14	44	58	195	50	0	29	7	58	37.7	11.1	3.2	10.8	.485
96-97	Utah	20	20	739	322	113	217	.521	19	50	.380	77	90	.856	18	60	78	191	52	0	33	5	62	37.0	16.1	3.9	9.6	.608
97-98	Utah	20	20	596	222	81	164	.494	9	26	.346	51	71	.718	16	44	60	155	54	0	31	3	48	29.8	11.1	3.0	7.8	.541
98-99	Utah	11	11	352	122	42	105	.400	4	12	.333	34	46	.739	11	25	36	92	32	0	18	1	31	32.0	11.1	3.3	8.4	.483
99-00	Utah	10	10	350	112	41	89	.461	7	18	.389	23	30	.767	7	23	30	103	30	0	13	2	26	35.0	11.2	3.0	10.3	.518
00-01	Utah	5	5	186	49	17	37	.459	0	8	.000	15	21	.714	11	17	28	57	19	0	10	3	7	37.2	9.8	5.6	11.4	.608
01-02	Utah	4	4	141	50	18	40	.450	2	7	.286	12	13	.923	3	13	16	40	16	1	11	1	8	35.3	12.5	4.0	10.0	.597
02-03	Utah	5	5	149	56	18	39	.462	0	1	.000	20	20	1.000	5	11	16	26	13	0	8	1	14	29.8	11.2	3.2	5.2	.466
NBA Playoff Totals		182	165	6398	2436	855	1809	.473	111	341	.326	615	759	.810	162	446	608	1839	539	1	338	50	517	35.2	13.4	3.3	10.1	....

• STOEFEN, Art

Arthur (Storke) Stoefen

Born: 1915. Height: 6'7". Weight: 215 lbs. Drafted: — College: Stanford

YEAR	TEAM	GP	GS	MIN	PTS	FGM	FGA	FG%	3PM	3PA	3P%	FTM	FTA	FT%	ORB	DRB	TRB	AST	PF	DQ	STL	BLK	TO	MPG	PPG	RPG	APG	PCM
46-47	Chicago-N	18	....	....	24	8	....	....	....	....	....	8	19	.421	....	....	....	....	....	....	....	....	....	....	1.3	....	....	....
NBL Season Totals		18	....	....	24	8	....	....	....	....	....	8	19	....	....	....	....	....	....	....	....	....	....	....	1.3	....	....	....
46-47	Chicago-N	2	....	....	0	0	....	....	....	....	....	0	1	.000	....	....	....	....	....	....	....	....	....	....	0.0	....	....	....
NBL Playoff Totals		2	....	....	0	0	....	....	....	....	....	0	1	....	....	....	....	....	....	....	....	....	....	....	0.0	....	....	....

• STOJAKOVIC, Predrag

Predrag Stojakovic

Born: June 9, 1977. Belgrade, Yugoslavia. Height: 6'9". Weight: 220 lbs. Drafted: 1996 College: POAK (Greece)

YEAR	TEAM	GP	GS	MIN	PTS	FGM	FGA	FG%	3PM	3PA	3P%	FTM	FTA	FT%	ORB	DRB	TRB	AST	PF	DQ	STL	BLK	TO	MPG	PPG	RPG	APG	PCM
98-99	Sacramento	48	1	1025	402	141	373	.378	57	178	.320	63	74	.851	43	100	143	72	43	0	41	7	53	21.4	8.4	3.0	1.5	.365
99-00	Sacramento	74	11	1749	877	321	717	.448	100	267	.375	135	153	.882	74	202	276	106	97	0	52	7	88	23.6	11.9	3.7	1.4	.460
00-01	Sacramento	75	75	2905	1529	559	1189	.470	144	360	.400	267	312	.856	93	341	434	164	144	0	91	13	146	38.7	20.4	5.8	2.2	.486
01-02	Sacramento	71	71	2649	1506	547	1130	.484	129	310	.416	283	323	.876	72	301	373	175	120	0	81	14	140	37.3	21.2	5.3	2.5	.526
02-03	Sacramento	72	72	2449	1380	497	1034	.481	155	406	.382	231	264	.875	61	336	397	141	143	1	72	5	101	34.0	19.2	5.5	2.0	.533
NBA Season Totals		340	230	10777	5694	2065	4443	.465	585	1521	.385	979	1126	.869	343	1280	1623	658	547	1	337	46	528	31.7	16.7	4.8	1.9	....
98-99	Sacramento	5	0	108	24	9	26	.346	3	14	.214	3	3	1.000	12	7	19	2	7	0	3	0	6	21.6	4.8	3.8	0.4	.206
99-00	Sacramento	5	0	129	44	16	40	.400	6	13	.462	6	9	.667	2	15	17	3	7	0	4	0	5	25.8	8.8	3.4	0.6	.275
00-01	Sacramento	8	8	307	173	52	128	.406	9	26	.346	60	62	.968	17	34	51	3	17	0	5	3	18	38.4	21.6	6.4	0.4	.444
01-02	Sacramento	10	7	338	148	50	134	.373	13	49	.265	35	39	.897	16	47	63	10	22	0	5	0	19	33.8	14.8	6.3	1.0	.342
02-03	Sacramento	12	12	486	277	97	202	.480	32	70	.457	51	60	.850	17	66	83	30	34	0	10	5	12	40.5	23.1	6.9	2.5	.562
NBA Playoff Totals		40	27	1368	666	224	530	.423	63	172	.366	155	173	.896	64	169	233	48	87	0	27	8	60	34.2	16.7	5.8	1.2	....

• STOKES, Ed

Edward Kobie Stokes

Born: Sept. 3, 1971. Syracuse, NY, United States. Height: 7' Weight: 264 lbs. Drafted: 1993 College: Arizona

YEAR	TEAM	GP	GS	MIN	PTS	FGM	FGA	FG%	3PM	3PA	3P%	FTM	FTA	FT%	ORB	DRB	TRB	AST	PF	DQ	STL	BLK	TO	MPG	PPG	RPG	APG	PCM
97-98	Toronto	4	0	17	3	1	3	.333	0	0	.000	1	2	.500	1	3	4	1	4	0	1	2	2	4.3	0.8	1.0	0.3	.267
NBA Season Totals		4	0	17	3	1	3	.333	0	0	.000	1	2	.500	1	3	4	1	4	0	1	2	2	4.3	0.8	1.0	0.3	....

YEAR	TEAM	GP	GS	MIN	PTS	FGM	FGA	FG%	3PM	3PA	3P%	FTM	FTA	FT%	ORB	DRB	TRB	AST	PF	DQ	STL	BLK	TO	MPG	PPG	RPG	APG	PCM

• STOKES, Greg

Gregory Lewis Stokes

Born: Aug. 5, 1963. New Haven, CT, United States. Height: 6'10". Weight: 220 lbs. Drafted: 1985 College: Iowa

YEAR	TEAM	GP	GS	MIN	PTS	FGM	FGA	FG%	3PM	3PA	3P%	FTM	FTA	FT%	ORB	DRB	TRB	AST	PF	DQ	STL	BLK	TO	MPG	PPG	RPG	APG	PCM
85-86	Philadelphia	31	13	350	126	56	119	.471	0	1	.000	14	21	.667	27	30	57	17	56	0	14	11	19	11.3	4.1	1.8	0.5	.328
89-90	Sacramento	11	0	34	4	1	9	.111	0	0	.000	2	2	1.000	2	3	5	0	8	0	0	0	3	3.1	0.4	0.5	0.0	-.158
NBA Season Totals		42	13	384	130	57	128	.445	0	1	.000	16	23	.696	29	33	62	17	64	0	14	11	22	9.1	3.1	1.5	0.4	....
85-86	Philadelphia	7	7	90	27	8	28	.286	0	0	.000	11	13	.846	6	7	13	4	12	0	2	6	4	12.9	3.9	1.9	0.6	.244
NBA Playoff Totals		7	7	90	27	8	28	.286	0	0	.000	11	13	.846	6	7	13	4	12	0	2	6	4	12.9	3.9	1.9	0.6	....

• STOKES, Maurice

Maurice Stokes

Born: June 17, 1933. Pittsburgh, PA, United States. Died: Apr.6, 1970. Height: 6'7". Weight: 232 lbs. Drafted: 1955 College: St. Francis (PA)

YEAR	TEAM	GP	GS	MIN	PTS	FGM	FGA	FG%	3PM	3PA	3P%	FTM	FTA	FT%	ORB	DRB	TRB	AST	PF	DQ	STL	BLK	TO	MPG	PPG	RPG	APG	PCM
55-56	Rochester	67	....	2323	1125	403	1137	.354	....	....	....	319	447	.714	....	....	1094	328	276	11	....	....	....	34.7	16.8	**16.3**	4.9	.711
56-57	Rochester	72	....	2761	1124	434	1249	.347	....	....	....	256	385	.665	....	....	**1256**	331	287	12	....	....	....	38.3	15.6	**17.4**	4.6	.620
57-58	Cincinnati	63	....	2460	1066	414	1181	.351	....	....	....	238	333	.715	....	....	1142	403	226	9	....	....	....	39.0	16.9	18.1	6.4	.705
NBA Season Totals		202	....	7544	3315	1251	3567	.351	....	....	....	813	1165	.698	....	....	3492	1062	789	32	....	....	....	37.3	16.4	17.3	5.3	....
57-58	Cincinnati	1	....	39	12	3	12	.250	....	....	....	6	7	.857	....	....	15	2	3	0	....	....	....	39.0	12.0	15.0	2.0	.448
NBA Playoff Totals		1	....	39	12	3	12	.250	....	....	....	6	7	.857	....	....	15	2	3	0	....	....	....	39.0	12.0	15.0	2.0	....

• STOLKEY, Art

Arthur F. Stolkey

Born: Oct. 23, 1920. Height: 6'1". Weight: 180 lbs. Drafted: — College: Detroit

YEAR	TEAM	GP	GS	MIN	PTS	FGM	FGA	FG%	3PM	3PA	3P%	FTM	FTA	FT%	ORB	DRB	TRB	AST	PF	DQ	STL	BLK	TO	MPG	PPG	RPG	APG	PCM
46-47	Detroit	23	....	....	102	36	164	.220	....	....	....	30	44	.682	....	....	....	38	72	....	....	....	....	....	4.4	....	1.7	....
NBA Season Totals		23	....	....	102	36	164	.220	....	....	....	30	44	.682	....	....	....	38	72	....	....	....	....	....	4.4	....	1.7	....

• STOLL, Randy

Randy C. Stoll

Born: 1945. Seattle, WA, United States. Height: 6'7". Weight: 235 lbs. Drafted: — College: Washington State

YEAR	TEAM	GP	GS	MIN	PTS	FGM	FGA	FG%	3PM	3PA	3P%	FTM	FTA	FT%	ORB	DRB	TRB	AST	PF	DQ	STL	BLK	TO	MPG	PPG	RPG	APG	PCM
67-68	Anaheim-A	25	....	403	142	66	138	.478	0	0	.000	10	25	.400	....	....	91	12	42	0	....	....	28	16.1	5.7	3.6	0.5	.368
ABA Season Totals		25	....	403	142	66	138	.478	0	0	.000	10	25	.400	....	....	91	12	42	0	....	....	28	16.1	5.7	3.6	0.5	....

• STONE, George

George (Radar, Rocky) Stone

Born: Feb. 9, 1946. Murray, KY, United States. Height: 6'7". Weight: 195 lbs. Drafted: 1968 College: Marshall

YEAR	TEAM	GP	GS	MIN	PTS	FGM	FGA	FG%	3PM	3PA	3P%	FTM	FTA	FT%	ORB	DRB	TRB	AST	PF	DQ	STL	BLK	TO	MPG	PPG	RPG	APG	PCM
68-69	Los Angeles-A	74	....	2199	1163	437	964	.453	28	74	.378	261	337	.774	155	349	504	57	254	8	....	....	124	29.7	15.7	6.8	0.8	.485
69-70	Los Angeles-A	83	....	2639	1328	512	1194	.429	65	206	.316	239	306	.781	165	386	551	145	280	4	....	....	155	31.8	16.0	6.6	1.7	.467
70-71	Utah-A	78	....	1734	915	372	808	.460	50	157	.318	121	156	.776	94	269	363	106	173	0	....	....	72	22.2	11.7	4.7	1.4	.519
71-72	Carolina-A	16	....	239	72	28	75	.373	0	5	.000	16	17	.941	6	33	39	21	23	0	....	....	16	14.9	4.5	2.4	1.3	.326
71-72	Utah-A	8	....	142	52	21	48	.438	1	4	.250	9	11	.818	7	16	23	4	17	0	....	....	6	17.8	6.5	2.9	0.5	.314
ABA Season Totals		259	....	6953	3530	1370	3089	.444	144	446	.323	646	827	.781	427	1053	1480	333	747	12	....	....	373	26.8	13.6	5.7	1.3	....
69-70	Los Angeles-A	17	....	724	402	165	388	.425	14	55	.255	58	77	.753	....	....	158	42	....	0	....	....	43	42.6	23.6	9:3	2.5	....
70-71	Utah-A	18	....	424	207	84	209	.402	4	28	.143	35	41	.854	28	76	104	29	45	0	....	....	21	23.6	11.5	5.8	1.6	.482
ABA Playoff Totals		35	....	1148	609	249	597	.417	18	83	.217	93	118	.788	28	76	262	71	45	0	....	....	64	32.8	17.4	7.5	2.0	....

• STOUDAMIRE, Damon

Damon Lamon Stoudamire

Born: Sept. 3, 1973. Portland, OR, United States. Height: 5'10". Weight: 171 lbs. Drafted: 1995 College: Arizona

YEAR	TEAM	GP	GS	MIN	PTS	FGM	FGA	FG%	3PM	3PA	3P%	FTM	FTA	FT%	ORB	DRB	TRB	AST	PF	DQ	STL	BLK	TO	MPG	PPG	RPG	APG	PCM
95-96	Toronto	70	70	2865	1331	481	1129	.426	133	337	.395	236	296	.797	59	222	281	653	166	0	98	19	266	40.9	19.0	4.0	9.3	.500
96-97	Toronto	81	81	3311	1634	564	1407	.401	176	496	.355	330	401	.823	86	244	330	709	162	1	123	13	292	40.9	20.2	4.1	8.8	.501
97-98	Toronto	49	49	2033	952	354	833	.425	65	205	.317	179	212	.844	63	154	217	399	112	0	80	5	157	41.5	19.4	4.4	8.1	.498
97-98	Portland	22	22	806	273	94	258	.364	26	99	.263	59	75	.787	24	57	81	181	38	0	33	2	64	36.6	12.4	3.7	8.2	.425
98-99	Portland	50	50	1673	631	249	629	.396	44	142	.310	89	122	.730	41	126	167	312	81	0	49	4	110	33.5	12.6	3.3	6.2	.411
99-00	Portland	78	78	2372	974	386	894	.432	80	212	.377	122	145	.841	61	182	243	405	173	0	77	1	149	30.4	12.5	3.1	5.2	.431
00-01	Portland	82	82	2655	1066	406	935	.434	82	219	.374	172	207	.831	69	234	303	468	202	1	106	8	191	32.4	13.0	3.7	5.7	.453
01-02	Portland	75	71	2796	1016	369	918	.402	104	295	.353	174	196	.888	78	214	292	490	153	0	67	7	149	37.3	13.5	3.9	6.5	.419
02-03	Portland	59	27	1315	409	156	415	.376	44	114	.386	53	67	.791	40	115	155	204	67	0	39	6	82	22.3	6.9	2.6	3.5	.355
NBA Season Totals		566	530	19826	8286	3059	7418	.412	754	2119	.356	1414	1721	.822	521	1548	2069	3821	1154	2	672	65	1460	35.0	14.6	3.7	6.8	....
97-98	Portland	4	4	166	71	25	63	.397	8	22	.364	13	13	1.000	6	11	17	38	13	0	5	1	16	41.5	17.8	4.3	9.5	.469
98-99	Portland	13	13	403	132	49	129	.380	10	22	.455	24	34	.706	7	34	41	73	31	0	8	1	38	31.0	10.2	3.2	5.6	.334
99-00	Portland	16	16	447	142	56	135	.415	10	30	.333	20	24	.833	8	34	42	58	43	1	8	4	19	27.9	8.9	2.6	3.6	.322
00-01	Portland	3	3	114	53	19	46	.413	2	13	.154	13	13	1.000	1	8	9	13	6	0	2	1	9	38.0	17.7	3.0	4.3	.378
01-02	Portland	3	3	99	15	5	22	.227	3	4	.750	2	3	.667	1	6	7	10	5	0	2	0	4	33.0	5.0	2.3	3.3	.125
02-03	Portland	7	6	232	107	36	79	.456	15	31	.484	20	21	.952	7	29	36	39	22	0	6	2	12	33.1	15.3	5.1	5.6	.557
NBA Playoff Totals		46	45	1461	520	190	474	.401	48	122	.393	92	108	.852	30	122	152	231	120	1	31	9	98	31.8	11.3	3.3	5.0	....

• STOUDEMIRE, Amare

Amare Carsares (STAT) Stoudemire

Born: Nov. 16, 1982. Lake Wells, FL, United States. Height: 6'10". Weight: 245 lbs. Drafted: 2002 College: none (HS: Cypress Creek, FL)

YEAR	TEAM	GP	GS	MIN	PTS	FGM	FGA	FG%	3PM	3PA	3P%	FTM	FTA	FT%	ORB	DRB	TRB	AST	PF	DQ	STL	BLK	TO	MPG	PPG	RPG	APG	PCM
02-03	Phoenix	82	71	2570	1106	392	830	.472	2	10	.200	320	484	.661	250	471	721	78	269	3	62	87	189	31.3	13.5	8.8	1.0	.473
NBA Season Totals		82	71	2570	1106	392	830	.472	2	10	.200	320	484	.661	250	471	721	78	269	3	62	87	189	31.3	13.5	8.8	1.0	....
02-03	Phoenix	6	6	203	85	34	65	.523	1	1	1.000	16	28	.571	16	31	47	7	28	1	10	9	19	33.8	14.2	7.8	1.2	.438
NBA Playoff Totals		6	6	203	85	34	65	.523	1	1	1.000	16	28	.571	16	31	47	7	28	1	10	9	19	33.8	14.2	7.8	1.2	....

YEAR	TEAM	GP	GS	MIN	PTS	FGM	FGA	FG%	3PM	3PA	3P%	FTM	FTA	FT%	ORB	DRB	TRB	AST	PF	DQ	STL	BLK	TO	MPG	PPG	RPG	APG	PCM

• STOUT, Marvin
Marvin Stout

Born: 1915. Height: 5'11". Weight: 155 lbs. Drafted: — College: Ball State

YEAR	TEAM	GP	GS	MIN	PTS	FGM	FGA	FG%	3PM	3PA	3P%	FTM	FTA	FT%	ORB	DRB	TRB	AST	PF	DQ	STL	BLK	TO	MPG	PPG	RPG	APG	PCM
39-40	Indianapolis-N	1	....	....	2	1	....	....	....	....	....	0	....	....	....	....	....	....	....	....	....	....	....	....	2.0	....	....	....
NBL Season Totals		1	....	....	2	1	....	....	....	....	....	0	....	....	....	....	....	....	....	....	....	....	....	....	2.0	....	....	....

• STOVALL, Paul
Paul L. Stovall

Born: Aug. 16, 1948. Died: Jan.9, 1978. Height: 6'4". Weight: 215 lbs. Drafted: 1972 College: Arizona State

YEAR	TEAM	GP	GS	MIN	PTS	FGM	FGA	FG%	3PM	3PA	3P%	FTM	FTA	FT%	ORB	DRB	TRB	AST	PF	DQ	STL	BLK	TO	MPG	PPG	RPG	APG	PCM
72-73	Phoenix	25	....	211	76	26	76	.342	....	....	....	24	38	.632	....	....	61	13	37	0	....	....	....	8.4	3.0	2.4	0.5	.372
73-74	San Diego-A	13	....	194	100	36	73	.493	0	0	.000	28	44	.636	21	37	58	12	32	....	4	6	21	14.9	7.7	4.5	0.9	.573
NBA Season Totals		25	....	211	76	26	76	.342	....	....	....	24	38	.632	....	....	61	13	37	0	....	....	....	8.4	3.0	2.4	0.5	....
ABA Season Totals		13	....	194	100	36	73	.493	0	0	.000	28	44	.636	21	37	58	12	32	....	4	6	21	14.9	7.7	4.5	0.9	....
Career Totals		38	....	405	176	62	149	.416	0	0	.000	52	82	.634	21	37	119	25	69	0	4	6	21	10.7	4.6	3.1	0.7	....

• STRACK, Dave
David H. Strack

Born: 1923. Height: 5'11". Weight: — Drafted: — College: Michigan

YEAR	TEAM	GP	GS	MIN	PTS	FGM	FGA	FG%	3PM	3PA	3P%	FTM	FTA	FT%	ORB	DRB	TRB	AST	PF	DQ	STL	BLK	TO	MPG	PPG	RPG	APG	PCM
45-46	Indianapolis-N	2	....	....	5	2	....	....	....	....	....	1	....	....	....	....	....	....	....	....	....	....	....	....	2.5	....	....	....
NBL Season Totals		2	....	....	5	2	....	....	....	....	....	1	....	....	....	....	....	....	....	....	....	....	....	....	2.5	....	....	....

• STRAIN, Ted
Ted Strain

Born: 1917. Height: 6' Weight: 155 lbs. Drafted: — College: Wisconsin

YEAR	TEAM	GP	GS	MIN	PTS	FGM	FGA	FG%	3PM	3PA	3P%	FTM	FTA	FT%	ORB	DRB	TRB	AST	PF	DQ	STL	BLK	TO	MPG	PPG	RPG	APG	PCM
41-42	Chicago-N	1	....	....	0	0	....	....	....	....	....	0	....	....	....	....	....	....	....	....	....	....	....	....	0.0	....	....	....
NBL Season Totals		1	....	....	0	0	....	....	....	....	....	0	....	....	....	....	....	....	....	....	....	....	....	....	0.0	....	....	....

• STRAND, Reno
Reno Strand

Born: May 14, 1909. Died: June27, 1988. Height: 6' Weight: 195 lbs. Drafted: — College: none

YEAR	TEAM	GP	GS	MIN	PTS	FGM	FGA	FG%	3PM	3PA	3P%	FTM	FTA	FT%	ORB	DRB	TRB	AST	PF	DQ	STL	BLK	TO	MPG	PPG	RPG	APG	PCM
38-39	Cleveland-N	15	....	....	42	17	....	....	....	....	....	8	....	....	....	....	....	....	....	....	....	....	....	....	2.8	....	....	....
NBL Season Totals		15	....	....	42	17	....	....	....	....	....	8	....	....	....	....	....	....	....	....	....	....	....	....	2.8	....	....	....

• STRAWDER, Joe
Joe Tom Strawder

Born: Sept. 21, 1940. Belle Glade, FL, United States. Height: 6'10". Weight: 235 lbs. Drafted: 1964 College: Bradley

YEAR	TEAM	GP	GS	MIN	PTS	FGM	FGA	FG%	3PM	3PA	3P%	FTM	FTA	FT%	ORB	DRB	TRB	AST	PF	DQ	STL	BLK	TO	MPG	PPG	RPG	APG	PCM
65-66	Detroit	79	....	2180	676	250	613	.408	....	....	....	176	256	.688	....	....	820	78	305	10	....	....	....	27.6	8.6	10.4	1.0	.449
66-67	Detroit	79	....	2156	750	281	660	.426	....	....	....	188	262	.718	....	....	791	82	**344**	**19**	....	....	....	27.3	9.5	10.0	1.0	.469
67-68	Detroit	73	....	2029	551	206	456	.452	....	....	....	139	215	.647	....	....	685	85	312	**18**	....	....	....	27.8	7.5	9.4	1.2	.417
NBA Season Totals		231	....	6365	1977	737	1729	.426	....	....	....	503	733	.686	....	....	2296	245	961	47	....	....	....	27.6	8.6	9.9	1.1	....
67-68	Detroit	6	....	177	42	14	42	.333	....	....	....	14	22	.636	....	....	65	9	27	1	....	....	....	29.5	7.0	10.8	1.5	.386
NBA Playoff Totals		6	....	177	42	14	42	.333	....	....	....	14	22	.636	....	....	65	9	27	1	....	....	....	29.5	7.0	10.8	1.5	....

• STRICKER, Bill
William Louis Stricker

Born: Jan. 22, 1948. Height: 6'9". Weight: 210 lbs. Drafted: 1970 College: Pacific

YEAR	TEAM	GP	GS	MIN	PTS	FGM	FGA	FG%	3PM	3PA	3P%	FTM	FTA	FT%	ORB	DRB	TRB	AST	PF	DQ	STL	BLK	TO	MPG	PPG	RPG	APG	PCM
70-71	Portland	1	....	2	4	2	3	.667	....	....	....	0	0	.000	....	....	0	0	1	0	....	....	....	2.0	4.0	0.0	0.0	1.355
NBA Season Totals		1	....	2	4	2	3	.667	....	....	....	0	0	.000	....	....	0	0	1	0	....	....	....	2.0	4.0	0.0	0.0	....

• STRICKLAND, Erick
Demerick Montae (Erick) Strickland

Born: Nov. 25, 1973. Opelika, AL, United States. Height: 6'3". Weight: 210 lbs. Drafted: — College: Nebraska

YEAR	TEAM	GP	GS	MIN	PTS	FGM	FGA	FG%	3PM	3PA	3P%	FTM	FTA	FT%	ORB	DRB	TRB	AST	PF	DQ	STL	BLK	TO	MPG	PPG	RPG	APG	PCM
96-97	Dallas	28	15	759	297	102	256	.398	28	92	.304	65	80	.813	21	69	90	68	75	3	27	5	67	27.1	10.6	3.2	2.4	.310
97-98	Dallas	67	19	1505	511	199	558	.357	48	163	.294	65	84	.774	35	126	161	167	140	1	56	8	107	22.5	7.6	2.4	2.5	.265
98-99	Dallas	33	2	567	249	89	221	.403	18	59	.305	53	65	.815	12	71	83	64	44	0	40	2	36	17.2	7.5	2.5	1.9	.453
99-00	Dallas	68	67	2025	867	316	730	.433	73	186	.392	162	195	.831	69	254	323	211	190	3	105	13	102	29.8	12.8	4.8	3.1	.458
00-01	New York	28	0	421	140	40	131	.305	16	47	.340	24	28	.857	9	43	52	29	46	0	22	1	21	15.0	4.3	1.9	1.0	.229
00-01	Vancouver	22	0	409	140	41	136	.301	14	48	.292	44	51	.863	9	67	76	66	42	0	22	1	27	18.6	6.4	3.5	3.0	.416
01-02	Boston	79	4	1643	606	190	488	.389	95	247	.385	131	155	.845	22	191	213	184	145	1	56	1	94	20.8	7.7	2.7	2.3	.377
02-03	Indiana	71	10	1275	458	163	380	.429	62	160	.388	70	87	.805	23	122	145	209	111	0	38	7	98	18.0	6.5	2.0	2.9	.404
NBA Season Totals		396	117	8604	3248	1140	2900	.393	354	1002	.353	614	745	.824	200	943	1143	998	793	8	366	38	552	21.7	8.2	2.9	2.5	....
01-02	Boston	12	0	118	35	11	39	.282	4	20	.200	9	9	1.000	2	11	13	17	15	0	5	1	9	9.8	2.9	1.1	1.4	.258
02-03	Indiana	5	0	42	21	6	14	.429	1	5	.200	8	10	.800	3	4	7	8	3	0	1	0	1	8.4	4.2	1.4	1.6	.632
NBA Playoff Totals		17	0	160	56	17	53	.321	5	25	.200	17	19	.895	5	15	20	25	18	0	6	1	10	9.4	3.3	1.2	1.5	....

• STRICKLAND, Mark
Mark Strickland

Born: July 14, 1970. Atlanta, GA, United States. Height: 6'9". Weight: 210 lbs. Drafted: — College: Temple

YEAR	TEAM	GP	GS	MIN	PTS	FGM	FGA	FG%	3PM	3PA	3P%	FTM	FTA	FT%	ORB	DRB	TRB	AST	PF	DQ	STL	BLK	TO	MPG	PPG	RPG	APG	PCM
94-95	Indiana	4	0	9	3	1	3	.333	0	0	.000	1	2	.500	2	2	4	0	0	0	0	1	1	2.3	0.8	1.0	0.0	.490
96-97	Miami	31	0	153	62	25	60	.417	0	1	.000	12	21	.571	16	21	37	1	17	0	4	10	16	4.9	2.0	1.2	0.0	.333
97-98	Miami	51	8	847	349	145	269	.539	0	1	.000	59	82	.720	80	133	213	26	87	0	18	34	46	16.6	6.8	4.2	0.5	.489
98-99	Miami	32	1	357	119	50	101	.495	0	1	.000	19	26	.731	26	52	78	9	28	0	7	8	13	11.2	3.7	2.4	0.3	.390

YEAR	TEAM	GP	GS	MIN	PTS	FGM	FGA	FG%	3PM	3PA	3P%	FTM	FTA	FT%	ORB	DRB	TRB	AST	PF	DQ	STL	BLK	TO	MPG	PPG	RPG	APG	PCM
99-00	Miami	58	5	663	284	122	224	.545	0	0	.000	40	56	.714	44	96	140	22	68	0	15	18	24	11.4	4.9	2.4	0.4	.471
00-01	Denver	46	2	517	201	82	185	.443	0	1	.000	37	59	.627	43	77	120	17	58	0	12	19	24	11.2	4.4	2.6	0.4	.397
00-01	New Jersey	9	0	202	51	21	54	.389	1	1	1.000	8	11	.727	11	30	41	7	14	0	4	3	10	22.4	5.7	4.6	0.8	.275
01-02	Atlanta	46	10	654	208	91	204	.446	1	4	.250	25	44	.568	41	90	131	20	48	0	19	17	28	14.2	4.5	2.8	0.4	.341
02-03	Dallas	4	0	13	4	2	5	.400	0	0	.000	0	0	.000	5	2	7	0	1	0	0	0	1	3.3	1.0	1.8	0.0	.482
NBA Season Totals		281	26	3415	1281	539	1105	.488	2	9	.222	201	301	.668	268	503	771	102	321	0	79	110	163	12.2	4.6	2.7	0.4	....
96-97	Miami	4	0	16	8	4	8	.500	0	0	.000	0	2	.000	0	3	3	1	0	0	1	0	2	4.0	2.0	0.8	0.3	.392
97-98	Miami	3	0	28	9	4	5	.800	0	0	.000	1	2	.500	2	5	7	0	4	0	0	1	0	9.3	3.0	2.3	0.0	.468
98-99	Miami	2	0	8	4	1	2	.500	0	0	.000	2	2	1.000	1	2	3	0	0	0	1	0	1	4.0	2.0	1.5	0.0	.722
99-00	Miami	1	0	10	2	1	3	.333	0	0	.000	0	2	.000	0	0	0	0	0	0	2	0	1	10.0	2.0	0.0	0.0	.018
NBA Playoff Totals		10	0	62	23	10	18	.556	0	0	.000	3	8	.375	3	10	13	1	4	0	4	1	4	6.2	2.3	1.3	0.1	....

• STRICKLAND, Rod

Rodney (Hot Rod) Strickland

Born: July 11, 1966. Bronx, NY, United States. Height: 6'3". Weight: 175 lbs. Drafted: 1988 College: DePaul

YEAR	TEAM	GP	GS	MIN	PTS	FGM	FGA	FG%	3PM	3PA	3P%	FTM	FTA	FT%	ORB	DRB	TRB	AST	PF	DQ	STL	BLK	TO	MPG	PPG	RPG	APG	PCM
88-89	New York	81	10	1358	721	265	567	.467	19	59	.322	172	231	.745	51	109	160	319	142	2	98	3	146	16.8	8.9	2.0	3.9	.585
89-90	New York	51	0	1019	429	170	386	.440	6	21	.286	83	130	.638	43	83	126	219	71	0	70	8	87	20.0	8.4	2.5	4.3	.504
89-90	San Antonio	31	24	1121	439	173	370	.468	2	9	.222	91	148	.615	47	86	133	249	89	3	57	6	84	36.2	14.2	4.3	8.0	.496
90-91	San Antonio	58	56	2076	800	314	651	.482	11	33	.333	161	211	.763	57	162	219	463	125	0	117	11	157	35.8	13.8	3.8	8.0	.518
91-92	San Antonio	57	54	2053	787	300	659	.455	5	15	.333	182	265	.687	92	173	265	491	122	0	118	17	160	36.0	13.8	4.6	8.6	.539
92-93	Portland	78	35	2474	1069	396	816	.485	4	30	.133	273	381	.717	120	217	337	559	153	1	131	24	203	31.7	13.7	4.3	7.2	.575
93-94	Portland	82	58	2889	1411	528	1093	.483	2	10	.200	353	471	.749	122	248	370	740	171	0	147	24	254	35.2	17.2	4.5	9.0	.632
94-95	Portland	64	61	2267	1211	441	946	.466	46	123	.374	283	380	.745	73	244	317	562	118	0	123	9	211	35.4	18.9	5.0	8.8	.643
95-96	Portland	67	63	2526	1256	471	1023	.460	38	111	.342	276	423	.652	89	208	297	640	135	2	97	16	255	37.7	18.7	4.4	9.6	.566
96-97	Washington	82	81	2997	1410	515	1105	.466	13	77	.169	367	497	.738	95	240	335	727	166	2	143	14	271	36.5	17.2	4.1	8.9	.569
97-98	Washington	76	76	3020	1349	490	1130	.434	12	48	.250	357	492	.726	112	293	405	**801**	182	2	126	25	266	39.7	17.8	5.3	**10.5**	**.580**
98-99	Washington	44	43	1632	690	251	603	.416	12	42	.286	176	236	.746	56	156	212	434	91	0	76	5	142	37.1	15.7	4.8	9.9	.568
99-00	Washington	69	67	2188	869	327	762	.429	1	21	.048	214	305	.702	73	186	259	519	147	1	94	18	187	31.7	12.6	3.8	7.5	.503
00-01	Washington	33	28	1020	401	141	331	.426	4	16	.250	115	147	.782	25	80	105	231	55	0	43	4	83	30.9	12.2	3.2	7.0	.498
00-01	Portland	21	0	351	97	41	98	.418	0	1	.000	15	26	.577	11	24	35	72	21	0	10	1	24	16.7	4.6	1.7	3.4	.372
01-02	Miami	76	64	2294	794	316	714	.443	8	26	.308	154	201	.766	49	183	232	463	114	0	82	11	159	30.2	10.4	3.1	6.1	.444
02-03	Minnesota	47	8	955	320	120	278	.432	1	11	.091	79	107	.738	20	75	95	215	55	0	46	6	76	20.3	6.8	2.0	4.6	.459
NBA Season Totals		1017	728	32240	14053	5259	11532	.456	184	653	.282	3351	4651	.720	1135	2767	3902	7704	1957	13	1578	202	2765	31.7	13.8	3.8	7.6	....
88-89	New York	9	0	111	54	22	49	.449	1	1	1.000	9	17	.529	6	7	13	25	21	0	4	1	13	12.3	6.0	1.4	2.8	.422
89-90	San Antonio	10	10	384	123	54	127	.425	0	7	.000	15	27	.556	22	31	53	112	30	2	14	0	34	38.4	12.3	5.3	11.2	.482
90-91	San Antonio	4	4	168	75	29	67	.433	0	6	.000	17	21	.810	5	16	21	35	14	0	9	0	13	42.0	18.8	5.3	8.8	.502
91-92	San Antonio	2	2	80	31	13	22	.591	0	0	.000	5	8	.625	0	7	7	19	8	0	3	2	6	40.0	15.5	3.5	9.5	.543
92-93	Portland	4	4	156	54	22	52	.423	0	1	.000	10	12	.833	9	17	26	37	10	0	5	2	7	39.0	13.5	6.5	9.3	.539
93-94	Portland	4	4	154	94	36	72	.500	0	1	.000	22	27	.815	3	13	16	39	13	0	4	2	10	38.5	23.5	4.0	9.8	.688
94-95	Portland	3	3	126	70	27	65	.415	2	5	.400	14	18	.778	1	11	12	37	11	0	3	2	10	42.0	23.3	4.0	12.3	.581
95-96	Portland	5	5	202	103	37	84	.440	6	12	.500	23	36	.639	12	19	31	42	14	0	5	0	12	40.4	20.6	6.2	8.4	.560
96-97	Washington	3	3	124	59	22	52	.423	1	2	.500	14	19	.737	5	13	18	25	8	0	3	0	11	41.3	19.7	6.0	8.3	.492
00-01	Portland	2	0	19	8	2	6	.333	0	0	.000	4	6	.667	2	2	4	2	1	0	2	0	1	9.5	4.0	2.0	1.0	.513
02-03	Minnesota	6	0	73	28	11	21	.524	0	0	.000	6	6	1.000	0	6	6	17	5	0	4	2	8	12.2	4.7	1.0	2.8	.532
NBA Playoff Totals		52	35	1597	699	275	617	.446	10	35	.286	139	197	.706	65	142	207	390	135	2	56	11	125	30.7	13.4	4.0	7.5	....

• STRICKLAND, Roger

Roger (The Rifle) Strickland

Born: Sept. 4, 1940. Jacksonville, FL, United States. Height: 6'5". Weight: 200 lbs. Drafted: 1963 College: Jacksonville

YEAR	TEAM	GP	GS	MIN	PTS	FGM	FGA	FG%	3PM	3PA	3P%	FTM	FTA	FT%	ORB	DRB	TRB	AST	PF	DQ	STL	BLK	TO	MPG	PPG	RPG	APG	PCM
63-64	Baltimore	1	....	4	2	1	3	.333	....	....	....	0	0	.000	....	....	0	0	1	0	....	....	....	4.0	2.0	0.0	0.0	.014
NBA Season Totals		1	....	4	2	1	3	.333	....	....	....	0	0	.000	....	....	0	0	1	0	....	....	....	4.0	2.0	0.0	0.0	....

• STROEDER, John

John Stroeder

Born: July 24, 1958. Bremerton, WA, United States. Height: 6'10". Weight: 260 lbs. Drafted: 1980 College: Montana

YEAR	TEAM	GP	GS	MIN	PTS	FGM	FGA	FG%	3PM	3PA	3P%	FTM	FTA	FT%	ORB	DRB	TRB	AST	PF	DQ	STL	BLK	TO	MPG	PPG	RPG	APG	PCM
87-88	Milwaukee	41	0	271	78	29	79	.367	0	2	.000	20	30	.667	24	47	71	20	48	0	3	12	25	6.6	1.9	1.7	0.5	.305
88-89	San Antonio	1	0	2	0	0	0	.000	0	0	.000	0	0	.000	0	0	0	0	2	0	0	0	1	2.0	0.0	0.0	0.0	-.930
88-89	Golden State	4	0	20	4	2	5	.400	0	0	.000	0	0	.000	5	9	14	3	1	0	0	2	2	5.0	1.0	3.5	0.8	.849
NBA Season Totals		46	0	293	82	31	84	.369	0	2	.000	20	30	.667	29	56	85	23	51	0	3	14	28	6.4	1.8	1.8	0.5	....
87-88	Milwaukee	1	0	1	3	1	1	1.000	1	1	1.000	0	0	.000	0	0	0	0	0	0	0	0	0	1.0	3.0	0.0	0.0	3.000
NBA Playoff Totals		1	0	1	3	1	1	1.000	1	1	1.000	0	0	.000	0	0	0	0	0	0	0	0	0	1.0	3.0	0.0	0.0	....

• STRONG, Derek

Derek Lamar Strong

Born: Feb. 9, 1968. Los Angeles, CA, United States. Height: 6'8". Weight: 220 lbs. Drafted: 1990 College: Xavier (OH)

YEAR	TEAM	GP	GS	MIN	PTS	FGM	FGA	FG%	3PM	3PA	3P%	FTM	FTA	FT%	ORB	DRB	TRB	AST	PF	DQ	STL	BLK	TO	MPG	PPG	RPG	APG	PCM
91-92	Washington	1	0	12	3	0	4	.000	0	0	.000	3	4	.750	1	4	5	1	1	0	0	0	1	12.0	3.0	5.0	1.0	.262
92-93	Milwaukee	23	0	339	156	42	92	.457	4	8	.500	68	85	.800	40	75	115	14	20	0	11	1	14	14.7	6.8	5.0	0.6	.627
93-94	Milwaukee	67	11	1131	444	141	341	.413	3	13	.231	159	206	.772	109	172	281	48	69	1	38	14	60	16.9	6.6	4.2	0.7	.451
94-95	Boston	70	24	1344	441	149	329	.453	2	7	.286	141	172	.820	136	239	375	44	143	0	24	13	77	19.2	6.3	5.4	0.6	.410
95-96	LA Lakers	63	0	746	214	72	169	.426	1	9	.111	69	85	.812	60	118	178	32	80	1	18	12	19	11.8	3.4	2.8	0.5	.388
96-97	Orlando	82	21	2004	699	262	586	.447	0	13	.000	175	218	.803	174	345	519	73	196	2	47	20	98	24.4	8.5	6.3	0.9	.408
97-98	Orlando	58	8	1638	736	259	617	.420	0	4	.000	218	279	.781	152	275	427	51	122	0	31	24	75	28.2	12.7	7.4	0.9	.459
98-99	Orlando	44	0	695	223	76	180	.422	0	2	.000	71	99	.717	66	95	161	17	64	0	15	7	37	15.8	5.1	3.7	0.4	.343
99-00	Orlando	20	0	148	54	21	48	.438	1	4	.250	11	14	.786	11	33	44	4	15	0	5	2	12	7.4	2.7	2.2	0.2	.413
00-01	LA Clippers	28	8	491	118	45	117	.385	0	1	.000	28	37	.757	34	74	108	7	30	0	14	1	22	17.5	4.2	3.9	0.3	.273
NBA Season Totals		456	72	8548	3088	1067	2483	.430	11	61	.180	943	1199	.786	783	1430	2213	291	740	4	203	94	415	18.7	6.8	4.9	0.6	....

YEAR	TEAM	GP	GS	MIN	PTS	FGM	FGA	FG%	3PM	3PA	3P%	FTM	FTA	FT%	ORB	DRB	TRB	AST	PF	DQ	STL	BLK	TO	MPG	PPG	RPG	APG	PCM
94-95	Boston	4	1	81	11	4	12	.333	0	0	.000	3	6	.500	13	11	24	3	7	0	3	1	5	20.3	2.8	6.0	0.8	.291
96-97	Orlando	5	5	195	61	21	40	.525	0	1	.000	19	25	.760	20	30	50	4	20	1	2	2	14	39.0	12.2	10.0	0.8	.373
98-99	Orlando	1	0	16	4	1	2	.500	0	0	.000	2	2	1.000	0	0	0	0	2	0	1	0	1	16.0	4.0	0.0	0.0	.139
NBA Playoff Totals		**10**	**6**	**292**	**76**	**26**	**54**	**.481**	**0**	**1**	**.000**	**24**	**33**	**.727**	**33**	**41**	**74**	**7**	**29**	**1**	**6**	**3**	**20**	**29.2**	**7.6**	**7.4**	**0.7**	**....**

• STRONG, Ted
Ted R. Strong

Born: Jan. 2, 1917. South Bend, IN, United States. Died: 1951.   Height: 6'3".   Weight: 210 lbs.   Drafted: —   College: none

YEAR	TEAM	GP	GS	MIN	PTS	FGM	FGA	FG%	3PM	3PA	3P%	FTM	FTA	FT%	ORB	DRB	TRB	AST	PF	DQ	STL	BLK	TO	MPG	PPG	RPG	APG	PCM
42-43	Chicago-N	10	....	....	36	13	....	....	....	....	....	10	....	....	....	....	....	....	....	....	....	....	....	....	3.6	....	....	....
NBL Season Totals		**10**	**....**	**....**	**36**	**13**	**....**	**....**	**....**	**....**	**....**	**10**	**....**	**....**	**....**	**....**	**....**	**....**	**....**	**....**	**....**	**....**	**....**	**....**	**3.6**	**....**	**....**	**....**
42-43	Chicago-N	3	....	....	8	2	....	....	....	....	....	4	....	....	....	....	....	....	....	....	....	....	....	....	2.7	....	....	....
NBL Playoff Totals		**3**	**....**	**....**	**8**	**2**	**....**	**....**	**....**	**....**	**....**	**4**	**....**	**....**	**....**	**....**	**....**	**....**	**....**	**....**	**....**	**....**	**....**	**....**	**2.7**	**....**	**....**	**....**

• STROTHERS, Lamont
William Lamont Strothers

Born: May 10, 1968. Nansemond Co., VA, United States.   Height: 6'4".   Weight: 190 lbs.   Drafted: 1991   College: Christopher Newport

YEAR	TEAM	GP	GS	MIN	PTS	FGM	FGA	FG%	3PM	3PA	3P%	FTM	FTA	FT%	ORB	DRB	TRB	AST	PF	DQ	STL	BLK	TO	MPG	PPG	RPG	APG	PCM
91-92	Portland	4	0	17	10	4	12	.333	0	2	.000	2	4	.500	1	0	1	1	2	0	1	1	2	4.3	2.5	0.3	0.3	.159
92-93	Dallas	9	0	138	50	20	61	.328	2	13	.154	8	10	.800	8	6	14	13	13	0	8	0	15	15.3	5.6	1.6	1.4	.182
NBA Season Totals		**13**	**0**	**155**	**60**	**24**	**73**	**.329**	**2**	**15**	**.133**	**10**	**14**	**.714**	**9**	**6**	**15**	**14**	**15**	**0**	**9**	**1**	**17**	**11.9**	**4.6**	**1.2**	**1.1**	**....**

• STROUD, John
John Busby Stroud

Born: Oct. 29, 1957. New Albany, MS, United States.   Height: 6'7".   Weight: 215 lbs.   Drafted: 1980   College: Mississippi

YEAR	TEAM	GP	GS	MIN	PTS	FGM	FGA	FG%	3PM	3PA	3P%	FTM	FTA	FT%	ORB	DRB	TRB	AST	PF	DQ	STL	BLK	TO	MPG	PPG	RPG	APG	PCM
80-81	Houston	9	....	88	25	11	34	.324	0	0	.000	3	4	.750	7	6	13	9	7	0	1	0	4	9.8	2.8	1.4	1.0	.219
NBA Season Totals		**9**	**....**	**88**	**25**	**11**	**34**	**.324**	**0**	**0**	**.000**	**3**	**4**	**.750**	**7**	**6**	**13**	**9**	**7**	**0**	**1**	**0**	**4**	**9.8**	**2.8**	**1.4**	**1.0**	**....**

• STROUD, Red
William D. (Red) Stroud

Born: May 2, 1941.   Height: 6'   Weight: 160 lbs.   Drafted: 1963   College: Mississippi State

YEAR	TEAM	GP	GS	MIN	PTS	FGM	FGA	FG%	3PM	3PA	3P%	FTM	FTA	FT%	ORB	DRB	TRB	AST	PF	DQ	STL	BLK	TO	MPG	PPG	RPG	APG	PCM
67-68	New Orleans-A	7	....	33	20	5	11	.455	1	1	1.000	9	10	.900	....	....	2	1	7	0	....	....	9	4.7	2.9	0.3	0.1	.440
ABA Season Totals		**7**	**....**	**33**	**20**	**5**	**11**	**.455**	**1**	**1**	**1.000**	**9**	**10**	**.900**	**....**	**....**	**2**	**1**	**7**	**0**	**....**	**....**	**9**	**4.7**	**2.9**	**0.3**	**0.1**	**....**

• STRUMILLO, Chester
Chester Strumillo

Born: 1924.   Height: 5'11".   Weight: 175 lbs.   Drafted: —   College: Northwestern

YEAR	TEAM	GP	GS	MIN	PTS	FGM	FGA	FG%	3PM	3PA	3P%	FTM	FTA	FT%	ORB	DRB	TRB	AST	PF	DQ	STL	BLK	TO	MPG	PPG	RPG	APG	PCM
44-45	Chicago-N	1	....	....	0	0	....	....	....	....	....	0	....	....	....	....	....	....	....	....	....	....	....	....	0.0	....	....	....
NBL Season Totals		**1**	**....**	**....**	**0**	**0**	**....**	**....**	**....**	**....**	**....**	**0**	**....**	**....**	**....**	**....**	**....**	**....**	**....**	**....**	**....**	**....**	**....**	**....**	**0.0**	**....**	**....**	**....**

• STUMP, Gene
Eugene Andrew Stump

Born: Nov. 13, 1923.   Height: 6'2".   Weight: 185 lbs.   Drafted: 1947   College: DePaul

YEAR	TEAM	GP	GS	MIN	PTS	FGM	FGA	FG%	3PM	3PA	3P%	FTM	FTA	FT%	ORB	DRB	TRB	AST	PF	DQ	STL	BLK	TO	MPG	PPG	RPG	APG	PCM
47-48	Boston	43	....	....	142	59	247	.239	....	....	....	24	38	.632	....	....	....	18	66	....	....	....	....	....	3.3	....	0.4	....
48-49	Boston	56	....	....	478	193	580	.333	....	....	....	92	129	.713	....	....	....	56	102	....	....	....	....	....	8.5	....	1.0	....
49-50	Minneapolis	23	....	....	61	27	95	.284	....	....	....	7	14	.500	....	....	....	23	32	....	....	....	....	....	2.7	....	1.0	....
49-50	Waterloo	26	....	....	102	36	118	.305	....	....	....	30	40	.750	....	....	....	21	27	....	....	....	....	....	3.9	....	0.8	....
NBA Season Totals		**148**	**....**	**....**	**783**	**315**	**1040**	**.303**	**....**	**....**	**....**	**153**	**221**	**.692**	**....**	**....**	**....**	**118**	**227**	**....**	**....**	**....**	**....**	**....**	**5.3**	**....**	**0.8**	**....**
47-48	Boston	3	....	....	2	1	3	.333	....	....	....	0	0	.000	....	....	....	0	2	....	....	....	....	....	0.7	....	0.0	....
NBA Playoff Totals		**3**	**....**	**....**	**2**	**1**	**3**	**.333**	**....**	**....**	**....**	**0**	**0**	**.000**	**....**	**....**	**....**	**0**	**2**	**....**	**....**	**....**	**....**	**....**	**0.7**	**....**	**0.0**	**....**

• STUTZ, Stan
Stanley J. Stutz   aka.: Stanley J. Modzelewski

Born: Apr. 14, 1920. Worcester, MA, United States. Died: Oct.28, 1975.   Height: 5'10".   Weight: 170 lbs.   Drafted: —   College: Rhode Island

YEAR	TEAM	GP	GS	MIN	PTS	FGM	FGA	FG%	3PM	3PA	3P%	FTM	FTA	FT%	ORB	DRB	TRB	AST	PF	DQ	STL	BLK	TO	MPG	PPG	RPG	APG	PCM
46-47	New York	60	....	....	477	172	641	.268	....	....	....	133	170	.782	....	....	....	49	127	....	....	....	....	....	8.0	....	0.8	....
47-48	New York	47	....	....	331	109	501	.218	....	....	....	113	135	.837	....	....	....	57	121	....	....	....	....	....	7.0	....	1.2	....
48-49	Baltimore	59	....	....	373	121	431	.281	....	....	....	131	159	.824	....	....	....	82	149	....	....	....	....	....	6.3	....	1.4	....
NBA Season Totals		**166**	**....**	**....**	**1181**	**402**	**1573**	**.256**	**....**	**....**	**....**	**377**	**464**	**.813**	**....**	**....**	**....**	**188**	**397**	**....**	**....**	**....**	**....**	**....**	**7.1**	**....**	**1.1**	**....**
46-47	New York	5	....	....	84	28	101	.277	....	....	....	28	32	.875	....	....	....	7	13	....	....	....	....	....	16.8	....	1.4	....
47-48	New York	3	....	....	15	3	11	.273	....	....	....	9	11	.818	....	....	....	1	9	....	....	....	....	....	5.0	....	0.3	....
48-49	Baltimore	3	....	....	5	1	5	.200	....	....	....	3	6	.500	....	....	....	0	9	....	....	....	....	....	1.7	....	0.0	....
NBA Playoff Totals		**11**	**....**	**....**	**104**	**32**	**117**	**.274**	**....**	**....**	**....**	**40**	**49**	**.816**	**....**	**....**	**....**	**8**	**31**	**....**	**....**	**....**	**....**	**....**	**9.5**	**....**	**0.7**	**....**

• STYLER, John
John Styler

Born: 1916.   Height: 6'6".   Weight: 225 lbs.   Drafted: —   College: none

YEAR	TEAM	GP	GS	MIN	PTS	FGM	FGA	FG%	3PM	3PA	3P%	FTM	FTA	FT%	ORB	DRB	TRB	AST	PF	DQ	STL	BLK	TO	MPG	PPG	RPG	APG	PCM
44-45	Chicago-N	16	....	....	22	10	....	....	....	....	....	2	....	....	....	....	....	....	....	....	....	....	....	....	1.4	....	....	....
45-46	Indianapolis-N	4	....	....	12	5	....	....	....	....	....	2	....	....	....	....	....	....	....	....	....	....	....	....	3.0	....	....	....
NBL Season Totals		**20**	**....**	**....**	**34**	**15**	**....**	**....**	**....**	**....**	**....**	**4**	**....**	**....**	**....**	**....**	**....**	**....**	**....**	**....**	**....**	**....**	**....**	**....**	**1.7**	**....**	**....**	**....**
44-45	Chicago-N	1	....	....	0	0	....	....	....	....	....	0	....	....	....	....	....	....	....	....	....	....	....	....	0.0	....	....	....
NBL Playoff Totals		**1**	**....**	**....**	**0**	**0**	**....**	**....**	**....**	**....**	**....**	**0**	**....**	**....**	**....**	**....**	**....**	**....**	**....**	**....**	**....**	**....**	**....**	**....**	**0.0**	**....**	**....**	**....**

YEAR	TEAM	GP	GS	MIN	PTS	FGM	FGA	FG%	3PM	3PA	3P%	FTM	FTA	FT%	ORB	DRB	TRB	AST	PF	DQ	STL	BLK	TO	MPG	PPG	RPG	APG	PCM

• SUDDITH, Arnold
Arnold Suddith

Born: Dec. 26, 1910. Died: Sept.1984. Height: 6'1". Weight: 170 lbs. Drafted: — College: Indiana

YEAR	TEAM	GP	GS	MIN	PTS	FGM	FGA	FG%	3PM	3PA	3P%	FTM	FTA	FT%	ORB	DRB	TRB	AST	PF	DQ	STL	BLK	TO	MPG	PPG	RPG	APG	PCM
39-40	Indianapolis-N	6	....	....	14	5	....	....	....	....	....	4	....	....	....	....	....	....	....	....	....	....	....	....	2.3	....	....	....
NBL Season Totals		6	....	....	14	5	....	....	....	....	....	4	....	....	....	....	....	....	....	....	....	....	....	....	2.3	....	....	....

• SUESENS, Kenny
Kenny Suesens

Born: Oct. 23, 1916. Burlington, IA, United States. Died: May29, 1992. Height: 6'1". Weight: 175 lbs. Drafted: — College: Iowa

YEAR	TEAM	GP	GS	MIN	PTS	FGM	FGA	FG%	3PM	3PA	3P%	FTM	FTA	FT%	ORB	DRB	TRB	AST	PF	DQ	STL	BLK	TO	MPG	PPG	RPG	APG	PCM
38-39	Sheboygan-N	10	....	....	15	4	....	....	....	....	....	7	....	....	....	....	....	....	....	....	....	....	....	....	1.5	....	....	....
39-40	Sheboygan-N	28	....	....	66	19	....	....	....	....	....	28	....	....	....	....	....	....	....	....	....	....	....	....	2.4	....	....	....
40-41	Sheboygan-N	24	....	....	77	18	....	....	....	....	....	41	....	....	....	....	....	....	....	....	....	....	....	....	3.2	....	....	....
41-42	Sheboygan-N	24	....	....	79	30	....	....	....	....	....	19	....	....	....	....	....	....	....	....	....	....	....	....	3.3	....	....	....
42-43	Sheboygan-N	23	....	....	85	32	....	....	....	....	....	21	....	....	....	....	....	....	....	....	....	....	....	....	3.7	....	....	....
43-44	Sheboygan-N	21	....	....	100	34	....	....	....	....	....	32	....	....	....	....	....	....	....	....	....	....	....	....	4.8	....	....	....
45-46	Sheboygan-N	4	....	....	3	1	....	....	....	....	....	1	....	....	....	....	....	....	....	....	....	....	....	....	0.8	....	....	....
46-47	Sheboygan-N	37	....	....	62	14	....	....	....	....	....	34	73	.466	....	....	....	....	75	....	....	....	....	....	1.7	....	....	....
47-48	Sheboygan-N	11	....	....	11	3	....	....	....	....	....	5	15	.333	....	....	....	....	....	....	....	....	....	....	1.0	....	....	....
48-49	Sheboygan-N	26	....	....	16	3	....	....	....	....	....	10	18	.556	....	....	....	....	17	....	....	....	....	....	0.6	....	....	....
NBL Season Totals		208	....	....	514	158	....	....	....	....	....	198	106		....	....	....	....	92	....	....	....	....	....	2.5	....	....	....
39-40	Sheboygan-N	3	....	....	15	5	....	....	....	....	....	5	....	....	....	....	....	....	....	....	....	....	....	....	5.0	....	....	....
40-41	Sheboygan-N	6	....	....	14	3	....	....	....	....	....	8	....	....	....	....	....	....	....	....	....	....	....	....	2.3	....	....	....
42-43	Sheboygan-N	5	....	....	23	9	....	....	....	....	....	5	....	....	....	....	....	....	....	....	....	....	....	....	4.6	....	....	....
43-44	Sheboygan-N	6	....	....	24	6	....	....	....	....	....	12	....	....	....	....	....	....	....	....	....	....	....	....	4.0	....	....	....
45-46	Sheboygan-N	5	....	....	12	5	....	....	....	....	....	2	5	.400	....	....	....	....	....	....	....	....	....	....	2.4	....	....	....
46-47	Sheboygan-N	4	....	....	3	1	....	....	....	....	....	1	3	.333	....	....	....	....	....	....	....	....	....	....	0.8	....	....	....
NBL Playoff Totals		29	....	....	91	29	....	....	....	....	....	33	8		....	....	....	....	....	....	....	....	....	....	3.1	....	....	....

• SUITER, Gary
Gary G. Suiter

Born: Jan. 18, 1945. Height: 6'9". Weight: 225 lbs. Drafted: — College: Midwestern State

YEAR	TEAM	GP	GS	MIN	PTS	FGM	FGA	FG%	3PM	3PA	3P%	FTM	FTA	FT%	ORB	DRB	TRB	AST	PF	DQ	STL	BLK	TO	MPG	PPG	RPG	APG	PCM
70-71	Cleveland	30	....	140	42	19	54	.352	....	....	....	4	9	.444	....	....	41	2	20	0	....	....	....	4.7	1.4	1.4	0.1	.276
NBA Season Totals		30	....	140	42	19	54	.352	....	....	....	4	9	.444	....	....	41	2	20	0	....	....	....	4.7	1.4	1.4	0.1	

• SULLIVAN, Bob
Robert Sullivan

Born: 1921. Height: 6'. Weight: 180 lbs. Drafted: — College: Wisconsin

YEAR	TEAM	GP	GS	MIN	PTS	FGM	FGA	FG%	3PM	3PA	3P%	FTM	FTA	FT%	ORB	DRB	TRB	AST	PF	DQ	STL	BLK	TO	MPG	PPG	RPG	APG	PCM
43-44	Oshkosh-N	3	....	....	13	6	....	....	....	....	....	1	....	....	....	....	....	....	....	....	....	....	....	....	4.3	....	....	....
45-46	Oshkosh-N	30	....	....	102	34	....	....	....	....	....	34	50	.680	....	....	....	....	....	....	....	....	....	....	3.4	....	....	....
46-47	Oshkosh-N	41	....	....	138	45	....	....	....	....	....	48	60	.800	....	....	....	....	59	....	....	....	....	....	3.4	....	....	....
47-48	Oshkosh-N	13	....	....	12	4	....	....	....	....	....	4	5	.800	....	....	....	....	....	....	....	....	....	....	0.9	....	....	....
NBL Season Totals		87	....	....	265	89	....	....	....	....	....	87	115		....	....	....	....	59	....	....	....	....	....	3.0	....	....	....
45-46	Oshkosh-N	5	....	....	17	5	....	....	....	....	....	7	9	.778	....	....	....	....	....	....	....	....	....	....	3.4	....	....	....
46-47	Oshkosh-N	5	....	....	6	3	....	....	....	....	....	0	2	.000	....	....	....	....	....	....	....	....	....	....	1.2	....	....	....
NBL Playoff Totals		10	....	....	23	8	....	....	....	....	....	7	11		....	....	....	....	....	....	....	....	....	....	2.3	....	....	....

• SULLIVAN, Jack
Jack Sullivan

Born: 1916. Height: 6'1". Weight: 182 lbs. Drafted: — College: Notre Dame

YEAR	TEAM	GP	GS	MIN	PTS	FGM	FGA	FG%	3PM	3PA	3P%	FTM	FTA	FT%	ORB	DRB	TRB	AST	PF	DQ	STL	BLK	TO	MPG	PPG	RPG	APG	PCM
37-38	Columbus-N	2	....	....	3	1	....	....	....	....	....	1	....	....	....	....	....	....	....	....	....	....	....	....	1.5	....	....	....
NBL Season Totals		2	....	....	3	1	....	....	....	....	....	1	....	....	....	....	....	....	....	....	....	....	....	....	1.5	....	....	....

• SUMMERS, Bill
Bill Summers

Born: —. Height: — Weight: — Drafted: — College: —

YEAR	TEAM	GP	GS	MIN	PTS	FGM	FGA	FG%	3PM	3PA	3P%	FTM	FTA	FT%	ORB	DRB	TRB	AST	PF	DQ	STL	BLK	TO	MPG	PPG	RPG	APG	PCM
40-41	Hammond-N	1	....	....	2	1	....	....	....	....	....	0	....	....	....	....	....	....	....	....	....	....	....	....	2.0	....	....	....
NBL Season Totals		1	....	....	2	1	....	....	....	....	....	0	....	....	....	....	....	....	....	....	....	....	....	....	2.0	....	....	....

• SUMPTER, Barry
Barry Sumpter

Born: Nov. 11, 1965. Brooklyn, IL, United States. Height: 6'11". Weight: 215 lbs. Drafted: 1988 College: Austin Peay

YEAR	TEAM	GP	GS	MIN	PTS	FGM	FGA	FG%	3PM	3PA	3P%	FTM	FTA	FT%	ORB	DRB	TRB	AST	PF	DQ	STL	BLK	TO	MPG	PPG	RPG	APG	PCM
88-89	LA Clippers	1	0	1	0	0	1	.000	0	0	.000	0	0	.000	0	0	0	0	0	0	0	0	0	1.0	0.0	0.0	0.0	-.930
NBA Season Totals		1	0	1	0	0	1	.000	0	0	.000	0	0	.000	0	0	0	0	0	0	0	0	0	1.0	0.0	0.0	0.0	....

• SUNDERLAGE, Don
Don J. Sunderlage

Born: Dec. 20, 1929. Roselle, IL, United States. Died: July15, 1961. Height: 6'1". Weight: 180 lbs. Drafted: 1951 College: Illinois

YEAR	TEAM	GP	GS	MIN	PTS	FGM	FGA	FG%	3PM	3PA	3P%	FTM	FTA	FT%	ORB	DRB	TRB	AST	PF	DQ	STL	BLK	TO	MPG	PPG	RPG	APG	PCM
53-54	Milwaukee	68	....	2232	760	254	748	.340	....	....	....	252	337	.748	....	....	225	187	263	8	....	....	....	32.8	11.2	3.3	2.8	.308
54-55	Minneapolis	45	....	404	114	33	133	.248	....	....	....	48	73	.658	....	....	56	37	57	0	....	....	....	9.0	2.5	1.2	0.8	.238
NBA Season Totals		113	....	2636	874	287	881	.326	....	....	....	300	410	.732	....	....	281	224	320	8	....	....	....	23.3	7.7	2.5	2.0	....

YEAR	TEAM	GP	GS	MIN	PTS	FGM	FGA	FG%	3PM	3PA	3P%	FTM	FTA	FT%	ORB	DRB	TRB	AST	PF	DQ	STL	BLK	TO	MPG	PPG	RPG	APG	PCM

• SUNDOV, Bruno

Bruno Sundov

Born: Feb. 10, 1980. Split, Croatia.   Height: 7'2".   Weight: 220 lbs.   Drafted: 1998   College: —

YEAR	TEAM	GP	GS	MIN	PTS	FGM	FGA	FG%	3PM	3PA	3P%	FTM	FTA	FT%	ORB	DRB	TRB	AST	PF	DQ	STL	BLK	TO	MPG	PPG	RPG	APG	PCM
98-99	Dallas	3	0	11	4	2	7	.286	0	0	.000	0	0	.000	0	0	0	1	4	0	0	0	1	3.7	1.3	0.0	0.3	-.182
99-00	Dallas	14	0	61	26	12	31	.387	0	0	.000	2	2	1.000	5	7	12	2	16	0	2	4	4	4.4	1.9	0.9	0.1	.239
00-01	Indiana	11	4	120	43	20	41	.488	0	4	.000	3	5	.600	4	19	23	2	21	1	2	4	3	10.9	3.9	2.1	0.2	.328
01-02	Indiana	22	0	88	32	16	40	.400	0	1	.000	0	2	.000	7	14	21	3	16	0	3	3	4	4.0	1.5	1.0	0.1	.298
02-03	Boston	26	0	138	32	14	56	.250	4	16	.250	0	2	.000	8	20	28	7	24	0	6	3	9	5.3	1.2	1.1	0.3	.110
NBA Season Totals		76	4	418	137	64	175	.366	4	21	.190	5	11	.455	24	60	84	15	81	1	13	12	21	5.5	1.8	1.1	0.2	....
01-02	Indiana	1	0	2	2	1	1	1.000	0	0	.000	0	0	.000	0	0	0	0	0	0	0	0	0	2.0	2.0	0.0	0.0	1.000
NBA Playoff Totals		1	0	2	2	1	1	1.000	0	0	.000	0	0	.000	0	0	0	0	0	0	0	0	0	2.0	2.0	0.0	0.0	....

• SUNDVOLD, Jon

Jon Thomas (Sunny) Sundvold

Born: July 2, 1961. Sioux Falls, SD, United States.   Height: 6'2".   Weight: 170 lbs.   Drafted: 1983   College: Missouri

YEAR	TEAM	GP	GS	MIN	PTS	FGM	FGA	FG%	3PM	3PA	3P%	FTM	FTA	FT%	ORB	DRB	TRB	AST	PF	DQ	STL	BLK	TO	MPG	PPG	RPG	APG	PCM
83-84	Seattle	73	2	1284	507	217	488	.445	9	37	.243	64	72	.889	23	68	91	239	81	0	29	1	80	17.6	6.9	1.2	3.3	.395
84-85	Seattle	73	1	1150	400	170	400	.425	12	38	.316	48	59	.814	17	53	70	206	87	0	36	1	88	15.8	5.5	1.0	2.8	.328
85-86	San Antonio	70	4	1150	500	220	476	.462	21	60	.350	39	48	.813	22	58	80	261	110	0	34	0	84	16.4	7.1	1.1	3.7	.447
86-87	San Antonio	76	42	1765	850	365	751	.486	50	149	.336	70	84	.833	20	78	98	315	109	1	35	0	99	23.2	11.2	1.3	4.1	.454
87-88	San Antonio	52	12	1024	421	176	379	.464	26	64	.406	43	48	.896	14	34	48	183	54	0	27	2	57	19.7	8.1	0.9	3.5	.409
88-89	Miami	68	8	1338	709	307	675	.455	48	92	.522	47	57	.825	18	69	87	137	78	0	27	1	88	19.7	10.4	1.3	2.0	.372
89-90	Miami	63	2	867	384	148	363	.408	44	100	.440	44	52	.846	15	56	71	102	69	0	25	0	50	13.8	6.1	1.1	1.6	.344
90-91	Miami	24	0	225	112	43	107	.402	15	35	.429	11	11	1.000	3	6	9	24	11	0	7	0	17	9.4	4.7	0.4	1.0	.319
91-92	Miami	3	0	8	3	1	3	.333	1	1	1.000	0	0	.000	0	0	0	2	2	0	0	0	0	2.7	1.0	0.0	0.7	.294
NBA Season Totals		502	71	8811	3886	1647	3642	.452	226	576	.392	366	431	.849	132	422	554	1469	601	1	220	5	563	17.6	7.7	1.1	2.9	....
83-84	Seattle	3	0	22	8	3	8	.375	0	3	.000	2	2	1.000	1	1	2	5	1	0	0	0	1	7.3	2.7	0.7	1.7	.417
85-86	San Antonio	3	0	43	16	7	18	.389	1	6	.167	1	1	1.000	0	1	1	5	1	0	0	0	5	14.3	5.3	0.3	1.7	.162
87-88	San Antonio	3	3	90	35	15	30	.500	3	9	.333	2	3	.667	1	3	4	15	3	0	4	0	3	30.0	11.7	1.3	5.0	.443
91-92	Miami	1	0	2	0	0	1	.000	0	0	.000	0	0	.000	0	0	0	0	1	0	0	0	0	2.0	0.0	0.0	0.0	-.697
NBA Playoff Totals		10	3	157	59	25	57	.439	4	18	.222	5	6	.833	2	5	7	25	6	0	4	0	9	15.7	5.9	0.7	2.5	....

• SURA, Bob

Robert (Bob) Sura Jr.

Born: Mar. 25, 1973. Wilkes-Barre, PA, United States.   Height: 6'5".   Weight: 200 lbs.   Drafted: 1995   College: Florida State

YEAR	TEAM	GP	GS	MIN	PTS	FGM	FGA	FG%	3PM	3PA	3P%	FTM	FTA	FT%	ORB	DRB	TRB	AST	PF	DQ	STL	BLK	TO	MPG	PPG	RPG	APG	PCM
95-96	Cleveland	79	3	1150	422	148	360	.411	27	78	.346	99	141	.702	34	101	135	233	126	1	56	21	119	14.6	5.3	1.7	2.9	.416
96-97	Cleveland	82	23	2269	755	253	587	.431	53	164	.323	196	319	.614	76	232	308	390	218	3	90	33	180	27.7	9.2	3.8	4.8	.412
97-98	Cleveland	46	4	942	267	87	231	.377	19	60	.317	74	131	.565	25	69	94	171	113	0	44	7	92	20.5	5.8	2.0	3.7	.309
98-99	Cleveland	50	6	841	214	70	210	.333	9	45	.200	65	103	.631	21	81	102	152	98	1	46	14	67	16.8	4.3	2.0	3.0	.336
99-00	Cleveland	73	45	2216	1009	356	815	.437	122	332	.367	175	251	.697	50	238	288	284	201	0	91	19	148	30.4	13.8	3.9	3.9	.453
00-01	Golden State	53	42	1684	586	202	518	.390	47	172	.273	135	189	.714	54	173	227	242	127	0	54	8	160	31.8	11.1	4.3	4.6	.358
01-02	Golden State	78	5	1779	778	250	590	.424	42	133	.316	236	328	.720	89	167	256	275	160	1	88	17	133	22.8	10.0	3.3	3.5	.485
02-03	Golden State	55	0	1130	401	135	328	.412	28	85	.329	103	148	.696	58	109	167	177	108	0	45	2	82	20.5	7.3	3.0	3.2	.415
NBA Season Totals		516	128	12011	4432	1501	3639	.412	347	1069	.325	1083	1610	.673	407	1170	1577	1924	1151	6	514	121	981	23.3	8.6	3.1	3.7	....
95-96	Cleveland	3	0	18	4	2	3	.667	0	0	.000	0	0	.000	0	1	1	3	4	0	1	0	4	6.0	1.3	0.3	1.0	.138
97-98	Cleveland	3	0	31	4	1	5	.200	0	2	.000	2	3	.667	0	3	3	4	4	0	1	0	2	10.3	1.3	1.0	1.3	.136
NBA Playoff Totals		6	0	49	8	3	8	.375	0	2	.000	2	3	.667	0	4	4	7	8	0	2	0	6	8.2	1.3	0.7	1.2	....

• SURHOFF, Dick

Richard C. Surhoff Jr.

Born: Nov. 16, 1929. Died: May 1, 1987.   Height: 6'4".   Weight: 210 lbs.   Drafted: 1952   College: Long Island University

YEAR	TEAM	GP	GS	MIN	PTS	FGM	FGA	FG%	3PM	3PA	3P%	FTM	FTA	FT%	ORB	DRB	TRB	AST	PF	DQ	STL	BLK	TO	MPG	PPG	RPG	APG	PCM
52-53	New York	26	....	187	45	13	61	.213	....	....	....	19	30	.633	....	....	25	9	36	1	....	....	....	7.2	1.7	1.0	0.3	.122
53-54	Milwaukee	32	....	358	133	43	129	.333	....	....	....	47	62	.758	....	....	69	23	53	0	....	....	....	11.2	4.2	2.2	0.7	.353
NBA Season Totals		58	....	545	178	56	190	.295	....	....	....	66	92	.717	....	....	94	32	89	1	....	....	....	9.4	3.1	1.6	0.6	....
52-53	New York	4	....	13	4	2	4	.500	....	....	....	0	0	.000	....	....	2	2	2	0	....	....	....	3.3	1.0	0.5	0.5	.448
NBA Playoff Totals		4	....	13	4	2	4	.500	....	....	....	0	0	.000	....	....	2	2	2	0	....	....	....	3.3	1.0	0.5	0.5	....

• SUTOR, George

George Joseph Sutor

Born: Sept. 14, 1943. Philadelphia, PA, United States.   Height: 6'8".   Weight: 235 lbs.   Drafted: —   College: LaSalle

YEAR	TEAM	GP	GS	MIN	PTS	FGM	FGA	FG%	3PM	3PA	3P%	FTM	FTA	FT%	ORB	DRB	TRB	AST	PF	DQ	STL	BLK	TO	MPG	PPG	RPG	APG	PCM
67-68	Kentucky-A	1	....	5	0	0	0	.000	0	0	.000	0	0	.000	....	....	1	0	2	0	....	....	0	5.0	0.0	1.0	0.0	.000
68-69	Minnesota-A	64	....	886	349	139	397	.350	0	0	.000	71	114	.623	175	173	348	27	170	8	....	....	60	13.8	5.5	5.4	0.4	.413
69-70	Carolina-A	11	....	135	31	12	41	.293	1	1	1.000	7	15	.467	21	30	51	2	29	0	....	....	11	12.3	2.8	4.6	0.2	.269
69-70	Miami-A	3	....	12	0	0	5	.000	0	0	.000	0	2	.000	2	2	4	1	2	0	....	....	0	4.0	0.0	1.3	0.3	-.119
ABA Season Totals		79	....	1038	380	151	443	.341	0	1	.000	78	131	.595	198	205	404	30	203	8	....	....	71	13.1	4.8	5.1	0.4	....
68-69	Minnesota-A	1	....	3	0	0	1	.000	0	0	.000	0	1	.000	....	....	0	0	2	0	....	....	1	3.0	0.0	0.0	0.0	-.715
ABA Playoff Totals		1	....	3	0	0	1	.000	0	0	.000	0	1	.000	....	....	0	0	2	0	....	....	1	3.0	0.0	0.0	0.0	....

• SUTTLE, Dane

Dane Lee Suttle

Born: Aug. 9, 1961. Los Angeles, CA, United States.   Height: 6'3".   Weight: 190 lbs.   Drafted: 1983   College: Pepperdine

YEAR	TEAM	GP	GS	MIN	PTS	FGM	FGA	FG%	3PM	3PA	3P%	FTM	FTA	FT%	ORB	DRB	TRB	AST	PF	DQ	STL	BLK	TO	MPG	PPG	RPG	APG	PCM
83-84	Kansas City	40	1	469	258	109	214	.509	0	3	.000	40	47	.851	21	25	46	46	46	0	20	0	32	11.7	6.5	1.2	1.2	.462
84-85	Kansas City	6	0	24	14	6	13	.462	0	1	.000	2	2	1.000	0	3	3	2	3	0	1	0	1	4.0	2.3	0.5	0.3	.459
NBA Season Totals		46	1	493	272	115	227	.507	0	4	.000	42	49	.857	21	28	49	48	49	0	21	0	33	10.7	5.9	1.1	1.0	....

YEAR	TEAM	GP	GS	MIN	PTS	FGM	FGA	FG%	3PM	3PA	3P%	FTM	FTA	FT%	ORB	DRB	TRB	AST	PF	DQ	STL	BLK	TO	MPG	PPG	RPG	APG	PCM

• SUTTON, Greg
Gregory Ray Sutton

Born: Dec. 3, 1967. Santa Cruz, CA, United States.　Height: 6'2".　Weight: 170 lbs.　Drafted: 1991　College: Oral Roberts

YEAR	TEAM	GP	GS	MIN	PTS	FGM	FGA	FG%	3PM	3PA	3P%	FTM	FTA	FT%	ORB	DRB	TRB	AST	PF	DQ	STL	BLK	TO	MPG	PPG	RPG	APG	PCM
91-92	San Antonio	67	2	601	246	93	240	.388	26	89	.292	34	45	.756	6	41	47	91	111	0	26	9	67	9.0	3.7	0.7	1.4	.273
94-95	Charlotte	53	4	690	263	94	230	.409	43	115	.374	32	45	.711	8	48	56	91	114	0	33	2	53	13.0	5.0	1.1	1.7	.302
95-96	Charlotte	18	0	190	62	20	50	.400	7	21	.333	15	19	.789	4	11	15	39	36	0	8	0	16	10.6	3.4	0.8	2.2	.331
95-96	Philadelphia	30	2	465	190	65	167	.389	40	96	.417	20	27	.741	4	31	35	63	56	0	17	2	45	15.5	6.3	1.2	2.1	.301
NBA Season Totals		168	8	1946	761	272	687	.396	116	321	.361	101	136	.743	22	131	153	284	317	0	84	13	181	11.6	4.5	0.9	1.7	....
91-92	San Antonio	2	0	15	7	2	6	.333	0	2	.000	3	3	1.000	0	0	0	2	3	0	1	1	0	7.5	3.5	0.0	1.0	.393
94-95	Charlotte	3	0	23	0	0	7	.000	0	5	.000	0	0	.000	3	2	5	3	1	0	0	0	1	7.7	0.0	1.7	1.0	-.004
NBA Playoff Totals		5	0	38	7	2	13	.154	0	7	.000	3	3	1.000	3	2	5	5	4	0	1	1	1	7.6	1.4	1.0	1.0	....

• SVENDSEN, George
George Peter Svendsen Jr.

Born: Mar. 22, 1913. Minneapolis, MN, United States. Died: Aug.6, 1995.　Height: 6'4".　Weight: 230 lbs.　Drafted: —　College: Minnesota

YEAR	TEAM	GP	GS	MIN	PTS	FGM	FGA	FG%	3PM	3PA	3P%	FTM	FTA	FT%	ORB	DRB	TRB	AST	PF	DQ	STL	BLK	TO	MPG	PPG	RPG	APG	PCM
37-38	Oshkosh-N	11	....	....	45	18	....	....	....	....	....	9	....	....	....	....	....	....	....	....	....	....	....	....	4.1	....	....	....
NBL Season Totals		11	....	....	45	18	....	....	....	....	....	9	....	....	....	....	....	....	....	....	....	....	....	....	4.1	....	....	....
37-38	Oshkosh-N	1	....	....	0	0	....	....	....	....	....	0	....	....	....	....	....	....	....	....	....	....	....	....	0.0	....	....	....
NBL Playoff Totals		1	....	....	0	0	....	....	....	....	....	0	....	....	....	....	....	....	....	....	....	....	....	....	0.0	....	....	....

• SWAGERTY, Keith
Keith M. Swagerty

Born: Oct. 30, 1945. San Jose, CA, United States.　Height: 6'7".　Weight: 235 lbs.　Drafted: 1967　College: Pacific

YEAR	TEAM	GP	GS	MIN	PTS	FGM	FGA	FG%	3PM	3PA	3P%	FTM	FTA	FT%	ORB	DRB	TRB	AST	PF	DQ	STL	BLK	TO	MPG	PPG	RPG	APG	PCM
68-69	Houston-A	77	....	2447	980	362	883	.410	0	5	.000	256	421	.608	326	496	822	92	238	5	....	....	112	31.8	12.7	10.7	1.2	.478
69-70	Kentucky-A	3	....	30	7	2	9	.222	0	1	.000	3	3	1.000	1	5	6	3	4	0	....	....	2	10.0	2.3	2.0	1.0	.262
ABA Season Totals		80	....	2477	987	364	892	.408	0	6	.000	259	424	.611	327	501	828	95	242	5	....	....	114	31.0	12.3	10.4	1.2	....

• SWAIN, Bennie
Bennie S. Swain

Born: Dec. 16, 1933.　Height: 6'8".　Weight: 220 lbs.　Drafted: 1958　College: Texas Southern

YEAR	TEAM	GP	GS	MIN	PTS	FGM	FGA	FG%	3PM	3PA	3P%	FTM	FTA	FT%	ORB	DRB	TRB	AST	PF	DQ	STL	BLK	TO	MPG	PPG	RPG	APG	PCM
58-59	Boston	58	....	708	265	99	244	.406	....	....	....	67	110	.609	....	....	262	29	127	3	....	....	....	12.2	4.6	4.5	0.5	.459
NBA Season Totals		58	....	708	265	99	244	.406	....	....	....	67	110	.609	....	....	262	29	127	3	....	....	....	12.2	4.6	4.5	0.5	....
58-59	Boston	5	....	27	5	2	6	.333	....	....	....	1	2	.500	....	....	14	1	4	0	....	....	....	5.4	1.0	2.8	0.2	.440
NBA Playoff Totals		5	....	27	5	2	6	.333	....	....	....	1	2	.500	....	....	14	1	4	0	....	....	....	5.4	1.0	2.8	0.2	....

• SWANK, Everett
Everett Swank

Born: Feb. 17, 1913. Died: June1, 2000.　Height: 5'11".　Weight: 165 lbs.　Drafted: —　College: Indiana Central

YEAR	TEAM	GP	GS	MIN	PTS	FGM	FGA	FG%	3PM	3PA	3P%	FTM	FTA	FT%	ORB	DRB	TRB	AST	PF	DQ	STL	BLK	TO	MPG	PPG	RPG	APG	PCM
37-38	Indianapolis-N	4	....	....	10	4	....	....	....	....	....	2	....	....	....	....	....	....	....	....	....	....	....	....	2.5	....	....	....
38-39	Indianapolis-N	9	....	....	10	3	....	....	....	....	....	4	....	....	....	....	....	....	....	....	....	....	....	....	1.1	....	....	....
NBL Season Totals		13	....	....	20	7	....	....	....	....	....	6	....	....	....	....	....	....	....	....	....	....	....	....	1.5	....	....	....

• SWANSON, George
George Swanson

Born: —.　Height: —　Weight: —　Drafted: —　College: Toledo

YEAR	TEAM	GP	GS	MIN	PTS	FGM	FGA	FG%	3PM	3PA	3P%	FTM	FTA	FT%	ORB	DRB	TRB	AST	PF	DQ	STL	BLK	TO	MPG	PPG	RPG	APG	PCM
39-40	Sheboygan-N	11	....	....	13	4	....	....	....	....	....	5	....	....	....	....	....	....	....	....	....	....	....	....	1.2	....	....	....
NBL Season Totals		11	....	....	13	4	....	....	....	....	....	5	....	....	....	....	....	....	....	....	....	....	....	....	1.2	....	....	....
39-40	Sheboygan-N	1	....	....	1	0	....	....	....	....	....	1	....	....	....	....	....	....	....	....	....	....	....	....	1.0	....	....	....
NBL Playoff Totals		1	....	....	1	0	....	....	....	....	....	1	....	....	....	....	....	....	....	....	....	....	....	....	1.0	....	....	....

• SWANSON, Hale
Hale Swanson

Born: 1914.　Height: 6'3".　Weight: 200 lbs.　Drafted: —　College: Illinois

YEAR	TEAM	GP	GS	MIN	PTS	FGM	FGA	FG%	3PM	3PA	3P%	FTM	FTA	FT%	ORB	DRB	TRB	AST	PF	DQ	STL	BLK	TO	MPG	PPG	RPG	APG	PCM
39-40	Hammond-N	2	....	....	0	0	....	....	....	....	....	0	....	....	....	....	....	....	....	....	....	....	....	....	0.0	....	....	....
NBL Season Totals		2	....	....	0	0	....	....	....	....	....	0	....	....	....	....	....	....	....	....	....	....	....	....	0.0	....	....	....

• SWANSON, Norm
Norman P. Swanson

Born: Oct. 4, 1930.　Height: 6'6".　Weight: 210 lbs.　Drafted: 1953　College: Detroit

YEAR	TEAM	GP	GS	MIN	PTS	FGM	FGA	FG%	3PM	3PA	3P%	FTM	FTA	FT%	ORB	DRB	TRB	AST	PF	DQ	STL	BLK	TO	MPG	PPG	RPG	APG	PCM
53-54	Rochester	63	....	611	100	31	137	.226	....	....	....	38	64	.594	....	....	110	33	91	3	....	....	....	9.7	1.6	1.7	0.5	.170
NBA Season Totals		63	....	611	100	31	137	.226	....	....	....	38	64	.594	....	....	110	33	91	3	....	....	....	9.7	1.6	1.7	0.5	....
53-54	Rochester	6	....	23	8	3	7	.429	....	....	....	2	3	.667	....	....	5	0	5	0	....	....	....	3.8	1.3	0.8	0.0	.286
NBA Playoff Totals		6	....	23	8	3	7	.429	....	....	....	2	3	.667	....	....	5	0	5	0	....	....	....	3.8	1.3	0.8	0.0	....

YEAR	TEAM	GP	GS	MIN	PTS	FGM	FGA	FG%	3PM	3PA	3P%	FTM	FTA	FT%	ORB	DRB	TRB	AST	PF	DQ	STL	BLK	TO	MPG	PPG	RPG	APG	PCM

• SWARTZ, Dan
Daniel S. (Dogpatch) Swartz

Born: Dec. 23, 1934. Owingsville, KY, United States. Height: 6'4". Weight: 215 lbs. Drafted: 1956 College: Morehead State

62-63	Boston	39	....	335	175	57	150	.380	....	....	....	61	72	.847	....	....	88	21	92	0	....	....	....	8.6	4.5	2.3	0.5	.465
NBA Season Totals		39	....	335	175	57	150	.380	....	....	....	61	72	.847	....	....	88	21	92	0	....	....	....	8.6	4.5	2.3	0.5	....
62-63	Boston	1	....	4	0	0	0	.000	....	....	....	0	0	.000	....	....	0	0	0	0	....	....	....	4.0	0.0	0.0	0.0	.000
NBA Playoff Totals		1	....	4	0	0	0	.000	....	....	....	0	0	.000	....	....	0	0	0	0	....	....	....	4.0	0.0	0.0	0.0	....

• SWIFT, Skeeter
Harley E. (Skeeter) Swift Jr.

Born: June 19, 1946. Alexandria, VA, United States. Height: 6'3". Weight: 204 lbs. Drafted: 1969 College: East Tennessee State

69-70	New Orleans-A	66	....	1089	607	215	546	.394	38	125	.304	139	168	.827	21	79	100	77	208	4	....	....	101	16.5	9.2	1.5	1.2	.363
70-71	Memphis-A	28	....	507	339	128	313	.409	13	65	.200	70	88	.795	18	38	56	44	79	0	....	....	60	18.1	12.1	2.0	1.6	.492
70-71	Pittsburgh-A	52	....	1627	710	274	582	.471	26	85	.306	136	158	.861	42	135	177	225	185	1	....	....	138	31.3	13.7	3.4	4.3	.487
71-72	Pittsburgh-A	79	....	2340	1059	401	856	.468	33	100	.330	224	265	.845	48	152	200	309	277	6	....	....	252	29.6	13.4	2.5	3.9	.445
72-73	Dallas-A	42	....	1123	501	177	374	.473	19	49	.388	128	149	.859	20	62	82	150	140	1	....	....	136	26.7	11.9	2.0	3.6	.437
73-74	San Antonio-A	16	....	153	63	23	67	.343	1	12	.083	16	20	.800	5	11	16	15	26	....	3	0	13	9.6	3.9	1.0	0.9	.283
ABA Season Totals		283	....	6839	3279	1218	2738	.445	130	436	.298	713	848	.841	154	477	631	820	915	12	3	0	700	24.2	11.6	2.2	2.9	....

• SWIFT, Stromile
Stromile Swift

Born: Nov. 21, 1979. Shreveport, LA, United States. Height: 6'9". Weight: 225 lbs. Drafted: 2000 College: Louisiana State

00-01	Vancouver	80	6	1312	391	153	339	.451	0	4	.000	85	141	.603	109	175	284	28	160	0	62	82	64	16.4	4.9	3.6	0.4	.369
01-02	Memphis	68	14	1804	803	293	611	.480	0	3	.000	217	305	.711	161	269	430	50	178	3	53	113	122	26.5	11.8	6.3	0.7	.487
02-03	Memphis	67	26	1478	647	235	489	.481	0	2	.000	177	245	.722	114	270	384	45	152	3	55	104	99	22.1	9.7	5.7	0.7	.520
NBA Season Totals		215	46	4594	1841	681	1439	.473	0	9	.000	479	691	.693	384	714	1098	123	490	6	170	299	285	21.4	8.6	5.1	0.6	....

• SWIHART, Willard
Willard Swihart

Born: 1914. Height: 6'3". Weight: 190 lbs. Drafted: — College: Toledo

43-44	Cleveland-N	15	....	....	39	14	....	....	....	....	....	11	....	....	....	....	....	....	....	....	....	....	....	2.6	....	....	....	....
NBL Season Totals		15	....	....	39	14	....	....	....	....	....	11	....	....	....	....	....	....	....	....	....	....	....	2.6	....	....	....	....
43-44	Cleveland-N	2	....	....	1	0	....	....	....	....	....	1	....	....	....	....	....	....	....	....	....	....	....	0.5	....	....	....	....
NBL Playoff Totals		2	....	....	1	0	....	....	....	....	....	1	....	....	....	....	....	....	....	....	....	....	....	0.5	....	....	....	....

• SWINSON, Aaron
Aaron Anthony Swinson

Born: Jan. 9, 1971. Brunswick, GA, United States. Height: 6'5". Weight: 230 lbs. Drafted: — College: Auburn

94-95	Phoenix	9	0	51	24	10	18	.556	0	0	.000	4	5	.800	3	5	8	3	8	0	1	0	5	5.7	2.7	0.9	0.3	.377
NBA Season Totals		9	0	51	24	10	18	.556	0	0	.000	4	5	.800	3	5	8	3	8	0	1	0	5	5.7	2.7	0.9	0.3	....

• SYDNOR, Buck
Wallace B. (Buck) Sydnor

Born: Sept. 19, 1921. Height: 5'10". Weight: 175 lbs. Drafted: — College: Western Kentucky

46-47	Chicago	15	....	....	15	5	26	.192	....	....	....	5	10	.500	....	....	0	6	....	....	....	....	....	1.0	....	0.0	....	....
NBA Season Totals		15	....	....	15	5	26	.192	....	....	....	5	10	.500	....	....	0	6	....	....	....	....	....	1.0	....	0.0	....	....

• SYKES, Larry
Larry Sykes

Born: Apr. 11, 1973. Toledo, OH, United States. Height: 6'9". Weight: 255 lbs. Drafted: — College: Xavier

95-96	Boston	1	0	2	0	0	0	.000	0	0	.000	0	0	.000	1	1	2	0	0	0	0	0	1	2.0	0.0	2.0	0.0	.470
NBA Season Totals		1	0	2	0	0	0	.000	0	0	.000	0	0	.000	1	1	2	0	0	0	0	0	1	2.0	0.0	2.0	0.0	....

• SYNNOTT, Bob
Robert Synnott

Born: 1912. Height: 6'3". Weight: 190 lbs. Drafted: — College: none

44-45	Fort Wayne-N	30	....	....	75	32	....	....	....	....	....	11	....	....	....	....	....	....	....	....	....	....	....	2.5	....	....	....	....
45-46	Fort Wayne-N	24	....	....	48	24	....	....	....	....	....	0	....	....	....	....	....	....	....	....	....	....	....	2.0	....	....	....	....
46-47	Chicago-N	1	....	....	0	0	....	....	....	....	....	0	0	.000	....	....	....	....	....	....	....	....	....	0.0	....	....	....	....
46-47	Syracuse-N	4	....	....	16	6	....	....	....	....	....	4	6	.667	....	....	....	....	....	....	....	....	....	4.0	....	....	....	....
NBL Season Totals		59	....	....	139	62	....	....	....	....	....	15	6	....	....	....	....	....	....	....	....	....	....	2.4	....	....	....	....
44-45	Fort Wayne-N	6	....	....	19	7	....	....	....	....	....	5	....	....	....	....	....	....	....	....	....	....	....	3.2	....	....	....	....
NBL Playoff Totals		6	....	....	19	7	....	....	....	....	....	5	....	....	....	....	....	....	....	....	....	....	....	3.2	....	....	....	....

• SZABO, Brett
Brett Leon Szabo

Born: Feb. 1, 1968. Postville, IA, United States. Height: 6'11". Weight: 230 lbs. Drafted: — College: Augustana

96-97	Boston	70	24	662	153	54	121	.446	0	1	.000	45	61	.738	56	109	165	17	119	0	16	32	42	9.5	2.2	2.4	0.2	.310
NBA Season Totals		70	24	662	153	54	121	.446	0	1	.000	45	61	.738	56	109	165	17	119	0	16	32	42	9.5	2.2	2.4	0.2	....

YEAR	TEAM	GP	GS	MIN	PTS	FGM	FGA	FG%	3PM	3PA	3P%	FTM	FTA	FT%	ORB	DRB	TRB	AST	PF	DQ	STL	BLK	TO	MPG	PPG	RPG	APG	PCM

• SZCZERBIAK, Wally

Walter Robert Szczerbiak

Born: Mar. 5, 1977. Madrid, Spain.   Height: 6'7".   Weight: 244 lbs.   Drafted: 1999   College: Miami (OH)

YEAR	TEAM	GP	GS	MIN	PTS	FGM	FGA	FG%	3PM	3PA	3P%	FTM	FTA	FT%	ORB	DRB	TRB	AST	PF	DQ	STL	BLK	TO	MPG	PPG	RPG	APG	PCM
99-00	Minnesota	73	53	2171	845	342	669	.511	28	78	.359	133	161	.826	89	183	272	201	175	3	58	23	83	29.7	11.6	3.7	2.8	.424
00-01	Minnesota	82	82	2856	1145	469	920	.510	26	77	.338	181	208	.870	133	314	447	260	226	4	59	33	138	34.8	14.0	5.5	3.2	.446
01-02	Minnesota	82	82	3117	1531	609	1200	.508	87	191	.455	226	272	.831	120	271	391	257	188	1	66	21	181	38.0	18.7	4.8	3.1	.462
02-03	Minnesota	52	42	1836	913	351	729	.481	61	145	.421	150	173	.867	53	188	241	136	123	0	44	22	87	35.3	17.6	4.6	2.6	.464
NBA Season Totals		289	259	9980	4434	1771	3518	.503	202	491	.411	690	814	.848	395	956	1351	854	712	8	227	99	489	34.5	15.3	4.7	3.0	....
99-00	Minnesota	4	4	94	24	12	30	.400	0	3	.000	0	0	.000	2	6	8	2	7	0	3	1	1	23.5	6.0	2.0	0.5	.177
00-01	Minnesota	4	4	143	56	18	37	.486	0	1	.000	20	25	.800	4	14	18	10	6	0	5	3	12	35.8	14.0	4.5	2.5	.403
01-02	Minnesota	3	3	131	60	21	44	.477	2	9	.222	16	18	.889	9	12	21	6	8	0	2	0	8	43.7	20.0	7.0	2.0	.418
02-03	Minnesota	6	6	252	87	29	61	.475	3	14	.214	26	30	.867	6	24	30	13	19	0	6	1	18	42.0	14.5	5.0	2.2	.313
NBA Playoff Totals		17	17	620	227	80	172	.465	5	27	.185	62	73	.849	21	56	77	31	40	0	16	5	39	36.5	13.4	4.5	1.8	....

• SZCZERBIAK, Walt

Walter Szczerbiak

Born: Aug. 21, 1949. Pittsburgh, PA, United States.   Height: 6'6".   Weight: 210 lbs.   Drafted: —   College: George Washington

YEAR	TEAM	GP	GS	MIN	PTS	FGM	FGA	FG%	3PM	3PA	3P%	FTM	FTA	FT%	ORB	DRB	TRB	AST	PF	DQ	STL	BLK	TO	MPG	PPG	RPG	APG	PCM
71-72	Pittsburgh-A	53	....	598	333	149	237	.629	0	2	.000	35	53	.660	82	68	150	41	100	0	....	....	50	11.3	6.3	2.8	0.8	.638
ABA Season Totals		53	....	598	333	149	237	.629	0	2	.000	35	53	.660	82	68	150	41	100	0	....	....	50	11.3	6.3	2.8	0.8	....

• SZUKALA, Stan

Stanley Szukala

Born: 1918.   Height: 6'   Weight: 175 lbs.   Drafted: —   College: DePaul

YEAR	TEAM	GP	GS	MIN	PTS	FGM	FGA	FG%	3PM	3PA	3P%	FTM	FTA	FT%	ORB	DRB	TRB	AST	PF	DQ	STL	BLK	TO	MPG	PPG	RPG	APG	PCM
40-41	Chicago-N	24	....	....	102	45	....	....	....	....	....	12	....	....	....	....	....	....	....	....	....	....	....	....	4.3	....	....	....
41-42	Chicago-N	6	....	....	10	5	....	....	....	....	....	0	....	....	....	....	....	....	....	....	....	....	....	....	1.7	....	....	....
45-46	Chicago-N	19	....	....	121	52	....	....	....	....	....	17	33	.515	....	....	....	....	....	....	....	....	....	....	6.4	....	....	....
46-47	Chicago-N	38	....	....	129	56	....	....	....	....	....	17	27	.630	....	....	....	70	....	....	....	....	....	....	3.4	....	....	....
NBL Season Totals		87	....	....	362	158	....	....	....	....	....	46	60	....	....	....	....	70	....	....	....	....	....	....	4.2	....	....	....
46-47	Chicago-N	7	....	....	8	2	....	....	....	....	....	4	5	.800	....	....	....	....	....	....	....	....	....	....	1.1	....	....	....
NBL Playoff Totals		7	....	....	8	2	....	....	....	....	....	4	5	....	....	....	....	....	....	....	....	....	....	....	1.1	....	....	....

• TABAK, Zan

Zan Tabak

Born: June 15, 1970. Split, Croatia.   Height: 7'   Weight: 245 lbs.   Drafted: 1991   College: none (HS: Split, CRO)

YEAR	TEAM	GP	GS	MIN	PTS	FGM	FGA	FG%	3PM	3PA	3P%	FTM	FTA	FT%	ORB	DRB	TRB	AST	PF	DQ	STL	BLK	TO	MPG	PPG	RPG	APG	PCM
94-95	Houston	37	0	182	75	24	53	.453	0	1	.000	27	44	.614	23	34	57	4	37	0	2	7	19	4.9	2.0	1.5	0.1	.389
95-96	Toronto	67	18	1332	514	225	414	.543	0	1	.000	64	114	.561	117	203	320	62	204	2	24	31	101	19.9	7.7	4.8	0.9	.406
96-97	Toronto	13	4	218	84	32	71	.451	0	0	.000	20	29	.690	20	29	49	14	35	0	6	11	21	16.8	6.5	3.8	1.1	.386
97-98	Toronto	39	29	752	248	116	249	.466	0	1	.000	16	48	.333	59	95	154	36	117	1	15	27	43	19.3	6.4	3.9	0.9	.315
97-98	Boston	18	5	232	59	26	55	.473	0	0	.000	7	13	.538	25	33	58	12	46	1	5	11	16	12.9	3.3	3.2	0.7	.322
99-00	Indiana	18	0	114	37	16	34	.471	0	0	.000	5	8	.625	16	16	32	4	13	0	3	9	11	6.3	2.1	1.8	0.2	.419
00-01	Indiana	55	14	777	216	98	186	.527	0	0	.000	20	47	.426	65	148	213	33	125	0	10	30	57	14.1	3.9	3.9	0.6	.362
NBA Season Totals		247	70	3607	1233	537	1062	.506	0	3	.000	159	303	.525	325	558	883	165	577	4	65	126	268	14.6	5.0	3.6	0.7	....
94-95	Houston	8	0	31	6	2	5	.400	0	0	.000	2	2	1.000	1	0	1	1	5	0	1	3	2	3.9	0.8	0.1	0.1	.152
99-00	Indiana	10	0	47	12	4	8	.500	0	0	.000	4	4	1.000	4	12	16	0	10	0	0	2	1	4.7	1.2	1.6	0.0	.410
00-01	Indiana	2	2	10	1	0	4	.000	0	0	.000	1	2	.500	3	0	3	0	2	0	0	0	0	5.0	0.5	1.5	0.0	-.125
NBA Playoff Totals		20	2	88	19	6	17	.353	0	0	.000	7	8	.875	8	12	20	1	17	0	1	5	3	4.4	1.0	1.0	0.1	....

• TAMAGNO, Chelso

Chelso Tamagno

Born: Mar. 20, 1912. Died: Apr.1986.   Height: 5'10".   Weight: 185 lbs.   Drafted: —   College: Michigan

YEAR	TEAM	GP	GS	MIN	PTS	FGM	FGA	FG%	3PM	3PA	3P%	FTM	FTA	FT%	ORB	DRB	TRB	AST	PF	DQ	STL	BLK	TO	MPG	PPG	RPG	APG	PCM
37-38	Wingfoots-N	17	....	....	38	17	....	....	....	....	....	4	....	....	....	....	....	....	....	....	....	....	....	....	2.2	....	....	....
38-39	Wingfoots-N	11	....	....	15	6	....	....	....	....	....	3	....	....	....	....	....	....	....	....	....	....	....	....	1.4	....	....	....
NBL Season Totals		28	....	....	53	23	....	....	....	....	....	7	....	....	....	....	....	....	....	....	....	....	....	....	1.9	....	....	....
37-38	Wingfoots-N	5	....	....	5	2	....	....	....	....	....	1	....	....	....	....	....	....	....	....	....	....	....	....	1.0	....	....	....
NBL Playoff Totals		5	....	....	5	2	....	....	....	....	....	1	....	....	....	....	....	....	....	....	....	....	....	....	1.0	....	....	....

• TANNENBAUM, Sid

Sidney Tannenbaum

Born: Oct. 8, 1925. Brooklyn, NY, United States. Died: Sept.4, 1986.   Height: 6'   Weight: 160 lbs.   Drafted: —   College: New York University

YEAR	TEAM	GP	GS	MIN	PTS	FGM	FGA	FG%	3PM	3PA	3P%	FTM	FTA	FT%	ORB	DRB	TRB	AST	PF	DQ	STL	BLK	TO	MPG	PPG	RPG	APG	PCM
47-48	New York	24	....	....	242	90	360	.250	....	....	....	62	74	.838	....	....	....	37	33	....	....	....	....	10.1	....	1.5	....
48-49	New York	32	....	....	257	96	339	.283	....	....	....	65	77	.844	....	....	....	71	53	....	....	....	....	8.0	....	2.2	....
48-49	Baltimore	14	....	....	134	50	162	.309	....	....	....	34	43	.791	....	....	....	54	21	....	....	....	....	9.6	....	3.9	....
NBA Season Totals		70	....	....	633	236	861	.274	....	....	....	161	194	.830	....	....	....	162	107	....	....	....	....	9.0	....	2.3	....
47-48	New York	3	....	....	30	11	33	.333	....	....	....	8	11	.727	....	....	....	4	8	....	....	....	....	10.0	....	1.3	....
48-49	Baltimore	3	....	....	17	6	29	.207	....	....	....	5	5	1.000	....	....	....	10	5	....	....	....	....	5.7	....	3.3	....
NBA Playoff Totals		6	....	....	47	17	62	.274	....	....	....	13	16	.813	....	....	....	14	13	....	....	....	....	7.8	....	2.3	....

• TARLAC, Dragan

Dragan Tarlac

Born: May 9, 1973. Belgrade, Yugoslavia.   Height: 6'10".   Weight: 260 lbs.   Drafted: 1995   College: none

YEAR	TEAM	GP	GS	MIN	PTS	FGM	FGA	FG%	3PM	3PA	3P%	FTM	FTA	FT%	ORB	DRB	TRB	AST	PF	DQ	STL	BLK	TO	MPG	PPG	RPG	APG	PCM
00-01	Chicago	43	12	598	103	39	99	.394	0	0	.000	25	33	.758	37	85	122	31	95	2	7	19	38	13.9	2.4	2.8	0.7	.227
NBA Season Totals		43	12	598	103	39	99	.394	0	0	.000	25	33	.758	37	85	122	31	95	2	7	19	38	13.9	2.4	2.8	0.7	....

• TARPLEY, Roy

Roy James Tarpley Jr.

Born: Nov. 28, 1964. New York, NY, United States. Height: 6'11". Weight: 230 lbs. Drafted: 1986 College: Michigan

YEAR	TEAM	GP	GS	MIN	PTS	FGM	FGA	FG%	3PM	3PA	3P%	FTM	FTA	FT%	ORB	DRB	TRB	AST	PF	DQ	STL	BLK	TO	MPG	PPG	RPG	APG	PCM
86-87	Dallas	75	1	1405	561	233	499	.467	0	3	.333	94	139	.676	180	353	533	52	232	3	56	79	98	18.7	7.5	7.1	0.7	.549
87-88	Dallas	81	9	2307	1093	444	888	.500	0	5	.000	205	277	.740	360	599	959	86	313	8	103	86	170	28.5	13.5	11.8	1.1	.652
88-89	Dallas	19	6	591	328	131	242	.541	0	1	.000	66	96	.688	77	141	218	17	70	2	28	30	46	31.1	17.3	11.5	0.9	.694
89-90	Dallas	45	35	1648	758	314	696	.451	0	6	.000	130	172	.756	189	400	589	67	160	0	79	70	117	36.6	16.8	13.1	1.5	.582
90-91	Dallas	5	5	171	102	43	79	.544	0	1	.000	16	18	.889	16	39	55	12	20	0	6	9	13	34.2	20.4	11.0	2.4	.726
94-95	Dallas	55	1	1354	691	292	610	.479	5	18	.278	102	122	.836	142	307	449	58	155	2	45	55	110	24.6	12.6	8.2	1.1	.579
NBA Season Totals		280	57	7476	3533	1457	3014	.483	6	34	.176	613	824	.744	964	1839	2803	292	950	15	317	329	554	26.7	12.6	10.0	1.0	....
86-87	Dallas	4	1	114	53	24	48	.500	0	0	.000	5	7	.714	18	24	42	1	18	1	1	7	7	28.5	13.3	10.5	0.3	.548
87-88	Dallas	17	0	563	304	125	241	.519	0	3	.000	54	73	.740	88	131	219	30	69	3	21	26	32	33.1	17.9	12.9	1.8	.719
89-90	Dallas	3	3	129	50	22	46	.478	0	1	.000	6	12	.500	9	37	46	1	12	0	7	10	9	43.0	16.7	15.3	0.3	.548
NBA Playoff Totals		24	4	806	407	171	335	.510	0	4	.000	65	92	.707	115	192	307	32	99	4	29	43	48	33.6	17.0	12.8	1.3	....

• TART, Levern

Levern Donihue (Doc) Tart

Born: June 1, 1942. Marion, SC, United States. Height: 6'2". Weight: 195 lbs. Drafted: 1964 College: Bradley

YEAR	TEAM	GP	GS	MIN	PTS	FGM	FGA	FG%	3PM	3PA	3P%	FTM	FTA	FT%	ORB	DRB	TRB	AST	PF	DQ	STL	BLK	TO	MPG	PPG	RPG	APG	PCM
67-68	New Jersey-A	31	....	1085	589	212	517	.410	0	3	.000	165	199	.829	....	....	120	102	89	0	....	....	82	35.0	19.0	3.9	3.3	.464
67-68	Oakland-A	42	....	1768	1129	421	983	.428	1	12	.083	286	367	.779	....	....	274	147	123	0	....	....	195	42.1	26.9	6.5	3.5	.553
68-69	Denver-A	20	....	345	154	56	159	.352	0	2	.000	42	56	.750	25	26	51	44	40	1	....	....	42	17.3	7.7	2.6	2.2	.396
68-69	Houston-A	6	....	138	74	28	63	.444	0	0	.000	18	29	.621	7	9	16	12	16	0	....	....	19	23.0	12.3	2.7	2.0	.433
68-69	New York-A	35	....	920	513	190	427	.445	0	1	.000	133	170	.782	68	60	128	87	85	1	....	....	88	26.3	14.7	3.7	2.5	.507
69-70	New York-A	80	....	3210	1935	756	1528	.495	11	35	.314	412	526	.783	252	294	546	264	268	4	....	....	248	40.1	24.2	6.8	3.3	.585
70-71	New York-A	27	....	985	490	192	453	.424	4	9	.444	102	133	.767	52	54	106	73	84	0	....	....	87	36.5	18.1	3.9	2.7	.414
70-71	Texas-A	33	....	821	432	165	409	.403	6	25	.240	96	120	.800	51	82	133	101	87	0	....	....	80	24.9	13.1	4.0	3.1	.511
ABA Season Totals		274	....	9272	5316	2020	4539	.445	22	87	.253	1254	1600	.784	455	525	1374	830	792	6	....	....	841	33.8	19.4	5.0	3.0	....
69-70	New York-A	7	....	313	187	70	143	.490	2	6	.333	45	52	.865	....	....	30	36	....	0	....	....	....	44.7	26.7	4.3	5.1	....
70-71	Texas-A	4	....	101	80	32	87	.368	2	12	.167	14	20	.700	11	12	23	33	12	0	....	....	8	25.3	20.0	5.8	8.3	.859
ABA Playoff Totals		11	....	414	267	102	230	.443	4	18	.222	59	72	.819	11	12	53	69	12	0	....	....	8	37.6	24.3	4.8	6.3	....

• TATUM, Earl

William Earl Tatum

Born: July 26, 1953. Mount Vernon, NY, United States. Height: 6'5". Weight: 185 lbs. Drafted: 1976 College: Marquette

YEAR	TEAM	GP	GS	MIN	PTS	FGM	FGA	FG%	3PM	3PA	3P%	FTM	FTA	FT%	ORB	DRB	TRB	AST	PF	DQ	STL	BLK	TO	MPG	PPG	RPG	APG	PCM
76-77	LA Lakers	68	....	1249	638	283	607	.466	....	....	....	72	100	.720	83	153	236	118	168	1	85	22	....	18.4	9.4	3.5	1.7	.490
77-78	LA Lakers	25	....	663	351	153	314	.487	....	....	....	45	59	.763	23	67	90	70	85	1	37	10	53	26.5	14.0	3.6	2.8	.481
77-78	Indiana	57	....	1859	822	357	773	.462	....	....	....	108	137	.788	56	149	205	226	172	4	103	30	131	32.6	14.4	3.6	4.0	.433
78-79	Boston	3	....	38	20	8	20	.400	....	....	....	4	5	.800	1	3	4	1	7	0	0	1	3	12.7	6.7	1.3	0.3	.224
78-79	Detroit	76	....	1195	592	272	607	.448	....	....	....	48	66	.727	40	81	121	72	158	3	78	33	84	15.7	7.8	1.6	0.9	.355
79-80	Cleveland	33	....	225	85	36	94	.383	2	6	.333	11	19	.579	11	15	26	20	29	0	16	5	17	6.8	2.6	0.8	0.6	.288
NBA Season Totals		262	....	5229	2508	1109	2415	.459	2	6	.333	288	386	.746	214	468	682	507	619	9	319	101	288	20.0	9.6	2.6	1.9	....
76-77	LA Lakers	11	....	356	150	67	134	.500	....	....	....	16	24	.667	16	38	54	27	34	2	15	9	....	32.4	13.6	4.9	2.5	.425
NBA Playoff Totals		11	....	356	150	67	134	.500	....	....	....	16	24	.667	16	38	54	27	34	2	15	9	....	32.4	13.6	4.9	2.5	....

• TAYLOR, Anthony

Anthony Paul Taylor

Born: Nov. 30, 1965. Los Angeles, CA, United States. Height: 6'4". Weight: 175 lbs. Drafted: 1988 College: Oregon

YEAR	TEAM	GP	GS	MIN	PTS	FGM	FGA	FG%	3PM	3PA	3P%	FTM	FTA	FT%	ORB	DRB	TRB	AST	PF	DQ	STL	BLK	TO	MPG	PPG	RPG	APG	PCM
88-89	Miami	21	7	368	144	60	151	.397	0	2	.000	24	32	.750	11	23	34	43	37	0	22	5	21	17.5	6.9	1.6	2.0	.331
NBA Season Totals		21	7	368	144	60	151	.397	0	2	.000	24	32	.750	11	23	34	43	37	0	22	5	21	17.5	6.9	1.6	2.0	....

• TAYLOR, Brian

Brian Dwight Taylor

Born: June 9, 1951. Perth Amboy, NJ, United States. Height: 6'2". Weight: 185 lbs. Drafted: 1972 College: Princeton

YEAR	TEAM	GP	GS	MIN	PTS	FGM	FGA	FG%	3PM	3PA	3P%	FTM	FTA	FT%	ORB	DRB	TRB	AST	PF	DQ	STL	BLK	TO	MPG	PPG	RPG	APG	PCM
72-73	New York-A	63	....	2038	962	395	767	.515	4	25	.160	168	226	.743	77	126	203	175	219	5	....	....	137	32.3	15.3	3.2	2.8	.431
73-74	New York-A	75	....	2505	834	363	762	.476	8	29	.276	100	143	.699	92	122	214	341	192	....	154	22	164	33.4	11.1	2.9	4.5	.385
74-75	New York-A	79	....	2611	1104	472	920	.513	10	46	.217	150	196	.765	86	146	232	282	216	....	221	26	152	33.1	14.0	2.9	3.6	.425
75-76	New York-A	54	....	1733	904	354	722	.490	32	76	.421	164	207	.792	70	92	162	204	138	....	152	22	153	32.1	16.7	3.0	3.8	.500
76-77	Kansas City	72	....	2488	1227	501	995	.504	....	....	....	225	275	.818	88	150	238	320	206	1	199	16	....	34.6	17.0	3.3	4.4	.506
77-78	Denver	39	....	1222	452	182	403	.452	....	....	....	88	115	.765	30	68	98	132	120	1	71	9	78	31.3	11.6	2.5	3.4	.352
78-79	San Diego	20	....	212	76	30	83	.361	....	....	....	16	18	.889	13	13	26	20	34	0	24	0	16	10.6	3.8	1.3	1.0	.306
79-80	San Diego	78	....	2754	1056	418	895	.467	90	239	.377	130	162	.802	76	112	188	335	246	6	147	25	112	35.3	13.5	2.4	4.3	.387
80-81	San Diego	80	....	2312	810	310	591	.525	44	115	**.383**	146	185	.789	58	93	151	440	212	0	118	23	112	28.9	10.1	1.9	5.5	.468
81-82	San Diego	41	40	1274	443	165	328	.503	23	63	.365	90	110	.818	26	70	96	229	113	1	47	9	82	31.1	10.8	2.3	5.6	.426
NBA Season Totals		330	40	10262	4064	1606	3295	.487	157	417	.376	695	865	.803	291	506	797	1476	931	9	606	82	428	31.1	12.3	2.4	4.5	....
ABA Season Totals		271	....	8887	3804	1584	3171	.500	54	176	.307	582	772	.754	325	486	811	1002	765	5	500	70	606	32.8	14.0	3.0	3.7	....
Career Totals		601	40	19149	7868	3190	6466	.493	211	593	.356	1277	1637	.780	616	992	1608	2478	1696	14	1106	152	1034	31.9	13.1	2.7	4.1	....
72-73	New York-A	5	....	166	68	28	58	.483	0	1	.000	12	15	.800	3	13	16	11	14	1	....	....	10	33.2	13.6	3.2	2.2	.361
73-74	New York-A	14	....	507	197	86	166	.518	2	3	.667	23	30	.767	32	29	61	62	45	....	33	4	32	36.2	14.1	4.4	4.4	.452
74-75	New York-A	5	....	186	31	13	36	.361	1	3	.333	4	4	1.000	4	8	12	14	21	....	7	1	8	37.2	6.2	2.4	2.8	.148
75-76	New York-A	13	....	475	205	81	213	.380	9	30	.300	34	46	.739	15	19	34	46	37	....	26	3	31	36.5	15.8	2.6	3.5	.309
ABA Playoff Totals		37	....	1334	501	208	473	.440	12	37	.324	73	95	.768	54	69	123	133	117	1	66	8	81	36.1	13.5	3.3	3.6	....

YEAR	TEAM	GP	GS	MIN	PTS	FGM	FGA	FG%	3PM	3PA	3P%	FTM	FTA	FT%	ORB	DRB	TRB	AST	PF	DQ	STL	BLK	TO	MPG	PPG	RPG	APG	PCM

• TAYLOR, Fatty
Roland Morris (Fatty) Taylor

Born: Mar. 13, 1946. Washington, DC, United States.   Height: 6'   Weight: 175 lbs.   Drafted: 1969   College: LaSalle

YEAR	TEAM	GP	GS	MIN	PTS	FGM	FGA	FG%	3PM	3PA	3P%	FTM	FTA	FT%	ORB	DRB	TRB	AST	PF	DQ	STL	BLK	TO	MPG	PPG	RPG	APG	PCM
69-70	Washington-A	83	....	1994	665	243	520	.467	1	6	.167	178	264	.674	176	201	377	201	285	4	....	....	157	24.0	8.0	4.5	2.4	.412
70-71	Virginia-A	84	....	1629	539	180	393	.458	4	22	.182	175	256	.684	102	161	263	225	228	3	....	....	142	19.4	6.4	3.1	2.3	.445
71-72	Virginia-A	84	....	2669	777	306	680	.450	1	15	.067	164	258	.636	178	238	416	321	302	3	....	....	206	31.8	9.3	5.0	3.8	.375
72-73	Virginia-A	78	....	2553	785	316	679	.465	3	7	.429	150	248	.605	137	181	318	374	266	3	210	....	237	32.7	10.1	4.1	4.8	.389
73-74	Virginia-A	80	....	2812	772	292	709	.412	3	19	.158	185	256	.723	124	253	377	416	270	....	215	15	279	35.2	9.7	4.7	5.2	.379
74-75	Denver-A	76	....	2018	637	251	586	.428	6	21	.286	129	172	.750	85	136	221	337	238	....	172	16	248	26.6	8.4	2.9	4.4	.389
75-76	Virginia-A	76	....	2483	622	243	600	.405	11	51	.216	125	173	.723	117	224	341	401	212	....	206	16	247	32.7	8.2	4.5	5.3	.377
76-77	Denver	79	....	1548	301	132	314	.420	....	....	....	37	65	.569	90	121	211	288	202	0	132	9	....	19.6	3.8	2.7	3.6	.358
NBA Season Totals		79	....	1548	301	132	314	.420	....	....	....	37	65	.569	90	121	211	288	202	0	132	9	....	19.6	3.8	2.7	3.6	....
ABA Season Totals		561	....	16158	4797	1831	4167	.439	29	141	.206	1106	1627	.680	919	1394	2313	2275	1801	13	**803**	47	1516	28.8	8.6	4.1	4.1	....
Career Totals		640	....	17706	5098	1963	4481	.438	29	141	.206	1143	1692	.676	1009	1515	2524	2563	2003	13	**935**	56	1516	27.7	8.0	3.9	4.0	....
69-70	Washington-A	7	....	129	10	5	11	.455	0	0	.000	0	0	.000	....	....	22	19	....	0	....	....	6	18.4	1.4	3.1	2.7	....
70-71	Virginia-A	12	....	214	53	17	40	.425	0	2	.000	19	28	.679	18	19	37	27	37	1	....	....	18	17.8	4.4	3.1	2.3	.365
71-72	Virginia-A	11	....	382	115	47	106	.443	1	3	.333	20	30	.667	15	42	57	45	41	0	....	....	39	34.7	10.5	5.2	4.1	.370
72-73	Virginia-A	5	....	169	41	13	38	.342	1	2	.500	14	15	.933	4	17	21	14	19	0	....	....	18	33.8	8.2	4.2	2.8	.259
73-74	Virginia-A	5	....	167	39	16	54	.296	1	6	.167	6	11	.545	12	13	25	25	11	....	8	3	17	33.4	7.8	5.0	5.0	.297
74-75	Denver-A	13	....	275	73	29	64	.453	0	1	.000	15	19	.789	16	22	38	37	36	....	27	2	15	21.2	5.6	2.9	2.8	.360
76-77	Denver	1	....	1	0	0	0	.000	....	....	....	0	0	.000	0	0	0	0	0	0	0	0	....	1.0	0.0	0.0	0.0	.000
NBA Playoff Totals		1	....	1	0	0	0	.000	....	....	....	0	0	.000	0	0	0	0	0	0	0	0	....	1.0	0.0	0.0	0.0	....
ABA Playoff Totals		53	....	1336	331	127	313	.406	3	14	.214	74	103	.718	65	113	200	167	144	1	35	5	113	25.2	6.2	3.8	3.2	....
Career Playoff Totals		54	....	1337	331	127	313	.406	3	14	.214	74	103	.718	65	113	200	167	144	1	35	5	113	24.8	6.1	3.7	3.1	....

• TAYLOR, Fred
Fredrick Ollie Taylor

Born: Feb. 5, 1948. Houston, TX, United States.   Height: 6'5".   Weight: 180 lbs.   Drafted: 1970   College: Pan American

YEAR	TEAM	GP	GS	MIN	PTS	FGM	FGA	FG%	3PM	3PA	3P%	FTM	FTA	FT%	ORB	DRB	TRB	AST	PF	DQ	STL	BLK	TO	MPG	PPG	RPG	APG	PCM
70-71	Phoenix	54	....	552	298	110	284	.387	....	....	....	78	125	.624	....	....	86	51	113	0	....	....	....	10.2	5.5	1.6	0.9	.383
71-72	Phoenix	13	....	69	16	6	27	.222	....	....	....	4	13	.308	....	....	17	7	8	0	....	....	....	5.3	1.2	1.3	0.5	.191
71-72	Cincinnati	21	....	214	71	30	90	.333	....	....	....	11	19	.579	....	....	37	11	32	0	....	....	....	10.2	3.4	1.8	0.5	.217
NBA Season Totals		88	....	835	385	146	401	.364	....	....	....	93	157	.592	....	....	140	69	153	0	....	....	....	9.5	4.4	1.6	0.8	....

• TAYLOR, Jay
Cornelius F. (Jay) Taylor

Born: Oct. 3, 1967. Aurora, IL, United States.   Height: 6'3".   Weight: 190 lbs.   Drafted: —   College: Eastern Illinois

YEAR	TEAM	GP	GS	MIN	PTS	FGM	FGA	FG%	3PM	3PA	3P%	FTM	FTA	FT%	ORB	DRB	TRB	AST	PF	DQ	STL	BLK	TO	MPG	PPG	RPG	APG	PCM
89-90	New Jersey	17	0	114	51	21	52	.404	3	13	.231	6	9	.667	5	6	11	5	9	0	5	3	10	6.7	3.0	0.6	0.3	.264
NBA Season Totals		17	0	114	51	21	52	.404	3	13	.231	6	9	.667	5	6	11	5	9	0	5	3	10	6.7	3.0	0.6	0.3	....

• TAYLOR, Jeff
Jeffrey Taylor

Born: Jan. 1, 1960. Blytheville, AR, United States.   Height: 6'4".   Weight: 175 lbs.   Drafted: 1982   College: Texas Tech

YEAR	TEAM	GP	GS	MIN	PTS	FGM	FGA	FG%	3PM	3PA	3P%	FTM	FTA	FT%	ORB	DRB	TRB	AST	PF	DQ	STL	BLK	TO	MPG	PPG	RPG	APG	PCM
82-83	Houston	44	5	774	158	64	160	.400	0	1	.000	30	46	.652	25	53	78	110	82	1	40	15	62	17.6	3.6	1.8	2.5	.274
86-87	Detroit	12	0	44	21	6	10	.600	0	0	.000	9	10	.900	1	3	4	3	4	0	2	1	8	3.7	1.8	0.3	0.3	.391
NBA Season Totals		56	5	818	179	70	170	.412	0	1	.000	39	56	.696	26	56	82	113	86	1	42	16	70	14.6	3.2	1.5	2.0	....

• TAYLOR, Johnny
Johnny Antonio Taylor

Born: June 4, 1974. Chattanooga, TN, United States.   Height: 6'9".   Weight: 220 lbs.   Drafted: 1997   College: Tennessee (Chatanooga)

YEAR	TEAM	GP	GS	MIN	PTS	FGM	FGA	FG%	3PM	3PA	3P%	FTM	FTA	FT%	ORB	DRB	TRB	AST	PF	DQ	STL	BLK	TO	MPG	PPG	RPG	APG	PCM
97-98	Orlando	12	0	108	38	13	37	.351	1	2	.500	11	16	.688	4	9	13	1	22	0	3	2	8	9.0	3.2	1.1	0.1	.129
98-99	Denver	36	9	724	207	82	198	.414	26	68	.382	17	23	.739	30	71	101	24	97	1	28	17	34	20.1	5.8	2.8	0.7	.255
99-00	Denver	1	0	5	0	0	2	.000	0	0	.000	0	0	.000	0	1	1	0	1	0	0	0	0	5.0	0.0	1.0	0.0	-.272
99-00	Orlando	5	0	29	11	5	12	.417	1	1	1.000	0	0	.000	2	3	5	1	4	0	1	1	2	5.8	2.2	1.0	0.2	.292
NBA Season Totals		54	9	866	256	100	249	.402	28	71	.394	28	39	.718	36	84	120	26	124	1	32	20	44	16.0	4.7	2.2	0.5	....

• TAYLOR, Leonard
Leonard Chester Taylor Jr.

Born: May 2, 1966. Los Angeles, CA, United States.   Height: 6'8".   Weight: 220 lbs.   Drafted: —   College: California

YEAR	TEAM	GP	GS	MIN	PTS	FGM	FGA	FG%	3PM	3PA	3P%	FTM	FTA	FT%	ORB	DRB	TRB	AST	PF	DQ	STL	BLK	TO	MPG	PPG	RPG	APG	PCM
89-90	Golden State	10	0	37	11	0	6	.000	0	1	.000	11	16	.688	4	8	12	1	4	0	0	0	5	3.7	1.1	1.2	0.1	.237
NBA Season Totals		10	0	37	11	0	6	.000	0	1	.000	11	16	.688	4	8	12	1	4	0	0	0	5	3.7	1.1	1.2	0.1	....

• TAYLOR, Maurice
Maurice De Shawn Taylor

Born: Oct. 30, 1976. Detroit, MI, United States.   Height: 6'9".   Weight: 260 lbs.   Drafted: 1997   College: Michigan

YEAR	TEAM	GP	GS	MIN	PTS	FGM	FGA	FG%	3PM	3PA	3P%	FTM	FTA	FT%	ORB	DRB	TRB	AST	PF	DQ	STL	BLK	TO	MPG	PPG	RPG	APG	PCM
97-98	LA Clippers	71	3	1513	815	321	675	.476	0	1	.000	173	244	.709	118	178	296	53	222	7	34	40	107	21.3	11.5	4.2	0.7	.433
98-99	LA Clippers	46	45	1505	773	311	675	.461	1	6	.167	150	206	.728	100	142	242	67	179	5	16	29	120	32.7	16.8	5.3	1.5	.377
99-00	LA Clippers	62	60	2227	1060	458	988	.464	1	8	.125	143	201	.711	96	304	400	101	217	4	51	48	169	35.9	17.1	6.5	1.6	.388
00-01	Houston	69	69	1972	899	390	797	.489	0	4	.000	119	162	.735	109	269	378	104	208	3	28	38	125	28.6	13.0	5.5	1.5	.417
02-03	Houston	67	9	1377	562	231	535	.432	0	2	.000	100	138	.725	95	143	238	66	151	0	22	22	100	20.6	8.4	3.6	1.0	.318
NBA Season Totals		315	186	8594	4109	1711	3670	.466	2	21	.095	685	951	.720	518	1036	1554	391	977	19	151	177	621	27.3	13.0	4.9	1.2	....

YEAR	TEAM	GP	GS	MIN	PTS	FGM	FGA	FG%	3PM	3PA	3P%	FTM	FTA	FT%	ORB	DRB	TRB	AST	PF	DQ	STL	BLK	TO	MPG	PPG	RPG	APG	PCM

• TAYLOR, Oliver

Oliver Harold Taylor

Born: Mar. 7, 1947. New York, NY, United States. Height: 6'2". Weight: 194 lbs. Drafted: 1970 College: Houston

YEAR	TEAM	GP	GS	MIN	PTS	FGM	FGA	FG%	3PM	3PA	3P%	FTM	FTA	FT%	ORB	DRB	TRB	AST	PF	DQ	STL	BLK	TO	MPG	PPG	RPG	APG	PCM
70-71	New York-A	80	....	1617	694	251	496	.506	5	12	.417	187	277	.675	111	196	307	146	231	2	....	....	162	20.2	8.7	3.8	1.8	.489
71-72	New York-A	82	....	1891	708	245	542	.452	0	6	.000	218	308	.708	128	202	330	153	213	2	....	....	153	23.1	8.6	4.0	1.9	.410
72-73	San Diego-A	69	....	2121	947	325	757	.429	11	55	.200	286	425	.673	156	209	365	275	191	1	....	....	207	30.7	13.7	5.3	4.0	.491
73-74	Carolina-A	23	....	443	162	56	126	.444	1	3	.333	49	71	.690	29	45	74	44	54	....	17	6	49	19.3	7.0	3.2	1.9	.413
73-74	New York-A	8	....	76	28	9	24	.375	1	1	1.000	9	15	.600	5	9	14	10	9	....	3	0	9	9.5	3.5	1.8	1.3	.423
ABA Season Totals		262	....	6148	2539	886	1945	.456	18	77	.234	749	1096	.683	429	661	1090	628	698	5	20	6	580	23.5	9.7	4.2	2.4	....
70-71	New York-A	6	....	128	53	15	31	.484	1	2	.500	22	29	.759	7	8	15	13	18	0	....	....	10	21.3	8.8	2.5	2.2	.451
71-72	New York-A	19	....	702	211	79	180	.439	0	1	.000	53	72	.736	....	....	100	47	60	....	....	....	68	36.9	11.1	5.3	2.5	.325
72-73	San Diego-A	4	....	139	49	20	52	.385	2	6	.333	7	14	.500	15	15	30	12	12	0	....	....	17	34.8	12.3	7.5	3.0	.373
73-74	Carolina-A	2	....	25	9	4	7	.571	0	0	.000	1	1	1.000	3	0	3	1	2	....	2	0	2	12.5	4.5	1.5	0.5	.371
ABA Playoff Totals		31	....	994	322	118	270	.437	3	9	.333	83	116	.716	25	23	148	73	92	0	2	0	97	32.1	10.4	4.8	2.4	....

• TAYLOR, Ronald

Ronald (Lurch) Taylor

Born: Nov. 21, 1947. Torrance, CA, United States. Height: 7'1". Weight: 265 lbs. Drafted: 1969 College: USC

YEAR	TEAM	GP	GS	MIN	PTS	FGM	FGA	FG%	3PM	3PA	3P%	FTM	FTA	FT%	ORB	DRB	TRB	AST	PF	DQ	STL	BLK	TO	MPG	PPG	RPG	APG	PCM
69-70	New York-A	72	....	873	360	153	318	.481	0	0	.000	54	97	.557	119	167	286	64	207	11	....	....	120	12.1	5.0	4.0	0.9	.492
69-70	Washington-A	3	....	37	9	3	9	.333	0	0	.000	3	5	.600	1	6	7	0	11	0	....	....	4	12.3	3.0	2.3	0.0	.116
70-71	Virginia-A	1	....	25	2	1	9	.111	0	0	.000	0	1	.000	0	0	0	4	6	0	....	....	0	25.0	2.0	0.0	4.0	-.097
71-72	Pittsburgh-A	1	....	4	0	0	1	.000	0	0	.000	0	0	.000	1	0	1	0	5	0	....	....	1	4.0	0.0	1.0	0.0	-.549
ABA Season Totals		77	....	939	371	157	337	.466	0	0	.000	57	103	.553	121	173	294	68	229	11	....	....	125	12.2	4.8	3.8	0.9	....
69-70	New York-A	2	....	5	0	0	4	.000	0	0	.000	0	1	.000	....	....	2	0	....	0	....	....	....	2.5	0.0	1.0	0.0	....
ABA Playoff Totals		2	....	5	0	0	4	.000	0	0	.000	0	1	.000	....	....	2	0	....	0	....	....	....	2.5	0.0	1.0	0.0	....

• TAYLOR, Vince

Vincent Caldwell Taylor

Born: Sept. 11, 1960. Lexington, KY, United States. Height: 6'5". Weight: 180 lbs. Drafted: 1982 College: Duke

YEAR	TEAM	GP	GS	MIN	PTS	FGM	FGA	FG%	3PM	3PA	3P%	FTM	FTA	FT%	ORB	DRB	TRB	AST	PF	DQ	STL	BLK	TO	MPG	PPG	RPG	APG	PCM
82-83	New York	31	0	321	95	37	102	.363	0	0	.000	21	32	.656	19	17	36	41	54	1	20	2	31	10.4	3.1	1.2	1.3	.238
NBA Season Totals		31	0	321	95	37	102	.363	0	0	.000	21	32	.656	19	17	36	41	54	1	20	2	31	10.4	3.1	1.2	1.3	....

• TEAGLE, Terry

Terry Michael Teagle

Born: Apr. 10, 1960. Broaddus, TX, United States. Height: 6'5". Weight: 195 lbs. Drafted: 1982 College: Baylor

YEAR	TEAM	GP	GS	MIN	PTS	FGM	FGA	FG%	3PM	3PA	3P%	FTM	FTA	FT%	ORB	DRB	TRB	AST	PF	DQ	STL	BLK	TO	MPG	PPG	RPG	APG	PCM
82-83	Houston	73	44	1708	761	332	776	.428	10	29	.345	87	125	.696	74	120	194	150	171	0	53	18	139	23.4	10.4	2.7	2.1	.319
83-84	Houston	68	0	616	340	148	315	.470	7	27	.259	37	44	.841	28	50	78	63	81	1	13	4	61	9.1	5.0	1.1	0.9	.394
84-85	Detroit	2	0	5	2	1	2	.500	0	0	.000	0	0	.000	0	0	0	0	2	0	0	0	1	2.5	1.0	0.0	0.0	-.159
84-85	Golden State	19	3	344	173	73	135	.541	2	4	.500	25	35	.714	22	21	43	14	34	0	13	5	13	18.1	9.1	2.3	0.7	.449
85-86	Golden State	82	52	2158	1165	475	958	.496	4	25	.160	211	265	.796	96	139	235	115	241	2	71	34	139	26.3	14.2	2.9	1.4	.412
86-87	Golden State	82	0	1650	922	370	808	.458	0	10	.000	182	234	.778	68	107	175	105	190	0	68	13	115	20.1	11.2	2.1	1.3	.391
87-88	Golden State	47	4	958	594	248	546	.454	1	9	.111	97	121	.802	41	40	81	61	95	0	32	4	80	20.4	12.6	1.7	1.3	.376
88-89	Golden State	66	41	1569	1002	409	859	.476	2	12	.167	182	225	.809	110	153	263	96	173	2	79	17	119	23.8	15.2	4.0	1.5	.516
89-90	Golden State	82	49	2376	1323	538	1122	.480	3	14	.214	244	294	.830	114	253	367	155	231	3	91	15	148	29.0	16.1	4.5	1.9	.469
90-91	LA Lakers	82	0	1498	815	335	757	.443	0	9	.000	145	177	.819	82	99	181	82	165	1	31	8	82	18.3	9.9	2.2	1.0	.364
91-92	LA Lakers	82	0	1602	880	364	805	.452	1	4	.250	151	197	.766	91	92	183	113	148	0	66	9	115	19.5	10.7	2.2	1.4	.396
92-93	Houston	2	0	25	5	2	7	.286	0	0	.000	1	2	.500	0	3	3	2	1	0	0	0	1	12.5	2.5	1.5	1.0	.136
NBA Season Totals		687	193	14509	7982	3295	7090	.465	30	143	.210	1362	1719	.792	726	1077	1803	956	1532	9	517	127	1013	21.1	11.6	2.6	1.4	....
86-87	Golden State	10	0	233	144	57	124	.460	0	2	.000	30	38	.789	13	7	20	13	27	0	8	1	14	23.3	14.4	2.0	1.3	.400
88-89	Golden State	8	0	240	158	70	141	.496	0	2	.000	18	22	.818	15	22	37	10	27	0	8	3	13	30.0	19.8	4.6	1.3	.503
90-91	LA Lakers	18	1	274	119	47	125	.376	0	0	.000	25	32	.781	8	20	28	11	31	0	8	4	16	15.2	6.6	1.6	0.6	.229
91-92	LA Lakers	4	2	126	70	27	55	.491	0	0	.000	16	20	.800	3	10	13	8	18	1	5	2	8	31.5	17.5	3.3	2.0	.424
92-93	Houston	5	0	12	4	2	5	.400	0	0	.000	0	2	.000	0	0	0	0	1	0	0	0	3	2.4	0.8	0.0	0.0	-.250
NBA Playoff Totals		45	3	885	495	203	450	.451	0	4	.000	89	114	.781	39	59	98	42	104	1	29	10	54	19.7	11.0	2.2	0.9	....

• TEMPLE, Collis

Collis Temple Jr.

Born: Nov. 8, 1952. Kentwood, LA, United States. Height: 6'8". Weight: 220 lbs. Drafted: 1974 College: Louisiana State

YEAR	TEAM	GP	GS	MIN	PTS	FGM	FGA	FG%	3PM	3PA	3P%	FTM	FTA	FT%	ORB	DRB	TRB	AST	PF	DQ	STL	BLK	TO	MPG	PPG	RPG	APG	PCM
74-75	San Antonio-A	24	....	102	42	17	41	.415	0	1	.000	8	10	.800	14	17	31	15	29	....	4	4	12	4.3	1.8	1.3	0.6	.501
ABA Season Totals		24	....	102	42	17	41	.415	0	1	.000	8	10	.800	14	17	31	15	29	....	4	4	12	4.3	1.8	1.3	0.6	....

• TERJESEN, Irving

Irving Terjesen

Born: Mar. 4, 1915. Died: Apr.12, 1990. Height: 6'3". Weight: 195 lbs. Drafted: — College: New York University

YEAR	TEAM	GP	GS	MIN	PTS	FGM	FGA	FG%	3PM	3PA	3P%	FTM	FTA	FT%	ORB	DRB	TRB	AST	PF	DQ	STL	BLK	TO	MPG	PPG	RPG	APG	PCM
38-39	Non-Skids-N	25	....	....	99	38	....	....	....	....	....	23	....	....	....	....	....	....	....	....	....	....	....	....	4.0	....	....	....
39-40	Non-Skids-N	26	....	....	81	31	....	....	....	....	....	19	....	....	....	....	....	....	....	....	....	....	....	....	3.1	....	....	....
40-41	Non-Skids-N	11	....	....	15	6	....	....	....	....	....	3	....	....	....	....	....	....	....	....	....	....	....	....	1.4	....	....	....
NBL Season Totals		62	....	....	195	75	....	....	....	....	....	45	....	....	....	....	....	....	....	....	....	....	....	....	3.1	....	....	....
38-39	Non-Skids-N	5	....	....	13	5	....	....	....	....	....	3	....	....	....	....	....	....	....	....	....	....	....	....	2.6	....	....	....
39-40	Non-Skids-N	7	....	....	5	2	....	....	....	....	....	1	....	....	....	....	....	....	....	....	....	....	....	....	0.7	....	....	....
40-41	Non-Skids-N	1	....	....	4	2	....	....	....	....	....	0	....	....	....	....	....	....	....	....	....	....	....	....	4.0	....	....	....
NBL Playoff Totals		13	....	....	22	9	....	....	....	....	....	4	....	....	....	....	....	....	....	....	....	....	....	....	1.7	....	....	....

YEAR	TEAM	GP	GS	MIN	PTS	FGM	FGA	FG%	3PM	3PA	3P%	FTM	FTA	FT%	ORB	DRB	TRB	AST	PF	DQ	STL	BLK	TO	MPG	PPG	RPG	APG	PCM

● TERRELL, Ira

Ira Edmondson Terrell

Born: June 19, 1954. Dallas, TX, United States. Height: 6'8". Weight: 200 lbs. Drafted: 1976 College: Southern Methodist

YEAR	TEAM	GP	GS	MIN	PTS	FGM	FGA	FG%	3PM	3PA	3P%	FTM	FTA	FT%	ORB	DRB	TRB	AST	PF	DQ	STL	BLK	TO	MPG	PPG	RPG	APG	PCM
76-77	Phoenix	78	....	1751	665	277	545	.508	....	....	....	111	176	.631	99	288	387	103	165	0	41	47	....	22.4	8.5	5.0	1.3	.449
78-79	New Orleans	31	....	572	153	63	144	.438	....	....	....	27	38	.711	34	75	109	26	73	0	15	22	37	18.5	4.9	3.5	0.8	.296
78-79	Portland	18	....	160	68	30	54	.556	....	....	....	8	15	.533	10	27	37	15	27	0	7	6	16	8.9	3.8	2.1	0.8	.489
NBA Season Totals		127	....	2483	886	370	743	.498	....	....	....	146	229	.638	143	390	533	144	265	0	63	75	53	19.6	7.0	4.2	1.1	
78-79	Portland	1	....	6	0	0	4	.000	....	....	....	0	0	.000	0	2	2	0	0	0	0	0	0	6.0	0.0	2.0	0.0	-.299
NBA Playoff Totals		1	....	6	0	0	4	.000	....	....	....	0	0	.000	0	2	2	0	0	0	0	0	0	6.0	0.0	2.0	0.0	....

● TERRY, Carlos

Carlos Fernando Terry

Born: June 22, 1956. Lexington, NC, United States. Died: Mar.12, 1989. Height: 6'5". Weight: 210 lbs. Drafted: 1978 College: Winston-Salem State

YEAR	TEAM	GP	GS	MIN	PTS	FGM	FGA	FG%	3PM	3PA	3P%	FTM	FTA	FT%	ORB	DRB	TRB	AST	PF	DQ	STL	BLK	TO	MPG	PPG	RPG	APG	PCM
80-81	Washington	26	....	504	188	80	160	.500	0	6	.000	28	42	.667	43	73	116	70	68	1	27	13	57	19.4	7.2	4.5	2.7	.485
81-82	Washington	13	0	60	9	3	15	.200	0	3	.000	3	4	.750	5	7	12	8	15	0	3	1	5	4.6	0.7	0.9	0.6	.156
82-83	Washington	55	3	514	88	39	106	.368	0	2	.000	10	15	.667	27	72	99	46	79	1	24	13	22	9.3	1.6	1.8	0.8	.278
NBA Season Totals		94	3	1078	285	122	281	.434	0	11	.000	41	61	.672	75	152	227	124	162	2	54	27	84	11.5	3.0	2.4	1.3	....
81-82	Washington	3	0	5	0	0	0	.000	0	0	.000	0	0	.000	0	1	1	0	0	0	0	0	0	1.7	0.0	0.3	0.0	.184
NBA Playoff Totals		3	0	5	0	0	0	.000	0	0	.000	0	0	.000	0	1	1	0	0	0	0	0	0	1.7	0.0	0.3	0.0	....

● TERRY, Chuck

Allen Charles (Teen Angel, Carlos) Terry

Born: Sept. 27, 1950. Long Beach, CA, United States. Height: 6'6". Weight: 215 lbs. Drafted: 1972 College: Long Beach State

YEAR	TEAM	GP	GS	MIN	PTS	FGM	FGA	FG%	3PM	3PA	3P%	FTM	FTA	FT%	ORB	DRB	TRB	AST	PF	DQ	STL	BLK	TO	MPG	PPG	RPG	APG	PCM
72-73	Milwaukee	67	....	693	127	55	162	.340	....	....	....	17	24	.708	....	....	145	40	116	1	....	....	....	10.3	1.9	2.2	0.6	.220
73-74	San Antonio-A	61	....	1093	301	132	294	.449	1	2	.500	36	41	.878	67	99	166	72	139	....	18	5	33	17.9	4.9	2.7	1.2	.297
73-74	Milwaukee	7	....	32	8	4	12	.333	....	....	....	0	0	.000	1	2	3	4	4	0	2	0	....	4.6	1.1	0.4	0.6	.207
74-75	San Antonio-A	79	....	1186	338	148	313	.473	3	8	.375	39	53	.736	77	140	217	69	146	....	37	3	.37	15.0	4.3	2.7	0.9	.329
75-76	New York-A	66	....	970	220	96	246	.390	6	21	.286	22	29	.759	45	99	144	38	116	....	36	6	21	14.7	3.3	2.2	0.6	.208
76-77	New York	61	....	1075	304	128	318	.403	....	....	....	48	62	.774	43	100	143	39	120	0	58	10	....	17.6	5.0	2.3	0.6	.233
NBA Season Totals		135	....	1800	439	187	492	.380	....	....	....	65	86	.756	44	102	291	83	240	1	60	10	....	13.3	3.3	2.2	0.6	
ABA Season Totals		206	....	3249	859	376	853	.441	10	31	.323	97	123	.789	189	338	527	179	401	....	91	14	91	15.8	4.2	2.6	0.9	
Career Totals		341	....	5049	1298	563	1345	.419	10	31	.323	162	209	.775	233	440	818	262	641	1	151	24	91	14.8	3.8	2.4	0.8	....
72-73	Milwaukee	5	....	18	8	4	5	.800	....	....	....	0	0	.000	....	....	3	1	2	0	....	....	....	3.6	1.6	0.6	0.2	.556
73-74	San Antonio-A	7	....	112	26	11	24	.458	0	0	.000	4	6	.667	10	14	24	7	9	....	0	0	3	16.0	3.7	3.4	1.0	.346
74-75	San Antonio-A	5	....	123	27	12	25	.480	0	0	.000	3	4	.750	2	17	19	2	14	....	3	1	1	24.6	5.4	3.8	0.4	.227
75-76	New York-A	4	....	23	0	0	7	.000	0	2	.000	0	0	.000	1	1	2	1	7	....	0	0	5	5.8	0.0	0.5	0.3	-.281
NBA Playoff Totals		5	....	18	8	4	5	.800	....	....	....	0	0	.000	....	....	3	1	2	0	....	....	....	3.6	1.6	0.6	0.2	
ABA Playoff Totals		16	....	258	53	23	56	.411	0	2	.000	7	10	.700	13	32	45	10	30	....	3	1	9	16.1	3.3	2.8	0.6	
Career Playoff Totals		21	....	276	61	27	61	.443	0	2	.000	7	10	.700	13	32	48	11	32	0	3	1	9	13.1	2.9	2.3	0.5	....

● TERRY, Claude

Claude Lewis Terry

Born: Jan. 12, 1950. Salida, CA, United States. Height: 6'4". Weight: 195 lbs. Drafted: 1972 College: Stanford

YEAR	TEAM	GP	GS	MIN	PTS	FGM	FGA	FG%	3PM	3PA	3P%	FTM	FTA	FT%	ORB	DRB	TRB	AST	PF	DQ	STL	BLK	TO	MPG	PPG	RPG	APG	PCM
72-73	Denver-A	68	....	667	324	120	285	.421	10	24	.417	74	114	.649	45	30	75	62	111	0	....	....	69	9.8	4.8	1.1	0.9	.365
73-74	Denver-A	60	....	587	300	113	255	.443	14	35	.400	60	69	.870	26	45	71	73	64	....	12	3	57	9.8	5.0	1.2	1.2	.496
74-75	Denver-A	70	....	989	466	193	364	.530	10	25	.400	70	92	.761	57	83	140	111	82	....	33	2	80	14.1	6.7	2.0	1.6	.521
75-76	Denver-A	79	....	1349	557	232	500	.464	13	55	.236	80	89	.899	42	110	152	146	116	....	40	5	96	17.1	7.1	1.9	1.8	.415
76-77	Buffalo	33	....	304	116	49	104	.471	....	....	....	18	23	.783	4	24	28	33	27	0	11	0	....	9.2	3.5	0.8	1.0	.383
76-77	Atlanta	12	....	241	112	47	87	.540	....	....	....	18	21	.857	8	10	18	25	21	0	9	1	....	20.1	9.3	1.5	2.1	.461
77-78	Atlanta	27	....	166	59	25	68	.368	....	....	....	9	11	.818	3	12	15	7	14	0	6	0	8	6.1	2.2	0.6	0.3	.203
NBA Season Totals		72	....	711	287	121	259	.467	....	....	....	45	55	.818	15	46	61	65	62	0	26	1	8	9.9	4.0	0.8	0.9	....
ABA Season Totals		277	....	3592	1647	658	1404	.469	47	139	.338	284	364	.780	170	268	438	392	373	0	85	10	302	13.0	5.9	1.6	1.4	
Career Totals		349	....	4303	1934	779	1663	.468	47	139	.338	329	419	.785	185	314	499	457	435	0	111	11	310	12.3	5.5	1.4	1.3	....
72-73	Denver-A	4	....	36	5	2	9	.222	0	2	.000	1	1	1.000	1	2	3	2	5	0	....	....	4	9.0	1.3	0.8	0.5	.038
74-75	Denver-A	12	....	135	50	23	58	.397	1	10	.100	3	5	.600	5	8	13	13	18	....	1	1	4	11.3	4.2	1.1	1.1	.267
75-76	Denver-A	12	....	159	49	18	50	.360	0	7	.000	13	17	.765	4	17	21	17	15	....	7	1	15	13.3	4.1	1.8	1.4	.312
ABA Playoff Totals		28	....	330	104	43	117	.368	1	19	.053	17	23	.739	10	27	37	32	38	0	8	2	23	11.8	3.7	1.3	1.1	....

● TERRY, Jason

Jason Eugene Terry

Born: Sept. 15, 1977. Seattle, WA, United States. Height: 6'2". Weight: 176 lbs. Drafted: 1999 College: Arizona

YEAR	TEAM	GP	GS	MIN	PTS	FGM	FGA	FG%	3PM	3PA	3P%	FTM	FTA	FT%	ORB	DRB	TRB	AST	PF	DQ	STL	BLK	TO	MPG	PPG	RPG	APG	PCM
99-00	Atlanta	81	27	1888	657	249	600	.415	46	157	.293	113	140	.807	24	142	166	346	133	0	90	10	156	23.3	8.1	2.0	4.3	.394
00-01	Atlanta	82	77	3089	1619	596	1367	.436	124	314	.395	303	358	.846	42	227	269	403	204	2	104	12	239	37.7	19.7	3.3	4.9	.449
01-02	Atlanta	78	78	2967	1504	524	1219	.430	172	444	.387	284	340	.835	40	230	270	444	156	0	144	13	181	38.0	19.3	3.5	5.7	.501
02-03	Atlanta	81	81	3081	1395	488	1141	.428	160	431	.371	259	292	.887	37	242	279	600	175	2	126	14	249	38.0	17.2	3.4	7.4	.492
NBA Season Totals		322	263	11025	5175	1857	4327	.429	502	1346	.373	959	1130	.849	143	841	984	1793	668	4	464	49	825	34.2	16.1	3.1	5.6	....

● TERZYNSKI, Ray

Ray Terzynski

Born: Nov. 27, 1919. Died: Aug.1983. Height: 6'1". Weight: 180 lbs. Drafted: — College: Wisconsin (Stevens Point)

YEAR	TEAM	GP	GS	MIN	PTS	FGM	FGA	FG%	3PM	3PA	3P%	FTM	FTA	FT%	ORB	DRB	TRB	AST	PF	DQ	STL	BLK	TO	MPG	PPG	RPG	APG	PCM
43-44	Oshkosh-N	19	....	....	64	23	....	....	....	....	....	18	....	....	....	....	....	....	....	....	....	....	....	....	3.4	....	....	....
44-45	Oshkosh-N	29	....	....	127	41	....	....	....	....	....	45	....	....	....	....	....	....	....	....	....	....	....	....	4.4	....	....	....

YEAR	TEAM	GP	GS	MIN	PTS	FGM	FGA	FG%	3PM	3PA	3P%	FTM	FTA	FT%	ORB	DRB	TRB	AST	PF	DQ	STL	BLK	TO	MPG	PPG	RPG	APG	PCM
45-46	Oshkosh-N	4	....	....	0	0	....	....	....	....	....	0	0	.000	....	....	....	....	....	....	....	....	....	....	0.0	....	....	....
NBL Season Totals		52	....	....	191	64	....	....	....	....	....	63	0	....	....	....	....	....	....	....	....	....	....	....	3.7	....	....	....
43-44	Oshkosh-N	3	....	....	5	1	....	....	....	....	....	3	....	....	....	....	....	....	....	....	....	....	....	....	1.7	....	....	....
NBL Playoff Totals		3	....	....	5	1	....	....	....	....	....	3	....	....	....	....	....	....	....	....	....	....	....	....	1.7	....	....	....

• THACKER, Tom

Thomas Porter (Tack) Thacker

Born: Nov. 2, 1939. Covington, KY, United States. Height: 6'2". Weight: 170 lbs. Drafted: 1963 College: Cincinnati

YEAR	TEAM	GP	GS	MIN	PTS	FGM	FGA	FG%	3PM	3PA	3P%	FTM	FTA	FT%	ORB	DRB	TRB	AST	PF	DQ	STL	BLK	TO	MPG	PPG	RPG	APG	PCM
63-64	Cincinnati	48	....	457	132	53	181	.293	....	....	....	26	53	.491	....	....	115	51	51	0	....	....	....	9.5	2.8	2.4	1.1	.337
64-65	Cincinnati	55	....	470	135	56	168	.333	....	....	....	23	47	.489	....	....	127	41	64	0	....	....	....	8.5	2.5	2.3	0.7	.347
65-66	Cincinnati	50	....	478	183	84	207	.406	....	....	....	15	38	.395	....	....	119	61	85	0	....	....	....	9.6	3.7	2.4	1.2	.443
67-68	Boston	65	....	782	271	114	272	.419	....	....	....	43	84	.512	....	....	161	69	165	2	....	....	....	12.0	4.2	2.5	1.1	.351
68-69	Indiana-A	18	....	346	98	40	117	.342	0	2	.000	18	31	.581	31	36	67	52	51	0	....	....	26	19.2	5.4	3.7	2.9	.351
69-70	Indiana-A	70	....	1016	188	70	212	.330	10	39	.256	38	69	.551	91	120	211	185	177	2	....	....	115	14.5	2.7	3.0	2.6	.363
70-71	Indiana-A	8	....	92	13	6	17	.353	0	3	.000	1	1	1.000	7	15	22	7	18	0	....	....	8	11.5	1.6	2.8	0.9	.250
NBA Season Totals		218	....	2187	721	307	828	.371	....	....	....	107	222	.482	....	....	522	222	365	2	....	....	....	10.0	3.3	2.4	1.0	....
ABA Season Totals		96	....	1454	299	116	346	.335	10	44	.227	57	101	.564	129	171	300	244	246	2	....	....	149	15.1	3.1	3.1	2.5	....
Career Totals		314	....	3641	1020	423	1174	.360	10	44	.227	164	323	.508	129	171	822	466	611	4	....	....	149	11.6	3.2	2.6	1.5	....
63-64	Cincinnati	6	....	43	13	6	23	.261	....	....	....	1	4	.250	....	....	13	3	4	0	....	....	....	7.2	2.2	2.2	0.5	.252
64-65	Cincinnati	4	....	47	13	5	13	.385	....	....	....	3	4	.750	....	....	12	3	8	0	....	....	....	11.8	3.3	3.0	0.8	.347
65-66	Cincinnati	4	....	46	17	7	22	.318	....	....	....	3	4	.750	....	....	9	5	11	0	....	....	....	11.5	4.3	2.3	1.3	.297
67-68	Boston	17	....	81	16	7	24	.292	....	....	....	2	7	.286	....	....	17	8	23	0	....	....	....	4.8	0.9	1.0	0.5	.178
68-69	Indiana-A	16	....	391	100	36	117	.308	0	5	.000	28	47	.596	....	....	77	59	53	1	....	....	33	24.4	6.3	4.8	3.7	.340
69-70	Indiana-A	14	....	187	33	12	38	.316	3	11	.273	6	11	.545	16	32	48	36	37	0	....	....	20	13.4	2.4	3.4	2.6	.401
NBA Playoff Totals		31	....	217	59	25	82	.305	....	....	....	9	19	.474	....	....	51	19	46	0	....	....	....	7.0	1.9	1.6	0.6	....
ABA Playoff Totals		30	....	578	133	48	155	.310	3	16	.188	34	58	.586	16	32	125	95	90	1	....	....	53	19.3	4.4	4.2	3.2	....
Career Playoff Totals		61	....	795	192	73	237	.308	3	16	.188	43	77	.558	16	32	176	114	136	1	....	....	53	13.0	3.1	2.9	1.9	....

• THEARD, Floyd

Floyd Theard

Born: Sept. 5, 1944. Died: Apr.11, 1985. Height: 6'1". Weight: 170 lbs. Drafted: — College: Kentucky

YEAR	TEAM	GP	GS	MIN	PTS	FGM	FGA	FG%	3PM	3PA	3P%	FTM	FTA	FT%	ORB	DRB	TRB	AST	PF	DQ	STL	BLK	TO	MPG	PPG	RPG	APG	PCM
69-70	Denver-A	25	....	406	96	39	113	.345	0	1	.000	18	28	.643	8	43	51	44	49	1	....	....	45	16.2	3.8	2.0	1.8	.249
ABA Season Totals		25	....	406	96	39	113	.345	0	1	.000	18	28	.643	8	43	51	44	49	1	....	....	45	16.2	3.8	2.0	1.8	....

• THEUS, Reggie

Reggie Wayne Theus

Born: Oct. 13, 1957. Inglewood, CA, United States. Height: 6'7". Weight: 190 lbs. Drafted: 1978 College: UNLV

YEAR	TEAM	GP	GS	MIN	PTS	FGM	FGA	FG%	3PM	3PA	3P%	FTM	FTA	FT%	ORB	DRB	TRB	AST	PF	DQ	STL	BLK	TO	MPG	PPG	RPG	APG	PCM
78-79	Chicago	82	....	2753	1338	537	1119	.480	....	....	....	264	347	.761	92	136	228	429	270	2	93	18	303	33.6	16.3	2.8	5.2	.422
79-80	Chicago	82	....	3029	1660	566	1172	.483	28	105	.267	500	597	.838	143	186	329	515	262	4	114	20	344	36.9	20.2	4.0	6.3	.535
80-81	Chicago	82	....	2820	1549	543	1097	.495	18	90	.200	445	550	.809	124	163	287	426	258	1	122	20	262	34.4	18.9	3.5	5.2	.530
81-82	Chicago	82	82	2838	1508	560	1194	.469	25	100	.250	363	449	.808	115	197	312	476	243	1	87	16	279	34.6	18.4	3.8	5.8	.497
82-83	Chicago	82	81	2856	1953	749	1567	.478	21	91	.231	434	542	.801	91	209	300	484	281	6	143	17	320	34.8	23.8	3.7	5.9	.594
83-84	Chicago	31	6	601	271	92	237	.388	3	15	.200	84	108	.778	21	25	46	142	78	2	21	3	59	19.4	8.7	1.5	4.6	.417
83-84	Kansas City	30	29	897	474	170	388	.438	4	27	.148	130	173	.751	29	54	83	210	93	1	29	9	96	29.9	15.8	2.8	7.0	.508
84-85	Kansas City	82	80	2543	1341	501	1029	.487	5	38	.132	334	387	.863	106	164	270	656	250	0	95	18	303	31.0	16.4	3.3	8.0	.583
85-86	Sacramento	82	82	2919	1503	546	1137	.480	6	35	.171	405	490	.827	73	231	304	788	231	3	112	20	328	35.6	18.3	3.7	9.6	.600
86-87	Sacramento	79	76	2872	1600	577	1223	.472	17	78	.218	429	495	.867	86	180	266	692	208	3	78	16	292	36.4	20.3	3.4	8.8	.583
87-88	Sacramento	73	73	2653	1574	619	1318	.470	16	59	.271	320	385	.831	72	160	232	463	173	0	59	16	234	36.3	21.6	3.2	6.3	.518
88-89	Atlanta	82	82	2517	1296	497	1067	.466	17	58	.293	285	335	.851	86	156	242	387	236	0	108	16	197	30.7	15.8	3.0	4.7	.478
89-90	Orlando	76	71	2350	1438	517	1178	.439	26	105	.248	378	443	.853	75	146	221	407	194	1	60	12	228	30.9	18.9	2.9	5.4	.507
90-91	New Jersey	81	81	2955	1510	583	1247	.468	52	144	.361	292	343	.851	69	160	229	378	231	0	85	35	251	36.5	18.6	2.8	4.7	.424
NBA Season Totals		1026	743	34603	19015	7057	14973	.471	238	945	.252	4663	5644	.826	1182	2167	3349	6453	3008	24	1206	236	3496	33.7	18.5	3.3	6.3	....
80-81	Chicago	6	....	232	119	40	90	.444	2	9	.222	37	43	.860	7	14	21	38	22	0	15	0	15	38.7	19.8	3.5	6.3	.522
83-84	Kansas City	3	3	81	43	17	43	.395	0	3	.000	9	10	.900	4	7	11	16	9	0	5	0	9	27.0	14.3	3.7	5.3	.467
85-86	Sacramento	3	3	102	45	18	46	.391	0	1	.000	9	12	.750	3	5	8	19	9	0	3	2	14	34.0	15.0	2.7	6.3	.322
88-89	Atlanta	5	5	127	37	14	38	.368	0	2	.000	9	12	.750	3	4	7	24	18	1	1	0	10	25.4	7.4	1.4	4.8	.226
NBA Playoff Totals		17	11	542	244	89	217	.410	2	15	.133	64	77	.831	17	30	47	97	58	1	24	2	48	31.9	14.4	2.8	5.7	....

• THIBEAUX, Peter

Peter C. Thibeaux

Born: Oct. 3, 1961. Los Angeles, CA, United States. Height: 6'7". Weight: 210 lbs. Drafted: 1983 College: St. Mary's (CA)

YEAR	TEAM	GP	GS	MIN	PTS	FGM	FGA	FG%	3PM	3PA	3P%	FTM	FTA	FT%	ORB	DRB	TRB	AST	PF	DQ	STL	BLK	TO	MPG	PPG	RPG	APG	PCM
84-85	Golden State	51	1	461	231	94	195	.482	0	2	.000	43	67	.642	29	40	69	17	85	1	11	17	36	9.0	4.5	1.4	0.3	.349
85-86	Golden State	42	8	531	231	100	233	.429	2	5	.400	29	48	.604	28	47	75	28	82	1	23	15	38	12.6	5.5	1.8	0.7	.302
NBA Season Totals		93	9	992	462	194	428	.453	2	7	.286	72	115	.626	57	87	144	45	167	2	34	32	74	10.7	5.0	1.5	0.5	....

• THIEBEN, Bill

William Bernhard Thieben

Born: Mar. 28, 1935. Height: 6'7". Weight: 215 lbs. Drafted: 1956 College: Hofstra

YEAR	TEAM	GP	GS	MIN	PTS	FGM	FGA	FG%	3PM	3PA	3P%	FTM	FTA	FT%	ORB	DRB	TRB	AST	PF	DQ	STL	BLK	TO	MPG	PPG	RPG	APG	PCM
56-57	Fort Wayne	58	....	633	237	90	256	.352	....	....	....	57	87	.655	....	....	207	17	78	0	....	....	....	10.9	4.1	3.6	0.3	.393
57-58	Detroit	27	....	243	100	42	143	.294	....	....	....	16	27	.593	....	....	65	7	44	0	....	....	....	9.0	3.7	2.4	0.3	.258
NBA Season Totals		85	....	876	337	132	399	.331	....	....	....	73	114	.640	....	....	272	24	122	0	....	....	....	10.3	4.0	3.2	0.3	....
56-57	Fort Wayne	2	....	28	14	6	7	.857	....	....	....	2	6	.333	....	....	6	3	5	0	....	....	....	14.0	7.0	3.0	1.5	.648
NBA Playoff Totals		2	....	28	14	6	7	.857	....	....	....	2	6	.333	....	....	6	3	5	0	....	....	....	14.0	7.0	3.0	1.5	....

YEAR	TEAM	GP	GS	MIN	PTS	FGM	FGA	FG%	3PM	3PA	3P%	FTM	FTA	FT%	ORB	DRB	TRB	AST	PF	DQ	STL	BLK	TO	MPG	PPG	RPG	APG	PCM

• THIGPEN, Justus — Justus Thigpen

Born: Aug. 13, 1947. Height: 6'1". Weight: 160 lbs. Drafted: 1969 College: Weber State

YEAR	TEAM	GP	GS	MIN	PTS	FGM	FGA	FG%	3PM	3PA	3P%	FTM	FTA	FT%	ORB	DRB	TRB	AST	PF	DQ	STL	BLK	TO	MPG	PPG	RPG	APG	PCM
69-70	Pittsburgh-A	3	....	58	11	5	19	.263	0	0	.000	1	3	.333	4	4	8	4	14	1	....	....	1	19.3	3.7	2.7	1.3	.061
72-73	Detroit	18	....	99	46	23	57	.404	....	....	....	0	0	.000	....	....	9	8	18	0	0	0	....	5.5	2.6	0.5	0.4	.262
73-74	Omaha	1	....	2	2	1	3	.333	....	....	....	0	0	.000	1	0	1	0	0	0	0	0	....	2.0	2.0	1.0	0.0	.575
NBA Season Totals		19	....	101	48	24	60	.400	....	....	....	0	0	.000	1	0	10	8	18	0	0	0	....	5.3	2.5	0.5	0.4	....
ABA Season Totals		3	....	58	11	5	19	.263	0	0	.000	1	3	.333	4	4	8	4	14	1	....	....	1	19.3	3.7	2.7	1.3	....
Career Totals		22	....	159	59	29	79	.367	0	0	.000	1	3	.333	5	4	18	12	32	1	0	0	1	7.2	2.7	0.8	0.5	....

• THIRDKILL, David — David Thirdkill

Born: Apr. 12, 1960. St. Louis, MO, United States. Height: 6'7". Weight: 195 lbs. Drafted: 1982 College: Bradley

YEAR	TEAM	GP	GS	MIN	PTS	FGM	FGA	FG%	3PM	3PA	3P%	FTM	FTA	FT%	ORB	DRB	TRB	AST	PF	DQ	STL	BLK	TO	MPG	PPG	RPG	APG	PCM
82-83	Phoenix	49	2	521	194	74	170	.435	1	7	.143	45	78	.577	28	44	72	36	93	1	19	4	49	10.6	4.0	1.5	0.7	.253
83-84	Detroit	46	0	291	77	31	72	.431	0	1	.000	15	31	.484	9	22	31	27	44	0	10	3	18	6.3	1.7	0.7	0.6	.220
84-85	Detroit	10	1	115	29	12	23	.522	0	1	.000	5	11	.455	4	4	8	1	16	0	3	2	12	11.5	2.9	0.8	0.1	.091
84-85	Milwaukee	6	0	16	7	3	4	.750	0	0	.000	1	2	.500	1	1	2	0	1	0	0	0	0	2.7	1.2	0.3	0.0	.438
84-85	San Antonio	2	2	52	15	5	11	.455	0	0	.000	5	6	.833	5	2	7	3	5	0	2	1	2	26.0	7.5	3.5	1.5	.332
85-86	Boston	49	0	385	163	54	110	.491	0	1	.000	55	88	.625	27	43	70	15	55	0	11	3	20	7.9	3.3	1.4	0.3	.378
86-87	Boston	17	0	89	25	10	24	.417	0	1	.000	5	16	.313	5	14	19	2	12	0	2	0	5	5.2	1.5	1.1	0.1	.206
NBA Season Totals		179	5	1469	510	189	414	.457	1	11	.091	131	232	.565	79	130	209	84	226	1	47	13	106	8.2	2.8	1.2	0.5	....
84-85	San Antonio	5	0	22	4	1	4	.250	0	2	.000	2	4	.500	0	2	2	2	4	0	0	0	4	4.4	0.8	0.4	0.4	-.060
85-86	Boston	13	0	47	17	6	18	.333	0	1	.000	5	11	.455	1	7	8	3	5	0	2	0	3	3.6	1.3	0.6	0.2	.223
NBA Playoff Totals		18	0	69	21	7	22	.318	0	3	.000	7	15	.467	1	9	10	5	9	0	2	0	7	3.8	1.2	0.6	0.3	....

• THOMAS, Carl — Carl Thomas

Born: Oct. 3, 1969. Dayton, OH, United States. Height: 6'4". Weight: 175 lbs. Drafted: — College: Eastern Michigan

YEAR	TEAM	GP	GS	MIN	PTS	FGM	FGA	FG%	3PM	3PA	3P%	FTM	FTA	FT%	ORB	DRB	TRB	AST	PF	DQ	STL	BLK	TO	MPG	PPG	RPG	APG	PCM
91-92	Sacramento	1	0	31	12	5	12	.417	1	2	.500	1	2	.500	0	0	0	1	3	0	1	0	1	31.0	12.0	0.0	1.0	.152
96-97	Cleveland	19	0	77	21	9	24	.375	2	12	.167	1	1	1.000	3	10	13	8	7	0	2	1	6	4.1	1.1	0.7	0.4	.281
97-98	Golden State	10	0	139	62	25	65	.385	5	21	.238	7	10	.700	4	6	10	9	12	0	5	1	6	13.9	6.2	1.0	0.9	.269
97-98	Orlando	4	0	15	9	4	5	.800	0	0	.000	1	2	.500	0	0	0	1	0	0	0	1	0	3.8	2.3	0.0	0.3	.642
97-98	Cleveland	29	0	272	77	27	70	.386	15	38	.395	8	13	.615	6	31	37	9	27	0	16	5	12	9.4	2.7	1.3	0.3	.275
NBA Season Totals		63	0	534	181	70	176	.398	23	73	.315	18	28	.643	13	47	60	28	49	0	24	8	25	8.5	2.9	1.0	0.4	....
97-98	Cleveland	1	0	11	2	0	1	.000	0	0	.000	2	3	.667	1	0	1	0	2	0	0	0	0	11.0	2.0	1.0	0.0	.057
NBA Playoff Totals		1	0	11	2	0	1	.000	0	0	.000	2	3	.667	1	0	1	0	2	0	0	0	0	11.0	2.0	1.0	0.0	....

• THOMAS, Charles — Charles Thomas

Born: Oct. 3, 1969. Dayton, OH, United States. Height: 6'3". Weight: 175 lbs. Drafted: — College: Eastern Michigan

YEAR	TEAM	GP	GS	MIN	PTS	FGM	FGA	FG%	3PM	3PA	3P%	FTM	FTA	FT%	ORB	DRB	TRB	AST	PF	DQ	STL	BLK	TO	MPG	PPG	RPG	APG	PCM
91-92	Detroit	37	0	156	48	18	51	.353	2	17	.118	10	15	.667	6	16	22	22	20	0	4	1	18	4.2	1.3	0.6	0.6	.241
NBA Season Totals		37	0	156	48	18	51	.353	2	17	.118	10	15	.667	6	16	22	22	20	0	4	1	18	4.2	1.3	0.6	0.6	....

• THOMAS, Earle — Earle Thomas

Born: 1915. Height: 6'4". Weight: 205 lbs. Drafted: — College: Ohio State

YEAR	TEAM	GP	GS	MIN	PTS	FGM	FGA	FG%	3PM	3PA	3P%	FTM	FTA	FT%	ORB	DRB	TRB	AST	PF	DQ	STL	BLK	TO	MPG	PPG	RPG	APG	PCM
37-38	Cincinnati-N	3	....	....	8	4	....	....	....	....	....	0	....	....	....	....	....	....	....	....	....	....	....	....	2.7	....	....	....
38-39	Indianapolis-N	6	....	....	1	0	....	....	....	....	....	1	....	....	....	....	....	....	....	....	....	....	....	....	0.2	....	....	....
NBL Season Totals		9	....	....	9	4	....	....	....	....	....	1	....	....	....	....	....	....	....	....	....	....	....	....	1.0	....	....	....

• THOMAS, Etan — Dedreck Etan Thomas

Born: Apr. 1, 1978. Harlem, NY, United States. Height: 6'9". Weight: 256 lbs. Drafted: 2000 College: Syracuse

YEAR	TEAM	GP	GS	MIN	PTS	FGM	FGA	FG%	3PM	3PA	3P%	FTM	FTA	FT%	ORB	DRB	TRB	AST	PF	DQ	STL	BLK	TO	MPG	PPG	RPG	APG	PCM
01-02	Washington	47	0	618	203	81	151	.536	0	0	.000	41	74	.554	55	126	181	6	76	0	17	35	26	13.1	4.3	3.9	0.1	.460
02-03	Washington	38	0	513	182	61	124	.492	0	0	.000	60	94	.638	70	95	165	3	66	0	8	23	33	13.5	4.8	4.3	0.1	.450
NBA Season Totals		85	0	1131	385	142	275	.516	0	0	.000	101	168	.601	125	221	346	9	142	0	25	58	59	13.3	4.5	4.1	0.1	....

• THOMAS, Irving — Irving Thomas

Born: Jan. 2, 1966. Brooklyn, NY, United States. Height: 6'8". Weight: 225 lbs. Drafted: — College: Florida State

YEAR	TEAM	GP	GS	MIN	PTS	FGM	FGA	FG%	3PM	3PA	3P%	FTM	FTA	FT%	ORB	DRB	TRB	AST	PF	DQ	STL	BLK	TO	MPG	PPG	RPG	APG	PCM
90-91	LA Lakers	26	0	108	46	17	50	.340	0	0	.000	12	21	.571	14	17	31	10	24	0	4	1	13	4.2	1.8	1.2	0.4	.296
NBA Season Totals		26	0	108	46	17	50	.340	0	0	.000	12	21	.571	14	17	31	10	24	0	4	1	13	4.2	1.8	1.2	0.4	....
90-91	LA Lakers	3	0	5	2	1	1	1.000	0	0	.000	0	0	.000	0	0	0	0	0	0	0	0	0	1.7	0.7	0.0	0.0	.400
NBA Playoff Totals		3	0	5	2	1	1	1.000	0	0	.000	0	0	.000	0	0	0	0	0	0	0	0	0	1.7	0.7	0.0	0.0	....

• THOMAS, Isiah — Isiah Lord Thomas III

Born: Apr. 30, 1961. Chicago, IL, United States. Height: 6'1". Weight: 180 lbs. Drafted: 1981 College: Indiana   HOF: 2000

YEAR	TEAM	GP	GS	MIN	PTS	FGM	FGA	FG%	3PM	3PA	3P%	FTM	FTA	FT%	ORB	DRB	TRB	AST	PF	DQ	STL	BLK	TO	MPG	PPG	RPG	APG	PCM
81-82	Detroit	72	72	2433	1225	453	1068	.424	17	59	.288	302	429	.704	57	152	209	565	253	2	150	17	**302**	33.8	17.0	2.9	7.8	.477
82-83	Detroit	81	81	**3093**	1854	725	1537	.472	36	125	.288	368	518	.710	105	223	328	634	318	8	199	29	324	**38.2**	22.9	4.0	7.8	.587
83-84	Detroit	82	82	3007	1748	669	1448	.462	22	65	.338	388	529	.733	103	224	327	**914**	324	8	204	33	303	36.7	21.3	4.0	11.1	**.674**
84-85	Detroit	81	81	3089	1720	646	1410	.458	29	113	.257	399	493	.809	114	247	361	**1123**	288	8	187	25	300	38.1	21.2	4.5	**13.9**	**.739**
85-86	Detroit	77	77	2790	1609	609	1248	.488	26	84	.310	365	462	.790	83	194	277	830	245	9	171	20	293	36.2	20.9	3.6	10.8	.684

YEAR	TEAM	GP	GS	MIN	PTS	FGM	FGA	FG%	3PM	3PA	3P%	FTM	FTA	FT%	ORB	DRB	TRB	AST	PF	DQ	STL	BLK	TO	MPG	PPG	RPG	APG	PCM
86-87	Detroit	81	81	3013	1671	626	1353	.463	19	98	.194	400	521	.768	82	237	319	813	251	5	153	20	340	37.2	20.6	3.9	10.0	.608
87-88	Detroit	81	81	2927	1577	621	1341	.463	30	97	.309	305	394	.774	64	214	278	678	217	0	141	17	275	36.1	19.5	3.4	8.4	.559
88-89	Detroit	80	76	2924	1458	569	1227	.464	33	121	.273	287	351	.818	49	224	273	663	209	0	133	20	296	36.6	18.2	3.4	8.3	.530
89-90	Detroit	81	81	2993	1492	579	1322	.438	42	136	.309	292	377	.775	74	234	308	765	206	0	139	19	**324**	37.0	18.4	3.8	9.4	.536
90-91	Detroit	48	46	1657	776	289	665	.435	19	65	.292	179	229	.782	35	125	160	446	118	4	75	10	187	34.5	16.2	3.3	9.3	.529
91-92	Detroit	78	78	2918	1445	564	1264	.446	25	86	.291	292	378	.772	68	179	247	560	194	2	118	15	250	37.4	18.5	3.2	7.2	.475
92-93	Detroit	79	79	2922	1391	526	1258	.418	61	198	.308	278	377	.737	71	161	232	671	222	2	123	18	284	37.0	17.6	2.9	8.5	.465
93-94	Detroit	58	56	1750	856	318	763	.417	39	126	.310	181	258	.702	46	113	159	399	126	0	68	6	203	30.2	14.8	2.7	6.9	.465
NBA Season Totals		979	971	35516	18822	7194	15904	.452	398	1373	.290	4036	5316	.759	951	2527	3478	9061	2971	48	1861	249	3681	36.3	19.2	3.6	9.3	....
83-84	Detroit	5	5	198	107	39	83	.470	2	6	.333	27	35	.771	7	12	19	55	22	1	13	6	23	39.6	21.4	3.8	11.0	.631
84-85	Detroit	9	9	355	219	83	166	.500	6	15	.400	47	62	.758	11	36	47	101	39	2	19	4	30	39.4	24.3	5.2	11.2	.737
85-86	Detroit	4	4	163	106	41	91	.451	0	5	.000	24	36	.667	8	14	22	48	17	0	9	3	17	40.8	26.5	5.5	12.0	.695
86-87	Detroit	15	15	562	361	134	297	.451	10	33	.303	83	110	.755	21	46	67	130	51	1	39	4	42	37.5	24.1	4.5	8.7	.668
87-88	Detroit	23	23	911	504	183	419	.437	13	44	.295	125	151	.828	26	81	107	201	71	2	66	8	85	39.6	21.9	4.7	8.7	.596
88-89	Detroit	17	17	633	309	115	279	.412	8	30	.267	71	96	.740	24	49	73	141	39	0	27	4	43	37.2	18.2	4.3	8.3	.528
89-90	Detroit	20	20	758	409	148	320	.463	32	68	.471	81	102	.794	21	88	109	163	65	1	43	7	72	37.9	20.5	5.5	8.2	.610
90-91	Detroit	13	11	436	176	60	149	.403	6	22	.273	50	69	.725	13	41	54	111	41	1	13	2	41	33.5	13.5	4.2	8.5	.481
91-92	Detroit	5	5	200	70	22	65	.338	4	11	.364	22	28	.786	3	23	26	37	18	0	5	0	16	40.0	14.0	5.2	7.4	.362
NBA Playoff Totals		111	109	4216	2261	825	1869	.441	81	234	.346	530	689	.769	134	390	524	987	363	8	234	38	369	38.0	20.4	4.7	8.9	....

• THOMAS, Jamel

Jamel Thomas

Born: Mar. 25, 1973. Brooklyn, NY, United States.   Height: 6'6".   Weight: 215 lbs.   Drafted: —   College: Providence

YEAR	TEAM	GP	GS	MIN	PTS	FGM	FGA	FG%	3PM	3PA	3P%	FTM	FTA	FT%	ORB	DRB	TRB	AST	PF	DQ	STL	BLK	TO	MPG	PPG	RPG	APG	PCM
99-00	Boston	3	0	19	11	5	10	.500	0	1	.000	1	1	1.000	0	2	2	2	0	0	0	0	1	6.3	3.7	0.7	0.7	.503
99-00	Golden State	4	0	27	6	3	8	.375	0	2	.000	0	0	.000	1	2	3	4	2	0	1	0	4	6.8	1.5	0.8	1.0	.182
00-01	New Jersey	5	0	56	13	6	19	.316	1	3	.333	0	0	.000	4	5	9	0	6	0	3	0	6	11.2	2.6	1.8	0.0	.072
NBA Season Totals		12	0	102	30	14	37	.378	1	6	.167	1	1	1.000	5	9	14	6	8	0	4	0	11	8.5	2.5	1.2	0.5	....

• THOMAS, Jim

James Edward Thomas

Born: Oct. 19, 1960. Lakeland, FL, United States.   Height: 6'3".   Weight: 190 lbs.   Drafted: 1983   College: Indiana

YEAR	TEAM	GP	GS	MIN	PTS	FGM	FGA	FG%	3PM	3PA	3P%	FTM	FTA	FT%	ORB	DRB	TRB	AST	PF	DQ	STL	BLK	TO	MPG	PPG	RPG	APG	PCM
83-84	Indiana	72	15	1219	455	187	403	.464	1	11	.091	80	110	.727	59	90	149	130	115	1	60	6	72	16.9	6.3	2.1	1.8	.376
84-85	Indiana	80	52	2059	885	347	726	.478	8	42	.190	183	234	.782	74	187	261	234	195	2	76	5	128	25.7	11.1	3.3	2.9	.421
85-86	LA Clippers	6	0	69	13	6	15	.400	0	0	.000	1	2	.500	3	5	8	12	12	0	5	1	9	11.5	2.2	1.3	2.0	.233
90-91	Minnesota	3	0	14	2	1	4	.250	0	0	.000	0	0	.000	0	0	0	1	0	0	1	0	1	4.7	0.7	0.0	0.3	.019
NBA Season Totals		161	67	3361	1355	541	1148	.471	9	53	.170	264	346	.763	136	282	418	377	322	3	142	12	210	20.9	8.4	2.6	2.3	....

• THOMAS, Joe

Joseph Randle Thomas

Born: Mar. 9, 1948. Canton, GA, United States.   Height: 6'6".   Weight: 205 lbs.   Drafted: 1970   College: Marquette

YEAR	TEAM	GP	GS	MIN	PTS	FGM	FGA	FG%	3PM	3PA	3P%	FTM	FTA	FT%	ORB	DRB	TRB	AST	PF	DQ	STL	BLK	TO	MPG	PPG	RPG	APG	PCM
70-71	Phoenix	39	....	204	55	23	86	.267	....	....	....	9	20	.450	....	....	43	17	19	0	....	....	....	5.2	1.4	1.1	0.4	.217
NBA Season Totals		39	....	204	55	23	86	.267	....	....	....	9	20	.450	....	....	43	17	19	0	....	....	....	5.2	1.4	1.1	0.4	

• THOMAS, John

John Thomas

Born: Sept. 8, 1975. Minneapolis, MN, United States.   Height: 6'9".   Weight: 265 lbs.   Drafted: 1997   College: Minnesota

YEAR	TEAM	GP	GS	MIN	PTS	FGM	FGA	FG%	3PM	3PA	3P%	FTM	FTA	FT%	ORB	DRB	TRB	AST	PF	DQ	STL	BLK	TO	MPG	PPG	RPG	APG	PCM
97-98	Boston	33	2	368	108	41	80	.513	0	0	.000	26	33	.788	32	38	70	13	65	0	19	9	33	11.2	3.3	2.1	0.4	.307
97-98	Toronto	21	0	167	43	14	33	.424	0	0	.000	15	21	.714	16	20	36	4	32	0	3	3	13	8.0	2.0	1.7	0.2	.234
98-99	Toronto	39	11	593	169	71	123	.577	0	1	.000	27	48	.563	65	69	134	15	82	0	17	9	21	15.2	4.3	3.4	0.4	.366
99-00	Toronto	55	6	477	114	49	107	.458	0	1	.000	16	41	.390	37	38	75	9	106	1	12	14	14	8.7	2.1	1.4	0.2	.190
NBA Season Totals		148	19	1605	434	175	343	.510	0	2	.000	84	143	.587	150	165	315	41	285	1	51	35	81	10.8	2.9	2.1	0.3	....
99-00	Toronto	1	0	1	0	0	0	.000	0	0	.000	0	0	.000	0	0	0	0	0	0	0	0	0	1.0	0.0	0.0	0.0	.000
NBA Playoff Totals		1	0	1	0	0	0	.000	0	0	.000	0	0	.000	0	0	0	0	0	0	0	0	0	1.0	0.0	0.0	0.0	....

• THOMAS, Kenny

Kenneth Cornelius Thomas

Born: July 25, 1977. Atlanta, GA, United States.   Height: 6'7".   Weight: 261 lbs.   Drafted: 1999   College: New Mexico

YEAR	TEAM	GP	GS	MIN	PTS	FGM	FGA	FG%	3PM	3PA	3P%	FTM	FTA	FT%	ORB	DRB	TRB	AST	PF	DQ	STL	BLK	TO	MPG	PPG	RPG	APG	PCM
99-00	Houston	72	29	1797	594	212	531	.399	32	122	.262	138	209	.660	147	290	437	113	167	0	54	22	112	25.0	8.3	6.1	1.6	.381
00-01	Houston	74	21	1820	528	206	465	.443	25	92	.272	91	126	.722	122	295	417	77	178	4	40	43	116	24.6	7.1	5.6	1.0	.346
01-02	Houston	72	71	2484	1015	396	829	.478	0	16	.000	223	336	.664	158	358	516	137	195	5	85	66	143	34.5	14.1	7.2	1.9	.446
02-03	Houston	20	14	586	197	82	190	.432	0	0	.000	33	45	.733	45	92	137	39	49	0	16	6	40	29.3	9.9	6.9	2.0	.379
02-03	Philadelphia	46	28	1392	470	178	369	.482	0	0	.000	114	152	.750	140	252	392	73	120	2	46	22	76	30.3	10.2	8.5	1.6	.469
NBA Season Totals		284	163	8079	2804	1074	2384	.451	57	230	.248	599	868	.690	612	1287	1899	439	709	11	241	159	487	28.4	9.9	6.7	1.5	....
02-03	Philadelphia	12	12	389	127	54	101	.535	0	0	.000	19	29	.655	42	70	112	11	42	1	8	5	19	32.4	10.6	9.3	0.9	.434
NBA Playoff Totals		12	12	389	127	54	101	.535	0	0	.000	19	29	.655	42	70	112	11	42	1	8	5	19	32.4	10.6	9.3	0.9	....

• THOMAS, Kurt

Kurt Vincent Thomas

Born: Oct. 4, 1972. Dallas, TX, United States.   Height: 6'9".   Weight: 230 lbs.   Drafted: 1995   College: Texas Christian

YEAR	TEAM	GP	GS	MIN	PTS	FGM	FGA	FG%	3PM	3PA	3P%	FTM	FTA	FT%	ORB	DRB	TRB	AST	PF	DQ	STL	BLK	TO	MPG	PPG	RPG	APG	PCM
95-96	Miami	74	42	1655	666	274	547	.501	0	2	.000	118	178	.663	122	317	439	46	271	7	47	36	96	22.4	9.0	5.9	0.6	.425
96-97	Miami	18	9	374	113	39	105	.371	0	1	.000	35	46	.761	31	76	107	9	67	3	12	9	25	20.8	6.3	5.9	0.5	.323
97-98	Dallas	5	0	73	37	17	45	.378	0	0	.000	3	3	1.000	8	16	24	3	19	1	1	0	10	14.6	7.4	4.8	0.6	.269
98-99	New York	50	44	1182	406	170	368	.462	0	1	.000	66	108	.611	82	204	286	55	159	3	45	17	73	23.6	8.1	5.7	1.1	.378
99-00	New York	80	21	1971	641	270	535	.505	1	3	.333	100	128	.781	144	361	505	82	278	6	51	42	105	24.6	8.0	6.3	1.0	.405

YEAR	TEAM	GP	GS	MIN	PTS	FGM	FGA	FG%	3PM	3PA	3P%	FTM	FTA	FT%	ORB	DRB	TRB	AST	PF	DQ	STL	BLK	TO	MPG	PPG	RPG	APG	PCM
00-01	New York	77	29	2125	800	314	614	.511	1	3	.333	171	210	.814	172	343	515	63	287	6	61	69	99	27.6	10.4	6.7	0.8	.444
01-02	New York	82	82	2771	1143	463	938	.494	1	6	.167	216	265	.815	214	533	747	87	**341**	8	71	79	153	33.8	13.9	9.1	1.1	.471
02-03	New York	81	81	2576	1134	497	1028	.483	2	3	.667	138	184	.750	160	477	637	162	**344**	**12**	81	97	138	31.8	14.0	7.9	2.0	.492
NBA Season Totals		467	308	12727	4940	2044	4180	.489	5	19	.263	847	1122	.755	933	2327	3260	507	1766	46	369	349	699	27.3	10.6	7.0	1.1	....
95-96	Miami	3	3	60	12	4	10	.400	0	0	.000	4	4	1.000	4	12	16	3	13	1	2	1	5	20.0	4.0	5.3	1.0	.277
98-99	New York	20	12	419	106	45	118	.381	0	0	.000	16	23	.696	38	72	110	7	76	0	15	12	19	21.0	5.3	5.5	0.4	.279
99-00	New York	16	0	251	69	31	61	.508	0	0	.000	7	10	.700	18	32	50	5	44	1	3	6	14	15.7	4.3	3.1	0.3	.266
00-01	New York	5	5	186	72	25	47	.532	0	0	.000	22	31	.710	17	39	56	9	26	1	2	5	9	37.2	14.4	11.2	1.8	.510
NBA Playoff Totals		44	20	916	259	105	236	.445	0	0	.000	49	68	.721	77	155	232	24	159	3	22	24	47	20.8	5.9	5.3	0.5	....

• THOMAS, Ronald

Ronald Morton (The Plumber) Thomas

Born: Nov. 19, 1950. Louisville, KY, United States.   Height: 6'6".   Weight: 215 lbs.   Drafted: 1972   College: Louisville

YEAR	TEAM	GP	GS	MIN	PTS	FGM	FGA	FG%	3PM	3PA	3P%	FTM	FTA	FT%	ORB	DRB	TRB	AST	PF	DQ	STL	BLK	TO	MPG	PPG	RPG	APG	PCM
72-73	Kentucky-A	31	....	369	145	62	132	.470	0	2	.000	21	41	.512	53	62	115	23	73	2	....	....	21	11.9	4.7	3.7	0.7	.458
73-74	Kentucky-A	71	....	976	294	128	273	.469	1	7	.143	37	63	.587	112	177	289	62	156	....	48	7	71	13.7	4.1	4.1	0.9	.420
74-75	Kentucky-A	79	....	830	288	115	256	.449	1	3	.333	57	119	.479	124	176	300	46	133	....	51	14	71	10.5	3.6	3.8	0.6	.474
75-76	Kentucky-A	83	....	1117	324	134	277	.484	1	2	.500	55	94	.585	148	223	371	67	168	....	61	18	71	13.5	3.9	4.5	0.8	.456
ABA Season Totals		264	....	3292	1051	439	938	.468	3	14	.214	170	317	.536	437	638	1075	198	530	2	160	39	234	12.5	4.0	4.1	0.8	....
72-73	Kentucky-A	17	....	247	85	38	77	.494	0	1	.000	9	23	.391	28	47	75	13	44	2	....	....	24	14.5	5.0	4.4	0.8	.428
73-74	Kentucky-A	8	....	109	36	15	28	.536	0	0	.000	6	10	.600	13	24	37	4	14	....	3	3	3	13.6	4.5	4.6	0.5	.490
74-75	Kentucky-A	15	....	167	62	25	42	.595	0	0	.000	12	16	.750	26	30	56	11	25	....	11	0	10	11.1	4.1	3.7	0.7	.575
75-76	Kentucky-A	10	....	142	45	20	41	.488	0	0	.000	5	13	.385	18	36	54	9	23	....	4	3	8	14.2	4.5	5.4	0.9	.497
ABA Playoff Totals		50	....	665	228	98	188	.521	0	1	.000	32	62	.516	85	137	222	37	106	2	18	6	45	13.3	4.6	4.4	0.7	....

• THOMAS, Terry

Terry C. Thomas

Born: Aug. 20, 1953. Detroit, MI, United States.   Height: 6'8".   Weight: 220 lbs.   Drafted: 1975   College: Detroit

YEAR	TEAM	GP	GS	MIN	PTS	FGM	FGA	FG%	3PM	3PA	3P%	FTM	FTA	FT%	ORB	DRB	TRB	AST	PF	DQ	STL	BLK	TO	MPG	PPG	RPG	APG	PCM
75-76	Detroit	28	....	136	77	28	65	.431	....	....	....	21	29	.724	15	21	36	3	21	1	4	2	....	4.9	2.8	1.3	0.1	.494
NBA Season Totals		28	....	136	77	28	65	.431	....	....	....	21	29	.724	15	21	36	3	21	1	4	2	....	4.9	2.8	1.3	0.1	
75-76	Detroit	4	....	6	0	0	5	.000	....	....	....	0	0	.000	1	0	1	0	1	0	0	0	....	1.5	0.0	0.3	0.0	-.644
NBA Playoff Totals		4	....	6	0	0	5	.000	....	....	....	0	0	.000	1	0	1	0	1	0	0	0	....	1.5	0.0	0.3	0.0	

• THOMAS, Tim

Timothy Mark Thomas

Born: Feb. 26, 1977. Paterson, NJ, United States.   Height: 6'10".   Weight: 230 lbs.   Drafted: 1997   College: Villanova

YEAR	TEAM	GP	GS	MIN	PTS	FGM	FGA	FG%	3PM	3PA	3P%	FTM	FTA	FT%	ORB	DRB	TRB	AST	PF	DQ	STL	BLK	TO	MPG	PPG	RPG	APG	PCM
97-98	Philadelphia	77	48	1779	845	306	684	.447	62	171	.363	171	231	.740	107	181	288	90	185	2	54	17	116	23.1	11.0	3.7	1.2	.397
98-99	Philadelphia	17	0	188	78	27	67	.403	5	19	.263	19	24	.792	7	26	33	15	21	0	3	3	15	11.1	4.6	1.9	0.9	.366
98-99	Milwaukee	33	26	624	280	105	212	.495	16	49	.327	54	88	.614	42	51	93	31	86	2	23	9	31	18.9	8.5	2.8	0.9	.400
99-00	Milwaukee	80	1	2093	945	347	753	.461	63	182	.346	188	243	.774	100	232	332	113	227	3	59	31	129	26.2	11.8	4.2	1.4	.400
00-01	Milwaukee	76	16	2086	954	326	758	.430	107	260	.412	195	253	.771	79	234	313	138	194	3	78	45	114	27.4	12.6	4.1	1.8	.429
01-02	Milwaukee	74	22	1987	869	316	753	.420	95	291	.326	142	179	.793	64	236	300	105	200	3	65	32	127	26.9	11.7	4.1	1.4	.365
02-03	Milwaukee	80	70	2359	1066	412	930	.443	97	265	.366	145	186	.780	97	292	389	102	257	5	70	49	133	29.5	13.3	4.9	1.3	.387
NBA Season Totals		437	183	11116	5037	1839	4157	.442	445	1237	.360	914	1204	.759	496	1252	1748	594	1170	20	352	186	665	25.4	11.5	4.0	1.4	....
98-99	Milwaukee	3	3	60	23	8	18	.444	0	2	.000	7	12	.583	4	8	12	1	11	0	1	1	5	20.0	7.7	4.0	0.3	.269
99-00	Milwaukee	5	0	142	77	29	59	.492	5	15	.333	14	17	.824	6	18	24	10	14	0	1	4	1	28.4	15.4	4.8	2.0	.552
00-01	Milwaukee	18	0	479	203	64	143	.448	22	51	.431	53	65	.815	22	59	81	29	52	1	9	10	21	26.6	11.3	4.5	1.6	.431
02-03	Milwaukee	6	5	191	107	36	78	.462	12	21	.571	23	32	.719	8	21	29	8	27	2	3	6	8	31.8	17.8	4.8	1.3	.463
NBA Playoff Totals		32	8	872	410	137	298	.460	39	89	.438	97	126	.770	40	106	146	48	104	3	14	21	35	27.3	12.8	4.6	1.5	....

• THOMAS, Willis

Willis (Lefty) Thomas

Born: 1937.   Height: 6'2".   Weight: 185 lbs.   Drafted: —   College: Tennessee State

YEAR	TEAM	GP	GS	MIN	PTS	FGM	FGA	FG%	3PM	3PA	3P%	FTM	FTA	FT%	ORB	DRB	TRB	AST	PF	DQ	STL	BLK	TO	MPG	PPG	RPG	APG	PCM
67-68	Anaheim-A	38	....	525	261	107	245	.437	0	1	.000	47	61	.770	....	....	56	30	62	0	....	....	43	13.8	6.9	1.5	0.8	.374
67-68	Denver-A	24	....	542	294	136	305	.446	0	2	.000	22	32	.688	....	....	58	25	45	1	....	....	51	22.6	12.3	2.4	1.0	.384
ABA Season Totals		62	....	1067	555	243	550	.442	0	3	.000	69	93	.742	....	....	114	55	107	1	....	....	94	17.2	9.0	1.8	0.9	....

• THOMPSON, Bernard

Bernard Thompson

Born: Aug. 30, 1962. Phoenix, AZ, United States.   Height: 6'6".   Weight: 210 lbs.   Drafted: 1984   College: Fresno State

YEAR	TEAM	GP	GS	MIN	PTS	FGM	FGA	FG%	3PM	3PA	3P%	FTM	FTA	FT%	ORB	DRB	TRB	AST	PF	DQ	STL	BLK	TO	MPG	PPG	RPG	APG	PCM
84-85	Portland	59	0	535	197	79	212	.373	0	8	.000	39	51	.765	37	39	76	52	79	0	31	10	35	9.1	3.3	1.3	0.9	.304
85-86	Phoenix	61	20	1281	517	195	399	.489	0	2	.000	127	157	.809	58	83	141	132	151	0	51	10	92	21.0	8.5	2.3	2.2	.380
86-87	Phoenix	24	2	331	111	42	105	.400	0	3	.000	27	33	.818	20	11	31	18	53	0	11	5	17	13.8	4.6	1.3	0.8	.218
87-88	Phoenix	37	7	566	191	74	159	.465	0	2	.000	43	60	.717	40	36	76	51	75	1	21	1	22	15.3	5.2	2.1	1.4	.343
88-89	Houston	23	0	222	62	20	59	.339	0	2	.000	22	26	.846	9	19	28	13	33	0	13	1	18	9.7	2.7	1.2	0.6	.202
NBA Season Totals		204	29	2935	1078	410	934	.439	0	17	.000	258	327	.789	164	188	352	266	391	1	127	27	184	14.4	5.3	1.7	1.3	....
84-85	Portland	2	0	10	2	0	5	.000	0	0	.000	2	2	1.000	1	2	3	2	1	0	0	1	0	5.0	1.0	1.5	1.0	.274
NBA Playoff Totals		2	0	10	2	0	5	.000	0	0	.000	2	2	1.000	1	2	3	2	1	0	0	1	0	5.0	1.0	1.5	1.0	....

YEAR	TEAM	GP	GS	MIN	PTS	FGM	FGA	FG%	3PM	3PA	3P%	FTM	FTA	FT%	ORB	DRB	TRB	AST	PF	DQ	STL	BLK	TO	MPG	PPG	RPG	APG	PCM

• THOMPSON, Bill Bill Thompson

Born: —. Height: 6'4". Weight: — Drafted: — College: St. John's (OH)

YEAR	TEAM	GP	GS	MIN	PTS	FGM	FGA	FG%	3PM	3PA	3P%	FTM	FTA	FT%	ORB	DRB	TRB	AST	PF	DQ	STL	BLK	TO	MPG	PPG	RPG	APG	PCM
41-42	Toledo-N	16	....	....	59	25	....	....	....	....	....	9	...	...	...	...	...	...	...	...	...	...	...	...	3.7	...	...	...
NBL Season Totals		16	....	....	59	25	....	....	....	....	....	9	...	...	...	...	...	...	...	...	...	...	...	...	3.7	...	...	...

• THOMPSON, Billy William Stansbury (B.T. Express) Thompson

Born: Dec. 1, 1963. Camden, NJ, United States. Height: 6'7". Weight: 195 lbs. Drafted: 1986 College: Louisville

YEAR	TEAM	GP	GS	MIN	PTS	FGM	FGA	FG%	3PM	3PA	3P%	FTM	FTA	FT%	ORB	DRB	TRB	AST	PF	DQ	STL	BLK	TO	MPG	PPG	RPG	APG	PCM
86-87	LA Lakers	59	0	762	332	142	261	.544	0	1	.000	48	74	.649	69	102	171	60	148	1	15	30	59	12.9	5.6	2.9	1.0	.460
87-88	LA Lakers	9	0	38	14	3	13	.231	0	0	.000	8	10	.800	2	7	9	1	11	0	1	0	6	4.2	1.6	1.0	0.1	.090
88-89	Miami	79	58	2273	854	349	716	.487	0	4	.000	156	224	.696	241	331	572	176	260	8	56	105	190	28.8	10.8	7.2	2.2	.463
89-90	Miami	79	45	2142	867	375	727	.516	2	4	.500	115	185	.622	238	313	551	166	237	1	54	89	158	27.1	11.0	7.0	2.1	.500
90-91	Miami	73	46	1481	499	205	411	.499	0	4	.000	89	124	.718	120	192	312	111	161	3	32	48	117	20.3	6.8	4.3	1.5	.399
91-92	Golden State	1	0	1	0	0	0	.000	0	0	.000	0	0	.000	0	0	0	0	0	0	0	0	0	1.0	0.0	0.0	0.0	.000
NBA Season Totals		300	149	6697	2566	1074	2128	.505	2	13	.154	416	617	.674	670	945	1615	514	817	13	158	272	530	22.3	8.6	5.4	1.7	....
86-87	LA Lakers	3	0	27	14	6	11	.545	0	0	.000	2	2	1.000	3	3	6	2	2	0	4	0	0	9.0	4.7	2.0	0.7	.736
NBA Playoff Totals		3	0	27	14	6	11	.545	0	0	.000	2	2	1.000	3	3	6	2	2	0	4	0	0	9.0	4.7	2.0	0.7	

• THOMPSON, Brooks Brooks James Thompson

Born: July 19, 1970. Dallas, TX, United States. Height: 6'4". Weight: 193 lbs. Drafted: 1994 College: Oklahoma State

YEAR	TEAM	GP	GS	MIN	PTS	FGM	FGA	FG%	3PM	3PA	3P%	FTM	FTA	FT%	ORB	DRB	TRB	AST	PF	DQ	STL	BLK	TO	MPG	PPG	RPG	APG	PCM
94-95	Orlando	38	2	246	116	45	114	.395	18	58	.310	8	12	.667	7	16	23	43	46	1	10	2	27	6.5	3.1	0.6	1.1	.329
95-96	Orlando	33	0	246	140	48	103	.466	25	64	.391	19	27	.704	4	20	24	31	35	0	12	0	23	7.5	4.2	0.7	0.9	.460
96-97	Utah	2	0	8	0	0	1	.000	0	0	.000	0	0	.000	0	0	0	1	1	0	0	0	1	4.0	0.0	0.0	0.5	-.158
96-97	Denver	65	6	1047	445	162	405	.400	97	244	.398	24	38	.632	18	78	96	179	125	0	55	2	85	16.1	6.8	1.5	2.8	.390
97-98	Phoenix	13	0	46	26	10	27	.370	5	16	.313	1	3	.333	1	4	5	3	6	0	4	0	5	3.5	2.0	0.4	0.2	.298
97-98	New York	17	0	121	33	13	29	.448	4	14	.286	3	5	.600	0	10	10	24	16	0	6	1	10	7.1	1.9	0.6	1.4	.352
NBA Season Totals		168	8	1714	760	278	679	.409	149	396	.376	55	85	.647	30	128	158	281	229	1	87	5	151	10.2	4.5	0.9	1.7	....
94-95	Orlando	3	0	11	12	3	4	.750	3	4	.750	3	4	.750	1	1	2	3	1	0	0	1	2	3.7	4.0	0.7	1.0	1.295
95-96	Orlando	5	0	48	26	10	21	.476	1	6	.167	5	7	.714	3	2	5	7	7	0	0	1	9	9.6	5.2	1.0	1.4	.334
NBA Playoff Totals		8	0	59	38	13	25	.520	4	10	.400	8	11	.727	4	3	7	10	8	0	0	2	11	7.4	4.8	0.9	1.3	....

• THOMPSON, Corny Cornelius Allen Thompson

Born: Feb. 5, 1960. Middletown, CT, United States. Height: 6'8". Weight: 225 lbs. Drafted: 1982 College: Connecticut

YEAR	TEAM	GP	GS	MIN	PTS	FGM	FGA	FG%	3PM	3PA	3P%	FTM	FTA	FT%	ORB	DRB	TRB	AST	PF	DQ	STL	BLK	TO	MPG	PPG	RPG	APG	PCM
82-83	Dallas	44	2	520	122	43	137	.314	0	0	.000	36	46	.783	41	79	120	34	92	0	12	7	31	11.8	2.8	2.7	0.8	.242
NBA Season Totals		44	2	520	122	43	137	.314	0	0	.000	36	46	.783	41	79	120	34	92	0	12	7	31	11.8	2.8	2.7	0.8	....

• THOMPSON, David David O'Neil Thompson

Born: July 13, 1954. Shelby, NC, United States. Height: 6'4". Weight: 195 lbs. Drafted: 1975 College: North Carolina State HOF: 1996

YEAR	TEAM	GP	GS	MIN	PTS	FGM	FGA	FG%	3PM	3PA	3P%	FTM	FTA	FT%	ORB	DRB	TRB	AST	PF	DQ	STL	BLK	TO	MPG	PPG	RPG	APG	PCM
75-76	Denver-A	83	....	3101	2158	807	1567	.515	3	19	.158	541	681	.794	228	297	525	308	282	....	136	102	250	37.4	26.0	6.3	3.7	.678
76-77	Denver	82	....	3001	2125	824	1626	.507	....	....	.....	477	623	.766	138	196	334	337	236	1	114	53	.....	36.6	25.9	4.1	4.1	.646
77-78	Denver	80	....	3025	2172	826	1584	.521	....	....	.....	520	668	.778	156	234	390	362	213	1	92	99	248	37.8	27.2	4.9	4.5	.678
78-79	Denver	76	....	2670	1825	693	1353	.512	....	....	.....	439	583	.753	109	165	274	225	180	2	70	82	182	35.1	24.0	3.6	3.0	.582
79-80	Denver	39	....	1239	839	289	617	.468	7	19	.368	254	335	.758	56	118	174	124	106	0	39	38	117	31.8	21.5	4.5	3.2	.577
80-81	Denver	77	....	2620	1967	734	1451	.506	10	39	.256	489	615	.795	107	180	287	231	231	3	53	60	246	34.0	25.5	3.7	3.0	.589
81-82	Denver	61	5	1246	906	313	644	.486	4	14	.286	276	339	.814	57	91	148	117	149	1	34	29	140	20.4	14.9	2.4	1.9	.558
82-83	Seattle	75	64	2155	1190	445	925	.481	2	10	.200	298	380	.784	96	174	270	222	142	0	47	33	165	28.7	15.9	3.6	3.0	.495
83-84	Seattle	19	0	349	240	89	165	.539	0	1	.000	62	73	.849	18	26	44	13	30	0	10	13	27	18.4	12.6	2.3	0.7	.577
NBA Season Totals		509	69	16305	11264	4213	8365	.504	23	83	.277	2815	3616	.778	737	1184	1921	1631	1287	8	459	407	1125	32.0	22.1	3.8	3.2	....
ABA Season Totals		83	....	3101	2158	807	1567	.515	3	19	.158	541	681	.794	228	297	525	308	282	....	136	102	250	37.4	26.0	6.3	3.7	....
Career Totals		592	69	19406	13422	5020	9932	.505	26	102	.255	3356	4297	.781	965	1481	2446	1939	1569	8	595	509	1375	32.8	22.7	4.1	3.3	....
75-76	Denver-A	13	....	508	343	127	237	.536	1	4	.250	88	105	.838	32	51	83	39	54	....	16	5	50	39.1	26.4	6.4	3.0	.651
76-77	Denver	6	....	237	148	56	121	.463	....	....	.....	36	53	.679	13	18	31	24	22	1	9	4	....	39.5	24.7	5.2	4.0	.545
77-78	Denver	13	....	481	328	131	291	.450	....	....	.....	66	80	.825	18	35	53	52	34	0	9	21	39	37.0	25.2	4.1	4.0	.549
78-79	Denver	3	....	122	84	38	69	.551	....	....	.....	8	11	.727	7	14	21	12	12	0	4	1	12	40.7	28.0	7.0	4.0	.617
81-82	Denver	3	....	66	35	15	33	.455	1	3	.333	4	7	.571	4	6	10	6	8	0	1	0	8	22.0	11.7	3.3	2.0	.342
82-83	Seattle	2	2	65	24	9	25	.360	0	0	.000	6	10	.600	0	0	0	7	7	0	1	1	4	32.5	12.0	0.0	3.5	.161
NBA Playoff Totals		27	2	971	619	249	539	.462	1	3	.333	120	161	.745	42	73	115	101	83	1	24	27	63	36.0	22.9	4.3	3.7	....
ABA Playoff Totals		13	....	508	343	127	237	.536	1	4	.250	88	105	.838	32	51	83	39	54	....	16	5	50	39.1	26.4	6.4	3.0	....
Career Playoff Totals		40	2	1479	962	376	776	.485	2	7	.286	208	266	.782	74	124	198	140	137	1	40	32	113	37.0	24.1	5.0	3.5	....

• THOMPSON, George George (Tip, Tipper) Thompson

Born: Nov. 29, 1947. Brooklyn, NY, United States. Height: 6'2". Weight: 200 lbs. Drafted: 1969 College: Marquette

YEAR	TEAM	GP	GS	MIN	PTS	FGM	FGA	FG%	3PM	3PA	3P%	FTM	FTA	FT%	ORB	DRB	TRB	AST	PF	DQ	STL	BLK	TO	MPG	PPG	RPG	APG	PCM
69-70	Pittsburgh-A	54	....	1017	701	259	587	.441	7	32	.219	176	260	.677	47	47	94	73	109	0	....	....	84	18.8	13.0	1.7	1.4	.492
70-71	Pittsburgh-A	82	....	2470	1520	575	1220	.471	23	90	.256	347	485	.715	129	162	291	207	217	3	....	....	198	30.1	18.5	3.5	2.5	.544
71-72	Pittsburgh-A	70	....	2904	1888	696	1448	.481	41	132	.311	455	584	.779	155	198	353	257	201	2	....	....	217	41.5	27.0	5.0	3.7	.579
72-73	Memphis-A	80	....	2925	1727	579	1269	.456	20	73	.274	549	700	.784	95	170	265	403	246	1	....	....	245	36.6	21.6	3.3	5.0	.550

YEAR TEAM	GP	GS	MIN	PTS	FGM	FGA	FG%	3PM	3PA	3P%	FTM	FTA	FT%	ORB	DRB	TRB	AST	PF	DQ	STL	BLK	TO	MPG	PPG	RPG	APG	PCM
73-74 Memphis-A	78	....	2732	1498	539	1134	.475	10	54	.185	410	519	.790	93	180	273	396	234	....	117	24	210	35.0	19.2	3.5	5.1	.559
74-75 Milwaukee	73	....	1983	780	306	691	.443	....	....	....	168	214	.785	50	131	181	225	203	5	66	6	....	27.2	10.7	2.5	3.1	.382
NBA Season Totals	73	....	1983	780	306	691	.443	....	....	....	168	214	.785	50	131	181	225	203	5	66	6	....	27.2	10.7	2.5	3.1	....
ABA Season Totals	364	....	12048	7334	2648	5658	.468	101	381	.265	1937	2548	.760	519	757	1276	1336	1007	6	117	24	954	33.1	20.1	3.5	3.7	....
Career Totals	437	....	14031	8114	2954	6349	.465	101	381	.265	2105	2762	.762	569	888	1457	1561	1210	11	183	30	954	32.1	18.6	3.3	3.6	....

• THOMPSON, Homer

Homer Thompson

Born: 1916. Jeffersonville, IN, United States. Height: 6'4". Weight: 215 lbs. Drafted: — College: Kentucky

YEAR TEAM	GP	GS	MIN	PTS	FGM	FGA	FG%	3PM	3PA	3P%	FTM	FTA	FT%	ORB	DRB	TRB	AST	PF	DQ	STL	BLK	TO	MPG	PPG	RPG	APG	PCM
39-40 Indianapolis-N	24	....	....	106	27	....	....	....	....	....	52	....	....	....	....	....	....	....	....	....	....	....	....	4.4	....	....	....
46-47 Indianapolis-N	1	....	....	2	1	....	....	....	....	....	0	1	.000	....	....	....	....	3	....	....	....	....	....	2.0	....	....	....
46-47 Sheboygan-N	3	....	....	6	2	....	....	....	....	....	2	3	.667	....	....	....	....	....	....	....	....	....	....	2.0	....	....	....
NBL Season Totals	28	....	....	114	30	....	....	....	....	....	54	4	....	....	....	....	....	3	....	....	....	....	....	4.1	....	....	....

• THOMPSON, Jack

John Sigred Thompson

Born: Mar. 26, 1946. New York, NY, United States. Height: 6'1". Weight: 185 lbs. Drafted: 1968 College: South Carolina

YEAR TEAM	GP	GS	MIN	PTS	FGM	FGA	FG%	3PM	3PA	3P%	FTM	FTA	FT%	ORB	DRB	TRB	AST	PF	DQ	STL	BLK	TO	MPG	PPG	RPG	APG	PCM
68-69 Indiana-A	2	....	4	2	1	3	.333	0	1	.000	0	0	.000	1	0	1	2	0	0	....	....	2	2.0	1.0	0.5	1.0	.857
ABA Season Totals	2	....	4	2	1	3	.333	0	1	.000	0	0	.000	1	0	1	2	0	0	....	....	2	2.0	1.0	0.5	1.0	....

• THOMPSON, John

John R. Thompson Jr.

Born: Sept. 2, 1941. Washington, DC, United States. Height: 6'10". Weight: 225 lbs. Drafted: 1964 College: Providence

YEAR TEAM	GP	GS	MIN	PTS	FGM	FGA	FG%	3PM	3PA	3P%	FTM	FTA	FT%	ORB	DRB	TRB	AST	PF	DQ	STL	BLK	TO	MPG	PPG	RPG	APG	PCM
64-65 Boston	64	....	699	230	84	209	.402	....	....	....	62	105	.590	....	....	230	16	141	1	....	....	....	10.9	3.6	3.6	0.3	.372
65-66 Boston	10	....	72	32	14	30	.467	....	....	....	4	6	.667	....	....	30	3	15	0	....	....	....	7.2	3.2	3.0	0.3	.555
NBA Season Totals	74	....	771	262	98	239	.410	....	....	....	66	111	.595	....	....	260	19	156	1	....	....	....	10.4	3.5	3.5	0.3	....
64-65 Boston	3	....	21	11	2	7	.286	....	....	....	7	7	1.000	....	....	12	1	2	0	....	....	....	7.0	3.7	4.0	0.3	.802
65-66 Boston	3	....	11	2	1	7	.143	....	....	....	0	0	.000	....	....	4	0	2	0	....	....	....	3.7	0.7	1.3	0.0	-.032
NBA Playoff Totals	6	....	32	13	3	14	.214	....	....	....	7	7	1.000	....	....	16	1	4	0	....	....	....	5.3	2.2	2.7	0.2	....

• THOMPSON, Kevin

Kevin Lamont Thompson

Born: Feb. 7, 1971. Winston-Salem, NC, United States. Height: 6'11". Weight: 260 lbs. Drafted: 1993 College: North Carolina State

YEAR TEAM	GP	GS	MIN	PTS	FGM	FGA	FG%	3PM	3PA	3P%	FTM	FTA	FT%	ORB	DRB	TRB	AST	PF	DQ	STL	BLK	TO	MPG	PPG	RPG	APG	PCM
93-94 Portland	14	0	58	13	6	14	.429	0	1	.000	1	2	.500	7	6	13	3	11	0	0	2	6	4.1	0.9	0.9	0.2	.201
NBA Season Totals	14	0	58	13	6	14	.429	0	1	.000	1	2	.500	7	6	13	3	11	0	0	2	6	4.1	0.9	0.9	0.2	....

• THOMPSON, LaSalle

LaSalle (Tank) Thompson III

Born: June 23, 1961. Cincinnati, OH, United States. Height: 6'10". Weight: 245 lbs. Drafted: 1982 College: Texas

YEAR TEAM	GP	GS	MIN	PTS	FGM	FGA	FG%	3PM	3PA	3P%	FTM	FTA	FT%	ORB	DRB	TRB	AST	PF	DQ	STL	BLK	TO	MPG	PPG	RPG	APG	PCM
82-83 Kansas City	71	3	987	383	147	287	.512	0	1	.000	89	137	.650	133	242	375	33	186	1	40	61	99	13.9	5.4	5.3	0.5	.534
83-84 Kansas City	80	38	1915	826	333	637	.523	0	0	.000	160	223	.717	260	449	709	86	327	8	71	145	168	23.9	10.3	8.9	1.1	.605
84-85 Kansas City	82	77	2458	965	369	695	.531	0	0	.000	227	315	.721	274	580	854	130	328	4	98	128	205	30.0	11.8	10.4	1.6	.578
85-86 Sacramento	80	64	2377	1024	411	794	.518	0	1	.000	202	276	.732	252	518	770	168	295	8	71	109	184	29.7	12.8	9.6	2.1	.584
86-87 Sacramento	82	53	2166	912	362	752	.481	0	5	.000	188	255	.737	237	450	687	122	290	6	69	126	139	26.4	11.1	8.4	1.5	.556
87-88 Sacramento	69	9	1257	550	215	456	.471	2	5	.400	118	164	.720	138	289	427	68	217	1	54	73	110	18.2	8.0	6.2	1.0	.548
88-89 Sacramento	43	42	1276	646	247	536	.461	0	1	.000	152	188	.809	120	272	392	44	153	6	46	55	116	29.7	15.0	9.1	1.0	.538
88-89 Indiana	33	29	1053	413	169	314	.538	0	0	.000	75	93	.806	104	222	326	37	132	6	33	39	63	31.9	12.5	9.9	1.1	.531
89-90 Indiana	82	60	2126	554	223	471	.473	1	5	.200	107	134	.799	175	455	630	106	313	**11**	65	71	148	25.9	6.8	7.7	1.3	.402
90-91 Indiana	82	77	1946	625	276	565	.488	1	5	.200	72	104	.692	154	409	563	147	265	4	63	63	164	23.7	7.6	6.9	1.8	.444
91-92 Indiana	80	49	1299	394	168	359	.468	0	2	.000	58	71	.817	98	283	381	102	207	0	52	34	96	16.2	4.9	4.8	1.3	.437
92-93 Indiana	63	0	730	237	104	213	.488	0	1	.000	29	39	.744	55	123	178	34	137	0	29	24	44	11.6	3.8	2.8	0.5	.380
93-94 Indiana	30	1	282	70	27	77	.351	0	0	.000	16	30	.533	26	49	75	16	59	1	10	8	24	9.4	2.3	2.5	0.5	.253
94-95 Indiana	38	3	453	112	49	118	.415	0	0	.000	14	16	.875	28	61	89	18	76	0	18	10	34	11.9	2.9	2.3	0.5	.238
95-96 Philadelphia	44	11	773	85	33	83	.398	0	0	.000	19	24	.792	62	137	199	26	125	5	19	20	35	17.6	1.9	4.5	0.6	.253
96-97 Denver	17	0	105	7	3	16	.188	0	0	.000	1	2	.500	5	21	26	0	26	0	3	6	7	6.2	0.4	1.5	0.0	.080
96-97 Indiana	9	0	35	3	0	3	.000	0	0	.000	3	4	.750	2	6	8	2	7	0	0	0	2	3.9	0.3	0.9	0.2	.120
NBA Season Totals	985	516	21238	7806	3136	6376	.492	4	26	.154	1530	2075	.737	2123	4566	6689	1139	3143	61	741	972	1638	21.6	7.9	6.8	1.2	....
83-84 Kansas City	3	3	93	45	18	40	.450	0	0	.000	9	11	.818	11	19	30	4	14	0	3	4	5	31.0	15.0	10.0	1.3	.550
85-86 Sacramento	3	3	99	29	11	32	.344	0	0	.000	7	12	.583	14	21	35	2	8	0	2	6	4	33.0	9.7	11.7	0.7	.422
89-90 Indiana	3	0	54	18	7	15	.467	0	0	.000	4	4	1.000	6	9	15	2	13	0	0	1	7	18.0	6.0	5.0	0.7	.277
90-91 Indiana	5	5	126	45	19	39	.487	0	0	.000	7	7	1.000	6	25	31	8	15	0	4	7	10	25.2	9.0	6.2	1.6	.458
91-92 Indiana	3	3	63	16	7	11	.636	0	0	.000	2	2	1.000	2	11	13	4	11	0	1	4	3	21.0	5.3	4.3	1.3	.403
92-93 Indiana	4	0	73	15	5	15	.333	0	0	.000	5	6	.833	7	7	14	3	9	0	3	2	4	18.3	3.8	3.5	0.8	.249
93-94 Indiana	7	0	39	10	4	11	.364	0	0	.000	2	3	.667	3	7	10	5	9	0	3	1	4	5.6	1.4	1.4	0.7	.348
NBA Playoff Totals	28	14	547	178	71	163	.436	0	0	.000	36	45	.800	49	99	148	28	79	0	16	25	37	19.5	6.4	5.3	1.0	....

• THOMPSON, Mychal

Mychal George Thompson

Born: Jan. 30, 1955. Nassau, Bahamas. Height: 6'10". Weight: 226 lbs. Drafted: 1978 College: Minnesota

YEAR TEAM	GP	GS	MIN	PTS	FGM	FGA	FG%	3PM	3PA	3P%	FTM	FTA	FT%	ORB	DRB	TRB	AST	PF	DQ	STL	BLK	TO	MPG	PPG	RPG	APG	PCM
78-79 Portland	73	....	2144	1074	460	938	.490	....	....	....	154	269	.572	198	406	604	176	270	10	67	134	204	29.4	14.7	8.3	2.4	.562
80-81 Portland	79	....	2790	1345	569	1151	.494	0	1	.000	207	323	.641	223	463	686	284	260	5	62	170	245	35.3	17.0	8.7	3.6	.561
81-82 Portland	79	78	3129	1642	681	1303	.523	0	0	.000	280	446	.628	258	663	921	319	233	2	69	107	245	39.6	20.8	11.7	4.0	.644
82-83 Portland	80	80	3017	1259	505	1033	.489	0	1	.000	249	401	.621	183	570	753	380	213	1	68	110	280	37.7	15.7	9.4	4.8	.538
83-84 Portland	79	74	2648	1240	487	929	.524	0	2	.000	266	399	.667	235	453	688	308	237	2	84	108	237	33.5	15.7	8.7	3.9	.598
84-85 Portland	79	55	2616	1451	572	1111	.515	0	0	.000	307	449	.684	211	407	618	205	216	0	78	104	229	33.1	18.4	7.8	2.6	.586
85-86 Portland	82	78	2569	1204	503	1011	.498	0	0	.000	198	309	.641	181	427	608	176	267	5	76	35	197	31.3	14.7	7.4	2.1	.479

YEAR	TEAM	GP	GS	MIN	PTS	FGM	FGA	FG%	3PM	3PA	3P%	FTM	FTA	FT%	ORB	DRB	TRB	AST	PF	DQ	STL	BLK	TO	MPG	PPG	RPG	APG	PCM
86-87	San Antonio	49	6	1210	605	230	528	.436	1	1	1.000	144	196	.735	91	185	276	87	117	0	31	41	78	24.7	12.3	5.6	1.8	.490
86-87	LA Lakers	33	1	680	333	129	269	.480	0	1	.000	75	101	.743	47	89	136	28	85	1	14	30	56	20.6	10.1	4.1	0.8	.436
87-88	LA Lakers	80	0	2007	925	370	722	.512	0	3	.000	185	292	.634	198	291	489	66	251	1	38	79	112	25.1	11.6	6.1	0.8	.479
88-89	LA Lakers	80	8	1994	738	291	521	.559	0	0	.000	156	230	.678	157	310	467	48	224	0	58	59	96	24.9	9.2	5.8	0.6	.447
89-90	LA Lakers	70	70	1883	706	281	562	.500	0	0	.000	144	204	.706	173	304	477	43	207	0	33	73	77	26.9	10.1	6.8	0.6	.445
90-91	LA Lakers	72	4	1077	288	113	228	.496	0	2	.000	62	88	.705	74	154	228	21	112	0	23	23	50	15.0	4.0	3.2	0.3	.323
NBA Season Totals		935	454	27764	12810	5191	10306	.504	1	12	.083	2427	3707	.655	2229	4722	6951	2141	2692	27	701	1073	2106	29.7	13.7	7.4	2.3	....
78-79	Portland	3	....	121	59	27	54	.500	....	....	....	5	10	.500	9	22	31	6	11	0	2	5	5	40.3	19.7	10.3	2.0	.527
80-81	Portland	3	....	132	75	31	51	.608	0	0	.000	13	18	.722	5	18	23	4	10	0	3	9	7	44.0	25.0	7.7	1.3	.605
82-83	Portland	7	7	284	105	40	85	.471	0	0	.000	25	38	.658	16	40	56	39	24	0	6	8	28	40.6	15.0	8.0	5.6	.452
83-84	Portland	4	4	121	61	22	44	.500	0	0	.000	17	22	.773	9	20	29	15	11	0	5	3	6	30.3	15.3	7.3	3.8	.644
84-85	Portland	9	0	250	133	50	102	.490	0	0	.000	33	49	.673	25	47	72	14	32	2	7	12	19	27.8	14.8	8.0	1.6	.577
85-86	Portland	4	4	140	76	31	54	.574	0	0	.000	14	26	.538	11	22	33	14	13	0	1	3	10	35.0	19.0	8.3	3.5	.594
86-87	LA Lakers	18	0	401	158	62	137	.453	0	0	.000	34	50	.680	29	59	88	9	50	0	7	17	16	22.3	8.8	4.9	0.5	.390
87-88	LA Lakers	24	0	615	232	98	191	.513	0	0	.000	36	62	.581	63	107	170	12	70	1	17	21	33	25.6	9.7	7.1	0.5	.450
88-89	LA Lakers	15	0	377	171	65	128	.508	0	0	.000	41	60	.683	39	38	77	11	52	1	6	12	14	25.1	11.4	5.1	0.7	.442
89-90	LA Lakers	9	8	225	58	21	44	.477	0	0	.000	16	26	.615	15	24	39	2	26	0	2	13	17	25.0	6.4	4.3	0.2	.251
90-91	LA Lakers	8	0	42	4	2	7	.286	0	0	.000	0	0	.000	3	6	9	0	10	0	0	3	1	5.3	0.5	1.1	0.0	.117
NBA Playoff Totals		104	23	2708	1132	449	897	.501	0	0	.000	234	361	.648	224	403	627	126	309	4	56	106	156	26.0	10.9	6.0	1.2	....

• THOMPSON, Paul

Paul Stanford Thompson

Born: May 25, 1961. Smyrna, TN, United States.   Height: 6'6".   Weight: 210 lbs.   Drafted: 1983   College: Tulane

YEAR	TEAM	GP	GS	MIN	PTS	FGM	FGA	FG%	3PM	3PA	3P%	FTM	FTA	FT%	ORB	DRB	TRB	AST	PF	DQ	STL	BLK	TO	MPG	PPG	RPG	APG	PCM
83-84	Cleveland	82	10	1731	742	309	662	.467	9	39	.231	115	149	.772	120	192	312	122	192	2	70	37	74	21.1	9.0	3.8	1.5	.439
84-85	Cleveland	33	27	715	347	148	354	.418	6	23	.261	45	53	.849	36	80	116	58	77	1	41	20	43	21.7	10.5	3.5	1.8	.389
84-85	Milwaukee	16	0	227	106	41	105	.390	0	7	.000	24	34	.706	21	21	42	20	42	0	15	5	14	14.2	6.6	2.6	1.3	.389
85-86	Philadelphia	23	8	432	179	70	194	.361	2	12	.167	37	43	.860	27	36	63	24	49	1	15	17	30	18.8	7.8	2.7	1.0	.288
NBA Season Totals		154	45	3105	1374	568	1315	.432	17	81	.210	221	279	.792	204	329	533	224	360	4	141	79	161	20.2	8.9	3.5	1.5	....
84-85	Milwaukee	3	0	34	13	5	12	.417	0	2	.000	3	5	.600	1	4	5	2	3	0	4	1	4	11.3	4.3	1.7	0.7	.349
NBA Playoff Totals		3	0	34	13	5	12	.417	0	2	.000	3	5	.600	1	4	5	2	3	0	4	1	4	11.3	4.3	1.7	0.7	....

• THOMPSON, Stephen

Stephen M. Thompson

Born: Dec. 2, 1968. Los Angeles, CA, United States.   Height: 6'4".   Weight: 185 lbs.   Drafted: —   College: Syracuse

YEAR	TEAM	GP	GS	MIN	PTS	FGM	FGA	FG%	3PM	3PA	3P%	FTM	FTA	FT%	ORB	DRB	TRB	AST	PF	DQ	STL	BLK	TO	MPG	PPG	RPG	APG	PCM
91-92	Orlando	1	0	15	2	1	3	.333	0	0	.000	0	0	.000	0	1	1	1	2	0	0	0	2	15.0	2.0	1.0	1.0	-.043
91-92	Sacramento	18	0	76	29	13	34	.382	0	1	.000	3	8	.375	11	7	18	7	7	0	6	3	4	4.2	1.6	1.0	0.4	.431
NBA Season Totals		19	0	91	31	14	37	.378	0	1	.000	3	8	.375	11	8	19	8	9	0	6	3	6	4.8	1.6	1.0	0.4	....

• THOREN, Skip

Duane W. (Skip) Thoren

Born: Apr. 5, 1943. Rockford, IL, United States.   Height: 6'10".   Weight: 230 lbs.   Drafted: 1965   College: Illinois

YEAR	TEAM	GP	GS	MIN	PTS	FGM	FGA	FG%	3PM	3PA	3P%	FTM	FTA	FT%	ORB	DRB	TRB	AST	PF	DQ	STL	BLK	TO	MPG	PPG	RPG	APG	PCM
67-68	Minnesota-A	63	....	1203	514	206	475	.434	0	1	.000	102	164	.622	....	....	436	59	124	3	....	....	77	19.1	8.2	6.9	0.9	.536
68-69	Miami-A	78	....	2645	1305	532	1100	.484	0	2	.000	241	392	.615	**391**	655	1046	195	324	11	....	....	180	33.9	16.7	13.4	2.5	.656
69-70	Miami-A	29	....	1020	420	164	364	.451	0	2	.000	92	155	.594	109	284	393	75	112	2	....	....	91	35.2	14.5	13.6	2.6	.584
ABA Season Totals		170	....	4868	2239	902	1939	.465	0	5	.000	435	711	.612	500	939	1875	329	560	16	....	....	348	28.6	13.2	11.0	1.9	....
67-68	Minnesota-A	2	....	52	35	14	28	.500	0	0	.000	7	12	.583	....	....	27	4	5	0	....	....	7	26.0	17.5	13.5	2.0	.891
68-69	Miami-A	12	....	402	157	61	129	.473	0	0	.000	35	61	.574	42	113	155	17	48	3	....	....	25	33.5	13.1	12.9	1.4	.546
ABA Playoff Totals		14	....	454	192	75	157	.478	0	0	.000	42	73	.575	42	113	182	21	53	3	....	....	32	32.4	13.7	13.0	1.5	....

• THORN, Rod

Rodney King Thorn

Born: May 23, 1941. Princeton, WV, United States.   Height: 6'4".   Weight: 195 lbs.   Drafted: 1963   College: West Virginia

YEAR	TEAM	GP	GS	MIN	PTS	FGM	FGA	FG%	3PM	3PA	3P%	FTM	FTA	FT%	ORB	DRB	TRB	AST	PF	DQ	STL	BLK	TO	MPG	PPG	RPG	APG	PCM
63-64	Baltimore	75	....	2594	1080	411	1015	.405	....	....	....	258	353	.731	....	....	360	281	187	3	....	....	....	34.6	14.4	4.8	3.7	.433
64-65	Detroit	74	....	1770	816	320	750	.427	....	....	....	176	243	.724	....	....	266	161	122	0	....	....	....	23.9	11.0	3.6	2.2	.461
65-66	Detroit	27	....	815	376	143	343	.417	....	....	....	90	123	.732	....	....	101	64	67	0	....	....	....	30.2	13.9	3.7	2.4	.414
65-66	St. Louis	46	....	924	404	163	385	.423	....	....	....	78	113	.690	....	....	109	81	77	0	....	....	....	20.1	8.8	2.4	1.8	.400
66-67	St. Louis	67	....	1166	591	233	524	.445	....	....	....	125	172	.727	....	....	160	118	88	0	....	....	....	17.4	8.8	2.4	1.8	.493
67-68	Seattle	66	....	1668	1006	377	835	.451	....	....	....	252	342	.737	....	....	265	230	117	1	....	....	....	25.3	15.2	4.0	3.5	.627
68-69	Seattle	29	....	567	333	131	283	.463	....	....	....	71	97	.732	....	....	83	80	58	0	....	....	....	19.6	11.5	2.9	2.8	.588
69-70	Seattle	19	....	105	55	20	45	.444	....	....	....	15	24	.625	....	....	16	17	8	0	....	....	....	5.5	2.9	0.8	0.9	.558
70-71	Seattle	63	....	767	351	141	299	.472	....	....	....	69	102	.676	....	....	103	182	60	0	....	....	....	12.2	5.6	1.6	2.9	.614
NBA Season Totals		466	....	10376	5012	1939	4479	.433	....	....	....	1134	1569	.723	....	....	1463	1214	784	4	....	....	....	22.3	10.8	3.1	2.6	....
65-66	St. Louis	10	....	119	38	12	39	.308	....	....	....	14	18	.778	....	....	17	10	9	0	....	....	....	11.9	3.8	1.7	1.0	.313
66-67	St. Louis	9	....	156	91	33	77	.429	....	....	....	25	27	.926	....	....	28	11	13	0	....	....	....	17.3	10.1	3.1	1.2	.548
NBA Playoff Totals		19	....	275	129	45	116	.388	....	....	....	39	45	.867	....	....	45	21	22	0	....	....	....	14.5	6.8	2.4	1.1	....

• THORNTON, —

Thornton

Born: —.   Height: —   Weight: —   Drafted: —   College: —

YEAR	TEAM	GP	GS	MIN	PTS	FGM	FGA	FG%	3PM	3PA	3P%	FTM	FTA	FT%	ORB	DRB	TRB	AST	PF	DQ	STL	BLK	TO	MPG	PPG	RPG	APG	PCM
38-39	Hammond-N	1	....	....	2	1	....	....	....	....	....	0	....	....	....	....	....	....	....	....	....	....	....	....	2.0	....	....	....
NBL Season Totals		1	....	....	2	1	....	....	....	....	....	0	....	....	....	....	....	....	....	....	....	....	....	....	2.0	....	....	....

• THORNTON, Bob

Robert George Thornton

Born: July 10, 1962. Los Angeles, CA, United States. Height: 6'10". Weight: 225 lbs. Drafted: 1984 College: California (Irvine)

YEAR	TEAM	GP	GS	MIN	PTS	FGM	FGA	FG%	3PM	3PA	3P%	FTM	FTA	FT%	ORB	DRB	TRB	AST	PF	DQ	STL	BLK	TO	MPG	PPG	RPG	APG	PCM
85-86	New York	71	23	1323	336	125	274	.456	0	0	.000	86	162	.531	113	177	290	43	209	5	30	7	85	18.6	4.7	4.1	0.6	.254
86-87	New York	33	4	282	71	29	67	.433	0	1	.000	13	20	.650	18	38	56	8	48	0	4	3	23	8.5	2.2	1.7	0.2	.198
87-88	New York	7	0	85	17	6	19	.316	0	0	.000	5	8	.625	5	8	13	4	23	0	2	0	8	12.1	2.4	1.9	0.6	.042
87-88	Philadelphia	41	2	508	147	59	111	.532	0	2	.000	29	47	.617	41	58	99	11	80	1	9	3	29	12.4	3.6	2.4	0.3	.278
88-89	Philadelphia	54	0	449	127	47	111	.423	1	3	.333	32	60	.533	36	56	92	15	87	0	8	7	22	8.3	2.4	1.7	0.3	.243
89-90	Philadelphia	56	0	592	123	48	112	.429	1	3	.333	26	51	.510	45	88	133	17	105	1	20	12	34	10.6	2.2	2.4	0.3	.241
90-91	Minnesota	12	1	110	16	4	13	.308	0	0	.000	8	10	.800	1	14	15	1	18	0	0	3	10	9.2	1.3	1.3	0.1	.062
91-92	Utah	2	0	6	4	1	7	.143	0	0	.000	2	2	1.000	2	0	2	0	1	0	0	0	0	3.0	2.0	1.0	0.0	-.030
95-96	Washington	7	0	31	3	1	6	.167	0	0	.000	1	2	.500	6	6	12	0	7	0	1	0	1	4.4	0.4	1.7	0.0	.188
NBA Season Totals		283	30	3386	844	320	720	.444	2	9	.222	202	362	.558	267	445	712	99	578	7	74	35	212	12.0	3.0	2.5	0.3	....
89-90	Philadelphia	9	0	89	19	7	18	.389	0	0	.000	5	10	.500	11	4	15	4	22	0	2	1	2	9.9	2.1	1.7	0.4	.172
91-92	Utah	7	0	32	7	2	5	.400	0	0	.000	3	4	.750	4	5	9	1	3	0	0	0	1	4.6	1.0	1.3	0.1	.339
NBA Playoff Totals		16	0	121	26	9	23	.391	0	0	.000	8	14	.571	15	9	24	5	25	0	2	1	3	7.6	1.6	1.5	0.3	....

• THORNTON, Dallas

Dallas (Big D) Thornton

Born: Sept. 1, 1946. Louisville, KY, United States. Height: 6'4". Weight: 190 lbs. Drafted: 1968 College: Kentucky Wesleyan

YEAR	TEAM	GP	GS	MIN	PTS	FGM	FGA	FG%	3PM	3PA	3P%	FTM	FTA	FT%	ORB	DRB	TRB	AST	PF	DQ	STL	BLK	TO	MPG	PPG	RPG	APG	PCM
68-69	Miami-A	45	....	756	297	108	249	.434	2	9	.222	79	125	.632	38	81	119	63	92	1	....	....	80	16.8	6.6	2.6	1.4	.385
69-70	Miami-A	5	....	114	44	15	35	.429	0	2	.000	14	17	.824	5	17	22	11	14	0	....	....	18	22.8	8.8	4.4	2.2	.447
ABA Season Totals		50	....	870	341	123	284	.433	2	11	.182	93	142	.655	43	98	141	74	106	1	....	....	98	17.4	6.8	2.8	1.5	....
68-69	Miami-A	7	....	118	67	23	59	.390	0	7	.000	21	34	.618	....	....	23	6	9	0	....	....	8	16.9	9.6	3.3	0.9	.451
ABA Playoff Totals		7	....	118	67	23	59	.390	0	7	.000	21	34	.618	....	....	23	6	9	0	....	....	8	16.9	9.6	3.3	0.9	....

• THORNTON, Jack

Jack Thornton

Born: 1914. Height: 6'5". Weight: 200 lbs. Drafted: — College: Texas Wesleyan

YEAR	TEAM	GP	GS	MIN	PTS	FGM	FGA	FG%	3PM	3PA	3P%	FTM	FTA	FT%	ORB	DRB	TRB	AST	PF	DQ	STL	BLK	TO	MPG	PPG	RPG	APG	PCM
41-42	Sheboygan-N	2	....	....	3	0	....	....	....	....	....	3	....	....	....	....	....	....	....	....	....	....	....	....	1.5	....	....	....
NBL Season Totals		2	....	....	3	0	....	....	....	....	....	3	....	....	....	....	....	....	....	....	....	....	....	....	1.5	....	....	....

• THORPE, Otis

Otis Henry Thorpe

Born: Aug. 5, 1962. Boynton Beach, FL, United States. Height: 6'9". Weight: 225 lbs. Drafted: 1984 College: Providence

YEAR	TEAM	GP	GS	MIN	PTS	FGM	FGA	FG%	3PM	3PA	3P%	FTM	FTA	FT%	ORB	DRB	TRB	AST	PF	DQ	STL	BLK	TO	MPG	PPG	RPG	APG	PCM
84-85	Kansas City	82	23	1918	1052	411	685	.600	0	2	.000	230	371	.620	187	369	556	111	256	2	34	37	189	23.4	12.8	6.8	1.4	.594
85-86	Sacramento	75	18	1675	742	289	492	.587	0	0	.000	164	248	.661	137	283	420	84	233	3	35	34	120	22.3	9.9	5.6	1.1	.501
86-87	Sacramento	82	82	2956	1547	567	1050	.540	0	3	.000	413	543	.761	259	560	819	201	292	11	46	60	189	36.0	18.9	10.0	2.5	.609
87-88	Sacramento	82	82	3072	1704	622	1226	.507	0	6	.000	460	609	.755	279	558	837	266	264	3	62	56	230	37.5	20.8	10.2	3.2	.621
88-89	Houston	82	82	3135	1370	521	961	.542	0	2	.000	328	450	.729	272	515	787	202	259	6	82	37	221	38.2	16.7	9.6	2.5	.522
89-90	Houston	82	82	2947	1401	547	998	.548	0	10	.000	307	446	.688	258	476	734	261	270	5	66	24	230	35.9	17.1	9.0	3.2	.550
90-91	Houston	82	82	3039	1435	549	988	.556	3	7	.429	334	480	.696	287	559	846	197	278	10	73	20	213	37.1	17.5	10.3	2.4	.564
91-92	Houston	82	82	3056	1420	558	943	.592	0	7	.000	304	463	.657	285	577	862	250	307	7	52	37	238	37.3	17.3	10.5	3.0	.581
92-93	Houston	72	69	2357	923	385	690	.558	0	2	.000	153	256	.598	219	370	589	181	234	3	43	19	151	32.7	12.8	8.2	2.5	.484
93-94	Houston	82	82	2909	1149	449	801	.561	0	2	.000	251	382	.657	271	599	870	189	253	1	66	28	189	35.5	14.0	10.6	2.3	.538
94-95	Houston	36	35	1188	479	206	366	.563	0	3	.000	67	127	.528	113	209	322	58	102	1	22	13	76	33.0	13.3	8.9	1.6	.487
94-95	Portland	34	0	908	458	179	315	.568	0	4	.000	100	154	.649	89	147	236	54	122	2	19	15	54	26.7	13.5	6.9	1.6	.559
95-96	Detroit	82	82	2841	1161	452	853	.530	0	4	.000	257	362	.710	211	477	688	158	**300**	7	53	39	197	34.6	14.2	8.4	1.9	.461
96-97	Detroit	79	79	2661	1036	419	787	.532	0	2	.000	198	303	.653	226	396	622	133	298	7	59	17	142	33.7	13.1	7.9	1.7	.438
97-98	Vancouver	47	46	1574	528	205	430	.477	0	4	.000	118	170	.694	100	271	371	161	158	3	30	23	113	33.5	11.2	7.9	3.4	.435
97-98	Sacramento	27	20	623	224	89	194	.459	0	1	.000	46	70	.657	51	115	166	61	80	1	18	7	38	23.1	8.3	6.1	2.3	.460
98-99	Washington	49	38	1539	554	240	440	.545	0	2	.000	74	106	.698	96	238	334	101	196	**9**	42	19	88	31.4	11.3	6.8	2.1	.429
99-00	Miami	51	1	777	279	125	243	.514	0	3	.000	29	48	.604	56	110	166	33	136	4	26	9	59	15.2	5.5	3.3	0.6	.343
00-01	Charlotte	49	4	647	138	59	131	.450	0	0	.000	20	24	.833	50	95	145	29	108	0	12	7	32	13.2	2.8	3.0	0.6	.268
NBA Season Totals		1257	989	39822	17600	6872	12593	.546	3	64	.047	3853	5612	.687	3446	6924	10370	2730	4146	85	840	501	2769	31.7	14.0	8.2	2.2	....
85-86	Sacramento	3	0	35	12	3	13	.231	0	0	.000	6	13	.462	8	4	12	0	4	0	0	1	1	11.7	4.0	4.0	0.0	.250
88-89	Houston	4	4	152	64	24	37	.649	0	0	.000	16	21	.762	6	14	20	12	17	1	5	1	15	38.0	16.0	5.0	3.0	.426
89-90	Houston	4	4	164	80	27	45	.600	0	0	.000	26	38	.684	14	19	33	7	12	0	5	0	9	41.0	20.0	8.3	1.8	.527
90-91	Houston	3	3	116	47	22	38	.579	0	0	.000	3	6	.500	7	18	25	8	8	0	2	0	6	38.7	15.7	8.3	2.7	.475
92-93	Houston	12	12	419	174	73	115	.635	0	0	.000	28	43	.651	36	67	103	31	35	0	6	1	17	34.9	14.5	8.6	2.6	.552
93-94	Houston	23	23	854	261	111	194	.572	1	2	.500	38	67	.567	68	160	228	54	86	2	13	10	37	37.1	11.3	9.9	2.3	.453
94-95	Portland	3	0	66	31	12	21	.571	0	0	.000	7	10	.700	5	8	13	2	12	1	0	0	3	22.0	10.3	4.3	0.7	.410
95-96	Detroit	3	3	101	35	13	24	.542	0	0	.000	9	12	.750	14	21	35	7	9	0	0	0	7	33.7	11.7	11.7	2.3	.522
96-97	Detroit	5	5	152	49	21	41	.512	0	0	.000	7	9	.778	12	20	32	4	21	0	2	0	9	30.4	9.8	6.4	0.8	.311
99-00	Miami	10	0	136	33	13	27	.481	0	1	.000	7	14	.500	6	23	29	3	29	0	0	2	11	13.6	3.3	2.9	0.3	.187
00-01	Charlotte	8	0	57	4	2	9	.222	0	0	.000	0	0	.000	6	11	17	0	8	0	0	0	2	7.1	0.5	2.1	0.0	.133
NBA Playoff Totals		78	54	2252	790	321	564	.569	1	3	.333	147	233	.631	182	365	547	128	241	4	33	15	117	28.9	10.1	7.0	1.6	....

• THREATT, Sedale

Sedale Eugene Threatt

Born: Sept. 10, 1961. Atlanta, GA, United States. Height: 6'2". Weight: 175 lbs. Drafted: 1983 College: West Virginia Tech

YEAR	TEAM	GP	GS	MIN	PTS	FGM	FGA	FG%	3PM	3PA	3P%	FTM	FTA	FT%	ORB	DRB	TRB	AST	PF	DQ	STL	BLK	TO	MPG	PPG	RPG	APG	PCM
83-84	Philadelphia	45	0	464	148	62	148	.419	1	8	.125	23	28	.821	17	23	40	41	65	1	13	2	32	10.3	3.3	0.9	0.9	.217
84-85	Philadelphia	82	0	1304	446	188	416	.452	4	22	.182	66	90	.733	21	78	99	175	171	2	80	16	98	15.9	5.4	1.2	2.1	.322
85-86	Philadelphia	70	27	1754	696	310	684	.453	1	24	.042	75	90	.833	21	100	121	193	157	1	93	5	105	25.1	9.9	1.7	2.8	.331
86-87	Philadelphia	28	8	668	265	108	261	.414	7	16	.438	42	53	.792	18	39	57	82	76	0	32	4	48	23.9	9.5	2.0	2.9	.317
86-87	Chicago	40	0	778	315	131	273	.480	0	16	.000	53	66	.803	8	43	51	177	88	0	42	9	44	19.5	7.9	1.3	4.4	.487
87-88	Chicago	45	0	701	298	132	263	.502	2	20	.100	32	41	.780	12	43	55	107	71	0	27	3	45	15.6	6.6	1.2	2.4	.414
87-88	Seattle	26	0	354	194	84	162	.519	1	7	.143	25	30	.833	11	22	33	53	29	0	33	5	18	13.6	7.5	1.3	2.0	.597

YEAR	TEAM	GP	GS	MIN	PTS	FGM	FGA	FG%	3PM	3PA	3P%	FTM	FTA	FT%	ORB	DRB	TRB	AST	PF	DQ	STL	BLK	TO	MPG	PPG	RPG	APG	PCM
88-89	Seattle	63	0	1220	544	235	476	.494	11	30	.367	63	77	.818	31	86	117	238	155	0	83	4	76	19.4	8.6	1.9	3.8	.504
89-90	Seattle	65	18	1481	744	303	599	.506	8	32	.250	130	157	.828	43	72	115	216	164	0	65	8	78	22.8	11.4	1.8	3.3	.479
90-91	Seattle	80	57	2066	1013	433	835	.519	10	35	.286	137	173	.792	25	74	99	273	191	0	113	8	136	25.8	12.7	1.2	3.4	.436
91-92	LA Lakers	82	82	3070	1240	509	1041	.489	20	62	.323	202	243	.831	43	210	253	593	231	1	168	16	180	37.4	15.1	3.1	7.2	.486
92-93	LA Lakers	82	82	2893	1235	522	1028	.508	14	53	.264	177	215	.823	47	226	273	564	248	1	142	11	172	35.3	15.1	3.3	6.9	.508
93-94	LA Lakers	81	20	2278	965	411	852	.482	5	33	.152	138	155	.890	28	125	153	344	186	1	110	19	105	28.1	11.9	1.9	4.2	.440
94-95	LA Lakers	59	2	1384	558	217	437	.497	36	95	.379	88	111	.793	21	103	124	248	139	1	54	12	71	23.5	9.5	2.1	4.2	.470
95-96	LA Lakers	82	8	1687	596	241	526	.458	60	169	.355	54	71	.761	20	75	95	269	178	0	68	11	74	20.6	7.3	1.2	3.3	.365
96-97	Houston	21	0	334	70	28	74	.378	8	20	.400	6	8	.750	5	19	24	40	29	0	15	3	13	15.9	3.3	1.1	1.9	.247
NBA Season Totals		951	304	22436	9327	3914	8075	.485	188	642	.293	1311	1608	.815	371	1338	1709	3613	2178	8	1138	136	1295	23.6	9.8	1.8	3.8	....
83-84	Philadelphia	3	0	6	2	1	3	.333	0	2	.000	0	0	.000	1	1	2	1	0	0	1	0	2	2.0	0.7	0.7	0.3	.357
84-85	Philadelphia	4	0	28	4	2	7	.286	0	0	.000	0	0	.000	1	0	1	5	2	0	1	0	3	7.0	1.0	0.3	1.3	.101
85-86	Philadelphia	12	0	312	160	67	143	.469	0	2	.000	26	33	.788	6	19	25	42	35	0	23	2	15	26.0	13.3	2.1	3.5	.472
86-87	Chicago	3	0	70	20	8	17	.471	0	0	.000	4	4	1.000	2	3	5	16	11	0	1	0	2	23.3	6.7	1.7	5.3	.390
87-88	Seattle	5	0	80	32	14	34	.412	0	1	.000	4	4	1.000	2	9	11	11	7	0	1	0	5	16.0	6.4	2.2	2.2	.355
88-89	Seattle	8	1	201	96	39	82	.476	1	4	.250	17	20	.850	3	10	13	49	22	0	17	0	11	25.1	12.0	1.6	6.1	.570
90-91	Seattle	5	5	136	73	30	56	.536	4	11	.364	9	10	.900	1	7	8	17	14	0	5	0	8	27.2	14.6	1.6	3.4	.475
91-92	LA Lakers	4	4	162	59	24	46	.522	2	3	.667	9	12	.750	0	8	8	17	11	0	2	0	11	40.5	14.8	2.0	4.3	.305
92-93	LA Lakers	5	5	205	90	39	89	.438	3	13	.231	9	12	.750	3	14	17	40	19	1	13	1	12	41.0	18.0	3.4	8.0	.456
94-95	LA Lakers	1	0	11	2	1	4	.250	0	2	.000	0	0	.000	0	0	0	2	2	0	1	0	0	11.0	2.0	0.0	2.0	.119
95-96	LA Lakers	4	0	57	10	4	18	.222	2	11	.182	0	0	.000	1	2	3	4	4	0	2	0	3	14.3	2.5	0.8	1.0	.019
96-97	Houston	16	0	266	59	22	56	.393	9	30	.300	6	8	.750	2	15	17	48	35	0	6	4	12	16.6	3.7	1.1	3.0	.283
NBA Playoff Totals		70	15	1534	607	251	555	.452	21	79	.266	84	103	.816	22	88	110	252	162	1	73	7	84	21.9	8.7	1.6	3.6	....

• THURMOND, Nate

Nathaniel (Nate the Great) Thurmond

Born: July 25, 1941. Akron, OH, United States. Height: 6'11". Weight: 225 lbs. Drafted: 1963 College: Bowling Green HOF: 1985

YEAR	TEAM	GP	GS	MIN	PTS	FGM	FGA	FG%	3PM	3PA	3P%	FTM	FTA	FT%	ORB	DRB	TRB	AST	PF	DQ	STL	BLK	TO	MPG	PPG	RPG	APG	PCM
63-64	San Francisco	76	....	1966	533	219	554	.395	....	....	....	95	173	.549	....	....	790	86	184	2	....	....	....	25.9	7.0	10.4	1.1	.453
64-65	San Francisco	77	....	3173	1273	519	1240	.419	....	....	....	235	357	.658	....	....	1395	157	232	3	....	....	....	41.2	16.5	18.1	2.0	.582
65-66	San Francisco	73	....	2891	1188	454	1119	.406	....	....	....	280	428	.654	....	....	1312	111	223	7	....	....	....	39.6	16.3	18.0	1.5	.583
66-67	San Francisco	65	....	2755	1214	467	1068	.437	....	....	....	280	445	.629	....	....	1382	166	183	3	....	....	....	42.4	18.7	21.3	2.6	.689
67-68	San Francisco	51	....	2222	1046	382	929	.411	....	....	....	282	438	.644	....	....	1121	215	137	1	....	....	....	43.6	20.5	22.0	4.2	.741
68-69	San Francisco	71	....	3208	1524	571	1394	.410	....	....	....	382	621	.615	....	....	1402	253	171	0	....	....	....	45.2	21.5	19.7	3.6	.664
69-70	San Francisco	43	....	1919	943	341	824	.414	....	....	....	261	346	.754	....	....	762	150	110	1	....	....	....	44.6	21.9	**17.7**	3.5	.662
70-71	San Francisco	82	....	3351	1641	623	1401	.445	....	....	....	395	541	.730	....	....	1128	257	192	1	....	....	....	40.9	20.0	13.8	3.1	.624
71-72	Golden State	78	....	3362	1673	628	1454	.432	....	....	....	417	561	.743	....	....	1252	230	214	1	....	....	....	43.1	21.4	16.1	2.9	.639
72-73	Golden State	79	....	3419	1349	517	1159	.446	....	....	....	315	439	.718	....	....	1349	280	240	2	....	....	....	43.3	17.1	17.1	3.5	.620
73-74	Golden State	62	....	2463	807	308	694	.444	....	....	....	191	287	.666	249	629	878	165	179	4	41	179	....	39.7	13.0	14.2	2.7	.527
74-75	Chicago	80	....	2756	632	250	686	.364	....	....	....	132	224	.589	259	645	904	328	271	6	46	195	....	34.5	7.9	11.3	4.1	.454
75-76	Chicago	13	....	260	48	20	45	.444	....	....	....	8	18	.444	14	57	71	26	15	0	4	12	....	20.0	3.7	5.5	2.0	.409
75-76	Cleveland	65	....	1133	298	122	292	.418	....	....	....	54	105	.514	101	243	344	68	145	1	18	86	....	17.4	4.6	5.3	1.0	.389
76-77	Cleveland	49	....	997	268	100	246	.407	....	....	....	68	106	.642	121	253	374	83	128	2	16	81	....	20.3	5.5	7.6	1.7	.489
NBA Season Totals		964	....	35875	14437	5521	13105	.421	....	....	....	3395	5089	.667	744	1827	14464	2575	2624	34	125	553	....	37.2	15.0	15.0	2.7	....
63-64	San Francisco	12	....	410	120	42	96	.438	....	....	....	36	53	.679	....	....	148	10	46	0	....	....	....	34.2	10.0	12.3	0.8	.441
66-67	San Francisco	15	....	690	238	93	215	.433	....	....	....	52	91	.571	....	....	346	47	52	1	....	....	....	46.0	15.9	23.1	3.1	.633
68-69	San Francisco	6	....	263	100	40	102	.392	....	....	....	20	34	.588	....	....	117	28	18	0	....	....	....	43.8	16.7	19.5	4.7	.628
70-71	San Francisco	5	....	192	88	36	97	.371	....	....	....	16	20	.800	....	....	51	15	20	0	....	....	....	38.4	17.6	10.2	3.0	.449
71-72	Golden State	5	....	230	127	53	122	.434	....	....	....	21	28	.750	....	....	89	26	12	0	....	....	....	46.0	25.4	17.8	5.2	.720
72-73	Golden State	11	....	460	160	64	161	.398	....	....	....	32	40	.800	....	....	145	40	30	1	....	....	....	41.8	14.5	13.2	3.6	.501
74-75	Chicago	13	....	254	46	14	38	.368	....	....	....	18	37	.486	24	63	87	31	36	0	5	21	....	19.5	3.5	6.7	2.4	.440
75-76	Cleveland	13	....	375	87	37	79	.468	....	....	....	13	32	.406	38	79	117	28	52	2	6	29	....	28.8	6.7	9.0	2.2	.408
76-77	Cleveland	1	....	1	0	0	0	.000	....	....	....	0	0	.000	0	1	1	0	0	0	0	1	....	1.0	0.0	1.0	0.0	.863
NBA Playoff Totals		81	....	2875	966	379	910	.416	....	....	....	208	335	.621	62	143	1101	225	266	4	11	51	....	35.5	11.9	13.6	2.8	....

• THURSTON, Mel

John Melvin Thurston

Born: Jan. 16, 1919. Died: Oct.8, 1997. Height: 6' Weight: 175 lbs. Drafted: — College: Canisius

YEAR	TEAM	GP	GS	MIN	PTS	FGM	FGA	FG%	3PM	3PA	3P%	FTM	FTA	FT%	ORB	DRB	TRB	AST	PF	DQ	STL	BLK	TO	MPG	PPG	RPG	APG	PCM
46-47	Tri-Cities-N	39	....	....	114	39	....	....	....	....	....	36	59	.610	....	....	....	....	62	....	....	....	....	....	2.9	....	....	....
47-48	Tri-Cities-N	34	....	....	110	36	....	....	....	....	....	38	61	.623	....	....	....	....	....	....	....	....	....	....	3.2	....	....	....
47-48	Providence	14	....	....	78	32	113	.283	....	....	....	14	28	.500	....	....	....	4	42	....	....	....	....	....	5.6	....	0.3	....
NBA Season Totals		14	....	....	78	32	113	.283	....	....	....	14	28	.500	....	....	....	4	42	....	....	....	....	....	5.6	....	0.3	....
NBL Season Totals		73	....	....	224	75	....	....	....	....	....	74	120	....	....	....	....	....	62	....	....	....	....	....	3.1	....	....	....
Career Totals		87	....	....	302	107	113	....	....	....	....	88	148	....	....	....	....	4	104	....	....	....	....	....	3.5	....	0.0	....

• TICCO, Milt

Milton M. Ticco

Born: Sept. 22, 1922. Jenkins, KY, United States. Died: Jan.26, 2002. Height: 6'3". Weight: 205 lbs. Drafted: — College: Kentucky

YEAR	TEAM	GP	GS	MIN	PTS	FGM	FGA	FG%	3PM	3PA	3P%	FTM	FTA	FT%	ORB	DRB	TRB	AST	PF	DQ	STL	BLK	TO	MPG	PPG	RPG	APG	PCM
46-47	Youngstown-N	36	....	....	406	180	....	....	....	....	....	46	63	.730	....	....	....	....	79	....	....	....	....	....	11.3	....	....	....
47-48	Flint-N	30	....	....	173	74	....	....	....	....	....	25	35	.714	....	....	....	....	....	....	....	....	....	....	5.8	....	....	....
47-48	Indianapolis-N	10	....	....	9	3	....	....	....	....	....	3	3	1.000	....	....	....	....	....	....	....	....	....	....	0.9	....	....	....
47-48	Sheboygan-N	20	....	....	82	35	....	....	....	....	....	12	13	.923	....	....	....	....	....	....	....	....	....	....	4.1	....	....	....
NBL Season Totals		96	....	....	670	292	....	....	....	....	....	86	114	....	....	....	....	....	79	....	....	....	....	....	7.0	....	....	....

• TIDRICK, Hal

Howard Benjamin Tidrick

Born: Aug. 4, 1915. Died: Apr.2, 1974. Height: 6'1". Weight: 190 lbs. Drafted: — College: Washington & Jefferson

YEAR	TEAM	GP	GS	MIN	PTS	FGM	FGA	FG%	3PM	3PA	3P%	FTM	FTA	FT%	ORB	DRB	TRB	AST	PF	DQ	STL	BLK	TO	MPG	PPG	RPG	APG	PCM
44-45	Sheboygan-N	1	....	....	0	0	....	....	....	....	....	0	....	....	....	....	....	....	....	....	....	....	....	....	0.0	....	....	....
46-47	Toledo-N	44	....	....	579	**232**	....	....	....	....	....	115	165	.697	....	....	....	....	105	....	....	....	....	....	13.2	....	....	....
47-48	Toledo-N	59	....	....	723	267	....	....	....	....	....	189	243	**.778**	....	....	....	....	149	....	....	....	....	....	12.3	....	....	....

YEAR	TEAM	GP	GS	MIN	PTS	FGM	FGA	FG%	3PM	3PA	3P%	FTM	FTA	FT%	ORB	DRB	TRB	AST	PF	DQ	STL	BLK	TO	MPG	PPG	RPG	APG	PCM
48-49	Indianapolis	8	....	....	38	12	67	.179	....	....	....	14	18	.778	....	....	....	11	18	....	....	....	....	4.8	....	1.4	....
48-49	Baltimore	53	....	....	514	182	549	.332	....	....	....	150	187	.802	....	....	....	90	173	....	....	....	....	9.7	....	1.7	....
NBA Season Totals		61	....	....	552	194	616	.315	....	....	....	164	205	.800	....	....	....	101	191	....	....	....	....	9.0	....	1.7	....
NBL Season Totals		104	....	....	1302	499	....	....	....	....	....	304	408	....	....	....	....	....	254	....	....	....	....	12.5	....	....	....
Career Totals		165	....	....	1854	693	616	....	....	....	....	468	613	....	....	....	....	101	445	....	....	....	....	11.2	....	0.6	....
46-47	Toledo-N	5	....	....	51	19	....	....	....	....	....	13	21	.619	....	....	....	....	....	....	....	....	....	10.2	....	....	....
48-49	Baltimore	3	....	....	13	5	19	.263	....	....	....	3	5	.600	....	....	....	1	16	....	....	....	....	4.3	....	0.3	....
NBA Playoff Totals		3	....	....	13	5	19	.263	....	....	....	3	5	.600	....	....	....	1	16	....	....	....	....	4.3	....	0.3	....
NBL Playoff Totals		5	....	....	51	19	....	....	....	....	....	13	21	....	....	....	....	....	....	....	....	....	....	10.2	....	....	....
Career Playoff Totals		8	....	....	64	24	19	....	....	....	....	16	26	....	....	....	....	1	16	....	....	....	....	8.0	....	0.1	....

• TIEMAN, Dan

Daniel Theodore Tieman

Born: Nov. 30, 1940. Height: 6'. Weight: 185 lbs. Drafted: — College: Villa Madonna

YEAR	TEAM	GP	GS	MIN	PTS	FGM	FGA	FG%	3PM	3PA	3P%	FTM	FTA	FT%	ORB	DRB	TRB	AST	PF	DQ	STL	BLK	TO	MPG	PPG	RPG	APG	PCM
62-63	Cincinnati	29	....	176	34	15	57	.263	....	....	....	4	10	.400	....	....	22	27	18	0	....	....	....	6.1	1.2	0.8	0.9	.235
NBA Season Totals		29	....	176	34	15	57	.263	....	....	....	4	10	.400	....	....	22	27	18	0	....	....	....	6.1	1.2	0.8	0.9	

• TILLIS, Darren

Darren Tillis

Born: Feb. 23, 1960. Dallas, TX, United States. Height: 6'11". Weight: 215 lbs. Drafted: 1982 College: Cleveland State

YEAR	TEAM	GP	GS	MIN	PTS	FGM	FGA	FG%	3PM	3PA	3P%	FTM	FTA	FT%	ORB	DRB	TRB	AST	PF	DQ	STL	BLK	TO	MPG	PPG	RPG	APG	PCM
82-83	Boston	15	0	44	16	7	23	.304	0	1	.000	2	6	.333	4	5	9	2	8	0	0	2	5	2.9	1.1	0.6	0.1	.086
82-83	Cleveland	37	4	482	152	69	158	.437	0	0	.000	14	22	.636	37	84	121	16	86	3	8	28	19	13.0	4.1	3.3	0.4	.356
83-84	Golden State	72	1	730	257	108	254	.425	0	2	.000	41	63	.651	75	109	184	24	176	1	12	60	50	10.1	3.6	2.6	0.3	.338
NBA Season Totals		124	5	1256	425	184	435	.423	0	3	.000	57	91	.626	116	198	314	42	270	4	20	90	74	10.1	3.4	2.5	0.3	....

• TINGLE, Jack

Robert Jackson Tingle

Born: Dec. 30, 1924. Bedford, KY, United States. Died: Sept.22, 1958. Height: 6'4". Weight: 205 lbs. Drafted: 1947 College: Kentucky

YEAR	TEAM	GP	GS	MIN	PTS	FGM	FGA	FG%	3PM	3PA	3P%	FTM	FTA	FT%	ORB	DRB	TRB	AST	PF	DQ	STL	BLK	TO	MPG	PPG	RPG	APG	PCM
47-48	Washington	37	....	....	89	36	137	.263	....	....	....	17	33	.515	....	....	....	7	45	....	....	....	....	2.4	....	0.2	....
48-49	Minneapolis	2	....	....	2	1	6	.167	....	....	....	0	0	.000	....	....	....	1	2	....	....	....	....	1.0	....	0.5	....
NBA Season Totals		39	....	....	91	37	143	.259	....	....	....	17	33	.515	....	....	....	8	47	....	....	....	....	2.3	....	0.2	....

• TINSLEY, George

George T. Tinsley

Born: Sept. 19, 1946. Louisville, KY, United States. Height: 6'5". Weight: 205 lbs. Drafted: 1969 College: Kentucky Wesleyan

YEAR	TEAM	GP	GS	MIN	PTS	FGM	FGA	FG%	3PM	3PA	3P%	FTM	FTA	FT%	ORB	DRB	TRB	AST	PF	DQ	STL	BLK	TO	MPG	PPG	RPG	APG	PCM
69-70	Kentucky-A	77	....	1419	506	173	400	.433	1	8	.125	159	214	.743	146	175	321	76	189	3	....	....	95	18.4	6.6	4.2	1.0	.401
69-70	Washington-A	5	....	27	7	2	7	.286	0	0	.000	3	4	.750	1	3	4	0	3	0	....	....	3	5.4	1.4	0.8	0.0	.164
71-72	Florida-A	51	....	418	191	70	174	.402	5	22	.227	46	62	.742	30	30	60	38	79	0	....	....	26	8.2	3.7	1.2	0.7	.366
ABA Season Totals		133	....	1864	704	245	581	.422	6	30	.200	208	280	.743	177	208	385	114	271	3	....	....	124	14.0	5.3	2.9	0.9	....
69-70	Kentucky-A	12	....	270	116	41	91	.451	2	5	.400	32	44	.727	28	36	64	16	....	0	....	....	16	22.5	9.7	5.3	1.3	....
71-72	Florida-A	3	....	14	6	3	5	.600	0	2	.000	0	0	.000	....	....	1	3	3	....	....	....	2	4.7	2.0	0.3	1.0	.512
ABA Playoff Totals		15	....	284	122	44	96	.458	2	7	.286	32	44	.727	28	36	65	19	3	0	....	....	18	18.9	8.1	4.3	1.3	....

• TINSLEY, Jamaal

Jamaal Tinsley

Born: Feb. 28, 1978. Brooklyn, NY, United States. Height: 6'3". Weight: 195 lbs. Drafted: 2001 College: Iowa State

YEAR	TEAM	GP	GS	MIN	PTS	FGM	FGA	FG%	3PM	3PA	3P%	FTM	FTA	FT%	ORB	DRB	TRB	AST	PF	DQ	STL	BLK	TO	MPG	PPG	RPG	APG	PCM
01-02	Indiana	80	78	2442	751	289	760	.380	42	175	.240	131	186	.704	78	220	298	647	248	9	138	40	270	30.5	9.4	3.7	8.1	.443
02-03	Indiana	73	69	2237	566	220	556	.396	46	166	.277	80	112	.714	58	202	260	548	201	2	125	18	192	30.6	7.8	3.6	7.5	.423
NBA Season Totals		153	147	4679	1317	509	1316	.387	88	341	.258	211	298	.708	136	422	558	1195	449	11	263	58	462	30.6	8.6	3.6	7.8	....
01-02	Indiana	5	5	88	18	8	19	.421	0	1	.000	2	3	.667	2	8	10	25	12	0	2	0	12	17.6	3.6	2.0	5.0	.335
02-03	Indiana	6	6	185	51	20	35	.571	8	13	.615	3	6	.500	6	12	18	39	20	0	4	0	8	30.8	8.5	3.0	6.5	.445
NBA Playoff Totals		11	11	273	69	28	54	.519	8	14	.571	5	9	.556	8	20	28	64	32	0	6	0	20	24.8	6.3	2.5	5.8	....

• TISDALE, Wayman

Wayman Lawrence Tisdale

Born: June 9, 1964. Tulsa, OK, United States. Height: 6'9". Weight: 240 lbs. Drafted: 1985 College: Oklahoma

YEAR	TEAM	GP	GS	MIN	PTS	FGM	FGA	FG%	3PM	3PA	3P%	FTM	FTA	FT%	ORB	DRB	TRB	AST	PF	DQ	STL	BLK	TO	MPG	PPG	RPG	APG	PCM
85-86	Indiana	81	60	2277	1192	516	1002	.515	0	2	.000	160	234	.684	191	393	584	79	290	3	32	44	186	28.1	14.7	7.2	1.0	.482
86-87	Indiana	81	15	2159	1174	458	892	.513	0	2	.000	258	364	.709	217	258	475	117	293	9	50	26	138	26.7	14.5	5.9	1.4	.507
87-88	Indiana	79	57	2378	1268	511	998	.512	0	2	.000	246	314	.783	168	323	491	103	274	5	54	34	142	30.1	16.1	6.2	1.3	.493
88-89	Indiana	48	5	1326	768	285	564	.505	0	4	.000	198	250	.792	99	211	310	75	181	5	35	32	106	27.6	16.0	6.5	1.6	.552
88-89	Sacramento	31	30	1108	613	247	472	.523	0	0	.000	119	160	.744	88	211	299	53	109	2	20	20	65	35.7	19.8	9.6	1.7	.583
89-90	Sacramento	79	79	2937	1758	726	1383	.525	0	6	.000	306	391	.783	185	410	595	108	251	3	54	54	150	37.2	22.3	7.5	1.4	.551
90-91	Sacramento	33	31	1116	660	262	542	.483	0	1	.000	136	170	.800	75	178	253	66	99	0	23	28	83	33.8	20.0	7.7	2.0	.550
91-92	Sacramento	72	71	2521	1195	522	1043	.500	0	2	.000	151	198	.763	135	334	469	106	248	6	55	79	122	35.0	16.6	6.5	1.5	.450
92-93	Sacramento	76	75	2283	1263	544	1068	.509	0	2	.000	175	231	.758	127	373	500	108	277	8	52	47	114	30.0	16.6	6.6	1.4	.520
93-94	Sacramento	79	77	2557	1319	552	1102	.501	0	0	.000	215	266	.808	159	401	560	139	290	4	37	52	126	32.4	16.7	7.1	1.8	.504
94-95	Phoenix	65	13	1276	650	278	574	.484	0	0	.000	94	122	.770	83	164	247	45	190	3	29	27	65	19.6	10.0	3.8	0.7	.424
95-96	Phoenix	63	6	1152	672	279	564	.495	0	0	.000	114	149	.765	55	159	214	58	188	2	15	36	63	18.3	10.7	3.4	0.9	.478
96-97	Phoenix	53	15	778	346	158	371	.426	0	0	.000	30	48	.625	35	85	120	20	111	0	8	21	37	14.7	6.5	2.3	0.4	.274
NBA Season Totals		840	534	23868	12878	5338	10575	.505	0	21	.000	2202	2897	.760	1617	3500	5117	1077	2801	47	464	500	1397	28.4	15.3	6.1	1.3	....

YEAR	TEAM	GP	GS	MIN	PTS	FGM	FGA	FG%	3PM	3PA	3P%	FTM	FTA	FT%	ORB	DRB	TRB	AST	PF	DQ	STL	BLK	TO	MPG	PPG	RPG	APG	PCM
86-87	Indiana	4	0	108	51	19	31	.613	0	0	.000	13	23	.565	5	11	16	9	17	1	1	0	5	27.0	12.8	4.0	2.3	.445
94-95	Phoenix	10	0	170	73	32	71	.451	0	1	.000	9	14	.643	6	24	30	11	32	1	0	4	6	17.0	7.3	3.0	1.1	.335
95-96	Phoenix	4	0	67	21	10	30	.333	0	0	.000	1	2	.500	3	1	4	2	7	0	1	1	1	16.8	5.3	1.0	0.5	.079
96-97	Phoenix	4	4	36	12	6	15	.400	0	0	.000	0	0	.000	2	5	7	0	5	0	0	0	1	9.0	3.0	1.8	0.0	.191
NBA Playoff Totals		22	4	381	157	67	147	.456	0	1	.000	23	39	.590	16	41	57	22	61	2	2	5	13	17.3	7.1	2.6	1.0	....

• TOBIN, Paul

Paul Tobin

Born: —.   Height: 5'9".   Weight: 170 lbs.   Drafted: —   College: Akron

YEAR	TEAM	GP	GS	MIN	PTS	FGM	FGA	FG%	3PM	3PA	3P%	FTM	FTA	FT%	ORB	DRB	TRB	AST	PF	DQ	STL	BLK	TO	MPG	PPG	RPG	APG	PCM
37-38	Non-Skids-N	14	....	....	62	20	....	....	....	....	....	22	....	....	....	....	....	....	....	....	....	....	....	4.4	....	....	....	
38-39	Non-Skids-N	15	....	....	48	21	....	....	....	....	....	6	....	....	....	....	....	....	....	....	....	....	....	3.2	....	....	....	
39-40	Non-Skids-N	13	....	....	9	4	....	....	....	....	....	1	....	....	....	....	....	....	....	....	....	....	....	0.7	....	....	....	
NBL Season Totals		42	....	....	119	45	....	....	....	....	....	29	....	....	....	....	....	....	....	....	....	....	....	2.8	....	....	....	
37-38	Non-Skids-N	2	....	....	3	0	....	....	....	....	....	3	....	....	....	....	....	....	....	....	....	....	....	1.5	....	....	....	
38-39	Non-Skids-N	5	....	....	7	2	....	....	....	....	....	3	....	....	....	....	....	....	....	....	....	....	....	1.4	....	....	....	
39-40	Non-Skids-N	2	....	....	0	0	....	....	....	....	....	0	....	....	....	....	....	....	....	....	....	....	....	0.0	....	....	....	
NBL Playoff Totals		9	....	....	10	2	....	....	....	....	....	6	....	....	....	....	....	....	....	....	....	....	....	1.1	....	....	....	

• TODOROVICH, Mike

Marko John Todorovich

Born: June 11, 1923. Died: June24, 2000.   Height: 6'5".   Weight: 220 lbs.   Drafted: —   College: Wyoming

YEAR	TEAM	GP	GS	MIN	PTS	FGM	FGA	FG%	3PM	3PA	3P%	FTM	FTA	FT%	ORB	DRB	TRB	AST	PF	DQ	STL	BLK	TO	MPG	PPG	RPG	APG	PCM
47-48	Sheboygan-N	60	....	....	777	277	....	....	....	....	....	223	343	.650	....	....	182	....	....	....	....	....	....	13.0	....	....	....	
48-49	Sheboygan-N	60	....	....	648	239	....	....	....	....	....	170	281	.605	....	....	183	....	....	....	....	....	....	10.8	....	....	....	
49-50	St. Louis	14	....	....	97	31	116	.267	....	....	....	35	56	.625	....	....	19	47	....	....	....	....	....	6.9	....	1.4		
49-50	Tri-Cities	51	....	....	695	232	736	.315	....	....	....	231	314	.736	....	....	188	183	....	....	....	....	....	13.6	....	3.7		
50-51	Tri-Cities	66	....	....	653	221	715	.309	....	....	....	211	301	.701	....	455	179	197	5	....	....	....	....	9.9	6.9	2.7		
NBA Season Totals		131	....	....	1445	484	1567	.309	....	....	....	477	671	.711	....	455	386	427	5	....	....	....	....	11.0	3.5	2.9		
NBL Season Totals		120	....	....	1425	516	....	....	....	....	....	393	624	....	....	....	365	....	....	....	....	....	....	11.9	....	....	....	
Career Totals		251	....	....	2870	1000	1567	....	....	....	....	870	1295	....	....	455	386	792	5	....	....	....	....	11.4	1.8	1.5		
49-50	Tri-Cities	3	....	....	31	6	31	.194	....	....	....	19	24	.792	....	....	8	14	....	....	....	....	....	10.3	....	2.7		
NBA Playoff Totals		3	....	....	31	6	31	.194	....	....	....	19	24	.792	....	....	8	14	....	....	....	....	....	10.3	....	2.7		

• TOLBERT, Ray

Raymond Lee Tolbert

Born: Sept. 10, 1958. Anderson, IN, United States.   Height: 6'9".   Weight: 225 lbs.   Drafted: 1981   College: Indiana

YEAR	TEAM	GP	GS	MIN	PTS	FGM	FGA	FG%	3PM	3PA	3P%	FTM	FTA	FT%	ORB	DRB	TRB	AST	PF	DQ	STL	BLK	TO	MPG	PPG	RPG	APG	PCM
81-82	New Jersey	12	0	115	44	20	44	.455	0	1	.000	4	8	.500	11	16	27	8	19	0	4	2	12	9.6	3.7	2.3	0.7	.342
81-82	Seattle	52	0	492	175	80	158	.506	0	1	.000	15	27	.556	39	60	99	25	64	0	8	14	31	9.5	3.4	1.9	0.5	.362
82-83	Seattle	45	2	712	224	100	190	.526	0	2	.000	24	44	.545	46	105	151	31	97	1	16	24	50	15.8	5.0	3.4	0.7	.353
82-83	Detroit	28	0	395	142	57	124	.460	0	1	.000	28	59	.475	26	65	91	19	56	0	10	23	31	14.1	5.1	3.3	0.7	.372
83-84	Detroit	49	0	475	151	64	121	.529	0	1	.000	23	45	.511	45	53	98	26	88	1	12	20	25	9.7	3.1	2.0	0.5	.363
87-88	New York	11	0	177	47	19	41	.463	0	0	.000	9	17	.529	14	21	35	5	25	0	5	2	10	16.1	4.3	3.2	0.5	.261
87-88	LA Lakers	14	0	82	42	16	28	.571	0	0	.000	10	13	.769	9	11	20	5	14	0	3	1	11	5.9	3.0	1.4	0.4	.515
88-89	Atlanta	50	0	341	103	40	94	.426	0	0	.000	23	37	.622	31	57	88	16	55	0	13	13	35	6.8	2.1	1.8	0.3	.326
NBA Season Totals		261	2	2789	928	396	800	.495	0	6	.000	136	250	.544	221	388	609	135	418	2	71	101	205	10.7	3.6	2.3	0.5	....
81-82	Seattle	4	0	31	10	3	5	.600	0	0	.000	4	8	.500	1	4	5	1	7	0	4	0	0	7.8	2.5	1.3	0.3	.402
83-84	Detroit	1	0	2	0	0	0	.000	0	0	.000	0	0	.000	0	0	0	0	0	0	0	0	0	2.0	0.0	0.0	0.0	.000
NBA Playoff Totals		5	0	33	10	3	5	.600	0	0	.000	4	8	.500	1	4	5	1	7	0	4	0	0	6.6	2.0	1.0	0.2	....

• TOLBERT, Tom

Byron Thomas (Fabian) Tolbert

Born: Oct. 16, 1965. Long Beach, CA, United States.   Height: 6'7".   Weight: 235 lbs.   Drafted: 1988   College: Arizona

YEAR	TEAM	GP	GS	MIN	PTS	FGM	FGA	FG%	3PM	3PA	3P%	FTM	FTA	FT%	ORB	DRB	TRB	AST	PF	DQ	STL	BLK	TO	MPG	PPG	RPG	APG	PCM
88-89	Charlotte	14	0	117	40	17	37	.459	0	3	.000	6	12	.500	7	14	21	7	20	0	2	4	1	8.4	2.9	1.5	0.5	.350
89-90	Golden State	70	21	1347	616	218	442	.493	5	18	.278	175	241	.726	122	241	363	58	191	0	23	25	77	19.2	8.8	5.2	0.8	.490
90-91	Golden State	62	32	1371	500	183	433	.423	7	21	.333	127	172	.738	87	188	275	76	195	4	35	38	81	22.1	8.1	4.4	1.2	.354
91-92	Golden State	35	0	310	90	33	86	.384	2	8	.250	22	40	.550	14	41	55	21	73	0	10	6	21	8.9	2.6	1.6	0.6	.218
92-93	Orlando	72	61	1838	583	226	454	.498	9	28	.321	122	168	.726	133	279	412	91	192	4	33	21	122	25.5	8.1	5.7	1.3	.368
93-94	LA Clippers	49	6	640	187	74	177	.418	6	16	.375	33	45	.733	36	72	108	30	61	0	13	15	39	13.1	3.8	2.2	0.6	.282
94-95	Charlotte	10	0	57	14	6	18	.333	0	4	.000	2	2	1.000	7	10	17	2	9	0	0	0	3	5.7	1.4	1.7	0.2	.242
NBA Season Totals		312	120	5680	2030	757	1647	.460	29	98	.296	487	680	.716	406	845	1251	285	741	8	116	109	344	18.2	6.5	4.0	0.9	....
90-91	Golden State	9	0	116	32	14	33	.424	1	3	.333	3	11	.273	0	18	18	8	29	0	3	4	4	12.9	3.6	2.0	0.9	.217
NBA Playoff Totals		9	0	116	32	14	33	.424	1	3	.333	3	11	.273	0	18	18	8	29	0	3	4	4	12.9	3.6	2.0	0.9	....

• TOLLSTAM, Chet

Chester Tollstam

Born: 1918.   Height: 6'2".   Weight: 180 lbs.   Drafted: —   College: DePaul

YEAR	TEAM	GP	GS	MIN	PTS	FGM	FGA	FG%	3PM	3PA	3P%	FTM	FTA	FT%	ORB	DRB	TRB	AST	PF	DQ	STL	BLK	TO	MPG	PPG	RPG	APG	PCM
40-41	Hammond-N	11	....	....	32	13	....	....	....	....	....	6	....	....	....	....	....	....	....	....	....	....	....	2.9	....	....	....	
NBL Season Totals		11	....	....	32	13	....	....	....	....	....	6	....	....	....	....	....	....	....	....	....	....	....	2.9	....	....	....	

YEAR	TEAM	GP	GS	MIN	PTS	FGM	FGA	FG%	3PM	3PA	3P%	FTM	FTA	FT%	ORB	DRB	TRB	AST	PF	DQ	STL	BLK	TO	MPG	PPG	RPG	APG	PCM

• TOLSON, Dean
Byron Dean Tolson

Born: Nov. 25, 1951. Kansas City, KS, United States.   Height: 6'8".   Weight: 190 lbs.   Drafted: 1974   College: Arkansas

YEAR	TEAM	GP	GS	MIN	PTS	FGM	FGA	FG%	3PM	3PA	3P%	FTM	FTA	FT%	ORB	DRB	TRB	AST	PF	DQ	STL	BLK	TO	MPG	PPG	RPG	APG	PCM
74-75	Seattle	19	....	87	43	16	37	.432	....	....	....	11	17	.647	12	10	22	5	12	0	4	6	....	4.6	2.3	1.2	0.3	.482
76-77	Seattle	60	....	587	359	137	242	.566	....	....	....	85	159	.535	73	84	157	27	83	0	32	21	....	9.8	6.0	2.6	0.5	.625
77-78	Seattle	1	....	7	0	0	1	.000	....	....	....	0	0	.000	0	0	0	2	2	0	0	0	1	7.0	0.0	0.0	2.0	-.054
NBA Season Totals		80	....	681	402	153	280	.546	....	....	....	96	176	.545	85	94	179	34	97	0	36	27	1	8.5	5.0	2.2	0.4	
74-75	Seattle	4	....	22	4	1	8	.125	....	....	....	2	2	1.000	4	3	7	1	3	0	0	0	....	5.5	1.0	1.8	0.3	.176
NBA Playoff Totals		4	....	22	4	1	8	.125	....	....	....	2	2	1.000	4	3	7	1	3	0	0	0	....	5.5	1.0	1.8	0.3	

• TOMJANOVICH, Rudy
Rudolph (Rudy T.) Tomjanovich

Born: Nov. 24, 1948. Hamtramck, MI, United States.   Height: 6'8".   Weight: 218 lbs.   Drafted: 1970   College: Michigan

YEAR	TEAM	GP	GS	MIN	PTS	FGM	FGA	FG%	3PM	3PA	3P%	FTM	FTA	FT%	ORB	DRB	TRB	AST	PF	DQ	STL	BLK	TO	MPG	PPG	RPG	APG	PCM
70-71	San Diego	77	....	1062	409	168	439	.383	....	....	....	73	112	.652	....	....	381	73	124	0	....	....	....	13.8	5.3	4.9	0.9	.487
71-72	Houston	78	....	2689	1172	500	1010	.495	....	....	....	172	238	.723	....	....	923	117	193	2	....	....	....	34.5	15.0	11.8	1.5	.576
72-73	Houston	81	....	2972	1560	655	1371	.478	....	....	....	250	335	.746	....	....	938	178	225	1	....	....	....	36.7	19.3	11.6	2.2	.613
73-74	Houston	80	....	3227	1961	788	1470	.536	....	....	....	385	454	.848	230	487	717	250	230	0	89	66	....	40.3	24.5	9.0	3.1	.667
74-75	Houston	81	....	3134	1677	694	1323	.525	....	....	....	289	366	.790	184	429	613	236	230	1	76	24	....	38.7	20.7	7.6	2.9	.575
75-76	Houston	79	....	2912	1465	622	1202	.517	....	....	....	221	288	.767	167	499	666	188	206	1	42	19	....	36.9	18.5	8.4	2.4	.562
76-77	Houston	81	....	3130	1753	733	1437	.510	....	....	....	287	342	.839	172	512	684	172	198	1	57	27	....	38.6	21.6	8.4	2.1	.582
77-78	Houston	23	....	849	495	217	447	.485	....	....	....	61	81	.753	40	98	138	32	63	0	15	5	39	36.9	21.5	6.0	1.4	.468
78-79	Houston	74	....	2641	1408	620	1200	.517	....	....	....	168	221	.760	170	402	572	137	186	0	44	18	141	35.7	19.0	7.7	1.9	.520
79-80	Houston	62	....	1834	880	370	778	.476	22	79	.278	118	147	.803	132	226	358	109	161	2	32	10	99	29.6	14.2	5.8	1.8	.445
80-81	Houston	52	....	1264	603	263	563	.467	12	51	.235	65	82	.793	78	130	208	81	121	0	19	6	57	24.3	11.6	4.0	1.6	.408
NBA Season Totals		768	....	25714	13383	5630	11240	.501	34	130	.262	2089	2666	.784	1173	2783	6198	1573	1937	8	374	175	336	33.5	17.4	8.1	2.0	
74-75	Houston	8	....	304	184	72	128	.563	....	....	....	40	48	.833	22	42	64	23	17	0	1	4	....	38.0	23.0	8.0	2.9	.679
76-77	Houston	12	....	457	243	107	212	.505	....	....	....	29	37	.784	24	41	65	24	36	0	7	3	....	38.1	20.3	5.4	2.0	.474
78-79	Houston	2	....	64	20	9	23	.391	....	....	....	2	5	.400	7	7	14	2	1	0	1	1	1	32.0	10.0	7.0	1.0	.333
79-80	Houston	7	....	185	58	24	64	.375	1	7	.143	9	13	.692	12	28	40	10	21	1	2	0	14	26.4	8.3	5.7	1.4	.253
80-81	Houston	8	....	31	6	1	9	.111	0	3	.000	4	6	.667	2	4	6	0	3	0	0	0	2	3.9	0.8	0.8	0.0	.003
NBA Playoff Totals		37	....	1041	511	213	436	.489	1	10	.100	84	109	.771	67	122	189	59	78	1	11	8	17	28.1	13.8	5.1	1.6	

• TONEY, Andrew
Andrew Toney

Born: Nov. 23, 1957. Birmingham, AL, United States.   Height: 6'3".   Weight: 178 lbs.   Drafted: 1980   College: Southwestern Louisiana

YEAR	TEAM	GP	GS	MIN	PTS	FGM	FGA	FG%	3PM	3PA	3P%	FTM	FTA	FT%	ORB	DRB	TRB	AST	PF	DQ	STL	BLK	TO	MPG	PPG	RPG	APG	PCM
80-81	Philadelphia	75	....	1768	968	399	806	.495	9	29	.310	161	226	.712	32	111	143	273	234	5	59	10	218	23.6	12.9	1.9	3.6	.426
81-82	Philadelphia	77	1	1909	1274	511	979	.522	25	59	.424	227	306	.742	43	91	134	283	269	5	64	17	216	24.8	16.5	1.7	3.7	.517
82-83	Philadelphia	81	81	2474	1598	626	1250	.501	22	76	.289	324	411	.788	42	183	225	365	255	0	80	17	267	30.5	19.7	2.8	4.5	.538
83-84	Philadelphia	78	72	2556	1588	593	1125	.527	12	38	.316	390	465	.839	57	136	193	373	251	1	70	23	296	32.8	20.4	2.5	4.8	.521
84-85	Philadelphia	70	65	2237	1245	450	914	.492	39	105	.371	306	355	.862	35	142	177	363	211	1	65	24	224	32.0	17.8	2.5	5.2	.500
85-86	Philadelphia	6	0	84	25	11	36	.306	0	2	.000	3	8	.375	2	3	5	12	6	0	2	0	7	14.0	4.2	0.8	2.0	.102
86-87	Philadelphia	52	12	1058	549	197	437	.451	22	67	.328	133	167	.796	16	69	85	188	78	0	18	8	114	20.3	10.6	1.6	3.6	.446
87-88	Philadelphia	29	15	522	211	72	171	.421	9	27	.333	58	72	.806	8	39	47	108	35	0	11	6	49	18.0	7.3	1.6	3.7	.431
NBA Season Totals		468	246	12608	7458	2859	5718	.500	138	403	.342	1602	2010	.797	235	774	1009	1965	1341	12	369	105	1391	26.9	15.9	2.2	4.2	
80-81	Philadelphia	16	....	356	221	77	180	.428	1	9	.111	66	81	.815	10	27	37	54	50	0	11	7	54	22.3	13.8	2.3	3.4	.442
81-82	Philadelphia	21	19	707	457	185	365	.507	5	15	.333	82	103	.796	20	31	51	102	86	1	18	2	67	33.7	21.8	2.4	4.9	.503
82-83	Philadelphia	12	12	357	226	87	185	.470	2	5	.000	52	69	.754	11	17	28	55	43	1	11	1	45	29.8	18.8	2.3	4.6	.466
83-84	Philadelphia	5	5	180	103	40	77	.519	0	5	.000	23	30	.767	5	6	11	19	24	0	4	1	25	36.0	20.6	2.2	3.8	.367
84-85	Philadelphia	13	13	442	219	83	174	.477	6	14	.429	47	61	.770	8	24	32	66	46	0	12	5	50	34.0	16.8	2.5	5.1	.398
86-87	Philadelphia	5	0	104	28	13	34	.382	0	3	.000	2	2	1.000	2	7	9	27	16	1	2	2	16	20.8	5.6	1.8	5.4	.260
NBA Playoff Totals		72	49	2146	1254	485	1015	.478	12	51	.235	272	346	.786	56	112	168	323	265	3	58	18	257	29.8	17.4	2.3	4.5	

• TONEY, Sedric
Sedric Andre Toney

Born: Apr. 13, 1962. Columbus, MS, United States.   Height: 6'2".   Weight: 178 lbs.   Drafted: 1985   College: Dayton

YEAR	TEAM	GP	GS	MIN	PTS	FGM	FGA	FG%	3PM	3PA	3P%	FTM	FTA	FT%	ORB	DRB	TRB	AST	PF	DQ	STL	BLK	TO	MPG	PPG	RPG	APG	PCM
85-86	Atlanta	3	0	24	5	2	7	.286	0	0	.000	1	1	1.000	0	2	2	0	6	0	1	0	3	8.0	1.7	0.7	0.0	-.101
85-86	Phoenix	10	0	206	75	26	59	.441	3	10	.300	20	30	.667	3	20	23	26	18	0	5	0	19	20.6	7.5	2.3	2.6	.328
87-88	New York	21	0	139	57	21	48	.438	5	14	.357	10	11	.909	3	5	8	24	20	0	9	1	13	6.6	2.7	0.4	1.1	.377
88-89	Indiana	2	0	9	2	1	5	.200	0	3	.000	0	1	.000	1	1	2	0	1	0	0	0	2	4.5	1.0	1.0	0.0	-.294
89-90	Atlanta	32	0	286	88	30	72	.417	7	13	.538	21	25	.840	3	11	14	52	35	0	10	0	22	8.9	2.8	0.4	1.6	.306
89-90	Sacramento	32	9	682	176	57	178	.320	16	50	.320	46	58	.793	11	35	46	122	71	0	23	0	51	21.3	5.5	1.4	3.8	.250
93-94	Cleveland	12	0	64	6	2	12	.167	0	1	.000	2	2	1.000	1	2	3	11	8	0	0	0	5	5.3	0.5	0.3	0.9	.051
NBA Season Totals		112	9	1410	409	139	381	.365	31	91	.341	100	128	.781	22	76	98	235	159	1	48	1	115	12.6	3.7	0.9	2.1	
87-88	New York	3	0	15	11	3	6	.500	3	6	.500	2	2	1.000	0	0	0	2	4	0	1	0	2	5.0	3.7	0.0	0.7	.503
NBA Playoff Totals		3	0	15	11	3	6	.500	3	6	.500	2	2	1.000	0	0	0	2	4	0	1	0	2	5.0	3.7	0.0	0.7	

• TONKOVICH, Andy
Andrew Edward Tonkovich

Born: Nov. 1, 1922.   Height: 6'1".   Weight: 185 lbs.   Drafted: 1948   College: Marshall

YEAR	TEAM	GP	GS	MIN	PTS	FGM	FGA	FG%	3PM	3PA	3P%	FTM	FTA	FT%	ORB	DRB	TRB	AST	PF	DQ	STL	BLK	TO	MPG	PPG	RPG	APG	PCM
48-49	Providence	17	....	....	44	19	71	.268	....	....	....	6	9	.667	....	....	....	10	12	....	....	....	....	....	2.6	....	0.6	....
NBA Season Totals		17	....	....	44	19	71	.268	....	....	....	6	9	.667	....	....	....	10	12	....	....	....	....	....	2.6	....	0.6	....

YEAR	TEAM	GP	GS	MIN	PTS	FGM	FGA	FG%	3PM	3PA	3P%	FTM	FTA	FT%	ORB	DRB	TRB	AST	PF	DQ	STL	BLK	TO	MPG	PPG	RPG	APG	PCM

• TOOLSON, Andy

Andrew K. Toolson

Born: Jan. 19, 1966. Chicago, IL, United States. Height: 6'6". Weight: 210 lbs. Drafted: — College: Brigham Young

YEAR	TEAM	GP	GS	MIN	PTS	FGM	FGA	FG%	3PM	3PA	3P%	FTM	FTA	FT%	ORB	DRB	TRB	AST	PF	DQ	STL	BLK	TO	MPG	PPG	RPG	APG	PCM
90-91	Utah	47	15	470	137	50	124	.403	12	32	.375	25	33	.758	32	35	67	31	58	0	14	2	24	10.0	2.9	1.4	0.7	.267
95-96	Utah	13	0	53	22	8	22	.364	3	12	.250	3	4	.750	0	6	6	1	12	0	0	0	3	4.1	1.7	0.5	0.1	.125
NBA Season Totals		60	15	523	159	58	146	.397	15	44	.341	28	37	.757	32	41	73	32	70	0	14	2	27	8.7	2.7	1.2	0.5	....
90-91	Utah	2	0	4	0	0	2	.000	0	1	.000	0	0	.000	0	0	0	1	0	0	1	0	0	2.0	0.0	0.0	0.5	.034
NBA Playoff Totals		2	0	4	0	0	2	.000	0	1	.000	0	0	.000	0	0	0	1	0	0	1	0	0	2.0	0.0	0.0	0.5	

• TOOMAY, Jack

John C. Toomay

Born: Aug. 9, 1922. Height: 6'6". Weight: 215 lbs. Drafted: — College: College of Pacific

YEAR	TEAM	GP	GS	MIN	PTS	FGM	FGA	FG%	3PM	3PA	3P%	FTM	FTA	FT%	ORB	DRB	TRB	AST	PF	DQ	STL	BLK	TO	MPG	PPG	RPG	APG	PCM
47-48	Chicago	9	....	....	29	9	47	.191	....	....	....	11	20	.550	....	....	....	2	22	....	....	....	....		3.2	....	0.2	....
47-48	Providence	14	....	....	153	52	144	.361	....	....	....	49	71	.690	....	....	....	5	49	....	....	....	....		10.9	....	0.4	....
48-49	Baltimore	23	....	....	75	24	63	.381	....	....	....	27	41	.659	....	....	....	11	49	....	....	....	....		3.3	....	0.5	....
48-49	Washington	13	....	....	25	8	21	.381	....	....	....	9	12	.750	....	....	....	1	16	....	....	....	....		1.9	....	0.1	....
49-50	Denver	62	....	....	594	204	514	.397	....	....	....	186	264	.705	....	....	....	94	213	....	....	....	....		9.6	....	1.5	....
NBA Season Totals		121	....	....	876	297	789	.376	....	....	....	282	408	.691	....	....	....	113	349	....	....	....	....		7.2	....	0.9	....
48-49	Baltimore	1	....	....	7	1	5	.200	....	....	....	5	7	.714	....	....	....	0	6	....	....	....	....		7.0	....	....	....
NBA Playoff Totals		1	....	....	7	1	5	.200	....	....	....	5	7	.714	....	....	....	0	6	....	....	....	....		7.0	....	0.0	

• TOONE, Bernard

Bernard Toone

Born: July 14, 1956. Yonkers, NY, United States. Height: 6'9". Weight: 210 lbs. Drafted: 1979 College: Marquette

YEAR	TEAM	GP	GS	MIN	PTS	FGM	FGA	FG%	3PM	3PA	3P%	FTM	FTA	FT%	ORB	DRB	TRB	AST	PF	DQ	STL	BLK	TO	MPG	PPG	RPG	APG	PCM
79-80	Philadelphia	23	....	124	55	23	64	.359	1	7	.143	8	10	.800	12	22	34	12	20	0	4	5	16	5.4	2.4	1.5	0.5	.367
NBA Season Totals		23	....	124	55	23	64	.359	1	7	.143	8	10	.800	12	22	34	12	20	0	4	5	16	5.4	2.4	1.5	0.5	....
79-80	Philadelphia	4	....	6	0	0	4	.000	0	1	.000	0	0	.000	0	1	1	1	1	0	0	0	0	1.5	0.0	0.3	0.3	-.345
NBA Playoff Totals		4	....	6	0	0	4	.000	0	1	.000	0	0	.000	0	1	1	1	1	0	0	0	0	1.5	0.0	0.3	0.3	....

• TORGOFF, Irv

Irving Torgoff

Born: Mar. 6, 1917. Died: Oct.21, 1993. Height: 6'2". Weight: 192 lbs. Drafted: — College: Long Island University

YEAR	TEAM	GP	GS	MIN	PTS	FGM	FGA	FG%	3PM	3PA	3P%	FTM	FTA	FT%	ORB	DRB	TRB	AST	PF	DQ	STL	BLK	TO	MPG	PPG	RPG	APG	PCM
39-40	Detroit-N	26	....	....	171	64	....	....	....	....	....	43	....	....	....	....	....	....	....	....	....	....		6.6	....	....	....
46-47	Washington	58	....	....	490	187	684	.273	....	....	....	116	159	.730	....	....	....	30	173	....	....	....	....		8.4	....	0.5	....
47-48	Washington	47	....	....	339	111	541	.205	....	....	....	117	144	.813	....	....	....	32	153	....	....	....	....		7.2	....	0.7	....
48-49	Baltimore	29	....	....	133	45	178	.253	....	....	....	43	56	.768	....	....	....	32	77	....	....	....	....		4.6	....	1.1	....
48-49	Philadelphia	13	....	....	35	14	48	.292	....	....	....	7	8	.875	....	....	....	12	33	....	....	....	....		2.7	....	0.9	....
NBA Season Totals		147	....	....	997	357	1451	.246	....	....	....	283	367	.771	....	....	....	106	436	....	....	....	....		6.8	....	0.7	....
NBL Season Totals		26	....	....	171	64	....	....	....	....	....	43	....	....	....	....	....	....	....	....	....	....	....		6.6	....	....	....
Career Totals		173	....	....	1168	421	1451		....	....	....	326	367	....	....	....	....	106	436	....	....	....	....		6.8	....	0.6	....
39-40	Detroit-N	3	....	....	27	10	....	....	....	....	....	7	....	....	....	....	....	....	....	....	....	....	....		9.0	....	....	....
46-47	Washington	6	....	....	39	13	81	.160	....	....	....	13	19	.684	....	....	....	5	23	....	....	....	....		6.5	....	0.8	....
48-49	Philadelphia	2	....	....	0	0	3	.000	....	....	....	0	0	.000	....	....	....	2	2	....	....	....	....		0.0	....	1.0	....
NBA Playoff Totals		8	....	....	39	13	84	.155	....	....	....	13	19	.684	....	....	....	7	25	....	....	....	....		4.9	....	0.9	....
NBL Playoff Totals		3	....	....	27	10	....	....	....	....	....	7	....	....	....	....	....	....	....	....	....	....	....		9.0	....	....	....
Career Playoff Totals		11	....	....	66	23	84		....	....	....	20	19	....	....	....	....	7	25	....	....	....	....		6.0	....	0.6	....

• TORMOHLEN, Bumper

Eugene R. (Bumper) Tormohlen

Born: May 12, 1937. Height: 6'8". Weight: 230 lbs. Drafted: 1959 College: Tennessee

YEAR	TEAM	GP	GS	MIN	PTS	FGM	FGA	FG%	3PM	3PA	3P%	FTM	FTA	FT%	ORB	DRB	TRB	AST	PF	DQ	STL	BLK	TO	MPG	PPG	RPG	APG	PCM
62-63	St. Louis	7	....	47	12	5	10	.500	....	....	....	2	10	.200	....	....	15	5	11	0	....	....	....	6.7	1.7	2.1	0.7	.392
63-64	St. Louis	51	....	640	210	94	250	.376	....	....	....	22	46	.478	....	....	216	50	128	3	....	....	....	12.5	4.1	4.2	1.0	.404
65-66	St. Louis	71	....	775	342	144	324	.444	....	....	....	54	82	.659	....	....	314	60	138	3	....	....	....	10.9	4.8	4.4	0.8	.587
66-67	St. Louis	63	....	1036	394	172	403	.427	....	....	....	50	84	.595	....	....	347	73	177	4	....	....	....	16.4	6.3	5.5	1.2	.473
67-68	St. Louis	77	....	714	229	98	262	.374	....	....	....	33	56	.589	....	....	226	68	94	0	....	....	....	9.3	3.0	2.9	0.9	.439
69-70	Atlanta	2	....	11	4	2	4	.500	....	....	....	0	0	.000	....	....	4	1	3	0	....	....	....	5.5	2.0	2.0	0.5	.505
NBA Season Totals		271	....	3223	1191	515	1253	.411	....	....	....	161	278	.579	....	....	1122	257	551	10	....	....	....	11.9	4.4	4.1	0.9	....
62-63	St. Louis	5	....	15	8	4	10	.400	....	....	....	0	0	.000	....	....	5	3	6	0	....	....	....	3.0	1.6	1.0	0.6	.564
63-64	St. Louis	6	....	39	13	5	13	.385	....	....	....	3	5	.600	....	....	14	9	12	0	....	....	....	6.5	2.2	2.3	1.5	.595
65-66	St. Louis	6	....	38	7	2	10	.200	....	....	....	3	4	.750	....	....	18	6	7	0	....	....	....	6.3	1.2	3.0	1.0	.500
66-67	St. Louis	6	....	52	24	11	21	.524	....	....	....	2	5	.400	....	....	22	2	11	0	....	....	....	8.7	4.0	3.7	0.3	.584
67-68	St. Louis	3	....	25	7	2	6	.333	....	....	....	3	4	.750	....	....	6	5	4	0	....	....	....	8.3	2.3	2.0	1.7	.504
NBA Playoff Totals		26	....	169	59	24	60	.400	....	....	....	11	18	.611	....	....	65	25	40	0	....	....	....	6.5	2.3	2.5	1.0	....

• TORRES, Oscar

Oscar Jose Torres

Born: Dec. 18, 1976. Caracas, Venezuela. Height: 6'6". Weight: 210 lbs. Drafted: — College: none

YEAR	TEAM	GP	GS	MIN	PTS	FGM	FGA	FG%	3PM	3PA	3P%	FTM	FTA	FT%	ORB	DRB	TRB	AST	PF	DQ	STL	BLK	TO	MPG	PPG	RPG	APG	PCM
01-02	Houston	65	13	1075	389	135	341	.396	37	126	.294	82	105	.781	47	75	122	40	64	0	25	9	49	16.5	6.0	1.9	0.6	.282
02-03	Golden State	17	0	109	53	16	36	.444	7	13	.538	14	20	.700	3	9	12	3	9	0	4	2	8	6.4	3.1	0.7	0.2	.371
NBA Season Totals		82	13	1184	442	151	377	.401	44	139	.317	96	125	.768	50	84	134	43	73	0	29	11	57	14.4	5.4	1.6	0.5	....

• TOSHEFF, Bill

William Mark Tosheff

Born: June 2, 1926. Height: 6'1". Weight: 175 lbs. Drafted: 1951 College: Indiana

YEAR TEAM	GP	GS	MIN	PTS	FGM	FGA	FG%	3PM	3PA	3P%	FTM	FTA	FT%	ORB	DRB	TRB	AST	PF	DQ	STL	BLK	TO	MPG	PPG	RPG	APG	PCM
51-52 Indianapolis	65	....	2055	608	213	651	.327	....	....	....	182	221	.824	....	....	216	222	204	7	....	....	....	31.6	9.4	3.3	3.4	.316
52-53 Indianapolis	67	....	2459	759	253	783	.323	....	....	....	253	314	.806	....	....	229	243	243	5	....	....	....	36.7	11.3	3.4	3.6	.301
53-54 Milwaukee	71	....	1825	492	168	578	.291	....	....	....	156	210	.743	....	....	163	196	207	3	....	....	....	25.7	6.9	2.3	2.8	.261
NBA Season Totals	203	....	6339	1859	634	2012	.315	....	....	....	591	745	.793	....	....	608	661	654	15	....	....	....	31.2	9.2	3.0	3.3	....
51-52 Indianapolis	2	....	68	7	2	18	.111	....	....	....	3	3	1.000	....	....	6	7	9	0	....	....	....	34.0	3.5	3.0	3.5	.084
52-53 Indianapolis	2	....	66	9	1	16	.063	....	....	....	7	7	1.000	....	....	5	4	5	0	....	....	....	33.0	4.5	2.5	2.0	.077
NBA Playoff Totals	4	....	134	16	3	34	.088	....	....	....	10	10	1.000	....	....	11	11	14	0	....	....	....	33.5	4.0	2.8	2.8	....

• TOUGH, Bob

Robert (Red) Tough

Born: Aug. 28, 1920. Died: Apr.7, 1999. Height: 6' Weight: 185 lbs. Drafted: — College: St. John's (NY)

YEAR TEAM	GP	GS	MIN	PTS	FGM	FGA	FG%	3PM	3PA	3P%	FTM	FTA	FT%	ORB	DRB	TRB	AST	PF	DQ	STL	BLK	TO	MPG	PPG	RPG	APG	PCM
45-46 Fort Wayne-N	5	....	....	29	12	....	....	....	....	....	5	....	....	....	....	....	....	....	....	....	....	....	....	5.8	....	....	....
46-47 Fort Wayne-N	44	....	....	303	124	....	....	....	....	....	55	81	.679	....	....	....	....	73	....	....	....	....	....	6.9	....	....	....
47-48 Fort Wayne-N	60	....	....	306	129	....	....	....	....	....	48	71	.676	....	....	....	....	98	....	....	....	....	....	5.1	....	....	....
48-49 Fort Wayne	53	....	....	466	183	661	.277	....	....	....	100	138	.725	....	....	....	99	101	....	....	....	....	....	8.8	....	1.9	....
49-50 Baltimore	8	....	....	27	11	39	.282	....	....	....	5	6	.833	....	....	....	2	15	....	....	....	....	....	3.4	....	0.3	....
49-50 Waterloo	21	....	....	96	32	114	.281	....	....	....	32	34	.941	....	....	....	36	25	....	....	....	....	....	4.6	....	1.7	....
NBA Season Totals	82	....	....	589	226	814	.278	....	....	....	137	178	.770	....	....	....	137	141	....	....	....	....	....	7.2	....	1.7	....
NBL Season Totals	109	....	....	638	265	....	....	....	....	....	108	152	....	....	....	....	....	171	....	....	....	....	....	5.9	....	....	....
Career Totals	191	....	....	1227	491	814	....	....	....	....	245	330	....	....	....	....	137	312	....	....	....	....	....	6.4	....	0.7	....
45-46 Fort Wayne-N	4	....	....	22	9	....	....	....	....	....	4	8	.500	....	....	....	....	....	....	....	....	....	....	5.5	....	....	....
46-47 Fort Wayne-N	8	....	....	50	17	....	....	....	....	....	16	19	.842	....	....	....	....	....	....	....	....	....	....	6.3	....	....	....
47-48 Fort Wayne-N	4	....	....	21	9	....	....	....	....	....	3	4	.750	....	....	....	....	....	....	....	....	....	....	5.3	....	....	....
NBL Playoff Totals	16	....	....	93	35	....	....	....	....	....	23	31	....	....	....	....	....	....	....	....	....	....	....	5.8	....	....	....

• TOWE, Monty

Monte Corwin Towe

Born: Sept. 27, 1953. Marion, IN, United States. Height: 5'7". Weight: 150 lbs. Drafted: 1975 College: North Carolina State

YEAR TEAM	GP	GS	MIN	PTS	FGM	FGA	FG%	3PM	3PA	3P%	FTM	FTA	FT%	ORB	DRB	TRB	AST	PF	DQ	STL	BLK	TO	MPG	PPG	RPG	APG	PCM
75-76 Denver-A	64	....	576	189	72	179	.402	9	42	.214	36	44	.818	6	49	55	136	84	....	37	5	81	9.0	3.0	0.9	2.1	.438
76-77 Denver	51	....	409	130	56	138	.406	....	....	....	18	25	.720	8	26	34	87	61	0	16	0	....	8.0	2.5	0.7	1.7	.387
NBA Season Totals	51	....	409	130	56	138	.406	....	....	....	18	25	.720	8	26	34	87	61	0	16	0	....	8.0	2.5	0.7	1.7	....
ABA Season Totals	64	....	576	189	72	179	.402	9	42	.214	36	44	.818	6	49	55	136	84	....	37	5	81	9.0	3.0	0.9	2.1	....
Career Totals	115	....	985	319	128	317	.404	9	42	.214	54	69	.783	14	75	89	223	145	0	53	5	81	8.6	2.8	0.8	1.9	....
75-76 Denver-A	4	....	30	10	3	8	.375	0	0	.000	4	5	.800	0	0	0	6	6	....	1	0	5	7.5	2.5	0.0	1.5	.303
76-77 Denver	1	....	6	4	2	3	.667	....	....	....	0	0	.000	0	0	0	1	0	0	0	0	....	6.0	4.0	0.0	1.0	.712
NBA Playoff Totals	1	....	6	4	2	3	.667	....	....	....	0	0	.000	0	0	0	1	0	0	0	0	....	6.0	4.0	0.0	1.0	....
ABA Playoff Totals	4	....	30	10	3	8	.375	0	0	.000	4	5	.800	0	0	0	6	6	....	1	0	5	7.5	2.5	0.0	1.5	....
Career Playoff Totals	5	....	36	14	5	11	.455	0	0	.000	4	5	.800	0	0	0	7	6	0	1	0	5	7.2	2.8	0.0	1.4	....

• TOWER, Keith

Keith Raymond Tower

Born: May 15, 1970. Libby, MT, United States. Height: 6'11". Weight: 250 lbs. Drafted: — College: Notre Dame

YEAR TEAM	GP	GS	MIN	PTS	FGM	FGA	FG%	3PM	3PA	3P%	FTM	FTA	FT%	ORB	DRB	TRB	AST	PF	DQ	STL	BLK	TO	MPG	PPG	RPG	APG	PCM
93-94 Orlando	11	0	32	8	4	9	.444	0	0	.000	0	0	.000	0	6	6	1	6	0	0	0	0	2.9	0.7	0.5	0.1	.227
94-95 Orlando	3	0	7	1	0	2	.000	0	0	.000	1	2	.500	1	2	3	0	1	0	0	0	1	2.3	0.3	1.0	0.0	.009
95-96 LA Clippers	34	1	305	82	32	72	.444	0	1	.000	18	26	.692	22	29	51	5	50	1	4	11	17	9.0	2.4	1.5	0.1	.225
96-97 Milwaukee	5	1	72	7	3	8	.375	0	0	.000	1	8	.125	2	7	9	1	12	0	2	1	2	14.4	1.4	1.8	0.2	.054
NBA Season Totals	53	2	416	98	39	91	.429	0	1	.000	20	36	.556	25	44	69	7	69	1	6	12	20	7.8	1.8	1.3	0.1	....

• TOWERY, Blackie

William Carlisle (Blackie) Towery

Born: June 20, 1920. Height: 6'4". Weight: 210 lbs. Drafted: — College: Western Kentucky

YEAR TEAM	GP	GS	MIN	PTS	FGM	FGA	FG%	3PM	3PA	3P%	FTM	FTA	FT%	ORB	DRB	TRB	AST	PF	DQ	STL	BLK	TO	MPG	PPG	RPG	APG	PCM
41-42 Fort Wayne-N	24	....	....	163	64	....	....	....	....	....	35	....	....	....	....	....	....	....	....	....	....	....	....	6.8	....	....	....
42-43 Fort Wayne-N	23	....	....	139	53	....	....	....	....	....	33	....	....	....	....	....	....	....	....	....	....	....	....	6.0	....	....	....
43-44 Fort Wayne-N	22	....	....	129	48	....	....	....	....	....	33	....	....	....	....	....	....	....	....	....	....	....	....	5.9	....	....	....
44-45 Fort Wayne-N	1	....	....	1	0	....	....	....	....	....	1	....	....	....	....	....	....	....	....	....	....	....	....	1.0	....	....	....
46-47 Fort Wayne-N	41	....	....	280	100	....	....	....	....	....	80	134	.597	....	....	....	....	123	....	....	....	....	....	6.8	....	....	....
47-48 Fort Wayne-N	59	....	....	407	139	....	....	....	....	....	129	187	.690	....	....	....	....	194	....	....	....	....	....	6.9	....	....	....
48-49 Fort Wayne	22	....	....	164	56	216	.259	....	....	....	52	73	.712	....	....	....	35	79	....	....	....	....	....	7.5	....	1.6	....
48-49 Indianapolis	38	....	....	437	147	555	.265	....	....	....	143	190	.753	....	....	....	136	164	....	....	....	....	....	11.5	....	3.6	....
49-50 Baltimore	68	....	....	597	222	678	.327	....	....	....	153	202	.757	....	....	....	142	244	....	....	....	....	....	8.8	....	2.1	....
NBA Season Totals	128	....	....	1198	425	1449	.293	....	....	....	348	465	.748	....	....	....	313	487	....	....	....	....	....	9.4	....	2.4	....
NBL Season Totals	170	....	....	1119	404	....	....	....	....	....	311	321	....	....	....	....	....	317	....	....	....	....	....	6.6	....	....	....
Career Totals	298	....	....	2317	829	1449	....	....	....	....	659	786	....	....	....	....	313	804	....	....	....	....	....	7.8	....	1.1	....
41-42 Fort Wayne-N	6	....	....	47	17	....	....	....	....	....	13	....	....	....	....	....	....	....	....	....	....	....	....	7.8	....	....	....
42-43 Fort Wayne-N	6	....	....	25	9	....	....	....	....	....	7	....	....	....	....	....	....	....	....	....	....	....	....	4.2	....	....	....
43-44 Fort Wayne-N	5	....	....	31	14	....	....	....	....	....	3	....	....	....	....	....	....	....	....	....	....	....	....	6.2	....	....	....
46-47 Fort Wayne-N	8	....	....	37	15	....	....	....	....	....	7	15	.467	....	....	....	....	....	....	....	....	....	....	4.6	....	....	....
47-48 Fort Wayne-N	4	....	....	19	7	....	....	....	....	....	5	10	.500	....	....	....	....	....	....	....	....	....	....	4.8	....	....	....
NBL Playoff Totals	29	....	....	159	62	....	....	....	....	....	35	25	....	....	....	....	....	....	....	....	....	....	....	5.5	....	....	....

• TOWNES, Linton

Linton Rodney Townes

Born: Nov. 30, 1959. Richmond, VA, United States. Height: 6'7". Weight: 190 lbs. Drafted: 1982 College: James Madison

YEAR TEAM	GP	GS	MIN	PTS	FGM	FGA	FG%	3PM	3PA	3P%	FTM	FTA	FT%	ORB	DRB	TRB	AST	PF	DQ	STL	BLK	TO	MPG	PPG	RPG	APG	PCM
82-83 Portland	55	0	516	247	105	234	.449	9	25	.360	28	38	.737	30	35	65	31	81	0	19	5	33	9.4	4.5	1.2	0.6	.338
83-84 Milwaukee	2	0	2	2	1	1	1.000	0	0	.000	0	0	.000	0	0	0	0	1	0	0	0	0	1.0	1.0	0.0	0.0	.768
83-84 San Diego	2	0	17	6	3	7	.429	0	0	.000	0	0	.000	0	1	1	1	3	0	1	2	1	8.5	3.0	0.5	0.5	.279
84-85 San Antonio	1	0	8	2	0	6	.000	0	0	.000	2	2	1.000	1	0	1	0	1	0	0	0	0	8.0	2.0	1.0	0.0	-.391
NBA Season Totals	60	0	543	257	109	248	.440	9	25	.360	30	40	.750	31	36	67	32	86	0	20	7	34	9.1	4.3	1.1	0.5	....
82-83 Portland	6	0	60	33	13	27	.481	1	3	.333	6	7	.857	2	1	3	5	11	0	0	0	3	10.0	5.5	0.5	0.8	.341
84-85 San Antonio	2	0	6	8	4	8	.500	0	1	.000	0	0	.000	2	1	3	0	1	0	0	0	0	3.0	4.0	1.5	0.0	1.100
NBA Playoff Totals	8	0	66	41	17	35	.486	1	4	.250	6	7	.857	4	2	6	5	12	0	0	0	3	8.3	5.1	0.8	0.6	....

• TOWNSEND, John

John (Houdini of the Hardwood) Townsend

Born: Sept. 20, 1916. Indianapolis, IN, United States. Died: Dec.2001. Height: 6'4". Weight: 208 lbs. Drafted: — College: Michigan

YEAR TEAM	GP	GS	MIN	PTS	FGM	FGA	FG%	3PM	3PA	3P%	FTM	FTA	FT%	ORB	DRB	TRB	AST	PF	DQ	STL	BLK	TO	MPG	PPG	RPG	APG	PCM
38-39 Hammond-N	5	....	....	43	14	....	....	....	....	....	15	....	....	....	....	....	....	....	....	....	....	....	....	8.6	....	....	....
41-42 Indianapolis-N	22	....	....	169	53	....	....	....	....	....	63	....	....	....	....	....	....	....	....	....	....	....	....	7.7	....	....	....
42-43 Oshkosh-N	5	....	....	18	4	....	....	....	....	....	10	....	....	....	....	....	....	....	....	....	....	....	....	3.6	....	....	....
42-43 Toledo-N	2	....	....	16	6	....	....	....	....	....	4	....	....	....	....	....	....	....	....	....	....	....	....	8.0	....	....	....
NBL Season Totals	34	....	....	246	77	....	....	....	....	....	92	....	....	....	....	....	....	....	....	....	....	....	....	7.2	....	....	....
41-42 Indianapolis-N	2	....	....	23	6	....	....	....	....	....	11	....	....	....	....	....	....	....	....	....	....	....	....	11.5	....	....	....
NBL Playoff Totals	2	....	....	23	6	....	....	....	....	....	11	....	....	....	....	....	....	....	....	....	....	....	....	11.5	....	....	....

• TOWNSEND, Raymond

Raymond Anthony Townsend

Born: Dec. 20, 1955. San Jose, CA, United States. Height: 6'3". Weight: 175 lbs. Drafted: 1978 College: UCLA

YEAR TEAM	GP	GS	MIN	PTS	FGM	FGA	FG%	3PM	3PA	3P%	FTM	FTA	FT%	ORB	DRB	TRB	AST	PF	DQ	STL	BLK	TO	MPG	PPG	RPG	APG	PCM
78-79 Golden State	65	....	771	304	127	289	.439	....	....	....	50	68	.735	11	44	55	91	70	0	27	6	52	11.9	4.7	0.8	1.4	.326
79-80 Golden State	75	....	1159	406	171	421	.406	4	26	.154	60	84	.714	33	56	89	116	113	0	60	4	68	15.5	5.4	1.2	1.5	.278
81-82 Indiana	14	0	95	35	11	41	.268	2	9	.222	11	20	.550	2	11	13	10	18	0	3	0	6	6.8	2.5	0.9	0.7	.157
NBA Season Totals	154	0	2025	745	309	751	.411	6	35	.171	121	172	.703	46	111	157	217	201	0	90	10	126	13.1	4.8	1.0	1.4	....

• TRAPP, George

George Trapp

Born: July 11, 1948. Detroit, MI, United States. Died: Jan.21, 2002. Height: 6'8". Weight: 205 lbs. Drafted: 1971 College: Long Beach State

YEAR TEAM	GP	GS	MIN	PTS	FGM	FGA	FG%	3PM	3PA	3P%	FTM	FTA	FT%	ORB	DRB	TRB	AST	PF	DQ	STL	BLK	TO	MPG	PPG	RPG	APG	PCM
71-72 Atlanta	60	....	890	393	144	388	.371	....	....	....	105	139	.755	....	....	183	51	144	2	....	....	....	14.8	6.6	3.1	0.9	.361
72-73 Atlanta	77	....	1853	868	359	824	.436	....	....	....	150	194	.773	....	....	455	127	274	11	....	....	....	24.1	11.3	5.9	1.6	.468
73-74 Detroit	82	....	1489	765	333	693	.481	....	....	....	99	134	.739	97	216	313	81	226	2	47	33	....	18.2	9.3	3.8	1.0	.475
74-75 Detroit	78	....	1472	675	288	652	.442	....	....	....	99	131	.756	71	205	276	63	210	1	37	14	....	18.9	8.7	3.5	0.8	.387
75-76 Detroit	76	....	1091	619	278	602	.462	....	....	....	63	88	.716	79	150	229	50	167	3	33	23	....	14.4	8.1	3.0	0.7	.469
76-77 Detroit	6	....	68	33	15	29	.517	....	....	....	3	4	.750	4	6	10	3	13	0	0	1	....	11.3	5.5	1.7	0.5	.396
NBA Season Totals	379	....	6863	3353	1417	3188	.444	....	....	....	519	690	.752	251	577	1466	375	1034	19	117	71	....	18.1	8.8	3.9	1.0	....
71-72 Atlanta	6	....	66	41	19	44	.432	....	....	....	3	8	.375	....	....	18	5	13	0	....	....	....	11.0	6.8	3.0	0.8	.498
72-73 Atlanta	6	....	99	25	11	32	.344	....	....	....	3	5	.600	....	....	21	3	21	0	....	....	....	16.5	4.2	3.5	0.5	.187
73-74 Detroit	7	....	119	62	30	51	.588	....	....	....	2	2	1.000	4	18	22	2	23	1	0	5	....	17.0	8.9	3.1	0.3	.465
74-75 Detroit	3	....	81	41	18	33	.545	....	....	....	5	7	.714	5	17	22	4	6	0	0	0	....	27.0	13.7	7.3	1.3	.594
75-76 Detroit	9	....	153	89	37	89	.416	....	....	....	15	18	.833	12	23	35	9	26	0	4	4	....	17.0	9.9	3.9	1.0	.472
NBA Playoff Totals	31	....	518	258	115	249	.462	....	....	....	28	40	.700	21	58	118	23	89	1	4	9	....	16.7	8.3	3.8	0.7	....

• TRAPP, John

John Quincy (John Q.) Trapp

Born: Oct. 2, 1945. Detroit, MI, United States. Height: 6'7". Weight: 210 lbs. Drafted: 1968 College: UNLV

YEAR TEAM	GP	GS	MIN	PTS	FGM	FGA	FG%	3PM	3PA	3P%	FTM	FTA	FT%	ORB	DRB	TRB	AST	PF	DQ	STL	BLK	TO	MPG	PPG	RPG	APG	PCM
68-69 San Diego	25	....	142	77	29	80	.363	....	....	....	19	29	.655	....	....	49	5	38	0	....	....	....	5.7	3.1	2.0	0.2	.430
69-70 San Diego	70	....	1025	442	185	434	.426	....	....	....	72	104	.692	....	....	309	49	200	3	....	....	....	14.6	6.3	4.4	0.7	.437
70-71 San Diego	82	....	2080	786	322	766	.420	....	....	....	142	188	.755	....	....	510	138	337	**16**	....	....	....	25.4	9.6	6.2	1.7	.402
71-72 LA Lakers	58	....	759	329	139	314	.443	....	....	....	51	73	.699	....	....	180	42	130	3	....	....	....	13.1	5.7	3.1	0.7	.416
72-73 Denver-A	25	....	342	127	54	128	.422	0	2	.000	19	32	.594	27	45	72	20	76	1	....	....	25	13.7	5.1	2.9	0.8	.313
72-73 LA Lakers	5	....	35	13	3	12	.250	....	....	....	7	10	.700	....	....	14	2	10	0	....	....	....	7.0	2.6	2.8	0.4	.400
72-73 Philadelphia	39	....	854	419	168	408	.412	....	....	....	83	112	.741	....	....	186	47	140	0	....	....	....	21.9	10.7	4.8	1.2	.414
NBA Season Totals	279	....	4895	2066	846	2014	.420	....	....	....	374	516	.725	....	....	1248	283	855	22	....	....	....	17.5	7.4	4.5	1.0	....
ABA Season Totals	25	....	342	127	54	128	.422	0	2	.000	19	32	.594	27	45	72	20	76	1	....	....	25	13.7	5.1	2.9	0.8	....
Career Totals	304	....	5237	2193	900	2142	.420	0	2	.000	393	548	.717	27	45	1320	303	931	23	....	....	25	17.2	7.2	4.3	1.0	....
71-72 LA Lakers	10	....	71	20	8	33	.242	....	....	....	4	7	.571	....	....	16	5	9	0	....	....	....	7.1	2.0	1.6	0.5	.179
72-73 Denver-A	5	....	51	22	7	16	.438	0	0	.000	8	12	.667	4	3	7	2	13	0	....	....	1	10.2	4.4	1.4	0.4	.289
NBA Playoff Totals	10	....	71	20	8	33	.242	....	....	....	4	7	.571	....	....	16	5	9	0	....	....	....	7.1	2.0	1.6	0.5	....
ABA Playoff Totals	5	....	51	22	7	16	.438	0	0	.000	8	12	.667	4	3	7	2	13	0	....	....	1	10.2	4.4	1.4	0.4	....
Career Playoff Totals	15	....	122	42	15	49	.306	0	0	.000	12	19	.632	4	3	23	7	22	0	....	....	1	8.1	2.8	1.5	0.5	....

• TRAYLOR, Robert

Robert DeShaun (Tractor) Traylor

Born: Feb. 1, 1977. Detroit, MI, United States. Height: 6'8". Weight: 284 lbs. Drafted: 1998 College: Michigan

YEAR TEAM	GP	GS	MIN	PTS	FGM	FGA	FG%	3PM	3PA	3P%	FTM	FTA	FT%	ORB	DRB	TRB	AST	PF	DQ	STL	BLK	TO	MPG	PPG	RPG	APG	PCM
98-99 Milwaukee	49	43	786	259	108	201	.537	0	1	.000	43	80	.538	80	102	182	38	140	4	44	44	42	16.0	5.3	3.7	0.8	.436
99-00 Milwaukee	44	16	447	157	58	122	.475	0	4	.000	41	68	.603	50	65	115	20	79	0	25	25	27	10.2	3.6	2.6	0.5	.443
00-01 Cleveland	70	7	1212	402	161	324	.497	0	2	.000	80	141	.567	124	176	300	63	204	3	49	76	98	17.3	5.7	4.3	0.9	.412
01-02 Charlotte	61	1	679	228	87	204	.426	1	1	1.000	53	84	.631	67	120	187	37	127	1	24	37	45	11.1	3.7	3.1	0.6	.405

YEAR	TEAM	GP	GS	MIN	PTS	FGM	FGA	FG%	3PM	3PA	3P%	FTM	FTA	FT%	ORB	DRB	TRB	AST	PF	DQ	STL	BLK	TO	MPG	PPG	RPG	APG	PCM
02-03	New Orleans	69	0	851	268	105	237	.443	1	3	.333	57	88	.648	108	154	262	50	153	1	45	37	53	12.3	3.9	3.8	0.7	.451
NBA Season Totals		293	67	3975	1314	519	1088	.477	2	11	.182	274	461	.594	429	617	1046	208	703	9	187	219	265	13.6	4.5	3.6	0.7	....
98-99	Milwaukee	3	1	45	16	7	9	.778	0	0	.000	2	4	.500	6	6	12	2	15	1	2	4	4	15.0	5.3	4.0	0.7	.474
99-00	Milwaukee	1	0	4	0	0	1	.000	0	0	.000	0	0	.000	1	1	2	1	2	0	0	1	0	4.0	0.0	2.0	1.0	.500
01-02	Charlotte	8	0	62	18	7	20	.350	0	1	.000	4	6	.667	4	12	16	3	15	0	2	2	4	7.8	2.3	2.0	0.4	.263
02-03	New Orleans	6	0	94	21	10	22	.455	0	0	.000	1	4	.250	11	19	30	4	17	0	3	5	6	15.7	3.5	5.0	0.7	.366
NBA Playoff Totals		18	1	205	55	24	52	.462	0	1	.000	7	14	.500	22	38	60	10	49	1	7	12	14	11.4	3.1	3.3	0.6	....

• TRENT, Gary

Gary Dajaun Trent

Born: Sept. 22, 1974. Columbus, OH, United States. Height: 6'8". Weight: 250 lbs. Drafted: 1995 College: Ohio University

YEAR	TEAM	GP	GS	MIN	PTS	FGM	FGA	FG%	3PM	3PA	3P%	FTM	FTA	FT%	ORB	DRB	TRB	AST	PF	DQ	STL	BLK	TO	MPG	PPG	RPG	APG	PCM
95-96	Portland	69	10	1219	518	220	429	.513	0	9	.000	78	141	.553	84	154	238	50	116	0	25	11	90	17.7	7.5	3.4	0.7	.380
96-97	Portland	82	28	1918	882	361	674	.536	0	11	.000	160	229	.699	156	272	428	87	186	2	48	35	131	23.4	10.8	5.2	1.1	.479
97-98	Portland	41	13	1005	471	177	359	.493	4	9	.444	113	163	.693	80	154	234	58	115	2	27	19	74	24.5	11.5	5.7	1.4	.478
97-98	Toronto	13	7	355	159	64	146	.438	0	3	.000	31	49	.633	43	61	104	14	46	1	8	8	22	27.3	12.2	8.0	1.1	.449
98-99	Dallas	45	23	1362	719	287	602	.477	0	5	.000	145	235	.617	127	224	351	77	122	1	29	23	66	30.3	16.0	7.8	1.7	.536
99-00	Dallas	11	11	301	151	70	142	.493	0	2	.000	11	21	.524	20	32	52	22	28	0	8	3	25	27.4	13.7	4.7	2.0	.422
00-01	Dallas	33	4	319	133	57	130	.438	0	1	.000	19	36	.528	39	53	92	10	52	0	13	8	22	9.7	4.0	2.8	0.3	.405
01-02	Minnesota	64	10	1140	478	193	381	.507	0	2	.000	92	144	.639	104	166	270	60	160	0	21	27	58	17.8	7.5	4.2	0.9	.450
02-03	Minnesota	80	22	1221	476	208	389	.535	0	2	.000	60	101	.594	106	185	291	77	142	0	32	23	59	15.3	6.0	3.6	1.0	.469
NBA Season Totals		438	128	8840	3987	1637	3252	.503	4	44	.091	709	1119	.634	759	1301	2060	455	967	6	211	157	547	20.2	9.1	4.7	1.0	....
95-96	Portland	2	0	10	2	1	4	.250	0	0	.000	0	0	.000	0	1	1	0	3	0	1	0	0	5.0	1.0	0.5	0.0	-.035
96-97	Portland	4	0	61	32	13	29	.448	0	1	.000	6	11	.545	5	7	12	4	11	0	0	1	6	15.3	8.0	3.0	1.0	.335
01-02	Minnesota	3	0	48	19	8	16	.500	0	0	.000	3	6	.500	5	4	9	1	8	0	0	0	3	16.0	6.3	3.0	0.3	.277
02-03	Minnesota	6	0	42	14	5	14	.357	0	0	.000	4	6	.667	4	3	7	1	6	0	1	0	4	7.0	2.3	1.2	0.2	.165
NBA Playoff Totals		15	0	161	67	27	63	.429	0	1	.000	13	23	.565	14	15	29	6	28	0	2	1	13	10.7	4.5	1.9	0.4	....

• TREPAGNIER, Jeff

Jeffery Trepagnier

Born: July 11, 1979. Los Angeles, CA, United States. Height: 6'4". Weight: 200 lbs. Drafted: 2001 College: Southern California

YEAR	TEAM	GP	GS	MIN	PTS	FGM	FGA	FG%	3PM	3PA	3P%	FTM	FTA	FT%	ORB	DRB	TRB	AST	PF	DQ	STL	BLK	TO	MPG	PPG	RPG	APG	PCM
01-02	Cleveland	12	0	77	18	7	23	.304	0	1	.000	4	7	.571	3	9	12	12	8	0	8	4	11	6.4	1.5	1.0	1.0	.304
02-03	Denver	8	0	98	45	17	40	.425	4	8	.500	7	7	1.000	8	8	16	6	5	0	8	0	8	12.3	5.6	2.0	0.8	.438
NBA Season Totals		20	0	175	63	24	63	.381	4	9	.444	11	14	.786	11	17	28	18	13	0	16	4	19	8.8	3.2	1.4	0.9	....

• TRESVANT, John

John B. Tresvant

Born: Nov. 6, 1939. Height: 6'7". Weight: 215 lbs. Drafted: 1964 College: Seattle

YEAR	TEAM	GP	GS	MIN	PTS	FGM	FGA	FG%	3PM	3PA	3P%	FTM	FTA	FT%	ORB	DRB	TRB	AST	PF	DQ	STL	BLK	TO	MPG	PPG	RPG	APG	PCM
64-65	St. Louis	4	....	35	14	4	11	.364	....	....	....	6	9	.667	....	....	18	6	9	0	....	....	....	8.8	3.5	4.5	1.5	.721
65-66	St. Louis	15	....	213	101	37	78	.474	....	....	....	27	32	.844	....	....	85	10	43	0	....	....	....	14.2	6.7	5.7	0.7	.605
65-66	Detroit	46	....	756	383	134	322	.416	....	....	....	115	158	.728	....	....	279	62	136	2	....	....	....	16.4	8.3	6.1	1.3	.608
66-67	Detroit	68	....	1553	676	256	585	.438	....	....	....	164	234	.701	....	....	483	88	246	8	....	....	....	22.8	9.9	7.1	1.3	.501
67-68	Detroit	55	....	1671	733	275	597	.461	....	....	....	183	278	.658	....	....	540	114	239	**15**	....	....	....	30.4	13.3	9.8	2.1	.545
67-68	Cincinnati	30	....	802	309	121	270	.448	....	....	....	67	106	.632	....	....	169	46	105	**3**	....	....	....	26.7	10.3	5.6	1.5	.402
68-69	Cincinnati	51	....	1681	608	239	531	.450	....	....	....	130	223	.583	....	....	419	103	193	5	....	....	....	33.0	11.9	8.2	2.0	.425
68-69	Seattle	26	....	801	354	141	289	.488	....	....	....	72	107	.673	....	....	267	63	107	4	....	....	....	30.8	13.6	10.3	2.4	.584
69-70	Seattle	49	....	1278	617	217	507	.428	....	....	....	183	249	.735	....	....	362	95	164	4	....	....	....	26.1	12.6	7.4	1.9	.536
69-70	LA Lakers	20	....	221	117	47	88	.534	....	....	....	23	35	.657	....	....	63	17	40	0	....	....	....	11.1	5.9	3.2	0.9	.600
70-71	LA Lakers	8	....	66	43	18	35	.514	....	....	....	7	10	.700	....	....	23	10	11	0	....	....	....	8.3	5.4	2.9	1.3	.811
70-71	Baltimore	67	....	1451	507	184	401	.459	....	....	....	139	195	.713	....	....	359	76	185	1	....	....	....	21.7	7.6	5.4	1.1	.422
71-72	Baltimore	65	....	1227	445	162	360	.450	....	....	....	121	148	.818	....	....	323	83	175	6	....	....	....	18.9	6.8	5.0	1.3	.456
72-73	Baltimore	55	....	541	211	85	182	.467	....	....	....	41	59	.695	....	....	156	33	101	0	....	....	....	9.8	3.8	2.8	0.6	.459
NBA Season Totals		559	....	12296	5118	1920	4256	.451	....	....	....	1278	1843	.693	....	....	3546	806	1754	48	....	....	....	22.0	9.2	6.3	1.4	....
69-70	LA Lakers	11	....	148	65	23	51	.451	....	....	....	19	23	.826	....	....	38	16	22	1	....	....	....	13.5	5.9	3.5	1.5	.542
70-71	Baltimore	18	....	484	150	56	137	.409	....	....	....	38	57	.667	....	....	134	19	64	1	....	....	....	26.9	8.3	7.4	1.1	.375
71-72	Baltimore	6	....	180	47	20	48	.417	....	....	....	7	11	.636	....	....	58	6	23	1	....	....	....	30.0	7.8	9.7	1.0	.378
72-73	Baltimore	5	....	50	12	5	15	.333	....	....	....	2	4	.500	....	....	16	3	6	0	....	....	....	10.0	2.4	3.2	0.6	.343
NBA Playoff Totals		40	....	862	274	104	251	.414	....	....	....	66	95	.695	....	....	246	44	115	3	....	....	....	21.6	6.9	6.2	1.1	....

• TRIPTOW, Dick

Richard Floyd (Tiptoe) Triptow

Born: Nov. 3, 1922. Height: 6' Weight: 170 lbs. Drafted: — College: DePaul

YEAR	TEAM	GP	GS	MIN	PTS	FGM	FGA	FG%	3PM	3PA	3P%	FTM	FTA	FT%	ORB	DRB	TRB	AST	PF	DQ	STL	BLK	TO	MPG	PPG	RPG	APG	PCM
44-45	Chicago-N	30	....	....	299	113	....	....	....	....	....	73	....	....	....	....	....	....	....	....	....	....	....	....	10.0	....	....	....
45-46	Chicago-N	34	....	....	221	68	....	....	....	....	....	85	127	.669	....	....	....	....	....	....	....	....	....	....	6.5	....	....	....
46-47	Chicago-N	44	....	....	178	59	....	....	....	....	....	60	90	.667	....	....	....	....	71	....	....	....	....	....	4.0	....	....	....
47-48	Fort Wayne-N	48	....	....	223	74	....	....	....	....	....	75	119	.630	....	....	....	....	....	....	....	....	....	....	4.6	....	....	....
47-48	Tri-Cities-N	9	....	....	48	18	....	....	....	....	....	12	19	.632	....	....	....	....	....	....	....	....	....	....	5.3	....	....	....
48-49	Fort Wayne	55	....	....	334	116	417	.278	....	....	....	102	141	.723	....	....	....	96	107	....	....	....	....	....	6.1	....	1.7	....
49-50	Baltimore	4	....	....	2	0	5	.000	....	....	....	2	2	1.000	....	....	....	1	5	....	....	....	....	....	0.5	....	0.3	....
NBA Season Totals		59	....	....	336	116	422	.275	....	....	....	104	143	.727	....	....	....	97	112	....	....	....	....	....	5.7	....	1.6	....
NBL Season Totals		165	....	....	969	332	....	....	....	....	....	305	355	....	....	....	....	....	71	....	....	....	....	....	5.9	....	....	....
Career Totals		224	....	....	1305	448	422	....	....	....	....	409	498	....	....	....	....	97	183	....	....	....	....	....	5.8	....	0.4	....
44-45	Chicago-N	3	....	....	28	11	....	....	....	....	....	6	....	....	....	....	....	....	....	....	....	....	....	....	9.3	....	....	....
46-47	Chicago-N	11	....	....	53	19	....	....	....	....	....	15	22	.682	....	....	....	....	....	....	....	....	....	....	4.8	....	....	....
47-48	Fort Wayne-N	4	....	....	19	9	....	....	....	....	....	1	3	.333	....	....	....	....	....	....	....	....	....	....	4.8	....	....	....
NBL Playoff Totals		18	....	....	100	39	....	....	....	....	....	22	25	....	....	....	....	....	....	....	....	....	....	....	5.6	....	....	....

YEAR	TEAM	GP	GS	MIN	PTS	FGM	FGA	FG%	3PM	3PA	3P%	FTM	FTA	FT%	ORB	DRB	TRB	AST	PF	DQ	STL	BLK	TO	MPG	PPG	RPG	APG	PCM

• TRIPUCKA, Kelly

Peter Kelly Tripucka

Born: Feb. 16, 1959. Glen Ridge, NJ, United States.   Height: 6'6".   Weight: 220 lbs.   Drafted: 1981   College: Notre Dame

YEAR	TEAM	GP	GS	MIN	PTS	FGM	FGA	FG%	3PM	3PA	3P%	FTM	FTA	FT%	ORB	DRB	TRB	AST	PF	DQ	STL	BLK	TO	MPG	PPG	RPG	APG	PCM
81-82	Detroit	82	82	3077	1772	636	1281	.496	5	22	.227	495	621	.797	219	224	443	270	241	0	89	16	279	37.5	21.6	5.4	3.3	.503
82-83	Detroit	58	58	2252	1536	565	1156	.489	14	37	.378	392	464	.845	126	138	264	237	157	0	67	20	186	38.8	26.5	4.6	4.1	.581
83-84	Detroit	76	75	2493	1618	595	1296	.459	2	17	.118	426	523	.815	119	187	306	228	190	0	65	17	190	32.8	21.3	4.0	3.0	.506
84-85	Detroit	55	43	1675	1049	396	831	.477	2	5	.400	255	288	.885	66	152	218	135	118	1	49	14	116	30.5	19.1	4.0	2.5	.520
85-86	Detroit	81	81	2626	1622	615	1236	.498	12	25	.480	380	444	.856	116	232	348	265	167	0	93	10	186	32.4	20.0	4.3	3.3	.559
86-87	Utah	79	76	1865	798	291	621	.469	19	52	.365	197	226	.872	54	188	242	243	147	0	85	11	166	23.6	10.1	3.1	3.1	.444
87-88	Utah	49	21	976	368	139	303	.459	31	74	.419	59	68	.868	30	87	117	105	68	1	34	4	69	19.9	7.5	2.4	2.1	.381
88-89	Charlotte	71	65	2302	1606	568	1215	.467	30	84	.357	440	508	.866	79	188	267	224	196	0	88	16	234	32.4	22.6	3.8	3.2	.542
89-90	Charlotte	79	73	2404	1232	442	1029	.430	38	104	.365	310	351	.883	82	240	322	224	220	1	75	16	174	30.4	15.6	4.1	2.8	.425
90-91	Charlotte	77	1	1289	541	187	412	.454	15	45	.333	152	167	.910	46	130	176	159	130	0	33	13	92	16.7	7.0	2.3	2.1	.430
NBA Season Totals		707	575	20959	12142	4434	9380	.473	168	465	.361	3106	3660	.849	937	1766	2703	2090	1634	3	678	137	1692	29.6	17.2	3.8	3.0	....
83-84	Detroit	5	5	208	137	48	102	.471	0	1	.000	41	51	.804	10	13	23	15	22	1	11	0	18	41.6	27.4	4.6	3.0	.494
84-85	Detroit	9	9	288	133	49	118	.415	0	1	.000	35	40	.875	19	20	39	29	22	0	4	3	19	32.0	14.8	4.3	3.2	.390
85-86	Detroit	4	4	175	87	33	71	.465	0	0	.000	21	23	.913	10	13	23	9	14	1	3	2	16	43.8	21.8	5.8	2.3	.372
86-87	Utah	5	5	70	32	14	20	.700	0	3	.000	4	4	1.000	1	6	7	3	6	0	4	0	7	14.0	6.4	1.4	0.6	.436
87-88	Utah	2	0	9	2	1	3	.333	0	0	.000	0	0	.000	1	0	1	1	1	0	0	0	1	4.5	1.0	0.5	0.5	.082
NBA Playoff Totals		25	23	750	391	145	314	.462	0	5	.000	101	118	.856	41	52	93	57	65	2	22	5	61	30.0	15.6	3.7	2.3	....

• TRUITT, Ansley

Ansley Hoover Truitt

Born: Aug. 24, 1950. West Point, GA, United States.   Height: 6'9".   Weight: 215 lbs.   Drafted: 1972   College: California (Berkeley)

YEAR	TEAM	GP	GS	MIN	PTS	FGM	FGA	FG%	3PM	3PA	3P%	FTM	FTA	FT%	ORB	DRB	TRB	AST	PF	DQ	STL	BLK	TO	MPG	PPG	RPG	APG	PCM
72-73	Dallas-A	16	....	86	39	18	42	.429	0	0	.000	3	9	.333	10	28	38	2	9	0	....	....	7	5.4	2.4	2.4	0.1	.547
ABA Season Totals		16	....	86	39	18	42	.429	0	0	.000	3	9	.333	10	28	38	2	9	0	....	....	7	5.4	2.4	2.4	0.1	....

• TRYBANSKI, Cezary

Cezary Trybanski

Born: Sept. 22, 1979. Warsaw, Poland.   Height: 7'2".   Weight: 240 lbs.   Drafted: —   College: none

YEAR	TEAM	GP	GS	MIN	PTS	FGM	FGA	FG%	3PM	3PA	3P%	FTM	FTA	FT%	ORB	DRB	TRB	AST	PF	DQ	STL	BLK	TO	MPG	PPG	RPG	APG	PCM
02-03	Memphis	15	0	86	14	5	20	.250	0	0	.000	4	10	.400	6	8	14	1	13	0	0	6	8	5.7	0.9	0.9	0.1	.044
NBA Season Totals		15	0	86	14	5	20	.250	0	0	.000	4	10	.400	6	8	14	1	13	0	0	6	8	5.7	0.9	0.9	0.1	....

• TSAKALIDIS, Jake

Iakovos (Jake) Tsakalidis

Born: June 10, 1979. Rustavi, Soviet Union.   Height: 7'2".   Weight: 285 lbs.   Drafted: 2000   College: none

YEAR	TEAM	GP	GS	MIN	PTS	FGM	FGA	FG%	3PM	3PA	3P%	FTM	FTA	FT%	ORB	DRB	TRB	AST	PF	DQ	STL	BLK	TO	MPG	PPG	RPG	APG	PCM
00-01	Phoenix	57	39	947	256	101	215	.470	0	0	.000	54	91	.593	83	159	242	19	137	1	10	55	66	16.6	4.5	4.2	0.3	.330
01-02	Phoenix	67	47	1582	491	190	400	.475	0	1	.000	111	159	.698	130	243	373	23	193	4	23	69	78	23.6	7.3	5.6	0.3	.359
02-03	Phoenix	33	27	542	161	61	135	.452	0	0	.000	39	58	.672	45	77	122	13	80	1	6	17	26	16.4	4.9	3.7	0.4	.316
NBA Season Totals		157	113	3071	908	352	750	.469	0	1	.000	204	308	.662	258	479	737	55	410	6	39	141	170	19.6	5.8	4.7	0.4	....
00-01	Phoenix	4	4	75	12	6	16	.375	0	0	.000	0	0	.000	10	18	28	0	11	0	0	7	1	18.8	3.0	7.0	0.0	.382
NBA Playoff Totals		4	4	75	12	6	16	.375	0	0	.000	0	0	.000	10	18	28	0	11	0	0	7	1	18.8	3.0	7.0	0.0	....

• TSCHOGL, John

John Mark Tschogl

Born: Apr. 25, 1950. Chula Vista, CA, United States.   Height: 6'6".   Weight: 206 lbs.   Drafted: 1972   College: Santa Barbara

YEAR	TEAM	GP	GS	MIN	PTS	FGM	FGA	FG%	3PM	3PA	3P%	FTM	FTA	FT%	ORB	DRB	TRB	AST	PF	DQ	STL	BLK	TO	MPG	PPG	RPG	APG	PCM
72-73	Atlanta	10	....	94	30	14	40	.350	....	....	....	2	4	.500	....	....	21	6	25	0	....	....	....	9.4	3.0	2.1	0.6	.223
73-74	Atlanta	64	....	499	128	59	166	.355	....	....	....	10	17	.588	33	43	76	33	69	0	17	20	....	7.8	2.0	1.2	0.5	.215
74-75	Philadelphia	39	....	623	119	53	148	.358	....	....	....	13	22	.591	52	59	111	30	80	2	25	25	....	16.0	3.1	2.8	0.8	.207
NBA Season Totals		113	....	1216	277	126	354	.356	....	....	....	25	43	.581	85	102	208	69	174	2	42	45	....	10.8	2.5	1.8	0.6	....
72-73	Atlanta	3	....	11	10	5	8	.625	....	....	....	0	0	.000	....	....	4	1	0	0	....	....	....	3.7	3.3	1.3	0.3	1.091
NBA Playoff Totals		3	....	11	10	5	8	.625	....	....	....	0	0	.000	....	....	4	1	0	0	....	....	....	3.7	3.3	1.3	0.3	....

• TSIOROPOULOS, Lou

Louis C. Tsioropoulos

Born: Aug. 31, 1930. Lynn, MA, United States.   Height: 6'5".   Weight: 190 lbs.   Drafted: 1953   College: Kentucky

YEAR	TEAM	GP	GS	MIN	PTS	FGM	FGA	FG%	3PM	3PA	3P%	FTM	FTA	FT%	ORB	DRB	TRB	AST	PF	DQ	STL	BLK	TO	MPG	PPG	RPG	APG	PCM
56-57	Boston	52	....	670	227	79	256	.309	....	....	....	69	89	.775	....	....	207	33	135	6	....	....	....	12.9	4.4	4.0	0.6	.348
57-58	Boston	70	....	1819	538	198	624	.317	....	....	....	142	207	.686	....	....	434	112	242	8	....	....	....	26.0	7.7	6.2	1.6	.316
58-59	Boston	35	....	488	145	60	190	.316	....	....	....	25	33	.758	....	....	110	20	74	0	....	....	....	13.9	4.1	3.1	0.6	.254
NBA Season Totals		157	....	2977	910	337	1070	.315	....	....	....	236	329	.717	....	....	751	165	451	14	....	....	....	19.0	5.8	4.8	1.1	....
57-58	Boston	11	....	239	69	25	85	.294	....	....	....	19	29	.655	....	....	64	14	40	4	....	....	....	21.7	6.3	5.8	1.3	.299
NBA Playoff Totals		11	....	239	69	25	85	.294	....	....	....	19	29	.655	....	....	64	14	40	4	....	....	....	21.7	6.3	5.8	1.3	....

• TSKITISHVILI, Nik

Nikoloz Tskitishvili

Born: Apr. 14, 1983. Tbilisi, Georgia.   Height: 7'.   Weight: 225 lbs.   Drafted: 2002   College: none

YEAR	TEAM	GP	GS	MIN	PTS	FGM	FGA	FG%	3PM	3PA	3P%	FTM	FTA	FT%	ORB	DRB	TRB	AST	PF	DQ	STL	BLK	TO	MPG	PPG	RPG	APG	PCM
02-03	Denver	81	16	1326	315	115	393	.293	37	152	.243	48	65	.738	64	117	181	91	136	1	31	29	84	16.4	3.9	2.2	1.1	.177
NBA Season Totals		81	16	1326	315	115	393	.293	37	152	.243	48	65	.738	64	117	181	91	136	1	31	29	84	16.4	3.9	2.2	1.1	....

• TUCKER, Al

Albert Ames (Tuck) Tucker

Born: Feb. 24, 1943. Dayton, OH, United States. Died: May 7, 2001.   Height: 6'8".   Weight: 190 lbs.   Drafted: 1967   College: Oklahoma Baptist

YEAR	TEAM	GP	GS	MIN	PTS	FGM	FGA	FG%	3PM	3PA	3P%	FTM	FTA	FT%	ORB	DRB	TRB	AST	PF	DQ	STL	BLK	TO	MPG	PPG	RPG	APG	PCM
67-68	Seattle	81	....	2368	1060	437	989	.442	....	....	....	186	263	.707	....	....	605	111	262	6	....	....	....	29.2	13.1	7.5	1.4	.465
68-69	Seattle	56	....	1259	579	235	544	.432	....	....	....	109	171	.637	....	....	317	55	111	0	....	....	....	22.5	10.3	5.7	1.0	.459
68-69	Cincinnati	28	....	626	301	126	265	.475	....	....	....	49	73	.671	....	....	122	19	75	2	....	....	....	22.4	10.8	4.4	0.7	.427
69-70	Chicago	33	....	557	231	97	189	.513	....	....	....	37	45	.822	....	....	113	31	52	0	....	....	....	16.9	7.0	3.4	0.9	.463
69-70	Baltimore	28	....	262	131	49	96	.510	....	....	....	33	42	.786	....	....	53	7	34	0	....	....	....	9.4	4.7	1.9	0.3	.478
70-71	Florida-A	14	....	331	169	66	149	.443	3	7	.429	34	42	.810	19	46	65	12	40	1	....	....	25	23.6	12.1	4.6	0.9	.452
70-71	Baltimore	31	....	276	129	52	115	.452	....	....	....	25	31	.806	....	....	73	7	33	0	....	....	....	8.9	4.2	2.4	0.2	.467
71-72	Florida-A	81	....	1799	941	377	810	.465	30	82	.366	157	199	.789	91	301	392	100	205	3	....	....	129	22.2	11.6	4.8	1.2	.505
NBA Season Totals		257	....	5348	2431	996	2198	.453	....	....	....	439	625	.702	....	....	1283	230	567	8	....	....	....	20.8	9.5	5.0	0.9	....
ABA Season Totals		95	....	2130	1110	443	959	.462	33	89	.371	191	241	.793	110	347	457	112	245	4	....	....	154	22.4	11.7	4.8	1.2	....
Career Totals		352	....	7478	3541	1439	3157	.456	33	89	.371	630	866	.727	110	347	1740	342	812	12	....	....	154	21.2	10.1	4.9	1.0	....
69-70	Baltimore	4	....	5	4	2	2	1.000	....	....	....	0	0	.000	....	....	0	0	0	0	....	....	....	1.3	1.0	0.0	0.0	.800
70-71	Florida-A	6	....	165	76	28	65	.431	1	6	.167	19	23	.826	4	28	32	12	20	0	....	....	11	27.5	12.7	5.3	2.0	.465
71-72	Florida-A	3	....	51	10	5	20	.250	0	1	.000	0	1	.000	....	....	14	4	8	....	....	....	3	17.0	3.3	4.7	1.3	.189
NBA Playoff Totals		4	....	5	4	2	2	1.000	....	....	....	0	0	.000	....	....	0	0	0	0	....	....	....	1.3	1.0	0.0	0.0	....
ABA Playoff Totals		9	....	216	86	33	85	.388	1	7	.143	19	24	.792	4	28	46	16	28	0	....	....	14	24.0	9.6	5.1	1.8	....
Career Playoff Totals		13	....	221	90	35	87	.402	1	7	.143	19	24	.792	4	28	46	16	28	0	....	....	14	17.0	6.9	3.5	1.2	....

• TUCKER, Anthony

Anthony Glenn Tucker

Born: Apr. 4, 1969. Washington, DC, United States.   Height: 6'8".   Weight: 220 lbs.   Drafted: —   College: Wake Forest

YEAR	TEAM	GP	GS	MIN	PTS	FGM	FGA	FG%	3PM	3PA	3P%	FTM	FTA	FT%	ORB	DRB	TRB	AST	PF	DQ	STL	BLK	TO	MPG	PPG	RPG	APG	PCM
94-95	Washington	62	13	982	243	96	210	.457	0	1	.000	51	83	.614	44	126	170	68	129	0	46	11	56	15.8	3.9	2.7	1.1	.299
NBA Season Totals		62	13	982	243	96	210	.457	0	1	.000	51	83	.614	44	126	170	68	129	0	46	11	56	15.8	3.9	2.7	1.1	....

• TUCKER, Jim

James D. Tucker

Born: Dec. 11, 1932. Paris, KY, United States.   Height: 6'7".   Weight: 185 lbs.   Drafted: 1954   College: Duquesne

YEAR	TEAM	GP	GS	MIN	PTS	FGM	FGA	FG%	3PM	3PA	3P%	FTM	FTA	FT%	ORB	DRB	TRB	AST	PF	DQ	STL	BLK	TO	MPG	PPG	RPG	APG	PCM
54-55	Syracuse	20	....	287	105	39	116	.336	....	....	....	27	38	.711	....	....	97	12	50	0	....	....	....	14.4	5.3	4.9	0.6	.391
55-56	Syracuse	70	....	895	268	101	290	.348	....	....	....	66	83	.795	....	....	232	38	166	2	....	....	....	12.8	3.8	3.3	0.5	.311
56-57	Syracuse	9	....	119	34	17	44	.386	....	....	....	0	1	.000	....	....	20	2	26	0	....	....	....	13.2	3.8	2.2	0.2	.178
NBA Season Totals		99	....	1301	407	157	450	.349	....	....	....	93	122	.762	....	....	349	52	242	2	....	....	....	13.1	4.1	3.5	0.5	....
54-55	Syracuse	9	....	59	24	8	27	.296	....	....	....	8	9	.889	....	....	15	1	13	0	....	....	....	6.6	2.7	1.7	0.1	.288
55-56	Syracuse	6	....	72	32	13	34	.382	....	....	....	6	8	.750	....	....	25	2	15	0	....	....	....	12.0	5.3	4.2	0.3	.431
NBA Playoff Totals		15	....	131	56	21	61	.344	....	....	....	14	17	.824	....	....	40	3	28	0	....	....	....	8.7	3.7	2.7	0.2	....

• TUCKER, Trent

Kelvin Trent (Doc) Tucker

Born: Dec. 20, 1959. Tarboro, NC, United States.   Height: 6'5".   Weight: 193 lbs.   Drafted: 1982   College: Minnesota

YEAR	TEAM	GP	GS	MIN	PTS	FGM	FGA	FG%	3PM	3PA	3P%	FTM	FTA	FT%	ORB	DRB	TRB	AST	PF	DQ	STL	BLK	TO	MPG	PPG	RPG	APG	PCM
82-83	New York	78	59	1830	655	299	647	.462	14	30	.467	43	64	.672	75	141	216	195	235	1	56	6	70	23.5	8.4	2.8	2.5	.343
83-84	New York	63	21	1228	481	225	450	.500	6	16	.375	25	33	.758	43	87	130	138	124	0	63	8	57	19.5	7.6	2.1	2.2	.401
84-85	New York	77	46	1819	653	293	606	.483	29	72	.403	38	48	.792	74	114	188	199	195	0	75	15	62	23.6	8.5	2.4	2.6	.374
85-86	New York	77	23	1788	818	349	740	.472	41	91	.451	79	100	.790	70	99	169	192	167	0	65	8	69	23.2	10.6	2.2	2.5	.410
86-87	New York	70	15	1691	795	325	691	.470	68	161	.422	77	101	.762	49	86	135	166	169	1	116	13	77	24.2	11.4	1.9	2.4	.423
87-88	New York	71	4	1248	506	193	455	.424	69	167	.413	51	71	.718	32	87	119	117	158	3	53	6	50	17.6	7.1	1.7	1.6	.339
88-89	New York	81	24	1824	687	263	579	.454	118	296	.399	43	55	.782	55	121	176	132	163	0	88	6	57	22.5	8.5	2.2	1.6	.357
89-90	New York	81	2	1725	667	253	606	.417	95	245	.388	66	86	.767	57	117	174	173	159	0	74	8	73	21.3	8.2	2.1	2.1	.352
90-91	New York	65	13	1194	463	191	434	.440	64	153	.418	17	27	.630	33	72	105	111	120	0	44	9	46	18.4	7.1	1.6	1.7	.334
91-92	San Antonio	24	0	415	155	60	129	.465	19	48	.396	16	20	.800	8	29	37	27	39	0	21	3	14	17.3	6.5	1.5	1.1	.346
92-93	Chicago	69	0	909	357	143	295	.485	53	131	.405	18	22	.818	16	55	71	82	65	0	24	6	21	13.2	5.2	1.0	1.2	.380
NBA Season Totals		756	207	15671	6237	2594	5632	.461	576	1410	.409	473	627	.754	512	1008	1520	1532	1594	5	679	88	596	20.7	8.3	2.0	2.0	....
82-83	New York	6	0	85	26	9	15	.600	1	2	.500	7	10	.700	2	7	9	5	7	0	2	0	2	14.2	4.3	1.5	0.8	.349
83-84	New York	12	6	254	91	42	84	.500	1	5	.200	6	10	.600	6	12	18	27	32	0	11	3	12	21.2	7.6	1.5	2.3	.326
87-88	New York	4	0	71	25	8	19	.421	6	13	.462	3	4	.750	0	2	2	4	4	0	3	0	1	17.8	6.3	0.5	1.0	.288
88-89	New York	9	0	159	71	27	58	.466	15	32	.469	2	4	.500	9	10	19	14	20	0	10	2	6	17.7	7.9	2.1	1.6	.441
89-90	New York	10	0	178	60	22	55	.400	10	27	.370	6	6	1.000	5	9	14	20	19	0	10	0	6	17.8	6.0	1.4	2.0	.328
90-91	New York	3	2	66	24	9	25	.360	4	10	.400	2	2	1.000	3	9	12	9	7	0	1	0	1	22.0	8.0	4.0	3.0	.403
91-92	San Antonio	3	0	38	14	6	14	.429	1	5	.200	1	1	1.000	1	2	3	2	3	0	0	0	3	12.7	4.7	1.0	0.7	.193
92-93	Chicago	19	0	208	53	19	46	.413	12	26	.462	3	6	.500	4	13	17	19	15	0	7	0	7	10.9	2.8	0.9	1.0	.267
NBA Playoff Totals		66	8	1059	364	142	316	.449	50	120	.417	30	43	.698	30	64	94	100	107	0	44	5	38	16.0	5.5	1.4	1.5	....

• TURKCAN, Mirsad

Mirsad Turkcan

Born: June 7, 1976. Yugoslavia.   Height: 6'9".   Weight: 236 lbs.   Drafted: 1998   College: —

YEAR	TEAM	GP	GS	MIN	PTS	FGM	FGA	FG%	3PM	3PA	3P%	FTM	FTA	FT%	ORB	DRB	TRB	AST	PF	DQ	STL	BLK	TO	MPG	PPG	RPG	APG	PCM
99-00	New York	7	0	25	4	2	10	.200	0	2	.000	0	0	.000	2	8	10	1	4	0	2	0	1	3.6	0.6	1.4	0.1	.240
99-00	Milwaukee	10	0	65	29	12	28	.429	0	4	.000	5	8	.625	11	12	23	4	10	0	1	1	7	6.5	2.9	2.3	0.4	.450
NBA Season Totals		17	0	90	33	14	38	.368	0	6	.000	5	8	.625	13	20	33	5	14	0	3	1	8	5.3	1.9	1.9	0.3	....
99-00	Milwaukee	2	0	10	4	1	5	.200	0	1	.000	2	2	1.000	0	2	2	0	1	0	0	0	3	5.0	2.0	1.0	0.0	-.099
NBA Playoff Totals		2	0	10	4	1	5	.200	0	1	.000	2	2	1.000	0	2	2	0	1	0	0	0	3	5.0	2.0	1.0	0.0	....

YEAR	TEAM	GP	GS	MIN	PTS	FGM	FGA	FG%	3PM	3PA	3P%	FTM	FTA	FT%	ORB	DRB	TRB	AST	PF	DQ	STL	BLK	TO	MPG	PPG	RPG	APG	PCM

• TURKOGLU, Hidayet

Hidayet (Hedo) Turkoglu

Born: Mar. 19, 1979. Istanbul, Turkey.   Height: 6'8".   Weight: 220 lbs.   Drafted: 2000   College: none

YEAR	TEAM	GP	GS	MIN	PTS	FGM	FGA	FG%	3PM	3PA	3P%	FTM	FTA	FT%	ORB	DRB	TRB	AST	PF	DQ	STL	BLK	TO	MPG	PPG	RPG	APG	PCM
00-01	Sacramento	74	7	1245	391	138	335	.412	28	86	.326	87	112	.777	49	161	210	69	139	1	52	24	55	16.8	5.3	2.8	0.9	.341
01-02	Sacramento	80	10	1970	810	290	687	.422	63	171	.368	167	230	.726	63	300	363	163	184	0	57	31	81	24.6	10.1	4.5	2.0	.432
02-03	Sacramento	67	11	1175	447	165	391	.422	29	78	.372	88	110	.800	35	153	188	87	125	0	25	12	50	17.5	6.7	2.8	1.3	.365
NBA Season Totals		221	28	4390	1648	593	1413	.420	120	335	.358	342	452	.757	147	614	761	319	448	1	134	67	186	19.9	7.5	3.4	1.4	....
00-01	Sacramento	8	0	141	60	20	46	.435	8	14	.571	12	12	1.000	7	21	28	11	18	0	3	1	6	17.6	7.5	3.5	1.4	.454
01-02	Sacramento	16	8	443	138	55	137	.401	12	34	.353	16	31	.516	17	66	83	23	49	0	6	9	23	27.7	8.6	5.2	1.4	.289
02-03	Sacramento	10	5	174	53	18	50	.360	4	14	.286	13	18	.722	5	24	29	14	19	0	12	5	5	17.4	5.3	2.9	1.4	.377
NBA Playoff Totals		34	13	758	251	93	233	.399	24	62	.387	41	61	.672	29	111	140	48	86	0	21	15	34	22.3	7.4	4.1	1.4	....

• TURNER, Andre

Andre D. Turner

Born: Dec. 13, 1964. Memphis, TN, United States.   Height: 5'11".   Weight: 160 lbs.   Drafted: 1986   College: Memphis State

YEAR	TEAM	GP	GS	MIN	PTS	FGM	FGA	FG%	3PM	3PA	3P%	FTM	FTA	FT%	ORB	DRB	TRB	AST	PF	DQ	STL	BLK	TO	MPG	PPG	RPG	APG	PCM
86-87	Boston	3	0	18	4	2	5	.400	0	1	.000	0	0	.000	1	1	2	1	1	0	0	0	5	6.0	1.3	0.7	0.3	-.055
87-88	Houston	12	0	99	35	12	34	.353	1	7	.143	10	14	.714	4	4	8	23	13	0	7	1	12	8.3	2.9	0.7	1.9	.352
88-89	Milwaukee	4	0	13	6	3	6	.500	0	0	.000	0	0	.000	0	3	3	0	2	0	2	0	4	3.3	1.5	0.8	0.0	.247
89-90	LA Clippers	3	0	31	4	2	13	.154	0	1	.000	0	0	.000	3	2	5	3	1	0	1	0	4	10.3	1.3	1.7	1.0	-.055
89-90	Charlotte	8	0	84	22	9	25	.360	0	1	.000	4	4	1.000	1	2	3	20	5	0	7	0	8	10.5	2.8	0.4	2.5	.331
90-91	Philadelphia	70	1	1407	412	168	383	.439	12	33	.364	64	87	.736	36	116	152	311	124	0	63	0	98	20.1	5.9	2.2	4.4	.415
91-92	Washington	70	3	871	284	111	261	.425	1	16	.063	61	77	.792	17	73	90	177	59	0	57	2	84	12.4	4.1	1.3	2.5	.413
NBA Season Totals		170	4	2523	767	307	727	.422	14	59	.237	139	182	.764	62	201	263	535	205	0	137	3	215	14.8	4.5	1.5	3.1	....
90-91	Philadelphia	8	0	189	58	21	48	.438	3	9	.333	13	16	.813	2	11	13	35	12	0	11	0	8	23.6	7.3	1.6	4.4	.413
NBA Playoff Totals		8	0	189	58	21	48	.438	3	9	.333	13	16	.813	2	11	13	35	12	0	11	0	8	23.6	7.3	1.6	4.4	....

• TURNER, Bill

William R. Turner III

Born: Feb. 18, 1944.   Height: 6'7".   Weight: 220 lbs.   Drafted: —   College: Akron

YEAR	TEAM	GP	GS	MIN	PTS	FGM	FGA	FG%	3PM	3PA	3P%	FTM	FTA	FT%	ORB	DRB	TRB	AST	PF	DQ	STL	BLK	TO	MPG	PPG	RPG	APG	PCM
67-68	San Francisco	42	....	482	172	68	157	.433	....	....	....	36	60	.600			155	16	74	1	....	....		11.5	4.1	3.7	0.4	.425
68-69	San Francisco	79	....	1486	619	222	535	.415	....	....	....	175	230	.761			380	67	231	6	....	....		18.8	7.8	4.8	0.8	.426
69-70	San Francisco	3	....	75	23	9	17	.529	....	....	....	5	10	.500			14	1	7	0	....	....		25.0	7.7	4.7	0.3	.322
69-70	Cincinnati	69	....	1095	494	188	451	.417	....	....	....	118	157	.752			290	42	187	3	....	....		15.9	7.2	4.2	0.6	.425
70-71	San Francisco	18	....	200	65	26	82	.317	....	....	....	13	20	.650			42	8	24	0	....	....		11.1	3.6	2.3	0.4	.244
71-72	Golden State	62	....	597	182	71	181	.392	....	....	....	40	53	.755			131	22	67	1	....	....		9.6	2.9	2.1	0.4	.319
72-73	Portland	2	....	8	4	2	6	.333	....	....	....	0	0	.000			2	0	3	0	....	....		4.0	2.0	1.0	0.0	.125
72-73	LA Lakers	19	....	117	38	17	52	.327	....	....	....	4	7	.571			25	11	13	0	....	....		6.2	2.0	1.3	0.6	.300
NBA Season Totals		294	....	4060	1597	603	1481	.407	....	....	....	391	537	.728			1039	167	606	11	....	....		13.8	5.4	3.5	0.6	....
67-68	San Francisco	9	....	148	47	19	40	.475	....	....	....	9	12	.750			29	10	30	2	....	....		16.4	5.2	3.2	1.1	.353
68-69	San Francisco	6	....	96	33	13	35	.371	....	....	....	7	11	.636			25	7	14	0	....	....		16.0	5.5	4.2	1.2	.376
70-71	San Francisco	2	....	18	6	1	5	.200	....	....	....	4	6	.667			3	1	2	0	....	....		9.0	3.0	1.5	0.5	.253
71-72	Golden State	3	....	9	4	2	2	1.000	....	....	....	0	0	.000			3	0	0	0	....	....		3.0	1.3	1.0	0.0	.732
72-73	LA Lakers	2	....	13	6	2	5	.400	....	....	....	2	2	1.000			2	0	1	0	....	....		6.5	3.0	1.0	0.0	.363
NBA Playoff Totals		22	....	284	96	37	87	.425	....	....	....	22	31	.710			62	18	47	2	....	....		12.9	4.4	2.8	0.8	....

• TURNER, Elston

Elston Howard Turner

Born: June 10, 1959. Knoxville, TN, United States.   Height: 6'5".   Weight: 190 lbs.   Drafted: 1981   College: Mississippi

YEAR	TEAM	GP	GS	MIN	PTS	FGM	FGA	FG%	3PM	3PA	3P%	FTM	FTA	FT%	ORB	DRB	TRB	AST	PF	DQ	STL	BLK	TO	MPG	PPG	RPG	APG	PCM
81-82	Dallas	80	62	1996	661	282	639	.441	0	4	.000	97	138	.703	143	158	301	189	182	1	75	2	112	25.0	8.3	3.8	2.4	.340
82-83	Dallas	59	16	879	214	96	238	.403	2	3	.667	20	30	.667	68	84	152	88	75	0	47	0	59	14.9	3.6	2.6	1.5	.308
83-84	Dallas	47	1	536	137	54	150	.360	1	9	.111	28	34	.824	42	51	93	59	40	0	26	0	28	11.4	2.9	2.0	1.3	.325
84-85	Denver	81	2	1491	414	181	388	.466	1	6	.167	51	65	.785	88	128	216	158	152	0	96	7	73	18.4	5.1	2.7	2.0	.363
85-86	Denver	73	0	1324	369	165	379	.435	0	9	.000	39	53	.736	64	137	201	165	150	1	70	6	80	18.1	5.1	2.8	2.3	.343
86-87	Chicago	70	4	936	248	112	252	.444	1	8	.125	23	31	.742	34	81	115	102	97	1	30	4	28	13.4	3.5	1.6	1.5	.310
87-88	Chicago	17	0	98	17	8	30	.267	0	0	.000	1	2	.500	8	2	10	9	5	0	8	0	10	5.8	1.0	0.6	0.5	.110
88-89	Denver	78	12	1746	337	151	353	.428	2	7	.286	33	56	.589	109	178	287	144	209	2	90	8	62	22.4	4.3	3.7	1.8	.284
NBA Season Totals		505	97	9006	2397	1049	2429	.432	7	46	.152	292	409	.714	556	819	1375	914	910	5	442	27	452	17.8	4.7	2.7	1.8	....
83-84	Dallas	8	0	53	14	7	20	.350	0	0	.000	0	0	.000	5	5	10	8	4	0	6	1	3	6.6	1.8	1.3	1.0	.408
84-85	Denver	15	4	358	114	50	102	.490	2	2	1.000	12	19	.632	30	43	73	46	42	0	17	1	26	23.9	7.6	4.9	3.1	.426
85-86	Denver	10	0	196	66	29	54	.537	1	1	1.000	7	8	.875	12	17	29	22	19	1	7	0	5	19.6	6.6	2.9	2.2	.438
86-87	Chicago	3	0	25	8	4	5	.800	0	0	.000	0	0	.000	1	1	2	1	3	0	2	0	0	8.3	2.7	0.7	0.3	.419
87-88	Chicago	4	0	29	2	1	6	.167	0	0	.000	0	0	.000	1	4	5	6	2	0	0	0	1	7.3	0.5	1.3	1.5	.226
88-89	Denver	3	0	74	14	6	13	.462	0	1	.000	2	6	.333	2	9	11	3	9	0	1	0	0	24.7	4.7	3.7	1.0	.214
NBA Playoff Totals		43	4	735	218	97	200	.485	3	4	.750	21	33	.636	51	79	130	86	79	1	33	2	35	17.1	5.1	3.0	2.0	....

• TURNER, Gary

Gary D. Turner

Born: 1945.   Height: 6'7".   Weight: 200 lbs.   Drafted: 1966   College: Texas Christian

YEAR	TEAM	GP	GS	MIN	PTS	FGM	FGA	FG%	3PM	3PA	3P%	FTM	FTA	FT%	ORB	DRB	TRB	AST	PF	DQ	STL	BLK	TO	MPG	PPG	RPG	APG	PCM
67-68	Houston-A	2	....	21	6	2	2	1.000	0	0	.000	2	3	.667	....	....	3	0	2	0	....	....	2	10.5	3.0	1.5	0.0	.345
ABA Season Totals		2	....	21	6	2	2	1.000	0	0	.000	2	3	.667	....	....	3	0	2	0	....	....	2	10.5	3.0	1.5	0.0	....

YEAR	TEAM	GP	GS	MIN	PTS	FGM	FGA	FG%	3PM	3PA	3P%	FTM	FTA	FT%	ORB	DRB	TRB	AST	PF	DQ	STL	BLK	TO	MPG	PPG	RPG	APG	PCM

• TURNER, Henry

Henry Turner

Born: Aug. 18, 1966. Oakland, CA, United States.   Height: 6'7".   Weight: 200 lbs.   Drafted: —   College: Cal State Fullerton

YEAR	TEAM	GP	GS	MIN	PTS	FGM	FGA	FG%	3PM	3PA	3P%	FTM	FTA	FT%	ORB	DRB	TRB	AST	PF	DQ	STL	BLK	TO	MPG	PPG	RPG	APG	PCM
89-90	Sacramento	36	1	315	156	58	122	.475	0	3	.000	40	65	.615	22	28	50	22	40	0	17	7	25	8.8	4.3	1.4	0.6	.428
94-95	Sacramento	30	0	149	68	23	57	.404	2	5	.400	20	35	.571	17	11	28	7	20	0	8	1	12	5.0	2.3	0.9	0.2	.339
NBA Season Totals		66	1	464	224	81	179	.453	2	8	.250	60	100	.600	39	39	78	29	60	0	25	8	37	7.0	3.4	1.2	0.4	....

• TURNER, Herschell

Herschell C. (H.T.) Turner

Born: Mar. 29, 1938.   Height: 6'2".   Weight: 195 lbs.   Drafted: 1960   College: Nebraska

YEAR	TEAM	GP	GS	MIN	PTS	FGM	FGA	FG%	3PM	3PA	3P%	FTM	FTA	FT%	ORB	DRB	TRB	AST	PF	DQ	STL	BLK	TO	MPG	PPG	RPG	APG	PCM
67-68	Anaheim-A	32	....	435	115	45	138	.326	5	25	.200	20	41	.488	....	....	68	40	62	1	....	....	38	13.6	3.6	2.1	1.3	.245
67-68	Pittsburgh-A	9	....	65	16	6	21	.286	1	1	1.000	3	6	.500	....	....	6	5	10	0	....	....	7	7.2	1.8	0.7	0.6	.138
ABA Season Totals		41	....	500	131	51	159	.321	6	26	.231	23	47	.489	....	....	74	45	72	1	....	....	45	12.2	3.2	1.8	1.1	

• TURNER, Jack

Jackie Lee Turner

Born: June 29, 1930. Bedford, IN, United States.   Height: 6'4".   Weight: 170 lbs.   Drafted: 1954   College: Western Kentucky

YEAR	TEAM	GP	GS	MIN	PTS	FGM	FGA	FG%	3PM	3PA	3P%	FTM	FTA	FT%	ORB	DRB	TRB	AST	PF	DQ	STL	BLK	TO	MPG	PPG	RPG	APG	PCM
54-55	New York	65	....	922	282	111	308	.360	....	....	....	60	76	.789	....	....	154	77	76	0	....	....	....	14.2	4.3	2.4	1.2	.337
NBA Season Totals		65	....	922	282	111	308	.360	....	....	....	60	76	.789	....	....	154	77	76	0	....	....	....	14.2	4.3	2.4	1.2	
54-55	New York	2	....	16	5	2	6	.333	....	....	....	1	3	.333	....	....	4	2	1	0	....	....	....	8.0	2.5	2.0	1.0	.398
NBA Playoff Totals		2	....	16	5	2	6	.333	....	....	....	1	3	.333	....	....	4	2	1	0	....	....	....	8.0	2.5	2.0	1.0	

• TURNER, Jack

John F. Turner

Born: June 5, 1939.   Height: 6'5".   Weight: 200 lbs.   Drafted: 1961   College: Louisville

YEAR	TEAM	GP	GS	MIN	PTS	FGM	FGA	FG%	3PM	3PA	3P%	FTM	FTA	FT%	ORB	DRB	TRB	AST	PF	DQ	STL	BLK	TO	MPG	PPG	RPG	APG	PCM
61-62	Chicago	42	....	567	200	84	221	.380	....	....	....	32	42	.762	....	....	85	44	51	0	....	....	....	13.5	4.8	2.0	1.0	.334
NBA Season Totals		42	....	567	200	84	221	.380	....	....	....	32	42	.762	....	....	85	44	51	0	....	....	....	13.5	4.8	2.0	1.0	

• TURNER, Jeff

Jeffrey Steven Turner

Born: Apr. 9, 1962. Bangor, ME, United States.   Height: 6'9".   Weight: 230 lbs.   Drafted: 1984   College: Vanderbilt

YEAR	TEAM	GP	GS	MIN	PTS	FGM	FGA	FG%	3PM	3PA	3P%	FTM	FTA	FT%	ORB	DRB	TRB	AST	PF	DQ	STL	BLK	TO	MPG	PPG	RPG	APG	PCM
84-85	New Jersey	72	36	1429	421	171	377	.454	0	3	.000	79	92	.859	88	130	218	108	243	8	29	7	94	19.8	5.8	3.0	1.5	.262
85-86	New Jersey	53	1	650	226	84	171	.491	0	1	.000	58	78	.744	45	92	137	14	125	4	21	3	48	12.3	4.3	2.6	0.3	.304
86-87	New Jersey	76	22	1003	378	151	325	.465	0	1	.000	76	104	.731	80	117	197	60	200	6	33	13	84	13.2	5.0	2.6	0.8	.321
89-90	Orlando	60	15	1105	308	132	308	.429	2	10	.200	42	54	.778	52	175	227	53	161	4	23	12	60	18.4	5.1	3.8	0.9	.278
90-91	Orlando	71	43	1683	609	259	532	.487	6	15	.400	85	112	.759	108	255	363	97	234	5	29	10	128	23.7	8.6	5.1	1.4	.352
91-92	Orlando	75	42	1591	530	225	499	.451	1	8	.125	79	114	.693	62	184	246	92	229	6	24	16	105	21.2	7.1	3.3	1.2	.264
92-93	Orlando	75	20	1479	528	231	437	.529	10	17	.588	56	70	.800	74	178	252	107	192	2	19	9	68	19.7	7.0	3.4	1.4	.373
93-94	Orlando	68	51	1536	451	199	426	.467	18	55	.327	35	45	.778	79	192	271	60	239	1	23	11	75	22.6	6.6	4.0	0.9	.263
94-95	Orlando	49	5	576	199	73	178	.410	27	75	.360	26	29	.897	23	74	97	38	102	2	12	3	20	11.8	4.1	2.0	0.8	.309
95-96	Orlando	13	0	192	47	18	51	.353	9	27	.333	2	2	1.000	10	18	28	6	33	2	2	1	10	14.8	3.6	2.2	0.5	.138
NBA Season Totals		612	235	11244	3697	1543	3304	.467	73	212	.344	538	700	.769	621	1415	2036	635	1758	40	215	85	692	18.4	6.0	3.3	1.0	
84-85	New Jersey	3	0	21	4	2	5	.400	0	0	.000	0	0	.000	2	2	4	2	6	0	0	0	0	7.0	1.3	1.3	0.7	.203
85-86	New Jersey	3	0	18	3	1	3	.333	0	0	.000	1	1	1.000	0	3	3	3	7	0	0	0	4	6.0	1.0	1.0	1.0	.010
94-95	Orlando	18	0	179	49	17	40	.425	11	22	.500	4	4	1.000	4	21	25	11	44	0	4	3	6	9.9	2.7	1.4	0.6	.239
NBA Playoff Totals		24	0	218	56	20	48	.417	11	22	.500	5	5	1.000	6	26	32	16	57	0	4	3	10	9.1	2.3	1.3	0.7	

• TURNER, John

John L. Turner

Born: Nov. 30, 1967. Washington, DC, United States.   Height: 6'8".   Weight: 245 lbs.   Drafted: 1991   College: Phillips

YEAR	TEAM	GP	GS	MIN	PTS	FGM	FGA	FG%	3PM	3PA	3P%	FTM	FTA	FT%	ORB	DRB	TRB	AST	PF	DQ	STL	BLK	TO	MPG	PPG	RPG	APG	PCM
91-92	Houston	42	0	345	117	43	98	.439	0	0	.000	31	59	.525	38	40	78	12	40	0	6	4	34	8.2	2.8	1.9	0.3	.282
NBA Season Totals		42	0	345	117	43	98	.439	0	0	.000	31	59	.525	38	40	78	12	40	0	6	4	34	8.2	2.8	1.9	0.3	

• TURNER, Wayne

Wayne Keon Turner

Born: Mar. 22, 1976. Boston, MA, United States.   Height: 6'2".   Weight: 190 lbs.   Drafted: —   College: Kentucky

YEAR	TEAM	GP	GS	MIN	PTS	FGM	FGA	FG%	3PM	3PA	3P%	FTM	FTA	FT%	ORB	DRB	TRB	AST	PF	DQ	STL	BLK	TO	MPG	PPG	RPG	APG	PCM
99-00	Boston	3	0	41	4	1	6	.167	0	0	.000	2	6	.333	1	2	3	5	4	0	0	0	3	13.7	1.3	1.0	1.7	.031
NBA Season Totals		3	0	41	4	1	6	.167	0	0	.000	2	6	.333	1	2	3	5	4	0	0	0	3	13.7	1.3	1.0	1.7	

• TURPIN, Melvin

Melvin Harrison Turpin

Born: Dec. 28, 1960. Lexington, KY, United States.   Height: 6'11".   Weight: 240 lbs.   Drafted: 1984   College: Kentucky

YEAR	TEAM	GP	GS	MIN	PTS	FGM	FGA	FG%	3PM	3PA	3P%	FTM	FTA	FT%	ORB	DRB	TRB	AST	PF	DQ	STL	BLK	TO	MPG	PPG	RPG	APG	PCM
84-85	Cleveland	79	45	1949	835	363	711	.511	0	0	.000	109	139	.784	155	297	452	36	211	3	38	87	119	24.7	10.6	5.7	0.5	.443
85-86	Cleveland	80	69	2292	1097	456	838	.544	0	4	.000	185	228	.811	182	374	556	55	260	6	65	106	136	28.7	13.7	7.0	0.7	.528
86-87	Cleveland	64	0	801	393	169	366	.462	0	0	.000	55	77	.714	62	128	190	33	90	1	11	40	64	12.5	6.1	3.0	0.5	.446
87-88	Utah	79	0	1011	470	199	389	.512	1	3	.333	71	98	.724	88	148	236	32	157	2	26	68	71	12.8	5.9	3.0	0.4	.477
89-90	Washington	59	12	818	276	110	209	.526	0	2	.000	56	71	.789	88	133	221	27	135	0	15	47	47	13.9	4.7	3.7	0.5	.444
NBA Season Totals		361	127	6871	3071	1297	2513	.516	1	9	.111	476	613	.777	575	1080	1655	183	853	12	155	348	437	19.0	8.5	4.6	0.5	
84-85	Cleveland	4	0	45	25	12	19	.632	0	0	.000	1	2	.500	3	5	8	0	3	0	4	1	5	11.3	6.3	2.0	0.0	.535
87-88	Utah	7	0	31	8	3	9	.333	0	0	.000	2	2	1.000	3	3	6	2	5	0	1	4	2	4.4	1.1	0.9	0.3	.342
NBA Playoff Totals		11	0	76	33	15	28	.536	0	0	.000	3	4	.750	6	8	14	2	8	0	5	5	7	6.9	3.0	1.3	0.2	

• TWARDZIK, Dave

Dave John (Pinball) Twardzik

Born: Sept. 20, 1950. Hershey, PA, United States. Height: 6'1". Weight: 175 lbs. Drafted: 1972 College: Old Dominion

YEAR	TEAM	GP	GS	MIN	PTS	FGM	FGA	FG%	3PM	3PA	3P%	FTM	FTA	FT%	ORB	DRB	TRB	AST	PF	DQ	STL	BLK	TO	MPG	PPG	RPG	APG	PCM
72-73	Virginia-A	80	....	1357	462	141	306	.461	2	9	.222	178	212	.840	45	113	158	184	202	1	....	....	122	17.0	5.8	2.0	2.3	.407
73-74	Virginia-A	57	....	1413	497	163	343	.475	3	15	.200	168	214	.785	52	129	181	170	173	....	60	8	118	24.8	8.7	3.2	3.0	.423
74-75	Virginia-A	76	....	2679	1036	359	657	.546	1	6	.167	317	384	.826	94	153	247	404	238	....	132	11	266	35.3	13.6	3.3	5.3	.487
75-76	Virginia-A	43	....	871	316	100	216	.463	3	16	.188	113	139	.813	28	61	89	125	107	....	62	3	93	20.3	7.3	2.1	2.9	.426
76-77	Portland	74	....	1937	765	263	430	.612	....	....	....	239	284	.842	75	127	202	247	228	6	128	15	....	26.2	10.3	2.7	3.3	.495
77-78	Portland	75	....	1820	667	242	409	.592	....	....	....	183	234	.782	36	98	134	244	186	2	107	4	158	24.3	8.9	1.8	3.3	.422
78-79	Portland	64	....	1570	667	203	381	.533	....	....	....	261	299	.873	39	80	119	176	185	5	84	4	128	24.5	10.4	1.9	2.8	.428
79-80	Portland	67	....	1594	567	183	394	.464	4	7	.571	197	252	.782	52	104	156	273	149	2	77	1	134	23.8	8.5	2.3	4.1	.422
NBA Season Totals		280	....	6921	2666	891	1614	.552	4	7	.571	880	1069	.823	202	409	611	940	748	15	396	24	420	24.7	9.5	2.2	3.4	....
ABA Season Totals		256	....	6320	2311	763	1522	.501	9	46	.196	776	949	.818	219	456	675	883	720	1	254	22	599	24.7	9.0	2.6	3.4	....
Career Totals		536	....	13241	4977	1654	3136	.527	13	53	.245	1656	2018	.821	421	865	1286	1823	1468	16	650	46	1019	24.7	9.3	2.4	3.4	....
72-73	Virginia-A	2	....	29	12	3	7	.429	0	0	.000	6	6	1.000	0	1	1	3	3	0	....	....	1	14.5	6.0	0.5	1.5	.388
73-74	Virginia-A	5	....	83	25	7	17	.412	0	1	.000	11	15	.733	7	7	14	5	12	....	3	0	6	16.6	5.0	2.8	1.0	.329
76-77	Portland	14	....	354	153	55	93	.591	....	....	....	43	59	.729	4	20	24	39	47	2	16	2	....	25.3	10.9	1.7	2.8	.447
77-78	Portland	6	....	108	36	11	23	.478	....	....	....	14	14	1.000	1	3	4	11	16	0	7	0	10	18.0	6.0	0.7	1.8	.294
78-79	Portland	3	....	77	25	7	14	.500	....	....	....	11	12	.917	4	3	7	10	14	0	5	0	9	25.7	8.3	2.3	3.3	.334
79-80	Portland	2	....	20	2	1	4	.250	0	0	.000	0	0	.000	1	3	4	2	2	0	2	0	3	10.0	1.0	2.0	1.0	.164
NBA Playoff Totals		25	....	559	216	74	134	.552	0	0	.000	68	85	.800	10	29	39	62	79	2	30	2	22	22.4	8.6	1.6	2.5	....
ABA Playoff Totals		7	....	112	37	10	24	.417	0	1	.000	17	21	.810	7	8	15	8	15	0	3	0	7	16.0	5.3	2.1	1.1	....
Career Playoff Totals		32	....	671	253	84	158	.532	0	1	.000	85	106	.802	17	37	54	70	94	2	33	2	29	21.0	7.9	1.7	2.2	....

• TWYMAN, Jack

John Kennedy Twyman

Born: May 11, 1934. Pittsburgh, PA, United States. Height: 6'6". Weight: 210 lbs. Drafted: 1955 College: Cincinnati HOF: 1983

YEAR	TEAM	GP	GS	MIN	PTS	FGM	FGA	FG%	3PM	3PA	3P%	FTM	FTA	FT%	ORB	DRB	TRB	AST	PF	DQ	STL	BLK	TO	MPG	PPG	RPG	APG	PCM
55-56	Rochester	72	....	2186	1038	417	987	.422	....	....	....	204	298	.685	....	....	466	171	239	4	....	....	....	30.4	14.4	6.5	2.4	.478
56-57	Rochester	72	....	2338	1174	449	1023	.439	....	....	....	276	363	.760	....	....	354	123	251	4	....	....	....	32.5	16.3	4.9	1.7	.444
57-58	Cincinnati	72	....	2178	1237	465	1028	**.452**	....	....	....	307	396	.775	....	....	464	110	224	3	....	....	....	30.3	17.2	6.4	1.5	.547
58-59	Cincinnati	72	....	2713	1857	710	**1691**	.420	....	....	....	437	558	.783	....	....	653	209	277	6	....	....	....	37.7	25.8	9.1	2.9	.635
59-60	Cincinnati	75	....	3023	2338	870	2063	.422	....	....	....	**598**	762	.785	....	....	664	260	275	10	....	....	....	40.3	31.2	8.9	3.5	.693
60-61	Cincinnati	79	....	2920	1997	796	1632	.488	....	....	....	405	554	.731	....	....	672	225	279	5	....	....	....	37.0	25.3	8.5	2.8	.681
61-62	Cincinnati	80	....	2991	1831	739	1542	.479	....	....	....	353	435	.811	....	....	638	215	323	5	....	....	....	37.4	22.9	8.0	2.7	.604
62-63	Cincinnati	80	....	2623	1586	641	1335	.480	....	....	....	304	375	.811	....	....	598	214	286	7	....	....	....	32.8	19.8	7.5	2.7	.621
63-64	Cincinnati	68	....	1996	1083	447	993	.450	....	....	....	189	228	.829	....	....	364	137	267	7	....	....	....	29.4	15.9	5.4	2.0	.496
64-65	Cincinnati	80	....	2236	1156	479	1081	.443	....	....	....	198	239	.828	....	....	383	137	239	4	....	....	....	28.0	14.5	4.8	1.7	.469
65-66	Cincinnati	73	....	943	543	224	498	.450	....	....	....	95	117	.812	....	....	168	60	122	1	....	....	....	12.9	7.4	2.3	0.8	.505
NBA Season Totals		823	....	26147	15840	6237	13873	.450	....	....	....	3366	4325	.778	....	....	5424	1861	2782	56	....	....	....	31.8	19.2	6.6	2.3	....
57-58	Cincinnati	2	....	74	37	15	45	.333	....	....	....	7	12	.583	....	....	22	1	6	0	....	....	....	37.0	18.5	11.0	0.5	.384
61-62	Cincinnati	4	....	149	76	34	78	.436	....	....	....	8	8	1.000	....	....	29	12	18	0	....	....	....	37.3	19.0	7.3	3.0	.482
62-63	Cincinnati	12	....	410	249	92	205	.449	....	....	....	65	77	.844	....	....	98	30	47	1	....	....	....	34.2	20.8	8.2	2.5	.610
63-64	Cincinnati	10	....	354	205	83	176	.472	....	....	....	39	49	.796	....	....	87	16	41	1	....	....	....	35.4	20.5	8.7	1.6	.565
64-65	Cincinnati	4	....	97	49	19	48	.396	....	....	....	11	11	1.000	....	....	17	3	16	0	....	....	....	24.3	12.3	4.3	0.8	.385
65-66	Cincinnati	2	....	11	5	2	4	.500	....	....	....	1	2	.500	....	....	2	0	3	0	....	....	....	5.5	2.5	1.0	0.0	.312
NBA Playoff Totals		34	....	1095	621	245	556	.441	....	....	....	131	159	.824	....	....	255	62	131	2	....	....	....	32.2	18.3	7.5	1.8	....

• TYLER, B.J.

Brandon Joel Tyler

Born: Apr. 30, 1971. Galveston, TX, United States. Height: 6'1". Weight: 185 lbs. Drafted: 1994 College: Texas

YEAR	TEAM	GP	GS	MIN	PTS	FGM	FGA	FG%	3PM	3PA	3P%	FTM	FTA	FT%	ORB	DRB	TRB	AST	PF	DQ	STL	BLK	TO	MPG	PPG	RPG	APG	PCM
94-95	Philadelphia	55	8	809	195	72	189	.381	16	51	.314	35	50	.700	13	49	62	174	58	0	36	2	99	14.7	3.5	1.1	3.2	.293
NBA Season Totals		55	8	809	195	72	189	.381	16	51	.314	35	50	.700	13	49	62	174	58	0	36	2	99	14.7	3.5	1.1	3.2	....

• TYLER, Terry

Terry Christopher Tyler

Born: Oct. 30, 1956. Detroit, MI, United States. Height: 6'7". Weight: 215 lbs. Drafted: 1978 College: Detroit

YEAR	TEAM	GP	GS	MIN	PTS	FGM	FGA	FG%	3PM	3PA	3P%	FTM	FTA	FT%	ORB	DRB	TRB	AST	PF	DQ	STL	BLK	TO	MPG	PPG	RPG	APG	PCM
78-79	Detroit	82	....	2560	1056	456	946	.482	....	....	....	144	219	.658	211	437	648	89	254	3	104	201	139	31.2	12.9	7.9	1.1	.507
79-80	Detroit	82	....	2670	1005	430	925	.465	2	12	.167	143	187	.765	228	399	627	129	237	3	107	220	172	32.6	12.3	7.6	1.6	.479
80-81	Detroit	82	....	2549	1100	476	895	.532	0	8	.000	148	250	.592	198	369	567	136	215	2	112	180	164	31.1	13.4	6.9	1.7	.532
81-82	Detroit	82	0	1989	815	336	643	.523	1	4	.250	142	192	.740	154	339	493	126	182	1	77	160	123	24.3	9.9	6.0	1.5	.563
82-83	Detroit	82	56	2543	990	421	880	.478	2	15	.133	146	196	.745	180	360	540	157	221	3	103	160	123	31.0	12.1	6.6	1.9	.487
83-84	Detroit	82	7	1602	722	313	691	.453	2	13	.154	94	132	.712	104	181	285	76	151	1	63	59	82	19.5	8.8	3.5	0.9	.416
84-85	Detroit	82	53	2004	950	422	855	.494	0	8	.000	106	148	.716	148	275	423	63	192	0	49	90	74	24.4	11.6	5.2	0.8	.479
85-86	Sacramento	71	52	1651	674	295	649	.455	0	3	.000	84	112	.750	109	204	313	94	159	0	64	108	92	23.3	9.5	4.4	1.3	.439
86-87	Sacramento	82	48	1930	760	329	664	.495	1	3	.333	101	140	.721	116	212	328	73	151	1	55	78	82	23.5	9.3	4.0	0.9	.410
87-88	Sacramento	74	28	1185	410	184	407	.452	1	7	.143	41	64	.641	87	155	242	56	85	0	43	47	44	16.0	5.5	3.3	0.8	.405
88-89	Dallas	70	11	1057	386	169	360	.469	1	9	.111	47	62	.758	74	135	209	40	90	0	24	39	49	15.1	5.5	3.0	0.6	.388
NBA Season Totals		871	255	21740	8868	3831	7915	.484	10	82	.122	1196	1702	.703	1609	3066	4675	1039	1937	14	801	1342	1144	25.0	10.2	5.4	1.2	....
83-84	Detroit	5	0	42	25	10	24	.417	0	0	.000	5	9	.556	5	2	7	1	4	0	0	3	1	8.4	5.0	1.4	0.2	.421
84-85	Detroit	9	0	179	120	49	100	.490	0	1	.000	22	27	.815	15	25	40	3	17	0	6	4	9	19.9	13.3	4.4	0.3	.579
85-86	Sacramento	3	2	51	8	2	10	.200	0	0	.000	4	4	1.000	3	5	8	4	5	0	2	3	1	17.0	2.7	2.7	1.3	.268
NBA Playoff Totals		17	2	272	153	61	134	.455	0	1	.000	31	40	.775	23	32	55	8	26	0	8	10	11	16.0	9.0	3.2	0.5	....

• TYRA, Charlie

Charles E. (Moose) Tyra

Born: Aug. 16, 1935. Louisville, KY, United States. Height: 6'8". Weight: 230 lbs. Drafted: 1957 College: Louisville

YEAR	TEAM	GP	GS	MIN	PTS	FGM	FGA	FG%	3PM	3PA	3P%	FTM	FTA	FT%	ORB	DRB	TRB	AST	PF	DQ	STL	BLK	TO	MPG	PPG	RPG	APG	PCM
57-58	New York	68	....	1182	500	175	490	.357	....	....	....	150	224	.670	....	....	480	34	175	3	....	....	....	17.4	7.4	7.1	0.5	.485
58-59	New York	69	....	1586	609	240	606	.396	....	....	....	129	190	.679	....	....	485	33	180	2	....	....	....	23.0	8.8	7.0	0.5	.409
59-60	New York	74	....	2033	945	406	942	.431	....	....	....	133	189	.704	....	....	598	80	258	8	....	....	....	27.5	12.8	8.1	1.1	.478
60-61	New York	59	....	1384	518	199	549	.362	....	....	....	120	173	.694	....	....	394	82	164	7	....	....	....	23.5	8.8	6.7	1.4	.412
61-62	Chicago	78	....	1606	519	193	534	.361	....	....	....	133	214	.621	....	....	610	86	210	7	....	....	....	20.6	6.7	7.8	1.1	.448
NBA Season Totals		348	....	7791	3091	1213	3121	.389	....	....	....	665	990	.672	....	....	2567	315	987	27	....	....	....	22.4	8.9	7.4	0.9	....
58-59	New York	2	....	55	30	12	28	.429	....	....	....	6	9	.667	....	....	31	1	5	0	....	....	....	27.5	15.0	15.5	0.5	.719
NBA Playoff Totals		2	....	55	30	12	28	.429	....	....	....	6	9	.667	....	....	31	1	5	0	....	....	....	27.5	15.0	15.5	0.5	....

• UDALL, Morris

Morris King (Mo) Udall

Born: June 15, 1922. St. Johns, AZ, United States. Died: Dec.12, 1998. Height: 6'5". Weight: 200 lbs. Drafted: — College: Arizona

YEAR	TEAM	GP	GS	MIN	PTS	FGM	FGA	FG%	3PM	3PA	3P%	FTM	FTA	FT%	ORB	DRB	TRB	AST	PF	DQ	STL	BLK	TO	MPG	PPG	RPG	APG	PCM
48-49	Denver-N	57	....	....	371	125	....	....	....	....	....	121	171	.708	....	....	....	....	123	....	....	....	....	....	6.5	....	....	....
NBL Season Totals		57	....	....	371	125	....	....	....	....	....	121	171	....	....	....	....	....	123	....	....	....	....	....	6.5	....	....	....

• UNSELD, Wes

Westley Sissel Unseld

Born: Mar. 14, 1946. Louisville, KY, United States. Height: 6'7". Weight: 245 lbs. Drafted: 1968 College: Louisville HOF: 1988

YEAR	TEAM	GP	GS	MIN	PTS	FGM	FGA	FG%	3PM	3PA	3P%	FTM	FTA	FT%	ORB	DRB	TRB	AST	PF	DQ	STL	BLK	TO	MPG	PPG	RPG	APG	PCM
68-69	Baltimore	82	....	2970	1131	427	897	.476	....	....	....	277	458	.605	....	....	1491	213	276	4	....	....	....	36.2	13.8	18.2	2.6	.687
69-70	Baltimore	82	....	3234	1325	526	1015	.518	....	....	....	273	428	.638	....	....	1370	291	250	2	....	....	....	39.4	16.2	16.7	3.5	.695
70-71	Baltimore	74	....	2904	1047	424	846	.501	....	....	....	199	303	.657	....	....	1253	293	235	2	....	....	....	39.2	14.1	16.9	4.0	.671
71-72	Baltimore	76	....	3171	989	409	822	.498	....	....	....	171	272	.629	....	....	1336	278	218	1	....	....	....	41.7	13.0	17.6	3.7	.620
72-73	Baltimore	79	....	3085	991	421	854	.493	....	....	....	149	212	.703	....	....	1260	347	168	0	....	....	....	39.1	12.5	15.9	4.4	.648
73-74	Washington	56	....	1727	328	146	333	.438	....	....	....	36	55	.655	152	365	517	159	121	1	56	16	....	30.8	5.9	9.2	2.8	.424
74-75	Washington	73	....	2904	672	273	544	.502	....	....	....	126	184	.685	318	759	1077	297	180	1	115	68	....	39.8	9.2	**14.8**	4.1	.551
75-76	Washington	78	....	2922	750	318	567	**.561**	....	....	....	114	195	.585	271	765	1036	404	203	3	84	59	....	37.5	9.6	13.3	5.2	.604
76-77	Washington	82	....	2860	640	270	551	.490	....	....	....	100	166	.602	243	634	877	363	253	5	87	45	....	34.9	7.8	10.7	4.4	.500
77-78	Washington	80	....	2644	607	257	491	.523	....	....	....	93	173	.538	286	669	955	326	234	2	98	45	176	33.1	7.6	11.9	4.1	.544
78-79	Washington	77	....	2406	843	346	600	.577	....	....	....	151	235	.643	274	556	830	315	204	2	71	37	154	31.2	10.9	10.8	4.1	.639
79-80	Washington	82	....	2973	794	327	637	.513	1	2	.500	139	209	.665	334	760	1094	366	249	5	65	61	156	36.3	9.7	13.3	4.5	.583
80-81	Washington	63	....	2032	507	225	429	.524	2	4	.500	55	86	.640	207	466	673	170	171	1	52	36	95	32.3	8.0	10.7	2.7	.502
NBA Season Totals		984	....	35832	10624	4369	8586	.509	3	6	.500	1883	2976	.633	2085	4974	13769	3822	2762	29	628	367	581	36.4	10.8	14.0	3.9	....
68-69	Baltimore	4	....	165	75	30	57	.526	....	....	....	15	19	.789	....	....	74	5	14	0	....	....	....	41.3	18.8	18.5	1.3	.682
69-70	Baltimore	7	....	289	73	29	70	.414	....	....	....	15	19	.789	....	....	165	24	25	1	....	....	....	41.3	10.4	23.6	3.4	.679
70-71	Baltimore	18	....	759	238	96	208	.462	....	....	....	46	81	.568	....	....	339	69	60	0	....	....	....	42.2	13.2	18.8	3.8	.621
71-72	Baltimore	6	....	266	74	32	65	.492	....	....	....	10	19	.526	....	....	75	25	22	0	....	....	....	44.3	12.3	12.5	4.2	.471
72-73	Baltimore	5	....	201	49	20	48	.417	....	....	....	9	19	.474	....	....	76	17	12	0	....	....	....	40.2	9.8	15.2	3.4	.498
73-74	Washington	7	....	297	71	31	63	.492	....	....	....	9	15	.600	22	63	85	27	15	0	4	1	....	42.4	10.1	12.1	3.9	.465
74-75	Washington	17	....	734	182	71	130	.546	....	....	....	40	61	.656	65	211	276	64	39	0	15	20	....	43.2	10.7	16.2	3.8	.565
75-76	Washington	7	....	310	49	18	39	.462	....	....	....	13	24	.542	26	59	85	28	19	0	6	4	....	44.3	7.0	12.1	4.0	.397
76-77	Washington	9	....	368	67	30	54	.556	....	....	....	7	12	.583	24	81	105	44	32	0	8	6	....	40.9	7.4	11.7	4.9	.465
77-78	Washington	18	....	677	169	71	134	.530	....	....	....	27	46	.587	72	144	216	79	62	2	17	7	36	37.6	9.4	12.0	4.4	.511
78-79	Washington	19	....	736	195	78	158	.494	....	....	....	39	64	.609	90	163	253	64	66	2	17	14	30	38.7	10.3	13.3	3.4	.518
79-80	Washington	2	....	87	18	7	14	.500	0	1	.000	4	6	.667	7	21	28	7	5	0	0	3	3	43.5	9.0	14.0	3.5	.477
NBA Playoff Totals		119	....	4889	1260	513	1040	.493	0	1	.000	234	385	.608	306	742	1777	453	371	5	67	55	69	41.1	10.6	14.9	3.8	....

• UPLINGER, Hal

Harold F. Uplinger

Born: Sept. 30, 1929. Height: 6'4". Weight: 185 lbs. Drafted: — College: Long Island University

YEAR	TEAM	GP	GS	MIN	PTS	FGM	FGA	FG%	3PM	3PA	3P%	FTM	FTA	FT%	ORB	DRB	TRB	AST	PF	DQ	STL	BLK	TO	MPG	PPG	RPG	APG	PCM
53-54	Baltimore	23	....	268	86	33	94	.351	....	....	....	20	22	.909	....	....	31	26	42	0	....	....	....	11.7	3.7	1.3	1.1	.308
NBA Season Totals		23	....	268	86	33	94	.351	....	....	....	20	22	.909	....	....	31	26	42	0	....	....	....	11.7	3.7	1.3	1.1	....

• UPSHAW, Kelvin

Kelvin Parnell Upshaw

Born: Jan. 24, 1963. Chicago, IL, United States. Height: 6'2". Weight: 180 lbs. Drafted: — College: Utah

YEAR	TEAM	GP	GS	MIN	PTS	FGM	FGA	FG%	3PM	3PA	3P%	FTM	FTA	FT%	ORB	DRB	TRB	AST	PF	DQ	STL	BLK	TO	MPG	PPG	RPG	APG	PCM
88-89	Miami	9	0	144	57	26	63	.413	1	5	.200	4	6	.667	4	9	13	20	18	0	7	0	13	16.0	6.3	1.4	2.2	.286
88-89	Boston	23	0	473	162	73	149	.490	2	10	.200	14	20	.700	6	30	36	97	62	1	19	3	41	20.6	7.0	1.6	4.2	.379
89-90	Boston	14	0	131	30	12	39	.308	2	5	.400	4	6	.667	3	10	13	28	19	0	2	1	13	9.4	2.1	0.9	2.0	.209
89-90	Dallas	3	0	4	2	1	3	.333	0	1	.000	0	0	.000	0	0	0	0	0	0	0	0	0	1.3	0.7	0.0	0.0	.032
89-90	Golden State	23	0	252	128	51	104	.490	2	9	.222	24	31	.774	6	22	28	26	34	0	25	0	16	11.0	5.6	1.2	1.1	.482
90-91	Dallas	48	1	514	270	104	231	.450	7	29	.241	55	64	.859	20	35	55	86	77	0	28	5	38	10.7	5.6	1.1	1.8	.486
NBA Season Totals		120	1	1518	649	267	589	.453	14	59	.237	101	127	.795	39	106	145	257	210	1	81	9	121	12.7	5.4	1.2	2.1	....
88-89	Boston	3	0	24	10	5	12	.417	0	0	.000	0	0	.000	0	2	2	5	4	0	1	0	1	8.0	3.3	0.7	1.7	.368
NBA Playoff Totals		3	0	24	10	5	12	.417	0	0	.000	0	0	.000	0	2	2	5	4	0	1	0	1	8.0	3.3	0.7	1.7	....

• URSO, Joe

Joseph Urso

Born: 1916. Height: 5'10". Weight: 170 lbs. Drafted: — College: Duquesne

YEAR	TEAM	GP	GS	MIN	PTS	FGM	FGA	FG%	3PM	3PA	3P%	FTM	FTA	FT%	ORB	DRB	TRB	AST	PF	DQ	STL	BLK	TO	MPG	PPG	RPG	APG	PCM
44-45	Pittsburgh-N	29	....	....	202	81	....	....	....	....	....	40	....	....	....	....	....	....	....	....	....	....	....	....	7.0	....	....	....
45-46	Youngstown-N	15	....	....	43	16	....	....	....	....	....	11	....	....	....	....	....	....	....	....	....	....	....	....	2.9	....	....	....
NBL Season Totals		44	....	....	245	97	....	....	....	....	....	51	....	....	....	....	....	....	....	....	....	....	....	....	5.6	....	....	....

USRY, Jim
James L. Usry

Born: 1922. Athens, GA, United States. Died: Jan.2002. Height: 6'4". Weight: 225 lbs. Drafted: — College: Lincoln (MO)

YEAR TEAM	GP	GS	MIN	PTS	FGM	FGA	FG%	3PM	3PA	3P%	FTM	FTA	FT%	ORB	DRB	TRB	AST	PF	DQ	STL	BLK	TO	MPG	PPG	RPG	APG	PCM
48-49 Dayton-N	36	....	....	329	129	....	....	....	....	....	....	71	134	.530	....	....	....	....	....	....	....	....	....	....	9.1	....	....	....
NBL Season Totals	36			329	129							71	134												9.1			

VACENDAK, Stephen
Stephen T. Vacendak

Born: Aug. 15, 1944. Scranton, PA, United States. Height: 6'1". Weight: 185 lbs. Drafted: 1966 College: Duke

YEAR TEAM	GP	GS	MIN	PTS	FGM	FGA	FG%	3PM	3PA	3P%	FTM	FTA	FT%	ORB	DRB	TRB	AST	PF	DQ	STL	BLK	TO	MPG	PPG	RPG	APG	PCM
67-68 Pittsburgh-A	9	....	73	36	13	35	.371	0	0	.000	10	15	.667	....	....	15	8	14	0	....	....	9	8.1	4.0	1.7	0.9	.434
68-69 Minnesota-A	60	....	1589	745	288	716	.402	2	8	.250	167	215	.777	90	120	210	166	158	1	....	....	139	26.5	12.4	3.5	2.8	.415
69-70 Miami-A	12	....	137	37	13	46	.283	0	2	.000	11	20	.550	4	8	12	17	18	0	....	....	8	11.4	3.1	1.0	1.4	.196
69-70 Pittsburgh-A	2	....	36	6	2	13	.154	0	0	.000	2	2	1.000	1	0	1	3	4	0	....	....	2	18.0	3.0	0.5	1.5	-.024
ABA Season Totals	83	....	1835	824	316	810	.390	2	10	.200	190	252	.754	95	128	238	194	194	1	....	....	158	22.1	9.9	2.9	2.3	....
67-68 Pittsburgh-A	7	....	16	4	2	7	.286	0	0	.000	0	0	.000	....	....	3	2	2	0	....	....	1	2.3	0.6	0.4	0.3	.241
68-69 Minnesota-A	7	....	214	115	39	85	.459	0	0	.000	37	41	.902	....	....	17	12	24	0	....	....	16	30.6	16.4	2.4	1.7	.429
ABA Playoff Totals	14	....	230	119	41	92	.446	0	0	.000	37	41	.902			20	14	26	0	....	....	17	16.4	8.5	1.4	1.0	....

VALENTINE, Darnell
Darnell Terrell Valentine

Born: Feb. 3, 1959. Chicago, IL, United States. Height: 6'1". Weight: 183 lbs. Drafted: 1981 College: Kansas

YEAR TEAM	GP	GS	MIN	PTS	FGM	FGA	FG%	3PM	3PA	3P%	FTM	FTA	FT%	ORB	DRB	TRB	AST	PF	DQ	STL	BLK	TO	MPG	PPG	RPG	APG	PCM
81-82 Portland	82	14	1387	526	187	453	.413	0	9	.000	152	200	.760	48	101	149	270	187	1	94	3	123	16.9	6.4	1.8	3.3	.416
82-83 Portland	47	36	1298	587	209	460	.454	0	1	.000	169	213	.793	34	83	117	293	139	1	101	5	132	27.6	12.5	2.5	6.2	.525
83-84 Portland	68	60	1893	696	251	561	.447	0	3	.000	194	246	.789	49	78	127	395	179	1	107	6	150	27.8	10.2	1.9	5.8	.426
84-85 Portland	75	59	2278	872	321	679	.473	0	2	.000	230	290	.793	54	165	219	522	189	1	143	5	195	30.4	11.6	2.9	7.0	.500
85-86 Portland	28	27	734	256	92	206	.447	1	3	.333	71	100	.710	20	52	72	139	78	0	49	1	59	26.2	9.1	2.6	5.0	.419
85-86 LA Clippers	34	2	483	200	69	182	.379	3	11	.273	59	75	.787	12	41	53	107	45	0	23	1	58	14.2	5.9	1.6	3.1	.412
86-87 LA Clippers	65	52	1759	726	275	671	.410	13	56	.232	163	200	.815	38	112	150	447	148	3	116	10	169	27.1	11.2	2.3	6.9	.482
87-88 LA Clippers	79	31	1636	562	223	533	.418	15	33	.455	101	136	.743	37	119	156	382	135	0	122	8	150	20.7	7.1	2.0	4.8	.445
88-89 Cleveland	77	4	1086	366	136	319	.426	3	14	.214	91	112	.813	22	81	103	174	88	0	57	7	85	14.1	4.8	1.3	2.3	.375
90-91 Cleveland	65	60	1841	609	230	496	.464	6	25	.240	143	172	.831	37	135	172	351	170	2	98	12	124	28.3	9.4	2.6	5.4	.429
NBA Season Totals	620	345	14395	5400	1993	4560	.437	41	157	.261	1373	1744	.787	351	967	1318	3080	1358	9	910	58	1245	23.2	8.7	2.1	5.0	....
82-83 Portland	7	7	205	85	34	80	.425	1	2	.500	16	21	.762	5	10	15	61	21	0	10	3	19	29.3	12.1	2.1	8.7	.521
83-84 Portland	5	5	178	92	30	60	.500	0	0	.000	32	35	.914	3	8	11	42	23	2	9	1	11	35.6	18.4	2.2	8.4	.597
84-85 Portland	9	9	244	115	43	88	.489	0	0	.000	29	31	.935	6	11	17	58	28	1	16	0	21	27.1	12.8	1.9	6.4	.542
88-89 Cleveland	5	0	80	21	7	20	.350	0	0	.000	7	8	.875	3	4	7	16	7	0	5	0	5	16.0	4.2	1.4	3.2	.360
NBA Playoff Totals	26	21	707	313	114	248	.460	1	2	.500	84	95	.884	17	33	50	177	79	3	40	4	56	27.2	12.0	1.9	6.8	....

VALENTINE, Ronnie
Ronnie L. Valentine

Born: Nov. 27, 1957. Norfolk, VA, United States. Height: 6'7". Weight: 210 lbs. Drafted: 1980 College: Old Dominion

YEAR TEAM	GP	GS	MIN	PTS	FGM	FGA	FG%	3PM	3PA	3P%	FTM	FTA	FT%	ORB	DRB	TRB	AST	PF	DQ	STL	BLK	TO	MPG	PPG	RPG	APG	PCM
80-81 Denver	24	....	123	84	37	98	.378	1	2	.500	9	19	.474	10	20	30	7	23	0	7	4	17	5.1	3.5	1.3	0.3	.349
NBA Season Totals	24	....	123	84	37	98	.378	1	2	.500	9	19	.474	10	20	30	7	23	0	7	4	17	5.1	3.5	1.3	0.3	....

VALLELY, John
John Stephen Vallely

Born: Oct. 3, 1948. Height: 6'3". Weight: 185 lbs. Drafted: 1970 College: UCLA

YEAR TEAM	GP	GS	MIN	PTS	FGM	FGA	FG%	3PM	3PA	3P%	FTM	FTA	FT%	ORB	DRB	TRB	AST	PF	DQ	STL	BLK	TO	MPG	PPG	RPG	APG	PCM
70-71 Atlanta	51	....	430	191	73	204	.358	....	....	....	45	59	.763			34	47	50	0	....	....	....	8.4	3.7	0.7	0.9	.311
71-72 Atlanta	9	....	110	53	20	43	.465	....	....	....	13	20	.650			11	9	13	0	....	....	....	12.2	5.9	1.2	1.0	.402
71-72 Houston	40	....	256	115	49	128	.383	....	....	....	17	25	.680			21	28	37	0	....	....	....	6.4	2.9	0.5	0.7	.302
NBA Season Totals	100	....	796	359	142	375	.379	....	....	....	75	104	.721			66	84	100	0	....	....	....	8.0	3.6	0.7	0.8	....

VAN ARSDALE, Dick
Richard Albert Van Arsdale

Born: Feb. 22, 1943. Indianapolis, IN, United States. Height: 6'5". Weight: 210 lbs. Drafted: 1965 College: Indiana

YEAR TEAM	GP	GS	MIN	PTS	FGM	FGA	FG%	3PM	3PA	3P%	FTM	FTA	FT%	ORB	DRB	TRB	AST	PF	DQ	STL	BLK	TO	MPG	PPG	RPG	APG	PCM
65-66 New York	79	....	2289	969	359	838	.428	....	....	....	251	351	.715	....	....	376	184	235	5	....	....	....	29.0	12.3	4.8	2.3	.428
66-67 New York	79	....	2892	1191	410	913	.449	....	....	....	371	509	.729	....	....	555	247	264	3	....	....	....	36.6	15.1	7.0	3.1	.474
67-68 New York	78	....	2348	859	316	725	.436	....	....	....	227	339	.670	....	....	424	230	225	0	....	....	....	30.1	11.0	5.4	2.9	.431
68-69 Phoenix	80	....	3388	1678	612	1386	.442	....	....	....	454	644	.705	....	....	548	385	245	2	....	....	....	42.4	21.0	6.9	4.8	.518
69-70 Phoenix	77	....	2966	1643	592	1166	.508	....	....	....	459	575	.798	....	....	264	338	282	5	....	....	....	38.5	21.3	3.4	4.4	.531
70-71 Phoenix	81	....	3157	1771	609	1346	.452	....	....	....	553	682	.811	....	....	316	329	246	1	....	....	....	39.0	21.9	3.9	4.1	.514
71-72 Phoenix	82	....	3096	1619	545	1178	.463	....	....	....	529	626	.845	....	....	334	297	232	1	....	....	....	37.8	19.7	4.1	3.6	.503
72-73 Phoenix	81	....	2979	1490	532	1118	.476	....	....	....	426	496	.859	....	....	326	268	221	2	....	....	....	36.8	18.4	4.0	3.3	.486
73-74 Phoenix	78	....	2832	1389	514	1028	.500	....	....	....	361	423	.853	66	155	221	324	241	2	96	17	....	36.3	17.8	2.8	4.2	.488
74-75 Phoenix	70	....	2419	1124	421	895	.470	....	....	....	282	339	.832	52	137	189	195	177	2	81	11	....	34.6	16.1	2.7	2.8	.415
75-76 Phoenix	58	....	1870	747	276	570	.484	....	....	....	195	235	.830	39	98	137	140	113	2	52	11	....	32.2	12.9	2.4	2.4	.378
76-77 Phoenix	78	....	1535	599	227	498	.456	....	....	....	145	166	.873	31	86	117	120	94	0	35	5	....	19.7	7.7	1.5	1.5	.360
NBA Season Totals	921	....	31771	15079	5413	11661	.464	....	....	....	4253	5385	.790	188	476	3807	3057	2575	25	264	44	....	34.5	16.4	4.1	3.3	....
66-67 New York	4	....	153	46	15	47	.319	....	....	....	16	22	.727	....	....	25	14	16	1	....	....	....	38.3	11.5	6.3	3.5	.317
67-68 New York	4	....	88	13	5	22	.227	....	....	....	3	4	.750	....	....	16	13	9	0	....	....	....	22.0	3.3	4.0	3.3	.271
69-70 Phoenix	7	....	255	115	43	100	.430	....	....	....	29	33	.879	....	....	18	29	23	0	....	....	....	36.4	16.4	2.6	4.1	.397
75-76 Phoenix	19	....	472	162	61	125	.488	....	....	....	40	46	.870	10	13	23	38	41	0	13	2	....	24.8	8.5	1.2	2.0	.318
NBA Playoff Totals	34	....	968	336	124	294	.422	....	....	....	88	105	.838	10	13	82	94	89	1	13	2	....	28.5	9.9	2.4	2.8	....

• VAN ARSDALE, Tom

Thomas Arthur Van Arsdale

Born: Feb. 22, 1943. Indianapolis, IN, United States. Height: 6'5". Weight: 202 lbs. Drafted: 1965 College: Indiana

YEAR	TEAM	GP	GS	MIN	PTS	FGM	FGA	FG%	3PM	3PA	3P%	FTM	FTA	FT%	ORB	DRB	TRB	AST	PF	DQ	STL	BLK	TO	MPG	PPG	RPG	APG	PCM
65-66	Detroit	79	....	2041	833	312	834	.374	....	....	....	209	290	.721	....	....	309	205	251	1	....	....	....	25.8	10.5	3.9	2.6	.385
66-67	Detroit	79	....	2134	966	347	887	.391	....	....	....	272	347	.784	....	....	341	193	241	3	....	....	....	27.0	12.2	4.3	2.4	.428
67-68	Detroit	50	....	832	329	114	307	.371	....	....	....	101	136	.743	....	....	132	79	119	3	....	....	....	16.6	6.6	2.6	1.6	.377
67-68	Cincinnati	27	....	682	281	97	238	.408	....	....	....	87	116	.750	....	....	93	76	83	2	....	....	....	25.3	10.4	3.4	2.8	.424
68-69	Cincinnati	77	....	3059	1492	547	1233	.444	....	....	....	398	533	.747	....	....	356	208	300	6	....	....	....	39.7	19.4	4.6	2.7	.417
69-70	Cincinnati	71	....	2544	1621	620	1376	.451	....	....	....	381	492	.774	....	....	463	155	247	3	....	....	....	35.8	22.8	6.5	2.2	.542
70-71	Cincinnati	82	....	3146	1875	749	1642	.456	....	....	....	377	523	.721	....	....	499	181	294	3	....	....	....	38.4	22.9	6.1	2.2	.494
71-72	Cincinnati	73	....	2598	1399	550	1205	.456	....	....	....	299	396	.755	....	....	350	198	241	1	....	....	....	35.6	19.2	4.8	2.7	.467
72-73	Omaha	49	....	1282	610	250	547	.457	....	....	....	110	140	.786	....	....	173	90	123	0	....	....	....	26.2	12.4	3.5	1.8	.422
72-73	Philadelphia	30	....	1029	530	195	496	.393	....	....	....	140	168	.833	....	....	185	62	101	0	....	....	....	34.3	17.7	6.2	2.1	.433
73-74	Philadelphia	78	....	3041	1526	614	1433	.428	....	....	....	298	350	.851	88	305	393	202	300	6	62	3	....	39.0	19.6	5.0	2.6	.410
74-75	Philadelphia	9	....	273	126	49	116	.422	....	....	....	28	41	.683	7	22	29	16	26	0	13	0	....	30.3	14.0	3.2	1.8	.349
74-75	Atlanta	73	....	2570	1382	544	1269	.429	....	....	....	294	383	.768	70	179	249	207	231	5	78	3	....	35.2	18.9	3.4	2.8	.419
75-76	Atlanta	75	....	2026	818	346	785	.441	....	....	....	126	166	.759	35	151	186	146	202	5	57	7	....	27.0	10.9	2.5	1.9	.328
76-77	Phoenix	77	....	1425	444	171	395	.433	....	....	....	102	145	.703	47	137	184	67	163	0	20	3	....	18.5	5.8	2.4	0.9	.278
NBA Season Totals		929	....	28682	14232	5505	12763	.431	....	....	....	3222	4226	.762	247	794	3942	2085	2922	38	230	16	....	30.9	15.3	4.2	2.2	....

• VAN BREDA KOLFF, Butch

Willem Hendrik (Butch) Van Breda Kolff

Born: Oct. 28, 1922. Glen Ridge, NJ, United States. Height: 6'3". Weight: 185 lbs. Drafted: — College: New York University

YEAR	TEAM	GP	GS	MIN	PTS	FGM	FGA	FG%	3PM	3PA	3P%	FTM	FTA	FT%	ORB	DRB	TRB	AST	PF	DQ	STL	BLK	TO	MPG	PPG	RPG	APG	PCM
46-47	New York	16	....	....	25	7	34	.206	....	....	....	11	17	.647	....	....	....	6	10	....	....	....	....	....	1.6	....	0.4	....
47-48	New York	44	....	....	180	53	192	.276	....	....	....	74	120	.617	....	....	....	29	81	....	....	....	....	....	4.1	....	0.7	....
48-49	New York	59	....	....	415	127	401	.317	....	....	....	161	240	.671	....	....	....	143	148	....	....	....	....	....	7.0	....	2.4	....
49-50	New York	56	....	....	206	55	167	.329	....	....	....	96	134	.716	....	....	....	78	111	....	....	....	....	....	3.7	....	1.4	....
NBA Season Totals		175	....	....	826	242	794	.305	....	....	....	342	511	.669	....	....	....	256	350	....	....	....	....	....	4.7	....	1.5	....
46-47	New York	5	....	....	21	7	32	.219	....	....	....	7	13	.538	....	....	....	4	5	....	....	....	....	....	4.2	....	0.8	....
47-48	New York	3	....	....	22	6	16	.375	....	....	....	10	14	.714	....	....	....	2	8	....	....	....	....	....	7.3	....	0.7	....
48-49	New York	6	....	....	49	15	40	.375	....	....	....	19	23	.826	....	....	....	7	14	....	....	....	....	....	8.2	....	1.2	....
49-50	New York	1	....	....	0	0	0	.000	....	....	....	0	0	.000	....	....	....	0	2	....	....	....	....	....	0.0	....	0.0	....
NBA Playoff Totals		15	....	....	92	28	88	.318	....	....	....	36	50	.720	....	....	....	13	29	....	....	....	....	....	6.1	....	0.9	....

• VAN BREDA KOLFF, Jan

Jan Michael (V.B.K.) Van Breda Kolff

Born: Dec. 16, 1951. Palos Verdes, CA, United States. Height: 6'7". Weight: 195 lbs. Drafted: 1974 College: Vanderbilt

YEAR	TEAM	GP	GS	MIN	PTS	FGM	FGA	FG%	3PM	3PA	3P%	FTM	FTA	FT%	ORB	DRB	TRB	AST	PF	DQ	STL	BLK	TO	MPG	PPG	RPG	APG	PCM
74-75	Denver-A	84	....	1639	487	155	342	.453	0	3	.000	177	211	.839	121	237	358	181	164	....	48	43	122	19.5	5.8	4.3	2.2	.459
75-76	Kentucky-A	43	....	861	247	95	192	.495	1	2	.500	56	68	.824	63	132	195	81	87	....	29	42	64	20.0	5.7	4.5	1.9	.441
75-76	Virginia-A	37	....	1117	366	128	296	.432	1	4	.250	109	130	.838	81	160	241	101	77	....	36	54	80	30.2	9.9	6.5	2.7	.447
76-77	New York	72	....	2398	737	271	609	.445	....	....	....	195	228	.855	156	304	460	117	205	2	74	68	....	33.3	10.2	6.4	1.6	.364
77-78	New Jersey	68	....	1419	301	107	292	.366	....	....	....	87	123	.707	66	178	244	105	192	7	52	46	75	20.9	4.4	3.6	1.5	.276
78-79	New Jersey	80	....	1998	538	196	423	.463	....	....	....	146	183	.798	108	274	382	180	235	4	85	74	136	25.0	6.7	4.8	2.3	.387
79-80	New Jersey	82	....	2399	561	212	458	.463	7	20	.350	130	155	.839	103	326	429	247	307	11	100	76	156	29.3	6.8	5.2	3.0	.361
80-81	New Jersey	78	....	1426	300	100	245	.408	2	8	.250	98	117	.838	48	154	202	129	214	3	38	50	109	18.3	3.8	2.6	1.7	.257
81-82	New Jersey	41	0	452	144	41	82	.500	0	2	.000	62	76	.816	17	31	48	32	63	1	12	13	29	11.0	3.5	1.2	0.8	.323
82-83	New Jersey	13	0	63	15	5	14	.357	0	0	.000	5	6	.833	2	11	13	5	9	0	2	2	3	4.8	1.2	1.0	0.4	.325
NBA Season Totals		434	0	10155	2596	932	2123	.439	9	30	.300	723	888	.814	500	1278	1778	815	1225	28	363	329	508	23.4	6.0	4.1	1.9	....
ABA Season Totals		164	....	3617	1100	378	830	.455	2	9	.222	342	409	.836	265	529	794	363	328	....	113	139	266	22.1	6.7	4.8	2.2	....
Career Totals		598	0	13772	3696	1310	2953	.444	11	39	.282	1065	1297	.821	765	1807	2572	1178	1553	28	476	468	774	23.0	6.2	4.3	2.0	....
74-75	Denver-A	12	....	192	63	17	40	.425	0	0	.000	29	31	.935	18	22	40	15	27	....	4	6	14	16.0	5.3	3.3	1.3	.427
75-76	Kentucky-A	10	....	186	53	21	40	.525	0	0	.000	11	14	.786	17	19	36	16	12	....	6	5	11	18.6	5.3	3.6	1.6	.426
78-79	New Jersey	2	....	81	21	8	20	.400	....	....	....	5	6	.833	11	9	20	7	9	0	0	3	5	40.5	10.5	10.0	3.5	.366
81-82	New Jersey	2	0	16	0	0	1	.000	0	0	.000	0	0	.000	0	3	3	0	0	0	2	1	1	8.0	0.0	1.5	0.0	.230
NBA Playoff Totals		4	0	97	21	8	21	.381	0	0	.000	5	6	.833	11	12	23	7	9	0	2	4	6	24.3	5.3	5.8	1.8	....
ABA Playoff Totals		22	....	378	116	38	80	.475	0	0	.000	40	45	.889	35	41	76	31	39	....	10	11	25	17.2	5.3	3.5	1.4	....
Career Playoff Totals		26	0	475	137	46	101	.455	0	0	.000	45	51	.882	46	53	99	38	48	0	12	15	31	18.3	5.3	3.8	1.5	....

• VAN EXEL, Nick

Nickey Maxwell Van Exel

Born: Nov. 27, 1971. Kenosha, WI, United States. Height: 6'1". Weight: 170 lbs. Drafted: 1993 College: Cincinnati

YEAR	TEAM	GP	GS	MIN	PTS	FGM	FGA	FG%	3PM	3PA	3P%	FTM	FTA	FT%	ORB	DRB	TRB	AST	PF	DQ	STL	BLK	TO	MPG	PPG	RPG	APG	PCM
93-94	LA Lakers	81	80	2700	1099	413	1049	.394	123	364	.338	150	192	.781	47	191	238	466	154	1	85	8	146	33.3	13.6	2.9	5.8	.407
94-95	LA Lakers	80	80	2944	1348	465	1107	.420	183	511	.358	235	300	.783	27	196	223	660	157	0	97	6	224	36.8	16.9	2.8	8.3	.489
95-96	LA Lakers	74	74	2513	1099	396	950	.417	144	403	.357	163	204	.799	29	152	181	509	115	0	70	10	155	34.0	14.9	2.4	6.9	.455
96-97	LA Lakers	79	79	2937	1206	432	1075	.402	177	468	.378	165	200	.825	44	182	226	672	110	0	75	10	213	37.2	15.3	2.9	8.5	.459
97-98	LA Lakers	64	46	2053	881	311	743	.419	123	316	.389	136	172	.791	31	163	194	442	120	0	64	6	102	32.1	13.8	3.0	6.9	.508
98-99	Denver	50	50	1802	826	306	769	.398	72	234	.308	142	175	.811	14	99	113	368	90	0	40	3	121	36.0	16.5	2.3	7.4	.444
99-00	Denver	79	79	2950	1275	473	1213	.390	133	401	.332	196	240	.817	34	277	311	714	148	0	68	11	221	37.3	16.1	3.9	9.0	.491
00-01	Denver	71	70	2688	1259	460	1112	.414	135	358	.377	204	249	.819	44	197	241	600	109	1	61	18	165	37.9	17.7	3.4	8.5	.523
01-02	Denver	45	44	1739	965	372	912	.408	85	252	.337	136	174	.782	19	150	169	365	69	0	30	7	116	38.6	21.4	3.8	8.1	.522
01-02	Dallas	27	2	757	357	129	314	.411	34	98	.347	65	77	.844	9	76	85	113	35	0	14	4	40	28.0	13.2	3.1	4.2	.461
02-03	Dallas	73	1	2026	912	342	831	.412	118	312	.378	110	144	.764	35	173	208	312	86	1	42	4	121	27.8	12.5	2.8	4.3	.432
NBA Season Totals		723	605	25109	11227	4099	10075	.407	1327	3717	.357	1702	2127	.800	333	1856	2189	5221	1193	3	646	87	1624	34.7	15.5	3.0	7.2	....
94-95	LA Lakers	10	10	464	200	67	162	.414	21	66	.318	45	59	.763	9	29	38	73	33	0	21	3	22	46.4	20.0	3.8	7.3	.439
95-96	LA Lakers	4	4	137	47	16	54	.296	5	16	.313	10	13	.769	4	12	16	27	10	0	2	0	11	34.3	11.8	4.0	6.8	.295
96-97	LA Lakers	9	9	353	130	45	119	.378	12	44	.273	28	34	.824	6	25	31	58	19	0	10	0	18	39.2	14.4	3.4	6.4	.376

YEAR	TEAM	GP	GS	MIN	PTS	FGM	FGA	FG%	3PM	3PA	3P%	FTM	FTA	FT%	ORB	DRB	TRB	AST	PF	DQ	STL	BLK	TO	MPG	PPG	RPG	APG	PCM
97-98	LA Lakers	13	0	367	151	50	151	.331	22	70	.314	29	40	.725	9	23	32	54	30	0	8	1	22	28.2	11.6	2.5	4.2	.316
01-02	Dallas	8	1	264	89	37	101	.366	7	34	.206	8	12	.667	7	17	24	31	26	0	8	0	12	33.0	11.1	3.0	3.9	.263
02-03	Dallas	20	3	672	389	150	326	.460	44	112	.393	45	64	.703	18	50	68	82	47	0	12	0	39	33.6	19.5	3.4	4.1	.485
NBA Playoff Totals		64	27	2257	1006	365	913	.400	111	342	.325	165	222	.743	53	156	209	325	165	0	61	4	124	35.3	15.7	3.3	5.1	....

• VAN HORN, Keith

Keith Adam Van Horn

Born: Oct. 23, 1975. Fullerton, CA, United States. Height: 6'10". Weight: 220 lbs. Drafted: 1997 College: Utah

97-98	New Jersey	62	62	2325	1219	446	1047	.426	69	224	.308	258	305	.846	142	266	408	106	216	0	64	25	161	37.5	19.7	6.6	1.7	.418
98-99	New Jersey	42	42	1576	916	322	752	.428	16	53	.302	256	298	.859	114	244	358	65	134	2	43	53	133	37.5	21.8	8.5	1.5	.516
99-00	New Jersey	80	80	2782	1535	559	1257	.445	84	228	.368	333	393	.847	200	476	676	158	258	5	64	60	245	34.8	19.2	8.5	2.0	.515
00-01	New Jersey	49	47	1733	831	308	708	.435	65	170	.382	150	186	.806	78	269	347	82	150	4	40	20	103	35.4	17.0	7.1	1.7	.434
01-02	New Jersey	81	81	2465	1199	471	1089	.433	101	293	.345	156	195	.800	137	472	609	164	221	1	63	42	146	30.4	14.8	7.5	2.0	.493
02-03	Philadelphia	74	73	2337	1176	459	952	.482	65	176	.369	193	240	.804	159	365	524	93	251	7	63	30	150	31.6	15.9	7.1	1.3	.479
NBA Season Totals		388	385	13218	6876	2565	5805	.442	400	1144	.350	1346	1617	.832	830	2092	2922	668	1230	19	337	230	938	34.1	17.7	7.5	1.7	....
97-98	New Jersey	3	3	77	38	13	29	.448	0	2	.000	12	15	.800	2	7	9	1	7	0	0	0	2	25.7	12.7	3.0	0.3	.341
01-02	New Jersey	20	20	643	266	97	241	.402	37	84	.440	35	49	.714	32	101	133	41	56	2	19	9	35	32.2	13.3	6.7	2.1	.409
02-03	Philadelphia	12	12	401	125	42	110	.382	14	32	.438	27	30	.900	24	66	90	9	41	1	10	2	26	33.4	10.4	7.5	0.8	.305
NBA Playoff Totals		35	35	1121	429	152	380	.400	51	118	.432	74	94	.787	58	174	232	51	104	3	29	11	63	32.0	12.3	6.6	1.5	....

• VAN LIER, Norm

Norman Allen (Stormin' Norman) Van Lier III

Born: Apr. 1, 1947. East Liverpool, OH, United States. Height: 6'1". Weight: 173 lbs. Drafted: 1969 College: St. Francis (PA)

69-70	Cincinnati	81	....	2895	770	302	749	.403	....	....	....	166	224	.741	....	....	409	500	329	**18**	....	....	....	35.7	9.5	5.0	6.2	.389
70-71	Cincinnati	82	....	3324	1315	478	1138	.420	....	....	....	359	440	.816	....	....	583	**832**	343	12	....	....	....	40.5	16.0	7.1	**10.1**	**.606**
71-72	Cincinnati	10	....	275	73	28	90	.311	....	....	....	17	22	.773	....	....	58	51	32	1	....	....	....	27.5	7.3	5.8	5.1	.405
71-72	Chicago	69	....	2140	832	306	671	.456	....	....	....	220	278	.791	....	....	299	491	207	4	....	....	....	31.0	12.1	4.3	7.1	.569
72-73	Chicago	80	....	2882	1114	474	1064	.445	....	....	....	166	211	.787	....	....	438	567	269	5	....	....	....	36.0	13.9	5.5	7.1	.519
73-74	Chicago	80	....	2863	1142	427	1051	.406	....	....	....	288	370	.778	114	263	377	548	282	4	162	7	....	35.8	14.3	4.7	6.9	.491
74-75	Chicago	70	....	2590	1050	407	970	.420	....	....	....	236	298	.792	86	242	328	403	246	5	139	14	....	37.0	15.0	4.7	5.8	.456
75-76	Chicago	76	....	3026	957	361	987	.366	....	....	....	235	319	.737	138	272	410	500	298	9	150	26	....	39.8	12.6	5.4	6.6	.390
76-77	Chicago	82	....	3097	838	300	729	.412	....	....	....	238	306	.778	108	262	370	636	268	3	129	16	....	37.8	10.2	4.5	7.8	.441
77-78	Chicago	78	....	2524	572	200	477	.419	....	....	....	172	229	.751	86	198	284	531	279	9	144	5	203	32.4	7.3	3.6	6.8	.389
78-79	Milwaukee	38	....	555	107	30	77	.390	....	....	....	47	52	.904	8	32	40	158	108	4	43	3	49	14.6	2.8	1.1	4.2	.399
NBA Season Totals		746	....	26171	8770	3313	8003	.414	....	....	....	2144	2749	.780	540	1269	3596	5217	2661	74	767	71	252	35.1	11.8	4.8	7.0	....
71-72	Chicago	4	....	144	56	22	53	.415	....	....	....	12	14	.857	....	....	25	33	15	0	....	....	....	36.0	14.0	6.3	8.3	.562
72-73	Chicago	7	....	258	101	45	129	.349	....	....	....	11	15	.733	....	....	37	36	32	3	....	....	....	36.9	14.4	5.3	5.1	.335
73-74	Chicago	11	....	466	161	61	144	.424	....	....	....	39	47	.830	11	36	47	75	41	0	17	3	....	42.4	14.6	4.3	6.8	.420
74-75	Chicago	13	....	547	196	67	164	.409	....	....	....	62	83	.747	18	49	67	61	52	1	20	5	....	42.1	15.1	5.2	4.7	.383
76-77	Chicago	3	....	134	16	3	19	.158	....	....	....	10	12	.833	5	10	15	29	14	1	10	1	....	44.7	5.3	5.0	9.7	.308
NBA Playoff Totals		38	....	1549	530	198	509	.389	....	....	....	134	171	.784	34	95	191	234	154	5	47	9	....	40.8	13.9	5.0	6.2	....

• VAN ZANT, Dennis

Dennis Van Zant

Born: June 1, 1952. Height: 6'9". Weight: 210 lbs. Drafted: 1974 College: Azusa Pacific

75-76	San Antonio-A	1	....	2	2	0	0	.000	0	0	.000	2	2	1.000	0	1	1	0	1	....	0	0	0	2.0	2.0	1.0	0.0	1.223
ABA Season Totals		1	....	2	2	0	0	.000	0	0	.000	2	2	1.000	0	1	1	0	1	....	0	0	0	2.0	2.0	1.0	0.0	....

• VANCE, Gene

Ellis Eugene Vance

Born: Feb. 25, 1923. Height: 6'3". Weight: 195 lbs. Drafted: 1947 College: Illinois

47-48	Chicago	48	....	....	402	163	617	.264	....	....	....	76	126	.603	....	....	....	49	193	....	....	....	....	....	8.4	....	1.0	....
48-49	Chicago	56	....	....	575	222	657	.338	....	....	....	131	181	.724	....	....	....	167	217	....	....	....	....	....	10.3	....	3.0	....
49-50	Tri-Cities	35	....	....	306	110	325	.338	....	....	....	86	120	.717	....	....	....	121	145	....	....	....	....	....	8.7	....	3.5	....
50-51	Tri-Cities	28	....	....	131	44	110	.400	....	....	....	43	61	.705	....	....	88	53	91	0	....	....	....	....	4.7	3.1	1.9	....
51-52	Milwaukee	7	....	118	23	7	26	.269	....	....	....	9	14	.643	....	....	15	9	18	0	....	....	....	16.9	3.3	2.1	1.3	.200
NBA Season Totals		174	....	118	1437	546	1735	.315	....	....	....	345	502	.687	....	....	103	399	664	0	....	....	....	0.7	8.3	0.6	2.3	....
47-48	Chicago	5	....	....	47	17	66	.258	....	....	....	13	17	.765	....	....	....	1	15	....	....	....	....	....	9.4	....	0.2	....
48-49	Chicago	2	....	....	21	8	35	.229	....	....	....	5	6	.833	....	....	....	7	11	....	....	....	....	....	10.5	....	3.5	....
49-50	Tri-Cities	3	....	....	19	7	31	.226	....	....	....	5	10	.500	....	....	....	9	17	....	....	....	....	....	6.3	....	3.0	....
NBA Playoff Totals		10	....	....	87	32	132	.242	....	....	....	23	33	.697	....	....	....	17	43	....	....	....	....	....	8.7	....	1.7	....

• VANDER MEULEN, Augie

Augie Vander Meulen

Born: Nov. 6, 1909. Died: Dec.2, 1993. Height: 6'4". Weight: 175 lbs. Drafted: — College: Carroll (WI)

37-38	Oshkosh-N	10	....	....	77	29	....	....	....	....	....	19	....	....	....	....	....	....	....	....	....	....	....	....	7.7	....	....	....
38-39	Oshkosh-N	7	....	....	28	10	....	....	....	....	....	8	....	....	....	....	....	....	....	....	....	....	....	....	4.0	....	....	....
NBL Season Totals		17	....	....	105	39	....	....	....	....	....	27	....	....	....	....	....	....	....	....	....	....	....	....	6.2	....	....	....
37-38	Oshkosh-N	5	....	....	24	6	....	....	....	....	....	12	....	....	....	....	....	....	....	....	....	....	....	....	4.8	....	....	....
38-39	Oshkosh-N	3	....	....	8	2	....	....	....	....	....	4	....	....	....	....	....	....	....	....	....	....	....	....	2.7	....	....	....
NBL Playoff Totals		8	....	....	32	8	....	....	....	....	....	16	....	....	....	....	....	....	....	....	....	....	....	....	4.0	....	....	....

• VANDER VELDEN, Logan

Logan Vander Velden

Born: Apr. 3, 1971. Valders, WI, United States. Height: 6'8". Weight: 215 lbs. Drafted: — College: Wisconsin (Green Bay)

YEAR	TEAM	GP	GS	MIN	PTS	FGM	FGA	FG%	3PM	3PA	3P%	FTM	FTA	FT%	ORB	DRB	TRB	AST	PF	DQ	STL	BLK	TO	MPG	PPG	RPG	APG	PCM
95-96	LA Clippers	15	0	31	9	3	14	.214	0	5	.000	3	4	.750	1	5	6	1	4	0	0	0	0	2.1	0.6	0.4	0.1	.097
NBA Season Totals		15	0	31	9	3	14	.214	0	5	.000	3	4	.750	1	5	6	1	4	0	0	0	0	2.1	0.6	0.4	0.1	....

• VANDEWEGHE, Ernie

Ernest Maurice (Doc) Vandeweghe Jr.

Born: Sept. 12, 1928. Montreal, QU, Canada. Height: 6'3". Weight: 195 lbs. Drafted: 1949 College: Colgate

YEAR	TEAM	GP	GS	MIN	PTS	FGM	FGA	FG%	3PM	3PA	3P%	FTM	FTA	FT%	ORB	DRB	TRB	AST	PF	DQ	STL	BLK	TO	MPG	PPG	RPG	APG	PCM
49-50	New York	42	....	....	421	164	390	.421	....	....	....	93	140	.664	....	....	....	78	126	....	....	....	....	....	10.0	....	1.9	....
50-51	New York	44	....	....	338	135	336	.402	....	....	....	68	97	.701	....	....	195	121	144	6	....	....	....	....	7.7	4.4	2.8	....
51-52	New York	57	....	1507	524	200	457	.438	....	....	....	124	160	.775	....	....	264	164	188	3	....	....	....	26.4	9.2	4.6	2.9	.438
52-53	New York	61	....	1745	731	272	625	.435	....	....	....	187	244	.766	....	....	342	144	242	11	....	....	....	28.6	12.0	5.6	2.4	.458
53-54	New York	15	....	271	99	37	103	.359	....	....	....	25	31	.806	....	....	20	29	38	1	....	....	....	18.1	6.6	1.3	1.9	.325
55-56	New York	5	....	77	22	10	31	.323	....	....	....	2	2	1.000	....	....	13	12	15	0	....	....	....	15.4	4.4	2.6	2.4	.326
NBA Season Totals		224	....	3600	2135	818	1942	.421	....	....	....	499	674	.740	....	....	834	548	753	21	....	....	....	16.1	9.5	3.7	2.4	....
49-50	New York	4	....	....	32	9	26	.346	....	....	....	14	16	.875	....	....	....	3	16	....	....	....	....	....	8.0	....	0.8	....
50-51	New York	14	....	....	101	37	91	.407	....	....	....	27	37	.730	....	....	66	34	55	4	....	....	....	....	7.2	4.7	2.4	....
51-52	New York	14	....	414	151	51	118	.432	....	....	....	49	60	.817	....	....	69	27	58	1	....	....	....	29.6	10.8	4.9	1.9	.393
52-53	New York	11	....	340	144	49	112	.438	....	....	....	46	61	.754	....	....	64	27	50	0	....	....	....	30.9	13.1	5.8	2.5	.458
NBA Playoff Totals		43	....	754	428	146	347	.421	....	....	....	136	174	.782	....	....	199	91	179	5	....	....	....	17.5	10.0	4.6	2.1	....

• VANDEWEGHE, Kiki

Ernest Maurice (Kiki) Vandeweghe III

Born: Aug. 1, 1958. Weisbaden, Germany. Height: 6'8". Weight: 220 lbs. Drafted: 1980 College: UCLA

YEAR	TEAM	GP	GS	MIN	PTS	FGM	FGA	FG%	3PM	3PA	3P%	FTM	FTA	FT%	ORB	DRB	TRB	AST	PF	DQ	STL	BLK	TO	MPG	PPG	RPG	APG	PCM
80-81	Denver	51	....	1376	588	229	537	.426	0	7	.000	130	159	.818	86	184	270	94	116	0	29	24	87	27.0	11.5	5.3	1.8	.406
81-82	Denver	82	78	2775	1760	706	1260	.560	1	13	.077	347	405	.857	149	312	461	247	217	1	52	29	189	33.8	21.5	5.6	3.0	.618
82-83	Denver	82	79	2909	2186	841	1537	.547	15	51	.294	489	559	.875	124	313	437	203	198	0	66	38	180	35.5	26.7	5.3	2.5	.683
83-84	Denver	78	71	2734	2295	895	1603	.558	11	30	.367	494	580	.852	84	289	373	238	187	1	53	50	156	35.1	29.4	4.8	3.1	.754
84-85	Portland	72	69	2502	1616	618	1158	.534	11	33	.333	369	412	.896	74	154	228	106	116	0	37	22	115	34.8	22.4	3.2	1.5	.524
85-86	Portland	79	76	2791	1962	719	1332	.540	1	8	.125	523	602	.869	92	124	216	187	161	0	54	17	174	35.3	24.8	2.7	2.4	.568
86-87	Portland	79	79	3029	2122	808	1545	.523	39	81	**.481**	467	527	.886	86	165	251	220	137	0	52	17	142	38.3	26.9	3.2	2.8	.576
87-88	Portland	37	7	1038	747	283	557	.508	22	58	.379	159	181	.878	36	73	109	71	68	0	21	7	48	28.1	20.2	2.9	1.9	.586
88-89	Portland	18	1	432	251	103	217	.475	16	38	.421	29	33	.879	11	24	35	34	40	0	7	4	13	24.0	13.9	1.9	1.9	.443
88-89	New York	27	0	502	248	97	209	.464	3	10	.300	51	56	.911	15	21	36	35	38	0	12	7	27	18.6	9.2	1.3	1.3	.373
89-90	New York	22	13	563	258	102	231	.442	10	19	.526	44	48	.917	15	38	53	41	28	0	15	3	26	25.6	11.7	2.4	1.9	.369
90-91	New York	75	72	2420	1226	458	927	.494	51	141	.362	259	288	.899	78	102	180	110	122	0	42	10	105	32.3	16.3	2.4	1.5	.394
91-92	New York	67	0	956	467	188	383	.491	26	66	.394	65	81	.802	31	57	88	57	87	0	15	8	27	14.3	7.0	1.3	0.9	.394
92-93	LA Clippers	41	3	494	254	92	203	.453	12	37	.324	58	66	.879	12	36	48	25	45	0	13	7	21	12.0	6.2	1.2	0.6	.397
NBA Season Totals		810	548	24521	15980	6139	11699	.525	218	592	.368	3484	3997	.872	893	1892	2785	1668	1560	2	468	243	1310	30.3	19.7	3.4	2.1	....
81-82	Denver	3	3	109	68	25	43	.581	0	0	.000	18	18	1.000	4	14	18	9	7	0	2	4	6	36.3	22.7	6.0	3.0	.683
82-83	Denver	8	8	317	214	87	160	.544	0	4	.000	40	50	.800	6	46	52	32	16	0	4	7	12	39.6	26.8	6.5	4.0	.686
83-84	Denver	5	5	180	127	49	96	.510	2	5	.400	27	28	.964	6	17	23	20	14	1	9	5	10	36.0	25.4	4.6	4.0	.682
84-85	Portland	9	9	311	202	85	158	.538	1	7	.143	31	33	.939	14	13	27	17	23	0	8	3	12	34.6	22.4	3.0	1.9	.530
85-86	Portland	4	4	149	112	40	69	.580	0	2	.000	32	32	1.000	2	3	5	8	12	0	2	2	9	37.3	28.0	1.3	2.0	.591
86-87	Portland	4	4	174	99	38	71	.535	1	4	.250	22	26	.846	5	8	13	11	10	0	1	1	11	43.5	24.8	3.3	2.8	.444
87-88	Portland	4	0	72	31	11	40	.275	0	5	.000	9	9	1.000	3	10	13	7	8	0	1	0	3	18.0	7.8	3.3	1.8	.250
88-89	New York	9	0	159	73	25	49	.510	3	8	.375	20	21	.952	2	9	11	7	10	0	3	2	5	17.7	8.1	1.2	0.8	.398
89-90	New York	10	10	236	76	31	74	.419	6	13	.462	8	10	.800	7	5	12	14	14	0	5	2	7	23.6	7.6	1.2	1.4	.230
90-91	New York	3	3	99	51	13	32	.406	3	5	.600	22	25	.880	1	7	8	4	8	0	1	0	12	33.0	17.0	2.7	1.3	.299
91-92	New York	8	0	75	36	13	24	.542	4	5	.800	6	7	.857	3	3	6	4	10	0	2	1	1	9.4	4.5	0.8	0.5	.432
92-93	LA Clippers	1	0	9	4	2	6	.333	0	0	.000	0	0	.000	0	0	0	1	0	0	1	0	1	9.0	4.0	0.0	1.0	.148
NBA Playoff Totals		68	46	1890	1093	419	822	.510	20	58	.345	235	259	.907	53	135	188	134	132	1	39	27	89	27.8	16.1	2.8	2.0	....

• VANIEL, Matt

Matt Vaniel

Born: Nov. 14, 1919. Died: Jan.1981. Height: 6'3". Weight: 170 lbs. Drafted: — College: none

YEAR	TEAM	GP	GS	MIN	PTS	FGM	FGA	FG%	3PM	3PA	3P%	FTM	FTA	FT%	ORB	DRB	TRB	AST	PF	DQ	STL	BLK	TO	MPG	PPG	RPG	APG	PCM
44-45	Pittsburgh-N	24	....	....	179	78	....	....	....	....	....	23	....	....	....	....	....	....	....	....	....	....	....	....	7.5	....	....	....
NBL Season Totals		24	....	....	179	78	....	....	....	....	....	23	....	....	....	....	....	....	....	....	....	....	....	....	7.5	....	....	....

• VANOS, Nick

Nicholas Vanos

Born: Apr. 13, 1963. San Mateo, CA, United States. Died: Aug.16, 1987. Height: 7'1". Weight: 255 lbs. Drafted: 1985 College: Santa Clara

YEAR	TEAM	GP	GS	MIN	PTS	FGM	FGA	FG%	3PM	3PA	3P%	FTM	FTA	FT%	ORB	DRB	TRB	AST	PF	DQ	STL	BLK	TO	MPG	PPG	RPG	APG	PCM
85-86	Phoenix	11	0	202	54	23	72	.319	0	0	.000	8	23	.348	21	39	60	16	34	0	2	5	20	18.4	4.9	5.5	1.5	.230
86-87	Phoenix	57	14	640	168	65	158	.411	0	2	.000	38	59	.644	67	113	180	43	94	0	19	23	46	11.2	2.9	3.2	0.8	.371
NBA Season Totals		68	14	842	222	88	230	.383	0	2	.000	46	82	.561	88	152	240	59	128	0	21	28	66	12.4	3.3	3.5	0.9	....

• VANTERPOOL, David

David Vanterpool

Born: Mar. 31, 1973. Daytona Beach, FL, United States. Height: 6'5". Weight: 200 lbs. Drafted: — College: St. Bonaventure

YEAR	TEAM	GP	GS	MIN	PTS	FGM	FGA	FG%	3PM	3PA	3P%	FTM	FTA	FT%	ORB	DRB	TRB	AST	PF	DQ	STL	BLK	TO	MPG	PPG	RPG	APG	PCM
00-01	Washington	22	0	411	122	46	110	.418	0	6	.000	30	50	.600	15	22	37	66	44	0	23	3	37	18.7	5.5	1.7	3.0	.321
NBA Season Totals		22	0	411	122	46	110	.418	0	6	.000	30	50	.600	15	22	37	66	44	0	23	3	37	18.7	5.5	1.7	3.0	....

• VARDA, Ratko

Ratko Varda

Born: May 6, 1979. Bosanska Gradiska, Bosnia. Height: 7'1". Weight: 260 lbs. Drafted: — College: none

YEAR	TEAM	GP	GS	MIN	PTS	FGM	FGA	FG%	3PM	3PA	3P%	FTM	FTA	FT%	ORB	DRB	TRB	AST	PF	DQ	STL	BLK	TO	MPG	PPG	RPG	APG	PCM
01-02	Detroit	1	0	6	5	2	3	.667	0	0	.000	1	1	1.000	0	1	1	0	3	0	0	0	1	6.0	5.0	1.0	0.0	.456
NBA Season Totals		1	0	6	5	2	3	.667	0	0	.000	1	1	1.000	0	1	1	0	3	0	0	0	1	6.0	5.0	1.0	0.0	....

• VAUGHN, Chico

Charles (Chico) Vaughn

Born: Feb. 19, 1940. Portland, OR, United States. Height: 6'2". Weight: 190 lbs. Drafted: 1962 College: Southern Illinois

YEAR	TEAM	GP	GS	MIN	PTS	FGM	FGA	FG%	3PM	3PA	3P%	FTM	FTA	FT%	ORB	DRB	TRB	AST	PF	DQ	STL	BLK	TO	MPG	PPG	RPG	APG	PCM
62-63	St. Louis	77	....	1845	778	295	708	.417	....	....	....	188	261	.720	....	....	258	252	201	3	....	....	....	24.0	10.1	3.4	3.3	.462
63-64	St. Louis	68	....	1340	583	238	538	.442	....	....	....	107	148	.723	....	....	126	129	166	0	....	....	....	19.7	8.6	1.9	1.9	.392
64-65	St. Louis	75	....	1965	870	344	811	.424	....	....	....	182	242	.752	....	....	173	157	192	2	....	....	....	26.2	11.6	2.3	2.1	.377
65-66	St. Louis	19	....	445	190	72	192	.375	....	....	....	46	62	.742	....	....	46	36	39	1	....	....	....	23.4	10.0	2.4	1.9	.347
65-66	Detroit	37	....	774	280	110	282	.390	....	....	....	60	82	.732	....	....	63	104	60	0	....	....	....	20.9	7.6	1.7	2.8	.373
66-67	Detroit	51	....	680	220	85	226	.376	....	....	....	50	74	.676	....	....	67	75	54	0	....	....	....	13.3	4.3	1.3	1.5	.324
67-68	Pittsburgh-A	74	....	2858	1469	512	1350	.379	137	410	.334	308	416	.740	....	....	298	142	203	0	....	....	171	38.6	19.9	4.0	1.9	.370
68-69	Minnesota-A	69	....	2301	1228	415	1170	.355	145	523	.277	253	329	.769	44	121	165	107	178	1	....	....	150	33.3	17.8	2.4	1.6	.319
69-70	Pittsburgh-A	21	....	401	204	66	180	.367	24	82	.293	48	70	.686	17	11	28	22	53	1	....	....	23	19.1	9.7	1.3	1.0	.307
NBA Season Totals		327	....	7049	2921	1144	2757	.415	....	....	....	633	869	.728	....	....	733	753	712	6	....	....	....	21.6	8.9	2.2	2.3	....
ABA Season Totals		164	....	5560	2901	993	2700	.368	306	1015	.301	609	815	.747	61	132	491	271	434	2	....	....	344	33.9	17.7	3.0	1.7	....
Career Totals		491	....	12609	5822	2137	5457	.392	306	1015	.301	1242	1684	.738	61	132	1224	1024	1146	8	....	....	344	25.7	11.9	2.5	2.1	....
62-63	St. Louis	11	....	314	110	46	96	.479	....	....	....	18	27	.667	....	....	31	31	46	2	....	....	....	28.5	10.0	2.8	2.8	.353
63-64	St. Louis	12	....	242	105	43	101	.426	....	....	....	19	26	.731	....	....	25	21	31	0	....	....	....	20.2	8.8	2.1	1.8	.373
64-65	St. Louis	4	....	75	25	9	29	.310	....	....	....	7	8	.875	....	....	6	10	14	0	....	....	....	18.8	6.3	1.5	2.5	.277
67-68	Pittsburgh-A	15	....	576	266	90	256	.352	24	93	.258	62	78	.795	....	....	53	44	53	1	....	....	34	38.4	17.7	3.5	2.9	.339
68-69	Minnesota-A	5	....	57	34	11	37	.297	6	21	.286	6	7	.857	....	....	6	1	5	0	....	....	1	11.4	6.8	1.2	0.2	.270
NBA Playoff Totals		27	....	631	240	98	226	.434	....	....	....	44	61	.721	....	....	62	62	91	2	....	....	....	23.4	8.9	2.3	2.3	....
ABA Playoff Totals		20	....	633	300	101	293	.345	30	114	.263	68	85	.800	....	....	59	45	58	1	....	....	35	31.7	15.0	3.0	2.3	....
Career Playoff Totals		47	....	1264	540	199	519	.383	30	114	.263	112	146	.767	....	....	121	107	149	3	....	....	35	26.9	11.5	2.6	2.3	....

• VAUGHN, David

David Vaughn III

Born: Mar. 23, 1973. Tulsa, OK, United States. Height: 6'9". Weight: 240 lbs. Drafted: 1995 College: Memphis

YEAR	TEAM	GP	GS	MIN	PTS	FGM	FGA	FG%	3PM	3PA	3P%	FTM	FTA	FT%	ORB	DRB	TRB	AST	PF	DQ	STL	BLK	TO	MPG	PPG	RPG	APG	PCM
95-96	Orlando	33	0	266	64	27	80	.338	0	1	.000	10	18	.556	33	47	80	8	68	2	6	15	17	8.1	1.9	2.4	0.2	.248
96-97	Orlando	35	6	298	81	31	72	.431	0	0	.000	19	30	.633	35	60	95	7	43	0	8	15	28	8.5	2.3	2.7	0.2	.366
97-98	Golden State	22	0	322	114	46	114	.404	0	1	.000	22	34	.647	34	68	102	18	48	1	10	6	31	14.6	5.2	4.6	0.8	.383
97-98	Chicago	3	0	6	4	1	1	1.000	0	0	.000	2	4	.500	0	1	1	0	1	0	0	0	0	2.0	1.3	0.3	0.0	.590
97-98	New Jersey	15	2	161	44	19	33	.576	0	0	.000	6	9	.667	19	30	49	2	34	0	5	4	9	10.7	2.9	3.3	0.1	.381
98-99	New Jersey	10	0	103	34	13	24	.542	0	0	.000	8	10	.800	13	21	34	1	22	0	2	8	11	10.3	3.4	3.4	0.1	.427
NBA Season Totals		118	8	1156	341	137	324	.423	0	2	.000	67	105	.638	134	227	361	36	216	3	31	48	96	9.8	2.9	3.1	0.3	....
97-98	New Jersey	1	0	1	0	0	0	.000	0	0	.000	0	0	.000	0	0	0	0	0	0	0	1	0	1.0	0.0	0.0	0.0	.915
NBA Playoff Totals		1	0	1	0	0	0	.000	0	0	.000	0	0	.000	0	0	0	0	0	0	0	1	0	1.0	0.0	0.0	0.0	....

• VAUGHN, David

David Vaughn

Born: June 4, 1952. Nashville, TN, United States. Height: 6'11". Weight: 220 lbs. Drafted: 1975 College: Oral Roberts

YEAR	TEAM	GP	GS	MIN	PTS	FGM	FGA	FG%	3PM	3PA	3P%	FTM	FTA	FT%	ORB	DRB	TRB	AST	PF	DQ	STL	BLK	TO	MPG	PPG	RPG	APG	PCM
74-75	Virginia-A	83	....	2507	969	422	998	.423	0	2	.000	125	229	.546	276	618	894	132	274	....	79	126	195	30.2	11.7	10.8	1.6	.491
75-76	Virginia-A	10	....	86	29	12	33	.364	0	0	.000	5	8	.625	8	11	19	3	15	....	0	2	5	8.6	2.9	1.9	0.3	.262
ABA Season Totals		93	....	2593	998	434	1031	.421	0	2	.000	130	237	.549	284	629	913	135	289	....	79	128	200	27.9	10.7	9.8	1.5	....

• VAUGHN, Jacque

Jacque Vaughn

Born: Feb. 11, 1975. Los Angeles, CA, United States. Height: 6'1". Weight: 190 lbs. Drafted: 1997 College: Kansas

YEAR	TEAM	GP	GS	MIN	PTS	FGM	FGA	FG%	3PM	3PA	3P%	FTM	FTA	FT%	ORB	DRB	TRB	AST	PF	DQ	STL	BLK	TO	MPG	PPG	RPG	APG	PCM
97-98	Utah	45	0	419	139	44	122	.361	3	8	.375	48	68	.706	4	34	38	84	63	1	9	1	54	9.3	3.1	0.8	1.9	.275
98-99	Utah	19	0	87	44	11	30	.367	2	8	.250	20	24	.833	1	10	11	12	14	0	5	0	14	4.6	2.3	0.6	0.6	.393
99-00	Utah	78	0	884	289	109	262	.416	14	34	.412	57	76	.750	11	54	65	121	92	0	32	0	77	11.3	3.7	0.8	1.6	.283
00-01	Utah	82	0	1620	498	170	393	.433	30	78	.385	128	164	.780	18	132	150	323	145	0	48	3	129	19.8	6.1	1.8	3.9	.393
01-02	Atlanta	82	16	1856	540	206	438	.470	24	54	.444	104	126	.825	18	150	168	349	183	0	65	2	112	22.6	6.6	2.0	4.3	.393
02-03	Orlando	80	48	1686	473	184	411	.448	8	34	.235	97	125	.776	26	92	118	232	169	1	64	2	97	21.1	5.9	1.5	2.9	.302
NBA Season Totals		386	64	6552	1983	724	1656	.437	81	216	.375	454	583	.779	78	472	550	1121	666	2	223	8	483	17.0	5.1	1.4	2.9	....
97-98	Utah	7	0	24	7	2	10	.200	1	2	.500	2	2	1.000	0	3	3	4	0	0	0	0	4	3.4	1.0	0.4	0.6	.129
98-99	Utah	2	0	6	3	1	2	.500	1	1	1.000	0	0	.000	0	0	0	2	2	0	0	0	0	3.0	1.5	0.0	1.0	.574
99-00	Utah	7	0	67	28	10	28	.357	1	2	.500	7	8	.875	4	8	12	11	5	0	4	1	9	9.6	4.0	1.7	1.6	.421
00-01	Utah	5	0	57	3	1	10	.100	1	2	.500	0	0	.000	0	2	2	8	13	0	0	1	1	11.4	0.6	0.4	1.6	-.005
02-03	Orlando	7	6	131	34	12	33	.364	0	1	.000	10	13	.769	1	5	6	25	18	0	4	1	9	18.7	4.9	0.9	3.6	.263
NBA Playoff Totals		28	6	285	75	26	83	.313	4	8	.500	19	23	.826	5	18	23	50	38	0	8	3	23	10.2	2.7	0.8	1.8	....

• VAUGHN, Ralph

Ralph Lincoln Vaughn

Born: Feb. 12, 1918. Frankfort, IN, United States. Died: June7, 1980. Height: 6'1". Weight: 175 lbs. Drafted: — College: Southern California

YEAR	TEAM	GP	GS	MIN	PTS	FGM	FGA	FG%	3PM	3PA	3P%	FTM	FTA	FT%	ORB	DRB	TRB	AST	PF	DQ	STL	BLK	TO	MPG	PPG	RPG	APG	PCM
40-41	Chicago-N	3	....	....	16	5	....	....	....	....	....	6	....	....	....	....	....	....	....	....	....	....	....	....	5.3	....	....	....
40-41	Hammond-N	20	....	....	179	64	....	....	....	....	....	51	....	....	....	....	....	....	....	....	....	....	....	....	9.0	....	....	....
41-42	Chicago-N	21	....	....	190	72	....	....	....	....	....	46	....	....	....	....	....	....	....	....	....	....	....	....	9.0	....	....	....

YEAR	TEAM	GP	GS	MIN	PTS	FGM	FGA	FG%	3PM	3PA	3P%	FTM	FTA	FT%	ORB	DRB	TRB	AST	PF	DQ	STL	BLK	TO	MPG	PPG	RPG	APG	PCM
42-43	Oshkosh-N	22	....	....	222	86	....	....	....	....	....	50	....	....	....	....	....	....	....	....	....	....	....	....	10.1	....	....	....
46-47	Oshkosh-N	35	....	....	201	76	....	....	....	....	....	49	64	.766	....	....	....	....	33	....	....	....	....	....	5.7	....	....	....
NBL Season Totals		101	....	....	808	303						202	64						33						8.0			
42-43	Oshkosh-N	2	....	....	14	7	....	....	....	....	....	0	....	....											7.0			
46-47	Oshkosh-N	7	....	....	61	25	....	....	....	....	....	11	16	.688											8.7			
NBL Playoff Totals		9	....	....	75	32						11	16												8.3			

• VAUGHN, Virgil
Virgil V. Vaughn

Born: May 15, 1918.   Height: 6'4".   Weight: 205 lbs.   Drafted: —   College: Western Kentucky

YEAR	TEAM	GP	GS	MIN	PTS	FGM	FGA	FG%	3PM	3PA	3P%	FTM	FTA	FT%	ORB	DRB	TRB	AST	PF	DQ	STL	BLK	TO	MPG	PPG	RPG	APG	PCM
46-47	Boston	17	....	....	45	15	78	.192	....	....	....	15	28	.536	....	....	....	....	10	18	....	....	....	....	2.6	....	0.6	
47-48	Syracuse-N	11	....	....	63	29	....	....	....	....	....	5	9	.556											5.7			
NBA Season Totals		17	....	....	45	15	78	.192				15	28	.536					10	18					2.6		0.6	
NBL Season Totals		11	....	....	63	29						5	9												5.7			
Career Totals		28	....	....	108	44	78					20	37						10	18					3.9		0.4	
47-48	Syracuse-N	3	....	....	10	2	....	....	....	....	....	6	11	.545											3.3			
NBL Playoff Totals		3	....	....	10	2						6	11												3.3			

• VAUGHT, Loy
Loy Stephen Vaught

Born: Feb. 27, 1968. Grand Rapids, MI, United States.   Height: 6'9".   Weight: 230 lbs.   Drafted: 1990   College: Michigan

YEAR	TEAM	GP	GS	MIN	PTS	FGM	FGA	FG%	3PM	3PA	3P%	FTM	FTA	FT%	ORB	DRB	TRB	AST	PF	DQ	STL	BLK	TO	MPG	PPG	RPG	APG	PCM
90-91	LA Clippers	73	0	1178	399	175	359	.487	0	2	.000	49	74	.662	124	225	349	40	135	2	20	23	51	16.1	5.5	4.8	0.5	.436
91-92	LA Clippers	79	38	1687	601	271	551	.492	4	5	.800	55	69	.797	160	352	512	71	165	1	37	31	63	21.4	7.6	6.5	0.9	.483
92-93	LA Clippers	79	4	1653	743	313	616	.508	1	4	.250	116	155	.748	164	328	492	54	172	2	55	39	87	20.9	9.4	6.2	0.7	.535
93-94	LA Clippers	75	56	2118	877	373	695	.537	0	5	.000	131	182	.720	218	438	656	74	221	5	76	22	98	28.2	11.7	8.7	1.0	.538
94-95	LA Clippers	80	79	2966	1401	609	1185	.514	7	33	.212	176	248	.710	261	511	772	139	243	4	104	29	168	37.1	17.5	9.7	1.7	.523
95-96	LA Clippers	80	78	2966	1298	571	1087	.525	7	19	.368	149	205	.727	204	604	808	112	241	4	87	40	160	37.1	16.2	10.1	1.4	.513
96-97	LA Clippers	82	82	2838	1220	542	1084	.500	2	12	.167	134	191	.702	222	595	817	110	241	3	85	25	139	34.6	14.9	10.0	1.3	.503
97-98	LA Clippers	10	6	265	75	36	84	.429	0	2	.000	3	8	.375	16	49	65	7	33	0	4	2	13	26.5	7.5	6.5	0.7	.281
98-99	Detroit	37	10	481	127	59	155	.381	0	1	.000	9	14	.643	36	110	146	11	54	0	15	6	17	13.0	3.4	3.9	0.3	.335
99-00	Detroit	43	0	292	75	32	89	.360	0	3	.000	11	16	.688	26	65	91	11	45	0	6	4	11	6.8	1.7	2.1	0.3	.323
00-01	Dallas	37	1	392	114	55	121	.455	0	0	.000	4	6	.667	35	88	123	16	61	0	15	5	18	10.6	3.1	3.3	0.4	.399
00-01	Washington	14	0	157	54	25	48	.521	0	0	.000	4	4	1.000	16	34	50	7	13	0	6	2	8	11.2	3.9	3.6	0.5	.510
NBA Season Totals		689	354	16993	6984	3061	6074	.504	21	86	.244	841	1172	.718	1482	3399	4881	652	1624	21	510	228	833	24.7	10.1	7.1	0.9	....
91-92	LA Clippers	5	0	36	17	7	11	.636	1	1	1.000	2	2	1.000	2	10	12	4	3	0	1	1	1	7.2	3.4	2.4	0.8	.785
92-93	LA Clippers	3	0	50	16	6	15	.400	0	0	.000	4	5	.800	4	14	18	0	7	0	4	1	3	16.7	5.3	6.0	0.0	.451
96-97	LA Clippers	3	3	90	45	19	31	.613	1	3	.333	6	9	.667	5	22	27	2	12	1	3	2	6	30.0	15.0	9.0	0.7	.591
98-99	Detroit	2	0	15	4	2	4	.500	0	0	.000	0	0	.000	0	1	1	0	1	0	1	0	0	7.5	2.0	0.5	0.0	.237
99-00	Detroit	2	0	16	0	0	3	.000	0	0	.000	0	0	.000	1	5	6	0	1	0	2	0	1	8.0	0.0	3.0	0.0	.199
NBA Playoff Totals		15	3	207	82	34	64	.531	2	4	.500	12	16	.750	12	52	64	6	24	1	11	4	11	13.8	5.5	4.3	0.4	....

• VERGA, Bob
Robert Bruce Verga

Born: Sept. 7, 1945. Neptune, NJ, United States.   Height: 6'1".   Weight: 190 lbs.   Drafted: 1967   College: Duke

YEAR	TEAM	GP	GS	MIN	PTS	FGM	FGA	FG%	3PM	3PA	3P%	FTM	FTA	FT%	ORB	DRB	TRB	AST	PF	DQ	STL	BLK	TO	MPG	PPG	RPG	APG	PCM
67-68	Dallas-A	31	....	1285	735	280	633	.442	13	50	.260	162	218	.743	....	....	138	74	93	1	....	....	95	41.5	23.7	4.5	2.4	.452
68-69	Denver-A	6	....	150	67	24	77	.312	1	3	.333	18	28	.643	10	11	21	11	16	0	....	....	25	25.0	11.2	3.5	1.8	.273
68-69	Houston-A	33	....	1133	814	293	656	.447	13	47	.277	215	282	.762	89	55	144	136	116	0	....	....	119	34.3	24.7	4.4	4.1	.620
68-69	New York-A	24	....	521	306	99	273	.363	5	18	.278	103	144	.715	27	41	68	41	68	1	....	....	51	21.7	12.8	2.8	1.7	.413
69-70	Carolina-A	82	....	3411	2258	867	1984	.437	66	215	.307	458	565	.811	176	254	430	290	268	3	....	....	313	41.6	27.5	5.2	3.5	.539
70-71	Carolina-A	75	....	2009	1412	550	1202	.458	10	44	.227	302	419	.721	167	113	280	182	223	2	....	....	164	26.8	18.8	3.7	2.4	.595
71-72	Carolina-A	8	....	127	59	23	59	.390	3	10	.300	10	13	.769	5	3	8	10	20	0	....	....	12	15.9	7.4	1.0	1.3	.279
71-72	Pittsburgh-A	62	....	1902	1163	436	987	.442	16	42	.381	275	385	.714	91	138	229	243	178	1	....	....	212	30.7	18.8	3.7	3.9	.539
73-74	Portland	21	....	216	104	42	93	.452	....	....	....	20	32	.625	11	7	18	17	22	0	12	0	....	10.3	5.0	0.9	0.8	.375
NBA Season Totals		21	....	216	104	42	93	.452	....	....	....	20	32	.625	11	7	18	17	22	0	12	0	....	10.3	5.0	0.9	0.8	
ABA Season Totals		321	....	10538	6814	2572	5871	.438	127	429	.296	1543	2054	.751	565	615	1318	987	982	8	....	....	991	32.8	21.2	4.1	3.1	
Career Totals		342	....	10754	6918	2614	5964	.438	127	429	.296	1563	2086	.749	576	622	1336	1004	1004	8	12	0	991	31.4	20.2	3.9	2.9	
69-70	Carolina-A	4	....	156	108	48	102	.471	4	16	.250	8	11	.727	....	....	11	10	....	....	....	....	....	39.0	27.0	2.8	2.5	
ABA Playoff Totals		4	....	156	108	48	102	.471	4	16	.250	8	11	.727	....	....	11	10	....	....	....	....	....	39.0	27.0	2.8	2.5	

• VERHOEVEN, Pete
Peter Gerard Verhoeven

Born: Feb. 15, 1959. Hanford, CA, United States.   Height: 6'9".   Weight: 215 lbs.   Drafted: 1981   College: Fresno State

YEAR	TEAM	GP	GS	MIN	PTS	FGM	FGA	FG%	3PM	3PA	3P%	FTM	FTA	FT%	ORB	DRB	TRB	AST	PF	DQ	STL	BLK	TO	MPG	PPG	RPG	APG	PCM
81-82	Portland	71	22	1207	349	149	296	.503	0	0	.000	51	72	.708	106	148	254	52	215	4	42	22	57	17.0	4.9	3.6	0.7	.333
82-83	Portland	48	0	527	195	87	171	.509	0	1	.000	21	31	.677	44	52	96	32	95	2	18	9	38	11.0	4.1	2.0	0.7	.349
83-84	Portland	43	0	327	117	50	100	.500	0	1	.000	17	25	.680	27	34	61	20	75	0	22	11	22	7.6	2.7	1.4	0.5	.368
84-85	Kansas City	54	0	366	123	51	108	.472	0	0	.000	21	25	.840	28	35	63	17	85	1	15	7	22	6.8	2.3	1.2	0.3	.288
85-86	Golden State	61	5	749	206	90	167	.539	1	2	.500	25	43	.581	65	95	160	29	141	3	29	17	31	12.3	3.4	2.6	0.5	.339
86-87	Indiana	5	0	44	10	5	14	.357	0	0	.000	0	0	.000	2	5	7	2	11	1	2	1	0	8.8	2.0	1.4	0.4	.181
NBA Season Totals		282	27	3220	1000	432	856	.505	1	4	.250	135	196	.689	272	369	641	152	622	11	128	67	170	11.4	3.5	2.3	0.5	
83-84	Portland	3	0	19	2	0	0	.000	0	0	.000	2	2	1.000	0	0	0	0	10	0	1	0	1	6.3	0.7	0.0	0.0	-.139
NBA Playoff Totals		3	0	19	2	0	0	.000	0	0	.000	2	2	1.000	0	0	0	0	10	0	1	0	1	6.3	0.7	0.0	0.0	

VETRA, Gundars

Gundars Vetra

Born: May 22, 1967. Ventspils, Latvia.   Height: 6'6".   Weight: 195 lbs.   Drafted: —   College: none

YEAR TEAM	GP	GS	MIN	PTS	FGM	FGA	FG%	3PM	3PA	3P%	FTM	FTA	FT%	ORB	DRB	TRB	AST	PF	DQ	STL	BLK	TO	MPG	PPG	RPG	APG	PCM
92-93 Minnesota	13	0	89	45	19	40	.475	3	3	1.000	4	6	.667	4	4	8	6	12	0	2	0	3	6.8	3.5	0.6	0.5	.357
NBA Season Totals	13	0	89	45	19	40	.475	3	3	1.000	4	6	.667	4	4	8	6	12	0	2	0	3	6.8	3.5	0.6	0.5	....

VIANNA, Joao

Joao Jose Vianna

Born: Nov. 15, 1966. Trabajara, Brazil.   Height: 6'9".   Weight: 215 lbs.   Drafted: —   College: none

YEAR TEAM	GP	GS	MIN	PTS	FGM	FGA	FG%	3PM	3PA	3P%	FTM	FTA	FT%	ORB	DRB	TRB	AST	PF	DQ	STL	BLK	TO	MPG	PPG	RPG	APG	PCM
91-92 Dallas	1	0	9	2	1	2	.500	0	0	.000	0	0	.000	0	0	0	2	3	0	0	0	1	9.0	2.0	0.0	2.0	.099
NBA Season Totals	1	0	9	2	1	2	.500	0	0	.000	0	0	.000	0	0	0	2	3	0	0	0	1	9.0	2.0	0.0	2.0	....

VINCENT, Jay

Jay Fletcher Vincent

Born: June 10, 1959. Kalamazoo, MI, United States.   Height: 6'7".   Weight: 220 lbs.   Drafted: 1981   College: Michigan State

YEAR TEAM	GP	GS	MIN	PTS	FGM	FGA	FG%	3PM	3PA	3P%	FTM	FTA	FT%	ORB	DRB	TRB	AST	PF	DQ	STL	BLK	TO	MPG	PPG	RPG	APG	PCM
81-82 Dallas	81	62	2626	1732	719	1448	.497	1	4	.250	293	409	.716	182	383	565	176	308	8	89	22	194	32.4	21.4	7.0	2.2	.571
82-83 Dallas	81	73	2726	1513	622	1272	.489	0	3	.000	269	343	.784	217	375	592	212	295	3	70	45	186	33.7	18.7	7.3	2.6	.537
83-84 Dallas	61	5	1421	672	252	579	.435	0	1	.000	168	215	.781	81	166	247	114	159	1	30	10	116	23.3	11.0	4.0	1.9	.389
84-85 Dallas	79	47	2543	1441	545	1138	.479	0	4	.000	351	420	.836	185	519	704	169	226	0	48	22	174	32.2	18.2	8.9	2.1	.586
85-86 Dallas	80	3	1994	1106	442	919	.481	0	3	.000	222	274	.810	107	261	368	180	193	2	66	21	144	24.9	13.8	4.6	2.3	.517
86-87 Washington	51	17	1386	678	274	613	.447	0	3	.000	130	169	.769	69	141	210	85	127	0	40	17	77	27.2	13.3	4.1	1.7	.399
87-88 Denver	73	8	1755	1124	446	958	.466	1	4	.250	231	287	.805	80	229	309	143	198	1	46	26	139	24.0	15.4	4.2	2.0	.517
88-89 Denver	5	1	95	32	13	38	.342	1	2	.500	5	9	.556	2	16	18	5	11	0	1	1	5	19.0	6.4	3.6	1.0	.222
88-89 San Antonio	24	3	551	217	91	219	.416	0	1	.000	35	51	.686	36	56	92	22	52	0	5	3	36	23.0	9.0	3.8	0.9	.271
89-90 Philadelphia	17	5	259	124	45	105	.429	1	1	1.000	33	37	.892	13	23	36	8	23	0	10	2	14	15.2	7.3	2.1	0.5	.369
89-90 LA Lakers	24	1	200	90	41	78	.526	0	1	.000	8	12	.667	7	19	26	10	29	0	8	3	19	8.3	3.8	1.1	0.4	.337
NBA Season Totals	576	225	15556	8729	3490	7367	.474	4	27	.148	1745	2226	.784	979	2188	3167	1124	1621	15	413	172	1104	27.0	15.2	5.5	2.0	....
83-84 Dallas	10	10	353	152	48	124	.387	0	1	.000	56	62	.903	29	41	70	19	36	1	7	1	25	35.3	15.2	7.0	1.9	.372
84-85 Dallas	4	2	134	62	20	56	.357	0	0	.000	22	29	.759	9	13	22	3	16	0	6	3	11	33.5	15.5	5.5	0.8	.295
85-86 Dallas	10	0	204	106	38	99	.384	0	0	.000	30	34	.882	15	24	39	15	19	0	4	1	17	20.4	10.6	3.9	1.5	.391
86-87 Washington	3	0	72	30	11	30	.367	0	1	.000	8	9	.889	2	7	9	3	10	0	2	0	4	24.0	10.0	3.0	1.0	.235
87-88 Denver	8	0	200	140	53	104	.510	0	1	.000	34	40	.850	10	27	37	6	25	0	5	4	14	25.0	17.5	4.6	0.8	.571
89-90 LA Lakers	3	0	8	0	0	2	.000	0	0	.000	0	0	.000	0	0	0	0	1	0	0	0	2	2.7	0.0	0.0	0.0	-.527
NBA Playoff Totals	38	12	971	490	170	415	.410	0	2	.000	150	174	.862	65	112	177	46	107	1	24	9	73	25.6	12.9	4.7	1.2	....

VINCENT, Sam

James Samuel Vincent

Born: May 18, 1963. Lansing, MI, United States.   Height: 6'2".   Weight: 185 lbs.   Drafted: 1985   College: Michigan State

YEAR TEAM	GP	GS	MIN	PTS	FGM	FGA	FG%	3PM	3PA	3P%	FTM	FTA	FT%	ORB	DRB	TRB	AST	PF	DQ	STL	BLK	TO	MPG	PPG	RPG	APG	PCM
85-86 Boston	57	0	432	184	59	162	.364	1	4	.250	65	70	.929	11	37	48	69	59	0	17	4	51	7.6	3.2	0.8	1.2	.345
86-87 Boston	46	5	374	171	60	136	.441	0	0	.000	51	55	.927	5	22	27	59	33	0	13	1	32	8.1	3.7	0.6	1.3	.413
87-88 Seattle	43	0	548	195	72	152	.474	5	13	.385	46	60	.767	17	32	49	137	63	0	21	4	52	12.7	4.5	1.1	3.2	.459
87-88 Chicago	29	27	953	378	138	309	.447	3	8	.375	99	107	.925	18	85	103	244	82	0	34	12	84	32.9	13.0	3.6	8.4	.522
88-89 Chicago	70	56	1703	656	274	566	.484	2	17	.118	106	129	.822	34	156	190	335	124	0	53	10	140	24.3	9.4	2.7	4.8	.458
89-90 Orlando	63	45	1657	705	258	564	.457	1	14	.071	188	214	.879	37	157	194	354	108	1	65	20	132	26.3	11.2	3.1	5.6	.525
90-91 Orlando	49	17	975	406	152	353	.431	3	19	.158	99	120	.825	17	90	107	197	74	0	30	5	93	19.9	8.3	2.2	4.0	.441
91-92 Orlando	39	18	885	411	150	349	.430	1	13	.077	110	130	.846	19	82	101	148	55	1	35	4	70	22.7	10.5	2.6	3.8	.469
NBA Season Totals	396	168	7527	3106	1163	2591	.449	16	88	.182	764	885	.863	158	661	819	1543	598	2	268	60	654	19.0	7.8	2.1	3.9	....
85-86 Boston	9	0	41	22	8	28	.286	0	1	.000	6	6	1.000	1	6	7	5	9	0	2	0	4	4.6	2.4	0.8	0.6	.225
86-87 Boston	17	0	141	74	23	56	.411	1	2	.500	27	35	.771	3	9	12	19	13	0	3	2	10	8.3	4.4	0.7	1.1	.428
87-88 Chicago	10	10	251	102	41	110	.373	0	3	.000	20	25	.800	6	13	19	44	23	0	8	1	27	25.1	10.2	1.9	4.4	.289
88-89 Chicago	16	0	113	29	10	33	.303	0	2	.000	9	12	.750	4	4	8	19	9	0	3	1	6	7.1	1.8	0.5	1.2	.247
NBA Playoff Totals	52	10	546	227	82	227	.361	1	8	.125	62	78	.795	14	32	46	87	54	0	16	4	47	10.5	4.4	0.9	1.7	....

VINSON, Fred

Frederick O'Neal Vinson

Born: Jan. 28, 1971. Murfreesboro, NC, United States.   Height: 6'4".   Weight: 190 lbs.   Drafted: —   College: Georgia Tech

YEAR TEAM	GP	GS	MIN	PTS	FGM	FGA	FG%	3PM	3PA	3P%	FTM	FTA	FT%	ORB	DRB	TRB	AST	PF	DQ	STL	BLK	TO	MPG	PPG	RPG	APG	PCM
94-95 Atlanta	5	0	27	4	1	7	.143	1	6	.167	1	1	1.000	0	0	0	1	4	0	0	0	2	5.4	0.8	0.0	0.2	-.160
99-00 Seattle	8	0	40	13	5	17	.294	2	7	.286	1	2	.500	0	1	1	0	2	0	3	0	4	5.0	1.6	0.1	0.0	.019
NBA Season Totals	13	0	67	17	6	24	.250	3	13	.231	2	3	.667	0	1	1	1	6	0	3	0	6	5.2	1.3	0.1	0.1	....

VIRDEN, Claude

Claude Felton Virden

Born: Nov. 25, 1947. Akron, OH, United States.   Height: 6'6".   Weight: 195 lbs.   Drafted: 1970   College: Murray State

YEAR TEAM	GP	GS	MIN	PTS	FGM	FGA	FG%	3PM	3PA	3P%	FTM	FTA	FT%	ORB	DRB	TRB	AST	PF	DQ	STL	BLK	TO	MPG	PPG	RPG	APG	PCM
72-73 Kentucky-A	31	....	825	306	130	327	.398	0	2	.000	46	59	.780	49	105	154	74	84	0	....	....	49	26.6	9.9	5.0	2.4	.370
ABA Season Totals	31	....	825	306	130	327	.398	0	2	.000	46	59	.780	49	105	154	74	84	0	....	....	49	26.6	9.9	5.0	2.4	....

VOCE, Gary

Gary Anthony Voce

Born: Nov. 24, 1965. Jamaica.   Height: 6'9".   Weight: 240 lbs.   Drafted: —   College: Notre Dame

YEAR TEAM	GP	GS	MIN	PTS	FGM	FGA	FG%	3PM	3PA	3P%	FTM	FTA	FT%	ORB	DRB	TRB	AST	PF	DQ	STL	BLK	TO	MPG	PPG	RPG	APG	PCM
89-90 Cleveland	1	0	4	2	1	3	.333	0	0	.000	0	0	.000	2	0	2	0	0	0	0	0	0	4.0	2.0	2.0	0.0	.500
NBA Season Totals	1	0	4	2	1	3	.333	0	0	.000	0	0	.000	2	0	2	0	0	0	0	0	0	4.0	2.0	2.0	0.0	....

VOCKE, Howard
Howard Vocke

Born: 1915.   Height: 6'3".   Weight: 190 lbs.   Drafted: —   College: St. John's (NY)

YEAR	TEAM	GP	GS	MIN	PTS	FGM	FGA	FG%	3PM	3PA	3P%	FTM	FTA	FT%	ORB	DRB	TRB	AST	PF	DQ	STL	BLK	TO	MPG	PPG	RPG	APG	PCM
39-40	Wingfoots-N	27	....	....	140	49	....	....	....	....	....	42	....	....	....	....	....	....	....	....	....	....	....	5.2	....	....	....	....
40-41	Wingfoots-N	24	....	....	113	48	....	....	....	....	....	17	....	....	....	....	....	....	....	....	....	....	....	4.7	....	....	....	....
41-42	Wingfoots-N	24	....	....	81	34	....	....	....	....	....	13	....	....	....	....	....	....	....	....	....	....	....	3.4	....	....	....	....
NBL Season Totals		75	....	....	334	131	....	....	....	....	....	72	....	....	....	....	....	....	....	....	....	....	....	4.5	....	....	....	....
41-42	Wingfoots-N	3	....	....	13	5	....	....	....	....	....	3	....	....	....	....	....	....	....	....	....	....	....	4.3	....	....	....	....
NBL Playoff Totals		3	....	....	13	5	....	....	....	....	....	3	....	....	....	....	....	....	....	....	....	....	....	4.3	....	....	....	....

VOLKER, Floyd
Floyd W. Volker

Born: June 21, 1921. Casper, WY, United States. Died: Jan.5, 1995.   Height: 6'4".   Weight: 205 lbs.   Drafted: —   College: Wyoming

YEAR	TEAM	GP	GS	MIN	PTS	FGM	FGA	FG%	3PM	3PA	3P%	FTM	FTA	FT%	ORB	DRB	TRB	AST	PF	DQ	STL	BLK	TO	MPG	PPG	RPG	APG	PCM
47-48	Oshkosh-N	57	....	....	235	102	....	....	....	....	....	31	66	.470	....	....	133	....	....	....	....	....	....	4.1	....	....	....
48-49	Oshkosh-N	64	....	....	410	166	....	....	....	....	....	78	134	.582	....	....	190	....	....	....	....	....	....	6.4	....	....	....
49-50	Indianapolis	17	....	....	41	17	53	.321	....	....	....	7	18	.389	....	....	....	7	32	....	....	....	....	2.4	....	0.4	....
49-50	Denver	37	....	....	356	146	474	.308	....	....	....	64	111	.577	....	....	....	105	137	....	....	....	....	9.6	....	2.8	....
NBA Season Totals		54	....	....	397	163	527	.309	....	....	....	71	129	.550	....	....	....	112	169	....	....	....	....	7.4	....	2.1	....
NBL Season Totals		121	....	....	645	268	....	....	....	....	....	109	200	....	....	....	323	....	....	....	....	....	....	5.3	....	....	....
Career Totals		175	....	....	1042	431	527	....	....	....	....	180	329	....	....	....	112	492	....	....	....	....	....	6.0	....	0.6	....
47-48	Oshkosh-N	4	....	....	28	12	....	....	....	....	....	4	5	.800	....	....	....	....	....	....	....	....	....	7.0	....	....	....
48-49	Oshkosh-N	7	....	....	53	22	....	....	....	....	....	9	17	.529	....	....	....	....	....	....	....	....	....	7.6	....	....	....
NBL Playoff Totals		11	....	....	81	34	....	....	....	....	....	13	22	....	....	....	....	....	....	....	....	....	....	7.4	....	....	....

VOLKOV, Alexander
Alexander Volkov

Born: Mar. 29, 1964. Omsk, Soviet Union.   Height: 6'10".   Weight: 218 lbs.   Drafted: —   College: Kiev Institute (Ukraine)

YEAR	TEAM	GP	GS	MIN	PTS	FGM	FGA	FG%	3PM	3PA	3P%	FTM	FTA	FT%	ORB	DRB	TRB	AST	PF	DQ	STL	BLK	TO	MPG	PPG	RPG	APG	PCM
89-90	Atlanta	72	4	937	357	137	284	.482	13	34	.382	70	120	.583	52	67	119	83	166	3	36	22	50	13.0	5.0	1.7	1.2	.347
91-92	Atlanta	77	27	1516	662	251	569	.441	35	110	.318	125	198	.631	103	162	265	250	178	2	66	30	100	19.7	8.6	3.4	3.2	.501
NBA Season Totals		149	31	2453	1019	388	853	.455	48	144	.333	195	318	.613	155	229	384	333	344	5	102	52	150	16.5	6.8	2.6	2.2	....

VON NIEDA, Whitey
Stanley L. (Whitey) Von Nieda Jr.

Born: June 19, 1922.   Height: 6'1".   Weight: 170 lbs.   Drafted: —   College: Penn State

YEAR	TEAM	GP	GS	MIN	PTS	FGM	FGA	FG%	3PM	3PA	3P%	FTM	FTA	FT%	ORB	DRB	TRB	AST	PF	DQ	STL	BLK	TO	MPG	PPG	RPG	APG	PCM
47-48	Tri-Cities-N	60	....	....	726	276	....	....	....	....	....	174	287	.606	....	....	144	....	....	....	....	....	....	12.1	....	....	....
48-49	Tri-Cities-N	64	....	....	641	247	....	....	....	....	....	147	226	.650	....	....	141	....	....	....	....	....	....	10.0	....	....	....
49-50	Tri-Cities	26	....	....	109	40	116	.345	....	....	....	29	46	.630	....	....	36	48	....	....	....	....	....	4.2	....	1.4	....
49-50	Baltimore	33	....	....	204	80	220	.364	....	....	....	44	69	.638	....	....	107	79	....	....	....	....	....	6.2	....	3.2	....
NBA Season Totals		59	....	....	313	120	336	.357	....	....	....	73	115	.635	....	....	143	127	....	....	....	....	....	5.3	....	2.4	....
NBL Season Totals		124	....	....	1367	523	....	....	....	....	....	321	513	....	....	....	285	....	....	....	....	....	....	11.0	....	....	....
Career Totals		183	....	....	1680	643	336	....	....	....	....	394	628	....	....	....	143	412	....	....	....	....	....	9.2	....	0.8	....
47-48	Tri-Cities-N	6	....	....	97	41	....	....	....	....	....	15	28	.536	....	....	....	....	....	....	....	....	....	16.2	....	....	....
48-49	Tri-Cities-N	6	....	....	53	20	....	....	....	....	....	13	24	.542	....	....	....	....	....	....	....	....	....	8.8	....	....	....
NBL Playoff Totals		12	....	....	150	61	....	....	....	....	....	28	52	....	....	....	....	....	....	....	....	....	....	12.5	....	....	....

VOORHEIS, Bernie
Bernard Voorheis

Born: 1922. Spencerport, NY, United States.   Height: 5'10".   Weight: 150 lbs.   Drafted: —   College: Cornell

YEAR	TEAM	GP	GS	MIN	PTS	FGM	FGA	FG%	3PM	3PA	3P%	FTM	FTA	FT%	ORB	DRB	TRB	AST	PF	DQ	STL	BLK	TO	MPG	PPG	RPG	APG	PCM
45-46	Rochester-N	8	....	....	0	0	....	....	....	....	....	0	....	....	....	....	....	....	....	....	....	....	....	0.0	....	....	....
NBL Season Totals		8	....	....	0	0	....	....	....	....	....	0	....	....	....	....	....	....	....	....	....	....	....	0.0	....	....	....
45-46	Rochester-N	1	....	....	0	0	....	....	....	....	....	0	....	....	....	....	....	....	....	....	....	....	....	0.0	....	....	....
NBL Playoff Totals		1	....	....	0	0	....	....	....	....	....	0	....	....	....	....	....	....	....	....	....	....	....	0.0	....	....	....

VOSKUHL, Jake
Robert Jake Voskuhl

Born: Nov. 1, 1977. Tulsa, OK, United States.   Height: 6'11".   Weight: 245 lbs.   Drafted: 2000   College: Connecticut

YEAR	TEAM	GP	GS	MIN	PTS	FGM	FGA	FG%	3PM	3PA	3P%	FTM	FTA	FT%	ORB	DRB	TRB	AST	PF	DQ	STL	BLK	TO	MPG	PPG	RPG	APG	PCM
00-01	Chicago	16	2	143	30	11	25	.440	0	0	.000	8	14	.571	12	22	34	5	38	0	5	6	12	8.9	1.9	2.1	0.3	.229
01-02	Phoenix	59	34	900	296	107	193	.554	0	0	.000	82	109	.752	103	147	250	18	139	1	11	23	48	15.3	5.0	4.2	0.3	.418
02-03	Phoenix	65	1	947	248	92	163	.564	0	0	.000	64	96	.667	97	128	225	36	172	0	18	29	48	14.6	3.8	3.5	0.6	.352
NBA Season Totals		140	37	1990	574	210	381	.551	0	0	.000	154	219	.703	212	297	509	59	349	1	34	58	108	14.2	4.1	3.6	0.4	....
02-03	Phoenix	6	0	98	36	12	17	.706	0	0	.000	12	13	.923	9	13	22	2	21	0	4	4	6	16.3	6.0	3.7	0.3	.464
NBA Playoff Totals		6	0	98	36	12	17	.706	0	0	.000	12	13	.923	9	13	22	2	21	0	4	4	6	16.3	6.0	3.7	0.3	....

VRANES, Danny
Daniel LaDrew Vranes

Born: Oct. 29, 1958. Salt Lake City, UT, United States.   Height: 6'7".   Weight: 210 lbs.   Drafted: 1981   College: Utah

YEAR	TEAM	GP	GS	MIN	PTS	FGM	FGA	FG%	3PM	3PA	3P%	FTM	FTA	FT%	ORB	DRB	TRB	AST	PF	DQ	STL	BLK	TO	MPG	PPG	RPG	APG	PCM
81-82	Seattle	77	1	1075	375	143	262	.546	0	1	.000	89	148	.601	71	127	198	56	150	0	28	21	69	14.0	4.9	2.6	0.7	.366
82-83	Seattle	82	73	2054	567	226	429	.527	0	1	.000	115	209	.550	177	248	425	120	254	2	53	49	98	25.0	6.9	5.2	1.5	.363
83-84	Seattle	80	72	2174	669	258	495	.521	0	1	.000	153	236	.648	150	245	395	132	263	4	51	54	120	27.2	8.4	4.9	1.7	.360
84-85	Seattle	76	70	2163	440	186	402	.463	1	4	.250	67	127	.528	154	282	436	152	256	4	76	57	122	28.5	5.8	5.7	2.0	.310

YEAR	TEAM	GP	GS	MIN	PTS	FGM	FGA	FG%	3PM	3PA	3P%	FTM	FTA	FT%	ORB	DRB	TRB	AST	PF	DQ	STL	BLK	TO	MPG	PPG	RPG	APG	PCM
85-86	Seattle	80	19	1569	301	131	284	.461	0	4	.000	39	75	.520	115	166	281	68	218	3	63	31	56	19.6	3.8	3.5	0.9	.261
86-87	Philadelphia	58	6	817	140	59	138	.428	1	5	.200	21	45	.467	51	95	146	30	127	0	35	25	23	14.1	2.4	2.5	0.5	.243
87-88	Philadelphia	57	5	772	121	53	121	.438	0	3	.000	15	35	.429	45	72	117	36	100	0	27	33	23	13.5	2.1	2.1	0.6	.238
NBA Season Totals		510	246	10624	2613	1056	2131	.496	2	19	.105	499	875	.570	763	1235	1998	594	1368	13	333	270	511	20.8	5.1	3.9	1.2	....
81-82	Seattle	6	0	29	3	1	5	.200	0	0	.000	1	2	.500	1	1	2	0	2	0	1	0	2	4.8	0.5	0.3	0.0	-.039
82-83	Seattle	2	2	56	12	6	17	.353	0	0	.000	0	0	.000	9	10	19	1	7	0	0	1	1	28.0	6.0	9.5	0.5	.306
83-84	Seattle	5	5	147	36	16	39	.410	0	1	.000	4	7	.571	16	22	38	11	24	1	3	6	5	29.4	7.2	7.6	2.2	.360
86-87	Philadelphia	2	0	3	0	0	0	.000	0	0	.000	0	0	.000	0	3	3	0	1	0	0	0	0	1.5	0.0	1.5	0.0	.776
NBA Playoff Totals		15	7	235	51	23	61	.377	0	1	.000	5	9	.556	26	36	62	12	34	1	4	7	8	15.7	3.4	4.1	0.8	....

• VRANKOVIC, Stojko
Stojan (Stojko) Vrankovic

Born: Jan. 22, 1964. Drnis, Yugoslavia. Height: 7'2". Weight: 260 lbs. Drafted: — College: none

YEAR	TEAM	GP	GS	MIN	PTS	FGM	FGA	FG%	3PM	3PA	3P%	FTM	FTA	FT%	ORB	DRB	TRB	AST	PF	DQ	STL	BLK	TO	MPG	PPG	RPG	APG	PCM
90-91	Boston	31	0	166	58	24	52	.462	0	0	.000	10	18	.556	15	36	51	4	43	1	1	29	25	5.4	1.9	1.6	0.1	.389
91-92	Boston	19	0	110	37	15	32	.469	0	0	.000	7	12	.583	8	20	28	5	22	0	0	17	10	5.8	1.9	1.5	0.3	.423
96-97	Minnesota	53	35	766	181	78	139	.561	0	0	.000	25	37	.676	57	111	168	14	121	1	10	67	53	14.5	3.4	3.2	0.3	.334
97-98	LA Clippers	65	38	996	195	79	186	.425	0	0	.000	37	65	.569	71	192	263	36	130	3	11	66	46	15.3	3.0	4.0	0.6	.334
98-99	LA Clippers	2	0	12	2	1	4	.250	0	0	.000	0	0	.000	4	2	6	0	2	0	0	0	0	6.0	1.0	3.0	0.0	.315
NBA Season Totals		170	73	2050	473	197	413	.477	0	0	.000	79	132	.598	155	361	516	59	318	5	22	179	134	12.1	2.8	3.0	0.3	....
90-91	Boston	1	0	4	2	1	1	1.000	0	0	.000	0	1	.000	0	2	2	0	2	0	0	0	1	4.0	2.0	2.0	0.0	.383
91-92	Boston	1	0	3	2	1	1	1.000	0	0	.000	0	0	.000	0	0	0	1	0	0	0	0	0	3.0	2.0	0.0	1.0	1.024
96-97	Minnesota	1	0	6	0	0	2	.000	0	0	.000	0	0	.000	1	0	1	0	0	0	0	0	0	6.0	0.0	1.0	0.0	-.155
NBA Playoff Totals		3	0	13	4	2	4	.500	0	0	.000	0	1	.000	1	2	3	1	2	0	0	0	1	4.3	1.3	1.0	0.3	....

• VROMAN, Brett
Brett Grant Vroman

Born: Dec. 25, 1955. Hollywood, CA, United States. Height: 7' Weight: 220 lbs. Drafted: 1978 College: UNLV

YEAR	TEAM	GP	GS	MIN	PTS	FGM	FGA	FG%	3PM	3PA	3P%	FTM	FTA	FT%	ORB	DRB	TRB	AST	PF	DQ	STL	BLK	TO	MPG	PPG	RPG	APG	PCM
80-81	Utah	11	....	93	34	10	27	.370	0	1	.000	14	19	.737	7	18	25	9	26	1	5	5	9	8.5	3.1	2.3	0.8	.407
NBA Season Totals		11	....	93	34	10	27	.370	0	1	.000	14	19	.737	7	18	25	9	26	1	5	5	9	8.5	3.1	2.3	0.8	....

• VUKOSIC, Frank
Frank Vukosic

Born: Apr. 8, 1915. Died: May17, 1989. Height: — Weight: — Drafted: — College: none

YEAR	TEAM	GP	GS	MIN	PTS	FGM	FGA	FG%	3PM	3PA	3P%	FTM	FTA	FT%	ORB	DRB	TRB	AST	PF	DQ	STL	BLK	TO	MPG	PPG	RPG	APG	PCM
44-45	Pittsburgh-N	4	....	....	0	0	....	....	....	....	....	0	....	....	....	....	....	....	....	....	....	....	....	0.0	....	....	....	....
NBL Season Totals		4	....	....	0	0	....	....	....	....	....	0	....	....	....	....	....	....	....	....	....	....	....	0.0	....	....	....	....

• WADDELL, Vaughn
Vaughn Waddell

Born: Sept. 29, 1910. Died: Mar.1980. Height: 6'1". Weight: 190 lbs. Drafted: — College: none

YEAR	TEAM	GP	GS	MIN	PTS	FGM	FGA	FG%	3PM	3PA	3P%	FTM	FTA	FT%	ORB	DRB	TRB	AST	PF	DQ	STL	BLK	TO	MPG	PPG	RPG	APG	PCM
46-47	Detroit-N	8	....	....	25	10	....	....	....	....	....	5	8	.625	....	....	....	....	....	....	....	....	....	3.1	....	....	....	....
NBL Season Totals		8	....	....	25	10	....	....	....	....	....	5	8	....	....	....	....	....	....	....	....	....	....	3.1	....	....	....	....

• WADE, Mark
Mark A. Wade

Born: Oct. 15, 1965. Torrance, CA, United States. Height: 5'11". Weight: 160 lbs. Drafted: — College: UNLV

YEAR	TEAM	GP	GS	MIN	PTS	FGM	FGA	FG%	3PM	3PA	3P%	FTM	FTA	FT%	ORB	DRB	TRB	AST	PF	DQ	STL	BLK	TO	MPG	PPG	RPG	APG	PCM
87-88	Golden State	11	0	123	8	3	20	.150	0	2	.000	2	4	.500	3	12	15	34	13	0	7	1	13	11.2	0.7	1.4	3.1	.250
89-90	Dallas	1	0	3	0	0	0	.000	0	0	.000	0	0	.000	0	0	0	2	0	0	0	0	0	3.0	0.0	0.0	2.0	.709
NBA Season Totals		12	0	126	8	3	20	.150	0	2	.000	2	4	.500	3	12	15	36	13	0	7	1	13	10.5	0.7	1.3	3.0	....

• WAGER, Clint
Clinton B. Wager

Born: Jan. 20, 1920. Winona, MN, United States. Died: Feb.29, 1996. Height: 6'6". Weight: 210 lbs. Drafted: — College: St. Mary's (MN)

YEAR	TEAM	GP	GS	MIN	PTS	FGM	FGA	FG%	3PM	3PA	3P%	FTM	FTA	FT%	ORB	DRB	TRB	AST	PF	DQ	STL	BLK	TO	MPG	PPG	RPG	APG	PCM
43-44	Oshkosh-N	22	....	....	230	79	....	....	....	....	....	72	....	....	....	....	....	....	....	....	....	....	....	10.5	....	....	....	....
44-45	Oshkosh-N	27	....	....	168	70	....	....	....	....	....	28	....	....	....	....	....	....	....	....	....	....	....	6.2	....	....	....	....
45-46	Oshkosh-N	34	....	....	167	68	....	....	....	....	....	31	48	.646	....	....	....	....	....	....	....	....	....	4.9	....	....	....	....
46-47	Oshkosh-N	44	....	....	186	68	....	....	....	....	....	50	69	.725	....	....	....	....	142	....	....	....	....	4.2	....	....	....	....
47-48	Oshkosh-N	59	....	....	236	90	....	....	....	....	....	56	93	.602	....	....	....	....	169	....	....	....	....	4.0	....	....	....	....
48-49	Hammond-N	61	....	....	332	125	....	....	....	....	....	82	146	.562	....	....	....	....	**236**	....	....	....	....	5.4	....	....	....	....
49-50	Fort Wayne	63	....	....	143	57	203	.281	....	....	....	29	47	.617	....	....	....	90	175	....	....	....	....	2.3	....	1.4	....	....
NBA Season Totals		63	....	....	143	57	203	.281	....	....	....	29	47	.617	....	....	....	90	175	....	....	....	....	2.3	....	1.4	....	....
NBL Season Totals		247	....	....	1319	500	....	....	....	....	....	319	356	....	....	....	....	....	547	....	....	....	....	5.3	....	....	....	....
Career Totals		310	....	....	1462	557	203	....	....	....	....	348	403	....	....	....	....	90	722	....	....	....	....	4.7	....	0.3	....	....
43-44	Oshkosh-N	3	....	....	21	8	....	....	....	....	....	5	....	....	....	....	....	....	....	....	....	....	....	7.0	....	....	....	....
45-46	Oshkosh-N	5	....	....	32	13	....	....	....	....	....	6	7	.857	....	....	....	....	....	....	....	....	....	6.4	....	....	....	....
46-47	Oshkosh-N	7	....	....	40	15	....	....	....	....	....	10	12	.833	....	....	....	....	....	....	....	....	....	5.7	....	....	....	....
47-48	Oshkosh-N	3	....	....	4	2	....	....	....	....	....	0	2	.000	....	....	....	....	....	....	....	....	....	1.3	....	....	....	....
48-49	Hammond-N	2	....	....	9	3	....	....	....	....	....	3	7	.429	....	....	....	....	....	....	....	....	....	4.5	....	....	....	....
49-50	Fort Wayne	4	....	....	30	11	25	.440	....	....	....	8	10	.800	....	....	....	8	22	....	....	....	....	7.5	....	2.0	....	....
NBA Playoff Totals		4	....	....	30	11	25	.440	....	....	....	8	10	.800	....	....	....	8	22	....	....	....	....	7.5	....	2.0	....	....
NBL Playoff Totals		20	....	....	106	41	....	....	....	....	....	24	28	....	....	....	....	....	....	....	....	....	....	5.3	....	....	....	....
Career Playoff Totals		24	....	....	136	52	25	....	....	....	....	32	38	....	....	....	....	8	22	....	....	....	....	5.7	....	0.3	....	....

YEAR	TEAM	GP	GS	MIN	PTS	FGM	FGA	FG%	3PM	3PA	3P%	FTM	FTA	FT%	ORB	DRB	TRB	AST	PF	DQ	STL	BLK	TO	MPG	PPG	RPG	APG	PCM

• WAGNER, Dajuan   Dajuan Marquett Wagner

Born: Feb. 4, 1983. Camden, NJ, United States.   Height: 6'2".   Weight: 200 lbs.   Drafted: 2002   College: Memphis

YEAR	TEAM	GP	GS	MIN	PTS	FGM	FGA	FG%	3PM	3PA	3P%	FTM	FTA	FT%	ORB	DRB	TRB	AST	PF	DQ	STL	BLK	TO	MPG	PPG	RPG	APG	PCM
02-03	Cleveland	47	24	1385	629	223	605	.369	55	174	.316	128	160	.800	20	62	82	130	107	2	38	7	85	29.5	13.4	1.7	2.8	.288
NBA Season Totals		47	24	1385	629	223	605	.369	55	174	.316	128	160	.800	20	62	82	130	107	2	38	7	85	29.5	13.4	1.7	2.8	....

• WAGNER, Danny   Daniel Earnest (Dan) Wagner

Born: Aug. 1, 1922.   Height: 6'   Weight: 170 lbs.   Drafted: —   College: Texas

YEAR	TEAM	GP	GS	MIN	PTS	FGM	FGA	FG%	3PM	3PA	3P%	FTM	FTA	FT%	ORB	DRB	TRB	AST	PF	DQ	STL	BLK	TO	MPG	PPG	RPG	APG	PCM
47-48	Flint-N	50	....	....	251	96	....	....	....	....	....	59	92	.641	....	....	....	....	82	....	....	....	....	....	5.0	....	....	....
48-49	Sheboygan-N	62	....	....	331	111	....	....	....	....	....	109	146	.747	....	....	....	....	120	....	....	....	....	....	5.3	....	....	....
49-50	Sheboygan	11	....	....	69	19	54	.352	....	....	....	31	35	.886	....	....	....	18	22	....	....	....	....	....	6.3	....	1.6	....
NBA Season Totals		11	....	....	69	19	54	.352	....	....	....	31	35	.886	....	....	....	18	22	....	....	....	....	....	6.3	....	1.6	....
NBL Season Totals		112	....	....	582	207	....	....	....	....	....	168	238		....	....	....	....	202	....	....	....	....	....	5.2	....	....	....
Career Totals		123	....	....	651	226	54		....	....	....	199	273		....	....	....	18	224	....	....	....	....	....	5.3	....	0.1	....
48-49	Sheboygan-N	2	....	....	7	3	....	....	....	....	....	1	1	1.000	....	....	....	....	....	....	....	....	....	....	3.5	....	....	....
NBL Playoff Totals		2	....	....	7	3	....	....	....	....	....	1	1		....	....	....	....	....	....	....	....	....	....	3.5	....	....	....

• WAGNER, Milt   Milton Wagner Jr.

Born: Feb. 20, 1963. Camden, NJ, United States.   Height: 6'5".   Weight: 185 lbs.   Drafted: 1986   College: Louisville

YEAR	TEAM	GP	GS	MIN	PTS	FGM	FGA	FG%	3PM	3PA	3P%	FTM	FTA	FT%	ORB	DRB	TRB	AST	PF	DQ	STL	BLK	TO	MPG	PPG	RPG	APG	PCM
87-88	LA Lakers	40	4	380	152	62	147	.422	2	10	.200	26	29	.897	4	24	28	61	42	0	6	4	24	9.5	3.8	0.7	1.5	.342
90-91	Miami	13	1	116	63	24	57	.421	6	17	.353	9	11	.818	0	7	7	15	14	0	2	3	12	8.9	4.8	0.5	1.2	.351
NBA Season Totals		53	5	496	215	86	204	.422	8	27	.296	35	40	.875	4	31	35	76	56	0	8	7	36	9.4	4.1	0.7	1.4	....
87-88	LA Lakers	5	0	14	6	2	5	.400	0	1	.000	2	2	1.000	0	2	2	3	3	0	0	1	0	2.8	1.2	0.4	0.6	.558
NBA Playoff Totals		5	0	14	6	2	5	.400	0	1	.000	2	2	1.000	0	2	2	3	3	0	0	1	0	2.8	1.2	0.4	0.6	....

• WAGNER, Norm   Norman Wagner

Born: 1912.   Height: 6'5".   Weight: 200 lbs.   Drafted: —   College: Missouri

YEAR	TEAM	GP	GS	MIN	PTS	FGM	FGA	FG%	3PM	3PA	3P%	FTM	FTA	FT%	ORB	DRB	TRB	AST	PF	DQ	STL	BLK	TO	MPG	PPG	RPG	APG	PCM
37-38	Cincinnati-N	4	....	....	20	9	....	....	....	....	....	2	....	....	....	....	....	....	....	....	....	....	....	....	5.0	....	....	....
37-38	Columbus-N	3	....	....	9	3	....	....	....	....	....	3	....	....	....	....	....	....	....	....	....	....	....	....	3.0	....	....	....
37-38	Dayton-N	1	....	....	5	2	....	....	....	....	....	1	....	....	....	....	....	....	....	....	....	....	....	....	5.0	....	....	....
NBL Season Totals		8	....	....	34	14	....	....	....	....	....	6	....	....	....	....	....	....	....	....	....	....	....	....	4.3	....	....	....

• WAGNER, Phillip   Phillip C. Wagner

Born: Dec. 18, 1945.   Height: 6'2".   Weight: 190 lbs.   Drafted: 1968   College: Georgia Tech

YEAR	TEAM	GP	GS	MIN	PTS	FGM	FGA	FG%	3PM	3PA	3P%	FTM	FTA	FT%	ORB	DRB	TRB	AST	PF	DQ	STL	BLK	TO	MPG	PPG	RPG	APG	PCM
68-69	Indiana-A	12	....	180	36	11	41	.268	1	4	.250	13	17	.765	8	15	23	14	28	0	....	....	18	15.0	3.0	1.9	1.2	.179
ABA Season Totals		12	....	180	36	11	41	.268	1	4	.250	13	17	.765	8	15	23	14	28	0	....	....	18	15.0	3.0	1.9	1.2	....

• WAITERS, Granville   Granville S. Waiters

Born: Jan. 8, 1961. Columbus, OH, United States.   Height: 6'11".   Weight: 225 lbs.   Drafted: 1983   College: Ohio State

YEAR	TEAM	GP	GS	MIN	PTS	FGM	FGA	FG%	3PM	3PA	3P%	FTM	FTA	FT%	ORB	DRB	TRB	AST	PF	DQ	STL	BLK	TO	MPG	PPG	RPG	APG	PCM
83-84	Indiana	78	8	1040	277	123	238	.517	0	1	.000	31	51	.608	64	163	227	60	164	2	24	85	62	13.3	3.6	2.9	0.8	.388
84-85	Indiana	62	5	703	199	85	190	.447	0	1	.000	29	50	.580	57	113	170	30	107	2	16	44	56	11.3	3.2	2.7	0.5	.335
85-86	Houston	43	0	156	27	13	39	.333	0	1	.000	1	6	.167	15	13	28	8	30	0	4	10	13	3.6	0.6	0.7	0.2	.142
86-87	Chicago	44	26	534	85	40	93	.430	0	1	.000	5	9	.556	38	49	87	22	83	1	10	31	18	12.1	1.9	2.0	0.5	.227
87-88	Chicago	22	0	114	18	9	29	.310	0	1	.000	0	2	.000	9	19	28	1	26	0	2	15	7	5.2	0.8	1.3	0.0	.200
NBA Season Totals		249	39	2547	606	270	589	.458	0	5	.000	66	118	.559	183	357	540	121	410	5	56	185	156	10.2	2.4	2.2	0.5	....
85-86	Houston	11	0	26	8	4	7	.571	0	0	.000	0	0	.000	2	3	5	0	3	0	1	3	1	2.4	0.7	0.5	0.0	.433
86-87	Chicago	2	0	8	0	0	0	.000	0	0	.000	0	0	.000	0	1	1	0	1	0	0	1	0	4.0	0.0	0.5	0.0	.175
NBA Playoff Totals		13	0	34	8	4	7	.571	0	0	.000	0	0	.000	2	4	6	0	4	0	1	4	1	2.6	0.6	0.5	0.0	....

• WAKEFIELD, Andre   Andre Wakefield

Born: Jan. 11, 1955. Chicago, IL, United States.   Height: 6'3".   Weight: 175 lbs.   Drafted: 1978   College: Loyola (IL)

YEAR	TEAM	GP	GS	MIN	PTS	FGM	FGA	FG%	3PM	3PA	3P%	FTM	FTA	FT%	ORB	DRB	TRB	AST	PF	DQ	STL	BLK	TO	MPG	PPG	RPG	APG	PCM
78-79	Chicago	2	....	8	0	0	1	.000	....	....	....	0	0	.000	0	0	0	1	2	0	0	0	2	4.0	0.0	0.0	0.5	-.311
78-79	Detroit	71	....	578	172	62	176	.352	....	....	....	48	69	.696	25	51	76	69	68	0	19	2	71	8.1	2.4	1.1	1.0	.223
79-80	Utah	8	....	47	15	6	15	.400	0	0	.000	3	3	1.000	0	4	4	3	13	0	1	0	8	5.9	1.9	0.5	0.4	.033
NBA Season Totals		81	....	633	187	68	192	.354	0	0	.000	51	72	.708	25	55	80	73	83	0	20	2	81	7.8	2.3	1.0	0.9	....

• WALK, Neal   Neal Eugene Walk

Born: July 29, 1948. Cleveland, OH, United States.   Height: 6'10".   Weight: 220 lbs.   Drafted: 1969   College: Florida

YEAR	TEAM	GP	GS	MIN	PTS	FGM	FGA	FG%	3PM	3PA	3P%	FTM	FTA	FT%	ORB	DRB	TRB	AST	PF	DQ	STL	BLK	TO	MPG	PPG	RPG	APG	PCM
69-70	Phoenix	82	....	1394	669	257	547	.470	....	....	....	155	242	.640	....	....	455	80	225	2	....	....	....	17.0	8.2	5.5	1.0	.550
70-71	Phoenix	82	....	2033	1057	426	945	.451	....	....	....	205	268	.765	....	....	674	117	282	8	....	....	....	24.8	12.9	8.2	1.4	.578
71-72	Phoenix	81	....	2142	1268	506	1057	.479	....	....	....	256	344	.744	....	....	665	151	295	9	....	....	....	26.4	15.7	8.2	1.9	.641
72-73	Phoenix	81	....	3114	1635	678	1455	.466	....	....	....	279	355	.786	....	....	1006	287	**323**	11	....	....	....	38.4	20.2	12.4	3.5	.638
73-74	Phoenix	82	....	2549	1381	573	1245	.460	....	....	....	235	297	.791	235	602	837	331	255	8	73	57	....	31.1	16.8	10.2	4.0	.693
74-75	New Orleans	37	....	851	366	151	358	.422	....	....	....	64	80	.800	73	189	262	101	122	3	30	20	....	23.0	9.9	7.1	2.7	.552

YEAR	TEAM	GP	GS	MIN	PTS	FGM	FGA	FG%	3PM	3PA	3P%	FTM	FTA	FT%	ORB	DRB	TRB	AST	PF	DQ	STL	BLK	TO	MPG	PPG	RPG	APG	PCM
74-75	New York	30	....	274	116	47	115	.409	....	....	....	22	25	.880	18	59	77	22	55	0	7	3	....	9.1	3.9	2.6	0.7	.453
75-76	New York	82	....	1340	603	262	607	.432	....	....	....	79	99	.798	98	291	389	119	209	3	26	22	....	16.3	7.4	4.7	1.5	.506
76-77	New York	11	....	135	62	28	57	.491	....	....	....	6	7	.857	5	22	27	6	22	0	4	3	....	12.3	5.6	2.5	0.5	.423
NBA Season Totals		568	....	13832	7157	2928	6386	.459	....	....	....	1301	1717	.758	429	1163	4392	1214	1788	44	140	105	....	24.4	12.6	7.7	2.1	
69-70	Phoenix	5	....	63	40	17	43	.395	....	....	....	6	8	.750		35	2	13	0	....	....	....		12.6	8.0	7.0	0.4	.691
74-75	New York	3	....	39	10	5	10	.500	....	....	....	0	0	.000	0	5	5	2	4	0	1	2	....	13.0	3.3	1.7	0.7	.271
NBA Playoff Totals		8	....	102	50	22	53	.415	....	....	....	6	8	.750	0	5	40	4	17	0	1	2	....	12.8	6.3	5.0	0.5	

• WALKER, Andy
Andrew Martin Walker

Born: Mar. 25, 1955. Long Island City, NY, United States.   Height: 6'4".   Weight: 190 lbs.   Drafted: 1976   College: Niagara

YEAR	TEAM	GP	GS	MIN	PTS	FGM	FGA	FG%	3PM	3PA	3P%	FTM	FTA	FT%	ORB	DRB	TRB	AST	PF	DQ	STL	BLK	TO	MPG	PPG	RPG	APG	PCM
76-77	New Orleans	40	....	438	180	72	156	.462	....	....	....	36	47	.766	23	52	75	32	59	0	20	7	....	11.0	4.5	1.9	0.8	.407
NBA Season Totals		40	....	438	180	72	156	.462	....	....	....	36	47	.766	23	52	75	32	59	0	20	7	....	11.0	4.5	1.9	0.8	

• WALKER, Antoine
Antoine Devon Walker

Born: Aug. 12, 1976. Chicago, IL, United States.   Height: 6'8".   Weight: 224 lbs.   Drafted: 1996   College: Kentucky

YEAR	TEAM	GP	GS	MIN	PTS	FGM	FGA	FG%	3PM	3PA	3P%	FTM	FTA	FT%	ORB	DRB	TRB	AST	PF	DQ	STL	BLK	TO	MPG	PPG	RPG	APG	PCM
96-97	Boston	82	68	2970	1435	576	1354	.425	52	159	.327	231	366	.631	288	453	741	262	271	1	105	53	230	36.2	17.5	9.0	3.2	.479
97-98	Boston	82	82	3268	1840	722	1705	.423	91	292	.312	305	473	.645	270	566	836	273	262	2	142	60	**295**	39.9	22.4	10.2	3.3	.526
98-99	Boston	42	41	1549	784	303	735	.412	65	176	.369	113	202	.559	106	253	359	130	142	2	63	28	119	36.9	18.7	8.5	3.1	.475
99-00	Boston	82	82	3003	1680	648	1506	.430	73	285	.256	311	445	.699	199	453	652	305	263	4	117	32	259	36.6	20.5	8.0	3.7	.515
00-01	Boston	81	81	3396	1892	711	1720	.413	**221**	**603**	.367	249	348	.716	151	568	719	445	251	2	138	49	301	41.9	23.4	8.9	5.5	.548
01-02	Boston	81	81	**3406**	1794	666	**1689**	.394	222	**645**	.344	240	324	.741	150	564	714	407	237	2	122	38	251	42.0	22.1	8.8	5.0	.508
02-03	Boston	78	78	3235	1570	603	1554	.388	188	**582**	.323	176	286	.615	99	464	563	373	221	4	116	31	260	41.5	20.1	7.2	4.8	.424
NBA Season Totals		528	513	20827	10995	4229	10263	.412	912	2742	.333	1625	2444	.665	1263	3321	4584	2195	1647	17	803	291	1715	39.4	20.8	8.7	4.2	....
01-02	Boston	16	16	704	354	131	319	.411	42	109	.385	50	64	.781	23	115	138	52	56	2	24	6	55	44.0	22.1	8.6	3.3	.442
02-03	Boston	10	10	440	173	73	176	.415	16	45	.356	11	22	.500	20	67	87	43	44	3	17	4	37	44.0	17.3	8.7	4.3	.377
NBA Playoff Totals		26	26	1144	527	204	495	.412	58	154	.377	61	86	.709	43	182	225	95	100	5	41	10	92	44.0	20.3	8.7	3.7	....

• WALKER, Brady
Brady W. Walker

Born: Mar. 15, 1921. Provo, UT, United States.   Height: 6'6".   Weight: 205 lbs.   Drafted: 1948   College: Brigham Young

YEAR	TEAM	GP	GS	MIN	PTS	FGM	FGA	FG%	3PM	3PA	3P%	FTM	FTA	FT%	ORB	DRB	TRB	AST	PF	DQ	STL	BLK	TO	MPG	PPG	RPG	APG	PCM
48-49	Providence	59	....	....	491	202	556	.363	....	....	....	87	155	.561	....	....	68	100	....	....	....	....		8.3	....	1.2		
49-50	Boston	68	....	....	508	218	583	.374	....	....	....	72	114	.632	....	....	109	100	....	....	....	....		7.5	....	1.6		
50-51	Bos/Bal	66	....	....	400	164	416	.394	....	....	....	72	103	.699	....	354	111	82	2	....	....	....		6.1	5.4	1.7		
51-52	Baltimore	35	....	699	204	89	217	.410	....	....	....	26	34	.765	....	195	40	38	0	....	....	....		20.0	5.8	5.6	1.1	.410
NBA Season Totals		228	....	699	1603	673	1772	.380	....	....	....	257	406	.633	....	....	549	328	320	2	....	....	....	3.1	7.0	2.4	1.4	....

• WALKER, Chet
Chester (The Jet) Walker

Born: Feb. 22, 1940. Benton Harbor, MI, United States.   Height: 6'6".   Weight: 212 lbs.   Drafted: 1962   College: Bradley

YEAR	TEAM	GP	GS	MIN	PTS	FGM	FGA	FG%	3PM	3PA	3P%	FTM	FTA	FT%	ORB	DRB	TRB	AST	PF	DQ	STL	BLK	TO	MPG	PPG	RPG	APG	PCM
62-63	Syracuse	78	....	1992	957	352	751	.469	....	....	....	253	362	.699	....	....	561	83	220	3	....	....	....	25.5	12.3	7.2	1.1	.530
63-64	Philadelphia	76	....	2775	1314	492	1118	.440	....	....	....	330	464	.711	....	....	784	124	232	3	....	....	....	36.5	17.3	10.3	1.6	.521
64-65	Philadelphia	79	....	2187	1042	377	936	.403	....	....	....	288	388	.742	....	....	528	132	200	2	....	....	....	27.7	13.2	6.7	1.7	.487
65-66	Philadelphia	80	....	2603	1221	443	982	.451	....	....	....	335	468	.716	....	....	636	201	238	3	....	....	....	32.5	15.3	8.0	2.5	.536
66-67	Philadelphia	81	....	2691	1567	561	1150	.488	....	....	....	445	581	.766	....	....	660	188	232	4	....	....	....	33.2	19.3	8.1	2.3	.633
67-68	Philadelphia	82	....	2623	1465	539	1172	.460	....	....	....	387	533	.726	....	....	607	157	252	3	....	....	....	32.0	17.9	7.4	1.9	.562
68-69	Philadelphia	82	....	2753	1477	554	1145	.484	....	....	....	369	459	.804	....	....	640	144	244	0	....	....	....	33.6	18.0	7.8	1.8	.562
69-70	Chicago	78	....	2726	1675	596	1249	.477	....	....	....	483	568	.850	....	....	604	192	203	1	....	....	....	34.9	21.5	7.7	2.5	.631
70-71	Chicago	81	....	2927	1780	650	1398	.465	....	....	....	480	559	**.859**	....	....	588	179	187	2	....	....	....	36.1	22.0	7.3	2.2	.592
71-72	Chicago	78	....	2588	1719	619	1225	.505	....	....	....	481	568	.847	....	....	473	178	171	0	....	....	....	33.2	22.0	6.1	2.3	.655
72-73	Chicago	79	....	2455	1570	597	1248	.478	....	....	....	376	452	.832	....	....	395	179	166	1	....	....	....	31.1	19.9	5.0	2.3	.591
73-74	Chicago	82	....	2661	1583	572	1178	.486	....	....	....	439	502	.875	131	275	406	200	201	1	68	4	....	32.5	19.3	5.0	2.4	.575
74-75	Chicago	76	....	2452	1461	524	1076	.487	....	....	....	413	480	.860	114	318	432	169	181	0	49	6	....	32.3	19.2	5.7	2.2	.590
NBA Season Totals		1032	....	33433	18831	6876	14628	.470	....	....	....	5079	6384	.796	245	593	7314	2126	2727	23	117	10	....	32.4	18.2	7.1	2.1	....
62-63	Syracuse	5	....	130	76	27	53	.509	....	....	....	22	30	.733	....	....	47	9	8	0	....	....	....	26.0	15.2	9.4	1.8	.747
63-64	Philadelphia	5	....	190	94	30	77	.390	....	....	....	34	46	.739	....	....	52	13	15	0	....	....	....	38.0	18.8	10.4	2.6	.544
64-65	Philadelphia	11	....	469	223	83	173	.480	....	....	....	57	75	.760	....	....	79	18	38	0	....	....	....	42.6	20.3	7.2	1.6	.459
65-66	Philadelphia	5	....	181	73	24	64	.375	....	....	....	25	31	.806	....	....	37	15	18	0	....	....	....	36.2	14.6	7.4	3.0	.439
66-67	Philadelphia	15	....	551	326	115	246	.467	....	....	....	96	119	.807	....	....	114	32	44	0	....	....	....	36.7	21.7	7.6	2.1	.588
67-68	Philadelphia	13	....	485	248	86	210	.410	....	....	....	76	112	.679	....	....	96	24	44	1	....	....	....	37.3	19.1	7.4	1.8	.459
68-69	Philadelphia	4	....	109	54	23	43	.535	....	....	....	8	12	.667	....	....	23	8	5	0	....	....	....	27.3	13.5	5.8	2.0	.569
69-70	Chicago	5	....	178	97	35	83	.422	....	....	....	27	33	.818	....	....	42	11	14	0	....	....	....	35.6	19.4	8.4	2.2	.535
70-71	Chicago	7	....	234	105	44	100	.440	....	....	....	17	24	.708	....	....	50	22	20	0	....	....	....	33.4	15.0	7.1	3.1	.484
71-72	Chicago	4	....	97	45	16	38	.421	....	....	....	13	16	.813	....	....	14	4	7	0	....	....	....	24.3	11.3	3.5	1.0	.395
72-73	Chicago	7	....	229	117	42	121	.347	....	....	....	33	37	.892	....	....	62	14	15	0	....	....	....	32.7	16.7	8.9	2.0	.481
73-74	Chicago	11	....	403	230	81	159	.509	....	....	....	68	79	.861	26	35	61	18	26	0	10	1	....	36.6	20.9	5.5	1.6	.547
74-75	Chicago	13	....	432	228	81	164	.494	....	....	....	66	75	.880	10	50	60	24	32	2	13	1	....	33.2	17.5	4.6	1.8	.506
NBA Playoff Totals		105	....	3688	1916	687	1531	.449	....	....	....	542	689	.787	36	85	737	212	286	3	23	2	....	35.1	18.2	7.0	2.0	....

• WALKER, Darrell
Darrell Walker

Born: Mar. 9, 1961. Chicago, IL, United States.   Height: 6'4".   Weight: 180 lbs.   Drafted: 1983   College: Arkansas

YEAR	TEAM	GP	GS	MIN	PTS	FGM	FGA	FG%	3PM	3PA	3P%	FTM	FTA	FT%	ORB	DRB	TRB	AST	PF	DQ	STL	BLK	TO	MPG	PPG	RPG	APG	PCM
83-84	New York	82	0	1324	644	216	518	.417	4	15	.267	208	263	.791	74	93	167	284	202	1	127	15	197	16.1	7.9	2.0	3.5	.492
84-85	New York	82	66	2489	1103	430	989	.435	0	17	.000	243	347	.700	128	150	278	408	244	2	167	21	205	30.4	13.5	3.4	5.0	.441
85-86	New York	81	35	2023	838	324	753	.430	0	10	.000	190	277	.686	100	120	220	337	216	1	146	36	194	25.0	10.3	2.7	4.2	.422
86-87	Denver	81	25	2020	988	358	742	.482	0	4	.000	272	365	.745	157	170	327	282	229	0	120	37	186	24.9	12.2	4.0	3.5	.525

YEAR	TEAM	GP	GS	MIN	PTS	FGM	FGA	FG%	3PM	3PA	3P%	FTM	FTA	FT%	ORB	DRB	TRB	AST	PF	DQ	STL	BLK	TO	MPG	PPG	RPG	APG	PCM
87-88	Washington	52	0	940	310	114	291	.392	0	6	.000	82	105	.781	43	84	127	100	105	2	62	10	68	18.1	6.0	2.4	1.9	.334
88-89	Washington	79	78	2565	714	286	681	.420	0	9	.000	142	184	.772	135	372	507	496	215	2	155	23	182	32.5	9.0	6.4	6.3	.478
89-90	Washington	81	81	2883	772	316	696	.454	2	21	.095	138	201	.687	173	541	714	652	220	1	139	30	170	35.6	9.5	8.8	8.0	.570
90-91	Washington	71	65	2305	553	230	535	.430	0	9	.000	93	154	.604	140	358	498	459	199	2	78	33	156	32.5	7.8	7.0	6.5	.460
91-92	Detroit	74	4	1541	387	161	381	.423	0	10	.000	65	105	.619	85	153	238	205	134	0	63	18	81	20.8	5.2	3.2	2.8	.352
92-93	Detroit	9	2	144	8	3	19	.158	0	1	.000	2	6	.333	4	15	19	9	12	0	10	0	13	16.0	0.9	2.1	1.0	.070
92-93	Chicago	28	0	367	72	31	77	.403	0	0	.000	10	20	.500	18	21	39	44	51	0	23	2	11	13.1	2.6	1.4	1.6	.264
NBA Season Totals		720	356	18601	6389	2469	5682	.435	6	102	.059	1445	2027	.713	1057	2077	3134	3276	1827	11	1090	225	1463	25.8	8.9	4.4	4.6	....
83-84	New York	12	0	195	82	27	73	.370	0	0	.000	28	46	.609	20	15	35	20	29	0	24	2	32	16.3	6.8	2.9	1.7	.337
86-87	Denver	3	3	68	26	11	34	.324	0	0	.000	4	7	.571	3	7	10	5	4	0	2	0	4	22.7	8.7	3.3	1.7	.208
87-88	Washington	5	0	155	55	22	54	.407	0	1	.000	11	16	.688	9	15	24	14	18	0	7	4	9	31.0	11.0	4.8	2.8	.346
91-92	Detroit	5	0	68	10	3	9	.333	0	0	.000	4	4	1.000	5	7	12	4	7	0	1	0	5	13.6	2.0	2.4	0.8	.190
92-93	Chicago	9	0	22	4	1	4	.250	0	0	.000	2	3	.667	0	1	1	5	0	0	0	0	1	2.4	0.4	0.1	0.6	.276
NBA Playoff Totals		34	3	508	177	64	174	.368	0	1	.000	49	76	.645	37	45	82	48	58	0	34	6	51	14.9	5.2	2.4	1.4	....

• WALKER, Foots

Clarence (Foots) Walker

Born: May 21, 1951. Southampton, NY, United States. Height: 6' Weight: 172 lbs. Drafted: 1974 College: West Georgia

YEAR	TEAM	GP	GS	MIN	PTS	FGM	FGA	FG%	3PM	3PA	3P%	FTM	FTA	FT%	ORB	DRB	TRB	AST	PF	DQ	STL	BLK	TO	MPG	PPG	RPG	APG	PCM
74-75	Cleveland	72	....	1070	302	111	275	.404	....	....	....	80	117	.684	47	99	146	192	126	0	80	7	....	14.9	4.2	2.0	2.7	.409
75-76	Cleveland	81	....	1280	370	143	369	.388	....	....	....	84	108	.778	53	129	182	288	136	0	98	5	....	15.8	4.6	2.2	3.6	.463
76-77	Cleveland	62	....	1216	403	157	349	.450	....	....	....	89	115	.774	55	105	160	254	124	1	83	4	....	19.6	6.5	2.6	4.1	.493
77-78	Cleveland	81	....	2496	733	287	641	.448	....	....	....	159	221	.719	76	218	294	453	218	0	176	24	178	30.8	9.0	3.6	5.6	.435
78-79	Cleveland	55	....	1753	553	208	448	.464	....	....	....	137	175	.783	59	139	198	321	153	0	130	18	127	31.9	10.1	3.6	5.8	.458
79-80	Cleveland	76	....	2422	712	258	568	.454	1	9	.111	195	243	.802	78	209	287	607	202	2	155	12	160	31.9	9.4	3.8	8.0	.516
80-81	New Jersey	41	....	1172	234	72	169	.426	2	9	.222	88	111	.793	22	80	102	253	105	0	52	1	86	28.6	5.7	2.5	6.2	.363
81-82	New Jersey	77	54	1861	456	156	378	.413	3	9	.333	141	194	.727	31	119	150	398	179	1	120	6	108	24.2	5.9	1.9	5.2	.392
82-83	New Jersey	79	10	1388	346	114	250	.456	2	12	.167	116	149	.779	30	106	136	264	134	1	78	3	103	17.6	4.4	1.7	3.3	.390
83-84	New Jersey	34	0	378	90	32	90	.356	2	5	.400	24	27	.889	8	23	31	81	37	0	20	3	31	11.1	2.6	0.9	2.4	.332
NBA Season Totals		658	64	15036	4199	1538	3537	.435	10	44	.227	1113	1460	.762	459	1227	1686	3111	1414	5	992	83	793	22.9	6.4	2.6	4.7	....
75-76	Cleveland	13	....	125	30	11	27	.407	....	....	....	8	10	.800	5	11	16	23	17	0	7	1	....	9.6	2.3	1.2	1.8	.385
76-77	Cleveland	3	....	95	47	18	37	.486	....	....	....	11	15	.733	4	8	12	20	12	0	4	1	....	31.7	15.7	4.0	6.7	.598
77-78	Cleveland	2	....	70	25	10	26	.385	....	....	....	5	5	1.000	5	2	7	10	7	0	3	2	6	35.0	12.5	3.5	5.0	.349
82-83	New Jersey	2	0	36	7	2	6	.333	0	0	.000	3	3	1.000	0	0	0	11	1	0	0	0	2	18.0	3.5	0.0	5.5	.367
83-84	New Jersey	2	0	4	0	0	1	.000	0	0	.000	0	0	.000	0	0	0	0	0	0	0	0	0	2.0	0.0	0.0	0.0	-.233
NBA Playoff Totals		22	0	330	109	41	97	.423	0	0	.000	27	33	.818	14	21	35	64	37	0	14	4	8	15.0	5.0	1.6	2.9	....

• WALKER, Horace

Horace Walker

Born: Apr. 17, 1938. Height: 6'3". Weight: 210 lbs. Drafted: 1960 College: Michigan State

YEAR	TEAM	GP	GS	MIN	PTS	FGM	FGA	FG%	3PM	3PA	3P%	FTM	FTA	FT%	ORB	DRB	TRB	AST	PF	DQ	STL	BLK	TO	MPG	PPG	RPG	APG	PCM
61-62	Chicago	65	....	1331	438	149	439	.339	....	....	....	140	193	.725	....	....	466	69	194	2	....	....	....	20.5	6.7	7.2	1.1	.423
NBA Season Totals		65	....	1331	438	149	439	.339	....	....	....	140	193	.725	....	....	466	69	194	2	....	....	....	20.5	6.7	7.2	1.1	....

• WALKER, Jimmy

James Walker

Born: Apr. 8, 1944. Amherst, VA, United States. Height: 6'3". Weight: 195 lbs. Drafted: 1967 College: Providence

YEAR	TEAM	GP	GS	MIN	PTS	FGM	FGA	FG%	3PM	3PA	3P%	FTM	FTA	FT%	ORB	DRB	TRB	AST	PF	DQ	STL	BLK	TO	MPG	PPG	RPG	APG	PCM
67-68	Detroit	81	....	1585	712	289	733	.394	....	....	....	134	175	.766	....	....	135	226	204	1	....	....	....	19.6	8.8	1.7	2.8	.403
68-69	Detroit	69	....	1639	806	312	670	.466	....	....	....	182	229	.795	....	....	157	221	172	1	....	....	....	23.8	11.7	2.3	3.2	.490
69-70	Detroit	81	....	2869	1687	666	1394	.478	....	....	....	355	440	.807	....	....	242	248	203	4	....	....	....	35.4	20.8	3.0	3.1	.492
70-71	Detroit	79	....	2765	1392	524	1201	.436	....	....	....	344	414	.831	....	....	207	268	173	0	....	....	....	35.0	17.6	2.6	3.4	.430
71-72	Detroit	78	....	3083	1665	634	1386	.457	....	....	....	397	480	.827	....	....	231	315	198	2	....	....	....	39.5	21.3	3.0	4.0	.471
72-73	Houston	81	....	3079	1454	605	1301	.465	....	....	....	244	276	.884	....	....	268	442	207	0	....	....	....	38.0	18.0	3.3	5.5	.484
73-74	Houston	3	....	38	14	7	12	.583	....	....	....	0	1	.000	0	2	2	4	4	0	0	0	....	12.7	4.7	0.7	1.3	.366
73-74	Omaha	72	....	2920	1423	575	1228	.468	....	....	....	273	332	.822	39	163	202	303	166	0	81	9	....	40.6	19.8	2.8	4.2	.442
74-75	Omaha	81	....	3122	1353	553	1164	.475	....	....	....	247	289	.855	51	188	239	226	222	2	85	13	....	38.5	16.7	3.0	2.8	.379
75-76	Kansas City	73	....	2490	1149	459	950	.483	....	....	....	231	267	.865	49	128	177	176	186	2	87	14	....	34.1	15.7	2.4	2.4	.396
NBA Season Totals		698	....	23590	11655	4624	10039	.461	....	....	....	2407	2903	.829	139	481	1860	2429	1735	12	253	36	....	33.8	16.7	2.7	3.5	....
67-68	Detroit	6	....	121	76	31	67	.463	....	....	....	14	17	.824	....	....	9	9	17	1	....	....	....	20.2	12.7	1.5	1.5	.473
74-75	Omaha	6	....	225	92	39	84	.464	....	....	....	14	18	.778	1	9	10	17	12	0	5	1	....	37.5	15.3	1.7	2.8	.333
NBA Playoff Totals		12	....	346	168	70	151	.464	....	....	....	28	35	.800	1	9	19	26	29	1	5	1	....	28.8	14.0	1.6	2.2	....

• WALKER, Kenny

Kenneth (Sky) Walker

Born: Aug. 18, 1964. Roberta, GA, United States. Height: 6'8". Weight: 210 lbs. Drafted: 1986 College: Kentucky

YEAR	TEAM	GP	GS	MIN	PTS	FGM	FGA	FG%	3PM	3PA	3P%	FTM	FTA	FT%	ORB	DRB	TRB	AST	PF	DQ	STL	BLK	TO	MPG	PPG	RPG	APG	PCM
86-87	New York	68	64	1719	710	285	581	.491	0	4	.000	140	185	.757	118	220	338	75	236	7	49	49	75	25.3	10.4	5.0	1.1	.419
87-88	New York	82	61	2139	826	344	728	.473	0	1	.000	138	178	.775	192	197	389	86	290	5	63	59	82	26.1	10.1	4.7	1.0	.377
88-89	New York	79	2	1163	419	174	356	.489	5	20	.250	66	85	.776	101	129	230	36	190	1	41	45	47	14.7	5.3	2.9	0.5	.379
89-90	New York	68	21	1595	535	204	384	.531	2	5	.400	125	173	.723	131	212	343	49	178	1	33	52	61	23.5	7.9	5.0	0.7	.412
90-91	New York	54	8	771	230	83	191	.435	0	1	.000	64	82	.780	63	94	157	13	92	0	18	30	32	14.3	4.3	2.9	0.2	.328
93-94	Washington	73	4	1397	351	132	274	.482	0	3	.000	87	125	.696	118	171	289	33	156	1	26	59	44	19.1	4.8	4.0	0.5	.337
94-95	Washington	24	0	266	57	18	42	.429	0	0	.000	21	28	.750	19	28	47	7	42	0	5	5	14	11.1	2.4	2.0	0.3	.223
NBA Season Totals		448	160	9050	3128	1240	2556	.485	7	34	.206	641	856	.749	742	1051	1793	299	1184	15	235	299	355	20.2	7.0	4.0	0.7	....
87-88	New York	4	2	80	18	8	24	.333	0	0	.000	2	2	1.000	3	6	9	5	11	0	2	3	1	20.0	4.5	2.3	1.3	.193
88-89	New York	9	0	90	20	3	13	.231	0	0	.000	14	19	.737	5	11	16	2	22	0	1	3	4	10.0	2.2	1.8	0.2	.169
89-90	New York	10	2	154	41	16	29	.552	0	1	.000	9	14	.643	7	18	25	6	22	0	0	4	1	15.4	4.1	2.5	0.6	.317
90-91	New York	3	0	31	10	4	8	.500	0	0	.000	2	2	1.000	2	5	7	2	8	0	1	1	3	10.3	3.3	2.3	0.7	.331
NBA Playoff Totals		26	4	355	89	31	74	.419	0	1	.000	27	37	.730	17	40	57	15	63	0	4	11	9	13.7	3.4	2.2	0.6	....

YEAR	TEAM	GP	GS	MIN	PTS	FGM	FGA	FG%	3PM	3PA	3P%	FTM	FTA	FT%	ORB	DRB	TRB	AST	PF	DQ	STL	BLK	TO	MPG	PPG	RPG	APG	PCM

• WALKER, Phil
Phillip B. Walker

Born: Mar. 20, 1956. Philadelphia, PA, United States. Height: 6'3". Weight: 180 lbs. Drafted: 1977 College: Millersville State (PA)

YEAR	TEAM	GP	GS	MIN	PTS	FGM	FGA	FG%	3PM	3PA	3P%	FTM	FTA	FT%	ORB	DRB	TRB	AST	PF	DQ	STL	BLK	TO	MPG	PPG	RPG	APG	PCM
77-78	Washington	40	....	384	178	57	161	.354	....	....	....	64	96	.667	21	31	52	54	39	0	14	5	64	9.6	4.5	1.3	1.4	.320
NBA Season Totals		40	....	384	178	57	161	.354	....	....	....	64	96	.667	21	31	52	54	39	0	14	5	64	9.6	4.5	1.3	1.4	....
77-78	Washington	4	....	17	6	1	8	.125	....	....	....	4	5	.800	1	1	2	2	5	0	0	0	3	4.3	1.5	0.5	0.5	-.081
NBA Playoff Totals		4	....	17	6	1	8	.125	....	....	....	4	5	.800	1	1	2	2	5	0	0	0	3	4.3	1.5	0.5	0.5	....

• WALKER, Samaki
Samaki Ijuma Walker

Born: Feb. 25, 1976. Columbus, OH, United States. Height: 6'9". Weight: 240 lbs. Drafted: 1996 College: Louisville

YEAR	TEAM	GP	GS	MIN	PTS	FGM	FGA	FG%	3PM	3PA	3P%	FTM	FTA	FT%	ORB	DRB	TRB	AST	PF	DQ	STL	BLK	TO	MPG	PPG	RPG	APG	PCM
96-97	Dallas	43	12	602	214	83	187	.444	0	1	.000	48	74	.649	47	100	147	17	71	0	15	22	39	14.0	5.0	3.4	0.4	.374
97-98	Dallas	41	19	1027	365	156	321	.486	0	1	.000	53	97	.546	96	206	302	24	127	2	30	40	62	25.0	8.9	7.4	0.6	.434
98-99	Dallas	39	2	568	229	88	190	.463	0	1	.000	53	98	.541	46	97	143	6	87	3	9	16	37	14.6	5.9	3.7	0.2	.357
99-00	San Antonio	71	7	980	360	137	305	.449	0	0	.000	86	126	.683	77	195	272	38	108	1	10	35	64	13.8	5.1	3.8	0.5	.420
00-01	San Antonio	61	1	963	321	121	252	.480	1	3	.333	78	124	.629	67	176	243	29	103	0	10	41	68	15.8	5.3	4.0	0.5	.386
01-02	LA Lakers	69	63	1655	460	187	365	.512	0	0	.000	86	129	.667	129	352	481	64	170	1	28	88	53	24.0	6.7	7.0	0.9	.462
02-03	LA Lakers	67	39	1245	296	115	274	.420	0	1	.000	66	101	.653	115	253	368	64	143	4	20	55	56	18.6	4.4	5.5	1.0	.395
NBA Season Totals		391	143	7040	2245	887	1894	.468	1	7	.143	470	749	.628	577	1379	1956	242	809	11	122	297	379	18.0	5.7	5.0	0.6	....
99-00	San Antonio	4	4	121	36	14	31	.452	0	0	.000	8	12	.667	13	32	45	2	13	0	1	12	8	30.3	9.0	11.3	0.5	.499
00-01	San Antonio	12	0	76	14	5	15	.333	0	0	.000	4	8	.500	5	9	14	3	12	0	1	1	1	6.3	1.2	1.2	0.3	.192
01-02	LA Lakers	19	5	240	62	24	52	.462	1	1	1.000	13	17	.765	32	46	78	4	42	0	2	6	12	12.6	3.3	4.1	0.2	.363
02-03	LA Lakers	9	0	49	4	2	5	.400	0	0	.000	0	0	.000	4	9	13	2	11	0	1	2	3	5.4	0.4	1.4	0.2	.210
NBA Playoff Totals		44	9	486	116	45	103	.437	1	1	1.000	25	37	.676	54	96	150	11	78	0	5	21	24	11.0	2.6	3.4	0.3	....

• WALKER, Wally
Walter Frederick Walker

Born: July 18, 1954. Millersville, PA, United States. Height: 6'7". Weight: 190 lbs. Drafted: 1976 College: Virginia

YEAR	TEAM	GP	GS	MIN	PTS	FGM	FGA	FG%	3PM	3PA	3P%	FTM	FTA	FT%	ORB	DRB	TRB	AST	PF	DQ	STL	BLK	TO	MPG	PPG	RPG	APG	PCM
76-77	Portland	66	....	627	341	137	305	.449	....	....	....	67	100	.670	45	63	108	51	92	0	14	2	....	9.5	5.2	1.6	0.8	.468
77-78	Portland	9	....	101	43	19	41	.463	....	....	....	5	8	.625	7	10	17	8	13	0	2	0	11	11.2	4.8	1.9	0.9	.324
77-78	Seattle	68	....	1003	440	185	420	.440	....	....	....	70	112	.625	80	122	202	69	125	1	24	10	68	14.8	6.5	3.0	1.0	.385
78-79	Seattle	60	....	969	394	168	343	.490	....	....	....	58	96	.604	66	111	177	69	127	0	12	26	66	16.2	6.6	3.0	1.2	.385
79-80	Seattle	70	....	844	326	139	274	.507	0	0	.000	48	64	.750	64	106	170	53	102	0	21	4	49	12.1	4.7	2.4	0.8	.404
80-81	Seattle	82	....	1796	689	290	626	.463	0	3	.000	109	169	.645	105	210	315	122	168	1	53	15	115	21.9	8.4	3.8	1.5	.365
81-82	Seattle	70	70	1965	694	302	629	.480	0	2	.000	90	134	.672	108	197	305	218	215	2	36	28	112	28.1	9.9	4.4	3.1	.379
82-83	Houston	82	59	2251	797	362	806	.449	1	4	.250	72	116	.621	137	236	373	199	202	3	37	22	148	27.5	9.7	4.5	2.4	.338
83-84	Houston	58	18	612	244	118	241	.490	2	6	.333	6	18	.333	26	66	92	55	65	0	17	4	35	10.6	4.2	1.6	0.9	.368
NBA Season Totals		565	147	10168	3968	1720	3685	.467	3	15	.200	525	817	.643	638	1121	1759	844	1109	7	216	111	604	18.0	7.0	3.1	1.5	....
76-77	Portland	10	....	83	43	20	36	.556	....	....	....	3	7	.429	2	5	7	8	20	1	3	0	....	8.3	4.3	0.7	0.8	.409
77-78	Seattle	20	....	261	93	36	85	.424	....	....	....	21	26	.808	20	18	38	12	51	0	8	4	18	13.1	4.7	1.9	0.6	.257
78-79	Seattle	13	....	85	14	6	16	.375	....	....	....	2	4	.500	7	10	17	2	19	0	0	0	4	6.5	1.1	1.3	0.2	.111
79-80	Seattle	13	....	157	54	18	35	.514	0	0	.000	18	24	.750	15	14	29	7	20	0	1	3	5	12.1	4.2	2.2	0.5	.381
81-82	Seattle	8	8	157	39	19	45	.422	0	0	.000	1	4	.250	12	20	32	15	26	0	4	4	7	19.6	4.9	4.0	1.9	.308
NBA Playoff Totals		64	8	743	243	99	217	.456	0	0	.000	45	65	.692	56	67	123	44	136	1	16	11	34	11.6	3.8	1.9	0.7	....

• WALLACE, Ben
Ben Wallace

Born: Sept. 10, 1974. White Hall, AL, United States. Height: 6'9". Weight: 240 lbs. Drafted: — College: Virginia Union

YEAR	TEAM	GP	GS	MIN	PTS	FGM	FGA	FG%	3PM	3PA	3P%	FTM	FTA	FT%	ORB	DRB	TRB	AST	PF	DQ	STL	BLK	TO	MPG	PPG	RPG	APG	PCM
96-97	Washington	34	0	197	38	16	46	.348	0	0	.000	6	20	.300	25	33	58	2	27	0	8	11	17	5.8	1.1	1.7	0.1	.249
97-98	Washington	67	16	1124	205	85	164	.518	0	0	.000	35	98	.357	112	212	324	18	116	1	61	72	27	16.8	3.1	4.8	0.3	.413
98-99	Washington	46	16	1231	277	115	199	.578	0	0	.000	47	132	.356	137	247	384	18	111	0	50	90	36	26.8	6.0	8.3	0.4	.462
99-00	Orlando	81	81	1951	389	166	330	.503	0	0	.000	57	117	.487	209	441	650	67	164	0	71	130	71	24.1	4.8	8.0	0.8	.471
00-01	Detroit	80	80	2760	511	215	439	.490	1	4	.250	80	238	.336	303	**749**	**1052**	123	192	0	107	186	117	34.5	6.4	13.2	1.5	.504
01-02	Detroit	80	80	2921	609	255	480	.531	0	3	.000	99	234	.423	318	721	1039	115	178	2	138	278	70	36.5	7.6	**13.0**	1.4	.563
02-03	Detroit	73	73	2872	506	210	437	.481	1	6	.167	85	189	.450	**293**	833	**1126**	120	179	0	104	230	88	39.3	6.9	**15.4**	1.6	.539
NBA Season Totals		461	346	13056	2535	1062	2095	.507	2	13	.154	409	1028	.398	1397	3236	4633	463	967	3	539	997	426	28.3	5.5	10.0	1.0	....
01-02	Detroit	10	10	408	73	28	59	.475	0	0	.000	17	39	.436	48	113	161	12	24	0	19	26	19	40.8	7.3	16.1	1.2	.506
02-03	Detroit	17	17	722	151	53	109	.486	0	1	.000	45	101	.446	86	191	277	28	50	0	42	52	15	42.5	8.9	16.3	1.6	.562
NBA Playoff Totals		27	27	1130	224	81	168	.482	0	1	.000	62	140	.443	134	304	438	40	74	0	61	78	34	41.9	8.3	16.2	1.5	....

• WALLACE, Gerald
Gerald Jermaine Wallace

Born: July 23, 1982. Sylacauga, AL, United States. Height: 6'7". Weight: 215 lbs. Drafted: 2001 College: Alabama

YEAR	TEAM	GP	GS	MIN	PTS	FGM	FGA	FG%	3PM	3PA	3P%	FTM	FTA	FT%	ORB	DRB	TRB	AST	PF	DQ	STL	BLK	TO	MPG	PPG	RPG	APG	PCM
01-02	Sacramento	54	1	430	173	75	175	.429	0	7	.000	23	46	.500	49	40	89	27	46	0	19	6	22	8.0	3.2	1.6	0.5	.381
02-03	Sacramento	47	7	570	220	90	183	.492	1	4	.250	39	74	.527	38	90	128	23	68	0	23	15	44	12.1	4.7	2.7	0.5	.394
NBA Season Totals		101	8	1000	393	165	358	.461	1	11	.091	62	120	.517	87	130	217	50	114	0	42	21	66	9.9	3.9	2.1	0.5	....
01-02	Sacramento	5	0	14	4	0	1	.000	0	0	.000	4	4	1.000	1	0	1	1	3	0	0	1	2	2.8	0.8	0.2	0.2	.202
02-03	Sacramento	7	0	18	6	2	5	.400	0	0	.000	2	2	1.000	0	5	5	0	4	0	0	1	2	2.6	0.9	0.7	0.0	.283
NBA Playoff Totals		12	0	32	10	2	6	.333	0	0	.000	6	6	1.000	1	5	6	1	7	0	0	2	4	2.7	0.8	0.5	0.1	....

YEAR	TEAM	GP	GS	MIN	PTS	FGM	FGA	FG%	3PM	3PA	3P%	FTM	FTA	FT%	ORB	DRB	TRB	AST	PF	DQ	STL	BLK	TO	MPG	PPG	RPG	APG	PCM

• WALLACE, John
John Wallace

Born: Feb. 9, 1974. Rochester, NY, United States.　　Height: 6'8".　　Weight: 225 lbs.　　Drafted: 1996　　College: Syracuse

YEAR	TEAM	GP	GS	MIN	PTS	FGM	FGA	FG%	3PM	3PA	3P%	FTM	FTA	FT%	ORB	DRB	TRB	AST	PF	DQ	STL	BLK	TO	MPG	PPG	RPG	APG	PCM
96-97	New York	68	6	787	325	122	236	.517	2	4	.500	79	110	.718	51	104	155	37	102	0	21	25	75	11.6	4.8	2.3	0.5	.399
97-98	Toronto	82	36	2361	1147	468	979	.478	1	2	.500	210	293	.717	117	256	373	110	239	7	62	101	172	28.8	14.0	4.5	1.3	.417
98-99	Toronto	48	3	812	411	153	354	.432	0	0	.000	105	150	.700	54	117	171	46	92	0	12	43	70	16.9	8.6	3.6	1.0	.445
99-00	New York	60	0	798	392	155	332	.467	0	3	.000	82	102	.804	42	93	135	22	103	0	10	14	63	13.3	6.5	2.3	0.4	.359
00-01	Detroit	40	0	527	237	100	236	.424	2	15	.133	35	45	.778	25	58	83	23	72	1	13	16	36	13.2	5.9	2.1	0.6	.326
01-02	Phoenix	46	0	490	231	93	214	.435	5	13	.385	40	46	.870	27	58	85	29	60	0	11	9	29	10.7	5.0	1.8	0.6	.392
NBA Season Totals		344	45	5775	2743	1091	2351	.464	10	37	.270	551	746	.739	316	686	1002	267	668	8	129	208	445	16.8	8.0	2.9	0.8	....
96-97	New York	4	1	40	10	4	15	.267	0	1	.000	2	2	1.000	2	5	7	5	6	0	1	2	2	10.0	2.5	1.8	1.3	.244
99-00	New York	1	0	4	0	0	2	.000	0	0	.000	0	0	.000	0	1	1	0	1	0	1	0	1	4.0	0.0	1.0	0.0	-.341
NBA Playoff Totals		5	1	44	10	4	17	.235	0	1	.000	2	2	1.000	2	6	8	5	7	0	2	2	3	8.8	2.0	1.6	1.0	....

• WALLACE, Paul
Paul Wallace

Born: —.　　Height: —　　Weight: —　　Drafted: —　　College: Toledo

YEAR	TEAM	GP	GS	MIN	PTS	FGM	FGA	FG%	3PM	3PA	3P%	FTM	FTA	FT%	ORB	DRB	TRB	AST	PF	DQ	STL	BLK	TO	MPG	PPG	RPG	APG	PCM
41-42	Toledo-N	1	....	....	0	0	....	....	....	....	....	0	....	....	....	....	....	....	....	....	....	....	....	0.0	....	....	....
NBL Season Totals		1	....	....	0	0	....	....	....	....	....	0	....	....	....	....	....	....	....	....	....	....	....	0.0	....	....	....

• WALLACE, Rasheed
Rasheed Abdul Wallace

Born: Sept. 17, 1974. Philadelphia, PA, United States.　　Height: 6'10".　　Weight: 225 lbs.　　Drafted: 1995　　College: North Carolina

YEAR	TEAM	GP	GS	MIN	PTS	FGM	FGA	FG%	3PM	3PA	3P%	FTM	FTA	FT%	ORB	DRB	TRB	AST	PF	DQ	STL	BLK	TO	MPG	PPG	RPG	APG	PCM
95-96	Washington	65	51	1788	655	275	565	.487	27	82	.329	78	120	.650	93	210	303	85	206	4	42	54	104	27.5	10.1	4.7	1.3	.354
96-97	Portland	62	56	1892	938	380	681	.558	9	33	.273	169	265	.638	122	297	419	74	198	1	48	59	112	30.5	15.1	6.8	1.2	.521
97-98	Portland	77	77	2896	1124	466	875	.533	8	39	.205	184	278	.662	132	346	478	195	268	6	75	88	169	37.6	14.6	6.2	2.5	.424
98-99	Portland	49	18	1414	628	242	476	.508	13	31	.419	131	179	.732	57	184	241	60	175	6	48	54	80	28.9	12.8	4.9	1.2	.439
99-00	Portland	81	77	2845	1325	542	1045	.519	8	50	.160	233	331	.704	129	437	566	142	216	2	87	107	157	35.1	16.4	7.0	1.8	.502
00-01	Portland	77	75	2940	1477	590	1178	.501	52	162	.321	245	320	.766	147	455	602	212	206	2	90	135	158	38.2	19.2	7.8	2.8	.564
01-02	Portland	79	79	2963	1521	603	1287	.469	114	317	.360	201	274	.734	136	509	645	152	212	0	101	101	131	37.5	19.3	8.2	1.9	.536
02-03	Portland	74	74	2684	1340	515	1094	.471	110	307	.358	200	272	.735	113	435	548	153	223	2	70	77	140	36.3	18.1	7.4	2.1	.503
NBA Season Totals		564	507	19422	9008	3613	7201	.502	341	1021	.334	1441	2039	.707	929	2873	3802	1073	1704	23	561	675	1051	34.4	16.0	6.7	1.9	....
96-97	Portland	4	4	148	79	33	56	.589	2	5	.400	11	20	.550	8	16	24	6	17	1	2	2	6	37.0	19.8	6.0	1.5	.489
97-98	Portland	4	4	157	58	23	47	.489	4	5	.800	8	16	.500	7	12	19	11	16	0	2	2	5	39.3	14.5	4.8	2.8	.341
98-99	Portland	13	13	468	193	75	146	.514	1	9	.111	42	58	.724	17	46	63	20	50	1	20	11	16	36.0	14.8	4.8	1.5	.410
99-00	Portland	16	16	605	286	110	225	.489	8	13	.615	58	75	.773	31	72	103	28	52	0	15	20	23	37.8	17.9	6.4	1.8	.471
00-01	Portland	3	3	128	50	19	51	.373	4	11	.364	8	14	.571	5	19	24	7	9	0	1	3	4	42.7	16.7	8.0	2.3	.342
01-02	Portland	3	3	125	76	28	69	.406	7	17	.412	13	16	.813	10	27	37	5	12	0	2	2	2	41.7	25.3	12.3	1.7	.583
02-03	Portland	7	7	260	122	44	97	.454	14	35	.400	20	28	.714	10	26	36	18	26	1	4	5	6	37.1	17.4	5.1	2.6	.437
NBA Playoff Totals		50	50	1891	864	332	691	.480	40	95	.421	160	227	.705	88	218	306	95	182	3	46	45	62	37.8	17.3	6.1	1.9	....

• WALLACE, Red
Michael John (Red) Wallace

Born: July 12, 1918. Died: July7, 1977.　　Height: 6'1".　　Weight: 185 lbs.　　Drafted: —　　College: Scranton

YEAR	TEAM	GP	GS	MIN	PTS	FGM	FGA	FG%	3PM	3PA	3P%	FTM	FTA	FT%	ORB	DRB	TRB	AST	PF	DQ	STL	BLK	TO	MPG	PPG	RPG	APG	PCM
46-47	Boston	24	....	....	131	55	224	.246	....	....	....	21	48	.438	....	....	....	20	42	....	....	....	....	5.5	....	0.8	....
46-47	Toronto	37	....	....	425	170	585	.291	....	....	....	85	148	.574	....	....	....	38	125	....	....	....	....	11.5	....	1.0	....
NBA Season Totals		61	....	....	556	225	809	.278	....	....	....	106	196	.541	....	....	....	58	167	....	....	....	....	9.1	....	1.0	....

• WALLER, Dwight
Dwight Waller

Born: Oct. 5, 1945. Brownsville, TN, United States.　　Height: 6'6".　　Weight: 220 lbs.　　Drafted: 1968　　College: Tennessee State

YEAR	TEAM	GP	GS	MIN	PTS	FGM	FGA	FG%	3PM	3PA	3P%	FTM	FTA	FT%	ORB	DRB	TRB	AST	PF	DQ	STL	BLK	TO	MPG	PPG	RPG	APG	PCM
68-69	Atlanta	11	....	29	7	2	9	.222	....	....	....	3	7	.429	....	....	10	1	8	0	....	....	....	2.6	0.6	0.9	0.1	.195
69-70	Denver-A	7	....	87	29	10	24	.417	0	1	.000	9	19	.474	16	22	38	4	12	0	....	....	16	12.4	4.1	5.4	0.6	.514
71-72	Denver-A	2	....	10	4	2	4	.500	0	0	.000	0	0	.000	1	4	5	1	3	0	....	....	1	5.0	2.0	2.5	0.5	.644
NBA Season Totals		11	....	29	7	2	9	.222	....	....	....	3	7	.429	....	....	10	1	8	0	....	....	....	2.6	0.6	0.9	0.1	....
ABA Season Totals		9	....	97	33	12	28	.429	0	1	.000	9	19	.474	17	26	43	5	15	0	....	....	17	10.8	3.7	4.8	0.6	....
Career Totals		20	....	126	40	14	37	.378	0	1	.000	12	26	.462	17	26	53	6	23	0	....	....	17	6.3	2.0	2.7	0.3	....

• WALLER, Jamie
Jamie Antonio Waller

Born: Nov. 20, 1964. South Boston, VA, United States.　　Height: 6'4".　　Weight: 215 lbs.　　Drafted: 1987　　College: Virginia Union

YEAR	TEAM	GP	GS	MIN	PTS	FGM	FGA	FG%	3PM	3PA	3P%	FTM	FTA	FT%	ORB	DRB	TRB	AST	PF	DQ	STL	BLK	TO	MPG	PPG	RPG	APG	PCM
87-88	New Jersey	9	0	91	42	16	40	.400	0	2	.000	10	18	.556	9	4	13	3	13	0	4	1	11	10.1	4.7	1.4	0.3	.215
NBA Season Totals		9	0	91	42	16	40	.400	0	2	.000	10	18	.556	9	4	13	3	13	0	4	1	11	10.1	4.7	1.4	0.3	....

• WALSH, Don
Donald Walsh

Born: —.　　Height: —　　Weight: —　　Drafted: —　　College: Gallagher Business

YEAR	TEAM	GP	GS	MIN	PTS	FGM	FGA	FG%	3PM	3PA	3P%	FTM	FTA	FT%	ORB	DRB	TRB	AST	PF	DQ	STL	BLK	TO	MPG	PPG	RPG	APG	PCM
37-38	Kankakee-N	4	....	....	4	2	....	....	....	....	....	0	....	....	....	....	....	....	....	....	....	....	....	1.0	....	....	....
NBL Season Totals		4	....	....	4	2	....	....	....	....	....	0	....	....	....	....	....	....	....	....	....	....	....	1.0	....	....	....

• WALSH, Jim
James Patrick Walsh

Born: Aug. 29, 1930. San Francisco, CA, United States. Died: Mar.4, 1976. Height: 6'4". Weight: 195 lbs. Drafted: 1952 College: Stanford

YEAR	TEAM	GP	GS	MIN	PTS	FGM	FGA	FG%	3PM	3PA	3P%	FTM	FTA	FT%	ORB	DRB	TRB	AST	PF	DQ	STL	BLK	TO	MPG	PPG	RPG	APG	PCM
57-58	Philadelphia	10	....	72	20	5	27	.185	....	....	....	10	17	.588	....	....	15	8	9	0	....	....	....	7.2	2.0	1.5	0.8	.267
NBA Season Totals		10	....	72	20	5	27	.185	....	....	....	10	17	.588	....	....	15	8	9	0	....	....	....	7.2	2.0	1.5	0.8	....

• WALTERS, Ken
Ken Walters

Born: 1922. Height: 6' Weight: 170 lbs. Drafted: — College: Ohio University

YEAR	TEAM	GP	GS	MIN	PTS	FGM	FGA	FG%	3PM	3PA	3P%	FTM	FTA	FT%	ORB	DRB	TRB	AST	PF	DQ	STL	BLK	TO	MPG	PPG	RPG	APG	PCM
47-48	Syracuse-N	1	....	....	0	0	....	....	....	....	....	0	0	.000	....	....	....	....	0	....	....	....	....	....	0.0	....	....	....
NBL Season Totals		1	....	....	0	0	....	....	....	....	....	0	0	....	....	....	....	....	0	....	....	....	....	....	0.0	....	....	....

• WALTERS, Rex
Rex Andrew Walters

Born: Mar. 12, 1970. Omaha, NE, United States. Height: 6'4". Weight: 190 lbs. Drafted: 1993 College: Kansas

YEAR	TEAM	GP	GS	MIN	PTS	FGM	FGA	FG%	3PM	3PA	3P%	FTM	FTA	FT%	ORB	DRB	TRB	AST	PF	DQ	STL	BLK	TO	MPG	PPG	RPG	APG	PCM
93-94	New Jersey	48	0	386	162	60	115	.522	14	28	.500	28	34	.824	6	32	38	71	41	0	15	3	29	8.0	3.4	0.8	1.5	.497
94-95	New Jersey	80	30	1435	523	206	469	.439	71	196	.362	40	52	.769	18	75	93	121	135	0	37	16	72	17.9	6.5	1.2	1.5	.282
95-96	New Jersey	11	0	87	33	12	33	.364	3	12	.250	6	6	1.000	2	5	7	11	4	0	3	0	7	7.9	3.0	0.6	1.0	.297
95-96	Philadelphia	33	8	523	153	49	115	.426	19	54	.352	36	46	.783	11	37	48	95	49	0	22	4	33	15.8	4.6	1.5	2.9	.387
96-97	Philadelphia	59	16	1041	402	148	325	.455	57	148	.385	49	62	.790	21	86	107	113	75	1	28	3	59	17.6	6.8	1.8	1.9	.375
97-98	Philadelphia	19	0	127	42	11	29	.379	3	14	.214	17	17	1.000	3	6	9	21	17	0	5	0	17	6.7	2.2	0.5	1.1	.298
97-98	Miami	19	0	108	38	13	24	.542	3	8	.375	9	11	.818	2	13	15	14	11	0	3	1	10	5.7	2.0	0.8	0.7	.420
98-99	Miami	33	13	506	101	35	95	.368	12	38	.316	19	23	.826	10	40	50	58	63	0	10	3	32	15.3	3.1	1.5	1.8	.217
99-00	Miami	33	0	389	93	38	91	.418	5	20	.250	12	16	.750	8	28	36	65	44	0	6	0	29	11.8	2.8	1.1	2.0	.272
NBA Season Totals		335	67	4602	1547	572	1296	.441	187	518	.361	216	267	.809	81	322	403	569	439	1	129	30	288	13.7	4.6	1.2	1.7	....
93-94	New Jersey	1	0	1	2	1	1	1.000	0	0	.000	0	0	.000	0	0	0	0	0	0	0	0	0	1.0	2.0	0.0	0.0	2.000
98-99	Miami	3	0	13	0	0	3	.000	0	2	.000	0	0	.000	0	0	0	4	0	0	0	0	0	4.3	0.0	0.0	1.3	.137
NBA Playoff Totals		4	0	14	2	1	4	.250	0	2	.000	0	0	.000	0	0	0	4	0	0	0	0	0	3.5	0.5	0.0	1.0	....

• WALTHER, Paul
Paul G. (Lefty) Walther

Born: Mar. 23, 1927. Height: 6'2". Weight: 160 lbs. Drafted: — College: Tennessee

YEAR	TEAM	GP	GS	MIN	PTS	FGM	FGA	FG%	3PM	3PA	3P%	FTM	FTA	FT%	ORB	DRB	TRB	AST	PF	DQ	STL	BLK	TO	MPG	PPG	RPG	APG	PCM
49-50	Minneapolis	22	....	....	75	32	80	.400	....	....	....	11	21	.524	....	....	....	10	39	....	....	....	....	....	3.4	....	0.5	....
49-50	Indianapolis	31	....	....	216	82	210	.390	....	....	....	52	88	.591	....	....	....	46	84	....	....	....	....	....	7.0	....	1.5	....
50-51	Indianapolis	63	....	....	571	213	634	.336	....	....	....	145	209	.694	....	....	226	225	201	8	....	....	....	....	9.1	3.6	3.6	....
51-52	Indianapolis	55	....	1903	671	220	549	.401	....	....	....	231	308	.750	....	....	246	137	171	6	....	....	....	34.6	12.2	4.5	2.5	.368
52-53	Indianapolis	67	....	2468	718	227	645	.352	....	....	....	264	354	.746	....	....	284	205	260	7	....	....	....	36.8	10.7	4.2	3.1	.306
53-54	Philadelphia	64	....	2067	421	138	392	.352	....	....	....	145	206	.704	....	....	257	220	199	5	....	....	....	32.3	6.6	4.0	3.4	.297
54-55	Fort Wayne	68	....	820	166	56	161	.348	....	....	....	54	88	.614	....	....	155	131	115	1	....	....	....	12.1	2.4	2.3	1.9	.379
NBA Season Totals		370	....	7258	2838	968	2671	.362	....	....	....	902	1274	.708	....	....	1168	974	1069	27	....	....	....	19.6	7.7	3.2	2.6	....
49-50	Indianapolis	6	....	....	33	12	41	.293	....	....	....	9	19	.474	....	....	....	8	17	....	....	....	....	....	5.5	....	1.3	....
50-51	Indianapolis	3	....	....	17	3	7	.429	....	....	....	11	15	.733	....	....	5	9	6	0	....	....	....	....	5.7	1.7	3.0	....
51-52	Indianapolis	2	....	85	32	8	16	.500	....	....	....	16	18	.889	....	....	7	6	8	0	....	....	....	42.5	16.0	3.5	3.0	.417
52-53	Indianapolis	2	....	75	26	5	20	.250	....	....	....	16	17	.941	....	....	8	4	8	1	....	....	....	37.5	13.0	4.0	2.0	.304
54-55	Fort Wayne	10	....	95	35	12	22	.545	....	....	....	11	18	.611	....	....	20	8	20	0	....	....	....	9.5	3.5	2.0	0.8	.446
NBA Playoff Totals		23	....	255	143	40	106	.377	....	....	....	63	87	.724	....	....	40	35	59	1	....	....	....	11.1	6.2	1.7	1.5	....

• WALTHOUR, Isaac
Isaac (Rabbit) Walthour

Born: 1928. Height: 5'11". Weight: 163 lbs. Drafted: — College: none (HS: Benjamin Franklin, NY)

YEAR	TEAM	GP	GS	MIN	PTS	FGM	FGA	FG%	3PM	3PA	3P%	FTM	FTA	FT%	ORB	DRB	TRB	AST	PF	DQ	STL	BLK	TO	MPG	PPG	RPG	APG	PCM
53-54	Milwaukee	4	....	30	2	1	6	.167	....	....	....	0	0	.000	....	....	1	2	6	0	....	....	....	7.5	0.5	0.3	0.5	-.013
NBA Season Totals		4	....	30	2	1	6	.167	....	....	....	0	0	.000	....	....	1	2	6	0	....	....	....	7.5	0.5	0.3	0.5	....

• WALTON, Bill
William Theodore Walton III

Born: Nov. 5, 1952. La Mesa, CA, United States. Height: 6'11". Weight: 210 lbs. Drafted: 1974 College: UCLA HOF: 1993

YEAR	TEAM	GP	GS	MIN	PTS	FGM	FGA	FG%	3PM	3PA	3P%	FTM	FTA	FT%	ORB	DRB	TRB	AST	PF	DQ	STL	BLK	TO	MPG	PPG	RPG	APG	PCM
74-75	Portland	35	....	1153	448	177	345	.513	....	....	....	94	137	.686	92	349	441	167	115	4	29	94	....	32.9	12.8	12.6	4.8	.698
75-76	Portland	51	....	1687	823	345	732	.471	....	....	....	133	228	.583	132	549	681	220	144	3	49	82	....	33.1	16.1	13.4	4.3	.726
76-77	Portland	65	....	2264	1210	491	930	.528	....	....	....	228	327	.697	211	723	934	245	174	5	66	211	....	34.8	18.6	**14.4**	3.8	.794
77-78	Portland	58	....	1929	1097	460	882	.522	....	....	....	177	246	.720	118	648	766	291	145	3	60	146	209	33.3	18.9	13.2	5.0	.845
79-80	San Diego	14	....	337	194	81	161	.503	0	0	.000	32	54	.593	28	98	126	34	37	0	8	38	36	24.1	13.9	9.0	2.4	.757
82-83	San Diego	33	32	1099	465	200	379	.528	0	0	.000	65	117	.556	75	248	323	120	113	0	34	119	106	33.3	14.1	9.8	3.6	.632
83-84	San Diego	55	46	1476	668	288	518	.556	0	2	.000	92	154	.597	132	345	477	183	153	1	45	88	176	26.8	12.1	8.7	3.3	.646
84-85	LA Clippers	67	37	1647	676	269	516	.521	0	2	.000	138	203	.680	168	432	600	156	184	0	50	140	174	24.6	10.1	9.0	2.3	.650
85-86	Boston	80	2	1546	606	231	411	.562	0	0	.000	144	202	.713	136	408	544	165	210	1	38	106	152	19.3	7.6	6.8	2.1	.640
86-87	Boston	10	0	112	28	10	26	.385	0	0	.000	8	15	.533	11	20	31	9	23	0	1	10	15	11.2	2.8	3.1	0.9	.303
NBA Season Totals		468	117	13250	6215	2552	4900	.521	0	4	.000	1111	1683	.660	1103	3820	4923	1590	1298	17	380	1034	868	28.3	13.3	10.5	3.4	....
76-77	Portland	19	....	755	345	153	302	.507	....	....	....	39	57	.684	56	232	288	104	80	3	20	64	....	39.7	18.2	15.2	5.5	.716
77-78	Portland	2	....	49	27	11	18	.611	....	....	....	5	7	.714	5	17	22	4	1	0	3	3	6	24.5	13.5	11.0	2.0	.884
85-86	Boston	16	0	291	127	54	93	.581	0	1	.000	19	23	.826	25	78	103	27	45	1	6	12	22	18.2	7.9	6.4	1.7	.649
86-87	Boston	12	0	102	29	12	25	.480	0	0	.000	5	14	.357	9	22	31	10	23	0	3	4	8	8.5	2.4	2.6	0.8	.398
NBA Playoff Totals		49	0	1197	528	230	438	.525	0	1	.000	68	101	.673	95	349	444	145	149	4	32	83	36	24.4	10.8	9.1	3.0	....

• WALTON, Jack

Jack Walton

Born: 1923. Markle, IN, United States. Height: 6'2". Weight: 190 lbs. Drafted: — College: Oklahoma State

YEAR	TEAM	GP	GS	MIN	PTS	FGM	FGA	FG%	3PM	3PA	3P%	FTM	FTA	FT%	ORB	DRB	TRB	AST	PF	DQ	STL	BLK	TO	MPG	PPG	RPG	APG	PCM
48-49	Anderson-N	8	....	....	14	5	....	....	....	....	....	4	5	.800	....	....	....	....	18	....	....	....	....	....	1.8	....	....	....
NBL Season Totals		8	....	....	14	5	....	....	....	....	....	4	5	....	....	....	....	....	18	....	....	....	....	....	1.8	....	....	....

• WALTON, Lloyd

Lloyd Walton

Born: Nov. 23, 1953. Chicago, IL, United States. Height: 6' Weight: 160 lbs. Drafted: 1976 College: Marquette

YEAR	TEAM	GP	GS	MIN	PTS	FGM	FGA	FG%	3PM	3PA	3P%	FTM	FTA	FT%	ORB	DRB	TRB	AST	PF	DQ	STL	BLK	TO	MPG	PPG	RPG	APG	PCM
76-77	Milwaukee	53	....	678	229	88	188	.468	....	....	....	53	65	.815	15	36	51	141	52	0	40	2	....	12.8	4.3	1.0	2.7	.471
77-78	Milwaukee	76	....	1264	362	154	344	.448	....	....	....	54	83	.651	26	50	76	253	94	0	77	13	106	16.6	4.8	1.0	3.3	.379
78-79	Milwaukee	75	....	1381	375	157	327	.480	....	....	....	61	90	.678	34	70	104	356	103	0	72	9	120	18.4	5.0	1.4	4.7	.444
79-80	Milwaukee	76	....	1243	270	110	242	.455	1	3	.333	49	71	.690	33	58	91	285	68	0	43	2	114	16.4	3.6	1.2	3.8	.355
80-81	Kansas City	61	....	821	206	90	218	.413	0	1	.000	26	33	.788	13	35	48	208	45	0	32	2	79	13.5	3.4	0.8	3.4	.359
NBA Season Totals		341	....	5387	1442	599	1319	.454	1	4	.250	243	342	.711	121	249	370	1243	362	0	264	28	419	15.8	4.2	1.1	3.6	....
77-78	Milwaukee	9	....	124	42	17	35	.486	....	....	....	8	13	.615	1	3	4	37	8	0	8	3	14	13.8	4.7	0.4	4.1	.509
79-80	Milwaukee	1	....	4	0	0	1	.000	0	0	.000	0	0	.000	0	1	1	1	0	0	0	1	1	4.0	0.0	1.0	1.0	.274
80-81	Kansas City	8	....	73	11	4	15	.267	0	1	.000	3	4	.750	3	4	7	19	6	0	4	0	9	9.1	1.4	0.9	2.4	.278
NBA Playoff Totals		18	....	201	53	21	51	.412	0	1	.000	11	17	.647	4	8	12	57	14	0	12	4	24	11.2	2.9	0.7	3.2	....

• WANZER, Bobby

Robert Francis (Hooks) Wanzer

Born: June 4, 1921. Brooklyn, NY, United States. Height: 6' Weight: 170 lbs. Drafted: 1948 College: Seton Hall HOF: 1987

YEAR	TEAM	GP	GS	MIN	PTS	FGM	FGA	FG%	3PM	3PA	3P%	FTM	FTA	FT%	ORB	DRB	TRB	AST	PF	DQ	STL	BLK	TO	MPG	PPG	RPG	APG	PCM
47-48	Rochester-N	40	....	....	167	55	....	....	....	....	....	57	69	.826	....	....	....	....	38	....	....	....	....	....	4.2	....	....	....
48-49	Rochester	60	....	....	613	202	533	.379	....	....	....	209	254	.823	....	....	....	186	132	....	....	....	....	....	10.2	....	3.1	....
49-50	Rochester	67	....	....	791	254	614	.414	....	....	....	283	351	.806	....	....	....	214	102	....	....	....	....	....	11.8	....	3.2	....
50-51	Rochester	68	....	....	736	252	628	.401	....	....	....	232	273	.850	....	....	232	181	129	0	....	....	....	....	10.8	3.4	2.7	....
51-52	Rochester	66	....	2498	1033	328	772	.425	....	....	....	377	417	**.904**	....	....	333	262	201	5	....	....	....	37.8	15.7	5.0	4.0	.483
52-53	Rochester	70	....	2577	1020	318	866	.367	....	....	....	384	473	.812	....	....	351	252	206	7	....	....	....	36.8	14.6	5.0	3.6	.424
53-54	Rochester	72	....	2538	958	322	835	.386	....	....	....	314	428	.734	....	....	392	254	171	2	....	....	....	35.3	13.3	5.4	3.5	.433
54-55	Rochester	72	....	2376	942	324	820	.395	....	....	....	294	374	.786	....	....	374	247	163	2	....	....	....	33.0	13.1	5.2	3.4	.449
55-56	Rochester	72	....	1980	749	245	651	.376	....	....	....	259	360	.719	....	....	272	225	151	0	....	....	....	27.5	10.4	3.8	3.1	.419
56-57	Rochester	21	....	159	82	23	49	.469	....	....	....	36	46	.783	....	....	25	9	20	0	....	....	....	7.6	3.9	1.2	0.4	.512
NBA Season Totals		568	....	12128	6924	2268	5768	.393	....	....	....	2388	2976	.802	....	....	1979	1830	1275	16	....	....	....	21.4	12.2	3.5	3.2	....
NBL Season Totals		40	....	....	167	55	....	....	....	....	....	57	69	....	....	....	....	....	38	....	....	....	....	....	4.2	....	....	....
Career Totals		608	....	12128	7091	2323	5768	....	....	....	....	2445	3045	....	....	....	1979	1830	1313	16	....	....	....	19.9	11.7	3.3	3.0	....
47-48	Rochester-N	11	....	....	66	21	....	....	....	....	....	24	28	.857	....	....	....	....	....	....	....	....	....	....	6.0	....	....	....
48-49	Rochester	4	....	....	38	13	41	.317	....	....	....	12	17	.706	....	....	....	9	9	....	....	....	....	....	9.5	....	2.3	....
49-50	Rochester	2	....	....	27	8	17	.471	....	....	....	11	13	.846	....	....	....	4	7	....	....	....	....	....	13.5	....	2.0	....
50-51	Rochester	14	....	....	175	57	121	.471	....	....	....	61	67	.910	....	....	71	59	45	1	....	....	....	....	12.5	5.1	4.2	....
51-52	Rochester	6	....	249	113	33	77	.429	....	....	....	47	49	.959	....	....	38	19	23	2	....	....	....	41.5	18.8	6.3	3.2	.499
52-53	Rochester	3	....	116	51	14	37	.378	....	....	....	23	27	.852	....	....	21	9	13	0	....	....	....	38.7	17.0	7.0	3.0	.473
53-54	Rochester	6	....	245	96	30	74	.405	....	....	....	36	44	.818	....	....	35	26	18	0	....	....	....	40.8	16.0	5.8	4.3	.465
54-55	Rochester	3	....	100	54	16	35	.457	....	....	....	22	24	.917	....	....	21	8	8	0	....	....	....	33.3	18.0	7.0	2.7	.617
NBA Playoff Totals		38	....	710	554	171	402	.425	....	....	....	212	241	.880	....	....	186	134	123	3	....	....	....	18.7	14.6	4.9	3.5	....
NBL Playoff Totals		11	....	....	66	21	....	....	....	....	....	24	28	....	....	....	....	....	....	....	....	....	....	....	6.0	....	....	....
Career Playoff Totals		49	....	710	620	192	402	....	....	....	....	236	269	....	....	....	186	134	123	3	....	....	....	14.5	12.7	3.8	2.7	....

• WARBINGTON, Perry

Perry Warbington

Born: Sept. 7, 1952. Atlabta, GA, United States. Height: 6'2". Weight: 165 lbs. Drafted: 1974 College: Georgia Southern

YEAR	TEAM	GP	GS	MIN	PTS	FGM	FGA	FG%	3PM	3PA	3P%	FTM	FTA	FT%	ORB	DRB	TRB	AST	PF	DQ	STL	BLK	TO	MPG	PPG	RPG	APG	PCM
74-75	Philadelphia	5	....	70	10	4	21	.190	....	....	....	2	2	1.000	2	6	8	16	16	0	0	0	....	14.0	2.0	1.6	3.2	.198
NBA Season Totals		5	....	70	10	4	21	.190	....	....	....	2	2	1.000	2	6	8	16	16	0	0	0	....	14.0	2.0	1.6	3.2	....

• WARD, Charlie

Charlie Ward Jr.

Born: Oct. 12, 1970. Thomasville, GA, United States. Height: 6'2". Weight: 190 lbs. Drafted: 1994 College: Florida State

YEAR	TEAM	GP	GS	MIN	PTS	FGM	FGA	FG%	3PM	3PA	3P%	FTM	FTA	FT%	ORB	DRB	TRB	AST	PF	DQ	STL	BLK	TO	MPG	PPG	RPG	APG	PCM
94-95	New York	10	0	44	16	4	19	.211	1	10	.100	7	10	.700	1	5	6	4	7	0	2	0	8	4.4	1.6	0.6	0.4	.034
95-96	New York	62	1	787	244	87	218	.399	33	99	.333	37	54	.685	29	73	102	132	98	0	54	6	81	12.7	3.9	1.6	2.1	.359
96-97	New York	79	21	1763	409	133	337	.395	48	154	.312	95	125	.760	45	175	220	326	188	2	83	15	150	22.3	5.2	2.8	4.1	.353
97-98	New York	82	82	2317	642	235	516	.455	81	215	.377	91	113	.805	32	242	274	466	195	3	144	37	172	28.3	7.8	3.3	5.7	.453
98-99	New York	50	50	1556	378	135	334	.404	53	149	.356	55	78	.705	23	149	172	271	105	0	103	8	131	31.1	7.6	3.4	5.4	.373
99-00	New York	72	69	1986	528	189	447	.423	102	264	.386	48	58	.828	22	206	228	300	176	3	95	16	102	27.6	7.3	3.2	4.2	.379
00-01	New York	61	33	1492	433	155	373	.416	67	175	.383	56	70	.800	32	127	159	273	132	0	70	10	112	24.5	7.1	2.6	4.5	.393
01-02	New York	63	0	1058	326	113	303	.373	53	164	.323	47	58	.810	15	112	127	203	100	0	68	14	75	16.8	5.2	2.0	3.2	.423
02-03	New York	66	6	1466	472	165	414	.399	101	267	.378	41	53	.774	25	152	177	306	146	1	78	11	95	22.2	7.2	2.7	4.6	.453
NBA Season Totals		545	262	12469	3448	1216	2961	.411	539	1497	.360	477	619	.771	224	1241	1465	2281	1147	9	697	117	926	22.9	6.3	2.7	4.2	....
95-96	New York	7	0	92	32	13	27	.481	3	12	.250	3	7	.429	2	7	9	17	9	0	11	0	6	13.1	4.6	1.3	2.4	.477
96-97	New York	9	0	182	20	8	27	.296	1	9	.111	3	4	.750	3	22	25	39	18	1	13	0	15	20.2	2.2	2.8	4.3	.311
97-98	New York	10	10	261	66	23	55	.418	9	21	.429	11	16	.688	3	25	28	60	24	0	20	2	17	26.1	6.6	2.8	6.0	.455
98-99	New York	20	20	494	92	34	93	.366	18	56	.321	6	8	.750	12	34	46	75	45	0	35	3	24	24.7	4.6	2.3	3.8	.314
99-00	New York	16	16	439	150	57	113	.504	21	53	.396	15	21	.714	11	57	68	65	40	1	22	5	20	27.4	9.4	4.3	4.1	.495
00-01	New York	5	0	86	25	8	27	.296	3	12	.250	6	6	1.000	2	5	7	7	8	0	2	0	8	17.2	5.0	1.4	1.4	.151
NBA Playoff Totals		67	46	1554	385	143	342	.418	55	163	.337	44	62	.710	33	150	183	263	144	2	103	10	90	23.2	5.7	2.7	3.9	....

YEAR	TEAM	GP	GS	MIN	PTS	FGM	FGA	FG%	3PM	3PA	3P%	FTM	FTA	FT%	ORB	DRB	TRB	AST	PF	DQ	STL	BLK	TO	MPG	PPG	RPG	APG	PCM

• WARD, Gerry
Gerald W. Ward

Born: Sept. 6, 1941.　　Height: 6'4".　　Weight: 195 lbs.　　Drafted: 1963　　College: Boston College

YEAR	TEAM	GP	GS	MIN	PTS	FGM	FGA	FG%	3PM	3PA	3P%	FTM	FTA	FT%	ORB	DRB	TRB	AST	PF	DQ	STL	BLK	TO	MPG	PPG	RPG	APG	PCM
63-64	St. Louis	24	....	139	43	16	53	.302	....	....	....	11	17	.647	....	....	21	21	26	0	....	....	....	5.8	1.8	0.9	0.9	.315
64-65	Boston	3	....	30	5	2	18	.111	....	....	....	1	1	1.000	....	....	5	6	6	0	....	....	....	10.0	1.7	1.7	2.0	.055
65-66	Philadelphia	66	....	838	173	67	189	.354	....	....	....	39	60	.650	....	....	89	80	163	3	....	....	....	12.7	2.6	1.3	1.2	.206
66-67	Chicago	76	....	1042	321	117	307	.381	....	....	....	87	138	.630	....	....	179	130	169	2	....	....	....	13.7	4.2	2.4	1.7	.366
NBA Season Totals		169	....	2049	542	202	567	.356	....	....	....	138	216	.639	....	....	294	237	364	5	....	....	....	12.1	3.2	1.7	1.4	....
63-64	St. Louis	6	....	16	11	5	10	.500	....	....	....	1	1	1.000	....	....	0	2	5	0	....	....	....	2.7	1.8	0.0	0.3	.476
65-66	Philadelphia	5	....	44	4	2	8	.250	....	....	....	0	1	.000	....	....	5	1	11	0	....	....	....	8.8	0.8	1.0	0.2	-.006
66-67	Chicago	3	....	38	24	10	22	.455	....	....	....	4	5	.800	....	....	10	2	7	0	....	....	....	12.7	8.0	3.3	0.7	.569
NBA Playoff Totals		14	....	98	39	17	40	.425	....	....	....	5	7	.714	....	....	15	5	23	0	....	....	....	7.0	2.8	1.1	0.4	....

• WARD, Henry
Henry Lorette Ward

Born: Jan. 30, 1952. Jackson, MS, United States.　　Height: 6'4".　　Weight: 195 lbs.　　Drafted: 1975　　College: Jackson State

YEAR	TEAM	GP	GS	MIN	PTS	FGM	FGA	FG%	3PM	3PA	3P%	FTM	FTA	FT%	ORB	DRB	TRB	AST	PF	DQ	STL	BLK	TO	MPG	PPG	RPG	APG	PCM
75-76	San Antonio-A	61	....	688	330	148	310	.477	18	23	**.783**	16	27	.593	45	95	140	35	99	....	16	10	45	11.3	5.4	2.3	0.6	.436
76-77	San Antonio	27	....	171	83	34	90	.378	....	....	....	15	17	.882	10	23	33	6	30	0	6	5	....	6.3	3.1	1.2	0.2	.328
NBA Season Totals		27	....	171	83	34	90	.378	....	....	....	15	17	.882	10	23	33	6	30	0	6	5	....	6.3	3.1	1.2	0.2	....
ABA Season Totals		61	....	688	330	148	310	.477	18	23	.783	16	27	.593	45	95	140	35	99	....	16	10	45	11.3	5.4	2.3	0.6	....
Career Totals		88	....	859	413	182	400	.455	18	23	.783	31	44	.705	55	118	173	41	129	0	22	15	45	9.8	4.7	2.0	0.5	....
75-76	San Antonio-A	5	....	18	10	4	12	.333	2	2	1.000	0	0	.000	1	1	2	0	6	....	1	1	1	3.6	2.0	0.4	0.0	.110
76-77	San Antonio	1	....	1	4	2	3	.667	....	....	....	0	0	.000	0	0	0	0	0	0	0	0	....	1.0	4.0	0.0	0.0	3.137
NBA Playoff Totals		1	....	1	4	2	3	.667	....	....	....	0	0	.000	0	0	0	0	0	0	0	0	....	1.0	4.0	0.0	0.0	....
ABA Playoff Totals		5	....	18	10	4	12	.333	2	2	1.000	0	0	.000	1	1	2	0	6	....	1	1	1	3.6	2.0	0.4	0.0	....
Career Playoff Totals		6	....	19	14	6	15	.400	2	2	1.000	0	0	.000	1	1	2	0	6	0	1	1	1	3.2	2.3	0.3	0.0	....

• WARE, Jim
James Edward Ware

Born: May 2, 1944. Natchez, MS, United States.　　Height: 6'7".　　Weight: 210 lbs.　　Drafted: 1966　　College: Oklahoma City

YEAR	TEAM	GP	GS	MIN	PTS	FGM	FGA	FG%	3PM	3PA	3P%	FTM	FTA	FT%	ORB	DRB	TRB	AST	PF	DQ	STL	BLK	TO	MPG	PPG	RPG	APG	PCM
66-67	Cincinnati	33	....	201	70	30	97	.309	....	....	....	10	17	.588	....	....	69	6	35	0	....	....	....	6.1	2.1	2.1	0.2	.309
67-68	San Diego	30	....	228	73	25	97	.258	....	....	....	23	34	.676	....	....	77	7	28	1	....	....	....	7.6	2.4	2.6	0.2	.306
68-69	Dallas-A	1	....	15	7	3	4	.750	0	0	.000	1	2	.500	2	5	7	1	4	0	....	....	1	15.0	7.0	7.0	1.0	.743
NBA Season Totals		63	....	429	143	55	194	.284	....	....	....	33	51	.647	....	....	146	13	63	1	....	....	....	6.8	2.3	2.3	0.2	....
ABA Season Totals		1	....	15	7	3	4	.750	0	0	.000	1	2	.500	2	5	7	1	4	0	....	....	1	15.0	7.0	7.0	1.0	....
Career Totals		64	....	444	150	58	198	.293	0	0	.000	34	53	.642	2	5	153	14	67	1	....	....	1	6.9	2.3	2.4	0.2	....
66-67	Cincinnati	3	....	13	10	5	13	.385	....	....	....	0	0	.000	....	....	2	0	1	0	....	....	....	4.3	3.3	0.7	0.0	.371
NBA Playoff Totals		3	....	13	10	5	13	.385	....	....	....	0	0	.000	....	....	2	0	1	0	....	....	....	4.3	3.3	0.7	0.0	....

• WAREHAM, Dave
David Wareham

Born: 1924.　　Height: 6'1".　　Weight: 185 lbs.　　Drafted: —　　College: Loras

YEAR	TEAM	GP	GS	MIN	PTS	FGM	FGA	FG%	3PM	3PA	3P%	FTM	FTA	FT%	ORB	DRB	TRB	AST	PF	DQ	STL	BLK	TO	MPG	PPG	RPG	APG	PCM
48-49	Waterloo-N	4	....	....	3	1	....	....	....	....	....	1	3	.333	....	....	....	....	2	....	....	....	....	0.8	....	....	....
NBL Season Totals		4	....	....	3	1	....	....	....	....	....	1	3	....	....	....	....	....	2	....	....	....	....	0.8	....	....	....

• WARLEY, Ben
Benjamin Vallentina Warley

Born: Sept. 4, 1936. Washington, DC, United States.　　Height: 6'5".　　Weight: 200 lbs.　　Drafted: 1961　　College: Tennessee State

YEAR	TEAM	GP	GS	MIN	PTS	FGM	FGA	FG%	3PM	3PA	3P%	FTM	FTA	FT%	ORB	DRB	TRB	AST	PF	DQ	STL	BLK	TO	MPG	PPG	RPG	APG	PCM
62-63	Syracuse	26	....	206	125	50	111	.450	....	....	....	25	35	.714	....	....	86	4	42	1	....	....	....	7.9	4.8	3.3	0.2	.626
63-64	Philadelphia	79	....	1740	650	215	494	.435	....	....	....	220	305	.721	....	....	619	71	274	5	....	....	....	22.0	8.2	7.8	0.9	.495
64-65	Philadelphia	65	....	900	312	94	253	.372	....	....	....	124	176	.705	....	....	277	53	170	6	....	....	....	13.8	4.8	4.3	0.8	.425
65-66	Philadelphia	1	....	6	2	1	3	.333	....	....	....	0	0	.000	....	....	2	0	1	0	....	....	....	6.0	2.0	2.0	0.0	.268
65-66	Baltimore	56	....	767	294	115	281	.409	....	....	....	64	97	.660	....	....	215	25	128	2	....	....	....	13.7	5.3	3.8	0.4	.391
66-67	Baltimore	62	....	1037	384	125	312	.401	....	....	....	134	170	.788	....	....	325	51	176	6	....	....	....	16.7	6.2	5.2	0.8	.454
67-68	Anaheim-A	71	....	2297	1235	435	985	.442	52	166	.313	313	389	.805	....	....	608	96	276	12	161	32.4	17.4	8.6	1.4	.544
68-69	Los Angeles-A	35	....	876	491	172	423	.407	31	121	.256	116	155	.748	51	143	194	26	127	6	....	....	53	25.0	14.0	5.5	0.7	.457
69-70	Denver-A	42	....	475	193	60	170	.353	15	58	.259	58	76	.763	26	84	110	30	98	0	....	....	36	11.3	4.6	2.6	0.7	.374
NBA Season Totals		289	....	4656	1767	600	1454	.413	....	....	....	567	783	.724	....	....	1524	204	791	20	....	....	....	16.1	6.1	5.3	0.7	....
ABA Season Totals		148	....	3648	1919	667	1578	.423	98	345	.284	487	620	.785	77	227	912	152	501	18	....	....	250	24.6	13.0	6.2	1.0	....
Career Totals		437	....	8304	3686	1267	3032	.418	98	345	.284	1054	1403	.751	77	227	2436	356	1292	38	....	....	250	19.0	8.4	5.6	0.8	....
62-63	Syracuse	2	....	9	2	0	4	.000	....	....	....	2	4	.500	....	....	3	0	2	0	....	....	....	4.5	1.0	1.5	0.0	-.041
63-64	Philadelphia	4	....	85	28	9	23	.391	....	....	....	10	15	.667	....	....	33	2	11	0	....	....	....	21.3	7.0	8.3	0.5	.459
64-65	Philadelphia	2	....	6	0	0	1	.000	....	....	....	0	0	.000	....	....	1	1	1	0	....	....	....	3.0	0.0	0.5	0.5	.141
65-66	Baltimore	2	....	9	1	0	4	.000	....	....	....	1	1	1.000	....	....	2	0	2	0	....	....	....	4.5	0.5	1.0	0.0	-.150
69-70	Denver-A	10	....	129	45	16	38	.421	7	16	.438	6	10	.600	5	24	29	11	27	1	....	....	9	12.9	4.5	2.9	1.1	.390
NBA Playoff Totals		10	....	109	31	9	32	.281	....	....	....	13	20	.650	....	....	39	3	16	0	....	....	....	10.9	3.1	3.9	0.3	....
ABA Playoff Totals		10	....	129	45	16	38	.421	7	16	.438	6	10	.600	5	24	29	11	27	1	....	....	9	12.9	4.5	2.9	1.1	....
Career Playoff Totals		20	....	238	76	25	70	.357	7	16	.438	19	30	.633	5	24	68	14	43	1	....	....	9	11.9	3.8	3.4	0.7	....

WARLICK, Bob
Robert Lee Warlick

Born: Mar. 20, 1941. Hickory, NC, United States. Height: 6'5". Weight: 200 lbs. Drafted: — College: Denver

YEAR	TEAM	GP	GS	MIN	PTS	FGM	FGA	FG%	3PM	3PA	3P%	FTM	FTA	FT%	ORB	DRB	TRB	AST	PF	DQ	STL	BLK	TO	MPG	PPG	RPG	APG	PCM
65-66	Detroit	10	....	78	24	11	38	.289	....	....	....	2	6	.333	....	....	16	10	8	0	....	....	....	7.8	2.4	1.6	1.0	.293
66-67	San Francisco	12	....	65	36	15	52	.288	....	....	....	6	11	.545	....	....	20	10	4	0	....	....	....	5.4	3.0	1.7	0.8	.475
67-68	San Francisco	69	....	1320	611	257	610	.421	....	....	....	97	171	.567	....	....	264	159	164	1	....	....	....	19.1	8.9	3.8	2.3	.482
68-69	Milwaukee	3	....	22	6	1	8	.125	....	....	....	4	5	.800	....	....	1	1	3	0	....	....	....	7.3	2.0	0.3	0.3	.022
68-69	Phoenix	63	....	975	507	212	501	.423	....	....	....	83	137	.606	....	....	151	131	119	0	....	....	....	15.5	8.0	2.4	2.1	.484
69-70	Los Angeles-A	29	....	711	289	112	309	.362	0	1	.000	65	96	.677	51	63	114	76	70	0	....	....	57	24.5	10.0	3.9	2.6	.367
NBA Season Totals		157		2460	1184	496	1209	.410				192	330	.582			452	311	298	1				15.7	7.5	2.9	2.0	
ABA Season Totals		29		711	289	112	309	.362	0	1	.000	65	96	.677	51	63	114	76	70	0			57	24.5	10.0	3.9	2.6	
Career Totals		186		3171	1473	608	1518	.401	0	1	.000	257	426	.603	51	63	566	387	368	1			57	17.0	7.9	3.0	2.1	
66-67	San Francisco	2	....	8	0	0	2	.000	....	....	....	0	0	.000	....	....	0	1	0	0	....	....	....	4.0	0.0	0.0	0.5	-.049
67-68	San Francisco	10	....	226	138	55	118	.466	....	....	....	28	37	.757	....	....	53	24	26	2	....	....	....	22.6	13.8	5.3	2.4	.641
NBA Playoff Totals		12		234	138	55	120	.458				28	37	.757			53	25	26	2				19.5	11.5	4.4	2.1	

WARNER, Cornell
Cornell Warner

Born: Aug. 12, 1948. Jackson, MS, United States. Height: 6'9". Weight: 220 lbs. Drafted: 1970 College: Jackson State

YEAR	TEAM	GP	GS	MIN	PTS	FGM	FGA	FG%	3PM	3PA	3P%	FTM	FTA	FT%	ORB	DRB	TRB	AST	PF	DQ	STL	BLK	TO	MPG	PPG	RPG	APG	PCM
70-71	Buffalo	65	....	1293	391	156	376	.415				79	143	.552			452	53	140	2				19.9	6.0	7.0	0.8	.436
71-72	Buffalo	62	....	1239	382	162	366	.443				58	78	.744			379	54	125	2				20.0	6.2	6.1	0.9	.429
72-73	Buffalo	4	....	47	17	8	17	.471				1	2	.500			15	6	6	0				11.8	4.3	3.8	1.5	.553
72-73	Cleveland	68	....	1323	390	166	404	.411				58	88	.659			507	66	172	0				19.5	5.7	7.5	1.0	.461
73-74	Cleveland	5	....	49	8	2	13	.154				4	4	1.000	5	12	17	4	7	0	0	2		9.8	1.6	3.4	0.8	.300
73-74	Milwaukee	67	....	1356	425	172	336	.512				81	110	.736	101	279	380	67	197	2	27	40		20.2	6.3	5.7	1.0	.435
74-75	Milwaukee	79	....	2519	602	248	541	.458				106	155	.684	238	574	812	127	267	8	49	54		31.9	7.6	10.3	1.6	.419
75-76	LA Lakers	81	....	2512	591	251	524	.479				89	128	.695	223	499	722	106	283	3	55	46		31.0	7.3	8.9	1.3	.382
76-77	LA Lakers	14	....	170	54	25	53	.472				4	6	.667	21	48	69	11	28	0	1	2		12.1	3.9	4.9	0.8	.523
NBA Season Totals		445		10508	2860	1190	2630	.452				480	714	.672	588	1412	3353	494	1225	15	132	144		23.6	6.4	7.5	1.1	
73-74	Milwaukee	16	....	505	107	47	111	.423				13	19	.684	35	128	163	20	70	3	7	14		31.6	6.7	10.2	1.3	.360
76-77	LA Lakers	5	....	56	14	7	12	.583				0	0	.000	2	7	9	6	11	0	1	0		11.2	2.8	1.8	1.2	.349
NBA Playoff Totals		21		561	121	54	123	.439				13	19	.684	37	135	172	26	81	3	8	14		26.7	5.8	8.2	1.2	

WARNKE, Donald
Donald L. Warnke

Born: Apr. 8, 1921. Died: Apr.1970. Height: 6'10". Weight: 200 lbs. Drafted: — College: Valparaiso

YEAR	TEAM	GP	GS	MIN	PTS	FGM	FGA	FG%	3PM	3PA	3P%	FTM	FTA	FT%	ORB	DRB	TRB	AST	PF	DQ	STL	BLK	TO	MPG	PPG	RPG	APG	PCM
44-45	Cleveland-N	20	....	....	29	10	....	....	....	....	....	9	....	....	....	....	....	....	....	....	....	....	....	1.5	....	....	....	
45-46	Youngstown-N	1	....	....	0	0	....	....	....	....	....	0	0	.000	....	....	....	....	....	....	....	....	....	0.0	....	....	....	
NBL Season Totals		21			29	10						9	0											1.4				

WARREN, Bob
Robert G. (Colonel) Warren

Born: July 17, 1946. Murray, KY, United States. Height: 6'5". Weight: 190 lbs. Drafted: 1968 College: Vanderbilt

YEAR	TEAM	GP	GS	MIN	PTS	FGM	FGA	FG%	3PM	3PA	3P%	FTM	FTA	FT%	ORB	DRB	TRB	AST	PF	DQ	STL	BLK	TO	MPG	PPG	RPG	APG	PCM
68-69	Los Angeles-A	76	....	2045	898	285	645	.442	31	89	.348	297	385	.771	147	202	349	155	252	6	....	....	175	26.9	11.8	4.6	2.0	.450
69-70	Los Angeles-A	72	....	1672	733	266	647	.411	25	107	.234	176	238	.739	119	158	277	141	190	1	....	....	148	23.2	10.2	3.8	2.0	.417
70-71	Memphis-A	46	....	763	420	146	367	.398	21	81	.259	107	133	.805	69	75	144	85	87	0	....	....	73	16.6	9.1	3.1	1.8	.544
71-72	Carolina-A	37	....	501	188	73	167	.437	3	17	.176	39	49	.796	19	35	54	46	59	1	....	....	34	13.5	5.1	1.5	1.2	.347
71-72	Memphis-A	38	....	1300	662	240	540	.444	8	38	.211	174	219	.795	120	85	205	136	106	0	....	....	106	34.2	17.4	5.4	3.6	.511
72-73	Carolina-A	17	....	353	157	54	106	.509	0	0	.000	49	60	.817	26	39	65	22	43	0	....	....	33	20.8	9.2	3.8	1.3	.478
72-73	Dallas-A	9	....	172	70	20	53	.377	1	1	1.000	29	34	.853	9	13	22	16	25	0	....	....	16	19.1	7.8	2.4	1.8	.374
72-73	Utah-A	51	....	1046	502	170	345	.493	4	18	.222	158	180	.878	57	98	155	109	144	2	....	....	94	20.5	9.8	3.0	2.1	.506
73-74	San Antonio-A	36	....	486	154	61	134	.455	0	1	.000	32	35	.914	26	35	61	38	40	0	9	5	30	13.5	4.3	1.7	1.1	.347
73-74	Utah-A	23	....	313	129	49	121	.405	0	5	.000	31	38	.816	27	16	43	36	33	0	12	8	32	13.6	5.6	1.9	1.6	.409
74-75	San Antonio-A	71	....	992	333	127	265	.479	2	7	.286	77	91	.846	42	70	112	91	109	0	35	9	68	14.0	4.7	1.6	1.3	.359
75-76	San Diego-A	10	....	265	101	36	81	.444	1	3	.333	28	32	.875	27	32	59	23	35	....	9	6	23	26.5	10.1	5.9	2.3	.459
ABA Season Totals		486	....	9908	4347	1527	3471	.440	96	367	.262	1197	1494	.801	688	858	1546	898	1123	10	65	28	832	20.4	8.9	3.2	1.8	....
69-70	Los Angeles-A	17	....	576	256	96	223	.430	15	54	.278	49	64	.766	....	....	127	67	....	0	....	....	38	33.9	15.1	7.5	3.9	
72-73	Utah-A	10	....	221	95	32	68	.471	2	4	.500	29	32	.906	14	25	39	16	33	0	....	....	20	22.1	9.5	3.9	1.6	.449
73-74	San Antonio-A	7	....	133	36	14	29	.483	0	0	.000	8	8	1.000	9	12	21	9	21	....	2	2	9	19.0	5.1	3.0	1.3	.319
74-75	San Antonio-A	1	....	5	0	0	1	.000	0	0	.000	0	0	.000	0	0	0	0	0	....	0	0	1	5.0	0.0	0.0	0.0	-.178
ABA Playoff Totals		35	....	935	387	142	321	.442	17	58	.293	86	104	.827	23	37	187	92	54	0	2	2	68	26.7	11.1	5.3	2.6	

WARREN, John
John Warren II

Born: July 7, 1947. Sparta, GA, United States. Height: 6'3". Weight: 180 lbs. Drafted: 1969 College: St. John's (NY)

YEAR	TEAM	GP	GS	MIN	PTS	FGM	FGA	FG%	3PM	3PA	3P%	FTM	FTA	FT%	ORB	DRB	TRB	AST	PF	DQ	STL	BLK	TO	MPG	PPG	RPG	APG	PCM
69-70	New York	44	....	272	112	44	108	.407				24	35	.686			40	30	53	0				6.2	2.5	0.9	0.7	.354
70-71	Cleveland	82	....	2610	940	380	899	.423				180	217	.829			344	347	299	13				31.8	11.5	4.2	4.2	.399
71-72	Cleveland	68	....	969	337	144	345	.417				49	58	.845			133	91	92	0				14.3	5.0	2.0	1.3	.349
72-73	Cleveland	40	....	290	126	54	111	.486				18	19	.947			42	34	45	0				7.3	3.2	1.1	0.9	.456
73-74	Cleveland	69	....	790	299	132	291	.454				35	41	.854	42	86	128	62	117	1	27	6		11.4	4.3	1.9	0.9	.369
NBA Season Totals		303		4931	1814	754	1754	.430				306	370	.827	42	86	687	564	606	14	27	6		16.3	6.0	2.3	1.9	
69-70	New York	10	....	22	4	2	5	.400				0	0	.000			3	2	6	0				2.2	0.4	0.3	0.2	.164
NBA Playoff Totals		10		22	4	2	5	.400				0	0	.000			3	2	6	0				2.2	0.4	0.3	0.2	

• WARRICK, Bryan
Bryan Anthony Warrick

Born: July 22, 1959. Moses Lake, WA, United States. Height: 6'5". Weight: 195 lbs. Drafted: 1982 College: St. Joseph's (PA)

YEAR TEAM	GP	GS	MIN	PTS	FGM	FGA	FG%	3PM	3PA	3P%	FTM	FTA	FT%	ORB	DRB	TRB	AST	PF	DQ	STL	BLK	TO	MPG	PPG	RPG	APG	PCM
82-83 Washington	43	20	727	172	65	171	.380	0	5	.000	42	57	.737	15	54	69	126	103	5	21	8	73	16.9	4.0	1.6	2.9	.253
83-84 Washington	32	0	254	63	27	66	.409	1	3	.333	8	16	.500	5	17	22	43	37	0	9	3	19	7.9	2.0	0.7	1.3	.259
84-85 LA Clippers	58	1	713	215	85	173	.491	1	4	.250	44	57	.772	10	48	58	153	85	0	23	6	70	12.3	3.7	1.0	2.6	.374
85-86 Milwaukee	5	0	27	10	4	10	.400	1	2	.500	1	1	1.000	0	3	3	6	3	0	2	0	5	5.4	2.0	0.6	1.2	.350
85-86 Indiana	31	5	658	217	81	172	.471	2	10	.200	53	67	.791	10	56	66	109	76	0	25	2	47	21.2	7.0	2.1	3.5	.380
NBA Season Totals	169	26	2379	677	262	592	.443	5	24	.208	148	198	.747	40	178	218	437	304	5	80	19	214	14.1	4.0	1.3	2.6	....

• WASHBURN, Chris
Christopher Scott Washburn

Born: May 13, 1965. Hickory, NC, United States. Height: 6'11". Weight: 225 lbs. Drafted: 1986 College: North Carolina State

YEAR TEAM	GP	GS	MIN	PTS	FGM	FGA	FG%	3PM	3PA	3P%	FTM	FTA	FT%	ORB	DRB	TRB	AST	PF	DQ	STL	BLK	TO	MPG	PPG	RPG	APG	PCM
86-87 Golden State	35	2	385	132	57	145	.393	0	1	.000	18	51	.353	36	65	101	16	51	0	6	8	39	11.0	3.8	2.9	0.5	.257
87-88 Golden State	8	0	86	33	14	32	.438	0	0	.000	5	8	.625	9	11	20	3	10	0	1	0	7	10.8	4.1	2.5	0.4	.307
87-88 Atlanta	29	0	174	57	22	49	.449	0	0	.000	13	23	.565	19	36	55	3	19	0	4	8	9	6.0	2.0	1.9	0.1	.434
NBA Season Totals	72	2	645	222	93	226	.412	0	1	.000	36	82	.439	64	112	176	22	80	0	11	16	55	9.0	3.1	2.4	0.3	....
86-87 Golden State	5	0	29	11	3	7	.429	0	0	.000	5	6	.833	0	1	1	2	2	0	0	0	4	5.8	2.2	0.2	0.4	.180
87-88 Atlanta	1	0	2	0	0	0	.000	0	0	.000	0	0	.000	0	0	0	0	0	0	0	0	0	2.0	0.0	0.0	0.0	.000
NBA Playoff Totals	6	0	31	11	3	7	.429	0	0	.000	5	6	.833	0	1	1	2	2	0	0	0	4	5.2	1.8	0.2	0.3	....

• WASHINGTON, Bobby
Robert Washington

Born: July 11, 1947. Height: 5'11". Weight: 175 lbs. Drafted: — College: Eastern Kentucky

YEAR TEAM	GP	GS	MIN	PTS	FGM	FGA	FG%	3PM	3PA	3P%	FTM	FTA	FT%	ORB	DRB	TRB	AST	PF	DQ	STL	BLK	TO	MPG	PPG	RPG	APG	PCM
69-70 Kentucky-A	2	....	5	0	0	1	.000	0	0	.000	0	0	.000	0	0	0	0	0	0	....	....	1	2.5	0.0	0.0	0.0	-.172
70-71 Cleveland	47	....	823	350	123	310	.397	....	....	....	104	140	.743	....	....	105	190	105	0	....	....	....	17.5	7.4	2.2	4.0	.529
71-72 Cleveland	69	....	967	350	123	309	.398	....	....	....	104	128	.813	....	....	129	223	135	1	....	....	....	14.0	5.1	1.9	3.2	.502
NBA Season Totals	116	....	1790	700	246	619	.397	....	....	....	208	268	.776	....	....	234	413	240	1	....	....	....	15.4	6.0	2.0	3.6	....
ABA Season Totals	2	....	5	0	0	1	.000	0	0	.000	0	0	.000	0	0	0	0	0	0	....	....	1	2.5	0.0	0.0	0.0	....
Career Totals	118	....	1795	700	246	620	.397	0	0	.000	208	268	.776	0	0	234	413	240	1	....	....	1	15.2	5.9	2.0	3.5	....

• WASHINGTON, Donald
Donald Maurice Washington Jr.

Born: Apr. 22, 1952. Washington, DC, United States. Height: 6'8". Weight: 210 lbs. Drafted: 1975 College: North Carolina

YEAR TEAM	GP	GS	MIN	PTS	FGM	FGA	FG%	3PM	3PA	3P%	FTM	FTA	FT%	ORB	DRB	TRB	AST	PF	DQ	STL	BLK	TO	MPG	PPG	RPG	APG	PCM
74-75 Denver-A	50	....	438	196	79	183	.432	0	2	.000	38	56	.679	41	48	89	30	92	....	12	19	49	8.8	3.9	1.8	0.6	.382
75-76 Utah-A	6	....	58	24	12	18	.667	0	0	.000	0	0	.000	4	9	13	3	19	....	1	1	3	9.7	4.0	2.2	0.5	.433
ABA Season Totals	56	....	496	220	91	201	.453	0	2	.000	38	56	.679	45	57	102	33	111	....	13	20	52	8.9	3.9	1.8	0.6	....
74-75 Denver-A	4	....	26	11	5	10	.500	0	0	.000	1	1	1.000	2	4	6	2	9	....	1	2	4	6.5	2.8	1.5	0.5	.389
ABA Playoff Totals	4	....	26	11	5	10	.500	0	0	.000	1	1	1.000	2	4	6	2	9	....	1	2	4	6.5	2.8	1.5	0.5	....

• WASHINGTON, Duane
Duane E. Washington

Born: Aug. 31, 1964. Eschwege, Germany. Height: 6'4". Weight: 195 lbs. Drafted: 1987 College: Middle Tennessee State

YEAR TEAM	GP	GS	MIN	PTS	FGM	FGA	FG%	3PM	3PA	3P%	FTM	FTA	FT%	ORB	DRB	TRB	AST	PF	DQ	STL	BLK	TO	MPG	PPG	RPG	APG	PCM
87-88 New Jersey	15	0	156	54	18	42	.429	2	4	.500	16	20	.800	5	17	22	34	23	0	12	0	9	10.4	3.6	1.5	2.3	.504
92-93 LA Clippers	4	0	28	0	0	5	.000	0	0	.000	0	0	.000	0	2	2	5	2	0	1	0	2	7.0	0.0	0.5	1.3	.024
NBA Season Totals	19	0	184	54	18	47	.383	2	4	.500	16	20	.800	5	19	24	39	25	0	13	0	11	9.7	2.8	1.3	2.1	....

• WASHINGTON, Eric
Eric Maurice Washington

Born: Mar. 23, 1974. Pearl, MS, United States. Height: 6'4". Weight: 190 lbs. Drafted: 1997 College: Alabama

YEAR TEAM	GP	GS	MIN	PTS	FGM	FGA	FG%	3PM	3PA	3P%	FTM	FTA	FT%	ORB	DRB	TRB	AST	PF	DQ	STL	BLK	TO	MPG	PPG	RPG	APG	PCM
97-98 Denver	66	36	1539	511	201	498	.404	44	137	.321	65	83	.783	47	80	127	78	143	0	53	25	73	23.3	7.7	1.9	1.2	.241
98-99 Denver	38	6	761	205	73	184	.397	37	97	.381	22	32	.688	35	54	89	30	87	2	25	18	34	20.0	5.4	2.3	0.8	.241
NBA Season Totals	104	42	2300	716	274	682	.402	81	234	.346	87	115	.757	82	134	216	108	230	2	78	43	107	22.1	6.9	2.1	1.0	....

• WASHINGTON, Jim
James H. Washington

Born: July 1, 1943. Philadelphia, PA, United States. Height: 6'6". Weight: 210 lbs. Drafted: 1965 College: Villanova

YEAR TEAM	GP	GS	MIN	PTS	FGM	FGA	FG%	3PM	3PA	3P%	FTM	FTA	FT%	ORB	DRB	TRB	AST	PF	DQ	STL	BLK	TO	MPG	PPG	RPG	APG	PCM
65-66 St. Louis	65	....	1104	384	158	393	.402	....	....	....	68	120	.567	....	....	353	43	176	5	....	....	....	17.0	5.9	5.4	0.7	.398
66-67 Chicago	77	....	1475	592	252	604	.417	....	....	....	88	159	.553	....	....	468	56	181	1	....	....	....	19.2	7.7	6.1	0.7	.442
67-68 Chicago	82	....	2525	1023	418	915	.457	....	....	....	187	274	.682	....	....	825	113	233	1	....	....	....	30.8	12.5	10.1	1.4	.512
68-69 Chicago	80	....	2705	1121	440	1023	.430	....	....	....	241	356	.677	....	....	847	104	226	0	....	....	....	33.8	14.0	10.6	1.3	.488
69-70 Philadelphia	79	....	2459	1006	401	842	.476	....	....	....	204	273	.747	....	....	734	104	262	5	....	....	....	31.1	12.7	9.3	1.3	.502
70-71 Philadelphia	78	....	2501	1049	395	829	.476	....	....	....	259	340	.762	....	....	747	97	258	6	....	....	....	32.1	13.4	9.6	1.2	.513
71-72 Philadelphia	17	....	545	191	68	156	.436	....	....	....	55	67	.821	....	....	135	25	59	3	....	....	....	32.1	11.2	7.9	1.5	.421
71-72 Atlanta	67	....	2416	851	325	729	.446	....	....	....	201	256	.785	....	....	601	121	217	0	....	....	....	36.1	12.7	9.0	1.8	.431
72-73 Atlanta	75	....	2833	779	308	713	.432	....	....	....	163	224	.728	....	....	801	174	252	5	....	....	....	37.8	10.4	10.7	2.3	.418
73-74 Atlanta	73	....	2519	728	297	612	.485	....	....	....	134	196	.684	207	528	735	156	249	5	49	74	....	34.5	10.0	10.1	2.1	.450
74-75 Atlanta	38	....	905	269	114	259	.440	....	....	....	41	55	.745	52	141	193	68	86	2	23	13	....	23.8	7.1	5.1	1.8	.382
74-75 Buffalo	42	....	674	175	77	162	.475	....	....	....	21	38	.553	58	139	197	43	81	3	11	13	....	16.0	4.2	4.7	1.0	.413
75-76 Buffalo	1	....	7	0	0	1	.000	....	....	....	0	0	.000	1	0	1	1	0	0	0	0	....	7.0	0.0	1.0	1.0	.163
NBA Season Totals	774	....	22668	8168	3253	7238	.449	....	....	....	1662	2358	.705	318	808	6637	1105	2280	36	83	100	....	29.3	10.6	8.6	1.4	....
65-66 St. Louis	4	....	6	4	2	4	.500	....	....	....	0	0	.000	....	....	3	0	2	0	....	....	....	1.5	1.0	0.8	0.0	.667
66-67 Chicago	3	....	58	14	6	16	.375	....	....	....	2	4	.500	....	....	5	8	11	0	....	....	....	19.3	4.7	1.7	2.7	.249
67-68 Chicago	5	....	205	86	38	85	.447	....	....	....	10	15	.667	....	....	75	10	15	0	....	....	....	41.0	17.2	15.0	2.0	.548
69-70 Philadelphia	5	....	167	63	25	57	.439	....	....	....	13	23	.565	....	....	49	9	18	0	....	....	....	33.4	12.6	9.8	1.8	.453

YEAR	TEAM	GP	GS	MIN	PTS	FGM	FGA	FG%	3PM	3PA	3P%	FTM	FTA	FT%	ORB	DRB	TRB	AST	PF	DQ	STL	BLK	TO	MPG	PPG	RPG	APG	PCM
70-71	Philadelphia	7	....	216	80	27	61	.443	....	....	....	26	36	.722	....	....	48	10	24	1	....	....	....	30.9	11.4	6.9	1.4	.411
71-72	Atlanta	6	....	209	65	28	58	.483	....	....	....	9	16	.563	....	....	48	10	20	0	....	....	....	34.8	10.8	8.0	1.7	.384
72-73	Atlanta	6	....	226	43	19	48	.396	....	....	....	5	17	.294	....	....	60	14	19	1	....	....	....	37.7	7.2	10.0	2.3	.320
74-75	Buffalo	6	....	39	4	2	5	.400	....	....	....	0	0	.000	3	4	7	3	5	0	0	0	....	6.5	0.7	1.2	0.5	.224
NBA Playoff Totals		42	....	1126	359	147	334	.440	....	....	....	65	111	.586	3	4	295	64	114	2	0	0	....	26.8	8.5	7.0	1.5	....

• WASHINGTON, Kermit

Kermit Alan (Special K) Washington

Born: Sept. 17, 1951. Washington, DC, United States. Height: 6'8". Weight: 230 lbs. Drafted: 1973 College: American

YEAR	TEAM	GP	GS	MIN	PTS	FGM	FGA	FG%	3PM	3PA	3P%	FTM	FTA	FT%	ORB	DRB	TRB	AST	PF	DQ	STL	BLK	TO	MPG	PPG	RPG	APG	PCM
73-74	LA Lakers	45	....	400	172	73	151	.483	....	....	....	26	49	.531	62	85	147	19	77	0	21	18	....	8.9	3.8	3.3	0.4	.525
74-75	LA Lakers	55	....	949	246	87	207	.420	....	....	....	72	122	.590	106	244	350	66	155	2	25	32	....	17.3	4.5	6.4	1.2	.454
75-76	LA Lakers	36	....	492	123	39	90	.433	....	....	....	45	66	.682	51	114	165	20	76	0	11	26	....	13.7	3.4	4.6	0.6	.411
76-77	LA Lakers	53	....	1342	514	191	380	.503	....	....	....	132	187	.706	182	310	492	48	183	1	43	52	....	25.3	9.7	9.3	0.9	.542
77-78	LA Lakers	25	....	751	288	110	244	.451	....	....	....	68	110	.618	110	169	279	30	74	1	19	24	53	30.0	11.5	11.2	1.2	.518
77-78	Boston	32	....	866	376	137	263	.521	....	....	....	102	136	.750	105	230	335	42	114	2	28	40	54	27.1	11.8	10.5	1.3	.639
78-79	San Diego	82	....	2764	927	350	623	.562	....	....	....	227	330	.688	296	504	800	125	317	11	85	121	189	33.7	11.3	9.8	1.5	.494
79-80	Portland	80	....	2657	1073	421	761	.553	0	3	.000	231	360	.642	325	517	842	167	307	8	73	131	168	33.2	13.4	10.5	2.1	.582
80-81	Portland	73	....	2120	831	325	571	.569	0	1	.000	181	288	.628	236	450	686	149	258	5	85	86	146	29.0	11.4	9.4	2.0	.590
81-82	Portland	20	4	418	100	38	78	.487	0	0	.000	24	41	.585	40	77	117	29	56	0	9	16	18	20.9	5.0	5.9	1.5	.419
87-88	Golden State	6	1	56	16	7	14	.500	0	0	.000	2	2	1.000	9	10	19	0	13	0	4	4	4	9.3	2.7	3.2	0.0	.444
NBA Season Totals		507	5	12815	4666	1778	3382	.526	0	4	.000	1110	1691	.656	1522	2710	4232	695	1630	30	403	550	632	25.3	9.2	8.3	1.4	....
73-74	LA Lakers	3	....	14	15	5	11	.455	....	....	....	5	7	.714	9	1	10	1	0	0	1	0	....	4.7	5.0	3.3	0.3	1.336
79-80	Portland	3	....	121	31	13	26	.500	0	1	.000	5	8	.625	12	19	31	6	9	0	1	4	4	40.3	10.3	10.3	2.0	.408
80-81	Portland	3	....	128	26	12	23	.522	0	1	.000	2	2	1.000	14	38	52	7	9	0	8	2	7	42.7	8.7	17.3	2.3	.544
NBA Playoff Totals		9	....	263	72	30	60	.500	0	2	.000	12	17	.706	35	58	93	14	18	0	10	6	11	29.2	8.0	10.3	1.6	....

• WASHINGTON, Pearl

Dwayne Alonzo (Pearl) Washington

Born: Jan. 6, 1964. Brooklyn, NY, United States. Height: 6'2". Weight: 190 lbs. Drafted: 1986 College: Syracuse

YEAR	TEAM	GP	GS	MIN	PTS	FGM	FGA	FG%	3PM	3PA	3P%	FTM	FTA	FT%	ORB	DRB	TRB	AST	PF	DQ	STL	BLK	TO	MPG	PPG	RPG	APG	PCM
86-87	New Jersey	72	61	1600	616	257	538	.478	4	24	.167	98	125	.784	37	92	129	301	184	5	92	7	173	22.2	8.6	1.8	4.2	.393
87-88	New Jersey	68	10	1379	633	245	547	.448	11	49	.224	132	189	.698	54	64	118	206	163	2	91	4	143	20.3	9.3	1.7	3.0	.387
88-89	Miami	54	8	1065	411	164	387	.424	1	14	.071	82	104	.788	49	74	123	226	101	0	73	4	124	19.7	7.6	2.3	4.2	.431
NBA Season Totals		194	79	4044	1660	666	1472	.452	16	87	.184	312	418	.746	140	230	370	733	448	7	256	15	440	20.8	8.6	1.9	3.8	....

• WASHINGTON, Richard

Richard Lee Washington

Born: July 15, 1955. Portland, OR, United States. Height: 6'11". Weight: 220 lbs. Drafted: 1976 College: UCLA

YEAR	TEAM	GP	GS	MIN	PTS	FGM	FGA	FG%	3PM	3PA	3P%	FTM	FTA	FT%	ORB	DRB	TRB	AST	PF	DQ	STL	BLK	TO	MPG	PPG	RPG	APG	PCM
76-77	Kansas City	82	....	2265	1069	446	1034	.431	....	....	....	177	254	.697	201	497	698	85	324	13	63	90	....	27.6	13.0	8.5	1.0	.480
77-78	Kansas City	78	....	2231	1000	425	891	.477	....	....	....	150	199	.754	188	466	654	118	324	12	74	73	187	28.6	12.8	8.4	1.5	.493
78-79	Kansas City	18	....	161	38	14	41	.341	....	....	....	10	16	.625	11	37	48	7	31	0	7	3	14	8.9	2.1	2.7	0.4	.276
79-80	Milwaukee	75	....	1092	440	197	421	.468	0	0	.000	46	76	.605	95	181	276	55	166	2	26	48	60	14.6	5.9	3.7	0.7	.432
80-81	Dallas	11	....	307	119	51	117	.436	0	0	.000	17	23	.739	25	59	84	16	37	0	5	7	21	27.9	10.8	7.6	1.5	.407
80-81	Cleveland	69	....	1505	681	289	630	.459	1	2	.500	102	136	.750	133	236	369	113	246	3	41	54	110	21.8	9.9	5.3	1.6	.457
81-82	Cleveland	18	2	313	109	50	115	.435	0	2	.000	9	15	.600	32	43	75	15	51	0	8	2	34	17.4	6.1	4.2	0.8	.275
NBA Season Totals		351	2	7874	3456	1472	3249	.453	1	4	.250	511	719	.711	685	1519	2204	409	1179	30	224	277	426	22.4	9.8	6.3	1.2	....
78-79	Kansas City	4	....	52	24	11	20	.550	....	....	....	2	2	1.000	3	10	13	0	17	1	1	1	1	13.0	6.0	3.3	0.0	.401
79-80	Milwaukee	7	....	112	51	25	47	.532	0	0	.000	1	4	.250	7	13	20	3	22	0	4	8	8	16.0	7.3	2.9	0.4	.400
NBA Playoff Totals		11	....	164	75	36	67	.537	0	0	.000	3	6	.500	10	23	33	3	39	1	5	9	9	14.9	6.8	3.0	0.3	....

• WASHINGTON, Stan

Stanley Washington

Born: Jan. 23, 1952. Washington, DC, United States. Height: 6'4". Weight: 190 lbs. Drafted: 1974 College: San Diego

YEAR	TEAM	GP	GS	MIN	PTS	FGM	FGA	FG%	3PM	3PA	3P%	FTM	FTA	FT%	ORB	DRB	TRB	AST	PF	DQ	STL	BLK	TO	MPG	PPG	RPG	APG	PCM
74-75	Washington	1	....	4	0	0	1	.000	....	....	....	0	0	.000	0	0	0	0	1	0	0	0	....	4.0	0.0	0.0	0.0	-.320
NBA Season Totals		1	....	4	0	0	1	.000	....	....	....	0	0	.000	0	0	0	0	1	0	0	0	....	4.0	0.0	0.0	0.0	....

• WASHINGTON, Trooper

Thomas (Trooper) Washington

Born: Apr. 21, 1944. Philadelphia, PA, United States. Height: 6'7". Weight: 215 lbs. Drafted: — College: Cheyney State

YEAR	TEAM	GP	GS	MIN	PTS	FGM	FGA	FG%	3PM	3PA	3P%	FTM	FTA	FT%	ORB	DRB	TRB	AST	PF	DQ	STL	BLK	TO	MPG	PPG	RPG	APG	PCM
67-68	Pittsburgh-A	63	....	1844	732	312	596	**.523**	2	2	1.000	106	186	.570	303	369	672	102	189	4	....	....	110	29.3	11.6	10.7	1.6	.576
68-69	Minnesota-A	69	....	2625	1032	421	839	.502	0	6	.000	190	316	.601	367	501	868	178	239	2	....	....	190	38.0	15.0	12.6	2.6	.558
69-70	Los Angeles-A	37	....	1104	377	155	274	**.566**	1	3	.333	66	99	.667	160	218	378	80	144	5	....	....	73	29.8	10.2	10.2	2.2	.557
69-70	Pittsburgh-A	44	....	1249	422	165	308	**.536**	3	5	.600	89	141	.631	152	292	444	116	141	3	....	....	104	28.4	9.6	10.1	2.6	.584
70-71	Florida-A	57	....	1876	534	216	426	.507	0	2	.000	102	167	.611	194	412	606	187	184	5	....	....	208	32.9	9.4	10.6	3.3	.520
71-72	New York-A	80	....	2510	881	387	678	.571	0	0	.000	107	166	.645	281	469	750	161	291	4	....	....	188	31.4	11.0	9.4	2.0	.522
72-73	New York-A	76	....	2027	521	229	425	.539	0	0	.000	63	101	.624	174	379	553	203	242	5	....	....	183	26.7	6.9	7.3	2.7	.464
ABA Season Totals		426	....	13235	4499	1885	3546	.532	6	18	.333	723	1176	.615	1631	2640	4271	1027	1430	28	....	....	1056	31.1	10.6	10.0	2.4	....
67-68	Pittsburgh-A	15	....	610	218	95	179	.531	0	2	.000	28	57	.491	102	159	261	42	60	3	....	....	39	40.7	14.5	17.4	2.8	.618
68-69	Minnesota-A	6	....	230	67	26	62	.419	0	0	.000	15	21	.714	30	49	79	14	17	0	....	....	15	38.3	11.2	13.2	2.3	.478
69-70	Los Angeles-A	17	....	471	126	58	93	.624	0	0	.000	10	25	.400	66	122	188	45	....	2	....	....	28	27.7	7.4	11.1	2.6	....
70-71	Florida-A	6	....	88	17	7	20	.350	0	0	.000	3	8	.375	9	20	29	14	10	0	....	....	4	14.7	2.8	4.8	2.3	.461
71-72	New York-A	18	....	548	142	64	107	.598	0	0	.000	14	24	.583	73	100	173	43	63	....	....	....	26	30.4	7.9	9.6	2.4	.497
72-73	New York-A	4	....	68	15	6	11	.545	0	0	.000	3	4	.750	4	14	18	3	8	0	....	....	2	17.0	3.8	4.5	0.8	.382
ABA Playoff Totals		66	....	2015	585	256	472	.542	0	2	.000	73	139	.525	284	464	748	161	158	5	....	....	114	30.5	8.9	11.3	2.4	....

YEAR	TEAM	GP	GS	MIN	PTS	FGM	FGA	FG%	3PM	3PA	3P%	FTM	FTA	FT%	ORB	DRB	TRB	AST	PF	DQ	STL	BLK	TO	MPG	PPG	RPG	APG	PCM

• WASHINGTON, Wilson
Wilson Washington Jr.

Born: Aug. 3, 1955. Norfolk, VA, United States.   Height: 6'9".   Weight: 227 lbs.   Drafted: 1977   College: Old Dominion

YEAR	TEAM	GP	GS	MIN	PTS	FGM	FGA	FG%	3PM	3PA	3P%	FTM	FTA	FT%	ORB	DRB	TRB	AST	PF	DQ	STL	BLK	TO	MPG	PPG	RPG	APG	PCM
77-78	Philadelphia	14	....	38	19	8	19	.421	....	....	....	3	6	.500	2	12	14	1	3	0	1	2	10	2.7	1.4	1.0	0.1	.368
77-78	New Jersey	24	....	523	210	92	187	.492	....	....	....	26	47	.553	48	94	142	9	72	2	17	35	53	21.8	8.8	5.9	0.4	.420
78-79	New Jersey	62	....	1139	502	218	434	.502	....	....	....	66	104	.635	88	206	294	47	186	5	31	67	99	18.4	8.1	4.7	0.8	.459
NBA Season Totals		100	....	1700	731	318	640	.497	....	....	....	95	157	.605	138	312	450	57	261	7	49	104	162	17.0	7.3	4.5	0.6	....

• WAST, Zano
Zano Wast

Born: Aug. 20, 1916. Died: May21, 1988.   Height: 6'2".   Weight: 175 lbs.   Drafted: —   College: Toledo

YEAR	TEAM	GP	GS	MIN	PTS	FGM	FGA	FG%	3PM	3PA	3P%	FTM	FTA	FT%	ORB	DRB	TRB	AST	PF	DQ	STL	BLK	TO	MPG	PPG	RPG	APG	PCM
42-43	Toledo-N	1	....	....	0	0	....	....	....	....	....	0	....	....	....	....	....	....	....	....	....	....	....	0.0	....	....	....	
NBL Season Totals		1	....	....	0	0	....	....	....	....	....	0	....	....	....	....	....	....	....	....	....	....	....	0.0	....	....	....	

• WATKINS, Jack
Jack Watkins

Born: 1923.   Height: 6'2".   Weight: 180 lbs.   Drafted: —   College: Oklahoma

YEAR	TEAM	GP	GS	MIN	PTS	FGM	FGA	FG%	3PM	3PA	3P%	FTM	FTA	FT%	ORB	DRB	TRB	AST	PF	DQ	STL	BLK	TO	MPG	PPG	RPG	APG	PCM
48-49	Sheboygan-N	7	....	....	5	1	....	....	....	....	....	3	4	.750	....	....	....	....	....	....	....	....	....	0.7	....	....	....	
NBL Season Totals		7	....	....	5	1	....	....	....	....	....	3	4		....	....	....	....	....	....	....	....	....	0.7	....	....	....	

• WATSON, Bobby
Robert E. Watson

Born: Mar. 22, 1930. Owensboro, KY, United States.   Height: 6'   Weight: 160 lbs.   Drafted: 1952   College: Kentucky

YEAR	TEAM	GP	GS	MIN	PTS	FGM	FGA	FG%	3PM	3PA	3P%	FTM	FTA	FT%	ORB	DRB	TRB	AST	PF	DQ	STL	BLK	TO	MPG	PPG	RPG	APG	PCM
54-55	Min/Mil	63	....	702	175	72	223	.323	....	....	....	31	45	.689	....	....	87	79	67	0	....	....	....	11.1	2.8	1.4	1.3	.278
NBA Season Totals		63	....	702	175	72	223	.323	....	....	....	31	45	.689	....	....	87	79	67	0	....	....	....	11.1	2.8	1.4	1.3	....

• WATSON, Chub
Chub Watson

Born: 1916.   Height: 6'2".   Weight: —   Drafted: —   College: Marshall

YEAR	TEAM	GP	GS	MIN	PTS	FGM	FGA	FG%	3PM	3PA	3P%	FTM	FTA	FT%	ORB	DRB	TRB	AST	PF	DQ	STL	BLK	TO	MPG	PPG	RPG	APG	PCM
38-39	Pittsburgh-N	1	....	....	16	8	....	....	....	....	....	0	....	....	....	....	....	....	....	....	....	....	....	16.0	....	....	....	
NBL Season Totals		1	....	....	16	8	....	....	....	....	....	0	....	....	....	....	....	....	....	....	....	....	....	16.0	....	....	....	

• WATSON, Earl
Earl Joseph Watson

Born: June 12, 1979. Kansas City, KS, United States.   Height: 6'1".   Weight: 195 lbs.   Drafted: 2001   College: UCLA

YEAR	TEAM	GP	GS	MIN	PTS	FGM	FGA	FG%	3PM	3PA	3P%	FTM	FTA	FT%	ORB	DRB	TRB	AST	PF	DQ	STL	BLK	TO	MPG	PPG	RPG	APG	PCM
01-02	Seattle	64	0	964	231	96	212	.453	16	44	.364	23	36	.639	31	52	83	125	93	0	60	5	51	15.1	3.6	1.3	2.0	.314
02-03	Memphis	79	2	1367	433	170	391	.435	31	91	.341	62	86	.721	46	118	164	225	138	0	89	14	88	17.3	5.5	2.1	2.8	.415
NBA Season Totals		143	2	2331	664	266	603	.441	47	135	.348	85	122	.697	77	170	247	350	231	0	149	19	139	16.3	4.6	1.7	2.4	....

• WATSON, Jamie
Jamie Lovell Watson

Born: Feb. 23, 1972. Elm City, NC, United States.   Height: 6'7".   Weight: 190 lbs.   Drafted: 1994   College: South Carolina

YEAR	TEAM	GP	GS	MIN	PTS	FGM	FGA	FG%	3PM	3PA	3P%	FTM	FTA	FT%	ORB	DRB	TRB	AST	PF	DQ	STL	BLK	TO	MPG	PPG	RPG	APG	PCM
94-95	Utah	60	1	673	195	76	152	.500	5	19	.263	38	56	.679	16	58	74	59	86	0	35	11	48	11.2	3.3	1.2	1.0	.305
95-96	Utah	16	0	217	48	18	43	.419	3	7	.429	9	13	.692	5	22	27	24	30	0	8	2	18	13.6	3.0	1.7	1.5	.239
96-97	Utah	13	0	129	33	11	25	.440	1	3	.333	10	12	.833	4	14	18	10	16	0	11	2	9	9.9	2.5	1.4	0.8	.331
96-97	Dallas	10	6	211	45	20	47	.426	3	9	.333	2	4	.500	14	15	29	23	18	0	11	2	15	21.1	4.5	2.9	2.3	.286
98-99	Miami	3	0	18	2	1	2	.500	0	0	.000	0	0	.000	0	1	1	1	1	0	0	0	1	6.0	0.7	0.3	0.3	.099
NBA Season Totals		102	7	1248	323	126	269	.468	12	38	.316	59	85	.694	39	110	149	117	151	0	65	17	91	12.2	3.2	1.5	1.1	....
94-95	Utah	5	0	57	12	6	9	.667	0	0	.000	0	0	.000	1	0	1	3	12	0	2	1	6	11.4	2.4	0.2	0.6	.085
NBA Playoff Totals		5	0	57	12	6	9	.667	0	0	.000	0	0	.000	1	0	1	3	12	0	2	1	6	11.4	2.4	0.2	0.6	....

• WATTS, Ron
Ronald Michael Watts

Born: May 21, 1943.   Height: 6'6".   Weight: 210 lbs.   Drafted: 1965   College: Wake Forest

YEAR	TEAM	GP	GS	MIN	PTS	FGM	FGA	FG%	3PM	3PA	3P%	FTM	FTA	FT%	ORB	DRB	TRB	AST	PF	DQ	STL	BLK	TO	MPG	PPG	RPG	APG	PCM
65-66	Boston	1	....	3	2	1	2	.500	....	....	....	0	0	.000	....	....	1	1	1	0	....	....	....	3.0	2.0	1.0	1.0	.941
66-67	Boston	27	....	89	38	11	44	.250	....	....	....	16	23	.696	....	....	38	1	16	0	....	....	....	3.3	1.4	1.4	0.0	.382
NBA Season Totals		28	....	92	40	12	46	.261	....	....	....	16	23	.696	....	....	39	2	17	0	....	....	....	3.3	1.4	1.4	0.1	....
66-67	Boston	1	....	5	3	1	6	.167	....	....	....	1	2	.500	....	....	2	0	3	0	....	....	....	5.0	3.0	2.0	0.0	-.197
NBA Playoff Totals		1	....	5	3	1	6	.167	....	....	....	1	2	.500	....	....	2	0	3	0	....	....	....	5.0	3.0	2.0	0.0	....

• WATTS, Samuel
Samuel D. Watts

Born: Mar. 14, 1948.   Height: 6'3".   Weight: 185 lbs.   Drafted: —   College: Florida A&M

YEAR	TEAM	GP	GS	MIN	PTS	FGM	FGA	FG%	3PM	3PA	3P%	FTM	FTA	FT%	ORB	DRB	TRB	AST	PF	DQ	STL	BLK	TO	MPG	PPG	RPG	APG	PCM
70-71	Pittsburgh-A	54	....	650	281	109	287	.380	14	41	.341	49	67	.731	45	54	99	45	106	0	....	....	68	12.0	5.2	1.8	0.8	.342
ABA Season Totals		54	....	650	281	109	287	.380	14	41	.341	49	67	.731	45	54	99	45	106	0	....	....	68	12.0	5.2	1.8	0.8	....

• WATTS, Slick
Donald Earl (Slick) Watts

Born: July 22, 1951. Rolling Ford, MS, United States.   Height: 6'1".   Weight: 175 lbs.   Drafted: —   College: Xavier (LA)

YEAR	TEAM	GP	GS	MIN	PTS	FGM	FGA	FG%	3PM	3PA	3P%	FTM	FTA	FT%	ORB	DRB	TRB	AST	PF	DQ	STL	BLK	TO	MPG	PPG	RPG	APG	PCM
73-74	Seattle	62	....	1424	496	198	510	.388	....	....	....	100	155	.645	72	110	182	351	207	8	115	13	....	23.0	8.0	2.9	5.7	.476
74-75	Seattle	82	....	2056	557	232	551	.421	....	....	....	93	153	.608	95	167	262	499	254	7	190	12	....	25.1	6.8	3.2	6.1	.461
75-76	Seattle	82	....	2776	1065	433	1015	.427	....	....	....	199	344	.578	112	253	365	**661**	270	3	**261**	16	....	33.9	13.0	4.5	**8.1**	.524

YEAR	TEAM	GP	GS	MIN	PTS	FGM	FGA	FG%	3PM	3PA	3P%	FTM	FTA	FT%	ORB	DRB	TRB	AST	PF	DQ	STL	BLK	TO	MPG	PPG	RPG	APG	PCM
76-77	Seattle	79	....	2627	1028	428	1015	.422	....	....	....	172	293	.587	81	226	307	630	256	5	214	25	....	33.3	13.0	3.9	8.0	.510
77-78	Seattle	32	....	809	250	110	272	.404	....	....	....	30	53	.566	21	60	81	133	88	1	53	14	93	25.3	7.8	2.5	4.2	.318
77-78	New Orleans	39	....	775	280	109	286	.381	....	....	....	62	103	.602	39	59	98	161	96	0	55	17	74	19.9	7.2	2.5	4.1	.426
78-79	Houston	61	....	1046	225	92	227	.405	....	....	....	41	67	.612	35	68	103	243	143	1	73	14	73	17.1	3.7	1.7	4.0	.383
NBA Season Totals		437	....	11513	3901	1602	3876	.413	....	....	....	697	1168	.597	455	943	1398	2678	1314	25	961	111	240	26.3	8.9	3.2	6.1	....
74-75	Seattle	9	....	282	100	43	93	.462	....	....	....	14	26	.538	10	23	33	64	30	0	27	4	....	31.3	11.1	3.7	7.1	.500
75-76	Seattle	6	....	197	71	30	69	.435	....	....	....	11	23	.478	5	13	18	49	28	1	12	2	....	32.8	11.8	3.0	8.2	.466
78-79	Houston	2	....	43	14	6	15	.400	....	....	....	2	3	.667	4	3	7	7	8	0	4	1	7	21.5	7.0	3.5	3.5	.327
NBA Playoff Totals		17	....	522	185	79	177	.446	....	....	....	27	52	.519	19	39	58	120	66	1	43	7	7	30.7	10.9	3.4	7.1	....

• WAXMAN, Stan

Stan Waxman

Born: 1922. Height: 5'11". Weight: 180 lbs. Drafted: — College: Long Island University

YEAR	TEAM	GP	GS	MIN	PTS	FGM	FGA	FG%	3PM	3PA	3P%	FTM	FTA	FT%	ORB	DRB	TRB	AST	PF	DQ	STL	BLK	TO	MPG	PPG	RPG	APG	PCM
46-47	Tri-Cities-N	18	....	....	128	59	....	....	....	....	....	10	17	.588	....	....	....	....	....	....	....	....	....	....	7.1	....	....	....
NBL Season Totals		18	....	....	128	59	....	....	....	....	....	10	17	....	....	....	....	....	....	....	....	....	....	....	7.1	....	....	....

• WEATHERSPOON, Clarence

Clarence (Baby Barkley) Weatherspoon

Born: Sept. 8, 1970. Crawford, MS, United States. Height: 6'6". Weight: 240 lbs. Drafted: 1992 College: Southern Mississippi

YEAR	TEAM	GP	GS	MIN	PTS	FGM	FGA	FG%	3PM	3PA	3P%	FTM	FTA	FT%	ORB	DRB	TRB	AST	PF	DQ	STL	BLK	TO	MPG	PPG	RPG	APG	PCM
92-93	Philadelphia	82	82	2654	1280	494	1053	.469	1	4	.250	291	408	.713	179	410	589	147	188	1	85	67	172	32.4	15.6	7.2	1.8	.491
93-94	Philadelphia	82	82	3147	1506	602	1246	.483	4	17	.235	298	430	.693	254	578	832	192	152	0	100	116	197	38.4	18.4	10.1	2.3	.564
94-95	Philadelphia	76	76	2991	1373	543	1238	.439	4	21	.190	283	377	.751	144	382	526	215	195	1	115	67	190	39.4	18.1	6.9	2.8	.435
95-96	Philadelphia	78	75	3096	1300	491	1015	.484	0	2	.000	318	426	.746	237	516	753	158	214	3	112	108	179	39.7	16.7	9.7	2.0	.507
96-97	Philadelphia	82	82	2949	1003	398	811	.491	1	6	.167	206	279	.738	219	460	679	140	187	0	74	86	139	36.0	12.2	8.3	1.7	.440
97-98	Philadelphia	48	18	1290	405	141	331	.426	0	0	.000	123	174	.707	109	227	336	40	108	1	43	52	67	26.9	8.4	7.0	0.8	.415
97-98	Golden State	31	31	1035	331	127	277	.458	0	0	.000	77	103	.748	89	169	258	49	86	1	42	22	50	33.4	10.7	8.3	1.6	.430
98-99	Miami	49	3	1040	397	141	264	.534	0	0	.000	115	143	.804	72	171	243	34	107	0	28	17	61	21.2	8.1	5.0	0.7	.449
99-00	Miami	78	2	1615	565	215	419	.513	0	0	.000	135	183	.738	128	321	449	93	165	1	51	49	100	20.7	7.2	5.8	1.2	.491
00-01	Cleveland	82	82	2774	924	347	692	.501	0	0	.000	230	291	.790	223	573	796	103	171	0	85	105	112	33.8	11.3	9.7	1.3	.508
01-02	New York	56	41	1727	494	189	452	.418	0	0	.000	116	146	.795	149	311	460	60	132	0	37	48	47	30.8	8.8	8.2	1.1	.405
02-03	New York	79	19	2024	521	186	414	.449	0	0	.000	149	194	.768	214	385	599	68	174	0	69	36	63	25.6	6.6	7.6	0.9	.430
NBA Season Totals		823	593	26342	10099	3874	8212	.472	10	50	.200	2341	3154	.742	2017	4503	6520	1299	1879	8	841	773	1377	32.0	12.3	7.9	1.6	....
98-99	Miami	5	0	112	29	9	26	.346	0	0	.000	11	17	.647	4	17	21	2	8	0	7	1	3	22.4	5.8	4.2	0.4	.295
99-00	Miami	10	0	170	64	25	60	.417	0	0	.000	14	24	.583	18	23	41	1	23	0	4	3	8	17.0	6.4	4.1	0.1	.321
NBA Playoff Totals		15	0	282	93	34	86	.395	0	0	.000	25	41	.610	22	40	62	3	31	0	11	4	11	18.8	6.2	4.1	0.2	....

• WEATHERSPOON, Nick

Nick Levoter (Spoon) Weatherspoon

Born: July 20, 1950. Greenwood, MS, United States. Height: 6'7". Weight: 195 lbs. Drafted: 1973 College: Illinois

YEAR	TEAM	GP	GS	MIN	PTS	FGM	FGA	FG%	3PM	3PA	3P%	FTM	FTA	FT%	ORB	DRB	TRB	AST	PF	DQ	STL	BLK	TO	MPG	PPG	RPG	APG	PCM
73-74	Washington	65	....	1216	494	199	483	.412	....	....	....	96	139	.691	133	264	397	38	179	1	48	16	....	18.7	7.6	6.1	0.6	.444
74-75	Washington	82	....	1347	615	256	562	.456	....	....	....	103	138	.746	132	214	346	51	212	2	65	21	....	16.4	7.5	4.2	0.6	.447
75-76	Washington	64	....	1083	532	218	458	.476	....	....	....	96	137	.701	85	189	274	55	172	2	46	16	....	16.9	8.3	4.3	0.9	.492
76-77	Washington	11	....	152	59	27	76	.355	....	....	....	5	8	.625	11	13	24	2	19	0	3	5	....	13.8	5.4	2.2	0.2	.199
76-77	Seattle	51	....	1505	652	283	614	.461	....	....	....	86	136	.632	109	295	404	51	149	1	49	23	....	29.5	12.8	7.9	1.0	.457
77-78	Chicago	41	....	611	209	86	194	.443	....	....	....	37	42	.881	57	68	125	32	74	0	19	10	49	14.9	5.1	3.0	0.8	.340
78-79	San Diego	82	....	2642	1134	479	998	.480	....	....	....	176	238	.739	179	275	454	135	287	6	80	37	180	32.2	13.8	5.5	1.6	.383
79-80	San Diego	57	....	1124	391	164	378	.434	0	0	.000	63	91	.692	83	125	208	54	136	1	34	17	86	19.7	6.9	3.6	0.9	.301
NBA Season Totals		453	....	9680	4086	1712	3763	.455	0	0	.000	662	929	.713	789	1443	2232	418	1228	13	344	145	315	21.4	9.0	4.9	0.9	....
73-74	Washington	7	....	87	20	9	19	.474	....	....	....	2	5	.400	11	16	27	0	11	0	2	2	....	12.4	2.9	3.9	0.0	.328
74-75	Washington	17	....	404	175	70	136	.515	....	....	....	35	43	.814	25	56	81	16	56	0	14	2	....	23.8	10.3	4.8	0.9	.443
75-76	Washington	7	....	224	86	36	80	.450	....	....	....	14	25	.560	10	32	42	10	28	1	2	4	....	32.0	12.3	6.0	1.4	.353
NBA Playoff Totals		31	....	715	281	115	235	.489	....	....	....	51	73	.699	46	104	150	26	95	1	18	8	....	23.1	9.1	4.8	0.8	....

• WEBB, Jeff

Jeffrey William Webb

Born: July 6, 1948. Height: 6'4". Weight: 170 lbs. Drafted: — College: Kansas State

YEAR	TEAM	GP	GS	MIN	PTS	FGM	FGA	FG%	3PM	3PA	3P%	FTM	FTA	FT%	ORB	DRB	TRB	AST	PF	DQ	STL	BLK	TO	MPG	PPG	RPG	APG	PCM
70-71	Milwaukee	29	....	300	65	27	78	.346	....	....	....	11	15	.733	....	....	24	19	33	0	....	....	....	10.3	2.2	0.8	0.7	.158
71-72	Milwaukee	19	....	109	29	9	35	.257	....	....	....	11	13	.846	....	....	18	7	8	0	....	....	....	5.7	1.5	0.9	0.4	.236
71-72	Phoenix	27	....	129	67	31	65	.477	....	....	....	5	10	.500	....	....	17	16	21	0	....	....	....	4.8	2.5	0.6	0.6	.459
NBA Season Totals		75	....	538	161	67	178	.376	....	....	....	27	38	.711	....	....	59	42	62	0	....	....	....	7.2	2.1	0.8	0.6	....
70-71	Milwaukee	9	....	23	11	4	7	.571	....	....	....	3	3	1.000	....	....	1	2	2	0	....	....	....	2.6	1.2	0.1	0.2	.465
NBA Playoff Totals		9	....	23	11	4	7	.571	....	....	....	3	3	1.000	....	....	1	2	2	0	....	....	....	2.6	1.2	0.1	0.2	....

• WEBB, Marcus

Marcus L. Webb

Born: May 9, 1970. Montgomery, AL, United States. Height: 6'9". Weight: 255 lbs. Drafted: — College: Alabama

YEAR	TEAM	GP	GS	MIN	PTS	FGM	FGA	FG%	3PM	3PA	3P%	FTM	FTA	FT%	ORB	DRB	TRB	AST	PF	DQ	STL	BLK	TO	MPG	PPG	RPG	APG	PCM
92-93	Boston	9	0	51	39	13	25	.520	0	1	.000	13	21	.619	5	5	10	2	11	0	1	2	5	5.7	4.3	1.1	0.2	.560
NBA Season Totals		9	0	51	39	13	25	.520	0	1	.000	13	21	.619	5	5	10	2	11	0	1	2	5	5.7	4.3	1.1	0.2	....

• WEBB, Spud

Anthony Jerome (Spud) Webb

Born: July 13, 1963. Dallas, TX, United States. Height: 5'6". Weight: 133 lbs. Drafted: 1985 College: North Carolina State

YEAR	TEAM	GP	GS	MIN	PTS	FGM	FGA	FG%	3PM	3PA	3P%	FTM	FTA	FT%	ORB	DRB	TRB	AST	PF	DQ	STL	BLK	TO	MPG	PPG	RPG	APG	PCM
85-86	Atlanta	79	8	1229	616	199	412	.483	2	11	.182	216	275	.785	27	96	123	337	164	1	82	5	158	15.6	7.8	1.6	4.3	.589
86-87	Atlanta	33	0	532	223	71	162	.438	1	6	.167	80	105	.762	6	54	60	167	65	1	34	2	69	16.1	6.8	1.8	5.1	.564
87-88	Atlanta	82	1	1347	490	191	402	.475	1	19	.053	107	131	.817	16	130	146	337	125	0	63	12	131	16.4	6.0	1.8	4.1	.496

YEAR	TEAM	GP	GS	MIN	PTS	FGM	FGA	FG%	3PM	3PA	3P%	FTM	FTA	FT%	ORB	DRB	TRB	AST	PF	DQ	STL	BLK	TO	MPG	PPG	RPG	APG	PCM
88-89	Atlanta	81	6	1219	319	133	290	.459	1	22	.045	52	60	.867	21	102	123	284	104	0	70	6	81	15.0	3.9	1.5	3.5	.438
89-90	Atlanta	82	46	2184	751	294	616	.477	1	19	.053	162	186	.871	38	163	201	477	185	0	105	12	139	26.6	9.2	2.5	5.8	.470
90-91	Atlanta	75	64	2197	1003	359	803	.447	54	168	.321	231	266	.868	41	133	174	417	180	0	118	6	143	29.3	13.4	2.3	5.6	.491
91-92	Sacramento	77	77	2724	1231	448	1006	.445	73	199	.367	262	305	.859	30	193	223	547	193	1	125	24	231	35.4	16.0	2.9	7.1	.485
92-93	Sacramento	69	68	2335	1000	342	789	.433	37	135	.274	279	328	.851	44	149	193	481	177	0	104	6	193	33.8	14.5	2.8	7.0	.468
93-94	Sacramento	79	62	2567	1005	373	810	.460	55	164	.335	204	251	.813	44	178	222	528	182	1	93	23	166	32.5	12.7	2.8	6.7	.479
94-95	Sacramento	76	76	2458	878	302	689	.438	48	145	.331	226	242	**.934**	29	145	174	468	148	0	75	8	182	32.3	11.6	2.3	6.2	.409
95-96	Atlanta	51	0	817	300	104	222	.468	18	57	.316	74	87	.851	19	41	60	140	68	0	27	2	51	16.0	5.9	1.2	2.7	.410
95-96	Minnesota	26	21	645	244	82	208	.394	29	72	.403	51	58	.879	7	33	40	154	41	0	25	5	60	24.8	9.4	1.5	5.9	.427
97-98	Orlando	4	0	34	12	5	12	.417	0	1	.000	2	2	1.000	2	1	3	5	6	0	1	0	7	8.5	3.0	0.8	1.3	.163
NBA Season Totals		814	429	20288	8072	2903	6421	.452	320	1018	.314	1946	2296	.848	324	1418	1742	4342	1638	4	922	111	1611	24.9	9.9	2.1	5.3	....
85-86	Atlanta	9	0	183	110	42	81	.519	0	2	.000	26	33	.788	6	25	31	65	13	0	4	1	10	20.3	12.2	3.4	7.2	.865
86-87	Atlanta	8	1	122	31	9	19	.474	0	1	.000	13	17	.765	1	7	8	38	10	0	6	0	18	15.3	3.9	1.0	4.8	.427
87-88	Atlanta	12	0	211	106	35	81	.432	2	8	.250	34	37	.919	4	16	20	56	22	0	9	0	10	17.6	8.8	1.7	4.7	.611
88-89	Atlanta	5	0	55	8	3	11	.273	0	0	.000	2	2	1.000	0	4	4	15	6	0	4	0	0	11.0	1.6	0.8	3.0	.387
90-91	Atlanta	5	5	154	66	25	57	.439	5	12	.417	11	16	.688	8	14	22	24	13	0	7	1	13	30.8	13.2	4.4	4.8	.449
NBA Playoff Totals		39	6	725	321	114	249	.458	7	23	.304	86	105	.819	19	66	85	198	64	0	30	2	51	18.6	8.2	2.2	5.1	....

• WEBBER, Chris

Mayce Edward Christopher Webber III

Born: Mar. 1, 1973. Detroit, MI, United States. Height: 6'9". Weight: 245 lbs. Drafted: 1993 College: Michigan

YEAR	TEAM	GP	GS	MIN	PTS	FGM	FGA	FG%	3PM	3PA	3P%	FTM	FTA	FT%	ORB	DRB	TRB	AST	PF	DQ	STL	BLK	TO	MPG	PPG	RPG	APG	PCM
93-94	Golden State	76	76	2438	1333	572	1037	.552	0	14	.000	189	355	.532	305	389	694	272	247	4	93	164	205	32.1	17.5	9.1	3.6	.696
94-95	Washington	54	52	2067	1085	464	938	.495	40	145	.276	117	233	.502	200	318	518	256	186	2	83	85	167	38.3	20.1	9.6	4.7	.608
95-96	Washington	15	15	558	356	150	276	.543	15	34	.441	41	69	.594	37	77	114	75	51	1	27	9	50	37.2	23.7	7.6	5.0	.670
96-97	Washington	72	72	2806	1445	604	1167	.518	60	151	.397	177	313	.565	238	505	743	331	258	6	122	137	230	39.0	20.1	10.3	4.6	.645
97-98	Washington	71	71	2809	1555	647	1341	.482	65	205	.317	196	333	.589	176	498	674	273	269	4	111	124	185	39.6	21.9	9.5	3.8	.603
98-99	Sacramento	42	42	1719	839	378	778	.486	4	34	.118	79	174	.454	149	396	545	173	145	1	60	89	148	40.9	20.0	**13.0**	4.1	.613
99-00	Sacramento	75	75	2880	1834	748	1548	.483	27	95	.284	311	414	.751	190	598	788	345	264	7	120	128	218	38.4	24.5	10.5	4.6	.715
00-01	Sacramento	70	70	2836	1898	786	1635	.481	2	28	.071	324	461	.703	179	598	777	294	226	1	93	118	195	40.5	27.1	11.1	4.2	.708
01-02	Sacramento	54	54	2071	1322	532	1075	.495	5	19	.263	253	338	.749	150	396	546	258	181	1	90	76	158	38.4	24.5	10.1	4.8	.721
02-03	Sacramento	67	67	2622	1542	661	1433	.461	5	21	.238	215	354	.607	160	544	704	364	204	1	106	88	215	39.1	23.0	10.5	5.4	.649
NBA Season Totals		596	594	22806	13209	5542	11228	.494	223	746	.299	1902	3044	.625	1784	4319	6103	2641	2031	28	905	1018	1771	38.3	22.2	10.2	4.4	....
93-94	Golden State	3	3	109	47	22	40	.550	0	2	.000	3	10	.300	13	13	26	27	11	0	3	9	9	36.3	15.7	8.7	9.0	.716
96-97	Washington	3	3	106	47	19	30	.633	5	11	.455	4	8	.500	7	17	24	10	18	3	2	7	16	35.3	15.7	8.0	3.3	.500
98-99	Sacramento	5	5	192	74	31	80	.388	2	7	.286	10	25	.400	13	34	47	20	20	1	9	5	20	38.4	14.8	9.4	4.0	.383
99-00	Sacramento	5	5	196	122	47	110	.427	1	5	.200	27	34	.794	14	34	48	27	14	1	8	10	8	39.2	24.4	9.6	5.4	.701
00-01	Sacramento	8	8	348	186	76	196	.388	0	1	.000	34	49	.694	34	58	92	25	29	0	9	8	31	43.5	23.3	11.5	3.1	.449
01-02	Sacramento	16	16	667	379	160	319	.502	0	4	.000	59	99	.596	49	124	173	75	64	2	14	25	46	41.7	23.7	10.8	4.7	.630
02-03	Sacramento	7	7	246	166	67	135	.496	0	3	.000	32	49	.653	18	40	58	25	25	1	10	8	23	35.1	23.7	8.3	3.6	.653
NBA Playoff Totals		47	47	1864	1021	422	910	.464	8	33	.242	169	274	.617	148	320	468	209	181	8	55	72	153	39.7	21.7	10.0	4.4	....

• WEBER, Jake

Forest John Weber

Born: Mar. 18, 1918. Died: Jan.6, 1990. Height: 6'6". Weight: 225 lbs. Drafted: — College: Purdue

YEAR	TEAM	GP	GS	MIN	PTS	FGM	FGA	FG%	3PM	3PA	3P%	FTM	FTA	FT%	ORB	DRB	TRB	AST	PF	DQ	STL	BLK	TO	MPG	PPG	RPG	APG	PCM
45-46	Indianapolis-N	5	....	....	18	7	....	....	....	....	....	4	....	....	....	....	....	....	....	....	....	....	....	....	3.6	....	....	....
46-47	New York	11	....	....	20	7	24	.292	....	....	....	6	8	.750	....	....	....	1	20	....	....	....	....	....	1.8	....	0.1	....
46-47	Providence	39	....	....	153	52	178	.292	....	....	....	49	71	.690	....	....	....	3	91	....	....	....	....	....	3.9	....	0.1	....
NBA Season Totals		50	....	....	173	59	202	.292	....	....	....	55	79	.696	....	....	....	4	111	....	....	....	....	....	3.5	....	0.1	....
NBL Season Totals		5	....	....	18	7	....	....	....	....	....	4	....	....	....	....	....	....	....	....	....	....	....	....	3.6	....	....	....
Career Totals		55	....	....	191	66	202		....	....	....	59	79		....	....	....	4	111	....	....	....	....	....	3.5	....	0.1	....

• WEBSTER, Elnardo

Elnardo Webster

Born: Mar. 6, 1948. Jersey City, NJ, United States. Height: 6'5". Weight: 190 lbs. Drafted: 1969 College: St. Peter's

YEAR	TEAM	GP	GS	MIN	PTS	FGM	FGA	FG%	3PM	3PA	3P%	FTM	FTA	FT%	ORB	DRB	TRB	AST	PF	DQ	STL	BLK	TO	MPG	PPG	RPG	APG	PCM
71-72	Memphis-A	16	....	223	116	47	103	.456	1	4	.250	21	27	.778	15	28	43	15	37	0	....	....	33	13.9	7.3	2.7	0.9	.460
71-72	New York-A	3	....	14	6	3	6	.500	0	0	.000	0	2	.000	0	1	1	1	2	0	....	....	2	4.7	2.0	0.3	0.3	.258
ABA Season Totals		19	....	237	122	50	109	.459	1	4	.250	21	29	.724	15	29	44	16	39	0	....	....	35	12.5	6.4	2.3	0.8	....

• WEBSTER, Jeff

Jeffrey Tyrone Webster

Born: Feb. 19, 1971. Pine Bluff, AR, United States. Height: 6'8". Weight: 232 lbs. Drafted: 1994 College: Oklahoma

YEAR	TEAM	GP	GS	MIN	PTS	FGM	FGA	FG%	3PM	3PA	3P%	FTM	FTA	FT%	ORB	DRB	TRB	AST	PF	DQ	STL	BLK	TO	MPG	PPG	RPG	APG	PCM
95-96	Washington	11	0	58	18	8	23	.348	2	6	.333	0	0	.000	2	5	7	3	7	0	4	0	3	5.3	1.6	0.6	0.3	.195
NBA Season Totals		11	0	58	18	8	23	.348	2	6	.333	0	0	.000	2	5	7	3	7	0	4	0	3	5.3	1.6	0.6	0.3	....

• WEBSTER, Marvin

Marvin Nathaniel (The Human Eraser, Marvin the Magnificent) Webster

Born: Apr. 13, 1952. Baltimore, MD, United States. Height: 7'1". Weight: 225 lbs. Drafted: 1975 College: Morgan State

YEAR	TEAM	GP	GS	MIN	PTS	FGM	FGA	FG%	3PM	3PA	3P%	FTM	FTA	FT%	ORB	DRB	TRB	AST	PF	DQ	STL	BLK	TO	MPG	PPG	RPG	APG	PCM
75-76	Denver-A	38	....	398	165	55	120	.458	0	1	.000	55	78	.705	63	111	174	30	60	....	9	52	38	10.5	4.3	4.6	0.8	.649
76-77	Denver	80	....	1276	539	198	400	.495	....	....	....	143	220	.650	152	332	484	62	149	2	23	118	....	16.0	6.7	6.1	0.8	.592
77-78	Seattle	82	....	2910	1144	427	851	.502	....	....	....	290	461	.629	361	674	1035	203	262	8	48	162	254	35.5	14.0	12.6	2.5	.577
78-79	New York	60	....	2027	678	264	558	.473	....	....	....	150	262	.573	198	457	655	172	183	6	24	112	168	33.8	11.3	10.9	2.9	.508
79-80	New York	20	....	298	88	38	79	.481	0	0	.000	12	16	.750	28	52	80	9	39	1	3	11	20	14.9	4.4	4.0	0.5	.363
80-81	New York	82	....	1708	423	159	341	.466	1	4	.250	104	163	.638	162	303	465	72	187	2	27	97	107	20.8	5.2	5.7	0.9	.388
81-82	New York	82	32	1883	506	199	405	.491	0	0	.000	108	170	.635	184	306	490	99	211	2	22	91	90	23.0	6.2	6.0	1.2	.409

YEAR	TEAM	GP	GS	MIN	PTS	FGM	FGA	FG%	3PM	3PA	3P%	FTM	FTA	FT%	ORB	DRB	TRB	AST	PF	DQ	STL	BLK	TO	MPG	PPG	RPG	APG	PCM
82-83	New York	82	0	1472	442	168	331	.508	0	1	.000	106	180	.589	176	267	443	49	210	3	35	131	98	18.0	5.4	5.4	0.6	.463
83-84	New York	76	5	1290	290	112	239	.469	0	0	.000	66	117	.564	146	220	366	53	187	2	34	100	84	17.0	3.8	4.8	0.7	.391
86-87	Milwaukee	15	0	102	27	10	19	.526	1	1	1.000	6	8	.750	12	14	26	3	17	0	3	7	8	6.8	1.8	1.7	0.2	.383
NBA Season Totals		579	37	12966	4137	1575	3223	.489	2	6	.333	985	1597	.617	1419	2625	4044	722	1445	26	219	829	829	22.4	7.1	7.0	1.2	
ABA Season Totals		38	....	398	165	55	120	.458	0	1	.000	55	78	.705	63	111	174	30	60	....	9	52	38	10.5	4.3	4.6	0.8	
Career Totals		617	37	13364	4302	1630	3343	.488	2	7	.286	1040	1675	.621	1482	2736	4218	752	1505	26	228	881	867	21.7	7.0	6.8	1.2	
75-76	Denver-A	13	....	155	57	21	50	.420	0	0	.000	15	28	.536	24	47	71	9	28	....	1	14	15	11.9	4.4	5.5	0.7	.556
76-77	Denver	6	....	96	30	13	26	.500	....	....	....	4	6	.667	14	26	40	3	12	0	2	11	....	16.0	5.0	6.7	0.5	.528
77-78	Seattle	22	....	904	355	137	280	.489	....	....	....	81	120	.675	95	194	289	58	76	2	6	58	74	41.1	16.1	13.1	2.6	.541
80-81	New York	2	....	63	12	6	12	.500	0	0	.000	0	4	.000	4	6	10	1	6	0	0	1	3	31.5	6.0	5.0	0.5	.164
82-83	New York	6	0	115	28	7	18	.389	0	0	.000	14	22	.636	13	15	28	3	18	0	0	7	4	19.2	4.7	4.7	0.5	.327
83-84	New York	12	0	204	37	14	29	.483	0	0	.000	9	15	.600	24	32	56	3	32	0	4	17	2	17.0	3.1	4.7	0.3	.384
NBA Playoff Totals		48	0	1382	462	177	365	.485	0	0	.000	108	167	.647	150	273	423	68	144	2	12	94	83	28.8	9.6	8.8	1.4	
ABA Playoff Totals		13	....	155	57	21	50	.420	0	0	.000	15	28	.536	24	47	71	9	28	....	1	14	15	11.9	4.4	5.5	0.7	
Career Playoff Totals		61	0	1537	519	198	415	.477	0	0	.000	123	195	.631	174	320	494	77	172	2	13	108	98	25.2	8.5	8.1	1.3	

• WEDMAN, Scott

Scott Dean Wedman

Born: July 29, 1952. Harper, KS, United States.   Height: 6'7".   Weight: 215 lbs.   Drafted: 1974   College: Colorado

YEAR	TEAM	GP	GS	MIN	PTS	FGM	FGA	FG%	3PM	3PA	3P%	FTM	FTA	FT%	ORB	DRB	TRB	AST	PF	DQ	STL	BLK	TO	MPG	PPG	RPG	APG	PCM
74-75	Omaha	80	....	2554	889	375	806	.465	....	....	....	139	170	.818	202	288	490	129	270	2	81	27	....	31.9	11.1	6.1	1.6	.375
75-76	Kansas City	82	....	2968	1267	538	1181	.456	....	....	....	191	245	.780	199	407	606	199	280	8	103	36	....	36.2	15.5	7.4	2.4	.444
76-77	Kansas City	81	....	2743	1248	521	1133	.460	....	....	....	206	241	.855	187	319	506	227	226	3	100	23	....	33.9	15.4	6.2	2.8	.475
77-78	Kansas City	81	....	2961	1435	607	1192	.509	....	....	....	221	254	.870	144	319	463	201	242	2	99	22	162	36.6	17.7	5.7	2.5	.472
78-79	Kansas City	73	....	2498	1338	561	1050	.534	....	....	....	216	271	.797	135	251	386	144	239	4	76	30	110	34.2	18.3	5.3	2.0	.508
79-80	Kansas City	68	....	2347	1290	569	1112	.512	7	22	.318	145	181	.801	114	272	386	145	230	1	84	45	109	34.5	19.0	5.7	2.1	.513
80-81	Kansas City	81	....	2902	1535	685	1437	.477	25	77	.325	140	204	.686	128	305	433	226	294	4	97	46	162	35.8	19.0	5.3	2.8	.451
81-82	Cleveland	54	39	1638	591	260	589	.441	5	23	.217	66	90	.733	128	176	304	133	189	4	73	14	76	30.3	10.9	5.6	2.5	.381
82-83	Cleveland	35	35	1290	634	280	583	.480	9	22	.409	65	77	.844	69	139	208	86	145	5	23	11	95	36.9	18.1	5.9	2.5	.401
82-83	Boston	40	0	503	209	94	205	.459	1	10	.100	20	30	.667	29	45	74	31	83	1	20	6	32	12.6	5.2	1.9	0.8	.323
83-84	Boston	68	5	916	327	148	333	.444	2	13	.154	29	35	.829	41	98	139	67	107	0	27	7	41	13.5	4.8	2.0	1.0	.324
84-85	Boston	78	5	1127	499	220	460	.478	17	34	.500	42	55	.764	57	102	159	94	111	0	23	10	47	14.4	6.4	2.0	1.2	.402
85-86	Boston	79	19	1402	634	286	605	.473	17	48	.354	45	68	.662	66	126	192	83	127	0	38	22	55	17.7	8.0	2.4	1.1	.385
86-87	Boston	6	2	78	20	9	27	.333	1	2	.500	1	2	.500	3	6	9	6	6	0	2	2	3	13.0	3.3	1.5	1.0	.201
NBA Season Totals		906	105	25927	11916	5153	10713	.481	84	251	.335	1526	1923	.794	1502	2853	4355	1771	2549	34	846	301	892	28.6	13.2	4.8	2.0	
74-75	Omaha	6	....	230	66	27	68	.397	....	....	....	12	18	.667	10	25	35	16	17	0	6	3	....	38.3	11.0	5.8	2.7	.302
78-79	Kansas City	5	....	174	96	36	78	.462	....	....	....	24	32	.750	13	24	37	9	18	0	9	3	14	34.8	19.2	7.4	1.8	.506
79-80	Kansas City	3	....	116	68	29	64	.453	2	3	.667	8	11	.727	6	15	21	9	9	0	1	3	2	38.7	22.7	7.0	3.0	.531
80-81	Kansas City	15	....	657	307	129	297	.434	9	32	.281	40	56	.714	16	71	87	58	51	0	18	8	39	43.8	20.5	5.8	3.9	.387
82-83	Boston	6	0	66	29	14	24	.583	0	2	.000	1	2	.500	3	11	14	0	11	0	1	0	4	11.0	4.8	2.3	0.0	.371
83-84	Boston	17	1	226	89	40	96	.417	4	7	.571	5	10	.500	24	23	47	17	19	0	6	0	13	13.3	5.2	2.8	1.0	.359
84-85	Boston	21	1	350	182	73	134	.545	10	22	.455	26	38	.684	22	37	59	33	50	1	13	0	12	16.7	8.7	2.8	1.6	.535
85-86	Boston	12	0	142	45	20	51	.392	2	4	.500	3	4	.750	11	11	22	8	14	0	9	3	6	11.8	3.8	1.8	0.7	.309
NBA Playoff Totals		85	2	1961	882	368	812	.453	27	70	.386	119	171	.696	105	217	322	150	189	1	63	20	90	23.1	10.4	3.8	1.8	

• WEHR, Dick

Richard Wade Wehr

Born: Dec. 9, 1925.   Height: 6'4".   Weight: 180 lbs.   Drafted: 1948   College: Indiana

YEAR	TEAM	GP	GS	MIN	PTS	FGM	FGA	FG%	3PM	3PA	3P%	FTM	FTA	FT%	ORB	DRB	TRB	AST	PF	DQ	STL	BLK	TO	MPG	PPG	RPG	APG	PCM
48-49	Indianapolis	9	....	....	12	5	21	.238	....	....	....	2	6	.333	....	....	....	3	12	....	....	....	....	1.3	....	0.3	....	
NBA Season Totals		9	....	....	12	5	21	.238	....	....	....	2	6	.333	....	....	....	3	12	....	....	....	....	1.3	....	0.3	....	

• WEIDNER, Brant

Brant Clifford Weidner

Born: Oct. 28, 1960. Orefield, PA, United States.   Height: 6'9".   Weight: 230 lbs.   Drafted: 1983   College: William & Mary

YEAR	TEAM	GP	GS	MIN	PTS	FGM	FGA	FG%	3PM	3PA	3P%	FTM	FTA	FT%	ORB	DRB	TRB	AST	PF	DQ	STL	BLK	TO	MPG	PPG	RPG	APG	PCM
83-84	San Antonio	8	0	38	8	2	9	.222	0	0	.000	4	4	1.000	4	7	11	0	5	0	0	2	2	4.8	1.0	1.4	0.0	.247
NBA Season Totals		8	0	38	8	2	9	.222	0	0	.000	4	4	1.000	4	7	11	0	5	0	0	2	2	4.8	1.0	1.4	0.0	

• WEIGANDT, Bob

Robert Weigandt

Born: 1914.   Height: 5'10".   Weight: 190 lbs.   Drafted: —   College: Wisconsin

YEAR	TEAM	GP	GS	MIN	PTS	FGM	FGA	FG%	3PM	3PA	3P%	FTM	FTA	FT%	ORB	DRB	TRB	AST	PF	DQ	STL	BLK	TO	MPG	PPG	RPG	APG	PCM
38-39	Oshkosh-N	1	....	....	0	0	....	....	....	....	....	0	....	....	....	....	....	....	....	....	....	....	....	0.0	....	....	....	
NBL Season Totals		1	....	....	0	0	....	....	....	....	....	0	....	....	....	....	....	....	....	....	....	....	....	0.0	....	....	....	

• WEISS, Bob

Robert William Weiss

Born: May 7, 1942. Easton, PA, United States.   Height: 6'2".   Weight: 180 lbs.   Drafted: 1965   College: Penn State

YEAR	TEAM	GP	GS	MIN	PTS	FGM	FGA	FG%	3PM	3PA	3P%	FTM	FTA	FT%	ORB	DRB	TRB	AST	PF	DQ	STL	BLK	TO	MPG	PPG	RPG	APG	PCM
65-66	Philadelphia	7	....	30	6	3	9	.333	....	....	....	0	0	.000	....	....	7	4	10	0	....	....	....	4.3	0.9	1.0	0.6	.258
66-67	Philadelphia	6	....	29	12	5	10	.500	....	....	....	2	5	.400	....	....	3	10	8	0	....	....	....	4.8	2.0	0.5	1.7	.623
67-68	Seattle	82	....	1614	803	295	686	.430	....	....	....	213	254	.839	....	....	150	342	137	0	....	....	....	19.7	9.8	1.8	4.2	.589
68-69	Milwaukee	15	....	242	99	36	114	.316	....	....	....	27	34	.794	....	....	27	27	24	1	....	....	....	16.1	6.6	1.8	1.8	.309
68-69	Chicago	62	....	1236	407	153	385	.397	....	....	....	101	126	.802	....	....	135	172	150	0	....	....	....	19.9	6.6	2.2	2.8	.366
69-70	Chicago	82	....	2544	943	365	855	.427	....	....	....	213	253	.842	....	....	227	474	206	0	....	....	....	31.0	11.5	2.8	5.8	.446
70-71	Chicago	82	....	2237	782	278	659	.422	....	....	....	226	269	.840	....	....	189	387	216	1	....	....	....	27.3	9.5	2.3	4.7	.423
71-72	Chicago	82	....	2450	928	358	832	.430	....	....	....	212	254	.835	....	....	170	377	212	1	....	....	....	29.9	11.3	2.1	4.6	.402
72-73	Chicago	82	....	2086	717	279	655	.426	....	....	....	159	189	.841	....	....	148	295	151	1	....	....	....	25.4	8.7	1.8	3.6	.374
73-74	Chicago	79	....	1708	668	263	564	.466	....	....	....	142	170	.835	32	71	103	303	156	0	104	12	....	21.6	8.5	1.3	3.8	.450

YEAR	TEAM	GP	GS	MIN	PTS	FGM	FGA	FG%	3PM	3PA	3P%	FTM	FTA	FT%	ORB	DRB	TRB	AST	PF	DQ	STL	BLK	TO	MPG	PPG	RPG	APG	PCM
74-75	Buffalo	76	....	1338	258	102	261	.391	....	....	....	54	67	.806	21	83	104	260	146	0	82	19	....	17.6	3.4	1.4	3.4	.330
75-76	Buffalo	66	....	995	213	89	183	.486	....	....	....	35	48	.729	13	53	66	150	94	0	48	14	....	15.1	3.2	1.0	2.3	.316
76-77	Washington	62	....	768	153	62	133	.466	....	....	....	29	37	.784	15	54	69	130	66	0	53	7	....	12.4	2.5	1.1	2.1	.348
NBA Season Totals		783	....	17277	5989	2288	5346	.428	....	....	....	1413	1706	.828	81	261	1398	2931	1576	4	287	52	....	22.1	7.6	1.8	3.7	....
66-67	Philadelphia	1	....	4	4	2	3	.667	....	....	....	0	0	.000	....	....	2	2	1	0	....	....	....	4.0	4.0	2.0	2.0	1.701
69-70	Chicago	5	....	121	58	25	59	.424	....	....	....	8	10	.800	....	....	6	24	11	0	....	....	....	24.2	11.6	1.2	4.8	.451
70-71	Chicago	7	....	250	110	42	92	.457	....	....	....	26	30	.867	....	....	18	57	19	0	....	....	....	35.7	15.7	2.6	8.1	.550
71-72	Chicago	4	....	119	55	24	49	.490	....	....	....	7	8	.875	....	....	13	12	15	1	....	....	....	29.8	13.8	3.3	3.0	.432
72-73	Chicago	7	....	175	84	34	79	.430	....	....	....	16	21	.762	....	....	16	15	20	0	....	....	....	25.0	12.0	2.3	2.1	.374
73-74	Chicago	11	....	251	52	23	74	.311	....	....	....	6	6	1.000	5	15	20	32	20	0	7	1	....	22.8	4.7	1.8	2.9	.215
74-75	Buffalo	7	....	113	30	11	23	.478	....	....	....	8	12	.667	2	5	7	17	15	0	4	1	....	16.1	4.3	1.0	2.4	.329
75-76	Buffalo	7	....	36	8	3	8	.375	....	....	....	2	3	.667	0	4	4	3	5	0	2	0	....	5.1	1.1	0.6	0.4	.222
76-77	Washington	4	....	34	6	3	5	.600	....	....	....	0	1	.000	1	2	3	2	5	0	1	0	....	8.5	1.5	0.8	0.5	.193
NBA Playoff Totals		53	....	1103	407	167	392	.426	....	....	....	73	91	.802	8	26	89	164	111	1	14	2	....	20.8	7.7	1.7	3.1	....

• WEISS, Herm

Herm Weiss   Herman Weiss

Born: 1916.   Height: 6'   Weight: 180 lbs.   Drafted: —   College: Case Reserve

YEAR	TEAM	GP	GS	MIN	PTS	FGM	FGA	FG%	3PM	3PA	3P%	FTM	FTA	FT%	ORB	DRB	TRB	AST	PF	DQ	STL	BLK	TO	MPG	PPG	RPG	APG	PCM
44-45	Cleveland-N	3	....	....	4	2						0													1.3			
NBL Season Totals		3	....	....	4	2						0													1.3			

• WEITZMAN, Rick

Richard L. Weitzman

Born: Apr. 30, 1946.   Height: 6'2".   Weight: 175 lbs.   Drafted: 1967   College: Northeastern

YEAR	TEAM	GP	GS	MIN	PTS	FGM	FGA	FG%	3PM	3PA	3P%	FTM	FTA	FT%	ORB	DRB	TRB	AST	PF	DQ	STL	BLK	TO	MPG	PPG	RPG	APG	PCM
67-68	Boston	25	....	75	33	12	46	.261	....	....	....	9	13	.692	....	....	10	8	8	0	....	....	....	3.0	1.3	0.4	0.3	.249
NBA Season Totals		25	....	75	33	12	46	.261	....	....	....	9	13	.692	....	....	10	8	8	0	....	....	....	3.0	1.3	0.4	0.3	....
67-68	Boston	3	....	5	4	2	3	.667	....	....	....	0	0	.000	....	....	1	1	0	0	....	....	....	1.7	1.3	0.3	0.3	1.040
NBA Playoff Totals		3	....	5	4	2	3	.667	....	....	....	0	0	.000	....	....	1	1	0	0	....	....	....	1.7	1.3	0.3	0.3	....

• WELLS, Bonzi

Gawen Deangelo (Bonzi) Wells

Born: Sept. 20, 1976. Muncie, IN, United States.   Height: 6'5".   Weight: 210 lbs.   Drafted: 1998   College: Ball State

YEAR	TEAM	GP	GS	MIN	PTS	FGM	FGA	FG%	3PM	3PA	3P%	FTM	FTA	FT%	ORB	DRB	TRB	AST	PF	DQ	STL	BLK	TO	MPG	PPG	RPG	APG	PCM
98-99	Portland	7	0	35	31	11	20	.550	1	3	.333	8	18	.444	4	5	9	3	5	0	1	1	6	5.0	4.4	1.3	0.4	.689
99-00	Portland	66	0	1162	580	236	480	.492	20	53	.377	88	129	.682	78	104	182	97	153	3	69	12	97	17.6	8.8	2.8	1.5	.454
00-01	Portland	75	46	1995	950	387	726	.533	17	50	.340	159	240	.663	120	247	367	208	203	1	94	20	169	26.6	12.7	4.9	2.8	.515
01-02	Portland	74	69	2347	1255	487	1039	.469	66	172	.384	215	290	.741	121	323	444	204	208	0	113	25	191	31.7	17.0	6.0	2.8	.513
02-03	Portland	75	65	2397	1138	437	990	.441	38	130	.292	226	313	.722	98	296	394	246	220	2	123	18	215	32.0	15.2	5.3	3.3	.440
NBA Season Totals		297	180	7936	3954	1558	3255	.479	142	408	.348	696	990	.703	421	975	1396	758	789	6	400	76	678	26.7	13.3	4.7	2.6	....
99-00	Portland	14	0	188	105	37	83	.446	2	10	.200	29	41	.707	12	23	35	13	33	0	7	0	16	13.4	7.5	2.5	0.9	.429
01-02	Portland	3	3	106	37	14	38	.368	0	7	.000	9	13	.692	4	8	12	13	11	1	6	1	11	35.3	12.3	4.0	4.3	.282
02-03	Portland	7	7	268	133	49	124	.395	9	30	.300	26	39	.667	14	34	48	26	30	1	15	3	21	38.3	19.0	6.9	3.7	.428
NBA Playoff Totals		24	10	562	275	100	245	.408	11	47	.234	64	93	.688	30	65	95	52	74	2	28	4	48	23.4	11.5	4.0	2.2	....

• WELLS, Bubba

Charles Richard (Bubba) Wells

Born: July 26, 1974. Russellville, KY, United States.   Height: 6'5".   Weight: 230 lbs.   Drafted: 1997   College: Austin Peay

YEAR	TEAM	GP	GS	MIN	PTS	FGM	FGA	FG%	3PM	3PA	3P%	FTM	FTA	FT%	ORB	DRB	TRB	AST	PF	DQ	STL	BLK	TO	MPG	PPG	RPG	APG	PCM
97-98	Dallas	39	2	395	128	48	116	.414	1	6	.167	31	43	.721	22	46	68	34	40	1	15	4	31	10.1	3.3	1.7	0.9	.329
NBA Season Totals		39	2	395	128	48	116	.414	1	6	.167	31	43	.721	22	46	68	34	40	1	15	4	31	10.1	3.3	1.7	0.9	....

• WELLS, Owen

Owen Wells

Born: Dec. 9, 1950. Providence, RI, United States.   Height: 6'7".   Weight: 200 lbs.   Drafted: 1974   College: Detroit

YEAR	TEAM	GP	GS	MIN	PTS	FGM	FGA	FG%	3PM	3PA	3P%	FTM	FTA	FT%	ORB	DRB	TRB	AST	PF	DQ	STL	BLK	TO	MPG	PPG	RPG	APG	PCM
74-75	Houston	33	....	214	99	42	100	.420	....	....	....	15	22	.682	12	23	35	22	38	0	9	3	....	6.5	3.0	1.1	0.7	.399
NBA Season Totals		33	....	214	99	42	100	.420	....	....	....	15	22	.682	12	23	35	22	38	0	9	3	....	6.5	3.0	1.1	0.7	....
74-75	Houston	4	....	5	6	3	5	.600	....	....	....	0	0	.000	0	1	1	1	1	0	0	0	....	1.3	1.5	0.3	0.3	1.174
NBA Playoff Totals		4	....	5	6	3	5	.600	....	....	....	0	0	.000	0	1	1	1	1	0	0	0	....	1.3	1.5	0.3	0.3	....

• WELLS, Ralph

Ralph E. Wells

Born: Sept. 3, 1940. Died: Aug.2, 1968.   Height: 6'1".   Weight: 180 lbs.   Drafted: —   College: Northwestern

YEAR	TEAM	GP	GS	MIN	PTS	FGM	FGA	FG%	3PM	3PA	3P%	FTM	FTA	FT%	ORB	DRB	TRB	AST	PF	DQ	STL	BLK	TO	MPG	PPG	RPG	APG	PCM
62-63	Chicago	3	....	48	2	1	7	.143	....	....	....	0	7	.000	....	....	6	7	6	0	....	....	....	16.0	0.7	2.0	2.3	.111
NBA Season Totals		3	....	48	2	1	7	.143	....	....	....	0	7	.000	....	....	6	7	6	0	....	....	....	16.0	0.7	2.0	2.3	....

• WELP, Chris

Christian Ansgar Welp

Born: Jan. 2, 1964. Delmenhorst, Germany.   Height: 7'   Weight: 245 lbs.   Drafted: 1987   College: Washington

YEAR	TEAM	GP	GS	MIN	PTS	FGM	FGA	FG%	3PM	3PA	3P%	FTM	FTA	FT%	ORB	DRB	TRB	AST	PF	DQ	STL	BLK	TO	MPG	PPG	RPG	APG	PCM
87-88	Philadelphia	10	0	132	48	18	31	.581	0	0	.000	12	18	.667	11	13	24	5	25	0	5	5	9	13.2	4.8	2.4	0.5	.379
88-89	Philadelphia	72	0	843	246	99	222	.446	0	1	.000	48	73	.658	59	134	193	29	176	0	23	41	43	11.7	3.4	2.7	0.4	.318

YEAR	TEAM	GP	GS	MIN	PTS	FGM	FGA	FG%	3PM	3PA	3P%	FTM	FTA	FT%	ORB	DRB	TRB	AST	PF	DQ	STL	BLK	TO	MPG	PPG	RPG	APG	PCM
89-90	San Antonio	13	1	56	15	7	23	.304	0	0	.000	1	2	.500	7	5	12	5	21	0	1	0	7	4.3	1.2	0.9	0.4	.011
89-90	Golden State	14	2	142	50	16	38	.421	0	0	.000	18	23	.783	11	25	36	4	37	0	5	8	8	10.1	3.6	2.6	0.3	.369
NBA Season Totals		109	3	1173	359	140	314	.446	0	1	.000	79	116	.681	88	177	265	43	259	0	34	54	67	10.8	3.3	2.4	0.4	....
88-89	Philadelphia	3	0	22	2	1	3	.333	0	0	.000	0	2	.000	0	7	7	0	7	0	0	0	1	7.3	0.7	2.3	0.0	.070
NBA Playoff Totals		3	0	22	2	1	3	.333	0	0	.000	0	2	.000	0	7	7	0	7	0	0	0	1	7.3	0.7	2.3	0.0	....

• WELSCH, Jiri
Welsch Welsch

Born: Jan. 27, 1980. Pardubice, Czech Rep.. Height: 6'7". Weight: 208 lbs. Drafted: 2002 College: none

YEAR	TEAM	GP	GS	MIN	PTS	FGM	FGA	FG%	3PM	3PA	3P%	FTM	FTA	FT%	ORB	DRB	TRB	AST	PF	DQ	STL	BLK	TO	MPG	PPG	RPG	APG	PCM
02-03	Golden State	37	0	234	61	19	75	.253	1	4	.250	22	29	.759	12	16	28	27	32	1	8	2	19	6.3	1.6	0.8	0.7	.167
NBA Season Totals		37	0	234	61	19	75	.253	1	4	.250	22	29	.759	12	16	28	27	32	1	8	2	19	6.3	1.6	0.8	0.7	....

• WENDT, Bill
William Wendt

Born: 1915. Height: 6'3". Weight: 180 lbs. Drafted: — College: DePaul

YEAR	TEAM	GP	GS	MIN	PTS	FGM	FGA	FG%	3PM	3PA	3P%	FTM	FTA	FT%	ORB	DRB	TRB	AST	PF	DQ	STL	BLK	TO	MPG	PPG	RPG	APG	PCM
38-39	Hammond-N	8	....	....	20	8	....	....				4													2.5	....	....	....
NBL Season Totals		8		....	20	8	....					4													2.5	....	....	....

• WENNINGTON, Bill
William Percey Wennington

Born: Dec. 26, 1963. Montreal, QU, Canada. Height: 7' Weight: 245 lbs. Drafted: 1985 College: St. John's (NY)

YEAR	TEAM	GP	GS	MIN	PTS	FGM	FGA	FG%	3PM	3PA	3P%	FTM	FTA	FT%	ORB	DRB	TRB	AST	PF	DQ	STL	BLK	TO	MPG	PPG	RPG	APG	PCM
85-86	Dallas	56	3	562	189	72	153	.471	0	4	.000	45	62	.726	32	100	132	21	83	0	11	22	22	10.0	3.4	2.4	0.4	.396
86-87	Dallas	58	0	560	157	56	132	.424	0	2	.000	45	60	.750	53	76	129	24	95	0	13	10	41	9.7	2.7	2.2	0.4	.293
87-88	Dallas	30	0	125	63	25	49	.510	1	2	.500	12	19	.632	14	25	39	4	33	0	5	9	9	4.2	2.1	1.3	0.1	.538
88-89	Dallas	65	9	1074	300	119	275	.433	1	9	.111	61	82	.744	82	204	286	46	211	3	16	35	52	16.5	4.6	4.4	0.7	.336
89-90	Dallas	60	2	814	270	105	234	.449	0	4	.000	60	75	.800	64	134	198	41	144	2	20	21	48	13.6	4.5	3.3	0.7	.365
90-91	Sacramento	77	23	1455	437	181	415	.436	1	5	.200	74	94	.787	101	239	340	69	230	4	46	59	54	18.9	5.7	4.4	0.9	.371
93-94	Chicago	76	0	1371	542	235	482	.488	0	2	.000	72	88	.818	117	236	353	70	214	4	43	29	76	18.0	7.1	4.6	0.9	.442
94-95	Chicago	73	1	956	363	156	317	.492	0	4	.000	51	63	.810	64	126	190	40	198	5	22	17	37	13.1	5.0	2.6	0.5	.352
95-96	Chicago	71	20	1065	376	169	343	.493	1	1	1.000	37	43	.860	58	116	174	46	171	1	21	16	36	15.0	5.3	2.5	0.6	.322
96-97	Chicago	61	19	783	280	118	237	.498	0	2	.000	44	53	.830	46	83	129	41	132	1	10	11	31	12.8	4.6	2.1	0.7	.330
97-98	Chicago	48	8	467	167	75	172	.436	0	0	.000	17	21	.810	32	48	80	19	77	1	4	5	14	9.7	3.5	1.7	0.4	.279
98-99	Chicago	38	3	451	143	62	178	.348	1	1	1.000	18	22	.818	20	59	79	18	79	1	13	12	17	11.9	3.8	2.1	0.5	.222
99-00	Sacramento	7	0	56	14	6	20	.300	0	0	.000	2	2	1.000	5	14	19	1	13	0	2	2	1	8.0	2.0	2.7	0.1	.294
NBA Season Totals		720	88	9739	3301	1379	3007	.459	5	36	.139	538	684	.787	688	1460	2148	440	1680	22	226	248	438	13.5	4.6	3.0	0.6	....
85-86	Dallas	6	0	18	7	2	6	.333	1	1	1.000	2	2	1.000	4	1	5	0	4	0	0	0	0	3.0	1.2	0.8	0.0	.337
86-87	Dallas	4	0	47	15	6	12	.500	0	0	.000	3	5	.600	4	6	10	4	9	0	0	3	3	11.8	3.8	2.5	1.0	.380
87-88	Dallas	6	0	14	0	0	4	.000	0	0	.000	0	0	.000	3	1	4	1	5	0	1	0	1	2.3	0.0	0.7	0.2	-.090
88-89	Dallas	3	0	25	2	1	5	.200	0	0	.000	0	0	.000	0	3	3	1	5	0	0	1	2	8.3	0.7	1.0	0.3	-.046
93-94	Chicago	7	0	47	8	3	6	.500	0	0	.000	2	3	.667	4	3	7	4	14	0	0	1	1	6.7	1.1	1.0	0.6	.194
94-95	Chicago	10	0	133	48	21	51	.412	0	0	.000	6	6	1.000	12	16	28	3	32	0	3	3	8	13.3	4.8	2.8	0.3	.244
95-96	Chicago	18	0	169	54	26	50	.520	0	1	.000	2	4	.500	11	19	30	9	30	0	4	1	5	9.4	3.0	1.7	0.5	.320
97-98	Chicago	16	0	119	44	20	38	.526	0	0	.000	4	8	.500	3	11	14	3	23	1	6	2	8	7.4	2.8	0.9	0.2	.263
NBA Playoff Totals		70	0	572	178	79	172	.459	1	2	.500	19	28	.679	41	60	101	25	122	1	14	11	28	8.2	2.5	1.4	0.4	....

• WENSTROM, Matt
Matthew William Wenstrom

Born: Nov. 4, 1970. Minneapolis, MN, United States. Height: 7'1". Weight: 250 lbs. Drafted: — College: North Carolina

YEAR	TEAM	GP	GS	MIN	PTS	FGM	FGA	FG%	3PM	3PA	3P%	FTM	FTA	FT%	ORB	DRB	TRB	AST	PF	DQ	STL	BLK	TO	MPG	PPG	RPG	APG	PCM
93-94	Boston	11	0	37	18	6	10	.600	0	0	.000	6	10	.600	6	6	12	0	7	0	0	2	4	3.4	1.6	1.1	0.0	.499
NBA Season Totals		11	0	37	18	6	10	.600	0	0	.000	6	10	.600	6	6	12	0	7	0	0	2	4	3.4	1.6	1.1	0.0	....

• WERDANN, Robert
Robert Werdann

Born: Sept. 12, 1970. Sunnyside, NY, United States. Height: 6'11". Weight: 250 lbs. Drafted: — College: St. John's (NY)

YEAR	TEAM	GP	GS	MIN	PTS	FGM	FGA	FG%	3PM	3PA	3P%	FTM	FTA	FT%	ORB	DRB	TRB	AST	PF	DQ	STL	BLK	TO	MPG	PPG	RPG	APG	PCM
92-93	Denver	28	0	149	53	18	59	.305	0	1	.000	17	31	.548	23	29	52	7	38	1	6	4	11	5.3	1.9	1.9	0.3	.306
95-96	New Jersey	13	0	93	39	16	32	.500	0	0	.000	7	13	.538	5	18	23	2	17	0	5	3	7	7.2	3.0	1.8	0.2	.407
96-97	New Jersey	6	0	31	9	3	7	.429	0	0	.000	3	3	1.000	3	3	6	0	10	0	2	1	2	5.2	1.5	1.0	0.0	.230
NBA Season Totals		47	0	273	101	37	98	.378	0	1	.000	27	47	.574	31	50	81	9	65	1	13	8	20	5.8	2.1	1.7	0.2	....

• WERTIS, Ray
Raymond A. Wertis

Born: Jan. 1, 1922. Height: 5'11". Weight: — Drafted: — College: St. John's (NY)

YEAR	TEAM	GP	GS	MIN	PTS	FGM	FGA	FG%	3PM	3PA	3P%	FTM	FTA	FT%	ORB	DRB	TRB	AST	PF	DQ	STL	BLK	TO	MPG	PPG	RPG	APG	PCM
46-47	Toronto	18	....	....	99	38	171	.222	....	....	....	23	37	.622	....	....	....	18	29	....	....	....	....	5.5	....	1.0	....	
46-47	Cleveland	43	....	....	115	41	195	.210	....	....	....	33	54	.611	....	....	....	21	53	....	....	....	....	2.7	....	0.5	....	
47-48	Providence	7	....	....	32	13	72	.181	....	....	....	6	14	.429	....	....	....	6	13	....	....	....	....	4.6	....	0.9	....	
NBA Season Totals		68	....	....	246	92	438	.210	....	....	....	62	105	.590	....	....	....	45	95	....	....	....	....	3.6	....	0.7	....	
46-47	Cleveland	3	....	....	16	6	26	.231	....	....	....	4	5	.800	....	....	....	6	6	....	....	....	....	5.3	....	2.0	....	
NBA Playoff Totals		3	....	....	16	6	26	.231	....	....	....	4	5	.800	....	....	....	6	6	....	....	....	....	5.3	....	2.0	....	

• WESLEY, David
David Barakau Wesley

Born: Nov. 14, 1970. San Antonio, TX, United States. Height: 6' Weight: 190 lbs. Drafted: — College: Baylor

YEAR	TEAM	GP	GS	MIN	PTS	FGM	FGA	FG%	3PM	3PA	3P%	FTM	FTA	FT%	ORB	DRB	TRB	AST	PF	DQ	STL	BLK	TO	MPG	PPG	RPG	APG	PCM
93-94	New Jersey	60	0	542	183	64	174	.368	11	47	.234	44	53	.830	10	34	44	123	47	0	38	4	54	9.0	3.1	0.7	2.1	.404
94-95	Boston	51	36	1380	378	128	313	.409	51	119	.429	71	94	.755	31	86	117	266	144	0	82	9	87	27.1	7.4	2.3	5.2	.378

YEAR	TEAM	GP	GS	MIN	PTS	FGM	FGA	FG%	3PM	3PA	3P%	FTM	FTA	FT%	ORB	DRB	TRB	AST	PF	DQ	STL	BLK	TO	MPG	PPG	RPG	APG	PCM
95-96	Boston	82	53	2104	1009	338	736	.459	116	272	.426	217	288	.753	68	196	264	390	207	0	100	11	156	25.7	12.3	3.2	4.8	.534
96-97	Boston	74	73	2991	1240	456	974	.468	103	286	.360	225	288	.781	67	197	264	537	221	1	162	13	215	40.4	16.8	3.6	7.3	.470
97-98	Charlotte	81	81	2845	1054	383	864	.443	59	170	.347	229	288	.795	49	164	213	529	229	3	140	30	227	35.1	13.0	2.6	6.5	.421
98-99	Charlotte	50	50	1848	706	243	545	.446	61	170	.359	159	191	.832	23	138	161	322	130	2	100	10	142	37.0	14.1	3.2	6.4	.453
99-00	Charlotte	82	82	2760	1116	407	955	.426	88	248	.355	214	275	.778	39	186	225	463	186	2	109	11	159	33.7	13.6	2.7	5.6	.428
00-01	Charlotte	82	82	3106	1414	523	1239	.422	97	258	.376	271	339	.799	64	160	224	361	220	2	128	16	171	37.9	17.2	2.7	4.4	.392
01-02	Charlotte	67	63	2487	951	364	910	.400	85	256	.332	138	188	.734	44	99	143	236	147	0	74	15	119	37.1	14.2	2.1	3.5	.293
02-03	New Orleans	73	73	2710	1217	449	1037	.433	134	316	.424	185	237	.781	38	137	175	251	173	0	109	9	132	37.1	16.7	2.4	3.4	.369
NBA Season Totals		702	593	22773	9268	3355	7747	.433	805	2142	.376	1753	2241	.782	433	1397	1830	3478	1704	10	1042	128	1462	32.4	13.2	2.6	5.0	....
93-94	New Jersey	3	0	18	9	3	7	.429	1	4	.250	2	2	1.000	0	0	0	3	0	0	2	0	4	6.0	3.0	0.0	1.0	.375
97-98	Charlotte	9	9	285	90	33	83	.398	9	21	.429	15	21	.714	5	13	18	60	25	0	7	0	19	31.7	10.0	2.0	6.7	.353
99-00	Charlotte	4	4	152	44	16	48	.333	3	10	.300	9	9	1.000	3	9	12	19	17	0	8	0	6	38.0	11.0	3.0	4.8	.268
00-01	Charlotte	10	10	394	170	63	134	.470	13	33	.394	31	41	.756	4	26	30	39	28	0	16	1	14	39.4	17.0	3.0	3.9	.411
01-02	Charlotte	9	9	377	142	52	129	.403	17	38	.447	21	23	.913	3	14	17	31	30	0	10	2	21	41.9	15.8	1.9	3.4	.262
02-03	New Orleans	6	6	185	79	29	72	.403	14	34	.412	7	7	1.000	1	6	7	13	23	1	5	1	15	30.8	13.2	1.2	2.2	.226
NBA Playoff Totals		41	38	1411	534	196	473	.414	57	140	.407	85	103	.825	16	68	84	165	123	1	48	4	79	34.4	13.0	2.0	4.0	....

• WESLEY, Walt

Walter Wesley

Born: Jan. 25, 1945. Fort Myers, FL, United States. Height: 6'11". Weight: 220 lbs. Drafted: 1966 College: Kansas

YEAR	TEAM	GP	GS	MIN	PTS	FGM	FGA	FG%	3PM	3PA	3P%	FTM	FTA	FT%	ORB	DRB	TRB	AST	PF	DQ	STL	BLK	TO	MPG	PPG	RPG	APG	PCM
66-67	Cincinnati	64	....	909	314	131	333	.393	....	....	....	52	123	.423	....	....	329	19	161	2	....	....	....	14.2	4.9	5.1	0.3	.380
67-68	Cincinnati	66	....	918	452	188	404	.465	....	....	....	76	152	.500	....	....	281	34	168	2	....	....	....	13.9	6.8	4.3	0.5	.487
68-69	Cincinnati	82	....	1334	624	245	534	.459	....	....	....	134	207	.647	....	....	403	47	191	0	....	....	....	16.3	7.6	4.9	0.6	.497
69-70	Chicago	72	....	1407	685	270	648	.417	....	....	....	145	219	.662	....	....	455	68	184	1	....	....	....	19.5	9.5	6.3	0.9	.508
70-71	Cleveland	82	....	2425	1455	565	1241	.455	....	....	....	325	473	.687	....	....	713	83	295	5	....	....	....	29.6	17.7	8.7	1.0	.574
71-72	Cleveland	82	....	2185	1020	412	1006	.410	....	....	....	196	291	.674	....	....	711	76	245	4	....	....	....	26.6	12.4	8.7	0.9	.485
72-73	Cleveland	12	....	110	36	14	47	.298	....	....	....	8	12	.667	....	....	38	7	21	0	....	....	....	9.2	3.0	3.2	0.6	.341
72-73	Phoenix	45	....	364	144	63	155	.406	....	....	....	18	34	.529	....	....	113	24	56	0	....	....	....	8.1	3.2	2.5	0.5	.436
73-74	Washington	39	....	400	168	71	151	.470	....	....	....	26	43	.605	63	73	136	14	74	1	9	20	....	10.3	4.3	3.5	0.4	.483
74-75	Philadelphia	4	....	33	12	5	9	.556	....	....	....	2	4	.500	4	4	8	1	8	0	0	0	....	8.3	3.0	2.0	0.3	.373
74-75	Milwaukee	41	....	214	88	37	84	.440	....	....	....	14	23	.609	14	41	55	11	43	0	7	5	....	5.2	2.1	1.3	0.3	.398
75-76	LA Lakers	1	....	7	4	1	2	.500	....	....	....	2	4	.500	0	1	1	1	2	0	0	0	....	7.0	4.0	1.0	1.0	.489
NBA Season Totals		590	....	10306	5002	2002	4614	.434	....	....	....	998	1585	.630	81	119	3243	385	1448	15	16	25	....	17.5	8.5	5.5	0.7	....
66-67	Cincinnati	3	....	23	4	2	10	.200	....	....	....	0	0	.000	....	....	9	0	7	0	....	....	....	7.7	1.3	3.0	0.0	.087
69-70	Chicago	4	....	59	38	16	31	.516	....	....	....	6	12	.500	....	....	19	2	9	0	....	....	....	14.8	9.5	4.8	0.5	.630
73-74	Washington	1	....	1	0	0	0	.000	....	....	....	0	0	.000	0	0	0	0	0	0	0	0	....	1.0	0.0	0.0	0.0	.000
NBA Playoff Totals		8	....	83	42	18	41	.439	....	....	....	6	12	.500	0	0	28	2	16	0	0	0	....	10.4	5.3	3.5	0.3	....

• WEST, Doug

Jeffery Douglas (Fresh) West

Born: May 27, 1967. Altoona, PA, United States. Height: 6'6". Weight: 200 lbs. Drafted: 1989 College: Villanova

YEAR	TEAM	GP	GS	MIN	PTS	FGM	FGA	FG%	3PM	3PA	3P%	FTM	FTA	FT%	ORB	DRB	TRB	AST	PF	DQ	STL	BLK	TO	MPG	PPG	RPG	APG	PCM
89-90	Minnesota	52	0	378	135	53	135	.393	3	11	.273	26	32	.813	24	46	70	18	61	0	10	6	31	7.3	2.6	1.3	0.3	.258
90-91	Minnesota	75	1	824	294	118	246	.480	0	1	.000	58	84	.690	56	80	136	48	115	0	35	23	38	11.0	3.9	1.8	0.6	.371
91-92	Minnesota	80	72	2540	1116	463	894	.518	4	23	.174	186	231	.805	107	150	257	281	239	1	66	26	120	31.8	14.0	3.2	3.5	.432
92-93	Minnesota	80	80	3104	1543	646	1249	.517	2	23	.087	249	296	.841	89	158	247	235	279	1	85	21	168	38.8	19.3	3.1	2.9	.403
93-94	Minnesota	72	61	2182	1056	434	891	.487	1	8	.125	187	231	.810	61	170	231	172	236	3	65	24	137	30.3	14.7	3.2	2.4	.395
94-95	Minnesota	71	65	2328	919	351	762	.461	11	61	.180	206	246	.837	60	167	227	185	250	4	65	24	128	32.8	12.9	3.2	2.6	.331
95-96	Minnesota	73	16	1639	465	175	393	.445	1	13	.077	114	144	.792	48	113	161	119	228	2	30	17	80	22.5	6.4	2.2	1.6	.235
96-97	Minnesota	68	66	1920	531	226	484	.467	15	45	.333	64	94	.681	37	111	148	113	218	3	61	24	68	28.2	7.8	2.2	1.7	.234
97-98	Minnesota	38	10	688	157	64	171	.374	0	2	.000	29	40	.725	23	59	82	45	97	1	11	5	23	18.1	4.1	2.2	1.2	.185
98-99	Vancouver	14	2	294	81	31	65	.477	0	2	.000	19	25	.760	5	20	25	19	38	1	16	7	12	21.0	5.8	1.8	1.4	.287
99-00	Vancouver	38	0	581	152	59	145	.407	0	3	.000	34	40	.850	18	53	71	43	80	0	12	8	19	15.3	4.0	1.9	1.1	.253
00-01	Vancouver	15	6	171	28	11	38	.289	0	2	.000	6	7	.857	4	11	15	14	21	0	3	4	4	11.4	1.9	1.0	0.9	.149
NBA Season Totals		676	379	16649	6477	2631	5473	.481	37	194	.191	1178	1470	.801	532	1138	1670	1292	1862	16	459	189	828	24.6	9.6	2.5	1.9	....
96-97	Minnesota	3	3	87	33	12	22	.545	0	2	.000	9	9	1.000	0	4	4	6	11	0	2	1	1	29.0	11.0	1.3	2.0	.351
NBA Playoff Totals		3	3	87	33	12	22	.545	0	2	.000	9	9	1.000	0	4	4	6	11	0	2	1	1	29.0	11.0	1.3	2.0	....

• WEST, Jerry

Jerry Alan (Mr. Clutch, Zeke from Cabin Creek) West

Born: May 28, 1938. Cheylan, WV, United States. Height: 6'2". Weight: 175 lbs. Drafted: 1960 College: West Virginia HOF: 1980

YEAR	TEAM	GP	GS	MIN	PTS	FGM	FGA	FG%	3PM	3PA	3P%	FTM	FTA	FT%	ORB	DRB	TRB	AST	PF	DQ	STL	BLK	TO	MPG	PPG	RPG	APG	PCM
60-61	LA Lakers	79	....	2797	1389	529	1264	.419	....	....	....	331	497	.666	....	....	611	333	213	1	....	....	....	35.4	17.6	7.7	4.2	.559
61-62	LA Lakers	75	....	3087	2310	799	1795	.445	....	....	....	712	926	.769	....	....	591	402	173	4	....	....	....	41.2	30.8	7.9	5.4	.756
62-63	LA Lakers	55	....	2163	1489	559	1213	.461	....	....	....	371	477	.778	....	....	384	307	150	1	....	....	....	39.3	27.1	7.0	5.6	.714
63-64	LA Lakers	72	....	2906	2064	740	1529	.484	....	....	....	584	702	.832	....	....	433	403	200	2	....	....	....	40.4	28.7	6.0	5.6	.742
64-65	LA Lakers	74	....	3066	2292	822	1655	.497	....	....	....	648	789	.821	....	....	447	364	221	2	....	....	....	41.4	31.0	6.0	4.9	.752
65-66	LA Lakers	79	....	3218	2476	818	1731	.473	....	....	....	**840**	**977**	.860	....	....	562	480	243	1	....	....	....	40.7	31.3	7.1	6.1	.819
66-67	LA Lakers	66	....	2670	1892	645	1389	.464	....	....	....	602	686	.878	....	....	392	447	160	1	....	....	....	40.5	28.7	5.9	6.8	.769
67-68	LA Lakers	51	....	1919	1343	476	926	.514	....	....	....	391	482	.811	....	....	294	310	152	1	....	....	....	37.6	26.3	5.8	6.1	.779
68-69	LA Lakers	61	....	2394	1580	545	1156	.471	....	....	....	490	597	.821	....	....	262	423	156	1	....	....	....	39.2	25.9	4.3	6.9	.698
69-70	LA Lakers	74	....	3106	2309	831	1673	.497	....	....	....	**647**	**785**	.824	....	....	338	554	160	3	....	....	....	42.0	**31.2**	4.6	7.5	.758
70-71	LA Lakers	69	....	2845	1859	667	1351	.494	....	....	....	525	631	.832	....	....	320	655	180	0	....	....	....	41.2	26.9	4.6	9.5	.763
71-72	LA Lakers	77	....	2973	1985	735	1540	.477	....	....	....	515	633	.814	....	....	327	747	209	0	....	....	....	38.6	25.8	4.2	**9.7**	.767
72-73	LA Lakers	69	....	2460	1575	618	1291	.479	....	....	....	339	421	.805	....	....	289	607	138	0	....	....	....	35.7	22.8	4.2	8.8	.750
73-74	LA Lakers	31	....	967	629	232	519	.447	....	....	....	165	198	.833	30	86	116	206	80	0	81	23	....	31.2	20.3	3.7	6.6	.695
NBA Season Totals		932	....	36571	25192	9016	19032	.474	....	....	....	7160	8801	.814	30	86	5366	6238	2435	17	81	23	....	39.2	27.0	5.8	6.7	....
60-61	LA Lakers	12	....	461	275	99	202	.490	....	....	....	77	106	.726	....	....	104	66	39	0	....	....	....	38.4	22.9	8.7	5.5	.719
61-62	LA Lakers	13	....	557	409	144	310	.465	....	....	....	121	150	.807	....	....	88	57	38	0	....	....	....	42.8	31.5	6.8	4.4	.703
62-63	LA Lakers	13	....	538	362	144	286	.503	....	....	....	74	100	.740	....	....	106	61	34	0	....	....	....	41.4	27.8	8.2	4.7	.713
63-64	LA Lakers	5	....	206	156	57	115	.496	....	....	....	42	53	.792	....	....	36	17	20	0	....	....	....	41.2	31.2	7.2	3.4	.717

YEAR	TEAM	GP	GS	MIN	PTS	FGM	FGA	FG%	3PM	3PA	3P%	FTM	FTA	FT%	ORB	DRB	TRB	AST	PF	DQ	STL	BLK	TO	MPG	PPG	RPG	APG	PCM
64-65	LA Lakers	11	....	470	447	155	351	.442	....	....	....	137	154	.890	....	....	63	58	37	0	....	....	....	42.7	40.6	5.7	5.3	.842
65-66	LA Lakers	14	....	619	479	185	357	.518	....	....	....	109	125	.872	....	....	88	79	40	0	....	....	....	44.2	34.2	6.3	5.6	.787
66-67	LA Lakers	1	....	1	0	0	0	.000	....	....	....	0	0	.000	....	....	1	0	0	0	....	....	....	1.0	0.0	1.0	0.0	.797
67-68	LA Lakers	15	....	622	462	165	313	.527	....	....	....	132	169	.781	....	....	81	82	47	0	....	....	....	41.5	30.8	5.4	5.5	.761
68-69	LA Lakers	18	....	757	556	196	423	.463	....	....	....	164	204	.804	....	....	71	135	52	1	....	....	....	42.1	30.9	3.9	7.5	.719
69-70	LA Lakers	18	....	830	562	196	418	.469	....	....	....	170	212	.802	....	....	66	151	55	1	....	....	....	46.1	31.2	3.7	8.4	.664
71-72	LA Lakers	15	....	608	344	128	340	.376	....	....	....	88	106	.830	....	....	73	134	39	0	....	....	....	40.5	22.9	4.9	8.9	.578
72-73	LA Lakers	17	....	638	401	151	336	.449	....	....	....	99	127	.780	....	....	76	132	49	1	....	....	....	37.5	23.6	4.5	7.8	.666
73-74	LA Lakers	1	....	14	4	2	9	.222	....	....	....	0	0	.000	0	2	2	1	1	0	0	0	....	14.0	4.0	2.0	1.0	.033
NBA Playoff Totals		153	....	6321	4457	1622	3460	.469	....	....	....	1213	1506	.805	0	2	855	973	451	3	0	0	....	41.3	29.1	5.6	6.4	....

• WEST, Mark

Mark Andre West

Born: Nov. 5, 1960. Petersburg, VA, United States. Height: 6'10". Weight: 230 lbs. Drafted: 1983 College: Old Dominion

YEAR	TEAM	GP	GS	MIN	PTS	FGM	FGA	FG%	3PM	3PA	3P%	FTM	FTA	FT%	ORB	DRB	TRB	AST	PF	DQ	STL	BLK	TO	MPG	PPG	RPG	APG	PCM
83-84	Dallas	34	0	202	37	15	42	.357	0	0	.000	7	22	.318	19	27	46	13	55	0	1	15	14	5.9	1.1	1.4	0.4	.188
84-85	Milwaukee	1	0	6	2	0	1	.000	0	0	.000	2	2	1.000	1	0	1	0	4	0	0	1	2	6.0	2.0	1.0	0.0	-.133
84-85	Cleveland	65	25	882	253	106	193	.549	0	1	.000	41	85	.482	89	161	250	15	193	7	13	48	59	13.6	3.9	3.8	0.2	.354
85-86	Cleveland	67	26	1172	280	113	209	.541	0	0	.000	54	103	.524	97	225	322	20	235	6	27	62	94	17.5	4.2	4.8	0.3	.320
86-87	Cleveland	78	13	1333	507	209	385	.543	0	2	.000	89	173	.514	126	213	339	41	229	5	22	81	109	17.1	6.5	4.3	0.5	.414
87-88	Cleveland	54	12	1183	459	182	316	.576	0	0	.000	95	153	.621	83	198	281	50	158	2	25	79	92	21.9	8.5	5.2	0.9	.473
87-88	Phoenix	29	29	915	343	134	257	.521	0	1	.000	75	132	.568	82	160	242	24	107	2	22	68	81	31.6	11.8	8.3	0.8	.450
88-89	Phoenix	82	32	2019	594	243	372	.653	0	0	.000	108	202	.535	167	384	551	39	273	4	35	187	107	24.6	7.2	6.7	0.5	.478
89-90	Phoenix	82	79	2399	861	331	530	**.625**	0	0	.000	199	288	.691	212	516	728	45	277	5	36	184	123	29.3	10.5	8.9	0.5	.552
90-91	Phoenix	82	64	1957	629	247	382	.647	0	0	.000	135	206	.655	171	393	564	37	266	2	32	161	82	23.9	7.7	6.9	0.5	.519
91-92	Phoenix	82	11	1436	501	196	310	.632	0	0	.000	109	171	.637	134	238	372	22	239	2	14	80	82	17.5	6.1	4.5	0.3	.443
92-93	Phoenix	82	82	1558	436	175	285	.614	0	0	.000	86	166	.518	153	305	458	29	243	3	16	103	90	19.0	5.3	5.6	0.4	.429
93-94	Phoenix	82	50	1236	382	162	286	.566	0	0	.000	58	116	.500	112	183	295	33	214	4	31	109	74	15.1	4.7	3.6	0.4	.413
94-95	Detroit	67	58	1543	500	217	390	.556	0	0	.000	66	138	.478	160	248	408	18	247	8	27	102	87	23.0	7.5	6.1	0.3	.408
95-96	Detroit	47	21	682	150	61	126	.484	0	0	.000	28	45	.622	49	84	133	6	135	2	6	37	33	14.5	3.2	2.8	0.1	.232
96-97	Cleveland	70	43	959	227	100	180	.556	0	0	.000	27	56	.482	69	117	186	19	142	0	11	55	49	13.7	3.2	2.7	0.3	.294
97-98	Indiana	15	1	105	23	10	21	.476	0	0	.000	3	6	.500	6	9	15	2	15	0	2	4	8	7.0	1.5	1.0	0.1	.179
98-99	Atlanta	49	0	499	60	22	59	.373	0	0	.000	16	45	.356	49	76	125	13	81	0	4	22	17	10.2	1.2	2.6	0.3	.224
99-00	Phoenix	22	2	127	15	5	12	.417	0	0	.000	5	8	.625	6	25	31	2	23	0	2	4	6	5.8	0.7	1.4	0.1	.214
NBA Season Totals		1090	548	20213	6259	2528	4356	.580	0	4	.000	1203	2117	.568	1785	3562	5347	428	3136	52	326	1402	1209	18.5	5.7	4.9	0.4	....
83-84	Dallas	4	0	32	12	5	9	.556	0	0	.000	2	3	.667	0	7	7	3	11	1	0	3	3	8.0	3.0	1.8	0.8	.388
84-85	Cleveland	4	4	68	8	3	5	.600	0	0	.000	2	5	.400	5	13	18	4	19	0	2	0	5	17.0	2.0	4.5	1.0	.208
88-89	Phoenix	12	12	227	74	32	50	.640	0	0	.000	10	14	.714	21	32	53	6	36	1	7	19	13	18.9	6.2	4.4	0.5	.469
89-90	Phoenix	16	16	544	177	75	130	.577	0	0	.000	27	50	.540	53	111	164	5	73	3	4	41	26	34.0	11.1	10.3	0.3	.473
90-91	Phoenix	4	4	93	23	9	15	.600	0	0	.000	5	7	.714	8	10	18	2	15	0	2	10	3	23.3	5.8	4.5	0.5	.396
91-92	Phoenix	8	0	96	32	14	19	.737	0	0	.000	4	8	.500	8	9	17	2	21	1	2	4	2	12.0	4.0	2.1	0.3	.390
92-93	Phoenix	24	24	469	114	43	79	.544	0	0	.000	28	46	.609	36	63	99	11	69	2	4	33	17	19.5	4.8	4.1	0.5	.347
93-94	Phoenix	7	6	69	17	5	15	.333	0	0	.000	7	10	.700	11	9	20	0	19	0	0	7	4	9.9	2.4	2.9	0.0	.273
95-96	Detroit	3	3	78	28	11	21	.524	0	0	.000	6	13	.462	6	10	16	1	12	0	1	1	2	26.0	9.3	5.3	0.3	.330
97-98	Indiana	4	0	11	3	1	2	.500	0	0	.000	1	3	.333	1	0	1	0	4	0	0	0	0	2.8	0.8	0.3	0.0	.023
98-99	Atlanta	9	0	68	8	3	10	.300	0	0	.000	2	4	.500	3	6	9	2	14	0	2	1	6	7.6	0.9	1.0	0.2	.033
NBA Playoff Totals		95	69	1755	496	201	355	.566	0	0	.000	94	163	.577	152	270	422	36	293	8	24	119	81	18.5	5.2	4.4	0.4	....

• WEST, Roland

Roland D. West

Born: June 6, 1944. Height: 6'4". Weight: 178 lbs. Drafted: 1967 College: Cincinnati

YEAR	TEAM	GP	GS	MIN	PTS	FGM	FGA	FG%	3PM	3PA	3P%	FTM	FTA	FT%	ORB	DRB	TRB	AST	PF	DQ	STL	BLK	TO	MPG	PPG	RPG	APG	PCM
67-68	Baltimore	4	....	14	4	2	5	.400	....	....	....	0	0	.000	....	....	5	0	3	0	....	....	....	3.5	1.0	1.3	0.0	.314
NBA Season Totals		4	....	14	4	2	5	.400	....	....	....	0	0	.000	....	....	5	0	3	0	....	....	....	3.5	1.0	1.3	0.0	....

• WESTBROOK, Dexter

Dexter Westbrook

Born: 1943. Height: 6'8". Weight: 190 lbs. Drafted: 1967 College: Providence

YEAR	TEAM	GP	GS	MIN	PTS	FGM	FGA	FG%	3PM	3PA	3P%	FTM	FTA	FT%	ORB	DRB	TRB	AST	PF	DQ	STL	BLK	TO	MPG	PPG	RPG	APG	PCM
67-68	New Jersey-A	7	....	59	31	12	19	.632	0	0	.000	7	9	.778	....	....	9	2	16	0	....	....	7	8.4	4.4	1.3	0.3	.467
67-68	Pittsburgh-A	5	....	68	17	7	20	.350	0	0	.000	3	5	.600	....	....	14	3	14	0	....	....	6	13.6	3.4	2.8	0.6	.216
ABA Season Totals		12	....	127	48	19	39	.487	0	0	.000	10	14	.714	....	....	23	5	30	0	....	....	13	10.6	4.0	1.9	0.4	....

• WESTPHAL, Paul

Paul Douglas Westphal

Born: Nov. 30, 1950. Torrance, CA, United States. Height: 6'4". Weight: 195 lbs. Drafted: 1972 College: USC

YEAR	TEAM	GP	GS	MIN	PTS	FGM	FGA	FG%	3PM	3PA	3P%	FTM	FTA	FT%	ORB	DRB	TRB	AST	PF	DQ	STL	BLK	TO	MPG	PPG	RPG	APG	PCM
72-73	Boston	60	....	482	245	89	212	.420	....	....	....	67	86	.779	....	....	67	69	88	0	....	....	....	8.0	4.1	1.1	1.2	.477
73-74	Boston	82	....	1165	588	238	475	.501	....	....	....	112	153	.732	49	94	143	171	173	1	39	34	....	14.2	7.2	1.7	2.1	.527
74-75	Boston	82	....	1581	803	342	670	.510	....	....	....	119	156	.763	44	119	163	235	192	0	78	33	....	19.3	9.8	2.0	2.9	.528
75-76	Phoenix	82	....	2960	1679	657	1329	.494	....	....	....	365	440	.830	74	185	259	440	218	3	210	38	....	36.1	20.5	3.2	5.4	.575
76-77	Phoenix	81	....	2600	1726	682	1317	.518	....	....	....	362	439	.825	57	133	190	459	171	1	134	21	....	32.1	21.3	2.3	5.7	.676
77-78	Phoenix	80	....	2481	2014	809	1568	.516	....	....	....	396	487	.813	41	123	164	437	162	0	138	31	280	31.0	25.2	2.1	5.5	.716
78-79	Phoenix	81	....	2641	1941	801	1496	.535	....	....	....	339	405	.837	35	124	159	529	159	2	111	26	235	32.6	24.0	2.0	6.5	.702
79-80	Phoenix	82	....	2665	1792	692	1317	.525	26	93	.280	382	443	.862	46	141	187	416	162	0	119	35	205	32.5	21.9	2.3	5.1	.639
80-81	Seattle	36	....	1078	601	221	500	.442	6	25	.240	153	184	.832	11	57	68	148	70	0	46	14	79	29.9	16.7	1.9	4.1	.470
81-82	New York	18	12	451	210	86	194	.443	2	8	.250	36	47	.766	9	13	22	100	61	1	19	8	47	25.1	11.7	1.2	5.6	.415
82-83	New York	80	59	1978	798	318	693	.459	14	48	.292	148	184	.804	19	96	115	439	180	1	87	16	200	24.7	10.0	1.4	5.5	.435
83-84	Phoenix	59	2	865	412	144	313	.460	7	26	.269	117	142	.824	8	35	43	148	69	0	41	6	77	14.7	7.0	0.7	2.5	.441
NBA Season Totals		823	73	20947	12809	5079	10084	.504	55	200	.275	2596	3166	.820	393	1120	1580	3591	1705	9	1022	262	1123	25.5	15.6	1.9	4.4	....
72-73	Boston	11	....	109	43	19	39	.487	....	....	....	5	7	.714	....	....	7	9	24	1	....	....	....	9.9	3.9	0.6	0.8	.284
73-74	Boston	18	....	241	103	46	100	.460	....	....	....	11	15	.733	6	15	21	31	37	0	8	2	....	13.4	5.7	1.2	1.7	.386
74-75	Boston	11	....	183	88	38	81	.469	....	....	....	12	18	.667	5	8	13	32	21	0	6	2	....	16.6	8.0	1.2	2.9	.479
75-76	Phoenix	19	....	685	401	165	323	.511	....	....	....	71	93	.763	14	33	47	96	61	1	34	9	....	36.1	21.1	2.5	5.1	.554

YEAR	TEAM	GP	GS	MIN	PTS	FGM	FGA	FG%	3PM	3PA	3P%	FTM	FTA	FT%	ORB	DRB	TRB	AST	PF	DQ	STL	BLK	TO	MPG	PPG	RPG	APG	PCM
77-78	Phoenix	2	....	66	52	22	47	.468	....	....	....	8	9	.889	3	3	6	19	4	0	1	0	5	33.0	26.0	3.0	9.5	.774
78-79	Phoenix	15	....	534	336	142	287	.495	....	....	....	52	66	.788	7	26	33	64	38	0	15	5	38	35.6	22.4	2.2	4.3	.499
79-80	Phoenix	8	....	253	167	69	142	.486	1	12	.083	28	32	.875	2	8	10	31	20	0	11	3	13	31.6	20.9	1.3	3.9	.530
82-83	New York	6	6	156	57	22	50	.440	3	8	.375	10	13	.769	0	8	8	34	13	0	2	2	9	26.0	9.5	1.3	5.7	.414
83-84	Phoenix	17	2	222	90	30	80	.375	2	9	.222	28	32	.875	3	5	8	37	23	0	12	0	24	13.1	5.3	0.5	2.2	.301
NBA Playoff Totals		107	8	2449	1337	553	1149	.481	6	29	.207	225	285	.789	40	106	153	353	241	2	89	23	89	22.9	12.5	1.4	3.3	....

• WETZEL, John

John Francis Wetzel

Born: Oct. 22, 1944. Waynesboro, VA, United States.   Height: 6'5".   Weight: 190 lbs.   Drafted: 1966   College: Virginia Tech

YEAR	TEAM	GP	GS	MIN	PTS	FGM	FGA	FG%	3PM	3PA	3P%	FTM	FTA	FT%	ORB	DRB	TRB	AST	PF	DQ	STL	BLK	TO	MPG	PPG	RPG	APG	PCM
67-68	LA Lakers	38	....	434	139	52	119	.437	....	....	....	35	46	.761	....	....	84	51	55	0	....	....	....	11.4	3.7	2.2	1.3	.432
70-71	Phoenix	70	....	1091	331	124	288	.431	....	....	....	83	101	.822	....	....	153	114	156	1	....	....	....	15.6	4.7	2.2	1.6	.345
71-72	Phoenix	51	....	419	86	31	82	.378	....	....	....	24	30	.800	....	....	65	56	71	0	....	....	....	8.2	1.7	1.3	1.1	.307
72-73	Atlanta	28	....	504	98	42	94	.447	....	....	....	14	17	.824	....	....	58	39	41	1	....	....	....	18.0	3.5	2.1	1.4	.256
73-74	Atlanta	70	....	1232	255	107	252	.425	....	....	....	41	57	.719	39	131	170	138	147	1	73	19	....	17.6	3.6	2.4	2.0	.297
74-75	Atlanta	63	....	785	242	87	204	.426	....	....	....	68	77	.883	34	80	114	77	108	1	51	8	....	12.5	3.8	1.8	1.2	.354
75-76	Phoenix	37	....	249	64	22	46	.478	....	....	....	20	24	.833	8	30	38	19	30	0	9	3	....	6.7	1.7	1.0	0.5	.334
NBA Season Totals		357	....	4714	1215	465	1085	.429	....	....	....	285	352	.810	81	241	682	494	608	4	133	30	....	13.2	3.4	1.9	1.4	....
72-73	Atlanta	3	....	33	6	3	7	.429	....	....	....	0	0	.000	....	....	2	4	6	0	....	....	....	11.0	2.0	0.7	1.3	.190
75-76	Phoenix	2	....	5	2	0	0	.000	....	....	....	2	2	1.000	0	2	2	0	2	0	0	0	....	2.5	1.0	1.0	0.0	.572
NBA Playoff Totals		5	....	38	8	3	7	.429	....	....	....	2	2	1.000	0	2	4	4	8	0	0	0	....	7.6	1.6	0.8	0.8	....

• WHATLEY, Ennis

Ennis Whatley

Born: Aug. 11, 1962. Birmingham, AL, United States.   Height: 6'3".   Weight: 177 lbs.   Drafted: 1983   College: Alabama

YEAR	TEAM	GP	GS	MIN	PTS	FGM	FGA	FG%	3PM	3PA	3P%	FTM	FTA	FT%	ORB	DRB	TRB	AST	PF	DQ	STL	BLK	TO	MPG	PPG	RPG	APG	PCM
83-84	Chicago	80	73	2159	668	261	556	.469	0	2	.000	146	200	.730	63	134	197	662	223	4	119	17	272	27.0	8.4	2.5	8.3	.477
84-85	Chicago	70	44	1385	349	140	313	.447	1	9	.111	68	86	.791	34	67	101	381	141	1	66	10	147	19.8	5.0	1.4	5.4	.396
85-86	Cleveland	8	0	66	22	9	19	.474	0	0	.000	4	7	.571	2	5	7	13	8	0	5	0	6	8.3	2.8	0.9	1.6	.411
85-86	Washington	4	0	27	11	5	14	.357	0	0	.000	1	3	.333	2	5	7	7	1	0	1	0	6	6.8	2.8	1.8	1.8	.599
85-86	San Antonio	2	1	14	2	1	2	.500	0	0	.000	0	0	.000	0	0	0	3	1	0	0	0	4	7.0	1.0	0.0	1.5	.007
86-87	Washington	73	72	1816	618	246	515	.478	0	2	.000	126	165	.764	58	136	194	392	172	0	92	10	139	24.9	8.5	2.7	5.4	.460
87-88	Atlanta	5	0	24	11	4	9	.444	0	0	.000	3	4	.750	0	4	4	2	3	0	2	0	4	4.8	2.2	0.8	0.4	.353
88-89	LA Clippers	8	0	90	34	12	33	.364	0	0	.000	10	11	.909	2	14	16	22	15	0	7	1	11	11.3	4.3	2.0	2.8	.474
91-92	Portland	23	0	209	69	21	51	.412	0	4	.000	27	31	.871	6	15	21	34	12	0	14	3	14	9.1	3.0	0.9	1.5	.442
93-94	Atlanta	82	1	1004	292	120	236	.508	0	6	.000	52	66	.788	22	77	99	181	93	0	59	2	82	12.2	3.6	1.2	2.2	.403
94-95	Atlanta	27	2	292	70	24	53	.453	2	8	.250	20	32	.625	9	21	30	54	37	0	19	0	19	10.8	2.6	1.1	2.0	.361
96-97	Portland	3	0	22	4	2	4	.500	0	0	.000	0	0	.000	0	3	3	3	5	0	0	0	1	7.3	1.3	1.0	1.0	.222
NBA Season Totals		385	193	7108	2150	845	1805	.468	3	31	.097	457	605	.755	198	481	679	1754	711	5	383	44	699	18.5	5.6	1.8	4.6	....
86-87	Washington	2	0	32	6	3	12	.250	0	0	.000	0	0	.000	1	2	3	6	2	0	2	0	8	16.0	3.0	1.5	3.0	.010
91-92	Portland	15	0	96	16	6	20	.300	0	1	.000	4	4	1.000	0	10	10	13	11	0	7	0	4	6.4	1.1	0.7	0.9	.249
93-94	Atlanta	11	0	113	24	9	28	.321	0	0	.000	6	8	.750	3	11	14	12	18	0	7	0	9	10.3	2.2	1.3	1.1	.189
94-95	Atlanta	3	0	19	0	0	4	.000	0	0	.000	0	0	.000	1	3	4	1	2	0	0	0	0	6.3	0.0	1.3	0.3	.007
NBA Playoff Totals		31	2	260	46	18	64	.281	0	1	.000	10	12	.833	5	26	31	32	33	0	16	0	21	8.4	1.5	1.0	1.0	....

• WHEAT, DeJuan

DeJuan Shontez Wheat

Born: Oct. 14, 1973. Louisville, KY, United States.   Height: 6'   Weight: 165 lbs.   Drafted: 1997   College: Louisville

YEAR	TEAM	GP	GS	MIN	PTS	FGM	FGA	FG%	3PM	3PA	3P%	FTM	FTA	FT%	ORB	DRB	TRB	AST	PF	DQ	STL	BLK	TO	MPG	PPG	RPG	APG	PCM
97-98	Minnesota	34	0	150	57	20	50	.400	8	17	.471	9	15	.600	3	8	11	25	12	0	6	1	10	4.4	1.7	0.3	0.7	.372
98-99	Vancouver	46	0	590	208	73	193	.378	22	60	.367	40	55	.727	11	34	45	102	59	0	26	2	48	12.8	4.5	1.0	2.2	.346
NBA Season Totals		80	0	740	265	93	243	.383	30	77	.390	49	70	.700	14	42	56	127	71	0	32	3	58	9.3	3.3	0.7	1.6	....
97-98	Minnesota	1	0	3	2	1	2	.500	0	0	.000	0	0	.000	0	1	1	0	0	0	1	0	0	3.0	2.0	1.0	0.0	.972
NBA Playoff Totals		1	0	3	2	1	2	.500	0	0	.000	0	0	.000	0	1	1	0	0	0	1	0	0	3.0	2.0	1.0	0.0	....

• WHEELER, Clinton

Clinton Wheeler

Born: Oct. 27, 1959. Neptune, NJ, United States.   Height: 6'1".   Weight: 185 lbs.   Drafted: 1981   College: William Paterson

YEAR	TEAM	GP	GS	MIN	PTS	FGM	FGA	FG%	3PM	3PA	3P%	FTM	FTA	FT%	ORB	DRB	TRB	AST	PF	DQ	STL	BLK	TO	MPG	PPG	RPG	APG	PCM
87-88	Indiana	59	0	513	149	62	132	.470	0	0	.000	25	34	.735	19	21	40	103	37	0	36	2	53	8.7	2.5	0.7	1.7	.381
88-89	Miami	8	0	143	56	24	42	.571	0	0	.000	8	10	.800	5	7	12	21	9	0	8	0	6	17.9	7.0	1.5	2.6	.487
88-89	Portland	20	0	211	49	21	45	.467	0	1	.000	7	10	.700	12	7	19	33	17	0	19	0	18	10.6	2.5	1.0	1.7	.338
NBA Season Totals		87	0	867	254	107	219	.489	0	1	.000	40	54	.741	36	35	71	157	63	0	63	2	77	10.0	2.9	0.8	1.8	....

• WHEELER, Tyson

Tyson Aaron Wheeler

Born: Oct. 8, 1975. New Britain, CT, United States.   Height: 5'10".   Weight: 165 lbs.   Drafted: 1998   College: Rhode Island

YEAR	TEAM	GP	GS	MIN	PTS	FGM	FGA	FG%	3PM	3PA	3P%	FTM	FTA	FT%	ORB	DRB	TRB	AST	PF	DQ	STL	BLK	TO	MPG	PPG	RPG	APG	PCM
98-99	Denver	1	0	3	4	1	1	1.000	1	1	1.000	1	2	.500	0	0	0	2	1	0	0	0	0	3.0	4.0	0.0	2.0	1.778
NBA Season Totals		1	0	3	4	1	1	1.000	1	1	1.000	1	2	.500	0	0	0	2	1	0	0	0	0	3.0	4.0	0.0	2.0	....

• WHITAKER, Skippy

Lucian Cary (Skippy) Whitaker

Born: Aug. 29, 1930. Louisville, KY, United States.   Height: 6'1".   Weight: 180 lbs.   Drafted: 1952   College: Kentucky

YEAR	TEAM	GP	GS	MIN	PTS	FGM	FGA	FG%	3PM	3PA	3P%	FTM	FTA	FT%	ORB	DRB	TRB	AST	PF	DQ	STL	BLK	TO	MPG	PPG	RPG	APG	PCM
54-55	Boston	3	....	15	2	1	6	.167	....	....	....	0	0	.000	....	....	1	1	4	0	....	....	....	5.0	0.7	0.3	0.3	-.084
NBA Season Totals		3	....	15	2	1	6	.167	....	....	....	0	0	.000	....	....	1	1	4	0	....	....	....	5.0	0.7	0.3	0.3	....

YEAR TEAM	GP	GS	MIN	PTS	FGM	FGA	FG%	3PM	3PA	3P%	FTM	FTA	FT%	ORB	DRB	TRB	AST	PF	DQ	STL	BLK	TO	MPG	PPG	RPG	APG	PCM

• WHITE, Dean

Dean White

Born: 1923. Height: 6'7". Weight: 220 lbs. Drafted: — College: Valparaiso

YEAR TEAM	GP	GS	MIN	PTS	FGM	FGA	FG%	3PM	3PA	3P%	FTM	FTA	FT%	ORB	DRB	TRB	AST	PF	DQ	STL	BLK	TO	MPG	PPG	RPG	APG	PCM
46-47 Sheboygan-N	5	....	....	21	7	....	....	....	....	....	7	9	.778	....	....	....	....	5	....	....	....	....	....	4.2	....	....	....
NBL Season Totals	5	....	....	21	7	....	....	....	....	....	7	9	....	....	....	....	....	5	....	....	....	....	....	4.2	....	....	....
46-47 Sheboygan-N	1	....	....	2	1	....	....	....	....	....	0	0	.000	....	....	....	....	....	....	....	....	....	....	2.0	....	....	....
NBL Playoff Totals	1	....	....	2	1	....	....	....	....	....	0	0	....	....	....	....	....	....	....	....	....	....	....	2.0	....	....	....

• WHITE, Eric

Eric Lance White

Born: Dec. 30, 1965. San Francisco, CA, United States. Height: 6'8". Weight: 200 lbs. Drafted: 1987 College: Pepperdine

YEAR TEAM	GP	GS	MIN	PTS	FGM	FGA	FG%	3PM	3PA	3P%	FTM	FTA	FT%	ORB	DRB	TRB	AST	PF	DQ	STL	BLK	TO	MPG	PPG	RPG	APG	PCM
87-88 LA Clippers	17	4	352	178	66	124	.532	1	1	1.000	45	57	.789	31	31	62	9	32	0	7	3	20	20.7	10.5	3.6	0.5	.459
88-89 Utah	1	0	2	0	0	1	.000	0	0	.000	0	0	.000	0	0	0	0	1	0	0	0	0	2.0	0.0	0.0	0.0	-.698
88-89 LA Clippers	37	0	434	158	62	119	.521	0	0	.000	34	42	.810	34	36	70	17	39	0	10	1	26	11.7	4.3	1.9	0.5	.351
NBA Season Totals	55	4	788	336	128	244	.525	1	1	1.000	79	99	.798	65	67	132	26	72	0	17	4	46	14.3	6.1	2.4	0.5	....

• WHITE, Herb

Herbert Thomas White

Born: June 15, 1948. Height: 6'2". Weight: 195 lbs. Drafted: 1970 College: Georgia

YEAR TEAM	GP	GS	MIN	PTS	FGM	FGA	FG%	3PM	3PA	3P%	FTM	FTA	FT%	ORB	DRB	TRB	AST	PF	DQ	STL	BLK	TO	MPG	PPG	RPG	APG	PCM
70-71 Atlanta	38	....	315	90	34	84	.405	....	....	....	22	39	.564	....	....	48	47	62	2	....	....	....	8.3	2.4	1.3	1.2	.343
NBA Season Totals	38	....	315	90	34	84	.405	....	....	....	22	39	.564	....	....	48	47	62	2	....	....	....	8.3	2.4	1.3	1.2	....

• WHITE, Hubie

Hubert (Hubie) White Jr.

Born: Jan. 26, 1940. Height: 6'4". Weight: 205 lbs. Drafted: 1962 College: Villanova

YEAR TEAM	GP	GS	MIN	PTS	FGM	FGA	FG%	3PM	3PA	3P%	FTM	FTA	FT%	ORB	DRB	TRB	AST	PF	DQ	STL	BLK	TO	MPG	PPG	RPG	APG	PCM
62-63 San Francisco	29	....	271	92	40	111	.360	....	....	....	12	18	.667	....	....	35	28	47	0	....	....	....	9.3	3.2	1.2	1.0	.282
63-64 Philadelphia	23	....	196	79	31	105	.295	....	....	....	17	28	.607	....	....	42	12	28	0	....	....	....	8.5	3.4	1.8	0.5	.273
69-70 Miami-A	54	....	824	361	146	363	.402	7	43	.163	62	84	.738	70	85	155	56	147	2	....	....	59	15.3	6.7	2.9	1.0	.363
70-71 Pittsburgh-A	14	....	166	46	17	61	.279	2	7	.286	10	13	.769	10	22	32	14	28	0	....	....	10	11.9	3.3	2.3	1.0	.246
NBA Season Totals	52	....	467	171	71	216	.329	....	....	....	29	46	.630	....	....	77	40	75	0	....	....	....	9.0	3.3	1.5	0.8	....
ABA Season Totals	68	....	990	407	163	424	.384	9	50	.180	72	97	.742	80	107	187	70	175	2	....	....	69	14.6	6.0	2.8	1.0	....
Career Totals	120	....	1457	578	234	640	.366	9	50	.180	101	143	.706	80	107	264	110	250	2	....	....	69	12.1	4.8	2.2	0.9	....

• WHITE, Jahidi

Jahidi White

Born: Feb. 19, 1976. St. Louis, MO, United States. Height: 6'9". Weight: 290 lbs. Drafted: 1998 College: Georgetown

YEAR TEAM	GP	GS	MIN	PTS	FGM	FGA	FG%	3PM	3PA	3P%	FTM	FTA	FT%	ORB	DRB	TRB	AST	PF	DQ	STL	BLK	TO	MPG	PPG	RPG	APG	PCM
98-99 Washington	20	0	191	49	17	32	.531	0	0	.000	15	35	.429	23	35	58	1	39	1	3	11	16	9.6	2.5	2.9	0.1	.316
99-00 Washington	80	59	1537	569	228	450	.507	0	0	.000	113	211	.536	202	351	553	15	234	0	31	83	94	19.2	7.1	6.9	0.2	.490
00-01 Washington	68	56	1609	583	203	408	.498	0	1	.000	177	312	.567	178	343	521	20	211	3	32	111	136	23.7	8.6	7.7	0.3	.460
01-02 Washington	71	69	1346	383	150	279	.538	0	0	.000	83	154	.539	159	285	444	17	163	0	25	75	65	19.0	5.4	6.3	0.2	.455
02-03 Washington	16	8	230	67	25	53	.472	0	0	.000	17	25	.680	37	36	73	2	33	1	1	12	9	14.4	4.2	4.6	0.1	.413
NBA Season Totals	255	192	4913	1651	623	1222	.510	0	1	.000	405	737	.550	599	1050	1649	55	680	5	92	292	320	19.3	6.5	6.5	0.2	....

• WHITE, Jo Jo

Joseph Henry (Jo Jo) White

Born: Nov. 16, 1946. St. Louis, MO, United States. Height: 6'3". Weight: 190 lbs. Drafted: 1969 College: Kansas

YEAR TEAM	GP	GS	MIN	PTS	FGM	FGA	FG%	3PM	3PA	3P%	FTM	FTA	FT%	ORB	DRB	TRB	AST	PF	DQ	STL	BLK	TO	MPG	PPG	RPG	APG	PCM
69-70 Boston	60	....	1328	729	309	684	.452	....	....	....	111	135	.822	....	....	169	145	132	1	....	....	....	22.1	12.2	2.8	2.4	.483
70-71 Boston	75	....	2787	1601	693	1494	.464	....	....	....	215	269	.799	....	....	376	361	255	5	....	....	....	37.2	21.3	5.0	4.8	.543
71-72 Boston	79	....	3261	1825	770	1788	.431	....	....	....	285	343	.831	....	....	446	416	227	1	....	....	....	41.3	23.1	5.6	5.3	.515
72-73 Boston	82	....	3250	1612	717	1655	.433	....	....	....	178	228	.781	....	....	414	498	185	2	....	....	....	39.6	19.7	5.0	6.1	.502
73-74 Boston	82	....	3238	1488	649	1445	.449	....	....	....	190	227	.837	100	251	351	448	185	1	105	25	....	39.5	18.1	4.3	5.5	.472
74-75 Boston	82	....	3220	1502	658	1440	.457	....	....	....	186	223	.834	84	227	311	458	207	1	128	17	....	39.3	18.3	3.8	5.6	.473
75-76 Boston	82	....	3257	1552	670	1492	.449	....	....	....	212	253	.838	61	252	313	445	183	2	107	20	....	39.7	18.9	3.8	5.4	.469
76-77 Boston	82	....	3333	1609	638	1488	.429	....	....	....	333	383	.869	87	296	383	492	193	5	118	22	....	40.6	19.6	4.7	6.0	.498
77-78 Boston	46	....	1641	681	289	690	.419	....	....	....	103	120	.858	53	127	180	209	109	2	49	7	115	35.7	14.8	3.9	4.5	.375
78-79 Boston	47	....	1455	589	255	596	.428	....	....	....	79	89	.888	22	106	128	214	100	1	54	4	141	31.0	12.5	2.7	4.6	.350
78-79 Golden State	29	....	883	358	149	314	.475	....	....	....	60	69	.870	20	52	72	133	73	0	26	3	70	30.4	12.3	2.5	4.6	.393
79-80 Golden State	78	....	2052	770	336	706	.476	1	6	.167	97	114	.851	42	139	181	239	186	0	88	13	156	26.3	9.9	2.3	3.1	.350
80-81 Kansas City	13	....	236	83	36	82	.439	0	0	.000	11	18	.611	3	18	21	37	21	0	11	1	18	18.2	6.4	1.6	2.8	.349
NBA Season Totals	837	....	29941	14399	6169	13874	.445	1	6	.167	2060	2471	.834	472	1468	3345	4095	2056	21	686	112	500	35.8	17.2	4.0	4.9	....
71-72 Boston	11	....	432	258	109	220	.495	....	....	....	40	48	.833	....	....	59	58	31	0	....	....	....	39.3	23.5	5.4	5.3	.607
72-73 Boston	13	....	583	319	135	300	.450	....	....	....	49	54	.907	....	....	54	83	44	2	....	....	....	44.8	24.5	4.2	6.4	.510
73-74 Boston	18	....	765	298	132	310	.426	....	....	....	34	46	.739	17	58	75	98	56	1	15	2	....	42.5	16.6	4.2	5.4	.384
74-75 Boston	11	....	462	227	100	227	.441	....	....	....	27	33	.818	18	32	50	63	32	0	11	4	....	42.0	20.6	4.5	5.7	.471
75-76 Boston	18	....	791	408	165	371	.445	....	....	....	78	95	.821	12	59	71	98	51	0	23	1	....	43.9	22.7	3.9	5.4	.474
76-77 Boston	9	....	395	210	91	201	.453	....	....	....	28	33	.848	10	29	39	52	27	0	14	0	....	43.9	23.3	4.3	5.8	.491
NBA Playoff Totals	80	....	3428	1720	732	1629	.449	....	....	....	256	309	.828	57	178	348	452	241	3	63	7	....	42.9	21.5	4.4	5.7	....

• WHITE, Randy

Randy (Bird) White

Born: Nov. 4, 1967. Shreveport, LA, United States. Height: 6'8". Weight: 240 lbs. Drafted: 1989 College: Louisiana Tech

YEAR TEAM	GP	GS	MIN	PTS	FGM	FGA	FG%	3PM	3PA	3P%	FTM	FTA	FT%	ORB	DRB	TRB	AST	PF	DQ	STL	BLK	TO	MPG	PPG	RPG	APG	PCM
89-90 Dallas	55	2	707	237	93	252	.369	1	14	.071	50	89	.562	78	95	173	21	124	0	24	6	50	12.9	4.3	3.1	0.4	.251
90-91 Dallas	79	29	1901	695	265	665	.398	6	37	.162	159	225	.707	173	331	504	63	308	6	81	44	134	24.1	8.8	6.4	0.8	.356
91-92 Dallas	65	12	1021	418	145	382	.380	4	27	.148	124	162	.765	96	140	236	31	157	1	31	22	65	15.7	6.4	3.6	0.5	.341

YEAR	TEAM	GP	GS	MIN	PTS	FGM	FGA	FG%	3PM	3PA	3P%	FTM	FTA	FT%	ORB	DRB	TRB	AST	PF	DQ	STL	BLK	TO	MPG	PPG	RPG	APG	PCM
92-93	Dallas	64	20	1433	618	235	540	.435	10	42	.238	138	184	.750	154	216	370	49	226	4	63	45	109	22.4	9.7	5.8	0.8	.421
93-94	Dallas	18	3	320	115	45	112	.402	6	20	.300	19	33	.576	30	53	83	11	46	0	10	10	18	17.8	6.4	4.6	0.6	.362
NBA Season Totals		281	66	5382	2083	783	1951	.401	27	140	.193	490	693	.707	531	835	1366	175	861	11	209	127	376	19.2	7.4	4.9	0.6	....
89-90	Dallas	1	0	2	0	0	0	.000	0	0	.000	0	0	.000	0	0	0	0	0	0	0	0	0	2.0	0.0	0.0	0.0	.000
NBA Playoff Totals		1	0	2	0	0	0	.000	0	0	.000	0	0	.000	0	0	0	0	0	0	0	0	0	2.0	0.0	0.0	0.0	....

• WHITE, Rodney

Rodney Charles White

Born: June 28, 1980. Philadelpia, PA, United States.   Height: 6'9".   Weight: 238 lbs.   Drafted: 2001   College: North Carolina (Charlotte)

YEAR	TEAM	GP	GS	MIN	PTS	FGM	FGA	FG%	3PM	3PA	3P%	FTM	FTA	FT%	ORB	DRB	TRB	AST	PF	DQ	STL	BLK	TO	MPG	PPG	RPG	APG	PCM
01-02	Detroit	16	0	129	56	21	60	.350	2	9	.222	12	14	.857	2	16	18	12	6	0	9	2	14	8.1	3.5	1.1	0.8	.339
02-03	Denver	72	19	1563	650	260	638	.408	32	134	.239	98	125	.784	43	170	213	121	134	1	45	32	156	21.7	9.0	3.0	1.7	.312
NBA Season Totals		88	19	1692	706	281	698	.403	34	143	.238	110	139	.791	45	186	231	133	140	1	54	34	170	19.2	8.0	2.6	1.5	....
01-02	Detroit	1	0	3	0	0	1	.000	0	0	.000	0	0	.000	0	0	0	0	0	0	0	0	1	3.0	0.0	0.0	0.0	-.604
NBA Playoff Totals		1	0	3	0	0	1	.000	0	0	.000	0	0	.000	0	0	0	0	0	0	0	0	1	3.0	0.0	0.0	0.0	....

• WHITE, Rory

Rory Wilbur White

Born: Aug. 16, 1959. Tuskegee, AL, United States.   Height: 6'8".   Weight: 210 lbs.   Drafted: 1982   College: South Alabama

YEAR	TEAM	GP	GS	MIN	PTS	FGM	FGA	FG%	3PM	3PA	3P%	FTM	FTA	FT%	ORB	DRB	TRB	AST	PF	DQ	STL	BLK	TO	MPG	PPG	RPG	APG	PCM
82-83	Phoenix	65	0	626	324	127	234	.543	0	1	.000	70	109	.642	47	58	105	30	54	0	16	2	52	9.6	5.0	1.6	0.5	.451
83-84	Phoenix	22	2	308	162	69	144	.479	0	0	.000	24	42	.571	30	32	62	14	25	0	13	2	18	14.0	7.4	2.8	0.6	.461
83-84	Milwaukee	8	0	45	16	7	17	.412	0	0	.000	2	5	.400	5	3	8	1	3	0	2	1	5	5.6	2.0	1.0	0.1	.235
83-84	San Diego	6	0	19	8	4	9	.444	0	0	.000	0	0	.000	2	2	4	0	3	0	0	0	1	3.2	1.3	0.7	0.0	.250
84-85	LA Clippers	80	14	1106	378	144	279	.516	0	0	.000	90	130	.692	94	101	195	34	115	0	35	20	88	13.8	4.7	2.4	0.4	.332
85-86	LA Clippers	75	30	1761	875	355	684	.519	1	9	.111	164	222	.739	82	99	181	74	161	2	74	8	98	23.5	11.7	2.4	1.0	.398
86-87	LA Clippers	68	35	1545	624	265	552	.480	0	3	.000	94	144	.653	90	104	194	79	159	1	47	19	75	22.7	9.2	2.9	1.2	.334
NBA Season Totals		324	81	5410	2387	971	1919	.506	1	13	.077	444	652	.681	350	399	749	232	520	3	187	52	337	16.7	7.4	2.3	0.7	....
82-83	Phoenix	3	0	40	16	7	14	.500	0	1	.000	2	4	.500	1	9	10	0	4	0	0	0	1	13.3	5.3	3.3	0.0	.377
NBA Playoff Totals		3	0	40	16	7	14	.500	0	1	.000	2	4	.500	1	9	10	0	4	0	0	0	1	13.3	5.3	3.3	0.0	....

• WHITE, Rudy

Rudolph White

Born: June 23, 1953. Silver City, NM, United States.   Height: 6'2".   Weight: 195 lbs.   Drafted: 1975   College: Arizona State

YEAR	TEAM	GP	GS	MIN	PTS	FGM	FGA	FG%	3PM	3PA	3P%	FTM	FTA	FT%	ORB	DRB	TRB	AST	PF	DQ	STL	BLK	TO	MPG	PPG	RPG	APG	PCM
75-76	Houston	32	....	284	102	42	102	.412	....	....	....	18	25	.720	13	25	38	30	32	0	19	5	....	8.9	3.2	1.2	0.9	.354
76-77	Houston	46	....	368	109	47	106	.443	....	....	....	15	25	.600	13	28	41	35	39	0	11	1	....	8.0	2.4	0.9	0.8	.305
77-78	Houston	21	....	219	76	31	85	.365	....	....	....	14	18	.778	8	13	21	22	24	0	8	0	21	10.4	3.6	1.0	1.0	.220
79-80	Houston	9	....	106	36	13	24	.542	0	0	.000	10	13	.769	9	5	8	0	5	0	8	11.8	4.0	1.0	0.6	.302		
80-81	Golden State	4	....	43	22	9	18	.500	0	0	.000	4	4	1.000	0	0	0	2	7	0	4	0	3	10.8	5.5	0.0	0.5	.319
80-81	Seattle	12	....	165	39	14	47	.298	0	1	.000	11	12	.917	1	10	11	18	16	0	5	1	10	13.8	3.3	0.9	1.5	.165
NBA Season Totals		124	....	1185	384	156	382	.408	0	1	.000	72	97	.742	35	85	120	112	126	0	52	7	42	9.6	3.1	1.0	0.9	....
76-77	Houston	1	....	2	2	1	3	.333	....	....	....	0	0	.000	1	0	1	0	0	0	1	0	....	2.0	2.0	1.0	0.0	.569
NBA Playoff Totals		1	....	2	2	1	3	.333	....	....	....	0	0	.000	1	0	1	0	0	0	1	0	....	2.0	2.0	1.0	0.0	....

• WHITE, Tony

Tony F. White

Born: Feb. 15, 1965. Charlotte, NC, United States.   Height: 6'2".   Weight: 170 lbs.   Drafted: 1987   College: Tennessee

YEAR	TEAM	GP	GS	MIN	PTS	FGM	FGA	FG%	3PM	3PA	3P%	FTM	FTA	FT%	ORB	DRB	TRB	AST	PF	DQ	STL	BLK	TO	MPG	PPG	RPG	APG	PCM
87-88	Chicago	2	0	2	0	0	0	.000	0	0	.000	0	0	.000	0	0	0	0	0	0	0	0	0	1.0	0.0	0.0	0.0	.000
87-88	New York	12	0	117	43	17	46	.370	0	1	.000	9	13	.692	1	2	3	10	14	0	1	0	13	9.8	3.6	0.3	0.8	.084
87-88	Golden State	35	0	462	218	94	203	.463	0	5	.000	30	41	.732	11	17	28	49	43	0	19	2	35	13.2	6.2	0.8	1.4	.339
NBA Season Totals		49	0	581	261	111	249	.446	0	6	.000	39	54	.722	12	19	31	59	57	0	20	2	48	11.9	5.3	0.6	1.2	....

• WHITE, Willie

Willie White

Born: Aug. 20, 1962. Memphis, TN, United States.   Height: 6'3".   Weight: 195 lbs.   Drafted: 1984   College: Tennessee (Chatanooga)

YEAR	TEAM	GP	GS	MIN	PTS	FGM	FGA	FG%	3PM	3PA	3P%	FTM	FTA	FT%	ORB	DRB	TRB	AST	PF	DQ	STL	BLK	TO	MPG	PPG	RPG	APG	PCM
84-85	Denver	39	0	234	129	52	124	.419	4	11	.364	21	31	.677	15	21	36	29	24	0	5	2	31	6.0	3.3	0.9	0.7	.377
85-86	Denver	43	4	343	173	74	168	.440	6	21	.286	19	23	.826	17	27	44	53	24	0	18	2	26	8.0	4.0	1.0	1.2	.480
NBA Season Totals		82	4	577	302	126	292	.432	10	32	.313	40	54	.741	32	48	80	82	48	0	23	4	57	7.0	3.7	1.0	1.0	....
84-85	Denver	10	3	123	63	27	57	.474	2	3	.667	7	12	.583	9	8	17	17	6	0	5	0	16	12.3	6.3	1.7	1.7	.436
85-86	Denver	4	0	21	5	2	7	.286	1	4	.250	0	0	.000	1	2	3	6	4	0	1	0	2	5.3	1.3	0.8	1.5	.323
NBA Playoff Totals		14	3	144	68	29	64	.453	3	7	.429	7	12	.583	10	10	20	23	10	0	6	0	18	10.3	4.9	1.4	1.6	....

• WHITEHEAD, Jerome

Jerome Clay Whitehead

Born: Sept. 30, 1956. Waukegan, IL, United States.   Height: 6'10".   Weight: 220 lbs.   Drafted: 1978   College: Marquette

YEAR	TEAM	GP	GS	MIN	PTS	FGM	FGA	FG%	3PM	3PA	3P%	FTM	FTA	FT%	ORB	DRB	TRB	AST	PF	DQ	STL	BLK	TO	MPG	PPG	RPG	APG	PCM
78-79	San Diego	31	....	152	38	15	34	.441	....	....	....	8	18	.444	16	34	50	7	29	0	3	4	12	4.9	1.2	1.6	0.2	.339
79-80	San Diego	18	....	225	59	27	45	.600	0	0	.000	5	18	.278	29	41	70	6	32	0	1	6	7	12.5	3.3	3.9	0.3	.410
79-80	Utah	32	....	328	67	31	69	.449	0	0	.000	5	17	.294	27	70	97	18	65	3	7	11	29	10.3	2.1	3.0	0.6	.291
80-81	Dallas	7	....	118	37	16	38	.421	0	0	.000	5	11	.455	8	20	28	2	16	0	4	1	11	16.9	5.3	4.0	0.3	.247
80-81	Cleveland	3	....	8	2	1	3	.333	0	0	.000	0	0	.000	2	1	3	0	6	0	1	0	0	2.7	0.7	1.0	0.0	.136
80-81	San Diego	38	....	562	155	66	139	.475	0	1	.000	23	45	.511	48	135	183	24	100	2	15	8	46	14.8	4.1	4.8	0.6	.364
81-82	San Diego	72	63	2214	996	406	726	.559	0	0	.000	184	241	.763	231	433	664	102	290	16	48	44	144	30.8	13.8	9.2	1.4	.549
82-83	San Diego	46	23	905	400	164	306	.536	0	0	.000	72	87	.828	105	156	261	42	139	2	21	15	64	19.7	8.7	5.7	0.9	.507
83-84	San Diego	70	1	921	376	144	294	.490	0	0	.000	88	107	.822	94	151	245	19	159	2	17	12	56	13.2	5.4	3.5	0.3	.409
84-85	Golden State	79	78	2536	1026	421	825	.510	0	0	.000	184	235	.783	219	403	622	53	322	8	45	43	142	32.1	13.0	7.9	0.7	.419

YEAR	TEAM	GP	GS	MIN	PTS	FGM	FGA	FG%	3PM	3PA	3P%	FTM	FTA	FT%	ORB	DRB	TRB	AST	PF	DQ	STL	BLK	TO	MPG	PPG	RPG	APG	PCM
85-86	Golden State	81	3	1079	312	126	294	.429	0	0	.000	60	97	.619	94	234	328	19	176	2	18	19	65	13.3	3.9	4.0	0.2	.330
86-87	Golden State	73	1	937	373	147	327	.450	0	1	.000	79	113	.699	110	152	262	24	175	1	16	12	51	12.8	5.1	3.6	0.3	.380
87-88	Golden State	72	27	1221	407	174	360	.483	0	0	.000	59	82	.720	109	212	321	39	209	3	32	21	50	17.0	5.7	4.5	0.5	.384
88-89	Golden State	5	0	42	7	3	6	.500	0	0	.000	1	2	.500	0	5	5	2	8	0	1	0	2	8.4	1.4	1.0	0.4	.140
88-89	San Antonio	52	4	580	168	69	176	.392	0	0	.000	30	45	.667	49	80	129	17	107	1	22	4	21	11.2	3.2	2.5	0.3	.267
NBA Season Totals		679	200	11828	4423	1810	3642	.497	0	2	.000	803	1118	.718	1141	2127	3268	374	1833	40	251	200	700	17.4	6.5	4.8	0.6	....
86-87	Golden State	10	0	100	22	9	27	.333	0	0	.000	4	10	.400	5	9	14	3	22	1	2	2	1	10.0	2.2	1.4	0.3	.112
NBA Playoff Totals		10	0	100	22	9	27	.333	0	0	.000	4	10	.400	5	9	14	3	22	1	2	2	1	10.0	2.2	1.4	0.3	....

• WHITESIDE, Donald
Donald Whiteside

Born: Apr. 25, 1969. Chicago, IL, United States.　Height: 5'10".　Weight: 160 lbs.　Drafted: —　College: Northern Illinois

YEAR	TEAM	GP	GS	MIN	PTS	FGM	FGA	FG%	3PM	3PA	3P%	FTM	FTA	FT%	ORB	DRB	TRB	AST	PF	DQ	STL	BLK	TO	MPG	PPG	RPG	APG	PCM
96-97	Toronto	27	1	259	59	18	55	.327	12	36	.333	11	15	.733	2	10	12	36	23	0	11	0	16	9.6	2.2	0.4	1.3	.220
97-98	Atlanta	3	0	16	2	1	2	.500	0	1	.000	0	2	.000	0	1	1	1	0	0	0	0	1	5.3	0.7	0.3	0.3	.078
NBA Season Totals		30	1	275	61	19	57	.333	12	37	.324	11	17	.647	2	11	13	37	23	0	11	0	17	9.2	2.0	0.4	1.2	....

• WHITFIELD, Dwayne
Dwayne Whitfield

Born: Aug. 21, 1972. Aberdeen, MS, United States.　Height: 6'9".　Weight: 240 lbs.　Drafted: 1995　College: Jackson State

YEAR	TEAM	GP	GS	MIN	PTS	FGM	FGA	FG%	3PM	3PA	3P%	FTM	FTA	FT%	ORB	DRB	TRB	AST	PF	DQ	STL	BLK	TO	MPG	PPG	RPG	APG	PCM
95-96	Toronto	8	1	122	40	13	30	.433	0	0	.000	14	22	.636	9	16	25	2	14	0	3	2	8	15.3	5.0	3.1	0.3	.299
NBA Season Totals		8	1	122	40	13	30	.433	0	0	.000	14	22	.636	9	16	25	2	14	0	3	2	8	15.3	5.0	3.1	0.3	....

• WHITLINGER, Warren
Warren Whitlinger

Born: 1914.　Height: 5'9".　Weight: 170 lbs.　Drafted: —　College: Ohio State

YEAR	TEAM	GP	GS	MIN	PTS	FGM	FGA	FG%	3PM	3PA	3P%	FTM	FTA	FT%	ORB	DRB	TRB	AST	PF	DQ	STL	BLK	TO	MPG	PPG	RPG	APG	PCM
37-38	Non-Skids-N	13	....	....	59	17	....	....	....	....	....	25	....	....	....	....	....	....	....	....	....	....	....	4.5	....	....	....	....
NBL Season Totals		13	....	....	59	17	....	....	....	....	....	25	....	....	....	....	....	....	....	....	....	....	....	4.5	....	....	....	....
37-38	Non-Skids-N	2	....	....	4	2	....	....	....	....	....	0	....	....	....	....	....	....	....	....	....	....	....	2.0	....	....	....	....
NBL Playoff Totals		2	....	....	4	2	....	....	....	....	....	0	....	....	....	....	....	....	....	....	....	....	....	2.0	....	....	....	....

• WHITNEY, Chris
Christopher Antoine Whitney

Born: Oct. 5, 1971. Hopkinsville, KY, United States.　Height: 6'　Weight: 168 lbs.　Drafted: 1993　College: Clemson

YEAR	TEAM	GP	GS	MIN	PTS	FGM	FGA	FG%	3PM	3PA	3P%	FTM	FTA	FT%	ORB	DRB	TRB	AST	PF	DQ	STL	BLK	TO	MPG	PPG	RPG	APG	PCM
93-94	San Antonio	40	4	339	72	25	82	.305	10	30	.333	12	15	.800	5	24	29	53	53	0	11	1	36	8.5	1.8	0.7	1.3	.165
94-95	San Antonio	25	0	179	42	14	47	.298	3	19	.158	11	11	1.000	4	9	13	28	34	1	4	0	18	7.2	1.7	0.5	1.1	.134
95-96	Washington	21	0	335	150	45	99	.455	19	44	.432	41	44	.932	2	31	33	51	46	0	18	1	23	16.0	7.1	1.6	2.4	.470
96-97	Washington	82	1	1117	430	139	330	.421	58	163	.356	94	113	.832	13	91	104	182	100	0	49	4	66	13.6	5.2	1.3	2.2	.426
97-98	Washington	82	6	1073	422	126	355	.355	52	169	.308	118	129	.915	16	99	115	196	106	0	34	6	66	13.1	5.1	1.4	2.4	.422
98-99	Washington	39	1	441	187	64	156	.410	32	95	.337	27	31	.871	8	39	47	69	49	0	18	2	36	11.3	4.8	1.2	1.8	.421
99-00	Washington	82	15	1627	642	217	521	.417	96	255	.376	112	132	.848	20	114	134	313	166	0	55	5	107	19.8	7.8	1.6	3.8	.432
00-01	Washington	59	31	1532	558	182	470	.387	93	248	.375	101	113	.894	12	94	106	248	150	5	55	3	103	26.0	9.5	1.8	4.2	.362
01-02	Washington	82	81	2171	833	274	656	.418	131	323	.406	154	175	.880	11	141	152	314	182	1	72	6	85	26.5	10.2	1.9	3.8	.401
02-03	Denver	29	20	762	277	94	261	.360	43	128	.336	46	57	.807	1	45	46	124	77	1	17	1	55	26.3	9.6	1.6	4.3	.301
02-03	Orlando	22	1	290	78	30	88	.341	7	36	.194	11	12	.917	2	19	21	21	15	0	12	1	16	13.2	3.5	1.0	1.0	.198
NBA Season Totals		563	160	9866	3691	1210	3065	.395	544	1510	.360	727	832	.874	94	706	800	1599	978	8	345	30	611	17.5	6.6	1.4	2.8	....
96-97	Washington	3	0	20	7	2	5	.400	2	4	.500	1	1	1.000	0	2	2	2	1	0	0	0	5	6.7	2.3	0.7	0.7	.154
02-03	Orlando	7	0	111	22	8	21	.381	4	9	.444	2	2	1.000	3	8	11	7	21	1	2	2	2	15.9	3.1	1.6	1.0	.181
NBA Playoff Totals		10	0	131	29	10	26	.385	6	13	.462	3	3	1.000	3	10	13	9	22	1	2	2	7	13.1	2.9	1.3	0.9	....

• WHITNEY, Hank
Henry Lee Whitney

Born: Apr. 28, 1939. Brooklyn, NY, United States.　Height: 6'7".　Weight: 230 lbs.　Drafted: —　College: Iowa State

YEAR	TEAM	GP	GS	MIN	PTS	FGM	FGA	FG%	3PM	3PA	3P%	FTM	FTA	FT%	ORB	DRB	TRB	AST	PF	DQ	STL	BLK	TO	MPG	PPG	RPG	APG	PCM
67-68	New Jersey-A	37	....	1159	591	217	552	.393	0	0	.000	157	220	.714	....	....	477	56	158	3	....	....	54	31.3	16.0	12.9	1.5	.589
68-69	Houston-A	18	....	249	83	27	81	.333	0	1	.000	29	48	.604	20	53	73	18	54	0	....	....	21	13.8	4.6	4.1	1.0	.356
68-69	New York-A	31	....	643	268	104	248	.419	0	0	.000	60	82	.732	64	117	181	38	90	1	....	....	51	20.7	8.6	5.8	1.2	.459
69-70	Carolina-A	59	....	981	397	170	403	.422	0	0	.000	57	88	.648	127	244	371	56	200	4	....	....	80	16.6	6.7	6.3	0.9	.490
ABA Season Totals		145	....	3032	1339	518	1284	.403	0	1	.000	303	438	.692	211	414	1102	168	502	8	....	....	206	20.9	9.2	7.6	1.2	....
69-70	Carolina-A	4	....	60	38	17	33	.515	0	0	.000	4	9	.444	....	....	21	0	....	....	....	....	....	15.0	9.5	5.3	0.0	....
ABA Playoff Totals		4	....	60	38	17	33	.515	0	0	.000	4	9	.444	....	....	21	0	....	....	....	....	....	15.0	9.5	5.3	0.0	....

• WHITNEY, Hawkeye
Charles Vincent (Hawkeye) Whitney

Born: June 22, 1957. Washington, DC, United States.　Height: 6'5".　Weight: 235 lbs.　Drafted: 1980　College: North Carolina State

YEAR	TEAM	GP	GS	MIN	PTS	FGM	FGA	FG%	3PM	3PA	3P%	FTM	FTA	FT%	ORB	DRB	TRB	AST	PF	DQ	STL	BLK	TO	MPG	PPG	RPG	APG	PCM
80-81	Kansas City	47	....	782	350	149	306	.487	2	6	.333	50	65	.769	29	77	106	68	98	0	47	6	47	16.6	7.4	2.3	1.4	.424
81-82	Kansas City	23	4	266	54	25	71	.352	0	1	.000	4	7	.571	13	27	40	19	31	0	12	1	14	11.6	2.3	1.7	0.8	.197
NBA Season Totals		70	4	1048	404	174	377	.462	2	7	.286	54	72	.750	42	104	146	87	129	0	59	7	61	15.0	5.8	2.1	1.2	....

• WICKS, Sidney
Sidney Wicks

Born: Sept. 19, 1949. Los Angeles, CA, United States.　Height: 6'8".　Weight: 225 lbs.　Drafted: 1971　College: UCLA

YEAR	TEAM	GP	GS	MIN	PTS	FGM	FGA	FG%	3PM	3PA	3P%	FTM	FTA	FT%	ORB	DRB	TRB	AST	PF	DQ	STL	BLK	TO	MPG	PPG	RPG	APG	PCM
71-72	Portland	82	....	3245	2009	784	1837	.427	....	....	....	441	621	.710	....	....	943	350	186	1	....	....	....	39.6	24.5	11.5	4.3	.664
72-73	Portland	80	....	3152	1906	761	1684	.452	....	....	....	384	531	.723	....	....	870	440	253	3	....	....	....	39.4	23.8	10.9	5.5	.695
73-74	Portland	75	....	2853	1684	685	1492	.459	....	....	....	314	412	.762	196	488	684	326	214	2	90	63	....	38.0	22.5	9.1	4.3	.638

YEAR	TEAM	GP	GS	MIN	PTS	FGM	FGA	FG%	3PM	3PA	3P%	FTM	FTA	FT%	ORB	DRB	TRB	AST	PF	DQ	STL	BLK	TO	MPG	PPG	RPG	APG	PCM
74-75	Portland	82	....	3162	1778	692	1391	.497	....	....	....	394	558	.706	231	646	877	287	289	5	108	80	....	38.6	21.7	10.7	3.5	.653
75-76	Portland	79	....	3044	1505	580	1201	.483	....	....	....	345	512	.674	245	467	712	244	250	5	77	53	....	38.5	19.1	9.0	3.1	.553
76-77	Boston	82	....	2642	1238	464	1012	.458	....	....	....	310	464	.668	268	556	824	169	331	14	64	61	....	32.2	15.1	10.0	2.1	.552
77-78	Boston	81	....	2413	1083	433	927	.467	....	....	....	217	329	.660	223	450	673	171	318	9	67	46	227	29.8	13.4	8.3	2.1	.474
78-79	San Diego	79	....	2022	771	312	676	.462	....	....	....	147	226	.650	159	246	405	126	274	4	70	36	182	25.6	9.8	5.1	1.6	.356
79-80	San Diego	71	....	2146	503	210	496	.423	0	1	.000	83	152	.546	138	271	409	213	241	5	76	52	170	30.2	7.1	5.8	3.0	.312
80-81	San Diego	49	....	1083	326	125	286	.437	0	1	.000	76	150	.507	79	144	223	111	168	3	40	40	93	22.1	6.7	4.6	2.3	.352
NBA Season Totals		760	....	25762	12803	5046	11002	.459	0	2	.000	2711	3955	.685	1539	3268	6620	2437	2524	51	592	431	672	33.9	16.8	8.7	3.2	....
76-77	Boston	9	....	261	118	42	81	.519	....	....	....	34	47	.723	26	57	83	16	37	2	13	3	....	29.0	13.1	9.2	1.8	.585
NBA Playoff Totals		9	....	261	118	42	81	.519	....	....	....	34	47	.723	26	57	83	16	37	2	13	3	....	29.0	13.1	9.2	1.8	

• WIDBY, Ron
George Ronald Widby

Born: Mar. 9, 1945. Knoxville, TN, United States.   Height: 6'4".   Weight: 210 lbs.   Drafted: 1967   College: Tennessee

YEAR	TEAM	GP	GS	MIN	PTS	FGM	FGA	FG%	3PM	3PA	3P%	FTM	FTA	FT%	ORB	DRB	TRB	AST	PF	DQ	STL	BLK	TO	MPG	PPG	RPG	APG	PCM
67-68	New Orleans-A	20	....	137	58	27	70	.386	0	3	.000	4	7	.571			45	4	18	0	....	....	7	6.9	2.9	2.3	0.2	.406
ABA Season Totals		20	....	137	58	27	70	.386	0	3	.000	4	7	.571			45	4	18	0	....	....	7	6.9	2.9	2.3	0.2	
67-68	New Orleans-A	6	....	31	18	8	19	.421	2	3	.667	0	2	.000			17	1	5	0	....	....	2	5.2	3.0	2.8	0.2	.685
ABA Playoff Totals		6	....	31	18	8	19	.421	2	3	.667	0	2	.000			17	1	5	0	....	....	2	5.2	3.0	2.8	0.2	

• WIDOWITZ, Paul
Paul Widowitz

Born: 1917.   Height: 6'1".   Weight: 170 lbs.   Drafted: —   College: Duquesne

YEAR	TEAM	GP	GS	MIN	PTS	FGM	FGA	FG%	3PM	3PA	3P%	FTM	FTA	FT%	ORB	DRB	TRB	AST	PF	DQ	STL	BLK	TO	MPG	PPG	RPG	APG	PCM
45-46	Cleveland-N	16	....	....	114	52	....	....	....	....	....	10	19	.526					....					7.1	....	....		
NBL Season Totals		16	....	....	114	52	....	....	....	....	....	10	19						....					7.1	....	....		

• WIER, Murray
Murray Neal (Rampaging Redhead, Wizard Wier) Wier

Born: Dec. 12, 1926. Grand View, IA, United States.   Height: 5'9".   Weight: 155 lbs.   Drafted: 1948   College: Iowa

YEAR	TEAM	GP	GS	MIN	PTS	FGM	FGA	FG%	3PM	3PA	3P%	FTM	FTA	FT%	ORB	DRB	TRB	AST	PF	DQ	STL	BLK	TO	MPG	PPG	RPG	APG	PCM
48-49	Tri-Cities-N	60	....	....	239	80	....	....	....	....	....	79	113	.699			....	91	....	....				4.0	....	....		
49-50	Tri-Cities	56	....	....	429	157	480	.327	....	....	....	115	166	.693			107	141	....	....				7.7	....	1.9		
NBA Season Totals		56	....	....	429	157	480	.327	....	....	....	115	166	.693			107	141	....	....				7.7	....	1.9		
NBL Season Totals		60	....	....	239	80	....	....	....	....	....	79	113					91	....	....				4.0	....	....		
Career Totals		116	....	....	668	237	480		....	....	....	194	279				107	232	....	....				5.8	....	0.9		
48-49	Tri-Cities-N	6	....	....	35	13	....	....	....	....	....	9	13	.692					....	....				5.8	....	....		
49-50	Tri-Cities	3	....	....	10	3	9	.333	....	....	....	4	8	.500			0	4	....	....				3.3	....	0.0		
NBA Playoff Totals		3	....	....	10	3	9	.333	....	....	....	4	8	.500			0	4	....	....				3.3	....	0.0		
NBL Playoff Totals		6	....	....	35	13	....	....	....	....	....	9	13						....	....				5.8	....	....		
Career Playoff Totals		9	....	....	45	16	9	....	....	....	....	13	21				0	4	....	....				5.0	....	0.0		

• WIESENHAHN, Bob
Robert B. Wiesenhahn Jr.

Born: Dec. 22, 1938.   Height: 6'4".   Weight: 215 lbs.   Drafted: 1961   College: Cincinnati

YEAR	TEAM	GP	GS	MIN	PTS	FGM	FGA	FG%	3PM	3PA	3P%	FTM	FTA	FT%	ORB	DRB	TRB	AST	PF	DQ	STL	BLK	TO	MPG	PPG	RPG	APG	PCM
61-62	Cincinnati	60	....	326	119	51	161	.317				17	30	.567		....	112	23	50	0		....		5.4	2.0	1.9	0.4	.380
NBA Season Totals		60	....	326	119	51	161	.317				17	30	.567		....	112	23	50	0		....		5.4	2.0	1.9	0.4	
61-62	Cincinnati	2	....	6	3	1	4	.250				1	1	1.000		....	2	0	0	0		....		3.0	1.5	1.0	0.0	.370
NBA Playoff Totals		2	....	6	3	1	4	.250				1	1	1.000		....	2	0	0	0		....		3.0	1.5	1.0	0.0	

• WIETHE, John
John Albert (Socko) Wiethe

Born: Oct. 17, 1912. Cincinnati, OH, United States. Died: May 3, 1989.   Height: 6'   Weight: 198 lbs.   Drafted: —   College: Xavier (OH)

YEAR	TEAM	GP	GS	MIN	PTS	FGM	FGA	FG%	3PM	3PA	3P%	FTM	FTA	FT%	ORB	DRB	TRB	AST	PF	DQ	STL	BLK	TO	MPG	PPG	RPG	APG	PCM
37-38	Cincinnati-N	6	....	....	32	10	....	....	....	....	....	12	....					....	....	....				5.3	....	....		
NBL Season Totals		6	....	....	32	10	....	....	....	....	....	12	....						....	....				5.3	....	....		

• WIGGERS, John
John Wiggers

Born: 1917.   Height: 6'9".   Weight: 200 lbs.   Drafted: —   College: Morehead State

YEAR	TEAM	GP	GS	MIN	PTS	FGM	FGA	FG%	3PM	3PA	3P%	FTM	FTA	FT%	ORB	DRB	TRB	AST	PF	DQ	STL	BLK	TO	MPG	PPG	RPG	APG	PCM
40-41	Wingfoots-N	5	....	....	3	1	....	....	....	....	....	1	....					....	....	....				0.6	....	....		
NBL Season Totals		5	....	....	3	1	....	....	....	....	....	1	....						....	....				0.6	....	....		

• WIGGINS, Mitchell
Mitchell Lee Wiggins

Born: Sept. 28, 1959. Lenoir County, NC, United States.   Height: 6'4".   Weight: 185 lbs.   Drafted: 1983   College: Florida State

YEAR	TEAM	GP	GS	MIN	PTS	FGM	FGA	FG%	3PM	3PA	3P%	FTM	FTA	FT%	ORB	DRB	TRB	AST	PF	DQ	STL	BLK	TO	MPG	PPG	RPG	APG	PCM
83-84	Chicago	82	40	2123	1018	399	890	.448	7	29	.241	213	287	.742	138	190	328	187	278	8	106	11	139	25.9	12.4	4.0	2.3	.416
84-85	Houston	82	24	1575	738	318	657	.484	6	23	.261	96	131	.733	110	125	235	119	195	1	83	13	90	19.2	9.0	2.9	1.5	.423
85-86	Houston	78	0	1198	531	222	489	.454	1	12	.083	86	118	.729	87	72	159	101	155	1	59	5	62	15.4	6.8	2.0	1.3	.379
86-87	Houston	32	19	788	355	153	350	.437	0	5	.000	49	65	.754	74	59	133	76	82	1	44	3	51	24.6	11.1	4.2	2.4	.415
89-90	Houston	66	52	1852	1024	416	853	.488	0	3	.000	192	237	.810	133	153	286	104	165	0	85	1	86	28.1	15.5	4.3	1.6	.483
91-92	Philadelphia	49	0	569	211	88	229	.384	0	1	.000	35	51	.686	43	51	94	22	67	0	20	1	25	11.6	4.3	1.9	0.4	.261
NBA Season Totals		389	135	8105	3877	1596	3468	.460	14	73	.192	671	889	.755	585	650	1235	609	942	11	397	34	453	20.8	10.0	3.2	1.6	....

YEAR	TEAM	GP	GS	MIN	PTS	FGM	FGA	FG%	3PM	3PA	3P%	FTM	FTA	FT%	ORB	DRB	TRB	AST	PF	DQ	STL	BLK	TO	MPG	PPG	RPG	APG	PCM
84-85	Houston	5	0	45	18	9	18	.500	0	0	.000	0	0	.000	3	1	4	1	6	0	4	0	3	9.0	3.6	0.8	0.2	.279
85-86	Houston	20	0	443	199	89	179	.497	0	3	.000	21	28	.750	38	38	76	31	44	0	14	3	27	22.2	10.0	3.8	1.6	.420
89-90	Houston	4	0	51	16	7	15	.467	0	0	.000	2	3	.667	4	9	13	2	5	0	1	0	4	12.8	4.0	3.3	0.5	.337
NBA Playoff Totals		29	0	539	233	105	212	.495	0	3	.000	23	31	.742	45	48	93	34	55	0	19	3	34	18.6	8.0	3.2	1.2	....

• WILBURN, Ken

Kenneth Wilburn

Born: June 8, 1944. River Rouge, MI, United States.　　Height: 6'6".　　Weight: 195 lbs.　　Drafted: 1966　　College: Central State (OH)

YEAR	TEAM	GP	GS	MIN	PTS	FGM	FGA	FG%	3PM	3PA	3P%	FTM	FTA	FT%	ORB	DRB	TRB	AST	PF	DQ	STL	BLK	TO	MPG	PPG	RPG	APG	PCM
67-68	Chicago	3	....	26	11	5	9	.556				1	4	.250	....	....	10	2	4	0	....	....	....	8.7	3.7	3.3	0.7	.592
68-69	Denver-A	37	....	409	174	72	181	.398	0	0	.000	30	57	.526	80	97	177	22	56	1	....	....	37	11.1	4.7	4.8	0.6	.542
68-69	Minnesota-A	6	....	34	6	2	9	.222	0	0	.000	2	5	.400	6	12	18	2	6	0	....	....	6	5.7	1.0	3.0	0.3	.408
68-69	New York-A	4	....	22	10	2	8	.250	0	0	.000	6	9	.667	1	3	4	2	6	0	....	....	4	5.5	2.5	1.0	0.5	.305
68-69	Chicago	4	....	14	7	3	8	.375	....	....	....	1	4	.250	....	....	3	1	1	0	....	....	....	3.5	1.8	0.8	0.3	.344
NBA Season Totals		7	....	40	18	8	17	.471	....	....	....	2	8	.250	....	....	13	3	5	0	....	....	....	5.7	2.6	1.9	0.4	....
ABA Season Totals		47	....	465	190	76	198	.384	0	0	.000	38	71	.535	87	112	199	26	68	1	....	....	47	9.9	4.0	4.2	0.6	....
Career Totals		54	....	505	208	84	215	.391	0	0	.000	40	79	.506	87	112	212	29	73	1	....	....	47	9.4	3.9	3.9	0.5	....
68-69	Denver-A	7	....	93	36	16	33	.485	0	0	.000	4	16	.250	....	....	32	5	21	0	....	....	11	13.3	5.1	4.6	0.7	.435
ABA Playoff Totals		7	....	93	36	16	33	.485	0	0	.000	4	16	.250	....	....	32	5	21	0	....	....	11	13.3	5.1	4.6	0.7	....

• WILCOX, Chris

Chris Ray Wilcox

Born: Aug. 3, 1982. Raleigh, NC, United States.　　Height: 6'10".　　Weight: 221 lbs.　　Drafted: 2002　　College: Maryland

YEAR	TEAM	GP	GS	MIN	PTS	FGM	FGA	FG%	3PM	3PA	3P%	FTM	FTA	FT%	ORB	DRB	TRB	AST	PF	DQ	STL	BLK	TO	MPG	PPG	RPG	APG	PCM
02-03	LA Clippers	46	3	480	171	73	140	.521	0	0	.000	25	50	.500	32	72	104	21	65	2	7	12	26	10.4	3.7	2.3	0.5	.376
NBA Season Totals		46	3	480	171	73	140	.521	0	0	.000	25	50	.500	32	72	104	21	65	2	7	12	26	10.4	3.7	2.3	0.5	....

• WILCUTT, D.C.

D. C. (Dixie) Wilcutt

Born: Mar. 25, 1923. Patton, AL, United States.　　Height: 6'2".　　Weight: 165 lbs.　　Drafted: 1948　　College: St. Louis

YEAR	TEAM	GP	GS	MIN	PTS	FGM	FGA	FG%	3PM	3PA	3P%	FTM	FTA	FT%	ORB	DRB	TRB	AST	PF	DQ	STL	BLK	TO	MPG	PPG	RPG	APG	PCM
48-49	St. Louis	22	....	....	51	18	51	.353	....	....	....	15	18	.833	....	....	31	9	....	....	....	....	....	2.3	....	1.4		
49-50	St. Louis	37	....	....	77	24	73	.329	....	....	....	29	42	.690	....	....	49	27	....	....	....	....	....	2.1	....	1.3		
NBA Season Totals		59	....	....	128	42	124	.339	....	....	....	44	60	.733	....	....	80	36	....	....	....	....	....	2.2	....	1.4		
48-49	St. Louis	2	....	....	6	3	7	.429	....	....	....	0	0	.000	....	....	4	2	....	....	....	....	....	3.0	....	2.0		
NBA Playoff Totals		2	....	....	6	3	7	.429	....	....	....	0	0	.000	....	....	4	2	....	....	....	....	....	3.0	....	2.0		

• WILEY, Gene

Eugene Wiley

Born: Nov. 12, 1937.　　Height: 6'10".　　Weight: 210 lbs.　　Drafted: 1962　　College: Wichita

YEAR	TEAM	GP	GS	MIN	PTS	FGM	FGA	FG%	3PM	3PA	3P%	FTM	FTA	FT%	ORB	DRB	TRB	AST	PF	DQ	STL	BLK	TO	MPG	PPG	RPG	APG	PCM
62-63	LA Lakers	75	....	1488	241	109	236	.462	....	....	....	23	68	.338	....	....	504	40	180	4	....	....	....	19.8	3.2	6.7	0.5	.335
63-64	LA Lakers	78	....	1510	337	146	273	.535	....	....	....	45	75	.600	....	....	510	44	225	4	....	....	....	19.4	4.3	6.5	0.6	.390
64-65	LA Lakers	80	....	2002	406	175	376	.465	....	....	....	56	111	.505	....	....	690	105	235	11	....	....	....	25.0	5.1	8.6	1.3	.399
65-66	LA Lakers	67	....	1386	289	123	289	.426	....	....	....	43	76	.566	....	....	490	63	171	3	....	....	....	20.7	4.3	7.3	0.9	.389
67-68	Dallas-A	1	....	21	1	0	1	.000	0	0	.000	1	3	.333	....	....	3	0	3	0	....	....	2	21.0	1.0	3.0	0.0	.028
67-68	Oakland-A	8	....	64	17	7	19	.368	0	0	.000	3	5	.600	....	....	17	2	7	0	....	....	0	8.0	2.1	2.1	0.3	.309
NBA Season Totals		300	....	6386	1273	553	1174	.471	....	....	....	167	330	.506	....	....	2194	252	811	22	....	....	....	21.3	4.2	7.3	0.8	....
ABA Season Totals		9	....	85	18	7	20	.350	0	0	.000	4	8	.500	....	....	20	2	10	0	....	....	2	9.4	2.0	2.2	0.2	....
Career Totals		309	....	6471	1291	560	1194	.469	0	0	.000	171	338	.506	....	....	2214	254	821	22	....	....	2	20.9	4.2	7.2	0.8	....
62-63	LA Lakers	9	....	278	30	14	35	.400	....	....	....	2	15	.133	....	....	97	11	29	1	....	....	....	30.9	3.3	10.8	1.2	.312
63-64	LA Lakers	5	....	48	13	5	8	.625	....	....	....	3	3	1.000	....	....	16	0	9	1	....	....	....	9.6	2.6	3.2	0.0	.409
64-65	LA Lakers	11	....	379	77	33	59	.559	....	....	....	11	19	.579	....	....	158	23	41	0	....	....	....	34.5	7.0	14.4	2.1	.496
65-66	LA Lakers	2	....	5	0	0	1	.000	....	....	....	0	0	.000	....	....	1	0	1	0	....	....	....	2.5	0.0	0.5	0.0	-.078
NBA Playoff Totals		27	....	710	120	52	103	.505	....	....	....	16	37	.432	....	....	272	34	80	2	....	....	....	26.3	4.4	10.1	1.3	....

• WILEY, Michael

Michael Anthony Wiley

Born: Oct. 16, 1957. Long Beach, CA, United States.　　Height: 6'9".　　Weight: 200 lbs.　　Drafted: 1980　　College: Long Beach State

YEAR	TEAM	GP	GS	MIN	PTS	FGM	FGA	FG%	3PM	3PA	3P%	FTM	FTA	FT%	ORB	DRB	TRB	AST	PF	DQ	STL	BLK	TO	MPG	PPG	RPG	APG	PCM
80-81	San Antonio	33	....	271	188	76	138	.551	0	2	.000	36	48	.750	22	42	64	11	38	1	8	6	26	8.2	5.7	1.9	0.3	.620
81-82	San Diego	61	1	1013	504	203	359	.565	0	5	.000	98	141	.695	67	115	182	52	127	1	40	16	73	16.6	8.3	3.0	0.9	.484
NBA Season Totals		94	1	1284	692	279	497	.561	0	7	.000	134	189	.709	89	157	246	63	165	2	48	22	99	13.7	7.4	2.6	0.7	....
80-81	San Antonio	3	....	5	2	0	1	.000	0	0	.000	2	2	1.000	0	0	0	0	2	0	0	0	0	1.7	0.7	0.0	0.0	.036
NBA Playoff Totals		3	....	5	2	0	1	.000	0	0	.000	2	2	1.000	0	0	0	0	2	0	0	0	0	1.7	0.7	0.0	0.0	....

• WILEY, Morlon

Morlon David Wiley

Born: Sept. 24, 1966. New Orleans, LA, United States.　　Height: 6'4".　　Weight: 185 lbs.　　Drafted: 1988　　College: Long Beach State

YEAR	TEAM	GP	GS	MIN	PTS	FGM	FGA	FG%	3PM	3PA	3P%	FTM	FTA	FT%	ORB	DRB	TRB	AST	PF	DQ	STL	BLK	TO	MPG	PPG	RPG	APG	PCM
88-89	Dallas	51	1	408	111	46	114	.404	6	24	.250	13	16	.813	13	34	47	76	61	0	25	6	36	8.0	2.2	0.9	1.5	.339
89-90	Orlando	40	2	638	229	92	208	.442	17	46	.370	28	38	.737	13	39	52	114	65	0	45	3	64	16.0	5.7	1.3	2.9	.376
90-91	Orlando	34	0	350	113	45	108	.417	6	12	.500	17	25	.680	4	13	17	73	37	1	24	0	34	10.3	3.3	0.5	2.1	.336
91-92	Orlando	9	0	90	21	9	28	.321	0	4	.000	3	5	.600	2	5	7	13	13	0	4	0	8	10.0	2.3	0.8	1.4	.145
91-92	San Antonio	3	0	13	6	3	5	.600	0	0	.000	0	0	.000	0	1	1	1	3	0	0	0	0	4.3	2.0	0.3	0.3	.365
91-92	Atlanta	41	19	767	177	71	160	.444	14	38	.368	21	30	.700	22	51	73	166	73	0	43	3	53	18.7	4.3	1.8	4.0	.385
92-93	Atlanta	25	2	354	72	26	81	.321	15	51	.294	5	8	.625	9	26	35	81	49	0	26	2	30	14.2	2.9	1.4	3.2	.321
92-93	Dallas	33	13	641	191	70	173	.405	39	103	.379	12	18	.667	20	36	56	100	78	2	39	1	50	19.4	5.8	1.7	3.0	.320
93-94	Miami	4	0	34	7	3	8	.375	1	4	.250	0	0	.000	0	4	4	7	4	0	2	0	6	8.5	1.8	1.0	1.8	.240

YEAR	TEAM	GP	GS	MIN	PTS	FGM	FGA	FG%	3PM	3PA	3P%	FTM	FTA	FT%	ORB	DRB	TRB	AST	PF	DQ	STL	BLK	TO	MPG	PPG	RPG	APG	PCM
93-94	Dallas	12	0	124	14	6	21	.286	2	6	.333	0	0	.000	0	6	6	16	17	0	13	0	11	10.3	1.2	0.5	1.3	.138
94-95	Dallas	38	2	407	130	47	111	.423	29	75	.387	7	10	.700	6	33	39	69	44	0	21	1	19	10.7	3.4	1.0	1.8	.395
94-95	Atlanta	5	0	17	7	3	6	.500	1	4	.250	0	0	.000	0	4	4	6	0	0	1	1	4	3.4	1.4	0.8	1.2	.731
NBA Season Totals		295	39	3843	1078	421	1023	.412	130	367	.354	106	150	.707	89	252	341	722	444	3	243	17	315	13.0	3.7	1.2	2.4	....

• WILFONG, Win

Alva Winfred (Win) Wilfong

Born: Mar. 18, 1933. Died: May18, 1985.   Height:. 6'2".   Weight: 185 lbs.   Drafted: 1957   College: Missouri

YEAR	TEAM	GP	GS	MIN	PTS	FGM	FGA	FG%	3PM	3PA	3P%	FTM	FTA	FT%	ORB	DRB	TRB	AST	PF	DQ	STL	BLK	TO	MPG	PPG	RPG	APG	PCM
57-58	St. Louis	71	....	1360	555	196	543	.361	....	....	....	163	238	.685	....	....	290	163	199	3	....	....	....	19.2	7.8	4.1	2.3	.456
58-59	St. Louis	63	....	741	260	99	285	.347	....	....	....	62	82	.756	....	....	121	50	102	0	....	....	....	11.8	4.1	1.9	0.8	.307
59-60	Cincinnati	72	....	1992	727	283	764	.370	....	....	....	161	207	.778	....	....	352	265	229	1	....	....	....	27.7	10.1	4.9	3.7	.429
60-61	Cincinnati	62	....	717	284	106	305	.348	....	....	....	72	89	.809	....	....	147	87	119	1	....	....	....	11.6	4.6	2.4	1.4	.419
NBA Season Totals		268	....	4810	1826	684	1897	.361	....	....	....	458	616	.744	....	....	910	565	649	5	....	....	....	17.9	6.8	3.4	2.1	....
57-58	St. Louis	11	....	162	61	19	69	.275	....	....	....	23	33	.697	....	....	41	25	24	0	....	....	....	14.7	5.5	3.7	2.3	.456
58-59	St. Louis	5	....	46	19	7	19	.368	....	....	....	5	6	.833	....	....	6	3	7	0	....	....	....	9.2	3.8	1.2	0.6	.331
NBA Playoff Totals		16	....	208	80	26	88	.295	....	....	....	28	39	.718	....	....	47	28	31	0	....	....	....	13.0	5.0	2.9	1.8	....

• WILKENS, Lenny

Leonard Randolph Wilkens

Born: Oct. 28, 1937. Brooklyn, NY, United States.   Height: 6'1".   Weight: 180 lbs.   Drafted: 1960   College: Providence   HOF: 1989

YEAR	TEAM	GP	GS	MIN	PTS	FGM	FGA	FG%	3PM	3PA	3P%	FTM	FTA	FT%	ORB	DRB	TRB	AST	PF	DQ	STL	BLK	TO	MPG	PPG	RPG	APG	PCM
60-61	St. Louis	75	....	1898	880	333	783	.425	....	....	....	214	300	.713	....	....	335	212	215	5	....	....	....	25.3	11.7	4.5	2.8	.496
61-62	St. Louis	20	....	870	364	140	364	.385	....	....	....	84	110	.764	....	....	131	116	63	0	....	....	....	43.5	18.2	6.6	5.8	.457
62-63	St. Louis	75	....	2569	888	333	834	.399	....	....	....	222	319	.696	....	....	403	381	256	6	....	....	....	34.3	11.8	5.4	5.1	.440
63-64	St. Louis	78	....	2526	938	334	808	.413	....	....	....	270	365	.740	....	....	335	359	287	7	....	....	....	32.4	12.0	4.3	4.6	.443
64-65	St. Louis	78	....	2854	1284	434	1048	.414	....	....	....	416	558	.746	....	....	365	431	283	7	....	....	....	36.6	16.5	4.7	5.5	.512
65-66	St. Louis	69	....	2692	1244	411	954	.431	....	....	....	422	532	.793	....	....	322	429	248	4	....	....	....	39.0	18.0	4.7	6.2	.539
66-67	St. Louis	78	....	2974	1355	448	1036	.432	....	....	....	459	583	.787	....	....	412	442	280	6	....	....	....	38.1	17.4	5.3	5.7	.533
67-68	St. Louis	82	....	3169	1638	546	1246	.438	....	....	....	546	711	.768	....	....	438	679	255	3	....	....	....	38.6	20.0	5.3	8.3	.656
68-69	Seattle	82	....	3463	1835	644	1462	.440	....	....	....	547	710	.770	....	....	511	674	294	8	....	....	....	42.2	22.4	6.2	8.2	.627
69-70	Seattle	75	....	2802	1334	448	1066	.420	....	....	....	438	556	.788	....	....	378	**683**	212	5	....	....	....	37.4	17.8	5.0	**9.1**	**.622**
70-71	Seattle	71	....	2641	1403	471	1125	.419	....	....	....	461	574	.803	....	....	319	654	201	3	....	....	....	37.2	19.8	4.5	9.2	.653
71-72	Seattle	80	....	2989	1438	479	1027	.466	....	....	....	480	620	.774	....	....	338	**766**	209	4	....	....	....	37.4	18.0	4.2	9.6	**.661**
72-73	Cleveland	75	....	2973	1538	572	1275	.449	....	....	....	394	476	.828	....	....	346	628	221	2	....	....	....	39.6	20.5	4.6	8.4	.612
73-74	Cleveland	74	....	2483	1213	462	994	.465	....	....	....	289	361	.801	80	197	277	522	165	2	97	17	....	33.6	16.4	3.7	7.1	.602
74-75	Portland	65	....	1161	420	134	305	.439	....	....	....	152	198	.768	38	82	120	235	96	1	77	9	....	17.9	6.5	1.8	3.6	.504
NBA Season Totals		1077	....	38064	17772	6189	14327	.432	....	....	....	5394	6973	.774	118	279	5030	7211	3285	63	174	26	....	35.3	16.5	4.7	6.7	....
60-61	St. Louis	12	....	437	170	63	166	.380	....	....	....	44	58	.759	....	....	72	42	51	4	....	....	....	36.4	14.2	6.0	3.5	.398
62-63	St. Louis	11	....	400	151	57	154	.370	....	....	....	37	49	.755	....	....	69	69	51	2	....	....	....	36.4	13.7	6.3	6.3	.468
63-64	St. Louis	12	....	413	172	64	143	.448	....	....	....	44	58	.759	....	....	60	64	42	0	....	....	....	34.4	14.3	5.0	5.3	.517
64-65	St. Louis	4	....	147	64	20	57	.351	....	....	....	24	29	.828	....	....	12	15	14	0	....	....	....	36.8	16.0	3.0	3.8	.381
65-66	St. Louis	10	....	391	171	57	143	.399	....	....	....	57	83	.687	....	....	54	70	43	0	....	....	....	39.1	17.1	5.4	7.0	.522
66-67	St. Louis	9	....	378	193	58	145	.400	....	....	....	77	90	.856	....	....	68	65	34	0	....	....	....	42.0	21.4	7.6	7.2	.628
67-68	St. Louis	6	....	237	110	40	91	.440	....	....	....	30	40	.750	....	....	38	47	23	1	....	....	....	39.5	18.3	6.3	7.8	.603
NBA Playoff Totals		64	....	2403	1031	359	899	.399	....	....	....	313	407	.769	....	....	373	372	258	7	....	....	....	37.5	16.1	5.8	5.8	....

• WILKERSON, Bob

Robert Lee (Bobby) Wilkerson

Born: Aug. 15, 1954. Anderson, IN, United States.   Height: 6'6".   Weight: 195 lbs.   Drafted: 1976   College: Indiana

YEAR	TEAM	GP	GS	MIN	PTS	FGM	FGA	FG%	3PM	3PA	3P%	FTM	FTA	FT%	ORB	DRB	TRB	AST	PF	DQ	STL	BLK	TO	MPG	PPG	RPG	APG	PCM
76-77	Seattle	78	....	1552	526	221	573	.386	....	....	....	84	122	.689	96	162	258	171	136	0	72	8	....	19.9	6.7	3.3	2.2	.364
77-78	Denver	81	....	2780	921	382	936	.408	....	....	....	157	210	.748	98	376	474	439	275	3	126	21	292	34.3	11.4	5.9	5.4	.387
78-79	Denver	80	....	2425	911	396	869	.456	....	....	....	119	173	.688	100	314	414	284	190	0	118	21	200	30.3	11.4	5.2	3.6	.415
79-80	Denver	75	....	2381	1033	430	1030	.417	7	34	.206	166	222	.748	85	231	316	243	194	1	93	27	195	31.7	13.8	4.2	3.2	.362
80-81	Chicago	80	....	2238	798	330	715	.462	1	10	.100	137	163	.840	86	196	282	272	170	0	102	23	176	28.0	10.0	3.5	3.4	.386
81-82	Cleveland	65	38	1805	716	284	679	.418	3	18	.167	145	185	.784	60	190	250	237	188	3	92	25	137	27.8	11.0	3.8	3.6	.396
82-83	Cleveland	77	11	1702	519	213	511	.417	0	4	.000	93	124	.750	62	180	242	189	157	0	68	16	162	22.1	6.7	3.1	2.5	.306
NBA Season Totals		536	49	14883	5424	2256	5313	.425	11	66	.167	901	1199	.751	587	1649	2236	1835	1310	7	671	141	1162	27.8	10.1	4.2	3.4	....
77-78	Denver	13	....	426	120	47	127	.370	....	....	....	26	42	.619	20	51	71	78	55	2	19	4	25	32.8	9.2	5.5	6.0	.392
78-79	Denver	3	....	101	29	14	34	.412	....	....	....	1	3	.333	7	19	26	15	7	0	3	1	6	33.7	9.7	8.7	5.0	.446
80-81	Chicago	6	....	152	55	25	59	.424	0	1	.000	5	5	1.000	6	10	16	14	13	0	5	1	11	25.3	9.2	2.7	2.3	.285
NBA Playoff Totals		22	....	679	204	86	220	.391	0	1	.000	32	50	.640	33	80	113	107	75	2	27	6	42	30.9	9.3	5.1	4.9	....

• WILKES, Jamaal

Jamaal Abdul-Lateef (Silk) Wilkes   aka.: Jackson Keith Wilkes

Born: May 2, 1953. Berkeley, CA, United States.   Height: 6'6".   Weight: 190 lbs.   Drafted: 1974   College: UCLA

YEAR	TEAM	GP	GS	MIN	PTS	FGM	FGA	FG%	3PM	3PA	3P%	FTM	FTA	FT%	ORB	DRB	TRB	AST	PF	DQ	STL	BLK	TO	MPG	PPG	RPG	APG	PCM
74-75	Golden State	82	....	2515	1164	502	1135	.442	....	....	....	160	218	.734	203	468	671	183	222	0	107	22	....	30.7	14.2	8.2	2.2	.512
75-76	Golden State	82	....	2716	1461	617	1334	.463	....	....	....	227	294	.772	193	527	720	167	222	0	102	31	....	33.1	17.8	8.8	2.0	.563
76-77	Golden State	76	....	2579	1343	548	1147	.478	....	....	....	247	310	.797	155	423	578	211	222	1	127	16	....	33.9	17.7	7.6	2.8	.559
77-78	LA Lakers	51	....	1490	660	277	630	.440	....	....	....	106	148	.716	113	267	380	182	162	1	77	22	107	29.2	12.9	7.5	3.6	.532
78-79	LA Lakers	82	....	2915	1524	626	1242	.504	....	....	....	272	362	.751	164	445	609	227	275	2	134	27	221	35.5	18.6	7.4	2.8	.532
79-80	LA Lakers	82	....	3111	1644	726	1358	.535	3	17	.176	189	234	.808	176	349	525	250	220	1	129	28	156	37.9	20.0	6.4	3.0	.547
80-81	LA Lakers	81	....	3028	1827	786	1495	.526	1	13	.077	254	335	.758	146	289	435	235	223	1	121	29	211	37.4	22.6	5.4	2.9	.541
81-82	LA Lakers	82	82	2906	1734	744	1417	.525	0	4	.000	246	336	.732	153	240	393	143	240	1	89	24	164	35.4	21.1	4.8	1.7	.493
82-83	LA Lakers	80	80	2552	1571	684	1290	.530	0	6	.000	203	268	.757	146	197	343	182	221	0	65	17	152	31.9	19.6	4.3	2.3	.526
83-84	LA Lakers	75	74	2507	1294	542	1055	.514	2	8	.250	208	280	.743	130	210	340	214	205	0	72	41	135	33.4	17.3	4.5	2.9	.484
84-85	LA Lakers	42	8	761	347	148	303	.488	0	1	.000	51	66	.773	35	59	94	41	65	0	19	3	50	18.1	8.3	2.2	1.0	.356
85-86	LA Clippers	13	1	195	75	26	65	.400	1	3	.333	22	27	.815	13	16	29	15	19	0	7	2	16	15.0	5.8	2.2	1.2	.329
NBA Season Totals		828	245	27275	14644	6226	12471	.499	7	52	.135	2185	2878	.759	1627	3490	5117	2050	2296	7	1049	262	1212	32.9	17.7	6.2	2.5	....

YEAR	TEAM	GP	GS	MIN	PTS	FGM	FGA	FG%	3PM	3PA	3P%	FTM	FTA	FT%	ORB	DRB	TRB	AST	PF	DQ	STL	BLK	TO	MPG	PPG	RPG	APG	PCM
74-75	Golden State	17	....	503	255	111	249	.446	....	....	....	33	47	.702	30	89	119	28	53	1	26	14	....	29.6	15.0	7.0	1.6	.482
75-76	Golden State	13	....	450	207	86	200	.430	....	....	....	35	45	.778	25	78	103	29	33	1	12	8	....	34.6	15.9	7.9	2.2	.472
76-77	Golden State	10	....	346	155	66	154	.429	....	....	....	23	28	.821	18	62	80	16	23	0	16	6	....	34.6	15.5	8.0	1.6	.446
77-78	LA Lakers	3	....	108	36	15	32	.469	....	....	....	6	11	.545	9	17	26	8	14	1	3	1	11	36.0	12.0	8.7	2.7	.356
78-79	LA Lakers	8	....	307	147	61	128	.477	....	....	....	25	37	.676	20	48	68	16	21	0	15	2	15	38.4	18.4	8.5	2.0	.497
79-80	LA Lakers	16	....	652	324	140	294	.476	0	1	.000	44	54	.815	53	75	128	48	51	0	24	5	35	40.8	20.3	8.0	3.0	.491
80-81	LA Lakers	3	....	113	54	21	48	.438	0	1	.000	12	18	.667	4	4	8	4	10	0	1	1	4	37.7	18.0	2.7	1.3	.283
81-82	LA Lakers	14	14	535	280	121	241	.502	0	1	.000	38	49	.776	40	30	70	37	43	0	16	3	40	38.2	20.0	5.0	2.6	.429
82-83	LA Lakers	15	15	589	299	136	273	.498	0	2	.000	27	44	.614	42	48	90	51	51	0	20	11	33	39.3	19.9	6.0	3.4	.476
83-84	LA Lakers	14	0	196	63	28	70	.400	0	1	.000	7	11	.636	10	16	26	9	27	0	4	2	7	14.0	4.5	1.9	0.6	.216
NBA Playoff Totals		113	29	3799	1820	785	1689	.465	0	6	.000	250	344	.727	251	467	718	246	326	3	137	53	145	33.6	16.1	6.4	2.2	....

• WILKES, James

James Robert Wilkes

Born: Mar. 12, 1958. Nashville, TN, United States. Height: 6'7". Weight: 195 lbs. Drafted: 1980 College: UCLA

YEAR	TEAM	GP	GS	MIN	PTS	FGM	FGA	FG%	3PM	3PA	3P%	FTM	FTA	FT%	ORB	DRB	TRB	AST	PF	DQ	STL	BLK	TO	MPG	PPG	RPG	APG	PCM
80-81	Chicago	48	....	540	199	85	184	.462	0	1	.000	29	42	.690	36	60	96	30	86	0	25	12	34	11.3	4.1	2.0	0.6	.346
81-82	Chicago	57	22	862	314	128	266	.481	0	1	.000	58	80	.725	62	97	159	64	112	0	30	18	63	15.1	5.5	2.8	1.1	.379
82-83	Detroit	9	0	129	34	11	34	.324	0	1	.000	12	15	.800	9	10	19	10	22	0	3	1	5	14.3	3.8	2.1	1.1	.226
NBA Season Totals		114	22	1531	547	224	484	.463	0	3	.000	99	137	.723	107	167	274	104	220	0	58	31	102	13.4	4.8	2.4	0.9	....
80-81	Chicago	2	....	5	0	0	1	.000	0	0	.000	0	0	.000	0	1	1	1	0	0	1	0	2	2.5	0.0	0.5	0.5	.036
NBA Playoff Totals		2	....	5	0	0	1	.000	0	0	.000	0	0	.000	0	1	1	1	0	0	1	0	2	2.5	0.0	0.5	0.5	....

• WILKINS, Dominique

Jacques Dominique (the Human Highlight Film) Wilkins

Born: Jan. 12, 1960. Paris, France. Height: 6'7". Weight: 200 lbs. Drafted: 1982 College: Georgia

YEAR	TEAM	GP	GS	MIN	PTS	FGM	FGA	FG%	3PM	3PA	3P%	FTM	FTA	FT%	ORB	DRB	TRB	AST	PF	DQ	STL	BLK	TO	MPG	PPG	RPG	APG	PCM
82-83	Atlanta	82	82	2697	1434	601	1220	.493	2	11	.182	230	337	.682	226	252	478	129	210	1	84	63	180	32.9	17.5	5.8	1.6	.473
83-84	Atlanta	81	81	2961	1750	684	1429	.479	0	11	.000	382	496	.770	254	328	582	126	197	1	117	87	219	36.6	21.6	7.2	1.6	.532
84-85	Atlanta	81	81	3023	2217	853	**1891**	.451	25	81	.309	486	603	.806	226	331	557	200	170	0	135	54	227	37.3	27.4	6.9	2.5	.600
85-86	Atlanta	78	78	3049	2366	888	**1897**	.468	13	70	.186	577	705	.818	261	357	618	206	170	0	138	49	250	39.1	**30.3**	7.9	2.6	.665
86-87	Atlanta	79	79	2969	2294	828	1787	.463	31	106	.292	607	742	.818	210	284	494	261	149	0	117	51	213	37.6	29.0	6.3	3.3	.662
87-88	Atlanta	78	76	2948	2397	909	1957	.464	38	129	.295	541	655	.826	211	291	502	224	162	0	103	47	218	37.8	30.7	6.4	2.9	.657
88-89	Atlanta	80	80	2997	2099	814	1756	.464	29	105	.276	442	524	.844	256	297	553	211	138	0	117	52	184	37.5	26.2	6.9	2.6	.616
89-90	Atlanta	80	79	2888	2138	810	1672	.484	59	183	.322	459	569	.807	217	304	521	200	141	0	126	47	176	36.1	26.7	6.5	2.5	.662
90-91	Atlanta	81	81	3078	2101	770	1640	.470	85	249	.341	476	574	.829	261	471	732	265	156	0	123	65	203	38.0	25.9	9.0	3.3	.690
91-92	Atlanta	42	42	1601	1179	424	914	.464	37	128	.289	294	352	.835	103	192	295	158	77	0	52	24	122	38.1	28.1	7.0	3.8	.663
92-93	Atlanta	71	70	2647	2121	741	1584	.468	120	316	.380	519	627	.828	187	295	482	227	116	0	70	27	185	37.3	29.9	6.8	3.2	.695
93-94	Atlanta	49	49	1687	1196	430	996	.432	61	198	.308	275	322	.854	119	186	305	114	87	0	63	22	118	34.4	24.4	6.2	2.3	.586
93-94	LA Clippers	25	25	948	727	268	592	.453	24	97	.247	167	200	.835	63	113	176	55	39	0	29	8	53	37.9	29.1	7.0	2.2	.636
94-95	Boston	77	64	2423	1370	496	1169	.424	112	289	.388	266	340	.782	157	244	401	166	130	0	61	14	169	31.5	17.8	5.2	2.2	.457
96-97	San Antonio	63	26	1945	1145	397	953	.417	70	239	.293	281	350	.803	169	233	402	119	100	0	39	31	132	30.9	18.2	6.4	1.9	.510
98-99	Orlando	27	2	252	134	50	132	.379	5	19	.263	29	42	.690	30	41	71	16	19	0	4	1	23	9.3	5.0	2.6	0.6	.444
NBA Season Totals		1074	995	38113	26668	9963	21589	.461	711	2231	.319	6031	7438	.811	2950	4219	7169	2677	2061	2	1378	642	2672	35.5	24.8	6.7	2.5	....
82-83	Atlanta	3	3	109	47	17	42	.405	1	1	1.000	12	14	.857	8	7	15	1	9	0	2	1	10	36.3	15.7	5.0	0.3	.255
83-84	Atlanta	5	5	197	96	35	84	.417	0	1	.000	26	31	.839	21	20	41	11	13	0	12	1	15	39.4	19.2	8.2	2.2	.457
85-86	Atlanta	9	9	360	257	94	217	.433	1	5	.200	68	79	.861	20	34	54	25	24	0	9	2	30	40.0	28.6	6.0	2.8	.516
86-87	Atlanta	9	9	360	241	86	210	.410	3	10	.300	66	74	.892	27	43	70	25	25	0	16	8	26	40.0	26.8	7.8	2.8	.556
87-88	Atlanta	12	12	473	374	137	300	.457	4	18	.222	96	125	.768	37	40	77	34	24	0	16	6	30	39.4	31.2	6.4	2.8	.630
88-89	Atlanta	5	5	212	136	52	116	.448	5	17	.294	27	38	.711	10	17	27	17	5	0	4	8	12	42.4	27.2	5.4	3.4	.530
90-91	Atlanta	5	5	195	104	35	94	.372	2	15	.133	32	35	.914	6	26	32	13	8	0	9	5	11	39.0	20.8	6.4	2.6	.463
92-93	Atlanta	3	3	113	90	32	75	.427	3	12	.250	23	30	.767	12	4	16	9	8	0	3	1	10	37.7	30.0	5.3	3.0	.547
94-95	Boston	4	4	150	76	26	61	.426	8	17	.471	16	18	.889	17	26	43	8	7	0	2	3	9	37.5	19.0	10.8	2.0	.560
98-99	Orlando	1	0	3	2	1	2	.500	0	0	.000	0	0	.000	0	0	0	0	0	0	0	0	0	3.0	2.0	0.0	0.0	.370
NBA Playoff Totals		56	55	2172	1423	515	1201	.429	27	96	.281	366	444	.824	158	217	375	143	123	0	73	35	153	38.8	25.4	6.7	2.6	....

• WILKINS, Eddie Lee

Eddie Lee (Easy) Wilkins

Born: May 7, 1962. Cartersville, GA, United States. Height: 6'10". Weight: 220 lbs. Drafted: 1984 College: Gardner-Webb

YEAR	TEAM	GP	GS	MIN	PTS	FGM	FGA	FG%	3PM	3PA	3P%	FTM	FTA	FT%	ORB	DRB	TRB	AST	PF	DQ	STL	BLK	TO	MPG	PPG	RPG	APG	PCM
84-85	New York	54	16	917	298	116	233	.498	0	2	.000	66	122	.541	86	176	262	16	155	3	21	16	65	17.0	5.5	4.9	0.3	.355
86-87	New York	24	10	454	139	56	127	.441	0	1	.000	27	58	.466	45	62	107	6	67	1	9	2	29	18.9	5.8	4.5	0.3	.257
88-89	New York	71	2	584	289	114	245	.465	0	1	.000	61	111	.550	72	76	148	7	110	1	10	16	57	8.2	4.1	2.1	0.1	.358
89-90	New York	79	0	972	371	141	310	.455	0	2	.000	89	147	.605	114	151	265	16	152	1	18	18	71	12.3	4.7	3.4	0.2	.357
90-91	New York	68	1	668	279	114	255	.447	0	1	.000	51	90	.567	69	111	180	15	91	0	17	7	48	9.8	4.1	2.6	0.2	.372
92-93	Philadelphia	26	0	192	158	55	97	.567	0	2	.000	48	78	.615	14	26	40	2	34	1	7	1	18	7.4	6.1	1.5	0.1	.620
NBA Season Totals		322	29	3787	1534	596	1267	.470	0	9	.000	342	606	.564	400	602	1002	62	609	7	82	60	288	11.8	4.8	3.1	0.2	....
88-89	New York	7	0	26	15	5	11	.455	0	0	.000	5	10	.500	5	6	11	0	3	0	0	0	4	3.7	2.1	1.6	0.0	.470
89-90	New York	7	0	54	24	9	18	.500	0	0	.000	6	11	.545	5	6	11	0	7	0	2	0	2	7.7	3.4	1.6	0.0	.375
90-91	New York	1	0	13	9	4	6	.667	0	0	.000	1	2	.500	2	0	2	0	4	0	0	0	2	13.0	9.0	2.0	0.0	.369
NBA Playoff Totals		15	0	93	48	18	35	.514	0	0	.000	12	23	.522	12	12	24	0	14	0	2	0	8	6.2	3.2	1.6	0.0	....

• WILKINS, Gerald

Gerald Bernard (Doug E. Fresh) Wilkins

Born: Sept. 11, 1963. Atlanta, GA, United States. Height: 6'6". Weight: 185 lbs. Drafted: 1985 College: Tennessee (Chatanooga)

YEAR	TEAM	GP	GS	MIN	PTS	FGM	FGA	FG%	3PM	3PA	3P%	FTM	FTA	FT%	ORB	DRB	TRB	AST	PF	DQ	STL	BLK	TO	MPG	PPG	RPG	APG	PCM
85-86	New York	81	53	2025	1013	437	934	.468	7	25	.280	132	237	.557	92	116	208	161	155	0	68	9	154	25.0	12.5	2.6	2.0	.358
86-87	New York	80	73	2758	1527	633	1302	.486	26	74	.351	235	335	.701	120	174	294	354	165	0	88	18	216	34.5	19.1	3.7	4.4	.482
87-88	New York	81	78	2703	1412	591	1324	.446	39	129	.302	191	243	.786	106	164	270	326	183	1	90	22	211	33.4	17.4	3.3	4.0	.417
88-89	New York	81	58	2414	1161	462	1025	.451	51	172	.297	186	246	.756	95	149	244	274	166	1	115	22	170	29.8	14.3	3.0	3.4	.423
89-90	New York	82	80	2609	1191	472	1032	.457	39	125	.312	208	259	.803	133	238	371	330	188	0	95	21	197	31.8	14.5	4.5	4.0	.451
90-91	New York	68	56	2164	938	380	804	.473	9	43	.209	169	206	.820	78	129	207	275	181	0	82	23	163	31.8	13.8	3.0	4.0	.403
91-92	New York	82	82	2344	1016	431	964	.447	38	108	.352	116	159	.730	74	132	206	219	195	4	76	17	115	28.6	12.4	2.5	2.7	.348

YEAR	TEAM	GP	GS	MIN	PTS	FGM	FGA	FG%	3PM	3PA	3P%	FTM	FTA	FT%	ORB	DRB	TRB	AST	PF	DQ	STL	BLK	TO	MPG	PPG	RPG	APG	PCM
92-93	Cleveland	80	35	2079	890	361	797	.453	16	58	.276	152	181	.840	74	140	214	183	154	1	78	18	96	26.0	11.1	2.7	2.3	.381
93-94	Cleveland	82	82	2768	1170	446	975	.457	84	212	.396	194	250	.776	106	197	303	255	186	0	105	38	131	33.8	14.3	3.7	3.1	.411
95-96	Vancouver	28	14	738	188	77	205	.376	14	64	.219	20	23	.870	22	43	65	68	55	0	22	2	36	26.4	6.7	2.3	2.4	.220
96-97	Orlando	80	26	2202	848	323	759	.426	66	203	.325	136	190	.716	59	114	173	173	144	0	54	12	120	27.5	10.6	2.2	2.2	.293
97-98	Orlando	72	16	1252	380	141	434	.325	29	109	.266	69	98	.704	16	74	90	78	78	0	34	6	79	17.4	5.3	1.3	1.1	.155
98-99	Orlando	3	0	28	2	0	9	.000	0	0	.000	2	2	1.000	0	1	1	1	3	0	0	0	3	9.3	0.7	0.3	0.3	-.286
NBA Season Totals		900	653	26084	11736	4754	10564	.450	418	1322	.316	1810	2429	.745	975	1671	2646	2697	1853	7	907	208	1691	29.0	13.0	2.9	3.0	....
87-88	New York	4	4	149	80	33	69	.478	2	4	.500	12	14	.857	1	7	8	19	12	0	4	0	11	37.3	20.0	2.0	4.8	.410
88-89	New York	9	9	290	145	63	131	.481	1	10	.100	18	23	.783	9	24	33	42	27	1	12	3	22	32.2	16.1	3.7	4.7	.469
89-90	New York	10	10	319	146	63	137	.460	2	8	.250	18	22	.818	14	22	36	52	23	0	14	1	18	31.9	14.6	3.6	5.2	.471
90-91	New York	3	1	78	32	14	38	.368	2	7	.286	2	2	1.000	2	6	8	5	11	0	5	1	8	26.0	10.7	2.7	1.7	.198
91-92	New York	12	12	344	107	45	109	.413	1	13	.077	16	23	.696	12	18	30	34	35	0	5	1	15	28.7	8.9	2.5	2.8	.244
92-93	Cleveland	9	2	236	93	38	87	.437	4	12	.333	13	17	.765	6	10	16	24	16	0	9	2	11	26.2	10.3	1.8	2.7	.333
93-94	Cleveland	3	3	126	61	20	45	.444	7	16	.438	14	16	.875	3	10	13	10	6	0	3	0	3	42.0	20.3	4.3	3.3	.454
96-97	Orlando	5	0	144	47	16	45	.356	3	9	.333	12	14	.857	3	6	9	4	7	0	0	2	3	28.8	9.4	1.8	0.8	.191
NBA Playoff Totals		55	41	1686	711	292	661	.442	22	79	.278	105	131	.802	50	103	153	190	137	1	52	10	91	30.7	12.9	2.8	3.5	....

• WILKINS, Jeff

Jeffrey Wilkins

Born: Mar. 9, 1955. Chicago, IL, United States. Height: 6'11". Weight: 230 lbs. Drafted: 1977 College: Illinois State

YEAR	TEAM	GP	GS	MIN	PTS	FGM	FGA	FG%	3PM	3PA	3P%	FTM	FTA	FT%	ORB	DRB	TRB	AST	PF	DQ	STL	BLK	TO	MPG	PPG	RPG	APG	PCM
80-81	Utah	56	....	1058	261	117	260	.450	0	0	.000	27	40	.675	62	212	274	40	169	3	32	46	62	18.9	4.7	4.9	0.7	.336
81-82	Utah	82	62	2274	765	314	718	.437	0	3	.000	137	176	.778	120	491	611	90	248	4	32	77	131	27.7	9.3	7.5	1.1	.396
82-83	Utah	81	34	2307	934	389	816	.477	0	3	.000	156	200	.780	154	442	596	132	251	4	41	42	186	28.5	11.5	7.4	1.6	.436
83-84	Utah	81	1	1734	632	249	520	.479	0	3	.000	134	182	.736	109	346	455	73	205	1	27	42	105	21.4	7.8	5.6	0.9	.421
84-85	Utah	79	0	1505	631	285	582	.490	0	1	.000	61	80	.763	78	288	366	81	173	0	35	18	95	19.1	8.0	4.6	1.0	.434
85-86	Utah	48	0	604	222	96	240	.400	0	0	.000	30	47	.638	40	105	145	28	86	0	3	11	34	12.6	4.6	3.0	0.6	.309
85-86	San Antonio	27	4	522	130	51	134	.381	0	0	.000	28	46	.609	34	93	127	18	71	1	8	10	19	19.3	4.8	4.7	0.7	.283
NBA Season Totals		454	101	10004	3575	1501	3270	.459	0	10	.000	573	771	.743	597	1977	2574	462	1203	13	178	246	632	22.0	7.9	5.7	1.0	....
83-84	Utah	11	1	205	77	30	57	.526	0	0	.000	17	22	.773	10	39	49	5	32	0	0	5	11	18.6	7.0	4.5	0.5	.390
84-85	Utah	10	0	257	129	51	118	.432	0	1	.000	27	35	.771	13	50	63	13	27	0	4	5	15	25.7	12.9	6.3	1.3	.456
85-86	San Antonio	3	0	16	0	0	1	.000	0	0	.000	0	0	.000	0	3	3	0	6	0	0	2	0	5.3	0.0	1.0	0.0	.058
NBA Playoff Totals		24	1	478	206	81	176	.460	0	1	.000	44	57	.772	23	92	115	18	65	0	4	12	26	19.9	8.6	4.8	0.8	....

• WILKINS, Russell

Russell Wilkins

Born: 1920. Height: 6'1". Weight: 190 lbs. Drafted: — College: Tri-State

YEAR	TEAM	GP	GS	MIN	PTS	FGM	FGA	FG%	3PM	3PA	3P%	FTM	FTA	FT%	ORB	DRB	TRB	AST	PF	DQ	STL	BLK	TO	MPG	PPG	RPG	APG	PCM
46-47	Anderson-N	5	....	....	5	2	....	....	....	....	....	1	2	.500	....	....	....	....	....	....	....	....	....	....	1.0	....	....	....
NBL Season Totals		5	....	....	5	2	....	....	....	....	....	1	2	....	....	....	....	....	....	....	....	....	....	....	1.0	....	....	....

• WILKINSON, Dale

Dale Wayne Wilkinson

Born: Mar. 18, 1960. Pocatello, ID, United States. Height: 6'10". Weight: 220 lbs. Drafted: 1982 College: Idaho State

YEAR	TEAM	GP	GS	MIN	PTS	FGM	FGA	FG%	3PM	3PA	3P%	FTM	FTA	FT%	ORB	DRB	TRB	AST	PF	DQ	STL	BLK	TO	MPG	PPG	RPG	APG	PCM
84-85	Detroit	2	0	7	0	0	2	.000	0	0	.000	0	0	.000	0	1	1	0	2	0	0	0	0	3.5	0.0	0.5	0.0	-.266
84-85	LA Clippers	10	0	38	14	4	14	.286	0	1	.000	6	7	.857	1	2	3	2	8	0	0	0	4	3.8	1.4	0.3	0.2	.044
NBA Season Totals		12	0	45	14	4	16	.250	0	1	.000	6	7	.857	1	3	4	2	10	0	0	0	4	3.8	1.2	0.3	0.2	....

• WILKS, Mike

Michael Wilks

Born: May 7, 1979. Milwaukee, WI, United States. Height: 5'10". Weight: 185 lbs. Drafted: — College: Rice

YEAR	TEAM	GP	GS	MIN	PTS	FGM	FGA	FG%	3PM	3PA	3P%	FTM	FTA	FT%	ORB	DRB	TRB	AST	PF	DQ	STL	BLK	TO	MPG	PPG	RPG	APG	PCM
02-03	Atlanta	15	7	364	85	29	81	.358	6	17	.353	21	29	.724	9	32	41	42	38	0	16	1	16	24.3	5.7	2.7	2.8	.277
02-03	Minnesota	31	0	324	62	21	67	.313	4	18	.222	16	18	.889	11	19	30	50	31	0	11	3	12	10.5	2.0	1.0	1.6	.274
NBA Season Totals		46	7	688	147	50	148	.338	10	35	.286	37	47	.787	20	51	71	92	69	0	27	4	28	15.0	3.2	1.5	2.0	....
02-03	Minnesota	4	0	7	3	1	2	.500	1	1	1.000	0	0	.000	0	0	0	0	0	0	0	0	0	1.8	0.8	0.0	0.0	.299
NBA Playoff Totals		4	0	7	3	1	2	.500	1	1	1.000	0	0	.000	0	0	0	0	0	0	0	0	0	1.8	0.8	0.0	0.0	....

• WILLETT, —

Willett

Born: —. Height: — Weight: — Drafted: — College: —

YEAR	TEAM	GP	GS	MIN	PTS	FGM	FGA	FG%	3PM	3PA	3P%	FTM	FTA	FT%	ORB	DRB	TRB	AST	PF	DQ	STL	BLK	TO	MPG	PPG	RPG	APG	PCM
38-39	Hammond-N	2	....	....	0	0	....	....	....	....	....	0	....	....	....	....	....	....	....	....	....	....	....	....	0.0	....	....	....
NBL Season Totals		2	....	....	0	0	....	....	....	....	....	0	....	....	....	....	....	....	....	....	....	....	....	....	0.0	....	....	....

• WILLIAMS, Aaron

Aaron Williams

Born: Oct. 2, 1971. Evanston, IL, United States. Height: 6'9". Weight: 220 lbs. Drafted: — College: Xavier

YEAR	TEAM	GP	GS	MIN	PTS	FGM	FGA	FG%	3PM	3PA	3P%	FTM	FTA	FT%	ORB	DRB	TRB	AST	PF	DQ	STL	BLK	TO	MPG	PPG	RPG	APG	PCM
93-94	Utah	6	0	12	4	2	8	.250	0	0	.000	0	1	.000	1	2	3	1	4	0	0	0	1	2.0	0.7	0.5	0.2	-.073
94-95	Milwaukee	15	0	72	24	8	24	.333	0	1	.000	8	12	.667	5	14	19	0	14	0	2	6	8	4.8	1.6	1.3	0.0	.255
96-97	Denver	1	0	10	6	3	5	.600	0	0	.000	0	0	.000	2	3	5	0	0	0	0	3	4	10.0	6.0	5.0	0.0	.786
96-97	Vancouver	32	1	553	197	82	143	.573	0	1	.000	33	49	.673	60	78	138	15	72	1	16	26	29	17.3	6.2	4.3	0.5	.463
97-98	Seattle	65	9	757	296	115	220	.523	0	1	.000	66	85	.776	48	99	147	14	119	0	19	38	52	11.6	4.6	2.3	0.2	.384
98-99	Seattle	40	2	458	158	52	123	.423	0	1	.000	54	74	.730	54	74	128	22	75	1	14	24	30	11.5	4.0	3.2	0.6	.432
99-00	Washington	81	0	1545	616	235	450	.522	0	3	.000	146	201	.726	159	250	409	58	234	1	43	92	80	19.1	7.6	5.0	0.7	.501
00-01	New Jersey	82	25	2336	838	297	650	.457	0	2	.000	244	310	.787	211	379	590	88	**319**	9	59	113	132	28.5	10.2	7.2	1.1	.433
01-02	New Jersey	82	13	1547	592	231	439	.526	0	2	.000	130	186	.699	115	224	339	77	212	5	29	76	79	18.9	7.2	4.1	0.9	.451
02-03	New Jersey	81	0	1597	500	199	439	.453	0	1	.000	102	130	.785	137	194	331	88	206	5	27	57	85	19.7	6.2	4.1	1.1	.358
NBA Season Totals		485	50	8887	3231	1224	2501	.489	0	12	.000	783	1048	.747	792	1317	2109	363	1255	22	209	435	500	18.3	6.7	4.3	0.7	....

YEAR	TEAM	GP	GS	MIN	PTS	FGM	FGA	FG%	3PM	3PA	3P%	FTM	FTA	FT%	ORB	DRB	TRB	AST	PF	DQ	STL	BLK	TO	MPG	PPG	RPG	APG	PCM
97-98	Seattle	3	0	7	2	0	3	.000	0	0	.000	2	2	1.000	1	0	1	0	0	0	0	1	1	2.3	0.7	0.3	0.0	.024
01-02	New Jersey	20	0	416	130	46	96	.479	0	1	.000	38	46	.826	24	46	70	16	78	5	8	16	23	20.8	6.5	3.5	0.8	.307
02-03	New Jersey	19	0	340	123	50	106	.472	0	0	.000	23	31	.742	33	54	87	18	54	0	6	17	13	17.9	6.5	4.6	0.9	.446
NBA Playoff Totals		42	0	763	255	96	205	.468	0	1	.000	63	79	.797	58	100	158	34	132	5	14	34	37	18.2	6.1	3.8	0.8	....

• WILLIAMS, Al
Alfred Williams

Born: Jan. 3, 1948.   Height: 6'6".   Weight: 200 lbs.   Drafted: 1970   College: Drake

YEAR	TEAM	GP	GS	MIN	PTS	FGM	FGA	FG%	3PM	3PA	3P%	FTM	FTA	FT%	ORB	DRB	TRB	AST	PF	DQ	STL	BLK	TO	MPG	PPG	RPG	APG	PCM
70-71	Kentucky-A	11	....	70	43	19	43	.442	0	0	.000	5	10	.500	9	17	26	5	13	0	....	....	7	6.4	3.9	2.4	0.5	.620
ABA Season Totals		11	....	70	43	19	43	.442	0	0	.000	5	10	.500	9	17	26	5	13	0	....	....	7	6.4	3.9	2.4	0.5	....

• WILLIAMS, Alvin
Alvin Leon Williams

Born: Aug. 6, 1974. Philadelphia, PA, United States.   Height: 6'5".   Weight: 185 lbs.   Drafted: 1997   College: Villanova

YEAR	TEAM	GP	GS	MIN	PTS	FGM	FGA	FG%	3PM	3PA	3P%	FTM	FTA	FT%	ORB	DRB	TRB	AST	PF	DQ	STL	BLK	TO	MPG	PPG	RPG	APG	PCM
97-98	Portland	41	10	864	283	109	238	.458	7	24	.292	58	79	.734	19	41	60	83	60	0	30	2	49	21.1	6.9	1.5	2.0	.298
97-98	Toronto	13	13	207	41	16	44	.364	2	4	.500	7	11	.636	5	16	21	20	19	0	8	1	8	15.9	3.2	1.6	1.5	.226
98-99	Toronto	50	45	1051	248	95	237	.401	14	42	.333	44	52	.846	19	63	82	130	94	1	51	12	56	21.0	5.0	1.6	2.6	.285
99-00	Toronto	55	28	779	292	114	287	.397	16	55	.291	48	65	.738	27	58	85	126	78	0	34	11	47	14.2	5.3	1.5	2.3	.391
00-01	Toronto	82	34	2394	802	330	767	.430	33	108	.306	109	145	.752	50	162	212	407	171	1	123	26	103	29.2	9.8	2.6	5.0	.416
01-02	Toronto	82	82	2927	971	403	971	.415	21	103	.321	140	188	.745	58	223	281	468	191	1	135	26	150	35.7	11.8	3.4	5.7	.386
02-03	Toronto	78	78	2640	1027	396	905	.438	48	146	.329	187	239	.782	55	190	245	416	170	0	111	21	128	33.8	13.2	3.1	5.3	.433
NBA Season Totals		401	280	10862	3664	1463	3449	.424	182	572	.318	556	731	.761	233	753	986	1650	783	3	492	99	541	27.1	9.1	2.5	4.1	....
99-00	Toronto	1	0	1	0	0	0	.000	0	0	.000	0	0	.000	0	0	0	0	0	0	0	0	0	1.0	0.0	0.0	0.0	.000
00-01	Toronto	12	12	486	165	69	160	.431	10	28	.357	17	25	.680	6	29	35	50	34	0	15	8	16	40.5	13.8	2.9	4.2	.324
01-02	Toronto	5	5	196	60	24	75	.320	3	14	.214	9	11	.818	2	22	24	28	12	0	6	2	8	39.2	12.0	4.8	5.6	.305
NBA Playoff Totals		18	17	683	225	93	235	.396	13	42	.310	26	36	.722	8	51	59	78	46	0	21	10	24	37.9	12.5	3.3	4.3	....

• WILLIAMS, Art
Arthur T. (Hambone) Williams

Born: Sept. 29, 1939. Bonham, TX, United States.   Height: 6'1".   Weight: 180 lbs.   Drafted: —   College: California Poly

YEAR	TEAM	GP	GS	MIN	PTS	FGM	FGA	FG%	3PM	3PA	3P%	FTM	FTA	FT%	ORB	DRB	TRB	AST	PF	DQ	STL	BLK	TO	MPG	PPG	RPG	APG	PCM
67-68	San Diego	79	....	1739	643	265	718	.369	....	....	....	113	165	.685	....	....	286	391	204	0	....	....	....	22.0	8.1	3.6	4.9	.505
68-69	San Diego	79	....	1987	559	227	592	.383	....	....	....	105	149	.705	....	....	364	524	238	0	....	....	....	25.2	7.1	4.6	6.6	.529
69-70	San Diego	80	....	1545	466	189	464	.407	....	....	....	88	118	.746	....	....	292	503	168	0	....	....	....	19.3	5.8	3.7	6.3	.620
70-71	Boston	74	....	1141	360	150	330	.455	....	....	....	60	83	.723	....	....	205	233	182	1	....	....	....	15.4	4.9	2.8	3.1	.490
71-72	Boston	81	....	1326	412	161	339	.475	....	....	....	90	119	.756	....	....	256	327	204	2	....	....	....	16.4	5.1	3.2	4.0	.566
72-73	Boston	81	....	974	263	110	261	.421	....	....	....	43	56	.768	....	....	182	236	136	1	....	....	....	12.0	3.2	2.2	2.9	.508
73-74	Boston	67	....	617	173	73	168	.435	....	....	....	27	32	.844	20	95	115	163	100	0	44	3	....	9.2	2.6	1.7	2.4	.539
74-75	San Diego-A	7	....	89	16	8	12	.667	0	0	.000	0	0	.000	3	9	12	20	15	....	7	0	10	12.7	2.3	1.7	2.9	.435
NBA Season Totals		541	....	9329	2876	1175	2872	.409	....	....	....	526	722	.729	20	95	1700	2377	1232	4	44	3	....	17.2	5.3	3.1	4.4	....
ABA Season Totals		7	....	89	16	8	12	.667	0	0	.000	0	0	.000	3	9	12	20	15	....	7	0	10	12.7	2.3	1.7	2.9	....
Career Totals		548	....	9418	2892	1183	2884	.410	0	0	.000	526	722	.729	23	104	1712	2397	1247	4	51	3	10	17.2	5.3	3.1	4.4	....
68-69	San Diego	6	....	102	27	12	25	.480	....	....	....	3	7	.429	....	....	17	32	15	0	....	....	....	17.0	4.5	2.8	5.3	.585
71-72	Boston	11	....	173	65	25	64	.391	....	....	....	15	20	.750	....	....	28	33	30	0	....	....	....	15.7	5.9	2.5	3.0	.450
72-73	Boston	10	....	156	48	21	47	.447	....	....	....	6	8	.750	....	....	27	41	31	1	....	....	....	15.6	4.8	2.7	4.1	.523
73-74	Boston	12	....	96	27	10	27	.370	....	....	....	7	8	.875	4	19	23	29	14	0	7	0	....	8.0	2.3	1.9	2.4	.615
NBA Playoff Totals		39	....	527	167	68	163	.417	....	....	....	31	43	.721	4	19	95	135	90	1	7	0	....	13.5	4.3	2.4	3.5	....

• WILLIAMS, Bernie
Bernard Williams

Born: Dec. 30, 1945. Washington, DC, United States.   Height: 6'3".   Weight: 175 lbs.   Drafted: 1969   College: LaSalle

YEAR	TEAM	GP	GS	MIN	PTS	FGM	FGA	FG%	3PM	3PA	3P%	FTM	FTA	FT%	ORB	DRB	TRB	AST	PF	DQ	STL	BLK	TO	MPG	PPG	RPG	APG	PCM
69-70	San Diego	72	....	1228	598	251	641	.392	....	....	....	96	122	.787	....	....	155	165	124	0	....	....	....	17.1	8.3	2.2	2.3	.415
70-71	San Diego	56	....	708	292	112	338	.331	....	....	....	68	81	.840	....	....	85	113	76	1	....	....	....	12.6	5.2	1.5	2.0	.369
71-72	Virginia-A	78	....	1667	829	349	816	.428	18	65	.277	113	142	.796	51	103	154	134	178	0	....	....	123	21.4	10.6	2.0	1.7	.368
72-73	Virginia-A	71	....	1513	888	356	831	.428	10	58	.172	166	193	.860	60	65	125	137	150	0	....	....	136	21.3	12.5	1.8	1.9	.426
73-74	Virginia-A	6	....	51	15	6	19	.316	1	2	.500	2	2	1.000	0	4	4	7	3	....	1	0	5	8.5	2.5	0.7	1.2	.274
NBA Season Totals		128	....	1936	890	363	979	.371	....	"....	....	164	203	.808	....	....	240	278	200	1	....	....	....	15.1	7.0	1.9	2.2	....
ABA Season Totals		155	....	3231	1732	711	1666	.427	29	125	.232	281	337	.834	111	172	283	278	331	0	1	0	264	20.8	11.2	1.8	1.8	....
Career Totals		283	....	5167	2622	1074	2645	.406	29	125	.232	445	540	.824	111	172	523	556	531	1	1	0	264	18.3	9.3	1.8	2.0	....
71-72	Virginia-A	11	....	356	189	84	190	.442	2	4	.500	19	27	.704	17	30	47	23	38	1	....	....	28	32.4	17.2	4.3	2.1	.401
72-73	Virginia-A	3	....	24	7	3	8	.375	0	1	.000	1	1	1.000	0	0	0	1	4	0	....	....	7	8.0	2.3	0.0	0.3	.075
ABA Playoff Totals		14	....	380	196	87	198	.439	2	5	.400	20	28	.714	17	30	47	24	42	1	....	....	35	27.1	14.0	3.4	1.7	....

• WILLIAMS, Bob
Robert L. Williams

Born: May 12, 1931.   Height: 6'6".   Weight: 230 lbs.   Drafted: —   College: Florida A&M

YEAR	TEAM	GP	GS	MIN	PTS	FGM	FGA	FG%	3PM	3PA	3P%	FTM	FTA	FT%	ORB	DRB	TRB	AST	PF	DQ	STL	BLK	TO	MPG	PPG	RPG	APG	PCM
55-56	Minneapolis	20	....	173	66	21	46	.457	....	....	....	24	45	.533	....	....	54	7	36	1	....	....	....	8.7	3.3	2.7	0.4	.434
56-57	Minneapolis	4	....	20	4	1	4	.250	....	....	....	2	3	.667	....	....	5	0	2	0	....	....	....	5.0	1.0	1.3	0.0	.219
NBA Season Totals		24	....	193	70	22	50	.440	....	....	....	26	48	.542	....	....	59	7	38	1	....	....	....	8.0	2.9	2.5	0.3	....

• WILLIAMS, Brandon

Brandon Williams

Born: Feb. 27, 1975. Collinston, LA, United States. Height: 6'6". Weight: 215 lbs. Drafted: — College: Davidson

YEAR	TEAM	GP	GS	MIN	PTS	FGM	FGA	FG%	3PM	3PA	3P%	FTM	FTA	FT%	ORB	DRB	TRB	AST	PF	DQ	STL	BLK	TO	MPG	PPG	RPG	APG	PCM
97-98	Golden State	9	2	140	37	16	50	.320	3	9	.333	2	4	.500	4	11	15	3	18	0	6	3	9	15.6	4.1	1.7	0.3	.098
98-99	San Antonio	3	0	4	2	0	0	.000	0	0	.000	2	4	.500	1	0	1	0	0	0	0	0	0	1.3	0.7	0.3	0.0	.500
02-03	Atlanta	6	0	19	2	1	7	.143	0	1	.000	0	0	.000	2	0	2	0	4	0	2	0	3	3.2	0.3	0.3	0.0	-.229
NBA Season Totals		18	2	163	41	17	57	.298	3	10	.300	4	8	.500	7	11	18	3	22	0	8	3	12	9.1	2.3	1.0	0.2	....

• WILLIAMS, Buck

Charles Linwood (Buck) Williams

Born: Mar. 8, 1960. Rocky Mount, NC, United States. Height: 6'8". Weight: 215 lbs. Drafted: 1981 College: Maryland

YEAR	TEAM	GP	GS	MIN	PTS	FGM	FGA	FG%	3PM	3PA	3P%	FTM	FTA	FT%	ORB	DRB	TRB	AST	PF	DQ	STL	BLK	TO	MPG	PPG	RPG	APG	PCM
81-82	New Jersey	82	82	2825	1268	513	881	.582	0	1	.000	242	388	.624	347	658	1005	107	285	5	84	84	238	34.5	15.5	12.3	1.3	.604
82-83	New Jersey	82	82	2961	1396	536	912	.588	0	4	.000	324	523	.620	365	662	1027	125	270	4	91	110	246	36.1	17.0	12.5	1.5	.631
83-84	New Jersey	81	81	3003	1274	495	926	.535	0	4	.000	284	498	.570	**355**	645	1000	130	298	3	81	125	235	37.1	15.7	12.3	1.6	.559
84-85	New Jersey	82	82	**3182**	1491	577	1089	.530	1	4	.250	336	538	.625	323	682	1005	167	293	7	63	110	238	38.8	18.2	12.3	2.0	.577
85-86	New Jersey	82	82	3070	1301	500	956	.523	0	2	.000	301	445	.676	329	657	986	131	294	9	73	96	246	37.4	15.9	12.0	1.6	.540
86-87	New Jersey	82	82	2976	1472	521	936	.557	0	1	.000	430	588	.731	322	701	1023	129	315	8	78	91	279	36.3	18.0	12.5	1.6	.623
87-88	New Jersey	70	70	2637	1279	466	832	.560	1	1	1.000	346	518	.668	298	536	834	109	266	5	68	44	189	37.7	18.3	11.9	1.6	.590
88-89	New Jersey	74	72	2446	959	373	702	.531	0	3	.000	213	320	.666	249	447	696	78	223	0	61	36	141	33.1	13.0	9.4	1.1	.486
89-90	Portland	82	82	2801	1114	413	754	.548	0	1	.000	288	408	.706	250	550	800	116	285	4	69	39	164	34.2	13.6	9.8	1.4	.509
90-91	Portland	80	80	2582	933	358	595	**.602**	0	0	.000	217	308	.705	227	524	751	97	247	2	47	47	136	32.3	11.7	9.4	1.2	.511
91-92	Portland	80	80	2519	901	340	563	**.604**	0	1	.000	221	293	.754	260	444	704	108	244	4	62	41	128	31.5	11.3	8.8	1.4	.514
92-93	Portland	82	82	2498	678	270	528	.511	0	1	.000	138	214	.645	232	458	690	75	270	0	81	61	98	30.5	8.3	8.4	0.9	.417
93-94	Portland	81	81	2636	783	291	524	.555	0	1	.000	201	296	.679	315	528	843	80	239	1	58	47	113	32.5	9.7	10.4	1.0	.481
94-95	Portland	82	82	2422	757	309	604	.512	1	2	.500	138	205	.673	251	418	669	78	254	2	67	69	123	29.5	9.2	8.2	1.0	.434
95-96	Portland	70	10	1672	511	192	384	.500	2	3	.667	125	187	.668	159	245	404	42	187	1	40	47	91	23.9	7.3	5.8	0.6	.379
96-97	New York	74	4	1496	465	175	326	.537	0	1	.000	115	179	.642	166	231	397	53	204	2	40	38	81	20.2	6.3	5.4	0.7	.417
97-98	New York	41	6	738	202	75	149	.503	0	0	.000	52	71	.732	78	105	183	21	93	1	17	15	37	18.0	4.9	4.5	0.5	.364
NBA Season Totals		1307	1140	42464	16784	6404	11661	.549	5	30	.167	3971	5979	.664	4526	8491	13017	1646	4267	58	1080	1100	2783	32.5	12.8	10.0	1.3	....
81-82	New Jersey	2	2	79	35	14	26	.538	0	0	.000	7	15	.467	11	10	21	3	7	0	1	2	4	39.5	17.5	10.5	1.5	.490
82-83	New Jersey	2	2	85	38	11	22	.500	0	0	.000	16	20	.800	9	14	23	4	12	2	2	2	5	42.5	19.0	11.5	2.0	.531
83-84	New Jersey	11	11	473	171	63	130	.485	0	0	.000	45	81	.556	57	98	155	16	44	2	15	17	29	43.0	15.5	14.1	1.5	.498
84-85	New Jersey	3	3	123	74	26	40	.650	0	0	.000	22	30	.733	14	18	32	1	12	0	3	5	6	41.0	24.7	10.7	0.3	.686
85-86	New Jersey	3	3	126	62	21	29	.724	0	0	.000	20	26	.769	12	19	31	2	15	1	6	1	6	42.0	20.7	10.3	0.7	.609
89-90	Portland	21	21	776	273	101	199	.508	0	0	.000	71	105	.676	67	126	193	39	74	1	13	6	41	37.0	13.0	9.2	1.9	.428
90-91	Portland	16	16	572	165	65	130	.500	0	0	.000	35	58	.603	53	90	143	14	55	1	10	4	24	35.8	10.3	8.9	0.9	.362
91-92	Portland	21	21	758	201	66	130	.508	0	0	.000	69	91	.758	61	118	179	22	73	1	27	17	45	36.1	9.6	8.5	1.0	.378
92-93	Portland	4	4	119	35	11	23	.478	0	0	.000	13	19	.684	12	17	29	1	12	1	1	3	6	29.8	8.8	7.3	0.3	.350
93-94	Portland	4	4	125	51	19	28	.679	0	0	.000	13	15	.867	14	21	35	2	11	0	4	2	8	31.3	12.8	8.8	0.5	.554
94-95	Portland	3	3	103	25	9	15	.600	0	0	.000	7	11	.636	8	11	19	1	14	1	4	2	4	34.3	8.3	6.3	0.3	.308
95-96	Portland	5	1	133	24	9	23	.391	1	2	.500	5	7	.714	13	12	25	1	18	0	1	4	5	26.6	4.8	5.0	0.2	.195
96-97	New York	10	1	193	43	17	35	.486	0	0	.000	9	17	.529	13	27	40	6	34	0	3	4	4	19.3	4.3	4.0	0.6	.275
97-98	New York	3	0	45	14	4	9	.444	0	0	.000	6	8	.750	7	9	16	1	5	0	0	1	3	15.0	4.7	5.3	0.3	.447
NBA Playoff Totals		108	92	3710	1211	436	839	.520	1	2	.500	338	503	.672	351	590	941	113	386	10	90	70	190	34.4	11.2	8.7	1.0	....

• WILLIAMS, Charles

Charles E. (Toothpick) Williams

Born: Sept. 5, 1943. Colorado Springs, CO, United States. Height: 6' Weight: 165 lbs. Drafted: — College: Seattle

YEAR	TEAM	GP	GS	MIN	PTS	FGM	FGA	FG%	3PM	3PA	3P%	FTM	FTA	FT%	ORB	DRB	TRB	AST	PF	DQ	STL	BLK	TO	MPG	PPG	RPG	APG	PCM
67-68	Pittsburgh-A	78	....	3042	1625	642	1573	.408	51	178	.287	290	429	.676	....	....	377	173	295	6	....	....	270	39.0	20.8	4.8	2.2	.390
68-69	Minnesota-A	66	....	2282	1237	484	1298	.373	66	212	.311	203	286	.710	110	136	246	163	222	6	....	....	204	34.6	18.7	3.7	2.5	.353
69-70	Pittsburgh-A	26	....	925	506	193	537	.359	16	75	.213	104	135	.770	25	53	78	94	80	1	....	....	80	35.6	19.5	3.0	3.6	.365
70-71	Memphis-A	56	....	1269	767	308	759	.406	23	99	.232	128	183	.699	47	80	127	123	142	2	....	....	100	22.7	13.7	2.3	2.2	.454
70-71	Pittsburgh-A	32	....	973	472	193	458	.421	10	37	.270	76	108	.704	25	58	83	127	101	0	....	....	127	30.4	14.8	2.6	4.0	.437
71-72	Memphis-A	82	....	2583	1295	480	1258	.382	41	174	.236	294	395	.744	85	143	228	253	250	5	....	....	233	31.5	15.8	2.8	3.1	.364
72-73	Memphis-A	10	....	219	72	25	75	.333	3	14	.214	19	26	.731	2	10	12	42	31	1	....	....	24	21.9	7.2	1.2	4.2	.306
72-73	Utah-A	22	....	151	46	12	40	.300	0	6	.000	22	31	.710	2	4	6	17	23	0	....	....	10	6.9	2.1	0.3	0.8	.202
ABA Season Totals		372	....	11444	6020	2337	5998	.390	210	795	.264	1136	1593	.713	296	484	1157	992	1144	21	....	....	1048	30.8	16.2	3.1	2.7	....
67-68	Pittsburgh-A	15	....	626	356	145	336	.432	6	35	.171	60	82	.732	....	....	64	37	61	3	....	....	56	41.7	23.7	4.3	2.5	.414
68-69	Minnesota-A	7	....	255	120	41	112	.366	11	38	.289	27	39	.692	....	....	24	14	28	1	....	....	19	36.4	17.1	3.4	2.0	.308
70-71	Memphis-A	4	....	129	77	31	74	.419	2	6	.333	13	18	.722	6	8	14	8	15	0	....	....	4	32.3	19.3	3.5	2.0	.429
72-73	Utah-A	4	....	12	2	1	5	.200	0	0	.000	0	0	.000	0	1	1	1	3	0	....	....	1	3.0	0.5	0.3	0.3	-.079
ABA Playoff Totals		30	....	1022	555	218	527	.414	19	79	.241	100	139	.719	6	9	103	60	107	4	....	....	80	34.1	18.5	3.4	2.0	....

• WILLIAMS, Chuck

Edward (Chuck) Williams

Born: June 6, 1946. Boulder, CO, United States. Height: 6'2". Weight: 175 lbs. Drafted: 1968 College: Colorado

YEAR	TEAM	GP	GS	MIN	PTS	FGM	FGA	FG%	3PM	3PA	3P%	FTM	FTA	FT%	ORB	DRB	TRB	AST	PF	DQ	STL	BLK	TO	MPG	PPG	RPG	APG	PCM
70-71	Pittsburgh-A	83	....	1795	786	268	613	.437	1	4	.250	249	317	.785	90	95	185	170	161	4	....	....	151	21.6	9.5	2.2	2.0	.429
71-72	Denver-A	84	....	1580	731	263	583	.451	0	4	.000	205	275	.745	62	95	157	160	144	1	....	....	98	18.8	8.7	1.9	1.9	.426
72-73	San Diego-A	83	....	3074	1470	488	1020	.478	1	7	.143	493	623	.791	71	158	229	**582**	275	8	....	....	231	37.0	17.7	2.8	7.0	**.539**
73-74	Kentucky-A	33	....	922	291	109	256	.426	1	3	.333	72	97	.742	19	57	76	170	67	....	26	3	86	27.9	8.8	2.3	5.2	.417
73-74	San Diego-A	57	....	1954	822	296	662	.447	3	9	.333	227	285	.796	61	113	174	387	131	....	63	8	170	34.3	14.4	3.1	6.8	.521
74-75	Memphis-A	81	....	3171	1174	476	963	.494	10	24	.417	212	260	.815	60	160	220	**576**	165	....	115	18	171	39.1	14.5	2.7	7.1	**.468**
75-76	Denver-A	79	....	2529	866	339	660	.514	0	4	.000	188	231	.814	41	169	210	375	215	....	115	7	180	32.0	11.0	2.7	4.7	.422
76-77	Denver	21	....	311	100	35	93	.376	....	....	....	30	39	.769	8	26	34	44	26	0	8	0	....	14.8	4.8	1.6	2.1	.367
76-77	Buffalo	44	....	556	124	43	117	.368	....	....	....	38	48	.792	18	49	67	88	34	0	24	3	....	12.6	2.8	1.5	2.0	.358
77-78	Buffalo	73	....	2002	530	208	436	.477	....	....	....	114	138	.826	29	108	137	317	137	0	48	4	153	27.4	7.3	1.9	4.3	.324
NBA Season Totals		138	....	2869	754	286	646	.443	....	....	....	182	225	.809	55	183	238	449	197	0	80	7	153	20.8	5.5	1.7	3.3	....
ABA Season Totals		500	....	15025	6140	2239	4757	.471	16	55	.291	1646	2088	.788	404	847	1251	2420	1158	13	319	36	1087	30.1	12.3	2.5	4.8	....
Career Totals		638	....	17894	6894	2525	5403	.467	16	55	.291	1828	2313	.790	459	1030	1489	2869	1355	13	399	43	1240	28.0	10.8	2.3	4.5	....

YEAR	TEAM	GP	GS	MIN	PTS	FGM	FGA	FG%	3PM	3PA	3P%	FTM	FTA	FT%	ORB	DRB	TRB	AST	PF	DQ	STL	BLK	TO	MPG	PPG	RPG	APG	PCM
71-72	Denver-A	7	....	108	45	18	42	.429	0	0	.000	9	12	.750	....	....	19	6	14	0	....	....	6	15.4	6.4	2.7	0.9	.369
72-73	San Diego-A	4	....	158	77	27	61	.443	0	0	.000	23	30	.767	4	6	10	21	12	0	....	....	16	39.5	19.3	2.5	5.3	.443
73-74	Kentucky-A	8	....	213	67	22	54	.407	0	0	.000	23	24	.958	7	13	20	44	12	....	9	2	28	26.6	8.4	2.5	5.5	.476
74-75	Memphis-A	5	....	210	88	33	59	.559	0	0	.000	22	24	.917	1	7	8	33	13	....	6	2	12	42.0	17.6	1.6	6.6	.486
75-76	Denver-A	13	....	444	164	62	132	.470	1	3	.333	39	43	.907	11	37	48	48	31	....	6	5	26	34.2	12.6	3.7	3.7	.410
ABA Playoff Totals		37	....	1133	441	162	348	.466	1	3	.333	116	133	.872	23	63	105	152	82	0	21	9	88	30.6	11.9	2.8	4.1	....

• WILLIAMS, Chuckie
Charles Leon (Chuckie) Williams

Born: Dec. 31, 1953. Columbus, OH, United States.   Height: 6'3".   Weight: 180 lbs.   Drafted: 1976   College: Kansas State

YEAR	TEAM	GP	GS	MIN	PTS	FGM	FGA	FG%	3PM	3PA	3P%	FTM	FTA	FT%	ORB	DRB	TRB	AST	PF	DQ	STL	BLK	TO	MPG	PPG	RPG	APG	PCM
76-77	Cleveland	22	....	65	37	14	47	.298	....	....	....	9	12	.750	3	1	4	7	7	0	1	0	....	3.0	1.7	0.2	0.3	.240
NBA Season Totals		22	....	65	37	14	47	.298	....	....	....	9	12	.750	3	1	4	7	7	0	1	0	....	3.0	1.7	0.2	0.3	....

• WILLIAMS, Cliff
Clifford L. Williams

Born: Apr. 15, 1945.   Height: 6'3".   Weight: 180 lbs.   Drafted: —   College: Bowling Green

YEAR	TEAM	GP	GS	MIN	PTS	FGM	FGA	FG%	3PM	3PA	3P%	FTM	FTA	FT%	ORB	DRB	TRB	AST	PF	DQ	STL	BLK	TO	MPG	PPG	RPG	APG	PCM
68-69	Detroit	3	....	18	4	2	9	.222	....	....	....	0	0	.000	....	....	3	2	7	0	....	....	....	6.0	1.3	1.0	0.7	.003
NBA Season Totals		3	....	18	4	2	9	.222	....	....	....	0	0	.000	....	....	3	2	7	0	....	....	....	6.0	1.3	1.0	0.7	....

• WILLIAMS, Corey
Corey Williams

Born: Apr. 24, 1970. Twiggs, GA, United States.   Height: 6'2".   Weight: 190 lbs.   Drafted: 1992   College: Oklahoma State

YEAR	TEAM	GP	GS	MIN	PTS	FGM	FGA	FG%	3PM	3PA	3P%	FTM	FTA	FT%	ORB	DRB	TRB	AST	PF	DQ	STL	BLK	TO	MPG	PPG	RPG	APG	PCM
92-93	Chicago	35	0	242	81	31	85	.365	1	3	.333	18	22	.818	19	12	31	23	24	0	4	1	11	6.9	2.3	0.9	0.7	.270
93-94	Minnesota	4	0	46	11	5	13	.385	0	1	.000	1	1	1.000	1	5	6	6	6	0	2	0	2	11.5	2.8	1.5	1.5	.281
NBA Season Totals		39	0	288	92	36	98	.367	1	4	.250	19	23	.826	20	17	37	29	30	0	6	1	13	7.4	2.4	0.9	0.7	....

• WILLIAMS, Dave
David Williams

Born: 1914.   Height: 6'3".   Weight: 210 lbs.   Drafted: —   College: Indiana Central

YEAR	TEAM	GP	GS	MIN	PTS	FGM	FGA	FG%	3PM	3PA	3P%	FTM	FTA	FT%	ORB	DRB	TRB	AST	PF	DQ	STL	BLK	TO	MPG	PPG	RPG	APG	PCM
38-39	Indianapolis-N	18	....	....	58	24	....	....	....	....	....	10	....	....	....	....	....	....	....	....	....	....	....	3.2	....	....	....	....
39-40	Indianapolis-N	7	....	....	10	3	....	....	....	....	....	4	....	....	....	....	....	....	....	....	....	....	....	1.4	....	....	....	....
41-42	Toledo-N	7	....	....	24	9	....	....	....	....	....	6	....	....	....	....	....	....	....	....	....	....	....	3.4	....	....	....	....
NBL Season Totals		32	....	....	92	36	....	....	....	....	....	20	....	....	....	....	....	....	....	....	....	....	....	2.9	....	....	....	....

• WILLIAMS, Duck
Donald Edgar (Duck) Williams

Born: Aug. 2, 1956. Demopolis, AL, United States.   Height: 6'2".   Weight: 180 lbs.   Drafted: 1978   College: Notre Dame

YEAR	TEAM	GP	GS	MIN	PTS	FGM	FGA	FG%	3PM	3PA	3P%	FTM	FTA	FT%	ORB	DRB	TRB	AST	PF	DQ	STL	BLK	TO	MPG	PPG	RPG	APG	PCM
79-80	Utah	77	....	1794	506	232	519	.447	0	12	.000	42	60	.700	21	85	106	183	166	0	100	11	108	23.3	6.6	1.4	2.4	.258
NBA Season Totals		77	....	1794	506	232	519	.447	0	12	.000	42	60	.700	21	85	106	183	166	0	100	11	108	23.3	6.6	1.4	2.4	....

• WILLIAMS, Earl
Earl (The Twirl) Williams

Born: Mar. 24, 1951. Levittown, PA, United States.   Height: 6'7".   Weight: 230 lbs.   Drafted: 1974   College: Winston-Salem

YEAR	TEAM	GP	GS	MIN	PTS	FGM	FGA	FG%	3PM	3PA	3P%	FTM	FTA	FT%	ORB	DRB	TRB	AST	PF	DQ	STL	BLK	TO	MPG	PPG	RPG	APG	PCM
74-75	Phoenix	79	....	1040	371	163	394	.414	....	....	....	45	103	.437	156	300	456	95	146	0	28	32	....	13.2	4.7	5.8	1.2	.562
75-76	Detroit	46	....	562	168	73	152	.480	....	....	....	22	44	.500	103	148	251	18	81	0	22	20	....	12.2	3.7	5.5	0.4	.519
76-77	New York	1	....	7	3	0	2	.000	....	....	....	3	6	.500	1	1	2	1	2	0	0	1	....	7.0	3.0	2.0	1.0	.283
78-79	Boston	20	....	273	122	54	123	.439	....	....	....	14	24	.583	41	64	105	12	41	0	12	9	20	13.7	6.1	5.3	0.6	.533
NBA Season Totals		146	....	1882	664	290	671	.432	....	....	....	84	177	.475	301	513	814	126	270	0	62	62	20	12.9	4.5	5.6	0.9	....

• WILLIAMS, Eric
Eric C. Williams

Born: July 17, 1972. Newark, NJ, United States.   Height: 6'8".   Weight: 220 lbs.   Drafted: 1995   College: Providence

YEAR	TEAM	GP	GS	MIN	PTS	FGM	FGA	FG%	3PM	3PA	3P%	FTM	FTA	FT%	ORB	DRB	TRB	AST	PF	DQ	STL	BLK	TO	MPG	PPG	RPG	APG	PCM
95-96	Boston	64	6	1470	685	241	546	.441	3	10	.300	200	298	.671	92	125	217	70	147	1	56	11	90	23.0	10.7	3.4	1.1	.367
96-97	Boston	72	67	2435	1078	374	820	.456	2	8	.250	328	436	.752	126	203	329	129	213	0	72	13	137	33.8	15.0	4.6	1.8	.373
97-98	Denver	4	4	145	79	24	61	.393	0	0	.000	31	45	.689	10	11	21	12	9	0	4	0	9	36.3	19.8	5.3	3.0	.430
98-99	Denver	38	8	780	277	80	219	.365	6	26	.231	111	139	.799	34	47	81	37	76	0	27	8	49	20.5	7.3	2.1	1.0	.267
99-00	Boston	68	17	1378	489	165	386	.427	25	72	.347	134	169	.793	55	101	156	93	165	3	44	16	66	20.3	7.2	2.3	1.4	.316
00-01	Boston	81	11	1745	535	162	448	.362	46	139	.331	165	231	.714	64	143	207	112	179	1	64	13	76	21.5	6.6	2.6	1.4	.274
01-02	Boston	74	30	1747	472	144	385	.374	24	86	.279	160	219	.731	58	163	221	109	179	1	77	8	95	23.6	6.4	3.0	1.5	.261
02-03	Boston	82	79	2351	746	254	575	.442	37	110	.336	201	268	.750	143	239	382	140	234	0	86	19	97	28.7	9.1	4.7	1.7	.351
NBA Season Totals		483	222	12051	4361	1444	3440	.420	143	451	.317	1330	1805	.737	582	1032	1614	702	1202	6	430	88	619	25.0	9.0	3.3	1.5	....
01-02	Boston	16	16	487	125	47	94	.500	14	30	.467	17	23	.739	18	52	70	21	53	1	25	4	11	30.4	7.8	4.4	1.3	.325
02-03	Boston	10	2	310	96	33	88	.375	3	15	.200	27	34	.794	12	20	32	17	42	2	9	0	12	31.0	9.6	3.2	1.7	.222
NBA Playoff Totals		26	18	797	221	80	182	.440	17	45	.378	44	57	.772	30	72	102	38	95	3	34	4	23	30.7	8.5	3.9	1.5	....

• WILLIAMS, Fly
James (Fly) Williams

Born: Feb. 18, 1953. Brooklyn, NY, United States.   Height: 6'5".   Weight: 200 lbs.   Drafted: 1976   College: Austin Peay

YEAR	TEAM	GP	GS	MIN	PTS	FGM	FGA	FG%	3PM	3PA	3P%	FTM	FTA	FT%	ORB	DRB	TRB	AST	PF	DQ	STL	BLK	TO	MPG	PPG	RPG	APG	PCM
74-75	St. Louis-A	71	....	1239	665	297	643	.462	2	14	.143	69	101	.683	72	109	181	142	156	....	64	10	177	17.5	9.4	2.5	2.0	.479
ABA Season Totals		71	....	1239	665	297	643	.462	2	14	.143	69	101	.683	72	109	181	142	156	....	64	10	177	17.5	9.4	2.5	2.0	....
74-75	St. Louis-A	2	....	8	2	1	5	.200	0	1	.000	0	0	.000	0	1	1	0	2	....	0	0	1	4.0	1.0	0.5	0.0	-.194
ABA Playoff Totals		2	....	8	2	1	5	.200	0	1	.000	0	0	.000	0	1	1	0	2	....	0	0	1	4.0	1.0	0.5	0.0	....

• WILLIAMS, Frank

Frank Lowell Williams

Born: Feb. 25, 1980. Peoria, IL, United States. Height: 6'3". Weight: 212 lbs. Drafted: 2002 College: Illinois

YEAR	TEAM	GP	GS	MIN	PTS	FGM	FGA	FG%	3PM	3PA	3P%	FTM	FTA	FT%	ORB	DRB	TRB	AST	PF	DQ	STL	BLK	TO	MPG	PPG	RPG	APG	PCM
02-03	New York	21	0	167	28	9	33	.273	6	16	.375	4	6	.667	3	15	18	34	20	0	7	2	17	8.0	1.3	0.9	1.6	.254
NBA Season Totals		21	0	167	28	9	33	.273	6	16	.375	4	6	.667	3	15	18	34	20	0	7	2	17	8.0	1.3	0.9	1.6	....

• WILLIAMS, Freeman

Freeman Williams Jr.

Born: May 15, 1956. Los Angeles, CA, United States. Height: 6'4". Weight: 190 lbs. Drafted: 1978 College: Portland State

YEAR	TEAM	GP	GS	MIN	PTS	FGM	FGA	FG%	3PM	3PA	3P%	FTM	FTA	FT%	ORB	DRB	TRB	AST	PF	DQ	STL	BLK	TO	MPG	PPG	RPG	APG	PCM
78-79	San Diego	72	....	1195	746	335	683	.490	....	....	....	76	98	.776	48	50	98	83	88	0	42	2	101	16.6	10.4	1.4	1.2	.429
79-80	San Diego	82	....	2118	1526	645	1343	.480	42	128	.328	194	238	.815	103	89	192	166	145	0	72	9	172	25.8	18.6	2.3	2.0	.511
80-81	San Diego	82	....	1976	1585	642	1381	.465	48	141	.340	253	297	.852	75	54	129	164	157	0	91	5	164	24.1	19.3	1.6	2.0	.534
81-82	San Diego	37	10	808	610	234	513	.456	24	74	.324	118	140	.843	21	29	50	67	85	1	23	0	89	21.8	16.5	1.4	1.8	.447
81-82	Atlanta	23	0	189	110	42	110	.382	4	20	.200	22	26	.846	2	10	12	19	18	0	6	0	18	8.2	4.8	0.5	0.8	.306
82-83	Utah	18	3	210	92	36	101	.356	2	7	.286	18	25	.720	3	14	17	10	30	0	6	1	13	11.7	5.1	0.9	0.6	.179
85-86	Washington	9	0	110	69	25	67	.373	7	14	.500	12	17	.706	4	8	12	7	10	0	7	1	13	12.2	7.7	1.3	0.8	.336
NBA Season Totals		323	13	6606	4738	1959	4198	.467	127	384	.331	693	841	.824	256	254	510	516	533	1	247	18	570	20.5	14.7	1.6	1.6	....
81-82	Atlanta	1	0	4	0	0	2	.000	0	1	.000	0	0	.000	0	0	0	0	0	0	0	0	0	4.0	0.0	0.0	0.0	-.461
NBA Playoff Totals		1	0	4	0	0	2	.000	0	1	.000	0	0	.000	0	0	0	0	0	0	0	0	0	4.0	0.0	0.0	0.0	....

• WILLIAMS, Gene

Eugene Williams

Born: Apr. 1, 1947. San Francisco, CA, United States. Height: 6'7". Weight: 235 lbs. Drafted: 1969 College: Kansas State

YEAR	TEAM	GP	GS	MIN	PTS	FGM	FGA	FG%	3PM	3PA	3P%	FTM	FTA	FT%	ORB	DRB	TRB	AST	PF	DQ	STL	BLK	TO	MPG	PPG	RPG	APG	PCM
69-70	Kentucky-A	1	....	8	0	0	1	.000	0	0	.000	0	0	.000	0	0	0	0	2	0	....	....	2	8.0	0.0	0.0	0.0	-.215
ABA Season Totals		1	....	8	0	0	1	.000	0	0	.000	0	0	.000	0	0	0	0	2	0	....	....	2	8.0	0.0	0.0	0.0	....

• WILLIAMS, Gus

Gus (The Wizard) Williams

Born: Oct. 10, 1953. Mount Vernon, NY, United States. Height: 6'2". Weight: 175 lbs. Drafted: 1975 College: USC

YEAR	TEAM	GP	GS	MIN	PTS	FGM	FGA	FG%	3PM	3PA	3P%	FTM	FTA	FT%	ORB	DRB	TRB	AST	PF	DQ	STL	BLK	TO	MPG	PPG	RPG	APG	PCM
75-76	Golden State	77	....	1728	903	365	853	.428	....	....	....	173	233	.742	62	97	159	240	143	2	140	26	....	22.4	11.7	2.1	3.1	.467
76-77	Golden State	82	....	1930	762	325	701	.464	....	....	....	112	150	.747	72	161	233	292	218	4	121	19	....	23.5	9.3	2.8	3.6	.446
77-78	Seattle	79	....	2572	1431	602	1335	.451	....	....	....	227	278	.817	83	173	256	294	198	2	185	41	190	32.6	18.1	3.2	3.7	.493
78-79	Seattle	76	....	2266	1457	606	1224	.495	....	....	....	245	316	.775	111	134	245	307	162	3	158	29	190	29.8	19.2	3.2	4.0	.597
79-80	Seattle	82	....	2969	1816	739	1533	.482	7	36	.194	331	420	.788	127	148	275	397	160	1	200	37	180	36.2	22.1	3.4	4.8	.579
81-82	Seattle	80	80	2876	1875	773	1592	.486	9	40	.225	320	436	.734	92	152	244	549	163	0	172	36	200	36.0	23.4	3.1	6.9	.632
82-83	Seattle	80	80	2761	1600	660	1384	.477	2	43	.047	278	370	.751	72	133	205	643	117	0	182	26	232	34.5	20.0	2.6	8.0	.624
83-84	Seattle	80	80	2818	1497	598	1306	.458	4	25	.160	297	396	.750	67	137	204	675	151	0	189	25	232	35.2	18.7	2.6	8.4	.574
84-85	Washington	79	78	2960	1578	638	1483	.430	51	176	.290	251	346	.725	72	123	195	608	159	1	178	32	213	37.5	20.0	2.5	7.7	.507
85-86	Washington	77	67	2284	1036	434	1013	.428	30	116	.259	138	188	.734	52	114	166	453	113	0	96	15	162	29.7	13.5	2.2	5.9	.444
86-87	Atlanta	33	0	481	138	53	146	.363	5	18	.278	27	40	.675	8	32	40	139	53	0	17	5	53	14.6	4.2	1.2	4.2	.369
NBA Season Totals		825	385	25645	14093	5793	12570	.461	108	454	.238	2399	3173	.756	818	1404	2222	4597	1637	13	1638	291	1652	31.1	17.1	2.7	5.6	....
75-76	Golden State	11	....	178	74	30	85	.353	....	....	....	14	21	.667	5	9	14	26	22	0	11	0	....	16.2	6.7	1.3	2.4	.315
76-77	Golden State	10	....	184	88	35	70	.500	....	....	....	18	21	.857	9	6	15	25	30	1	8	1	....	18.4	8.8	1.5	2.5	.462
77-78	Seattle	22	....	701	403	163	342	.477	....	....	....	77	106	.726	30	56	86	88	70	2	45	12	54	31.9	18.3	3.9	4.0	.542
78-79	Seattle	17	....	609	452	181	382	.474	....	....	....	90	127	.709	36	34	70	63	42	1	34	11	42	35.8	26.6	4.1	3.7	.609
79-80	Seattle	15	....	564	355	146	284	.514	1	5	.200	62	86	.721	30	30	60	84	38	0	34	7	47	37.6	23.7	4.0	5.6	.608
81-82	Seattle	8	8	315	210	82	186	.441	2	6	.333	44	56	.786	12	14	26	65	13	0	13	5	18	39.4	26.3	3.3	8.1	.625
82-83	Seattle	2	2	81	65	26	47	.553	0	2	.000	13	15	.867	4	3	7	8	5	0	5	0	6	40.5	32.5	3.5	4.0	.705
83-84	Seattle	5	5	215	117	50	98	.510	2	6	.333	15	21	.714	2	10	12	57	7	0	8	3	14	43.0	23.4	2.4	11.4	.631
84-85	Washington	4	4	159	72	30	71	.423	3	10	.300	9	12	.750	4	4	8	20	5	0	5	1	13	39.8	18.0	2.0	5.0	.329
85-86	Washington	5	5	199	91	38	79	.481	1	10	.100	14	18	.778	4	6	10	33	11	0	11	0	7	39.8	18.2	2.0	6.6	.474
NBA Playoff Totals		99	24	3205	1927	781	1644	.475	9	39	.231	356	483	.737	136	172	308	469	243	4	174	40	201	32.4	19.5	3.1	4.7	....

• WILLIAMS, Guy

Guy Bernard Williams

Born: July 1, 1960. Los Angeles, CA, United States. Height: 6'9". Weight: 200 lbs. Drafted: 1983 College: Washington State

YEAR	TEAM	GP	GS	MIN	PTS	FGM	FGA	FG%	3PM	3PA	3P%	FTM	FTA	FT%	ORB	DRB	TRB	AST	PF	DQ	STL	BLK	TO	MPG	PPG	RPG	APG	PCM
84-85	Washington	21	0	119	61	29	63	.460	1	4	.250	2	5	.400	15	12	27	9	17	0	5	2	8	5.7	2.9	1.3	0.4	.452
85-86	Golden State	5	0	25	7	2	5	.400	0	0	.000	3	6	.500	0	6	6	0	7	1	1	2	0	5.0	1.4	1.2	0.0	.317
NBA Season Totals		26	0	144	68	31	68	.456	1	4	.250	5	11	.455	15	18	33	9	24	1	6	4	8	5.5	2.6	1.3	0.3	....

• WILLIAMS, Hank

Henry Williams

Born: Apr. 28, 1952. Norristown, PA, United States. Height: 6'5". Weight: 210 lbs. Drafted: 1975 College: Jacksonville

YEAR	TEAM	GP	GS	MIN	PTS	FGM	FGA	FG%	3PM	3PA	3P%	FTM	FTA	FT%	ORB	DRB	TRB	AST	PF	DQ	STL	BLK	TO	MPG	PPG	RPG	APG	PCM
74-75	Utah-A	40	....	468	173	76	173	.439	3	22	.136	18	23	.783	31	65	96	26	74	....	14	4	32	11.7	4.3	2.4	0.7	.355
ABA Season Totals		40	....	468	173	76	173	.439	3	22	.136	18	23	.783	31	65	96	26	74	....	14	4	32	11.7	4.3	2.4	0.7	....
74-75	Utah-A	2	....	7	4	2	6	.333	0	0	.000	0	0	.000	1	1	2	0	2	....	0	0	0	3.5	2.0	1.0	0.0	.191
ABA Playoff Totals		2	....	7	4	2	6	.333	0	0	.000	0	0	.000	1	1	2	0	2	....	0	0	0	3.5	2.0	1.0	0.0	....

• WILLIAMS, Herb

Herbert L. Williams

Born: Feb. 16, 1958. Columbus, OH, United States. Height: 6'10". Weight: 242 lbs. Drafted: 1981 College: Ohio State

YEAR	TEAM	GP	GS	MIN	PTS	FGM	FGA	FG%	3PM	3PA	3P%	FTM	FTA	FT%	ORB	DRB	TRB	AST	PF	DQ	STL	BLK	TO	MPG	PPG	RPG	APG	PCM
81-82	Indiana	82	75	2277	942	407	854	.477	2	7	.286	126	188	.670	175	430	605	139	200	0	53	178	139	27.8	11.5	7.4	1.7	.528
82-83	Indiana	78	74	2513	1315	580	1163	.499	0	7	.000	155	220	.705	151	432	583	262	230	4	54	171	226	32.2	16.9	7.5	3.4	.584
83-84	Indiana	69	53	2279	1029	411	860	.478	0	4	.000	207	295	.702	154	400	554	215	193	4	60	108	207	33.0	14.9	8.0	3.1	.522
84-85	Indiana	75	70	2557	1375	575	1211	.475	1	9	.111	224	341	.657	154	480	634	252	218	1	54	134	263	34.1	18.3	8.5	3.4	.554

YEAR	TEAM	GP	GS	MIN	PTS	FGM	FGA	FG%	3PM	3PA	3P%	FTM	FTA	FT%	ORB	DRB	TRB	AST	PF	DQ	STL	BLK	TO	MPG	PPG	RPG	APG	PCM
85-86	Indiana	78	74	2770	1549	627	1275	.492	1	12	.083	294	403	.730	172	538	710	174	244	2	50	184	211	35.5	19.9	9.1	2.2	.596
86-87	Indiana	74	67	2526	1101	451	939	.480	0	9	.000	199	269	.740	143	400	543	174	255	9	59	93	148	34.1	14.9	7.3	2.4	.471
87-88	Indiana	75	37	1966	748	311	732	.425	0	6	.000	126	171	.737	116	353	469	98	244	1	37	146	120	26.2	10.0	6.3	1.3	.418
88-89	Indiana	46	46	1567	578	244	542	.450	0	3	.000	90	126	.714	87	309	396	88	156	3	31	80	106	34.1	12.6	8.6	1.9	.433
88-89	Dallas	30	20	903	199	78	197	.396	0	2	.000	43	68	.632	48	149	197	36	80	2	15	54	42	30.1	6.6	6.6	1.2	.317
89-90	Dallas	81	0	2199	700	295	665	.444	2	9	.222	108	159	.679	76	315	391	119	243	4	51	106	105	27.1	8.6	4.8	1.5	.344
90-91	Dallas	60	36	1832	747	332	655	.507	0	4	.000	83	130	.638	86	271	357	95	197	3	30	88	114	30.5	12.5	6.0	1.6	.420
91-92	Dallas	75	26	2040	859	367	851	.431	1	6	.167	124	171	.725	106	348	454	94	189	2	35	98	113	27.2	11.5	6.1	1.3	.412
92-93	New York	55	0	571	158	72	175	.411	0	0	.000	14	21	.667	44	102	146	19	78	0	21	28	22	10.4	2.9	2.7	0.3	.357
93-94	New York	70	3	774	233	103	233	.442	0	1	.000	27	42	.643	56	126	182	28	108	1	18	43	42	11.1	3.3	2.6	0.4	.351
94-95	New York	56	3	743	187	82	180	.456	0	0	.000	23	37	.622	23	109	132	27	108	0	13	45	39	13.3	3.3	2.4	0.5	.280
95-96	Toronto	1	0	31	6	3	8	.375	0	0	.000	0	0	.000	1	7	8	0	4	0	1	2	0	31.0	6.0	8.0	0.0	.315
95-96	New York	43	2	540	132	59	144	.410	1	4	.250	13	20	.650	14	68	82	27	75	0	13	31	22	12.6	3.1	1.9	0.6	.259
96-97	New York	21	2	184	39	18	46	.391	0	1	.000	3	4	.750	9	22	31	5	18	0	4	5	4	8.8	1.9	1.5	0.2	.233
97-98	New York	27	0	178	37	18	43	.419	0	0	.000	1	8	.125	6	23	29	4	34	0	6	9	5	6.6	1.4	1.1	0.1	.199
98-99	New York	6	0	34	10	4	8	.500	0	0	.000	2	2	1.000	3	3	6	0	2	0	0	2	2	5.7	1.7	1.0	0.0	.320
NBA Season Totals		1102	588	28484	11944	5037	10781	.467	8	84	.095	1862	2675	.696	1624	4885	6509	1856	2876	36	605	1605	1930	25.8	10.8	5.9	1.7	....
86-87	Indiana	4	4	134	47	20	34	.588	0	0	.000	7	13	.538	3	17	20	7	12	0	0	1	11	33.5	11.8	5.0	1.8	.316
89-90	Dallas	3	0	81	41	14	23	.609	0	0	.000	13	16	.813	4	9	13	5	16	1	1	2	3	27.0	13.7	4.3	1.7	.508
92-93	New York	7	0	69	14	5	14	.357	0	0	.000	4	4	1.000	5	9	14	2	13	0	1	4	2	9.9	2.0	2.0	0.3	.254
93-94	New York	19	0	127	28	13	31	.419	0	0	.000	2	3	.667	10	10	20	3	19	0	3	11	7	6.7	1.5	1.1	0.2	.239
94-95	New York	8	0	55	8	3	13	.231	0	0	.000	2	2	1.000	3	4	7	0	13	0	5	5	1	6.9	1.0	0.9	0.0	.137
95-96	New York	5	0	33	9	3	5	.600	0	0	.000	3	4	.750	0	0	0	0	3	0	0	2	1	6.6	1.8	0.0	0.0	.187
96-97	New York	3	0	23	4	2	5	.400	0	0	.000	0	0	.000	0	1	1	0	4	0	0	0	0	7.7	1.3	0.3	0.0	.012
98-99	New York	8	0	16	2	1	5	.200	0	0	.000	0	0	.000	0	3	3	0	3	0	0	0	0	2.0	0.3	0.4	0.0	-.014
NBA Playoff Totals		57	4	538	153	61	130	.469	0	0	.000	31	42	.738	25	53	78	17	83	1	10	25	25	9.4	2.7	1.4	0.3	....

• WILLIAMS, Hot Rod

John (Hot Rod) Williams

Born: Aug. 9, 1962. Sorrento, LA, United States. Height: 6'11". Weight: 215 lbs. Drafted: 1985 College: Tulane

YEAR	TEAM	GP	GS	MIN	PTS	FGM	FGA	FG%	3PM	3PA	3P%	FTM	FTA	FT%	ORB	DRB	TRB	AST	PF	DQ	STL	BLK	TO	MPG	PPG	RPG	APG	PCM
86-87	Cleveland	80	0	2714	1168	435	897	.485	0	1	.000	298	400	.745	222	407	629	154	197	0	58	167	136	33.9	14.6	7.9	1.9	.528
87-88	Cleveland	77	0	2106	843	316	663	.477	0	1	.000	211	279	.756	159	347	506	103	203	2	61	145	108	27.4	10.9	6.6	1.3	.506
88-89	Cleveland	82	0	2125	948	356	700	.509	1	4	.250	235	314	.748	173	304	477	108	188	1	77	134	98	25.9	11.6	5.8	1.3	.550
89-90	Cleveland	82	0	2776	1381	528	1070	.493	0	0	.000	325	440	.739	220	443	663	168	214	2	86	167	139	33.9	16.8	8.1	2.0	.586
90-91	Cleveland	43	14	1293	505	199	430	.463	0	1	.000	107	164	.652	111	179	290	100	126	2	36	69	65	30.1	11.7	6.7	2.3	.478
91-92	Cleveland	80	12	2432	952	341	678	.503	0	4	.000	270	359	.752	228	379	607	196	191	2	60	182	80	30.4	11.9	7.6	2.5	.589
92-93	Cleveland	67	13	2055	738	263	560	.470	0	0	.000	212	296	.716	127	288	415	157	171	2	48	105	114	30.7	11.0	6.2	2.3	.454
93-94	Cleveland	76	72	2660	1040	394	825	.478	0	0	.000	252	346	.728	207	368	575	193	219	3	78	130	137	35.0	13.7	7.6	2.5	.490
94-95	Cleveland	74	73	2641	929	366	810	.452	1	5	.200	196	286	.685	173	334	507	192	211	2	83	101	148	35.7	12.6	6.9	2.6	.411
95-96	Phoenix	62	58	1652	455	180	397	.453	0	1	.000	95	130	.731	129	243	372	62	170	2	46	90	62	26.6	7.3	6.0	1.0	.387
96-97	Phoenix	68	66	2137	541	204	416	.490	0	2	.000	133	198	.672	178	384	562	100	176	1	67	88	68	31.4	8.0	8.3	1.5	.441
97-98	Phoenix	71	30	1333	255	95	202	.470	0	0	.000	65	93	.699	107	205	312	49	138	2	33	60	28	18.8	3.6	4.4	0.7	.360
98-99	Dallas	25	11	403	29	11	33	.333	0	0	.000	7	10	.700	36	47	83	15	49	0	13	18	13	16.1	1.2	3.3	0.6	.230
NBA Season Totals		887	349	26327	9784	3688	7681	.480	2	19	.105	2406	3315	.726	2070	3928	5998	1597	2253	21	746	1456	1196	29.7	11.0	6.8	1.8	....
87-88	Cleveland	5	0	133	46	20	40	.500	0	0	.000	6	13	.462	13	16	29	4	13	0	3	7	4	26.6	9.2	5.8	0.8	.413
88-89	Cleveland	5	2	161	55	21	45	.467	0	0	.000	13	18	.722	7	27	34	10	12	0	2	7	11	32.2	11.0	6.8	2.0	.405
89-90	Cleveland	5	0	174	95	39	70	.557	0	0	.000	17	22	.773	14	32	46	11	23	1	2	5	7	34.8	19.0	9.2	2.2	.619
91-92	Cleveland	17	0	567	255	84	154	.545	0	0	.000	87	109	.798	50	80	130	42	58	2	24	17	31	33.4	15.0	7.6	2.5	.578
92-93	Cleveland	9	0	237	81	30	75	.400	0	0	.000	21	28	.750	12	29	41	17	26	1	5	14	11	26.3	9.0	4.6	1.9	.369
94-95	Cleveland	4	4	144	27	12	42	.286	0	1	.000	3	8	.375	3	22	25	11	11	0	9	3	10	36.0	6.8	6.3	2.8	.197
95-96	Phoenix	4	4	115	36	14	32	.438	0	0	.000	8	12	.667	11	15	26	1	17	1	0	7	6	28.8	9.0	6.5	0.3	.310
96-97	Phoenix	5	5	105	20	8	15	.533	0	0	.000	4	10	.400	10	13	23	3	12	0	2	8	5	21.0	4.0	4.6	0.6	.328
97-98	Phoenix	3	0	33	6	2	7	.286	0	0	.000	2	3	.667	2	2	4	1	8	0	0	2	0	11.0	2.0	1.3	0.3	.118
NBA Playoff Totals		57	15	1669	621	230	480	.479	0	1	.000	161	223	.722	122	236	358	100	180	5	47	70	85	29.3	10.9	6.3	1.8	....

• WILLIAMS, Jason

Jason Chandler Williams

Born: Nov. 18, 1975. Belle, WV, United States. Height: 6'1". Weight: 190 lbs. Drafted: 1998 College: Florida

YEAR	TEAM	GP	GS	MIN	PTS	FGM	FGA	FG%	3PM	3PA	3P%	FTM	FTA	FT%	ORB	DRB	TRB	AST	PF	DQ	STL	BLK	TO	MPG	PPG	RPG	APG	PCM
98-99	Sacramento	50	50	1805	641	231	617	.374	100	323	.310	79	105	.752	14	139	153	299	91	0	95	1	143	36.1	12.8	3.1	6.0	.372
99-00	Sacramento	81	81	2760	999	363	973	.373	145	505	.287	128	170	.753	22	208	230	589	140	0	117	8	296	34.1	12.3	2.8	7.3	.384
00-01	Sacramento	77	77	2290	720	281	690	.407	98	311	.315	60	76	.789	19	166	185	416	114	0	94	9	160	29.7	9.4	2.4	5.4	.379
01-02	Memphis	65	65	2236	959	376	985	.382	127	430	.295	80	101	.792	22	173	195	519	102	0	111	7	214	34.4	14.8	3.0	8.0	.451
02-03	Memphis	76	76	2406	919	333	859	.388	143	404	.354	110	131	.840	25	187	212	631	130	0	91	10	168	31.7	12.1	2.8	8.3	.496
NBA Season Totals		349	349	11497	4238	1584	4124	.384	613	1973	.311	457	583	.784	102	873	975	2454	577	0	508	35	981	32.9	12.1	2.8	7.0	....
98-99	Sacramento	5	5	163	50	16	45	.356	9	29	.310	9	9	1.000	2	16	18	20	15	0	8	1	13	32.6	10.0	3.6	4.0	.320
99-00	Sacramento	5	5	145	52	18	48	.375	8	25	.320	8	10	.800	1	7	8	12	8	0	3	0	8	29.0	10.4	1.6	2.4	.249
00-01	Sacramento	8	8	191	70	26	61	.426	11	30	.367	7	7	1.000	0	18	18	23	14	0	8	0	21	23.9	8.8	2.3	2.9	.325
NBA Playoff Totals		18	18	499	172	60	154	.390	28	84	.333	24	26	.923	3	41	44	55	37	0	19	1	42	27.7	9.6	2.4	3.1	....

• WILLIAMS, Jay

Jason Williams

Born: Sept. 10, 1981. Plainfield, NJ, United States. Height: 6'2". Weight: 195 lbs. Drafted: 2002 College: Duke

YEAR	TEAM	GP	GS	MIN	PTS	FGM	FGA	FG%	3PM	3PA	3P%	FTM	FTA	FT%	ORB	DRB	TRB	AST	PF	DQ	STL	BLK	TO	MPG	PPG	RPG	APG	PCM
02-03	Chicago	75	54	1961	714	273	685	.399	65	202	.322	103	161	.640	27	168	195	350	179	1	86	17	171	26.1	9.5	2.6	4.7	.372
NBA Season Totals		75	54	1961	714	273	685	.399	65	202	.322	103	161	.640	27	168	195	350	179	1	86	17	171	26.1	9.5	2.6	4.7	....

• WILLIAMS, Jayson

Jayson Williams

Born: Feb. 22, 1968. Ritter, SC, United States. Height: 6'9". Weight: 240 lbs. Drafted: 1990 College: St. John's (NY)

YEAR	TEAM	GP	GS	MIN	PTS	FGM	FGA	FG%	3PM	3PA	3P%	FTM	FTA	FT%	ORB	DRB	TRB	AST	PF	DQ	STL	BLK	TO	MPG	PPG	RPG	APG	PCM
90-91	Philadelphia	52	1	508	182	72	161	.447	1	2	.500	37	56	.661	41	70	111	16	92	1	9	6	42	9.8	3.5	2.1	0.3	.281
91-92	Philadelphia	50	8	646	206	75	206	.364	0	0	.000	56	88	.636	62	83	145	12	110	1	20	20	45	12.9	4.1	2.9	0.2	.250
92-93	New Jersey	12	2	139	49	21	46	.457	0	0	.000	7	18	.389	22	19	41	0	24	0	4	4	8	11.6	4.1	3.4	0.0	.342
93-94	New Jersey	70	0	877	322	125	293	.427	0	0	.000	72	119	.605	109	154	263	26	140	1	17	36	35	12.5	4.6	3.8	0.4	.420
94-95	New Jersey	75	6	982	363	149	323	.461	0	5	.000	65	122	.533	179	246	425	35	160	2	26	33	60	13.1	4.8	5.7	0.5	.543
95-96	New Jersey	80	6	1858	721	279	660	.423	2	7	.286	161	272	.592	342	461	803	47	238	4	35	57	104	23.2	9.0	10.0	0.6	.534
96-97	New Jersey	41	40	1432	550	221	540	.409	0	4	.000	108	183	.590	242	311	553	51	158	5	24	36	82	34.9	13.4	13.5	1.2	.484
97-98	New Jersey	65	65	2343	837	321	645	.498	0	4	.000	195	293	.666	**443**	440	883	67	236	7	45	49	98	36.0	12.9	13.6	1.0	.540
98-99	New Jersey	30	30	1020	242	97	218	.445	0	2	.000	48	85	.565	147	213	360	33	126	3	24	60	46	34.0	8.1	12.0	1.1	.444
NBA Season Totals		475	158	9805	3472	1360	3092	.440	3	24	.125	749	1236	.606	1587	1997	3584	287	1284	24	204	301	520	20.6	7.3	7.5	0.6	....
90-91	Philadelphia	4	0	10	8	4	5	.800	0	0	.000	0	0	.000	2	2	4	0	1	0	0	0	1	2.5	2.0	1.0	0.0	.940
93-94	New Jersey	2	0	17	1	0	3	.000	0	0	.000	1	2	.500	3	0	3	0	5	0	0	0	2	8.5	0.5	1.5	0.0	-.211
97-98	New Jersey	3	2	116	21	9	21	.429	0	0	.000	3	6	.500	20	22	42	5	8	0	2	3	2	38.7	7.0	14.0	1.7	.445
NBA Playoff Totals		9	2	143	30	13	29	.448	0	0	.000	4	8	.500	25	24	49	5	14	0	2	3	5	15.9	3.3	5.4	0.6	....

• WILLIAMS, Jerome

Jerome (Junk Yard Dog) Williams

Born: May 10, 1973. Washington, DC, United States. Height: 6'9". Weight: 206 lbs. Drafted: 1996 College: Georgetown

YEAR	TEAM	GP	GS	MIN	PTS	FGM	FGA	FG%	3PM	3PA	3P%	FTM	FTA	FT%	ORB	DRB	TRB	AST	PF	DQ	STL	BLK	TO	MPG	PPG	RPG	APG	PCM
96-97	Detroit	33	0	177	49	20	51	.392	0	0	.000	9	17	.529	22	28	50	7	18	0	13	1	13	5.4	1.5	1.5	0.2	.356
97-98	Detroit	77	3	1305	410	151	288	.524	0	1	.000	108	166	.651	170	209	379	48	144	1	51	10	62	16.9	5.3	4.9	0.6	.452
98-99	Detroit	50	10	1154	355	124	248	.500	0	0	.000	107	159	.673	158	191	349	23	108	0	63	7	41	23.1	7.1	7.0	0.5	.464
99-00	Detroit	82	1	2102	689	257	456	.564	0	3	.000	175	284	.616	277	512	789	68	196	0	95	21	105	25.6	8.4	9.6	0.8	.557
00-01	Detroit	33	2	804	241	88	201	.438	0	2	.000	65	90	.722	98	180	278	32	81	0	39	10	47	24.4	7.3	8.4	1.0	.471
00-01	Toronto	26	0	378	131	48	93	.516	0	1	.000	35	45	.778	35	69	104	13	43	0	18	10	16	14.5	5.0	4.0	0.5	.490
01-02	Toronto	68	32	1641	518	190	388	.490	0	0	.000	138	204	.676	165	221	386	75	153	0	78	25	68	24.1	7.6	5.7	1.1	.428
02-03	Toronto	71	63	2346	691	267	535	.499	1	6	.167	156	281	.555	231	419	650	95	197	2	116	26	98	33.0	9.7	9.2	1.3	.441
NBA Season Totals		440	111	9907	3084	1145	2260	.507	1	13	.077	793	1246	.636	1156	1829	2985	361	940	3	473	110	450	22.5	7.0	6.8	0.8	....
96-97	Detroit	1	0	5	4	2	2	1.000	0	0	.000	0	0	.000	0	3	3	0	0	0	1	0	1	5.0	4.0	3.0	0.0	1.359
98-99	Detroit	5	5	123	31	12	27	.444	0	0	.000	7	9	.778	12	20	32	4	7	0	4	0	4	24.6	6.2	6.4	0.8	.379
99-00	Detroit	3	0	73	15	7	14	.500	0	0	.000	1	8	.125	7	14	21	2	8	0	3	0	3	24.3	5.0	7.0	0.7	.316
00-01	Toronto	11	0	164	35	12	24	.500	0	0	.000	11	22	.500	20	25	45	9	23	0	10	6	6	14.9	3.2	4.1	0.8	.416
01-02	Toronto	5	1	143	36	14	33	.424	0	0	.000	8	12	.667	16	17	33	7	19	0	9	1	4	28.6	7.2	6.6	1.4	.359
NBA Playoff Totals		25	6	508	121	47	100	.470	0	0	.000	27	51	.529	55	79	134	22	57	0	27	7	18	20.3	4.8	5.4	0.9	....

• WILLIAMS, John

John Sam (Rock) Williams

Born: Oct. 26, 1966. Los Angeles, CA, United States. Height: 6'8". Weight: 235 lbs. Drafted: 1986 College: Louisiana State

YEAR	TEAM	GP	GS	MIN	PTS	FGM	FGA	FG%	3PM	3PA	3P%	FTM	FTA	FT%	ORB	DRB	TRB	AST	PF	DQ	STL	BLK	TO	MPG	PPG	RPG	APG	PCM
86-87	Washington	78	0	1773	718	283	624	.454	8	36	.222	144	223	.646	130	236	366	191	173	1	129	30	125	22.7	9.2	4.7	2.4	.485
87-88	Washington	82	0	2428	1047	427	910	.469	5	38	.132	188	256	.734	127	317	444	232	217	3	117	34	148	29.6	12.8	5.4	2.8	.465
88-89	Washington	82	0	2413	1120	438	940	.466	19	71	.268	225	290	.776	158	415	573	356	213	1	142	70	156	29.4	13.7	7.0	4.3	.617
89-90	Washington	18	0	632	327	130	274	.474	2	18	.111	65	84	.774	27	109	136	84	33	0	21	9	43	35.1	18.2	7.6	4.7	.589
90-91	Washington	33	11	941	411	164	393	.417	10	41	.244	73	97	.753	42	135	177	133	63	0	39	6	69	28.5	12.5	5.4	4.0	.469
92-93	LA Clippers	74	8	1638	492	205	477	.430	12	53	.226	70	129	.543	88	228	316	142	188	1	83	23	81	22.1	6.6	4.3	1.9	.362
93-94	LA Clippers	34	6	725	191	81	188	.431	5	20	.250	24	36	.667	37	90	127	97	85	1	25	10	34	21.3	5.6	3.7	2.9	.374
94-95	Indiana	34	0	402	100	41	115	.357	4	12	.333	14	25	.560	23	39	62	27	48	0	10	2	34	11.8	2.9	1.8	0.8	.172
NBA Season Totals		435	25	10952	4406	1769	3921	.451	65	289	.225	803	1140	.704	632	1569	2201	1262	1020	7	566	184	690	25.2	10.1	5.1	2.9	....
86-87	Washington	3	0	49	20	8	14	.571	0	1	.000	4	7	.571	4	7	11	2	3	0	2	0	2	16.3	6.7	3.7	0.7	.490
87-88	Washington	5	5	185	65	23	48	.479	0	1	.000	19	32	.594	11	18	29	21	18	1	8	4	12	37.0	13.0	5.8	4.2	.415
92-93	LA Clippers	5	0	98	11	4	18	.222	2	3	.667	1	2	.500	5	9	14	7	17	1	5	0	6	19.6	2.2	2.8	1.4	.093
NBA Playoff Totals		13	5	332	96	35	80	.438	2	5	.400	24	41	.585	20	34	54	30	38	2	15	4	20	25.5	7.4	4.2	2.3	....

• WILLIAMS, Kenny

Kenneth Ray Williams

Born: June 9, 1969. Elizabeth City, NC, United States. Height: 6'9". Weight: 205 lbs. Drafted: 1990 College: Elizabeth City State(DNP)

YEAR	TEAM	GP	GS	MIN	PTS	FGM	FGA	FG%	3PM	3PA	3P%	FTM	FTA	FT%	ORB	DRB	TRB	AST	PF	DQ	STL	BLK	TO	MPG	PPG	RPG	APG	PCM
90-91	Indiana	75	0	527	220	93	179	.520	0	3	.000	34	50	.680	56	75	131	31	81	0	11	31	38	7.0	2.9	1.7	0.4	.481
91-92	Indiana	60	6	565	252	113	218	.518	0	4	.000	26	43	.605	64	65	129	40	99	0	20	41	24	9.4	4.2	2.2	0.7	.527
92-93	Indiana	57	0	844	348	150	282	.532	0	3	.000	48	68	.706	102	126	228	38	87	1	21	44	29	14.8	6.1	4.0	0.7	.547
93-94	Indiana	68	1	982	427	191	391	.488	0	4	.000	45	64	.703	93	112	205	52	99	0	24	49	48	14.4	6.3	3.0	0.8	.465
NBA Season Totals		260	7	2918	1247	547	1070	.511	0	14	.000	153	225	.680	315	378	693	161	366	1	76	165	139	11.2	4.8	2.7	0.6	....
90-91	Indiana	2	0	2	0	0	0	.000	0	0	.000	0	2	.000	0	0	0	0	1	0	0	0	0	1.0	0.0	0.0	0.0	-.700
91-92	Indiana	1	0	1	0	0	0	.000	0	0	.000	0	0	.000	0	0	0	0	0	0	1	0	0	1.0	0.0	0.0	0.0	.929
92-93	Indiana	2	0	11	2	1	1	1.000	0	0	.000	0	2	.000	0	0	0	2	1	0	0	2	1	5.5	1.0	0.0	1.0	.333
93-94	Indiana	12	0	91	20	9	25	.360	0	0	.000	2	2	1.000	6	11	17	5	18	0	5	3	5	7.6	1.7	1.4	0.4	.229
NBA Playoff Totals		17	0	105	22	10	26	.385	0	0	.000	2	6	.333	6	11	17	7	20	0	6	5	6	6.2	1.3	1.0	0.4	....

• WILLIAMS, Kevin

Kevin Eugene Williams

Born: Sept. 11, 1961. New York, NY, United States. Height: 6'2". Weight: 175 lbs. Drafted: 1983 College: St. John's (NY)

YEAR	TEAM	GP	GS	MIN	PTS	FGM	FGA	FG%	3PM	3PA	3P%	FTM	FTA	FT%	ORB	DRB	TRB	AST	PF	DQ	STL	BLK	TO	MPG	PPG	RPG	APG	PCM
83-84	San Antonio	19	0	200	75	25	58	.431	0	1	.000	25	32	.781	4	9	13	43	42	1	8	4	23	10.5	3.9	0.7	2.3	.347
84-85	Cleveland	46	4	413	163	58	134	.433	0	5	.000	47	64	.734	19	44	63	61	86	1	22	4	51	9.0	3.5	1.4	1.3	.350
86-87	Seattle	65	0	703	319	132	296	.446	0	7	.000	55	66	.833	47	36	83	66	154	1	45	8	65	10.8	4.9	1.3	1.0	.322

YEAR	TEAM	GP	GS	MIN	PTS	FGM	FGA	FG%	3PM	3PA	3P%	FTM	FTA	FT%	ORB	DRB	TRB	AST	PF	DQ	STL	BLK	TO	MPG	PPG	RPG	APG	PCM
87-88	Seattle	80	9	1084	502	199	450	.442	1	7	.143	103	122	.844	61	66	127	96	207	1	62	7	64	13.6	6.3	1.6	1.2	.358
88-89	New Jersey	41	0	433	175	67	168	.399	1	6	.167	40	51	.784	19	31	50	36	74	0	25	8	41	10.6	4.3	1.2	0.9	.275
88-89	LA Clippers	9	0	114	34	14	32	.438	0	0	.000	6	8	.750	9	11	20	17	17	0	5	3	10	12.7	3.8	2.2	1.9	.380
NBA Season Totals		260	13	2947	1268	495	1138	.435	2	26	.077	276	343	.805	159	197	356	319	580	4	167	34	254	11.3	4.9	1.4	1.2	....
84-85	Cleveland	2	0	7	2	1	2	.500	0	0	.000	0	0	.000	0	0	0	1	1	0	0	0	0	3.5	1.0	0.0	0.5	.239
86-87	Seattle	14	0	255	120	45	94	.479	0	2	.000	30	40	.750	19	15	34	30	44	0	16	1	10	18.2	8.6	2.4	2.1	.469
87-88	Seattle	5	0	70	14	7	16	.438	0	2	.000	0	0	.000	6	2	8	9	15	0	3	0	4	14.0	2.8	1.6	1.8	.211
NBA Playoff Totals		21	0	332	136	53	112	.473	0	4	.000	30	40	.750	25	17	42	40	60	0	19	1	14	15.8	6.5	2.0	1.9	....

• WILLIAMS, Lorenzo

Lorenzo Williams

Born: July 15, 1969. Ocala, FL, United States.   Height: 6'9".   Weight: 200 lbs.   Drafted: —   College: Stetson

YEAR	TEAM	GP	GS	MIN	PTS	FGM	FGA	FG%	3PM	3PA	3P%	FTM	FTA	FT%	ORB	DRB	TRB	AST	PF	DQ	STL	BLK	TO	MPG	PPG	RPG	APG	PCM
92-93	Charlotte	2	0	18	2	1	3	.333	0	0	.000	0	0	.000	3	6	9	0	4	0	0	2	2	9.0	1.0	4.5	0.0	.370
92-93	Orlando	3	0	10	0	0	2	.000	0	0	.000	0	0	.000	1	1	2	0	2	0	1	1	0	3.3	0.0	0.7	0.0	.093
92-93	Boston	22	7	151	34	16	31	.516	0	0	.000	2	7	.286	13	31	44	5	23	0	4	14	7	6.9	1.5	2.0	0.2	.421
93-94	Orlando	3	0	19	2	1	6	.167	0	1	.000	0	0	.000	3	1	4	2	3	0	2	3	0	6.3	0.7	1.3	0.7	.340
93-94	Charlotte	1	0	19	0	0	1	.000	0	0	.000	0	0	.000	0	4	4	0	2	0	1	2	1	19.0	0.0	4.0	0.0	.193
93-94	Dallas	34	11	678	108	48	103	.466	0	0	.000	12	28	.429	92	117	209	23	87	0	15	41	20	19.9	3.2	6.1	0.7	.383
94-95	Dallas	82	81	2383	328	145	304	.477	0	0	.000	38	101	.376	291	399	690	124	306	6	52	148	107	29.1	4.0	8.4	1.5	.366
95-96	Dallas	65	61	1806	198	87	214	.407	0	1	.000	24	70	.343	234	287	521	85	226	9	48	122	78	27.8	3.0	8.0	1.3	.342
96-97	Washington	19	0	264	45	20	31	.645	0	0	.000	5	7	.714	28	41	69	4	49	0	6	8	17	13.9	2.4	3.6	0.2	.291
97-98	Washington	14	6	111	26	13	17	.765	0	0	.000	0	2	.000	16	10	26	3	17	0	2	3	1	7.9	1.9	1.9	0.2	.400
99-00	Washington	8	0	76	14	7	9	.778	0	0	.000	0	0	.000	12	13	25	1	13	0	3	6	3	9.5	1.8	3.1	0.1	.467
NBA Season Totals		253	166	5535	757	338	721	.469	0	2	.000	81	215	.377	693	910	1603	247	732	15	134	350	236	21.9	3.0	6.3	1.0	....
92-93	Boston	1	0	3	2	1	1	1.000	0	0	.000	0	0	.000	1	0	1	0	0	0	0	0	0	3.0	2.0	1.0	0.0	.978
96-97	Washington	2	0	5	0	0	0	.000	0	0	.000	0	0	.000	0	0	0	0	1	0	0	0	0	2.5	0.0	0.0	0.0	-.093
NBA Playoff Totals		3	0	8	2	1	1	1.000	0	0	.000	0	0	.000	1	0	1	0	1	0	0	0	0	2.7	0.7	0.3	0.0	....

• WILLIAMS, Micheal

Micheal Douglas Williams

Born: July 23, 1966. Dallas, TX, United States.   Height: 6'2".   Weight: 175 lbs.   Drafted: 1988   College: Baylor

YEAR	TEAM	GP	GS	MIN	PTS	FGM	FGA	FG%	3PM	3PA	3P%	FTM	FTA	FT%	ORB	DRB	TRB	AST	PF	DQ	STL	BLK	TO	MPG	PPG	RPG	APG	PCM
88-89	Detroit	49	0	358	127	47	129	.364	2	9	.222	31	47	.660	9	18	27	70	44	0	13	3	44	7.3	2.6	0.6	1.4	.270
89-90	Phoenix	6	0	26	5	2	10	.200	0	0	.000	1	2	.500	1	0	1	4	0	0	0	0	5	4.3	0.8	0.2	0.7	-.095
89-90	Charlotte	22	1	303	151	58	109	.532	0	3	.000	35	44	.795	11	20	31	77	39	0	22	1	29	13.8	6.9	1.4	3.5	.614
90-91	Indiana	73	37	1706	813	261	523	.499	1	7	.143	290	330	.879	49	127	176	348	202	1	150	17	153	23.4	11.1	2.4	4.8	.589
91-92	Indiana	79	76	2750	1188	404	824	.490	8	33	.242	372	427	.871	73	209	282	647	262	7	233	22	237	34.8	15.0	3.6	8.2	.590
92-93	Minnesota	76	76	2661	1151	353	791	.446	26	107	.243	419	462	.907	84	189	273	661	268	7	165	23	228	35.0	15.1	3.6	8.7	.571
93-94	Minnesota	71	66	2206	971	314	687	.457	10	45	.222	333	397	.839	67	154	221	512	193	3	118	24	206	31.1	13.7	3.1	7.2	.548
94-95	Minnesota	1	1	28	6	1	4	.250	0	0	.000	4	5	.800	0	1	1	3	3	0	2	0	3	28.0	6.0	1.0	3.0	.161
95-96	Minnesota	9	7	189	55	13	40	.325	1	3	.333	28	33	.848	3	20	23	31	37	0	5	3	23	21.0	6.1	2.6	3.4	.266
97-98	Minnesota	25	0	161	64	16	48	.333	0	4	.000	32	33	.970	2	12	14	32	24	0	9	2	15	6.4	2.6	0.6	1.3	.417
98-99	Toronto	2	0	15	2	1	5	.200	0	0	.000	0	0	.000	1	0	1	0	1	0	0	0	1	7.5	1.0	0.5	0.0	-.133
NBA Season Totals		413	264	10403	4533	1470	3170	.464	48	211	.227	1545	1780	.868	300	750	1050	2385	1073	18	717	95	944	25.2	11.0	2.5	5.8	....
88-89	Detroit	4	0	6	2	0	0	.000	0	0	.000	2	2	1.000	1	1	2	2	1	0	1	0	0	1.5	0.5	0.5	0.5	1.078
90-91	Indiana	5	5	183	103	30	65	.462	0	1	.000	43	48	.896	7	9	16	42	23	2	14	0	12	36.6	20.6	3.2	8.4	.650
91-92	Indiana	3	3	106	50	18	43	.419	3	9	.333	11	15	.733	1	7	8	24	12	0	9	0	7	35.3	16.7	2.7	8.0	.513
97-98	Minnesota	4	0	58	20	6	15	.400	1	2	.500	7	9	.778	2	7	9	11	14	0	3	1	3	14.5	5.0	2.3	2.8	.440
NBA Playoff Totals		16	8	353	175	54	123	.439	4	12	.333	63	74	.851	11	24	35	79	50	2	27	1	22	22.1	10.9	2.2	4.9	....

• WILLIAMS, Mike

Michael George Williams

Born: Aug. 14, 1963. Chicago, IL, United States.   Height: 6'8".   Weight: 255 lbs.   Drafted: 1986   College: Bradley

YEAR	TEAM	GP	GS	MIN	PTS	FGM	FGA	FG%	3PM	3PA	3P%	FTM	FTA	FT%	ORB	DRB	TRB	AST	PF	DQ	STL	BLK	TO	MPG	PPG	RPG	APG	PCM
89-90	Sacramento	16	0	88	15	6	14	.429	0	1	.000	3	6	.500	5	17	22	2	28	0	3	7	3	5.5	0.9	1.4	0.1	.253
89-90	Atlanta	5	0	14	0	0	4	.000	0	0	.000	0	0	.000	0	1	1	0	2	0	0	0	0	2.8	0.0	0.2	0.0	-.268
NBA Season Totals		21	0	102	15	6	18	.333	0	1	.000	3	6	.500	5	18	23	2	30	0	3	7	3	4.9	0.7	1.1	0.1	....

• WILLIAMS, Milt

Milton Williams

Born: Nov. 22, 1945. Seattle, WA, United States.   Height: 6'2".   Weight: 182 lbs.   Drafted: 1968   College: Lincoln (MO)

YEAR	TEAM	GP	GS	MIN	PTS	FGM	FGA	FG%	3PM	3PA	3P%	FTM	FTA	FT%	ORB	DRB	TRB	AST	PF	DQ	STL	BLK	TO	MPG	PPG	RPG	APG	PCM
70-71	New York	5	....	13	4	1	1	1.000	....	....	....	2	3	.667	....	....	0	2	3	0	....	....	....	2.6	0.8	0.0	0.4	.351
71-72	Atlanta	10	....	127	67	23	53	.434	....	....	....	21	29	.724	....	....	4	20	18	0	....	....	....	12.7	6.7	0.4	2.0	.441
73-74	Seattle	53	....	505	165	62	149	.416	....	....	....	41	63	.651	19	28	47	103	82	1	25	0	....	9.5	3.1	0.9	1.9	.406
74-75	St. Louis-A	4	....	95	22	11	19	.579	0	0	.000	0	0	.000	4	9	13	12	10	....	10	0	10	23.8	5.5	3.3	3.0	.372
NBA Season Totals		68	....	645	236	86	203	.424	....	....	....	64	95	.674	19	28	51	125	103	1	25	0	....	9.5	3.5	0.8	1.8	....
ABA Season Totals		4	....	95	22	11	19	.579	0	0	.000	0	0	.000	4	9	13	12	10	....	10	0	10	23.8	5.5	3.3	3.0	....
Career Totals		72	....	740	258	97	222	.437	0	0	.000	64	95	.674	23	37	64	137	113	1	35	0	10	10.3	3.6	0.9	1.9	....

• WILLIAMS, Monty

Tavares Montgomery Williams

Born: Oct. 8, 1971. Fredericksburg, VA, United States.   Height: 6'8".   Weight: 225 lbs.   Drafted: 1994   College: Notre Dame

YEAR	TEAM	GP	GS	MIN	PTS	FGM	FGA	FG%	3PM	3PA	3P%	FTM	FTA	FT%	ORB	DRB	TRB	AST	PF	DQ	STL	BLK	TO	MPG	PPG	RPG	APG	PCM
94-95	New York	41	23	503	137	60	133	.451	0	8	.000	17	38	.447	42	56	98	49	87	0	20	4	41	12.3	3.3	2.4	1.2	.290
95-96	New York	14	0	62	19	7	22	.318	0	0	.000	5	8	.625	9	8	17	4	9	0	2	0	6	4.4	1.4	1.2	0.3	.254
95-96	San Antonio	17	0	122	49	20	46	.435	0	1	.000	9	12	.750	11	12	23	4	17	0	4	2	14	7.2	2.9	1.4	0.2	.275
96-97	San Antonio	65	26	1345	588	234	460	.509	0	1	.000	120	186	.645	98	108	206	91	161	1	55	52	117	20.7	9.0	3.2	1.4	.410
97-98	San Antonio	72	16	1314	453	165	368	.448	1	2	.500	122	182	.670	67	112	179	89	133	1	34	24	79	18.3	6.3	2.5	1.2	.320
98-99	Denver	1	0	6	1	0	2	.000	0	1	.000	1	2	.500	0	0	0	0	0	0	0	0	0	6.0	1.0	0.0	0.0	-.204
99-00	Orlando	75	23	1501	651	263	538	.489	2	5	.400	123	166	.741	96	154	250	106	187	1	46	17	109	20.0	8.7	3.3	1.4	.398

YEAR	TEAM	GP	GS	MIN	PTS	FGM	FGA	FG%	3PM	3PA	3P%	FTM	FTA	FT%	ORB	DRB	TRB	AST	PF	DQ	STL	BLK	TO	MPG	PPG	RPG	APG	PCM
00-01	Orlando	82	0	1211	410	162	364	.445	1	13	.077	85	133	.639	86	157	243	79	136	1	29	16	85	14.8	5.0	3.0	1.0	.343
01-02	Orlando	68	19	1284	484	198	362	.547	0	4	.000	88	134	.657	80	155	235	96	134	1	49	17	86	18.9	7.1	3.5	1.4	.431
02-03	Philadelphia	21	2	276	92	34	80	.425	0	2	.000	24	32	.750	12	33	45	26	33	0	12	5	17	13.1	4.4	2.1	1.2	.365
NBA Season Totals		**456**	**109**	**7624**	**2884**	**1143**	**2375**	**.481**	**4**	**36**	**.111**	**594**	**893**	**.665**	**501**	**795**	**1296**	**544**	**897**	**5**	**251**	**137**	**554**	**16.7**	**6.3**	**2.8**	**1.2**	....
94-95	New York	1	0	4	4	2	2	1.000	0	0	.000	0	0	.000	0	0	0	0	1	0	0	0	0	4.0	4.0	0.0	0.0	.883
95-96	San Antonio	7	0	29	7	2	9	.222	0	0	.000	3	6	.500	3	4	7	0	4	0	0	0	4	4.1	1.0	1.0	0.0	-.002
97-98	San Antonio	5	0	28	12	5	8	.625	0	0	.000	2	3	.667	2	4	6	1	2	0	0	0	4	5.6	2.4	1.2	0.2	.386
00-01	Orlando	3	0	14	7	3	4	.750	0	0	.000	1	3	.333	4	2	6	0	2	0	0	2	1	4.7	2.3	2.0	0.0	.757
01-02	Orlando	4	3	93	34	14	27	.519	0	1	.000	6	10	.600	7	15	22	9	8	0	3	0	5	23.3	8.5	5.5	2.3	.481
02-03	Philadelphia	10	0	96	19	8	23	.348	0	1	.000	3	4	.750	7	8	15	0	12	0	2	0	4	9.6	1.9	1.5	0.0	.118
NBA Playoff Totals		**30**	**3**	**264**	**83**	**34**	**73**	**.466**	**0**	**2**	**.000**	**15**	**26**	**.577**	**23**	**33**	**56**	**10**	**29**	**0**	**5**	**2**	**18**	**8.8**	**2.8**	**1.9**	**0.3**	....

• WILLIAMS, Nate

Nathaniel Russell Williams

Born: May 2, 1950. Columbia, LA, United States. Height: 6'5". Weight: 215 lbs. Drafted: 1971 College: Utah State

YEAR	TEAM	GP	GS	MIN	PTS	FGM	FGA	FG%	3PM	3PA	3P%	FTM	FTA	FT%	ORB	DRB	TRB	AST	PF	DQ	STL	BLK	TO	MPG	PPG	RPG	APG	PCM
71-72	Cincinnati	81	....	2173	963	418	968	.432	....	....	....	127	172	.738	....	....	372	174	300	11	....	....	....	26.8	11.9	4.6	2.1	.395
72-73	Omaha	80	....	1079	940	417	874	.477	....	....	....	106	133	.797	....	....	339	128	272	9	....	....	....	13.5	11.8	4.2	1.6	.794
73-74	Omaha	82	....	2513	1269	538	1165	.462	....	....	....	193	236	.818	118	226	344	182	290	5	149	34	....	30.6	15.5	4.2	2.2	.436
74-75	Omaha	50	....	1131	627	265	584	.454	....	....	....	97	118	.822	58	121	179	78	152	2	53	24	....	22.6	12.5	3.6	1.6	.463
74-75	New Orleans	35	....	814	502	209	404	.517	....	....	....	84	102	.824	44	114	158	67	99	1	44	6	....	23.3	14.3	4.5	1.9	.611
75-76	New Orleans	81	....	1935	1039	421	948	.444	....	....	....	197	239	.824	135	225	360	107	253	6	109	17	....	23.9	12.8	4.4	1.3	.461
76-77	New Orleans	79	....	1776	974	414	917	.451	....	....	....	146	194	.753	107	199	306	92	200	0	76	16	....	22.5	12.3	3.9	1.2	.451
77-78	New Orleans	27	....	434	211	90	214	.421	....	....	....	31	37	.838	27	63	90	34	61	1	21	12	24	16.1	7.8	3.3	1.3	.456
77-78	Golden State	46	....	815	514	222	510	.435	....	....	....	70	84	.833	38	76	114	40	120	2	36	22	60	17.7	11.2	2.5	0.9	.425
78-79	Golden State	81	....	1299	670	284	567	.501	....	....	....	102	117	.872	68	139	207	61	169	0	55	5	89	16.0	8.3	2.6	0.8	.431
NBA Season Totals		**642**	....	**13969**	**7709**	**3278**	**7151**	**.458**	....	....	....	**1153**	**1432**	**.805**	**595**	**1163**	**2469**	**963**	**1916**	**37**	**543**	**136**	**173**	**21.8**	**12.0**	**3.8**	**1.5**	....

• WILLIAMS, Pete

Robert Eric Williams

Born: Mar. 10, 1965. Harbor City, CA, United States. Height: 6'7". Weight: 190 lbs. Drafted: 1985 College: Arizona

YEAR	TEAM	GP	GS	MIN	PTS	FGM	FGA	FG%	3PM	3PA	3P%	FTM	FTA	FT%	ORB	DRB	TRB	AST	PF	DQ	STL	BLK	TO	MPG	PPG	RPG	APG	PCM
85-86	Denver	53	11	573	151	67	111	.604	0	0	.000	17	40	.425	47	99	146	14	68	1	19	23	21	10.8	2.8	2.8	0.3	.415
86-87	Denver	5	0	10	2	1	2	.500	0	0	.000	0	0	.000	0	1	1	1	1	0	0	0	1	2.0	0.4	0.2	0.2	.167
NBA Season Totals		**58**	**11**	**583**	**153**	**68**	**113**	**.602**	**0**	**0**	**.000**	**17**	**40**	**.425**	**47**	**100**	**147**	**15**	**69**	**1**	**19**	**23**	**22**	**10.1**	**2.6**	**2.5**	**0.3**	....
85-86	Denver	4	0	18	4	2	4	.500	0	1	.000	0	0	.000	1	3	4	3	2	0	0	0	0	4.5	1.0	1.0	0.8	.452
NBA Playoff Totals		**4**	**0**	**18**	**4**	**2**	**4**	**.500**	**0**	**1**	**.000**	**0**	**0**	**.000**	**1**	**3**	**4**	**3**	**2**	**0**	**0**	**0**	**0**	**4.5**	**1.0**	**1.0**	**0.8**	....

• WILLIAMS, Ray

Thomas Ray Williams

Born: Oct. 14, 1954. Mount Vernon, NY, United States. Height: 6'3". Weight: 188 lbs. Drafted: 1977 College: Minnesota

YEAR	TEAM	GP	GS	MIN	PTS	FGM	FGA	FG%	3PM	3PA	3P%	FTM	FTA	FT%	ORB	DRB	TRB	AST	PF	DQ	STL	BLK	TO	MPG	PPG	RPG	APG	PCM
77-78	New York	81	....	1550	756	305	689	.443	....	....	....	146	207	.705	85	124	209	363	211	4	108	15	243	19.1	9.3	2.6	4.5	.508
78-79	New York	81	....	2370	1401	575	1257	.457	....	....	....	251	313	.802	104	187	291	504	274	4	128	19	284	29.3	17.3	3.6	6.2	.562
79-80	New York	82	....	2582	1714	687	1384	.496	7	37	.189	333	423	.787	149	263	412	512	295	5	167	24	254	31.5	20.9	5.0	6.2	.692
80-81	New York	79	....	2742	1560	616	1335	.461	16	68	.235	312	382	.817	122	199	321	432	270	4	185	37	237	34.7	19.7	4.1	5.5	.547
81-82	New Jersey	82	69	2732	1674	639	1383	.462	9	54	.167	387	465	.832	117	208	325	488	302	9	199	43	287	33.3	20.4	4.0	6.0	.585
82-83	Kansas City	72	68	2170	1109	419	1068	.392	15	74	.203	256	333	.769	93	234	327	569	248	3	120	26	**338**	30.1	15.4	4.5	7.9	.518
83-84	New York	76	63	2230	1124	418	939	.445	25	81	.309	263	318	.827	67	200	267	449	274	5	162	26	220	29.3	14.8	3.5	5.9	.532
84-85	Boston	23	5	459	147	55	143	.385	6	23	.261	31	46	.674	16	41	57	90	56	1	30	5	41	20.0	6.4	2.5	3.9	.382
85-86	Atlanta	19	13	367	159	57	143	.399	4	11	.364	41	48	.854	19	26	45	67	48	1	28	1	42	19.3	8.4	2.4	3.5	.422
85-86	San Antonio	23	8	397	164	50	131	.382	2	6	.333	62	64	.969	13	24	37	111	64	1	28	3	51	17.3	7.1	1.6	4.8	.486
85-86	New Jersey	5	0	63	32	10	32	.313	0	2	.000	12	14	.857	3	1	4	9	12	0	5	0	9	12.6	6.4	0.8	1.8	.233
86-87	New Jersey	32	14	800	318	131	290	.452	7	28	.250	49	60	.817	26	49	75	185	111	4	38	9	93	25.0	9.9	2.3	5.8	.422
NBA Season Totals		**655**	**240**	**18462**	**10158**	**3962**	**8794**	**.451**	**91**	**384**	**.237**	**2143**	**2673**	**.802**	**814**	**1556**	**2370**	**3779**	**2165**	**41**	**1198**	**208**	**2099**	**28.2**	**15.5**	**3.6**	**5.8**	....
77-78	New York	6	....	140	105	41	78	.526	....	....	....	23	26	.885	6	9	15	31	25	0	6	0	17	23.3	17.5	2.5	5.2	.705
80-81	New York	2	....	84	43	18	41	.439	1	3	.333	6	11	.545	3	5	8	9	10	1	4	0	9	42.0	21.5	4.0	4.5	.330
81-82	New Jersey	2	2	77	34	14	47	.298	2	5	.400	4	5	.800	8	4	12	14	10	0	4	0	6	38.5	17.0	6.0	7.0	.297
83-84	New York	11	6	310	123	46	130	.354	2	12	.167	29	39	.744	8	31	39	88	39	1	17	1	41	28.2	11.2	3.5	8.0	.423
84-85	Boston	19	0	278	120	47	116	.405	2	15	.133	24	25	.960	14	22	36	60	44	0	12	1	33	14.6	6.3	1.9	3.2	.409
NBA Playoff Totals		**40**	**8**	**889**	**425**	**166**	**412**	**.403**	**7**	**35**	**.200**	**86**	**106**	**.811**	**39**	**71**	**110**	**202**	**128**	**2**	**43**	**2**	**106**	**22.2**	**10.6**	**2.8**	**5.1**	....

• WILLIAMS, Reggie

Reggie (Silk) Williams

Born: Mar. 5, 1964. Baltimore, MD, United States. Height: 6'7". Weight: 190 lbs. Drafted: 1987 College: Georgetown

YEAR	TEAM	GP	GS	MIN	PTS	FGM	FGA	FG%	3PM	3PA	3P%	FTM	FTA	FT%	ORB	DRB	TRB	AST	PF	DQ	STL	BLK	TO	MPG	PPG	RPG	APG	PCM
87-88	LA Clippers	35	0	857	365	152	427	.356	13	58	.224	48	66	.727	55	63	118	58	108	1	29	21	63	24.5	10.4	3.4	1.7	.245
88-89	LA Clippers	63	0	1303	642	260	594	.438	30	104	.288	92	122	.754	70	109	179	103	181	1	81	29	113	20.7	10.2	2.8	1.6	.389
89-90	LA Clippers	5	5	133	60	21	57	.368	0	5	.000	18	21	.857	8	7	15	10	7	0	9	1	9	26.6	12.0	3.0	2.0	.355
89-90	Cleveland	32	12	542	218	91	239	.381	6	27	.222	30	41	.732	17	43	60	38	79	2	22	10	32	16.9	6.8	1.9	1.2	.247
89-90	San Antonio	10	0	68	42	19	42	.452	0	5	.000	4	6	.667	3	5	8	5	16	0	1	3	4	6.8	4.2	0.8	0.5	.365
90-91	San Antonio	22	0	354	171	61	127	.480	14	26	.538	35	41	.854	17	42	59	46	64	2	20	11	35	16.1	7.8	2.7	2.1	.500
90-91	Denver	51	46	1542	820	323	728	.444	43	131	.328	131	156	.840	116	131	247	87	189	7	93	30	77	30.2	16.1	4.8	1.7	.459
91-92	Denver	81	80	2623	1474	601	1277	.471	56	156	.359	216	269	.803	145	260	405	235	270	4	148	68	170	32.4	18.2	5.0	2.9	.521
92-93	Denver	79	79	2722	1341	535	1167	.458	33	122	.270	238	296	.804	132	296	428	295	284	6	126	76	198	34.5	17.0	5.4	3.7	.481
93-94	Denver	82	68	2654	1065	418	1014	.412	64	230	.278	165	225	.733	98	294	392	300	288	3	117	66	164	32.4	13.0	4.8	3.7	.400
94-95	Denver	74	70	2198	993	388	846	.459	85	266	.320	132	174	.759	94	235	329	231	264	4	114	67	126	29.7	13.4	4.4	3.1	.467
95-96	Denver	52	5	817	241	94	254	.370	20	89	.225	33	39	.846	25	97	122	74	137	1	34	21	52	15.7	4.6	2.3	1.4	.268
96-97	Indiana	2	0	33	5	2	9	.222	0	1	.000	1	2	.500	1	6	7	2	5	0	0	0	2	16.5	2.5	3.5	1.0	.075
96-97	New Jersey	11	0	167	71	27	67	.403	9	33	.273	8	10	.800	4	20	24	8	28	0	8	4	10	15.2	6.5	2.2	0.7	.314
NBA Season Totals		**599**	**365**	**16013**	**7508**	**2992**	**6848**	**.437**	**373**	**1253**	**.298**	**1151**	**1468**	**.784**	**785**	**1608**	**2393**	**1492**	**1920**	**31**	**802**	**407**	**1055**	**26.7**	**12.5**	**4.0**	**2.5**	....

YEAR	TEAM	GP	GS	MIN	PTS	FGM	FGA	FG%	3PM	3PA	3P%	FTM	FTA	FT%	ORB	DRB	TRB	AST	PF	DQ	STL	BLK	TO	MPG	PPG	RPG	APG	PCM
89-90	San Antonio	9	0	49	20	9	27	.333	0	2	.000	2	2	1.000	5	6	11	3	8	0	2	0	5	5.4	2.2	1.2	0.3	.206
93-94	Denver	12	12	405	171	62	149	.416	20	50	.400	27	35	.771	18	43	61	42	53	1	9	12	28	33.8	14.3	5.1	3.5	.391
94-95	Denver	3	3	84	26	8	36	.222	4	13	.308	6	6	1.000	5	11	16	12	11	0	3	1	3	28.0	8.7	5.3	4.0	.277
NBA Playoff Totals		**24**	**15**	**538**	**217**	**79**	**212**	**.373**	**24**	**65**	**.369**	**35**	**43**	**.814**	**28**	**60**	**88**	**57**	**72**	**1**	**14**	**13**	**36**	**22.4**	**9.0**	**3.7**	**2.4**	**....**

• WILLIAMS, Rickey

Richard C. Williams

Born: Mar. 12, 1957. Buffalo, NY, United States.   Height: 6'1".   Weight: 175 lbs.   Drafted: 1978   College: Long Beach State

YEAR	TEAM	GP	GS	MIN	PTS	FGM	FGA	FG%	3PM	3PA	3P%	FTM	FTA	FT%	ORB	DRB	TRB	AST	PF	DQ	STL	BLK	TO	MPG	PPG	RPG	APG	PCM
82-83	Utah	44	0	346	147	56	135	.415	0	3	.000	35	53	.660	15	23	38	37	42	0	20	4	40	7.9	3.3	0.9	0.8	.315
NBA Season Totals		**44**	**0**	**346**	**147**	**56**	**135**	**.415**	**0**	**3**	**.000**	**35**	**53**	**.660**	**15**	**23**	**38**	**37**	**42**	**0**	**20**	**4**	**40**	**7.9**	**3.3**	**0.9**	**0.8**	**....**

• WILLIAMS, Rob

Robert Aaron Williams

Born: May 5, 1961. Houston, TX, United States.   Height: 6'2".   Weight: 175 lbs.   Drafted: 1982   College: Houston

YEAR	TEAM	GP	GS	MIN	PTS	FGM	FGA	FG%	3PM	3PA	3P%	FTM	FTA	FT%	ORB	DRB	TRB	AST	PF	DQ	STL	BLK	TO	MPG	PPG	RPG	APG	PCM
82-83	Denver	74	33	1443	515	191	468	.408	2	15	.133	131	174	.753	37	99	136	361	221	4	89	12	185	19.5	7.0	1.8	4.9	.408
83-84	Denver	79	66	1924	804	309	671	.461	15	47	.319	171	209	.818	54	140	194	464	268	4	84	5	166	24.4	10.2	2.5	5.9	.484
NBA Season Totals		**153**	**99**	**3367**	**1319**	**500**	**1139**	**.439**	**17**	**62**	**.274**	**302**	**383**	**.789**	**91**	**239**	**330**	**825**	**489**	**8**	**173**	**17**	**351**	**22.0**	**8.6**	**2.2**	**5.4**	**....**
82-83	Denver	7	7	134	57	24	54	.444	2	3	.667	7	7	1.000	2	11	13	37	27	1	8	1	19	19.1	8.1	1.9	5.3	.456
83-84	Denver	5	4	149	57	21	47	.447	5	13	.385	10	12	.833	5	14	19	24	19	1	3	1	8	29.8	11.4	3.8	4.8	.421
NBA Playoff Totals		**12**	**11**	**283**	**114**	**45**	**101**	**.446**	**7**	**16**	**.438**	**17**	**19**	**.895**	**7**	**25**	**32**	**61**	**46**	**2**	**11**	**2**	**27**	**23.6**	**9.5**	**2.7**	**5.1**	**....**

• WILLIAMS, Ron

Ronald Robert (Fritz) Williams

Born: Sept. 24, 1944. Weirton, WV, United States.   Height: 6'3".   Weight: 188 lbs.   Drafted: 1968   College: West Virginia

YEAR	TEAM	GP	GS	MIN	PTS	FGM	FGA	FG%	3PM	3PA	3P%	FTM	FTA	FT%	ORB	DRB	TRB	AST	PF	DQ	STL	BLK	TO	MPG	PPG	RPG	APG	PCM
68-69	San Francisco	75	....	1472	585	238	567	.420	....	....	....	109	142	.768	....	....	178	247	176	3	....	....	....	19.6	7.8	2.4	3.3	.448
69-70	San Francisco	80	....	2435	1181	452	1046	.432	....	....	....	277	337	.822	....	....	190	424	287	7	....	....	....	30.4	14.8	2.4	5.3	.471
70-71	San Francisco	82	....	2809	1183	426	977	.436	....	....	....	331	392	.844	....	....	244	480	301	9	....	....	....	34.3	14.4	3.0	5.9	.467
71-72	Golden State	80	....	1932	777	291	614	.474	....	....	....	195	234	.833	....	....	147	308	232	1	....	....	....	24.2	9.7	1.8	3.9	.444
72-73	Golden State	73	....	1016	435	180	409	.440	....	....	....	75	83	.904	....	....	81	114	108	0	....	....	....	13.9	6.0	1.1	1.6	.382
73-74	Milwaukee	71	....	1130	444	192	393	.489	....	....	....	60	68	.882	19	50	69	153	114	1	49	2	....	15.9	6.3	1.0	2.2	.403
74-75	Milwaukee	46	....	526	148	62	165	.376	....	....	....	24	29	.828	10	33	43	71	70	2	23	2	....	11.4	3.2	0.9	1.5	.278
75-76	LA Lakers	9	....	158	44	17	43	.395	....	....	....	10	13	.769	2	17	19	21	15	0	3	0	....	17.6	4.9	2.1	2.3	.343
NBA Season Totals		**516**	**....**	**11478**	**4797**	**1858**	**4214**	**.441**	**....**	**....**	**....**	**1081**	**1298**	**.833**	**31**	**100**	**971**	**1818**	**1303**	**23**	**75**	**4**	**....**	**22.2**	**9.3**	**1.9**	**3.5**	**....**
68-69	San Francisco	4	....	42	24	10	26	.385	....	....	....	4	4	1.000	....	....	4	3	4	0	....	....	....	10.5	6.0	1.0	0.8	.376
70-71	San Francisco	5	....	172	65	24	63	.381	....	....	....	17	19	.895	....	....	17	29	19	1	....	....	....	34.4	13.0	3.4	5.8	.408
71-72	Golden State	5	....	83	32	9	31	.290	....	....	....	14	15	.933	....	....	8	10	12	0	....	....	....	16.6	6.4	1.6	2.0	.309
72-73	Golden State	3	....	20	9	4	6	.667	....	....	....	1	1	1.000	....	....	1	5	1	0	....	....	....	6.7	3.0	0.3	1.7	.671
73-74	Milwaukee	15	....	354	130	57	122	.467	....	....	....	16	20	.800	6	21	27	47	40	1	9	3	....	23.6	8.7	1.8	3.1	.376
NBA Playoff Totals		**32**	**....**	**671**	**260**	**104**	**248**	**.419**	**....**	**....**	**....**	**52**	**59**	**.881**	**6**	**21**	**57**	**94**	**76**	**2**	**9**	**3**	**....**	**21.0**	**8.1**	**1.8**	**2.9**	**....**

• WILLIAMS, Sam

Samuel Keith Williams

Born: Mar. 7, 1959. Los Angeles, CA, United States.   Height: 6'8".   Weight: 210 lbs.   Drafted: 1981   College: Arizona State

YEAR	TEAM	GP	GS	MIN	PTS	FGM	FGA	FG%	3PM	3PA	3P%	FTM	FTA	FT%	ORB	DRB	TRB	AST	PF	DQ	STL	BLK	TO	MPG	PPG	RPG	APG	PCM
81-82	Golden State	59	22	1073	357	154	277	.556	0	0	.000	49	89	.551	91	217	308	38	156	0	45	76	65	18.2	6.1	5.2	0.6	.494
82-83	Golden State	75	28	1533	627	252	479	.526	0	1	.000	123	171	.719	153	240	393	45	244	4	71	89	98	20.4	8.4	5.2	0.6	.489
83-84	Golden State	7	0	59	28	11	26	.423	0	0	.000	6	7	.857	4	9	13	2	6	0	6	3	3	8.4	4.0	1.9	0.3	.519
83-84	Philadelphia	70	12	1375	472	193	405	.477	0	1	.000	86	133	.647	117	209	326	60	203	3	62	103	98	19.6	6.7	4.7	0.9	.428
84-85	Philadelphia	46	8	488	144	58	148	.392	0	1	.000	28	47	.596	38	68	106	11	92	1	26	26	46	10.6	3.1	2.3	0.2	.255
NBA Season Totals		**257**	**70**	**4528**	**1628**	**668**	**1335**	**.500**	**0**	**3**	**.000**	**292**	**447**	**.653**	**403**	**743**	**1146**	**156**	**701**	**8**	**210**	**297**	**310**	**17.6**	**6.3**	**4.5**	**0.6**	**....**
83-84	Philadelphia	4	0	55	5	2	8	.250	0	0	.000	1	2	.500	1	5	6	3	7	0	2	6	5	13.8	1.3	1.5	0.8	.132
84-85	Philadelphia	5	0	26	5	1	6	.167	0	0	.000	3	10	.300	4	8	12	0	2	0	0	0	4	5.2	1.0	2.4	0.0	.139
NBA Playoff Totals		**9**	**0**	**81**	**10**	**3**	**14**	**.214**	**0**	**0**	**.000**	**4**	**12**	**.333**	**5**	**13**	**18**	**3**	**9**	**0**	**2**	**6**	**9**	**9.0**	**1.1**	**2.0**	**0.3**	**....**

• WILLIAMS, Sam

Samuel H. Williams

Born: Jan. 22, 1945.   Height: 6'3".   Weight: 180 lbs.   Drafted: 1968   College: Iowa

YEAR	TEAM	GP	GS	MIN	PTS	FGM	FGA	FG%	3PM	3PA	3P%	FTM	FTA	FT%	ORB	DRB	TRB	AST	PF	DQ	STL	BLK	TO	MPG	PPG	RPG	APG	PCM
68-69	Milwaukee	55	....	628	228	78	228	.342	....	....	....	72	134	.537	....	....	109	61	106	1	....	....	....	11.4	4.1	2.0	1.1	.310
69-70	Milwaukee	11	....	44	27	11	24	.458	....	....	....	5	11	.455	....	....	7	3	5	0	....	....	....	4.0	2.5	0.6	0.3	.460
NBA Season Totals		**66**	**....**	**672**	**255**	**89**	**252**	**.353**	**....**	**....**	**....**	**77**	**145**	**.531**	**....**	**....**	**116**	**64**	**111**	**1**	**....**	**....**	**....**	**10.2**	**3.9**	**1.8**	**1.0**	**....**
69-70	Milwaukee	2	....	16	8	4	7	.571	....	....	....	0	2	.000	....	....	4	1	5	0	....	....	....	8.0	4.0	2.0	0.5	.433
NBA Playoff Totals		**2**	**....**	**16**	**8**	**4**	**7**	**.571**	**....**	**....**	**....**	**0**	**2**	**.000**	**....**	**....**	**4**	**1**	**5**	**0**	**....**	**....**	**....**	**8.0**	**4.0**	**2.0**	**0.5**	**....**

• WILLIAMS, Scott

Scott Christopher (Tank) Williams

Born: Mar. 21, 1968. Hacienda Heights, CA, United States.   Height: 6'10".   Weight: 230 lbs.   Drafted: —   College: North Carolina

YEAR	TEAM	GP	GS	MIN	PTS	FGM	FGA	FG%	3PM	3PA	3P%	FTM	FTA	FT%	ORB	DRB	TRB	AST	PF	DQ	STL	BLK	TO	MPG	PPG	RPG	APG	PCM
90-91	Chicago	51	0	337	127	53	104	.510	1	2	.500	20	28	.714	42	56	98	16	51	0	12	13	26	6.6	2.5	1.9	0.3	.473
91-92	Chicago	63	0	690	214	83	172	.483	0	3	.000	48	74	.649	90	157	247	50	122	0	13	36	38	11.0	3.4	3.9	0.8	.516
92-93	Chicago	71	5	1369	422	166	356	.466	0	7	.000	90	126	.714	168	283	451	68	230	3	55	65	71	19.3	5.9	6.4	1.0	.482
93-94	Chicago	38	11	638	289	114	236	.483	1	5	.200	60	98	.612	69	112	181	39	112	1	16	21	46	16.8	7.6	4.8	1.0	.483
94-95	Philadelphia	77	43	1781	491	206	434	.475	0	7	.000	79	107	.738	173	312	485	59	237	4	71	40	85	23.1	6.4	6.3	0.8	.390
95-96	Philadelphia	13	1	193	40	15	29	.517	0	2	.000	10	12	.833	13	33	46	5	27	0	6	7	8	14.8	3.1	3.5	0.4	.344
96-97	Philadelphia	62	52	1317	362	162	318	.509	0	2	.000	38	55	.691	155	242	397	41	206	5	44	41	50	21.2	5.8	6.4	0.7	.425
97-98	Philadelphia	58	7	801	237	93	213	.437	0	5	.000	51	63	.810	87	124	211	29	132	0	17	21	29	13.8	4.1	3.6	0.5	.367
98-99	Philadelphia	2	0	17	0	0	2	.000	0	0	.000	0	0	.000	1	1	2	1	4	0	2	1	2	8.5	0.0	1.0	0.5	.013
98-99	Milwaukee	5	0	29	14	5	15	.333	0	0	.000	4	7	.571	2	10	12	0	5	0	1	1	2	5.8	2.8	2.4	0.0	.421

YEAR	TEAM	GP	GS	MIN	PTS	FGM	FGA	FG%	3PM	3PA	3P%	FTM	FTA	FT%	ORB	DRB	TRB	AST	PF	DQ	STL	BLK	TO	MPG	PPG	RPG	APG	PCM
99-00	Milwaukee	68	46	1488	518	212	425	.499	0	0	.000	94	129	.729	177	271	448	28	230	3	40	66	65	21.9	7.6	6.6	0.4	.456
00-01	Milwaukee	66	31	1272	403	171	361	.474	1	4	.250	60	70	.857	97	267	364	35	178	1	48	32	41	19.3	6.1	5.5	0.5	.431
01-02	Denver	41	16	736	202	86	217	.396	0	2	.000	30	41	.732	82	127	209	13	98	1	17	33	35	18.0	4.9	5.1	0.3	.341
02-03	Phoenix	69	33	872	273	120	292	.411	0	2	.000	33	42	.786	72	121	193	22	159	2	27	21	32	12.6	4.0	2.8	0.3	.292
NBA Season Totals		684	245	11540	3592	1486	3174	.468	3	41	.073	617	852	.724	1228	2116	3344	406	1791	20	369	398	530	16.9	5.3	4.9	0.6	....
90-91	Chicago	12	0	72	23	6	13	.462	0	1	.000	11	20	.550	4	16	20	3	15	0	1	3	4	6.0	1.9	1.7	0.3	.377
91-92	Chicago	22	0	321	88	34	70	.486	0	1	.000	20	28	.714	33	62	95	7	65	0	6	18	15	14.6	4.0	4.3	0.3	.389
92-93	Chicago	19	0	395	104	44	87	.506	0	2	.000	16	29	.552	40	71	111	26	58	2	7	17	24	20.8	5.5	5.8	1.4	.410
93-94	Chicago	10	0	151	63	24	57	.421	0	0	.000	15	21	.714	15	24	39	7	23	0	7	3	9	15.1	6.3	3.9	0.7	.422
99-00	Milwaukee	5	0	93	51	23	36	.639	0	0	.000	5	6	.833	9	19	28	2	16	0	2	5	4	18.6	10.2	5.6	0.4	.665
00-01	Milwaukee	17	17	378	134	59	120	.492	0	0	.000	16	28	.571	45	77	122	12	57	1	11	24	12	22.2	7.9	7.2	0.7	.507
02-03	Phoenix	6	6	83	24	11	32	.344	0	0	.000	2	2	1.000	6	9	15	1	17	0	4	3	1	13.8	4.0	2.5	0.2	.209
NBA Playoff Totals		91	23	1493	487	201	415	.484	0	4	.000	85	134	.634	152	278	430	58	251	3	38	73	69	16.4	5.4	4.7	0.6	....

• WILLIAMS, Shammond

Shammond Omar Williams

Born: Apr. 5, 1975. Bronx, NY, United States. Height: 6'1". Weight: 201 lbs. Drafted: 1998 College: North Carolina

98-99	Atlanta	2	0	4	3	0	1	.000	0	0	.000	3	4	.750	0	0	0	1	0	0	0	0	0	2.0	1.5	0.0	0.5	.694
99-00	Seattle	43	5	517	225	84	225	.373	24	81	.296	33	51	.647	12	40	52	78	39	0	18	0	40	12.0	5.2	1.2	1.8	.355
00-01	Seattle	69	6	1238	467	161	368	.438	61	133	.459	84	96	.875	34	98	132	190	83	0	31	4	82	17.9	6.8	1.9	2.8	.423
01-02	Seattle	50	2	603	221	81	193	.420	28	75	.373	31	39	.795	16	47	63	83	35	0	21	2	35	12.1	4.4	1.3	1.7	.393
02-03	Boston	51	2	1169	372	134	338	.396	56	159	.352	48	57	.842	12	98	110	128	84	0	61	3	61	22.9	7.3	2.2	2.5	.331
02-03	Denver	27	9	712	255	94	241	.390	37	102	.363	30	45	.667	12	49	61	138	56	0	16	3	53	26.4	9.4	2.3	5.1	.371
NBA Season Totals		242	24	4243	1543	554	1366	.406	206	550	.375	229	292	.784	86	332	418	618	297	0	147	12	271	17.5	6.4	1.7	2.6	....
99-00	Seattle	5	2	99	51	18	33	.545	7	11	.636	8	11	.727	2	9	11	18	3	0	8	0	6	19.8	10.2	2.2	3.6	.668
01-02	Seattle	3	0	38	16	6	14	.429	2	4	.500	2	3	.667	1	3	4	3	1	0	2	0	4	12.7	5.3	1.3	1.0	.341
NBA Playoff Totals		8	2	137	67	24	47	.511	9	15	.600	10	14	.714	3	12	15	21	4	0	10	0	10	17.1	8.4	1.9	2.6	....

• WILLIAMS, Sly

Sylvester (Sly, The Garbage Man) Williams

Born: Jan. 26, 1958. New Haven, CT, United States. Height: 6'7". Weight: 210 lbs. Drafted: 1979 College: Rhode Island

79-80	New York	57	....	556	266	104	267	.390	0	4	.000	58	90	.644	65	56	121	36	73	0	19	8	51	9.8	4.7	2.1	0.6	.356
80-81	New York	67	....	1976	885	349	708	.493	2	8	.250	185	268	.690	159	257	416	180	199	0	116	18	141	29.5	13.2	6.2	2.7	.505
81-82	New York	60	27	1521	831	349	628	.556	2	9	.222	131	173	.757	100	127	227	142	153	0	77	16	114	25.4	13.9	3.8	2.4	.544
82-83	New York	68	6	1385	806	314	647	.485	2	19	.105	176	259	.680	94	196	290	133	166	3	73	3	136	20.4	11.9	4.3	2.0	.539
83-84	Atlanta	13	1	258	105	34	114	.298	1	9	.111	36	46	.783	19	31	50	16	33	0	14	1	18	19.8	8.1	3.8	1.2	.277
84-85	Atlanta	34	20	867	417	167	380	.439	4	15	.267	79	123	.642	45	123	168	94	83	1	28	8	78	25.5	12.3	4.9	2.8	.435
85-86	Boston	6	0	54	17	5	21	.238	0	4	.000	7	12	.583	7	8	15	2	15	0	1	1	7	9.0	2.8	2.5	0.3	.079
NBA Season Totals		305	54	6617	3327	1322	2765	.478	11	68	.162	672	971	.692	489	798	1287	603	722	4	328	55	545	21.7	10.9	4.2	2.0	....
80-81	New York	2	....	56	26	13	18	.722	0	0	.000	0	0	.000	4	5	9	5	7	0	3	0	3	28.0	13.0	4.5	2.5	.570
82-83	New York	5	0	82	36	16	41	.390	1	1	1.000	3	3	1.000	10	11	21	6	4	0	3	1	12	16.4	7.2	4.2	1.2	.365
NBA Playoff Totals		7	0	138	62	29	59	.492	1	1	1.000	3	3	1.000	14	16	30	11	11	0	6	1	15	19.7	8.9	4.3	1.6	....

• WILLIAMS, Travis

Travis Williams

Born: May 27, 1969. Columbia, SC, United States. Height: 6'6". Weight: 215 lbs. Drafted: — College: South Carolina State

97-98	Charlotte	39	0	365	136	56	119	.471	0	1	.000	24	46	.522	53	39	92	20	55	0	18	5	31	9.4	3.5	2.4	0.5	.388
98-99	Charlotte	8	0	62	15	6	13	.462	0	0	.000	3	4	.750	6	13	19	2	10	0	2	1	6	7.8	1.9	2.4	0.3	.328
NBA Season Totals		47	0	427	151	62	132	.470	0	1	.000	27	50	.540	59	52	111	22	65	0	20	6	37	9.1	3.2	2.4	0.5	....
97-98	Charlotte	4	0	18	5	1	3	.333	0	0	.000	3	4	.750	1	4	5	0	3	0	1	1	0	4.5	1.3	1.3	0.0	.430
NBA Playoff Totals		4	0	18	5	1	3	.333	0	0	.000	3	4	.750	1	4	5	0	3	0	1	1	0	4.5	1.3	1.3	0.0	....

• WILLIAMS, Walt

Walter Ander (The Wizard) Williams

Born: Apr. 16, 1970. Washington, DC, United States. Height: 6'8". Weight: 219 lbs. Drafted: 1992 College: Maryland

92-93	Sacramento	59	26	1673	1001	358	823	.435	61	191	.319	224	302	.742	115	150	265	178	209	6	66	29	177	28.4	17.0	4.5	3.0	.475
93-94	Sacramento	57	4	1356	638	226	580	.390	38	132	.288	148	233	.635	71	164	235	132	200	6	52	23	143	23.8	11.2	4.1	2.3	.353
94-95	Sacramento	77	77	2739	1259	445	998	.446	103	296	.348	266	364	.731	100	245	345	316	265	3	123	63	246	35.6	16.4	4.5	4.1	.428
95-96	Sacramento	45	45	1381	658	235	540	.435	58	170	.341	130	172	.756	62	145	207	165	151	0	53	42	104	30.7	14.6	4.6	3.7	.465
95-96	Miami	28	28	788	337	124	268	.463	56	123	.455	33	60	.550	37	75	112	65	87	0	32	16	48	28.1	12.0	4.0	2.3	.409
96-97	Toronto	73	73	2647	1199	419	982	.427	175	437	.400	186	243	.765	103	264	367	197	282	**11**	97	62	175	36.3	16.4	5.0	2.7	.398
97-98	Toronto	28	16	876	348	125	319	.392	49	129	.380	49	60	.817	27	91	118	69	100	2	40	23	53	31.3	12.4	4.2	2.5	.356
97-98	Portland	31	1	594	260	85	225	.378	31	90	.344	59	65	.908	23	59	82	53	61	0	19	12	40	19.2	8.4	2.6	1.7	.380
98-99	Portland	48	16	1044	446	147	347	.424	63	144	.438	89	107	.832	36	107	143	80	101	2	37	28	63	21.8	9.3	3.0	1.7	.415
99-00	Houston	76	66	1859	827	312	681	.458	102	261	.391	101	123	.821	69	237	306	157	190	2	49	44	113	24.5	10.9	4.0	2.1	.445
00-01	Houston	72	31	1583	599	202	513	.394	98	248	.395	97	126	.770	31	214	245	97	153	2	30	28	73	22.0	8.3	3.4	1.3	.348
01-02	Houston	48	25	1117	450	166	396	.419	78	183	.426	40	51	.784	37	125	162	69	106	0	18	10	53	23.3	9.4	3.4	1.4	.348
02-03	Dallas	66	1	1161	363	134	341	.393	64	171	.374	31	50	.620	53	154	207	59	141	0	42	26	35	17.6	5.5	3.1	0.9	.331
NBA Season Totals		708	409	18818	8385	2978	7013	.425	976	2575	.379	1453	1956	.743	764	2030	2794	1637	2046	34	658	406	1323	26.6	11.8	3.9	2.3	....
95-96	Miami	3	3	70	14	6	18	.333	1	9	.111	1	2	.500	3	9	12	5	4	0	1	1	3	23.3	4.7	4.0	1.7	.229
97-98	Portland	4	0	102	53	17	31	.548	8	15	.533	11	14	.786	3	11	14	9	18	2	1	0	1	25.5	13.3	3.5	2.3	.521
98-99	Portland	13	0	185	63	21	58	.362	13	32	.406	8	14	.571	5	11	16	11	27	0	7	3	11	14.2	4.8	1.2	0.8	.222
02-03	Dallas	15	3	227	85	32	81	.395	14	41	.341	7	7	1.000	12	31	43	15	28	0	5	12	17	15.1	5.7	2.9	1.0	.367
NBA Playoff Totals		35	6	584	215	76	188	.404	36	97	.371	27	37	.730	23	62	85	40	77	2	14	16	32	16.7	6.1	2.4	1.1	....

• WILLIAMS, Ward
Ward M. Williams

Born: June 26, 1923. Height: 6'4". Weight: 195 lbs. Drafted: 1948 College: Indiana

YEAR	TEAM	GP	GS	MIN	PTS	FGM	FGA	FG%	3PM	3PA	3P%	FTM	FTA	FT%	ORB	DRB	TRB	AST	PF	DQ	STL	BLK	TO	MPG	PPG	RPG	APG	PCM
48-49	Fort Wayne	53	....	....	215	61	257	.237	....	....	....	93	124	.750	....	....	....	82	158	....	....	....	....	....	4.1	....	1.5	....
NBA Season Totals		53	....	....	215	61	257	.237	....	....	....	93	124	.750	....	....	....	82	158	....	....	....	....	....	4.1	....	1.5	....

• WILLIAMS, Willie
Willie Earl Williams

Born: July 28, 1946. Height: 6'7". Weight: 200 lbs. Drafted: 1970 College: Florida State

YEAR	TEAM	GP	GS	MIN	PTS	FGM	FGA	FG%	3PM	3PA	3P%	FTM	FTA	FT%	ORB	DRB	TRB	AST	PF	DQ	STL	BLK	TO	MPG	PPG	RPG	APG	PCM
70-71	Boston	16	....	56	15	6	32	.188	....	....	....	3	5	.600	....	....	10	2	8	0	....	....	....	3.5	0.9	0.6	0.1	-.014
70-71	Cincinnati	9	....	49	8	4	10	.400	....	....	....	0	0	.000	....	....	13	6	6	0	....	....	....	5.4	0.9	1.4	0.7	.373
NBA Season Totals		25	....	105	23	10	42	.238	....	....	....	3	5	.600	....	....	23	8	14	0	....	....	....	4.2	0.9	0.9	0.3	....

• WILLIAMSON, Corliss
Corliss Mondari (Big Nasty) Williamson

Born: Dec. 4, 1973. Russellville, AR, United States. Height: 6'7". Weight: 245 lbs. Drafted: 1995 College: Arkansas

YEAR	TEAM	GP	GS	MIN	PTS	FGM	FGA	FG%	3PM	3PA	3P%	FTM	FTA	FT%	ORB	DRB	TRB	AST	PF	DQ	STL	BLK	TO	MPG	PPG	RPG	APG	PCM
95-96	Sacramento	53	3	609	297	125	268	.466	0	3	.000	47	84	.560	56	58	114	23	115	2	11	9	74	11.5	5.6	2.2	0.4	.282
96-97	Sacramento	79	31	1992	915	371	745	.498	0	3	.000	173	251	.689	139	187	326	124	263	4	60	49	158	25.2	11.6	4.1	1.6	.401
97-98	Sacramento	79	75	2819	1401	561	1134	.495	0	9	.000	279	443	.630	162	284	446	230	252	4	76	48	198	35.7	17.7	5.6	2.9	.453
98-99	Sacramento	50	50	1374	659	269	555	.485	1	5	.200	120	188	.638	85	121	206	66	118	1	30	8	75	27.5	13.2	4.1	1.3	.397
99-00	Sacramento	76	76	1707	785	311	622	.500	0	0	.000	163	212	.769	122	168	290	82	192	0	38	19	110	22.5	10.3	3.8	1.1	.409
00-01	Toronto	42	31	886	390	153	325	.471	0	2	.000	84	130	.646	57	96	153	33	98	0	15	13	65	21.1	9.3	3.6	0.8	.351
00-01	Detroit	27	9	800	411	172	322	.534	0	0	.000	67	107	.626	53	115	168	28	87	0	35	8	45	29.6	15.2	6.2	1.0	.499
01-02	Detroit	78	7	1702	1063	411	806	.510	1	5	.200	240	298	.805	117	202	319	94	226	1	49	26	137	21.8	13.6	4.1	1.2	.536
02-03	Detroit	82	1	2061	987	374	826	.453	2	11	.182	237	300	.790	147	211	358	104	238	1	44	27	126	25.1	12.0	4.4	1.3	.402
NBA Season Totals		566	283	13950	6908	2747	5603	.490	4	38	.105	1410	2013	.700	938	1442	2380	784	1589	13	358	207	988	24.6	12.2	4.2	1.4	....
95-96	Sacramento	1	0	2	1	0	1	.000	0	0	.000	1	1	1.000	0	0	0	0	0	0	0	0	0	2.0	1.0	0.0	0.0	.030
98-99	Sacramento	5	5	130	53	23	40	.575	0	0	.000	7	10	.700	7	9	16	6	13	0	2	1	6	26.0	10.6	3.2	1.2	.377
99-00	Sacramento	5	5	87	33	11	16	.688	0	0	.000	11	12	.917	4	11	15	1	8	0	1	0	5	17.4	6.6	3.0	0.2	.408
01-02	Detroit	10	0	269	133	52	112	.464	0	2	.000	29	38	.763	19	34	53	10	31	0	9	2	22	26.9	13.3	5.3	1.0	.407
02-03	Detroit	15	0	233	117	37	90	.411	0	0	.000	43	58	.741	13	20	33	15	38	1	4	3	20	15.5	7.8	2.2	1.0	.341
NBA Playoff Totals		36	10	721	337	123	259	.475	0	2	.000	91	119	.765	43	74	117	32	90	1	16	6	53	20.0	9.4	3.3	0.9	....

• WILLIAMSON, John
John Lee (Super John) Williamson

Born: Nov. 10, 1951. New Haven, CT, United States. Died: Nov.30, 1996. Height: 6'2". Weight: 185 lbs. Drafted: 1973 College: New Mexico State

YEAR	TEAM	GP	GS	MIN	PTS	FGM	FGA	FG%	3PM	3PA	3P%	FTM	FTA	FT%	ORB	DRB	TRB	AST	PF	DQ	STL	BLK	TO	MPG	PPG	RPG	APG	PCM
73-74	New York-A	77	....	2264	1116	482	982	.491	2	11	.182	150	190	.789	68	145	213	243	254	....	86	27	208	29.4	14.5	2.8	3.2	.451
74-75	New York-A	75	....	1872	866	370	768	.482	3	13	.231	123	147	.837	51	98	149	197	188	....	61	23	148	25.0	11.5	2.0	2.6	.411
75-76	New York-A	76	....	2255	1233	519	1153	.450	8	42	.190	187	232	.806	70	120	190	188	224	....	76	33	185	29.7	16.2	2.5	2.5	.411
76-77	New York	42	....	1426	875	357	803	.445	....	....	....	161	204	.789	24	95	119	90	143	3	59	6	....	34.0	20.8	2.8	2.1	.431
76-77	Indiana	30	....	1055	620	261	544	.480	....	....	....	98	125	.784	18	56	74	111	103	1	48	7	....	35.2	20.7	2.5	3.7	.483
77-78	Indiana	42	....	1449	804	335	795	.421	....	....	....	134	161	.832	34	86	120	132	131	4	47	0	126	34.5	19.1	2.9	3.1	.357
77-78	New Jersey	33	....	1282	973	388	854	.454	....	....	....	197	230	.857	32	75	107	82	105	2	47	10	102	38.8	29.5	3.2	2.5	.508
78-79	New Jersey	74	....	2451	1643	635	1367	.465	....	....	....	373	437	.854	53	143	196	255	215	3	89	12	229	33.1	22.2	2.6	3.4	.491
79-80	New Jersey	28	....	771	496	206	461	.447	8	19	.421	76	88	.864	24	30	54	87	71	1	26	9	42	27.5	17.7	1.9	3.1	.474
79-80	Washington	30	....	603	349	153	356	.430	3	16	.188	40	50	.800	14	31	45	39	66	0	10	10	48	20.1	11.6	1.5	1.3	.313
80-81	Washington	9	....	112	42	18	56	.321	1	6	.167	5	6	.833	0	7	7	17	13	0	4	1	12	12.4	4.7	0.8	1.9	.174
NBA Season Totals		288	....	9149	5802	2353	5236	.449	12	41	.293	1084	1301	.833	199	523	722	813	847	14	330	55	559	31.8	20.1	2.5	2.8	....
ABA Season Totals		228	....	6391	3215	1371	2903	.472	13	66	.197	460	569	.808	189	363	552	628	666	....	223	83	541	28.0	14.1	2.4	2.8	....
Career Totals		516	....	15540	9017	3724	8139	.458	25	107	.234	1544	1870	.826	388	886	1274	1441	1513	14	553	138	1100	30.1	17.5	2.5	2.8	....
73-74	New York-A	14	....	425	166	72	160	.450	0	3	.000	22	27	.815	17	29	46	40	44	....	10	6	33	30.4	11.9	3.3	2.9	.364
74-75	New York-A	5	....	118	60	26	43	.605	0	1	.000	8	13	.615	3	7	10	10	21	....	1	3	10	23.6	12.0	2.0	2.0	.452
75-76	New York-A	10	....	360	222	94	189	.497	2	6	.333	32	46	.696	11	13	24	26	36	....	10	3	29	36.0	22.2	2.4	2.6	.459
78-79	New Jersey	2	....	92	59	23	62	.371	....	....	....	13	16	.813	3	3	6	8	8	0	4	0	14	46.0	29.5	3.0	4.0	.264
79-80	Washington	2	....	31	27	11	19	.579	2	6	.333	3	3	1.000	1	1	2	1	7	0	0	0	4	15.5	13.5	1.0	0.5	.512
NBA Playoff Totals		4	....	123	86	34	81	.420	2	6	.333	16	19	.842	4	4	8	9	15	0	4	0	18	30.8	21.5	2.0	2.3	....
ABA Playoff Totals		29	....	903	448	192	392	.490	2	10	.200	62	86	.721	31	49	80	76	101	....	21	12	72	31.1	15.4	2.8	2.6	....
Career Playoff Totals		33	....	1026	534	226	473	.478	4	16	.250	78	105	.743	35	53	88	85	116	0	25	12	90	31.1	16.2	2.7	2.6	....

• WILLIFORD, Vann
Duncan Vann Williford

Born: Jan. 26, 1948. Height: 6'6". Weight: 195 lbs. Drafted: 1970 College: North Carolina State

YEAR	TEAM	GP	GS	MIN	PTS	FGM	FGA	FG%	3PM	3PA	3P%	FTM	FTA	FT%	ORB	DRB	TRB	AST	PF	DQ	STL	BLK	TO	MPG	PPG	RPG	APG	PCM
70-71	Carolina-A	38	....	295	148	62	141	.440	3	9	.333	21	37	.568	28	40	68	15	34	0	....	....	21	7.8	3.9	1.8	0.4	.465
ABA Season Totals		38	....	295	148	62	141	.440	3	9	.333	21	37	.568	28	40	68	15	34	0	....	....	21	7.8	3.9	1.8	0.4	....

• WILLIS, Kevin
Kevin Alvin (Devo, Fresh) Willis

Born: Sept. 6, 1962. Los Angeles, CA, United States. Height: 7' Weight: 220 lbs. Drafted: 1984 College: Michigan State

YEAR	TEAM	GP	GS	MIN	PTS	FGM	FGA	FG%	3PM	3PA	3P%	FTM	FTA	FT%	ORB	DRB	TRB	AST	PF	DQ	STL	BLK	TO	MPG	PPG	RPG	APG	PCM
84-85	Atlanta	82	19	1785	765	322	690	.467	2	9	.222	119	181	.657	177	345	522	36	226	4	31	49	107	21.8	9.3	6.4	0.4	.441
85-86	Atlanta	82	59	2300	1010	419	811	.517	0	6	.000	172	263	.654	243	461	704	45	294	6	66	44	180	28.0	12.3	8.6	0.5	.480
86-87	Atlanta	81	81	2626	1304	538	1003	.536	1	4	.250	227	320	.709	321	528	849	62	313	4	65	61	170	32.4	16.1	10.5	0.8	.570
87-88	Atlanta	75	55	2091	871	356	687	.518	0	2	.000	159	245	.649	235	312	547	28	240	2	68	41	135	27.9	11.6	7.3	0.4	.443
89-90	Atlanta	81	51	2273	1006	418	805	.519	2	7	.286	168	246	.683	253	392	645	57	259	4	63	47	146	28.1	12.4	8.0	0.7	.491
90-91	Atlanta	80	80	2373	1051	444	881	.504	4	10	.400	159	238	.668	259	445	704	99	235	2	60	40	152	29.7	13.1	8.8	1.2	.510
91-92	Atlanta	81	80	2962	1480	591	1224	.483	6	37	.162	292	363	.804	418	840	1258	173	223	0	72	54	194	36.6	18.3	15.5	2.1	.691
92-93	Atlanta	80	80	2878	1435	616	1218	.506	7	29	.241	196	300	.653	335	693	1028	165	264	1	68	41	216	36.0	17.9	12.9	2.1	.604
93-94	Atlanta	80	80	2867	1531	627	1257	.499	9	24	.375	268	376	.713	335	628	963	150	250	2	79	38	192	35.8	19.1	12.0	1.9	.616

YEAR	TEAM	GP	GS	MIN	PTS	FGM	FGA	FG%	3PM	3PA	3P%	FTM	FTA	FT%	ORB	DRB	TRB	AST	PF	DQ	STL	BLK	TO	MPG	PPG	RPG	APG	PCM
94-95	Atlanta	2	2	89	42	16	41	.390	0	1	.000	10	15	.667	10	26	36	3	7	0	1	3	7	44.5	21.0	18.0	1.5	.529
94-95	Miami	65	61	2301	1112	457	974	.469	3	14	.214	195	282	.691	217	479	696	83	208	3	59	33	156	35.4	17.1	10.7	1.3	.508
95-96	Miami	47	42	1357	479	195	412	.473	0	5	.000	89	125	.712	134	286	420	34	158	4	19	25	99	28.9	10.2	8.9	0.7	.415
95-96	Golden State	28	18	778	315	130	300	.433	1	4	.250	54	77	.701	74	144	218	19	95	0	13	16	62	27.8	11.3	7.8	0.7	.378
96-97	Houston	75	32	1964	842	350	728	.481	2	14	.143	140	202	.693	146	415	561	71	216	1	42	32	120	26.2	11.2	7.5	0.9	.466
97-98	Houston	81	74	2528	1305	531	1041	.510	1	7	.143	242	305	.793	232	447	679	78	235	1	55	38	170	31.2	16.1	8.4	1.0	.529
98-99	Toronto	42	38	1216	504	187	447	.418	0	2	.000	130	155	.839	109	241	350	67	134	1	28	28	86	29.0	12.0	8.3	1.6	.461
99-00	Toronto	79	1	1679	604	236	569	.415	1	3	.333	131	164	.799	201	281	482	49	256	3	36	48	98	21.3	7.6	6.1	0.6	.386
00-01	Toronto	35	9	771	309	124	269	.461	0	2	.000	61	81	.753	68	155	223	21	78	0	19	21	40	22.0	8.8	6.4	0.6	.465
00-01	Denver	43	13	1059	413	180	421	.428	1	4	.250	52	66	.788	109	200	309	29	138	0	38	31	47	24.6	9.6	7.2	0.7	.432
01-02	Houston	52	5	866	315	125	284	.440	0	1	.000	65	87	.747	105	194	299	14	98	0	25	23	41	16.7	6.1	5.8	0.3	.472
02-03	San Antonio	71	6	841	297	123	257	.479	0	2	.000	51	83	.614	83	143	226	24	120	1	20	20	60	11.8	4.2	3.2	0.3	.380
NBA Season Totals		1342	886	37604	16990	6985	14319	.488	40	187	.214	2980	4174	.714	4064	7655	11719	1307	4047	39	927	733	2478	28.0	12.7	8.7	1.0	....
85-86	Atlanta	9	9	280	125	55	98	.561	0	0	.000	15	23	.652	31	34	65	5	38	2	7	8	15	31.1	13.9	7.2	0.6	.462
86-87	Atlanta	9	9	356	141	60	115	.522	0	0	.000	21	31	.677	33	50	83	6	33	0	9	7	17	39.6	15.7	9.2	0.7	.428
87-88	Atlanta	12	12	462	194	80	138	.580	0	1	.000	34	50	.680	36	72	108	11	51	1	10	10	25	38.5	16.2	9.0	0.9	.469
90-91	Atlanta	5	5	159	77	27	67	.403	2	3	.667	21	30	.700	18	27	45	5	22	0	3	1	2	31.8	15.4	9.0	1.0	.468
92-93	Atlanta	3	3	103	50	21	45	.467	0	1	.000	8	14	.571	13	13	26	3	13	0	2	0	7	34.3	16.7	8.7	1.0	.403
93-94	Atlanta	11	11	362	134	59	129	.457	0	5	.000	16	21	.762	38	81	119	11	37	0	8	5	19	32.9	12.2	10.8	1.0	.459
96-97	Houston	16	0	295	102	38	95	.400	0	1	.000	26	38	.684	22	53	75	11	47	0	9	4	22	18.4	6.4	4.7	0.7	.321
97-98	Houston	5	5	168	56	22	55	.400	0	1	.000	12	16	.750	18	35	53	5	21	0	8	3	12	33.6	11.2	10.6	1.0	.401
99-00	Toronto	3	0	76	39	12	33	.364	0	0	.000	15	20	.750	6	20	26	1	11	0	2	0	2	25.3	13.0	8.7	0.3	.492
02-03	San Antonio	18	0	91	46	21	40	.525	1	1	1.000	3	3	1.000	19	12	31	2	16	0	1	1	8	5.1	2.6	1.7	0.1	.510
NBA Playoff Totals		91	54	2352	964	395	815	.485	3	13	.231	171	246	.695	234	397	631	60	289	3	59	39	129	25.8	10.6	6.9	0.7	....

• WILLOUGHBY, Bill

William Wesley (Willow) Willoughby

Born: May 20, 1957. Englewood, NJ, United States. Height: 6'8". Weight: 205 lbs. Drafted: 1975 College: none (HS: Dwight Morrow, NJ)

YEAR	TEAM	GP	GS	MIN	PTS	FGM	FGA	FG%	3PM	3PA	3P%	FTM	FTA	FT%	ORB	DRB	TRB	AST	PF	DQ	STL	BLK	TO	MPG	PPG	RPG	APG	PCM
75-76	Atlanta	62	....	870	292	113	284	.398	....	....	....	66	100	.660	103	185	288	31	87	0	37	29	....	14.0	4.7	4.6	0.5	.432
76-77	Atlanta	39	....	549	193	75	169	.444	....	....	....	43	63	.683	65	105	170	13	64	1	19	23	....	14.1	4.9	4.4	0.3	.432
77-78	Buffalo	56	....	1079	376	156	363	.430	....	....	....	64	80	.800	76	143	219	38	131	2	24	47	56	19.3	6.7	3.9	0.7	.350
79-80	Cleveland	78	....	1447	535	219	457	.479	1	9	.111	96	127	.756	122	207	329	72	189	0	32	62	70	18.6	6.9	4.2	0.9	.427
80-81	Houston	55	....	1145	349	150	287	.523	0	0	.000	49	64	.766	74	153	227	64	102	0	18	31	72	20.8	6.3	4.1	1.2	.372
81-82	Houston	69	42	1475	539	240	464	.517	3	7	.429	56	77	.727	107	157	264	75	146	1	31	59	76	21.4	7.8	3.8	1.1	.402
82-83	San Antonio	52	0	1062	319	136	295	.461	6	13	.462	41	53	.774	61	129	190	56	123	0	24	16	52	20.4	6.1	3.7	1.1	.317
82-83	New Jersey	10	0	84	24	11	29	.379	0	1	.000	2	2	1.000	2	9	11	8	16	0	1	1	7	8.4	2.4	1.1	0.8	.176
83-84	New Jersey	67	2	936	303	124	258	.481	0	7	.000	55	63	.873	75	118	193	56	106	0	23	24	54	14.0	4.5	2.9	0.8	.383
NBA Season Totals		488	44	8647	2930	1224	2606	.470	10	37	.270	472	629	.750	685	1206	1891	413	964	4	209	292	387	17.7	6.0	3.9	0.8	....
80-81	Houston	19	....	417	114	42	116	.362	0	1	.000	30	40	.750	28	57	85	22	42	0	14	19	23	21.9	6.0	4.5	1.2	.320
81-82	Houston	2	0	17	4	1	2	.500	0	0	.000	2	2	1.000	2	4	6	1	1	0	0	0	1	8.5	2.0	3.0	0.5	.488
83-84	New Jersey	3	0	13	2	1	3	.333	0	0	.000	0	0	.000	3	0	3	0	2	0	0	0	0	4.3	0.7	1.0	0.0	.154
NBA Playoff Totals		24	0	447	120	44	121	.364	0	1	.000	32	42	.762	33	61	94	23	45	0	14	19	24	18.6	5.0	3.9	1.0	....

• WILLOUGHBY, Dedric

Dedric Demond Willoughby

Born: May 27, 1974. New Orleans, LA, United States. Height: 6'3". Weight: 180 lbs. Drafted: — College: Iowa State

YEAR	TEAM	GP	GS	MIN	PTS	FGM	FGA	FG%	3PM	3PA	3P%	FTM	FTA	FT%	ORB	DRB	TRB	AST	PF	DQ	STL	BLK	TO	MPG	PPG	RPG	APG	PCM
99-00	Chicago	25	1	508	190	61	179	.341	29	98	.296	39	51	.765	11	40	51	66	32	0	23	2	37	20.3	7.6	2.0	2.6	.335
NBA Season Totals		25	1	508	190	61	179	.341	29	98	.296	39	51	.765	11	40	51	66	32	0	23	2	37	20.3	7.6	2.0	2.6	....

• WILSON, Bob

Robert Wilson Jr.

Born: Mar. 8, 1926. Height: 6'4". Weight: 185 lbs. Drafted: — College: West Virginia State

YEAR	TEAM	GP	GS	MIN	PTS	FGM	FGA	FG%	3PM	3PA	3P%	FTM	FTA	FT%	ORB	DRB	TRB	AST	PF	DQ	STL	BLK	TO	MPG	PPG	RPG	APG	PCM
51-52	Milwaukee	63	....	1308	236	79	264	.299	....	....	....	78	135	.578	....	....	210	108	172	8	....	....	....	20.8	3.7	3.3	1.7	.238
NBA Season Totals		63	....	1308	236	79	264	.299	....	....	....	78	135	.578	....	....	210	108	172	8	....	....	....	20.8	3.7	3.3	1.7	....

• WILSON, Bobby

Robert E. Wilson

Born: Jan. 15, 1951. Indianapolis, IN, United States. Height: 6'3". Weight: 175 lbs. Drafted: 1974 College: Wichita State

YEAR	TEAM	GP	GS	MIN	PTS	FGM	FGA	FG%	3PM	3PA	3P%	FTM	FTA	FT%	ORB	DRB	TRB	AST	PF	DQ	STL	BLK	TO	MPG	PPG	RPG	APG	PCM
74-75	Chicago	48	....	425	276	115	225	.511	....	....	....	46	58	.793	18	34	52	36	54	1	22	1	....	8.9	5.8	1.1	0.8	.564
75-76	Chicago	58	....	856	437	197	489	.403	....	....	....	43	58	.741	32	62	94	52	96	1	25	2	....	14.8	7.5	1.6	0.9	.326
76-77	Boston	25	....	131	49	19	59	.322	....	....	....	11	13	.846	3	6	9	14	19	0	3	0	....	5.2	2.0	0.4	0.6	.222
77-78	Indiana	12	....	86	30	14	36	.389	....	....	....	2	3	.667	6	6	12	8	16	0	2	1	6	7.2	2.5	1.0	0.7	.235
NBA Season Totals		143	....	1498	792	345	809	.426	....	....	....	102	132	.773	59	108	167	110	185	2	52	4	6	10.5	5.5	1.2	0.8	....
74-75	Chicago	10	....	93	44	17	41	.415	....	....	....	10	12	.833	2	9	11	4	10	0	4	0	....	9.3	4.4	1.1	0.4	.348
NBA Playoff Totals		10	....	93	44	17	41	.415	....	....	....	10	12	.833	2	9	11	4	10	0	4	0	....	9.3	4.4	1.1	0.4	....

• WILSON, Bobby

Robert F. Wilson

Born: 1944. Height: 6'8". Weight: 215 lbs. Drafted: — College: Kansas

YEAR	TEAM	GP	GS	MIN	PTS	FGM	FGA	FG%	3PM	3PA	3P%	FTM	FTA	FT%	ORB	DRB	TRB	AST	PF	DQ	STL	BLK	TO	MPG	PPG	RPG	APG	PCM
67-68	Dallas-A	69	....	1562	616	226	581	.389	1	2	.500	163	265	.615	....	....	450	55	209	8	....	....	127	22.6	8.9	6.5	0.8	.403
ABA Season Totals		69	....	1562	616	226	581	.389	1	2	.500	163	265	.615	....	....	450	55	209	8	....	....	127	22.6	8.9	6.5	0.8	....
67-68	Dallas-A	6	....	50	21	7	25	.280	1	1	1.000	6	13	.462	....	....	26	2	12	1	....	....	7	8.3	3.5	4.3	0.3	.442
ABA Playoff Totals		6	....	50	21	7	25	.280	1	1	1.000	6	13	.462	....	....	26	2	12	1	....	....	7	8.3	3.5	4.3	0.3	....

YEAR	TEAM	GP	GS	MIN	PTS	FGM	FGA	FG%	3PM	3PA	3P%	FTM	FTA	FT%	ORB	DRB	TRB	AST	PF	DQ	STL	BLK	TO	MPG	PPG	RPG	APG	PCM

• WILSON, Bubba

Thomas E. (Bubba) Wilson

Born: Aug. 7, 1955. Gastonia, NC, United States.   Height: 6'3".   Weight: 175 lbs.   Drafted: 1978   College: Western

YEAR	TEAM	GP	GS	MIN	PTS	FGM	FGA	FG%	3PM	3PA	3P%	FTM	FTA	FT%	ORB	DRB	TRB	AST	PF	DQ	STL	BLK	TO	MPG	PPG	RPG	APG	PCM
79-80	Golden State	16	....	143	17	7	25	.280	0	0	.000	3	6	.500	6	10	16	12	11	0	2	0	8	8.9	1.1	1.0	0.8	.116
NBA Season Totals		16	....	143	17	7	25	.280	0	0	.000	3	6	.500	6	10	16	12	11	0	2	0	8	8.9	1.1	1.0	0.8	....

• WILSON, George

George (Jiff) Wilson

Born: May 9, 1942. Meridian, MS, United States.   Height: 6'8".   Weight: 225 lbs.   Drafted: 1964   College: Cincinnati

YEAR	TEAM	GP	GS	MIN	PTS	FGM	FGA	FG%	3PM	3PA	3P%	FTM	FTA	FT%	ORB	DRB	TRB	AST	PF	DQ	STL	BLK	TO	MPG	PPG	RPG	APG	PCM
64-65	Cincinnati	39	....	288	91	41	155	.265	....	....	....	9	30	.300	....	....	102	11	59	0	....	....	....	7.4	2.3	2.6	0.3	.224
65-66	Cincinnati	47	....	276	135	54	138	.391	....	....	....	27	42	.643	....	....	98	17	56	0	....	....	....	5.9	2.9	2.1	0.4	.503
66-67	Cincinnati	12	....	125	29	8	41	.195	....	....	....	13	16	.813	....	....	43	0	19	0	....	....	....	10.4	2.4	3.6	0.0	.226
66-67	Chicago	43	....	448	199	77	193	.399	....	....	....	45	70	.643	....	....	163	15	73	0	....	....	....	10.4	4.6	3.8	0.3	.481
67-68	Seattle	77	....	1236	467	179	498	.359	....	....	....	109	155	.703	....	....	470	56	218	1	....	....	....	16.1	6.1	6.1	0.7	.445
68-69	Phoenix	41	....	1294	475	191	481	.397	....	....	....	93	151	.616	....	....	505	76	145	4	....	....	....	31.6	11.6	12.3	1.9	.509
68-69	Philadelphia	38	....	552	222	81	182	.445	....	....	....	60	84	.714	....	....	216	32	87	1	....	....	....	14.5	5.8	5.7	0.8	.560
69-70	Philadelphia	67	....	836	358	118	304	.388	....	....	....	122	172	.709	....	....	317	52	145	3	....	....	....	12.5	5.3	4.7	0.8	.533
70-71	Buffalo	46	....	713	240	92	269	.342	....	....	....	56	69	.812	....	....	230	48	99	1	....	....	....	15.5	5.2	5.0	1.0	.410
NBA Season Totals		410	....	5768	2216	841	2261	.372	....	....	....	534	789	.677	....	....	2144	307	901	10	....	....	....	14.1	5.4	5.2	0.7	....
64-65	Cincinnati	2	....	3	2	1	1	1.000	....	....	....	0	0	.000	....	....	2	1	1	0	....	....	....	1.5	1.0	1.0	0.5	1.461
65-66	Cincinnati	1	....	3	2	1	1	1.000	....	....	....	0	0	.000	....	....	1	0	1	0	....	....	....	3.0	2.0	1.0	0.0	.797
66-67	Chicago	2	....	27	7	2	9	.222	....	....	....	3	6	.500	....	....	9	0	5	0	....	....	....	13.5	3.5	4.5	0.0	.200
68-69	Philadelphia	5	....	45	3	0	7	.000	....	....	....	3	4	.750	....	....	18	8	9	0	....	....	....	9.0	0.6	3.6	1.6	.385
69-70	Philadelphia	2	....	23	9	4	13	.308	....	....	....	1	1	1.000	....	....	12	1	4	0	....	....	....	11.5	4.5	6.0	0.5	.478
NBA Playoff Totals		12	....	101	23	8	31	.258	....	....	....	7	11	.636	....	....	42	10	20	0	....	....	....	8.4	1.9	3.5	0.8	....

• WILSON, George

George William (Ducky) Wilson

Born: Feb. 3, 1914. Chicago, IL, United States. Died: Nov.23, 1978.   Height: 6'1".   Weight: 190 lbs.   Drafted: —   College: Northwestern

YEAR	TEAM	GP	GS	MIN	PTS	FGM	FGA	FG%	3PM	3PA	3P%	FTM	FTA	FT%	ORB	DRB	TRB	AST	PF	DQ	STL	BLK	TO	MPG	PPG	RPG	APG	PCM
39-40	Chicago-N	16	....	....	18	5	....	....	....	....	....	8	....	....	....	....	....	....	....	....	....	....	....	1.1	....	....	....	....
NBL Season Totals		16	....	....	18	5	....	....	....	....	....	8	....	....	....	....	....	....	....	....	....	....	....	1.1	....	....	....	....

• WILSON, Harlan

Harlan Wilson

Born: 1914.   Height: 5'11".   Weight: 160 lbs.   Drafted: —   College: Indiana Central

YEAR	TEAM	GP	GS	MIN	PTS	FGM	FGA	FG%	3PM	3PA	3P%	FTM	FTA	FT%	ORB	DRB	TRB	AST	PF	DQ	STL	BLK	TO	MPG	PPG	RPG	APG	PCM
37-38	Indianapolis-N	11	....	....	72	24	....	....	....	....	....	24	....	....	....	....	....	....	....	....	....	....	....	6.5	....	....	....	....
NBL Season Totals		11	....	....	72	24	....	....	....	....	....	24	....	....	....	....	....	....	....	....	....	....	....	6.5	....	....	....	....

• WILSON, Isaiah

Isáiah (Bunny) Wilson

Born: May 31, 1948.   Height: 6'2".   Weight: 175 lbs.   Drafted: 1971   College: Baltimore

YEAR	TEAM	GP	GS	MIN	PTS	FGM	FGA	FG%	3PM	3PA	3P%	FTM	FTA	FT%	ORB	DRB	TRB	AST	PF	DQ	STL	BLK	TO	MPG	PPG	RPG	APG	PCM
71-72	Detroit	48	....	322	167	63	177	.356	....	....	....	41	56	.732	....	....	47	41	32	0	....	....	....	6.7	3.5	1.0	0.9	.420
72-73	Memphis-A	30	....	386	190	68	159	.428	3	8	.375	51	64	.797	18	21	39	72	46	0	....	....	41	12.9	6.3	1.3	2.4	.508
NBA Season Totals		48	....	322	167	63	177	.356	....	....	....	41	56	.732	....	....	47	41	32	0	....	....	....	6.7	3.5	1.0	0.9	....
ABA Season Totals		30	....	386	190	68	159	.428	3	8	.375	51	64	.797	18	21	39	72	46	0	....	....	41	12.9	6.3	1.3	2.4	....
Career Totals		78	....	708	357	131	336	.390	3	8	.375	92	120	.767	18	21	86	113	78	0	....	....	41	9.1	4.6	1.1	1.4	....

• WILSON, Jasper

Jasper Wilson

Born: July 12, 1947. Camden, AR, United States.   Height: 6'6".   Weight: 200 lbs.   Drafted: 1968   College: Southern University

YEAR	TEAM	GP	GS	MIN	PTS	FGM	FGA	FG%	3PM	3PA	3P%	FTM	FTA	FT%	ORB	DRB	TRB	AST	PF	DQ	STL	BLK	TO	MPG	PPG	RPG	APG	PCM
68-69	New Orleans-A	66	....	756	343	128	339	.378	5	12	.417	82	127	.646	61	112	173	43	127	1	....	....	63	11.5	5.2	2.6	0.7	.378
69-70	New Orleans-A	4	....	59	23	8	21	.381	1	2	.500	6	8	.750	2	12	14	2	6	0	....	....	4	14.8	5.8	3.5	0.5	.385
ABA Season Totals		70	....	815	366	136	360	.378	6	14	.429	88	135	.652	63	124	187	45	133	1	....	....	67	11.6	5.2	2.7	0.6	....
68-69	New Orleans-A	10	....	92	39	11	42	.262	0	5	.000	17	23	.739	....	....	26	2	20	0	....	....	4	9.2	3.9	2.6	0.2	.281
ABA Playoff Totals		10	....	92	39	11	42	.262	0	5	.000	17	23	.739	....	....	26	2	20	0	....	....	4	9.2	3.9	2.6	0.2	....

• WILSON, Jim

James Wilson

Born: 1948.   Height: 5'10".   Weight: 175 lbs.   Drafted: 1970   College: Cheyney State

YEAR	TEAM	GP	GS	MIN	PTS	FGM	FGA	FG%	3PM	3PA	3P%	FTM	FTA	FT%	ORB	DRB	TRB	AST	PF	DQ	STL	BLK	TO	MPG	PPG	RPG	APG	PCM
70-71	Pittsburgh-A	6	....	44	6	1	8	.125	0	0	.000	4	6	.667	1	5	6	8	3	0	....	:...	5	7.3	1.0	1.0	1.3	.291
ABA Season Totals		6	....	44	6	1	8	.125	0	0	.000	4	6	.667	1	5	6	8	3	0	....	....	5	7.3	1.0	1.0	1.3	....

• WILSON, Michael

Michael Wilson

Born: Sept. 15, 1959. Memphis, TN, United States.   Height: 6'4".   Weight: 175 lbs.   Drafted: 1982   College: Marquette

YEAR	TEAM	GP	GS	MIN	PTS	FGM	FGA	FG%	3PM	3PA	3P%	FTM	FTA	FT%	ORB	DRB	TRB	AST	PF	DQ	STL	BLK	TO	MPG	PPG	RPG	APG	PCM
83-84	Washington	6	0	26	1	0	2	.000	0	1	.000	1	2	.500	1	0	1	3	5	0	0	0	3	4.3	0.2	0.2	0.5	-.088
84-85	Cleveland	11	0	175	77	27	54	.500	0	0	.000	23	30	.767	10	8	18	24	14	0	10	3	15	15.9	7.0	1.6	2.2	.472
84-85	New Jersey	8	0	92	22	9	23	.391	0	0	.000	4	6	.667	4	9	13	11	7	0	4	2	5	11.5	2.8	1.6	1.4	.321
86-87	New Jersey	5	0	43	8	3	8	.375	0	0	.000	2	2	1.000	1	3	4	6	9	0	1	0	4	8.6	1.6	0.8	1.2	.151
86-87	Atlanta	2	0	2	0	0	2	.000	0	0	.000	0	0	.000	0	0	0	1	1	0	0	0	1	1.0	0.0	0.0	0.5	-1.09
NBA Season Totals		32	0	338	108	39	89	.438	0	1	.000	30	40	.750	16	20	36	45	36	0	15	5	28	10.6	3.4	1.1	1.4	....

WILSON, Nikita
Nikita Franciscus Wilson

Born: Feb. 25, 1964. Pineville, LA, United States.   Height: 6'8".   Weight: 200 lbs.   Drafted: 1987   College: Louisiana State

YEAR TEAM	GP	GS	MIN	PTS	FGM	FGA	FG%	3PM	3PA	3P%	FTM	FTA	FT%	ORB	DRB	TRB	AST	PF	DQ	STL	BLK	TO	MPG	PPG	RPG	APG	PCM
87-88 Portland	15	0	54	19	7	23	.304	0	0	.000	5	6	.833	2	9	11	3	7	0	0	0	5	3.6	1.3	0.7	0.2	.170
NBA Season Totals	15	0	54	19	7	23	.304	0	0	.000	5	6	.833	2	9	11	3	7	0	0	0	5	3.6	1.3	0.7	0.2	....

WILSON, Othell
Coatlen Othell Wilson

Born: Oct. 26, 1961. Alexandria, VA, United States.   Height: 6'   Weight: 190 lbs.   Drafted: 1984   College: Virginia

YEAR TEAM	GP	GS	MIN	PTS	FGM	FGA	FG%	3PM	3PA	3P%	FTM	FTA	FT%	ORB	DRB	TRB	AST	PF	DQ	STL	BLK	TO	MPG	PPG	RPG	APG	PCM
84-85 Golden State	74	23	1260	325	134	291	.460	3	16	.188	54	76	.711	35	96	131	217	122	0	77	12	96	17.0	4.4	1.8	2.9	.364
86-87 Sacramento	53	2	789	210	82	185	.443	3	18	.167	43	54	.796	28	53	81	207	67	0	42	4	80	14.9	4.0	1.5	3.9	.435
NBA Season Totals	127	25	2049	535	216	476	.454	6	34	.176	97	130	.746	63	149	212	424	189	0	119	16	176	16.1	4.2	1.7	3.3	....

WILSON, Rick
Richard Wilson

Born: Feb. 7, 1956. Louisville, KY, United States.   Height: 6'5".   Weight: 200 lbs.   Drafted: 1978   College: Louisville

YEAR TEAM	GP	GS	MIN	PTS	FGM	FGA	FG%	3PM	3PA	3P%	FTM	FTA	FT%	ORB	DRB	TRB	AST	PF	DQ	STL	BLK	TO	MPG	PPG	RPG	APG	PCM
78-79 Atlanta	61	....	589	186	81	197	.411	....	....	....	24	44	.545	20	56	76	72	66	1	30	8	43	9.7	3.0	1.2	1.2	.316
79-80 Atlanta	5	....	59	8	2	14	.143	0	0	.000	4	6	.667	2	1	3	11	3	0	4	1	8	11.8	1.6	0.6	2.2	.117
NBA Season Totals	66	....	648	194	83	211	.393	0	0	.000	28	50	.560	22	57	79	83	69	1	34	9	51	9.8	2.9	1.2	1.3	....
78-79 Atlanta	1	....	1	0	0	0	.000	....	....	....	0	0	.000	0	0	0	0	0	0	0	0	0	1.0	0.0	0.0	0.0	.000
NBA Playoff Totals	1	....	1	0	0	0	.000	....	....	....	0	0	.000	0	0	0	0	0	0	0	0	0	1.0	0.0	0.0	0.0	....

WILSON, Ricky
Ricky Wilson

Born: July 16, 1964. Hampton, VA, United States.   Height: 6'3".   Weight: 195 lbs.   Drafted: 1986   College: George Mason

YEAR TEAM	GP	GS	MIN	PTS	FGM	FGA	FG%	3PM	3PA	3P%	FTM	FTA	FT%	ORB	DRB	TRB	AST	PF	DQ	STL	BLK	TO	MPG	PPG	RPG	APG	PCM
87-88 New Jersey	6	0	47	21	7	11	.636	1	1	1.000	6	11	.545	1	0	1	6	6	0	6	0	4	7.8	3.5	0.2	1.0	.454
87-88 San Antonio	18	1	373	104	36	99	.364	9	25	.360	23	29	.793	1	25	26	63	34	0	17	3	22	20.7	5.8	1.4	3.5	.312
NBA Season Totals	24	1	420	125	43	110	.391	10	26	.385	29	40	.725	2	25	27	69	40	0	23	3	26	17.5	5.2	1.1	2.9	....
87-88 San Antonio	2	0	9	0	0	2	.000	0	0	.000	0	0	.000	0	0	0	1	2	0	0	0	1	4.5	0.0	0.0	0.5	-.296
NBA Playoff Totals	2	0	9	0	0	2	.000	0	0	.000	0	0	.000	0	0	0	1	2	0	0	0	1	4.5	0.0	0.0	0.5	....

WILSON, Stephen
Stephen Earl Wilson

Born: Oct. 16, 1948. Richmond, IN, United States.   Height: 6'5".   Weight: 185 lbs.   Drafted: 1970   College: Hanover

YEAR TEAM	GP	GS	MIN	PTS	FGM	FGA	FG%	3PM	3PA	3P%	FTM	FTA	FT%	ORB	DRB	TRB	AST	PF	DQ	STL	BLK	TO	MPG	PPG	RPG	APG	PCM
70-71 Denver-A	39	....	261	134	53	132	.402	6	33	.182	22	41	.537	22	26	48	29	43	1	....	....	30	6.7	3.4	1.2	0.7	.456
71-72 Denver-A	9	....	36	14	5	23	.217	0	2	.000	4	7	.571	3	1	4	6	9	0	....	....	3	4.0	1.6	0.4	0.7	.087
ABA Season Totals	48	....	297	148	58	155	.374	6	35	.171	26	48	.542	25	27	52	35	52	1	....	....	33	6.2	3.1	1.1	0.7	....

WILSON, Trevor
Trevor Wilson

Born: Mar. 16, 1968. Los Angeles, CA, United States.   Height: 6'7".   Weight: 210 lbs.   Drafted: 1990   College: UCLA

YEAR TEAM	GP	GS	MIN	PTS	FGM	FGA	FG%	3PM	3PA	3P%	FTM	FTA	FT%	ORB	DRB	TRB	AST	PF	DQ	STL	BLK	TO	MPG	PPG	RPG	APG	PCM
90-91 Atlanta	25	0	162	55	21	70	.300	0	2	.000	13	26	.500	16	24	40	11	13	0	5	1	18	6.5	2.2	1.6	0.4	.216
93-94 LA Lakers	5	4	126	51	19	39	.487	0	0	.000	13	25	.520	12	16	28	12	17	0	5	1	6	25.2	10.2	5.6	2.4	.461
93-94 Sacramento	52	9	1095	415	168	349	.481	0	2	.000	79	141	.560	108	137	245	60	106	0	33	10	88	21.1	8.0	4.7	1.2	.384
94-95 Sacramento	15	0	147	47	18	40	.450	0	0	.000	11	14	.786	10	16	26	12	12	0	4	2	6	9.8	3.1	1.7	0.8	.384
95-96 Philadelphia	6	0	79	23	10	20	.500	0	0	.000	3	4	.750	7	7	14	4	9	0	3	0	1	13.2	3.8	2.3	0.7	.357
NBA Season Totals	103	13	1609	591	236	518	.456	0	4	.000	119	210	.567	153	200	353	99	157	0	50	14	119	15.6	5.7	3.4	1.0	....

WINCHESTER, Kennard
Kennard Norman Winchester Jr.

Born: Sept. 3, 1966. Chestertown, MD, United States.   Height: 6'5".   Weight: 210 lbs.   Drafted: —   College: Averett

YEAR TEAM	GP	GS	MIN	PTS	FGM	FGA	FG%	3PM	3PA	3P%	FTM	FTA	FT%	ORB	DRB	TRB	AST	PF	DQ	STL	BLK	TO	MPG	PPG	RPG	APG	PCM
90-91 Houston	64	1	607	239	98	245	.400	8	20	.400	35	45	.778	34	33	67	25	70	0	16	13	32	9.5	3.7	1.0	0.4	.249
91-92 Houston	4	0	17	2	1	3	.333	0	0	.000	0	0	.000	0	0	0	1	0	0	0	0	0	4.3	0.5	0.0	0.0	-.019
91-92 New York	15	0	64	33	12	27	.444	1	2	.500	8	10	.800	6	9	15	8	4	0	2	2	2	4.3	2.2	1.0	0.5	.635
92-93 Houston	39	0	340	143	61	139	.439	4	19	.211	17	22	.773	17	32	49	13	40	0	10	10	16	8.7	3.7	1.3	0.3	.331
NBA Season Totals	122	1	1028	417	172	414	.415	13	41	.317	60	77	.779	57	74	131	46	115	0	28	25	50	8.4	3.4	1.1	0.4	....
91-92 New York	3	0	11	6	3	5	.600	0	0	.000	0	1	.000	0	0	0	2	0	0	0	0	1	3.7	2.0	0.0	0.7	.445
NBA Playoff Totals	3	0	11	6	3	5	.600	0	0	.000	0	1	.000	0	0	0	2	0	0	0	0	1	3.7	2.0	0.0	0.7	....

WINDIS, Tony
Tony John Windis

Born: Jan. 27, 1933.   Height: 6'1".   Weight: 160 lbs.   Drafted: 1959   College: Wyoming

YEAR TEAM	GP	GS	MIN	PTS	FGM	FGA	FG%	3PM	3PA	3P%	FTM	FTA	FT%	ORB	DRB	TRB	AST	PF	DQ	STL	BLK	TO	MPG	PPG	RPG	APG	PCM
59-60 Detroit	9	....	193	36	16	60	.267	....	....	....	4	6	.667	....	....	47	32	20	0	....	....	....	21.4	4.0	5.2	3.6	.361
NBA Season Totals	9	....	193	36	16	60	.267	....	....	....	4	6	.667	....	....	47	32	20	0	....	....	....	21.4	4.0	5.2	3.6	....

WINDSOR, John
John T. Windsor

Born: Apr. 3, 1940.   Height: 6'8".   Weight: 215 lbs.   Drafted: 1962   College: Stanford

YEAR TEAM	GP	GS	MIN	PTS	FGM	FGA	FG%	3PM	3PA	3P%	FTM	FTA	FT%	ORB	DRB	TRB	AST	PF	DQ	STL	BLK	TO	MPG	PPG	RPG	APG	PCM
63-64 San Francisco	11	....	68	27	10	27	.370	....	....	....	7	8	.875	....	....	26	2	13	0	....	....	....	6.2	2.5	2.4	0.2	.456
NBA Season Totals	11	....	68	27	10	27	.370	....	....	....	7	8	.875	....	....	26	2	13	0	....	....	....	6.2	2.5	2.4	0.2	....

YEAR	TEAM	GP	GS	MIN	PTS	FGM	FGA	FG%	3PM	3PA	3P%	FTM	FTA	FT%	ORB	DRB	TRB	AST	PF	DQ	STL	BLK	TO	MPG	PPG	RPG	APG	PCM

• WINFIELD, Lee

Leroy Winfield

Born: Feb. 4, 1947. St. Louis, MO, United States.   Height: 6'2".   Weight: 174 lbs.   Drafted: 1969   College: North Texas State

YEAR	TEAM	GP	GS	MIN	PTS	FGM	FGA	FG%	3PM	3PA	3P%	FTM	FTA	FT%	ORB	DRB	TRB	AST	PF	DQ	STL	BLK	TO	MPG	PPG	RPG	APG	PCM
69-70	Seattle	64	....	771	363	138	288	.479	....	....	....	87	116	.750	....	....	98	102	95	0	....	....	....	12.0	5.7	1.5	1.6	.489
70-71	Seattle	79	....	1605	830	334	716	.466	....	....	....	162	244	.664	....	....	193	225	135	1	....	....	....	20.3	10.5	2.4	2.8	.518
71-72	Seattle	81	....	2040	861	343	692	.496	....	....	....	175	262	.668	....	....	218	290	198	1	....	....	....	25.2	10.6	2.7	3.6	.468
72-73	Seattle	53	....	1061	348	143	332	.431	....	....	....	62	108	.574	....	....	126	186	92	3	....	....	....	20.0	6.6	2.4	3.5	.421
73-74	Buffalo	36	....	433	107	37	105	.352	....	....	....	33	52	.635	19	24	43	47	42	0	15	5	....	12.0	3.0	1.2	1.3	.263
74-75	Buffalo	68	....	1259	377	164	312	.526	....	....	....	49	68	.721	45	81	126	134	106	1	43	30	....	18.5	5.5	1.9	2.0	.364
75-76	Kansas City	22	....	214	73	32	66	.485	....	....	....	9	14	.643	8	16	24	19	14	0	10	6	....	9.7	3.3	1.1	0.9	.364
NBA Season Totals		403	....	7383	2959	1191	2511	.474	....	....	....	577	864	.668	72	121	828	1003	682	6	68	41	....	18.3	7.3	2.1	2.5	....
73-74	Buffalo	1	....	12	1	0	2	.000	....	....	....	1	2	.500	0	3	3	2	0	0	1	0	....	12.0	1.0	3.0	2.0	.310
74-75	Buffalo	6	....	65	17	7	16	.438	....	....	....	3	5	.600	5	3	8	9	10	1	2	1	....	10.8	2.8	1.3	1.5	.328
NBA Playoff Totals		7	....	77	18	7	18	.389	....	....	....	4	7	.571	5	6	11	11	10	1	3	1	....	11.0	2.6	1.6	1.6	....

• WINGATE, David

David Grover Stacey Wingate Jr.

Born: Dec. 15, 1963. Baltimore, MD, United States.   Height: 6'5".   Weight: 185 lbs.   Drafted: 1986   College: Georgetown

YEAR	TEAM	GP	GS	MIN	PTS	FGM	FGA	FG%	3PM	3PA	3P%	FTM	FTA	FT%	ORB	DRB	TRB	AST	PF	DQ	STL	BLK	TO	MPG	PPG	RPG	APG	PCM
86-87	Philadelphia	77	0	1612	680	259	602	.430	13	52	.250	149	201	.741	70	86	156	155	169	1	93	19	131	20.9	8.8	2.0	2.0	.342
87-88	Philadelphia	61	0	1419	545	218	545	.400	10	40	.250	99	132	.750	44	57	101	119	125	0	47	22	104	23.3	8.9	1.7	2.0	.250
88-89	Philadelphia	33	0	372	137	54	115	.470	2	6	.333	27	34	.794	12	25	37	73	43	0	9	2	36	11.3	4.2	1.1	2.2	.393
89-90	San Antonio	78	0	1856	527	220	491	.448	0	13	.000	87	112	.777	62	133	195	208	154	2	89	18	125	23.8	6.8	2.5	2.7	.310
90-91	San Antonio	25	0	563	136	53	138	.384	1	9	.111	29	41	.707	24	51	75	46	66	0	19	5	43	22.5	5.4	3.0	1.8	.216
91-92	Washington	81	72	2127	638	266	572	.465	1	18	.056	105	146	.719	80	189	269	247	162	1	123	21	122	26.3	7.9	3.3	3.0	.373
92-93	Charlotte	72	55	1471	440	180	336	.536	1	6	.167	79	107	.738	49	125	174	183	135	1	66	9	86	20.4	6.1	2.4	2.5	.385
93-94	Charlotte	50	36	1005	310	136	283	.481	4	12	.333	34	51	.667	30	104	134	104	85	0	42	6	55	20.1	6.2	2.7	2.1	.356
94-95	Charlotte	52	9	515	122	50	122	.410	4	22	.182	18	24	.750	11	49	60	56	60	0	19	6	26	9.9	2.3	1.2	1.1	.269
95-96	Seattle	60	3	695	223	88	212	.415	15	34	.441	32	41	.780	17	39	56	58	66	0	20	4	42	11.6	3.7	0.9	1.0	.242
96-97	Seattle	65	2	929	236	89	214	.416	25	71	.352	33	40	.825	23	51	74	80	108	0	44	5	39	14.3	3.6	1.1	1.2	.247
97-98	Seattle	58	2	546	150	66	140	.471	3	7	.429	15	29	.517	19	60	79	37	58	0	21	3	35	9.4	2.6	1.4	0.6	.278
98-99	New York	20	0	92	14	7	16	.438	0	0	.000	0	0	.000	3	5	8	5	10	0	4	0	6	4.6	0.7	0.4	0.3	.135
99-00	New York	7	0	32	2	1	9	.111	0	0	.000	0	0	.000	1	1	2	3	7	0	1	2	2	4.6	0.3	0.3	0.4	-.076
00-01	Seattle	1	0	9	6	3	3	1.000	0	0	.000	0	0	.000	0	0	0	2	1	0	0	0	0	9.0	6.0	0.0	2.0	.862
NBA Season Totals		740	179	13243	4166	1690	3798	.445	79	290	.272	707	958	.738	445	975	1420	1376	1249	5	597	122	852	17.9	5.6	1.9	1.9	....
86-87	Philadelphia	5	0	90	41	15	37	.405	2	2	1.000	9	14	.643	5	7	12	9	11	1	5	1	9	18.0	8.2	2.4	1.8	.345
89-90	San Antonio	10	0	293	91	40	77	.519	2	3	.667	9	12	.750	9	28	37	38	34	1	18	3	14	29.3	9.1	3.7	3.8	.412
90-91	San Antonio	3	0	38	14	6	12	.500	0	0	.000	2	3	.667	1	2	3	1	8	1	1	0	1	12.7	4.7	1.0	0.3	.212
92-93	Charlotte	9	0	117	19	8	22	.364	0	0	.000	3	8	.375	4	8	12	15	9	0	4	1	1	13.0	2.1	1.3	1.7	.259
94-95	Charlotte	4	4	73	32	13	27	.481	2	6	.333	4	6	.667	3	3	6	15	14	0	4	0	4	18.3	8.0	1.5	3.8	.451
95-96	Seattle	13	0	68	19	7	16	.438	1	2	.500	4	4	1.000	1	2	3	0	16	0	0	0	4	5.2	1.5	0.2	0.0	.031
96-97	Seattle	12	0	192	77	28	66	.424	12	31	.387	9	13	.692	13	24	37	14	22	0	5	3	9	16.0	6.4	3.1	1.2	.406
97-98	Seattle	3	0	13	8	2	5	.400	0	0	.000	4	6	.667	2	2	4	2	1	0	1	0	1	4.3	2.7	1.3	0.7	.747
NBA Playoff Totals		59	4	884	301	119	262	.454	19	44	.432	44	66	.667	38	76	114	94	115	3	38	8	43	15.0	5.1	1.9	1.6	....

• WINGFIELD, Dontonio

Dontonio Wingfield

Born: June 23, 1974. Albany, GA, United States.   Height: 6'8".   Weight: 256 lbs.   Drafted: 1994   College: Cincinnati

YEAR	TEAM	GP	GS	MIN	PTS	FGM	FGA	FG%	3PM	3PA	3P%	FTM	FTA	FT%	ORB	DRB	TRB	AST	PF	DQ	STL	BLK	TO	MPG	PPG	RPG	APG	PCM
94-95	Seattle	20	0	81	46	18	51	.353	2	12	.167	8	10	.800	11	19	30	3	15	0	5	3	8	4.1	2.3	1.5	0.2	.474
95-96	Portland	44	2	487	165	60	157	.382	19	63	.302	26	34	.765	45	59	104	28	73	1	20	6	31	11.1	3.8	2.4	0.6	.325
96-97	Portland	47	0	569	211	79	193	.409	26	77	.338	27	40	.675	63	74	137	45	101	1	14	6	47	12.1	4.5	2.9	1.0	.355
97-98	Portland	3	0	9	1	0	3	.000	0	0	.000	1	2	.500	2	2	4	0	2	0	0	0	1	3.0	0.3	1.3	0.0	-.041
NBA Season Totals		114	2	1146	423	157	404	.389	47	152	.309	62	86	.721	121	154	275	76	191	2	39	15	87	10.1	3.7	2.4	0.7	....
95-96	Portland	5	0	62	24	8	21	.381	6	10	.600	2	6	.333	10	4	14	4	10	0	0	0	3	12.4	4.8	2.8	0.8	.319
96-97	Portland	3	0	16	8	2	2	1.000	0	0	.000	4	4	1.000	0	2	2	1	3	0	1	0	2	5.3	2.7	0.7	0.3	.538
NBA Playoff Totals		8	0	78	32	10	23	.435	6	10	.600	6	10	.600	10	6	16	5	13	0	1	0	5	9.8	4.0	2.0	0.6	....

• WINGO, Harthorne

Harthorne Nathaniel (Wingy) Wingo

Born: Sept. 9, 1947. Tryon, NC, United States.   Height: 6'6".   Weight: 210 lbs.   Drafted: —   College: Friendship JC

YEAR	TEAM	GP	GS	MIN	PTS	FGM	FGA	FG%	3PM	3PA	3P%	FTM	FTA	FT%	ORB	DRB	TRB	AST	PF	DQ	STL	BLK	TO	MPG	PPG	RPG	APG	PCM
72-73	New York	13	....	59	20	9	22	.409	....	....	....	2	6	.333	....	....	16	1	9	0	....	....	....	4.5	1.5	1.2	0.1	.307
73-74	New York	60	....	536	212	82	172	.477	....	....	....	48	76	.632	72	94	166	25	85	0	7	14	....	8.9	3.5	2.8	0.4	.480
74-75	New York	82	....	1686	607	233	506	.460	....	....	....	141	187	.754	163	293	456	84	215	2	48	35	....	20.6	7.4	5.6	1.0	.444
75-76	New York	57	....	533	184	72	163	.442	....	....	....	40	60	.667	46	61	107	18	59	0	19	8	....	9.4	3.2	1.9	0.3	.346
NBA Season Totals		212	....	2814	1023	396	863	.459	....	....	....	231	329	.702	281	448	745	128	368	2	74	57	....	13.3	4.8	3.5	0.6	....
72-73	New York	3	....	12	11	5	13	.385	....	....	....	1	2	.500	....	....	7	0	1	0	....	....	....	4.0	3.7	2.3	0.0	.774
73-74	New York	5	....	16	12	6	11	.545	....	....	....	0	0	.000	2	1	3	1	2	0	1	0	....	3.2	2.4	0.6	0.2	.662
74-75	New York	3	....	76	27	10	23	.435	....	....	....	7	10	.700	9	13	22	7	7	0	4	0	....	25.3	9.0	7.3	2.3	.506
NBA Playoff Totals		11	....	104	50	21	47	.447	....	....	....	8	12	.667	11	14	32	8	10	0	5	0	....	9.5	4.5	2.9	0.7	....

YEAR	TEAM	GP	GS	MIN	PTS	FGM	FGA	FG%	3PM	3PA	3P%	FTM	FTA	FT%	ORB	DRB	TRB	AST	PF	DQ	STL	BLK	TO	MPG	PPG	RPG	APG	PCM

• WINKLER, Marv
Marvin Winkler

Born: Feb. 18, 1948. Height: 6'1". Weight: 164 lbs. Drafted: 1970 College: Southwestern Louisiana

YEAR	TEAM	GP	GS	MIN	PTS	FGM	FGA	FG%	3PM	3PA	3P%	FTM	FTA	FT%	ORB	DRB	TRB	AST	PF	DQ	STL	BLK	TO	MPG	PPG	RPG	APG	PCM
70-71	Milwaukee	3	....	14	8	3	10	.300	....	....	....	2	2	1.000	....	....	4	2	3	0	....	....	....	4.7	2.7	1.3	0.7	.458
71-72	Indiana-A	20	....	155	40	15	54	.278	2	4	.500	8	14	.571	7	9	16	12	16	0	....	....	12	7.8	2.0	0.8	0.6	.152
NBA Season Totals		3	....	14	8	3	10	.300	....	....	....	2	2	1.000	....	....	4	2	3	0	....	....	....	4.7	2.7	1.3	0.7	....
ABA Season Totals		20	....	155	40	15	54	.278	2	4	.500	8	14	.571	7	9	16	12	16	0	....	....	12	7.8	2.0	0.8	0.6	....
Career Totals		23	....	169	48	18	64	.281	2	4	.500	10	16	.625	7	9	20	14	19	0	....	....	12	7.3	2.1	0.9	0.6	....
70-71	Milwaukee	5	....	8	0	0	4	.000	....	....	....	0	0	.000	....	....	0	1	3	0	....	....	....	1.6	0.0	0.0	0.2	-.449
NBA Playoff Totals		5	....	8	0	0	4	.000	....	....	....	0	0	.000	....	....	0	1	3	0	....	....	....	1.6	0.0	0.0	0.2	....

• WINSLOW, Rickie
Rickie O'Neal Winslow

Born: July 26, 1964. Houston, TX, United States. Height: 6'8". Weight: 225 lbs. Drafted: 1987 College: Houston

YEAR	TEAM	GP	GS	MIN	PTS	FGM	FGA	FG%	3PM	3PA	3P%	FTM	FTA	FT%	ORB	DRB	TRB	AST	PF	DQ	STL	BLK	TO	MPG	PPG	RPG	APG	PCM
87-88	Milwaukee	7	0	45	7	3	13	.231	0	1	.000	1	2	.500	3	4	7	2	9	0	1	0	4	6.4	1.0	1.0	0.3	-.025
NBA Season Totals		7	0	45	7	3	13	.231	0	1	.000	1	2	.500	3	4	7	2	9	0	1	0	4	6.4	1.0	1.0	0.3	....

• WINTER, Trevor
Trevor Winter

Born: Jan. 7, 1974. Slayton, MN, United States. Height: 7' Weight: 275 lbs. Drafted: — College: Minnesota

YEAR	TEAM	GP	GS	MIN	PTS	FGM	FGA	FG%	3PM	3PA	3P%	FTM	FTA	FT%	ORB	DRB	TRB	AST	PF	DQ	STL	BLK	TO	MPG	PPG	RPG	APG	PCM
98-99	Minnesota	1	0	5	0	0	0	.000	0	0	.000	0	0	.000	1	2	3	0	5	0	0	0	0	5.0	0.0	3.0	0.0	.089
NBA Season Totals		1	0	5	0	0	0	.000	0	0	.000	0	0	.000	1	2	3	0	5	0	0	0	0	5.0	0.0	3.0	0.0	....

• WINTERMUTE, Urgel
Urgel (Slim) Wintermute

Born: July 9, 1917. Portland, OR, United States. Height: 6'8". Weight: 200 lbs. Drafted: — College: Oregon

YEAR	TEAM	GP	GS	MIN	PTS	FGM	FGA	FG%	3PM	3PA	3P%	FTM	FTA	FT%	ORB	DRB	TRB	AST	PF	DQ	STL	BLK	TO	MPG	PPG	RPG	APG	PCM
39-40	Detroit-N	25	....	....	180	65	....	....	....	....	....	50	....	....	....	....	....	....	....	....	....	....	....	7.2	....	....	....
NBL Season Totals		25	....	....	180	65	....	....	....	....	....	50	....	....	....	....	....	....	....	....	....	....	....	7.2	....	....	....
39-40	Detroit-N	2	....	....	6	3	....	....	....	....	....	0	....	....	....	....	....	....	....	....	....	....	....	3.0	....	....	....
NBL Playoff Totals		2	....	....	6	3	....	....	....	....	....	0	....	....	....	....	....	....	....	....	....	....	....	3.0	....	....	....

• WINTERS, Brian
Brian Joseph Winters

Born: Mar. 1, 1952. Rockaway, NY, United States. Height: 6'4". Weight: 185 lbs. Drafted: 1974 College: South Carolina

YEAR	TEAM	GP	GS	MIN	PTS	FGM	FGA	FG%	3PM	3PA	3P%	FTM	FTA	FT%	ORB	DRB	TRB	AST	PF	DQ	STL	BLK	TO	MPG	PPG	RPG	APG	PCM
74-75	LA Lakers	68	....	1516	794	359	810	.443	....	....	....	76	92	.826	39	99	138	195	168	1	74	18	....	22.3	11.7	2.0	2.9	.443
75-76	Milwaukee	78	....	2795	1416	618	1333	.464	....	....	....	180	217	.829	66	183	249	366	240	0	124	25	....	35.8	18.2	3.2	4.7	.471
76-77	Milwaukee	78	....	2717	1509	652	1308	.498	....	....	....	205	242	.847	64	167	231	337	228	1	114	29	....	34.8	19.3	3.0	4.3	.519
77-78	Milwaukee	80	....	2751	1594	674	1457	.463	....	....	....	246	293	.840	87	163	250	393	239	4	124	27	240	34.4	19.9	3.1	4.9	.497
78-79	Milwaukee	79	....	2575	1561	662	1343	.493	....	....	....	237	277	.856	48	129	177	383	243	1	83	40	261	32.6	19.8	2.2	4.8	.497
79-80	Milwaukee	80	....	2623	1292	535	1116	.479	38	102	.373	184	214	.860	48	175	223	362	208	0	101	28	184	32.8	16.2	2.8	4.5	.460
80-81	Milwaukee	69	....	1771	799	331	697	.475	18	51	.353	119	137	.869	32	108	140	229	185	2	70	10	138	25.7	11.6	2.0	3.3	.394
81-82	Milwaukee	61	13	1829	967	404	806	.501	36	93	.387	123	156	.788	51	119	170	253	187	1	57	9	116	30.0	15.9	2.8	4.1	.481
82-83	Milwaukee	57	12	1361	605	255	587	.434	22	68	.324	73	85	.859	35	75	110	156	132	2	45	4	80	23.9	10.6	1.9	2.7	.355
NBA Season Totals		650	25	19938	10537	4490	9457	.475	114	314	.363	1443	1713	.842	470	1218	1688	2674	1830	12	792	190	1019	30.7	16.2	2.6	4.1	....
75-76	Milwaukee	3	....	126	82	39	62	.629	....	....	....	4	5	.800	3	4	7	15	11	1	5	2	....	42.0	27.3	2.3	5.0	.637
77-78	Milwaukee	9	....	305	184	82	165	.497	....	....	....	20	27	.741	4	26	30	58	20	0	12	8	29	33.9	20.4	3.3	6.4	.601
79-80	Milwaukee	7	....	268	111	46	100	.460	9	21	.429	10	10	1.000	4	17	21	37	25	1	11	0	16	38.3	15.9	3.0	5.3	.395
80-81	Milwaukee	7	....	181	70	28	61	.459	2	6	.333	12	16	.750	4	19	23	22	22	1	10	1	12	25.9	10.0	3.3	3.1	.398
81-82	Milwaukee	6	6	232	101	38	77	.494	5	10	.500	20	24	.833	4	11	15	28	23	0	8	1	22	38.7	16.8	2.5	4.7	.365
82-83	Milwaukee	9	3	240	89	36	84	.429	3	11	.273	14	17	.824	7	15	22	32	22	0	6	4	17	26.7	9.9	2.4	3.6	.346
NBA Playoff Totals		41	9	1352	637	269	549	.490	19	48	.396	80	99	.808	26	92	118	192	123	3	52	16	96	33.0	15.5	2.9	4.7	....

• WINTERS, Voise
Voise Lee Winters

Born: Oct. 12, 1962. Chicago, IL, United States. Height: 6'8". Weight: 200 lbs. Drafted: 1985 College: Bradley

YEAR	TEAM	GP	GS	MIN	PTS	FGM	FGA	FG%	3PM	3PA	3P%	FTM	FTA	FT%	ORB	DRB	TRB	AST	PF	DQ	STL	BLK	TO	MPG	PPG	RPG	APG	PCM
85-86	Philadelphia	4	0	17	6	3	13	.231	0	1	.000	0	0	.000	1	2	3	0	1	0	1	0	2	4.3	1.5	0.8	0.0	-.112
NBA Season Totals		4	0	17	6	3	13	.231	0	1	.000	0	0	.000	1	2	3	0	1	0	1	0	2	4.3	1.5	0.8	0.0	....

• WISBAR, Eddie
Edward Wisbar

Born: May 3, 1916. Died: Apr.1967. Height: 6'6". Weight: 200 lbs. Drafted: — College: none

YEAR	TEAM	GP	GS	MIN	PTS	FGM	FGA	FG%	3PM	3PA	3P%	FTM	FTA	FT%	ORB	DRB	TRB	AST	PF	DQ	STL	BLK	TO	MPG	PPG	RPG	APG	PCM
37-38	Pittsburgh-N	13	....	....	76	27	....	....	....	....	....	22	....	....	....	....	....	....	....	....	....	....	....	5.8	....	....	....
NBL Season Totals		13	....	....	76	27	....	....	....	....	....	22	....	....	....	....	....	....	....	....	....	....	....	5.8	....	....	....

• WISE, Skip
Allen Harper (Skip) Wise Jr.

Born: July 25, 1955. Height: 6'2". Weight: 170 lbs. Drafted: — College: Clemson

YEAR	TEAM	GP	GS	MIN	PTS	FGM	FGA	FG%	3PM	3PA	3P%	FTM	FTA	FT%	ORB	DRB	TRB	AST	PF	DQ	STL	BLK	TO	MPG	PPG	RPG	APG	PCM
75-76	San Antonio-A	2	....	10	4	2	4	.500	0	0	.000	0	0	.000	1	2	3	1	4	....	0	0	2	5.0	2.0	1.5	0.5	.422
ABA Season Totals		2	....	10	4	2	4	.500	0	0	.000	0	0	.000	1	2	3	1	4	....	0	0	2	5.0	2.0	1.5	0.5	....

• WISE, Willie

Willie M. (Wondrous Willie) Wise

Born: Mar. 3, 1947. San Francisco, CA, United States. Height: 6'5". Weight: 210 lbs. Drafted: 1969 College: Drake

YEAR	TEAM	GP	GS	MIN	PTS	FGM	FGA	FG%	3PM	3PA	3P%	FTM	FTA	FT%	ORB	DRB	TRB	AST	PF	DQ	STL	BLK	TO	MPG	PPG	RPG	APG	PCM
69-70	Los Angeles-A	82	....	2709	1248	483	1014	.476	4	17	.235	278	427	.651	283	669	952	204	301	8	....	....	186	33.0	15.2	11.6	2.5	.609
70-71	Utah-A	82	....	2676	1299	491	1059	.464	5	17	.294	312	467	.668	307	500	807	204	297	5	....	....	179	32.6	15.8	9.8	2.5	.581
71-72	Utah-A	84	....	3300	1951	743	1471	.505	6	18	.333	459	633	.725	282	612	894	286	299	3	....	....	282	39.3	23.2	10.6	3.4	.670
72-73	Utah-A	83	....	3131	1823	672	1404	.479	3	18	.167	476	607	.784	217	465	682	277	278	5	....	....	236	37.7	22.0	8.2	3.3	.607
73-74	Utah-A	82	....	3292	1826	714	1458	.490	2	16	.125	396	501	.790	170	453	623	302	246	....	118	43	202	40.1	22.3	7.6	3.7	.582
74-75	Virginia-A	16	....	574	334	128	296	.432	1	4	.250	77	111	.694	32	70	102	54	50	....	26	3	45	35.9	20.9	6.4	3.4	.519
75-76	Virginia-A	46	....	1343	629	247	595	.415	0	6	.000	135	175	.771	89	173	262	125	135	....	53	13	125	29.2	13.7	5.7	2.7	.456
76-77	Denver	75	....	1403	616	237	513	.462	....	....	....	142	218	.651	76	177	253	142	180	2	60	18	....	18.7	8.2	3.4	1.9	.461
77-78	Seattle	2	....	10	1	0	3	.000	....	....	....	1	4	.250	2	1	3	0	2	0	0	0	0	5.0	0.5	1.5	0.0	-.119
NBA Season Totals		77	....	1413	617	237	516	.459	....	....	....	143	222	.644	78	178	256	142	182	2	60	18	0	18.4	8.0	3.3	1.8	....
ABA Season Totals		475	....	17025	9110	3478	7297	.477	21	96	.219	2133	2921	.730	1380	2942	4322	1452	1606	21	197	59	1255	35.8	19.2	9.1	3.1	....
Career Totals		552	....	18438	9727	3715	7813	.475	21	96	.219	2276	3143	.724	1458	3120	4578	1594	1788	23	257	77	1255	33.4	17.6	8.3	2.9	....
69-70	Los Angeles-A	12	....	237	115	50	97	.515	0	2	.000	15	31	.484	....	....	64	23	....	1	....	....	17	19.8	9.6	5.3	1.9	....
70-71	Utah-A	17	....	691	359	139	271	.513	0	2	.000	81	116	.698	57	163	220	82	65	1	....	....	49	40.6	21.1	12.9	4.8	.706
71-72	Utah-A	11	....	458	278	112	199	.563	0	1	.000	54	80	.675	29	99	128	33	44	2	....	....	38	41.6	25.3	11.6	3.0	.699
72-73	Utah-A	10	....	414	250	92	181	.508	1	3	.333	65	83	.783	27	56	83	38	33	1	....	....	35	41.4	25.0	8.3	3.8	.637
73-74	Utah-A	18	....	792	420	171	372	.460	1	2	.500	77	101	.762	38	111	149	48	51	....	25	10	51	44.0	23.3	8.3	2.7	.503
76-77	Denver	6	....	106	45	14	41	.341	....	....	....	17	25	.680	6	22	28	3	16	0	0	1	....	17.7	7.5	4.7	0.5	.367
NBA Playoff Totals		6	....	106	45	14	41	.341	....	....	....	17	25	.680	6	22	28	3	16	0	0	1	....	17.7	7.5	4.7	0.5	....
ABA Playoff Totals		68	....	2592	1422	564	1120	.504	2	10	.200	292	411	.710	151	429	644	224	193	5	25	10	190	38.1	20.9	9.5	3.3	....
Career Playoff Totals		74	....	2698	1467	578	1161	.498	2	10	.200	309	436	.709	157	451	672	227	209	5	25	11	190	36.5	19.8	9.1	3.1	....

• WITASEK, Herm

Herman J. Witasek

Born: 1913. Lankin, ND, United States. Height: 6'3". Weight: 210 lbs. Drafted: — College: North Dakota

YEAR	TEAM	GP	GS	MIN	PTS	FGM	FGA	FG%	3PM	3PA	3P%	FTM	FTA	FT%	ORB	DRB	TRB	AST	PF	DQ	STL	BLK	TO	MPG	PPG	RPG	APG	PCM
37-38	Oshkosh-N	13	....	....	69	29	....	....	....	....	....	11	....	....	....	....	....	....	....	....	....	....	....	....	5.3	....	....	....
38-39	Oshkosh-N	28	....	....	141	56	....	....	....	....	....	29	....	....	....	....	....	....	....	....	....	....	....	....	5.0	....	....	....
39-40	Oshkosh-N	28	....	....	162	62	....	....	....	....	....	38	....	....	....	....	....	....	....	....	....	....	....	....	5.8	....	....	....
40-41	Oshkosh-N	24	....	....	136	54	....	....	....	....	....	28	....	....	....	....	....	....	....	....	....	....	....	....	5.7	....	....	....
41-42	Oshkosh-N	21	....	....	70	25	....	....	....	....	....	20	....	....	....	....	....	....	....	....	....	....	....	....	3.3	....	....	....
NBL Season Totals		114	....	....	578	226	....	....	....	....	....	126	....	....	....	....	....	....	....	....	....	....	....	....	5.1	....	....	....
37-38	Oshkosh-N	5	....	....	9	4	....	....	....	....	....	1	....	....	....	....	....	....	....	....	....	....	....	....	1.8	....	....	....
38-39	Oshkosh-N	5	....	....	35	15	....	....	....	....	....	5	....	....	....	....	....	....	....	....	....	....	....	....	7.0	....	....	....
39-40	Oshkosh-N	8	....	....	44	16	....	....	....	....	....	12	....	....	....	....	....	....	....	....	....	....	....	....	5.5	....	....	....
40-41	Oshkosh-N	5	....	....	28	11	....	....	....	....	....	6	....	....	....	....	....	....	....	....	....	....	....	....	5.6	....	....	....
NBL Playoff Totals		23	....	....	116	46	....	....	....	....	....	24	....	....	....	....	....	....	....	....	....	....	....	....	5.0	....	....	....

• WITTE, Luke

Luke Witte

Born: Oct. 19, 1950. Philadelphia, PA, United States. Height: 7' Weight: 235 lbs. Drafted: 1973 College: Ohio State

YEAR	TEAM	GP	GS	MIN	PTS	FGM	FGA	FG%	3PM	3PA	3P%	FTM	FTA	FT%	ORB	DRB	TRB	AST	PF	DQ	STL	BLK	TO	MPG	PPG	RPG	APG	PCM
73-74	Cleveland	57	....	728	256	105	243	.432	....	....	....	46	62	.742	80	147	227	41	91	0	8	22	....	12.8	4.5	4.0	0.7	.458
74-75	Cleveland	39	....	271	85	33	96	.344	....	....	....	19	31	.613	38	54	92	15	42	0	4	22	....	6.9	2.2	2.4	0.4	.383
75-76	Cleveland	22	....	99	31	11	32	.344	....	....	....	9	15	.600	9	29	38	4	14	0	1	1	....	4.5	1.4	1.7	0.2	.420
NBA Season Totals		118	....	1098	372	149	371	.402	....	....	....	74	108	.685	127	230	357	60	147	0	13	45	....	9.3	3.2	3.0	0.5	....
75-76	Cleveland	7	....	28	16	6	11	.545	....	....	....	4	4	1.000	4	5	9	4	4	0	0	0	....	4.0	2.3	1.3	0.6	.796
NBA Playoff Totals		7	....	28	16	6	11	.545	....	....	....	4	4	1.000	4	5	9	4	4	0	0	0	....	4.0	2.3	1.3	0.6	....

• WITTMAN, Greg

H. Gregory Wittman

Born: May 10, 1947. Rockingham, NC, United States. Height: 6'8". Weight: 210 lbs. Drafted: 1969 College: Western Carolina

YEAR	TEAM	GP	GS	MIN	PTS	FGM	FGA	FG%	3PM	3PA	3P%	FTM	FTA	FT%	ORB	DRB	TRB	AST	PF	DQ	STL	BLK	TO	MPG	PPG	RPG	APG	PCM
69-70	Denver-A	50	....	453	196	80	204	.392	4	17	.235	32	59	.542	30	68	98	15	87	2	....	....	36	9.1	3.9	2.0	0.3	.313
70-71	Florida-A	5	....	40	8	2	12	.167	0	0	.000	4	7	.571	5	5	10	0	14	1	....	....	4	8.0	1.6	2.0	0.0	.030
70-71	Texas-A	5	....	30	8	4	13	.308	0	1	.000	0	2	.000	4	5	9	0	7	0	....	....	4	6.0	1.6	1.8	0.0	.147
ABA Season Totals		60	....	523	212	86	229	.376	4	18	.222	36	68	.529	39	78	117	15	108	3	....	....	44	8.7	3.5	2.0	0.3	....
69-70	Denver-A	2	....	4	4	1	2	.500	1	1	1.000	1	3	.333	0	0	0	0	2	0	....	....	0	2.0	2.0	0.0	0.0	.357
ABA Playoff Totals		2	....	4	4	1	2	.500	1	1	1.000	1	3	.333	0	0	0	0	2	0	....	....	0	2.0	2.0	0.0	0.0	....

• WITTMAN, Randy

Randy Scott Wittman

Born: Oct. 28, 1959. Indianapolis, IN, United States. Height: 6'6". Weight: 210 lbs. Drafted: 1983 College: Indiana

YEAR	TEAM	GP	GS	MIN	PTS	FGM	FGA	FG%	3PM	3PA	3P%	FTM	FTA	FT%	ORB	DRB	TRB	AST	PF	DQ	STL	BLK	TO	MPG	PPG	RPG	APG	PCM
83-84	Atlanta	78	1	1071	350	160	318	.503	2	5	.400	28	46	.609	14	57	71	71	82	0	17	0	31	13.7	4.5	0.9	0.9	.267
84-85	Atlanta	41	22	1168	406	187	352	.531	2	7	.286	30	41	.732	16	57	73	125	58	0	28	7	57	28.5	9.9	1.8	3.0	.343
85-86	Atlanta	81	79	2760	1043	467	881	.530	5	16	.313	104	135	.770	51	119	170	306	118	0	81	14	113	34.1	12.9	2.1	3.8	.383
86-87	Atlanta	71	65	2049	900	398	792	.503	4	12	.333	100	127	.787	30	94	124	211	107	0	39	16	85	28.9	12.7	1.7	3.0	.383
87-88	Atlanta	82	82	2412	823	376	787	.478	0	0	.000	71	89	.798	39	131	170	302	117	0	50	18	82	29.4	10.0	2.1	3.7	.350
88-89	Sacramento	31	2	416	118	50	117	.427	2	4	.500	16	22	.727	6	20	26	32	12	0	10	0	12	13.4	3.8	0.8	1.0	.250
88-89	Indiana	33	11	704	173	80	169	.473	1	2	.500	12	19	.632	20	34	54	79	31	0	13	2	20	21.3	5.2	1.6	2.4	.288
89-90	Indiana	61	0	544	130	62	122	.508	1	2	.500	5	6	.833	4	26	30	39	21	0	7	4	24	8.9	2.1	0.5	0.6	.222
90-91	Indiana	41	0	355	74	35	79	.443	0	5	.000	4	6	.667	6	27	33	25	9	0	10	4	8	8.7	1.8	0.8	0.6	.256
91-92	Indiana	24	0	115	17	8	19	.421	0	0	.000	1	2	.500	1	8	9	11	4	0	2	0	2	4.8	0.7	0.4	0.5	.214
NBA Season Totals		543	262	11594	4034	1823	3636	.501	17	53	.321	371	493	.753	187	573	760	1201	559	0	257	65	434	21.4	7.4	1.4	2.2	....

YEAR	TEAM	GP	GS	MIN	PTS	FGM	FGA	FG%	3PM	3PA	3P%	FTM	FTA	FT%	ORB	DRB	TRB	AST	PF	DQ	STL	BLK	TO	MPG	PPG	RPG	APG	PCM
83-84	Atlanta	5	0	96	40	20	37	.541	0	0	.000	0	0	.000	5	4	9	11	5	0	1	0	4	19.2	8.0	1.8	2.2	.408
85-86	Atlanta	9	9	348	160	71	135	.526	0	2	.000	18	26	.692	4	20	24	30	16	0	10	1	13	38.7	17.8	2.7	3.3	.408
86-87	Atlanta	9	9	300	148	67	121	.554	0	0	.000	14	17	.824	3	15	18	30	22	0	4	4	12	33.3	16.4	2.0	3.3	.437
87-88	Atlanta	12	12	344	137	66	122	.541	0	0	.000	5	7	.714	9	17	26	43	24	0	7	1	13	28.7	11.4	2.2	3.6	.402
89-90	Indiana	2	0	11	0	0	0	.000	0	0	.000	0	0	.000	0	1	1	0	0	0	0	0	0	5.5	0.0	0.5	0.0	.000
90-91	Indiana	1	0	6	2	1	1	1.000	0	0	.000	0	0	.000	0	0	0	1	1	0	0	0	0	6.0	2.0	0.0	1.0	.433
NBA Playoff Totals		38	30	1105	487	225	417	.540	0	2	.000	37	50	.740	21	57	78	115	68	0	22	6	42	29.1	12.8	2.1	3.0	....

• WITTS, Garry

Garrett David Witts

Born: July 3, 1959. Elizabeth, NJ, United States.　Height: 6'7".　Weight: 190 lbs.　Drafted: 1981　College: Holy Cross

YEAR	TEAM	GP	GS	MIN	PTS	FGM	FGA	FG%	3PM	3PA	3P%	FTM	FTA	FT%	ORB	DRB	TRB	AST	PF	DQ	STL	BLK	TO	MPG	PPG	RPG	APG	PCM
81-82	Washington	46	0	493	132	49	84	.583	1	2	.500	33	40	.825	29	33	62	38	74	1	17	4	37	10.7	2.9	1.3	0.8	.296
NBA Season Totals		46	0	493	132	49	84	.583	1	2	.500	33	40	.825	29	33	62	38	74	1	17	4	37	10.7	2.9	1.3	0.8	....
81-82	Washington	4	0	28	5	2	2	1.000	0	0	.000	1	2	.500	2	1	3	2	6	0	1	0	0	7.0	1.3	0.8	0.5	.272
NBA Playoff Totals		4	0	28	5	2	2	1.000	0	0	.000	1	2	.500	2	1	3	2	6	0	1	0	0	7.0	1.3	0.8	0.5	....

• WNOROWSKI, Kayo

Kayo Wnorowski

Born: 1921.　Height: 6'　Weight: 215 lbs.　Drafted: —　College: Siena

YEAR	TEAM	GP	GS	MIN	PTS	FGM	FGA	FG%	3PM	3PA	3P%	FTM	FTA	FT%	ORB	DRB	TRB	AST	PF	DQ	STL	BLK	TO	MPG	PPG	RPG	APG	PCM
48-49	Denver-N	19	....	....	31	14	....	....	0	0	....	3	8	.375	....	....	....	....	17	....	....	....	....	....	1.6	....	....	....
NBL Season Totals		19	....	....	31	14	....	....				3	8		....	....	....	....	17	....	....	....	....	....	1.6	....	....	....

• WOHL, Dave

David Bruce Wohl

Born: Nov. 2, 1949. Flushing, NY, United States.　Height: 6'2".　Weight: 185 lbs.　Drafted: 1971　College: Pennsylvania

YEAR	TEAM	GP	GS	MIN	PTS	FGM	FGA	FG%	3PM	3PA	3P%	FTM	FTA	FT%	ORB	DRB	TRB	AST	PF	DQ	STL	BLK	TO	MPG	PPG	RPG	APG	PCM
71-72	Philadelphia	79	....	1628	642	243	567	.429	....	....	....	156	206	.757	....	150	228	229	2	....	....	....	....	20.6	8.1	1.9	2.9	.387
72-73	Portland	22	....	393	118	47	114	.412	....	....	....	24	33	.727	....	20	68	45	0	....	....	....	....	17.9	5.4	0.9	3.1	.336
72-73	Buffalo	56	....	1540	493	207	454	.456	....	....	....	79	100	.790	....	89	258	182	0	....	....	....	....	27.5	8.8	1.6	4.6	.367
73-74	Buffalo	41	....	606	162	60	150	.400	....	....	....	42	60	.700	7	22	29	127	72	0	33	1	....	14.8	4.0	0.7	3.1	.359
73-74	Houston	26	....	449	155	61	127	.480	....	....	....	33	42	.786	4	13	17	109	64	0	43	1	....	17.3	6.0	0.7	4.2	.462
74-75	Houston	75	....	1722	485	203	462	.439	....	....	....	79	106	.745	26	86	112	340	184	1	75	9	....	23.0	6.5	1.5	4.5	.383
75-76	Houston	50	....	700	170	66	163	.405	....	....	....	38	49	.776	9	47	56	112	112	2	26	1	....	14.0	3.4	1.1	2.2	.300
76-77	Houston	14	....	62	18	7	17	.412	....	....	....	4	4	1.000	1	4	5	15	18	1	0	0	....	4.4	1.3	0.4	1.1	.371
76-77	New York	37	....	924	275	109	273	.399	....	....	....	57	85	.671	15	61	76	127	97	1	39	6	....	25.0	7.4	2.1	3.4	.313
77-78	New Jersey	10	....	118	35	12	34	.353	....	....	....	11	12	.917	1	3	4	13	24	0	3	0	16	11.8	3.5	0.4	1.3	.098
NBA Season Totals		410	....	8142	2553	1015	2361	.430	....	....	....	523	697	.750	63	236	558	1397	1027	7	219	18	16	19.9	6.2	1.4	3.4	....
74-75	Houston	4	....	8	6	3	3	1.000	....	....	....	0	0	.000	0	1	1	2	2	0	1	0	....	2.0	1.5	0.3	0.5	1.037
NBA Playoff Totals		4	....	8	6	3	3	1.000	....	....	....	0	0	.000	0	1	1	2	2	0	1	0	....	2.0	1.5	0.3	0.5	....

• WOLF, Joe

Joseph James Wolf

Born: Dec. 17, 1964. Kohler, WI, United States.　Height: 6'11".　Weight: 230 lbs.　Drafted: 1987　College: North Carolina

YEAR	TEAM	GP	GS	MIN	PTS	FGM	FGA	FG%	3PM	3PA	3P%	FTM	FTA	FT%	ORB	DRB	TRB	AST	PF	DQ	STL	BLK	TO	MPG	PPG	RPG	APG	PCM
87-88	LA Clippers	42	0	1137	320	136	334	.407	3	15	.200	45	54	.833	51	136	187	98	139	8	38	16	76	27.1	7.6	4.5	2.3	.286
88-89	LA Clippers	66	0	1450	386	170	402	.423	2	14	.143	44	64	.688	83	188	271	113	152	1	32	16	92	22.0	5.8	4.1	1.7	.291
89-90	LA Clippers	77	0	1325	370	155	392	.395	5	25	.200	55	71	.775	63	169	232	62	129	0	30	24	77	17.2	4.8	3.0	0.8	.258
90-91	Denver	74	38	1593	539	234	519	.451	2	15	.133	69	83	.831	136	264	400	107	244	8	60	31	96	21.5	7.3	5.4	1.4	.399
91-92	Denver	67	0	1160	254	100	277	.361	1	11	.091	53	66	.803	97	143	240	61	124	1	32	14	60	17.3	3.8	3.6	0.9	.260
92-93	Boston	2	0	9	1	0	1	.000	0	0	.000	1	2	.500	1	2	3	0	2	0	0	1	2	4.5	0.5	1.5	0.0	.059
92-93	Portland	21	0	156	52	20	43	.465	0	1	.000	12	14	.857	13	32	45	5	22	0	7	0	4	7.4	2.5	2.1	0.2	.445
94-95	Charlotte	63	6	583	90	38	81	.469	2	6	.333	12	16	.750	34	95	129	37	101	0	9	6	19	9.3	1.4	2.0	0.6	.269
95-96	Charlotte	1	0	18	0	0	1	.000	0	0	.000	0	0	.000	0	2	2	0	2	0	2	0	2	18.0	0.0	2.0	0.0	.000
95-96	Orlando	63	8	1047	291	135	262	.515	0	6	.000	21	29	.724	49	136	185	63	161	4	13	5	38	16.6	4.6	2.9	1.0	.300
96-97	Milwaukee	56	7	525	95	40	89	.449	1	7	.143	14	19	.737	32	80	112	20	105	0	14	11	17	9.4	1.7	2.0	0.4	.250
97-98	Denver	57	8	621	87	40	121	.331	2	10	.200	5	10	.500	36	90	126	30	92	0	20	7	23	10.9	1.5	2.2	0.5	.193
98-99	Charlotte	3	0	12	0	0	1	.000	0	0	.000	0	2	.000	0	1	1	0	6	0	0	0	0	4.0	0.0	0.3	0.0	-.296
NBA Season Totals		592	67	9636	2485	1068	2523	.423	18	110	.164	331	430	.770	595	1338	1933	596	1279	22	257	131	506	16.3	4.2	3.3	1.0	....
92-93	Portland	2	0	20	2	1	2	.500	0	0	.000	0	0	.000	2	2	4	0	1	0	0	1	0	10.0	1.0	2.0	0.0	.263
94-95	Charlotte	1	0	3	0	0	0	.000	0	0	.000	0	0	.000	0	0	0	0	0	0	0	0	0	3.0	0.0	0.0	0.0	.000
95-96	Orlando	11	0	85	20	8	23	.348	1	3	.333	3	4	.750	1	5	6	2	19	0	1	0	4	7.7	1.8	0.5	0.2	.017
NBA Playoff Totals		14	0	108	22	9	25	.360	1	3	.333	3	4	.750	3	7	10	2	20	0	1	1	4	7.7	1.6	0.7	0.1	....

• WOLKOWYSKI, Ruben

Ruben Wolkowyski

Born: Sept. 30, 1973. Buenos Aries, Argentina.　Height: 6'10".　Weight: 270 lbs.　Drafted: —　College: none

YEAR	TEAM	GP	GS	MIN	PTS	FGM	FGA	FG%	3PM	3PA	3P%	FTM	FTA	FT%	ORB	DRB	TRB	AST	PF	DQ	STL	BLK	TO	MPG	PPG	RPG	APG	PCM
00-01	Seattle	34	1	305	75	25	79	.316	0	2	.000	25	34	.735	12	34	46	3	38	0	6	18	12	9.0	2.2	1.4	0.1	.199
02-03	Boston	7	0	24	5	2	4	.500	0	1	.000	1	4	.250	0	1	1	1	3	0	0	0	1	3.4	0.7	0.1	0.1	.065
NBA Season Totals		41	1	329	80	27	83	.325	0	3	.000	26	38	.684	12	35	47	4	41	0	6	18	13	8.0	2.0	1.1	0.1	....

• WOLLEN, Eddie

Edward Wollen

Born: —.　Height: —　Weight: —　Drafted: —　College: none

YEAR	TEAM	GP	GS	MIN	PTS	FGM	FGA	FG%	3PM	3PA	3P%	FTM	FTA	FT%	ORB	DRB	TRB	AST	PF	DQ	STL	BLK	TO	MPG	PPG	RPG	APG	PCM
48-49	Dayton-N	1	....	....	0	0	....	....	0	0	....	0	0	.000	....	....	....	....	....	....	....	....	....	....	0.0	....	....	....
NBL Season Totals		1	....	....	0	0	....	....				0	0		....	....	....	....	....	....	....	....	....	....	0.0	....	....	....

YEAR	TEAM	GP	GS	MIN	PTS	FGM	FGA	FG%	3PM	3PA	3P%	FTM	FTA	FT%	ORB	DRB	TRB	AST	PF	DQ	STL	BLK	TO	MPG	PPG	RPG	APG	PCM

• WOLTZEN, Tarzan

Tarzan Woltzen

Born: 1918.   Height: —   Weight: —   Drafted: —   College: —

YEAR	TEAM	GP	GS	MIN	PTS	FGM	FGA	FG%	3PM	3PA	3P%	FTM	FTA	FT%	ORB	DRB	TRB	AST	PF	DQ	STL	BLK	TO	MPG	PPG	RPG	APG	PCM
37-38	Kankakee-N	8	....	....	0	0	....	....	....	....	....	....	0	....	....	....	....	....	....	....	....	....	....	....	0.0	....	....	....
NBL Season Totals		8	....	....	0	0	....	....	....	....	....	....	0	....	....	....	....	....	....	....	....	....	....	....	0.0	....	....	....

• WOOD, Al

Martin Alphonzo Wood

Born: June 2, 1958. Gray, GA, United States.   Height: 6'6".   Weight: 193 lbs.   Drafted: 1981   College: North Carolina

YEAR	TEAM	GP	GS	MIN	PTS	FGM	FGA	FG%	3PM	3PA	3P%	FTM	FTA	FT%	ORB	DRB	TRB	AST	PF	DQ	STL	BLK	TO	MPG	PPG	RPG	APG	PCM
81-82	Atlanta	19	0	238	92	36	105	.343	0	6	.000	20	28	.714	22	22	44	11	34	0	9	1	11	12.5	4.8	2.3	0.6	.255
81-82	San Diego	29	5	692	362	143	276	.518	3	18	.167	73	91	.802	29	61	90	47	74	4	22	8	61	23.9	12.5	3.1	1.6	.437
82-83	San Diego	76	47	1822	825	343	740	.464	15	50	.300	124	161	.770	96	140	236	134	188	5	55	36	114	24.0	10.9	3.1	1.8	.387
83-84	Seattle	81	81	2236	1160	467	945	.494	3	21	.143	223	271	.823	94	181	275	166	207	1	64	32	130	27.6	14.3	3.4	2.0	.447
84-85	Seattle	80	79	2545	1203	515	1061	.485	7	33	.212	166	214	.776	99	180	279	236	187	3	84	52	120	31.8	15.0	3.5	3.0	.437
85-86	Seattle	78	34	1749	902	355	817	.435	5	37	.135	187	239	.782	80	164	244	114	171	2	57	19	109	22.4	11.6	3.1	1.5	.393
86-87	Dallas	54	0	657	358	121	310	.390	7	25	.280	109	139	.784	39	55	94	34	83	0	19	11	32	12.2	6.6	1.7	0.6	.383
NBA Season Totals		417	246	9939	4902	1980	4254	.465	40	190	.211	902	1143	.789	459	803	1262	742	944	15	310	159	577	23.8	11.8	3.0	1.8	....
83-84	Seattle	5	5	157	60	26	56	.464	0	1	.000	8	12	.667	7	27	34	10	16	0	1	1	7	31.4	12.0	6.8	2.0	.385
NBA Playoff Totals		5	5	157	60	26	56	.464	0	1	.000	8	12	.667	7	27	34	10	16	0	1	1	7	31.4	12.0	6.8	2.0	

• WOOD, Bob

Robert A. Wood

Born: Oct. 7, 1921.   Height: 5'10".   Weight: —   Drafted: —   College: DeKalb Teachers

YEAR	TEAM	GP	GS	MIN	PTS	FGM	FGA	FG%	3PM	3PA	3P%	FTM	FTA	FT%	ORB	DRB	TRB	AST	PF	DQ	STL	BLK	TO	MPG	PPG	RPG	APG	PCM
49-50	Sheboygan	6	....	....	7	3	14	.214	....	....	....	1	1	1.000	....	....	....	1	6	....	....	....	....	....	1.2	....	0.2	....
NBA Season Totals		6	....	....	7	3	14	.214	....	....	....	1	1	1.000	....	....	....	1	6	....	....	....	....	....	1.2	....	0.2	....

• WOOD, David

David Leroy Wood

Born: Nov. 30, 1964. Spokane, WA, United States.   Height: 6'9".   Weight: 227 lbs.   Drafted: —   College: Nevada-Reno

YEAR	TEAM	GP	GS	MIN	PTS	FGM	FGA	FG%	3PM	3PA	3P%	FTM	FTA	FT%	ORB	DRB	TRB	AST	PF	DQ	STL	BLK	TO	MPG	PPG	RPG	APG	PCM
88-89	Chicago	2	0	2	0	0	0	.000	0	0	.000	0	0	.000	0	0	0	0	0	0	0	0	0	1.0	0.0	0.0	0.0	.000
90-91	Houston	82	13	1421	432	148	349	.424	28	90	.311	108	133	.812	107	139	246	94	236	4	58	16	90	17.3	5.3	3.0	1.1	.308
92-93	San Antonio	64	2	598	155	52	117	.444	5	21	.238	46	55	.836	38	59	97	34	93	1	13	12	32	9.3	2.4	1.5	0.5	.279
93-94	Detroit	78	3	1182	322	119	259	.459	22	49	.449	62	82	.756	104	135	239	51	201	3	39	19	31	15.2	4.1	3.1	0.7	.331
94-95	Golden State	78	13	1336	428	153	326	.469	31	91	.341	91	117	.778	83	158	241	65	217	4	28	13	55	17.1	5.5	3.1	0.8	.325
95-96	Golden State	21	0	96	22	7	14	.500	1	3	.333	7	8	.875	7	9	16	5	23	0	2	1	2	4.6	1.0	0.8	0.2	.265
95-96	Phoenix	4	0	34	4	1	6	.167	0	0	.000	2	2	1.000	2	3	5	2	9	0	1	0	2	8.5	1.0	1.3	0.5	.028
95-96	Dallas	37	0	642	182	67	154	.435	19	59	.322	29	40	.725	42	91	133	27	118	5	16	9	19	17.4	4.9	3.6	0.7	.310
96-97	Milwaukee	46	0	240	57	20	38	.526	5	15	.333	12	18	.667	5	22	27	13	36	0	7	6	5	5.2	1.2	0.6	0.3	.280
NBA Season Totals		412	31	5551	1602	567	1263	.449	111	328	.338	357	455	.785	388	616	1004	291	933	17	164	76	236	13.5	3.9	2.4	0.7	....
90-91	Houston	3	0	44	7	2	3	.667	1	1	1.000	2	4	.500	1	4	5	3	8	0	3	0	1	14.7	2.3	1.7	1.0	.253
92-93	San Antonio	5	0	20	5	2	4	.500	1	1	1.000	0	0	.000	1	2	3	1	7	0	0	0	0	4.0	1.0	0.6	0.2	.187
NBA Playoff Totals		8	0	64	12	4	7	.571	2	2	1.000	2	4	.500	2	6	8	4	15	0	3	0	1	8.0	1.5	1.0	0.5	....

• WOOD, Howard

James Howard Wood

Born: May 20, 1959. Southhampton, NY, United States.   Height: 6'7".   Weight: 235 lbs.   Drafted: 1981   College: Tennessee

YEAR	TEAM	GP	GS	MIN	PTS	FGM	FGA	FG%	3PM	3PA	3P%	FTM	FTA	FT%	ORB	DRB	TRB	AST	PF	DQ	STL	BLK	TO	MPG	PPG	RPG	APG	PCM
81-82	Utah	42	3	342	144	55	120	.458	0	1	.000	34	52	.654	22	43	65	9	37	0	8	6	17	8.1	3.4	1.5	0.2	.367
NBA Season Totals		42	3	342	144	55	120	.458	0	1	.000	34	52	.654	22	43	65	9	37	0	8	6	17	8.1	3.4	1.5	0.2	....

• WOOD, Leon

Osie Leon Wood III

Born: Mar. 25, 1962. Columbia, SC, United States.   Height: 6'3".   Weight: 185 lbs.   Drafted: 1984   College: Cal State Fullerton

YEAR	TEAM	GP	GS	MIN	PTS	FGM	FGA	FG%	3PM	3PA	3P%	FTM	FTA	FT%	ORB	DRB	TRB	AST	PF	DQ	STL	BLK	TO	MPG	PPG	RPG	APG	PCM
84-85	Philadelphia	38	1	269	122	50	134	.373	4	30	.133	18	26	.692	3	15	18	45	17	0	8	0	27	7.1	3.2	0.5	1.2	.294
85-86	Philadelphia	29	1	455	154	57	136	.419	13	29	.448	27	34	.794	9	18	27	75	24	0	14	0	20	15.7	5.3	0.9	2.6	.365
85-86	Washington	39	0	743	378	127	330	.385	28	85	.329	96	121	.793	16	47	63	107	46	0	20	0	66	19.1	9.7	1.6	2.7	.386
86-87	New Jersey	76	7	1733	557	187	501	.373	60	200	.300	123	154	.799	23	97	120	370	126	0	48	3	106	22.8	7.3	1.6	4.9	.374
87-88	San Antonio	38	8	830	352	120	282	.426	43	108	.398	69	91	.758	16	35	51	155	44	0	22	1	34	21.8	9.3	1.3	4.1	.449
87-88	Atlanta	14	0	79	48	16	30	.533	9	19	.474	7	8	.875	1	5	6	19	6	0	4	0	6	5.6	3.4	0.4	1.4	.705
89-90	New Jersey	28	2	200	50	16	49	.327	4	21	.190	14	16	.875	1	11	12	47	16	0	6	0	8	7.1	1.8	0.4	1.7	.350
90-91	Sacramento	12	0	222	81	25	63	.397	12	38	.316	19	21	.905	5	14	19	49	10	0	5	0	12	18.5	6.8	1.6	4.1	.466
NBA Season Totals		274	19	4531	1742	598	1525	.392	173	530	.326	373	471	.792	74	242	316	867	289	0	127	4	279	16.5	6.4	1.2	3.2	....
84-85	Philadelphia	5	0	15	14	4	9	.444	0	1	.000	6	8	.750	0	1	1	2	0	0	0	0	3	3.0	2.8	0.2	0.4	.579
85-86	Washington	1	0	2	5	1	5	.200	1	1	1.000	2	2	1.000	0	0	0	0	0	0	0	0	0	2.0	5.0	0.0	0.0	.642
87-88	Atlanta	4	0	4	3	1	1	1.000	1	1	1.000	0	0	.000	0	0	0	1	0	0	0	0	0	1.0	0.8	0.0	0.3	1.017
NBA Playoff Totals		10	0	21	22	6	15	.400	2	3	.667	8	10	.800	0	1	1	3	0	0	0	0	3	2.1	2.2	0.1	0.3	....

• WOODEN, John

John Robert (the India Rubber Man) Wooden

Born: Oct. 14, 1910. Centerton, IN, United States.   Height: 5'10".   Weight: 183 lbs.   Drafted: —   College: Purdue

HOF: 1960

YEAR	TEAM	GP	GS	MIN	PTS	FGM	FGA	FG%	3PM	3PA	3P%	FTM	FTA	FT%	ORB	DRB	TRB	AST	PF	DQ	STL	BLK	TO	MPG	PPG	RPG	APG	PCM
37-38	Whiting-N	13	....	....	143	52	....	....	....	....	....	....	39	....	....	....	....	....	....	....	....	....	....	....	11.0	....	....	....
38-39	Hammond-N	5	....	....	32	10	....	....	....	....	....	....	12	....	....	....	....	....	....	....	....	....	....	....	6.4	....	....	....
38-39	Indianapolis-N	5	....	....	39	14	....	....	....	....	....	....	11	....	....	....	....	....	....	....	....	....	....	....	7.8	....	....	....
NBL Season Totals		23	....	....	'214	76	....	....	....	....	....	....	62	....	....	....	....	....	....	....	....	....	....	....	9.3	....	....	....

YEAR TEAM	GP	GS	MIN	PTS	FGM	FGA	FG%	3PM	3PA	3P%	FTM	FTA	FT%	ORB	DRB	TRB	AST	PF	DQ	STL	BLK	TO	MPG	PPG	RPG	APG	PCM
37-38 Whiting-N	2	....	....	33	8	....	....	....	....	....	17	....	....	....	....	....	....	....	....	....	....	....	....	16.5	....	....	....
NBL Playoff Totals	2	....	....	33	8	....	....	....	....	....	17	....	....	....	....	....	....	....	....	....	....	....	....	16.5	....	....	....

• WOODS, Loren
Loren Gerald Woods

Born: June 21, 1978. St. Louis, MO, United States.   Height: 7'1".   Weight: 245 lbs.   Drafted: 2001   College: Arizona

YEAR TEAM	GP	GS	MIN	PTS	FGM	FGA	FG%	3PM	3PA	3P%	FTM	FTA	FT%	ORB	DRB	TRB	AST	PF	DQ	STL	BLK	TO	MPG	PPG	RPG	APG	PCM
01-02 Minnesota	60	0	516	110	33	96	.344	0	2	.000	44	60	.733	46	76	122	22	60	0	17	34	36	8.6	1.8	2.0	0.4	.323
02-03 Minnesota	38	11	353	80	29	76	.382	1	3	.333	21	27	.778	27	68	95	19	37	0	10	13	23	9.3	2.1	2.5	0.5	.354
NBA Season Totals	98	11	869	190	62	172	.360	1	5	.200	65	87	.747	73	144	217	41	97	0	27	47	59	8.9	1.9	2.2	0.4	....
02-03 Minnesota	2	0	2	2	1	3	.333	0	0	.000	0	0	.000	1	0	1	0	0	0	0	0	0	1.0	1.0	0.5	0.0	.546
NBA Playoff Totals	2	0	2	2	1	3	.333	0	0	.000	0	0	.000	1	0	1	0	0	0	0	0	0	1.0	1.0	0.5	0.0	....

• WOODS, Qyntel
Qyntel Deon Woods

Born: Feb. 16, 1981. Memphis, TN, United States.   Height: 6'8".   Weight: 221 lbs.   Drafted: 2002   College: Northeast Mississippi CC

YEAR TEAM	GP	GS	MIN	PTS	FGM	FGA	FG%	3PM	3PA	3P%	FTM	FTA	FT%	ORB	DRB	TRB	AST	PF	DQ	STL	BLK	TO	MPG	PPG	RPG	APG	PCM
02-03 Portland	53	0	334	128	59	118	.500	3	9	.333	7	20	.350	15	38	53	12	36	1	15	1	23	6.3	2.4	1.0	0.2	.321
NBA Season Totals	53	0	334	128	59	118	.500	3	9	.333	7	20	.350	15	38	53	12	36	1	15	1	23	6.3	2.4	1.0	0.2	....
02-03 Portland	4	0	18	7	3	9	.333	0	1	.000	1	2	.500	1	1	2	0	3	0	0	0	1	4.5	1.8	0.5	0.0	.036
NBA Playoff Totals	4	0	18	7	3	9	.333	0	1	.000	1	2	.500	1	1	2	0	3	0	0	0	1	4.5	1.8	0.5	0.0	....

• WOODS, Randy
Randolph Woods

Born: Sept. 23, 1970. Philadelphia, PA, United States.   Height: 5'10".   Weight: 185 lbs.   Drafted: 1992   College: LaSalle

YEAR TEAM	GP	GS	MIN	PTS	FGM	FGA	FG%	3PM	3PA	3P%	FTM	FTA	FT%	ORB	DRB	TRB	AST	PF	DQ	STL	BLK	TO	MPG	PPG	RPG	APG	PCM
92-93 LA Clippers	41	1	174	68	23	66	.348	3	14	.214	19	26	.731	6	8	14	40	26	0	14	1	16	4.2	1.7	0.3	1.0	.387
93-94 LA Clippers	40	0	352	145	49	133	.368	27	78	.346	20	35	.571	13	16	29	71	40	0	24	2	32	8.8	3.6	0.7	1.8	.400
94-95 LA Clippers	62	3	495	124	37	117	.316	22	74	.297	28	38	.737	10	34	44	134	87	0	41	0	56	8.0	2.0	0.7	2.2	.349
95-96 Denver	8	0	72	19	6	22	.273	5	21	.238	2	2	1.000	3	3	6	12	13	0	6	1	5	9.0	2.4	0.8	1.5	.251
NBA Season Totals	151	4	1093	356	115	338	.340	57	187	.305	69	101	.683	32	61	93	257	166	0	85	4	109	7.2	2.4	0.6	1.7	....

• WOODS, Sonny
Robert (Sonny) Woods

Born: 1923. Died: July 11, 1970.   Height: 5'11".   Weight: 195 lbs.   Drafted: —   College: none

YEAR TEAM	GP	GS	MIN	PTS	FGM	FGA	FG%	3PM	3PA	3P%	FTM	FTA	FT%	ORB	DRB	TRB	AST	PF	DQ	STL	BLK	TO	MPG	PPG	RPG	APG	PCM
48-49 Dayton-N	40	....	....	266	105	....	....	....	....	....	56	98	.571	....	....	....	....	....	....	....	....	....	6.7	....	....	....
NBL Season Totals	40	....	....	266	105	....	....	....	....	....	56	98	....	....	....	....	....	....	....	....	....	....	6.7	....	....	....

• WOODS, Tommy
James Thomas Woods Jr.

Born: June 10, 1943.   Height: 6'7".   Weight: 210 lbs.   Drafted: —   College: East Tennessee State

YEAR TEAM	GP	GS	MIN	PTS	FGM	FGA	FG%	3PM	3PA	3P%	FTM	FTA	FT%	ORB	DRB	TRB	AST	PF	DQ	STL	BLK	TO	MPG	PPG	RPG	APG	PCM
67-68 Kentucky-A	18	....	184	42	14	43	.326	0	1	.000	14	16	.875	....	....	55	4	25	0	....	....	9	10.2	2.3	3.1	0.2	.310
ABA Season Totals	18	....	184	42	14	43	.326	0	1	.000	14	16	.875	....	....	55	4	25	0	....	....	9	10.2	2.3	3.1	0.2	....

• WOODSON, Mike
Michael Dean Woodson

Born: Mar. 24, 1958. Indianapolis, IN, United States.   Height: 6'5".   Weight: 195 lbs.   Drafted: 1980   College: Indiana

YEAR TEAM	GP	GS	MIN	PTS	FGM	FGA	FG%	3PM	3PA	3P%	FTM	FTA	FT%	ORB	DRB	TRB	AST	PF	DQ	STL	BLK	TO	MPG	PPG	RPG	APG	PCM
80-81 New York	81	....	949	380	165	373	.442	1	5	.200	49	64	.766	33	64	97	75	95	0	36	12	57	11.7	4.7	1.2	0.9	.318
81-82 New Jersey	7	0	145	83	30	68	.441	0	1	.000	23	32	.719	5	8	13	16	21	1	7	2	9	20.7	11.9	1.9	2.3	.437
81-82 Kansas City	76	74	2186	1221	508	1001	.507	7	24	.292	198	254	.780	97	137	234	206	199	2	135	33	144	28.8	16.1	3.1	2.7	.508
82-83 Kansas City	81	3	2426	1473	584	1154	.506	7	33	.212	298	377	.790	84	164	248	254	203	0	137	59	170	30.0	18.2	3.1	3.1	.560
83-84 Kansas City	71	12	1838	1027	389	816	.477	2	8	.250	247	302	.818	62	113	175	175	174	2	83	28	114	25.9	14.5	2.5	2.5	.474
84-85 Kansas City	78	3	1998	1329	530	1068	.496	5	21	.238	264	330	.800	69	129	198	143	216	1	117	28	140	25.6	17.0	2.5	1.8	.520
85-86 Sacramento	81	51	2417	1264	510	1073	.475	2	13	.154	242	289	.837	94	132	226	197	215	0	92	37	146	29.8	15.6	2.8	2.4	.424
86-87 LA Clippers	74	66	2126	1262	494	1130	.437	34	123	.276	240	290	.828	68	94	162	196	201	1	100	16	170	28.7	17.1	2.2	2.6	.406
87-88 LA Clippers	80	77	2534	1438	562	1263	.445	18	78	.231	296	341	.868	64	126	190	273	210	1	109	26	184	31.7	18.0	2.4	3.4	.430
88-89 Houston	81	79	2259	1046	410	936	.438	31	89	.348	195	237	.823	51	143	194	206	195	1	89	18	138	27.9	12.9	2.4	2.5	.362
89-90 Houston	61	11	972	394	160	405	.395	12	41	.293	62	86	.721	25	63	88	66	100	1	42	11	49	15.9	6.5	1.4	1.1	.270
90-91 Houston	11	3	125	53	21	54	.389	1	6	.167	10	12	.833	2	9	11	10	11	0	5	4	7	11.4	4.8	1.0	0.9	.312
90-91 Cleveland	4	0	46	11	5	23	.217	0	1	.000	1	1	1.000	1	1	2	5	7	0	0	1	5	11.5	2.8	0.5	1.3	-.122
NBA Season Totals	786	379	20021	10981	4368	9364	.466	120	443	.271	2125	2615	.813	655	1183	1838	1822	1847	11	952	275	1333	25.5	14.0	2.3	2.3	....
80-81 New York	2	....	8	4	1	3	.333	0	0	.000	2	2	1.000	2	0	2	0	3	0	0	0	3	4.0	2.0	1.0	0.0	.329
83-84 Kansas City	3	0	87	49	18	44	.409	0	1	.000	13	15	.867	4	4	8	9	11	0	2	0	3	29.0	16.3	2.7	3.0	.401
85-86 Sacramento	3	3	110	56	22	49	.449	0	2	.000	12	12	1.000	7	4	11	5	13	0	4	2	11	36.7	18.7	3.7	1.7	.326
88-89 Houston	4	4	137	47	17	49	.347	3	9	.333	10	12	.833	4	5	9	18	7	0	4	2	9	34.3	11.8	2.3	4.5	.277
89-90 Houston	1	0	6	2	1	3	.333	0	1	.000	0	0	.000	0	0	0	2	1	0	0	0	0	6.0	2.0	0.0	2.0	.297
NBA Playoff Totals	13	7	348	158	59	148	.399	3	13	.231	37	41	.902	17	13	30	34	35	0	10	4	23	26.8	12.2	2.3	2.6	....

• WOOLLARD, Bob
John George Woollard

Born: July 27, 1940.   Height: 6'10".   Weight: 225 lbs.   Drafted: —   College: Wake Forest

YEAR TEAM	GP	GS	MIN	PTS	FGM	FGA	FG%	3PM	3PA	3P%	FTM	FTA	FT%	ORB	DRB	TRB	AST	PF	DQ	STL	BLK	TO	MPG	PPG	RPG	APG	PCM
69-70 Miami-A	19	....	234	84	32	82	.390	0	1	.000	20	25	.800	25	44	69	6	42	1	....	....	16	12.3	4.4	3.6	0.3	.372
ABA Season Totals	19	....	234	84	32	82	.390	0	1	.000	20	25	.800	25	44	69	6	42	1	....	....	16	12.3	4.4	3.6	0.3	....

• WOOLRIDGE, Orlando

Loren Vernada Woolridge

Born: Dec. 16, 1959. Bernice, LA, United States. Height: 6'9". Weight: 215 lbs. Drafted: 1981 College: Notre Dame

YEAR	TEAM	GP	GS	MIN	PTS	FGM	FGA	FG%	3PM	3PA	3P%	FTM	FTA	FT%	ORB	DRB	TRB	AST	PF	DQ	STL	BLK	TO	MPG	PPG	RPG	APG	PCM
81-82	Chicago	75	12	1188	548	202	394	.513	0	3	.000	144	206	.699	82	145	227	81	152	1	23	24	105	15.8	7.3	3.0	1.1	.434
82-83	Chicago	57	38	1627	939	361	622	.580	0	3	.000	217	340	.638	122	176	298	97	177	1	38	44	160	28.5	16.5	5.2	1.7	.537
83-84	Chicago	75	74	2544	1444	570	1086	.525	1	2	.500	303	424	.715	130	239	369	136	253	6	71	60	188	33.9	19.3	4.9	1.8	.482
84-85	Chicago	77	76	2816	1767	679	1225	.554	0	5	.000	409	521	.785	158	277	435	135	185	0	58	38	177	36.6	22.9	5.6	1.8	.566
85-86	Chicago	70	59	2248	1448	540	1090	.495	4	23	.174	364	462	.788	150	200	350	213	186	2	49	47	175	32.1	20.7	5.0	3.0	.572
86-87	New Jersey	75	53	2638	1551	556	1067	.521	1	8	.125	438	564	.777	118	249	367	261	243	4	54	86	210	35.2	20.7	4.9	3.5	.553
87-88	New Jersey	19	12	622	312	110	247	.445	0	2	.000	92	130	.708	31	60	91	71	73	2	13	20	48	32.7	16.4	4.8	3.7	.449
88-89	LA Lakers	74	0	1491	715	231	494	.468	0	1	.000	253	343	.738	81	189	270	58	130	0	30	65	104	20.1	9.7	3.6	0.8	.451
89-90	LA Lakers	62	2	1421	788	306	550	.556	0	5	.000	176	240	.733	49	136	185	96	160	2	39	46	74	22.9	12.7	3.0	1.5	.521
90-91	Denver	53	50	1823	1330	490	983	.498	0	4	.000	350	439	.797	141	220	361	119	145	2	69	23	154	34.4	25.1	6.8	2.2	.640
91-92	Detroit	82	61	2113	1146	452	907	.498	1	9	.111	241	353	.683	109	151	260	88	154	0	41	33	131	25.8	14.0	3.2	1.1	.418
92-93	Detroit	50	47	1477	655	271	566	.479	0	9	.000	113	168	.673	84	92	176	112	114	1	26	25	75	29.5	13.1	3.5	2.2	.381
92-93	Milwaukee	8	0	78	43	18	33	.545	0	0	.000	7	9	.778	3	6	9	3	8	0	1	2	6	9.8	5.4	1.1	0.4	.425
93-94	Philadelphia	74	1	1955	937	364	773	.471	1	14	.071	208	302	.689	103	195	298	139	186	1	41	56	141	26.4	12.7	4.0	1.9	.418
NBA Season Totals		851	485	24041	13623	5150	10037	.513	8	88	.091	3315	4501	.737	1361	2335	3696	1609	2166	22	553	569	1748	28.3	16.0	4.3	1.9	....
84-85	Chicago	4	4	167	82	34	68	.500	0	0	.000	14	18	.778	6	7	13	8	19	1	6	1	12	41.8	20.5	3.3	2.0	.333
85-86	Chicago	3	3	135	63	25	62	.403	0	1	.000	13	15	.867	6	8	14	4	12	0	3	1	4	45.0	21.0	4.7	1.3	.292
88-89	LA Lakers	15	0	276	122	39	75	.520	0	0	.000	44	62	.710	20	50	70	17	35	0	2	15	22	18.4	8.1	4.7	1.1	.516
89-90	LA Lakers	9	0	199	106	40	70	.571	0	1	.000	26	37	.703	6	17	23	10	25	1	8	8	11	22.1	11.8	2.6	1.1	.492
91-92	Detroit	5	5	128	55	23	52	.442	0	0	.000	9	16	.563	5	5	10	3	14	0	1	1	6	25.6	11.0	2.0	0.6	.212
NBA Playoff Totals		36	12	905	428	161	327	.492	0	2	.000	106	148	.716	43	87	130	42	105	2	20	26	55	25.1	11.9	3.6	1.2	....

• WORKMAN, Haywoode

Haywoode Wilvon Workman

Born: Jan. 23, 1966. Charlotte, NC, United States. Height: 6'2". Weight: 180 lbs. Drafted: 1989 College: Oral Roberts

YEAR	TEAM	GP	GS	MIN	PTS	FGM	FGA	FG%	3PM	3PA	3P%	FTM	FTA	FT%	ORB	DRB	TRB	AST	PF	DQ	STL	BLK	TO	MPG	PPG	RPG	APG	PCM
89-90	Atlanta	6	0	16	6	2	3	.667	0	0	.000	2	2	1.000	0	3	3	2	3	0	3	0	0	2.7	1.0	0.5	0.3	.713
90-91	Washington	73	56	2034	581	234	515	.454	12	50	.240	101	133	.759	51	191	242	353	162	1	87	7	131	27.9	8.0	3.3	4.8	.391
93-94	Indiana	65	52	1714	501	195	460	.424	18	56	.321	93	116	.802	32	172	204	404	152	0	85	4	150	26.4	7.7	3.1	6.2	.435
94-95	Indiana	69	14	1028	292	101	269	.375	35	98	.357	55	74	.743	21	90	111	194	115	0	59	5	76	14.9	4.2	1.6	2.8	.360
95-96	Indiana	77	4	1164	279	101	259	.390	23	71	.324	54	73	.740	27	97	124	213	152	0	65	4	92	15.1	3.6	1.6	2.8	.319
96-97	Indiana	4	2	81	22	11	20	.550	0	3	.000	0	1	.000	4	3	7	11	10	0	3	0	5	20.3	5.5	1.8	2.8	.307
98-99	Milwaukee	29	29	815	200	73	170	.429	17	47	.362	37	47	.787	14	88	102	172	53	0	32	1	63	28.1	6.9	3.5	5.9	.418
99-00	Milwaukee	23	1	248	66	23	62	.371	11	29	.379	9	13	.692	1	16	17	44	23	0	11	0	14	10.8	2.9	0.7	1.9	.319
99-00	Toronto	13	1	102	20	8	28	.286	3	14	.214	1	2	.500	0	9	9	17	14	1	9	0	4	7.8	1.5	0.7	1.3	.258
NBA Season Totals		359	159	7202	1967	748	1786	.419	119	368	.323	352	461	.764	150	669	819	1410	684	2	354	21	535	20.1	5.5	2.3	3.9	....
93-94	Indiana	16	15	511	128	45	131	.344	6	21	.286	32	38	.842	11	40	51	112	40	0	28	1	38	31.9	8.0	3.2	7.0	.368
94-95	Indiana	17	0	275	77	24	67	.358	2	18	.111	27	32	.844	5	23	28	46	45	0	11	0	16	16.2	4.5	1.6	2.7	.304
95-96	Indiana	5	0	53	19	7	16	.438	3	5	.600	2	2	1.000	1	2	3	2	5	0	2	0	2	10.6	3.8	0.6	0.4	.248
98-99	Milwaukee	3	0	53	13	4	11	.364	0	3	.000	5	6	.833	1	2	3	7	7	0	3	0	7	17.7	4.3	1.0	2.3	.191
NBA Playoff Totals		41	15	892	237	80	225	.356	11	47	.234	66	78	.846	18	67	85	167	97	0	44	1	63	21.8	5.8	2.1	4.1	....

• WORKMAN, Mark

Mark Cecil Workman

Born: Mar. 10, 1930. Charleston, WV, United States. Died: Dec.21, 1983. Height: 6'9". Weight: 215 lbs. Drafted: 1952 College: West Virginia

YEAR	TEAM	GP	GS	MIN	PTS	FGM	FGA	FG%	3PM	3PA	3P%	FTM	FTA	FT%	ORB	DRB	TRB	AST	PF	DQ	STL	BLK	TO	MPG	PPG	RPG	APG	PCM
52-53	Mil/Phi	65	....	1030	330	130	408	.319	....	....	....	70	113	.619	....	....	193	37	166	5	....	....	....	15.8	5.1	3.0	0.6	.233
53-54	Baltimore	14	....	151	56	25	60	.417	....	....	....	6	10	.600	....	....	37	7	31	0	....	....	....	10.8	4.0	2.6	0.5	.358
NBA Season Totals		79	....	1181	386	155	468	.331	....	....	....	76	123	.618	....	....	230	44	197	5	....	....	....	14.9	4.9	2.9	0.6	....

• WORKMAN, Tom

Thomas Edwin (Hawk) Workman

Born: Nov. 14, 1944. Seattle, WA, United States. Height: 6'7". Weight: 218 lbs. Drafted: 1967 College: Seattle

YEAR	TEAM	GP	GS	MIN	PTS	FGM	FGA	FG%	3PM	3PA	3P%	FTM	FTA	FT%	ORB	DRB	TRB	AST	PF	DQ	STL	BLK	TO	MPG	PPG	RPG	APG	PCM
67-68	St. Louis	19	....	85	55	19	38	.500	....	....	....	17	22	.773	....	....	24	3	14	0	....	....	....	4.5	2.9	1.3	0.2	.647
67-68	Baltimore	1	....	10	1	0	2	.000	....	....	....	1	1	1.000	....	....	1	0	3	0	....	....	....	10.0	1.0	1.0	0.0	-.100
68-69	Baltimore	21	....	86	53	22	54	.407	....	....	....	9	15	.600	....	....	27	2	16	0	....	....	....	4.1	2.5	1.3	0.1	.488
69-70	Los Angeles-A	26	....	445	310	116	251	.462	1	4	.250	77	98	.786	44	50	94	22	69	0	....	....	33	17.1	11.9	3.6	0.8	.587
69-70	Detroit	2	....	6	0	0	1	.000	....	....	....	0	0	.000	....	....	0	0	1	0	....	....	....	3.0	0.0	0.0	0.0	-.220
70-71	Denver-A	39	....	489	236	89	199	.447	1	11	.091	57	68	.838	39	94	133	37	81	0	....	....	52	12.5	6.1	3.4	0.9	.536
70-71	Utah-A	17	....	190	119	44	104	.423	2	8	.250	29	37	.784	18	28	46	11	32	1	....	....	26	11.2	7.0	2.7	0.6	.552
NBA Season Totals		43	....	187	109	41	95	.432	....	....	....	27	38	.711	....	....	52	5	34	0	....	....	....	4.3	2.5	1.2	0.1	....
ABA Season Totals		82	....	1124	665	249	554	.449	4	23	.174	163	203	.803	101	172	273	70	182	1	....	....	111	13.7	8.1	3.3	0.9	....
Career Totals		125	....	1311	774	290	649	.447	4	23	.174	190	241	.788	101	172	325	75	216	1	....	....	111	10.5	6.2	2.6	0.6	....
68-69	Baltimore	1	....	2	0	0	1	.000	....	....	....	0	0	.000	....	....	1	0	0	0	....	....	....	2.0	0.0	1.0	0.0	.000
69-70	Los Angeles-A	3	....	9	6	3	7	.429	0	0	.000	0	0	.000	....	....	3	0	....	0	....	....	2	3.0	2.0	1.0	0.0	....
NBA Playoff Totals		1	....	2	0	0	1	.000	....	....	....	0	0	.000	....	....	1	0	0	0	....	....	....	2.0	0.0	1.0	0.0	....
ABA Playoff Totals		3	....	9	6	3	7	.429	0	0	.000	0	0	.000	....	....	3	0	....	0	....	....	2	3.0	2.0	1.0	0.0	....
Career Playoff Totals		4	....	11	6	3	8	.375	0	0	.000	0	0	.000	....	....	4	0	0	0	....	....	2	2.8	1.5	1.0	0.0	....

• WORSLEY, Willie

Willie James Worsley

Born: Nov. 13, 1945. Bronx, NY, United States. Height: 5'9". Weight: 175 lbs. Drafted: — College: Texas Western

YEAR	TEAM	GP	GS	MIN	PTS	FGM	FGA	FG%	3PM	3PA	3P%	FTM	FTA	FT%	ORB	DRB	TRB	AST	PF	DQ	STL	BLK	TO	MPG	PPG	RPG	APG	PCM
68-69	New York-A	24	....	460	145	36	123	.293	10	30	.333	63	84	.750	6	29	35	39	48	0	....	....	32	19.2	6.0	1.5	1.6	.251
ABA Season Totals		24	....	460	145	36	123	.293	10	30	.333	63	84	.750	6	29	35	39	48	0	....	....	32	19.2	6.0	1.5	1.6	....

YEAR	TEAM	GP	GS	MIN	PTS	FGM	FGA	FG%	3PM	3PA	3P%	FTM	FTA	FT%	ORB	DRB	TRB	AST	PF	DQ	STL	BLK	TO	MPG	PPG	RPG	APG	PCM

• WORTHEN, Sam

Samuel Lee Worthen

Born: Jan. 17, 1958. Brooklyn, NY, United States.   Height: 6'5".   Weight: 195 lbs.   Drafted: 1980   College: Marquette

YEAR	TEAM	GP	GS	MIN	PTS	FGM	FGA	FG%	3PM	3PA	3P%	FTM	FTA	FT%	ORB	DRB	TRB	AST	PF	DQ	STL	BLK	TO	MPG	PPG	RPG	APG	PCM
80-81	Chicago	64	....	945	235	95	192	.495	0	4	.000	45	60	.750	22	93	115	115	115	0	57	6	90	14.8	3.7	1.8	1.8	.310
81-82	Utah	5	0	22	4	2	5	.400	0	0	.000	0	0	.000	1	0	1	3	3	0	0	0	2	4.4	0.8	0.2	0.6	.099
NBA Season Totals		69	0	967	239	97	197	.492	0	4	.000	45	60	.750	23	93	116	118	118	0	57	6	92	14.0	3.5	1.7	1.7	....
80-81	Chicago	1	....	1	0	0	0	.000	0	0	.000	0	0	.000	0	0	0	0	0	0	0	0	0	1.0	0.0	0.0	0.0	.000
NBA Playoff Totals		1	....	1	0	0	0	.000	0	0	.000	0	0	.000	0	0	0	0	0	0	0	0	0	1.0	0.0	0.0	0.0	....

• WORTHY, James

James Ager Worthy

Born: Feb. 27, 1961. Gastonia, NC, United States.   Height: 6'9".   Weight: 225 lbs.   Drafted: 1982   College: North Carolina

HOF: 2003

YEAR	TEAM	GP	GS	MIN	PTS	FGM	FGA	FG%	3PM	3PA	3P%	FTM	FTA	FT%	ORB	DRB	TRB	AST	PF	DQ	STL	BLK	TO	MPG	PPG	RPG	APG	PCM
82-83	LA Lakers	77	1	1970	1033	447	772	.579	1	4	.250	138	221	.624	157	242	399	132	221	2	91	64	177	25.6	13.4	5.2	1.7	.552
83-84	LA Lakers	82	53	2415	1185	495	890	.556	0	6	.000	195	257	.759	157	358	515	207	244	5	77	70	180	29.5	14.5	6.3	2.5	.557
84-85	LA Lakers	80	76	2696	1410	610	1066	.572	0	7	.000	190	245	.776	169	342	511	201	196	0	87	67	200	33.7	17.6	6.4	2.5	.562
85-86	LA Lakers	75	73	2454	1500	629	1086	.579	0	13	.000	242	314	.771	136	251	387	201	195	0	82	77	150	32.7	20.0	5.2	2.7	.625
86-87	LA Lakers	82	82	2819	1594	651	1207	.539	0	13	.000	292	389	.751	158	308	466	226	206	0	108	83	164	34.4	19.4	5.7	2.8	.580
87-88	LA Lakers	75	72	2655	1478	617	1161	.531	2	16	.125	242	304	.796	129	245	374	289	175	1	72	55	158	35.4	19.7	5.0	3.9	.561
88-89	LA Lakers	81	81	2960	1657	702	1282	.548	2	23	.087	251	321	.782	169	320	489	288	175	0	108	56	178	36.5	20.5	6.0	3.6	.592
89-90	LA Lakers	80	80	2960	1685	711	1298	.548	15	49	.306	248	317	.782	160	318	478	288	190	0	99	49	160	37.0	21.1	6.0	3.6	.593
90-91	LA Lakers	78	74	3008	1670	716	1455	.492	26	90	.289	212	266	.797	107	249	356	275	117	0	104	35	125	38.6	21.4	4.6	3.5	.512
91-92	LA Lakers	54	54	2108	1075	450	1007	.447	9	43	.209	166	204	.814	98	207	305	252	89	0	76	23	130	39.0	19.9	5.6	4.7	.485
92-93	LA Lakers	82	69	2359	1221	510	1142	.447	30	111	.270	171	211	.810	73	174	247	278	87	0	92	27	139	28.8	14.9	3.0	3.4	.458
93-94	LA Lakers	80	2	1597	812	340	838	.406	32	111	.288	100	135	.741	48	133	181	154	80	0	45	18	96	20.0	10.2	2.3	1.9	.379
NBA Season Totals		926	717	30001	16320	6878	13204	.521	117	486	.241	2447	3184	.769	1561	3147	4708	2791	1975	8	1041	624	1857	32.4	17.6	5.1	3.0	....
83-84	LA Lakers	21	8	708	371	164	274	.599	1	2	.500	42	69	.609	36	69	105	56	57	0	27	11	39	33.7	17.7	5.0	2.7	.546
84-85	LA Lakers	19	19	626	408	166	267	.622	1	2	.500	75	111	.676	35	61	96	41	53	1	17	13	26	32.9	21.5	5.1	2.2	.654
85-86	LA Lakers	14	14	539	274	121	217	.558	0	4	.000	32	47	.681	22	43	65	45	43	0	16	10	36	38.5	19.6	4.6	3.2	.477
86-87	LA Lakers	18	18	681	425	176	298	.591	0	2	.000	73	97	.753	31	70	101	63	42	1	28	22	40	37.8	23.6	5.6	3.5	.663
87-88	LA Lakers	24	24	896	506	204	390	.523	1	9	.111	97	128	.758	53	86	139	106	58	0	33	19	55	37.3	21.1	5.8	4.4	.593
88-89	LA Lakers	15	15	600	372	153	270	.567	3	8	.375	63	80	.788	37	64	101	42	36	0	18	16	33	40.0	24.8	6.7	2.8	.631
89-90	LA Lakers	9	9	366	218	90	181	.497	2	8	.250	36	43	.837	11	39	50	27	18	0	14	3	22	40.7	24.2	5.6	3.0	.524
90-91	LA Lakers	18	18	733	379	161	346	.465	4	24	.167	53	72	.736	25	48	73	70	34	0	19	2	40	40.7	21.1	4.1	3.9	.418
92-93	LA Lakers	5	0	148	69	32	86	.372	2	8	.250	3	5	.600	7	10	17	13	11	0	5	0	7	29.6	13.8	3.4	2.6	.273
NBA Playoff Totals		143	125	5297	3022	1267	2329	.544	14	67	.209	474	652	.727	257	490	747	463	352	2	177	96	298	37.0	21.1	5.2	3.2	....

• WRIGHT, Brad

Bradford William Wright

Born: Mar. 26, 1962. Hollywood, CA, United States.   Height: 6'11".   Weight: 225 lbs.   Drafted: 1985   College: UCLA

YEAR	TEAM	GP	GS	MIN	PTS	FGM	FGA	FG%	3PM	3PA	3P%	FTM	FTA	FT%	ORB	DRB	TRB	AST	PF	DQ	STL	BLK	TO	MPG	PPG	RPG	APG	PCM
86-87	New York	14	0	138	52	20	46	.435	0	1	.000	12	28	.429	25	28	53	1	20	0	3	6	13	9.9	3.7	3.8	0.1	.418
87-88	Denver	2	0	7	2	1	5	.200	0	0	.000	0	0	.000	0	1	1	0	3	0	0	0	2	3.5	1.0	0.5	0.0	-.580
NBA Season Totals		16	0	145	54	21	51	.412	0	1	.000	12	28	.429	25	29	54	1	23	0	3	6	15	9.1	3.4	3.4	0.1	....

• WRIGHT, Howard

Paul Gregory Wright

Born: Dec. 20, 1967. San Diego, CA, United States.   Height: 6'8".   Weight: 220 lbs.   Drafted: —   College: Stanford

YEAR	TEAM	GP	GS	MIN	PTS	FGM	FGA	FG%	3PM	3PA	3P%	FTM	FTA	FT%	ORB	DRB	TRB	AST	PF	DQ	STL	BLK	TO	MPG	PPG	RPG	APG	PCM
90-91	Atlanta	4	0	20	5	2	3	.667	0	0	.000	1	1	1.000	1	5	6	0	3	0	0	0	2	5.0	1.3	1.5	0.0	.320
90-91	Orlando	8	0	136	43	15	41	.366	0	0	.000	13	21	.619	10	27	37	3	23	0	3	5	9	17.0	5.4	4.6	0.4	.302
90-91	Dallas	3	0	8	6	2	3	.667	0	1	.000	2	2	1.000	1	1	2	0	2	0	1	0	0	2.7	2.0	0.7	0.0	.867
92-93	Orlando	4	0	10	8	4	5	.800	0	0	.000	0	2	.000	1	1	2	0	0	0	0	0	0	2.5	2.0	0.5	0.0	.800
NBA Season Totals		19	0	174	62	23	52	.442	0	1	.000	16	26	.615	13	34	47	3	28	0	4	5	11	9.2	3.3	2.5	0.2	....

• WRIGHT, Howie

Howard L. Wright

Born: Feb. 22, 1947. Louisville, KY, United States.   Height: 6'3".   Weight: 185 lbs.   Drafted: 1970   College: Austin Peay

YEAR	TEAM	GP	GS	MIN	PTS	FGM	FGA	FG%	3PM	3PA	3P%	FTM	FTA	FT%	ORB	DRB	TRB	AST	PF	DQ	STL	BLK	TO	MPG	PPG	RPG	APG	PCM
70-71	Kentucky-A	52	....	612	237	94	245	.384	9	42	.214	40	49	.816	23	57	80	63	89	0	....	....	59	11.8	4.6	1.5	1.2	.354
71-72	Kentucky-A	1	....	4	0	0	0	.000	0	0	.000	0	1	1.000	0	0	0	0	0	0	....	....	1	4.0	0.0	0.0	0.0	-.110
ABA Season Totals		53	....	616	237	94	245	.384	9	42	.214	40	50	.800	23	57	80	63	89	0	....	....	60	11.6	4.5	1.5	1.2	....
70-71	Kentucky-A	5	....	36	20	7	20	.350	2	8	.250	4	9	.444	0	2	2	4	6	0	....	....	1	7.2	4.0	0.4	0.8	.322
ABA Playoff Totals		5	....	36	20	7	20	.350	2	8	.250	4	9	.444	0	2	2	4	6	0	....	....	1	7.2	4.0	0.4	0.8	....

• WRIGHT, Joby

Joseph A. Wright

Born: Sept. 5, 1950.   Height: 6'8".   Weight: 220 lbs.   Drafted: 1972   College: Indiana

YEAR	TEAM	GP	GS	MIN	PTS	FGM	FGA	FG%	3PM	3PA	3P%	FTM	FTA	FT%	ORB	DRB	TRB	AST	PF	DQ	STL	BLK	TO	MPG	PPG	RPG	APG	PCM
72-73	Seattle	77	....	931	303	133	278	.478	....	....	....	37	89	.416	....	....	218	36	164	0	....	....	....	12.1	3.9	2.8	0.5	.337
73-74	Memphis-A	3	....	31	12	5	16	.313	0	0	.000	2	2	1.000	9	5	14	0	7	....	0	1	4	10.3	4.0	4.7	0.0	.373
75-76	San Diego-A	10	....	105	36	16	27	.593	0	0	.000	4	10	.400	7	15	22	0	22	....	4	2	11	10.5	3.6	2.2	0.0	.317
75-76	Virginia-A	13	....	200	85	34	82	.415	0	0	.000	17	28	.607	22	15	37	2	32	....	1	2	13	15.4	6.5	2.8	0.2	.291
NBA Season Totals		77	....	931	303	133	278	.478	....	....	....	37	89	.416	....	....	218	36	164	0	....	....	....	12.1	3.9	2.8	0.5	....
ABA Season Totals		26	....	336	133	55	125	.440	0	0	.000	23	40	.575	38	35	73	2	61	....	5	5	28	12.9	5.1	2.8	0.1	....
Career Totals		103	....	1267	436	188	403	.467	0	0	.000	60	129	.465	38	35	291	38	225	0	5	5	28	12.3	4.2	2.8	0.4	....

YEAR	TEAM	GP	GS	MIN	PTS	FGM	FGA	FG%	3PM	3PA	3P%	FTM	FTA	FT%	ORB	DRB	TRB	AST	PF	DQ	STL	BLK	TO	MPG	PPG	RPG	APG	PCM

• WRIGHT, John
John Wright

Born: —.   Height: 6'1".   Weight: —   Drafted: —   College: George Washington

YEAR	TEAM	GP	GS	MIN	PTS	FGM	FGA	FG%	3PM	3PA	3P%	FTM	FTA	FT%	ORB	DRB	TRB	AST	PF	DQ	STL	BLK	TO	MPG	PPG	RPG	APG	PCM
45-46	Youngstown-N	2	....	....	11	3	....	....	....	....	....	5	....	....	....	....	....	....	....	....	....	....	....	....	5.5	....	....	....
NBL Season Totals		2	....	....	11	3	....	....	....	....	....	5	....	....	....	....	....	....	....	....	....	....	....	....	5.5	....	....	....

• WRIGHT, Larry
Larry Glenn Wright

Born: Nov. 23, 1954. Monroe, LA, United States.   Height: 6'1".   Weight: 160 lbs.   Drafted: 1976   College: Grambling

YEAR	TEAM	GP	GS	MIN	PTS	FGM	FGA	FG%	3PM	3PA	3P%	FTM	FTA	FT%	ORB	DRB	TRB	AST	PF	DQ	STL	BLK	TO	MPG	PPG	RPG	APG	PCM
76-77	Washington	78	....	1421	612	262	595	.440	....	....	....	88	115	.765	32	66	98	232	170	0	55	5	....	18.2	7.8	1.3	3.0	.414
77-78	Washington	70	....	1466	642	283	570	.496	....	....	....	76	107	.710	31	71	102	260	195	3	68	15	133	20.9	9.2	1.5	3.7	.430
78-79	Washington	73	....	1658	677	276	589	.469	....	....	....	125	168	.744	48	92	140	298	166	3	69	13	117	22.7	9.3	1.9	4.1	.437
79-80	Washington	76	....	1286	558	229	500	.458	4	16	.250	96	108	.889	40	82	122	222	144	3	49	16	106	16.9	7.3	1.6	2.9	.436
80-81	Detroit	45	....	997	335	140	303	.462	2	7	.286	53	66	.803	26	62	88	153	114	1	42	7	72	22.2	7.4	2.0	3.4	.356
81-82	Detroit	1	0	6	0	0	1	.000	0	0	.000	0	0	.000	0	0	0	0	2	0	0	0	1	6.0	0.0	0.0	0.0	-.461
NBA Season Totals		343	0	6834	2824	1190	2558	.465	6	23	.261	438	564	.777	177	373	550	1165	791	10	283	58	429	19.9	8.2	1.6	3.4	....
76-77	Washington	8	....	104	53	19	39	.487	....	....	....	15	21	.714	1	6	7	16	18	1	7	1	....	13.0	6.6	0.9	2.0	.477
77-78	Washington	21	....	402	171	76	163	.466	....	....	....	19	25	.760	7	24	31	67	58	1	17	2	25	19.1	8.1	1.5	3.2	.408
78-79	Washington	18	....	331	151	62	129	.481	....	....	....	27	30	.900	12	13	25	44	49	0	10	4	27	18.4	8.4	1.4	2.4	.383
79-80	Washington	2	....	33	22	9	17	.529	0	1	.000	4	5	.800	1	1	2	6	6	0	3	0	3	16.5	11.0	1.0	3.0	.605
NBA Playoff Totals		49	....	870	397	166	348	.477	0	1	.000	65	81	.802	21	44	65	133	131	2	37	7	55	17.8	8.1	1.3	2.7	....

• WRIGHT, Leroy
James Leroy Wright

Born: May 6, 1938. New York, NY, United States.   Height: 6'9".   Weight: 215 lbs.   Drafted: 1960   College: Pacific

YEAR	TEAM	GP	GS	MIN	PTS	FGM	FGA	FG%	3PM	3PA	3P%	FTM	FTA	FT%	ORB	DRB	TRB	AST	PF	DQ	STL	BLK	TO	MPG	PPG	RPG	APG	PCM
67-68	Pittsburgh-A	17	....	331	57	24	60	.400	0	0	.000	9	22	.409			108	14	49	1	....	....	20	19.5	3.4	6.4	0.8	.325
68-69	Minnesota-A	10	....	95	8	4	13	.308	0	0	.000	0	5	.000	12	18	30	1	15	0	....	....	2	9.5	0.8	3.0	0.1	.196
ABA Season Totals		27	....	426	65	28	73	.384	0	0	.000	9	27	.333	12	18	138	15	64	1	....	....	22	15.8	2.4	5.1	0.6	....
67-68	Pittsburgh-A	13	....	190	26	9	28	.321	0	1	.000	8	22	.364	....	....	73	8	30	2	....	....	8	14.6	2.0	5.6	0.6	.326
68-69	Minnesota-A	1	....	5	0	0	3	.000	0	0	.000	0	0	.000	....	....	0	0	2	0	....	....	0	5.0	0.0	0.0	0.0	-.686
ABA Playoff Totals		14	....	195	26	9	31	.290	0	1	.000	8	22	.364	....	....	73	8	32	2	....	....	8	13.9	1.9	5.2	0.6	....

• WRIGHT, Lonnie
Lawrence Wright

Born: Jan. 23, 1944. Newark, NJ, United States.   Height: 6'2".   Weight: 205 lbs.   Drafted: 1966   College: Colorado State

YEAR	TEAM	GP	GS	MIN	PTS	FGM	FGA	FG%	3PM	3PA	3P%	FTM	FTA	FT%	ORB	DRB	TRB	AST	PF	DQ	STL	BLK	TO	MPG	PPG	RPG	APG	PCM
67-68	Denver-A	38	....	896	373	146	346	.422	2	9	.222	79	121	.653	....	....	96	68	96	0	....	....	43	23.6	9.8	2.5	1.8	.345
68-69	Denver-A	69	....	2538	1130	453	1089	.416	19	86	.221	205	276	.743	50	240	290	175	250	2	....	....	160	36.8	16.4	4.2	2.5	.353
69-70	Denver-A	79	....	2237	961	393	952	.413	54	193	.280	121	175	.691	49	167	216	149	278	7	....	....	97	28.3	12.2	2.7	1.9	.310
70-71	Denver-A	41	....	769	264	98	328	.299	15	56	.268	53	77	.688	36	53	89	61	86	1	....	....	43	18.8	6.4	2.2	1.5	.234
70-71	Florida-A	31	....	629	244	101	230	.439	2	18	.111	40	56	.714	19	45	64	55	76	1	....	....	32	20.3	7.9	2.1	1.8	.351
71-72	Florida-A	77	....	1638	618	252	599	.421	19	73	.260	95	117	.812	45	113	158	133	197	0	....	....	89	21.3	8.0	2.1	1.7	.308
ABA Season Totals		335	....	8707	3590	1443	3544	.407	111	435	.255	593	822	.721	199	618	913	641	983	11	....	....	464	26.0	10.7	2.7	1.9	....
67-68	Denver-A	5	....	149	36	13	50	.260	1	4	.250	9	14	.643	....	....	13	10	9	0	....	....	17	29.8	7.2	2.6	2.0	.147
68-69	Denver-A	7	....	224	84	31	86	.360	2	8	.250	20	28	.714	....	....	37	14	24	0	....	....	7	32.0	12.0	5.3	2.0	.316
69-70	Denver-A	11	....	334	84	32	109	.294	2	8	.250	18	23	.783	13	19	32	44	33	0	....	....	11	30.4	7.6	2.9	4.0	.238
70-71	Florida-A	6	....	105	37	15	45	.333	1	10	.100	6	7	.857	2	7	9	3	15	0	....	....	3	17.5	6.2	1.5	0.5	.165
71-72	Florida-A	4	....	93	42	19	45	.422	0	4	.000	4	4	1.000	....	....	9	7	7	....	....	....	2	23.3	10.5	2.3	1.8	.342
ABA Playoff Totals		33	....	905	283	110	335	.328	6	34	.176	57	76	.750	15	26	100	78	88	0	....	....	40	27.4	8.6	3.0	2.4	....

• WRIGHT, Loren
Loren Wright

Born: —.   Height: —   Weight: —   Drafted: —   College: —

YEAR	TEAM	GP	GS	MIN	PTS	FGM	FGA	FG%	3PM	3PA	3P%	FTM	FTA	FT%	ORB	DRB	TRB	AST	PF	DQ	STL	BLK	TO	MPG	PPG	RPG	APG	PCM
37-38	Cincinnati-N	4	....	....	4	2	....	....	....	....	....	0	....	....	....	....	....	....	....	....	....	....	....	....	1.0	....	....	....
NBL Season Totals		4	....	....	4	2	....	....	....	....	....	0	....	....	....	....	....	....	....	....	....	....	....	....	1.0	....	....	....

• WRIGHT, Lorenzen
Lorenzen Vern-Gagne Wright

Born: Nov. 4, 1975. Memphis, TN, United States.   Height: 6'11".   Weight: 225 lbs.   Drafted: 1996   College: Memphis

YEAR	TEAM	GP	GS	MIN	PTS	FGM	FGA	FG%	3PM	3PA	3P%	FTM	FTA	FT%	ORB	DRB	TRB	AST	PF	DQ	STL	BLK	TO	MPG	PPG	RPG	APG	PCM
96-97	LA Clippers	77	51	1936	561	236	491	.481	1	4	.250	88	150	.587	206	265	471	49	211	2	48	60	77	25.1	7.3	6.1	0.6	.370
97-98	LA Clippers	69	38	2067	623	241	542	.445	0	2	.000	141	214	.659	180	426	606	55	237	2	55	87	83	30.0	9.0	8.8	0.8	.423
98-99	LA Clippers	48	15	1135	319	119	260	.458	0	1	.000	81	117	.692	142	219	361	33	162	2	26	36	48	23.6	6.6	7.5	0.7	.419
99-00	Atlanta	75	0	1205	448	180	361	.499	1	3	.333	87	135	.644	117	188	305	21	203	9	29	40	66	16.1	6.0	4.1	0.3	.392
00-01	Atlanta	71	46	1988	881	363	811	.448	0	2	.000	155	216	.718	180	355	535	87	232	2	42	63	125	28.0	12.4	7.5	1.2	.455
01-02	Memphis	43	33	1252	516	223	486	.459	0	2	.000	70	123	.569	130	275	405	44	126	0	30	23	72	29.1	12.0	9.4	1.0	.475
02-03	Memphis	70	49	1982	797	325	716	.454	0	5	.000	147	223	.659	170	358	528	80	209	7	51	54	110	28.3	11.4	7.5	1.1	.441
NBA Season Totals		453	232	11565	4145	1687	3667	.460	2	19	.105	769	1178	.653	1125	2086	3211	369	1380	18	281	363	581	25.5	9.2	7.1	0.8	....
96-97	LA Clippers	3	3	92	31	13	32	.406	0	0	.000	5	5	1.000	7	15	22	2	6	0	3	2	1	30.7	10.3	7.3	0.7	.401
NBA Playoff Totals		3	3	92	31	13	32	.406	0	0	.000	5	5	1.000	7	15	22	2	6	0	3	2	1	30.7	10.3	7.3	0.7	....

• WRIGHT, Luther

Luther A. Wright Jr.

Born: Sept. 22, 1971. Jersey City, NJ, United States. Height: 7'2". Weight: 270 lbs. Drafted: 1993 College: Seton Hall

YEAR	TEAM	GP	GS	MIN	PTS	FGM	FGA	FG%	3PM	3PA	3P%	FTM	FTA	FT%	ORB	DRB	TRB	AST	PF	DQ	STL	BLK	TO	MPG	PPG	RPG	APG	PCM
93-94	Utah	15	2	92	19	8	23	.348	0	1	.000	3	4	.750	6	4	10	0	21	0	1	2	6	6.1	1.3	0.7	0.0	.017
NBA Season Totals		15	2	92	19	8	23	.348	0	1	.000	3	4	.750	6	4	10	0	21	0	1	2	6	6.1	1.3	0.7	0.0	....

• WRIGHT, Sharone

Sharone Addaryl Wright

Born: Jan. 30, 1973. Macon, GA, United States. Height: 6'11". Weight: 260 lbs. Drafted: 1994 College: Clemson

YEAR	TEAM	GP	GS	MIN	PTS	FGM	FGA	FG%	3PM	3PA	3P%	FTM	FTA	FT%	ORB	DRB	TRB	AST	PF	DQ	STL	BLK	TO	MPG	PPG	RPG	APG	PCM
94-95	Philadelphia	79	49	2044	904	361	776	.465	0	8	.000	182	282	.645	191	281	472	48	246	5	37	104	150	25.9	11.4	6.0	0.6	.410
95-96	Philadelphia	46	32	1136	483	183	384	.477	0	0	.000	117	186	.629	124	175	299	27	125	2	24	39	83	24.7	10.5	6.5	0.6	.435
95-96	Toronto	11	6	298	181	65	128	.508	1	3	.333	50	73	.685	24	33	57	11	38	2	6	10	28	27.1	16.5	5.2	1.0	.494
96-97	Toronto	60	28	1009	390	161	403	.400	0	1	.000	68	133	.511	79	107	186	28	146	3	15	50	96	16.8	6.5	3.1	0.5	.238
97-98	Toronto	7	0	44	16	7	14	.500	0	0	.000	2	4	.500	1	8	9	4	7	0	0	0	2	6.3	2.3	1.3	0.6	.369
NBA Season Totals		203	115	4531	1974	777	1705	.456	1	12	.083	419	678	.618	419	604	1023	118	562	12	82	203	359	22.3	9.7	5.0	0.6	....

• WUKOVITS, Tom

Tom Wukovits

Born: Feb. 4, 1916. Died: Nov.13, 1991. Height: 5'11". Weight: 165 lbs. Drafted: — College: Notre Dame

YEAR	TEAM	GP	GS	MIN	PTS	FGM	FGA	FG%	3PM	3PA	3P%	FTM	FTA	FT%	ORB	DRB	TRB	AST	PF	DQ	STL	BLK	TO	MPG	PPG	RPG	APG	PCM
39-40	Non-Skids-N	22	....	....	51	18	....	....	....	....	....	15	....	....	....	....	....	....	....	....	....	....	....	....	2.3	....	....	....
40-41	Non-Skids-N	24	....	....	153	54	....	....	....	....	....	45	....	....	....	....	....	....	....	....	....	....	....	....	6.4	....	....	....
41-42	Toledo-N	3	....	....	4	2	....	....	....	....	....	0	....	....	....	....	....	....	....	....	....	....	....	....	1.3	....	....	....
44-45	Cleveland-N	26	....	....	244	85	....	....	....	....	....	74	....	....	....	....	....	....	....	....	....	....	....	....	9.4	....	....	....
45-46	Cleveland-N	33	....	....	231	76	....	....	....	....	....	79	124	.637	....	....	....	....	....	....	....	....	....	....	7.0	....	....	....
NBL Season Totals		108	....	....	683	235	....	....	....	....	....	213	124	....	....	....	....	....	....	....	....	....	....	....	6.3	....	....	....
39-40	Non-Skids-N	8	....	....	33	14	....	....	....	....	....	5	....	....	....	....	....	....	....	....	....	....	....	....	4.1	....	....	....
40-41	Non-Skids-N	2	....	....	9	3	....	....	....	....	....	3	....	....	....	....	....	....	....	....	....	....	....	....	4.5	....	....	....
44-45	Cleveland-N	2	....	....	22	5	....	....	....	....	....	12	....	....	....	....	....	....	....	....	....	....	....	....	11.0	....	....	....
NBL Playoff Totals		12	....	....	64	22	....	....	....	....	....	20	....	....	....	....	....	....	....	....	....	....	....	....	5.3	....	....	....

• WUYCIK, Dennis

Dennis Mark Wuycik

Born: Mar. 29, 1950. Ambridge, PA, United States. Height: 6'6". Weight: 215 lbs. Drafted: 1972 College: North Carolina

YEAR	TEAM	GP	GS	MIN	PTS	FGM	FGA	FG%	3PM	3PA	3P%	FTM	FTA	FT%	ORB	DRB	TRB	AST	PF	DQ	STL	BLK	TO	MPG	PPG	RPG	APG	PCM
72-73	Carolina-A	83	....	973	377	151	329	.459	0	4	.000	75	108	.694	69	110	179	79	165	3	....	....	116	11.7	4.5	2.2	1.0	.386
73-74	Carolina-A	49	....	492	228	88	190	.463	1	2	.500	51	77	.662	51	55	106	31	88	....	16	4	40	10.0	4.7	2.2	0.6	.443
74-75	St. Louis-A	25	....	219	79	34	74	.459	0	1	.000	11	19	.579	17	21	38	18	40	....	6	1	25	8.8	3.2	1.5	0.7	.347
ABA Season Totals		157	....	1684	684	273	593	.460	1	7	.143	137	204	.672	137	186	323	128	293	3	22	5	181	10.7	4.4	2.1	0.8	....
72-73	Carolina-A	12	....	81	20	7	20	.350	0	1	.000	6	10	.600	6	10	16	2	14	0	....	....	8	6.8	1.7	1.3	0.2	.208
73-74	Carolina-A	3	....	13	4	1	4	.250	0	0	.000	2	2	1.000	1	2	3	1	0	....	0	0	1	4.3	1.3	1.0	0.3	.396
ABA Playoff Totals		15	....	94	24	8	24	.333	0	1	.000	8	12	.667	7	12	19	3	14	0	0	0	9	6.3	1.6	1.3	0.2	....

• WYNDER, A.J.

Arthur J. Wynder

Born: Sept. 11, 1964. Bronx, NY, United States. Height: 6'2". Weight: 180 lbs. Drafted: — College: Fairfield

YEAR	TEAM	GP	GS	MIN	PTS	FGM	FGA	FG%	3PM	3PA	3P%	FTM	FTA	FT%	ORB	DRB	TRB	AST	PF	DQ	STL	BLK	TO	MPG	PPG	RPG	APG	PCM
90-91	Boston	6	0	39	12	3	12	.250	0	1	.000	6	8	.750	1	2	3	8	1	0	1	0	4	6.5	2.0	0.5	1.3	.275
NBA Season Totals		6	0	39	12	3	12	.250	0	1	.000	6	8	.750	1	2	3	8	1	0	1	0	4	6.5	2.0	0.5	1.3	....

• YARBROUGH, Vincent

Vincent Raymond Yarbrough

Born: Mar. 21, 1981. Cleveland, TN, United States. Height: 6'7". Weight: 210 lbs. Drafted: 2002 College: Tennessee

YEAR	TEAM	GP	GS	MIN	PTS	FGM	FGA	FG%	3PM	3PA	3P%	FTM	FTA	FT%	ORB	DRB	TRB	AST	PF	DQ	STL	BLK	TO	MPG	PPG	RPG	APG	PCM
02-03	Denver	59	39	1381	406	168	428	.393	21	78	.269	49	62	.790	36	126	162	130	145	2	57	33	81	23.4	6.9	2.7	2.2	.286
NBA Season Totals		59	39	1381	406	168	428	.393	21	78	.269	49	62	.790	36	126	162	130	145	2	57	33	81	23.4	6.9	2.7	2.2	....

• YARDLEY, George

George Harry (Bird) Yardley III

Born: Nov. 3, 1928. Hollywood, CA, United States. Height: 6'5". Weight: 190 lbs. Drafted: 1950 College: Stanford HOF: 1996

YEAR	TEAM	GP	GS	MIN	PTS	FGM	FGA	FG%	3PM	3PA	3P%	FTM	FTA	FT%	ORB	DRB	TRB	AST	PF	DQ	STL	BLK	TO	MPG	PPG	RPG	APG	PCM
53-54	Fort Wayne	63	....	1489	564	209	492	.425	....	....	....	146	205	.712	....	....	407	99	166	3	....	....	....	23.6	9.0	6.5	1.6	.470
54-55	Fort Wayne	60	....	2150	1036	363	869	.418	....	....	....	310	416	.745	....	....	594	126	205	7	....	....	....	35.8	17.3	9.9	2.1	.531
55-56	Fort Wayne	71	....	2353	1233	434	1067	.407	....	....	....	365	492	.742	....	....	686	159	212	2	....	....	....	33.1	17.4	9.7	2.2	.570
56-57	Fort Wayne	72	....	2691	1547	522	1273	.410	....	....	....	503	639	.787	....	....	755	147	231	2	....	....	....	37.4	21.5	10.5	2.0	.594
57-58	Detroit	72	....	2843	**2001**	673	**1624**	.414	....	....	....	**655**	**808**	.811	....	....	768	97	226	3	....	....	....	39.5	**27.8**	10.7	1.3	.652
58-59	Detroit	46	....	1419	958	350	843	.415	....	....	....	258	316	.816	....	....	327	40	122	2	....	....	....	30.8	20.8	7.1	0.9	.575
58-59	Syracuse	15	....	420	251	96	199	.482	....	....	....	59	91	.648	....	....	104	25	37	0	....	....	....	28.0	16.7	6.9	1.7	.612
59-60	Syracuse	73	....	2402	1473	546	1205	.453	....	....	....	381	467	.816	....	....	579	122	227	3	....	....	....	32.9	20.2	7.9	1.7	.602
NBA Season Totals		472	....	15767	9063	3193	7572	.422	....	....	....	2677	3434	.780	....	....	4220	815	1426	22	....	....	....	33.4	19.2	8.9	1.7	....
53-54	Fort Wayne	4	....	107	42	16	33	.485	....	....	....	10	12	.833	....	....	24	3	10	0	....	....	....	26.8	10.5	6.0	0.8	.435
54-55	Fort Wayne	11	....	420	174	57	143	.399	....	....	....	60	79	.759	....	....	99	36	37	2	....	....	....	38.2	15.8	9.0	3.3	.494
55-56	Fort Wayne	10	....	406	230	77	183	.421	....	....	....	76	98	.776	....	....	139	26	25	0	....	....	....	40.6	23.0	13.9	2.6	.664
56-57	Fort Wayne	2	....	85	57	24	53	.453	....	....	....	9	11	.818	....	....	19	8	7	0	....	....	....	42.5	28.5	9.5	4.0	.661
57-58	Detroit	7	....	254	164	52	127	.409	....	....	....	60	67	.896	....	....	72	17	26	0	....	....	....	36.3	23.4	10.3	2.4	.675
58-59	Syracuse	9	....	333	226	83	189	.439	....	....	....	60	70	.857	....	....	87	21	29	0	....	....	....	37.0	25.1	9.7	2.3	.670
59-60	Syracuse	3	....	88	40	15	39	.385	....	....	....	10	12	.833	....	....	17	1	9	0	....	....	....	29.3	13.3	5.7	0.3	.361
NBA Playoff Totals		46	....	1693	933	324	767	.422	....	....	....	285	349	.817	....	....	457	112	143	2	....	....	....	36.8	20.3	9.9	2.4	....

YEAR	TEAM	GP	GS	MIN	PTS	FGM	FGA	FG%	3PM	3PA	3P%	FTM	FTA	FT%	ORB	DRB	TRB	AST	PF	DQ	STL	BLK	TO	MPG	PPG	RPG	APG	PCM

• YATES, Barry — Barry Yates

Born: Jan. 30, 1946. Height: 6'7". Weight: 215 lbs. Drafted: 1971 College: Maryland

YEAR	TEAM	GP	GS	MIN	PTS	FGM	FGA	FG%	3PM	3PA	3P%	FTM	FTA	FT%	ORB	DRB	TRB	AST	PF	DQ	STL	BLK	TO	MPG	PPG	RPG	APG	PCM
71-72	Philadelphia	24	....	144	69	31	83	.373	....	....	....	7	11	.636	....	....	40	7	14	0	....	....	....	6.0	2.9	1.7	0.3	.408
NBA Season Totals		24	....	144	69	31	83	.373	....	....	....	7	11	.636	....	....	40	7	14	0	....	....	....	6.0	2.9	1.7	0.3	....

• YATES, Wayne — Wayne E. Yates

Born: Nov. 7, 1937. Height: 6'8". Weight: 235 lbs. Drafted: 1961 College: Memphis State

YEAR	TEAM	GP	GS	MIN	PTS	FGM	FGA	FG%	3PM	3PA	3P%	FTM	FTA	FT%	ORB	DRB	TRB	AST	PF	DQ	STL	BLK	TO	MPG	PPG	RPG	APG	PCM
61-62	LA Lakers	37	....	263	72	31	105	.295	....	....	....	10	22	.455	....	....	94	16	72	1	....	....	....	7.1	1.9	2.5	0.4	.283
NBA Season Totals		37	....	263	72	31	105	.295	....	....	....	10	22	.455	....	....	94	16	72	1	....	....	....	7.1	1.9	2.5	0.4	....
61-62	LA Lakers	4	....	12	7	3	8	.375	....	....	....	1	2	.500	....	....	5	1	2	0	....	....	....	3.0	1.8	1.3	0.3	.587
NBA Playoff Totals		4	....	12	7	3	8	.375	....	....	....	1	2	.500	....	....	5	1	2	0	....	....	....	3.0	1.8	1.3	0.3	....

• YELVERTON, Charlie — Charles W. Yelverton

Born: Dec. 5, 1948. Height: 6'2". Weight: 190 lbs. Drafted: 1971 College: Fordham

YEAR	TEAM	GP	GS	MIN	PTS	FGM	FGA	FG%	3PM	3PA	3P%	FTM	FTA	FT%	ORB	DRB	TRB	AST	PF	DQ	STL	BLK	TO	MPG	PPG	RPG	APG	PCM
71-72	Portland	69	....	1227	545	206	530	.389	....	....	....	133	188	.707	....	....	201	81	145	2	....	....	....	17.8	7.9	2.9	1.2	.362
NBA Season Totals		69	....	1227	545	206	530	.389	....	....	....	133	188	.707	....	....	201	81	145	2	....	....	....	17.8	7.9	2.9	1.2	....

• YESAWICH, Paul — Paul J. (Hooks) Yesawich Jr.

Born: 1923. Height: 6'2". Weight: 190 lbs. Drafted: — College: Niagara

YEAR	TEAM	GP	GS	MIN	PTS	FGM	FGA	FG%	3PM	3PA	3P%	FTM	FTA	FT%	ORB	DRB	TRB	AST	PF	DQ	STL	BLK	TO	MPG	PPG	RPG	APG	PCM
48-49	Syracuse-N	5	....	....	8	2	....	....	....	....	....	4	5	.800	....	....	....	4	....	....	....	....	....	1.6	....	....	....	....
NBL Season Totals		5	....	....	8	2	....	....	....	....	....	4	5	....	....	....	....	4	....	....	....	....	....	1.6	....	....	....	....

• YONAKOR, Rich — Richard Robert Yonakor

Born: Oct. 3, 1958. Euclid, OH, United States. Height: 6'9". Weight: 220 lbs. Drafted: 1980 College: North Carolina

YEAR	TEAM	GP	GS	MIN	PTS	FGM	FGA	FG%	3PM	3PA	3P%	FTM	FTA	FT%	ORB	DRB	TRB	AST	PF	DQ	STL	BLK	TO	MPG	PPG	RPG	APG	PCM
81-82	San Antonio	10	0	70	33	14	26	.538	0	0	.000	5	7	.714	13	14	27	3	7	0	1	2	2	7.0	3.3	2.7	0.3	.669
NBA Season Totals		10	0	70	33	14	26	.538	0	0	.000	5	7	.714	13	14	27	3	7	0	1	2	2	7.0	3.3	2.7	0.3	....
81-82	San Antonio	2	0	4	2	1	2	.500	0	0	.000	0	0	.000	0	1	1	1	1	0	1	0	0	2.0	1.0	0.5	0.5	.885
NBA Playoff Totals		2	0	4	2	1	2	.500	0	0	.000	0	0	.000	0	1	1	1	1	0	1	0	0	2.0	1.0	0.5	0.5	....

• YOST, Nicholas — Nicholas Yost

Born: 1915. Height: 6'4". Weight: 220 lbs. Drafted: — College: DePaul

YEAR	TEAM	GP	GS	MIN	PTS	FGM	FGA	FG%	3PM	3PA	3P%	FTM	FTA	FT%	ORB	DRB	TRB	AST	PF	DQ	STL	BLK	TO	MPG	PPG	RPG	APG	PCM
38-39	Hammond-N	9	....	....	81	36	....	....	....	....	....	9	....	....	....	....	....	....	....	....	....	....	....	9.0	....	....	....	....
39-40	Hammond-N	8	....	....	43	18	....	....	....	....	....	7	....	....	....	....	....	....	....	....	....	....	....	5.4	....	....	....	....
NBL Season Totals		17	....	....	124	54	....	....	....	....	....	16	....	....	....	....	....	....	....	....	....	....	....	7.3	....	....	....	....

• YOUNG, Danny — Danny Richardson Young

Born: July 26, 1962. Raleigh, NC, United States. Height: 6'3". Weight: 175 lbs. Drafted: 1984 College: Wake Forest

YEAR	TEAM	GP	GS	MIN	PTS	FGM	FGA	FG%	3PM	3PA	3P%	FTM	FTA	FT%	ORB	DRB	TRB	AST	PF	DQ	STL	BLK	TO	MPG	PPG	RPG	APG	PCM
84-85	Seattle	3	0	26	4	2	10	.200	0	1	.000	0	0	.000	0	3	3	2	2	0	3	0	2	8.7	1.3	1.0	0.7	.057
85-86	Seattle	82	0	1901	568	227	449	.506	24	74	.324	90	106	.849	29	91	120	303	113	0	110	9	90	23.2	6.9	1.5	3.7	.402
86-87	Seattle	73	0	1482	352	132	288	.458	29	79	.367	59	71	.831	23	90	113	353	72	0	74	3	88	20.3	4.8	1.5	4.8	.432
87-88	Seattle	77	0	949	243	89	218	.408	22	77	.286	43	53	.811	18	57	75	218	69	0	52	2	39	12.3	3.2	1.0	2.8	.424
88-89	Portland	48	0	952	297	115	250	.460	17	50	.340	50	64	.781	17	57	74	123	50	0	55	3	43	19.8	6.2	1.5	2.6	.374
89-90	Portland	82	0	1393	383	138	328	.421	16	59	.271	91	112	.813	29	93	122	231	84	0	82	4	82	17.0	4.7	1.5	2.8	.373
90-91	Portland	75	1	897	283	103	271	.380	36	104	.346	41	45	.911	22	53	75	141	49	0	50	7	53	12.0	3.8	1.0	1.9	.363
91-92	Portland	18	0	134	45	16	40	.400	3	10	.300	10	14	.714	0	9	9	20	6	0	6	0	5	7.4	2.5	0.5	1.1	.364
91-92	LA Clippers	44	5	889	235	84	215	.391	20	60	.333	47	53	.887	16	50	66	152	47	0	40	4	44	20.2	5.3	1.5	3.5	.352
92-93	Detroit	65	2	836	188	69	167	.413	22	68	.324	28	32	.875	13	34	47	119	36	0	31	5	33	12.9	2.9	0.7	1.8	.301
94-95	Milwaukee	7	0	77	24	9	17	.529	5	12	.417	1	1	1.000	1	4	5	12	8	0	4	0	4	11.0	3.4	0.7	1.7	.392
NBA Season Totals		574	8	9536	2622	984	2253	.437	194	594	.327	460	551	.835	168	541	709	1674	536	0	507	37	483	16.6	4.6	1.2	2.9	....
86-87	Seattle	14	0	208	57	21	52	.404	5	16	.313	10	10	1.000	4	12	16	48	21	1	15	0	7	14.9	4.1	1.1	3.4	.442
87-88	Seattle	5	0	95	32	11	21	.524	0	3	.000	10	10	1.000	3	7	10	19	7	0	2	2	7	19.0	6.4	2.0	3.8	.487
88-89	Portland	3	0	66	28	12	26	.462	3	8	.375	1	2	.500	2	2	4	12	2	0	1	0	2	22.0	9.3	1.3	4.0	.443
89-90	Portland	21	0	294	86	28	72	.389	11	29	.379	19	27	.704	11	19	30	32	29	0	14	2	17	14.0	4.1	1.4	1.5	.301
90-91	Portland	7	0	36	12	6	11	.545	0	1	.000	0	0	.000	0	0	0	7	0	0	0	0	2	5.1	1.7	0.0	1.0	.359
91-92	LA Clippers	3	0	11	4	2	4	.500	0	2	.000	0	0	.000	0	0	0	1	0	0	0	0	2	3.7	1.3	0.0	0.3	.123
NBA Playoff Totals		53	1	710	219	80	186	.430	19	59	.322	40	49	.816	20	40	60	119	59	1	32	4	37	13.4	4.1	1.1	2.2	....

• YOUNG, Jewell — Jewell Young

Born: Jan. 18, 1913. Hedrick, IN, United States. Died: Apr.16, 2003. Height: 6' Weight: 160 lbs. Drafted: — College: Purdue

YEAR	TEAM	GP	GS	MIN	PTS	FGM	FGA	FG%	3PM	3PA	3P%	FTM	FTA	FT%	ORB	DRB	TRB	AST	PF	DQ	STL	BLK	TO	MPG	PPG	RPG	APG	PCM
38-39	Indianapolis-N	26	....	....	264	96	....	....	....	....	....	72	....	....	....	....	....	....	....	....	....	....	....	10.2	....	....	....	....
39-40	Indianapolis-N	28	....	....	260	95	....	....	....	....	....	70	....	....	....	....	....	....	....	....	....	....	....	9.3	....	....	....	....
41-42	Indianapolis-N	23	....	....	263	93	....	....	....	....	....	77	....	....	....	....	....	....	....	....	....	....	....	11.4	....	....	....	....

YEAR	TEAM	GP	GS	MIN	PTS	FGM	FGA	FG%	3PM	3PA	3P%	FTM	FTA	FT%	ORB	DRB	TRB	AST	PF	DQ	STL	BLK	TO	MPG	PPG	RPG	APG	PCM
42-43	Oshkosh-N	3	....	....	7	3	....	....	....	....	....	1	....	....	....	....	....	....	....	....	....	....	....	....	2.3	....	....	....
45-46	Indianapolis-N	8	....	....	9	3	....	....	....	....	....	3	....	....	....	....	....	....	....	....	....	....	....	....	1.1	....	....	....
NBL Season Totals		88	....	....	803	290	....	....	....	....	....	223	....	....	....	....	....	....	....	....	....	....	....	....	9.1	....	....	....
41-42	Indianapolis-N	2	....	....	35	12	....	....	....	....	....	11	....	....	....	....	....	....	....	....	....	....	....	....	17.5	....	....	....
NBL Playoff Totals		2	....	....	35	12	....	....	....	....	....	11	....	....	....	....	....	....	....	....	....	....	....	....	17.5	....	....	....

• YOUNG, Michael

Michael Wayne Young

Born: Jan. 2, 1961. Houston, TX, United States. Height: 6'7". Weight: 220 lbs. Drafted: 1984 College: Houston

YEAR	TEAM	GP	GS	MIN	PTS	FGM	FGA	FG%	3PM	3PA	3P%	FTM	FTA	FT%	ORB	DRB	TRB	AST	PF	DQ	STL	BLK	TO	MPG	PPG	RPG	APG	PCM
84-85	Phoenix	2	0	11	4	2	6	.333	0	1	.000	0	0	.000	1	1	2	0	0	0	0	0	0	5.5	2.0	1.0	0.0	.194
85-86	Philadelphia	2	0	2	0	0	2	.000	0	0	.000	0	0	.000	0	0	0	0	0	0	0	0	0	1.0	0.0	0.0	0.0	-.929
89-90	LA Clippers	45	2	459	219	92	194	.474	8	26	.308	27	38	.711	36	50	86	24	47	0	25	3	14	10.2	4.9	1.9	0.5	.469
NBA Season Totals		49	2	472	223	94	202	.465	8	27	.296	27	38	.711	37	51	88	24	47	0	25	3	14	9.6	4.6	1.8	0.5	....
85-86	Philadelphia	3	0	3	2	1	4	.250	0	0	.000	0	0	.000	1	0	1	0	0	0	0	0	0	1.0	0.7	0.3	0.0	.047
NBA Playoff Totals		3	0	3	2	1	4	.250	0	0	.000	0	0	.000	1	0	1	0	0	0	0	0	0	1.0	0.7	0.3	0.0	....

• YOUNG, Perry

Perry Young

Born: Aug. 4, 1963. Baltimore, MD, United States. Height: 6'5". Weight: 210 lbs. Drafted: 1985 College: Virginia Tech

YEAR	TEAM	GP	GS	MIN	PTS	FGM	FGA	FG%	3PM	3PA	3P%	FTM	FTA	FT%	ORB	DRB	TRB	AST	PF	DQ	STL	BLK	TO	MPG	PPG	RPG	APG	PCM
86-87	Chicago	5	0	20	5	2	4	.500	0	0	.000	1	2	.500	0	1	1	0	3	0	1	0	1	4.0	1.0	0.2	0.0	.110
86-87	Portland	4	0	52	8	4	17	.235	0	0	.000	0	0	.000	3	4	7	7	11	0	4	1	3	13.0	2.0	1.8	1.8	.128
NBA Season Totals		9	0	72	13	6	21	.286	0	0	.000	1	2	.500	3	5	8	7	14	0	5	1	4	8.0	1.4	0.9	0.8	....

• YOUNG, Suntino

Suntino Korleone Young

Born: Dec. 31, 1978. Wichita, KS, United States. Height: 6'7". Weight: 213 lbs. Drafted: 1998 College: none (HS: Hargrave Military Academy, VA)

YEAR	TEAM	GP	GS	MIN	PTS	FGM	FGA	FG%	3PM	3PA	3P%	FTM	FTA	FT%	ORB	DRB	TRB	AST	PF	DQ	STL	BLK	TO	MPG	PPG	RPG	APG	PCM
98-99	Detroit	3	0	15	13	5	10	.500	1	4	.250	2	2	1.000	2	2	4	1	3	0	0	0	1	5.0	4.3	1.3	0.3	.733
NBA Season Totals		3	0	15	13	5	10	.500	1	4	.250	2	2	1.000	2	2	4	1	3	0	0	0	1	5.0	4.3	1.3	0.3	....

• YOUNG, Tim

Tim Aaron Young

Born: Feb. 6, 1976. Santa Cruz, CA, United States. Height: 7' Weight: 220 lbs. Drafted: 1999 College: Stanford

YEAR	TEAM	GP	GS	MIN	PTS	FGM	FGA	FG%	3PM	3PA	3P%	FTM	FTA	FT%	ORB	DRB	TRB	AST	PF	DQ	STL	BLK	TO	MPG	PPG	RPG	APG	PCM
99-00	Golden State	25	0	137	54	13	39	.333	0	0	.000	28	36	.778	13	22	35	5	18	0	2	1	9	5.5	2.2	1.4	0.2	.368
NBA Season Totals		25	0	137	54	13	39	.333	0	0	.000	28	36	.778	13	22	35	5	18	0	2	1	9	5.5	2.2	1.4	0.2	....

• YOUNG, Willie

William Young

Born: —. Height: — Weight: — Drafted: — College: Wisconsin

YEAR	TEAM	GP	GS	MIN	PTS	FGM	FGA	FG%	3PM	3PA	3P%	FTM	FTA	FT%	ORB	DRB	TRB	AST	PF	DQ	STL	BLK	TO	MPG	PPG	RPG	APG	PCM
37-38	Whiting-N	2	....	....	0	0	....	....	....	....	....	0	....	....	....	....	....	....	....	....	....	....	....	....	0.0	....	....	....
NBL Playoff Totals		2	....	....	0	0	....	....	....	....	....	0	....	....	....	....	....	....	....	....	....	....	....	....	0.0	....	....	....

• YOURIST, Abe

Abe Yourist

Born: 1911. Height: 6'2". Weight: 210 lbs. Drafted: — College: Heidelberg

YEAR	TEAM	GP	GS	MIN	PTS	FGM	FGA	FG%	3PM	3PA	3P%	FTM	FTA	FT%	ORB	DRB	TRB	AST	PF	DQ	STL	BLK	TO	MPG	PPG	RPG	APG	PCM
41-42	Toledo-N	1	....	....	0	0	....	....	....	....	....	0	....	....	....	....	....	....	....	....	....	....	....	....	0.0	....	....	....
NBL Season Totals		1	....	....	0	0	....	....	....	....	....	0	....	....	....	....	....	....	....	....	....	....	....	....	0.0	....	....	....

• ZADEL, Stan

Stan Zadel

Born: Apr. 8, 1916. Died: Oct.1982. Height: 6'5". Weight: 215 lbs. Drafted: — College: none

YEAR	TEAM	GP	GS	MIN	PTS	FGM	FGA	FG%	3PM	3PA	3P%	FTM	FTA	FT%	ORB	DRB	TRB	AST	PF	DQ	STL	BLK	TO	MPG	PPG	RPG	APG	PCM
38-39	Sheboygan-N	10	....	....	31	9	....	....	....	....	....	13	....	....	....	....	....	....	....	....	....	....	....	....	3.1	....	....	....
39-40	Chicago-N	18	....	....	108	42	....	....	....	....	....	24	....	....	....	....	....	....	....	....	....	....	....	....	6.0	....	....	....
NBL Season Totals		28	....	....	139	51	....	....	....	....	....	37	....	....	....	....	....	....	....	....	....	....	....	....	5.0	....	....	....

• ZASLOFSKY, Max

Max (Slats, The Touch) Zaslofsky

Born: Dec. 7, 1925. Brooklyn, NY, United States. Died: Oct.15, 1985. Height: 6'2". Weight: 170 lbs. Drafted: — College: St. John's (NY)

YEAR	TEAM	GP	GS	MIN	PTS	FGM	FGA	FG%	3PM	3PA	3P%	FTM	FTA	FT%	ORB	DRB	TRB	AST	PF	DQ	STL	BLK	TO	MPG	PPG	RPG	APG	PCM
46-47	Chicago	61	....	....	877	336	1020	.329	....	....	....	205	278	.737	....	....	....	40	121	....	....	....	....	....	14.4	....	0.7	....
47-48	Chicago	48	....	....	**1007**	**373**	1156	.323	....	....	....	261	333	.784	....	....	....	29	125	....	....	....	....	....	21.0	....	0.6	....
48-49	Chicago	58	....	....	1197	425	1216	.350	....	....	....	347	413	.840	....	....	....	149	156	....	....	....	....	....	20.6	....	2.6	....
49-50	Chicago	68	....	....	1115	397	1132	.351	....	....	....	321	381	**.843**	....	....	....	155	185	....	....	....	....	....	16.4	....	2.3	....
50-51	New York	66	....	....	835	302	853	.354	....	....	....	231	298	.775	....	....	228	136	150	3	....	....	....	....	12.7	3.5	2.1	....
51-52	New York	66	....	2113	931	322	958	.336	....	....	....	287	380	.755	....	....	194	156	183	5	....	....	....	32.0	14.1	2.9	2.4	.341
52-53	New York	29	....	722	344	123	320	.384	....	....	....	98	142	.690	....	....	75	55	81	1	....	....	....	24.9	11.9	2.6	1.9	.389
53-54	Bal/Mil/FtW	65	....	1881	811	278	756	.368	....	....	....	255	357	.714	....	....	160	154	142	1	....	....	....	28.9	12.5	2.5	2.4	.371
54-55	Fort Wayne	70	....	1862	785	269	821	.328	....	....	....	247	352	.702	....	....	191	203	142	0	....	....	....	26.6	11.2	2.7	2.9	.364
55-56	Fort Wayne	9	....	182	88	29	81	.358	....	....	....	30	35	.857	....	....	16	16	18	1	....	....	....	20.2	9.8	1.8	1.8	.394
NBA Season Totals		540	....	6760	7990	2854	8313	.343	....	....	....	2282	2969	.769	....	....	864	1093	1291	11	....	....	....	12.5	14.8	1.6	2.0	....
46-47	Chicago	11	....	....	149	60	199	.302	....	....	....	29	44	.659	....	....	....	4	26	....	....	....	....	....	13.5	....	0.4	....
47-48	Chicago	5	....	....	97	30	88	.341	....	....	....	37	47	.787	....	....	....	0	17	....	....	....	....	....	19.4	....	0.0	....
48-49	Chicago	2	....	....	44	15	49	.306	....	....	....	14	18	.778	....	....	....	6	3	....	....	....	....	....	22.0	....	3.0	....
49-50	Chicago	2	....	....	45	15	32	.469	....	....	....	15	18	.833	....	....	....	6	7	....	....	....	....	....	22.5	....	3.0	....

YEAR	TEAM	GP	GS	MIN	PTS	FGM	FGA	FG%	3PM	3PA	3P%	FTM	FTA	FT%	ORB	DRB	TRB	AST	PF	DQ	STL	BLK	TO	MPG	PPG	RPG	APG	PCM
50-51	New York	14	....	....	250	88	217	.406	....	....	....	74	100	.740	....	....	58	38	43	2	....	....	....	....	17.9	4.1	2.7	
51-52	New York	14	....	506	227	69	185	.373	....	....	....	89	110	.809	....	....	44	23	51	1	....	....	....	36.1	16.2	3.1	1.6	.355
53-54	Fort Wayne	4	....	98	35	11	36	.306	....	....	....	13	15	.867	....	....	3	6	7	0	....	....	....	24.5	8.8	0.8	1.5	.244
54-55	Fort Wayne	11	....	129	52	18	44	.409	....	....	....	16	20	.800	....	....	16	18	20	0	....	....	....	11.7	4.7	1.5	1.6	.449
NBA Playoff Totals		63	....	733	899	306	850	.360	....	....	....	287	372	.772	....	....	121	101	174	3	....	....	....	11.6	14.3	1.9	1.6	

• ZAWOLUK, Zeke

Robert Michael (Zeke) Zawoluk

Born: Oct. 13, 1930. Brooklyn, NY, United States.   Height: 6'7".   Weight: 215 lbs.   Drafted: 1952   College: St. John's (NY)

YEAR	TEAM	GP	GS	MIN	PTS	FGM	FGA	FG%	3PM	3PA	3P%	FTM	FTA	FT%	ORB	DRB	TRB	AST	PF	DQ	STL	BLK	TO	MPG	PPG	RPG	APG	PCM
52-53	Indianapolis	41	....	622	187	55	150	.367	....	....	....	77	116	.664	....	....	146	31	83	1	....	....	....	15.2	4.6	3.6	0.8	.353
53-54	Philadelphia	71	....	1795	592	203	540	.376	....	....	....	186	230	.809	....	....	330	99	220	6	....	....	....	25.3	8.3	4.6	1.4	.346
54-55	Philadelphia	67	....	1117	431	138	375	.368	....	....	....	155	199	.779	....	....	256	87	147	3	....	....	....	16.7	6.4	3.8	1.3	.432
NBA Season Totals		179	....	3534	1210	396	1065	.372	....	....	....	418	545	.767	....	....	732	217	450	10	....	....	....	19.7	6.8	4.1	1.2	
52-53	Indianapolis	2	....	18	2	1	6	.167	....	....	....	0	2	.000	....	....	2	0	5	0	....	....	....	9.0	1.0	1.0	0.0	-.150
NBA Playoff Totals		2	....	18	2	1	6	.167	....	....	....	0	2	.000	....	....	2	0	5	0	....	....	....	9.0	1.0	1.0	0.0	

• ZELLER, Dave

David A. Zeller

Born: June 8, 1939.   Height: 6'1".   Weight: 175 lbs.   Drafted: 1961   College: Miami (OH)

YEAR	TEAM	GP	GS	MIN	PTS	FGM	FGA	FG%	3PM	3PA	3P%	FTM	FTA	FT%	ORB	DRB	TRB	AST	PF	DQ	STL	BLK	TO	MPG	PPG	RPG	APG	PCM
61-62	Cincinnati	61	....	278	90	36	102	.353	....	....	....	18	24	.750	....	....	27	58	37	0	....	....	....	4.6	1.5	0.4	1.0	.408
NBA Season Totals		61	....	278	90	36	102	.353	....	....	....	18	24	.750	....	....	27	58	37	0	....	....	....	4.6	1.5	0.4	1.0	
61-62	Cincinnati	2	....	5	2	1	2	.500	....	....	....	0	0	.000	....	....	1	1	0	0	....	....	....	2.5	1.0	0.5	0.5	.644
NBA Playoff Totals		2	....	5	2	1	2	.500	....	....	....	0	0	.000	....	....	1	1	0	0	....	....	....	2.5	1.0	0.5	0.5	

• ZELLER, Gary

Gary Lynn Zeller

Born: Nov. 20, 1947. Died: Feb.5, 1996.   Height: 6'3".   Weight: 205 lbs.   Drafted: 1970   College: Drake

YEAR	TEAM	GP	GS	MIN	PTS	FGM	FGA	FG%	3PM	3PA	3P%	FTM	FTA	FT%	ORB	DRB	TRB	AST	PF	DQ	STL	BLK	TO	MPG	PPG	RPG	APG	PCM
70-71	Baltimore	50	....	226	83	34	115	.296	....	....	....	15	28	.536	....	....	27	7	43	0	....	....	....	4.5	1.7	0.5	0.1	.091
71-72	New York-A	12	....	82	18	7	30	.233	0	1	.000	4	6	.667	5	5	10	2	16	0	....	....	9	6.8	1.5	0.8	0.2	.011
71-72	Baltimore	28	....	471	188	83	229	.362	....	....	....	22	35	.629	....	....	65	30	62	0	....	....	....	16.8	6.7	2.3	1.1	.254
NBA Season Totals		78	....	697	271	117	344	.340	....	....	....	37	63	.587	....	....	92	37	105	0	....	....	....	8.9	3.5	1.2	0.5	
ABA Season Totals		12	....	82	18	7	30	.233	0	1	.000	4	6	.667	5	5	10	2	16	0	....	....	9	6.8	1.5	0.8	0.2	
Career Totals		90	....	779	289	124	374	.332	0	1	.000	41	69	.594	5	5	102	39	121	0	....	....	9	8.7	3.2	1.1	0.4	
70-71	Baltimore	15	....	67	26	12	35	.343	....	....	....	2	7	.286	....	....	13	4	15	0	....	....	....	4.5	1.7	0.9	0.3	.199
71-72	New York-A	3	....	9	2	1	1	1.000	0	0	.000	0	1	.000	....	....	1	0	7	....	....	....	3	3.0	0.7	0.3	0.0	-.071
NBA Playoff Totals		15	....	67	26	12	35	.343	....	....	....	2	7	.286	....	....	13	4	15	0	....	....	....	4.5	1.7	0.9	0.3	
ABA Playoff Totals		3	....	9	2	1	1	1.000	0	0	.000	0	1	.000	....	....	1	0	7	....	....	....	3	3.0	0.7	0.3	0.0	
Career Playoff Totals		18	....	76	28	13	36	.361	0	0	.000	2	8	.250	....	....	14	4	22	0	....	....	3	4.2	1.6	0.8	0.2	

• ZELLER, Harry

Harry Raymond Zeller

Born: July 10, 1918.   Height: 6'4".   Weight: 210 lbs.   Drafted: —   College: Washington & Jefferson

YEAR	TEAM	GP	GS	MIN	PTS	FGM	FGA	FG%	3PM	3PA	3P%	FTM	FTA	FT%	ORB	DRB	TRB	AST	PF	DQ	STL	BLK	TO	MPG	PPG	RPG	APG	PCM
46-47	Pittsburgh	48	....	....	362	120	382	.314	....	....	....	122	177	.689	....	....	31	177	....	....	....	....	....	7.5	....	0.6		
NBA Season Totals		48	....	....	362	120	382	.314	....	....	....	122	177	.689	....	....	31	177	....	....	....	....	....	7.5	....	0.6		

• ZENO, Tony

Anthony Michael Zeno

Born: Oct. 1, 1957. New Orleans, LA, United States.   Height: 6'8".   Weight: 210 lbs.   Drafted: 1979   College: Arizona State

YEAR	TEAM	GP	GS	MIN	PTS	FGM	FGA	FG%	3PM	3PA	3P%	FTM	FTA	FT%	ORB	DRB	TRB	AST	PF	DQ	STL	BLK	TO	MPG	PPG	RPG	APG	PCM
79-80	Indiana	8	....	59	14	6	21	.286	0	0	.000	2	2	1.000	3	11	14	1	13	0	4	3	9	7.4	1.8	1.8	0.1	.110
NBA Season Totals		8	....	59	14	6	21	.286	0	0	.000	2	2	1.000	3	11	14	1	13	0	4	3	9	7.4	1.8	1.8	0.1	

• ZERAVICH, Jim

Jim Zeravich

Born: Feb. 17, 1920. Died: Aug.16, 1998.   Height: 6'7".   Weight: —   Drafted: —   College: Washington & Jefferson

YEAR	TEAM	GP	GS	MIN	PTS	FGM	FGA	FG%	3PM	3PA	3P%	FTM	FTA	FT%	ORB	DRB	TRB	AST	PF	DQ	STL	BLK	TO	MPG	PPG	RPG	APG	PCM
46-47	Syracuse-N	2	....	....	5	1	....	....	....	....	....	3	5	.600	....	....	....	....	....	....	....	....	....	2.5	....	....		
NBL Season Totals		2	....	....	5	1	....	....	....	....	....	3	5		....	....	....	....	....	....	....	....	....	2.5	....	....		

• ZEVENBERGEN, Phil

Phil Zevenbergen

Born: Apr. 13, 1964. Seattle, WA, United States.   Height: 6'10".   Weight: 230 lbs.   Drafted: 1987   College: Washington

YEAR	TEAM	GP	GS	MIN	PTS	FGM	FGA	FG%	3PM	3PA	3P%	FTM	FTA	FT%	ORB	DRB	TRB	AST	PF	DQ	STL	BLK	TO	MPG	PPG	RPG	APG	PCM
87-88	San Antonio	8	0	58	30	15	27	.556	0	0	.000	0	2	.000	4	9	13	3	12	0	3	1	4	7.3	3.8	1.6	0.4	.476
NBA Season Totals		8	0	58	30	15	27	.556	0	0	.000	0	2	.000	4	9	13	3	12	0	3	1	4	7.3	3.8	1.6	0.4	
87-88	San Antonio	1	0	1	0	0	0	.000	0	0	.000	0	0	.000	0	0	0	0	0	0	0	0	0	1.0	0.0	0.0	0.0	.000
NBA Playoff Totals		1	0	1	0	0	0	.000	0	0	.000	0	0	.000	0	0	0	0	0	0	0	0	0	1.0	0.0	0.0	0.0	

YEAR	TEAM	GP	GS	MIN	PTS	FGM	FGA	FG%	3PM	3PA	3P%	FTM	FTA	FT%	ORB	DRB	TRB	AST	PF	DQ	STL	BLK	TO	MPG	PPG	RPG	APG	PCM

• ZHIZHI, Wang

Wang Zhizhi

Born: July 8, 1977. Beijing, China.   Height: 7'   Weight: 255 lbs.   Drafted: 1999   College: Beijing

YEAR	TEAM	GP	GS	MIN	PTS	FGM	FGA	FG%	3PM	3PA	3P%	FTM	FTA	FT%	ORB	DRB	TRB	AST	PF	DQ	STL	BLK	TO	MPG	PPG	RPG	APG	PCM
00-01	Dallas	5	0	38	24	8	19	.421	0	2	.000	8	10	.800	1	6	7	0	8	0	0	0	1	7.6	4.8	1.4	0.0	.395
01-02	Dallas	55	0	598	308	109	248	.440	48	116	.414	42	57	.737	19	92	111	22	84	0	11	12	25	10.9	5.6	2.0	0.4	.435
02-03	LA Clippers	41	1	412	182	62	162	.383	16	46	.348	42	58	.724	26	51	77	11	41	0	8	10	31	10.0	4.4	1.9	0.3	.329
NBA Season Totals		101	1	1048	514	179	429	.417	64	164	.390	92	125	.736	46	149	195	33	133	0	19	22	57	10.4	5.1	1.9	0.3	....
00-01	Dallas	5	0	23	10	3	8	.375	1	2	.500	3	3	1.000	0	2	2	1	1	0	1	1	1	4.6	2.0	0.4	0.2	.385
01-02	Dallas	8	0	44	20	7	16	.438	3	6	.500	3	6	.500	5	3	8	3	11	0	0	1	0	5.5	2.5	1.0	0.4	.385
NBA Playoff Totals		13	0	67	30	10	24	.417	4	8	.500	6	9	.667	5	5	10	4	12	0	1	2	1	5.2	2.3	0.8	0.3	....

• ZIDEK, George

Jiri Zidek

Born: Aug. 2, 1973. Zlin, Czechoslovakia.   Height: 7'   Weight: 250 lbs.   Drafted: 1995   College: UCLA

YEAR	TEAM	GP	GS	MIN	PTS	FGM	FGA	FG%	3PM	3PA	3P%	FTM	FTA	FT%	ORB	DRB	TRB	AST	PF	DQ	STL	BLK	TO	MPG	PPG	RPG	APG	PCM
95-96	Charlotte	71	21	888	281	105	248	.423	0	0	.000	71	93	.763	69	114	183	16	170	2	9	7	36	12.5	4.0	2.6	0.2	.255
96-97	Charlotte	36	2	288	91	33	85	.388	0	2	.000	25	32	.781	25	38	63	9	44	0	4	3	22	8.0	2.5	1.8	0.3	.254
96-97	Denver	16	0	88	52	16	33	.485	0	0	.000	20	25	.800	10	13	23	5	17	0	1	0	5	5.5	3.3	1.4	0.3	.556
97-98	Denver	6	0	42	18	4	15	.267	0	0	.000	10	12	.833	4	9	13	1	5	0	0	2	3	7.0	3.0	2.2	0.2	.400
97-98	Seattle	6	0	22	11	3	14	.214	1	2	.500	4	4	1.000	0	4	4	1	5	0	0	0	1	3.7	1.8	0.7	0.2	.113
NBA Season Totals		135	23	1328	453	161	395	.408	1	4	.250	130	166	.783	108	178	286	32	241	2	14	12	67	9.8	3.4	2.1	0.2	....

• ZIEGENHORN, Babe

Maurice Ziegenhorn

Born: Nov. 21, 1918.   Died: Aug. 1970.   Height: 6'   Weight: 185 lbs.   Drafted: —   College: Notre Dame

YEAR	TEAM	GP	GS	MIN	PTS	FGM	FGA	FG%	3PM	3PA	3P%	FTM	FTA	FT%	ORB	DRB	TRB	AST	PF	DQ	STL	BLK	TO	MPG	PPG	RPG	APG	PCM
41-42	Sheboygan-N	15	....	....	40	17	....	....	....	....	....	6	....	....	....	....	....	....	....	....	....	....	....	2.7	....	....	....
45-46	Sheboygan-N	7	....	....	5	2	....	....	....	....	....	1	....	....	....	....	....	....	....	....	....	....	....	0.7	....	....	....
NBL Season Totals		22	....	....	45	19	....	....	....	....	....	7	....	....	....	....	....	....	....	....	....	....	....	2.0	....	....	....

• ZOET, Jim

Jim Zoet

Born: Dec. 20, 1953. Uxbridge, ON, Canada.   Height: 7'1".   Weight: 240 lbs.   Drafted: —   College: Kent State

YEAR	TEAM	GP	GS	MIN	PTS	FGM	FGA	FG%	3PM	3PA	3P%	FTM	FTA	FT%	ORB	DRB	TRB	AST	PF	DQ	STL	BLK	TO	MPG	PPG	RPG	APG	PCM
82-83	Detroit	7	0	30	2	1	5	.200	0	0	.000	0	0	.000	3	5	8	1	9	0	1	3	4	4.3	0.3	1.1	0.1	.088
NBA Season Totals		7	0	30	2	1	5	.200	0	0	.000	0	0	.000	3	5	8	1	9	0	1	3	4	4.3	0.3	1.1	0.1	....

• ZOPF, Bill

William Charles (Zip) Zopf Jr.

Born: June 7, 1948.   Height: 6'1".   Weight: 170 lbs.   Drafted: 1970   College: Duquesne

YEAR	TEAM	GP	GS	MIN	PTS	FGM	FGA	FG%	3PM	3PA	3P%	FTM	FTA	FT%	ORB	DRB	TRB	AST	PF	DQ	STL	BLK	TO	MPG	PPG	RPG	APG	PCM
70-71	Milwaukee	53	....	398	118	49	135	.363	....	....	....	20	36	.556	....	....	46	73	34	0	....	....	....	7.5	2.2	0.9	1.4	.365
NBA Season Totals		53	....	398	118	49	135	.363	....	....	....	20	36	.556	....	....	46	73	34	0	....	....	....	7.5	2.2	0.9	1.4	....

• ZUNIC, Matt

Matthew (Mad Matt) Zunic

Born: Dec. 19, 1919.   Height: 6'3".   Weight: 195 lbs.   Drafted: 1947   College: George Washington

YEAR	TEAM	GP	GS	MIN	PTS	FGM	FGA	FG%	3PM	3PA	3P%	FTM	FTA	FT%	ORB	DRB	TRB	AST	PF	DQ	STL	BLK	TO	MPG	PPG	RPG	APG	PCM
47-48	Flint-N	57	....	....	331	123	....	....	....	....	....	85	128	.664	....	....	....	209	....	....	....	....	....	5.8	....	....	....
48-49	Washington	56	....	....	273	98	323	.303	....	....	....	77	109	.706	....	....	50	182	....	....	....	....	....	4.9	....	0.9	....
NBA Season Totals		56	....	....	273	98	323	.303	....	....	....	77	109	.706	....	....	50	182	....	....	....	....	....	4.9	....	0.9	....
NBL Season Totals		57	....	....	331	123	....	....	....	....	....	85	128	....	....	....	....	209	....	....	....	....	....	5.8	....	....	....
Career Totals		113	....	....	604	221	323	....	....	....	....	162	237	....	....	....	50	391	....	....	....	....	....	5.3	....	0.4	....
48-49	Washington	9	....	....	26	7	39	.179	....	....	....	12	19	.632	....	....	6	26	....	....	....	....	....	2.9	....	0.7	....
NBA Playoff Totals		9	....	....	26	7	39	.179	....	....	....	12	19	.632	....	....	6	26	....	....	....	....	....	2.9	....	0.7	....

Chapter 54

The NBA Coaching Register

Season Team	Reg. Season W	L	Playoffs W	L
Adelman, Rik				
88-89 Portland	14	21	0	3
89-90 Portland	59	23	12	9
90-91 Portland	63	19	9	7
91-92 Portland	57	25	13	8
92-93 Portland	51	31	1	3
93-94 Portland	47	35	1	3
95-96 Golden State	36	46	—	—
96-97 Golden State	30	52	—	—
98-99 Sacramento	27	23	2	3
99-00 Sacramento	44	38	2	3
00-01 Sacramento	55	27	3	5
01-02 Sacramento	61	21	4	6
02-03 Sacramento	59	23	7	5
Totals	603	384	54	55
Adubato, Richie				
79-80 Detroit	12	58	—	—
89-90 Dallas	42	29	0	3
90-91 Dallas	28	54	—	—
91-92 Dallas	22	60	—	—
92-93 Dallas	2	27	—	—
96-97 Orlando	21	12	2	3
Totals	127	240	2	6
Ainge, Danny				
96-97 Phoenix	40	34	2	3
97-98 Phoenix	56	26	1	3
98-99 Phoenix	27	23	0	3
99-00 Phoenix	13	7	—	—
Totals	136	90	3	9
Albeck, Stan				
79-80 Cleveland	37	45	—	—
80-81 San Antonio	52	30	3	4
81-82 San Antonio	48	34	4	5
82-83 San Antonio	53	29	6	5
83-84 New Jersey	45	37	5	6
84-85 New Jersey	42	40	0	3
85-86 Chicago	30	52	0	3
Totals	307	267	18	26
Armstrong, Curly				
48-49 Fort Wayne	22	32	—	—
Totals	22	32	—	—
Attles, Al				
69-70 S.F. Warriors	8	22	—	—
70-71 S.F. Warriors	41	41	1	4
71-72 Golden State	51	31	1	4
72-73 Golden State	47	35	5	6
73-74 Golden State	44	38	—	—
74-75 Golden State	**48**	**34**	**12**	**5**
75-76 Golden State	59	23	7	6
76-77 Golden State	46	36	5	5
77-78 Golden State	43	39	—	—
78-79 Golden State	38	44	—	—
79-80 Golden State	18	43	—	—
80-81 Golden State	39	43	—	—
81-82 Golden State	45	37	—	—
82-83 Golden State	30	52	—	—
Totals	557	518	31	30

Season Team	Reg. Season W	L	Playoffs W	L
Auerbach, Red				
46-47 Wash. Capitols	49	11	2	4
47-48 Wash. Capitols	28	20	—	—
48-49 Wash. Capitols	38	22	6	5
49-50 Tri-Cities	28	29	1	2
50-51 Boston	39	30	0	2
51-52 Boston	39	27	1	2
52-53 Boston	46	25	3	3
53-54 Boston	42	30	2	4
54-55 Boston	36	36	1	3
55-56 Boston	39	33	1	2
56-57 Boston	**44**	**28**	**7**	**3**
57-58 Boston	49	23	6	5
58-59 Boston	**52**	**20**	**8**	**3**
59-60 Boston	**59**	**16**	**8**	**5**
60-61 Boston	**57**	**22**	**8**	**2**
61-62 Boston	**60**	**20**	**8**	**6**
62-63 Boston	**58**	**22**	**8**	**5**
63-64 Boston	**59**	**21**	**8**	**2**
64-65 Boston	**62**	**18**	**8**	**4**
65-66 Boston	**54**	**26**	**11**	**6**
Totals	938	479	97	68
Bach, Johnny				
79-80 Golden State	6	15	—	—
83-84 Golden State	37	45	—	—
84-85 Golden State	22	60	—	—
85-86 Golden State	30	52	—	—
Totals	95	172	—	—
Badger, Ed				
76-77 Chicago	44	38	1	2
77-78 Chicago	40	42	—	—
Totals	84	80	1	2
Barker, Cliff				
49-50 Ind. Olympians	39	25	3	3
50-51 Ind. Olympians	24	32	—	—
Totals	63	57	3	3
Barthelme, Al				
54-55 Baltimore Bullets	1	2	—	—
Totals	1	2	—	—
Bass, Bob				
79-80 San Antonio	8	8	1	2
83-84 San Antonio	26	25	—	—
91-92 San Antonio	26	18	0	3
Totals	60	51	1	5
Baylor, Elgin				
74-75 New Orleans	0	1	—	—
76-77 New Orleans	21	35	—	—
77-78 New Orleans	39	43	—	—
78-79 New Orleans	26	56	—	—
Totals	86	135	—	—
Beard, Butch				
94-95 New Jersey	30	52	—	—
95-96 New Jersey	30	52	—	—
Totals	60	104	—	—
Bee, Clair				
52-53 Baltimore Bullets	16	51	0	2
53-54 Baltimore Bullets	16	56	—	—
54-55 Baltimore Bullets	2	9	—	—
Totals	34	116	0	2
Bennett, Carl				
48-49 Fort Wayne	0	6	—	—
Totals	0	6	—	—
Berry, Bill				
01-02 Chicago	0	2	—	—
Totals	0	2	—	—

Season Team	Reg. Season W	L	Playoffs W	L
Bertka, Bill				
93-94 LA Lakers	1	1	—	—
98-99 LA Lakers	1	0	—	—
Totals	2	1	—	—
Bianchi, Al				
67-68 Seattle	23	59	—	—
68-69 Seattle	30	52	—	—
Totals	53	111	—	—
Bickerstaff, Bernie				
85-86 Seattle	31	51	—	—
86-87 Seattle	39	43	7	7
87-88 Seattle	44	38	2	3
88-89 Seattle	46	30	3	5
89-90 Seattle	41	41	—	—
94-95 Denver	20	12	—	—
95-96 Denver	35	47	—	—
96-97 Denver	4	9	—	—
96-97 Washington	22	13	0	3
97-98 Washington	42	40	—	—
98-99 Washington	13	19	—	—
Totals	337	343	12	18
Birch, Paul				
46-47 Pittsburgh	15	45	—	—
51-52 Fort Wayne	29	37	0	2
52-53 Fort Wayne	36	33	4	4
53-54 Fort Wayne	40	32	0	4
Totals	120	147	4	10
Bird, Larry				
97-98 Indianapolis	58	24	9	4
98-99 Indianapolis	33	17	9	4
99-00 Indianapolis	56	26	13	10
Totals	147	67	31	18
Blair, Bill				
82-83 New Jersey	2	4	0	2
94-95 Minnesota	21	61	—	—
95-96 Minnesota	6	14	—	—
Totals	29	79	0	2
Boryla, Vince				
55-56 New York	9	12	—	—
56-57 New York	36	36	—	—
57-58 New York	35	37	—	—
Totals	80	85	—	—
Braun, Carl				
59-60 New York	19	29	—	—
60-61 New York	21	58	—	—
Totals	40	87	—	—
Bristow, Allan				
91-92 Charlotte	31	51	—	—
92-93 Charlotte	44	38	4	5
93-94 Charlotte	41	41	—	—
94-95 Charlotte	50	32	1	3
95-96 Charlotte	41	41	—	—
Totals	207	203	5	8
Brovelli, Jim				
98-99 Washington	5	13	—	—
Totals	5	13	—	—
Brown, Herb				
75-76 Detroit	19	21	4	5
76-77 Detroit	44	38	—	—
77-78 Detroit	9	15	—	—
Totals	72	74	4	5

Boldface = NBA championship season

Season	Team	Reg. Season W	L	Playoffs W	L
Brown, Hubie					
76-77	Atlanta	31	51	—	—
77-78	Atlanta	41	41	0	2
78-79	Atlanta	46	36	5	4
79-80	Atlanta	50	32	—	—
80-81	Atlanta	31	48	—	—
82-83	New York	44	38	2	4
83-84	New York	47	35	6	6
84-85	New York	24	58	—	—
85-86	New York	23	59	—	—
86-87	New York	4	12	—	—
02-03	Memphis	28	46	—	—
Totals		369	456	13	16
Brown, Larry					
76-77	Denver	50	32	2	4
77-78	Denver	48	34	6	7
78-79	Denver	28	25	—	—
81-82	New Jersey	44	38	0	2
82-83	New Jersey	47	29	—	—
88-89	San Antonio	21	61	—	—
89-90	San Antonio	56	26	6	4
90-91	San Antonio	55	27	1	3
91-92	San Antonio	21	17	—	—
91-92	LA Clippers	23	12	2	3
92-93	LA Clippers	41	41	2	3
93-94	Indianapolis	47	35	10	7
94-95	Indianapolis	52	30	2	3
95-96	Indianapolis	52	30	—	—
96-97	Indianapolis	39	43	10	6
97-98	Philadelphia	31	51	—	—
98-99	Philadelphia	28	22	3	5
99-00	Philadelphia	49	33	5	5
00-01	Philadelphia	56	26	12	11
01-02	Philadelphia	43	39	2	3
02-03	Philadelphia	48	34	4	6
Totals		879	685	67	72
Brownstein, Phil					
48-49	Chicago Stags	10	1	—	—
49-50	Chicago Stags	40	28	0	3
Totals		50	29	0	3
Buckner, Quinn					
93-94	Dallas	13	69	—	—
Totals		13	69	—	—
Buckwalter, Bucky					
72-73	Seattle	13	24	—	—
Totals		13	24	—	—
Budko, Walt					
50-51	Baltimore Bullets	10	19	—	—
Totals		10	19	—	—
Butcher, Donnie					
66-67	Detroit	2	6	—	—
67-68	Detroit	40	42	2	4
68-69	Detroit	10	12	—	—
Totals		52	60	2	4
Bzdelik, Jeff					
02-03	Denver	17	65	—	—
Totals		17		—	—
Calipari, John					
96-97	New Jersey	26	56	—	—
97-98	New Jersey	43	39	0	3
98-99	New Jersey	3	17	—	—
Totals		72	112	0	3
Calvin, Mack					
91-92	LA Clippers	1	1	—	—
Totals		1	1	—	—
Carlesimo, P.J.					
94-95	Portland	44	38	0	3
95-96	Portland	44	38	2	3
96-97	Portland	49	33	1	3
97-98	Golden State	19	63	—	—
98-99	Golden State	21	29	—	—
99-00	Golden State	6	21	—	—
Totals		183	222	3	9
Carlisle, Rick					
01-02	Detroit	50	32	4	6
02-03	Detroit	50	32	14	6
Totals		100	64	18	12

Season	Team	Reg. Season W	L	Playoffs W	L
Carr, M.L.					
95-96	Boston	33	49	—	—
96-97	Boston	15	67	—	—
Totals		48	116	—	—
Carter, Butch					
97-98	Toronto	5	28	—	—
98-99	Toronto	23	27	—	—
99-00	Toronto	45	37	0	3
Totals		73	92	0	3
Carter, Fred					
92-93	Philadelphia	7	19	—	—
93-94	Philadelphia	25	57	—	—
Totals		32	76	—	—
Cartwright, Bill					
01-02	Chicago	17	38	—	—
02-03	Chicago	30	52	—	—
Totals		47	90	—	—
Casey, Don					
88-89	LA Clippers	11	33	—	—
89-90	LA Clippers	30	52	—	—
98-99	New Jersey	13	17	—	—
99-00	New Jersey	31	51	—	—
Totals		85	153	—	—
Castellani, John					
59-60	Minneapolis	11	25	—	—
Totals		11	25	—	—
Cervi, Al					
49-50	Syracuse	51	13	6	5
50-51	Syracuse	32	34	4	3
51-52	Syracuse	40	26	3	4
52-53	Syracuse	47	24	0	2
53-54	Syracuse	42	30	9	4
54-55	**Syracuse**	**43**	**29**	**7**	**4**
55-56	Syracuse	35	37	5	4
56-57	Syracuse	4	8	—	—
58-59	Phil. Warriors	32	40	—	—
Totals		326	241	34	26
Chaney, Don					
84-85	LA Clippers	9	12	—	—
85-86	LA Clippers	32	50	—	—
86-87	LA Clippers	12	70	—	—
88-89	Houston	45	37	1	3
89-90	Houston	41	41	1	3
90-91	Houston	52	30	0	3
91-92	Houston	26	26	—	—
93-94	Detroit	20	62	—	—
94-95	Detroit	28	54	—	—
01-02	New York	20	43	—	—
02-03	New York	37	45	2	4
Totals		322	470	4	13
Cheeks, Maurice					
01-02	Portland	49	33	0	3
02-03	Portland	50	32	3	4
Totals		99	65	3	7
Cleamons, Jim					
96-97	Dallas	24	58	—	—
97-98	Dallas	4	12	—	—
Totals		28	70	—	—
Clifford, Roy					
46-47	Cleveland Rebels	13	10	1	2
Totals		13	10	1	2
Cohalan, Neil					
46-47	New York	33	27	2	3
Totals		33	27	2	3
Colangelo, Jerry					
69-70	Phoenix	24	20	3	4
72-73	Phoenix	35	40	—	—
Totals		59	60	3	4
Collins, Doug					
86-87	Chicago	40	42	0	3
87-88	Chicago	50	32	4	6
88-89	Chicago	47	35	9	8
95-96	Detroit	46	36	0	3
96-97	Detroit	54	28	2	3
97-98	Detroit	21	24	—	—
01-02	Washington	37	45	—	—
02-03	Washington	37	45	2	4
Totals		332	287	17	27

Season	Team	Reg. Season W	L	Playoffs W	L
Costello, Larry					
68-69	Milwaukee	27	55	—	—
69-70	Milwaukee	56	26	5	5
70-71	**Milwaukee**	**66**	**16**	**12**	**2**
71-72	Milwaukee	63	19	6	5
72-73	Milwaukee	60	22	2	4
73-74	Milwaukee	59	23	11	5
74-75	Milwaukee	38	44	—	—
75-76	Milwaukee	38	44	1	2
76-77	Milwaukee	3	15	—	—
78-79	Chicago	20	36	—	—
Totals		430	300	37	23
Cousy, Bob					
69-70	Cincinnati	36	46	—	—
70-71	Cincinnati	33	49	—	—
71-72	Cincinnati	30	52	—	—
72-73	KC-Omaha	36	46	—	—
73-74	KC-Omaha	6	16	—	—
Totals		141	209	—	—
Cowens, Dave					
78-79	Boston	27	41	—	—
96-97	Charlotte	54	28	0	3
97-98	Charlotte	51	31	4	5
98-99	Charlotte	4	11	—	—
00-01	Golden State	17	65	—	—
01-02	Golden State	8	15	—	—
Totals		161	191	4	8
Cunningham, Billy					
77-78	Philadelphia	53	23	6	4
78-79	Philadelphia	47	35	5	4
79-80	Philadelphia	59	23	12	6
80-81	Philadelphia	62	20	9	7
81-82	Philadelphia	58	24	12	9
82-83	**Philadelphia**	**65**	**17**	**12**	**1**
83-84	Philadelphia	52	30	2	3
84-85	Philadelphia	58	24	8	5
Totals		454	196	66	39
Curtis, Glenn					
46-47	Detroit Falcons	12	22	—	—
Totals		12	22	—	—
Daly, Chuck					
81-82	Cleveland	9	32	—	—
83-84	Detroit	49	33	2	3
84-85	Detroit	46	36	5	4
85-86	Detroit	46	36	1	3
86-87	Detroit	52	30	10	5
87-88	Detroit	54	28	14	9
88-89	**Detroit**	**63**	**19**	**15**	**2**
89-90	**Detroit**	**59**	**23**	**15**	**5**
90-91	Detroit	50	32	7	8
91-92	Detroit	48	34	2	3
92-93	New Jersey	43	39	2	3
93-94	New Jersey	45	37	1	3
97-98	Orlando	41	41	—	—
98-99	Orlando	33	17	1	3
Totals		638	437	75	51
Daniels, Mel					
88-89	Indianapolis	0	2	—	—
Totals		0	2	—	—
D'Antoni, Mike					
98-99	Denver	14	36	—	—
Totals		14	36	—	—
Darden, Jimmy					
49-50	Denver (I)	11	51	—	—
Totals		11	51	—	—
Davis, Johnny					
	Philadelphia	22	60	—	—
Total		22	60	—	—
DeBusschere, Dave					
64-65	Detroit	29	40	—	—
65-66	Detroit	22	58	—	—
66-67	Detroit	28	45	—	—
Totals		79	143	—	—
Dehnert, Red					
46-47	Cleveland Rebels	17	20	—	—
Totals		17	20	—	—

Season	Team	W	L	W	L
Delaney, Don					
80-81	Cleveland	3	8	—	—
81-82	Cleveland	4	11	—	—
Totals		7	19	—	—
Dischinger, Terry					
71-72	Detroit	0	2	—	—
Totals		0	2	—	—
Donovan, Eddie					
61-62	New York	29	51	—	—
62-63	New York	21	59	—	—
63-64	New York	22	58	—	—
64-65	New York	12	26	—	—
Totals		84	194	—	—
Duffie, Ike					
49-50	Anderson	1	2	4	4
Totals		1	2	4	4
Dunleavy, Mike					
90-91	LA Lakers	58	24	12	7
91-92	LA Lakers	43	39	1	3
92-93	Milwaukee	28	54	—	—
93-94	Milwaukee	20	62	—	—
94-95	Milwaukee	34	48	—	—
95-96	Milwaukee	25	57	—	—
97-98	Portland	46	36	1	3
98-99	Portland	35	15	7	6
99-00	Portland	59	23	10	8
00-01	Portland	50	32	0	3
Totals		398	390	31	30
Eckman, Charlie					
54-55	Fort Wayne	43	29	6	5
55-56	Fort Wayne	37	35	4	6
56-57	Fort Wayne	34	38	0	3
57-58	Detroit	9	16	—	—
Totals		123	118	10	14
Egan, Johnny					
72-73	Houston	16	19	—	—
73-74	Houston	32	50	—	—
74-75	Houston	41	41	3	5
75-76	Houston	40	42	—	—
Totals		129	152	3	5
Evans, Mike					
01-02	Denver	18	38	—	—
Totals		18	38	—	—
Farmer, Mike					
66-67	Baltimore	1	8	—	—
Totals		1	8	—	—
Feerick, Bob					
49-50	Wash. Capitols	32	36	0	2
62-63	S.F. Warriors	31	49	—	—
Totals		63	85	0	2
Fitch, Bill					
70-71	Cleveland	15	67	—	—
71-72	Cleveland	23	59	—	—
72-73	Cleveland	32	50	—	—
73-74	Cleveland	29	53	—	—
74-75	Cleveland	40	42	—	—
75-76	Cleveland	49	33	6	7
76-77	Cleveland	43	39	1	2
77-78	Cleveland	43	39	0	2
78-79	Cleveland	30	52	—	—
79-80	Boston	61	21	5	4
80-81	Boston	62	20	12	5
81-82	**Boston**	**63**	**19**	**7**	**5**
82-83	Boston	56	26	2	5
83-84	Houston	29	53	—	—
84-85	Houston	48	34	2	3
85-86	Houston	51	31	13	7
86-87	Houston	42	40	5	5
87-88	Houston	46	36	1	3
89-90	New Jersey	17	65	—	—
90-91	New Jersey	26	56	—	—
91-92	New Jersey	40	42	1	3
94-95	LA Clippers	17	65	—	—
95-96	LA Clippers	29	53	—	—
96-97	LA Clippers	36	46	0	3
97-98	LA Clippers	17	65	—	—
Totals		944	1106	55	54

Season	Team	W	L	W	L
Fitzgerald, Dick					
46-47	Toronto Huskies	2	1	—	—
Totals		2	1	—	—
Fitzsimmons, Cotton					
70-71	Phoenix	48	34	—	—
71-72	Phoenix	49	33	—	—
72-73	Atlanta	46	36	2	4
73-74	Atlanta	35	47	—	—
74-75	Atlanta	31	51	—	—
75-76	Atlanta	28	46	—	—
77-78	Buffalo	27	55	—	—
78-79	Kansas City	48	34	1	4
79-80	Kansas City	47	35	1	2
80-81	Kansas City	40	42	7	8
81-82	Kansas City	30	52	—	—
82-83	Kansas City	45	37	—	—
83-84	Kansas City	38	44	0	3
84-85	San Antonio	41	41	2	3
85-86	San Antonio	35	47	0	3
88-89	Phoenix	55	27	7	5
89-90	Phoenix	54	28	9	7
90-91	Phoenix	55	27	1	3
91-92	Phoenix	53	29	4	4
95-96	Phoenix	27	22	1	3
96-97	Phoenix	0	8	—	—
Totals		832	775	35	49
Floyd, Tim					
98-99	Chicago	13	37	—	—
99-00	Chicago	17	65	—	—
00-01	Chicago	15	67	—	—
01-02	Chicago	4	21	—	—
Totals		49	190	—	—
Ford, Chris					
90-91	Boston	56	26	5	6
91-92	Boston	51	31	6	4
92-93	Boston	48	34	1	3
93-94	Boston	32	50	—	—
94-95	Boston	35	47	1	3
96-97	Milwaukee	33	49	—	—
97-98	Milwaukee	36	46	—	—
98-99	LA Clippers	9	41	—	—
99-00	LA Clippers	11	34	—	—
Totals		311	358	13	16
Fratello, Mike					
80-81	Atlanta	0	3	—	—
83-84	Atlanta	40	42	2	3
84-85	Atlanta	34	48	—	—
85-86	Atlanta	50	32	4	5
86-87	Atlanta	57	25	4	5
87-88	Atlanta	50	32	6	6
88-89	Atlanta	52	30	2	3
89-90	Atlanta	41	41	—	—
93-94	Cleveland	47	35	0	3
94-95	Cleveland	43	39	1	3
95-96	Cleveland	47	35	0	3
96-97	Cleveland	42	40	—	—
97-98	Cleveland	47	35	1	3
98-99	Cleveland	22	28	—	—
Totals		572	465	20	34
Friddle, Burl					
48-49	Indianapolis Jets	14	29	—	—
Totals		14	29	—	—
Gallatin, Harry					
62-63	St. Louis	48	32	6	5
63-64	St. Louis	46	34	6	6
64-65	New York	19	23	—	—
64-65	St. Louis	17	16	—	—
65-66	New York	6	15	—	—
Totals		136	120	12	11
Gentry, Alvin					
94-95	Miami	15	21	—	—
97-98	Detroit	16	21	—	—
98-99	Detroit	29	21	2	3
99-00	Detroit	42	40	0	3
00-01	LA Clippers	31	51	—	—
01-02	LA Clippers	39	43	—	—
02-03	LA Clippers	19	39	—	—
Totals		191	236	2	6

Season	Team	W	L	W	L
Gottlieb, Eddie					
46-47	**Phil. Warriors**	**35**	**25**	**8**	**2**
47-48	Phil. Warriors	27	21	6	7
48-49	Phil. Warriors	28	32	0	2
49-50	Phil. Warriors	26	42	0	2
50-51	Phil. Warriors	40	26	0	2
51-52	Phil. Warriors	33	33	1	2
52-53	Phil. Warriors	12	57	—	—
53-54	Phil. Warriors	29	43	—	—
54-55	Phil. Warriors	33	39	—	—
Totals		263	318	15	17
Gregory, Ed					
87-88	Golden State	4	14	—	—
Totals		4	14	—	—
Guerin, Richie					
64-65	St. Louis	28	19	1	3
65-66	St. Louis	36	44	6	4
66-67	St. Louis	39	42	5	4
67-68	St. Louis	56	26	2	4
68-69	Atlanta	48	34	5	6
69-70	Atlanta	48	34	4	5
70-71	Atlanta	36	46	1	4
71-72	Atlanta	36	46	2	4
Totals		327	291	26	34
Guokas, Matt					
85-86	Philadelphia	54	28	6	6
86-87	Philadelphia	45	37	2	3
87-88	Philadelphia	20	23	—	—
89-90	Orlando	18	64	—	—
90-91	Orlando	31	51	—	—
91-92	Orlando	21	61	—	—
92-93	Orlando	41	41	—	—
Totals		230	305	8	9
Hale, Bruce					
48-49	Indianapolis Jets	4	13	—	—
Totals		4	13	—	—
Hamblen, Frank					
91-92	Milwaukee	23	42	—	—
Totals		23	42	—	—
Hamilton, Leonard					
00-01	Washington	19	63	—	—
Totals		19	63	—	—
Hannum, Alex					
56-57	St. Louis	15	16	8	4
57-58	**St. Louis**	**41**	**31**	**8**	**3**
60-61	Syracuse	38	41	4	4
61-62	Syracuse	41	39	2	3
62-63	Syracuse	48	32	2	3
63-64	S.F. Warriors	48	32	5	7
64-65	S.F. Warriors	17	63	—	—
65-66	S.F. Warriors	35	45	—	—
66-67	**Philadelphia**	**68**	**13**	**11**	**4**
67-68	Philadelphia	62	20	7	6
69-70	San Diego Rockets	18	38	—	—
70-71	San Diego Rockets	40	42	—	—
Totals		471	412	47	34
Hanzlik, Bill					
97-98	Denver	11	71	—	—
Totals		11	71	—	—
Harris, Del					
79-80	Houston	41	41	2	5
80-81	Houston	40	42	12	9
81-82	Houston	46	36	1	2
82-83	Houston	14	68	—	—
87-88	Milwaukee	42	40	2	3
88-89	Milwaukee	49	33	3	6
89-90	Milwaukee	44	38	1	3
90-91	Milwaukee	48	34	0	3
91-92	Milwaukee	8	9	—	—
94-95	LA Lakers	48	34	5	5
95-96	LA Lakers	53	29	1	3
96-97	LA Lakers	56	26	4	5
97-98	LA Lakers	61	21	7	6
98-99	LA Lakers	6	6	—	—
Totals		556	457	38	50

Season	Team	Reg. Season W	L	Playoffs W	L
Harrison, Les					
48-49	Rochester	45	15	2	2
49-50	Rochester	51	17	0	2
50-51	**Rochester**	**41**	**27**	**9**	**5**
51-52	Rochester	41	25	3	3
52-53	Rochester	44	26	1	5
53-54	Rochester	44	28	3	3
54-55	Rochester	29	43	1	2
Totals		295	181	19	22
Harter, Dick					
88-89	Charlotte	20	62	—	—
89-90	Charlotte	8	32	—	—
Totals		28	94	—	—
Hayman, Lew					
46-47	Toronto Huskies	0	1	—	—
Totals		0	1	—	—
Heard, Gar					
92-93	Dallas	9	44	—	—
99-00	Washington	14	30	—	—
Totals		23	74	—	—
Heinsohn, Tom					
69-70	Boston	34	48	—	—
70-71	Boston	44	38	—	—
71-72	Boston	56	26	5	6
72-73	Boston	68	14	7	6
73-74	**Boston**	**56**	**26**	**12**	**6**
74-75	Boston	60	22	6	5
75-76	**Boston**	**54**	**28**	**12**	**6**
76-77	Boston	44	38	5	4
77-78	Boston	11	23	—	—
Totals		427	263	47	33
Hickey, Nat					
47-48	Providence	4	25	—	—
Totals		4	25	—	—
Hill, Bob					
86-87	New York	20	46	—	—
90-91	Indianapolis	32	25	2	3
91-92	Indianapolis	40	42	1	3
92-93	Indianapolis	41	41	10	6
94-95	San Antonio	62	20	9	6
95-96	San Antonio	59	23	5	5
96-97	San Antonio	3	15	—	—
Totals		257	212	27	23
Hill, Brian					
93-94	Orlando	50	32	0	3
94-95	Orlando	57	25	11	10
95-96	Orlando	60	22	7	5
96-97	Orlando	24	25	—	—
97-98	Vancouver	19	63	—	—
98-99	Vancouver	8	42	—	—
99-00	Vancouver	22	60	—	—
Totals		240	269	18	18
Holzman, Red					
53-54	Milwaukee Hawks	10	16	—	—
54-55	Milwaukee Hawks	26	46	—	—
55-56	St. Louis	33	39	4	5
56-57	St. Louis	14	19	—	—
67-68	New York	28	17	2	4
68-69	New York	54	28	6	4
69-70	**New York**	**60**	**22**	**12**	**7**
70-71	New York	52	30	7	5
71-72	New York	48	34	9	7
72-73	**New York**	**57**	**25**	**12**	**5**
73-74	New York	49	33	5	7
74-75	New York	40	42	1	2
75-76	New York	38	44	—	—
76-77	New York	40	42	—	—
78-79	New York	25	43	—	—
79-80	New York	39	43	—	—
80-81	New York	50	32	0	2
81-82	New York	33	49	—	—
Totals		696	604	58	48
Hopkins, Bob					
77-78	Seattle	5	17	—	—
Totals		5	17	—	—
Hughes, Rex					
91-92	Sacramento	22	35	—	—
92-93	San Antonio	1	0	—	—
Totals		23	35	—	—

Season	Team	Reg. Season W	L	Playoffs W	L
Inman, Stu					
71-72	Portland	6	20	—	—
Totals		6	20	—	—
Irvine, George					
84-85	Indianapolis	22	60	—	—
85-86	Indianapolis	26	56	—	—
88-89	Indianapolis	6	14	—	—
99-00	Detroit	14	10	—	—
00-01	Detroit	32	50	—	—
Totals		100	190	—	—
Issel, Dan					
92-93	Denver	36	46	—	—
93-94	Denver	42	40	6	6
94-95	Denver	18	16	—	—
99-01	Denver	35	47	—	—
00-01	Denver	40	42	—	—
01-02	Denver	9	17	—	—
Totals		180	208	6	6
Jackson, Phil					
89-90	Chicago	55	27	10	6
90-91	**Chicago**	**61**	**21**	**15**	**2**
91-92	**Chicago**	**67**	**15**	**15**	**7**
92-93	**Chicago**	**57**	**25**	**15**	**4**
93-94	Chicago	55	27	6	4
94-95	Chicago	47	35	5	5
95-96	**Chicago**	**72**	**10**	**15**	**3**
96-97	**Chicago**	**69**	**13**	**15**	**4**
97-98	**Chicago**	**62**	**20**	**15**	**6**
99-00	**LA Lakers**	**67**	**15**	**15**	**8**
00-01	**LA Lakers**	**56**	**26**	**15**	**1**
01-02	**LA Lakers**	**58**	**24**	**11**	**4**
02-03	LA Lakers	50	32	6	6
Totals		776	290	158	60
Jackson, Stu					
89-90	New York	45	37	4	6
90-91	New York	7	8	—	—
96-97	Vancouver	6	33	—	—
Totals		58	78	4	6
Jeannette, Buddy					
47-48	**Baltimore Bullets**	**28**	**20**	**9**	**3**
48-49	Baltimore Bullets	29	31	1	2
49-50	Baltimore Bullets	25	43	—	—
50-51	Baltimore Bullets	14	23	—	—
64-65	Baltimore	37	43	5	5
66-67	Baltimore	3	13	—	—
Totals		136	173	15	10
Johnson, Dennis					
02-03	LA Clippers	8	16	—	—
Totals		8	16	—	—
Johnson, Frank					
01-02	Phoenix	11	20	—	—
02-03	Phoenix	44	38	2	4
Totals		55	58	2	4
Johnson, Magic					
93-94	LA Lakers	5	11	—	—
Totals		5	11	—	—
Johnson, Phil					
73-74	KC-Omaha	27	30	—	—
74-75	KC-Omaha	44	38	—	—
75-76	Kansas City	31	51	—	—
76-77	Kansas City	40	42	—	—
77-78	Kansas City	13	24	—	—
81-82	Chicago	0	1	—	—
84-85	Kansas City	30	43	0	3
85-86	Sacramento	37	45	0	3
86-87	Sacramento	14	32	—	—
Totals		236	306	0	6
Johnston, Neil					
59-60	Phil. Warriors	49	26	4	5
60-61	Phil. Warriors	46	33	0	3
Totals		95	59	4	8

Season	Team	Reg. Season W	L	Playoffs W	L
Jones, K.C.					
73-74	Capital Bullets	47	35	3	4
74-75	Washington	60	22	8	9
75-76	Washington	48	34	3	4
83-84	**Boston**	**62**	**20**	**15**	**8**
84-85	Boston	63	19	13	8
85-86	**Boston**	**67**	**15**	**15**	**3**
86-87	Boston	59	23	13	10
87-88	Boston	57	25	9	8
90-91	Seattle	41	41	2	3
91-92	Seattle	18	18	—	—
Totals		522	252	81	57
Jones, Wah Wah					
50-51	Ind. Olympians	7	5	1	2
Totals		7	5	1	2
Jordan, Eddie					
96-97	Sacramento	6	9	—	—
97-98	Sacramento	7	55	—	—
Totals		33	64	—	—
Jucker, Ed					
67-68	Cincinnati	39	43	—	—
68-69	Cincinnati	41	41	—	—
Totals		80	84	—	—
Julian, Doggie					
48-49	Boston	25	35	—	—
49-50	Boston	22	46	—	—
Totals		47	81	—	—
Karl, George					
84-85	Cleveland	36	46	1	3
85-86	Cleveland	25	42	—	—
86-87	Golden State	42	40	4	6
87-88	Golden State	16	48	—	—
91-92	Seattle	27	15	4	5
92-93	Seattle	55	27	10	9
93-94	Seattle	63	19	2	3
94-95	Seattle	57	25	1	3
95-96	Seattle	64	18	13	8
96-97	Seattle	57	25	6	6
97-98	Seattle	61	21	4	6
98-99	Milwaukee	28	22	0	3
99-00	Milwaukee	42	40	2	3
00-01	Milwaukee	52	30	10	8
01-02	Milwaukee	41	41	—	—
02-03	Milwaukee	42	40	8	9
Totals		708	499	65	72
Kauffman, Bob					
77-78	Detroit	29	29	—	—
Totals		29	29	—	—
Kerr, Red					
66-67	Chicago	33	48	0	3
67-68	Chicago	29	53	1	4
68-69	Phoenix	16	66	—	—
69-70	Phoenix	15	23	—	—
Totals		93	190	1	7
Kloppenburg, Bob					
81-82	Cleveland	0	3	—	—
88-89	Seattle	1	4	—	—
91-92	Seattle	2	2	—	—
Totals		3	9	—	—
Kruger, Lon					
00-01	Atlanta	25	57	—	—
01-02	Atlanta	33	49	—	—
02-03	Atlanta	11	16	—	—
Totals		69	122	—	—
Kundla, Johnny					
48-49	**Minneapolis**	**44**	**16**	**8**	**2**
49-50	**Minneapolis**	**51**	**17**	**10**	**2**
50-51	Minneapolis	44	24	3	4
51-52	**Minneapolis**	**40**	**26**	**9**	**4**
52-53	**Minneapolis**	**48**	**22**	**9**	**3**
53-54	**Minneapolis**	**46**	**26**	**9**	**4**
54-55	Minneapolis	40	32	3	4
55-56	Minneapolis	33	39	1	2
56-57	Minneapolis	34	38	2	3
57-58	Minneapolis	10	23	—	—
58-59	Minneapolis	33	39	6	7
Totals		423	302	60	35

Lanier, Bob

Season Team	Reg. Season W	L	Playoffs W	L
94-95 Golden State	12	25	—	—
Totals	12	25	—	—

Lapchick, Joe

Season Team	Reg. Season W	L	Playoffs W	L
47-48 New York	26	22	1	2
48-49 New York	32	28	3	3
49-50 New York	40	28	3	2
50-51 New York	36	30	8	6
51-52 New York	37	29	8	6
52-53 New York	47	23	6	5
53-54 New York	44	28	0	4
54-55 New York	38	34	1	2
55-56 New York	26	25	—	—
Totals	326	247	30	30

Layden, Frank

Season Team	W	L	W	L
81-82 Utah	17	45	—	—
82-83 Utah	30	52	—	—
83-84 Utah	45	37	5	6
84-85 Utah	41	41	4	6
85-86 Utah	42	40	1	3
86-87 Utah	44	38	2	3
87-88 Utah	47	35	6	5
88-89 Utah	11	6	—	—
Totals	277	294	18	23

Lee, George

Season Team	W	L	W	L
68-69 S.F. Warriors	41	41	2	4
69-70 S.F. Warriors	22	30	—	—
Totals	63	71	2	4

Leonard, Slick

Season Team	W	L	W	L
62-63 Chicago Zephyrs	13	29	—	—
63-64 Baltimore	31	49	—	—
76-77 Indianapolis	36	46	—	—
77-78 Indianapolis	31	51	—	—
78-79 Indianapolis	38	44	—	—
79-80 Indianapolis	37	45	—	—
Totals	186	264	—	—

Levane, Andrew

Season Team	W	L	W	L
52-53 Milwaukee Hawks	27	44	—	—
53-54 Milwaukee Hawks	11	35	—	—
58-59 New York	40	32	0	2
59-60 New York	8	19	—	—
61-62 St. Louis	20	40	—	—
Totals	106	170	0	2

Lewis, Grady

Season Team	W	L	W	L
48-49 St. Louis Bombers	29	31	0	2
49-50 St. Louis Bombers	26	42	—	—
Totals	55	73	0	2

Littles, Gene

Season Team	W	L	W	L
85-86 Cleveland	4	11	—	—
89-90 Charlotte	11	31	—	—
90-91 Charlotte	26	56	—	—
94-95 Denver	3	13	0	3
Totals	44	111	0	3

Lloyd, Earl

Season Team	W	L	W	L
71-72 Detroit	20	50	—	—
72-73 Detroit	2	5	—	—
Totals	22	55	—	—

Locke, Tates

Season Team	W	L	W	L
76-77 Buffalo	16	30	—	—
Totals	16	30	—	—

Loeffler, Ken

Season Team	W	L	W	L
46-47 St. Louis Bombers	38	23	1	2
47-48 St. Louis Bombers	29	19	3	4
48-49 Providence	12	48	—	—
Totals	79	90	4	6

Logan, John

Season Team	W	L	W	L
50-51 Tri-Cities	2	1	—	—
Totals	2	1	—	—

Loughery, Kevin

Season Team	Reg. Season W	L	Playoffs W	L
72-73 Philadelphia	5	26	—	—
76-77 New York Nets	22	60	—	—
77-78 New Jersey	24	58	—	—
78-79 New Jersey	37	45	0	2
79-80 New Jersey	34	48	—	—
80-81 New Jersey	12	23	—	—
81-82 Atlanta	42	40	0	2
82-83 Atlanta	43	39	1	2
83-84 Chicago	27	55	—	—
84-85 Chicago	38	44	1	3
85-86 Washington	7	6	2	3
86-87 Washington	42	40	0	3
87-88 Washington	8	19	—	—
91-92 Miami	38	44	0	3
92-93 Miami	36	46	—	—
93-94 Miami	42	40	2	3
94-95 Miami	17	29	—	—
Totals	474	662	6	21

Lowe, Sidney

Season Team	W	L	W	L
92-93 Minnesota	13	40	—	—
93-94 Minnesota	20	62	—	—
00-01 Vancouver	23	59	—	—
01-02 Memphis	23	59	—	—
02-03 Memphis	0	8	—	—
Totals	79	228	—	—

Lucas, John

Season Team	W	L	W	L
92-93 San Antonio	39	22	5	5
93-94 San Antonio	55	27	1	3
94-95 Philadelphia	24	58	—	—
95-96 Philadelphia	18	64	—	—
01-02 Cleveland	29	53	—	—
02-03 Cleveland	8	34	—	—
Totals	173	258	6	8

Lynam, Jim

Season Team	W	L	W	L
83-84 San Diego	30	52	—	—
84-85 LA Clippers	22	39	—	—
87-88 Philadelphia	16	23	—	—
88-89 Philadelphia	46	36	0	3
89-90 Philadelphia	53	29	4	6
90-91 Philadelphia	44	38	4	4
91-92 Philadelphia	35	47	—	—
94-95 Washington	21	61	—	—
95-96 Washington	39	43	—	—
96-97 Washington	22	24	—	—
Totals	328	392	8	13

Macauley, Ed

Season Team	W	L	W	L
58-59 St. Louis	43	19	2	4
59-60 St. Louis	46	29	7	7
Totals	89	48	9	11

MacKinnon, Bob

Season Team	W	L	W	L
76-77 Buffalo	3	4	—	—
80-81 New Jersey	12	25	—	—
87-88 New Jersey	10	29	—	—
Totals	25	58	—	—

MacLeod, John

Season Team	W	L	W	L
73-74 Phoenix	30	52	—	—
74-75 Phoenix	32	50	—	—
75-76 Phoenix	42	40	10	9
76-77 Phoenix	34	48	—	—
77-78 Phoenix	49	33	0	2
78-79 Phoenix	50	32	9	6
79-80 Phoenix	55	27	3	5
80-81 Phoenix	57	25	3	4
81-82 Phoenix	46	36	2	5
82-83 Phoenix	53	29	1	2
83-84 Phoenix	41	41	9	8
84-85 Phoenix	36	46	0	3
85-86 Phoenix	32	50	—	—
86-87 Phoenix	22	34	—	—
87-88 Dallas	53	29	10	7
88-89 Dallas	38	44	—	—
89-90 Dallas	5	6	—	—
90-91 New York	32	35	0	3
Totals	707	657	47	54

Malone, Brendan

Season Team	W	L	W	L
95-96 Toronto	21	61	—	—
Totals	21	61	—	—

Marshall, Tom

Season Team	W	L	W	L
58-59 Cincinnati	16	38	—	—
59-60 Cincinnati	19	56	—	—
Totals	35	94	—	—

Martin, Dugie

Season Team	Reg. Season W	L	Playoffs W	L
56-57 St. Louis	5	3	—	—
Totals	5	3	—	—

McCarthy, Johnny

Season Team	W	L	W	L
71-72 Buffalo	22	50	—	—
Totals	22	50	—	—

McCloskey, Jack

Season Team	W	L	W	L
72-73 Portland	21	61	—	—
73-74 Portland	27	55	—	—
Totals	48	116	—	—

McGuire, Dick

Season Team	W	L	W	L
59-60 Detroit	17	24	0	2
60-61 Detroit	34	45	2	3
61-62 Detroit	37	43	5	5
62-63 Detroit	34	46	—	—
65-66 New York	24	35	—	—
66-67 New York	36	45	1	3
67-68 New York	15	22	—	—
Totals	197	260	8	13

McGuire, Frank

Season Team	W	L	W	L
61-62 Phil. Warriors	49	31	6	6
Totals	49	31	6	6

McHone, Morris

Season Team	W	L	W	L
83-84 San Antonio	11	20	—	—
Totals	11	20	—	—

McKinney, Bones

Season Team	W	L	W	L
50-51 Wash. Capitols	10	25	—	—
Totals	10	25	—	—

McKinney, Jack

Season Team	W	L	W	L
79-80 LA Lakers	10	4	—	—
80-81 Indianapolis	44	38	0	2
81-82 Indianapolis	35	47	—	—
82-83 Indianapolis	20	62	—	—
83-84 Indianapolis	26	56	—	—
84-85 Kansas City	1	8	—	—
Totals	136	215	0	2

McMahon, Jack

Season Team	W	L	W	L
62-63 Chicago Zephyrs	12	26	—	—
63-64 Cincinnati	55	25	4	6
64-65 Cincinnati	48	32	1	3
65-66 Cincinnati	45	35	2	3
66-67 Cincinnati	39	42	1	3
67-68 San Diego Rockets	15	67	—	—
68-69 San Diego Rockets	37	45	2	4
69-70 San Diego Rockets	9	17	—	—
Totals	260	289	10	19

McMillan, Dave

Season Team	W	L	W	L
50-51 Tri-Cities	9	14	—	—
Totals	9	14	—	—

McMillan, Nate

Season Team	W	L	W	L
00-01 Seattle	38	29	—	—
01-02 Seattle	45	37	2	3
02-03 Seattle	40	42	—	—
Totals	123	108	2	3

Mendenhall, Murray

Season Team	W	L	W	L
49-50 Fort Wayne	40	28	3	2
50-51 Fort Wayne	32	36	1	2
Totals	72	64	4	4

Mikan, George

Season Team	W	L	W	L
57-58 Minneapolis	9	30	—	—
Totals	9	30	—	—

Moe, Douglas

Season Team	W	L	W	L
76-77 San Antonio	44	38	—	2
77-78 San Antonio	52	30	2	4
78-79 San Antonio	48	34	7	7
79-80 San Antonio	33	33	—	—
80-81 Denver	26	25	—	—
81-82 Denver	46	36	1	2
82-83 Denver	45	37	3	5
83-84 Denver	38	44	2	3
84-85 Denver	52	30	8	7
85-86 Denver	47	35	5	5
86-87 Denver	37	45	0	3
87-88 Denver	54	28	5	6
88-89 Denver	44	38	0	3
89-90 Denver	43	39	0	3
92-93 Philadelphia	19	37	—	—
Totals	628	529	33	50

Season	Team	Reg. Season W	Reg. Season L	Playoffs W	Playoffs L
Moore, Doxie					
49-50	Anderson	15	11	—	—
51-52	Milwaukee Hawks	17	49	—	—
Totals		32	60	—	—
More, Doug					
76-77	San Antonio	44	38	0	2
77-78	San Antonio	52	30	2	4
78-79	San Antonio	48	34	7	7
79-80	San Antonio	33	33	—	—
Totals		177	135	9	13
Morris, Bob					
46-47	Providence	28	32	—	—
Totals		28	32	—	—
Motta, Dick					
68-69	Chicago	33	49	—	—
69-70	Chicago	39	43	1	4
70-71	Chicago	51	31	3	4
71-72	Chicago	57	25	0	4
72-73	Chicago	51	31	3	4
73-74	Chicago	54	28	4	7
74-75	Chicago	47	35	7	6
75-76	Chicago	24	58	—	—
76-77	Washington	48	34	4	5
77-78	**Washington**	**44**	**38**	**14**	**7**
78-79	Washington	54	28	9	10
79-80	Washington	39	43	0	2
80-81	Dallas	15	67	—	—
81-82	Dallas	28	54	—	—
82-83	Dallas	38	44	—	—
83-84	Dallas	43	39	4	6
84-85	Dallas	44	38	1	3
85-86	Dallas	44	38	5	5
86-87	Dallas	55	27	1	3
89-90	Sacramento	16	38	—	—
90-91	Sacramento	25	57	—	—
91-92	Sacramento	7	18	—	—
94-95	Dallas	36	46	—	—
95-96	Dallas	26	56	—	—
96-97	Denver	17	52	—	—
Totals		935	1017	56	70
Mullaney, Joe					
69-70	LA Lakers	46	36	11	7
70-71	LA Lakers	48	34	5	7
76-77	Buffalo	11	18	—	—
Totals		105	88	16	14
Musselman, Bill					
80-81	Cleveland	25	46	—	—
81-82	Cleveland	2	21	—	—
89-90	Minnesota	22	60	—	—
90-91	Minnesota	29	53	—	—
02-03	Golden State	38	44	—	—
Totals		116	224	—	—
Nelson, Don					
76-77	Milwaukee	27	37	—	—
77-78	Milwaukee	44	38	5	4
78-79	Milwaukee	38	44	—	—
79-80	Milwaukee	49	33	3	4
80-81	Milwaukee	60	22	3	4
81-82	Milwaukee	55	27	2	4
82-83	Milwaukee	51	31	5	4
83-84	Milwaukee	50	32	8	8
84-85	Milwaukee	59	23	3	5
85-86	Milwaukee	57	25	7	7
86-87	Milwaukee	50	32	6	6
88-89	Golden State	43	39	4	4
89-90	Golden State	37	45	—	—
90-91	Golden State	44	38	4	5
91-92	Golden State	55	27	1	3
92-93	Golden State	34	48	—	—
93-94	Golden State	50	32	0	3
94-95	Golden State	14	31	—	—
95-96	New York	34	25	—	—
97-98	Dallas	16	50	—	—
98-99	Dallas	19	31	—	—
99-00	Dallas	40	42	—	—
00-01	Dallas	53	29	4	6
01-02	Dallas	57	25	4	4
02-03	Dallas	60	22	10	10
Totals		1096	828	69	81

Season	Team	Reg. Season W	Reg. Season L	Playoffs W	Playoffs L
Newell, Tom					
88-89	Seattle	0	1	—	—
Totals		0	1	—	—
Nissalke, Tom					
72-73	Seattle	13	32	—	—
76-77	Houston	49	33	6	6
77-78	Houston	28	54	—	—
78-79	Houston	47	35	0	2
79-80	Utah	24	58	—	—
80-81	Utah	28	54	—	—
81-82	Utah	8	12	—	—
82-83	Cleveland	23	59	—	—
83-84	Cleveland	28	54	—	—
Totals		248	391	6	8
O'Brien, Jim					
00-01	Boston	24	24	—	—
01-02	Boston	49	33	9	7
02-03	Boston	44	38	—	—
Totals		117	95	9	7
Olsen, Ole					
46-47	Chicago Stags	39	22	5	6
47-48	Chicago Stags	28	20	3	4
48-49	Chicago Stags	28	21	0	2
Totals		95	63	8	12
Pettit, Bob					
61-62	St. Louis	4	2	—	—
Totals		4	2	—	—
Pfund, Randy					
92-93	LA Lakers	39	43	2	3
93-94	LA Lakers	27	37	—	—
Totals		66	80	2	3
Phillip, Andy					
58-59	St. Louis	6	4	—	—
Totals		6	4	—	—
Pitino, Rick					
87-88	New York	38	44	1	3
88-89	New York	52	30	5	4
97-98	Boston	36	46	—	—
98-99	Boston	19	31	—	—
99-00	Boston	35	47	—	—
00-01	Boston	12	22	—	—
Totals		192	220	6	7
Pollard, Jim					
59-60	Minneapolis	14	25	5	4
61-62	Chicago Packers	18	62	—	—
Totals		32	87	5	4
Popovich, Gregg					
96-97	San Antonio	17	47	—	—
97-98	San Antonio	56	26	4	5
98-99	**San Antonio**	**37**	**13**	**15**	**2**
99-00	San Antonio	53	29	1	3
00-01	San Antonio	58	24	7	6
01-02	Sacramento	61	21	10	6
02-03	San Antonio	60	22	16	8
Totals		342	182	53	30
Potter, Roger					
49-50	Tri-Cities	1	6	—	—
Totals		1	6	—	—
Rambis, Kurt					
98-99	LA Lakers	24	13	3	5
Totals		24	13	3	5

Season	Team	Reg. Season W	Reg. Season L	Playoffs W	Playoffs L
Ramsay, Jack					
68-69	Philadelphia	55	27	1	4
69-70	Philadelphia	42	40	1	4
70-71	Philadelphia	47	35	3	4
71-72	Philadelphia	30	52	—	—
72-73	Buffalo	21	61	—	—
73-74	Buffalo	42	40	2	4
74-75	Buffalo	49	33	3	4
75-76	Buffalo	46	36	4	5
76-77	**Portland**	**49**	**33**	**14**	**5**
77-78	Portland	58	24	2	4
78-79	Portland	45	37	1	2
79-80	Portland	38	44	1	2
80-81	Portland	45	37	1	2
81-82	Portland	42	40	—	—
82-83	Portland	46	36	3	4
83-84	Portland	48	34	2	3
84-85	Portland	42	40	4	5
85-86	Portland	40	42	1	3
86-87	Indianapolis	41	41	1	3
87-88	Indianapolis	38	44	—	—
88-89	Indianapolis	0	7	—	—
Totals		864	783	44	58
Reed, Willis					
77-78	New York	43	39	2	4
78-79	New York	6	8	—	—
87-88	New Jersey	7	21	—	—
88-89	New Jersey	26	56	—	—
Totals		82	124	2	4
Reiser, Chick					
51-52	Baltimore Bullets	8	19	—	—
52-53	Baltimore Bullets	0	3	—	—
Totals		8	22	—	—
Reynolds, Jerry					
86-87	Sacramento	15	21	—	—
87-88	Sacramento	7	17	—	—
88-89	Sacramento	27	55	—	—
89-90	Sacramento	7	21	—	—
Totals		56	114	—	—
Riley, Pat					
81-82	**LA Lakers**	**50**	**21**	**12**	**2**
82-83	LA Lakers	58	24	8	7
83-84	LA Lakers	54	28	14	7
84-85	**LA Lakers**	**62**	**20**	**15**	**4**
85-86	LA Lakers	62	20	8	6
86-87	**LA Lakers**	**65**	**17**	**15**	**3**
87-88	**LA Lakers**	**62**	**20**	**15**	**9**
88-89	LA Lakers	57	25	11	4
89-90	LA Lakers	63	19	4	5
91-92	New York	51	31	6	6
92-93	New York	60	22	9	6
93-94	New York	57	25	14	11
94-95	New York	55	27	6	5
95-96	Miami	42	40	0	3
96-97	Miami	61	21	8	9
97-98	Miami	55	27	2	3
98-99	Miami	33	17	2	3
99-00	Miami	52	30	6	4
00-01	Miami	50	32	0	3
01-02	Miami	36	46	—	—
02-03	Miami	25	57	—	—
		1110	569	155	100
Rivers, Doc					
99-00	Orlando	41	41	—	—
00-01	Orlando	43	39	1	3
01-02	Orlando	44	38	1	3
02-03	Orlando	42	40	—	—
Totals		170	158	2	6
Robertson, Scotty					
74-75	New Orleans	1	14	—	—
78-79	Chicago	11	15	—	—
80-81	Detroit	21	61	—	—
81-82	Detroit	39	43	—	—
82-83	Detroit	37	45	—	—
Totals		109	178	—	—
Rocha, Red					
57-58	Detroit	24	23	3	4
58-59	Detroit	28	44	1	2
59-60	Detroit	13	21	4	6
Totals		65	88	—	—

Season Team	Reg. Season W	L	Playoffs W	L
Rodgers, Jimmy				
88-89 Boston	42	40	0	3
89-90 Boston	52	30	2	3
91-92 Minnesota	15	67	—	—
92-93 Minnesota	6	23	—	—
Totals	115	160	2	6
Rolfe, Red				
46-47 Toronto Huskies	17	27	—	—
Totals	17	27	—	—
Rothstein, Ron				
88-89 Miami	15	67	—	—
89-90 Miami	18	64	—	—
90-91 Miami	24	58	—	—
92-93 Detroit	40	42	—	—
Totals	97	231	—	—
Rubin, Roy				
72-73 Philadelphia	4	47	—	—
Totals	4	47	—	—
Russell, Bill				
66-67 Boston	60	21	4	5
67-68 Boston	**54**	**28**	**12**	**7**
68-69 Boston	**48**	**34**	**12**	**6**
73-74 Seattle	36	46	—	—
74-75 Seattle	43	39	4	5
75-76 Seattle	43	39	2	4
76-77 Seattle	40	42	—	—
87-88 Sacramento	17	41	—	—
Totals	341	290	34	27
Russell, Honey				
46-47 Boston	22	38	—	—
47-48 Boston	20	28	1	2
Totals	42	66	1	2
Sachs, Ed				
46-47 Detroit Falcons	8	18	—	—
Totals	8	18	—	—
Sadowski, Ed				
46-47 Toronto Huskies	3	9	—	—
Totals	3	9	—	—
Sanders, Tom				
77-78 Boston	21	27	—	—
78-79 Boston	2	12	—	—
Totals	23	39	—	—
Saunders, Flip				
95-96 Minnesota	20	42	—	—
96-97 Minnesota	40	42	0	3
97-98 Minnesota	45	37	2	3
98-99 Minnesota	25	25	1	3
99-00 Minnesota	50	32	1	3
00-01 Minnesota	47	35	1	3
01-02 Minnesota	50	32	0	3
02-03 Minnesota	51	31	2	4
Totals	328	276	7	22
Schaefer, Herm				
51-52 Ind. Olympians	34	32	0	2
52-53 Ind. Olympians	28	43	0	2
Totals	62	75	0	4
Schaus, Fred				
60-61 LA Lakers	36	43	6	6
61-62 LA Lakers	54	26	7	6
62-63 LA Lakers	53	27	6	7
63-64 LA Lakers	42	38	2	3
64-65 LA Lakers	49	31	5	6
65-66 LA Lakers	45	35	7	7
66-67 LA Lakers	36	45	0	3
Totals	315	245	33	38
Schayes, Dolph				
63-64 Philadelphia	34	46	2	3
64-65 Philadelphia	40	40	6	5
65-66 Philadelphia	55	25	1	4
70-71 Buffalo	22	60	—	—
71-72 Buffalo	0	1	—	—
Totals	151	172	9	12

Season Team	Reg. Season W	L	Playoffs W	L
Schuler, Mike				
86-87 Portland	49	33	1	3
87-88 Portland	53	29	1	3
88-89 Portland	25	22	—	—
90-91 LA Clippers	31	51	—	—
91-92 LA Clippers	21	24	—	—
Totals	179	159	2	6
Schultz, Howie				
49-50 Anderson	21	14	—	—
Totals	21	14	—	—
Scolari, Fred				
51-52 Baltimore Bullets	12	27	—	—
Totals	12	27	—	—
Scott, Bryon				
00-01 New Jersey	26	56	—	—
01-02 New Jersey	52	30	11	5
02-03 New Jersey	49	33	6	6
Totals	127	119	17	11
Scott, Ray				
72-73 Detroit	38	37	—	—
73-74 Detroit	52	30	3	4
74-75 Detroit	40	42	1	2
75-76 Detroit	17	25	—	—
Totals	147	134	4	6
Senesky, George				
55-56 Phil. Warriors	**45**	**27**	**7**	**3**
56-57 Phil. Warriors	37	35	0	2
57-58 Phil. Warriors	37	35	3	5
Totals	119	97	10	10
Seymour, Paul				
56-57 Syracuse	34	26	2	3
57-58 Syracuse	41	31	1	2
58-59 Syracuse	35	37	5	4
59-60 Syracuse	45	30	1	2
60-61 St. Louis	51	28	5	7
61-62 St. Louis	5	9	—	—
65-66 Baltimore	38	42	0	3
68-69 Detroit	22	38	—	—
Totals	271	241	14	21
Sharman, Bill				
66-67 S.F. Warriors	44	37	9	6
67-68 S.F. Warriors	43	39	4	6
71-72 LA Lakers	**69**	**13**	**12**	**3**
72-73 LA Lakers	60	22	9	8
73-74 LA Lakers	47	35	1	4
74-75 LA Lakers	30	52	—	—
75-76 LA Lakers	40	42	—	—
Totals	333	240	35	27
Shipp, Charley				
49-50 Waterloo	8	27	—	—
Totals	8	27	—	—
Shue, Gene				
66-67 Baltimore	16	40	—	—
67-68 Baltimore	36	46	—	—
68-69 Baltimore	57	25	0	4
69-70 Baltimore	50	32	3	4
70-71 Baltimore	42	40	8	10
71-72 Baltimore	38	44	2	4
72-73 Baltimore	52	30	1	4
73-74 Philadelphia	25	57	—	—
74-75 Philadelphia	34	48	—	—
75-76 Philadelphia	46	36	1	2
76-77 Philadelphia	50	32	10	9
77-78 Philadelphia	2	4	—	—
78-79 San Diego	43	39	—	—
79-80 San Diego	35	47	—	—
80-81 Washington	39	43	—	—
81-82 Washington	43	39	3	4
82-83 Washington	42	40	—	—
83-84 Washington	35	47	1	3
84-85 Washington	40	42	1	3
85-86 Washington	32	37	—	—
87-88 LA Clippers	17	65	—	—
88-89 LA Clippers	10	28	—	—
Totals	784	861	30	47

Season Team	Reg. Season W	L	Playoffs W	L
Silas, Paul				
80-81 San Diego	36	46	—	—
81-82 San Diego	17	65	—	—
82-83 San Diego	25	57	—	—
98-99 Charlotte	22	13	—	—
99-00 Charlotte	49	33	1	3
00-01 Charlotte	46	36	6	4
01-02 Charlotte	44	38	4	5
02-03 New Orleans	47	35	—	—
Totals	286	323	11	12
Skiles, Scott				
99-00 Phoenix	40	16	4	5
00-01 Phoenix	51	31	1	3
01-02 Phoenix	25	26	—	—
Totals	116	73	5	8
Sloan, Jerry				
79-80 Chicago	30	52	—	—
80-81 Chicago	45	37	2	4
81-82 Chicago	19	32	—	—
88-89 Utah	40	25	0	3
89-90 Utah	55	27	2	3
90-91 Utah	54	28	4	5
91-92 Utah	55	27	9	7
92-93 Utah	47	35	2	3
93-94 Utah	53	29	8	8
94-95 Utah	60	22	2	3
95-96 Utah	55	27	10	8
96-97 Utah	64	18	13	7
97-98 Utah	62	20	13	7
98-99 Utah	37	13	5	6
99-00 Utah	55	27	4	6
00-01 Utah	53	29	2	3
01-02 Utah	44	38	1	3
02-03 Utah	47	35	1	4
Totals	875	521	78	80
Smart, Keith				
02-03 Cleveland	9	31	—	—
Totals	9	31	—	—
Smiley, Jack				
49-50 Waterloo	11	16	—	—
Totals	11	16	—	—
Soar, Hank				
47-48 Providence	2	17	—	—
Totals	2	17	—	—
St.Jean, Garry				
92-93 Sacramento	25	57	—	—
93-94 Sacramento	28	54	—	—
94-95 Sacramento	39	43	—	—
95-96 Sacramento	39	43	1	3
96-97 Sacramento	28	39	—	—
Totals	159	236	1	3
Staak, Bob				
96-97 Washington	0	1	—	—
Totals	0	1	—	—
Staverman, Larry				
77-78 Kansas City	18	27	—	—
Totals	18	27	—	—
Stotts, Terry				
02-03 Atlanta	24	31	2	4
Totals	24	31	2	4
Suesens, Kenny				
49-50 Sheboygan	22	40	1	2
Totals	22	40	1	2
Tarkanian, Jerry				
92-93 San Antonio	9	11	—	—
Totals	9	11	—	—
Thomas, Isiah				
00-01 Indianapolis	41	41	1	3
01-02 Indianapolis	42	40	2	3
02-03 Indianapolis	48	34	3	4
Totals	131	115	6	10
Thorn, Rod				
81-82 Chicago	15	15	—	—
Totals	15	15	—	—

Season	Team	Reg. Season W	L	Playoffs W	L
Todd, Roland					
70-71	Portland	29	53	—	—
71-72	Portland	12	44	—	—
Totals		41	97	—	—
Todorovich, Mike					
50-51	Tri-Cities	14	28	—	—
Totals		14	28	—	—
Tomjanovich, Rudy					
91-92	Houston	16	14	—	—
92-93	Houston	55	27	6	6
93-94	**Houston**	**58**	**24**	**15**	**8**
94-95	**Houston**	**47**	**35**	**15**	**7**
95-96	Houston	48	34	3	5
96-97	Houston	57	25	9	7
97-98	Houston	41	41	2	3
98-99	Houston	31	19	1	3
99-00	Houston	34	48	—	—
00-01	Houston	45	37	—	—
01-02	Houston	28	54	—	—
02-03	Houston	43	39	—	—
Totals		503	397	51	39
Tormohlen, Bumper					
75-76	Atlanta	1	7	—	—
Totals		1	7	—	—
Unseld, Wes					
87-88	Washington	30	25	2	3
88-89	Washington	40	42	—	—
89-90	Washington	31	51	—	—
90-91	Washington	30	52	—	—
91-92	Washington	25	57	—	—
92-93	Washington	22	60	—	—
93-94	Washington	24	58	—	—
Totals		202	345	2	3
Van Arsdale, Dick					
86-87	Phoenix	14	12	—	—
Totals		14	12	—	—
Van Breda Kolff, Bill 'Butch'					
67-68	LA Lakers	52	30	10	5
68-69	LA Lakers	55	27	11	7
69-70	Detroit	31	51	—	—
70-71	Detroit	45	37	—	—
71-72	Detroit	6	4	—	—
72-73	Phoenix	3	4	—	—
74-75	New Orleans	22	44	—	—
75-76	New Orleans	38	44	—	—
76-77	New Orleans	14	12	—	—
Totals		266	253	21	12
Van Gundy, Jeff					
95-96	New York	13	10	4	4
96-97	New York	57	25	6	4
97-98	New York	43	39	4	6
98-99	New York	27	23	12	8
99-00	New York	50	32	9	7
00-01	New York	48	34	2	3
01-02	New York	10	9	—	—
Totals		248	172	37	32

Season	Team	Reg. Season W	L	Playoffs W	L
Versace, Dick					
88-89	Indianapolis	22	31	—	—
89-90	Indianapolis	42	40	0	3
90-91	Indianapolis	9	16	—	—
Totals		73	87	0	3
Vitale, Dick					
78-79	Detroit	30	52	—	—
79-80	Detroit	4	8	—	—
Totals		34	60	—	—
Walker, Darrell					
96-97	Toronto	30	52	—	—
97-98	Toronto	11	38	—	—
99-00	Washington	5	33	—	—
Totals		46	123	—	—
Walsh, Don					
78-79	Denver	19	10	1	2
79-80	Denver	30	52	—	—
80-81	Denver	11	20	—	—
Totals		60	82	1	2
Wanzer, Bobby					
55-56	Rochester	31	41	—	—
56-57	Rochester	31	41	—	—
57-58	Cincinnati	33	39	0	2
58-59	Cincinnati	3	15	—	—
Totals		98	136	0	2
Weiss, Bob					
86-87	San Antonio	28	54	—	—
87-88	San Antonio	31	51	0	3
90-91	Atlanta	43	39	2	3
91-92	Atlanta	38	44	—	—
92-93	Atlanta	43	39	0	3
93-94	LA Clippers	27	55	—	—
Totals		210	282	2	9
West, Jerry					
76-77	LA Lakers	53	29	4	7
77-78	LA Lakers	45	37	1	2
78-79	LA Lakers	47	35	3	5
		145	101	8	14
Westhead, Paul					
79-80	**LA Lakers**	**50**	**18**	**12**	**4**
80-81	LA Lakers	54	28	1	2
81-82	LA Lakers	7	4	—	—
82-83	Chicago	28	54	—	—
90-91	Denver	20	62	—	—
91-92	Denver	24	58	—	—
Totals		183	224	13	6
Westphal, Paul					
92-93	Phoenix	62	20	13	11
93-94	Phoenix	56	26	6	4
94-95	Phoenix	59	23	6	4
95-96	Phoenix	14	19	—	—
98-99	Seattle	25	25	—	—
99-00	Seattle	45	37	2	3
00-01	Seattle	6	9	—	—
Totals		267	159	27	22
Wetzel, John					
87-88	Phoenix	28	54	—	—
Totals		28	54	—	—

Season	Team	Reg. Season W	L	Playoffs W	L
Wilkens, Lenny					
69-70	Seattle	36	46	—	—
70-71	Seattle	38	44	—	—
71-72	Seattle	47	35	—	—
74-75	Portland	38	44	—	—
75-76	Portland	37	45	—	—
77-78	Seattle	42	18	13	9
78-79	**Seattle**	**52**	**30**	**12**	**5**
79-80	Seattle	56	26	7	8
80-81	Seattle	34	48	—	—
81-82	Seattle	52	30	3	5
82-83	Seattle	48	34	0	2
83-84	Seattle	42	40	2	3
84-85	Seattle	31	51	—	—
86-87	Cleveland	31	51	—	—
87-88	Cleveland	42	40	2	3
88-89	Cleveland	57	25	2	3
89-90	Cleveland	42	40	2	3
90-91	Cleveland	33	49	—	—
91-92	Cleveland	57	25	9	8
92-93	Cleveland	54	28	3	6
93-94	Atlanta	57	25	5	6
94-95	Atlanta	42	40	0	3
95-96	Atlanta	46	36	4	6
96-97	Atlanta	56	26	4	6
97-98	Atlanta	50	32	1	3
98-99	Atlanta	31	19	3	6
99-00	Atlanta	28	54	—	—
00-01	Toronto	47	35	6	6
01-02	Toronto	42	40	2	3
02-03	Toronto	24	58	—	—
Totals		1292	1114	80	94
Winter, Tex					
71-72	Houston	34	48	—	—
72-73	Houston	17	30	—	—
Totals		51	78	—	—
Winters, Brian					
95-96	Vancouver	15	67	—	—
96-97	Vancouver	8	35	—	—
01-02	Golden State	13	46	—	—
Totals		36	148	—	—
Wittman, Randy					
99-00	Cleveland	32	50	—	—
00-01	Cleveland	30	52	—	—
Totals		62	102	—	—
Wohl, Dave					
85-86	New Jersey	39	43	0	3
86-87	New Jersey	24	58	—	—
87-88	New Jersey	2	13	—	—
Totals		65	114	0	3
Wolf, Charlie					
60-61	Cincinnati	33	46	—	—
61-62	Cincinnati	43	37	1	3
62-63	Cincinnati	42	38	6	6
63-64	Detroit	23	57	—	—
64-65	Detroit	2	9	—	—
Totals		143	187	7	9
Young, Draff					
73-74	KC-Omaha	0	3	—	—
Totals		0	3	—	—

Appendix

Magic Johnson, 1989
Magic Johnson was honored as *SPORT* magazine's Athlete of the Decade for the 1980s.

The NBA Entry Draft

Drafting players in the NBA used to be so simple. Small scouting staffs kept tabs on the top college players in the land and passed along reports to their general managers. In turn, the GMs would plug into their own network of contacts and, by the time draft day arrived, there was little doubt about which college prospects were the best in the land. And so they gathered on draft day and, with little hoopla, divvied up the young talent.

But not any more.

Today, teams prepare by sending out large scouting staffs on a world-wide talent search. In addition to scouring the college campuses, they must find their way around high-school gyms and on to overseas flights bound for Europe and Asia. They file detailed reports and leave it to the GMs to figure out how to compare the relative merits of a kid in high school vs. a college senior vs. an 18-year-old playing pro ball in Europe vs. an apparent phenom playing amateur ball in China. And then comes the hoopla—weeks of advance hype followed by a live, prime-time television broadcast of the draft itself.

Just look at the 2003 draft. The top three picks—LeBron James, Darko Milicic and Carmelo Anthony—came out of high school, Europe and U.S. college respectively. A year earlier, the No. 1 pick, Yao Ming, was discovered in China. In 2001 Kwame Brown became the first high schooler selected first overall. After providing the No. 1 pick for 54 consecutive years—including such current stars as Allen Iverson and Shaq O'Neal, plus Hall of Famers (to name just three) Lew Alcindor, Oscar Robertson and Elgin Baylor—U.S. colleges have been shut out of the top spot since 2000.

If anything, the addition in recent years of high schoolers and foreign-born players has made the draft an even bigger crapshoot. Not that it was ever a sure thing. If so, Portland Trail Blazers wouldn't have passed on Michael Jordan in 1984 to select Sam Bowie (or, in the same year, 15 players wouldn't have been taken before Utah grabbed John Stockton). Or how would you like to have been one of the five GMs who passed on Larry Bird in 1978? But the addition of teenagers to the draft pool has no doubt complicated matters. In 1996, 12 players were selected before Charlotte took high-schooler Kobe Bryant. A year later, Tracy McGrady went ninth, to Toronto. Ouch!

The draft has been a work in progress since its inauguration in 1947. Pittsburgh made Clifton Neeley of Texas Western the first player ever selected in a draft that included Baltimore, Boston, Chicago, New York, Philadelphia, Providence, St. Louis, Toronto and Washington. Until 1965, teams were allowed to exchange a first-round pick for a territorial selection, allowing them to secure the rights of a top local player. The Celtics employed this option in 1956 to acquire Tom Heinsohn from Holy Cross and in 1959 the Philadelphia Warriors

David Stern and LeBron James
The NBA Commissioner welcomes the No. 1 pick of the 2003 NBA Draft, chosen by the Cleveland Cavaliers straight from high school.

grabbed Wilt Chamberlain who played high school ball in the area before attending Kansas.

For almost four decades, the draft order was based on the regular-season standings, with teams drafting in the inverse order of finish. In 1985, responding to concerns that non-playoff teams could deliberately try to finish lower in the standings to improve their draft position, the league instituted a lottery system. For the first round, the order of selection for all teams that missed the playoffs was determined by a lottery. In the first lottery draft, the New York Knicks won top pick and selected Patrick Ewing.

A year later, the lottery was amended so that only the first three picks were determined by a lottery. The change assured that the worst team in the league would pick no higher than fourth.

The length of the draft has undergone several changes. In the early years, teams were allowed to keep picking until the

talent pool had dried up. From 1974 to 1985 the draft was restricted to 10 rounds. For the next two years, it was limited to seven rounds, in 1988 it was three rounds, and then in 1989 it was reduced to just two rounds, allowing undrafted players to try to catch on with the team of their choice.

In 1990 the lottery was amended again. To accommodate the growth of the league through expansion, a weighted system was introduced in order to increase the likelihood of the weakest teams acquiring a top pick. The system was further amended in 1994 and, after Toronto and Vancouver came into the league, again in 1996, to further increase the chances of the worst teams getting one of the top three picks.

It works like this: By numbering 14 ping-pong balls 1 through 14, there are 1,001 possible combinations created. The 1,001 combinations are assigned to non-playoff teams, with the worst team receiving the most combinations, the second worst getting the second most, and so on. Four balls are drawn from a drum. The numbers on the balls are compared to the numbers that have been pre-assigned. The team that has the winning combination receives the first pick. The process is then repeated until the order of selection has been established for the first three picks, after which teams draft in the inverse order of the final standings. The worst team has a 25% chance of winning the No. 1 pick.

All players who have completed their college eligibility plus international players who turn 22 during the draft year are automatically eligible for the draft. In addition, other players may enter the draft by notifying the league 45 days before draft day.

THE NBA ENTRY DRAFT

2003

First Round

1	Cleveland	LeBron James	St.Vincent-St.Mary H.S (OH)
2	Detroit	Darko Milicic	Hemofarm Vrsac, Yugoslavia
3	Denver	Carmelo Anthony	Syracuse
4	Toronto	Chris Bosh	Georgia Tech
5	Miami	Dwyane Wade	Marquette
6	LA Clippers	Chris Kaman	Central Michigan
7	Chicago	Kirk Hinrich	Kansas
8	Milwaukee	T.J. Ford	Texas
9	New York	Mike Sweetney	Georgetown
10	Washington	Jarvis Hayes	Georgia
11	Golden State	Mickael Pietrus	Pau Orthez, France
12	Seattle	Nick Collison	Kansas
13	Memphis	Marcus Banks	UNLV
14	Seattle	Luke Ridnour	Oregon
15	Orlando	Reece Gaines	Louisville
16	Boston	Troy Bell	Boston College
17	Phoenix	Zarko Cabarkapa	Buducnost, Serbia
18	New Orleans	David West	Xavier
19	Utah	Aleksandar Pavlovic	Buducnost, Serbia
20	Boston	Dahntay Jones	Duke
21	Atlanta	Boris Diaw	Pau Orthez, France
22	New Jersey	Zoran Planinic	Cibona Zagreb
23	Portland	Travis Outlaw	Starkville H.S. (MS)
24	LA Lakers	Brian Cook	Illinois
25	Detroit	Carlos Delfino	Skipper Bologna, Italy
26	Minnesota	Ndudi Ebi	Westbury Christian H.S. (TX)
27	Memphis	Kendrick Perkins	Clifton J.Ozen H.S. (TX)
28	San Antonio	Leandro Barbosa	Baura Tilibra, Brazil
29	Dallas	Josh Howard	Wake Forest

Second Round

30	New York	Maciej Lampe	Universiade Computense, Spain
31	Cleveland	Jason Kapono	UCLA
32	LA Lakers	Luke Walton	Arizona
33	Miami	Jerome Beasley	North Dakota
34	LA Clippers	Sofoklis Schortsanitis	Iraklis, Greece
35	Milwaukee	Szymon Szewczyk	Braunschweig, Poland
36	Chicago	Mario Austin	Mississippi State
37	Atlanta	Travis Hansen	Brigham Young
38	Washington	Steve Blake	Maryland
39	New York	Slavko Vranes	Buducnost, Yugoslavia
40	Golden State	Derrick Zimmerman	Mississippi State
41	Seattle	Willie Green	Detroit
42	Orlando	Zaur Pachulia	Ulker, Turkey
43	Milwaukee	Keith Bogans	Kentucky
44	Houston	Malick Badiane	Langen, Germany
45	Chicago	Matt Bonner	Florida
46	Denver	Sani Becirovic	Serbia
47	Utah	Maurice Williams	Alabama
48	New Orleans	James Lang	Central Park Christian H.S. (AL)
49	Indiana	James Jones	Miami
50	Philadelphia	Paccelis Morlende	Dijon, France
51	New Jersey	Kyle Korver	Creighton
52	Toronto	Remon Van de Hare	Spain
53	Miami	Tommy Smith	Arizona State
54	Portland	Nedzad Simanovic	Bosnia
55	Minnesota	Rick Rickert	Minnesota
56	Boston	Brandon Hunter	Ohio
57	Dallas	Xue Yuyang	China
58	Detroit	Andreas Glynaidakis	Greece

2002

First Round

1	Houston	Yao Ming	Shanghai Sharks, China
2	Chicago	Jay Williams	Duke
3	Golden State	Mike Dunleavy	Duke
4	Memphis	Drew Gooden	Kansas
5	Denver	Nikoloz Tskitishvili	Benetton Treviso, Italy
6	Cleveland	Dajuan Wagner	Memphis
7	New York	Maybyner "Nene" Hilario	Vasco da Gama, Brazil
8	LA Clippers	Chris Wilcox	Maryland
9	Phoenix	Amare Stoudemire	Cypress Creek H.S. (FL)
10	Miami	Caron Butler	Connecticut
11	Washington	Jared Jeffries	Indiana
12	LA Clippers	Melvin Ely	Fresno St.
13	Milwaukee	Marcus Haislip	Tennessee
14	Indiana	Freddie Jones	Oregon
15	Houston	Bostjan Nachbar	Benetton Treviso, Italy
16	Philadelphia	Jiri Welsch	Olympia Lubliana, Slovenia
17	Washington	Juan Dixon	Maryland
18	Orlando	Curtis Borchardt	Stanford
19	Utah	Ryan Humphrey	Notre Dame
20	Toronto	Kareem Rush	Missouri
21	Portland	Qyntel Woods	Northeast Mississippi CC
22	Phoenix	Casey Jacobsen	Stanford
23	Detroit	Tayshaun Prince	Kentucky
24	New Jersey	Nenad Krstic	Partizan Belgrade
25	Denver	Frank Williams	Illinois
26	San Antonio	John Salmons	Miami
27	LA Lakers	Chris Jefferies	Fresno St.
28	Sacramento	Dan Dickau	Gonzaga
29	Minnesota	Forfeited	

Second Round

30	Golden State	Steve Logan	Cincinnati
31	Chicago	Roger Mason Jr.	Virginia
32	Memphis	Robert Archibald	Illinois
33	Denver	Vincent Yarbrough	Tennessee
34	Milwaukee	Dan Gadzuric	UCLA
35	Cleveland	Carlos Boozer	Duke
36	New York	Milos Vujanic	Yugoslavia
37	Atlanta	David Andersen	Kinder Bologna, Italy
38	Houston	Tito Maddox	Fresno St.
39	Washington	Rod Grizzard	Alabama
40	Washington	Juan Carlos Navarro	Spain
41	LA Clippers	Mario Kasun	Croatia
42	Milwaukee	Ron Murray	Shaw (NC)
43	Portland	Jason Jennings	Arkansas St.
44	Chicago	Lonny Baxter	Maryland
45	Phoenix	Sam Clancy	USC
46	Memphis	Matt Barnes	UCLA
47	Utah	Jamal Sampson	California
48	Milwaukee	Chris Owens	Texas
49	Seattle	Peter Fehse	Germany
50	Boston	Darius Songaila	Wake Forest
51	Portland	Federico Kammerichs	Argentina
52	Minnesota	Marcus Taylor	Michigan St.
53	Miami	Rasual Butler	La Salle
54	New Jersey	Tamar Slay	Marshall
55	Dallas	Mladen Sekularac	FMP Zeleznik, Yugoslavia
56	San Antonio	Luis Scola	Tau Ceramica, Spain
57	San Antonio	Randy Holcomb	San-Diego St.
58	Sacramento	Corsley Edwards	Central Connecticut St.

2001

First Round

1	Washington	Kwame Brown	Glynn Academy HS (GA)
2	LA Clippers	Tyson Chandler	Dominguez HS (CA)
3	Atlanta	Pau Gasol	Spain
4	Chicago	Eddy Curry	Thornwood HS (IL)
5	Golden State	Jason Richardson	Michigan State
6	Vancouver	Shane Battier	Duke
7	New Jersey	Eddie Griffin	Seton Hall
8	Cleveland	DeSagana Diop	Oak Hill Academy HS (VA)
9	Detroit	Rodney White	Charlotte
10	Boston	Joe Johnson	Arkansas
11	Boston	Kedrick Brown	Okaloosa-Walton CC
12	Seattle	Vladimir Radmanovic	Yugoslavia
13	Houston	Richard Jefferson	Arizona
14	Golden State	Troy Murphy	Notre Dame
15	Orlando	Steven Hunter	DePaul
16	Charlotte	Kirk Haston	Indiana
17	Toronto	Michael Bradley	Villanova
18	Houston	Jason Collins	Stanford
19	Portland	Zach Randolph	Michigan State
20	Cleveland	Brendan Haywood	North Carolina
21	Boston	Joseph Forte	North Carolina
22	Orlando	Jeryl Sasser	Southern Methodist
23	Houston	Brandon Armstrong	Pepperdine
24	Utah	Raul Lopez	Spain
25	Sacramento	Gerald Wallace	Alabama
26	Philadelphia	Samuel Dalembert	Seton Hall
27	Vancouver	Jamaal Tinsley	Iowa State
28	San Antonio	Tony Parker	France
29	Minnesota	Forfeited	

Second Round

30	Chicago	Trenton Hassell	Austin Peay
31	Golden State	Gilbert Arenas	Arizona
32	Orlando	Omar Cook	St. John's, NY
33	Vancouver	Will Solomon	Clemson
34	Atlanta	Terence Morris	Maryland
35	New Jersey	Brian Scalabrine	USC
36	Cleveland	Jeff Trepagnier	USC
37	Philadelphia	Damone Brown	Syracuse
38	Detroit	Mehmet Okur	Turkey
39	New York	Michael Wright	Arizona
40	Seattle	Earl Watson	UCLA
41	Indiana	Jamison Brewer	Auburn
42	Seattle	Bobby Simmons	DePaul
43	New York	Eric Chenowith	Kansas
44	Dallas	Kyle Hill	Eastern Illinois
45	Chicago	Sean Lampley	California
46	Minnesota	Loren Woods	Arizona
47	Denver	Ousmane Cisse	St. Jude HS (AL)
48	Vancouver	Antonio Fotsis	Greece
49	Miami	Ken Johnson	Ohio State
50	Portland	Ruben Boumtje-Boumtje	Georetown
51	Phoenix	Alton Ford	Houston
52	Milwaukee	Andre Hutson	Michigan State
53	Utah	Jarron Collins	Stanford
54	Dallas	Kenny Satterfield	Cincinnati
55	Sacramento	Maurice Jeffers	St. Louis
56	San Antonio	Robertas Javtokas	Lithuania
57	Philadelphia	Alvin Jones	Georgia Tech
58	San Antonio	Bryan Bracey	Oregon

2000

First Round

1	New Jersey	Kenyon Martin	Cincinnati
2	Vancouver	Stromile Swift	Louisiana State
3	LA Clippers	Darius Miles	East Saint Louis HS (IL)
4	Chicago	Marcus Fizer	Iowa State
5	Orlando	Mike Miller	Florida
6	Atlanta	DerMarr Johnson	Cincinnati
7	Chicago	Chris Mihm	Texas
8	Cleveland	Jamal Crawford	Michigan
9	Houston	Joel Przybilla	Minnesota
10	Orlando	Keyon Dooling	Missouri
11	Boston	Jerome Moiso	UCLA
12	Dallas	Etan Thomas	Syracuse
13	Orlando	Courtney Alexander	Fresno State
14	Detroit	Mateen Cleaves	Michigan State
15	Milwaukee	Jason Collier	Georgia Tech
16	Sacramento	Hidayet Turkoglu	Turkey
17	Seattle	Desmond Mason	Oklahoma State
18	LA Clippers	Quentin Richardson	Depaul
19	Charlotte	Jamaal Magloire	Kentucky
20	Philadelphia	Craig Claxton	Hofstra

21	Toronto	Morris Peterson	Michigan State
22	New York	Donnell Harvey	Florida
23	Utah	DeShawn Stevenson	Washington Union HS (CA)
24	Chicago	Dalibor Bagaric	Croatia
25	Phoenix	Iakovos Tsakalidis	Republic of Georgia
26	Denver	Mamadou N'diaye	Auburn
27	Indiana	Primoz Brezec	Slovenia
28	Portland	Erick Barkley	St. John's
29	LA Laker	Mark Madsen	Stanford

Second Round

30	LA Clippers	Marko Jaric	Greece
31	Dallas	Dan Langhi	Vanderbilt
32	Chicago	A.J. Guyton	Indiana
33	Chicago	Jake Voskuhl	Connecticut
34	Chicago	Khalid El-Amin	Connecticut
35	Washington	Mike Smith	Louisiana-Monroe
36	New Jersey	Soumaila Samake	Mali
37	Miami	Eddie House	Arizona State
38	Houston	Eduardo Najera	Oklahoma
39	New York	Lavor Postell	St. John's
40	Atlanta	Hanno Mottola	Utah
41	San Antonio	Chris Carrawell	Duke
42	Seattle	Olumide Oyedeji	Nigeria
43	Milwaukee	Michael Redd	Ohio State
44	Detroit	Brian Cardinal	Purdue
45	Sacramento	Jabari Smith	Louisiana State
46	Toronto	DeeAndre Hulett	College of the Sequoias (CA)
47	Seattle	Josip Sesar	Croatia
48	Philadelphia	Mark Karcher	Temple
49	Milwaukee	Jason Hart	Syracuse
50	Utah	Kaniel Dickens	Idaho
51	Minnesota	Igor Rakocevic	Yugoslavia
52	Miami	Ernest Brown	Indian Hill CC
53	Denver	Dan McClintock	Northern Arizona
54	San Antonio	Cory Hightower	Indian Hill CC
55	Golden State	Chris Porter	Auburn
56	Indiana	Jaquay Walls	Colorado
57	Atlanta	Scoonie Penn	Ohio State
58	Dallas	Pete Mickeal	Cincinnati

1999

First Round

1	Chicago	Elton Brand	Duke
2	Vancouver	Steve Francis	Maryland
3	Charlotte	Baron Davis	UCLA
4	LA Clippers	Lamar Odom	Rhode Island
5	Toronto	Jonathan Bender	Picayune HS (MS)
6	Minnesota	Wally Szczerbiak	Miami Ohio
7	Washington	Richard Hamilton	Conneticut
8	Cleveland	Andre Miller	Utah
9	Phoenix	Shawn Marion	Nevada-Las Vegas
10	Atlanta	Jason Terry	Arizona
11	Cleveland	Trajan Langdon	Duke
12	Toronto	Alek Radojevic	Barton County CC
13	Orlando	Corey Maggette	Duke
14	Minnesota	William Avery	Duke
15	New York	Frederic Weis	France
16	Chicago	Ron Artest	St. John's
17	Atlanta	Cal Bowdler	Old Dominion
18	Denver	James Posey	Xavier (OH)
19	Utah	Quincy Lewis	Minnesota
20	Atlanta	Dion Glover	Georgia Tech
21	Indiana	Jeff Foster	SouthWest Texas State
22	Houston	Kenny Thomas	New Mexico
23	LA Lakers	Devean George	Augsburg (MN)
24	Utah	Andrei Kirilenko	Russia
25	Miami	Tim James	Miami
26	Golden State	Vonteego Cummings	Pittsburgh
27	Philadelphia	Jumaine Jones	Georgia
28	Utah	Scott Padgett	Kentucky
29	Dallas	Leon Smith	Martin Luther King HS (IL)

Second Round

30	LA Lakers	John Celestand	Villanova
31	LA Clippers	Rico Hill	Illinois State
32	Chicago	Michael Ruffin	Tulsa
33	Denver	Chris Herren	Fresno State
34	New Jersey	Evan Eschmeyer	Northwestern
35	Washington	Calvin Booth	Penn State
36	Dallas	Wang Zhi-Zhi	China
37	Vancouver	Obinna Ekezie	Maryland
38	Orlando	Laron Profit	Maryland
39	Cleveland	A.J. Bramlett	Arizona
40	San Antonio	Gordan Giricek	Croatia
41	Denver	Francisco Elson	California
42	Minnesota	Louis Bullock	Michigan
43	Charlotte	Lee Nailon	Texas Christian

44	Houston	Tyrone Washington	Mississippi State
45	Sacramento	Ryan Robertson	Kansas
46	New York	J.R. Koch	Iowa
47	Philadelphia	Todd MacCulloch	Washington
48	Milwaukee	Galen Young	UNC-Charlotte
49	Chicago	Lari Ketner	Massachusetts
50	Houston	Venson Hamilton	Nebraska
51	Vancouver	Antwain Smith	St Paul's (VA)
52	Portland	Roberto Bergersen	Boise State
53	Miami	Rodney Buford	Creighton
54	Detroit	Melvin Levett	Cincinnati
55	Boston	Kris Clack	Texas
56	Golden State	Tim Young	Stanford
57	San Antonio	Emmanuel Ginobili	Italy
58	Utah	Eddie Lucas	Virginia Tech

1998

First Round

1	LA Clippers	Michael Olowokandi	Pacific
2	Vancouver	Mike Bibby	Arizona
3	Denver	Raef LaFrentz	Kansas
4	Toronto	Antawn Jamison	North Carolina
5	Golden State	Vince Carter	North Carolina
6	Dallas	Robert Traylor	Michigan
7	Sacramento	Jason Williams	Florida
8	Philadelphia	Larry Hughes	Saint Louis
9	Milwaukee	Dirk Nowitzki	Germany
10	Boston	Paul Pierce	Kansas
11	Detroit	Bonzi Wells	Ball State
12	Orlando	Michael Doleac	Utah
13	Orlando	Keon Clark	Nevada-Las Vegas
14	Houston	Michael Dickerson	Arizona
15	Orlando	Matt Harpring	Georgia Tech
16	Houston	Bryce Drew	Valparaiso
17	Minnesota	Radoslav Nesterovic	Slovenia
18	Houston	Mirsad Turkcan	Turkey
19	Milwaukee	Pat Garrity	Notre Dame
20	Atlanta	Roshown McLeod	Duke
21	Charlotte	Ricky Davis	Iowa
22	LA Clippers	Brian Skinner	Baylor
23	Denver	Tyronn Lue	Nebraska
24	San Antonio	Felipe Lopez	St John's
25	Indiana	Al Harrington	St Patrick's HS
26	LA Lakers	Sam Jacobson	Minnesota
27	Seattle	Vladimir Stepania	Slovenia
28	Chicago	Corey Benjamin	Oregon State
29	Utah	Nazr Mohammed	Kentucky

Second Round

30	Dallas	Ansu Sesay	Mississippi
31	LA Lakers	Ruben Patterson	Cincinnati
32	Seattle	Rashard Lewis	Alief Elsik HS
33	Seattle	Jelani McCoy	UCLA
34	Chicago	Shammond Williams	North Carolina
35	Dallas	Bruno Sundov	Croatia
36	Sacramento	Jerome James	Florida A&M
37	Philadelphia	Casey Shaw	Toledo
38	New York	DeMarco Johnson	UNC-Charlotte
39	Milwaukee	Rafer Alston	Fresno State
40	Detroit	Korleone Young	Hargrave Military Acadamy
41	Houston	Cuttino Mobley	Rhode Island
42	Orlando	Miles Simon	Arizona
43	Washington	Jahidi White	Georgetown
44	New York	Sean Marks	California
45	LA Lakers	Toby Bailey	UCLA
46	Minnesota	Andrae Patterson	Indiana
47	Toronto	Tyson Wheeler	Rhode Island
48	Cleveland	Ryan Stack	South Carolina
49	Atlanta	Cory Carr	Texas Tech
50	Charlotte	Andrew Betts	Long Beach State
51	Miami	Corey Brewer	Oklahoma
52	San Antonio	Derrick Dial	Michigan
53	Dallas	Greg Buckner	Clemson
54	Denver	Tremaine Fowlkes	Fresno State
55	Denver	Ryan Bowen	Iowa
56	Vancouver	J.R. Henderson	UCLA
57	Utah	Torraye Braggs	Xavier (OH)
58	Chicago	Maceo Baston	Michigan

1997

First Round

1	San Antonio	Tim Duncan	Wake Forest
2	New Jersey	Keith Van Horn	Utah
3	Boston	Chauncey Billups	Colorado
4	Vancouver	Antonio Daniels	Bowling Green
5	Denver	Tony Battie	Texas Tech

6	Boston	Ron Mercer	Kentucky
7	New Jersey	Tim Thomas	Villanova
8	Golden State	Adonal Foyle	Colgate
9	Toronto	Tracy McGrady	Mount Zion Academy (NC)
10	Milwaukee	Danny Fortson	Cincinnati
11	Sacramento	Olivier Saint-Jean	San Jose State
12	Indiana	Austin Croshere	Providence
13	Cleveland	Derek Anderson	Kentucky
14	LA Clippers	Maurice Taylor	Michigan
15	Dallas	Kelvin Cato	Iowa State
16	Cleveland	Brevin Knight	Stanford
17	Orlando	Johnny Taylor	Tennessee-Chattanooga
18	Portland	Chris Anstey	Australia
19	Detroit	Scot Pollard	Kansas
20	Minnesota	Paul Grant	Wisconsin
21	New Jersey	Anthony Parker	Bradley
22	Atlanta	Ed Gray	California
23	Seattle	Bobby Jackson	Minnesota
24	Houston	Rodrick Rhodes	Southern Cal
25	New York	John Thomas	Minnesota
26	Miami	Charles Smith	New Mexico
27	Utah	Jacque Vaughn	Kansas
28	Chicago	Keith Booth	Maryland

Second Round

29	Houston	Serge Zwikker	North Carolina
30	Miami	Mark Sanford	Washington
31	Detroit	Charles O'Bannon	UCLA
32	Denver	James Cotton	Long Beach State
33	Philadelphia	Marko Milic	Slovenia
34	Dallas	Bubba Wells	Austin Peay
35	Philadelphia	Kebu Stewart	Cal State Bakersfield
36	Philadelphia	James Collins	Florida State
37	Golden State	Marc Jackson	Temple
38	Milwaukee	Jerald Honeycutt	Tulane
39	Sacramento	Anthony Johnson	College of Charleston
40	Seattle	Eddie Elisma	Georgia Tech
41	Denver	Jason Lawson	Villanova
42	Phoenix	Stephen Jackson	Butler County CC (KS)
43	Minnesota	Gordon Malone	West Virginia
44	Cleveland	Cedric Henderson	Memphis
45	Washington	God Shammgod	Providence
46	Orlando	Eric Washington	Alabama
47	Portland	Alvin Williams	Villanova
48	Washington	Predrag Drobnjak	Partizan-Belgrade
49	Atlanta	Alein Digbeu	Villeurbanne-France
50	Atlanta	Chris Crawford	Marquette
51	LA Lakers	DeJuan Wheat	Louisville
52	Vancouver	C.J Bruton	Indian Hills CC (IA)
53	LA Lakers	Paul Rogers	Gonzaga
54	Seattle	Mark Blount	Pittsburgh
55	Boston	Ben Pepper	Australia
56	Utah	Nate Erdmann	Oklahoma
57	Chicago	Roberto Duenas	FC Barcelona-Spain

1996

First Round

1	Philadelphia	Allen Iverson	Georgetown
2	Toronto	Marcus Camby	Massachusetts
3	Vancouver	Shareef Abdur-Rahim	California
4	Milwaukee	Stephon Marbury	Georgia Tech
5	Minnesota	Ray Allen	Connecticut
6	Boston	Antoine Walker	Kentucky
7	LA Clippers	Lorenzen Wright	Memphis (TN)
8	New Jersey	Kerry Kittles	Villanova
9	Dallas	Samaki Walker	Louisville
10	Indiana	Erick Dampier	Mississippi State
11	Golden State	Todd Fuller	North Carolina State
12	Cleveland	Vitaly Potapenko	Wright State
13	LA Lakers	Kobe Bryant	Lower Merion HS (PA)
14	Sacramento	Predrag Stojakovic	PAOK Greece
15	Phoenix	Steve Nash	Santa Clara
16	Charlotte	Tony Delk	Kentucky
17	Portland	Jermaine O'Neal	Eau Claire HS (SC)
18	New York	John Wallace	Syracuse
19	New York	Walter McCarty	Kentucky
20	Cleveland	Zydrunas Ilgauskas	Lithuania
21	New York	Dontae' Jones	Mississippi State
22	Vancouver	Roy Rogers	Alabama
23	Denver	Efthimis Rentzias	PAOK Greece
24	LA Lakers	Derek Fisher	Arkansas-Little Rock
25	Utah	Martin Muursepp	Kalev Tallin (Estonia)
26	Detroit	Jerome Williams	Georgetown
27	Orlando	Brian Evans	Indiana
28	Atlanta	Priest Lauderdale	Central St/Greece
29	Chicago	Travis Knight	Connecticut

Second Round

30	Houston	Othella Harrington	Georgetown
31	Philadelphia	Mark Hendrickson	Washington State
32	Philadelphia	Ryan Minor	Oklahoma
33	Milwaukee	Moochie Norris	West Florida
34	Dallas	Shawn Harvey	West Virginia State
35	Seattle	Joseph Blair	Arizona
36	LA Clippers	Doron Sheffer	Connecticut
37	Denver	Jeff McInnis	North Carolina
38	Boston	Steve Hamer	Tennessee
39	Phoenix	Russ Millard	Iowa
40	Golden State	Marcus Mann	Mississippi Valley St
41	Sacramento	Jason Sasser	Texas Tech
42	Houston	Randy Livingston	Louisiana State
43	Phoenix	Ben Davis	Arizona
44	Charlotte	Malik Rose	Drexel
45	Seattle	Joe Vogel	Colorado State
46	Portland	Marcus Brown	Murray State
47	Seattle	Ron Riley	Arizona State
48	Philadelphia	Jamie Feick	Michigan State
49	Orlando	Amal McCaskill	Marquette
50	Houston	Terrell Bell	Georgia
51	Vancouver	Chris Robinson	Western Kentucky
52	Indiana	Mark Pope	Kentucky
53	Milwaukee	Jeff Nordgaard	Wisconsin-Green Bay
54	Utah	Shandon Anderson	Georgia
55	Washington	Ronnie Henderson	Louisiana State
56	Cleveland	Reggie Geary	Arizona
57	Seattle	Drew Barry	Georgia Tech
58	Dallas	Darnell Robinson	Arkansas

1995
First Round

1	Golden State	Joe Smith	Maryland
2	LA Clippers	Antonio McDyess	Alabama
3	Philadelphia	Jerry Stackhouse	North Carolina
4	Washington	Rasheed Wallace	North Carolina
5	Minnesota	Kevin Garnett	Farragut Academy (IL)
6	Vancouver	Bryant Reeves	Oklahoma State
7	Toronto	Damon Stoudamire	Arizona
8	Portland	Shawn Respert	Michigan State
9	New Jersey	Ed O'Bannon	UCLA
10	Miami	Kurt Thomas	Texas Christian
11	Milwaukee	Gary Trent	Ohio University
12	Dallas	Cherokee Parks	Duke
13	Sacramento	Corliss Williamson	Arkansas
14	Boston	Eric Williams	Providence
15	Denver	Brent Barry	Oregon State
16	Atlanta	Alan Henderson	Indiana
17	Cleveland	Bob Sura	Florida State
18	Detroit	Theo Ratliff	Wyoming
19	Detroit	Randolph Childress	Georgia Tech
20	Chicago	Jason Caffey	Alabama
21	Phoenix	Michael Finley	Wisconsin
22	Charlotte	George Zidek	UCLA
23	Indiana	Travis Best	Georgia Tech
24	Dallas	Loren Meyer	Iowa State
25	Orlando	David Vaughn	Memphis
26	Seattle	Sherrell Ford	Illinois-Chicago
27	Phoenix	Mario Bennett	Arizona State
28	Utah	Greg Ostertag	Kansas
29	San Antonio	Cory Alexander	Virginia

Second Round

30	Detroit	Lou Roe	Massachusetts
31	Chicago	Dragan Tarlac	Greece
32	Washington	Terrence Rencher	Texas
33	Boston	Junior Burrough	Virginia
34	Golden State	Andrew DeClerq	Florida
35	Toronto	Jimmy King	Michigan
36	Vancouver	Lawrence Moten	Syracuse
37	LA Lakers	Frankie King	Western Carolina
38	Milwaukee	Rashard Griffith	Wisconsin
39	Cleveland	Donny Marshall	Connecticut
40	Golden State	Dwayne Whitfield	Jackson State
41	Houston	Erik Meek	Duke
42	Atlanta	Donnie Boyce	Colorado
43	Milwaukee	Eric Snow	Michigan State
44	Denver	Anthony Pelle	Fresno State
45	Atlanta	Troy Brown	Providence
46	Miami	George Banks	Texas-El Paso
47	Sacramento	Tyus Edney	UCLA
48	Minnesota	Mark Davis	Texas Tech
49	Minnesota	Jerome Allen	Pennsylvania
50	Golden State	Martin Lewis	Seward Couty CC
51	Sacramento	Dejan Bodiroga	Italy
52	Indiana	Fred Hoiberg	Indiana

53	LA Clippers	Constantin Popa	Miami (FL)
54	Seattle	Aurelijius Zukauskas	Lithuania
55	Golden State	Michael McDonald	New Orleans
56	Phoenix	Chris Carr	Southern Illinois
57	Atlanta	Cuonzo Martin	Purdue
58	Detroit	Don Reid	Georgetown (DC)

1994
First Round

1	Milwaukee	Glenn Robinson	Purdue
2	Dallas	Jason Kidd	California
3	Detroit	Grant Hill	Duke
4	Minnesota	Donyell Marshall	Connecticut
5	Washington	Juwan Howard	Michigan
6	Philadelphia	Sharone Wright	Clemson
7	LA Clippers	Lamond Murray	California
8	Sacramento	Brian Grant	Xavier (OH)
9	Boston	Eric Montross	North Carolina
10	LA Lakers	Eddie Jones	Temple
11	Seattle	Carlos Rogers	Tennessee State
12	Miami	Khalid Reeves	Arizona
13	Denver	Jalen Rose	Michigan
14	New Jersey	Yinka Dare	George Washington
15	Indiana	Eric Piatkowski	Nebraska
16	Golden State	Clifford Rozier	Louisville
17	Portland	Aaron McKie	Temple
18	Milwaukee	Eric Mobley	Pittsburgh
19	Dallas	Tony Dumas	Missouri-Kansas City
20	Philadelphia	B.J Tyler	Texas
21	Chicago	Dickey Simpkins	Providence
22	San Antonio	Bill Curley	Boston College
23	Phoenix	Wesley Person	Auburn
24	New York	Monty Williams	Notre Dame
25	LA Clippers	Greg Minor	Louisville
26	New York	Charlie Ward	Florida State
27	Orlando	Brooks Thompson	Oklahoma State

Second Round

28	Dallas	Deon Thomas	Illinois
29	Phoenix	Antonio Lang	Duke
30	Minnesota	Howard Eisley	Boston College
31	Orlando	Rodney Dent	Kentucky
32	Washington	Jim McIlvaine	Marquette
33	Philadelphia	Derrick Alston	Duquesne
34	Atlanta	Gaylon Nickerson	NW Oklahoma State
35	Sacramento	Michael Smith	Providence
36	Boston	Andrei Fetisov	Russia
37	Seattle	Dontonio Wingfield	Cincinnati
38	Charlotte	Darrin Hancock	Kansas
39	Golden State	Anthony Miller	Michigan State
40	Miami	Jeff Webster	Oklahoma
41	Indiana	William Njoku	St Mary's (Canada)
42	Cleveland	Gary Collier	Tulsa
43	Portland	Shawnelle Scott	St John's
44	Indiana	Damon Bailey	Indiana
45	Golden State	Dwayne Morton	Louisville
46	Milwaukee	Voshon Lenard	Minnesota
47	Utah	Jamie Watson	South Carolina
48	Detroit	Jevon Crudup	Missouri
49	Chicago	Kris Bruton	Benedict (SC)
50	Phoenix	Charles Claxton	Georgia
51	Sacramento	Lawrence Funderburke	Ohio St
52	Phoenix	Anthony Goldwire	Houston
53	Houston	Albert Burditt	Texas
54	Seattle	Zelko Rebraca	Belgrade (Yugoslavia)

1993
First Round

1	Orlando	Chris Webber	Michigan
2	Philadelphia	Shawn Bradley	Brigham Young
3	Golden State	Anfernee Hardaway	Memphis State
4	Dallas	Jamal Mashburn	Kentucky
5	Minnesota	Isaiah Rider	Nevada-Las Vegas
6	Washington	Calbert Cheaney	Indiana
7	Sacramento	Bobby Hurley	Duke
8	Milwaukee	Vin Baker	Hartford
9	Denver	Rodney Rogers	Wake Forest
10	Detroit	Lindsey Hunter	Jackson State
11	Detroit	Allan Houston	Tennessee
12	LA Lakers	George Lynch	North Carolina
13	LA Clippers	Terry Dehere	Seton Hall
14	Indiana	Scott Haskin	Oregon State
15	Atlanta	Doug Edwards	Florida State
16	New Jersey	Rex Walters	Kansas
17	Charlotte	Greg Graham	Indiana
18	Utah	Luther Wright	Seton Hall

19	Boston	Acie Earl	Iowa
20	Charlotte	Scott Burrell	Connecticut
21	Portland	James Robinson	Alabama
22	Cleveland	Chris Mills	Arizona
23	Seattle	Ervin Johnson	New Orleans
24	Houston	Sam Cassell	Florida State
25	Chicago	Corie Blount	Cincinnati
26	Orlando	Geert Hammink	Louisiana State
27	Phoenix	Malcolm Mackey	Georgia Tech

Second Round

28	Dallas	Lucious Harris	Long Beach State
29	Minnesota	Sherron Mills	Virginia Commonwealth
30	Washington	Gheorghe Muresan	Pau Orthez, France
31	Sacramento	Evers Burns	Maryland
32	Philadelphia	Alphonso Ford	Mississippi Valley State
33	Dallas	Eric Riley	Michigan
34	Golden State	Darnell Mee	Western Kentucky
35	Miami	Ed Stokes	Arizona
36	New Jersey	John Best	Tennessee Tech
37	LA Lakers	Nick Van Exel	Cincinnati
38	Washington	Conrad McRae	Syracuse
39	Indiana	Thomas Hill	Duke
40	Atlanta	Richard Manning	Washington
41	Chicago	Anthony Reed	Tulane
42	Seattle	Adonis Jordan	Kansas
43	Denver	Josh Grant	Utah
44	Sacramento	Alex Holcombe	Baylor
45	Utah	Bryon Russell	Long Beach State
46	Houston	Richard Petruska	UCLA
47	San Antonio	Chris Whitney	Clemson
48	Portland	Kevin Thompson	North Carolina State
49	Phoenix	Mark Buford	Mississippi Valley State
50	Houston	Marcelo Nicola	Argentina
51	Indiana	Spencer Dunkley	Delaware
52	Sacramento	Mike Peplowski	Michigan State
53	LA Clippers	Leonard White	Southern
54	Phoenix	Byron Wilson	Utah

1992

First Round

1	Orlando	Shaquille O'Neal	Louisiana State
2	Charlotte	Alonzo Mourning	Georgetown
3	Minnesota	Christian Laettner	Duke
4	Dallas	Jimmy Jackson	Ohio State
5	Denver	LaPhonso Ellis	Notre Dame
6	Washington	Tom Gugliotta	North Carolina State
7	Sacramento	Walt Williams	Maryland
8	Milwaukee	Todd Day	Arkansas
9	Philadelphia	Clarence Weatherspoon	Southern Mississippi
10	Atlanta	Adam Keefe	Stanford
11	Houston	Robert Horry	Alabama
12	Miami	Harold Miner	USC
13	Denver	Bryant Stith	Virginia
14	Indiana	Malik Sealy	St. John's
15	LA Lakers	Anthony Peeler	Missouri
16	LA Clippers	Randy Woods	La Salle
17	Seattle	Doug Christie	Pepperdine
18	San Antonio	Tracy Murray	UCLA
19	Detroit	Don MacLean	UCLA
20	New York	Hubert Davis	North Carolina
21	Boston	Jon Barry	Georgia Tech
22	Phoenix	Oliver Miller	Arkansas
23	Milwaukee	Lee Mayberry	Arkansas
24	Golden State	Latrell Sprewell	Alabama
25	LA Clippers	Elmore Spencer	Nevada-Las Vegas
26	Portland	David Johnson	Syracuse
27	Chicago	Byron Houston	Oklahoma State

Second Round

28	Minnesota	Marlon Maxey	Texas-El Paso
29	New Jersey	P. J. Brown	Louisiana Tech
30	Dallas	Sean Rooks	Arizona
31	Portland	Reggie Smith	Texas Christian
32	Washington	Brent Price	Oklahoma
33	Chicago	Corey Williams	Oklahoma State
34	Minnesota	Chris Smith	Connecticut
35	Charlotte	Tony Bennett	Wisconsin-Green Bay
36	LA Lakers	Duane Cooper	USC
37	Miami	Isaiah Morris	Arkansas
38	Atlanta	Elmer Bennett	Notre Dame
39	Chicago	Litterial Green	Georgia
40	New Jersey	Steve Rogers	Alabama State
41	Houston	Ronald Jones	Murray State
42	Miami	Matt Geiger	Georgia Tech
43	Golden State	Predrag Danilovic	Partizan
44	San Antonio	Henry Williams	North Carolina-Charlotte
45	Seattle	Chris King	Wake Forest

46	Denver	Robert Verdann	St. John's
47	Boston	Darren Morningstar	Pittsburgh
48	Phoenix	Brian Davis	Duke
49	Phoenix	Ron Ellis	Louisiana Tech
50	Golden State	Matt Fish	North Carolina-Wilmington
51	Minnesota	Tim Burroughs	Jacksonville
52	Chicago	Matt Steigenga	Michigan State
53	Houston	Curtus Blair	Richmond
54	Sacramento	Brett Roberts	Morehead State

1991

First Round

1	Charlotte	Larry Johnson	Nevada-Las Vegas
2	New Jersey	Kenny Anderson	Georgia Tech
3	Sacramento	Billy Owens	Syracuse
4	Denver	Dikembe Mutombo	Georgetown
5	Miami	Steve Smith	Michigan State
6	Dallas	Doug Smith	Missouri
7	Minnesota	Luc Longley	New Mexico
8	Denver	Mark Macon	Temple
9	Atlanta	Stacey Augmon	Nevada-Las Vegas
10	Orlando	Brian Williams	Arizona
11	Cleveland	Terrell Brandon	Oregon
12	New York	Greg Anthony	Nevada-Las Vegas
13	Indiana	Dale Davis	Clemson
14	Seattle	Rich King	Nebraska
15	Atlanta	Anthony Avent	Seton Hall
16	Golden State	Chris Gatling	Old Dominion
17	Golden State	Victor Alexander	Iowa State
18	Milwaukee	Kevin Brooks	SW Louisiana
19	Washington	LaBradford Smith	Louisville
20	Houston	John Turner	Phillips
21	Utah	Eric Murdock	Providence
22	LA Clippers	LeRon Ellis	Syracuse
23	Orlando	Stanley Roberts	Louisiana State
24	Boston	Rick Fox	North Carolina
25	Golden State	Shaun Vandiver	Colorado
26	Chicago	Mark Randall	Kansas
27	Sacramento	Pete Chilcutt	North Carolina

Second Round

28	Charlotte	Kevin Lynch	Minnesota
29	Miami	George Ackles	Nevada-Las Vegas
30	Atlanta	Rodney Monroe	North Carolina State
31	Sacramento	Randy Brown	New Mexico State
32	Phoenix	Chad Gallagher	Creighton
33	Dallas	Donald Hodge	Temple
34	Minnesota	Myron Brown	Slippery Rock
35	Dallas	Mike Iuzzolino	St. Francis (PA)
36	Orlando	Chris Corchiani	North Carolina State
37	LA Clippers	Elliot Perry	Memphis State
38	LA Clippers	Joe Wylie	Miami (FL)
39	Cleveland	Jimmy Oliver	Purdue
40	Detroit	Doug Overton	La Salle
41	Indiana	Sean Green	Iona
42	Sacramento	Steve Hood	James Madison
43	Golden State	Lamont Strothers	Christopher Newport
44	Philadelphia	Alvaro Teheran	Houston
45	Milwaukee	Bobby Phills	Southern
46	Phoenix	Richard Dumas	Oklahoma State
47	Houston	Keith Hughes	Rutgers
48	Utah	Isaac Austin	Arizona State
49	San Antonio	Greg Sutton	Oral Roberts
50	Phoenix	Joey Wright	Texas
51	Houston	Zan Tabak	Yugoslavia
52	LA Lakers	Anthony Jones	Oral Roberts
53	New Jersey	Von McDade	Wisconsin-Milwaukee
54	Portland	Marcus Kennedy	Eastern Michigan

1990

First Round

1	New Jersey	Derrick Coleman	Syracuse
2	Seattle	Gary Payton	Oregon State
3	Denver	Chris Jackson	Louisiana State
4	Orlando	Dennis Scott	Georgia Tech
5	Charlotte	Kendall Gill	Illinois
6	Minnesota	Felton Spencer	Louisville
7	Sacramento	Lionel Simmons	La Salle
8	LA Clippers	Bo Kimble	Loyola Marymount
9	Miami	Willie Burton	Minnesota
10	Atlanta	Rumeal Robinson	Michigan
11	Golden State	Tyrone Hill	Xavier (OH)
12	Houston	Alec Kessler	Georgia
13	LA Clippers	Loy Vaught	Michigan
14	Sacramento	Travis Mays	Texas
15	Miami	Dave Jamerson	Ohio

16	Milwaukee	Terry Mills	Michigan
17	New York	Jerrod Mustaf	Maryland
18	Sacramento	Duane Causwell	Temple
19	Boston	Dee Brown	Jacksonville
20	Minnesota	Gerald Glass	Mississippi
21	Phoenix	Jayson Williams	St. John's
22	New Jersey	Tate George	Connecticut
23	Sacramento	Anthony Bonner	St. Louis
24	San Antonio	Dwayne Schintzius	Florida
25	Portland	Alaa Abdelnaby	Duke
26	Detroit	Lance Banks	Texas
27	LA Lakers	Elden Campbell	Clemson

Second Round

28	Golden State	Les Jepsen	Clemson
29	Chicago	Toni Kukoc	Iowa
30	Miami	Carl Herrera	Houston
31	Phoenix	Negele Knight	Houston
32	Philadelphia	Brian Oliver	Dayton
33	Utah	Walter Palmer	Georgia Tech
34	Golden State	Kevin Pritchard	Dartmouth
35	Washington	Greg Foster	Kansas
36	Atlanta	Trevor Wilson	UTEP
37	Washington	A.J. English	UCLA
38	Seattle	Jud Buechler	Virginia Union
39	Charlotte	Steve Scheffler	Arizona
40	Sacramento	Bimbo Coles	Purdue
41	Atlanta	Steve Bardo	Illinois
42	Denver	Marcus Liberty	Illinois
43	San Antonio	Tony Massenburg	Maryland
44	Milwaukee	Steve Henson	Kansas State
45	Indiana	Antonio Davis	Texas-El Paso
46	Indiana	Kenny Williams	Elizabeth City State
47	Philadelphia	Derek Strong	Xavier (OH)
48	Phoenix	Cedric Ceballos	Cal State-Fullerton
49	Dallas	Phil Henderson	Duke
50	Phoenix	Milos Babic	Tennessee Tech
51	LA Lakers	Tony Smith	Marquette
52	Cleveland	Stephano Rusconi	None (Italy)
53	Seattle	Abdul Shamsid-Deen	Providence
54	San Antonio	Sean Higgins	Michigan

1989
First Round

1	Sacramento	Pervis Ellison	Louisville
2	LA Clippers	Danny Ferry	Duke
3	San Antonio	Sean Elliott	Arizona
4	Miami	Glen Rice	Michigan
5	Charlotte	J.R. Reid	North Carolina
6	Chicago	Stacey King	Oklahoma
7	Indiana	George McCloud	Florida State
8	Dallas	Randy White	Louisiana Tech
9	Washington	Tom Hammonds	Georgia Tech
10	Minnesota	Pooh Richardson	UCLA
11	Orlando	Nick Anderson	Illinois
12	New Jersey	Mookie Blaylock	Oklahoma
13	Boston	Michael Smith	Brigham Young
14	Golden State	Tim Hardaway	Texas-El Paso
15	Denver	Todd Lichti	Stanford
16	Seattle	Dana Barros	Boston College
17	Seattle	Shawn Kemp	Trinity Valley
18	Chicago	B.J. Armstrong	Iowa
19	Philadelphia	Kenny Payne	Louisville
20	Chicago	Jeff Sanders	Georgia Southern
21	Utah	Blue Edwards	East Carolina
22	Portland	Byron Irvin	Missouri
23	Atlanta	Roy Marble	Iowa
24	Phoenix	Anthony Cook	Arizona
25	Cleveland	John Morton	Seton Hall
26	LA Lakers	Vlade Divac	None (Yugoslavia)
27	Detroit	Kenny Battle	Illinois

Second Round

28	Miami	Sherman Douglas	Syracuse
29	Charlotte	Dyron Nix	Tennessee
30	Milwaukee	Frank Kornet	Vanderbilt
31	LA Clippers	Jeff Martin	Murray State
32	New Jersey	Stanley Brundy	DePaul
33	LA Clippers	Jay Edwards	Indiana
34	Minnesota	Gary Leonard	Missouri
35	Dallas	Pat Durham	Colorado State
36	Portland	Cliff Robinson	Connecticut
37	Orlando	Michael Ansley	Alabama
38	Minnesota	Doug West	Villanova
39	Washington	Ed Horton	Iowa
40	Boston	Dino Radja	Virtus Roma, Yugoslavia
41	Washington	Doug Roth	Tennessee
42	Denver	Michael Cutright	McNeese State

43	Cleveland	Chucky Brown	North Carolina State
44	Philadelphia	Reggie Cross	Hawaii
45	Miami	Scott Haffner	Evansville
46	Phoenix	Ricky Blanton	Louisiana State
47	Denver	Reggie Turner	Alabama-Birmingham
48	Utah	Junie Lewis	South Alabama
49	Atlanta	Haywoode Workman	Oral Roberts
50	New York	Brian Quinnett	Washington State
51	Phoenix	Mike Morrison	Loyola (MD)
52	Phoenix	Greg Grant	Trenton State
53	Dallas	Jeff Hodge	South Alabama
54	Philadelphia	Toney Mack	Georgia

NBA drafts held between 1957 and 1988 consisted of anywhere from three to 21 rounds; results of the first two rounds plus territorial picks are represented below.

1988
First Round
1. LAC, Danny Manning, Kansas; 2. Ind, Rik Smits, Marist; 3. Phil, Charles Smith, Pittsburgh; 4. NJ, Chris Morris, Auburn; 5. GS, Mitch Richmond, Kansas State; 6. LAC, Hersey Hawkins, Bradley; 7. Phoe, Tim Perry, Temple; 8. Char, Rex Chapman, Kentucky; 9. Mia, Rony Seikaly, Syracuse; 10. SA, Willie Anderson, Georgia; 11. Chi, Will Perdue, Vanderbilt; 12. Wash, Harvey Grant, Oklahoma; 13. Mil, Jeff Grayer, Iowa State; 14. Phoe, Dan Majerle, Central Michigan; 15. Sea, Gary Grant, Michigan; 16. Hous, Derrick Chievous, Missouri; 17. Utah, Eric Leckner, Wyoming; 18. Sac, Rick Berry, San Jose State; 19. NY, Rod Strickland, DePaul; 20. Mia, Kevin Edwards, DePaul; 21. Port, Mark Bryant, Seton Hall; 22. Clev, Randolph Keys, Southern Mississippi; 23. Den, Jerome Lane, Pittsburgh; 24. Bos, Brian Shaw, UC Santa Barbara; 25. LAL, David Rivers, Notre Dame.

Second Round
1. Port, Rolando Ferreira, Houston; 2. SA, Shelton Jones, St. John's; 3. Phoe, Andrew Lang, Arkansas; 4. Sac, Vinny Del Negro, North Carolina State; 5. Det, Fennis Dembo, Wyoming; 6. Phil, Everette Stephens, Purdue; 7. NJ, Charles Shackleford, North Carolina State; 8. Mia, Grant Long, Eastern Michigan; 9. Char, Tom Tolbert, Arizona; 10. Mia, Sylvester Gray, Memphis State; 11. Wash, Ledell Eackles, New Orleans; 12. NY, Greg Butler, Stanford; 13. Phoe, Dean Garrett, Indiana; 14. Mil, Tito Horford, Miami (FL); 15. Mia, Orlando Graham, Auburn; 16. GS, Keith Smart, Indiana; 17. Utah, Jeff Moe, Iowa; 18. Den, Todd Mitchell, Purdue; 19. Atl, Anthony Taylor, Oregon; 20. LAC, Tom Garrick, Rhode Island; 21. Dall, Morlon Wiley, Long Beach State; 22. Den, Vernon Maxwell, Florida; 23. Det, Micheal Williams, Baylor; 24. Dall, Jose Vargas, Louisiana State; 25. Phoe, Steve Kerr, Arizona.

1987
First Round
1. SA, David Robinson, Navy; 2. Phoe, Armon Gilliam, Nevada-Las Vegas; 3. NJ, Dennis Hopson, Ohio State; 4. LAC, Reggie Williams, Georgetown; 5. Sea, Scottie Pippen, Central Arkansas; 6. Sac, Kenny Smith, North Carolina; 7. Clev, Kevin Johnson, California; 8. Chi, Olden Polynice, Virginia; 9. Sea, Derrick McKey, Alabama; 10. Chi, Horace Grant, Clemson; 11. Ind, Reggie Miller, UCLA; 12. Wash, Tyrone Bogues, Wake Forest; 13. LAC, Joe Wolf, North Carolina; 14. GS, Tellis Frank, Western Kentucky; 15. Utah, Jose Ortiz, Oregon State; 16. Phil, Christian Welp, Washington; 17. Port, Ronnie Murphy, Jacksonville; 18. NY, Mark Jackson, St. John's; 19. LAC, Ken Norman, Illinois; 20. Dall, Jim Farmer, Alabama; 21. Atl, Dallas Comegys, DePaul; 22. Bos, Reggie Lewis, Northeastern; 23. SA, Greg Anderson, Houston.

Second Round
1. Det, Fred Banks, Nevada-Las Vegas; 2. NY, Ron Moore, West Virginia State; 3. Dall, Steve Alford, Indiana; 4. SA, Nate Blackwell, Temple; 5. Chi, Rickie Winslow, Houston; 6. Port, Lester Fonville, Jackson State; 7. NJ, Nikita Wilson, Louisiana State; 8. Den, Andre Moore, Loyola (IL); 9. Mil, Bob McCann, Morehead State; 10. Chi, Tony White, Tennessee; 11. Ind, Brian Rowsom, North Carolina-Wilmington; 12. Hous, Doug Lee, Purdue; 13. Wash, Duane Washington, Middle Tennessee State; 14. Wash, Derrick Dowell, USC; 15. LAC, Norris Coleman, Kansas State; 16. Phil, Vincent Askew, Memphis State; 17. Mil, Winston Garland, SW Missouri State; 18. Clev, Kannard Johnson, Western Kentucky; 19. Atl, Terence Bailey, Wagner; 20. Phil, Andrew Kennedy, Virginia; 21. Atl, Terry Coner, Alabama; 22. Bos, Brad Lohaus, Iowa; 23. Phoe, Bruce Dalrymple, Georgia Tech.

1986
First Round
1. Clev, Brad Daugherty, North Carolina; 2. Bos, Len Bias, Maryland; 3. GS, Chris Washburn, North Carolina State; 4. Ind, Chuck Person, Auburn; 5. NY, Kenny Walker, Kentucky; 6. Phoe, William Bedford, Memphis State; 7. Dall, Roy Tarpley, Michigan; 8. Clev, Ron Harper, Miami (OH); 9. Chi, Brad Sellers, Ohio State; 10. SA, Johnny Dawkins, Duke; 11. Det, John Salley, Georgia Tech; 12. Wash, John Williams, Louisiana State; 13. NJ, Dwayne Washington, Syracuse; 14. Port, Walter Berry, St. John's; 15. Utah, Dell Curry, Virginia Tech; 16. Den, Mo Martin, St. Joseph's; 17. Sac, Harold Pressley, Villanova; 18. Den, Mark Alarie, Duke; 19. Atl, Billy Thompson, Louisville; 20. Hous, Buck Johnson, Alabama; 21. Wash, Anthony Jones, Nevada-Las Vegas; 22. Mil, Scott Skiles, Michigan State; 23. LAL, Ken Barlow, Notre Dame; 24. Port, Arvidas Sabonis, None (Soviet Union).

Second Round
1. Dall, Mark Price, Georgia Tech; 2. Ind, Greg Dreiling, Kansas; 3. Det, Dennis

Rodman, SE Oklahoma State; 4. Chi, Larry Krystkowiak, Montana; 5. Clev, Johnny Newman, Richmond; 6. Sea, Nate McMillan, North Carolina State; 7. Phoe, Joe Ward, Georgia; 8. Atl, Cedric Henderson, Georgia; 9. SA, Kevin Duckworth, Eastern Illinois; 10. Sac, Johnny Rogers, California-Irvine; 11. Dall, Milt Wagner, Louisville; 12. Wash, Steve Mitchell, Alabama-Birmingham; 13. Port, Parragiotis Fasoulas, North Carolina State; 14. Sea, Lemone Lampley, DePaul; 15. Phoe, Rafael Addison, Syracuse; 16. Atl, Augusto Binelli, None (Italy); 17. Den, Otis Smith, Jacksonville; 18. Atl, Ron Kellogg, Kansas; 19. Hous, Dave Feitl, Texas-El Paso; 20. Phil, David Wingate, Georgetown; 21. Mil, Keith Smith, Loyola Marymount; 22. Phoe, Jeff Hornacek, Iowa State; 23. NY, Michael Jackson, Georgetown.

1985

First Round

1. NY, Patrick Ewing, Georgetown; 2. Ind, Wayman Tisdale, Oklahoma; 3. LAC, Benoit Benjamin, Creighton; 4. Sea, Xavier McDaniel, Wichita State; 5. Atl, Jon Koncak, Southern Methodist; 6. Sac, Joe Kleine, Arkansas; 7. GS, Chris Mullin, St. John's; 8. Dall, Detlef Schrempf, Washington; 9. Clev, Charles Oakley, Virginia Union; 10. Phoe, Ed Pinckney, Villanova; 11. Chi, Keith Lee, Memphis State; 12. Wash, Kenny Green, Wake Forest; 13. Utah, Karl Malone, Louisiana Tech; 14. SA, Alfredrick Hughes, Loyola (IL); 15. Den, Blair Rasmussen, Oregon; 16. Dall, Bill Wennington, St. John's; 17. Dall, Uwe Blab, Indiana; 18. Det, Joe Dumars, McNeese State; 19. Hous, Steve Harris, Tulsa; 20. Bos, Sam Vincent, Michigan State; 21. Phil, Terry Catledge, South Alabama; 22. Mil, Jerry Reynolds, Louisiana State; 23. LAL, A.C. Green, Oregon State; 24. Port, Terry Porter, Wisconsin-Stevens Point.

Second Round

1. Port, Mike Smrek, Canisius; 2. Ind, Bill Martin, Georgetown; 3. Ind, Dwayne McClain, Villanova; 4. Chi, Ken Johnson, Michigan State; 5. SA, Mike Brittain, South Carolina; 6. Clev, Calvin Duncan, Virginia Commonwealth; 7. Wash, Manute Bol, Bridgeport; 8. Phoe, Nick Vanos, Santa Clara; 9. Phil, Greg Stokes, Iowa; 10. Chi, Aubrey Sherrod, Wichita State; 11. SA, Tyrone Corbin, DePaul; 12. NJ, Yvon Joseph, Georgia Tech; 13. Utah, Carey Scurry, Long Island; 14. NJ, Fernando Martin, Madrid (Spain); 15. Port, George Montgomery, Illinois; 16. Dall, Mark Acres, Oral Roberts; 17. Atl, Lorenzo Charles, North Carolina State; 18. GS, Bobby Lee Hurt, Alabama; 19. Den, Barry Stevens, Iowa State; 20. Phil, Voise Winters, Bradley; 21. Clev, John Williams, Tulane; 22. Chi, Adrian Branch, Maryland; 23. NY, Gerald Wilkins, Tennessee-Chattanooga.

1984

First Round

1. Hous, Akeem Olajuwon, Houston; 2. Port, Sam Bowie, Kentucky; 3. Chi, Michael Jordan, North Carolina; 4. Dall, Sam Perkins, North Carolina; 5. Phil, Charles Barkley, Auburn; 6. Wash, Mel Turpin, Kentucky; 7. SA, Alvin Robertson, Arkansas; 8. LAC, Lancaster Gordon, Louisville; 9. KC, Otis Thorpe, Providence; 10. Phil, Leon Wood, Cal State-Fullerton; 11. Atl, Kevin Willis, Michigan State; 12. Clev, Tim McCormick, Michigan; 13. Phoe, Jay Humphries, Colorado; 14. LAC, Michael Cage, San Diego State; 15. Dall, Terence Stansbury, Temple; 16. Utah, John Stockton, Gonzaga; 17. NJ, Jeff Turner, Vanderbilt; 18. Ind, Vern Fleming, Georgia; 19. Port, Bernard Thompson, Fresno State; 20. Det, Tony Campbell, Ohio State; 21. Mil, Kenny Fields, UCLA; 22. Phil, Tom Sewell, Lamar; 23. LAL, Earl Jones, District of Columbia; 24. Bos, Michael Young, Houston.

Second Round

1. Ind, Devin Durrant, Brigham Young; 2. Port, Victor Fleming, Xavier (OH); 3. Clev, Ron Anderson, Fresno State; 4. Sea, Cory Blackwell, Wisconsin; 5. Ind, Stuart Gray, UCLA; 6. GS, Steve Burtt, Iona; 7. GS, Jay Murphy, Boston College; 8. Det, Eric Turner, Michigan; 9. Port, Steve Colter, New Mexico State; 10. Wash, Tony Costner, St. Joseph's; 11. GS, Othell Wilson, Virginia; 12. Phoe, Charles Jones, Louisville; 13. Chi, Ben Coleman, Maryland; 14. Dall, Charles Sitton, Oregon State; 15. Sea, Danny Young, Wake Forest; 16. Dall, Anthony Teachey, Wake Forest; 17. Dall, Tom Sluby, Notre Dame; 18. Den, Willie White, Tennessee-Chattanooga; 19. Chi, Greg Wiltjer, Victoria (Canada); 20. Wash, Fred Raynolds, Texas-El Paso; 21. GS, Gary Plummer, Boston U; 22. Port, Jerome Kersey, Longwood (VA); 23. Bos, Ronnie Williams, Florida.

1983

First Round

1. Hous, Ralph Sampson, Virginia; 2. Ind, Steve Stipanovich, Missouri; 3. Hous, Rodney McCray, Louisville; 4. SD, Byron Scott, Arizona State; 5. Chi, Sidney Green, Nevada-Las Vegas; 6. GS, Russell Cross, Purdue; 7. Utah, Thurl Bailey, North Carolina State; 8. Det, Antoine Carr, Wichita State; 9. Dall, Dale Ellis, Tennessee; 10. Wash, Jeff Malone, Mississippi State; 11. Dall, Derek Harper, Illinois; 12. NY, Darrell Walker, Arkansas; 13. KC, Ennis Whatley, Alabama; 14. Port, Clyde Drexler, Houston; 15. Den, Howard Carter, Louisiana State; 16. Sea, Jon Sundvold, Missouri; 17. Phil, Leo Rautins, Syracuse; 18. Mil, Randy Breuer, Minnesota; 19. SA, John Paxson, Notre Dame; 20. Clev, Roy Hinson, Rutgers; 21. Bos, Greg Kite, Brigham Young; 22. Wash, Randy Wittman, Indiana; 23. Ind, Mitchell Wiggins, Florida State; 24. Clev, Stewart Granger, Villanova.

Second Round

1. Chi, Sidney Lowe, North Carolina State; 2. Ind, Leroy Combs, Oklahoma State; 3. Clev, John Garris, Boston College; 4. Phoe, Rod Foster, UCLA; 5. Chi, Larry Micheaux, Houston; 6. Dall, Mark West, Old Dominion; 7. Atl, James Banks, Georgetown; 8. Wash, Michael Britt, District of Columbia; 9. Dall, Dirk Minniefield, Kentucky; 10. Wash, Guy Williams, Washington State; 11. SA, Darrell Lockhart,

Auburn; 12. Sea, Scooter McCray, Louisville; 13. Den, David Russell, St. John's; 14. KC, Chris McNealy, San Jose State; 15. Port, Granville Waiters, Ohio State; 16. Ind, James Thomas, Indiana; 17. Mil, Ted Kitchel, Indiana; 18. Mil, Mike Davis, Alabama; 19. GS, Pace Mannion, Utah; 20. NJ, Horace Owens, Rhode Island; 21. Phoe, Paul Williams, Arizona State; 22. SA, Kevin Williams, St. John's; 23. Phil, Ken Lyons, North Texas State.

1982

First Round

1. LAL, James Worthy, North Carolina; 2. SD, Terry Cummings, DePaul; 3. Utah, Dominique Wilkins, Georgia; 4. Dall, Bill Garnett, Wyoming; 5. KC, LaSalle Thompson, Texas; 6. NY, Trent Tucker, Minnesota; 7. Chi, Quintin Dailey, San Francisco; 8. Ind, Clark Kellogg, Ohio State; 9. Det, Cliff Levingston, Wichita State; 10. Atl, Keith Edmonson, Purdue; 11. Port, Lafayette Lever, Arizona State; 12. Clev, John Bagley, Boston College; 13. NJ, Eric Floyd, Georgetown; 14. GS, Lester Conner, Oregon State; 15. Phoe, David Thirdkill, Bradley; 16. Hous, Terry Teagle, Baylor; 17. KC, Brook Steppe, Georgia Tech; 18. Det, Ricky Pierce, Rice; 19. Den, Rob Williams, Houston; 20. Mil, Paul Pressey, Tulsa; 21. NJ, Eddie Phillips, Alabama; 22. Phil, Mark McNamara, California; 23. Bos, Darren Tillis, Cleveland State.

Second Round

1. SA, Oliver Robinson, Alabama-Birmingham; 2. Wash, Bryan Warrick, St. Joseph's; 3. Chi, Ricky Frazier, Missouri; 4. Mil, Fred Roberts, Brigham Young; 5. Clev, David Magley, Kansas; 6. NY, Scott Hastings, Arkansas; 7. Chi, Wallace Bryant, San Francisco; 8. Chi, Rod Higgins, Fresno State; 9. SD, Richard Anderson, UC Santa Barbara; 10. Port, Linton Townes, James Madison; 11. NY, Vince Taylor, Duke; 12. GS, Derek Smith, Louisville; 13. Phil, Mitchell Anderson, Bradley; 14. Port, Audie Norris, Jackson State; 15. GS, Wayne Sappleton, Loyola (IL); 16. Phoe, Kevin Magee, California-Irvine; 17. Ind, Guy Morgan, Wake Forest; 18. Wash, Dwight Anderson, USC; 19. Hous, Jeff Taylor, Texas Tech; 20. Ind, Jose Slaughter, Portland; 21. Wash, Mike Gibson, S. Carolina-Spartanburg; 22. Phil, Russ Schoene, Tennessee-Chattanooga; 23. Bos, Tony Guy, Kansas.

1981

First Round

1. Dall, Mark Aguirre, DePaul; 2. Det, Isiah Thomas, Indiana; 3. NJ, Buck Williams, Maryland; 4. Atl, Al Wood, North Carolina; 5. Sea, Danny Vranes, Utah; 6. Chi, Orlando Woolridge, Notre Dame; 7. KC, Steve Johnson, Oregon State; 8. SD, Tom Chambers, Utah; 9. Dall, Rolando Blackman, Kansas; 10. NJ, Albert King, Maryland; 11. Wash, Frank Johnson, Wake Forest; 12. Det, Kelly Tripucka, Notre Dame; 13. Utah, Danny Schayes, Syracuse; 14. Ind, Herb Williams, Ohio State; 15. Port, Jeff Lamp, Virginia; 16. Port, Darnell Valentine, Kansas; 17. KC, Kevin Loder, Alabama State; 18. NJ, Ray Tolbert, Indiana; 19. LAL, Mike McGee, Michigan; 20. Phoe, Larry Nance, Clemson; 21. Mil, Alton Lister, Arizona State; 22. Phil, Franklin Edwards, Cleveland State; 23. Bos, Charles Bradley, Wyoming.

Second Round

1. Dall, Jay Vincent, Michigan State; 2. Bos, Tracy Jackson, Notre Dame; 3. Port, Brian Jackson, Utah State; 4. Utah, Howard Wood, Tennessee; 5. SA, Gene Banks, Duke; 6. KC, Eddie Johnson, Illinois; 7. SA, Ed Rains, South Alabama; 8. Bos, Danny Ainge, Brigham Young; 9. Chi, Mike Olliver, Lamar; 10. GS, Sam Williams, Arizona State; 11. Den, Kenneth Green, Pan American; 12. Wash, Charles Davis, Vanderbilt; 13. Ind, Ray Blume, Oregon State; 14. Ind, Al Leslie, Bucknell; 15. Atl, Clyde Bradshaw, DePaul; 16. LAL, Harvey Knuckles, Toledo; 17. NY, Greg Cook, Louisiana State; 18. Wash, Claude Gregory, Wisconsin; 19. LAL, Elvis Rolle, Florida State; 20. Dall, Elston Turner, Mississippi; 21. Wash, Steve Lingenfelter, South Dakota State; 22. Hous, Ed Turner, Texas A&I; 23. Phil, Vernon Smith, Texas A&M.

1980

First Round

1. GS, Joe Barry Carroll, Purdue; 2. Utah, Darrell Griffith, Louisville; 3. Bos, Kevin McHale, Minnesota; 4. Chi, Kelvin Ransey, Ohio State; 5. Den, James Ray, Jacksonville; 6. NJ, Mike O'Koren, North Carolina; 7. NJ, Mike Gminski, Duke; 8. Phil, Andrew Toney, SW Louisiana; 9. SD, Michael Brooks, La Salle; 10. Port, Ronnie Lester, Iowa; 11. Dall, Kiki Vandeweghe, UCLA; 12. NY, Mike Woodson, Indiana; 13. GS, Rickey Brown, Mississippi State; 14. Wash, Wes Matthews, Wisconsin; 15. SA, Reggie Johnson, Tennessee; 16. KC, Hawkeye Whitney, North Carolina State; 17. Det, Larry Drew, Missouri; 18. Atl, Don Collins, Washington State; 19. Utah, John Duren, Georgetown; 20. Sea, Bill Hanzlik, Notre Dame; 21. Phil, Monti Davis, Tennessee State; 22. Clev, Chad Kinch, North Carolina-Charlotte; 23. Den, Carl Nicks, Indiana State.

Second Round

1. GS, Larry Smith, Alcorn State; 2. GS, Jeff Ruland, Iona; 3. Chi, Sam Worthen, Marquette; 4. Hous, John Stroud, Mississippi; 5. Atl, Craig Shelton, Georgetown; 6. Ind, Louis Orr, Syracuse; 7. Ind, Kenny Natt, NE Louisiana; 8. LAL, Wayne Robinson, Virginia Tech; 9. Port, David Lawrence, McNeese State; 10. Port, Bruce Collins, Weber State; 11. Dall, Roosevelt Bouie, Syracuse; 12. Wash, Ricky Mahorn, Hampton Institute; 13. NY, DeWayne Scales, Louisiana State; 14. LAL, Butch Carter, Indiana; 15. Hous, Terry Stotts, Oklahoma; 16. SA, Michael Wiley, Long Beach State; 17. Ind, Dick Miller, Toledo; 18. Den, Jawann Oldham, Seattle; 19. Phoe, Kimberly Belton, Stanford; 20. Hous, Billy Williams, Clemson; 21. Phil, Clyde Austin, North Carolina State; 22. Det, Brad Branson, Southern Methodist; 23. Bos, Arnette Hallman, Purdue.

1979

First Round

1. LAL, Earvin Johnson, Michigan State; 2. Chi, David Greenwood, UCLA; 3. NY, Bill Cartwright, San Francisco; 4. Det, Greg Kelser, Michigan State; 5. Mil, Sidney Moncrief, Arkansas; 6. Sea, James Bailey, Rutgers; 7. Sea, Vinnie Johnson, Baylor; 8. NJ, Calvin Natt, NE Louisiana; 9. NY, Larry Demic, Arizona; 10. Det, Roy Hamilton, UCLA; 11. NJ, Cliff Robinson, USC; 12. Port, Jim Paxson, Dayton; 13. Ind, Dudley Bradley, North Carolina; 14. LAL, Brad Holland, UCLA; 15. Det, Phil Hubbard, Michigan; 16. Phil, Jim Spanarkel, Duke; 17. Hous, Lee Johnson, East Texas State; 18. KC, Reggie King, Alabama; 19. SA, Wiley Peck, Mississippi State; 20. Utah, Larry Knight, Loyola (IL); 21. NY, Sylvester Williams, Rhode Island; 22. Phoe, Kyle Macy, Kentucky.

Second Round

1. Utah, Tico Brown, Georgia Tech; 2. Phoe, Johnny High, Nevada-Reno; 3. LAL, Oliver Mack, East Carolina; 4. Clev, Bruce Flowers, Notre Dame; 5. NY, Reggie Carter, St. John's; 6. GS, Danny Salisbury, Pan American; 7. Det, Tony Price, Penn; 8. Den, Gary Garland, DePaul; 9. Mil, Edgar Jones, Nevada-Reno; 10. Ind, Tony Zeno, Arizona State; 11. Chi, Lawrence Butler, Idaho State; 12. NY, Kim Goetz, San Diego State; 13. Atl, James Bradley, Memphis State; 14. Phil, Clint Richardson, Seattle; 15. Phil, Bernard Toone, Marquette; 16. Atl, Larry Wilson, Nicholls State; 17. LAL, Victor King, Louisiana Tech; 18. Port, Andrew Fields, Cheyney State; 19. LAL, Mark Young, Fairfield; 20. Hous, Paul Mokeski, Kansas; 21. Sea, John Moore, Texas; 22. Wash, Joe DeSantis, Fairfield.

1978

First Round

1. Port, Mychal Thompson, Minnesota; 2. KC, Phil Ford, North Carolina; 3. Ind, Rick Robey, Kentucky; 4. NY, Micheal Ray Richardson, Montana; 5. GS, Purvis Short, Jackson State; 6. Bos, Larry Bird, Indiana State; 7. Port, Ron Brewer, Arkansas; 8. Bos, Freeman Williams, Portland State; 9. Chi, Reggie Theus, Nevada-Las Vegas; 10. Atl, Butch Lee, Marquette; 11. NO, James Hardy, San Francisco; 12. Mil, George Johnson, St. John's; 13. NJ, Winford Boynes, San Francisco; 14. Wash, Roger Phegley, Bradley; 15. Clev, Mike Mitchell, Auburn; 16. Atl, Jack Givens, Kentucky; 17. Den, Rod Griffin, Wake Forest; 18. Wash, Dave Corzine, DePaul; 19. Phoe, Marty Byrnes, Syracuse; 20. SA, Frank Sanders, Southern; 21. Den, Mike Evans, Kansas State; 22. GS, Ray Townsend, UCLA.

Second Round

1. Det, Terry Tyler, Detroit; 2. Port, Keith Herron, Villanova; 3. Atl, Rick Wilson, Louisville; 4. LAL, Ron Carter, Virginia Military; 5. Ind, Wayne Radford, Indiana; 6. Hous, Buster Matheney, Utah; 7. Det, John Long, Detroit; 8. Bos, Jeff Judkins, Utah; 9. Chi, Marvin Johnson, New Mexico; 10. NY, John Rudd, McNeese State; 11. Clev, Harry Davis, Florida State; 12. NY, Greg Bunch, Cal State-Fullerton; 13. NO, Tom Green, Southern; 14. Phil, Maurice Cheeks, West Texas State; 15. Wash, Terry Sykes, Grambling; 16. LAL, Lew Massey, North Carolina-Charlotte; 17. Sea, James Lee, Kentucky; 18. GS, Wayne Cooper, New Orleans; 19. Buff, Jerome Whitehead, Marquette; 20. Sea, Kevin McDonald, Penn; 21. Phil, Glenn Hagan, St. Bonaventure; 22. Port, Clemon Johnson, Florida A&M.

1977

First Round

1. Mil, Kent Benson, Indiana; 2. KC, Otis Birdsong, Houston; 3. Mil, Marques Johnson, UCLA; 4. Wash, Greg Ballard, Oregon; 5. Phoe, Walter Davis, North Carolina; 6. LAL, Kenny Carr, North Carolina St.; 7. NYN, Bernard King, Tennessee; 8. Sea, Jack Sikma, Illinois Wesleyan; 9. Den, Tom LaGarde, North Carolina; 10. NY, Ray Williams, Minnesota; 11. Mil, Ernie Grunfeld, Tennessee; 12. Bos, Cedric Maxwell, North Carolina-Charlotte; 13. Chi, Tate Armstrong, Duke; 14. Atl, Tree Rollins, Clemson; 15. LAL, Brad Davis, Maryland; 16. GS, Rickey Green, Michigan; 17. Wash, Bo Ellis, Marquette; 18. GS, Wesley Cox, Louisville; 19. Port, Rich Laurel, Hofstra; 20. Phil, Glenn Mosley, Seton Hall; 21. Den, Anthony Roberts, Oral Roberts; 22. LAL, Norm Nixon, Duquesne.

Second Round

1. Chi, Mike Glenn, Southern Illinois; 2. Buff, Larry Johnson, Kentucky; 3. Phil, Wilson Washington, Old Dominion; 4. NY, Glen Gondrezick, Nevada-Las Vegas; 5. Mil, Glenn Williams, St. John's; 6. Port, Kim Anderson, Missouri; 7. Ind, Alonzo Bradley, Texas Southern; 8. Chi, Steve Sheppard, Maryland; 9. KC, Eddie Owens, Nevada-Las Vegas; 10. NY, Toby Knight, Notre Dame; 11. Clev, Ed Jordan, Rutgers; 12. Hous, Larry Moffett, Nevada-Las Vegas; 13. Chi, Mark Landsberger, Arizona State; 14. Det, Ben Poquette, Central Michigan; 15. SA, Jeff Wilkins, Illinois State; 16. GS, Ricky Love, Alabama-Huntsville; 17. Wash, Phil Walker, Millersville; 18. Hous, Robert Reid, St. Mary's (TX); 19. Port, T.R. Dunn, Alabama; 20. Phil, Bob Elliott, Arizona; 21. Phil, Herm Harris, Arizona; 22. NO, Essie Hollis, St. Bonaventure.

1976

First Round

1. Hous, John Lucas, Maryland; 2. Chi, Scott May, Indiana; 3. KC, Richard Washington, UCLA; 4. Det, Leon Douglas, Alabama; 5. Port, Wally Walker, Virginia; 6. Buff, Adrian Dantley, Notre Dame; 7. Mil, Quinn Buckner, Indiana; 8. GS, Robert Parish, Centenary; 9. Atl, Armond Hill, Princeton; 10. Phoe, Ron Lee, Oregon; 11. Sea, Bob Wilkerson, Indiana; 12. Phil, Terry Furlow, Michigan State; 13. Wash, Mitch Kupchak, North Carolina; 14. Wash, Larry Wright, Grambling; 15. Clev, Chuckie Williams, Kansas State; 16. Bos, Norman Cook, Kansas; 17. GS, Sonny

Parker, Texas A&M.

Second Round

1. Chi, Willie Smith, Missouri; 2. Sea, Bayard Forrest, Grand Canyon; 3. Port, Major Jones, Albany State (GA); 4. LAL, Earl Tatum, Marquette; 5. Port, John Davis, Dayton; 6. Mil, Alex English, South Carolina; 7. Mil, Scott Lloyd, Arizona State; 8. NY, Lonnie Shelton, Oregon State; 9. NO, Jacky Dorsey, Georgia; 10. Hous, Phil Hicks, Tulane; 11. Atl, Bob Carrington, Boston College; 12. Sea, Dennis Johnson, Pepperdine; 13. Phoe, Al Fleming, Arizona; 14. Wash, Joe Pace, Coppin State; 15. Clev, Mo Howard, Maryland; 16. Phoe, Butch Feher, Vanderbilt; 17. GS, Marshall Rogers, Pan American.

1975

First Round

1. Atl, David Thompson, North Carolina State; 2. LAL, David Meyers, UCLA; 3. Atl, Marvin Webster, Morgan State; 4. Phoe, Alvan Adams, Oklahoma; 5. Phil, Darryl Dawkins, None; 6. Port, Lionel Hollins, Arizona State; 7. NO, Rich Kelley, Stanford; 8. LAL, Junior Bridgeman, Louisville; 9. NY, Eugene Short, Jackson State; 10. KC-O, Bill Robinzine, DePaul; 11. Hous, Joe Meriweather, Southern Illinois; 12. Sea, Frank Oleynick, Seattle; 13. KC-O, Bob Bigelow, Pennsylvania; 14. GS, Joe Bryant, La Salle; 15. Clev, John Lambert, USC; 16. Phoe, Ricky Sobers, Nevada-Las Vegas; 17. Bos, Tom Boswell, South Carolina; 18. Wash, Kevin Grevey, Kentucky.

Second Round

1. Atl, Bill Willoughby, None; 2. GS, Gus Williams, USC; 3. Sea, Bruce Seals, Xavier (LA); 4. Mil, Clyde Mayes, Furman; 5. Phil, Lloyd Free, Guilford; 6. Mil, Cornelius Cash, Bowling Green; 7. Port, Bob Gross, Long Beach State; 8. NY, Luther Burden, Utah; 9. Det, Walter Luckett, Ohio; 10. Clev, Dan Roundfield, Central Michigan; 11. Hous, Jim Blanks, Gardner-Webb; 12. Chi, Steve Green, Indiana; 13. KC-O, Glenn Hansen, Louisiana State; 14. Chi, John Laskowski, Indiana; 15. Clev, Mel Utley, St. John's; 16. NY, Larry Fogle, Canisius; 17. Phoe, Allen Murphy, Louisville; 18. Phoe, Jimmy Dan Conner, Kentucky.

1974

First Round

1. Port, Bill Walton, UCLA; 2. Phil, Marvin Barnes, Providence; 3. Sea, Tom Burleson, North Carolina State; 4. Phoe, John Shumate, Notre Dame; 5. Hous, Bobby Jones, North Carolina; 6. KC-O, Scott Wedman, Colorado; 7. Atl, Tom Henderson, Hawaii; 8. Clev, Campy Russell, Michigan; 9. Buff, Tom McMillen, Maryland; 10. Atl, Mike Sojourner, Utah; 11. GS, Keith Wilkes, UCLA; 12. LAL, Brian Winters, South Carolina; 13. Wash, Len Elmore, Maryland; 14. Chi, Maurice Lucas, Marquette; 15. Det, Al Eberhard, Missouri; 16. Chi, Cliff Pondexter, Long Beach State; 17. Bos, Glenn McDonald, Long Beach State; 18. Mil, Gary Brokaw, Notre Dame.

Second Round

1. Phil, Don Smith, Dayton; 2. Port, Jan van Breda Kolff, Vanderbilt; 3. LAL, Billy Knight, Pittsburgh; 4. Wash, Truck Robinson, Tennessee State; 5. Hous, Gus Bailey, Texas-El Paso; 6. KC-O, Len Kosmalski, Tennessee; 7. Atl, John Drew, Gardner-Webb; 8. Sea, Leonard Gray, Long Beach State; 9. Chi, Leon Benbow, Jacksonville; 10. NO, Aaron James, Grambling; 11. GS, Phil Smith, San Francisco; 12. Wash, Dennis DuVal, Syracuse; 13. Phoe, Fred Saunders, Syracuse; 14. NY, Jesse Dark, Virginia Commonwealth; 15. Det, Eric Money, Arizona; 16. Port, Phil Lumpkin, Miami (OH); 17. Bos, Kevin Stacom, Providence; 18. Port, Rubin Collins, Maryland-Eastern Shore.

1973

First Round

1. Phil, Doug Collins, Illinois State; 2. Clev, Jim Brewer, Minnesota; 3. Buff, Ernie DiGregorio, Providence; 4. Sea, Mike Green, Louisiana Tech; 5. LAL, Kermit Washington, American; 6. Hous, Ed Ratleff, Long Beach State; 7. KC-O, Ron Behagen, Minnesota; 8. Phoe, Mike Bantom, St. Joseph's; 9. Atl, Dwight Jones, Houston; 10. Atl, John Brown, Missouri; 11. GS, Kevin Joyce, South Carolina; 12. Chi, Kevin Kunnert, Iowa; 13. Cap, Nick Weatherspoon, Illinois; 14. NY, Mel Davis, St. John's; 15. Port, Barry Parkhill, Virginia; 16. Mil, Swen Nater, UCLA; 17. Bos, Steve Downing, Indiana; 18. Phil, Raymond Lewis, Cal State-Los Angeles.

Second Round

1. Cap, Louis Nelson, Washington; 2. KC-O, Mike D'Antoni, Marshall; 3. Phil, Allan Bristow, Virginia Tech; 4. Phil, George McGinnis, Indiana; 5. LAL, Bill Schaeffer, St. John's; 6. Chi, Kevin Stacom, Providence; 7. KC-O, Larry McNeill, Marquette; 8. Clev, Allan Hornyak, Ohio State; 9. Atl, Tom Ingelsby, Villanova; 10. NY, Pat McFarland, St. Joseph's; 11. GS, Derrek Dickey, Cincinnati; 12. Chi, Wendell Hudson, Alabama; 13. LAL, Jim Chones, Marquette; 14. Phil, Caldwell Jones, Albany State (GA); 15. Phoe, Gary Melchionni, Duke; 16. LAL, John Perry, Pan American; 17. Bos, Phil Hankinson, Penn.

1972

First Round

1. Port, LaRue Martin, Loyola (IL); 2. Buff, Bob McAdoo, North Carolina; 3. Clev, Dwight Davis, Houston; 4. Phoe, Corky Calhoun, Pennsylvania; 5. Phil, Fred Boyd, Oregon State; 6. Mil, Russell Lee, Marshall; 7. Sea, Bud Stallworth, Kansas; 8. NY, Tom Riker, South Carolina; 9. Det, Bob Nash, Hawaii; 10. Bos, Paul Westphal, USC; 11. Chi, Ralph Simpson, Michigan State; 12. Mil, Julius Erving, Massachusetts; 13. LAL, Travis Grant, Kentucky State.

Second Round

1. Port, Bob Davis, Weber State; 2. Buff, Harold Fox, Jacksonville; 3. LAL, Jim Price, Louisville; 4. Det, Chris Ford, Villanova; 5. Sea, Joby Wright, Indiana; 6. Cin, Sam Sibert, Kentucky State; 7. Hous, John Gianelli, Pacific; 8. Atl, Steve Bracey, Tulsa; 9. LAL, Paul Stovall, Arizona State; 10. Sea, Brian Taylor, Princeton; 11. Clev, Steve Hawes, Washington; 12. Balt, Tom Patterson, Ouachita Baptist; 13. Port, Dave Twardzik, Old Dominion; 14. Bos, Dennis Wuycik, North Carolina; 15. Cin, Mike Ratliff, Eau Claire State; 16. Mil, Chuck Terry, Long Beach State; 17. Port, Ollie Johnson, Temple.

1971

First Round

1. Clev, Austin Carr, Notre Dame; 2. Port, Sidney Wicks, UCLA; 3. Buff, Elmore Smith, Kentucky State; 4. Cin, Ken Durrett, La Salle; 5. Atl, George Trapp, Long Beach State; 6. Sea, Fred Brown, Iowa; 7. SD, Cliff Meely, Colorado; 8. SF, Darnell Hillman, San Jose State; 9. Balt, Stan Love, Oregon; 10. Bos, Clarence Glover, Western Kentucky; 11. Det, Curtis Rowe, UCLA; 12. Phil, Dana Lewis, Tulsa; 13. LAL, Jim Cleamons, Ohio State; 14. Phoe, John Roche, South Carolina; 15. Chi, Kennedy McIntosh, Eastern Michigan; 16. NY, Dean Meminger, Marquette; 17. Mil, Collis Jones, Notre Dame.

Second Round

1. Clev, Steve Patterson, UCLA; 2. Buff, Fred Hilton, Grambling; 3. Chi, Willie Sojourner, Weber State; 4. Cin, John Mengelt, Auburn; 5. Atl, Ted McClain, Tennessee State; 6. Sea, Jim McDaniels, Western Kentucky; 7. SD, Mike Newlin, Utah; 8. Port, Charles Yelverton, Fordham; 9. Buff, Amos Thomas, SW Oklahoma State; 10. Port, Rick Fisher, Colorado State; 11. Bos, Jim Rose, Western Kentucky; 12. Det, Isaiah Wilson, Baltimore; 13. Buff, Spencer Haywood, Detroit; 14. Cin, Joe Bergman, Creighton; 15. Chi, Howard Porter, Villanova; 16. Phil, Marvin Stewart, Nebraska; 17. NY, Gregg Northington, Alabama State; 18. Clev, Willie Long, New Mexico.

1970

First Round

1. Det, Bob Lanier, St. Bonaventure; 2. SD, Rudy Tomjanovich, Michigan; 3. Atl, Pete Maravich, Louisiana State; 4. Bos, Dave Cowens, Florida State; 5. Cin, Sam Lacey, New Mexico State; 6. Sea, Jim Ard, Cincinnati; 7. Clev, John Johnson, Iowa; 8. Port, Geoff Petrie, Princeton; 9. Balt, George Johnson, Stephen F. Austin; 10. Phoe, Greg Howard, New Mexico; 11. Chi, Jimmy Collins, New Mexico State; 12. Phil, Al Henry, Wisconsin; 13. LAL, Jim McMillian, Columbia; 14. Atl, John Vallely, UCLA; 15. Buff, John Hummer, Princeton; 16. Mil, Gary Freeman, Oregon State; 17. NY, Mike Price, Illinois.

Second Round

1. SD, Calvin Murphy, Niagara; 2. Cin, Nate Archibald, Texas–El Paso; 3. Sea, Jake Ford, Maryland State; 4. Bos, Rex Morgan, Jacksonville; 5. Cin, Doug Cook, Davidson; 6. Sea, Pete Cross, San Francisco; 7. Buff, Cornell Warner, Jackson State; 8. Port, Walt Gilmore, Fort Valley State; 9. Clev, Dave Sorenson, Ohio State; 10. Phoe, Fred Taylor, Pan American; 11. Chi, Paul Ruffner, Brigham Young; 12. Phoe, Joe DePre, St. John's; 13. LAL, Earnest Killum, Stetson; 14. Atl, Dan Hester, Louisiana State; 15. Det, Ken Warzynski, DePaul; 16. Mil, Bill Zopf, Duquesne; 17. NY, Howie Wright, Austin Peay.

1969

First Round

1. Mil, Lew Alcindor, UCLA; 2. Phoe, Neal Walk, Florida; 3. Sea, Lucius Allen, UCLA; 4. Det, Terry Driscoll, Boston College; 5. Chi, Larry Cannon, La Salle; 6. SD, Bobby Smith, Tulsa; 7. SF, Bob Portman, Creighton; 8. Cin, Herm Gilliam, Purdue; 9. Bos, Jo Jo White, Kansas; 10. Atl, Butch Beard, Louisville; 11. NY, John Warren, St. John's; 12. LAL, Willie McCarter, Drake; 13. Phil, Bud Ogden, Santa Clara; 14. Balt, Mike Davis, Virginia Union; 15. LAL, Rick Roberson, Cincinnati.

Second Round

1. Chi, Simmie Hill, West Texas State; 2. Mil, Bob Greacen, Rutgers; 3. Sea, Ron Taylor, USC; 4. Det, Willie Norwood, Alcorn A&M; 5. Chi, Kenny Spain, Houston; 6. SD, Bernie Williams, La Salle; 7. SF, Ed Siudet, Holy Cross; 8. Chi, John Baum, Temple; 9. Phoe, Gene Williams, Kansas State; 10. Atl, Wally Anderzunas, Creighton; 11. NY, Bill Bunting, North Carolina; 12. LAL, Dick Garrett, Southern Illinois; 13. Phil, Willie Taylor, LeMoyne; 14. Balt, Willie Scott, Alabama State.

1968

First Round

1. SD, Elvin Hayes, Houston; 2. Balt, Wes Unseld, Louisville; 3. Sea, Bob Kauffman, Guilford; 4. Chi, Tom Boerwinkle, Tennessee; 5. Cin, Don Smith, Iowa State; 6. Det, Otto Moore, Pan American; 7. Mil, Charles Paulk, NE Oklahoma; 8. Phoe, Gary Gregor, South Carolina; 9. SF, Ron Williams, West Virginia; 10. NY, Bill Hosket, Ohio State; 11. LAL, Bill Hewitt, USC; 12. Bos, Don Chaney, Houston; 13. Atl, Skip Harlicka, South Carolina; 14. Phil, Shaler Halimon, Utah State.

Second Round

1. SD, John Trapp, Nevada–Las Vegas; 2. Sea, Art Harris, Stanford; 3. Chi, Loy Petersen, Oregon State; 4. Balt, Bob Quick, Xavier (OH); 5. Chi, Ron Dunlap, Illinois; 6. Det, Manny Leaks, Niagara; 7. Phoe, Dick Cunningham, Murray State; 8. Mil, Eugene Moore, St. Louis.

1967

First Round

1. Det, Jimmy Walker, turnebil01; 2. Balt, Earl Monroe, Winston-Salem; 3. Chi, Clem Haskins, Western Kentucky; 4. Det, Sonny Dove, St. John's; 5. NY, Walt Frazier, Southern Illinois; 6. Sea, Al Tucker, Oklahoma Baptist; 7. SD, Pat Riley, Kentucky; 8. StL, Tom Workman, Seattle; 9. Cin, Mel Daniels, New Mexico; 10. SF, Dave Lattin, Texas–El Paso; 11. Bos, Mal Graham, New York University; 12. Phil, Craig Raymond, Brigham Young.

Second Round

1. Balt, James Jones, Grambling; 2. Det, Steve Sullivan, Georgetown; 3. Chi, Byron Beck, Denver; 4. LAL, Randy Mahaffey, Clemson; 5. NY, Phil Jackson, North Dakota; 6. SD, Bob Netolicky, Drake; 7. Sea, Bob Rule, Colorado State.

1966

First Round

1. NY, Cazzie Russell, Michigan; 2. Det, Dave Bing, Syracuse; 3. SF, Clyde Lee, Vanderbilt; 4. StL, Lou Hudson, Minnesota; 5. Balt, Jack Marin, Duke; 6. Cin, Walt Wesley, Kansas; 7. LAL, Jerry Chambers, Utah; 8. Bos, Jim Barnett, Oregon; 9. Phil, Matt Guokas, St. Joseph's (PA); 10. Chi, Dave Schellhase, Purdue.

Second Round

1. NY, Henry Akin, Morehead State; 2. Det, Dorie Murrey, Detroit; 3. SF, Joe Ellis, San Francisco; 4. StL, Dick Snyder, Davidson; 5. Balt, Neil Johnson, Creighton; 6. Cin, Jerry Lee Wells, Oklahoma City; 7. LAL, Henry Finkel, Dayton; 8. Bos, Leon Clark, Wyoming; 9. Phil, Bill Melchionni, Villanova; 10. Chi, Erwin Mueller, San Francisco.

1965

First Round

1. SF, Fred Hetzel, Davidson; 2. SF, Rick Barry, Miami (FL); 3. NY, Dave Stallworth, Wichita State; 4. Balt, Jerry Sloan, Evansville; 5. Phil, Bill Cunningham, North Carolina; 6. StL, Jim Washington, Villanova; 7. Cin, Nate Bowman, Wichita State; 9. Bos, Ollie Johnson, San Francisco.

Second Round

1. SF, Wilbert Frazier, Grambling; 2. NY, Dick Van Arsdale, Indiana; 3. Det, Tom Van Arsdale, Indiana; 4. Balt, Tal Brody, Illinois; 5. Phil, Jesse Branson, Elon; 6. NY, Hal Blevins, Arkansas A&M; 7. Cin, Flynn Robinson, Wyoming; 8. LAL, John Fairchild, Brigham Young; 9. Bos, Ronnie Watts, Wake Forest.

Territorial Picks

NY: Bill Bradley, Princeton; Det: Bill Buntin, Michigan; LAL: Gail Goodrich, UCLA.

1964

First Round

1. NY, Jim Barnes, Texas Western; 2. Det, Joe Caldwell, Arizona State; 3. Balt, Gary Bradds, Ohio State; 4. Phil, Lucious Jackson, Pan American; 5. LAL, Walt Hazzard, UCLA; 6. StL, Jeff Mullins, Duke; 7. SF, Barry Kramer, New York University; 8. Bos, Mel Counts, Oregon State.

Second Round

1. NY, Willis Reed, Grambling; 2. Det, Les Hunter, Loyola (IL); 3. StL, Paul Silas, Creighton; 4. Phil, Ira Harge, New Mexico; 5. LAL, Cotton Nash, Kentucky; 6. NY, Howard Komives, Bowling Green; 7. SF, Bud Koper, Oklahoma City; 8. Cin, Bill Chmielewski, Dayton; 9. Bos, Ron Bonham, Cincinnati.

Territorial Picks

Cin: George Wilson, Cincinnati.

1963

First Round

1. NY, Art Heyman, Duke; 2. Balt, Rod Thorn, West Virginia; 3. SF, Nate Thurmond, Bowling Green; 4. Det, Ed Miles, Seattle; 5. StL, Gerry Ward, Boston College; 6. Syr, Tom Hoover, Villanova; 7. LAL, Roger Strickland, Jacksonville; 8. Bos, Bill Green, Colorado State.

Second Round

1. NY, Jerry Harkness, Loyola (IL); 2. Balt, Gus Johnson, Idaho; 3. SF, Gary Hill, Oklahoma City; 4. Det, Jerry Smith, Furman; 5. LAL, Jim King, Tulsa; 6. StL, Leland Mitchell, Mississippi State; 7. Syr, Hershell West, Grambling; 8. LAL, Mel Gibson, Western Carolina; 9. StL, Ken Saylors, Arkansas Tech.

Territorial Picks

Cin: Tom Thacker, Cincinnati.

1962

First Round

1. Chi, Bill McGill, Utah; 2. NY, Paul Hogue, Cincinnati; 3. StL, Zelmo Beaty, Prairie View; 4. Syr, Len Chappell, Wake Forest; 5. Phil, Wayne Hightower, Kansas; 6. LAL, Leroy Ellis, St. John's; 7. Bos, John Havlicek, Ohio State.

Second Round

1. Chi, Terry Dischinger, Purdue; 2. NY, John Rudometkin, USC; 3. StL, Bob Duffy, Colgate; 4. Det, Kevin Loughery, St. John's; 5. Syr, Chet Walker, Bradley; 6. Cin, Enoch Olsen, Louisville; 7. Phil, Hubie White, Villanova; 8. LAL, Gene Wiley, Wichita State; 9. Bos, Jack Foley, Holy Cross.

Territorial Picks

Det: Dave Debusschere, Detroit; Cin: Jerry Lucas, Ohio State.

1961

First Round
1. Chi, Walt Bellamy, Indiana; 2. NY, Tom Stith, St. Bonaventure; 3. Cin, Larry Siegfried, Ohio State; 4. Det, Ray Scott, Portland; 5. LAL, Wayne Yates, Memphis State; 6. Syr, Ben Warley, Tennessee State; 7. Phil, Tom Meschery, St. Mary's (CA); 8. StL, Cleo Hill, Winston-Salem; 9. Bos, Gary Phillips, Houston.

Second Round
1. NY, Ronald Martin, St. Bonaventure; 2. Cin, Bob Wiesenhahn, Cincinnati; 3. Det, Johnny Egan, Providence; 4. LAL, Fred Sawyer, Louisville; 5. Syr, Chris Smith, Virginia Tech; 6. Phil, Ted Luckenbill, Houston; 7. StL, Ron Horn, Indiana; 8. Bos, Al Butler, Niagara; 9. Chi, Jack Turner, Louisville; 10. Chi, Jerry Graves, Mississippi State; 11. Chi, York Larese, North Carolina; 12. Chi, Don Kojis, Marquette; 13. Chi, Doug Moe, North Carolina; 14. Chi, Jeff Cohen, William & Mary.

1960

First Round
1. Mpls, Jerry West, West Virginia; 2. NY, Darrall Imhoff, California; 3. Det, Jack Moreland, Louisiana Tech; 4. Syr, Lee Shaffer, North Carolina; 5. StL, Lenny Wilkens, Providence; 6. Phil, Al Bunge, Maryland; 7. Bos, Tom Sanders, New York University.

Second Round
1. Cin, Jay Arnette, Texas; 2. NY, Dave Budd, Wake Forest; 3. NY, Kelly Coleman, Kentucky Wesleyan; 4. Det, Ron Johnson, Minnesota; 5. Syr, Wilbur Trosch, St. Francis (PA); 6. StL, Horace Walker, Michigan State; 7. Phil, Bill Kennedy, Temple; 8. Bos, Leroy Wright, College of Pacific.

Territorial Picks
Cin: Oscar Robertson, Cincinnati.

1959

First Round
1. Cin, Bob Boozer, Kansas State; 2. Det, Bailey Howell, Mississippi State; 3. Mpls, Tom Hawkins, Notre Dame; 4. Syr, Dick Barnett, Tennessee State; 5. NY, Johnny Green, Michigan State; 6. Bos, John Richter, North Carolina State.

Second Round
1. Det, Tom Robitaille, Rice; 2. Det, Don Goldstein, Louisville; 3. Phil, Joe Ruklick, Northwestern; 4. Mpls, Rudy LaRusso, Dartmouth; 5. Syr, Gene Tormohlen, Tennessee; 6. StL, Alan Seiden, St. John's; 7. StL, Cal Ramsey, New York University; 8. Bos, Gene Guarilia, George Washington.

Territorial Picks
Phil: Wilt Chamberlain, Kansas; StL: Bob Ferry, St. Louis.

1958

First Round
1. Mpls, Elgin Baylor, Seattle; 2. Cin, Archie Dees, Indiana; 3. NY, Mike Farmer, San Francisco; 4. NY, Pete Brennan, North Carolina; 5. Syr, Connie Dierking, Cincinnati; 6. StL, Dave Gambee, Oregon State; 7. Bos, Ben Swain, Texas Southern.

Second Round
·1. Mpls, Steve Hamilton, Morehead State; 2. Cin, Vern Hatton, Kentucky; 3. Det, Barney Cable, Bradley; 4. NY, Joe Quigg, North Carolina; 5. Phil, Lamar Sharrar, West Virginia; 6. Syr, Hal Greer, Marshall; 7. StL, Hub Reed, Oklahoma City; 8. Bos, Jimmy Smith, Steubenville.

Territorial Picks
Phil: Guy Rodgers, Temple.

1957

First Round
1. Cin, Rod Hundley, West Virginia; 2. Det, Charles Tyra, Louisville; 3. Mpls, Jim Krebs, Southern Methodist; 4. StL, Win Wilfong, Memphis State; 5. NY, Brendan McCann, St. Bonaventure; 6. Phil, Len Rosenbluth, North Carolina; 7. Syr, George BonSalle, Illinois; 8. Bos, Sam Jones, North Carolina Central.

Second Round
1. Cin, Dick Duckett, St. John's; 2. Det, Bob McCoy, Grambling; 3. Mpls, Harvey Schmidt, Illinois; 4. StL, Jim Palmer, Dayton; 5. NY, Larry Friend, California; 6. Phil, Jack Sullivan, Mount St. Mary's; 7. Syr, Jim Morgan, Louisville; 8. Bos, Dick O'Neal, Texas Christian.

NBA drafts held between 1947 and 1956 consisted of up to 17 rounds; results of the first round plus territorial picks are represented below.

1956

First Round
1. Roc, Si Green, Duquesne; 2. StL, Bill Russell, San Francisco; 3. Mpls, Jim Paxson, Dayton; 4. NY, Ronnie Shavlik, North Carolina State; 5. Syr, Joe Holup, George Washington; 6. FtW, Ron Sobie, DePaul; 7. Phi, Hal Lear, Temple.

Territorial Picks
Bos: Tom Heinsohn, Holy Cross.

1955

First Round
1. Mil, Dick Ricketts, Duquesne; 2. Roch, Maurice Stokes, St. Francis (PA); 3. Bos, Jim Loscutoff, Oregon; 4. NY, Ken Sears, Santa Clara; 5. FtW, John Horan, Dayton; 7. Syr, Ed Conlin, Fordham.

Territorial Picks
Mpls: Dick Garmaker, Minnesota; Phil: Tom Gola, La Salle.

1954

First Round
1. Balt, Frank Selvy, Furman; 2. Mil, Bob Pettit, Louisiana State; 3. Phil, Gene Shue, Maryland; 4. FtW, Dick Rosenthal, Notre Dame; 5. Bos, Togo Palazzi, Holy Cross; 6. Syr, John Kerr, Illinois; 7. Roch, Tom Marshall, Western Kentucky; 8. NY, Jack Turner, Western Kentucky; 9. Mpls, Ed Kalafat, Minnesota.

1953

First Round
1. Bal, Ray Felix, Long Island; 2. Mil, Bob Houbregs, Washington; 3. FTW, Jack Molinas, Columbia; 4. Roc, Richie Regan, Seton Hall; 5. Bos, Frank Ramsey, Kentucky; 6. Syr, James Neal, Wofford; 7. Min, Jim Fritsche, Hamline.

Territorial Picks
Phi: Ernie Beck, Pennsylvania; NY: Walter Dukes, Seton Hall.

1952

First Round
1. Mil, Mark Workman, West Virginia; 2. Bal, Jim Baechtold, Eastern Kentucky; 3. FTW, Dick Groat, Duke; 4. Ind, Joe Dean, Louisiana State; 5. NY, Ralph Polson, Whitworth; 6. Bos, Bill Stauffer, Missouri; 7. Syr, Bob Luchmueller, Lousiville; 8. Roc, Chuck Darling, Iowa; 9. Min, Clyde Lovellette, Kansas.

Territorial Picks
Phi: Walter Davis, Texas A&M.

1951

First Round
1. Balt, Gene Melchiorre, Bradley; 2. TriC, Mel Hutchins, Brigham Young; 3. Inds, Marcus Freiberger, Oklahoma; 4. FtW, Zeke Sinicola, Niagara; 5. Syr, John McConathy, NW Louisiana; 6. NY, Ed Smith, Harvard; 7. Bos, Ernie Barrett, Kansas State; 8. Roch, Sam Ranzino, North Carolina State; 9. Phil, Don Sunderlage, Illinois.

Territorial Picks
Mpls: Whitey Skoog, Minnesota.

1950

First Round
1. Bos, Charlie Share, Bowling Green; 2. Bal, Don Rehfeldt, Wisconsin; 3. Tri, Bob Cousy, Holy Cross; 4. Was, Dick Schnittker, Ohio State; 5. Chi, Larry Foust, La Salle; 6. NY, Irwin Dambrot, CCNY; 7. FtW, George Yardley, Stanford; 8. Ind, Bob Lavoy, Western Kentucky; 9. Roc, Joe McNamee, San Francisco; 10. Min, Kevin O'Shea, Notre Dame; 11. Syr, Don Lofgran, San Francisco.

Territorial Picks
Phi: Paul Arizin, Villanova.

1949

First Round
1. Pro, Howie Shannon, Kansas State; 2. Ind, Alex Groza, Kentucky; 3. FTW, Bob Harris, Oklahoma State; 5. Phi, Vern Gardner, Utah; 6. Bal, Ron Livingstone, Wyoming; 7. NY, Dick McGuire, St. John's; 9. Chi, Jack Kerris, Loyola (IL); 9. Was, Wallace Jones, Kentucky; 10. Roc, Frank Saul, Seton Hall.

Territorial Picks
StL: Ed Macauley, St. Louis; Min: Vern Mikkelsen, Hamline.

1948

First Round
1. Pro, Andy Tonkovich, Marshall; 2. Ind, George Kok, Arkansas; 3. Bos, George Hauptfuhrer, Harvard; 4. NY, Adolph Schayes, New York University; 5. Chi, Ed Mikan, DePaul; 6. Bal, Walter Budko, Columbia; 7. StL, Robert Gale, Cornell; 8. FTW, Ward Williams, Indiana; 9. Min, Chuck Hanger, California; 10. Roc, Robert Wanzer, Seton Hall; 11. Phi, Don Ray, Western Kentucky; 12. Was, Jack Nichols, Washington.

1947

First Round
1. Pit, Clifton McNeeley, Texas Western; 2. Tor, Glen Selbo, Wisconsin; 3. Bos, Ed Ehlers, Purdue; 4. NY, Walt Dropo, Connecticut; 5. NY, Dick Holub, Long Island; 6. Phi, Frank Crossin, Pennsylvania; 7. StL, Jack Underman, Ohio State; 8. Chi, Paul Huston, Ohio State; 9. Was, Dick O'Keefe, Santa Clara; 10. Bal, Larry Killick, Vermont.

Contributors

Christian Anderson wrote several articles for this book.

Bob Bellotti, who developed the Points Created™ rating system in 1987, has been a statistical analyst for NBA teams since 1988. He also manages his company, Bellotti Basketball, which publishes custom statistical player reports and written analyses, including video breakdown, for professional and college basketball teams. Bellotti has written five books about basketball statistics, including *The Points Created Pro Basketball Book* (Night Work Publishing). He also has written for *The Sporting News, Basketball America,* and other national publications. He has been a professional writer since 1981.

Phil Berger is the author of *Miracle on 33rd Street: The New York Knickerbockers' Championship Season, 1969-1970* and *Knight Fall: Bobby Knight, The Truth Behind America's Most Controversial Coach.* Phil was a sportswriter for *The New York Times* and author of more than a dozen books and boxing reporter for *The Times* from 1986-92. He was a former associate editor at *SPORT* magazine. Phil died in March 2001.

Peter Bjarkman has written dozens of basketball and baseball books, including *The Boston Celtics Encyclopedia* and *Hoopla: A Century of College Basketball.*

Robert Bradley is the founder and president of the Association for Professional Basketball Research, an Internet-based (www.APBR.org) historical society of over 500 members. Organized in 1998, the APBR has provided help to numerous authors, sportswriters and organizations including The Children's Television Workshop, Total Sports, Turner Sports, Sportsline.com, *Sports Illustrated* and ESPN. Author of *The Compendium of Professional Basketball* (Xaler Press, 1999), Bradley has worked for the Phoenix Public Library since 1980 and is a member of the Professional Football Researchers Association and the Hockey Research Association.

Morgan Brenner is a retired life insurance company executive turned sports historian. He wrote *College Basketball's National Championships: The Complete Record of Every Tournament Ever Played* (Scarecrow Press, 1999). The tome includes the results of 598 tournaments. He followed that book with *The Encyclopedia of College & University Name Histories* (Scarecrow Press, 2003), which contains the name and location histories of 1,304 United States institutions. In the spring of 2004, he expects publication of *The Majors: The Complete Results of Golf's Most Prestigious Tournaments.* A native of York, Pennsylvania, he resides in Havertown, PA.

Ted Brock wrote several articles for this book and also wrote for *Total Football.*

Mike Douchant is author of the *Encyclopedia of College Basketball* and *Tourney Time* with Dick Vitale. He was an editor who was on the ground floor in helping create periodicals such as *The Sporting News Basketball Yearbooks, Official NBA Register* and *Lindy's College Basketball Yearbook.*

Joe Gergen is a sports columnist for *New York Newsday.* He has written several sports books, including *Final Four.*

John Grasso was born in Queens, NY and lives in Guilford, NY. He is the author of three books: *505 Boxing Questions Your Friends Can't Answer* and *The 100 Greatest Boxers of All Time,* both with Bert Sugar, and *The Olympic Games Boxing Record Book.* He was also the Olympics editor for *The Ring Record Book* and is currently working on *The Olympic Games Basketball History and Record Book.* He is a member of the Association for Professional Basketball Research.

Gary D. Hailey is a partner at Venable, Baetjer, Howard & Civiletti in Washington, D.C., where he spends most of his time reviewing print, television, and Internet advertising. He is a graduate of Rice University (1974) and Harvard Law School (1977), and recently passed the International Association of Approved Basketball Officials exam and became a referee.

Bill Heller is the author of *Playing Tall: The Ten Shortest Players in NBA History.*

Dave Hereen is the creator of TENDEX, the oldest and most widely used system for rating basketball players. As a sportswriter for the South Florida *Sun-Sentinel,* Hereen has won 13 state and national writing awards. He has written basketball columns for *The Sporting News, CBS Sportsline* and *Basketball Times.* He has written five basketball books and currently has a novel under contract to be published.

Mikhail Horowitz is the author of *Big League Poets* (City Lights, 1978) and a contributor to both the *Biographical Encyclopedia of Baseball* and the seventh edition of *Total Baseball.* He was formerly a senior editor at Total Sports and is currently an editor in the Publications Office at Bard College, Annandale-on-Hudson, NY.

Leonard Koppett, a member of the writers' wing in the Halls of Fame of baseball and basketball, authored 17 books, including *24 Seconds to Shoot: The Birth and Improbable Rise of the NBA,* during a career that spanned six decades and included stints at the *New York Times, New York Herald Tribune* and the *New York Post* before a second career in California at the *Palo Alto Times* and *Oakland Tribune.* Koppett also did extensive magazine, radio and television work, as well as teaching university courses in journalism, sports law, business and current affairs. He died on June 22, 2003 at the age of 79, two weeks after completing *The Rise and Fall of the Press Box* (SPORTClassic Books, 2003).

Sean Lahman is the author of the annual *Pro Football Prospectus,* and has edited or contributed to a number of sports reference books, including *Total Baseball, Sports Illustrated Sports Almanac, Total Tennis,* and *Baseball: The Biographical Encyclopedia.* Over the past ten years, he has led the effort to make sports statistics available to the general public, developing or contributing to a number of pioneering web sites. He attended the University of Cincinnati and lives in upstate New York.

Roland Lazenby has written extensively about pro and college basketball, including the publication of numerous books. His work includes *Mad Game, The NBA Education of Kobe Bryant,* and a biography of coach Phil Jackson. Lazenby's 1997 title *Bull Run!* was named the sports book of the year by the Independent Publishers Association. He also authored *Blood On The Horns, The Long Strange Ride of Michael Jordan's Chicago Bulls,* the inside story of the break-up of the six-time world champions. Lazenby also helped produce the nationally syndicated documentary *Kobe Bryant, Destiny's Child* for Intersport TV in Chicago. Kareem Abdul-Jabbar declared that Lazenby's 1993 book *The Lakers, A Basketball Journey* was "the best, most in-depth book ever written on the team." Lazenby's work has appeared in the *Chicago Sun-Times, Sporting News, SPORT,* and numerous other publications. He is the editor of *Lindy's Pro Basketball Annual* and a regular contributor to Japan's leading basketball magazine, *Dunkshoot.*

Roger Meyer has been a sports enthusiast since childhood. He played baseball and basketball in high school and ran track in college. He has compiled numerous research projects on pro basketball, baseball, football, hockey and boxing. He has built a large sports publication library, which is still growing today. He has been married to Joan for 40 years and has two children, four grandchildren and resides in Foxboro, MA.

George Pattison is a writer living in Woodstock, NY.

Robert Peterson is a freelance writer and the author of three sports histories: *Only The Ball Was White: The Story of the Segregated Negro Baseball Leagues Before Jackie Robinson* (1970); *Cages to Jump Shots: Pro Basketball's Early Years* (1990); and *Pigskin: The Early Years of Pro Football* (1997).

Terry Pluto is a columnist for the *Akron Beacon Journal* and also writes two religion columns per month. Seven times he has been named "Ohio Sportswriter of the Year," including 2002 and 2003. He is the author of 19 books, including two classic basketball oral histories: *Loose Balls: The Short, Wild Life of the American Basketball Association* (named the top sports book of 1989 by *USA Today*) and *Tall Tales: The Glory Years of the NBA in the Words of the Men who Played, Coached, and Built Pro Basketball.* In 1997, the *Chicago Tribune* referred to Pluto as "America's finest author of sports books." He also wrote *The Curse of Rocky Colavito: A Loving Look at a Thirty-Year Slump,* named one of the nation's top five sports books for 1994 by *The New York Times.* Pluto has twice been nominated for the Pulitzer Prize for commentary and has been the winner of more than 60 national and state writing awards.

Steve Popper has spent the last four years at *The New York Times,* covering many assignments, including the NBA. Prior to coming to *The Times,* Steve spent two seasons covering the New York Knicks for the *New York Post.* He also writes a weekly column for MSGNetwork.com.

Bob Ryan, a 35-year veteran of the *Boston Globe,* covered the NBA Celtics for several years before winning acclaim as a general sports columnist. He is the author of 11 books, including a bestseller with former Celtics star Larry Bird, *Drive: The Story of My Life.* In 1997 he was awarded the prestigious Curt Gowdy Media Award by the Basketball Hall of Fame. He is a member of the Naismith Basketball Hall of Fame and the College Basketball Writers Hall of Fame, as well as being a charter member of the New England Basketball Hall of Fame. He is a regular on ESPN's *The Sports Reporters* and an occasional host of ESPN's *Pardon the Interruption.*

Alex Sachare is the author, co-author or editor of nine books on basketball and a former editor of *Hoop* magazine, and has contributed to numerous other books and periodicals. His books include *The Complete Idiot's Guide to Basketball,* with Walt Frazier; *America's Dream Team,* with Chuck Daly; *The Official NBA Basketball Encyclopedia,* second edition; and *The Chicago Bulls Encyclopedia.* Sachare was a sports writer and pro basketball editor for the Associated Press for 10 years before joining the NBA under commissioners Larry O'Brien and David Stern. Sachare resigned as the NBA's vice president, editorial, in 1996 and later returned to his alma mater as director of communications and editor of *Columbia College Today.*

Charles Salzburg is the author of *From Set Shots to Slam Dunks: The Glory Days of Basketball in the Words of Those Who Played It.*

Ken Shouler is editor as well as a key contributor for *Total Basketball.* He runs Wordsworth Writing & Editing, a ghostwriting and editing firm. He wrote *The Experts Pick Basketball's Best 50 Players in the Last 50 Years* and is the author of several baseball books. He has been a feature writer for *Cigar Aficionado* magazine since 1993 and has also written for *TV Guide, Street and Smith's* annuals, *Philosophy Now,* and dozens of other publications. He has been interviewed on Fox, NBC, The History Channel, MSNBC, National Public Radio, The Score in Chicago, WFAN in New York and many other radio and television stations. He teaches philosophy at Westchester Community College and lives in Harrison, NY with his wife, Rose Marie.

Sam Smith has been with the *Chicago Tribune* since 1979 as a political, business and sports writer. He has been a basketball writer since 1984 and is now the pro basketball columnist. He is the author of two books on Michael Jordan and the Chicago Bulls, *The New York Times* best seller *The Jordan Rules* and *The Second Coming.* He is a regular contributor to ESPN radio, *ESPN The Magazine* and ESPN.com.

Jed Thorn has worked as an editor on several sports publications, including autobiographies, novels, and reference volumes. He lives in Cincinnati, OH, where he is studying ancient Greek history at the University of Cincinnati.

Stew Thornley is a sports historian and an award-winning author of more than 30 books, including *Basketball's Original Dynasty: The History of the Lakers* and *Land of the Giants: New York's Polo Grounds.* He lives in Roseville, MN, with his wife, Brenda Himrich, and is currently working on a book on Minnesota baseball as well as one on the gravesites of notable Minnesotans. Thornley, who has visited the graves of 184 members of the Baseball Hall of Fame across the United States and in Cuba, also has a pictorial book in the works on the graves of these greats.

Nate Trela is a reporter for the *Detroit Free Press.* He began his career as a sportswriter in 1998 with *The News-Sentinel* of Fort Wayne, IN, where his duties included covering the CBA, college football, and college basketball. Trela has also worked as an education reporter for the South Bend (Ind.) *Tribune* and is a member of APBR. He attended the University of Missouri and resides in Sterling Heights, MI, with his wife, Michelle, and their daughter, Mairead.

Photographs and Illustrations

AFP/CORBIS/Magmaphoto.com: Front cover, pp. 253, 259, 262, 265, Insert pp. 4, 11 (top left).

The Associated Press: pp. x, 113, 235, 244, 247, 256, 268, 365, 558, 641, 643, 656, 1457, Insert pp. 8, 11 (top right), 13 (top left; top right), 18 (lower left), 24 (top left; bottom).

Bettman/CORBIS/Magmaphoto.com: p. 226, 229, 238.

Collection of Naismith Memorial Basketball Hall of Fame: pp. 1, 3, 12, 22, 27, 375, 383.

Reuters New Media Inc./CORBIS/Magmaphoto.com: pp. 232, 465, Insert pp. 12 (bottom), 13 (top left; top right) 20 (top right), 24 (top right).

The SPORT Collection: pp. 44, 55, 59, 63, 65 (M. Blumenthal), 66, 71, 74, 77, 80 (O. Sweet), 83 (G. Heyer), 86 (G. Heyer), 89, 92 (M. Blumenthal), 95 (G. Heyer), 98 (M. Blumenthal), 101 (M. Blumenthal), 104 (H. Scharfman), 107 (M. Newman), 110 (K. Fitzgerald), 116, 119 (M. Emmons), 122, 125 (M. Emmons), 128 (M. Emmons), 131 (M. Blumenthal), 134 (M. Emmons), 137, 140 (M. Blumenthal), 144 (M. Blumenthal), 150, 156 (M. Blumenthal), 162, 169 (M. Blumenthal), 171 (L. Berman), 172 (K. Fitzgerald), 175 (M. Blumenthal), 178 (M. Blumenthal), 181 (K. Fitzgerald), 184, 187, 190 (A. Neste), 193, 196 (B. Jennaro), 199 (N. Hogue), 202 (K. Fitzgerald), 205 (C. Skalak Jr.), 208, 211 (M. Blumenthal), 214, 217, 220, 223 (L. Raynor), 241, 250 (R. Widner), 271, 276 (I. Wyman), 281, 283 (M. Newman), 311, 321, 328, 338, 340, 345 (R. Widner), 351 (F. Kaplan), 360, 381 (K. Fitzgerald), 425, 428, 433 (K. Fitzgerald), 444, 446, 448 (D. Norenberg), 450, 452 (M. Emmons), 454 (M. Blumenthal), 456 (K. Fitzgerald), 458 (K. Fitzgerald), 460 (K. Fitzgerald), 511 (D. Sparks), 513 (K. Fitzgerald), 531 (M. Blumenthal), 541, 551, 561 (M. Blumenthal), 563 (M. Blumenthal), 569 (K. Fitzgerald), 661 (L. Schiller), 663, 670, 751, 1455, Insert pp. 1 (Illustration by J.C. Murphy), 2 (M. Newman), 3 (M. Blumenthal, top; D. Norenberg, bottom), 5 (Illustration by A.S. Tobey, top left; G. Heyer, top right; M. Blumenthal, lower left), 6 (J. Zehrt, top left; M. Blumenthal, lower left; D. Sutton, lower right), 9 (top; R. Berard, bottom), 10, 12 (lower left) 13 (M. Blumenthal, lower right), 14, 15 (H. Peskin), 16 (M. Blumenthal, top, lower left, lower right), 17 (M. Blumenthal), 18 (M. Rubio, top left; top right; C. Campbell, lower right), 19 (F. Kaplan, top left; M. Blumenthal, top right; lower left), 20 (K. Fitzgerald, top left; K. Fitzgerald, bottom right), 21 (top left; P. Burchman, top right; M. Newman, lower left), 22 (L. Stuart, left; lower right), 23 (N. Leifer, top; J. Zehrt, bottom).

The Ozzie Sweet Collection: Insert p. 7, Back cover.

Team Abbreviations

AND	Anderson Packers	IND	Indiana Pacers	POR	Portland Trail Blazers
ATL	Atlanta Hawks	INJ	Indianapolis Jets	PRO	Providence Steamrollers
BAL	Baltimore Bullets (1947-54)	INO	Indianapolis Olympians	ROC	Rochester Royals
BLB	Baltimore Bullets (1963-73)	KCK	Kansas City Kings	SAC	Sacramento Kings
BOS	Boston Celtics	KCO	Kansas City-Omaha Kings	SAS	San Antonio Spurs
BUF	Buffalo Braves	LAC	Los Angeles Clippers	SCS	San Diego Clippers
CAP	Capital Bullets	LAL	Los Angeles Lakers	SDR	San Diego Rockets
CHA	Charlotte Hornets	MEM	Memphis Grizzlies	SEA	Seattle SuperSonics
CHI	Chicago Bulls	MIA	Miami Heat	SFW	San Francisco Warriors
CHP	Chicago Packers	MIL	Milwaukee Bucks	SHE	Sheboygan Redskins
CHS	Chicago Stags	MIN	Minnesota Timberwolves	SLB	St. Louis Bombers
CHZ	Chicago Zephyrs	MLH	Milwaukee Hawks	STL	St. Louis Hawks
CIN	Cincinnati Royals	MPL	Minneapolis Lakers	SYR	Syracuse Nationals
CLE	Cleveland Cavaliers	NJN	New Jersey Nets	TOR	Toronto Raptors
CLR	Cleveland Rebels	NOH	New Orleans Hornets	TRH	Toronto Huskies
DAL	Dallas Mavericks	NOJ	New Orelans Jazz	TRI	Tri-Cities Blackhawks
DEN	Denver Nuggets (1976-present)	NYK	New York Knickerbockers	UTJ	Utah Jazz
DET	Detroit Pistons	NYN	New York Nets	VAN	Vancouver Grizzlies
DNN	Denver Nuggets (1949-50)	ORL	Orlando Magic	WAS	Washington Wizards
DTF	Detroit Falcons	PHI	Philadelphia 76ers	WAT	Waterloo Hawks
FTW	Fort Wayne Pistons	PHO	Phoenix Suns	WSB	Washington Bullets
GST	Golden State Warriors	PHW	Philadelphia Warriors	WSC	Washington Capitols
HOU	Houston Rockets	PIT	Pittsburgh Ironmen		

www.sportclassicbooks.com